THE BAR COUNCIL

THE BAR DIRECTORY

2013 EDITION

SWEET & MAXWELL

*Published in 2012 by Sweet & Maxwell, 100 Avenue Road, London NW3 3PF
part of Thomson Reuters (Professional) UK Limited
(Registered in England & Wales, Company No 1679046.
Registered Office and address for service:
Aldgate House, 33 Aldgate High Street, London EC3N 1DL)*

*For further information on our products and services, visit
www.sweetandmaxwell.co.uk*

Set by Interactive Sciences Ltd, Gloucester
Printed and bound by CPI Group (UK) Ltd, Croydon CR0 4YY
No natural forests were destroyed to make this product; only
farmed timber was used and replanted.

British Library Cataloguing in Publication Data

A CIP catalogue record for this book
is available from the British Library

ISBN 978 041402488 5

The information in this Directory was supplied in part by chambers and individual barristers directly to the publishers (for Parts A, B, I and J), and in part by the General Council of the Bar Records Office (for Parts C, F, G and H). Parts D and E were drawn from information supplied by the Bar Council in the first instance and supplemented with information from chambers and individual barristers.

The General Council of the Bar information on chambers and individual barristers dates up to 17 August 2012. Sweet & Maxwell accepted applications for bronze, silver and gold chambers and individual barristers entries up to 17 August 2012. Information for Part C, the Public Access Directory, dates up to 17 August 2012.

The Bar of England and Wales is a unique profession of specialist advocates and advisers. The modern Bar takes a flexible and mobile approach to advising a wide range of clients using the latest technology. Barristers are independent and very well placed to offer solutions to any legal problem, providing good value for money. Instructing a barrister directly, or via a solicitor, early on can help resolve a problem swiftly and efficiently - well before a case is heard before a judge. But if the dispute continues, barristers have the advocacy skills to represent their client's best interests, whether in court or at tribunal, or in arbitration or through mediation. Recent rule changes to barristers' working methods mean that the Bar is more accessible than ever.

There are now over 15,000 practising barristers, employed and self-employed, in England and Wales. The Directory contains the details, locations and specialisms of many of these barristers. It is an extremely valuable resource, which is supplemented by the information on the Bar Council's website at www.barcouncil.org.uk

Access to justice is a vital part of our daily life. It demands client choice and an assurance that clients will receive high quality representation. Using this Directory is a first step to ensuring that access to justice is both informed and effective.

Michael Todd QC

Chairman of the Bar Council of England and Wales

June 2012

CONTENTS

GUIDE TO USING THE DIRECTORY

This Directory has been compiled from information supplied by chambers and individual barristers directly to the publishers (for Parts A, B, I and J), and by the General Council of the Bar Records Office (for Parts C, F, G and H). Information in Parts D and E was supplied by the Bar Council in the first instance and supplemented with information from chambers and individual barristers.

The General Council of the Bar information on chambers and individual barristers dates up to 17 August 2012. Sweet & Maxwell accepted applications for bronze, silver and gold chambers and individual barrister entries up to 17 August 2012. Information for Part C, the Public Access Directory, dates up to 17 August 2012. The introductory pages include information on the Bar of England and Wales, the General Council of the Bar, the Circuits of the Bar and Licensed Access. This information was supplied by the General Council of the Bar. The Directory is divided into nine parts as follows:

Part A Types of Work by Chambers

Part A lists chambers by the type of work they do and by the town or city where they are located. The types of work undertaken by chambers are listed in alphabetical order. Within these main categories, chambers are listed alphabetically under the town or city in which they practise. For example, a reader wishing to locate a Birmingham-based chambers specialising in trademarks would be able to look under 'T' for Trademarks and find under that heading the details of any chambers in Birmingham which offer their services in this field. A complete list of the types of work can be found at the front of Part A.

Each listing provides the name and telephone number. The first point of contact in each instance will be the clerk. (Details of clerks can be found in *Part D Chambers by Location*).

Please note that chambers are only listed in this section if information on specialisms has been supplied by them.

The symbol • indicates that chambers have an expanded entry in *Part D Chambers by Location*.

Part B Types of Work by Individual Barristers

Part B lists individual barristers by the types of work in which they specialise. The areas of work are listed in alphabetical order. Within these main categories, individual barristers are listed alphabetically by surname. For example, a reader wishing to locate a particular barrister specialising in trademarks would be able to look under 'T' for Trademarks and find under that heading those barristers who offer their services in this field. A complete list of the types of work can be found at the front of Part B.

Each listing provides the name of the individual barrister, their chambers' address and chambers' telephone number. The first point of contact in each instance will be the clerk. (Details of clerks can be found in *Part D Chambers by Location*)

Please note that barristers are only listed in this section if the information on specialisms has been supplied by them.

Part C Public Access Directory

Part C lists barristers who have undertaken appropriate training to accept instructions from members of the public without a solicitor having been instructed also. The section is comprised of an index by types of work undertaken and an alphabetical listing of the barristers containing their contact details.

Part D Chambers by Location

Part D lists chambers in England and Wales by the town or city in which they are located. The town/city names are in alphabetical order and under those main headings chambers are listed alphabetically, thus 7 King's Bench Walk would be listed before 4 Pump Court under London.

Information for each set of chambers includes full contact details. Some chambers have opted to include additional information about themselves in this part of the Directory. Additional information includes the names of barristers practising from that chambers, date chambers were established, opening times, chambers' facilities, disability access, languages spoken, details regarding fees and a list of the types of work undertaken including details of the number of counsel practising in each area. Please note that details of the types of work undertaken by those chambers which have chosen not to include this information in Part D may be found in *Part A Types of Work by Chambers*.

The following symbols indicate that barristers are:
† Recorders
* Door Tenants/Associate Members

Part E Individual Barristers Self-Employed

Part E lists self-employed barristers. Individuals are listed alphabetically by surname, and details include the chambers at which they practise, year of call to the Bar, Inn of Court and academic qualifications.

Some individual barristers have opted to include additional information about themselves in this part of the Directory, such as other qualifications, membership of foreign bars, other professional experience, languages spoken, publications, reported cases and a list of the types of work they undertake.

Part F Individual Barristers in Employment

Part F lists those barristers who are in employment. Barristers are listed alphabetically by surname, and details include their date of call to the Bar, academic qualifications and details of their position of employment with a full address, where supplied.

Part G Individual Barristers Unregistered

This section lists those barristers who are unregistered. Barristers are listed alphabetically by surname, and details include their date of call to the Bar, their Inn of Court and academic qualifications.

Note: for barristers in this section, information has been supplied by the Bar Council based on payment of the Member's Services Fee.

Part H Index of Languages Spoken

Part I is an index of all languages spoken by chambers and individual barristers. The languages are listed alphabetically, as are chambers and individuals.

All chambers in this section have an expanded entry in *Part D Chambers by Location* and all individual barristers in this section have an expanded entry in *Part E Individual Barristers in Private Practice*.

Part I A–Z Index of Chambers

Part J lists all the chambers from *Part D Chambers by Location* alphabetically with the Part D page reference.

Bar Directory Website

Information in Parts A, B, D, E, F and G of the book is also available online at: www.legalhub.co.uk

The Bar Council publishes an electronic version of the Public Access directory on its website at:
www.barcouncil.org.uk

Updating of Information

Information about chambers or individual barristers which needs updating should in the first instance be discussed with the Records Office at the Bar Council on the following number:
Telephone: 020 7242 0934

Any comments regarding *The Bar Directory* or requests for updating on *The Bar Directory* which can be found on the Legal Hub website should be directed in the first instance to:

The Bar Directory
Editorial Department
Sweet & Maxwell
100 Avenue Road
London NW3 3PF
Telephone: 020 7393 7000

THE BAR OF ENGLAND AND WALES

The Bar of England and Wales is a unique legal profession of specialist advocates and advisers. There are now over 15,000 practising barristers in England and Wales. More than 12,000 are self-employed, and over 3,000 are employed.

The Bar provides solutions to any legal problem and is very good value for money. Relatively recent rule changes to the way in which barristers work mean that the Bar is more accessible than ever through Public Access and Licensed Access, as well as remaining a predominantly referral profession.

Self-employed barristers are independent and objective. Their highly competitive training in litigation and advocacy, together with their specialist knowledge and experience in and out of court, can make a substantial difference to the outcome of a case, whether criminal or civil. Whatever the nature of the legal problem, it is important at an early stage to decide whether to bring in a barrister.

Broad areas of specialisation include: Construction, Commercial, Company, Criminal (including extradition), Defamation, Employment, Environment, Family, Housing, Immigration, Insolvency, Insurance, Personal Injury, Property, Equity, Wills and Trusts. These can be subdivided further into more than 300 categories of expertise.

Through their grouping in chambers, or in some cases working as sole practitioners, barristers are able to operate with low overheads and to offer competitive rates. Legal Aid will often cover the services of a barrister, and sometimes a Queen's Counsel. For those not eligible for Legal Aid, solicitors can help the lay client by negotiating an affordable fee, which includes a number of different types of agreement.

In addition to barristers in self-employed practice, employed barristers, who might work for the Government or in industry for example, are playing an increasingly important role. Following the Access to Justice Act 1999 which amended the Courts and Legal Services Act 1990, employed barristers were permitted by the Bar Council to conduct litigation.

Barristers who have completed appropriate training are able to take instructions directly from members of the public (the Public Access Scheme). In addition, members of certain professional bodies, some overseas clients, or organisations with licences from the Bar Council, are able to seek advice directly from Counsel or they may instruct Counsel in non-court litigation (the Licensed Access

Scheme). In some cases, members of the Bar provide their services on a pro bono basis, for example through the Free Representation Unit or the Bar Pro Bono Unit. There is a rich history of barristers working on a pro bono basis in human rights cases. For more information visit: www.barprobono.org.uk.

In addition to being either employed or self-employed, the Legal Services Act 2007 has precipitated further liberalising changes to the Bar's Code of Conduct and the ways in which barristers are permitted to practise. From 2010, barristers may be managers and partners with other lawyers and non-lawyers in Legal Disciplinary Practices (LDPs) regulated by the Solicitors Regulation Authority (SRA), in other 'recognised bodies' regulated by the Council for Licensed Conveyancers (CLC) and also act in a 'dual capacity' as both self-employed and employed at the same time (though not in the same case), subject to certain provisos. They may investigate or collect evidence and take witness statements, conduct correspondence, share premises and office facilities with any other person (subject to certain conditions), and attend on clients at police stations. Further reforms may follow as more of the Act is implemented.

The modern Bar is committed to excellence in advocacy, advisory services and in the way in which it carries out and offers its service. Barristers take a flexible and mobile approach to advising a wide range of clients using the latest technology.

THE BAR COUNCIL

The Bar Council, more formally known as the General Council of the Bar, represents barristers in England and Wales.

The Bar Council promotes the Bar's high quality specialist advocacy and advisory services; fair access to justice for all; the highest standards of ethics, equality and diversity across the profession, and the development of business opportunities for barristers at home and abroad. It represents the interests of the Bar on all matters relating to the profession, whether trade union, disciplinary, public interest or in any way affecting the administration of justice.

It is also the Approved Regulator of the Bar of England and Wales, discharging its regulatory functions through the independent Bar Standards Board.

Its range of services, member benefits, online advice and practical guidance for all types of barristers provides support to the profession. It is the Bar Council's role to get the best and brightest minds across England and Wales, regardless of background or ethnicity, to help secure the future of the Bar.

The work of the Bar Council is undertaken by an executive and a number of committees of practitioners. The Bar Council officers are elected by Bar Council members in May, and serve for one calendar year.

In its representative capacity, the Bar Council executive provides support to the Chairman's office as well as a number of representative committees, sub-committees and working groups. The executive supports the Bar Council's work by:

- Communicating regularly with the profession about key matters affecting its interests
- Influencing the development of public policy and legislation affecting the provision of specialist advocacy and advisory services and, more widely, in the profession's and the public interest, and
- Developing and promoting the work (and the values) of the Bar at home and abroad to governments, legislatures, the media and other stakeholders, helping to make entry to the profession open to all with the requisite ability to provide rewarding careers and to sustain the long-term future of the Bar.

The General Council of the Bar

Main Office:

289–293 High Holborn, London WC1V 7HZ
Telephone: 020 7242 0082
Fax: 020 7831 9217
DX 240 LDE

Records Office:

289–293 High Holborn, London WC1V 7HZ
Telephone: 020 7242 0934
Email: Records@BarCouncil.org.uk
DX 240 LDE

Brussels Office:

Avenue des Nerviens 85, B-1040 Brussels
Belgium
Telephone: 00 322 230 4810
Email: BrusselsOffice@barcouncil.org.uk
Fax: 00 322 230 4596

Website: www.barcouncil.org.uk

Bar Standards Board

The Board comprises 15 people. The Board has a lay majority with eight lay members and seven barristers. None of our members are members of the Bar Council or any of its representational committees. All members are appointed to work in the public interest.

The Board runs its work through eight committees each of which reports to the Board. The Board is responsible for regulating the education and training of barristers, and for the rules of professional conduct which they must obey. It is responsible for quality assurance and compliance, and the provision of a disciplinary system.

289–293 High Holborn, London, WC1V 7HZ
Telephone: 020 7611 1444
Complaints line: 020 7611 1445
Fax: 020 7831 9217
Email: Contactus@barstandardsboard.org.uk
Website: www.BarStandardsBoard.org.uk

CIRCUITS OF THE BAR COUNCIL

The Bar in England and Wales is divided into six regions, which are more commonly known as "Circuits". The Circuits provide important sources of support, advice and representation for barristers practising in those areas. They provide a range of services to the members in their respective geographical areas, maintain lines of communication with all parts of the legal system, including the courts, and are represented on the Bar Council through the Circuit Leaders. They liaise closely with the local court service, Crown Prosecution Service and other bodies as well as providing important training and social events for barristers.

In England and Wales, the Circuits, in alphabetical order, are: Midland, Northern, North Eastern, South Eastern, Wales and Chester and Western. The Midland Circuit covers central England from the east to Wales. The Northern Circuit covers northern England to the west of the Pennines and the North Eastern Circuit, the east of that area. The Wales and Chester covers the whole of Wales. The South Eastern Circuit encompasses London, the Home Counties and East Anglia and the Western Circuit from just west of Guildford to Truro and includes Winchester, Bristol and Exeter. Barristers that practise in the courts of the Circuit are represented by a Circuit Leader.

Each Circuit has its own presiding High Court Judge who, with resident Circuit Judges, takes responsibility for every aspect of the administration of the court system.

Circuits provide a wide range of services for their members, including continuing education seminars, advocacy courses, new practitioner programmes and the provision of information. They also liaise closely with Her Majesty's Courts and Tribunal Service to ensure they play an active and relevant role in the administration of justice in their region.

The Circuits still play an important part in the maintenance of access to justice. As constraints on public funds continue to increase, the Circuits have assisted in the setting-up and extension of free representation schemes in different parts of the country, often working closely with Citizens Advice Bureaux.

The Circuits have proved their capacity to accommodate change, as demonstrated by the establishment of the 'European Circuit' for barristers of England and Wales who practise mainly in the EU.

SPECIALIST BAR ASSOCIATIONS

These associations are groups of barristers in independent practice in specialist fields. Their memberships often overlap. The associations concern themselves with the law and procedure in their fields, advise on law reform, look after their members' interests and help them to keep up-to-date with new developments. Many also provide extensive continuing professional education and many publish their own directories.

Bar Association for Commerce, Finance and Industry (BACFI)

BACFI was established in 1965 to promote the interests of barristers working in-house or providing legal services outside chambers. The Association's membership includes employed and non practising barristers working in commerce, finance and industry (the CFI Bar), overseas lawyers working in the UK, law students and retired barristers.

BACFI's President is Lord Hoffman of Chedworth. The Association aims to provide representation, education and support to its members. It is governed by a General Committee of elected members, runs a full annual programme of CPD seminars and networking events and maintains a Professional Issues sub-committee.

BACFI has several elected and nominated members on the General Council of the Bar and is represented on various Bar Council and BSB committees, to ensure that the voice of its members is heard. Visit www.bacfi.org for details of forthcoming events, quarterly newsletter and professional consultation responses. Join in discussions on LinkedIn by joining the BACFI Group.

Any member who has the time and energy to help with the Association is invited to contact the Chairman: Tricia Howse, CBE (tricia.howse@hotmail.co.uk).

For further information on membership or any other enquiries please contact our administrator Sandra Janes at membership@bacfi.org or on 01525 222 244 or in writing to PO Box 4352, Edlesborough, Dunstable, Beds, LU6 9EF.

Bar Association for Local Government and the Public Service

The main objectives of the association include the protection and promotion of the professional rights and interests of barristers employed in the public sector by giving advice to barristers seeking a career in the public sector, making representations to the Bar Council and elsewhere relating to training, rights of audience, direct access to counsel and by promoting professional knowledge.

Further details about the Association and an application form for membership can be obtained from the association's website or from the Chairman.

Chairman: Dr Mirza Ahmad LLD (Hon), LLM, MBA, Barrister, c/o St Philips Chambers, 55 Temple Row, Birmingham B2 5LS; email: chairman@balgps.org.uk

Website: www.balgps.org.uk

Bar European Group

The BEG was set up more than 30 years ago to promote interest in, and knowledge of, Community law. The group holds a yearly conference in a European country and a number of other lectures and seminars in the UK. Open to all interested barristers or Bar students, with associate membership for non-barristers. Membership includes barristers interested in Community Law and human rights who advise and appear in the UK courts, before the Luxembourg courts, the Strasbourg Court and before the EU Commission.

Chairman: Tom de la Mare, Blackstone House, Temple, London EC4Y 9BW (DX: 281 London, Chancery Lane, telephone 020 7583 1770, email TomdelaMare@blackstone chambers.com)

Vice-Chairman: Tim Ward QC, Monkton Chambers 1 & 2 Raymond Buildings, Gray's Inn, London WC1R 5NR (DX 257 LDE, telephone 020 7405 7211, email tward@monckon. com)

Hon Secretary: Julie Anderson, 20 Essex Street, London WC2R 3AL (DX 0009 LDE, telephone 07710 218285, email janderson@20essexst.com)

Treasurer: Nicholas Paines QC, Monckton Chambers, 1 & 2 Raymond Buildings, Gray's Inn, London WC1R 5NR (DX 257 LDE, telephone 020 7405 7211, email npaines @monckton.com)

Chancery Bar Association

The Chancery Bar offers an unrivalled breadth and depth of legal expertise across the whole spectrum of finance, property and business law. A detailed list of the kinds of work that Chancery barristers undertake can be seen at http:/ /www.chba.org.uk/chancery_work/the_chancery_bar.
Members of the Chancery Bar specialise in providing high quality advocacy in all courts and tribunals in England and Wales and many courts abroad. Members appear regularly in the Chancery Division but are equally at home and practise in the Queen's Bench Division, the Commercial Court and the Technology and Construction Court and in other specialist tribunals and arbitrations. Their practices involve the giving of specialist advice on commercial, property and private client transactions and disputes.

The Chancery Bar Association, which was established in 1935, is the oldest specialist bar association, as well as one of the largest. It represents the interests of about 1,300 members on the Bar Council. The main functions of the Association are to provide lectures, seminars and an annual conference during the year for the continuing professional development of its members; to promote the practices of its members both nationally and internationally; to liaise with other professional bodies in relation to the work of Chancery barristers; to respond to consultations issued by the Government, the judiciary, the Bar Council, and the regulators of the Bar, and to further equality and diversity initiatives of the profession and the pro bono activities of charitable bodies.

Contacts:

Francesca Compton, Administrator, Chancery Bar Association, 294B Queens Road, London SE14 5JN. Email: admin @chba.org.uk Tel: 07791 398254

Website: www.chba.org.uk

Commercial Bar Association (COMBAR)

COMBAR was founded in 1989. The commercial Bar serves the specialist needs of commerce, including international commercial litigation and arbitration. The experience of the commercial Bar extends across the fields of international trade, shipping and aviation, banking and financial services, insurance and reinsurance, commodity transactions, insolvency, oil & gas/energy law, mergers and acquisitions, competition law, intellectual property, professional negligence, licensing, judicial review of government acts, employment, European Community matters, private and public international law and beyond.

COMBAR liaises with other associations, authorities and bodies on matters of common interest, comments on proposed legislation and initiatives affecting the commercial field, offers a continuing programme of lectures and seminars and promotes good practice at the commercial Bar (including in the areas of equal opportunity, diversity and recruitment). COMBAR actively encourages close working links with lawyers practising in other jurisdictions, particularly in Europe, the Channel Islands, North America, the Commonwealth, Africa, India and the Far East. COMBAR promotes the commercial Bar nationally and internationally.

Contact: Veronica Kendall, Administrator, The Commercial Bar Association (COMBAR), 3 Verulam Buildings, Gray's Inn, London WC1R 5NT (telephone 020 7404 2022; website www.combar.com; e-mail admin@combar.com)

Constitutional and Administrative Law Bar Association (ALBA)

Membership is open to all members of the Bar, and associate membership to other lawyers, students and those with an interest in public law. The Association is concerned with the legal issues arising between individuals on the one hand and national and local government and public bodies on the other, including issues arising under the Human Rights Act. Members provide specialist advice and representation for and against public bodies, particularly in the field of judicial review and human rights. ALBA has a full programme of meetings, seminars and conferences, and has a regular newsletter. It fosters a knowledge of public and human rights law and its practice amongst its membership, and for the Bar as a whole, in its continuing education programme. It is regularly consulted by the Ministry of Justice and the Courts Service about matters affecting practice and procedure in the Administrative Court. Attendance at ALBA's functions attracts credits under the continuing education programme.

Further information can be obtained from the Association's website: www.adminlaw.org.uk

Criminal Bar Association

The Criminal Bar Association was founded in 1969. It is the largest of the Specialist Bar Associations with about 3,800 members. It aims to represent the views of the members of the independent criminal Bar in England and Wales. These members are principally engaged in providing advocacy and advice in the criminal courts, but are also instructed in extradition, regulatory, disciplinary and other 'quasi-criminal' proceedings. The CBA is invariably consulted in, and asked to make submissions to, any significant review affecting the criminal justice system. It also responds to initiatives and proposals from the European Commission. The CBA provides continuing education for criminal barristers at all levels of practice. A series of topical lectures delivered at the Old Bailey every autumn and winter by eminent judges, academics and practising lawyers is recorded and distributed to all Circuits. A full day conference is held every spring which addresses issues of present and future significance to the profession. Lectures and seminars covering all new major legislation are provided both in London and on Circuit. The CBA newsletter is published quarterly with a circulation of over 4,500.

The committee, elected by the membership, includes three representatives from each of the five circuits outside the South East.

CBA Secretariat: Mr Aaron J Dolan (telephone 0207 611 1475; email: aaron.dolan@criminalbar.com)

Website: www.criminalbar.com

Employment Law Bar Association

The Employment Law Bar Association represents and supports barristers working in employment law. ELBA organises regular CPD accredited speaker meetings addressed by leading members of the profession and judiciary, as well as by many other distinguished speakers. ELBA supports pupils and recently qualified barristers seeking to specialise in employment law through its meetings and advocacy training. ELBA is the forum for consultation with the employment Bar. Members socialise after meetings when refreshments are provided, at the annual dinner and at joint events with organisations such as the Employment Lawyers Association.

Formed in 1994, the association currently has over 1,000 members. Membership of ELBA is open to barristers practising in employment law, whether in independent practice or employed. Associate membership is open to the judiciary, pupils and students with an interest in employment law.

Website: www.elba.org.uk

To make contact: enquiries@elba.org.uk

Chair: Damian Brown, Littleton Chambers, 3 King's Bench Walk North, Temple, London EC4Y 7HR (telephone 020 7797 8600)

Secretary: Gavin Mansfield, Littleton Chambers, 3 King's Bench Walk North, Temple, London EC4Y 7HR (telephone 020 7797 8600)

Family Law Bar Association

The FLBA is the Specialist Bar Association for family barristers. With over 2,500 members it is one of the largest SBAs. The work of the family law practitioner falls principally into two areas:

Matrimonial and similar disputes

These cover the entire spectrum of disputes relating to relationship breakdown whether between married couples or not. Common types of litigation include:

- Every type of financial and property dispute including child support
- Disputes about the future arrangements for children after marriage or relationship breakdown
- All types of injunctive relief for domestic violence
- International jurisdiction issues
- Recognition of foreign marriages and divorces
- Post-death financial provision for impecunious surviving spouses and other dependants

Children

These disputes do not always involve divorce or relationship breakdown. Decisions may lead to the removal of children from their parents, either for fostering or adoption.

Such disputes frequently involve child abuse of differing kinds. It is here that the family law barrister meets the medical profession, police, local authorities and other public bodies. Perhaps in this area of the law, more than any other, the practitioner needs to be alert to human rights issues as they develop.

Membership of the FLBA is open to any member of the Bar, whether in independent practice, employment or pupillage. The Association has an active regional network comprising nearly one half of its members practising out of some 30 court centres. It organises residential weekend conferences in London and the provinces, together with seminars, meetings, continuing education programmes and social activities. The FLBA produces a newsletter Family Affairs to keep its members up to date with events around the country and the more important changes in the law and procedure.

On matters of law and procedural reform the Association is always consulted by government departments and a wide range of other public bodies.

All barristers with an interest in this field are encouraged to join the FLBA. Answers to any questions involving practice at the family law Bar should be sought from the Secretary. Enquiries concerning membership should be addressed to the Administrator.

Secretary: Philip Marshall QC, 1 King's Bench Walk, Temple, London EC4Y 7DB (telephone 020 7936 1500; email pmarshall@lkbw.co.uk)

Administrator: Carol Harris, FLBA Administration Office, General Council of the Bar, 289-293 High Holborn, London WC1V 7HZ (telephone 020 7242 1289; email charris@barcouncil.org.uk)

Website: www.flba.co.uk

FDA CPS Section

The FDA (formerly First Division Association) is the trade union that looks after the interests of senior public servants and has a significant membership of lawyers within the Crown Prosecution Service (CPS). The FDA is recognised by the CPS for negotiating terms and conditions and provides representation in industrial relations problems. It has an active CPS section committee which offers a collective view of professional issues which affect the service.

Convenor: Roland Zollner

Contact: Paul Whiteman, FDA Head Office, 8 Leake Street, London, SE1 7NN (telephone 020 7401 5555 or email paul@fda.org.uk)

Intellectual Property Bar Association (formerly Patent Bar Association)

The Intellectual Property Bar Association is the Specialist Bar Association for barristers practising in all areas of intellectual property law, including: patents, trademarks, passing off, copyright, registered and unregistered designs, performer's rights, trade secrets, breach of confidence, privacy and data protection. Most members have considerable scientific or technical expertise and are also regularly instructed in commercial cases and arbitrations with a technical content.

In addition to appearing in the High Court and the Patents County Court, members appear in the Patent Office, Trade Marks Registry, the European Patent Office, the Community Trade Marks and Design Office (known as the Office for the Harmonisation of Internal Markets) and the European Court of Justice, including the CFI.

Membership of the IPBA comprises the members of all the main intellectual property chambers, together with a number of individual practitioners based elsewhere.

A list of members and their Chambers is available at the IPBA's website: www.ipba.co.uk.

Chairman: Henry Carr QC, 11 South Square, Gray's Inn, London WC1R 5EY. (Tel: 020 7405 1222, email hcarr@ 11southsquare.com.

Secretary: Miles Copeland, 3 New Square, Lincoln's Inn London WC2A 3RS. (Tel: 0207 405 1111, email copeland@ 3newsquare.com).

The International Bar Association

The International Bar Association (IBA), established in 1947, is the world's leading organisation of international legal practitioners, bar associations and law societies. The IBA influences the development of international law reform and shapes the future of the legal profession throughout the world. It has a membership of 45,000 individual lawyers and more than 200 Bar Associations and Law Societies spanning all continents.

Grouped into two Divisions - the Legal Practice Division and the Public and the Professional Interest Division - the IBA covers all practice areas and professional interests, providing members with access to leading experts and up-to-date information. Through the various Committees of the Divisions, the IBA enables an interchange of information and views as to laws, practices and professional responsibilities relating to the practice of law around the globe. Additionally, the IBA's high quality publications and world-class conferences provide unrivalled professional development and network-building opportunities for international legal practitioners and professional associates.

The IBA's Bar Issues Commission provides an invaluable forum for the IBA's member Bar associations and law societies to discuss all matters relating to law at an international level.

The International Bar Association's Human Rights Institute works to promote, protect and enforce human rights under a just rule of law, and preserve the independence of the judiciary and the legal profession worldwide.

In partnership with the Open Society Initiative for Southern Africa, the IBA created the Southern Africa Litigation Centre, based in Johannesburg, South Africa, to promote human rights and the Rule of Law in Angola, Botswana, the Democratic Republic of Congo, Lesotho, Malawi, Mozambique, Namibia, Swaziland, Zambia and Zimbabwe.

Also, the IBA was instrumental in establishing the International Legal Assistance Consortium in Stockholm, Sweden. This global consortium of non-governmental organisations provides technical legal assistance to post-conflict countries.

Executive Director: Mark Ellis, International Bar Association, 4th Floor, 10 St Bride Street, London EC4 4AD. Telephone +44 (0)20 7842 0090; fax +44 (0)20 7842 0091; email: member@int-bar.org; website: www.ibanet.org

Justices' Clerks' Society

The Society was founded in 1839 and incorporated in 1903. It is a professional body representing legal advisers to lay magistrates in England and Wales and it is committed to improving the quality of justice in Magistrates' Courts. One of the main objects of the Society is to keep under review the operation of the law, especially that administered by Magistrates' Courts in England and Wales, to point out its defects and to support proposals for improvement. Through the members of its national Council, assisted by the specialist networks, the Society takes an active part in the development of all aspects of the law relating to Magistrates' Courts and is able to respond to a wide range of proposals emanating from government departments, agencies and other professional bodies. Members of the Society also play an active role in numerous bodies in addition to developing their own initiatives and innovations.

Contact: Jayne Skeates, HMCTS Head of Legal Services, Her Majesty's Courts and Tribunals Service, 3rd Floor, Temple Court, 35 Bull Street, Birmingham, B4 6EQ (telephone 0121 250 6307, email jcs@hmcts.gsi.gov.uk)

London Common Law and Commercial Bar Association (LCLCBA)

The LCLCBA dates back to 1966 and now has approximately 1,500 members. Membership is open to any member of the Bar whose practice is predominantly civil law within the High Court including the Commercial Court and the County Courts in and around London. It represents the interests of practitioners whose practices range from general common law to purely commercial as well as those who specialise in such diverse areas as construction, personal injury, professional negligence, employment, revenue, defamation, environmental and EC. Because of its broadly-based and large membership, it is in a strong position to protect and advance the interests of its members and to influence developments in civil law and practice.

Its current Chairman is Michael Kent QC and Vice-Chairman is Gregory Mitchell QC.

The LCLCBA represents its members' interests on the Bar Council, the South Eastern Circuit Committee and the Commercial Court Committee; produces papers at the request of the Bar Council, the Law Commission, the Bar Standards Board and the Ministry of Justice on matters of substantive and procedural law; organises regular seminars and lectures on topics of interest/concern to its members; offers an arbitration scheme; and liaises with other Specialist Bar Associations and the London Solicitors' Litigation Association.

Recent initiatives include installing a computerised database system to allow swift electronic communication with its membership and setting up a professional conduct complaints guidance facility for any members facing such complaints. It has a sub-committee dedicated to considering ways of improving equal opportunities at the Bar and has a mentoring scheme designed to help women return to the Bar after having had children. Another sub-committee focuses on the facilities offered by the courts in London to users with a view to seeking to improve these for the Association's members.

The Association has a website which can be found at www.lclcba.com. For more information, contact Michelle Stevens-Hoare (Secretary), Hardwicke Building, Lincoln's Inn, London, WC2A 3SB (telephone 020 7242 2523; email michelle.stevens-hoare@hardwicke.co.uk). To join, contact Amy Thompson, the Association's Administrator, at Hardwicke, New Square, Lincoln's Inn, London WCA 3SB (telephone: 020 7242 2523; email: lclcba@hardwicke.co.uk)

Northern Chancery Bar Association

The Northern Chancery Bar Association was set up by practitioners in the 1980s to advance the development of practice at the Chancery Bar in the North of England. Its purpose is to act as a forum for debate on matters of common interest, and as a medium for facilitating communication between practitioners, the judiciary, and Court staff about the administration of Chancery matters in the area.

We currently have over 100 members in sets of Chambers located in Liverpool, Manchester, Leeds, Newcastle-upon-Tyne and elsewhere. One of the Association's past chairmen is Mr Justice Peter Smith who sits permanently in the Chancery Division. We hold seminars from time to time on topics of interest to members and an annual dinner, which the local Judges who exercise jurisdiction in Chancery matters are invited to attend.

Chancery practice in the North continues to grow, displaying a substantial increase in both the volume and calibre of work. The increasing weight of work, and the importance attached to dealing with local disputes in the locality, is reflected in the number and quality of judges available to hear such cases. The jurisdiction is headed by the Vice-Chancellor of the County Palatine of Lancaster. Mr Justice Briggs has recently been appointed to this office, succeeding Mr Justice David Richards. He is assisted by several Circuit Judges sitting in the cities mentioned above with power under section 9 Supreme Court Act 1981 to hear High Court work on a full-time or semi-full time basis together with a number of specialist District Judges; all of whom deal with Chancery. It is anticipated that the work of the Association will continue to expand.

Any enquiries may be directed to David Mohyuddin, The Secretary, The Northern Chancery Bar Association, Exchange Chambers, 7 Ralli Court, West Riverside, Manchester M3 5PT (telephone 0161 833 2722, fax 0161 833 2789, DX: 14330 Manchester 1).

Chair: Lesley Anderson QC, Kings Chambers - Leeds and Manchester (telephone 0161 832 9082, fax 0161 835 2139, DX: 718188 Manchester 3).

Treasurer: Brad Pomfret, St James's Chambers (telephone 0161 834 7000,
fax 0161 834 2341 and DX: 14350 Manchester 1

http://www.nchba.co.uk

Northern Circuit Commercial Bar Association

NCCBA is an association of over 100 members, all of whom practise commercial law on the Northern Circuit. Founded in 1998, the Association provides an online directory of members' specialisms, provides a programme of CPD Events for members and solicitors and a specific programme of events for new practitioners. It also fosters links with other professionals in the Northwest. Details of all NCCBA events can be obtained from the Administrator, Sara Brett, PO Box 569, Bury BL8 9JF, tel 07776 339538, email admin@nccba.org.uk, and from the NCCBA's website at www.nccba.org.uk

Parliamentary Bar Mess

Members of this long-standing Bar association appear before parliamentary select committees in both Houses of Parliament at the committee stage of private and hybrid bills.

Members are normally instructed by Parliamentary Agents acting on behalf of local authorities or other government agencies, statutory undertakers or private promoters seeking statutory powers for major public works. They also appear for petitioners (for example local authorities, private individuals or environmental associations etc.) against the grant of powers for the carrying out of such works. Members of the Mess also appear at inquiries held under the Transport and Works Act 1992 and, in addition, many practise in the field of Town and Country Planning and National Infrastructure Planning. The Mess has assisted in the debate on parliamentary procedure and large infrastructure projects. Examples of recent bills promoted in hybrid and private parliamentary proceedings are the Crossrail Bill and the London Local Authorities Bill. A list of members may be obtained from the Treasurer.

Leader: Patrick Clarkson QC, Landmark Chambers, 180 Fleet Street, London EC4A 2HG (Tel: 020 7430 1221).

Treasurer: Timothy Comyn, Francis Taylor Building, Temple, London EC4Y 7BY (Tel: 020 7353 8415)

Personal Injuries Bar Association (PIBA)

Established in 1995, PIBA has grown to be one of the largest Specialist Bar Associations, with over 1,500 members drawn equally from barristers representing claimants and defendants. Membership of PIBA is open to any barrister or pupil barrister who practises or has an interest in the field of personal injuries, including clinical negligence, and to any student interested in developing a personal injury practice at the Bar. Chambers' schemes (group memberships) are also available. Membership is free for pupil barristers and barristers up to three years' call.

Membership of PIBA brings the following benefits:

- Access to the PIBA website, which contains news and updates on current legal developments, articles of interest, information on membership, events, etc.
- Regular email updates, informing members of news and events
- A varied continuing education programme, CPD accredited and heavily subsidised especially for younger members including:
  - Regular free evening seminars in London;
  - An annual residential conference in Oxford;

- A one-day conference on the Northern Circuit;
- Other events on other circuits;
- An annual lecture with keynote speaker, usually from the Judiciary.

Under the auspices of PIBA, a Personal Injuries Handbook has been published. PIBA proactively participates in consultations over reforms to legal services, costs and other areas which impact on personal injury work. PIBA representatives play a full and significant role on the Bar Council.

Chair: Charlie Cory-Wright QC, 39 Essex Street, London

Vice-Chair: Andrew Ritchie QC, 9 Gough Square, London

Secretary: Steven Snowden, Crown Office Chambers, London

Treasurer: Nigel Spencer Ley, Farrar's Building, London

Membership & Administration: Mrs Sarah Wilks, 9 Faircroft Avenue, Walmley, West Midlands, B76 1HQ Tel: 0121 240 8448 email admin@piba.org.uk

Website: www.piba.org.uk

Planning and Environment Bar Association (PEBA)

PEBA is the Specialist Bar Association for barristers who specialise in planning, environment, compulsory purchase, highways, housing, rating and other aspects of local government and administrative law. Membership of PEBA is only open to practising barristers (employed as well as those in independent practice) who demonstrate that they genuinely specialise in the areas.

PEBA runs a National Conference, as well as seminars for members, and publishes occasional newsletters. It also represents members both in responding to consultation papers, and in maintaining good relations with other professions relevant to the practices of its members.

Further information can be obtained from the Association's website: www.peba.info.

Secretary: Mr Christopher Boyle, Landmark Chambers, 180 Fleet Street, London, EC4A 2HG
(email peba.administrator@cptevents.co.uk)

Professional Negligence Bar Association

Formed in November 1990 to promote the idea of a professional negligence speciality, this Association is concerned mostly with lectures, seminars and continuing professional education generally. Members are recruited from widely different parts of the Bar, as the Association covers clinical, financial, construction and legal professional negligence. The PNBA is open to practising employed and non-practising barristers who have an interest in the subject. There are no categories of pupil or student membership although pupils of members may attend PNBA functions.

Further information can be obtained from the Association's website: www.pnba.co.uk

Secretary: Victoria Woodbridge, Crown Office Chambers, 2 Crown Office Row, Temple, London EC4Y 7HJ, DX: 80 London Chancery Lane, Tel: 020 7797 8100, Email: woodbridge @crownofficechambers.com

Property Bar Association

A body of specialists in property or property-related work founded to give voice to the opinions of specialist property lawyers on questions of law reform and practice, to provide a pool of expertise and a forum for discussion, education and training, raise the profile of property barristers and to develop innovative services to lay and professional clients.

The Association is recognised by the Bar Standards Board and the Bar Council for education and training purposes. Full details of members and events can be obtained from the Association's website www.propertybar.org.uk. All enquiries should be addressed to the Administrator.

Chairman: John Furber QC, Wilberforce Chambers, 8 New Square, Lincoln's Inn, London, WC2A 3QP

Secretary: Toby Watkin, Landmark Chambers, 180 Fleet Street, London, EC4A 2HG

Administrator: Amy Thomson, Hardwicke Building, New Square, Lincoln's Inn, London WC2A 3SB

All enquiries to: propertybarassociation@googlemail.com or 020 7691 0302

Public Access Bar Association (PABA)

This Specialist Bar Association comprises a large group of barristers who specialise in the growing area of Public Access work. Under the Bar scheme launched in July 2004, members of the public and businesses may instruct barristers directly and without the intervention of a solicitor.

PABA acts as an organ of communication of the views of PA barristers on matters of policy. It holds seminars featuring specialist speakers on interesting topics. It is trying to improve public awareness of PA work. PABA has its own Mediation panel for ADR in Public Access cases.

There are about 2,000 barristers now registered for PA work. They are acting in numerous areas of practice. Direct instruction can - and often does - save clients the unnecessary cost of using two lawyers, in the very many situations where direct instruction of the Bar is possible.

Chairman: Marc Beaumont, Windsor Chambers, Castle Hill House, 12 Castle Hill, Windsor SL4 1PD, mcb@windsorchambers.com, mc.beaumont@virgin.net

Vice Chairman: James Corbett QC, Kobre & Kim LLP, 60 Gresham St, London EC2V 7BB, james.corbett@kobrekim.com

Treasurer: Andrew Granville Stafford, 4 King's Bench Walk, 2nd Floor, 2 King's BenchWalk, London EC4Y 7DL, ags@4kbw.co.uk

Events: Timothy Becker, Clerksroom Chambers, 218 Strand, London WC2R 1AT, becker@clerksroom.com

Secretary: Jonathan Maskew, jonathan@footstepsms.co.uk

Administrator: Rebecca Hutt, becca.hutt@gmail.com

For PABA's programme of events and membership information, please see www.paba.org.uk

Revenue Bar Association

Members provide specialist tax advice and advocacy in relation to tax matters. The majority are tax specialists. The others have mixed practices, often Chancery work concentrating on the tax affecting trusts, estates and property. Members advise on technical points of tax law, planning, dealing with HMRC, as well as advocacy in the Tax Chamber of the First-tier and Upper Tax Tribunals, the Court of Appeal, the Supreme Court and the ECJ. Some members also have rights of audience in foreign courts.

Secretary: Richard Vallat, Pump Court Tax Chambers, 16 Bedford Row, London WC1R 4EF (telephone 020 7414 8080; website www.revenue-bar.org; email rba@pumptax.com)

Technology and Construction Bar Association (TECBAR)

TECBAR is the specialist bar association for employed or self-employed barristers who practise in the Technology and Construction Court, or before adjudicators, arbitrators and other tribunals, in cases relating to construction, civil engineering, information technology, telecommunications, oil and gas, chemical plants and ship-building.

To apply for membership, please contact the Secretary: Lynne McCafferty, 4 Pump Court, Temple, London EC4Y 7AN. Telephone: 020 7842 5555.

TECBAR Adjudicator and Mediator Appointments: contact the clerks at Atkin Chambers, 1 Atkin Building, Gray's Inn, London WC1R 5AT (telephone 020 7404 0102; email clerks@atkinchambers.com)

Website: www.tecbar.org

LICENSED ACCESS

Licensed Access is a scheme which enables organisations with the necessary skills and experience to instruct the Bar directly. The Bar Standards Board grants licences which are individually tailored to suit the particular needs and skills of the licensees and cover the spectrum of work at the Bar. This includes not only advisory and other non-contentious work but also contentious matters.

Members of professional bodies who were granted Direct Professional Access are now deemed to hold licensed access. A list of licensees and Direct Professional Access bodies is available from the Bar Standards Board.

Queries regarding the scheme should be addressed to Joanne Dixon, The Bar Standards Board, 289–293 High Holborn, London WC1V 7HZ. Telephone: 020 7611 1444.

PUBLIC ACCESS

In 2004, the rules were changed to allow barristers who had undertaken appropriate training to accept instructions from members of the public, business and other organisations without a solicitor also being instructed. A barrister will only be able to accept the work if satisfied that the interests of the client and the interests of justice do not require a solicitor to be involved. In April 2010 changes to the Code resulted in a barrister being allowed to accept work on this basis in all matters that are privately funded including contentious criminal, immigration or family matters. At present, around 5,000 barristers have undertaken the necessary training.

This directory contains a list of those who have undertaken the training. Up-to-date information can be found on the Bar Council website:
www.barcouncil.org.uk/publicaccess

For further details please contact:
Telephone: 020 7611 1472
Email: PAenquiry@BarCouncil.org.uk

BARMARK/BAR BUSINESS STANDARD

BARMARK is the Bar Council's "kite marking scheme". It is a voluntary scheme for those chambers who wish to demonstrate their effectiveness and, in particular, that they comply with the Bar Council's Practice Management Guidelines and the associated Quality Assurance Checklist. The Bar Council is currently updating the BarMark standard, and the new Bar Business Standard is due to be launched in the Autumn of 2012.

Further information about the BARMARK scheme/Bar Business Standard can be obtained from the Bar Council website: www.barcouncil.org.uk

PART A

A

Types of Work by Chambers

This section lists chambers by the type of work they do and by the town or city where they are located. The types of work undertaken by chambers are listed in alphabetical order. Within these main categories, chambers are listed alphabetically under the town or city in which they practise. For example, a reader wishing to locate a Birmingham-based chambers specialising in trademarks would be able to look under 'T' for Trademarks and find under that heading the details of any chambers in Birmingham which offer their services in this field. A complete list of the types of work can be found overleaf.

Each listing provides the chambers' name and chambers' telephone number. The first point of contact in each instance will be the clerk. (Details of clerks can be found in *Part D Chambers by Location*).

Please note that chambers are only listed in this section if information on specialisms has been supplied by them.

The symbol • indicates that chambers have an expanded entry in *Part D Chambers by Location*.

A

Type of Work

Bournemouth	3 PB Barristers	01202 292102
Bristol	3 PB Barristers	0117 928 1520
London	Erskine Chambers	020 7242 5532
	•One Essex Court	020 7583 2000
	•13 Old Square Chambers	020 7831 4445
	3 PB Barristers	020 7583 8055
Manchester	18 St John Street	0161 278 1800
Oxford	3 PB Barristers	01865 793 736
Winchester	3 PB Barristers	01962 868884

ADJUDICATION

Bournemouth	3 PB Barristers	01202 292102
Bristol	3 PB Barristers	0117 928 1520
	Queen Square Chambers	0117 921 1966
London	Arbitration Chambers	020 7267 2137
	Atkin Chambers	020 7404 0102
	•Crown Office Chambers	020 7797 8100
	Keating Chambers	020 7544 2600
	3 PB Barristers	020 7583 8055
Manchester	18 St John Street	0161 278 1800
Oxford	3 PB Barristers	01865 793 736
Winchester	3 PB Barristers	01962 868884

ADMINISTRATIVE LAW

Birmingham	•No5 Chambers	0845 210 5555
	•St Philips Chambers	0121 246 7000
Bournemouth	3 PB Barristers	01202 292102
Bristol	No5 Chambers	0845 210 5555
	3 PB Barristers	0117 928 1520
	St John's Chambers	0117 923 4700
Chichester	Pallant Chambers	01243 784538
Exeter	Rougemont Chambers	01392 208484
Leeds	Kings Chambers	0845 034 3444
	Park Court Chambers	0113 243 3277
London	•Arden Chambers	020 7242 4244
	Atlas Chambers	020 7269 7980
	•2 Bedford Row	020 7440 8888
	42 Bedford Row	020 7831 0222
	•9-12 Bell Yard	020 7400 1800
	Blackstone Chambers	020 7583 1770
	Brick Court Chambers	020 7379 3550
	Chambers of Mr Patrick Ground QC	020 7736 0131
	1 Chancery Lane	0845 634 6666
	•Cornerstone Barristers	020 7242 4986
	1 Crown Office Row	020 7797 7500
	•Devereux Chambers	020 7353 7534
	Doughty Street Chambers	020 7404 1313
	•One Essex Court	020 7583 2000
	Essex Court Chambers	020 7813 8000
	20 Essex Street	020 7842 1200
	•39 Essex Street	020 7832 1111
	•Farrar's Building	020 7583 9241
	Farringdon Chambers	020 7089 5700
	Five Paper	020 7815 3200
	Fountain Court Chambers	020 7583 3335
	Francis Taylor Building	020 7353 8415
	•Goldsmith Chambers	020 7353 6802
	Gough Square Chambers	020 7353 0924
	•4-5 Gray's Inn Square	020 7404 5252
	Great James Street Chambers	020 7440 4949
	Hailsham Chambers	020 7643 5000
	Harcourt Chambers	0844 561 7135
	•Henderson Chambers	020 7583 9020

A

	•1 KBW Chambers	020 7936 1500
	2 King's Bench Walk	020 7353 1746
	11 King's Bench Walk	020 7632 8500
	13 King's Bench Walk	020 7353 7204
	Lamb Chambers	020 7797 8300
	•Maitland Chambers	020 7406 1200
	Matrix Chambers	020 7404 3447
	•Monckton Chambers	020 7405 7211
	New Square Chambers	020 7419 8000
	No5 Chambers	0845 210 5555
	•13 Old Square Chambers	020 7831 4445
	3 PB Barristers	020 7583 8055
	1 Pump Court	020 7842 7070
	•5 Pump Court	020 7353 2532
	6 Pump Court	020 7797 8400
	•3 Raymond Buildings	020 7400 6400
	Serle Court	020 7242 6105
	•Tanfield Chambers	020 7421 5300
	•Temple Garden Chambers	020 7583 1315
	Tooks Chambers	020 7842 7575
	3 Verulam Buildings	020 7831 8441
Maidstone	6 Pump Court Chambers	01622 688094
Manchester	Central Chambers	0161 236 1133
	Chambers of Ian Macdonald QC	0161 236 1840
	•Cobden House Chambers	0161 833 6000
	Kenworthy's Chambers	0161 832 4036
	Kings Chambers	0845 034 3444
	St James's Chambers	0161 834 7000
	18 St John Street	0161 278 1800
	•St Johns Buildings	0161 214 1500
Middlesbrough	Old Court Chambers	01642 232523
Newcastle Upon Tyne	Cathedral Chambers	0191 232 1311
	Dere Street Barristers	0844 3351551
Oxford	Harcourt Chambers	0844 561 7135
	3 PB Barristers	01865 793 736
Southampton	•College Chambers	023 8023 0338
Winchester	3 PB Barristers	01962 868884

ADMIRALTY

London	Brick Court Chambers	020 7379 3550
	20 Essex Street	020 7842 1200
	Fountain Court Chambers	020 7583 3335
	•4-5 Gray's Inn Square	020 7404 5252
Plymouth	Devon Chambers	01752 661659
Portsmouth	Portsmouth Barristers' Chambers	023 9283 1292

ADOPTION

Birmingham	St Ive's Chambers	0121 236 0863
	•St Philips Chambers	0121 246 7000
Bournemouth	3 PB Barristers	01202 292102
Bristol	3 PB Barristers	0117 928 1520
	Queen Square Chambers	0117 921 1966
Exeter	Rougemont Chambers	01392 208484
Faringdon	Faringdon Chambers	01367 240598
London	•29 Bedford Row Chambers	020 7404 1044
	Bell Yard Chambers	020 7306 9292
	•Goldsmith Chambers	020 7353 6802
	•1 KBW Chambers	020 7936 1500
	•4 Paper Buildings	020 7427 5200
	3 PB Barristers	020 7583 8055
	Renaissance Chambers	020 7404 1111
	•Tanfield Chambers	020 7421 5300
Manchester	18 St John Street	0161 278 1800
Middlesbrough	Amicus Chambers	01642 876334

• Expanded entry in Part D

Newcastle Upon Tyne	Dere Street Barristers	0844 3351551
Oxford	3 PB Barristers	01865 793 736
Portsmouth	Guildhall Chambers Portsmouth	023 9275 2400
Southampton	•College Chambers	023 8023 0338
Winchester	3 PB Barristers	01962 868884

AGENCY

London	Five Paper	020 7815 3200
Newcastle Upon Tyne	Dere Street Barristers	0844 3351551
Portsmouth	Portsmouth Barristers'Chambers	023 9283 1292
Southampton	•College Chambers	023 8023 0338

AGRICULTURE

Birmingham	•No5 Chambers	0845 210 5555
Bristol	No5 Chambers	0845 210 5555
	St John's Chambers	0117 923 4700
Chester	Linenhall Chambers	01244 348282
Exeter	Rougemont Chambers	01392 208484
	Walnut House	01392 279751
Ipswich	East Anglian Chambers	01473 214481
Leeds	Chancery House Chambers	0113 244 6691
	Enterprise Chambers	0113 246 0391
	Zenith Chambers	0113 245 5438
Liverpool	Atlantic Chambers	0151 236 4421
London	Brick Court Chambers	020 7379 3550
	Enterprise Chambers	020 7405 9471
	Essex Court Chambers	020 7813 8000
	Falcon Chambers	020 7353 2484
	Five Paper	020 7815 3200
	Hailsham Chambers	020 7643 5000
	•Maitland Chambers	020 7406 1200
	•Monckton Chambers	020 7405 7211
	No5 Chambers	0845 210 5555
	•13 Old Square Chambers	020 7831 4445
	Radcliffe Chambers	020 7831 0081
	•9 Stone Buildings	020 7404 5055
	3 Verulam Buildings	020 7831 8441
Manchester	•Cobden House Chambers	0161 833 6000
	St James's Chambers	0161 834 7000
	18 St John Street	0161 278 1800
	•St Johns Buildings	0161 214 1500
Middlesbrough	•Trinity Chambers	01642 247569
Newcastle Upon Tyne	Dere Street Barristers	0844 3351551
	Enterprise Chambers	0191 222 3344
	•Trinity Chambers	0191 232 1927
Plymouth	Devon Chambers	01752 661659
Swansea	Iscoed Chambers	01792 652988

ALTERNATIVE DISPUTE RESOLUTION

Birmingham	•No5 Chambers	0845 210 5555
	•St Philips Chambers	0121 246 7000
Bournemouth	3 PB Barristers	01202 292102
Bristol	3 PB Barristers	0117 928 1520
Exeter	Rougemont Chambers	01392 208484
London	Atkin Chambers	020 7404 0102
	Bell Yard Chambers	020 7306 9292
	Blackstone Chambers	020 7583 1770
	•Cornerstone Barristers	020 7242 4986
	•One Essex Court	020 7583 2000
	Five Paper	020 7815 3200
	•Henderson Chambers	020 7583 9020
	•1 KBW Chambers	020 7936 1500
	Keating Chambers	020 7544 2600
	•Maitland Chambers	020 7406 1200

	3 PB Barristers	020 7583 8055
	•Pump Court Tax Chambers	020 7414 8080
	•Tanfield Chambers	020 7421 5300
	XXIV Old Buildings	020 7691 2424
Manchester	18 St John Street	0161 278 1800
Oxford	3 PB Barristers	01865 793 736
Portsmouth	Portsmouth Barristers'Chambers	023 9283 1292
Winchester	3 PB Barristers	01962 868884

AMERICAN LAW

Exeter	Rougemont Chambers	01392 208484

ANCILLARY RELIEF

Birmingham	St Ive's Chambers	0121 236 0863
Bournemouth	3 PB Barristers	01202 292102
Bristol	3 PB Barristers	0117 928 1520
	Queen Square Chambers	0117 921 1966
Exeter	Rougemont Chambers	01392 208484
Faringdon	Faringdon Chambers	01367 240598
Liverpool	•Oriel Chambers	0151 236 7191
London	•29 Bedford Row Chambers	020 7404 1044
	Bell Yard Chambers	020 7306 9292
	Five Paper	020 7815 3200
	•1 KBW Chambers	020 7936 1500
	•4 Paper Buildings	020 7427 5200
	3 PB Barristers	020 7583 8055
	Renaissance Chambers	020 7404 1111
	•Tanfield Chambers	020 7421 5300
	The Chambers of Grahame Aldous QC	020 7832 0500
Manchester	18 St John Street	0161 278 1800
Middlesbrough	Amicus Chambers	01642 876334
Newcastle Upon Tyne	Dere Street Barristers	0844 3351551
Northampton	Northampton Chambers	01604 636271
Oxford	3 PB Barristers	01865 793 736
Portsmouth	Guildhall Chambers Portsmouth	023 9275 2400
	Portsmouth Barristers'Chambers	023 9283 1292
Sheffield	Bank House Chambers	0114 275 1223
Southampton	•College Chambers	023 8023 0338
Winchester	3 PB Barristers	01962 868884

ANIMAL RIGHTS LAW

London	The Chambers of Grahame Aldous QC	020 7832 0500
Manchester	18 St John Street	0161 278 1800
Newcastle Upon Tyne	Dere Street Barristers	0844 3351551

ANIMALS

Birmingham	St Ive's Chambers	0121 236 0863
Bournemouth	3 PB Barristers	01202 292102
Brighton	Crown Office Row Chambers	01273 625625
Bristol	3 PB Barristers	0117 928 1520
Exeter	Walnut House	01392 279751
London	3 PB Barristers	020 7583 8055
	The Chambers of Grahame Aldous QC	020 7832 0500
Manchester	18 St John Street	0161 278 1800
	•St Johns Buildings	0161 214 1500
Newcastle Upon Tyne	Dere Street Barristers	0844 3351551
Oxford	3 PB Barristers	01865 793 736
Winchester	3 PB Barristers	01962 868884

ANTI-DUMPING

Manchester	18 St John Street	0161 278 1800

ANTI-SOCIAL BEHAVIOUR ORDERS

Birmingham	St Ive's Chambers	0121 236 0863
Bristol	Queen Square Chambers	0117 921 1966

• Expanded entry in Part D

Exeter	Walnut House	01392 279751
Leeds	KBW	0113 297 1200
London	Bell Yard Chambers	020 7306 9292
	•Cornerstone Barristers	020 7242 4986
	•23 Essex Street	020 7413 0353
	Five Paper	020 7815 3200
	•187 Fleet Street	020 7430 7430
	•1 KBW Chambers	020 7936 1500
	15 New Bridge Street	020 7842 1900
	18 Red Lion Court	020 7520 6000
	The Chambers of Grahame Aldous QC	020 7832 0500
Manchester	Chambers of Ian Macdonald QC	0161 236 1840
	Kenworthy's Chambers	0161 832 4036
	18 St John Street	0161 278 1800
	•St Johns Buildings	0161 214 1500
Middlesbrough	•Trinity Chambers	01642 247569
Newcastle Upon Tyne	Dere Street Barristers	0844 3351551
	•Trinity Chambers	0191 232 1927
Portsmouth	Guildhall Chambers Portsmouth	023 9275 2400

ARAB COMMERCIAL LAW

Bournemouth	3 PB Barristers	01202 292102
Bristol	3 PB Barristers	0117 928 1520
London	3 PB Barristers	020 7583 8055
	Serle Court	020 7242 6105
Oxford	3 PB Barristers	01865 793 736
Winchester	3 PB Barristers	01962 868884

ARAB LAW

Bournemouth	3 PB Barristers	01202 292102
Bristol	3 PB Barristers	0117 928 1520
London	3 PB Barristers	020 7583 8055
	Serle Court	020 7242 6105
	•Tanfield Chambers	020 7421 5300
Oxford	3 PB Barristers	01865 793 736
Winchester	3 PB Barristers	01962 868884

ARBITRATION

Birmingham	No 8 Chambers	0121 236 5514
	•No5 Chambers	0845 210 5555
	•St Philips Chambers	0121 246 7000
Bournemouth	3 PB Barristers	01202 292102
Bristol	No5 Chambers	0845 210 5555
	3 PB Barristers	0117 928 1520
	Queen Square Chambers	0117 921 1966
	St John's Chambers	0117 923 4700
Chester	Linenhall Chambers	01244 348282
Exeter	Rougemont Chambers	01392 208484
Leeds	Enterprise Chambers	0113 246 0391
	KBW	0113 297 1200
	Kings Chambers	0845 034 3444
	Park Court Chambers	0113 243 3277
	•Sovereign Chambers	0113 245 1841
	Zenith Chambers	0113 245 5438
Liverpool	Atlantic Chambers	0151 236 4421
London	Arbitration Chambers	020 7267 2137
	Atkin Chambers	020 7404 0102
	Bell Yard Chambers	020 7306 9292
	Blackstone Chambers	020 7583 1770
	Brick Court Chambers	020 7379 3550
	•Chambers of Mr Ami Feder	020 7797 7788
	•Cornerstone Barristers	020 7242 4986
	•Crown Office Chambers	020 7797 8100
	•Devereux Chambers	020 7353 7534

• Expanded entry in Part D

A

	Enterprise Chambers	020 7405 9471
	Erskine Chambers	020 7242 5532
	•One Essex Court	020 7583 2000
	Essex Court Chambers	020 7813 8000
	20 Essex Street	020 7842 1200
	•39 Essex Street	020 7832 1111
	Falcon Chambers	020 7353 2484
	Fountain Court Chambers	020 7583 3335
	•Goldsmith Chambers	020 7353 6802
	•4-5 Gray's Inn Square	020 7404 5252
	Hailsham Chambers	020 7643 5000
	•Henderson Chambers	020 7583 9020
	4 KBW	020 7822 8822
	Keating Chambers	020 7544 2600
	11 King's Bench Walk	020 7632 8500
	Lamb Chambers	020 7797 8300
	•Maitland Chambers	020 7406 1200
	Matrix Chambers	020 7404 3447
	•Monckton Chambers	020 7405 7211
	New Square Chambers	020 7419 8000
	No5 Chambers	0845 210 5555
	•13 Old Square Chambers	020 7831 4445
	Outer Temple Chambers	020 7353 6381
	3 PB Barristers	020 7583 8055
	Prince Henry's Chambers	020 7837 1645
	4 Pump Court	020 7842 5555
	•5 Pump Court	020 7353 2532
	•Pump Court Chambers	020 7353 0711
	Radcliffe Chambers	020 7831 0081
	Selborne Chambers	020 7420 9500
	Serle Court	020 7242 6105
	•South Square	020 7696 9900
	3 Stone Buildings	020 7242 4937
	•9 Stone Buildings	020 7404 5055
	11 Stone Buildings	020 7831 6381
	•Tanfield Chambers	020 7421 5300
	•Three New Square IP	020 7405 1111
	3 Verulam Buildings	020 7831 8441
	XXIV Old Buildings	020 7691 2424
Manchester	Byrom Street Chambers	0161 829 2100
	•Cobden House Chambers	0161 833 6000
	Deans Court Chambers	0161 214 6000
	Kings Chambers	0845 034 3444
	St James's Chambers	0161 834 7000
	18 St John Street	0161 278 1800
	•St Johns Buildings	0161 214 1500
Middlesbrough	Old Court Chambers	01642 232523
	•Trinity Chambers	01642 247569
Newcastle Upon Tyne	Dere Street Barristers	0844 3351551
	Enterprise Chambers	0191 222 3344
	•Trinity Chambers	0191 232 1927
Northampton	Chartlands Chambers	01604 603322
Norwich	Octagon House	01603 623186
Oxford	3 PB Barristers	01865 793 736
Plymouth	Devon Chambers	01752 661659
Portsmouth	Guildhall Chambers Portsmouth	023 9275 2400
	Portsmouth Barristers'Chambers	023 9283 1292
Preston	Deans Court Chambers	01772 565 600
Sheffield	Bank House Chambers	0114 275 1223
Swindon	Pump Court Chambers	01793 539899
Winchester	3 PB Barristers	01962 868884
	Pump Court Chambers	01962 868 161

• Expanded entry in Part D

ART

London	Serle Court	020 7242 6105

ASBESTOS-RELATED DISEASES

Birmingham	St Ive's Chambers	0121 236 0863
Bournemouth	3 PB Barristers	01202 292102
Bristol	3 PB Barristers	0117 928 1520
	Queen Square Chambers	0117 921 1966
London	•Henderson Chambers	020 7583 9020
	3 PB Barristers	020 7583 8055
	•Tanfield Chambers	020 7421 5300
	The Chambers of Grahame Aldous QC	020 7832 0500
Manchester	Byrom Street Chambers	0161 829 2100
	Chambers of Ian Macdonald QC	0161 236 1840
	•Lincoln House Chambers	0161 832 5701
	18 St John Street	0161 278 1800
Newcastle Upon Tyne	Dere Street Barristers	0844 3351551
Oxford	3 PB Barristers	01865 793 736
Southampton	•College Chambers	023 8023 0338
Winchester	3 PB Barristers	01962 868884

ASSESSMENT OF COSTS

London	Five Paper	020 7815 3200
Manchester	18 St John Street	0161 278 1800
Newcastle Upon Tyne	Dere Street Barristers	0844 3351551
Southampton	•College Chambers	023 8023 0338

ASSET FINANCE

Birmingham	•No5 Chambers	0845 210 5555
Bristol	No5 Chambers	0845 210 5555
Liverpool	•Oriel Chambers	0151 236 7191
London	Brick Court Chambers	020 7379 3550
	Erskine Chambers	020 7242 5532
	Five Paper	020 7815 3200
	Fountain Court Chambers	020 7583 3335
	No5 Chambers	0845 210 5555
	•South Square	020 7696 9900
Manchester	18 St John Street	0161 278 1800

ASSET FORFEITURE

Bournemouth	3 PB Barristers	01202 292102
Bristol	3 PB Barristers	0117 928 1520
	Queen Square Chambers	0117 921 1966
London	•2 Bedford Row	020 7440 8888
	•23 Essex Street	020 7413 0353
	•187 Fleet Street	020 7430 7430
	•Furnival Chambers	020 7405 3232
	•1 KBW Chambers	020 7936 1500
	15 New Bridge Street	020 7842 1900
	3 PB Barristers	020 7583 8055
	•3 Raymond Buildings	020 7400 6400
	18 Red Lion Court	020 7520 6000
	The Chambers of Grahame Aldous QC	020 7832 0500
Manchester	Chambers of Ian Macdonald QC	0161 236 1840
	18 St John Street	0161 278 1800
Middlesbrough	•Trinity Chambers	01642 247569
Newcastle Upon Tyne	Dere Street Barristers	0844 3351551
	•Trinity Chambers	0191 232 1927
Oxford	3 PB Barristers	01865 793 736
Winchester	3 PB Barristers	01962 868884

ASSET RECOVERY

Birmingham	•St Philips Chambers	0121 246 7000
Bournemouth	3 PB Barristers	01202 292102
Bristol	3 PB Barristers	0117 928 1520

• Expanded entry in Part D

	Queen Square Chambers	0117 921 1966
Exeter	Walnut House	01392 279751
London	•2 Bedford Row	020 7440 8888
	Essex Court Chambers	020 7813 8000
	•23 Essex Street	020 7413 0353
	Five Paper	020 7815 3200
	•187 Fleet Street	020 7430 7430
	•1 KBW Chambers	020 7936 1500
	•Maitland Chambers	020 7406 1200
	15 New Bridge Street	020 7842 1900
	Outer Temple Chambers	020 7353 6381
	3 PB Barristers	020 7583 8055
	•3 Raymond Buildings	020 7400 6400
	18 Red Lion Court	020 7520 6000
Manchester	Chambers of Ian Macdonald QC	0161 236 1840
	18 St John Street	0161 278 1800
	•St Johns Buildings	0161 214 1500
Middlesbrough	•Trinity Chambers	01642 247569
Newcastle Upon Tyne	Dere Street Barristers	0844 3351551
	•Trinity Chambers	0191 232 1927
Oxford	3 PB Barristers	01865 793 736
Winchester	3 PB Barristers	01962 868884

ASYLUM

Birmingham	St Ive's Chambers	0121 236 0863
Exeter	Rougemont Chambers	01392 208484
	Walnut House	01392 279751
London	Bell Yard Chambers	020 7306 9292
	Blackstone Chambers	020 7583 1770
	1 Crown Office Row	020 7797 7500
	The Chambers of Grahame Aldous QC	020 7832 0500
Manchester	Chambers of Ian Macdonald QC	0161 236 1840
	Kenworthy's Chambers	0161 832 4036
	18 St John Street	0161 278 1800
	•St Johns Buildings	0161 214 1500
Newcastle Upon Tyne	Dere Street Barristers	0844 3351551
Northampton	Chartlands Chambers	01604 603322

AUDITING

London	•One Essex Court	020 7583 2000
Manchester	18 St John Street	0161 278 1800

AVIATION

London	Blackstone Chambers	020 7583 1770
	Essex Court Chambers	020 7813 8000
	20 Essex Street	020 7842 1200
	•23 Essex Street	020 7413 0353
	Fountain Court Chambers	020 7583 3335
	•4-5 Gray's Inn Square	020 7404 5252
	•1 Paper Buildings	020 7353 3728
	XXIV Old Buildings	020 7691 2424

BAHAMAS LAW

London	Radcliffe Chambers	020 7831 0081
	XXIV Old Buildings	020 7691 2424

BANKING

Birmingham	•No5 Chambers	0845 210 5555
	•St Philips Chambers	0121 246 7000
Bournemouth	3 PB Barristers	01202 292102
Bristol	No5 Chambers	0845 210 5555
	3 PB Barristers	0117 928 1520
	St John's Chambers	0117 923 4700
Exeter	Rougemont Chambers	01392 208484
Leeds	Chancery House Chambers	0113 244 6691

• Expanded entry in Part D

A

	Enterprise Chambers	0113 246 0391
	Kings Chambers	0845 034 3444
Liverpool	Atlantic Chambers	0151 236 4421
	•Oriel Chambers	0151 236 7191
London	•Argent Chambers	020 7556 5500
	Blackstone Chambers	020 7583 1770
	Brick Court Chambers	020 7379 3550
	Enterprise Chambers	020 7405 9471
	Erskine Chambers	020 7242 5532
	•One Essex Court	020 7583 2000
	Essex Court Chambers	020 7813 8000
	20 Essex Street	020 7842 1200
	Five Paper	020 7815 3200
	Fountain Court Chambers	020 7583 3335
	Gough Square Chambers	020 7353 0924
	•4-5 Gray's Inn Square	020 7404 5252
	4 KBW	020 7822 8822
	13 King's Bench Walk	020 7353 7204
	Lamb Chambers	020 7797 8300
	•Maitland Chambers	020 7406 1200
	New Square Chambers	020 7419 8000
	No5 Chambers	0845 210 5555
	•13 Old Square Chambers	020 7831 4445
	3 PB Barristers	020 7583 8055
	4 Pump Court	020 7842 5555
	Radcliffe Chambers	020 7831 0081
	Selborne Chambers	020 7420 9500
	Serle Court	020 7242 6105
	•South Square	020 7696 9900
	3 Stone Buildings	020 7242 4937
	4 Stone Buildings	020 7242 5524
	•9 Stone Buildings	020 7404 5055
	•Tanfield Chambers	020 7421 5300
	Ten Old Square	020 7405 0758
	3 Verulam Buildings	020 7831 8441
	•Wilberforce Chambers	020 7306 0102
	XXIV Old Buildings	020 7691 2424
Manchester	•Cobden House Chambers	0161 833 6000
	Deans Court Chambers	0161 214 6000
	Kings Chambers	0845 034 3444
	St James's Chambers	0161 834 7000
	9 St John Street	0161 955 9000
	18 St John Street	0161 278 1800
	•St Johns Buildings	0161 214 1500
Newcastle Upon Tyne	Enterprise Chambers	0191 222 3344
Oxford	3 PB Barristers	01865 793 736
Portsmouth	Portsmouth Barristers' Chambers	023 9283 1292
Preston	Deans Court Chambers	01772 565 600
Winchester	3 PB Barristers	01962 868884

BANKING AND FINANCE

Birmingham	St Ive's Chambers	0121 236 0863
	•St Philips Chambers	0121 246 7000
Exeter	Walnut House	01392 279751
London	11 Stone Buildings	020 7831 6381
	XXIV Old Buildings	020 7691 2424

BILLS OF EXCHANGE

Bournemouth	3 PB Barristers	01202 292102
Bristol	3 PB Barristers	0117 928 1520
London	•One Essex Court	020 7583 2000
	Five Paper	020 7815 3200
	3 PB Barristers	020 7583 8055
Oxford	3 PB Barristers	01865 793 736

Winchester	3 PB Barristers	01962 868884

BLOODSTOCK

London	The Chambers of Grahame Aldous QC	020 7832 0500
Manchester	18 St John Street	0161 278 1800
Newcastle Upon Tyne	Dere Street Barristers	0844 3351551

BOATING

Portsmouth	Portsmouth Barristers'Chambers	023 9283 1292

BOUNDARIES

Birmingham	St Ive's Chambers	0121 236 0863
Bournemouth	3 PB Barristers	01202 292102
Bristol	3 PB Barristers	0117 928 1520
	Queen Square Chambers	0117 921 1966
Exeter	Rougemont Chambers	01392 208484
London	•Arden Chambers	020 7242 4244
	•Cornerstone Barristers	020 7242 4986
	Five Paper	020 7815 3200
	•Henderson Chambers	020 7583 9020
	Keating Chambers	020 7544 2600
	•Maitland Chambers	020 7406 1200
	3 PB Barristers	020 7583 8055
	•5 Pump Court	020 7353 2532
	•Tanfield Chambers	020 7421 5300
	The Chambers of Grahame Aldous QC	020 7832 0500
Manchester	18 St John Street	0161 278 1800
Newcastle Upon Tyne	Dere Street Barristers	0844 3351551
Oxford	3 PB Barristers	01865 793 736
Portsmouth	Guildhall Chambers Portsmouth	023 9275 2400
	Portsmouth Barristers'Chambers	023 9283 1292
Southampton	•College Chambers	023 8023 0338
Winchester	3 PB Barristers	01962 868884

BREACH OF CONFIDENCE

London	Bell Yard Chambers	020 7306 9292
	•Maitland Chambers	020 7406 1200
	•8 New Square	020 7405 4321
	•13 Old Square Chambers	020 7831 4445
Manchester	18 St John Street	0161 278 1800
Portsmouth	Portsmouth Barristers'Chambers	023 9283 1292

BRITISH VIRGIN ISLANDS LAW

London	•Tanfield Chambers	020 7421 5300
	XXIV Old Buildings	020 7691 2424

BUILDING

Bournemouth	3 PB Barristers	01202 292102
Bristol	3 PB Barristers	0117 928 1520
	Queen Square Chambers	0117 921 1966
Chichester	Pallant Chambers	01243 784538
Exeter	Rougemont Chambers	01392 208484
London	Arbitration Chambers	020 7267 2137
	Chambers of Mr Patrick Ground QC	020 7736 0131
	Keating Chambers	020 7544 2600
	3 PB Barristers	020 7583 8055
Manchester	18 St John Street	0161 278 1800
Newcastle Upon Tyne	Dere Street Barristers	0844 3351551
Oxford	3 PB Barristers	01865 793 736
Portsmouth	Portsmouth Barristers'Chambers	023 9283 1292
Southampton	•College Chambers	023 8023 0338
Winchester	3 PB Barristers	01962 868884

BUILDING SOCIETIES

Manchester	•St Johns Buildings	0161 214 1500

• Expanded entry in Part D

CANON LAW (RC)

Newcastle Upon Tyne	Dere Street Barristers	0844 3351551

CAPITAL MARKETS

London	Erskine Chambers	020 7242 5532
	XXIV Old Buildings	020 7691 2424

CAPITAL TAX

Birmingham	No 8 Chambers	0121 236 5514
	•No5 Chambers	0845 210 5555
	•St Philips Chambers	0121 246 7000
Bradford	Broadway House Chambers	01274 722560
Bristol	No5 Chambers	0845 210 5555
	St John's Chambers	0117 923 4700
Leeds	Broadway House Chambers	0113 246 2600
	Chancery House Chambers	0113 244 6691
	Kings Chambers	0845 034 3444
	Zenith Chambers	0113 245 5438
Liverpool	Atlantic Chambers	0151 236 4421
London	Atlas Chambers	020 7269 7980
	•Devereux Chambers	020 7353 7534
	Gough Square Chambers	020 7353 0924
	•Maitland Chambers	020 7406 1200
	New Square Chambers	020 7419 8000
	No5 Chambers	0845 210 5555
	Prince Henry's Chambers	020 7837 1645
	•Pump Court Tax Chambers	020 7414 8080
	Radcliffe Chambers	020 7831 0081
	3 Stone Buildings	020 7242 4937
	•9 Stone Buildings	020 7404 5055
	Taxchambers	020 7242 2744
	Temple Tax Chambers	020 7353 7884
	Ten Old Square	020 7405 0758
	•Wilberforce Chambers	020 7306 0102
Manchester	•Cobden House Chambers	0161 833 6000
	Kings Chambers	0845 034 3444
	St James's Chambers	0161 834 7000
	18 St John Street	0161 278 1800
	•St Johns Buildings	0161 214 1500
Newcastle Upon Tyne	Dere Street Barristers	0844 3351551

CARE PROCEEDINGS

Birmingham	Cornwall Street Chambers	0121 233 7500
	No 8 Chambers	0121 236 5514
	St Ive's Chambers	0121 236 0863
	•St Philips Chambers	0121 246 7000
Bournemouth	3 PB Barristers	01202 292102
Bradford	Broadway House Chambers	01274 722560
Brighton	Crown Office Row Chambers	01273 625625
Bristol	Albion Chambers	0117 927 2144
	Queen Square Chambers	0117 921 1966
	St John's Chambers	0117 923 4700
	Unity Street Chambers	0117 906 9789
Canterbury	Becket Chambers	01227 786331
Chelmsford	Trinity Chambers	01245 605040
Chester	Linenhall Chambers	01244 348282
Chichester	Pallant Chambers	01243 784538
Exeter	Rougemont Chambers	01392 208484
	Walnut House	01392 279751
Faringdon	Faringdon Chambers	01367 240598
Hull	Wilberforce Chambers	01482 323264
Ipswich	East Anglian Chambers	01473 214481
Leeds	Broadway House Chambers	0113 246 2600
	KBW	0113 297 1200

• Expanded entry in Part D

	Park Court Chambers	0113 243 3277
	37 Park Square Chambers	0113 243 9422
	•Sovereign Chambers	0113 245 1841
	Zenith Chambers	0113 245 5438
Lewes	Westgate Chambers	01273 480510
Liverpool	Atlantic Chambers	0151 236 4421
	Chavasse Court Chambers	0151 229 2030
	•Oriel Chambers	0151 236 7191
London	42 Bedford Row	020 7831 0222
	•29 Bedford Row Chambers	020 7404 1044
	Bell Yard Chambers	020 7306 9292
	•Chambers of Mr Ami Feder	020 7797 7788
	•3 Dr Johnson's Buildings	020 7353 4854
	1 Garden Court Family Law Chambers	020 7797 7900
	•Goldsmith Chambers	020 7353 6802
	14 Gray's Inn Square	020 7242 0858
	Harcourt Chambers	0844 561 7135
	•1 KBW Chambers	020 7936 1500
	•New Court	020 7583 5123
	Outer Temple Chambers	020 7353 6381
	3 PB Barristers	020 7583 8055
	1 Pump Court	020 7842 7070
	•5 Pump Court	020 7353 2532
	6 Pump Court	020 7797 8400
	•Pump Court Chambers	020 7353 0711
	Queen Elizabeth Building	020 7797 7837
	Renaissance Chambers	020 7404 1111
	•Tanfield Chambers	020 7421 5300
	The Chambers of Grahame Aldous QC	020 7832 0500
	Tooks Chambers	020 7842 7575
Maidstone	6 Pump Court Chambers	01622 688094
Manchester	Central Chambers	0161 236 1133
	•Cobden House Chambers	0161 833 6000
	Deans Court Chambers	0161 214 6000
	Kenworthy's Chambers	0161 832 4036
	9 St John Street	0161 955 9000
	18 St John Street	0161 278 1800
	•St Johns Buildings	0161 214 1500
Middlesbrough	Amicus Chambers	01642 876334
	Fountain Chambers	01642 804040
	Old Court Chambers	01642 232523
	•Trinity Chambers	01642 247569
Newcastle Upon Tyne	Cathedral Chambers	0191 232 1311
	Dere Street Barristers	0844 3351551
	•Trinity Chambers	0191 232 1927
Northampton	Chartlands Chambers	01604 603322
	Northampton Chambers	01604 636271
Norwich	Octagon House	01603 623186
Nottingham	KCH Garden Square	0115 941 8851
Oxford	Harcourt Chambers	0844 561 7135
	3 PB Barristers	01865 793 736
Plymouth	Devon Chambers	01752 661659
Portsmouth	Guildhall Chambers Portsmouth	023 9275 2400
Preston	Deans Court Chambers	01772 565 600
Sheffield	Bank House Chambers	0114 275 1223
	St Johns Buildings	0114 273 8951
Southampton	•College Chambers	023 8023 0338
Stoke On Trent	Regent Chambers	01782 286666
Swindon	Pump Court Chambers	01793 539899
Taunton	Octagon Chambers	01823 331919
Winchester	3 PB Barristers	01962 868884
	Pump Court Chambers	01962 868 161

• Expanded entry in Part D

CHANCERY

Birmingham	St Ive's Chambers	0121 236 0863
	•St Philips Chambers	0121 246 7000
Bristol	Queen Square Chambers	0117 921 1966
Exeter	Walnut House	01392 279751
London	•Crown Office Chambers	020 7797 8100
	Five Paper	020 7815 3200
	•South Square	020 7696 9900
Manchester	18 St John Street	0161 278 1800
	•St Johns Buildings	0161 214 1500

CHANCERY (COMMERCIAL)

Birmingham	St Ive's Chambers	0121 236 0863
Bournemouth	3 PB Barristers	01202 292102
Bristol	3 PB Barristers	0117 928 1520
	Queen Square Chambers	0117 921 1966
Exeter	Rougemont Chambers	01392 208484
	Walnut House	01392 279751
Leeds	Enterprise Chambers	0113 246 0391
London	•Cornerstone Barristers	020 7242 4986
	Enterprise Chambers	020 7405 9471
	Erskine Chambers	020 7242 5532
	Five Paper	020 7815 3200
	•Maitland Chambers	020 7406 1200
	3 PB Barristers	020 7583 8055
	XXIV Old Buildings	020 7691 2424
Manchester	18 St John Street	0161 278 1800
Middlesbrough	•Trinity Chambers	01642 247569
Newcastle Upon Tyne	Dere Street Barristers	0844 3351551
	Enterprise Chambers	0191 222 3344
	•Trinity Chambers	0191 232 1927
Oxford	3 PB Barristers	01865 793 736
Portsmouth	Guildhall Chambers Portsmouth	023 9275 2400
	Portsmouth Barristers'Chambers	023 9283 1292
Winchester	3 PB Barristers	01962 868884

CHANCERY (GENERAL)

Birmingham	St Ive's Chambers	0121 236 0863
	•St Philips Chambers	0121 246 7000
Bournemouth	3 PB Barristers	01202 292102
Bristol	3 PB Barristers	0117 928 1520
	Queen Square Chambers	0117 921 1966
	St John's Chambers	0117 923 4700
	Unity Street Chambers	0117 906 9789
Chelmsford	Trinity Chambers	01245 605040
Chester	Linenhall Chambers	01244 348282
Chichester	Pallant Chambers	01243 784538
Exeter	Rougemont Chambers	01392 208484
	Walnut House	01392 279751
Faringdon	Faringdon Chambers	01367 240598
Hull	Wilberforce Chambers	01482 323264
Leeds	Chancery House Chambers	0113 244 6691
	Enterprise Chambers	0113 246 0391
	KBW	0113 297 1200
	Kings Chambers	0845 034 3444
	Park Court Chambers	0113 243 3277
	37 Park Square Chambers	0113 243 9422
	•Sovereign Chambers	0113 245 1841
	Zenith Chambers	0113 245 5438
Liverpool	Atlantic Chambers	0151 236 4421
	•Oriel Chambers	0151 236 7191
London	Atlas Chambers	020 7269 7980
	42 Bedford Row	020 7831 0222
	Blackstone Chambers	020 7583 1770

A

	Brick Court Chambers	020 7379 3550
	•Chambers of Mr Ami Feder	020 7797 7788
	•Charter Chambers	020 7618 4400
	•Cornerstone Barristers	020 7242 4986
	•3 Dr Johnson's Buildings	020 7353 4854
	Enterprise Chambers	020 7405 9471
	•Farrar's Building	020 7583 9241
	Five Paper	020 7815 3200
	Fountain Court Chambers	020 7583 3335
	•Goldsmith Chambers	020 7353 6802
	Gough Square Chambers	020 7353 0924
	4 KBW	020 7822 8822
	13 King's Bench Walk	020 7353 7204
	Lamb Chambers	020 7797 8300
	•Maitland Chambers	020 7406 1200
	New Square Chambers	020 7419 8000
	•13 Old Square Chambers	020 7831 4445
	3 PB Barristers	020 7583 8055
	1 Pump Court	020 7842 7070
	4 Pump Court	020 7842 5555
	•5 Pump Court	020 7353 2532
	Radcliffe Chambers	020 7831 0081
	Selborne Chambers	020 7420 9500
	Serle Court	020 7242 6105
	•South Square	020 7696 9900
	3 Stone Buildings	020 7242 4937
	•9 Stone Buildings	020 7404 5055
	11 Stone Buildings	020 7831 6381
	•Tanfield Chambers	020 7421 5300
	Ten Old Square	020 7405 0758
	•Wilberforce Chambers	020 7306 0102
	XXIV Old Buildings	020 7691 2424
Manchester	•Cobden House Chambers	0161 833 6000
	Deans Court Chambers	0161 214 6000
	Kings Chambers	0845 034 3444
	St James's Chambers	0161 834 7000
	9 St John Street	0161 955 9000
	18 St John Street	0161 278 1800
	•St Johns Buildings	0161 214 1500
Middlesbrough	•Trinity Chambers	01642 247569
Newcastle Upon Tyne	Cathedral Chambers	0191 232 1311
	Dere Street Barristers	0844 3351551
	Enterprise Chambers	0191 222 3344
	•Trinity Chambers	0191 232 1927
Norwich	Octagon House	01603 623186
Nottingham	KCH Garden Square	0115 941 8851
Oxford	3 PB Barristers	01865 793 736
Portsmouth	Guildhall Chambers Portsmouth	023 9275 2400
	Portsmouth Barristers'Chambers	023 9283 1292
Preston	Deans Court Chambers	01772 565 600
Sheffield	Bank House Chambers	0114 275 1223
	St Johns Buildings	0114 273 8951
Southampton	•College Chambers	023 8023 0338
Stoke On Trent	Regent Chambers	01782 286666
Swansea	Iscoed Chambers	01792 652988
Winchester	3 PB Barristers	01962 868884

CHANCERY (LAND LAW)

Birmingham	No 8 Chambers	0121 236 5514
	St Ive's Chambers	0121 236 0863
	•St Philips Chambers	0121 246 7000
Bournemouth	3 PB Barristers	01202 292102
Bristol	Albion Chambers	0117 927 2144
	3 PB Barristers	0117 928 1520

• Expanded entry in Part D

	Queen Square Chambers	0117 921 1966
	St John's Chambers	0117 923 4700
	Unity Street Chambers	0117 906 9789
Chichester	Pallant Chambers	01243 784538
Exeter	Rougemont Chambers	01392 208484
	Walnut House	01392 279751
Leeds	Chancery House Chambers	0113 244 6691
	KBW	0113 297 1200
	Kings Chambers	0845 034 3444
	Zenith Chambers	0113 245 5438
Liverpool	Atlantic Chambers	0151 236 4421
London	•Arden Chambers	020 7242 4244
	42 Bedford Row	020 7831 0222
	•Chambers of Mr Ami Feder	020 7797 7788
	1 Chancery Lane	0845 634 6666
	•Cornerstone Barristers	020 7242 4986
	Falcon Chambers	020 7353 2484
	Five Paper	020 7815 3200
	•Goldsmith Chambers	020 7353 6802
	Gough Square Chambers	020 7353 0924
	Harcourt Chambers	0844 561 7135
	Lamb Chambers	020 7797 8300
	•Maitland Chambers	020 7406 1200
	New Square Chambers	020 7419 8000
	•13 Old Square Chambers	020 7831 4445
	3 PB Barristers	020 7583 8055
	1 Pump Court	020 7842 7070
	•5 Pump Court	020 7353 2532
	•Pump Court Chambers	020 7353 0711
	Radcliffe Chambers	020 7831 0081
	Selborne Chambers	020 7420 9500
	3 Stone Buildings	020 7242 4937
	•9 Stone Buildings	020 7404 5055
	•Tanfield Chambers	020 7421 5300
	Ten Old Square	020 7405 0758
	•Wilberforce Chambers	020 7306 0102
	XXIV Old Buildings	020 7691 2424
Manchester	•Cobden House Chambers	0161 833 6000
	Deans Court Chambers	0161 214 6000
	Kings Chambers	0845 034 3444
	St James's Chambers	0161 834 7000
	18 St John Street	0161 278 1800
Middlesbrough	•Trinity Chambers	01642 247569
Newcastle Upon Tyne	Dere Street Barristers	0844 3351551
	•Trinity Chambers	0191 232 1927
Oxford	Harcourt Chambers	0844 561 7135
	3 PB Barristers	01865 793 736
Portsmouth	Portsmouth Barristers'Chambers	023 9283 1292
Preston	Deans Court Chambers	01772 565 600
Swindon	Pump Court Chambers	01793 539899
Winchester	3 PB Barristers	01962 868884
	Pump Court Chambers	01962 868 161

CHARITIES

Birmingham	•St Philips Chambers	0121 246 7000
Bristol	St John's Chambers	0117 923 4700
Exeter	Rougemont Chambers	01392 208484
Ipswich	East Anglian Chambers	01473 214481
Leeds	Kings Chambers	0845 034 3444
	Zenith Chambers	0113 245 5438
London	•Maitland Chambers	020 7406 1200
	New Square Chambers	020 7419 8000
	•13 Old Square Chambers	020 7831 4445
	Radcliffe Chambers	020 7831 0081

	Serle Court	020 7242 6105
	3 Stone Buildings	020 7242 4937
	•9 Stone Buildings	020 7404 5055
	Taxchambers	020 7242 2744
	Ten Old Square	020 7405 0758
	•Wilberforce Chambers	020 7306 0102
	Wynne Chambers	020 3239 6964
	XXIV Old Buildings	020 7691 2424
Manchester	•Cobden House Chambers	0161 833 6000
	Kings Chambers	0845 034 3444
	St James's Chambers	0161 834 7000
	18 St John Street	0161 278 1800
	•St Johns Buildings	0161 214 1500
Middlesbrough	•Trinity Chambers	01642 247569
Newcastle Upon Tyne	Dere Street Barristers	0844 3351551
	•Trinity Chambers	0191 232 1927
Southampton	•College Chambers	023 8023 0338

CHILD ABDUCTION

Birmingham	St Ive's Chambers	0121 236 0863
Bristol	Queen Square Chambers	0117 921 1966
Exeter	Rougemont Chambers	01392 208484
Faringdon	Faringdon Chambers	01367 240598
London	•29 Bedford Row Chambers	020 7404 1044
	•23 Essex Street	020 7413 0353
	•1 KBW Chambers	020 7936 1500
	•4 Paper Buildings	020 7427 5200
	Renaissance Chambers	020 7404 1111
	The Chambers of Grahame Aldous QC	020 7832 0500
Manchester	18 St John Street	0161 278 1800
Middlesbrough	Amicus Chambers	01642 876334
Newcastle Upon Tyne	Dere Street Barristers	0844 3351551
Portsmouth	Guildhall Chambers Portsmouth	023 9275 2400
Southampton	•College Chambers	023 8023 0338

CHILD ABUSE

Birmingham	St Ive's Chambers	0121 236 0863
Bristol	Queen Square Chambers	0117 921 1966
Faringdon	Faringdon Chambers	01367 240598
London	•23 Essex Street	020 7413 0353
	•1 KBW Chambers	020 7936 1500
	15 New Bridge Street	020 7842 1900
	•Nine Bedford Row	020 7489 2727
	•4 Paper Buildings	020 7427 5200
	18 Red Lion Court	020 7520 6000
	The Chambers of Grahame Aldous QC	020 7832 0500
Manchester	18 St John Street	0161 278 1800
Middlesbrough	Amicus Chambers	01642 876334
Newcastle Upon Tyne	Dere Street Barristers	0844 3351551
Portsmouth	Guildhall Chambers Portsmouth	023 9275 2400
Southampton	•College Chambers	023 8023 0338

CHILD CARE LAW

Birmingham	St Ive's Chambers	0121 236 0863
Bournemouth	3 PB Barristers	01202 292102
Bristol	3 PB Barristers	0117 928 1520
	Queen Square Chambers	0117 921 1966
Exeter	Rougemont Chambers	01392 208484
Faringdon	Faringdon Chambers	01367 240598
London	Bell Yard Chambers	020 7306 9292
	•Goldsmith Chambers	020 7353 6802
	•1 KBW Chambers	020 7936 1500
	•4 Paper Buildings	020 7427 5200
	3 PB Barristers	020 7583 8055

• Expanded entry in Part D

	The Chambers of Grahame Aldous QC	020 7832 0500
Manchester	18 St John Street	0161 278 1800
Middlesbrough	Amicus Chambers	01642 876334
Newcastle Upon Tyne	Dere Street Barristers	0844 3351551
Oxford	3 PB Barristers	01865 793 736
Portsmouth	Guildhall Chambers Portsmouth	023 9275 2400
Southampton	•College Chambers	023 8023 0338
Winchester	3 PB Barristers	01962 868884

CHILD SUPPORT

Birmingham	St Ive's Chambers	0121 236 0863
Bristol	Queen Square Chambers	0117 921 1966
Faringdon	Faringdon Chambers	01367 240598
London	•29 Bedford Row Chambers	020 7404 1044
	•1 KBW Chambers	020 7936 1500
	•4 Paper Buildings	020 7427 5200
	The Chambers of Grahame Aldous QC	020 7832 0500
Manchester	18 St John Street	0161 278 1800
Middlesbrough	Amicus Chambers	01642 876334
Newcastle Upon Tyne	Dere Street Barristers	0844 3351551
Southampton	•College Chambers	023 8023 0338

CHILDREN

Birmingham	Cornwall Street Chambers	0121 233 7500
	St Ive's Chambers	0121 236 0863
	•St Philips Chambers	0121 246 7000
Bournemouth	3 PB Barristers	01202 292102
Brighton	Crown Office Row Chambers	01273 625625
Bristol	3 PB Barristers	0117 928 1520
	Queen Square Chambers	0117 921 1966
Exeter	Rougemont Chambers	01392 208484
	Walnut House	01392 279751
London	•29 Bedford Row Chambers	020 7404 1044
	Bell Yard Chambers	020 7306 9292
	Five Paper	020 7815 3200
	•1 KBW Chambers	020 7936 1500
	•4 Paper Buildings	020 7427 5200
	3 PB Barristers	020 7583 8055
	Renaissance Chambers	020 7404 1111
	The Chambers of Grahame Aldous QC	020 7832 0500
Manchester	Kenworthy's Chambers	0161 832 4036
	18 St John Street	0161 278 1800
	•St Johns Buildings	0161 214 1500
Newcastle Upon Tyne	Dere Street Barristers	0844 3351551
Oxford	3 PB Barristers	01865 793 736
Portsmouth	Guildhall Chambers Portsmouth	023 9275 2400
Southampton	•College Chambers	023 8023 0338
Winchester	3 PB Barristers	01962 868884

CHINESE LAW

London	Essex Court Chambers	020 7813 8000
	Serle Court	020 7242 6105

CIVIL ACTIONS AGAINST THE POLICE

Bournemouth	3 PB Barristers	01202 292102
Bristol	3 PB Barristers	0117 928 1520
	Queen Square Chambers	0117 921 1966
Chester	Linenhall Chambers	01244 348282
Leeds	KBW	0113 297 1200
London	•Argent Chambers	020 7556 5500
	Bell Yard Chambers	020 7306 9292
	Doughty Street Chambers	020 7404 1313
	•23 Essex Street	020 7413 0353
	•187 Fleet Street	020 7430 7430
	•Henderson Chambers	020 7583 9020

	•1 KBW Chambers	020 7936 1500
	Matrix Chambers	020 7404 3447
	15 New Bridge Street	020 7842 1900
	3 PB Barristers	020 7583 8055
	•Tanfield Chambers	020 7421 5300
	The Chambers of Grahame Aldous QC	020 7832 0500
Manchester	Chambers of Ian Macdonald QC	0161 236 1840
	Kenworthy's Chambers	0161 832 4036
	•Lincoln House Chambers	0161 832 5701
	18 St John Street	0161 278 1800
Newcastle Upon Tyne	Dere Street Barristers	0844 3351551
Oxford	3 PB Barristers	01865 793 736
Portsmouth	Guildhall Chambers Portsmouth	023 9275 2400
Winchester	3 PB Barristers	01962 868884

CIVIL FRAUD

Birmingham	St Ive's Chambers	0121 236 0863
Bristol	Queen Square Chambers	0117 921 1966
	St John's Chambers	0117 923 4700
Exeter	Walnut House	01392 279751
Leeds	•Sovereign Chambers	0113 245 1841
London	Blackstone Chambers	020 7583 1770
	•Cornerstone Barristers	020 7242 4986
	Five Paper	020 7815 3200
	•187 Fleet Street	020 7430 7430
	Gough Square Chambers	020 7353 0924
	3 Hare Court	020 7415 7800
	•Maitland Chambers	020 7406 1200
	•13 Old Square Chambers	020 7831 4445
	Serle Court	020 7242 6105
	•South Square	020 7696 9900
	4 Stone Buildings	020 7242 5524
	11 Stone Buildings	020 7831 6381
	The Chambers of Grahame Aldous QC	020 7832 0500
	XXIV Old Buildings	020 7691 2424
Manchester	18 St John Street	0161 278 1800
	•St Johns Buildings	0161 214 1500
Newcastle Upon Tyne	Dere Street Barristers	0844 3351551
Portsmouth	Guildhall Chambers Portsmouth	023 9275 2400
	Portsmouth Barristers'Chambers	023 9283 1292

CIVIL LAW

Birmingham	St Ive's Chambers	0121 236 0863
Exeter	Rougemont Chambers	01392 208484
	Walnut House	01392 279751
Leeds	37 Park Square Chambers	0113 243 9422
London	Bell Yard Chambers	020 7306 9292
	4 Brick Court	020 7832 3200
	•Cornerstone Barristers	020 7242 4986
	•One Essex Court	020 7583 2000
	Five Paper	020 7815 3200
	Middle Temple Lane Chambers	020 7583 4352
Manchester	Chambers of Ian Macdonald QC	0161 236 1840
	18 St John Street	0161 278 1800
	•St Johns Buildings	0161 214 1500
Newcastle Upon Tyne	Dere Street Barristers	0844 3351551
Sheffield	Bank House Chambers	0114 275 1223
Southampton	•College Chambers	023 8023 0338

CIVIL LIBERTIES

Bristol	St John's Chambers	0117 923 4700
Leeds	Park Court Chambers	0113 243 3277
	•Sovereign Chambers	0113 245 1841
Lewes	Westgate Chambers	01273 480510

• Expanded entry in Part D

A

Liverpool	Atlantic Chambers	0151 236 4421
London	25 Bedford Row	020 7067 1500
	•9-12 Bell Yard	020 7400 1800
	Blackstone Chambers	020 7583 1770
	1 Chancery Lane	0845 634 6666
	•Devereux Chambers	020 7353 7534
	Doughty Street Chambers	020 7404 1313
	Essex Court Chambers	020 7813 8000
	20 Essex Street	020 7842 1200
	•39 Essex Street	020 7832 1111
	•Farrar's Building	020 7583 9241
	•Goldsmith Chambers	020 7353 6802
	•4-5 Gray's Inn Square	020 7404 5252
	Hailsham Chambers	020 7643 5000
	Matrix Chambers	020 7404 3447
	•Monckton Chambers	020 7405 7211
	15 New Bridge Street	020 7842 1900
	New Square Chambers	020 7419 8000
	1 Pump Court	020 7842 7070
	•Pump Court Chambers	020 7353 0711
	•3 Raymond Buildings	020 7400 6400
	18 Red Lion Court	020 7520 6000
	Tooks Chambers	020 7842 7575
Manchester	Central Chambers	0161 236 1133
	Chambers of Ian Macdonald QC	0161 236 1840
	St James's Chambers	0161 834 7000
	9 St John Street	0161 955 9000
	•St Johns Buildings	0161 214 1500
Middlesbrough	Old Court Chambers	01642 232523
Newcastle Upon Tyne	Dere Street Barristers	0844 3351551
Plymouth	Devon Chambers	01752 661659
Portsmouth	Guildhall Chambers Portsmouth	023 9275 2400
Swansea	Iscoed Chambers	01792 652988
Swindon	Pump Court Chambers	01793 539899
Winchester	Pump Court Chambers	01962 868 161

CIVIL LITIGATION

Birmingham	St Ive's Chambers	0121 236 0863
Bristol	Queen Square Chambers	0117 921 1966
Exeter	Walnut House	01392 279751
London	Five Paper	020 7815 3200
	XXIV Old Buildings	020 7691 2424
Manchester	•St Johns Buildings	0161 214 1500
Pitstone	Victor House Chambers	01296 664043

CIVIL PARTNERSHIPS

Birmingham	St Ive's Chambers	0121 236 0863
Bournemouth	3 PB Barristers	01202 292102
Bristol	3 PB Barristers	0117 928 1520
	Queen Square Chambers	0117 921 1966
Exeter	Walnut House	01392 279751
Faringdon	Faringdon Chambers	01367 240598
London	Five Paper	020 7815 3200
	•1 KBW Chambers	020 7936 1500
	3 PB Barristers	020 7583 8055
Manchester	18 St John Street	0161 278 1800
	•St Johns Buildings	0161 214 1500
Newcastle Upon Tyne	Dere Street Barristers	0844 3351551
Oxford	3 PB Barristers	01865 793 736
Portsmouth	Portsmouth Barristers'Chambers	023 9283 1292
Southampton	•College Chambers	023 8023 0338
Winchester	3 PB Barristers	01962 868884

• Expanded entry in Part D

A

CIVIL RECOVERY		
London	Five Paper	020 7815 3200
Manchester	•St Johns Buildings	0161 214 1500
CLINICAL NEGLIGENCE		
Birmingham	No 8 Chambers	0121 236 5514
	•No5 Chambers	0845 210 5555
	St Ive's Chambers	0121 236 0863
Bournemouth	3 PB Barristers	01202 292102
Bristol	No5 Chambers	0845 210 5555
	3 PB Barristers	0117 928 1520
	Queen Square Chambers	0117 921 1966
	St John's Chambers	0117 923 4700
	Unity Street Chambers	0117 906 9789
Chelmsford	Trinity Chambers	01245 605040
Chichester	Pallant Chambers	01243 784538
Exeter	Rougemont Chambers	01392 208484
Ipswich	East Anglian Chambers	01473 214481
Leeds	Chancery House Chambers	0113 244 6691
	Kings Chambers	0845 034 3444
	Park Court Chambers	0113 243 3277
	37 Park Square Chambers	0113 243 9422
	Zenith Chambers	0113 245 5438
Liverpool	Atlantic Chambers	0151 236 4421
	•Oriel Chambers	0151 236 7191
London	•Chambers of Mr Ami Feder	020 7797 7788
	•Cornerstone Barristers	020 7242 4986
	•Crown Office Chambers	020 7797 8100
	1 Crown Office Row	020 7797 7500
	•39 Essex Street	020 7832 1111
	•Farrar's Building	020 7583 9241
	Fountain Court Chambers	020 7583 3335
	•Goldsmith Chambers	020 7353 6802
	Hailsham Chambers	020 7643 5000
	•Henderson Chambers	020 7583 9020
	12 King's Bench Walk	020 7583 0811
	13 King's Bench Walk	020 7353 7204
	No5 Chambers	0845 210 5555
	Outer Temple Chambers	020 7353 6381
	3 PB Barristers	020 7583 8055
	Queen Elizabeth Building	020 7797 7837
	•Tanfield Chambers	020 7421 5300
	•Temple Garden Chambers	020 7583 1315
	The Chambers of Grahame Aldous QC	020 7832 0500
Manchester	Central Chambers	0161 236 1133
	Deans Court Chambers	0161 214 6000
	Kings Chambers	0845 034 3444
	•Lincoln House Chambers	0161 832 5701
	18 St John Street	0161 278 1800
Middlesbrough	Fountain Chambers	01642 804040
Newcastle Upon Tyne	Dere Street Barristers	0844 3351551
Oxford	3 PB Barristers	01865 793 736
Portsmouth	Guildhall Chambers Portsmouth	023 9275 2400
	Portsmouth Barristers'Chambers	023 9283 1292
Preston	Deans Court Chambers	01772 565 600
Sheffield	St Johns Buildings	0114 273 8951
Southampton	•College Chambers	023 8023 0338
Winchester	3 PB Barristers	01962 868884
COHABITATION		
Birmingham	St Ive's Chambers	0121 236 0863
Bournemouth	3 PB Barristers	01202 292102
Bristol	3 PB Barristers	0117 928 1520
	Queen Square Chambers	0117 921 1966

• Expanded entry in Part D

Exeter	Rougemont Chambers	01392 208484
Faringdon	Faringdon Chambers	01367 240598
London	•29 Bedford Row Chambers	020 7404 1044
	Five Paper	020 7815 3200
	•1 KBW Chambers	020 7936 1500
	3 PB Barristers	020 7583 8055
Manchester	18 St John Street	0161 278 1800
	•St Johns Buildings	0161 214 1500
Middlesbrough	Amicus Chambers	01642 876334
Newcastle Upon Tyne	Dere Street Barristers	0844 3351551
Northampton	Northampton Chambers	01604 636271
Oxford	3 PB Barristers	01865 793 736
Portsmouth	Guildhall Chambers Portsmouth	023 9275 2400
	Portsmouth Barristers'Chambers	023 9283 1292
Southampton	•College Chambers	023 8023 0338
Winchester	3 PB Barristers	01962 868884

COMMERCIAL CONTRACTS

Birmingham	St Ive's Chambers	0121 236 0863
Bournemouth	3 PB Barristers	01202 292102
Bristol	3 PB Barristers	0117 928 1520
Exeter	Rougemont Chambers	01392 208484
London	•Arden Chambers	020 7242 4244
	Chambers of Mr Patrick Ground QC	020 7736 0131
	Five Paper	020 7815 3200
	Gough Square Chambers	020 7353 0924
	Keating Chambers	020 7544 2600
	•Maitland Chambers	020 7406 1200
	3 PB Barristers	020 7583 8055
	The Chambers of Grahame Aldous QC	020 7832 0500
	XXIV Old Buildings	020 7691 2424
Maidstone	Maidstone Chambers	01622 688592
Manchester	18 St John Street	0161 278 1800
Middlesbrough	•Trinity Chambers	01642 247569
Newcastle Upon Tyne	Dere Street Barristers	0844 3351551
	•Trinity Chambers	0191 232 1927
Oxford	3 PB Barristers	01865 793 736
Pitstone	Victor House Chambers	01296 664043
Portsmouth	Portsmouth Barristers'Chambers	023 9283 1292
Southampton	•College Chambers	023 8023 0338
Winchester	3 PB Barristers	01962 868884

COMMERCIAL FRAUD

Bournemouth	3 PB Barristers	01202 292102
Bristol	3 PB Barristers	0117 928 1520
	Queen Square Chambers	0117 921 1966
Exeter	Walnut House	01392 279751
London	Blackstone Chambers	020 7583 1770
	Erskine Chambers	020 7242 5532
	Essex Court Chambers	020 7813 8000
	Five Paper	020 7815 3200
	Gough Square Chambers	020 7353 0924
	•Henderson Chambers	020 7583 9020
	•Maitland Chambers	020 7406 1200
	15 New Bridge Street	020 7842 1900
	•Nine Bedford Row	020 7489 2727
	3 PB Barristers	020 7583 8055
	18 Red Lion Court	020 7520 6000
	3 Verulam Buildings	020 7831 8441
	XXIV Old Buildings	020 7691 2424
Manchester	18 St John Street	0161 278 1800
	•St Johns Buildings	0161 214 1500
Middlesbrough	•Trinity Chambers	01642 247569
Newcastle Upon Tyne	Dere Street Barristers	0844 3351551

• Expanded entry in Part D

	•Trinity Chambers	0191 232 1927
Oxford	3 PB Barristers	01865 793 736
Portsmouth	Portsmouth Barristers'Chambers	023 9283 1292
Winchester	3 PB Barristers	01962 868884

COMMERCIAL LAW

Birmingham	Cornwall Street Chambers	0121 233 7500
	No 8 Chambers	0121 236 5514
	•No5 Chambers	0845 210 5555
Bournemouth	3 PB Barristers	01202 292102
Bristol	No5 Chambers	0845 210 5555
	3 PB Barristers	0117 928 1520
	St John's Chambers	0117 923 4700
	Unity Street Chambers	0117 906 9789
Canterbury	Becket Chambers	01227 786331
Chelmsford	Trinity Chambers	01245 605040
Chester	Linenhall Chambers	01244 348282
Chichester	Pallant Chambers	01243 784538
Exeter	Rougemont Chambers	01392 208484
	Walnut House	01392 279751
Ipswich	East Anglian Chambers	01473 214481
Leeds	Chancery House Chambers	0113 244 6691
	Enterprise Chambers	0113 246 0391
	Kings Chambers	0845 034 3444
	Park Court Chambers	0113 243 3277
	Zenith Chambers	0113 245 5438
Liverpool	•Number 7 Harrington Street Chambers	0151 242 0707
London	•Argent Chambers	020 7556 5500
	Atkin Chambers	020 7404 0102
	Blackstone Chambers	020 7583 1770
	•Crown Office Chambers	020 7797 8100
	Enterprise Chambers	020 7405 9471
	Erskine Chambers	020 7242 5532
	•One Essex Court	020 7583 2000
	20 Essex Street	020 7842 1200
	Five Paper	020 7815 3200
	Fountain Court Chambers	020 7583 3335
	•4-5 Gray's Inn Square	020 7404 5252
	Great James Street Chambers	020 7440 4949
	Hailsham Chambers	020 7643 5000
	3 Hare Court	020 7415 7800
	•Henderson Chambers	020 7583 9020
	11 King's Bench Walk	020 7632 8500
	•Maitland Chambers	020 7406 1200
	Matrix Chambers	020 7404 3447
	Middle Temple Lane Chambers	020 7583 4352
	•Monckton Chambers	020 7405 7211
	No5 Chambers	0845 210 5555
	•13 Old Square Chambers	020 7831 4445
	Outer Temple Chambers	020 7353 6381
	3 PB Barristers	020 7583 8055
	4 Pump Court	020 7842 5555
	•5 Pump Court	020 7353 2532
	6 Pump Court	020 7797 8400
	•Pump Court Chambers	020 7353 0711
	Radcliffe Chambers	020 7831 0081
	Selborne Chambers	020 7420 9500
	Serle Court	020 7242 6105
	•South Square	020 7696 9900
	11 Stone Buildings	020 7831 6381
	•Tanfield Chambers	020 7421 5300
	•Wilberforce Chambers	020 7306 0102
	XXIV Old Buildings	020 7691 2424
Maidstone	Maidstone Chambers	01622 688592

• Expanded entry in Part D

	6 Pump Court Chambers	01622 688094
Manchester	Central Chambers	0161 236 1133
	Kenworthy's Chambers	0161 832 4036
	Kings Chambers	0845 034 3444
	•Lincoln House Chambers	0161 832 5701
	9 St John Street	0161 955 9000
	18 St John Street	0161 278 1800
	•St Johns Buildings	0161 214 1500
Middlesbrough	•Trinity Chambers	01642 247569
Newcastle Upon Tyne	Dere Street Barristers	0844 3351551
	Enterprise Chambers	0191 222 3344
	•Trinity Chambers	0191 232 1927
Oxford	3 PB Barristers	01865 793 736
Portsmouth	Guildhall Chambers Portsmouth	023 9275 2400
	Portsmouth Barristers'Chambers	023 9283 1292
Southampton	•College Chambers	023 8023 0338
Swindon	Pump Court Chambers	01793 539899
Winchester	3 PB Barristers	01962 868884
	Pump Court Chambers	01962 868 161

COMMERCIAL LITIGATION

Birmingham	•No5 Chambers	0845 210 5555
	St Ive's Chambers	0121 236 0863
	•St Philips Chambers	0121 246 7000
Bournemouth	3 PB Barristers	01202 292102
Bradford	Broadway House Chambers	01274 722560
Bristol	No5 Chambers	0845 210 5555
	3 PB Barristers	0117 928 1520
	St John's Chambers	0117 923 4700
	Unity Street Chambers	0117 906 9789
Chelmsford	Trinity Chambers	01245 605040
Exeter	Rougemont Chambers	01392 208484
	Walnut House	01392 279751
Ipswich	East Anglian Chambers	01473 214481
Leeds	Broadway House Chambers	0113 246 2600
	Chancery House Chambers	0113 244 6691
	Enterprise Chambers	0113 246 0391
	KBW	0113 297 1200
	Kings Chambers	0845 034 3444
	Park Court Chambers	0113 243 3277
	Zenith Chambers	0113 245 5438
Liverpool	Atlantic Chambers	0151 236 4421
	•Number 7 Harrington Street Chambers	0151 242 0707
	•Oriel Chambers	0151 236 7191
London	Atkin Chambers	020 7404 0102
	•9-12 Bell Yard	020 7400 1800
	Blackstone Chambers	020 7583 1770
	Brick Court Chambers	020 7379 3550
	1 Chancery Lane	0845 634 6666
	•Devereux Chambers	020 7353 7534
	Enterprise Chambers	020 7405 9471
	Erskine Chambers	020 7242 5532
	20 Essex Street	020 7842 1200
	•39 Essex Street	020 7832 1111
	•Farrar's Building	020 7583 9241
	Farringdon Chambers	020 7089 5700
	Five Paper	020 7815 3200
	Fountain Court Chambers	020 7583 3335
	•Goldsmith Chambers	020 7353 6802
	Gough Square Chambers	020 7353 0924
	•Henderson Chambers	020 7583 9020
	4 KBW	020 7822 8822
	Keating Chambers	020 7544 2600
	11 King's Bench Walk	020 7632 8500

A

	Lamb Chambers	020 7797 8300
	•Maitland Chambers	020 7406 1200
	Matrix Chambers	020 7404 3447
	•Monckton Chambers	020 7405 7211
	New Square Chambers	020 7419 8000
	No5 Chambers	0845 210 5555
	•13 Old Square Chambers	020 7831 4445
	Outer Temple Chambers	020 7353 6381
	3 PB Barristers	020 7583 8055
	4 Pump Court	020 7842 5555
	•5 Pump Court	020 7353 2532
	6 Pump Court	020 7797 8400
	•Pump Court Chambers	020 7353 0711
	Radcliffe Chambers	020 7831 0081
	Selborne Chambers	020 7420 9500
	Serle Court	020 7242 6105
	•South Square	020 7696 9900
	3 Stone Buildings	020 7242 4937
	4 Stone Buildings	020 7242 5524
	•9 Stone Buildings	020 7404 5055
	11 Stone Buildings	020 7831 6381
	•Tanfield Chambers	020 7421 5300
	•Temple Garden Chambers	020 7583 1315
	Ten Old Square	020 7405 0758
	3 Verulam Buildings	020 7831 8441
	•Wilberforce Chambers	020 7306 0102
	XXIV Old Buildings	020 7691 2424
Maidstone	6 Pump Court Chambers	01622 688094
Manchester	Byrom Street Chambers	0161 829 2100
	•Cobden House Chambers	0161 833 6000
	Deans Court Chambers	0161 214 6000
	Kings Chambers	0845 034 3444
	•Lincoln House Chambers	0161 832 5701
	9 St John Street	0161 955 9000
	18 St John Street	0161 278 1800
	•St Johns Buildings	0161 214 1500
Middlesbrough	Fountain Chambers	01642 804040
	•Trinity Chambers	01642 247569
Newcastle Upon Tyne	Dere Street Barristers	0844 3351551
	Enterprise Chambers	0191 222 3344
	•Trinity Chambers	0191 232 1927
Nottingham	KCH Garden Square	0115 941 8851
Oxford	3 PB Barristers	01865 793 736
Portsmouth	Guildhall Chambers Portsmouth	023 9275 2400
	Portsmouth Barristers'Chambers	023 9283 1292
Preston	Deans Court Chambers	01772 565 600
Southampton	•College Chambers	023 8023 0338
Swindon	Pump Court Chambers	01793 539899
Winchester	3 PB Barristers	01962 868884
	Pump Court Chambers	01962 868 161

COMMERCIAL PLANNING

London	•Cornerstone Barristers	020 7242 4986
Manchester	18 St John Street	0161 278 1800
Middlesbrough	•Trinity Chambers	01642 247569
Newcastle Upon Tyne	•Trinity Chambers	0191 232 1927

COMMERCIAL PROPERTY

Birmingham	No 8 Chambers	0121 236 5514
	•No5 Chambers	0845 210 5555
	St Ive's Chambers	0121 236 0863
	•St Philips Chambers	0121 246 7000
Bournemouth	3 PB Barristers	01202 292102
Bristol	No5 Chambers	0845 210 5555

• Expanded entry in Part D

	3 PB Barristers	0117 928 1520
	Queen Square Chambers	0117 921 1966
	St John's Chambers	0117 923 4700
	Unity Street Chambers	0117 906 9789
Exeter	Rougemont Chambers	01392 208484
Leeds	Chancery House Chambers	0113 244 6691
	Enterprise Chambers	0113 246 0391
	Kings Chambers	0845 034 3444
	Park Court Chambers	0113 243 3277
Liverpool	Atlantic Chambers	0151 236 4421
London	•Arden Chambers	020 7242 4244
	•Cornerstone Barristers	020 7242 4986
	•Devereux Chambers	020 7353 7534
	Enterprise Chambers	020 7405 9471
	Falcon Chambers	020 7353 2484
	Five Paper	020 7815 3200
	•Henderson Chambers	020 7583 9020
	Lamb Chambers	020 7797 8300
	•Maitland Chambers	020 7406 1200
	New Square Chambers	020 7419 8000
	No5 Chambers	0845 210 5555
	•13 Old Square Chambers	020 7831 4445
	3 PB Barristers	020 7583 8055
	•Pump Court Chambers	020 7353 0711
	Radcliffe Chambers	020 7831 0081
	Selborne Chambers	020 7420 9500
	Serle Court	020 7242 6105
	3 Stone Buildings	020 7242 4937
	•9 Stone Buildings	020 7404 5055
	11 Stone Buildings	020 7831 6381
	•Tanfield Chambers	020 7421 5300
	Ten Old Square	020 7405 0758
	The Chambers of Grahame Aldous QC	020 7832 0500
	3 Verulam Buildings	020 7831 8441
	•Wilberforce Chambers	020 7306 0102
	XXIV Old Buildings	020 7691 2424
Manchester	•Cobden House Chambers	0161 833 6000
	Kings Chambers	0845 034 3444
	St James's Chambers	0161 834 7000
	9 St John Street	0161 955 9000
	18 St John Street	0161 278 1800
Middlesbrough	•Trinity Chambers	01642 247569
Newcastle Upon Tyne	Dere Street Barristers	0844 3351551
	Enterprise Chambers	0191 222 3344
	•Trinity Chambers	0191 232 1927
Nottingham	KCH Garden Square	0115 941 8851
Oxford	3 PB Barristers	01865 793 736
Portsmouth	Guildhall Chambers Portsmouth	023 9275 2400
	Portsmouth Barristers'Chambers	023 9283 1292
Southampton	•College Chambers	023 8023 0338
Swansea	Iscoed Chambers	01792 652988
Swindon	Pump Court Chambers	01793 539899
Winchester	3 PB Barristers	01962 868884
	Pump Court Chambers	01962 868 161

COMMERCIAL REGULATION

London	Blackstone Chambers	020 7583 1770
	Gough Square Chambers	020 7353 0924
	•Henderson Chambers	020 7583 9020
Manchester	18 St John Street	0161 278 1800
Middlesbrough	•Trinity Chambers	01642 247569
Newcastle Upon Tyne	•Trinity Chambers	0191 232 1927

• Expanded entry in Part D

COMMODITIES

London	Blackstone Chambers	020 7583 1770
	Brick Court Chambers	020 7379 3550
	•One Essex Court	020 7583 2000
	Essex Court Chambers	020 7813 8000
	20 Essex Street	020 7842 1200
	Hailsham Chambers	020 7643 5000
	•South Square	020 7696 9900
	•Tanfield Chambers	020 7421 5300
	3 Verulam Buildings	020 7831 8441
Manchester	18 St John Street	0161 278 1800
	•St Johns Buildings	0161 214 1500

COMMON LAND

Birmingham	St Ive's Chambers	0121 236 0863
Bournemouth	3 PB Barristers	01202 292102
Bristol	3 PB Barristers	0117 928 1520
	Queen Square Chambers	0117 921 1966
	St John's Chambers	0117 923 4700
Chelmsford	Trinity Chambers	01245 605040
Chester	Linenhall Chambers	01244 348282
Exeter	Rougemont Chambers	01392 208484
	Walnut House	01392 279751
Leeds	Kings Chambers	0845 034 3444
Liverpool	Atlantic Chambers	0151 236 4421
London	Falcon Chambers	020 7353 2484
	Five Paper	020 7815 3200
	Francis Taylor Building	020 7353 8415
	Lamb Chambers	020 7797 8300
	•Maitland Chambers	020 7406 1200
	New Square Chambers	020 7419 8000
	•13 Old Square Chambers	020 7831 4445
	3 PB Barristers	020 7583 8055
	Radcliffe Chambers	020 7831 0081
	Selborne Chambers	020 7420 9500
	•9 Stone Buildings	020 7404 5055
	•Tanfield Chambers	020 7421 5300
	XXIV Old Buildings	020 7691 2424
Manchester	•Cobden House Chambers	0161 833 6000
	Kings Chambers	0845 034 3444
	St James's Chambers	0161 834 7000
	18 St John Street	0161 278 1800
Middlesbrough	•Trinity Chambers	01642 247569
Newcastle Upon Tyne	Dere Street Barristers	0844 3351551
	•Trinity Chambers	0191 232 1927
Oxford	3 PB Barristers	01865 793 736
Plymouth	Devon Chambers	01752 661659
Sheffield	St Johns Buildings	0114 273 8951
Southampton	•College Chambers	023 8023 0338
Swansea	Iscoed Chambers	01792 652988

COMMON LAW (GENERAL)

Birmingham	Cornwall Street Chambers	0121 233 7500
	Equity Chambers	0121 236 5007
	No 8 Chambers	0121 236 5514
	St Ive's Chambers	0121 236 0863
	•St Philips Chambers	0121 246 7000
Bournemouth	3 PB Barristers	01202 292102
Bradford	Broadway House Chambers	01274 722560
Brighton	Crown Office Row Chambers	01273 625625
Bristol	Albion Chambers	0117 927 2144
	3 PB Barristers	0117 928 1520
	Queen Square Chambers	0117 921 1966
	St John's Chambers	0117 923 4700

• Expanded entry in Part D

	Unity Street Chambers	0117 906 9789
Canterbury	Becket Chambers	01227 786331
Chelmsford	Trinity Chambers	01245 605040
Chester	Linenhall Chambers	01244 348282
Chichester	Pallant Chambers	01243 784538
Exeter	Rougemont Chambers	01392 208484
	Walnut House	01392 279751
Hull	Wilberforce Chambers	01482 323264
Ipswich	East Anglian Chambers	01473 214481
Leeds	Broadway House Chambers	0113 246 2600
	Chancery House Chambers	0113 244 6691
	KBW	0113 297 1200
	Kings Chambers	0845 034 3444
	Park Court Chambers	0113 243 3277
	Zenith Chambers	0113 245 5438
Lewes	Westgate Chambers	01273 480510
Liverpool	Chavasse Court Chambers	0151 229 2030
	•Oriel Chambers	0151 236 7191
London	42 Bedford Row	020 7831 0222
	•29 Bedford Row Chambers	020 7404 1044
	Bell Yard Chambers	020 7306 9292
	•9-12 Bell Yard	020 7400 1800
	Brick Court Chambers	020 7379 3550
	•Chambers of Mr Ami Feder	020 7797 7788
	1 Chancery Lane	0845 634 6666
	•Charter Chambers	020 7618 4400
	1 Crown Office Row	020 7797 7500
	•Devereux Chambers	020 7353 7534
	Doughty Street Chambers	020 7404 1313
	•2 Dr Johnson's Buildings	020 7936 2613
	•3 Dr Johnson's Buildings	020 7353 4854
	•39 Essex Street	020 7832 1111
	•Farrar's Building	020 7583 9241
	Farringdon Chambers	020 7089 5700
	Five Paper	020 7815 3200
	Fountain Court Chambers	020 7583 3335
	•Goldsmith Chambers	020 7353 6802
	14 Gray's Inn Square	020 7242 0858
	•Henderson Chambers	020 7583 9020
	2 King's Bench Walk	020 7353 1746
	4 King's Bench Walk	020 7822 7000
	13 King's Bench Walk	020 7353 7204
	Lamb Chambers	020 7797 8300
	New Square Chambers	020 7419 8000
	•13 Old Square Chambers	020 7831 4445
	Outer Temple Chambers	020 7353 6381
	3 PB Barristers	020 7583 8055
	1 Pump Court	020 7842 7070
	4 Pump Court	020 7842 5555
	•5 Pump Court	020 7353 2532
	6 Pump Court	020 7797 8400
	Radcliffe Chambers	020 7831 0081
	•3 Raymond Buildings	020 7400 6400
	Selborne Chambers	020 7420 9500
	•Tanfield Chambers	020 7421 5300
	•Temple Garden Chambers	020 7583 1315
	The Chambers of Grahame Aldous QC	020 7832 0500
	3 Verulam Buildings	020 7831 8441
Maidstone	6 Pump Court Chambers	01622 688094
Manchester	Byrom Street Chambers	0161 829 2100
	Chambers of Ian Macdonald QC	0161 236 1840
	•Cobden House Chambers	0161 833 6000
	Deans Court Chambers	0161 214 6000
	Kenworthy's Chambers	0161 832 4036

	Kings Chambers	0845 034 3444
	•Lincoln House Chambers	0161 832 5701
	St James's Chambers	0161 834 7000
	9 St John Street	0161 955 9000
	18 St John Street	0161 278 1800
	•St Johns Buildings	0161 214 1500
Middlesbrough	Fountain Chambers	01642 804040
	Old Court Chambers	01642 232523
	•Trinity Chambers	01642 247569
Newcastle Upon Tyne	Cathedral Chambers	0191 232 1311
	Dere Street Barristers	0844 3351551
	•Trinity Chambers	0191 232 1927
Northampton	Chartlands Chambers	01604 603322
	Northampton Chambers	01604 636271
Norwich	Octagon House	01603 623186
Nottingham	KCH Garden Square	0115 941 8851
Oxford	3 PB Barristers	01865 793 736
Plymouth	Devon Chambers	01752 661659
Portsmouth	Guildhall Chambers Portsmouth	023 9275 2400
	Portsmouth Barristers'Chambers	023 9283 1292
Preston	Deans Court Chambers	01772 565 600
Sheffield	Bank House Chambers	0114 275 1223
	St Johns Buildings	0114 273 8951
Southampton	•College Chambers	023 8023 0338
Stoke On Trent	Regent Chambers	01782 286666
Swansea	Iscoed Chambers	01792 652988
Taunton	Octagon Chambers	01823 331919
Winchester	3 PB Barristers	01962 868884

COMMUNITY CARE

London	•Arden Chambers	020 7242 4244
	•39 Essex Street	020 7832 1111
	Five Paper	020 7815 3200
	Matrix Chambers	020 7404 3447
	Renaissance Chambers	020 7404 1111
Manchester	Chambers of Ian Macdonald QC	0161 236 1840
	18 St John Street	0161 278 1800
Newcastle Upon Tyne	Dere Street Barristers	0844 3351551
Southampton	•College Chambers	023 8023 0338

COMPANY, COMMERCIAL AND COMPETITION

Birmingham	•No5 Chambers	0845 210 5555
	•St Philips Chambers	0121 246 7000
Bournemouth	3 PB Barristers	01202 292102
Bristol	No5 Chambers	0845 210 5555
	3 PB Barristers	0117 928 1520
	St John's Chambers	0117 923 4700
	Unity Street Chambers	0117 906 9789
Chelmsford	Trinity Chambers	01245 605040
Chester	Linenhall Chambers	01244 348282
Exeter	Rougemont Chambers	01392 208484
	Walnut House	01392 279751
Kew	Kew Chambers	0844 8099991
Leeds	Chancery House Chambers	0113 244 6691
	KBW	0113 297 1200
	Kings Chambers	0845 034 3444
	Park Court Chambers	0113 243 3277
	•Sovereign Chambers	0113 245 1841
	Zenith Chambers	0113 245 5438
Liverpool	Atlantic Chambers	0151 236 4421
London	42 Bedford Row	020 7831 0222
	Brick Court Chambers	020 7379 3550
	•Chambers of Mr Ami Feder	020 7797 7788
	•Devereux Chambers	020 7353 7534

• Expanded entry in Part D

	Fountain Court Chambers	020 7583 3335
	•Goldsmith Chambers	020 7353 6802
	Gough Square Chambers	020 7353 0924
	Harcourt Chambers	0844 561 7135
	13 King's Bench Walk	020 7353 7204
	Lamb Chambers	020 7797 8300
	•Maitland Chambers	020 7406 1200
	•Monckton Chambers	020 7405 7211
	New Square Chambers	020 7419 8000
	No5 Chambers	0845 210 5555
	•13 Old Square Chambers	020 7831 4445
	3 PB Barristers	020 7583 8055
	•Pump Court Chambers	020 7353 0711
	Radcliffe Chambers	020 7831 0081
	Selborne Chambers	020 7420 9500
	Serle Court	020 7242 6105
	•South Square	020 7696 9900
	3 Stone Buildings	020 7242 4937
	4 Stone Buildings	020 7242 5524
	•9 Stone Buildings	020 7404 5055
	11 Stone Buildings	020 7831 6381
	•Tanfield Chambers	020 7421 5300
	Ten Old Square	020 7405 0758
	3 Verulam Buildings	020 7831 8441
	•Wilberforce Chambers	020 7306 0102
	XXIV Old Buildings	020 7691 2424
Manchester	•Cobden House Chambers	0161 833 6000
	Kings Chambers	0845 034 3444
	•Lincoln House Chambers	0161 832 5701
	St James's Chambers	0161 834 7000
	9 St John Street	0161 955 9000
	•St Johns Buildings	0161 214 1500
Middlesbrough	•Trinity Chambers	01642 247569
Newcastle Upon Tyne	•Trinity Chambers	0191 232 1927
Oxford	Harcourt Chambers	0844 561 7135
	3 PB Barristers	01865 793 736
Portsmouth	Guildhall Chambers Portsmouth	023 9275 2400
	Portsmouth Barristers'Chambers	023 9283 1292
Southampton	•College Chambers	023 8023 0338
Swindon	Pump Court Chambers	01793 539899
Winchester	3 PB Barristers	01962 868884
	Pump Court Chambers	01962 868 161

COMPANY LAW

Birmingham	St Ive's Chambers	0121 236 0863
Exeter	Rougemont Chambers	01392 208484
	Walnut House	01392 279751
Leeds	Enterprise Chambers	0113 246 0391
London	•Argent Chambers	020 7556 5500
	Blackstone Chambers	020 7583 1770
	Enterprise Chambers	020 7405 9471
	Erskine Chambers	020 7242 5532
	•One Essex Court	020 7583 2000
	Essex Court Chambers	020 7813 8000
	Five Paper	020 7815 3200
	•South Square	020 7696 9900
	XXIV Old Buildings	020 7691 2424
Manchester	18 St John Street	0161 278 1800
	•St Johns Buildings	0161 214 1500
Newcastle Upon Tyne	Dere Street Barristers	0844 3351551
	Enterprise Chambers	0191 222 3344
Southampton	•College Chambers	023 8023 0338

COMPANY WINDING UP APPLICATIONS

Birmingham	St Ive's Chambers	0121 236 0863
London	Five Paper	020 7815 3200

COMPETITION LAW

Bristol	St John's Chambers	0117 923 4700
Exeter	Walnut House	01392 279751
Leeds	Chancery House Chambers	0113 244 6691
	Kings Chambers	0845 034 3444
	Park Court Chambers	0113 243 3277
London	•Argent Chambers	020 7556 5500
	Blackstone Chambers	020 7583 1770
	Brick Court Chambers	020 7379 3550
	•One Essex Court	020 7583 2000
	20 Essex Street	020 7842 1200
	Fountain Court Chambers	020 7583 3335
	•4-5 Gray's Inn Square	020 7404 5252
	•Henderson Chambers	020 7583 9020
	Lamb Chambers	020 7797 8300
	•Maitland Chambers	020 7406 1200
	Matrix Chambers	020 7404 3447
	•Monckton Chambers	020 7405 7211
	•8 New Square	020 7405 4321
Manchester	•Cobden House Chambers	0161 833 6000
	Kings Chambers	0845 034 3444
	18 St John Street	0161 278 1800
	•St Johns Buildings	0161 214 1500

COMPULSORY PURCHASE

COMPUTER CONTRACTS

Bournemouth	•3 PB Barristers	01202 292102
Bristol	3 PB Barristers	0117 928 1520
London	•Henderson Chambers	020 7583 9020
	Keating Chambers	020 7544 2600
	•8 New Square	020 7405 4321
	3 PB Barristers	020 7583 8055
Manchester	18 St John Street	0161 278 1800
Oxford	3 PB Barristers	01865 793 736
Winchester	3 PB Barristers	01962 868884

COMPUTER CRIME

Birmingham	St Ive's Chambers	0121 236 0863
Bournemouth	3 PB Barristers	01202 292102
Bristol	3 PB Barristers	0117 928 1520
	Queen Square Chambers	0117 921 1966
Exeter	Walnut House	01392 279751
London	•2 Bedford Row	020 7440 8888
	Bell Yard Chambers	020 7306 9292
	•23 Essex Street	020 7413 0353
	•187 Fleet Street	020 7430 7430
	•Henderson Chambers	020 7583 9020
	15 New Bridge Street	020 7842 1900
	3 PB Barristers	020 7583 8055
	The Chambers of Grahame Aldous QC	020 7832 0500
Manchester	Chambers of Ian Macdonald QC	0161 236 1840
	18 St John Street	0161 278 1800
	•St Johns Buildings	0161 214 1500
Newcastle Upon Tyne	Dere Street Barristers	0844 3351551
Oxford	3 PB Barristers	01865 793 736
Winchester	3 PB Barristers	01962 868884

COMPUTER LITIGATION

Bournemouth	3 PB Barristers	01202 292102
Bristol	3 PB Barristers	0117 928 1520

• Expanded entry in Part D

London	Essex Court Chambers	020 7813 8000
	•Henderson Chambers	020 7583 9020
	Keating Chambers	020 7544 2600
	•8 New Square	020 7405 4321
	3 PB Barristers	020 7583 8055
	•Tanfield Chambers	020 7421 5300
Manchester	18 St John Street	0161 278 1800
Oxford	3 PB Barristers	01865 793 736
Winchester	3 PB Barristers	01962 868884

CONCILIATION

London	Arbitration Chambers	020 7267 2137
	Bell Yard Chambers	020 7306 9292
	Five Paper	020 7815 3200
	•Tanfield Chambers	020 7421 5300
Manchester	18 St John Street	0161 278 1800
Portsmouth	Portsmouth Barristers'Chambers	023 9283 1292

CONFIDENTIAL INFORMATION

Exeter	Walnut House	01392 279751
London	Bell Yard Chambers	020 7306 9292
	Blackstone Chambers	020 7583 1770
	•8 New Square	020 7405 4321
Manchester	18 St John Street	0161 278 1800
	•St Johns Buildings	0161 214 1500
Portsmouth	Portsmouth Barristers'Chambers	023 9283 1292

CONFISCATION

Bournemouth	3 PB Barristers	01202 292102
Bristol	3 PB Barristers	0117 928 1520
Exeter	Rougemont Chambers	01392 208484
Leeds	KBW	0113 297 1200
Liverpool	Atlantic Chambers	0151 236 4421
London	Atkinson Bevan Chambers	020 7353 2112
	•2 Bedford Row	020 7440 8888
	25 Bedford Row	020 7067 1500
	•23 Essex Street	020 7413 0353
	Farringdon Chambers	020 7089 5700
	Five Paper	020 7815 3200
	•187 Fleet Street	020 7430 7430
	•Furnival Chambers	020 7405 3232
	Gough Square Chambers	020 7353 0924
	15 New Bridge Street	020 7842 1900
	•Nine Bedford Row	020 7489 2727
	•1 Paper Buildings	020 7353 3728
	3 PB Barristers	020 7583 8055
	•QEB Hollis Whiteman	020 7933 8855
	18 Red Lion Court	020 7520 6000
	The Chambers of Grahame Aldous QC	020 7832 0500
Manchester	Chambers of Ian Macdonald QC	0161 236 1840
	•Lincoln House Chambers	0161 832 5701
	18 St John Street	0161 278 1800
Middlesbrough	•Trinity Chambers	01642 247569
Newcastle Upon Tyne	Dere Street Barristers	0844 3351551
	•Trinity Chambers	0191 232 1927
Oxford	3 PB Barristers	01865 793 736
Portsmouth	Guildhall Chambers Portsmouth	023 9275 2400
Southampton	•College Chambers	023 8023 0338
Winchester	3 PB Barristers	01962 868884

CONFISCATION OF THE PROCEEDS OF CRIME

Birmingham	•No5 Chambers	0845 210 5555
	St Ive's Chambers	0121 236 0863
Bristol	Queen Square Chambers	0117 921 1966
Liverpool	Atlantic Chambers	0151 236 4421

London	Bell Yard Chambers	020 7306 9292
	•1 KBW Chambers	020 7936 1500
	Middle Temple Lane Chambers	020 7583 4352
	•3 Raymond Buildings	020 7400 6400
Newcastle Upon Tyne	Dere Street Barristers	0844 3351551

CONFLICT OF LAWS

Bournemouth	3 PB Barristers	01202 292102
Bristol	3 PB Barristers	0117 928 1520
Leeds	Chancery House Chambers	0113 244 6691
London	Blackstone Chambers	020 7583 1770
	Brick Court Chambers	020 7379 3550
	1 Chancery Lane	0845 634 6666
	•One Essex Court	020 7583 2000
	Essex Court Chambers	020 7813 8000
	20 Essex Street	020 7842 1200
	•Goldsmith Chambers	020 7353 6802
	Great James Street Chambers	020 7440 4949
	Hailsham Chambers	020 7643 5000
	•Maitland Chambers	020 7406 1200
	•Monckton Chambers	020 7405 7211
	New Square Chambers	020 7419 8000
	•13 Old Square Chambers	020 7831 4445
	3 PB Barristers	020 7583 8055
	Selborne Chambers	020 7420 9500
	3 Stone Buildings	020 7242 4937
	•9 Stone Buildings	020 7404 5055
	•Tanfield Chambers	020 7421 5300
	Ten Old Square	020 7405 0758
	3 Verulam Buildings	020 7831 8441
	XXIV Old Buildings	020 7691 2424
Manchester	18 St John Street	0161 278 1800
	•St Johns Buildings	0161 214 1500
Newcastle Upon Tyne	Dere Street Barristers	0844 3351551
Oxford	3 PB Barristers	01865 793 736
Winchester	3 PB Barristers	01962 868884

CONSTITUTIONAL AND ADMINISTRATIVE LAW

Exeter	Rougemont Chambers	01392 208484
	Walnut House	01392 279751
London	•Arden Chambers	020 7242 4244
	•Argent Chambers	020 7556 5500
	•Cornerstone Barristers	020 7242 4986
	3 Hare Court	020 7415 7800
	•Henderson Chambers	020 7583 9020
Manchester	Byrom Street Chambers	0161 829 2100
	Chambers of Ian Macdonald QC	0161 236 1840

CONSTITUTIONAL LAW

London	Blackstone Chambers	020 7583 1770
Manchester	18 St John Street	0161 278 1800
	•St Johns Buildings	0161 214 1500

CONSTRUCTION LAW

Birmingham	•No5 Chambers	0845 210 5555
	•St Philips Chambers	0121 246 7000
Bournemouth	3 PB Barristers	01202 292102
Bristol	No5 Chambers	0845 210 5555
	3 PB Barristers	0117 928 1520
	Queen Square Chambers	0117 921 1966
	St John's Chambers	0117 923 4700
	Unity Street Chambers	0117 906 9789
Chichester	Pallant Chambers	01243 784538
Exeter	Rougemont Chambers	01392 208484
Ipswich	East Anglian Chambers	01473 214481

• Expanded entry in Part D

Leeds	Chancery House Chambers	0113 244 6691
	Kings Chambers	0845 034 3444
	•Sovereign Chambers	0113 245 1841
	Zenith Chambers	0113 245 5438
Liverpool	•Oriel Chambers	0151 236 7191
London	Arbitration Chambers	020 7267 2137
	Atkin Chambers	020 7404 0102
	42 Bedford Row	020 7831 0222
	Brick Court Chambers	020 7379 3550
	•Chambers of Mr Ami Feder	020 7797 7788
	1 Chancery Lane	0845 634 6666
	1 Crown Office Row	020 7797 7500
	•Devereux Chambers	020 7353 7534
	Essex Court Chambers	020 7813 8000
	20 Essex Street	020 7842 1200
	•39 Essex Street	020 7832 1111
	Fountain Court Chambers	020 7583 3335
	•Goldsmith Chambers	020 7353 6802
	Hailsham Chambers	020 7643 5000
	•Henderson Chambers	020 7583 9020
	Keating Chambers	020 7544 2600
	Lamb Chambers	020 7797 8300
	•Monckton Chambers	020 7405 7211
	No5 Chambers	0845 210 5555
	3 PB Barristers	020 7583 8055
	Prince Henry's Chambers	020 7837 1645
	4 Pump Court	020 7842 5555
	•5 Pump Court	020 7353 2532
	•Pump Court Chambers	020 7353 0711
	•Tanfield Chambers	020 7421 5300
	Ten Old Square	020 7405 0758
	3 Verulam Buildings	020 7831 8441
	XXIV Old Buildings	020 7691 2424
Maidstone	Maidstone Chambers	01622 688592
Manchester	Deans Court Chambers	0161 214 6000
	Kings Chambers	0845 034 3444
	St James's Chambers	0161 834 7000
	9 St John Street	0161 955 9000
	18 St John Street	0161 278 1800
	•St Johns Buildings	0161 214 1500
Newcastle Upon Tyne	Dere Street Barristers	0844 3351551
Oxford	3 PB Barristers	01865 793 736
Plymouth	Devon Chambers	01752 661659
Portsmouth	Portsmouth Barristers'Chambers	023 9283 1292
Preston	Deans Court Chambers	01772 565 600
Sheffield	St Johns Buildings	0114 273 8951
Southampton	•College Chambers	023 8023 0338
Swansea	Iscoed Chambers	01792 652988
Swindon	Pump Court Chambers	01793 539899
Winchester	3 PB Barristers	01962 868884
	Pump Court Chambers	01962 868 161

CONSUMER CREDIT

Birmingham	St Ive's Chambers	0121 236 0863
Bournemouth	3 PB Barristers	01202 292102
Bristol	3 PB Barristers	0117 928 1520
Exeter	Rougemont Chambers	01392 208484
London	•Cornerstone Barristers	020 7242 4986
	Five Paper	020 7815 3200
	Gough Square Chambers	020 7353 0924
	•Henderson Chambers	020 7583 9020
	Middle Temple Lane Chambers	020 7583 4352
	3 PB Barristers	020 7583 8055
	•5 Pump Court	020 7353 2532

Manchester	18 St John Street	0161 278 1800
	•St Johns Buildings	0161 214 1500
Newcastle Upon Tyne	Dere Street Barristers	0844 3351551
Oxford	3 PB Barristers	01865 793 736
Portsmouth	Guildhall Chambers Portsmouth	023 9275 2400
Winchester	3 PB Barristers	01962 868884

CONSUMER LAW

Birmingham	No 8 Chambers	0121 236 5514
	St Ive's Chambers	0121 236 0863
	•St Philips Chambers	0121 246 7000
Bournemouth	3 PB Barristers	01202 292102
Bristol	3 PB Barristers	0117 928 1520
	Queen Square Chambers	0117 921 1966
	St John's Chambers	0117 923 4700
	Unity Street Chambers	0117 906 9789
Chester	Linenhall Chambers	01244 348282
Exeter	Rougemont Chambers	01392 208484
	Walnut House	01392 279751
Ipswich	East Anglian Chambers	01473 214481
Leeds	Chancery House Chambers	0113 244 6691
	Kings Chambers	0845 034 3444
	Park Court Chambers	0113 243 3277
London	•Chambers of Mr Ami Feder	020 7797 7788
	1 Chancery Lane	0845 634 6666
	•Cornerstone Barristers	020 7242 4986
	•Devereux Chambers	020 7353 7534
	Francis Taylor Building	020 7353 8415
	•Goldsmith Chambers	020 7353 6802
	Gough Square Chambers	020 7353 0924
	Hailsham Chambers	020 7643 5000
	•Henderson Chambers	020 7583 9020
	Lamb Chambers	020 7797 8300
	3 PB Barristers	020 7583 8055
	4 Pump Court	020 7842 5555
	6 Pump Court	020 7797 8400
	Selborne Chambers	020 7420 9500
	•Tanfield Chambers	020 7421 5300
	•Temple Garden Chambers	020 7583 1315
Maidstone	6 Pump Court Chambers	01622 688094
Manchester	Kings Chambers	0845 034 3444
	9 St John Street	0161 955 9000
	18 St John Street	0161 278 1800
	•St Johns Buildings	0161 214 1500
Middlesbrough	Fountain Chambers	01642 804040
	•Trinity Chambers	01642 247569
Newcastle Upon Tyne	Dere Street Barristers	0844 3351551
	•Trinity Chambers	0191 232 1927
Oxford	3 PB Barristers	01865 793 736
Winchester	3 PB Barristers	01962 868884

CONTAMINATED LAND

Bristol	Queen Square Chambers	0117 921 1966
London	•Cornerstone Barristers	020 7242 4986
	•23 Essex Street	020 7413 0353
	Five Paper	020 7815 3200
	Francis Taylor Building	020 7353 8415
	•Henderson Chambers	020 7583 9020
	•Maitland Chambers	020 7406 1200
Manchester	18 St John Street	0161 278 1800
Newcastle Upon Tyne	Dere Street Barristers	0844 3351551

CONTRACTS

Birmingham	St Ive's Chambers	0121 236 0863

• Expanded entry in Part D

Bournemouth	3 PB Barristers	01202 292102
Bristol	3 PB Barristers	0117 928 1520
Exeter	Rougemont Chambers	01392 208484
	Walnut House	01392 279751
Leeds	37 Park Square Chambers	0113 243 9422
London	•Cornerstone Barristers	020 7242 4986
	Five Paper	020 7815 3200
	Keating Chambers	020 7544 2600
	4 King's Bench Walk	020 7822 7000
	•Maitland Chambers	020 7406 1200
	3 PB Barristers	020 7583 8055
	•South Square	020 7696 9900
	XXIV Old Buildings	020 7691 2424
Manchester	18 St John Street	0161 278 1800
	•St Johns Buildings	0161 214 1500
Newcastle Upon Tyne	Dere Street Barristers	0844 3351551
Oxford	3 PB Barristers	01865 793 736
Portsmouth	Guildhall Chambers Portsmouth	023 9275 2400
	Portsmouth Barristers'Chambers	023 9283 1292
Southampton	•College Chambers	023 8023 0338
Winchester	3 PB Barristers	01962 868884

CONVEYANCING

Birmingham	•No5 Chambers	0845 210 5555
	•St Philips Chambers	0121 246 7000
Bristol	No5 Chambers	0845 210 5555
Exeter	Rougemont Chambers	01392 208484
Leeds	Chancery House Chambers	0113 244 6691
	Enterprise Chambers	0113 246 0391
	Kings Chambers	0845 034 3444
Liverpool	Atlantic Chambers	0151 236 4421
London	42 Bedford Row	020 7831 0222
	Enterprise Chambers	020 7405 9471
	Falcon Chambers	020 7353 2484
	Five Paper	020 7815 3200
	•Maitland Chambers	020 7406 1200
	New Square Chambers	020 7419 8000
	No5 Chambers	0845 210 5555
	•13 Old Square Chambers	020 7831 4445
	Radcliffe Chambers	020 7831 0081
	Selborne Chambers	020 7420 9500
	3 Stone Buildings	020 7242 4937
	•9 Stone Buildings	020 7404 5055
	Ten Old Square	020 7405 0758
Manchester	•Cobden House Chambers	0161 833 6000
	Kings Chambers	0845 034 3444
	St James's Chambers	0161 834 7000
	9 St John Street	0161 955 9000
	18 St John Street	0161 278 1800
Middlesbrough	•Trinity Chambers	01642 247569
Newcastle Upon Tyne	Dere Street Barristers	0844 3351551
	Enterprise Chambers	0191 222 3344
	•Trinity Chambers	0191 232 1927

COPYRIGHT

Birmingham	•No5 Chambers	0845 210 5555
Bournemouth	3 PB Barristers	01202 292102
Bristol	No5 Chambers	0845 210 5555
	3 PB Barristers	0117 928 1520
	St John's Chambers	0117 923 4700
Leeds	Chancery House Chambers	0113 244 6691
	Kings Chambers	0845 034 3444
	•Sovereign Chambers	0113 245 1841
	Zenith Chambers	0113 245 5438

Liverpool	Atlantic Chambers	0151 236 4421
London	Blackstone Chambers	020 7583 1770
	Doughty Street Chambers	020 7404 1313
	Fountain Court Chambers	020 7583 3335
	•Furnival Chambers	020 7405 3232
	Lamb Chambers	020 7797 8300
	•8 New Square	020 7405 4321
	No5 Chambers	0845 210 5555
	3 PB Barristers	020 7583 8055
	Serle Court	020 7242 6105
	11 South Square	020 7405 1222
	3 Stone Buildings	020 7242 4937
	•9 Stone Buildings	020 7404 5055
	•Three New Square IP	020 7405 1111
Manchester	•Cobden House Chambers	0161 833 6000
	Kings Chambers	0845 034 3444
	St James's Chambers	0161 834 7000
	18 St John Street	0161 278 1800
	•St Johns Buildings	0161 214 1500
Newcastle Upon Tyne	Dere Street Barristers	0844 3351551
Nottingham	KCH Garden Square	0115 941 8851
Oxford	3 PB Barristers	01865 793 736
Portsmouth	Portsmouth Barristers'Chambers	023 9283 1292
Winchester	3 PB Barristers	01962 868884

COPYRIGHT THEFT

London	•23 Essex Street	020 7413 0353
	•QEB Hollis Whiteman	020 7933 8855
Manchester	18 St John Street	0161 278 1800
Newcastle Upon Tyne	Dere Street Barristers	0844 3351551

COPYRIGHT TRIBUNAL

London	•23 Essex Street	020 7413 0353
Manchester	18 St John Street	0161 278 1800

CORONERS

Birmingham	•St Philips Chambers	0121 246 7000
Bristol	Queen Square Chambers	0117 921 1966
Exeter	Walnut House	01392 279751
London	•2 Bedford Row	020 7440 8888
	•Cornerstone Barristers	020 7242 4986
	1 Crown Office Row	020 7797 7500
	•23 Essex Street	020 7413 0353
	•187 Fleet Street	020 7430 7430
	•1 KBW Chambers	020 7936 1500
	15 New Bridge Street	020 7842 1900
	18 Red Lion Court	020 7520 6000
	•Temple Garden Chambers	020 7583 1315
Manchester	Chambers of Ian Macdonald QC	0161 236 1840
	18 St John Street	0161 278 1800
	•St Johns Buildings	0161 214 1500
Newcastle Upon Tyne	Dere Street Barristers	0844 3351551
Pitstone	Victor House Chambers	01296 664043

CORONER'S INQUESTS

Bristol	Queen Square Chambers	0117 921 1966
Exeter	Rougemont Chambers	01392 208484
Leeds	37 Park Square Chambers	0113 243 9422
London	•2 Bedford Row	020 7440 8888
	•Cornerstone Barristers	020 7242 4986
	•23 Essex Street	020 7413 0353
	•187 Fleet Street	020 7430 7430
	•Henderson Chambers	020 7583 9020
	•1 KBW Chambers	020 7936 1500
	15 New Bridge Street	020 7842 1900

	•5 Pump Court	020 7353 2532
	•3 Raymond Buildings	020 7400 6400
	18 Red Lion Court	020 7520 6000
Manchester	Chambers of Ian Macdonald QC	0161 236 1840
Newcastle Upon Tyne	Dere Street Barristers	0844 3351551
Portsmouth	Guildhall Chambers Portsmouth	023 9275 2400

CORPORATE FINANCE

Birmingham	•No5 Chambers	0845 210 5555
Bournemouth	3 PB Barristers	01202 292102
Bristol	No5 Chambers	0845 210 5555
	3 PB Barristers	0117 928 1520
Exeter	Rougemont Chambers	01392 208484
Leeds	Chancery House Chambers	0113 244 6691
	KBW	0113 297 1200
	Kings Chambers	0845 034 3444
London	Blackstone Chambers	020 7583 1770
	Erskine Chambers	020 7242 5532
	Fountain Court Chambers	020 7583 3335
	•Henderson Chambers	020 7583 9020
	•Maitland Chambers	020 7406 1200
	New Square Chambers	020 7419 8000
	No5 Chambers	0845 210 5555
	•13 Old Square Chambers	020 7831 4445
	3 PB Barristers	020 7583 8055
	•South Square	020 7696 9900
	4 Stone Buildings	020 7242 5524
	•9 Stone Buildings	020 7404 5055
	Taxchambers	020 7242 2744
	Ten Old Square	020 7405 0758
	XXIV Old Buildings	020 7691 2424
Manchester	Kings Chambers	0845 034 3444
	9 St John Street	0161 955 9000
	18 St John Street	0161 278 1800
	•St Johns Buildings	0161 214 1500
Oxford	3 PB Barristers	01865 793 736
Portsmouth	Portsmouth Barristers'Chambers	023 9283 1292
Winchester	3 PB Barristers	01962 868884

CORPORATE FRAUD

Birmingham	Equity Chambers	0121 236 5007
	No 8 Chambers	0121 236 5514
	•No5 Chambers	0845 210 5555
	•St Philips Chambers	0121 246 7000
Bournemouth	3 PB Barristers	01202 292102
Brighton	Crown Office Row Chambers	01273 625625
Bristol	No5 Chambers	0845 210 5555
	3 PB Barristers	0117 928 1520
	Queen Square Chambers	0117 921 1966
	St John's Chambers	0117 923 4700
Chelmsford	Trinity Chambers	01245 605040
Chester	Linenhall Chambers	01244 348282
Exeter	Rougemont Chambers	01392 208484
	Walnut House	01392 279751
Ipswich	East Anglian Chambers	01473 214481
Leeds	KBW	0113 297 1200
	Kings Chambers	0845 034 3444
	Park Court Chambers	0113 243 3277
	•Sovereign Chambers	0113 245 1841
Liverpool	Atlantic Chambers	0151 236 4421
	•Number 7 Harrington Street Chambers	0151 242 0707
London	•Argent Chambers	020 7556 5500
	Atkinson Bevan Chambers	020 7353 2112
	•2 Bedford Row	020 7440 8888

A

	25 Bedford Row	020 7067 1500
	Bell Yard Chambers	020 7306 9292
	•9-12 Bell Yard	020 7400 1800
	Carmelite Chambers	020 7936 6300
	•Chambers of Mr Ami Feder	020 7797 7788
	•Cornerstone Barristers	020 7242 4986
	•Devereux Chambers	020 7353 7534
	Doughty Street Chambers	020 7404 1313
	•23 Essex Street	020 7413 0353
	Farringdon Chambers	020 7089 5700
	•187 Fleet Street	020 7430 7430
	•Furnival Chambers	020 7405 3232
	•Goldsmith Chambers	020 7353 6802
	Gough Square Chambers	020 7353 0924
	•4-5 Gray's Inn Square	020 7404 5252
	Great James Street Chambers	020 7440 4949
	4 KBW	020 7822 8822
	•1 KBW Chambers	020 7936 1500
	13 King's Bench Walk	020 7353 7204
	Lombard Chambers	020 7107 2100
	Matrix Chambers	020 7404 3447
	15 New Bridge Street	020 7842 1900
	New Square Chambers	020 7419 8000
	•Nine Bedford Row	020 7489 2727
	No5 Chambers	0845 210 5555
	Outer Temple Chambers	020 7353 6381
	•1 Paper Buildings	020 7353 3728
	3 PB Barristers	020 7583 8055
	1 Pump Court	020 7842 7070
	6 Pump Court	020 7797 8400
	•Pump Court Chambers	020 7353 0711
	•QEB Hollis Whiteman	020 7933 8855
	•3 Raymond Buildings	020 7400 6400
	18 Red Lion Court	020 7520 6000
	Serle Court	020 7242 6105
	•9 Stone Buildings	020 7404 5055
	11 Stone Buildings	020 7831 6381
	The Chambers of Grahame Aldous QC	020 7832 0500
Maidstone	6 Pump Court Chambers	01622 688094
Manchester	Central Chambers	0161 236 1133
	Chambers of Ian Macdonald QC	0161 236 1840
	•Cobden House Chambers	0161 833 6000
	Deans Court Chambers	0161 214 6000
	Kenworthy's Chambers	0161 832 4036
	Kings Chambers	0845 034 3444
	•Lincoln House Chambers	0161 832 5701
	9 St John Street	0161 955 9000
	18 St John Street	0161 278 1800
	•St Johns Buildings	0161 214 1500
Middlesbrough	Fountain Chambers	01642 804040
	•Trinity Chambers	01642 247569
Newcastle Upon Tyne	Dere Street Barristers	0844 3351551
	•Trinity Chambers	0191 232 1927
Nottingham	1 High Pavement	0115 941 8218
Oxford	3 PB Barristers	01865 793 736
Plymouth	Devon Chambers	01752 661659
Preston	Deans Court Chambers	01772 565 600
Sheffield	Bank House Chambers	0114 275 1223
Stoke On Trent	Regent Chambers	01782 286666
Swansea	Iscoed Chambers	01792 652988
Swindon	Pump Court Chambers	01793 539899
Taunton	Octagon Chambers	01823 331919
Winchester	3 PB Barristers	01962 868884
	Pump Court Chambers	01962 868 161

• Expanded entry in Part D

CORPORATE GOVERNANCE

Bournemouth	3 PB Barristers	01202 292102
Bristol	3 PB Barristers	0117 928 1520
London	Erskine Chambers	020 7242 5532
	Five Paper	020 7815 3200
	3 PB Barristers	020 7583 8055
Manchester	18 St John Street	0161 278 1800
Newcastle Upon Tyne	Dere Street Barristers	0844 3351551
Oxford	3 PB Barristers	01865 793 736
Winchester	3 PB Barristers	01962 868884

CORPORATE INSOLVENCY

Bournemouth	3 PB Barristers	01202 292102
Bristol	3 PB Barristers	0117 928 1520
London	Erskine Chambers	020 7242 5532
	Five Paper	020 7815 3200
	•Maitland Chambers	020 7406 1200
	3 PB Barristers	020 7583 8055
	•South Square	020 7696 9900
Manchester	18 St John Street	0161 278 1800
Newcastle Upon Tyne	Dere Street Barristers	0844 3351551
Oxford	3 PB Barristers	01865 793 736
Southampton	•College Chambers	023 8023 0338
Winchester	3 PB Barristers	01962 868884

CORPORATE LIABILITY

Bournemouth	3 PB Barristers	01202 292102
Bristol	3 PB Barristers	0117 928 1520
London	•2 Bedford Row	020 7440 8888
	Erskine Chambers	020 7242 5532
	Five Paper	020 7815 3200
	•Henderson Chambers	020 7583 9020
	3 PB Barristers	020 7583 8055
	XXIV Old Buildings	020 7691 2424
Manchester	18 St John Street	0161 278 1800
Newcastle Upon Tyne	Dere Street Barristers	0844 3351551
Oxford	3 PB Barristers	01865 793 736
Winchester	3 PB Barristers	01962 868884

CORPORATE MANSLAUGHTER

Bournemouth	3 PB Barristers	01202 292102
Bristol	3 PB Barristers	0117 928 1520
	Queen Square Chambers	0117 921 1966
Exeter	Walnut House	01392 279751
London	•2 Bedford Row	020 7440 8888
	Bell Yard Chambers	020 7306 9292
	•Cornerstone Barristers	020 7242 4986
	•23 Essex Street	020 7413 0353
	•187 Fleet Street	020 7430 7430
	•Henderson Chambers	020 7583 9020
	•1 KBW Chambers	020 7936 1500
	15 New Bridge Street	020 7842 1900
	•Nine Bedford Row	020 7489 2727
	Outer Temple Chambers	020 7353 6381
	3 PB Barristers	020 7583 8055
	•3 Raymond Buildings	020 7400 6400
	18 Red Lion Court	020 7520 6000
	The Chambers of Grahame Aldous QC	020 7832 0500
Manchester	Chambers of Ian Macdonald QC	0161 236 1840
	•Lincoln House Chambers	0161 832 5701
	18 St John Street	0161 278 1800
	•St Johns Buildings	0161 214 1500
Middlesbrough	•Trinity Chambers	01642 247569
Newcastle Upon Tyne	Dere Street Barristers	0844 3351551

A

	•Trinity Chambers	0191 232 1927
Oxford	3 PB Barristers	01865 793 736
Portsmouth	Guildhall Chambers Portsmouth	023 9275 2400
Winchester	3 PB Barristers	01962 868884

CORPORATE RECOVERY

Bournemouth	3 PB Barristers	01202 292102
Bristol	3 PB Barristers	0117 928 1520
London	Erskine Chambers	020 7242 5532
	Essex Court Chambers	020 7813 8000
	Five Paper	020 7815 3200
	•Maitland Chambers	020 7406 1200
	3 PB Barristers	020 7583 8055
	•South Square	020 7696 9900
Manchester	18 St John Street	0161 278 1800
Newcastle Upon Tyne	Dere Street Barristers	0844 3351551
Oxford	3 PB Barristers	01865 793 736
Southampton	•College Chambers	023 8023 0338
Winchester	3 PB Barristers	01962 868884

CORPORATION TAX

Birmingham	•No5 Chambers	0845 210 5555
	•St Philips Chambers	0121 246 7000
Bradford	Broadway House Chambers	01274 722560
Bristol	No5 Chambers	0845 210 5555
	St John's Chambers	0117 923 4700
Leeds	Broadway House Chambers	0113 246 2600
	Chancery House Chambers	0113 244 6691
	Kings Chambers	0845 034 3444
Liverpool	Atlantic Chambers	0151 236 4421
London	•Maitland Chambers	020 7406 1200
	New Square Chambers	020 7419 8000
	No5 Chambers	0845 210 5555
	Prince Henry's Chambers	020 7837 1645
	•Pump Court Tax Chambers	020 7414 8080
	3 Stone Buildings	020 7242 4937
	•9 Stone Buildings	020 7404 5055
	Taxchambers	020 7242 2744
	Temple Tax Chambers	020 7353 7884
	Ten Old Square	020 7405 0758
Manchester	Kings Chambers	0845 034 3444
	St James's Chambers	0161 834 7000
	18 St John Street	0161 278 1800
Newcastle Upon Tyne	Dere Street Barristers	0844 3351551

COSTS

Birmingham	•No5 Chambers	0845 210 5555
Bournemouth	3 PB Barristers	01202 292102
Bristol	3 PB Barristers	0117 928 1520
Leeds	Kings Chambers	0845 034 3444
London	•Crown Office Chambers	020 7797 8100
	1 Crown Office Row	020 7797 7500
	•39 Essex Street	020 7832 1111
	•Farrar's Building	020 7583 9241
	Five Paper	020 7815 3200
	Hailsham Chambers	020 7643 5000
	3 PB Barristers	020 7583 8055
	•Temple Garden Chambers	020 7583 1315
Manchester	Kenworthy's Chambers	0161 832 4036
	Kings Chambers	0845 034 3444
	18 St John Street	0161 278 1800
	•St Johns Buildings	0161 214 1500
Newcastle Upon Tyne	Dere Street Barristers	0844 3351551
Oxford	3 PB Barristers	01865 793 736

• Expanded entry in Part D

Southampton	•College Chambers	023 8023 0338
Winchester	3 PB Barristers	01962 868884

COUNCIL TAX

Exeter	Walnut House	01392 279751
London	Five Paper	020 7815 3200
Manchester	•St Johns Buildings	0161 214 1500

COUNCILLORS AND STANDARDS

London	•23 Essex Street	020 7413 0353
	Five Paper	020 7815 3200
Manchester	18 St John Street	0161 278 1800
Newcastle Upon Tyne	Dere Street Barristers	0844 3351551

COURT OF PROTECTION

Birmingham	•No5 Chambers	0845 210 5555
	St Ive's Chambers	0121 236 0863
Bournemouth	3 PB Barristers	01202 292102
Bristol	No5 Chambers	0845 210 5555
	3 PB Barristers	0117 928 1520
London	Five Paper	020 7815 3200
	No5 Chambers	0845 210 5555
	•13 Old Square Chambers	020 7831 4445
	3 PB Barristers	020 7583 8055
	Radcliffe Chambers	020 7831 0081
	The Chambers of Grahame Aldous QC	020 7832 0500
Manchester	Chambers of Ian Macdonald QC	0161 236 1840
	18 St John Street	0161 278 1800
Newcastle Upon Tyne	Dere Street Barristers	0844 3351551
Oxford	3 PB Barristers	01865 793 736
Portsmouth	Guildhall Chambers Portsmouth	023 9275 2400
Southampton	•College Chambers	023 8023 0338
Winchester	3 PB Barristers	01962 868884

COURTS MARTIAL

Birmingham	No 8 Chambers	0121 236 5514
	St Ive's Chambers	0121 236 0863
	•St Philips Chambers	0121 246 7000
Bournemouth	3 PB Barristers	01202 292102
Bristol	Albion Chambers	0117 927 2144
	3 PB Barristers	0117 928 1520
	St John's Chambers	0117 923 4700
Chester	Linenhall Chambers	01244 348282
Exeter	Rougemont Chambers	01392 208484
	Walnut House	01392 279751
Ipswich	East Anglian Chambers	01473 214481
Leeds	KBW	0113 297 1200
	Park Court Chambers	0113 243 3277
	37 Park Square Chambers	0113 243 9422
	Zenith Chambers	0113 245 5438
Liverpool	Atlantic Chambers	0151 236 4421
London	•Argent Chambers	020 7556 5500
	Atkinson Bevan Chambers	020 7353 2112
	•2 Bedford Row	020 7440 8888
	•9-12 Bell Yard	020 7400 1800
	Carmelite Chambers	020 7936 6300
	•Chambers of Marion Smullen and Kerim Fuad QC	020 7427 4400
	•Chambers of Mr Ami Feder	020 7797 7788
	•Charter Chambers	020 7618 4400
	•Cornerstone Barristers	020 7242 4986
	•23 Essex Street	020 7413 0353
	•Furnival Chambers	020 7405 3232
	•Goldsmith Chambers	020 7353 6802
	Great James Street Chambers	020 7440 4949

A

	15 New Bridge Street	020 7842 1900
	•1 Paper Buildings	020 7353 3728
	3 PB Barristers	020 7583 8055
	•Pump Court Chambers	020 7353 0711
	•QEB Hollis Whiteman	020 7933 8855
	•3 Raymond Buildings	020 7400 6400
	18 Red Lion Court	020 7520 6000
	The Chambers of Grahame Aldous QC	020 7832 0500
Manchester	Chambers of Ian Macdonald QC	0161 236 1840
	•Cobden House Chambers	0161 833 6000
	18 St John Street	0161 278 1800
Middlesbrough	Fountain Chambers	01642 804040
	Old Court Chambers	01642 232523
	•Trinity Chambers	01642 247569
Newcastle Upon Tyne	Cathedral Chambers	0191 232 1311
	Dere Street Barristers	0844 3351551
	•Trinity Chambers	0191 232 1927
Nottingham	KCH Garden Square	0115 941 8851
Oxford	3 PB Barristers	01865 793 736
Plymouth	Devon Chambers	01752 661659
Sheffield	Bank House Chambers	0114 275 1223
	St Johns Buildings	0114 273 8951
Swindon	Pump Court Chambers	01793 539899
Taunton	Octagon Chambers	01823 331919
Winchester	3 PB Barristers	01962 868884
	Pump Court Chambers	01962 868 161

CRIME

Birmingham	Cornwall Street Chambers	0121 233 7500
	Equity Chambers	0121 236 5007
	No 8 Chambers	0121 236 5514
	•No5 Chambers	0845 210 5555
	St Ive's Chambers	0121 236 0863
	•St Philips Chambers	0121 246 7000
Bournemouth	3 PB Barristers	01202 292102
Bradford	Broadway House Chambers	01274 722560
Brighton	Crown Office Row Chambers	01273 625625
Bristol	Albion Chambers	0117 927 2144
	No5 Chambers	0845 210 5555
	3 PB Barristers	0117 928 1520
	Queen Square Chambers	0117 921 1966
	St John's Chambers	0117 923 4700
	Unity Street Chambers	0117 906 9789
Canterbury	Becket Chambers	01227 786331
Chester	Linenhall Chambers	01244 348282
Chichester	Pallant Chambers	01243 784538
Exeter	Rougemont Chambers	01392 208484
	Walnut House	01392 279751
Hull	Wilberforce Chambers	01482 323264
Ipswich	East Anglian Chambers	01473 214481
Leeds	Broadway House Chambers	0113 246 2600
	KBW	0113 297 1200
	Park Court Chambers	0113 243 3277
	37 Park Square Chambers	0113 243 9422
	•Sovereign Chambers	0113 245 1841
	Zenith Chambers	0113 245 5438
Lewes	Westgate Chambers	01273 480510
Liverpool	Atlantic Chambers	0151 236 4421
	Chavasse Court Chambers	0151 229 2030
	•Oriel Chambers	0151 236 7191
London	•Argent Chambers	020 7556 5500
	Atkinson Bevan Chambers	020 7353 2112
	25 Bedford Row	020 7067 1500
	Bell Yard Chambers	020 7306 9292

• Expanded entry in Part D

A

	•9-12 Bell Yard	020 7400 1800
	4 Brick Court	020 7832 3200
	Carmelite Chambers	020 7936 6300
	•Chambers of Marion Smullen and Kerim Fuad QC	020 7427 4400
	•Chambers of Mr Ami Feder	020 7797 7788
	•Charter Chambers	020 7618 4400
	•Cornerstone Barristers	020 7242 4986
	1 Crown Office Row	020 7797 7500
	Doughty Street Chambers	020 7404 1313
	•2 Dr Johnson's Buildings	020 7936 2613
	•Farrar's Building	020 7583 9241
	Farringdon Chambers	020 7089 5700
	•187 Fleet Street	020 7430 7430
	•Furnival Chambers	020 7405 3232
	•Goldsmith Chambers	020 7353 6802
	Great James Street Chambers	020 7440 4949
	•1 KBW Chambers	020 7936 1500
	2 King's Bench Walk	020 7353 1746
	4 King's Bench Walk	020 7822 7000
	13 King's Bench Walk	020 7353 7204
	Lombard Chambers	020 7107 2100
	Matrix Chambers	020 7404 3447
	Middle Temple Lane Chambers	020 7583 4352
	15 New Bridge Street	020 7842 1900
	•Nine Bedford Row	020 7489 2727
	No5 Chambers	0845 210 5555
	12 Old Square Chambers	020 7404 0875
	Outer Temple Chambers	020 7353 6381
	•1 Paper Buildings	020 7353 3728
	3 PB Barristers	020 7583 8055
	1 Pump Court	020 7842 7070
	•5 Pump Court	020 7353 2532
	6 Pump Court	020 7797 8400
	•Pump Court Chambers	020 7353 0711
	•QEB Hollis Whiteman	020 7933 8855
	•3 Raymond Buildings	020 7400 6400
	18 Red Lion Court	020 7520 6000
	The Chambers of Grahame Aldous QC	020 7832 0500
	Tooks Chambers	020 7842 7575
Maidstone	Maidstone Chambers	01622 688592
	6 Pump Court Chambers	01622 688094
Manchester	Central Chambers	0161 236 1133
	Chambers of Ian Macdonald QC	0161 236 1840
	•Cobden House Chambers	0161 833 6000
	Deans Court Chambers	0161 214 6000
	Kenworthy's Chambers	0161 832 4036
	•Lincoln House Chambers	0161 832 5701
	9 St John Street	0161 955 9000
	18 St John Street	0161 278 1800
	•St Johns Buildings	0161 214 1500
Middlesbrough	Fountain Chambers	01642 804040
	Old Court Chambers	01642 232523
	•Trinity Chambers	01642 247569
Newcastle Upon Tyne	Cathedral Chambers	0191 232 1311
	Dere Street Barristers	0844 3351551
	•Trinity Chambers	0191 232 1927
Northampton	Northampton Chambers	01604 636271
Norwich	Octagon House	01603 623186
Nottingham	1 High Pavement	0115 941 8218
	KCH Garden Square	0115 941 8851
Oxford	3 PB Barristers	01865 793 736
Plymouth	Devon Chambers	01752 661659
Portsmouth	Guildhall Chambers Portsmouth	023 9275 2400

 • Expanded entry in Part D

A

Preston	Deans Court Chambers	01772 565 600
Sheffield	Bank House Chambers	0114 275 1223
	St Johns Buildings	0114 273 8951
Southampton	•College Chambers	023 8023 0338
Stoke On Trent	Regent Chambers	01782 286666
Swansea	Iscoed Chambers	01792 652988
Swindon	Pump Court Chambers	01793 539899
Taunton	Octagon Chambers	01823 331919
Winchester	3 PB Barristers	01962 868884
	Pump Court Chambers	01962 868 161

CRIME AND CRIMINAL DUE PROCESS

Birmingham	•St Philips Chambers	0121 246 7000
Bournemouth	3 PB Barristers	01202 292102
Bristol	3 PB Barristers	0117 928 1520
	Queen Square Chambers	0117 921 1966
Exeter	Walnut House	01392 279751
London	•2 Bedford Row	020 7440 8888
	Bell Yard Chambers	020 7306 9292
	•23 Essex Street	020 7413 0353
	•187 Fleet Street	020 7430 7430
	•1 KBW Chambers	020 7936 1500
	15 New Bridge Street	020 7842 1900
	3 PB Barristers	020 7583 8055
	18 Red Lion Court	020 7520 6000
	The Chambers of Grahame Aldous QC	020 7832 0500
Manchester	Chambers of Ian Macdonald QC	0161 236 1840
	18 St John Street	0161 278 1800
	•St Johns Buildings	0161 214 1500
Middlesbrough	•Trinity Chambers	01642 247569
Newcastle Upon Tyne	Dere Street Barristers	0844 3351551
	•Trinity Chambers	0191 232 1927
Oxford	3 PB Barristers	01865 793 736
Winchester	3 PB Barristers	01962 868884

CRIMINAL JUDICIAL REVIEW

Bournemouth	3 PB Barristers	01202 292102
Bristol	3 PB Barristers	0117 928 1520
	Queen Square Chambers	0117 921 1966
Exeter	Rougemont Chambers	01392 208484
	Walnut House	01392 279751
London	•2 Bedford Row	020 7440 8888
	25 Bedford Row	020 7067 1500
	Bell Yard Chambers	020 7306 9292
	•Cornerstone Barristers	020 7242 4986
	•23 Essex Street	020 7413 0353
	•187 Fleet Street	020 7430 7430
	•1 KBW Chambers	020 7936 1500
	15 New Bridge Street	020 7842 1900
	3 PB Barristers	020 7583 8055
	•3 Raymond Buildings	020 7400 6400
	18 Red Lion Court	020 7520 6000
	The Chambers of Grahame Aldous QC	020 7832 0500
Manchester	Chambers of Ian Macdonald QC	0161 236 1840
	18 St John Street	0161 278 1800
	•St Johns Buildings	0161 214 1500
Middlesbrough	•Trinity Chambers	01642 247569
Newcastle Upon Tyne	Dere Street Barristers	0844 3351551
	•Trinity Chambers	0191 232 1927
Oxford	3 PB Barristers	01865 793 736
Portsmouth	Guildhall Chambers Portsmouth	023 9275 2400
Winchester	3 PB Barristers	01962 868884

• Expanded entry in Part D

CROSS-BORDER LITIGATION AND REMEDIES

Bournemouth	3 PB Barristers	01202 292102
Bristol	3 PB Barristers	0117 928 1520
London	1 Chancery Lane	0845 634 6666
	Erskine Chambers	020 7242 5532
	•Henderson Chambers	020 7583 9020
	3 PB Barristers	020 7583 8055
	•South Square	020 7696 9900
	•Tanfield Chambers	020 7421 5300
	XXIV Old Buildings	020 7691 2424
Manchester	•St Johns Buildings	0161 214 1500
Newcastle Upon Tyne	Dere Street Barristers	0844 3351551
Oxford	3 PB Barristers	01865 793 736
Winchester	3 PB Barristers	01962 868884

CULTURAL PROPERTY LAW

London	3 Stone Buildings	020 7242 4937

CUSTOMS

Birmingham	St Ive's Chambers	0121 236 0863
London	•Cornerstone Barristers	020 7242 4986
	•Maitland Chambers	020 7406 1200
	•Monckton Chambers	020 7405 7211
	15 New Bridge Street	020 7842 1900
	Prince Henry's Chambers	020 7837 1645
	•Pump Court Tax Chambers	020 7414 8080
	Temple Tax Chambers	020 7353 7884
Manchester	•Lincoln House Chambers	0161 832 5701
	18 St John Street	0161 278 1800
	•St Johns Buildings	0161 214 1500
Portsmouth	Guildhall Chambers Portsmouth	023 9275 2400

DAMAGES

Bournemouth	3 PB Barristers	01202 292102
Bristol	3 PB Barristers	0117 928 1520
London	Five Paper	020 7815 3200
	Hailsham Chambers	020 7643 5000
	3 PB Barristers	020 7583 8055
Manchester	18 St John Street	0161 278 1800
Middlesbrough	•Trinity Chambers	01642 247569
Newcastle Upon Tyne	Dere Street Barristers	0844 3351551
	•Trinity Chambers	0191 232 1927
Oxford	3 PB Barristers	01865 793 736
Portsmouth	Guildhall Chambers Portsmouth	023 9275 2400
Southampton	•College Chambers	023 8023 0338
Winchester	3 PB Barristers	01962 868884

DATA PROTECTION

London	Blackstone Chambers	020 7583 1770
	•Cornerstone Barristers	020 7242 4986
	•Henderson Chambers	020 7583 9020
	11 King's Bench Walk	020 7632 8500
	Matrix Chambers	020 7404 3447
	•8 New Square	020 7405 4321
Manchester	18 St John Street	0161 278 1800
	•St Johns Buildings	0161 214 1500
Newcastle Upon Tyne	Dere Street Barristers	0844 3351551

DEFAMATION

Birmingham	No 8 Chambers	0121 236 5514
Bristol	Queen Square Chambers	0117 921 1966
	St John's Chambers	0117 923 4700
Chester	Linenhall Chambers	01244 348282
Leeds	KBW	0113 297 1200
Liverpool	Atlantic Chambers	0151 236 4421

A

London	Blackstone Chambers	020 7583 1770
	One Brick Court	020 7353 8845
	Brick Court Chambers	020 7379 3550
	•Cornerstone Barristers	020 7242 4986
	Doughty Street Chambers	020 7404 1313
	Fountain Court Chambers	020 7583 3335
	•4-5 Gray's Inn Square	020 7404 5252
	4 King's Bench Walk	020 7822 7000
	Matrix Chambers	020 7404 3447
Manchester	•Cobden House Chambers	0161 833 6000
	Kenworthy's Chambers	0161 832 4036
	St James's Chambers	0161 834 7000
	18 St John Street	0161 278 1800
Middlesbrough	•Trinity Chambers	01642 247569
Newcastle Upon Tyne	Dere Street Barristers	0844 3351551
	•Trinity Chambers	0191 232 1927
Southampton	•College Chambers	023 8023 0338

DERIVATIVES

London	•One Essex Court	020 7583 2000
	Essex Court Chambers	020 7813 8000
	Five Paper	020 7815 3200

DESIGN

Manchester	18 St John Street	0161 278 1800
	•St Johns Buildings	0161 214 1500
Portsmouth	Portsmouth Barristers'Chambers	023 9283 1292

DIRECTORS' DISQUALIFICATION

Birmingham	St Ive's Chambers	0121 236 0863
Exeter	Rougemont Chambers	01392 208484
London	Erskine Chambers	020 7242 5532
	•One Essex Court	020 7583 2000
	Five Paper	020 7815 3200
	•Henderson Chambers	020 7583 9020
	•Maitland Chambers	020 7406 1200
	•13 Old Square Chambers	020 7831 4445
	•Tanfield Chambers	020 7421 5300
	XXIV Old Buildings	020 7691 2424
Newcastle Upon Tyne	Dere Street Barristers	0844 3351551
Southampton	•College Chambers	023 8023 0338

DISABILITY AND HEALTH

Exeter	Rougemont Chambers	01392 208484
London	•Cornerstone Barristers	020 7242 4986
	The Chambers of Grahame Aldous QC	020 7832 0500
Manchester	Central Chambers	0161 236 1133
	18 St John Street	0161 278 1800

DISABILITY DISCRIMINATION

Birmingham	St Ive's Chambers	0121 236 0863
Bournemouth	3 PB Barristers	01202 292102
Bristol	3 PB Barristers	0117 928 1520
	Queen Square Chambers	0117 921 1966
London	Bell Yard Chambers	020 7306 9292
	Five Paper	020 7815 3200
	•Henderson Chambers	020 7583 9020
	3 PB Barristers	020 7583 8055
	The Chambers of Grahame Aldous QC	020 7832 0500
Manchester	Chambers of Ian Macdonald QC	0161 236 1840
	18 St John Street	0161 278 1800
Newcastle Upon Tyne	Dere Street Barristers	0844 3351551
Oxford	3 PB Barristers	01865 793 736
Southampton	•College Chambers	023 8023 0338
Winchester	3 PB Barristers	01962 868884

• Expanded entry in Part D

DISASTERS

Bournemouth	3 PB Barristers	01202 292102
Bristol	3 PB Barristers	0117 928 1520
London	•Cornerstone Barristers	020 7242 4986
	•Henderson Chambers	020 7583 9020
	3 PB Barristers	020 7583 8055
	The Chambers of Grahame Aldous QC	020 7832 0500
Manchester	•St Johns Buildings	0161 214 1500
Oxford	3 PB Barristers	01865 793 736
Winchester	3 PB Barristers	01962 868884

DISCIPLINARY PROCEDURES

Birmingham	St Ive's Chambers	0121 236 0863
Bournemouth	3 PB Barristers	01202 292102
Bristol	3 PB Barristers	0117 928 1520
	Queen Square Chambers	0117 921 1966
Exeter	Walnut House	01392 279751
London	Bell Yard Chambers	020 7306 9292
	Five Paper	020 7815 3200
	•Henderson Chambers	020 7583 9020
	3 PB Barristers	020 7583 8055
	18 Red Lion Court	020 7520 6000
	•Tanfield Chambers	020 7421 5300
	The Chambers of Grahame Aldous QC	020 7832 0500
Manchester	Chambers of Ian Macdonald QC	0161 236 1840
	18 St John Street	0161 278 1800
	•St Johns Buildings	0161 214 1500
Newcastle Upon Tyne	Dere Street Barristers	0844 3351551
Oxford	3 PB Barristers	01865 793 736
Portsmouth	Guildhall Chambers Portsmouth	023 9275 2400
Southampton	•College Chambers	023 8023 0338
Winchester	3 PB Barristers	01962 868884

DISCIPLINARY TRIBUNALS

Birmingham	St Ive's Chambers	0121 236 0863
Bournemouth	3 PB Barristers	01202 292102
Bristol	3 PB Barristers	0117 928 1520
	Queen Square Chambers	0117 921 1966
London	Bell Yard Chambers	020 7306 9292
	Chambers of Mr Patrick Ground QC	020 7736 0131
	•Cornerstone Barristers	020 7242 4986
	•23 Essex Street	020 7413 0353
	Five Paper	020 7815 3200
	Hailsham Chambers	020 7643 5000
	•Henderson Chambers	020 7583 9020
	•13 Old Square Chambers	020 7831 4445
	Outer Temple Chambers	020 7353 6381
	3 PB Barristers	020 7583 8055
	18 Red Lion Court	020 7520 6000
	•Tanfield Chambers	020 7421 5300
	The Chambers of Grahame Aldous QC	020 7832 0500
Manchester	Chambers of Ian Macdonald QC	0161 236 1840
	•Lincoln House Chambers	0161 832 5701
	18 St John Street	0161 278 1800
Newcastle Upon Tyne	Dere Street Barristers	0844 3351551
Oxford	3 PB Barristers	01865 793 736
Portsmouth	Guildhall Chambers Portsmouth	023 9275 2400
Southampton	•College Chambers	023 8023 0338
Winchester	3 PB Barristers	01962 868884

DISCRIMINATION

Birmingham	No 8 Chambers	0121 236 5514
	St Ive's Chambers	0121 236 0863
	•St Philips Chambers	0121 246 7000

 • Expanded entry in Part D

Bournemouth	3 PB Barristers	01202 292102
Bradford	Broadway House Chambers	01274 722560
Bristol	Albion Chambers	0117 927 2144
	3 PB Barristers	0117 928 1520
	Queen Square Chambers	0117 921 1966
	St John's Chambers	0117 923 4700
Chester	Linenhall Chambers	01244 348282
Exeter	Rougemont Chambers	01392 208484
	Walnut House	01392 279751
Ipswich	East Anglian Chambers	01473 214481
Leeds	Broadway House Chambers	0113 246 2600
	Chancery House Chambers	0113 244 6691
	Kings Chambers	0845 034 3444
	Park Court Chambers	0113 243 3277
Liverpool	Atlantic Chambers	0151 236 4421
	•Oriel Chambers	0151 236 7191
London	•Arden Chambers	020 7242 4244
	Bell Yard Chambers	020 7306 9292
	Blackstone Chambers	020 7583 1770
	•Chambers of Mr Ami Feder	020 7797 7788
	1 Chancery Lane	0845 634 6666
	1 Crown Office Row	020 7797 7500
	•Devereux Chambers	020 7353 7534
	Doughty Street Chambers	020 7404 1313
	•39 Essex Street	020 7832 1111
	Farringdon Chambers	020 7089 5700
	Five Paper	020 7815 3200
	•Goldsmith Chambers	020 7353 6802
	•4-5 Gray's Inn Square	020 7404 5252
	•Henderson Chambers	020 7583 9020
	12 King's Bench Walk	020 7583 0811
	Lamb Chambers	020 7797 8300
	Matrix Chambers	020 7404 3447
	3 PB Barristers	020 7583 8055
	1 Pump Court	020 7842 7070
	•Tanfield Chambers	020 7421 5300
	The Chambers of Grahame Aldous QC	020 7832 0500
	Tooks Chambers	020 7842 7575
	Wynne Chambers	020 3239 6964
Manchester	Central Chambers	0161 236 1133
	Chambers of Ian Macdonald QC	0161 236 1840
	Kings Chambers	0845 034 3444
	St James's Chambers	0161 834 7000
	9 St John Street	0161 955 9000
	18 St John Street	0161 278 1800
	•St Johns Buildings	0161 214 1500
Middlesbrough	Fountain Chambers	01642 804040
	Old Court Chambers	01642 232523
Newcastle Upon Tyne	Dere Street Barristers	0844 3351551
Nottingham	KCH Garden Square	0115 941 8851
Oxford	3 PB Barristers	01865 793 736
Southampton	•College Chambers	023 8023 0338
Winchester	3 PB Barristers	01962 868884

DISPUTE RESOLUTION

Exeter	Walnut House	01392 279751
London	Arbitration Chambers	020 7267 2137
	Bell Yard Chambers	020 7306 9292
	Blackstone Chambers	020 7583 1770
	Erskine Chambers	020 7242 5532
	•39 Essex Street	020 7832 1111
	Five Paper	020 7815 3200
	•Goldsmith Chambers	020 7353 6802
	•Henderson Chambers	020 7583 9020

• Expanded entry in Part D

	•Maitland Chambers	020 7406 1200
	Outer Temple Chambers	020 7353 6381
	XXIV Old Buildings	020 7691 2424
Manchester	18 St John Street	0161 278 1800
	•St Johns Buildings	0161 214 1500
Newcastle Upon Tyne	Dere Street Barristers	0844 3351551
Portsmouth	Portsmouth Barristers'Chambers	023 9283 1292

DISPUTE RESOLUTION AND ARBITRATION

Exeter	Walnut House	01392 279751
London	Bell Yard Chambers	020 7306 9292
	4 Pump Court	020 7842 5555
Southampton	•College Chambers	023 8023 0338

DIVORCE

Birmingham	St Ive's Chambers	0121 236 0863
Bournemouth	3 PB Barristers	01202 292102
Bristol	3 PB Barristers	0117 928 1520
	Queen Square Chambers	0117 921 1966
Exeter	Rougemont Chambers	01392 208484
Faringdon	Faringdon Chambers	01367 240598
London	•29 Bedford Row Chambers	020 7404 1044
	Bell Yard Chambers	020 7306 9292
	1 Crown Office Row	020 7797 7500
	Five Paper	020 7815 3200
	•1 KBW Chambers	020 7936 1500
	3 PB Barristers	020 7583 8055
Manchester	18 St John Street	0161 278 1800
Middlesbrough	Amicus Chambers	01642 876334
Newcastle Upon Tyne	Dere Street Barristers	0844 3351551
Northampton	Northampton Chambers	01604 636271
Oxford	3 PB Barristers	01865 793 736
Portsmouth	Guildhall Chambers Portsmouth	023 9275 2400
Southampton	•College Chambers	023 8023 0338
Winchester	3 PB Barristers	01962 868884

DOMESTIC VIOLENCE INJUNCTIONS

Birmingham	St Ive's Chambers	0121 236 0863
Bournemouth	3 PB Barristers	01202 292102
Bristol	3 PB Barristers	0117 928 1520
	Queen Square Chambers	0117 921 1966
Exeter	Rougemont Chambers	01392 208484
	Walnut House	01392 279751
Faringdon	Faringdon Chambers	01367 240598
London	•29 Bedford Row Chambers	020 7404 1044
	•1 KBW Chambers	020 7936 1500
	3 PB Barristers	020 7583 8055
Manchester	18 St John Street	0161 278 1800
	•St Johns Buildings	0161 214 1500
Middlesbrough	Amicus Chambers	01642 876334
Newcastle Upon Tyne	Dere Street Barristers	0844 3351551
Northampton	Northampton Chambers	01604 636271
Oxford	3 PB Barristers	01865 793 736
Portsmouth	Guildhall Chambers Portsmouth	023 9275 2400
Southampton	•College Chambers	023 8023 0338
Winchester	3 PB Barristers	01962 868884

DRINK DRIVING

Birmingham	St Ive's Chambers	0121 236 0863
Bristol	Queen Square Chambers	0117 921 1966
London	•Goldsmith Chambers	020 7353 6802

DRY SHIPPING

London	Atkin Chambers	020 7404 0102
Portsmouth	Portsmouth Barristers'Chambers	023 9283 1292

A

EC COMPETITION LAW

Birmingham	•St Philips Chambers	0121 246 7000
Bristol	St John's Chambers	0117 923 4700
Leeds	Chancery House Chambers	0113 244 6691
	Kings Chambers	0845 034 3444
	•Sovereign Chambers	0113 245 1841
London	Blackstone Chambers	020 7583 1770
	Brick Court Chambers	020 7379 3550
	20 Essex Street	020 7842 1200
	•39 Essex Street	020 7832 1111
	Falcon Chambers	020 7353 2484
	Fountain Court Chambers	020 7583 3335
	•4-5 Gray's Inn Square	020 7404 5252
	•Henderson Chambers	020 7583 9020
	Lamb Chambers	020 7797 8300
	•Maitland Chambers	020 7406 1200
	Matrix Chambers	020 7404 3447
	•8 New Square	020 7405 4321
	•Tanfield Chambers	020 7421 5300
	•Three New Square IP	020 7405 1111
	3 Verulam Buildings	020 7831 8441
Manchester	Kings Chambers	0845 034 3444
	•Lincoln House Chambers	0161 832 5701
	18 St John Street	0161 278 1800
	•St Johns Buildings	0161 214 1500

ECCLESIASTICAL LAW

Bournemouth	3 PB Barristers	01202 292102
Bristol	3 PB Barristers	0117 928 1520
	St John's Chambers	0117 923 4700
Chester	Linenhall Chambers	01244 348282
Faringdon	Faringdon Chambers	01367 240598
Leeds	37 Park Square Chambers	0113 243 9422
	Zenith Chambers	0113 245 5438
Liverpool	Atlantic Chambers	0151 236 4421
London	Francis Taylor Building	020 7353 8415
	Harcourt Chambers	0844 561 7135
	3 PB Barristers	020 7583 8055
	•Pump Court Chambers	020 7353 0711
	Radcliffe Chambers	020 7831 0081
	Serle Court	020 7242 6105
	Ten Old Square	020 7405 0758
	•Wilberforce Chambers	020 7306 0102
	XXIV Old Buildings	020 7691 2424
Manchester	Byrom Street Chambers	0161 829 2100
Newcastle Upon Tyne	Dere Street Barristers	0844 3351551
Oxford	Harcourt Chambers	0844 561 7135
	3 PB Barristers	01865 793 736
Swindon	Pump Court Chambers	01793 539899
Winchester	3 PB Barristers	01962 868884
	Pump Court Chambers	01962 868 161

ECHR

Exeter	Rougemont Chambers	01392 208484
London	•2 Bedford Row	020 7440 8888
	25 Bedford Row	020 7067 1500
	Blackstone Chambers	020 7583 1770
	Five Paper	020 7815 3200
	•Monckton Chambers	020 7405 7211
	15 New Bridge Street	020 7842 1900
	•3 Raymond Buildings	020 7400 6400
	18 Red Lion Court	020 7520 6000
Manchester	Chambers of Ian Macdonald QC	0161 236 1840
	•St Johns Buildings	0161 214 1500

• Expanded entry in Part D

Newcastle Upon Tyne	Dere Street Barristers	0844 3351551

E-COMMERCE

London	Essex Court Chambers	020 7813 8000
	•Henderson Chambers	020 7583 9020
	•8 New Square	020 7405 4321
Manchester	18 St John Street	0161 278 1800

ECONOMIC TORTS

Bournemouth	3 PB Barristers	01202 292102
Bristol	3 PB Barristers	0117 928 1520
London	•One Essex Court	020 7583 2000
	Five Paper	020 7815 3200
	3 PB Barristers	020 7583 8055
	The Chambers of Grahame Aldous QC	020 7832 0500
Manchester	18 St John Street	0161 278 1800
Newcastle Upon Tyne	Dere Street Barristers	0844 3351551
Oxford	3 PB Barristers	01865 793 736
Portsmouth	Portsmouth Barristers'Chambers	023 9283 1292
Southampton	•College Chambers	023 8023 0338
Winchester	3 PB Barristers	01962 868884

EDUCATION

Birmingham	St Ive's Chambers	0121 236 0863
	•St Philips Chambers	0121 246 7000
Bournemouth	3 PB Barristers	01202 292102
Bristol	3 PB Barristers	0117 928 1520
	St John's Chambers	0117 923 4700
Chelmsford	Trinity Chambers	01245 605040
Chester	Linenhall Chambers	01244 348282
Exeter	Rougemont Chambers	01392 208484
	Walnut House	01392 279751
Leeds	Chancery House Chambers	0113 244 6691
	Kings Chambers	0845 034 3444
	Park Court Chambers	0113 243 3277
	37 Park Square Chambers	0113 243 9422
Liverpool	Atlantic Chambers	0151 236 4421
London	Atlas Chambers	020 7269 7980
	42 Bedford Row	020 7831 0222
	Blackstone Chambers	020 7583 1770
	Chambers of Mr Patrick Ground QC	020 7736 0131
	1 Chancery Lane	0845 634 6666
	•Cornerstone Barristers	020 7242 4986
	•Devereux Chambers	020 7353 7534
	Doughty Street Chambers	020 7404 1313
	•3 Dr Johnson's Buildings	020 7353 4854
	•39 Essex Street	020 7832 1111
	Francis Taylor Building	020 7353 8415
	1 Garden Court Family Law Chambers	020 7797 7900
	•Goldsmith Chambers	020 7353 6802
	•4-5 Gray's Inn Square	020 7404 5252
	Harcourt Chambers	0844 561 7135
	2 King's Bench Walk	020 7353 1746
	4 King's Bench Walk	020 7822 7000
	•Maitland Chambers	020 7406 1200
	Matrix Chambers	020 7404 3447
	12 Old Square Chambers	020 7404 0875
	3 PB Barristers	020 7583 8055
	1 Pump Court	020 7842 7070
	•5 Pump Court	020 7353 2532
	Radcliffe Chambers	020 7831 0081
	•Tanfield Chambers	020 7421 5300
	Ten Old Square	020 7405 0758
	Tooks Chambers	020 7842 7575

Manchester	Central Chambers	0161 236 1133
	Chambers of Ian Macdonald QC	0161 236 1840
	Kings Chambers	0845 034 3444
	St James's Chambers	0161 834 7000
	18 St John Street	0161 278 1800
	•St Johns Buildings	0161 214 1500
Middlesbrough	Fountain Chambers	01642 804040
	Old Court Chambers	01642 232523
Newcastle Upon Tyne	Dere Street Barristers	0844 3351551
Oxford	Harcourt Chambers	0844 561 7135
	3 PB Barristers	01865 793 736
Plymouth	Devon Chambers	01752 661659
Sheffield	St Johns Buildings	0114 273 8951
Southampton	•College Chambers	023 8023 0338
Winchester	3 PB Barristers	01962 868884

ELECTION LAW

Bournemouth	3 PB Barristers	01202 292102
Bristol	3 PB Barristers	0117 928 1520
London	Blackstone Chambers	020 7583 1770
	•Cornerstone Barristers	020 7242 4986
	•Henderson Chambers	020 7583 9020
	Matrix Chambers	020 7404 3447
	3 PB Barristers	020 7583 8055
Manchester	18 St John Street	0161 278 1800
Oxford	3 PB Barristers	01865 793 736
Winchester	3 PB Barristers	01962 868884

EMPLOYEE BENEFIT TRUSTS

Exeter	Walnut House	01392 279751
London	Erskine Chambers	020 7242 5532
	•Pump Court Tax Chambers	020 7414 8080
	Temple Tax Chambers	020 7353 7884
Manchester	Chambers of Ian Macdonald QC	0161 236 1840
	18 St John Street	0161 278 1800
	•St Johns Buildings	0161 214 1500
Newcastle Upon Tyne	Dere Street Barristers	0844 3351551

EMPLOYMENT

Birmingham	Cornwall Street Chambers	0121 233 7500
	Equity Chambers	0121 236 5007
	No 8 Chambers	0121 236 5514
	•No5 Chambers	0845 210 5555
	•St Philips Chambers	0121 246 7000
Bournemouth	3 PB Barristers	01202 292102
Bradford	Broadway House Chambers	01274 722560
Brighton	Crown Office Row Chambers	01273 625625
Bristol	Albion Chambers	0117 927 2144
	No5 Chambers	0845 210 5555
	3 PB Barristers	0117 928 1520
	St John's Chambers	0117 923 4700
	Unity Street Chambers	0117 906 9789
Canterbury	Becket Chambers	01227 786331
Chelmsford	Trinity Chambers	01245 605040
Chester	Linenhall Chambers	01244 348282
Chichester	Pallant Chambers	01243 784538
Exeter	Rougemont Chambers	01392 208484
	Walnut House	01392 279751
Hull	Wilberforce Chambers	01482 323264
Ipswich	East Anglian Chambers	01473 214481
Kew	Kew Chambers	0844 8099991
Leeds	Broadway House Chambers	0113 246 2600
	Chancery House Chambers	0113 244 6691
	KBW	0113 297 1200

• Expanded entry in Part D

	Kings Chambers	0845 034 3444
	Park Court Chambers	0113 243 3277
	37 Park Square Chambers	0113 243 9422
	•Sovereign Chambers	0113 245 1841
	Zenith Chambers	0113 245 5438
Lewes	Westgate Chambers	01273 480510
Liverpool	Atlantic Chambers	0151 236 4421
	•Number 7 Harrington Street Chambers	0151 242 0707
	•Oriel Chambers	0151 236 7191
London	42 Bedford Row	020 7831 0222
	Bell Yard Chambers	020 7306 9292
	•9-12 Bell Yard	020 7400 1800
	Blackstone Chambers	020 7583 1770
	Brick Court Chambers	020 7379 3550
	•Chambers of Mr Ami Feder	020 7797 7788
	•Cornerstone Barristers	020 7242 4986
	1 Crown Office Row	020 7797 7500
	•Devereux Chambers	020 7353 7534
	Doughty Street Chambers	020 7404 1313
	•2 Dr Johnson's Buildings	020 7936 2613
	•3 Dr Johnson's Buildings	020 7353 4854
	•One Essex Court	020 7583 2000
	Essex Court Chambers	020 7813 8000
	•39 Essex Street	020 7832 1111
	•Farrar's Building	020 7583 9241
	Farringdon Chambers	020 7089 5700
	Five Paper	020 7815 3200
	Fountain Court Chambers	020 7583 3335
	Francis Taylor Building	020 7353 8415
	•Goldsmith Chambers	020 7353 6802
	•4-5 Gray's Inn Square	020 7404 5252
	Hailsham Chambers	020 7643 5000
	Harcourt Chambers	0844 561 7135
	3 Hare Court	020 7415 7800
	•Henderson Chambers	020 7583 9020
	4 KBW	020 7822 8822
	2 King's Bench Walk	020 7353 1746
	4 King's Bench Walk	020 7822 7000
	11 King's Bench Walk	020 7632 8500
	12 King's Bench Walk	020 7583 0811
	13 King's Bench Walk	020 7353 7204
	Lamb Chambers	020 7797 8300
	Matrix Chambers	020 7404 3447
	Middle Temple Lane Chambers	020 7583 4352
	•Monckton Chambers	020 7405 7211
	New Square Chambers	020 7419 8000
	No5 Chambers	0845 210 5555
	12 Old Square Chambers	020 7404 0875
	•13 Old Square Chambers	020 7831 4445
	Outer Temple Chambers	020 7353 6381
	3 PB Barristers	020 7583 8055
	1 Pump Court	020 7842 7070
	4 Pump Court	020 7842 5555
	•5 Pump Court	020 7353 2532
	6 Pump Court	020 7797 8400
	•Pump Court Chambers	020 7353 0711
	Radcliffe Chambers	020 7831 0081
	•9 Stone Buildings	020 7404 5055
	11 Stone Buildings	020 7831 6381
	•Tanfield Chambers	020 7421 5300
	•Temple Garden Chambers	020 7583 1315
	The Chambers of Grahame Aldous QC	020 7832 0500
	Tooks Chambers	020 7842 7575
	•Wilberforce Chambers	020 7306 0102

• Expanded entry in Part D

A

	Wynne Chambers	020 3239 6964
Maidstone	Maidstone Chambers	01622 688592
	6 Pump Court Chambers	01622 688094
Manchester	Byrom Street Chambers	0161 829 2100
	Central Chambers	0161 236 1133
	Chambers of Ian Macdonald QC	0161 236 1840
	•Cobden House Chambers	0161 833 6000
	Deans Court Chambers	0161 214 6000
	Kenworthy's Chambers	0161 832 4036
	Kings Chambers	0845 034 3444
	St James's Chambers	0161 834 7000
	9 St John Street	0161 955 9000
	18 St John Street	0161 278 1800
	•St Johns Buildings	0161 214 1500
Middlesbrough	Fountain Chambers	01642 804040
	Old Court Chambers	01642 232523
	•Trinity Chambers	01642 247569
Newcastle Upon Tyne	Cathedral Chambers	0191 232 1311
	Dere Street Barristers	0844 3351551
	•Trinity Chambers	0191 232 1927
Northampton	Northampton Chambers	01604 636271
Norwich	Octagon House	01603 623186
Nottingham	KCH Garden Square	0115 941 8851
Oxford	Harcourt Chambers	0844 561 7135
	3 PB Barristers	01865 793 736
Plymouth	Devon Chambers	01752 661659
Portsmouth	Guildhall Chambers Portsmouth	023 9275 2400
Preston	Deans Court Chambers	01772 565 600
Sheffield	Bank House Chambers	0114 275 1223
	St Johns Buildings	0114 273 8951
Southampton	•College Chambers	023 8023 0338
Stoke On Trent	Regent Chambers	01782 286666
Swansea	Iscoed Chambers	01792 652988
Swindon	Pump Court Chambers	01793 539899
Taunton	Octagon Chambers	01823 331919
Winchester	3 PB Barristers	01962 868884
	Pump Court Chambers	01962 868 161

ENERGY

Birmingham	•No5 Chambers	0845 210 5555
Bristol	No5 Chambers	0845 210 5555
	St John's Chambers	0117 923 4700
London	Arbitration Chambers	020 7267 2137
	Atkin Chambers	020 7404 0102
	Atlas Chambers	020 7269 7980
	•One Essex Court	020 7583 2000
	Essex Court Chambers	020 7813 8000
	20 Essex Street	020 7842 1200
	•39 Essex Street	020 7832 1111
	Fountain Court Chambers	020 7583 3335
	Francis Taylor Building	020 7353 8415
	Keating Chambers	020 7544 2600
	•Maitland Chambers	020 7406 1200
	No5 Chambers	0845 210 5555
	6 Pump Court	020 7797 8400
	Serle Court	020 7242 6105
	•Wilberforce Chambers	020 7306 0102
	XXIV Old Buildings	020 7691 2424
Maidstone	6 Pump Court Chambers	01622 688094
Manchester	•St Johns Buildings	0161 214 1500
Swansea	Iscoed Chambers	01792 652988

ENGINEERING DISPUTES

Birmingham	•No5 Chambers	0845 210 5555

• Expanded entry in Part D

A

Bournemouth	3 PB Barristers	01202 292102
Bristol	3 PB Barristers	0117 928 1520
	Queen Square Chambers	0117 921 1966
London	•Crown Office Chambers	020 7797 8100
	Essex Court Chambers	020 7813 8000
	Keating Chambers	020 7544 2600
	3 PB Barristers	020 7583 8055
Manchester	18 St John Street	0161 278 1800
Newcastle Upon Tyne	Dere Street Barristers	0844 3351551
Oxford	3 PB Barristers	01865 793 736
Portsmouth	Portsmouth Barristers'Chambers	023 9283 1292
Southampton	•College Chambers	023 8023 0338
Winchester	3 PB Barristers	01962 868884

ENTERTAINMENT

Leeds	Kings Chambers	0845 034 3444
London	Blackstone Chambers	020 7583 1770
	Brick Court Chambers	020 7379 3550
	•Devereux Chambers	020 7353 7534
	•3 Dr Johnson's Buildings	020 7353 4854
	•One Essex Court	020 7583 2000
	Essex Court Chambers	020 7813 8000
	•39 Essex Street	020 7832 1111
	Fountain Court Chambers	020 7583 3335
	•Maitland Chambers	020 7406 1200
	•8 New Square	020 7405 4321
	New Square Chambers	020 7419 8000
	•13 Old Square Chambers	020 7831 4445
	4 Pump Court	020 7842 5555
	Selborne Chambers	020 7420 9500
	3 Stone Buildings	020 7242 4937
	•9 Stone Buildings	020 7404 5055
	11 Stone Buildings	020 7831 6381
	•Three New Square IP	020 7405 1111
	3 Verulam Buildings	020 7831 8441
Manchester	Kings Chambers	0845 034 3444
	18 St John Street	0161 278 1800
	•St Johns Buildings	0161 214 1500

ENVIRONMENT

Birmingham	•No5 Chambers	0845 210 5555
	St Ive's Chambers	0121 236 0863
	•St Philips Chambers	0121 246 7000
Bradford	Broadway House Chambers	01274 722560
Brighton	Crown Office Row Chambers	01273 625625
Bristol	No5 Chambers	0845 210 5555
	Queen Square Chambers	0117 921 1966
	St John's Chambers	0117 923 4700
Canterbury	Becket Chambers	01227 786331
Chelmsford	Trinity Chambers	01245 605040
Chester	Linenhall Chambers	01244 348282
Exeter	Rougemont Chambers	01392 208484
	Walnut House	01392 279751
Leeds	Broadway House Chambers	0113 246 2600
	Chancery House Chambers	0113 244 6691
	Enterprise Chambers	0113 246 0391
	KBW	0113 297 1200
	Kings Chambers	0845 034 3444
	Park Court Chambers	0113 243 3277
	•Sovereign Chambers	0113 245 1841
	Zenith Chambers	0113 245 5438
Liverpool	•Oriel Chambers	0151 236 7191
London	•Arden Chambers	020 7242 4244
	Atkin Chambers	020 7404 0102

A

	Atlas Chambers	020 7269 7980
	•2 Bedford Row	020 7440 8888
	42 Bedford Row	020 7831 0222
	Blackstone Chambers	020 7583 1770
	Brick Court Chambers	020 7379 3550
	1 Chancery Lane	0845 634 6666
	•Cornerstone Barristers	020 7242 4986
	1 Crown Office Row	020 7797 7500
	•Devereux Chambers	020 7353 7534
	Doughty Street Chambers	020 7404 1313
	Enterprise Chambers	020 7405 9471
	Essex Court Chambers	020 7813 8000
	20 Essex Street	020 7842 1200
	•39 Essex Street	020 7832 1111
	Five Paper	020 7815 3200
	Francis Taylor Building	020 7353 8415
	Gough Square Chambers	020 7353 0924
	•4-5 Gray's Inn Square	020 7404 5252
	•Henderson Chambers	020 7583 9020
	13 King's Bench Walk	020 7353 7204
	Lamb Chambers	020 7797 8300
	Landmark Chambers	020 7430 1221
	Matrix Chambers	020 7404 3447
	•Monckton Chambers	020 7405 7211
	No5 Chambers	0845 210 5555
	1 Pump Court	020 7842 7070
	6 Pump Court	020 7797 8400
	•Pump Court Chambers	020 7353 0711
	Radcliffe Chambers	020 7831 0081
	•3 Raymond Buildings	020 7400 6400
	Selborne Chambers	020 7420 9500
	•Three New Square IP	020 7405 1111
Maidstone	6 Pump Court Chambers	01622 688094
Manchester	Byrom Street Chambers	0161 829 2100
	Central Chambers	0161 236 1133
	•Cobden House Chambers	0161 833 6000
	Deans Court Chambers	0161 214 6000
	Kings Chambers	0845 034 3444
	•Lincoln House Chambers	0161 832 5701
	St James's Chambers	0161 834 7000
	9 St John Street	0161 955 9000
	18 St John Street	0161 278 1800
	•St Johns Buildings	0161 214 1500
Middlesbrough	Fountain Chambers	01642 804040
	•Trinity Chambers	01642 247569
Newcastle Upon Tyne	Dere Street Barristers	0844 3351551
	Enterprise Chambers	0191 222 3344
	•Trinity Chambers	0191 232 1927
Plymouth	Devon Chambers	01752 661659
Preston	Deans Court Chambers	01772 565 600
Southampton	•College Chambers	023 8023 0338
Swansea	Iscoed Chambers	01792 652988
Swindon	Pump Court Chambers	01793 539899
Winchester	Pump Court Chambers	01962 868 161

EQUINE LAW

Bournemouth	3 PB Barristers	01202 292102
Bristol	3 PB Barristers	0117 928 1520
London	Middle Temple Lane Chambers	020 7583 4352
	3 PB Barristers	020 7583 8055
	The Chambers of Grahame Aldous QC	020 7832 0500
Manchester	18 St John Street	0161 278 1800
Newcastle Upon Tyne	Dere Street Barristers	0844 3351551
Oxford	3 PB Barristers	01865 793 736

• Expanded entry in Part D

A

Winchester	3 PB Barristers	01962 868884

EQUITY

Birmingham	No 8 Chambers	0121 236 5514
	•No5 Chambers	0845 210 5555
	•St Philips Chambers	0121 246 7000
Bournemouth	3 PB Barristers	01202 292102
Bradford	Broadway House Chambers	01274 722560
Bristol	Albion Chambers	0117 927 2144
	No5 Chambers	0845 210 5555
	3 PB Barristers	0117 928 1520
	St John's Chambers	0117 923 4700
	Unity Street Chambers	0117 906 9789
Chelmsford	Trinity Chambers	01245 605040
Chester	Linenhall Chambers	01244 348282
Chichester	Pallant Chambers	01243 784538
Exeter	Rougemont Chambers	01392 208484
Leeds	Broadway House Chambers	0113 246 2600
	Chancery House Chambers	0113 244 6691
	Enterprise Chambers	0113 246 0391
	KBW	0113 297 1200
	Kings Chambers	0845 034 3444
	Park Court Chambers	0113 243 3277
	37 Park Square Chambers	0113 243 9422
	•Sovereign Chambers	0113 245 1841
	Zenith Chambers	0113 245 5438
Liverpool	Atlantic Chambers	0151 236 4421
London	•Chambers of Mr Ami Feder	020 7797 7788
	Enterprise Chambers	020 7405 9471
	Five Paper	020 7815 3200
	•Goldsmith Chambers	020 7353 6802
	Gough Square Chambers	020 7353 0924
	Harcourt Chambers	0844 561 7135
	•1 KBW Chambers	020 7936 1500
	Lamb Chambers	020 7797 8300
	•Maitland Chambers	020 7406 1200
	New Square Chambers	020 7419 8000
	No5 Chambers	0845 210 5555
	•13 Old Square Chambers	020 7831 4445
	3 PB Barristers	020 7583 8055
	1 Pump Court	020 7842 7070
	Radcliffe Chambers	020 7831 0081
	Selborne Chambers	020 7420 9500
	Serle Court	020 7242 6105
	3 Stone Buildings	020 7242 4937
	4 Stone Buildings	020 7242 5524
	•9 Stone Buildings	020 7404 5055
	Ten Old Square	020 7405 0758
	•Wilberforce Chambers	020 7306 0102
	XXIV Old Buildings	020 7691 2424
Manchester	•Cobden House Chambers	0161 833 6000
	Deans Court Chambers	0161 214 6000
	Kings Chambers	0845 034 3444
	St James's Chambers	0161 834 7000
	9 St John Street	0161 955 9000
	18 St John Street	0161 278 1800
	•St Johns Buildings	0161 214 1500
Middlesbrough	Fountain Chambers	01642 804040
	•Trinity Chambers	01642 247569
Newcastle Upon Tyne	Dere Street Barristers	0844 3351551
	Enterprise Chambers	0191 222 3344
	•Trinity Chambers	0191 232 1927
Nottingham	KCH Garden Square	0115 941 8851
Oxford	Harcourt Chambers	0844 561 7135

• Expanded entry in Part D

	3 PB Barristers	01865 793 736
Portsmouth	Portsmouth Barristers'Chambers	023 9283 1292
Preston	Deans Court Chambers	01772 565 600
Swansea	Iscoed Chambers	01792 652988
Winchester	3 PB Barristers	01962 868884

A

EUROPEAN, FOREIGN AND INTERNATIONAL LAW

Exeter	Walnut House	01392 279751

EUROPEAN LAW

Exeter	Walnut House	01392 279751
London	•Argent Chambers	020 7556 5500
	25 Bedford Row	020 7067 1500
	Blackstone Chambers	020 7583 1770
	•One Essex Court	020 7583 2000
	Essex Court Chambers	020 7813 8000
	Francis Taylor Building	020 7353 8415
	•Henderson Chambers	020 7583 9020
	11 King's Bench Walk	020 7632 8500
	•Monckton Chambers	020 7405 7211
	•South Square	020 7696 9900
	•Tanfield Chambers	020 7421 5300
	XXIV Old Buildings	020 7691 2424

EUROPEAN UNION

London	•One Essex Court	020 7583 2000
	•Henderson Chambers	020 7583 9020
	Matrix Chambers	020 7404 3447
	•Pump Court Tax Chambers	020 7414 8080

EXCISE

Birmingham	St Ive's Chambers	0121 236 0863
Manchester	•St Johns Buildings	0161 214 1500

EXTRADITION

Bristol	Queen Square Chambers	0117 921 1966
Exeter	Walnut House	01392 279751
London	•2 Bedford Row	020 7440 8888
	25 Bedford Row	020 7067 1500
	Bell Yard Chambers	020 7306 9292
	•9-12 Bell Yard	020 7400 1800
	Doughty Street Chambers	020 7404 1313
	•23 Essex Street	020 7413 0353
	•187 Fleet Street	020 7430 7430
	Great James Street Chambers	020 7440 4949
	Matrix Chambers	020 7404 3447
	15 New Bridge Street	020 7842 1900
	•QEB Hollis Whiteman	020 7933 8855
	•3 Raymond Buildings	020 7400 6400
	18 Red Lion Court	020 7520 6000
	The Chambers of Grahame Aldous QC	020 7832 0500
Manchester	Chambers of Ian Macdonald QC	0161 236 1840
	18 St John Street	0161 278 1800
	•St Johns Buildings	0161 214 1500
Middlesbrough	•Trinity Chambers	01642 247569
Newcastle Upon Tyne	•Trinity Chambers	0191 232 1927

FACTORING

Bournemouth	3 PB Barristers	01202 292102
Bristol	3 PB Barristers	0117 928 1520
Liverpool	•Oriel Chambers	0151 236 7191
London	Five Paper	020 7815 3200
	3 PB Barristers	020 7583 8055
Oxford	3 PB Barristers	01865 793 736
Winchester	3 PB Barristers	01962 868884

• Expanded entry in Part D

FAMILY LAW

Birmingham	Cornwall Street Chambers	0121 233 7500
	Equity Chambers	0121 236 5007
	No 8 Chambers	0121 236 5514
	•No5 Chambers	0845 210 5555
	St Ive's Chambers	0121 236 0863
	•St Philips Chambers	0121 246 7000
Bournemouth	3 PB Barristers	01202 292102
Bradford	Broadway House Chambers	01274 722560
Brighton	Crown Office Row Chambers	01273 625625
Bristol	Albion Chambers	0117 927 2144
	No5 Chambers	0845 210 5555
	3 PB Barristers	0117 928 1520
	Queen Square Chambers	0117 921 1966
	St John's Chambers	0117 923 4700
	Unity Street Chambers	0117 906 9789
Canterbury	Becket Chambers	01227 786331
Chelmsford	Trinity Chambers	01245 605040
Chester	Linenhall Chambers	01244 348282
Chichester	Pallant Chambers	01243 784538
Exeter	Rougemont Chambers	01392 208484
	Walnut House	01392 279751
Faringdon	Faringdon Chambers	01367 240598
Hull	Wilberforce Chambers	01482 323264
Ipswich	East Anglian Chambers	01473 214481
Leeds	Broadway House Chambers	0113 246 2600
	KBW	0113 297 1200
	Park Court Chambers	0113 243 3277
	37 Park Square Chambers	0113 243 9422
	•Sovereign Chambers	0113 245 1841
	Zenith Chambers	0113 245 5438
Lewes	Westgate Chambers	01273 480510
Liverpool	Atlantic Chambers	0151 236 4421
	Chavasse Court Chambers	0151 229 2030
	•Number 7 Harrington Street Chambers	0151 242 0707
	•Oriel Chambers	0151 236 7191
London	•Argent Chambers	020 7556 5500
	42 Bedford Row	020 7831 0222
	•29 Bedford Row Chambers	020 7404 1044
	Bell Yard Chambers	020 7306 9292
	4 Brick Court	020 7832 3200
	•Chambers of Mr Ami Feder	020 7797 7788
	•Charter Chambers	020 7618 4400
	•2 Dr Johnson's Buildings	020 7936 2613
	•3 Dr Johnson's Buildings	020 7353 4854
	Five Paper	020 7815 3200
	1 Garden Court Family Law Chambers	020 7797 7900
	•Goldsmith Chambers	020 7353 6802
	14 Gray's Inn Square	020 7242 0858
	Harcourt Chambers	0844 561 7135
	•1 KBW Chambers	020 7936 1500
	2 King's Bench Walk	020 7353 1746
	4 King's Bench Walk	020 7822 7000
	13 King's Bench Walk	020 7353 7204
	Middle Temple Lane Chambers	020 7583 4352
	•New Court	020 7583 5123
	No5 Chambers	0845 210 5555
	12 Old Square Chambers	020 7404 0875
	•1 Paper Buildings	020 7353 3728
	•4 Paper Buildings	020 7427 5200
	3 PB Barristers	020 7583 8055
	1 Pump Court	020 7842 7070
	•5 Pump Court	020 7353 2532

• Expanded entry in Part D

	6 Pump Court	020 7797 8400
	•Pump Court Chambers	020 7353 0711
	Queen Elizabeth Building	020 7797 7837
	Renaissance Chambers	020 7404 1111
	•Tanfield Chambers	020 7421 5300
	The Chambers of Grahame Aldous QC	020 7832 0500
	Tooks Chambers	020 7842 7575
Maidstone	Maidstone Chambers	01622 688592
	6 Pump Court Chambers	01622 688094
Manchester	Central Chambers	0161 236 1133
	Chambers of Ian Macdonald QC	0161 236 1840
	•Cobden House Chambers	0161 833 6000
	Deans Court Chambers	0161 214 6000
	Kenworthy's Chambers	0161 832 4036
	9 St John Street	0161 955 9000
	18 St John Street	0161 278 1800
	•St Johns Buildings	0161 214 1500
Middlesbrough	Amicus Chambers	01642 876334
	Fountain Chambers	01642 804040
	Old Court Chambers	01642 232523
	•Trinity Chambers	01642 247569
Newcastle Upon Tyne	Cathedral Chambers	0191 232 1311
	Dere Street Barristers	0844 3351551
	•Trinity Chambers	0191 232 1927
Northampton	Chartlands Chambers	01604 603322
	Northampton Chambers	01604 636271
Norwich	Octagon House	01603 623186
Nottingham	KCH Garden Square	0115 941 8851
Oxford	Harcourt Chambers	0844 561 7135
	3 PB Barristers	01865 793 736
Pitstone	Victor House Chambers	01296 664043
Plymouth	Devon Chambers	01752 661659
Portsmouth	Guildhall Chambers Portsmouth	023 9275 2400
	Portsmouth Barristers'Chambers	023 9283 1292
Preston	Deans Court Chambers	01772 565 600
Sheffield	Bank House Chambers	0114 275 1223
	St Johns Buildings	0114 273 8951
Southampton	•College Chambers	023 8023 0338
Stoke On Trent	Regent Chambers	01782 286666
Swansea	Iscoed Chambers	01792 652988
Swindon	Pump Court Chambers	01793 539899
Taunton	Octagon Chambers	01823 331919
Winchester	3 PB Barristers	01962 868884
	Pump Court Chambers	01962 868 161

FAMILY PROVISION

Birmingham	No 8 Chambers	0121 236 5514
	•No5 Chambers	0845 210 5555
	St Ive's Chambers	0121 236 0863
	•St Philips Chambers	0121 246 7000
Bournemouth	3 PB Barristers	01202 292102
Bradford	Broadway House Chambers	01274 722560
Brighton	Crown Office Row Chambers	01273 625625
Bristol	Albion Chambers	0117 927 2144
	No5 Chambers	0845 210 5555
	3 PB Barristers	0117 928 1520
	St John's Chambers	0117 923 4700
	Unity Street Chambers	0117 906 9789
Canterbury	Becket Chambers	01227 786331
Chelmsford	Trinity Chambers	01245 605040
Chester	Linenhall Chambers	01244 348282
Chichester	Pallant Chambers	01243 784538
Exeter	Rougemont Chambers	01392 208484
	Walnut House	01392 279751

• Expanded entry in Part D

Faringdon	Faringdon Chambers	01367 240598
Hull	Wilberforce Chambers	01482 323264
Ipswich	East Anglian Chambers	01473 214481
Leeds	Broadway House Chambers	0113 246 2600
	KBW	0113 297 1200
	Park Court Chambers	0113 243 3277
	37 Park Square Chambers	0113 243 9422
	•Sovereign Chambers	0113 245 1841
	Zenith Chambers	0113 245 5438
Liverpool	Atlantic Chambers	0151 236 4421
	Chavasse Court Chambers	0151 229 2030
London	42 Bedford Row	020 7831 0222
	•29 Bedford Row Chambers	020 7404 1044
	•Chambers of Mr Ami Feder	020 7797 7788
	•Charter Chambers	020 7618 4400
	•3 Dr Johnson's Buildings	020 7353 4854
	Five Paper	020 7815 3200
	1 Garden Court Family Law Chambers	020 7797 7900
	•Goldsmith Chambers	020 7353 6802
	14 Gray's Inn Square	020 7242 0858
	Harcourt Chambers	0844 561 7135
	•1 KBW Chambers	020 7936 1500
	•Maitland Chambers	020 7406 1200
	•New Court	020 7583 5123
	New Square Chambers	020 7419 8000
	No5 Chambers	0845 210 5555
	•13 Old Square Chambers	020 7831 4445
	•4 Paper Buildings	020 7427 5200
	3 PB Barristers	020 7583 8055
	1 Pump Court	020 7842 7070
	4 Pump Court	020 7842 5555
	•5 Pump Court	020 7353 2532
	6 Pump Court	020 7797 8400
	•Pump Court Chambers	020 7353 0711
	Queen Elizabeth Building	020 7797 7837
	Radcliffe Chambers	020 7831 0081
	Renaissance Chambers	020 7404 1111
	3 Stone Buildings	020 7242 4937
	•9 Stone Buildings	020 7404 5055
	•Tanfield Chambers	020 7421 5300
	Ten Old Square	020 7405 0758
	•Wilberforce Chambers	020 7306 0102
	XXIV Old Buildings	020 7691 2424
Maidstone	6 Pump Court Chambers	01622 688094
Manchester	Central Chambers	0161 236 1133
	•Cobden House Chambers	0161 833 6000
	Deans Court Chambers	0161 214 6000
	Kenworthy's Chambers	0161 832 4036
	St James's Chambers	0161 834 7000
	9 St John Street	0161 955 9000
	18 St John Street	0161 278 1800
	•St Johns Buildings	0161 214 1500
Middlesbrough	Fountain Chambers	01642 804040
	Old Court Chambers	01642 232523
	•Trinity Chambers	01642 247569
Newcastle Upon Tyne	Cathedral Chambers	0191 232 1311
	Dere Street Barristers	0844 3351551
	•Trinity Chambers	0191 232 1927
Northampton	Chartlands Chambers	01604 603322
	Northampton Chambers	01604 636271
Norwich	Octagon House	01603 623186
Nottingham	KCH Garden Square	0115 941 8851
Oxford	Harcourt Chambers	0844 561 7135
	3 PB Barristers	01865 793 736

• Expanded entry in Part D

A

Plymouth	Devon Chambers	01752 661659
Portsmouth	Guildhall Chambers Portsmouth	023 9275 2400
	Portsmouth Barristers'Chambers	023 9283 1292
Preston	Deans Court Chambers	01772 565 600
Sheffield	St Johns Buildings	0114 273 8951
Stoke On Trent	Regent Chambers	01782 286666
Swansea	Iscoed Chambers	01792 652988
Swindon	Pump Court Chambers	01793 539899
Winchester	3 PB Barristers	01962 868884
	Pump Court Chambers	01962 868 161

FINANCIAL INSTRUMENTS

London	Erskine Chambers	020 7242 5532
	Five Paper	020 7815 3200
	XXIV Old Buildings	020 7691 2424
Manchester	•St Johns Buildings	0161 214 1500

FINANCIAL PROVISION

Birmingham	St Ive's Chambers	0121 236 0863
Bournemouth	3 PB Barristers	01202 292102
Bristol	3 PB Barristers	0117 928 1520
	Queen Square Chambers	0117 921 1966
Exeter	Rougemont Chambers	01392 208484
Faringdon	Faringdon Chambers	01367 240598
London	•29 Bedford Row Chambers	020 7404 1044
	Five Paper	020 7815 3200
	•1 KBW Chambers	020 7936 1500
	3 PB Barristers	020 7583 8055
Manchester	18 St John Street	0161 278 1800
Middlesbrough	Amicus Chambers	01642 876334
Newcastle Upon Tyne	Dere Street Barristers	0844 3351551
Oxford	3 PB Barristers	01865 793 736
Portsmouth	Portsmouth Barristers'Chambers	023 9283 1292
Southampton	•College Chambers	023 8023 0338
Winchester	3 PB Barristers	01962 868884

FINANCIAL PROVISION FOR CHILDREN

Birmingham	St Ive's Chambers	0121 236 0863
Bristol	Queen Square Chambers	0117 921 1966
Faringdon	Faringdon Chambers	01367 240598
London	Five Paper	020 7815 3200

FINANCIAL SERVICES

Birmingham	•No5 Chambers	0845 210 5555
	•St Philips Chambers	0121 246 7000
Bournemouth	3 PB Barristers	01202 292102
Bristol	No5 Chambers	0845 210 5555
	3 PB Barristers	0117 928 1520
	St John's Chambers	0117 923 4700
Exeter	Walnut House	01392 279751
Leeds	Chancery House Chambers	0113 244 6691
	Kings Chambers	0845 034 3444
	Park Court Chambers	0113 243 3277
London	•2 Bedford Row	020 7440 8888
	Blackstone Chambers	020 7583 1770
	Brick Court Chambers	020 7379 3550
	Erskine Chambers	020 7242 5532
	•One Essex Court	020 7583 2000
	Essex Court Chambers	020 7813 8000
	20 Essex Street	020 7842 1200
	•23 Essex Street	020 7413 0353
	Fountain Court Chambers	020 7583 3335
	•4-5 Gray's Inn Square	020 7404 5252
	•Henderson Chambers	020 7583 9020
	Lamb Chambers	020 7797 8300

• Expanded entry in Part D

	Lombard Chambers	020 7107 2100
	•Maitland Chambers	020 7406 1200
	New Square Chambers	020 7419 8000
	No5 Chambers	0845 210 5555
	•13 Old Square Chambers	020 7831 4445
	Outer Temple Chambers	020 7353 6381
	3 PB Barristers	020 7583 8055
	4 Pump Court	020 7842 5555
	Radcliffe Chambers	020 7831 0081
	Selborne Chambers	020 7420 9500
	Serle Court	020 7242 6105
	•South Square	020 7696 9900
	3 Stone Buildings	020 7242 4937
	4 Stone Buildings	020 7242 5524
	•9 Stone Buildings	020 7404 5055
	Ten Old Square	020 7405 0758
	3 Verulam Buildings	020 7831 8441
	•Wilberforce Chambers	020 7306 0102
	XXIV Old Buildings	020 7691 2424
Manchester	Kings Chambers	0845 034 3444
	St James's Chambers	0161 834 7000
	9 St John Street	0161 955 9000
	•St Johns Buildings	0161 214 1500
Oxford	3 PB Barristers	01865 793 736
Portsmouth	Portsmouth Barristers'Chambers	023 9283 1292
Swansea	Iscoed Chambers	01792 652988
Winchester	3 PB Barristers	01962 868884

FIRE AND OTHER PROPERTY DAMAGE CLAIMS

Bristol	Queen Square Chambers	0117 921 1966
London	1 Chancery Lane	0845 634 6666
	•39 Essex Street	020 7832 1111
	•Henderson Chambers	020 7583 9020
	Keating Chambers	020 7544 2600
Manchester	18 St John Street	0161 278 1800
	•St Johns Buildings	0161 214 1500
Newcastle Upon Tyne	Dere Street Barristers	0844 3351551

FIRE PRECAUTIONS

Manchester	18 St John Street	0161 278 1800

FIREARMS

Birmingham	St Ive's Chambers	0121 236 0863
Bournemouth	3 PB Barristers	01202 292102
Bristol	3 PB Barristers	0117 928 1520
	Queen Square Chambers	0117 921 1966
Exeter	Rougemont Chambers	01392 208484
	Walnut House	01392 279751
Leeds	37 Park Square Chambers	0113 243 9422
London	•2 Bedford Row	020 7440 8888
	25 Bedford Row	020 7067 1500
	Bell Yard Chambers	020 7306 9292
	•23 Essex Street	020 7413 0353
	•187 Fleet Street	020 7430 7430
	•1 KBW Chambers	020 7936 1500
	15 New Bridge Street	020 7842 1900
	3 PB Barristers	020 7583 8055
	18 Red Lion Court	020 7520 6000
	The Chambers of Grahame Aldous QC	020 7832 0500
Manchester	Chambers of Ian Macdonald QC	0161 236 1840
	18 St John Street	0161 278 1800
	•St Johns Buildings	0161 214 1500
Middlesbrough	•Trinity Chambers	01642 247569
Newcastle Upon Tyne	Dere Street Barristers	0844 3351551

• Expanded entry in Part D

A

	•Trinity Chambers	0191 232 1927
Oxford	3 PB Barristers	01865 793 736
Winchester	3 PB Barristers	01962 868884

FOOD LAW

Birmingham	St Ive's Chambers	0121 236 0863
Bristol	Queen Square Chambers	0117 921 1966
London	•Cornerstone Barristers	020 7242 4986
	Gough Square Chambers	020 7353 0924
	•Henderson Chambers	020 7583 9020
	6 Pump Court	020 7797 8400
	The Chambers of Grahame Aldous QC	020 7832 0500
Maidstone	6 Pump Court Chambers	01622 688094
Manchester	18 St John Street	0161 278 1800

FORCED MARRIAGE

Birmingham	St Ive's Chambers	0121 236 0863
Bristol	Queen Square Chambers	0117 921 1966
Faringdon	Faringdon Chambers	01367 240598
London	•4 Paper Buildings	020 7427 5200

FOREIGN LAW

Birmingham	No 8 Chambers	0121 236 5514
Bournemouth	3 PB Barristers	01202 292102
Bristol	3 PB Barristers	0117 928 1520
Exeter	Rougemont Chambers	01392 208484
	Walnut House	01392 279751
Leeds	Chancery House Chambers	0113 244 6691
London	•Argent Chambers	020 7556 5500
	25 Bedford Row	020 7067 1500
	Brick Court Chambers	020 7379 3550
	•Chambers of Mr Ami Feder	020 7797 7788
	•3 Dr Johnson's Buildings	020 7353 4854
	•Goldsmith Chambers	020 7353 6802
	Hailsham Chambers	020 7643 5000
	New Square Chambers	020 7419 8000
	3 PB Barristers	020 7583 8055
	•Pump Court Chambers	020 7353 0711
	•9 Stone Buildings	020 7404 5055
	XXIV Old Buildings	020 7691 2424
Oxford	3 PB Barristers	01865 793 736
Swindon	Pump Court Chambers	01793 539899
Winchester	3 PB Barristers	01962 868884
	Pump Court Chambers	01962 868 161

FORFEITURE

Birmingham	St Ive's Chambers	0121 236 0863
Bristol	Queen Square Chambers	0117 921 1966
London	•2 Bedford Row	020 7440 8888
	Bell Yard Chambers	020 7306 9292
	•23 Essex Street	020 7413 0353
	Five Paper	020 7815 3200
	•187 Fleet Street	020 7430 7430
	•1 KBW Chambers	020 7936 1500
	15 New Bridge Street	020 7842 1900
	18 Red Lion Court	020 7520 6000
	The Chambers of Grahame Aldous QC	020 7832 0500
Manchester	Chambers of Ian Macdonald QC	0161 236 1840
	18 St John Street	0161 278 1800
Newcastle Upon Tyne	Dere Street Barristers	0844 3351551

FOSTERING

Birmingham	St Ive's Chambers	0121 236 0863
Bristol	Queen Square Chambers	0117 921 1966
Faringdon	Faringdon Chambers	01367 240598

• Expanded entry in Part D

London	•Goldsmith Chambers	020 7353 6802

FRANCHISING

Birmingham	•St Philips Chambers	0121 246 7000
Bournemouth	3 PB Barristers	01202 292102
Bristol	3 PB Barristers	0117 928 1520
	St John's Chambers	0117 923 4700
Exeter	Rougemont Chambers	01392 208484
Leeds	Chancery House Chambers	0113 244 6691
	Kings Chambers	0845 034 3444
London	1 Chancery Lane	0845 634 6666
	Gough Square Chambers	020 7353 0924
	3 PB Barristers	020 7583 8055
	Selborne Chambers	020 7420 9500
	•Tanfield Chambers	020 7421 5300
	•Three New Square IP	020 7405 1111
Manchester	Kings Chambers	0845 034 3444
	St James's Chambers	0161 834 7000
Oxford	3 PB Barristers	01865 793 736
Portsmouth	Portsmouth Barristers'Chambers	023 9283 1292
Swansea	Iscoed Chambers	01792 652988
Winchester	3 PB Barristers	01962 868884

FRAUD

Birmingham	Equity Chambers	0121 236 5007
	•No5 Chambers	0845 210 5555
	St Ive's Chambers	0121 236 0863
	•St Philips Chambers	0121 246 7000
Bournemouth	3 PB Barristers	01202 292102
Bristol	3 PB Barristers	0117 928 1520
	Queen Square Chambers	0117 921 1966
Exeter	Rougemont Chambers	01392 208484
	Walnut House	01392 279751
London	•2 Bedford Row	020 7440 8888
	Bell Yard Chambers	020 7306 9292
	Carmelite Chambers	020 7936 6300
	•Cornerstone Barristers	020 7242 4986
	•One Essex Court	020 7583 2000
	•23 Essex Street	020 7413 0353
	•187 Fleet Street	020 7430 7430
	•1 KBW Chambers	020 7936 1500
	Middle Temple Lane Chambers	020 7583 4352
	15 New Bridge Street	020 7842 1900
	3 PB Barristers	020 7583 8055
	6 Pump Court	020 7797 8400
	•QEB Hollis Whiteman	020 7933 8855
	•3 Raymond Buildings	020 7400 6400
	18 Red Lion Court	020 7520 6000
	The Chambers of Grahame Aldous QC	020 7832 0500
Maidstone	6 Pump Court Chambers	01622 688094
Manchester	Chambers of Ian Macdonald QC	0161 236 1840
	•Lincoln House Chambers	0161 832 5701
	18 St John Street	0161 278 1800
	•St Johns Buildings	0161 214 1500
Middlesbrough	•Trinity Chambers	01642 247569
Newcastle Upon Tyne	Dere Street Barristers	0844 3351551
	•Trinity Chambers	0191 232 1927
Oxford	3 PB Barristers	01865 793 736
Portsmouth	Guildhall Chambers Portsmouth	023 9275 2400
Winchester	3 PB Barristers	01962 868884

FREEDOM OF EXPRESSION

London	Matrix Chambers	020 7404 3447
Manchester	•St Johns Buildings	0161 214 1500

A

FREEDOM OF INFORMATION

London	Blackstone Chambers	020 7583 1770
	Five Paper	020 7815 3200
	•Henderson Chambers	020 7583 9020
	11 King's Bench Walk	020 7632 8500
Manchester	Chambers of Ian Macdonald QC	0161 236 1840
	18 St John Street	0161 278 1800
Newcastle Upon Tyne	Dere Street Barristers	0844 3351551
Southampton	•College Chambers	023 8023 0338

FREEZING ORDERS

Birmingham	St Ive's Chambers	0121 236 0863
Bournemouth	3 PB Barristers	01202 292102
Bristol	3 PB Barristers	0117 928 1520
London	Blackstone Chambers	020 7583 1770
	Erskine Chambers	020 7242 5532
	•23 Essex Street	020 7413 0353
	Five Paper	020 7815 3200
	•Henderson Chambers	020 7583 9020
	•Maitland Chambers	020 7406 1200
	15 New Bridge Street	020 7842 1900
	3 PB Barristers	020 7583 8055
	•Tanfield Chambers	020 7421 5300
	XXIV Old Buildings	020 7691 2424
Manchester	18 St John Street	0161 278 1800
	•St Johns Buildings	0161 214 1500
Middlesbrough	•Trinity Chambers	01642 247569
Newcastle Upon Tyne	•Trinity Chambers	0191 232 1927
Oxford	3 PB Barristers	01865 793 736
Portsmouth	Guildhall Chambers Portsmouth	023 9275 2400
	Portsmouth Barristers'Chambers	023 9283 1292
Winchester	3 PB Barristers	01962 868884

FUND MANAGEMENT

London	Erskine Chambers	020 7242 5532
	•One Essex Court	020 7583 2000

FUNDING ARRANGEMENTS

London	Five Paper	020 7815 3200
Manchester	18 St John Street	0161 278 1800
	•St Johns Buildings	0161 214 1500
Newcastle Upon Tyne	Dere Street Barristers	0844 3351551

GAMBLING

London	Erskine Chambers	020 7242 5532
	•One Essex Court	020 7583 2000
	•Tanfield Chambers	020 7421 5300
Manchester	18 St John Street	0161 278 1800
Southampton	•College Chambers	023 8023 0338

GAMING AND LOTTERIES

London	Blackstone Chambers	020 7583 1770
	•Cornerstone Barristers	020 7242 4986
	Erskine Chambers	020 7242 5532
	Francis Taylor Building	020 7353 8415
	•Tanfield Chambers	020 7421 5300
	3 Verulam Buildings	020 7831 8441
Manchester	18 St John Street	0161 278 1800
	•St Johns Buildings	0161 214 1500
Southampton	•College Chambers	023 8023 0338

GERMAN LAW

London	•Chambers of Mr Ami Feder	020 7797 7788
	•South Square	020 7696 9900

• Expanded entry in Part D

GROUP LITIGATION

London	Five Paper	020 7815 3200
	•Henderson Chambers	020 7583 9020
	XXIV Old Buildings	020 7691 2424
Manchester	18 St John Street	0161 278 1800
	•St Johns Buildings	0161 214 1500
Newcastle Upon Tyne	Dere Street Barristers	0844 3351551

GUARANTEES

Birmingham	St Ive's Chambers	0121 236 0863
Bournemouth	3 PB Barristers	01202 292102
Bristol	3 PB Barristers	0117 928 1520
London	Erskine Chambers	020 7242 5532
	•One Essex Court	020 7583 2000
	Five Paper	020 7815 3200
	3 PB Barristers	020 7583 8055
	•South Square	020 7696 9900
Manchester	18 St John Street	0161 278 1800
	•St Johns Buildings	0161 214 1500
Oxford	3 PB Barristers	01865 793 736
Portsmouth	Portsmouth Barristers'Chambers	023 9283 1292
Winchester	3 PB Barristers	01962 868884

HEALTH AND SAFETY

Birmingham	No 8 Chambers	0121 236 5514
	•St Philips Chambers	0121 246 7000
Bournemouth	3 PB Barristers	01202 292102
Bristol	3 PB Barristers	0117 928 1520
	Queen Square Chambers	0117 921 1966
	Unity Street Chambers	0117 906 9789
Exeter	Rougemont Chambers	01392 208484
	Walnut House	01392 279751
Hull	Wilberforce Chambers	01482 323264
Leeds	Chancery House Chambers	0113 244 6691
	Kings Chambers	0845 034 3444
	Park Court Chambers	0113 243 3277
	37 Park Square Chambers	0113 243 9422
	Zenith Chambers	0113 245 5438
London	•2 Bedford Row	020 7440 8888
	Carmelite Chambers	020 7936 6300
	•Cornerstone Barristers	020 7242 4986
	1 Crown Office Row	020 7797 7500
	•Devereux Chambers	020 7353 7534
	•39 Essex Street	020 7832 1111
	•Farrar's Building	020 7583 9241
	Five Paper	020 7815 3200
	Francis Taylor Building	020 7353 8415
	Gough Square Chambers	020 7353 0924
	•Henderson Chambers	020 7583 9020
	Outer Temple Chambers	020 7353 6381
	•1 Paper Buildings	020 7353 3728
	3 PB Barristers	020 7583 8055
	6 Pump Court	020 7797 8400
	•QEB Hollis Whiteman	020 7933 8855
	•3 Raymond Buildings	020 7400 6400
	18 Red Lion Court	020 7520 6000
	•Temple Garden Chambers	020 7583 1315
	The Chambers of Grahame Aldous QC	020 7832 0500
Maidstone	6 Pump Court Chambers	01622 688094
Manchester	Byrom Street Chambers	0161 829 2100
	Central Chambers	0161 236 1133
	Chambers of Ian Macdonald QC	0161 236 1840
	Deans Court Chambers	0161 214 6000
	Kenworthy's Chambers	0161 832 4036

A

	Kings Chambers	0845 034 3444
	•Lincoln House Chambers	0161 832 5701
	9 St John Street	0161 955 9000
	18 St John Street	0161 278 1800
	•St Johns Buildings	0161 214 1500
Middlesbrough	Fountain Chambers	01642 804040
	•Trinity Chambers	01642 247569
Newcastle Upon Tyne	Dere Street Barristers	0844 3351551
	•Trinity Chambers	0191 232 1927
Oxford	3 PB Barristers	01865 793 736
Plymouth	Devon Chambers	01752 661659
Portsmouth	Guildhall Chambers Portsmouth	023 9275 2400
Preston	Deans Court Chambers	01772 565 600
Sheffield	Bank House Chambers	0114 275 1223
Southampton	•College Chambers	023 8023 0338
Stoke On Trent	Regent Chambers	01782 286666
Winchester	3 PB Barristers	01962 868884

HEALTHCARE LAW

Bristol	Queen Square Chambers	0117 921 1966
Exeter	Walnut House	01392 279751
London	1 Chancery Lane	0845 634 6666
	•Crown Office Chambers	020 7797 8100
	1 Crown Office Row	020 7797 7500
	•Henderson Chambers	020 7583 9020
	11 King's Bench Walk	020 7632 8500
	Matrix Chambers	020 7404 3447
Manchester	18 St John Street	0161 278 1800
	•St Johns Buildings	0161 214 1500
Southampton	•College Chambers	023 8023 0338

HIGHWAYS

Exeter	Walnut House	01392 279751
London	1 Chancery Lane	0845 634 6666
	•Cornerstone Barristers	020 7242 4986
	Francis Taylor Building	020 7353 8415
	The Chambers of Grahame Aldous QC	020 7832 0500
Manchester	18 St John Street	0161 278 1800
	•St Johns Buildings	0161 214 1500
Newcastle Upon Tyne	Dere Street Barristers	0844 3351551
Southampton	•College Chambers	023 8023 0338

HINDU LAW

London	•Tanfield Chambers	020 7421 5300

HOLIDAY INJURY AND DAMAGES

Bournemouth	3 PB Barristers	01202 292102
Bristol	3 PB Barristers	0117 928 1520
	Queen Square Chambers	0117 921 1966
London	•Henderson Chambers	020 7583 9020
	3 PB Barristers	020 7583 8055
	•Tanfield Chambers	020 7421 5300
	The Chambers of Grahame Aldous QC	020 7832 0500
Manchester	18 St John Street	0161 278 1800
Newcastle Upon Tyne	Dere Street Barristers	0844 3351551
Oxford	3 PB Barristers	01865 793 736
Southampton	•College Chambers	023 8023 0338
Winchester	3 PB Barristers	01962 868884

HOLIDAY LAW

Manchester	18 St John Street	0161 278 1800
Newcastle Upon Tyne	Dere Street Barristers	0844 3351551

HOMICIDE

Birmingham	St Ive's Chambers	0121 236 0863

• Expanded entry in Part D

Bournemouth	3 PB Barristers	01202 292102
Bristol	3 PB Barristers	0117 928 1520
	Queen Square Chambers	0117 921 1966
Exeter	Walnut House	01392 279751
London	•2 Bedford Row	020 7440 8888
	25 Bedford Row	020 7067 1500
	Bell Yard Chambers	020 7306 9292
	•23 Essex Street	020 7413 0353
	•187 Fleet Street	020 7430 7430
	•1 KBW Chambers	020 7936 1500
	15 New Bridge Street	020 7842 1900
	3 PB Barristers	020 7583 8055
	•3 Raymond Buildings	020 7400 6400
	18 Red Lion Court	020 7520 6000
	The Chambers of Grahame Aldous QC	020 7832 0500
Manchester	Chambers of Ian Macdonald QC	0161 236 1840
	18 St John Street	0161 278 1800
	•St Johns Buildings	0161 214 1500
Middlesbrough	•Trinity Chambers	01642 247569
Newcastle Upon Tyne	Dere Street Barristers	0844 3351551
	•Trinity Chambers	0191 232 1927
Oxford	3 PB Barristers	01865 793 736
Winchester	3 PB Barristers	01962 868884

HONG KONG LAW

London	Essex Court Chambers	020 7813 8000
	•13 Old Square Chambers	020 7831 4445

HOUSING

Birmingham	No 8 Chambers	0121 236 5514
	St Ive's Chambers	0121 236 0863
	•St Philips Chambers	0121 246 7000
Bournemouth	3 PB Barristers	01202 292102
Bradford	Broadway House Chambers	01274 722560
Brighton	Crown Office Row Chambers	01273 625625
Bristol	3 PB Barristers	0117 928 1520
	Queen Square Chambers	0117 921 1966
	St John's Chambers	0117 923 4700
	Unity Street Chambers	0117 906 9789
Chester	Linenhall Chambers	01244 348282
Chichester	Pallant Chambers	01243 784538
Exeter	Rougemont Chambers	01392 208484
	Walnut House	01392 279751
Leeds	Broadway House Chambers	0113 246 2600
	Chancery House Chambers	0113 244 6691
	Enterprise Chambers	0113 246 0391
	Kings Chambers	0845 034 3444
	Park Court Chambers	0113 243 3277
	•Sovereign Chambers	0113 245 1841
	Zenith Chambers	0113 245 5438
Lewes	Westgate Chambers	01273 480510
Liverpool	Atlantic Chambers	0151 236 4421
	•Oriel Chambers	0151 236 7191
London	•Arden Chambers	020 7242 4244
	Atlas Chambers	020 7269 7980
	42 Bedford Row	020 7831 0222
	•Chambers of Mr Ami Feder	020 7797 7788
	1 Chancery Lane	0845 634 6666
	•Cornerstone Barristers	020 7242 4986
	Doughty Street Chambers	020 7404 1313
	•3 Dr Johnson's Buildings	020 7353 4854
	Enterprise Chambers	020 7405 9471
	Falcon Chambers	020 7353 2484
	Five Paper	020 7815 3200

	Francis Taylor Building	020 7353 8415
	•Goldsmith Chambers	020 7353 6802
	14 Gray's Inn Square	020 7242 0858
	•4-5 Gray's Inn Square	020 7404 5252
	Hailsham Chambers	020 7643 5000
	•Henderson Chambers	020 7583 9020
	Lamb Chambers	020 7797 8300
	•Maitland Chambers	020 7406 1200
	New Square Chambers	020 7419 8000
	12 Old Square Chambers	020 7404 0875
	•13 Old Square Chambers	020 7831 4445
	3 PB Barristers	020 7583 8055
	1 Pump Court	020 7842 7070
	•5 Pump Court	020 7353 2532
	Radcliffe Chambers	020 7831 0081
	•9 Stone Buildings	020 7404 5055
	•Tanfield Chambers	020 7421 5300
	The Chambers of Grahame Aldous QC	020 7832 0500
Manchester	Central Chambers	0161 236 1133
	Chambers of Ian Macdonald QC	0161 236 1840
	•Cobden House Chambers	0161 833 6000
	Kenworthy's Chambers	0161 832 4036
	Kings Chambers	0845 034 3444
	•Lincoln House Chambers	0161 832 5701
	St James's Chambers	0161 834 7000
	9 St John Street	0161 955 9000
	18 St John Street	0161 278 1800
	•St Johns Buildings	0161 214 1500
Middlesbrough	Fountain Chambers	01642 804040
	Old Court Chambers	01642 232523
	•Trinity Chambers	01642 247569
Newcastle Upon Tyne	Cathedral Chambers	0191 232 1311
	Dere Street Barristers	0844 3351551
	Enterprise Chambers	0191 222 3344
	•Trinity Chambers	0191 232 1927
Nottingham	KCH Garden Square	0115 941 8851
Oxford	3 PB Barristers	01865 793 736
Plymouth	Devon Chambers	01752 661659
Sheffield	Bank House Chambers	0114 275 1223
Southampton	•College Chambers	023 8023 0338
Stoke On Trent	Regent Chambers	01782 286666
Swansea	Iscoed Chambers	01792 652988
Winchester	3 PB Barristers	01962 868884

HUMAN RIGHTS

Birmingham	Equity Chambers	0121 236 5007
	No 8 Chambers	0121 236 5514
	•No5 Chambers	0845 210 5555
	•St Philips Chambers	0121 246 7000
Bristol	No5 Chambers	0845 210 5555
	Unity Street Chambers	0117 906 9789
Canterbury	Becket Chambers	01227 786331
Chelmsford	Trinity Chambers	01245 605040
Exeter	Rougemont Chambers	01392 208484
Leeds	Chancery House Chambers	0113 244 6691
	Park Court Chambers	0113 243 3277
London	•Arden Chambers	020 7242 4244
	•Argent Chambers	020 7556 5500
	Atlas Chambers	020 7269 7980
	25 Bedford Row	020 7067 1500
	Blackstone Chambers	020 7583 1770
	•Chambers of Mr Ami Feder	020 7797 7788
	1 Chancery Lane	0845 634 6666
	•Cornerstone Barristers	020 7242 4986

• Expanded entry in Part D

	1 Crown Office Row	020 7797 7500
	•Devereux Chambers	020 7353 7534
	Doughty Street Chambers	020 7404 1313
	Essex Court Chambers	020 7813 8000
	20 Essex Street	020 7842 1200
	•39 Essex Street	020 7832 1111
	Farringdon Chambers	020 7089 5700
	Francis Taylor Building	020 7353 8415
	Great James Street Chambers	020 7440 4949
	•Henderson Chambers	020 7583 9020
	2 King's Bench Walk	020 7353 1746
	11 King's Bench Walk	020 7632 8500
	Matrix Chambers	020 7404 3447
	Middle Temple Lane Chambers	020 7583 4352
	•Monckton Chambers	020 7405 7211
	No5 Chambers	0845 210 5555
	•13 Old Square Chambers	020 7831 4445
	1 Pump Court	020 7842 7070
	6 Pump Court	020 7797 8400
	18 Red Lion Court	020 7520 6000
	Renaissance Chambers	020 7404 1111
	Serle Court	020 7242 6105
	•Temple Garden Chambers	020 7583 1315
Maidstone	6 Pump Court Chambers	01622 688094
Manchester	Byrom Street Chambers	0161 829 2100
	Central Chambers	0161 236 1133
	Chambers of Ian Macdonald QC	0161 236 1840
	Kenworthy's Chambers	0161 832 4036
	•Lincoln House Chambers	0161 832 5701
Middlesbrough	Fountain Chambers	01642 804040
Newcastle Upon Tyne	Cathedral Chambers	0191 232 1311

IMMIGRATION

Birmingham	Cornwall Street Chambers	0121 233 7500
	Equity Chambers	0121 236 5007
	No 8 Chambers	0121 236 5514
	•No5 Chambers	0845 210 5555
	•St Philips Chambers	0121 246 7000
Bradford	Broadway House Chambers	01274 722560
Bristol	No5 Chambers	0845 210 5555
Chelmsford	Trinity Chambers	01245 605040
Exeter	Rougemont Chambers	01392 208484
Leeds	Broadway House Chambers	0113 246 2600
	Chancery House Chambers	0113 244 6691
	KBW	0113 297 1200
	Kings Chambers	0845 034 3444
	Park Court Chambers	0113 243 3277
	37 Park Square Chambers	0113 243 9422
	•Sovereign Chambers	0113 245 1841
Liverpool	Atlantic Chambers	0151 236 4421
London	•Argent Chambers	020 7556 5500
	Bell Yard Chambers	020 7306 9292
	Blackstone Chambers	020 7583 1770
	4 Brick Court	020 7832 3200
	•Chambers of Mr Ami Feder	020 7797 7788
	•Cornerstone Barristers	020 7242 4986
	1 Crown Office Row	020 7797 7500
	Doughty Street Chambers	020 7404 1313
	•2 Dr Johnson's Buildings	020 7936 2613
	Essex Court Chambers	020 7813 8000
	20 Essex Street	020 7842 1200
	•39 Essex Street	020 7832 1111
	Francis Taylor Building	020 7353 8415
	•Goldsmith Chambers	020 7353 6802

A

	•4-5 Gray's Inn Square	020 7404 5252
	Great James Street Chambers	020 7440 4949
	•Henderson Chambers	020 7583 9020
	4 King's Bench Walk	020 7822 7000
	11 King's Bench Walk	020 7632 8500
	13 King's Bench Walk	020 7353 7204
	Matrix Chambers	020 7404 3447
	Middle Temple Lane Chambers	020 7583 4352
	15 New Bridge Street	020 7842 1900
	No5 Chambers	0845 210 5555
	12 Old Square Chambers	020 7404 0875
	1 Pump Court	020 7842 7070
	•5 Pump Court	020 7353 2532
	Renaissance Chambers	020 7404 1111
	•Temple Garden Chambers	020 7583 1315
	Tooks Chambers	020 7842 7575
Manchester	Central Chambers	0161 236 1133
	Chambers of Ian Macdonald QC	0161 236 1840
	Kenworthy's Chambers	0161 832 4036
	Kings Chambers	0845 034 3444
	•Lincoln House Chambers	0161 832 5701
	18 St John Street	0161 278 1800
Middlesbrough	Amicus Chambers	01642 876334
	Old Court Chambers	01642 232523
	•Trinity Chambers	01642 247569
Newcastle Upon Tyne	Cathedral Chambers	0191 232 1311
	•Trinity Chambers	0191 232 1927
Northampton	Chartlands Chambers	01604 603322
Plymouth	Devon Chambers	01752 661659
Sheffield	Bank House Chambers	0114 275 1223
	St Johns Buildings	0114 273 8951
Southampton	•College Chambers	023 8023 0338
Stoke On Trent	Regent Chambers	01782 286666

INCOME TAX

Birmingham	No 8 Chambers	0121 236 5514
	•No5 Chambers	0845 210 5555
	•St Philips Chambers	0121 246 7000
Bradford	Broadway House Chambers	01274 722560
Bristol	No5 Chambers	0845 210 5555
	St John's Chambers	0117 923 4700
Leeds	Broadway House Chambers	0113 246 2600
	Chancery House Chambers	0113 244 6691
	Kings Chambers	0845 034 3444
	Zenith Chambers	0113 245 5438
Liverpool	Atlantic Chambers	0151 236 4421
London	Atlas Chambers	020 7269 7980
	•Devereux Chambers	020 7353 7534
	•Maitland Chambers	020 7406 1200
	New Square Chambers	020 7419 8000
	No5 Chambers	0845 210 5555
	Prince Henry's Chambers	020 7837 1645
	•Pump Court Tax Chambers	020 7414 8080
	Radcliffe Chambers	020 7831 0081
	3 Stone Buildings	020 7242 4937
	•9 Stone Buildings	020 7404 5055
	Taxchambers	020 7242 2744
	Temple Tax Chambers	020 7353 7884
	•Wilberforce Chambers	020 7306 0102
Manchester	•Cobden House Chambers	0161 833 6000
	Kings Chambers	0845 034 3444
	St James's Chambers	0161 834 7000
	18 St John Street	0161 278 1800
	•St Johns Buildings	0161 214 1500

• Expanded entry in Part D

Newcastle Upon Tyne	Dere Street Barristers	0844 3351551

INDUSTRIAL DEAFNESS

Birmingham	St Ive's Chambers	0121 236 0863
Bournemouth	3 PB Barristers	01202 292102
Bristol	3 PB Barristers	0117 928 1520
	Queen Square Chambers	0117 921 1966
London	•Cornerstone Barristers	020 7242 4986
	3 PB Barristers	020 7583 8055
	The Chambers of Grahame Aldous QC	020 7832 0500
Manchester	•Lincoln House Chambers	0161 832 5701
	18 St John Street	0161 278 1800
Newcastle Upon Tyne	Dere Street Barristers	0844 3351551
Oxford	3 PB Barristers	01865 793 736
Southampton	•College Chambers	023 8023 0338
Winchester	3 PB Barristers	01962 868884

INDUSTRIAL DISEASES

Birmingham	•No5 Chambers	0845 210 5555
	St Ive's Chambers	0121 236 0863
Bournemouth	3 PB Barristers	01202 292102
Bristol	No5 Chambers	0845 210 5555
	3 PB Barristers	0117 928 1520
	Queen Square Chambers	0117 921 1966
Leeds	37 Park Square Chambers	0113 243 9422
	Zenith Chambers	0113 245 5438
London	•Cornerstone Barristers	020 7242 4986
	•Crown Office Chambers	020 7797 8100
	•39 Essex Street	020 7832 1111
	•Henderson Chambers	020 7583 9020
	12 King's Bench Walk	020 7583 0811
	No5 Chambers	0845 210 5555
	3 PB Barristers	020 7583 8055
	The Chambers of Grahame Aldous QC	020 7832 0500
Manchester	Byrom Street Chambers	0161 829 2100
	Chambers of Ian Macdonald QC	0161 236 1840
	•Lincoln House Chambers	0161 832 5701
	18 St John Street	0161 278 1800
Newcastle Upon Tyne	Dere Street Barristers	0844 3351551
Oxford	3 PB Barristers	01865 793 736
Southampton	•College Chambers	023 8023 0338
Winchester	3 PB Barristers	01962 868884

INDUSTRIAL RELATIONS LAW

Bristol	Queen Square Chambers	0117 921 1966
Exeter	Rougemont Chambers	01392 208484
	Walnut House	01392 279751
London	•Cornerstone Barristers	020 7242 4986
	•Henderson Chambers	020 7583 9020
	•Tanfield Chambers	020 7421 5300
	The Chambers of Grahame Aldous QC	020 7832 0500
Manchester	Chambers of Ian Macdonald QC	0161 236 1840
	18 St John Street	0161 278 1800
	•St Johns Buildings	0161 214 1500
Newcastle Upon Tyne	Dere Street Barristers	0844 3351551
Southampton	•College Chambers	023 8023 0338

INFORMATION TECHNOLOGY

Birmingham	•No5 Chambers	0845 210 5555
Bournemouth	3 PB Barristers	01202 292102
Bristol	No5 Chambers	0845 210 5555
	3 PB Barristers	0117 928 1520
	Unity Street Chambers	0117 906 9789
Leeds	Chancery House Chambers	0113 244 6691
	Kings Chambers	0845 034 3444

A

London	Atkin Chambers	020 7404 0102
	Brick Court Chambers	020 7379 3550
	•Devereux Chambers	020 7353 7534
	•One Essex Court	020 7583 2000
	Fountain Court Chambers	020 7583 3335
	Hailsham Chambers	020 7643 5000
	•Henderson Chambers	020 7583 9020
	4 KBW	020 7822 8822
	Keating Chambers	020 7544 2600
	Lamb Chambers	020 7797 8300
	•8 New Square	020 7405 4321
	No5 Chambers	0845 210 5555
	3 PB Barristers	020 7583 8055
	4 Pump Court	020 7842 5555
	Selborne Chambers	020 7420 9500
	11 South Square	020 7405 1222
	•9 Stone Buildings	020 7404 5055
	11 Stone Buildings	020 7831 6381
	•Tanfield Chambers	020 7421 5300
	•Three New Square IP	020 7405 1111
	3 Verulam Buildings	020 7831 8441
Manchester	•Cobden House Chambers	0161 833 6000
	Deans Court Chambers	0161 214 6000
	Kings Chambers	0845 034 3444
	St James's Chambers	0161 834 7000
	9 St John Street	0161 955 9000
	18 St John Street	0161 278 1800
	•St Johns Buildings	0161 214 1500
Oxford	3 PB Barristers	01865 793 736
Plymouth	Devon Chambers	01752 661659
Preston	Deans Court Chambers	01772 565 600
Winchester	3 PB Barristers	01962 868884

INHERITANCE

Birmingham	St Ive's Chambers	0121 236 0863
Bournemouth	3 PB Barristers	01202 292102
Bristol	Queen Square Chambers	0117 921 1966
Faringdon	Faringdon Chambers	01367 240598
London	Five Paper	020 7815 3200

INHERITANCE AND COHABITEES

Birmingham	St Ive's Chambers	0121 236 0863
Bristol	3 PB Barristers	0117 928 1520
Exeter	Rougemont Chambers	01392 208484
Faringdon	Faringdon Chambers	01367 240598
London	Five Paper	020 7815 3200
	3 PB Barristers	020 7583 8055
	•Pump Court Chambers	020 7353 0711
Manchester	18 St John Street	0161 278 1800
Newcastle Upon Tyne	Dere Street Barristers	0844 3351551
Northampton	Northampton Chambers	01604 636271
Oxford	3 PB Barristers	01865 793 736
Portsmouth	Portsmouth Barristers'Chambers	023 9283 1292
Swindon	Pump Court Chambers	01793 539899
Winchester	3 PB Barristers	01962 868884
	Pump Court Chambers	01962 868 161

INQUESTS

Bournemouth	3 PB Barristers	01202 292102
Bristol	Albion Chambers	0117 927 2144
	3 PB Barristers	0117 928 1520
	Queen Square Chambers	0117 921 1966
Exeter	Rougemont Chambers	01392 208484
Leeds	KBW	0113 297 1200

• Expanded entry in Part D

London	•2 Bedford Row	020 7440 8888
	25 Bedford Row	020 7067 1500
	•9-12 Bell Yard	020 7400 1800
	•Chambers of Marion Smullen and Kerim Fuad QC	020 7427 4400
	•Charter Chambers	020 7618 4400
	•Cornerstone Barristers	020 7242 4986
	•23 Essex Street	020 7413 0353
	Farringdon Chambers	020 7089 5700
	•187 Fleet Street	020 7430 7430
	•Henderson Chambers	020 7583 9020
	•1 KBW Chambers	020 7936 1500
	15 New Bridge Street	020 7842 1900
	3 PB Barristers	020 7583 8055
	6 Pump Court	020 7797 8400
	18 Red Lion Court	020 7520 6000
	The Chambers of Grahame Aldous QC	020 7832 0500
Maidstone	6 Pump Court Chambers	01622 688094
Manchester	Chambers of Ian Macdonald QC	0161 236 1840
	Kenworthy's Chambers	0161 832 4036
	•Lincoln House Chambers	0161 832 5701
	18 St John Street	0161 278 1800
Newcastle Upon Tyne	Dere Street Barristers	0844 3351551
Oxford	3 PB Barristers	01865 793 736
Portsmouth	Guildhall Chambers Portsmouth	023 9275 2400
Winchester	3 PB Barristers	01962 868884

INSOLVENCY

Birmingham	Cornwall Street Chambers	0121 233 7500
	No 8 Chambers	0121 236 5514
	•No5 Chambers	0845 210 5555
	St Ive's Chambers	0121 236 0863
	•St Philips Chambers	0121 246 7000
Bournemouth	3 PB Barristers	01202 292102
Brighton	Crown Office Row Chambers	01273 625625
Bristol	No5 Chambers	0845 210 5555
	3 PB Barristers	0117 928 1520
	St John's Chambers	0117 923 4700
Chelmsford	Trinity Chambers	01245 605040
Chichester	Pallant Chambers	01243 784538
Exeter	Rougemont Chambers	01392 208484
	Walnut House	01392 279751
Ipswich	East Anglian Chambers	01473 214481
Leeds	Chancery House Chambers	0113 244 6691
	Enterprise Chambers	0113 246 0391
	KBW	0113 297 1200
	Kings Chambers	0845 034 3444
	Park Court Chambers	0113 243 3277
	•Sovereign Chambers	0113 245 1841
Liverpool	Atlantic Chambers	0151 236 4421
	•Number 7 Harrington Street Chambers	0151 242 0707
	•Oriel Chambers	0151 236 7191
London	42 Bedford Row	020 7831 0222
	Blackstone Chambers	020 7583 1770
	•Chambers of Mr Ami Feder	020 7797 7788
	•Charter Chambers	020 7618 4400
	Enterprise Chambers	020 7405 9471
	Erskine Chambers	020 7242 5532
	•One Essex Court	020 7583 2000
	Essex Court Chambers	020 7813 8000
	20 Essex Street	020 7842 1200
	Falcon Chambers	020 7353 2484
	Five Paper	020 7815 3200
	Fountain Court Chambers	020 7583 3335

A

	•Goldsmith Chambers	020 7353 6802
	Gough Square Chambers	020 7353 0924
	3 Hare Court	020 7415 7800
	4 KBW	020 7822 8822
	Lamb Chambers	020 7797 8300
	•Maitland Chambers	020 7406 1200
	New Square Chambers	020 7419 8000
	No5 Chambers	0845 210 5555
	•13 Old Square Chambers	020 7831 4445
	3 PB Barristers	020 7583 8055
	Radcliffe Chambers	020 7831 0081
	Selborne Chambers	020 7420 9500
	Serle Court	020 7242 6105
	•South Square	020 7696 9900
	3 Stone Buildings	020 7242 4937
	4 Stone Buildings	020 7242 5524
	•9 Stone Buildings	020 7404 5055
	11 Stone Buildings	020 7831 6381
	•Tanfield Chambers	020 7421 5300
	Ten Old Square	020 7405 0758
	3 Verulam Buildings	020 7831 8441
	•Wilberforce Chambers	020 7306 0102
	XXIV Old Buildings	020 7691 2424
Manchester	Central Chambers	0161 236 1133
	•Cobden House Chambers	0161 833 6000
	Deans Court Chambers	0161 214 6000
	Kings Chambers	0845 034 3444
	St James's Chambers	0161 834 7000
	9 St John Street	0161 955 9000
	18 St John Street	0161 278 1800
	•St Johns Buildings	0161 214 1500
Middlesbrough	•Trinity Chambers	01642 247569
Newcastle Upon Tyne	Cathedral Chambers	0191 232 1311
	Dere Street Barristers	0844 3351551
	Enterprise Chambers	0191 222 3344
	•Trinity Chambers	0191 232 1927
Nottingham	KCH Garden Square	0115 941 8851
Oxford	3 PB Barristers	01865 793 736
Plymouth	Devon Chambers	01752 661659
Portsmouth	Guildhall Chambers Portsmouth	023 9275 2400
	Portsmouth Barristers'Chambers	023 9283 1292
Preston	Deans Court Chambers	01772 565 600
Southampton	•College Chambers	023 8023 0338
Swansea	Iscoed Chambers	01792 652988
Winchester	3 PB Barristers	01962 868884

INSURANCE

Birmingham	No 8 Chambers	0121 236 5514
	•No5 Chambers	0845 210 5555
	•St Philips Chambers	0121 246 7000
Bournemouth	3 PB Barristers	01202 292102
Bristol	No5 Chambers	0845 210 5555
	3 PB Barristers	0117 928 1520
	St John's Chambers	0117 923 4700
Chichester	Pallant Chambers	01243 784538
Leeds	Chancery House Chambers	0113 244 6691
	Kings Chambers	0845 034 3444
	Park Court Chambers	0113 243 3277
Liverpool	Atlantic Chambers	0151 236 4421
	•Oriel Chambers	0151 236 7191
London	Atkin Chambers	020 7404 0102
	42 Bedford Row	020 7831 0222
	Blackstone Chambers	020 7583 1770
	Brick Court Chambers	020 7379 3550

• Expanded entry in Part D

	1 Chancery Lane	0845 634 6666
	•Devereux Chambers	020 7353 7534
	•One Essex Court	020 7583 2000
	Essex Court Chambers	020 7813 8000
	20 Essex Street	020 7842 1200
	•39 Essex Street	020 7832 1111
	Fountain Court Chambers	020 7583 3335
	•4-5 Gray's Inn Square	020 7404 5252
	Hailsham Chambers	020 7643 5000
	•Henderson Chambers	020 7583 9020
	Keating Chambers	020 7544 2600
	12 King's Bench Walk	020 7583 0811
	13 King's Bench Walk	020 7353 7204
	Lamb Chambers	020 7797 8300
	•Maitland Chambers	020 7406 1200
	No5 Chambers	0845 210 5555
	•13 Old Square Chambers	020 7831 4445
	3 PB Barristers	020 7583 8055
	4 Pump Court	020 7842 5555
	Selborne Chambers	020 7420 9500
	Serle Court	020 7242 6105
	•South Square	020 7696 9900
	3 Stone Buildings	020 7242 4937
	4 Stone Buildings	020 7242 5524
	•9 Stone Buildings	020 7404 5055
	11 Stone Buildings	020 7831 6381
	•Tanfield Chambers	020 7421 5300
	•Temple Garden Chambers	020 7583 1315
	3 Verulam Buildings	020 7831 8441
Manchester	Byrom Street Chambers	0161 829 2100
	Deans Court Chambers	0161 214 6000
	Kings Chambers	0845 034 3444
	St James's Chambers	0161 834 7000
	9 St John Street	0161 955 9000
Oxford	3 PB Barristers	01865 793 736
Portsmouth	Guildhall Chambers Portsmouth	023 9275 2400
Preston	Deans Court Chambers	01772 565 600
Winchester	3 PB Barristers	01962 868884

INSURANCE (LONG TERM)

London	Erskine Chambers	020 7242 5532
Manchester	•St Johns Buildings	0161 214 1500

INTELLECTUAL PROPERTY

Birmingham	•No5 Chambers	0845 210 5555
	•St Philips Chambers	0121 246 7000
Bournemouth	3 PB Barristers	01202 292102
Bristol	No5 Chambers	0845 210 5555
	3 PB Barristers	0117 928 1520
	St John's Chambers	0117 923 4700
Exeter	Walnut House	01392 279751
Leeds	Chancery House Chambers	0113 244 6691
	Kings Chambers	0845 034 3444
	Park Court Chambers	0113 243 3277
	•Sovereign Chambers	0113 245 1841
	Zenith Chambers	0113 245 5438
Liverpool	Atlantic Chambers	0151 236 4421
London	Blackstone Chambers	020 7583 1770
	Doughty Street Chambers	020 7404 1313
	•One Essex Court	020 7583 2000
	Essex Court Chambers	020 7813 8000
	20 Essex Street	020 7842 1200
	Fountain Court Chambers	020 7583 3335
	13 King's Bench Walk	020 7353 7204

A

	Lamb Chambers	020 7797 8300
	•Maitland Chambers	020 7406 1200
	•Monckton Chambers	020 7405 7211
	•8 New Square	020 7405 4321
	New Square Chambers	020 7419 8000
	No5 Chambers	0845 210 5555
	12 Old Square Chambers	020 7404 0875
	•13 Old Square Chambers	020 7831 4445
	3 PB Barristers	020 7583 8055
	Serle Court	020 7242 6105
	11 South Square	020 7405 1222
	•9 Stone Buildings	020 7404 5055
	11 Stone Buildings	020 7831 6381
	•Three New Square IP	020 7405 1111
	3 Verulam Buildings	020 7831 8441
	•Wilberforce Chambers	020 7306 0102
Manchester	•Cobden House Chambers	0161 833 6000
	Kings Chambers	0845 034 3444
	St James's Chambers	0161 834 7000
	9 St John Street	0161 955 9000
	18 St John Street	0161 278 1800
Nottingham	KCH Garden Square	0115 941 8851
Oxford	3 PB Barristers	01865 793 736
Portsmouth	Guildhall Chambers Portsmouth	023 9275 2400
	Portsmouth Barristers'Chambers	023 9283 1292
Southampton	•College Chambers	023 8023 0338
Winchester	3 PB Barristers	01962 868884

INTERNATIONAL ARBITRATION

Birmingham	•No5 Chambers	0845 210 5555
Bournemouth	3 PB Barristers	01202 292102
Bristol	No5 Chambers	0845 210 5555
	3 PB Barristers	0117 928 1520
London	Blackstone Chambers	020 7583 1770
	•39 Essex Street	020 7832 1111
	Fountain Court Chambers	020 7583 3335
	Keating Chambers	020 7544 2600
	•Maitland Chambers	020 7406 1200
	No5 Chambers	0845 210 5555
	3 PB Barristers	020 7583 8055
	•Tanfield Chambers	020 7421 5300
Oxford	3 PB Barristers	01865 793 736
Winchester	3 PB Barristers	01962 868884

INTERNATIONAL COMMERCIAL ARBITRATION

Bournemouth	3 PB Barristers	01202 292102
Bristol	3 PB Barristers	0117 928 1520
London	Atkin Chambers	020 7404 0102
	Blackstone Chambers	020 7583 1770
	Essex Court Chambers	020 7813 8000
	Keating Chambers	020 7544 2600
	3 PB Barristers	020 7583 8055
	•Tanfield Chambers	020 7421 5300
Oxford	3 PB Barristers	01865 793 736
Winchester	3 PB Barristers	01962 868884

INTERNATIONAL CRIMINAL LAW

Bristol	Queen Square Chambers	0117 921 1966
Exeter	Walnut House	01392 279751
London	•2 Bedford Row	020 7440 8888
	25 Bedford Row	020 7067 1500
	Bell Yard Chambers	020 7306 9292
	•187 Fleet Street	020 7430 7430
	•1 KBW Chambers	020 7936 1500

• Expanded entry in Part D

	15 New Bridge Street	020 7842 1900
	•3 Raymond Buildings	020 7400 6400
	18 Red Lion Court	020 7520 6000
Manchester	Chambers of Ian Macdonald QC	0161 236 1840
	18 St John Street	0161 278 1800
	•St Johns Buildings	0161 214 1500
Middlesbrough	•Trinity Chambers	01642 247569
Newcastle Upon Tyne	•Trinity Chambers	0191 232 1927

INTERNATIONAL FRAUD AND ASSET TRACING

Bournemouth	3 PB Barristers	01202 292102
Bristol	3 PB Barristers	0117 928 1520
	Queen Square Chambers	0117 921 1966
London	•2 Bedford Row	020 7440 8888
	•23 Essex Street	020 7413 0353
	•187 Fleet Street	020 7430 7430
	•1 KBW Chambers	020 7936 1500
	•Maitland Chambers	020 7406 1200
	15 New Bridge Street	020 7842 1900
	3 PB Barristers	020 7583 8055
	•3 Raymond Buildings	020 7400 6400
	18 Red Lion Court	020 7520 6000
	The Chambers of Grahame Aldous QC	020 7832 0500
Manchester	Chambers of Ian Macdonald QC	0161 236 1840
	18 St John Street	0161 278 1800
Newcastle Upon Tyne	Dere Street Barristers	0844 3351551
Oxford	3 PB Barristers	01865 793 736
Winchester	3 PB Barristers	01962 868884

INTERNATIONAL HUMAN RIGHTS LAW

London	•2 Bedford Row	020 7440 8888
	25 Bedford Row	020 7067 1500
	Blackstone Chambers	020 7583 1770
	15 New Bridge Street	020 7842 1900
	•3 Raymond Buildings	020 7400 6400
	18 Red Lion Court	020 7520 6000
Manchester	Chambers of Ian Macdonald QC	0161 236 1840

INTERNATIONAL LAW

Leeds	Chancery House Chambers	0113 244 6691
London	•Argent Chambers	020 7556 5500
	Blackstone Chambers	020 7583 1770
	Brick Court Chambers	020 7379 3550
	Doughty Street Chambers	020 7404 1313
	Essex Court Chambers	020 7813 8000
	20 Essex Street	020 7842 1200
	•4-5 Gray's Inn Square	020 7404 5252
	•Maitland Chambers	020 7406 1200
	Matrix Chambers	020 7404 3447
	•Monckton Chambers	020 7405 7211
	New Square Chambers	020 7419 8000
	Serle Court	020 7242 6105
	3 Verulam Buildings	020 7831 8441
	XXIV Old Buildings	020 7691 2424

INTERNATIONAL TAX

London	Taxchambers	020 7242 2744

INTERNATIONAL TRADE

Birmingham	•No5 Chambers	0845 210 5555
Bristol	No5 Chambers	0845 210 5555
Exeter	Rougemont Chambers	01392 208484
Leeds	Chancery House Chambers	0113 244 6691
	Kings Chambers	0845 034 3444
London	Blackstone Chambers	020 7583 1770

A

	Brick Court Chambers	020 7379 3550
	Essex Court Chambers	020 7813 8000
	20 Essex Street	020 7842 1200
	Five Paper	020 7815 3200
	Fountain Court Chambers	020 7583 3335
	Lamb Chambers	020 7797 8300
	•Maitland Chambers	020 7406 1200
	•Monckton Chambers	020 7405 7211
	No5 Chambers	0845 210 5555
	4 Pump Court	020 7842 5555
	Selborne Chambers	020 7420 9500
	•South Square	020 7696 9900
	•9 Stone Buildings	020 7404 5055
	3 Verulam Buildings	020 7831 8441
	XXIV Old Buildings	020 7691 2424
Manchester	Kings Chambers	0845 034 3444
Portsmouth	Portsmouth Barristers'Chambers	023 9283 1292

INTERNET CRIME

Birmingham	St Ive's Chambers	0121 236 0863
Bristol	Queen Square Chambers	0117 921 1966
London	•2 Bedford Row	020 7440 8888
	Bell Yard Chambers	020 7306 9292
	Essex Court Chambers	020 7813 8000
	•23 Essex Street	020 7413 0353
	•187 Fleet Street	020 7430 7430
	15 New Bridge Street	020 7842 1900
	The Chambers of Grahame Aldous QC	020 7832 0500
Manchester	Chambers of Ian Macdonald QC	0161 236 1840
	18 St John Street	0161 278 1800
Newcastle Upon Tyne	Dere Street Barristers	0844 3351551

INTERNET GAMING AND LICENSING

London	•Cornerstone Barristers	020 7242 4986
	•Tanfield Chambers	020 7421 5300

INTERNET LAW

London	•Henderson Chambers	020 7583 9020
Manchester	•St Johns Buildings	0161 214 1500

INVESTMENTS

London	Erskine Chambers	020 7242 5532
	XXIV Old Buildings	020 7691 2424
Manchester	•St Johns Buildings	0161 214 1500

ISLAMIC FAMILY LAW

Bournemouth	3 PB Barristers	01202 292102
Bristol	3 PB Barristers	0117 928 1520
London	3 PB Barristers	020 7583 8055
Oxford	3 PB Barristers	01865 793 736
Winchester	3 PB Barristers	01962 868884

ISLAMIC LAW

Bournemouth	3 PB Barristers	01202 292102
Bristol	3 PB Barristers	0117 928 1520
London	Essex Court Chambers	020 7813 8000
	Outer Temple Chambers	020 7353 6381
	3 PB Barristers	020 7583 8055
	•Tanfield Chambers	020 7421 5300
	Wynne Chambers	020 3239 6964
Oxford	3 PB Barristers	01865 793 736
Winchester	3 PB Barristers	01962 868884

ISRAELI LAW

London	•Chambers of Mr Ami Feder	020 7797 7788

• Expanded entry in Part D

JUDICIAL REVIEW

Birmingham	Equity Chambers	0121 236 5007
	•No5 Chambers	0845 210 5555
	St Ive's Chambers	0121 236 0863
Bournemouth	3 PB Barristers	01202 292102
Bristol	No5 Chambers	0845 210 5555
	3 PB Barristers	0117 928 1520
Exeter	Rougemont Chambers	01392 208484
Leeds	37 Park Square Chambers	0113 243 9422
Liverpool	Atlantic Chambers	0151 236 4421
	•Oriel Chambers	0151 236 7191
London	•Arden Chambers	020 7242 4244
	•Argent Chambers	020 7556 5500
	•2 Bedford Row	020 7440 8888
	Blackstone Chambers	020 7583 1770
	•Cornerstone Barristers	020 7242 4986
	1 Crown Office Row	020 7797 7500
	•3 Dr Johnson's Buildings	020 7353 4854
	•23 Essex Street	020 7413 0353
	•39 Essex Street	020 7832 1111
	Five Paper	020 7815 3200
	Francis Taylor Building	020 7353 8415
	•Henderson Chambers	020 7583 9020
	15 New Bridge Street	020 7842 1900
	No5 Chambers	0845 210 5555
	3 PB Barristers	020 7583 8055
	6 Pump Court	020 7797 8400
	•3 Raymond Buildings	020 7400 6400
Maidstone	6 Pump Court Chambers	01622 688094
Manchester	Central Chambers	0161 236 1133
	Chambers of Ian Macdonald QC	0161 236 1840
	Kenworthy's Chambers	0161 832 4036
	•Lincoln House Chambers	0161 832 5701
	18 St John Street	0161 278 1800
Newcastle Upon Tyne	Dere Street Barristers	0844 3351551
Oxford	3 PB Barristers	01865 793 736
Portsmouth	Guildhall Chambers Portsmouth	023 9275 2400
Sheffield	St Johns Buildings	0114 273 8951
Southampton	•College Chambers	023 8023 0338
Winchester	3 PB Barristers	01962 868884

LABOUR ARBITRATION

London	•Henderson Chambers	020 7583 9020
Manchester	Chambers of Ian Macdonald QC	0161 236 1840
	18 St John Street	0161 278 1800
	•St Johns Buildings	0161 214 1500
Newcastle Upon Tyne	Dere Street Barristers	0844 3351551

LAND COMPENSATION

London	•Arden Chambers	020 7242 4244
	•Cornerstone Barristers	020 7242 4986
	Francis Taylor Building	020 7353 8415
	•Henderson Chambers	020 7583 9020
	•Maitland Chambers	020 7406 1200
Manchester	18 St John Street	0161 278 1800
Newcastle Upon Tyne	Dere Street Barristers	0844 3351551

LANDLORD AND TENANT

Birmingham	No 8 Chambers	0121 236 5514
	•No5 Chambers	0845 210 5555
	St Ive's Chambers	0121 236 0863
	•St Philips Chambers	0121 246 7000
Bournemouth	3 PB Barristers	01202 292102
Bradford	Broadway House Chambers	01274 722560

A

Brighton	Crown Office Row Chambers	01273 625625
Bristol	Albion Chambers	0117 927 2144
	No5 Chambers	0845 210 5555
	3 PB Barristers	0117 928 1520
	Queen Square Chambers	0117 921 1966
	St John's Chambers	0117 923 4700
	Unity Street Chambers	0117 906 9789
Canterbury	Becket Chambers	01227 786331
Chelmsford	Trinity Chambers	01245 605040
Chester	Linenhall Chambers	01244 348282
Chichester	Pallant Chambers	01243 784538
Exeter	Rougemont Chambers	01392 208484
	Walnut House	01392 279751
Hull	Wilberforce Chambers	01482 323264
Ipswich	East Anglian Chambers	01473 214481
Leeds	Broadway House Chambers	0113 246 2600
	Chancery House Chambers	0113 244 6691
	Enterprise Chambers	0113 246 0391
	KBW	0113 297 1200
	Kings Chambers	0845 034 3444
	Park Court Chambers	0113 243 3277
	37 Park Square Chambers	0113 243 9422
	•Sovereign Chambers	0113 245 1841
	Zenith Chambers	0113 245 5438
Lewes	Westgate Chambers	01273 480510
Liverpool	Atlantic Chambers	0151 236 4421
	•Oriel Chambers	0151 236 7191
London	•Arden Chambers	020 7242 4244
	42 Bedford Row	020 7831 0222
	•Chambers of Mr Ami Feder	020 7797 7788
	Chambers of Mr Patrick Ground QC	020 7736 0131
	1 Chancery Lane	0845 634 6666
	•Cornerstone Barristers	020 7242 4986
	Doughty Street Chambers	020 7404 1313
	•3 Dr Johnson's Buildings	020 7353 4854
	Enterprise Chambers	020 7405 9471
	Falcon Chambers	020 7353 2484
	•Farrar's Building	020 7583 9241
	Five Paper	020 7815 3200
	Francis Taylor Building	020 7353 8415
	•Goldsmith Chambers	020 7353 6802
	Gough Square Chambers	020 7353 0924
	14 Gray's Inn Square	020 7242 0858
	•4-5 Gray's Inn Square	020 7404 5252
	Hailsham Chambers	020 7643 5000
	•Henderson Chambers	020 7583 9020
	•1 KBW Chambers	020 7936 1500
	4 King's Bench Walk	020 7822 7000
	13 King's Bench Walk	020 7353 7204
	Lamb Chambers	020 7797 8300
	•Maitland Chambers	020 7406 1200
	Middle Temple Lane Chambers	020 7583 4352
	New Square Chambers	020 7419 8000
	No5 Chambers	0845 210 5555
	12 Old Square Chambers	020 7404 0875
	•13 Old Square Chambers	020 7831 4445
	3 PB Barristers	020 7583 8055
	Prince Henry's Chambers	020 7837 1645
	1 Pump Court	020 7842 7070
	4 Pump Court	020 7842 5555
	•5 Pump Court	020 7353 2532
	6 Pump Court	020 7797 8400
	•Pump Court Chambers	020 7353 0711
	Radcliffe Chambers	020 7831 0081

• Expanded entry in Part D

	Selborne Chambers	020 7420 9500
	Serle Court	020 7242 6105
	3 Stone Buildings	020 7242 4937
	•9 Stone Buildings	020 7404 5055
	•Tanfield Chambers	020 7421 5300
	•Temple Garden Chambers	020 7583 1315
	Ten Old Square	020 7405 0758
	The Chambers of Grahame Aldous QC	020 7832 0500
	•Wilberforce Chambers	020 7306 0102
	XXIV Old Buildings	020 7691 2424
Maidstone	Maidstone Chambers	01622 688592
	6 Pump Court Chambers	01622 688094
Manchester	Central Chambers	0161 236 1133
	Chambers of Ian Macdonald QC	0161 236 1840
	•Cobden House Chambers	0161 833 6000
	Deans Court Chambers	0161 214 6000
	Kenworthy's Chambers	0161 832 4036
	Kings Chambers	0845 034 3444
	St James's Chambers	0161 834 7000
	9 St John Street	0161 955 9000
	18 St John Street	0161 278 1800
	•St Johns Buildings	0161 214 1500
Middlesbrough	Fountain Chambers	01642 804040
	Old Court Chambers	01642 232523
	•Trinity Chambers	01642 247569
Newcastle Upon Tyne	Cathedral Chambers	0191 232 1311
	Dere Street Barristers	0844 3351551
	Enterprise Chambers	0191 222 3344
	•Trinity Chambers	0191 232 1927
Northampton	Chartlands Chambers	01604 603322
Norwich	Octagon House	01603 623186
Nottingham	KCH Garden Square	0115 941 8851
Oxford	3 PB Barristers	01865 793 736
Pitstone	Victor House Chambers	01296 664043
Plymouth	Devon Chambers	01752 661659
Portsmouth	Guildhall Chambers Portsmouth	023 9275 2400
	Portsmouth Barristers'Chambers	023 9283 1292
Preston	Deans Court Chambers	01772 565 600
Sheffield	Bank House Chambers	0114 275 1223
	St Johns Buildings	0114 273 8951
Southampton	•College Chambers	023 8023 0338
Stoke On Trent	Regent Chambers	01782 286666
Swansea	Iscoed Chambers	01792 652988
Swindon	Pump Court Chambers	01793 539899
Winchester	3 PB Barristers	01962 868884
	Pump Court Chambers	01962 868 161

LANDS TRIBUNAL

Birmingham	St Ive's Chambers	0121 236 0863
Bournemouth	3 PB Barristers	01202 292102
Bristol	3 PB Barristers	0117 928 1520
Exeter	Rougemont Chambers	01392 208484
London	•Cornerstone Barristers	020 7242 4986
	Five Paper	020 7815 3200
	Francis Taylor Building	020 7353 8415
	•Henderson Chambers	020 7583 9020
	Keating Chambers	020 7544 2600
	•Maitland Chambers	020 7406 1200
	3 PB Barristers	020 7583 8055
	•Tanfield Chambers	020 7421 5300
Manchester	18 St John Street	0161 278 1800
Newcastle Upon Tyne	Dere Street Barristers	0844 3351551
Oxford	3 PB Barristers	01865 793 736
Southampton	•College Chambers	023 8023 0338

• Expanded entry in Part D

Winchester	3 PB Barristers	01962 868884
LEASEHOLD ENFRANCHISEMENT		
Bristol	Queen Square Chambers	0117 921 1966
London	•Cornerstone Barristers	020 7242 4986
	Five Paper	020 7815 3200
	•Maitland Chambers	020 7406 1200
	•Tanfield Chambers	020 7421 5300
Manchester	18 St John Street	0161 278 1800
Newcastle Upon Tyne	Dere Street Barristers	0844 3351551
Southampton	•College Chambers	023 8023 0338
LEAVE TO REMOVE		
Birmingham	St Ive's Chambers	0121 236 0863
Bristol	Queen Square Chambers	0117 921 1966
Faringdon	Faringdon Chambers	01367 240598
London	•4 Paper Buildings	020 7427 5200
LEGAL ADVICE		
London	Five Paper	020 7815 3200
Manchester	18 St John Street	0161 278 1800
	•St Johns Buildings	0161 214 1500
Newcastle Upon Tyne	Dere Street Barristers	0844 3351551
LEGAL AID COSTS		
London	Five Paper	020 7815 3200
Manchester	18 St John Street	0161 278 1800
Newcastle Upon Tyne	Dere Street Barristers	0844 3351551
Southampton	•College Chambers	023 8023 0338
LETTERS OF CREDIT		
London	•One Essex Court	020 7583 2000
	Five Paper	020 7815 3200
LICENSING		
Birmingham	Cornwall Street Chambers	0121 233 7500
	Equity Chambers	0121 236 5007
	No 8 Chambers	0121 236 5514
	•No5 Chambers	0845 210 5555
	St Ive's Chambers	0121 236 0863
	•St Philips Chambers	0121 246 7000
Bournemouth	3 PB Barristers	01202 292102
Bradford	Broadway House Chambers	01274 722560
Brighton	Crown Office Row Chambers	01273 625625
Bristol	No5 Chambers	0845 210 5555
	3 PB Barristers	0117 928 1520
	Queen Square Chambers	0117 921 1966
	St John's Chambers	0117 923 4700
Canterbury	Becket Chambers	01227 786331
Chelmsford	Trinity Chambers	01245 605040
Chester	Linenhall Chambers	01244 348282
Chichester	Pallant Chambers	01243 784538
Exeter	Rougemont Chambers	01392 208484
	Walnut House	01392 279751
Ipswich	East Anglian Chambers	01473 214481
Leeds	Broadway House Chambers	0113 246 2600
	Enterprise Chambers	0113 246 0391
	KBW	0113 297 1200
	Kings Chambers	0845 034 3444
	Park Court Chambers	0113 243 3277
	37 Park Square Chambers	0113 243 9422
	•Sovereign Chambers	0113 245 1841
	Zenith Chambers	0113 245 5438
Liverpool	Atlantic Chambers	0151 236 4421
	•Number 7 Harrington Street Chambers	0151 242 0707

• Expanded entry in Part D

A

London	•Argent Chambers	020 7556 5500
	Atkinson Bevan Chambers	020 7353 2112
	42 Bedford Row	020 7831 0222
	•9-12 Bell Yard	020 7400 1800
	•Chambers of Mr Ami Feder	020 7797 7788
	•Cornerstone Barristers	020 7242 4986
	Enterprise Chambers	020 7405 9471
	•One Essex Court	020 7583 2000
	•23 Essex Street	020 7413 0353
	Farringdon Chambers	020 7089 5700
	Five Paper	020 7815 3200
	Francis Taylor Building	020 7353 8415
	•Goldsmith Chambers	020 7353 6802
	Gough Square Chambers	020 7353 0924
	Great James Street Chambers	020 7440 4949
	Hailsham Chambers	020 7643 5000
	•1 KBW Chambers	020 7936 1500
	13 King's Bench Walk	020 7353 7204
	•Maitland Chambers	020 7406 1200
	No5 Chambers	0845 210 5555
	12 Old Square Chambers	020 7404 0875
	3 PB Barristers	020 7583 8055
	1 Pump Court	020 7842 7070
	4 Pump Court	020 7842 5555
	•5 Pump Court	020 7353 2532
	6 Pump Court	020 7797 8400
	•Pump Court Chambers	020 7353 0711
	•QEB Hollis Whiteman	020 7933 8855
	Radcliffe Chambers	020 7831 0081
	•3 Raymond Buildings	020 7400 6400
	•Tanfield Chambers	020 7421 5300
	•Three New Square IP	020 7405 1111
Maidstone	6 Pump Court Chambers	01622 688094
Manchester	•Cobden House Chambers	0161 833 6000
	Deans Court Chambers	0161 214 6000
	Kenworthy's Chambers	0161 832 4036
	Kings Chambers	0845 034 3444
	•Lincoln House Chambers	0161 832 5701
	St James's Chambers	0161 834 7000
	9 St John Street	0161 955 9000
	18 St John Street	0161 278 1800
	•St Johns Buildings	0161 214 1500
Middlesbrough	Fountain Chambers	01642 804040
	Old Court Chambers	01642 232523
	•Trinity Chambers	01642 247569
Newcastle Upon Tyne	Dere Street Barristers	0844 3351551
	Enterprise Chambers	0191 222 3344
	•Trinity Chambers	0191 232 1927
Northampton	Chartlands Chambers	01604 603322
Norwich	Octagon House	01603 623186
Nottingham	1 High Pavement	0115 941 8218
	KCH Garden Square	0115 941 8851
Oxford	3 PB Barristers	01865 793 736
Plymouth	Devon Chambers	01752 661659
Portsmouth	Guildhall Chambers Portsmouth	023 9275 2400
Preston	Deans Court Chambers	01772 565 600
Sheffield	St Johns Buildings	0114 273 8951
Southampton	•College Chambers	023 8023 0338
Stoke On Trent	Regent Chambers	01782 286666
Swansea	Iscoed Chambers	01792 652988
Swindon	Pump Court Chambers	01793 539899
Taunton	Octagon Chambers	01823 331919
Winchester	3 PB Barristers	01962 868884
	Pump Court Chambers	01962 868 161

A

LIMITED PARTNERSHIPS

Birmingham	St Ive's Chambers	0121 236 0863
London	48 Bedford Row	020 7430 2005
	Erskine Chambers	020 7242 5532
	Five Paper	020 7815 3200
	•Maitland Chambers	020 7406 1200
Manchester	18 St John Street	0161 278 1800
Newcastle Upon Tyne	Dere Street Barristers	0844 3351551
Southampton	•College Chambers	023 8023 0338

LITIGATION

Birmingham	•St Philips Chambers	0121 246 7000
Bristol	Queen Square Chambers	0117 921 1966
Exeter	Walnut House	01392 279751
London	•Argent Chambers	020 7556 5500
	Bell Yard Chambers	020 7306 9292
	11 King's Bench Walk	020 7632 8500
	•5 Pump Court	020 7353 2532
Maidstone	Maidstone Chambers	01622 688592
Manchester	Chambers of Ian Macdonald QC	0161 236 1840
Northampton	Northampton Chambers	01604 636271
Southampton	•College Chambers	023 8023 0338

LOCAL AUTHORITIES

Birmingham	St Ive's Chambers	0121 236 0863
Bristol	Albion Chambers	0117 927 2144
	St John's Chambers	0117 923 4700
	Unity Street Chambers	0117 906 9789
Canterbury	Becket Chambers	01227 786331
Chelmsford	Trinity Chambers	01245 605040
Chester	Linenhall Chambers	01244 348282
Exeter	Rougemont Chambers	01392 208484
	Walnut House	01392 279751
Ipswich	East Anglian Chambers	01473 214481
Leeds	Kings Chambers	0845 034 3444
	Park Court Chambers	0113 243 3277
	•Sovereign Chambers	0113 245 1841
London	•Arden Chambers	020 7242 4244
	Atlas Chambers	020 7269 7980
	42 Bedford Row	020 7831 0222
	•9-12 Bell Yard	020 7400 1800
	Blackstone Chambers	020 7583 1770
	Brick Court Chambers	020 7379 3550
	•Chambers of Mr Ami Feder	020 7797 7788
	Chambers of Mr Patrick Ground QC	020 7736 0131
	•Charter Chambers	020 7618 4400
	•Cornerstone Barristers	020 7242 4986
	•Devereux Chambers	020 7353 7534
	Doughty Street Chambers	020 7404 1313
	•39 Essex Street	020 7832 1111
	Five Paper	020 7815 3200
	Francis Taylor Building	020 7353 8415
	1 Garden Court Family Law Chambers	020 7797 7900
	•Goldsmith Chambers	020 7353 6802
	•4-5 Gray's Inn Square	020 7404 5252
	Harcourt Chambers	0844 561 7135
	•Henderson Chambers	020 7583 9020
	•1 KBW Chambers	020 7936 1500
	Keating Chambers	020 7544 2600
	13 King's Bench Walk	020 7353 7204
	Lamb Chambers	020 7797 8300
	•Maitland Chambers	020 7406 1200
	Matrix Chambers	020 7404 3447
	New Square Chambers	020 7419 8000

• Expanded entry in Part D

	Outer Temple Chambers	020 7353 6381
	1 Pump Court	020 7842 7070
	6 Pump Court	020 7797 8400
	Radcliffe Chambers	020 7831 0081
	•Tanfield Chambers	020 7421 5300
	•Wilberforce Chambers	020 7306 0102
Maidstone	6 Pump Court Chambers	01622 688094
Manchester	Byrom Street Chambers	0161 829 2100
	Kings Chambers	0845 034 3444
	•Lincoln House Chambers	0161 832 5701
	18 St John Street	0161 278 1800
	•St Johns Buildings	0161 214 1500
Middlesbrough	Old Court Chambers	01642 232523
	•Trinity Chambers	01642 247569
Newcastle Upon Tyne	Dere Street Barristers	0844 3351551
	•Trinity Chambers	0191 232 1927
Oxford	Harcourt Chambers	0844 561 7135
Plymouth	Devon Chambers	01752 661659
Southampton	•College Chambers	023 8023 0338
Swansea	Iscoed Chambers	01792 652988

LOCAL AUTHORITY CLAIMS

Bristol	Queen Square Chambers	0117 921 1966
London	•Arden Chambers	020 7242 4244
	1 Chancery Lane	0845 634 6666
	•Cornerstone Barristers	020 7242 4986
	Five Paper	020 7815 3200
	•Henderson Chambers	020 7583 9020
Manchester	18 St John Street	0161 278 1800
Newcastle Upon Tyne	Dere Street Barristers	0844 3351551

LOCAL AUTHORITY LIABILITY

Bristol	Queen Square Chambers	0117 921 1966
London	•Cornerstone Barristers	020 7242 4986
	Five Paper	020 7815 3200
	•Henderson Chambers	020 7583 9020
	The Chambers of Grahame Aldous QC	020 7832 0500
Manchester	18 St John Street	0161 278 1800
Newcastle Upon Tyne	Dere Street Barristers	0844 3351551

LOCAL GOVERNMENT AND PUBLIC SERVICES

Birmingham	•St Philips Chambers	0121 246 7000
Exeter	Walnut House	01392 279751
London	•Argent Chambers	020 7556 5500
	11 King's Bench Walk	020 7632 8500
	Matrix Chambers	020 7404 3447
Manchester	Chambers of Ian Macdonald QC	0161 236 1840
Southampton	•College Chambers	023 8023 0338

LOCAL GOVERNMENT FINANCE

London	•Cornerstone Barristers	020 7242 4986
	Five Paper	020 7815 3200
	•Henderson Chambers	020 7583 9020
Manchester	18 St John Street	0161 278 1800
Newcastle Upon Tyne	Dere Street Barristers	0844 3351551

MALICIOUS FALSEHOOD

Bristol	Queen Square Chambers	0117 921 1966
London	•8 New Square	020 7405 4321
Manchester	18 St John Street	0161 278 1800
Newcastle Upon Tyne	Dere Street Barristers	0844 3351551
Southampton	•College Chambers	023 8023 0338

MALICIOUS PROSECUTION

Bristol	Queen Square Chambers	0117 921 1966

A

Exeter	Walnut House	01392 279751
London	Bell Yard Chambers	020 7306 9292
	•Charter Chambers	020 7618 4400
	•23 Essex Street	020 7413 0353
	•187 Fleet Street	020 7430 7430
	•1 KBW Chambers	020 7936 1500
	15 New Bridge Street	020 7842 1900
	The Chambers of Grahame Aldous QC	020 7832 0500
Manchester	Chambers of Ian Macdonald QC	0161 236 1840
	18 St John Street	0161 278 1800
	•St Johns Buildings	0161 214 1500
Newcastle Upon Tyne	Dere Street Barristers	0844 3351551

MARKETS AND FAIRS

Manchester	•St Johns Buildings	0161 214 1500
Newcastle Upon Tyne	Dere Street Barristers	0844 3351551

MATRIMONIAL

Birmingham	St Ive's Chambers	0121 236 0863
Brighton	Crown Office Row Chambers	01273 625625
Bristol	Queen Square Chambers	0117 921 1966
Exeter	Rougemont Chambers	01392 208484
	Walnut House	01392 279751
Faringdon	Faringdon Chambers	01367 240598
London	•29 Bedford Row Chambers	020 7404 1044
	Bell Yard Chambers	020 7306 9292
	Five Paper	020 7815 3200
	•1 KBW Chambers	020 7936 1500
Manchester	18 St John Street	0161 278 1800
	•St Johns Buildings	0161 214 1500
Newcastle Upon Tyne	Dere Street Barristers	0844 3351551
Portsmouth	Guildhall Chambers Portsmouth	023 9275 2400
	Portsmouth Barristers'Chambers	023 9283 1292
Sheffield	Bank House Chambers	0114 275 1223
Southampton	•College Chambers	023 8023 0338

MATRIMONIAL FINANCE

Birmingham	St Ive's Chambers	0121 236 0863
	•St Philips Chambers	0121 246 7000
Bournemouth	3 PB Barristers	01202 292102
Bristol	3 PB Barristers	0117 928 1520
	Queen Square Chambers	0117 921 1966
Exeter	Rougemont Chambers	01392 208484
Faringdon	Faringdon Chambers	01367 240598
Leeds	37 Park Square Chambers	0113 243 9422
London	•29 Bedford Row Chambers	020 7404 1044
	Bell Yard Chambers	020 7306 9292
	1 Crown Office Row	020 7797 7500
	Five Paper	020 7815 3200
	•1 KBW Chambers	020 7936 1500
	3 PB Barristers	020 7583 8055
	The Chambers of Grahame Aldous QC	020 7832 0500
Manchester	18 St John Street	0161 278 1800
Newcastle Upon Tyne	Dere Street Barristers	0844 3351551
Oxford	3 PB Barristers	01865 793 736
Portsmouth	Guildhall Chambers Portsmouth	023 9275 2400
	Portsmouth Barristers'Chambers	023 9283 1292
Southampton	•College Chambers	023 8023 0338
Winchester	3 PB Barristers	01962 868884

MEDIA

London	•Argent Chambers	020 7556 5500
	•One Essex Court	020 7583 2000
	Essex Court Chambers	020 7813 8000
	•23 Essex Street	020 7413 0353

• Expanded entry in Part D

	4 King's Bench Walk	020 7822 7000
	•Maitland Chambers	020 7406 1200
	Matrix Chambers	020 7404 3447
	11 Stone Buildings	020 7831 6381
Manchester	18 St John Street	0161 278 1800
	•St Johns Buildings	0161 214 1500

MEDIA AND ENTERTAINMENT

Birmingham	Cornwall Street Chambers	0121 233 7500
London	Blackstone Chambers	020 7583 1770
	Brick Court Chambers	020 7379 3550
	Doughty Street Chambers	020 7404 1313
	•39 Essex Street	020 7832 1111
	Fountain Court Chambers	020 7583 3335
	•Maitland Chambers	020 7406 1200
	•8 New Square	020 7405 4321
	Serle Court	020 7242 6105
	3 Stone Buildings	020 7242 4937
	•9 Stone Buildings	020 7404 5055
	•Three New Square IP	020 7405 1111
Manchester	18 St John Street	0161 278 1800
	•St Johns Buildings	0161 214 1500

MEDIATION

Birmingham	St Ive's Chambers	0121 236 0863
Bournemouth	3 PB Barristers	01202 292102
Brighton	Crown Office Row Chambers	01273 625625
Bristol	3 PB Barristers	0117 928 1520
	Queen Square Chambers	0117 921 1966
Canterbury	Becket Chambers	01227 786331
Exeter	Rougemont Chambers	01392 208484
Leeds	Enterprise Chambers	0113 246 0391
London	Arbitration Chambers	020 7267 2137
	Bell Yard Chambers	020 7306 9292
	Blackstone Chambers	020 7583 1770
	•Chambers of Mr Ami Feder	020 7797 7788
	•Crown Office Chambers	020 7797 8100
	1 Crown Office Row	020 7797 7500
	Enterprise Chambers	020 7405 9471
	•One Essex Court	020 7583 2000
	•39 Essex Street	020 7832 1111
	Five Paper	020 7815 3200
	•Henderson Chambers	020 7583 9020
	•1 KBW Chambers	020 7936 1500
	Matrix Chambers	020 7404 3447
	•13 Old Square Chambers	020 7831 4445
	3 PB Barristers	020 7583 8055
	•5 Pump Court	020 7353 2532
	6 Pump Court	020 7797 8400
	•Pump Court Tax Chambers	020 7414 8080
	Serle Court	020 7242 6105
	3 Stone Buildings	020 7242 4937
	•Tanfield Chambers	020 7421 5300
	The Chambers of Grahame Aldous QC	020 7832 0500
	XXIV Old Buildings	020 7691 2424
Maidstone	6 Pump Court Chambers	01622 688094
Manchester	Byrom Street Chambers	0161 829 2100
	18 St John Street	0161 278 1800
Middlesbrough	•Trinity Chambers	01642 247569
Newcastle Upon Tyne	Enterprise Chambers	0191 222 3344
Nottingham	KCH Garden Square	0115 941 8851
Oxford	3 PB Barristers	01865 793 736
Portsmouth	Portsmouth Barristers'Chambers	023 9283 1292
Southampton	•College Chambers	023 8023 0338

Winchester	3 PB Barristers	01962 868884

MEDICAL LAW

Exeter	Rougemont Chambers	01392 208484
London	1 Crown Office Row	020 7797 7500
	Hailsham Chambers	020 7643 5000
	•Henderson Chambers	020 7583 9020
	13 King's Bench Walk	020 7353 7204
Manchester	Byrom Street Chambers	0161 829 2100
	18 St John Street	0161 278 1800
Middlesbrough	•Trinity Chambers	01642 247569
Newcastle Upon Tyne	•Trinity Chambers	0191 232 1927
Southampton	•College Chambers	023 8023 0338

MEDICAL NEGLIGENCE

Birmingham	No 8 Chambers	0121 236 5514
	•St Philips Chambers	0121 246 7000
Bournemouth	3 PB Barristers	01202 292102
Bradford	Broadway House Chambers	01274 722560
Bristol	3 PB Barristers	0117 928 1520
	Queen Square Chambers	0117 921 1966
	St John's Chambers	0117 923 4700
	Unity Street Chambers	0117 906 9789
Chelmsford	Trinity Chambers	01245 605040
Chester	Linenhall Chambers	01244 348282
Chichester	Pallant Chambers	01243 784538
Exeter	Rougemont Chambers	01392 208484
	Walnut House	01392 279751
Ipswich	East Anglian Chambers	01473 214481
Leeds	Broadway House Chambers	0113 246 2600
	Chancery House Chambers	0113 244 6691
	KBW	0113 297 1200
	Kings Chambers	0845 034 3444
	Park Court Chambers	0113 243 3277
	37 Park Square Chambers	0113 243 9422
	•Sovereign Chambers	0113 245 1841
	Zenith Chambers	0113 245 5438
Lewes	Westgate Chambers	01273 480510
Liverpool	Atlantic Chambers	0151 236 4421
	•Number 7 Harrington Street Chambers	0151 242 0707
London	42 Bedford Row	020 7831 0222
	•Chambers of Mr Ami Feder	020 7797 7788
	1 Chancery Lane	0845 634 6666
	•Charter Chambers	020 7618 4400
	•Devereux Chambers	020 7353 7534
	Doughty Street Chambers	020 7404 1313
	•39 Essex Street	020 7832 1111
	Fountain Court Chambers	020 7583 3335
	Hailsham Chambers	020 7643 5000
	Harcourt Chambers	0844 561 7135
	•Henderson Chambers	020 7583 9020
	•1 KBW Chambers	020 7936 1500
	Lamb Chambers	020 7797 8300
	New Square Chambers	020 7419 8000
	12 Old Square Chambers	020 7404 0875
	3 PB Barristers	020 7583 8055
	4 Pump Court	020 7842 5555
	6 Pump Court	020 7797 8400
	•Pump Court Chambers	020 7353 0711
	•9 Stone Buildings	020 7404 5055
	•Tanfield Chambers	020 7421 5300
	The Chambers of Grahame Aldous QC	020 7832 0500
Maidstone	6 Pump Court Chambers	01622 688094
Manchester	Byrom Street Chambers	0161 829 2100

• Expanded entry in Part D

	•Cobden House Chambers	0161 833 6000
	Deans Court Chambers	0161 214 6000
	Kings Chambers	0845 034 3444
	•Lincoln House Chambers	0161 832 5701
	St James's Chambers	0161 834 7000
	9 St John Street	0161 955 9000
	18 St John Street	0161 278 1800
	•St Johns Buildings	0161 214 1500
Middlesbrough	Fountain Chambers	01642 804040
	Old Court Chambers	01642 232523
	•Trinity Chambers	01642 247569
Newcastle Upon Tyne	Dere Street Barristers	0844 3351551
	•Trinity Chambers	0191 232 1927
Nottingham	KCH Garden Square	0115 941 8851
Oxford	Harcourt Chambers	0844 561 7135
	3 PB Barristers	01865 793 736
Plymouth	Devon Chambers	01752 661659
Portsmouth	Guildhall Chambers Portsmouth	023 9275 2400
	Portsmouth Barristers'Chambers	023 9283 1292
Preston	Deans Court Chambers	01772 565 600
Southampton	•College Chambers	023 8023 0338
Swansea	Iscoed Chambers	01792 652988
Swindon	Pump Court Chambers	01793 539899
Taunton	Octagon Chambers	01823 331919
Winchester	3 PB Barristers	01962 868884
	Pump Court Chambers	01962 868 161

MEDICINES ACT

London	•Henderson Chambers	020 7583 9020
	The Chambers of Grahame Aldous QC	020 7832 0500
Manchester	18 St John Street	0161 278 1800
Middlesbrough	•Trinity Chambers	01642 247569
Newcastle Upon Tyne	•Trinity Chambers	0191 232 1927

MENTAL HEALTH

Birmingham	Cornwall Street Chambers	0121 233 7500
	St Ive's Chambers	0121 236 0863
	•St Philips Chambers	0121 246 7000
Bradford	Broadway House Chambers	01274 722560
Bristol	Albion Chambers	0117 927 2144
	St John's Chambers	0117 923 4700
Chelmsford	Trinity Chambers	01245 605040
Exeter	Rougemont Chambers	01392 208484
	Walnut House	01392 279751
Ipswich	East Anglian Chambers	01473 214481
Leeds	Broadway House Chambers	0113 246 2600
	Park Court Chambers	0113 243 3277
	Zenith Chambers	0113 245 5438
Liverpool	Atlantic Chambers	0151 236 4421
London	•Arden Chambers	020 7242 4244
	Atkinson Bevan Chambers	020 7353 2112
	42 Bedford Row	020 7831 0222
	•9-12 Bell Yard	020 7400 1800
	•Chambers of Marion Smullen and Kerim Fuad QC	020 7427 4400
	•Chambers of Mr Ami Feder	020 7797 7788
	1 Chancery Lane	0845 634 6666
	1 Crown Office Row	020 7797 7500
	•Devereux Chambers	020 7353 7534
	Doughty Street Chambers	020 7404 1313
	•39 Essex Street	020 7832 1111
	Farringdon Chambers	020 7089 5700
	Five Paper	020 7815 3200
	1 Garden Court Family Law Chambers	020 7797 7900

	•Goldsmith Chambers	020 7353 6802
	14 Gray's Inn Square	020 7242 0858
	Hailsham Chambers	020 7643 5000
	•1 KBW Chambers	020 7936 1500
	Lamb Chambers	020 7797 8300
	Matrix Chambers	020 7404 3447
	New Square Chambers	020 7419 8000
	1 Pump Court	020 7842 7070
	•5 Pump Court	020 7353 2532
	Renaissance Chambers	020 7404 1111
Manchester	Byrom Street Chambers	0161 829 2100
	Central Chambers	0161 236 1133
	Chambers of Ian Macdonald QC	0161 236 1840
	Kenworthy's Chambers	0161 832 4036
	•Lincoln House Chambers	0161 832 5701
	St James's Chambers	0161 834 7000
	9 St John Street	0161 955 9000
	18 St John Street	0161 278 1800
	•St Johns Buildings	0161 214 1500
Middlesbrough	Fountain Chambers	01642 804040
	Old Court Chambers	01642 232523
	•Trinity Chambers	01642 247569
Newcastle Upon Tyne	Dere Street Barristers	0844 3351551
	•Trinity Chambers	0191 232 1927
Northampton	Chartlands Chambers	01604 603322
	Northampton Chambers	01604 636271
Nottingham	KCH Garden Square	0115 941 8851
Plymouth	Devon Chambers	01752 661659
Southampton	•College Chambers	023 8023 0338
Taunton	Octagon Chambers	01823 331919

MERGERS AND ACQUISITIONS

London	Erskine Chambers	020 7242 5532
	•One Essex Court	020 7583 2000
Manchester	18 St John Street	0161 278 1800

MIDDLE EASTERN LAW

Bournemouth	3 PB Barristers	01202 292102
Bristol	3 PB Barristers	0117 928 1520
London	3 PB Barristers	020 7583 8055
	•Tanfield Chambers	020 7421 5300
Oxford	3 PB Barristers	01865 793 736
Winchester	3 PB Barristers	01962 868884

MILITARY LAW

Birmingham	St Ive's Chambers	0121 236 0863
Bournemouth	3 PB Barristers	01202 292102
Bristol	3 PB Barristers	0117 928 1520
Exeter	Walnut House	01392 279751
London	1 Crown Office Row	020 7797 7500
	•23 Essex Street	020 7413 0353
	15 New Bridge Street	020 7842 1900
	3 PB Barristers	020 7583 8055
Manchester	Chambers of Ian Macdonald QC	0161 236 1840
	18 St John Street	0161 278 1800
	•St Johns Buildings	0161 214 1500
Newcastle Upon Tyne	Dere Street Barristers	0844 3351551
Oxford	3 PB Barristers	01865 793 736
Winchester	3 PB Barristers	01962 868884

MINERAL RIGHTS

London	•Cornerstone Barristers	020 7242 4986
Newcastle Upon Tyne	Dere Street Barristers	0844 3351551

• Expanded entry in Part D

MINING

London	•Cornerstone Barristers	020 7242 4986
	•Maitland Chambers	020 7406 1200
	Radcliffe Chambers	020 7831 0081
Manchester	•St Johns Buildings	0161 214 1500
Newcastle Upon Tyne	Dere Street Barristers	0844 3351551

MONEY LAUNDERING

Birmingham	•St Philips Chambers	0121 246 7000
Bristol	Queen Square Chambers	0117 921 1966
London	•2 Bedford Row	020 7440 8888
	•23 Essex Street	020 7413 0353
	•Furnival Chambers	020 7405 3232
	Middle Temple Lane Chambers	020 7583 4352
	15 New Bridge Street	020 7842 1900
	Outer Temple Chambers	020 7353 6381
	•3 Raymond Buildings	020 7400 6400
	XXIV Old Buildings	020 7691 2424
Manchester	18 St John Street	0161 278 1800
	•St Johns Buildings	0161 214 1500
Middlesbrough	•Trinity Chambers	01642 247569
Newcastle Upon Tyne	•Trinity Chambers	0191 232 1927

MORTGAGES

London	•Arden Chambers	020 7242 4244
	Five Paper	020 7815 3200
	•Henderson Chambers	020 7583 9020
	•Maitland Chambers	020 7406 1200
	11 Stone Buildings	020 7831 6381
	•Tanfield Chambers	020 7421 5300
Manchester	Chambers of Ian Macdonald QC	0161 236 1840
	18 St John Street	0161 278 1800
Newcastle Upon Tyne	Dere Street Barristers	0844 3351551
Portsmouth	Portsmouth Barristers' Chambers	023 9283 1292
Southampton	•College Chambers	023 8023 0338

MOTOR VEHICLES

Birmingham	St Ive's Chambers	0121 236 0863
Bristol	Queen Square Chambers	0117 921 1966
London	Bell Yard Chambers	020 7306 9292
	•23 Essex Street	020 7413 0353
	•187 Fleet Street	020 7430 7430
	•Henderson Chambers	020 7583 9020
	15 New Bridge Street	020 7842 1900
	The Chambers of Grahame Aldous QC	020 7832 0500
Manchester	Chambers of Ian Macdonald QC	0161 236 1840
	18 St John Street	0161 278 1800
Newcastle Upon Tyne	Dere Street Barristers	0844 3351551
Portsmouth	Guildhall Chambers Portsmouth	023 9275 2400

MULTI-PARTY LITIGATION

Bournemouth	3 PB Barristers	01202 292102
Bristol	3 PB Barristers	0117 928 1520
London	Five Paper	020 7815 3200
	•Henderson Chambers	020 7583 9020
	3 PB Barristers	020 7583 8055
	XXIV Old Buildings	020 7691 2424
Manchester	18 St John Street	0161 278 1800
	•St Johns Buildings	0161 214 1500
Newcastle Upon Tyne	Dere Street Barristers	0844 3351551
Oxford	3 PB Barristers	01865 793 736
Portsmouth	Portsmouth Barristers' Chambers	023 9283 1292
Winchester	3 PB Barristers	01962 868884

A

NATIONAL INSURANCE

London	Prince Henry's Chambers	020 7837 1645
	•Pump Court Tax Chambers	020 7414 8080
Manchester	•St Johns Buildings	0161 214 1500

NATURAL RESOURCES

London	6 Pump Court	020 7797 8400
Maidstone	6 Pump Court Chambers	01622 688094

NEPALESE LAW

London	•Tanfield Chambers	020 7421 5300

NHS INQUIRIES

London	•Henderson Chambers	020 7583 9020
	The Chambers of Grahame Aldous QC	020 7832 0500
Manchester	18 St John Street	0161 278 1800

NIGER LAW

London	•Tanfield Chambers	020 7421 5300

NIGERIAN LAW

London	Middle Temple Lane Chambers	020 7583 4352

OCCUPATIONAL DISEASES

Bournemouth	3 PB Barristers	01202 292102
Bristol	3 PB Barristers	0117 928 1520
	Queen Square Chambers	0117 921 1966
Leeds	KBW	0113 297 1200
	37 Park Square Chambers	0113 243 9422
London	•Henderson Chambers	020 7583 9020
	3 PB Barristers	020 7583 8055
	The Chambers of Grahame Aldous QC	020 7832 0500
Manchester	18 St John Street	0161 278 1800
Newcastle Upon Tyne	Dere Street Barristers	0844 3351551
Oxford	3 PB Barristers	01865 793 736
Southampton	•College Chambers	023 8023 0338
Winchester	3 PB Barristers	01962 868884

OFFSHORE FINANCE

London	Erskine Chambers	020 7242 5532
	•Maitland Chambers	020 7406 1200
	XXIV Old Buildings	020 7691 2424

OFFSHORE INVESTMENT

London	Erskine Chambers	020 7242 5532
	•Maitland Chambers	020 7406 1200
	XXIV Old Buildings	020 7691 2424

OFFSHORE TRUST LITIGATION

London	•Maitland Chambers	020 7406 1200
	XXIV Old Buildings	020 7691 2424
Manchester	•St Johns Buildings	0161 214 1500
Newcastle Upon Tyne	Dere Street Barristers	0844 3351551
Southampton	•College Chambers	023 8023 0338

OIL AND GAS LAW

London	•Henderson Chambers	020 7583 9020
	•Tanfield Chambers	020 7421 5300

OMBUDSMAN

London	Five Paper	020 7815 3200
	•Henderson Chambers	020 7583 9020
Manchester	Chambers of Ian Macdonald QC	0161 236 1840
	18 St John Street	0161 278 1800
Newcastle Upon Tyne	Dere Street Barristers	0844 3351551

• Expanded entry in Part D

Southampton	•College Chambers	023 8023 0338
OVERSEAS ACCIDENTS		
London	•Cornerstone Barristers	020 7242 4986
	•Henderson Chambers	020 7583 9020
	The Chambers of Grahame Aldous QC	020 7832 0500
Manchester	18 St John Street	0161 278 1800
Newcastle Upon Tyne	Dere Street Barristers	0844 3351551
Southampton	•College Chambers	023 8023 0338
PARLIAMENTARY		
Exeter	Rougemont Chambers	01392 208484
Leeds	Kings Chambers	0845 034 3444
London	•Cornerstone Barristers	020 7242 4986
	•39 Essex Street	020 7832 1111
	Francis Taylor Building	020 7353 8415
	•Goldsmith Chambers	020 7353 6802
	•4-5 Gray's Inn Square	020 7404 5252
	•Henderson Chambers	020 7583 9020
	•1 KBW Chambers	020 7936 1500
	New Square Chambers	020 7419 8000
	6 Pump Court	020 7797 8400
	Serle Court	020 7242 6105
Maidstone	6 Pump Court Chambers	01622 688094
Manchester	Kings Chambers	0845 034 3444
	•St Johns Buildings	0161 214 1500
PARTNERSHIPS		
Birmingham	•No5 Chambers	0845 210 5555
	St Ive's Chambers	0121 236 0863
	•St Philips Chambers	0121 246 7000
Bournemouth	3 PB Barristers	01202 292102
Bradford	Broadway House Chambers	01274 722560
Bristol	No5 Chambers	0845 210 5555
	3 PB Barristers	0117 928 1520
	St John's Chambers	0117 923 4700
	Unity Street Chambers	0117 906 9789
Canterbury	Becket Chambers	01227 786331
Chester	Linenhall Chambers	01244 348282
Chichester	Pallant Chambers	01243 784538
Exeter	Rougemont Chambers	01392 208484
	Walnut House	01392 279751
Leeds	Broadway House Chambers	0113 246 2600
	Chancery House Chambers	0113 244 6691
	Enterprise Chambers	0113 246 0391
	KBW	0113 297 1200
	Kings Chambers	0845 034 3444
	Park Court Chambers	0113 243 3277
	37 Park Square Chambers	0113 243 9422
	•Sovereign Chambers	0113 245 1841
	Zenith Chambers	0113 245 5438
Liverpool	Atlantic Chambers	0151 236 4421
London	Atlas Chambers	020 7269 7980
	42 Bedford Row	020 7831 0222
	48 Bedford Row	020 7430 2005
	Blackstone Chambers	020 7583 1770
	•Chambers of Mr Ami Feder	020 7797 7788
	Enterprise Chambers	020 7405 9471
	Erskine Chambers	020 7242 5532
	•One Essex Court	020 7583 2000
	Five Paper	020 7815 3200
	•Goldsmith Chambers	020 7353 6802
	Hailsham Chambers	020 7643 5000
	13 King's Bench Walk	020 7353 7204

	Lamb Chambers	020 7797 8300
	•Maitland Chambers	020 7406 1200
	New Square Chambers	020 7419 8000
	No5 Chambers	0845 210 5555
	•13 Old Square Chambers	020 7831 4445
	Outer Temple Chambers	020 7353 6381
	•4 Paper Buildings	020 7427 5200
	3 PB Barristers	020 7583 8055
	•5 Pump Court	020 7353 2532
	Radcliffe Chambers	020 7831 0081
	Selborne Chambers	020 7420 9500
	Serle Court	020 7242 6105
	•South Square	020 7696 9900
	3 Stone Buildings	020 7242 4937
	4 Stone Buildings	020 7242 5524
	•9 Stone Buildings	020 7404 5055
	•Tanfield Chambers	020 7421 5300
	Ten Old Square	020 7405 0758
	3 Verulam Buildings	020 7831 8441
	XXIV Old Buildings	020 7691 2424
Manchester	•Cobden House Chambers	0161 833 6000
	Kings Chambers	0845 034 3444
	St James's Chambers	0161 834 7000
	18 St John Street	0161 278 1800
	•St Johns Buildings	0161 214 1500
Middlesbrough	•Trinity Chambers	01642 247569
Newcastle Upon Tyne	Dere Street Barristers	0844 3351551
	Enterprise Chambers	0191 222 3344
	•Trinity Chambers	0191 232 1927
Northampton	Chartlands Chambers	01604 603322
Nottingham	KCH Garden Square	0115 941 8851
Oxford	3 PB Barristers	01865 793 736
Portsmouth	Guildhall Chambers Portsmouth	023 9275 2400
	Portsmouth Barristers'Chambers	023 9283 1292
Southampton	•College Chambers	023 8023 0338
Swansea	Iscoed Chambers	01792 652988
Winchester	3 PB Barristers	01962 868884

PASSING OFF

Bournemouth	3 PB Barristers	01202 292102
Bristol	3 PB Barristers	0117 928 1520
London	Blackstone Chambers	020 7583 1770
	•Maitland Chambers	020 7406 1200
	•8 New Square	020 7405 4321
	•13 Old Square Chambers	020 7831 4445
	3 PB Barristers	020 7583 8055
	•Tanfield Chambers	020 7421 5300
Manchester	18 St John Street	0161 278 1800
	•St Johns Buildings	0161 214 1500
Newcastle Upon Tyne	Dere Street Barristers	0844 3351551
Oxford	3 PB Barristers	01865 793 736
Portsmouth	Portsmouth Barristers'Chambers	023 9283 1292
Winchester	3 PB Barristers	01962 868884

PATENTS

Birmingham	•No5 Chambers	0845 210 5555
Bristol	No5 Chambers	0845 210 5555
	St John's Chambers	0117 923 4700
Leeds	Chancery House Chambers	0113 244 6691
	Kings Chambers	0845 034 3444
	•Sovereign Chambers	0113 245 1841
London	Fountain Court Chambers	020 7583 3335
	•8 New Square	020 7405 4321
	No5 Chambers	0845 210 5555

• Expanded entry in Part D

	11 South Square	020 7405 1222
	•Three New Square IP	020 7405 1111
Manchester	•Cobden House Chambers	0161 833 6000
	Kings Chambers	0845 034 3444
	St James's Chambers	0161 834 7000
	18 St John Street	0161 278 1800
	•St Johns Buildings	0161 214 1500

PENSIONS

Birmingham	Cornwall Street Chambers	0121 233 7500
	No 8 Chambers	0121 236 5514
	•St Philips Chambers	0121 246 7000
Bristol	Queen Square Chambers	0117 921 1966
	St John's Chambers	0117 923 4700
Exeter	Walnut House	01392 279751
Leeds	KBW	0113 297 1200
	Kings Chambers	0845 034 3444
Liverpool	Atlantic Chambers	0151 236 4421
London	•29 Bedford Row Chambers	020 7404 1044
	•Devereux Chambers	020 7353 7534
	•One Essex Court	020 7583 2000
	Five Paper	020 7815 3200
	•Goldsmith Chambers	020 7353 6802
	Gough Square Chambers	020 7353 0924
	•Maitland Chambers	020 7406 1200
	New Square Chambers	020 7419 8000
	Outer Temple Chambers	020 7353 6381
	Radcliffe Chambers	020 7831 0081
	Selborne Chambers	020 7420 9500
	•South Square	020 7696 9900
	3 Stone Buildings	020 7242 4937
	Taxchambers	020 7242 2744
	Temple Tax Chambers	020 7353 7884
	Ten Old Square	020 7405 0758
	3 Verulam Buildings	020 7831 8441
	•Wilberforce Chambers	020 7306 0102
	XXIV Old Buildings	020 7691 2424
Manchester	Chambers of Ian Macdonald QC	0161 236 1840
	•Cobden House Chambers	0161 833 6000
	Kings Chambers	0845 034 3444
	St James's Chambers	0161 834 7000
	18 St John Street	0161 278 1800
	•St Johns Buildings	0161 214 1500
Newcastle Upon Tyne	Dere Street Barristers	0844 3351551
Portsmouth	Portsmouth Barristers'Chambers	023 9283 1292

PERFORMANCE BONDS

London	•One Essex Court	020 7583 2000
	Keating Chambers	020 7544 2600
Manchester	18 St John Street	0161 278 1800

PERSONAL INJURY

Birmingham	Cornwall Street Chambers	0121 233 7500
	Equity Chambers	0121 236 5007
	No 8 Chambers	0121 236 5514
	•No5 Chambers	0845 210 5555
	St Ive's Chambers	0121 236 0863
	•St Philips Chambers	0121 246 7000
Bournemouth	3 PB Barristers	01202 292102
Bradford	Broadway House Chambers	01274 722560
Brighton	Crown Office Row Chambers	01273 625625
Bristol	Albion Chambers	0117 927 2144
	No5 Chambers	0845 210 5555
	3 PB Barristers	0117 928 1520

A

	Queen Square Chambers	0117 921 1966
	St John's Chambers	0117 923 4700
	Unity Street Chambers	0117 906 9789
Canterbury	Becket Chambers	01227 786331
Chelmsford	Trinity Chambers	01245 605040
Chester	Linenhall Chambers	01244 348282
Chichester	Pallant Chambers	01243 784538
Exeter	Rougemont Chambers	01392 208484
	Walnut House	01392 279751
Hull	Wilberforce Chambers	01482 323264
Ipswich	East Anglian Chambers	01473 214481
Kew	Kew Chambers	0844 8099991
Leeds	Broadway House Chambers	0113 246 2600
	Chancery House Chambers	0113 244 6691
	KBW	0113 297 1200
	Kings Chambers	0845 034 3444
	Park Court Chambers	0113 243 3277
	37 Park Square Chambers	0113 243 9422
	•Sovereign Chambers	0113 245 1841
	Zenith Chambers	0113 245 5438
Lewes	Westgate Chambers	01273 480510
Liverpool	Atlantic Chambers	0151 236 4421
	•Number 7 Harrington Street Chambers	0151 242 0707
	•Oriel Chambers	0151 236 7191
London	•Argent Chambers	020 7556 5500
	42 Bedford Row	020 7831 0222
	•9-12 Bell Yard	020 7400 1800
	1 Chancery Lane	0845 634 6666
	•Charter Chambers	020 7618 4400
	•Cornerstone Barristers	020 7242 4986
	•Crown Office Chambers	020 7797 8100
	1 Crown Office Row	020 7797 7500
	•Devereux Chambers	020 7353 7534
	Doughty Street Chambers	020 7404 1313
	•2 Dr Johnson's Buildings	020 7936 2613
	•3 Dr Johnson's Buildings	020 7353 4854
	•39 Essex Street	020 7832 1111
	•Farrar's Building	020 7583 9241
	•Goldsmith Chambers	020 7353 6802
	14 Gray's Inn Square	020 7242 0858
	Hailsham Chambers	020 7643 5000
	Harcourt Chambers	0844 561 7135
	•Henderson Chambers	020 7583 9020
	•1 KBW Chambers	020 7936 1500
	4 King's Bench Walk	020 7822 7000
	12 King's Bench Walk	020 7583 0811
	13 King's Bench Walk	020 7353 7204
	Lamb Chambers	020 7797 8300
	Middle Temple Lane Chambers	020 7583 4352
	No5 Chambers	0845 210 5555
	12 Old Square Chambers	020 7404 0875
	Outer Temple Chambers	020 7353 6381
	3 PB Barristers	020 7583 8055
	1 Pump Court	020 7842 7070
	4 Pump Court	020 7842 5555
	•5 Pump Court	020 7353 2532
	6 Pump Court	020 7797 8400
	•Pump Court Chambers	020 7353 0711
	•9 Stone Buildings	020 7404 5055
	•Tanfield Chambers	020 7421 5300
	•Temple Garden Chambers	020 7583 1315
	The Chambers of Grahame Aldous QC	020 7832 0500
Maidstone	Maidstone Chambers	01622 688592
	6 Pump Court Chambers	01622 688094

• Expanded entry in Part D

Manchester	Byrom Street Chambers	0161 829 2100
	Central Chambers	0161 236 1133
	Chambers of Ian Macdonald QC	0161 236 1840
	•Cobden House Chambers	0161 833 6000
	Deans Court Chambers	0161 214 6000
	Kenworthy's Chambers	0161 832 4036
	Kings Chambers	0845 034 3444
	•Lincoln House Chambers	0161 832 5701
	St James's Chambers	0161 834 7000
	9 St John Street	0161 955 9000
	18 St John Street	0161 278 1800
	•St Johns Buildings	0161 214 1500
Middlesbrough	Fountain Chambers	01642 804040
	Old Court Chambers	01642 232523
	•Trinity Chambers	01642 247569
Newcastle Upon Tyne	Cathedral Chambers	0191 232 1311
	Dere Street Barristers	0844 3351551
	•Trinity Chambers	0191 232 1927
Northampton	Chartlands Chambers	01604 603322
	Northampton Chambers	01604 636271
Norwich	Octagon House	01603 623186
Nottingham	KCH Garden Square	0115 941 8851
Oxford	Harcourt Chambers	0844 561 7135
	3 PB Barristers	01865 793 736
Pitstone	Victor House Chambers	01296 664043
Plymouth	Devon Chambers	01752 661659
Portsmouth	Guildhall Chambers Portsmouth	023 9275 2400
	Portsmouth Barristers'Chambers	023 9283 1292
Preston	Deans Court Chambers	01772 565 600
Sheffield	Bank House Chambers	0114 275 1223
	St Johns Buildings	0114 273 8951
Southampton	•College Chambers	023 8023 0338
Stoke On Trent	Regent Chambers	01782 286666
Swansea	Iscoed Chambers	01792 652988
Swindon	Pump Court Chambers	01793 539899
Taunton	Octagon Chambers	01823 331919
Winchester	3 PB Barristers	01962 868884
	Pump Court Chambers	01962 868 161

PERSONAL INJURY AND TORTS

Exeter	Walnut House	01392 279751

PERSONAL INSOLVENCY

Birmingham	No 8 Chambers	0121 236 5514
	•No5 Chambers	0845 210 5555
	•St Philips Chambers	0121 246 7000
Bournemouth	3 PB Barristers	01202 292102
Bradford	Broadway House Chambers	01274 722560
Brighton	Crown Office Row Chambers	01273 625625
Bristol	No5 Chambers	0845 210 5555
	3 PB Barristers	0117 928 1520
	St John's Chambers	0117 923 4700
Canterbury	Becket Chambers	01227 786331
Chelmsford	Trinity Chambers	01245 605040
Chichester	Pallant Chambers	01243 784538
Exeter	Rougemont Chambers	01392 208484
Leeds	Broadway House Chambers	0113 246 2600
	Chancery House Chambers	0113 244 6691
	Enterprise Chambers	0113 246 0391
	Kings Chambers	0845 034 3444
	Park Court Chambers	0113 243 3277
	37 Park Square Chambers	0113 243 9422
	Zenith Chambers	0113 245 5438
Liverpool	Atlantic Chambers	0151 236 4421

	•Oriel Chambers	0151 236 7191
London	42 Bedford Row	020 7831 0222
	•Chambers of Mr Ami Feder	020 7797 7788
	Enterprise Chambers	020 7405 9471
	Five Paper	020 7815 3200
	Fountain Court Chambers	020 7583 3335
	•Goldsmith Chambers	020 7353 6802
	•1 KBW Chambers	020 7936 1500
	Lamb Chambers	020 7797 8300
	•Maitland Chambers	020 7406 1200
	New Square Chambers	020 7419 8000
	No5 Chambers	0845 210 5555
	•13 Old Square Chambers	020 7831 4445
	3 PB Barristers	020 7583 8055
	•5 Pump Court	020 7353 2532
	Radcliffe Chambers	020 7831 0081
	Renaissance Chambers	020 7404 1111
	Selborne Chambers	020 7420 9500
	•South Square	020 7696 9900
	3 Stone Buildings	020 7242 4937
	4 Stone Buildings	020 7242 5524
	•9 Stone Buildings	020 7404 5055
	•Tanfield Chambers	020 7421 5300
	Ten Old Square	020 7405 0758
	XXIV Old Buildings	020 7691 2424
Manchester	•Cobden House Chambers	0161 833 6000
	Deans Court Chambers	0161 214 6000
	Kings Chambers	0845 034 3444
	St James's Chambers	0161 834 7000
	18 St John Street	0161 278 1800
	•St Johns Buildings	0161 214 1500
Middlesbrough	Fountain Chambers	01642 804040
	•Trinity Chambers	01642 247569
Newcastle Upon Tyne	Dere Street Barristers	0844 3351551
	Enterprise Chambers	0191 222 3344
	•Trinity Chambers	0191 232 1927
Nottingham	KCH Garden Square	0115 941 8851
Oxford	3 PB Barristers	01865 793 736
Plymouth	Devon Chambers	01752 661659
Portsmouth	Guildhall Chambers Portsmouth	023 9275 2400
Preston	Deans Court Chambers	01772 565 600
Sheffield	Bank House Chambers	0114 275 1223
Southampton	•College Chambers	023 8023 0338
Swansea	Iscoed Chambers	01792 652988
Winchester	3 PB Barristers	01962 868884

PHARMACEUTICALS

London	•23 Essex Street	020 7413 0353
	•Henderson Chambers	020 7583 9020

PLANNING

Birmingham	•No5 Chambers	0845 210 5555
	St Ive's Chambers	0121 236 0863
	•St Philips Chambers	0121 246 7000
Bournemouth	3 PB Barristers	01202 292102
Brighton	Crown Office Row Chambers	01273 625625
Bristol	No5 Chambers	0845 210 5555
	3 PB Barristers	0117 928 1520
	St John's Chambers	0117 923 4700
Canterbury	Becket Chambers	01227 786331
Chelmsford	Trinity Chambers	01245 605040
Chester	Linenhall Chambers	01244 348282
Exeter	Rougemont Chambers	01392 208484
	Walnut House	01392 279751

• Expanded entry in Part D

Ipswich	East Anglian Chambers	01473 214481
Leeds	Chancery House Chambers	0113 244 6691
	Kings Chambers	0845 034 3444
	Park Court Chambers	0113 243 3277
	37 Park Square Chambers	0113 243 9422
	•Sovereign Chambers	0113 245 1841
	Zenith Chambers	0113 245 5438
Liverpool	Atlantic Chambers	0151 236 4421
	•Number 7 Harrington Street Chambers	0151 242 0707
London	•Arden Chambers	020 7242 4244
	Atlas Chambers	020 7269 7980
	42 Bedford Row	020 7831 0222
	•9-12 Bell Yard	020 7400 1800
	Blackstone Chambers	020 7583 1770
	•Chambers of Mr Ami Feder	020 7797 7788
	Chambers of Mr Patrick Ground QC	020 7736 0131
	•Cornerstone Barristers	020 7242 4986
	•39 Essex Street	020 7832 1111
	Falcon Chambers	020 7353 2484
	Francis Taylor Building	020 7353 8415
	•4-5 Gray's Inn Square	020 7404 5252
	Harcourt Chambers	0844 561 7135
	Lamb Chambers	020 7797 8300
	Landmark Chambers	020 7430 1221
	New Square Chambers	020 7419 8000
	No5 Chambers	0845 210 5555
	•13 Old Square Chambers	020 7831 4445
	3 PB Barristers	020 7583 8055
	6 Pump Court	020 7797 8400
	•Pump Court Chambers	020 7353 0711
	Radcliffe Chambers	020 7831 0081
	•9 Stone Buildings	020 7404 5055
	•Wilberforce Chambers	020 7306 0102
Maidstone	6 Pump Court Chambers	01622 688094
Manchester	Kings Chambers	0845 034 3444
	9 St John Street	0161 955 9000
	18 St John Street	0161 278 1800
	•St Johns Buildings	0161 214 1500
Middlesbrough	•Trinity Chambers	01642 247569
Newcastle Upon Tyne	Dere Street Barristers	0844 3351551
	•Trinity Chambers	0191 232 1927
Nottingham	KCH Garden Square	0115 941 8851
Oxford	Harcourt Chambers	0844 561 7135
	3 PB Barristers	01865 793 736
Plymouth	Devon Chambers	01752 661659
Portsmouth	Guildhall Chambers Portsmouth	023 9275 2400
Sheffield	St Johns Buildings	0114 273 8951
Southampton	•College Chambers	023 8023 0338
Swansea	Iscoed Chambers	01792 652988
Swindon	Pump Court Chambers	01793 539899
Taunton	Octagon Chambers	01823 331919
Winchester	3 PB Barristers	01962 868884
	Pump Court Chambers	01962 868 161

POLICE

Birmingham	Cornwall Street Chambers	0121 233 7500
	St Ive's Chambers	0121 236 0863
	•St Philips Chambers	0121 246 7000
Bournemouth	3 PB Barristers	01202 292102
Bristol	3 PB Barristers	0117 928 1520
	Queen Square Chambers	0117 921 1966
Exeter	Walnut House	01392 279751
London	25 Bedford Row	020 7067 1500
	Bell Yard Chambers	020 7306 9292

	Blackstone Chambers	020 7583 1770
	1 Chancery Lane	0845 634 6666
	•23 Essex Street	020 7413 0353
	•187 Fleet Street	020 7430 7430
	•Henderson Chambers	020 7583 9020
	•1 KBW Chambers	020 7936 1500
	15 New Bridge Street	020 7842 1900
	3 PB Barristers	020 7583 8055
	18 Red Lion Court	020 7520 6000
Manchester	Chambers of Ian Macdonald QC	0161 236 1840
	18 St John Street	0161 278 1800
	•St Johns Buildings	0161 214 1500
Newcastle Upon Tyne	Dere Street Barristers	0844 3351551
Oxford	3 PB Barristers	01865 793 736
Winchester	3 PB Barristers	01962 868884

POLICE DISCIPLINE

Birmingham	•No5 Chambers	0845 210 5555
Bristol	Queen Square Chambers	0117 921 1966
Leeds	•Sovereign Chambers	0113 245 1841
London	•2 Bedford Row	020 7440 8888
	•23 Essex Street	020 7413 0353
	•187 Fleet Street	020 7430 7430
	•1 KBW Chambers	020 7936 1500
	15 New Bridge Street	020 7842 1900
	•3 Raymond Buildings	020 7400 6400
	The Chambers of Grahame Aldous QC	020 7832 0500
Manchester	Chambers of Ian Macdonald QC	0161 236 1840
	18 St John Street	0161 278 1800
Newcastle Upon Tyne	Dere Street Barristers	0844 3351551
Sheffield	St Johns Buildings	0114 273 8951

POLLUTION

Bristol	Queen Square Chambers	0117 921 1966
London	•Cornerstone Barristers	020 7242 4986
	•23 Essex Street	020 7413 0353
	Five Paper	020 7815 3200
	Francis Taylor Building	020 7353 8415
	•Henderson Chambers	020 7583 9020
Manchester	•Lincoln House Chambers	0161 832 5701
	18 St John Street	0161 278 1800
Newcastle Upon Tyne	Dere Street Barristers	0844 3351551

PRISON LAW

Birmingham	•No5 Chambers	0845 210 5555
	St Ive's Chambers	0121 236 0863
	•St Philips Chambers	0121 246 7000
Bristol	No5 Chambers	0845 210 5555
	Queen Square Chambers	0117 921 1966
Exeter	Rougemont Chambers	01392 208484
	Walnut House	01392 279751
Leeds	•Sovereign Chambers	0113 245 1841
London	•Argent Chambers	020 7556 5500
	25 Bedford Row	020 7067 1500
	Bell Yard Chambers	020 7306 9292
	Blackstone Chambers	020 7583 1770
	•Chambers of Marion Smullen and Kerim Fuad QC	020 7427 4400
	1 Crown Office Row	020 7797 7500
	•23 Essex Street	020 7413 0353
	Farringdon Chambers	020 7089 5700
	•187 Fleet Street	020 7430 7430
	•Goldsmith Chambers	020 7353 6802
	•1 KBW Chambers	020 7936 1500

• Expanded entry in Part D

	13 King's Bench Walk	020 7353 7204
	Matrix Chambers	020 7404 3447
	Middle Temple Lane Chambers	020 7583 4352
	15 New Bridge Street	020 7842 1900
	No5 Chambers	0845 210 5555
	•5 Pump Court	020 7353 2532
	18 Red Lion Court	020 7520 6000
	Tooks Chambers	020 7842 7575
Manchester	Chambers of Ian Macdonald QC	0161 236 1840
	Kenworthy's Chambers	0161 832 4036
	18 St John Street	0161 278 1800
	•St Johns Buildings	0161 214 1500
Middlesbrough	•Trinity Chambers	01642 247569
Newcastle Upon Tyne	Dere Street Barristers	0844 3351551
	•Trinity Chambers	0191 232 1927
Sheffield	Bank House Chambers	0114 275 1223

PRISONERS' RIGHTS

Birmingham	St Ive's Chambers	0121 236 0863
Bristol	Queen Square Chambers	0117 921 1966
London	Doughty Street Chambers	020 7404 1313
	•23 Essex Street	020 7413 0353
	•187 Fleet Street	020 7430 7430
	•1 KBW Chambers	020 7936 1500
	15 New Bridge Street	020 7842 1900
	18 Red Lion Court	020 7520 6000
Manchester	Central Chambers	0161 236 1133

PRIVACY

London	Blackstone Chambers	020 7583 1770
	15 New Bridge Street	020 7842 1900
Manchester	Chambers of Ian Macdonald QC	0161 236 1840
	•St Johns Buildings	0161 214 1500

PRIVATE CHILDREN LAW

Birmingham	St Ive's Chambers	0121 236 0863
Bristol	Queen Square Chambers	0117 921 1966
Exeter	Rougemont Chambers	01392 208484
Faringdon	Faringdon Chambers	01367 240598
London	Bell Yard Chambers	020 7306 9292
	Five Paper	020 7815 3200
	•1 KBW Chambers	020 7936 1500
	•Tanfield Chambers	020 7421 5300
	The Chambers of Grahame Aldous QC	020 7832 0500
Manchester	18 St John Street	0161 278 1800
Middlesbrough	Amicus Chambers	01642 876334
Newcastle Upon Tyne	Dere Street Barristers	0844 3351551
Northampton	Northampton Chambers	01604 636271
Portsmouth	Guildhall Chambers Portsmouth	023 9275 2400
Southampton	•College Chambers	023 8023 0338

PRIVATE CLIENT

Exeter	Walnut House	01392 279751
London	•Maitland Chambers	020 7406 1200
	•Pump Court Tax Chambers	020 7414 8080
	XXIV Old Buildings	020 7691 2424

PRIVY COUNCIL

London	•Cornerstone Barristers	020 7242 4986
	Erskine Chambers	020 7242 5532
	Five Paper	020 7815 3200
	•Henderson Chambers	020 7583 9020
	•South Square	020 7696 9900
	XXIV Old Buildings	020 7691 2424

PRIVY COUNCIL APPEALS		
London	•2 Bedford Row	020 7440 8888
	•Chambers of Mr Ami Feder	020 7797 7788
	•Cornerstone Barristers	020 7242 4986
	Erskine Chambers	020 7242 5532
	Five Paper	020 7815 3200
	•Maitland Chambers	020 7406 1200
	18 Red Lion Court	020 7520 6000
PROCUREMENT		
London	•Arden Chambers	020 7242 4244
	Atkin Chambers	020 7404 0102
	Blackstone Chambers	020 7583 1770
	•Cornerstone Barristers	020 7242 4986
	Francis Taylor Building	020 7353 8415
	•Henderson Chambers	020 7583 9020
	Keating Chambers	020 7544 2600
	•Monckton Chambers	020 7405 7211
Manchester	•St Johns Buildings	0161 214 1500
Newcastle Upon Tyne	Dere Street Barristers	0844 3351551
PRODUCT LIABILITY		
Birmingham	St Ive's Chambers	0121 236 0863
Bournemouth	3 PB Barristers	01202 292102
Bristol	3 PB Barristers	0117 928 1520
	Queen Square Chambers	0117 921 1966
London	•Crown Office Chambers	020 7797 8100
	Essex Court Chambers	020 7813 8000
	•39 Essex Street	020 7832 1111
	•Henderson Chambers	020 7583 9020
	3 PB Barristers	020 7583 8055
	The Chambers of Grahame Aldous QC	020 7832 0500
Manchester	18 St John Street	0161 278 1800
Oxford	3 PB Barristers	01865 793 736
Winchester	3 PB Barristers	01962 868884
PRODUCT SAFETY		
Birmingham	St Ive's Chambers	0121 236 0863
Bristol	Queen Square Chambers	0117 921 1966
London	•Cornerstone Barristers	020 7242 4986
	Gough Square Chambers	020 7353 0924
	•Henderson Chambers	020 7583 9020
	The Chambers of Grahame Aldous QC	020 7832 0500
Manchester	18 St John Street	0161 278 1800
PROFESSIONAL NEGLIGENCE		
Birmingham	•No5 Chambers	0845 210 5555
	St Ive's Chambers	0121 236 0863
	•St Philips Chambers	0121 246 7000
Bournemouth	3 PB Barristers	01202 292102
Bradford	Broadway House Chambers	01274 722560
Brighton	Crown Office Row Chambers	01273 625625
Bristol	Albion Chambers	0117 927 2144
	3 PB Barristers	0117 928 1520
	Queen Square Chambers	0117 921 1966
	St John's Chambers	0117 923 4700
	Unity Street Chambers	0117 906 9789
Canterbury	Becket Chambers	01227 786331
Chelmsford	Trinity Chambers	01245 605040
Chester	Linenhall Chambers	01244 348282
Chichester	Pallant Chambers	01243 784538
Exeter	Rougemont Chambers	01392 208484
	Walnut House	01392 279751
Hull	Wilberforce Chambers	01482 323264
Ipswich	East Anglian Chambers	01473 214481

• Expanded entry in Part D

Leeds	Broadway House Chambers	0113 246 2600
	Chancery House Chambers	0113 244 6691
	Enterprise Chambers	0113 246 0391
	KBW	0113 297 1200
	Kings Chambers	0845 034 3444
	Park Court Chambers	0113 243 3277
	37 Park Square Chambers	0113 243 9422
	•Sovereign Chambers	0113 245 1841
	Zenith Chambers	0113 245 5438
Liverpool	Atlantic Chambers	0151 236 4421
	•Oriel Chambers	0151 236 7191
London	Atkin Chambers	020 7404 0102
	Atlas Chambers	020 7269 7980
	42 Bedford Row	020 7831 0222
	•29 Bedford Row Chambers	020 7404 1044
	•9-12 Bell Yard	020 7400 1800
	Blackstone Chambers	020 7583 1770
	Brick Court Chambers	020 7379 3550
	•Chambers of Mr Ami Feder	020 7797 7788
	Chambers of Mr Patrick Ground QC	020 7736 0131
	1 Chancery Lane	0845 634 6666
	•Charter Chambers	020 7618 4400
	•Cornerstone Barristers	020 7242 4986
	•Crown Office Chambers	020 7797 8100
	1 Crown Office Row	020 7797 7500
	•Devereux Chambers	020 7353 7534
	Doughty Street Chambers	020 7404 1313
	Enterprise Chambers	020 7405 9471
	Erskine Chambers	020 7242 5532
	•One Essex Court	020 7583 2000
	Essex Court Chambers	020 7813 8000
	20 Essex Street	020 7842 1200
	•39 Essex Street	020 7832 1111
	Falcon Chambers	020 7353 2484
	•Farrar's Building	020 7583 9241
	Farringdon Chambers	020 7089 5700
	Five Paper	020 7815 3200
	Fountain Court Chambers	020 7583 3335
	•Goldsmith Chambers	020 7353 6802
	Gough Square Chambers	020 7353 0924
	•4-5 Gray's Inn Square	020 7404 5252
	Hailsham Chambers	020 7643 5000
	Harcourt Chambers	0844 561 7135
	3 Hare Court	020 7415 7800
	•Henderson Chambers	020 7583 9020
	•1 KBW Chambers	020 7936 1500
	Keating Chambers	020 7544 2600
	4 King's Bench Walk	020 7822 7000
	12 King's Bench Walk	020 7583 0811
	13 King's Bench Walk	020 7353 7204
	Lamb Chambers	020 7797 8300
	•Maitland Chambers	020 7406 1200
	New Square Chambers	020 7419 8000
	•13 Old Square Chambers	020 7831 4445
	Outer Temple Chambers	020 7353 6381
	3 PB Barristers	020 7583 8055
	Prince Henry's Chambers	020 7837 1645
	1 Pump Court	020 7842 7070
	4 Pump Court	020 7842 5555
	•5 Pump Court	020 7353 2532
	6 Pump Court	020 7797 8400
	•Pump Court Chambers	020 7353 0711
	•Pump Court Tax Chambers	020 7414 8080
	Queen Elizabeth Building	020 7797 7837

 • Expanded entry in Part D

A

	Radcliffe Chambers	020 7831 0081
	Selborne Chambers	020 7420 9500
	Serle Court	020 7242 6105
	•South Square	020 7696 9900
	3 Stone Buildings	020 7242 4937
	4 Stone Buildings	020 7242 5524
	•9 Stone Buildings	020 7404 5055
	11 Stone Buildings	020 7831 6381
	•Tanfield Chambers	020 7421 5300
	•Temple Garden Chambers	020 7583 1315
	Ten Old Square	020 7405 0758
	The Chambers of Grahame Aldous QC	020 7832 0500
	•Three New Square IP	020 7405 1111
	3 Verulam Buildings	020 7831 8441
	•Wilberforce Chambers	020 7306 0102
	XXIV Old Buildings	020 7691 2424
Maidstone	6 Pump Court Chambers	01622 688094
Manchester	Byrom Street Chambers	0161 829 2100
	Central Chambers	0161 236 1133
	•Cobden House Chambers	0161 833 6000
	Deans Court Chambers	0161 214 6000
	Kenworthy's Chambers	0161 832 4036
	Kings Chambers	0845 034 3444
	•Lincoln House Chambers	0161 832 5701
	St James's Chambers	0161 834 7000
	9 St John Street	0161 955 9000
	18 St John Street	0161 278 1800
	•St Johns Buildings	0161 214 1500
Middlesbrough	Fountain Chambers	01642 804040
	Old Court Chambers	01642 232523
	•Trinity Chambers	01642 247569
Newcastle Upon Tyne	Dere Street Barristers	0844 3351551
	Enterprise Chambers	0191 222 3344
	•Trinity Chambers	0191 232 1927
Northampton	Chartlands Chambers	01604 603322
Nottingham	KCH Garden Square	0115 941 8851
Oxford	Harcourt Chambers	0844 561 7135
	3 PB Barristers	01865 793 736
Plymouth	Devon Chambers	01752 661659
Portsmouth	Guildhall Chambers Portsmouth	023 9275 2400
	Portsmouth Barristers'Chambers	023 9283 1292
Preston	Deans Court Chambers	01772 565 600
Sheffield	St Johns Buildings	0114 273 8951
Southampton	•College Chambers	023 8023 0338
Swansea	Iscoed Chambers	01792 652988
Swindon	Pump Court Chambers	01793 539899
Taunton	Octagon Chambers	01823 331919
Winchester	3 PB Barristers	01962 868884
	Pump Court Chambers	01962 868 161

PROPERTY

Birmingham	•No5 Chambers	0845 210 5555
	St Ive's Chambers	0121 236 0863
	•St Philips Chambers	0121 246 7000
Bristol	No5 Chambers	0845 210 5555
Chichester	Pallant Chambers	01243 784538
Exeter	Walnut House	01392 279751
Leeds	Zenith Chambers	0113 245 5438
London	12 King's Bench Walk	020 7583 0811
	Landmark Chambers	020 7430 1221
	Middle Temple Lane Chambers	020 7583 4352
	No5 Chambers	0845 210 5555
	Serle Court	020 7242 6105
	Ten Old Square	020 7405 0758

• Expanded entry in Part D

	XXIV Old Buildings	020 7691 2424
Manchester	Chambers of Ian Macdonald QC	0161 236 1840

PUBLIC ACCESS

Birmingham	St Ive's Chambers	0121 236 0863
Bristol	Queen Square Chambers	0117 921 1966
Exeter	Walnut House	01392 279751
London	•Charter Chambers	020 7618 4400
	Five Paper	020 7815 3200
	•187 Fleet Street	020 7430 7430
Manchester	Central Chambers	0161 236 1133
	Kenworthy's Chambers	0161 832 4036
	•St Johns Buildings	0161 214 1500
Northampton	Northampton Chambers	01604 636271
Nottingham	KCH Garden Square	0115 941 8851

PUBLIC HEALTH

Exeter	Walnut House	01392 279751
London	•Henderson Chambers	020 7583 9020
Manchester	•St Johns Buildings	0161 214 1500
Middlesbrough	•Trinity Chambers	01642 247569
Newcastle Upon Tyne	Dere Street Barristers	0844 3351551
	•Trinity Chambers	0191 232 1927

PUBLIC INQUIRIES

London	•2 Bedford Row	020 7440 8888
	Blackstone Chambers	020 7583 1770
	•Cornerstone Barristers	020 7242 4986
	•23 Essex Street	020 7413 0353
	Five Paper	020 7815 3200
	Francis Taylor Building	020 7353 8415
	•Henderson Chambers	020 7583 9020
	•Maitland Chambers	020 7406 1200
	Outer Temple Chambers	020 7353 6381
	6 Pump Court	020 7797 8400
	•3 Raymond Buildings	020 7400 6400
	18 Red Lion Court	020 7520 6000
	The Chambers of Grahame Aldous QC	020 7832 0500
Maidstone	6 Pump Court Chambers	01622 688094
Manchester	Chambers of Ian Macdonald QC	0161 236 1840
	•Lincoln House Chambers	0161 832 5701
	18 St John Street	0161 278 1800
Newcastle Upon Tyne	Dere Street Barristers	0844 3351551
Portsmouth	Guildhall Chambers Portsmouth	023 9275 2400
Southampton	•College Chambers	023 8023 0338

PUBLIC LAW

Birmingham	•No5 Chambers	0845 210 5555
Bournemouth	3 PB Barristers	01202 292102
Bristol	No5 Chambers	0845 210 5555
	3 PB Barristers	0117 928 1520
Exeter	Rougemont Chambers	01392 208484
Liverpool	Atlantic Chambers	0151 236 4421
London	•Arden Chambers	020 7242 4244
	Blackstone Chambers	020 7583 1770
	•Chambers of Mr Ami Feder	020 7797 7788
	•Cornerstone Barristers	020 7242 4986
	1 Crown Office Row	020 7797 7500
	Doughty Street Chambers	020 7404 1313
	•One Essex Court	020 7583 2000
	Francis Taylor Building	020 7353 8415
	3 Hare Court	020 7415 7800
	•Henderson Chambers	020 7583 9020
	4 King's Bench Walk	020 7822 7000
	13 King's Bench Walk	020 7353 7204

A

	Landmark Chambers	020 7430 1221
	•Monckton Chambers	020 7405 7211
	No5 Chambers	0845 210 5555
	3 PB Barristers	020 7583 8055
	•Temple Garden Chambers	020 7583 1315
Manchester	Chambers of Ian Macdonald QC	0161 236 1840
	18 St John Street	0161 278 1800
	•St Johns Buildings	0161 214 1500
Newcastle Upon Tyne	Dere Street Barristers	0844 3351551
Northampton	Northampton Chambers	01604 636271
Oxford	3 PB Barristers	01865 793 736
Portsmouth	Guildhall Chambers Portsmouth	023 9275 2400
Sheffield	Bank House Chambers	0114 275 1223
	St Johns Buildings	0114 273 8951
Winchester	3 PB Barristers	01962 868884

PUBLISHING

London	•8 New Square	020 7405 4321
Manchester	18 St John Street	0161 278 1800
	•St Johns Buildings	0161 214 1500

RAILWAYS

London	•Cornerstone Barristers	020 7242 4986
	Essex Court Chambers	020 7813 8000
	Francis Taylor Building	020 7353 8415
	•Henderson Chambers	020 7583 9020
	Keating Chambers	020 7544 2600

RATING AND CPO

London	•Arden Chambers	020 7242 4244
	•Cornerstone Barristers	020 7242 4986
	Francis Taylor Building	020 7353 8415
	Landmark Chambers	020 7430 1221
Manchester	•St Johns Buildings	0161 214 1500
Newcastle Upon Tyne	Dere Street Barristers	0844 3351551

REAL PROPERTY

Birmingham	St Ive's Chambers	0121 236 0863
Bournemouth	3 PB Barristers	01202 292102
Brighton	Crown Office Row Chambers	01273 625625
Bristol	3 PB Barristers	0117 928 1520
Exeter	Rougemont Chambers	01392 208484
	Walnut House	01392 279751
Leeds	Enterprise Chambers	0113 246 0391
London	•Arden Chambers	020 7242 4244
	1 Chancery Lane	0845 634 6666
	•Cornerstone Barristers	020 7242 4986
	Enterprise Chambers	020 7405 9471
	Falcon Chambers	020 7353 2484
	Five Paper	020 7815 3200
	•Goldsmith Chambers	020 7353 6802
	•Henderson Chambers	020 7583 9020
	4 King's Bench Walk	020 7822 7000
	13 King's Bench Walk	020 7353 7204
	•Maitland Chambers	020 7406 1200
	3 PB Barristers	020 7583 8055
	•5 Pump Court	020 7353 2532
	•Tanfield Chambers	020 7421 5300
Maidstone	Maidstone Chambers	01622 688592
Manchester	18 St John Street	0161 278 1800
	•St Johns Buildings	0161 214 1500
Newcastle Upon Tyne	Dere Street Barristers	0844 3351551
	Enterprise Chambers	0191 222 3344
Oxford	3 PB Barristers	01865 793 736
Portsmouth	Guildhall Chambers Portsmouth	023 9275 2400

• Expanded entry in Part D

	Portsmouth Barristers'Chambers	023 9283 1292
Winchester	3 PB Barristers	01962 868884

REGISTERED DESIGNS

London	•8 New Square	020 7405 4321
Manchester	18 St John Street	0161 278 1800
Portsmouth	Portsmouth Barristers'Chambers	023 9283 1292

REGULATORY AND DISCIPLINARY LAW

Birmingham	Cornwall Street Chambers	0121 233 7500
	•No5 Chambers	0845 210 5555
	St Ive's Chambers	0121 236 0863
	•St Philips Chambers	0121 246 7000
Bournemouth	3 PB Barristers	01202 292102
Bristol	3 PB Barristers	0117 928 1520
	Queen Square Chambers	0117 921 1966
Exeter	Walnut House	01392 279751
Leeds	Kings Chambers	0845 034 3444
	•Sovereign Chambers	0113 245 1841
London	•2 Bedford Row	020 7440 8888
	Bell Yard Chambers	020 7306 9292
	•9-12 Bell Yard	020 7400 1800
	Blackstone Chambers	020 7583 1770
	•Chambers of Marion Smullen and Kerim Fuad QC	020 7427 4400
	•Charter Chambers	020 7618 4400
	•Cornerstone Barristers	020 7242 4986
	•Crown Office Chambers	020 7797 8100
	1 Crown Office Row	020 7797 7500
	Doughty Street Chambers	020 7404 1313
	•23 Essex Street	020 7413 0353
	•39 Essex Street	020 7832 1111
	Five Paper	020 7815 3200
	Gough Square Chambers	020 7353 0924
	•Henderson Chambers	020 7583 9020
	•Nine Bedford Row	020 7489 2727
	•1 Paper Buildings	020 7353 3728
	3 PB Barristers	020 7583 8055
	•5 Pump Court	020 7353 2532
	•QEB Hollis Whiteman	020 7933 8855
	•3 Raymond Buildings	020 7400 6400
	18 Red Lion Court	020 7520 6000
	Serle Court	020 7242 6105
	The Chambers of Grahame Aldous QC	020 7832 0500
Manchester	Byrom Street Chambers	0161 829 2100
	Central Chambers	0161 236 1133
	Chambers of Ian Macdonald QC	0161 236 1840
	•Cobden House Chambers	0161 833 6000
	Kings Chambers	0845 034 3444
	18 St John Street	0161 278 1800
	•St Johns Buildings	0161 214 1500
Newcastle Upon Tyne	Dere Street Barristers	0844 3351551
Oxford	3 PB Barristers	01865 793 736
Southampton	•College Chambers	023 8023 0338
Winchester	3 PB Barristers	01962 868884

REGULATORY CRIME

Birmingham	St Ive's Chambers	0121 236 0863
Bristol	Queen Square Chambers	0117 921 1966
Exeter	Walnut House	01392 279751
London	•187 Fleet Street	020 7430 7430
	Francis Taylor Building	020 7353 8415
	•3 Raymond Buildings	020 7400 6400
Manchester	•St Johns Buildings	0161 214 1500

• Expanded entry in Part D

A

REMEDIES

Bristol	Queen Square Chambers	0117 921 1966
London	Five Paper	020 7815 3200
	XXIV Old Buildings	020 7691 2424
Manchester	18 St John Street	0161 278 1800
	•St Johns Buildings	0161 214 1500
Newcastle Upon Tyne	Dere Street Barristers	0844 3351551
Portsmouth	Portsmouth Barristers'Chambers	023 9283 1292
Southampton	•College Chambers	023 8023 0338

RESTITUTION

London	•One Essex Court	020 7583 2000
	Five Paper	020 7815 3200
	Francis Taylor Building	020 7353 8415
Manchester	18 St John Street	0161 278 1800
Newcastle Upon Tyne	Dere Street Barristers	0844 3351551
Southampton	•College Chambers	023 8023 0338

RESTRAINT OF TRADE

London	Blackstone Chambers	020 7583 1770
	•One Essex Court	020 7583 2000
	Farringdon Chambers	020 7089 5700
	Five Paper	020 7815 3200
	11 King's Bench Walk	020 7632 8500
Manchester	18 St John Street	0161 278 1800
Portsmouth	Portsmouth Barristers'Chambers	023 9283 1292

RIGHTS OF LIGHT

Bournemouth	3 PB Barristers	01202 292102
Bristol	3 PB Barristers	0117 928 1520
	Queen Square Chambers	0117 921 1966
London	Five Paper	020 7815 3200
	Francis Taylor Building	020 7353 8415
	•Henderson Chambers	020 7583 9020
	3 PB Barristers	020 7583 8055
	Radcliffe Chambers	020 7831 0081
	•Tanfield Chambers	020 7421 5300
Manchester	18 St John Street	0161 278 1800
Newcastle Upon Tyne	Dere Street Barristers	0844 3351551
Oxford	3 PB Barristers	01865 793 736
Portsmouth	Portsmouth Barristers'Chambers	023 9283 1292
Southampton	•College Chambers	023 8023 0338
Winchester	3 PB Barristers	01962 868884

RIGHTS OF WAY

Birmingham	St Ive's Chambers	0121 236 0863
Bournemouth	3 PB Barristers	01202 292102
Bristol	3 PB Barristers	0117 928 1520
	Queen Square Chambers	0117 921 1966
Exeter	Rougemont Chambers	01392 208484
London	•Cornerstone Barristers	020 7242 4986
	Five Paper	020 7815 3200
	•Henderson Chambers	020 7583 9020
	3 PB Barristers	020 7583 8055
	•Tanfield Chambers	020 7421 5300
Manchester	18 St John Street	0161 278 1800
Newcastle Upon Tyne	Dere Street Barristers	0844 3351551
Oxford	3 PB Barristers	01865 793 736
Portsmouth	Portsmouth Barristers'Chambers	023 9283 1292
Southampton	•College Chambers	023 8023 0338
Winchester	3 PB Barristers	01962 868884

ROAD HAULAGE

Birmingham	No 8 Chambers	0121 236 5514
	St Ive's Chambers	0121 236 0863

• Expanded entry in Part D

Bristol	Queen Square Chambers	0117 921 1966
London	•23 Essex Street	020 7413 0353
	Gough Square Chambers	020 7353 0924
	•Henderson Chambers	020 7583 9020
	15 New Bridge Street	020 7842 1900
	The Chambers of Grahame Aldous QC	020 7832 0500
Manchester	Chambers of Ian Macdonald QC	0161 236 1840
	18 St John Street	0161 278 1800
Newcastle Upon Tyne	Dere Street Barristers	0844 3351551
Portsmouth	Guildhall Chambers Portsmouth	023 9275 2400

ROAD TRAFFIC

Birmingham	St Ive's Chambers	0121 236 0863
	•St Philips Chambers	0121 246 7000
Bournemouth	3 PB Barristers	01202 292102
Brighton	Crown Office Row Chambers	01273 625625
Bristol	3 PB Barristers	0117 928 1520
	Queen Square Chambers	0117 921 1966
Exeter	Rougemont Chambers	01392 208484
	Walnut House	01392 279751
London	Bell Yard Chambers	020 7306 9292
	•Cornerstone Barristers	020 7242 4986
	1 Crown Office Row	020 7797 7500
	Essex Court Chambers	020 7813 8000
	•23 Essex Street	020 7413 0353
	•187 Fleet Street	020 7430 7430
	Francis Taylor Building	020 7353 8415
	•Henderson Chambers	020 7583 9020
	Middle Temple Lane Chambers	020 7583 4352
	15 New Bridge Street	020 7842 1900
	3 PB Barristers	020 7583 8055
	•3 Raymond Buildings	020 7400 6400
Manchester	Central Chambers	0161 236 1133
	Chambers of Ian Macdonald QC	0161 236 1840
	•Lincoln House Chambers	0161 832 5701
	18 St John Street	0161 278 1800
	•St Johns Buildings	0161 214 1500
Middlesbrough	•Trinity Chambers	01642 247569
Newcastle Upon Tyne	Dere Street Barristers	0844 3351551
	•Trinity Chambers	0191 232 1927
Northampton	Northampton Chambers	01604 636271
Oxford	3 PB Barristers	01865 793 736
Pitstone	Victor House Chambers	01296 664043
Portsmouth	Guildhall Chambers Portsmouth	023 9275 2400
Winchester	3 PB Barristers	01962 868884

ROAD TRAFFIC OFFENCES

Birmingham	St Ive's Chambers	0121 236 0863
Bristol	Queen Square Chambers	0117 921 1966
London	•2 Bedford Row	020 7440 8888
	Bell Yard Chambers	020 7306 9292
	•23 Essex Street	020 7413 0353
	•187 Fleet Street	020 7430 7430
	•Henderson Chambers	020 7583 9020
	15 New Bridge Street	020 7842 1900
	18 Red Lion Court	020 7520 6000
	The Chambers of Grahame Aldous QC	020 7832 0500
Manchester	Chambers of Ian Macdonald QC	0161 236 1840
	18 St John Street	0161 278 1800
Newcastle Upon Tyne	Dere Street Barristers	0844 3351551
Northampton	Northampton Chambers	01604 636271
Portsmouth	Guildhall Chambers Portsmouth	023 9275 2400

A

SALE AND CARRIAGE OF GOODS

Birmingham	No 8 Chambers	0121 236 5514
	•St Philips Chambers	0121 246 7000
Bournemouth	3 PB Barristers	01202 292102
Bradford	Broadway House Chambers	01274 722560
Bristol	3 PB Barristers	0117 928 1520
	St John's Chambers	0117 923 4700
	Unity Street Chambers	0117 906 9789
Chelmsford	Trinity Chambers	01245 605040
Chester	Linenhall Chambers	01244 348282
Chichester	Pallant Chambers	01243 784538
Leeds	Broadway House Chambers	0113 246 2600
	Chancery House Chambers	0113 244 6691
	Kings Chambers	0845 034 3444
	Zenith Chambers	0113 245 5438
Liverpool	Atlantic Chambers	0151 236 4421
	•Oriel Chambers	0151 236 7191
London	42 Bedford Row	020 7831 0222
	Blackstone Chambers	020 7583 1770
	Brick Court Chambers	020 7379 3550
	•Chambers of Mr Ami Feder	020 7797 7788
	1 Crown Office Row	020 7797 7500
	•Devereux Chambers	020 7353 7534
	•One Essex Court	020 7583 2000
	Essex Court Chambers	020 7813 8000
	20 Essex Street	020 7842 1200
	•39 Essex Street	020 7832 1111
	•Farrar's Building	020 7583 9241
	Five Paper	020 7815 3200
	Fountain Court Chambers	020 7583 3335
	•Goldsmith Chambers	020 7353 6802
	Gough Square Chambers	020 7353 0924
	Hailsham Chambers	020 7643 5000
	•Henderson Chambers	020 7583 9020
	Lamb Chambers	020 7797 8300
	•Maitland Chambers	020 7406 1200
	New Square Chambers	020 7419 8000
	3 PB Barristers	020 7583 8055
	4 Pump Court	020 7842 5555
	Selborne Chambers	020 7420 9500
	•Tanfield Chambers	020 7421 5300
	Ten Old Square	020 7405 0758
	•Three New Square IP	020 7405 1111
	3 Verulam Buildings	020 7831 8441
Manchester	Byrom Street Chambers	0161 829 2100
	•Cobden House Chambers	0161 833 6000
	Deans Court Chambers	0161 214 6000
	Kings Chambers	0845 034 3444
	St James's Chambers	0161 834 7000
	9 St John Street	0161 955 9000
Middlesbrough	Old Court Chambers	01642 232523
	•Trinity Chambers	01642 247569
Newcastle Upon Tyne	Dere Street Barristers	0844 3351551
	•Trinity Chambers	0191 232 1927
Northampton	Chartlands Chambers	01604 603322
Nottingham	KCH Garden Square	0115 941 8851
Oxford	3 PB Barristers	01865 793 736
Plymouth	Devon Chambers	01752 661659
Portsmouth	Guildhall Chambers Portsmouth	023 9275 2400
	Portsmouth Barristers'Chambers	023 9283 1292
Preston	Deans Court Chambers	01772 565 600
Southampton	•College Chambers	023 8023 0338
Swansea	Iscoed Chambers	01792 652988

• Expanded entry in Part D

Winchester	3 PB Barristers	01962 868884

SALE OF BUSINESS

Exeter	Rougemont Chambers	01392 208484
London	Erskine Chambers	020 7242 5532
	•One Essex Court	020 7583 2000
	Five Paper	020 7815 3200
Manchester	18 St John Street	0161 278 1800
Newcastle Upon Tyne	Dere Street Barristers	0844 3351551
Portsmouth	Portsmouth Barristers'Chambers	023 9283 1292

SCHOOL SITES

Birmingham	St Ive's Chambers	0121 236 0863
Newcastle Upon Tyne	Dere Street Barristers	0844 3351551
Southampton	•College Chambers	023 8023 0338

SCIENTIFIC CASES

London	•Henderson Chambers	020 7583 9020
Newcastle Upon Tyne	Dere Street Barristers	0844 3351551

SECURITIES LAW AND REGULATION

London	Erskine Chambers	020 7242 5532
	Essex Court Chambers	020 7813 8000
	•South Square	020 7696 9900
Manchester	18 St John Street	0161 278 1800
	•St Johns Buildings	0161 214 1500

SERIAL CRIME

Birmingham	St Ive's Chambers	0121 236 0863
Bournemouth	3 PB Barristers	01202 292102
Bristol	3 PB Barristers	0117 928 1520
	Queen Square Chambers	0117 921 1966
Exeter	Walnut House	01392 279751
London	•2 Bedford Row	020 7440 8888
	25 Bedford Row	020 7067 1500
	Bell Yard Chambers	020 7306 9292
	•23 Essex Street	020 7413 0353
	•187 Fleet Street	020 7430 7430
	•1 KBW Chambers	020 7936 1500
	15 New Bridge Street	020 7842 1900
	•Nine Bedford Row	020 7489 2727
	3 PB Barristers	020 7583 8055
	18 Red Lion Court	020 7520 6000
	The Chambers of Grahame Aldous QC	020 7832 0500
Manchester	Chambers of Ian Macdonald QC	0161 236 1840
	18 St John Street	0161 278 1800
	•St Johns Buildings	0161 214 1500
Middlesbrough	•Trinity Chambers	01642 247569
Newcastle Upon Tyne	Dere Street Barristers	0844 3351551
	•Trinity Chambers	0191 232 1927
Oxford	3 PB Barristers	01865 793 736
Winchester	3 PB Barristers	01962 868884

SERIOUS FRAUD

Birmingham	•No5 Chambers	0845 210 5555
	St Ive's Chambers	0121 236 0863
Bournemouth	3 PB Barristers	01202 292102
Bristol	3 PB Barristers	0117 928 1520
	Queen Square Chambers	0117 921 1966
Leeds	37 Park Square Chambers	0113 243 9422
London	•2 Bedford Row	020 7440 8888
	25 Bedford Row	020 7067 1500
	Bell Yard Chambers	020 7306 9292
	•Cornerstone Barristers	020 7242 4986
	•23 Essex Street	020 7413 0353

	•187 Fleet Street	020 7430 7430
	•1 KBW Chambers	020 7936 1500
	15 New Bridge Street	020 7842 1900
	•Nine Bedford Row	020 7489 2727
	3 PB Barristers	020 7583 8055
	•QEB Hollis Whiteman	020 7933 8855
	18 Red Lion Court	020 7520 6000
	The Chambers of Grahame Aldous QC	020 7832 0500
Manchester	Chambers of Ian Macdonald QC	0161 236 1840
	18 St John Street	0161 278 1800
Middlesbrough	•Trinity Chambers	01642 247569
Newcastle Upon Tyne	Dere Street Barristers	0844 3351551
	•Trinity Chambers	0191 232 1927
Oxford	3 PB Barristers	01865 793 736
Winchester	3 PB Barristers	01962 868884

SEXUAL OFFENCES

Birmingham	St Ive's Chambers	0121 236 0863
Bristol	Queen Square Chambers	0117 921 1966
Exeter	Walnut House	01392 279751
London	Bell Yard Chambers	020 7306 9292
	•187 Fleet Street	020 7430 7430
	•1 KBW Chambers	020 7936 1500
	15 New Bridge Street	020 7842 1900
	•3 Raymond Buildings	020 7400 6400
	18 Red Lion Court	020 7520 6000
Manchester	Kenworthy's Chambers	0161 832 4036
	•St Johns Buildings	0161 214 1500
Newcastle Upon Tyne	Dere Street Barristers	0844 3351551

SHARE OPTIONS

Leeds	Chancery House Chambers	0113 244 6691
	Kings Chambers	0845 034 3444
London	Erskine Chambers	020 7242 5532
	•Maitland Chambers	020 7406 1200
	New Square Chambers	020 7419 8000
	Selborne Chambers	020 7420 9500
	•South Square	020 7696 9900
	•9 Stone Buildings	020 7404 5055
	XXIV Old Buildings	020 7691 2424
Manchester	Kings Chambers	0845 034 3444
	St James's Chambers	0161 834 7000
	18 St John Street	0161 278 1800
Portsmouth	Portsmouth Barristers'Chambers	023 9283 1292

SHAREHOLDER AGREEMENTS

Bournemouth	3 PB Barristers	01202 292102
Bristol	3 PB Barristers	0117 928 1520
London	Erskine Chambers	020 7242 5532
	•One Essex Court	020 7583 2000
	Five Paper	020 7815 3200
	•Henderson Chambers	020 7583 9020
	•Maitland Chambers	020 7406 1200
	3 PB Barristers	020 7583 8055
	•Tanfield Chambers	020 7421 5300
Manchester	18 St John Street	0161 278 1800
Newcastle Upon Tyne	Dere Street Barristers	0844 3351551
Oxford	3 PB Barristers	01865 793 736
Portsmouth	Portsmouth Barristers'Chambers	023 9283 1292
Winchester	3 PB Barristers	01962 868884

SHIP BUILDING

London	Keating Chambers	020 7544 2600

• Expanded entry in Part D

SHIPPING

Exeter	Walnut House	01392 279751
London	Arbitration Chambers	020 7267 2137
	Brick Court Chambers	020 7379 3550
	Essex Court Chambers	020 7813 8000
	20 Essex Street	020 7842 1200
	Fountain Court Chambers	020 7583 3335
	•4-5 Gray's Inn Square	020 7404 5252
	Serle Court	020 7242 6105
	3 Verulam Buildings	020 7831 8441
Middlesbrough	•Trinity Chambers	01642 247569
Newcastle Upon Tyne	•Trinity Chambers	0191 232 1927
Plymouth	Devon Chambers	01752 661659
Portsmouth	Portsmouth Barristers'Chambers	023 9283 1292

SOCIAL SECURITY

London	•Arden Chambers	020 7242 4244
	•Cornerstone Barristers	020 7242 4986
	Prince Henry's Chambers	020 7837 1645
Manchester	Chambers of Ian Macdonald QC	0161 236 1840
	18 St John Street	0161 278 1800
Middlesbrough	•Trinity Chambers	01642 247569
Newcastle Upon Tyne	Dere Street Barristers	0844 3351551
	•Trinity Chambers	0191 232 1927
Southampton	•College Chambers	023 8023 0338

SOCIAL SERVICES

London	•Arden Chambers	020 7242 4244
	•Cornerstone Barristers	020 7242 4986
Manchester	Chambers of Ian Macdonald QC	0161 236 1840
	18 St John Street	0161 278 1800
Newcastle Upon Tyne	Dere Street Barristers	0844 3351551
Southampton	•College Chambers	023 8023 0338

SOCIAL WELFARE

Exeter	Walnut House	01392 279751
London	1 Chancery Lane	0845 634 6666
	Five Paper	020 7815 3200
Manchester	Chambers of Ian Macdonald QC	0161 236 1840
	18 St John Street	0161 278 1800
	•St Johns Buildings	0161 214 1500
Middlesbrough	•Trinity Chambers	01642 247569
Newcastle Upon Tyne	Dere Street Barristers	0844 3351551
	•Trinity Chambers	0191 232 1927

SOCIETY OF LLOYD'S

London	•Henderson Chambers	020 7583 9020
Manchester	•St Johns Buildings	0161 214 1500

SOLICITOR'S INDEMNITY

London	•Henderson Chambers	020 7583 9020
Newcastle Upon Tyne	Dere Street Barristers	0844 3351551
Portsmouth	Portsmouth Barristers'Chambers	023 9283 1292
Southampton	•College Chambers	023 8023 0338

SOUTH ASIAN LAW

London	Essex Court Chambers	020 7813 8000

SOUTH EAST ASIAN LAW

London	Essex Court Chambers	020 7813 8000

SPECIAL GUARDIANSHIP

Birmingham	St Ive's Chambers	0121 236 0863
Bristol	Queen Square Chambers	0117 921 1966
Exeter	Walnut House	01392 279751

Faringdon	Faringdon Chambers	01367 240598
London	•1 KBW Chambers	020 7936 1500
Manchester	•St Johns Buildings	0161 214 1500
Middlesbrough	Amicus Chambers	01642 876334
Newcastle Upon Tyne	Dere Street Barristers	0844 3351551
Southampton	•College Chambers	023 8023 0338

SPEEDING

Birmingham	St Ive's Chambers	0121 236 0863
Bristol	Queen Square Chambers	0117 921 1966
London	•Goldsmith Chambers	020 7353 6802

SPORT

Birmingham	•No5 Chambers	0845 210 5555
	•St Philips Chambers	0121 246 7000
Bristol	No5 Chambers	0845 210 5555
	St John's Chambers	0117 923 4700
Leeds	Kings Chambers	0845 034 3444
London	•Argent Chambers	020 7556 5500
	•2 Bedford Row	020 7440 8888
	•9-12 Bell Yard	020 7400 1800
	Blackstone Chambers	020 7583 1770
	Brick Court Chambers	020 7379 3550
	•Chambers of Mr Ami Feder	020 7797 7788
	1 Chancery Lane	0845 634 6666
	•Cornerstone Barristers	020 7242 4986
	1 Crown Office Row	020 7797 7500
	•Devereux Chambers	020 7353 7534
	•One Essex Court	020 7583 2000
	Essex Court Chambers	020 7813 8000
	•39 Essex Street	020 7832 1111
	•Farrar's Building	020 7583 9241
	•187 Fleet Street	020 7430 7430
	Fountain Court Chambers	020 7583 3335
	•4-5 Gray's Inn Square	020 7404 5252
	Hailsham Chambers	020 7643 5000
	•Henderson Chambers	020 7583 9020
	11 King's Bench Walk	020 7632 8500
	12 King's Bench Walk	020 7583 0811
	•Maitland Chambers	020 7406 1200
	Matrix Chambers	020 7404 3447
	•Monckton Chambers	020 7405 7211
	•8 New Square	020 7405 4321
	No5 Chambers	0845 210 5555
	•13 Old Square Chambers	020 7831 4445
	•1 Paper Buildings	020 7353 3728
	4 Pump Court	020 7842 5555
	•Pump Court Chambers	020 7353 0711
	•QEB Hollis Whiteman	020 7933 8855
	Queen Elizabeth Building	020 7797 7837
	•3 Raymond Buildings	020 7400 6400
	Selborne Chambers	020 7420 9500
	Serle Court	020 7242 6105
	•South Square	020 7696 9900
	3 Stone Buildings	020 7242 4937
	11 Stone Buildings	020 7831 6381
	3 Verulam Buildings	020 7831 8441
	•Wilberforce Chambers	020 7306 0102
Manchester	Byrom Street Chambers	0161 829 2100
	Kings Chambers	0845 034 3444
Plymouth	Devon Chambers	01752 661659
Swindon	Pump Court Chambers	01793 539899
Winchester	Pump Court Chambers	01962 868 161

• Expanded entry in Part D

SPORTS MEDICINE

Location	Chambers	Telephone
Bristol	Queen Square Chambers	0117 921 1966
London	•Henderson Chambers	020 7583 9020
	The Chambers of Grahame Aldous QC	020 7832 0500
Newcastle Upon Tyne	Dere Street Barristers	0844 3351551
Southampton	•College Chambers	023 8023 0338

STAMP DUTY

Location	Chambers	Telephone
London	•Pump Court Tax Chambers	020 7414 8080
	Taxchambers	020 7242 2744
	Temple Tax Chambers	020 7353 7884
Manchester	•St Johns Buildings	0161 214 1500

STATE AID

Location	Chambers	Telephone
London	Blackstone Chambers	020 7583 1770
Manchester	18 St John Street	0161 278 1800

STRATEGIC ALLIANCES

Location	Chambers	Telephone
London	•One Essex Court	020 7583 2000
Manchester	18 St John Street	0161 278 1800

SUCCESSION

Location	Chambers	Telephone
Birmingham	•No5 Chambers	0845 210 5555
	St Ive's Chambers	0121 236 0863
	•St Philips Chambers	0121 246 7000
Bournemouth	3 PB Barristers	01202 292102
Bristol	Albion Chambers	0117 927 2144
	No5 Chambers	0845 210 5555
	3 PB Barristers	0117 928 1520
	St John's Chambers	0117 923 4700
Chester	Linenhall Chambers	01244 348282
Exeter	Rougemont Chambers	01392 208484
	Walnut House	01392 279751
Faringdon	Faringdon Chambers	01367 240598
Leeds	Chancery House Chambers	0113 244 6691
	Enterprise Chambers	0113 246 0391
	KBW	0113 297 1200
	Kings Chambers	0845 034 3444
	Park Court Chambers	0113 243 3277
	Zenith Chambers	0113 245 5438
Liverpool	Atlantic Chambers	0151 236 4421
London	•Chambers of Mr Ami Feder	020 7797 7788
	Enterprise Chambers	020 7405 9471
	Five Paper	020 7815 3200
	•Goldsmith Chambers	020 7353 6802
	•Maitland Chambers	020 7406 1200
	New Square Chambers	020 7419 8000
	No5 Chambers	0845 210 5555
	•13 Old Square Chambers	020 7831 4445
	3 PB Barristers	020 7583 8055
	•Pump Court Chambers	020 7353 0711
	Radcliffe Chambers	020 7831 0081
	Selborne Chambers	020 7420 9500
	3 Stone Buildings	020 7242 4937
	•9 Stone Buildings	020 7404 5055
	11 Stone Buildings	020 7831 6381
	•Tanfield Chambers	020 7421 5300
	Ten Old Square	020 7405 0758
	•Wilberforce Chambers	020 7306 0102
	XXIV Old Buildings	020 7691 2424
Manchester	•Cobden House Chambers	0161 833 6000
	Kings Chambers	0845 034 3444
	St James's Chambers	0161 834 7000
	9 St John Street	0161 955 9000
	18 St John Street	0161 278 1800

	•St Johns Buildings	0161 214 1500
Middlesbrough	•Trinity Chambers	01642 247569
Newcastle Upon Tyne	Cathedral Chambers	0191 232 1311
	Dere Street Barristers	0844 3351551
	Enterprise Chambers	0191 222 3344
	•Trinity Chambers	0191 232 1927
Nottingham	KCH Garden Square	0115 941 8851
Oxford	3 PB Barristers	01865 793 736
Swansea	Iscoed Chambers	01792 652988
Swindon	Pump Court Chambers	01793 539899
Winchester	3 PB Barristers	01962 868884
	Pump Court Chambers	01962 868 161

TAX

Birmingham	•No5 Chambers	0845 210 5555
Bournemouth	3 PB Barristers	01202 292102
Bristol	3 PB Barristers	0117 928 1520
Exeter	Walnut House	01392 279751
London	25 Bedford Row	020 7067 1500
	•One Essex Court	020 7583 2000
	•23 Essex Street	020 7413 0353
	Matrix Chambers	020 7404 3447
	Middle Temple Lane Chambers	020 7583 4352
	3 PB Barristers	020 7583 8055
	Serle Court	020 7242 6105
	Temple Tax Chambers	020 7353 7884
Manchester	18 St John Street	0161 278 1800
	•St Johns Buildings	0161 214 1500
Newcastle Upon Tyne	Dere Street Barristers	0844 3351551
Oxford	3 PB Barristers	01865 793 736
Winchester	3 PB Barristers	01962 868884

TAX INVESTIGATIONS

London	Temple Tax Chambers	020 7353 7884
Manchester	18 St John Street	0161 278 1800
Newcastle Upon Tyne	Dere Street Barristers	0844 3351551

TAXATION AND DUTIES

Birmingham	•St Philips Chambers	0121 246 7000
Exeter	Walnut House	01392 279751
London	Essex Court Chambers	020 7813 8000
	•39 Essex Street	020 7832 1111
	•Maitland Chambers	020 7406 1200
	18 Red Lion Court	020 7520 6000
	Temple Tax Chambers	020 7353 7884

TECHNICAL CONTRACTS

London	Arbitration Chambers	020 7267 2137
	Keating Chambers	020 7544 2600
	The Chambers of Grahame Aldous QC	020 7832 0500
Manchester	18 St John Street	0161 278 1800
Newcastle Upon Tyne	Dere Street Barristers	0844 3351551
Portsmouth	Portsmouth Barristers'Chambers	023 9283 1292

TECHNOLOGY AND CONSTRUCTION COURT

Bournemouth	3 PB Barristers	01202 292102
Bristol	3 PB Barristers	0117 928 1520
London	3 PB Barristers	020 7583 8055
	•Tanfield Chambers	020 7421 5300
Manchester	18 St John Street	0161 278 1800
Newcastle Upon Tyne	Dere Street Barristers	0844 3351551
Oxford	3 PB Barristers	01865 793 736
Portsmouth	Portsmouth Barristers'Chambers	023 9283 1292
Winchester	3 PB Barristers	01962 868884

• Expanded entry in Part D

TELECOMMUNICATIONS

London	Atkin Chambers	020 7404 0102
	Blackstone Chambers	020 7583 1770
	Brick Court Chambers	020 7379 3550
	•Devereux Chambers	020 7353 7534
	•One Essex Court	020 7583 2000
	Fountain Court Chambers	020 7583 3335
	•4-5 Gray's Inn Square	020 7404 5252
	•Henderson Chambers	020 7583 9020
	Keating Chambers	020 7544 2600
	•Maitland Chambers	020 7406 1200
	•Monckton Chambers	020 7405 7211
	•8 New Square	020 7405 4321
	4 Pump Court	020 7842 5555
	Serle Court	020 7242 6105
	•Three New Square IP	020 7405 1111
	3 Verulam Buildings	020 7831 8441
Manchester	St James's Chambers	0161 834 7000
	18 St John Street	0161 278 1800
	•St Johns Buildings	0161 214 1500

TERRORISM

Birmingham	St Ive's Chambers	0121 236 0863
Bristol	Queen Square Chambers	0117 921 1966
London	Bell Yard Chambers	020 7306 9292
	•187 Fleet Street	020 7430 7430
	15 New Bridge Street	020 7842 1900
	•3 Raymond Buildings	020 7400 6400
	18 Red Lion Court	020 7520 6000
Manchester	•St Johns Buildings	0161 214 1500
Newcastle Upon Tyne	Dere Street Barristers	0844 3351551

TIMESHARE

London	Five Paper	020 7815 3200
	Gough Square Chambers	020 7353 0924
Manchester	18 St John Street	0161 278 1800
Newcastle Upon Tyne	Dere Street Barristers	0844 3351551
Southampton	•College Chambers	023 8023 0338

TITLE TO LAND

Bristol	Queen Square Chambers	0117 921 1966
London	Five Paper	020 7815 3200
Manchester	18 St John Street	0161 278 1800
Newcastle Upon Tyne	Dere Street Barristers	0844 3351551
Portsmouth	Portsmouth Barristers'Chambers	023 9283 1292
Southampton	•College Chambers	023 8023 0338

TORTS

Birmingham	St Ive's Chambers	0121 236 0863
	•St Philips Chambers	0121 246 7000
Bournemouth	3 PB Barristers	01202 292102
Bristol	3 PB Barristers	0117 928 1520
	Queen Square Chambers	0117 921 1966
Exeter	Rougemont Chambers	01392 208484
	Walnut House	01392 279751
London	Five Paper	020 7815 3200
	4 King's Bench Walk	020 7822 7000
	3 PB Barristers	020 7583 8055
	The Chambers of Grahame Aldous QC	020 7832 0500
Manchester	18 St John Street	0161 278 1800
	•St Johns Buildings	0161 214 1500
Middlesbrough	•Trinity Chambers	01642 247569
Newcastle Upon Tyne	Dere Street Barristers	0844 3351551
	•Trinity Chambers	0191 232 1927
Oxford	3 PB Barristers	01865 793 736

Portsmouth	Guildhall Chambers Portsmouth	023 9275 2400
	Portsmouth Barristers'Chambers	023 9283 1292
Southampton	•College Chambers	023 8023 0338
Winchester	3 PB Barristers	01962 868884

TRADE DESCRIPTIONS ACT

Birmingham	St Ive's Chambers	0121 236 0863
Bristol	Queen Square Chambers	0117 921 1966
London	•Cornerstone Barristers	020 7242 4986
	Gough Square Chambers	020 7353 0924
	•Henderson Chambers	020 7583 9020
Manchester	18 St John Street	0161 278 1800

TRADE SECRETS

London	•8 New Square	020 7405 4321
Manchester	•St Johns Buildings	0161 214 1500
Portsmouth	Portsmouth Barristers'Chambers	023 9283 1292

TRADEMARKS

Birmingham	•No5 Chambers	0845 210 5555
	St Ive's Chambers	0121 236 0863
Bristol	No5 Chambers	0845 210 5555
	St John's Chambers	0117 923 4700
Chester	Linenhall Chambers	01244 348282
Exeter	Walnut House	01392 279751
Leeds	Chancery House Chambers	0113 244 6691
	Kings Chambers	0845 034 3444
	•Sovereign Chambers	0113 245 1841
London	•23 Essex Street	020 7413 0353
	Gough Square Chambers	020 7353 0924
	Lamb Chambers	020 7797 8300
	•Maitland Chambers	020 7406 1200
	•8 New Square	020 7405 4321
	No5 Chambers	0845 210 5555
	11 South Square	020 7405 1222
	•Three New Square IP	020 7405 1111
Manchester	•Cobden House Chambers	0161 833 6000
	Kings Chambers	0845 034 3444
	St James's Chambers	0161 834 7000
	18 St John Street	0161 278 1800
	•St Johns Buildings	0161 214 1500
Portsmouth	Portsmouth Barristers'Chambers	023 9283 1292

TRADING STANDARDS

Birmingham	St Ive's Chambers	0121 236 0863
	•St Philips Chambers	0121 246 7000
Bristol	Queen Square Chambers	0117 921 1966
London	•Arden Chambers	020 7242 4244
	•2 Bedford Row	020 7440 8888
	•Cornerstone Barristers	020 7242 4986
	•23 Essex Street	020 7413 0353
	Gough Square Chambers	020 7353 0924
	•Henderson Chambers	020 7583 9020
	6 Pump Court	020 7797 8400
	•3 Raymond Buildings	020 7400 6400
Maidstone	6 Pump Court Chambers	01622 688094
Manchester	18 St John Street	0161 278 1800
Newcastle Upon Tyne	Dere Street Barristers	0844 3351551

TRANSPORT AND WORKS ACT INQUIRIES

London	•Cornerstone Barristers	020 7242 4986
Manchester	18 St John Street	0161 278 1800
Newcastle Upon Tyne	Dere Street Barristers	0844 3351551
Southampton	•College Chambers	023 8023 0338

• Expanded entry in Part D

TRAVEL LAW

Birmingham	•No5 Chambers	0845 210 5555
	•St Philips Chambers	0121 246 7000
Exeter	Walnut House	01392 279751
London	1 Chancery Lane	0845 634 6666
	3 Hare Court	020 7415 7800
	•Henderson Chambers	020 7583 9020
	Outer Temple Chambers	020 7353 6381
	XXIV Old Buildings	020 7691 2424
Manchester	18 St John Street	0161 278 1800
	•St Johns Buildings	0161 214 1500
Newcastle Upon Tyne	Dere Street Barristers	0844 3351551

TRUST LITIGATION

Bournemouth	3 PB Barristers	01202 292102
Bristol	3 PB Barristers	0117 928 1520
London	Five Paper	020 7815 3200
	•Maitland Chambers	020 7406 1200
	3 PB Barristers	020 7583 8055
	XXIV Old Buildings	020 7691 2424
Manchester	18 St John Street	0161 278 1800
	•St Johns Buildings	0161 214 1500
Newcastle Upon Tyne	Dere Street Barristers	0844 3351551
Oxford	3 PB Barristers	01865 793 736
Portsmouth	Portsmouth Barristers'Chambers	023 9283 1292
Southampton	•College Chambers	023 8023 0338
Winchester	3 PB Barristers	01962 868884

TRUSTS

Birmingham	Cornwall Street Chambers	0121 233 7500
	No 8 Chambers	0121 236 5514
	•No5 Chambers	0845 210 5555
	St Ive's Chambers	0121 236 0863
	•St Philips Chambers	0121 246 7000
Bournemouth	3 PB Barristers	01202 292102
Bradford	Broadway House Chambers	01274 722560
Brighton	Crown Office Row Chambers	01273 625625
Bristol	Albion Chambers	0117 927 2144
	No5 Chambers	0845 210 5555
	3 PB Barristers	0117 928 1520
	St John's Chambers	0117 923 4700
	Unity Street Chambers	0117 906 9789
Chelmsford	Trinity Chambers	01245 605040
Chester	Linenhall Chambers	01244 348282
Chichester	Pallant Chambers	01243 784538
Exeter	Rougemont Chambers	01392 208484
	Walnut House	01392 279751
Faringdon	Faringdon Chambers	01367 240598
Ipswich	East Anglian Chambers	01473 214481
Leeds	Broadway House Chambers	0113 246 2600
	Chancery House Chambers	0113 244 6691
	Enterprise Chambers	0113 246 0391
	KBW	0113 297 1200
	Kings Chambers	0845 034 3444
	Park Court Chambers	0113 243 3277
	37 Park Square Chambers	0113 243 9422
	•Sovereign Chambers	0113 245 1841
	Zenith Chambers	0113 245 5438
Liverpool	Atlantic Chambers	0151 236 4421
London	•Arden Chambers	020 7242 4244
	•Chambers of Mr Ami Feder	020 7797 7788
	Enterprise Chambers	020 7405 9471
	Five Paper	020 7815 3200
	•Goldsmith Chambers	020 7353 6802

	Gough Square Chambers	020 7353 0924
	Hailsham Chambers	020 7643 5000
	Harcourt Chambers	0844 561 7135
	•1 KBW Chambers	020 7936 1500
	Lamb Chambers	020 7797 8300
	•Maitland Chambers	020 7406 1200
	New Square Chambers	020 7419 8000
	No5 Chambers	0845 210 5555
	•13 Old Square Chambers	020 7831 4445
	Outer Temple Chambers	020 7353 6381
	3 PB Barristers	020 7583 8055
	1 Pump Court	020 7842 7070
	•Pump Court Tax Chambers	020 7414 8080
	Radcliffe Chambers	020 7831 0081
	Selborne Chambers	020 7420 9500
	Serle Court	020 7242 6105
	•South Square	020 7696 9900
	3 Stone Buildings	020 7242 4937
	4 Stone Buildings	020 7242 5524
	•9 Stone Buildings	020 7404 5055
	11 Stone Buildings	020 7831 6381
	•Tanfield Chambers	020 7421 5300
	Taxchambers	020 7242 2744
	Temple Tax Chambers	020 7353 7884
	Ten Old Square	020 7405 0758
	The Chambers of Grahame Aldous QC	020 7832 0500
	•Wilberforce Chambers	020 7306 0102
	Wynne Chambers	020 3239 6964
	XXIV Old Buildings	020 7691 2424
Manchester	•Cobden House Chambers	0161 833 6000
	Deans Court Chambers	0161 214 6000
	Kings Chambers	0845 034 3444
	St James's Chambers	0161 834 7000
	9 St John Street	0161 955 9000
	18 St John Street	0161 278 1800
	•St Johns Buildings	0161 214 1500
Middlesbrough	Fountain Chambers	01642 804040
	•Trinity Chambers	01642 247569
Newcastle Upon Tyne	Dere Street Barristers	0844 3351551
	Enterprise Chambers	0191 222 3344
	•Trinity Chambers	0191 232 1927
Nottingham	KCH Garden Square	0115 941 8851
Oxford	Harcourt Chambers	0844 561 7135
	3 PB Barristers	01865 793 736
Preston	Deans Court Chambers	01772 565 600
Southampton	•College Chambers	023 8023 0338
Swansea	Iscoed Chambers	01792 652988
Winchester	3 PB Barristers	01962 868884

UNINCORPORATED ASSOCIATIONS

London	•Cornerstone Barristers	020 7242 4986
	Erskine Chambers	020 7242 5532
	13 King's Bench Walk	020 7353 7204
Manchester	18 St John Street	0161 278 1800
	•St Johns Buildings	0161 214 1500
Portsmouth	Portsmouth Barristers'Chambers	023 9283 1292

UNIT TRUSTS

London	Erskine Chambers	020 7242 5532

UNMARRIED COUPLES

Birmingham	St Ive's Chambers	0121 236 0863
Bristol	Queen Square Chambers	0117 921 1966
Exeter	Rougemont Chambers	01392 208484

	Walnut House	01392 279751
Faringdon	Faringdon Chambers	01367 240598
London	•29 Bedford Row Chambers	020 7404 1044
	Five Paper	020 7815 3200
	•1 KBW Chambers	020 7936 1500
	•4 Paper Buildings	020 7427 5200
	Renaissance Chambers	020 7404 1111
Manchester	18 St John Street	0161 278 1800
	•St Johns Buildings	0161 214 1500
Newcastle Upon Tyne	Dere Street Barristers	0844 3351551
Portsmouth	Guildhall Chambers Portsmouth	023 9275 2400
	Portsmouth Barristers'Chambers	023 9283 1292
Southampton	•College Chambers	023 8023 0338

UNREGISTERED DESIGNS

London	•8 New Square	020 7405 4321
Manchester	18 St John Street	0161 278 1800
Portsmouth	Portsmouth Barristers'Chambers	023 9283 1292

UTILITIES

London	•Cornerstone Barristers	020 7242 4986
	•One Essex Court	020 7583 2000
	Essex Court Chambers	020 7813 8000
	•39 Essex Street	020 7832 1111
	Francis Taylor Building	020 7353 8415
	•Henderson Chambers	020 7583 9020
	Keating Chambers	020 7544 2600
Manchester	•St Johns Buildings	0161 214 1500
Plymouth	Devon Chambers	01752 661659

VAT

Exeter	Walnut House	01392 279751
Leeds	KBW	0113 297 1200
London	25 Bedford Row	020 7067 1500
	1 Crown Office Row	020 7797 7500
	•23 Essex Street	020 7413 0353
	•187 Fleet Street	020 7430 7430
	•Monckton Chambers	020 7405 7211
	Prince Henry's Chambers	020 7837 1645
	•Pump Court Tax Chambers	020 7414 8080
	Temple Tax Chambers	020 7353 7884
Manchester	•Lincoln House Chambers	0161 832 5701
	18 St John Street	0161 278 1800
	•St Johns Buildings	0161 214 1500
Newcastle Upon Tyne	Dere Street Barristers	0844 3351551

WAR CRIMES TRIBUNALS

London	•2 Bedford Row	020 7440 8888
	•Goldsmith Chambers	020 7353 6802
	•Pump Court Chambers	020 7353 0711
	•3 Raymond Buildings	020 7400 6400
Middlesbrough	•Trinity Chambers	01642 247569
Newcastle Upon Tyne	•Trinity Chambers	0191 232 1927
Swindon	Pump Court Chambers	01793 539899
Winchester	Pump Court Chambers	01962 868 161

WARDSHIP

Birmingham	St Ive's Chambers	0121 236 0863
Bournemouth	3 PB Barristers	01202 292102
Bristol	3 PB Barristers	0117 928 1520
	Queen Square Chambers	0117 921 1966
Exeter	Rougemont Chambers	01392 208484
London	•29 Bedford Row Chambers	020 7404 1044
	•1 KBW Chambers	020 7936 1500
	3 PB Barristers	020 7583 8055

A

	Renaissance Chambers	020 7404 1111
	The Chambers of Grahame Aldous QC	020 7832 0500
Manchester	18 St John Street	0161 278 1800
Middlesbrough	Amicus Chambers	01642 876334
Newcastle Upon Tyne	Dere Street Barristers	0844 3351551
Oxford	3 PB Barristers	01865 793 736
Portsmouth	Guildhall Chambers Portsmouth	023 9275 2400
Southampton	•College Chambers	023 8023 0338
Winchester	3 PB Barristers	01962 868884

WARRANTY CLAIMS

London	Erskine Chambers	020 7242 5532
	•One Essex Court	020 7583 2000
	Five Paper	020 7815 3200
	•Henderson Chambers	020 7583 9020
	•Maitland Chambers	020 7406 1200
Portsmouth	Portsmouth Barristers'Chambers	023 9283 1292

WATER

London	•Cornerstone Barristers	020 7242 4986
	•Henderson Chambers	020 7583 9020
Manchester	18 St John Street	0161 278 1800
	•St Johns Buildings	0161 214 1500
Newcastle Upon Tyne	Dere Street Barristers	0844 3351551

WILLS

Birmingham	Cornwall Street Chambers	0121 233 7500
	No 8 Chambers	0121 236 5514
	•No5 Chambers	0845 210 5555
	St Ive's Chambers	0121 236 0863
Bournemouth	3 PB Barristers	01202 292102
Bradford	Broadway House Chambers	01274 722560
Bristol	Albion Chambers	0117 927 2144
	No5 Chambers	0845 210 5555
	3 PB Barristers	0117 928 1520
	St John's Chambers	0117 923 4700
	Unity Street Chambers	0117 906 9789
Chelmsford	Trinity Chambers	01245 605040
Chester	Linenhall Chambers	01244 348282
Chichester	Pallant Chambers	01243 784538
Exeter	Rougemont Chambers	01392 208484
Faringdon	Faringdon Chambers	01367 240598
Ipswich	East Anglian Chambers	01473 214481
Leeds	Broadway House Chambers	0113 246 2600
	Chancery House Chambers	0113 244 6691
	Enterprise Chambers	0113 246 0391
	KBW	0113 297 1200
	Kings Chambers	0845 034 3444
	Park Court Chambers	0113 243 3277
	37 Park Square Chambers	0113 243 9422
	•Sovereign Chambers	0113 245 1841
	Zenith Chambers	0113 245 5438
Liverpool	Atlantic Chambers	0151 236 4421
London	•Arden Chambers	020 7242 4244
	•Chambers of Mr Ami Feder	020 7797 7788
	Enterprise Chambers	020 7405 9471
	Five Paper	020 7815 3200
	•Goldsmith Chambers	020 7353 6802
	Gough Square Chambers	020 7353 0924
	Harcourt Chambers	0844 561 7135
	Lamb Chambers	020 7797 8300
	•Maitland Chambers	020 7406 1200
	New Square Chambers	020 7419 8000
	No5 Chambers	0845 210 5555

• Expanded entry in Part D

	•13 Old Square Chambers	020 7831 4445
	3 PB Barristers	020 7583 8055
	1 Pump Court	020 7842 7070
	•Pump Court Tax Chambers	020 7414 8080
	Radcliffe Chambers	020 7831 0081
	Selborne Chambers	020 7420 9500
	Serle Court	020 7242 6105
	3 Stone Buildings	020 7242 4937
	4 Stone Buildings	020 7242 5524
	•9 Stone Buildings	020 7404 5055
	11 Stone Buildings	020 7831 6381
	Taxchambers	020 7242 2744
	Ten Old Square	020 7405 0758
	•Wilberforce Chambers	020 7306 0102
	Wynne Chambers	020 3239 6964
	XXIV Old Buildings	020 7691 2424
Manchester	•Cobden House Chambers	0161 833 6000
	Deans Court Chambers	0161 214 6000
	Kings Chambers	0845 034 3444
	St James's Chambers	0161 834 7000
	9 St John Street	0161 955 9000
	18 St John Street	0161 278 1800
Middlesbrough	Fountain Chambers	01642 804040
	•Trinity Chambers	01642 247569
Newcastle Upon Tyne	Dere Street Barristers	0844 3351551
	Enterprise Chambers	0191 222 3344
	•Trinity Chambers	0191 232 1927
Nottingham	KCH Garden Square	0115 941 8851
Oxford	Harcourt Chambers	0844 561 7135
	3 PB Barristers	01865 793 736
Portsmouth	Portsmouth Barristers'Chambers	023 9283 1292
Preston	Deans Court Chambers	01772 565 600
Swansea	Iscoed Chambers	01792 652988
Winchester	3 PB Barristers	01962 868884

• Expanded entry in Part D

PART B

Types of Work by Individual Barristers

This section lists individual barristers by the types of work in which they specialise. The areas of work are listed in alphabetical order. Within these main categoties, individual barristers are listed alphabetically by surname. For example, a reader wishing to locate a particular barrister specialising in trademarks would be able to look under 'T' for Trademarks and find under that heading those barristers who offer their services in this field. A complete list of the types of work can be found overleaf.

Each listing provides the name of the individual barrister and contact details. The first point of contact will be the clerk. (Details of clerks can be found in *Part D Chambers by Location*).

Please note that barristers are only listed in this section if information on specialisms has been supplied by them.

B

Type of Work

B

Name	Chambers	Telephone
Laney Miss Anna Marie	Crown Office Chambers, London	020 7797 8100
Smith Miss Joanna Angela	Wilberforce Chambers, London	020 7306 0102

ADMINISTRATIVE LAW

Name	Chambers	Telephone
Alesbury Mr Alun	Cornerstone Barristers, London	020 7242 4986
	12 Old Square Chambers, London	020 7404 0875
Beard Mr Mark Christopher	6 Pump Court, London	020 7797 8400
	6 Pump Court Chambers, Maidstone	01622 688094
Cornwell Dr James Matthew	11 King's Bench Walk, London	020 7632 8500
Daly Mr David	Heathway Chambers, London	020 8293 0509
Dingemans Mr James Michael	3 Hare Court, London	020 7415 7800
Dowley Mr Dominic Myles	Serle Court, London	020 7242 6105
Druce Mr Michael James	Cornerstone Barristers, London	020 7242 4986
Dutton Mr Timothy James	Fountain Court Chambers, London	020 7583 3335
Edington Mrs Fiona Anne Rider	Thomas More Chambers, London	020 7404 7000
Francis Mr Robert Anthony	3 Serjeants Inn, London	020 7427 5000
Giffin Mr Nigel Dyson	11 King's Bench Walk, London	020 7632 8500
Goudie Mr James	11 King's Bench Walk, London	020 7632 8500
Hockman Mr Stephen Alexander	6 Pump Court, London	020 7797 8400
	6 Pump Court Chambers, Maidstone	01622 688094
	Regency Chambers, Peterborough	01733 315215
Jones Mr Kelvin Mcallister	Templis Chambers, London	020 7649 9808
Nardell Mr Gordon Lawrence	39 Essex Street, London	020 7832 1111
	82 King Street, Manchester	0161 870 9969
O'Sullivan Mr Richard John	1215 Chambers, London	020 3291 1215
Rhodes Mr Robert Elliott	Outer Temple Chambers, London	020 7353 6381
	Principal Chambers, Sevenoaks	0845 209 8080
	St Philips Chambers, Birmingham	0121 246 7000
Roots Mr Guy Robert Godfrey	12 College Place, Southampton	023 8032 0320
	Francis Taylor Building, London	020 7353 8415
Sandham Mr James Andrew	Arden Chambers, London	020 7242 4244
Straker Mr Timothy Derrick	4-5 Gray's Inn Square, London	020 7404 5252
Williams Ms Heather Jean	Doughty Street Chambers, Bristol	01179 058 717
	Doughty Street Chambers, London	020 7404 1313
	Doughty Street Chambers, Manchester	0161 618 1066

ADMIRALTY

Name	Chambers	Telephone
Collett Mr Michael John	20 Essex Street, London	020 7842 1200
Selvaratnam Miss Vasanti Emily Indrani	Stone Chambers, London	020 7440 6900

ADOPTION

Name	Chambers	Telephone
Delahunty Ms Johanne Erica	4 Paper Buildings, London	020 7427 5200
	Park Lane Plowden, Leeds	0113 228 5049
	St Ive's Chambers, Birmingham	0121 236 0863
Harvey Miss Louise	College Chambers, Southampton	023 8023 0338
Purdie Mr Robert Anthony James	Faringdon Chambers, Faringdon	01367 240598
	4 King's Bench Walk, London	020 7822 7000

AGENCY

Name	Chambers	Telephone
Lowenstein Mr Paul David	3 Verulam Buildings, London	020 7831 8441

AGRICULTURE

Name	Chambers	Telephone
Cole Mr Edward Arthur	Falcon Chambers, London	020 7353 2484
Denyer-Green Mr Barry Peter Douglas	Falcon Chambers, London	020 7353 2484
Hutton Miss Caroline	Enterprise Chambers, Leeds	0113 246 0391
	Enterprise Chambers, London	020 7405 9471
	Enterprise Chambers, Newcastle Upon Tyne	0191 222 3344
Jourdan Mr Stephen Eric	Falcon Chambers, London	020 7353 2484
Newsom Mr George Lucien	Guildhall Chambers, Bristol	0117 930 9000
Peters Mr Edward James Hedley	Falcon Chambers, London	020 7353 2484
Rodger Mr Martin Owen	Falcon Chambers, London	020 7353 2484

Stevenson Dr Simon John	Park Lane Plowden, Leeds	0113 228 5049
Taskis Ms Catherine Louise	Falcon Chambers, London	020 7353 2484
Windsor Miss Emily May	Falcon Chambers, London	020 7353 2484

ALTERNATIVE DISPUTE RESOLUTION

Boyle Mr Alan Gordon	Serle Court, London	020 7242 6105
Laney Miss Anna Marie	Crown Office Chambers, London	020 7797 8100
Lowenstein Mr Paul David	3 Verulam Buildings, London	020 7831 8441
Tompkinson Miss Deborah Ann	Clerksroom (London), London	0845 083 3000
	Clerksroom (Taunton), Taunton	0845 083 3000

AMERICAN LAW

Moore Mr George Crawford Jackson	11 King's Bench Walk, London	020 7632 8500

ANCILLARY RELIEF

Ford Mr Gerard James	Old Court Chambers, Middlesbrough	01642 232523
Purdie Mr Robert Anthony James	Faringdon Chambers, Faringdon	01367 240598
	4 King's Bench Walk, London	020 7822 7000

ANGUILLA LAW

Moore Mr George Crawford Jackson	11 King's Bench Walk, London	020 7632 8500

ANIMALS

Menzies Mr Richard Mark	Lamb Chambers, London	020 7797 8300

ANTIGUA AND BARBUDA LAW

Moore Mr George Crawford Jackson	11 King's Bench Walk, London	020 7632 8500

ARBITRATION

Bellamy Mr Jonathan Mark	39 Essex Street, London	020 7832 1111
	82 King Street, Manchester	0161 870 9969
Boyle Mr Alan Gordon	Serle Court, London	020 7242 6105
Cole Mr Edward Arthur	Falcon Chambers, London	020 7353 2484
Collett Mr Michael John	20 Essex Street, London	020 7842 1200
De Verneuil Smith Mr Peter Robert	3 Verulam Buildings, London	020 7831 8441
Dowding Mr Nicholas Alan Tatham	Falcon Chambers, London	020 7353 2484
Dowley Mr Dominic Myles	Serle Court, London	020 7242 6105
Dutton Mr Timothy James	Fountain Court Chambers, London	020 7583 3335
Hutton Miss Caroline	Enterprise Chambers, Leeds	0113 246 0391
	Enterprise Chambers, London	020 7405 9471
	Enterprise Chambers, Newcastle Upon Tyne	0191 222 3344
Jess Dr Digby Charles	Exchange Chambers, Leeds	0113 203 1970
	Exchange Chambers, Liverpool	0151 236 7747
	Exchange Chambers, Manchester	0161 833 2722
Laney Miss Anna Marie	Crown Office Chambers, London	020 7797 8100
Lavender Mr Nicholas	Serle Court, London	020 7242 6105
McCredie Miss Fionnuala Mary Constance	Keating Chambers, London	020 7544 2600
Mold Mr Andrew Matthew Stephen	Wilberforce Chambers, London	020 7306 0102
Newsom Mr George Lucien	Guildhall Chambers, Bristol	0117 930 9000
Orr Mr Craig Wyndham	One Essex Court, London	020 7583 2000
Reeds Mr Gareth David	Canary Wharf Chambers, London	020 7183 8011
Reynolds Mr Kirk	Falcon Chambers, London	020 7353 2484
Selvaratnam Miss Vasanti Emily Indrani	Stone Chambers, London	020 7440 6900
Smith Miss Joanna Angela	Wilberforce Chambers, London	020 7306 0102
Thorley Mr Simon Joe	Three New Square IP, London	020 7405 1111
Trace Mr Anthony John	Maitland Chambers, London	020 7406 1200

Windsor Miss Emily May	Falcon Chambers, London	020 7353 2484

ARCHAEOLOGY

Lowenstein Mr Paul David	3 Verulam Buildings, London	020 7831 8441

ART

Lowenstein Mr Paul David	3 Verulam Buildings, London	020 7831 8441

ASBESTOS-RELATED DISEASES

Hodson Mr Peter David	Chambers of Ian Macdonald QC, Manchester	0161 236 1840
Phillips Mr Matthew James	Outer Temple Chambers, London	020 7353 6381

ASSESSMENT OF COSTS

Harvey Miss Louise	College Chambers, Southampton	023 8023 0338

ASSET FINANCE

Goodfellow Mr Giles William Jeremy	Pump Court Tax Chambers, London	020 7414 8080
Rushton Ms Nicola Jane	Five Paper, London	020 7815 3200

ASSET FORFEITURE

Dudley-Jones Ms Elizabeth Sarah	Deans Court Chambers, Manchester	0161 214 6000
	Deans Court Chambers, Preston	01772 565 600
Evans Mr Martin Alan Langham	Chambers of Andrew Mitchell QC, London	020 7440 9950
Fisher Mr Jonathan Simon	Devereux Chambers, London	020 7353 7534

ASSET RECOVERY

Douglas-Jones Mr Benjamin Timothy	Apex, Cardiff	02920 232 032
	Five Paper Buildings, London	020 7583 6117
Dudley-Jones Ms Elizabeth Sarah	Deans Court Chambers, Manchester	0161 214 6000
	Deans Court Chambers, Preston	01772 565 600
Fisher Mr Jonathan Simon	Devereux Chambers, London	020 7353 7534

AVIATION

Collett Mr Michael John	20 Essex Street, London	020 7842 1200
Howells Miss Katherine Jane	Old Square Chambers, Bristol	0117 930 5100
	Old Square Chambers, London	020 7269 0300
Lowenstein Mr Paul David	3 Verulam Buildings, London	020 7831 8441
Orr Mr Craig Wyndham	One Essex Court, London	020 7583 2000

BANKING

Acton Mr Stephen Neil	Radcliffe Chambers, London	020 7831 0081
Boyle Mr Alan Gordon	Serle Court, London	020 7242 6105
Collett Mr Michael John	20 Essex Street, London	020 7842 1200
De Verneuil Smith Mr Peter Robert	3 Verulam Buildings, London	020 7831 8441
Dowley Mr Dominic Myles	Serle Court, London	020 7242 6105
Lavender Mr Nicholas	Serle Court, London	020 7242 6105
Lowenstein Mr Paul David	3 Verulam Buildings, London	020 7831 8441
McCann Miss Sarah Jane	Hardwicke, London	020 7242 2523
Mold Mr Andrew Matthew Stephen	Wilberforce Chambers, London	020 7306 0102
Orr Mr Craig Wyndham	One Essex Court, London	020 7583 2000
Selvaratnam Miss Vasanti Emily Indrani	Stone Chambers, London	020 7440 6900
Sen Mr Aditya Kumar	Coram Chambers, London	020 7092 3700
Toube Ms Felicity Rosalind	South Square, London	020 7696 9900
Trace Mr Anthony John	Maitland Chambers, London	020 7406 1200
Walsh Mr Steven James Franklyn	Five Paper, London	020 7815 3200
Wardell Mr John David Meredith	Wilberforce Chambers, London	020 7306 0102
Waters Mr Malcolm Ian	Radcliffe Chambers, London	020 7831 0081
Wilson Mr Graham James	Gray's Inn Tax Chambers, London	020 7242 2642

Zelin Mr Geoffrey Andrew	Enterprise Chambers, Leeds	0113 246 0391
	Enterprise Chambers, London	020 7405 9471
	Enterprise Chambers, Newcastle Upon Tyne	0191 222 3344

BANKING AND FINANCE

Boyle Mr Alan Gordon	Serle Court, London	020 7242 6105
Fisher Mr Jonathan Simon	Devereux Chambers, London	020 7353 7534

BIOTECHNOLOGY

Campbell Mr Douglas James	Three New Square IP, London	020 7405 1111
Delaney Mr Joe	Three New Square IP, London	020 7405 1111
Jamal Miss Isabel Leila	8 New Square, London	020 7405 4321
Mitcheson Mr Thomas George Moseley	Three New Square IP, London	020 7405 1111
Thorley Mr Simon Joe	Three New Square IP, London	020 7405 1111

BOUNDARIES

Bignell Miss Janet Susan	Falcon Chambers, London	020 7353 2484
Butler Mr Andrew	Tanfield Chambers, London	020 7421 5300
Chapman Mr Vivian Robert	New Street Chambers, Leicester	0116 262 5906
	9 Stone Buildings, London	020 7404 5055
Dray Mr Martin Benedict Antony	Falcon Chambers, London	020 7353 2484
Harpum Mr Charles	Falcon Chambers, London	020 7353 2484
Karas Mr Jonathan Marcus	Wilberforce Chambers, London	020 7306 0102
Ross Martyn Mr John Greaves	New Square Chambers, London	020 7419 8000
	Octagon House, Norwich	01603 623186
Stevenson Dr Simon John	Park Lane Plowden, Leeds	0113 228 5049
Tanney Mr Anthony	Falcon Chambers, London	020 7353 2484
Tozer Miss Stephanie	Falcon Chambers, London	020 7353 2484

BREACH OF CONFIDENCE

Abrahams Mr James	8 New Square, London	020 7405 4321
Alexander Mr Daniel Sakyi	8 New Square, London	020 7405 4321
Baldwin Mr John Paul	8 New Square, London	020 7405 4321
Berkeley Miss Iona Sarah Caroline	8 New Square, London	020 7405 4321
Campbell Mr Douglas James	Three New Square IP, London	020 7405 1111
Chacksfield Mr Mark Andrew	8 New Square, London	020 7405 4321
Clark Miss Fiona Jane Stewart	8 New Square, London	020 7405 4321
Delaney Mr Joe	Three New Square IP, London	020 7405 1111
Hill Mr Jonathan	8 New Square, London	020 7405 4321
Howe Mr Martin Russell Thomson	8 New Square, London	020 7405 4321
Jamal Miss Isabel Leila	8 New Square, London	020 7405 4321
Jones Mr Kelvin Mcallister	Templis Chambers, London	020 7649 9808
Lane Ms Lindsay Ruth Busfield	8 New Square, London	020 7405 4321
Lawrence Dr Heather Bunting Elizabeth	11 South Square, London	020 7405 1222
Lowenstein Mr Paul David	3 Verulam Buildings, London	020 7831 8441
Lykiardopoulos Mr Andrew Nicolas	8 New Square, London	020 7405 4321
May Miss Charlotte Louisa	8 New Square, London	020 7405 4321
Meade Mr Richard David	8 New Square, London	020 7405 4321
Mellor Mr Edward James Wilson	8 New Square, London	020 7405 4321
Mitcheson Mr Thomas George Moseley	Three New Square IP, London	020 7405 1111
Moody-Stuart Mr Thomas	8 New Square, London	020 7405 4321
Onslow Mr Robert Denzil	8 New Square, London	020 7405 4321
Platts-Mills Mr Mark Fortescue	8 New Square, London	020 7405 4321
Speck Mr Adrian	8 New Square, London	020 7405 4321
St Ville Mr Laurence James	8 New Square, London	020 7405 4321
Tappin Mr Michael John	8 New Square, London	020 7405 4321
Thorley Mr Simon Joe	Three New Square IP, London	020 7405 1111
Ward Mr Robin Henry	8 New Square, London	020 7405 4321

Whyte Dr James Richard Cleland | 8 New Square, London | 020 7405 4321

BRITISH VIRGIN ISLANDS LAW

Moore Mr George Crawford Jackson | 11 King's Bench Walk, London | 020 7632 8500

BRITISH WEST INDIES LAW

Moore Mr George Crawford Jackson | 11 King's Bench Walk, London | 020 7632 8500

BUILDING

Smith Miss Joanna Angela | Wilberforce Chambers, London | 020 7306 0102

BUILDING SOCIETIES

Ovey Miss Elizabeth Helen	Radcliffe Chambers, London	020 7831 0081
Waters Mr Malcolm Ian	Radcliffe Chambers, London	020 7831 0081

CAPITAL TAX

Aaronson Mr Graham Raphael	Pump Court Tax Chambers, London	020 7414 8080
Baldry Mr Rupert Patrick Craig	Pump Court Tax Chambers, London	020 7414 8080
Bradley Mr Charles Edward May	Pump Court Tax Chambers, London	020 7414 8080
Bremner Mr Jonathan Sinclair Grant	Pump Court Tax Chambers, London	020 7414 8080
Bryant Miss Judith Anne	Wilberforce Chambers, London	020 7306 0102
Campbell Miss Emily Charlotte	Wilberforce Chambers, London	020 7306 0102
Chacko Mr Thomas Joseph	Pump Court Tax Chambers, London	020 7414 8080
Child Mr John Frederick	Wilberforce Chambers, London	020 7306 0102
Choudhury Miss Sadiya Asghar	Pump Court Tax Chambers, London	020 7414 8080
Conolly Dr Oliver Stephen	Pump Court Tax Chambers, London	020 7414 8080
Dunn Ms Sarah Patricia Quincey	Pump Court Tax Chambers, London	020 7414 8080
Ewart Mr David Scott	Pump Court Tax Chambers, London	020 7414 8080
Frawley Ms Lyndsey Anne	Quorum Chambers, St Albans	01727 884516
	Quorum Tax Chambers, London	020 7043 5189
Furness Mr Michael James	Wilberforce Chambers, London	020 7306 0102
Ghosh Mr Indranil Julian	Pump Court Tax Chambers, London	020 7414 8080
Goodfellow Mr Giles William Jeremy	Pump Court Tax Chambers, London	020 7414 8080
Green Mr Brian Russell	Wilberforce Chambers, London	020 7306 0102
Henderson Mr James Thomas	Kings Chambers, Leeds	0845 034 3444
	Kings Chambers, Manchester	0845 034 3444
	Pump Court Tax Chambers, London	020 7414 8080
Herbert Mr Mark Jeremy	5 Stone Buildings, London	020 7242 6201
Hilliard Mr Jonathan Adam	Wilberforce Chambers, London	020 7306 0102
Massey Mr William Greville Sale	Pump Court Tax Chambers, London	020 7414 8080
Matthews Mr Janek Paul	Pump Court Tax Chambers, London	020 7414 8080
Milne Mr David Calder	Pump Court Tax Chambers, London	020 7414 8080
Mold Mr Andrew Matthew Stephen	Wilberforce Chambers, London	020 7306 0102
Nugee Mr Edward George	Wilberforce Chambers, London	020 7306 0102
Poots Miss Laura Jill	Pump Court Tax Chambers, London	020 7414 8080
Prosser Mr Kevin John	Pump Court Tax Chambers, London	020 7414 8080
Richards Mr Ian	Pump Court Tax Chambers, London	020 7414 8080
Rivett Mr James Peter	Pump Court Tax Chambers, London	020 7414 8080
Southern Mr David Boardman	Temple Tax Chambers, London	020 7353 7884
Tallon Mr John Mark	Pump Court Tax Chambers, London	020 7414 8080
Thomas Mr Roger Christopher	Pump Court Tax Chambers, London	020 7414 8080
Thornhill Mr Andrew Robert	Albion Chambers, Bristol	0117 927 2144
	Pump Court Tax Chambers, London	020 7414 8080
Vallat Mr Richard Justin	Pump Court Tax Chambers, London	020 7414 8080
Wilson Miss Mary Elizabeth Frances	Pump Court Tax Chambers, London	020 7414 8080
Wilson Mr Graham James	Gray's Inn Tax Chambers, London	020 7242 2642
Woolf The Hon Jeremy Richard George	Pump Court Tax Chambers, London	020 7414 8080
Yang Dr Zizhen	Pump Court Tax Chambers, London	020 7414 8080
Yates Mr David James Francis	Pump Court Tax Chambers, London	020 7414 8080

CARE PROCEEDINGS

Carrodus Miss Gail Caroline | Huntercombe Chambers, Henley-On-Thames | 01491 641934

Delahunty Ms Johanne Erica	4 Paper Buildings, London	020 7427 5200
	Park Lane Plowden, Leeds	0113 228 5049
	St Ive's Chambers, Birmingham	0121 236 0863
Ford Mr Gerard James	Old Court Chambers, Middlesbrough	01642 232523
Harvey Miss Louise	College Chambers, Southampton	023 8023 0338
Pope Mrs Heather	1 Hare Court, London	020 7797 7070
Purdie Mr Robert Anthony James	Faringdon Chambers, Faringdon	01367 240598
	4 King's Bench Walk, London	020 7822 7000

CHANCERY

Boyle Mr Alan Gordon	Serle Court, London	020 7242 6105
Carr Mr Adrian James Selden	Tanfield Chambers, London	020 7421 5300
Ferber Ms Iris	42 Bedford Row, London	020 7831 0222
Fetherstonhaugh Mr Guy Cuthbert Charles	Falcon Chambers, London	020 7353 2484
Ross Martyn Mr John Greaves	New Square Chambers, London	020 7419 8000
	Octagon House, Norwich	01603 623186

CHANCERY (COMMERCIAL)

Bacon Mr Nicholas Michael	Four New Square, London	020 7822 2000
Boyle Mr Alan Gordon	Serle Court, London	020 7242 6105
Butler Mr Andrew	Tanfield Chambers, London	020 7421 5300
Hattan Mr Simon Justin	Serle Court, London	020 7242 6105
Jones Mr Kelvin Mcallister	Templis Chambers, London	020 7649 9808
Lightman Mr Daniel	Serle Court, London	020 7242 6105
Lowenstein Mr Paul David	3 Verulam Buildings, London	020 7831 8441
Rushton Ms Nicola Jane	Five Paper, London	020 7815 3200
Smith Miss Joanna Angela	Wilberforce Chambers, London	020 7306 0102
Stallworthy Mr Nicolas Kyd	Outer Temple Chambers, London	020 7353 6381

CHANCERY (GENERAL)

Acton Mr Stephen Neil	Radcliffe Chambers, London	020 7831 0081
Asplin Miss Sarah Jane	3 Stone Buildings, London	020 7242 4937
Berkley Mr Michael Stuart	Rougemont Chambers, Exeter	01392 208484
Bloch Mr Michael Gordon	Wilberforce Chambers, London	020 7306 0102
Bornman Miss Kerry	3 Stone Buildings, London	020 7242 4937
Boyle Mr Alan Gordon	Serle Court, London	020 7242 6105
Bryant Miss Judith Anne	Wilberforce Chambers, London	020 7306 0102
Butler Mr Andrew	Tanfield Chambers, London	020 7421 5300
Campbell Miss Emily Charlotte	Wilberforce Chambers, London	020 7306 0102
Chapman Mr Vivian Robert	New Street Chambers, Leicester	0116 262 5906
	9 Stone Buildings, London	020 7404 5055
Child Mr John Frederick	Wilberforce Chambers, London	020 7306 0102
Cowen Mr Gary Adam	Falcon Chambers, London	020 7353 2484
Daly Mr David	Heathway Chambers, London	020 8293 0509
Dutton Mr Timothy James	Fountain Court Chambers, London	020 7583 3335
Fancourt Mr Timothy Miles	Falcon Chambers, London	020 7353 2484
Francis Mr Andrew James	Serle Court, London	020 7242 6105
	Zenith Chambers, Leeds	0113 245 5438
Frawley Ms Lyndsey Anne	Quorum Chambers, St Albans	01727 884516
	Quorum Tax Chambers, London	020 7043 5189
Furness Mr Michael James	Wilberforce Chambers, London	020 7306 0102
Green Mr Brian Russell	Wilberforce Chambers, London	020 7306 0102
Ham Mr Robert Wallace	Wilberforce Chambers, London	020 7306 0102
Harpum Mr Charles	Falcon Chambers, London	020 7353 2484
Heather Mr Christopher Mark	Tanfield Chambers, London	020 7421 5300
Herbert Mr Mark Jeremy	5 Stone Buildings, London	020 7242 6201
Hilliard Mr Jonathan Adam	Wilberforce Chambers, London	020 7306 0102
Hinks Mr Frank Peter	Serle Court, London	020 7242 6105
Hochberg Mr Daniel Alan	Wilberforce Chambers, London	020 7306 0102
Jackson Mr Nicholas David Kingsley	Atlantic Chambers, Liverpool	0151 236 4421
Lightman Mr Daniel	Serle Court, London	020 7242 6105
Lloyd Mr Stephen James George	13 Old Square Chambers, London	020 7831 4445
Lowe Mr Thomas William Gordon	Wilberforce Chambers, London	020 7306 0102

Martin Mr John Vandeleur	Wilberforce Chambers, London	020 7306 0102
McCann Miss Sarah Jane	Hardwicke, London	020 7242 2523
Mold Mr Andrew Matthew Stephen	Wilberforce Chambers, London	020 7306 0102
Newsom Mr George Lucien	Guildhall Chambers, Bristol	0117 930 9000
Nugee Mr Christopher George	Wilberforce Chambers, London	020 7306 0102
Nugee Mr Edward George	Wilberforce Chambers, London	020 7306 0102
O'Mahony Mr Jonathan Solomon	9 Stone Buildings, London	020 7404 5055
O'Sullivan Mr Michael Morton	5 Stone Buildings, London	020 7242 6201
Ovey Miss Elizabeth Helen	Radcliffe Chambers, London	020 7831 0081
Purdie Mr Robert Anthony James	Faringdon Chambers, Faringdon	01367 240598
	4 King's Bench Walk, London	020 7822 7000
Reeds Mr Gareth David	Canary Wharf Chambers, London	020 7183 8011
Rodger Mr Martin Owen	Falcon Chambers, London	020 7353 2484
Ross Martyn Mr John Greaves	New Square Chambers, London	020 7419 8000
	Octagon House, Norwich	01603 623186
Rowley Mr Keith Nigel	Radcliffe Chambers, London	020 7831 0081
Sandham Mr James Andrew	Arden Chambers, London	020 7242 4244
Sawyer Mr Edward Humphrey	Wilberforce Chambers, London	020 7306 0102
Sen Mr Aditya Kumar	Coram Chambers, London	020 7092 3700
Smith Miss Joanna Angela	Wilberforce Chambers, London	020 7306 0102
Stevenson Dr Simon John	Park Lane Plowden, Leeds	0113 228 5049
Studer Mr Mark Edgar Walter	Wilberforce Chambers, London	020 7306 0102
Thomas-Symonds Mr Nicklaus	Civitas Chambers, Cardiff	0845 0713 007
Toube Ms Felicity Rosalind	South Square, London	020 7696 9900
Tozer Miss Stephanie	Falcon Chambers, London	020 7353 2484
Trace Mr Anthony John	Maitland Chambers, London	020 7406 1200
Tunkel Mr Alan Michael	3 Stone Buildings, London	020 7242 4937
Walsh Mr Steven James Franklyn	Five Paper, London	020 7815 3200
Wardell Mr John David Meredith	Wilberforce Chambers, London	020 7306 0102
West Mr Mark	Radcliffe Chambers, London	020 7831 0081
Wicks Ms Joanne	Wilberforce Chambers, London	020 7306 0102
Windsor Miss Emily May	Falcon Chambers, London	020 7353 2484
Zelin Mr Geoffrey Andrew	Enterprise Chambers, Leeds	0113 246 0391
	Enterprise Chambers, London	020 7405 9471
	Enterprise Chambers, Newcastle Upon Tyne	0191 222 3344

CHANCERY (LAND LAW)

Acton Mr Stephen Neil	Radcliffe Chambers, London	020 7831 0081
Berkley Mr Michael Stuart	Rougemont Chambers, Exeter	01392 208484
Bignell Miss Janet Susan	Falcon Chambers, London	020 7353 2484
Bornman Miss Kerry	3 Stone Buildings, London	020 7242 4937
Boyle Mr Alan Gordon	Serle Court, London	020 7242 6105
Buckpitt Mr Michael David	Tanfield Chambers, London	020 7421 5300
Butler Mr Andrew	Tanfield Chambers, London	020 7421 5300
Campbell Miss Emily Charlotte	Wilberforce Chambers, London	020 7306 0102
Chapman Mr Vivian Robert	New Street Chambers, Leicester	0116 262 5906
	9 Stone Buildings, London	020 7404 5055
Clark Mr Wayne Vincent	Falcon Chambers, London	020 7353 2484
Cole Mr Edward Arthur	Falcon Chambers, London	020 7353 2484
Cowen Mr Gary Adam	Falcon Chambers, London	020 7353 2484
Daly Mr David	Heathway Chambers, London	020 8293 0509
Denyer-Green Mr Barry Peter Douglas	Falcon Chambers, London	020 7353 2484
Dowding Mr Nicholas Alan Tatham	Falcon Chambers, London	020 7353 2484
Dray Mr Martin Benedict Antony	Falcon Chambers, London	020 7353 2484
Fain Mr Carl Ian	Tanfield Chambers, London	020 7421 5300
Fancourt Mr Timothy Miles	Falcon Chambers, London	020 7353 2484
Fitzgerald Miss Elizabeth Helen	Falcon Chambers, London	020 7353 2484
Francis Mr Andrew James	Serle Court, London	020 7242 6105
	Zenith Chambers, Leeds	0113 245 5438
Frawley Ms Lyndsey Anne	Quorum Chambers, St Albans	01727 884516
	Quorum Tax Chambers, London	020 7043 5189
Gallagher Mr Stanley Harold	Tanfield Chambers, London	020 7421 5300

Harpum Mr Charles	Falcon Chambers, London	020 7353 2484
Heather Mr Christopher Mark	Tanfield Chambers, London	020 7421 5300
Hilliard Mr Jonathan Adam	Wilberforce Chambers, London	020 7306 0102
Hinks Mr Frank Peter	Serle Court, London	020 7242 6105
Hochberg Mr Daniel Alan	Wilberforce Chambers, London	020 7306 0102
Hutchings Mr Martin Anthony	Wilberforce Chambers, London	020 7306 0102
Hutton Miss Caroline	Enterprise Chambers, Leeds	0113 246 0391
	Enterprise Chambers, London	020 7405 9471
	Enterprise Chambers, Newcastle Upon Tyne	0191 222 3344
Jourdan Mr Stephen Eric	Falcon Chambers, London	020 7353 2484
Karas Mr Jonathan Marcus	Wilberforce Chambers, London	020 7306 0102
Lloyd Mr Stephen James George	13 Old Square Chambers, London	020 7831 4445
Loveday Mr Mark Alan	Tanfield Chambers, London	020 7421 5300
Martin Mr John Vandeleur	Wilberforce Chambers, London	020 7306 0102
McCann Miss Sarah Jane	Hardwicke, London	020 7242 2523
Mold Mr Andrew Matthew Stephen	Wilberforce Chambers, London	020 7306 0102
Nugee Mr Christopher George	Wilberforce Chambers, London	020 7306 0102
Nugee Mr Edward George	Wilberforce Chambers, London	020 7306 0102
O'Sullivan Mr Michael Morton	5 Stone Buildings, London	020 7242 6201
O'Sullivan Mr Richard John	1215 Chambers, London	020 3291 1215
Peters Mr Edward James Hedley	Falcon Chambers, London	020 7353 2484
Radevsky Mr Anthony Eric	Falcon Chambers, London	020 7353 2484
Reynolds Mr Kirk	Falcon Chambers, London	020 7353 2484
Rodger Mr Martin Owen	Falcon Chambers, London	020 7353 2484
Ross Martyn Mr John Greaves	New Square Chambers, London	020 7419 8000
	Octagon House, Norwich	01603 623186
Sandham Mr James Andrew	Arden Chambers, London	020 7242 4244
Sawyer Mr Edward Humphrey	Wilberforce Chambers, London	020 7306 0102
Stevenson Dr Simon John	Park Lane Plowden, Leeds	0113 228 5049
Studer Mr Mark Edgar Walter	Wilberforce Chambers, London	020 7306 0102
Tanney Mr Anthony	Falcon Chambers, London	020 7353 2484
Taskis Ms Catherine Louise	Falcon Chambers, London	020 7353 2484
Tozer Miss Stephanie	Falcon Chambers, London	020 7353 2484
Trace Mr Anthony John	Maitland Chambers, London	020 7406 1200
Tunkel Mr Alan Michael	3 Stone Buildings, London	020 7242 4937
Waters Mr Malcolm Ian	Radcliffe Chambers, London	020 7831 0081
West Mr Mark	Radcliffe Chambers, London	020 7831 0081
Wicks Ms Joanne	Wilberforce Chambers, London	020 7306 0102
Windsor Miss Emily May	Falcon Chambers, London	020 7353 2484
Zelin Mr Geoffrey Andrew	Enterprise Chambers, Leeds	0113 246 0391
	Enterprise Chambers, London	020 7405 9471
	Enterprise Chambers, Newcastle Upon Tyne	0191 222 3344

CHARITIES

Bryant Miss Judith Anne	Wilberforce Chambers, London	020 7306 0102
Campbell Miss Emily Charlotte	Wilberforce Chambers, London	020 7306 0102
Chapman Mr Vivian Robert	New Street Chambers, Leicester	0116 262 5906
	9 Stone Buildings, London	020 7404 5055
Child Mr John Frederick	Wilberforce Chambers, London	020 7306 0102
Furness Mr Michael James	Wilberforce Chambers, London	020 7306 0102
Green Mr Brian Russell	Wilberforce Chambers, London	020 7306 0102
Ham Mr Robert Wallace	Wilberforce Chambers, London	020 7306 0102
Hochberg Mr Daniel Alan	Wilberforce Chambers, London	020 7306 0102
Lloyd Mr Stephen James George	13 Old Square Chambers, London	020 7831 4445
Mold Mr Andrew Matthew Stephen	Wilberforce Chambers, London	020 7306 0102
Newsom Mr George Lucien	Guildhall Chambers, Bristol	0117 930 9000
Nugee Mr Edward George	Wilberforce Chambers, London	020 7306 0102
Quint Ms Joan Francesca Rae	Radcliffe Chambers, London	020 7831 0081
Reeds Mr Gareth David	Canary Wharf Chambers, London	020 7183 8011
Ross Martyn Mr John Greaves	New Square Chambers, London	020 7419 8000
	Octagon House, Norwich	01603 623186
Smith Dr Peter Michael	Radcliffe Chambers, London	020 7831 0081

Stevenson Dr Simon John	Park Lane Plowden, Leeds	0113 228 5049
Studer Mr Mark Edgar Walter	Wilberforce Chambers, London	020 7306 0102
Thomson Mr Martin Haldane Ahmad	Wynne Chambers, London	020 3239 6964
Tunkel Mr Alan Michael	3 Stone Buildings, London	020 7242 4937
West Mr Mark	Radcliffe Chambers, London	020 7831 0081

CHILD ABDUCTION

Purdie Mr Robert Anthony James	Faringdon Chambers, Faringdon	01367 240598
	4 King's Bench Walk, London	020 7822 7000

CHILD ABUSE

Purdie Mr Robert Anthony James	Faringdon Chambers, Faringdon	01367 240598
	4 King's Bench Walk, London	020 7822 7000

CHILD CARE LAW

Purdie Mr Robert Anthony James	Faringdon Chambers, Faringdon	01367 240598
	4 King's Bench Walk, London	020 7822 7000

CHILD SUPPORT

Purdie Mr Robert Anthony James	Faringdon Chambers, Faringdon	01367 240598
	4 King's Bench Walk, London	020 7822 7000

CHILDREN

Delahunty Ms Johanne Erica	4 Paper Buildings, London	020 7427 5200
	Park Lane Plowden, Leeds	0113 228 5049
	St Ive's Chambers, Birmingham	0121 236 0863
Harvey Miss Louise	College Chambers, Southampton	023 8023 0338
Pope Mrs Heather	1 Hare Court, London	020 7797 7070

CIVIL ACTIONS AGAINST THE POLICE

Barton Miss Fiona	5 Essex Court, London	020 7410 2000
Bassett Mr John Stewart Britten	5 Essex Court, London	020 7410 2000
Rogers Mr Kenneth Edward	Assize Court Chambers, Bristol	0117 926 4587
	Invictus Chambers London, London	
Tompkinson Miss Deborah Ann	Clerksroom (London), London	0845 083 3000
	Clerksroom (Taunton), Taunton	0845 083 3000
Williams Ms Heather Jean	Doughty Street Chambers, Bristol	01179 058 717
	Doughty Street Chambers, London	020 7404 1313
	Doughty Street Chambers, Manchester	0161 618 1066

CIVIL FRAUD

Boyle Mr Alan Gordon	Serle Court, London	020 7242 6105
Butler Mr Andrew	Tanfield Chambers, London	020 7421 5300
Fisher Mr Jonathan Simon	Devereux Chambers, London	020 7353 7534
Lightman Mr Daniel	Serle Court, London	020 7242 6105
Rushton Ms Nicola Jane	Five Paper, London	020 7815 3200
Selvaratnam Miss Vasanti Emily Indrani	Stone Chambers, London	020 7440 6900
Walford Mr Richard Henry Howard	Serle Court, London	020 7242 6105

CIVIL LAW

Butler Mr Andrew	Tanfield Chambers, London	020 7421 5300
Tompkinson Miss Deborah Ann	Clerksroom (London), London	0845 083 3000
	Clerksroom (Taunton), Taunton	0845 083 3000

CIVIL LIBERTIES

Bassett Mr John Stewart Britten	5 Essex Court, London	020 7410 2000
Dingemans Mr James Michael	3 Hare Court, London	020 7415 7800
Finch Ms Nadine Elizabeth	Garden Court Chambers, London	020 7993 7600
Giffin Mr Nigel Dyson	11 King's Bench Walk, London	020 7632 8500
Nardell Mr Gordon Lawrence	39 Essex Street, London	020 7832 1111
	82 King Street, Manchester	0161 870 9969
Straker Mr Timothy Derrick	4-5 Gray's Inn Square, London	020 7404 5252
Thomas-Symonds Mr Nicklaus	Civitas Chambers, Cardiff	0845 0713 007

Williams Ms Heather Jean	Doughty Street Chambers, Bristol	01179 058 717
	Doughty Street Chambers, London	020 7404 1313
	Doughty Street Chambers, Manchester	0161 618 1066

CIVIL LITIGATION

Lavender Mr Nicholas	Serle Court, London	020 7242 6105

CIVIL PARTNERSHIPS

Carrodus Miss Gail Caroline	Huntercombe Chambers, Henley-On-Thames	01491 641934
Purdie Mr Robert Anthony James	Faringdon Chambers, Faringdon	01367 240598
	4 King's Bench Walk, London	020 7822 7000

CIVIL RECOVERY

Evans Mr Martin Alan Langham	Chambers of Andrew Mitchell QC, London	020 7440 9950

CLINICAL NEGLIGENCE

Badenoch Mr James Forster	1 Crown Office Row, London	020 7797 7500
Boyd Miss Kerstin Margaret	Tanfield Chambers, London	020 7421 5300
Briden Mr Timothy John	Lamb Chambers, London	020 7797 8300
Cherry Mr John Mitchell	Lamb Chambers, London	020 7797 8300
Furniss Mr Richard Alexander	42 Bedford Row, London	020 7831 0222
Howells Miss Katherine Jane	Old Square Chambers, Bristol	0117 930 5100
	Old Square Chambers, London	020 7269 0300
Jerram Ms Harriet Anne	Outer Temple Chambers, London	020 7353 6381
Latimer-Sayer Mr William Laurence	Cloisters, London	020 7827 4000
Menzies Mr Richard Mark	Lamb Chambers, London	020 7797 8300
Michael Mr Simon Laurence	No5 Chambers, Birmingham	0845 210 5555
	No5 Chambers, Bristol	0845 210 5555
	No5 Chambers, London	0845 210 5555
Phillips Mr Matthew James	Outer Temple Chambers, London	020 7353 6381
Pitchers Mr Henry William Stodart	No5 Chambers, Birmingham	0845 210 5555
	No5 Chambers, Bristol	0845 210 5555
	No5 Chambers, London	0845 210 5555
Tavares Mr Nathan Warren	Outer Temple Chambers, London	020 7353 6381

COHABITATION

Carrodus Miss Gail Caroline	Huntercombe Chambers, Henley-On-Thames	01491 641934
Purdie Mr Robert Anthony James	Faringdon Chambers, Faringdon	01367 240598
	4 King's Bench Walk, London	020 7822 7000

COMMERCIAL CONTRACTS

Jamal Miss Isabel Leila	8 New Square, London	020 7405 4321
Lowenstein Mr Paul David	3 Verulam Buildings, London	020 7831 8441
Smith Miss Joanna Angela	Wilberforce Chambers, London	020 7306 0102
Stallworthy Mr Nicolas Kyd	Outer Temple Chambers, London	020 7353 6381

COMMERCIAL FRAUD

Boyle Mr Alan Gordon	Serle Court, London	020 7242 6105
Hattan Mr Simon Justin	Serle Court, London	020 7242 6105
Lowe Mr Thomas William Gordon	Wilberforce Chambers, London	020 7306 0102
Lowenstein Mr Paul David	3 Verulam Buildings, London	020 7831 8441
Rhodes Mr Robert Elliott	Outer Temple Chambers, London	020 7353 6381
	Principal Chambers, Sevenoaks	0845 209 8080
	St Philips Chambers, Birmingham	0121 246 7000

COMMERCIAL LAW

Bloch Mr Michael Gordon	Wilberforce Chambers, London	020 7306 0102
Child Mr John Frederick	Wilberforce Chambers, London	020 7306 0102
Collett Mr Michael John	20 Essex Street, London	020 7842 1200
Cornwell Dr James Matthew	11 King's Bench Walk, London	020 7632 8500
Dowley Mr Dominic Myles	Serle Court, London	020 7242 6105
Dutton Mr Timothy James	Fountain Court Chambers, London	020 7583 3335

Ferber Ms Iris	42 Bedford Row, London	020 7831 0222
Lowenstein Mr Paul David	3 Verulam Buildings, London	020 7831 8441
McCann Miss Sarah Jane	Hardwicke, London	020 7242 2523
McPherson Mr Graeme Paul	Four New Square, London	020 7822 2000
Mold Mr Andrew Matthew Stephen	Wilberforce Chambers, London	020 7306 0102
Moser Mr Philip Curt Harold	Monckton Chambers, London	020 7405 7211
Orr Mr Craig Wyndham	One Essex Court, London	020 7583 2000
Reeds Mr Gareth David	Canary Wharf Chambers, London	020 7183 8011
Rhodes Mr Robert Elliott	Outer Temple Chambers, London	020 7353 6381
	Principal Chambers, Sevenoaks	0845 209 8080
	St Philips Chambers, Birmingham	0121 246 7000
Rushton Ms Nicola Jane	Five Paper, London	020 7815 3200
Sawyer Mr Edward Humphrey	Wilberforce Chambers, London	020 7306 0102
Selvaratnam Miss Vasanti Emily Indrani	Stone Chambers, London	020 7440 6900
Smith Miss Joanna Angela	Wilberforce Chambers, London	020 7306 0102
Stoner Mr Christopher Paul	Serle Court, London	020 7242 6105
Thomas-Symonds Mr Nicklaus	Civitas Chambers, Cardiff	0845 0713 007
Toube Ms Felicity Rosalind	South Square, London	020 7696 9900
Trace Mr Anthony John	Maitland Chambers, London	020 7406 1200
Treasure Mr Francis Seton	42 Bedford Row, London	020 7831 0222
Tunkel Mr Alan Michael	3 Stone Buildings, London	020 7242 4937

COMMERCIAL LITIGATION

Acton Mr Stephen Neil	Radcliffe Chambers, London	020 7831 0081
Bellamy Mr Jonathan Mark	39 Essex Street, London	020 7832 1111
	82 King Street, Manchester	0161 870 9969
Berkley Mr Michael Stuart	Rougemont Chambers, Exeter	01392 208484
Bloch Mr Michael Gordon	Wilberforce Chambers, London	020 7306 0102
Boyd Mr Stephen James Harvey	Selborne Chambers, London	020 7420 9500
Boyle Mr Alan Gordon	Serle Court, London	020 7242 6105
Butler Mr Andrew	Tanfield Chambers, London	020 7421 5300
Carr Miss Sue Lascelles	Four New Square, London	020 7822 2000
Collett Mr Michael John	20 Essex Street, London	020 7842 1200
De Verneuil Smith Mr Peter Robert	3 Verulam Buildings, London	020 7831 8441
Dingemans Mr James Michael	3 Hare Court, London	020 7415 7800
Dowley Mr Dominic Myles	Serle Court, London	020 7242 6105
Dutton Mr Timothy James	Fountain Court Chambers, London	020 7583 3335
Fain Mr Carl Ian	Tanfield Chambers, London	020 7421 5300
Fancourt Mr Timothy Miles	Falcon Chambers, London	020 7353 2484
Frawley Ms Lyndsey Anne	Quorum Chambers, St Albans	01727 884516
	Quorum Tax Chambers, London	020 7043 5189
Giffin Mr Nigel Dyson	11 King's Bench Walk, London	020 7632 8500
Goudie Mr James	11 King's Bench Walk, London	020 7632 8500
Hattan Mr Simon Justin	Serle Court, London	020 7242 6105
Hilliard Mr Jonathan Adam	Wilberforce Chambers, London	020 7306 0102
Hochberg Mr Daniel Alan	Wilberforce Chambers, London	020 7306 0102
Hutchings Mr Martin Anthony	Wilberforce Chambers, London	020 7306 0102
Jackson Mr Nicholas David Kingsley	Atlantic Chambers, Liverpool	0151 236 4421
Jess Dr Digby Charles	Exchange Chambers, Leeds	0113 203 1970
	Exchange Chambers, Liverpool	0151 236 7747
	Exchange Chambers, Manchester	0161 833 2722
Jones Mr Kelvin Mcallister	Templis Chambers, London	020 7649 9808
Laney Miss Anna Marie	Crown Office Chambers, London	020 7797 8100
Lightman Mr Daniel	Serle Court, London	020 7242 6105
Lowe Mr Thomas William Gordon	Wilberforce Chambers, London	020 7306 0102
Lowenstein Mr Paul David	3 Verulam Buildings, London	020 7831 8441
MacNab Mr Alexander Andrew	Monckton Chambers, London	020 7405 7211
Martin Mr John Vandeleur	Wilberforce Chambers, London	020 7306 0102
McCann Miss Sarah Jane	Hardwicke, London	020 7242 2523
McCredie Miss Fionnuala Mary Constance	Keating Chambers, London	020 7544 2600
McPherson Mr Graeme Paul	Four New Square, London	020 7822 2000
Mold Mr Andrew Matthew Stephen	Wilberforce Chambers, London	020 7306 0102

Nardell Mr Gordon Lawrence	39 Essex Street, London	020 7832 1111
	82 King Street, Manchester	0161 870 9969
Nugee Mr Christopher George	Wilberforce Chambers, London	020 7306 0102
Orr Mr Craig Wyndham	One Essex Court, London	020 7583 2000
Reed Mr Jeremy Nigel	Hogarth Chambers, London	020 7404 0404
Reeds Mr Gareth David	Canary Wharf Chambers, London	020 7183 8011
Rushton Ms Nicola Jane	Five Paper, London	020 7815 3200
Selvaratnam Miss Vasanti Emily Indrani	Stone Chambers, London	020 7440 6900
Sen Mr Aditya Kumar	Coram Chambers, London	020 7092 3700
Smith Miss Joanna Angela	Wilberforce Chambers, London	020 7306 0102
Stallworthy Mr Nicolas Kyd	Outer Temple Chambers, London	020 7353 6381
Stoner Mr Christopher Paul	Serle Court, London	020 7242 6105
Tompkinson Miss Deborah Ann	Clerksroom (London), London	0845 083 3000
	Clerksroom (Taunton), Taunton	0845 083 3000
Toube Ms Felicity Rosalind	South Square, London	020 7696 9900
Trace Mr Anthony John	Maitland Chambers, London	020 7406 1200
Tunkel Mr Alan Michael	3 Stone Buildings, London	020 7242 4937
Walford Mr Richard Henry Howard	Serle Court, London	020 7242 6105
Walsh Mr Steven James Franklyn	Five Paper, London	020 7815 3200
Wardell Mr John David Meredith	Wilberforce Chambers, London	020 7306 0102
West Mr Mark	Radcliffe Chambers, London	020 7831 0081
Wicks Ms Joanne	Wilberforce Chambers, London	020 7306 0102
Windsor Miss Emily May	Falcon Chambers, London	020 7353 2484

B

COMMERCIAL PLANNING

Boyle Mr Alan Gordon	Serle Court, London	020 7242 6105

COMMERCIAL PROPERTY

Acton Mr Stephen Neil	Radcliffe Chambers, London	020 7831 0081
Barnes Mr Michael	Wilberforce Chambers, London	020 7306 0102
Berkley Mr Michael Stuart	Rougemont Chambers, Exeter	01392 208484
Bignell Miss Janet Susan	Falcon Chambers, London	020 7353 2484
Butler Mr Andrew	Tanfield Chambers, London	020 7421 5300
Chapman Mr Vivian Robert	New Street Chambers, Leicester	0116 262 5906
	9 Stone Buildings, London	020 7404 5055
Clark Mr Wayne Vincent	Falcon Chambers, London	020 7353 2484
Cole Mr Edward Arthur	Falcon Chambers, London	020 7353 2484
Cowen Mr Gary Adam	Falcon Chambers, London	020 7353 2484
Denyer-Green Mr Barry Peter Douglas	Falcon Chambers, London	020 7353 2484
Dowding Mr Nicholas Alan Tatham	Falcon Chambers, London	020 7353 2484
Dray Mr Martin Benedict Antony	Falcon Chambers, London	020 7353 2484
Fancourt Mr Timothy Miles	Falcon Chambers, London	020 7353 2484
Fitzgerald Miss Elizabeth Helen	Falcon Chambers, London	020 7353 2484
Francis Mr Andrew James	Serle Court, London	020 7242 6105
	Zenith Chambers, Leeds	0113 245 5438
Gallagher Mr Stanley Harold	Tanfield Chambers, London	020 7421 5300
Harpum Mr Charles	Falcon Chambers, London	020 7353 2484
Heather Mr Christopher Mark	Tanfield Chambers, London	020 7421 5300
Hilliard Mr Jonathan Adam	Wilberforce Chambers, London	020 7306 0102
Hochberg Mr Daniel Alan	Wilberforce Chambers, London	020 7306 0102
Hutchings Mr Martin Anthony	Wilberforce Chambers, London	020 7306 0102
Hutton Miss Caroline	Enterprise Chambers, Leeds	0113 246 0391
	Enterprise Chambers, London	020 7405 9471
	Enterprise Chambers, Newcastle Upon Tyne	0191 222 3344
Jackson Mr Nicholas David Kingsley	Atlantic Chambers, Liverpool	0151 236 4421
Jourdan Mr Stephen Eric	Falcon Chambers, London	020 7353 2484
Karas Mr Jonathan Marcus	Wilberforce Chambers, London	020 7306 0102
Loveday Mr Mark Alan	Tanfield Chambers, London	020 7421 5300
Martin Mr John Vandeleur	Wilberforce Chambers, London	020 7306 0102
McCann Miss Sarah Jane	Hardwicke, London	020 7242 2523
Mold Mr Andrew Matthew Stephen	Wilberforce Chambers, London	020 7306 0102

Nugee Mr Christopher George	Wilberforce Chambers, London	020 7306 0102
Nugee Mr Edward George	Wilberforce Chambers, London	020 7306 0102
Radevsky Mr Anthony Eric	Falcon Chambers, London	020 7353 2484
Reeds Mr Gareth David	Canary Wharf Chambers, London	020 7183 8011
Reynolds Mr Kirk	Falcon Chambers, London	020 7353 2484
Rodger Mr Martin Owen	Falcon Chambers, London	020 7353 2484
Rowley Mr Keith Nigel	Radcliffe Chambers, London	020 7831 0081
Sandham Mr James Andrew	Arden Chambers, London	020 7242 4244
Tanney Mr Anthony	Falcon Chambers, London	020 7353 2484
Tozer Miss Stephanie	Falcon Chambers, London	020 7353 2484
Trace Mr Anthony John	Maitland Chambers, London	020 7406 1200
Tunkel Mr Alan Michael	3 Stone Buildings, London	020 7242 4937
Wardell Mr John David Meredith	Wilberforce Chambers, London	020 7306 0102
West Mr Mark	Radcliffe Chambers, London	020 7831 0081
Wicks Ms Joanne	Wilberforce Chambers, London	020 7306 0102
Windsor Miss Emily May	Falcon Chambers, London	020 7353 2484
Zelin Mr Geoffrey Andrew	Enterprise Chambers, Leeds	0113 246 0391
	Enterprise Chambers, London	020 7405 9471
	Enterprise Chambers, Newcastle Upon Tyne	0191 222 3344

COMMERCIAL REGULATION

Boyle Mr Alan Gordon	Serle Court, London	020 7242 6105
Rhodes Mr Robert Elliott	Outer Temple Chambers, London	020 7353 6381
	Principal Chambers, Sevenoaks	0845 209 8080
	St Philips Chambers, Birmingham	0121 246 7000

COMMODITIES

Collett Mr Michael John	20 Essex Street, London	020 7842 1200
Dowley Mr Dominic Myles	Serle Court, London	020 7242 6105
Lowenstein Mr Paul David	3 Verulam Buildings, London	020 7831 8441
Selvaratnam Miss Vasanti Emily Indrani	Stone Chambers, London	020 7440 6900

COMMON LAND

Acton Mr Stephen Neil	Radcliffe Chambers, London	020 7831 0081
Alesbury Mr Alun	Cornerstone Barristers, London	020 7242 4986
	12 Old Square Chambers, London	020 7404 0875
Bignell Miss Janet Susan	Falcon Chambers, London	020 7353 2484
Chapman Mr Vivian Robert	New Street Chambers, Leicester	0116 262 5906
	9 Stone Buildings, London	020 7404 5055
Cowen Mr Gary Adam	Falcon Chambers, London	020 7353 2484
Denyer-Green Mr Barry Peter Douglas	Falcon Chambers, London	020 7353 2484
Druce Mr Michael James	Cornerstone Barristers, London	020 7242 4986
Ellis Miss Rosalind Morag	Cornerstone Barristers, London	020 7242 4986
Harpum Mr Charles	Falcon Chambers, London	020 7353 2484
Hinks Mr Frank Peter	Serle Court, London	020 7242 6105
Hutton Miss Caroline	Enterprise Chambers, Leeds	0113 246 0391
	Enterprise Chambers, London	020 7405 9471
	Enterprise Chambers, Newcastle Upon Tyne	0191 222 3344
Jourdan Mr Stephen Eric	Falcon Chambers, London	020 7353 2484
Karas Mr Jonathan Marcus	Wilberforce Chambers, London	020 7306 0102
Newsom Mr George Lucien	Guildhall Chambers, Bristol	0117 930 9000
Nugee Mr Edward George	Wilberforce Chambers, London	020 7306 0102
Rodger Mr Martin Owen	Falcon Chambers, London	020 7353 2484
Sandham Mr James Andrew	Arden Chambers, London	020 7242 4244
Stevenson Dr Simon John	Park Lane Plowden, Leeds	0113 228 5049
Tozer Miss Stephanie	Falcon Chambers, London	020 7353 2484

COMMON LAW (GENERAL)

Bassett Mr John Stewart Britten	5 Essex Court, London	020 7410 2000
Berkley Mr Michael Stuart	Rougemont Chambers, Exeter	01392 208484

Boyd Mr Stephen James Harvey	Selborne Chambers, London	020 7420 9500
Dingemans Mr James Michael	3 Hare Court, London	020 7415 7800
Fain Mr Carl Ian	Tanfield Chambers, London	020 7421 5300
Ford Mr Gerard James	Old Court Chambers, Middlesbrough	01642 232523
Francis Mr Robert Anthony	3 Serjeants Inn, London	020 7427 5000
Harvey Miss Louise	College Chambers, Southampton	023 8023 0338
Hockman Mr Stephen Alexander	6 Pump Court, London	020 7797 8400
	6 Pump Court Chambers, Maidstone	01622 688094
	Regency Chambers, Peterborough	01733 315215
Howells Miss Katherine Jane	Old Square Chambers, Bristol	0117 930 5100
	Old Square Chambers, London	020 7269 0300
Jess Dr Digby Charles	Exchange Chambers, Leeds	0113 203 1970
	Exchange Chambers, Liverpool	0151 236 7747
	Exchange Chambers, Manchester	0161 833 2722
Mawhinney Mr Richard Martin	Outer Temple Chambers, London	020 7353 6381
	St John's Chambers, Bristol	0117 923 4700
McCann Miss Sarah Jane	Hardwicke, London	020 7242 2523
Rogers Mr Kenneth Edward	Assize Court Chambers, Bristol	0117 926 4587
	Invictus Chambers London, London	
Sandham Mr James Andrew	Arden Chambers, London	020 7242 4244
Tavares Mr Nathan Warren	Outer Temple Chambers, London	020 7353 6381
Tompkinson Miss Deborah Ann	Clerksroom (London), London	0845 083 3000
	Clerksroom (Taunton), Taunton	0845 083 3000
Treasure Mr Francis Seton	42 Bedford Row, London	020 7831 0222
West Mr Mark	Radcliffe Chambers, London	020 7831 0081

B

COMMUNICATIONS

Campbell Mr Douglas James	Three New Square IP, London	020 7405 1111
Whyte Dr James Richard Cleland	8 New Square, London	020 7405 4321

COMMUNITY CARE

Finch Ms Nadine Elizabeth	Garden Court Chambers, London	020 7993 7600
O'Sullivan Mr Richard John	1215 Chambers, London	020 3291 1215

COMPANY, COMMERCIAL AND COMPETITION

Acton Mr Stephen Neil	Radcliffe Chambers, London	020 7831 0081
Bloch Mr Michael Gordon	Wilberforce Chambers, London	020 7306 0102
Boyle Mr Alan Gordon	Serle Court, London	020 7242 6105
Campbell Mr Douglas James	Three New Square IP, London	020 7405 1111
Lloyd Mr Stephen James George	13 Old Square Chambers, London	020 7831 4445
Martin Mr John Vandeleur	Wilberforce Chambers, London	020 7306 0102
Mold Mr Andrew Matthew Stephen	Wilberforce Chambers, London	020 7306 0102
Orr Mr Craig Wyndham	One Essex Court, London	020 7583 2000
Reeds Mr Gareth David	Canary Wharf Chambers, London	020 7183 8011
Rowley Mr Keith Nigel	Radcliffe Chambers, London	020 7831 0081
Sen Mr Aditya Kumar	Coram Chambers, London	020 7092 3700
Toube Ms Felicity Rosalind	South Square, London	020 7696 9900
Trace Mr Anthony John	Maitland Chambers, London	020 7406 1200
Tunkel Mr Alan Michael	3 Stone Buildings, London	020 7242 4937
Walsh Mr Steven James Franklyn	Five Paper, London	020 7815 3200
West Mr Mark	Radcliffe Chambers, London	020 7831 0081
Wilson Mr Graham James	Gray's Inn Tax Chambers, London	020 7242 2642
Zelin Mr Geoffrey Andrew	Enterprise Chambers, Leeds	0113 246 0391
	Enterprise Chambers, London	020 7405 9471
	Enterprise Chambers, Newcastle Upon Tyne	0191 222 3344

COMPANY LAW

Boyle Mr Alan Gordon	Serle Court, London	020 7242 6105
Lightman Mr Daniel	Serle Court, London	020 7242 6105

COMPETITION LAW

Abrahams Mr James	8 New Square, London	020 7405 4321
Alexander Mr Daniel Sakyi	8 New Square, London	020 7405 4321
Baldwin Mr John Paul	8 New Square, London	020 7405 4321

Chacksfield Mr Mark Andrew	8 New Square, London	020 7405 4321
Clark Miss Fiona Jane Stewart	8 New Square, London	020 7405 4321
Hamer Mr George Clemens	8 New Square, London	020 7405 4321
Hill Mr Jonathan	8 New Square, London	020 7405 4321
Howe Mr Martin Russell Thomson	8 New Square, London	020 7405 4321
Jamal Miss Isabel Leila	8 New Square, London	020 7405 4321
Jones Mr Kelvin Mcallister	Templis Chambers, London	020 7649 9808
MacNab Mr Alexander Andrew	Monckton Chambers, London	020 7405 7211
Meade Mr Richard David	8 New Square, London	020 7405 4321
Mellor Mr Edward James Wilson	8 New Square, London	020 7405 4321
Moody-Stuart Mr Thomas	8 New Square, London	020 7405 4321
Onslow Mr Robert Denzil	8 New Square, London	020 7405 4321
Platts-Mills Mr Mark Fortescue	8 New Square, London	020 7405 4321
Reeds Mr Gareth David	Canary Wharf Chambers, London	020 7183 8011
Selvaratnam Miss Vasanti Emily Indrani	Stone Chambers, London	020 7440 6900
Speck Mr Adrian	8 New Square, London	020 7405 4321
St Ville Mr Laurence James	8 New Square, London	020 7405 4321
Stevenson Dr Simon John	Park Lane Plowden, Leeds	0113 228 5049
Ward Mr Robin Henry	8 New Square, London	020 7405 4321

COMPULSORY PURCHASE

Alesbury Mr Alun	Cornerstone Barristers, London	020 7242 4986
	12 Old Square Chambers, London	020 7404 0875
Barnes Mr Michael	Wilberforce Chambers, London	020 7306 0102
Chapman Mr Vivian Robert	New Street Chambers, Leicester	0116 262 5906
	9 Stone Buildings, London	020 7404 5055
Cowen Mr Gary Adam	Falcon Chambers, London	020 7353 2484
Denyer-Green Mr Barry Peter Douglas	Falcon Chambers, London	020 7353 2484
Druce Mr Michael James	Cornerstone Barristers, London	020 7242 4986
Karas Mr Jonathan Marcus	Wilberforce Chambers, London	020 7306 0102
Newsom Mr George Lucien	Guildhall Chambers, Bristol	0117 930 9000
Roots Mr Guy Robert Godfrey	12 College Place, Southampton	023 8032 0320
	Francis Taylor Building, London	020 7353 8415

COMPUTER CONTRACTS

Campbell Mr Douglas James	Three New Square IP, London	020 7405 1111
Jones Mr Kelvin Mcallister	Templis Chambers, London	020 7649 9808
Whyte Dr James Richard Cleland	8 New Square, London	020 7405 4321

COMPUTER CRIME

Dudley-Jones Ms Elizabeth Sarah	Deans Court Chambers, Manchester	0161 214 6000
	Deans Court Chambers, Preston	01772 565 600
Fisher Mr Jonathan Simon	Devereux Chambers, London	020 7353 7534

COMPUTER LITIGATION

Alexander Mr Daniel Sakyi	8 New Square, London	020 7405 4321
Baldwin Mr John Paul	8 New Square, London	020 7405 4321
Campbell Mr Douglas James	Three New Square IP, London	020 7405 1111
Howe Mr Martin Russell Thomson	8 New Square, London	020 7405 4321
Jones Mr Kelvin Mcallister	Templis Chambers, London	020 7649 9808
Lawrence Dr Heather Bunting Elizabeth	11 South Square, London	020 7405 1222
Lowenstein Mr Paul David	3 Verulam Buildings, London	020 7831 8441
Meade Mr Richard David	8 New Square, London	020 7405 4321
Mellor Mr Edward James Wilson	8 New Square, London	020 7405 4321
Moody-Stuart Mr Thomas	8 New Square, London	020 7405 4321
Onslow Mr Robert Denzil	8 New Square, London	020 7405 4321
Platts-Mills Mr Mark Fortescue	8 New Square, London	020 7405 4321
St Ville Mr Laurence James	8 New Square, London	020 7405 4321

Whyte Dr James Richard Cleland	8 New Square, London	020 7405 4321

CONCILIATION

Boyle Mr Alan Gordon	Serle Court, London	020 7242 6105

CONFIDENTIAL INFORMATION

Berkeley Miss Iona Sarah Caroline	8 New Square, London	020 7405 4321
Bowhill Miss Jessie Kate	8 New Square, London	020 7405 4321
Campbell Mr Douglas James	Three New Square IP, London	020 7405 1111
Hamer Mr George Clemens	8 New Square, London	020 7405 4321
Hill Mr Jonathan	8 New Square, London	020 7405 4321
Jamal Miss Isabel Leila	8 New Square, London	020 7405 4321
Jones Mr Kelvin Mcallister	Templis Chambers, London	020 7649 9808
Lowenstein Mr Paul David	3 Verulam Buildings, London	020 7831 8441
Lykiardopoulos Mr Andrew Nicolas	8 New Square, London	020 7405 4321
Mitcheson Mr Thomas George Moseley	Three New Square IP, London	020 7405 1111
Reed Mr Jeremy Nigel	Hogarth Chambers, London	020 7404 0404
Thorley Mr Simon Joe	Three New Square IP, London	020 7405 1111
Whyte Dr James Richard Cleland	8 New Square, London	020 7405 4321

CONFISCATION

Evans Mr Martin Alan Langham	Chambers of Andrew Mitchell QC, London	020 7440 9950
Fisher Mr Jonathan Simon	Devereux Chambers, London	020 7353 7534
Rhodes Mr Robert Elliott	Outer Temple Chambers, London	020 7353 6381
	Principal Chambers, Sevenoaks	0845 209 8080
	St Philips Chambers, Birmingham	0121 246 7000

CONFISCATION OF THE PROCEEDS OF CRIME

Dudley-Jones Ms Elizabeth Sarah	Deans Court Chambers, Manchester	0161 214 6000
	Deans Court Chambers, Preston	01772 565 600

CONFLICT OF LAWS

Alexander Mr Daniel Sakyi	8 New Square, London	020 7405 4321
Bryant Miss Judith Anne	Wilberforce Chambers, London	020 7306 0102
Campbell Miss Emily Charlotte	Wilberforce Chambers, London	020 7306 0102
Child Mr John Frederick	Wilberforce Chambers, London	020 7306 0102
Collett Mr Michael John	20 Essex Street, London	020 7842 1200
Dowley Mr Dominic Myles	Serle Court, London	020 7242 6105
Lowenstein Mr Paul David	3 Verulam Buildings, London	020 7831 8441
Mold Mr Andrew Matthew Stephen	Wilberforce Chambers, London	020 7306 0102
Moser Mr Philip Curt Harold	Monckton Chambers, London	020 7405 7211
Reeds Mr Gareth David	Canary Wharf Chambers, London	020 7183 8011
Selvaratnam Miss Vasanti Emily Indrani	Stone Chambers, London	020 7440 6900
Walsh Mr Steven James Franklyn	Five Paper, London	020 7815 3200

CONSTITUTIONAL AND ADMINISTRATIVE LAW

Edington Mrs Fiona Anne Rider	Thomas More Chambers, London	020 7404 7000
Jones Mr Kelvin Mcallister	Templis Chambers, London	020 7649 9808
O'Sullivan Mr Richard John	1215 Chambers, London	020 3291 1215

CONSTRUCTION LAW

Bellamy Mr Jonathan Mark	39 Essex Street, London	020 7832 1111
	82 King Street, Manchester	0161 870 9969
Dowley Mr Dominic Myles	Serle Court, London	020 7242 6105
Jess Dr Digby Charles	Exchange Chambers, Leeds	0113 203 1970
	Exchange Chambers, Liverpool	0151 236 7747
	Exchange Chambers, Manchester	0161 833 2722
Laney Miss Anna Marie	Crown Office Chambers, London	020 7797 8100
McCann Miss Sarah Jane	Hardwicke, London	020 7242 2523
McCredie Miss Fionnuala Mary Constance	Keating Chambers, London	020 7544 2600
Smith Miss Joanna Angela	Wilberforce Chambers, London	020 7306 0102

Thomas-Symonds Mr Nicklaus	Civitas Chambers, Cardiff	0845 0713 007

CONSUMER CREDIT

Waters Mr Malcolm Ian	Radcliffe Chambers, London	020 7831 0081

CONSUMER LAW

Ford Mr Gerard James	Old Court Chambers, Middlesbrough	01642 232523
Reeds Mr Gareth David	Canary Wharf Chambers, London	020 7183 8011
Tompkinson Miss Deborah Ann	Clerksroom (London), London	0845 083 3000
	Clerksroom (Taunton), Taunton	0845 083 3000

CONTRACTS

Frawley Ms Lyndsey Anne	Quorum Chambers, St Albans	01727 884516
	Quorum Tax Chambers, London	020 7043 5189
Jones Mr Kelvin Mcallister	Templis Chambers, London	020 7649 9808
Smith Miss Joanna Angela	Wilberforce Chambers, London	020 7306 0102
Tavares Mr Nathan Warren	Outer Temple Chambers, London	020 7353 6381

CONVEYANCING

Acton Mr Stephen Neil	Radcliffe Chambers, London	020 7831 0081
Bignell Miss Janet Susan	Falcon Chambers, London	020 7353 2484
Chapman Mr Vivian Robert	New Street Chambers, Leicester	0116 262 5906
	9 Stone Buildings, London	020 7404 5055
Clark Mr Wayne Vincent	Falcon Chambers, London	020 7353 2484
Cowen Mr Gary Adam	Falcon Chambers, London	020 7353 2484
Denyer-Green Mr Barry Peter Douglas	Falcon Chambers, London	020 7353 2484
Dowding Mr Nicholas Alan Tatham	Falcon Chambers, London	020 7353 2484
Dray Mr Martin Benedict Antony	Falcon Chambers, London	020 7353 2484
Francis Mr Andrew James	Serle Court, London	020 7242 6105
	Zenith Chambers, Leeds	0113 245 5438
Gallagher Mr Stanley Harold	Tanfield Chambers, London	020 7421 5300
Harpum Mr Charles	Falcon Chambers, London	020 7353 2484
Hutton Miss Caroline	Enterprise Chambers, Leeds	0113 246 0391
	Enterprise Chambers, London	020 7405 9471
	Enterprise Chambers, Newcastle Upon Tyne	0191 222 3344
Jourdan Mr Stephen Eric	Falcon Chambers, London	020 7353 2484
Karas Mr Jonathan Marcus	Wilberforce Chambers, London	020 7306 0102
Lloyd Mr Stephen James George	13 Old Square Chambers, London	020 7831 4445
Nugee Mr Edward George	Wilberforce Chambers, London	020 7306 0102
O'Sullivan Mr Michael Morton	5 Stone Buildings, London	020 7242 6201
Radevsky Mr Anthony Eric	Falcon Chambers, London	020 7353 2484
Ross Martyn Mr John Greaves	New Square Chambers, London	020 7419 8000
	Octagon House, Norwich	01603 623186
Sandham Mr James Andrew	Arden Chambers, London	020 7242 4244
Studer Mr Mark Edgar Walter	Wilberforce Chambers, London	020 7306 0102
Tanney Mr Anthony	Falcon Chambers, London	020 7353 2484
Tunkel Mr Alan Michael	3 Stone Buildings, London	020 7242 4937
Waters Mr Malcolm Ian	Radcliffe Chambers, London	020 7831 0081
West Mr Mark	Radcliffe Chambers, London	020 7831 0081
Wicks Ms Joanne	Wilberforce Chambers, London	020 7306 0102

COPYRIGHT

Abrahams Mr James	8 New Square, London	020 7405 4321
Alexander Mr Daniel Sakyi	8 New Square, London	020 7405 4321
Baldwin Mr John Paul	8 New Square, London	020 7405 4321
Berkeley Miss Iona Sarah Caroline	8 New Square, London	020 7405 4321
Bloch Mr Michael Gordon	Wilberforce Chambers, London	020 7306 0102
Bowhill Miss Jessie Kate	8 New Square, London	020 7405 4321
Campbell Mr Douglas James	Three New Square IP, London	020 7405 1111
Chacksfield Mr Mark Andrew	8 New Square, London	020 7405 4321
Clark Miss Fiona Jane Stewart	8 New Square, London	020 7405 4321
Colley Dr Peter Mclean	Hogarth Chambers, London	020 7404 0404
Delaney Mr Joe	Three New Square IP, London	020 7405 1111

Douglas-Jones Mr Benjamin Timothy	Apex, Cardiff	02920 232 032
	Five Paper Buildings, London	020 7583 6117
Hamer Mr George Clemens	8 New Square, London	020 7405 4321
Hill Mr Jonathan	8 New Square, London	020 7405 4321
Howe Mr Martin Russell Thomson	8 New Square, London	020 7405 4321
Jackson Mr Nicholas David Kingsley	Atlantic Chambers, Liverpool	0151 236 4421
Jamal Miss Isabel Leila	8 New Square, London	020 7405 4321
Jones Mr Kelvin Mcallister	Templis Chambers, London	020 7649 9808
Lane Ms Lindsay Ruth Busfield	8 New Square, London	020 7405 4321
Lawrence Dr Heather Bunting Elizabeth	11 South Square, London	020 7405 1222
Lowe Mr Thomas William Gordon	Wilberforce Chambers, London	020 7306 0102
Lykiardopoulos Mr Andrew Nicolas	8 New Square, London	020 7405 4321
Mawhinney Mr Richard Martin	Outer Temple Chambers, London	020 7353 6381
	St John's Chambers, Bristol	0117 923 4700
May Miss Charlotte Louisa	8 New Square, London	020 7405 4321
Meade Mr Richard David	8 New Square, London	020 7405 4321
Mellor Mr Edward James Wilson	8 New Square, London	020 7405 4321
Mitcheson Mr Thomas George Moseley	Three New Square IP, London	020 7405 1111
Moody-Stuart Mr Thomas	8 New Square, London	020 7405 4321
Onslow Mr Robert Denzil	8 New Square, London	020 7405 4321
Platts-Mills Mr Mark Fortescue	8 New Square, London	020 7405 4321
Reed Mr Jeremy Nigel	Hogarth Chambers, London	020 7404 0404
Speck Mr Adrian	8 New Square, London	020 7405 4321
St Ville Mr Laurence James	8 New Square, London	020 7405 4321
Stevenson Dr Simon John	Park Lane Plowden, Leeds	0113 228 5049
Tappin Mr Michael John	8 New Square, London	020 7405 4321
Thorley Mr Simon Joe	Three New Square IP, London	020 7405 1111
Ward Mr Robin Henry	8 New Square, London	020 7405 4321
Whyte Dr James Richard Cleland	8 New Square, London	020 7405 4321

COPYRIGHT THEFT

Abrahams Mr James	8 New Square, London	020 7405 4321
Alexander Mr Daniel Sakyi	8 New Square, London	020 7405 4321
Baldwin Mr John Paul	8 New Square, London	020 7405 4321
Howe Mr Martin Russell Thomson	8 New Square, London	020 7405 4321
Jamal Miss Isabel Leila	8 New Square, London	020 7405 4321
Jones Mr Kelvin Mcallister	Templis Chambers, London	020 7649 9808
Lane Ms Lindsay Ruth Busfield	8 New Square, London	020 7405 4321
May Miss Charlotte Louisa	8 New Square, London	020 7405 4321
Meade Mr Richard David	8 New Square, London	020 7405 4321
Mellor Mr Edward James Wilson	8 New Square, London	020 7405 4321
Moody-Stuart Mr Thomas	8 New Square, London	020 7405 4321
Platts-Mills Mr Mark Fortescue	8 New Square, London	020 7405 4321
Tappin Mr Michael John	8 New Square, London	020 7405 4321

COPYRIGHT TRIBUNAL

Abrahams Mr James	8 New Square, London	020 7405 4321
Alexander Mr Daniel Sakyi	8 New Square, London	020 7405 4321
Baldwin Mr John Paul	8 New Square, London	020 7405 4321
Clark Miss Fiona Jane Stewart	8 New Square, London	020 7405 4321
Howe Mr Martin Russell Thomson	8 New Square, London	020 7405 4321
Jamal Miss Isabel Leila	8 New Square, London	020 7405 4321
Jones Mr Kelvin Mcallister	Templis Chambers, London	020 7649 9808
Lane Ms Lindsay Ruth Busfield	8 New Square, London	020 7405 4321
Lawrence Dr Heather Bunting Elizabeth	11 South Square, London	020 7405 1222
May Miss Charlotte Louisa	8 New Square, London	020 7405 4321
Meade Mr Richard David	8 New Square, London	020 7405 4321
Mellor Mr Edward James Wilson	8 New Square, London	020 7405 4321
Moody-Stuart Mr Thomas	8 New Square, London	020 7405 4321
Onslow Mr Robert Denzil	8 New Square, London	020 7405 4321

Name	Chambers	Telephone
Platts-Mills Mr Mark Fortescue	8 New Square, London	020 7405 4321
Reed Mr Jeremy Nigel	Hogarth Chambers, London	020 7404 0404
Speck Mr Adrian	8 New Square, London	020 7405 4321
St Ville Mr Laurence James	8 New Square, London	020 7405 4321
Tappin Mr Michael John	8 New Square, London	020 7405 4321
Thorley Mr Simon Joe	Three New Square IP, London	020 7405 1111
Whyte Dr James Richard Cleland	8 New Square, London	020 7405 4321

CORONERS

Name	Chambers	Telephone
Douglas-Jones Mr Benjamin Timothy	Apex, Cardiff	02920 232 032
	Five Paper Buildings, London	020 7583 6117
Dudley-Jones Ms Elizabeth Sarah	Deans Court Chambers, Manchester	0161 214 6000
	Deans Court Chambers, Preston	01772 565 600

CORONER'S INQUESTS

Name	Chambers	Telephone
Dudley-Jones Ms Elizabeth Sarah	Deans Court Chambers, Manchester	0161 214 6000
	Deans Court Chambers, Preston	01772 565 600
Tompkinson Miss Deborah Ann	Clerksroom (London), London	0845 083 3000
	Clerksroom (Taunton), Taunton	0845 083 3000

CORPORATE FINANCE

Name	Chambers	Telephone
Dowley Mr Dominic Myles	Serle Court, London	020 7242 6105
Orr Mr Craig Wyndham	One Essex Court, London	020 7583 2000
Wilson Mr Graham James	Gray's Inn Tax Chambers, London	020 7242 2642

CORPORATE FRAUD

Name	Chambers	Telephone
Altman Mr Brian	2 Bedford Row, London	020 7440 8888
Douglas-Jones Mr Benjamin Timothy	Apex, Cardiff	02920 232 032
	Five Paper Buildings, London	020 7583 6117
Dudley-Jones Ms Elizabeth Sarah	Deans Court Chambers, Manchester	0161 214 6000
	Deans Court Chambers, Preston	01772 565 600
Fisher Mr Jonathan Simon	Devereux Chambers, London	020 7353 7534
Katz Mr Philip Alec Jackson	9-12 Bell Yard, London	020 7400 1800
Lawrence Sir Ivan John	5 Pump Court, London	020 7353 2532
Sen Mr Aditya Kumar	Coram Chambers, London	020 7092 3700

CORPORATE GOVERNANCE

Name	Chambers	Telephone
Boyle Mr Alan Gordon	Serle Court, London	020 7242 6105

CORPORATE INSOLVENCY

Name	Chambers	Telephone
Boyle Mr Alan Gordon	Serle Court, London	020 7242 6105
Lightman Mr Daniel	Serle Court, London	020 7242 6105

CORPORATE LIABILITY

Name	Chambers	Telephone
Nicholls Mr Peter John	5 Pump Court, London	020 7353 2532

CORPORATE MANSLAUGHTER

Name	Chambers	Telephone
Dudley-Jones Ms Elizabeth Sarah	Deans Court Chambers, Manchester	0161 214 6000
	Deans Court Chambers, Preston	01772 565 600
Fisher Mr Jonathan Simon	Devereux Chambers, London	020 7353 7534
Katz Mr Philip Alec Jackson	9-12 Bell Yard, London	020 7400 1800

CORPORATION TAX

Name	Chambers	Telephone
Aaronson Mr Graham Raphael	Pump Court Tax Chambers, London	020 7414 8080
Baldry Mr Rupert Patrick Craig	Pump Court Tax Chambers, London	020 7414 8080
Bradley Mr Charles Edward May	Pump Court Tax Chambers, London	020 7414 8080
Bremner Mr Jonathan Sinclair Grant	Pump Court Tax Chambers, London	020 7414 8080
Chacko Mr Thomas Joseph	Pump Court Tax Chambers, London	020 7414 8080
Choudhury Miss Sadiya Asghar	Pump Court Tax Chambers, London	020 7414 8080
Conolly Dr Oliver Stephen	Pump Court Tax Chambers, London	020 7414 8080
Ewart Mr David Scott	Pump Court Tax Chambers, London	020 7414 8080
Frawley Ms Lyndsey Anne	Quorum Chambers, St Albans	01727 884516
	Quorum Tax Chambers, London	020 7043 5189

Ghosh Mr Indranil Julian	Pump Court Tax Chambers, London	020 7414 8080
Goodfellow Mr Giles William Jeremy	Pump Court Tax Chambers, London	020 7414 8080
Hamilton Mrs Penelope Ann	Pump Court Tax Chambers, London	020 7414 8080
Henderson Mr James Thomas	Kings Chambers, Leeds	0845 034 3444
	Kings Chambers, Manchester	0845 034 3444
	Pump Court Tax Chambers, London	020 7414 8080
Hitchmough Mr Andrew John	Pump Court Tax Chambers, London	020 7414 8080
Massey Mr William Greville Sale	Pump Court Tax Chambers, London	020 7414 8080
Matthews Mr Janek Paul	Pump Court Tax Chambers, London	020 7414 8080
Milne Mr David Calder	Pump Court Tax Chambers, London	020 7414 8080
Poots Miss Laura Jill	Pump Court Tax Chambers, London	020 7414 8080
Prosser Mr Kevin John	Pump Court Tax Chambers, London	020 7414 8080
Rivett Mr James Peter	Pump Court Tax Chambers, London	020 7414 8080
Southern Mr David Boardman	Temple Tax Chambers, London	020 7353 7884
Tallon Mr John Mark	Pump Court Tax Chambers, London	020 7414 8080
Thomas Mr Roger Christopher	Pump Court Tax Chambers, London	020 7414 8080
Thornhill Mr Andrew Robert	Albion Chambers, Bristol	0117 927 2144
	Pump Court Tax Chambers, London	020 7414 8080
Vallat Mr Richard Justin	Pump Court Tax Chambers, London	020 7414 8080
White Mr Jeremy Barry	Pump Court Tax Chambers, London	020 7414 8080
Wilson Miss Mary Elizabeth Frances	Pump Court Tax Chambers, London	020 7414 8080
Wilson Mr Graham James	Gray's Inn Tax Chambers, London	020 7242 2642
Woolf The Hon Jeremy Richard George	Pump Court Tax Chambers, London	020 7414 8080
Yang Dr Zizhen	Pump Court Tax Chambers, London	020 7414 8080
Yates Mr David James Francis	Pump Court Tax Chambers, London	020 7414 8080

COSTS

Bacon Mr Nicholas Michael	Four New Square, London	020 7822 2000
Ford Mr Gerard James	Old Court Chambers, Middlesbrough	01642 232523
Mawhinney Mr Richard Martin	Outer Temple Chambers, London	020 7353 6381
	St John's Chambers, Bristol	0117 923 4700
Rushton Ms Nicola Jane	Five Paper, London	020 7815 3200
Windsor Miss Emily May	Falcon Chambers, London	020 7353 2484

COURT OF PROTECTION

Delahunty Ms Johanne Erica	4 Paper Buildings, London	020 7427 5200
	Park Lane Plowden, Leeds	0113 228 5049
	St Ive's Chambers, Birmingham	0121 236 0863
O'Sullivan Mr Michael Morton	5 Stone Buildings, London	020 7242 6201
Stevenson Dr Simon John	Park Lane Plowden, Leeds	0113 228 5049
Studer Mr Mark Edgar Walter	Wilberforce Chambers, London	020 7306 0102

COURTS MARTIAL

Edington Mrs Fiona Anne Rider	Thomas More Chambers, London	020 7404 7000

CRIME

Altman Mr Brian	2 Bedford Row, London	020 7440 8888
Douglas-Jones Mr Benjamin Timothy	Apex, Cardiff	02920 232 032
	Five Paper Buildings, London	020 7583 6117
Dudley-Jones Ms Elizabeth Sarah	Deans Court Chambers, Manchester	0161 214 6000
	Deans Court Chambers, Preston	01772 565 600
Edington Mrs Fiona Anne Rider	Thomas More Chambers, London	020 7404 7000
Fisher Mr Jonathan Simon	Devereux Chambers, London	020 7353 7534
Hockman Mr Stephen Alexander	6 Pump Court, London	020 7797 8400
	6 Pump Court Chambers, Maidstone	01622 688094
	Regency Chambers, Peterborough	01733 315215
Katz Mr Philip Alec Jackson	9-12 Bell Yard, London	020 7400 1800
Lawrence Sir Ivan John	5 Pump Court, London	020 7353 2532
Rhodes Mr Robert Elliott	Outer Temple Chambers, London	020 7353 6381
	Principal Chambers, Sevenoaks	0845 209 8080
	St Philips Chambers, Birmingham	0121 246 7000

Rogers Mr Kenneth Edward	Assize Court Chambers, Bristol	0117 926 4587
	Invictus Chambers London, London	

CRIME AND CRIMINAL DUE PROCESS

Dudley-Jones Ms Elizabeth Sarah	Deans Court Chambers, Manchester	0161 214 6000
	Deans Court Chambers, Preston	01772 565 600
Katz Mr Philip Alec Jackson	9-12 Bell Yard, London	020 7400 1800

CRIMINAL JUDICIAL REVIEW

Fisher Mr Jonathan Simon	Devereux Chambers, London	020 7353 7534

CROSS-BORDER LITIGATION AND REMEDIES

Lowenstein Mr Paul David	3 Verulam Buildings, London	020 7831 8441

CULTURAL PROPERTY LAW

Jamal Miss Isabel Leila	8 New Square, London	020 7405 4321
Lowenstein Mr Paul David	3 Verulam Buildings, London	020 7831 8441

CUSTOMS

Bradley Mr Charles Edward May	Pump Court Tax Chambers, London	020 7414 8080
Chacko Mr Thomas Joseph	Pump Court Tax Chambers, London	020 7414 8080
Hamilton Mrs Penelope Ann	Pump Court Tax Chambers, London	020 7414 8080
Hitchmough Mr Andrew John	Pump Court Tax Chambers, London	020 7414 8080
Rogers Mr Kenneth Edward	Assize Court Chambers, Bristol	0117 926 4587
	Invictus Chambers London, London	
Southern Mr David Boardman	Temple Tax Chambers, London	020 7353 7884
Vallat Mr Richard Justin	Pump Court Tax Chambers, London	020 7414 8080
White Mr Jeremy Barry	Pump Court Tax Chambers, London	020 7414 8080
Yang Dr Zizhen	Pump Court Tax Chambers, London	020 7414 8080

DAMAGES

Chapman Mr Vivian Robert	New Street Chambers, Leicester	0116 262 5906
	9 Stone Buildings, London	020 7404 5055
Tompkinson Miss Deborah Ann	Clerksroom (London), London	0845 083 3000
	Clerksroom (Taunton), Taunton	0845 083 3000

DATA PROTECTION

Abrahams Mr James	8 New Square, London	020 7405 4321
Alexander Mr Daniel Sakyi	8 New Square, London	020 7405 4321
Baldwin Mr John Paul	8 New Square, London	020 7405 4321
Bassett Mr John Stewart Britten	5 Essex Court, London	020 7410 2000
Bowhill Miss Jessie Kate	8 New Square, London	020 7405 4321
Campbell Mr Douglas James	Three New Square IP, London	020 7405 1111
Chacksfield Mr Mark Andrew	8 New Square, London	020 7405 4321
Cornwell Dr James Matthew	11 King's Bench Walk, London	020 7632 8500
Hill Mr Jonathan	8 New Square, London	020 7405 4321
Howe Mr Martin Russell Thomson	8 New Square, London	020 7405 4321
Jones Mr Kelvin Mcallister	Templis Chambers, London	020 7649 9808
Lane Ms Lindsay Ruth Busfield	8 New Square, London	020 7405 4321
Lawrence Dr Heather Bunting Elizabeth	11 South Square, London	020 7405 1222
May Miss Charlotte Louisa	8 New Square, London	020 7405 4321
Onslow Mr Robert Denzil	8 New Square, London	020 7405 4321
St Ville Mr Laurence James	8 New Square, London	020 7405 4321
Whyte Dr James Richard Cleland	8 New Square, London	020 7405 4321

DEFAMATION

Hamer Mr George Clemens	8 New Square, London	020 7405 4321
Lawrence Sir Ivan John	5 Pump Court, London	020 7353 2532

DESIGN

Abrahams Mr James	8 New Square, London	020 7405 4321
Alexander Mr Daniel Sakyi	8 New Square, London	020 7405 4321
Baldwin Mr John Paul	8 New Square, London	020 7405 4321
Berkeley Miss Iona Sarah Caroline	8 New Square, London	020 7405 4321

B

Campbell Mr Douglas James	Three New Square IP, London	020 7405 1111
Clark Miss Fiona Jane Stewart	8 New Square, London	020 7405 4321
Colley Dr Peter Mclean	Hogarth Chambers, London	020 7404 0404
Hamer Mr George Clemens	8 New Square, London	020 7405 4321
Howe Mr Martin Russell Thomson	8 New Square, London	020 7405 4321
Jamal Miss Isabel Leila	8 New Square, London	020 7405 4321
Jones Mr Kelvin Mcallister	Templis Chambers, London	020 7649 9808
Lane Ms Lindsay Ruth Busfield	8 New Square, London	020 7405 4321
Lawrence Dr Heather Bunting Elizabeth	11 South Square, London	020 7405 1222
Lykiardopoulos Mr Andrew Nicolas	8 New Square, London	020 7405 4321
May Miss Charlotte Louisa	8 New Square, London	020 7405 4321
Meade Mr Richard David	8 New Square, London	020 7405 4321
Mellor Mr Edward James Wilson	8 New Square, London	020 7405 4321
Mitcheson Mr Thomas George Moseley	Three New Square IP, London	020 7405 1111
Moody-Stuart Mr Thomas	8 New Square, London	020 7405 4321
Onslow Mr Robert Denzil	8 New Square, London	020 7405 4321
Platts-Mills Mr Mark Fortescue	8 New Square, London	020 7405 4321
Reed Mr Jeremy Nigel	Hogarth Chambers, London	020 7404 0404
Speck Mr Adrian	8 New Square, London	020 7405 4321
St Ville Mr Laurence James	8 New Square, London	020 7405 4321
Tappin Mr Michael John	8 New Square, London	020 7405 4321
Whyte Dr James Richard Cleland	8 New Square, London	020 7405 4321

B

DISABILITY AND HEALTH

Dudley-Jones Ms Elizabeth Sarah	Deans Court Chambers, Manchester	0161 214 6000
	Deans Court Chambers, Preston	01772 565 600

DISASTERS

Butler Mr Andrew	Tanfield Chambers, London	020 7421 5300

DISCIPLINARY PROCEDURES

Badenoch Mr James Forster	1 Crown Office Row, London	020 7797 7500
Cornwell Dr James Matthew	11 King's Bench Walk, London	020 7632 8500

DISCRIMINATION

Brown Mr Damian Robert	Littleton Chambers, London	020 7797 8600
Cornwell Dr James Matthew	11 King's Bench Walk, London	020 7632 8500
Daly Mr David	Heathway Chambers, London	020 8293 0509
Giffin Mr Nigel Dyson	11 King's Bench Walk, London	020 7632 8500
Goudie Mr James	11 King's Bench Walk, London	020 7632 8500
Jeans Mr Christopher James Marwood	11 King's Bench Walk, London	020 7632 8500
Kempster Mr Ivor Toby Chalmers	Old Square Chambers, Bristol	0117 930 5100
	Old Square Chambers, London	020 7269 0300
Linstead Mr Peter James	Tanfield Chambers, London	020 7421 5300
MacLaren Miss Catriona Longueville	Tanfield Chambers, London	020 7421 5300
Sheppard Mr Timothy Derie	No5 Chambers, Birmingham	0845 210 5555
	No5 Chambers, Bristol	0845 210 5555
	No5 Chambers, London	0845 210 5555
Straker Mr Timothy Derrick	4-5 Gray's Inn Square, London	020 7404 5252
Thomson Mr Martin Haldane Ahmad	Wynne Chambers, London	020 3239 6964
Williams Ms Heather Jean	Doughty Street Chambers, Bristol	01179 058 717
	Doughty Street Chambers, London	020 7404 1313
	Doughty Street Chambers, Manchester	0161 618 1066

DISPUTE RESOLUTION

Boyle Mr Alan Gordon	Serle Court, London	020 7242 6105
Newsom Mr George Lucien	Guildhall Chambers, Bristol	0117 930 9000
Rhodes Mr Robert Elliott	Outer Temple Chambers, London	020 7353 6381
	Principal Chambers, Sevenoaks	0845 209 8080
	St Philips Chambers, Birmingham	0121 246 7000
Smith Miss Joanna Angela	Wilberforce Chambers, London	020 7306 0102

Windsor Miss Emily May	Falcon Chambers, London	020 7353 2484

DISPUTE RESOLUTION AND ARBITRATION

Boyle Mr Alan Gordon	Serle Court, London	020 7242 6105
Cole Mr Edward Arthur	Falcon Chambers, London	020 7353 2484
Ross Martyn Mr John Greaves	New Square Chambers, London	020 7419 8000
	Octagon House, Norwich	01603 623186

DIVORCE

Carrodus Miss Gail Caroline	Huntercombe Chambers, Henley-On-Thames	01491 641934
Purdie Mr Robert Anthony James	Faringdon Chambers, Faringdon	01367 240598
	4 King's Bench Walk, London	020 7822 7000

DOMESTIC VIOLENCE INJUNCTIONS

Harvey Miss Louise	College Chambers, Southampton	023 8023 0338
Purdie Mr Robert Anthony James	Faringdon Chambers, Faringdon	01367 240598
	4 King's Bench Walk, London	020 7822 7000

EC COMPETITION LAW

Abrahams Mr James	8 New Square, London	020 7405 4321
Alexander Mr Daniel Sakyi	8 New Square, London	020 7405 4321
Baldwin Mr John Paul	8 New Square, London	020 7405 4321
Chacksfield Mr Mark Andrew	8 New Square, London	020 7405 4321
Clark Miss Fiona Jane Stewart	8 New Square, London	020 7405 4321
Colley Dr Peter Mclean	Hogarth Chambers, London	020 7404 0404
Hamer Mr George Clemens	8 New Square, London	020 7405 4321
Howe Mr Martin Russell Thomson	8 New Square, London	020 7405 4321
Jones Mr Kelvin Mcallister	Templis Chambers, London	020 7649 9808
May Miss Charlotte Louisa	8 New Square, London	020 7405 4321
Meade Mr Richard David	8 New Square, London	020 7405 4321
Mellor Mr Edward James Wilson	8 New Square, London	020 7405 4321
Mitcheson Mr Thomas George Moseley	Three New Square IP, London	020 7405 1111
Moody-Stuart Mr Thomas	8 New Square, London	020 7405 4321
Moser Mr Philip Curt Harold	Monckton Chambers, London	020 7405 7211
Nardell Mr Gordon Lawrence	39 Essex Street, London	020 7832 1111
	82 King Street, Manchester	0161 870 9969
Onslow Mr Robert Denzil	8 New Square, London	020 7405 4321
Platts-Mills Mr Mark Fortescue	8 New Square, London	020 7405 4321
Reed Mr Jeremy Nigel	Hogarth Chambers, London	020 7404 0404
Reeds Mr Gareth David	Canary Wharf Chambers, London	020 7183 8011
Selvaratnam Miss Vasanti Emily Indrani	Stone Chambers, London	020 7440 6900
Speck Mr Adrian	8 New Square, London	020 7405 4321
St Ville Mr Laurence James	8 New Square, London	020 7405 4321
Thorley Mr Simon Joe	Three New Square IP, London	020 7405 1111
Ward Mr Robin Henry	8 New Square, London	020 7405 4321
Wilson Mr Graham James	Gray's Inn Tax Chambers, London	020 7242 2642

ECCLESIASTICAL LAW

Briden Mr Timothy John	Lamb Chambers, London	020 7797 8300
Newsom Mr George Lucien	Guildhall Chambers, Bristol	0117 930 9000
Nugee Mr Edward George	Wilberforce Chambers, London	020 7306 0102
Purdie Mr Robert Anthony James	Faringdon Chambers, Faringdon	01367 240598
	4 King's Bench Walk, London	020 7822 7000
Smith Dr Peter Michael	Radcliffe Chambers, London	020 7831 0081

E-COMMERCE

Abrahams Mr James	8 New Square, London	020 7405 4321
Alexander Mr Daniel Sakyi	8 New Square, London	020 7405 4321
Baldwin Mr John Paul	8 New Square, London	020 7405 4321
Boyle Mr Alan Gordon	Serle Court, London	020 7242 6105
Howe Mr Martin Russell Thomson	8 New Square, London	020 7405 4321
Jones Mr Kelvin Mcallister	Templis Chambers, London	020 7649 9808

Lane Ms Lindsay Ruth Busfield	8 New Square, London	020 7405 4321
May Miss Charlotte Louisa	8 New Square, London	020 7405 4321
Mellor Mr Edward James Wilson	8 New Square, London	020 7405 4321
Moody-Stuart Mr Thomas	8 New Square, London	020 7405 4321
Onslow Mr Robert Denzil	8 New Square, London	020 7405 4321
Speck Mr Adrian	8 New Square, London	020 7405 4321
St Ville Mr Laurence James	8 New Square, London	020 7405 4321

ECONOMIC TORTS

Smith Miss Joanna Angela	Wilberforce Chambers, London	020 7306 0102

EDUCATION

Cornwell Dr James Matthew	11 King's Bench Walk, London	020 7632 8500
Giffin Mr Nigel Dyson	11 King's Bench Walk, London	020 7632 8500
Goudie Mr James	11 King's Bench Walk, London	020 7632 8500
Straker Mr Timothy Derrick	4-5 Gray's Inn Square, London	020 7404 5252

ELECTION LAW

Straker Mr Timothy Derrick	4-5 Gray's Inn Square, London	020 7404 5252

EMPLOYEE BENEFIT TRUSTS

Baldry Mr Rupert Patrick Craig	Pump Court Tax Chambers, London	020 7414 8080
Dunn Ms Sarah Patricia Quincey	Pump Court Tax Chambers, London	020 7414 8080
Goodfellow Mr Giles William Jeremy	Pump Court Tax Chambers, London	020 7414 8080
Henderson Mr James Thomas	Kings Chambers, Leeds	0845 034 3444
	Kings Chambers, Manchester	0845 034 3444
	Pump Court Tax Chambers, London	020 7414 8080
Matthews Mr Janek Paul	Pump Court Tax Chambers, London	020 7414 8080
Stallworthy Mr Nicolas Kyd	Outer Temple Chambers, London	020 7353 6381
Tallon Mr John Mark	Pump Court Tax Chambers, London	020 7414 8080
Thornhill Mr Andrew Robert	Albion Chambers, Bristol	0117 927 2144
	Pump Court Tax Chambers, London	020 7414 8080
Vallat Mr Richard Justin	Pump Court Tax Chambers, London	020 7414 8080
Wilson Miss Mary Elizabeth Frances	Pump Court Tax Chambers, London	020 7414 8080
Woolf The Hon Jeremy Richard George	Pump Court Tax Chambers, London	020 7414 8080

EMPLOYMENT

Boyd Mr Stephen James Harvey	Selborne Chambers, London	020 7420 9500
Brown Mr Damian Robert	Littleton Chambers, London	020 7797 8600
Cornwell Dr James Matthew	11 King's Bench Walk, London	020 7632 8500
Daly Mr David	Heathway Chambers, London	020 8293 0509
Ferber Ms Iris	42 Bedford Row, London	020 7831 0222
Frawley Ms Lyndsey Anne	Quorum Chambers, St Albans	01727 884516
	Quorum Tax Chambers, London	020 7043 5189
Giffin Mr Nigel Dyson	11 King's Bench Walk, London	020 7632 8500
Goudie Mr James	11 King's Bench Walk, London	020 7632 8500
Jeans Mr Christopher James Marwood	11 King's Bench Walk, London	020 7632 8500
Jones Mr Kelvin Mcallister	Templis Chambers, London	020 7649 9808
Kempster Mr Ivor Toby Chalmers	Old Square Chambers, Bristol	0117 930 5100
	Old Square Chambers, London	020 7269 0300
Linstead Mr Peter James	Tanfield Chambers, London	020 7421 5300
MacLaren Miss Catriona Longueville	Tanfield Chambers, London	020 7421 5300
Mawhinney Mr Richard Martin	Outer Temple Chambers, London	020 7353 6381
	St John's Chambers, Bristol	0117 923 4700
Quickfall Mr Roger Mark	Park Lane Plowden, Leeds	0113 228 5049
Reeds Mr Gareth David	Canary Wharf Chambers, London	020 7183 8011
Scott Mr Ian Richard	Old Square Chambers, Bristol	0117 930 5100
	Old Square Chambers, London	020 7269 0300
Sheppard Mr Timothy Derie	No5 Chambers, Birmingham	0845 210 5555
	No5 Chambers, Bristol	0845 210 5555
	No5 Chambers, London	0845 210 5555
Thomson Mr Martin Haldane Ahmad	Wynne Chambers, London	020 3239 6964

Tompkinson Miss Deborah Ann	Clerksroom (London), London	0845 083 3000
	Clerksroom (Taunton), Taunton	0845 083 3000
Williams Ms Heather Jean	Doughty Street Chambers, Bristol	01179 058 717
	Doughty Street Chambers, London	020 7404 1313
	Doughty Street Chambers, Manchester	0161 618 1066

ENERGY

Alesbury Mr Alun	Cornerstone Barristers, London	020 7242 4986
	12 Old Square Chambers, London	020 7404 0875
Druce Mr Michael James	Cornerstone Barristers, London	020 7242 4986
Hockman Mr Stephen Alexander	6 Pump Court, London	020 7797 8400
	6 Pump Court Chambers, Maidstone	01622 688094
	Regency Chambers, Peterborough	01733 315215
Lowenstein Mr Paul David	3 Verulam Buildings, London	020 7831 8441
McCredie Miss Fionnuala Mary Constance	Keating Chambers, London	020 7544 2600
Nugee Mr Christopher George	Wilberforce Chambers, London	020 7306 0102
Roots Mr Guy Robert Godfrey	12 College Place, Southampton	023 8032 0320
	Francis Taylor Building, London	020 7353 8415

ENGINEERING DISPUTES

Laney Miss Anna Marie	Crown Office Chambers, London	020 7797 8100
Smith Miss Joanna Angela	Wilberforce Chambers, London	020 7306 0102

ENTERTAINMENT

Abrahams Mr James	8 New Square, London	020 7405 4321
Alexander Mr Daniel Sakyi	8 New Square, London	020 7405 4321
Baldwin Mr John Paul	8 New Square, London	020 7405 4321
Berkeley Miss Iona Sarah Caroline	8 New Square, London	020 7405 4321
Bowhill Miss Jessie Kate	8 New Square, London	020 7405 4321
Campbell Mr Douglas James	Three New Square IP, London	020 7405 1111
Chacksfield Mr Mark Andrew	8 New Square, London	020 7405 4321
Clark Miss Fiona Jane Stewart	8 New Square, London	020 7405 4321
Goudie Mr James	11 King's Bench Walk, London	020 7632 8500
Hamer Mr George Clemens	8 New Square, London	020 7405 4321
Hill Mr Jonathan	8 New Square, London	020 7405 4321
Howe Mr Martin Russell Thomson	8 New Square, London	020 7405 4321
Jones Mr Kelvin Mcallister	Templis Chambers, London	020 7649 9808
Lane Ms Lindsay Ruth Busfield	8 New Square, London	020 7405 4321
Lowenstein Mr Paul David	3 Verulam Buildings, London	020 7831 8441
May Miss Charlotte Louisa	8 New Square, London	020 7405 4321
Meade Mr Richard David	8 New Square, London	020 7405 4321
Mellor Mr Edward James Wilson	8 New Square, London	020 7405 4321
Mitcheson Mr Thomas George Moseley	Three New Square IP, London	020 7405 1111
Moody-Stuart Mr Thomas	8 New Square, London	020 7405 4321
Onslow Mr Robert Denzil	8 New Square, London	020 7405 4321
Platts-Mills Mr Mark Fortescue	8 New Square, London	020 7405 4321
Speck Mr Adrian	8 New Square, London	020 7405 4321
St Ville Mr Laurence James	8 New Square, London	020 7405 4321
Tappin Mr Michael John	8 New Square, London	020 7405 4321
Thorley Mr Simon Joe	Three New Square IP, London	020 7405 1111
Ward Mr Robin Henry	8 New Square, London	020 7405 4321
Whyte Dr James Richard Cleland	8 New Square, London	020 7405 4321

ENVIRONMENT

Alesbury Mr Alun	Cornerstone Barristers, London	020 7242 4986
	12 Old Square Chambers, London	020 7404 0875
Beard Mr Mark Christopher	6 Pump Court, London	020 7797 8400
	6 Pump Court Chambers, Maidstone	01622 688094
Cowen Mr Gary Adam	Falcon Chambers, London	020 7353 2484
Druce Mr Michael James	Cornerstone Barristers, London	020 7242 4986
Giffin Mr Nigel Dyson	11 King's Bench Walk, London	020 7632 8500
Goudie Mr James	11 King's Bench Walk, London	020 7632 8500

Hockman Mr Stephen Alexander	6 Pump Court, London	020 7797 8400
	6 Pump Court Chambers, Maidstone	01622 688094
	Regency Chambers, Peterborough	01733 315215
Howell Williams Mr Craig	Francis Taylor Building, London	020 7353 8415
McCredie Miss Fionnuala Mary Constance	Keating Chambers, London	020 7544 2600
Nardell Mr Gordon Lawrence	39 Essex Street, London	020 7832 1111
	82 King Street, Manchester	0161 870 9969
Roots Mr Guy Robert Godfrey	12 College Place, Southampton	023 8032 0320
	Francis Taylor Building, London	020 7353 8415
Sheppard Mr Timothy Derie	No5 Chambers, Birmingham	0845 210 5555
	No5 Chambers, Bristol	0845 210 5555
	No5 Chambers, London	0845 210 5555
Straker Mr Timothy Derrick	4-5 Gray's Inn Square, London	020 7404 5252
Windsor Miss Emily May	Falcon Chambers, London	020 7353 2484

EQUITY

Acton Mr Stephen Neil	Radcliffe Chambers, London	020 7831 0081
Asplin Miss Sarah Jane	3 Stone Buildings, London	020 7242 4937
Berkley Mr Michael Stuart	Rougemont Chambers, Exeter	01392 208484
Bornman Miss Kerry	3 Stone Buildings, London	020 7242 4937
Boyle Mr Alan Gordon	Serle Court, London	020 7242 6105
Bremner Mr Jonathan Sinclair Grant	Pump Court Tax Chambers, London	020 7414 8080
Bryant Miss Judith Anne	Wilberforce Chambers, London	020 7306 0102
Campbell Miss Emily Charlotte	Wilberforce Chambers, London	020 7306 0102
Chapman Mr Vivian Robert	New Street Chambers, Leicester	0116 262 5906
	9 Stone Buildings, London	020 7404 5055
Child Mr John Frederick	Wilberforce Chambers, London	020 7306 0102
Choudhury Miss Sadiya Asghar	Pump Court Tax Chambers, London	020 7414 8080
Conolly Dr Oliver Stephen	Pump Court Tax Chambers, London	020 7414 8080
Daly Mr David	Heathway Chambers, London	020 8293 0509
Dray Mr Martin Benedict Antony	Falcon Chambers, London	020 7353 2484
Dunn Ms Sarah Patricia Quincey	Pump Court Tax Chambers, London	020 7414 8080
Ewart Mr David Scott	Pump Court Tax Chambers, London	020 7414 8080
Francis Mr Andrew James	Serle Court, London	020 7242 6105
	Zenith Chambers, Leeds	0113 245 5438
Furness Mr Michael James	Wilberforce Chambers, London	020 7306 0102
Goodfellow Mr Giles William Jeremy	Pump Court Tax Chambers, London	020 7414 8080
Green Mr Brian Russell	Wilberforce Chambers, London	020 7306 0102
Ham Mr Robert Wallace	Wilberforce Chambers, London	020 7306 0102
Henderson Mr James Thomas	Kings Chambers, Leeds	0845 034 3444
	Kings Chambers, Manchester	0845 034 3444
	Pump Court Tax Chambers, London	020 7414 8080
Herbert Mr Mark Jeremy	5 Stone Buildings, London	020 7242 6201
Hilliard Mr Jonathan Adam	Wilberforce Chambers, London	020 7306 0102
Hinks Mr Frank Peter	Serle Court, London	020 7242 6105
Hochberg Mr Daniel Alan	Wilberforce Chambers, London	020 7306 0102
Jackson Mr Nicholas David Kingsley	Atlantic Chambers, Liverpool	0151 236 4421
Lightman Mr Daniel	Serle Court, London	020 7242 6105
Lloyd Mr Stephen James George	13 Old Square Chambers, London	020 7831 4445
Lowe Mr Thomas William Gordon	Wilberforce Chambers, London	020 7306 0102
Martin Mr John Vandeleur	Wilberforce Chambers, London	020 7306 0102
Massey Mr William Greville Sale	Pump Court Tax Chambers, London	020 7414 8080
Matthews Mr Janek Paul	Pump Court Tax Chambers, London	020 7414 8080
McCann Miss Sarah Jane	Hardwicke, London	020 7242 2523
Mold Mr Andrew Matthew Stephen	Wilberforce Chambers, London	020 7306 0102
Newsom Mr George Lucien	Guildhall Chambers, Bristol	0117 930 9000
Nugee Mr Christopher George	Wilberforce Chambers, London	020 7306 0102
Nugee Mr Edward George	Wilberforce Chambers, London	020 7306 0102
O'Sullivan Mr Michael Morton	5 Stone Buildings, London	020 7242 6201
Ovey Miss Elizabeth Helen	Radcliffe Chambers, London	020 7831 0081
Poots Miss Laura Jill	Pump Court Tax Chambers, London	020 7414 8080
Quint Ms Joan Francesca Rae	Radcliffe Chambers, London	020 7831 0081
Richards Mr Ian	Pump Court Tax Chambers, London	020 7414 8080

Rivett Mr James Peter	Pump Court Tax Chambers, London	020 7414 8080
Ross Martyn Mr John Greaves	New Square Chambers, London	020 7419 8000
	Octagon House, Norwich	01603 623186
Sandham Mr James Andrew	Arden Chambers, London	020 7242 4244
Sawyer Mr Edward Humphrey	Wilberforce Chambers, London	020 7306 0102
Stevenson Dr Simon John	Park Lane Plowden, Leeds	0113 228 5049
Studer Mr Mark Edgar Walter	Wilberforce Chambers, London	020 7306 0102
Tallon Mr John Mark	Pump Court Tax Chambers, London	020 7414 8080
Tanney Mr Anthony	Falcon Chambers, London	020 7353 2484
Thomas Mr Roger Christopher	Pump Court Tax Chambers, London	020 7414 8080
Thornhill Mr Andrew Robert	Albion Chambers, Bristol	0117 927 2144
	Pump Court Tax Chambers, London	020 7414 8080
Trace Mr Anthony John	Maitland Chambers, London	020 7406 1200
Tunkel Mr Alan Michael	3 Stone Buildings, London	020 7242 4937
Vallat Mr Richard Justin	Pump Court Tax Chambers, London	020 7414 8080
Walford Mr Richard Henry Howard	Serle Court, London	020 7242 6105
Walsh Mr Steven James Franklyn	Five Paper, London	020 7815 3200
Waters Mr Malcolm Ian	Radcliffe Chambers, London	020 7831 0081
West Mr Mark	Radcliffe Chambers, London	020 7831 0081
Wicks Ms Joanne	Wilberforce Chambers, London	020 7306 0102
Wilson Miss Mary Elizabeth Frances	Pump Court Tax Chambers, London	020 7414 8080
Wilson Mr Graham James	Gray's Inn Tax Chambers, London	020 7242 2642
Windsor Miss Emily May	Falcon Chambers, London	020 7353 2484
Woolf The Hon Jeremy Richard George	Pump Court Tax Chambers, London	020 7414 8080
Yates Mr David James Francis	Pump Court Tax Chambers, London	020 7414 8080

EUROPEAN LAW

Edington Mrs Fiona Anne Rider	Thomas More Chambers, London	020 7404 7000

EUROPEAN UNION

Ghosh Mr Indranil Julian	Pump Court Tax Chambers, London	020 7414 8080
McCredie Miss Fionnuala Mary Constance	Keating Chambers, London	020 7544 2600
Moser Mr Philip Curt Harold	Monckton Chambers, London	020 7405 7211
Stevenson Dr Simon John	Park Lane Plowden, Leeds	0113 228 5049

EXCISE

Bradley Mr Charles Edward May	Pump Court Tax Chambers, London	020 7414 8080
Chacko Mr Thomas Joseph	Pump Court Tax Chambers, London	020 7414 8080
MacNab Mr Alexander Andrew	Monckton Chambers, London	020 7405 7211
Yang Dr Zizhen	Pump Court Tax Chambers, London	020 7414 8080

EXTRADITION

Rhodes Mr Robert Elliott	Outer Temple Chambers, London	020 7353 6381
	Principal Chambers, Sevenoaks	0845 209 8080
	St Philips Chambers, Birmingham	0121 246 7000

FACTORING

Jones Mr Kelvin Mcallister	Templis Chambers, London	020 7649 9808

FAMILY LAW

Amaouche Miss Sassa-Ann	29 Bedford Row Chambers, London	020 7404 1044
Bancroft Miss Anna Louise	Deans Court Chambers, Manchester	0161 214 6000
	Deans Court Chambers, Preston	01772 565 600
Boyd Miss Kerstin Margaret	Tanfield Chambers, London	020 7421 5300
Delahunty Ms Johanne Erica	4 Paper Buildings, London	020 7427 5200
	Park Lane Plowden, Leeds	0113 228 5049
	St Ive's Chambers, Birmingham	0121 236 0863
Edington Mrs Fiona Anne Rider	Thomas More Chambers, London	020 7404 7000
Finch Ms Nadine Elizabeth	Garden Court Chambers, London	020 7993 7600
Ford Mr Gerard James	Old Court Chambers, Middlesbrough	01642 232523
Francis Mr Nicholas	29 Bedford Row Chambers, London	020 7404 1044
Harvey Miss Louise	College Chambers, Southampton	023 8023 0338
Pope Mrs Heather	1 Hare Court, London	020 7797 7070

Purdie Mr Robert Anthony James	Faringdon Chambers, Faringdon	01367 240598
	4 King's Bench Walk, London	020 7822 7000

FAMILY PROVISION

Acton Mr Stephen Neil	Radcliffe Chambers, London	020 7831 0081
Amaouche Miss Sassa-Ann	29 Bedford Row Chambers, London	020 7404 1044
Bornman Miss Kerry	3 Stone Buildings, London	020 7242 4937
Boyle Mr Alan Gordon	Serle Court, London	020 7242 6105
Bryant Miss Judith Anne	Wilberforce Chambers, London	020 7306 0102
Carrodus Miss Gail Caroline	Huntercombe Chambers, Henley-On-Thames	01491 641934
Chapman Mr Vivian Robert	New Street Chambers, Leicester	0116 262 5906
	9 Stone Buildings, London	020 7404 5055
Daly Mr David	Heathway Chambers, London	020 8293 0509
Ford Mr Gerard James	Old Court Chambers, Middlesbrough	01642 232523
Francis Mr Andrew James	Serle Court, London	020 7242 6105
	Zenith Chambers, Leeds	0113 245 5438
Jackson Mr Nicholas David Kingsley	Atlantic Chambers, Liverpool	0151 236 4421
Lloyd Mr Stephen James George	13 Old Square Chambers, London	020 7831 4445
MacLaren Miss Catriona Longueville	Tanfield Chambers, London	020 7421 5300
O'Sullivan Mr Michael Morton	5 Stone Buildings, London	020 7242 6201
Purdie Mr Robert Anthony James	Faringdon Chambers, Faringdon	01367 240598
	4 King's Bench Walk, London	020 7822 7000
Quint Ms Joan Francesca Rae	Radcliffe Chambers, London	020 7831 0081
Ross Martyn Mr John Greaves	New Square Chambers, London	020 7419 8000
	Octagon House, Norwich	01603 623186
Stevenson Dr Simon John	Park Lane Plowden, Leeds	0113 228 5049
Studer Mr Mark Edgar Walter	Wilberforce Chambers, London	020 7306 0102
Tunkel Mr Alan Michael	3 Stone Buildings, London	020 7242 4937
West Mr Mark	Radcliffe Chambers, London	020 7831 0081

FINANCIAL PROVISION

Carrodus Miss Gail Caroline	Huntercombe Chambers, Henley-On-Thames	01491 641934
Purdie Mr Robert Anthony James	Faringdon Chambers, Faringdon	01367 240598
	4 King's Bench Walk, London	020 7822 7000

FINANCIAL PROVISION FOR CHILDREN

Purdie Mr Robert Anthony James	Faringdon Chambers, Faringdon	01367 240598
	4 King's Bench Walk, London	020 7822 7000

FINANCIAL SERVICES

Boyle Mr Alan Gordon	Serle Court, London	020 7242 6105
Burling Mr Julian Michael	Serle Court, London	020 7242 6105
Dowley Mr Dominic Myles	Serle Court, London	020 7242 6105
Hattan Mr Simon Justin	Serle Court, London	020 7242 6105
Lavender Mr Nicholas	Serle Court, London	020 7242 6105
Lowe Mr Thomas William Gordon	Wilberforce Chambers, London	020 7306 0102
McCann Miss Sarah Jane	Hardwicke, London	020 7242 2523
McPherson Mr Graeme Paul	Four New Square, London	020 7822 2000
Mold Mr Andrew Matthew Stephen	Wilberforce Chambers, London	020 7306 0102
Nardell Mr Gordon Lawrence	39 Essex Street, London	020 7832 1111
	82 King Street, Manchester	0161 870 9969
Nugee Mr Edward George	Wilberforce Chambers, London	020 7306 0102
Orr Mr Craig Wyndham	One Essex Court, London	020 7583 2000
Ovey Miss Elizabeth Helen	Radcliffe Chambers, London	020 7831 0081
Reeds Mr Gareth David	Canary Wharf Chambers, London	020 7183 8011
Rhodes Mr Robert Elliott	Outer Temple Chambers, London	020 7353 6381
	Principal Chambers, Sevenoaks	0845 209 8080
	St Philips Chambers, Birmingham	0121 246 7000
Stallworthy Mr Nicolas Kyd	Outer Temple Chambers, London	020 7353 6381
Wardell Mr John David Meredith	Wilberforce Chambers, London	020 7306 0102
Waters Mr Malcolm Ian	Radcliffe Chambers, London	020 7831 0081

Wilson Mr Graham James	Gray's Inn Tax Chambers, London	020 7242 2642

FIRE AND OTHER PROPERTY DAMAGE CLAIMS

Butler Mr Andrew	Tanfield Chambers, London	020 7421 5300
Laney Miss Anna Marie	Crown Office Chambers, London	020 7797 8100

FORCED MARRIAGE

Purdie Mr Robert Anthony James	Faringdon Chambers, Faringdon	01367 240598
	4 King's Bench Walk, London	020 7822 7000

FOREIGN LAW

Edington Mrs Fiona Anne Rider	Thomas More Chambers, London	020 7404 7000
Mold Mr Andrew Matthew Stephen	Wilberforce Chambers, London	020 7306 0102
Moore Mr George Crawford Jackson	11 King's Bench Walk, London	020 7632 8500
Reeds Mr Gareth David	Canary Wharf Chambers, London	020 7183 8011
Sen Mr Aditya Kumar	Coram Chambers, London	020 7092 3700

FORFEITURE

Dudley-Jones Ms Elizabeth Sarah	Deans Court Chambers, Manchester	0161 214 6000
	Deans Court Chambers, Preston	01772 565 600
Fisher Mr Jonathan Simon	Devereux Chambers, London	020 7353 7534

FOSTERING

Purdie Mr Robert Anthony James	Faringdon Chambers, Faringdon	01367 240598
	4 King's Bench Walk, London	020 7822 7000

FRANCHISING

Abrahams Mr James	8 New Square, London	020 7405 4321
Boyd Mr Stephen James Harvey	Selborne Chambers, London	020 7420 9500
Campbell Mr Douglas James	Three New Square IP, London	020 7405 1111
Chacksfield Mr Mark Andrew	8 New Square, London	020 7405 4321
Clark Miss Fiona Jane Stewart	8 New Square, London	020 7405 4321
Hamer Mr George Clemens	8 New Square, London	020 7405 4321
Howe Mr Martin Russell Thomson	8 New Square, London	020 7405 4321
Onslow Mr Robert Denzil	8 New Square, London	020 7405 4321
Platts-Mills Mr Mark Fortescue	8 New Square, London	020 7405 4321
St Ville Mr Laurence James	8 New Square, London	020 7405 4321

FRAUD

De Verneuil Smith Mr Peter Robert	3 Verulam Buildings, London	020 7831 8441
Dowley Mr Dominic Myles	Serle Court, London	020 7242 6105
Dudley-Jones Ms Elizabeth Sarah	Deans Court Chambers, Manchester	0161 214 6000
	Deans Court Chambers, Preston	01772 565 600
Evans Mr Martin Alan Langham	Chambers of Andrew Mitchell QC, London	020 7440 9950
Fisher Mr Jonathan Simon	Devereux Chambers, London	020 7353 7534
Rogers Mr Kenneth Edward	Assize Court Chambers, Bristol	0117 926 4587
	Invictus Chambers London, London	
Sawyer Mr Edward Humphrey	Wilberforce Chambers, London	020 7306 0102
Trace Mr Anthony John	Maitland Chambers, London	020 7406 1200

FREEDOM OF INFORMATION

Cornwell Dr James Matthew	11 King's Bench Walk, London	020 7632 8500
Jones Mr Kelvin Mcallister	Templis Chambers, London	020 7649 9808

FREEZING ORDERS

Boyle Mr Alan Gordon	Serle Court, London	020 7242 6105
Jones Mr Kelvin Mcallister	Templis Chambers, London	020 7649 9808
Lowenstein Mr Paul David	3 Verulam Buildings, London	020 7831 8441
Rushton Ms Nicola Jane	Five Paper, London	020 7815 3200

Name	Chambers	Telephone
Tompkinson Miss Deborah Ann	Clerksroom (London), London	0845 083 3000
	Clerksroom (Taunton), Taunton	0845 083 3000

GERMAN LAW

Name	Chambers	Telephone
Reeds Mr Gareth David	Canary Wharf Chambers, London	020 7183 8011

GRENADA LAW

Name	Chambers	Telephone
Moore Mr George Crawford Jackson	11 King's Bench Walk, London	020 7632 8500

GUARANTEES

Name	Chambers	Telephone
Lowenstein Mr Paul David	3 Verulam Buildings, London	020 7831 8441

HEALTH AND SAFETY

Name	Chambers	Telephone
Briden Mr Timothy John	Lamb Chambers, London	020 7797 8300
Douglas-Jones Mr Benjamin Timothy	Apex, Cardiff	02920 232 032
	Five Paper Buildings, London	020 7583 6117
Hockman Mr Stephen Alexander	6 Pump Court, London	020 7797 8400
	6 Pump Court Chambers, Maidstone	01622 688094
	Regency Chambers, Peterborough	01733 315215
Hodson Mr Peter David	Chambers of Ian Macdonald QC, Manchester	0161 236 1840
Howells Miss Katherine Jane	Old Square Chambers, Bristol	0117 930 5100
	Old Square Chambers, London	020 7269 0300
McCredie Miss Fionnuala Mary Constance	Keating Chambers, London	020 7544 2600
Nicholls Mr Peter John	5 Pump Court, London	020 7353 2532
Pitchers Mr Henry William Stodart	No5 Chambers, Birmingham	0845 210 5555
	No5 Chambers, Bristol	0845 210 5555
	No5 Chambers, London	0845 210 5555
Quickfall Mr Roger Mark	Park Lane Plowden, Leeds	0113 228 5049
Rhodes Mr Robert Elliott	Outer Temple Chambers, London	020 7353 6381
	Principal Chambers, Sevenoaks	0845 209 8080
	St Philips Chambers, Birmingham	0121 246 7000

HEALTHCARE LAW

Name	Chambers	Telephone
Dudley-Jones Ms Elizabeth Sarah	Deans Court Chambers, Manchester	0161 214 6000
	Deans Court Chambers, Preston	01772 565 600
Jerram Ms Harriet Anne	Outer Temple Chambers, London	020 7353 6381
Mawhinney Mr Richard Martin	Outer Temple Chambers, London	020 7353 6381
	St John's Chambers, Bristol	0117 923 4700

HIGHWAYS

Name	Chambers	Telephone
Alesbury Mr Alun	Cornerstone Barristers, London	020 7242 4986
	12 Old Square Chambers, London	020 7404 0875
Chapman Mr Vivian Robert	New Street Chambers, Leicester	0116 262 5906
	9 Stone Buildings, London	020 7404 5055
Ellis Miss Rosalind Morag	Cornerstone Barristers, London	020 7242 4986
Howells Miss Katherine Jane	Old Square Chambers, Bristol	0117 930 5100
	Old Square Chambers, London	020 7269 0300
Karas Mr Jonathan Marcus	Wilberforce Chambers, London	020 7306 0102
Newsom Mr George Lucien	Guildhall Chambers, Bristol	0117 930 9000
Windsor Miss Emily May	Falcon Chambers, London	020 7353 2484

HOLIDAY INJURY AND DAMAGES

Name	Chambers	Telephone
Howells Miss Katherine Jane	Old Square Chambers, Bristol	0117 930 5100
	Old Square Chambers, London	020 7269 0300
Tompkinson Miss Deborah Ann	Clerksroom (London), London	0845 083 3000
	Clerksroom (Taunton), Taunton	0845 083 3000

HOLIDAY LAW

Name	Chambers	Telephone
Howells Miss Katherine Jane	Old Square Chambers, Bristol	0117 930 5100
	Old Square Chambers, London	020 7269 0300

HOUSING

Name	Chambers	Telephone
Cole Mr Edward Arthur	Falcon Chambers, London	020 7353 2484

Cowen Mr Gary Adam	Falcon Chambers, London	020 7353 2484
Daly Mr David	Heathway Chambers, London	020 8293 0509
Ferber Ms Iris	42 Bedford Row, London	020 7831 0222
Ford Mr Gerard James	Old Court Chambers, Middlesbrough	01642 232523
Glen Mr Philip Alexander	12 College Place, Southampton	023 8032 0320
O'Sullivan Mr Richard John	1215 Chambers, London	020 3291 1215
Rodger Mr Martin Owen	Falcon Chambers, London	020 7353 2484
Sandham Mr James Andrew	Arden Chambers, London	020 7242 4244
Straker Mr Timothy Derrick	4-5 Gray's Inn Square, London	020 7404 5252
Windsor Miss Emily May	Falcon Chambers, London	020 7353 2484

HUMAN RIGHTS

Badenoch Mr James Forster	1 Crown Office Row, London	020 7797 7500
Brown Mr Damian Robert	Littleton Chambers, London	020 7797 8600
Cornwell Dr James Matthew	11 King's Bench Walk, London	020 7632 8500
Daly Mr David	Heathway Chambers, London	020 8293 0509
Dingemans Mr James Michael	3 Hare Court, London	020 7415 7800
Edington Mrs Fiona Anne Rider	Thomas More Chambers, London	020 7404 7000
Finch Ms Nadine Elizabeth	Garden Court Chambers, London	020 7993 7600
Giffin Mr Nigel Dyson	11 King's Bench Walk, London	020 7632 8500
O'Sullivan Mr Richard John	1215 Chambers, London	020 3291 1215
Rhodes Mr Robert Elliott	Outer Temple Chambers, London	020 7353 6381
	Principal Chambers, Sevenoaks	0845 209 8080
	St Philips Chambers, Birmingham	0121 246 7000
Sandham Mr James Andrew	Arden Chambers, London	020 7242 4244

IMMIGRATION

Cornwell Dr James Matthew	11 King's Bench Walk, London	020 7632 8500
Finch Ms Nadine Elizabeth	Garden Court Chambers, London	020 7993 7600

INCOME TAX

Aaronson Mr Graham Raphael	Pump Court Tax Chambers, London	020 7414 8080
Baldry Mr Rupert Patrick Craig	Pump Court Tax Chambers, London	020 7414 8080
Bradley Mr Charles Edward May	Pump Court Tax Chambers, London	020 7414 8080
Bremner Mr Jonathan Sinclair Grant	Pump Court Tax Chambers, London	020 7414 8080
Campbell Miss Emily Charlotte	Wilberforce Chambers, London	020 7306 0102
Chacko Mr Thomas Joseph	Pump Court Tax Chambers, London	020 7414 8080
Child Mr John Frederick	Wilberforce Chambers, London	020 7306 0102
Choudhury Miss Sadiya Asghar	Pump Court Tax Chambers, London	020 7414 8080
Conolly Dr Oliver Stephen	Pump Court Tax Chambers, London	020 7414 8080
Dunn Ms Sarah Patricia Quincey	Pump Court Tax Chambers, London	020 7414 8080
Ewart Mr David Scott	Pump Court Tax Chambers, London	020 7414 8080
Frawley Ms Lyndsey Anne	Quorum Chambers, St Albans	01727 884516
	Quorum Tax Chambers, London	020 7043 5189
Furness Mr Michael James	Wilberforce Chambers, London	020 7306 0102
Ghosh Mr Indranil Julian	Pump Court Tax Chambers, London	020 7414 8080
Goodfellow Mr Giles William Jeremy	Pump Court Tax Chambers, London	020 7414 8080
Green Mr Brian Russell	Wilberforce Chambers, London	020 7306 0102
Henderson Mr James Thomas	Kings Chambers, Leeds	0845 034 3444
	Kings Chambers, Manchester	0845 034 3444
	Pump Court Tax Chambers, London	020 7414 8080
Herbert Mr Mark Jeremy	5 Stone Buildings, London	020 7242 6201
Hilliard Mr Jonathan Adam	Wilberforce Chambers, London	020 7306 0102
Massey Mr William Greville Sale	Pump Court Tax Chambers, London	020 7414 8080
Matthews Mr Janek Paul	Pump Court Tax Chambers, London	020 7414 8080
Milne Mr David Calder	Pump Court Tax Chambers, London	020 7414 8080
Mold Mr Andrew Matthew Stephen	Wilberforce Chambers, London	020 7306 0102
Nugee Mr Edward George	Wilberforce Chambers, London	020 7306 0102
Poots Miss Laura Jill	Pump Court Tax Chambers, London	020 7414 8080
Prosser Mr Kevin John	Pump Court Tax Chambers, London	020 7414 8080
Richards Mr Ian	Pump Court Tax Chambers, London	020 7414 8080
Rivett Mr James Peter	Pump Court Tax Chambers, London	020 7414 8080
Southern Mr David Boardman	Temple Tax Chambers, London	020 7353 7884
Tallon Mr John Mark	Pump Court Tax Chambers, London	020 7414 8080

Thomas Mr Roger Christopher	Pump Court Tax Chambers, London	020 7414 8080
Thornhill Mr Andrew Robert	Albion Chambers, Bristol	0117 927 2144
	Pump Court Tax Chambers, London	020 7414 8080
Vallat Mr Richard Justin	Pump Court Tax Chambers, London	020 7414 8080
Wilson Miss Mary Elizabeth Frances	Pump Court Tax Chambers, London	020 7414 8080
Wilson Mr Graham James	Gray's Inn Tax Chambers, London	020 7242 2642
Woolf The Hon Jeremy Richard George	Pump Court Tax Chambers, London	020 7414 8080
Yang Dr Zizhen	Pump Court Tax Chambers, London	020 7414 8080
Yates Mr David James Francis	Pump Court Tax Chambers, London	020 7414 8080

INDIAN LAW

Sen Mr Aditya Kumar	Coram Chambers, London	020 7092 3700

INDUSTRIAL DEAFNESS

Howells Miss Katherine Jane	Old Square Chambers, Bristol	0117 930 5100
	Old Square Chambers, London	020 7269 0300

INDUSTRIAL DISEASES

Hodson Mr Peter David	Chambers of Ian Macdonald QC, Manchester	0161 236 1840
Howells Miss Katherine Jane	Old Square Chambers, Bristol	0117 930 5100
	Old Square Chambers, London	020 7269 0300
Linstead Mr Peter James	Tanfield Chambers, London	020 7421 5300

INFORMATION TECHNOLOGY

Abrahams Mr James	8 New Square, London	020 7405 4321
Alexander Mr Daniel Sakyi	8 New Square, London	020 7405 4321
Baldwin Mr John Paul	8 New Square, London	020 7405 4321
Berkeley Miss Iona Sarah Caroline	8 New Square, London	020 7405 4321
Bloch Mr Michael Gordon	Wilberforce Chambers, London	020 7306 0102
Campbell Mr Douglas James	Three New Square IP, London	020 7405 1111
Chacksfield Mr Mark Andrew	8 New Square, London	020 7405 4321
Clark Miss Fiona Jane Stewart	8 New Square, London	020 7405 4321
Dowley Mr Dominic Myles	Serle Court, London	020 7242 6105
Hamer Mr George Clemens	8 New Square, London	020 7405 4321
Hill Mr Jonathan	8 New Square, London	020 7405 4321
Howe Mr Martin Russell Thomson	8 New Square, London	020 7405 4321
Jones Mr Kelvin Mcallister	Templis Chambers, London	020 7649 9808
Lane Ms Lindsay Ruth Busfield	8 New Square, London	020 7405 4321
Lawrence Dr Heather Bunting Elizabeth	11 South Square, London	020 7405 1222
Lowenstein Mr Paul David	3 Verulam Buildings, London	020 7831 8441
Lykiardopoulos Mr Andrew Nicolas	8 New Square, London	020 7405 4321
May Miss Charlotte Louisa	8 New Square, London	020 7405 4321
Meade Mr Richard David	8 New Square, London	020 7405 4321
Mellor Mr Edward James Wilson	8 New Square, London	020 7405 4321
Mitcheson Mr Thomas George Moseley	Three New Square IP, London	020 7405 1111
Moody-Stuart Mr Thomas	8 New Square, London	020 7405 4321
Onslow Mr Robert Denzil	8 New Square, London	020 7405 4321
Platts-Mills Mr Mark Fortescue	8 New Square, London	020 7405 4321
Reed Mr Jeremy Nigel	Hogarth Chambers, London	020 7404 0404
Speck Mr Adrian	8 New Square, London	020 7405 4321
St Ville Mr Laurence James	8 New Square, London	020 7405 4321
Ward Mr Robin Henry	8 New Square, London	020 7405 4321
Whyte Dr James Richard Cleland	8 New Square, London	020 7405 4321

INHERITANCE

Purdie Mr Robert Anthony James	Faringdon Chambers, Faringdon	01367 240598
	4 King's Bench Walk, London	020 7822 7000
Stevenson Dr Simon John	Park Lane Plowden, Leeds	0113 228 5049

INHERITANCE AND COHABITEES

Bornman Miss Kerry	3 Stone Buildings, London	020 7242 4937

B

Boyle Mr Alan Gordon	Serle Court, London	020 7242 6105
Bryant Miss Judith Anne	Wilberforce Chambers, London	020 7306 0102
Newsom Mr George Lucien	Guildhall Chambers, Bristol	0117 930 9000
Purdie Mr Robert Anthony James	Faringdon Chambers, Faringdon	01367 240598
	4 King's Bench Walk, London	020 7822 7000
Ross Martyn Mr John Greaves	New Square Chambers, London	020 7419 8000
	Octagon House, Norwich	01603 623186
Studer Mr Mark Edgar Walter	Wilberforce Chambers, London	020 7306 0102

INQUESTS

Barton Miss Fiona	5 Essex Court, London	020 7410 2000
Bassett Mr John Stewart Britten	5 Essex Court, London	020 7410 2000
Dudley-Jones Ms Elizabeth Sarah	Deans Court Chambers, Manchester	0161 214 6000
	Deans Court Chambers, Preston	01772 565 600

INSOLVENCY

Acton Mr Stephen Neil	Radcliffe Chambers, London	020 7831 0081
Bloch Mr Michael Gordon	Wilberforce Chambers, London	020 7306 0102
Boyle Mr Alan Gordon	Serle Court, London	020 7242 6105
Butler Mr Andrew	Tanfield Chambers, London	020 7421 5300
Fain Mr Carl Ian	Tanfield Chambers, London	020 7421 5300
Jackson Mr Nicholas David Kingsley	Atlantic Chambers, Liverpool	0151 236 4421
Jourdan Mr Stephen Eric	Falcon Chambers, London	020 7353 2484
Lightman Mr Daniel	Serle Court, London	020 7242 6105
Lloyd Mr Stephen James George	13 Old Square Chambers, London	020 7831 4445
Lowe Mr Thomas William Gordon	Wilberforce Chambers, London	020 7306 0102
McCann Miss Sarah Jane	Hardwicke, London	020 7242 2523
Mold Mr Andrew Matthew Stephen	Wilberforce Chambers, London	020 7306 0102
O'Sullivan Mr Richard John	1215 Chambers, London	020 3291 1215
Reeds Mr Gareth David	Canary Wharf Chambers, London	020 7183 8011
Rushton Ms Nicola Jane	Five Paper, London	020 7815 3200
Toube Ms Felicity Rosalind	South Square, London	020 7696 9900
Trace Mr Anthony John	Maitland Chambers, London	020 7406 1200
Tunkel Mr Alan Michael	3 Stone Buildings, London	020 7242 4937
West Mr Mark	Radcliffe Chambers, London	020 7831 0081
Wilson Mr Graham James	Gray's Inn Tax Chambers, London	020 7242 2642
Zelin Mr Geoffrey Andrew	Enterprise Chambers, Leeds	0113 246 0391
	Enterprise Chambers, London	020 7405 9471
	Enterprise Chambers, Newcastle Upon Tyne	0191 222 3344

INSURANCE

Acton Mr Stephen Neil	Radcliffe Chambers, London	020 7831 0081
Bacon Mr Nicholas Michael	Four New Square, London	020 7822 2000
Bellamy Mr Jonathan Mark	39 Essex Street, London	020 7832 1111
	82 King Street, Manchester	0161 870 9969
Briden Mr Timothy John	Lamb Chambers, London	020 7797 8300
Burling Mr Julian Michael	Serle Court, London	020 7242 6105
Butler Mr Andrew	Tanfield Chambers, London	020 7421 5300
Carr Miss Sue Lascelles	Four New Square, London	020 7822 2000
Collett Mr Michael John	20 Essex Street, London	020 7842 1200
De Verneuil Smith Mr Peter Robert	3 Verulam Buildings, London	020 7831 8441
Dingemans Mr James Michael	3 Hare Court, London	020 7415 7800
Dowley Mr Dominic Myles	Serle Court, London	020 7242 6105
Dutton Mr Timothy James	Fountain Court Chambers, London	020 7583 3335
Jess Dr Digby Charles	Exchange Chambers, Leeds	0113 203 1970
	Exchange Chambers, Liverpool	0151 236 7747
	Exchange Chambers, Manchester	0161 833 2722
Lavender Mr Nicholas	Serle Court, London	020 7242 6105
Lowenstein Mr Paul David	3 Verulam Buildings, London	020 7831 8441
McCann Miss Sarah Jane	Hardwicke, London	020 7242 2523
McPherson Mr Graeme Paul	Four New Square, London	020 7822 2000
Orr Mr Craig Wyndham	One Essex Court, London	020 7583 2000

B

Selvaratnam Miss Vasanti Emily Indrani	Stone Chambers, London	020 7440 6900
Tompkinson Miss Deborah Ann	Clerksroom (London), London	0845 083 3000
	Clerksroom (Taunton), Taunton	0845 083 3000
Toube Ms Felicity Rosalind	South Square, London	020 7696 9900
Trace Mr Anthony John	Maitland Chambers, London	020 7406 1200
Wilson Mr Graham James	Gray's Inn Tax Chambers, London	020 7242 2642

INTELLECTUAL PROPERTY

Abrahams Mr James	8 New Square, London	020 7405 4321
Alexander Mr Daniel Sakyi	8 New Square, London	020 7405 4321
Baldwin Mr John Paul	8 New Square, London	020 7405 4321
Berkeley Miss Iona Sarah Caroline	8 New Square, London	020 7405 4321
Bloch Mr Michael Gordon	Wilberforce Chambers, London	020 7306 0102
Bowhill Miss Jessie Kate	8 New Square, London	020 7405 4321
Campbell Mr Douglas James	Three New Square IP, London	020 7405 1111
Chacksfield Mr Mark Andrew	8 New Square, London	020 7405 4321
Clark Miss Fiona Jane Stewart	8 New Square, London	020 7405 4321
Colley Dr Peter Mclean	Hogarth Chambers, London	020 7404 0404
Delaney Mr Joe	Three New Square IP, London	020 7405 1111
Douglas-Jones Mr Benjamin Timothy	Apex, Cardiff	02920 232 032
	Five Paper Buildings, London	020 7583 6117
Hamer Mr George Clemens	8 New Square, London	020 7405 4321
Hill Mr Jonathan	8 New Square, London	020 7405 4321
Howe Mr Martin Russell Thomson	8 New Square, London	020 7405 4321
Jones Mr Kelvin Mcallister	Templis Chambers, London	020 7649 9808
Lane Ms Lindsay Ruth Busfield	8 New Square, London	020 7405 4321
Lawrence Dr Heather Bunting Elizabeth	11 South Square, London	020 7405 1222
Lykiardopoulos Mr Andrew Nicolas	8 New Square, London	020 7405 4321
Mawhinney Mr Richard Martin	Outer Temple Chambers, London	020 7353 6381
	St John's Chambers, Bristol	0117 923 4700
May Miss Charlotte Louisa	8 New Square, London	020 7405 4321
Meade Mr Richard David	8 New Square, London	020 7405 4321
Mellor Mr Edward James Wilson	8 New Square, London	020 7405 4321
Mitcheson Mr Thomas George Moseley	Three New Square IP, London	020 7405 1111
Moody-Stuart Mr Thomas	8 New Square, London	020 7405 4321
Onslow Mr Robert Denzil	8 New Square, London	020 7405 4321
Platts-Mills Mr Mark Fortescue	8 New Square, London	020 7405 4321
Reed Mr Jeremy Nigel	Hogarth Chambers, London	020 7404 0404
Speck Mr Adrian	8 New Square, London	020 7405 4321
St Ville Mr Laurence James	8 New Square, London	020 7405 4321
Stevenson Dr Simon John	Park Lane Plowden, Leeds	0113 228 5049
Tappin Mr Michael John	8 New Square, London	020 7405 4321
Thorley Mr Simon Joe	Three New Square IP, London	020 7405 1111
Ward Mr Robin Henry	8 New Square, London	020 7405 4321

INTERNATIONAL ARBITRATION

Boyle Mr Alan Gordon	Serle Court, London	020 7242 6105
Dingemans Mr James Michael	3 Hare Court, London	020 7415 7800
Walford Mr Richard Henry Howard	Serle Court, London	020 7242 6105

INTERNATIONAL COMMERCIAL ARBITRATION

Bellamy Mr Jonathan Mark	39 Essex Street, London	020 7832 1111
	82 King Street, Manchester	0161 870 9969
Boyle Mr Alan Gordon	Serle Court, London	020 7242 6105

INTERNATIONAL FRAUD AND ASSET TRACING

Dudley-Jones Ms Elizabeth Sarah	Deans Court Chambers, Manchester	0161 214 6000
	Deans Court Chambers, Preston	01772 565 600

B

Fisher Mr Jonathan Simon	Devereux Chambers, London	020 7353 7534

INTERNATIONAL LAW

Edington Mrs Fiona Anne Rider	Thomas More Chambers, London	020 7404 7000
Moore Mr George Crawford Jackson	11 King's Bench Walk, London	020 7632 8500

INTERNATIONAL TRADE

Collett Mr Michael John	20 Essex Street, London	020 7842 1200
Dowley Mr Dominic Myles	Serle Court, London	020 7242 6105
Lowenstein Mr Paul David	3 Verulam Buildings, London	020 7831 8441
Orr Mr Craig Wyndham	One Essex Court, London	020 7583 2000
Selvaratnam Miss Vasanti Emily Indrani	Stone Chambers, London	020 7440 6900
Sen Mr Aditya Kumar	Coram Chambers, London	020 7092 3700

INTERNET CRIME

Dudley-Jones Ms Elizabeth Sarah	Deans Court Chambers, Manchester	0161 214 6000
	Deans Court Chambers, Preston	01772 565 600

INTERNET LAW

Campbell Mr Douglas James	Three New Square IP, London	020 7405 1111
Jones Mr Kelvin Mcallister	Templis Chambers, London	020 7649 9808
Lowenstein Mr Paul David	3 Verulam Buildings, London	020 7831 8441
May Miss Charlotte Louisa	8 New Square, London	020 7405 4321
Speck Mr Adrian	8 New Square, London	020 7405 4321
Whyte Dr James Richard Cleland	8 New Square, London	020 7405 4321

ISLAMIC LAW

Thomson Mr Martin Haldane Ahmad	Wynne Chambers, London	020 3239 6964

JAMAICA LAW

Moore Mr George Crawford Jackson	11 King's Bench Walk, London	020 7632 8500

JUDICIAL REVIEW

Barton Miss Fiona	5 Essex Court, London	020 7410 2000
Cornwell Dr James Matthew	11 King's Bench Walk, London	020 7632 8500
O'Sullivan Mr Richard John	1215 Chambers, London	020 3291 1215

LAND COMPENSATION

Alesbury Mr Alun	Cornerstone Barristers, London	020 7242 4986
	12 Old Square Chambers, London	020 7404 0875
Barnes Mr Michael	Wilberforce Chambers, London	020 7306 0102
Chapman Mr Vivian Robert	New Street Chambers, Leicester	0116 262 5906
	9 Stone Buildings, London	020 7404 5055
Cowen Mr Gary Adam	Falcon Chambers, London	020 7353 2484
Denyer-Green Mr Barry Peter Douglas	Falcon Chambers, London	020 7353 2484
Druce Mr Michael James	Cornerstone Barristers, London	020 7242 4986
Karas Mr Jonathan Marcus	Wilberforce Chambers, London	020 7306 0102
Newsom Mr George Lucien	Guildhall Chambers, Bristol	0117 930 9000
Roots Mr Guy Robert Godfrey	12 College Place, Southampton	023 8032 0320
	Francis Taylor Building, London	020 7353 8415

LANDLORD AND TENANT

Acton Mr Stephen Neil	Radcliffe Chambers, London	020 7831 0081
Barnes Mr Michael	Wilberforce Chambers, London	020 7306 0102
Berkley Mr Michael Stuart	Rougemont Chambers, Exeter	01392 208484
Bignell Miss Janet Susan	Falcon Chambers, London	020 7353 2484
Boyd Mr Stephen James Harvey	Selborne Chambers, London	020 7420 9500
Buckpitt Mr Michael David	Tanfield Chambers, London	020 7421 5300
Butler Mr Andrew	Tanfield Chambers, London	020 7421 5300
Carr Mr Adrian James Selden	Tanfield Chambers, London	020 7421 5300
Chapman Mr Vivian Robert	New Street Chambers, Leicester	0116 262 5906
	9 Stone Buildings, London	020 7404 5055
Clark Mr Wayne Vincent	Falcon Chambers, London	020 7353 2484

Name	Chambers	Telephone
Cole Mr Edward Arthur	Falcon Chambers, London	020 7353 2484
Cowen Mr Gary Adam	Falcon Chambers, London	020 7353 2484
Daly Mr David	Heathway Chambers, London	020 8293 0509
Denyer-Green Mr Barry Peter Douglas	Falcon Chambers, London	020 7353 2484
Dowding Mr Nicholas Alan Tatham	Falcon Chambers, London	020 7353 2484
Dray Mr Martin Benedict Antony	Falcon Chambers, London	020 7353 2484
Fain Mr Carl Ian	Tanfield Chambers, London	020 7421 5300
Fancourt Mr Timothy Miles	Falcon Chambers, London	020 7353 2484
Ferber Ms Iris	42 Bedford Row, London	020 7831 0222
Fetherstonhaugh Mr Guy Cuthbert Charles	Falcon Chambers, London	020 7353 2484
Fitzgerald Miss Elizabeth Helen	Falcon Chambers, London	020 7353 2484
Ford Mr Gerard James	Old Court Chambers, Middlesbrough	01642 232523
Francis Mr Andrew James	Serle Court, London	020 7242 6105
	Zenith Chambers, Leeds	0113 245 5438
Gallagher Mr Stanley Harold	Tanfield Chambers, London	020 7421 5300
Glen Mr Philip Alexander	12 College Place, Southampton	023 8032 0320
Harpum Mr Charles	Falcon Chambers, London	020 7353 2484
Heather Mr Christopher Mark	Tanfield Chambers, London	020 7421 5300
Hilliard Mr Jonathan Adam	Wilberforce Chambers, London	020 7306 0102
Hochberg Mr Daniel Alan	Wilberforce Chambers, London	020 7306 0102
Hutchings Mr Martin Anthony	Wilberforce Chambers, London	020 7306 0102
Hutton Miss Caroline	Enterprise Chambers, Leeds	0113 246 0391
	Enterprise Chambers, London	020 7405 9471
	Enterprise Chambers, Newcastle Upon Tyne	0191 222 3344
Jackson Mr Nicholas David Kingsley	Atlantic Chambers, Liverpool	0151 236 4421
Jourdan Mr Stephen Eric	Falcon Chambers, London	020 7353 2484
Karas Mr Jonathan Marcus	Wilberforce Chambers, London	020 7306 0102
Lloyd Mr Stephen James George	13 Old Square Chambers, London	020 7831 4445
Loveday Mr Mark Alan	Tanfield Chambers, London	020 7421 5300
Martin Mr John Vandeleur	Wilberforce Chambers, London	020 7306 0102
McCann Miss Sarah Jane	Hardwicke, London	020 7242 2523
Mold Mr Andrew Matthew Stephen	Wilberforce Chambers, London	020 7306 0102
Newsom Mr George Lucien	Guildhall Chambers, Bristol	0117 930 9000
Nugee Mr Christopher George	Wilberforce Chambers, London	020 7306 0102
Nugee Mr Edward George	Wilberforce Chambers, London	020 7306 0102
O'Sullivan Mr Richard John	1215 Chambers, London	020 3291 1215
Peters Mr Edward James Hedley	Falcon Chambers, London	020 7353 2484
Radevsky Mr Anthony Eric	Falcon Chambers, London	020 7353 2484
Reeds Mr Gareth David	Canary Wharf Chambers, London	020 7183 8011
Reynolds Mr Kirk	Falcon Chambers, London	020 7353 2484
Rodger Mr Martin Owen	Falcon Chambers, London	020 7353 2484
Ross Martyn Mr John Greaves	New Square Chambers, London	020 7419 8000
	Octagon House, Norwich	01603 623186
Rowley Mr Keith Nigel	Radcliffe Chambers, London	020 7831 0081
Sandham Mr James Andrew	Arden Chambers, London	020 7242 4244
Sawyer Mr Edward Humphrey	Wilberforce Chambers, London	020 7306 0102
Stevenson Dr Simon John	Park Lane Plowden, Leeds	0113 228 5049
Tanney Mr Anthony	Falcon Chambers, London	020 7353 2484
Taskis Ms Catherine Louise	Falcon Chambers, London	020 7353 2484
Tozer Miss Stephanie	Falcon Chambers, London	020 7353 2484
Trace Mr Anthony John	Maitland Chambers, London	020 7406 1200
Tunkel Mr Alan Michael	3 Stone Buildings, London	020 7242 4937
Wardell Mr John David Meredith	Wilberforce Chambers, London	020 7306 0102
West Mr Mark	Radcliffe Chambers, London	020 7831 0081
Wicks Ms Joanne	Wilberforce Chambers, London	020 7306 0102
Windsor Miss Emily May	Falcon Chambers, London	020 7353 2484

Zelin Mr Geoffrey Andrew	Enterprise Chambers, Leeds	0113 246 0391
	Enterprise Chambers, London	020 7405 9471
	Enterprise Chambers, Newcastle Upon Tyne	0191 222 3344

LANDS TRIBUNAL

Bignell Miss Janet Susan	Falcon Chambers, London	020 7353 2484
Chapman Mr Vivian Robert	New Street Chambers, Leicester	0116 262 5906
	9 Stone Buildings, London	020 7404 5055
Gallagher Mr Stanley Harold	Tanfield Chambers, London	020 7421 5300
Karas Mr Jonathan Marcus	Wilberforce Chambers, London	020 7306 0102
Newsom Mr George Lucien	Guildhall Chambers, Bristol	0117 930 9000
Tanney Mr Anthony	Falcon Chambers, London	020 7353 2484

LEASEHOLD ENFRANCHISEMENT

Buckpitt Mr Michael David	Tanfield Chambers, London	020 7421 5300
Dray Mr Martin Benedict Antony	Falcon Chambers, London	020 7353 2484
Gallagher Mr Stanley Harold	Tanfield Chambers, London	020 7421 5300
Heather Mr Christopher Mark	Tanfield Chambers, London	020 7421 5300
Karas Mr Jonathan Marcus	Wilberforce Chambers, London	020 7306 0102
Loveday Mr Mark Alan	Tanfield Chambers, London	020 7421 5300
Radevsky Mr Anthony Eric	Falcon Chambers, London	020 7353 2484
Tanney Mr Anthony	Falcon Chambers, London	020 7353 2484

LEAVE TO REMOVE

Purdie Mr Robert Anthony James	Faringdon Chambers, Faringdon	01367 240598
	4 King's Bench Walk, London	020 7822 7000

LEGAL ADVICE

Tompkinson Miss Deborah Ann	Clerksroom (London), London	0845 083 3000
	Clerksroom (Taunton), Taunton	0845 083 3000

LEGAL AID COSTS

Rushton Ms Nicola Jane	Five Paper, London	020 7815 3200

LICENSING

Alesbury Mr Alun	Cornerstone Barristers, London	020 7242 4986
	12 Old Square Chambers, London	020 7404 0875
Harvey Miss Louise	College Chambers, Southampton	023 8023 0338
Thorley Mr Simon Joe	Three New Square IP, London	020 7405 1111

LIMITED LIABILITY PARTNERSHIPS

Banks Mr Roderick Charles I'Anson	48 Bedford Row, London	020 7430 2005

LIMITED PARTNERSHIPS

Banks Mr Roderick Charles I'Anson	48 Bedford Row, London	020 7430 2005

LITIGATION

Bignell Miss Janet Susan	Falcon Chambers, London	020 7353 2484
Boyle Mr Alan Gordon	Serle Court, London	020 7242 6105
Butler Mr Andrew	Tanfield Chambers, London	020 7421 5300
Fetherstonhaugh Mr Guy Cuthbert Charles	Falcon Chambers, London	020 7353 2484
Fisher Mr Jonathan Simon	Devereux Chambers, London	020 7353 7534
Hinks Mr Frank Peter	Serle Court, London	020 7242 6105

LOCAL AUTHORITIES

Alesbury Mr Alun	Cornerstone Barristers, London	020 7242 4986
	12 Old Square Chambers, London	020 7404 0875
Barnes Mr Michael	Wilberforce Chambers, London	020 7306 0102
Beard Mr Mark Christopher	6 Pump Court, London	020 7797 8400
	6 Pump Court Chambers, Maidstone	01622 688094
Cornwell Dr James Matthew	11 King's Bench Walk, London	020 7632 8500
Daly Mr David	Heathway Chambers, London	020 8293 0509
Denyer-Green Mr Barry Peter Douglas	Falcon Chambers, London	020 7353 2484

Druce Mr Michael James	Cornerstone Barristers, London	020 7242 4986
Ellis Miss Rosalind Morag	Cornerstone Barristers, London	020 7242 4986
Giffin Mr Nigel Dyson	11 King's Bench Walk, London	020 7632 8500
Goudie Mr James	11 King's Bench Walk, London	020 7632 8500
Hockman Mr Stephen Alexander	6 Pump Court, London	020 7797 8400
	6 Pump Court Chambers, Maidstone	01622 688094
	Regency Chambers, Peterborough	01733 315215
Karas Mr Jonathan Marcus	Wilberforce Chambers, London	020 7306 0102
Roots Mr Guy Robert Godfrey	12 College Place, Southampton	023 8032 0320
	Francis Taylor Building, London	020 7353 8415
Sandham Mr James Andrew	Arden Chambers, London	020 7242 4244
Straker Mr Timothy Derrick	4-5 Gray's Inn Square, London	020 7404 5252

LOCAL AUTHORITY CLAIMS

Dudley-Jones Ms Elizabeth Sarah	Deans Court Chambers, Manchester	0161 214 6000
	Deans Court Chambers, Preston	01772 565 600
Howells Miss Katherine Jane	Old Square Chambers, Bristol	0117 930 5100
	Old Square Chambers, London	020 7269 0300

LOCAL AUTHORITY LIABILITY

Dudley-Jones Ms Elizabeth Sarah	Deans Court Chambers, Manchester	0161 214 6000
	Deans Court Chambers, Preston	01772 565 600
Howells Miss Katherine Jane	Old Square Chambers, Bristol	0117 930 5100
	Old Square Chambers, London	020 7269 0300

LOCAL GOVERNMENT AND PUBLIC SERVICES

Ellis Miss Rosalind Morag	Cornerstone Barristers, London	020 7242 4986
O'Sullivan Mr Richard John	1215 Chambers, London	020 3291 1215

MALICIOUS FALSEHOOD

Abrahams Mr James	8 New Square, London	020 7405 4321
Alexander Mr Daniel Sakyi	8 New Square, London	020 7405 4321
Baldwin Mr John Paul	8 New Square, London	020 7405 4321
Bowhill Miss Jessie Kate	8 New Square, London	020 7405 4321
Campbell Mr Douglas James	Three New Square IP, London	020 7405 1111
Chacksfield Mr Mark Andrew	8 New Square, London	020 7405 4321
Clark Miss Fiona Jane Stewart	8 New Square, London	020 7405 4321
Hamer Mr George Clemens	8 New Square, London	020 7405 4321
Lane Ms Lindsay Ruth Busfield	8 New Square, London	020 7405 4321
Lykiardopoulos Mr Andrew Nicolas	8 New Square, London	020 7405 4321
May Miss Charlotte Louisa	8 New Square, London	020 7405 4321
Meade Mr Richard David	8 New Square, London	020 7405 4321
Mellor Mr Edward James Wilson	8 New Square, London	020 7405 4321
Moody-Stuart Mr Thomas	8 New Square, London	020 7405 4321
Onslow Mr Robert Denzil	8 New Square, London	020 7405 4321
Platts-Mills Mr Mark Fortescue	8 New Square, London	020 7405 4321
Speck Mr Adrian	8 New Square, London	020 7405 4321
St Ville Mr Laurence James	8 New Square, London	020 7405 4321
Tappin Mr Michael John	8 New Square, London	020 7405 4321
Ward Mr Robin Henry	8 New Square, London	020 7405 4321

MARKETS AND FAIRS

Chapman Mr Vivian Robert	New Street Chambers, Leicester	0116 262 5906
	9 Stone Buildings, London	020 7404 5055

MATRIMONIAL

Pope Mrs Heather	1 Hare Court, London	020 7797 7070
Purdie Mr Robert Anthony James	Faringdon Chambers, Faringdon	01367 240598
	4 King's Bench Walk, London	020 7822 7000

MATRIMONIAL FINANCE

Carrodus Miss Gail Caroline	Huntercombe Chambers, Henley-On-Thames	01491 641934

Purdie Mr Robert Anthony James	Faringdon Chambers, Faringdon 4 King's Bench Walk, London	01367 240598 020 7822 7000

MEDIA

Abrahams Mr James	8 New Square, London	020 7405 4321
Alexander Mr Daniel Sakyi	8 New Square, London	020 7405 4321
Baldwin Mr John Paul	8 New Square, London	020 7405 4321
Campbell Mr Douglas James	Three New Square IP, London	020 7405 1111
Clark Miss Fiona Jane Stewart	8 New Square, London	020 7405 4321
Hill Mr Jonathan	8 New Square, London	020 7405 4321
Howe Mr Martin Russell Thomson	8 New Square, London	020 7405 4321
Lane Ms Lindsay Ruth Busfield	8 New Square, London	020 7405 4321
May Miss Charlotte Louisa	8 New Square, London	020 7405 4321
Meade Mr Richard David	8 New Square, London	020 7405 4321
Mellor Mr Edward James Wilson	8 New Square, London	020 7405 4321
Moody-Stuart Mr Thomas	8 New Square, London	020 7405 4321
Onslow Mr Robert Denzil	8 New Square, London	020 7405 4321
Platts-Mills Mr Mark Fortescue	8 New Square, London	020 7405 4321
Speck Mr Adrian	8 New Square, London	020 7405 4321
Tappin Mr Michael John	8 New Square, London	020 7405 4321
Whyte Dr James Richard Cleland	8 New Square, London	020 7405 4321

MEDIA AND ENTERTAINMENT

Abrahams Mr James	8 New Square, London	020 7405 4321
Alexander Mr Daniel Sakyi	8 New Square, London	020 7405 4321
Baldwin Mr John Paul	8 New Square, London	020 7405 4321
Bowhill Miss Jessie Kate	8 New Square, London	020 7405 4321
Campbell Mr Douglas James	Three New Square IP, London	020 7405 1111
Chacksfield Mr Mark Andrew	8 New Square, London	020 7405 4321
Clark Miss Fiona Jane Stewart	8 New Square, London	020 7405 4321
Dowley Mr Dominic Myles	Serle Court, London	020 7242 6105
Hamer Mr George Clemens	8 New Square, London	020 7405 4321
Hill Mr Jonathan	8 New Square, London	020 7405 4321
Howe Mr Martin Russell Thomson	8 New Square, London	020 7405 4321
Jones Mr Kelvin Mcallister	Templis Chambers, London	020 7649 9808
Lane Ms Lindsay Ruth Busfield	8 New Square, London	020 7405 4321
Lowe Mr Thomas William Gordon	Wilberforce Chambers, London	020 7306 0102
Lowenstein Mr Paul David	3 Verulam Buildings, London	020 7831 8441
Lykiardopoulos Mr Andrew Nicolas	8 New Square, London	020 7405 4321
May Miss Charlotte Louisa	8 New Square, London	020 7405 4321
Meade Mr Richard David	8 New Square, London	020 7405 4321
Mellor Mr Edward James Wilson	8 New Square, London	020 7405 4321
Moody-Stuart Mr Thomas	8 New Square, London	020 7405 4321
Onslow Mr Robert Denzil	8 New Square, London	020 7405 4321
Platts-Mills Mr Mark Fortescue	8 New Square, London	020 7405 4321
Reed Mr Jeremy Nigel	Hogarth Chambers, London	020 7404 0404
Speck Mr Adrian	8 New Square, London	020 7405 4321
St Ville Mr Laurence James	8 New Square, London	020 7405 4321
Tappin Mr Michael John	8 New Square, London	020 7405 4321
Thorley Mr Simon Joe	Three New Square IP, London	020 7405 1111
Ward Mr Robin Henry	8 New Square, London	020 7405 4321
Whyte Dr James Richard Cleland	8 New Square, London	020 7405 4321

MEDIATION

Boyd Mr Stephen James Harvey	Selborne Chambers, London	020 7420 9500
Boyle Mr Alan Gordon	Serle Court, London	020 7242 6105
Butler Mr Andrew	Tanfield Chambers, London	020 7421 5300
Carrodus Miss Gail Caroline	Huntercombe Chambers, Henley-On-Thames	01491 641934
Daly Mr David	Heathway Chambers, London	020 8293 0509
Lowenstein Mr Paul David	3 Verulam Buildings, London	020 7831 8441
Meade Mr Richard David	8 New Square, London	020 7405 4321
Ross Martyn Mr John Greaves	New Square Chambers, London Octagon House, Norwich	020 7419 8000 01603 623186

B

Tompkinson Miss Deborah Ann	Clerksroom (London), London	0845 083 3000
	Clerksroom (Taunton), Taunton	0845 083 3000
Tozer Miss Stephanie	Falcon Chambers, London	020 7353 2484

MEDICAL LAW

Dudley-Jones Ms Elizabeth Sarah	Deans Court Chambers, Manchester	0161 214 6000
	Deans Court Chambers, Preston	01772 565 600

MEDICAL NEGLIGENCE

Francis Mr Robert Anthony	3 Serjeants Inn, London	020 7427 5000
Howells Miss Katherine Jane	Old Square Chambers, Bristol	0117 930 5100
	Old Square Chambers, London	020 7269 0300
Jerram Ms Harriet Anne	Outer Temple Chambers, London	020 7353 6381

MEDICINES ACT

Dudley-Jones Ms Elizabeth Sarah	Deans Court Chambers, Manchester	0161 214 6000
	Deans Court Chambers, Preston	01772 565 600

MENTAL HEALTH

Badenoch Mr James Forster	1 Crown Office Row, London	020 7797 7500
Dudley-Jones Ms Elizabeth Sarah	Deans Court Chambers, Manchester	0161 214 6000
	Deans Court Chambers, Preston	01772 565 600
Francis Mr Robert Anthony	3 Serjeants Inn, London	020 7427 5000
O'Sullivan Mr Richard John	1215 Chambers, London	020 3291 1215
Tavares Mr Nathan Warren	Outer Temple Chambers, London	020 7353 6381

B

MILITARY LAW

Edington Mrs Fiona Anne Rider	Thomas More Chambers, London	020 7404 7000

MINERAL RIGHTS

Bignell Miss Janet Susan	Falcon Chambers, London	020 7353 2484
Chapman Mr Vivian Robert	New Street Chambers, Leicester	0116 262 5906
	9 Stone Buildings, London	020 7404 5055
Harpum Mr Charles	Falcon Chambers, London	020 7353 2484
Peters Mr Edward James Hedley	Falcon Chambers, London	020 7353 2484

MINING

Chapman Mr Vivian Robert	New Street Chambers, Leicester	0116 262 5906
	9 Stone Buildings, London	020 7404 5055
Fetherstonhaugh Mr Guy Cuthbert Charles	Falcon Chambers, London	020 7353 2484
Rodger Mr Martin Owen	Falcon Chambers, London	020 7353 2484

MONEY LAUNDERING

Evans Mr Martin Alan Langham	Chambers of Andrew Mitchell QC, London	020 7440 9950
Fisher Mr Jonathan Simon	Devereux Chambers, London	020 7353 7534
Rhodes Mr Robert Elliott	Outer Temple Chambers, London	020 7353 6381
	Principal Chambers, Sevenoaks	0845 209 8080
	St Philips Chambers, Birmingham	0121 246 7000

MONTSERRAT LAW

Moore Mr George Crawford Jackson	11 King's Bench Walk, London	020 7632 8500

MORTGAGES

Bignell Miss Janet Susan	Falcon Chambers, London	020 7353 2484
Chapman Mr Vivian Robert	New Street Chambers, Leicester	0116 262 5906
	9 Stone Buildings, London	020 7404 5055
Clark Mr Wayne Vincent	Falcon Chambers, London	020 7353 2484
Dray Mr Martin Benedict Antony	Falcon Chambers, London	020 7353 2484
Harpum Mr Charles	Falcon Chambers, London	020 7353 2484
Heather Mr Christopher Mark	Tanfield Chambers, London	020 7421 5300
Ross Martyn Mr John Greaves	New Square Chambers, London	020 7419 8000
	Octagon House, Norwich	01603 623186
Tozer Miss Stephanie	Falcon Chambers, London	020 7353 2484

Waters Mr Malcolm Ian	Radcliffe Chambers, London	020 7831 0081
MULTI-PARTY LITIGATION		
Lowenstein Mr Paul David	3 Verulam Buildings, London	020 7831 8441
NATIONAL INSURANCE		
Aaronson Mr Graham Raphael	Pump Court Tax Chambers, London	020 7414 8080
Baldry Mr Rupert Patrick Craig	Pump Court Tax Chambers, London	020 7414 8080
Bradley Mr Charles Edward May	Pump Court Tax Chambers, London	020 7414 8080
Bremner Mr Jonathan Sinclair Grant	Pump Court Tax Chambers, London	020 7414 8080
Chacko Mr Thomas Joseph	Pump Court Tax Chambers, London	020 7414 8080
Choudhury Miss Sadiya Asghar	Pump Court Tax Chambers, London	020 7414 8080
Conolly Dr Oliver Stephen	Pump Court Tax Chambers, London	020 7414 8080
Dunn Ms Sarah Patricia Quincey	Pump Court Tax Chambers, London	020 7414 8080
Ewart Mr David Scott	Pump Court Tax Chambers, London	020 7414 8080
Ghosh Mr Indranil Julian	Pump Court Tax Chambers, London	020 7414 8080
Goodfellow Mr Giles William Jeremy	Pump Court Tax Chambers, London	020 7414 8080
Henderson Mr James Thomas	Kings Chambers, Leeds	0845 034 3444
	Kings Chambers, Manchester	0845 034 3444
	Pump Court Tax Chambers, London	020 7414 8080
Massey Mr William Greville Sale	Pump Court Tax Chambers, London	020 7414 8080
Matthews Mr Janek Paul	Pump Court Tax Chambers, London	020 7414 8080
Milne Mr David Calder	Pump Court Tax Chambers, London	020 7414 8080
Poots Miss Laura Jill	Pump Court Tax Chambers, London	020 7414 8080
Prosser Mr Kevin John	Pump Court Tax Chambers, London	020 7414 8080
Rivett Mr James Peter	Pump Court Tax Chambers, London	020 7414 8080
Tallon Mr John Mark	Pump Court Tax Chambers, London	020 7414 8080
Thomas Mr Roger Christopher	Pump Court Tax Chambers, London	020 7414 8080
Thornhill Mr Andrew Robert	Albion Chambers, Bristol	0117 927 2144
	Pump Court Tax Chambers, London	020 7414 8080
Vallat Mr Richard Justin	Pump Court Tax Chambers, London	020 7414 8080
Wilson Miss Mary Elizabeth Frances	Pump Court Tax Chambers, London	020 7414 8080
Woolf The Hon Jeremy Richard George	Pump Court Tax Chambers, London	020 7414 8080
Yang Dr Zizhen	Pump Court Tax Chambers, London	020 7414 8080
Yates Mr David James Francis	Pump Court Tax Chambers, London	020 7414 8080
NEW YORK LAW		
Reeds Mr Gareth David	Canary Wharf Chambers, London	020 7183 8011
OCCUPATIONAL DISEASES		
Howells Miss Katherine Jane	Old Square Chambers, Bristol	0117 930 5100
	Old Square Chambers, London	020 7269 0300
OFFSHORE TRUST LITIGATION		
Boyle Mr Alan Gordon	Serle Court, London	020 7242 6105
Bryant Miss Judith Anne	Wilberforce Chambers, London	020 7306 0102
Chamberlain Ms Emma Jane Mary	Pump Court Tax Chambers, London	020 7414 8080
Hinks Mr Frank Peter	Serle Court, London	020 7242 6105
Lowe Mr Thomas William Gordon	Wilberforce Chambers, London	020 7306 0102
OVERSEAS ACCIDENTS		
Howells Miss Katherine Jane	Old Square Chambers, Bristol	0117 930 5100
	Old Square Chambers, London	020 7269 0300
PARLIAMENTARY		
Alesbury Mr Alun	Cornerstone Barristers, London	020 7242 4986
	12 Old Square Chambers, London	020 7404 0875
Druce Mr Michael James	Cornerstone Barristers, London	020 7242 4986
Nardell Mr Gordon Lawrence	39 Essex Street, London	020 7832 1111
	82 King Street, Manchester	0161 870 9969

Roots Mr Guy Robert Godfrey	12 College Place, Southampton	023 8032 0320
	Francis Taylor Building, London	020 7353 8415

PARTNERSHIPS

Acton Mr Stephen Neil	Radcliffe Chambers, London	020 7831 0081
Banks Mr Roderick Charles I'Anson	48 Bedford Row, London	020 7430 2005
Berkley Mr Michael Stuart	Rougemont Chambers, Exeter	01392 208484
Boyd Mr Stephen James Harvey	Selborne Chambers, London	020 7420 9500
Chapman Mr Vivian Robert	New Street Chambers, Leicester	0116 262 5906
	9 Stone Buildings, London	020 7404 5055
Dowley Mr Dominic Myles	Serle Court, London	020 7242 6105
Dutton Mr Timothy James	Fountain Court Chambers, London	020 7583 3335
Francis Mr Andrew James	Serle Court, London	020 7242 6105
	Zenith Chambers, Leeds	0113 245 5438
Hinks Mr Frank Peter	Serle Court, London	020 7242 6105
Hochberg Mr Daniel Alan	Wilberforce Chambers, London	020 7306 0102
Jackson Mr Nicholas David Kingsley	Atlantic Chambers, Liverpool	0151 236 4421
Lloyd Mr Stephen James George	13 Old Square Chambers, London	020 7831 4445
Mawhinney Mr Richard Martin	Outer Temple Chambers, London	020 7353 6381
	St John's Chambers, Bristol	0117 923 4700
McCann Miss Sarah Jane	Hardwicke, London	020 7242 2523
Mold Mr Andrew Matthew Stephen	Wilberforce Chambers, London	020 7306 0102
Newsom Mr George Lucien	Guildhall Chambers, Bristol	0117 930 9000
Nugee Mr Edward George	Wilberforce Chambers, London	020 7306 0102
Rodger Mr Martin Owen	Falcon Chambers, London	020 7353 2484
Ross Martyn Mr John Greaves	New Square Chambers, London	020 7419 8000
	Octagon House, Norwich	01603 623186
Sen Mr Aditya Kumar	Coram Chambers, London	020 7092 3700
Smith Miss Joanna Angela	Wilberforce Chambers, London	020 7306 0102
Stevenson Dr Simon John	Park Lane Plowden, Leeds	0113 228 5049
Stoner Mr Christopher Paul	Serle Court, London	020 7242 6105
Trace Mr Anthony John	Maitland Chambers, London	020 7406 1200
Tunkel Mr Alan Michael	3 Stone Buildings, London	020 7242 4937
West Mr Mark	Radcliffe Chambers, London	020 7831 0081
Zelin Mr Geoffrey Andrew	Enterprise Chambers, Leeds	0113 246 0391
	Enterprise Chambers, London	020 7405 9471
	Enterprise Chambers, Newcastle Upon Tyne	0191 222 3344

PASSING OFF

Abrahams Mr James	8 New Square, London	020 7405 4321
Alexander Mr Daniel Sakyi	8 New Square, London	020 7405 4321
Baldwin Mr John Paul	8 New Square, London	020 7405 4321
Campbell Mr Douglas James	Three New Square IP, London	020 7405 1111
Clark Miss Fiona Jane Stewart	8 New Square, London	020 7405 4321
Delaney Mr Joe	Three New Square IP, London	020 7405 1111
Howe Mr Martin Russell Thomson	8 New Square, London	020 7405 4321
Jackson Mr Nicholas David Kingsley	Atlantic Chambers, Liverpool	0151 236 4421
Jamal Miss Isabel Leila	8 New Square, London	020 7405 4321
Jones Mr Kelvin Mcallister	Templis Chambers, London	020 7649 9808
Lane Ms Lindsay Ruth Busfield	8 New Square, London	020 7405 4321
Lawrence Dr Heather Bunting Elizabeth	11 South Square, London	020 7405 1222
May Miss Charlotte Louisa	8 New Square, London	020 7405 4321
Meade Mr Richard David	8 New Square, London	020 7405 4321
Mellor Mr Edward James Wilson	8 New Square, London	020 7405 4321
Mitcheson Mr Thomas George Moseley	Three New Square IP, London	020 7405 1111
Moody-Stuart Mr Thomas	8 New Square, London	020 7405 4321
Onslow Mr Robert Denzil	8 New Square, London	020 7405 4321
Platts-Mills Mr Mark Fortescue	8 New Square, London	020 7405 4321
Reed Mr Jeremy Nigel	Hogarth Chambers, London	020 7404 0404
Speck Mr Adrian	8 New Square, London	020 7405 4321
St Ville Mr Laurence James	8 New Square, London	020 7405 4321

Tappin Mr Michael John	8 New Square, London	020 7405 4321
Thorley Mr Simon Joe	Three New Square IP, London	020 7405 1111
Whyte Dr James Richard Cleland	8 New Square, London	020 7405 4321

PATENTS

Abrahams Mr James	8 New Square, London	020 7405 4321
Alexander Mr Daniel Sakyi	8 New Square, London	020 7405 4321
Baldwin Mr John Paul	8 New Square, London	020 7405 4321
Berkeley Miss Iona Sarah Caroline	8 New Square, London	020 7405 4321
Bloch Mr Michael Gordon	Wilberforce Chambers, London	020 7306 0102
Bowhill Miss Jessie Kate	8 New Square, London	020 7405 4321
Campbell Mr Douglas James	Three New Square IP, London	020 7405 1111
Chacksfield Mr Mark Andrew	8 New Square, London	020 7405 4321
Clark Miss Fiona Jane Stewart	8 New Square, London	020 7405 4321
Colley Dr Peter Mclean	Hogarth Chambers, London	020 7404 0404
Delaney Mr Joe	Three New Square IP, London	020 7405 1111
Hamer Mr George Clemens	8 New Square, London	020 7405 4321
Hill Mr Jonathan	8 New Square, London	020 7405 4321
Howe Mr Martin Russell Thomson	8 New Square, London	020 7405 4321
Jamal Miss Isabel Leila	8 New Square, London	020 7405 4321
Jones Mr Kelvin Mcallister	Templis Chambers, London	020 7649 9808
Lane Ms Lindsay Ruth Busfield	8 New Square, London	020 7405 4321
Lawrence Dr Heather Bunting Elizabeth	11 South Square, London	020 7405 1222
Lykiardopoulos Mr Andrew Nicolas	8 New Square, London	020 7405 4321
May Miss Charlotte Louisa	8 New Square, London	020 7405 4321
Meade Mr Richard David	8 New Square, London	020 7405 4321
Mellor Mr Edward James Wilson	8 New Square, London	020 7405 4321
Mitcheson Mr Thomas George Moseley	Three New Square IP, London	020 7405 1111
Moody-Stuart Mr Thomas	8 New Square, London	020 7405 4321
Onslow Mr Robert Denzil	8 New Square, London	020 7405 4321
Platts-Mills Mr Mark Fortescue	8 New Square, London	020 7405 4321
Reed Mr Jeremy Nigel	Hogarth Chambers, London	020 7404 0404
Speck Mr Adrian	8 New Square, London	020 7405 4321
St Ville Mr Laurence James	8 New Square, London	020 7405 4321
Tappin Mr Michael John	8 New Square, London	020 7405 4321
Thorley Mr Simon Joe	Three New Square IP, London	020 7405 1111
Ward Mr Robin Henry	8 New Square, London	020 7405 4321
Whyte Dr James Richard Cleland	8 New Square, London	020 7405 4321

PENSIONS

Asplin Miss Sarah Jane	3 Stone Buildings, London	020 7242 4937
Campbell Miss Emily Charlotte	Wilberforce Chambers, London	020 7306 0102
Furness Mr Michael James	Wilberforce Chambers, London	020 7306 0102
Green Mr Brian Russell	Wilberforce Chambers, London	020 7306 0102
Ham Mr Robert Wallace	Wilberforce Chambers, London	020 7306 0102
Hilliard Mr Jonathan Adam	Wilberforce Chambers, London	020 7306 0102
Mold Mr Andrew Matthew Stephen	Wilberforce Chambers, London	020 7306 0102
Nugee Mr Christopher George	Wilberforce Chambers, London	020 7306 0102
Nugee Mr Edward George	Wilberforce Chambers, London	020 7306 0102
Ovey Miss Elizabeth Helen	Radcliffe Chambers, London	020 7831 0081
Rowley Mr Keith Nigel	Radcliffe Chambers, London	020 7831 0081
Stallworthy Mr Nicolas Kyd	Outer Temple Chambers, London	020 7353 6381
Stevenson Dr Simon John	Park Lane Plowden, Leeds	0113 228 5049

PERSONAL INJURY

Badenoch Mr James Forster	1 Crown Office Row, London	020 7797 7500
Bassett Mr John Stewart Britten	5 Essex Court, London	020 7410 2000
Boyd Miss Kerstin Margaret	Tanfield Chambers, London	020 7421 5300
Briden Mr Timothy John	Lamb Chambers, London	020 7797 8300
Cherry Mr John Mitchell	Lamb Chambers, London	020 7797 8300
Dingemans Mr James Michael	3 Hare Court, London	020 7415 7800
Ford Mr Gerard James	Old Court Chambers, Middlesbrough	01642 232523

Francis Mr Robert Anthony	3 Serjeants Inn, London	020 7427 5000
Furniss Mr Richard Alexander	42 Bedford Row, London	020 7831 0222
Hockman Mr Stephen Alexander	6 Pump Court, London	020 7797 8400
	6 Pump Court Chambers, Maidstone	01622 688094
	Regency Chambers, Peterborough	01733 315215
Hodson Mr Peter David	Chambers of Ian Macdonald QC, Manchester	0161 236 1840
Howells Miss Katherine Jane	Old Square Chambers, Bristol	0117 930 5100
	Old Square Chambers, London	020 7269 0300
Jerram Ms Harriet Anne	Outer Temple Chambers, London	020 7353 6381
Kempster Mr Ivor Toby Chalmers	Old Square Chambers, Bristol	0117 930 5100
	Old Square Chambers, London	020 7269 0300
Latimer-Sayer Mr William Laurence	Cloisters, London	020 7827 4000
Mawhinney Mr Richard Martin	Outer Temple Chambers, London	020 7353 6381
	St John's Chambers, Bristol	0117 923 4700
Menzies Mr Richard Mark	Lamb Chambers, London	020 7797 8300
Michael Mr Simon Laurence	No5 Chambers, Birmingham	0845 210 5555
	No5 Chambers, Bristol	0845 210 5555
	No5 Chambers, London	0845 210 5555
Nicholls Mr Peter John	5 Pump Court, London	020 7353 2532
Phillips Mr Matthew James	Outer Temple Chambers, London	020 7353 6381
Pitchers Mr Henry William Stodart	No5 Chambers, Birmingham	0845 210 5555
	No5 Chambers, Bristol	0845 210 5555
	No5 Chambers, London	0845 210 5555
Quickfall Mr Roger Mark	Park Lane Plowden, Leeds	0113 228 5049
Scott Mr Ian Richard	Old Square Chambers, Bristol	0117 930 5100
	Old Square Chambers, London	020 7269 0300
Tavares Mr Nathan Warren	Outer Temple Chambers, London	020 7353 6381
Tompkinson Miss Deborah Ann	Clerksroom (London), London	0845 083 3000
	Clerksroom (Taunton), Taunton	0845 083 3000
Treasure Mr Francis Seton	42 Bedford Row, London	020 7831 0222

PERSONAL INSOLVENCY

Acton Mr Stephen Neil	Radcliffe Chambers, London	020 7831 0081
Carrodus Miss Gail Caroline	Huntercombe Chambers, Henley-On-Thames	01491 641934
Lightman Mr Daniel	Serle Court, London	020 7242 6105
Lloyd Mr Stephen James George	13 Old Square Chambers, London	020 7831 4445
McCann Miss Sarah Jane	Hardwicke, London	020 7242 2523
Reeds Mr Gareth David	Canary Wharf Chambers, London	020 7183 8011
Toube Ms Felicity Rosalind	South Square, London	020 7696 9900
Trace Mr Anthony John	Maitland Chambers, London	020 7406 1200
Tunkel Mr Alan Michael	3 Stone Buildings, London	020 7242 4937
Walsh Mr Steven James Franklyn	Five Paper, London	020 7815 3200
West Mr Mark	Radcliffe Chambers, London	020 7831 0081
Zelin Mr Geoffrey Andrew	Enterprise Chambers, Leeds	0113 246 0391
	Enterprise Chambers, London	020 7405 9471
	Enterprise Chambers, Newcastle Upon Tyne	0191 222 3344

PHARMACEUTICALS

Abrahams Mr James	8 New Square, London	020 7405 4321
Alexander Mr Daniel Sakyi	8 New Square, London	020 7405 4321
Baldwin Mr John Paul	8 New Square, London	020 7405 4321
Campbell Mr Douglas James	Three New Square IP, London	020 7405 1111
Delaney Mr Joe	Three New Square IP, London	020 7405 1111
Hill Mr Jonathan	8 New Square, London	020 7405 4321
Howe Mr Martin Russell Thomson	8 New Square, London	020 7405 4321
Jamal Miss Isabel Leila	8 New Square, London	020 7405 4321
May Miss Charlotte Louisa	8 New Square, London	020 7405 4321
Meade Mr Richard David	8 New Square, London	020 7405 4321
Mellor Mr Edward James Wilson	8 New Square, London	020 7405 4321
Mitcheson Mr Thomas George Moseley	Three New Square IP, London	020 7405 1111

Moody-Stuart Mr Thomas	8 New Square, London	020 7405 4321
Onslow Mr Robert Denzil	8 New Square, London	020 7405 4321
Speck Mr Adrian	8 New Square, London	020 7405 4321
St Ville Mr Laurence James	8 New Square, London	020 7405 4321
Tappin Mr Michael John	8 New Square, London	020 7405 4321
Thorley Mr Simon Joe	Three New Square IP, London	020 7405 1111
Whyte Dr James Richard Cleland	8 New Square, London	020 7405 4321

PLANNING

Alesbury Mr Alun	Cornerstone Barristers, London	020 7242 4986
	12 Old Square Chambers, London	020 7404 0875
Barnes Mr Michael	Wilberforce Chambers, London	020 7306 0102
Beard Mr Mark Christopher	6 Pump Court, London	020 7797 8400
	6 Pump Court Chambers, Maidstone	01622 688094
Daly Mr David	Heathway Chambers, London	020 8293 0509
Denyer-Green Mr Barry Peter Douglas	Falcon Chambers, London	020 7353 2484
Druce Mr Michael James	Cornerstone Barristers, London	020 7242 4986
Ellis Miss Rosalind Morag	Cornerstone Barristers, London	020 7242 4986
Hockman Mr Stephen Alexander	6 Pump Court, London	020 7797 8400
	6 Pump Court Chambers, Maidstone	01622 688094
	Regency Chambers, Peterborough	01733 315215
Howell Williams Mr Craig	Francis Taylor Building, London	020 7353 8415
Jackson Mr Nicholas David Kingsley	Atlantic Chambers, Liverpool	0151 236 4421
Karas Mr Jonathan Marcus	Wilberforce Chambers, London	020 7306 0102
Nardell Mr Gordon Lawrence	39 Essex Street, London	020 7832 1111
	82 King Street, Manchester	0161 870 9969
Newsom Mr George Lucien	Guildhall Chambers, Bristol	0117 930 9000
Roots Mr Guy Robert Godfrey	12 College Place, Southampton	023 8032 0320
	Francis Taylor Building, London	020 7353 8415
Sheppard Mr Timothy Derie	No5 Chambers, Birmingham	0845 210 5555
	No5 Chambers, Bristol	0845 210 5555
	No5 Chambers, London	0845 210 5555
Straker Mr Timothy Derrick	4-5 Gray's Inn Square, London	020 7404 5252

POLICE

Barton Miss Fiona	5 Essex Court, London	020 7410 2000
Bassett Mr John Stewart Britten	5 Essex Court, London	020 7410 2000

POLICE DISCIPLINE

Barton Miss Fiona	5 Essex Court, London	020 7410 2000
Bassett Mr John Stewart Britten	5 Essex Court, London	020 7410 2000

PRIVACY

Alexander Mr Daniel Sakyi	8 New Square, London	020 7405 4321
Hill Mr Jonathan	8 New Square, London	020 7405 4321
Reed Mr Jeremy Nigel	Hogarth Chambers, London	020 7404 0404
St Ville Mr Laurence James	8 New Square, London	020 7405 4321

PRIVATE CHILDREN LAW

Carrodus Miss Gail Caroline	Huntercombe Chambers, Henley-On-Thames	01491 641934
Harvey Miss Louise	College Chambers, Southampton	023 8023 0338
Pope Mrs Heather	1 Hare Court, London	020 7797 7070
Purdie Mr Robert Anthony James	Faringdon Chambers, Faringdon	01367 240598
	4 King's Bench Walk, London	020 7822 7000

PRIVATE CLIENT

Baldry Mr Rupert Patrick Craig	Pump Court Tax Chambers, London	020 7414 8080
Boyle Mr Alan Gordon	Serle Court, London	020 7242 6105
Bradley Mr Charles Edward May	Pump Court Tax Chambers, London	020 7414 8080
Bremner Mr Jonathan Sinclair Grant	Pump Court Tax Chambers, London	020 7414 8080
Chacko Mr Thomas Joseph	Pump Court Tax Chambers, London	020 7414 8080
Chamberlain Ms Emma Jane Mary	Pump Court Tax Chambers, London	020 7414 8080
Child Mr John Frederick	Wilberforce Chambers, London	020 7306 0102

Choudhury Miss Sadiya Asghar	Pump Court Tax Chambers, London	020 7414 8080
Conolly Dr Oliver Stephen	Pump Court Tax Chambers, London	020 7414 8080
Dunn Ms Sarah Patricia Quincey	Pump Court Tax Chambers, London	020 7414 8080
Ewart Mr David Scott	Pump Court Tax Chambers, London	020 7414 8080
Goodfellow Mr Giles William Jeremy	Pump Court Tax Chambers, London	020 7414 8080
Henderson Mr James Thomas	Kings Chambers, Leeds	0845 034 3444
	Kings Chambers, Manchester	0845 034 3444
	Pump Court Tax Chambers, London	020 7414 8080
Hinks Mr Frank Peter	Serle Court, London	020 7242 6105
Massey Mr William Greville Sale	Pump Court Tax Chambers, London	020 7414 8080
Matthews Mr Janek Paul	Pump Court Tax Chambers, London	020 7414 8080
Poots Miss Laura Jill	Pump Court Tax Chambers, London	020 7414 8080
Rivett Mr James Peter	Pump Court Tax Chambers, London	020 7414 8080
Tallon Mr John Mark	Pump Court Tax Chambers, London	020 7414 8080
Thomas Mr Roger Christopher	Pump Court Tax Chambers, London	020 7414 8080
Thornhill Mr Andrew Robert	Albion Chambers, Bristol	0117 927 2144
	Pump Court Tax Chambers, London	020 7414 8080
Vallat Mr Richard Justin	Pump Court Tax Chambers, London	020 7414 8080
Wilson Miss Mary Elizabeth Frances	Pump Court Tax Chambers, London	020 7414 8080
Woolf The Hon Jeremy Richard George	Pump Court Tax Chambers, London	020 7414 8080
Yang Dr Zizhen	Pump Court Tax Chambers, London	020 7414 8080
Yates Mr David James Francis	Pump Court Tax Chambers, London	020 7414 8080

B

PROCUREMENT

Giffin Mr Nigel Dyson	11 King's Bench Walk, London	020 7632 8500
McCredie Miss Fionnuala Mary Constance	Keating Chambers, London	020 7544 2600

PRODUCT LIABILITY

Baldwin Mr John Paul	8 New Square, London	020 7405 4321
Bellamy Mr Jonathan Mark	39 Essex Street, London	020 7832 1111
	82 King Street, Manchester	0161 870 9969
Platts-Mills Mr Mark Fortescue	8 New Square, London	020 7405 4321

PROFESSIONAL NEGLIGENCE

Acton Mr Stephen Neil	Radcliffe Chambers, London	020 7831 0081
Asplin Miss Sarah Jane	3 Stone Buildings, London	020 7242 4937
Bacon Mr Nicholas Michael	Four New Square, London	020 7822 2000
Badenoch Mr James Forster	1 Crown Office Row, London	020 7797 7500
Bassett Mr John Stewart Britten	5 Essex Court, London	020 7410 2000
Bellamy Mr Jonathan Mark	39 Essex Street, London	020 7832 1111
	82 King Street, Manchester	0161 870 9969
Berkley Mr Michael Stuart	Rougemont Chambers, Exeter	01392 208484
Bornman Miss Kerry	3 Stone Buildings, London	020 7242 4937
Boyd Mr Stephen James Harvey	Selborne Chambers, London	020 7420 9500
Bryant Miss Judith Anne	Wilberforce Chambers, London	020 7306 0102
Butler Mr Andrew	Tanfield Chambers, London	020 7421 5300
Campbell Miss Emily Charlotte	Wilberforce Chambers, London	020 7306 0102
Carr Miss Sue Lascelles	Four New Square, London	020 7822 2000
Chapman Mr Vivian Robert	New Street Chambers, Leicester	0116 262 5906
	9 Stone Buildings, London	020 7404 5055
Cherry Mr John Mitchell	Lamb Chambers, London	020 7797 8300
Child Mr John Frederick	Wilberforce Chambers, London	020 7306 0102
Clark Mr Wayne Vincent	Falcon Chambers, London	020 7353 2484
Cole Mr Edward Arthur	Falcon Chambers, London	020 7353 2484
Daly Mr David	Heathway Chambers, London	020 8293 0509
De Verneuil Smith Mr Peter Robert	3 Verulam Buildings, London	020 7831 8441
Dowding Mr Nicholas Alan Tatham	Falcon Chambers, London	020 7353 2484
Dowley Mr Dominic Myles	Serle Court, London	020 7242 6105
Dray Mr Martin Benedict Antony	Falcon Chambers, London	020 7353 2484
Dudley-Jones Ms Elizabeth Sarah	Deans Court Chambers, Manchester	0161 214 6000
	Deans Court Chambers, Preston	01772 565 600
Dutton Mr Timothy James	Fountain Court Chambers, London	020 7583 3335

Ewart Mr David Scott	Pump Court Tax Chambers, London	020 7414 8080
Fancourt Mr Timothy Miles	Falcon Chambers, London	020 7353 2484
Francis Mr Andrew James	Serle Court, London	020 7242 6105
	Zenith Chambers, Leeds	0113 245 5438
Furness Mr Michael James	Wilberforce Chambers, London	020 7306 0102
Furniss Mr Richard Alexander	42 Bedford Row, London	020 7831 0222
Goodfellow Mr Giles William Jeremy	Pump Court Tax Chambers, London	020 7414 8080
Green Mr Brian Russell	Wilberforce Chambers, London	020 7306 0102
Hamer Mr George Clemens	8 New Square, London	020 7405 4321
Hattan Mr Simon Justin	Serle Court, London	020 7242 6105
Herbert Mr Mark Jeremy	5 Stone Buildings, London	020 7242 6201
Hilliard Mr Jonathan Adam	Wilberforce Chambers, London	020 7306 0102
Hochberg Mr Daniel Alan	Wilberforce Chambers, London	020 7306 0102
Hutchings Mr Martin Anthony	Wilberforce Chambers, London	020 7306 0102
Jackson Mr Nicholas David Kingsley	Atlantic Chambers, Liverpool	0151 236 4421
Jerram Ms Harriet Anne	Outer Temple Chambers, London	020 7353 6381
Jess Dr Digby Charles	Exchange Chambers, Leeds	0113 203 1970
	Exchange Chambers, Liverpool	0151 236 7747
	Exchange Chambers, Manchester	0161 833 2722
Jourdan Mr Stephen Eric	Falcon Chambers, London	020 7353 2484
Laney Miss Anna Marie	Crown Office Chambers, London	020 7797 8100
Lightman Mr Daniel	Serle Court, London	020 7242 6105
Lloyd Mr Stephen James George	13 Old Square Chambers, London	020 7831 4445
Loveday Mr Mark Alan	Tanfield Chambers, London	020 7421 5300
Lowe Mr Thomas William Gordon	Wilberforce Chambers, London	020 7306 0102
Lowenstein Mr Paul David	3 Verulam Buildings, London	020 7831 8441
MacNab Mr Alexander Andrew	Monckton Chambers, London	020 7405 7211
Martin Mr John Vandeleur	Wilberforce Chambers, London	020 7306 0102
Massey Mr William Greville Sale	Pump Court Tax Chambers, London	020 7414 8080
Mawhinney Mr Richard Martin	Outer Temple Chambers, London	020 7353 6381
	St John's Chambers, Bristol	0117 923 4700
McCann Miss Sarah Jane	Hardwicke, London	020 7242 2523
McCredie Miss Fionnuala Mary Constance	Keating Chambers, London	020 7544 2600
McPherson Mr Graeme Paul	Four New Square, London	020 7822 2000
Menzies Mr Richard Mark	Lamb Chambers, London	020 7797 8300
Michael Mr Simon Laurence	No5 Chambers, Birmingham	0845 210 5555
	No5 Chambers, Bristol	0845 210 5555
	No5 Chambers, London	0845 210 5555
Mold Mr Andrew Matthew Stephen	Wilberforce Chambers, London	020 7306 0102
Nicholls Mr Peter John	5 Pump Court, London	020 7353 2532
Nugee Mr Christopher George	Wilberforce Chambers, London	020 7306 0102
Orr Mr Craig Wyndham	One Essex Court, London	020 7583 2000
O'Sullivan Mr Michael Morton	5 Stone Buildings, London	020 7242 6201
Ovey Miss Elizabeth Helen	Radcliffe Chambers, London	020 7831 0081
Pitchers Mr Henry William Stodart	No5 Chambers, Birmingham	0845 210 5555
	No5 Chambers, Bristol	0845 210 5555
	No5 Chambers, London	0845 210 5555
Radevsky Mr Anthony Eric	Falcon Chambers, London	020 7353 2484
Reynolds Mr Kirk	Falcon Chambers, London	020 7353 2484
Rhodes Mr Robert Elliott	Outer Temple Chambers, London	020 7353 6381
	Principal Chambers, Sevenoaks	0845 209 8080
	St Philips Chambers, Birmingham	0121 246 7000
Rodger Mr Martin Owen	Falcon Chambers, London	020 7353 2484
Ross Martyn Mr John Greaves	New Square Chambers, London	020 7419 8000
	Octagon House, Norwich	01603 623186
Rowley Mr Keith Nigel	Radcliffe Chambers, London	020 7831 0081
Sawyer Mr Edward Humphrey	Wilberforce Chambers, London	020 7306 0102
Sen Mr Aditya Kumar	Coram Chambers, London	020 7092 3700
Smith Miss Joanna Angela	Wilberforce Chambers, London	020 7306 0102
Stallworthy Mr Nicolas Kyd	Outer Temple Chambers, London	020 7353 6381
Stevenson Dr Simon John	Park Lane Plowden, Leeds	0113 228 5049
Studer Mr Mark Edgar Walter	Wilberforce Chambers, London	020 7306 0102
Tallon Mr John Mark	Pump Court Tax Chambers, London	020 7414 8080

B

Tanney Mr Anthony	Falcon Chambers, London	020 7353 2484
Tavares Mr Nathan Warren	Outer Temple Chambers, London	020 7353 6381
Tompkinson Miss Deborah Ann	Clerksroom (London), London	0845 083 3000
	Clerksroom (Taunton), Taunton	0845 083 3000
Toube Ms Felicity Rosalind	South Square, London	020 7696 9900
Tozer Miss Stephanie	Falcon Chambers, London	020 7353 2484
Trace Mr Anthony John	Maitland Chambers, London	020 7406 1200
Treasure Mr Francis Seton	42 Bedford Row, London	020 7831 0222
Tunkel Mr Alan Michael	3 Stone Buildings, London	020 7242 4937
Vallat Mr Richard Justin	Pump Court Tax Chambers, London	020 7414 8080
Walford Mr Richard Henry Howard	Serle Court, London	020 7242 6105
Walsh Mr Steven James Franklyn	Five Paper, London	020 7815 3200
Wardell Mr John David Meredith	Wilberforce Chambers, London	020 7306 0102
West Mr Mark	Radcliffe Chambers, London	020 7831 0081
Wicks Ms Joanne	Wilberforce Chambers, London	020 7306 0102
Wilson Miss Mary Elizabeth Frances	Pump Court Tax Chambers, London	020 7414 8080
Windsor Miss Emily May	Falcon Chambers, London	020 7353 2484
Woolf The Hon Jeremy Richard George	Pump Court Tax Chambers, London	020 7414 8080
Yates Mr David James Francis	Pump Court Tax Chambers, London	020 7414 8080
Zelin Mr Geoffrey Andrew	Enterprise Chambers, Leeds	0113 246 0391
	Enterprise Chambers, London	020 7405 9471
	Enterprise Chambers, Newcastle Upon Tyne	0191 222 3344

B

PROPERTY

Cole Mr Edward Arthur	Falcon Chambers, London	020 7353 2484
Ferber Ms Iris	42 Bedford Row, London	020 7831 0222
Fetherstonhaugh Mr Guy Cuthbert Charles	Falcon Chambers, London	020 7353 2484
Hinks Mr Frank Peter	Serle Court, London	020 7242 6105
Loveday Mr Mark Alan	Tanfield Chambers, London	020 7421 5300
O'Sullivan Mr Richard John	1215 Chambers, London	020 3291 1215

PUBLIC INQUIRIES

Badenoch Mr James Forster	1 Crown Office Row, London	020 7797 7500
Barton Miss Fiona	5 Essex Court, London	020 7410 2000
Chapman Mr Vivian Robert	New Street Chambers, Leicester	0116 262 5906
	9 Stone Buildings, London	020 7404 5055
Edington Mrs Fiona Anne Rider	Thomas More Chambers, London	020 7404 7000
Francis Mr Robert Anthony	3 Serjeants Inn, London	020 7427 5000
Jerram Ms Harriet Anne	Outer Temple Chambers, London	020 7353 6381

PUBLIC LAW

Cornwell Dr James Matthew	11 King's Bench Walk, London	020 7632 8500
Dingemans Mr James Michael	3 Hare Court, London	020 7415 7800
Dutton Mr Timothy James	Fountain Court Chambers, London	020 7583 3335
Ferber Ms Iris	42 Bedford Row, London	020 7831 0222
O'Sullivan Mr Richard John	1215 Chambers, London	020 3291 1215
Rhodes Mr Robert Elliott	Outer Temple Chambers, London	020 7353 6381
	Principal Chambers, Sevenoaks	0845 209 8080
	St Philips Chambers, Birmingham	0121 246 7000
Sheppard Mr Timothy Derie	No5 Chambers, Birmingham	0845 210 5555
	No5 Chambers, Bristol	0845 210 5555
	No5 Chambers, London	0845 210 5555

PUBLISHING

Jones Mr Kelvin Mcallister	Templis Chambers, London	020 7649 9808
Whyte Dr James Richard Cleland	8 New Square, London	020 7405 4321

RATING AND CPO

Alesbury Mr Alun	Cornerstone Barristers, London	020 7242 4986
	12 Old Square Chambers, London	020 7404 0875

Roots Mr Guy Robert Godfrey	12 College Place, Southampton	023 8032 0320
	Francis Taylor Building, London	020 7353 8415

REAL PROPERTY

Bignell Miss Janet Susan	Falcon Chambers, London	020 7353 2484
Boyd Mr Stephen James Harvey	Selborne Chambers, London	020 7420 9500
Butler Mr Andrew	Tanfield Chambers, London	020 7421 5300
Carr Mr Adrian James Selden	Tanfield Chambers, London	020 7421 5300
Chapman Mr Vivian Robert	New Street Chambers, Leicester	0116 262 5906
	9 Stone Buildings, London	020 7404 5055
Clark Mr Wayne Vincent	Falcon Chambers, London	020 7353 2484
Cole Mr Edward Arthur	Falcon Chambers, London	020 7353 2484
Dray Mr Martin Benedict Antony	Falcon Chambers, London	020 7353 2484
Fain Mr Carl Ian	Tanfield Chambers, London	020 7421 5300
Fancourt Mr Timothy Miles	Falcon Chambers, London	020 7353 2484
Fetherstonhaugh Mr Guy Cuthbert Charles	Falcon Chambers, London	020 7353 2484
Fitzgerald Miss Elizabeth Helen	Falcon Chambers, London	020 7353 2484
Glen Mr Philip Alexander	12 College Place, Southampton	023 8032 0320
Harpum Mr Charles	Falcon Chambers, London	020 7353 2484
Heather Mr Christopher Mark	Tanfield Chambers, London	020 7421 5300
Hinks Mr Frank Peter	Serle Court, London	020 7242 6105
Jackson Mr Nicholas David Kingsley	Atlantic Chambers, Liverpool	0151 236 4421
Karas Mr Jonathan Marcus	Wilberforce Chambers, London	020 7306 0102
Newsom Mr George Lucien	Guildhall Chambers, Bristol	0117 930 9000
Peters Mr Edward James Hedley	Falcon Chambers, London	020 7353 2484
Radevsky Mr Anthony Eric	Falcon Chambers, London	020 7353 2484
Ross Martyn Mr John Greaves	New Square Chambers, London	020 7419 8000
	Octagon House, Norwich	01603 623186
Sandham Mr James Andrew	Arden Chambers, London	020 7242 4244
Stevenson Dr Simon John	Park Lane Plowden, Leeds	0113 228 5049
Studer Mr Mark Edgar Walter	Wilberforce Chambers, London	020 7306 0102
Tanney Mr Anthony	Falcon Chambers, London	020 7353 2484
Taskis Ms Catherine Louise	Falcon Chambers, London	020 7353 2484
Walford Mr Richard Henry Howard	Serle Court, London	020 7242 6105
West Mr Mark	Radcliffe Chambers, London	020 7831 0081
Windsor Miss Emily May	Falcon Chambers, London	020 7353 2484

REGISTERED DESIGNS

Berkeley Miss Iona Sarah Caroline	8 New Square, London	020 7405 4321
Campbell Mr Douglas James	Three New Square IP, London	020 7405 1111
Jamal Miss Isabel Leila	8 New Square, London	020 7405 4321
Jones Mr Kelvin Mcallister	Templis Chambers, London	020 7649 9808
Whyte Dr James Richard Cleland	8 New Square, London	020 7405 4321

REGULATORY AND DISCIPLINARY LAW

Dudley-Jones Ms Elizabeth Sarah	Deans Court Chambers, Manchester	0161 214 6000
	Deans Court Chambers, Preston	01772 565 600
Dutton Mr Timothy James	Fountain Court Chambers, London	020 7583 3335
Jerram Ms Harriet Anne	Outer Temple Chambers, London	020 7353 6381
Jess Dr Digby Charles	Exchange Chambers, Leeds	0113 203 1970
	Exchange Chambers, Liverpool	0151 236 7747
	Exchange Chambers, Manchester	0161 833 2722
Rhodes Mr Robert Elliott	Outer Temple Chambers, London	020 7353 6381
	Principal Chambers, Sevenoaks	0845 209 8080
	St Philips Chambers, Birmingham	0121 246 7000
Tavares Mr Nathan Warren	Outer Temple Chambers, London	020 7353 6381

REMEDIES

Lowenstein Mr Paul David	3 Verulam Buildings, London	020 7831 8441
Windsor Miss Emily May	Falcon Chambers, London	020 7353 2484

RESTITUTION

Chapman Mr Vivian Robert	New Street Chambers, Leicester	0116 262 5906
	9 Stone Buildings, London	020 7404 5055

B

Tompkinson Miss Deborah Ann	Clerksroom (London), London	0845 083 3000
	Clerksroom (Taunton), Taunton	0845 083 3000
West Mr Mark	Radcliffe Chambers, London	020 7831 0081

RESTRAINT OF TRADE

Jones Mr Kelvin Mcallister	Templis Chambers, London	020 7649 9808

RIGHTS OF LIGHT

Bignell Miss Janet Susan	Falcon Chambers, London	020 7353 2484
Chapman Mr Vivian Robert	New Street Chambers, Leicester	0116 262 5906
	9 Stone Buildings, London	020 7404 5055
Dray Mr Martin Benedict Antony	Falcon Chambers, London	020 7353 2484
Francis Mr Andrew James	Serle Court, London	020 7242 6105
	Zenith Chambers, Leeds	0113 245 5438
Karas Mr Jonathan Marcus	Wilberforce Chambers, London	020 7306 0102
Ross Martyn Mr John Greaves	New Square Chambers, London	020 7419 8000
	Octagon House, Norwich	01603 623186
Tozer Miss Stephanie	Falcon Chambers, London	020 7353 2484

RIGHTS OF WAY

Bignell Miss Janet Susan	Falcon Chambers, London	020 7353 2484
Butler Mr Andrew	Tanfield Chambers, London	020 7421 5300
Chapman Mr Vivian Robert	New Street Chambers, Leicester	0116 262 5906
	9 Stone Buildings, London	020 7404 5055
Dray Mr Martin Benedict Antony	Falcon Chambers, London	020 7353 2484
Harpum Mr Charles	Falcon Chambers, London	020 7353 2484
Karas Mr Jonathan Marcus	Wilberforce Chambers, London	020 7306 0102
Radevsky Mr Anthony Eric	Falcon Chambers, London	020 7353 2484
Ross Martyn Mr John Greaves	New Square Chambers, London	020 7419 8000
	Octagon House, Norwich	01603 623186
Tanney Mr Anthony	Falcon Chambers, London	020 7353 2484
Tozer Miss Stephanie	Falcon Chambers, London	020 7353 2484

SALE AND CARRIAGE OF GOODS

Acton Mr Stephen Neil	Radcliffe Chambers, London	020 7831 0081
Boyd Mr Stephen James Harvey	Selborne Chambers, London	020 7420 9500
Collett Mr Michael John	20 Essex Street, London	020 7842 1200
Dowley Mr Dominic Myles	Serle Court, London	020 7242 6105
Ford Mr Gerard James	Old Court Chambers, Middlesbrough	01642 232523
Lowenstein Mr Paul David	3 Verulam Buildings, London	020 7831 8441
McCann Miss Sarah Jane	Hardwicke, London	020 7242 2523
McPherson Mr Graeme Paul	Four New Square, London	020 7822 2000
Selvaratnam Miss Vasanti Emily Indrani	Stone Chambers, London	020 7440 6900
Tompkinson Miss Deborah Ann	Clerksroom (London), London	0845 083 3000
	Clerksroom (Taunton), Taunton	0845 083 3000

SALE OF BUSINESS

Boyle Mr Alan Gordon	Serle Court, London	020 7242 6105
Jones Mr Kelvin Mcallister	Templis Chambers, London	020 7649 9808
Lowenstein Mr Paul David	3 Verulam Buildings, London	020 7831 8441

SCHOOL SITES

Chapman Mr Vivian Robert	New Street Chambers, Leicester	0116 262 5906
	9 Stone Buildings, London	020 7404 5055

SCIENTIFIC AND TECHNICAL DISPUTES

Abrahams Mr James	8 New Square, London	020 7405 4321
Alexander Mr Daniel Sakyi	8 New Square, London	020 7405 4321
Baldwin Mr John Paul	8 New Square, London	020 7405 4321
Campbell Mr Douglas James	Three New Square IP, London	020 7405 1111
Clark Miss Fiona Jane Stewart	8 New Square, London	020 7405 4321
Colley Dr Peter Mclean	Hogarth Chambers, London	020 7404 0404
Delaney Mr Joe	Three New Square IP, London	020 7405 1111
Howe Mr Martin Russell Thomson	8 New Square, London	020 7405 4321

Jamal Miss Isabel Leila	8 New Square, London	020 7405 4321
Jones Mr Kelvin Mcallister	Templis Chambers, London	020 7649 9808
Lane Ms Lindsay Ruth Busfield	8 New Square, London	020 7405 4321
Lawrence Dr Heather Bunting Elizabeth	11 South Square, London	020 7405 1222
Lykiardopoulos Mr Andrew Nicolas	8 New Square, London	020 7405 4321
May Miss Charlotte Louisa	8 New Square, London	020 7405 4321
Meade Mr Richard David	8 New Square, London	020 7405 4321
Mellor Mr Edward James Wilson	8 New Square, London	020 7405 4321
Moody-Stuart Mr Thomas	8 New Square, London	020 7405 4321
Onslow Mr Robert Denzil	8 New Square, London	020 7405 4321
Platts-Mills Mr Mark Fortescue	8 New Square, London	020 7405 4321
Reed Mr Jeremy Nigel	Hogarth Chambers, London	020 7404 0404
Speck Mr Adrian	8 New Square, London	020 7405 4321
St Ville Mr Laurence James	8 New Square, London	020 7405 4321
Tappin Mr Michael John	8 New Square, London	020 7405 4321
Whyte Dr James Richard Cleland	8 New Square, London	020 7405 4321

SCIENTIFIC CASES

Hill Mr Jonathan	8 New Square, London	020 7405 4321
Jones Mr Kelvin Mcallister	Templis Chambers, London	020 7649 9808

SECURITIES LAW AND REGULATION

Fisher Mr Jonathan Simon	Devereux Chambers, London	020 7353 7534

SERIAL CRIME

Dudley-Jones Ms Elizabeth Sarah	Deans Court Chambers, Manchester	0161 214 6000
	Deans Court Chambers, Preston	01772 565 600

SERIOUS FRAUD

Dudley-Jones Ms Elizabeth Sarah	Deans Court Chambers, Manchester	0161 214 6000
	Deans Court Chambers, Preston	01772 565 600
Fisher Mr Jonathan Simon	Devereux Chambers, London	020 7353 7534
Katz Mr Philip Alec Jackson	9-12 Bell Yard, London	020 7400 1800

SEXUAL OFFENCES

Dudley-Jones Ms Elizabeth Sarah	Deans Court Chambers, Manchester	0161 214 6000
	Deans Court Chambers, Preston	01772 565 600

SHARE OPTIONS

Nugee Mr Edward George	Wilberforce Chambers, London	020 7306 0102
Wilson Mr Graham James	Gray's Inn Tax Chambers, London	020 7242 2642

SHAREHOLDER AGREEMENTS

Boyle Mr Alan Gordon	Serle Court, London	020 7242 6105

SHIPPING

Collett Mr Michael John	20 Essex Street, London	020 7842 1200
Selvaratnam Miss Vasanti Emily Indrani	Stone Chambers, London	020 7440 6900

SOCIAL WELFARE

Cornwell Dr James Matthew	11 King's Bench Walk, London	020 7632 8500
O'Sullivan Mr Richard John	1215 Chambers, London	020 3291 1215

SOCIETY OF LLOYD'S

Child Mr John Frederick	Wilberforce Chambers, London	020 7306 0102

SOLICITOR'S INDEMNITY

Smith Miss Joanna Angela	Wilberforce Chambers, London	020 7306 0102
Tompkinson Miss Deborah Ann	Clerksroom (London), London	0845 083 3000
	Clerksroom (Taunton), Taunton	0845 083 3000

Wicks Ms Joanne | Wilberforce Chambers, London | 020 7306 0102

SPECIAL GUARDIANSHIP

Purdie Mr Robert Anthony James	Faringdon Chambers, Faringdon	01367 240598
	4 King's Bench Walk, London	020 7822 7000

SPORT

Bellamy Mr Jonathan Mark	39 Essex Street, London	020 7832 1111
	82 King Street, Manchester	0161 870 9969
Bloch Mr Michael Gordon	Wilberforce Chambers, London	020 7306 0102
Boyd Mr Stephen James Harvey	Selborne Chambers, London	020 7420 9500
Boyle Mr Alan Gordon	Serle Court, London	020 7242 6105
Brown Mr Damian Robert	Littleton Chambers, London	020 7797 8600
Goudie Mr James	11 King's Bench Walk, London	020 7632 8500
Hamer Mr George Clemens	8 New Square, London	020 7405 4321
Jones Mr Kelvin Mcallister	Templis Chambers, London	020 7649 9808
McPherson Mr Graeme Paul	Four New Square, London	020 7822 2000
Trace Mr Anthony John	Maitland Chambers, London	020 7406 1200

ST LUCIA LAW

Moore Mr George Crawford Jackson	11 King's Bench Walk, London	020 7632 8500

STAMP DUTY

Baldry Mr Rupert Patrick Craig	Pump Court Tax Chambers, London	020 7414 8080
Bradley Mr Charles Edward May	Pump Court Tax Chambers, London	020 7414 8080
Bremner Mr Jonathan Sinclair Grant	Pump Court Tax Chambers, London	020 7414 8080
Chacko Mr Thomas Joseph	Pump Court Tax Chambers, London	020 7414 8080
Choudhury Miss Sadiya Asghar	Pump Court Tax Chambers, London	020 7414 8080
Conolly Dr Oliver Stephen	Pump Court Tax Chambers, London	020 7414 8080
Ewart Mr David Scott	Pump Court Tax Chambers, London	020 7414 8080
Ghosh Mr Indranil Julian	Pump Court Tax Chambers, London	020 7414 8080
Goodfellow Mr Giles William Jeremy	Pump Court Tax Chambers, London	020 7414 8080
Henderson Mr James Thomas	Kings Chambers, Leeds	0845 034 3444
	Kings Chambers, Manchester	0845 034 3444
	Pump Court Tax Chambers, London	020 7414 8080
Massey Mr William Greville Sale	Pump Court Tax Chambers, London	020 7414 8080
Matthews Mr Janek Paul	Pump Court Tax Chambers, London	020 7414 8080
Milne Mr David Calder	Pump Court Tax Chambers, London	020 7414 8080
Poots Miss Laura Jill	Pump Court Tax Chambers, London	020 7414 8080
Prosser Mr Kevin John	Pump Court Tax Chambers, London	020 7414 8080
Rivett Mr James Peter	Pump Court Tax Chambers, London	020 7414 8080
Southern Mr David Boardman	Temple Tax Chambers, London	020 7353 7884
Tallon Mr John Mark	Pump Court Tax Chambers, London	020 7414 8080
Thomas Mr Roger Christopher	Pump Court Tax Chambers, London	020 7414 8080
Thornhill Mr Andrew Robert	Albion Chambers, Bristol	0117 927 2144
	Pump Court Tax Chambers, London	020 7414 8080
Vallat Mr Richard Justin	Pump Court Tax Chambers, London	020 7414 8080
Wilson Miss Mary Elizabeth Frances	Pump Court Tax Chambers, London	020 7414 8080
Woolf The Hon Jeremy Richard George	Pump Court Tax Chambers, London	020 7414 8080
Yang Dr Zizhen	Pump Court Tax Chambers, London	020 7414 8080
Yates Mr David James Francis	Pump Court Tax Chambers, London	020 7414 8080

SUCCESSION

Acton Mr Stephen Neil	Radcliffe Chambers, London	020 7831 0081
Berkley Mr Michael Stuart	Rougemont Chambers, Exeter	01392 208484
Bornman Miss Kerry	3 Stone Buildings, London	020 7242 4937
Boyd Mr Stephen James Harvey	Selborne Chambers, London	020 7420 9500
Boyle Mr Alan Gordon	Serle Court, London	020 7242 6105
Campbell Miss Emily Charlotte	Wilberforce Chambers, London	020 7306 0102
Carr Mr Adrian James Selden	Tanfield Chambers, London	020 7421 5300
Chamberlain Ms Emma Jane Mary	Pump Court Tax Chambers, London	020 7414 8080
Chapman Mr Vivian Robert	New Street Chambers, Leicester	0116 262 5906
	9 Stone Buildings, London	020 7404 5055
Child Mr John Frederick	Wilberforce Chambers, London	020 7306 0102

Daly Mr David	Heathway Chambers, London	020 8293 0509
Francis Mr Andrew James	Serle Court, London	020 7242 6105
	Zenith Chambers, Leeds	0113 245 5438
Green Mr Brian Russell	Wilberforce Chambers, London	020 7306 0102
Ham Mr Robert Wallace	Wilberforce Chambers, London	020 7306 0102
Herbert Mr Mark Jeremy	5 Stone Buildings, London	020 7242 6201
Hinks Mr Frank Peter	Serle Court, London	020 7242 6105
Hochberg Mr Daniel Alan	Wilberforce Chambers, London	020 7306 0102
Jackson Mr Nicholas David Kingsley	Atlantic Chambers, Liverpool	0151 236 4421
Lloyd Mr Stephen James George	13 Old Square Chambers, London	020 7831 4445
Mold Mr Andrew Matthew Stephen	Wilberforce Chambers, London	020 7306 0102
Nugee Mr Edward George	Wilberforce Chambers, London	020 7306 0102
O'Sullivan Mr Michael Morton	5 Stone Buildings, London	020 7242 6201
Ovey Miss Elizabeth Helen	Radcliffe Chambers, London	020 7831 0081
Purdie Mr Robert Anthony James	Faringdon Chambers, Faringdon	01367 240598
	4 King's Bench Walk, London	020 7822 7000
Quint Ms Joan Francesca Rae	Radcliffe Chambers, London	020 7831 0081
Ross Martyn Mr John Greaves	New Square Chambers, London	020 7419 8000
	Octagon House, Norwich	01603 623186
Stevenson Dr Simon John	Park Lane Plowden, Leeds	0113 228 5049
Studer Mr Mark Edgar Walter	Wilberforce Chambers, London	020 7306 0102
Trace Mr Anthony John	Maitland Chambers, London	020 7406 1200
Tunkel Mr Alan Michael	3 Stone Buildings, London	020 7242 4937
West Mr Mark	Radcliffe Chambers, London	020 7831 0081
Wilson Mr Graham James	Gray's Inn Tax Chambers, London	020 7242 2642

TAX

Bornman Miss Kerry	3 Stone Buildings, London	020 7242 4937
Chamberlain Ms Emma Jane Mary	Pump Court Tax Chambers, London	020 7414 8080
Fisher Mr Jonathan Simon	Devereux Chambers, London	020 7353 7534
Stevenson Dr Simon John	Park Lane Plowden, Leeds	0113 228 5049

TAX INVESTIGATIONS

Bradley Mr Charles Edward May	Pump Court Tax Chambers, London	020 7414 8080
Chacko Mr Thomas Joseph	Pump Court Tax Chambers, London	020 7414 8080
Fisher Mr Jonathan Simon	Devereux Chambers, London	020 7353 7534
Rhodes Mr Robert Elliott	Outer Temple Chambers, London	020 7353 6381
	Principal Chambers, Sevenoaks	0845 209 8080
	St Philips Chambers, Birmingham	0121 246 7000
Southern Mr David Boardman	Temple Tax Chambers, London	020 7353 7884
Yang Dr Zizhen	Pump Court Tax Chambers, London	020 7414 8080

TAX TRIBUNAL

Bradley Mr Charles Edward May	Pump Court Tax Chambers, London	020 7414 8080
Chacko Mr Thomas Joseph	Pump Court Tax Chambers, London	020 7414 8080
Yang Dr Zizhen	Pump Court Tax Chambers, London	020 7414 8080

TAXATION AND DUTIES

Fisher Mr Jonathan Simon	Devereux Chambers, London	020 7353 7534
Frawley Ms Lyndsey Anne	Quorum Chambers, St Albans	01727 884516
	Quorum Tax Chambers, London	020 7043 5189

TECHNICAL CONTRACTS

Campbell Mr Douglas James	Three New Square IP, London	020 7405 1111
Jamal Miss Isabel Leila	8 New Square, London	020 7405 4321
Jones Mr Kelvin Mcallister	Templis Chambers, London	020 7649 9808
Lowenstein Mr Paul David	3 Verulam Buildings, London	020 7831 8441
Smith Miss Joanna Angela	Wilberforce Chambers, London	020 7306 0102

TECHNOLOGY AND CONSTRUCTION COURT

Smith Miss Joanna Angela	Wilberforce Chambers, London	020 7306 0102

TELECOMMUNICATIONS

Alexander Mr Daniel Sakyi	8 New Square, London	020 7405 4321
Baldwin Mr John Paul	8 New Square, London	020 7405 4321

Campbell Mr Douglas James	Three New Square IP, London	020 7405 1111
Cole Mr Edward Arthur	Falcon Chambers, London	020 7353 2484
Hamer Mr George Clemens	8 New Square, London	020 7405 4321
Hill Mr Jonathan	8 New Square, London	020 7405 4321
Howe Mr Martin Russell Thomson	8 New Square, London	020 7405 4321
Lowenstein Mr Paul David	3 Verulam Buildings, London	020 7831 8441
Mellor Mr Edward James Wilson	8 New Square, London	020 7405 4321
Mitcheson Mr Thomas George Moseley	Three New Square IP, London	020 7405 1111
Moody-Stuart Mr Thomas	8 New Square, London	020 7405 4321
Nardell Mr Gordon Lawrence	39 Essex Street, London	020 7832 1111
	82 King Street, Manchester	0161 870 9969
Onslow Mr Robert Denzil	8 New Square, London	020 7405 4321
Thorley Mr Simon Joe	Three New Square IP, London	020 7405 1111
Whyte Dr James Richard Cleland	8 New Square, London	020 7405 4321

TERRORISM

Dudley-Jones Ms Elizabeth Sarah	Deans Court Chambers, Manchester	0161 214 6000
	Deans Court Chambers, Preston	01772 565 600

TITLE TO LAND

Bignell Miss Janet Susan	Falcon Chambers, London	020 7353 2484
Chapman Mr Vivian Robert	New Street Chambers, Leicester	0116 262 5906
	9 Stone Buildings, London	020 7404 5055
Dray Mr Martin Benedict Antony	Falcon Chambers, London	020 7353 2484
Harpum Mr Charles	Falcon Chambers, London	020 7353 2484
Karas Mr Jonathan Marcus	Wilberforce Chambers, London	020 7306 0102
Ross Martyn Mr John Greaves	New Square Chambers, London	020 7419 8000
	Octagon House, Norwich	01603 623186
Tanney Mr Anthony	Falcon Chambers, London	020 7353 2484
Tozer Miss Stephanie	Falcon Chambers, London	020 7353 2484

TORTS

Campbell Mr Douglas James	Three New Square IP, London	020 7405 1111
Smith Miss Joanna Angela	Wilberforce Chambers, London	020 7306 0102
Tompkinson Miss Deborah Ann	Clerksroom (London), London	0845 083 3000
	Clerksroom (Taunton), Taunton	0845 083 3000

TRADE DESCRIPTIONS ACT

Alexander Mr Daniel Sakyi	8 New Square, London	020 7405 4321
Baldwin Mr John Paul	8 New Square, London	020 7405 4321
Clark Miss Fiona Jane Stewart	8 New Square, London	020 7405 4321
Howe Mr Martin Russell Thomson	8 New Square, London	020 7405 4321
Lane Ms Lindsay Ruth Busfield	8 New Square, London	020 7405 4321
May Miss Charlotte Louisa	8 New Square, London	020 7405 4321
Meade Mr Richard David	8 New Square, London	020 7405 4321
Moody-Stuart Mr Thomas	8 New Square, London	020 7405 4321
Onslow Mr Robert Denzil	8 New Square, London	020 7405 4321
Platts-Mills Mr Mark Fortescue	8 New Square, London	020 7405 4321

TRADE SECRETS

Abrahams Mr James	8 New Square, London	020 7405 4321
Alexander Mr Daniel Sakyi	8 New Square, London	020 7405 4321
Baldwin Mr John Paul	8 New Square, London	020 7405 4321
Bowhill Miss Jessie Kate	8 New Square, London	020 7405 4321
Campbell Mr Douglas James	Three New Square IP, London	020 7405 1111
Chacksfield Mr Mark Andrew	8 New Square, London	020 7405 4321
Clark Miss Fiona Jane Stewart	8 New Square, London	020 7405 4321
Hamer Mr George Clemens	8 New Square, London	020 7405 4321
Howe Mr Martin Russell Thomson	8 New Square, London	020 7405 4321
Jamal Miss Isabel Leila	8 New Square, London	020 7405 4321
Lane Ms Lindsay Ruth Busfield	8 New Square, London	020 7405 4321
Lowenstein Mr Paul David	3 Verulam Buildings, London	020 7831 8441
Lykiardopoulos Mr Andrew Nicolas	8 New Square, London	020 7405 4321
May Miss Charlotte Louisa	8 New Square, London	020 7405 4321

Meade Mr Richard David	8 New Square, London	020 7405 4321
Mellor Mr Edward James Wilson	8 New Square, London	020 7405 4321
Moody-Stuart Mr Thomas	8 New Square, London	020 7405 4321
Onslow Mr Robert Denzil	8 New Square, London	020 7405 4321
Platts-Mills Mr Mark Fortescue	8 New Square, London	020 7405 4321
Reed Mr Jeremy Nigel	Hogarth Chambers, London	020 7404 0404
Speck Mr Adrian	8 New Square, London	020 7405 4321
St Ville Mr Laurence James	8 New Square, London	020 7405 4321
Tappin Mr Michael John	8 New Square, London	020 7405 4321
Ward Mr Robin Henry	8 New Square, London	020 7405 4321
Whyte Dr James Richard Cleland	8 New Square, London	020 7405 4321

TRADEMARKS

Abrahams Mr James	8 New Square, London	020 7405 4321
Alexander Mr Daniel Sakyi	8 New Square, London	020 7405 4321
Baldwin Mr John Paul	8 New Square, London	020 7405 4321
Berkeley Miss Iona Sarah Caroline	8 New Square, London	020 7405 4321
Bloch Mr Michael Gordon	Wilberforce Chambers, London	020 7306 0102
Bowhill Miss Jessie Kate	8 New Square, London	020 7405 4321
Campbell Mr Douglas James	Three New Square IP, London	020 7405 1111
Chacksfield Mr Mark Andrew	8 New Square, London	020 7405 4321
Clark Miss Fiona Jane Stewart	8 New Square, London	020 7405 4321
Colley Dr Peter Mclean	Hogarth Chambers, London	020 7404 0404
Delaney Mr Joe	Three New Square IP, London	020 7405 1111
Douglas-Jones Mr Benjamin Timothy	Apex, Cardiff	02920 232 032
	Five Paper Buildings, London	020 7583 6117
Hamer Mr George Clemens	8 New Square, London	020 7405 4321
Hill Mr Jonathan	8 New Square, London	020 7405 4321
Howe Mr Martin Russell Thomson	8 New Square, London	020 7405 4321
Jackson Mr Nicholas David Kingsley	Atlantic Chambers, Liverpool	0151 236 4421
Jamal Miss Isabel Leila	8 New Square, London	020 7405 4321
Jones Mr Kelvin Mcallister	Templis Chambers, London	020 7649 9808
Lane Ms Lindsay Ruth Busfield	8 New Square, London	020 7405 4321
Lawrence Dr Heather Bunting Elizabeth	11 South Square, London	020 7405 1222
Lykiardopoulos Mr Andrew Nicolas	8 New Square, London	020 7405 4321
May Miss Charlotte Louisa	8 New Square, London	020 7405 4321
Meade Mr Richard David	8 New Square, London	020 7405 4321
Mellor Mr Edward James Wilson	8 New Square, London	020 7405 4321
Mitcheson Mr Thomas George Moseley	Three New Square IP, London	020 7405 1111
Moody-Stuart Mr Thomas	8 New Square, London	020 7405 4321
Onslow Mr Robert Denzil	8 New Square, London	020 7405 4321
Platts-Mills Mr Mark Fortescue	8 New Square, London	020 7405 4321
Reed Mr Jeremy Nigel	Hogarth Chambers, London	020 7404 0404
Speck Mr Adrian	8 New Square, London	020 7405 4321
St Ville Mr Laurence James	8 New Square, London	020 7405 4321
Tappin Mr Michael John	8 New Square, London	020 7405 4321
Thorley Mr Simon Joe	Three New Square IP, London	020 7405 1111
Ward Mr Robin Henry	8 New Square, London	020 7405 4321
Whyte Dr James Richard Cleland	8 New Square, London	020 7405 4321

TRANSPORT AND WORKS ACT INQUIRIES

Alesbury Mr Alun	Cornerstone Barristers, London	020 7242 4986
	12 Old Square Chambers, London	020 7404 0875

TRAVEL LAW

Howells Miss Katherine Jane	Old Square Chambers, Bristol	0117 930 5100
	Old Square Chambers, London	020 7269 0300

TRUST LITIGATION

Bornman Miss Kerry	3 Stone Buildings, London	020 7242 4937
Boyle Mr Alan Gordon	Serle Court, London	020 7242 6105

Bryant Miss Judith Anne	Wilberforce Chambers, London	020 7306 0102
Chamberlain Ms Emma Jane Mary	Pump Court Tax Chambers, London	020 7414 8080
Chapman Mr Vivian Robert	New Street Chambers, Leicester	0116 262 5906
	9 Stone Buildings, London	020 7404 5055
Hattan Mr Simon Justin	Serle Court, London	020 7242 6105
Hinks Mr Frank Peter	Serle Court, London	020 7242 6105
Ross Martyn Mr John Greaves	New Square Chambers, London	020 7419 8000
	Octagon House, Norwich	01603 623186
Stallworthy Mr Nicolas Kyd	Outer Temple Chambers, London	020 7353 6381
Studer Mr Mark Edgar Walter	Wilberforce Chambers, London	020 7306 0102

TRUSTS

Acton Mr Stephen Neil	Radcliffe Chambers, London	020 7831 0081
Asplin Miss Sarah Jane	3 Stone Buildings, London	020 7242 4937
Berkley Mr Michael Stuart	Rougemont Chambers, Exeter	01392 208484
Bornman Miss Kerry	3 Stone Buildings, London	020 7242 4937
Boyd Mr Stephen James Harvey	Selborne Chambers, London	020 7420 9500
Bradley Mr Charles Edward May	Pump Court Tax Chambers, London	020 7414 8080
Bremner Mr Jonathan Sinclair Grant	Pump Court Tax Chambers, London	020 7414 8080
Bryant Miss Judith Anne	Wilberforce Chambers, London	020 7306 0102
Campbell Miss Emily Charlotte	Wilberforce Chambers, London	020 7306 0102
Carr Mr Adrian James Selden	Tanfield Chambers, London	020 7421 5300
Chacko Mr Thomas Joseph	Pump Court Tax Chambers, London	020 7414 8080
Chamberlain Ms Emma Jane Mary	Pump Court Tax Chambers, London	020 7414 8080
Chapman Mr Vivian Robert	New Street Chambers, Leicester	0116 262 5906
	9 Stone Buildings, London	020 7404 5055
Child Mr John Frederick	Wilberforce Chambers, London	020 7306 0102
Choudhury Miss Sadiya Asghar	Pump Court Tax Chambers, London	020 7414 8080
Conolly Dr Oliver Stephen	Pump Court Tax Chambers, London	020 7414 8080
Daly Mr David	Heathway Chambers, London	020 8293 0509
Dunn Ms Sarah Patricia Quincey	Pump Court Tax Chambers, London	020 7414 8080
Ewart Mr David Scott	Pump Court Tax Chambers, London	020 7414 8080
Francis Mr Andrew James	Serle Court, London	020 7242 6105
	Zenith Chambers, Leeds	0113 245 5438
Furness Mr Michael James	Wilberforce Chambers, London	020 7306 0102
Goodfellow Mr Giles William Jeremy	Pump Court Tax Chambers, London	020 7414 8080
Green Mr Brian Russell	Wilberforce Chambers, London	020 7306 0102
Ham Mr Robert Wallace	Wilberforce Chambers, London	020 7306 0102
Henderson Mr James Thomas	Kings Chambers, Leeds	0845 034 3444
	Kings Chambers, Manchester	0845 034 3444
	Pump Court Tax Chambers, London	020 7414 8080
Herbert Mr Mark Jeremy	5 Stone Buildings, London	020 7242 6201
Hilliard Mr Jonathan Adam	Wilberforce Chambers, London	020 7306 0102
Hinks Mr Frank Peter	Serle Court, London	020 7242 6105
Hochberg Mr Daniel Alan	Wilberforce Chambers, London	020 7306 0102
Jackson Mr Nicholas David Kingsley	Atlantic Chambers, Liverpool	0151 236 4421
Lloyd Mr Stephen James George	13 Old Square Chambers, London	020 7831 4445
Lowe Mr Thomas William Gordon	Wilberforce Chambers, London	020 7306 0102
Martin Mr John Vandeleur	Wilberforce Chambers, London	020 7306 0102
Massey Mr William Greville Sale	Pump Court Tax Chambers, London	020 7414 8080
Matthews Mr Janek Paul	Pump Court Tax Chambers, London	020 7414 8080
McCann Miss Sarah Jane	Hardwicke, London	020 7242 2523
Milne Mr David Calder	Pump Court Tax Chambers, London	020 7414 8080
Mold Mr Andrew Matthew Stephen	Wilberforce Chambers, London	020 7306 0102
Newsom Mr George Lucien	Guildhall Chambers, Bristol	0117 930 9000
Nugee Mr Christopher George	Wilberforce Chambers, London	020 7306 0102
Nugee Mr Edward George	Wilberforce Chambers, London	020 7306 0102
O'Sullivan Mr Michael Morton	5 Stone Buildings, London	020 7242 6201
O'Sullivan Mr Richard John	1215 Chambers, London	020 3291 1215
Ovey Miss Elizabeth Helen	Radcliffe Chambers, London	020 7831 0081
Poots Miss Laura Jill	Pump Court Tax Chambers, London	020 7414 8080
Purdie Mr Robert Anthony James	Faringdon Chambers, Faringdon	01367 240598
	4 King's Bench Walk, London	020 7822 7000
Quint Ms Joan Francesca Rae	Radcliffe Chambers, London	020 7831 0081

Richards Mr Ian	Pump Court Tax Chambers, London	020 7414 8080
Rivett Mr James Peter	Pump Court Tax Chambers, London	020 7414 8080
Ross Martyn Mr John Greaves	New Square Chambers, London	020 7419 8000
	Octagon House, Norwich	01603 623186
Sandham Mr James Andrew	Arden Chambers, London	020 7242 4244
Sawyer Mr Edward Humphrey	Wilberforce Chambers, London	020 7306 0102
Smith Dr Peter Michael	Radcliffe Chambers, London	020 7831 0081
Stallworthy Mr Nicolas Kyd	Outer Temple Chambers, London	020 7353 6381
Stevenson Dr Simon John	Park Lane Plowden, Leeds	0113 228 5049
Stoner Mr Christopher Paul	Serle Court, London	020 7242 6105
Studer Mr Mark Edgar Walter	Wilberforce Chambers, London	020 7306 0102
Tallon Mr John Mark	Pump Court Tax Chambers, London	020 7414 8080
Tanney Mr Anthony	Falcon Chambers, London	020 7353 2484
Thomas Mr Roger Christopher	Pump Court Tax Chambers, London	020 7414 8080
Thomson Mr Martin Haldane Ahmad	Wynne Chambers, London	020 3239 6964
Thornhill Mr Andrew Robert	Albion Chambers, Bristol	0117 927 2144
	Pump Court Tax Chambers, London	020 7414 8080
Trace Mr Anthony John	Maitland Chambers, London	020 7406 1200
Tunkel Mr Alan Michael	3 Stone Buildings, London	020 7242 4937
Vallat Mr Richard Justin	Pump Court Tax Chambers, London	020 7414 8080
Walsh Mr Steven James Franklyn	Five Paper, London	020 7815 3200
West Mr Mark	Radcliffe Chambers, London	020 7831 0081
Wicks Ms Joanne	Wilberforce Chambers, London	020 7306 0102
Wilson Miss Mary Elizabeth Frances	Pump Court Tax Chambers, London	020 7414 8080
Wilson Mr Graham James	Gray's Inn Tax Chambers, London	020 7242 2642
Windsor Miss Emily May	Falcon Chambers, London	020 7353 2484
Woolf The Hon Jeremy Richard George	Pump Court Tax Chambers, London	020 7414 8080
Yang Dr Zizhen	Pump Court Tax Chambers, London	020 7414 8080
Yates Mr David James Francis	Pump Court Tax Chambers, London	020 7414 8080

TURKS AND CAICOS ISLANDS LAW

Moore Mr George Crawford Jackson	11 King's Bench Walk, London	020 7632 8500

UNIT TRUSTS

Nugee Mr Edward George	Wilberforce Chambers, London	020 7306 0102

UNMARRIED COUPLES

Purdie Mr Robert Anthony James	Faringdon Chambers, Faringdon	01367 240598
	4 King's Bench Walk, London	020 7822 7000

UNREGISTERED DESIGNS

Campbell Mr Douglas James	Three New Square IP, London	020 7405 1111
Jamal Miss Isabel Leila	8 New Square, London	020 7405 4321
Jones Mr Kelvin Mcallister	Templis Chambers, London	020 7649 9808
Whyte Dr James Richard Cleland	8 New Square, London	020 7405 4321

VAT

Baldry Mr Rupert Patrick Craig	Pump Court Tax Chambers, London	020 7414 8080
Bradley Mr Charles Edward May	Pump Court Tax Chambers, London	020 7414 8080
Bremner Mr Jonathan Sinclair Grant	Pump Court Tax Chambers, London	020 7414 8080
Chacko Mr Thomas Joseph	Pump Court Tax Chambers, London	020 7414 8080
Choudhury Miss Sadiya Asghar	Pump Court Tax Chambers, London	020 7414 8080
Conolly Dr Oliver Stephen	Pump Court Tax Chambers, London	020 7414 8080
Dunn Ms Sarah Patricia Quincey	Pump Court Tax Chambers, London	020 7414 8080
Ewart Mr David Scott	Pump Court Tax Chambers, London	020 7414 8080
Frawley Ms Lyndsey Anne	Quorum Chambers, St Albans	01727 884516
	Quorum Tax Chambers, London	020 7043 5189
Ghosh Mr Indranil Julian	Pump Court Tax Chambers, London	020 7414 8080
Goodfellow Mr Giles William Jeremy	Pump Court Tax Chambers, London	020 7414 8080
Hamilton Mrs Penelope Ann	Pump Court Tax Chambers, London	020 7414 8080
Henderson Mr James Thomas	Kings Chambers, Leeds	0845 034 3444
	Kings Chambers, Manchester	0845 034 3444
	Pump Court Tax Chambers, London	020 7414 8080
Hitchmough Mr Andrew John	Pump Court Tax Chambers, London	020 7414 8080

MacNab Mr Alexander Andrew	Monckton Chambers, London	020 7405 7211
Massey Mr William Greville Sale	Pump Court Tax Chambers, London	020 7414 8080
Matthews Mr Janek Paul	Pump Court Tax Chambers, London	020 7414 8080
Milne Mr David Calder	Pump Court Tax Chambers, London	020 7414 8080
Poots Miss Laura Jill	Pump Court Tax Chambers, London	020 7414 8080
Prosser Mr Kevin John	Pump Court Tax Chambers, London	020 7414 8080
Rivett Mr James Peter	Pump Court Tax Chambers, London	020 7414 8080
Southern Mr David Boardman	Temple Tax Chambers, London	020 7353 7884
Tallon Mr John Mark	Pump Court Tax Chambers, London	020 7414 8080
Thomas Mr Roger Christopher	Pump Court Tax Chambers, London	020 7414 8080
Thornhill Mr Andrew Robert	Albion Chambers, Bristol	0117 927 2144
	Pump Court Tax Chambers, London	020 7414 8080
Vallat Mr Richard Justin	Pump Court Tax Chambers, London	020 7414 8080
White Mr Jeremy Barry	Pump Court Tax Chambers, London	020 7414 8080
Wilson Miss Mary Elizabeth Frances	Pump Court Tax Chambers, London	020 7414 8080
Woolf The Hon Jeremy Richard George	Pump Court Tax Chambers, London	020 7414 8080
Yang Dr Zizhen	Pump Court Tax Chambers, London	020 7414 8080
Yates Mr David James Francis	Pump Court Tax Chambers, London	020 7414 8080

WAR CRIMES TRIBUNALS

Edington Mrs Fiona Anne Rider	Thomas More Chambers, London	020 7404 7000
Lawrence Sir Ivan John	5 Pump Court, London	020 7353 2532

WARRANTY CLAIMS

Boyle Mr Alan Gordon	Serle Court, London	020 7242 6105
Lowenstein Mr Paul David	3 Verulam Buildings, London	020 7831 8441

WATER

Bignell Miss Janet Susan	Falcon Chambers, London	020 7353 2484
Chapman Mr Vivian Robert	New Street Chambers, Leicester	0116 262 5906
	9 Stone Buildings, London	020 7404 5055
Fetherstonhaugh Mr Guy Cuthbert Charles	Falcon Chambers, London	020 7353 2484
Harpum Mr Charles	Falcon Chambers, London	020 7353 2484
Hockman Mr Stephen Alexander	6 Pump Court, London	020 7797 8400
	6 Pump Court Chambers, Maidstone	01622 688094
	Regency Chambers, Peterborough	01733 315215
Karas Mr Jonathan Marcus	Wilberforce Chambers, London	020 7306 0102

WILLS

Acton Mr Stephen Neil	Radcliffe Chambers, London	020 7831 0081
Asplin Miss Sarah Jane	3 Stone Buildings, London	020 7242 4937
Berkley Mr Michael Stuart	Rougemont Chambers, Exeter	01392 208484
Bornman Miss Kerry	3 Stone Buildings, London	020 7242 4937
Boyd Mr Stephen James Harvey	Selborne Chambers, London	020 7420 9500
Boyle Mr Alan Gordon	Serle Court, London	020 7242 6105
Bremner Mr Jonathan Sinclair Grant	Pump Court Tax Chambers, London	020 7414 8080
Bryant Miss Judith Anne	Wilberforce Chambers, London	020 7306 0102
Campbell Miss Emily Charlotte	Wilberforce Chambers, London	020 7306 0102
Chapman Mr Vivian Robert	New Street Chambers, Leicester	0116 262 5906
	9 Stone Buildings, London	020 7404 5055
Child Mr John Frederick	Wilberforce Chambers, London	020 7306 0102
Choudhury Miss Sadiya Asghar	Pump Court Tax Chambers, London	020 7414 8080
Conolly Dr Oliver Stephen	Pump Court Tax Chambers, London	020 7414 8080
Daly Mr David	Heathway Chambers, London	020 8293 0509
Dunn Ms Sarah Patricia Quincey	Pump Court Tax Chambers, London	020 7414 8080
Ewart Mr David Scott	Pump Court Tax Chambers, London	020 7414 8080
Francis Mr Andrew James	Serle Court, London	020 7242 6105
	Zenith Chambers, Leeds	0113 245 5438
Furness Mr Michael James	Wilberforce Chambers, London	020 7306 0102
Goodfellow Mr Giles William Jeremy	Pump Court Tax Chambers, London	020 7414 8080
Green Mr Brian Russell	Wilberforce Chambers, London	020 7306 0102
Ham Mr Robert Wallace	Wilberforce Chambers, London	020 7306 0102

Henderson Mr James Thomas	Kings Chambers, Leeds	0845 034 3444
	Kings Chambers, Manchester	0845 034 3444
	Pump Court Tax Chambers, London	020 7414 8080
Herbert Mr Mark Jeremy	5 Stone Buildings, London	020 7242 6201
Hilliard Mr Jonathan Adam	Wilberforce Chambers, London	020 7306 0102
Hinks Mr Frank Peter	Serle Court, London	020 7242 6105
Hochberg Mr Daniel Alan	Wilberforce Chambers, London	020 7306 0102
Jackson Mr Nicholas David Kingsley	Atlantic Chambers, Liverpool	0151 236 4421
Lightman Mr Daniel	Serle Court, London	020 7242 6105
Lloyd Mr Stephen James George	13 Old Square Chambers, London	020 7831 4445
Lowe Mr Thomas William Gordon	Wilberforce Chambers, London	020 7306 0102
Martin Mr John Vandeleur	Wilberforce Chambers, London	020 7306 0102
Massey Mr William Greville Sale	Pump Court Tax Chambers, London	020 7414 8080
Matthews Mr Janek Paul	Pump Court Tax Chambers, London	020 7414 8080
Mold Mr Andrew Matthew Stephen	Wilberforce Chambers, London	020 7306 0102
Newsom Mr George Lucien	Guildhall Chambers, Bristol	0117 930 9000
Nugee Mr Christopher George	Wilberforce Chambers, London	020 7306 0102
Nugee Mr Edward George	Wilberforce Chambers, London	020 7306 0102
O'Sullivan Mr Michael Morton	5 Stone Buildings, London	020 7242 6201
Ovey Miss Elizabeth Helen	Radcliffe Chambers, London	020 7831 0081
Poots Miss Laura Jill	Pump Court Tax Chambers, London	020 7414 8080
Purdie Mr Robert Anthony James	Faringdon Chambers, Faringdon	01367 240598
	4 King's Bench Walk, London	020 7822 7000
Quint Ms Joan Francesca Rae	Radcliffe Chambers, London	020 7831 0081
Richards Mr Ian	Pump Court Tax Chambers, London	020 7414 8080
Rivett Mr James Peter	Pump Court Tax Chambers, London	020 7414 8080
Ross Martyn Mr John Greaves	New Square Chambers, London	020 7419 8000
	Octagon House, Norwich	01603 623186
Sawyer Mr Edward Humphrey	Wilberforce Chambers, London	020 7306 0102
Stevenson Dr Simon John	Park Lane Plowden, Leeds	0113 228 5049
Stoner Mr Christopher Paul	Serle Court, London	020 7242 6105
Studer Mr Mark Edgar Walter	Wilberforce Chambers, London	020 7306 0102
Tallon Mr John Mark	Pump Court Tax Chambers, London	020 7414 8080
Thomas Mr Roger Christopher	Pump Court Tax Chambers, London	020 7414 8080
Thomson Mr Martin Haldane Ahmad	Wynne Chambers, London	020 3239 6964
Thornhill Mr Andrew Robert	Albion Chambers, Bristol	0117 927 2144
	Pump Court Tax Chambers, London	020 7414 8080
Trace Mr Anthony John	Maitland Chambers, London	020 7406 1200
Tunkel Mr Alan Michael	3 Stone Buildings, London	020 7242 4937
Vallat Mr Richard Justin	Pump Court Tax Chambers, London	020 7414 8080
Walsh Mr Steven James Franklyn	Five Paper, London	020 7815 3200
West Mr Mark	Radcliffe Chambers, London	020 7831 0081
Wilson Miss Mary Elizabeth Frances	Pump Court Tax Chambers, London	020 7414 8080
Wilson Mr Graham James	Gray's Inn Tax Chambers, London	020 7242 2642
Windsor Miss Emily May	Falcon Chambers, London	020 7353 2484
Woolf The Hon Jeremy Richard George	Pump Court Tax Chambers, London	020 7414 8080
Yates Mr David James Francis	Pump Court Tax Chambers, London	020 7414 8080

B

PART C

Public Access Directory Types of Work by Individual Barrister

The information contained in this list of barristers undertaking public access work applies as at 17 August 2012. Regularly updated information can be found on the Bar Council website: www.barcouncil.org.uk/about/find-a-barrister.

The section is comprised of an index by types of work undertaken and an alphabetical listing of the barristers containing their contact details.

Type of Work

C

Abasheikh Mr Omar Said Imam	Paragon Chambers, London	020 3318 9988
Adewale Mr Remi Adetokunbo Sanni	Chambers of G. D. Tetteh, London	020 7353 7095
	Chambers of Mr R. A. Adewale, Address withheld	020 7231 2814
Ahluwalia Mr Navtej Singh	Garden Court Chambers, London	020 7993 7600
Ahmad Mr Kashif Zubair	Blenheim Chambers, Hounslow	07588 608288
Ahmed Mr Nazir	Centurion Chambers, West Bromwich	0121 553 4613
Aina Mr Benjamin Adejowon Olufemi	Old Bailey Chambers, London	020 3008 6404
Albutt Mr Ian Leslie	Cornerstone Barristers, London	020 7242 4986
	Heavenwood Chambers, Stroud	01453 873444
Algazy Mr Jacques Max	Cloisters, London	020 7827 4000
Allwood Mrs Gina Louisa	Seven Bedford Row, London	020 7242 3555
Alomo Mr Richard Olusoji	14 Gray's Inn Square, London	020 7242 0858
Altaras Mr David Maurice	36 Bedford Row, London	020 7421 8000
Amraoui Mr Thomas	4-5 Gray's Inn Square, London	020 7404 5252
Anderson Mr Jack Duthie	4-5 Gray's Inn Square, London	020 7404 5252
Andre Mr Roger Louis	Sovereign Chambers, Leeds	0113 245 1841
Arkhurst Mr Reginald Leon	4 King's Bench Walk, London	020 7822 7000
Arnold Mr Graham John	Farringdon Chambers, London	020 7089 5700
Arshad Miss Farrhat	Doughty Street Chambers, Bristol	01179 058 717
	Doughty Street Chambers, London	020 7404 1313
	Doughty Street Chambers, Manchester	0161 618 1066
Artesi Miss Desiree Allison Ann	Thomas More Chambers, London	020 7404 7000
Ashford-Thom Mr Ian	3 PB Barristers, London	020 7583 8055
	Temple Garden Chambers, London	020 7583 1315
Askey Mr Robert John	Palmyra Chambers, Warrington	01925 444919
Auburn Mr Jonathan Walter	4-5 Gray's Inn Square, London	020 7404 5252
Bagchi Mr Andrew Kumar	1 Garden Court Family Law Chambers, London	020 7797 7900
Baldwin Dr Timothy John	Garden Court Chambers, London	020 7993 7600
Banks Miss Fiona Jane	Monckton Chambers, London	020 7405 7211
Barker Mr Kerry	Guildhall Chambers, Bristol	0117 930 9000
Barnes Ms Rachel Ann	3 Raymond Buildings, London	020 7400 6400
Bates Mr Alan Twan	Monckton Chambers, London	020 7405 7211
Beaumont Mr Marc Clifford	9 Stone Buildings, London	020 7404 5055
	Windsor Barristers' Chambers, Windsor	01753 839321
Bedloe Mr Giles Robert	Dyers Chambers, London	020 7404 1881
Beloff Mr Rupert Joseph Alexei	No5 Chambers, Birmingham	0845 210 5555
	No5 Chambers, Bristol	0845 210 5555
	No5 Chambers, London	0845 210 5555
Berry Mr Adrian Christopher	Garden Court Chambers, London	020 7993 7600
Bhanji Mr Shiraz Musa	4 Bingham Place, London	020 7486 5347
	1 Gray's Inn Square, London	020 7405 0001
Birnbaum Mr Michael Ian	9-12 Bell Yard, London	020 7400 1800
Bishop Mr Malcolm Leslie	Argent Chambers, London	020 7556 5500
	Equity Chambers, Birmingham	0121 236 5007
	30 Park Place, Cardiff	029 2039 8421
Booth Mr Alexander Henry Spencer	Francis Taylor Building, London	020 7353 8415
Bourne Mr Charles Gregory	4-5 Gray's Inn Square, London	020 7404 5252
Bowen Mr Nicholas James Hugh	Doughty Street Chambers, Bristol	01179 058 717
	Doughty Street Chambers, London	020 7404 1313
	Doughty Street Chambers, Manchester	0161 618 1066
Bowers Mr Rupert John	Doughty Street Chambers, London	020 7404 1313
Bowsher Mr Michael Frederick Thomas	Monckton Chambers, London	020 7405 7211
Bradshaw Mr Mark Kieran	No5 Chambers, Birmingham	0845 210 5555
	No5 Chambers, Bristol	0845 210 5555
	No5 Chambers, London	0845 210 5555
Bragge Mr Thomas Hereward	Stour Chambers, Canterbury	01227 764899
Braier Mr Jason Dean	Field Court Chambers, London	020 7405 6114
Brewin Mr Carl Patrick	3 PB Barristers, London	020 7583 8055

Broatch Mr Donald	Five Paper, London	020 7815 3200
Brown Mr Philip Stephen	9 Stone Buildings, London	020 7404 5055
Brown Mr Roger Charles Arthur	Kenworthy's Chambers, Manchester	0161 832 4036
Brown Mr Sam Clement	Atkinson Bevan Chambers, London	020 7353 2112
Bryden Mr Christopher James Yuen Kang	4 King's Bench Walk, London	020 7822 7000
Bunting Mr Daniel Alexander James	2 Dr Johnson's Buildings, London	020 7936 2613
Bunting Mr Jude James	Tooks Chambers, London	020 7842 7575
Burnett Mr Iain	4 King's Bench Walk, London	020 7822 7000
Burrett Mr Alex	1 Gray's Inn Square, London	020 7405 0001
Burton Mr James William	39 Essex Street, London	020 7832 1111
	82 King Street, Manchester	0161 870 9969
Butler Mr Simon David	The Chambers of Grahame Aldous QC, London	020 7832 0500
Caldwell Mr Peter Hugh Coyles	Dyers Chambers, London	020 7404 1881
Caplan Mr Jonathan Michael	Five Paper Buildings, London	020 7583 6117
	Riverview Chambers, London	0844 225 3999
Carrion Benitez Ms Miriam	36 Bedford Row, London	020 7421 8000
Cartwright Mr Ivan Matthew	KCH Garden Square, Nottingham	0115 941 8851
Cecil Miss Joanne Michelle	1 Pump Court, London	020 7842 7070
Charalambides Mr Leonidas	Francis Taylor Building, London	020 7353 8415
Chowdhary Mr Islamuddin	Cassian Chambers, Ilford	07796 262641
Christie Mr Iain Robert	5RB, London	020 7242 2902
Clark Mr Dingle	Goldsmith Chambers, London	020 7353 6802
Clarke Mr Rory James	Cornerstone Barristers, London	020 7242 4986
Clay Mr Jonathan Roger	Cornerstone Barristers, London	020 7242 4986
Coster Mr Ronald David	42 Bedford Row, London	020 7831 0222
Crawford Mr Lincoln Santo	12 King's Bench Walk, London	020 7583 0811
Curtis Mr Michael Alexander	Crown Office Chambers, London	020 7797 8100
Dagg Mr John Douglas	Trinity Chambers, Chelmsford	01245 605040
Dalby Mr Joseph Francis	4-5 Gray's Inn Square, London	020 7404 5252
Daly Mr David	Heathway Chambers, London	020 8293 0509
Darroch Miss Fiona Culverwell	Clerksroom (London), London	0845 083 3000
	Clerksroom (Taunton), Taunton	0845 083 3000
	King's Lynn Chambers, King's Lynn	01553 672 085
Davies Mr Henry Olusola	Trinity Chambers, Birmingham	0121 346 4672
Davies Ms Elizabeth Mary	Garden Court Chambers, London	020 7993 7600
Davies Ms Samantha Teresa	Chambers of Ms Samantha Davies, Milton Keynes	0845 123 1234
	Warwick House Chambers, London	020 7430 2323
De Mello Mr Rembert Joseph Julius	No5 Chambers, Birmingham	0845 210 5555
	No5 Chambers, Bristol	0845 210 5555
	No5 Chambers, London	0845 210 5555
Dean Mr James Patrick	Goldsmith Chambers, London	020 7353 6802
Dean Mr Peter Thomas	36 Bedford Row, London	020 7421 8000
Devlin Mr Bernard Joseph	Five St Andrew's Hill, London	020 7332 5400
Dhaliwal Miss Davinder Kaur	No 8 Chambers, Birmingham	0121 236 5514
Diamond Mr Paul	Chambers of Mr Paul Diamond, Cambridge	01223 264544
Doerfel Mr Jan Hendrik Jamison	1215 Chambers, London	020 3291 1215
	Chambers of Mr J H Doerfel, Richmond	0845 123 1234
Doran Mr Gerard Patrick	Lincoln House Chambers, Manchester	0161 832 5701
Dos Santos Mr Alexander	Charter Chambers, London	020 7618 4400
Dowden Mr Andrew Philip	Castle Chambers, Harrow-on-the-Hill	020 8423 6579
	Melbury House, Leicester	07801 037802
Earle Mr James Christopher Reginald St John	Fenners Chambers, Cambridge	01223 368761
Eaton Mr Tobias Barnaby	Staple Inn Chambers, London	020 7242 5240
Edwards Mr Denis	Francis Taylor Building, London	020 7353 8415
Edwards Mr Martin Richard	39 Essex Street, London	020 7832 1111
	82 King Street, Manchester	0161 870 9969
Egleton Mr Richard Wildman	Pallant Chambers, Chichester	01243 784538

C

Engelman Mr Philip	Cloisters, London	020 7827 4000
	Trinity Chambers, Middlesbrough	01642 247569
	Trinity Chambers, Newcastle Upon Tyne	0191 232 1927
Facenna Mr Gerald Carlo	Monckton Chambers, London	020 7405 7211
Fagborun Bennett Ms Morayo Abosede	Hardwicke, London	020 7242 2523
Falkowski Mr Damian	4-5 Gray's Inn Square, London	020 7404 5252
Farbey Miss Judith Sarah	Doughty Street Chambers, Bristol	01179 058 717
	Doughty Street Chambers, London	020 7404 1313
	Doughty Street Chambers, Manchester	0161 618 1066
Fender Mr Carl David	Regency Chambers, Cambridge	01223 301517
	Regency Chambers, Peterborough	01733 315215
Fielden Dr Christa Maria	1 Mitre Court Buildings, London	020 7452 8900
Fisher Mr Jonathan Simon	Devereux Chambers, London	020 7353 7534
Fitzmaurice Mr Guy Edward Christian	Staple Inn Chambers, London	020 7242 5240
Foster Mr Julien Andrew Stewart	1 Garden Court Family Law Chambers, London	020 7797 7900
Fraser-Urquhart Mr Andrew	4-5 Gray's Inn Square, London	020 7404 5252
Gallagher Ms Caoilfhionn Anna	Doughty Street Chambers, Bristol	01179 058 717
	Doughty Street Chambers, London	020 7404 1313
	Doughty Street Chambers, Manchester	0161 618 1066
Galway-Cooper Dr Philip Anthony	Five St Andrew's Hill, London	020 7332 5400
Ganesan Mr Muthupandi Peter	Furnival Chambers, London	020 7405 3232
Gardner Mr James Piers	Monckton Chambers, London	020 7405 7211
Gasztowicz Mr Steven	Cornerstone Barristers, London	020 7242 4986
	New Street Chambers, Leicester	0116 262 5906
Gayan Mr Anil Kumarsingh	Clapham Law Chambers, London	020 7978 8482
Gersch Mr Adam Nissen	Argent Chambers, London	020 7556 5500
Gledhill Mr Lee Andre	Alexander Chambers, London	0845 652 0451/0854 652 0451
	Trident Barristers Chambers, Manchester	0161 663 3123
Goodman Mr Alexander David Edmund	Atlas Chambers, London	020 7269 7980
	4-5 Gray's Inn Square, London	020 7404 5252
Goodman Mr Andrew David	1 Chancery Lane, London	0845 634 6666
Gore Mr Andrew Roger	Fenners Chambers, Cambridge	01223 368761
Gore Mrs Harriet Nkechi Adimora	Kensington Chambers, London	020 7373 2217
Gore Ms Sally Elizabeth	14 Gray's Inn Square, London	020 7242 0858
Goudie Mr William Martin Phillip	Charter Chambers, London	020 7618 4400
Graham-Wells Miss Alison Christine	Exchange Chambers, Leeds	0113 203 1970
	Exchange Chambers, Liverpool	0151 236 7747
	Exchange Chambers, Manchester	0161 833 2722
Gray Mr Justin Henry Walford	Trinity Chambers, Middlesbrough	01642 247569
	Trinity Chambers, Newcastle Upon Tyne	0191 232 1927
Greatorex Mr Paul	4-5 Gray's Inn Square, London	020 7404 5252
Green Mr Patrick Curtis	Henderson Chambers, London	020 7583 9020
Griffin Mr Nicholas John	Five Paper Buildings, London	020 7583 6117
Ground Mr Patrick	Chambers of Mr Patrick Ground QC, London	020 7736 0131
Guy Mr Richard Perran	Chambers of Mr Ami Feder, London	020 7797 7788
	King's Bench and Godolphin (KBG)Chambers, Plymouth	01752 221551
	Southernhay Chambers, Exeter	01392 255777
Hanif Miss Saima Naz	4-5 Gray's Inn Square, London	020 7404 5252
Harris Mr Paul	Doughty Street Chambers, Bristol	01179 058 717
	Doughty Street Chambers, London	020 7404 1313
	Doughty Street Chambers, Manchester	0161 618 1066
Harrison Mr Peter John	6 Pump Court, London	020 7797 8400
	6 Pump Court Chambers, Maidstone	01622 688094
Harwood Mr Richard John	39 Essex Street, London	020 7832 1111
	82 King Street, Manchester	0161 870 9969

Hawkin Mr Benjamin	1 Mitre Court Buildings, London	020 7452 8900
Hays Mr William Stormont	6 King's Bench Walk, London	020 7583 0410
Henderson Miss Josephine	Five Paper, London	020 7815 3200
Hewson Ms Barbara Mary	Hardwicke, London	020 7242 2523
Hill Mr Piers Nicholas	37 Park Square Chambers, Leeds	0113 243 9422
Hill Ms Eleanor Mary Henrietta	Doughty Street Chambers, Bristol	01179 058 717
	Doughty Street Chambers, London	020 7404 1313
	Doughty Street Chambers, Manchester	0161 618 1066
Hoar Mr Francis John Patrick	Field Court Chambers, London	020 7405 6114
Hobson Mr John Graham	4-5 Gray's Inn Square, London	020 7404 5252
Hollis Mrs Kim	25 Bedford Row, London	020 7067 1500
Honey Mr Richard Arthur	Francis Taylor Building, London	020 7353 8415
Horne-Roberts Mrs Jennifer	Goldsmith Chambers, London	020 7353 6802
Horton Mr Matthew Bethell	39 Essex Street, London	020 7832 1111
	82 King Street, Manchester	0161 870 9969
Hossain Mr Mohammed Monwar	No. 3 Fleet Street Chambers, London	020 7936 4474
Humphreys Mr Richard William	Francis Taylor Building, London	020 7353 8415
	No5 Chambers, Birmingham	0845 210 5555
	No5 Chambers, Bristol	0845 210 5555
	No5 Chambers, London	0845 210 5555
Hussain Mr Muhammad Altaf	Chambers of Mr M A Hussain, London	020 8679 2398
Hussain Mr Mukhtar	Lincoln House Chambers, Manchester	0161 832 5701
Hussain Mr Tasaddat	Broadway House Chambers, Bradford	01274 722560
	Broadway House Chambers, Leeds	0113 246 2600
Hutchinson Mr Colin Thomas	Garden Court Chambers, London	020 7993 7600
Irwin Mr Gavin David	Dyers Chambers, London	020 7404 1881
Islam-Choudhury Mr Mugni	No5 Chambers, Birmingham	0845 210 5555
	No5 Chambers, Bristol	0845 210 5555
	No5 Chambers, London	0845 210 5555
Ismail Miss Nazmun Nisha	Central Chambers, Manchester	0161 236 1133
	No5 Chambers, Birmingham	0845 210 5555
	No5 Chambers, Bristol	0845 210 5555
	No5 Chambers, London	0845 210 5555
Jackson Mr Andrew Fraser	5 Pump Court, London	020 7353 2532
Jafferji Mr Zainulabedin Hatim	Chambers of Mr Jafferji, Leicester	07957 198777
Joffe Ms Natasha Juliet Louise	Outer Temple Chambers, London	020 7353 6381
John Miss Laura Elizabeth	Monckton Chambers, London	020 7405 7211
Johnson Miss Laura Wendy	1 Chancery Lane, London	0845 634 6666
Johnson Mr Phillip Michael	Chambers of Mr P Johnson, London	020 7288 2256
Jones Mr Kelvin Mcallister	Templis Chambers, London	020 7649 9808
Joseph Mr Sellappah Job	Chambers of Mr S J Joseph, London	020 8809 3083/020 8802 9889
Juss Prof Satvinder Singh	3 Hare Court, London	020 7415 7800
Keen Mr Spencer John	Pump Court Chambers, Swindon	01793 539899
	Pump Court Chambers, Winchester	01962 868 161
	Riverview Chambers, London	0844 225 3999
Kelly Mr Matthias John	39 Essex Street, London	020 7832 1111
Kent Mr Michael Harcourt	Crown Office Chambers, London	020 7797 8100
Khalique Miss Nageena	No5 Chambers, Birmingham	0845 210 5555
	No5 Chambers, Bristol	0845 210 5555
	No5 Chambers, London	0845 210 5555
Khan Mr Arfan	Field Court Chambers, London	020 7405 6114
Khan Mr Forz	Chambers of Mr F Khan, London	07854 109584
	6 King's Bench Walk, London	020 7353 4931
Khan Mr Mahmood Shafi	Luton Chambers, Luton	01582 598394
	Willesden Chambers, London	020 3273 1042
King Mr Charles Granville	Chambers of Mr C G King, Stroud	07949 461717
Knight Mr Benjamin James	Central Chambers, Manchester	0161 236 1133
Kohli Mr Ryan Singh	Cornerstone Barristers, London	020 7242 4986
Kramer Mr Philip Anthony	Park Lane Plowden, Newcastle Upon Tyne	0191 211 4087
Krause Ms Florence	Meritz Chambers, Hebben Bridge	0845 094 0856
Krushner Mr Damian Mark	Oakwood Chambers, London	07789 435485
Lahiffe Mr Martin Patrick Joseph	3 Temple Gardens, London	020 7353 3102

Lal Mr Sanjay	4 King's Bench Walk, London	020 7822 7000
Leigh Mr Kevin	No5 Chambers, Birmingham	0845 210 5555
	No5 Chambers, Bristol	0845 210 5555
	No5 Chambers, London	0845 210 5555
Leonard Mr James Alexander	Outer Temple Chambers, London	020 7353 6381
Levinson Miss Jemma	1 Mitre Court Buildings, London	020 7452 8900
Lewiecki Miss Marie	Old Bailey Chambers, London	020 3008 6404
Lewis Mr Dominic	Five Paper Buildings, London	020 7583 6117
Lissack Mr Richard Anthony	Outer Temple Chambers, London	020 7353 6381
	Riverview Chambers, London	0844 225 3999
Littman Mr Jeffrey James	Chambers of Mr Jeffrey Littman, London	020 8922 6844
	9 Park Place, Cardiff	029 2038 2731
Lloyd Mr Benjamin John	6 King's Bench Walk, London	020 7583 0410
Lloyd Mr John Nesbitt	Rougemont Chambers, Exeter	01392 208484
Lock Mr David Anthony	No5 Chambers, Birmingham	0845 210 5555
	No5 Chambers, Bristol	0845 210 5555
	No5 Chambers, London	0845 210 5555
Lodge Mr Hugo Daniel Paul	Atkinson Bevan Chambers, London	020 7353 2112
Lonsdale Miss Marion Mary	Academy Chambers, London	020 8455 2503
Lopez Mr Juan Nemesio	Francis Taylor Building, London	020 7353 8415
Lorenzo Ms Claudia	Pump Court Chambers, London	020 7353 0711
	Pump Court Chambers, Swindon	01793 539899
	Pump Court Chambers, Winchester	01962 868 161
Loveday Mr David Robert	4-5 Gray's Inn Square, London	020 7404 5252
Luh Miss Shu Shin	Garden Court Chambers, London	020 7993 7600
Macpherson Mr Duncan Charles Stewart	One Essex Court, London	020 7936 3030
Mahmood Mr Abid	Central Chambers, Manchester	0161 236 1133
	No5 Chambers, Birmingham	0845 210 5555
	No5 Chambers, Bristol	0845 210 5555
	No5 Chambers, London	0845 210 5555
Maka Mr Isaac	Chambers of Mr Isaac Maka, Ilford	07973 308 301
	4 King's Bench Walk, London	020 7822 7000
Malone Mr David John	1 Gray's Inn Square, London	020 7405 0001
Mandalia Mr Vinesh Lalji	St Philips Chambers, Birmingham	0121 246 7000
Mannion Ms Amy Elisabeth	9-12 Bell Yard, London	020 7400 1800
	1 Crown Office Row, London	020 7797 7500
Marcus Mr Peter	Zenith Chambers, Leeds	0113 245 5438
Markus Ms Kate	Doughty Street Chambers, Bristol	01179 058 717
	Doughty Street Chambers, London	020 7404 1313
	Doughty Street Chambers, Manchester	0161 618 1066
Marler Lieutenant Colonel Lee Gary	Bretton Woods Law, London	
	18 Red Lion Court, London	020 7520 6000
Masters Mr Alan Bruce Raymond	1 Pump Court, London	020 7842 7070
Mather Mr Nicholas Ian Stewart	Furnival Chambers, London	020 7405 3232
Matthias Mr David Huw	Francis Taylor Building, London	020 7353 8415
Mawrey Mr Richard Brooks	Henderson Chambers, London	020 7583 9020
McCombie Mr Fergus Alexander Paul	1 Gray's Inn Square, London	020 7405 0001
McCracken Mr Robert Henry Joy	Francis Taylor Building, London	020 7353 8415
McDonald Ms Melanie Sharon	No5 Chambers, Birmingham	0845 210 5555
	No5 Chambers, Bristol	0845 210 5555
	No5 Chambers, London	0845 210 5555
McDonnell Mr John Beresford William	13 Old Square Chambers, London	020 7831 4445
McGowan Miss Maura Patricia	2 Bedford Row, London	020 7440 8888
	Lincoln House Chambers, Manchester	0161 832 5701
McKendrick Mr John Dempster	Outer Temple Chambers, London	020 7353 6381
McLinden Mr John Vincent Barry	Field Court Chambers, London	020 7405 6114
Metcalfe Dr Eric William	Monckton Chambers, London	020 7405 7211
Middleton Mr Joseph	Doughty Street Chambers, Bristol	01179 058 717
	Doughty Street Chambers, London	020 7404 1313
	Doughty Street Chambers, Manchester	0161 618 1066
Miller Mr Peter Owen Michael	Cornerstone Barristers, London	020 7242 4986

C

Mishcon Mr Oliver Zebedee	Chambers of Mr Oliver Mishcon, London	020 7993 8890
Moffett Mr Jonathan Keith	4-5 Gray's Inn Square, London	020 7404 5252
Mohammad Mr Nazar	Legis Chambers, Aylesbury	01296 431125
	No. 3 Fleet Street Chambers, London	020 7936 4474
Monnington Mr Bruce Gilbert	Fenners Chambers, Cambridge	01223 368761
Mooney Mr Stephen John	Albion Chambers, Bristol	0117 927 2144
Morgan Dr Austen Jude	33 Bedford Row, London	020 7242 6476
Mullins Mr Mark Lovel Rupert	Five St Andrew's Hill, London	020 7332 5400
Muman Mr Vijay Kumar	43 Temple Row Chambers, Birmingham	0121 237 6035
Munir Dr Ashley Edward	Five St Andrew's Hill, London	020 7332 5400
Muquit Mr Mohammed Shuyeb	1 Mitre Court Buildings, London	020 7452 8900
Murphy Mr Michael Patrick	Central Chambers, Manchester	0161 236 1133
	10 King's Bench Walk, London	020 7353 7742
Mustakim Mr Abdul Yunus Al	Chambers of Mr Mustakim, London	
Myers Mr Benjamin John	Exchange Chambers, Liverpool	0151 236 7747
	Exchange Chambers, Manchester	0161 833 2722
Newman Mr Alan Ronald Harvey	Argent Chambers, London	020 7556 5500
Newsom Mr George Lucien	Guildhall Chambers, Bristol	0117 930 9000
Nicol Mr Nicholas Keith	1 Pump Court, London	020 7842 7070
O'Brien Mr Nicholas William Wattebot	10 King's Bench Walk, London	020 7353 7742
O'Connor Mr Patrick Michael Joseph	Doughty Street Chambers, Bristol	01179 058 717
	Doughty Street Chambers, London	020 7404 1313
	Doughty Street Chambers, Manchester	0161 618 1066
O'Donoghue Mr Hugh Vincent	Carmelite Chambers, London	020 7936 6300
Offer Mr Alexander	Garden Court Chambers, London	020 7993 7600
	Park Court Chambers, Leeds	0113 243 3277
Onipede Dr Victor Olusegun	Chambers of Dr V O Onipede, London	07956 207159
Oommen Mr Jacob	Chambers of Mr Jacob Oommen, East Barnet	07958 680272
Orme Miss Emily Charlotte	Arden Chambers, London	020 7242 4244
Ornsby Miss Suzanne Doreen	Francis Taylor Building, London	020 7353 8415
	St John's Chambers, Bristol	0117 923 4700
O'Sullivan Mr Richard John	1215 Chambers, London	020 3291 1215
Otwal Mr Mukhtiar Singh	42 Bedford Row, London	020 7831 0222
Owen Mr Timothy Wynn	Matrix Chambers, London	020 7404 3447
Ozin Mr Paul David	23 Essex Street, London	020 7413 0353
Padfield Mr Nicholas David	Chambers of Nicholas Padfield QC, London	020 7351 1961
Paget Mr Michael Rodborough	Garden Court Chambers, London	020 7993 7600
Palmer Mr Robert Henry	Monckton Chambers, London	020 7405 7211
Paraskos Mr Paraskevakis Christakis	11 Gray's Inn Square Chambers, London	020 7405 6879
Pascoe Ms Soraya	1 Gray's Inn Square, London	020 7405 0001
Patel Miss Gita	Kenworthy's Chambers, Manchester	0161 832 4036
Peretz Mr George Michael John	Monckton Chambers, London	020 7405 7211
Peterson Miss Geraldine Shelda	Chambers of Mr Ami Feder, London	020 7797 7788
	Chambers of Mr Ami Feder, London	020 7797 7788
	Lamb Building, Brighton	01273 820490
Plimmer Miss Melanie Ann	Kings Chambers, Birmingham	0845 034 3444
	Kings Chambers, Leeds	0845 034 3444
	Kings Chambers, Manchester	0845 034 3444
Purchas Mr Robin Michael	Francis Taylor Building, London	020 7353 8415
Rana Mr Mohammed Akram	Clapham Law Chambers, London	020 7978 8482
Rayment Mr Benedick Michael	Monckton Chambers, London	020 7405 7211
Read Mr Simon Eric	Zenith Chambers, Leeds	0113 245 5438
Record Mrs Celia Saint Claire	Chambers of Lawrence Jones, London	020 7831 1444
Rhodes Mr Robert Elliott	Outer Temple Chambers, London	020 7353 6381
	Principal Chambers, Sevenoaks	0845 209 8080
	St Philips Chambers, Birmingham	0121 246 7000

Richards Mr Duncan James	Chambers of Mr Ami Feder, London	020 7797 7788
	Chambers of Mr Ami Feder, London	020 7797 7788
	Principal Chambers, Sevenoaks	0845 209 8080
Richardson Mr Alistair Paul George	6 King's Bench Walk, London	020 7583 0410
Richardson Mr Garth Douglas Anthony	Devon Chambers, Plymouth	01752 661659
	Rougemont Chambers, Exeter	01392 208484
Rimmer Mr Anthony Michael	187 Fleet Street, London	020 7430 7430
Rivalland Mr Marc-Edouard	1 Chancery Lane, London	0845 634 6666
Riza Mr Alper Ali	Goldsmith Chambers, London	020 7353 6802
Roche Mr Patrick Richard Redmond	Tooks Chambers, London	020 7842 7575
Rogers Mr Ian Paul	Monckton Chambers, London	020 7405 7211
Rothwell Mrs Joanne Lesley	No5 Chambers, Birmingham	0845 210 5555
	No5 Chambers, Bristol	0845 210 5555
	No5 Chambers, London	0845 210 5555
Rubens Miss Jacqueline Ann	1 Pump Court, London	020 7842 7070
Rule Mr Philip David	Castle Chambers, Harrow-on-the-Hill	020 8423 6579
Sadiq Mr Muhammad Faisel	Ely Place Chambers, London	020 7400 9600
Scally Miss Josephine Theresa Sarah	Palmyra Chambers, Warrington	01925 444919
Scolding Miss Fiona Kate	Hardwicke, London	020 7242 2523
Seeboruth Mr Royln Jean-Paul	Chambers of Royln Seeboruth, Aylesbury	01296 393329
Shaw Mr Michael John	9-12 Bell Yard, London	020 7400 1800
Sheikh Ms Saira Kabir	Francis Taylor Building, London	020 7353 8415
Sheppard Mr Timothy Derie	No5 Chambers, Birmingham	0845 210 5555
	No5 Chambers, Bristol	0845 210 5555
	No5 Chambers, London	0845 210 5555
Sikand Miss Maya	Garden Court Chambers, London	020 7993 7600
Simpson Mr David Joseph	196 Temple Chamber, London	020 7099 9257
Sinclair Mr Graham Kelso	East Anglian Chambers, Colchester	01473 214481
	East Anglian Chambers, Ipswich	01473 214481
	East Anglian Chambers, Norwich	01473 214481
Singarajah Mr Frederico	1 Gray's Inn Square, London	020 7405 0001
Skelt Mr Ian Stuart	KBW, Leeds	0113 297 1200
Skinner Mr Samuel Richard Edward	KCH Garden Square, Nottingham	0115 941 8851
Smith Miss Eileen Joan	Trinity Chambers, Middlesbrough	01642 247569
	Trinity Chambers, Newcastle Upon Tyne	0191 232 1927
Smith Mr Alisdair Robert Macsorley	9-12 Bell Yard, London	020 7400 1800
Sood Mrs Usha Rani	Trent Chambers, Nottingham	0115 941 9596
Soto-Miranda Mr Diego Fernando	One Essex Court, London	020 7936 3030
Southey Mr David Hugh	Tooks Chambers, London	020 7842 7575
Speaight Mr Anthony Hugh	4 Pump Court, London	020 7842 5555
Spencer Mr Paul Anthony	3 Serjeants Inn, London	020 7427 5000
Stagg Mr Paul Andrew	1 Chancery Lane, London	0845 634 6666
Stanbury Mr Matthew Francis	Chambers of Ian Macdonald QC, Manchester	0161 236 1840
Stanford Mr Tony James	Old Bailey Chambers, London	020 3008 6404
Stedman Mr Aryan John	Chambers of Mr A J Stedman, Cliftonville	07702 870575
Steel Mr John Brychan	4-5 Gray's Inn Square, London	020 7404 5252
Stevenson Mr Paul Anthony	Tanfield Chambers, London	020 7421 5300
Stewart Mr Nicholas John Cameron	Ely Place Chambers, London	020 7400 9600
Stinchcombe Mr Paul David	4-5 Gray's Inn Square, London	020 7404 5252
Storrie Mr Timothy James	Lincoln House Chambers, Manchester	0161 832 5701
Strong Mr Adrian Peter Ciaran	KBW, Leeds	0113 297 1200
Stubbs Mr Richard John Morris	Trinity Chambers, Middlesbrough	01642 247569
	Trinity Chambers, Newcastle Upon Tyne	0191 232 1927
Symes Mr Mark Adrian	Garden Court Chambers, London	020 7993 7600
Tabari Mr Ali-Reza	St Philips Chambers, Birmingham	0121 246 7000
Thomas Miss Megan Moira	6 Pump Court, London	020 7797 8400
	6 Pump Court Chambers, Maidstone	01622 688094

Thomas Mr Andrew Martin	Lincoln House Chambers, Manchester	0161 832 5701
	Linenhall Chambers, Chester	01244 348282
Thompson Mr Andrew Edward Courtney	Tanfield Chambers, London	020 7421 5300
Tompkins Miss Kate	36 Bedford Row, London	020 7421 8000
Traversi Mr John David Stephen Antona	Nine Bedford Row, London	020 7489 2727
Tregidgo Mr Marc Gordon	4 King's Bench Walk, London	020 7822 7000
Treverton-Jones Mr Gregory Dennis	39 Essex Street, London	020 7832 1111
	82 King Street, Manchester	0161 870 9969
Trumpington Mr John Henry	Staple Inn Chambers, London	020 7242 5240
Tucker Mr James Eckhord	Queen Square Chambers, Bristol	0117 921 1966
Twist Mr Stephen John	Dere Street Barristers, Newcastle Upon Tyne	0844 3351551
Upton Mr John Stewart	4 King's Bench Walk, London	020 7822 7000
Van Overdijk Miss Claire Orit	No5 Chambers, Birmingham	0845 210 5555
	No5 Chambers, Bristol	0845 210 5555
	No5 Chambers, London	0845 210 5555
Vanhegan Mr Toby Bartholomew	Arden Chambers, London	020 7242 4244
Vassall-Adams Mr Guy Luke	Doughty Street Chambers, Bristol	01179 058 717
	Doughty Street Chambers, London	020 7404 1313
	Doughty Street Chambers, Manchester	0161 618 1066
Vaughan Mr Anthony	Garden Court Chambers, London	020 7993 7600
Wadsley Mr Peter John Campbell	St John's Chambers, Bristol	0117 923 4700
Wald Mr Richard Daniel	39 Essex Street, London	020 7832 1111
	82 King Street, Manchester	0161 870 9969
	Riverview Chambers, London	0844 225 3999
Warner Mr David Alexander	St Philips Chambers, Birmingham	0121 246 7000
Watson Mr Benjamin Turquand	3 Raymond Buildings, London	020 7400 6400
Weatherby Mr Peter Francis	Chambers of Ian Macdonald QC, Manchester	0161 236 1840
	Garden Court Chambers, London	020 7993 7600
Wenban-Smith Mr Mungo William	4-5 Gray's Inn Square, London	020 7404 5252
West Dr Ewan Donald	Monckton Chambers, London	020 7405 7211
Whale Mr Stephen John	4-5 Gray's Inn Square, London	020 7404 5252
White Mr Oliver Zachary	Littleton Chambers, London	020 7797 8600
Wigley Miss Jenny	No5 Chambers, Birmingham	0845 210 5555
	No5 Chambers, Bristol	0845 210 5555
	No5 Chambers, London	0845 210 5555
Wiktorowski-Solecki Miss Tamara	Middle Temple Lane Chambers, London	020 7583 4352
Williams Mr Ben Dylan	Kings Chambers, Birmingham	0845 034 3444
	Kings Chambers, Leeds	0845 034 3444
	Kings Chambers, Manchester	0845 034 3444
Williams Mr Rhodri John	Henderson Chambers, London	020 7583 9020
	30 Park Place, Cardiff	029 2039 8421
Wills Miss Alexandra Itari	Christ Church Chambers, London	020 7409 5278/07788 512787
Wise Mr Ian	Doughty Street Chambers, Bristol	01179 058 717
	Doughty Street Chambers, London	020 7404 1313
	Doughty Street Chambers, Manchester	0161 618 1066
Woolf The Hon Jeremy Richard George	Pump Court Tax Chambers, London	020 7414 8080
Wragg Mr Jonathan Robert	Highgate Chambers, London	020 8340 6031
Yeo Mr Nicholas	3 Raymond Buildings, London	020 7400 6400

ADMIRALTY

Ahmed Mr Ishfaq	Stone Chambers, London	020 7440 6900
Anderson Mr Richard Neil Macdiarmid	Arbitration Chambers, London	020 7267 2137
Aswani Mr Ravi Girdharilal	Stone Chambers, London	020 7440 6900
Bullock Mr Robert Gustaf	The Chambers of Mr Bullock, Brighton	01273 321050
Charkham Mr Graham Harold	20 Essex Street, London	020 7842 1200
Gibbons Miss Mary Regina	Stone Chambers, London	020 7440 6900

C

Henderson Mr Neil John	Stone Chambers, London	020 7440 6900
Howells Mr Stephen John	Stone Chambers, London	020 7440 6900
McTague Miss Meghann Rose	2 Temple Gardens, London	020 7822 1200
Parsons Mr Andrew James	Portsmouth Barristers'Chambers, Portsmouth	023 9283 1292
Selvaratnam Miss Vasanti Emily Indrani	Stone Chambers, London	020 7440 6900
Shirley Mr James Patrick	Stone Chambers, London	020 7440 6900
Temmink Mr Robert-Jan	Quadrant Chambers, London	020 7583 4444
Watthey Mr James Robertson	Hardwicke, London	020 7242 2523
Wills Miss Alexandra Itari	Christ Church Chambers, London	020 7409 5278/07788 512787

AGRICULTURE

Andrews Mr Paul Leslie	Great James Street Chambers, London	020 7440 4949
Batstone Mr William Harold Fitzherbert	Guildhall Chambers, Bristol	0117 930 9000
Blohm Mr Leslie Adrian	St John's Chambers, Bristol	0117 923 4700
Brook Mr Paul Antony	Park Lane Plowden, Leeds	0113 228 5049
	Park Lane Plowden, Newcastle Upon Tyne	0191 211 4087
Castle Mr Peter Bolton	13 Old Square Chambers, London	020 7831 4445
Collett Mr Gavin Charles	Rougemont Chambers, Exeter	01392 208484
Cotterell Mr David William	Albion Chambers, Bristol	0117 927 2144
Darroch Miss Fiona Culverwell	Clerksroom (London), London	0845 083 3000
	Clerksroom (Taunton), Taunton	0845 083 3000
	King's Lynn Chambers, King's Lynn	01553 672 085
Dean Mr Peter Thomas	36 Bedford Row, London	020 7421 8000
Devereux-Cooke Mr Richard Charles	13 Old Square Chambers, London	020 7831 4445
Dowell Mr Gregory Hamilton	Principal Chambers, Sevenoaks	0845 209 8080
Facenna Mr Gerald Carlo	Monckton Chambers, London	020 7405 7211
Felton Mr Timothy John Fowler	Rougemont Chambers, Exeter	01392 208484
Gerry Miss Felicity Ruth	36 Bedford Row, London	020 7421 8000
Gore Mr Andrew Roger	Fenners Chambers, Cambridge	01223 368761
Harwood Mr Richard John	39 Essex Street, London	020 7832 1111
	82 King Street, Manchester	0161 870 9969
Hill Mr Michael Gordon	Trinity Chambers, Middlesbrough	01642 247569
	Trinity Chambers, Newcastle Upon Tyne	0191 232 1927
Jackson Mr Christopher Marshall	Liverpool Civil Law, Liverpool	0151 242 0500
Lyon Mrs Shane Valerie	King's Bench and Godolphin (KBG)Chambers, Plymouth	01752 221551
Mainwaring Mr Robert Paul Clason	Portal Chambers, Llandysul	01559 395 292
Marsden Mr Andrew Guy	East Anglian Chambers, Chelmsford	01473 214481
	East Anglian Chambers, Colchester	01473 214481
	East Anglian Chambers, Ipswich	01473 214481
	East Anglian Chambers, Norwich	01473 214481
Matthias Mr David Huw	Francis Taylor Building, London	020 7353 8415
Mitchell Mr David John	No5 Chambers, Birmingham	0845 210 5555
	No5 Chambers, Bristol	0845 210 5555
	No5 Chambers, London	0845 210 5555
Monnington Mr Bruce Gilbert	Fenners Chambers, Cambridge	01223 368761
Newsom Mr George Lucien	Guildhall Chambers, Bristol	0117 930 9000
Ohrenstein Mr Dov	Radcliffe Chambers, London	020 7831 0081
Osborne Mr James Robert	Clerksroom (London), London	0845 083 3000
Parry Mr Charles Robert	Pump Court Chambers, London	020 7353 0711
	Pump Court Chambers, Swindon	01793 539899
	Pump Court Chambers, Winchester	01962 868 161
Pearce Mr Robert Edgar	Radcliffe Chambers, London	020 7831 0081
Peretz Mr George Michael John	Monckton Chambers, London	020 7405 7211
Powell Mr William Rhys	Regency Chambers, Cambridge	01223 301517
	Regency Chambers, Peterborough	01733 315215
Sellers Mr Graham	Atlantic Chambers, Liverpool	0151 236 4421

Smith Miss Eileen Joan	Trinity Chambers, Middlesbrough	01642 247569
	Trinity Chambers, Newcastle Upon Tyne	0191 232 1927
Stewart Mr Nicholas John Cameron	Ely Place Chambers, London	020 7400 9600
Sweeney Mr Noel Christopher	Veritas Chambers, Worle	01934 853 382
Taylor Mrs Susan	Trinity Chambers, Middlesbrough	01642 247569
	Trinity Chambers, Newcastle Upon Tyne	0191 232 1927
Wignall Mr Edward Gordon	No5 Chambers, Birmingham	0845 210 5555
	No5 Chambers, Bristol	0845 210 5555
	No5 Chambers, London	0845 210 5555
Wilkinson Mr Marc Ashley	No5 Chambers, Birmingham	0845 210 5555
	No5 Chambers, Bristol	0845 210 5555
	No5 Chambers, London	0845 210 5555
Wilson Mr Richard Carver	36 Bedford Row, London	020 7421 8000

ANCILLARY RELIEF

Ajaz Mr Mohammad Arshad	Eastmans Chambers, Reading	0118 966 9094
Akman Miss Mercy Louise	36 Bedford Row, London	020 7421 8000
Anderson Mr Nicholas Guy	1 KBW Chambers, London	020 7936 1500
	King's Bench Chambers, Lewes	01273 402600
Atkinson Mr Jody Roy	St John's Chambers, Bristol	0117 923 4700
Bailey Mr Charles Andrew Stuart	Trinity Chambers, Chelmsford	01245 605040
Bailey Mr Michael Robert	Tanfield Chambers, London	020 7421 5300
Banks Mr Francis Andrew	Atlantic Chambers, Liverpool	0151 236 4421
Barratt Mr Dominic Anthony	East Anglian Chambers, Chelmsford	01473 214481
	East Anglian Chambers, Colchester	01473 214481
	East Anglian Chambers, Ipswich	01473 214481
	East Anglian Chambers, Norwich	01473 214481
Beattie Ms Annabel Dorothy	Park Court Chambers, Leeds	0113 243 3277
Bennet Ms Pauline Agnes	Regency Chambers, Peterborough	01733 315215
Bezzam Miss Jayashree	Hampton Court Chambers, West Molesey	020 8979 0381
Bhachu Miss Sharanjeet Kaur	4 Brick Court, London	020 7832 3200
Bhanji Mr Shiraz Musa	4 Bingham Place, London	020 7486 5347
	1 Gray's Inn Square, London	020 7405 0001
Bojarski Mr Andrzej Leonard	36 Bedford Row, London	020 7421 8000
Bowe Mr Patrick Joseph	KCH Garden Square, Nottingham	0115 941 8851
Bray Miss Helen Lorna	Walnut House, Exeter	01392 279751
Buck Mr John	Tanfield Chambers, London	020 7421 5300
Buckhaven Mr Simon	Hardwicke, London	020 7242 2523
Buswell Mr Richard Thomas	Hardwicke, London	020 7242 2523
Carr Mr Christopher Sean	36 Bedford Row, London	020 7421 8000
Carron Mr Richard Byron	Queen Square Chambers, Bristol	0117 921 1966
Cellan-Jones Mr Deiniol James	1 KBW Chambers, London	020 7936 1500
	King's Bench Chambers, Lewes	01273 402600
Chatterjee Miss Adreeja Julia	No5 Chambers, Birmingham	0845 210 5555
	No5 Chambers, Bristol	0845 210 5555
	No5 Chambers, London	0845 210 5555
Clark Mr Dingle	Goldsmith Chambers, London	020 7353 6802
Da Costa-Waldman Mrs Elissa Josephine	Clerksroom (London), London	0845 083 3000
	Clerksroom (Taunton), Taunton	0845 083 3000
	King's Lynn Chambers, King's Lynn	01553 672 085
De Burgos Mr Jamie Michael Abulafia	36 Bedford Row, London	020 7421 8000
Dean Mr James Patrick	Goldsmith Chambers, London	020 7353 6802
Dhadli Mrs Perminder	KCH Garden Square, Nottingham	0115 941 8851
Dhaliwal Miss Davinder Kaur	No 8 Chambers, Birmingham	0121 236 5514
Edington Mrs Fiona Anne Rider	Thomas More Chambers, London	020 7404 7000
Edwards Mr Nigel Royston	St Paul's Chambers, Leeds	0113 245 5866

C

Name	Chambers	Telephone
Elcombe Mr Nicholas John	East Anglian Chambers, Chelmsford	01473 214481
	East Anglian Chambers, Colchester	01473 214481
	East Anglian Chambers, Ipswich	01473 214481
	East Anglian Chambers, Norwich	01473 214481
Elliott Mr Mark Daniel	3 PB Barristers, Bournemouth	01202 292102
	3 PB Barristers, Bristol	0117 928 1520
	3 PB Barristers, London	020 7583 8055
	3 PB Barristers, Oxford	01865 793 736
	3 PB Barristers, Winchester	01962 868884
Fairbank Mr Nicholas James	4 Paper Buildings, London	020 7427 5200
Fama Mrs Gudrun Hildegard	Middle Temple Lane Chambers, London	020 7583 4352
Fletcher Mr Christopher Michael	Octagon House, Norwich	01603 623186
Gill Miss Baljinder	10 King's Bench Walk, London	020 7353 7742
Gillan Mrs Dominique Lye-Ping	Guildford Chambers, Guildford	01483 539131
Gillman Miss Rachel Mary	1 Garden Court Family Law Chambers, London	020 7797 7900
Gillott Mr Paul Alan Ashley	15 Winckley Square, Preston	01772 252828
Glaser Mr Michael Samson	14 Gray's Inn Square, London	020 7242 0858
Glover Mr Stephen Julian	37 Park Square Chambers, Leeds	0113 243 9422
Goodall Miss Rachael Jane	3 PB Barristers, Bournemouth	01202 292102
	3 PB Barristers, Bristol	0117 928 1520
	3 PB Barristers, London	020 7583 8055
	3 PB Barristers, Oxford	01865 793 736
	3 PB Barristers, Winchester	01962 868884
Gore Mr Andrew Julian Mark	37 Park Square Chambers, Leeds	0113 243 9422
Hale Mr Charles Stanley	4 Paper Buildings, London	020 7427 5200
Harris Mr David Robert	St Albans Chambers, St Albans	01727 843383
Hasan Miss Ayesha	3 Dr Johnson's Buildings, London	020 7353 4854
Hay Mr Malcolm John Marshall	3 Dr Johnson's Buildings, London	020 7353 4854
Hillas Miss Samantha	Atlantic Chambers, Liverpool	0151 236 4421
Hillier Mr William	New Street Chambers, Leicester	0116 262 5906
Hughes Mrs Kathryn Sally	Chavasse Court Chambers, Liverpool	0151 229 2030
James Mr George Christopher Mohun	No5 Chambers, Birmingham	0845 210 5555
	No5 Chambers, Bristol	0845 210 5555
	No5 Chambers, London	0845 210 5555
Japheth Miss Bethan	Linenhall Chambers, Chester	01244 348282
Johnstone Mr Mark Anthony	4 Paper Buildings, London	020 7427 5200
Josty Mr David Stephen	College Chambers, Southampton	023 8023 0338
Kenny Mr Martin William	Walnut House, Exeter	01392 279751
Khalid Mr James	Goulds Green Chambers, Uxbridge	01895 422574
	Goulds Green Chambers, Uxbridge	01895 422574
Khan Mr Imran	St Albans Chambers, St Albans	01727 843383
Kidd Mr Peter William	Number 7 Harrington Street Chambers, Liverpool	0151 242 0707
Leonard Mr Charles Robert Weston	Hardwicke, London	020 7242 2523
Lloyd Ms Rhiannon	4 Paper Buildings, London	020 7427 5200
Loeb Miss Dinah Yolande	Westgate Chambers, Lewes	01273 480510
MacKenzie Miss Julie Fiona	Pump Court Chambers, London	020 7353 0711
	Pump Court Chambers, Swindon	01793 539899
	Pump Court Chambers, Winchester	01962 868 161
Marks Miss Gillian	14 Gray's Inn Square, London	020 7242 0858
Marsden Mr Andrew Guy	East Anglian Chambers, Chelmsford	01473 214481
	East Anglian Chambers, Colchester	01473 214481
	East Anglian Chambers, Ipswich	01473 214481
	East Anglian Chambers, Norwich	01473 214481
Mayhew Miss Judith	3 Dr Johnson's Buildings, London	020 7353 4854
McCabe Miss Louise Anne	St Philips Chambers, Birmingham	0121 246 7000
McKay Mr Christopher Alexander	Cathedral Chambers, Newport	01633 215112
Meachin Miss Vanessa Veronica	St Philips Chambers, Birmingham	0121 246 7000
Melville-Shreeve Mr Michael David	Walnut House, Exeter	01392 279751
Milsom Mrs Catherine Mary	Argent Chambers, London	020 7556 5500

Name	Chambers	Telephone
Moore Mr Jonathan Guy	Cathedral Chambers, Cardiff	02920 660129
	Cathedral Chambers, Newport	01633 215112
Moore Mrs Therese Finola	4 Brick Court, London	020 7832 3200
Nall-Cain The Hon Richard Christopher Philip	St Albans Chambers, St Albans	01727 843383
Nichols Mr Stuart Richard	1 Garden Court Family Law Chambers, London	020 7797 7900
Nickless Mr Jason Alan	College Chambers, Southampton	023 8023 0338
O'Brien Mr David	Trinity Chambers, Chelmsford	01245 605040
Oommen Mr Jacob	Chambers of Mr Jacob Oommen, East Barnet	07958 680272
O'Sullivan Mr Richard John	1215 Chambers, London	020 3291 1215
Pettitt Mr Robert	Northampton Chambers, Northampton	01604 636271
Procter Mr Alfred George Haydn	1 Garden Court Family Law Chambers, London	020 7797 7900
Rai Miss Puneet Kaur	Thomas More Chambers, London	020 7404 7000
Rana Mr Mohammed Akram	Clapham Law Chambers, London	020 7978 8482
Rawal Miss Anita	Chambers of Mr Ami Feder, London	020 7797 7788
	Chambers of Mr Ami Feder, London	020 7797 7788
	Lamb Building, Brighton	01273 820490
Reid Miss Claudette Patricia	Chambers of Miss Claudette Reid, London	
Rhodes Miss Amanda Louise	Unity Street Chambers, Bristol	0117 906 9789
Richman Mrs Helene Pines	Eighteen Carlton Crescent, Southampton	023 8063 9001
	9 Stone Buildings, London	020 7404 5055
	Stour Chambers, Canterbury	01227 764899
Roberts Mr Huw Eifion	Linenhall Chambers, Chester	01244 348282
Roberts Mr James Mcclintock	1 KBW Chambers, London	020 7936 1500
	King's Bench Chambers, Lewes	01273 402600
Rowlinson Miss Wendy Julia	Pallant Chambers, Chichester	01243 784538
Rudd Mr Matthew Allan	Broadway House Chambers, Bradford	01274 722560
	Broadway House Chambers, Leeds	0113 246 2600
Seeboruth Mr Royln Jean-Paul	Chambers of Royln Seeboruth, Aylesbury	01296 393329
Sharp Mr David Ian	Tanfield Chambers, London	020 7421 5300
Shaw Ms Nicola Jane Duckworth	Trinity Chambers, Middlesbrough	01642 247569
	Trinity Chambers, Newcastle Upon Tyne	0191 232 1927
	15 Winckley Square, Preston	01772 252828
Smout Mr William Kingsley	Guildford Chambers, Guildford	01483 539131
Southern Miss Emma Catherine	12 College Place, Southampton	023 8032 0320
Spencer Mr Shaun Anthony	St Johns Buildings, Chester	01244 323070
	St Johns Buildings, Manchester	0161 214 1500
	16 Winckley Square, Preston	01772 256100
Stirling Mr Christopher William	Field Court Chambers, London	020 7405 6114
Styles Mr Clive Richard	Becket Chambers, Canterbury	01227 786331
Thomas Mr Gareth	Atlantic Chambers, Liverpool	0151 236 4421
Tresman Mr Lewis Robert Simon	Staple Inn Chambers, London	020 7242 5240
Turnbull Mrs Linda Angela	1 Gray's Inn Square, London	020 7405 0001
Twist Mr Stephen John	Dere Street Barristers, Newcastle Upon Tyne	0844 3351551
Tyler Mr Thomas Geoffrey	3 PB Barristers, Bournemouth	01202 292102
	3 PB Barristers, Bristol	0117 928 1520
	3 PB Barristers, London	020 7583 8055
	3 PB Barristers, Oxford	01865 793 736
	3 PB Barristers, Winchester	01962 868884
Vencatachellum Ms Glenda Roxande	Rowchester Chambers, Birmingham	0121 233 2327
Villarosa Miss Annunziata	Clerksroom (London), London	0845 083 3000
	Clerksroom (Taunton), Taunton	0845 083 3000
Vollenweider Mr Amiot Marcus Ellerton	Thomas More Chambers, London	020 7404 7000
Wagstaff Mr Andrew Martin Nicholas	Westgate Chambers, Lewes	01273 480510

Watson Mr Duncan Allen	Westgate Chambers, Lewes	01273 480510
Wheaton Mr Ian Malcolm James	Eighteen Carlton Crescent, Southampton	023 8063 9001
Whyatt Mr Michael George	15 Winckley Square, Preston	01772 252828
Williams Miss Anna	Trinity Chambers, Chelmsford	01245 605040
Wills Miss Alexandra Itari	Christ Church Chambers, London	020 7409 5278/07788 512787
Winslett Mr Frank	Westgate Chambers, Lewes	01273 480510
Wood Ms Katie Anne	4 Paper Buildings, London	020 7427 5200

ARBITRATION

Abasheikh Mr Omar Said Imam	Paragon Chambers, London	020 3318 9988
Aeberli Mr Peter Dolph	3 PB Barristers, Bournemouth	01202 292102
	3 PB Barristers, Bristol	0117 928 1520
	3 PB Barristers, London	020 7583 8055
	3 PB Barristers, Oxford	01865 793 736
	3 PB Barristers, Winchester	01962 868884
Ahmed Mr Ishfaq	Stone Chambers, London	020 7440 6900
Akinsanya Mr Stephen Olubunmi	Old Bailey Chambers, London	020 3008 6404
Akman Miss Mercy Louise	36 Bedford Row, London	020 7421 8000
Ali Mrs Shamim	Chambers of Mrs Shamim Ali, Hatfield	01707 276737
Aliker Mr Phillip Bliss	Tanfield Chambers, London	020 7421 5300
Almihdar Mr Ali Hamed	Outer Temple Chambers, London	020 7353 6381
Alomo Mr Richard Olusoji	14 Gray's Inn Square, London	020 7242 0858
Altaras Mr David Maurice	36 Bedford Row, London	020 7421 8000
Anderson Mr Richard Neil Macdiarmid	Arbitration Chambers, London	020 7267 2137
Arkhurst Mr Reginald Leon	4 King's Bench Walk, London	020 7822 7000
Artesi Miss Desiree Allison Ann	Thomas More Chambers, London	020 7404 7000
Asprey Mr Nicholas	Clock Chambers, Wolverhampton	01902 313444
	Serle Court, London	020 7242 6105
Aswani Mr Ravi Girdharilal	Stone Chambers, London	020 7440 6900
Barrett Mr Kevin John	No5 Chambers, Birmingham	0845 210 5555
	No5 Chambers, Bristol	0845 210 5555
	No5 Chambers, London	0845 210 5555
Barwise Miss Stephanie Nicola	Atkin Chambers, London	020 7404 0102
Beaumont Mr Benjamin	Chambers of Dr Michael Arnheim, London	020 7833 5093
	Middle Temple Lane Chambers, London	020 7583 4352
Beaumont Mr Marc Clifford	9 Stone Buildings, London	020 7404 5055
	Windsor Barristers' Chambers, Windsor	01753 839321
Bellamy Mr Jonathan Mark	39 Essex Street, London	020 7832 1111
	82 King Street, Manchester	0161 870 9969
Bezzam Miss Jayashree	Hampton Court Chambers, West Molesey	020 8979 0381
Bhanji Mr Shiraz Musa	4 Bingham Place, London	020 7486 5347
	1 Gray's Inn Square, London	020 7405 0001
Bhattacharyya Mr Ardhendu	Slough Barristers Chamber, Slough	01753 553806
Bishop Mr Malcolm Leslie	Argent Chambers, London	020 7556 5500
	Equity Chambers, Birmingham	0121 236 5007
	30 Park Place, Cardiff	029 2039 8421
Boulding Mr Philip Vincent	Keating Chambers, London	020 7544 2600
Bourne Mr Geoffrey Robert	13 Old Square Chambers, London	020 7831 4445
Bowsher Mr Michael Frederick Thomas	Monckton Chambers, London	020 7405 7211
Brook Mr Paul Antony	Park Lane Plowden, Leeds	0113 228 5049
	Park Lane Plowden, Newcastle Upon Tyne	0191 211 4087
Buchan Miss Caroline Venetia	Chambers of Miss C Buchan, Haywards Heath	01444 482222
Bueno Mr Antonio De Padua Jose Maria	Clerksroom (Taunton), Taunton	0845 083 3000

C

Name	Chambers	Telephone
Bullock Mr Robert Gustaf	The Chambers of Mr Bullock, Brighton	01273 321050
Burr Mr Andrew Charles	Atkin Chambers, London	020 7404 0102
Castle Mr Peter Bolton	13 Old Square Chambers, London	020 7831 4445
Chambers Miss Gaynor Marie	Keating Chambers, London	020 7544 2600
Charkham Mr Graham Harold	20 Essex Street, London	020 7842 1200
Clark Miss Geraldine	Serle Court, London	020 7242 6105
Cohen Mr Edward Mervyn	11 Stone Buildings, London	020 7831 6381
Colbey Mr Richard	Guildhall Chambers Portsmouth, Portsmouth	023 9275 2400
	Lamb Chambers, London	020 7797 8300
Collett Mr Gavin Charles	Rougemont Chambers, Exeter	01392 208484
Coster Mr Ronald David	42 Bedford Row, London	020 7831 0222
Crawshaw Mr Simon Richard	Atkin Chambers, London	020 7404 0102
Crowley Mr Daniel John	2 Temple Gardens, London	020 7822 1200
Curtis Mr Michael Alexander	Crown Office Chambers, London	020 7797 8100
Darling Mr Paul Antony	Keating Chambers, London	020 7544 2600
De Waal Mr John Henry Lowndes	Hardwicke, London	020 7242 2523
Denbin Mr Jack Arnold	Greenway, Sonning-on-Thames	0118 969 2484
Devine Mr Michael Buxton	Rougemont Chambers, Exeter	01392 208484
di Mambro Mr David Jesse Andrew	Pallant Chambers, Chichester	01243 784538
	Radcliffe Chambers, London	020 7831 0081
Dillon Mr Thomas William Matthew	Chambers of Thomas Dillon, London	020 7692 2722
Doerries Miss Chantal-Aimée Renee Aemelia An	Atkin Chambers, London	020 7404 0102
Du Toit Sc Mr Johan Ignatius	Selborne Chambers, London	020 7420 9500
	St Philips Chambers, Birmingham	0121 246 7000
Dyer Mr Allen Gordon	4 Pump Court, London	020 7842 5555
Edwards Mr Anthony	Chancery House Chambers, Leeds	0113 244 6691
Edwards Mr Nigel Royston	St Paul's Chambers, Leeds	0113 245 5866
Elliott Mr Timothy Stanley	Keating Chambers, London	020 7544 2600
Engelman Mr Philip	Cloisters, London	020 7827 4000
	Trinity Chambers, Middlesbrough	01642 247569
	Trinity Chambers, Newcastle Upon Tyne	0191 232 1927
Evans Mr Robert Jonathan	Keating Chambers, London	020 7544 2600
Falkowski Mr Damian	4-5 Gray's Inn Square, London	020 7404 5252
Fender Mr Carl David	Regency Chambers, Cambridge	01223 301517
	Regency Chambers, Peterborough	01733 315215
Finlay Mr Darren	Sovereign Chambers, Leeds	0113 245 1841
Francis Mr Nicholas	29 Bedford Row Chambers, London	020 7404 1044
Franklin Miss Kim	Crown Office Chambers, London	020 7797 8100
Friedman Mr David Peter	4 Pump Court, London	020 7842 5555
Furst Mr Stephen Andrew	Keating Chambers, London	020 7544 2600
Gainer Mr Richard St Clair	St Margaret's Chambers, Twickenham	020 8241 3516
Garrett Miss Lucy Margaret	Keating Chambers, London	020 7544 2600
Garvie Mr Carl Peter	St Philips Chambers, Birmingham	0121 246 7000
Gee Mr Steven Mark	Stone Chambers, London	020 7440 6900
Gelbart Mr Geoff Alan	1 Gray's Inn Square, London	020 7405 0001
Gibbons Miss Mary Regina	Stone Chambers, London	020 7440 6900
Gill Mr Manjit Singh	No5 Chambers, Birmingham	0845 210 5555
	No5 Chambers, Bristol	0845 210 5555
	No5 Chambers, London	0845 210 5555
Godwin Mr William George Henry	3 Hare Court, London	020 7415 7800
	St John's Chambers, Bristol	0117 923 4700
Gore Mr Andrew Roger	Fenners Chambers, Cambridge	01223 368761
Gough Miss Karen Louise	Arbitration Chambers, London	020 7267 2137
	39 Essex Street, London	020 7832 1111
	82 King Street, Manchester	0161 870 9969
Graham Mrs Alana Nicole	Chambers of Alana Graham, Halesowen	01384 894560
	9 Stone Buildings, London	020 7404 5055

Barrister	Chambers	Telephone
Graham-Wells Miss Alison Christine	Exchange Chambers, Leeds	0113 203 1970
	Exchange Chambers, Liverpool	0151 236 7747
	Exchange Chambers, Manchester	0161 833 2722
Griffiths Mr David	St Philips Chambers, Birmingham	0121 246 7000
Guy Mr John David Colin	Tanfield Chambers, London	020 7421 5300
Halden Mr Angus Robert	Queen Square Chambers, Bristol	0117 921 1966
Hannaford Miss Sarah Jane	Keating Chambers, London	020 7544 2600
Hargreaves Mr Simon John Robert	Keating Chambers, London	020 7544 2600
Harvey Mr John Gilbert	No5 Chambers, Birmingham	0845 210 5555
	No5 Chambers, Bristol	0845 210 5555
	No5 Chambers, London	0845 210 5555
Henderson Mr Neil John	Stone Chambers, London	020 7440 6900
Hendron Mr Henry Joseph Christopher	Strand Chambers, London	020 7117 6920
Higginson Mr Timothy Nicholas Bennett	Littleton Chambers, London	020 7797 8600
	St John's Chambers, Bristol	0117 923 4700
Hirst Mr Martin Lewis	13 KBW, Oxford	01865 311066
	13 King's Bench Walk, London	020 7353 7204
Holroyd Mr John James	Zenith Chambers, Leeds	0113 245 5438
Hood Mr David	Prince of Wales Chambers, London	020 7622 7415
Horne Mr Charles Hugh Wilson	Kings Chambers, Birmingham	0845 034 3444
	Kings Chambers, Leeds	0845 034 3444
	Kings Chambers, Manchester	0845 034 3444
Hossain Mr Ajmalul	Selborne Chambers, London	020 7420 9500
	St Philips Chambers, Birmingham	0121 246 7000
Howells Mr Stephen John	Stone Chambers, London	020 7440 6900
Hughes Mr Adrian Warwick	39 Essex Street, London	020 7832 1111
	82 King Street, Manchester	0161 870 9969
Hunt Mr Stephen	4 Stone Buildings, London	020 7242 5524
Irvin Mr Peter	Brick Court Chambers, London	020 7379 3550
Jackson Miss Rosemary Elizabeth	Keating Chambers, London	020 7544 2600
Jafar Mr Abdurahman Akhtar	Chambers of Mr Abdurahman Jafar, Ilford	07828 937338
Jinadu Mr Abdul-Lateef Abodurin Olayinka	Keating Chambers, London	020 7544 2600
Jones Mr Richard Frederick Thomas	Heavenwood Chambers, Stroud	01453 873444
Joseph Mr Charles Henry	Tanfield Chambers, London	020 7421 5300
Joseph Mr Paul Wolfe	No5 Chambers, Birmingham	0845 210 5555
	No5 Chambers, Bristol	0845 210 5555
	No5 Chambers, London	0845 210 5555
Keane Mr Owen Ashley	Design Chambers, London	020 7353 0747
Kennedy Mr Stuart Victor	3 PB Barristers, Bournemouth	01202 292102
	3 PB Barristers, Bristol	0117 928 1520
	3 PB Barristers, London	020 7583 8055
	3 PB Barristers, Oxford	01865 793 736
	3 PB Barristers, Winchester	01962 868884
Kent Mr Michael Harcourt	Crown Office Chambers, London	020 7797 8100
Khan Dr Alexander	Coral House, Manchester	
Khan Mr Arfan	Field Court Chambers, London	020 7405 6114
Khan Mr Zarif	Dyers Chambers, London	020 7404 1881
Kramer Mr Philip Anthony	Park Lane Plowden, Newcastle Upon Tyne	0191 211 4087
Lamont Mr Calum	Keating Chambers, London	020 7544 2600
Leabeater Mr James Ferguson	4 Pump Court, London	020 7842 5555
Lee Miss Krista Chui Lan	Keating Chambers, London	020 7544 2600
Lemon Miss Jane Katherine	Keating Chambers, London	020 7544 2600
Lenon Mr Andrew Ralph Fitzmaurice	One Essex Court, London	020 7583 2000
Lewiecki Miss Marie	Old Bailey Chambers, London	020 3008 6404
Lindsey Ms Susan	Crown Office Chambers, London	020 7797 8100
Lissack Mr Richard Anthony	Outer Temple Chambers, London	020 7353 6381
	Riverview Chambers, London	0844 225 3999
Machell Mr John William	Serle Court, London	020 7242 6105
Maher Ms Martha Johanna Dorothy	St John's Chambers, Bristol	0117 923 4700

Name	Chambers	Telephone
Mainwaring Mr Robert Paul Clason	Portal Chambers, Llandysul	01559 395 292
Marquand Mr Charles Nicholas Hilary	4 Stone Buildings, London	020 7242 5524
Marshall Mr Derek Stanley	College Chambers, Southampton	023 8023 0338
Matthias Mr David Huw	Francis Taylor Building, London	020 7353 8415
Mawrey Mr Richard Brooks	Henderson Chambers, London	020 7583 9020
McCafferty Miss Lynne	4 Pump Court, London	020 7842 5555
McCue Mr Donald	11 Stone Buildings, London	020 7831 6381
Medd Mr James Powys	Crown Office Chambers, London	020 7797 8100
Miller Mr Andrew	2 Temple Gardens, London	020 7822 1200
Morgan Dr Austen Jude	33 Bedford Row, London	020 7242 6476
Mort Mr Justin John Glasbrook	Keating Chambers, London	020 7544 2600
Murray Mr Charles Humphrey Stewart	Rougemont Chambers, Exeter	01392 208484
Mustakim Mr Abdul Yunus Al	Chambers of Mr Mustakim, London	
Newman Mr Paul	3 PB Barristers, Bournemouth	01202 292102
	3 PB Barristers, Bristol	0117 928 1520
	3 PB Barristers, London	020 7583 8055
	3 PB Barristers, Oxford	01865 793 736
	3 PB Barristers, Winchester	01962 868884
Newsom Mr George Lucien	Guildhall Chambers, Bristol	0117 930 9000
Nicholson Mr Jeremy Mark	4 Pump Court, London	020 7842 5555
Nissen Mr Alexander David	Keating Chambers, London	020 7544 2600
Noble Mr Andrew	Enterprise Chambers, Leeds	0113 246 0391
Normington Mr James Adam	Park Court Chambers, Leeds	0113 243 3277
Ojutiku Mrs Fadekemi Omotayo	4 King's Bench Walk, London	020 7822 7000
Okoye Miss Joy Nwamala	Chambers of Joy Okoye, London	07976 426871/020 7405 7011
Oommen Mr Jacob	Chambers of Mr Jacob Oommen, East Barnet	07958 680272
O'Sullivan Mr Richard John	1215 Chambers, London	020 3291 1215
O'Sullivan Mr Thomas Sean Patrick	4 Pump Court, London	020 7842 5555
Otwal Mr Mukhtiar Singh	42 Bedford Row, London	020 7831 0222
Owens Miss Elspeth Eluned	4 Pump Court, London	020 7842 5555
Parry Mr Charles Robert	Pump Court Chambers, London	020 7353 0711
	Pump Court Chambers, Swindon	01793 539899
	Pump Court Chambers, Winchester	01962 868 161
Parsons Mr Andrew James	Portsmouth Barristers'Chambers, Portsmouth	023 9283 1292
Pennicott Mr Ian	Keating Chambers, London	020 7544 2600
Pettican Mr Kevin	11 Stone Buildings, London	020 7831 6381
Platford Mr Graham Roy	Five Paper, London	020 7815 3200
Prior Mr Paul Stephen	36 Bedford Row, London	020 7421 8000
Pugh Mr John Bishop	John Pugh's Chambers, Liverpool	0151 236 5415
Quiney Mr Charles Benedictus Alexander	Crown Office Chambers, London	020 7797 8100
Quirke Mr Gerard Martin	Citadel Chambers, Birmingham	0121 233 8500
Reeds Mr Gareth David	Canary Wharf Chambers, London	020 7183 8011
Reffin Miss Clare Alyson	One Essex Court, London	020 7583 2000
Ridd Mr David Ian Mcgregor	Farrar's Building, London	020 7583 9241
Rifat Mr Maurice Alan	1 Gray's Inn Square, London	020 7405 0001
Rigney Mr Andrew James	Crown Office Chambers, London	020 7797 8100
Rinker Mr Andrew Stuart D'Artois	Chambers of Mr Andrew Rinker, London	020 7584 1091
Rippon Mr Simon John	Citadel Chambers, Birmingham	0121 233 8500
Ritchie Mr Andrew George	The Chambers of Grahame Aldous QC, London	020 7832 0500
Royce Mr Darryl Fraser	Atkin Chambers, London	020 7404 0102
Saini Mr Parminder Paul Singh	12 Old Square Chambers, London	020 7404 0875
Samuel Mr Richard Geoffrey Graham	3 Hare Court, London	020 7415 7800
Scott Holland Mr Gideon Silas	Keating Chambers, London	020 7544 2600
Sears Mr Robert David Murray	Four New Square, London	020 7822 2000
Selby Mr Lawrence Julian Catello	Nine Bedford Row, London	020 7489 2727
Sellers Mr Graham	Atlantic Chambers, Liverpool	0151 236 4421

Name	Chambers	Telephone
Selvaratnam Miss Vasanti Emily Indrani	Stone Chambers, London	020 7440 6900
Shamim Mr Mohammed	Clapham Law Chambers, London	020 7978 8482
Shapiro Mr Daniel Jonathan	Crown Office Chambers, London	020 7797 8100
Shaw Mr Jonathan Paul	No5 Chambers, Birmingham	0845 210 5555
	No5 Chambers, Bristol	0845 210 5555
	No5 Chambers, London	0845 210 5555
	Zenith Chambers, Leeds	0113 245 5438
Shirley Mr James Patrick	Stone Chambers, London	020 7440 6900
Singarajah Mr Frederico	1 Gray's Inn Square, London	020 7405 0001
Singer Mr Andrew Michael	Kings Chambers, Birmingham	0845 034 3444
	Kings Chambers, Leeds	0845 034 3444
	Kings Chambers, Manchester	0845 034 3444
Sjostrand Miss Ekaterina	13 Old Square Chambers, London	020 7831 4445
Sliwinski Mr Robert Andrew	SWL Chambers, Loudwater	01494 616007
Smith Mr Roger Gavin Abbey	1 Hare Court, London	020 7797 7070
Snow Mr Darren Mark	Charter Chambers, London	020 7618 4400
Spalton Mr George David John	Four New Square, London	020 7822 2000
Speaight Mr Anthony Hugh	4 Pump Court, London	020 7842 5555
Staddon Mr Paul	Tanfield Chambers, London	020 7421 5300
Stansfield Mr Piers Alistair	Keating Chambers, London	020 7544 2600
Stead Mr Richard James	St John's Chambers, Bristol	0117 923 4700
Stephens Miss Jessica	Keating Chambers, London	020 7544 2600
Stephens Mr Michael Allen	Design Chambers, London	020 7353 0747
	St Ive's Chambers, Birmingham	0121 236 0863
Stern Mr David Patrick Julian	King's Bench Chambers, Bournemouth	01202 250025
	11 Stone Buildings, London	020 7831 6381
Stewart Mr Nicholas John Cameron	Ely Place Chambers, London	020 7400 9600
Steynor Mr Alan Charles	Keating Chambers, London	020 7544 2600
Taylor Miss Eve Rebecca	St John's Chambers, Bristol	0117 923 4700
Temmink Mr Robert-Jan	Quadrant Chambers, London	020 7583 4444
Terry Mr Robert Jeffrey	Kings Chambers, Birmingham	0845 034 3444
	Kings Chambers, Leeds	0845 034 3444
	Kings Chambers, Manchester	0845 034 3444
	Lamb Chambers, London	020 7797 8300
Thompson Mr Michael James	Keating Chambers, London	020 7544 2600
Topal Mr Erol	Lamb Chambers, London	020 7797 8300
Townend Mr Samuel John	Keating Chambers, London	020 7544 2600
Tozzi Mr Nigel Kenneth	4 Pump Court, London	020 7842 5555
Turner Mr Alan Joseph	Melbeck Chambers, Dudley	020 7404 2166
Twist Mr Stephen John	Dere Street Barristers, Newcastle Upon Tyne	0844 3351551
Vaughan Mr Terence Paul	Fenners Chambers, Cambridge	01223 368761
Vaughan-Williams Mr Arthur Laurence	13 Old Square Chambers, London	020 7831 4445
Von Pommern-Peglow Dr Michael Alfred Herman Pr.	Brunswick Chambers, London	020 7353 1987
Walsh Mr Michael Patrick	Tanfield Chambers, London	020 7421 5300
Warner Mr David Alexander	St Philips Chambers, Birmingham	0121 246 7000
Watson-Gandy Prof Mark	13 Old Square Chambers, London	020 7831 4445
Watthey Mr James Robertson	Hardwicke, London	020 7242 2523
Wilcox Mr Jerome Carl Jean	Alexander Chambers, London	0845 652 0451/0854 652 0451
Williamson Mr Adrian John Gerard Hughes	Keating Chambers, London	020 7544 2600
Wills Miss Alexandra Itari	Christ Church Chambers, London	020 7409 5278/07788 512787
Winser Mr Crispin David Richard	Crown Office Chambers, London	020 7797 8100
Wise Mr Leslie Michael	10 King's Bench Walk, London	020 7353 7742
Wright Mr Alexander Paul	4 Pump Court, London	020 7842 5555
Wright Mr Frederick George Ian	Crown Office Chambers, London	020 7797 8100
Young Mr Lee Terence	Eighteen Carlton Crescent, Southampton	023 8063 9001

ASSET FINANCE

Name	Chambers	Telephone
Ajaz Mr Mohammad Arshad	Eastmans Chambers, Reading	0118 966 9094

C

Arthur Mr Stephen Joseph	Temple Tax Chambers, London	020 7353 7884
Askey Mr Robert John	Palmyra Chambers, Warrington	01925 444919
Beaumont Mr Marc Clifford	9 Stone Buildings, London	020 7404 5055
	Windsor Barristers' Chambers, Windsor	01753 839321
Bell Mr Thomas Capel	Hardwicke, London	020 7242 2523
Berriman Mr Trevor St John	43 Temple Row Chambers, Birmingham	0121 237 6035
Bowling Mr James Stuart	4 Pump Court, London	020 7842 5555
Bryden Mr Christopher James Yuen Kang	4 King's Bench Walk, London	020 7822 7000
Clegg Mr Simon Robert Jonathan	St Philips Chambers, Birmingham	0121 246 7000
Edwards Mr Nigel Royston	St Paul's Chambers, Leeds	0113 245 5866
Edwards Mr Paul	37 Park Square Chambers, Leeds	0113 243 9422
Fawcett Mr Neil	St Ive's Chambers, Birmingham	0121 236 0863
Gibbons Miss Mary Regina	Stone Chambers, London	020 7440 6900
Glasgow Mr Oliver Edwin James	2 Hare Court, London	020 7353 3982
Graham-Wells Miss Alison Christine	Exchange Chambers, Leeds	0113 203 1970
	Exchange Chambers, Liverpool	0151 236 7747
	Exchange Chambers, Manchester	0161 833 2722
Hollis Mrs Kim	25 Bedford Row, London	020 7067 1500
Keel Mr Douglas Vincent	11 Stone Buildings, London	020 7831 6381
Kenny Mr Martin William	Walnut House, Exeter	01392 279751
Mawrey Mr Richard Brooks	Henderson Chambers, London	020 7583 9020
Newbold Dr Anne Lorraine Elsie	Minerva Chambers, Ocean Village	00 350 20042779
O'Brien Mr Nicholas William Wattebot	10 King's Bench Walk, London	020 7353 7742
Owen Mr Timothy Wynn	Matrix Chambers, London	020 7404 3447
Pugh Mr John Bishop	John Pugh's Chambers, Liverpool	0151 236 5415
Reed Mr Julian Winn	9 Park Place, Cardiff	029 2038 2731
Rinker Mr Andrew Stuart D'Artois	Chambers of Mr Andrew Rinker, London	020 7584 1091
Rogers Mr Christopher Thomas	Five Paper, London	020 7815 3200
Sowler Mr Thomas Richard Holland	The Tax Chambers of Mr Richard Sowler TD, Douglas	07624 235000
Wilkinson Mr Marc Ashley	No5 Chambers, Birmingham	0845 210 5555
	No5 Chambers, Bristol	0845 210 5555
	No5 Chambers, London	0845 210 5555
Wills Miss Alexandra Itari	Christ Church Chambers, London	020 7409 5278/07788 512787

AVIATION

Ahmed Mr Ishfaq	Stone Chambers, London	020 7440 6900
Alexandra Miss Sebastiane	Holborn Chambers, London	020 7242 6060
Austins Mr Christopher John	Chambers of Mr Christopher Austins, Bristol	01761 221 208
	Clerksroom (Taunton), Taunton	0845 083 3000
	King's Lynn Chambers, King's Lynn	01553 672 085
Bezzam Miss Jayashree	Hampton Court Chambers, West Molesey	020 8979 0381
Colbey Mr Richard	Guildhall Chambers Portsmouth, Portsmouth	023 9275 2400
	Lamb Chambers, London	020 7797 8300
Dean Mr Paul Benjamin	Crown Office Chambers, London	020 7797 8100
Eaton Mr Tobias Barnaby	Staple Inn Chambers, London	020 7242 5240
Forlin Mr Gerard Emlyn	Cornerstone Barristers, London	020 7242 4986
Freeman Mr Peter Mark	Farrar's Building, London	020 7583 9241
Iyer Miss Shobana	Swan Chambers, Richmond	0845 123 1234
Miller Mr Andrew	2 Temple Gardens, London	020 7822 1200
O'Donoghue Mr Hugh Vincent	Carmelite Chambers, London	020 7936 6300
Ogunbusola Mr Victor Olaniyi	Chambers of Victor Ogumbusola, Basildon	07413 634231
Osborne Mr James Robert	Clerksroom (London), London	0845 083 3000
Perry Mr Christopher Edward	Palmyra Chambers, Warrington	01925 444919
Rahman Mr Anis	12 Old Square Chambers, London	020 7404 0875

Singarajah Mr Frederico	1 Gray's Inn Square, London	020 7405 0001
Snow Mr Darren Mark	Charter Chambers, London	020 7618 4400
Stebbings Mr Ian Anthony	1 Gray's Inn Square, London	020 7405 0001
Steel Mr John Brychan	4-5 Gray's Inn Square, London	020 7404 5252
Temmink Mr Robert-Jan	Quadrant Chambers, London	020 7583 4444
Watthey Mr James Robertson	Hardwicke, London	020 7242 2523

BANKING

Ahmed Mr Ishfaq	Stone Chambers, London	020 7440 6900
Ajaz Mr Mohammad Arshad	Eastmans Chambers, Reading	0118 966 9094
Alexandra Miss Sebastiane	Holborn Chambers, London	020 7242 6060
Aliker Mr Phillip Bliss	Tanfield Chambers, London	020 7421 5300
Antell Mr John Jason	King's Bench and Godolphin (KBG)Chambers, Plymouth	01752 221551
Askey Mr Robert John	Palmyra Chambers, Warrington	01925 444919
Aswani Mr Ravi Girdharilal	Stone Chambers, London	020 7440 6900
Barnard Mr James Philip	11 Stone Buildings, London	020 7831 6381
Beaumont Mr Benjamin	Chambers of Dr Michael Arnheim, London	020 7833 5093
	Middle Temple Lane Chambers, London	020 7583 4352
Beaumont Mr Marc Clifford	9 Stone Buildings, London	020 7404 5055
	Windsor Barristers' Chambers, Windsor	01753 839321
Bell Mr Thomas Capel	Hardwicke, London	020 7242 2523
Benson Mr Imran Michael Jafarey	Hailsham Chambers, London	020 7643 5000
Berkley Mr Michael Stuart	Rougemont Chambers, Exeter	01392 208484
Berry Mr Nicholas Michael	Rougemont Chambers, Exeter	01392 208484
Bishop Mr Malcolm Leslie	Argent Chambers, London	020 7556 5500
	Equity Chambers, Birmingham	0121 236 5007
	30 Park Place, Cardiff	029 2039 8421
Blackwood Mr Clive David	Lamb Chambers, London	020 7797 8300
Blohm Mr Leslie Adrian	St John's Chambers, Bristol	0117 923 4700
Bogle Mr James Stewart Lockhart	10 King's Bench Walk, London	020 7353 7742
Bourne Mr Geoffrey Robert	13 Old Square Chambers, London	020 7831 4445
Bowling Mr James Stuart	4 Pump Court, London	020 7842 5555
Boyd Mr Stephen James Harvey	Selborne Chambers, London	020 7420 9500
Bryden Mr Christopher James Yuen Kang	4 King's Bench Walk, London	020 7822 7000
Budworth Mr Martin James	Kings Chambers, Birmingham	0845 034 3444
	Kings Chambers, Leeds	0845 034 3444
	Kings Chambers, Manchester	0845 034 3444
Bueno Mr Antonio De Padua Jose Maria	Clerksroom (Taunton), Taunton	0845 083 3000
Bullock Mr Robert Gustaf	The Chambers of Mr Bullock, Brighton	01273 321050
Butler Mr Rupert James	3 Hare Court, London	020 7415 7800
Carlisle Mr Timothy St John Ogilvie	Field Court Chambers, London	020 7405 6114
Castle Mr Peter Bolton	13 Old Square Chambers, London	020 7831 4445
Charkham Mr Graham Harold	20 Essex Street, London	020 7842 1200
Chowdhary Mr Islamuddin	Cassian Chambers, Ilford	07796 262641
Christensen Mr Carlton	10 King's Bench Walk, London	020 7353 7742
Clark Miss Geraldine	Serle Court, London	020 7242 6105
Clayton Mr Nigel Garvin	Kings Chambers, Birmingham	0845 034 3444
	Kings Chambers, Leeds	0845 034 3444
	Kings Chambers, Manchester	0845 034 3444
Clegg Mr Simon Robert Jonathan	St Philips Chambers, Birmingham	0121 246 7000
Cohen Mr Edward Mervyn	11 Stone Buildings, London	020 7831 6381
Colbey Mr Richard	Guildhall Chambers Portsmouth, Portsmouth	023 9275 2400
	Lamb Chambers, London	020 7797 8300
Daniels Miss Philippa Catherine	36 Bedford Row, London	020 7421 8000
Devereux-Cooke Mr Richard Charles	13 Old Square Chambers, London	020 7831 4445
Devlin Mr Bernard Joseph	Five St Andrew's Hill, London	020 7332 5400

Name	Chambers	Telephone
Dickinson Mr John Finch Heneage	St John's Chambers, Bristol	0117 923 4700
Eilledge Miss Amanda Gail Caroline	11 Stone Buildings, London	020 7831 6381
Falkowski Mr Damian	4-5 Gray's Inn Square, London	020 7404 5252
Fawcett Mr Neil	St Ive's Chambers, Birmingham	0121 236 0863
Finlay Mr Darren	Sovereign Chambers, Leeds	0113 245 1841
Gee Mr Steven Mark	Stone Chambers, London	020 7440 6900
Gibbons Miss Mary Regina	Stone Chambers, London	020 7440 6900
Godfrey Mr Lauren John	Crown Office Row Chambers, Brighton	01273 625625
Godwin Mr William George Henry	3 Hare Court, London	020 7415 7800
	St John's Chambers, Bristol	0117 923 4700
Gold Mr Richard David	St John's Chambers, Bristol	0117 923 4700
Goodison Mr Adam Henry	South Square, London	020 7696 9900
Gun Cuninghame Mr Julian Arthur	Gough Square Chambers, London	020 7353 0924
Gupta Mr Amit	St Philips Chambers, Birmingham	0121 246 7000
Hall Mr James Edward	Cornwall Street Chambers, Birmingham	0121 233 7500
Hayes Mr Richard James	Lamb Chambers, London	020 7797 8300
Henderson Mr Neil John	Stone Chambers, London	020 7440 6900
Higginson Mr Timothy Nicholas Bennett	Littleton Chambers, London	020 7797 8600
	St John's Chambers, Bristol	0117 923 4700
Hill Mr Michael Gordon	Trinity Chambers, Middlesbrough	01642 247569
	Trinity Chambers, Newcastle Upon Tyne	0191 232 1927
Hirst Mr William Timothy John	Park Lane Plowden, Leeds	0113 228 5049
Horne Mr Charles Hugh Wilson	Kings Chambers, Birmingham	0845 034 3444
	Kings Chambers, Leeds	0845 034 3444
	Kings Chambers, Manchester	0845 034 3444
Hossain Mr Ajmalul	Selborne Chambers, London	020 7420 9500
	St Philips Chambers, Birmingham	0121 246 7000
Hurst Mr Brian	39 Park Square, Leeds	0113 245 6633
Iqbal Mr Mashood	London View Chambers, Sawbridgeworth	07788 912493
Irvin Mr Peter	Brick Court Chambers, London	020 7379 3550
Jarman Mr Samuel James Guthrie	4 KBW, London	020 7822 8822
	Lombard Chambers, London	020 7107 2100
Jayakrishnan Mr Harry Sisubalan	Trent Chambers, Nottingham	0115 941 9596
Jones Mr Geraint Anthony	New Walk Chambers, Leicester	0871 200 1298/0116 255 9144
	9 St John Street, Manchester	0161 955 9000
	Tanfield Chambers, London	020 7421 5300
Jones Mr Lawrence Victor	Chambers of Lawrence Jones, London	020 7831 1444
Kelly Mr Sean	Chancery House Chambers, Leeds	0113 244 6691
Lennard Mr Stephen Charles	Hardwicke, London	020 7242 2523
Lenon Mr Andrew Ralph Fitzmaurice	One Essex Court, London	020 7583 2000
Levy Mr Neil Howard	Guildhall Chambers, Bristol	0117 930 9000
	Guildhall Chambers, Bristol	0117 930 9000
Lowe Mr Mungo James	13 Old Square Chambers, London	020 7831 4445
MacKenzie Smith Mrs Catherine Joanna	10 King's Bench Walk, London	020 7353 7742
MacKenzie Mr Robert Sutherland	Middle Temple Lane Chambers, London	020 7583 4352
Macpherson Mr Duncan Charles Stewart	One Essex Court, London	020 7936 3030
Maguire Mr Andrew James	Exchange Chambers, Liverpool	0151 236 7747
	Exchange Chambers, Manchester	0161 833 2722
	St Philips Chambers, Birmingham	0121 246 7000
Mann Mr Christopher	13 KBW, Oxford	01865 311066
	13 King's Bench Walk, London	020 7353 7204
Matthias Mr David Huw	Francis Taylor Building, London	020 7353 8415
Mawrey Mr Richard Brooks	Henderson Chambers, London	020 7583 9020
McCue Mr Donald	11 Stone Buildings, London	020 7831 6381
McDonnell Mr John Beresford William	13 Old Square Chambers, London	020 7831 4445
McLinden Mr John Vincent Barry	Field Court Chambers, London	020 7405 6114

C

McNicholas Mr Christopher John	Goresbrook Chambers, Milton Keynes	0845 123 1234
Medcroft Mr Nicholas Julian	Outer Temple Chambers, London	020 7353 6381
Miller Mr Andrew	2 Temple Gardens, London	020 7822 1200
Mills Mr Simon Thomas	Five Paper, London	020 7815 3200
Morgan Dr Austen Jude	33 Bedford Row, London	020 7242 6476
Munro Mr Joshua Neil	Hailsham Chambers, London	020 7643 5000
Newbold Dr Anne Lorraine Elsie	Minerva Chambers, Ocean Village	00 350 20042779
Nolten Miss Sonia Jayne	2 Temple Gardens, London	020 7822 1200
Ogunbusola Mr Victor Olaniyi	Chambers of Victor Ogumbusola, Basildon	07413 634231
Ohrenstein Mr Dov	Radcliffe Chambers, London	020 7831 0081
Oliver Dr Peter James Robert	4 Pump Court, London	020 7842 5555
Onipede Dr Victor Olusegun	Chambers of Dr V O Onipede, London	07956 207159
Padfield Mr Nicholas David	Chambers of Nicholas Padfield QC, London	020 7351 1961
Payton Mr Clifford Coningsby	Alpha Court Chambers, Leamington Spa	01926 886412
Pettican Mr Kevin	11 Stone Buildings, London	020 7831 6381
Philpott Mr Anthony Luke	12 Old Square Chambers, London	020 7404 0875
Polli Mr Timothy James	Tanfield Chambers, London	020 7421 5300
Pugh Mr John Bishop	John Pugh's Chambers, Liverpool	0151 236 5415
Purves Mr Gavin Bowman	Swan House, London	020 8998 3035
Record Mrs Celia Saint Claire	Chambers of Lawrence Jones, London	020 7831 1444
Reffin Miss Clare Alyson	One Essex Court, London	020 7583 2000
Richman Mrs Helene Pines	Eighteen Carlton Crescent, Southampton	023 8063 9001
	9 Stone Buildings, London	020 7404 5055
	Stour Chambers, Canterbury	01227 764899
Ridd Mr David Ian Mcgregor	Farrar's Building, London	020 7583 9241
Rinker Mr Andrew Stuart D'Artois	Chambers of Mr Andrew Rinker, London	020 7584 1091
Rogers Mr Christopher Thomas	Five Paper, London	020 7815 3200
Rogers Mr Ian Paul	Monckton Chambers, London	020 7405 7211
Sellers Mr Graham	Atlantic Chambers, Liverpool	0151 236 4421
Selvaratnam Miss Vasanti Emily Indrani	Stone Chambers, London	020 7440 6900
Shirley Mr James Patrick	Stone Chambers, London	020 7440 6900
Sisley Mr Timothy Julian Crispin	9 Stone Buildings, London	020 7404 5055
Sjostrand Miss Ekaterina	13 Old Square Chambers, London	020 7831 4445
Sowler Mr Thomas Richard Holland	The Tax Chambers of Mr Richard Sowler TD, Douglas	07624 235000
Spalton Mr George David John	Four New Square, London	020 7822 2000
Staddon Mr Paul	Tanfield Chambers, London	020 7421 5300
Tabari Mr Ali-Reza	St Philips Chambers, Birmingham	0121 246 7000
Temmink Mr Robert-Jan	Quadrant Chambers, London	020 7583 4444
Temple Ms Eleanor Louise	Kings Chambers, Birmingham	0845 034 3444
	Kings Chambers, Leeds	0845 034 3444
	Kings Chambers, Manchester	0845 034 3444
Terry Mr Robert Jeffrey	Kings Chambers, Birmingham	0845 034 3444
	Kings Chambers, Leeds	0845 034 3444
	Kings Chambers, Manchester	0845 034 3444
	Lamb Chambers, London	020 7797 8300
Thornley Miss Hannah Elise	South Square, London	020 7696 9900
Thrower Mr James Simeon	Chambers of Simeon Thrower, London	020 8878 7374
Todd Mr Michael Alan	Erskine Chambers, London	020 7242 5532
Tozzi Mr Nigel Kenneth	4 Pump Court, London	020 7842 5555
Trompeter Mr Nicholas Simeon	Selborne Chambers, London	020 7420 9500
Van Tonder Mr Gerard Dirk	New Square Chambers, London	020 7419 8000
Vaughan-Williams Mr Arthur Laurence	13 Old Square Chambers, London	020 7831 4445
Vernon Mr Elliot Curt	No. 3 Fleet Street Chambers, London	020 7936 4474
Von Pommern-Peglow Dr Michael Alfred Herman Pr.	Brunswick Chambers, London	020 7353 1987
Waters Mr Malcolm Ian	Radcliffe Chambers, London	020 7831 0081

Watson-Gandy Prof Mark	13 Old Square Chambers, London	020 7831 4445
Watthey Mr James Robertson	Hardwicke, London	020 7242 2523
Wheatley Mr Geraint Rhys	Kings Chambers, Birmingham	0845 034 3444
	Kings Chambers, Leeds	0845 034 3444
	Kings Chambers, Manchester	0845 034 3444
Wiktorowski-Solecki Miss Tamara	Middle Temple Lane Chambers, London	020 7583 4352
Wilkinson Mr Marc Ashley	No5 Chambers, Birmingham	0845 210 5555
	No5 Chambers, Bristol	0845 210 5555
	No5 Chambers, London	0845 210 5555
Wills Miss Alexandra Itari	Christ Church Chambers, London	020 7409 5278/07788 512787
Wolman Mr Clive Richard	11 Stone Buildings, London	020 7831 6381
Yell Mr Nicholas Anthony	1 Chancery Lane, London	0845 634 6666

BANKRUPTCY

Ajaz Mr Mohammad Arshad	Eastmans Chambers, Reading	0118 966 9094
Allison Mr Simon Robert	Hardwicke, London	020 7242 2523
Ascroft Mr Richard Geoffrey	Guildhall Chambers, Bristol	0117 930 9000
Askey Mr Robert John	Palmyra Chambers, Warrington	01925 444919
Aswani Mr Ravi Girdharilal	Stone Chambers, London	020 7440 6900
Atkin Mrs Clare Catherine	Erimus Chambers, Bedford	01234 720952
Austin Mr Ian	Holborn Chambers, London	020 7242 6060
Barnard Mr James Philip	11 Stone Buildings, London	020 7831 6381
Beaumont Mr Marc Clifford	9 Stone Buildings, London	020 7404 5055
	Windsor Barristers' Chambers, Windsor	01753 839321
Becker Mr Timothy George Christie	Chambers of Mr Timothy Becker, Liverpool	0151 703 0319
	Clerksroom (London), London	0845 083 3000
Bedloe Mr Giles Robert	Dyers Chambers, London	020 7404 1881
Beloff Mr Rupert Joseph Alexei	No5 Chambers, Birmingham	0845 210 5555
	No5 Chambers, Bristol	0845 210 5555
	No5 Chambers, London	0845 210 5555
Berry Mr Nicholas Michael	Rougemont Chambers, Exeter	01392 208484
Bezzam Miss Jayashree	Hampton Court Chambers, West Molesey	020 8979 0381
Birch Mr Roger Allen	Five St Andrew's Hill, London	020 7332 5400
	Sovereign Chambers, Leeds	0113 245 1841
Blackwood Mr Clive David	Lamb Chambers, London	020 7797 8300
Bleasdale Miss Marie-Claire	Radcliffe Chambers, London	020 7831 0081
Bloomfield Mr Richard William	Chambers of Mr Richard Bloomfield, Whitley Bay	01670 360042
Bogle Mr James Stewart Lockhart	10 King's Bench Walk, London	020 7353 7742
Bowling Mr James Stuart	4 Pump Court, London	020 7842 5555
Boyd Mr Stephen James Harvey	Selborne Chambers, London	020 7420 9500
Bragge Mr Thomas Hereward	Stour Chambers, Canterbury	01227 764899
Bragiel Mr Edward Bronislaw Henryk	Hogarth Chambers, London	020 7404 0404
Brook Mr Paul Antony	Park Lane Plowden, Leeds	0113 228 5049
	Park Lane Plowden, Newcastle Upon Tyne	0191 211 4087
Brown Miss Susan Margaret	One Essex Court, London	020 7936 3030
Bryden Mr Christopher James Yuen Kang	4 King's Bench Walk, London	020 7822 7000
Buchan Miss Caroline Venetia	Chambers of Miss C Buchan, Haywards Heath	01444 482222
Budworth Mr Martin James	Kings Chambers, Birmingham	0845 034 3444
	Kings Chambers, Leeds	0845 034 3444
	Kings Chambers, Manchester	0845 034 3444
Butler Mr Andrew	Tanfield Chambers, London	020 7421 5300
Butler Mr Rupert James	3 Hare Court, London	020 7415 7800
Buttimore Mr Gabriel	13 KBW, Oxford	01865 311066
	13 King's Bench Walk, London	020 7353 7204
Calhaem Mr Simon Malcolm	29 Bedford Row Chambers, London	020 7404 1044

C

Capon Mr Philip Christopher William	East Anglian Chambers, Chelmsford	01473 214481
	East Anglian Chambers, Ipswich	01473 214481
	East Anglian Chambers, Norwich	01473 214481
	St Philips Chambers, Birmingham	0121 246 7000
Carlisle Mr Timothy St John Ogilvie	Field Court Chambers, London	020 7405 6114
Cartwright Mr Ivan Matthew	KCH Garden Square, Nottingham	0115 941 8851
Castle Mr Peter Bolton	13 Old Square Chambers, London	020 7831 4445
Cattermull Miss Emma Jayne	East Anglian Chambers, Chelmsford	01473 214481
	East Anglian Chambers, Ipswich	01473 214481
	East Anglian Chambers, Norwich	01473 214481
Cawsey Mr Barry Donald	Clerksroom (London), London	0845 083 3000
	Clerksroom (Taunton), Taunton	0845 083 3000
Chesner Mr Howard Michael	One Essex Court, London	020 7936 3030
Chowdhary Mr Islamuddin	Cassian Chambers, Ilford	07796 262641
Christensen Mr Carlton	10 King's Bench Walk, London	020 7353 7742
Clark Mr Dingle	Goldsmith Chambers, London	020 7353 6802
Clegg Mr Simon Robert Jonathan	St Philips Chambers, Birmingham	0121 246 7000
Colbey Mr Richard	Guildhall Chambers Portsmouth, Portsmouth	023 9275 2400
	Lamb Chambers, London	020 7797 8300
Coster Mr Ronald David	42 Bedford Row, London	020 7831 0222
Daniels Miss Philippa Catherine	36 Bedford Row, London	020 7421 8000
Davey Mr Charles	64 Bridge Street, Manchester	0845 083 3000
	Chambers of Mr C Davey, Bishop's Stortford	01279 506412
	Clerksroom (Taunton), Taunton	0845 083 3000
Davies Mr James Edwin	3 PB Barristers, Bournemouth	01202 292102
	3 PB Barristers, Bristol	0117 928 1520
	3 PB Barristers, London	020 7583 8055
	3 PB Barristers, Oxford	01865 793 736
	3 PB Barristers, Winchester	01962 868884
Degun Mr Jasvir Singh	One Essex Court, London	020 7936 3030
Devereux-Cooke Mr Richard Charles	13 Old Square Chambers, London	020 7831 4445
Edwards Mr Nigel Royston	St Paul's Chambers, Leeds	0113 245 5866
Egleton Mr Richard Wildman	Pallant Chambers, Chichester	01243 784538
Esprit Mr Benoit	Barristers Chambers, London	020 3417 6461
	Legis Chambers, Aylesbury	01296 431125
Falkowski Mr Damian	4-5 Gray's Inn Square, London	020 7404 5252
Finlay Mr Darren	Sovereign Chambers, Leeds	0113 245 1841
Fisher Mr David	New Square Chambers, London	020 7419 8000
Fowles Mr Jonathan James	Serle Court, London	020 7242 6105
French Mr Paul Beckinton	Guildhall Chambers, Bristol	0117 930 9000
Gainer Mr Richard St Clair	St Margaret's Chambers, Twickenham	020 8241 3516
Gair Mr Christopher	King's Bench Chambers, Bournemouth	01202 250025
Galway-Cooper Dr Philip Anthony	Five St Andrew's Hill, London	020 7332 5400
Garvie Mr Carl Peter	St Philips Chambers, Birmingham	0121 246 7000
Gelbart Mr Geoff Alan	1 Gray's Inn Square, London	020 7405 0001
Gibbons Miss Mary Regina	Stone Chambers, London	020 7440 6900
Glover Mr Marc Philip	Tanfield Chambers, London	020 7421 5300
Godfrey Mr Lauren John	Crown Office Row Chambers, Brighton	01273 625625
Gold Mr Richard David	St John's Chambers, Bristol	0117 923 4700
Goodfellow Mr Stephen John	East Anglian Chambers, Chelmsford	01473 214481
	East Anglian Chambers, Ipswich	01473 214481
	East Anglian Chambers, Norwich	01473 214481
Goodison Mr Adam Henry	South Square, London	020 7696 9900
Graham Mr Thomas Patrick Henry	New Square Chambers, London	020 7419 8000
Griffiths Mr David	St Philips Chambers, Birmingham	0121 246 7000
Gunstone Mr Robert Giles	KCH Garden Square, Nottingham	0115 941 8851
Gupta Mr Amit	St Philips Chambers, Birmingham	0121 246 7000
Guy Mr Richard Perran	Chambers of Mr Ami Feder, London	020 7797 7788
	King's Bench and Godolphin (KBG)Chambers, Plymouth	01752 221551
	Southernhay Chambers, Exeter	01392 255777
Hallett Miss Katherine Elizabeth	13 Old Square Chambers, London	020 7831 4445

Hammond Mr Tim Mark	Tanfield Chambers, London	020 7421 5300
Harris Mr David Robert	St Albans Chambers, St Albans	01727 843383
Harris Mr Melvyn	5 Essex Court, London	020 7410 2000
Hartman Mr Michael	One Essex Court, London	020 7936 3030
Henderson Mr Neil John	Stone Chambers, London	020 7440 6900
Hendron Mr Henry Joseph Christopher	Strand Chambers, London	020 7117 6920
Hicks Mr Edward Gordon David	Radcliffe Chambers, London	020 7831 0081
Hill Mr Michael Gordon	Trinity Chambers, Middlesbrough	01642 247569
	Trinity Chambers, Newcastle Upon Tyne	0191 232 1927
Hodgkiss Ms Suzanne Jane	43 Temple Row Chambers, Birmingham	0121 237 6035
Holmes-Milner Mr James Neil	The Chambers of Grahame Aldous QC, London	020 7832 0500
Hood Mr Nigel Anthony	New Square Chambers, London	020 7419 8000
Hornett Mr Stuart Ian	Selborne Chambers, London	020 7420 9500
Horton Mr Michael John Edward	Coram Chambers, London	020 7092 3700
Hubbard Mr Mark Iain	New Square Chambers, London	020 7419 8000
Huggins Mr Toby James	Unity Street Chambers, Bristol	0117 906 9789
Hunt Mr Stephen	4 Stone Buildings, London	020 7242 5524
Hussain Mr Muhammad Altaf	Chambers of Mr M A Hussain, London	020 8679 2398
Jones Mr Lawrence Victor	Chambers of Lawrence Jones, London	020 7831 1444
Jones Mr Rhys Charles Mansel	14 Gray's Inn Square, London	020 7242 0858
Jones Ms Cheryl Stephanie	No5 Chambers, Birmingham	0845 210 5555
	No5 Chambers, Bristol	0845 210 5555
	No5 Chambers, London	0845 210 5555
Joseph Dr Sandradee Theresa	13 Old Square Chambers, London	020 7831 4445
Joseph Mr Paul Wolfe	No5 Chambers, Birmingham	0845 210 5555
	No5 Chambers, Bristol	0845 210 5555
	No5 Chambers, London	0845 210 5555
Keel Mr Douglas Vincent	11 Stone Buildings, London	020 7831 6381
Kelly Mr Sean	Chancery House Chambers, Leeds	0113 244 6691
Khan Dr Alexander	Coral House, Manchester	
Kidd Mr Peter William	Number 7 Harrington Street Chambers, Liverpool	0151 242 0707
Kirk Mr Graeme Charles	One Essex Court, London	020 7936 3030
Knight Mr Keith Leslie Francis	4 King's Bench Walk, London	020 7822 7000
Kramer Mr Philip Anthony	Park Lane Plowden, Newcastle Upon Tyne	0191 211 4087
Kynoch Mr Duncan Stuart Sanderson	Selborne Chambers, London	020 7420 9500
Lane Mr Christopher Paul	No 8 Chambers, Birmingham	0121 236 5514
Lane Mr Simon Charles	Rougemont Chambers, Exeter	01392 208484
Learmonth Mr Alexander Robert Magnus	New Square Chambers, London	020 7419 8000
Leonard Mr Charles Robert Weston	Hardwicke, London	020 7242 2523
Lewiecki Miss Marie	Old Bailey Chambers, London	020 3008 6404
Lewis Mr Wayne Anthony	Access Lawyers, London	020 8801 2345
Lo Mr Bernard Norman	Field Court Chambers, London	020 7405 6114
Lowe Mr Mungo James	13 Old Square Chambers, London	020 7831 4445
Lyon Mrs Shane Valerie	King's Bench and Godolphin (KBG)Chambers, Plymouth	01752 221551
MacEvilly Mr Conn Jeremy	9 Stone Buildings, London	020 7404 5055
MacKenzie Smith Mrs Catherine Joanna	10 King's Bench Walk, London	020 7353 7742
MacKenzie Mr Robert Sutherland	Middle Temple Lane Chambers, London	020 7583 4352
Macpherson Mr Duncan Charles Stewart	One Essex Court, London	020 7936 3030
Maher Ms Martha Johanna Dorothy	St John's Chambers, Bristol	0117 923 4700
Mann Mr Christopher	13 KBW, Oxford	01865 311066
	13 King's Bench Walk, London	020 7353 7204

Marshall Mr Derek Stanley	College Chambers, Southampton	023 8023 0338
Matthias Mr David Huw	Francis Taylor Building, London	020 7353 8415
McDonnell Mr John Beresford William	13 Old Square Chambers, London	020 7831 4445
McLinden Mr John Vincent Barry	Field Court Chambers, London	020 7405 6114
McNae Mr Jonathan James	Selborne Chambers, London	020 7420 9500
Mendes Da Costa Mr David	Chambers of Mr D Mendes Da Costa, London	020 8747 4633
	MK Family Law Chambers, Milton Keynes	0845 123 1234
	No. 3 Fleet Street Chambers, London	020 7936 4474
Metzger Mr Kevin Albert	11 Gray's Inn Square Chambers, London	020 7405 6879
Michael Mr Nicholas	East Anglian Chambers, Chelmsford	01473 214481
	East Anglian Chambers, Colchester	01473 214481
	East Anglian Chambers, Ipswich	01473 214481
	East Anglian Chambers, Norwich	01473 214481
Mills Mr Kristian Anthony	Trinity Chambers, Middlesbrough	01642 247569
	Trinity Chambers, Newcastle Upon Tyne	0191 232 1927
Mullen Mr Mark Robert	Radcliffe Chambers, London	020 7831 0081
Murphy Mr Damian	Enterprise Chambers, Leeds	0113 246 0391
	Enterprise Chambers, London	020 7405 9471
	Enterprise Chambers, Newcastle Upon Tyne	0191 222 3344
Newman Mrs Veronica	Chambers of Mrs V Newman, Cardiff	029 2048 8797
Nicholls Mr David James	11 Stone Buildings, London	020 7831 6381
Nickless Mr Jason Alan	College Chambers, Southampton	023 8023 0338
O'Brien Mr Nicholas William Wattebot	10 King's Bench Walk, London	020 7353 7742
O'Donoghue Mr Hugh Vincent	Carmelite Chambers, London	020 7936 6300
Ohrenstein Mr Dov	Radcliffe Chambers, London	020 7831 0081
Oliver Dr Peter James Robert	4 Pump Court, London	020 7842 5555
O'Mahony Mr Jonathan Solomon	9 Stone Buildings, London	020 7404 5055
Oommen Mr Jacob	Chambers of Mr Jacob Oommen, East Barnet	07958 680272
Osborne Mr James Robert	Clerksroom (London), London	0845 083 3000
O'Sullivan Mr Richard John	1215 Chambers, London	020 3291 1215
Parker Miss Wendy	Hardwicke, London	020 7242 2523
Pascoe Ms Soraya	1 Gray's Inn Square, London	020 7405 0001
Pennington-Legh Mr Jonathan Piers	Field Court Chambers, London	020 7405 6114
Preston Mr Nicholas John Holman	Clerksroom (Taunton), Taunton	0845 083 3000
Puar Mr Mikhael	30 Park Place, Cardiff	029 2039 8421
Quirke Mr Gerard Martin	Citadel Chambers, Birmingham	0121 233 8500
Rainey Mr Philip Carslake	Tanfield Chambers, London	020 7421 5300
Rana Mr Mohammed Akram	Clapham Law Chambers, London	020 7978 8482
Record Mrs Celia Saint Claire	Chambers of Lawrence Jones, London	020 7831 1444
Reed Mr Simon John	New Walk Chambers, Leicester	0871 200 1298/0116 255 9144
Rifat Mr Maurice Alan	1 Gray's Inn Square, London	020 7405 0001
Ritchie Mr Richard Bulkeley	XXIV Old Buildings, London	020 7691 2424
Rivalland Mr Marc-Edouard	1 Chancery Lane, London	0845 634 6666
Roberts Mr Michael Charles	Chambers of Michael Roberts, Henley-On-Thames	01844 355 655
Roberts Mr Richard Vaughan	Henderson Chambers, London	020 7583 9020
Rogers Mr Christopher Thomas	Five Paper, London	020 7815 3200
Rowntree Mr Edward John Pickering	Hardwicke, London	020 7242 2523
Russell Mr Thomas Charles Welldon	KCH Garden Square, Nottingham	0115 941 8851
Sandham Mr James Andrew	Arden Chambers, London	020 7242 4244
Seal Mr Julius Damien	Chambers of Mr Julius Seal, London	020 7328 0158
Sefton-Smith Mr Lloyd	Lamb Chambers, London	020 7797 8300
Sellers Mr Graham	Atlantic Chambers, Liverpool	0151 236 4421
Sinclair Miss Lisa Anne	Chambers of Miss Lisa Sinclair, London	020 8946 7201
Singarajah Mr Frederico	1 Gray's Inn Square, London	020 7405 0001

Name	Chambers	Telephone
Sisley Mr Timothy Julian Crispin	9 Stone Buildings, London	020 7404 5055
Sjostrand Miss Ekaterina	13 Old Square Chambers, London	020 7831 4445
Skinner Mr Samuel Richard Edward	KCH Garden Square, Nottingham	0115 941 8851
Smith Mr Robert Clive	1 Paper Buildings, London	020 7353 3728
	RCS Chambers, Stainton	01709 814 147
Stenhouse Mr John Alexander	Nightingale Chambers, Wolverley	01562 851350
Sterling Mr Robert Alan	St James's Chambers, Manchester	0161 834 7000
	Zenith Chambers, Leeds	0113 245 5438
Stirling Mr Christopher William	Field Court Chambers, London	020 7405 6114
Stubbs Mr Richard John Morris	Trinity Chambers, Middlesbrough	01642 247569
	Trinity Chambers, Newcastle Upon Tyne	0191 232 1927
Swirsky Mr Adam Abraham Burl Bradbury	Lamb Chambers, London	020 7797 8300
Syril Mr George Carmel	Luton Chambers, Luton	01582 598394
	Willesden Chambers, London	020 3273 1042
Taylor Miss Araba Arba Kurankyiwa	Fenners Chambers, Cambridge	01223 368761
Taylor Mr Phillip Brian	Richmond Green Chambers, Richmond	020 8948 4801
Temmink Mr Robert-Jan	Quadrant Chambers, London	020 7583 4444
Tempest Mr Alistair Mark	Field Court Chambers, London	020 7405 6114
Temple Ms Eleanor Louise	Kings Chambers, Birmingham	0845 034 3444
	Kings Chambers, Leeds	0845 034 3444
	Kings Chambers, Manchester	0845 034 3444
Terry Mr Robert Jeffrey	Kings Chambers, Birmingham	0845 034 3444
	Kings Chambers, Leeds	0845 034 3444
	Kings Chambers, Manchester	0845 034 3444
	Lamb Chambers, London	020 7797 8300
Thornley Miss Hannah Elise	South Square, London	020 7696 9900
Trompeter Mr Nicholas Simeon	Selborne Chambers, London	020 7420 9500
Turnbull Miss Helen Mary	Lamb Chambers, London	020 7797 8300
Ume Mr Cyril Obiora	12 Old Square Chambers, London	020 7404 0875
Van Tonder Mr Gerard Dirk	New Square Chambers, London	020 7419 8000
Vasilescu Mr Andrei Constantin	Chambers of Martin Burr, London	0845 123 1234
Vaughan-Williams Mr Arthur Laurence	13 Old Square Chambers, London	020 7831 4445
Vernon Mr Elliot Curt	No. 3 Fleet Street Chambers, London	020 7936 4474
Warner Mr David Alexander	St Philips Chambers, Birmingham	0121 246 7000
Watson Mr Alaric	11 Stone Buildings, London	020 7831 6381
Watson Mr Duncan Allen	Westgate Chambers, Lewes	01273 480510
Wheaton Mr Ian Malcolm James	Eighteen Carlton Crescent, Southampton	023 8063 9001
Wiktorowski-Solecki Miss Tamara	Middle Temple Lane Chambers, London	020 7583 4352
Wilkinson Mr Marc Ashley	No5 Chambers, Birmingham	0845 210 5555
	No5 Chambers, Bristol	0845 210 5555
	No5 Chambers, London	0845 210 5555
Williams Miss June Cleo	No 8 Chambers, Birmingham	0121 236 5514
Wills Miss Alexandra Itari	Christ Church Chambers, London	020 7409 5278/07788 512787
Wise Mr Leslie Michael	10 King's Bench Walk, London	020 7353 7742
Wolman Mr Clive Richard	11 Stone Buildings, London	020 7831 6381
Yell Mr Nicholas Anthony	1 Chancery Lane, London	0845 634 6666

CARE PROCEEDINGS

Name	Chambers	Telephone
Adamson Miss Lilias Louisa	Becket Chambers, Canterbury	01227 786331
Adler Mr Jonathan	1 Pump Court, London	020 7842 7070
Ager Mr Richard Lawrence	Crown Office Row Chambers, Brighton	01273 625625
Ahern Mr Eugene Christopher	Trinity Chambers, Chelmsford	01245 605040
Ahmed Miss Amina	Renaissance Chambers, London	020 7404 1111
Ailes Mr John Ashley	Eighteen Carlton Crescent, Southampton	023 8063 9001
Ajaz Mr Mohammad Arshad	Eastmans Chambers, Reading	0118 966 9094
Akman Miss Mercy Louise	36 Bedford Row, London	020 7421 8000
Allen Mr Douglas Stephen	Harcourt Chambers, London	0844 561 7135

Barrister	Chambers	Telephone
Allwood Mrs Gina Louisa	Seven Bedford Row, London	020 7242 3555
Ameen Mr Danish	18 St John Street, Manchester	0161 278 1800
Andrews Miss Melanie Alexandra	Becket Chambers, Canterbury	01227 786331
Armbrister Mr Allan Ramsay	39 Park Square, Leeds	0113 245 6633
Atkinson Mr Jody Roy	St John's Chambers, Bristol	0117 923 4700
Austin Mr Ian	Holborn Chambers, London	020 7242 6060
Bagchi Mr Andrew Kumar	1 Garden Court Family Law Chambers, London	020 7797 7900
Bailey Mr Charles Andrew Stuart	Trinity Chambers, Chelmsford	01245 605040
Bailey Mr Michael Robert	Tanfield Chambers, London	020 7421 5300
Baker Mr Nicholas Michael Bridgman	Hardwicke, London	020 7242 2523
Barnett Miss Adrienne Elise	1 Pump Court, London	020 7842 7070
Barraclough Miss Lisa Ann	Colleton Chambers, Exeter	01392 274898
Barratt Mr Dominic Anthony	East Anglian Chambers, Chelmsford	01473 214481
	East Anglian Chambers, Colchester	01473 214481
	East Anglian Chambers, Ipswich	01473 214481
	East Anglian Chambers, Norwich	01473 214481
Batey Mr David Michael	Stour Chambers, Canterbury	01227 764899
Bennett Miss Angela Michelle	3 Dr Johnson's Buildings, London	020 7353 4854
Bhutta Miss Ayeesha Clare	Field Court Chambers, London	020 7405 6114
Bickler Mr Simon Lloyd	St Paul's Chambers, Leeds	0113 245 5866
Bisarya Mr Neil	Number 7 Harrington Street Chambers, Liverpool	0151 242 0707
Bishop Mr Malcolm Leslie	Argent Chambers, London	020 7556 5500
	Equity Chambers, Birmingham	0121 236 5007
	30 Park Place, Cardiff	029 2039 8421
Blackmore Miss Sarah Elizabeth	37 Park Square Chambers, Leeds	0113 243 9422
Bojarski Mr Andrzej Leonard	36 Bedford Row, London	020 7421 8000
Bowen Mr Nicholas James Hugh	Doughty Street Chambers, Bristol	01179 058 717
	Doughty Street Chambers, London	020 7404 1313
	Doughty Street Chambers, Manchester	0161 618 1066
Bowers Mr Rupert John	Doughty Street Chambers, London	020 7404 1313
Bradley Ms Sally Frances	Sovereign Chambers, Leeds	0113 245 1841
	18 St John Street, Manchester	0161 278 1800
	Trinity Chambers, Middlesbrough	01642 247569
	Trinity Chambers, Newcastle Upon Tyne	0191 232 1927
Bramwell Mr Christopher Paul	Regency Chambers, Cambridge	01223 301517
	Regency Chambers, Peterborough	01733 315215
Breen-Lawton Miss Denise	St Paul's Chambers, Leeds	0113 245 5866
Brereton Miss Joy	4 Paper Buildings, London	020 7427 5200
Briden Ms Sarah Louise	KCH Garden Square, Nottingham	0115 941 8851
Buck Mr John	Tanfield Chambers, London	020 7421 5300
Burdon Mr Michael Stewart	37 Park Square Chambers, Leeds	0113 243 9422
Butler Miss Judith Jane Scott	29 Bedford Row Chambers, London	020 7404 1044
Cabeza Miss Ruth Roberta Elizabeth	Field Court Chambers, London	020 7405 6114
Cade Mrs Diana	Trinity Chambers, Chelmsford	01245 605040
Carron Mr Richard Byron	Queen Square Chambers, Bristol	0117 921 1966
Chadwick Miss Joanna Ceridwen	No5 Chambers, Birmingham	0845 210 5555
	No5 Chambers, Bristol	0845 210 5555
	No5 Chambers, London	0845 210 5555
Chan Miss Rachel Siu Yee	Stour Chambers, Canterbury	01227 764899
Chatterjee Miss Adreeja Julia	No5 Chambers, Birmingham	0845 210 5555
	No5 Chambers, Bristol	0845 210 5555
	No5 Chambers, London	0845 210 5555
Chippeck Mr Stephen	5 King's Bench Walk, London	020 7353 5638
Chippendale Miss Emma Lorraine	37 Park Square Chambers, Leeds	0113 243 9422
Clegg Mr Adam Gordon	Stour Chambers, Canterbury	01227 764899
Cohen Mr Jonathan Lionel	4 Paper Buildings, London	020 7427 5200
Connolly Mrs Barbara Winifred	Seven Bedford Row, London	020 7242 3555
Cotterill Miss Suzannah	Field Court Chambers, London	020 7405 6114
Cox Ms Sita	Stour Chambers, Canterbury	01227 764899
Crossley Ms Joanne	St Paul's Chambers, Leeds	0113 245 5866

Name	Chambers	Telephone
Dassa Miss Regine	9 King's Bench Walk, London	020 7353 9564
Davies Miss Lindsay Jane	Fenners Chambers, Cambridge	01223 368761
Davies Miss Rebecca Lucinda	Westgate Chambers, Lewes	01273 480510
Davies Ms Samantha Teresa	Chambers of Ms Samantha Davies, Milton Keynes	0845 123 1234
	Warwick House Chambers, London	020 7430 2323
De Burgos Mr Jamie Michael Abulafia	36 Bedford Row, London	020 7421 8000
De Zonie Miss Jane	14 Gray's Inn Square, London	020 7242 0858
Dean Mr James Patrick	Goldsmith Chambers, London	020 7353 6802
Dean Mrs Christine Jacqueline	1 Pump Court, London	020 7842 7070
Degun Mr Jasvir Singh	One Essex Court, London	020 7936 3030
Dhadli Mrs Perminder	KCH Garden Square, Nottingham	0115 941 8851
Dhaliwal Miss Davinder Kaur	No 8 Chambers, Birmingham	0121 236 5514
Dodson Miss Joanna	Park Court Chambers, Leeds	0113 243 3277
	Renaissance Chambers, London	020 7404 1111
Dove Mr James Francis	The Chambers of Grahame Aldous QC, London	020 7832 0500
Dowell Mr Gregory Hamilton	Principal Chambers, Sevenoaks	0845 209 8080
Duffy Mr Derek James	St Paul's Chambers, Leeds	0113 245 5866
Dugdale Mr Jeremy Keith	Octagon House, Norwich	01603 623186
Edington Mrs Fiona Anne Rider	Thomas More Chambers, London	020 7404 7000
Edwards Mr Nigel Royston	St Paul's Chambers, Leeds	0113 245 5866
Elcombe Mr Nicholas John	East Anglian Chambers, Chelmsford	01473 214481
	East Anglian Chambers, Colchester	01473 214481
	East Anglian Chambers, Ipswich	01473 214481
	East Anglian Chambers, Norwich	01473 214481
Elliott Mr Edward Anthony John	Garden Court Chambers, London	020 7993 7600
Enright Ms Johanne	Chambers of Ms Johanne Enright, London	020 7287 7557
Ephraim-Adejumo Mrs Hilda Ekpo	12 Old Square Chambers, London	020 7404 0875
Fairbank Mr Nicholas James	4 Paper Buildings, London	020 7427 5200
Fairburn Mr George Edward Henry	Cornwall Street Chambers, Birmingham	0121 233 7500
	Cornwall Street Chambers, Shrewsbury	01743 363 611/0121 233 7500
Fairclough Miss Lucy Helen	Northampton Chambers, Northampton	01604 636271
Fama Mrs Gudrun Hildegard	Middle Temple Lane Chambers, London	020 7583 4352
Ferguson Mr Christopher Mark	Court Yard Chambers, London	020 7936 2710
	Sovereign Chambers, Leeds	0113 245 1841
	Unity Street Chambers, Bristol	0117 906 9789
Flood Mr Edward Albert	1 Garden Court Family Law Chambers, London	020 7797 7900
Forster Ms Sarah Judith	14 Gray's Inn Square, London	020 7242 0858
	Westgate Chambers, Lewes	01273 480510
Fortune Mr Peter Carl Michael	Guildhall Chambers Portsmouth, Portsmouth	023 9275 2400
	4 King's Bench Walk, London	020 7822 7000
Foster Mr Julien Andrew Stewart	1 Garden Court Family Law Chambers, London	020 7797 7900
Francis Mr Richard Maurice	9 Park Place, Cardiff	029 2038 2731
Frank Mr Ivor Richard Bainton	7 Bell Yard, London	020 7831 0636
Fry Mr Neil John	Coram Chambers, London	020 7092 3700
George Miss Susan Deborah	Coram Chambers, London	020 7092 3700
German Miss Kelly Anne	Eastbourne Chambers, Eastbourne	01323 642102
Gilbertson Mrs Helen Alison	Octagon House, Norwich	01603 623186
Gill Miss Baljinder	10 King's Bench Walk, London	020 7353 7742
Gillan Mrs Dominique Lye-Ping	Guildford Chambers, Guildford	01483 539131
Gillman Miss Rachel Mary	1 Garden Court Family Law Chambers, London	020 7797 7900
Giz Miss Alev Ayse	1 Garden Court Family Law Chambers, London	020 7797 7900

Gledhill Mr Lee Andre	Alexander Chambers, London	0845 652 0451/0854 652 0451
	Trident Barristers Chambers, Manchester	0161 663 3123
Gooderham Miss Elizabeth Ann	Northampton Chambers, Northampton	01604 636271
Gore Mr Andrew Julian Mark	37 Park Square Chambers, Leeds	0113 243 9422
Gore Ms Sally Elizabeth	14 Gray's Inn Square, London	020 7242 0858
Grant-Garwood Mr Joshua Dahren	1 Pump Court, London	020 7842 7070
Gray Mr Justin Henry Walford	Trinity Chambers, Middlesbrough	01642 247569
	Trinity Chambers, Newcastle Upon Tyne	0191 232 1927
Greenan Miss Sarah Octavia	Zenith Chambers, Leeds	0113 245 5438
Greenfield Mr Peter Charles	King's Bench Chambers, Bournemouth	01202 250025
Grundy Ms Clare	St Johns Buildings, Manchester	0161 214 1500
	St Johns Buildings Liverpool, Liverpool	0151 243 6000
	16 Winckley Square, Preston	01772 256100
Hall Mr Jeremy John	Becket Chambers, Canterbury	01227 786331
Hancock Ms Maria	Westgate Chambers, Lewes	01273 480510
Harrington Miss Tina Amanda	Trinity Chambers, Chelmsford	01245 605040
Harris Miss Katie Anne	Octagon House, Norwich	01603 623186
Henthorn Miss Kate Marie	7 Bell Yard, London	020 7831 0636
	18 St John Street, Manchester	0161 278 1800
Hepher Mr Paul Arthur Richard	4 Paper Buildings, London	020 7427 5200
Hewitt Miss Alexandra Helen	Linenhall Chambers, Chester	01244 348282
Hillas Miss Samantha	Atlantic Chambers, Liverpool	0151 236 4421
Hillier Mr William	New Street Chambers, Leicester	0116 262 5906
Hine Mr Charles Roderick John	King's Bench Chambers, Bournemouth	01202 250025
Hinton Mr Neil Pearse	King's Bench Chambers, Bournemouth	01202 250025
Holt Mrs Jane Rosemary	KCH Garden Square, Nottingham	0115 941 8851
Hornblower Mrs Sarah Patience	Rougemont Chambers, Exeter	01392 208484
Horton Mr Mark Varney	Colleton Chambers, Exeter	01392 274898
Howard Miss Amanda Jayne	Atlantic Chambers, Liverpool	0151 236 4421
	37 Park Square Chambers, Leeds	0113 243 9422
Howard Mr Steven James	3 PB Barristers, Bournemouth	01202 292102
	3 PB Barristers, London	020 7583 8055
Howe Mr Darren Francis	1 Garden Court Family Law Chambers, London	020 7797 7900
Howling Mr Rex Andrew	4 Paper Buildings, London	020 7427 5200
Hughes Dr Constance Mary	1 Pump Court, London	020 7842 7070
Hughes Mrs Kathryn Sally	Chavasse Court Chambers, Liverpool	0151 229 2030
Hunt Miss Alison Lorna	Regency Chambers, Cambridge	01223 301517
	Regency Chambers, Peterborough	01733 315215
Hussain Mr Muhammad Altaf	Chambers of Mr M A Hussain, London	020 8679 2398
Irving Miss Gillian	Linenhall Chambers, Chester	01244 348282
	9 St John Street, Manchester	0161 955 9000
	15 Winckley Square, Preston	01772 252828
Jacques Mr Gareth Edward	Regency Chambers, Peterborough	01733 315215
Japheth Miss Bethan	Linenhall Chambers, Chester	01244 348282
Jarman Mr Mark Christopher	4 Paper Buildings, London	020 7427 5200
Johnson Miss Melanie Jane	1 Pump Court, London	020 7842 7070
Johnson Mrs Carolyn Ann	Cobden House Chambers, Manchester	0161 833 6000
Jones Mr Rhys Charles Mansel	14 Gray's Inn Square, London	020 7242 0858
Josty Mr David Stephen	College Chambers, Southampton	023 8023 0338
Kabweru-Namulemu Miss Karen Hasasha	KCH Garden Square, Nottingham	0115 941 8851
Kenny Mr Martin William	Walnut House, Exeter	01392 279751
Ker-Reid Mr John	Pump Court Chambers, London	020 7353 0711
	Pump Court Chambers, Swindon	01793 539899
	Pump Court Chambers, Winchester	01962 868 161
Khan Mr Ayoub	Chambers of Mr Ayoub Khan, Birmingham	07930 987202
Kilvington Miss Sarah Elizabeth	18 St John Street, Manchester	0161 278 1800
King Miss Samantha Leonie	4 Paper Buildings, London	020 7427 5200

Kirby Miss Ruth Mary Anthony	4 Paper Buildings, London	020 7427 5200
Larizadeh Mr Cyrus Rais	4 Paper Buildings, London	020 7427 5200
Lau Miss Vanessa Hoi Chun	18 St John Street, Manchester	0161 278 1800
Le Fort Mr Michael Cameron Raoul	King's Bench Chambers, Bournemouth	01202 250025
Lee Miss Taryn Jane	37 Park Square Chambers, Leeds	0113 243 9422
Lee Mr Rosslyn Alexander	Dere Street Barristers, York	0844 3351551
	York Chambers, Newcastle Upon Tyne	0191 206 4677
Lenaghan Mr Anthony	Dyers Chambers, London	020 7404 1881
Lewis Mr Stuart John	New Walk Chambers, Leicester	0871 200 1298/0116 255 9144
Limbrey Mr Bernard Martin	3 Dr Johnson's Buildings, London	020 7353 4854
Littlewood Miss Rebecca Mae	1 Pump Court, London	020 7842 7070
Loeb Miss Dinah Yolande	Westgate Chambers, Lewes	01273 480510
Logan Miss Maura	St John's House Chambers, Altrincham	0161 980 7379
Lopez Mr Paul Anthony	St Ive's Chambers, Birmingham	0121 236 0863
Lorenzo Ms Claudia	Pump Court Chambers, London	020 7353 0711
	Pump Court Chambers, Swindon	01793 539899
	Pump Court Chambers, Winchester	01962 868 161
Love Miss Sharon Ann	Garden Court Chambers, London	020 7993 7600
Lugsdin Mr Martin	Kenworthy's Chambers, Manchester	0161 832 4036
MacKenzie Miss Julie Fiona	Pump Court Chambers, London	020 7353 0711
	Pump Court Chambers, Swindon	01793 539899
	Pump Court Chambers, Winchester	01962 868 161
Mackley Mr David John	18 St John Street, Manchester	0161 278 1800
Maddison Mr David Thomas James	Cobden House Chambers, Manchester	0161 833 6000
Magee Miss Rosein Moira	Pallant Chambers, Chichester	01243 784538
Mahmood Mr Abid	Central Chambers, Manchester	0161 236 1133
	No5 Chambers, Birmingham	0845 210 5555
	No5 Chambers, Bristol	0845 210 5555
	No5 Chambers, London	0845 210 5555
Malone Mr David John	1 Gray's Inn Square, London	020 7405 0001
Marks Miss Gillian	14 Gray's Inn Square, London	020 7242 0858
Martignetti Mr Ian	Regency Chambers, Cambridge	01223 301517
	Regency Chambers, Peterborough	01733 315215
Martin Mrs Dianne Joan Abegail	St John's Chambers, Bristol	0117 923 4700
Mather Miss Kate	1 Garden Court Family Law Chambers, London	020 7797 7900
Maynard Mr Matthew David	St Ive's Chambers, Birmingham	0121 236 0863
McCann Miss Katie	Atlantic Chambers, Liverpool	0151 236 4421
McCormack Mr Alan	Staple Inn Chambers, London	020 7242 5240
McCullough Miss Louise Clare	Chambers of Mr Ami Feder, London	020 7797 7788
	Chambers of Mr Ami Feder, London	020 7797 7788
	Lamb Building, Brighton	01273 820490
McMillan Mrs Carol Ann	Westgate Chambers, Lewes	01273 480510
McMullan Ms Laura Christina	Coram Chambers, London	020 7092 3700
Meachin Miss Vanessa Veronica	St Philips Chambers, Birmingham	0121 246 7000
Meichen Mr Jonathan Brian	St Philips Chambers, Birmingham	0121 246 7000
Miller Miss Catherine	East Anglian Chambers, Chelmsford	01473 214481
	East Anglian Chambers, Ipswich	01473 214481
	East Anglian Chambers, Norwich	01473 214481
Mills Miss Barbara	4 Paper Buildings, London	020 7427 5200
Milne Mrs Arlene Joan	Cobden House Chambers, Manchester	0161 833 6000
Mitropoulos Mr Christos	5 Pump Court, London	020 7353 2532
Moore Mr Jonathan Guy	Cathedral Chambers, Cardiff	02920 660129
	Cathedral Chambers, Newport	01633 215112
Moore Mrs Therese Finola	4 Brick Court, London	020 7832 3200
Moran Mr Christopher John	39 Park Square, Leeds	0113 245 6633
Morgan Mr Colin Thomas Patrick	Pallant Chambers, Chichester	01243 784538
Murkin Mrs Sandria	Becket Chambers, Canterbury	01227 786331
Mustakim Mr Abdul Yunus Al	Chambers of Mr Mustakim, London	
Mylvaganam Ms Tanoo	1 Gray's Inn Square, London	020 7405 0001
Newport Mr Ian Alun	College Chambers, Southampton	023 8023 0338
Noble Mr Philip Robert	Thomas More Chambers, London	020 7404 7000
Norton Mr Andrew David	1 Garden Court Family Law Chambers, London	020 7797 7900

C

Barrister	Chambers	Telephone
O'Brien Mr David	Trinity Chambers, Chelmsford	01245 605040
Ojutiku Mrs Fadekemi Omotayo	4 King's Bench Walk, London	020 7822 7000
Okoye Miss Joy Nwamala	Chambers of Joy Okoye, London	07976 426871/020 7405 7011
Oldham Mrs Frances Mary Theresa	36 Bedford Row, London	020 7421 8000
	37 Park Square Chambers, Leeds	0113 243 9422
O'Leary Ms Michele Ann	1 Pump Court, London	020 7842 7070
Ong Miss Grace Yu Mae	Argent Chambers, London	020 7556 5500
Papazian Miss Cliona Concepta	4 Paper Buildings, London	020 7427 5200
Parnell Mrs Cherie Eileen	East Anglian Chambers, Colchester	01473 214481
	East Anglian Chambers, Ipswich	01473 214481
	East Anglian Chambers, Norwich	01473 214481
Pascoe Ms Soraya	1 Gray's Inn Square, London	020 7405 0001
Peacock Miss Lisa Jayne	3 Dr Johnson's Buildings, London	020 7353 4854
Pearman Mr Lee Charles	4 Brick Court, London	020 7832 3200
Pears Mr Derrick Allan	Tanfield Chambers, London	020 7421 5300
Peddie Mr Ian James Crofton	Garden Court Chambers, London	020 7993 7600
	St Johns Buildings Liverpool, Liverpool	0151 243 6000
	Westgate Chambers, Lewes	01273 480510
Persaud Dr Marcia Chitroutie	1 Gray's Inn Square, London	020 7405 0001
Pettitt Mr Robert	Northampton Chambers, Northampton	01604 636271
Pickering Mr Simon Toby	Wilberforce Chambers, Hull	01482 323264
Preston Miss Kim Deborah	4 King's Bench Walk, London	020 7822 7000
Pritchard Mrs Teresa Julia	5 Pump Court, London	020 7353 2532
Pye Miss Margaret Jayne	Zenith Chambers, Leeds	0113 245 5438
Quirke Mr Gerard Martin	Citadel Chambers, Birmingham	0121 233 8500
Ramdas-Harsia Mr Rohan Mukesh	1 Pump Court, London	020 7842 7070
Reed Mr Julian Winn	9 Park Place, Cardiff	029 2038 2731
Reed Ms Lucy Emma	St John's Chambers, Bristol	0117 923 4700
Reynolds Mr John Adam	King's Bench Chambers, Bournemouth	01202 250025
Rhodes Miss Amanda Louise	Unity Street Chambers, Bristol	0117 906 9789
Rippon Mr Simon John	Citadel Chambers, Birmingham	0121 233 8500
Rosenblatt Mr Jeremy George	42 Bedford Row, London	020 7831 0222
Roy Mr Stefan Alexander Hiren	5 Pump Court, London	020 7353 2532
Rudd Miss Zoe Ann	College Chambers, Southampton	023 8023 0338
Sandford Mr Simon John Austin	5 King's Bench Walk, London	020 7353 5638
Sapstead Miss Louise Anne	KCH Garden Square, Nottingham	0115 941 8851
Savvides Miss Maria	Northampton Chambers, Northampton	01604 636271
Sayed Miss Ruby	1 Pump Court, London	020 7842 7070
Scott Ms Laura Louise	14 Gray's Inn Square, London	020 7242 0858
Seal Mr Julius Damien	Chambers of Mr Julius Seal, London	020 7328 0158
Sefton Mr Nicholas Edward	Linenhall Chambers, Chester	01244 348282
	Pendragon Chambers, Swansea	01792 411188
Self Mr Gary Peter	College Chambers, Southampton	023 8023 0338
	St David's Chambers, Swansea	01792 559924
Shaw Mr Julian	St Johns Buildings, Chester	01244 323070
	St Johns Buildings, Manchester	0161 214 1500
	St Johns Buildings Liverpool, Liverpool	0151 243 6000
Shield Miss Deborah	42 Bedford Row, London	020 7831 0222
Short Ms Mandy Lisa	14 Gray's Inn Square, London	020 7242 0858
Shuttleworth Mr Timothy William	Tanfield Chambers, London	020 7421 5300
Silverton Miss Catherine Anne	Sovereign Chambers, Leeds	0113 245 1841
Sleight Mr Nigel	Regency Chambers, Cambridge	01223 301517
	Regency Chambers, Peterborough	01733 315215
Small Mrs Arlene Annmarie	Clerksroom (London), London	0845 083 3000
	Clerksroom (Taunton), Taunton	0845 083 3000
	King's Lynn Chambers, King's Lynn	01553 672 085
Sofaer Miss Moira	Goldsmith Chambers, London	020 7353 6802
Sood Mrs Usha Rani	Trent Chambers, Nottingham	0115 941 9596
Spain Mr Timothy Harrisson	Trinity Chambers, Middlesbrough	01642 247569
	Trinity Chambers, Newcastle Upon Tyne	0191 232 1927
Sparrow Mrs Marie-Claire	Holborn Chambers, London	020 7242 6060

Name	Chambers	Telephone
Spencer Mr Shaun Anthony	St Johns Buildings, Chester	01244 323070
	St Johns Buildings, Manchester	0161 214 1500
	16 Winckley Square, Preston	01772 256100
Starr Mrs Teresa Margaret	Great James Street Chambers, London	020 7440 4949
Stringer Mr Leon Peter	15 Winckley Square, Preston	01772 252828
Strongman Mrs Carol Ann	No 8 Chambers, Birmingham	0121 236 5514
Stubbs Mr Andrew James	St Paul's Chambers, Leeds	0113 245 5866
Styles Mr Clive Richard	Becket Chambers, Canterbury	01227 786331
Swift Mr Jonathan Peter	29 Bedford Row Chambers, London	020 7404 1044
Symms Miss Kathryn Ann	Number 7 Harrington Street Chambers, Liverpool	0151 242 0707
Tansey Miss Anouska	2-3 Hind Court Chambers, London	020 7822 2150
Targett-Parker Miss Leanne Susan	No. 3 Fleet Street Chambers, London	020 7936 4474
	The Chambers of Miss Leanne Targett-Parker, London	020 8674 6694
Taylor Mrs Susan	Trinity Chambers, Middlesbrough	01642 247569
	Trinity Chambers, Newcastle Upon Tyne	0191 232 1927
Taylor Mrs Yvonne Marie	Trinity Chambers, Middlesbrough	01642 247569
	Trinity Chambers, Newcastle Upon Tyne	0191 232 1927
Taylor Ms Mary-Jane	Coram Chambers, London	020 7092 3700
Thomas Miss Jacqueline Louise	37 Park Square Chambers, Leeds	0113 243 9422
Thomas Mrs Felicity	Westgate Chambers, Lewes	01273 480510
Tompkins Miss Kate	36 Bedford Row, London	020 7421 8000
Tregidgo Mr Marc Gordon	4 King's Bench Walk, London	020 7822 7000
Tresman Mr Lewis Robert Simon	Staple Inn Chambers, London	020 7242 5240
Twist Mr Stephen John	Dere Street Barristers, Newcastle Upon Tyne	0844 3351551
Twydell Miss Cherry Louisa	Trinity Chambers, Chelmsford	01245 605040
Ume Mr Cyril Obiora	12 Old Square Chambers, London	020 7404 0875
Van Spall Ms Penelope-Jane	Chartlands Chambers, Northampton	01604 603322
Vavrecka Mr David Paul Frank	Coram Chambers, London	020 7092 3700
Vencatachellum Ms Glenda Roxande	Rowchester Chambers, Birmingham	0121 233 2327
Vollenweider Mr Amiot Marcus Ellerton	Thomas More Chambers, London	020 7404 7000
Wade Miss Rebecca Lucy	Northampton Chambers, Northampton	01604 636271
Waley Mr Eric Richard Thomas	Assize Court Chambers, Bristol	0117 926 4587
Wall Mr Christopher James Lynton	Becket Chambers, Canterbury	01227 786331
Ward Miss Kelly Jane	Pallant Chambers, Chichester	01243 784538
Watkins Miss Rachel Claire	Chartlands Chambers, Northampton	01604 603322
Watson Mr Duncan Allen	Westgate Chambers, Lewes	01273 480510
Webster Miss Sarah Mary	Staple Inn Chambers, London	020 7242 5240
Wheaton Mr Ian Malcolm James	Eighteen Carlton Crescent, Southampton	023 8063 9001
Whitehouse Mr Stuart Colin	Goldsmith Chambers, London	020 7353 6802
Wilkinson Mr Francis John	Field Court Chambers, London	020 7405 6114
Wilkinson Ms Tiffany Jodie	Trinity Chambers, Chelmsford	01245 605040
Williams Miss Micaila Teresa	Optimus Chambers, Braintree	01376 691 885/07736 283873
Wingert Miss Rachel Thomas	Renaissance Chambers, London	020 7404 1111
Winslett Mr Frank	Westgate Chambers, Lewes	01273 480510
Wood Miss Joanna Rachel	1 Pump Court, London	020 7842 7070
Wright Mrs Yasmin Tajdin	Cobden House Chambers, Manchester	0161 833 6000

CHANCERY (GENERAL)

Name	Chambers	Telephone
Adewale Mr Remi Adetokunbo Sanni	Chambers of G. D. Tetteh, London	020 7353 7095
	Chambers of Mr R. A. Adewale, Address withheld	020 7231 2814
Agnihotri Mr Naveen	12 College Place, Southampton	023 8032 0320
Ailes Mr John Ashley	Eighteen Carlton Crescent, Southampton	023 8063 9001
Ajaz Mr Mohammad Arshad	Eastmans Chambers, Reading	0118 966 9094
Alexandra Miss Sebastiane	Holborn Chambers, London	020 7242 6060
Altaras Mr David Maurice	36 Bedford Row, London	020 7421 8000

Name	Chambers	Telephone
Dovar Mr Daniel	Tanfield Chambers, London	020 7421 5300
Egleton Mr Richard Wildman	Pallant Chambers, Chichester	01243 784538
Eilledge Miss Amanda Gail Caroline	11 Stone Buildings, London	020 7831 6381
Engelman Mr Mark Trevor	Hardwicke, London	020 7242 2523
Esprit Mr Benoit	Barristers Chambers, London	020 3417 6461
	Legis Chambers, Aylesbury	01296 431125
Fain Mr Carl Ian	Tanfield Chambers, London	020 7421 5300
Falkowski Mr Damian	4-5 Gray's Inn Square, London	020 7404 5252
Fawcett Mr Neil	St Ive's Chambers, Birmingham	0121 236 0863
Ferber Ms Iris	42 Bedford Row, London	020 7831 0222
Fieldsend Mr James William	Tanfield Chambers, London	020 7421 5300
Finlay Mr Darren	Sovereign Chambers, Leeds	0113 245 1841
Fitzmaurice Mr Guy Edward Christian	Staple Inn Chambers, London	020 7242 5240
Follon Mr Daniel Richard Thomas	1 Gray's Inn Square, London	020 7405 0001
Fowles Mr Jonathan James	Serle Court, London	020 7242 6105
Francis Mr Andrew James	Serle Court, London	020 7242 6105
	Zenith Chambers, Leeds	0113 245 5438
Francis Mr Richard Maurice	9 Park Place, Cardiff	029 2038 2731
Gair Mr Christopher	King's Bench Chambers, Bournemouth	01202 250025
Gallivan Mr Terence John	Five Paper, London	020 7815 3200
Galway-Cooper Dr Philip Anthony	Five St Andrew's Hill, London	020 7332 5400
Gardiner Mr William David Hugh	Holborn Chambers, London	020 7242 6060
Garvie Mr Carl Peter	St Philips Chambers, Birmingham	0121 246 7000
Gasztowicz Mr Steven	Cornerstone Barristers, London	020 7242 4986
	New Street Chambers, Leicester	0116 262 5906
Gee Mr Steven Mark	Stone Chambers, London	020 7440 6900
George Mr Nicholas Frank Raymond	New Walk Chambers, Leicester	0871 200 1298/0116 255 9144
Gibbons Miss Mary Regina	Stone Chambers, London	020 7440 6900
Gibbons Ms Ellodie	Tanfield Chambers, London	020 7421 5300
Giles Mr David William	1 Gray's Inn Square, London	020 7405 0001
Glaser Mr Michael Samson	14 Gray's Inn Square, London	020 7242 0858
Gloag Mr Angus Robin	1 Gray's Inn Square, London	020 7405 0001
	Rougemont Chambers, Exeter	01392 208484
Glover Mr Marc Philip	Tanfield Chambers, London	020 7421 5300
Godfrey Mr Lauren John	Crown Office Row Chambers, Brighton	01273 625625
Gold Mr Richard David	St John's Chambers, Bristol	0117 923 4700
Goldberg Mr Simon Ian	Trinity Chambers, Middlesbrough	01642 247569
	Trinity Chambers, Newcastle Upon Tyne	0191 232 1927
Goldstein Mr Wayne Nathan	18 St John Street, Manchester	0161 278 1800
Goodall Mr Charles Vernon Machin-	Queen Square Chambers, Bristol	0117 921 1966
Goodison Mr Adam Henry	South Square, London	020 7696 9900
Gorasia Mr Paras Ravji	Kings Chambers, Birmingham	0845 034 3444
	Kings Chambers, Leeds	0845 034 3444
	Kings Chambers, Manchester	0845 034 3444
Gordon Mr Jeremy	Chambers of Mr Ami Feder, London	020 7797 7788
	Chambers of Mr Ami Feder, London	020 7797 7788
	Lamb Building, Brighton	01273 820490
Gore Mr Andrew Roger	Fenners Chambers, Cambridge	01223 368761
Graham Mrs Alana Nicole	Chambers of Alana Graham, Halesowen	01384 894560
	9 Stone Buildings, London	020 7404 5055
Graham-Wells Miss Alison Christine	Exchange Chambers, Leeds	0113 203 1970
	Exchange Chambers, Liverpool	0151 236 7747
	Exchange Chambers, Manchester	0161 833 2722
Grant Mr David Ericson	Outer Temple Chambers, London	020 7353 6381
Griffiths Mr David	St Philips Chambers, Birmingham	0121 246 7000
Gupta Mr Amit	St Philips Chambers, Birmingham	0121 246 7000
Guy Mr Richard Perran	Chambers of Mr Ami Feder, London	020 7797 7788
	King's Bench and Godolphin (KBG)Chambers, Plymouth	01752 221551
	Southernhay Chambers, Exeter	01392 255777

Name	Chambers	Telephone
Hall Mr James Edward	Cornwall Street Chambers, Birmingham	0121 233 7500
Hallett Miss Katherine Elizabeth	13 Old Square Chambers, London	020 7831 4445
Harris Mr David Robert	St Albans Chambers, St Albans	01727 843383
Harris Mr Melvyn	5 Essex Court, London	020 7410 2000
Haughty Mr Jeremy Nicholas	Chambers of Mr Ami Feder, London	020 7797 7788
	Chambers of Mr Ami Feder, London	020 7797 7788
	Rougemont Chambers, Exeter	01392 208484
Hayes Mr Richard James	Lamb Chambers, London	020 7797 8300
Haywood Dr Jennifer Margaret	Serle Court, London	020 7242 6105
Hendron Mr Henry Joseph Christopher	Strand Chambers, London	020 7117 6920
Hewson Ms Barbara Mary	Hardwicke, London	020 7242 2523
Hicks Mr Edward Gordon David	Radcliffe Chambers, London	020 7831 0081
Higginson Mr Timothy Nicholas Bennett	Littleton Chambers, London	020 7797 8600
	St John's Chambers, Bristol	0117 923 4700
Hill Mr Michael Gordon	Trinity Chambers, Middlesbrough	01642 247569
	Trinity Chambers, Newcastle Upon Tyne	0191 232 1927
Hill Mr Piers Nicholas	37 Park Square Chambers, Leeds	0113 243 9422
Hillas Miss Samantha	Atlantic Chambers, Liverpool	0151 236 4421
Hillman Mr Gerard Paul	Carmelite Chambers, London	020 7936 6300
Hilton Ms Saisampan	Holborn Chambers, London	020 7242 6060
Hirst Mr William Timothy John	Park Lane Plowden, Leeds	0113 228 5049
Hodgkiss Ms Suzanne Jane	43 Temple Row Chambers, Birmingham	0121 237 6035
Hodson Mr Matthew Paul	Farrar's Building, London	020 7583 9241
Hogben Mrs Helen Jane	Fountain Chambers, Middlesbrough	01642 804040
Holbech Mr Charles Edward	New Square Chambers, London	020 7419 8000
Holland Mr Charles Christopher	Francis Taylor Building, London	020 7353 8415
	Trinity Chambers, Middlesbrough	01642 247569
	Trinity Chambers, Newcastle Upon Tyne	0191 232 1927
Holmes-Milner Mr James Neil	The Chambers of Grahame Aldous QC, London	020 7832 0500
Hood Mr Nigel Anthony	New Square Chambers, London	020 7419 8000
Hormaeche Miss Alejandra	Tanfield Chambers, London	020 7421 5300
Horne Mr Charles Hugh Wilson	Kings Chambers, Birmingham	0845 034 3444
	Kings Chambers, Leeds	0845 034 3444
	Kings Chambers, Manchester	0845 034 3444
Hornett Mr Stuart Ian	Selborne Chambers, London	020 7420 9500
Howard Mr Robin William John	Fenners Chambers, Cambridge	01223 368761
Howells Mr Stephen John	Stone Chambers, London	020 7440 6900
Hubbard Mr Mark Iain	New Square Chambers, London	020 7419 8000
Huggins Mr Toby James	Unity Street Chambers, Bristol	0117 906 9789
Hughes-Deane Ms Charlotte Barbara	Atlantic Chambers, Liverpool	0151 236 4421
Hunt Mr Stephen	4 Stone Buildings, London	020 7242 5524
Hussain Mr Basharat	Cornwall Street Chambers, Birmingham	0121 233 7500
Hussain Mr Muhammad Altaf	Chambers of Mr M A Hussain, London	020 8679 2398
Hutchin Mr Edward Alister David	Temple Garden Chambers, London	020 7583 1315
Isaac Mr Nicholas Dudley	Tanfield Chambers, London	020 7421 5300
Iyer Miss Shobana	Swan Chambers, Richmond	0845 123 1234
Johnson Mr Phillip Michael	Chambers of Mr P Johnson, London	020 7288 2256
Jones Mr Alun	St Paul's Chambers, Leeds	0113 245 5866
Jones Mr Christopher David Harries	St John's Chambers, Bristol	0117 923 4700
Jones Mr Emyr Gweirydd	9 Park Place, Cardiff	029 2038 2731
Jones Mr Geraint Anthony	New Walk Chambers, Leicester	0871 200 1298/0116 255 9144
	9 St John Street, Manchester	0161 955 9000
	Tanfield Chambers, London	020 7421 5300
Jones Mr Kelvin Mcallister	Templis Chambers, London	020 7649 9808
Jones Mr Lawrence Victor	Chambers of Lawrence Jones, London	020 7831 1444

C

Name	Chambers	Telephone
Jones Mr Mark Simeon	3 Dr Johnson's Buildings, London	020 7353 4854
Jones Mr Rhys Charles Mansel	14 Gray's Inn Square, London	020 7242 0858
Jones Mr Richard Frederick Thomas	Heavenwood Chambers, Stroud	01453 873444
Joseph Dr Sandradee Theresa	13 Old Square Chambers, London	020 7831 4445
Joseph Mr Charles Henry	Tanfield Chambers, London	020 7421 5300
Joseph Mr Paul Wolfe	No5 Chambers, Birmingham	0845 210 5555
	No5 Chambers, Bristol	0845 210 5555
	No5 Chambers, London	0845 210 5555
Keel Mr Douglas Vincent	11 Stone Buildings, London	020 7831 6381
Kelly Mr Sean	Chancery House Chambers, Leeds	0113 244 6691
Kemp Mr James Rupert	Trinity Chambers, Middlesbrough	01642 247569
	Trinity Chambers, Newcastle Upon Tyne	0191 232 1927
Khan Dr Alexander	Coral House, Manchester	
Khan Mr Abdul Aleem	Gray's Chambers, Newbury	020 8518 2525
Khan Mr Arfan	Field Court Chambers, London	020 7405 6114
Kidd Mr Peter William	Number 7 Harrington Street Chambers, Liverpool	0151 242 0707
Kitzing Miss Susanna Loraine	Park Court Chambers, Leeds	0113 243 3277
Kramer Mr Philip Anthony	Park Lane Plowden, Newcastle Upon Tyne	0191 211 4087
Kynoch Mr Duncan Stuart Sanderson	Selborne Chambers, London	020 7420 9500
Lane Mr Simon Charles	Rougemont Chambers, Exeter	01392 208484
Le Poidevin Mr Nicholas Peter	New Square Chambers, London	020 7419 8000
Learmonth Mr Alexander Robert Magnus	New Square Chambers, London	020 7419 8000
Lee Miss Krista Chui Lan	Keating Chambers, London	020 7544 2600
Lennard Mr Stephen Charles	Hardwicke, London	020 7242 2523
Leonard Mr Charles Robert Weston	Hardwicke, London	020 7242 2523
Levy Miss Juliette	Selborne Chambers, London	020 7420 9500
Lewis Mr Wayne Anthony	Access Lawyers, London	020 8801 2345
Littman Mr Jeffrey James	Chambers of Mr Jeffrey Littman, London	020 8922 6844
	9 Park Place, Cardiff	029 2038 2731
Lonsdale Miss Marion Mary	Academy Chambers, London	020 8455 2503
Lonsdale Mr David James	33 Bedford Row, London	020 7242 6476
Lopez Mr Juan Nemesio	Francis Taylor Building, London	020 7353 8415
Lyons Miss Tara Yasmin	Pump Court Chambers, London	020 7353 0711
	Pump Court Chambers, Winchester	01962 868 161
	Riverview Chambers, London	0844 225 3999
MacEvilly Mr Conn Jeremy	9 Stone Buildings, London	020 7404 5055
Machell Mr John William	Serle Court, London	020 7242 6105
MacKenzie Smith Mrs Catherine Joanna	10 King's Bench Walk, London	020 7353 7742
MacKenzie Mr Robert Sutherland	Middle Temple Lane Chambers, London	020 7583 4352
Macpherson Mr Duncan Charles Stewart	One Essex Court, London	020 7936 3030
Maguire Mr Andrew James	Exchange Chambers, Liverpool	0151 236 7747
	Exchange Chambers, Manchester	0161 833 2722
	St Philips Chambers, Birmingham	0121 246 7000
Maher Ms Martha Johanna Dorothy	St John's Chambers, Bristol	0117 923 4700
Mainwaring Mr Robert Paul Clason	Portal Chambers, Llandysul	01559 395 292
Mann Mr Christopher	13 KBW, Oxford	01865 311066
	13 King's Bench Walk, London	020 7353 7204
Marks Mr Jonathan Clive	4 Pump Court, London	020 7842 5555
Marshall Mr Derek Stanley	College Chambers, Southampton	023 8023 0338
Matthias Mr David Huw	Francis Taylor Building, London	020 7353 8415
Mawrey Mr Richard Brooks	Henderson Chambers, London	020 7583 9020
McCarthy Mr William	Bridgewater Chambers, Manchester	0161 3877127
	1 Mitre Court Buildings, London	020 7452 8900
McCormack Mr Alan	Staple Inn Chambers, London	020 7242 5240
McCue Mr Donald	11 Stone Buildings, London	020 7831 6381

McDonnell Mr John Beresford William	13 Old Square Chambers, London	020 7831 4445
McGhee Mr Stuart Edward	College Chambers, Southampton	023 8023 0338
McLinden Mr John Vincent Barry	Field Court Chambers, London	020 7405 6114
McNae Mr Jonathan James	Selborne Chambers, London	020 7420 9500
Meager Mrs Rowena Elisabeth	No5 Chambers, Birmingham	0845 210 5555
	No5 Chambers, Bristol	0845 210 5555
	No5 Chambers, London	0845 210 5555
Meares Mr Nigel Leslie Vellacott	11 Stone Buildings, London	020 7831 6381
Menon Mr Harigovind	New Court Chambers, Newcastle Upon Tyne	0191 232 1980
	Park Lane Plowden, Newcastle Upon Tyne	0191 211 4087
Metzger Mr Kevin Albert	11 Gray's Inn Square Chambers, London	020 7405 6879
Michael Mr Nicholas	East Anglian Chambers, Chelmsford	01473 214481
	East Anglian Chambers, Colchester	01473 214481
	East Anglian Chambers, Ipswich	01473 214481
	East Anglian Chambers, Norwich	01473 214481
Miller Mr Ian Robertson	Broadway House Chambers, Bradford	01274 722560
	Broadway House Chambers, Leeds	0113 246 2600
Mills Mr Kristian Anthony	Trinity Chambers, Middlesbrough	01642 247569
	Trinity Chambers, Newcastle Upon Tyne	0191 232 1927
Mitchell Mr Alistair Stephen Fabian	49 Chambers, Bridgnorth	01746 761545
Mitchell Mr David John	No5 Chambers, Birmingham	0845 210 5555
	No5 Chambers, Bristol	0845 210 5555
	No5 Chambers, London	0845 210 5555
Mohammad Mr Nazar	Legis Chambers, Aylesbury	01296 431125
	No. 3 Fleet Street Chambers, London	020 7936 4474
Monnington Mr Bruce Gilbert	Fenners Chambers, Cambridge	01223 368761
Morgan Dr Austen Jude	33 Bedford Row, London	020 7242 6476
Morris Mr Phillip John	9 Park Place, Cardiff	029 2038 2731
Moss Mr Christopher Stephen	St Johns Buildings, Manchester	0161 214 1500
	St Johns Buildings Liverpool, Liverpool	0151 243 6000
	16 Winckley Square, Preston	01772 256100
Mullen Mr Mark Robert	Radcliffe Chambers, London	020 7831 0081
Muman Mr Vijay Kumar	43 Temple Row Chambers, Birmingham	0121 237 6035
Murphy Mr Damian	Enterprise Chambers, Leeds	0113 246 0391
	Enterprise Chambers, London	020 7405 9471
	Enterprise Chambers, Newcastle Upon Tyne	0191 222 3344
Murray Mr Charles Humphrey Stewart	Rougemont Chambers, Exeter	01392 208484
Mustakim Mr Abdul Yunus Al	Chambers of Mr Mustakim, London	
Mydeen Mr Kalandar	Chambers of Mr K Mydeen, Sutton	020 8643 3633
Newman Mr Paul	3 PB Barristers, Bournemouth	01202 292102
	3 PB Barristers, Bristol	0117 928 1520
	3 PB Barristers, London	020 7583 8055
	3 PB Barristers, Oxford	01865 793 736
	3 PB Barristers, Winchester	01962 868884
Newsom Mr George Lucien	Guildhall Chambers, Bristol	0117 930 9000
Nicholls Mr David James	11 Stone Buildings, London	020 7831 6381
Nickless Mr Jason Alan	College Chambers, Southampton	023 8023 0338
Noble Mr Andrew	Enterprise Chambers, Leeds	0113 246 0391
Noble Mr Philip Robert	Thomas More Chambers, London	020 7404 7000
Normington Mr James Adam	Park Court Chambers, Leeds	0113 243 3277
Norton Mr Giles	Enigma Chambers, Sheffield	07779 576499
	Holborn Chambers, London	020 7242 6060
Nurse Mr Gordon Bramwell William	Radcliffe Chambers, London	020 7831 0081
O'Brien Mr Nicholas William Wattebot	10 King's Bench Walk, London	020 7353 7742

C

Name	Chambers	Telephone
O'Donoghue Mr Hugh Vincent	Carmelite Chambers, London	020 7936 6300
Ohrenstein Mr Dov	Radcliffe Chambers, London	020 7831 0081
Oliver Mr David Keightley Rideal	13 Old Square Chambers, London	020 7831 4445
O'Mahony Mr Jonathan Solomon	9 Stone Buildings, London	020 7404 5055
O'Neill Mr Jonathan Norman	Rougemont Chambers, Exeter	01392 208484
Oommen Mr Jacob	Chambers of Mr Jacob Oommen, East Barnet	07958 680272
Osborne Mr James Robert	Clerksroom (London), London	0845 083 3000
O'Sullivan Mr Richard John	1215 Chambers, London	020 3291 1215
O'Toole Mr Bartholomew Vincent	5 King's Bench Walk, London	020 7353 5638
Otwal Mr Mukhtiar Singh	42 Bedford Row, London	020 7831 0222
Oulton Mr Richard Arthur Courtenay	5 Essex Court, London	020 7410 2000
Panton Mr Alastair Howard	10 King's Bench Walk, London	020 7353 7742
Paraskos Mr Paraskevakis Christakis	11 Gray's Inn Square Chambers, London	020 7405 6879
Parker Miss Wendy	Hardwicke, London	020 7242 2523
Parker Mrs Karen Lesley	Guildhall Chambers Portsmouth, Portsmouth	023 9275 2400
Parsons Mr Andrew James	Portsmouth Barristers'Chambers, Portsmouth	023 9283 1292
Paton Mr Ewan William	Guildhall Chambers, Bristol	0117 930 9000
Payton Mr Clifford Coningsby	Alpha Court Chambers, Leamington Spa	01926 886412
Pearce Mr Robert Edgar	Radcliffe Chambers, London	020 7831 0081
Pennock Mr Ian	Park Lane Plowden, Leeds	0113 228 5049
Penny Mr Timothy Charles	11 Stone Buildings, London	020 7831 6381
Pickering Mr Simon Toby	Wilberforce Chambers, Hull	01482 323264
Pithers Mr Clive Robert	Fenners Chambers, Cambridge	01223 368761
Polli Mr Timothy James	Tanfield Chambers, London	020 7421 5300
Power Mr Lawrence Imam	4 KBW, London	020 7822 8822
Pryke Mr Stuart	Fiduciary Legal, London	07814 495366
Purves Mr Gavin Bowman	Swan House, London	020 8998 3035
Quiney Mr Charles Benedictus Alexander	Crown Office Chambers, London	020 7797 8100
Quirke Mr Gerard Martin	Citadel Chambers, Birmingham	0121 233 8500
Rahman Mr Sami Ur	Field Court Chambers, London	020 7405 6114
Rana Mr Mohammed Akram	Clapham Law Chambers, London	020 7978 8482
Ratcliffe Miss Frances Anne	Radcliffe Chambers, London	020 7831 0081
Record Mrs Celia Saint Claire	Chambers of Lawrence Jones, London	020 7831 1444
Reed Mr Simon John	New Walk Chambers, Leicester	0871 200 1298/0116 255 9144
Reffin Miss Clare Alyson	One Essex Court, London	020 7583 2000
Richman Mrs Helene Pines	Eighteen Carlton Crescent, Southampton	023 8063 9001
	9 Stone Buildings, London	020 7404 5055
	Stour Chambers, Canterbury	01227 764899
Rickards Mr James	Outer Temple Chambers, London	020 7353 6381
Ridd Mr David Ian Mcgregor	Farrar's Building, London	020 7583 9241
Rifat Mr Maurice Alan	1 Gray's Inn Square, London	020 7405 0001
Rimmer Mr Anthony Michael	187 Fleet Street, London	020 7430 7430
Rinker Mr Andrew Stuart D'Artois	Chambers of Mr Andrew Rinker, London	020 7584 1091
Ritchie Mr Richard Bulkeley	XXIV Old Buildings, London	020 7691 2424
Riza Mr Alper Ali	Goldsmith Chambers, London	020 7353 6802
Roberts Mr Michael Charles	Chambers of Michael Roberts, Henley-On-Thames	01844 355 655
Robinson Miss Laura	Tanfield Chambers, London	020 7421 5300
Ross Mr Sidney David	11 Stone Buildings, London	020 7831 6381
Rowell Mr George Edward	St John's Chambers, Bristol	0117 923 4700
Rowntree Mr Edward John Pickering	Hardwicke, London	020 7242 2523
Roy Mr Stefan Alexander Hiren	5 Pump Court, London	020 7353 2532
Russell Mr Thomas Charles Welldon	KCH Garden Square, Nottingham	0115 941 8851
Sadiq Mr Muhammad Faisel	Ely Place Chambers, London	020 7400 9600
Saifee Mr Faisal Aftaab	Thomas More Chambers, London	020 7404 7000

Name	Chambers	Telephone
Sampson Dr Timothy Michael George	One Essex Court, London	020 7936 3030
Sandham Mr James Andrew	Arden Chambers, London	020 7242 4244
Seal Mr Julius Damien	Chambers of Mr Julius Seal, London	020 7328 0158
Seeboruth Mr Royln Jean-Paul	Chambers of Royln Seeboruth, Aylesbury	01296 393329
Sellers Mr Graham	Atlantic Chambers, Liverpool	0151 236 4421
Sen Mr Aditya Kumar	Coram Chambers, London	020 7092 3700
Sharples Mr John Edmund	St John's Chambers, Bristol	0117 923 4700
Sinclair Miss Lisa Anne	Chambers of Miss Lisa Sinclair, London	020 8946 7201
Sinclair Mr Graham Kelso	East Anglian Chambers, Colchester	01473 214481
	East Anglian Chambers, Ipswich	01473 214481
	East Anglian Chambers, Norwich	01473 214481
Singarajah Mr Frederico	1 Gray's Inn Square, London	020 7405 0001
Sisley Mr Timothy Julian Crispin	9 Stone Buildings, London	020 7404 5055
Sjostrand Miss Ekaterina	13 Old Square Chambers, London	020 7831 4445
Skelly Mr Andrew Jon	Hardwicke, London	020 7242 2523
Smith Mr Matthew Robert	Sovereign Chambers, Leeds	0113 245 1841
Smith Mr Roger Hugh Traylen	No5 Chambers, Birmingham	0845 210 5555
	No5 Chambers, Bristol	0845 210 5555
	No5 Chambers, London	0845 210 5555
Smithers Dr Roger Howard	Alexander Chambers, London	0845 652 0451/0854 652 0451
	Clerksroom (Taunton), Taunton	0845 083 3000
	Guildford Chambers, Guildford	01483 539131
Spratt Mr Christopher David Richard Dean	9 Stone Buildings, London	020 7404 5055
Spratt-Dawson Miss Josephine Margery	Trinity Chambers, Chelmsford	01245 605040
Staddon Mr Paul	Tanfield Chambers, London	020 7421 5300
Stenhouse Mr John Alexander	Nightingale Chambers, Wolverley	01562 851350
Sterling Mr Robert Alan	St James's Chambers, Manchester	0161 834 7000
	Zenith Chambers, Leeds	0113 245 5438
Stevenson Dr Simon John	Park Lane Plowden, Leeds	0113 228 5049
Stevenson Mr Paul Anthony	Tanfield Chambers, London	020 7421 5300
Stewart Mr Nicholas John Cameron	Ely Place Chambers, London	020 7400 9600
Stubbs Mr Richard John Morris	Trinity Chambers, Middlesbrough	01642 247569
	Trinity Chambers, Newcastle Upon Tyne	0191 232 1927
Swirsky Mr Adam Abraham Burl Bradbury	Lamb Chambers, London	020 7797 8300
Tabari Mr Ali-Reza	St Philips Chambers, Birmingham	0121 246 7000
Taylor Miss Araba Arba Kurankyiwa	Fenners Chambers, Cambridge	01223 368761
Temmink Mr Robert-Jan	Quadrant Chambers, London	020 7583 4444
Temple Ms Eleanor Louise	Kings Chambers, Birmingham	0845 034 3444
	Kings Chambers, Leeds	0845 034 3444
	Kings Chambers, Manchester	0845 034 3444
Terry Mr Robert Jeffrey	Kings Chambers, Birmingham	0845 034 3444
	Kings Chambers, Leeds	0845 034 3444
	Kings Chambers, Manchester	0845 034 3444
	Lamb Chambers, London	020 7797 8300
Thornley Miss Hannah Elise	South Square, London	020 7696 9900
Thrower Mr James Simeon	Chambers of Simeon Thrower, London	020 8878 7374
Trompeter Mr Nicholas Simeon	Selborne Chambers, London	020 7420 9500
Troup Mr Alexander William	St John's Chambers, Bristol	0117 923 4700
Trumpington Mr John Henry	Staple Inn Chambers, London	020 7242 5240
Tucker Mr Ashley Russell	Park Court Chambers, Leeds	0113 243 3277
Tucker Mr James William Richard	Teucro Chambers, Epsom	
Turnbull Miss Helen Mary	Lamb Chambers, London	020 7797 8300
Van Overdijk Miss Claire Orit	No5 Chambers, Birmingham	0845 210 5555
	No5 Chambers, Bristol	0845 210 5555
	No5 Chambers, London	0845 210 5555
Van Tonder Mr Gerard Dirk	New Square Chambers, London	020 7419 8000

Vane The Hon Christopher John Fletcher	Trinity Chambers, Middlesbrough	01642 247569
	Trinity Chambers, Newcastle Upon Tyne	0191 232 1927
Vaughan-Williams Mr Arthur Laurence	13 Old Square Chambers, London	020 7831 4445
Verduyn Dr Anthony James	St Philips Chambers, Birmingham	0121 246 7000
Vernon Mr Elliot Curt	No. 3 Fleet Street Chambers, London	020 7936 4474
Vitiello Mr Fabio Angelo-Giuseppe	Staple Inn Chambers, London	020 7242 5240
Wales Mr Matthew James	Guildhall Chambers, Bristol	0117 930 9000
Walford Mr Richard Henry Howard	Serle Court, London	020 7242 6105
Walsh Mr Michael Patrick	Tanfield Chambers, London	020 7421 5300
Warner Mr David Alexander	St Philips Chambers, Birmingham	0121 246 7000
Watson Mr Alaric	11 Stone Buildings, London	020 7831 6381
Watson Mr Duncan Allen	Westgate Chambers, Lewes	01273 480510
Watson Mr Ian David	3 Stone Buildings, London	020 7242 4937
Wheatley Mr Geraint Rhys	Kings Chambers, Birmingham	0845 034 3444
	Kings Chambers, Leeds	0845 034 3444
	Kings Chambers, Manchester	0845 034 3444
White Mr Steven James	Park Court Chambers, Leeds	0113 243 3277
Wightwick Mr Iain	Riverview Chambers, London	0844 225 3999
	Unity Street Chambers, Bristol	0117 906 9789
Wiktorowski-Solecki Miss Tamara	Middle Temple Lane Chambers, London	020 7583 4352
Wilcox Mr Jerome Carl Jean	Alexander Chambers, London	0845 652 0451/0854 652 0451
Wilkins Mr Christopher John	Pallant Chambers, Chichester	01243 784538
Wilkinson Mr Marc Ashley	No5 Chambers, Birmingham	0845 210 5555
	No5 Chambers, Bristol	0845 210 5555
	No5 Chambers, London	0845 210 5555
Willetts Mr Andrew Philip	King's Bench and Godolphin (KBG)Chambers, Plymouth	01752 221551
	New Walk Chambers, Leicester	0871 200 1298/0116 255 9144
Wills Miss Alexandra Itari	Christ Church Chambers, London	020 7409 5278/07788 512787
Wolman Mr Clive Richard	11 Stone Buildings, London	020 7831 6381
Wolstenholme Miss Janine	Sovereign Chambers, Leeds	0113 245 1841
Yell Mr Nicholas Anthony	1 Chancery Lane, London	0845 634 6666
Young Mr Martin Ford	9 Stone Buildings, London	020 7404 5055

CHANCERY (LAND LAW)

Adewale Mr Remi Adetokunbo Sanni	Chambers of G. D. Tetteh, London	020 7353 7095
	Chambers of Mr R. A. Adewale, Address withheld	020 7231 2814
Agnihotri Mr Naveen	12 College Place, Southampton	023 8032 0320
Ailes Mr John Ashley	Eighteen Carlton Crescent, Southampton	023 8063 9001
Ajaz Mr Mohammad Arshad	Eastmans Chambers, Reading	0118 966 9094
Aliker Mr Phillip Bliss	Tanfield Chambers, London	020 7421 5300
Allison Mr Simon Robert	Hardwicke, London	020 7242 2523
Allston Mr Anthony Stanley	3 Dr Johnson's Buildings, London	020 7353 4854
Alomo Mr Richard Olusoji	14 Gray's Inn Square, London	020 7242 0858
Altaras Mr David Maurice	36 Bedford Row, London	020 7421 8000
Ameen Mr Danish	18 St John Street, Manchester	0161 278 1800
Antell Mr John Jason	King's Bench and Godolphin (KBG)Chambers, Plymouth	01752 221551
Ash Mr Edward William	Chambers of Mr Edward Ash, Elsworth	01954 267674
Askey Mr Robert John	Palmyra Chambers, Warrington	01925 444919
Asprey Mr Nicholas	Clock Chambers, Wolverhampton	01902 313444
	Serle Court, London	020 7242 6105
Bailey Miss Rosana Henrietta	10 King's Bench Walk, London	020 7353 7742
Bailey Mr Charles Andrew Stuart	Trinity Chambers, Chelmsford	01245 605040
Bailey Mr Thomas Iain	Chambers of Mr Thomas Bailey, Milton Keynes	07983 447117
Baldwin Dr Timothy John	Garden Court Chambers, London	020 7993 7600

C

Name	Chambers	Telephone
Ballard Ms Appa	Cornwall Street Chambers, Birmingham	0121 233 7500
Barnes Mr Luke Clive	3 Dr Johnson's Buildings, London	020 7353 4854
Bastin Mr Alexander Charles	Hardwicke, London	020 7242 2523
Beaumont Mr Dean Andrew	KCH Garden Square, Nottingham	0115 941 8851
Beaumont Mr Marc Clifford	9 Stone Buildings, London	020 7404 5055
	Windsor Barristers' Chambers, Windsor	01753 839321
Becker Mr Timothy George Christie	Chambers of Mr Timothy Becker, Liverpool	0151 703 0319
	Clerksroom (London), London	0845 083 3000
Bedloe Mr Giles Robert	Dyers Chambers, London	020 7404 1881
Bell Miss Anne Margaret	Holborn Chambers, London	020 7242 6060
	Rougemont Chambers, Exeter	01392 208484
Bennion-Pedley Mr Edward	13 KBW, Oxford	01865 311066
	13 King's Bench Walk, London	020 7353 7204
Berkley Mr Michael Stuart	Rougemont Chambers, Exeter	01392 208484
Berry Mr Nicholas Michael	Rougemont Chambers, Exeter	01392 208484
Bezzam Miss Jayashree	Hampton Court Chambers, West Molesey	020 8979 0381
Blaker Mr Gary Mark	Selborne Chambers, London	020 7420 9500
Bleasdale Miss Marie-Claire	Radcliffe Chambers, London	020 7831 0081
Blohm Mr Leslie Adrian	St John's Chambers, Bristol	0117 923 4700
Bogle Mr James Stewart Lockhart	10 King's Bench Walk, London	020 7353 7742
Bojarski Mr Andrzej Leonard	36 Bedford Row, London	020 7421 8000
Bourne Mr Geoffrey Robert	13 Old Square Chambers, London	020 7831 4445
Boyd Mr Stephen James Harvey	Selborne Chambers, London	020 7420 9500
Bragiel Mr Edward Bronislaw Henryk	Hogarth Chambers, London	020 7404 0404
Branchflower Mr George	Zenith Chambers, Leeds	0113 245 5438
Bredemear Mr Zachary Charles	1 Chancery Lane, London	0845 634 6666
Brewin Mr Carl Patrick	3 PB Barristers, London	020 7583 8055
Brilliant Mr Simon Howard	Lamb Chambers, London	020 7797 8300
Brook Mr Paul Antony	Park Lane Plowden, Leeds	0113 228 5049
	Park Lane Plowden, Newcastle Upon Tyne	0191 211 4087
Brown Miss Susan Margaret	One Essex Court, London	020 7936 3030
Brown Mr Philip Stephen	9 Stone Buildings, London	020 7404 5055
Browne Mr James William	Lamb Chambers, London	020 7797 8300
Bruce Mr Andrew Jonathan	Serle Court, London	020 7242 6105
Bryden Mr Christopher James Yuen Kang	4 King's Bench Walk, London	020 7822 7000
Buckhaven Mr Simon	Hardwicke, London	020 7242 2523
Buckpitt Mr Michael David	Tanfield Chambers, London	020 7421 5300
Bullock Mr Robert Gustaf	The Chambers of Mr Bullock, Brighton	01273 321050
Burns Mr Jeremy Stuart	12 College Place, Southampton	023 8032 0320
Butler Mr Andrew	Tanfield Chambers, London	020 7421 5300
Butler Mr Rupert James	3 Hare Court, London	020 7415 7800
Butler Mr Simon David	The Chambers of Grahame Aldous QC, London	020 7832 0500
Buttimore Mr Gabriel	13 KBW, Oxford	01865 311066
	13 King's Bench Walk, London	020 7353 7204
Candlin Miss Naomi Helen	St Philips Chambers, Birmingham	0121 246 7000
Cant Mr Christopher Ian	9 Stone Buildings, London	020 7404 5055
Capon Mr Philip Christopher William	East Anglian Chambers, Chelmsford	01473 214481
	East Anglian Chambers, Ipswich	01473 214481
	East Anglian Chambers, Norwich	01473 214481
	St Philips Chambers, Birmingham	0121 246 7000
Carlisle Mr Timothy St John Ogilvie	Field Court Chambers, London	020 7405 6114
Carr Mr Adrian James Selden	Tanfield Chambers, London	020 7421 5300
Carr Mr Christopher Sean	36 Bedford Row, London	020 7421 8000
Cattermole Miss Rebecca Elke	Tanfield Chambers, London	020 7421 5300

Name	Chambers	Telephone
Cattermull Miss Emma Jayne	East Anglian Chambers, Chelmsford	01473 214481
	East Anglian Chambers, Ipswich	01473 214481
	East Anglian Chambers, Norwich	01473 214481
Caun Mr Lawrence	Lamb Chambers, London	020 7797 8300
Charalambides Mr Leonidas	Francis Taylor Building, London	020 7353 8415
Chatterjee Miss Adreeja Julia	No5 Chambers, Birmingham	0845 210 5555
	No5 Chambers, Bristol	0845 210 5555
	No5 Chambers, London	0845 210 5555
Chowdhary Mr Islamuddin	Cassian Chambers, Ilford	07796 262641
Christensen Mr Carlton	10 King's Bench Walk, London	020 7353 7742
Chute Ms Andrea Alexandra	Rougemont Chambers, Exeter	01392 208484
	Tooks Chambers, London	020 7842 7575
Clark Mr Andrew Richard	9 St John Street, Manchester	0161 955 9000
Clark Mr Dingle	Goldsmith Chambers, London	020 7353 6802
Clarke Mr George Robert Ivan	5 Pump Court, London	020 7353 2532
Clarke Mr Timothy John	Cornwall Street Chambers, Birmingham	0121 233 7500
Clayton Mr Nigel Garvin	Kings Chambers, Birmingham	0845 034 3444
	Kings Chambers, Leeds	0845 034 3444
	Kings Chambers, Manchester	0845 034 3444
Clegg Mr Simon Robert Jonathan	St Philips Chambers, Birmingham	0121 246 7000
Colbey Mr Richard	Guildhall Chambers Portsmouth, Portsmouth	023 9275 2400
	Lamb Chambers, London	020 7797 8300
Collett Mr Gavin Charles	Rougemont Chambers, Exeter	01392 208484
Cooper Miss Christine	Field Court Chambers, London	020 7405 6114
Coster Mr Ronald David	42 Bedford Row, London	020 7831 0222
Cotterell Mr David William	Albion Chambers, Bristol	0117 927 2144
Cramsie Mr James Sinclair Beresford	13 KBW, Oxford	01865 311066
	13 King's Bench Walk, London	020 7353 7204
Crew Miss Gillian Mary	Ely Place Chambers, London	020 7400 9600
Dagg Mr John Douglas	Trinity Chambers, Chelmsford	01245 605040
Dalby Mr Joseph Francis	4-5 Gray's Inn Square, London	020 7404 5252
Daly Mr David	Heathway Chambers, London	020 8293 0509
Daniels Miss Philippa Catherine	36 Bedford Row, London	020 7421 8000
Datta Mr Shomik	42 Bedford Row, London	020 7831 0222
Davies Miss Carol Elizabeth	College Chambers, Southampton	023 8023 0338
Davies Mr Max James	30 Park Place, Cardiff	029 2039 8421
Davies Ms Samantha Teresa	Chambers of Ms Samantha Davies, Milton Keynes	0845 123 1234
	Warwick House Chambers, London	020 7430 2323
De Waal Mr John Henry Lowndes	Hardwicke, London	020 7242 2523
Demachkie Mr Jamal	3 PB Barristers, London	020 7583 8055
Denbin Mr Jack Arnold	Greenway, Sonning-on-Thames	0118 969 2484
Devereux-Cooke Mr Richard Charles	13 Old Square Chambers, London	020 7831 4445
di Mambro Mr David Jesse Andrew	Pallant Chambers, Chichester	01243 784538
	Radcliffe Chambers, London	020 7831 0081
Dickinson Mr John Finch Heneage	St John's Chambers, Bristol	0117 923 4700
Dipré Mr Paul Nicholas Amadeus	Chambers of Mr P N Dipré, Address withheld	0845 123 1234
	MK Family Law Chambers, Milton Keynes	0845 123 1234
Dovar Mr Daniel	Tanfield Chambers, London	020 7421 5300
Egleton Mr Richard Wildman	Pallant Chambers, Chichester	01243 784538
Eilledge Miss Amanda Gail Caroline	11 Stone Buildings, London	020 7831 6381
Elliott Mr Colin Douglas	King's Bench and Godolphin (KBG)Chambers, Plymouth	01752 221551
Elliott Mr Edward Anthony John	Garden Court Chambers, London	020 7993 7600
Esprit Mr Benoit	Barristers Chambers, London	020 3417 6461
	Legis Chambers, Aylesbury	01296 431125
Fain Mr Carl Ian	Tanfield Chambers, London	020 7421 5300
Fairbank Mr Nicholas James	4 Paper Buildings, London	020 7427 5200
Falkowski Mr Damian	4-5 Gray's Inn Square, London	020 7404 5252

Fawcett Mr Neil	St Ive's Chambers, Birmingham	0121 236 0863
Feldman Mr Matthew Richard Bankes	42 Bedford Row, London	020 7831 0222
Fellows Mr Philip David Andrew	Hardwicke, London	020 7242 2523
Felton Mr Timothy John Fowler	Rougemont Chambers, Exeter	01392 208484
Ferber Ms Iris	42 Bedford Row, London	020 7831 0222
Fieldsend Mr James William	Tanfield Chambers, London	020 7421 5300
Finlay Mr Darren	Sovereign Chambers, Leeds	0113 245 1841
Fowles Mr Jonathan James	Serle Court, London	020 7242 6105
Francis Mr Andrew James	Serle Court, London	020 7242 6105
	Zenith Chambers, Leeds	0113 245 5438
Francis Mr Richard Maurice	9 Park Place, Cardiff	029 2038 2731
Fryer Mr Nigel Mccrae	Queen Square Chambers, Bristol	0117 921 1966
Gadd Mr Adam Brian	Pump Court Chambers, London	020 7353 0711
	Pump Court Chambers, Winchester	01962 868 161
	Riverview Chambers, London	0844 225 3999
Gallagher Mr Stanley Harold	Tanfield Chambers, London	020 7421 5300
Gallivan Mr Terence John	Five Paper, London	020 7815 3200
Galway-Cooper Dr Philip Anthony	Five St Andrew's Hill, London	020 7332 5400
Gasztowicz Mr Steven	Cornerstone Barristers, London	020 7242 4986
	New Street Chambers, Leicester	0116 262 5906
Gatty Mr Daniel Simon	Hardwicke, London	020 7242 2523
George Mr Michael David Roberts	St Philips Chambers, Birmingham	0121 246 7000
George Mr Nicholas Frank Raymond	New Walk Chambers, Leicester	0871 200 1298/0116 255 9144
Gibbons Miss Mary Regina	Stone Chambers, London	020 7440 6900
Gibbons Ms Ellodie	Tanfield Chambers, London	020 7421 5300
Giles Mr David William	1 Gray's Inn Square, London	020 7405 0001
Glaser Mr Michael Samson	14 Gray's Inn Square, London	020 7242 0858
Godfrey Mr Lauren John	Crown Office Row Chambers, Brighton	01273 625625
Gold Mr Richard David	St John's Chambers, Bristol	0117 923 4700
Goldstein Mr Wayne Nathan	18 St John Street, Manchester	0161 278 1800
Goodall Mr Charles Vernon Machin-	Queen Square Chambers, Bristol	0117 921 1966
Gordon Mr Jeremy	Chambers of Mr Ami Feder, London	020 7797 7788
	Chambers of Mr Ami Feder, London	020 7797 7788
	Lamb Building, Brighton	01273 820490
Gore Mr Andrew Roger	Fenners Chambers, Cambridge	01223 368761
Gourlay Miss Amanda Kirsten	Tanfield Chambers, London	020 7421 5300
Graham Mrs Alana Nicole	Chambers of Alana Graham, Halesowen	01384 894560
	9 Stone Buildings, London	020 7404 5055
Greenan Miss Sarah Octavia	Zenith Chambers, Leeds	0113 245 5438
Gunstone Mr Robert Giles	KCH Garden Square, Nottingham	0115 941 8851
Gupta Mr Amit	St Philips Chambers, Birmingham	0121 246 7000
Guy Mr Richard Perran	Chambers of Mr Ami Feder, London	020 7797 7788
	King's Bench and Godolphin (KBG)Chambers, Plymouth	01752 221551
	Southernhay Chambers, Exeter	01392 255777
Hall Mr James Edward	Cornwall Street Chambers, Birmingham	0121 233 7500
Hallett Miss Katherine Elizabeth	13 Old Square Chambers, London	020 7831 4445
Halstead Mr Robin Bernard	One Essex Court, London	020 7936 3030
Hansen Mr William Joseph	No5 Chambers, Birmingham	0845 210 5555
	No5 Chambers, Bristol	0845 210 5555
	No5 Chambers, London	0845 210 5555
Harris Mr David Robert	St Albans Chambers, St Albans	01727 843383
Harris Mr James	Five St Andrew's Hill, London	020 7332 5400
Harris Mr Melvyn	5 Essex Court, London	020 7410 2000
Harrison Mr John Foster	St Paul's Chambers, Leeds	0113 245 5866
Hayes Mr Richard James	Lamb Chambers, London	020 7797 8300
Heppinstall Mr Adam John	Henderson Chambers, London	020 7583 9020
Hicks Mr Edward Gordon David	Radcliffe Chambers, London	020 7831 0081
Hill Mr Piers Nicholas	37 Park Square Chambers, Leeds	0113 243 9422
Hillas Miss Samantha	Atlantic Chambers, Liverpool	0151 236 4421
Hillier Mr William	New Street Chambers, Leicester	0116 262 5906

Name	Chambers	Telephone
Hilton Ms Saisampan	Holborn Chambers, London	020 7242 6060
Hodgkiss Ms Suzanne Jane	43 Temple Row Chambers, Birmingham	0121 237 6035
Hodson Mr Matthew Paul	Farrar's Building, London	020 7583 9241
Holbech Mr Charles Edward	New Square Chambers, London	020 7419 8000
Holland Mr Charles Christopher	Francis Taylor Building, London	020 7353 8415
	Trinity Chambers, Middlesbrough	01642 247569
	Trinity Chambers, Newcastle Upon Tyne	0191 232 1927
Holland Mr Rowan Guy	Five Paper, London	020 7815 3200
Hormaeche Miss Alejandra	Tanfield Chambers, London	020 7421 5300
Horne Mr Charles Hugh Wilson	Kings Chambers, Birmingham	0845 034 3444
	Kings Chambers, Leeds	0845 034 3444
	Kings Chambers, Manchester	0845 034 3444
Hornett Mr Stuart Ian	Selborne Chambers, London	020 7420 9500
Horton Mr Michael John Edward	Coram Chambers, London	020 7092 3700
Hubbard Mr Mark Iain	New Square Chambers, London	020 7419 8000
Huggins Mr Toby James	Unity Street Chambers, Bristol	0117 906 9789
Hughes-Deane Ms Charlotte Barbara	Atlantic Chambers, Liverpool	0151 236 4421
Hunt Mr Stephen	4 Stone Buildings, London	020 7242 5524
Hussain Mr Muhammad Altaf	Chambers of Mr M A Hussain, London	020 8679 2398
Isaac Mr Nicholas Dudley	Tanfield Chambers, London	020 7421 5300
Jefferies Mr Thomas Robert	Landmark Chambers, London	020 7430 1221
Jones Mr Alun	St Paul's Chambers, Leeds	0113 245 5866
Jones Mr Christopher David Harries	St John's Chambers, Bristol	0117 923 4700
Jones Mr Emyr Gweirydd	9 Park Place, Cardiff	029 2038 2731
Jones Mr Geraint Anthony	New Walk Chambers, Leicester	0871 200 1298/0116 255 9144
	9 St John Street, Manchester	0161 955 9000
	Tanfield Chambers, London	020 7421 5300
Jones Mr Geraint Martyn	Fenners Chambers, Cambridge	01223 368761
Jones Mr Kelvin Mcallister	Templis Chambers, London	020 7649 9808
Jones Mr Mark Simeon	3 Dr Johnson's Buildings, London	020 7353 4854
Jones Mr Rhys Charles Mansel	14 Gray's Inn Square, London	020 7242 0858
Jones Mr Richard Frederick Thomas	Heavenwood Chambers, Stroud	01453 873444
Jones Ms Cheryl Stephanie	No5 Chambers, Birmingham	0845 210 5555
	No5 Chambers, Bristol	0845 210 5555
	No5 Chambers, London	0845 210 5555
Joseph Mr Charles Henry	Tanfield Chambers, London	020 7421 5300
Kelly Mr Sean	Chancery House Chambers, Leeds	0113 244 6691
Kelly Mrs Amy Louise	12 College Place, Southampton	023 8032 0320
Kemp Mr James Rupert	Trinity Chambers, Middlesbrough	01642 247569
	Trinity Chambers, Newcastle Upon Tyne	0191 232 1927
Khan Dr Alexander	Coral House, Manchester	
Khan Mr Abdul Aleem	Gray's Chambers, Newbury	020 8518 2525
Kilcoyne Mr Patrick Desmond Oliver	42 Bedford Row, London	020 7831 0222
Kilvington Miss Sarah Elizabeth	18 St John Street, Manchester	0161 278 1800
Kirk Mr Graeme Charles	One Essex Court, London	020 7936 3030
Knight Mr Keith Leslie Francis	4 King's Bench Walk, London	020 7822 7000
Kramer Mr Philip Anthony	Park Lane Plowden, Newcastle Upon Tyne	0191 211 4087
Kynoch Mr Duncan Stuart Sanderson	Selborne Chambers, London	020 7420 9500
Lane Mr Simon Charles	Rougemont Chambers, Exeter	01392 208484
Law Mr John Edward	The Chambers of Grahame Aldous QC, London	020 7832 0500
Le Poidevin Mr Nicholas Peter	New Square Chambers, London	020 7419 8000
Learmonth Mr Alexander Robert Magnus	New Square Chambers, London	020 7419 8000
Leigh Mr Kevin	No5 Chambers, Birmingham	0845 210 5555
	No5 Chambers, Bristol	0845 210 5555
	No5 Chambers, London	0845 210 5555
Lennard Mr Stephen Charles	Hardwicke, London	020 7242 2523

Leonard Mr Charles Robert Weston	Hardwicke, London	020 7242 2523
Leslie Miss Marie Rita	Albion Chambers, Bristol	0117 927 2144
Lippold Ms Sarah Ida Louise	13 KBW, Oxford	01865 311066
	13 King's Bench Walk, London	020 7353 7204
Littman Mr Jeffrey James	Chambers of Mr Jeffrey Littman, London	020 8922 6844
	9 Park Place, Cardiff	029 2038 2731
Lo Mr Bernard Norman	Field Court Chambers, London	020 7405 6114
Lopez Mr Juan Nemesio	Francis Taylor Building, London	020 7353 8415
Loveday Mr Mark Alan	Tanfield Chambers, London	020 7421 5300
MacEvilly Mr Conn Jeremy	9 Stone Buildings, London	020 7404 5055
Maguire Mr Andrew James	Exchange Chambers, Liverpool	0151 236 7747
	Exchange Chambers, Manchester	0161 833 2722
	St Philips Chambers, Birmingham	0121 246 7000
Mahmood Mr Abid	Central Chambers, Manchester	0161 236 1133
	No5 Chambers, Birmingham	0845 210 5555
	No5 Chambers, Bristol	0845 210 5555
	No5 Chambers, London	0845 210 5555
Maltz Mr Ben Daniel	Five Paper, London	020 7815 3200
Mann Mr Christopher	13 KBW, Oxford	01865 311066
	13 King's Bench Walk, London	020 7353 7204
Marcus Mr Peter	Zenith Chambers, Leeds	0113 245 5438
Marsden Mr Andrew Guy	East Anglian Chambers, Chelmsford	01473 214481
	East Anglian Chambers, Colchester	01473 214481
	East Anglian Chambers, Ipswich	01473 214481
	East Anglian Chambers, Norwich	01473 214481
Marshall Mr Derek Stanley	College Chambers, Southampton	023 8023 0338
Matthias Mr David Huw	Francis Taylor Building, London	020 7353 8415
McCann Miss Katie	Atlantic Chambers, Liverpool	0151 236 4421
McCormack Mr Alan	Staple Inn Chambers, London	020 7242 5240
McDonnell Mr John Beresford William	13 Old Square Chambers, London	020 7831 4445
McLinden Mr John Vincent Barry	Field Court Chambers, London	020 7405 6114
McNae Mr Jonathan James	Selborne Chambers, London	020 7420 9500
McNeill Mr David Martin	Five St Andrew's Hill, London	020 7332 5400
Meager Mrs Rowena Elisabeth	No5 Chambers, Birmingham	0845 210 5555
	No5 Chambers, Bristol	0845 210 5555
	No5 Chambers, London	0845 210 5555
Meares Mr Nigel Leslie Vellacott	11 Stone Buildings, London	020 7831 6381
Melville-Shreeve Mr Michael David	Walnut House, Exeter	01392 279751
Menon Mr Harigovind	New Court Chambers, Newcastle Upon Tyne	0191 232 1980
	Park Lane Plowden, Newcastle Upon Tyne	0191 211 4087
Michael Mr Nicholas	East Anglian Chambers, Chelmsford	01473 214481
	East Anglian Chambers, Colchester	01473 214481
	East Anglian Chambers, Ipswich	01473 214481
	East Anglian Chambers, Norwich	01473 214481
Miller Mr Ian Robertson	Broadway House Chambers, Bradford	01274 722560
	Broadway House Chambers, Leeds	0113 246 2600
Mitchell Mr David John	No5 Chambers, Birmingham	0845 210 5555
	No5 Chambers, Bristol	0845 210 5555
	No5 Chambers, London	0845 210 5555
Modgill Mr Alexander Jeffrey	Broadway House Chambers, Bradford	01274 722560
	Broadway House Chambers, Leeds	0113 246 2600
Monnington Mr Bruce Gilbert	Fenners Chambers, Cambridge	01223 368761
Moore Mr Jonathan Guy	Cathedral Chambers, Cardiff	02920 660129
	Cathedral Chambers, Newport	01633 215112
Morris Mr Phillip John	9 Park Place, Cardiff	029 2038 2731
Moss Mr Christopher Stephen	St Johns Buildings, Manchester	0161 214 1500
	St Johns Buildings Liverpool, Liverpool	0151 243 6000
	16 Winckley Square, Preston	01772 256100
Mullen Mr Mark Robert	Radcliffe Chambers, London	020 7831 0081

C

Name	Chambers	Telephone
Murray Mr Charles Humphrey Stewart	Rougemont Chambers, Exeter	01392 208484
Newman Mr Paul	3 PB Barristers, Bournemouth	01202 292102
	3 PB Barristers, Bristol	0117 928 1520
	3 PB Barristers, London	020 7583 8055
	3 PB Barristers, Oxford	01865 793 736
	3 PB Barristers, Winchester	01962 868884
Newsom Mr George Lucien	Guildhall Chambers, Bristol	0117 930 9000
Nicholls Mr David James	11 Stone Buildings, London	020 7831 6381
Nickless Mr Jason Alan	College Chambers, Southampton	023 8023 0338
Noble Mr Andrew	Enterprise Chambers, Leeds	0113 246 0391
Norman Mr Michael Charles	3 PB Barristers, Bournemouth	01202 292102
	3 PB Barristers, Bristol	0117 928 1520
	3 PB Barristers, London	020 7583 8055
	3 PB Barristers, Oxford	01865 793 736
	3 PB Barristers, Winchester	01962 868884
Normington Mr James Adam	Park Court Chambers, Leeds	0113 243 3277
Norton Mr Giles	Enigma Chambers, Sheffield	07779 576499
	Holborn Chambers, London	020 7242 6060
Nosworthy Mr Jonathan Alex	St Philips Chambers, Birmingham	0121 246 7000
Nurse Mr Gordon Bramwell William	Radcliffe Chambers, London	020 7831 0081
O'Brien Mr Nicholas William Wattebot	10 King's Bench Walk, London	020 7353 7742
Ohrenstein Mr Dov	Radcliffe Chambers, London	020 7831 0081
Oliver Mr David Keightley Rideal	13 Old Square Chambers, London	020 7831 4445
O'Mahony Mr Jonathan Solomon	9 Stone Buildings, London	020 7404 5055
O'Neill Mr Jonathan Norman	Rougemont Chambers, Exeter	01392 208484
O'Sullivan Mr Richard John	1215 Chambers, London	020 3291 1215
O'Toole Mr Simon Gerard	5 Pump Court, London	020 7353 2532
	Riverview Chambers, London	0844 225 3999
Otwal Mr Mukhtiar Singh	42 Bedford Row, London	020 7831 0222
Oulton Mr Richard Arthur Courtenay	5 Essex Court, London	020 7410 2000
Paget Mr Michael Rodborough	Garden Court Chambers, London	020 7993 7600
Panton Mr Alastair Howard	10 King's Bench Walk, London	020 7353 7742
Paraskos Mr Paraskevakis Christakis	11 Gray's Inn Square Chambers, London	020 7405 6879
Parker Mrs Karen Lesley	Guildhall Chambers Portsmouth, Portsmouth	023 9275 2400
Parsons Mr Andrew James	Portsmouth Barristers'Chambers, Portsmouth	023 9283 1292
Paton Mr Ewan William	Guildhall Chambers, Bristol	0117 930 9000
Payton Mr Clifford Coningsby	Alpha Court Chambers, Leamington Spa	01926 886412
Pearce Mr Robert Edgar	Radcliffe Chambers, London	020 7831 0081
Pennock Mr Ian	Park Lane Plowden, Leeds	0113 228 5049
Picarda Mr Hubert Alistair Paul	Chambers of Mr Hubert Picarda QC, London	020 7242 3566
Pigram Mr Christopher Stuart	East Anglian Chambers, Chelmsford	01473 214481
	East Anglian Chambers, Colchester	01473 214481
	East Anglian Chambers, Ipswich	01473 214481
Pithers Mr Clive Robert	Fenners Chambers, Cambridge	01223 368761
Platt Miss Heather Louise	Pump Court Chambers, London	020 7353 0711
	Pump Court Chambers, Swindon	01793 539899
	Riverview Chambers, London	0844 225 3999
Polli Mr Timothy James	Tanfield Chambers, London	020 7421 5300
Quirke Mr Gerard Martin	Citadel Chambers, Birmingham	0121 233 8500
Rahman Mr Sami Ur	Field Court Chambers, London	020 7405 6114
Rainey Mr Philip Carslake	Tanfield Chambers, London	020 7421 5300
Ratcliffe Miss Frances Anne	Radcliffe Chambers, London	020 7831 0081
Richman Mrs Helene Pines	Eighteen Carlton Crescent, Southampton	023 8063 9001
	9 Stone Buildings, London	020 7404 5055
	Stour Chambers, Canterbury	01227 764899

Rinker Mr Andrew Stuart D'Artois	Chambers of Mr Andrew Rinker, London	020 7584 1091
Risso-Gill Mr Edward David Charles	Thomas More Chambers, London	020 7404 7000
Ritchie Mr Richard Bulkeley	XXIV Old Buildings, London	020 7691 2424
Roberts Mr Huw Eifion	Linenhall Chambers, Chester	01244 348282
Roberts Mr Michael Charles	Chambers of Michael Roberts, Henley-On-Thames	01844 355 655
Robinson Miss Laura	Tanfield Chambers, London	020 7421 5300
Ross Mr Sidney David	11 Stone Buildings, London	020 7831 6381
Rowntree Mr Edward John Pickering	Hardwicke, London	020 7242 2523
Rubens Miss Jacqueline Ann	1 Pump Court, London	020 7842 7070
Sadiq Mr Muhammad Faisel	Ely Place Chambers, London	020 7400 9600
Sandham Mr James Andrew	Arden Chambers, London	020 7242 4244
Saunders Miss Zoe Alice	St John's Chambers, Bristol	0117 923 4700
Sefi Mr Benedict John	Harcourt Chambers, London	0844 561 7135
	Harcourt Chambers, Oxford	0844 561 7135
Sefton-Smith Mr Lloyd	Lamb Chambers, London	020 7797 8300
Sellers Mr Graham	Atlantic Chambers, Liverpool	0151 236 4421
Sharples Mr John Edmund	St John's Chambers, Bristol	0117 923 4700
Shaw Miss Joanna Elizabeth	One Essex Court, London	020 7936 3030
Shaw Ms Nicola Jane Duckworth	Trinity Chambers, Middlesbrough	01642 247569
	Trinity Chambers, Newcastle Upon Tyne	0191 232 1927
	15 Winckley Square, Preston	01772 252828
Sheftel Mr Andrew Lawson Baylies	Tanfield Chambers, London	020 7421 5300
Shuman Miss Karen Ann Elizabeth	1 Chancery Lane, London	0845 634 6666
	No 8 Chambers, Birmingham	0121 236 5514
Sinclair Miss Lisa Anne	Chambers of Miss Lisa Sinclair, London	020 8946 7201
Sinclair Mr Graham Kelso	East Anglian Chambers, Colchester	01473 214481
	East Anglian Chambers, Ipswich	01473 214481
	East Anglian Chambers, Norwich	01473 214481
Sisley Mr Timothy Julian Crispin	9 Stone Buildings, London	020 7404 5055
Sjostrand Miss Ekaterina	13 Old Square Chambers, London	020 7831 4445
Skelly Mr Andrew Jon	Hardwicke, London	020 7242 2523
Smith Mr Roger Hugh Traylen	No5 Chambers, Birmingham	0845 210 5555
	No5 Chambers, Bristol	0845 210 5555
	No5 Chambers, London	0845 210 5555
Smithers Dr Roger Howard	Alexander Chambers, London	0845 652 0451/0854 652 0451
	Clerksroom (Taunton), Taunton	0845 083 3000
	Guildford Chambers, Guildford	01483 539131
Speller Mr Bruce Christopher Norman	The White House, Battle	01424 777944
Spratt-Dawson Miss Josephine Margery	Trinity Chambers, Chelmsford	01245 605040
Staddon Mr Paul	Tanfield Chambers, London	020 7421 5300
Stenhouse Mr John Alexander	Nightingale Chambers, Wolverley	01562 851350
Sterling Mr Robert Alan	St James's Chambers, Manchester	0161 834 7000
	Zenith Chambers, Leeds	0113 245 5438
Stevens-Hoare Miss Michelle	Hardwicke, London	020 7242 2523
Stevenson Dr Simon John	Park Lane Plowden, Leeds	0113 228 5049
Stevenson Mr Paul Anthony	Tanfield Chambers, London	020 7421 5300
Stewart Mr Nicholas John Cameron	Ely Place Chambers, London	020 7400 9600
Stirling Mr Christopher William	Field Court Chambers, London	020 7405 6114
Stubbs Mr Richard John Morris	Trinity Chambers, Middlesbrough	01642 247569
	Trinity Chambers, Newcastle Upon Tyne	0191 232 1927
Styles Mrs Kay Margaret	Harcourt Chambers, London	0844 561 7135
	Harcourt Chambers, Oxford	0844 561 7135
Swirsky Mr Adam Abraham Burl Bradbury	Lamb Chambers, London	020 7797 8300
Taylor Miss Araba Arba Kurankyiwa	Fenners Chambers, Cambridge	01223 368761
Taylor Mr Rhys Steadman	30 Park Place, Cardiff	029 2039 8421

C

Terry Mr Robert Jeffrey	Kings Chambers, Birmingham	0845 034 3444
	Kings Chambers, Leeds	0845 034 3444
	Kings Chambers, Manchester	0845 034 3444
	Lamb Chambers, London	020 7797 8300
Thomas Mrs Felicity	Westgate Chambers, Lewes	01273 480510
Thrower Mr James Simeon	Chambers of Simeon Thrower, London	020 8878 7374
Tinnion Mr Antoine	Trinity Chambers, Middlesbrough	01642 247569
	Trinity Chambers, Newcastle Upon Tyne	0191 232 1927
Topal Mr Erol	Lamb Chambers, London	020 7797 8300
Treharne Mr Neil Simon	Dingle Chambers, Bristol	07818 827754
Trompeter Mr Nicholas Simeon	Selborne Chambers, London	020 7420 9500
Troup Mr Alexander William	St John's Chambers, Bristol	0117 923 4700
Trumpington Mr John Henry	Staple Inn Chambers, London	020 7242 5240
Tucker Mr James William Richard	Teucro Chambers, Epsom	
Turnbull Miss Helen Mary	Lamb Chambers, London	020 7797 8300
Upton Mr Jonathan Michael	Tanfield Chambers, London	020 7421 5300
Van Overdijk Miss Claire Orit	No5 Chambers, Birmingham	0845 210 5555
	No5 Chambers, Bristol	0845 210 5555
	No5 Chambers, London	0845 210 5555
Van Tonder Mr Gerard Dirk	New Square Chambers, London	020 7419 8000
Vane The Hon Christopher John Fletcher	Trinity Chambers, Middlesbrough	01642 247569
	Trinity Chambers, Newcastle Upon Tyne	0191 232 1927
Vanhegan Mr Toby Bartholomew	Arden Chambers, London	020 7242 4244
Vasilescu Mr Andrei Constantin	Chambers of Martin Burr, London	0845 123 1234
Vaughan-Williams Mr Arthur Laurence	13 Old Square Chambers, London	020 7831 4445
Verduyn Dr Anthony James	St Philips Chambers, Birmingham	0121 246 7000
Vernon Mr Elliot Curt	No. 3 Fleet Street Chambers, London	020 7936 4474
Vickery Mr Neil Michael	13 KBW, Oxford	01865 311066
	13 King's Bench Walk, London	020 7353 7204
Wales Mr Matthew James	Guildhall Chambers, Bristol	0117 930 9000
Walsh Mr Michael Patrick	Tanfield Chambers, London	020 7421 5300
Warner Mr David Alexander	St Philips Chambers, Birmingham	0121 246 7000
Watson Mr Alaric	11 Stone Buildings, London	020 7831 6381
Watson Mr Duncan Allen	Westgate Chambers, Lewes	01273 480510
Wheatley Mr Geraint Rhys	Kings Chambers, Birmingham	0845 034 3444
	Kings Chambers, Leeds	0845 034 3444
	Kings Chambers, Manchester	0845 034 3444
Wheaton Mr Ian Malcolm James	Eighteen Carlton Crescent, Southampton	023 8063 9001
White Mr Peter-John Spencer	Great Barford Chambers, Bedford	012134 870004
Wightwick Mr Iain	Riverview Chambers, London	0844 225 3999
	Unity Street Chambers, Bristol	0117 906 9789
Wilkinson Mr Marc Ashley	No5 Chambers, Birmingham	0845 210 5555
	No5 Chambers, Bristol	0845 210 5555
	No5 Chambers, London	0845 210 5555
Williams Mr Simon Paul	Radcliffe Chambers, London	020 7831 0081
Wolstenholme Miss Janine	Sovereign Chambers, Leeds	0113 245 1841
Worthley Mr Andrew Mark	Rougemont Chambers, Exeter	01392 208484
Young Mr Martin Ford	9 Stone Buildings, London	020 7404 5055

CHARITIES

Ajaz Mr Mohammad Arshad	Eastmans Chambers, Reading	0118 966 9094
Asprey Mr Nicholas	Clock Chambers, Wolverhampton	01902 313444
	Serle Court, London	020 7242 6105
Bennion-Pedley Mr Edward	13 KBW, Oxford	01865 311066
	13 King's Bench Walk, London	020 7353 7204
Birch Mr Roger Allen	Five St Andrew's Hill, London	020 7332 5400
	Sovereign Chambers, Leeds	0113 245 1841
Bragiel Mr Edward Bronislaw Henryk	Hogarth Chambers, London	020 7404 0404

C

Buchan Miss Caroline Venetia	Chambers of Miss C Buchan, Haywards Heath	01444 482222
Cant Mr Christopher Ian	9 Stone Buildings, London	020 7404 5055
Falkowski Mr Damian	4-5 Gray's Inn Square, London	020 7404 5252
Fowles Mr Jonathan James	Serle Court, London	020 7242 6105
Francis Mr Richard Maurice	9 Park Place, Cardiff	029 2038 2731
Godfrey Mr Lauren John	Crown Office Row Chambers, Brighton	01273 625625
Haywood Dr Jennifer Margaret	Serle Court, London	020 7242 6105
Holbech Mr Charles Edward	New Square Chambers, London	020 7419 8000
Hunt Mr Stephen	4 Stone Buildings, London	020 7242 5524
Hussain Mr Muhammad Altaf	Chambers of Mr M A Hussain, London	020 8679 2398
Iyer Miss Shobana	Swan Chambers, Richmond	0845 123 1234
Jones Mr Christopher David Harries	St John's Chambers, Bristol	0117 923 4700
Kessler Mr James Richard	Taxchambers, London	020 7242 2744
Khan Mr Abdul Aleem	Gray's Chambers, Newbury	020 8518 2525
Lewison Mr Josh	Radcliffe Chambers, London	020 7831 0081
Lloyd Mr John Nesbitt	Rougemont Chambers, Exeter	01392 208484
Lyon Mrs Shane Valerie	King's Bench and Godolphin (KBG)Chambers, Plymouth	01752 221551
Lyons Mr Timothy John	4-5 Gray's Inn Square, London	020 7404 5252
	St James's Chambers, Manchester	0161 834 7000
Matthias Mr David Huw	Francis Taylor Building, London	020 7353 8415
McDonnell Mr John Beresford William	13 Old Square Chambers, London	020 7831 4445
Meares Mr Nigel Leslie Vellacott	11 Stone Buildings, London	020 7831 6381
Monnington Mr Bruce Gilbert	Fenners Chambers, Cambridge	01223 368761
Mullen Mr Mark Robert	Radcliffe Chambers, London	020 7831 0081
Mustakim Mr Abdul Yunus Al	Chambers of Mr Mustakim, London	
Nasim Mr Zia-Ul-Mustafa	Milestone Chambers, London	
Newsom Mr George Lucien	Guildhall Chambers, Bristol	0117 930 9000
Nurse Mr Gordon Bramwell William	Radcliffe Chambers, London	020 7831 0081
Pearce Mr Robert Edgar	Radcliffe Chambers, London	020 7831 0081
Picarda Mr Hubert Alistair Paul	Chambers of Mr Hubert Picarda QC, London	020 7242 3566
Quirke Mr Gerard Martin	Citadel Chambers, Birmingham	0121 233 8500
Richman Mrs Helene Pines	Eighteen Carlton Crescent, Southampton	023 8063 9001
	9 Stone Buildings, London	020 7404 5055
	Stour Chambers, Canterbury	01227 764899
Roberts Mr Michael Charles	Chambers of Michael Roberts, Henley-On-Thames	01844 355 655
Silverton Miss Catherine Anne	Sovereign Chambers, Leeds	0113 245 1841
Skinner Mr Samuel Richard Edward	KCH Garden Square, Nottingham	0115 941 8851
Sowler Mr Thomas Richard Holland	The Tax Chambers of Mr Richard Sowler TD, Douglas	07624 235000
Sterling Mr Robert Alan	St James's Chambers, Manchester	0161 834 7000
	Zenith Chambers, Leeds	0113 245 5438
Stevenson Dr Simon John	Park Lane Plowden, Leeds	0113 228 5049
Stewart Mr Nicholas John Cameron	Ely Place Chambers, London	020 7400 9600
Taylor Miss Araba Arba Kurankyiwa	Fenners Chambers, Cambridge	01223 368761
Thomson Mr Martin Haldane Ahmad	Wynne Chambers, London	020 3239 6964

CHILDREN'S LAW

Ailes Mr John Ashley	Eighteen Carlton Crescent, Southampton	023 8063 9001
Ajaz Mr Mohammad Arshad	Eastmans Chambers, Reading	0118 966 9094
Akinbolu Miss Sandra Adwoa Anifa	Chambers of Mr Ami Feder, London	020 7797 7788
	Chambers of Mr Ami Feder, London	020 7797 7788
Akman Miss Mercy Louise	36 Bedford Row, London	020 7421 8000
Allen Miss Sylvia Delores	1 Mitre Court Buildings, London	020 7452 8900
Allwood Mrs Gina Louisa	Seven Bedford Row, London	020 7242 3555
Anderson Mr Nicholas Guy	1 KBW Chambers, London	020 7936 1500
	King's Bench Chambers, Lewes	01273 402600

C

Atkinson Mr Jody Roy	St John's Chambers, Bristol	0117 923 4700
Awodele Mr Olufemi Adetunji	Great James Street Chambers, London	020 7440 4949
Bailey Mr Michael Robert	Tanfield Chambers, London	020 7421 5300
Barratt Mr Dominic Anthony	East Anglian Chambers, Chelmsford	01473 214481
	East Anglian Chambers, Colchester	01473 214481
	East Anglian Chambers, Ipswich	01473 214481
	East Anglian Chambers, Norwich	01473 214481
Beattie Ms Annabel Dorothy	Park Court Chambers, Leeds	0113 243 3277
Bennet Ms Pauline Agnes	Regency Chambers, Peterborough	01733 315215
Bhutta Miss Ayeesha Clare	Field Court Chambers, London	020 7405 6114
Bojarski Mr Andrzej Leonard	36 Bedford Row, London	020 7421 8000
Bowen Mr Nicholas James Hugh	Doughty Street Chambers, Bristol	01179 058 717
	Doughty Street Chambers, London	020 7404 1313
	Doughty Street Chambers, Manchester	0161 618 1066
Briden Ms Sarah Louise	KCH Garden Square, Nottingham	0115 941 8851
Buckhaven Mr Simon	Hardwicke, London	020 7242 2523
Buswell Mr Richard Thomas	Hardwicke, London	020 7242 2523
Carron Mr Richard Byron	Queen Square Chambers, Bristol	0117 921 1966
Cellan-Jones Mr Deiniol James	1 KBW Chambers, London	020 7936 1500
	King's Bench Chambers, Lewes	01273 402600
Chippendale Miss Emma Lorraine	37 Park Square Chambers, Leeds	0113 243 9422
Clarke Mrs Amanda Lesley	Westgate Chambers, Lewes	01273 480510
Da Costa-Waldman Mrs Elissa Josephine	Clerksroom (London), London	0845 083 3000
	Clerksroom (Taunton), Taunton	0845 083 3000
	King's Lynn Chambers, King's Lynn	01553 672 085
Dale Miss Lucy-Ann Georgia	4 Brick Court, London	020 7832 3200
Dean Mr James Patrick	Goldsmith Chambers, London	020 7353 6802
Dhadli Mrs Perminder	KCH Garden Square, Nottingham	0115 941 8851
Dhaliwal Miss Davinder Kaur	No 8 Chambers, Birmingham	0121 236 5514
Dove Mr James Francis	The Chambers of Grahame Aldous QC, London	020 7832 0500
Dowell Mr Gregory Hamilton	Principal Chambers, Sevenoaks	0845 209 8080
Duffy Mr Derek James	St Paul's Chambers, Leeds	0113 245 5866
Earley Miss Sarah Jane	Pallant Chambers, Chichester	01243 784538
Edington Mrs Fiona Anne Rider	Thomas More Chambers, London	020 7404 7000
Edwards Mr Nigel Royston	St Paul's Chambers, Leeds	0113 245 5866
Elcombe Mr Nicholas John	East Anglian Chambers, Chelmsford	01473 214481
	East Anglian Chambers, Colchester	01473 214481
	East Anglian Chambers, Ipswich	01473 214481
	East Anglian Chambers, Norwich	01473 214481
Elliott Mr Mark Daniel	3 PB Barristers, Bournemouth	01202 292102
	3 PB Barristers, Bristol	0117 928 1520
	3 PB Barristers, London	020 7583 8055
	3 PB Barristers, Oxford	01865 793 736
	3 PB Barristers, Winchester	01962 868884
Ephraim-Adejumo Mrs Hilda Ekpo	12 Old Square Chambers, London	020 7404 0875
Fairbank Mr Nicholas James	4 Paper Buildings, London	020 7427 5200
Fairburn Mr George Edward Henry	Cornwall Street Chambers, Birmingham	0121 233 7500
	Cornwall Street Chambers, Shrewsbury	01743 363 611/0121 233 7500
Fama Mrs Gudrun Hildegard	Middle Temple Lane Chambers, London	020 7583 4352
Fletcher Mr Christopher Michael	Octagon House, Norwich	01603 623186
Gallagher Ms Caoilfhionn Anna	Doughty Street Chambers, Bristol	01179 058 717
	Doughty Street Chambers, London	020 7404 1313
	Doughty Street Chambers, Manchester	0161 618 1066
German Miss Kelly Anne	Eastbourne Chambers, Eastbourne	01323 642102
Gillan Mrs Dominique Lye-Ping	Guildford Chambers, Guildford	01483 539131
Gillman Miss Rachel Mary	1 Garden Court Family Law Chambers, London	020 7797 7900
Giz Miss Alev Ayse	1 Garden Court Family Law Chambers, London	020 7797 7900
Glaser Mr Michael Samson	14 Gray's Inn Square, London	020 7242 0858

C

Goodall Miss Rachael Jane	3 PB Barristers, Bournemouth	01202 292102
	3 PB Barristers, Bristol	0117 928 1520
	3 PB Barristers, London	020 7583 8055
	3 PB Barristers, Oxford	01865 793 736
	3 PB Barristers, Winchester	01962 868884
Griffin Mr Ian Ross	4 Brick Court, London	020 7832 3200
Hale Mr Charles Stanley	4 Paper Buildings, London	020 7427 5200
Harper Miss Helen Catherine	Renaissance Chambers, London	020 7404 1111
Harris Miss Katie Anne	Octagon House, Norwich	01603 623186
Harrison Dr Graeme	12 College Place, Southampton	023 8032 0320
Hartley Mrs Caroline Anne	Pump Court Chambers, London	020 7353 0711
	Pump Court Chambers, Swindon	01793 539899
	Pump Court Chambers, Winchester	01962 868 161
Hasan Miss Ayesha	3 Dr Johnson's Buildings, London	020 7353 4854
Hay Mr Malcolm John Marshall	3 Dr Johnson's Buildings, London	020 7353 4854
Hellens Mr Matthew James	3 Dr Johnson's Buildings, London	020 7353 4854
Hillas Miss Samantha	Atlantic Chambers, Liverpool	0151 236 4421
Hillier Mr William	New Street Chambers, Leicester	0116 262 5906
Hinton Mr Neil Pearse	King's Bench Chambers, Bournemouth	01202 250025
Ismail Miss Nazmun Nisha	Central Chambers, Manchester	0161 236 1133
	No5 Chambers, Birmingham	0845 210 5555
	No5 Chambers, Bristol	0845 210 5555
	No5 Chambers, London	0845 210 5555
Jamil Miss Yasmeen	4 Brick Court, London	020 7832 3200
Jarman Mr Mark Christopher	4 Paper Buildings, London	020 7427 5200
Johnson Mr Simon Nicholas	Stour Chambers, Canterbury	01227 764899
Johnstone Mr Mark Anthony	4 Paper Buildings, London	020 7427 5200
Josty Mr David Stephen	College Chambers, Southampton	023 8023 0338
Kenny Mr Martin William	Walnut House, Exeter	01392 279751
Kinnear Miss Elise	Field Court Chambers, London	020 7405 6114
Kirby Miss Ruth Mary Anthony	4 Paper Buildings, London	020 7427 5200
Lloyd Ms Rhiannon	4 Paper Buildings, London	020 7427 5200
Lugsdin Mr Martin	Kenworthy's Chambers, Manchester	0161 832 4036
Luh Miss Shu Shin	Garden Court Chambers, London	020 7993 7600
Mackley Mr David John	18 St John Street, Manchester	0161 278 1800
McCormack Mr Alan	Staple Inn Chambers, London	020 7242 5240
McGowan Miss Maura Patricia	2 Bedford Row, London	020 7440 8888
	Lincoln House Chambers, Manchester	0161 832 5701
Meachin Miss Vanessa Veronica	St Philips Chambers, Birmingham	0121 246 7000
Moore Mr Jonathan Guy	Cathedral Chambers, Cardiff	02920 660129
	Cathedral Chambers, Newport	01633 215112
Moore Mrs Therese Finola	4 Brick Court, London	020 7832 3200
Moran Mr Christopher John	39 Park Square, Leeds	0113 245 6633
Mustakim Mr Abdul Yunus Al	Chambers of Mr Mustakim, London	
Nickless Mr Jason Alan	College Chambers, Southampton	023 8023 0338
O'Brien Mr David	Trinity Chambers, Chelmsford	01245 605040
O'Donovan Mr Ronan Daniel James	14 Gray's Inn Square, London	020 7242 0858
Papazian Miss Cliona Concepta	4 Paper Buildings, London	020 7427 5200
Pemberton Miss Yolanda Erica	St Philips Chambers, Birmingham	0121 246 7000
Posner Miss Gabrielle Jan	Renaissance Chambers, London	020 7404 1111
Pritchard Mrs Teresa Julia	5 Pump Court, London	020 7353 2532
Procter Mr Alfred George Haydn	1 Garden Court Family Law Chambers, London	020 7797 7900
Rai Miss Puneet Kaur	Thomas More Chambers, London	020 7404 7000
Rawal Miss Anita	Chambers of Mr Ami Feder, London	020 7797 7788
	Chambers of Mr Ami Feder, London	020 7797 7788
	Lamb Building, Brighton	01273 820490
Rawcliffe Mr Anthony Mark Wilson	4 Brick Court, London	020 7832 3200
Rhodes Miss Amanda Louise	Unity Street Chambers, Bristol	0117 906 9789
Roberts Mr James Mcclintock	1 KBW Chambers, London	020 7936 1500
	King's Bench Chambers, Lewes	01273 402600
Rosenblatt Mr Jeremy George	42 Bedford Row, London	020 7831 0222
Sharp Mr David Ian	Tanfield Chambers, London	020 7421 5300

Shaw Mr Julian	St Johns Buildings, Chester	01244 323070
	St Johns Buildings, Manchester	0161 214 1500
	St Johns Buildings Liverpool, Liverpool	0151 243 6000
Shaw Ms Nicola Jane Duckworth	Trinity Chambers, Middlesbrough	01642 247569
	Trinity Chambers, Newcastle Upon Tyne	0191 232 1927
	15 Winckley Square, Preston	01772 252828
Smout Mr William Kingsley	Guildford Chambers, Guildford	01483 539131
Spencer Mr Shaun Anthony	St Johns Buildings, Chester	01244 323070
	St Johns Buildings, Manchester	0161 214 1500
	16 Winckley Square, Preston	01772 256100
Styles Mr Clive Richard	Becket Chambers, Canterbury	01227 786331
Sutton Mr Clive Raymond	Chambers of Mr Clive Sutton, Bruerne	07973 386702
Tresman Mr Lewis Robert Simon	Staple Inn Chambers, London	020 7242 5240
Turnbull Mrs Linda Angela	1 Gray's Inn Square, London	020 7405 0001
Twist Mr Stephen John	Dere Street Barristers, Newcastle Upon Tyne	0844 3351551
Tyler Mr William John	36 Bedford Row, London	020 7421 8000
Villarosa Miss Annunziata	Clerksroom (London), London	0845 083 3000
	Clerksroom (Taunton), Taunton	0845 083 3000
Vollenweider Mr Amiot Marcus Ellerton	Thomas More Chambers, London	020 7404 7000
Ward Miss Kelly Jane	Pallant Chambers, Chichester	01243 784538
White Ms Ceri Ann	4 Paper Buildings, London	020 7427 5200
Williams Miss Anna	Trinity Chambers, Chelmsford	01245 605040
Williams Miss June Cleo	No 8 Chambers, Birmingham	0121 236 5514
Winslett Mr Frank	Westgate Chambers, Lewes	01273 480510
Wood Ms Katie Anne	4 Paper Buildings, London	020 7427 5200

CIVIL LIBERTIES

Adewale Mr Remi Adetokunbo Sanni	Chambers of G. D. Tetteh, London	020 7353 7095
	Chambers of Mr R. A. Adewale, Address withheld	020 7231 2814
Akinbolu Miss Sandra Adwoa Anifa	Chambers of Mr Ami Feder, London	020 7797 7788
	Chambers of Mr Ami Feder, London	020 7797 7788
Algazy Mr Jacques Max	Cloisters, London	020 7827 4000
Ali Mrs Shamim	Chambers of Mrs Shamim Ali, Hatfield	01707 276737
Allwood Mrs Gina Louisa	Seven Bedford Row, London	020 7242 3555
Alomo Mr Richard Olusoji	14 Gray's Inn Square, London	020 7242 0858
Altaras Mr David Maurice	36 Bedford Row, London	020 7421 8000
Amraoui Mr Thomas	4-5 Gray's Inn Square, London	020 7404 5252
Arnheim Dr Michael Thomas Walter	Chambers of Dr Michael Arnheim, London	020 7833 5093
	Holborn Chambers, London	020 7242 6060
	Principal Chambers, Sevenoaks	0845 209 8080
Arnold Mr Graham John	Farringdon Chambers, London	020 7089 5700
Arshad Miss Farrhat	Doughty Street Chambers, Bristol	01179 058 717
	Doughty Street Chambers, London	020 7404 1313
	Doughty Street Chambers, Manchester	0161 618 1066
Auburn Mr Jonathan Walter	4-5 Gray's Inn Square, London	020 7404 5252
Badenoch Mr Tony David	6 King's Bench Walk, London	020 7583 0410
Bajwa Mr Ali Naseem	Garden Court Chambers, London	020 7993 7600
Baldwin Dr Timothy John	Garden Court Chambers, London	020 7993 7600
Bartfeld Mr Jason Maurice	187 Fleet Street, London	020 7430 7430
Barton Mr Hugh Geoffrey	Lincoln House Chambers, Manchester	0161 832 5701
Baruah Miss Rima	Thomas More Chambers, London	020 7404 7000
Beharrylal Mr Satyanand Sarju	15 New Bridge Street, London	020 7842 1900
Bell Mr Dominic Michael St. John	Chambers of Marion Smullen and Kerim Fuad QC, London	020 7427 4400
Berry Mr Adrian Christopher	Garden Court Chambers, London	020 7993 7600
Bhanji Mr Shiraz Musa	4 Bingham Place, London	020 7486 5347
	1 Gray's Inn Square, London	020 7405 0001
Bhatti Miss Balvinder	Citadel Chambers, Birmingham	0121 233 8500

C

Bicarregui Miss Anna Claire Victoria	4-5 Gray's Inn Square, London	020 7404 5252
Birkby Mr Richard Adam	Park Court Chambers, Leeds	0113 243 3277
Birnbaum Mr Michael Ian	9-12 Bell Yard, London	020 7400 1800
Bisarya Mr Neil	Number 7 Harrington Street Chambers, Liverpool	0151 242 0707
Bishop Mr Malcolm Leslie	Argent Chambers, London	020 7556 5500
	Equity Chambers, Birmingham	0121 236 5007
	30 Park Place, Cardiff	029 2039 8421
Blackwood Mr Clive David	Lamb Chambers, London	020 7797 8300
Bourne Mr Charles Gregory	4-5 Gray's Inn Square, London	020 7404 5252
Bowen Mr Nicholas James Hugh	Doughty Street Chambers, Bristol	01179 058 717
	Doughty Street Chambers, London	020 7404 1313
	Doughty Street Chambers, Manchester	0161 618 1066
Bowers Mr Rupert John	Doughty Street Chambers, London	020 7404 1313
Brown Mr Sam Clement	Atkinson Bevan Chambers, London	020 7353 2112
Brown Ms Grace	Tooks Chambers, London	020 7842 7575
Buchan Mr Andrew	Cloisters, London	020 7827 4000
Bullen Mrs Mary	The Chambers Of Mary Bullen, Wilton	01722 742204
Bunting Mr Daniel Alexander James	2 Dr Johnson's Buildings, London	020 7936 2613
Bunting Mr Jude James	Tooks Chambers, London	020 7842 7575
Burrett Mr Alex	1 Gray's Inn Square, London	020 7405 0001
Byrnes Miss Aisling Alice Elizabeth	25 Bedford Row, London	020 7067 1500
Caldwell Mr Peter Hugh Coyles	Dyers Chambers, London	020 7404 1881
Callery Mr Martin	Cobden House Chambers, Manchester	0161 833 6000
Carr Mr Christopher Sean	36 Bedford Row, London	020 7421 8000
Carrion Benitez Ms Miriam	36 Bedford Row, London	020 7421 8000
Casey Mr Paul Joseph	Chambers of Marion Smullen and Kerim Fuad QC, London	020 7427 4400
Cecil Miss Joanne Michelle	1 Pump Court, London	020 7842 7070
Chadwick Miss Joanna Ceridwen	No5 Chambers, Birmingham	0845 210 5555
	No5 Chambers, Bristol	0845 210 5555
	No5 Chambers, London	0845 210 5555
Chelvan Mr S	No5 Chambers, Birmingham	0845 210 5555
	No5 Chambers, Bristol	0845 210 5555
	No5 Chambers, London	0845 210 5555
	Trent Chambers, Nottingham	0115 941 9596
Chippeck Mr Stephen	5 King's Bench Walk, London	020 7353 5638
Chipperfield Mr Jeremy Steven	Cranford Chambers, London	020 7404 7454
Christie Mr Iain Robert	5RB, London	020 7242 2902
Christie Mr Richard Hamish	2 Pump Court, London	020 7353 5597
Clay Mr Jonathan Roger	Cornerstone Barristers, London	020 7242 4986
Comb Mr David William	Trinity Chambers, Middlesbrough	01642 247569
	Trinity Chambers, Newcastle Upon Tyne	0191 232 1927
Connolly Mr Dominic Regan	Five St Andrew's Hill, London	020 7332 5400
Coyle Mr Anthony Noel	Zenith Chambers, Leeds	0113 245 5438
Critchley Mr John Stephen	Field Court Chambers, London	020 7405 6114
Crosfill Mr John	Field Court Chambers, London	020 7405 6114
Davey Mr Charles	64 Bridge Street, Manchester	0845 083 3000
	Chambers of Mr C Davey, Bishop's Stortford	01279 506412
	Clerksroom (Taunton), Taunton	0845 083 3000
De Mello Mr Rembert Joseph Julius	No5 Chambers, Birmingham	0845 210 5555
	No5 Chambers, Bristol	0845 210 5555
	No5 Chambers, London	0845 210 5555
Del Fabbro Mr Oscar	23 Essex Street, London	020 7413 0353
Diamond Mr Paul	Chambers of Mr Paul Diamond, Cambridge	01223 264544
Doerfel Mr Jan Hendrik Jamison	1215 Chambers, London	020 3291 1215
	Chambers of Mr J H Doerfel, Richmond	0845 123 1234
Dos Santos Mr Alexander	Charter Chambers, London	020 7618 4400
Dubin Mr Joshua Charles	1 Pump Court, London	020 7842 7070

Eastwood Miss Philippa Clemency Anne	Doughty Street Chambers, London	020 7404 1313
Edwards Mr Denis	Francis Taylor Building, London	020 7353 8415
Elliott Mr Jason	Dere Street Barristers, Newcastle Upon Tyne	0844 3351551
Engelman Mr Philip	Cloisters, London	020 7827 4000
	Trinity Chambers, Middlesbrough	01642 247569
	Trinity Chambers, Newcastle Upon Tyne	0191 232 1927
Evans Mr Simeon Vaughan	St Johns Buildings, Manchester	0161 214 1500
	St Johns Buildings Liverpool, Liverpool	0151 243 6000
	16 Winckley Square, Preston	01772 256100
Facenna Mr Gerald Carlo	Monckton Chambers, London	020 7405 7211
Fishwick Mr Gregory David Philip Kyle	187 Fleet Street, London	020 7430 7430
Fitzmaurice Mr Guy Edward Christian	Staple Inn Chambers, London	020 7242 5240
Forster Ms Sarah Judith	14 Gray's Inn Square, London	020 7242 0858
	Westgate Chambers, Lewes	01273 480510
Frank Mr Ivor Richard Bainton	7 Bell Yard, London	020 7831 0636
Gallagher Ms Caoilfhionn Anna	Doughty Street Chambers, Bristol	01179 058 717
	Doughty Street Chambers, London	020 7404 1313
	Doughty Street Chambers, Manchester	0161 618 1066
Gallivan Mr Terence John	Five Paper, London	020 7815 3200
Gledhill Mr Lee Andre	Alexander Chambers, London	0845 652 0451/0854 652 0451
	Trident Barristers Chambers, Manchester	0161 663 3123
Glyn Mr Caspar Hilary Gordon	Cloisters, London	020 7827 4000
Godfrey Mr Lauren John	Crown Office Row Chambers, Brighton	01273 625625
Goldberg Mr Jonathan Jacob	Cobden House Chambers, Manchester	0161 833 6000
	North Square Chambers, London	020 8455 3735
Goodman Mr Alexander David Edmund	Atlas Chambers, London	020 7269 7980
	4-5 Gray's Inn Square, London	020 7404 5252
Gow Mr Henry	New Bailey Chambers, Liverpool	0151 236 9402
Grant Mr Gary Steven	Francis Taylor Building, London	020 7353 8415
Greatorex Mr Paul	4-5 Gray's Inn Square, London	020 7404 5252
Greenfield Mr Peter Charles	King's Bench Chambers, Bournemouth	01202 250025
Hanif Miss Saima Naz	4-5 Gray's Inn Square, London	020 7404 5252
Hanlon Mr James Tobias	Old Bailey Chambers, London	020 3008 6404
Hendron Mr Henry Joseph Christopher	Strand Chambers, London	020 7117 6920
Hewson Ms Barbara Mary	Hardwicke, London	020 7242 2523
Hill Mr Nicholas Mark	Pump Court Chambers, London	020 7353 0711
	Pump Court Chambers, Swindon	01793 539899
	St Philips Chambers, Birmingham	0121 246 7000
Hill Ms Eleanor Mary Henrietta	Doughty Street Chambers, Bristol	01179 058 717
	Doughty Street Chambers, London	020 7404 1313
	Doughty Street Chambers, Manchester	0161 618 1066
Hood Mr David	Prince of Wales Chambers, London	020 7622 7415
Horne-Roberts Mrs Jennifer	Goldsmith Chambers, London	020 7353 6802
Hossain Mr Mohammed Monwar	No. 3 Fleet Street Chambers, London	020 7936 4474
Hulse Mrs Cecilia Helen	Chambers of Mr Ami Feder, London	020 7797 7788
	Chambers of Mr Ami Feder, London	020 7797 7788
Hussain Miss Frida Khanam	Furnival Chambers, London	020 7405 3232
Hussain Mr Muhammad Altaf	Chambers of Mr M A Hussain, London	020 8679 2398
Hutchinson Mr Colin Thomas	Garden Court Chambers, London	020 7993 7600
Irwin Mr Gavin David	Dyers Chambers, London	020 7404 1881
Ismail Miss Nazmun Nisha	Central Chambers, Manchester	0161 236 1133
	No5 Chambers, Birmingham	0845 210 5555
	No5 Chambers, Bristol	0845 210 5555
	No5 Chambers, London	0845 210 5555

Jafar Mr Abdurahman Akhtar	Chambers of Mr Abdurahman Jafar, Ilford	07828 937338
Jarvis Mr Paul	6 King's Bench Walk, London	020 7583 0410
Jones Miss Jacinta Elizabeth Barrett	1 Mitre Court Buildings, London	020 7452 8900
Jones Mr Mark Andrew	St Ive's Chambers, Birmingham	0121 236 0863
Jones Ms Katie Laura	Lincoln House Chambers, Manchester	0161 832 5701
Juss Prof Satvinder Singh	3 Hare Court, London	020 7415 7800
Keith Mr Benjamin Charles Andrew	Five St Andrew's Hill, London	020 7332 5400
Kelly Mr Matthias John	39 Essex Street, London	020 7832 1111
Kent Mr Michael Harcourt	Crown Office Chambers, London	020 7797 8100
Khan Mr Forz	Chambers of Mr F Khan, London	07854 109584
	6 King's Bench Walk, London	020 7353 4931
Khan Mr Mahmood Shafi	Luton Chambers, Luton	01582 598394
	Willesden Chambers, London	020 3273 1042
King Mr John Patrick	Nine Bedford Row, London	020 7489 2727
Knight Mr Benjamin James	Central Chambers, Manchester	0161 236 1133
Kohli Mr Ryan Singh	Cornerstone Barristers, London	020 7242 4986
Krause Ms Florence	Meritz Chambers, Hebben Bridge	0845 094 0856
Kwiatkowski Mr Feliks Jerzy	Kew Chambers, Kew	0844 8099991
Lahiffe Mr Martin Patrick Joseph	3 Temple Gardens, London	020 7353 3102
Lal Mr Sanjay	4 King's Bench Walk, London	020 7822 7000
Leake Mr Stephen	Carmelite Chambers, London	020 7936 6300
Lemer Mr David James	Doughty Street Chambers, London	020 7404 1313
Lenaghan Mr Anthony	Dyers Chambers, London	020 7404 1881
Levinson Miss Jemma	1 Mitre Court Buildings, London	020 7452 8900
Lewiecki Miss Marie	Old Bailey Chambers, London	020 3008 6404
Lewis Mr Dominic	Five Paper Buildings, London	020 7583 6117
Lissack Mr Richard Anthony	Outer Temple Chambers, London	020 7353 6381
	Riverview Chambers, London	0844 225 3999
Lloyd Mr Benjamin John	6 King's Bench Walk, London	020 7583 0410
Lock Mr David Anthony	No5 Chambers, Birmingham	0845 210 5555
	No5 Chambers, Bristol	0845 210 5555
	No5 Chambers, London	0845 210 5555
Lodge Mr Hugo Daniel Paul	Atkinson Bevan Chambers, London	020 7353 2112
Lofthouse Mr James	1 Gray's Inn Square, London	020 7405 0001
Luh Miss Shu Shin	Garden Court Chambers, London	020 7993 7600
Lule Miss Jacqueline	1 Mitre Court Buildings, London	020 7452 8900
MacKenzie Mr Robert Sutherland	Middle Temple Lane Chambers, London	020 7583 4352
MacKie Ms Jeannie	Doughty Street Chambers, Bristol	01179 058 717
	Doughty Street Chambers, London	020 7404 1313
	Doughty Street Chambers, Manchester	0161 618 1066
Mahmood Mr Abid	Central Chambers, Manchester	0161 236 1133
	No5 Chambers, Birmingham	0845 210 5555
	No5 Chambers, Bristol	0845 210 5555
	No5 Chambers, London	0845 210 5555
Malone Mr David John	1 Gray's Inn Square, London	020 7405 0001
Mann Mr Jonathan Simon	25 Bedford Row, London	020 7067 1500
Mannion Ms Amy Elisabeth	9-12 Bell Yard, London	020 7400 1800
	1 Crown Office Row, London	020 7797 7500
Mantle Mr Peter John	Monckton Chambers, London	020 7405 7211
Marks Mr Jonathan Clive	4 Pump Court, London	020 7842 5555
Markus Ms Kate	Doughty Street Chambers, Bristol	01179 058 717
	Doughty Street Chambers, London	020 7404 1313
	Doughty Street Chambers, Manchester	0161 618 1066
Mather Mr Nicholas Ian Stewart	Furnival Chambers, London	020 7405 3232
Matthias Mr David Huw	Francis Taylor Building, London	020 7353 8415
McGowan Miss Maura Patricia	2 Bedford Row, London	020 7440 8888
	Lincoln House Chambers, Manchester	0161 832 5701
McKendrick Mr John Dempster	Outer Temple Chambers, London	020 7353 6381
McKiernan Mr Edward Joseph	Farringdon Chambers, London	020 7089 5700
McLinden Mr John Vincent Barry	Field Court Chambers, London	020 7405 6114
McTague Miss Meghann Rose	2 Temple Gardens, London	020 7822 1200
Menon Mr Rajiv	Garden Court Chambers, London	020 7993 7600

Metcalfe Dr Eric William	Monckton Chambers, London	020 7405 7211
Metzer Mr Anthony David Erwin	Argent Chambers, London	020 7556 5500
Middleton Mr Joseph	Doughty Street Chambers, Bristol	01179 058 717
	Doughty Street Chambers, London	020 7404 1313
	Doughty Street Chambers, Manchester	0161 618 1066
Millett Mr Kenneth James	2 Hare Court, London	020 7353 3982
Moran Mr Christopher John	39 Park Square, Leeds	0113 245 6633
Morris Mr Ben	Chavasse Court Chambers, Liverpool	0151 229 2030
Muller Mr Antonie Sean	Citadel Chambers, Birmingham	0121 233 8500
Muman Mr Vijay Kumar	43 Temple Row Chambers, Birmingham	0121 237 6035
Mustakim Mr Abdul Yunus Al	Chambers of Mr Mustakim, London	
Myers Mr Benjamin John	Exchange Chambers, Liverpool	0151 236 7747
	Exchange Chambers, Manchester	0161 833 2722
Mylvaganam Ms Tanoo	1 Gray's Inn Square, London	020 7405 0001
Newman Mr Alan Ronald Harvey	Argent Chambers, London	020 7556 5500
Nicholls Mr Colin Alfred Arthur	3 Raymond Buildings, London	020 7400 6400
O'Brien Mr Nicholas William Wattebot	10 King's Bench Walk, London	020 7353 7742
O'Connor Mr Patrick Michael Joseph	Doughty Street Chambers, Bristol	01179 058 717
	Doughty Street Chambers, London	020 7404 1313
	Doughty Street Chambers, Manchester	0161 618 1066
O'Donoghue Mr Hugh Vincent	Carmelite Chambers, London	020 7936 6300
Offer Mr Alexander	Garden Court Chambers, London	020 7993 7600
	Park Court Chambers, Leeds	0113 243 3277
Onalaja Mr James Oluwatosin	2 Pump Court, London	020 7353 5597
O'Neill Mr Brian Patrick	2 Hare Court, London	020 7353 3982
O'Sullivan Mr Richard John	1215 Chambers, London	020 3291 1215
Owen Mr Timothy Wynn	Matrix Chambers, London	020 7404 3447
Palmer Mr Robert Henry	Monckton Chambers, London	020 7405 7211
Panton Mr William Dwight	Amethyst Chambers, London	020 7936 4966
Paraskos Mr Paraskevakis Christakis	11 Gray's Inn Square Chambers, London	020 7405 6879
Pascoe Ms Soraya	1 Gray's Inn Square, London	020 7405 0001
Patel Mr Yasin Ahmed	25 Bedford Row, London	020 7067 1500
Penny Miss Abigail Sarah Prudence	4 Breams Buildings, London	020 7092 1900
Peretz Mr George Michael John	Monckton Chambers, London	020 7405 7211
Perian Mr Steven	3 Temple Gardens, London	020 7353 3102
Peterson Miss Geraldine Shelda	Chambers of Mr Ami Feder, London	020 7797 7788
	Chambers of Mr Ami Feder, London	020 7797 7788
	Lamb Building, Brighton	01273 820490
Pickup Mr James Kenneth	2 Hare Court, London	020 7353 3982
	Lincoln House Chambers, Manchester	0161 832 5701
Pipe Mr Adam	No 8 Chambers, Birmingham	0121 236 5514
Plimmer Miss Melanie Ann	Kings Chambers, Birmingham	0845 034 3444
	Kings Chambers, Leeds	0845 034 3444
	Kings Chambers, Manchester	0845 034 3444
Purnell Mr Paul Oliver	Farringdon Chambers, London	020 7089 5700
Qureshi Mr Tanveer Aftab	25 Bedford Row, London	020 7067 1500
Rahman Mr Anis	12 Old Square Chambers, London	020 7404 0875
Rai Mr Rajesh Kumar	1 Mitre Court Buildings, London	020 7452 8900
Rana Mr Mohammed Akram	Clapham Law Chambers, London	020 7978 8482
Rayment Mr Benedick Michael	Monckton Chambers, London	020 7405 7211
Rees Mr Robert Charles David	New Walk Chambers, Leicester	0871 200 1298/0116 255 9144
Rees Prof William Michael	1 Gray's Inn Square, London	020 7405 0001
Richards Mr Duncan James	Chambers of Mr Ami Feder, London	020 7797 7788
	Chambers of Mr Ami Feder, London	020 7797 7788
	Principal Chambers, Sevenoaks	0845 209 8080
Richardson Mr Alistair Paul George	6 King's Bench Walk, London	020 7583 0410
Rippon Mr Simon John	Citadel Chambers, Birmingham	0121 233 8500
Roche Mr Patrick Richard Redmond	Tooks Chambers, London	020 7842 7575
Rogers Mr Ian Paul	Monckton Chambers, London	020 7405 7211
Rose Miss Pamela Susan	1 Mitre Court Buildings, London	020 7452 8900

Rosemarine Mr Andrew Marc	Chambers of Mr A M Rosemarine, Manchester	0161 740 3861
Rule Mr Philip David	Castle Chambers, Harrow-on-the-Hill	020 8423 6579
Russell Mr Graham Alexander	Citadel Chambers, Birmingham	0121 233 8500
Russell-Mitra Miss Jessica Suparna	1 Mitre Court Buildings, London	020 7452 8900
Saifee Mr Faisal Aftaab	Thomas More Chambers, London	020 7404 7000
Scolding Miss Fiona Kate	Hardwicke, London	020 7242 2523
Scott Mr Andrew David Peter	Park Lane Plowden, Leeds	0113 228 5049
Seeboruth Mr Royln Jean-Paul	Chambers of Royln Seeboruth, Aylesbury	01296 393329
Sekar Mr Chandra	Angell Park Chambers, London	020 7737 5957
Shapiro Mr Selwyn	2 King's Bench Walk, London	020 7353 1746
Sharma Mr Sanjeev Mohan	Equity Chambers, Birmingham	0121 236 5007
Shaw Miss Joanna Elizabeth	One Essex Court, London	020 7936 3030
Sikand Miss Maya	Garden Court Chambers, London	020 7993 7600
Silverton Miss Catherine Anne	Sovereign Chambers, Leeds	0113 245 1841
Singarajah Mr Frederico	1 Gray's Inn Square, London	020 7405 0001
Skinner Mr Samuel Richard Edward	KCH Garden Square, Nottingham	0115 941 8851
Smith Mr Alisdair Robert Macsorley	9-12 Bell Yard, London	020 7400 1800
Solley Mr Stephen Malcolm	Charter Chambers, London	020 7618 4400
Sood Mrs Usha Rani	Trent Chambers, Nottingham	0115 941 9596
Spears Miss Katharine Sarah	Carmelite Chambers, London	020 7936 6300
Spencer Mr Paul Anthony	3 Serjeants Inn, London	020 7427 5000
Spicer Mr Robert Haden	Frederick Place Chambers, Bristol	0117 946 7059
Spooner Mr Henry Neville	Tolzey Chambers, Bristol	
	Westgate Chambers, Lewes	01273 480510
Spratt Mr Christopher David Richard Dean	9 Stone Buildings, London	020 7404 5055
St Louis Mr Brian Lloyd	15 New Bridge Street, London	020 7842 1900
Stagg Mr Paul Andrew	1 Chancery Lane, London	0845 634 6666
Stanage Mr Nick Sean	Doughty Street Chambers, Bristol	01179 058 717
	Doughty Street Chambers, London	020 7404 1313
	Doughty Street Chambers, Manchester	0161 618 1066
Stanbury Mr Matthew Francis	Chambers of Ian Macdonald QC, Manchester	0161 236 1840
Stanford Mr Tony James	Old Bailey Chambers, London	020 3008 6404
Stevens Mr Stuart Standish	Holborn Chambers, London	020 7242 6060
Stewart Mr Nicholas John Cameron	Ely Place Chambers, London	020 7400 9600
Stinchcombe Mr Paul David	4-5 Gray's Inn Square, London	020 7404 5252
Stone Mr Joseph	Doughty Street Chambers, Bristol	01179 058 717
	Doughty Street Chambers, London	020 7404 1313
	Doughty Street Chambers, Manchester	0161 618 1066
Storey Mr Richard Alexander	3 Temple Gardens, London	020 7353 3102
Storrie Mr Timothy James	Lincoln House Chambers, Manchester	0161 832 5701
Thomson Mr Martin Haldane Ahmad	Wynne Chambers, London	020 3239 6964
Tivadar Mr Daniel	3 Hare Court, London	020 7415 7800
Treverton-Jones Mr Gregory Dennis	39 Essex Street, London	020 7832 1111
	82 King Street, Manchester	0161 870 9969
Trowler Ms Rebecca	Doughty Street Chambers, Bristol	01179 058 717
	Doughty Street Chambers, London	020 7404 1313
	Doughty Street Chambers, Manchester	0161 618 1066
Twist Mr Stephen John	Dere Street Barristers, Newcastle Upon Tyne	0844 3351551
Uduje Mr Benjamin Elliott	42 Bedford Row, London	020 7831 0222
Upton Mr John Stewart	4 King's Bench Walk, London	020 7822 7000
Van Overdijk Miss Claire Orit	No5 Chambers, Birmingham	0845 210 5555
	No5 Chambers, Bristol	0845 210 5555
	No5 Chambers, London	0845 210 5555
Vassall-Adams Mr Guy Luke	Doughty Street Chambers, Bristol	01179 058 717
	Doughty Street Chambers, London	020 7404 1313
	Doughty Street Chambers, Manchester	0161 618 1066
Ward Mr Peter Mark	The Chambers of Peter Ward, London	020 3402 2152
Watson Mr Benjamin Turquand	3 Raymond Buildings, London	020 7400 6400
Watterson Ms Anna Elizabeth	1 Mitre Court Buildings, London	020 7452 8900

Weatherby Mr Peter Francis	Chambers of Ian Macdonald QC, Manchester	0161 236 1840
	Garden Court Chambers, London	020 7993 7600
Webster Mr Alistair Stevenson	Chambers of Andrew Mitchell QC, London	020 7440 9950
	Lincoln House Chambers, Manchester	0161 832 5701
Weekes Mr Mark Vincent	6 King's Bench Walk, London	020 7583 0410
Wells Mr Colin John	25 Bedford Row, London	020 7067 1500
White Mr Oliver Zachary	Littleton Chambers, London	020 7797 8600
Whitfield Mr Jonathan	Doughty Street Chambers, London	020 7404 1313
Wiktorowski-Solecki Miss Tamara	Middle Temple Lane Chambers, London	020 7583 4352
Wills Miss Alexandra Itari	Christ Church Chambers, London	020 7409 5278/07788 512787
Wise Mr Ian	Doughty Street Chambers, Bristol	01179 058 717
	Doughty Street Chambers, London	020 7404 1313
	Doughty Street Chambers, Manchester	0161 618 1066
Wood Mr James Alexander Douglas	Doughty Street Chambers, Bristol	01179 058 717
	Doughty Street Chambers, London	020 7404 1313
	Doughty Street Chambers, Manchester	0161 618 1066

CIVIL LITIGATION

Agnihotri Mr Naveen	12 College Place, Southampton	023 8032 0320
Ahluwalia Mr Navtej Singh	Garden Court Chambers, London	020 7993 7600
Ailes Mr John Ashley	Eighteen Carlton Crescent, Southampton	023 8063 9001
Ajaz Mr Mohammad Arshad	Eastmans Chambers, Reading	0118 966 9094
Akers Mr Robert Matthew Harry	St Johns Buildings, Chester	01244 323070
	St Johns Buildings, Manchester	0161 214 1500
	16 Winckley Square, Preston	01772 256100
Algazy Mr Jacques Max	Cloisters, London	020 7827 4000
Allison Mr Simon Robert	Hardwicke, London	020 7242 2523
Allwood Mrs Gina Louisa	Seven Bedford Row, London	020 7242 3555
Andre Mr Roger Louis	Sovereign Chambers, Leeds	0113 245 1841
Antell Mr John Jason	King's Bench and Godolphin (KBG)Chambers, Plymouth	01752 221551
Apthorp Mr George Charles	5 Essex Court, London	020 7410 2000
Arnold Mr Peter Matthew Miller	No5 Chambers, Birmingham	0845 210 5555
	No5 Chambers, Bristol	0845 210 5555
	No5 Chambers, London	0845 210 5555
Askey Mr Robert John	Palmyra Chambers, Warrington	01925 444919
Asprey Mr Nicholas	Clock Chambers, Wolverhampton	01902 313444
	Serle Court, London	020 7242 6105
Awodele Mr Olufemi Adetunji	Great James Street Chambers, London	020 7440 4949
Batey Mr David Michael	Stour Chambers, Canterbury	01227 764899
Beattie Ms Annabel Dorothy	Park Court Chambers, Leeds	0113 243 3277
Bezzam Miss Jayashree	Hampton Court Chambers, West Molesey	020 8979 0381
Bilsland Miss Alisan Margaret	St James's Chambers, Manchester	0161 834 7000
Bourne Mr Geoffrey Robert	13 Old Square Chambers, London	020 7831 4445
Bowen Mr Nicholas James Hugh	Doughty Street Chambers, Bristol	01179 058 717
	Doughty Street Chambers, London	020 7404 1313
	Doughty Street Chambers, Manchester	0161 618 1066
Branchflower Mr George	Zenith Chambers, Leeds	0113 245 5438
Bray Miss Helen Lorna	Walnut House, Exeter	01392 279751
Bredemear Mr Zachary Charles	1 Chancery Lane, London	0845 634 6666
Brown Miss Susan Margaret	One Essex Court, London	020 7936 3030
Buckhaven Mr Simon	Hardwicke, London	020 7242 2523
Butler Mr Simon David	The Chambers of Grahame Aldous QC, London	020 7832 0500
Buttimore Mr Gabriel	13 KBW, Oxford	01865 311066
	13 King's Bench Walk, London	020 7353 7204
Campbell Mr Oliver Edward Wilhelm	Henderson Chambers, London	020 7583 9020
Carr Mr Christopher Sean	36 Bedford Row, London	020 7421 8000
Cartwright Mr Ivan Matthew	KCH Garden Square, Nottingham	0115 941 8851

C

Caun Mr Lawrence	Lamb Chambers, London	020 7797 8300
Christensen Mr Carlton	10 King's Bench Walk, London	020 7353 7742
Coster Mr Ronald David	42 Bedford Row, London	020 7831 0222
Crew Miss Gillian Mary	Ely Place Chambers, London	020 7400 9600
Critchley Mr John Stephen	Field Court Chambers, London	020 7405 6114
Crosfill Mr John	Field Court Chambers, London	020 7405 6114
Croskell Mr Marcus James	East Anglian Chambers, Chelmsford	01473 214481
	East Anglian Chambers, Colchester	01473 214481
	East Anglian Chambers, Ipswich	01473 214481
	East Anglian Chambers, Norwich	01473 214481
Da Costa-Waldman Mrs Elissa Josephine	Clerksroom (London), London	0845 083 3000
	Clerksroom (Taunton), Taunton	0845 083 3000
	King's Lynn Chambers, King's Lynn	01553 672 085
Darroch Miss Fiona Culverwell	Clerksroom (London), London	0845 083 3000
	Clerksroom (Taunton), Taunton	0845 083 3000
	King's Lynn Chambers, King's Lynn	01553 672 085
Davies Miss Carol Elizabeth	College Chambers, Southampton	023 8023 0338
Davies Mr Henry Olusola	Trinity Chambers, Birmingham	0121 346 4672
Dovar Mr Daniel	Tanfield Chambers, London	020 7421 5300
Dowell Mr Gregory Hamilton	Principal Chambers, Sevenoaks	0845 209 8080
Dutt Miss Nisha	Middle Temple Lane Chambers, London	020 7583 4352
Engelman Mr Philip	Cloisters, London	020 7827 4000
	Trinity Chambers, Middlesbrough	01642 247569
	Trinity Chambers, Newcastle Upon Tyne	0191 232 1927
Ephraim-Adejumo Mrs Hilda Ekpo	12 Old Square Chambers, London	020 7404 0875
Facenna Mr Gerald Carlo	Monckton Chambers, London	020 7405 7211
Fairbank Mr Nicholas James	4 Paper Buildings, London	020 7427 5200
Falkowski Mr Damian	4-5 Gray's Inn Square, London	020 7404 5252
Field Mr Julian Nigel	Crown Office Chambers, London	020 7797 8100
Finlay Mr Darren	Sovereign Chambers, Leeds	0113 245 1841
Frawley Ms Lyndsey Anne	Quorum Chambers, St Albans	01727 884516
	Quorum Tax Chambers, London	020 7043 5189
Garvie Mr Carl Peter	St Philips Chambers, Birmingham	0121 246 7000
Gersch Mr Adam Nissen	Argent Chambers, London	020 7556 5500
Gill Miss Baljinder	10 King's Bench Walk, London	020 7353 7742
Gill Mr Satinderjit Singh	Five Paper, London	020 7815 3200
Glaser Mr Michael Samson	14 Gray's Inn Square, London	020 7242 0858
Gledhill Mr Lee Andre	Alexander Chambers, London	0845 652 0451/0854 652 0451
	Trident Barristers Chambers, Manchester	0161 663 3123
Gloag Mr Angus Robin	1 Gray's Inn Square, London	020 7405 0001
	Rougemont Chambers, Exeter	01392 208484
Glyn Mr Caspar Hilary Gordon	Cloisters, London	020 7827 4000
Goldberg Mr Simon Ian	Trinity Chambers, Middlesbrough	01642 247569
	Trinity Chambers, Newcastle Upon Tyne	0191 232 1927
Gow Mr Henry	New Bailey Chambers, Liverpool	0151 236 9402
Granville Stafford Mr Andrew	4 King's Bench Walk, London	020 7822 7000
Habib Miss Shysta	Kenworthy's Chambers, Manchester	0161 832 4036
Hanlon Mr James Tobias	Old Bailey Chambers, London	020 3008 6404
Harris Mr David Robert	St Albans Chambers, St Albans	01727 843383
Harris Mr James	Five St Andrew's Hill, London	020 7332 5400
Hillier Mr William	New Street Chambers, Leicester	0116 262 5906
Hinton Mr Neil Pearse	King's Bench Chambers, Bournemouth	01202 250025
Holland Mr Charles Christopher	Francis Taylor Building, London	020 7353 8415
	Trinity Chambers, Middlesbrough	01642 247569
	Trinity Chambers, Newcastle Upon Tyne	0191 232 1927
Hood Mr David	Prince of Wales Chambers, London	020 7622 7415
Hossain Mr Mohammed Monwar	No. 3 Fleet Street Chambers, London	020 7936 4474
Hughes-Deane Ms Charlotte Barbara	Atlantic Chambers, Liverpool	0151 236 4421

Ismail Miss Nazmun Nisha	Central Chambers, Manchester	0161 236 1133
	No5 Chambers, Birmingham	0845 210 5555
	No5 Chambers, Bristol	0845 210 5555
	No5 Chambers, London	0845 210 5555
Iyer Miss Shobana	Swan Chambers, Richmond	0845 123 1234
Jarratt Miss Alice Cordelia Betchworth	Carmelite Chambers, London	020 7936 6300
Jones Mr Emyr Gweirydd	9 Park Place, Cardiff	029 2038 2731
Jones Mr Richard Frederick Thomas	Heavenwood Chambers, Stroud	01453 873444
Jones Mrs Hettie Georgia	Liberty Chambers, Tenby	01834 844458
Kansal Miss Seema	12 Old Square Chambers, London	020 7404 0875
Kenny Mr Martin William	Walnut House, Exeter	01392 279751
Khan Dr Alexander	Coral House, Manchester	
Kidd Mr Peter William	Number 7 Harrington Street Chambers, Liverpool	0151 242 0707
Knight Mr Keith Leslie Francis	4 King's Bench Walk, London	020 7822 7000
Kramer Mr Philip Anthony	Park Lane Plowden, Newcastle Upon Tyne	0191 211 4087
Lane Mr Simon Charles	Rougemont Chambers, Exeter	01392 208484
Lewis Mr Wayne Anthony	Access Lawyers, London	020 8801 2345
Livingstone Mr Simon John	Thomas More Chambers, London	020 7404 7000
Lo Mr Bernard Norman	Field Court Chambers, London	020 7405 6114
Lopez Mr Juan Nemesio	Francis Taylor Building, London	020 7353 8415
Luh Miss Shu Shin	Garden Court Chambers, London	020 7993 7600
MacEvilly Mr Conn Jeremy	9 Stone Buildings, London	020 7404 5055
Maka Mr Isaac	Chambers of Mr Isaac Maka, Ilford	07973 308 301
	4 King's Bench Walk, London	020 7822 7000
Marsden Mr Andrew Guy	East Anglian Chambers, Chelmsford	01473 214481
	East Anglian Chambers, Colchester	01473 214481
	East Anglian Chambers, Ipswich	01473 214481
	East Anglian Chambers, Norwich	01473 214481
Matthias Mr David Huw	Francis Taylor Building, London	020 7353 8415
McCombie Mr Fergus Alexander Paul	1 Gray's Inn Square, London	020 7405 0001
McCulloch Miss Fiona Catharine Jane	Middle Temple Lane Chambers, London	020 7583 4352
McNae Mr Jonathan James	Selborne Chambers, London	020 7420 9500
Medcroft Mr Nicholas Julian	Outer Temple Chambers, London	020 7353 6381
Menon Mr Harigovind	New Court Chambers, Newcastle Upon Tyne	0191 232 1980
	Park Lane Plowden, Newcastle Upon Tyne	0191 211 4087
Metzger Mr Kevin Albert	11 Gray's Inn Square Chambers, London	020 7405 6879
Mitchell Mr Alistair Stephen Fabian	49 Chambers, Bridgnorth	01746 761545
Moffat Mr Russell Dean	Linenhall Chambers, Chester	01244 348282
Moran Mr Christopher John	39 Park Square, Leeds	0113 245 6633
Mullen Mr Mark Robert	Radcliffe Chambers, London	020 7831 0081
Muman Mr Vijay Kumar	43 Temple Row Chambers, Birmingham	0121 237 6035
Mustakim Mr Abdul Yunus Al	Chambers of Mr Mustakim, London	
Newman Mr Alan Ronald Harvey	Argent Chambers, London	020 7556 5500
Nickless Mr Jason Alan	College Chambers, Southampton	023 8023 0338
Norton Mr Giles	Enigma Chambers, Sheffield	07779 576499
	Holborn Chambers, London	020 7242 6060
O'Brien Mr Nicholas William Wattebot	10 King's Bench Walk, London	020 7353 7742
Onipede Dr Victor Olusegun	Chambers of Dr V O Onipede, London	07956 207159
Oommen Mr Jacob	Chambers of Mr Jacob Oommen, East Barnet	07958 680272
O'Sullivan Mr Richard John	1215 Chambers, London	020 3291 1215
Otchie Mr Andrew Akuafo	12 Old Square Chambers, London	020 7404 0875
Owen Mr Timothy Wynn	Matrix Chambers, London	020 7404 3447
Paraskos Mr Paraskevakis Christakis	11 Gray's Inn Square Chambers, London	020 7405 6879

Barrister	Chambers	Telephone
Peretz Mr George Michael John	Monckton Chambers, London	020 7405 7211
Perry Mr Christopher Edward	Palmyra Chambers, Warrington	01925 444919
Philipson Miss Amy Victoria	Sovereign Chambers, Leeds	0113 245 1841
Polli Mr Timothy James	Tanfield Chambers, London	020 7421 5300
Pugh Mr John Bishop	John Pugh's Chambers, Liverpool	0151 236 5415
Qureshi Miss Dilruba	Temple Court Chambers, London	020 7353 7888
Rahman Mr Anis	12 Old Square Chambers, London	020 7404 0875
Rahman Mr Leo Ferhanur	Chambers of Leo Rahman, Brighton	07814 004 790
Rai Miss Puneet Kaur	Thomas More Chambers, London	020 7404 7000
Rana Mr Mohammed Akram	Clapham Law Chambers, London	020 7978 8482
Reed Mr Simon John	New Walk Chambers, Leicester	0871 200 1298/0116 255 9144
Reid Miss Claudette Patricia	Chambers of Miss Claudette Reid, London	
Richman Mrs Helene Pines	Eighteen Carlton Crescent, Southampton	023 8063 9001
	9 Stone Buildings, London	020 7404 5055
	Stour Chambers, Canterbury	01227 764899
Rifat Mr Maurice Alan	1 Gray's Inn Square, London	020 7405 0001
Rinker Mr Andrew Stuart D'Artois	Chambers of Mr Andrew Rinker, London	020 7584 1091
Roberts Mr Huw Eifion	Linenhall Chambers, Chester	01244 348282
Russell Mr Thomas Charles Welldon	KCH Garden Square, Nottingham	0115 941 8851
Saini Mr Parminder Paul Singh	12 Old Square Chambers, London	020 7404 0875
Sefton-Smith Mr Lloyd	Lamb Chambers, London	020 7797 8300
Shamim Mr Mohammed	Clapham Law Chambers, London	020 7978 8482
Shaw Mr Julian	St Johns Buildings, Chester	01244 323070
	St Johns Buildings, Manchester	0161 214 1500
	St Johns Buildings Liverpool, Liverpool	0151 243 6000
Sinclair Miss Lisa Anne	Chambers of Miss Lisa Sinclair, London	020 8946 7201
Skelt Mr Ian Stuart	KBW, Leeds	0113 297 1200
Stead Mr Richard James	St John's Chambers, Bristol	0117 923 4700
Stebbings Mr Ian Anthony	1 Gray's Inn Square, London	020 7405 0001
Stevens-Hoare Miss Michelle	Hardwicke, London	020 7242 2523
Stirling Mr Christopher William	Field Court Chambers, London	020 7405 6114
Stuart Mr James William	Lamb Chambers, London	020 7797 8300
Swirsky Mr Adam Abraham Burl Bradbury	Lamb Chambers, London	020 7797 8300
Temmink Mr Robert-Jan	Quadrant Chambers, London	020 7583 4444
Treharne Mr Neil Simon	Dingle Chambers, Bristol	07818 827754
Tresman Mr Lewis Robert Simon	Staple Inn Chambers, London	020 7242 5240
Trumpington Mr John Henry	Staple Inn Chambers, London	020 7242 5240
Turnbull Miss Helen Mary	Lamb Chambers, London	020 7797 8300
Unigwe Mr Sylvester Emefiona	Essex House Chambers, London	020 7692 0677
	11 Gray's Inn Square Chambers, London	020 7405 6879
Van Tonder Mr Gerard Dirk	New Square Chambers, London	020 7419 8000
Vasilescu Mr Andrei Constantin	Chambers of Martin Burr, London	0845 123 1234
Victor-Mazeli Miss Jacqueline	Bell Yard Chambers, London	020 7306 9292
	Chambers of Martin Burr, London	0845 123 1234
Vitiello Mr Fabio Angelo-Giuseppe	Staple Inn Chambers, London	020 7242 5240
Walker Mr Adam Nigel	Seven Bedford Row, London	020 7242 3555
Walker-Nolan Mr Benjamin	Thomas More Chambers, London	020 7404 7000
Watson Mr Duncan Allen	Westgate Chambers, Lewes	01273 480510
Watterson Ms Anna Elizabeth	1 Mitre Court Buildings, London	020 7452 8900
Welch Mr David William	Alexander Chambers, London	0845 652 0451/0854 652 0451
	Warwick House Chambers, London	020 7430 2323
Whyatt Mr Michael George	15 Winckley Square, Preston	01772 252828
Whyte Miss Monica Patricia	42 Bedford Row, London	020 7831 0222
Wightwick Mr Iain	Riverview Chambers, London	0844 225 3999
	Unity Street Chambers, Bristol	0117 906 9789
Wilcox Mr Jerome Carl Jean	Alexander Chambers, London	0845 652 0451/0854 652 0451

Wilkinson Miss Katie	43 Temple Row Chambers, Birmingham	0121 237 6035
Williams Miss June Cleo	No 8 Chambers, Birmingham	0121 236 5514
Wills Miss Alexandra Itari	Christ Church Chambers, London	020 7409 5278/07788 512787
Winslett Mr Frank	Westgate Chambers, Lewes	01273 480510
Wolstenholme Miss Janine	Sovereign Chambers, Leeds	0113 245 1841
Woodward Miss Joanne Claire	9 St John Street, Manchester	0161 955 9000
Wragg Mr Jonathan Robert	Highgate Chambers, London	020 8340 6031

COMMERCIAL LITIGATION

Abasheikh Mr Omar Said Imam	Paragon Chambers, London	020 3318 9988
Adewale Mr Remi Adetokunbo Sanni	Chambers of G. D. Tetteh, London	020 7353 7095
	Chambers of Mr R. A. Adewale, Address withheld	020 7231 2814
Aeberli Mr Peter Dolph	3 PB Barristers, Bournemouth	01202 292102
	3 PB Barristers, Bristol	0117 928 1520
	3 PB Barristers, London	020 7583 8055
	3 PB Barristers, Oxford	01865 793 736
	3 PB Barristers, Winchester	01962 868884
Ahmed Mr Ishfaq	Stone Chambers, London	020 7440 6900
Ajaz Mr Mohammad Arshad	Eastmans Chambers, Reading	0118 966 9094
Alexandra Miss Sebastiane	Holborn Chambers, London	020 7242 6060
Algazy Mr Jacques Max	Cloisters, London	020 7827 4000
Aliker Mr Phillip Bliss	Tanfield Chambers, London	020 7421 5300
Alliott Mr George Beckles	Temple Garden Chambers, London	020 7583 1315
Allison Mr Simon Robert	Hardwicke, London	020 7242 2523
Almihdar Mr Ali Hamed	Outer Temple Chambers, London	020 7353 6381
Altaras Mr David Maurice	36 Bedford Row, London	020 7421 8000
Anderson Mr Mark Roger	No5 Chambers, Birmingham	0845 210 5555
	No5 Chambers, Bristol	0845 210 5555
	No5 Chambers, London	0845 210 5555
Anderson Mr Simon Peter Bede	Park Court Chambers, Leeds	0113 243 3277
Ansell Miss Rachel Louise	4 Pump Court, London	020 7842 5555
Antell Mr John Jason	King's Bench and Godolphin (KBG)Chambers, Plymouth	01752 221551
Arnold Mr James Matthew	Outer Temple Chambers, London	020 7353 6381
Artesi Miss Desiree Allison Ann	Thomas More Chambers, London	020 7404 7000
Ascroft Mr Richard Geoffrey	Guildhall Chambers, Bristol	0117 930 9000
Ashley Mr Neil Martin	East Anglian Chambers, Chelmsford	01473 214481
	East Anglian Chambers, Ipswich	01473 214481
	East Anglian Chambers, Norwich	01473 214481
Askey Mr Robert John	Palmyra Chambers, Warrington	01925 444919
Asprey Mr Nicholas	Clock Chambers, Wolverhampton	01902 313444
	Serle Court, London	020 7242 6105
Aswani Mr Ravi Girdharilal	Stone Chambers, London	020 7440 6900
Bailey Miss Rosana Henrietta	10 King's Bench Walk, London	020 7353 7742
Bailey Mr Russell Stuart	No5 Chambers, Birmingham	0845 210 5555
	No5 Chambers, Bristol	0845 210 5555
	No5 Chambers, London	0845 210 5555
Banks Miss Fiona Jane	Monckton Chambers, London	020 7405 7211
Barnard Mr James Philip	11 Stone Buildings, London	020 7831 6381
Barnes Miss Andrea Lynda	Clerksroom (Taunton), Taunton	0845 083 3000
	King's Lynn Chambers, King's Lynn	01553 672 085
Barnett Mr Jeremy Victor	2 Bedford Row, London	020 7440 8888
	St Paul's Chambers, Leeds	0113 245 5866
Barwise Miss Stephanie Nicola	Atkin Chambers, London	020 7404 0102
Bax Mr James Alexander	Rougemont Chambers, Exeter	01392 208484
Beaumont Mr Benjamin	Chambers of Dr Michael Arnheim, London	020 7833 5093
	Middle Temple Lane Chambers, London	020 7583 4352
Beaumont Mr Dean Andrew	KCH Garden Square, Nottingham	0115 941 8851

C

Beaumont Mr Marc Clifford	9 Stone Buildings, London	020 7404 5055
	Windsor Barristers' Chambers, Windsor	01753 839321
Becker Mr Timothy George Christie	Chambers of Mr Timothy Becker, Liverpool	0151 703 0319
	Clerksroom (London), London	0845 083 3000
Bell Mr Thomas Capel	Hardwicke, London	020 7242 2523
Bellamy Mr Jonathan Mark	39 Essex Street, London	020 7832 1111
	82 King Street, Manchester	0161 870 9969
Beloff Mr Rupert Joseph Alexei	No5 Chambers, Birmingham	0845 210 5555
	No5 Chambers, Bristol	0845 210 5555
	No5 Chambers, London	0845 210 5555
Bennett Miss Emma Louise	Exchange Chambers, Leeds	0113 203 1970
	Exchange Chambers, Liverpool	0151 236 7747
	Exchange Chambers, Manchester	0161 833 2722
Bennion-Pedley Mr Edward	13 KBW, Oxford	01865 311066
	13 King's Bench Walk, London	020 7353 7204
Benson Mr Imran Michael Jafarey	Hailsham Chambers, London	020 7643 5000
Berkin Mr Martyn David Maurice	Crown Office Chambers, London	020 7797 8100
Berkley Mr David Nahum	1 Gray's Inn Square, London	020 7405 0001
	St Johns Buildings, Chester	01244 323070
	St Johns Buildings, Manchester	0161 214 1500
	St Johns Buildings Liverpool, Liverpool	0151 243 6000
Berkley Mr Michael Stuart	Rougemont Chambers, Exeter	01392 208484
Berry Mr Nicholas Michael	Rougemont Chambers, Exeter	01392 208484
Bertram Mr Jonathan Peter	Seven Bedford Row, London	020 7242 3555
Bishop Mr Alan Richard	11 Stone Buildings, London	020 7831 6381
Bishop Mr Gordon William	Chambers of Gordon Bishop, Woking	01483 486 730
Bishop Mr Malcolm Leslie	Argent Chambers, London	020 7556 5500
	Equity Chambers, Birmingham	0121 236 5007
	30 Park Place, Cardiff	029 2039 8421
Blackmore Mr John Hugh	St John's Chambers, Bristol	0117 923 4700
Blackwood Mr Clive David	Lamb Chambers, London	020 7797 8300
Blohm Mr Leslie Adrian	St John's Chambers, Bristol	0117 923 4700
Bogle Mr James Stewart Lockhart	10 King's Bench Walk, London	020 7353 7742
Boulding Mr Philip Vincent	Keating Chambers, London	020 7544 2600
Bourne Mr Geoffrey Robert	13 Old Square Chambers, London	020 7831 4445
Bowen Mr Nicholas James Hugh	Doughty Street Chambers, Bristol	01179 058 717
	Doughty Street Chambers, London	020 7404 1313
	Doughty Street Chambers, Manchester	0161 618 1066
Bowling Mr James Stuart	4 Pump Court, London	020 7842 5555
Bowsher Mr Michael Frederick Thomas	Monckton Chambers, London	020 7405 7211
Boyd Mr Stephen James Harvey	Selborne Chambers, London	020 7420 9500
Bragge Mr Thomas Hereward	Stour Chambers, Canterbury	01227 764899
Bragiel Mr Edward Bronislaw Henryk	Hogarth Chambers, London	020 7404 0404
Braier Mr Jason Dean	Field Court Chambers, London	020 7405 6114
Branchflower Mr George	Zenith Chambers, Leeds	0113 245 5438
Bredemear Mr Zachary Charles	1 Chancery Lane, London	0845 634 6666
Brewin Mr Carl Patrick	3 PB Barristers, London	020 7583 8055
Brittain Mr Marc John	1 Gray's Inn Square, London	020 7405 0001
Brown Miss Susan Margaret	One Essex Court, London	020 7936 3030
Brown Mr Philip Stephen	9 Stone Buildings, London	020 7404 5055
Brown Mr Timothy William	13 KBW, Oxford	01865 311066
	13 King's Bench Walk, London	020 7353 7204
Bruce Mr Andrew Jonathan	Serle Court, London	020 7242 6105
Bryden Mr Christopher James Yuen Kang	4 King's Bench Walk, London	020 7822 7000
Buchan Miss Caroline Venetia	Chambers of Miss C Buchan, Haywards Heath	01444 482222
Buckhaven Mr Simon	Hardwicke, London	020 7242 2523
Buckpitt Mr Michael David	Tanfield Chambers, London	020 7421 5300

Name	Chambers	Telephone
Budworth Mr Martin James	Kings Chambers, Birmingham	0845 034 3444
	Kings Chambers, Leeds	0845 034 3444
	Kings Chambers, Manchester	0845 034 3444
Bueno Mr Antonio De Padua Jose Maria	Clerksroom (Taunton), Taunton	0845 083 3000
Bullock Mr Robert Gustaf	The Chambers of Mr Bullock, Brighton	01273 321050
Burgher Mr Benjimin George	Outer Temple Chambers, London	020 7353 6381
Burns Mr Jeremy Stuart	12 College Place, Southampton	023 8032 0320
Burr Mr Andrew Charles	Atkin Chambers, London	020 7404 0102
Busuttil Mr Godwin John Antoine	5RB, London	020 7242 2902
Butler Mr Andrew	Tanfield Chambers, London	020 7421 5300
Butler Mr Rupert James	3 Hare Court, London	020 7415 7800
Butler Mr Simon David	The Chambers of Grahame Aldous QC, London	020 7832 0500
Buttimore Mr Gabriel	13 KBW, Oxford	01865 311066
	13 King's Bench Walk, London	020 7353 7204
Byrne Mr Garrett Thomas	4-5 Gray's Inn Square, London	020 7404 5252
Campbell Mr Oliver Edward Wilhelm	Henderson Chambers, London	020 7583 9020
Cant Mr Christopher Ian	9 Stone Buildings, London	020 7404 5055
Capon Mr Philip Christopher William	East Anglian Chambers, Chelmsford	01473 214481
	East Anglian Chambers, Ipswich	01473 214481
	East Anglian Chambers, Norwich	01473 214481
	St Philips Chambers, Birmingham	0121 246 7000
Carlisle Mr Timothy St John Ogilvie	Field Court Chambers, London	020 7405 6114
Castle Mr Peter Bolton	13 Old Square Chambers, London	020 7831 4445
Cattermull Miss Emma Jayne	East Anglian Chambers, Chelmsford	01473 214481
	East Anglian Chambers, Ipswich	01473 214481
	East Anglian Chambers, Norwich	01473 214481
Cawsey Mr Barry Donald	Clerksroom (London), London	0845 083 3000
	Clerksroom (Taunton), Taunton	0845 083 3000
Challenger Mr Colin Westcott	Lamb Chambers, London	020 7797 8300
Charkham Mr Graham Harold	20 Essex Street, London	020 7842 1200
Chesner Mr Howard Michael	One Essex Court, London	020 7936 3030
Christensen Mr Carlton	10 King's Bench Walk, London	020 7353 7742
Christie Mr David Henderson	Seven Bedford Row, London	020 7242 3555
Christie Mr Iain Robert	5RB, London	020 7242 2902
Clark Miss Geraldine	Serle Court, London	020 7242 6105
Clark Mr Andrew Richard	9 St John Street, Manchester	0161 955 9000
Clark Ms Julia Elisabeth	Hogarth Chambers, London	020 7404 0404
Clegg Mr Simon Robert Jonathan	St Philips Chambers, Birmingham	0121 246 7000
Clement Mr Ryan Wayne	Conference Chambers, Harrow	020 8144 0134
Clifton Miss Jane April	Lamb Chambers, London	020 7797 8300
Cohen Mr Edward Mervyn	11 Stone Buildings, London	020 7831 6381
Colbey Mr Richard	Guildhall Chambers Portsmouth, Portsmouth	023 9275 2400
	Lamb Chambers, London	020 7797 8300
Constable Mr Adam Michael	Keating Chambers, London	020 7544 2600
Cooper Miss Christine	Field Court Chambers, London	020 7405 6114
Coster Mr Ronald David	42 Bedford Row, London	020 7831 0222
Coulter Mr Barry John	Clerksroom (London), London	0845 083 3000
	Clerksroom (Taunton), Taunton	0845 083 3000
	King's Lynn Chambers, King's Lynn	01553 672 085
Cox Miss Olivia Rodrigues	Atlantic Chambers, Liverpool	0151 236 4421
Cramsie Mr James Sinclair Beresford	13 KBW, Oxford	01865 311066
	13 King's Bench Walk, London	020 7353 7204
Crowley Mr Daniel John	2 Temple Gardens, London	020 7822 1200
Crystal Mr Jonathan	Argent Chambers, London	020 7556 5500
Culmer Miss Gabrielle Fiona	2 King's Bench Walk, London	020 7353 1746
Cunningham Mr Graham Taylor	Hardwicke, London	020 7242 2523
Curtis Mr Michael Alexander	Crown Office Chambers, London	020 7797 8100
Dalby Mr Joseph Francis	4-5 Gray's Inn Square, London	020 7404 5252
Daniels Miss Philippa Catherine	36 Bedford Row, London	020 7421 8000

Name	Chambers	Telephone
Darling Mr Paul Antony	Keating Chambers, London	020 7544 2600
Davey Mr Charles	64 Bridge Street, Manchester	0845 083 3000
	Chambers of Mr C Davey, Bishop's Stortford	01279 506412
	Clerksroom (Taunton), Taunton	0845 083 3000
Davies Miss Carol Elizabeth	College Chambers, Southampton	023 8023 0338
Davies Mr Jake Sebastian Hunter	Five Paper, London	020 7815 3200
Davies Mr James Edwin	3 PB Barristers, Bournemouth	01202 292102
	3 PB Barristers, Bristol	0117 928 1520
	3 PB Barristers, London	020 7583 8055
	3 PB Barristers, Oxford	01865 793 736
	3 PB Barristers, Winchester	01962 868884
Davis Mr Andrew Paul	Crown Office Chambers, London	020 7797 8100
De Jehan Mr David	Park Lane Plowden, Leeds	0113 228 5049
De Waal Mr John Henry Lowndes	Hardwicke, London	020 7242 2523
Deacon Mr Robert Murray	11 Stone Buildings, London	020 7831 6381
Demachkie Mr Jamal	3 PB Barristers, London	020 7583 8055
Devine Mr Michael Buxton	Rougemont Chambers, Exeter	01392 208484
Devlin Mr Bernard Joseph	Five St Andrew's Hill, London	020 7332 5400
di Mambro Mr David Jesse Andrew	Pallant Chambers, Chichester	01243 784538
	Radcliffe Chambers, London	020 7831 0081
Dickinson Mr John Finch Heneage	St John's Chambers, Bristol	0117 923 4700
Dipré Mr Paul Nicholas Amadeus	Chambers of Mr P N Dipré, Address withheld	0845 123 1234
	MK Family Law Chambers, Milton Keynes	0845 123 1234
Doerries Miss Chantal-Aimée Renee Aemelia An	Atkin Chambers, London	020 7404 0102
Dos Santos Mr Alexander	Charter Chambers, London	020 7618 4400
Drummond Mr Bruce Jonathon Hutcheon	Cornwall Street Chambers, Birmingham	0121 233 7500
	Palmyra Chambers, Warrington	01925 444919
Du Toit Sc Mr Johan Ignatius	Selborne Chambers, London	020 7420 9500
	St Philips Chambers, Birmingham	0121 246 7000
Dyer Mr Allen Gordon	4 Pump Court, London	020 7842 5555
Earle Mr James Christopher Reginald St John	Fenners Chambers, Cambridge	01223 368761
Edwards Mr Anthony	Chancery House Chambers, Leeds	0113 244 6691
Eilledge Miss Amanda Gail Caroline	11 Stone Buildings, London	020 7831 6381
Elliott Mr Timothy Stanley	Keating Chambers, London	020 7544 2600
Engelman Mr Philip	Cloisters, London	020 7827 4000
	Trinity Chambers, Middlesbrough	01642 247569
	Trinity Chambers, Newcastle Upon Tyne	0191 232 1927
Ensaff Mr Omar Sherif	No5 Chambers, Birmingham	0845 210 5555
	No5 Chambers, Bristol	0845 210 5555
	No5 Chambers, London	0845 210 5555
Ephraim-Adejumo Mrs Hilda Ekpo	12 Old Square Chambers, London	020 7404 0875
Evans Mr Robert Jonathan	Keating Chambers, London	020 7544 2600
Facenna Mr Gerald Carlo	Monckton Chambers, London	020 7405 7211
Fain Mr Carl Ian	Tanfield Chambers, London	020 7421 5300
Falkowski Mr Damian	4-5 Gray's Inn Square, London	020 7404 5252
Farrell Mr Simon Henry	3 Raymond Buildings, London	020 7400 6400
Fawcett Mr Neil	St Ive's Chambers, Birmingham	0121 236 0863
Ferber Ms Iris	42 Bedford Row, London	020 7831 0222
Ferm Mr Rodney Eric	Broadway House Chambers, Bradford	01274 722560
	Broadway House Chambers, Leeds	0113 246 2600
Field Mr Julian Nigel	Crown Office Chambers, London	020 7797 8100
Finlay Mr Darren	Sovereign Chambers, Leeds	0113 245 1841
Fisher Mr David	New Square Chambers, London	020 7419 8000
Fitzgerald Mr John Vincent	Ingenuity IP Chambers, Petts Wood	
Fitzmaurice Mr Guy Edward Christian	Staple Inn Chambers, London	020 7242 5240
Follon Mr Daniel Richard Thomas	1 Gray's Inn Square, London	020 7405 0001

C

Fowles Mr Jonathan James	Serle Court, London	020 7242 6105
Francis Mr Andrew James	Serle Court, London	020 7242 6105
	Zenith Chambers, Leeds	0113 245 5438
Fraser-Urquhart Mr Andrew	4-5 Gray's Inn Square, London	020 7404 5252
Frawley Ms Lyndsey Anne	Quorum Chambers, St Albans	01727 884516
	Quorum Tax Chambers, London	020 7043 5189
Friedman Mr David Peter	4 Pump Court, London	020 7842 5555
Fullerton Mr Michael Andrew	7 Bell Yard, London	020 7831 0636
	Chambers of Mr Michael Fullerton, Hove	01273 772050
Gadd Mr Adam Brian	Pump Court Chambers, London	020 7353 0711
	Pump Court Chambers, Winchester	01962 868 161
	Riverview Chambers, London	0844 225 3999
Gallivan Mr Terence John	Five Paper, London	020 7815 3200
Galway-Cooper Dr Philip Anthony	Five St Andrew's Hill, London	020 7332 5400
Garrett Miss Lucy Margaret	Keating Chambers, London	020 7544 2600
Garvie Mr Carl Peter	St Philips Chambers, Birmingham	0121 246 7000
Gasztowicz Mr Steven	Cornerstone Barristers, London	020 7242 4986
	New Street Chambers, Leicester	0116 262 5906
Gatty Mr Daniel Simon	Hardwicke, London	020 7242 2523
Gee Mr Steven Mark	Stone Chambers, London	020 7440 6900
Gelbart Mr Geoff Alan	1 Gray's Inn Square, London	020 7405 0001
George Mr Nicholas Frank Raymond	New Walk Chambers, Leicester	0871 200 1298/0116 255 9144
Gersch Mr Adam Nissen	Argent Chambers, London	020 7556 5500
Gibbons Miss Mary Regina	Stone Chambers, London	020 7440 6900
Gibbons Ms Ellodie	Tanfield Chambers, London	020 7421 5300
Gill Mr Manjit Singh	No5 Chambers, Birmingham	0845 210 5555
	No5 Chambers, Bristol	0845 210 5555
	No5 Chambers, London	0845 210 5555
Gillies Miss Jennie	4 Pump Court, London	020 7842 5555
Gilmore Miss Mary Seanin	Four New Square, London	020 7822 2000
Gladwell Mr Simon Mark	East Anglian Chambers, Ipswich	01473 214481
Gledhill Mr Lee Andre	Alexander Chambers, London	0845 652 0451/0854 652 0451
	Trident Barristers Chambers, Manchester	0161 663 3123
Gloag Mr Angus Robin	1 Gray's Inn Square, London	020 7405 0001
	Rougemont Chambers, Exeter	01392 208484
Glover Mr Marc Philip	Tanfield Chambers, London	020 7421 5300
Glover Mr Stephen Julian	37 Park Square Chambers, Leeds	0113 243 9422
Glyn Mr Caspar Hilary Gordon	Cloisters, London	020 7827 4000
Godfrey Mr Lauren John	Crown Office Row Chambers, Brighton	01273 625625
Godwin Mr William George Henry	3 Hare Court, London	020 7415 7800
	St John's Chambers, Bristol	0117 923 4700
Gold Mr Richard David	St John's Chambers, Bristol	0117 923 4700
Goldberg Mr Jonathan Jacob	Cobden House Chambers, Manchester	0161 833 6000
	North Square Chambers, London	020 8455 3735
Goldberg Mr Simon Ian	Trinity Chambers, Middlesbrough	01642 247569
	Trinity Chambers, Newcastle Upon Tyne	0191 232 1927
Goldrein Mr Iain Saville	7 Bell Yard, London	020 7831 0636
	Number 7 Harrington Street Chambers, Liverpool	0151 242 0707
Goldstein Mr Wayne Nathan	18 St John Street, Manchester	0161 278 1800
Goldstone Mr Simon Lewis	4 Pump Court, London	020 7842 5555
Goodison Mr Adam Henry	South Square, London	020 7696 9900
Goodman Mr Andrew David	1 Chancery Lane, London	0845 634 6666
Gorasia Mr Paras Ravji	Kings Chambers, Birmingham	0845 034 3444
	Kings Chambers, Leeds	0845 034 3444
	Kings Chambers, Manchester	0845 034 3444
Gough Miss Karen Louise	Arbitration Chambers, London	020 7267 2137
	39 Essex Street, London	020 7832 1111
	82 King Street, Manchester	0161 870 9969
Graham Mr Thomas Patrick Henry	New Square Chambers, London	020 7419 8000

Graham Mrs Alana Nicole	Chambers of Alana Graham, Halesowen	01384 894560
	9 Stone Buildings, London	020 7404 5055
Graham-Wells Miss Alison Christine	Exchange Chambers, Leeds	0113 203 1970
	Exchange Chambers, Liverpool	0151 236 7747
	Exchange Chambers, Manchester	0161 833 2722
Grant Mr David Ericson	Outer Temple Chambers, London	020 7353 6381
Granville Stafford Mr Andrew	4 King's Bench Walk, London	020 7822 7000
Greatorex Mr Paul	4-5 Gray's Inn Square, London	020 7404 5252
Green Mr Patrick Curtis	Henderson Chambers, London	020 7583 9020
Greenan Miss Sarah Octavia	Zenith Chambers, Leeds	0113 245 5438
Griffiths Mr David	St Philips Chambers, Birmingham	0121 246 7000
Ground Mr Patrick	Chambers of Mr Patrick Ground QC, London	020 7736 0131
Gupta Mr Amit	St Philips Chambers, Birmingham	0121 246 7000
Guy Mr John David Colin	Tanfield Chambers, London	020 7421 5300
Guy Mr Richard Perran	Chambers of Mr Ami Feder, London	020 7797 7788
	King's Bench and Godolphin (KBG)Chambers, Plymouth	01752 221551
	Southernhay Chambers, Exeter	01392 255777
Hackett Mr Philip George	Argent Chambers, London	020 7556 5500
Halden Mr Angus Robert	Queen Square Chambers, Bristol	0117 921 1966
Hall Mr James Edward	Cornwall Street Chambers, Birmingham	0121 233 7500
Hallett Miss Katherine Elizabeth	13 Old Square Chambers, London	020 7831 4445
Hamilton Mr Peter Bernard	4 Pump Court, London	020 7842 5555
Hammerton Mr Alastair Rolf	1 Chancery Lane, London	0845 634 6666
Hammond Mr Tim Mark	Tanfield Chambers, London	020 7421 5300
Hannaford Miss Sarah Jane	Keating Chambers, London	020 7544 2600
Hansen Mr William Joseph	No5 Chambers, Birmingham	0845 210 5555
	No5 Chambers, Bristol	0845 210 5555
	No5 Chambers, London	0845 210 5555
Hargreaves Mr Simon John Robert	Keating Chambers, London	020 7544 2600
Harris Mr James	Five St Andrew's Hill, London	020 7332 5400
Harris Mr Melvyn	5 Essex Court, London	020 7410 2000
Hartman Mr Michael	One Essex Court, London	020 7936 3030
Hatch Miss Lisa Sharmila	One Essex Court, London	020 7936 3030
Havenhand Mr John Barry	Clerksroom (London), London	0845 083 3000
	Clerksroom (Taunton), Taunton	0845 083 3000
	King's Lynn Chambers, King's Lynn	01553 672 085
Hayes Mr Richard James	Lamb Chambers, London	020 7797 8300
Haywood Dr Jennifer Margaret	Serle Court, London	020 7242 6105
Heal Mrs Madeleine	New Square Chambers, London	020 7419 8000
Henderson Mr Neil John	Stone Chambers, London	020 7440 6900
Hendron Mr Henry Joseph Christopher	Strand Chambers, London	020 7117 6920
Hewson Ms Barbara Mary	Hardwicke, London	020 7242 2523
Hicks Mr Edward Gordon David	Radcliffe Chambers, London	020 7831 0081
Higgins Mr Adrian John	13 KBW, Oxford	01865 311066
	13 King's Bench Walk, London	020 7353 7204
Higginson Mr Timothy Nicholas Bennett	Littleton Chambers, London	020 7797 8600
	St John's Chambers, Bristol	0117 923 4700
Hill Mr Michael Gordon	Trinity Chambers, Middlesbrough	01642 247569
	Trinity Chambers, Newcastle Upon Tyne	0191 232 1927
Hill Mr Nicholas Mark	Pump Court Chambers, London	020 7353 0711
	Pump Court Chambers, Swindon	01793 539899
	St Philips Chambers, Birmingham	0121 246 7000
Hirst Mr Martin Lewis	13 KBW, Oxford	01865 311066
	13 King's Bench Walk, London	020 7353 7204
Hirst Mr William Timothy John	Park Lane Plowden, Leeds	0113 228 5049
Hoar Mr Francis John Patrick	Field Court Chambers, London	020 7405 6114

Hodgkiss Ms Suzanne Jane	43 Temple Row Chambers, Birmingham	0121 237 6035
Hodkinson Mr Gary Stephen	Chambers of Mr Ami Feder, London	020 7797 7788
	Chambers of Mr Ami Feder, London	020 7797 7788
Hodson Mr Matthew Paul	Farrar's Building, London	020 7583 9241
Holland Mr Charles Christopher	Francis Taylor Building, London	020 7353 8415
	Trinity Chambers, Middlesbrough	01642 247569
	Trinity Chambers, Newcastle Upon Tyne	0191 232 1927
Hood Mr David	Prince of Wales Chambers, London	020 7622 7415
Hood Mr Nigel Anthony	New Square Chambers, London	020 7419 8000
Hormaeche Miss Alejandra	Tanfield Chambers, London	020 7421 5300
Hornett Mr Stuart Ian	Selborne Chambers, London	020 7420 9500
Hossain Mr Ajmalul	Selborne Chambers, London	020 7420 9500
	St Philips Chambers, Birmingham	0121 246 7000
Howells Mr Stephen John	Stone Chambers, London	020 7440 6900
Howlett Mr James Anthony	KCH Garden Square, Nottingham	0115 941 8851
Hubbard Mr Mark Iain	New Square Chambers, London	020 7419 8000
Hughes Mr Adrian Warwick	39 Essex Street, London	020 7832 1111
	82 King Street, Manchester	0161 870 9969
Hughes-Deane Ms Charlotte Barbara	Atlantic Chambers, Liverpool	0151 236 4421
Hurst Mr Brian	39 Park Square, Leeds	0113 245 6633
Hussain Mr Muhammad Altaf	Chambers of Mr M A Hussain, London	020 8679 2398
Hutchin Mr Edward Alister David	Temple Garden Chambers, London	020 7583 1315
Iqbal Mr Mashood	London View Chambers, Sawbridgeworth	07788 912493
Irvin Mr Peter	Brick Court Chambers, London	020 7379 3550
Iyer Miss Shobana	Swan Chambers, Richmond	0845 123 1234
Jackson Miss Rosemary Elizabeth	Keating Chambers, London	020 7544 2600
Jacobson Mr Lawrence	Five Paper, London	020 7815 3200
Jarman Mr Samuel James Guthrie	4 KBW, London	020 7822 8822
	Lombard Chambers, London	020 7107 2100
Jayakrishnan Mr Harry Sisubalan	Trent Chambers, Nottingham	0115 941 9596
Jinadu Mr Abdul-Lateef Abodurin Olayinka	Keating Chambers, London	020 7544 2600
Joffe Ms Natasha Juliet Louise	Outer Temple Chambers, London	020 7353 6381
Jones Mr Alun	St Paul's Chambers, Leeds	0113 245 5866
Jones Mr Christopher David Harries	St John's Chambers, Bristol	0117 923 4700
Jones Mr Geraint Anthony	New Walk Chambers, Leicester	0871 200 1298/0116 255 9144
	9 St John Street, Manchester	0161 955 9000
	Tanfield Chambers, London	020 7421 5300
Jones Mr Kelvin Mcallister	Templis Chambers, London	020 7649 9808
Jones Mr Mark Simeon	3 Dr Johnson's Buildings, London	020 7353 4854
Jones Mr Richard Frederick Thomas	Heavenwood Chambers, Stroud	01453 873444
Joseph Dr Sandradee Theresa	13 Old Square Chambers, London	020 7831 4445
Joseph Mr Charles Henry	Tanfield Chambers, London	020 7421 5300
Joseph Mr Paul Wolfe	No5 Chambers, Birmingham	0845 210 5555
	No5 Chambers, Bristol	0845 210 5555
	No5 Chambers, London	0845 210 5555
Joseph Mr Sellappah Job	Chambers of Mr S J Joseph, London	020 8809 3083/020 8802 9889
Josling Mr William Henry Charles	37 Park Square Chambers, Leeds	0113 243 9422
Keane Mr Owen Ashley	Design Chambers, London	020 7353 0747
Keeling Mr Adrian Francis	No5 Chambers, Birmingham	0845 210 5555
	No5 Chambers, Bristol	0845 210 5555
	No5 Chambers, London	0845 210 5555
Kelly Mr Sean	Chancery House Chambers, Leeds	0113 244 6691
Kenny Mr Martin William	Walnut House, Exeter	01392 279751
Kent Mr Michael Harcourt	Crown Office Chambers, London	020 7797 8100
Khan Dr Alexander	Coral House, Manchester	
Khan Mr Arfan	Field Court Chambers, London	020 7405 6114
Khan Mr Ayoub	Chambers of Mr Ayoub Khan, Birmingham	07930 987202

Khan Mr Mahmood Shafi	Luton Chambers, Luton	01582 598394
	Willesden Chambers, London	020 3273 1042
Kidd Mr Peter William	Number 7 Harrington Street Chambers, Liverpool	0151 242 0707
Kime Mr Matthew Jonathan	Cobden House Chambers, Manchester	0161 833 6000
	Ingenuity IP Chambers, Petts Wood	
	No. 3 Fleet Street Chambers, London	020 7936 4474
King Mr Charles Granville	Chambers of Mr C G King, Stroud	07949 461717
Kirk Mr Graeme Charles	One Essex Court, London	020 7936 3030
Kramer Mr Philip Anthony	Park Lane Plowden, Newcastle Upon Tyne	0191 211 4087
Kurji Ms Fatim Razahusein	No5 Chambers, Birmingham	0845 210 5555
	No5 Chambers, Bristol	0845 210 5555
	No5 Chambers, London	0845 210 5555
Kwiatkowski Mr Feliks Jerzy	Kew Chambers, Kew	0844 8099991
Kynoch Mr Duncan Stuart Sanderson	Selborne Chambers, London	020 7420 9500
Lamb Mr Jeffrey Thomas	Westgate Chambers, Lewes	01273 480510
Lamont Mr Calum	Keating Chambers, London	020 7544 2600
Lane Mr Simon Charles	Rougemont Chambers, Exeter	01392 208484
Law Mr John Edward	The Chambers of Grahame Aldous QC, London	020 7832 0500
Leabeater Mr James Ferguson	4 Pump Court, London	020 7842 5555
Lee Miss Krista Chui Lan	Keating Chambers, London	020 7544 2600
Lee Mr Rosslyn Alexander	Dere Street Barristers, York	0844 3351551
	York Chambers, Newcastle Upon Tyne	0191 206 4677
Lennard Mr Stephen Charles	Hardwicke, London	020 7242 2523
Lenon Mr Andrew Ralph Fitzmaurice	One Essex Court, London	020 7583 2000
Leonard Mr Charles Robert Weston	Hardwicke, London	020 7242 2523
Levy Miss Juliette	Selborne Chambers, London	020 7420 9500
Lewis Mr Jonathan Simon	Henderson Chambers, London	020 7583 9020
Lewis Mr Wayne Anthony	Access Lawyers, London	020 8801 2345
Lewis Mrs Pauline Grace	Holborn Chambers, London	020 7242 6060
Linstead Mr Peter James	Tanfield Chambers, London	020 7421 5300
Lissack Mr Richard Anthony	Outer Temple Chambers, London	020 7353 6381
	Riverview Chambers, London	0844 225 3999
Livingstone Mr Simon John	Thomas More Chambers, London	020 7404 7000
Lonsdale Miss Marion Mary	Academy Chambers, London	020 8455 2503
Lonsdale Mr David James	33 Bedford Row, London	020 7242 6476
Lopez Mr Juan Nemesio	Francis Taylor Building, London	020 7353 8415
Lowe Mr Mungo James	13 Old Square Chambers, London	020 7831 4445
Lule Miss Jacqueline	1 Mitre Court Buildings, London	020 7452 8900
MacBean Mr Andrew Hamish	Queen Square Chambers, Bristol	0117 921 1966
MacEvilly Mr Conn Jeremy	9 Stone Buildings, London	020 7404 5055
Machell Mr John William	Serle Court, London	020 7242 6105
MacKenzie Smith Mrs Catherine Joanna	10 King's Bench Walk, London	020 7353 7742
Macro Miss Morwenna Margaret	Five Paper, London	020 7815 3200
Maguire Mr Andrew James	Exchange Chambers, Liverpool	0151 236 7747
	Exchange Chambers, Manchester	0161 833 2722
	St Philips Chambers, Birmingham	0121 246 7000
Maher Ms Martha Johanna Dorothy	St John's Chambers, Bristol	0117 923 4700
Mann Mr Christopher	13 KBW, Oxford	01865 311066
	13 King's Bench Walk, London	020 7353 7204
Mannan Mr Charles Madani Fuad	Temple Court Chambers, London	020 7353 7888
Mantle Mr Peter John	Monckton Chambers, London	020 7405 7211
Margo Mr Saul Nicholas	Outer Temple Chambers, London	020 7353 6381
Marks Mr Jonathan Clive	4 Pump Court, London	020 7842 5555
Marsden Mr Andrew Charles	St John's Chambers, Bristol	0117 923 4700
Marshall Mr Derek Stanley	College Chambers, Southampton	023 8023 0338
Matthias Mr David Huw	Francis Taylor Building, London	020 7353 8415
Mawrey Mr Richard Brooks	Henderson Chambers, London	020 7583 9020
Maxwell Lewis Mr Cameron	Lamb Chambers, London	020 7797 8300
Maynard Mr Christopher Howard	Tanfield Chambers, London	020 7421 5300

C

McCafferty Miss Lynne	4 Pump Court, London	020 7842 5555
McCarthy Mr William	Bridgewater Chambers, Manchester	0161 3877127
	1 Mitre Court Buildings, London	020 7452 8900
McCombie Mr Fergus Alexander Paul	1 Gray's Inn Square, London	020 7405 0001
McCormick Mr William Thomas	Ely Place Chambers, London	020 7400 9600
McCracken Mr James	Cornwall Street Chambers, Birmingham	0121 233 7500
McCue Mr Donald	11 Stone Buildings, London	020 7831 6381
McDonnell Mr John Beresford William	13 Old Square Chambers, London	020 7831 4445
McLinden Mr John Vincent Barry	Field Court Chambers, London	020 7405 6114
McMorrow Mr Patrick Joseph	4 King's Bench Walk, London	020 7822 7000
McNae Mr Jonathan James	Selborne Chambers, London	020 7420 9500
McNeill Mr David Martin	Five St Andrew's Hill, London	020 7332 5400
McNicholas Mr Christopher John	Goresbrook Chambers, Milton Keynes	0845 123 1234
Meares Mr Nigel Leslie Vellacott	11 Stone Buildings, London	020 7831 6381
Medd Mr James Powys	Crown Office Chambers, London	020 7797 8100
Miah Mr Anawar Babul	Great James Street Chambers, London	020 7440 4949
Michalos Miss Christina Antigone Diana	5RB, London	020 7242 2902
Miles Mr Richard Iain	One Essex Court, London	020 7936 3030
Miller Mr Andrew	2 Temple Gardens, London	020 7822 1200
Mills Mr Simon Thomas	Five Paper, London	020 7815 3200
Mishcon Mr Oliver Zebedee	Chambers of Mr Oliver Mishcon, London	020 7993 8890
Mitchell Mr David John	No5 Chambers, Birmingham	0845 210 5555
	No5 Chambers, Bristol	0845 210 5555
	No5 Chambers, London	0845 210 5555
Moffat Mr Russell Dean	Linenhall Chambers, Chester	01244 348282
Morgan Dr Austen Jude	33 Bedford Row, London	020 7242 6476
Morgan Mr Jamie Peter	Trinity Chambers, Middlesbrough	01642 247569
	Trinity Chambers, Newcastle Upon Tyne	0191 232 1927
Moss Mr Christopher Stephen	St Johns Buildings, Manchester	0161 214 1500
	St Johns Buildings Liverpool, Liverpool	0151 243 6000
	16 Winckley Square, Preston	01772 256100
Munro Mr Joshua Neil	Hailsham Chambers, London	020 7643 5000
Murphy Mr Damian	Enterprise Chambers, Leeds	0113 246 0391
	Enterprise Chambers, London	020 7405 9471
	Enterprise Chambers, Newcastle Upon Tyne	0191 222 3344
Murray Mr Charles Humphrey Stewart	Rougemont Chambers, Exeter	01392 208484
Mustakim Mr Abdul Yunus Al	Chambers of Mr Mustakim, London	
Nabi Mr Sajjad	5 Pump Court, London	020 7353 2532
Neville Mr Joseph Richard	43 Temple Row Chambers, Birmingham	0121 237 6035
Newman Mr James Andrew	Ely Place Chambers, London	020 7400 9600
Newman Mr Paul	3 PB Barristers, Bournemouth	01202 292102
	3 PB Barristers, Bristol	0117 928 1520
	3 PB Barristers, London	020 7583 8055
	3 PB Barristers, Oxford	01865 793 736
	3 PB Barristers, Winchester	01962 868884
Newman Mrs Veronica	Chambers of Mrs V Newman, Cardiff	029 2048 8797
Nicholls Mr David James	11 Stone Buildings, London	020 7831 6381
Nicholson Mr Jeremy Mark	4 Pump Court, London	020 7842 5555
Nickless Mr Jason Alan	College Chambers, Southampton	023 8023 0338
Noble Mr Andrew	Enterprise Chambers, Leeds	0113 246 0391
Nolten Miss Sonia Jayne	2 Temple Gardens, London	020 7822 1200

Norman Mr Michael Charles	3 PB Barristers, Bournemouth	01202 292102
	3 PB Barristers, Bristol	0117 928 1520
	3 PB Barristers, London	020 7583 8055
	3 PB Barristers, Oxford	01865 793 736
	3 PB Barristers, Winchester	01962 868884
Normington Mr James Adam	Park Court Chambers, Leeds	0113 243 3277
Norton Mr Giles	Enigma Chambers, Sheffield	07779 576499
	Holborn Chambers, London	020 7242 6060
Nsugbe Mr Oba Eric	Pump Court Chambers, London	020 7353 0711
	Pump Court Chambers, Swindon	01793 539899
	Pump Court Chambers, Winchester	01962 868 161
Nurse Mr Gordon Bramwell William	Radcliffe Chambers, London	020 7831 0081
O'Donoghue Mr Hugh Vincent	Carmelite Chambers, London	020 7936 6300
Ogunbusola Mr Victor Olaniyi	Chambers of Victor Ogumbusola, Basildon	07413 634231
Ohrenstein Mr Dov	Radcliffe Chambers, London	020 7831 0081
Okoye Miss Joy Nwamala	Chambers of Joy Okoye, London	07976 426871/020 7405 7011
Oliver Dr Peter James Robert	4 Pump Court, London	020 7842 5555
Oliver Mr David Keightley Rideal	13 Old Square Chambers, London	020 7831 4445
Osborne Mr James Robert	Clerksroom (London), London	0845 083 3000
O'Sullivan Mr Richard John	1215 Chambers, London	020 3291 1215
O'Sullivan Mr Thomas Sean Patrick	4 Pump Court, London	020 7842 5555
O'Toole Mr Simon Gerard	5 Pump Court, London	020 7353 2532
	Riverview Chambers, London	0844 225 3999
Otwal Mr Mukhtiar Singh	42 Bedford Row, London	020 7831 0222
Owen Mr Timothy Wynn	Matrix Chambers, London	020 7404 3447
Owens Miss Elspeth Eluned	4 Pump Court, London	020 7842 5555
Owen-Thomas Mr Richard Matthew	13 KBW, Oxford	01865 311066
	13 King's Bench Walk, London	020 7353 7204
Padfield Mr Nicholas David	Chambers of Nicholas Padfield QC, London	020 7351 1961
Palmer Miss Claire Louise	Thomas More Chambers, London	020 7404 7000
Palmer Miss Suzanne Elizabeth Josephine	4 King's Bench Walk, London	020 7822 7000
Palmer Mr James Savill	Henderson Chambers, London	020 7583 9020
Panton Mr Alastair Howard	10 King's Bench Walk, London	020 7353 7742
Paraskos Mr Paraskevakis Christakis	11 Gray's Inn Square Chambers, London	020 7405 6879
Parker Mrs Karen Lesley	Guildhall Chambers Portsmouth, Portsmouth	023 9275 2400
Parsons Mr Andrew James	Portsmouth Barristers'Chambers, Portsmouth	023 9283 1292
Pascall Mr Matthew Stephen	Alexander Chambers, London	0845 652 0451/0854 652 0451
	Guildford Chambers, Guildford	01483 539131
Pearce Mr Robert Edgar	Radcliffe Chambers, London	020 7831 0081
Pearson Mr Christopher	Lamb Chambers, London	020 7797 8300
Pennicott Mr Ian	Keating Chambers, London	020 7544 2600
Pennington-Legh Mr Jonathan Piers	Field Court Chambers, London	020 7405 6114
Pennock Mr Ian	Park Lane Plowden, Leeds	0113 228 5049
Penny Mr Timothy Charles	11 Stone Buildings, London	020 7831 6381
Perry Miss Jacqueline Anne	2 Temple Gardens, London	020 7822 1200
Perry Mr Christopher Edward	Palmyra Chambers, Warrington	01925 444919
Pettican Mr Kevin	11 Stone Buildings, London	020 7831 6381
Phillips Mr Andrew Charles	Crown Office Chambers, London	020 7797 8100
Picarda Mr Hubert Alistair Paul	Chambers of Mr Hubert Picarda QC, London	020 7242 3566
Plant Mr James Richard	Farrar's Building, London	020 7583 9241
Platford Mr Graham Roy	Five Paper, London	020 7815 3200
Polli Mr Timothy James	Tanfield Chambers, London	020 7421 5300
Power Mr Lawrence Imam	4 KBW, London	020 7822 8822
Preston Mr Nicholas John Holman	Clerksroom (Taunton), Taunton	0845 083 3000
Pugh Mr John Bishop	John Pugh's Chambers, Liverpool	0151 236 5415
Purchas Mr James Alexander Francis	4 Pump Court, London	020 7842 5555

Quiney Mr Charles Benedictus Alexander	Crown Office Chambers, London	020 7797 8100
Rahman Mr Anis	12 Old Square Chambers, London	020 7404 0875
Rahman Mr Sami Ur	Field Court Chambers, London	020 7405 6114
Rai Mr Amarjit Singh	St Philips Chambers, Birmingham	0121 246 7000
Rainey Mr Philip Carslake	Tanfield Chambers, London	020 7421 5300
Ratcliffe Miss Frances Anne	Radcliffe Chambers, London	020 7831 0081
Rayment Mr Benedick Michael	Monckton Chambers, London	020 7405 7211
Record Mrs Celia Saint Claire	Chambers of Lawrence Jones, London	020 7831 1444
Reed Mr Simon John	New Walk Chambers, Leicester	0871 200 1298/0116 255 9144
Reeds Mr Gareth David	Canary Wharf Chambers, London	020 7183 8011
Rees Mr Hefin Ednyfed	39 Essex Street, London	020 7832 1111
Reffin Miss Clare Alyson	One Essex Court, London	020 7583 2000
Reid Miss Cheryl Louise Pegg	Temple Court Chambers, London	020 7353 7888
Reid Mr Sebastian Peter Scott	Tanfield Chambers, London	020 7421 5300
Rickards Mr James	Outer Temple Chambers, London	020 7353 6381
Ridd Mr David Ian Mcgregor	Farrar's Building, London	020 7583 9241
Rifat Mr Maurice Alan	1 Gray's Inn Square, London	020 7405 0001
Rigney Mr Andrew James	Crown Office Chambers, London	020 7797 8100
Rinker Mr Andrew Stuart D'Artois	Chambers of Mr Andrew Rinker, London	020 7584 1091
Ritchie Mr Richard Bulkeley	XXIV Old Buildings, London	020 7691 2424
Rivalland Mr Marc-Edouard	1 Chancery Lane, London	0845 634 6666
Roberts Mr Allan Calvin	Guildhall Chambers, Bristol	0117 930 9000
	Guildhall Chambers, Bristol	0117 930 9000
Roberts Mr Michael Charles	Chambers of Michael Roberts, Henley-On-Thames	01844 355 655
Roberts Mr Richard Vaughan	Henderson Chambers, London	020 7583 9020
Rogers Miss Christy Abigail	Ingenuity IP Chambers, Petts Wood	
	No. 3 Fleet Street Chambers, London	020 7936 4474
Rogers Mr Christopher Thomas	Five Paper, London	020 7815 3200
Rogers Mr Daniel James	Number 7 Harrington Street Chambers, Liverpool	0151 242 0707
Rogers Mr Ian Paul	Monckton Chambers, London	020 7405 7211
Rowntree Mr Edward John Pickering	Hardwicke, London	020 7242 2523
Roy Mr Stefan Alexander Hiren	5 Pump Court, London	020 7353 2532
Royce Mr Darryl Fraser	Atkin Chambers, London	020 7404 0102
Rushton Ms Nicola Jane	Five Paper, London	020 7815 3200
Russell Mr Thomas Charles Welldon	KCH Garden Square, Nottingham	0115 941 8851
Sadiq Mr Muhammad Faisel	Ely Place Chambers, London	020 7400 9600
Sampson Dr Timothy Michael George	One Essex Court, London	020 7936 3030
Samuel Mr Richard Geoffrey Graham	3 Hare Court, London	020 7415 7800
Sawtell Mr David Robert Fraser	4 King's Bench Walk, London	020 7822 7000
Scott Holland Mr Gideon Silas	Keating Chambers, London	020 7544 2600
Seal Mr Julius Damien	Chambers of Mr Julius Seal, London	020 7328 0158
Sears Mr Robert David Murray	Four New Square, London	020 7822 2000
Seeboruth Mr Royln Jean-Paul	Chambers of Royln Seeboruth, Aylesbury	01296 393329
Sefton-Smith Mr Lloyd	Lamb Chambers, London	020 7797 8300
Sellers Mr Graham	Atlantic Chambers, Liverpool	0151 236 4421
Selvaratnam Miss Vasanti Emily Indrani	Stone Chambers, London	020 7440 6900
Sen Mr Aditya Kumar	Coram Chambers, London	020 7092 3700
Serr Mr Ashley Barrie	Park Lane Plowden, Leeds	0113 228 5049
Shamim Mr Mohammed	Clapham Law Chambers, London	020 7978 8482
Shapiro Mr Daniel Jonathan	Crown Office Chambers, London	020 7797 8100
Shaw Mr Jonathan Paul	No5 Chambers, Birmingham	0845 210 5555
	No5 Chambers, Bristol	0845 210 5555
	No5 Chambers, London	0845 210 5555
	Zenith Chambers, Leeds	0113 245 5438

Shaw Mr Julian	St Johns Buildings, Chester	01244 323070
	St Johns Buildings, Manchester	0161 214 1500
	St Johns Buildings Liverpool, Liverpool	0151 243 6000
Sheftel Mr Andrew Lawson Baylies	Tanfield Chambers, London	020 7421 5300
Shirley Mr James Patrick	Stone Chambers, London	020 7440 6900
Silcock Mr Ian Peter	Hardwicke, London	020 7242 2523
Silverton Miss Catherine Anne	Sovereign Chambers, Leeds	0113 245 1841
Simon Mr Philipp Arnold Heinrich	4 KBW, London	020 7822 8822
Simpson Mr David Joseph	196 Temple Chamber, London	020 7099 9257
Singarajah Mr Frederico	1 Gray's Inn Square, London	020 7405 0001
Singer Mr Andrew Michael	Kings Chambers, Birmingham	0845 034 3444
	Kings Chambers, Leeds	0845 034 3444
	Kings Chambers, Manchester	0845 034 3444
Sisley Mr Timothy Julian Crispin	9 Stone Buildings, London	020 7404 5055
Sjostrand Miss Ekaterina	13 Old Square Chambers, London	020 7831 4445
Skelly Mr Andrew Jon	Hardwicke, London	020 7242 2523
Sliwinski Mr Robert Andrew	SWL Chambers, Loudwater	01494 616007
Small Mr John Robert	36 Bedford Row, London	020 7421 8000
Smith Mr Ian Alfio	11 Stone Buildings, London	020 7831 6381
Smith Mr Matthew Robert	Sovereign Chambers, Leeds	0113 245 1841
Smith Mr Robert Clive	1 Paper Buildings, London	020 7353 3728
	RCS Chambers, Stainton	01709 814 147
Smith Mr Robert Ian	St Paul's Chambers, Leeds	0113 245 5866
Smith Mr Roger Hugh Traylen	No5 Chambers, Birmingham	0845 210 5555
	No5 Chambers, Bristol	0845 210 5555
	No5 Chambers, London	0845 210 5555
Snow Mr Darren Mark	Charter Chambers, London	020 7618 4400
Sonaike Mr Kolarele Oladele Obafemi	One Essex Court, London	020 7936 3030
Soto-Miranda Mr Diego Fernando	One Essex Court, London	020 7936 3030
Sowler Mr Thomas Richard Holland	The Tax Chambers of Mr Richard Sowler TD, Douglas	07624 235000
Spalton Mr George David John	Four New Square, London	020 7822 2000
Speller Mr Bruce Christopher Norman	The White House, Battle	01424 777944
Spratt Mr Christopher David Richard Dean	9 Stone Buildings, London	020 7404 5055
Stenhouse Mr John Alexander	Nightingale Chambers, Wolverley	01562 851350
Stephens Mr Michael Allen	Design Chambers, London	020 7353 0747
	St Ive's Chambers, Birmingham	0121 236 0863
Sterling Mr Robert Alan	St James's Chambers, Manchester	0161 834 7000
	Zenith Chambers, Leeds	0113 245 5438
Stevens-Hoare Miss Michelle	Hardwicke, London	020 7242 2523
Stevenson Dr Simon John	Park Lane Plowden, Leeds	0113 228 5049
Stevenson Mr Paul Anthony	Tanfield Chambers, London	020 7421 5300
Stewart Mr Nicholas John Cameron	Ely Place Chambers, London	020 7400 9600
Stirling Mr Christopher William	Field Court Chambers, London	020 7405 6114
Stuart Mr James William	Lamb Chambers, London	020 7797 8300
Stubbs Mr Richard John Morris	Trinity Chambers, Middlesbrough	01642 247569
	Trinity Chambers, Newcastle Upon Tyne	0191 232 1927
Swirsky Mr Adam Abraham Burl Bradbury	Lamb Chambers, London	020 7797 8300
Tabari Mr Ali-Reza	St Philips Chambers, Birmingham	0121 246 7000
Taussig Mr Gurion	The Chambers of Grahame Aldous QC, London	020 7832 0500
Taylor Mr Michael Joseph Fitz	4 Pump Court, London	020 7842 5555
Taylor Mr Phillip Brian	Richmond Green Chambers, Richmond	020 8948 4801
Taylor Mr Simon	Chambers of Andrew Mitchell QC, London	020 7440 9950
Taylor Ms Karen Anne	Themis Chambers, London	07967 418976
Tee Mr Gregory James	Guildford Chambers, Guildford	01483 539131
Temmink Mr Robert-Jan	Quadrant Chambers, London	020 7583 4444

Name	Chambers	Telephone
Temple Ms Eleanor Louise	Kings Chambers, Birmingham	0845 034 3444
	Kings Chambers, Leeds	0845 034 3444
	Kings Chambers, Manchester	0845 034 3444
Terry Mr Robert Jeffrey	Kings Chambers, Birmingham	0845 034 3444
	Kings Chambers, Leeds	0845 034 3444
	Kings Chambers, Manchester	0845 034 3444
	Lamb Chambers, London	020 7797 8300
Thomas Mr Andrew Martin	Lincoln House Chambers, Manchester	0161 832 5701
	Linenhall Chambers, Chester	01244 348282
Thomas Mr Mark David	5 Essex Court, London	020 7410 2000
Thompson Mr Michael James	Keating Chambers, London	020 7544 2600
Thornley Miss Hannah Elise	South Square, London	020 7696 9900
Thrower Mr James Simeon	Chambers of Simeon Thrower, London	020 8878 7374
Ticciati Mr Oliver	4 Pump Court, London	020 7842 5555
Tinnion Mr Antoine	Trinity Chambers, Middlesbrough	01642 247569
	Trinity Chambers, Newcastle Upon Tyne	0191 232 1927
Tivadar Mr Daniel	3 Hare Court, London	020 7415 7800
Todd Mr Michael Alan	Erskine Chambers, London	020 7242 5532
Tompkinson Miss Deborah Ann	Clerksroom (London), London	0845 083 3000
	Clerksroom (Taunton), Taunton	0845 083 3000
Topal Mr Erol	Lamb Chambers, London	020 7797 8300
Townend Mr Samuel John	Keating Chambers, London	020 7544 2600
Tozzi Mr Nigel Kenneth	4 Pump Court, London	020 7842 5555
Trompeter Mr Nicholas Simeon	Selborne Chambers, London	020 7420 9500
Troup Mr Alexander William	St John's Chambers, Bristol	0117 923 4700
Trumpington Mr John Henry	Staple Inn Chambers, London	020 7242 5240
Tucker Mr Ashley Russell	Park Court Chambers, Leeds	0113 243 3277
Turnbull Miss Helen Mary	Lamb Chambers, London	020 7797 8300
Twine Miss Nicola	Park Lane Plowden, Leeds	0113 228 5049
Uduje Mr Benjamin Elliott	42 Bedford Row, London	020 7831 0222
Upton Mr Jonathan Michael	Tanfield Chambers, London	020 7421 5300
Van Der Leij Dr Martina	Field Court Chambers, London	020 7405 6114
Van Overdijk Miss Claire Orit	No5 Chambers, Birmingham	0845 210 5555
	No5 Chambers, Bristol	0845 210 5555
	No5 Chambers, London	0845 210 5555
Van Tonder Mr Gerard Dirk	New Square Chambers, London	020 7419 8000
Vasilescu Mr Andrei Constantin	Chambers of Martin Burr, London	0845 123 1234
Vaughan Mr Terence Paul	Fenners Chambers, Cambridge	01223 368761
Vaughan-Williams Mr Arthur Laurence	13 Old Square Chambers, London	020 7831 4445
Verduyn Dr Anthony James	St Philips Chambers, Birmingham	0121 246 7000
Vernon Mr Elliot Curt	No. 3 Fleet Street Chambers, London	020 7936 4474
Vickery Mr Neil Michael	13 KBW, Oxford	01865 311066
	13 King's Bench Walk, London	020 7353 7204
Vineall Mr Nicholas Edward John	4 Pump Court, London	020 7842 5555
Vitiello Mr Fabio Angelo-Giuseppe	Staple Inn Chambers, London	020 7242 5240
Von Pommern-Peglow Dr Michael Alfred Herman Pr.	Brunswick Chambers, London	020 7353 1987
Vonberg Mr Thomas Charles	Devereux Chambers, London	020 7353 7534
Wales Mr Matthew James	Guildhall Chambers, Bristol	0117 930 9000
Walford Mr Richard Henry Howard	Serle Court, London	020 7242 6105
Walker Mr Adam Nigel	Seven Bedford Row, London	020 7242 3555
Walsh Mr Michael Patrick	Tanfield Chambers, London	020 7421 5300
Warby Mr Mark David John	5RB, London	020 7242 2902
Ward Mr Martin Stuart	14 Gray's Inn Square, London	020 7242 0858
Warner Mr David Alexander	St Philips Chambers, Birmingham	0121 246 7000
Watson Mr Alaric	11 Stone Buildings, London	020 7831 6381
Watthey Mr James Robertson	Hardwicke, London	020 7242 2523
Webster Mr Keith	4 King's Bench Walk, London	020 7822 7000
Wells Mr Caspar John Mowlem	Goldsmith Chambers, London	020 7353 6802
Wheatley Mr Geraint Rhys	Kings Chambers, Birmingham	0845 034 3444
	Kings Chambers, Leeds	0845 034 3444
	Kings Chambers, Manchester	0845 034 3444

Wheaton Mr Ian Malcolm James	Eighteen Carlton Crescent, Southampton	023 8063 9001
White Mr Oliver Zachary	Littleton Chambers, London	020 7797 8600
White Mr Steven James	Park Court Chambers, Leeds	0113 243 3277
Widdett Ms Ceri Louise	Park Court Chambers, Leeds	0113 243 3277
Wightwick Mr Iain	Riverview Chambers, London	0844 225 3999
	Unity Street Chambers, Bristol	0117 906 9789
Wignall Mr Edward Gordon	No5 Chambers, Birmingham	0845 210 5555
	No5 Chambers, Bristol	0845 210 5555
	No5 Chambers, London	0845 210 5555
Wiktorowski-Solecki Miss Tamara	Middle Temple Lane Chambers, London	020 7583 4352
Wilcox Mr Jerome Carl Jean	Alexander Chambers, London	0845 652 0451/0854 652 0451
Wilkinson Mr Marc Ashley	No5 Chambers, Birmingham	0845 210 5555
	No5 Chambers, Bristol	0845 210 5555
	No5 Chambers, London	0845 210 5555
Willer Mr Robert Michael	Ely Place Chambers, London	020 7400 9600
Willetts Mr Andrew Philip	King's Bench and Godolphin (KBG)Chambers, Plymouth	01752 221551
	New Walk Chambers, Leicester	0871 200 1298/0116 255 9144
Williams Miss June Cleo	No 8 Chambers, Birmingham	0121 236 5514
Williams Mr Mark John	Queen Square Chambers, Bristol	0117 921 1966
Williams Mr Simon Paul	Radcliffe Chambers, London	020 7831 0081
Williamson Mr Adrian John Gerard Hughes	Keating Chambers, London	020 7544 2600
Wills Miss Alexandra Itari	Christ Church Chambers, London	020 7409 5278/07788 512787
Wilson Mr Richard Carver	36 Bedford Row, London	020 7421 8000
Winn-Smith Mr Matthew	Lamb Chambers, London	020 7797 8300
Winser Mr Crispin David Richard	Crown Office Chambers, London	020 7797 8100
Wise Mr Leslie Michael	10 King's Bench Walk, London	020 7353 7742
Wolman Mr Clive Richard	11 Stone Buildings, London	020 7831 6381
Wolstenholme Miss Janine	Sovereign Chambers, Leeds	0113 245 1841
Wright Mr Alexander Paul	4 Pump Court, London	020 7842 5555
Wright Mr Frederick George Ian	Crown Office Chambers, London	020 7797 8100
Wylie Mr Neil Richard	KCH Garden Square, Nottingham	0115 941 8851
Yell Mr Nicholas Anthony	1 Chancery Lane, London	0845 634 6666
Yeung Mr Stuart Roy	Northampton Chambers, Northampton	01604 636271
Young Mr Martin Ford	9 Stone Buildings, London	020 7404 5055

COMMERCIAL PROPERTY

Adewale Mr Remi Adetokunbo Sanni	Chambers of G. D. Tetteh, London	020 7353 7095
	Chambers of Mr R. A. Adewale, Address withheld	020 7231 2814
Aliker Mr Phillip Bliss	Tanfield Chambers, London	020 7421 5300
Allison Mr Simon Robert	Hardwicke, London	020 7242 2523
Allwood Mrs Gina Louisa	Seven Bedford Row, London	020 7242 3555
Artesi Miss Desiree Allison Ann	Thomas More Chambers, London	020 7404 7000
Ash Mr Edward William	Chambers of Mr Edward Ash, Elsworth	01954 267674
Askey Mr Robert John	Palmyra Chambers, Warrington	01925 444919
Asprey Mr Nicholas	Clock Chambers, Wolverhampton	01902 313444
	Serle Court, London	020 7242 6105
Badejo Mr Abimbola Rafiu	5 Pump Court, London	020 7353 2532
Bailey Miss Rosana Henrietta	10 King's Bench Walk, London	020 7353 7742
Bailey Mr Russell Stuart	No5 Chambers, Birmingham	0845 210 5555
	No5 Chambers, Bristol	0845 210 5555
	No5 Chambers, London	0845 210 5555
Barber Mr Phillip Arthur	Zenith Chambers, Leeds	0113 245 5438
Bastin Mr Alexander Charles	Hardwicke, London	020 7242 2523
Beaumont Mr Benjamin	Chambers of Dr Michael Arnheim, London	020 7833 5093
	Middle Temple Lane Chambers, London	020 7583 4352

C

Beaumont Mr Marc Clifford	9 Stone Buildings, London	020 7404 5055
	Windsor Barristers' Chambers, Windsor	01753 839321
Bennion-Pedley Mr Edward	13 KBW, Oxford	01865 311066
	13 King's Bench Walk, London	020 7353 7204
Berkley Mr David Nahum	1 Gray's Inn Square, London	020 7405 0001
	St Johns Buildings, Chester	01244 323070
	St Johns Buildings, Manchester	0161 214 1500
	St Johns Buildings Liverpool, Liverpool	0151 243 6000
Berkley Mr Michael Stuart	Rougemont Chambers, Exeter	01392 208484
Berry Mr Nicholas Michael	Rougemont Chambers, Exeter	01392 208484
Bhakar Mr Surinder Singh	4 King's Bench Walk, London	020 7822 7000
Blaker Mr Gary Mark	Selborne Chambers, London	020 7420 9500
Bleasdale Miss Marie-Claire	Radcliffe Chambers, London	020 7831 0081
Blohm Mr Leslie Adrian	St John's Chambers, Bristol	0117 923 4700
Boyd Mr Stephen James Harvey	Selborne Chambers, London	020 7420 9500
Bragiel Mr Edward Bronislaw Henryk	Hogarth Chambers, London	020 7404 0404
Bredemear Mr Zachary Charles	1 Chancery Lane, London	0845 634 6666
Brewin Mr Carl Patrick	3 PB Barristers, London	020 7583 8055
Brockley Mr Nigel Simon	No5 Chambers, Birmingham	0845 210 5555
	No5 Chambers, Bristol	0845 210 5555
	No5 Chambers, London	0845 210 5555
Brown Miss Susan Margaret	One Essex Court, London	020 7936 3030
Brown Mr Philip Stephen	9 Stone Buildings, London	020 7404 5055
Brown Mr Roger Charles Arthur	Kenworthy's Chambers, Manchester	0161 832 4036
Browne Mr James William	Lamb Chambers, London	020 7797 8300
Bruce Mr Andrew Jonathan	Serle Court, London	020 7242 6105
Bryden Mr Christopher James Yuen Kang	4 King's Bench Walk, London	020 7822 7000
Buchan Miss Caroline Venetia	Chambers of Miss C Buchan, Haywards Heath	01444 482222
Bullock Mr Robert Gustaf	The Chambers of Mr Bullock, Brighton	01273 321050
Butler Mr Rupert James	3 Hare Court, London	020 7415 7800
Butler Mr Simon David	The Chambers of Grahame Aldous QC, London	020 7832 0500
Buttimore Mr Gabriel	13 KBW, Oxford	01865 311066
	13 King's Bench Walk, London	020 7353 7204
Byrne Mr Garrett Thomas	4-5 Gray's Inn Square, London	020 7404 5252
Candlin Miss Naomi Helen	St Philips Chambers, Birmingham	0121 246 7000
Cant Mr Christopher Ian	9 Stone Buildings, London	020 7404 5055
Castle Mr Peter Bolton	13 Old Square Chambers, London	020 7831 4445
Cattermull Miss Emma Jayne	East Anglian Chambers, Chelmsford	01473 214481
	East Anglian Chambers, Ipswich	01473 214481
	East Anglian Chambers, Norwich	01473 214481
Caun Mr Lawrence	Lamb Chambers, London	020 7797 8300
Challenger Mr Colin Westcott	Lamb Chambers, London	020 7797 8300
Charalambides Mr Leonidas	Francis Taylor Building, London	020 7353 8415
Christensen Mr Carlton	10 King's Bench Walk, London	020 7353 7742
Clarke Mr George Robert Ivan	5 Pump Court, London	020 7353 2532
Clayton Mr Nigel Garvin	Kings Chambers, Birmingham	0845 034 3444
	Kings Chambers, Leeds	0845 034 3444
	Kings Chambers, Manchester	0845 034 3444
Cohen Mr Edward Mervyn	11 Stone Buildings, London	020 7831 6381
Colbey Mr Richard	Guildhall Chambers Portsmouth, Portsmouth	023 9275 2400
	Lamb Chambers, London	020 7797 8300
Collard Mr Michael David	5 Pump Court, London	020 7353 2532
Cooper Miss Christine	Field Court Chambers, London	020 7405 6114
Coster Mr Ronald David	42 Bedford Row, London	020 7831 0222
Cotterell Mr David William	Albion Chambers, Bristol	0117 927 2144
Crew Miss Gillian Mary	Ely Place Chambers, London	020 7400 9600
De Waal Mr John Henry Lowndes	Hardwicke, London	020 7242 2523

Demachkie Mr Jamal	3 PB Barristers, London	020 7583 8055
Denbin Mr Jack Arnold	Greenway, Sonning-on-Thames	0118 969 2484
Devlin Mr Bernard Joseph	Five St Andrew's Hill, London	020 7332 5400
di Mambro Mr David Jesse Andrew	Pallant Chambers, Chichester	01243 784538
	Radcliffe Chambers, London	020 7831 0081
Dovar Mr Daniel	Tanfield Chambers, London	020 7421 5300
Edwards Mr Martin Richard	39 Essex Street, London	020 7832 1111
	82 King Street, Manchester	0161 870 9969
Eilledge Miss Amanda Gail Caroline	11 Stone Buildings, London	020 7831 6381
England Mrs Lisa Johanna Louise	Guildhall Chambers Portsmouth, Portsmouth	023 9275 2400
Esprit Mr Benoit	Barristers Chambers, London	020 3417 6461
	Legis Chambers, Aylesbury	01296 431125
Fain Mr Carl Ian	Tanfield Chambers, London	020 7421 5300
Falkowski Mr Damian	4-5 Gray's Inn Square, London	020 7404 5252
Fawcett Mr Neil	St Ive's Chambers, Birmingham	0121 236 0863
Feldman Mr Matthew Richard Bankes	42 Bedford Row, London	020 7831 0222
Fieldsend Mr James William	Tanfield Chambers, London	020 7421 5300
Finlay Mr Darren	Sovereign Chambers, Leeds	0113 245 1841
Fitzmaurice Mr Guy Edward Christian	Staple Inn Chambers, London	020 7242 5240
Fowles Mr Jonathan James	Serle Court, London	020 7242 6105
Francis Mr Andrew James	Serle Court, London	020 7242 6105
	Zenith Chambers, Leeds	0113 245 5438
Gallagher Mr Stanley Harold	Tanfield Chambers, London	020 7421 5300
Gallivan Mr Terence John	Five Paper, London	020 7815 3200
Gasztowicz Mr Steven	Cornerstone Barristers, London	020 7242 4986
	New Street Chambers, Leicester	0116 262 5906
Gatty Mr Daniel Simon	Hardwicke, London	020 7242 2523
Gibbons Miss Mary Regina	Stone Chambers, London	020 7440 6900
Gibbons Ms Ellodie	Tanfield Chambers, London	020 7421 5300
Glover Mr Marc Philip	Tanfield Chambers, London	020 7421 5300
Godfrey Mr Lauren John	Crown Office Row Chambers, Brighton	01273 625625
Gold Mr Richard David	St John's Chambers, Bristol	0117 923 4700
Goldstone Mr Simon Lewis	4 Pump Court, London	020 7842 5555
Gore Mr Andrew Roger	Fenners Chambers, Cambridge	01223 368761
Griffiths Mr David	St Philips Chambers, Birmingham	0121 246 7000
Gupta Mr Amit	St Philips Chambers, Birmingham	0121 246 7000
Hallett Miss Katherine Elizabeth	13 Old Square Chambers, London	020 7831 4445
Hansen Mr William Joseph	No5 Chambers, Birmingham	0845 210 5555
	No5 Chambers, Bristol	0845 210 5555
	No5 Chambers, London	0845 210 5555
Harrap Mr Robert Philip	Five Paper, London	020 7815 3200
Harris Mr James	Five St Andrew's Hill, London	020 7332 5400
Hartman Mr Michael	One Essex Court, London	020 7936 3030
Haughty Mr Jeremy Nicholas	Chambers of Mr Ami Feder, London	020 7797 7788
	Chambers of Mr Ami Feder, London	020 7797 7788
	Rougemont Chambers, Exeter	01392 208484
Hayes Mr Richard James	Lamb Chambers, London	020 7797 8300
Hendron Mr Henry Joseph Christopher	Strand Chambers, London	020 7117 6920
Higginson Mr Timothy Nicholas Bennett	Littleton Chambers, London	020 7797 8600
	St John's Chambers, Bristol	0117 923 4700
Hill Mr Michael Gordon	Trinity Chambers, Middlesbrough	01642 247569
	Trinity Chambers, Newcastle Upon Tyne	0191 232 1927
Hill Mr Piers Nicholas	37 Park Square Chambers, Leeds	0113 243 9422
Hillier Mr William	New Street Chambers, Leicester	0116 262 5906
Hilton Ms Saisampan	Holborn Chambers, London	020 7242 6060
Holbech Mr Charles Edward	New Square Chambers, London	020 7419 8000

Barrister	Chambers	Telephone
Holland Mr Charles Christopher	Francis Taylor Building, London	020 7353 8415
	Trinity Chambers, Middlesbrough	01642 247569
	Trinity Chambers, Newcastle Upon Tyne	0191 232 1927
Holland Mr Rowan Guy	Five Paper, London	020 7815 3200
Hormaeche Miss Alejandra	Tanfield Chambers, London	020 7421 5300
Horne Mr Charles Hugh Wilson	Kings Chambers, Birmingham	0845 034 3444
	Kings Chambers, Leeds	0845 034 3444
	Kings Chambers, Manchester	0845 034 3444
Hornett Mr Stuart Ian	Selborne Chambers, London	020 7420 9500
Hossain Mr Ajmalul	Selborne Chambers, London	020 7420 9500
	St Philips Chambers, Birmingham	0121 246 7000
Howells Mr Stephen John	Stone Chambers, London	020 7440 6900
Hughes-Deane Ms Charlotte Barbara	Atlantic Chambers, Liverpool	0151 236 4421
Hunt Mr Stephen	4 Stone Buildings, London	020 7242 5524
Hussain Mr Muhammad Altaf	Chambers of Mr M A Hussain, London	020 8679 2398
Isaac Mr Nicholas Dudley	Tanfield Chambers, London	020 7421 5300
Iyer Miss Shobana	Swan Chambers, Richmond	0845 123 1234
Jefferies Mr Thomas Robert	Landmark Chambers, London	020 7430 1221
Jones Mr Christopher David Harries	St John's Chambers, Bristol	0117 923 4700
Jones Mr Geraint Anthony	New Walk Chambers, Leicester	0871 200 1298/0116 255 9144
	9 St John Street, Manchester	0161 955 9000
	Tanfield Chambers, London	020 7421 5300
Jones Mr Geraint Martyn	Fenners Chambers, Cambridge	01223 368761
Jones Mr Kelvin Mcallister	Templis Chambers, London	020 7649 9808
Jones Mr Mark Simeon	3 Dr Johnson's Buildings, London	020 7353 4854
Jones Mr Richard Frederick Thomas	Heavenwood Chambers, Stroud	01453 873444
Joseph Mr Charles Henry	Tanfield Chambers, London	020 7421 5300
Kelly Mr Sean	Chancery House Chambers, Leeds	0113 244 6691
Kelly Mrs Amy Louise	12 College Place, Southampton	023 8032 0320
Kenny Mr Martin William	Walnut House, Exeter	01392 279751
Khan Dr Alexander	Coral House, Manchester	
Khan Mr Abdul Aleem	Gray's Chambers, Newbury	020 8518 2525
Khan Mr Mahmood Shafi	Luton Chambers, Luton	01582 598394
	Willesden Chambers, London	020 3273 1042
Kilcoyne Mr Patrick Desmond Oliver	42 Bedford Row, London	020 7831 0222
Kirk Mr Graeme Charles	One Essex Court, London	020 7936 3030
Kramer Mr Philip Anthony	Park Lane Plowden, Newcastle Upon Tyne	0191 211 4087
Kynoch Mr Duncan Stuart Sanderson	Selborne Chambers, London	020 7420 9500
Lane Mr Christopher Paul	No 8 Chambers, Birmingham	0121 236 5514
Lane Mr Simon Charles	Rougemont Chambers, Exeter	01392 208484
Law Mr John Edward	The Chambers of Grahame Aldous QC, London	020 7832 0500
Lewis Mrs Pauline Grace	Holborn Chambers, London	020 7242 6060
Lopez Mr Juan Nemesio	Francis Taylor Building, London	020 7353 8415
Loveday Mr Mark Alan	Tanfield Chambers, London	020 7421 5300
Lowe Mr Mungo James	13 Old Square Chambers, London	020 7831 4445
Maguire Mr Andrew James	Exchange Chambers, Liverpool	0151 236 7747
	Exchange Chambers, Manchester	0161 833 2722
	St Philips Chambers, Birmingham	0121 246 7000
Maltz Mr Ben Daniel	Five Paper, London	020 7815 3200
Mann Mr Christopher	13 KBW, Oxford	01865 311066
	13 King's Bench Walk, London	020 7353 7204
Marsden Mr Andrew Guy	East Anglian Chambers, Chelmsford	01473 214481
	East Anglian Chambers, Colchester	01473 214481
	East Anglian Chambers, Ipswich	01473 214481
	East Anglian Chambers, Norwich	01473 214481
Matthias Mr David Huw	Francis Taylor Building, London	020 7353 8415
Maynard Mr Christopher Howard	Tanfield Chambers, London	020 7421 5300
McCarthy Mr William	Bridgewater Chambers, Manchester	0161 3877127
	1 Mitre Court Buildings, London	020 7452 8900

McCombie Mr Fergus Alexander Paul	1 Gray's Inn Square, London	020 7405 0001
McNae Mr Jonathan James	Selborne Chambers, London	020 7420 9500
Meares Mr Nigel Leslie Vellacott	11 Stone Buildings, London	020 7831 6381
Moss Mr Christopher Stephen	St Johns Buildings, Manchester	0161 214 1500
	St Johns Buildings Liverpool, Liverpool	0151 243 6000
	16 Winckley Square, Preston	01772 256100
Muir Miss Nicola Jane	Hardwicke, London	020 7242 2523
Mullen Mr Mark Robert	Radcliffe Chambers, London	020 7831 0081
Muman Mr Vijay Kumar	43 Temple Row Chambers, Birmingham	0121 237 6035
Newsom Mr George Lucien	Guildhall Chambers, Bristol	0117 930 9000
Nicholls Mr David James	11 Stone Buildings, London	020 7831 6381
Nickless Mr Jason Alan	College Chambers, Southampton	023 8023 0338
Noble Mr Andrew	Enterprise Chambers, Leeds	0113 246 0391
Normington Mr James Adam	Park Court Chambers, Leeds	0113 243 3277
Norton Mr Giles	Enigma Chambers, Sheffield	07779 576499
	Holborn Chambers, London	020 7242 6060
Nurse Mr Gordon Bramwell William	Radcliffe Chambers, London	020 7831 0081
O'Brien Mr Nicholas William Wattebot	10 King's Bench Walk, London	020 7353 7742
Ohrenstein Mr Dov	Radcliffe Chambers, London	020 7831 0081
Okoya Mr William Ebikise	Arden Chambers, London	020 7242 4244
O'Mahony Mr Jonathan Solomon	9 Stone Buildings, London	020 7404 5055
O'Sullivan Mr Richard John	1215 Chambers, London	020 3291 1215
Otwal Mr Mukhtiar Singh	42 Bedford Row, London	020 7831 0222
Oulton Mr Richard Arthur Courtenay	5 Essex Court, London	020 7410 2000
Panton Mr Alastair Howard	10 King's Bench Walk, London	020 7353 7742
Paraskos Mr Paraskevakis Christakis	11 Gray's Inn Square Chambers, London	020 7405 6879
Parker Mrs Karen Lesley	Guildhall Chambers Portsmouth, Portsmouth	023 9275 2400
Parsons Mr Andrew James	Portsmouth Barristers'Chambers, Portsmouth	023 9283 1292
Payton Mr Clifford Coningsby	Alpha Court Chambers, Leamington Spa	01926 886412
Pearce Mr Robert Edgar	Radcliffe Chambers, London	020 7831 0081
Pennock Mr Ian	Park Lane Plowden, Leeds	0113 228 5049
Petersen Mr Thomas James	Goldsmith Chambers, London	020 7353 6802
Philpott Mr Anthony Luke	12 Old Square Chambers, London	020 7404 0875
Polli Mr Timothy James	Tanfield Chambers, London	020 7421 5300
Rahman Mr Anis	12 Old Square Chambers, London	020 7404 0875
Rainey Mr Philip Carslake	Tanfield Chambers, London	020 7421 5300
Ratcliffe Miss Frances Anne	Radcliffe Chambers, London	020 7831 0081
Ridd Mr David Ian Mcgregor	Farrar's Building, London	020 7583 9241
Rifat Mr Maurice Alan	1 Gray's Inn Square, London	020 7405 0001
Risso-Gill Mr Edward David Charles	Thomas More Chambers, London	020 7404 7000
Roberts Mr Michael Charles	Chambers of Michael Roberts, Henley-On-Thames	01844 355 655
Roberts Mr Richard Vaughan	Henderson Chambers, London	020 7583 9020
Rowntree Mr Edward John Pickering	Hardwicke, London	020 7242 2523
Rushton Mr Jonathon Barker	36 Bedford Row, London	020 7421 8000
Sandham Mr James Andrew	Arden Chambers, London	020 7242 4244
Sawtell Mr David Robert Fraser	4 King's Bench Walk, London	020 7822 7000
Sellers Mr Graham	Atlantic Chambers, Liverpool	0151 236 4421
Sheftel Mr Andrew Lawson Baylies	Tanfield Chambers, London	020 7421 5300
Shuman Miss Karen Ann Elizabeth	1 Chancery Lane, London	0845 634 6666
	No 8 Chambers, Birmingham	0121 236 5514
Sinclair Miss Lisa Anne	Chambers of Miss Lisa Sinclair, London	020 8946 7201
Sisley Mr Timothy Julian Crispin	9 Stone Buildings, London	020 7404 5055
Sjostrand Miss Ekaterina	13 Old Square Chambers, London	020 7831 4445
Skelly Mr Andrew Jon	Hardwicke, London	020 7242 2523
Sliwinski Mr Robert Andrew	SWL Chambers, Loudwater	01494 616007

Smith Mr Roger Hugh Traylen	No5 Chambers, Birmingham	0845 210 5555
	No5 Chambers, Bristol	0845 210 5555
	No5 Chambers, London	0845 210 5555
Smyth Mr Christopher Julian Worsley	Queen Square Chambers, Bristol	0117 921 1966
Staddon Mr Paul	Tanfield Chambers, London	020 7421 5300
Stenhouse Mr John Alexander	Nightingale Chambers, Wolverley	01562 851350
Stephens Mr Michael Allen	Design Chambers, London	020 7353 0747
	St Ive's Chambers, Birmingham	0121 236 0863
Sterling Mr Robert Alan	St James's Chambers, Manchester	0161 834 7000
	Zenith Chambers, Leeds	0113 245 5438
Stevens-Hoare Miss Michelle	Hardwicke, London	020 7242 2523
Stevenson Mr Paul Anthony	Tanfield Chambers, London	020 7421 5300
Stewart Mr Nicholas John Cameron	Ely Place Chambers, London	020 7400 9600
Swirsky Mr Adam Abraham Burl Bradbury	Lamb Chambers, London	020 7797 8300
Temple Ms Eleanor Louise	Kings Chambers, Birmingham	0845 034 3444
	Kings Chambers, Leeds	0845 034 3444
	Kings Chambers, Manchester	0845 034 3444
Terry Mr Robert Jeffrey	Kings Chambers, Birmingham	0845 034 3444
	Kings Chambers, Leeds	0845 034 3444
	Kings Chambers, Manchester	0845 034 3444
	Lamb Chambers, London	020 7797 8300
Thomas Mrs Felicity	Westgate Chambers, Lewes	01273 480510
Thrower Mr James Simeon	Chambers of Simeon Thrower, London	020 8878 7374
Topal Mr Erol	Lamb Chambers, London	020 7797 8300
Trompeter Mr Nicholas Simeon	Selborne Chambers, London	020 7420 9500
Trumpington Mr John Henry	Staple Inn Chambers, London	020 7242 5240
Turnbull Miss Helen Mary	Lamb Chambers, London	020 7797 8300
Upton Mr Jonathan Michael	Tanfield Chambers, London	020 7421 5300
Van Overdijk Miss Claire Orit	No5 Chambers, Birmingham	0845 210 5555
	No5 Chambers, Bristol	0845 210 5555
	No5 Chambers, London	0845 210 5555
Van Tonder Mr Gerard Dirk	New Square Chambers, London	020 7419 8000
Vanhegan Mr Toby Bartholomew	Arden Chambers, London	020 7242 4244
Vaughan-Williams Mr Arthur Laurence	13 Old Square Chambers, London	020 7831 4445
Verduyn Dr Anthony James	St Philips Chambers, Birmingham	0121 246 7000
Vernon Mr Elliot Curt	No. 3 Fleet Street Chambers, London	020 7936 4474
Vickery Mr Neil Michael	13 KBW, Oxford	01865 311066
	13 King's Bench Walk, London	020 7353 7204
Wales Mr Matthew James	Guildhall Chambers, Bristol	0117 930 9000
Walsh Mr Michael Patrick	Tanfield Chambers, London	020 7421 5300
Waritay Mr Samuel	Chambers of Mr Samuel Waritay, London	0845 803 7767
Warner Mr David Alexander	St Philips Chambers, Birmingham	0121 246 7000
Watson Mr Alaric	11 Stone Buildings, London	020 7831 6381
Wheatley Mr Geraint Rhys	Kings Chambers, Birmingham	0845 034 3444
	Kings Chambers, Leeds	0845 034 3444
	Kings Chambers, Manchester	0845 034 3444
Wiktorowski-Solecki Miss Tamara	Middle Temple Lane Chambers, London	020 7583 4352
Wilcox Mr Jerome Carl Jean	Alexander Chambers, London	0845 652 0451/0854 652 0451
Wilkinson Mr Marc Ashley	No5 Chambers, Birmingham	0845 210 5555
	No5 Chambers, Bristol	0845 210 5555
	No5 Chambers, London	0845 210 5555
Williams Mr Simon Paul	Radcliffe Chambers, London	020 7831 0081
Wills Miss Alexandra Itari	Christ Church Chambers, London	020 7409 5278/07788 512787
Woodward Mr Jeremy Paul	Pallant Chambers, Chichester	01243 784538
Young Mr Martin Ford	9 Stone Buildings, London	020 7404 5055

COMMODITIES

Allerhand Mr Ludwik Edmund	Chambers of Mr Ludwik Allerhand, London	020 8291 4356

Allwood Mrs Gina Louisa	Seven Bedford Row, London	020 7242 3555
Almihdar Mr Ali Hamed	Outer Temple Chambers, London	020 7353 6381
Aswani Mr Ravi Girdharilal	Stone Chambers, London	020 7440 6900
Buttimore Mr Gabriel	13 KBW, Oxford	01865 311066
	13 King's Bench Walk, London	020 7353 7204
Charkham Mr Graham Harold	20 Essex Street, London	020 7842 1200
Clark Miss Geraldine	Serle Court, London	020 7242 6105
Gee Mr Steven Mark	Stone Chambers, London	020 7440 6900
Godwin Mr William George Henry	3 Hare Court, London	020 7415 7800
	St John's Chambers, Bristol	0117 923 4700
Henderson Mr Neil John	Stone Chambers, London	020 7440 6900
Iyer Miss Shobana	Swan Chambers, Richmond	0845 123 1234
McDonnell Mr John Beresford William	13 Old Square Chambers, London	020 7831 4445
Meredith Mr Christopher William	Furnival Chambers, London	020 7405 3232
Newbold Dr Anne Lorraine Elsie	Minerva Chambers, Ocean Village	00 350 20042779
O'Sullivan Mr Thomas Sean Patrick	4 Pump Court, London	020 7842 5555
Reffin Miss Clare Alyson	One Essex Court, London	020 7583 2000
Seeboruth Mr Royln Jean-Paul	Chambers of Royln Seeboruth, Aylesbury	01296 393329
Selvaratnam Miss Vasanti Emily Indrani	Stone Chambers, London	020 7440 6900
Shirley Mr James Patrick	Stone Chambers, London	020 7440 6900
Singarajah Mr Frederico	1 Gray's Inn Square, London	020 7405 0001
Spalton Mr George David John	Four New Square, London	020 7822 2000
Watthey Mr James Robertson	Hardwicke, London	020 7242 2523
Wright Mr Alexander Paul	4 Pump Court, London	020 7842 5555

COMMON LAND

Alomo Mr Richard Olusoji	14 Gray's Inn Square, London	020 7242 0858
Asprey Mr Nicholas	Clock Chambers, Wolverhampton	01902 313444
	Serle Court, London	020 7242 6105
Bailey Mr Thomas Iain	Chambers of Mr Thomas Bailey, Milton Keynes	07983 447117
Berry Mr Nicholas Michael	Rougemont Chambers, Exeter	01392 208484
Blohm Mr Leslie Adrian	St John's Chambers, Bristol	0117 923 4700
Booth Mr Alexander Henry Spencer	Francis Taylor Building, London	020 7353 8415
Braithwaite Mr Thomas James	Serle Court, London	020 7242 6105
Bredemear Mr Zachary Charles	1 Chancery Lane, London	0845 634 6666
Brewin Mr Carl Patrick	3 PB Barristers, London	020 7583 8055
Bryden Mr Christopher James Yuen Kang	4 King's Bench Walk, London	020 7822 7000
Budworth Mr Richard Dutton	2-3 Hind Court Chambers, London	020 7822 2150
Bullock Mr Robert Gustaf	The Chambers of Mr Bullock, Brighton	01273 321050
Buttimore Mr Gabriel	13 KBW, Oxford	01865 311066
	13 King's Bench Walk, London	020 7353 7204
Charalambides Mr Leonidas	Francis Taylor Building, London	020 7353 8415
Chute Ms Andrea Alexandra	Rougemont Chambers, Exeter	01392 208484
	Tooks Chambers, London	020 7842 7575
Coster Mr Ronald David	42 Bedford Row, London	020 7831 0222
Cotterell Mr David William	Albion Chambers, Bristol	0117 927 2144
Davies Ms Samantha Teresa	Chambers of Ms Samantha Davies, Milton Keynes	0845 123 1234
	Warwick House Chambers, London	020 7430 2323
Devereux-Cooke Mr Richard Charles	13 Old Square Chambers, London	020 7831 4445
di Mambro Mr David Jesse Andrew	Pallant Chambers, Chichester	01243 784538
	Radcliffe Chambers, London	020 7831 0081
Douglass Miss Geraldine Maisie	Portal Chambers, Llandysul	01559 395 292
Dowell Mr Gregory Hamilton	Principal Chambers, Sevenoaks	0845 209 8080
Edwards Mr Martin Richard	39 Essex Street, London	020 7832 1111
	82 King Street, Manchester	0161 870 9969
Falkowski Mr Damian	4-5 Gray's Inn Square, London	020 7404 5252
Fawcett Mr Neil	St Ive's Chambers, Birmingham	0121 236 0863

Fellows Mr Philip David Andrew	Hardwicke, London	020 7242 2523
Felton Mr Timothy John Fowler	Rougemont Chambers, Exeter	01392 208484
Goodfellow Mr Stephen John	East Anglian Chambers, Chelmsford	01473 214481
	East Anglian Chambers, Ipswich	01473 214481
	East Anglian Chambers, Norwich	01473 214481
Goodman Mr Alexander David Edmund	Atlas Chambers, London	020 7269 7980
	4-5 Gray's Inn Square, London	020 7404 5252
Gore Mr Andrew Roger	Fenners Chambers, Cambridge	01223 368761
Greenan Miss Sarah Octavia	Zenith Chambers, Leeds	0113 245 5438
Guy Mr Richard Perran	Chambers of Mr Ami Feder, London	020 7797 7788
	King's Bench and Godolphin (KBG)Chambers, Plymouth	01752 221551
	Southernhay Chambers, Exeter	01392 255777
Harrison Mr Peter John	6 Pump Court, London	020 7797 8400
	6 Pump Court Chambers, Maidstone	01622 688094
Hobson Mr John Graham	4-5 Gray's Inn Square, London	020 7404 5252
Hodson Mr Matthew Paul	Farrar's Building, London	020 7583 9241
Hogben Mrs Helen Jane	Fountain Chambers, Middlesbrough	01642 804040
Holland Mr Charles Christopher	Francis Taylor Building, London	020 7353 8415
	Trinity Chambers, Middlesbrough	01642 247569
	Trinity Chambers, Newcastle Upon Tyne	0191 232 1927
Holroyd Mr John James	Zenith Chambers, Leeds	0113 245 5438
Honey Mr Richard Arthur	Francis Taylor Building, London	020 7353 8415
Horne Mr Charles Hugh Wilson	Kings Chambers, Birmingham	0845 034 3444
	Kings Chambers, Leeds	0845 034 3444
	Kings Chambers, Manchester	0845 034 3444
Horton Mr Matthew Bethell	39 Essex Street, London	020 7832 1111
	82 King Street, Manchester	0161 870 9969
Hunt Mr Stephen	4 Stone Buildings, London	020 7242 5524
Jones Mr Alun	St Paul's Chambers, Leeds	0113 245 5866
Jones Mr Rhys Charles Mansel	14 Gray's Inn Square, London	020 7242 0858
Kelly Mrs Amy Louise	12 College Place, Southampton	023 8032 0320
Kynoch Mr Duncan Stuart Sanderson	Selborne Chambers, London	020 7420 9500
Le Poidevin Mr Nicholas Peter	New Square Chambers, London	020 7419 8000
Lloyd Mr John Nesbitt	Rougemont Chambers, Exeter	01392 208484
Lopez Mr Juan Nemesio	Francis Taylor Building, London	020 7353 8415
Marsden Mr Andrew Guy	East Anglian Chambers, Chelmsford	01473 214481
	East Anglian Chambers, Colchester	01473 214481
	East Anglian Chambers, Ipswich	01473 214481
	East Anglian Chambers, Norwich	01473 214481
Marshall Mr Derek Stanley	College Chambers, Southampton	023 8023 0338
Masters Mr Alan Bruce Raymond	1 Pump Court, London	020 7842 7070
Matthias Mr David Huw	Francis Taylor Building, London	020 7353 8415
McDonnell Mr John Beresford William	13 Old Square Chambers, London	020 7831 4445
Meager Mrs Rowena Elisabeth	No5 Chambers, Birmingham	0845 210 5555
	No5 Chambers, Bristol	0845 210 5555
	No5 Chambers, London	0845 210 5555
Menon Mr Harigovind	New Court Chambers, Newcastle Upon Tyne	0191 232 1980
	Park Lane Plowden, Newcastle Upon Tyne	0191 211 4087
Monnington Mr Bruce Gilbert	Fenners Chambers, Cambridge	01223 368761
Montague Mrs Susan	Weald Chambers, Address withheld	01424 882 876
Mynors Dr Charles Baskerville	Francis Taylor Building, London	020 7353 8415
Newsom Mr George Lucien	Guildhall Chambers, Bristol	0117 930 9000
Normington Mr James Adam	Park Court Chambers, Leeds	0113 243 3277
Norton Mr Giles	Enigma Chambers, Sheffield	07779 576499
	Holborn Chambers, London	020 7242 6060
Ohrenstein Mr Dov	Radcliffe Chambers, London	020 7831 0081
Pearce Mr Robert Edgar	Radcliffe Chambers, London	020 7831 0081

Barrister	Chambers	Telephone
Quirke Mr Gerard Martin	Citadel Chambers, Birmingham	0121 233 8500
Reevell Mr Simon Justin	39 Park Square, Leeds	0113 245 6633
Roberts Mr Richard Vaughan	Henderson Chambers, London	020 7583 9020
Sadiq Mr Muhammad Faisel	Ely Place Chambers, London	020 7400 9600
Sandham Mr James Andrew	Arden Chambers, London	020 7242 4244
Sefi Mr Benedict John	Harcourt Chambers, London	0844 561 7135
	Harcourt Chambers, Oxford	0844 561 7135
Sinclair Mr Graham Kelso	East Anglian Chambers, Colchester	01473 214481
	East Anglian Chambers, Ipswich	01473 214481
	East Anglian Chambers, Norwich	01473 214481
Smith Mr Robert Clive	1 Paper Buildings, London	020 7353 3728
	RCS Chambers, Stainton	01709 814 147
Smyth Mr Christopher Julian Worsley	Queen Square Chambers, Bristol	0117 921 1966
Sood Mrs Usha Rani	Trent Chambers, Nottingham	0115 941 9596
Spratt Mr Christopher David Richard Dean	9 Stone Buildings, London	020 7404 5055
Sterling Mr Robert Alan	St James's Chambers, Manchester	0161 834 7000
	Zenith Chambers, Leeds	0113 245 5438
Thomas Mrs Felicity	Westgate Chambers, Lewes	01273 480510
Vasilescu Mr Andrei Constantin	Chambers of Martin Burr, London	0845 123 1234
Wightwick Mr Iain	Riverview Chambers, London	0844 225 3999
	Unity Street Chambers, Bristol	0117 906 9789
Wilkinson Mr Marc Ashley	No5 Chambers, Birmingham	0845 210 5555
	No5 Chambers, Bristol	0845 210 5555
	No5 Chambers, London	0845 210 5555
Wragg Mr Jonathan Robert	Highgate Chambers, London	020 8340 6031

COMMON LAW (GENERAL)

Barrister	Chambers	Telephone
Adamson Mr Alan	Kew Chambers, Kew	0844 8099991
Adewale Mr Remi Adetokunbo Sanni	Chambers of G. D. Tetteh, London	020 7353 7095
	Chambers of Mr R. A. Adewale, Address withheld	020 7231 2814
Aeberli Mr Peter Dolph	3 PB Barristers, Bournemouth	01202 292102
	3 PB Barristers, Bristol	0117 928 1520
	3 PB Barristers, London	020 7583 8055
	3 PB Barristers, Oxford	01865 793 736
	3 PB Barristers, Winchester	01962 868884
Agnihotri Mr Naveen	12 College Place, Southampton	023 8032 0320
Ahmad Mr Kashif Zubair	Blenheim Chambers, Hounslow	07588 608288
Ahmed Mr Ishfaq	Stone Chambers, London	020 7440 6900
Ailes Mr John Ashley	Eighteen Carlton Crescent, Southampton	023 8063 9001
Ajaz Mr Mohammad Arshad	Eastmans Chambers, Reading	0118 966 9094
Akinsanya Mr Stephen Olubunmi	Old Bailey Chambers, London	020 3008 6404
Alakija Mr Ayodele Hugh	No 8 Chambers, Birmingham	0121 236 5514
Alam Ms Jan	Ropewalk Chambers, Nottingham	0115 947 2581
Alexandra Miss Sebastiane	Holborn Chambers, London	020 7242 6060
Algazy Mr Jacques Max	Cloisters, London	020 7827 4000
Ali Mr Ishtiyaq	Chartlands Chambers, Northampton	01604 603322
Alliott Mr George Beckles	Temple Garden Chambers, London	020 7583 1315
Alloway Mr Tor Hugh	Talloway Chambers, London	020 7419 5047
Allston Mr Anthony Stanley	3 Dr Johnson's Buildings, London	020 7353 4854
Altaras Mr David Maurice	36 Bedford Row, London	020 7421 8000
Aly Miss Sheila	Warwick House Chambers, London	020 7430 2323
Ameen Mr Danish	18 St John Street, Manchester	0161 278 1800
Amraoui Mr Thomas	4-5 Gray's Inn Square, London	020 7404 5252
Anderson Mr Jack Duthie	4-5 Gray's Inn Square, London	020 7404 5252
Anderson Mr Simon Peter Bede	Park Court Chambers, Leeds	0113 243 3277
Andre Mr Roger Louis	Sovereign Chambers, Leeds	0113 245 1841
Andrews Mr Paul Leslie	Great James Street Chambers, London	020 7440 4949
Angammana Mr Gamini Bertram	Chambers of Gamini Angammana, London	020 8771 5205

Barrister	Chambers	Telephone
Antell Mr John Jason	King's Bench and Godolphin (KBG)Chambers, Plymouth	01752 221551
Appiah Miss Linda	Guildford Chambers, Guildford	01483 539131
Apthorp Mr George Charles	5 Essex Court, London	020 7410 2000
Argent Mr Gavin Richard	Westgate Chambers, Lewes	01273 480510
Aris Mr Jason Mark	Citadel Chambers, Birmingham	0121 233 8500
Armstrong Mr Stuart David	Arden Chambers, London	020 7242 4244
Arnheim Dr Michael Thomas Walter	Chambers of Dr Michael Arnheim, London	020 7833 5093
	Holborn Chambers, London	020 7242 6060
	Principal Chambers, Sevenoaks	0845 209 8080
Artesi Miss Desiree Allison Ann	Thomas More Chambers, London	020 7404 7000
Ash Mr Edward William	Chambers of Mr Edward Ash, Elsworth	01954 267674
Ashford-Thom Mr Ian	3 PB Barristers, London	020 7583 8055
	Temple Garden Chambers, London	020 7583 1315
Askey Mr Robert John	Palmyra Chambers, Warrington	01925 444919
Aswani Mr Ravi Girdharilal	Stone Chambers, London	020 7440 6900
Atkin Mrs Clare Catherine	Erimus Chambers, Bedford	01234 720952
Austin Mr Ian	Holborn Chambers, London	020 7242 6060
Austins Mr Christopher John	Chambers of Mr Christopher Austins, Bristol	01761 221 208
	Clerksroom (Taunton), Taunton	0845 083 3000
	King's Lynn Chambers, King's Lynn	01553 672 085
Badejo Mr Abimbola Rafiu	5 Pump Court, London	020 7353 2532
Bailey Mr Russell Stuart	No5 Chambers, Birmingham	0845 210 5555
	No5 Chambers, Bristol	0845 210 5555
	No5 Chambers, London	0845 210 5555
Bailey Mr Thomas Iain	Chambers of Mr Thomas Bailey, Milton Keynes	07983 447117
Balchin Mr Richard Alexander	New Court, London	020 7583 5123
Baldwin Dr Timothy John	Garden Court Chambers, London	020 7993 7600
Ball Mr Steven James	Number 7 Harrington Street Chambers, Liverpool	0151 242 0707
Barnard Mr James Philip	11 Stone Buildings, London	020 7831 6381
Barnes Miss Andrea Lynda	Clerksroom (Taunton), Taunton	0845 083 3000
	King's Lynn Chambers, King's Lynn	01553 672 085
Barnes Mr Luke Clive	3 Dr Johnson's Buildings, London	020 7353 4854
Barney Ms Helen	No5 Chambers, Birmingham	0845 210 5555
	No5 Chambers, Bristol	0845 210 5555
	No5 Chambers, London	0845 210 5555
Barrett Mr Robert Scott	2 Pump Court, London	020 7353 5597
Baruah Miss Rima	Thomas More Chambers, London	020 7404 7000
Bastin Mr Alexander Charles	Hardwicke, London	020 7242 2523
Batey Mr David Michael	Stour Chambers, Canterbury	01227 764899
Bath Mrs Baljinder Kaur	College Chambers, Southampton	023 8023 0338
Bax Mr James Alexander	Rougemont Chambers, Exeter	01392 208484
Beaumont Mr Marc Clifford	9 Stone Buildings, London	020 7404 5055
	Windsor Barristers' Chambers, Windsor	01753 839321
Becker Mr Timothy George Christie	Chambers of Mr Timothy Becker, Liverpool	0151 703 0319
	Clerksroom (London), London	0845 083 3000
Bedloe Mr Giles Robert	Dyers Chambers, London	020 7404 1881
Beharrylal Mr Satyanand Sarju	15 New Bridge Street, London	020 7842 1900
Bellamy Mr Jonathan Mark	39 Essex Street, London	020 7832 1111
	82 King Street, Manchester	0161 870 9969
Beloff Mr Rupert Joseph Alexei	No5 Chambers, Birmingham	0845 210 5555
	No5 Chambers, Bristol	0845 210 5555
	No5 Chambers, London	0845 210 5555
Bennett Miss Emma Louise	Exchange Chambers, Leeds	0113 203 1970
	Exchange Chambers, Liverpool	0151 236 7747
	Exchange Chambers, Manchester	0161 833 2722
Berkley Mr Michael Stuart	Rougemont Chambers, Exeter	01392 208484

Berry Mr Nicholas Michael	Rougemont Chambers, Exeter	01392 208484
Bezzam Miss Jayashree	Hampton Court Chambers, West Molesey	020 8979 0381
Bhakar Mr Surinder Singh	4 King's Bench Walk, London	020 7822 7000
Bhattacharyya Mr Ardhendu	Slough Barristers Chamber, Slough	01753 553806
Bisarya Mr Neil	Number 7 Harrington Street Chambers, Liverpool	0151 242 0707
Bishop Mr Alan Richard	11 Stone Buildings, London	020 7831 6381
Bishop Mr Gordon William	Chambers of Gordon Bishop, Woking	01483 486 730
Bishop Mr Malcolm Leslie	Argent Chambers, London	020 7556 5500
	Equity Chambers, Birmingham	0121 236 5007
	30 Park Place, Cardiff	029 2039 8421
Bishop Mr Stephen Anthony	Goldsmith Chambers, London	020 7353 6802
Blackwood Mr Clive David	Lamb Chambers, London	020 7797 8300
Blake Ms Penelope Natasha	1 Gray's Inn Square, London	020 7405 0001
Bleasdale Miss Marie-Claire	Radcliffe Chambers, London	020 7831 0081
Bloomfield Mr Richard William	Chambers of Mr Richard Bloomfield, Whitley Bay	01670 360042
Boaitey Miss Charlotte	12 Old Square Chambers, London	020 7404 0875
Bogle Mr James Stewart Lockhart	10 King's Bench Walk, London	020 7353 7742
Bojarski Mr Andrzej Leonard	36 Bedford Row, London	020 7421 8000
Bourne Mr Charles Gregory	4-5 Gray's Inn Square, London	020 7404 5252
Bourne Mr Geoffrey Robert	13 Old Square Chambers, London	020 7831 4445
Bowden Mr Guy Robert	4 Breams Buildings, London	020 7092 1900
Bowen Mr Nicholas James Hugh	Doughty Street Chambers, Bristol	01179 058 717
	Doughty Street Chambers, London	020 7404 1313
	Doughty Street Chambers, Manchester	0161 618 1066
Boyd Mr Stephen James Harvey	Selborne Chambers, London	020 7420 9500
Bragge Mr Thomas Hereward	Stour Chambers, Canterbury	01227 764899
Braier Mr Jason Dean	Field Court Chambers, London	020 7405 6114
Branchflower Mr George	Zenith Chambers, Leeds	0113 245 5438
Bredemear Mr Zachary Charles	1 Chancery Lane, London	0845 634 6666
Brewin Mr Carl Patrick	3 PB Barristers, London	020 7583 8055
Brittain Mr Marc John	1 Gray's Inn Square, London	020 7405 0001
Brockley Mr Nigel Simon	No5 Chambers, Birmingham	0845 210 5555
	No5 Chambers, Bristol	0845 210 5555
	No5 Chambers, London	0845 210 5555
Brown Mr Cameron Kennedy Duncan	9-12 Bell Yard, London	020 7400 1800
Brown Mr Philip Stephen	9 Stone Buildings, London	020 7404 5055
Brunt Mr Philip Edwin	No 8 Chambers, Birmingham	0121 236 5514
Bryden Mr Christopher James Yuen Kang	4 King's Bench Walk, London	020 7822 7000
Buchan Miss Caroline Venetia	Chambers of Miss C Buchan, Haywards Heath	01444 482222
Buck Mr John	Tanfield Chambers, London	020 7421 5300
Buckhaven Mr Simon	Hardwicke, London	020 7242 2523
Buckle Mr Jonathan	Regency Chambers, Cambridge	01223 301517
	Regency Chambers, Peterborough	01733 315215
Budworth Mr Richard Dutton	2-3 Hind Court Chambers, London	020 7822 2150
Bueno Mr Antonio De Padua Jose Maria	Clerksroom (Taunton), Taunton	0845 083 3000
Bullen Mrs Mary	The Chambers Of Mary Bullen, Wilton	01722 742204
Bullock Mr Robert Gustaf	The Chambers of Mr Bullock, Brighton	01273 321050
Burns Mr Jeremy Stuart	12 College Place, Southampton	023 8032 0320
Butler Mr Andrew	Tanfield Chambers, London	020 7421 5300
Butler Mr Rupert James	3 Hare Court, London	020 7415 7800
Butler Mr Simon David	The Chambers of Grahame Aldous QC, London	020 7832 0500
Buttimore Mr Gabriel	13 KBW, Oxford	01865 311066
	13 King's Bench Walk, London	020 7353 7204
Campbell Mr Oliver Edward Wilhelm	Henderson Chambers, London	020 7583 9020
Campbell Mr Stafford Graham	Westgate Chambers, Lewes	01273 480510

Capon Mr Philip Christopher William	East Anglian Chambers, Chelmsford	01473 214481
	East Anglian Chambers, Ipswich	01473 214481
	East Anglian Chambers, Norwich	01473 214481
	St Philips Chambers, Birmingham	0121 246 7000
Carlisle Mr Timothy St John Ogilvie	Field Court Chambers, London	020 7405 6114
Carrington Mr Dominic	Chambers of Martin Burr, London	0845 123 1234
Cartwright Mr Ivan Matthew	KCH Garden Square, Nottingham	0115 941 8851
Casey Mr Paul Joseph	Chambers of Marion Smullen and Kerim Fuad QC, London	020 7427 4400
Cattermull Miss Emma Jayne	East Anglian Chambers, Chelmsford	01473 214481
	East Anglian Chambers, Ipswich	01473 214481
	East Anglian Chambers, Norwich	01473 214481
Caun Mr Lawrence	Lamb Chambers, London	020 7797 8300
Cawsey Mr Barry Donald	Clerksroom (London), London	0845 083 3000
	Clerksroom (Taunton), Taunton	0845 083 3000
Chadwick Miss Joanna Ceridwen	No5 Chambers, Birmingham	0845 210 5555
	No5 Chambers, Bristol	0845 210 5555
	No5 Chambers, London	0845 210 5555
Chaffin-Laird Miss Olivia Carolyn	No5 Chambers, Birmingham	0845 210 5555
	No5 Chambers, Bristol	0845 210 5555
	No5 Chambers, London	0845 210 5555
Challenger Mr Colin Westcott	Lamb Chambers, London	020 7797 8300
Challinor Mr Thomas Michael	Citadel Chambers, Birmingham	0121 233 8500
Chan Miss Susan	13 KBW, Oxford	01865 311066
	13 King's Bench Walk, London	020 7353 7204
Chesner Mr Howard Michael	One Essex Court, London	020 7936 3030
Chippeck Mr Stephen	5 King's Bench Walk, London	020 7353 5638
Choudhuri Miss Gulshanah	Sen Barristers, Eastleigh	07706 936045
Chowdhary Mr Islamuddin	Cassian Chambers, Ilford	07796 262641
Christensen Mr Carlton	10 King's Bench Walk, London	020 7353 7742
Christie Mr Iain Robert	5RB, London	020 7242 2902
Christie Mr Richard Hamish	2 Pump Court, London	020 7353 5597
Chute Ms Andrea Alexandra	Rougemont Chambers, Exeter	01392 208484
	Tooks Chambers, London	020 7842 7575
Clarke Miss Lisa Tarin	Staple Inn Chambers, London	020 7242 5240
Clarke Mr George Robert Ivan	5 Pump Court, London	020 7353 2532
Clarke Mr Nikolas Michael	Field Court Chambers, London	020 7405 6114
Clegg Mr Adam Gordon	Stour Chambers, Canterbury	01227 764899
Clement Mr Ryan Wayne	Conference Chambers, Harrow	020 8144 0134
Clifton Miss Jane April	Lamb Chambers, London	020 7797 8300
Cline Mr Robert James	Atlantic Chambers, Liverpool	0151 236 4421
Coates Mr George Alexander Nigel	Guildford Chambers, Guildford	01483 539131
Collett Mr Gavin Charles	Rougemont Chambers, Exeter	01392 208484
Comerton Miss Julie Anne	4 KBW, London	020 7822 8822
Conlon Mr Michael John Patrick	Harcourt Chambers, Milton Keynes	0845 123 1234
Cooksey Mr Nicholas	River Chambers, Shrewsbury	01743 350505
Cooper Mr Paul Andrew	Portal Chambers, Llandysul	01559 395 292
Coster Mr Ronald David	42 Bedford Row, London	020 7831 0222
Coulter Mr Barry John	Clerksroom (London), London	0845 083 3000
	Clerksroom (Taunton), Taunton	0845 083 3000
	King's Lynn Chambers, King's Lynn	01553 672 085
Cox Miss Kerry Amanda	Park Lane Plowden, Newcastle Upon Tyne	0191 211 4087
Cox Miss Olivia Rodrigues	Atlantic Chambers, Liverpool	0151 236 4421
Cox Ms Sita	Stour Chambers, Canterbury	01227 764899
Coyle Mr Anthony Noel	Zenith Chambers, Leeds	0113 245 5438
Crangle Mr Thomas Peter	4 Pump Court, London	020 7842 5555
Crawley Mr Ross Alexander	Middle Temple Lane Chambers, London	020 7583 4352
Crew Miss Gillian Mary	Ely Place Chambers, London	020 7400 9600
Crinion Mr Charles Edward	1 Mitre Court Buildings, London	020 7452 8900
Critchley Mr John Stephen	Field Court Chambers, London	020 7405 6114

Croskell Mr Marcus James	East Anglian Chambers, Chelmsford	01473 214481
	East Anglian Chambers, Colchester	01473 214481
	East Anglian Chambers, Ipswich	01473 214481
	East Anglian Chambers, Norwich	01473 214481
Crouch Mr Stephen William Michael	The Chambers of S W M Crouch, Badby	01327 315 742
Crowe Mr Cameron	36 Bedford Row, London	020 7421 8000
Crowley Mr Daniel John	2 Temple Gardens, London	020 7822 1200
Culley Miss Laura Joan	Citadel Chambers, Birmingham	0121 233 8500
Currie Mr Fergus Hugh	Unity Street Chambers, Bristol	0117 906 9789
Curtis Mr Michael Alexander	Crown Office Chambers, London	020 7797 8100
Dalby Mr Joseph Francis	4-5 Gray's Inn Square, London	020 7404 5252
Daniels Mr David William	Rowchester Chambers, Birmingham	0121 233 2327
Darlington Miss Elizabeth	5 Pump Court, London	020 7353 2532
	Zenith Chambers, Leeds	0113 245 5438
Darroch Miss Fiona Culverwell	Clerksroom (London), London	0845 083 3000
	Clerksroom (Taunton), Taunton	0845 083 3000
	King's Lynn Chambers, King's Lynn	01553 672 085
Dassa Miss Regine	9 King's Bench Walk, London	020 7353 9564
Datta Mr Shomik	42 Bedford Row, London	020 7831 0222
Davey Mr Charles	64 Bridge Street, Manchester	0845 083 3000
	Chambers of Mr C Davey, Bishop's Stortford	01279 506412
	Clerksroom (Taunton), Taunton	0845 083 3000
Davies Miss Carol Elizabeth	College Chambers, Southampton	023 8023 0338
Davies Mr Henry Olusola	Trinity Chambers, Birmingham	0121 346 4672
Davies Mr Jake Sebastian Hunter	Five Paper, London	020 7815 3200
Davies Mr Jonathan Huw	Old Square Chambers, Bristol	0117 930 5100
	Old Square Chambers, London	020 7269 0300
Davies Ms Samantha Teresa	Chambers of Ms Samantha Davies, Milton Keynes	0845 123 1234
	Warwick House Chambers, London	020 7430 2323
Davis Mr Andrew Paul	Crown Office Chambers, London	020 7797 8100
De Mounteney Mr Jonathan Patrick	Chambers of Mr J P De Mounteney, Reading	0118 934 6822
De Zonie Miss Jane	14 Gray's Inn Square, London	020 7242 0858
Deacon Mr Robert Murray	11 Stone Buildings, London	020 7831 6381
Deal Mr Timothy John	Deal Chambers, London	020 8856 8738
Dean Mr James Patrick	Goldsmith Chambers, London	020 7353 6802
Dean Mr Paul Benjamin	Crown Office Chambers, London	020 7797 8100
Dean Mr Peter Thomas	36 Bedford Row, London	020 7421 8000
Deegan Mr Lawrence Jeffrey	Fenners Chambers, Cambridge	01223 368761
Degun Mr Jasvir Singh	One Essex Court, London	020 7936 3030
Del Fabbro Mr Oscar	23 Essex Street, London	020 7413 0353
Devereux-Cooke Mr Richard Charles	13 Old Square Chambers, London	020 7831 4445
Douthwaite Mr Charles Philip	Four New Square, London	020 7822 2000
Dovar Mr Daniel	Tanfield Chambers, London	020 7421 5300
Dowden Mr Andrew Philip	Castle Chambers, Harrow-on-the-Hill	020 8423 6579
	Melbury House, Leicester	07801 037802
Dowell Mr Gregory Hamilton	Principal Chambers, Sevenoaks	0845 209 8080
Downey Mr Neil James	Atlantic Chambers, Liverpool	0151 236 4421
Draycott Mr Simon Douglas	Citadel Chambers, Birmingham	0121 233 8500
	Five St Andrew's Hill, London	020 7332 5400
Dunne Mr Anthony James	KBW, Leeds	0113 297 1200
Dutt Miss Nisha	Middle Temple Lane Chambers, London	020 7583 4352
Earle Mr James Christopher Reginald St John	Fenners Chambers, Cambridge	01223 368761
Eaton Mr Tobias Barnaby	Staple Inn Chambers, London	020 7242 5240
Edge Mr Timothy Richard	Deans Court Chambers, Manchester	0161 214 6000
	Deans Court Chambers, Preston	01772 565 600
Edwards Mr Denis	Francis Taylor Building, London	020 7353 8415
Edwards Mr Dickon Harrison	5 Pump Court, London	020 7353 2532

Edwards Mr Martin Richard	39 Essex Street, London	020 7832 1111
	82 King Street, Manchester	0161 870 9969
Edwards Mr Nigel Royston	St Paul's Chambers, Leeds	0113 245 5866
Edwards Mr Paul	37 Park Square Chambers, Leeds	0113 243 9422
Egan Mr Patrick Manus Dermot	Thomas More Chambers, London	020 7404 7000
Egleton Mr Richard Wildman	Pallant Chambers, Chichester	01243 784538
Eilledge Miss Amanda Gail Caroline	11 Stone Buildings, London	020 7831 6381
Elliott Mr Edward Anthony John	Garden Court Chambers, London	020 7993 7600
Engelman Mr Philip	Cloisters, London	020 7827 4000
	Trinity Chambers, Middlesbrough	01642 247569
	Trinity Chambers, Newcastle Upon Tyne	0191 232 1927
England Mrs Lisa Johanna Louise	Guildhall Chambers Portsmouth, Portsmouth	023 9275 2400
Ephraim-Adejumo Mrs Hilda Ekpo	12 Old Square Chambers, London	020 7404 0875
Evans Mr Andrew David	St Philips Chambers, Birmingham	0121 246 7000
Fagborun Bennett Ms Morayo Abosede	Hardwicke, London	020 7242 2523
Fain Mr Carl Ian	Tanfield Chambers, London	020 7421 5300
Fairbank Mr Nicholas James	4 Paper Buildings, London	020 7427 5200
Falkowski Mr Damian	4-5 Gray's Inn Square, London	020 7404 5252
Fama Mrs Gudrun Hildegard	Middle Temple Lane Chambers, London	020 7583 4352
Fawcett Mr Neil	St Ive's Chambers, Birmingham	0121 236 0863
Feldman Mr Matthew Richard Bankes	42 Bedford Row, London	020 7831 0222
Fellows Mr Philip David Andrew	Hardwicke, London	020 7242 2523
Felton Mr Timothy John Fowler	Rougemont Chambers, Exeter	01392 208484
Fender Mr Carl David	Regency Chambers, Cambridge	01223 301517
	Regency Chambers, Peterborough	01733 315215
Ferm Mr Rodney Eric	Broadway House Chambers, Bradford	01274 722560
	Broadway House Chambers, Leeds	0113 246 2600
Field Mr Julian Nigel	Crown Office Chambers, London	020 7797 8100
Finlay Mr Darren	Sovereign Chambers, Leeds	0113 245 1841
Fisher Mr David	New Square Chambers, London	020 7419 8000
Fitzmaurice Mr Guy Edward Christian	Staple Inn Chambers, London	020 7242 5240
Fletcher Mr James Watford	Five St Andrew's Hill, London	020 7332 5400
Follon Mr Daniel Richard Thomas	1 Gray's Inn Square, London	020 7405 0001
Fortune Mr Peter Carl Michael	Guildhall Chambers Portsmouth, Portsmouth	023 9275 2400
	4 King's Bench Walk, London	020 7822 7000
Foster Mr Charles Andrew	Outer Temple Chambers, London	020 7353 6381
Found Mr Timothy Paul	Farrar's Building, London	020 7583 9241
Francis Mr Richard Maurice	9 Park Place, Cardiff	029 2038 2731
Fullerton Mr Michael Andrew	7 Bell Yard, London	020 7831 0636
	Chambers of Mr Michael Fullerton, Hove	01273 772050
Gadd Mr Adam Brian	Pump Court Chambers, London	020 7353 0711
	Pump Court Chambers, Winchester	01962 868 161
	Riverview Chambers, London	0844 225 3999
Gainer Mr Richard St Clair	St Margaret's Chambers, Twickenham	020 8241 3516
Gair Mr Christopher	King's Bench Chambers, Bournemouth	01202 250025
Gallivan Mr Terence John	Five Paper, London	020 7815 3200
Galway-Cooper Dr Philip Anthony	Five St Andrew's Hill, London	020 7332 5400
Garvie Mr Carl Peter	St Philips Chambers, Birmingham	0121 246 7000
Gasztowicz Mr Steven	Cornerstone Barristers, London	020 7242 4986
	New Street Chambers, Leicester	0116 262 5906
Gelbart Mr Geoff Alan	1 Gray's Inn Square, London	020 7405 0001
George Mr Nicholas Frank Raymond	New Walk Chambers, Leicester	0871 200 1298/0116 255 9144
Gersch Mr Adam Nissen	Argent Chambers, London	020 7556 5500
Gibbons Miss Mary Regina	Stone Chambers, London	020 7440 6900
Gibbons Ms Ellodie	Tanfield Chambers, London	020 7421 5300
Giles Mr David William	1 Gray's Inn Square, London	020 7405 0001

Barrister	Chambers	Telephone
Gillies Miss Jennie	4 Pump Court, London	020 7842 5555
Gilmore Miss Mary Seanin	Four New Square, London	020 7822 2000
Gladwell Mr Simon Mark	East Anglian Chambers, Ipswich	01473 214481
Glaser Mr Michael Samson	14 Gray's Inn Square, London	020 7242 0858
Gledhill Mr Lee Andre	Alexander Chambers, London	0845 652 0451/0854 652 0451
	Trident Barristers Chambers, Manchester	0161 663 3123
Gloag Mr Angus Robin	1 Gray's Inn Square, London	020 7405 0001
	Rougemont Chambers, Exeter	01392 208484
Glover Mr Marc Philip	Tanfield Chambers, London	020 7421 5300
Glover Mr Stephen Julian	37 Park Square Chambers, Leeds	0113 243 9422
Glyn Mr Caspar Hilary Gordon	Cloisters, London	020 7827 4000
Godfrey Mr Lauren John	Crown Office Row Chambers, Brighton	01273 625625
Gofur Mr Abdul	Thomas More Chambers, London	020 7404 7000
Gold Mr Richard David	St John's Chambers, Bristol	0117 923 4700
Goldberg Mr Jonathan Jacob	Cobden House Chambers, Manchester	0161 833 6000
	North Square Chambers, London	020 8455 3735
Goldrein Mr Iain Saville	7 Bell Yard, London	020 7831 0636
	Number 7 Harrington Street Chambers, Liverpool	0151 242 0707
Goldstein Mr Wayne Nathan	18 St John Street, Manchester	0161 278 1800
Goodfellow Mr Stephen John	East Anglian Chambers, Chelmsford	01473 214481
	East Anglian Chambers, Ipswich	01473 214481
	East Anglian Chambers, Norwich	01473 214481
Goodlad Mr Grant David	Farrar's Building, London	020 7583 9241
Gordon Mr Jeremy	Chambers of Mr Ami Feder, London	020 7797 7788
	Chambers of Mr Ami Feder, London	020 7797 7788
	Lamb Building, Brighton	01273 820490
Gough Miss Karen Louise	Arbitration Chambers, London	020 7267 2137
	39 Essex Street, London	020 7832 1111
	82 King Street, Manchester	0161 870 9969
Grant Mr Gary Steven	Francis Taylor Building, London	020 7353 8415
Grant Mr Marcus H James	Temple Garden Chambers, London	020 7583 1315
Granville Stafford Mr Andrew	4 King's Bench Walk, London	020 7822 7000
Greatorex Mr Paul	4-5 Gray's Inn Square, London	020 7404 5252
Green Mr Patrick Curtis	Henderson Chambers, London	020 7583 9020
Greenan Miss Sarah Octavia	Zenith Chambers, Leeds	0113 245 5438
Greenfield Mr Peter Charles	King's Bench Chambers, Bournemouth	01202 250025
Griffiths Miss Alison Clare	4 King's Bench Walk, London	020 7822 7000
Griffiths Mr Hugh Robert James	Furnival Chambers, London	020 7405 3232
Grundy Ms Clare	St Johns Buildings, Manchester	0161 214 1500
	St Johns Buildings Liverpool, Liverpool	0151 243 6000
	16 Winckley Square, Preston	01772 256100
Gunstone Mr Robert Giles	KCH Garden Square, Nottingham	0115 941 8851
Gupta Mr Amit	St Philips Chambers, Birmingham	0121 246 7000
Guy Mr John David Colin	Tanfield Chambers, London	020 7421 5300
Guy Mr Richard Perran	Chambers of Mr Ami Feder, London	020 7797 7788
	King's Bench and Godolphin (KBG)Chambers, Plymouth	01752 221551
	Southernhay Chambers, Exeter	01392 255777
Hall Mr James Edward	Cornwall Street Chambers, Birmingham	0121 233 7500
Hall Mr Jeremy John	Becket Chambers, Canterbury	01227 786331
Halstead Mr Robin Bernard	One Essex Court, London	020 7936 3030
Ham Mr Nicholas Treharne	Dyers Chambers, London	020 7404 1881
Hamilton Mr Nigel	Broadway House Chambers, Bradford	01274 722560
	Broadway House Chambers, Leeds	0113 246 2600
Hamilton Mr Peter Bernard	4 Pump Court, London	020 7842 5555
Hammond Mr Tim Mark	Tanfield Chambers, London	020 7421 5300
Hanlon Mr James Tobias	Old Bailey Chambers, London	020 3008 6404
Hannam Mr Timothy James	Citadel Chambers, Birmingham	0121 233 8500
Hannant Miss Lisa Diane	5 Pump Court, London	020 7353 2532
Harding Mr Christopher James	Thomas More Chambers, London	020 7404 7000

Hardyman Mr Matthew James	15 New Bridge Street, London	020 7842 1900
Hargreaves Mr Simon John Robert	Keating Chambers, London	020 7544 2600
Harrap Mr Robert Philip	Five Paper, London	020 7815 3200
Harrington Miss Clare Stephanie	13 KBW, Oxford	01865 311066
	13 King's Bench Walk, London	020 7353 7204
Harris Mr David Robert	St Albans Chambers, St Albans	01727 843383
Harris Mr James	Five St Andrew's Hill, London	020 7332 5400
Harrison Mr John Foster	St Paul's Chambers, Leeds	0113 245 5866
Harrison Mr Piers William Benedict	Tanfield Chambers, London	020 7421 5300
Hartley Mr Richard Anthony	Cobden House Chambers, Manchester	0161 833 6000
Harvey Mr John Gilbert	No5 Chambers, Birmingham	0845 210 5555
	No5 Chambers, Bristol	0845 210 5555
	No5 Chambers, London	0845 210 5555
Harvey Mr Stephen Frank	18 Red Lion Court, London	020 7520 6000
	18 Red Lion Court (Annexe), Chelmsford	01245 280880
Hatch Miss Lisa Sharmila	One Essex Court, London	020 7936 3030
Haughty Mr Jeremy Nicholas	Chambers of Mr Ami Feder, London	020 7797 7788
	Chambers of Mr Ami Feder, London	020 7797 7788
	Rougemont Chambers, Exeter	01392 208484
Healy Miss Alexandra	9-12 Bell Yard, London	020 7400 1800
Henderson Mr Neil John	Stone Chambers, London	020 7440 6900
Hendron Mr Henry Joseph Christopher	Strand Chambers, London	020 7117 6920
Heppinstall Mr Adam John	Henderson Chambers, London	020 7583 9020
Hicks Mr Edward Gordon David	Radcliffe Chambers, London	020 7831 0081
Higgins Mr Adrian John	13 KBW, Oxford	01865 311066
	13 King's Bench Walk, London	020 7353 7204
Hill Mr Michael Gordon	Trinity Chambers, Middlesbrough	01642 247569
	Trinity Chambers, Newcastle Upon Tyne	0191 232 1927
Hill Mr Nicholas Mark	Pump Court Chambers, London	020 7353 0711
	Pump Court Chambers, Swindon	01793 539899
	St Philips Chambers, Birmingham	0121 246 7000
Hill Mr Simon Michael	33 Bedford Row, London	020 7242 6476
Hillier Mr William	New Street Chambers, Leicester	0116 262 5906
Hillman Mr Gerard Paul	Carmelite Chambers, London	020 7936 6300
Hine Mr Charles Roderick John	King's Bench Chambers, Bournemouth	01202 250025
Hinton Mr Neil Pearse	King's Bench Chambers, Bournemouth	01202 250025
Hirst Mr Martin Lewis	13 KBW, Oxford	01865 311066
	13 King's Bench Walk, London	020 7353 7204
Hirst Mr William Timothy John	Park Lane Plowden, Leeds	0113 228 5049
Hobson Miss Laura Elise	Citadel Chambers, Birmingham	0121 233 8500
Hodgkiss Ms Suzanne Jane	43 Temple Row Chambers, Birmingham	0121 237 6035
Hodson Mr Matthew Paul	Farrar's Building, London	020 7583 9241
Holdsworth Mr James Arthur	Temple Garden Chambers, London	020 7583 1315
Holland Mr Charles Christopher	Francis Taylor Building, London	020 7353 8415
	Trinity Chambers, Middlesbrough	01642 247569
	Trinity Chambers, Newcastle Upon Tyne	0191 232 1927
Holmes-Milner Mr James Neil	The Chambers of Grahame Aldous QC, London	020 7832 0500
Holt Miss Abigail Claire	Lincoln House Chambers, Manchester	0161 832 5701
Hornblower Mrs Sarah Patience	Rougemont Chambers, Exeter	01392 208484
Howard Miss Amanda Jayne	Atlantic Chambers, Liverpool	0151 236 4421
	37 Park Square Chambers, Leeds	0113 243 9422
Howard Mr Robin William John	Fenners Chambers, Cambridge	01223 368761
Howells Mr Stephen John	Stone Chambers, London	020 7440 6900
Huggins Mr Toby James	Unity Street Chambers, Bristol	0117 906 9789
Hughes Mr William Lloyd	9-12 Bell Yard, London	020 7400 1800
Hulse Mrs Cecilia Helen	Chambers of Mr Ami Feder, London	020 7797 7788
	Chambers of Mr Ami Feder, London	020 7797 7788
Hurst Mr Brian	39 Park Square, Leeds	0113 245 6633

Hussain Mr Basharat	Cornwall Street Chambers, Birmingham	0121 233 7500
Hussain Mr Muhammad Altaf	Chambers of Mr M A Hussain, London	020 8679 2398
Hutchin Mr Edward Alister David	Temple Garden Chambers, London	020 7583 1315
Hutchinson Mr Colin Thomas	Garden Court Chambers, London	020 7993 7600
Hypolite-De-Souza Mrs Josephine Claudia	12 Old Square Chambers, London	020 7404 0875
Irvin Mr Peter	Brick Court Chambers, London	020 7379 3550
Isaac Mr Nicholas Dudley	Tanfield Chambers, London	020 7421 5300
Iyer Miss Shobana	Swan Chambers, Richmond	0845 123 1234
Jafar Mr Abdurahman Akhtar	Chambers of Mr Abdurahman Jafar, Ilford	07828 937338
Jaisri Mr Shashi Satyendra	1 Mitre Court Buildings, London	020 7452 8900
Jarratt Miss Alice Cordelia Betchworth	Carmelite Chambers, London	020 7936 6300
Jayakrishnan Mr Harry Sisubalan	Trent Chambers, Nottingham	0115 941 9596
Jenkins Mr David Crofton	2 King's Bench Walk, London	020 7353 1746
Joffe Ms Natasha Juliet Louise	Outer Temple Chambers, London	020 7353 6381
John Mr Thomas Huw	Goresbrook Chambers, Milton Keynes	0845 123 1234
Johnson Miss Laura Wendy	1 Chancery Lane, London	0845 634 6666
Jones Mr Alun	St Paul's Chambers, Leeds	0113 245 5866
Jones Mr Christopher David Harries	St John's Chambers, Bristol	0117 923 4700
Jones Mr Rhys Charles Mansel	14 Gray's Inn Square, London	020 7242 0858
Jones Mr Richard Frederick Thomas	Heavenwood Chambers, Stroud	01453 873444
Joshi Mr Pramod Kumar	One Essex Court, London	020 7936 3030
Josty Mr David Stephen	College Chambers, Southampton	023 8023 0338
Jowett Mr Timothy David Christian	9 Park Place, Cardiff	029 2038 2731
Kannangara Mr Harshaka Hemantha	Temple Court Chambers, London	020 7353 7888
Keane Mr Owen Ashley	Design Chambers, London	020 7353 0747
Kee Mr Peter William	Becket Chambers, Canterbury	01227 786331
Keeling Mr Adrian Francis	No5 Chambers, Birmingham	0845 210 5555
	No5 Chambers, Bristol	0845 210 5555
	No5 Chambers, London	0845 210 5555
Keith Mr Benjamin Charles Andrew	Five St Andrew's Hill, London	020 7332 5400
Kelly Mr Matthias John	39 Essex Street, London	020 7832 1111
Kelly Mrs Amy Louise	12 College Place, Southampton	023 8032 0320
Kemp Mr James Rupert	Trinity Chambers, Middlesbrough	01642 247569
	Trinity Chambers, Newcastle Upon Tyne	0191 232 1927
Kennedy Mr Christopher Laurence Paul	9 St John Street, Manchester	0161 955 9000
Kennedy Mr Peter Nicholas Dodgson	15 Winckley Square, Preston	01772 252828
Kennedy Mr Stuart Victor	3 PB Barristers, Bournemouth	01202 292102
	3 PB Barristers, Bristol	0117 928 1520
	3 PB Barristers, London	020 7583 8055
	3 PB Barristers, Oxford	01865 793 736
	3 PB Barristers, Winchester	01962 868884
Kenny Mr Martin William	Walnut House, Exeter	01392 279751
Kent Mr Michael Harcourt	Crown Office Chambers, London	020 7797 8100
Khalil Mr Karim Shakir	Octagon House, Norwich	01603 623186
	1 Paper Buildings, London	020 7353 3728
Khalique Miss Nageena	No5 Chambers, Birmingham	0845 210 5555
	No5 Chambers, Bristol	0845 210 5555
	No5 Chambers, London	0845 210 5555
Khan Mr Abdul Aleem	Gray's Chambers, Newbury	020 8518 2525
Khan Mr Ayoub	Chambers of Mr Ayoub Khan, Birmingham	07930 987202
Khan Mr Imran	St Albans Chambers, St Albans	01727 843383
Khan Mr Mahmood Shafi	Luton Chambers, Luton	01582 598394
	Willesden Chambers, London	020 3273 1042
Kidd Mr Peter William	Number 7 Harrington Street Chambers, Liverpool	0151 242 0707
King Mr Graham Anthony	1 Gray's Inn Square, London	020 7405 0001

Kirk Mr Graeme Charles	One Essex Court, London	020 7936 3030
Kitzing Miss Susanna Loraine	Park Court Chambers, Leeds	0113 243 3277
Knight Mr Benjamin James	Central Chambers, Manchester	0161 236 1133
Kramer Mr Philip Anthony	Park Lane Plowden, Newcastle Upon Tyne	0191 211 4087
Krause Ms Florence	Meritz Chambers, Hebben Bridge	0845 094 0856
Krushner Mr Damian Mark	Oakwood Chambers, London	07789 435485
Kwiatkowski Mr Feliks Jerzy	Kew Chambers, Kew	0844 8099991
Kynoch Mr Duncan Stuart Sanderson	Selborne Chambers, London	020 7420 9500
Lakha Mr Shabbir	Farrar's Building, London	020 7583 9241
Lam Mr Chuen Fat	Chambers of Martin Burr, London	0845 123 1234
Lambert Mrs Alison Janet	Trinity Chambers, Chelmsford	01245 605040
Lane Miss Rachael Caroline	2 King's Bench Walk, London	020 7353 1746
Lane Mr Christopher Paul	No 8 Chambers, Birmingham	0121 236 5514
Lane Mr Michael John	East Anglian Chambers, Colchester	01473 214481
	East Anglian Chambers, Ipswich	01473 214481
	East Anglian Chambers, Norwich	01473 214481
Lane Mr Simon Charles	Rougemont Chambers, Exeter	01392 208484
Lanson Miss Lauren Elizabeth	1 Gray's Inn Square, London	020 7405 0001
Laughland Mr James Russell	Temple Garden Chambers, London	020 7583 1315
Lavin Miss Mary Mandie Jane	196 Temple Chamber, London	020 7099 9257
Law Mr John Edward	The Chambers of Grahame Aldous QC, London	020 7832 0500
Lawrence Miss Anne Mary	Atlas Chambers, London	020 7269 7980
Le Fort Mr Michael Cameron Raoul	King's Bench Chambers, Bournemouth	01202 250025
Lemer Mr David James	Doughty Street Chambers, London	020 7404 1313
Lenaghan Mr Anthony	Dyers Chambers, London	020 7404 1881
Lennard Mr Stephen Charles	Hardwicke, London	020 7242 2523
Leonard Mr Charles Robert Weston	Hardwicke, London	020 7242 2523
Leonard Mr James Alexander	Outer Temple Chambers, London	020 7353 6381
Lewiecki Miss Marie	Old Bailey Chambers, London	020 3008 6404
Lewington Miss Francesca Anna	Crown Office Row Chambers, Brighton	01273 625625
Lewis Mr Jonathan Simon	Henderson Chambers, London	020 7583 9020
Lewis Mr Stuart John	New Walk Chambers, Leicester	0871 200 1298/0116 255 9144
Lewis Mr Wayne Anthony	Access Lawyers, London	020 8801 2345
Ley Mr Spencer	Farrar's Building, London	020 7583 9241
Limbrey Mr Bernard Martin	3 Dr Johnson's Buildings, London	020 7353 4854
Lippold Ms Sarah Ida Louise	13 KBW, Oxford	01865 311066
	13 King's Bench Walk, London	020 7353 7204
Livingstone Mr Simon John	Thomas More Chambers, London	020 7404 7000
Lo Mr Bernard Norman	Field Court Chambers, London	020 7405 6114
Lofthouse Mr James	1 Gray's Inn Square, London	020 7405 0001
Logan Miss Maura	St John's House Chambers, Altrincham	0161 980 7379
Lonsdale Mr David James	33 Bedford Row, London	020 7242 6476
Lopez Mr Juan Nemesio	Francis Taylor Building, London	020 7353 8415
Lule Miss Jacqueline	1 Mitre Court Buildings, London	020 7452 8900
Lycourgou Miss Olive	4 King's Bench Walk, London	020 7822 7000
Lyons Miss Tara Yasmin	Pump Court Chambers, London	020 7353 0711
	Pump Court Chambers, Winchester	01962 868 161
	Riverview Chambers, London	0844 225 3999
MacBean Mr Andrew Hamish	Queen Square Chambers, Bristol	0117 921 1966
MacKenzie Smith Mrs Catherine Joanna	10 King's Bench Walk, London	020 7353 7742
Maher Ms Martha Johanna Dorothy	St John's Chambers, Bristol	0117 923 4700
Mahmood Mr Abid	Central Chambers, Manchester	0161 236 1133
	No5 Chambers, Birmingham	0845 210 5555
	No5 Chambers, Bristol	0845 210 5555
	No5 Chambers, London	0845 210 5555
Mahmood Mr Imran Waseem	5 Pump Court, London	020 7353 2532
Mahtab Miss Sumita Laila-Al	7 Bell Yard, London	020 7831 0636
Mainwaring Mr Robert Paul Clason	Portal Chambers, Llandysul	01559 395 292
Maitland Jones Mr Mark Griffith	13 KBW, Oxford	01865 311066
	13 King's Bench Walk, London	020 7353 7204

Maitland Mr Marc Claude	King's Bench Chambers, Bournemouth	01202 250025
Maka Mr Isaac	Chambers of Mr Isaac Maka, Ilford	07973 308 301
	4 King's Bench Walk, London	020 7822 7000
Malik Miss Sarah	Hardwicke, London	020 7242 2523
Malone Mr David John	1 Gray's Inn Square, London	020 7405 0001
Mandalia Mr Vinesh Lalji	St Philips Chambers, Birmingham	0121 246 7000
Manyarara Miss Natsai	12 Old Square Chambers, London	020 7404 0875
Marcus Mr Peter	Zenith Chambers, Leeds	0113 245 5438
Marks Mr Jonathan Clive	4 Pump Court, London	020 7842 5555
Marsden Mr Andrew Guy	East Anglian Chambers, Chelmsford	01473 214481
	East Anglian Chambers, Colchester	01473 214481
	East Anglian Chambers, Ipswich	01473 214481
	East Anglian Chambers, Norwich	01473 214481
Marshall Mr Derek Stanley	College Chambers, Southampton	023 8023 0338
Martignetti Mr Ian	Regency Chambers, Cambridge	01223 301517
	Regency Chambers, Peterborough	01733 315215
Mason Mr Ian Douglas	Amethyst Chambers, London	020 7936 4966
Matthias Mr David Huw	Francis Taylor Building, London	020 7353 8415
Mawrey Mr Richard Brooks	Henderson Chambers, London	020 7583 9020
McCarthy Mr William	Bridgewater Chambers, Manchester	0161 3877127
	1 Mitre Court Buildings, London	020 7452 8900
McCombie Mr Fergus Alexander Paul	1 Gray's Inn Square, London	020 7405 0001
McCormack Mr Alan	Staple Inn Chambers, London	020 7242 5240
McCormick Mr William Thomas	Ely Place Chambers, London	020 7400 9600
McCulloch Miss Fiona Catharine Jane	Middle Temple Lane Chambers, London	020 7583 4352
McDonald Mr John William	2 Temple Gardens, London	020 7822 1200
McFarlane Miss Cynthia Julliett	10 King's Bench Walk, London	020 7353 7742
McKinney Miss Nicola Alexandra	4 KBW, London	020 7822 8822
McLinden Mr John Vincent Barry	Field Court Chambers, London	020 7405 6114
McNeill Mr David Martin	Five St Andrew's Hill, London	020 7332 5400
McNicholas Mr Christopher John	Goresbrook Chambers, Milton Keynes	0845 123 1234
McTague Miss Meghann Rose	2 Temple Gardens, London	020 7822 1200
Medd Mr James Powys	Crown Office Chambers, London	020 7797 8100
Melville-Shreeve Mr Michael David	Walnut House, Exeter	01392 279751
Menary Mr Alexander William Christopher	KBW, Leeds	0113 297 1200
Mendes Da Costa Mr David	Chambers of Mr D Mendes Da Costa, London	020 8747 4633
	MK Family Law Chambers, Milton Keynes	0845 123 1234
	No. 3 Fleet Street Chambers, London	020 7936 4474
Menon Mr Harigovind	New Court Chambers, Newcastle Upon Tyne	0191 232 1980
	Park Lane Plowden, Newcastle Upon Tyne	0191 211 4087
Meredith-Hardy Mr John Octavian	Farrar's Building, London	020 7583 9241
Metzer Mr Anthony David Erwin	Argent Chambers, London	020 7556 5500
Michael Mr Nicholas	East Anglian Chambers, Chelmsford	01473 214481
	East Anglian Chambers, Colchester	01473 214481
	East Anglian Chambers, Ipswich	01473 214481
	East Anglian Chambers, Norwich	01473 214481
Michalos Miss Christina Antigone Diana	5RB, London	020 7242 2902
Miles Mr Richard Iain	One Essex Court, London	020 7936 3030
Miller Mr Andrew	2 Temple Gardens, London	020 7822 1200
Miller Mr Ian Daukes Douglas	1 Chancery Lane, London	0845 634 6666
Miller Mr Ian Robertson	Broadway House Chambers, Bradford	01274 722560
	Broadway House Chambers, Leeds	0113 246 2600
Mills Mr Kristian Anthony	Trinity Chambers, Middlesbrough	01642 247569
	Trinity Chambers, Newcastle Upon Tyne	0191 232 1927
Mitchell Mr Alistair Stephen Fabian	49 Chambers, Bridgnorth	01746 761545

Mitchell Mr Jonathan	1 Gray's Inn Square, London	020 7405 0001
	Holborn Chambers, London	020 7242 6060
Modgill Mr Alexander Jeffrey	Broadway House Chambers, Bradford	01274 722560
	Broadway House Chambers, Leeds	0113 246 2600
Moffat Mr Russell Dean	Linenhall Chambers, Chester	01244 348282
Morgan Mr John	Bedlington Chambers, London	020 7831 1159
Morris Mr Philip James	39 Park Square, Leeds	0113 245 6633
Morris Mr Phillip John	9 Park Place, Cardiff	029 2038 2731
Morris Ms Johanna	Chambers of Marion Smullen and Kerim Fuad QC, London	020 7427 4400
Morrison Mr Christopher Quintin	Old Court Chambers, Middlesbrough	01642 232523
Moss Mr Christopher Stephen	St Johns Buildings, Manchester	0161 214 1500
	St Johns Buildings Liverpool, Liverpool	0151 243 6000
	16 Winckley Square, Preston	01772 256100
Moss Mr Richard John	4 King's Bench Walk, London	020 7822 7000
Moulder Mr Paul John	Alexander Chambers, London	0845 652 0451/0854 652 0451
	Guildford Chambers, Guildford	01483 539131
Mullarkey Mr Ian	KBW, Leeds	0113 297 1200
Muller Mr Antonie Sean	Citadel Chambers, Birmingham	0121 233 8500
Munir Dr Ashley Edward	Five St Andrew's Hill, London	020 7332 5400
Munro Mr Joshua Neil	Hailsham Chambers, London	020 7643 5000
Murkin Mrs Sandria	Becket Chambers, Canterbury	01227 786331
Murphy Mr Damian	Enterprise Chambers, Leeds	0113 246 0391
	Enterprise Chambers, London	020 7405 9471
	Enterprise Chambers, Newcastle Upon Tyne	0191 222 3344
Murray Mr Charles Humphrey Stewart	Rougemont Chambers, Exeter	01392 208484
Mustakim Mr Abdul Yunus Al	Chambers of Mr Mustakim, London	
Mutch Mr Iain Richard Alistair	Palmyra Chambers, Warrington	01925 444919
Mylvaganam Ms Tanoo	1 Gray's Inn Square, London	020 7405 0001
Nall-Cain The Hon Richard Christopher Philip	St Albans Chambers, St Albans	01727 843383
Nath Mr Rakesh	Strand Chambers, London	020 7117 6920
Newman Mr James Andrew	Ely Place Chambers, London	020 7400 9600
Newman Mr Paul	3 PB Barristers, Bournemouth	01202 292102
	3 PB Barristers, Bristol	0117 928 1520
	3 PB Barristers, London	020 7583 8055
	3 PB Barristers, Oxford	01865 793 736
	3 PB Barristers, Winchester	01962 868884
Nicholson Mr Jeremy Mark	4 Pump Court, London	020 7842 5555
Nickless Mr Jason Alan	College Chambers, Southampton	023 8023 0338
Noble Mr Philip Robert	Thomas More Chambers, London	020 7404 7000
Norman Mr Jared Simon Gregory	Field Court Chambers, London	020 7405 6114
Norman Mr Michael Charles	3 PB Barristers, Bournemouth	01202 292102
	3 PB Barristers, Bristol	0117 928 1520
	3 PB Barristers, London	020 7583 8055
	3 PB Barristers, Oxford	01865 793 736
	3 PB Barristers, Winchester	01962 868884
Norton Mr Giles	Enigma Chambers, Sheffield	07779 576499
	Holborn Chambers, London	020 7242 6060
Nsugbe Mr Oba Eric	Pump Court Chambers, London	020 7353 0711
	Pump Court Chambers, Swindon	01793 539899
	Pump Court Chambers, Winchester	01962 868 161
O'Brien Mr Nicholas William Wattebot	10 King's Bench Walk, London	020 7353 7742
O'Brien Mr Sean Timothy	St Philips Chambers, Birmingham	0121 246 7000
O'Connor Miss Hilda Ann	Kidby Chambers, Woodbridge	
O'Connor Mr Patrick Michael Joseph	Doughty Street Chambers, Bristol	01179 058 717
	Doughty Street Chambers, London	020 7404 1313
	Doughty Street Chambers, Manchester	0161 618 1066
O'Donoghue Mr Hugh Vincent	Carmelite Chambers, London	020 7936 6300

C

Barrister	Chambers	Telephone
Ogunbusola Mr Victor Olaniyi	Chambers of Victor Ogumbusola, Basildon	07413 634231
Okoye Miss Joy Nwamala	Chambers of Joy Okoye, London	07976 426871/020 7405 7011
Oommen Mr Jacob	Chambers of Mr Jacob Oommen, East Barnet	07958 680272
Osborne Mr David Thomas	Chambers of Mr D T Osborne, Taunton	01823 400 705
Osborne Mr James Robert	Clerksroom (London), London	0845 083 3000
O'Sullivan Mr Bernard Anthony	Henderson Chambers, London	020 7583 9020
O'Sullivan Mr Richard John	1215 Chambers, London	020 3291 1215
O'Toole Mr Bartholomew Vincent	5 King's Bench Walk, London	020 7353 5638
Otwal Mr Mukhtiar Singh	42 Bedford Row, London	020 7831 0222
Oulton Mr Richard Arthur Courtenay	5 Essex Court, London	020 7410 2000
Owen Mr Timothy Wynn	Matrix Chambers, London	020 7404 3447
Owens Miss Elspeth Eluned	4 Pump Court, London	020 7842 5555
Owen-Thomas Mr Richard Matthew	13 KBW, Oxford	01865 311066
	13 King's Bench Walk, London	020 7353 7204
Paget Mr Michael Rodborough	Garden Court Chambers, London	020 7993 7600
Paige Mr Richard Mark	Sovereign Chambers, Leeds	0113 245 1841
Pallo Mr Simon Russel	Bank House Chambers, Sheffield	0114 275 1223
Palmer Miss Claire Louise	Thomas More Chambers, London	020 7404 7000
Palmer Miss Suzanne Elizabeth Josephine	4 King's Bench Walk, London	020 7822 7000
Palmer Mr Edward James	Regent Chambers, Stoke On Trent	01782 286666
Palmer Mr James Savill	Henderson Chambers, London	020 7583 9020
Panton Mr Alastair Howard	10 King's Bench Walk, London	020 7353 7742
Panton Mr William Dwight	Amethyst Chambers, London	020 7936 4966
Paraskos Mr Paraskevakis Christakis	11 Gray's Inn Square Chambers, London	020 7405 6879
Parker Miss Wendy	Hardwicke, London	020 7242 2523
Parker Mrs Karen Lesley	Guildhall Chambers Portsmouth, Portsmouth	023 9275 2400
Parry Mr Charles Robert	Pump Court Chambers, London	020 7353 0711
	Pump Court Chambers, Swindon	01793 539899
	Pump Court Chambers, Winchester	01962 868 161
Parsons Mr Andrew James	Portsmouth Barristers'Chambers, Portsmouth	023 9283 1292
Pascoe Ms Soraya	1 Gray's Inn Square, London	020 7405 0001
Patterson Mr Stewart	Pump Court Chambers, London	020 7353 0711
	Pump Court Chambers, Swindon	01793 539899
	Pump Court Chambers, Winchester	01962 868 161
Payne Mr David James	No 8 Chambers, Birmingham	0121 236 5514
Payton Mr Clifford Coningsby	Alpha Court Chambers, Leamington Spa	01926 886412
Peckham Ms Jane Louise	1 Crown Office Row, London	020 7797 7500
	Crown Office Row Chambers, Brighton	01273 625625
Peretz Mr George Michael John	Monckton Chambers, London	020 7405 7211
Perry Miss Jacqueline Anne	2 Temple Gardens, London	020 7822 1200
Perry Mr Christopher Edward	Palmyra Chambers, Warrington	01925 444919
Petersen Mr Thomas James	Goldsmith Chambers, London	020 7353 6802
Phillips Miss Emma Louise	1 Pump Court, London	020 7842 7070
Phillips Mr Andrew Charles	Crown Office Chambers, London	020 7797 8100
Pickering Mr Simon Toby	Wilberforce Chambers, Hull	01482 323264
Pigram Mr Christopher Stuart	East Anglian Chambers, Chelmsford	01473 214481
	East Anglian Chambers, Colchester	01473 214481
	East Anglian Chambers, Ipswich	01473 214481
Pithers Mr Clive Robert	Fenners Chambers, Cambridge	01223 368761
Plant Mr James Richard	Farrar's Building, London	020 7583 9241
Polli Mr Timothy James	Tanfield Chambers, London	020 7421 5300
Potter Miss Alison Lisa	4 Pump Court, London	020 7842 5555
Powell Mr William Rhys	Regency Chambers, Cambridge	01223 301517
	Regency Chambers, Peterborough	01733 315215
Power Mr Lawrence Imam	4 KBW, London	020 7822 8822
Power Mr Richard Michael Arthur	Lamb Chambers, London	020 7797 8300

Preston Mr Nicholas John Holman	Clerksroom (Taunton), Taunton	0845 083 3000
Pretsell Mr James Davidson	Farrar's Building, London	020 7583 9241
Prokofiev Mr Sergey	Lincoln House Chambers, Manchester	0161 832 5701
Puar Mr Mikhael	30 Park Place, Cardiff	029 2039 8421
Pugh Mr John Bishop	John Pugh's Chambers, Liverpool	0151 236 5415
Purves Mr Gavin Bowman	Swan House, London	020 8998 3035
Quiney Mr Charles Benedictus Alexander	Crown Office Chambers, London	020 7797 8100
Quirke Mr Gerard Martin	Citadel Chambers, Birmingham	0121 233 8500
Rahman Mr Anis	12 Old Square Chambers, London	020 7404 0875
Rahman Mr Sami Ur	Field Court Chambers, London	020 7405 6114
Rai Miss Puneet Kaur	Thomas More Chambers, London	020 7404 7000
Rainey Mr Philip Carslake	Tanfield Chambers, London	020 7421 5300
Rana Mr Mohammed Akram	Clapham Law Chambers, London	020 7978 8482
Randolph Mr Paul Leslie	Field Court Chambers, London	020 7405 6114
Raw Mr Edward	Tanfield Chambers, London	020 7421 5300
Read Mr Daniel James	Farrar's Building, London	020 7583 9241
Read Mr Simon Eric	Zenith Chambers, Leeds	0113 245 5438
Reed Mr Julian Winn	9 Park Place, Cardiff	029 2038 2731
Reed Mr Simon John	New Walk Chambers, Leicester	0871 200 1298/0116 255 9144
Reeds Mr Gareth David	Canary Wharf Chambers, London	020 7183 8011
Rees Mr Hefin Ednyfed	39 Essex Street, London	020 7832 1111
Regan Mr David Robert	St John's Chambers, Bristol	0117 923 4700
Reid Miss Cheryl Louise Pegg	Temple Court Chambers, London	020 7353 7888
Reid Mr Sebastian Peter Scott	Tanfield Chambers, London	020 7421 5300
Reynolds Mr John Adam	King's Bench Chambers, Bournemouth	01202 250025
Rhodes Mr Robert Elliott	Outer Temple Chambers, London	020 7353 6381
	Principal Chambers, Sevenoaks	0845 209 8080
	St Philips Chambers, Birmingham	0121 246 7000
Richards Mr Duncan James	Chambers of Mr Ami Feder, London	020 7797 7788
	Chambers of Mr Ami Feder, London	020 7797 7788
	Principal Chambers, Sevenoaks	0845 209 8080
Rifat Mr Maurice Alan	1 Gray's Inn Square, London	020 7405 0001
Rigney Mr Andrew James	Crown Office Chambers, London	020 7797 8100
Rimmer Mr Anthony Michael	187 Fleet Street, London	020 7430 7430
Rippon Mr Simon John	Citadel Chambers, Birmingham	0121 233 8500
Risso-Gill Mr Edward David Charles	Thomas More Chambers, London	020 7404 7000
Ritchie Mr Andrew George	The Chambers of Grahame Aldous QC, London	020 7832 0500
Rivalland Mr Marc-Edouard	1 Chancery Lane, London	0845 634 6666
Riza Mr Alper Ali	Goldsmith Chambers, London	020 7353 6802
Roberts Mr Allan Calvin	Guildhall Chambers, Bristol	0117 930 9000
	Guildhall Chambers, Bristol	0117 930 9000
Roberts Mr Huw Eifion	Linenhall Chambers, Chester	01244 348282
Roberts Mr Michael Charles	Chambers of Michael Roberts, Henley-On-Thames	01844 355 655
Roberts Mr Richard Vaughan	Henderson Chambers, London	020 7583 9020
Roche Mr Patrick Richard Redmond	Tooks Chambers, London	020 7842 7575
Rogers Mr Daniel James	Number 7 Harrington Street Chambers, Liverpool	0151 242 0707
Rogers Mr Ian Paul	Monckton Chambers, London	020 7405 7211
Rogers Mr Michael Peter	Chambers of Mr Ami Feder, London	020 7797 7788
	Chambers of Mr Ami Feder, London	020 7797 7788
Rooke Mr Alexander John Giles	Argent Chambers, London	020 7556 5500
Ross Mr Simon Hadleigh	Zenith Chambers, Leeds	0113 245 5438
Rowe Miss Freya Emily Beatrice	Thomas More Chambers, London	020 7404 7000
Roy Mr Stefan Alexander Hiren	5 Pump Court, London	020 7353 2532
Rubens Miss Jacqueline Ann	1 Pump Court, London	020 7842 7070
Rudd Mr Michael	36 Bedford Row, London	020 7421 8000
Rule Mr Philip David	Castle Chambers, Harrow-on-the-Hill	020 8423 6579
Rushton Mr Jonathon Barker	36 Bedford Row, London	020 7421 8000
Russell Mr Graham Alexander	Citadel Chambers, Birmingham	0121 233 8500
Russell Mr Thomas Charles Welldon	KCH Garden Square, Nottingham	0115 941 8851
Russell-Mitra Miss Jessica Suparna	1 Mitre Court Buildings, London	020 7452 8900

Rustom Mr Shiraz Sam	1215 Chambers, London	020 3291 1215
	Cranford Chambers, London	020 7404 7454
	1 Mitre Court Buildings, London	020 7452 8900
Rutherford Miss Emma Victoria	No 8 Chambers, Birmingham	0121 236 5514
Saifee Mr Faisal Aftaab	Thomas More Chambers, London	020 7404 7000
Saini Mr Parminder Paul Singh	12 Old Square Chambers, London	020 7404 0875
Salter Mr Michael Richard	Ely Place Chambers, London	020 7400 9600
Sandham Mr James Andrew	Arden Chambers, London	020 7242 4244
Sapstead Miss Louise Anne	KCH Garden Square, Nottingham	0115 941 8851
Sawtell Mr David Robert Fraser	4 King's Bench Walk, London	020 7822 7000
Scally Miss Josephine Theresa Sarah	Palmyra Chambers, Warrington	01925 444919
Scott Mr Andrew David Peter	Park Lane Plowden, Leeds	0113 228 5049
Seal Mr Julius Damien	Chambers of Mr Julius Seal, London	020 7328 0158
Seeboruth Mr Royln Jean-Paul	Chambers of Royln Seeboruth, Aylesbury	01296 393329
Sefton-Smith Mr Lloyd	Lamb Chambers, London	020 7797 8300
Sekar Mr Chandra	Angell Park Chambers, London	020 7737 5957
Self Mr Gary Peter	College Chambers, Southampton	023 8023 0338
	St David's Chambers, Swansea	01792 559924
Sen Mr Aditya Kumar	Coram Chambers, London	020 7092 3700
Serr Mr Ashley Barrie	Park Lane Plowden, Leeds	0113 228 5049
Shamim Mr Mohammed	Clapham Law Chambers, London	020 7978 8482
Shapiro Mr Daniel Jonathan	Crown Office Chambers, London	020 7797 8100
Sharpe Mr Timothy James	Temple Garden Chambers, London	020 7583 1315
Shaw Miss Joanna Elizabeth	One Essex Court, London	020 7936 3030
Shaw Mr Julian	St Johns Buildings, Chester	01244 323070
	St Johns Buildings, Manchester	0161 214 1500
	St Johns Buildings Liverpool, Liverpool	0151 243 6000
Shield Miss Deborah	42 Bedford Row, London	020 7831 0222
Shirley Mr James Patrick	Stone Chambers, London	020 7440 6900
Silverton Miss Catherine Anne	Sovereign Chambers, Leeds	0113 245 1841
Simpson Mr David Joseph	196 Temple Chamber, London	020 7099 9257
Sinclair Mr Graham Kelso	East Anglian Chambers, Colchester	01473 214481
	East Anglian Chambers, Ipswich	01473 214481
	East Anglian Chambers, Norwich	01473 214481
Singarajah Mr Frederico	1 Gray's Inn Square, London	020 7405 0001
Singer Mr Richard Adam	1 Gray's Inn Square, London	020 7405 0001
Sisley Mr Timothy Julian Crispin	9 Stone Buildings, London	020 7404 5055
Skelly Mr Andrew Jon	Hardwicke, London	020 7242 2523
Skelt Mr Ian Stuart	KBW, Leeds	0113 297 1200
Skinner Mr Samuel Richard Edward	KCH Garden Square, Nottingham	0115 941 8851
Skyner Mr Robert Stephen	39 Park Square, Leeds	0113 245 6633
Sleight Mr Nigel	Regency Chambers, Cambridge	01223 301517
	Regency Chambers, Peterborough	01733 315215
Sliwinski Mr Robert Andrew	SWL Chambers, Loudwater	01494 616007
Smith Mr Julian Robert	Lincoln's Inn Fields Chambers, London	0845 123 1234
Smith Mr Robert Clive	1 Paper Buildings, London	020 7353 3728
	RCS Chambers, Stainton	01709 814 147
Smith Mr Robert Ian	St Paul's Chambers, Leeds	0113 245 5866
Smith Mr Roger Hugh Traylen	No5 Chambers, Birmingham	0845 210 5555
	No5 Chambers, Bristol	0845 210 5555
	No5 Chambers, London	0845 210 5555
Snow Mr Darren Mark	Charter Chambers, London	020 7618 4400
Sonaike Mr Kolarele Oladele Obafemi	One Essex Court, London	020 7936 3030
Sood Mrs Usha Rani	Trent Chambers, Nottingham	0115 941 9596
Soto-Miranda Mr Diego Fernando	One Essex Court, London	020 7936 3030
Speker Mr Adam Samuel Edward	5RB, London	020 7242 2902
Spencer Mr Martin Benedict	Hailsham Chambers, London	020 7643 5000
Spencer Mr Paul Anthony	3 Serjeants Inn, London	020 7427 5000
Spicer Mr Robert Haden	Frederick Place Chambers, Bristol	0117 946 7059

Barrister	Chambers	Telephone
Spooner Mr Henry Neville	Tolzey Chambers, Bristol	
	Westgate Chambers, Lewes	01273 480510
Spratt-Dawson Miss Josephine Margery	Trinity Chambers, Chelmsford	01245 605040
Stagg Mr Paul Andrew	1 Chancery Lane, London	0845 634 6666
Stanage Mr Nick Sean	Doughty Street Chambers, Bristol	01179 058 717
	Doughty Street Chambers, London	020 7404 1313
	Doughty Street Chambers, Manchester	0161 618 1066
Stanbury Mr Matthew Francis	Chambers of Ian Macdonald QC, Manchester	0161 236 1840
Stanford Mr Tony James	Old Bailey Chambers, London	020 3008 6404
Starcevic Mr Petar	St Philips Chambers, Birmingham	0121 246 7000
Starr Mrs Teresa Margaret	Great James Street Chambers, London	020 7440 4949
Stead Mr Richard James	St John's Chambers, Bristol	0117 923 4700
Stebbings Mr Ian Anthony	1 Gray's Inn Square, London	020 7405 0001
Stemp Mr Scott	12 College Place, Southampton	023 8032 0320
Stenhouse Mr John Alexander	Nightingale Chambers, Wolverley	01562 851350
Stephens Miss Jessica	Keating Chambers, London	020 7544 2600
Stephens Mr Michael Allen	Design Chambers, London	020 7353 0747
	St Ive's Chambers, Birmingham	0121 236 0863
Stevens Mr Stuart Standish	Holborn Chambers, London	020 7242 6060
Stevens Mrs Hazel Ann	East Anglian Chambers, Chelmsford	01473 214481
	East Anglian Chambers, Ipswich	01473 214481
	East Anglian Chambers, Norwich	01473 214481
Stevens-Hoare Miss Michelle	Hardwicke, London	020 7242 2523
Stewart Mr Nicholas John Cameron	Ely Place Chambers, London	020 7400 9600
Stirling Mr Christopher William	Field Court Chambers, London	020 7405 6114
Storey Mr Richard Alexander	3 Temple Gardens, London	020 7353 3102
Stranex Mr Andrew John	St Paul's Chambers, Leeds	0113 245 5866
Styles Mr Clive Richard	Becket Chambers, Canterbury	01227 786331
Swirsky Mr Adam Abraham Burl Bradbury	Lamb Chambers, London	020 7797 8300
Syril Mr George Carmel	Luton Chambers, Luton	01582 598394
	Willesden Chambers, London	020 3273 1042
Tapsell Mr Paul Richard	Becket Chambers, Canterbury	01227 786331
Targett-Parker Miss Leanne Susan	No. 3 Fleet Street Chambers, London	020 7936 4474
	The Chambers of Miss Leanne Targett-Parker, London	020 8674 6694
Taussig Mr Gurion	The Chambers of Grahame Aldous QC, London	020 7832 0500
Tavares Mr Nathan Warren	Outer Temple Chambers, London	020 7353 6381
Taylor Mr Michael Joseph Fitz	4 Pump Court, London	020 7842 5555
Taylor Mr Phillip Brian	Richmond Green Chambers, Richmond	020 8948 4801
Taylor Mr Simon	Chambers of Andrew Mitchell QC, London	020 7440 9950
Taylor Mrs Yvonne Marie	Trinity Chambers, Middlesbrough	01642 247569
	Trinity Chambers, Newcastle Upon Tyne	0191 232 1927
Temmink Mr Robert-Jan	Quadrant Chambers, London	020 7583 4444
Tempest Mr Alistair Mark	Field Court Chambers, London	020 7405 6114
Thomas Mr Andrew Martin	Lincoln House Chambers, Manchester	0161 832 5701
	Linenhall Chambers, Chester	01244 348282
Thomas Mr Mark David	5 Essex Court, London	020 7410 2000
Thomas Mrs Felicity	Westgate Chambers, Lewes	01273 480510
Thompson Mr Andrew Edward Courtney	Tanfield Chambers, London	020 7421 5300
Thornton Mr John Robert	Stour Chambers, Canterbury	01227 764899
Ticciati Mr Oliver	4 Pump Court, London	020 7842 5555
Tivadar Mr Daniel	3 Hare Court, London	020 7415 7800

Tomlinson Mr Michael James	3 PB Barristers, Bournemouth	01202 292102
	3 PB Barristers, Bristol	0117 928 1520
	3 PB Barristers, London	020 7583 8055
	3 PB Barristers, Oxford	01865 793 736
	3 PB Barristers, Winchester	01962 868884
Tompkinson Miss Deborah Ann	Clerksroom (London), London	0845 083 3000
	Clerksroom (Taunton), Taunton	0845 083 3000
Topal Mr Erol	Lamb Chambers, London	020 7797 8300
Tregidgo Mr Marc Gordon	4 King's Bench Walk, London	020 7822 7000
Treharne Mr Neil Simon	Dingle Chambers, Bristol	07818 827754
Treverton-Jones Mr Gregory Dennis	39 Essex Street, London	020 7832 1111
	82 King Street, Manchester	0161 870 9969
Trumpington Mr John Henry	Staple Inn Chambers, London	020 7242 5240
Tucker Mr James William Richard	Teucro Chambers, Epsom	
Turnbull Miss Helen Mary	Lamb Chambers, London	020 7797 8300
Turner Mr Justyn Robert Surtees	4 King's Bench Walk, London	020 7822 7000
Uduje Mr Benjamin Elliott	42 Bedford Row, London	020 7831 0222
Vaitilingam Mr Adam Skanda	Albion Chambers, Bristol	0117 927 2144
Valios Mr Nicholas Paul	4 Breams Buildings, London	020 7092 1900
	No 8 Chambers, Birmingham	0121 236 5514
Van Der Leij Dr Martina	Field Court Chambers, London	020 7405 6114
Vaughan Mr Terence Paul	Fenners Chambers, Cambridge	01223 368761
Vernon Mr Elliot Curt	No. 3 Fleet Street Chambers, London	020 7936 4474
Vitiello Mr Fabio Angelo-Giuseppe	Staple Inn Chambers, London	020 7242 5240
Vollenweider Mr Amiot Marcus Ellerton	Thomas More Chambers, London	020 7404 7000
Wagstaff Mr Andrew Martin Nicholas	Westgate Chambers, Lewes	01273 480510
Waley Mr Eric Richard Thomas	Assize Court Chambers, Bristol	0117 926 4587
Walji Miss Shabnam	Regency Chambers, Cambridge	01223 301517
	Regency Chambers, Peterborough	01733 315215
Ward Mr Martin Stuart	14 Gray's Inn Square, London	020 7242 0858
Ward Mr Peter Mark	The Chambers of Peter Ward, London	020 3402 2152
Waritay Mr Samuel	Chambers of Mr Samuel Waritay, London	0845 803 7767
Warner Mr David Alexander	St Philips Chambers, Birmingham	0121 246 7000
Watson Mr Alaric	11 Stone Buildings, London	020 7831 6381
Watson Mr Duncan Allen	Westgate Chambers, Lewes	01273 480510
Watterson Ms Anna Elizabeth	1 Mitre Court Buildings, London	020 7452 8900
Wayne Mr Nicholas	Argent Chambers, London	020 7556 5500
Webster Mr Keith	4 King's Bench Walk, London	020 7822 7000
Wells Mr Caspar John Mowlem	Goldsmith Chambers, London	020 7353 6802
Wenban-Smith Mr Mungo William	4-5 Gray's Inn Square, London	020 7404 5252
White Mr Daniel Edward Mills	Citadel Chambers, Birmingham	0121 233 8500
White Mr Matthew James	St John's Chambers, Bristol	0117 923 4700
White Mr Oliver Zachary	Littleton Chambers, London	020 7797 8600
White Mr Peter-John Spencer	Great Barford Chambers, Bedford	012134 870004
White Mr Steven James	Park Court Chambers, Leeds	0113 243 3277
White Mrs Tanya	Great Barford Chambers, Bedford	012134 870004
Whitehouse Mr Stuart Colin	Goldsmith Chambers, London	020 7353 6802
Whyte Miss Monica Patricia	42 Bedford Row, London	020 7831 0222
Widdett Ms Ceri Louise	Park Court Chambers, Leeds	0113 243 3277
Wightwick Mr Iain	Riverview Chambers, London	0844 225 3999
	Unity Street Chambers, Bristol	0117 906 9789
Wignall Mr Edward Gordon	No5 Chambers, Birmingham	0845 210 5555
	No5 Chambers, Bristol	0845 210 5555
	No5 Chambers, London	0845 210 5555
Wilcox Mr Jerome Carl Jean	Alexander Chambers, London	0845 652 0451/0854 652 0451
Wilkinson Miss Katie	43 Temple Row Chambers, Birmingham	0121 237 6035
Wilkinson Mr Marc Ashley	No5 Chambers, Birmingham	0845 210 5555
	No5 Chambers, Bristol	0845 210 5555
	No5 Chambers, London	0845 210 5555

Willetts Mr Andrew Philip	King's Bench and Godolphin (KBG)Chambers, Plymouth	01752 221551
	New Walk Chambers, Leicester	0871 200 1298/0116 255 9144
Williams Miss June Cleo	No 8 Chambers, Birmingham	0121 236 5514
Williams Mr Mark John	Queen Square Chambers, Bristol	0117 921 1966
Wills Miss Alexandra Itari	Christ Church Chambers, London	020 7409 5278/07788 512787
Wilson Mr Richard Carver	36 Bedford Row, London	020 7421 8000
Wilson Ms Charmaine Kimberley	Westgate Chambers, Lewes	01273 480510
Wilton Mr Simon Daniel	Hailsham Chambers, London	020 7643 5000
Winn-Smith Mr Matthew	Lamb Chambers, London	020 7797 8300
Winser Mr Crispin David Richard	Crown Office Chambers, London	020 7797 8100
Winslett Mr Frank	Westgate Chambers, Lewes	01273 480510
Wolstenholme Miss Janine	Sovereign Chambers, Leeds	0113 245 1841
Wood Miss Caroline Sarah	Sovereign Chambers, Leeds	0113 245 1841
Wood Miss Katherine Anne	Trinity Chambers, Middlesbrough	01642 247569
	Trinity Chambers, Newcastle Upon Tyne	0191 232 1927
Wood Mr James Alexander Douglas	Doughty Street Chambers, Bristol	01179 058 717
	Doughty Street Chambers, London	020 7404 1313
	Doughty Street Chambers, Manchester	0161 618 1066
Woodward Mr Jeremy Paul	Pallant Chambers, Chichester	01243 784538
Worrall Mr Philip George	Kew Chambers, Kew	0844 8099991
Wright Mr Stuart Graham	Crown Office Row Chambers, Brighton	01273 625625
Wrottesley Miss Angela Jane	Bank House Chambers, Sheffield	0114 275 1223
Wylie Mr Neil Richard	KCH Garden Square, Nottingham	0115 941 8851
Yell Mr Nicholas Anthony	1 Chancery Lane, London	0845 634 6666
Yeung Mr Stuart Roy	Northampton Chambers, Northampton	01604 636271
Zeitler Miss Barbara	3 Dr Johnson's Buildings, London	020 7353 4854

COMPANY & COMMERCIAL

Abasheikh Mr Omar Said Imam	Paragon Chambers, London	020 3318 9988
Ahmed Mr Ishfaq	Stone Chambers, London	020 7440 6900
Ajaz Mr Mohammad Arshad	Eastmans Chambers, Reading	0118 966 9094
Alexandra Miss Sebastiane	Holborn Chambers, London	020 7242 6060
Allerhand Mr Ludwik Edmund	Chambers of Mr Ludwik Allerhand, London	020 8291 4356
Anderson Mr Richard Neil Macdiarmid	Arbitration Chambers, London	020 7267 2137
Andre Mr Roger Louis	Sovereign Chambers, Leeds	0113 245 1841
Antell Mr John Jason	King's Bench and Godolphin (KBG)Chambers, Plymouth	01752 221551
Arthur Mr Stephen Joseph	Temple Tax Chambers, London	020 7353 7884
Ascroft Mr Richard Geoffrey	Guildhall Chambers, Bristol	0117 930 9000
Ashley Mr Neil Martin	East Anglian Chambers, Chelmsford	01473 214481
	East Anglian Chambers, Ipswich	01473 214481
	East Anglian Chambers, Norwich	01473 214481
Askey Mr Robert John	Palmyra Chambers, Warrington	01925 444919
Asprey Mr Nicholas	Clock Chambers, Wolverhampton	01902 313444
	Serle Court, London	020 7242 6105
Aswani Mr Ravi Girdharilal	Stone Chambers, London	020 7440 6900
Bailey Miss Rosana Henrietta	10 King's Bench Walk, London	020 7353 7742
Barnett Mr Jeremy Victor	2 Bedford Row, London	020 7440 8888
	St Paul's Chambers, Leeds	0113 245 5866
Beaumont Mr Marc Clifford	9 Stone Buildings, London	020 7404 5055
	Windsor Barristers' Chambers, Windsor	01753 839321
Becker Mr Timothy George Christie	Chambers of Mr Timothy Becker, Liverpool	0151 703 0319
	Clerksroom (London), London	0845 083 3000
Berkin Mr Martyn David Maurice	Crown Office Chambers, London	020 7797 8100
Berkley Mr Michael Stuart	Rougemont Chambers, Exeter	01392 208484
Berry Mr Nicholas Michael	Rougemont Chambers, Exeter	01392 208484
Bezzam Miss Jayashree	Hampton Court Chambers, West Molesey	020 8979 0381

Bishop Mr Malcolm Leslie	Argent Chambers, London	020 7556 5500
	Equity Chambers, Birmingham	0121 236 5007
	30 Park Place, Cardiff	029 2039 8421
Blackmore Mr John Hugh	St John's Chambers, Bristol	0117 923 4700
Blackwood Mr Clive David	Lamb Chambers, London	020 7797 8300
Bleasdale Miss Marie-Claire	Radcliffe Chambers, London	020 7831 0081
Blohm Mr Leslie Adrian	St John's Chambers, Bristol	0117 923 4700
Bragiel Mr Edward Bronislaw Henryk	Hogarth Chambers, London	020 7404 0404
Brockley Mr Nigel Simon	No5 Chambers, Birmingham	0845 210 5555
	No5 Chambers, Bristol	0845 210 5555
	No5 Chambers, London	0845 210 5555
Brook Mr Paul Antony	Park Lane Plowden, Leeds	0113 228 5049
	Park Lane Plowden, Newcastle Upon Tyne	0191 211 4087
Brown Miss Susan Margaret	One Essex Court, London	020 7936 3030
Brown Mr Philip Stephen	9 Stone Buildings, London	020 7404 5055
Bryden Mr Christopher James Yuen Kang	4 King's Bench Walk, London	020 7822 7000
Buchan Miss Caroline Venetia	Chambers of Miss C Buchan, Haywards Heath	01444 482222
Budworth Mr Martin James	Kings Chambers, Birmingham	0845 034 3444
	Kings Chambers, Leeds	0845 034 3444
	Kings Chambers, Manchester	0845 034 3444
Butler Mr Andrew	Tanfield Chambers, London	020 7421 5300
Butler Mr Rupert James	3 Hare Court, London	020 7415 7800
Butler Mr Simon David	The Chambers of Grahame Aldous QC, London	020 7832 0500
Buttimore Mr Gabriel	13 KBW, Oxford	01865 311066
	13 King's Bench Walk, London	020 7353 7204
Cant Mr Christopher Ian	9 Stone Buildings, London	020 7404 5055
Capon Mr Philip Christopher William	East Anglian Chambers, Chelmsford	01473 214481
	East Anglian Chambers, Ipswich	01473 214481
	East Anglian Chambers, Norwich	01473 214481
	St Philips Chambers, Birmingham	0121 246 7000
Carlisle Mr Timothy St John Ogilvie	Field Court Chambers, London	020 7405 6114
Carr Mr Adrian James Selden	Tanfield Chambers, London	020 7421 5300
Castle Mr Peter Bolton	13 Old Square Chambers, London	020 7831 4445
Cattermull Miss Emma Jayne	East Anglian Chambers, Chelmsford	01473 214481
	East Anglian Chambers, Ipswich	01473 214481
	East Anglian Chambers, Norwich	01473 214481
Chesner Mr Howard Michael	One Essex Court, London	020 7936 3030
Christensen Mr Carlton	10 King's Bench Walk, London	020 7353 7742
Christie Mr David Henderson	Seven Bedford Row, London	020 7242 3555
Clark Miss Geraldine	Serle Court, London	020 7242 6105
Clark Ms Julia Elisabeth	Hogarth Chambers, London	020 7404 0404
Clegg Mr Simon Robert Jonathan	St Philips Chambers, Birmingham	0121 246 7000
Clifton Miss Jane April	Lamb Chambers, London	020 7797 8300
Cohen Mr Edward Mervyn	11 Stone Buildings, London	020 7831 6381
Costello Mr Paul James	Chambers of Mr Paul J Costello, Biggleswade	07846 016 399
Coster Mr Ronald David	42 Bedford Row, London	020 7831 0222
Coulter Mr Barry John	Clerksroom (London), London	0845 083 3000
	Clerksroom (Taunton), Taunton	0845 083 3000
	King's Lynn Chambers, King's Lynn	01553 672 085
Crawley Mr Ross Alexander	Middle Temple Lane Chambers, London	020 7583 4352
Crawshaw Mr Simon Richard	Atkin Chambers, London	020 7404 0102
Crowley Mr Daniel John	2 Temple Gardens, London	020 7822 1200
Cunningham Mr Graham Taylor	Hardwicke, London	020 7242 2523
Dalby Mr Joseph Francis	4-5 Gray's Inn Square, London	020 7404 5252
Daniels Miss Philippa Catherine	36 Bedford Row, London	020 7421 8000
Devereux-Cooke Mr Richard Charles	13 Old Square Chambers, London	020 7831 4445
Devlin Mr Bernard Joseph	Five St Andrew's Hill, London	020 7332 5400
Dickinson Mr John Finch Heneage	St John's Chambers, Bristol	0117 923 4700

Dipré Mr Paul Nicholas Amadeus	Chambers of Mr P N Dipré, Address withheld	0845 123 1234
	MK Family Law Chambers, Milton Keynes	0845 123 1234
Du Toit Sc Mr Johan Ignatius	Selborne Chambers, London	020 7420 9500
	St Philips Chambers, Birmingham	0121 246 7000
Dyer Mr Allen Gordon	4 Pump Court, London	020 7842 5555
Earle Mr James Christopher Reginald St John	Fenners Chambers, Cambridge	01223 368761
Edwards Mr Nigel Royston	St Paul's Chambers, Leeds	0113 245 5866
Eilledge Miss Amanda Gail Caroline	11 Stone Buildings, London	020 7831 6381
Engelman Mr Philip	Cloisters, London	020 7827 4000
	Trinity Chambers, Middlesbrough	01642 247569
	Trinity Chambers, Newcastle Upon Tyne	0191 232 1927
Ephraim-Adejumo Mrs Hilda Ekpo	12 Old Square Chambers, London	020 7404 0875
Falkowski Mr Damian	4-5 Gray's Inn Square, London	020 7404 5252
Fawcett Mr Neil	St Ive's Chambers, Birmingham	0121 236 0863
Fellows Mr Philip David Andrew	Hardwicke, London	020 7242 2523
Ferm Mr Rodney Eric	Broadway House Chambers, Bradford	01274 722560
	Broadway House Chambers, Leeds	0113 246 2600
Finlay Mr Darren	Sovereign Chambers, Leeds	0113 245 1841
Fisher Mr David	New Square Chambers, London	020 7419 8000
Fowles Mr Jonathan James	Serle Court, London	020 7242 6105
Francis Mr Andrew James	Serle Court, London	020 7242 6105
	Zenith Chambers, Leeds	0113 245 5438
Galway-Cooper Dr Philip Anthony	Five St Andrew's Hill, London	020 7332 5400
Garvie Mr Carl Peter	St Philips Chambers, Birmingham	0121 246 7000
Gasztowicz Mr Steven	Cornerstone Barristers, London	020 7242 4986
	New Street Chambers, Leicester	0116 262 5906
Gayan Mr Anil Kumarsingh	Clapham Law Chambers, London	020 7978 8482
Gee Mr Steven Mark	Stone Chambers, London	020 7440 6900
George Mr Michael David Roberts	St Philips Chambers, Birmingham	0121 246 7000
George Mr Nicholas Frank Raymond	New Walk Chambers, Leicester	0871 200 1298/0116 255 9144
Gibbons Miss Mary Regina	Stone Chambers, London	020 7440 6900
Godfrey Mr Lauren John	Crown Office Row Chambers, Brighton	01273 625625
Godwin Mr William George Henry	3 Hare Court, London	020 7415 7800
	St John's Chambers, Bristol	0117 923 4700
Goodison Mr Adam Henry	South Square, London	020 7696 9900
Gordon Mr Jeremy	Chambers of Mr Ami Feder, London	020 7797 7788
	Chambers of Mr Ami Feder, London	020 7797 7788
	Lamb Building, Brighton	01273 820490
Graham Mr Thomas Patrick Henry	New Square Chambers, London	020 7419 8000
Graham Mrs Alana Nicole	Chambers of Alana Graham, Halesowen	01384 894560
	9 Stone Buildings, London	020 7404 5055
Grant Mr David Ericson	Outer Temple Chambers, London	020 7353 6381
Granville Stafford Mr Andrew	4 King's Bench Walk, London	020 7822 7000
Griffiths Miss Alison Clare	4 King's Bench Walk, London	020 7822 7000
Gupta Mr Amit	St Philips Chambers, Birmingham	0121 246 7000
Guy Mr John David Colin	Tanfield Chambers, London	020 7421 5300
Hallett Miss Katherine Elizabeth	13 Old Square Chambers, London	020 7831 4445
Hanif Miss Saima Naz	4-5 Gray's Inn Square, London	020 7404 5252
Harris Mr David Robert	St Albans Chambers, St Albans	01727 843383
Harris Mr James	Five St Andrew's Hill, London	020 7332 5400
Harris Mr Melvyn	5 Essex Court, London	020 7410 2000
Harrison Mr John Foster	St Paul's Chambers, Leeds	0113 245 5866
Hartman Mr Michael	One Essex Court, London	020 7936 3030
Hayes Mr Richard James	Lamb Chambers, London	020 7797 8300
Haywood Dr Jennifer Margaret	Serle Court, London	020 7242 6105
Henderson Mr Neil John	Stone Chambers, London	020 7440 6900
Hendron Mr Henry Joseph Christopher	Strand Chambers, London	020 7117 6920
Hilton Ms Saisampan	Holborn Chambers, London	020 7242 6060

Name	Chambers	Telephone
Hirst Mr Martin Lewis	13 KBW, Oxford	01865 311066
	13 King's Bench Walk, London	020 7353 7204
Hodson Mr Matthew Paul	Farrar's Building, London	020 7583 9241
Holland Mr Charles Christopher	Francis Taylor Building, London	020 7353 8415
	Trinity Chambers, Middlesbrough	01642 247569
	Trinity Chambers, Newcastle Upon Tyne	0191 232 1927
Hood Mr Nigel Anthony	New Square Chambers, London	020 7419 8000
Hornett Mr Stuart Ian	Selborne Chambers, London	020 7420 9500
Hossain Mr Ajmalul	Selborne Chambers, London	020 7420 9500
	St Philips Chambers, Birmingham	0121 246 7000
Huggins Mr Toby James	Unity Street Chambers, Bristol	0117 906 9789
Hughes Mr Adrian Warwick	39 Essex Street, London	020 7832 1111
	82 King Street, Manchester	0161 870 9969
Hunt Mr Stephen	4 Stone Buildings, London	020 7242 5524
Hussain Mr Muhammad Altaf	Chambers of Mr M A Hussain, London	020 8679 2398
Iyer Miss Shobana	Swan Chambers, Richmond	0845 123 1234
Jacobson Mr Lawrence	Five Paper, London	020 7815 3200
Jayakrishnan Mr Harry Sisubalan	Trent Chambers, Nottingham	0115 941 9596
Jones Mr Alun	St Paul's Chambers, Leeds	0113 245 5866
Jones Mr Christopher David Harries	St John's Chambers, Bristol	0117 923 4700
Jones Mr Lawrence Victor	Chambers of Lawrence Jones, London	020 7831 1444
Jones Mr Richard Frederick Thomas	Heavenwood Chambers, Stroud	01453 873444
Joseph Dr Sandradee Theresa	13 Old Square Chambers, London	020 7831 4445
Joseph Mr Charles Henry	Tanfield Chambers, London	020 7421 5300
Keane Mr Owen Ashley	Design Chambers, London	020 7353 0747
Keel Mr Douglas Vincent	11 Stone Buildings, London	020 7831 6381
Kenny Mr Martin William	Walnut House, Exeter	01392 279751
Khan Dr Alexander	Coral House, Manchester	
Khan Mr Arfan	Field Court Chambers, London	020 7405 6114
Kramer Mr Philip Anthony	Park Lane Plowden, Newcastle Upon Tyne	0191 211 4087
Kynoch Mr Duncan Stuart Sanderson	Selborne Chambers, London	020 7420 9500
Lamb Mr Jeffrey Thomas	Westgate Chambers, Lewes	01273 480510
Latymer Mr Tam	Chambers of Tam Latymer, London	020 7353 2795
Lee Miss Krista Chui Lan	Keating Chambers, London	020 7544 2600
Lenaghan Mr Anthony	Dyers Chambers, London	020 7404 1881
Lennard Mr Stephen Charles	Hardwicke, London	020 7242 2523
Lenon Mr Andrew Ralph Fitzmaurice	One Essex Court, London	020 7583 2000
Lewiecki Miss Marie	Old Bailey Chambers, London	020 3008 6404
Longhurst-Woods Ms Lesley	2 Louisa Close, London	020 8985 8716
Lowe Mr Mungo James	13 Old Square Chambers, London	020 7831 4445
Ludbrook Mr Timothy Vivian	13 Old Square Chambers, London	020 7831 4445
MacEvilly Mr Conn Jeremy	9 Stone Buildings, London	020 7404 5055
Machell Mr John William	Serle Court, London	020 7242 6105
Macpherson Mr Duncan Charles Stewart	One Essex Court, London	020 7936 3030
Macro Miss Morwenna Margaret	Five Paper, London	020 7815 3200
Maher Ms Martha Johanna Dorothy	St John's Chambers, Bristol	0117 923 4700
Mann Mr Christopher	13 KBW, Oxford	01865 311066
	13 King's Bench Walk, London	020 7353 7204
Marsden Mr Andrew Charles	St John's Chambers, Bristol	0117 923 4700
Marshall Mr Derek Stanley	College Chambers, Southampton	023 8023 0338
Mason Mr Stephen Charles Winston	Chambers of Mr S C W Mason, Biggleswade	01462 701 036
Matthias Mr David Huw	Francis Taylor Building, London	020 7353 8415
Mawrey Mr Richard Brooks	Henderson Chambers, London	020 7583 9020
McCombie Mr Fergus Alexander Paul	1 Gray's Inn Square, London	020 7405 0001
McDonnell Mr John Beresford William	13 Old Square Chambers, London	020 7831 4445
McLinden Mr John Vincent Barry	Field Court Chambers, London	020 7405 6114
McNae Mr Jonathan James	Selborne Chambers, London	020 7420 9500

Name	Chambers	Telephone
Meredith Mr Christopher William	Furnival Chambers, London	020 7405 3232
Meredith-Hardy Mr John Octavian	Farrar's Building, London	020 7583 9241
Michael Mr Nicholas	East Anglian Chambers, Chelmsford	01473 214481
	East Anglian Chambers, Colchester	01473 214481
	East Anglian Chambers, Ipswich	01473 214481
	East Anglian Chambers, Norwich	01473 214481
Miller Mr Andrew	2 Temple Gardens, London	020 7822 1200
Mills Mr Simon Thomas	Five Paper, London	020 7815 3200
Mishcon Mr Oliver Zebedee	Chambers of Mr Oliver Mishcon, London	020 7993 8890
Moffat Mr Russell Dean	Linenhall Chambers, Chester	01244 348282
Morgan Mr Jamie Peter	Trinity Chambers, Middlesbrough	01642 247569
	Trinity Chambers, Newcastle Upon Tyne	0191 232 1927
Mullen Mr Mark Robert	Radcliffe Chambers, London	020 7831 0081
Murphy Mr Damian	Enterprise Chambers, Leeds	0113 246 0391
	Enterprise Chambers, London	020 7405 9471
	Enterprise Chambers, Newcastle Upon Tyne	0191 222 3344
Nath Mr Rakesh	Strand Chambers, London	020 7117 6920
Newman Miss Rebecca Jane	Clerksroom (Taunton), Taunton	0845 083 3000
	King's Lynn Chambers, King's Lynn	01553 672 085
Noble Mr Andrew	Enterprise Chambers, Leeds	0113 246 0391
Normington Mr James Adam	Park Court Chambers, Leeds	0113 243 3277
Norton Mr Giles	Enigma Chambers, Sheffield	07779 576499
	Holborn Chambers, London	020 7242 6060
O'Brien Mr Nicholas William Wattebot	10 King's Bench Walk, London	020 7353 7742
O'Brien Mr Sean Timothy	St Philips Chambers, Birmingham	0121 246 7000
O'Connor Miss Hilda Ann	Kidby Chambers, Woodbridge	
O'Donoghue Mr Hugh Vincent	Carmelite Chambers, London	020 7936 6300
Ohrenstein Mr Dov	Radcliffe Chambers, London	020 7831 0081
Okoya Mr William Ebikise	Arden Chambers, London	020 7242 4244
Okoye Miss Joy Nwamala	Chambers of Joy Okoye, London	07976 426871/020 7405 7011
Oliver Mr David Keightley Rideal	13 Old Square Chambers, London	020 7831 4445
Osborne Mr James Robert	Clerksroom (London), London	0845 083 3000
O'Sullivan Mr Richard John	1215 Chambers, London	020 3291 1215
O'Toole Mr Simon Gerard	5 Pump Court, London	020 7353 2532
	Riverview Chambers, London	0844 225 3999
Otwal Mr Mukhtiar Singh	42 Bedford Row, London	020 7831 0222
Oulton Mr Richard Arthur Courtenay	5 Essex Court, London	020 7410 2000
Owens Miss Elspeth Eluned	4 Pump Court, London	020 7842 5555
Owen-Thomas Mr Richard Matthew	13 KBW, Oxford	01865 311066
	13 King's Bench Walk, London	020 7353 7204
Parker Mrs Karen Lesley	Guildhall Chambers Portsmouth, Portsmouth	023 9275 2400
Parsons Mr Andrew James	Portsmouth Barristers'Chambers, Portsmouth	023 9283 1292
Patterson Mr Stewart	Pump Court Chambers, London	020 7353 0711
	Pump Court Chambers, Swindon	01793 539899
	Pump Court Chambers, Winchester	01962 868 161
Payton Mr Clifford Coningsby	Alpha Court Chambers, Leamington Spa	01926 886412
Pearce Mr Robert Edgar	Radcliffe Chambers, London	020 7831 0081
Peat Mr Richard Colin	13 Old Square Chambers, London	020 7831 4445
Pennock Mr Ian	Park Lane Plowden, Leeds	0113 228 5049
Penny Mr Timothy Charles	11 Stone Buildings, London	020 7831 6381
Pettican Mr Kevin	11 Stone Buildings, London	020 7831 6381
Picarda Mr Hubert Alistair Paul	Chambers of Mr Hubert Picarda QC, London	020 7242 3566
Platford Mr Graham Roy	Five Paper, London	020 7815 3200
Preston Mr Nicholas John Holman	Clerksroom (Taunton), Taunton	0845 083 3000
Quiney Mr Charles Benedictus Alexander	Crown Office Chambers, London	020 7797 8100

Quirke Mr Gerard Martin	Citadel Chambers, Birmingham	0121 233 8500
Rahman Mr Anis	12 Old Square Chambers, London	020 7404 0875
Reeds Mr Gareth David	Canary Wharf Chambers, London	020 7183 8011
Rees Prof William Michael	1 Gray's Inn Square, London	020 7405 0001
Reffin Miss Clare Alyson	One Essex Court, London	020 7583 2000
Richman Mrs Helene Pines	Eighteen Carlton Crescent, Southampton	023 8063 9001
	9 Stone Buildings, London	020 7404 5055
	Stour Chambers, Canterbury	01227 764899
Rifat Mr Maurice Alan	1 Gray's Inn Square, London	020 7405 0001
Rinker Mr Andrew Stuart D'Artois	Chambers of Mr Andrew Rinker, London	020 7584 1091
Ritchie Mr Richard Bulkeley	XXIV Old Buildings, London	020 7691 2424
Rivalland Mr Marc-Edouard	1 Chancery Lane, London	0845 634 6666
Roberts Mr Michael Charles	Chambers of Michael Roberts, Henley-On-Thames	01844 355 655
Roberts Mr Richard Vaughan	Henderson Chambers, London	020 7583 9020
Rogers Mr Christopher Thomas	Five Paper, London	020 7815 3200
Rowell Mr George Edward	St John's Chambers, Bristol	0117 923 4700
Rowntree Mr Edward John Pickering	Hardwicke, London	020 7242 2523
Rushton Ms Nicola Jane	Five Paper, London	020 7815 3200
Sampson Dr Timothy Michael George	One Essex Court, London	020 7936 3030
Samuel Mr Richard Geoffrey Graham	3 Hare Court, London	020 7415 7800
Sawtell Mr David Robert Fraser	4 King's Bench Walk, London	020 7822 7000
Seal Mr Julius Damien	Chambers of Mr Julius Seal, London	020 7328 0158
Sellers Mr Graham	Atlantic Chambers, Liverpool	0151 236 4421
Sen Mr Aditya Kumar	Coram Chambers, London	020 7092 3700
Shapiro Mr Daniel Jonathan	Crown Office Chambers, London	020 7797 8100
Shaw Mr Julian	St Johns Buildings, Chester	01244 323070
	St Johns Buildings, Manchester	0161 214 1500
	St Johns Buildings Liverpool, Liverpool	0151 243 6000
Sheridan Mr Iain Douglas	London Scottish, Stratford Upon Avon	07971 681724
Singarajah Mr Frederico	1 Gray's Inn Square, London	020 7405 0001
Sisley Mr Timothy Julian Crispin	9 Stone Buildings, London	020 7404 5055
Sjostrand Miss Ekaterina	13 Old Square Chambers, London	020 7831 4445
Smith Mr Ian Alfio	11 Stone Buildings, London	020 7831 6381
Smith Mr Matthew Robert	Sovereign Chambers, Leeds	0113 245 1841
Smith Mr Robert Ian	St Paul's Chambers, Leeds	0113 245 5866
Smithers Dr Roger Howard	Alexander Chambers, London	0845 652 0451/0854 652 0451
	Clerksroom (Taunton), Taunton	0845 083 3000
	Guildford Chambers, Guildford	01483 539131
Sowler Mr Thomas Richard Holland	The Tax Chambers of Mr Richard Sowler TD, Douglas	07624 235000
Spalton Mr George David John	Four New Square, London	020 7822 2000
Spink Mr Andrew John Murray	Outer Temple Chambers, London	020 7353 6381
	Riverview Chambers, London	0844 225 3999
Stenhouse Mr John Alexander	Nightingale Chambers, Wolverley	01562 851350
Sterling Mr Robert Alan	St James's Chambers, Manchester	0161 834 7000
	Zenith Chambers, Leeds	0113 245 5438
Stevens Mrs Hazel Ann	East Anglian Chambers, Chelmsford	01473 214481
	East Anglian Chambers, Ipswich	01473 214481
	East Anglian Chambers, Norwich	01473 214481
Stevenson Dr Simon John	Park Lane Plowden, Leeds	0113 228 5049
Stewart Mr Nicholas John Cameron	Ely Place Chambers, London	020 7400 9600
Stringer Mr Leon Peter	15 Winckley Square, Preston	01772 252828
Tabari Mr Ali-Reza	St Philips Chambers, Birmingham	0121 246 7000
Taylor Mr Simon	Chambers of Andrew Mitchell QC, London	020 7440 9950
Temmink Mr Robert-Jan	Quadrant Chambers, London	020 7583 4444

Temple Ms Eleanor Louise	Kings Chambers, Birmingham	0845 034 3444
	Kings Chambers, Leeds	0845 034 3444
	Kings Chambers, Manchester	0845 034 3444
Terry Mr Robert Jeffrey	Kings Chambers, Birmingham	0845 034 3444
	Kings Chambers, Leeds	0845 034 3444
	Kings Chambers, Manchester	0845 034 3444
	Lamb Chambers, London	020 7797 8300
Thornley Miss Hannah Elise	South Square, London	020 7696 9900
Thrower Mr James Simeon	Chambers of Simeon Thrower, London	020 8878 7374
Todd Mr Michael Alan	Erskine Chambers, London	020 7242 5532
Trompeter Mr Nicholas Simeon	Selborne Chambers, London	020 7420 9500
Trumpington Mr John Henry	Staple Inn Chambers, London	020 7242 5240
Tucker Mr James William Richard	Teucro Chambers, Epsom	
Turnbull Miss Helen Mary	Lamb Chambers, London	020 7797 8300
Van Overdijk Miss Claire Orit	No5 Chambers, Birmingham	0845 210 5555
	No5 Chambers, Bristol	0845 210 5555
	No5 Chambers, London	0845 210 5555
Van Tonder Mr Gerard Dirk	New Square Chambers, London	020 7419 8000
Vasilescu Mr Andrei Constantin	Chambers of Martin Burr, London	0845 123 1234
Vernon Mr Elliot Curt	No. 3 Fleet Street Chambers, London	020 7936 4474
Vitiello Mr Fabio Angelo-Giuseppe	Staple Inn Chambers, London	020 7242 5240
Von Pommern-Peglow Dr Michael Alfred Herman Pr.	Brunswick Chambers, London	020 7353 1987
Vonberg Mr Thomas Charles	Devereux Chambers, London	020 7353 7534
Walford Mr Richard Henry Howard	Serle Court, London	020 7242 6105
Warner Mr David Alexander	St Philips Chambers, Birmingham	0121 246 7000
White Mr Oliver Zachary	Littleton Chambers, London	020 7797 8600
Wiktorowski-Solecki Miss Tamara	Middle Temple Lane Chambers, London	020 7583 4352
Wilcox Mr Jerome Carl Jean	Alexander Chambers, London	0845 652 0451/0854 652 0451
Wilkins Mr Christopher John	Pallant Chambers, Chichester	01243 784538
Wilkinson Mr Marc Ashley	No5 Chambers, Birmingham	0845 210 5555
	No5 Chambers, Bristol	0845 210 5555
	No5 Chambers, London	0845 210 5555
Williams Mr Simon Paul	Radcliffe Chambers, London	020 7831 0081
Wills Miss Alexandra Itari	Christ Church Chambers, London	020 7409 5278/07788 512787
Wise Mr Leslie Michael	10 King's Bench Walk, London	020 7353 7742
Wolman Mr Clive Richard	11 Stone Buildings, London	020 7831 6381
Yell Mr Nicholas Anthony	1 Chancery Lane, London	0845 634 6666
Young Mr Lee Terence	Eighteen Carlton Crescent, Southampton	023 8063 9001
Young Mr Martin Ford	9 Stone Buildings, London	020 7404 5055

COMPETITION

Banks Miss Fiona Jane	Monckton Chambers, London	020 7405 7211
Bates Mr Alan Twan	Monckton Chambers, London	020 7405 7211
Beaumont Mr Marc Clifford	9 Stone Buildings, London	020 7404 5055
	Windsor Barristers' Chambers, Windsor	01753 839321
Blackmore Mr John Hugh	St John's Chambers, Bristol	0117 923 4700
Bowsher Mr Michael Frederick Thomas	Monckton Chambers, London	020 7405 7211
Craig Mr Aubrey John	Chancery House Chambers, Leeds	0113 244 6691
	St Philips Chambers, Birmingham	0121 246 7000
Cunningham Mr Graham Taylor	Hardwicke, London	020 7242 2523
Dalby Mr Joseph Francis	4-5 Gray's Inn Square, London	020 7404 5252
Darbishire Mr Adrian Munro	QEB Hollis Whiteman, London	020 7933 8855
Engelman Mr Mark Trevor	Hardwicke, London	020 7242 2523
Facenna Mr Gerald Carlo	Monckton Chambers, London	020 7405 7211
Fern Mr Gary	7 Stones IP, London	020 7193 4033
Fitzgerald Mr John Vincent	Ingenuity IP Chambers, Petts Wood	
Gee Mr Steven Mark	Stone Chambers, London	020 7440 6900
Gibbons Miss Mary Regina	Stone Chambers, London	020 7440 6900
Godfrey Mr Lauren John	Crown Office Row Chambers, Brighton	01273 625625

Name	Chambers	Telephone
Green Mr Patrick Curtis	Henderson Chambers, London	020 7583 9020
Hamer Mr George Clemens	8 New Square, London	020 7405 4321
Heal Mrs Madeleine	New Square Chambers, London	020 7419 8000
Henderson Mr Neil John	Stone Chambers, London	020 7440 6900
Holmes Ms Elisa	Monckton Chambers, London	020 7405 7211
Iqbal Mr Mashood	London View Chambers, Sawbridgeworth	07788 912493
Iyer Miss Shobana	Swan Chambers, Richmond	0845 123 1234
John Miss Laura Elizabeth	Monckton Chambers, London	020 7405 7211
Jones Mr Kelvin Mcallister	Templis Chambers, London	020 7649 9808
Kenny Mr Martin William	Walnut House, Exeter	01392 279751
Lambert Miss Jane Elizabeth	NIPC, Huddersfield	0800 862 0055
Lane Ms Lindsay Ruth Busfield	8 New Square, London	020 7405 4321
Lindsay Mr Alistair David	Monckton Chambers, London	020 7405 7211
Lissack Mr Richard Anthony	Outer Temple Chambers, London	020 7353 6381
	Riverview Chambers, London	0844 225 3999
Ludbrook Mr Timothy Vivian	13 Old Square Chambers, London	020 7831 4445
Macpherson Mr Duncan Charles Stewart	One Essex Court, London	020 7936 3030
Matthias Mr David Huw	Francis Taylor Building, London	020 7353 8415
Mawrey Mr Richard Brooks	Henderson Chambers, London	020 7583 9020
McKiernan Mr Edward Joseph	Farringdon Chambers, London	020 7089 5700
O'Connor Miss Hilda Ann	Kidby Chambers, Woodbridge	
Onslow Mr Robert Denzil	8 New Square, London	020 7405 4321
Peretz Mr George Michael John	Monckton Chambers, London	020 7405 7211
Rayment Mr Benedick Michael	Monckton Chambers, London	020 7405 7211
Reeds Mr Gareth David	Canary Wharf Chambers, London	020 7183 8011
Rinker Mr Andrew Stuart D'Artois	Chambers of Mr Andrew Rinker, London	020 7584 1091
Rogers Miss Christy Abigail	Ingenuity IP Chambers, Petts Wood	
	No. 3 Fleet Street Chambers, London	020 7936 4474
Sampson Dr Timothy Michael George	One Essex Court, London	020 7936 3030
Singarajah Mr Frederico	1 Gray's Inn Square, London	020 7405 0001
Spratt Mr Christopher David Richard Dean	9 Stone Buildings, London	020 7404 5055
Von Pommern-Peglow Dr Michael Alfred Herman Pr.	Brunswick Chambers, London	020 7353 1987
West Dr Ewan Donald	Monckton Chambers, London	020 7405 7211

CONSTRUCTION

Name	Chambers	Telephone
Aeberli Mr Peter Dolph	3 PB Barristers, Bournemouth	01202 292102
	3 PB Barristers, Bristol	0117 928 1520
	3 PB Barristers, London	020 7583 8055
	3 PB Barristers, Oxford	01865 793 736
	3 PB Barristers, Winchester	01962 868884
Agnihotri Mr Naveen	12 College Place, Southampton	023 8032 0320
Ajaz Mr Mohammad Arshad	Eastmans Chambers, Reading	0118 966 9094
Alliott Mr George Beckles	Temple Garden Chambers, London	020 7583 1315
Allsop Mr Julian Eliseo	Guildhall Chambers, Bristol	0117 930 9000
Anderson Mr Richard Neil Macdiarmid	Arbitration Chambers, London	020 7267 2137
Andrews Mr Paul Leslie	Great James Street Chambers, London	020 7440 4949
Ansell Miss Rachel Louise	4 Pump Court, London	020 7842 5555
Antell Mr John Jason	King's Bench and Godolphin (KBG)Chambers, Plymouth	01752 221551
Askey Mr Robert John	Palmyra Chambers, Warrington	01925 444919
Barrett Mr Kevin John	No5 Chambers, Birmingham	0845 210 5555
	No5 Chambers, Bristol	0845 210 5555
	No5 Chambers, London	0845 210 5555
Barwise Miss Stephanie Nicola	Atkin Chambers, London	020 7404 0102

Barrister	Chambers	Telephone
Beaumont Mr Benjamin	Chambers of Dr Michael Arnheim, London	020 7833 5093
	Middle Temple Lane Chambers, London	020 7583 4352
Beaumont Mr Marc Clifford	9 Stone Buildings, London	020 7404 5055
	Windsor Barristers' Chambers, Windsor	01753 839321
Bellamy Mr Jonathan Mark	39 Essex Street, London	020 7832 1111
	82 King Street, Manchester	0161 870 9969
Bennion-Pedley Mr Edward	13 KBW, Oxford	01865 311066
	13 King's Bench Walk, London	020 7353 7204
Berry Mr Nicholas Michael	Rougemont Chambers, Exeter	01392 208484
Bingham Mr Anthony William	3 PB Barristers, Bournemouth	01202 292102
	3 PB Barristers, Bristol	0117 928 1520
	3 PB Barristers, London	020 7583 8055
	3 PB Barristers, Oxford	01865 793 736
	3 PB Barristers, Winchester	01962 868884
Blackwood Mr Clive David	Lamb Chambers, London	020 7797 8300
Boulding Mr Philip Vincent	Keating Chambers, London	020 7544 2600
Bowen Mr Nicholas James Hugh	Doughty Street Chambers, Bristol	01179 058 717
	Doughty Street Chambers, London	020 7404 1313
	Doughty Street Chambers, Manchester	0161 618 1066
Bowling Mr James Stuart	4 Pump Court, London	020 7842 5555
Bowsher Mr Michael Frederick Thomas	Monckton Chambers, London	020 7405 7211
Bredemear Mr Zachary Charles	1 Chancery Lane, London	0845 634 6666
Brunner Mr Peter Roland	Brick Court Chambers, London	020 7379 3550
Bryden Mr Christopher James Yuen Kang	4 King's Bench Walk, London	020 7822 7000
Buchan Miss Caroline Venetia	Chambers of Miss C Buchan, Haywards Heath	01444 482222
Bullock Mr Robert Gustaf	The Chambers of Mr Bullock, Brighton	01273 321050
Burr Mr Andrew Charles	Atkin Chambers, London	020 7404 0102
Buttimore Mr Gabriel	13 KBW, Oxford	01865 311066
	13 King's Bench Walk, London	020 7353 7204
Cawsey Mr Barry Donald	Clerksroom (London), London	0845 083 3000
	Clerksroom (Taunton), Taunton	0845 083 3000
Chaffin-Laird Miss Olivia Carolyn	No5 Chambers, Birmingham	0845 210 5555
	No5 Chambers, Bristol	0845 210 5555
	No5 Chambers, London	0845 210 5555
Chambers Miss Gaynor Marie	Keating Chambers, London	020 7544 2600
Chern Mr Cyril	Crown Office Chambers, London	020 7797 8100
Clarke Mr George Robert Ivan	5 Pump Court, London	020 7353 2532
Clement Mr Ryan Wayne	Conference Chambers, Harrow	020 8144 0134
Colbey Mr Richard	Guildhall Chambers Portsmouth, Portsmouth	023 9275 2400
	Lamb Chambers, London	020 7797 8300
Collard Mr Michael David	5 Pump Court, London	020 7353 2532
Constable Mr Adam Michael	Keating Chambers, London	020 7544 2600
Coster Mr Ronald David	42 Bedford Row, London	020 7831 0222
Coulter Mr Barry John	Clerksroom (London), London	0845 083 3000
	Clerksroom (Taunton), Taunton	0845 083 3000
	King's Lynn Chambers, King's Lynn	01553 672 085
Cox Miss Olivia Rodrigues	Atlantic Chambers, Liverpool	0151 236 4421
Crangle Mr Thomas Peter	4 Pump Court, London	020 7842 5555
Crawshaw Mr Simon Richard	Atkin Chambers, London	020 7404 0102
Crowley Mr Daniel John	2 Temple Gardens, London	020 7822 1200
Curtis Mr Michael Alexander	Crown Office Chambers, London	020 7797 8100
Darling Mr Paul Antony	Keating Chambers, London	020 7544 2600
Deacon Mr Robert Murray	11 Stone Buildings, London	020 7831 6381
Denbin Mr Jack Arnold	Greenway, Sonning-on-Thames	0118 969 2484

Name	Chambers	Telephone
Dipré Mr Paul Nicholas Amadeus	Chambers of Mr P N Dipré, Address withheld	0845 123 1234
	MK Family Law Chambers, Milton Keynes	0845 123 1234
Doerries Miss Chantal-Aimée Renee Aemelia An	Atkin Chambers, London	020 7404 0102
Douthwaite Mr Charles Philip	Four New Square, London	020 7822 2000
Dyer Mr Allen Gordon	4 Pump Court, London	020 7842 5555
Edwards Mr Anthony	Chancery House Chambers, Leeds	0113 244 6691
Elliott Mr Timothy Stanley	Keating Chambers, London	020 7544 2600
Engelman Mr Philip	Cloisters, London	020 7827 4000
	Trinity Chambers, Middlesbrough	01642 247569
	Trinity Chambers, Newcastle Upon Tyne	0191 232 1927
Ensaff Mr Omar Sherif	No5 Chambers, Birmingham	0845 210 5555
	No5 Chambers, Bristol	0845 210 5555
	No5 Chambers, London	0845 210 5555
Evans Mr Robert Jonathan	Keating Chambers, London	020 7544 2600
Falkowski Mr Damian	4-5 Gray's Inn Square, London	020 7404 5252
Fawcett Mr Neil	St Ive's Chambers, Birmingham	0121 236 0863
Field Mr Julian Nigel	Crown Office Chambers, London	020 7797 8100
Finlay Mr Darren	Sovereign Chambers, Leeds	0113 245 1841
Fisher Mr David	New Square Chambers, London	020 7419 8000
Frame Mr Stuart James	Staple Inn Chambers, London	020 7242 5240
Franklin Miss Kim	Crown Office Chambers, London	020 7797 8100
Friedman Mr David Peter	4 Pump Court, London	020 7842 5555
Furst Mr Stephen Andrew	Keating Chambers, London	020 7544 2600
Gair Mr Christopher	King's Bench Chambers, Bournemouth	01202 250025
Galway-Cooper Dr Philip Anthony	Five St Andrew's Hill, London	020 7332 5400
Garrett Miss Lucy Margaret	Keating Chambers, London	020 7544 2600
George Mr Nicholas Frank Raymond	New Walk Chambers, Leicester	0871 200 1298/0116 255 9144
Gillies Miss Jennie	4 Pump Court, London	020 7842 5555
Gilmore Miss Mary Seanin	Four New Square, London	020 7822 2000
Godfrey Mr Lauren John	Crown Office Row Chambers, Brighton	01273 625625
Godwin Mr William George Henry	3 Hare Court, London	020 7415 7800
	St John's Chambers, Bristol	0117 923 4700
Goldberg Mr Simon Ian	Trinity Chambers, Middlesbrough	01642 247569
	Trinity Chambers, Newcastle Upon Tyne	0191 232 1927
Goodfellow Mr Stephen John	East Anglian Chambers, Chelmsford	01473 214481
	East Anglian Chambers, Ipswich	01473 214481
	East Anglian Chambers, Norwich	01473 214481
Gough Miss Karen Louise	Arbitration Chambers, London	020 7267 2137
	39 Essex Street, London	020 7832 1111
	82 King Street, Manchester	0161 870 9969
Granville Stafford Mr Andrew	4 King's Bench Walk, London	020 7822 7000
Griffiths Mr David	St Philips Chambers, Birmingham	0121 246 7000
Ground Mr Patrick	Chambers of Mr Patrick Ground QC, London	020 7736 0131
Halden Mr Angus Robert	Queen Square Chambers, Bristol	0117 921 1966
Hamilton Mr Peter Bernard	4 Pump Court, London	020 7842 5555
Hannaford Miss Sarah Jane	Keating Chambers, London	020 7544 2600
Hargreaves Mr Simon John Robert	Keating Chambers, London	020 7544 2600
Harris Mr James	Five St Andrew's Hill, London	020 7332 5400
Harvey Mr John Gilbert	No5 Chambers, Birmingham	0845 210 5555
	No5 Chambers, Bristol	0845 210 5555
	No5 Chambers, London	0845 210 5555
Hendron Mr Henry Joseph Christopher	Strand Chambers, London	020 7117 6920
Hirst Mr Martin Lewis	13 KBW, Oxford	01865 311066
	13 King's Bench Walk, London	020 7353 7204
Hodson Mr Matthew Paul	Farrar's Building, London	020 7583 9241

Barrister	Chambers	Telephone
Holland Mr Charles Christopher	Francis Taylor Building, London	020 7353 8415
	Trinity Chambers, Middlesbrough	01642 247569
	Trinity Chambers, Newcastle Upon Tyne	0191 232 1927
Holroyd Mr John James	Zenith Chambers, Leeds	0113 245 5438
Hughes Mr Adrian Warwick	39 Essex Street, London	020 7832 1111
	82 King Street, Manchester	0161 870 9969
Hunt Mr Stephen	4 Stone Buildings, London	020 7242 5524
Jackson Miss Rosemary Elizabeth	Keating Chambers, London	020 7544 2600
Jinadu Mr Abdul-Lateef Abodurin Olayinka	Keating Chambers, London	020 7544 2600
Jones Mr Christopher David Harries	St John's Chambers, Bristol	0117 923 4700
Jones Mr Kelvin Mcallister	Templis Chambers, London	020 7649 9808
Jones Mr Richard Frederick Thomas	Heavenwood Chambers, Stroud	01453 873444
Joseph Mr Charles Henry	Tanfield Chambers, London	020 7421 5300
Kelly Mr Sean	Chancery House Chambers, Leeds	0113 244 6691
Kennedy Mr Stuart Victor	3 PB Barristers, Bournemouth	01202 292102
	3 PB Barristers, Bristol	0117 928 1520
	3 PB Barristers, London	020 7583 8055
	3 PB Barristers, Oxford	01865 793 736
	3 PB Barristers, Winchester	01962 868884
Kent Mr Michael Harcourt	Crown Office Chambers, London	020 7797 8100
Kynoch Mr Duncan Stuart Sanderson	Selborne Chambers, London	020 7420 9500
Lamb Mr Jeffrey Thomas	Westgate Chambers, Lewes	01273 480510
Lamont Mr Calum	Keating Chambers, London	020 7544 2600
Lane Mr Simon Charles	Rougemont Chambers, Exeter	01392 208484
Leabeater Mr James Ferguson	4 Pump Court, London	020 7842 5555
Lee Miss Krista Chui Lan	Keating Chambers, London	020 7544 2600
Lemon Miss Jane Katherine	Keating Chambers, London	020 7544 2600
Lindsey Ms Susan	Crown Office Chambers, London	020 7797 8100
Lord Mr Wayne Edward	Construction Chambers, Derby	01332 617 917
MacBean Mr Andrew Hamish	Queen Square Chambers, Bristol	0117 921 1966
Maguire Mr Andrew James	Exchange Chambers, Liverpool	0151 236 7747
	Exchange Chambers, Manchester	0161 833 2722
	St Philips Chambers, Birmingham	0121 246 7000
Mann Mr Christopher	13 KBW, Oxford	01865 311066
	13 King's Bench Walk, London	020 7353 7204
Marks Mr Jonathan Clive	4 Pump Court, London	020 7842 5555
Marsden Mr Andrew Guy	East Anglian Chambers, Chelmsford	01473 214481
	East Anglian Chambers, Colchester	01473 214481
	East Anglian Chambers, Ipswich	01473 214481
	East Anglian Chambers, Norwich	01473 214481
Marshall Mr Derek Stanley	College Chambers, Southampton	023 8023 0338
Matthias Mr David Huw	Francis Taylor Building, London	020 7353 8415
Mawrey Mr Richard Brooks	Henderson Chambers, London	020 7583 9020
McCue Mr Donald	11 Stone Buildings, London	020 7831 6381
McDonald Mr John William	2 Temple Gardens, London	020 7822 1200
McDonnell Mr John Beresford William	13 Old Square Chambers, London	020 7831 4445
McMorrow Mr Patrick Joseph	4 King's Bench Walk, London	020 7822 7000
Medd Mr James Powys	Crown Office Chambers, London	020 7797 8100
Michael Mr Nicholas	East Anglian Chambers, Chelmsford	01473 214481
	East Anglian Chambers, Colchester	01473 214481
	East Anglian Chambers, Ipswich	01473 214481
	East Anglian Chambers, Norwich	01473 214481
Miller Mr Andrew	2 Temple Gardens, London	020 7822 1200
Mitchell Mr Alistair Stephen Fabian	49 Chambers, Bridgnorth	01746 761545
Moffat Mr Russell Dean	Linenhall Chambers, Chester	01244 348282
Mort Mr Justin John Glasbrook	Keating Chambers, London	020 7544 2600
Moulder Mr Paul John	Alexander Chambers, London	0845 652 0451/0854 652 0451
	Guildford Chambers, Guildford	01483 539131

Name	Chambers	Telephone
Newman Mr Paul	3 PB Barristers, Bournemouth	01202 292102
	3 PB Barristers, Bristol	0117 928 1520
	3 PB Barristers, London	020 7583 8055
	3 PB Barristers, Oxford	01865 793 736
	3 PB Barristers, Winchester	01962 868884
Newsom Mr George Lucien	Guildhall Chambers, Bristol	0117 930 9000
Nicholson Mr Jeremy Mark	4 Pump Court, London	020 7842 5555
Nickless Mr Jason Alan	College Chambers, Southampton	023 8023 0338
Nissen Mr Alexander David	Keating Chambers, London	020 7544 2600
Noble Mr Andrew	Enterprise Chambers, Leeds	0113 246 0391
Nolten Miss Sonia Jayne	2 Temple Gardens, London	020 7822 1200
O'Brien Mr Nicholas William Wattebot	10 King's Bench Walk, London	020 7353 7742
Oliver Dr Peter James Robert	4 Pump Court, London	020 7842 5555
Osborne Mr James Robert	Clerksroom (London), London	0845 083 3000
Osborne Mr Richard	4 Pump Court, London	020 7842 5555
Owens Miss Elspeth Eluned	4 Pump Court, London	020 7842 5555
Padfield Mr Nicholas David	Chambers of Nicholas Padfield QC, London	020 7351 1961
Palmer Mr Howard William Arthur	2 Temple Gardens, London	020 7822 1200
Panton Mr Alastair Howard	10 King's Bench Walk, London	020 7353 7742
Paraskos Mr Paraskevakis Christakis	11 Gray's Inn Square Chambers, London	020 7405 6879
Parker Mrs Karen Lesley	Guildhall Chambers Portsmouth, Portsmouth	023 9275 2400
Parsons Mr Andrew James	Portsmouth Barristers'Chambers, Portsmouth	023 9283 1292
Pascall Mr Matthew Stephen	Alexander Chambers, London	0845 652 0451/0854 652 0451
	Guildford Chambers, Guildford	01483 539131
Patterson Mr Stewart	Pump Court Chambers, London	020 7353 0711
	Pump Court Chambers, Swindon	01793 539899
	Pump Court Chambers, Winchester	01962 868 161
Pennicott Mr Ian	Keating Chambers, London	020 7544 2600
Petersen Mr Thomas James	Goldsmith Chambers, London	020 7353 6802
Pettican Mr Kevin	11 Stone Buildings, London	020 7831 6381
Phillips Mr Andrew Charles	Crown Office Chambers, London	020 7797 8100
Philpott Mr Anthony Luke	12 Old Square Chambers, London	020 7404 0875
Pigott Mrs Frances Winifred	Atkin Chambers, London	020 7404 0102
	St Philips Chambers, Birmingham	0121 246 7000
Quiney Mr Charles Benedictus Alexander	Crown Office Chambers, London	020 7797 8100
Quirke Mr Gerard Martin	Citadel Chambers, Birmingham	0121 233 8500
Reeds Mr Gareth David	Canary Wharf Chambers, London	020 7183 8011
Ridd Mr David Ian Mcgregor	Farrar's Building, London	020 7583 9241
Rifat Mr Maurice Alan	1 Gray's Inn Square, London	020 7405 0001
Rigney Mr Andrew James	Crown Office Chambers, London	020 7797 8100
Roberts Mr Michael Charles	Chambers of Michael Roberts, Henley-On-Thames	01844 355 655
Royce Mr Darryl Fraser	Atkin Chambers, London	020 7404 0102
Sampson Mr Graeme William	3 PB Barristers, Bournemouth	01202 292102
	3 PB Barristers, Bristol	0117 928 1520
	3 PB Barristers, London	020 7583 8055
	3 PB Barristers, Oxford	01865 793 736
	3 PB Barristers, Winchester	01962 868884
Sandham Mr James Andrew	Arden Chambers, London	020 7242 4244
Scott Holland Mr Gideon Silas	Keating Chambers, London	020 7544 2600
Sears Mr Robert David Murray	Four New Square, London	020 7822 2000
Selby Mr Jonathan Lee	Keating Chambers, London	020 7544 2600
Sellers Mr Graham	Atlantic Chambers, Liverpool	0151 236 4421
Shapiro Mr Daniel Jonathan	Crown Office Chambers, London	020 7797 8100
Shaw Mr Jonathan Paul	No5 Chambers, Birmingham	0845 210 5555
	No5 Chambers, Bristol	0845 210 5555
	No5 Chambers, London	0845 210 5555
	Zenith Chambers, Leeds	0113 245 5438

Name	Chambers	Telephone
Shaw Mr Julian	St Johns Buildings, Chester	01244 323070
	St Johns Buildings, Manchester	0161 214 1500
	St Johns Buildings Liverpool, Liverpool	0151 243 6000
Sims Miss Alice Antonia	Keating Chambers, London	020 7544 2600
Sinclair Miss Lisa Anne	Chambers of Miss Lisa Sinclair, London	020 8946 7201
Singarajah Mr Frederico	1 Gray's Inn Square, London	020 7405 0001
Singer Mr Andrew Michael	Kings Chambers, Birmingham	0845 034 3444
	Kings Chambers, Leeds	0845 034 3444
	Kings Chambers, Manchester	0845 034 3444
Sisley Mr Timothy Julian Crispin	9 Stone Buildings, London	020 7404 5055
Sliwinski Mr Robert Andrew	SWL Chambers, Loudwater	01494 616007
Smith Mr Robert Clive	1 Paper Buildings, London	020 7353 3728
	RCS Chambers, Stainton	01709 814 147
Smith Mr Robert Ian	St Paul's Chambers, Leeds	0113 245 5866
Speaight Mr Anthony Hugh	4 Pump Court, London	020 7842 5555
Spratt Mr Christopher David Richard Dean	9 Stone Buildings, London	020 7404 5055
Stansfield Mr Piers Alistair	Keating Chambers, London	020 7544 2600
Stead Mr Richard James	St John's Chambers, Bristol	0117 923 4700
Stenhouse Mr John Alexander	Nightingale Chambers, Wolverley	01562 851350
Stephens Miss Jessica	Keating Chambers, London	020 7544 2600
Stephens Mr Michael Allen	Design Chambers, London	020 7353 0747
	St Ive's Chambers, Birmingham	0121 236 0863
Steynor Mr Alan Charles	Keating Chambers, London	020 7544 2600
Taylor Miss Eve Rebecca	St John's Chambers, Bristol	0117 923 4700
Taylor Mr Michael Joseph Fitz	4 Pump Court, London	020 7842 5555
Temmink Mr Robert-Jan	Quadrant Chambers, London	020 7583 4444
Terry Mr Robert Jeffrey	Kings Chambers, Birmingham	0845 034 3444
	Kings Chambers, Leeds	0845 034 3444
	Kings Chambers, Manchester	0845 034 3444
	Lamb Chambers, London	020 7797 8300
Thompson Mr Michael James	Keating Chambers, London	020 7544 2600
Ticciati Mr Oliver	4 Pump Court, London	020 7842 5555
Topal Mr Erol	Lamb Chambers, London	020 7797 8300
Townend Mr Samuel John	Keating Chambers, London	020 7544 2600
Tozzi Mr Nigel Kenneth	4 Pump Court, London	020 7842 5555
Turner Mr Alan Joseph	Melbeck Chambers, Dudley	020 7404 2166
Vaughan Mr Terence Paul	Fenners Chambers, Cambridge	01223 368761
Vineall Mr Nicholas Edward John	4 Pump Court, London	020 7842 5555
Wheaton Mr Ian Malcolm James	Eighteen Carlton Crescent, Southampton	023 8063 9001
White Mr Matthew James	St John's Chambers, Bristol	0117 923 4700
Wightwick Mr Iain	Riverview Chambers, London	0844 225 3999
	Unity Street Chambers, Bristol	0117 906 9789
Williams Mr Simon Paul	Radcliffe Chambers, London	020 7831 0081
Williamson Mr Adrian John Gerard Hughes	Keating Chambers, London	020 7544 2600
Wills Miss Alexandra Itari	Christ Church Chambers, London	020 7409 5278/07788 512787
Winser Mr Crispin David Richard	Crown Office Chambers, London	020 7797 8100
Woodward Mr Jeremy Paul	Pallant Chambers, Chichester	01243 784538
Wright Mr Alexander Paul	4 Pump Court, London	020 7842 5555
Wright Mr Frederick George Ian	Crown Office Chambers, London	020 7797 8100

CONSUMER

Name	Chambers	Telephone
Ajaz Mr Mohammad Arshad	Eastmans Chambers, Reading	0118 966 9094
Antell Mr John Jason	King's Bench and Godolphin (KBG)Chambers, Plymouth	01752 221551
Askey Mr Robert John	Palmyra Chambers, Warrington	01925 444919
Barry Mr Denis Fintan Patrick	Five Paper Buildings, London	020 7583 6117
Becker Mr Timothy George Christie	Chambers of Mr Timothy Becker, Liverpool	0151 703 0319
	Clerksroom (London), London	0845 083 3000

C

Barrister	Chambers	Telephone
Buttimore Mr Gabriel	13 KBW, Oxford	01865 311066
	13 King's Bench Walk, London	020 7353 7204
Christensen Mr Carlton	10 King's Bench Walk, London	020 7353 7742
Conlon Mr Michael John Patrick	Harcourt Chambers, Milton Keynes	0845 123 1234
Coster Mr Ronald David	42 Bedford Row, London	020 7831 0222
Dean Mr James Patrick	Goldsmith Chambers, London	020 7353 6802
Dowell Mr Gregory Hamilton	Principal Chambers, Sevenoaks	0845 209 8080
Edwards Mr Nigel Royston	St Paul's Chambers, Leeds	0113 245 5866
Ephraim-Adejumo Mrs Hilda Ekpo	12 Old Square Chambers, London	020 7404 0875
Facenna Mr Gerald Carlo	Monckton Chambers, London	020 7405 7211
Falkowski Mr Damian	4-5 Gray's Inn Square, London	020 7404 5252
Finlay Mr Darren	Sovereign Chambers, Leeds	0113 245 1841
Graham-Wells Miss Alison Christine	Exchange Chambers, Leeds	0113 203 1970
	Exchange Chambers, Liverpool	0151 236 7747
	Exchange Chambers, Manchester	0161 833 2722
Gun Cuninghame Mr Julian Arthur	Gough Square Chambers, London	020 7353 0924
Hillier Mr William	New Street Chambers, Leicester	0116 262 5906
Hinton Mr Neil Pearse	King's Bench Chambers, Bournemouth	01202 250025
Iyer Miss Shobana	Swan Chambers, Richmond	0845 123 1234
Jones Mr Richard Frederick Thomas	Heavenwood Chambers, Stroud	01453 873444
Kenny Mr Martin William	Walnut House, Exeter	01392 279751
Khalid Mr James	Goulds Green Chambers, Uxbridge	01895 422574
	Goulds Green Chambers, Uxbridge	01895 422574
Kramer Mr Philip Anthony	Park Lane Plowden, Newcastle Upon Tyne	0191 211 4087
Lo Mr Bernard Norman	Field Court Chambers, London	020 7405 6114
Macro Miss Morwenna Margaret	Five Paper, London	020 7815 3200
Maka Mr Isaac	Chambers of Mr Isaac Maka, Ilford	07973 308 301
	4 King's Bench Walk, London	020 7822 7000
Matthias Mr David Huw	Francis Taylor Building, London	020 7353 8415
McCulloch Miss Fiona Catharine Jane	Middle Temple Lane Chambers, London	020 7583 4352
Moffat Mr Russell Dean	Linenhall Chambers, Chester	01244 348282
Muman Mr Vijay Kumar	43 Temple Row Chambers, Birmingham	0121 237 6035
Neville Mr Joseph Richard	43 Temple Row Chambers, Birmingham	0121 237 6035
Nickless Mr Jason Alan	College Chambers, Southampton	023 8023 0338
Norton Mr Giles	Enigma Chambers, Sheffield	07779 576499
	Holborn Chambers, London	020 7242 6060
O'Brien Mr Nicholas William Wattebot	10 King's Bench Walk, London	020 7353 7742
Oommen Mr Jacob	Chambers of Mr Jacob Oommen, East Barnet	07958 680272
Paraskos Mr Paraskevakis Christakis	11 Gray's Inn Square Chambers, London	020 7405 6879
Peretz Mr George Michael John	Monckton Chambers, London	020 7405 7211
Pointing Mr John Eric	Chambers of Mr John Pointing, London	020 8997 2285
Reed Mr Simon John	New Walk Chambers, Leicester	0871 200 1298/0116 255 9144
Russell Mr Thomas Charles Welldon	KCH Garden Square, Nottingham	0115 941 8851
Scally Miss Josephine Theresa Sarah	Palmyra Chambers, Warrington	01925 444919
Scott Mr Andrew David Peter	Park Lane Plowden, Leeds	0113 228 5049
Stephens Mr Michael Allen	Design Chambers, London	020 7353 0747
	St Ive's Chambers, Birmingham	0121 236 0863
Treharne Mr Neil Simon	Dingle Chambers, Bristol	07818 827754
Turnbull Miss Helen Mary	Lamb Chambers, London	020 7797 8300
Walker Mr Adam Nigel	Seven Bedford Row, London	020 7242 3555
Wightwick Mr Iain	Riverview Chambers, London	0844 225 3999
	Unity Street Chambers, Bristol	0117 906 9789
Wilcox Mr Jerome Carl Jean	Alexander Chambers, London	0845 652 0451/0854 652 0451
Wilkinson Miss Katie	43 Temple Row Chambers, Birmingham	0121 237 6035

CONVEYANCING

Barrister	Chambers	Telephone
Ash Mr Edward William	Chambers of Mr Edward Ash, Elsworth	01954 267674
Askey Mr Robert John	Palmyra Chambers, Warrington	01925 444919
Asprey Mr Nicholas	Clock Chambers, Wolverhampton	01902 313444
	Serle Court, London	020 7242 6105
Austin Mr Ian	Holborn Chambers, London	020 7242 6060
Bailey Mr Thomas Iain	Chambers of Mr Thomas Bailey, Milton Keynes	07983 447117
Beaumont Mr Marc Clifford	9 Stone Buildings, London	020 7404 5055
	Windsor Barristers' Chambers, Windsor	01753 839321
Becker Mr Timothy George Christie	Chambers of Mr Timothy Becker, Liverpool	0151 703 0319
	Clerksroom (London), London	0845 083 3000
Bennion-Pedley Mr Edward	13 KBW, Oxford	01865 311066
	13 King's Bench Walk, London	020 7353 7204
Berry Mr Nicholas Michael	Rougemont Chambers, Exeter	01392 208484
Blaker Mr Gary Mark	Selborne Chambers, London	020 7420 9500
Bleasdale Miss Marie-Claire	Radcliffe Chambers, London	020 7831 0081
Boyd Mr Stephen James Harvey	Selborne Chambers, London	020 7420 9500
Bragiel Mr Edward Bronislaw Henryk	Hogarth Chambers, London	020 7404 0404
Bredemear Mr Zachary Charles	1 Chancery Lane, London	0845 634 6666
Brewin Mr Carl Patrick	3 PB Barristers, London	020 7583 8055
Brook Mr Paul Antony	Park Lane Plowden, Leeds	0113 228 5049
	Park Lane Plowden, Newcastle Upon Tyne	0191 211 4087
Buchan Miss Caroline Venetia	Chambers of Miss C Buchan, Haywards Heath	01444 482222
Buttimore Mr Gabriel	13 KBW, Oxford	01865 311066
	13 King's Bench Walk, London	020 7353 7204
Cant Mr Christopher Ian	9 Stone Buildings, London	020 7404 5055
Cattermull Miss Emma Jayne	East Anglian Chambers, Chelmsford	01473 214481
	East Anglian Chambers, Ipswich	01473 214481
	East Anglian Chambers, Norwich	01473 214481
Clayton Mr Nigel Garvin	Kings Chambers, Birmingham	0845 034 3444
	Kings Chambers, Leeds	0845 034 3444
	Kings Chambers, Manchester	0845 034 3444
Colbey Mr Richard	Guildhall Chambers Portsmouth, Portsmouth	023 9275 2400
	Lamb Chambers, London	020 7797 8300
Davies Ms Samantha Teresa	Chambers of Ms Samantha Davies, Milton Keynes	0845 123 1234
	Warwick House Chambers, London	020 7430 2323
Dovar Mr Daniel	Tanfield Chambers, London	020 7421 5300
Edwards Mr Nigel Royston	St Paul's Chambers, Leeds	0113 245 5866
Eilledge Miss Amanda Gail Caroline	11 Stone Buildings, London	020 7831 6381
Falkowski Mr Damian	4-5 Gray's Inn Square, London	020 7404 5252
Francis Mr Andrew James	Serle Court, London	020 7242 6105
	Zenith Chambers, Leeds	0113 245 5438
Gallivan Mr Terence John	Five Paper, London	020 7815 3200
Gore Mr Andrew Roger	Fenners Chambers, Cambridge	01223 368761
Hill Mr Piers Nicholas	37 Park Square Chambers, Leeds	0113 243 9422
Holbech Mr Charles Edward	New Square Chambers, London	020 7419 8000
Hormaeche Miss Alejandra	Tanfield Chambers, London	020 7421 5300
Horne Mr Charles Hugh Wilson	Kings Chambers, Birmingham	0845 034 3444
	Kings Chambers, Leeds	0845 034 3444
	Kings Chambers, Manchester	0845 034 3444
Hornett Mr Stuart Ian	Selborne Chambers, London	020 7420 9500
Hunt Mr Stephen	4 Stone Buildings, London	020 7242 5524
Hussain Mr Muhammad Altaf	Chambers of Mr M A Hussain, London	020 8679 2398

Jones Ms Cheryl Stephanie	No5 Chambers, Birmingham	0845 210 5555
	No5 Chambers, Bristol	0845 210 5555
	No5 Chambers, London	0845 210 5555
Joseph Mr Charles Henry	Tanfield Chambers, London	020 7421 5300
Kelly Mr Sean	Chancery House Chambers, Leeds	0113 244 6691
Khan Mr Abdul Aleem	Gray's Chambers, Newbury	020 8518 2525
Kynoch Mr Duncan Stuart Sanderson	Selborne Chambers, London	020 7420 9500
Lane Mr Simon Charles	Rougemont Chambers, Exeter	01392 208484
Lewis Mrs Pauline Grace	Holborn Chambers, London	020 7242 6060
Mainwaring Mr Robert Paul Clason	Portal Chambers, Llandysul	01559 395 292
Marsden Mr Andrew Guy	East Anglian Chambers, Chelmsford	01473 214481
	East Anglian Chambers, Colchester	01473 214481
	East Anglian Chambers, Ipswich	01473 214481
	East Anglian Chambers, Norwich	01473 214481
McDonnell Mr John Beresford William	13 Old Square Chambers, London	020 7831 4445
Meager Mrs Rowena Elisabeth	No5 Chambers, Birmingham	0845 210 5555
	No5 Chambers, Bristol	0845 210 5555
	No5 Chambers, London	0845 210 5555
Meares Mr Nigel Leslie Vellacott	11 Stone Buildings, London	020 7831 6381
Melville-Shreeve Mr Michael David	Walnut House, Exeter	01392 279751
Mitchell Mr David John	No5 Chambers, Birmingham	0845 210 5555
	No5 Chambers, Bristol	0845 210 5555
	No5 Chambers, London	0845 210 5555
Monnington Mr Bruce Gilbert	Fenners Chambers, Cambridge	01223 368761
Muir Miss Nicola Jane	Hardwicke, London	020 7242 2523
Newsom Mr George Lucien	Guildhall Chambers, Bristol	0117 930 9000
Nurse Mr Gordon Bramwell William	Radcliffe Chambers, London	020 7831 0081
Ohrenstein Mr Dov	Radcliffe Chambers, London	020 7831 0081
O'Toole Mr Simon Gerard	5 Pump Court, London	020 7353 2532
	Riverview Chambers, London	0844 225 3999
Panton Mr Alastair Howard	10 King's Bench Walk, London	020 7353 7742
Paton Mr Ewan William	Guildhall Chambers, Bristol	0117 930 9000
Pearce Mr Robert Edgar	Radcliffe Chambers, London	020 7831 0081
Polli Mr Timothy James	Tanfield Chambers, London	020 7421 5300
Quirke Mr Gerard Martin	Citadel Chambers, Birmingham	0121 233 8500
Risso-Gill Mr Edward David Charles	Thomas More Chambers, London	020 7404 7000
Roberts Mr Michael Charles	Chambers of Michael Roberts, Henley-On-Thames	01844 355 655
Ross Mr Sidney David	11 Stone Buildings, London	020 7831 6381
Sandham Mr James Andrew	Arden Chambers, London	020 7242 4244
Sefton-Smith Mr Lloyd	Lamb Chambers, London	020 7797 8300
Sellers Mr Graham	Atlantic Chambers, Liverpool	0151 236 4421
Sinclair Miss Lisa Anne	Chambers of Miss Lisa Sinclair, London	020 8946 7201
Skelly Mr Andrew Jon	Hardwicke, London	020 7242 2523
Spratt Mr Christopher David Richard Dean	9 Stone Buildings, London	020 7404 5055
Sterling Mr Robert Alan	St James's Chambers, Manchester	0161 834 7000
	Zenith Chambers, Leeds	0113 245 5438
Taylor Miss Araba Arba Kurankyiwa	Fenners Chambers, Cambridge	01223 368761
Tinnion Mr Antoine	Trinity Chambers, Middlesbrough	01642 247569
	Trinity Chambers, Newcastle Upon Tyne	0191 232 1927
Trompeter Mr Nicholas Simeon	Selborne Chambers, London	020 7420 9500
Van Tonder Mr Gerard Dirk	New Square Chambers, London	020 7419 8000
Vernon Mr Elliot Curt	No. 3 Fleet Street Chambers, London	020 7936 4474
Wilkinson Mr Marc Ashley	No5 Chambers, Birmingham	0845 210 5555
	No5 Chambers, Bristol	0845 210 5555
	No5 Chambers, London	0845 210 5555
Williams Mr Simon Paul	Radcliffe Chambers, London	020 7831 0081

Wills Miss Alexandra Itari	Christ Church Chambers, London	020 7409 5278/07788 512787

COPYRIGHT

Abrahams Mr James	8 New Square, London	020 7405 4321
Andrews Mr Paul Leslie	Great James Street Chambers, London	020 7440 4949
Bailey Miss Rosana Henrietta	10 King's Bench Walk, London	020 7353 7742
Bate Mr Stephen Robert De Breteuil	5RB, London	020 7242 2902
Bennett Mr Miles Alexander Fordham	Five Paper Buildings, London	020 7583 6117
Bishop Mr Gordon William	Chambers of Gordon Bishop, Woking	01483 486 730
Blackmore Mr John Hugh	St John's Chambers, Bristol	0117 923 4700
Bowhill Miss Jessie Kate	8 New Square, London	020 7405 4321
Bragiel Mr Edward Bronislaw Henryk	Hogarth Chambers, London	020 7404 0404
Browne Mr Desmond John Michael	5RB, London	020 7242 2902
Buchan Miss Caroline Venetia	Chambers of Miss C Buchan, Haywards Heath	01444 482222
Clark Ms Julia Elisabeth	Hogarth Chambers, London	020 7404 0404
Colbey Mr Richard	Guildhall Chambers Portsmouth, Portsmouth	023 9275 2400
	Lamb Chambers, London	020 7797 8300
Craig Mr Aubrey John	Chancery House Chambers, Leeds	0113 244 6691
	St Philips Chambers, Birmingham	0121 246 7000
Critchley Mr John Stephen	Field Court Chambers, London	020 7405 6114
Cunningham Mr Graham Taylor	Hardwicke, London	020 7242 2523
De Mounteney Mr Jonathan Patrick	Chambers of Mr J P De Mounteney, Reading	0118 934 6822
Deacon Mr Robert Murray	11 Stone Buildings, London	020 7831 6381
di Mambro Mr David Jesse Andrew	Pallant Chambers, Chichester	01243 784538
	Radcliffe Chambers, London	020 7831 0081
Dillon Mr Thomas William Matthew	Chambers of Thomas Dillon, London	020 7692 2722
Drummond Mr Bruce Jonathon Hutcheon	Cornwall Street Chambers, Birmingham	0121 233 7500
	Palmyra Chambers, Warrington	01925 444919
Edwards Mr Nigel Royston	St Paul's Chambers, Leeds	0113 245 5866
Engelman Mr Mark Trevor	Hardwicke, London	020 7242 2523
Fern Mr Gary	7 Stones IP, London	020 7193 4033
Fitzgerald Mr John Vincent	Ingenuity IP Chambers, Petts Wood	
Gersch Mr Adam Nissen	Argent Chambers, London	020 7556 5500
Griffin Miss Lynn Myfanwy	23 Essex Street, London	020 7413 0353
Hamer Mr George Clemens	8 New Square, London	020 7405 4321
Heal Mrs Madeleine	New Square Chambers, London	020 7419 8000
Hendron Mr Henry Joseph Christopher	Strand Chambers, London	020 7117 6920
Hill Mr Jonathan	8 New Square, London	020 7405 4321
Himsworth Miss Emma Katherine	One Essex Court, London	020 7583 2000
Hobbs Mr Geoffrey William	One Essex Court, London	020 7583 2000
Iqbal Mr Mashood	London View Chambers, Sawbridgeworth	07788 912493
Iyer Miss Shobana	Swan Chambers, Richmond	0845 123 1234
Johnson Mr Phillip Michael	Chambers of Mr P Johnson, London	020 7288 2256
Jolliffe Mrs Victoria Esther Jean	5RB, London	020 7242 2902
Jones Mr Christopher David Harries	St John's Chambers, Bristol	0117 923 4700
Jones Mr Kelvin Mcallister	Templis Chambers, London	020 7649 9808
Keane Mr Owen Ashley	Design Chambers, London	020 7353 0747
Khan Dr Alexander	Coral House, Manchester	
Kime Mr Matthew Jonathan	Cobden House Chambers, Manchester	0161 833 6000
	Ingenuity IP Chambers, Petts Wood	
	No. 3 Fleet Street Chambers, London	020 7936 4474
Lambert Miss Jane Elizabeth	NIPC, Huddersfield	0800 862 0055
Lane Ms Lindsay Ruth Busfield	8 New Square, London	020 7405 4321
Lawrence Dr Heather Bunting Elizabeth	11 South Square, London	020 7405 1222
Levett Miss Francesca Anna	Five St Andrew's Hill, London	020 7332 5400
Lewis Mr Wayne Anthony	Access Lawyers, London	020 8801 2345
Matthias Mr David Huw	Francis Taylor Building, London	020 7353 8415

Name	Chambers	Telephone
Maxwell Lewis Mr Cameron	Lamb Chambers, London	020 7797 8300
Michalos Miss Christina Antigone Diana	5RB, London	020 7242 2902
Munden Mr Richard Alexander John	5RB, London	020 7242 2902
Nicol Mr Stuart Henry David	13 King's Bench Walk, London	020 7353 7204
O'Donoghue Mr Hugh Vincent	Carmelite Chambers, London	020 7936 6300
Onslow Mr Robert Denzil	8 New Square, London	020 7405 4321
Paraskos Mr Paraskevakis Christakis	11 Gray's Inn Square Chambers, London	020 7405 6879
Parsons Mr Andrew James	Portsmouth Barristers'Chambers, Portsmouth	023 9283 1292
Pearson Mr Christopher	Lamb Chambers, London	020 7797 8300
Penny Mr Timothy Charles	11 Stone Buildings, London	020 7831 6381
Perian Mr Steven	3 Temple Gardens, London	020 7353 3102
Platts-Mills Mr Mark Fortescue	8 New Square, London	020 7405 4321
Powell Mr William Rhys	Regency Chambers, Cambridge	01223 301517
	Regency Chambers, Peterborough	01733 315215
Purves Mr Gavin Bowman	Swan House, London	020 8998 3035
Reed Mr Jeremy Nigel	Hogarth Chambers, London	020 7404 0404
Roberts Mr Michael Charles	Chambers of Michael Roberts, Henley-On-Thames	01844 355 655
Roberts Mr Philip Duncan	One Essex Court, London	020 7583 2000
Rogers Miss Christy Abigail	Ingenuity IP Chambers, Petts Wood	
	No. 3 Fleet Street Chambers, London	020 7936 4474
Roughton Mr Ashley Wentworth	Hogarth Chambers, London	020 7404 0404
Saini Mr Parminder Paul Singh	12 Old Square Chambers, London	020 7404 0875
Sampson Dr Timothy Michael George	One Essex Court, London	020 7936 3030
Seeboruth Mr Royln Jean-Paul	Chambers of Royln Seeboruth, Aylesbury	01296 393329
Singarajah Mr Frederico	1 Gray's Inn Square, London	020 7405 0001
Singh Mr Dapinderpaul	23 Essex Street, London	020 7413 0353
	Park Court Chambers, Leeds	0113 243 3277
Smith Miss Eileen Joan	Trinity Chambers, Middlesbrough	01642 247569
	Trinity Chambers, Newcastle Upon Tyne	0191 232 1927
Stein Mr Daniel Alexander	No5 Chambers, Birmingham	0845 210 5555
	No5 Chambers, Bristol	0845 210 5555
	No5 Chambers, London	0845 210 5555
Sterling Mr Robert Alan	St James's Chambers, Manchester	0161 834 7000
	Zenith Chambers, Leeds	0113 245 5438
Sumnall Miss Charlene Emma Louise	Five Paper Buildings, London	020 7583 6117
Tritton Mr Robert Guy Henton	Hogarth Chambers, London	020 7404 0404
Vasilescu Mr Andrei Constantin	Chambers of Martin Burr, London	0845 123 1234
Warby Mr Mark David John	5RB, London	020 7242 2902
Ward Mr Robin Henry	8 New Square, London	020 7405 4321

C

CORONERS INQUESTS

Name	Chambers	Telephone
Ajaz Mr Mohammad Arshad	Eastmans Chambers, Reading	0118 966 9094
Askey Mr Robert John	Palmyra Chambers, Warrington	01925 444919
Bowden Mr Guy Robert	4 Breams Buildings, London	020 7092 1900
Bowen Mr Nicholas James Hugh	Doughty Street Chambers, Bristol	01179 058 717
	Doughty Street Chambers, London	020 7404 1313
	Doughty Street Chambers, Manchester	0161 618 1066
Bryan Mr Robert John	1 Paper Buildings, London	020 7353 3728
Campbell Mr Oliver Edward Wilhelm	Henderson Chambers, London	020 7583 9020
Casey Mr Paul Joseph	Chambers of Marion Smullen and Kerim Fuad QC, London	020 7427 4400
Chipperfield Mr Jeremy Steven	Cranford Chambers, London	020 7404 7454
Clark Mr Dingle	Goldsmith Chambers, London	020 7353 6802
Clements Miss Paula Kate	Alexander Chambers, London	0845 652 0451/0854 652 0451
	Guildford Chambers, Guildford	01483 539131

Climie Mr Roger Stephen	King's Bench and Godolphin (KBG)Chambers, Plymouth	01752 221551
	Outer Temple Chambers, London	020 7353 6381
Coster Mr Ronald David	42 Bedford Row, London	020 7831 0222
Crew Miss Gillian Mary	Ely Place Chambers, London	020 7400 9600
Dixon Mr David Steven	Sovereign Chambers, Leeds	0113 245 1841
Dowden Mr Andrew Philip	Castle Chambers, Harrow-on-the-Hill	020 8423 6579
	Melbury House, Leicester	07801 037802
Dowell Mr Gregory Hamilton	Principal Chambers, Sevenoaks	0845 209 8080
Duffy Mr Derek James	St Paul's Chambers, Leeds	0113 245 5866
Edington Mrs Fiona Anne Rider	Thomas More Chambers, London	020 7404 7000
Edwards Mr Nigel Royston	St Paul's Chambers, Leeds	0113 245 5866
Falkowski Mr Damian	4-5 Gray's Inn Square, London	020 7404 5252
Finlay Mr Darren	Sovereign Chambers, Leeds	0113 245 1841
Foulkes Miss Rebecca	5 Pump Court, London	020 7353 2532
Gallagher Ms Caoilfhionn Anna	Doughty Street Chambers, Bristol	01179 058 717
	Doughty Street Chambers, London	020 7404 1313
	Doughty Street Chambers, Manchester	0161 618 1066
German Miss Kelly Anne	Eastbourne Chambers, Eastbourne	01323 642102
Gilchrist Miss Naomi Roberta	St Philips Chambers, Birmingham	0121 246 7000
Gledhill Mr Lee Andre	Alexander Chambers, London	0845 652 0451/0854 652 0451
	Trident Barristers Chambers, Manchester	0161 663 3123
Goodlad Mr Grant David	Farrar's Building, London	020 7583 9241
Griffin Mr Nicholas John	Five Paper Buildings, London	020 7583 6117
Gurden Miss Alison Louise	1 Gray's Inn Square, London	020 7405 0001
Hanlon Mr James Tobias	Old Bailey Chambers, London	020 3008 6404
Harrison Dr Graeme	12 College Place, Southampton	023 8032 0320
Harrison Mr John Foster	St Paul's Chambers, Leeds	0113 245 5866
Hassall Mr Craig Jonathan	Sovereign Chambers, Leeds	0113 245 1841
Hinton Mr Neil Pearse	King's Bench Chambers, Bournemouth	01202 250025
Hobson Miss Sally Anne	1 Paper Buildings, London	020 7353 3728
Jackson Mr Andrew Fraser	5 Pump Court, London	020 7353 2532
Jones Mr Mark Andrew	St Ive's Chambers, Birmingham	0121 236 0863
Keith Mr Benjamin Charles Andrew	Five St Andrew's Hill, London	020 7332 5400
Kenny Mr Martin William	Walnut House, Exeter	01392 279751
Kramer Mr Philip Anthony	Park Lane Plowden, Newcastle Upon Tyne	0191 211 4087
Linehan Mr Stephen John	St Philips Chambers, Birmingham	0121 246 7000
Marshall Miss Vanessa Juliette	Seven Bedford Row, London	020 7242 3555
Matthias Mr David Huw	Francis Taylor Building, London	020 7353 8415
May Mr Christopher John	Five St Andrew's Hill, London	020 7332 5400
McGowan Miss Maura Patricia	2 Bedford Row, London	020 7440 8888
	Lincoln House Chambers, Manchester	0161 832 5701
Nickless Mr Jason Alan	College Chambers, Southampton	023 8023 0338
Offer Mr Alexander	Garden Court Chambers, London	020 7993 7600
	Park Court Chambers, Leeds	0113 243 3277
Oommen Mr Jacob	Chambers of Mr Jacob Oommen, East Barnet	07958 680272
Owen Mr Timothy Wynn	Matrix Chambers, London	020 7404 3447
Perry Mr Christopher Edward	Palmyra Chambers, Warrington	01925 444919
Reed Mr Simon John	New Walk Chambers, Leicester	0871 200 1298/0116 255 9144
Ritchie Miss Shauna	2 Bedford Row, London	020 7440 8888
Rooke Mr Alexander John Giles	Argent Chambers, London	020 7556 5500
Rule Mr Philip David	Castle Chambers, Harrow-on-the-Hill	020 8423 6579
Rustom Mr Shiraz Sam	1215 Chambers, London	020 3291 1215
	Cranford Chambers, London	020 7404 7454
	1 Mitre Court Buildings, London	020 7452 8900
Sekar Mr Chandra	Angell Park Chambers, London	020 7737 5957
Skelt Mr Ian Stuart	KBW, Leeds	0113 297 1200
Stebbings Mr Ian Anthony	1 Gray's Inn Square, London	020 7405 0001
Stevenson Mr Robert Lloyd	Sovereign Chambers, Leeds	0113 245 1841
Strong Mr Adrian Peter Ciaran	KBW, Leeds	0113 297 1200
Stuart Mr Bruce Ian	Lombard Chambers, London	020 7107 2100

Tizzano Mr Franco Salvatore	Old Bailey Chambers, London	020 3008 6404
Treharne Mr Neil Simon	Dingle Chambers, Bristol	07818 827754
Tucker Mr Ashley Russell	Park Court Chambers, Leeds	0113 243 3277
Twist Mr Stephen John	Dere Street Barristers, Newcastle Upon Tyne	0844 3351551
Walker Mr Adam Nigel	Seven Bedford Row, London	020 7242 3555
Williams Mr Ben Dylan	Kings Chambers, Birmingham	0845 034 3444
	Kings Chambers, Leeds	0845 034 3444
	Kings Chambers, Manchester	0845 034 3444
Winslett Mr Frank	Westgate Chambers, Lewes	01273 480510
Wood Mr Michael Mure	Chambers of Mr Michael Wood QC, London	020 8874 3474

CORPORATE FINANCE

Ajaz Mr Mohammad Arshad	Eastmans Chambers, Reading	0118 966 9094
Bowling Mr James Stuart	4 Pump Court, London	020 7842 5555
Bueno Mr Antonio De Padua Jose Maria	Clerksroom (Taunton), Taunton	0845 083 3000
Drummond Mr Bruce Jonathon Hutcheon	Cornwall Street Chambers, Birmingham	0121 233 7500
	Palmyra Chambers, Warrington	01925 444919
Gibbons Miss Mary Regina	Stone Chambers, London	020 7440 6900
Goodison Mr Adam Henry	South Square, London	020 7696 9900
Hossain Mr Ajmalul	Selborne Chambers, London	020 7420 9500
	St Philips Chambers, Birmingham	0121 246 7000
Iqbal Mr Mashood	London View Chambers, Sawbridgeworth	07788 912493
Keel Mr Douglas Vincent	11 Stone Buildings, London	020 7831 6381
Kelly Mr Sean	Chancery House Chambers, Leeds	0113 244 6691
Lewiecki Miss Marie	Old Bailey Chambers, London	020 3008 6404
Lewis Mr Wayne Anthony	Access Lawyers, London	020 8801 2345
Liddiard Mr Martin Thomas	No5 Chambers, Birmingham	0845 210 5555
	No5 Chambers, Bristol	0845 210 5555
	No5 Chambers, London	0845 210 5555
Matthias Mr David Huw	Francis Taylor Building, London	020 7353 8415
Meredith Mr Christopher William	Furnival Chambers, London	020 7405 3232
Newbold Dr Anne Lorraine Elsie	Minerva Chambers, Ocean Village	00 350 20042779
Parsons Mr Andrew James	Portsmouth Barristers'Chambers, Portsmouth	023 9283 1292
Peat Mr Richard Colin	13 Old Square Chambers, London	020 7831 4445
Rinker Mr Andrew Stuart D'Artois	Chambers of Mr Andrew Rinker, London	020 7584 1091
Shamim Mr Mohammed	Clapham Law Chambers, London	020 7978 8482
Sowler Mr Thomas Richard Holland	The Tax Chambers of Mr Richard Sowler TD, Douglas	07624 235000
Todd Mr Michael Alan	Erskine Chambers, London	020 7242 5532
Trompeter Mr Nicholas Simeon	Selborne Chambers, London	020 7420 9500
Von Pommern-Peglow Dr Michael Alfred Herman Pr.	Brunswick Chambers, London	020 7353 1987
Watson-Gandy Prof Mark	13 Old Square Chambers, London	020 7831 4445
Wills Miss Alexandra Itari	Christ Church Chambers, London	020 7409 5278/07788 512787
Wolman Mr Clive Richard	11 Stone Buildings, London	020 7831 6381

COSTS

Ailes Mr John Ashley	Eighteen Carlton Crescent, Southampton	023 8063 9001
Ajaz Mr Mohammad Arshad	Eastmans Chambers, Reading	0118 966 9094
Allwood Mrs Gina Louisa	Seven Bedford Row, London	020 7242 3555
Askey Mr Robert John	Palmyra Chambers, Warrington	01925 444919
Asprey Mr Nicholas	Clock Chambers, Wolverhampton	01902 313444
	Serle Court, London	020 7242 6105
Becker Mr Timothy George Christie	Chambers of Mr Timothy Becker, Liverpool	0151 703 0319
	Clerksroom (London), London	0845 083 3000

C

Name	Chambers	Telephone
Brown Mr Simon Jonathan	Crown Office Chambers, London	020 7797 8100
Butler Mr Simon David	The Chambers of Grahame Aldous QC, London	020 7832 0500
Cartwright Mr Ivan Matthew	KCH Garden Square, Nottingham	0115 941 8851
Christensen Mr Carlton	10 King's Bench Walk, London	020 7353 7742
Christie Mr Richard Hamish	2 Pump Court, London	020 7353 5597
Crew Miss Gillian Mary	Ely Place Chambers, London	020 7400 9600
De Berry Mr Philip John	18 St John Street, Manchester	0161 278 1800
Esprit Mr Benoit	Barristers Chambers, London	020 3417 6461
	Legis Chambers, Aylesbury	01296 431125
Evans Mr Paul Hugh	No5 Chambers, Birmingham	0845 210 5555
	No5 Chambers, Bristol	0845 210 5555
	No5 Chambers, London	0845 210 5555
Finlay Mr Darren	Sovereign Chambers, Leeds	0113 245 1841
Gersch Mr Adam Nissen	Argent Chambers, London	020 7556 5500
Gun Cuninghame Mr Julian Arthur	Gough Square Chambers, London	020 7353 0924
Iyer Miss Shobana	Swan Chambers, Richmond	0845 123 1234
Jarratt Miss Alice Cordelia Betchworth	Carmelite Chambers, London	020 7936 6300
Jones Mr Richard Frederick Thomas	Heavenwood Chambers, Stroud	01453 873444
Joseph Mr Sellappah Job	Chambers of Mr S J Joseph, London	020 8809 3083/020 8802 9889
Lane Mr Simon Charles	Rougemont Chambers, Exeter	01392 208484
Macro Miss Morwenna Margaret	Five Paper, London	020 7815 3200
Matthias Mr David Huw	Francis Taylor Building, London	020 7353 8415
McCormack Mr Alan	Staple Inn Chambers, London	020 7242 5240
Miller Mr Andrew	2 Temple Gardens, London	020 7822 1200
Moffat Mr Russell Dean	Linenhall Chambers, Chester	01244 348282
Mustakim Mr Abdul Yunus Al	Chambers of Mr Mustakim, London	
Nickless Mr Jason Alan	College Chambers, Southampton	023 8023 0338
Perian Mr Steven	3 Temple Gardens, London	020 7353 3102
Perry Mr Christopher Edward	Palmyra Chambers, Warrington	01925 444919
Ralph Mr Craig	Kings Chambers, Birmingham	0845 034 3444
	Kings Chambers, Leeds	0845 034 3444
	Kings Chambers, Manchester	0845 034 3444
Rifat Mr Maurice Alan	1 Gray's Inn Square, London	020 7405 0001
Turnbull Miss Helen Mary	Lamb Chambers, London	020 7797 8300
Van Tonder Mr Gerard Dirk	New Square Chambers, London	020 7419 8000
Vollenweider Mr Amiot Marcus Ellerton	Thomas More Chambers, London	020 7404 7000
Walker Mr Adam Nigel	Seven Bedford Row, London	020 7242 3555
Webster Miss Shelley Anne	Carmelite Chambers, London	020 7936 6300
Williams Miss June Cleo	No 8 Chambers, Birmingham	0121 236 5514
Wills Miss Alexandra Itari	Christ Church Chambers, London	020 7409 5278/07788 512787

COURTS MARTIAL

Name	Chambers	Telephone
Abu-Mustafa Mr Jehad	1 Paper Buildings, London	020 7353 3728
Akinsanya Mr Stephen Olubunmi	Old Bailey Chambers, London	020 3008 6404
Akudolu Miss Nneka Veronica Anastesia	2 Pump Court, London	020 7353 5597
Alexandra Miss Sebastiane	Holborn Chambers, London	020 7242 6060
Alliott Mr George Beckles	Temple Garden Chambers, London	020 7583 1315
Andrews Mr Paul Leslie	Great James Street Chambers, London	020 7440 4949
Apfel Mr Freddy	37 Park Square Chambers, Leeds	0113 243 9422
Archer Miss Audrey Sybil Dorothy	3 PB Barristers, Bournemouth	01202 292102
	3 PB Barristers, Bristol	0117 928 1520
	3 PB Barristers, London	020 7583 8055
	3 PB Barristers, Oxford	01865 793 736
	3 PB Barristers, Winchester	01962 868884
Armstrong Mr Dean Paul	2 Bedford Row, London	020 7440 8888
Atkinson Mr Nicholas Jeremy	Atkinson Bevan Chambers, London	020 7353 2112
	Staple Inn Chambers, London	020 7242 5240
Bagley Miss Louisa Ellen	1 Paper Buildings, London	020 7353 3728
Bahra Miss Narita	9-12 Bell Yard, London	020 7400 1800
	2 Hare Court, London	020 7353 3982

Bajwa Mr Ali Naseem	Garden Court Chambers, London	020 7993 7600
Ball Mr Steven James	Number 7 Harrington Street Chambers, Liverpool	0151 242 0707
Banham Mr Matthew Ian	Nine Bedford Row, London	020 7489 2727
Barraclough Mr Nicholas Maylin	187 Fleet Street, London	020 7430 7430
Beharrylal Mr Satyanand Sarju	15 New Bridge Street, London	020 7842 1900
Bendall Mr Richard Giles	Furnival Chambers, London	020 7405 3232
Benjamin Mr Daniel Robert	2 Dr Johnson's Buildings, London	020 7936 2613
Bennett Mr Ieuan Gereint	9 Park Place, Cardiff	029 2038 2731
Bergenthal Mr Ronnie Mark	Old Bailey Chambers, London	020 3008 6404
Berriman Mr Trevor St John	43 Temple Row Chambers, Birmingham	0121 237 6035
Bhanji Mr Shiraz Musa	4 Bingham Place, London	020 7486 5347
	1 Gray's Inn Square, London	020 7405 0001
Birnbaum Mr Michael Ian	9-12 Bell Yard, London	020 7400 1800
Bishop Mr Malcolm Leslie	Argent Chambers, London	020 7556 5500
	Equity Chambers, Birmingham	0121 236 5007
	30 Park Place, Cardiff	029 2039 8421
Blain Mr Roderick Graham	12 College Place, Southampton	023 8032 0320
Blakey Mr Michael Charles	St Johns Buildings, Manchester	0161 214 1500
	St Johns Buildings Liverpool, Liverpool	0151 243 6000
	16 Winckley Square, Preston	01772 256100
Bleaney Mr Nicholas Simon	Atkinson Bevan Chambers, London	020 7353 2112
Bond Mr Richard Ian Winsor	Citadel Chambers, Birmingham	0121 233 8500
Bonehill Mr Nicholas Benjamin	4 Breams Buildings, London	020 7092 1900
Boswell Mr Andrew Timothy	13 KBW, Oxford	01865 311066
	13 King's Bench Walk, London	020 7353 7204
Bourne Mr Ian Maclean	Charter Chambers, London	020 7618 4400
Bourne-Arton Mr Simon Nicholas	Park Court Chambers, Leeds	0113 243 3277
Bowes Mr Michael Anthony	Cobden House Chambers, Manchester	0161 833 6000
	Outer Temple Chambers, London	020 7353 6381
Brady Mr Scott	3 Temple Gardens, London	020 7353 3102
Brown Mr Edward Francis Trevenen	QEB Hollis Whiteman, London	020 7933 8855
Brown Mr Sam Clement	Atkinson Bevan Chambers, London	020 7353 2112
Bryan Mr Robert John	1 Paper Buildings, London	020 7353 3728
Budworth Mr Richard Dutton	2-3 Hind Court Chambers, London	020 7822 2150
Bunting Mr Daniel Alexander James	2 Dr Johnson's Buildings, London	020 7936 2613
Byrnes Miss Aisling Alice Elizabeth	25 Bedford Row, London	020 7067 1500
Caldwell Mr Peter Hugh Coyles	Dyers Chambers, London	020 7404 1881
Callery Mr Martin	Cobden House Chambers, Manchester	0161 833 6000
Canning Mr Richard	39 Park Square, Leeds	0113 245 6633
Casey Mr Paul Joseph	Chambers of Marion Smullen and Kerim Fuad QC, London	020 7427 4400
Cassidy Mr Patrick Stephen	Kenworthy's Chambers, Manchester	0161 832 4036
Chalk Mr Alexander John Gervase	6 King's Bench Walk, London	020 7583 0410
Challinor Mr Jonathan Gerald	Cornwall Street Chambers, Birmingham	0121 233 7500
Chipperfield Mr Jeremy Steven	Cranford Chambers, London	020 7404 7454
Clark Mr Dingle	Goldsmith Chambers, London	020 7353 6802
Cockings Mr Giles Francis Sacheveral	Furnival Chambers, London	020 7405 3232
Coffey Mr John Joseph	39 Park Square, Leeds	0113 245 6633
	3 Temple Gardens, London	020 7353 3102
Coles-Harrington Ms Frances Julia	2 Pump Court, London	020 7353 5597
Collett Mr Gavin Charles	Rougemont Chambers, Exeter	01392 208484
Coltart Mr Christopher Mccallum	2 Hare Court, London	020 7353 3982
Conlon Mr Michael John Patrick	Harcourt Chambers, Milton Keynes	0845 123 1234
Connell Mr Edward Samuel	Five St Andrew's Hill, London	020 7332 5400
Connolly Mr Dominic Regan	Five St Andrew's Hill, London	020 7332 5400
Cotter Mr Mark James	Five St Andrew's Hill, London	020 7332 5400
Cousens Mr Michael Patrick	Carmelite Chambers, London	020 7936 6300

Croskell Mr Marcus James	East Anglian Chambers, Chelmsford	01473 214481
	East Anglian Chambers, Colchester	01473 214481
	East Anglian Chambers, Ipswich	01473 214481
	East Anglian Chambers, Norwich	01473 214481
Culver Mr Edward James	4 King's Bench Walk, London	020 7822 7000
Culverhouse Miss Emily Anna Louise	Chambers of Miss E Culverhouse, Chesham	07813 007503
Dashani Miss Sonal	15 New Bridge Street, London	020 7842 1900
Davey Mr Neil Martin	Old Court Chambers, Middlesbrough	01642 232523
	39 Park Square, Leeds	0113 245 6633
	3 Temple Gardens, London	020 7353 3102
Davidson Mr Andrew Edward	Citadel Chambers, Birmingham	0121 233 8500
Davies Mr Jonathan Norval	9-12 Bell Yard, London	020 7400 1800
Davis Mr Simon John	St Philips Chambers, Birmingham	0121 246 7000
Dean Mr James Patrick	Goldsmith Chambers, London	020 7353 6802
Del Fabbro Mr Oscar	23 Essex Street, London	020 7413 0353
Delamere Miss Isabel Sarah	4 Breams Buildings, London	020 7092 1900
Dempsey Miss Karen Marie	3 Temple Gardens, London	020 7353 3102
Dilliway-Parry Mr Guy William	5 King's Bench Walk, London	020 7353 5638
Doherty Mr Nicholas Brudenell	4 King's Bench Walk, London	020 7822 7000
Donne Mr Jeremy Nigel	QEB Hollis Whiteman, London	020 7933 8855
Dos Santos Mr Alexander	Charter Chambers, London	020 7618 4400
Duffy Mr Derek James	St Paul's Chambers, Leeds	0113 245 5866
Dunn Miss Katherine Louise	Trinity Chambers, Middlesbrough	01642 247569
	Trinity Chambers, Newcastle Upon Tyne	0191 232 1927
Earle Mr James Christopher Reginald St John	Fenners Chambers, Cambridge	01223 368761
Eastwood Miss Philippa Clemency Anne	Doughty Street Chambers, London	020 7404 1313
Edington Mrs Fiona Anne Rider	Thomas More Chambers, London	020 7404 7000
Edmonds Mr Michael Jonathan	4 Breams Buildings, London	020 7092 1900
Edwards Mr Matthew Stuart	East Anglian Chambers, Chelmsford	01473 214481
	East Anglian Chambers, Colchester	01473 214481
	East Anglian Chambers, Ipswich	01473 214481
Falk Mr Charles Morton James	3 PB Barristers, London	020 7583 8055
Ferry-Swainson Mr Richard Joseph	2 Bedford Row, London	020 7440 8888
Fisher Mr Jervis Andrew	Citadel Chambers, Birmingham	0121 233 8500
Fishwick Mr Gregory David Philip Kyle	187 Fleet Street, London	020 7430 7430
Forlin Mr Gerard Emlyn	Cornerstone Barristers, London	020 7242 4986
Freeman Miss Lisa Claire	Furnival Chambers, London	020 7405 3232
Frymann Mr Andrew Philip	187 Fleet Street, London	020 7430 7430
Gadd Mr Adam Brian	Pump Court Chambers, London	020 7353 0711
	Pump Court Chambers, Winchester	01962 868 161
	Riverview Chambers, London	0844 225 3999
Gaskin Mr Francis John Gerald	4 Breams Buildings, London	020 7092 1900
Gau Mr Justin Charles	Pump Court Chambers, London	020 7353 0711
	Pump Court Chambers, Swindon	01793 539899
	Pump Court Chambers, Winchester	01962 868 161
Gersch Mr Adam Nissen	Argent Chambers, London	020 7556 5500
Gilchrist Miss Naomi Roberta	St Philips Chambers, Birmingham	0121 246 7000
Gladwell Mr Simon Mark	East Anglian Chambers, Ipswich	01473 214481
Glasgow Mr Oliver Edwin James	2 Hare Court, London	020 7353 3982
Glass Mr Anthony Trevor	QEB Hollis Whiteman, London	020 7933 8855
Gledhill Mr Lee Andre	Alexander Chambers, London	0845 652 0451/0854 652 0451
	Trident Barristers Chambers, Manchester	0161 663 3123
Godfrey Mr Thomas William Netherton	23 Essex Street, London	020 7413 0353
Goldberg Mr Jonathan Jacob	Cobden House Chambers, Manchester	0161 833 6000
	North Square Chambers, London	020 8455 3735
Goudie Mr William Martin Phillip	Charter Chambers, London	020 7618 4400
Gow Mr Henry	New Bailey Chambers, Liverpool	0151 236 9402

Gray Mr Peter Henry St John	5 Pump Court, London	020 7353 2532
Green Mr Jonathan Paul	Dyers Chambers, London	020 7404 1881
Grego Mr Kevin Christopher	Citadel Chambers, Birmingham	0121 233 8500
Griffiths Mr Peter	2 Bedford Row, London	020 7440 8888
	30 Park Place, Cardiff	029 2039 8421
Grunwald Mr Henry Cyril	Charter Chambers, London	020 7618 4400
Guest Mr Peter Liam	187 Fleet Street, London	020 7430 7430
Hadrill Mr Keith Paul	Furnival Chambers, London	020 7405 3232
Hamilton-Shield Miss Anna-Maria	Charter Chambers, London	020 7618 4400
Harbage Mr William John Hirons	36 Bedford Row, London	020 7421 8000
	37 Park Square Chambers, Leeds	0113 243 9422
Harding Mr Christopher James	Thomas More Chambers, London	020 7404 7000
Hardyman Mr Matthew James	15 New Bridge Street, London	020 7842 1900
Harries Mr Mark Robert	Carmelite Chambers, London	020 7936 6300
Harris Miss Stella Cassandra Methven	Tooks Chambers, London	020 7842 7575
Harvey Mr Stephen Frank	18 Red Lion Court, London	020 7520 6000
	18 Red Lion Court (Annexe), Chelmsford	01245 280880
Hays Mr William Stormont	6 King's Bench Walk, London	020 7583 0410
Heyworth Mr James Edward Watson	Lincoln House Chambers, Manchester	0161 832 5701
Higgins Mr Daniel Malcolm Buhlea	Nine Bedford Row, London	020 7489 2727
Hillman Mr Basil	4 King's Bench Walk, London	020 7822 7000
Hine Mr Charles Roderick John	King's Bench Chambers, Bournemouth	01202 250025
Hinton Mr Neil Pearse	King's Bench Chambers, Bournemouth	01202 250025
Hollis Mrs Kim	25 Bedford Row, London	020 7067 1500
Hood Mr David	Prince of Wales Chambers, London	020 7622 7415
Hooper Mr Gopal Arthur John	Thomas More Chambers, London	020 7404 7000
Hugheston-Roberts Mr Charles Justin	4 Breams Buildings, London	020 7092 1900
Hutchings Mr Richard Peter Mark	Chambers of Marion Smullen and Kerim Fuad QC, London	020 7427 4400
Inyundo Mr Richard Kwame Swaka	6 King's Bench Walk, London	020 7583 0410
Irwin Mr Gavin David	Dyers Chambers, London	020 7404 1881
Jackson Mr Andrew Fraser	5 Pump Court, London	020 7353 2532
Jafferjee Mr Aftab Asger	Atkinson Bevan Chambers, London	020 7353 2112
James Mr Roderick Ian	Charter Chambers, London	020 7618 4400
Jarratt Miss Alice Cordelia Betchworth	Carmelite Chambers, London	020 7936 6300
Johnson Miss Zoe Elisabeth	QEB Hollis Whiteman, London	020 7933 8855
Jones Mr Mark Andrew	St Ive's Chambers, Birmingham	0121 236 0863
Joshi Mr Rajendra Jugatray	18 Red Lion Court, London	020 7520 6000
	18 Red Lion Court (Annexe), Chelmsford	01245 280880
Kearney Mr John	Furnival Chambers, London	020 7405 3232
Keith Mr Benjamin Charles Andrew	Five St Andrew's Hill, London	020 7332 5400
Kelly Mr Richard Bernard	East Anglian Chambers, Chelmsford	01473 214481
	East Anglian Chambers, Colchester	01473 214481
	East Anglian Chambers, Ipswich	01473 214481
	East Anglian Chambers, Norwich	01473 214481
Kennedy Mr Peter Nicholas Dodgson	15 Winckley Square, Preston	01772 252828
Kenny Mr Martin William	Walnut House, Exeter	01392 279751
Keogh Mr Richard Thomas	Farringdon Chambers, London	020 7089 5700
Kessling Mr Christopher David	Chambers of Mr Christopher Kessling, Leicester	01509 890690
Khan Mr Forz	Chambers of Mr F Khan, London	07854 109584
	6 King's Bench Walk, London	020 7353 4931
Khan Mr Zarif	Dyers Chambers, London	020 7404 1881
King Mr Gelaga Perry	2 Bedford Row, London	020 7440 8888
Lahiffe Mr Martin Patrick Joseph	3 Temple Gardens, London	020 7353 3102
Lamb Mr Jeffrey Thomas	Westgate Chambers, Lewes	01273 480510
Lambert Mr Nigel Robert Woolf	Carmelite Chambers, London	020 7936 6300
Lawrence Sir Ivan John	5 Pump Court, London	020 7353 2532

Barrister	Chambers	Telephone
Lawton Mr Paul Anthony	Lincoln House Chambers, Manchester	0161 832 5701
	18 Red Lion Court, London	020 7520 6000
Le Fort Mr Michael Cameron Raoul	King's Bench Chambers, Bournemouth	01202 250025
Leake Mr Stephen	Carmelite Chambers, London	020 7936 6300
Leonard Mr James Alexander	Outer Temple Chambers, London	020 7353 6381
Lewiecki Miss Marie	Old Bailey Chambers, London	020 3008 6404
Lewis Mr Andrew Simon	4 Breams Buildings, London	020 7092 1900
Lewis Mr Dominic	Five Paper Buildings, London	020 7583 6117
Liddiard Mr Martin Thomas	No5 Chambers, Birmingham	0845 210 5555
	No5 Chambers, Bristol	0845 210 5555
	No5 Chambers, London	0845 210 5555
Linehan Mr Stephen John	St Philips Chambers, Birmingham	0121 246 7000
Lodge Mr Hugo Daniel Paul	Atkinson Bevan Chambers, London	020 7353 2112
Logan Mr Graeme Alexander	4 Breams Buildings, London	020 7092 1900
	15 New Bridge Street, London	020 7842 1900
Lowe Mr Christopher John	KCH Garden Square, Nottingham	0115 941 8851
Lyons Mr David Wakefield	King's Bench Chambers, Bournemouth	01202 250025
	2 Pump Court, London	020 7353 5597
Magee Mr Samuel Cairns	2 Bedford Row, London	020 7440 8888
Maggs Mr Patrick Terence	15 New Bridge Street, London	020 7842 1900
Malone Mr David John	1 Gray's Inn Square, London	020 7405 0001
Masters Mr Alan Bruce Raymond	1 Pump Court, London	020 7842 7070
Mather Mr Nicholas Ian Stewart	Furnival Chambers, London	020 7405 3232
Matthias Mr David Huw	Francis Taylor Building, London	020 7353 8415
McCulloch Miss Fiona Catharine Jane	Middle Temple Lane Chambers, London	020 7583 4352
McGowan Miss Maura Patricia	2 Bedford Row, London	020 7440 8888
	Lincoln House Chambers, Manchester	0161 832 5701
McKone Mr Mark Desmond	Sovereign Chambers, Leeds	0113 245 1841
Meeke Mr Robert Martin James	Colleton Chambers, Exeter	01392 274898
Milne Mr Alexander Hugh	18 Red Lion Court, London	020 7520 6000
	18 Red Lion Court (Annexe), Chelmsford	01245 280880
Milne Mr Richard James	23 Essex Street, London	020 7413 0353
Milsom Mrs Catherine Mary	Argent Chambers, London	020 7556 5500
Molloy Mr Andrew Joseph	St Ive's Chambers, Birmingham	0121 236 0863
Mooney Mr Stephen John	Albion Chambers, Bristol	0117 927 2144
Moore Mr James Anthony	Goldsmith Chambers, London	020 7353 6802
	39 Park Square, Leeds	0113 245 6633
Moran Mr Patrick Michael	15 New Bridge Street, London	020 7842 1900
Morris Mr Ben	Chavasse Court Chambers, Liverpool	0151 229 2030
Morris Mr Ieuan John	9 Park Place, Cardiff	029 2038 2731
Morris Ms Johanna	Chambers of Marion Smullen and Kerim Fuad QC, London	020 7427 4400
Morrison Mr Christopher Quintin	Old Court Chambers, Middlesbrough	01642 232523
Mousley Mr William Howard	2 King's Bench Walk, London	020 7353 1746
Mullins Mr Mark Lovel Rupert	Five St Andrew's Hill, London	020 7332 5400
Newcomb Mr Quinton John	1 Paper Buildings, London	020 7353 3728
Newton-Price Mr James Edward	Pump Court Chambers, London	020 7353 0711
	Pump Court Chambers, Swindon	01793 539899
	Pump Court Chambers, Winchester	01962 868 161
Nicholls Mr Colin Alfred Arthur	3 Raymond Buildings, London	020 7400 6400
Oakley Miss Louise Michelle	2 Bedford Row, London	020 7440 8888
O'Connor Mr Patrick Michael Joseph	Doughty Street Chambers, Bristol	01179 058 717
	Doughty Street Chambers, London	020 7404 1313
	Doughty Street Chambers, Manchester	0161 618 1066
O'Donoghue Mr Hugh Vincent	Carmelite Chambers, London	020 7936 6300
Onalaja Mr James Oluwatosin	2 Pump Court, London	020 7353 5597
O'Neill Mr Brian Patrick	2 Hare Court, London	020 7353 3982
Ong Miss Grace Yu Mae	Argent Chambers, London	020 7556 5500
Owen Mr Timothy Wynn	Matrix Chambers, London	020 7404 3447
Panagiotopoulou Miss Tania	Staple Inn Chambers, London	020 7242 5240
Pardoe Mr Matthew James	Dyers Chambers, London	020 7404 1881
Paton Mr Ian Francis	QEB Hollis Whiteman, London	020 7933 8855

Patterson Mr Stewart	Pump Court Chambers, London	020 7353 0711
	Pump Court Chambers, Swindon	01793 539899
	Pump Court Chambers, Winchester	01962 868 161
Pawson-Pounds Mr Daniel James	6 King's Bench Walk, London	020 7583 0410
Potter Rev Harry Drummond	25 Bedford Row, London	020 7067 1500
Power Mr Archangelo Carlo	2 Bedford Row, London	020 7440 8888
Purnell Mr Paul Oliver	Farringdon Chambers, London	020 7089 5700
Pyne Mr Russell David	2 King's Bench Walk, London	020 7353 1746
Quinn Mr Tomas Anthony	4 King's Bench Walk, London	020 7822 7000
Raggatt Mr Timothy Walter Harold	4 King's Bench Walk, London	020 7822 7000
	St Philips Chambers, Birmingham	0121 246 7000
Ramasamy Mr Selvaraju	QEB Hollis Whiteman, London	020 7933 8855
Reevell Mr Simon Justin	39 Park Square, Leeds	0113 245 6633
Reevell Mrs Louise Marie	39 Park Square, Leeds	0113 245 6633
Rhodes Mr Nicholas Piers	Charter Chambers, London	020 7618 4400
Richards Mr David James Martin	3 PB Barristers, Bournemouth	01202 292102
	3 PB Barristers, Bristol	0117 928 1520
	3 PB Barristers, London	020 7583 8055
	3 PB Barristers, Oxford	01865 793 736
	3 PB Barristers, Winchester	01962 868884
Richardson Mr Alistair Paul George	6 King's Bench Walk, London	020 7583 0410
Rippon Mr Simon John	Citadel Chambers, Birmingham	0121 233 8500
Roberts Mr Timothy David	Fountain Chambers, Middlesbrough	01642 804040
	QEB Hollis Whiteman, London	020 7933 8855
Rooke Mr Alexander John Giles	Argent Chambers, London	020 7556 5500
Rosen Mr Jonathan Leon	1 Gray's Inn Square, London	020 7405 0001
Rouse Mr Justin Clive Douglas	Nine Bedford Row, London	020 7489 2727
Ruffell Mr Mark Beresford	Pump Court Chambers, London	020 7353 0711
	Pump Court Chambers, Swindon	01793 539899
	Pump Court Chambers, Winchester	01962 868 161
Rule Mr Philip David	Castle Chambers, Harrow-on-the-Hill	020 8423 6579
Russell Miss Marguerite	Garden Court Chambers, London	020 7993 7600
Rustom Mr Shiraz Sam	1215 Chambers, London	020 3291 1215
	Cranford Chambers, London	020 7404 7454
	1 Mitre Court Buildings, London	020 7452 8900
Sadler Miss Rhiannon Jane	Westgate Chambers, Lewes	01273 480510
Sallon Mr Christopher Robert	Doughty Street Chambers, Bristol	01179 058 717
	Doughty Street Chambers, London	020 7404 1313
	Doughty Street Chambers, Manchester	0161 618 1066
Sandford Mr Simon John Austin	5 King's Bench Walk, London	020 7353 5638
Scott Bell Mrs Rosalind Sara	Trinity Chambers, Middlesbrough	01642 247569
	Trinity Chambers, Newcastle Upon Tyne	0191 232 1927
Scott Mr Matthew John	Pump Court Chambers, London	020 7353 0711
	Pump Court Chambers, Swindon	01793 539899
	Pump Court Chambers, Winchester	01962 868 161
Scutt Mr David Robert	9-12 Bell Yard, London	020 7400 1800
Sekar Mr Chandra	Angell Park Chambers, London	020 7737 5957
Shapiro Mr Selwyn	2 King's Bench Walk, London	020 7353 1746
Shotton Ms Sophie Diana	15 New Bridge Street, London	020 7842 1900
Silverton Miss Catherine Anne	Sovereign Chambers, Leeds	0113 245 1841
Singer Mr Richard Adam	1 Gray's Inn Square, London	020 7405 0001
Skinner Mr Samuel Richard Edward	KCH Garden Square, Nottingham	0115 941 8851
Smith Miss Eileen Joan	Trinity Chambers, Middlesbrough	01642 247569
	Trinity Chambers, Newcastle Upon Tyne	0191 232 1927
Smith Mr Alisdair Robert Macsorley	9-12 Bell Yard, London	020 7400 1800
Smith Mr Clive Francis	Chambers of Marion Smullen and Kerim Fuad QC, London	020 7427 4400
Smith Mr Julian Robert	Lincoln's Inn Fields Chambers, London	0845 123 1234
Spears Miss Katharine Sarah	Carmelite Chambers, London	020 7936 6300
St Louis Mr Brian Lloyd	15 New Bridge Street, London	020 7842 1900
Stanford Mr Tony James	Old Bailey Chambers, London	020 3008 6404

Name	Chambers	Telephone
Stebbings Mr Ian Anthony	1 Gray's Inn Square, London	020 7405 0001
Stevens Mr Mark Nicholas	Chambers of Marion Smullen and Kerim Fuad QC, London	020 7427 4400
Storey Mr Richard Alexander	3 Temple Gardens, London	020 7353 3102
Stork Mr Brian Raymond	3 Temple Gardens, London	020 7353 3102
Storrie Mr Timothy James	Lincoln House Chambers, Manchester	0161 832 5701
Stranex Mr Andrew John	St Paul's Chambers, Leeds	0113 245 5866
Stuart Mr Bruce Ian	Lombard Chambers, London	020 7107 2100
Sugarman Mr Jason Ashley	9-12 Bell Yard, London	020 7400 1800
Summers Mr Benjamin Dylan James	3 Raymond Buildings, London	020 7400 6400
Sutton-Mattocks Mr Christopher John	5 King's Bench Walk, London	020 7353 5638
Tatford Mr Warwick Henry Patrick	9-12 Bell Yard, London	020 7400 1800
Taylor Mrs Yvonne Marie	Trinity Chambers, Middlesbrough	01642 247569
	Trinity Chambers, Newcastle Upon Tyne	0191 232 1927
Tomassi Mr Mark David	Charter Chambers, London	020 7618 4400
Treharne Mr Neil Simon	Dingle Chambers, Bristol	07818 827754
Upton Mr John Stewart	4 King's Bench Walk, London	020 7822 7000
Valios Mr Nicholas Paul	4 Breams Buildings, London	020 7092 1900
	No 8 Chambers, Birmingham	0121 236 5514
Vollenweider Mr Amiot Marcus Ellerton	Thomas More Chambers, London	020 7404 7000
Walker Mr Liam David	Doughty Street Chambers, London	020 7404 1313
Walker-Nolan Mr Benjamin	Thomas More Chambers, London	020 7404 7000
Watson Mr Benjamin Turquand	3 Raymond Buildings, London	020 7400 6400
Watson Mr Tom Bradley	Chavasse Court Chambers, Liverpool	0151 229 2030
Weaver Mr Brett	6 King's Bench Walk, London	020 7583 0410
Weekes Mr Mark Vincent	6 King's Bench Walk, London	020 7583 0410
Whitfield Mr Jonathan	Doughty Street Chambers, London	020 7404 1313
Williams Miss Micaila Teresa	Optimus Chambers, Braintree	01376 691 885/07736 283873
Williams Mr Ben Dylan	Kings Chambers, Birmingham	0845 034 3444
	Kings Chambers, Leeds	0845 034 3444
	Kings Chambers, Manchester	0845 034 3444
Wood Mr James Alexander Douglas	Doughty Street Chambers, Bristol	01179 058 717
	Doughty Street Chambers, London	020 7404 1313
	Doughty Street Chambers, Manchester	0161 618 1066
Woods Mr Terence Mccartan	187 Fleet Street, London	020 7430 7430

CRIME

Name	Chambers	Telephone
Abasheikh Mr Omar Said Imam	Paragon Chambers, London	020 3318 9988
Abu-Mustafa Mr Jehad	1 Paper Buildings, London	020 7353 3728
Addison Mr Kenneth Paul	5 Pump Court, London	020 7353 2532
Afzal Mr Fayyaz	No5 Chambers, Birmingham	0845 210 5555
	No5 Chambers, Bristol	0845 210 5555
	No5 Chambers, London	0845 210 5555
Ailes Mr John Ashley	Eighteen Carlton Crescent, Southampton	023 8063 9001
Akers Mr Robert Matthew Harry	St Johns Buildings, Chester	01244 323070
	St Johns Buildings, Manchester	0161 214 1500
	16 Winckley Square, Preston	01772 256100
Akin-Olugbade Mr Oluwajeminipe Babarinsade	Nexus Chambers, London	020 7404 1147/020 7831 8309
Akinsanya Mr Stephen Olubunmi	Old Bailey Chambers, London	020 3008 6404
Akudolu Miss Nneka Veronica Anastesia	2 Pump Court, London	020 7353 5597
Alakija Mr Ayodele Hugh	No 8 Chambers, Birmingham	0121 236 5514
Aleeson Mr Warwick Lan Grieg	187 Fleet Street, London	020 7430 7430
Ali Mr Zafar	23 Essex Street, London	020 7413 0353
Amis Mr Christopher Jocelyn	23 Essex Street, London	020 7413 0353
Anderson Mr Richard Neil Macdiarmid	Arbitration Chambers, London	020 7267 2137
Andrews Mr Paul Leslie	Great James Street Chambers, London	020 7440 4949
Apfel Mr Freddy	37 Park Square Chambers, Leeds	0113 243 9422

Appiah Miss Linda	Guildford Chambers, Guildford	01483 539131
Archer Miss Audrey Sybil Dorothy	3 PB Barristers, Bournemouth	01202 292102
	3 PB Barristers, Bristol	0117 928 1520
	3 PB Barristers, London	020 7583 8055
	3 PB Barristers, Oxford	01865 793 736
	3 PB Barristers, Winchester	01962 868884
Argent Mr Gavin Richard	Westgate Chambers, Lewes	01273 480510
Argyle Mr Brian John	Chambers of K A Williams-Howes, London	020 8704 1010
	187 Fleet Street, London	020 7430 7430
Aris Mr Jason Mark	Citadel Chambers, Birmingham	0121 233 8500
Armbrister Mr Allan Ramsay	39 Park Square, Leeds	0113 245 6633
Armstrong Mr Dean Paul	2 Bedford Row, London	020 7440 8888
Arnold Mr Graham John	Farringdon Chambers, London	020 7089 5700
Arnold Mr Peter Matthew Miller	No5 Chambers, Birmingham	0845 210 5555
	No5 Chambers, Bristol	0845 210 5555
	No5 Chambers, London	0845 210 5555
Arshad Miss Farrhat	Doughty Street Chambers, Bristol	01179 058 717
	Doughty Street Chambers, London	020 7404 1313
	Doughty Street Chambers, Manchester	0161 618 1066
Ashley-Norman Mr Jonathan Charles	3 Raymond Buildings, London	020 7400 6400
Atkins Mr Richard Paul	St Philips Chambers, Birmingham	0121 246 7000
Atkinson Mr Nicholas Jeremy	Atkinson Bevan Chambers, London	020 7353 2112
	Staple Inn Chambers, London	020 7242 5240
Austin Mr Ian	Holborn Chambers, London	020 7242 6060
Austin Mr Jonathan Edward Newns	Linenhall Chambers, Chester	01244 348282
Austins Mr Christopher John	Chambers of Mr Christopher Austins, Bristol	01761 221 208
	Clerksroom (Taunton), Taunton	0845 083 3000
	King's Lynn Chambers, King's Lynn	01553 672 085
Awodele Mr Olufemi Adetunji	Great James Street Chambers, London	020 7440 4949
Aylett Mr Kenneth George	4 Breams Buildings, London	020 7092 1900
	15 New Bridge Street, London	020 7842 1900
Aylott Mr Colin Christopher	Carmelite Chambers, London	020 7936 6300
Azhar Mr Ali Mohammad	9 King's Bench Walk, London	020 7353 9564
Badenoch Mr Tony David	6 King's Bench Walk, London	020 7583 0410
Badger Mr Christopher James	23 Essex Street, London	020 7413 0353
Bagley Miss Louisa Ellen	1 Paper Buildings, London	020 7353 3728
Bahra Miss Narita	9-12 Bell Yard, London	020 7400 1800
	2 Hare Court, London	020 7353 3982
Bailey Miss Sasha	2 Pump Court, London	020 7353 5597
Baird Mr James Stevenson	Bank House Chambers, Sheffield	0114 275 1223
Bajwa Mr Ali Naseem	Garden Court Chambers, London	020 7993 7600
Baker Miss Maureen Anne	Seven Bedford Row, London	020 7242 3555
Baki Mr Neil Farres	25 Bedford Row, London	020 7067 1500
Ball Mr Ian David	Cornwall Street Chambers, Birmingham	0121 233 7500
Ball Mr Steven James	Number 7 Harrington Street Chambers, Liverpool	0151 242 0707
Banerjee Mr Subhankar	Atkinson Bevan Chambers, London	020 7353 2112
Banham Mr Matthew Ian	Nine Bedford Row, London	020 7489 2727
Banks Mr Timothy James	15 New Bridge Street, London	020 7842 1900
Barclay Mr Robin Nicholas John	2 Hare Court, London	020 7353 3982
Barker Mr Kerry	Guildhall Chambers, Bristol	0117 930 9000
Barnes Mr Ashley James	Chambers of Mr Ashley Barnes, St Helens	01744 814072
	New Bailey Chambers, Liverpool	0151 236 9402
Barnes Mr David Jonathan	3 Temple Gardens, London	020 7353 3102
Barnes Ms Rachel Ann	3 Raymond Buildings, London	020 7400 6400
Barnett Mr Jeremy Victor	2 Bedford Row, London	020 7440 8888
	St Paul's Chambers, Leeds	0113 245 5866
Barraclough Mr Nicholas Maylin	187 Fleet Street, London	020 7430 7430
Barrett Mr Robert Scott	2 Pump Court, London	020 7353 5597
Barry Mr Kevin James	36 Bedford Row, London	020 7421 8000

Name	Chambers	Telephone
Bartfeld Mr Jason Maurice	187 Fleet Street, London	020 7430 7430
Barton Mr Hugh Geoffrey	Lincoln House Chambers, Manchester	0161 832 5701
Barton Ms Chloe Louise	Charter Chambers, London	020 7618 4400
Bashir Mr Mohammed Issrar	Chambers of M I Bashir, London	07932 948487
	12 Old Square Chambers, London	020 7404 0875
Bass Mr Timothy James	Farringdon Chambers, London	020 7089 5700
Batcup Mr David John	Charter Chambers, London	020 7618 4400
Baur Mr Christopher Thomas	Furnival Chambers, London	020 7405 3232
Baxter Miss Bernadette	Lincoln House Chambers, Manchester	0161 832 5701
Becker Mr Paul Antony	Chavasse Court Chambers, Liverpool	0151 229 2030
Beeson Mr Nigel Adrian Laurence	New Bailey Chambers, Liverpool	0151 236 9402
Beharrylal Mr Satyanand Sarju	15 New Bridge Street, London	020 7842 1900
Bell Mr Dominic Michael St. John	Chambers of Marion Smullen and Kerim Fuad QC, London	020 7427 4400
Bendall Mr Richard Giles	Furnival Chambers, London	020 7405 3232
Benjamin Mr Daniel Robert	2 Dr Johnson's Buildings, London	020 7936 2613
Bennett Miss Emma Louise	Exchange Chambers, Leeds	0113 203 1970
	Exchange Chambers, Liverpool	0151 236 7747
	Exchange Chambers, Manchester	0161 833 2722
Bennett Mr Ieuan Gereint	9 Park Place, Cardiff	029 2038 2731
Bennett Mr Miles Alexander Fordham	Five Paper Buildings, London	020 7583 6117
Benson Mr Jeremy Keith	18 Red Lion Court, London	020 7520 6000
Bentley Mr David Neil	Doughty Street Chambers, Bristol	01179 058 717
	Doughty Street Chambers, London	020 7404 1313
	Doughty Street Chambers, Manchester	0161 618 1066
Bergenthal Mr Ronnie Mark	Old Bailey Chambers, London	020 3008 6404
Berriman Mr Trevor St John	43 Temple Row Chambers, Birmingham	0121 237 6035
Berry Mr Nicholas	Citadel Chambers, Birmingham	0121 233 8500
Bertham Mr Anthony Christopher	3 Temple Gardens, London	020 7353 3102
Beswick Miss Kirstin Wendy	Central Chambers, Manchester	0161 236 1133
Betts Mr Stephen	Chambers of Mr S Betts, Marlow	07739 892093
Bex Miss Kate	2 Hare Court, London	020 7353 3982
Beyts Mr Chester Andoe Michael	25 Bedford Row, London	020 7067 1500
Bhattacharyya Mr Ardhendu	Slough Barristers Chamber, Slough	01753 553806
Bhatti Miss Balvinder	Citadel Chambers, Birmingham	0121 233 8500
Bickler Mr Simon Lloyd	St Paul's Chambers, Leeds	0113 245 5866
Birbeck Mr Alan Giles	Dyers Chambers, London	020 7404 1881
Birkby Mr Richard Adam	Park Court Chambers, Leeds	0113 243 3277
Birnbaum Mr Michael Ian	9-12 Bell Yard, London	020 7400 1800
Bisarya Mr Neil	Number 7 Harrington Street Chambers, Liverpool	0151 242 0707
Bisbey Miss Gayle Yvette Dawn	2 Dr Johnson's Buildings, London	020 7936 2613
Bishop Mr Malcolm Leslie	Argent Chambers, London	020 7556 5500
	Equity Chambers, Birmingham	0121 236 5007
	30 Park Place, Cardiff	029 2039 8421
Bishop Mr Stephen Anthony	Goldsmith Chambers, London	020 7353 6802
Blain Mr Roderick Graham	12 College Place, Southampton	023 8032 0320
Blair Mr Peter Michael	Guildhall Chambers, Bristol	0117 930 9000
	6 King's Bench Walk, London	020 7583 0410
Blake Mr Christopher Ian	5 King's Bench Walk, London	020 7353 5638
Blake Ms Penelope Natasha	1 Gray's Inn Square, London	020 7405 0001
Blakey Mr Michael Charles	St Johns Buildings, Manchester	0161 214 1500
	St Johns Buildings Liverpool, Liverpool	0151 243 6000
	16 Winckley Square, Preston	01772 256100
Bleaney Mr Nicholas Simon	Atkinson Bevan Chambers, London	020 7353 2112
Bloomfield Mr Richard William	Chambers of Mr Richard Bloomfield, Whitley Bay	01670 360042
Blunt Mr Oliver Simon Peter	Furnival Chambers, London	020 7405 3232
Bond Mr Richard Ian Winsor	Citadel Chambers, Birmingham	0121 233 8500
Bonehill Mr Nicholas Benjamin	4 Breams Buildings, London	020 7092 1900
Borrelli Mr Michael Francis Antony	187 Fleet Street, London	020 7430 7430

Boswell Mr Andrew Timothy	13 KBW, Oxford	01865 311066
	13 King's Bench Walk, London	020 7353 7204
Bourne Mr Ian Maclean	Charter Chambers, London	020 7618 4400
Bourne-Arton Mr James Luke	St Paul's Chambers, Leeds	0113 245 5866
Bourne-Arton Mr Simon Nicholas	Park Court Chambers, Leeds	0113 243 3277
Bowden Mr Guy Robert	4 Breams Buildings, London	020 7092 1900
Bowers Mr Rupert John	Doughty Street Chambers, London	020 7404 1313
Bowes Mr Michael Anthony	Cobden House Chambers, Manchester	0161 833 6000
	Outer Temple Chambers, London	020 7353 6381
Boyd Mr Phillip Joseph George	Lincoln House Chambers, Manchester	0161 832 5701
Braamskamp Ms Christine Jolanda	3 Raymond Buildings, London	020 7400 6400
Bradnock Mr Thomas Philip	Colleton Chambers, Exeter	01392 274898
Brady Mr Scott	3 Temple Gardens, London	020 7353 3102
Brain Miss Pamela Francis	Chambers of Marion Smullen and Kerim Fuad QC, London	020 7427 4400
Bramwell Miss Corinne Victoria	Nine Bedford Row, London	020 7489 2727
Brand Miss Rachel Rennie Virginia Ann	Citadel Chambers, Birmingham	0121 233 8500
Branston Mr Gareth Philip	23 Essex Street, London	020 7413 0353
Brassington Mr Stephen David	2 Hare Court, London	020 7353 3982
Braun Ms Minka Chaya	25 Bedford Row, London	020 7067 1500
Bray Miss Caroline Jane	36 Bedford Row, London	020 7421 8000
Breen-Lawton Miss Denise	St Paul's Chambers, Leeds	0113 245 5866
Brehan Ms Daire	Chambers of Ms D Brehan, London	07808 726877
Brickman Miss Laura Gillian	Carmelite Chambers, London	020 7936 6300
Bridge Mr Giles	Broadway House Chambers, Bradford	01274 722560
	Broadway House Chambers, Leeds	0113 246 2600
Bright Miss Rachel Zelda	4 Brick Court, London	020 7832 3200
	187 Fleet Street, London	020 7430 7430
Brimelow Miss Janine Kirsty	Doughty Street Chambers, Bristol	01179 058 717
	Doughty Street Chambers, London	020 7404 1313
	Doughty Street Chambers, Manchester	0161 618 1066
Broadley Mr John	Cobden House Chambers, Manchester	0161 833 6000
Brooke Mr David Michael Graham	KBW, Leeds	0113 297 1200
Brown Mr Cameron Kennedy Duncan	9-12 Bell Yard, London	020 7400 1800
Brown Mr Edward Francis Trevenen	QEB Hollis Whiteman, London	020 7933 8855
Brown Mr Roger Charles Arthur	Kenworthy's Chambers, Manchester	0161 832 4036
Brown Mr Sam Clement	Atkinson Bevan Chambers, London	020 7353 2112
Brunner Ms Catherine Jane	Albion Chambers, Bristol	0117 927 2144
	36 Bedford Row, London	020 7421 8000
Brunt Mr Philip Edwin	No 8 Chambers, Birmingham	0121 236 5514
Bryan Mr Robert John	1 Paper Buildings, London	020 7353 3728
Bryant-Heron Mr Mark Nicholas	9-12 Bell Yard, London	020 7400 1800
Buchanan Mr James Ian Charles	2 Hare Court, London	020 7353 3982
Bull Mr Nicholas David	Old Bailey Chambers, London	020 3008 6404
Bullen Mrs Mary	The Chambers Of Mary Bullen, Wilton	01722 742204
Bunting Mr Daniel Alexander James	2 Dr Johnson's Buildings, London	020 7936 2613
Butters Mr Richard John	37 Park Square Chambers, Leeds	0113 243 9422
Butterworth Mr Martin Frank	Citadel Chambers, Birmingham	0121 233 8500
Buxton Mr Thomas Justin	Charter Chambers, London	020 7618 4400
Byrne Mr Garrett Thomas	4-5 Gray's Inn Square, London	020 7404 5252
Byrnes Miss Aisling Alice Elizabeth	25 Bedford Row, London	020 7067 1500
Caddle Miss Sherrie Loretta	Charter Chambers, London	020 7618 4400
Cairns Ms Sally	No 8 Chambers, Birmingham	0121 236 5514
Caldwell Mr Peter Hugh Coyles	Dyers Chambers, London	020 7404 1881
Callery Mr Martin	Cobden House Chambers, Manchester	0161 833 6000
Cammerman Mr Gideon Saul	187 Fleet Street, London	020 7430 7430
Campbell Mr Alasdair James	St Paul's Chambers, Leeds	0113 245 5866
Canning Mr Richard	39 Park Square, Leeds	0113 245 6633
Carey Miss Jacqueline Anne	2 Bedford Row, London	020 7440 8888
Carey-Hughes Mr Richard John	Nine Bedford Row, London	020 7489 2727
Carne Mr Roger Enys	Nine Bedford Row, London	020 7489 2727
Carr Mr James Christopher Daniel	4 Breams Buildings, London	020 7092 1900

Carrasco Mr Glenn Lawrence	9-12 Bell Yard, London	020 7400 1800
Carrington Mr Dominic	Chambers of Martin Burr, London	0845 123 1234
Carter Miss Nathalie Veronique	1 Gray's Inn Square, London	020 7405 0001
Carter-Stephenson Mr George Anthony	25 Bedford Row, London	020 7067 1500
Casey Mr Paul Joseph	Chambers of Marion Smullen and Kerim Fuad QC, London	020 7427 4400
Cassidy Mr Patrick Stephen	Kenworthy's Chambers, Manchester	0161 832 4036
Caudle Mr John Arthur	2 Bedford Row, London	020 7440 8888
Cavender Ms Susan Penelope	Guildhall Chambers, Bristol	0117 930 9000
Cecil Miss Joanne Michelle	1 Pump Court, London	020 7842 7070
Chadwick Miss Joanna Ceridwen	No5 Chambers, Birmingham	0845 210 5555
	No5 Chambers, Bristol	0845 210 5555
	No5 Chambers, London	0845 210 5555
Chadwick Mr Daniel James	25 Bedford Row, London	020 7067 1500
Chalk Mr Alexander John Gervase	6 King's Bench Walk, London	020 7583 0410
Challinor Mr Jonathan Gerald	Cornwall Street Chambers, Birmingham	0121 233 7500
Challinor Mr Thomas Michael	Citadel Chambers, Birmingham	0121 233 8500
Chan Miss Rachel Siu Yee	Stour Chambers, Canterbury	01227 764899
Channon Miss Rebecca Anne	Dyers Chambers, London	020 7404 1881
Charles Ms Katrina Skevi	Farringdon Chambers, London	020 7089 5700
Charnley Miss Bethan Rebecca	Nine Bedford Row, London	020 7489 2727
Chawla Mr Mukul	9-12 Bell Yard, London	020 7400 1800
Checa-Dover Miss Olivia	KBW, Leeds	0113 297 1200
Cheema Miss Parmjit Kaur	2 Hare Court, London	020 7353 3982
Cherrett Mr Darryl Joseph	Carmelite Chambers, London	020 7936 6300
Chidgey Mr David Gareth	Albion Chambers, Bristol	0117 927 2144
Chippeck Mr Stephen	5 King's Bench Walk, London	020 7353 5638
Chipperfield Mr Jeremy Steven	Cranford Chambers, London	020 7404 7454
Chodha Mr Tejpal Singh	Chambers of Mr T Chodha, Gravesend	01474 326666
Christie Mr Richard Hamish	2 Pump Court, London	020 7353 5597
Christie Mr Simon Paul William	Chavasse Court Chambers, Liverpool	0151 229 2030
Clare Miss Allison Jean	18 Red Lion Court, London	020 7520 6000
Clark Mr Dingle	Goldsmith Chambers, London	020 7353 6802
Clarke Miss Jessica Alice	Westgate Chambers, Lewes	01273 480510
Clarke Mr Nicholas Patrick James	18 St John Street, Manchester	0161 278 1800
Clarkson Mr Stuart James Macgregor	St Ive's Chambers, Birmingham	0121 236 0863
Claxton Mr Elroy Geraldo	23 Essex Street, London	020 7413 0353
	Old Bailey Chambers, London	020 3008 6404
Clegg Mr William	2 Bedford Row, London	020 7440 8888
Cockings Mr Giles Francis Sacheveral	Furnival Chambers, London	020 7405 3232
Cocks Mr David John	18 Red Lion Court, London	020 7520 6000
	18 Red Lion Court (Annexe), Chelmsford	01245 280880
Coffey Mr John Joseph	39 Park Square, Leeds	0113 245 6633
	3 Temple Gardens, London	020 7353 3102
Coles-Harrington Ms Frances Julia	2 Pump Court, London	020 7353 5597
Collins Miss Siobhan Ellen	Citadel Chambers, Birmingham	0121 233 8500
Coltart Mr Christopher Mccallum	2 Hare Court, London	020 7353 3982
Comb Mr David William	Trinity Chambers, Middlesbrough	01642 247569
	Trinity Chambers, Newcastle Upon Tyne	0191 232 1927
Comerton Miss Julie Anne	4 KBW, London	020 7822 8822
Common Mr Hamish Andrew	23 Essex Street, London	020 7413 0353
Compton Mr Benjamin Edward Welstead	Outer Temple Chambers, London	020 7353 6381
Conlon Mr Michael John Patrick	Harcourt Chambers, Milton Keynes	0845 123 1234
Connell Mr Edward Samuel	Five St Andrew's Hill, London	020 7332 5400
Connolly Mr Dominic Regan	Five St Andrew's Hill, London	020 7332 5400
Connolly Ms Deirdre Joan	Old Bailey Chambers, London	020 3008 6404

Name	Chambers	Telephone
Conrad Mr Alan David	Lincoln House Chambers, Manchester	0161 832 5701
	St Ive's Chambers, Birmingham	0121 236 0863
Cook Mr Paul Graham Whalley	Albion Chambers, Bristol	0117 927 2144
Cooke Mr Duncan Matthew	Atkinson Bevan Chambers, London	020 7353 2112
Cooper Miss Danielle Sophie	Tooks Chambers, London	020 7842 7575
Cooper Mr John Gordon	25 Bedford Row, London	020 7067 1500
Cooper Mr Paul Andrew	Portal Chambers, Llandysul	01559 395 292
Cornwall Miss Virginia Margaret	Albion Chambers, Bristol	0117 927 2144
Corre Mr Neil Bernard	Redbourne Chambers, London	020 8346 8524
Corsellis Mr Nicholas Robert Alexander	3 Temple Gardens, London	020 7353 3102
Costello Mr Paul James	Chambers of Mr Paul J Costello, Biggleswade	07846 016 399
Cotcher Miss Ann Louise	Farringdon Chambers, London	020 7089 5700
Cotter Mr Mark James	Five St Andrew's Hill, London	020 7332 5400
Cotter Mr Nicholas Andrew James Horlor	1 Paper Buildings, London	020 7353 3728
Cotton Mrs Heidi Elizabeth	Bank House Chambers, Sheffield	0114 275 1223
Cowley Mr Robert	No 8 Chambers, Birmingham	0121 236 5514
Cox Mr Jonathan Edward	KCH Garden Square, Nottingham	0115 941 8851
Crabb Miss Samantha Jill	Citadel Chambers, Birmingham	0121 233 8500
Crawley Mr Ross Alexander	Middle Temple Lane Chambers, London	020 7583 4352
Crinion Mr Charles Edward	1 Mitre Court Buildings, London	020 7452 8900
Croskell Mr Marcus James	East Anglian Chambers, Chelmsford	01473 214481
	East Anglian Chambers, Colchester	01473 214481
	East Anglian Chambers, Ipswich	01473 214481
	East Anglian Chambers, Norwich	01473 214481
Cross Mr Anthony Maurice	Lincoln House Chambers, Manchester	0161 832 5701
Crowe Mr Cameron	36 Bedford Row, London	020 7421 8000
Crowther Mr Thomas Edward	Apex, Cardiff	02920 232 032
Crowther Ms Lucy Ellen	Apex, Cardiff	02920 232 032
Culley Miss Laura Joan	Citadel Chambers, Birmingham	0121 233 8500
Culver Mr Edward James	4 King's Bench Walk, London	020 7822 7000
Culverhouse Miss Emily Anna Louise	Chambers of Miss E Culverhouse, Chesham	07813 007503
Daly Miss Orla Maire	5 King's Bench Walk, London	020 7353 5638
Darbishire Mr Adrian Munro	QEB Hollis Whiteman, London	020 7933 8855
Dashani Miss Sonal	15 New Bridge Street, London	020 7842 1900
Dassa Miss Regine	9 King's Bench Walk, London	020 7353 9564
Dave Miss Priya	3 Temple Gardens, London	020 7353 3102
Davenport Mr Richard Ian	Citadel Chambers, Birmingham	0121 233 8500
Davey Mr Neil Martin	Old Court Chambers, Middlesbrough	01642 232523
	39 Park Square, Leeds	0113 245 6633
	3 Temple Gardens, London	020 7353 3102
Davidge Miss Justine Marie	4 King's Bench Walk, London	020 7822 7000
Davidson Mr Andrew Edward	Citadel Chambers, Birmingham	0121 233 8500
Davies Miss Claire Suzanne	Farringdon Chambers, London	020 7089 5700
Davies Mr Henry Olusola	Trinity Chambers, Birmingham	0121 346 4672
Davies Mr Jonathan Norval	9-12 Bell Yard, London	020 7400 1800
Davis Miss Lucy-Victoria	Pump Court Chambers, London	020 7353 0711
	Pump Court Chambers, Swindon	01793 539899
	Pump Court Chambers, Winchester	01962 868 161
Davis Mr Adam David	Dyers Chambers, London	020 7404 1881
Davis Mr Simon John	St Philips Chambers, Birmingham	0121 246 7000
Davis Mr William Neal	Charter Chambers, London	020 7618 4400
Dawson Mr Richard Jon Foster	Lincoln House Chambers, Manchester	0161 832 5701
Day Mr Douglas Henry	Farrar's Building, London	020 7583 9241
De Burgos Mr Jamie Michael Abulafia	36 Bedford Row, London	020 7421 8000
Dean Miss Elizabeth Catherine	3 Temple Gardens, London	020 7353 3102
Dean Mr James Patrick	Goldsmith Chambers, London	020 7353 6802
Del Fabbro Mr Oscar	23 Essex Street, London	020 7413 0353
Delamere Miss Isabel Sarah	4 Breams Buildings, London	020 7092 1900

Barrister	Chambers	Telephone
Delany Ms Francesca	1 Mitre Court Buildings, London	020 7452 8900
Dempsey Miss Karen Marie	3 Temple Gardens, London	020 7353 3102
Denney Mr Stuart Henry Macdonald	Deans Court Chambers, Manchester	0161 214 6000
	Deans Court Chambers, Preston	01772 565 600
	Thomas More Chambers, London	020 7404 7000
Dennis Mr Mark Jonathan	6 King's Bench Walk, London	020 7583 0410
Dent Mr Stephen Robert Charles	Guildhall Chambers, Bristol	0117 930 9000
Desmond Mr Denis John	Cornwall Street Chambers, Birmingham	0121 233 7500
Devlin Mr Timothy Robert	Furnival Chambers, London	020 7405 3232
Dilliway-Parry Mr Guy William	5 King's Bench Walk, London	020 7353 5638
Dix Miss Rebecca	2 Bedford Row, London	020 7440 8888
Dixey Mr Ian Roger	Guildhall Chambers, Bristol	0117 930 9000
Dixon Mr David Steven	Sovereign Chambers, Leeds	0113 245 1841
Dixon Mr James Malcolm	No5 Chambers, Birmingham	0845 210 5555
	No5 Chambers, Bristol	0845 210 5555
	No5 Chambers, London	0845 210 5555
Doherty Mr Nicholas Brudenell	4 King's Bench Walk, London	020 7822 7000
Donne Mr Jeremy Nigel	QEB Hollis Whiteman, London	020 7933 8855
Donnelly Mr Stephen John	Dyers Chambers, London	020 7404 1881
Doran Mr Gerard Patrick	Lincoln House Chambers, Manchester	0161 832 5701
Dos Santos Mr Alexander	Charter Chambers, London	020 7618 4400
Douglass Mr Paul Stephen	9 King's Bench Walk, London	020 7353 9564
Dowden Mr Andrew Philip	Castle Chambers, Harrow-on-the-Hill	020 8423 6579
	Melbury House, Leicester	07801 037802
Dowse Ms Clare Olivia Mary	3 Temple Gardens, London	020 7353 3102
Drake Miss Rachel Alexia	13 King's Bench Walk, London	020 7353 7204
Draycott Mr Simon Douglas	Citadel Chambers, Birmingham	0121 233 8500
	Five St Andrew's Hill, London	020 7332 5400
Drew Mr Simon Patrick	No5 Chambers, Birmingham	0845 210 5555
	No5 Chambers, Bristol	0845 210 5555
	No5 Chambers, London	0845 210 5555
Dsane Miss Victoria Tsotsoo	Chambers of Miss Victoria Dsane, Sutton	020 8722 0990
Duck Mr Michael Charles	No5 Chambers, Birmingham	0845 210 5555
	No5 Chambers, Bristol	0845 210 5555
	No5 Chambers, London	0845 210 5555
Duffy Mr Derek James	St Paul's Chambers, Leeds	0113 245 5866
Dunn Miss Katherine Louise	Trinity Chambers, Middlesbrough	01642 247569
	Trinity Chambers, Newcastle Upon Tyne	0191 232 1927
Dunne Mr Anthony James	KBW, Leeds	0113 297 1200
Dunning Mr Francis John Grove	37 Park Square Chambers, Leeds	0113 243 9422
Dunstan Mr James Peter	St Philips Chambers, Birmingham	0121 246 7000
Dutt Miss Nisha	Middle Temple Lane Chambers, London	020 7583 4352
Dyble Mr Steven John	18 Red Lion Court, London	020 7520 6000
	18 Red Lion Court (Annexe), Chelmsford	01245 280880
Dye Mr John Geoffrey	Goldsmith Chambers, London	020 7353 6802
Earle Mr James Christopher Reginald St John	Fenners Chambers, Cambridge	01223 368761
Eastwood Miss Philippa Clemency Anne	Doughty Street Chambers, London	020 7404 1313
Eaton Mr James Bernard	Thomas More Chambers, London	020 7404 7000
Edington Mrs Fiona Anne Rider	Thomas More Chambers, London	020 7404 7000
Edmonds Mr Michael Jonathan	4 Breams Buildings, London	020 7092 1900
Edwards Miss Jennifer Mary	13 KBW, Oxford	01865 311066
	13 King's Bench Walk, London	020 7353 7204
Edwards Mr Dickon Harrison	5 Pump Court, London	020 7353 2532
Edwards Mr Jonathan William	Westgate Chambers, Lewes	01273 480510
Edwards Mr Matthew Stuart	East Anglian Chambers, Chelmsford	01473 214481
	East Anglian Chambers, Colchester	01473 214481
	East Anglian Chambers, Ipswich	01473 214481

Name	Chambers	Telephone
Edwards Mr Nigel Royston	St Paul's Chambers, Leeds	0113 245 5866
Egerton Miss Christine Anne	KBW, Leeds	0113 297 1200
Eissa Mr Adrian Nadir	25 Bedford Row, London	020 7067 1500
Elder Miss Fiona Ann Morag	Albion Chambers, Bristol	0117 927 2144
Elias Mr David	9 Park Place, Cardiff	029 2038 2731
Elliott Mr Edward Anthony John	Garden Court Chambers, London	020 7993 7600
Elliott Mr Eric Alan	Sovereign Chambers, Leeds	0113 245 1841
	Trinity Chambers, Middlesbrough	01642 247569
	Trinity Chambers, Newcastle Upon Tyne	0191 232 1927
	York Chambers, Newcastle Upon Tyne	0191 206 4677
Elliott Mr Jason	Dere Street Barristers, Newcastle Upon Tyne	0844 3351551
Elliott Ms Sarah Julia	Doughty Street Chambers, Bristol	01179 058 717
	Doughty Street Chambers, London	020 7404 1313
	Doughty Street Chambers, Manchester	0161 618 1066
Enoch Mr Dafydd Huw	Apex, Cardiff	02920 232 032
	23 Essex Street, London	020 7413 0353
Esprit Mr Benoit	Barristers Chambers, London	020 3417 6461
	Legis Chambers, Aylesbury	01296 431125
Etherington Mr David Charles Lynch	18 Red Lion Court, London	020 7520 6000
	18 Red Lion Court (Annexe), Chelmsford	01245 280880
Evans Mr Andrew David	St Philips Chambers, Birmingham	0121 246 7000
Evans Mr David Howard	Aspect Chambers, Birmingham	0121 222 2447
	Chambers of Andrew Mitchell QC, London	020 7440 9950
Evans Mr Philip	QEB Hollis Whiteman, London	020 7933 8855
Evans Mr Simeon Vaughan	St Johns Buildings, Manchester	0161 214 1500
	St Johns Buildings Liverpool, Liverpool	0151 243 6000
	16 Winckley Square, Preston	01772 256100
Fairclough Miss Lucy Helen	Northampton Chambers, Northampton	01604 636271
Falk Mr Charles Morton James	3 PB Barristers, London	020 7583 8055
Fama Mrs Gudrun Hildegard	Middle Temple Lane Chambers, London	020 7583 4352
Fapohunda Mrs Olukemi	Furnival Chambers, London	020 7405 3232
Farley Mr David Dunbar	St Johns Buildings, Manchester	0161 214 1500
	St Johns Buildings Liverpool, Liverpool	0151 243 6000
	16 Winckley Square, Preston	01772 256100
Farr Mr Philip Edward	1 Paper Buildings, London	020 7353 3728
Farrell Mr Simon Henry	3 Raymond Buildings, London	020 7400 6400
Farrelly Miss Catherine Louise	5 King's Bench Walk, London	020 7353 5638
Faure Walker Miss Julia Frances	2 Hare Court, London	020 7353 3982
Feest Mr Adam Sebastian	3 PB Barristers, Bournemouth	01202 292102
	3 PB Barristers, Bristol	0117 928 1520
	3 PB Barristers, London	020 7583 8055
	3 PB Barristers, Oxford	01865 793 736
	3 PB Barristers, Winchester	01962 868884
Fenny Mr Ian Charles	Guildhall Chambers, Bristol	0117 930 9000
Ferguson Mr Craig Charles	2 Hare Court, London	020 7353 3982
Ferguson Mr Stephen Michael	2 Bedford Row, London	020 7440 8888
Ferm Mr Rodney Eric	Broadway House Chambers, Bradford	01274 722560
	Broadway House Chambers, Leeds	0113 246 2600
Ferry-Swainson Mr Richard Joseph	2 Bedford Row, London	020 7440 8888
Field Mr Stephen Anthony	1 Pump Court, London	020 7842 7070
Fielding Mr Janick Raphael Alexander	4 King's Bench Walk, London	020 7822 7000
Finnigan Mr Peter Anthony	QEB Hollis Whiteman, London	020 7933 8855
Finucane Mr Brendan Godfrey Eamonn	Outer Temple Chambers, London	020 7353 6381

Name	Chambers	Telephone
Fish Mr David Thomas	Deans Court Chambers, Manchester	0161 214 6000
	Deans Court Chambers, Preston	01772 565 600
	Goldsmith Chambers, London	020 7353 6802
Fisher Mr Jervis Andrew	Citadel Chambers, Birmingham	0121 233 8500
Fisher Mr Richard Alan	Doughty Street Chambers, Bristol	01179 058 717
	Doughty Street Chambers, London	020 7404 1313
	Doughty Street Chambers, Manchester	0161 618 1066
Fishwick Mr Gregory David Philip Kyle	187 Fleet Street, London	020 7430 7430
Fitzgerald Mr Benedict Andrew	QEB Hollis Whiteman, London	020 7933 8855
Fitzgibbon Mr Francis George Herbert Dillon	Doughty Street Chambers, Bristol	01179 058 717
	Doughty Street Chambers, London	020 7404 1313
	Doughty Street Chambers, Manchester	0161 618 1066
Fitzgibbon Mr Neil Kevin	Carmelite Chambers, London	020 7936 6300
Fitzmaurice Mr Guy Edward Christian	Staple Inn Chambers, London	020 7242 5240
Fitzpatrick Mr Steven Mark	2 Pump Court, London	020 7353 5597
Fletcher Mr James Watford	Five St Andrew's Hill, London	020 7332 5400
Foinette Mr Ian	Five St Andrew's Hill, London	020 7332 5400
Follon Mr Daniel Richard Thomas	1 Gray's Inn Square, London	020 7405 0001
Ford Mr Mark Steven	Lincoln House Chambers, Manchester	0161 832 5701
Forshaw Miss Sarah Anne	5 King's Bench Walk, London	020 7353 5638
Forsyth Miss Samantha	No5 Chambers, Birmingham	0845 210 5555
	No5 Chambers, Bristol	0845 210 5555
	No5 Chambers, London	0845 210 5555
Forte Mr Timothy Axel	Dyers Chambers, London	020 7404 1881
Fortune Mr Peter Carl Michael	Guildhall Chambers Portsmouth, Portsmouth	023 9275 2400
	4 King's Bench Walk, London	020 7822 7000
Foulkes Miss Rebecca	5 Pump Court, London	020 7353 2532
Foulkes Mr Christopher David	2 Hare Court, London	020 7353 3982
Frame Mr Stuart James	Staple Inn Chambers, London	020 7242 5240
Frank Mr Ivor Richard Bainton	7 Bell Yard, London	020 7831 0636
Fraser Mr Mark-Anthony	Dyers Chambers, London	020 7404 1881
Freeman Miss Lisa Claire	Furnival Chambers, London	020 7405 3232
Fridd Mr Nicholas Timothy	Albion Chambers, Bristol	0117 927 2144
	Bell Yard Chambers, London	020 7306 9292
Friend Mr Mark Owen	Lincoln House Chambers, Manchester	0161 832 5701
Fryer Mr Nigel Mccrae	Queen Square Chambers, Bristol	0117 921 1966
Fryman Mr Neil	Lincoln House Chambers, Manchester	0161 832 5701
Frymann Mr Andrew Philip	187 Fleet Street, London	020 7430 7430
Fuad Mr Kerim	Chambers of Marion Smullen and Kerim Fuad QC, London	020 7427 4400
Fudge Mrs Sally Ruth	Furnival Chambers, London	020 7405 3232
Fullerton Mr Michael Andrew	7 Bell Yard, London	020 7831 0636
	Chambers of Mr Michael Fullerton, Hove	01273 772050
Furlong Mr Richard Craven	25 Bedford Row, London	020 7067 1500
Gadd Mr Adam Brian	Pump Court Chambers, London	020 7353 0711
	Pump Court Chambers, Winchester	01962 868 161
	Riverview Chambers, London	0844 225 3999
Gainer Mr Richard St Clair	St Margaret's Chambers, Twickenham	020 8241 3516
Gair Mr Christopher	King's Bench Chambers, Bournemouth	01202 250025
Ganesan Mr Muthupandi Peter	Furnival Chambers, London	020 7405 3232
Garcha Mr Gurdeep Singh	Citadel Chambers, Birmingham	0121 233 8500
Garlick Mr Paul Richard	Furnival Chambers, London	020 7405 3232
Gaskin Miss Leila	Charter Chambers, London	020 7618 4400
Gaskin Mr Francis John Gerald	4 Breams Buildings, London	020 7092 1900
Gau Mr Justin Charles	Pump Court Chambers, London	020 7353 0711
	Pump Court Chambers, Swindon	01793 539899
	Pump Court Chambers, Winchester	01962 868 161
Gaunt Miss Sarah Levina	36 Bedford Row, London	020 7421 8000
Gelbart Mr Geoff Alan	1 Gray's Inn Square, London	020 7405 0001

Gent Mr Matthew Thomas	Sovereign Chambers, Leeds	0113 245 1841
Gerasimidis Mr Nicolas	Guildhall Chambers, Bristol	0117 930 9000
Germain Mr Richard	Nine Bedford Row, London	020 7489 2727
German Miss Kelly Anne	Eastbourne Chambers, Eastbourne	01323 642102
Gerry Miss Felicity Ruth	36 Bedford Row, London	020 7421 8000
Gersch Mr Adam Nissen	Argent Chambers, London	020 7556 5500
Gibbs Mr Philip Mark	KCH Garden Square, Nottingham	0115 941 8851
Gilchrist Miss Naomi Roberta	St Philips Chambers, Birmingham	0121 246 7000
Gill Mr Rajinder Singh	Charter Chambers, London	020 7618 4400
Gillespie Mr Christopher Michael	2 Hare Court, London	020 7353 3982
Gillet Ms Gemma Louise	Dyers Chambers, London	020 7404 1881
Gladwell Mr Simon Mark	East Anglian Chambers, Ipswich	01473 214481
Glasgow Mr Oliver Edwin James	2 Hare Court, London	020 7353 3982
Glass Mr Anthony Trevor	QEB Hollis Whiteman, London	020 7933 8855
Gledhill Mr Lee Andre	Alexander Chambers, London	0845 652 0451/0854 652 0451
	Trident Barristers Chambers, Manchester	0161 663 3123
Gledhill Mr Simon Christopher	Thomas More Chambers, London	020 7404 7000
Gobir Mr Nuhu Garba	9 Park Place, Cardiff	029 2038 2731
Goddard Miss Suzanne Hazel	Lincoln House Chambers, Manchester	0161 832 5701
Godfrey Mr Howard Anthony	2 Bedford Row, London	020 7440 8888
Godfrey Mr Thomas William Netherton	23 Essex Street, London	020 7413 0353
Gofur Mr Abdul	Thomas More Chambers, London	020 7404 7000
Goldberg Mr Jonathan Jacob	Cobden House Chambers, Manchester	0161 833 6000
	North Square Chambers, London	020 8455 3735
Goldstein Mr Wayne Nathan	18 St John Street, Manchester	0161 278 1800
Gomulka Mr Michael Svend	25 Bedford Row, London	020 7067 1500
Goodall Miss Emma	Dyers Chambers, London	020 7404 1881
Goode Mr Julian Leigh Alexander	St Johns Buildings, Manchester	0161 214 1500
	St Johns Buildings Liverpool, Liverpool	0151 243 6000
	16 Winckley Square, Preston	01772 256100
Gooderham Miss Elizabeth Ann	Northampton Chambers, Northampton	01604 636271
Goodwin Mr Michael	Old Bailey Chambers, London	020 3008 6404
Goose Mr Julian Nicholas	2 Hare Court, London	020 7353 3982
	Zenith Chambers, Leeds	0113 245 5438
Goudie Mr William Martin Phillip	Charter Chambers, London	020 7618 4400
Gow Mr Henry	New Bailey Chambers, Liverpool	0151 236 9402
Gozem Mr Gaias	Lincoln House Chambers, Manchester	0161 832 5701
Grant Mr Chudi Paul	Kenworthy's Chambers, Manchester	0161 832 4036
Grant Mr Gary Steven	Francis Taylor Building, London	020 7353 8415
Gray Miss Jennifer	Chambers of Mr Ami Feder, London	020 7797 7788
	Chambers of Mr Ami Feder, London	020 7797 7788
	Lamb Building, Brighton	01273 820490
Gray Mr Peter Henry St John	5 Pump Court, London	020 7353 2532
Green Mr Garry Anthony	Tooks Chambers, London	020 7842 7575
Green Mr Jonathan Paul	Dyers Chambers, London	020 7404 1881
Greenfield Mr Peter Charles	King's Bench Chambers, Bournemouth	01202 250025
Greenwood Mr Alexander Barton	Apex, Cardiff	02920 232 032
Gregg Mr William Jonathan	St Paul's Chambers, Leeds	0113 245 5866
Grego Mr Kevin Christopher	Citadel Chambers, Birmingham	0121 233 8500
Grennan Mr Barry Edward	Kenworthy's Chambers, Manchester	0161 832 4036
Grey Mr Michael Henry John	Citadel Chambers, Birmingham	0121 233 8500
Griffin Miss Lynn Myfanwy	23 Essex Street, London	020 7413 0353
Griffin Mr Nicholas John	Five Paper Buildings, London	020 7583 6117
Griffiths Mr Hugh Robert James	Furnival Chambers, London	020 7405 3232
Griffiths Mr Peter	2 Bedford Row, London	020 7440 8888
	30 Park Place, Cardiff	029 2039 8421
Griffiths Mr Robert Norton	12 College Place, Southampton	023 8032 0320
Grunwald Mr Henry Cyril	Charter Chambers, London	020 7618 4400
Guest Mr Peter Liam	187 Fleet Street, London	020 7430 7430
Gurden Miss Alison Louise	1 Gray's Inn Square, London	020 7405 0001
Hadgill Mr Clinton Alexander	St Albans Chambers, St Albans	01727 843383

Name	Chambers	Telephone
Hadrill Mr Keith Paul	Furnival Chambers, London	020 7405 3232
Hall Mr Nicholas	Westgate Chambers, Lewes	01273 480510
Halliday-Davis Ms Deborah Lee	Carmelite Chambers, London	020 7936 6300
Hallowes Mr Rupert John Michael	3 Temple Gardens, London	020 7353 3102
Ham Mr Nicholas Treharne	Dyers Chambers, London	020 7404 1881
Hamblin Mr Nicholas Howard	Westgate Chambers, Lewes	01273 480510
Hamer Mr Charles Henry	Citadel Chambers, Birmingham	0121 233 8500
Hamilton Mr Nigel	Broadway House Chambers, Bradford	01274 722560
	Broadway House Chambers, Leeds	0113 246 2600
Hamilton-Shield Miss Anna-Maria	Charter Chambers, London	020 7618 4400
Hammett Mr Michael Greville	9 Park Place, Cardiff	029 2038 2731
Hanlon Mr James Tobias	Old Bailey Chambers, London	020 3008 6404
Hannam Mr Timothy James	Citadel Chambers, Birmingham	0121 233 8500
Hannant Miss Lisa Diane	5 Pump Court, London	020 7353 2532
Haque Mr Gazi Mosta Gawsal	Dollis Hill Chambers, London	020 8208 1663
Harbage Mr William John Hirons	36 Bedford Row, London	020 7421 8000
	37 Park Square Chambers, Leeds	0113 243 9422
Harding Mr Christopher James	Thomas More Chambers, London	020 7404 7000
Harding Mr Matthew Austin	39 Park Square, Leeds	0113 245 6633
Hardy Mr Maximilian John Lee	Nine Bedford Row, London	020 7489 2727
Hardyman Mr Matthew James	15 New Bridge Street, London	020 7842 1900
Hargreaves Mr Benjamin Thomas	Carmelite Chambers, London	020 7936 6300
Harounoff Mr David	9-12 Bell Yard, London	020 7400 1800
Harries Mr Mark Robert	Carmelite Chambers, London	020 7936 6300
Harrington Mr Timothy Mark	Citadel Chambers, Birmingham	0121 233 8500
Harris Miss Stella Cassandra Methven	Tooks Chambers, London	020 7842 7575
Harris Mr Adrian David	23 Essex Street, London	020 7413 0353
Harris Mr David Robert	St Albans Chambers, St Albans	01727 843383
Harris Mr James	Five St Andrew's Hill, London	020 7332 5400
Harris Mr Julian Gilbert Vaughan	Citadel Chambers, Birmingham	0121 233 8500
Harris Mr Wilbert Arthurlyn	Rowchester Chambers, Birmingham	0121 233 2327
Harris Ms Rebecca Elizabeth	QEB Hollis Whiteman, London	020 7933 8855
Harrison Mr John Foster	St Paul's Chambers, Leeds	0113 245 5866
Harrison Mr Paul John	13 KBW, Oxford	01865 311066
	13 King's Bench Walk, London	020 7353 7204
Harrison Mr Peter John	6 Pump Court, London	020 7797 8400
	6 Pump Court Chambers, Maidstone	01622 688094
Harvey Mr Stephen Frank	18 Red Lion Court, London	020 7520 6000
	18 Red Lion Court (Annexe), Chelmsford	01245 280880
Hashim Mr Mu'Min Iran Muhammad	Chambers of Marion Smullen and Kerim Fuad QC, London	020 7427 4400
	Paragon Chambers, London	020 3318 9988
Hassall Mr Craig Jonathan	Sovereign Chambers, Leeds	0113 245 1841
Hawes Mr Neil Ashley	Charter Chambers, London	020 7618 4400
Hawkes Mr Malcolm Alexander	Dyers Chambers, London	020 7404 1881
Hays Mr William Stormont	6 King's Bench Walk, London	020 7583 0410
Healy Miss Alexandra	9-12 Bell Yard, London	020 7400 1800
Hearnden Mr Richard Christopher	Furnival Chambers, London	020 7405 3232
Heeley Miss Michelle Louise	No5 Chambers, Birmingham	0845 210 5555
	No5 Chambers, Bristol	0845 210 5555
	No5 Chambers, London	0845 210 5555
Hegarty Mr Kevin John	St Philips Chambers, Birmingham	0121 246 7000
Hellman Mr Stephen Geoffrey	Chambers of Andrew Mitchell QC, London	020 7440 9950
Henderson Mr Ian Francis	Farringdon Chambers, London	020 7089 5700
Henderson Mr Lawrence Mark	9-12 Bell Yard, London	020 7400 1800
Henley Mr Andrew Michael	Furnival Chambers, London	020 7405 3232
Henry Mr Delroy	Citadel Chambers, Birmingham	0121 233 8500
Henson Miss Christine Ruth	Crown Office Row Chambers, Brighton	01273 625625
Henstock-Turner Mrs Sarah Elizabeth	College Chambers, Southampton	023 8023 0338
Henthorn Miss Kate Marie	7 Bell Yard, London	020 7831 0636
	18 St John Street, Manchester	0161 278 1800

Hett Mr James	The Chambers Of Mr Hett, Nottingham	0115 9313958/07727 688337
Hewitt Mr David Edward Miles	Five St Andrew's Hill, London	020 7332 5400
Heyworth Mr James Edward Watson	Lincoln House Chambers, Manchester	0161 832 5701
Hicks Mr Martin Leslie Arthur	2 Hare Court, London	020 7353 3982
Higgins Mr Daniel Malcolm Buhlea	Nine Bedford Row, London	020 7489 2727
Higginson Mr Peter St George	Charter Chambers, London	020 7618 4400
Higgs Mr Jonathan Alexander Cameron	5 King's Bench Walk, London	020 7353 5638
Hill Mr Max Benjamin Rowland	18 Red Lion Court, London	020 7520 6000
	18 Red Lion Court (Annexe), Chelmsford	01245 280880
Hill Mr Michael Gordon	Trinity Chambers, Middlesbrough	01642 247569
	Trinity Chambers, Newcastle Upon Tyne	0191 232 1927
Hillman Mr Basil	4 King's Bench Walk, London	020 7822 7000
Hillman Mr Gerard Paul	Carmelite Chambers, London	020 7936 6300
Hills Mr Timothy James	Albion Chambers, Bristol	0117 927 2144
Hilton Mr Alan John Howard	QEB Hollis Whiteman, London	020 7933 8855
Himsworth Mr Mark Stephen	Dyers Chambers, London	020 7404 1881
Hindmarsh Mr Luke Edward Thomas	9-12 Bell Yard, London	020 7400 1800
Hine Mr Charles Roderick John	King's Bench Chambers, Bournemouth	01202 250025
Hines Mr James Philip	3 Raymond Buildings, London	020 7400 6400
Hingston Mr Joe	Carmelite Chambers, London	020 7936 6300
Hinton Mr Neil Pearse	King's Bench Chambers, Bournemouth	01202 250025
Hirst Miss Kathryn Anne	Furnival Chambers, London	020 7405 3232
Hirst Miss Rebecca Elisabeth	Cobden House Chambers, Manchester	0161 833 6000
Hislop Mr David Seymour	Doughty Street Chambers, Bristol	01179 058 717
	Doughty Street Chambers, London	020 7404 1313
	Doughty Street Chambers, Manchester	0161 618 1066
Hobson Miss Laura Elise	Citadel Chambers, Birmingham	0121 233 8500
Hobson Miss Sally Anne	1 Paper Buildings, London	020 7353 3728
Hodgkiss Ms Suzanne Jane	43 Temple Row Chambers, Birmingham	0121 237 6035
Hogg The Right Hon Douglas Martin	Carmelite Chambers, London	020 7936 6300
	Hailsham Chambers, London	020 7643 5000
	37 Park Square Chambers, Leeds	0113 243 9422
Holborn Mr David Reginald	18 Red Lion Court, London	020 7520 6000
	18 Red Lion Court (Annexe), Chelmsford	01245 280880
Holland Miss Charlotte Kate	Lincoln House Chambers, Manchester	0161 832 5701
Holland Mr Ricky John	Lincoln House Chambers, Manchester	0161 832 5701
Hollis Mrs Kim	25 Bedford Row, London	020 7067 1500
Hood Mr David	Prince of Wales Chambers, London	020 7622 7415
Hooper Mr Gopal Arthur John	Thomas More Chambers, London	020 7404 7000
Hope Miss Heather Rosalind	Goldsmith Chambers, London	020 7353 6802
Hopper Mr Stephen John	Five Paper Buildings, London	020 7583 6117
Hornblower Mrs Sarah Patience	Rougemont Chambers, Exeter	01392 208484
Hossain Mr Mohammad Mozammel	187 Fleet Street, London	020 7430 7430
Howard Miss Nicola	25 Bedford Row, London	020 7067 1500
Howell Ms Claire Elizabeth Siobhan	36 Bedford Row, London	020 7421 8000
Hughes Mr William Lloyd	9-12 Bell Yard, London	020 7400 1800
Hugheston-Roberts Mr Charles Justin	4 Breams Buildings, London	020 7092 1900
Hunter Mr Timothy Charles	Atkinson Bevan Chambers, London	020 7353 2112
Huntley Miss Clare Helen Patricia	9-12 Bell Yard, London	020 7400 1800
Hurst Mr Brian	39 Park Square, Leeds	0113 245 6633
Hussain Miss Frida Khanam	Furnival Chambers, London	020 7405 3232
Hussain Mr Ghulam	Crown Office Row Chambers, Brighton	01273 625625
Hussain Mr Muhammad Altaf	Chambers of Mr M A Hussain, London	020 8679 2398
Hussain Mr Mukhtar	Lincoln House Chambers, Manchester	0161 832 5701
Hutchings Mr Richard Peter Mark	Chambers of Marion Smullen and Kerim Fuad QC, London	020 7427 4400
Ingram Mr Nigel Colquhoun	2 Bedford Row, London	020 7440 8888

Inyundo Mr Richard Kwame Swaka	6 King's Bench Walk, London	020 7583 0410
Irwin Mr Gavin David	Dyers Chambers, London	020 7404 1881
Islam Mr Aminul Ruhul	Chambers of Mr Aminul R. Islam, London	020 7247 1977
Islam Mr Mohammad Fakrul	18 Red Lion Court, London	020 7520 6000
Ivill Mr Scott Ashley	2 Hare Court, London	020 7353 3982
Jackson Mr Andrew Fraser	5 Pump Court, London	020 7353 2532
Jackson Mr Mark Joseph	No 8 Chambers, Birmingham	0121 236 5514
Jaffa Mr Ronald Mervyn	25 Bedford Row, London	020 7067 1500
Jafferjee Mr Aftab Asger	Atkinson Bevan Chambers, London	020 7353 2112
James Mr Roderick Ian	Charter Chambers, London	020 7618 4400
Jameson Mr Daniel Robert	Furnival Chambers, London	020 7405 3232
Janner The Hon Daniel Joseph Mitchell	23 Essex Street, London	020 7413 0353
	Exchange Chambers, Manchester	0161 833 2722
	St Philips Chambers, Birmingham	0121 246 7000
Jarratt Miss Alice Cordelia Betchworth	Carmelite Chambers, London	020 7936 6300
Jarvis Mr Paul	6 King's Bench Walk, London	020 7583 0410
Jefferies Mr Andrew	Dyers Chambers, London	020 7404 1881
	Westgate Chambers, Lewes	01273 480510
Jenkins Mr David Crofton	2 King's Bench Walk, London	020 7353 1746
Jenkins Mr Thomas Alun	2 Bedford Row, London	020 7440 8888
	Queen Square Chambers, Bristol	0117 921 1966
Jeremy Mr David Hugh Thomas	QEB Hollis Whiteman, London	020 7933 8855
John Mr Thomas Huw	Goresbrook Chambers, Milton Keynes	0845 123 1234
Johnson Miss Amanda	Exchange Chambers, Leeds	0113 203 1970
	Exchange Chambers, Liverpool	0151 236 7747
	Exchange Chambers, Manchester	0161 833 2722
Johnson Miss Zoe Elisabeth	QEB Hollis Whiteman, London	020 7933 8855
Johnson Ms Kathryn Margaret	Lincoln House Chambers, Manchester	0161 832 5701
Johnston Miss Anne-Marie	Carmelite Chambers, London	020 7936 6300
Jones Miss Claire-Louise	Chavasse Court Chambers, Liverpool	0151 229 2030
Jones Miss Jacinta Elizabeth Barrett	1 Mitre Court Buildings, London	020 7452 8900
Jones Mr Alun	St Paul's Chambers, Leeds	0113 245 5866
Jones Mr Gareth Edward	Lincoln House Chambers, Manchester	0161 832 5701
Jones Mr Mark Andrew	St Ive's Chambers, Birmingham	0121 236 0863
Jones Mr William John	2 Hare Court, London	020 7353 3982
Jones Mrs Hettie Georgia	Liberty Chambers, Tenby	01834 844458
Jones Ms Katie Laura	Lincoln House Chambers, Manchester	0161 832 5701
Jory Mr Richard Norman	9-12 Bell Yard, London	020 7400 1800
Joseph Mr Sellappah Job	Chambers of Mr S J Joseph, London	020 8809 3083/020 8802 9889
Joshi Mr Rajendra Jugatray	18 Red Lion Court, London	020 7520 6000
	18 Red Lion Court (Annexe), Chelmsford	01245 280880
Jowett Mr Timothy David Christian	9 Park Place, Cardiff	029 2038 2731
Judge Miss Parveen	1 Mitre Court Buildings, London	020 7452 8900
Kapila Miss Rachel Prakash	3 Raymond Buildings, London	020 7400 6400
Karaiskos Miss Maria	Old Bailey Chambers, London	020 3008 6404
Katz Mr Philip Alec Jackson	9-12 Bell Yard, London	020 7400 1800
Kaul Miss Kalyani	9-12 Bell Yard, London	020 7400 1800
Kayne Mr Charles Adrian	Carmelite Chambers, London	020 7936 6300
Kearney Mr John	Furnival Chambers, London	020 7405 3232
Keating Mr Dermot John	25 Bedford Row, London	020 7067 1500
Keeling Mr Adrian Francis	No5 Chambers, Birmingham	0845 210 5555
	No5 Chambers, Bristol	0845 210 5555
	No5 Chambers, London	0845 210 5555
Keith Mr Benjamin Charles Andrew	Five St Andrew's Hill, London	020 7332 5400
Kelly Mr Richard Bernard	East Anglian Chambers, Chelmsford	01473 214481
	East Anglian Chambers, Colchester	01473 214481
	East Anglian Chambers, Ipswich	01473 214481
	East Anglian Chambers, Norwich	01473 214481
Kennedy Miss Lucy Julia	QEB Hollis Whiteman, London	020 7933 8855
Kennedy Mr Peter Nicholas Dodgson	15 Winckley Square, Preston	01772 252828

Name	Chambers	Telephone
Kenny Mr Martin William	Walnut House, Exeter	01392 279751
Kent Mr Alan Peter	23 Essex Street, London	020 7413 0353
	Maidstone Chambers, Maidstone	01622 688592
Keogh Mr Richard Thomas	Farringdon Chambers, London	020 7089 5700
Kerr Mr Christopher Richard	2 Pump Court, London	020 7353 5597
Kessling Mr Christopher David	Chambers of Mr Christopher Kessling, Leicester	01509 890690
Kettle-Williams Miss Alexandra Margaret	Chambers of Marion Smullen and Kerim Fuad QC, London	020 7427 4400
Khalid Mr James	Goulds Green Chambers, Uxbridge	01895 422574
	Goulds Green Chambers, Uxbridge	01895 422574
Khalil Mr Karim Shakir	Octagon House, Norwich	01603 623186
	1 Paper Buildings, London	020 7353 3728
Khan Miss Abdah	Dyers Chambers, London	020 7404 1881
Khan Mr Ayoub	Chambers of Mr Ayoub Khan, Birmingham	07930 987202
Khan Mr Forz	Chambers of Mr F Khan, London	07854 109584
	6 King's Bench Walk, London	020 7353 4931
Khan Mr Mahmood Shafi	Luton Chambers, Luton	01582 598394
	Willesden Chambers, London	020 3273 1042
Khan Mr Shahnawaz Zulfiquar	1 Gray's Inn Square, London	020 7405 0001
Khan Mr Tahir	Broadway House Chambers, Bradford	01274 722560
	Broadway House Chambers, Leeds	0113 246 2600
Khan Mr Tariq Ali	Chambers of Mr T A Khan, Coventry	02476 666 400
Khan Mr Zarif	Dyers Chambers, London	020 7404 1881
King Mr Adam Henry Peter	QEB Hollis Whiteman, London	020 7933 8855
King Mr Gelaga Perry	2 Bedford Row, London	020 7440 8888
King Mr Graham Anthony	1 Gray's Inn Square, London	020 7405 0001
King Mr John Patrick	Nine Bedford Row, London	020 7489 2727
Kinnear Mr Jonathan Shea	9-12 Bell Yard, London	020 7400 1800
Kitchen Mr Simon Dugald Owen Ralph	Dyers Chambers, London	020 7404 1881
Knight Mr Benjamin James	Central Chambers, Manchester	0161 236 1133
Knight Mr Graeme Edward Verdon	7 Bell Yard, London	020 7831 0636
	Carmelite Chambers, London	020 7936 6300
	The Barristers Chambers, Address withheld	07966 056368
Krikler Mr Alexander Richard	4 Breams Buildings, London	020 7092 1900
Krushner Mr Damian Mark	Oakwood Chambers, London	07789 435485
Ladenburg Mr Guy Alexander	3 Raymond Buildings, London	020 7400 6400
Lahiffe Mr Martin Patrick Joseph	3 Temple Gardens, London	020 7353 3102
Lake Mr James Edward	St Paul's Chambers, Leeds	0113 245 5866
Lakha Mr Abbas	Nine Bedford Row, London	020 7489 2727
Lamb Mr Jeffrey Thomas	Westgate Chambers, Lewes	01273 480510
Lamb Mr John Richard	1 Pump Court, London	020 7842 7070
Lambert Mr Nigel Robert Woolf	Carmelite Chambers, London	020 7936 6300
Lane Miss Rachael Caroline	2 King's Bench Walk, London	020 7353 1746
Langevad Miss Claire Theresa Manuela	Chambers of Marion Smullen and Kerim Fuad QC, London	020 7427 4400
Langley Mr Charles Howard	2 Bedford Row, London	020 7440 8888
Larkin Mr Sean	QEB Hollis Whiteman, London	020 7933 8855
Lasker Mr Jeremy Stewart	Lincoln House Chambers, Manchester	0161 832 5701
Latymer Mr Tam	Chambers of Tam Latymer, London	020 7353 2795
Lau Miss Vanessa Hoi Chun	18 St John Street, Manchester	0161 278 1800
Lawrence Sir Ivan John	5 Pump Court, London	020 7353 2532
Lawton Mr Paul Anthony	Lincoln House Chambers, Manchester	0161 832 5701
	18 Red Lion Court, London	020 7520 6000
Le Fevre Miss Sarah Margaret	3 Raymond Buildings, London	020 7400 6400
Le Fort Mr Michael Cameron Raoul	King's Bench Chambers, Bournemouth	01202 250025
Leake Mr Stephen	Carmelite Chambers, London	020 7936 6300
Ledward Miss Jocelyn Victoria	QEB Hollis Whiteman, London	020 7933 8855
Lenaghan Mr Anthony	Dyers Chambers, London	020 7404 1881
Lennon Mr John Francis	23 Essex Street, London	020 7413 0353
Leonard Mr James Alexander	Outer Temple Chambers, London	020 7353 6381

Levett Miss Francesca Anna	Five St Andrew's Hill, London	020 7332 5400
Levinson Miss Jemma	1 Mitre Court Buildings, London	020 7452 8900
Lewiecki Miss Marie	Old Bailey Chambers, London	020 3008 6404
Lewington Miss Francesca Anna	Crown Office Row Chambers, Brighton	01273 625625
Lewis Mr Andrew Simon	4 Breams Buildings, London	020 7092 1900
Liddiard Mr Martin Thomas	No5 Chambers, Birmingham	0845 210 5555
	No5 Chambers, Bristol	0845 210 5555
	No5 Chambers, London	0845 210 5555
Light Prof Roy Alan	St John's Chambers, Bristol	0117 923 4700
Lindsay Mr Jeremy Mark Henry	37 Park Square Chambers, Leeds	0113 243 9422
Linehan Mr Stephen John	St Philips Chambers, Birmingham	0121 246 7000
Livingstone Mr Simon John	Thomas More Chambers, London	020 7404 7000
Lloyd Mr Benjamin John	6 King's Bench Walk, London	020 7583 0410
Lloyd-Eley Mr Andrew James	Old Bailey Chambers, London	020 3008 6404
Lloyd-Jones Mr John Benedict	36 Bedford Row, London	020 7421 8000
Lodge Mr Hugo Daniel Paul	Atkinson Bevan Chambers, London	020 7353 2112
Lofthouse Mr James	1 Gray's Inn Square, London	020 7405 0001
Logan Mr Graeme Alexander	4 Breams Buildings, London	020 7092 1900
	15 New Bridge Street, London	020 7842 1900
Longhurst-Woods Ms Lesley	2 Louisa Close, London	020 8985 8716
Lopez Mr Juan Nemesio	Francis Taylor Building, London	020 7353 8415
Lowe Mr Christopher John	KCH Garden Square, Nottingham	0115 941 8851
Lowe Mr Rupert William Manley	Guildhall Chambers, Bristol	0117 930 9000
Lownds Mr Peter Alexander	Doughty Street Chambers, Bristol	01179 058 717
	Doughty Street Chambers, London	020 7404 1313
	Doughty Street Chambers, Manchester	0161 618 1066
Lucking Mrs Adrienne Simone	36 Bedford Row, London	020 7421 8000
Lule Miss Jacqueline	1 Mitre Court Buildings, London	020 7452 8900
Lynch Mr Jerome	Charter Chambers, London	020 7618 4400
Lyons Mr David Wakefield	King's Bench Chambers, Bournemouth	01202 250025
	2 Pump Court, London	020 7353 5597
MacFarlane Mr Andrew Lennox	Colleton Chambers, Exeter	01392 274898
MacKie Ms Jeannie	Doughty Street Chambers, Bristol	01179 058 717
	Doughty Street Chambers, London	020 7404 1313
	Doughty Street Chambers, Manchester	0161 618 1066
MacLean Watt Mr Hector William Grantham	4 Breams Buildings, London	020 7092 1900
Magee Mr Michael James	Fenners Chambers, Cambridge	01223 368761
Magee Mr Samuel Cairns	2 Bedford Row, London	020 7440 8888
Maggs Mr Patrick Terence	15 New Bridge Street, London	020 7842 1900
Maginn Miss Olivia Maria	New Walk Chambers, Leicester	0871 200 1298/0116 255 9144
Mahmood Mr Abid	Central Chambers, Manchester	0161 236 1133
	No5 Chambers, Birmingham	0845 210 5555
	No5 Chambers, Bristol	0845 210 5555
	No5 Chambers, London	0845 210 5555
Mahmood Mr Imran Waseem	5 Pump Court, London	020 7353 2532
Mahtab Miss Sumita Laila-Al	7 Bell Yard, London	020 7831 0636
Mainwaring Mr Robert Paul Clason	Portal Chambers, Llandysul	01559 395 292
Maitland Mr Marc Claude	King's Bench Chambers, Bournemouth	01202 250025
Malcolm Miss Helen Katharine Lucy	3 Raymond Buildings, London	020 7400 6400
Malone Mr David John	1 Gray's Inn Square, London	020 7405 0001
Mandalia Mr Vinesh Lalji	St Philips Chambers, Birmingham	0121 246 7000
Manley Miss Lesley Patrica	Chambers of Marion Smullen and Kerim Fuad QC, London	020 7427 4400
Manley Ms Hilary	St Paul's Chambers, Leeds	0113 245 5866
	16 Winckley Square, Preston	01772 256100
Mann Mr Jasvir Singh	No5 Chambers, Birmingham	0845 210 5555
	No5 Chambers, Bristol	0845 210 5555
	No5 Chambers, London	0845 210 5555
Mann Mr Jonathan Simon	25 Bedford Row, London	020 7067 1500
Mannion Mr John Dennis	Tolzey Chambers, Bristol	
Mannion Ms Amy Elisabeth	9-12 Bell Yard, London	020 7400 1800
	1 Crown Office Row, London	020 7797 7500
Mansell Mr Jason Francis Guy	Seven Bedford Row, London	020 7242 3555

Name	Chambers	Telephone
Maroof Ms Lara Anne	Charter Chambers, London	020 7618 4400
Marshall Miss Vanessa Juliette	Seven Bedford Row, London	020 7242 3555
Martin Mr James Stephen	5 King's Bench Walk, London	020 7353 5638
Maselli Mr Mauro	Chambers of Mr M Maselli, Peterborough	07786 320064
	Priestgate Chambers, Peterborough	01733 865 042
Massey Miss Stella Maria	Central Chambers, Manchester	0161 236 1133
Masters Mr Alan Bruce Raymond	1 Pump Court, London	020 7842 7070
Mather Mr Nicholas Ian Stewart	Furnival Chambers, London	020 7405 3232
Mawdsley Mr David John	Chambers of Mr David Mawdsley, Southport	01704 565 387
Mawrey Ms Eleanor Frances	The Chambers of Grahame Aldous QC, London	020 7832 0500
Maxwell Mr Adrian Robert John	St John's Chambers, Bristol	0117 923 4700
May Mr Christopher John	Five St Andrew's Hill, London	020 7332 5400
Mayo Mr Simon Peter	187 Fleet Street, London	020 7430 7430
McCarthy Miss Tara Mia Inger	Thomas More Chambers, London	020 7404 7000
McCarthy Mr Martin Raymond	Farringdon Chambers, London	020 7089 5700
McCulloch Miss Fiona Catharine Jane	Middle Temple Lane Chambers, London	020 7583 4352
McCullough Miss Louise Clare	Chambers of Mr Ami Feder, London	020 7797 7788
	Chambers of Mr Ami Feder, London	020 7797 7788
	Lamb Building, Brighton	01273 820490
McDonald Miss Janet	9 Park Place, Cardiff	029 2038 2731
McDonnell Mr John Beresford William	13 Old Square Chambers, London	020 7831 4445
McFarlane Miss Cynthia Julliett	10 King's Bench Walk, London	020 7353 7742
McGhee Mr Philip James	QEB Hollis Whiteman, London	020 7933 8855
McGowan Miss Maura Patricia	2 Bedford Row, London	020 7440 8888
	Lincoln House Chambers, Manchester	0161 832 5701
McKiernan Mr Edward Joseph	Farringdon Chambers, London	020 7089 5700
McKone Mr Mark Desmond	Sovereign Chambers, Leeds	0113 245 1841
McLinden Mr John Vincent Barry	Field Court Chambers, London	020 7405 6114
McNally Mr John Joseph	Dyers Chambers, London	020 7404 1881
McNeill Mr David Martin	Five St Andrew's Hill, London	020 7332 5400
McNicholas Mr Christopher John	Goresbrook Chambers, Milton Keynes	0845 123 1234
Meegan Mr Trevor Leo	Citadel Chambers, Birmingham	0121 233 8500
Meeke Mr Robert Martin James	Colleton Chambers, Exeter	01392 274898
Menary Mr Alexander William Christopher	KBW, Leeds	0113 297 1200
Mendelle Mr Paul Michael	25 Bedford Row, London	020 7067 1500
Menon Mr Rajiv	Garden Court Chambers, London	020 7993 7600
Meredith Mr Christopher William	Furnival Chambers, London	020 7405 3232
Merz Mr Richard James	9-12 Bell Yard, London	020 7400 1800
Metzer Mr Anthony David Erwin	Argent Chambers, London	020 7556 5500
Metzger Mr Kevin Albert	11 Gray's Inn Square Chambers, London	020 7405 6879
Miah Mr Anawar Babul	Great James Street Chambers, London	020 7440 4949
Midgley Miss Anna Victoria Jane	Albion Chambers, Bristol	0117 927 2144
Miller Miss Wendy Anne May	Citadel Chambers, Birmingham	0121 233 8500
Miller Mr David Robin	Furnival Chambers, London	020 7405 3232
Millett Mr Kenneth James	2 Hare Court, London	020 7353 3982
Milne Mr Alexander Hugh	18 Red Lion Court, London	020 7520 6000
	18 Red Lion Court (Annexe), Chelmsford	01245 280880
Milne Mr Richard James	23 Essex Street, London	020 7413 0353
Milroy Miss Caroline	Thomas More Chambers, London	020 7404 7000
Milsom Mrs Catherine Mary	Argent Chambers, London	020 7556 5500
Misner Mr Philip Lawrence Ian	4 Breams Buildings, London	020 7092 1900
Mitchell Mr Alistair Stephen Fabian	49 Chambers, Bridgnorth	01746 761545
Mitchell Mr Andrew Robert	Chambers of Andrew Mitchell QC, London	020 7440 9950
Mitchell Mr Jonathan Stuart	25 Bedford Row, London	020 7067 1500

C

Mitchell Mr Jonathan	1 Gray's Inn Square, London	020 7405 0001
	Holborn Chambers, London	020 7242 6060
Mitchell Mr Keith Arno	Chambers of Andrew Mitchell QC, London	020 7440 9950
Modgil Miss Sangita	Carmelite Chambers, London	020 7936 6300
Molloy Miss Siobhan Angela	Chambers of Marion Smullen and Kerim Fuad QC, London	020 7427 4400
Molloy Mr Andrew Joseph	St Ive's Chambers, Birmingham	0121 236 0863
Mooney Mr Stephen John	Albion Chambers, Bristol	0117 927 2144
Moore Mr James Anthony	Goldsmith Chambers, London	020 7353 6802
	39 Park Square, Leeds	0113 245 6633
Moorhouse Mr Brendon Scott	Guildhall Chambers, Bristol	0117 930 9000
Mootien Miss Davina Poollay	4 Breams Buildings, London	020 7092 1900
Moran Mr Christopher John	39 Park Square, Leeds	0113 245 6633
Moran Mr Patrick Michael	15 New Bridge Street, London	020 7842 1900
Morris Mr Ben	Chavasse Court Chambers, Liverpool	0151 229 2030
Morris Mr Ieuan John	9 Park Place, Cardiff	029 2038 2731
Morris Mr Philip James	39 Park Square, Leeds	0113 245 6633
Morris Ms Johanna	Chambers of Marion Smullen and Kerim Fuad QC, London	020 7427 4400
Morrison Mr Christopher Quintin	Old Court Chambers, Middlesbrough	01642 232523
Moses Mr Stephen Colin	Furnival Chambers, London	020 7405 3232
Moss Mr Richard John	4 King's Bench Walk, London	020 7822 7000
Mostafa Miss Margia	2 Pump Court, London	020 7353 5597
Mousley Mr William Howard	2 King's Bench Walk, London	020 7353 1746
Mullarkey Mr Ian	KBW, Leeds	0113 297 1200
Muller Mr Antonie Sean	Citadel Chambers, Birmingham	0121 233 8500
Mullins Mr Mark Lovel Rupert	Five St Andrew's Hill, London	020 7332 5400
Munir Dr Ashley Edward	Five St Andrew's Hill, London	020 7332 5400
Munro Mr David Philip	St Philips Chambers, Birmingham	0121 246 7000
Muquit Mr Mohammed Shuyeb	1 Mitre Court Buildings, London	020 7452 8900
Murphy Mr Michael Patrick	Central Chambers, Manchester	0161 236 1133
	10 King's Bench Walk, London	020 7353 7742
Murray Mr Daniel Evan Duncan	Old Bailey Chambers, London	020 3008 6404
Murray Mr Lance John Mole	Nexus Chambers, London	020 7404 1147/020 7831 8309
Mutch Mr Iain Richard Alistair	Palmyra Chambers, Warrington	01925 444919
Myers Mr Benjamin John	Exchange Chambers, Liverpool	0151 236 7747
	Exchange Chambers, Manchester	0161 833 2722
Mylvaganam Ms Tanoo	1 Gray's Inn Square, London	020 7405 0001
Mytton Mr Paul Vincent	St Philips Chambers, Birmingham	0121 246 7000
Nadim Mr Ahmed	Lincoln House Chambers, Manchester	0161 832 5701
Nasim Mr Zia-Ul-Mustafa	Milestone Chambers, London	
Needham Mrs Julia Cherry	10 King's Bench Walk, London	020 7353 7742
Newbold Mr Michael Paul	9-12 Bell Yard, London	020 7400 1800
Newcomb Mr Quinton John	1 Paper Buildings, London	020 7353 3728
Newman Mr Alan Ronald Harvey	Argent Chambers, London	020 7556 5500
Newton Mr Andrew David	187 Fleet Street, London	020 7430 7430
Newton-Price Mr James Edward	Pump Court Chambers, London	020 7353 0711
	Pump Court Chambers, Swindon	01793 539899
	Pump Court Chambers, Winchester	01962 868 161
Nicholls Mr Christopher Benjamin	Citadel Chambers, Birmingham	0121 233 8500
Nicholls Mr Clive Victor	3 Raymond Buildings, London	020 7400 6400
Nicholls Mr Colin Alfred Arthur	3 Raymond Buildings, London	020 7400 6400
Nicholson Mr Thomas Edward Cyril	Atkinson Bevan Chambers, London	020 7353 2112
Nixon Miss Abigail Lisa Barbara	Citadel Chambers, Birmingham	0121 233 8500
Norton Mr Giles	Enigma Chambers, Sheffield	07779 576499
	Holborn Chambers, London	020 7242 6060
Nsugbe Mr Oba Eric	Pump Court Chambers, London	020 7353 0711
	Pump Court Chambers, Swindon	01793 539899
	Pump Court Chambers, Winchester	01962 868 161
Nuttall Mr Andrew Peter	Lincoln House Chambers, Manchester	0161 832 5701
Nwosu Miss Sheryl Ada	4 Breams Buildings, London	020 7092 1900
Oakley Miss Louise Michelle	2 Bedford Row, London	020 7440 8888

O'Byrne Mr Andrew John Martin	St Johns Buildings, Manchester	0161 214 1500
	St Johns Buildings Liverpool, Liverpool	0151 243 6000
	16 Winckley Square, Preston	01772 256100
O'Connor Mr Patrick Michael Joseph	Doughty Street Chambers, Bristol	01179 058 717
	Doughty Street Chambers, London	020 7404 1313
	Doughty Street Chambers, Manchester	0161 618 1066
O'Connor Ms Charlotte Jane Andrews	Nine Bedford Row, London	020 7489 2727
O'Donoghue Mr Hugh Vincent	Carmelite Chambers, London	020 7936 6300
Offenbach Mr Roger Leon	25 Bedford Row, London	020 7067 1500
Offer Mr Alexander	Garden Court Chambers, London	020 7993 7600
	Park Court Chambers, Leeds	0113 243 3277
O'Gorman Mr Christopher Francis	Cornwall Street Chambers, Birmingham	0121 233 7500
Ogunbusola Mr Victor Olaniyi	Chambers of Victor Ogumbusola, Basildon	07413 634231
O'Kane Miss Sarah Caroline	Argent Chambers, London	020 7556 5500
Oldfield Miss Jane Lisa Catherine	18 Red Lion Court, London	020 7520 6000
	18 Red Lion Court (Annexe), Chelmsford	01245 280880
Oldham Mrs Frances Mary Theresa	36 Bedford Row, London	020 7421 8000
	37 Park Square Chambers, Leeds	0113 243 9422
Omideyi Miss Anuoluwapo Iyanu	Furnival Chambers, London	020 7405 3232
Onalaja Mr James Oluwatosin	2 Pump Court, London	020 7353 5597
O'Neill Miss Sally Jane	Furnival Chambers, London	020 7405 3232
O'Neill Mr Brian Patrick	2 Hare Court, London	020 7353 3982
Ong Miss Grace Yu Mae	Argent Chambers, London	020 7556 5500
Onipede Dr Victor Olusegun	Chambers of Dr V O Onipede, London	07956 207159
Oommen Mr Jacob	Chambers of Mr Jacob Oommen, East Barnet	07958 680272
Orchard Miss Cathlyn Esther	Citadel Chambers, Birmingham	0121 233 8500
Orchard Mr Anthony Edward	Carmelite Chambers, London	020 7936 6300
Osborne Mr David Thomas	Chambers of Mr D T Osborne, Taunton	01823 400 705
Ossack Mrs Tanya Rachelle Elise	3 Temple Gardens, London	020 7353 3102
Otchie Mr Andrew Akuafo	12 Old Square Chambers, London	020 7404 0875
O'Toole Mr Bartholomew Vincent	5 King's Bench Walk, London	020 7353 5638
Owen Miss Carys	18 Red Lion Court, London	020 7520 6000
	18 Red Lion Court (Annexe), Chelmsford	01245 280880
Owen Mr Timothy Wynn	Matrix Chambers, London	020 7404 3447
Owen Ms Elen Mai	Linenhall Chambers, Chester	01244 348282
Owusu-Yianoma Mr David Kwasi Dartey	1 Mitre Court Buildings, London	020 7452 8900
Ozin Mr Paul David	23 Essex Street, London	020 7413 0353
Page Mr Jonathan Rowland Thomas	Carmelite Chambers, London	020 7936 6300
Paley Ms Ruth Theresa Elizabeth	23 Essex Street, London	020 7413 0353
Pallo Mr Simon Russel	Bank House Chambers, Sheffield	0114 275 1223
Palmer Miss Claire Louise	Thomas More Chambers, London	020 7404 7000
Palmer Mr Edward James	Regent Chambers, Stoke On Trent	01782 286666
Palmer Mr Nathan Emmanuel	5 Pump Court, London	020 7353 2532
Panagiotopoulou Miss Tania	Staple Inn Chambers, London	020 7242 5240
Pande Miss Kakoly	2 Dr Johnson's Buildings, London	020 7936 2613
Panton Mr William Dwight	Amethyst Chambers, London	020 7936 4966
Paraskos Mr Paraskevakis Christakis	11 Gray's Inn Square Chambers, London	020 7405 6879
Pardoe Mr Matthew James	Dyers Chambers, London	020 7404 1881
Pardoe Mr Rupert Adam Corin	23 Essex Street, London	020 7413 0353
Pascoe Ms Soraya	1 Gray's Inn Square, London	020 7405 0001
Patel Mr Yasin Ahmed	25 Bedford Row, London	020 7067 1500
Paton Mr Ian Francis	QEB Hollis Whiteman, London	020 7933 8855

Name	Chambers	Telephone
Patterson Mr Stewart	Pump Court Chambers, London	020 7353 0711
	Pump Court Chambers, Swindon	01793 539899
	Pump Court Chambers, Winchester	01962 868 161
Pawson-Pounds Mr Daniel James	6 King's Bench Walk, London	020 7583 0410
Payne Mr Geoffrey Donald Stephen	25 Bedford Row, London	020 7067 1500
Peddie Mr Ian James Crofton	Garden Court Chambers, London	020 7993 7600
	St Johns Buildings Liverpool, Liverpool	0151 243 6000
	Westgate Chambers, Lewes	01273 480510
Pedro Mr Terry Adebisi	1 Pump Court, London	020 7842 7070
Peet Mr Andrew Geraint	Chambers of Mr Andrew Peet, Leicester	07966 238437
Penny Miss Abigail Sarah Prudence	4 Breams Buildings, London	020 7092 1900
Pentol Mr Simon Alex	25 Bedford Row, London	020 7067 1500
Perian Mr Steven	3 Temple Gardens, London	020 7353 3102
Perrins Mr Gregory Lloyd	1 Paper Buildings, London	020 7353 3728
Perry Mr Lewis Kenneth	Rowchester Chambers, Birmingham	0121 233 2327
Persaud Dr Marcia Chitroutie	1 Gray's Inn Square, London	020 7405 0001
Petersen Mr Thomas James	Goldsmith Chambers, London	020 7353 6802
Phillips Miss Emma Louise	1 Pump Court, London	020 7842 7070
Phillips Mr Simon Benjamin	Francis Taylor Building, London	020 7353 8415
	Park Court Chambers, Leeds	0113 243 3277
Pickup Mr James Kenneth	2 Hare Court, London	020 7353 3982
	Lincoln House Chambers, Manchester	0161 832 5701
Pierpoint Miss Katherine Anne	Lincoln House Chambers, Manchester	0161 832 5701
Pigot Miss Diana Marguerite	2 Pump Court, London	020 7353 5597
Pinkus Miss Molly Carla	Farringdon Chambers, London	020 7089 5700
Pitt-Lewis Mrs Janet Rebecca	Cornwall Street Chambers, Birmingham	0121 233 7500
	Cornwall Street Chambers, Shrewsbury	01743 363 611/0121 233 7500
Pitts Miss Emily Odette	Colleton Chambers, Exeter	01392 274898
Plowright Mr Joseph Edward	1 Gray's Inn Square, London	020 7405 0001
Polnay Mr Jonathan Samuel	5 King's Bench Walk, London	020 7353 5638
Pope Miss Anna	Linenhall Chambers, Chester	01244 348282
Pople Miss Alison Ruth	2 Bedford Row, London	020 7440 8888
Porter Mr Jamie Robert	King's Bench Chambers, Bournemouth	01202 250025
Potter Rev Harry Drummond	25 Bedford Row, London	020 7067 1500
Powell Mr Oliver Jonathan	3 PB Barristers, London	020 7583 8055
Power Mr Archangelo Carlo	2 Bedford Row, London	020 7440 8888
Power Ms Alexia Clare	Furnival Chambers, London	020 7405 3232
Powis Miss Samantha Inez	Citadel Chambers, Birmingham	0121 233 8500
Pownall Mr Stephen Orlando Fletcher	2 Hare Court, London	020 7353 3982
Preston Miss Kim Deborah	4 King's Bench Walk, London	020 7822 7000
Price Mr Albert John	23 Essex Street, London	020 7413 0353
Price Mr Andrew Robert	Dyers Chambers, London	020 7404 1881
Prior Mr Paul Stephen	36 Bedford Row, London	020 7421 8000
Prior Mrs Mary	36 Bedford Row, London	020 7421 8000
Prokofiev Mr Sergey	Lincoln House Chambers, Manchester	0161 832 5701
Puar Mr Mikhael	30 Park Place, Cardiff	029 2039 8421
Purnell Mr Paul Oliver	Farringdon Chambers, London	020 7089 5700
Pyne Mr Russell David	2 King's Bench Walk, London	020 7353 1746
Quinlan Mr Christopher John	Guildhall Chambers, Bristol	0117 930 9000
Quinn Mr Tomas Anthony	4 King's Bench Walk, London	020 7822 7000
Quirke Mr Gerard Martin	Citadel Chambers, Birmingham	0121 233 8500
Radford Mrs Nadine Poggioli	187 Fleet Street, London	020 7430 7430
Rafferty Miss Angela Margaret Mary	1 Paper Buildings, London	020 7353 3728
Rafter Miss Kathryn Michelle	KBW, Leeds	0113 297 1200
Raggatt Mr Timothy Walter Harold	4 King's Bench Walk, London	020 7822 7000
	St Philips Chambers, Birmingham	0121 246 7000
Rahman Mr Anis	12 Old Square Chambers, London	020 7404 0875
Rai Miss Puneet Kaur	Thomas More Chambers, London	020 7404 7000
Ramasamy Mr Selvaraju	QEB Hollis Whiteman, London	020 7933 8855
Ramble Mr Donald Robert Louis	Five St Andrew's Hill, London	020 7332 5400

Ramzan Mr Mohammed Anwar	Great James Street Chambers, London	020 7440 4949
Rana Mr Mohammed Akram	Clapham Law Chambers, London	020 7978 8482
Randall Mrs Rebecca	25 Bedford Row, London	020 7067 1500
Raw Mr Edward	Tanfield Chambers, London	020 7421 5300
Rawat Miss Houzla Bibi Mahmad	Carmelite Chambers, London	020 7936 6300
Real Miss Kirsty Nichola	Albion Chambers, Bristol	0117 927 2144
Reece Mr Brian Alfred William	187 Fleet Street, London	020 7430 7430
Rees Mr Jonathan David	2 Hare Court, London	020 7353 3982
Reevell Mr Simon Justin	39 Park Square, Leeds	0113 245 6633
Reevell Mrs Louise Marie	39 Park Square, Leeds	0113 245 6633
Reiff-Musgrove Miss Kaja	Dyers Chambers, London	020 7404 1881
Reiz Mr Stanley	Carmelite Chambers, London	020 7936 6300
Rendle Mr Jeremy Mark	9 King's Bench Walk, London	020 7353 9564
Renouf Mr Gerard John Peter	2 Pump Court, London	020 7353 5597
Renvoize Mr Edward Philip	No.6 Park Square, Leeds	0113 245 9763
	1 Paper Buildings, London	020 7353 3728
Reynolds Mr John Adam	King's Bench Chambers, Bournemouth	01202 250025
Rhodes Miss Amanda Louise	Unity Street Chambers, Bristol	0117 906 9789
Rhodes Mr Nicholas Piers	Charter Chambers, London	020 7618 4400
Rhodes Mr Robert Elliott	Outer Temple Chambers, London	020 7353 6381
	Principal Chambers, Sevenoaks	0845 209 8080
	St Philips Chambers, Birmingham	0121 246 7000
Richards Mr David James Martin	3 PB Barristers, Bournemouth	01202 292102
	3 PB Barristers, Bristol	0117 928 1520
	3 PB Barristers, London	020 7583 8055
	3 PB Barristers, Oxford	01865 793 736
	3 PB Barristers, Winchester	01962 868884
Richardson Mr Alistair Paul George	6 King's Bench Walk, London	020 7583 0410
Richardson Mr Paul Andrew	1 Gray's Inn Square, London	020 7405 0001
Richmond Mr Bernard Grant	Central Chambers, Manchester	0161 236 1133
	Chambers of Mr Ami Feder, London	020 7797 7788
	Chambers of Mr Ami Feder, London	020 7797 7788
Rickarby Mr William Edmund	Cornwall Street Chambers, Birmingham	0121 233 7500
Riggs Miss Samantha	25 Bedford Row, London	020 7067 1500
Rimmer Mr Anthony Michael	187 Fleet Street, London	020 7430 7430
Rimmer Mr Nicholas Patrick Edward	23 Essex Street, London	020 7413 0353
Rinder Mr Robert Michael	2 Hare Court, London	020 7353 3982
Rippon Mr Simon John	Citadel Chambers, Birmingham	0121 233 8500
Ritchie Miss Shauna	2 Bedford Row, London	020 7440 8888
Riza Mr Alper Ali	Goldsmith Chambers, London	020 7353 6802
Roberts Miss Lisa	Lincoln House Chambers, Manchester	0161 832 5701
Roberts Mr Timothy David	Fountain Chambers, Middlesbrough	01642 804040
	QEB Hollis Whiteman, London	020 7933 8855
Robertshaw Mr Martin Andrew	39 Park Square, Leeds	0113 245 6633
Robinson Miss Claire Maria	Charter Chambers, London	020 7618 4400
Robinson Mr Nicholas James Lansdale	3 PB Barristers, Bournemouth	01202 292102
	3 PB Barristers, Bristol	0117 928 1520
	3 PB Barristers, London	020 7583 8055
	3 PB Barristers, Oxford	01865 793 736
	3 PB Barristers, Winchester	01962 868884
Roche Mr Patrick Richard Redmond	Tooks Chambers, London	020 7842 7575
Rogers Mr Michael Peter	Chambers of Mr Ami Feder, London	020 7797 7788
	Chambers of Mr Ami Feder, London	020 7797 7788
Rooke Mr Alexander John Giles	Argent Chambers, London	020 7556 5500
Rooney Mr Paul	New Court Chambers, Newcastle Upon Tyne	0191 232 1980
	QEB Hollis Whiteman, London	020 7933 8855
Rose Miss Pamela Susan	1 Mitre Court Buildings, London	020 7452 8900
Rosen Mr Jonathan Leon	1 Gray's Inn Square, London	020 7405 0001
Ross Mr Gordon Macrae	3 Temple Gardens, London	020 7353 3102
Roughton Mr Ashley Wentworth	Hogarth Chambers, London	020 7404 0404
Rouse Mr Justin Clive Douglas	Nine Bedford Row, London	020 7489 2727

Row Mr Charles Philip	Queen Square Chambers, Bristol	0117 921 1966
Rowe Miss Freya Emily Beatrice	Thomas More Chambers, London	020 7404 7000
Roy Mr Stefan Alexander Hiren	5 Pump Court, London	020 7353 2532
Rudd Mr Michael	36 Bedford Row, London	020 7421 8000
Rudolf Mr Nathaniel David	25 Bedford Row, London	020 7067 1500
Ruffell Mr Mark Beresford	Pump Court Chambers, London	020 7353 0711
	Pump Court Chambers, Swindon	01793 539899
	Pump Court Chambers, Winchester	01962 868 161
Rule Mr Philip David	Castle Chambers, Harrow-on-the-Hill	020 8423 6579
Rush Mr Craig Peter	2 Bedford Row, London	020 7440 8888
Russell Miss Marguerite	Garden Court Chambers, London	020 7993 7600
Russell Mr Graham Alexander	Citadel Chambers, Birmingham	0121 233 8500
Russell Mr Guy Jonothon	Westgate Chambers, Lewes	01273 480510
Russell-Mitra Miss Jessica Suparna	1 Mitre Court Buildings, London	020 7452 8900
Rustom Mr Shiraz Sam	1215 Chambers, London	020 3291 1215
	Cranford Chambers, London	020 7404 7454
	1 Mitre Court Buildings, London	020 7452 8900
Rutherford Miss Emma Victoria	No 8 Chambers, Birmingham	0121 236 5514
Rutter Mr Gary Mark	Chambers of Marion Smullen and Kerim Fuad QC, London	020 7427 4400
Ryan Mr William	Corsham Barristers Chambers, Corsham	01225 582582
	Farringdon Chambers, London	020 7089 5700
Ryle Ms Kate Frances	5 Pump Court, London	020 7353 2532
Sadler Miss Rhiannon Jane	Westgate Chambers, Lewes	01273 480510
Sallon Mr Christopher Robert	Doughty Street Chambers, Bristol	01179 058 717
	Doughty Street Chambers, London	020 7404 1313
	Doughty Street Chambers, Manchester	0161 618 1066
Salter Miss Sibby Anne Victoria	3 Temple Gardens, London	020 7353 3102
Sandford Mr Robert Stanley	Bank House Chambers, Sheffield	0114 275 1223
Sandford Mr Simon John Austin	5 King's Bench Walk, London	020 7353 5638
Santamera Miss Louise Alexandria	New Bailey Chambers, Liverpool	0151 236 9402
Saunders Mr Neil	3 Raymond Buildings, London	020 7400 6400
Savvides Miss Maria	Northampton Chambers, Northampton	01604 636271
Saxby Mr Oliver Charles John	6 Pump Court, London	020 7797 8400
	6 Pump Court Chambers, Maidstone	01622 688094
Sayed Miss Nermine Abdel	Old Bailey Chambers, London	020 3008 6404
Schofield Mr Thomas Leon	No5 Chambers, Birmingham	0845 210 5555
	No5 Chambers, Bristol	0845 210 5555
	No5 Chambers, London	0845 210 5555
Scott Bell Mrs Rosalind Sara	Trinity Chambers, Middlesbrough	01642 247569
	Trinity Chambers, Newcastle Upon Tyne	0191 232 1927
Scutt Mr David Robert	9-12 Bell Yard, London	020 7400 1800
Sear Miss Joanne	13 KBW, Oxford	01865 311066
	13 King's Bench Walk, London	020 7353 7204
Seeboruth Mr Royln Jean-Paul	Chambers of Royln Seeboruth, Aylesbury	01296 393329
Sefton Mr Nicholas Edward	Linenhall Chambers, Chester	01244 348282
	Pendragon Chambers, Swansea	01792 411188
Sekar Mr Chandra	Angell Park Chambers, London	020 7737 5957
Sekhon Mr Narinder Singh	Sovereign Chambers, Leeds	0113 245 1841
Seymour Mr Mark William	9-12 Bell Yard, London	020 7400 1800
Shapiro Mr Selwyn	2 King's Bench Walk, London	020 7353 1746
Sharma Miss Sunyana	3 PB Barristers, Bournemouth	01202 292102
	3 PB Barristers, London	020 7583 8055
Sharma Mr Jamie	187 Fleet Street, London	020 7430 7430
Sharma Mr Sanjeev Mohan	Equity Chambers, Birmingham	0121 236 5007
Sharpe Mr Martin Laurence	Park Court Chambers, Leeds	0113 243 3277
Shaw Mr Michael John	9-12 Bell Yard, London	020 7400 1800
Sheikh Mr Irshad Ahmed	187 Fleet Street, London	020 7430 7430
Shepherd Mr Richard Andrew John	Albion Chambers, Bristol	0117 927 2144
Sheppard-Jones Miss Victoria Louise	Carmelite Chambers, London	020 7936 6300

Name	Chambers	Telephone
Sherborn Miss Natalie Louise	25 Bedford Row, London	020 7067 1500
Shirley Miss Lynne	East Anglian Chambers, Chelmsford	01473 214481
	East Anglian Chambers, Ipswich	01473 214481
	East Anglian Chambers, Norwich	01473 214481
Shorey Miss Carrie Lorrae	Nine Bedford Row, London	020 7489 2727
Short Mr Gary Peter	KCH Garden Square, Nottingham	0115 941 8851
Shotton Ms Sophie Diana	15 New Bridge Street, London	020 7842 1900
Sidhu Mr Navjot	25 Bedford Row, London	020 7067 1500
Sikand Miss Maya	Garden Court Chambers, London	020 7993 7600
Silcott Mr Tyrone John	Charter Chambers, London	020 7618 4400
Silverton Miss Catherine Anne	Sovereign Chambers, Leeds	0113 245 1841
Simpson Mr Graeme Michael	Citadel Chambers, Birmingham	0121 233 8500
Singer Mr Richard Adam	1 Gray's Inn Square, London	020 7405 0001
Singh Mr Dapinderpaul	23 Essex Street, London	020 7413 0353
	Park Court Chambers, Leeds	0113 243 3277
Sinker Mr Andrew Tennant	New Bailey Chambers, Liverpool	0151 236 9402
Sjolin Ms Catarina Marianne	36 Bedford Row, London	020 7421 8000
Skinner Mr Samuel Richard Edward	KCH Garden Square, Nottingham	0115 941 8851
Skyner Mr Robert Stephen	39 Park Square, Leeds	0113 245 6633
Small Miss Penelope Susan	Chambers of Andrew Mitchell QC, London	020 7440 9950
Smith Miss Eileen Joan	Trinity Chambers, Middlesbrough	01642 247569
	Trinity Chambers, Newcastle Upon Tyne	0191 232 1927
Smith Mr Alisdair Robert Macsorley	9-12 Bell Yard, London	020 7400 1800
Smith Mr Clive Francis	Chambers of Marion Smullen and Kerim Fuad QC, London	020 7427 4400
Smith Mr David Andrew	9-12 Bell Yard, London	020 7400 1800
Smith Mr James Alastair	9-12 Bell Yard, London	020 7400 1800
Smith Mr Mark William	Aegis Chambers, Wembley	
Smith Ms Rachel Catherine	Lincoln House Chambers, Manchester	0161 832 5701
Smitten Mr Ben James	25 Bedford Row, London	020 7067 1500
Smoker Miss Kathleen Mary	Heavenwood Chambers, Stroud	01453 873444
Smullen Mrs Marion	Chambers of Marion Smullen and Kerim Fuad QC, London	020 7427 4400
Smyth Mr Christopher Julian Worsley	Queen Square Chambers, Bristol	0117 921 1966
Snook Mr Harry Benedick	St Albans Chambers, St Albans	01727 843383
Snow Mr Darren Mark	Charter Chambers, London	020 7618 4400
Sparrow Mrs Marie-Claire	Holborn Chambers, London	020 7242 6060
Spears Miss Katharine Sarah	Carmelite Chambers, London	020 7936 6300
Spence Mr Simon Peter	18 Red Lion Court, London	020 7520 6000
	18 Red Lion Court (Annexe), Chelmsford	01245 280880
Spens Mr David Patrick	Garden Court Chambers, London	020 7993 7600
Spenwyn Ms Marie Ann	Carmelite Chambers, London	020 7936 6300
Spooner Mr Henry Neville	Tolzey Chambers, Bristol	
	Westgate Chambers, Lewes	01273 480510
Squirrell Mr Benjamin	Nine Bedford Row, London	020 7489 2727
St Louis Mr Brian Lloyd	15 New Bridge Street, London	020 7842 1900
Stanbury Mr Matthew Francis	Chambers of Ian Macdonald QC, Manchester	0161 236 1840
Standfast Mr Philip Arthur	St Paul's Chambers, Leeds	0113 245 5866
Stanford Mr Tony James	Old Bailey Chambers, London	020 3008 6404
Staples Miss Joanna Lida	Dyers Chambers, London	020 7404 1881
Starr Mrs Teresa Margaret	Great James Street Chambers, London	020 7440 4949
Stebbings Mr Ian Anthony	1 Gray's Inn Square, London	020 7405 0001
Stein Mr Daniel Alexander	No5 Chambers, Birmingham	0845 210 5555
	No5 Chambers, Bristol	0845 210 5555
	No5 Chambers, London	0845 210 5555
Stein Mr Samuel	Dyers Chambers, London	020 7404 1881
	Westgate Chambers, Lewes	01273 480510
Stelling Mr Nigel Roy	Citadel Chambers, Birmingham	0121 233 8500
Stemp Mr Scott	12 College Place, Southampton	023 8032 0320

Stern Mr David Patrick Julian	King's Bench Chambers, Bournemouth	01202 250025
	11 Stone Buildings, London	020 7831 6381
Stevens Mr Mark Nicholas	Chambers of Marion Smullen and Kerim Fuad QC, London	020 7427 4400
Stevens Mr Stuart Standish	Holborn Chambers, London	020 7242 6060
Stevens Mrs Hazel Ann	East Anglian Chambers, Chelmsford	01473 214481
	East Anglian Chambers, Ipswich	01473 214481
	East Anglian Chambers, Norwich	01473 214481
Stevenson Mr Daniel Keith	9-12 Bell Yard, London	020 7400 1800
Stevenson Mr Robert Lloyd	Sovereign Chambers, Leeds	0113 245 1841
Stimpson Mr Christopher Hugh	Atkinson Bevan Chambers, London	020 7353 2112
Stone Mr Joseph	Doughty Street Chambers, Bristol	01179 058 717
	Doughty Street Chambers, London	020 7404 1313
	Doughty Street Chambers, Manchester	0161 618 1066
Storey Mr Richard Alexander	3 Temple Gardens, London	020 7353 3102
Stork Mr Brian Raymond	3 Temple Gardens, London	020 7353 3102
Storrie Mr Timothy James	Lincoln House Chambers, Manchester	0161 832 5701
Stott Mr Philip Geoffrey	QEB Hollis Whiteman, London	020 7933 8855
Stranex Mr Andrew John	St Paul's Chambers, Leeds	0113 245 5866
Strong Mr Adrian Peter Ciaran	KBW, Leeds	0113 297 1200
Stuart Mr Bruce Ian	Lombard Chambers, London	020 7107 2100
Stubbs Mr Andrew James	St Paul's Chambers, Leeds	0113 245 5866
Sugarman Mr Jason Ashley	9-12 Bell Yard, London	020 7400 1800
Suggett Mr Iain Robert Ottar	Warwick Chambers, Birmingham	0121 382 9122
Sukul Mr Rabi Shankar	Balham Chambers, London	020 8675 4609
Sullivan Mr Geoffrey Charles Alexander	36 Bedford Row, London	020 7421 8000
Summers Miss Allison	36 Bedford Row, London	020 7421 8000
Summers Mr Benjamin Dylan James	3 Raymond Buildings, London	020 7400 6400
Sutherland Mr James More	Nexus Chambers, London	020 7404 1147/020 7831 8309
Sutton-Mattocks Mr Christopher John	5 King's Bench Walk, London	020 7353 5638
Sweeney Mr Noel Christopher	Veritas Chambers, Worle	01934 853 382
Swinnerton Mr David Michael	Cornwall Street Chambers, Birmingham	0121 233 7500
Syfret Mr Nicholas	Citadel Chambers, Birmingham	0121 233 8500
	13 KBW, Oxford	01865 311066
	13 King's Bench Walk, London	020 7353 7204
Tahta Miss Natasha Alexandra	QEB Hollis Whiteman, London	020 7933 8855
Talbot Mr Jack Richard	Dyers Chambers, London	020 7404 1881
Tapsell Mr Paul Richard	Becket Chambers, Canterbury	01227 786331
Targett-Parker Miss Leanne Susan	No. 3 Fleet Street Chambers, London	020 7936 4474
	The Chambers of Miss Leanne Targett-Parker, London	020 8674 6694
Tatford Mr Warwick Henry Patrick	9-12 Bell Yard, London	020 7400 1800
Tatlow Mr Nicholas Mark	Citadel Chambers, Birmingham	0121 233 8500
Taylor Mr Jason	Albion Chambers, Bristol	0117 927 2144
Taylor Mrs Yvonne Marie	Trinity Chambers, Middlesbrough	01642 247569
	Trinity Chambers, Newcastle Upon Tyne	0191 232 1927
Tetlow Mr Bernard Geoffrey	Charter Chambers, London	020 7618 4400
Thomas Mr Andrew Martin	Lincoln House Chambers, Manchester	0161 832 5701
	Linenhall Chambers, Chester	01244 348282
Thomas Mr James Austin	KCH Garden Square, Nottingham	0115 941 8851
Thomas Mr Timothy Nicholas	Lombard Chambers, London	020 7107 2100
Thompson Miss Pauline Sonita	5 King's Bench Walk, London	020 7353 5638
Thompson Mr Patrick Miles	KBW, Leeds	0113 297 1200
	St Johns Buildings, Manchester	0161 214 1500
	St Johns Buildings Liverpool, Liverpool	0151 243 6000
	16 Winckley Square, Preston	01772 256100
Thompson Mr Ryan Jerome	Dyers Chambers, London	020 7404 1881
Thornton Mr John Robert	Stour Chambers, Canterbury	01227 764899
Tizzano Mr Franco Salvatore	Old Bailey Chambers, London	020 3008 6404

Tomassi Mr Mark David	Charter Chambers, London	020 7618 4400
Tompkins Miss Kate	36 Bedford Row, London	020 7421 8000
Tonge Mr Christopher Paul	Bank House Chambers, Sheffield	0114 275 1223
Toomey Mr Kevin Ian	2 Bedford Row, London	020 7440 8888
Topal Mr Erol	Lamb Chambers, London	020 7797 8300
Traversi Mr John David Stephen Antona	Nine Bedford Row, London	020 7489 2727
Tregidgo Mr Marc Gordon	4 King's Bench Walk, London	020 7822 7000
Treharne Mr Neil Simon	Dingle Chambers, Bristol	07818 827754
Tresman Mr Lewis Robert Simon	Staple Inn Chambers, London	020 7242 5240
Trowler Ms Rebecca	Doughty Street Chambers, Bristol	01179 058 717
	Doughty Street Chambers, London	020 7404 1313
	Doughty Street Chambers, Manchester	0161 618 1066
Tucker Mr James Eckhord	Queen Square Chambers, Bristol	0117 921 1966
Tucker Mr James William Richard	Teucro Chambers, Epsom	
Turner Mr Jonathan James	Argent Chambers, London	020 7556 5500
Udom Miss Nancy Ini	Five St Andrew's Hill, London	020 7332 5400
Unigwe Mr Sylvester Emefiona	Essex House Chambers, London	020 7692 0677
	11 Gray's Inn Square Chambers, London	020 7405 6879
Upton Mr Alexander Stuart Allen	23 Essex Street, London	020 7413 0353
Upton Mr John Stewart	4 King's Bench Walk, London	020 7822 7000
Usher Mr Neil Morris	Lincoln House Chambers, Manchester	0161 832 5701
Vaitilingam Mr Adam Skanda	Albion Chambers, Bristol	0117 927 2144
Valios Mr Nicholas Paul	4 Breams Buildings, London	020 7092 1900
	No 8 Chambers, Birmingham	0121 236 5514
Vallance Mr Henry	Old Bailey Chambers, London	020 3008 6404
Valley Miss Helen Maria	25 Bedford Row, London	020 7067 1500
Varley Mr James Robert Kenrick	1 High Pavement, Nottingham	0115 941 8218
Vine Mr James Peter Stockman	Five St Andrew's Hill, London	020 7332 5400
Vine Ms Sarah Jane	2 Pump Court, London	020 7353 5597
Vollenweider Mr Amiot Marcus Ellerton	Thomas More Chambers, London	020 7404 7000
Vout Mr Andrew Paul	9-12 Bell Yard, London	020 7400 1800
	1 High Pavement, Nottingham	0115 941 8218
Wade Miss Rebecca Lucy	Northampton Chambers, Northampton	01604 636271
Wade Mr Ian	Five Paper Buildings, London	020 7583 6117
Wagstaff Mr Andrew Martin Nicholas	Westgate Chambers, Lewes	01273 480510
Wald Mr Richard Daniel	39 Essex Street, London	020 7832 1111
	82 King Street, Manchester	0161 870 9969
	Riverview Chambers, London	0844 225 3999
Waldman Mr Amos	Doughty Street Chambers, Bristol	01179 058 717
	Doughty Street Chambers, London	020 7404 1313
	Doughty Street Chambers, Manchester	0161 618 1066
Waley Mr Eric Richard Thomas	Assize Court Chambers, Bristol	0117 926 4587
Walker Mr Liam David	Doughty Street Chambers, London	020 7404 1313
Walker Mr Paul Christopher	5 King's Bench Walk, London	020 7353 5638
Walker-Nolan Mr Benjamin	Thomas More Chambers, London	020 7404 7000
Wall Mr Mark Arthur	Citadel Chambers, Birmingham	0121 233 8500
Wallace Mr Shaun Anthony	Great James Street Chambers, London	020 7440 4949
Walmsley Mr Alan	5 King's Bench Walk, London	020 7353 5638
Walton Miss Karen Tanya	Dyers Chambers, London	020 7404 1881
Ward Miss Alexandra	9-12 Bell Yard, London	020 7400 1800
Ward Mr Peter Mark	The Chambers of Peter Ward, London	020 3402 2152
Warner Mr Anthony Charles Broughton	Citadel Chambers, Birmingham	0121 233 8500
Warrington Mr John Edward Lawrence	Five St Andrew's Hill, London	020 7332 5400
Wasunna Mr Christian Christopher Peter	2 Dr Johnson's Buildings, London	020 7936 2613
Waters Mr David Ebsworth	2 Hare Court, London	020 7353 3982
Watkinson Mr Howard	9-12 Bell Yard, London	020 7400 1800
Watson Mr Anthony Dennis	Lincoln House Chambers, Manchester	0161 832 5701

Watson Mr Benjamin Turquand	3 Raymond Buildings, London	020 7400 6400
Watson Mr Mark Andrew	KCH Garden Square, Nottingham	0115 941 8851
Watson Mr Tom Bradley	Chavasse Court Chambers, Liverpool	0151 229 2030
Watson Ms Claire	East Anglian Chambers, Chelmsford	01473 214481
	East Anglian Chambers, Ipswich	01473 214481
	East Anglian Chambers, Norwich	01473 214481
Wayne Mr Nicholas	Argent Chambers, London	020 7556 5500
Weatherby Mr Peter Francis	Chambers of Ian Macdonald QC, Manchester	0161 236 1840
	Garden Court Chambers, London	020 7993 7600
Weaver Mr Brett	6 King's Bench Walk, London	020 7583 0410
Webber Mr Dominic Denzil Fernandez	5 King's Bench Walk, London	020 7353 5638
Webster Miss Shelley Anne	Carmelite Chambers, London	020 7936 6300
Webster Mr Alistair Stevenson	Chambers of Andrew Mitchell QC, London	020 7440 9950
	Lincoln House Chambers, Manchester	0161 832 5701
Webster Mr Keith	4 King's Bench Walk, London	020 7822 7000
Weekes Mr Mark Vincent	6 King's Bench Walk, London	020 7583 0410
Weetch Mr Oliver Peter Mccallum	Chambers of Marion Smullen and Kerim Fuad QC, London	020 7427 4400
Welch Mr Robert William	Unity Street Chambers, Bristol	0117 906 9789
Wells Mr Colin John	25 Bedford Row, London	020 7067 1500
Western Mr Adam John Brooks	Citadel Chambers, Birmingham	0121 233 8500
Whawell Miss Leesha Claire	3 Temple Gardens, London	020 7353 3102
White Mr Daniel Edward Mills	Citadel Chambers, Birmingham	0121 233 8500
Whitfield Mr Jonathan	Doughty Street Chambers, London	020 7404 1313
Wilcox Mr Jerome Carl Jean	Alexander Chambers, London	0845 652 0451/0854 652 0451
Wild Mr Simon Peter	9-12 Bell Yard, London	020 7400 1800
Wilkins Mr Andrew Lewis	Cornwall Street Chambers, Birmingham	0121 233 7500
Wilkins Mr Thomas Alexander	Atkinson Bevan Chambers, London	020 7353 2112
Williams Miss Micaila Teresa	Optimus Chambers, Braintree	01376 691 885/07736 283873
Williams Mr Owen David Parker	9 Park Place, Cardiff	029 2038 2731
Williams Mr Simon Christopher	12 Old Square Chambers, London	020 7404 0875
Williams Ms Sandra Alessandra Caroline	The Chambers Of Alessandra Williams, Tadworth	07941 944950
Willmer Mr Stephen James	Argent Chambers, London	020 7556 5500
Wilson Ms Charmaine Kimberley	Westgate Chambers, Lewes	01273 480510
Winship Mr Julian Abdulla	Furnival Chambers, London	020 7405 3232
Winslett Mr Frank	Westgate Chambers, Lewes	01273 480510
Wise Mr Leslie Michael	10 King's Bench Walk, London	020 7353 7742
Wiseman Mr Adam Philip Pasternak	18 Red Lion Court, London	020 7520 6000
	18 Red Lion Court (Annexe), Chelmsford	01245 280880
Wood Mr James Alexander Douglas	Doughty Street Chambers, Bristol	01179 058 717
	Doughty Street Chambers, London	020 7404 1313
	Doughty Street Chambers, Manchester	0161 618 1066
Wood Mr Michael Mure	Chambers of Mr Michael Wood QC, London	020 8874 3474
Wood Mr Richard James	9 King's Bench Walk, London	020 7353 9564
Wood Mr Richard Michael	East Anglian Chambers, Chelmsford	01473 214481
	East Anglian Chambers, Ipswich	01473 214481
	East Anglian Chambers, Norwich	01473 214481
Wood Mr Stephen	Broadway House Chambers, Bradford	01274 722560
	Broadway House Chambers, Leeds	0113 246 2600
Woods Mr Terence Mccartan	187 Fleet Street, London	020 7430 7430
Wraith Mr Nigel Patrick	Colleton Chambers, Exeter	01392 274898
Wrottesley Miss Angela Jane	Bank House Chambers, Sheffield	0114 275 1223
Yeo Mr Nicholas	3 Raymond Buildings, London	020 7400 6400
Yeung Mr Stuart Roy	Northampton Chambers, Northampton	01604 636271

CRIME (CORPORATE/FRAUD)

Abasheikh Mr Omar Said Imam	Paragon Chambers, London	020 3318 9988

C

Barrister	Chambers	Telephone
Abu-Mustafa Mr Jehad	1 Paper Buildings, London	020 7353 3728
Addison Mr Kenneth Paul	5 Pump Court, London	020 7353 2532
Afzal Mr Fayyaz	No5 Chambers, Birmingham	0845 210 5555
	No5 Chambers, Bristol	0845 210 5555
	No5 Chambers, London	0845 210 5555
Aina Mr Benjamin Adejowon Olufemi	Old Bailey Chambers, London	020 3008 6404
Ajaz Mr Mohammad Arshad	Eastmans Chambers, Reading	0118 966 9094
Akin-Olugbade Mr Oluwajeminipe Babarinsade	Nexus Chambers, London	020 7404 1147/020 7831 8309
Akinsanya Mr Stephen Olubunmi	Old Bailey Chambers, London	020 3008 6404
Aleeson Mr Warwick Lan Grieg	187 Fleet Street, London	020 7430 7430
Ali Mr Zafar	23 Essex Street, London	020 7413 0353
Anderson Mr Richard Neil Macdiarmid	Arbitration Chambers, London	020 7267 2137
Andrews Mr Paul Leslie	Great James Street Chambers, London	020 7440 4949
Apfel Mr Freddy	37 Park Square Chambers, Leeds	0113 243 9422
Archer Miss Audrey Sybil Dorothy	3 PB Barristers, Bournemouth	01202 292102
	3 PB Barristers, Bristol	0117 928 1520
	3 PB Barristers, London	020 7583 8055
	3 PB Barristers, Oxford	01865 793 736
	3 PB Barristers, Winchester	01962 868884
Argyle Mr Brian John	Chambers of K A Williams-Howes, London	020 8704 1010
	187 Fleet Street, London	020 7430 7430
Armbrister Mr Allan Ramsay	39 Park Square, Leeds	0113 245 6633
Armstrong Mr Dean Paul	2 Bedford Row, London	020 7440 8888
Arnold Mr Peter Matthew Miller	No5 Chambers, Birmingham	0845 210 5555
	No5 Chambers, Bristol	0845 210 5555
	No5 Chambers, London	0845 210 5555
Ashley-Norman Mr Jonathan Charles	3 Raymond Buildings, London	020 7400 6400
Askey Mr Robert John	Palmyra Chambers, Warrington	01925 444919
Atkins Mr Richard Paul	St Philips Chambers, Birmingham	0121 246 7000
Atkinson Mr Nicholas Jeremy	Atkinson Bevan Chambers, London	020 7353 2112
	Staple Inn Chambers, London	020 7242 5240
Austin Mr Ian	Holborn Chambers, London	020 7242 6060
Austin Mr Jonathan Edward Newns	Linenhall Chambers, Chester	01244 348282
Aylett Mr Kenneth George	4 Breams Buildings, London	020 7092 1900
	15 New Bridge Street, London	020 7842 1900
Aylott Mr Colin Christopher	Carmelite Chambers, London	020 7936 6300
Badenoch Mr Tony David	6 King's Bench Walk, London	020 7583 0410
Badger Mr Christopher James	23 Essex Street, London	020 7413 0353
Bagley Miss Louisa Ellen	1 Paper Buildings, London	020 7353 3728
Bahra Miss Narita	9-12 Bell Yard, London	020 7400 1800
	2 Hare Court, London	020 7353 3982
Baird Mr James Stevenson	Bank House Chambers, Sheffield	0114 275 1223
Bajwa Mr Ali Naseem	Garden Court Chambers, London	020 7993 7600
Baki Mr Neil Farres	25 Bedford Row, London	020 7067 1500
Banham Mr Matthew Ian	Nine Bedford Row, London	020 7489 2727
Barclay Mr Robin Nicholas John	2 Hare Court, London	020 7353 3982
Barker Mr Kerry	Guildhall Chambers, Bristol	0117 930 9000
Barnes Ms Rachel Ann	3 Raymond Buildings, London	020 7400 6400
Barnett Mr Jeremy Victor	2 Bedford Row, London	020 7440 8888
	St Paul's Chambers, Leeds	0113 245 5866
Barraclough Mr Nicholas Maylin	187 Fleet Street, London	020 7430 7430
Barrett Mr Robert Scott	2 Pump Court, London	020 7353 5597
Barry Mr Denis Fintan Patrick	Five Paper Buildings, London	020 7583 6117
Barry Mr Kevin James	36 Bedford Row, London	020 7421 8000
Bartfeld Mr Jason Maurice	187 Fleet Street, London	020 7430 7430
Barton Mr Hugh Geoffrey	Lincoln House Chambers, Manchester	0161 832 5701
Batcup Mr David John	Charter Chambers, London	020 7618 4400
Baur Mr Christopher Thomas	Furnival Chambers, London	020 7405 3232
Baxter Miss Bernadette	Lincoln House Chambers, Manchester	0161 832 5701
Becker Mr Paul Antony	Chavasse Court Chambers, Liverpool	0151 229 2030
Beharrylal Mr Satyanand Sarju	15 New Bridge Street, London	020 7842 1900

Bell Mr Dominic Michael St. John	Chambers of Marion Smullen and Kerim Fuad QC, London	020 7427 4400
Bendall Mr Richard Giles	Furnival Chambers, London	020 7405 3232
Benjamin Mr Daniel Robert	2 Dr Johnson's Buildings, London	020 7936 2613
Bennett Miss Emma Louise	Exchange Chambers, Leeds	0113 203 1970
	Exchange Chambers, Liverpool	0151 236 7747
	Exchange Chambers, Manchester	0161 833 2722
Bennett Mr Ieuan Gereint	9 Park Place, Cardiff	029 2038 2731
Benson Mr Jeremy Keith	18 Red Lion Court, London	020 7520 6000
Bentley Mr David Neil	Doughty Street Chambers, Bristol	01179 058 717
	Doughty Street Chambers, London	020 7404 1313
	Doughty Street Chambers, Manchester	0161 618 1066
Bergenthal Mr Ronnie Mark	Old Bailey Chambers, London	020 3008 6404
Berriman Mr Trevor St John	43 Temple Row Chambers, Birmingham	0121 237 6035
Berry Mr Nicholas	Citadel Chambers, Birmingham	0121 233 8500
Bertham Mr Anthony Christopher	3 Temple Gardens, London	020 7353 3102
Bertram Mr Jonathan Peter	Seven Bedford Row, London	020 7242 3555
Beswick Miss Kirstin Wendy	Central Chambers, Manchester	0161 236 1133
Bex Miss Kate	2 Hare Court, London	020 7353 3982
Beyts Mr Chester Andoe Michael	25 Bedford Row, London	020 7067 1500
Bickler Mr Simon Lloyd	St Paul's Chambers, Leeds	0113 245 5866
Birbeck Mr Alan Giles	Dyers Chambers, London	020 7404 1881
Birkby Mr Richard Adam	Park Court Chambers, Leeds	0113 243 3277
Birnbaum Mr Michael Ian	9-12 Bell Yard, London	020 7400 1800
Bisarya Mr Neil	Number 7 Harrington Street Chambers, Liverpool	0151 242 0707
Blain Mr Roderick Graham	12 College Place, Southampton	023 8032 0320
Blair Mr Peter Michael	Guildhall Chambers, Bristol	0117 930 9000
	6 King's Bench Walk, London	020 7583 0410
Blakey Mr Michael Charles	St Johns Buildings, Manchester	0161 214 1500
	St Johns Buildings Liverpool, Liverpool	0151 243 6000
	16 Winckley Square, Preston	01772 256100
Bleaney Mr Nicholas Simon	Atkinson Bevan Chambers, London	020 7353 2112
Bloomfield Mr Richard William	Chambers of Mr Richard Bloomfield, Whitley Bay	01670 360042
Bond Mr Richard Ian Winsor	Citadel Chambers, Birmingham	0121 233 8500
Bonehill Mr Nicholas Benjamin	4 Breams Buildings, London	020 7092 1900
Borrelli Mr Michael Francis Antony	187 Fleet Street, London	020 7430 7430
Boswell Mr Andrew Timothy	13 KBW, Oxford	01865 311066
	13 King's Bench Walk, London	020 7353 7204
Bourne Mr Ian Maclean	Charter Chambers, London	020 7618 4400
Bourne-Arton Mr James Luke	St Paul's Chambers, Leeds	0113 245 5866
Bourne-Arton Mr Simon Nicholas	Park Court Chambers, Leeds	0113 243 3277
Bowden Mr Guy Robert	4 Breams Buildings, London	020 7092 1900
Bowers Mr Rupert John	Doughty Street Chambers, London	020 7404 1313
Bowes Mr Michael Anthony	Cobden House Chambers, Manchester	0161 833 6000
	Outer Temple Chambers, London	020 7353 6381
Boyd Mr Phillip Joseph George	Lincoln House Chambers, Manchester	0161 832 5701
Braamskamp Ms Christine Jolanda	3 Raymond Buildings, London	020 7400 6400
Brady Mr Scott	3 Temple Gardens, London	020 7353 3102
Bramwell Miss Corinne Victoria	Nine Bedford Row, London	020 7489 2727
Brand Miss Rachel Rennie Virginia Ann	Citadel Chambers, Birmingham	0121 233 8500
Branston Mr Gareth Philip	23 Essex Street, London	020 7413 0353
Brassington Mr Stephen David	2 Hare Court, London	020 7353 3982
Breen-Lawton Miss Denise	St Paul's Chambers, Leeds	0113 245 5866
Brehan Ms Daire	Chambers of Ms D Brehan, London	07808 726877
Brickman Miss Laura Gillian	Carmelite Chambers, London	020 7936 6300
Bridge Mr Giles	Broadway House Chambers, Bradford	01274 722560
	Broadway House Chambers, Leeds	0113 246 2600
Bright Miss Rachel Zelda	4 Brick Court, London	020 7832 3200
	187 Fleet Street, London	020 7430 7430

Brimelow Miss Janine Kirsty	Doughty Street Chambers, Bristol	01179 058 717
	Doughty Street Chambers, London	020 7404 1313
	Doughty Street Chambers, Manchester	0161 618 1066
Broadley Mr John	Cobden House Chambers, Manchester	0161 833 6000
Brown Mr Edward Francis Trevenen	QEB Hollis Whiteman, London	020 7933 8855
Brown Mr Roger Charles Arthur	Kenworthy's Chambers, Manchester	0161 832 4036
Brown Mr Sam Clement	Atkinson Bevan Chambers, London	020 7353 2112
Brunner Ms Catherine Jane	Albion Chambers, Bristol	0117 927 2144
	36 Bedford Row, London	020 7421 8000
Brunt Mr Philip Edwin	No 8 Chambers, Birmingham	0121 236 5514
Bryan Mr Robert John	1 Paper Buildings, London	020 7353 3728
Bryant-Heron Mr Mark Nicholas	9-12 Bell Yard, London	020 7400 1800
Buchanan Mr James Ian Charles	2 Hare Court, London	020 7353 3982
Bull Mr Nicholas David	Old Bailey Chambers, London	020 3008 6404
Bunting Mr Daniel Alexander James	2 Dr Johnson's Buildings, London	020 7936 2613
Burton Mr John Malcolm	3 Temple Gardens, London	020 7353 3102
Butters Mr Richard John	37 Park Square Chambers, Leeds	0113 243 9422
Butterworth Mr Martin Frank	Citadel Chambers, Birmingham	0121 233 8500
Buxton Mr Thomas Justin	Charter Chambers, London	020 7618 4400
Byrne Mr Garrett Thomas	4-5 Gray's Inn Square, London	020 7404 5252
Byrnes Miss Aisling Alice Elizabeth	25 Bedford Row, London	020 7067 1500
Caddle Miss Sherrie Loretta	Charter Chambers, London	020 7618 4400
Caldwell Mr Peter Hugh Coyles	Dyers Chambers, London	020 7404 1881
Callery Mr Martin	Cobden House Chambers, Manchester	0161 833 6000
Cammerman Mr Gideon Saul	187 Fleet Street, London	020 7430 7430
Campbell Mr Alasdair James	St Paul's Chambers, Leeds	0113 245 5866
Campbell Mr Oliver Edward Wilhelm	Henderson Chambers, London	020 7583 9020
Canning Mr Richard	39 Park Square, Leeds	0113 245 6633
Caplan Mr Jonathan Michael	Five Paper Buildings, London	020 7583 6117
	Riverview Chambers, London	0844 225 3999
Carey Miss Jacqueline Anne	2 Bedford Row, London	020 7440 8888
Carey-Hughes Mr Richard John	Nine Bedford Row, London	020 7489 2727
Carne Mr Roger Enys	Nine Bedford Row, London	020 7489 2727
Carr Mr James Christopher Daniel	4 Breams Buildings, London	020 7092 1900
Carrasco Mr Glenn Lawrence	9-12 Bell Yard, London	020 7400 1800
Carter Miss Nathalie Veronique	1 Gray's Inn Square, London	020 7405 0001
Carter-Stephenson Mr George Anthony	25 Bedford Row, London	020 7067 1500
Casey Mr Paul Joseph	Chambers of Marion Smullen and Kerim Fuad QC, London	020 7427 4400
Cecil Miss Joanne Michelle	1 Pump Court, London	020 7842 7070
Chadwick Mr Daniel James	25 Bedford Row, London	020 7067 1500
Chalk Mr Alexander John Gervase	6 King's Bench Walk, London	020 7583 0410
Challinor Mr Thomas Michael	Citadel Chambers, Birmingham	0121 233 8500
Chawla Mr Mukul	9-12 Bell Yard, London	020 7400 1800
Chawla Mr Neil	No5 Chambers, Birmingham	0845 210 5555
	No5 Chambers, Bristol	0845 210 5555
	No5 Chambers, London	0845 210 5555
Cheema Miss Parmjit Kaur	2 Hare Court, London	020 7353 3982
Cherrett Mr Darryl Joseph	Carmelite Chambers, London	020 7936 6300
Chipperfield Mr Jeremy Steven	Cranford Chambers, London	020 7404 7454
Christie Mr Richard Hamish	2 Pump Court, London	020 7353 5597
Christie Mr Simon Paul William	Chavasse Court Chambers, Liverpool	0151 229 2030
Clare Miss Allison Jean	18 Red Lion Court, London	020 7520 6000
Clarke Mr Nicholas Patrick James	18 St John Street, Manchester	0161 278 1800
Claxton Mr Elroy Geraldo	23 Essex Street, London	020 7413 0353
	Old Bailey Chambers, London	020 3008 6404
Clegg Mr William	2 Bedford Row, London	020 7440 8888
Climie Mr Roger Stephen	King's Bench and Godolphin (KBG)Chambers, Plymouth	01752 221551
	Outer Temple Chambers, London	020 7353 6381
Cockings Mr Giles Francis Sacheveral	Furnival Chambers, London	020 7405 3232

C

Cocks Mr David John	18 Red Lion Court, London	020 7520 6000
	18 Red Lion Court (Annexe), Chelmsford	01245 280880
Coffey Mr John Joseph	39 Park Square, Leeds	0113 245 6633
	3 Temple Gardens, London	020 7353 3102
Coles-Harrington Ms Frances Julia	2 Pump Court, London	020 7353 5597
Coltart Mr Christopher Mccallum	2 Hare Court, London	020 7353 3982
Comb Mr David William	Trinity Chambers, Middlesbrough	01642 247569
	Trinity Chambers, Newcastle Upon Tyne	0191 232 1927
Comerton Miss Julie Anne	4 KBW, London	020 7822 8822
Common Mr Hamish Andrew	23 Essex Street, London	020 7413 0353
Compton Mr Benjamin Edward Welstead	Outer Temple Chambers, London	020 7353 6381
Conlon Mr Michael John Patrick	Harcourt Chambers, Milton Keynes	0845 123 1234
Connell Mr Edward Samuel	Five St Andrew's Hill, London	020 7332 5400
Connolly Mr Dominic Regan	Five St Andrew's Hill, London	020 7332 5400
Connolly Ms Deirdre Joan	Old Bailey Chambers, London	020 3008 6404
Conrad Mr Alan David	Lincoln House Chambers, Manchester	0161 832 5701
	St Ive's Chambers, Birmingham	0121 236 0863
Cooper Miss Danielle Sophie	Tooks Chambers, London	020 7842 7575
Cooper Mr John Gordon	25 Bedford Row, London	020 7067 1500
Corre Mr Neil Bernard	Redbourne Chambers, London	020 8346 8524
Corsellis Mr Nicholas Robert Alexander	3 Temple Gardens, London	020 7353 3102
Costello Mr Paul James	Chambers of Mr Paul J Costello, Biggleswade	07846 016 399
Cotter Mr Mark James	Five St Andrew's Hill, London	020 7332 5400
Cotter Mr Nicholas Andrew James Horlor	1 Paper Buildings, London	020 7353 3728
Cox Mr Jonathan Edward	KCH Garden Square, Nottingham	0115 941 8851
Crabb Miss Samantha Jill	Citadel Chambers, Birmingham	0121 233 8500
Cross Mr Anthony Maurice	Lincoln House Chambers, Manchester	0161 832 5701
Crowe Mr Cameron	36 Bedford Row, London	020 7421 8000
Crowther Ms Lucy Ellen	Apex, Cardiff	02920 232 032
Culley Miss Laura Joan	Citadel Chambers, Birmingham	0121 233 8500
Darbishire Mr Adrian Munro	QEB Hollis Whiteman, London	020 7933 8855
Darroch Miss Fiona Culverwell	Clerksroom (London), London	0845 083 3000
	Clerksroom (Taunton), Taunton	0845 083 3000
	King's Lynn Chambers, King's Lynn	01553 672 085
Dashani Miss Sonal	15 New Bridge Street, London	020 7842 1900
Davenport Mr Richard Ian	Citadel Chambers, Birmingham	0121 233 8500
Davidge Miss Justine Marie	4 King's Bench Walk, London	020 7822 7000
Davies Miss Claire Suzanne	Farringdon Chambers, London	020 7089 5700
Davies Mr Henry Olusola	Trinity Chambers, Birmingham	0121 346 4672
Davies Mr Jonathan Norval	9-12 Bell Yard, London	020 7400 1800
Davis Mr Adam David	Dyers Chambers, London	020 7404 1881
Davis Mr Simon John	St Philips Chambers, Birmingham	0121 246 7000
Davis Mr William Neal	Charter Chambers, London	020 7618 4400
Dawson Mr Richard Jon Foster	Lincoln House Chambers, Manchester	0161 832 5701
Day Mr Douglas Henry	Farrar's Building, London	020 7583 9241
De Burgos Mr Jamie Michael Abulafia	36 Bedford Row, London	020 7421 8000
De Jehan Mr David	Park Lane Plowden, Leeds	0113 228 5049
Dean Mr James Patrick	Goldsmith Chambers, London	020 7353 6802
Del Fabbro Mr Oscar	23 Essex Street, London	020 7413 0353
Delamere Miss Isabel Sarah	4 Breams Buildings, London	020 7092 1900
Dempsey Miss Karen Marie	3 Temple Gardens, London	020 7353 3102
Denney Mr Stuart Henry Macdonald	Deans Court Chambers, Manchester	0161 214 6000
	Deans Court Chambers, Preston	01772 565 600
	Thomas More Chambers, London	020 7404 7000
Dennis Miss Rebecca Louise	Queen Square Chambers, Bristol	0117 921 1966
Dennis Mr Mark Jonathan	6 King's Bench Walk, London	020 7583 0410
Dent Mr Stephen Robert Charles	Guildhall Chambers, Bristol	0117 930 9000

Desmond Mr Denis John	Cornwall Street Chambers, Birmingham	0121 233 7500
Dix Miss Rebecca	2 Bedford Row, London	020 7440 8888
Doherty Mr Nicholas Brudenell	4 King's Bench Walk, London	020 7822 7000
Donne Mr Jeremy Nigel	QEB Hollis Whiteman, London	020 7933 8855
Donnelly Mr Stephen John	Dyers Chambers, London	020 7404 1881
Doran Mr Gerard Patrick	Lincoln House Chambers, Manchester	0161 832 5701
Dos Santos Mr Alexander	Charter Chambers, London	020 7618 4400
Dowden Mr Andrew Philip	Castle Chambers, Harrow-on-the-Hill	020 8423 6579
	Melbury House, Leicester	07801 037802
Dowse Ms Clare Olivia Mary	3 Temple Gardens, London	020 7353 3102
Draycott Mr Simon Douglas	Citadel Chambers, Birmingham	0121 233 8500
	Five St Andrew's Hill, London	020 7332 5400
Drew Mr Simon Patrick	No5 Chambers, Birmingham	0845 210 5555
	No5 Chambers, Bristol	0845 210 5555
	No5 Chambers, London	0845 210 5555
Duck Mr Michael Charles	No5 Chambers, Birmingham	0845 210 5555
	No5 Chambers, Bristol	0845 210 5555
	No5 Chambers, London	0845 210 5555
Duffy Mr Derek James	St Paul's Chambers, Leeds	0113 245 5866
Dunning Mr Francis John Grove	37 Park Square Chambers, Leeds	0113 243 9422
Dutt Miss Nisha	Middle Temple Lane Chambers, London	020 7583 4352
Dyble Mr Steven John	18 Red Lion Court, London	020 7520 6000
	18 Red Lion Court (Annexe), Chelmsford	01245 280880
Dye Mr John Geoffrey	Goldsmith Chambers, London	020 7353 6802
Eastwood Miss Philippa Clemency Anne	Doughty Street Chambers, London	020 7404 1313
Eaton Mr James Bernard	Thomas More Chambers, London	020 7404 7000
Edmonds Mr Michael Jonathan	4 Breams Buildings, London	020 7092 1900
Edwards Mr Dickon Harrison	5 Pump Court, London	020 7353 2532
Edwards Mr Jonathan William	Westgate Chambers, Lewes	01273 480510
Edwards Mr Nigel Royston	St Paul's Chambers, Leeds	0113 245 5866
Eissa Mr Adrian Nadir	25 Bedford Row, London	020 7067 1500
Elder Miss Fiona Ann Morag	Albion Chambers, Bristol	0117 927 2144
Enoch Mr Dafydd Huw	Apex, Cardiff	02920 232 032
	23 Essex Street, London	020 7413 0353
Etherington Mr David Charles Lynch	18 Red Lion Court, London	020 7520 6000
	18 Red Lion Court (Annexe), Chelmsford	01245 280880
Evans Mr David Howard	Aspect Chambers, Birmingham	0121 222 2447
	Chambers of Andrew Mitchell QC, London	020 7440 9950
Evans Mr Philip	QEB Hollis Whiteman, London	020 7933 8855
Evans Mr Simeon Vaughan	St Johns Buildings, Manchester	0161 214 1500
	St Johns Buildings Liverpool, Liverpool	0151 243 6000
	16 Winckley Square, Preston	01772 256100
Falk Mr Charles Morton James	3 PB Barristers, London	020 7583 8055
Farley Mr David Dunbar	St Johns Buildings, Manchester	0161 214 1500
	St Johns Buildings Liverpool, Liverpool	0151 243 6000
	16 Winckley Square, Preston	01772 256100
Farrell Mr Simon Henry	3 Raymond Buildings, London	020 7400 6400
Faure Walker Miss Julia Frances	2 Hare Court, London	020 7353 3982
Feest Mr Adam Sebastian	3 PB Barristers, Bournemouth	01202 292102
	3 PB Barristers, Bristol	0117 928 1520
	3 PB Barristers, London	020 7583 8055
	3 PB Barristers, Oxford	01865 793 736
	3 PB Barristers, Winchester	01962 868884
Ferguson Mr Craig Charles	2 Hare Court, London	020 7353 3982
Ferguson Mr Stephen Michael	2 Bedford Row, London	020 7440 8888

Ferm Mr Rodney Eric	Broadway House Chambers, Bradford	01274 722560
	Broadway House Chambers, Leeds	0113 246 2600
Ferry-Swainson Mr Richard Joseph	2 Bedford Row, London	020 7440 8888
Fielding Mr Janick Raphael Alexander	4 King's Bench Walk, London	020 7822 7000
Finnigan Mr Peter Anthony	QEB Hollis Whiteman, London	020 7933 8855
Finucane Mr Brendan Godfrey Eamonn	Outer Temple Chambers, London	020 7353 6381
Fish Mr David Thomas	Deans Court Chambers, Manchester	0161 214 6000
	Deans Court Chambers, Preston	01772 565 600
	Goldsmith Chambers, London	020 7353 6802
Fisher Mr Jervis Andrew	Citadel Chambers, Birmingham	0121 233 8500
Fisher Mr Jonathan Simon	Devereux Chambers, London	020 7353 7534
Fisher Mr Richard Alan	Doughty Street Chambers, Bristol	01179 058 717
	Doughty Street Chambers, London	020 7404 1313
	Doughty Street Chambers, Manchester	0161 618 1066
Fishwick Mr Gregory David Philip Kyle	187 Fleet Street, London	020 7430 7430
Fitzgerald Mr Benedict Andrew	QEB Hollis Whiteman, London	020 7933 8855
Fitzgibbon Mr Francis George Herbert Dillon	Doughty Street Chambers, Bristol	01179 058 717
	Doughty Street Chambers, London	020 7404 1313
	Doughty Street Chambers, Manchester	0161 618 1066
Fitzmaurice Mr Guy Edward Christian	Staple Inn Chambers, London	020 7242 5240
Fletcher Mr James Watford	Five St Andrew's Hill, London	020 7332 5400
Follon Mr Daniel Richard Thomas	1 Gray's Inn Square, London	020 7405 0001
Ford Mr Mark Steven	Lincoln House Chambers, Manchester	0161 832 5701
Forlin Mr Gerard Emlyn	Cornerstone Barristers, London	020 7242 4986
Forsyth Miss Samantha	No5 Chambers, Birmingham	0845 210 5555
	No5 Chambers, Bristol	0845 210 5555
	No5 Chambers, London	0845 210 5555
Forte Mr Timothy Axel	Dyers Chambers, London	020 7404 1881
Foulkes Miss Rebecca	5 Pump Court, London	020 7353 2532
Foulkes Mr Christopher David	2 Hare Court, London	020 7353 3982
Fraser Mr Mark-Anthony	Dyers Chambers, London	020 7404 1881
Freeman Miss Lisa Claire	Furnival Chambers, London	020 7405 3232
Fryer Mr Nigel Mccrae	Queen Square Chambers, Bristol	0117 921 1966
Fryman Mr Neil	Lincoln House Chambers, Manchester	0161 832 5701
Frymann Mr Andrew Philip	187 Fleet Street, London	020 7430 7430
Fuad Mr Kerim	Chambers of Marion Smullen and Kerim Fuad QC, London	020 7427 4400
Fuller Mr Alan Peter	Albion Chambers, Bristol	0117 927 2144
Fullerton Mr Michael Andrew	7 Bell Yard, London	020 7831 0636
	Chambers of Mr Michael Fullerton, Hove	01273 772050
Furlong Mr Richard Craven	25 Bedford Row, London	020 7067 1500
Gadd Mr Adam Brian	Pump Court Chambers, London	020 7353 0711
	Pump Court Chambers, Winchester	01962 868 161
	Riverview Chambers, London	0844 225 3999
Ganesan Mr Muthupandi Peter	Furnival Chambers, London	020 7405 3232
Garlick Mr Paul Richard	Furnival Chambers, London	020 7405 3232
Gaskin Miss Leila	Charter Chambers, London	020 7618 4400
Gaskin Mr Francis John Gerald	4 Breams Buildings, London	020 7092 1900
Gau Mr Justin Charles	Pump Court Chambers, London	020 7353 0711
	Pump Court Chambers, Swindon	01793 539899
	Pump Court Chambers, Winchester	01962 868 161
Gelbart Mr Geoff Alan	1 Gray's Inn Square, London	020 7405 0001
Gerasimidis Mr Nicolas	Guildhall Chambers, Bristol	0117 930 9000
Gerry Miss Felicity Ruth	36 Bedford Row, London	020 7421 8000
Gersch Mr Adam Nissen	Argent Chambers, London	020 7556 5500
Gibbs Mr Philip Mark	KCH Garden Square, Nottingham	0115 941 8851
Gilchrist Miss Naomi Roberta	St Philips Chambers, Birmingham	0121 246 7000
Gillespie Mr Christopher Michael	2 Hare Court, London	020 7353 3982

Gladwell Mr Simon Mark	East Anglian Chambers, Ipswich	01473 214481
Glasgow Mr Oliver Edwin James	2 Hare Court, London	020 7353 3982
Glass Mr Anthony Trevor	QEB Hollis Whiteman, London	020 7933 8855
Gledhill Mr Lee Andre	Alexander Chambers, London	0845 652 0451/0854 652 0451
	Trident Barristers Chambers, Manchester	0161 663 3123
Goddard Miss Suzanne Hazel	Lincoln House Chambers, Manchester	0161 832 5701
Godfrey Mr Howard Anthony	2 Bedford Row, London	020 7440 8888
Godfrey Mr Thomas William Netherton	23 Essex Street, London	020 7413 0353
Gofur Mr Abdul	Thomas More Chambers, London	020 7404 7000
Goldberg Mr Jonathan Jacob	Cobden House Chambers, Manchester	0161 833 6000
	North Square Chambers, London	020 8455 3735
Gomulka Mr Michael Svend	25 Bedford Row, London	020 7067 1500
Goodall Miss Emma	Dyers Chambers, London	020 7404 1881
Goode Mr Julian Leigh Alexander	St Johns Buildings, Manchester	0161 214 1500
	St Johns Buildings Liverpool, Liverpool	0151 243 6000
	16 Winckley Square, Preston	01772 256100
Goodwin Mr Michael	Old Bailey Chambers, London	020 3008 6404
Goose Mr Julian Nicholas	2 Hare Court, London	020 7353 3982
	Zenith Chambers, Leeds	0113 245 5438
Goudie Mr William Martin Phillip	Charter Chambers, London	020 7618 4400
Gow Mr Henry	New Bailey Chambers, Liverpool	0151 236 9402
Gozem Mr Gaias	Lincoln House Chambers, Manchester	0161 832 5701
Grant Mr Chudi Paul	Kenworthy's Chambers, Manchester	0161 832 4036
Grant Mr Gary Steven	Francis Taylor Building, London	020 7353 8415
Gray Miss Jennifer	Chambers of Mr Ami Feder, London	020 7797 7788
	Chambers of Mr Ami Feder, London	020 7797 7788
	Lamb Building, Brighton	01273 820490
Gray Mr Peter Henry St John	5 Pump Court, London	020 7353 2532
Green Mr Jonathan Paul	Dyers Chambers, London	020 7404 1881
Green Mr Timothy Sinclair	St Philips Chambers, Birmingham	0121 246 7000
Greenfield Mr Peter Charles	King's Bench Chambers, Bournemouth	01202 250025
Grego Mr Kevin Christopher	Citadel Chambers, Birmingham	0121 233 8500
Grennan Mr Barry Edward	Kenworthy's Chambers, Manchester	0161 832 4036
Grey Mr Michael Henry John	Citadel Chambers, Birmingham	0121 233 8500
Griffin Miss Lynn Myfanwy	23 Essex Street, London	020 7413 0353
Griffin Mr Nicholas John	Five Paper Buildings, London	020 7583 6117
Griffiths Mr Hugh Robert James	Furnival Chambers, London	020 7405 3232
Griffiths Mr Peter	2 Bedford Row, London	020 7440 8888
	30 Park Place, Cardiff	029 2039 8421
Grunwald Mr Henry Cyril	Charter Chambers, London	020 7618 4400
Guest Mr Peter Liam	187 Fleet Street, London	020 7430 7430
Hackett Mr Philip George	Argent Chambers, London	020 7556 5500
Hadrill Mr Keith Paul	Furnival Chambers, London	020 7405 3232
Halden Mr Angus Robert	Queen Square Chambers, Bristol	0117 921 1966
Hall Mr Nicholas	Westgate Chambers, Lewes	01273 480510
Halliday-Davis Ms Deborah Lee	Carmelite Chambers, London	020 7936 6300
Hallowes Mr Rupert John Michael	3 Temple Gardens, London	020 7353 3102
Hamblin Mr Nicholas Howard	Westgate Chambers, Lewes	01273 480510
Hamilton Mr Nigel	Broadway House Chambers, Bradford	01274 722560
	Broadway House Chambers, Leeds	0113 246 2600
Hamilton-Shield Miss Anna-Maria	Charter Chambers, London	020 7618 4400
Hanlon Mr James Tobias	Old Bailey Chambers, London	020 3008 6404
Hannam Mr Timothy James	Citadel Chambers, Birmingham	0121 233 8500
Harbage Mr William John Hirons	36 Bedford Row, London	020 7421 8000
	37 Park Square Chambers, Leeds	0113 243 9422
Harding Mr Christopher James	Thomas More Chambers, London	020 7404 7000
Harding Mr Matthew Austin	39 Park Square, Leeds	0113 245 6633
Hardy Mr Maximilian John Lee	Nine Bedford Row, London	020 7489 2727
Hargreaves Mr Benjamin Thomas	Carmelite Chambers, London	020 7936 6300
Harounoff Mr David	9-12 Bell Yard, London	020 7400 1800
Harries Mr Mark Robert	Carmelite Chambers, London	020 7936 6300

Harris Miss Stella Cassandra Methven	Tooks Chambers, London	020 7842 7575
Harris Mr Adrian David	23 Essex Street, London	020 7413 0353
Harris Mr Wilbert Arthurlyn	Rowchester Chambers, Birmingham	0121 233 2327
Harris Ms Rebecca Elizabeth	QEB Hollis Whiteman, London	020 7933 8855
Harrison Mr John Foster	St Paul's Chambers, Leeds	0113 245 5866
Harvey Mr Stephen Frank	18 Red Lion Court, London	020 7520 6000
	18 Red Lion Court (Annexe), Chelmsford	01245 280880
Hassall Mr Craig Jonathan	Sovereign Chambers, Leeds	0113 245 1841
Hawes Mr Neil Ashley	Charter Chambers, London	020 7618 4400
Hawkes Mr Malcolm Alexander	Dyers Chambers, London	020 7404 1881
Hays Mr William Stormont	6 King's Bench Walk, London	020 7583 0410
Healy Miss Alexandra	9-12 Bell Yard, London	020 7400 1800
Hearnden Mr Richard Christopher	Furnival Chambers, London	020 7405 3232
Hegarty Mr Kevin John	St Philips Chambers, Birmingham	0121 246 7000
Henderson Mr Ian Francis	Farringdon Chambers, London	020 7089 5700
Henderson Mr Lawrence Mark	9-12 Bell Yard, London	020 7400 1800
Henley Mr Andrew Michael	Furnival Chambers, London	020 7405 3232
Hewitt Mr David Edward Miles	Five St Andrew's Hill, London	020 7332 5400
Hicks Mr Martin Leslie Arthur	2 Hare Court, London	020 7353 3982
Higgins Mr Daniel Malcolm Buhlea	Nine Bedford Row, London	020 7489 2727
Higginson Mr Peter St George	Charter Chambers, London	020 7618 4400
Hill Mr Max Benjamin Rowland	18 Red Lion Court, London	020 7520 6000
	18 Red Lion Court (Annexe), Chelmsford	01245 280880
Hill Mr Michael Gordon	Trinity Chambers, Middlesbrough	01642 247569
	Trinity Chambers, Newcastle Upon Tyne	0191 232 1927
Hillman Mr Basil	4 King's Bench Walk, London	020 7822 7000
Hilton Mr Alan John Howard	QEB Hollis Whiteman, London	020 7933 8855
Himsworth Mr Mark Stephen	Dyers Chambers, London	020 7404 1881
Hines Mr James Philip	3 Raymond Buildings, London	020 7400 6400
Hinton Mr Neil Pearse	King's Bench Chambers, Bournemouth	01202 250025
Hirst Miss Rebecca Elisabeth	Cobden House Chambers, Manchester	0161 833 6000
Hislop Mr David Seymour	Doughty Street Chambers, Bristol	01179 058 717
	Doughty Street Chambers, London	020 7404 1313
	Doughty Street Chambers, Manchester	0161 618 1066
Hobson Miss Laura Elise	Citadel Chambers, Birmingham	0121 233 8500
Hobson Miss Sally Anne	1 Paper Buildings, London	020 7353 3728
Holborn Mr David Reginald	18 Red Lion Court, London	020 7520 6000
	18 Red Lion Court (Annexe), Chelmsford	01245 280880
Holland Miss Charlotte Kate	Lincoln House Chambers, Manchester	0161 832 5701
Holland Mr Ricky John	Lincoln House Chambers, Manchester	0161 832 5701
Hood Mr David	Prince of Wales Chambers, London	020 7622 7415
Hooper Mr Gopal Arthur John	Thomas More Chambers, London	020 7404 7000
Hopper Mr Stephen John	Five Paper Buildings, London	020 7583 6117
Hossain Mr Mohammad Mozammel	187 Fleet Street, London	020 7430 7430
Howard Miss Nicola	25 Bedford Row, London	020 7067 1500
Howell Ms Claire Elizabeth Siobhan	36 Bedford Row, London	020 7421 8000
Hughes Mr William Lloyd	9-12 Bell Yard, London	020 7400 1800
Hugheston-Roberts Mr Charles Justin	4 Breams Buildings, London	020 7092 1900
Hurst Mr Brian	39 Park Square, Leeds	0113 245 6633
Hussain Miss Frida Khanam	Furnival Chambers, London	020 7405 3232
Hussain Mr Muhammad Altaf	Chambers of Mr M A Hussain, London	020 8679 2398
Hussain Mr Mukhtar	Lincoln House Chambers, Manchester	0161 832 5701
Ingram Mr Nigel Colquhoun	2 Bedford Row, London	020 7440 8888
Inyundo Mr Richard Kwame Swaka	6 King's Bench Walk, London	020 7583 0410
Irwin Mr Gavin David	Dyers Chambers, London	020 7404 1881
Islam Mr Mohammad Fakrul	18 Red Lion Court, London	020 7520 6000
Ivill Mr Scott Ashley	2 Hare Court, London	020 7353 3982

Jackson Mr Andrew Fraser	5 Pump Court, London	020 7353 2532
Jackson Mr Mark Joseph	No 8 Chambers, Birmingham	0121 236 5514
Jaffa Mr Ronald Mervyn	25 Bedford Row, London	020 7067 1500
Jafferjee Mr Aftab Asger	Atkinson Bevan Chambers, London	020 7353 2112
James Mr Roderick Ian	Charter Chambers, London	020 7618 4400
Jameson Mr Daniel Robert	Furnival Chambers, London	020 7405 3232
Janner The Hon Daniel Joseph Mitchell	23 Essex Street, London	020 7413 0353
	Exchange Chambers, Manchester	0161 833 2722
	St Philips Chambers, Birmingham	0121 246 7000
Jarratt Miss Alice Cordelia Betchworth	Carmelite Chambers, London	020 7936 6300
Jarvis Mr Paul	6 King's Bench Walk, London	020 7583 0410
Jefferies Mr Andrew	Dyers Chambers, London	020 7404 1881
	Westgate Chambers, Lewes	01273 480510
Jenkins Mr David Crofton	2 King's Bench Walk, London	020 7353 1746
Jenkins Mr Edward Nicholas	Five Paper Buildings, London	020 7583 6117
Jenkins Mr Hywel Iestyn	Outer Temple Chambers, London	020 7353 6381
Jenkins Mr Thomas Alun	2 Bedford Row, London	020 7440 8888
	Queen Square Chambers, Bristol	0117 921 1966
Jeremy Mr David Hugh Thomas	QEB Hollis Whiteman, London	020 7933 8855
Johnson Miss Amanda	Exchange Chambers, Leeds	0113 203 1970
	Exchange Chambers, Liverpool	0151 236 7747
	Exchange Chambers, Manchester	0161 833 2722
Johnson Ms Kathryn Margaret	Lincoln House Chambers, Manchester	0161 832 5701
Johnston Miss Anne-Marie	Carmelite Chambers, London	020 7936 6300
Jones Miss Jacinta Elizabeth Barrett	1 Mitre Court Buildings, London	020 7452 8900
Jones Mr Alun	St Paul's Chambers, Leeds	0113 245 5866
Jones Mr Gareth Edward	Lincoln House Chambers, Manchester	0161 832 5701
Jones Mr Mark Andrew	St Ive's Chambers, Birmingham	0121 236 0863
Jones Mr William John	2 Hare Court, London	020 7353 3982
Joshi Mr Rajendra Jugatray	18 Red Lion Court, London	020 7520 6000
	18 Red Lion Court (Annexe), Chelmsford	01245 280880
Jowett Mr Timothy David Christian	9 Park Place, Cardiff	029 2038 2731
Judge Miss Parveen	1 Mitre Court Buildings, London	020 7452 8900
Kapila Miss Rachel Prakash	3 Raymond Buildings, London	020 7400 6400
Karaiskos Miss Maria	Old Bailey Chambers, London	020 3008 6404
Katz Mr Philip Alec Jackson	9-12 Bell Yard, London	020 7400 1800
Kearney Mr John	Furnival Chambers, London	020 7405 3232
Keating Mr Dermot John	25 Bedford Row, London	020 7067 1500
Keeling Mr Adrian Francis	No5 Chambers, Birmingham	0845 210 5555
	No5 Chambers, Bristol	0845 210 5555
	No5 Chambers, London	0845 210 5555
Keith Mr Benjamin Charles Andrew	Five St Andrew's Hill, London	020 7332 5400
Kelly Mr Richard Bernard	East Anglian Chambers, Chelmsford	01473 214481
	East Anglian Chambers, Colchester	01473 214481
	East Anglian Chambers, Ipswich	01473 214481
	East Anglian Chambers, Norwich	01473 214481
Kennedy Miss Lucy Julia	QEB Hollis Whiteman, London	020 7933 8855
Kennedy Mr Peter Nicholas Dodgson	15 Winckley Square, Preston	01772 252828
Kenny Mr Martin William	Walnut House, Exeter	01392 279751
Keogh Mr Richard Thomas	Farringdon Chambers, London	020 7089 5700
Kerr Mr Christopher Richard	2 Pump Court, London	020 7353 5597
Kessling Mr Christopher David	Chambers of Mr Christopher Kessling, Leicester	01509 890690
Khalil Mr Karim Shakir	Octagon House, Norwich	01603 623186
	1 Paper Buildings, London	020 7353 3728
Khan Mr Ayoub	Chambers of Mr Ayoub Khan, Birmingham	07930 987202
Khan Mr Forz	Chambers of Mr F Khan, London	07854 109584
	6 King's Bench Walk, London	020 7353 4931
Khan Mr Imran	St Albans Chambers, St Albans	01727 843383

C

Khan Mr Tahir	Broadway House Chambers, Bradford	01274 722560
	Broadway House Chambers, Leeds	0113 246 2600
Khan Mr Zarif	Dyers Chambers, London	020 7404 1881
King Mr Adam Henry Peter	QEB Hollis Whiteman, London	020 7933 8855
King Mr Gelaga Perry	2 Bedford Row, London	020 7440 8888
King Mr John Patrick	Nine Bedford Row, London	020 7489 2727
Kinnear Mr Jonathan Shea	9-12 Bell Yard, London	020 7400 1800
Kitchen Mr Simon Dugald Owen Ralph	Dyers Chambers, London	020 7404 1881
Knight Mr Benjamin James	Central Chambers, Manchester	0161 236 1133
Knight Mr Graeme Edward Verdon	7 Bell Yard, London	020 7831 0636
	Carmelite Chambers, London	020 7936 6300
	The Barristers Chambers, Address withheld	07966 056368
Lahiffe Mr Martin Patrick Joseph	3 Temple Gardens, London	020 7353 3102
Lake Mr James Edward	St Paul's Chambers, Leeds	0113 245 5866
Lamb Mr Jeffrey Thomas	Westgate Chambers, Lewes	01273 480510
Lamb Mr John Richard	1 Pump Court, London	020 7842 7070
Lambert Mr Nigel Robert Woolf	Carmelite Chambers, London	020 7936 6300
Langley Mr Charles Howard	2 Bedford Row, London	020 7440 8888
Larkin Mr Sean	QEB Hollis Whiteman, London	020 7933 8855
Lasker Mr Jeremy Stewart	Lincoln House Chambers, Manchester	0161 832 5701
Lawrence Sir Ivan John	5 Pump Court, London	020 7353 2532
Lawton Mr Paul Anthony	Lincoln House Chambers, Manchester	0161 832 5701
	18 Red Lion Court, London	020 7520 6000
Le Fevre Miss Sarah Margaret	3 Raymond Buildings, London	020 7400 6400
Leake Mr Stephen	Carmelite Chambers, London	020 7936 6300
Ledward Miss Jocelyn Victoria	QEB Hollis Whiteman, London	020 7933 8855
Lenaghan Mr Anthony	Dyers Chambers, London	020 7404 1881
Lennon Mr John Francis	23 Essex Street, London	020 7413 0353
Leonard Mr James Alexander	Outer Temple Chambers, London	020 7353 6381
Levett Miss Francesca Anna	Five St Andrew's Hill, London	020 7332 5400
Lewiecki Miss Marie	Old Bailey Chambers, London	020 3008 6404
Lewington Miss Francesca Anna	Crown Office Row Chambers, Brighton	01273 625625
Liddiard Mr Martin Thomas	No5 Chambers, Birmingham	0845 210 5555
	No5 Chambers, Bristol	0845 210 5555
	No5 Chambers, London	0845 210 5555
Lindsay Mr Jeremy Mark Henry	37 Park Square Chambers, Leeds	0113 243 9422
Linehan Mr Stephen John	St Philips Chambers, Birmingham	0121 246 7000
Lissack Mr Richard Anthony	Outer Temple Chambers, London	020 7353 6381
	Riverview Chambers, London	0844 225 3999
Livingstone Mr Simon John	Thomas More Chambers, London	020 7404 7000
Lloyd Mr Benjamin John	6 King's Bench Walk, London	020 7583 0410
Lloyd-Eley Mr Andrew James	Old Bailey Chambers, London	020 3008 6404
Lloyd-Jones Mr John Benedict	36 Bedford Row, London	020 7421 8000
Lodge Mr Hugo Daniel Paul	Atkinson Bevan Chambers, London	020 7353 2112
Lowe Mr Christopher John	KCH Garden Square, Nottingham	0115 941 8851
Lowe Mr Rupert William Manley	Guildhall Chambers, Bristol	0117 930 9000
Lownds Mr Peter Alexander	Doughty Street Chambers, Bristol	01179 058 717
	Doughty Street Chambers, London	020 7404 1313
	Doughty Street Chambers, Manchester	0161 618 1066
Lule Miss Jacqueline	1 Mitre Court Buildings, London	020 7452 8900
Lynch Mr Jerome	Charter Chambers, London	020 7618 4400
Lyons Mr David Wakefield	King's Bench Chambers, Bournemouth	01202 250025
	2 Pump Court, London	020 7353 5597
MacFarlane Mr Andrew Lennox	Colleton Chambers, Exeter	01392 274898
MacKenzie Smith Mrs Catherine Joanna	10 King's Bench Walk, London	020 7353 7742
Magee Mr Michael James	Fenners Chambers, Cambridge	01223 368761
Magee Mr Samuel Cairns	2 Bedford Row, London	020 7440 8888
Maggs Mr Patrick Terence	15 New Bridge Street, London	020 7842 1900
Maginn Miss Olivia Maria	New Walk Chambers, Leicester	0871 200 1298/0116 255 9144

Mahmood Mr Abid	Central Chambers, Manchester	0161 236 1133
	No5 Chambers, Birmingham	0845 210 5555
	No5 Chambers, Bristol	0845 210 5555
	No5 Chambers, London	0845 210 5555
Malone Mr David John	1 Gray's Inn Square, London	020 7405 0001
Mann Mr Jonathan Simon	25 Bedford Row, London	020 7067 1500
Mannion Ms Amy Elisabeth	9-12 Bell Yard, London	020 7400 1800
	1 Crown Office Row, London	020 7797 7500
Mansell Mr Jason Francis Guy	Seven Bedford Row, London	020 7242 3555
Marler Lieutenant Colonel Lee Gary	Bretton Woods Law, London	
	18 Red Lion Court, London	020 7520 6000
Maroof Ms Lara Anne	Charter Chambers, London	020 7618 4400
Martin Mr James Stephen	5 King's Bench Walk, London	020 7353 5638
Matthias Mr David Huw	Francis Taylor Building, London	020 7353 8415
Mawdsley Mr David John	Chambers of Mr David Mawdsley, Southport	01704 565 387
Mawrey Ms Eleanor Frances	The Chambers of Grahame Aldous QC, London	020 7832 0500
Maxwell Mr Adrian Robert John	St John's Chambers, Bristol	0117 923 4700
May Mr Christopher John	Five St Andrew's Hill, London	020 7332 5400
Mayo Mr Simon Peter	187 Fleet Street, London	020 7430 7430
McCarthy Miss Tara Mia Inger	Thomas More Chambers, London	020 7404 7000
McCarthy Mr Martin Raymond	Farringdon Chambers, London	020 7089 5700
McCulloch Miss Fiona Catharine Jane	Middle Temple Lane Chambers, London	020 7583 4352
McDonald Miss Janet	9 Park Place, Cardiff	029 2038 2731
McGhee Mr Philip James	QEB Hollis Whiteman, London	020 7933 8855
McGowan Miss Maura Patricia	2 Bedford Row, London	020 7440 8888
	Lincoln House Chambers, Manchester	0161 832 5701
McKiernan Mr Edward Joseph	Farringdon Chambers, London	020 7089 5700
McKone Mr Mark Desmond	Sovereign Chambers, Leeds	0113 245 1841
McLinden Mr John Vincent Barry	Field Court Chambers, London	020 7405 6114
McNally Mr John Joseph	Dyers Chambers, London	020 7404 1881
McNeill Mr David Martin	Five St Andrew's Hill, London	020 7332 5400
Meeke Mr Robert Martin James	Colleton Chambers, Exeter	01392 274898
Mendelle Mr Paul Michael	25 Bedford Row, London	020 7067 1500
Menon Mr Rajiv	Garden Court Chambers, London	020 7993 7600
Meredith Mr Christopher William	Furnival Chambers, London	020 7405 3232
Metzer Mr Anthony David Erwin	Argent Chambers, London	020 7556 5500
Midgley Miss Anna Victoria Jane	Albion Chambers, Bristol	0117 927 2144
Miller Mr David Robin	Furnival Chambers, London	020 7405 3232
Miller Mr Peter Owen Michael	Cornerstone Barristers, London	020 7242 4986
Millett Mr Kenneth James	2 Hare Court, London	020 7353 3982
Milne Mr Alexander Hugh	18 Red Lion Court, London	020 7520 6000
	18 Red Lion Court (Annexe), Chelmsford	01245 280880
Milne Mr Richard James	23 Essex Street, London	020 7413 0353
Milroy Miss Caroline	Thomas More Chambers, London	020 7404 7000
Milsom Mrs Catherine Mary	Argent Chambers, London	020 7556 5500
Misner Mr Philip Lawrence Ian	4 Breams Buildings, London	020 7092 1900
Mitchell Mr Andrew Robert	Chambers of Andrew Mitchell QC, London	020 7440 9950
Mitchell Mr Jonathan Stuart	25 Bedford Row, London	020 7067 1500
Mitchell Mr Keith Arno	Chambers of Andrew Mitchell QC, London	020 7440 9950
Modgil Miss Sangita	Carmelite Chambers, London	020 7936 6300
Mooney Mr Stephen John	Albion Chambers, Bristol	0117 927 2144
Moorhouse Mr Brendon Scott	Guildhall Chambers, Bristol	0117 930 9000
Moran Mr Patrick Michael	15 New Bridge Street, London	020 7842 1900
Morris Mr Ben	Chavasse Court Chambers, Liverpool	0151 229 2030
Morris Mr Ieuan John	9 Park Place, Cardiff	029 2038 2731
Morris Ms Johanna	Chambers of Marion Smullen and Kerim Fuad QC, London	020 7427 4400
Moses Mr Stephen Colin	Furnival Chambers, London	020 7405 3232

C

Mostafa Miss Margia	2 Pump Court, London	020 7353 5597
Mousley Mr William Howard	2 King's Bench Walk, London	020 7353 1746
Muller Mr Antonie Sean	Citadel Chambers, Birmingham	0121 233 8500
Murray Mr Daniel Evan Duncan	Old Bailey Chambers, London	020 3008 6404
Mytton Mr Paul Vincent	St Philips Chambers, Birmingham	0121 246 7000
Nadim Mr Ahmed	Lincoln House Chambers, Manchester	0161 832 5701
Newbold Mr Michael Paul	9-12 Bell Yard, London	020 7400 1800
Newcomb Mr Quinton John	1 Paper Buildings, London	020 7353 3728
Newton-Price Mr James Edward	Pump Court Chambers, London	020 7353 0711
	Pump Court Chambers, Swindon	01793 539899
	Pump Court Chambers, Winchester	01962 868 161
Nicholls Mr Christopher Benjamin	Citadel Chambers, Birmingham	0121 233 8500
Nicholls Mr Colin Alfred Arthur	3 Raymond Buildings, London	020 7400 6400
Nicholson Mr Thomas Edward Cyril	Atkinson Bevan Chambers, London	020 7353 2112
Norton Mr Giles	Enigma Chambers, Sheffield	07779 576499
	Holborn Chambers, London	020 7242 6060
Nsugbe Mr Oba Eric	Pump Court Chambers, London	020 7353 0711
	Pump Court Chambers, Swindon	01793 539899
	Pump Court Chambers, Winchester	01962 868 161
Nuttall Mr Andrew Peter	Lincoln House Chambers, Manchester	0161 832 5701
Nwosu Miss Sheryl Ada	4 Breams Buildings, London	020 7092 1900
O'Byrne Mr Andrew John Martin	St Johns Buildings, Manchester	0161 214 1500
	St Johns Buildings Liverpool, Liverpool	0151 243 6000
	16 Winckley Square, Preston	01772 256100
O'Connor Mr Patrick Michael Joseph	Doughty Street Chambers, Bristol	01179 058 717
	Doughty Street Chambers, London	020 7404 1313
	Doughty Street Chambers, Manchester	0161 618 1066
O'Connor Ms Charlotte Jane Andrews	Nine Bedford Row, London	020 7489 2727
O'Donoghue Mr Hugh Vincent	Carmelite Chambers, London	020 7936 6300
Offenbach Mr Roger Leon	25 Bedford Row, London	020 7067 1500
Offer Mr Alexander	Garden Court Chambers, London	020 7993 7600
	Park Court Chambers, Leeds	0113 243 3277
Ogunbusola Mr Victor Olaniyi	Chambers of Victor Ogumbusola, Basildon	07413 634231
O'Kane Miss Sarah Caroline	Argent Chambers, London	020 7556 5500
Oldham Mrs Frances Mary Theresa	36 Bedford Row, London	020 7421 8000
	37 Park Square Chambers, Leeds	0113 243 9422
Omideyi Miss Anuoluwapo Iyanu	Furnival Chambers, London	020 7405 3232
Onalaja Mr James Oluwatosin	2 Pump Court, London	020 7353 5597
O'Neill Mr Brian Patrick	2 Hare Court, London	020 7353 3982
Ong Miss Grace Yu Mae	Argent Chambers, London	020 7556 5500
Orchard Mr Anthony Edward	Carmelite Chambers, London	020 7936 6300
Owen Miss Carys	18 Red Lion Court, London	020 7520 6000
	18 Red Lion Court (Annexe), Chelmsford	01245 280880
Owen Mr Timothy Wynn	Matrix Chambers, London	020 7404 3447
Owusu-Yianoma Mr David Kwasi Dartey	1 Mitre Court Buildings, London	020 7452 8900
Ozin Mr Paul David	23 Essex Street, London	020 7413 0353
Page Mr Jonathan Rowland Thomas	Carmelite Chambers, London	020 7936 6300
Paley Ms Ruth Theresa Elizabeth	23 Essex Street, London	020 7413 0353
Panagiotopoulou Miss Tania	Staple Inn Chambers, London	020 7242 5240
Pande Miss Kakoly	2 Dr Johnson's Buildings, London	020 7936 2613
Paraskos Mr Paraskevakis Christakis	11 Gray's Inn Square Chambers, London	020 7405 6879
Pardoe Mr Matthew James	Dyers Chambers, London	020 7404 1881
Pardoe Mr Rupert Adam Corin	23 Essex Street, London	020 7413 0353
Patel Mr Yasin Ahmed	25 Bedford Row, London	020 7067 1500
Paton Mr Ian Francis	QEB Hollis Whiteman, London	020 7933 8855
Patterson Mr Stewart	Pump Court Chambers, London	020 7353 0711
	Pump Court Chambers, Swindon	01793 539899
	Pump Court Chambers, Winchester	01962 868 161

Name	Chambers	Telephone
Pawson-Pounds Mr Daniel James	6 King's Bench Walk, London	020 7583 0410
Peet Mr Andrew Geraint	Chambers of Mr Andrew Peet, Leicester	07966 238437
Penny Miss Abigail Sarah Prudence	4 Breams Buildings, London	020 7092 1900
Pentol Mr Simon Alex	25 Bedford Row, London	020 7067 1500
Perian Mr Steven	3 Temple Gardens, London	020 7353 3102
Perrins Mr Gregory Lloyd	1 Paper Buildings, London	020 7353 3728
Perry Mr Lewis Kenneth	Rowchester Chambers, Birmingham	0121 233 2327
Phillips Miss Emma Louise	1 Pump Court, London	020 7842 7070
Phillips Mr Simon Benjamin	Francis Taylor Building, London	020 7353 8415
	Park Court Chambers, Leeds	0113 243 3277
Pickup Mr James Kenneth	2 Hare Court, London	020 7353 3982
	Lincoln House Chambers, Manchester	0161 832 5701
Pierpoint Miss Katherine Anne	Lincoln House Chambers, Manchester	0161 832 5701
Pinto Miss Amanda Eve	Five Paper Buildings, London	020 7583 6117
Polnay Mr Jonathan Samuel	5 King's Bench Walk, London	020 7353 5638
Pople Miss Alison Ruth	2 Bedford Row, London	020 7440 8888
Powell Mr Oliver Jonathan	3 PB Barristers, London	020 7583 8055
Power Mr Archangelo Carlo	2 Bedford Row, London	020 7440 8888
Power Mr Lawrence Imam	4 KBW, London	020 7822 8822
Power Ms Alexia Clare	Furnival Chambers, London	020 7405 3232
Price Mr Albert John	23 Essex Street, London	020 7413 0353
Price Mr Andrew Robert	Dyers Chambers, London	020 7404 1881
Prior Mr Paul Stephen	36 Bedford Row, London	020 7421 8000
Prior Mrs Mary	36 Bedford Row, London	020 7421 8000
Prokofiev Mr Sergey	Lincoln House Chambers, Manchester	0161 832 5701
Purnell Mr Paul Oliver	Farringdon Chambers, London	020 7089 5700
Quinn Mr Tomas Anthony	4 King's Bench Walk, London	020 7822 7000
Quirke Mr Gerard Martin	Citadel Chambers, Birmingham	0121 233 8500
Qureshi Mr Tanveer Aftab	25 Bedford Row, London	020 7067 1500
Radford Mrs Nadine Poggioli	187 Fleet Street, London	020 7430 7430
Raggatt Mr Timothy Walter Harold	4 King's Bench Walk, London	020 7822 7000
	St Philips Chambers, Birmingham	0121 246 7000
Rai Mr Rajesh Kumar	1 Mitre Court Buildings, London	020 7452 8900
Randall Mrs Rebecca	25 Bedford Row, London	020 7067 1500
Rawat Miss Houzla Bibi Mahmad	Carmelite Chambers, London	020 7936 6300
Real Miss Kirsty Nichola	Albion Chambers, Bristol	0117 927 2144
Reece Mr Brian Alfred William	187 Fleet Street, London	020 7430 7430
Rees Mr Jonathan David	2 Hare Court, London	020 7353 3982
Rees Mr Jonathan Elystan	Apex, Cardiff	02920 232 032
Reevell Mr Simon Justin	39 Park Square, Leeds	0113 245 6633
Reiff-Musgrove Miss Kaja	Dyers Chambers, London	020 7404 1881
Reiz Mr Stanley	Carmelite Chambers, London	020 7936 6300
Renvoize Mr Edward Philip	No.6 Park Square, Leeds	0113 245 9763
	1 Paper Buildings, London	020 7353 3728
Rhodes Mr Nicholas Piers	Charter Chambers, London	020 7618 4400
Rhodes Mr Robert Elliott	Outer Temple Chambers, London	020 7353 6381
	Principal Chambers, Sevenoaks	0845 209 8080
	St Philips Chambers, Birmingham	0121 246 7000
Richards Mr David James Martin	3 PB Barristers, Bournemouth	01202 292102
	3 PB Barristers, Bristol	0117 928 1520
	3 PB Barristers, London	020 7583 8055
	3 PB Barristers, Oxford	01865 793 736
	3 PB Barristers, Winchester	01962 868884
Richardson Mr Alistair Paul George	6 King's Bench Walk, London	020 7583 0410
Riggs Miss Samantha	25 Bedford Row, London	020 7067 1500
Rimmer Mr Nicholas Patrick Edward	23 Essex Street, London	020 7413 0353
Rinker Mr Andrew Stuart D'Artois	Chambers of Mr Andrew Rinker, London	020 7584 1091
Rippon Mr Simon John	Citadel Chambers, Birmingham	0121 233 8500
Ritchie Miss Shauna	2 Bedford Row, London	020 7440 8888
Roberts Miss Lisa	Lincoln House Chambers, Manchester	0161 832 5701
Roberts Mr Timothy David	Fountain Chambers, Middlesbrough	01642 804040
	QEB Hollis Whiteman, London	020 7933 8855

C

Robertshaw Mr Martin Andrew	39 Park Square, Leeds	0113 245 6633
Robinson Miss Claire Maria	Charter Chambers, London	020 7618 4400
Robinson Mr Nicholas James Lansdale	3 PB Barristers, Bournemouth	01202 292102
	3 PB Barristers, Bristol	0117 928 1520
	3 PB Barristers, London	020 7583 8055
	3 PB Barristers, Oxford	01865 793 736
	3 PB Barristers, Winchester	01962 868884
Rooke Mr Alexander John Giles	Argent Chambers, London	020 7556 5500
Rose Miss Pamela Susan	1 Mitre Court Buildings, London	020 7452 8900
Rosen Mr Jonathan Leon	1 Gray's Inn Square, London	020 7405 0001
Ross Mr Gordon Macrae	3 Temple Gardens, London	020 7353 3102
Roughton Mr Ashley Wentworth	Hogarth Chambers, London	020 7404 0404
Rouse Mr Justin Clive Douglas	Nine Bedford Row, London	020 7489 2727
Row Mr Charles Philip	Queen Square Chambers, Bristol	0117 921 1966
Rowe Miss Freya Emily Beatrice	Thomas More Chambers, London	020 7404 7000
Roy Mr Stefan Alexander Hiren	5 Pump Court, London	020 7353 2532
Rudd Mr Michael	36 Bedford Row, London	020 7421 8000
Rudolf Mr Nathaniel David	25 Bedford Row, London	020 7067 1500
Ruffell Mr Mark Beresford	Pump Court Chambers, London	020 7353 0711
	Pump Court Chambers, Swindon	01793 539899
	Pump Court Chambers, Winchester	01962 868 161
Rule Mr Philip David	Castle Chambers, Harrow-on-the-Hill	020 8423 6579
Rush Mr Craig Peter	2 Bedford Row, London	020 7440 8888
Russell Miss Marguerite	Garden Court Chambers, London	020 7993 7600
Russell Mr Graham Alexander	Citadel Chambers, Birmingham	0121 233 8500
Russell Mr Guy Jonothon	Westgate Chambers, Lewes	01273 480510
Russell-Mitra Miss Jessica Suparna	1 Mitre Court Buildings, London	020 7452 8900
Rustom Mr Shiraz Sam	1215 Chambers, London	020 3291 1215
	Cranford Chambers, London	020 7404 7454
	1 Mitre Court Buildings, London	020 7452 8900
Sadler Miss Rhiannon Jane	Westgate Chambers, Lewes	01273 480510
Sallon Mr Christopher Robert	Doughty Street Chambers, Bristol	01179 058 717
	Doughty Street Chambers, London	020 7404 1313
	Doughty Street Chambers, Manchester	0161 618 1066
Salmon Mr Jonathan Carl	St Philips Chambers, Birmingham	0121 246 7000
Sandford Mr Robert Stanley	Bank House Chambers, Sheffield	0114 275 1223
Sandford Mr Simon John Austin	5 King's Bench Walk, London	020 7353 5638
Sangster Mr Nigel	25 Bedford Row, London	020 7067 1500
Saunders Mr Neil	3 Raymond Buildings, London	020 7400 6400
Saunt Ms Linda Patricia	Chambers of Andrew Mitchell QC, London	020 7440 9950
Saxby Mr Oliver Charles John	6 Pump Court, London	020 7797 8400
	6 Pump Court Chambers, Maidstone	01622 688094
Sayed Miss Nermine Abdel	Old Bailey Chambers, London	020 3008 6404
Schofield Mr Thomas Leon	No5 Chambers, Birmingham	0845 210 5555
	No5 Chambers, Bristol	0845 210 5555
	No5 Chambers, London	0845 210 5555
Scott Bell Mrs Rosalind Sara	Trinity Chambers, Middlesbrough	01642 247569
	Trinity Chambers, Newcastle Upon Tyne	0191 232 1927
Scott Mr Matthew John	Pump Court Chambers, London	020 7353 0711
	Pump Court Chambers, Swindon	01793 539899
	Pump Court Chambers, Winchester	01962 868 161
Scutt Mr David Robert	9-12 Bell Yard, London	020 7400 1800
Sear Miss Joanne	13 KBW, Oxford	01865 311066
	13 King's Bench Walk, London	020 7353 7204
Sekar Mr Chandra	Angell Park Chambers, London	020 7737 5957
Sekhon Mr Narinder Singh	Sovereign Chambers, Leeds	0113 245 1841
Sen Mr Aditya Kumar	Coram Chambers, London	020 7092 3700
Seymour Mr Mark William	9-12 Bell Yard, London	020 7400 1800
Shapiro Mr Selwyn	2 King's Bench Walk, London	020 7353 1746
Sharma Miss Sunyana	3 PB Barristers, Bournemouth	01202 292102
	3 PB Barristers, London	020 7583 8055

Sharma Mr Jamie	187 Fleet Street, London	020 7430 7430
Sharma Mr Sanjeev Mohan	Equity Chambers, Birmingham	0121 236 5007
Sharpe Mr Martin Laurence	Park Court Chambers, Leeds	0113 243 3277
Shaw Mr Michael John	9-12 Bell Yard, London	020 7400 1800
Sheikh Mr Irshad Ahmed	187 Fleet Street, London	020 7430 7430
Sheppard-Jones Miss Victoria Louise	Carmelite Chambers, London	020 7936 6300
Sherborn Miss Natalie Louise	25 Bedford Row, London	020 7067 1500
Short Mr Gary Peter	KCH Garden Square, Nottingham	0115 941 8851
Shotton Ms Sophie Diana	15 New Bridge Street, London	020 7842 1900
Sidhu Mr Navjot	25 Bedford Row, London	020 7067 1500
Silverton Miss Catherine Anne	Sovereign Chambers, Leeds	0113 245 1841
Simpson Mr Graeme Michael	Citadel Chambers, Birmingham	0121 233 8500
Singarajah Mr Frederico	1 Gray's Inn Square, London	020 7405 0001
Singh Mr Dapinderpaul	23 Essex Street, London	020 7413 0353
	Park Court Chambers, Leeds	0113 243 3277
Singh-Tiwana Mr Ekwall	No5 Chambers, Birmingham	0845 210 5555
	No5 Chambers, Bristol	0845 210 5555
	No5 Chambers, London	0845 210 5555
Sinker Mr Andrew Tennant	New Bailey Chambers, Liverpool	0151 236 9402
Sjolin Ms Catarina Marianne	36 Bedford Row, London	020 7421 8000
Skinner Mr Samuel Richard Edward	KCH Garden Square, Nottingham	0115 941 8851
Small Miss Penelope Susan	Chambers of Andrew Mitchell QC, London	020 7440 9950
Smith Miss Eileen Joan	Trinity Chambers, Middlesbrough	01642 247569
	Trinity Chambers, Newcastle Upon Tyne	0191 232 1927
Smith Mr Alisdair Robert Macsorley	9-12 Bell Yard, London	020 7400 1800
Smith Mr Clive Francis	Chambers of Marion Smullen and Kerim Fuad QC, London	020 7427 4400
Smith Mr David Andrew	9-12 Bell Yard, London	020 7400 1800
Smith Mr Ian Alfio	11 Stone Buildings, London	020 7831 6381
Smith Mr James Alastair	9-12 Bell Yard, London	020 7400 1800
Smith Mr Mark William	Aegis Chambers, Wembley	
Smith Ms Rachel Catherine	Lincoln House Chambers, Manchester	0161 832 5701
Smitten Mr Ben James	25 Bedford Row, London	020 7067 1500
Smyth Mr Christopher Julian Worsley	Queen Square Chambers, Bristol	0117 921 1966
Snow Mr Darren Mark	Charter Chambers, London	020 7618 4400
Solley Mr Stephen Malcolm	Charter Chambers, London	020 7618 4400
Sparrow Mrs Marie-Claire	Holborn Chambers, London	020 7242 6060
Spears Miss Katharine Sarah	Carmelite Chambers, London	020 7936 6300
Spence Mr Simon Peter	18 Red Lion Court, London	020 7520 6000
	18 Red Lion Court (Annexe), Chelmsford	01245 280880
Spencer Mr Paul Anthony	3 Serjeants Inn, London	020 7427 5000
Spens Mr David Patrick	Garden Court Chambers, London	020 7993 7600
Spenwyn Ms Marie Ann	Carmelite Chambers, London	020 7936 6300
St Louis Mr Brian Lloyd	15 New Bridge Street, London	020 7842 1900
Stanford Mr Tony James	Old Bailey Chambers, London	020 3008 6404
Stein Mr Daniel Alexander	No5 Chambers, Birmingham	0845 210 5555
	No5 Chambers, Bristol	0845 210 5555
	No5 Chambers, London	0845 210 5555
Stein Mr Samuel	Dyers Chambers, London	020 7404 1881
	Westgate Chambers, Lewes	01273 480510
Stelling Mr Nigel Roy	Citadel Chambers, Birmingham	0121 233 8500
Stemp Mr Scott	12 College Place, Southampton	023 8032 0320
Stern Mr David Patrick Julian	King's Bench Chambers, Bournemouth	01202 250025
	11 Stone Buildings, London	020 7831 6381
Stevens Mr Mark Nicholas	Chambers of Marion Smullen and Kerim Fuad QC, London	020 7427 4400
Stevens Mr Stuart Standish	Holborn Chambers, London	020 7242 6060
Stevenson Mr Robert Lloyd	Sovereign Chambers, Leeds	0113 245 1841
Stimpson Mr Christopher Hugh	Atkinson Bevan Chambers, London	020 7353 2112

C

Barrister	Chambers	Telephone
Stone Mr Joseph	Doughty Street Chambers, Bristol	01179 058 717
	Doughty Street Chambers, London	020 7404 1313
	Doughty Street Chambers, Manchester	0161 618 1066
Storey Mr Richard Alexander	3 Temple Gardens, London	020 7353 3102
Stork Mr Brian Raymond	3 Temple Gardens, London	020 7353 3102
Storrie Mr Timothy James	Lincoln House Chambers, Manchester	0161 832 5701
Stott Mr Philip Geoffrey	QEB Hollis Whiteman, London	020 7933 8855
Stranex Mr Andrew John	St Paul's Chambers, Leeds	0113 245 5866
Strong Mr Adrian Peter Ciaran	KBW, Leeds	0113 297 1200
Stubbs Mr Andrew James	St Paul's Chambers, Leeds	0113 245 5866
Sugarman Mr Jason Ashley	9-12 Bell Yard, London	020 7400 1800
Suggett Mr Iain Robert Ottar	Warwick Chambers, Birmingham	0121 382 9122
Sullivan Mr Geoffrey Charles Alexander	36 Bedford Row, London	020 7421 8000
Summers Miss Allison	36 Bedford Row, London	020 7421 8000
Summers Mr Benjamin Dylan James	3 Raymond Buildings, London	020 7400 6400
Sumnall Miss Charlene Emma Louise	Five Paper Buildings, London	020 7583 6117
Sutherland Mr James More	Nexus Chambers, London	020 7404 1147/020 7831 8309
Sutton-Mattocks Mr Christopher John	5 King's Bench Walk, London	020 7353 5638
Sweeney Mr Noel Christopher	Veritas Chambers, Worle	01934 853 382
Syfret Mr Nicholas	Citadel Chambers, Birmingham	0121 233 8500
	13 KBW, Oxford	01865 311066
	13 King's Bench Walk, London	020 7353 7204
Talbot Mr Jack Richard	Dyers Chambers, London	020 7404 1881
Tatford Mr Warwick Henry Patrick	9-12 Bell Yard, London	020 7400 1800
Taylor Ms Karen Anne	Themis Chambers, London	07967 418976
Tetlow Mr Bernard Geoffrey	Charter Chambers, London	020 7618 4400
Thomas Mr Andrew Martin	Lincoln House Chambers, Manchester	0161 832 5701
	Linenhall Chambers, Chester	01244 348282
Thomas Mr James Austin	KCH Garden Square, Nottingham	0115 941 8851
Thomas Mr Timothy Nicholas	Lombard Chambers, London	020 7107 2100
Thompson Miss Pauline Sonita	5 King's Bench Walk, London	020 7353 5638
Thompson Mr Patrick Miles	KBW, Leeds	0113 297 1200
	St Johns Buildings, Manchester	0161 214 1500
	St Johns Buildings Liverpool, Liverpool	0151 243 6000
	16 Winckley Square, Preston	01772 256100
Thompson Mr Ryan Jerome	Dyers Chambers, London	020 7404 1881
Thornton Mr John Robert	Stour Chambers, Canterbury	01227 764899
Tizzano Mr Franco Salvatore	Old Bailey Chambers, London	020 3008 6404
Toomey Mr Kevin Ian	2 Bedford Row, London	020 7440 8888
Traversi Mr John David Stephen Antona	Nine Bedford Row, London	020 7489 2727
Treharne Mr Neil Simon	Dingle Chambers, Bristol	07818 827754
Trowler Ms Rebecca	Doughty Street Chambers, Bristol	01179 058 717
	Doughty Street Chambers, London	020 7404 1313
	Doughty Street Chambers, Manchester	0161 618 1066
Tucker Mr James Eckhord	Queen Square Chambers, Bristol	0117 921 1966
Tucker Mr James William Richard	Teucro Chambers, Epsom	
Turner Mr Jonathan James	Argent Chambers, London	020 7556 5500
Udom Miss Nancy Ini	Five St Andrew's Hill, London	020 7332 5400
Upton Mr Alexander Stuart Allen	23 Essex Street, London	020 7413 0353
Upton Mr John Stewart	4 King's Bench Walk, London	020 7822 7000
Usher Mr Neil Morris	Lincoln House Chambers, Manchester	0161 832 5701
Valios Mr Nicholas Paul	4 Breams Buildings, London	020 7092 1900
	No 8 Chambers, Birmingham	0121 236 5514
Valley Miss Helen Maria	25 Bedford Row, London	020 7067 1500
Vine Mr James Peter Stockman	Five St Andrew's Hill, London	020 7332 5400
Vollenweider Mr Amiot Marcus Ellerton	Thomas More Chambers, London	020 7404 7000
Vout Mr Andrew Paul	9-12 Bell Yard, London	020 7400 1800
	1 High Pavement, Nottingham	0115 941 8218

Waley Mr Eric Richard Thomas	Assize Court Chambers, Bristol	0117 926 4587
Walker Mr Liam David	Doughty Street Chambers, London	020 7404 1313
Walker Mr Paul Christopher	5 King's Bench Walk, London	020 7353 5638
Wall Mr Mark Arthur	Citadel Chambers, Birmingham	0121 233 8500
Walmsley Mr Alan	5 King's Bench Walk, London	020 7353 5638
Walters Miss Vivian Irene Elizabeth	Five St Andrew's Hill, London	020 7332 5400
Walton Miss Karen Tanya	Dyers Chambers, London	020 7404 1881
Ward Miss Alexandra	9-12 Bell Yard, London	020 7400 1800
Warner Mr Anthony Charles Broughton	Citadel Chambers, Birmingham	0121 233 8500
Warrington Mr John Edward Lawrence	Five St Andrew's Hill, London	020 7332 5400
Waters Mr David Ebsworth	2 Hare Court, London	020 7353 3982
Watkinson Mr Howard	9-12 Bell Yard, London	020 7400 1800
Watson Mr Anthony Dennis	Lincoln House Chambers, Manchester	0161 832 5701
Watson Mr Benjamin Turquand	3 Raymond Buildings, London	020 7400 6400
Watson Mr Mark Andrew	KCH Garden Square, Nottingham	0115 941 8851
Watson Mr Tom Bradley	Chavasse Court Chambers, Liverpool	0151 229 2030
Wayne Mr Nicholas	Argent Chambers, London	020 7556 5500
Weatherby Mr Peter Francis	Chambers of Ian Macdonald QC, Manchester	0161 236 1840
	Garden Court Chambers, London	020 7993 7600
Weaver Mr Brett	6 King's Bench Walk, London	020 7583 0410
Webster Miss Shelley Anne	Carmelite Chambers, London	020 7936 6300
Webster Mr Alistair Stevenson	Chambers of Andrew Mitchell QC, London	020 7440 9950
	Lincoln House Chambers, Manchester	0161 832 5701
Weekes Mr Mark Vincent	6 King's Bench Walk, London	020 7583 0410
Wells Mr Colin John	25 Bedford Row, London	020 7067 1500
Western Mr Adam John Brooks	Citadel Chambers, Birmingham	0121 233 8500
Whawell Miss Leesha Claire	3 Temple Gardens, London	020 7353 3102
Whitfield Mr Jonathan	Doughty Street Chambers, London	020 7404 1313
Wiktorowski-Solecki Miss Tamara	Middle Temple Lane Chambers, London	020 7583 4352
Wilcox Mr Jerome Carl Jean	Alexander Chambers, London	0845 652 0451/0854 652 0451
Wild Mr Simon Peter	9-12 Bell Yard, London	020 7400 1800
Williams Mr Ben Dylan	Kings Chambers, Birmingham	0845 034 3444
	Kings Chambers, Leeds	0845 034 3444
	Kings Chambers, Manchester	0845 034 3444
Willmer Mr Stephen James	Argent Chambers, London	020 7556 5500
Wilson Mr Scott	Themis Chambers, London	07967 418976
Wise Mr Leslie Michael	10 King's Bench Walk, London	020 7353 7742
Wiseman Mr Adam Philip Pasternak	18 Red Lion Court, London	020 7520 6000
	18 Red Lion Court (Annexe), Chelmsford	01245 280880
Wong Miss Natasha Pui-Wai	187 Fleet Street, London	020 7430 7430
Wood Mr James Alexander Douglas	Doughty Street Chambers, Bristol	01179 058 717
	Doughty Street Chambers, London	020 7404 1313
	Doughty Street Chambers, Manchester	0161 618 1066
Wood Mr Michael Mure	Chambers of Mr Michael Wood QC, London	020 8874 3474
Wood Mr Richard Michael	East Anglian Chambers, Chelmsford	01473 214481
	East Anglian Chambers, Ipswich	01473 214481
	East Anglian Chambers, Norwich	01473 214481
Woods Mr Terence Mccartan	187 Fleet Street, London	020 7430 7430
Yeo Mr Nicholas	3 Raymond Buildings, London	020 7400 6400
Zoest Ms Jacqueline Amy	Carmelite Chambers, London	020 7936 6300

DATA PROTECTION

Ajaz Mr Mohammad Arshad	Eastmans Chambers, Reading	0118 966 9094
Antell Mr John Jason	King's Bench and Godolphin (KBG)Chambers, Plymouth	01752 221551
Askey Mr Robert John	Palmyra Chambers, Warrington	01925 444919
Bicarregui Miss Anna Claire Victoria	4-5 Gray's Inn Square, London	020 7404 5252

Bowen Mr Nicholas James Hugh	Doughty Street Chambers, Bristol	01179 058 717
	Doughty Street Chambers, London	020 7404 1313
	Doughty Street Chambers, Manchester	0161 618 1066
Buchan Miss Caroline Venetia	Chambers of Miss C Buchan, Haywards Heath	01444 482222
Busuttil Mr Godwin John Antoine	5RB, London	020 7242 2902
Buttimore Mr Gabriel	13 KBW, Oxford	01865 311066
	13 King's Bench Walk, London	020 7353 7204
Coster Mr Ronald David	42 Bedford Row, London	020 7831 0222
Edwards Mr Denis	Francis Taylor Building, London	020 7353 8415
Engelman Mr Mark Trevor	Hardwicke, London	020 7242 2523
Engelman Mr Philip	Cloisters, London	020 7827 4000
	Trinity Chambers, Middlesbrough	01642 247569
	Trinity Chambers, Newcastle Upon Tyne	0191 232 1927
Facenna Mr Gerald Carlo	Monckton Chambers, London	020 7405 7211
Falkowski Mr Damian	4-5 Gray's Inn Square, London	020 7404 5252
Fern Mr Gary	7 Stones IP, London	020 7193 4033
Gledhill Mr Lee Andre	Alexander Chambers, London	0845 652 0451/0854 652 0451
	Trident Barristers Chambers, Manchester	0161 663 3123
Hanlon Mr James Tobias	Old Bailey Chambers, London	020 3008 6404
Iyer Miss Shobana	Swan Chambers, Richmond	0845 123 1234
Lopez Mr Juan Nemesio	Francis Taylor Building, London	020 7353 8415
Matthias Mr David Huw	Francis Taylor Building, London	020 7353 8415
Peretz Mr George Michael John	Monckton Chambers, London	020 7405 7211
Perian Mr Steven	3 Temple Gardens, London	020 7353 3102
Scott Mr Andrew David Peter	Park Lane Plowden, Leeds	0113 228 5049
Strong Mr Adrian Peter Ciaran	KBW, Leeds	0113 297 1200
Stuart Mr Bruce Ian	Lombard Chambers, London	020 7107 2100

DEFAMATION

Afeeva Mr Mark Kudzo Dzitosi	Matrix Chambers, London	020 7404 3447
Algazy Mr Jacques Max	Cloisters, London	020 7827 4000
Aly Miss Sheila	Warwick House Chambers, London	020 7430 2323
Anderson Mr Richard Neil Macdiarmid	Arbitration Chambers, London	020 7267 2137
Andre Mr Roger Louis	Sovereign Chambers, Leeds	0113 245 1841
Andrews Mr Paul Leslie	Great James Street Chambers, London	020 7440 4949
Angammana Mr Gamini Bertram	Chambers of Gamini Angammana, London	020 8771 5205
Arnheim Dr Michael Thomas Walter	Chambers of Dr Michael Arnheim, London	020 7833 5093
	Holborn Chambers, London	020 7242 6060
	Principal Chambers, Sevenoaks	0845 209 8080
Awodele Mr Olufemi Adetunji	Great James Street Chambers, London	020 7440 4949
Azhar Mr Ali Mohammad	9 King's Bench Walk, London	020 7353 9564
Beaumont Mr Marc Clifford	9 Stone Buildings, London	020 7404 5055
	Windsor Barristers' Chambers, Windsor	01753 839321
Birkby Mr Richard Adam	Park Court Chambers, Leeds	0113 243 3277
Bishop Mr Gordon William	Chambers of Gordon Bishop, Woking	01483 486 730
Bishop Mr Malcolm Leslie	Argent Chambers, London	020 7556 5500
	Equity Chambers, Birmingham	0121 236 5007
	30 Park Place, Cardiff	029 2039 8421
Brady Mr Scott	3 Temple Gardens, London	020 7353 3102
Browne Mr Desmond John Michael	5RB, London	020 7242 2902
Buchan Miss Caroline Venetia	Chambers of Miss C Buchan, Haywards Heath	01444 482222
Buckhaven Mr Simon	Hardwicke, London	020 7242 2523
Buckley Mr Peter Evered	Cobden House Chambers, Manchester	0161 833 6000
Bullock Mr Robert Gustaf	The Chambers of Mr Bullock, Brighton	01273 321050
Bunting Mr Jude James	Tooks Chambers, London	020 7842 7575

Name	Chambers	Telephone
Busuttil Mr Godwin John Antoine	5RB, London	020 7242 2902
Butler Mr Rupert James	3 Hare Court, London	020 7415 7800
Caplan Mr Jonathan Michael	Five Paper Buildings, London	020 7583 6117
	Riverview Chambers, London	0844 225 3999
Chalk Mr Alexander John Gervase	6 King's Bench Walk, London	020 7583 0410
Chowdhary Mr Islamuddin	Cassian Chambers, Ilford	07796 262641
Christie Mr Iain Robert	5RB, London	020 7242 2902
Cohen Mr Edward Mervyn	11 Stone Buildings, London	020 7831 6381
Connolly Mr Dominic Regan	Five St Andrew's Hill, London	020 7332 5400
Corsellis Mr Nicholas Robert Alexander	3 Temple Gardens, London	020 7353 3102
Coster Mr Ronald David	42 Bedford Row, London	020 7831 0222
Craig Mr Aubrey John	Chancery House Chambers, Leeds	0113 244 6691
	St Philips Chambers, Birmingham	0121 246 7000
Critchley Mr John Stephen	Field Court Chambers, London	020 7405 6114
Crystal Mr Jonathan	Argent Chambers, London	020 7556 5500
De Mounteney Mr Jonathan Patrick	Chambers of Mr J P De Mounteney, Reading	0118 934 6822
Deacon Mr Robert Murray	11 Stone Buildings, London	020 7831 6381
Dean Mr Jacob	5RB, London	020 7242 2902
Dean Mr James Patrick	Goldsmith Chambers, London	020 7353 6802
Draycott Mr Simon Douglas	Citadel Chambers, Birmingham	0121 233 8500
	Five St Andrew's Hill, London	020 7332 5400
Eaton Mr Tobias Barnaby	Staple Inn Chambers, London	020 7242 5240
Edwards Mr Jonathan William	Westgate Chambers, Lewes	01273 480510
Edwards Mr Nigel Royston	St Paul's Chambers, Leeds	0113 245 5866
Engelman Mr Mark Trevor	Hardwicke, London	020 7242 2523
Engelman Mr Philip	Cloisters, London	020 7827 4000
	Trinity Chambers, Middlesbrough	01642 247569
	Trinity Chambers, Newcastle Upon Tyne	0191 232 1927
Ferm Mr Rodney Eric	Broadway House Chambers, Bradford	01274 722560
	Broadway House Chambers, Leeds	0113 246 2600
Finlay Mr Darren	Sovereign Chambers, Leeds	0113 245 1841
Fitzgerald Mr John Vincent	Ingenuity IP Chambers, Petts Wood	
Gadd Mr Adam Brian	Pump Court Chambers, London	020 7353 0711
	Pump Court Chambers, Winchester	01962 868 161
	Riverview Chambers, London	0844 225 3999
Gerry Miss Felicity Ruth	36 Bedford Row, London	020 7421 8000
Glasgow Mr Oliver Edwin James	2 Hare Court, London	020 7353 3982
Gledhill Mr Lee Andre	Alexander Chambers, London	0845 652 0451/0854 652 0451
	Trident Barristers Chambers, Manchester	0161 663 3123
Goldberg Mr Jonathan Jacob	Cobden House Chambers, Manchester	0161 833 6000
	North Square Chambers, London	020 8455 3735
Graham Mr Thomas Patrick Henry	New Square Chambers, London	020 7419 8000
Gray Mr Peter Henry St John	5 Pump Court, London	020 7353 2532
Hendron Mr Henry Joseph Christopher	Strand Chambers, London	020 7117 6920
Hood Mr David	Prince of Wales Chambers, London	020 7622 7415
Hussain Mr Muhammad Altaf	Chambers of Mr M A Hussain, London	020 8679 2398
Iqbal Mr Mashood	London View Chambers, Sawbridgeworth	07788 912493
Iyer Miss Shobana	Swan Chambers, Richmond	0845 123 1234
Jolliffe Mrs Victoria Esther Jean	5RB, London	020 7242 2902
Jones Mr Christopher David Harries	St John's Chambers, Bristol	0117 923 4700
Jones Mr Lawrence Victor	Chambers of Lawrence Jones, London	020 7831 1444
Kenny Mr Martin William	Walnut House, Exeter	01392 279751
Khan Dr Alexander	Coral House, Manchester	
Lamb Mr Jeffrey Thomas	Westgate Chambers, Lewes	01273 480510
Lenaghan Mr Anthony	Dyers Chambers, London	020 7404 1881
Lissack Mr Richard Anthony	Outer Temple Chambers, London	020 7353 6381
	Riverview Chambers, London	0844 225 3999

C

Ludbrook Mr Timothy Vivian	13 Old Square Chambers, London	020 7831 4445
Matthias Mr David Huw	Francis Taylor Building, London	020 7353 8415
McCormick Mr William Thomas	Ely Place Chambers, London	020 7400 9600
McLinden Mr John Vincent Barry	Field Court Chambers, London	020 7405 6114
Metzer Mr Anthony David Erwin	Argent Chambers, London	020 7556 5500
Michalos Miss Christina Antigone Diana	5RB, London	020 7242 2902
Miller Mr Andrew	2 Temple Gardens, London	020 7822 1200
Munden Mr Richard Alexander John	5RB, London	020 7242 2902
Mustakim Mr Abdul Yunus Al	Chambers of Mr Mustakim, London	
Mylvaganam Ms Tanoo	1 Gray's Inn Square, London	020 7405 0001
Nabi Mr Sajjad	5 Pump Court, London	020 7353 2532
Newman Mr Alan Ronald Harvey	Argent Chambers, London	020 7556 5500
Norton Mr Giles	Enigma Chambers, Sheffield	07779 576499
	Holborn Chambers, London	020 7242 6060
O'Brien Mr Nicholas William Wattebot	10 King's Bench Walk, London	020 7353 7742
O'Donoghue Mr Hugh Vincent	Carmelite Chambers, London	020 7936 6300
Osborne Mr James Robert	Clerksroom (London), London	0845 083 3000
Page Miss Adrienne May	5RB, London	020 7242 2902
Paraskos Mr Paraskevakis Christakis	11 Gray's Inn Square Chambers, London	020 7405 6879
Parker Mrs Karen Lesley	Guildhall Chambers Portsmouth, Portsmouth	023 9275 2400
Pearson Mr Christopher	Lamb Chambers, London	020 7797 8300
Penny Miss Abigail Sarah Prudence	4 Breams Buildings, London	020 7092 1900
Rahman Mr Anis	12 Old Square Chambers, London	020 7404 0875
Rinker Mr Andrew Stuart D'Artois	Chambers of Mr Andrew Rinker, London	020 7584 1091
Rippon Mr Simon John	Citadel Chambers, Birmingham	0121 233 8500
Rogers Miss Christy Abigail	Ingenuity IP Chambers, Petts Wood	
	No. 3 Fleet Street Chambers, London	020 7936 4474
Rooke Mr Alexander John Giles	Argent Chambers, London	020 7556 5500
Saini Mr Parminder Paul Singh	12 Old Square Chambers, London	020 7404 0875
Shore Miss Victoria Louise	5RB, London	020 7242 2902
Silverton Miss Catherine Anne	Sovereign Chambers, Leeds	0113 245 1841
Singarajah Mr Frederico	1 Gray's Inn Square, London	020 7405 0001
Skinner Mr Samuel Richard Edward	KCH Garden Square, Nottingham	0115 941 8851
Soto-Miranda Mr Diego Fernando	One Essex Court, London	020 7936 3030
Speker Mr Adam Samuel Edward	5RB, London	020 7242 2902
Spooner Mr Henry Neville	Tolzey Chambers, Bristol	
	Westgate Chambers, Lewes	01273 480510
Stanford Mr Tony James	Old Bailey Chambers, London	020 3008 6404
Stevens Mr Stuart Standish	Holborn Chambers, London	020 7242 6060
Stewart Mr Nicholas John Cameron	Ely Place Chambers, London	020 7400 9600
Vassall-Adams Mr Guy Luke	Doughty Street Chambers, Bristol	01179 058 717
	Doughty Street Chambers, London	020 7404 1313
	Doughty Street Chambers, Manchester	0161 618 1066
Vollenweider Mr Amiot Marcus Ellerton	Thomas More Chambers, London	020 7404 7000
Warby Mr Mark David John	5RB, London	020 7242 2902
Wells Mr Caspar John Mowlem	Goldsmith Chambers, London	020 7353 6802
Wheaton Mr Ian Malcolm James	Eighteen Carlton Crescent, Southampton	023 8063 9001
Widdett Ms Ceri Louise	Park Court Chambers, Leeds	0113 243 3277
Wiktorowski-Solecki Miss Tamara	Middle Temple Lane Chambers, London	020 7583 4352
Wolman Mr Clive Richard	11 Stone Buildings, London	020 7831 6381

DISCIPLINARY TRIBUNALS

Ajaz Mr Mohammad Arshad	Eastmans Chambers, Reading	0118 966 9094
Algazy Mr Jacques Max	Cloisters, London	020 7827 4000
Allwood Mrs Gina Louisa	Seven Bedford Row, London	020 7242 3555
Apthorp Mr George Charles	5 Essex Court, London	020 7410 2000

Barrister	Chambers	Telephone
Askey Mr Robert John	Palmyra Chambers, Warrington	01925 444919
Aylott Mr Colin Christopher	Carmelite Chambers, London	020 7936 6300
Badejo Mr Abimbola Rafiu	5 Pump Court, London	020 7353 2532
Bagley Miss Louisa Ellen	1 Paper Buildings, London	020 7353 3728
Bicarregui Miss Anna Claire Victoria	4-5 Gray's Inn Square, London	020 7404 5252
Bilsland Miss Alisan Margaret	St James's Chambers, Manchester	0161 834 7000
Bowen Mr Nicholas James Hugh	Doughty Street Chambers, Bristol	01179 058 717
	Doughty Street Chambers, London	020 7404 1313
	Doughty Street Chambers, Manchester	0161 618 1066
Bryan Mr Robert John	1 Paper Buildings, London	020 7353 3728
Bryant-Heron Mr Mark Nicholas	9-12 Bell Yard, London	020 7400 1800
Carr Mr Christopher Sean	36 Bedford Row, London	020 7421 8000
Chipperfield Mr Jeremy Steven	Cranford Chambers, London	020 7404 7454
Clark Mr Dingle	Goldsmith Chambers, London	020 7353 6802
Claxton Mr Elroy Geraldo	23 Essex Street, London	020 7413 0353
	Old Bailey Chambers, London	020 3008 6404
Clements Miss Paula Kate	Alexander Chambers, London	0845 652 0451/0854 652 0451
	Guildford Chambers, Guildford	01483 539131
Comb Mr David William	Trinity Chambers, Middlesbrough	01642 247569
	Trinity Chambers, Newcastle Upon Tyne	0191 232 1927
Conlon Mr Michael John Patrick	Harcourt Chambers, Milton Keynes	0845 123 1234
Costello Mr Paul James	Chambers of Mr Paul J Costello, Biggleswade	07846 016 399
Coster Mr Ronald David	42 Bedford Row, London	020 7831 0222
Cotter Mr Nicholas Andrew James Horlor	1 Paper Buildings, London	020 7353 3728
Dean Mr James Patrick	Goldsmith Chambers, London	020 7353 6802
Desmond Mr Denis John	Cornwall Street Chambers, Birmingham	0121 233 7500
Doherty Mr Nicholas Brudenell	4 King's Bench Walk, London	020 7822 7000
Dowden Mr Andrew Philip	Castle Chambers, Harrow-on-the-Hill	020 8423 6579
	Melbury House, Leicester	07801 037802
Draycott Mr Simon Douglas	Citadel Chambers, Birmingham	0121 233 8500
	Five St Andrew's Hill, London	020 7332 5400
Duffy Mr Derek James	St Paul's Chambers, Leeds	0113 245 5866
Edwards Mr Nigel Royston	St Paul's Chambers, Leeds	0113 245 5866
Elliott Mr Eric Alan	Sovereign Chambers, Leeds	0113 245 1841
	Trinity Chambers, Middlesbrough	01642 247569
	Trinity Chambers, Newcastle Upon Tyne	0191 232 1927
	York Chambers, Newcastle Upon Tyne	0191 206 4677
Engelman Mr Philip	Cloisters, London	020 7827 4000
	Trinity Chambers, Middlesbrough	01642 247569
	Trinity Chambers, Newcastle Upon Tyne	0191 232 1927
Falkowski Mr Damian	4-5 Gray's Inn Square, London	020 7404 5252
Finlay Mr Darren	Sovereign Chambers, Leeds	0113 245 1841
Garvie Mr Carl Peter	St Philips Chambers, Birmingham	0121 246 7000
Gersch Mr Adam Nissen	Argent Chambers, London	020 7556 5500
Gibbs Mr Philip Mark	KCH Garden Square, Nottingham	0115 941 8851
Gledhill Mr Lee Andre	Alexander Chambers, London	0845 652 0451/0854 652 0451
	Trident Barristers Chambers, Manchester	0161 663 3123
Glyn Mr Caspar Hilary Gordon	Cloisters, London	020 7827 4000
Goodlad Mr Grant David	Farrar's Building, London	020 7583 9241
Graham-Wells Miss Alison Christine	Exchange Chambers, Leeds	0113 203 1970
	Exchange Chambers, Liverpool	0151 236 7747
	Exchange Chambers, Manchester	0161 833 2722
Granville Stafford Mr Andrew	4 King's Bench Walk, London	020 7822 7000
Green Mr Patrick Curtis	Henderson Chambers, London	020 7583 9020
Griffin Mr Nicholas John	Five Paper Buildings, London	020 7583 6117
Gurden Miss Alison Louise	1 Gray's Inn Square, London	020 7405 0001
Hanlon Mr James Tobias	Old Bailey Chambers, London	020 3008 6404

Harris Mr Adrian David	23 Essex Street, London	020 7413 0353
Hassall Mr Craig Jonathan	Sovereign Chambers, Leeds	0113 245 1841
Hinton Mr Neil Pearse	King's Bench Chambers, Bournemouth	01202 250025
Hood Mr David	Prince of Wales Chambers, London	020 7622 7415
Horton Mr Matthew Bethell	39 Essex Street, London	020 7832 1111
	82 King Street, Manchester	0161 870 9969
Jackson Mr Andrew Fraser	5 Pump Court, London	020 7353 2532
Jarratt Miss Alice Cordelia Betchworth	Carmelite Chambers, London	020 7936 6300
Jones Mr Richard Frederick Thomas	Heavenwood Chambers, Stroud	01453 873444
Keith Mr Benjamin Charles Andrew	Five St Andrew's Hill, London	020 7332 5400
Kenny Mr Martin William	Walnut House, Exeter	01392 279751
Lewis Mr Wayne Anthony	Access Lawyers, London	020 8801 2345
Linehan Mr Stephen John	St Philips Chambers, Birmingham	0121 246 7000
Livingstone Mr Simon John	Thomas More Chambers, London	020 7404 7000
Mallett Mr Simon Jeremy	KBW, Leeds	0113 297 1200
Marler Lieutenant Colonel Lee Gary	Bretton Woods Law, London	
	18 Red Lion Court, London	020 7520 6000
Matthias Mr David Huw	Francis Taylor Building, London	020 7353 8415
McCombie Mr Fergus Alexander Paul	1 Gray's Inn Square, London	020 7405 0001
McCracken Mr James	Cornwall Street Chambers, Birmingham	0121 233 7500
McGowan Miss Maura Patricia	2 Bedford Row, London	020 7440 8888
	Lincoln House Chambers, Manchester	0161 832 5701
Merz Mr Richard James	9-12 Bell Yard, London	020 7400 1800
Metzger Mr Kevin Albert	11 Gray's Inn Square Chambers, London	020 7405 6879
Monaghan Ms Susan Mary	No5 Chambers, Birmingham	0845 210 5555
	No5 Chambers, Bristol	0845 210 5555
	No5 Chambers, London	0845 210 5555
Murphy Mr Michael Patrick	Central Chambers, Manchester	0161 236 1133
	10 King's Bench Walk, London	020 7353 7742
Onipede Dr Victor Olusegun	Chambers of Dr V O Onipede, London	07956 207159
Oommen Mr Jacob	Chambers of Mr Jacob Oommen, East Barnet	07958 680272
Owen Mr Timothy Wynn	Matrix Chambers, London	020 7404 3447
Page Mr Jonathan Rowland Thomas	Carmelite Chambers, London	020 7936 6300
Paraskos Mr Paraskevakis Christakis	11 Gray's Inn Square Chambers, London	020 7405 6879
Perian Mr Steven	3 Temple Gardens, London	020 7353 3102
Plimmer Miss Melanie Ann	Kings Chambers, Birmingham	0845 034 3444
	Kings Chambers, Leeds	0845 034 3444
	Kings Chambers, Manchester	0845 034 3444
Rees Mr Jonathan Elystan	Apex, Cardiff	02920 232 032
Richardson Mr Alistair Paul George	6 King's Bench Walk, London	020 7583 0410
Ritchie Miss Shauna	2 Bedford Row, London	020 7440 8888
Rule Mr Philip David	Castle Chambers, Harrow-on-the-Hill	020 8423 6579
Scott Bell Mrs Rosalind Sara	Trinity Chambers, Middlesbrough	01642 247569
	Trinity Chambers, Newcastle Upon Tyne	0191 232 1927
Scott Mr Andrew David Peter	Park Lane Plowden, Leeds	0113 228 5049
Sekar Mr Chandra	Angell Park Chambers, London	020 7737 5957
Stebbings Mr Ian Anthony	1 Gray's Inn Square, London	020 7405 0001
Stephens Mr Michael Allen	Design Chambers, London	020 7353 0747
	St Ive's Chambers, Birmingham	0121 236 0863
Stevenson Mr Robert Lloyd	Sovereign Chambers, Leeds	0113 245 1841
Stuart Mr Bruce Ian	Lombard Chambers, London	020 7107 2100
Stuart Mr James William	Lamb Chambers, London	020 7797 8300
Suter Mr Erich George Bernard	Park Chambers, Weybridge Park	01932 820082
Thomas Mr Gareth	Atlantic Chambers, Liverpool	0151 236 4421
Treharne Mr Neil Simon	Dingle Chambers, Bristol	07818 827754
Tresman Mr Lewis Robert Simon	Staple Inn Chambers, London	020 7242 5240
Trumpington Mr John Henry	Staple Inn Chambers, London	020 7242 5240

Name	Chambers	Telephone
Twist Mr Stephen John	Dere Street Barristers, Newcastle Upon Tyne	0844 3351551
Unigwe Mr Sylvester Emefiona	Essex House Chambers, London	020 7692 0677
	11 Gray's Inn Square Chambers, London	020 7405 6879
Vickery Mr Neil Michael	13 KBW, Oxford	01865 311066
	13 King's Bench Walk, London	020 7353 7204
Watson Mr Graham	Colleton Chambers, Exeter	01392 274898
Webster Miss Shelley Anne	Carmelite Chambers, London	020 7936 6300
Wilcox Mr Jerome Carl Jean	Alexander Chambers, London	0845 652 0451/0854 652 0451
Williams Mr Ben Dylan	Kings Chambers, Birmingham	0845 034 3444
	Kings Chambers, Leeds	0845 034 3444
	Kings Chambers, Manchester	0845 034 3444
Williams Ms Sandra Alessandra Caroline	The Chambers Of Alessandra Williams, Tadworth	07941 944950
Wills Miss Alexandra Itari	Christ Church Chambers, London	020 7409 5278/07788 512787
Wood Mr Michael Mure	Chambers of Mr Michael Wood QC, London	020 8874 3474
Woodward Miss Joanne Claire	9 St John Street, Manchester	0161 955 9000
Zeitler Miss Barbara	3 Dr Johnson's Buildings, London	020 7353 4854

DISCRIMINATION

Name	Chambers	Telephone
Adewale Mr Remi Adetokunbo Sanni	Chambers of G. D. Tetteh, London	020 7353 7095
	Chambers of Mr R. A. Adewale, Address withheld	020 7231 2814
Afeeva Mr Mark Kudzo Dzitosi	Matrix Chambers, London	020 7404 3447
Agnihotri Mr Naveen	12 College Place, Southampton	023 8032 0320
Ahmad Ms Aysha	42 Bedford Row, London	020 7831 0222
Akers Mr Robert Matthew Harry	St Johns Buildings, Chester	01244 323070
	St Johns Buildings, Manchester	0161 214 1500
	16 Winckley Square, Preston	01772 256100
Algazy Mr Jacques Max	Cloisters, London	020 7827 4000
Alomo Mr Richard Olusoji	14 Gray's Inn Square, London	020 7242 0858
Aly Miss Sheila	Warwick House Chambers, London	020 7430 2323
Amraoui Mr Thomas	4-5 Gray's Inn Square, London	020 7404 5252
Anderson Mr Jamie Henrie	Trinity Chambers, Middlesbrough	01642 247569
	Trinity Chambers, Newcastle Upon Tyne	0191 232 1927
Antell Mr John Jason	King's Bench and Godolphin (KBG)Chambers, Plymouth	01752 221551
Apthorp Mr George Charles	5 Essex Court, London	020 7410 2000
Ashley Mr Neil Martin	East Anglian Chambers, Chelmsford	01473 214481
	East Anglian Chambers, Ipswich	01473 214481
	East Anglian Chambers, Norwich	01473 214481
Askey Mr Robert John	Palmyra Chambers, Warrington	01925 444919
Atkinson Mr Jody Roy	St John's Chambers, Bristol	0117 923 4700
Auburn Mr Jonathan Walter	4-5 Gray's Inn Square, London	020 7404 5252
Awodele Mr Olufemi Adetunji	Great James Street Chambers, London	020 7440 4949
Beaumont Mr Marc Clifford	9 Stone Buildings, London	020 7404 5055
	Windsor Barristers' Chambers, Windsor	01753 839321
Berry Mr Adrian Christopher	Garden Court Chambers, London	020 7993 7600
Bertram Mr Jonathan Peter	Seven Bedford Row, London	020 7242 3555
Bhanji Mr Shiraz Musa	4 Bingham Place, London	020 7486 5347
	1 Gray's Inn Square, London	020 7405 0001
Bourke Ms Sarah Victoria Norma	Tooks Chambers, London	020 7842 7575
Bourne Mr Charles Gregory	4-5 Gray's Inn Square, London	020 7404 5252
Bourne Mr Colin Peter	Kings Chambers, Birmingham	0845 034 3444
	Kings Chambers, Leeds	0845 034 3444
	Kings Chambers, Manchester	0845 034 3444
Braier Mr Jason Dean	Field Court Chambers, London	020 7405 6114
Brehan Ms Daire	Chambers of Ms D Brehan, London	07808 726877
Brown Mr Timothy William	13 KBW, Oxford	01865 311066
	13 King's Bench Walk, London	020 7353 7204

C

Barrister	Chambers	Telephone
Bryden Mr Christopher James Yuen Kang	4 King's Bench Walk, London	020 7822 7000
Buchan Miss Caroline Venetia	Chambers of Miss C Buchan, Haywards Heath	01444 482222
Budworth Mr Martin James	Kings Chambers, Birmingham	0845 034 3444
	Kings Chambers, Leeds	0845 034 3444
	Kings Chambers, Manchester	0845 034 3444
Bunting Mr Jude James	Tooks Chambers, London	020 7842 7575
Burgher Mr Benjimin George	Outer Temple Chambers, London	020 7353 6381
Burrett Mr Alex	1 Gray's Inn Square, London	020 7405 0001
Butler Mr Rupert James	3 Hare Court, London	020 7415 7800
Callan Ms Jane Elizabeth	Trinity Chambers, Middlesbrough	01642 247569
	Trinity Chambers, Newcastle Upon Tyne	0191 232 1927
Carrion Benitez Ms Miriam	36 Bedford Row, London	020 7421 8000
Cartwright Mr Ivan Matthew	KCH Garden Square, Nottingham	0115 941 8851
Cattermull Miss Emma Jayne	East Anglian Chambers, Chelmsford	01473 214481
	East Anglian Chambers, Ipswich	01473 214481
	East Anglian Chambers, Norwich	01473 214481
Chadwick Miss Joanna Ceridwen	No5 Chambers, Birmingham	0845 210 5555
	No5 Chambers, Bristol	0845 210 5555
	No5 Chambers, London	0845 210 5555
Chambers Ms Rachel Elizabeth	Cloisters, London	020 7827 4000
Chan Miss Susan	13 KBW, Oxford	01865 311066
	13 King's Bench Walk, London	020 7353 7204
Christie Mr Iain Robert	5RB, London	020 7242 2902
Chute Ms Andrea Alexandra	Rougemont Chambers, Exeter	01392 208484
	Tooks Chambers, London	020 7842 7575
Clarke Mr Nikolas Michael	Field Court Chambers, London	020 7405 6114
Clay Mr Jonathan Roger	Cornerstone Barristers, London	020 7242 4986
Conlon Mr Michael John Patrick	Harcourt Chambers, Milton Keynes	0845 123 1234
Cooksey Mr Nicholas	River Chambers, Shrewsbury	01743 350505
Cooper Miss Samantha Ann	Outer Temple Chambers, London	020 7353 6381
Costello Mr Paul James	Chambers of Mr Paul J Costello, Biggleswade	07846 016 399
Coster Mr Ronald David	42 Bedford Row, London	020 7831 0222
Coulter Mr Barry John	Clerksroom (London), London	0845 083 3000
	Clerksroom (Taunton), Taunton	0845 083 3000
	King's Lynn Chambers, King's Lynn	01553 672 085
Coyle Mr Anthony Noel	Zenith Chambers, Leeds	0113 245 5438
Crasnow Ms Rachel	Cloisters, London	020 7827 4000
Crawford Mr Lincoln Santo	12 King's Bench Walk, London	020 7583 0811
Crew Miss Gillian Mary	Ely Place Chambers, London	020 7400 9600
Cunningham Ms Naomi Brigid	Outer Temple Chambers, London	020 7353 6381
Currie Mr Fergus Hugh	Unity Street Chambers, Bristol	0117 906 9789
Daly Mr David	Heathway Chambers, London	020 8293 0509
Davey Mr Charles	64 Bridge Street, Manchester	0845 083 3000
	Chambers of Mr C Davey, Bishop's Stortford	01279 506412
	Clerksroom (Taunton), Taunton	0845 083 3000
Davies Mr Jonathan Huw	Old Square Chambers, Bristol	0117 930 5100
	Old Square Chambers, London	020 7269 0300
De Mello Mr Rembert Joseph Julius	No5 Chambers, Birmingham	0845 210 5555
	No5 Chambers, Bristol	0845 210 5555
	No5 Chambers, London	0845 210 5555
Dean Mr James Patrick	Goldsmith Chambers, London	020 7353 6802
Doerfel Mr Jan Hendrik Jamison	1215 Chambers, London	020 3291 1215
	Chambers of Mr J H Doerfel, Richmond	0845 123 1234
Doughty Mr Peter	12 College Place, Southampton	023 8032 0320
Downey Mr Neil James	Atlantic Chambers, Liverpool	0151 236 4421
Dracass Mr Timothy William	Pump Court Chambers, London	020 7353 0711
	Pump Court Chambers, Winchester	01962 868 161
	Riverview Chambers, London	0844 225 3999

Eaton Mr Tobias Barnaby	Staple Inn Chambers, London	020 7242 5240
Edwards Mr Denis	Francis Taylor Building, London	020 7353 8415
Egan Mr Patrick Manus Dermot	Thomas More Chambers, London	020 7404 7000
Egleton Mr Richard Wildman	Pallant Chambers, Chichester	01243 784538
Elesinnla Mr Ayoade	Igbobi Chambers, London	0203 2867626
Engelman Mr Philip	Cloisters, London	020 7827 4000
	Trinity Chambers, Middlesbrough	01642 247569
	Trinity Chambers, Newcastle Upon Tyne	0191 232 1927
Esprit Mr Benoit	Barristers Chambers, London	020 3417 6461
	Legis Chambers, Aylesbury	01296 431125
Facenna Mr Gerald Carlo	Monckton Chambers, London	020 7405 7211
Fagborun Bennett Ms Morayo Abosede	Hardwicke, London	020 7242 2523
Fender Mr Carl David	Regency Chambers, Cambridge	01223 301517
	Regency Chambers, Peterborough	01733 315215
Ferber Ms Iris	42 Bedford Row, London	020 7831 0222
Fetto Mr Niazi Peter	2 Temple Gardens, London	020 7822 1200
Finlay Mr Darren	Sovereign Chambers, Leeds	0113 245 1841
Fortune Mr Peter Carl Michael	Guildhall Chambers Portsmouth, Portsmouth	023 9275 2400
	4 King's Bench Walk, London	020 7822 7000
Frantzis Miss Roxanne	KBW, Leeds	0113 297 1200
Fraser-Urquhart Mr Andrew	4-5 Gray's Inn Square, London	020 7404 5252
Gadd Mr Adam Brian	Pump Court Chambers, London	020 7353 0711
	Pump Court Chambers, Winchester	01962 868 161
	Riverview Chambers, London	0844 225 3999
Galbraith-Marten Mr Jason Nicholas	Cloisters, London	020 7827 4000
Garner Miss Sophie Jane	St Philips Chambers, Birmingham	0121 246 7000
Gill Mr Satinderjit Singh	Five Paper, London	020 7815 3200
Gilroy Mr Paul	Old Square Chambers, London	020 7269 0300
	9 St John Street, Manchester	0161 955 9000
Gledhill Mr Lee Andre	Alexander Chambers, London	0845 652 0451/0854 652 0451
	Trident Barristers Chambers, Manchester	0161 663 3123
Glyn Mr Caspar Hilary Gordon	Cloisters, London	020 7827 4000
Godfrey Mr Lauren John	Crown Office Row Chambers, Brighton	01273 625625
Goldberg Mr Simon Ian	Trinity Chambers, Middlesbrough	01642 247569
	Trinity Chambers, Newcastle Upon Tyne	0191 232 1927
Goodfellow Mr Stephen John	East Anglian Chambers, Chelmsford	01473 214481
	East Anglian Chambers, Ipswich	01473 214481
	East Anglian Chambers, Norwich	01473 214481
Goodlad Mr Grant David	Farrar's Building, London	020 7583 9241
Gorasia Mr Paras Ravji	Kings Chambers, Birmingham	0845 034 3444
	Kings Chambers, Leeds	0845 034 3444
	Kings Chambers, Manchester	0845 034 3444
Gordon Mr Jeremy	Chambers of Mr Ami Feder, London	020 7797 7788
	Chambers of Mr Ami Feder, London	020 7797 7788
	Lamb Building, Brighton	01273 820490
Greatorex Mr Paul	4-5 Gray's Inn Square, London	020 7404 5252
Green Mr Patrick Curtis	Henderson Chambers, London	020 7583 9020
Grundy Ms Clare	St Johns Buildings, Manchester	0161 214 1500
	St Johns Buildings Liverpool, Liverpool	0151 243 6000
	16 Winckley Square, Preston	01772 256100
Gunstone Mr Robert Giles	KCH Garden Square, Nottingham	0115 941 8851
Gurden Miss Alison Louise	1 Gray's Inn Square, London	020 7405 0001
Hanif Miss Saima Naz	4-5 Gray's Inn Square, London	020 7404 5252
Harrap Mr Robert Philip	Five Paper, London	020 7815 3200
Harris Mr Melvyn	5 Essex Court, London	020 7410 2000
Harris Mr Paul	Doughty Street Chambers, Bristol	01179 058 717
	Doughty Street Chambers, London	020 7404 1313
	Doughty Street Chambers, Manchester	0161 618 1066

Name	Chambers	Telephone
Harris Mr Wilbert Arthurlyn	Rowchester Chambers, Birmingham	0121 233 2327
Harwood-Gray Mr Barry John	Kenworthy's Chambers, Manchester	0161 832 4036
Hendron Mr Henry Joseph Christopher	Strand Chambers, London	020 7117 6920
Hewson Ms Barbara Mary	Hardwicke, London	020 7242 2523
Hignett Mr Richard James	No5 Chambers, Birmingham	0845 210 5555
	No5 Chambers, Bristol	0845 210 5555
	No5 Chambers, London	0845 210 5555
Hill Ms Eleanor Mary Henrietta	Doughty Street Chambers, Bristol	01179 058 717
	Doughty Street Chambers, London	020 7404 1313
	Doughty Street Chambers, Manchester	0161 618 1066
Hodkinson Mr Gary Stephen	Chambers of Mr Ami Feder, London	020 7797 7788
	Chambers of Mr Ami Feder, London	020 7797 7788
Hornblower Mrs Sarah Patience	Rougemont Chambers, Exeter	01392 208484
Horne-Roberts Mrs Jennifer	Goldsmith Chambers, London	020 7353 6802
Hulse Mrs Cecilia Helen	Chambers of Mr Ami Feder, London	020 7797 7788
	Chambers of Mr Ami Feder, London	020 7797 7788
Hussain Mr Muhammad Altaf	Chambers of Mr M A Hussain, London	020 8679 2398
Hutchinson Mr Colin Thomas	Garden Court Chambers, London	020 7993 7600
Irvin Mr Peter	Brick Court Chambers, London	020 7379 3550
Islam-Choudhury Mr Mugni	No5 Chambers, Birmingham	0845 210 5555
	No5 Chambers, Bristol	0845 210 5555
	No5 Chambers, London	0845 210 5555
Iyer Miss Shobana	Swan Chambers, Richmond	0845 123 1234
Jayakrishnan Mr Harry Sisubalan	Trent Chambers, Nottingham	0115 941 9596
Joffe Ms Natasha Juliet Louise	Outer Temple Chambers, London	020 7353 6381
Jones Mr David Nicholas	Broadway House Chambers, Bradford	01274 722560
	Broadway House Chambers, Leeds	0113 246 2600
	Cloisters, London	020 7827 4000
Jones Mr Mark Andrew	St Ive's Chambers, Birmingham	0121 236 0863
Joshi Mr Rajendra Jugatray	18 Red Lion Court, London	020 7520 6000
	18 Red Lion Court (Annexe), Chelmsford	01245 280880
Khalid Mr James	Goulds Green Chambers, Uxbridge	01895 422574
	Goulds Green Chambers, Uxbridge	01895 422574
Kirk Mr Thomas Sean Robinson	12 College Place, Southampton	023 8032 0320
Kirtley Mr Paul George	Exchange Chambers, Leeds	0113 203 1970
	Exchange Chambers, Liverpool	0151 236 7747
	Littleton Chambers, London	020 7797 8600
Knight Mr Keith Leslie Francis	4 King's Bench Walk, London	020 7822 7000
Kramer Mr Philip Anthony	Park Lane Plowden, Newcastle Upon Tyne	0191 211 4087
Kwiatkowski Mr Feliks Jerzy	Kew Chambers, Kew	0844 8099991
Lakha Mr Shabbir	Farrar's Building, London	020 7583 9241
Lane Mr Christopher Paul	No 8 Chambers, Birmingham	0121 236 5514
Lane Mr Michael John	East Anglian Chambers, Colchester	01473 214481
	East Anglian Chambers, Ipswich	01473 214481
	East Anglian Chambers, Norwich	01473 214481
Lennard Mr Stephen Charles	Hardwicke, London	020 7242 2523
Lewis Mr Wayne Anthony	Access Lawyers, London	020 8801 2345
Lippold Ms Sarah Ida Louise	13 KBW, Oxford	01865 311066
	13 King's Bench Walk, London	020 7353 7204
Livesey Mr John William Allan	Albion Chambers, Bristol	0117 927 2144
Livingstone Mr Simon John	Thomas More Chambers, London	020 7404 7000
Lloyd Mr John Nesbitt	Rougemont Chambers, Exeter	01392 208484
Luh Miss Shu Shin	Garden Court Chambers, London	020 7993 7600
Lule Miss Jacqueline	1 Mitre Court Buildings, London	020 7452 8900
MacEvilly Mr Conn Jeremy	9 Stone Buildings, London	020 7404 5055
MacLaren Miss Catriona Longueville	Tanfield Chambers, London	020 7421 5300
Mahmood Mr Abid	Central Chambers, Manchester	0161 236 1133
	No5 Chambers, Birmingham	0845 210 5555
	No5 Chambers, Bristol	0845 210 5555
	No5 Chambers, London	0845 210 5555

Malik Miss Sarah	Hardwicke, London	020 7242 2523
Markus Ms Kate	Doughty Street Chambers, Bristol	01179 058 717
	Doughty Street Chambers, London	020 7404 1313
	Doughty Street Chambers, Manchester	0161 618 1066
Mason Mr David Hugh Rothwell	Dere Street Barristers, Newcastle Upon Tyne	0844 3351551
Massarella Mr David Peter	Cloisters, London	020 7827 4000
Matthias Mr David Huw	Francis Taylor Building, London	020 7353 8415
McCombie Mr Fergus Alexander Paul	1 Gray's Inn Square, London	020 7405 0001
McKiernan Mr Edward Joseph	Farringdon Chambers, London	020 7089 5700
McKinney Miss Nicola Alexandra	4 KBW, London	020 7822 8822
Meichen Mr Jonathan Brian	St Philips Chambers, Birmingham	0121 246 7000
Meredith-Hardy Mr John Octavian	Farrar's Building, London	020 7583 9241
Miller Mr Ian Robertson	Broadway House Chambers, Bradford	01274 722560
	Broadway House Chambers, Leeds	0113 246 2600
Milne Mrs Arlene Joan	Cobden House Chambers, Manchester	0161 833 6000
Mitchell Mr Alistair Stephen Fabian	49 Chambers, Bridgnorth	01746 761545
Morgan Dr Austen Jude	33 Bedford Row, London	020 7242 6476
Morton Mr Gary David	Pump Court Chambers, London	020 7353 0711
	Pump Court Chambers, Swindon	01793 539899
	Pump Court Chambers, Winchester	01962 868 161
Moulder Mr Paul John	Alexander Chambers, London	0845 652 0451/0854 652 0451
	Guildford Chambers, Guildford	01483 539131
Muman Mr Vijay Kumar	43 Temple Row Chambers, Birmingham	0121 237 6035
Mustakim Mr Abdul Yunus Al	Chambers of Mr Mustakim, London	
Mylvaganam Ms Tanoo	1 Gray's Inn Square, London	020 7405 0001
Nabi Mr Sajjad	5 Pump Court, London	020 7353 2532
Neville Mr Joseph Richard	43 Temple Row Chambers, Birmingham	0121 237 6035
Nicol Mr Nicholas Keith	1 Pump Court, London	020 7842 7070
O'Brien Mr Nicholas William Wattebot	10 King's Bench Walk, London	020 7353 7742
O'Brien Mr Sean Timothy	St Philips Chambers, Birmingham	0121 246 7000
O'Dair Mr David Richard Frazer	36 Bedford Row, London	020 7421 8000
Oommen Mr Jacob	Chambers of Mr Jacob Oommen, East Barnet	07958 680272
O'Toole Mr Bartholomew Vincent	5 King's Bench Walk, London	020 7353 5638
Oulton Mr Richard Arthur Courtenay	5 Essex Court, London	020 7410 2000
Owen-Thomas Mr Richard Matthew	13 KBW, Oxford	01865 311066
	13 King's Bench Walk, London	020 7353 7204
Palmer Miss Claire Louise	Thomas More Chambers, London	020 7404 7000
Palmer Miss Suzanne Elizabeth Josephine	4 King's Bench Walk, London	020 7822 7000
Palmer Mr Iain Franklyn	Renaissance Chambers, London	020 7404 1111
Panton Mr William Dwight	Amethyst Chambers, London	020 7936 4966
Paraskos Mr Paraskevakis Christakis	11 Gray's Inn Square Chambers, London	020 7405 6879
Parker Mrs Karen Lesley	Guildhall Chambers Portsmouth, Portsmouth	023 9275 2400
Peretz Mr George Michael John	Monckton Chambers, London	020 7405 7211
Perian Mr Steven	3 Temple Gardens, London	020 7353 3102
Persaud Dr Marcia Chitroutie	1 Gray's Inn Square, London	020 7405 0001
Philpott Mr Anthony Luke	12 Old Square Chambers, London	020 7404 0875
Platt Miss Heather Louise	Pump Court Chambers, London	020 7353 0711
	Pump Court Chambers, Swindon	01793 539899
	Riverview Chambers, London	0844 225 3999
Pretsell Mr James Davidson	Farrar's Building, London	020 7583 9241
Qureshi Mr Asif Hasan	Quadrant Chambers, London	020 7583 4444
Rahman Mr Anis	12 Old Square Chambers, London	020 7404 0875
Rahman Mr Luthfur	Chambers of Mr L Rahman, Rochester	07947 588362
Rahman Mr Sami Ur	Field Court Chambers, London	020 7405 6114
Reed Mr Simon John	New Walk Chambers, Leicester	0871 200 1298/0116 255 9144
Rees Mr Robert Charles David	New Walk Chambers, Leicester	0871 200 1298/0116 255 9144

Name	Chambers	Telephone
Rees Prof William Michael	1 Gray's Inn Square, London	020 7405 0001
Rippon Mr Simon John	Citadel Chambers, Birmingham	0121 233 8500
Riza Mr Alper Ali	Goldsmith Chambers, London	020 7353 6802
Roberts Mr Jack	Sheldan, Oswestry	01691 657635
Roberts Mr Michael Charles	Chambers of Michael Roberts, Henley-On-Thames	01844 355 655
Robinson Miss Laura	Tanfield Chambers, London	020 7421 5300
Robinson-Young Mr David Tilley	Dere Street Barristers, Newcastle Upon Tyne	0844 3351551
Rogers Mr Ian Paul	Monckton Chambers, London	020 7405 7211
Rubens Miss Jacqueline Ann	1 Pump Court, London	020 7842 7070
Ryan Mr William	Corsham Barristers Chambers, Corsham	01225 582582
	Farringdon Chambers, London	020 7089 5700
Sadiq Mr Tariq Mahmood	St Philips Chambers, Birmingham	0121 246 7000
Saifee Mr Faisal Aftaab	Thomas More Chambers, London	020 7404 7000
Sandham Mr James Andrew	Arden Chambers, London	020 7242 4244
Sawtell Mr David Robert Fraser	4 King's Bench Walk, London	020 7822 7000
Seeboruth Mr Royln Jean-Paul	Chambers of Royln Seeboruth, Aylesbury	01296 393329
Sekar Mr Chandra	Angell Park Chambers, London	020 7737 5957
Self Mr Gary Peter	College Chambers, Southampton	023 8023 0338
	St David's Chambers, Swansea	01792 559924
Serr Mr Ashley Barrie	Park Lane Plowden, Leeds	0113 228 5049
Shaw Miss Joanna Elizabeth	One Essex Court, London	020 7936 3030
Shepherd Miss Judith Elizabeth	42 Bedford Row, London	020 7831 0222
Sheppard Mr Timothy Derie	No5 Chambers, Birmingham	0845 210 5555
	No5 Chambers, Bristol	0845 210 5555
	No5 Chambers, London	0845 210 5555
Short Mr Andrew John	Outer Temple Chambers, London	020 7353 6381
	Riverview Chambers, London	0844 225 3999
Silverton Miss Catherine Anne	Sovereign Chambers, Leeds	0113 245 1841
Skelt Mr Ian Stuart	KBW, Leeds	0113 297 1200
Skinner Mr Samuel Richard Edward	KCH Garden Square, Nottingham	0115 941 8851
Small Mr John Robert	36 Bedford Row, London	020 7421 8000
Sonaike Mr Kolarele Oladele Obafemi	One Essex Court, London	020 7936 3030
Sood Mrs Usha Rani	Trent Chambers, Nottingham	0115 941 9596
Sparrow Mrs Marie-Claire	Holborn Chambers, London	020 7242 6060
Spicer Mr Robert Haden	Frederick Place Chambers, Bristol	0117 946 7059
Stagg Mr Paul Andrew	1 Chancery Lane, London	0845 634 6666
Standfast Mr Philip Arthur	St Paul's Chambers, Leeds	0113 245 5866
Starcevic Mr Petar	St Philips Chambers, Birmingham	0121 246 7000
Stebbings Mr Ian Anthony	1 Gray's Inn Square, London	020 7405 0001
Stephenson Mr David Matthew	1 Mitre Court Buildings, London	020 7452 8900
Stewart Mr Richard Paul	Lamb Chambers, London	020 7797 8300
Stuart Mr James William	Lamb Chambers, London	020 7797 8300
Suter Mr Erich George Bernard	Park Chambers, Weybridge Park	01932 820082
Swinnerton Mr David Michael	Cornwall Street Chambers, Birmingham	0121 233 7500
Tapsell Mr Paul Richard	Becket Chambers, Canterbury	01227 786331
Targett-Parker Miss Leanne Susan	No. 3 Fleet Street Chambers, London	020 7936 4474
	The Chambers of Miss Leanne Targett-Parker, London	020 8674 6694
Thomas Mr Mark David	5 Essex Court, London	020 7410 2000
Thomas Mrs Felicity	Westgate Chambers, Lewes	01273 480510
Thomson Mr Martin Haldane Ahmad	Wynne Chambers, London	020 3239 6964
Tinnion Mr Antoine	Trinity Chambers, Middlesbrough	01642 247569
	Trinity Chambers, Newcastle Upon Tyne	0191 232 1927
Tivadar Mr Daniel	3 Hare Court, London	020 7415 7800
Topal Mr Erol	Lamb Chambers, London	020 7797 8300
Treharne Mr Neil Simon	Dingle Chambers, Bristol	07818 827754
Tucker Mr Ashley Russell	Park Court Chambers, Leeds	0113 243 3277

Tunley Mr James Christopher Gordon	4 KBW, London	020 7822 8822
Twist Mr Stephen John	Dere Street Barristers, Newcastle Upon Tyne	0844 3351551
Uduje Mr Benjamin Elliott	42 Bedford Row, London	020 7831 0222
Vaughan Mr Anthony	Garden Court Chambers, London	020 7993 7600
Walker Mr Adam Nigel	Seven Bedford Row, London	020 7242 3555
Ward Mr Martin Stuart	14 Gray's Inn Square, London	020 7242 0858
Ward Mr Peter Mark	The Chambers of Peter Ward, London	020 3402 2152
Wenban-Smith Mr Mungo William	4-5 Gray's Inn Square, London	020 7404 5252
Wheaton Mr Ian Malcolm James	Eighteen Carlton Crescent, Southampton	023 8063 9001
White Mr Matthew James	St John's Chambers, Bristol	0117 923 4700
Williams Mr Ben Dylan	Kings Chambers, Birmingham	0845 034 3444
	Kings Chambers, Leeds	0845 034 3444
	Kings Chambers, Manchester	0845 034 3444
Wilson Mr Paul Richard	Broadway House Chambers, Bradford	01274 722560
Wilson Mr Richard Carver	36 Bedford Row, London	020 7421 8000
Wood Mr Richard Michael	East Anglian Chambers, Chelmsford	01473 214481
	East Anglian Chambers, Ipswich	01473 214481
	East Anglian Chambers, Norwich	01473 214481
Wright Mr Ian	Five Paper, London	020 7815 3200
Young Mr Martin Ford	9 Stone Buildings, London	020 7404 5055

EC & COMPETITION LAW

Abrahams Mr James	8 New Square, London	020 7405 4321
Ajaz Mr Mohammad Arshad	Eastmans Chambers, Reading	0118 966 9094
Algazy Mr Jacques Max	Cloisters, London	020 7827 4000
Banks Miss Fiona Jane	Monckton Chambers, London	020 7405 7211
Barry Mr Denis Fintan Patrick	Five Paper Buildings, London	020 7583 6117
Bates Mr Alan Twan	Monckton Chambers, London	020 7405 7211
Berry Mr Adrian Christopher	Garden Court Chambers, London	020 7993 7600
Blackwood Mr Clive David	Lamb Chambers, London	020 7797 8300
Bowsher Mr Michael Frederick Thomas	Monckton Chambers, London	020 7405 7211
Costello Mr Paul James	Chambers of Mr Paul J Costello, Biggleswade	07846 016 399
Craig Mr Aubrey John	Chancery House Chambers, Leeds	0113 244 6691
	St Philips Chambers, Birmingham	0121 246 7000
Cunningham Mr Graham Taylor	Hardwicke, London	020 7242 2523
Dalby Mr Joseph Francis	4-5 Gray's Inn Square, London	020 7404 5252
Darroch Miss Fiona Culverwell	Clerksroom (London), London	0845 083 3000
	Clerksroom (Taunton), Taunton	0845 083 3000
	King's Lynn Chambers, King's Lynn	01553 672 085
Devine Mr Michael Buxton	Rougemont Chambers, Exeter	01392 208484
Devlin Mr Timothy Robert	Furnival Chambers, London	020 7405 3232
Edwards Mr Denis	Francis Taylor Building, London	020 7353 8415
Egan Mr Patrick Manus Dermot	Thomas More Chambers, London	020 7404 7000
Engelman Mr Philip	Cloisters, London	020 7827 4000
	Trinity Chambers, Middlesbrough	01642 247569
	Trinity Chambers, Newcastle Upon Tyne	0191 232 1927
Facenna Mr Gerald Carlo	Monckton Chambers, London	020 7405 7211
Fern Mr Gary	7 Stones IP, London	020 7193 4033
Frawley Ms Lyndsey Anne	Quorum Chambers, St Albans	01727 884516
	Quorum Tax Chambers, London	020 7043 5189
Gardner Mr James Piers	Monckton Chambers, London	020 7405 7211
Gibbons Miss Mary Regina	Stone Chambers, London	020 7440 6900
Hackett Mr Philip George	Argent Chambers, London	020 7556 5500
Hamer Mr George Clemens	8 New Square, London	020 7405 4321
Hannaford Miss Sarah Jane	Keating Chambers, London	020 7544 2600
Heal Mrs Madeleine	New Square Chambers, London	020 7419 8000
Henderson Mr Neil John	Stone Chambers, London	020 7440 6900
Hewson Ms Barbara Mary	Hardwicke, London	020 7242 2523

Hill Mr Jonathan	8 New Square, London	020 7405 4321
Hussain Mr Muhammad Altaf	Chambers of Mr M A Hussain, London	020 8679 2398
Iqbal Mr Mashood	London View Chambers, Sawbridgeworth	07788 912493
Iyer Miss Shobana	Swan Chambers, Richmond	0845 123 1234
John Miss Laura Elizabeth	Monckton Chambers, London	020 7405 7211
Jones Mr Kelvin Mcallister	Templis Chambers, London	020 7649 9808
Kime Mr Matthew Jonathan	Cobden House Chambers, Manchester	0161 833 6000
	Ingenuity IP Chambers, Petts Wood	
	No. 3 Fleet Street Chambers, London	020 7936 4474
Lambert Miss Jane Elizabeth	NIPC, Huddersfield	0800 862 0055
Lane Ms Lindsay Ruth Busfield	8 New Square, London	020 7405 4321
Lindsay Mr Alistair David	Monckton Chambers, London	020 7405 7211
Lyons Mr Timothy John	4-5 Gray's Inn Square, London	020 7404 5252
	St James's Chambers, Manchester	0161 834 7000
MacEvilly Mr Conn Jeremy	9 Stone Buildings, London	020 7404 5055
MacKenzie Smith Mrs Catherine Joanna	10 King's Bench Walk, London	020 7353 7742
Mahmood Mr Abid	Central Chambers, Manchester	0161 236 1133
	No5 Chambers, Birmingham	0845 210 5555
	No5 Chambers, Bristol	0845 210 5555
	No5 Chambers, London	0845 210 5555
Mantle Mr Peter John	Monckton Chambers, London	020 7405 7211
Matthias Mr David Huw	Francis Taylor Building, London	020 7353 8415
Mawrey Mr Richard Brooks	Henderson Chambers, London	020 7583 9020
McKiernan Mr Edward Joseph	Farringdon Chambers, London	020 7089 5700
Metcalfe Dr Eric William	Monckton Chambers, London	020 7405 7211
Morgan Dr Austen Jude	33 Bedford Row, London	020 7242 6476
O'Connor Miss Hilda Ann	Kidby Chambers, Woodbridge	
O'Donoghue Mr Hugh Vincent	Carmelite Chambers, London	020 7936 6300
Oliver Mr David Keightley Rideal	13 Old Square Chambers, London	020 7831 4445
Onslow Mr Robert Denzil	8 New Square, London	020 7405 4321
Peretz Mr George Michael John	Monckton Chambers, London	020 7405 7211
Purves Mr Gavin Bowman	Swan House, London	020 8998 3035
Qureshi Mr Asif Hasan	Quadrant Chambers, London	020 7583 4444
Rai Mr Rajesh Kumar	1 Mitre Court Buildings, London	020 7452 8900
Rayment Mr Benedick Michael	Monckton Chambers, London	020 7405 7211
Reeds Mr Gareth David	Canary Wharf Chambers, London	020 7183 8011
Rogers Miss Christy Abigail	Ingenuity IP Chambers, Petts Wood	
	No. 3 Fleet Street Chambers, London	020 7936 4474
Rogers Mr Ian Paul	Monckton Chambers, London	020 7405 7211
Rosemarine Mr Andrew Marc	Chambers of Mr A M Rosemarine, Manchester	0161 740 3861
Roughton Mr Ashley Wentworth	Hogarth Chambers, London	020 7404 0404
Simon Mr Philipp Arnold Heinrich	4 KBW, London	020 7822 8822
Singarajah Mr Frederico	1 Gray's Inn Square, London	020 7405 0001
Sloane Miss Valentina	Monckton Chambers, London	020 7405 7211
Sparrow Mrs Marie-Claire	Holborn Chambers, London	020 7242 6060
Thompson Mr Michael James	Keating Chambers, London	020 7544 2600
Tritton Mr Robert Guy Henton	Hogarth Chambers, London	020 7404 0404
Von Pommern-Peglow Dr Michael Alfred Herman Pr.	Brunswick Chambers, London	020 7353 1987
West Dr Ewan Donald	Monckton Chambers, London	020 7405 7211
Wiktorowski-Solecki Miss Tamara	Middle Temple Lane Chambers, London	020 7583 4352
Williams Mr Rhodri John	Henderson Chambers, London	020 7583 9020
	30 Park Place, Cardiff	029 2039 8421
Wolman Mr Clive Richard	11 Stone Buildings, London	020 7831 6381

ECCLESIASTICAL

Atkinson Mr Nicholas Jeremy	Atkinson Bevan Chambers, London	020 7353 2112
	Staple Inn Chambers, London	020 7242 5240

Name	Chambers	Telephone
Clarke Mr Timothy John	Cornwall Street Chambers, Birmingham	0121 233 7500
Davies Ms Samantha Teresa	Chambers of Ms Samantha Davies, Milton Keynes	0845 123 1234
	Warwick House Chambers, London	020 7430 2323
Gau Mr Justin Charles	Pump Court Chambers, London	020 7353 0711
	Pump Court Chambers, Swindon	01793 539899
	Pump Court Chambers, Winchester	01962 868 161
Halden Mr Angus Robert	Queen Square Chambers, Bristol	0117 921 1966
Hill Mr Nicholas Mark	Pump Court Chambers, London	020 7353 0711
	Pump Court Chambers, Swindon	01793 539899
	St Philips Chambers, Birmingham	0121 246 7000
Howells Mr Stephen John	Stone Chambers, London	020 7440 6900
Jones Mr Ian Harvey	Holbrook Chambers, Leicester	07771 961962
Le Poidevin Mr Nicholas Peter	New Square Chambers, London	020 7419 8000
Matthias Mr David Huw	Francis Taylor Building, London	020 7353 8415
McCulloch Miss Fiona Catharine Jane	Middle Temple Lane Chambers, London	020 7583 4352
McNicholas Mr Christopher John	Goresbrook Chambers, Milton Keynes	0845 123 1234
Mynors Dr Charles Baskerville	Francis Taylor Building, London	020 7353 8415
Newsom Mr George Lucien	Guildhall Chambers, Bristol	0117 930 9000
Normington Mr James Adam	Park Court Chambers, Leeds	0113 243 3277
Payton Mr Clifford Coningsby	Alpha Court Chambers, Leamington Spa	01926 886412
Ruffell Mr Mark Beresford	Pump Court Chambers, London	020 7353 0711
	Pump Court Chambers, Swindon	01793 539899
	Pump Court Chambers, Winchester	01962 868 161
Sefton-Smith Mr Lloyd	Lamb Chambers, London	020 7797 8300
Stanford Mr Tony James	Old Bailey Chambers, London	020 3008 6404
Taylor Miss Araba Arba Kurankyiwa	Fenners Chambers, Cambridge	01223 368761
Wagstaff Mr Andrew Martin Nicholas	Westgate Chambers, Lewes	01273 480510

EDUCATION

Name	Chambers	Telephone
Adewale Mr Remi Adetokunbo Sanni	Chambers of G. D. Tetteh, London	020 7353 7095
	Chambers of Mr R. A. Adewale, Address withheld	020 7231 2814
Ajaz Mr Mohammad Arshad	Eastmans Chambers, Reading	0118 966 9094
Akers Mr Robert Matthew Harry	St Johns Buildings, Chester	01244 323070
	St Johns Buildings, Manchester	0161 214 1500
	16 Winckley Square, Preston	01772 256100
Alam Ms Jan	Ropewalk Chambers, Nottingham	0115 947 2581
Allwood Mrs Gina Louisa	Seven Bedford Row, London	020 7242 3555
Amraoui Mr Thomas	4-5 Gray's Inn Square, London	020 7404 5252
Andre Mr Roger Louis	Sovereign Chambers, Leeds	0113 245 1841
Askey Mr Robert John	Palmyra Chambers, Warrington	01925 444919
Auburn Mr Jonathan Walter	4-5 Gray's Inn Square, London	020 7404 5252
Bates Mr Alan Twan	Monckton Chambers, London	020 7405 7211
Beaumont Mr Marc Clifford	9 Stone Buildings, London	020 7404 5055
	Windsor Barristers' Chambers, Windsor	01753 839321
Berry Mr Adrian Christopher	Garden Court Chambers, London	020 7993 7600
Bhanji Mr Shiraz Musa	4 Bingham Place, London	020 7486 5347
	1 Gray's Inn Square, London	020 7405 0001
Bhattacharyya Mr Ardhendu	Slough Barristers Chamber, Slough	01753 553806
Bicarregui Miss Anna Claire Victoria	4-5 Gray's Inn Square, London	020 7404 5252
Birkby Mr Richard Adam	Park Court Chambers, Leeds	0113 243 3277
Bisarya Mr Neil	Number 7 Harrington Street Chambers, Liverpool	0151 242 0707
Bishop Mr Malcolm Leslie	Argent Chambers, London	020 7556 5500
	Equity Chambers, Birmingham	0121 236 5007
	30 Park Place, Cardiff	029 2039 8421
Booth Mr Alexander Henry Spencer	Francis Taylor Building, London	020 7353 8415

C

Name	Chambers	Telephone
Bowen Mr Nicholas James Hugh	Doughty Street Chambers, Bristol	01179 058 717
	Doughty Street Chambers, London	020 7404 1313
	Doughty Street Chambers, Manchester	0161 618 1066
Brown Ms Grace	Tooks Chambers, London	020 7842 7575
Buchan Miss Caroline Venetia	Chambers of Miss C Buchan, Haywards Heath	01444 482222
Burrett Mr Alex	1 Gray's Inn Square, London	020 7405 0001
Cassidy Mr Patrick Stephen	Kenworthy's Chambers, Manchester	0161 832 4036
Cattermull Miss Emma Jayne	East Anglian Chambers, Chelmsford	01473 214481
	East Anglian Chambers, Ipswich	01473 214481
	East Anglian Chambers, Norwich	01473 214481
Choudhuri Miss Gulshanah	Sen Barristers, Eastleigh	07706 936045
Clements Miss Paula Kate	Alexander Chambers, London	0845 652 0451/0854 652 0451
	Guildford Chambers, Guildford	01483 539131
Cooper Mr Paul Andrew	Portal Chambers, Llandysul	01559 395 292
Coster Mr Ronald David	42 Bedford Row, London	020 7831 0222
Cotter Mr Mark James	Five St Andrew's Hill, London	020 7332 5400
Cox Mr Jonathan Edward	KCH Garden Square, Nottingham	0115 941 8851
Coyle Mr Anthony Noel	Zenith Chambers, Leeds	0113 245 5438
Daly Mr David	Heathway Chambers, London	020 8293 0509
De Mello Mr Rembert Joseph Julius	No5 Chambers, Birmingham	0845 210 5555
	No5 Chambers, Bristol	0845 210 5555
	No5 Chambers, London	0845 210 5555
Dean Mrs Christine Jacqueline	1 Pump Court, London	020 7842 7070
Dempsey Miss Karen Marie	3 Temple Gardens, London	020 7353 3102
Dunning Mr Francis John Grove	37 Park Square Chambers, Leeds	0113 243 9422
Edwards Mr Denis	Francis Taylor Building, London	020 7353 8415
Egleton Mr Richard Wildman	Pallant Chambers, Chichester	01243 784538
Engelman Mr Philip	Cloisters, London	020 7827 4000
	Trinity Chambers, Middlesbrough	01642 247569
	Trinity Chambers, Newcastle Upon Tyne	0191 232 1927
Foulkes Miss Rebecca	5 Pump Court, London	020 7353 2532
Gallivan Mr Terence John	Five Paper, London	020 7815 3200
German Miss Kelly Anne	Eastbourne Chambers, Eastbourne	01323 642102
Gill Mr Manjit Singh	No5 Chambers, Birmingham	0845 210 5555
	No5 Chambers, Bristol	0845 210 5555
	No5 Chambers, London	0845 210 5555
Gledhill Mr Lee Andre	Alexander Chambers, London	0845 652 0451/0854 652 0451
	Trident Barristers Chambers, Manchester	0161 663 3123
Goldstein Mr Wayne Nathan	18 St John Street, Manchester	0161 278 1800
Gore Ms Sally Elizabeth	14 Gray's Inn Square, London	020 7242 0858
Greatorex Mr Paul	4-5 Gray's Inn Square, London	020 7404 5252
Gunstone Mr Robert Giles	KCH Garden Square, Nottingham	0115 941 8851
Guy Mr Richard Perran	Chambers of Mr Ami Feder, London	020 7797 7788
	King's Bench and Godolphin (KBG)Chambers, Plymouth	01752 221551
	Southernhay Chambers, Exeter	01392 255777
Hamilton Mr John Conrad	Field Court Chambers, London	020 7405 6114
Hanif Miss Saima Naz	4-5 Gray's Inn Square, London	020 7404 5252
Hanlon Mr James Tobias	Old Bailey Chambers, London	020 3008 6404
Haukeland Mr Martin Jonathan	42 Bedford Row, London	020 7831 0222
Hegarty Mr Kevin John	St Philips Chambers, Birmingham	0121 246 7000
Henthorn Miss Kate Marie	7 Bell Yard, London	020 7831 0636
	18 St John Street, Manchester	0161 278 1800
Hobson Mr John Graham	4-5 Gray's Inn Square, London	020 7404 5252
Hughes Dr Constance Mary	1 Pump Court, London	020 7842 7070
Hussain Mr Muhammad Altaf	Chambers of Mr M A Hussain, London	020 8679 2398
Johnson Miss Laura Wendy	1 Chancery Lane, London	0845 634 6666
Johnson Mr Simon Nicholas	Stour Chambers, Canterbury	01227 764899
Jones Mr Ian Harvey	Holbrook Chambers, Leicester	07771 961962
Jones Mr Mark Andrew	St Ive's Chambers, Birmingham	0121 236 0863

Barrister	Chambers	Telephone
Juss Prof Satvinder Singh	3 Hare Court, London	020 7415 7800
Kelly Mrs Amy Louise	12 College Place, Southampton	023 8032 0320
Lane Mr Michael John	East Anglian Chambers, Colchester	01473 214481
	East Anglian Chambers, Ipswich	01473 214481
	East Anglian Chambers, Norwich	01473 214481
Lavin Miss Mary Mandie Jane	196 Temple Chamber, London	020 7099 9257
Lawrence Miss Anne Mary	Atlas Chambers, London	020 7269 7980
Lee Miss Taryn Jane	37 Park Square Chambers, Leeds	0113 243 9422
Lee Mr Rosslyn Alexander	Dere Street Barristers, York	0844 3351551
	York Chambers, Newcastle Upon Tyne	0191 206 4677
Levett Miss Francesca Anna	Five St Andrew's Hill, London	020 7332 5400
Lippold Ms Sarah Ida Louise	13 KBW, Oxford	01865 311066
	13 King's Bench Walk, London	020 7353 7204
Lloyd Mr John Nesbitt	Rougemont Chambers, Exeter	01392 208484
Loveday Mr David Robert	4-5 Gray's Inn Square, London	020 7404 5252
Luh Miss Shu Shin	Garden Court Chambers, London	020 7993 7600
Manning Miss Ruth Margaret Hayes	No 8 Chambers, Birmingham	0121 236 5514
Markus Ms Kate	Doughty Street Chambers, Bristol	01179 058 717
	Doughty Street Chambers, London	020 7404 1313
	Doughty Street Chambers, Manchester	0161 618 1066
Martignetti Mr Ian	Regency Chambers, Cambridge	01223 301517
	Regency Chambers, Peterborough	01733 315215
Matthias Mr David Huw	Francis Taylor Building, London	020 7353 8415
McDonald Ms Melanie Sharon	No5 Chambers, Birmingham	0845 210 5555
	No5 Chambers, Bristol	0845 210 5555
	No5 Chambers, London	0845 210 5555
McKendrick Mr John Dempster	Outer Temple Chambers, London	020 7353 6381
McKinney Miss Nicola Alexandra	4 KBW, London	020 7822 8822
Miller Mr Andrew	2 Temple Gardens, London	020 7822 1200
Milsom Mrs Catherine Mary	Argent Chambers, London	020 7556 5500
Mitchell Mr Christian Richard	Alexander Chambers, London	0845 652 0451/0854 652 0451
	Guildford Chambers, Guildford	01483 539131
Moffett Mr Jonathan Keith	4-5 Gray's Inn Square, London	020 7404 5252
Moll Mr Christiaan Eric	Blackfriars Chambers, London	020 7353 7400
Monaghan Ms Susan Mary	No5 Chambers, Birmingham	0845 210 5555
	No5 Chambers, Bristol	0845 210 5555
	No5 Chambers, London	0845 210 5555
Moulder Mr Paul John	Alexander Chambers, London	0845 652 0451/0854 652 0451
	Guildford Chambers, Guildford	01483 539131
Mylvaganam Ms Tanoo	1 Gray's Inn Square, London	020 7405 0001
Needham Mrs Julia Cherry	10 King's Bench Walk, London	020 7353 7742
Osborne Mr James Robert	Clerksroom (London), London	0845 083 3000
Pascall Mr Matthew Stephen	Alexander Chambers, London	0845 652 0451/0854 652 0451
	Guildford Chambers, Guildford	01483 539131
Pascoe Ms Soraya	1 Gray's Inn Square, London	020 7405 0001
Penni Miss Sally Selorm-Juliet	Kenworthy's Chambers, Manchester	0161 832 4036
Powell Mr William Rhys	Regency Chambers, Cambridge	01223 301517
	Regency Chambers, Peterborough	01733 315215
Rawlings Mr Clive Patrick	Hardwicke, London	020 7242 2523
Reed Ms Lucy Emma	St John's Chambers, Bristol	0117 923 4700
Rees Prof William Michael	1 Gray's Inn Square, London	020 7405 0001
Rogers Mr Ian Paul	Monckton Chambers, London	020 7405 7211
Rubens Miss Jacqueline Ann	1 Pump Court, London	020 7842 7070
Russell-Mitra Miss Jessica Suparna	1 Mitre Court Buildings, London	020 7452 8900
Sandham Mr James Andrew	Arden Chambers, London	020 7242 4244
Scolding Miss Fiona Kate	Hardwicke, London	020 7242 2523
Scott Mr Stuart	1 Pump Court, London	020 7842 7070
Scott Ms Laura Louise	14 Gray's Inn Square, London	020 7242 0858
Short Ms Mandy Lisa	14 Gray's Inn Square, London	020 7242 0858
Silverton Miss Catherine Anne	Sovereign Chambers, Leeds	0113 245 1841
Skinner Mr Samuel Richard Edward	KCH Garden Square, Nottingham	0115 941 8851
Smith Miss Eileen Joan	Trinity Chambers, Middlesbrough	01642 247569
	Trinity Chambers, Newcastle Upon Tyne	0191 232 1927

Smith Mr Alisdair Robert Macsorley	9-12 Bell Yard, London	020 7400 1800
Sood Mrs Usha Rani	Trent Chambers, Nottingham	0115 941 9596
Stagg Mr Paul Andrew	1 Chancery Lane, London	0845 634 6666
Stanford Mr Tony James	Old Bailey Chambers, London	020 3008 6404
Stebbings Mr Ian Anthony	1 Gray's Inn Square, London	020 7405 0001
Stewart Mr Nicholas John Cameron	Ely Place Chambers, London	020 7400 9600
Stinchcombe Mr Paul David	4-5 Gray's Inn Square, London	020 7404 5252
Tautz Mr William Henry	Tooks Chambers, London	020 7842 7575
Thomas Mr Mark David	5 Essex Court, London	020 7410 2000
Thompson Mr Andrew Edward Courtney	Tanfield Chambers, London	020 7421 5300
Thornton Mr John Robert	Stour Chambers, Canterbury	01227 764899
Udom Miss Nancy Ini	Five St Andrew's Hill, London	020 7332 5400
Ume Mr Cyril Obiora	12 Old Square Chambers, London	020 7404 0875
Van Spall Ms Penelope-Jane	Chartlands Chambers, Northampton	01604 603322
Ward Mr Martin Stuart	14 Gray's Inn Square, London	020 7242 0858
Ward Mr Peter Mark	The Chambers of Peter Ward, London	020 3402 2152
Warnock Mr Andrew Ronald	1 Chancery Lane, London	0845 634 6666
Wenban-Smith Mr Mungo William	4-5 Gray's Inn Square, London	020 7404 5252
Williams Mr Ben Dylan	Kings Chambers, Birmingham	0845 034 3444
	Kings Chambers, Leeds	0845 034 3444
	Kings Chambers, Manchester	0845 034 3444
Wills Miss Alexandra Itari	Christ Church Chambers, London	020 7409 5278/07788 512787
Wise Mr Ian	Doughty Street Chambers, Bristol	01179 058 717
	Doughty Street Chambers, London	020 7404 1313
	Doughty Street Chambers, Manchester	0161 618 1066
Wolstenholme Miss Janine	Sovereign Chambers, Leeds	0113 245 1841
Wrottesley Miss Angela Jane	Bank House Chambers, Sheffield	0114 275 1223

EMPLOYMENT

Abasheikh Mr Omar Said Imam	Paragon Chambers, London	020 3318 9988
Adewale Mr Remi Adetokunbo Sanni	Chambers of G. D. Tetteh, London	020 7353 7095
	Chambers of Mr R. A. Adewale, Address withheld	020 7231 2814
Adjei Mr Cyril John	Five Paper, London	020 7815 3200
Adkin Mr Timothy Clive	42 Bedford Row, London	020 7831 0222
Afeeva Mr Mark Kudzo Dzitosi	Matrix Chambers, London	020 7404 3447
Agnihotri Mr Naveen	12 College Place, Southampton	023 8032 0320
Ahmad Ms Aysha	42 Bedford Row, London	020 7831 0222
Ahmed Mr Ishfaq	Stone Chambers, London	020 7440 6900
Ahmed Mr Saleem	Perivale Chambers, Perivale	020 8998 1935
Akudolu Miss Nneka Veronica Anastesia	2 Pump Court, London	020 7353 5597
Alam Ms Jan	Ropewalk Chambers, Nottingham	0115 947 2581
Algazy Mr Jacques Max	Cloisters, London	020 7827 4000
Alliott Mr George Beckles	Temple Garden Chambers, London	020 7583 1315
Alloway Mr Tor Hugh	Talloway Chambers, London	020 7419 5047
Allsop Mr Julian Eliseo	Guildhall Chambers, Bristol	0117 930 9000
Allwood Mrs Gina Louisa	Seven Bedford Row, London	020 7242 3555
Alomo Mr Richard Olusoji	14 Gray's Inn Square, London	020 7242 0858
Aly Miss Sheila	Warwick House Chambers, London	020 7430 2323
Amraoui Mr Thomas	4-5 Gray's Inn Square, London	020 7404 5252
Anderson Mr Jack Duthie	4-5 Gray's Inn Square, London	020 7404 5252
Anderson Mr Jamie Henrie	Trinity Chambers, Middlesbrough	01642 247569
	Trinity Chambers, Newcastle Upon Tyne	0191 232 1927
Anderson Mr Simon Peter Bede	Park Court Chambers, Leeds	0113 243 3277
Antell Mr John Jason	King's Bench and Godolphin (KBG)Chambers, Plymouth	01752 221551
Arnold Mr Graham John	Farringdon Chambers, London	020 7089 5700
Arnold Mr James Matthew	Outer Temple Chambers, London	020 7353 6381
Ashford-Thom Mr Ian	3 PB Barristers, London	020 7583 8055
	Temple Garden Chambers, London	020 7583 1315

C

Name	Chambers	Telephone
Ashley Mr Neil Martin	East Anglian Chambers, Chelmsford	01473 214481
	East Anglian Chambers, Ipswich	01473 214481
	East Anglian Chambers, Norwich	01473 214481
Askey Mr Robert John	Palmyra Chambers, Warrington	01925 444919
Atkinson Mr Jody Roy	St John's Chambers, Bristol	0117 923 4700
Austin Mr Ian	Holborn Chambers, London	020 7242 6060
Awodele Mr Olufemi Adetunji	Great James Street Chambers, London	020 7440 4949
Azib Ms Rehana	2 Temple Gardens, London	020 7822 1200
Bailey Mr Charles Andrew Stuart	Trinity Chambers, Chelmsford	01245 605040
Bailey Mr Russell Stuart	No5 Chambers, Birmingham	0845 210 5555
	No5 Chambers, Bristol	0845 210 5555
	No5 Chambers, London	0845 210 5555
Barney Ms Helen	No5 Chambers, Birmingham	0845 210 5555
	No5 Chambers, Bristol	0845 210 5555
	No5 Chambers, London	0845 210 5555
Bax Mr James Alexander	Rougemont Chambers, Exeter	01392 208484
Bean Mr Matthew Allen	KBW, Leeds	0113 297 1200
Beaumont Mr Dean Andrew	KCH Garden Square, Nottingham	0115 941 8851
Beaumont Mr Marc Clifford	9 Stone Buildings, London	020 7404 5055
	Windsor Barristers' Chambers, Windsor	01753 839321
Becker Mr Timothy George Christie	Chambers of Mr Timothy Becker, Liverpool	0151 703 0319
	Clerksroom (London), London	0845 083 3000
Bedloe Mr Giles Robert	Dyers Chambers, London	020 7404 1881
Berkley Mr David Nahum	1 Gray's Inn Square, London	020 7405 0001
	St Johns Buildings, Chester	01244 323070
	St Johns Buildings, Manchester	0161 214 1500
	St Johns Buildings Liverpool, Liverpool	0151 243 6000
Bertram Mr Jonathan Peter	Seven Bedford Row, London	020 7242 3555
Bewley Miss Suhayla	East Anglian Chambers, Chelmsford	01473 214481
	East Anglian Chambers, Colchester	01473 214481
	East Anglian Chambers, Ipswich	01473 214481
Bezzam Miss Jayashree	Hampton Court Chambers, West Molesey	020 8979 0381
Bhattacharyya Mr Ardhendu	Slough Barristers Chamber, Slough	01753 553806
Bhatti Miss Balvinder	Citadel Chambers, Birmingham	0121 233 8500
Bicarregui Miss Anna Claire Victoria	4-5 Gray's Inn Square, London	020 7404 5252
Bilsland Miss Alisan Margaret	St James's Chambers, Manchester	0161 834 7000
Bisarya Mr Neil	Number 7 Harrington Street Chambers, Liverpool	0151 242 0707
Bishop Mr Alan Richard	11 Stone Buildings, London	020 7831 6381
Bishop Mr Malcolm Leslie	Argent Chambers, London	020 7556 5500
	Equity Chambers, Birmingham	0121 236 5007
	30 Park Place, Cardiff	029 2039 8421
Bishop Mr Stephen Anthony	Goldsmith Chambers, London	020 7353 6802
Blackwood Mr Clive David	Lamb Chambers, London	020 7797 8300
Bogle Mr James Stewart Lockhart	10 King's Bench Walk, London	020 7353 7742
Borkowski Miss Gemma Francesca	Albion Chambers, Bristol	0117 927 2144
Bourke Ms Sarah Victoria Norma	Tooks Chambers, London	020 7842 7575
Bourne Mr Charles Gregory	4-5 Gray's Inn Square, London	020 7404 5252
Bourne Mr Colin Peter	Kings Chambers, Birmingham	0845 034 3444
	Kings Chambers, Leeds	0845 034 3444
	Kings Chambers, Manchester	0845 034 3444
Boyd Mr Stephen James Harvey	Selborne Chambers, London	020 7420 9500
Braier Mr Jason Dean	Field Court Chambers, London	020 7405 6114
Branchflower Mr George	Zenith Chambers, Leeds	0113 245 5438
Brehan Ms Daire	Chambers of Ms D Brehan, London	07808 726877
Brockley Mr Nigel Simon	No5 Chambers, Birmingham	0845 210 5555
	No5 Chambers, Bristol	0845 210 5555
	No5 Chambers, London	0845 210 5555
Brown Mr Cameron Kennedy Duncan	9-12 Bell Yard, London	020 7400 1800

Name	Chambers	Telephone
Brown Mr Philip Stephen	9 Stone Buildings, London	020 7404 5055
Brown Mr Simon Jonathan	Crown Office Chambers, London	020 7797 8100
Brown Mr Timothy William	13 KBW, Oxford	01865 311066
	13 King's Bench Walk, London	020 7353 7204
Brunner Ms Catherine Jane	Albion Chambers, Bristol	0117 927 2144
	36 Bedford Row, London	020 7421 8000
Brunt Mr Philip Edwin	No 8 Chambers, Birmingham	0121 236 5514
Bryant Mr Keith	Outer Temple Chambers, London	020 7353 6381
Bryden Mr Christopher James Yuen Kang	4 King's Bench Walk, London	020 7822 7000
Buchan Miss Caroline Venetia	Chambers of Miss C Buchan, Haywards Heath	01444 482222
Buchan Mr Andrew	Cloisters, London	020 7827 4000
Buckle Mr Jonathan	Regency Chambers, Cambridge	01223 301517
	Regency Chambers, Peterborough	01733 315215
Budworth Mr Martin James	Kings Chambers, Birmingham	0845 034 3444
	Kings Chambers, Leeds	0845 034 3444
	Kings Chambers, Manchester	0845 034 3444
Bullen Mrs Mary	The Chambers Of Mary Bullen, Wilton	01722 742204
Bullock Mr Robert Gustaf	The Chambers of Mr Bullock, Brighton	01273 321050
Bunting Mr Jude James	Tooks Chambers, London	020 7842 7575
Burgher Mr Benjimin George	Outer Temple Chambers, London	020 7353 6381
Burns Mr Jeremy Stuart	12 College Place, Southampton	023 8032 0320
Burton Mr John Malcolm	3 Temple Gardens, London	020 7353 3102
Butler Mr Rupert James	3 Hare Court, London	020 7415 7800
Callan Ms Jane Elizabeth	Trinity Chambers, Middlesbrough	01642 247569
	Trinity Chambers, Newcastle Upon Tyne	0191 232 1927
Calvert Mr David Edward	12 King's Bench Walk, London	020 7583 0811
	St James's Chambers, Manchester	0161 834 7000
Campbell Mr Oliver Edward Wilhelm	Henderson Chambers, London	020 7583 9020
Carr Mr Christopher Sean	36 Bedford Row, London	020 7421 8000
Carrion Benitez Ms Miriam	36 Bedford Row, London	020 7421 8000
Cartwright Mr Ivan Matthew	KCH Garden Square, Nottingham	0115 941 8851
Case Mr Richard John	No5 Chambers, Birmingham	0845 210 5555
	No5 Chambers, Bristol	0845 210 5555
	No5 Chambers, London	0845 210 5555
Casey Mr Paul Joseph	Chambers of Marion Smullen and Kerim Fuad QC, London	020 7427 4400
Cattermull Miss Emma Jayne	East Anglian Chambers, Chelmsford	01473 214481
	East Anglian Chambers, Ipswich	01473 214481
	East Anglian Chambers, Norwich	01473 214481
Chadwick Miss Joanna Ceridwen	No5 Chambers, Birmingham	0845 210 5555
	No5 Chambers, Bristol	0845 210 5555
	No5 Chambers, London	0845 210 5555
Chambers Ms Rachel Elizabeth	Cloisters, London	020 7827 4000
Chan Miss Susan	13 KBW, Oxford	01865 311066
	13 King's Bench Walk, London	020 7353 7204
Chawla Mr Neil	No5 Chambers, Birmingham	0845 210 5555
	No5 Chambers, Bristol	0845 210 5555
	No5 Chambers, London	0845 210 5555
Checa-Dover Miss Olivia	KBW, Leeds	0113 297 1200
Chesner Mr Howard Michael	One Essex Court, London	020 7936 3030
Chidgey Mr David Gareth	Albion Chambers, Bristol	0117 927 2144
Chippeck Mr Stephen	5 King's Bench Walk, London	020 7353 5638
Choongh Mr Satnam Singh	No5 Chambers, Birmingham	0845 210 5555
	No5 Chambers, Bristol	0845 210 5555
	No5 Chambers, London	0845 210 5555
Christie Mr David Henderson	Seven Bedford Row, London	020 7242 3555
Chute Ms Andrea Alexandra	Rougemont Chambers, Exeter	01392 208484
	Tooks Chambers, London	020 7842 7575
Cifonelli Mr Rossano Giuseppe	2 Dr Johnson's Buildings, London	020 7936 2613
Clarke Mr Nikolas Michael	Field Court Chambers, London	020 7405 6114

Name	Chambers	Telephone
Clay Mr Jonathan Roger	Cornerstone Barristers, London	020 7242 4986
Clegg Mr Adam Gordon	Stour Chambers, Canterbury	01227 764899
Clement Mr Ryan Wayne	Conference Chambers, Harrow	020 8144 0134
Colbey Mr Richard	Guildhall Chambers Portsmouth, Portsmouth	023 9275 2400
	Lamb Chambers, London	020 7797 8300
Coleclough Mrs Suzanne Maria	St Philips Chambers, Birmingham	0121 246 7000
Comerton Miss Julie Anne	4 KBW, London	020 7822 8822
Conlon Mr Michael John Patrick	Harcourt Chambers, Milton Keynes	0845 123 1234
Cook Mr Paul Graham Whalley	Albion Chambers, Bristol	0117 927 2144
Cooksey Mr Nicholas	River Chambers, Shrewsbury	01743 350505
Cooper Miss Samantha Ann	Outer Temple Chambers, London	020 7353 6381
Costello Mr Paul James	Chambers of Mr Paul J Costello, Biggleswade	07846 016 399
Coster Mr Ronald David	42 Bedford Row, London	020 7831 0222
Cotter Mr Mark James	Five St Andrew's Hill, London	020 7332 5400
Coulter Mr Barry John	Clerksroom (London), London	0845 083 3000
	Clerksroom (Taunton), Taunton	0845 083 3000
	King's Lynn Chambers, King's Lynn	01553 672 085
Coyle Mr Anthony Noel	Zenith Chambers, Leeds	0113 245 5438
Cramsie Mr James Sinclair Beresford	13 KBW, Oxford	01865 311066
	13 King's Bench Walk, London	020 7353 7204
Crasnow Ms Rachel	Cloisters, London	020 7827 4000
Crawford Mr Lincoln Santo	12 King's Bench Walk, London	020 7583 0811
Crawley Mr Ross Alexander	Middle Temple Lane Chambers, London	020 7583 4352
Crew Miss Gillian Mary	Ely Place Chambers, London	020 7400 9600
Crinion Mr Charles Edward	1 Mitre Court Buildings, London	020 7452 8900
Crosfill Mr John	Field Court Chambers, London	020 7405 6114
Crow Mr Charles Duncan Timothy	No5 Chambers, Birmingham	0845 210 5555
	No5 Chambers, Bristol	0845 210 5555
	No5 Chambers, London	0845 210 5555
Crowther Ms Lucy Ellen	Apex, Cardiff	02920 232 032
Culverhouse Miss Emily Anna Louise	Chambers of Miss E Culverhouse, Chesham	07813 007503
Cunningham Miss Elizabeth Alice	Albion Chambers, Bristol	0117 927 2144
Cunningham Ms Naomi Brigid	Outer Temple Chambers, London	020 7353 6381
Currie Mr Fergus Hugh	Unity Street Chambers, Bristol	0117 906 9789
Curwen Mr David Christian	Unity Street Chambers, Bristol	0117 906 9789
Dalal Mr Rajen Charles James	Cobden House Chambers, Manchester	0161 833 6000
	Derwent Chambers, Derby	01332 242425
Daly Mr David	Heathway Chambers, London	020 8293 0509
Davey Mr Charles	64 Bridge Street, Manchester	0845 083 3000
	Chambers of Mr C Davey, Bishop's Stortford	01279 506412
	Clerksroom (Taunton), Taunton	0845 083 3000
Davies Mr Henry Olusola	Trinity Chambers, Birmingham	0121 346 4672
Davies Mr Jake Sebastian Hunter	Five Paper, London	020 7815 3200
Davies Mr Jonathan Huw	Old Square Chambers, Bristol	0117 930 5100
	Old Square Chambers, London	020 7269 0300
Davis Miss Lucy-Victoria	Pump Court Chambers, London	020 7353 0711
	Pump Court Chambers, Swindon	01793 539899
	Pump Court Chambers, Winchester	01962 868 161
De Mounteney Mr Jonathan Patrick	Chambers of Mr J P De Mounteney, Reading	0118 934 6822
Dean Mr James Patrick	Goldsmith Chambers, London	020 7353 6802
Dean Mr Paul Benjamin	Crown Office Chambers, London	020 7797 8100
Dennis Miss Rebecca Louise	Queen Square Chambers, Bristol	0117 921 1966
Dhar Mr Zeeshan	Hardwicke, London	020 7242 2523
Dipré Mr Paul Nicholas Amadeus	Chambers of Mr P N Dipré, Address withheld	0845 123 1234
	MK Family Law Chambers, Milton Keynes	0845 123 1234

Dixon Mr David Steven	Sovereign Chambers, Leeds	0113 245 1841
Dixon Mr James Malcolm	No5 Chambers, Birmingham	0845 210 5555
	No5 Chambers, Bristol	0845 210 5555
	No5 Chambers, London	0845 210 5555
Doerfel Mr Jan Hendrik Jamison	1215 Chambers, London	020 3291 1215
	Chambers of Mr J H Doerfel, Richmond	0845 123 1234
Dos Santos Mr Alexander	Charter Chambers, London	020 7618 4400
Doswell Mr Rupert John	KBW, Leeds	0113 297 1200
Doughty Mr Peter	12 College Place, Southampton	023 8032 0320
Dowden Mr Andrew Philip	Castle Chambers, Harrow-on-the-Hill	020 8423 6579
	Melbury House, Leicester	07801 037802
Dowell Mr Gregory Hamilton	Principal Chambers, Sevenoaks	0845 209 8080
Downey Mr Neil James	Atlantic Chambers, Liverpool	0151 236 4421
Dracass Mr Timothy William	Pump Court Chambers, London	020 7353 0711
	Pump Court Chambers, Winchester	01962 868 161
	Riverview Chambers, London	0844 225 3999
Dsane Miss Victoria Tsotsoo	Chambers of Miss Victoria Dsane, Sutton	020 8722 0990
Dye Mr John Geoffrey	Goldsmith Chambers, London	020 7353 6802
Eaton Mr James Bernard	Thomas More Chambers, London	020 7404 7000
Edge Mr Timothy Richard	Deans Court Chambers, Manchester	0161 214 6000
	Deans Court Chambers, Preston	01772 565 600
Edwards Mr Denis	Francis Taylor Building, London	020 7353 8415
Egan Mr Patrick Manus Dermot	Thomas More Chambers, London	020 7404 7000
Egleton Mr Richard Wildman	Pallant Chambers, Chichester	01243 784538
Elder Miss Fiona Ann Morag	Albion Chambers, Bristol	0117 927 2144
Elesinnla Mr Ayoade	Igbobi Chambers, London	0203 2867626
Elfield Miss Laura Elaine	The Chambers of Grahame Aldous QC, London	020 7832 0500
Engelman Mr Philip	Cloisters, London	020 7827 4000
	Trinity Chambers, Middlesbrough	01642 247569
	Trinity Chambers, Newcastle Upon Tyne	0191 232 1927
Esprit Mr Benoit	Barristers Chambers, London	020 3417 6461
	Legis Chambers, Aylesbury	01296 431125
Evans Mr Andrew David	St Philips Chambers, Birmingham	0121 246 7000
Fagborun Bennett Ms Morayo Abosede	Hardwicke, London	020 7242 2523
Fama Mrs Gudrun Hildegard	Middle Temple Lane Chambers, London	020 7583 4352
Fapohunda Mrs Olukemi	Furnival Chambers, London	020 7405 3232
Farr Mr Philip Edward	1 Paper Buildings, London	020 7353 3728
Faryl Miss Alaha Begum	Central Chambers, Manchester	0161 236 1133
Fawcett Mr Neil	St Ive's Chambers, Birmingham	0121 236 0863
Feldschreiber Dr Peter	Four New Square, London	020 7822 2000
Fender Mr Carl David	Regency Chambers, Cambridge	01223 301517
	Regency Chambers, Peterborough	01733 315215
Ferber Ms Iris	42 Bedford Row, London	020 7831 0222
Fetto Mr Niazi Peter	2 Temple Gardens, London	020 7822 1200
Finlay Mr Darren	Sovereign Chambers, Leeds	0113 245 1841
Finn Mr Terence	Erimus Chambers, Bedford	01234 720952
	Forest Chambers, Boston	01775 840827
Fortune Mr Peter Carl Michael	Guildhall Chambers Portsmouth, Portsmouth	023 9275 2400
	4 King's Bench Walk, London	020 7822 7000
Found Mr Timothy Paul	Farrar's Building, London	020 7583 9241
Frame Mr Stuart James	Staple Inn Chambers, London	020 7242 5240
Frantzis Miss Roxanne	KBW, Leeds	0113 297 1200
Fraser-Urquhart Mr Andrew	4-5 Gray's Inn Square, London	020 7404 5252
Frawley Ms Lyndsey Anne	Quorum Chambers, St Albans	01727 884516
	Quorum Tax Chambers, London	020 7043 5189
Frazer Ms Alison	Queen Square Chambers, Bristol	0117 921 1966

Fridd Mr Nicholas Timothy	Albion Chambers, Bristol	0117 927 2144
	Bell Yard Chambers, London	020 7306 9292
Fuller Mr Alan Peter	Albion Chambers, Bristol	0117 927 2144
Gadd Mr Adam Brian	Pump Court Chambers, London	020 7353 0711
	Pump Court Chambers, Winchester	01962 868 161
	Riverview Chambers, London	0844 225 3999
Gainer Mr Richard St Clair	St Margaret's Chambers, Twickenham	020 8241 3516
Galbraith-Marten Mr Jason Nicholas	Cloisters, London	020 7827 4000
Gallivan Mr Terence John	Five Paper, London	020 7815 3200
Garcha Mr Gurdeep Singh	Citadel Chambers, Birmingham	0121 233 8500
Gardiner Miss Kerry Ann	Queen Square Chambers, Bristol	0117 921 1966
Garner Miss Sophie Jane	St Philips Chambers, Birmingham	0121 246 7000
Gasztowicz Mr Steven	Cornerstone Barristers, London	020 7242 4986
	New Street Chambers, Leicester	0116 262 5906
Gau Mr Justin Charles	Pump Court Chambers, London	020 7353 0711
	Pump Court Chambers, Swindon	01793 539899
	Pump Court Chambers, Winchester	01962 868 161
Gelbart Mr Geoff Alan	1 Gray's Inn Square, London	020 7405 0001
Gent Mr Matthew Thomas	Sovereign Chambers, Leeds	0113 245 1841
Gill Mr Manjit Singh	No5 Chambers, Birmingham	0845 210 5555
	No5 Chambers, Bristol	0845 210 5555
	No5 Chambers, London	0845 210 5555
Gill Mr Satinderjit Singh	Five Paper, London	020 7815 3200
Gilroy Mr Paul	Old Square Chambers, London	020 7269 0300
	9 St John Street, Manchester	0161 955 9000
Ginniff Mr Nigel Thomas	Atlantic Chambers, Liverpool	0151 236 4421
Gladwell Mr Simon Mark	East Anglian Chambers, Ipswich	01473 214481
Gledhill Mr Lee Andre	Alexander Chambers, London	0845 652 0451/0854 652 0451
	Trident Barristers Chambers, Manchester	0161 663 3123
Gloag Mr Angus Robin	1 Gray's Inn Square, London	020 7405 0001
	Rougemont Chambers, Exeter	01392 208484
Glyn Mr Caspar Hilary Gordon	Cloisters, London	020 7827 4000
Godfrey Mr Lauren John	Crown Office Row Chambers, Brighton	01273 625625
Goldberg Mr Simon Ian	Trinity Chambers, Middlesbrough	01642 247569
	Trinity Chambers, Newcastle Upon Tyne	0191 232 1927
Goldman Mrs Linda	Henderson Chambers, London	020 7583 9020
Goodfellow Mr Stephen John	East Anglian Chambers, Chelmsford	01473 214481
	East Anglian Chambers, Ipswich	01473 214481
	East Anglian Chambers, Norwich	01473 214481
Goodlad Mr Grant David	Farrar's Building, London	020 7583 9241
Gorasia Mr Paras Ravji	Kings Chambers, Birmingham	0845 034 3444
	Kings Chambers, Leeds	0845 034 3444
	Kings Chambers, Manchester	0845 034 3444
Gordon Mr Jeremy	Chambers of Mr Ami Feder, London	020 7797 7788
	Chambers of Mr Ami Feder, London	020 7797 7788
	Lamb Building, Brighton	01273 820490
Gore Mrs Harriet Nkechi Adimora	Kensington Chambers, London	020 7373 2217
Graham Mrs Alana Nicole	Chambers of Alana Graham, Halesowen	01384 894560
	9 Stone Buildings, London	020 7404 5055
Grant Mr David Ericson	Outer Temple Chambers, London	020 7353 6381
Grant Mr Murray Ross	13 KBW, Oxford	01865 311066
	13 King's Bench Walk, London	020 7353 7204
Grant-Garwood Mr Joshua Dahren	1 Pump Court, London	020 7842 7070
Granville Stafford Mr Andrew	4 King's Bench Walk, London	020 7822 7000
Greatorex Mr Paul	4-5 Gray's Inn Square, London	020 7404 5252
Green Mr Patrick Curtis	Henderson Chambers, London	020 7583 9020
Greenfield Mr Peter Charles	King's Bench Chambers, Bournemouth	01202 250025
Grundy Ms Clare	St Johns Buildings, Manchester	0161 214 1500
	St Johns Buildings Liverpool, Liverpool	0151 243 6000
	16 Winckley Square, Preston	01772 256100

C

Gun Cuninghame Mr Julian Arthur	Gough Square Chambers, London	020 7353 0924
Gunstone Mr Robert Giles	KCH Garden Square, Nottingham	0115 941 8851
Gurden Miss Alison Louise	1 Gray's Inn Square, London	020 7405 0001
Guy Mr Richard Perran	Chambers of Mr Ami Feder, London	020 7797 7788
	King's Bench and Godolphin (KBG)Chambers, Plymouth	01752 221551
	Southernhay Chambers, Exeter	01392 255777
Hadgill Mr Clinton Alexander	St Albans Chambers, St Albans	01727 843383
Halden Mr Angus Robert	Queen Square Chambers, Bristol	0117 921 1966
Hall Mr Jeremy John	Becket Chambers, Canterbury	01227 786331
Halliwell Mr Toby George	Unity Street Chambers, Bristol	0117 906 9789
Hamilton Miss Amanda Jean	Furnival Chambers, London	020 7405 3232
Hamilton-Shield Miss Anna-Maria	Charter Chambers, London	020 7618 4400
Hanif Miss Saima Naz	4-5 Gray's Inn Square, London	020 7404 5252
Hanlon Mr James Tobias	Old Bailey Chambers, London	020 3008 6404
Harrap Mr Robert Philip	Five Paper, London	020 7815 3200
Harrington Miss Clare Stephanie	13 KBW, Oxford	01865 311066
	13 King's Bench Walk, London	020 7353 7204
Harris Mr Melvyn	5 Essex Court, London	020 7410 2000
Harrison Mr Piers William Benedict	Tanfield Chambers, London	020 7421 5300
Hartman Mr Michael	One Essex Court, London	020 7936 3030
Harwood-Gray Mr Barry John	Kenworthy's Chambers, Manchester	0161 832 4036
Hashim Mr Mu'Min Iran Muhammad	Chambers of Marion Smullen and Kerim Fuad QC, London	020 7427 4400
	Paragon Chambers, London	020 3318 9988
Hassall Mr Craig Jonathan	Sovereign Chambers, Leeds	0113 245 1841
Hatch Miss Lisa Sharmila	One Essex Court, London	020 7936 3030
Haughty Mr Jeremy Nicholas	Chambers of Mr Ami Feder, London	020 7797 7788
	Chambers of Mr Ami Feder, London	020 7797 7788
	Rougemont Chambers, Exeter	01392 208484
Havenhand Mr John Barry	Clerksroom (London), London	0845 083 3000
	Clerksroom (Taunton), Taunton	0845 083 3000
	King's Lynn Chambers, King's Lynn	01553 672 085
Hayes Mr Richard James	Lamb Chambers, London	020 7797 8300
Heath Mr Stephen David	Tanfield Chambers, London	020 7421 5300
Hendron Mr Henry Joseph Christopher	Strand Chambers, London	020 7117 6920
Henstock-Turner Mrs Sarah Elizabeth	College Chambers, Southampton	023 8023 0338
Heppinstall Mr Adam John	Henderson Chambers, London	020 7583 9020
Hewson Ms Barbara Mary	Hardwicke, London	020 7242 2523
Higginson Mr Timothy Nicholas Bennett	Littleton Chambers, London	020 7797 8600
	St John's Chambers, Bristol	0117 923 4700
Hignett Mr Richard James	No5 Chambers, Birmingham	0845 210 5555
	No5 Chambers, Bristol	0845 210 5555
	No5 Chambers, London	0845 210 5555
Hill Ms Eleanor Mary Henrietta	Doughty Street Chambers, Bristol	01179 058 717
	Doughty Street Chambers, London	020 7404 1313
	Doughty Street Chambers, Manchester	0161 618 1066
Hilton Ms Saisampan	Holborn Chambers, London	020 7242 6060
Hinton Mr Neil Pearse	King's Bench Chambers, Bournemouth	01202 250025
Hoar Mr Francis John Patrick	Field Court Chambers, London	020 7405 6114
Hodgkiss Ms Suzanne Jane	43 Temple Row Chambers, Birmingham	0121 237 6035
Hodkinson Mr Gary Stephen	Chambers of Mr Ami Feder, London	020 7797 7788
	Chambers of Mr Ami Feder, London	020 7797 7788
Hodson Mr Matthew Paul	Farrar's Building, London	020 7583 9241
Hogben Mrs Helen Jane	Fountain Chambers, Middlesbrough	01642 804040
Holmes-Milner Mr James Neil	The Chambers of Grahame Aldous QC, London	020 7832 0500
Hornblower Mrs Sarah Patience	Rougemont Chambers, Exeter	01392 208484
Howard Mr Robin William John	Fenners Chambers, Cambridge	01223 368761
Howells Mr Stephen John	Stone Chambers, London	020 7440 6900
Howlett Mr James Anthony	KCH Garden Square, Nottingham	0115 941 8851

Hulse Mrs Cecilia Helen	Chambers of Mr Ami Feder, London	020 7797 7788
	Chambers of Mr Ami Feder, London	020 7797 7788
Hussain Mr Basharat	Cornwall Street Chambers, Birmingham	0121 233 7500
Hussain Mr Muhammad Altaf	Chambers of Mr M A Hussain, London	020 8679 2398
Hutchin Mr Edward Alister David	Temple Garden Chambers, London	020 7583 1315
Hutchinson Mr Colin Thomas	Garden Court Chambers, London	020 7993 7600
Hymanson Miss Deanna Susan	Cobden House Chambers, Manchester	0161 833 6000
Iqbal Mr Mashood	London View Chambers, Sawbridgeworth	07788 912493
Irvin Mr Peter	Brick Court Chambers, London	020 7379 3550
Islam-Choudhury Mr Mugni	No5 Chambers, Birmingham	0845 210 5555
	No5 Chambers, Bristol	0845 210 5555
	No5 Chambers, London	0845 210 5555
Iyer Miss Shobana	Swan Chambers, Richmond	0845 123 1234
Jackson Mr Christopher Marshall	Liverpool Civil Law, Liverpool	0151 242 0500
Jafferji Mr Zainulabedin Hatim	Chambers of Mr Jafferji, Leicester	07957 198777
Jay Mr Grenville Richard	Regent Chambers, Stoke On Trent	01782 286666
Jayakrishnan Mr Harry Sisubalan	Trent Chambers, Nottingham	0115 941 9596
Jeram Miss Kirti	Park Lane Plowden, Newcastle Upon Tyne	0191 211 4087
Joffe Ms Natasha Juliet Louise	Outer Temple Chambers, London	020 7353 6381
John Mr Thomas Huw	Goresbrook Chambers, Milton Keynes	0845 123 1234
Johnson Miss Sarah Susan	Kenworthy's Chambers, Manchester	0161 832 4036
Jones Miss Emily Louise	Temple Garden Chambers, London	020 7583 1315
Jones Mr David Nicholas	Broadway House Chambers, Bradford	01274 722560
	Broadway House Chambers, Leeds	0113 246 2600
	Cloisters, London	020 7827 4000
Jones Mr Kelvin Mcallister	Templis Chambers, London	020 7649 9808
Jones Mr Richard Frederick Thomas	Heavenwood Chambers, Stroud	01453 873444
Joseph Mr Sellappah-Job	Chambers of Mr S J Joseph, London	020 8809 3083/020 8802 9889
Josling Mr William Henry Charles	37 Park Square Chambers, Leeds	0113 243 9422
Judge Miss Parveen	1 Mitre Court Buildings, London	020 7452 8900
Kee Mr Peter William	Becket Chambers, Canterbury	01227 786331
Keen Mr Spencer John	Pump Court Chambers, Swindon	01793 539899
	Pump Court Chambers, Winchester	01962 868 161
	Riverview Chambers, London	0844 225 3999
Kelly Mr Matthias John	39 Essex Street, London	020 7832 1111
Kenny Mr Martin William	Walnut House, Exeter	01392 279751
Keogh Mr Richard Thomas	Farringdon Chambers, London	020 7089 5700
Kerr Mr Derek William	Lamb Chambers, London	020 7797 8300
Khan Dr Alexander	Coral House, Manchester	
Khan Mr Arfan	Field Court Chambers, London	020 7405 6114
Khan Mr Ayoub	Chambers of Mr Ayoub Khan, Birmingham	07930 987202
Khan Mr Forz	Chambers of Mr F Khan, London	07854 109584
	6 King's Bench Walk, London	020 7353 4931
King Mr Graham Anthony	1 Gray's Inn Square, London	020 7405 0001
Kirk Mr Graeme Charles	One Essex Court, London	020 7936 3030
Kirk Mr Thomas Sean Robinson	12 College Place, Southampton	023 8032 0320
Kirtley Mr Paul George	Exchange Chambers, Leeds	0113 203 1970
	Exchange Chambers, Liverpool	0151 236 7747
	Littleton Chambers, London	020 7797 8600
Knight Mr Keith Leslie Francis	4 King's Bench Walk, London	020 7822 7000
Korn Mr Anthony Henry	No5 Chambers, Birmingham	0845 210 5555
	No5 Chambers, Bristol	0845 210 5555
	No5 Chambers, London	0845 210 5555
Kramer Mr Philip Anthony	Park Lane Plowden, Newcastle Upon Tyne	0191 211 4087
Kurji Ms Fatim Razahusein	No5 Chambers, Birmingham	0845 210 5555
	No5 Chambers, Bristol	0845 210 5555
	No5 Chambers, London	0845 210 5555
Kwiatkowski Mr Feliks Jerzy	Kew Chambers, Kew	0844 8099991

C

Lakha Mr Shabbir	Farrar's Building, London	020 7583 9241
Lam Mr Chuen Fat	Chambers of Martin Burr, London	0845 123 1234
Lamb Mr Edward Charles	The Chambers of Grahame Aldous QC, London	020 7832 0500
Lamb Mr Jeffrey Thomas	Westgate Chambers, Lewes	01273 480510
Lane Mr Michael John	East Anglian Chambers, Colchester	01473 214481
	East Anglian Chambers, Ipswich	01473 214481
	East Anglian Chambers, Norwich	01473 214481
Lanson Miss Lauren Elizabeth	1 Gray's Inn Square, London	020 7405 0001
Law Mr John Edward	The Chambers of Grahame Aldous QC, London	020 7832 0500
Lawrence Miss Anne Mary	Atlas Chambers, London	020 7269 7980
Leach Mr Douglas Colin	Guildhall Chambers, Bristol	0117 930 9000
Lemer Mr David James	Doughty Street Chambers, London	020 7404 1313
Lenaghan Mr Anthony	Dyers Chambers, London	020 7404 1881
Lennard Mr Stephen Charles	Hardwicke, London	020 7242 2523
Levett Miss Francesca Anna	Five St Andrew's Hill, London	020 7332 5400
Lewiecki Miss Marie	Old Bailey Chambers, London	020 3008 6404
Lewis Mr Stuart John	New Walk Chambers, Leicester	0871 200 1298/0116 255 9144
Lewis Mr Wayne Anthony	Access Lawyers, London	020 8801 2345
Lewis Mrs Pauline Grace	Holborn Chambers, London	020 7242 6060
Ling Ms Naomi	Outer Temple Chambers, London	020 7353 6381
Linstead Mr Peter James	Tanfield Chambers, London	020 7421 5300
Lippold Ms Sarah Ida Louise	13 KBW, Oxford	01865 311066
	13 King's Bench Walk, London	020 7353 7204
Lissack Mr Richard Anthony	Outer Temple Chambers, London	020 7353 6381
	Riverview Chambers, London	0844 225 3999
Livesey Mr John William Allan	Albion Chambers, Bristol	0117 927 2144
Livingstone Mr Simon John	Thomas More Chambers, London	020 7404 7000
Lloyd Mr John Nesbitt	Rougemont Chambers, Exeter	01392 208484
Longhurst-Woods Ms Lesley	2 Louisa Close, London	020 8985 8716
Lule Miss Jacqueline	1 Mitre Court Buildings, London	020 7452 8900
Lyons Miss Tara Yasmin	Pump Court Chambers, London	020 7353 0711
	Pump Court Chambers, Winchester	01962 868 161
	Riverview Chambers, London	0844 225 3999
MacEvilly Mr Conn Jeremy	9 Stone Buildings, London	020 7404 5055
MacLaren Miss Catriona Longueville	Tanfield Chambers, London	020 7421 5300
Magee Mr Michael James	Fenners Chambers, Cambridge	01223 368761
Mahmood Mr Abid	Central Chambers, Manchester	0161 236 1133
	No5 Chambers, Birmingham	0845 210 5555
	No5 Chambers, Bristol	0845 210 5555
	No5 Chambers, London	0845 210 5555
Mahmood Mr Imran Waseem	5 Pump Court, London	020 7353 2532
Maitland Jones Mr Mark Griffith	13 KBW, Oxford	01865 311066
	13 King's Bench Walk, London	020 7353 7204
Malik Miss Sarah	Hardwicke, London	020 7242 2523
Mallett Mr Simon Jeremy	KBW, Leeds	0113 297 1200
Malone Mr Gerald Fergus	Farringdon Chambers, London	020 7089 5700
Mankau Mrs Louise	Tanfield Chambers, London	020 7421 5300
Mann Mr Christopher	13 KBW, Oxford	01865 311066
	13 King's Bench Walk, London	020 7353 7204
Mannan Mr Charles Madani Fuad	Temple Court Chambers, London	020 7353 7888
Mannion Mr John Dennis	Tolzey Chambers, Bristol	
Margo Mr Saul Nicholas	Outer Temple Chambers, London	020 7353 6381
Marks Mr Jonathan Clive	4 Pump Court, London	020 7842 5555
Marler Lieutenant Colonel Lee Gary	Bretton Woods Law, London	
	18 Red Lion Court, London	020 7520 6000
Marshall Mr Derek Stanley	College Chambers, Southampton	023 8023 0338
Martin Mr Piers James	4 King's Bench Walk, London	020 7822 7000
Mason Mr David Hugh Rothwell	Dere Street Barristers, Newcastle Upon Tyne	0844 3351551
Massarella Mr David Peter	Cloisters, London	020 7827 4000
Matthias Mr David Huw	Francis Taylor Building, London	020 7353 8415

C

Mawdsley Mr David John	Chambers of Mr David Mawdsley, Southport	01704 565 387
McCombie Mr Fergus Alexander Paul	1 Gray's Inn Square, London	020 7405 0001
McCormack Mr Alan	Staple Inn Chambers, London	020 7242 5240
McCormick Mr William Thomas	Ely Place Chambers, London	020 7400 9600
McCracken Mr James	Cornwall Street Chambers, Birmingham	0121 233 7500
McGrath Mr Andrew John	No5 Chambers, Birmingham	0845 210 5555
	No5 Chambers, Bristol	0845 210 5555
	No5 Chambers, London	0845 210 5555
McKiernan Mr Edward Joseph	Farringdon Chambers, London	020 7089 5700
McKinney Miss Nicola Alexandra	4 KBW, London	020 7822 8822
Meichen Mr Jonathan Brian	St Philips Chambers, Birmingham	0121 246 7000
Mellor Miss Rachel Elizabeth	Broadway House Chambers, Bradford	01274 722560
	Broadway House Chambers, Leeds	0113 246 2600
Menon Mr Harigovind	New Court Chambers, Newcastle Upon Tyne	0191 232 1980
	Park Lane Plowden, Newcastle Upon Tyne	0191 211 4087
Mensah Mr Martin Mintah	Atlantic Chambers, Liverpool	0151 236 4421
Meredith-Hardy Mr John Octavian	Farrar's Building, London	020 7583 9241
Michael Mr Nicholas	East Anglian Chambers, Chelmsford	01473 214481
	East Anglian Chambers, Colchester	01473 214481
	East Anglian Chambers, Ipswich	01473 214481
	East Anglian Chambers, Norwich	01473 214481
Miller Mr Ian Robertson	Broadway House Chambers, Bradford	01274 722560
	Broadway House Chambers, Leeds	0113 246 2600
Millin Mrs Leslie Marilyn	The Chambers of Mrs Leslie Millin, Wokingham	0118 978 8026
Mills Mr Kristian Anthony	Trinity Chambers, Middlesbrough	01642 247569
	Trinity Chambers, Newcastle Upon Tyne	0191 232 1927
Milne Mrs Arlene Joan	Cobden House Chambers, Manchester	0161 833 6000
Mitchell Mr Alistair Stephen Fabian	49 Chambers, Bridgnorth	01746 761545
Mitchell Mr Christian Richard	Alexander Chambers, London	0845 652 0451/0854 652 0451
	Guildford Chambers, Guildford	01483 539131
Mitchell Mr Jonathan	1 Gray's Inn Square, London	020 7405 0001
	Holborn Chambers, London	020 7242 6060
Modgill Mr Alexander Jeffrey	Broadway House Chambers, Bradford	01274 722560
	Broadway House Chambers, Leeds	0113 246 2600
Moffat Mr Russell Dean	Linenhall Chambers, Chester	01244 348282
Moll Mr Christiaan Eric	Blackfriars Chambers, London	020 7353 7400
Moller Ms Alice Christina	Alexander Chambers, London	0845 652 0451/0854 652 0451
	Chambers of Ms A C Moller, Address withheld	07966 448572
Mooney Mr Stephen John	Albion Chambers, Bristol	0117 927 2144
Morgan Mr Jamie Peter	Trinity Chambers, Middlesbrough	01642 247569
	Trinity Chambers, Newcastle Upon Tyne	0191 232 1927
Morgan Mr John	Bedlington Chambers, London	020 7831 1159
Morris Mr Phillip John	9 Park Place, Cardiff	029 2038 2731
Morris Ms Johanna	Chambers of Marion Smullen and Kerim Fuad QC, London	020 7427 4400
Morton Mr Gary David	Pump Court Chambers, London	020 7353 0711
	Pump Court Chambers, Swindon	01793 539899
	Pump Court Chambers, Winchester	01962 868 161
Mullarkey Mr Ian	KBW, Leeds	0113 297 1200
Muman Mr Vijay Kumar	43 Temple Row Chambers, Birmingham	0121 237 6035
Murray Mr Charles Humphrey Stewart	Rougemont Chambers, Exeter	01392 208484
Mustakim Mr Abdul Yunus Al	Chambers of Mr Mustakim, London	
Mylvaganam Ms Tanoo	1 Gray's Inn Square, London	020 7405 0001
Nabi Mr Sajjad	5 Pump Court, London	020 7353 2532

C

Neville Mr Joseph Richard	43 Temple Row Chambers, Birmingham	0121 237 6035
Newman Miss Rebecca Jane	Clerksroom (Taunton), Taunton	0845 083 3000
	King's Lynn Chambers, King's Lynn	01553 672 085
Newman Mrs Veronica	Chambers of Mrs V Newman, Cardiff	029 2048 8797
Norton Mr Giles	Enigma Chambers, Sheffield	07779 576499
	Holborn Chambers, London	020 7242 6060
O'Brien Mr Nicholas William Wattebot	10 King's Bench Walk, London	020 7353 7742
O'Brien Mr Sean Timothy	St Philips Chambers, Birmingham	0121 246 7000
O'Dair Mr David Richard Frazer	36 Bedford Row, London	020 7421 8000
O'Donovan Mr Kevin John	No5 Chambers, Birmingham	0845 210 5555
	No5 Chambers, Bristol	0845 210 5555
	No5 Chambers, London	0845 210 5555
Okoye Miss Joy Nwamala	Chambers of Joy Okoye, London	07976 426871/020 7405 7011
O'Neill Mr Jonathan Norman	Rougemont Chambers, Exeter	01392 208484
Onipede Dr Victor Olusegun	Chambers of Dr V O Onipede, London	07956 207159
Oommen Mr Jacob	Chambers of Mr Jacob Oommen, East Barnet	07958 680272
Otchie Mr Andrew Akuafo	12 Old Square Chambers, London	020 7404 0875
O'Toole Mr Bartholomew Vincent	5 King's Bench Walk, London	020 7353 5638
O'Toole Mr Simon Gerard	5 Pump Court, London	020 7353 2532
	Riverview Chambers, London	0844 225 3999
Oulton Mr Richard Arthur Courtenay	5 Essex Court, London	020 7410 2000
Owen-Thomas Mr Richard Matthew	13 KBW, Oxford	01865 311066
	13 King's Bench Walk, London	020 7353 7204
Pallo Mr Simon Russel	Bank House Chambers, Sheffield	0114 275 1223
Palmer Miss Claire Louise	Thomas More Chambers, London	020 7404 7000
Palmer Miss Suzanne Elizabeth Josephine	4 King's Bench Walk, London	020 7822 7000
Palmer Mr Iain Franklyn	Renaissance Chambers, London	020 7404 1111
Palmer Mr James Savill	Henderson Chambers, London	020 7583 9020
Pande Miss Kakoly	2 Dr Johnson's Buildings, London	020 7936 2613
Panton Mr William Dwight	Amethyst Chambers, London	020 7936 4966
Paraskos Mr Paraskevakis Christakis	11 Gray's Inn Square Chambers, London	020 7405 6879
Pardoe Mr Matthew James	Dyers Chambers, London	020 7404 1881
Parker Miss Wendy	Hardwicke, London	020 7242 2523
Parker Mrs Karen Lesley	Guildhall Chambers Portsmouth, Portsmouth	023 9275 2400
Parry Mr Charles Robert	Pump Court Chambers, London	020 7353 0711
	Pump Court Chambers, Swindon	01793 539899
	Pump Court Chambers, Winchester	01962 868 161
Pascall Mr Matthew Stephen	Alexander Chambers, London	0845 652 0451/0854 652 0451
	Guildford Chambers, Guildford	01483 539131
Pascoe Ms Soraya	1 Gray's Inn Square, London	020 7405 0001
Patel Mr Yasin Ahmed	25 Bedford Row, London	020 7067 1500
Penni Miss Sally Selorm-Juliet	Kenworthy's Chambers, Manchester	0161 832 4036
Persaud Dr Marcia Chitroutie	1 Gray's Inn Square, London	020 7405 0001
Petersen Mr Thomas James	Goldsmith Chambers, London	020 7353 6802
Pettican Mr Kevin	11 Stone Buildings, London	020 7831 6381
Philipson Miss Amy Victoria	Sovereign Chambers, Leeds	0113 245 1841
Phillips Miss Emma Louise	1 Pump Court, London	020 7842 7070
Philpott Mr Anthony Luke	12 Old Square Chambers, London	020 7404 0875
Pickering Mr Simon Toby	Wilberforce Chambers, Hull	01482 323264
Pigram Mr Christopher Stuart	East Anglian Chambers, Chelmsford	01473 214481
	East Anglian Chambers, Colchester	01473 214481
	East Anglian Chambers, Ipswich	01473 214481
Plant Mr James Richard	Farrar's Building, London	020 7583 9241
Platt Miss Heather Louise	Pump Court Chambers, London	020 7353 0711
	Pump Court Chambers, Swindon	01793 539899
	Riverview Chambers, London	0844 225 3999

Plimmer Miss Melanie Ann	Kings Chambers, Birmingham	0845 034 3444
	Kings Chambers, Leeds	0845 034 3444
	Kings Chambers, Manchester	0845 034 3444
Porter Mr Jamie Robert	King's Bench Chambers, Bournemouth	01202 250025
Preston Mr David Henry	Ely Place Chambers, London	020 7400 9600
Pretsell Mr James Davidson	Farrar's Building, London	020 7583 9241
Price Mr Charles John	No5 Chambers, Birmingham	0845 210 5555
	No5 Chambers, Bristol	0845 210 5555
	No5 Chambers, London	0845 210 5555
Prokofiev Mr Sergey	Lincoln House Chambers, Manchester	0161 832 5701
Puar Mr Mikhael	30 Park Place, Cardiff	029 2039 8421
Quickfall Mr Roger Mark	Park Lane Plowden, Leeds	0113 228 5049
Quigley Ms Louise	St Johns Buildings, Manchester	0161 214 1500
	St Johns Buildings Liverpool, Liverpool	0151 243 6000
	16 Winckley Square, Preston	01772 256100
Qureshi Mr Tanveer Aftab	25 Bedford Row, London	020 7067 1500
Rahman Mr Anis	12 Old Square Chambers, London	020 7404 0875
Rahman Mr Leo Ferhanur	Chambers of Leo Rahman, Brighton	07814 004 790
Rahman Mr Luthfur	Chambers of Mr L Rahman, Rochester	07947 588362
Rahman Mr Sami Ur	Field Court Chambers, London	020 7405 6114
Ramzan Mr Mohammed Anwar	Great James Street Chambers, London	020 7440 4949
Rana Mr Mohammed Akram	Clapham Law Chambers, London	020 7978 8482
Randolph Mr Paul Leslie	Field Court Chambers, London	020 7405 6114
Read Mr Daniel James	Farrar's Building, London	020 7583 9241
Record Mrs Celia Saint Claire	Chambers of Lawrence Jones, London	020 7831 1444
Reed Mr Simon John	New Walk Chambers, Leicester	0871 200 1298/0116 255 9144
Reeds Mr Gareth David	Canary Wharf Chambers, London	020 7183 8011
Rees Mr Hefin Ednyfed	39 Essex Street, London	020 7832 1111
Rees Mr Robert Charles David	New Walk Chambers, Leicester	0871 200 1298/0116 255 9144
Rees Prof William Michael	1 Gray's Inn Square, London	020 7405 0001
Reffin Miss Clare Alyson	One Essex Court, London	020 7583 2000
Regan Mr David Robert	St John's Chambers, Bristol	0117 923 4700
Reid Miss Claudette Patricia	Chambers of Miss Claudette Reid, London	
Rendle Mr Jeremy Mark	9 King's Bench Walk, London	020 7353 9564
Richardson Mr Garth Douglas Anthony	Devon Chambers, Plymouth	01752 661659
	Rougemont Chambers, Exeter	01392 208484
Ridd Mr David Ian Mcgregor	Farrar's Building, London	020 7583 9241
Rippon Mr Simon John	Citadel Chambers, Birmingham	0121 233 8500
Rivalland Mr Marc-Edouard	1 Chancery Lane, London	0845 634 6666
Roberts Mr Allan Calvin	Guildhall Chambers, Bristol	0117 930 9000
	Guildhall Chambers, Bristol	0117 930 9000
Roberts Mr Jack	Sheldan, Oswestry	01691 657635
Roberts Mr Michael Charles	Chambers of Michael Roberts, Henley-On-Thames	01844 355 655
Roberts Mr Richard Vaughan	Henderson Chambers, London	020 7583 9020
Robinson Miss Laura	Tanfield Chambers, London	020 7421 5300
Robinson Mr Nicholas James Lansdale	3 PB Barristers, Bournemouth	01202 292102
	3 PB Barristers, Bristol	0117 928 1520
	3 PB Barristers, London	020 7583 8055
	3 PB Barristers, Oxford	01865 793 736
	3 PB Barristers, Winchester	01962 868884
Robinson-Young Mr David Tilley	Dere Street Barristers, Newcastle Upon Tyne	0844 3351551
Rogers Mr Ian Paul	Monckton Chambers, London	020 7405 7211
Rogers Mr Michael Peter	Chambers of Mr Ami Feder, London	020 7797 7788
	Chambers of Mr Ami Feder, London	020 7797 7788
Rowell Mr George Edward	St John's Chambers, Bristol	0117 923 4700
Rudd Mr Matthew Allan	Broadway House Chambers, Bradford	01274 722560
	Broadway House Chambers, Leeds	0113 246 2600
Rudd Mr Michael	36 Bedford Row, London	020 7421 8000

C

Barrister	Chambers	Telephone
Russell Mr Graham Alexander	Citadel Chambers, Birmingham	0121 233 8500
Russell Mr Thomas Charles Welldon	KCH Garden Square, Nottingham	0115 941 8851
Ryan Mr William	Corsham Barristers Chambers, Corsham	01225 582582
	Farringdon Chambers, London	020 7089 5700
Sadiq Mr Tariq Mahmood	St Philips Chambers, Birmingham	0121 246 7000
Saifee Mr Faisal Aftaab	Thomas More Chambers, London	020 7404 7000
Saini Mr Parminder Paul Singh	12 Old Square Chambers, London	020 7404 0875
Salter Mr Michael Richard	Ely Place Chambers, London	020 7400 9600
Samra Miss Sharn	Broadway House Chambers, Bradford	01274 722560
	Broadway House Chambers, Leeds	0113 246 2600
Samuel Mr Richard Geoffrey Graham	3 Hare Court, London	020 7415 7800
Samuels Mr Leslie John	Pump Court Chambers, London	020 7353 0711
	Pump Court Chambers, Winchester	01962 868 161
	Riverview Chambers, London	0844 225 3999
Santamera Miss Louise Alexandria	New Bailey Chambers, Liverpool	0151 236 9402
Sawtell Mr David Robert Fraser	4 King's Bench Walk, London	020 7822 7000
Seeboruth Mr Royln Jean-Paul	Chambers of Royln Seeboruth, Aylesbury	01296 393329
Sekar Mr Chandra	Angell Park Chambers, London	020 7737 5957
Self Mr Gary Peter	College Chambers, Southampton	023 8023 0338
	St David's Chambers, Swansea	01792 559924
Serr Mr Ashley Barrie	Park Lane Plowden, Leeds	0113 228 5049
Shaw Miss Joanna Elizabeth	One Essex Court, London	020 7936 3030
Sheftel Mr Andrew Lawson Baylies	Tanfield Chambers, London	020 7421 5300
Shepherd Miss Judith Elizabeth	42 Bedford Row, London	020 7831 0222
Shepherd Mr Richard Andrew John	Albion Chambers, Bristol	0117 927 2144
Sheppard Mr Timothy Derie	No5 Chambers, Birmingham	0845 210 5555
	No5 Chambers, Bristol	0845 210 5555
	No5 Chambers, London	0845 210 5555
Short Mr Andrew John	Outer Temple Chambers, London	020 7353 6381
	Riverview Chambers, London	0844 225 3999
Silverton Miss Catherine Anne	Sovereign Chambers, Leeds	0113 245 1841
Simpson Miss Carol Monica	Amethyst Chambers, London	020 7936 4966
Singarajah Mr Frederico	1 Gray's Inn Square, London	020 7405 0001
Singer Mr Nicholas Paul	42 Bedford Row, London	020 7831 0222
Singer Mr Richard Adam	1 Gray's Inn Square, London	020 7405 0001
Skelt Mr Ian Stuart	KBW, Leeds	0113 297 1200
Skinner Mr Samuel Richard Edward	KCH Garden Square, Nottingham	0115 941 8851
Small Mr John Robert	36 Bedford Row, London	020 7421 8000
Smith Mr Julian Robert	Lincoln's Inn Fields Chambers, London	0845 123 1234
Smith Mr Robert Clive	1 Paper Buildings, London	020 7353 3728
	RCS Chambers, Stainton	01709 814 147
Snook Mr Harry Benedick	St Albans Chambers, St Albans	01727 843383
Sonaike Mr Kolarele Oladele Obafemi	One Essex Court, London	020 7936 3030
Sood Mrs Usha Rani	Trent Chambers, Nottingham	0115 941 9596
Sparrow Mrs Marie-Claire	Holborn Chambers, London	020 7242 6060
Speller Mr Bruce Christopher Norman	The White House, Battle	01424 777944
Spicer Mr Robert Haden	Frederick Place Chambers, Bristol	0117 946 7059
Spratt Mr Christopher David Richard Dean	9 Stone Buildings, London	020 7404 5055
Sproull Mr Nicholas	Albion Chambers, Bristol	0117 927 2144
St Louis Mr Brian Lloyd	15 New Bridge Street, London	020 7842 1900
Staddon Mr Paul	Tanfield Chambers, London	020 7421 5300
Stagg Mr Paul Andrew	1 Chancery Lane, London	0845 634 6666
Standfast Mr Philip Arthur	St Paul's Chambers, Leeds	0113 245 5866
Stanford Mr Tony James	Old Bailey Chambers, London	020 3008 6404
Stanzel Mrs Sarah Astrid	Tanfield Chambers, London	020 7421 5300
Starcevic Mr Petar	St Philips Chambers, Birmingham	0121 246 7000
Stebbings Mr Ian Anthony	1 Gray's Inn Square, London	020 7405 0001

Stedman Mr Aryan John	Chambers of Mr A J Stedman, Cliftonville	07702 870575
Stephenson Mr David Matthew	1 Mitre Court Buildings, London	020 7452 8900
Stevenson Mr Daniel Keith	9-12 Bell Yard, London	020 7400 1800
Stevenson Mr Paul Anthony	Tanfield Chambers, London	020 7421 5300
Stevenson Mr Robert Lloyd	Sovereign Chambers, Leeds	0113 245 1841
Stewart Mr Richard Paul	Lamb Chambers, London	020 7797 8300
Stirling Mr Christopher William	Field Court Chambers, London	020 7405 6114
Strelitz Mr Paul Stephen	East Anglian Chambers, Chelmsford	01473 214481
	East Anglian Chambers, Colchester	01473 214481
	East Anglian Chambers, Ipswich	01473 214481
Stride Mr Lionel Alexander	Temple Garden Chambers, London	020 7583 1315
Stringer Mr Leon Peter	15 Winckley Square, Preston	01772 252828
Stuart Mr James William	Lamb Chambers, London	020 7797 8300
Stubbs Mr Richard John Morris	Trinity Chambers, Middlesbrough	01642 247569
	Trinity Chambers, Newcastle Upon Tyne	0191 232 1927
Suter Mr Erich George Bernard	Park Chambers, Weybridge Park	01932 820082
Swinnerton Mr David Michael	Cornwall Street Chambers, Birmingham	0121 233 7500
Swirsky Mr Adam Abraham Burl Bradbury	Lamb Chambers, London	020 7797 8300
Syril Mr George Carmel	Luton Chambers, Luton	01582 598394
	Willesden Chambers, London	020 3273 1042
Taft Mr Christopher Heiton	St James's Chambers, Manchester	0161 834 7000
Tapsell Mr Paul Richard	Becket Chambers, Canterbury	01227 786331
Targett-Parker Miss Leanne Susan	No. 3 Fleet Street Chambers, London	020 7936 4474
	The Chambers of Miss Leanne Targett-Parker, London	020 8674 6694
Taylor Mr Jason	Albion Chambers, Bristol	0117 927 2144
Tether Ms Melanie Georgia Kim	Old Square Chambers, Bristol	0117 930 5100
	Old Square Chambers, London	020 7269 0300
Tharoo Mrs Safia	42 Bedford Row, London	020 7831 0222
Thomas Mr Andrew Martin	Lincoln House Chambers, Manchester	0161 832 5701
	Linenhall Chambers, Chester	01244 348282
Thomas Mr Gareth	Atlantic Chambers, Liverpool	0151 236 4421
Thomas Mr Mark David	5 Essex Court, London	020 7410 2000
Thomas Mrs Felicity	Westgate Chambers, Lewes	01273 480510
Thomas Ms Rebecca Jane	42 Bedford Row, London	020 7831 0222
Thompson Mr Andrew Edward Courtney	Tanfield Chambers, London	020 7421 5300
Thomson Mr Martin Haldane Ahmad	Wynne Chambers, London	020 3239 6964
Tinnion Mr Antoine	Trinity Chambers, Middlesbrough	01642 247569
	Trinity Chambers, Newcastle Upon Tyne	0191 232 1927
Tivadar Mr Daniel	3 Hare Court, London	020 7415 7800
Tizzano Mr Franco Salvatore	Old Bailey Chambers, London	020 3008 6404
Tompkinson Miss Deborah Ann	Clerksroom (London), London	0845 083 3000
	Clerksroom (Taunton), Taunton	0845 083 3000
Toone Mr Robert Francis	KBW, Leeds	0113 297 1200
Topal Mr Erol	Lamb Chambers, London	020 7797 8300
Tozzi Mr Nigel Kenneth	4 Pump Court, London	020 7842 5555
Treharne Mr Neil Simon	Dingle Chambers, Bristol	07818 827754
Tresman Mr Lewis Robert Simon	Staple Inn Chambers, London	020 7242 5240
Trotter Miss Helen Claire	Pump Court Chambers, London	020 7353 0711
	Pump Court Chambers, Swindon	01793 539899
	Pump Court Chambers, Winchester	01962 868 161
Tucker Mr Ashley Russell	Park Court Chambers, Leeds	0113 243 3277
Tunley Mr James Christopher Gordon	4 KBW, London	020 7822 8822
Turnill Mr Evan	Pallant Chambers, Chichester	01243 784538
Twine Miss Nicola	Park Lane Plowden, Leeds	0113 228 5049
Twist Mr Stephen John	Dere Street Barristers, Newcastle Upon Tyne	0844 3351551

Name	Chambers	Telephone
Uduje Mr Benjamin Elliott	42 Bedford Row, London	020 7831 0222
Unigwe Mr Sylvester Emefiona	Essex House Chambers, London	020 7692 0677
	11 Gray's Inn Square Chambers, London	020 7405 6879
Vaitilingam Mr Adam Skanda	Albion Chambers, Bristol	0117 927 2144
Vaughan Mr Anthony	Garden Court Chambers, London	020 7993 7600
Vickery Mr Neil Michael	13 KBW, Oxford	01865 311066
	13 King's Bench Walk, London	020 7353 7204
Von Wachter Lady Victoria Nora Cressida	5 Essex Court, London	020 7410 2000
Wagstaff Mr Andrew Martin Nicholas	Westgate Chambers, Lewes	01273 480510
Walker Mr Adam Nigel	Seven Bedford Row, London	020 7242 3555
Ward Mr Martin Stuart	14 Gray's Inn Square, London	020 7242 0858
Ward Mr Peter Mark	The Chambers of Peter Ward, London	020 3402 2152
Wastall Mr Andrew James Frederick	Park Court Chambers, Leeds	0113 243 3277
Watson Mr Alaric	11 Stone Buildings, London	020 7831 6381
Watson Mr Graham	Colleton Chambers, Exeter	01392 274898
Webster Mr Keith	4 King's Bench Walk, London	020 7822 7000
Welch Mr David William	Alexander Chambers, London	0845 652 0451/0854 652 0451
	Warwick House Chambers, London	020 7430 2323
Wenban-Smith Mr Mungo William	4-5 Gray's Inn Square, London	020 7404 5252
Wheaton Mr Ian Malcolm James	Eighteen Carlton Crescent, Southampton	023 8063 9001
White Mr Daniel Edward Mills	Citadel Chambers, Birmingham	0121 233 8500
White Mr Matthew James	St John's Chambers, Bristol	0117 923 4700
White Mr Oliver Zachary	Littleton Chambers, London	020 7797 8600
White Mr Steven James	Park Court Chambers, Leeds	0113 243 3277
Whyte Miss Monica Patricia	42 Bedford Row, London	020 7831 0222
Widdett Ms Ceri Louise	Park Court Chambers, Leeds	0113 243 3277
Wignall Mr Edward Gordon	No5 Chambers, Birmingham	0845 210 5555
	No5 Chambers, Bristol	0845 210 5555
	No5 Chambers, London	0845 210 5555
Williams Miss Micaila Teresa	Optimus Chambers, Braintree	01376 691 885/07736 283873
Williams Mr Ben Dylan	Kings Chambers, Birmingham	0845 034 3444
	Kings Chambers, Leeds	0845 034 3444
	Kings Chambers, Manchester	0845 034 3444
Williams Mr Mark John	Queen Square Chambers, Bristol	0117 921 1966
Williams Ms Sandra Alessandra Caroline	The Chambers Of Alessandra Williams, Tadworth	07941 944950
Wilson Mr Paul Richard	Broadway House Chambers, Bradford	01274 722560
Wilson Mr Richard Carver	36 Bedford Row, London	020 7421 8000
Wilson Mr Scott	Themis Chambers, London	07967 418976
Winstone The Hon Anne Hilary Welch	Old Square Chambers, Bristol	0117 930 5100
	Old Square Chambers, London	020 7269 0300
Wood Mr Richard Michael	East Anglian Chambers, Chelmsford	01473 214481
	East Anglian Chambers, Ipswich	01473 214481
	East Anglian Chambers, Norwich	01473 214481
Woodward Miss Joanne Claire	9 St John Street, Manchester	0161 955 9000
Worthley Mr Andrew Mark	Rougemont Chambers, Exeter	01392 208484
Wright Mr Ian	Five Paper, London	020 7815 3200
Wylie Mr Neil Richard	KCH Garden Square, Nottingham	0115 941 8851
Wynn Mr Toby	KBW, Leeds	0113 297 1200
Yell Mr Nicholas Anthony	1 Chancery Lane, London	0845 634 6666
Young Mr Martin Ford	9 Stone Buildings, London	020 7404 5055
Zeitler Miss Barbara	3 Dr Johnson's Buildings, London	020 7353 4854

ENERGY

Name	Chambers	Telephone
Ajaz Mr Mohammad Arshad	Eastmans Chambers, Reading	0118 966 9094
Almihdar Mr Ali Hamed	Outer Temple Chambers, London	020 7353 6381
Aswani Mr Ravi Girdharilal	Stone Chambers, London	020 7440 6900
Barnett Mr Jeremy Victor	2 Bedford Row, London	020 7440 8888
	St Paul's Chambers, Leeds	0113 245 5866

C

Booth Mr Alexander Henry Spencer	Francis Taylor Building, London	020 7353 8415
Boulding Mr Philip Vincent	Keating Chambers, London	020 7544 2600
Burr Mr Andrew Charles	Atkin Chambers, London	020 7404 0102
Coulter Mr Barry John	Clerksroom (London), London	0845 083 3000
	Clerksroom (Taunton), Taunton	0845 083 3000
	King's Lynn Chambers, King's Lynn	01553 672 085
Darling Mr Paul Antony	Keating Chambers, London	020 7544 2600
Darroch Miss Fiona Culverwell	Clerksroom (London), London	0845 083 3000
	Clerksroom (Taunton), Taunton	0845 083 3000
	King's Lynn Chambers, King's Lynn	01553 672 085
Doerries Miss Chantal-Aimée Renee Aemelia An	Atkin Chambers, London	020 7404 0102
Edwards Mr Nigel Royston	St Paul's Chambers, Leeds	0113 245 5866
Elliott Mr Timothy Stanley	Keating Chambers, London	020 7544 2600
Evans Mr Robert Jonathan	Keating Chambers, London	020 7544 2600
Facenna Mr Gerald Carlo	Monckton Chambers, London	020 7405 7211
Gallivan Mr Terence John	Five Paper, London	020 7815 3200
Gee Mr Steven Mark	Stone Chambers, London	020 7440 6900
Godwin Mr William George Henry	3 Hare Court, London	020 7415 7800
	St John's Chambers, Bristol	0117 923 4700
Hammerton Mr Alastair Rolf	1 Chancery Lane, London	0845 634 6666
Hargreaves Mr Simon John Robert	Keating Chambers, London	020 7544 2600
Harwood Mr Richard John	39 Essex Street, London	020 7832 1111
	82 King Street, Manchester	0161 870 9969
Hirst Mr Martin Lewis	13 KBW, Oxford	01865 311066
	13 King's Bench Walk, London	020 7353 7204
Horton Mr Matthew Bethell	39 Essex Street, London	020 7832 1111
	82 King Street, Manchester	0161 870 9969
Jackson Miss Rosemary Elizabeth	Keating Chambers, London	020 7544 2600
Jinadu Mr Abdul-Lateef Abodurin Olayinka	Keating Chambers, London	020 7544 2600
Lenon Mr Andrew Ralph Fitzmaurice	One Essex Court, London	020 7583 2000
Matthias Mr David Huw	Francis Taylor Building, London	020 7353 8415
McGee Dr Tristan Paul	Foxhill Chambers, Penrith	01768 482710
Miller Mr Andrew	2 Temple Gardens, London	020 7822 1200
Newbold Dr Anne Lorraine Elsie	Minerva Chambers, Ocean Village	00 350 20042779
Nicholson Mr Jeremy Mark	4 Pump Court, London	020 7842 5555
Noble Mr Andrew	Enterprise Chambers, Leeds	0113 246 0391
Ogunbusola Mr Victor Olaniyi	Chambers of Victor Ogumbusola, Basildon	07413 634231
O'Sullivan Mr Thomas Sean Patrick	4 Pump Court, London	020 7842 5555
Owens Miss Elspeth Eluned	4 Pump Court, London	020 7842 5555
Paraskos Mr Paraskevakis Christakis	11 Gray's Inn Square Chambers, London	020 7405 6879
Pennicott Mr Ian	Keating Chambers, London	020 7544 2600
Rai Mr Rajesh Kumar	1 Mitre Court Buildings, London	020 7452 8900
Reid Miss Cheryl Louise Pegg	Temple Court Chambers, London	020 7353 7888
Rinker Mr Andrew Stuart D'Artois	Chambers of Mr Andrew Rinker, London	020 7584 1091
Royce Mr Darryl Fraser	Atkin Chambers, London	020 7404 0102
Scott Holland Mr Gideon Silas	Keating Chambers, London	020 7544 2600
Sears Mr Robert David Murray	Four New Square, London	020 7822 2000
Sims Miss Alice Antonia	Keating Chambers, London	020 7544 2600
Singarajah Mr Frederico	1 Gray's Inn Square, London	020 7405 0001
Sliwinski Mr Robert Andrew	SWL Chambers, Loudwater	01494 616007
Stansfield Mr Piers Alistair	Keating Chambers, London	020 7544 2600
Thompson Mr Michael James	Keating Chambers, London	020 7544 2600
Townend Mr Samuel John	Keating Chambers, London	020 7544 2600
Von Pommern-Peglow Dr Michael Alfred Herman Pr.	Brunswick Chambers, London	020 7353 1987
Watthey Mr James Robertson	Hardwicke, London	020 7242 2523

C

Wills Miss Alexandra Itari	Christ Church Chambers, London	020 7409 5278/07788 512787

ENTERTAINMENT

Abrahams Mr James	8 New Square, London	020 7405 4321
Afeeva Mr Mark Kudzo Dzitosi	Matrix Chambers, London	020 7404 3447
Alexandra Miss Sebastiane	Holborn Chambers, London	020 7242 6060
Algazy Mr Jacques Max	Cloisters, London	020 7827 4000
Aly Miss Sheila	Warwick House Chambers, London	020 7430 2323
Andrews Mr Paul Leslie	Great James Street Chambers, London	020 7440 4949
Arnheim Dr Michael Thomas Walter	Chambers of Dr Michael Arnheim, London	020 7833 5093
	Holborn Chambers, London	020 7242 6060
	Principal Chambers, Sevenoaks	0845 209 8080
Awodele Mr Olufemi Adetunji	Great James Street Chambers, London	020 7440 4949
Bate Mr Stephen Robert De Breteuil	5RB, London	020 7242 2902
Becker Mr Timothy George Christie	Chambers of Mr Timothy Becker, Liverpool	0151 703 0319
	Clerksroom (London), London	0845 083 3000
Beloff Mr Rupert Joseph Alexei	No5 Chambers, Birmingham	0845 210 5555
	No5 Chambers, Bristol	0845 210 5555
	No5 Chambers, London	0845 210 5555
Berkley Mr David Nahum	1 Gray's Inn Square, London	020 7405 0001
	St Johns Buildings, Chester	01244 323070
	St Johns Buildings, Manchester	0161 214 1500
	St Johns Buildings Liverpool, Liverpool	0151 243 6000
Booth Mr Alexander Henry Spencer	Francis Taylor Building, London	020 7353 8415
Bowhill Miss Jessie Kate	8 New Square, London	020 7405 4321
Bragiel Mr Edward Bronislaw Henryk	Hogarth Chambers, London	020 7404 0404
Bryden Mr Christopher James Yuen Kang	4 King's Bench Walk, London	020 7822 7000
Bullock Mr Robert Gustaf	The Chambers of Mr Bullock, Brighton	01273 321050
Busuttil Mr Godwin John Antoine	5RB, London	020 7242 2902
Caplan Mr Jonathan Michael	Five Paper Buildings, London	020 7583 6117
	Riverview Chambers, London	0844 225 3999
Charalambides Mr Leonidas	Francis Taylor Building, London	020 7353 8415
Christie Mr Iain Robert	5RB, London	020 7242 2902
Clark Ms Julia Elisabeth	Hogarth Chambers, London	020 7404 0404
Cohen Mr Edward Mervyn	11 Stone Buildings, London	020 7831 6381
Coulter Mr Barry John	Clerksroom (London), London	0845 083 3000
	Clerksroom (Taunton), Taunton	0845 083 3000
	King's Lynn Chambers, King's Lynn	01553 672 085
Critchley Mr John Stephen	Field Court Chambers, London	020 7405 6114
Crystal Mr Jonathan	Argent Chambers, London	020 7556 5500
De Mounteney Mr Jonathan Patrick	Chambers of Mr J P De Mounteney, Reading	0118 934 6822
Deacon Mr Robert Murray	11 Stone Buildings, London	020 7831 6381
Dean Mr Jacob	5RB, London	020 7242 2902
Dillon Mr Thomas William Matthew	Chambers of Thomas Dillon, London	020 7692 2722
Doherty Mr Nicholas Brudenell	4 King's Bench Walk, London	020 7822 7000
Draycott Mr Simon Douglas	Citadel Chambers, Birmingham	0121 233 8500
	Five St Andrew's Hill, London	020 7332 5400
Drummond Mr Bruce Jonathon Hutcheon	Cornwall Street Chambers, Birmingham	0121 233 7500
	Palmyra Chambers, Warrington	01925 444919
Edwards Mr Jonathan William	Westgate Chambers, Lewes	01273 480510
Edwards Mr Nigel Royston	St Paul's Chambers, Leeds	0113 245 5866
Engelman Mr Mark Trevor	Hardwicke, London	020 7242 2523
Engelman Mr Philip	Cloisters, London	020 7827 4000
	Trinity Chambers, Middlesbrough	01642 247569
	Trinity Chambers, Newcastle Upon Tyne	0191 232 1927
Fern Mr Gary	7 Stones IP, London	020 7193 4033

Fitzgerald Mr John Vincent	Ingenuity IP Chambers, Petts Wood	
Gerasimidis Mr Nicolas	Guildhall Chambers, Bristol	0117 930 9000
Goldrein Mr Iain Saville	7 Bell Yard, London	020 7831 0636
	Number 7 Harrington Street Chambers, Liverpool	0151 242 0707
Halden Mr Angus Robert	Queen Square Chambers, Bristol	0117 921 1966
Hamer Mr George Clemens	8 New Square, London	020 7405 4321
Heal Mrs Madeleine	New Square Chambers, London	020 7419 8000
Hewson Ms Barbara Mary	Hardwicke, London	020 7242 2523
Higginson Mr Timothy Nicholas Bennett	Littleton Chambers, London	020 7797 8600
	St John's Chambers, Bristol	0117 923 4700
Hill Mr Jonathan	8 New Square, London	020 7405 4321
Howells Mr Stephen John	Stone Chambers, London	020 7440 6900
Ingram Mr Nigel Colquhoun	2 Bedford Row, London	020 7440 8888
Irvin Mr Peter	Brick Court Chambers, London	020 7379 3550
Iyer Miss Shobana	Swan Chambers, Richmond	0845 123 1234
Johnson Mr Phillip Michael	Chambers of Mr P Johnson, London	020 7288 2256
Jolliffe Mrs Victoria Esther Jean	5RB, London	020 7242 2902
Jones Mr Geraint Anthony	New Walk Chambers, Leicester	0871 200 1298/0116 255 9144
	9 St John Street, Manchester	0161 955 9000
	Tanfield Chambers, London	020 7421 5300
Jones Mr Kelvin Mcallister	Templis Chambers, London	020 7649 9808
Keane Mr Owen Ashley	Design Chambers, London	020 7353 0747
Khan Mr Arfan	Field Court Chambers, London	020 7405 6114
Kime Mr Matthew Jonathan	Cobden House Chambers, Manchester	0161 833 6000
	Ingenuity IP Chambers, Petts Wood	
	No. 3 Fleet Street Chambers, London	020 7936 4474
Lahiffe Mr Martin Patrick Joseph	3 Temple Gardens, London	020 7353 3102
Lamb Mr Jeffrey Thomas	Westgate Chambers, Lewes	01273 480510
Lambert Miss Jane Elizabeth	NIPC, Huddersfield	0800 862 0055
Lane Ms Lindsay Ruth Busfield	8 New Square, London	020 7405 4321
Lawrence Dr Heather Bunting Elizabeth	11 South Square, London	020 7405 1222
Lenaghan Mr Anthony	Dyers Chambers, London	020 7404 1881
Lewis Mr Wayne Anthony	Access Lawyers, London	020 8801 2345
Lissack Mr Richard Anthony	Outer Temple Chambers, London	020 7353 6381
	Riverview Chambers, London	0844 225 3999
Longhurst-Woods Ms Lesley	2 Louisa Close, London	020 8985 8716
Matthias Mr David Huw	Francis Taylor Building, London	020 7353 8415
Maxwell Lewis Mr Cameron	Lamb Chambers, London	020 7797 8300
McDonnell Mr John Beresford William	13 Old Square Chambers, London	020 7831 4445
Michalos Miss Christina Antigone Diana	5RB, London	020 7242 2902
Munden Mr Richard Alexander John	5RB, London	020 7242 2902
Oke Mr Olanrewaju Oladipupo	Kingsway Chambers, London	020 7404 2357
Omideyi Miss Anuoluwapo Iyanu	Furnival Chambers, London	020 7405 3232
Onslow Mr Robert Denzil	8 New Square, London	020 7405 4321
Osborne Mr James Robert	Clerksroom (London), London	0845 083 3000
Paraskos Mr Paraskevakis Christakis	11 Gray's Inn Square Chambers, London	020 7405 6879
Pearson Mr Christopher	Lamb Chambers, London	020 7797 8300
Penny Mr Timothy Charles	11 Stone Buildings, London	020 7831 6381
Platts-Mills Mr Mark Fortescue	8 New Square, London	020 7405 4321
Purves Mr Gavin Bowman	Swan House, London	020 8998 3035
Reed Mr Jeremy Nigel	Hogarth Chambers, London	020 7404 0404
Richardson Mr Alistair Paul George	6 King's Bench Walk, London	020 7583 0410
Roberts Mr Michael Charles	Chambers of Michael Roberts, Henley-On-Thames	01844 355 655
Rogers Miss Christy Abigail	Ingenuity IP Chambers, Petts Wood	
	No. 3 Fleet Street Chambers, London	020 7936 4474
Rogers Mr Ian Paul	Monckton Chambers, London	020 7405 7211
Roughton Mr Ashley Wentworth	Hogarth Chambers, London	020 7404 0404

C

Saini Mr Parminder Paul Singh	12 Old Square Chambers, London	020 7404 0875
Shirley Mr James Patrick	Stone Chambers, London	020 7440 6900
Shore Miss Victoria Louise	5RB, London	020 7242 2902
Silcock Mr Ian Peter	Hardwicke, London	020 7242 2523
Silverton Miss Catherine Anne	Sovereign Chambers, Leeds	0113 245 1841
Singarajah Mr Frederico	1 Gray's Inn Square, London	020 7405 0001
Smith Miss Eileen Joan	Trinity Chambers, Middlesbrough	01642 247569
	Trinity Chambers, Newcastle Upon Tyne	0191 232 1927
Speker Mr Adam Samuel Edward	5RB, London	020 7242 2902
Spratt Mr Christopher David Richard Dean	9 Stone Buildings, London	020 7404 5055
Staddon Mr Paul	Tanfield Chambers, London	020 7421 5300
Stanford Mr Tony James	Old Bailey Chambers, London	020 3008 6404
Stewart Mr Nicholas John Cameron	Ely Place Chambers, London	020 7400 9600
Tozzi Mr Nigel Kenneth	4 Pump Court, London	020 7842 5555
Treharne Mr Neil Simon	Dingle Chambers, Bristol	07818 827754
Tritton Mr Robert Guy Henton	Hogarth Chambers, London	020 7404 0404
Warby Mr Mark David John	5RB, London	020 7242 2902
Ward Mr Robin Henry	8 New Square, London	020 7405 4321

ENVIRONMENT

Akers Mr Robert Matthew Harry	St Johns Buildings, Chester	01244 323070
	St Johns Buildings, Manchester	0161 214 1500
	16 Winckley Square, Preston	01772 256100
Albutt Mr Ian Leslie	Cornerstone Barristers, London	020 7242 4986
	Heavenwood Chambers, Stroud	01453 873444
Almihdar Mr Ali Hamed	Outer Temple Chambers, London	020 7353 6381
Altaras Mr David Maurice	36 Bedford Row, London	020 7421 8000
Amraoui Mr Thomas	4-5 Gray's Inn Square, London	020 7404 5252
Andrews Mr Paul Leslie	Great James Street Chambers, London	020 7440 4949
Baldwin Dr Timothy John	Garden Court Chambers, London	020 7993 7600
Ball Mr Ian David	Cornwall Street Chambers, Birmingham	0121 233 7500
Barnett Mr Jeremy Victor	2 Bedford Row, London	020 7440 8888
	St Paul's Chambers, Leeds	0113 245 5866
Barry Mr Denis Fintan Patrick	Five Paper Buildings, London	020 7583 6117
Bates Mr Alan Twan	Monckton Chambers, London	020 7405 7211
Bates Mr John Hayward	Old Square Chambers, Bristol	0117 930 5100
	Old Square Chambers, London	020 7269 0300
Beaumont Mr Marc Clifford	9 Stone Buildings, London	020 7404 5055
	Windsor Barristers' Chambers, Windsor	01753 839321
Beyts Mr Chester Andoe Michael	25 Bedford Row, London	020 7067 1500
Birkby Mr Richard Adam	Park Court Chambers, Leeds	0113 243 3277
Blair Mr Peter Michael	Guildhall Chambers, Bristol	0117 930 9000
	6 King's Bench Walk, London	020 7583 0410
Booth Mr Alexander Henry Spencer	Francis Taylor Building, London	020 7353 8415
Boulding Mr Philip Vincent	Keating Chambers, London	020 7544 2600
Bradnock Mr Thomas Philip	Colleton Chambers, Exeter	01392 274898
Bridge Mr Giles	Broadway House Chambers, Bradford	01274 722560
	Broadway House Chambers, Leeds	0113 246 2600
Brown Mr Roger Charles Arthur	Kenworthy's Chambers, Manchester	0161 832 4036
Buchan Miss Caroline Venetia	Chambers of Miss C Buchan, Haywards Heath	01444 482222
Burton Mr James William	39 Essex Street, London	020 7832 1111
	82 King Street, Manchester	0161 870 9969
Butler Mr Simon David	The Chambers of Grahame Aldous QC, London	020 7832 0500
Byrne Mr Garrett Thomas	4-5 Gray's Inn Square, London	020 7404 5252
Cahill Mr Paul Jeremy	No5 Chambers, Birmingham	0845 210 5555
	No5 Chambers, Bristol	0845 210 5555
	No5 Chambers, London	0845 210 5555
Callery Mr Martin	Cobden House Chambers, Manchester	0161 833 6000

Name	Chambers	Telephone
Carter Miss Nathalie Veronique	1 Gray's Inn Square, London	020 7405 0001
Charalambides Mr Leonidas	Francis Taylor Building, London	020 7353 8415
Choongh Mr Satnam Singh	No5 Chambers, Birmingham	0845 210 5555
	No5 Chambers, Bristol	0845 210 5555
	No5 Chambers, London	0845 210 5555
Clarke Mr Rory James	Cornerstone Barristers, London	020 7242 4986
Clay Mr Jonathan Roger	Cornerstone Barristers, London	020 7242 4986
Climie Mr Roger Stephen	King's Bench and Godolphin (KBG)Chambers, Plymouth	01752 221551
	Outer Temple Chambers, London	020 7353 6381
Collett Mr Gavin Charles	Rougemont Chambers, Exeter	01392 208484
Cooper Mr John Michael	Crown Office Chambers, London	020 7797 8100
Costello Mr Paul James	Chambers of Mr Paul J Costello, Biggleswade	07846 016 399
Coster Mr Ronald David	42 Bedford Row, London	020 7831 0222
Crowley Mr Daniel John	2 Temple Gardens, London	020 7822 1200
Dagg Mr John Douglas	Trinity Chambers, Chelmsford	01245 605040
Daly Mr David	Heathway Chambers, London	020 8293 0509
Darling Mr Paul Antony	Keating Chambers, London	020 7544 2600
Darroch Miss Fiona Culverwell	Clerksroom (London), London	0845 083 3000
	Clerksroom (Taunton), Taunton	0845 083 3000
	King's Lynn Chambers, King's Lynn	01553 672 085
Davies Mr Jonathan Huw	Old Square Chambers, Bristol	0117 930 5100
	Old Square Chambers, London	020 7269 0300
Devereux-Cooke Mr Richard Charles	13 Old Square Chambers, London	020 7831 4445
Eastwood Miss Philippa Clemency Anne	Doughty Street Chambers, London	020 7404 1313
Edwards Mr Denis	Francis Taylor Building, London	020 7353 8415
Edwards Mr Martin Richard	39 Essex Street, London	020 7832 1111
	82 King Street, Manchester	0161 870 9969
Edwards Mr Nigel Royston	St Paul's Chambers, Leeds	0113 245 5866
Elliott Mr Timothy Stanley	Keating Chambers, London	020 7544 2600
Enoch Mr Dafydd Huw	Apex, Cardiff	02920 232 032
	23 Essex Street, London	020 7413 0353
Facenna Mr Gerald Carlo	Monckton Chambers, London	020 7405 7211
Falkowski Mr Damian	4-5 Gray's Inn Square, London	020 7404 5252
Felton Mr Timothy John Fowler	Rougemont Chambers, Exeter	01392 208484
Forlin Mr Gerard Emlyn	Cornerstone Barristers, London	020 7242 4986
Foulkes Miss Rebecca	5 Pump Court, London	020 7353 2532
Fraser-Urquhart Mr Andrew	4-5 Gray's Inn Square, London	020 7404 5252
Fryer Mr Nigel Mccrae	Queen Square Chambers, Bristol	0117 921 1966
Gallivan Mr Terence John	Five Paper, London	020 7815 3200
German Miss Kelly Anne	Eastbourne Chambers, Eastbourne	01323 642102
Gill Mr Rajinder Singh	Charter Chambers, London	020 7618 4400
Goodman Mr Alexander David Edmund	Atlas Chambers, London	020 7269 7980
	4-5 Gray's Inn Square, London	020 7404 5252
Gore Mr Andrew Roger	Fenners Chambers, Cambridge	01223 368761
Greatorex Mr Paul	4-5 Gray's Inn Square, London	020 7404 5252
Green Mr Timothy Sinclair	St Philips Chambers, Birmingham	0121 246 7000
Ground Mr Patrick	Chambers of Mr Patrick Ground QC, London	020 7736 0131
Hackett Mr Philip George	Argent Chambers, London	020 7556 5500
Ham Mr Nicholas Treharne	Dyers Chambers, London	020 7404 1881
Hamilton Mr Nigel	Broadway House Chambers, Bradford	01274 722560
	Broadway House Chambers, Leeds	0113 246 2600
Hanif Miss Saima Naz	4-5 Gray's Inn Square, London	020 7404 5252
Harris Mr James	Five St Andrew's Hill, London	020 7332 5400
Harrison Mr John Foster	St Paul's Chambers, Leeds	0113 245 5866
Harrison Mr Peter John	6 Pump Court, London	020 7797 8400
	6 Pump Court Chambers, Maidstone	01622 688094
Harvey Mr John Gilbert	No5 Chambers, Birmingham	0845 210 5555
	No5 Chambers, Bristol	0845 210 5555
	No5 Chambers, London	0845 210 5555

Barrister	Chambers	Telephone
Harvey Mr Stephen Frank	18 Red Lion Court, London	020 7520 6000
	18 Red Lion Court (Annexe), Chelmsford	01245 280880
Harwood Mr Richard John	39 Essex Street, London	020 7832 1111
	82 King Street, Manchester	0161 870 9969
Hassall Mr Craig Jonathan	Sovereign Chambers, Leeds	0113 245 1841
Hegarty Mr Kevin John	St Philips Chambers, Birmingham	0121 246 7000
Hill Mr Michael Gordon	Trinity Chambers, Middlesbrough	01642 247569
	Trinity Chambers, Newcastle Upon Tyne	0191 232 1927
Hobson Mr John Graham	4-5 Gray's Inn Square, London	020 7404 5252
Hodgkiss Ms Suzanne Jane	43 Temple Row Chambers, Birmingham	0121 237 6035
Holroyd Mr John James	Zenith Chambers, Leeds	0113 245 5438
Honey Mr Richard Arthur	Francis Taylor Building, London	020 7353 8415
Horton Mr Matthew Bethell	39 Essex Street, London	020 7832 1111
	82 King Street, Manchester	0161 870 9969
Howlett Mr James Anthony	KCH Garden Square, Nottingham	0115 941 8851
Hussain Mr Ghulam	Crown Office Row Chambers, Brighton	01273 625625
Hussain Mr Muhammad Altaf	Chambers of Mr M A Hussain, London	020 8679 2398
Iyer Miss Shobana	Swan Chambers, Richmond	0845 123 1234
Jackson Miss Rosemary Elizabeth	Keating Chambers, London	020 7544 2600
Jackson Mr Mark Joseph	No 8 Chambers, Birmingham	0121 236 5514
Jenkins Mr David Crofton	2 King's Bench Walk, London	020 7353 1746
Jenkins Mr Edward Nicholas	Five Paper Buildings, London	020 7583 6117
Jinadu Mr Abdul-Lateef Abodurin Olayinka	Keating Chambers, London	020 7544 2600
John Miss Laura Elizabeth	Monckton Chambers, London	020 7405 7211
Jones Mr Geraint Anthony	New Walk Chambers, Leicester	0871 200 1298/0116 255 9144
	9 St John Street, Manchester	0161 955 9000
	Tanfield Chambers, London	020 7421 5300
Jones Mr Mark Andrew	St Ive's Chambers, Birmingham	0121 236 0863
Kennedy Mr Christopher Laurence Paul	9 St John Street, Manchester	0161 955 9000
Khan Mr Tahir	Broadway House Chambers, Bradford	01274 722560
	Broadway House Chambers, Leeds	0113 246 2600
Le Fevre Miss Sarah Margaret	3 Raymond Buildings, London	020 7400 6400
Lloyd Mr John Nesbitt	Rougemont Chambers, Exeter	01392 208484
Lopez Mr Juan Nemesio	Francis Taylor Building, London	020 7353 8415
Loveday Mr David Robert	4-5 Gray's Inn Square, London	020 7404 5252
Lowe Mr Rupert William Manley	Guildhall Chambers, Bristol	0117 930 9000
Mainwaring Mr Robert Paul Clason	Portal Chambers, Llandysul	01559 395 292
Malone Mr David John	1 Gray's Inn Square, London	020 7405 0001
Markus Ms Kate	Doughty Street Chambers, Bristol	01179 058 717
	Doughty Street Chambers, London	020 7404 1313
	Doughty Street Chambers, Manchester	0161 618 1066
Marsden Mr Andrew Guy	East Anglian Chambers, Chelmsford	01473 214481
	East Anglian Chambers, Colchester	01473 214481
	East Anglian Chambers, Ipswich	01473 214481
	East Anglian Chambers, Norwich	01473 214481
Mason Mr Ian Douglas	Amethyst Chambers, London	020 7936 4966
Matthias Mr David Huw	Francis Taylor Building, London	020 7353 8415
McCracken Mr Robert Henry Joy	Francis Taylor Building, London	020 7353 8415
Meeke Mr Robert Martin James	Colleton Chambers, Exeter	01392 274898
Melville-Shreeve Mr Michael David	Walnut House, Exeter	01392 279751
Mendelle Mr Paul Michael	25 Bedford Row, London	020 7067 1500
Miller Mr Peter Owen Michael	Cornerstone Barristers, London	020 7242 4986
Monnington Mr Bruce Gilbert	Fenners Chambers, Cambridge	01223 368761
Moorhouse Mr Brendon Scott	Guildhall Chambers, Bristol	0117 930 9000
Muller Mr Antonie Sean	Citadel Chambers, Birmingham	0121 233 8500
Mynors Dr Charles Baskerville	Francis Taylor Building, London	020 7353 8415
Newsom Mr George Lucien	Guildhall Chambers, Bristol	0117 930 9000

Ornsby Miss Suzanne Doreen	Francis Taylor Building, London	020 7353 8415
	St John's Chambers, Bristol	0117 923 4700
Osborne Mr James Robert	Clerksroom (London), London	0845 083 3000
Ozin Mr Paul David	23 Essex Street, London	020 7413 0353
Parker Mrs Karen Lesley	Guildhall Chambers Portsmouth, Portsmouth	023 9275 2400
Pennicott Mr Ian	Keating Chambers, London	020 7544 2600
Phillips Mr Simon Benjamin	Francis Taylor Building, London	020 7353 8415
	Park Court Chambers, Leeds	0113 243 3277
Pointing Mr John Eric	Chambers of Mr John Pointing, London	020 8997 2285
Potter Miss Alison Lisa	4 Pump Court, London	020 7842 5555
Powell Mr Jonathan David	Atlas Chambers, London	020 7269 7980
Powell Mr Oliver Jonathan	3 PB Barristers, London	020 7583 8055
Prokofiev Mr Sergey	Lincoln House Chambers, Manchester	0161 832 5701
Purchas Mr Robin Michael	Francis Taylor Building, London	020 7353 8415
Purves Mr Gavin Bowman	Swan House, London	020 8998 3035
Rai Mr Rajesh Kumar	1 Mitre Court Buildings, London	020 7452 8900
Rickarby Mr William Edmund	Cornwall Street Chambers, Birmingham	0121 233 7500
Riggs Miss Samantha	25 Bedford Row, London	020 7067 1500
Roberts Mr Timothy David	Fountain Chambers, Middlesbrough	01642 804040
	QEB Hollis Whiteman, London	020 7933 8855
Rubens Miss Jacqueline Ann	1 Pump Court, London	020 7842 7070
Rudd Mr Michael	36 Bedford Row, London	020 7421 8000
Rushton Mr Jonathon Barker	36 Bedford Row, London	020 7421 8000
Saifee Mr Faisal Aftaab	Thomas More Chambers, London	020 7404 7000
Salmon Mr Jonathan Carl	St Philips Chambers, Birmingham	0121 246 7000
Scott Holland Mr Gideon Silas	Keating Chambers, London	020 7544 2600
Sefi Mr Benedict John	Harcourt Chambers, London	0844 561 7135
	Harcourt Chambers, Oxford	0844 561 7135
Shapiro Mr Selwyn	2 King's Bench Walk, London	020 7353 1746
Sheikh Ms Saira Kabir	Francis Taylor Building, London	020 7353 8415
Singarajah Mr Frederico	1 Gray's Inn Square, London	020 7405 0001
Skinner Mr Samuel Richard Edward	KCH Garden Square, Nottingham	0115 941 8851
Sliwinski Mr Robert Andrew	SWL Chambers, Loudwater	01494 616007
Smith Miss Eileen Joan	Trinity Chambers, Middlesbrough	01642 247569
	Trinity Chambers, Newcastle Upon Tyne	0191 232 1927
Smith Mr Alisdair Robert Macsorley	9-12 Bell Yard, London	020 7400 1800
Snow Mr Darren Mark	Charter Chambers, London	020 7618 4400
Solley Mr Stephen Malcolm	Charter Chambers, London	020 7618 4400
Spencer Mr Shaun Anthony	St Johns Buildings, Chester	01244 323070
	St Johns Buildings, Manchester	0161 214 1500
	16 Winckley Square, Preston	01772 256100
Stanford Mr Tony James	Old Bailey Chambers, London	020 3008 6404
Stebbings Mr Ian Anthony	1 Gray's Inn Square, London	020 7405 0001
Steel Mr John Brychan	4-5 Gray's Inn Square, London	020 7404 5252
Stein Mr Daniel Alexander	No5 Chambers, Birmingham	0845 210 5555
	No5 Chambers, Bristol	0845 210 5555
	No5 Chambers, London	0845 210 5555
Stemp Mr Scott	12 College Place, Southampton	023 8032 0320
Stenhouse Mr John Alexander	Nightingale Chambers, Wolverley	01562 851350
Stevenson Mr Daniel Keith	9-12 Bell Yard, London	020 7400 1800
Stevenson Mr Robert Lloyd	Sovereign Chambers, Leeds	0113 245 1841
Steynor Mr Alan Charles	Keating Chambers, London	020 7544 2600
Thomas Miss Megan Moira	6 Pump Court, London	020 7797 8400
	6 Pump Court Chambers, Maidstone	01622 688094
Thomas Mr Andrew Martin	Lincoln House Chambers, Manchester	0161 832 5701
	Linenhall Chambers, Chester	01244 348282
Townend Mr Samuel John	Keating Chambers, London	020 7544 2600
Townsend Mrs Harriet Caroline Jane	Cornerstone Barristers, London	020 7242 4986
Turner Mr Alan Joseph	Melbeck Chambers, Dudley	020 7404 2166

Wald Mr Richard Daniel	39 Essex Street, London	020 7832 1111
	82 King Street, Manchester	0161 870 9969
	Riverview Chambers, London	0844 225 3999
Whale Mr Stephen John	4-5 Gray's Inn Square, London	020 7404 5252
Wigley Miss Jenny	No5 Chambers, Birmingham	0845 210 5555
	No5 Chambers, Bristol	0845 210 5555
	No5 Chambers, London	0845 210 5555
Wignall Mr Edward Gordon	No5 Chambers, Birmingham	0845 210 5555
	No5 Chambers, Bristol	0845 210 5555
	No5 Chambers, London	0845 210 5555
Wilkins Mr Andrew Lewis	Cornwall Street Chambers, Birmingham	0121 233 7500
Williams Mr Ben Dylan	Kings Chambers, Birmingham	0845 034 3444
	Kings Chambers, Leeds	0845 034 3444
	Kings Chambers, Manchester	0845 034 3444
Wills Miss Alexandra Itari	Christ Church Chambers, London	020 7409 5278/07788 512787
Wraith Mr Nigel Patrick	Colleton Chambers, Exeter	01392 274898
Wrottesley Miss Angela Jane	Bank House Chambers, Sheffield	0114 275 1223
Zwart Mr Auberon Christiaan Conrad	39 Essex Street, London	020 7832 1111
	82 King Street, Manchester	0161 870 9969

EQUITY, WILLS & TRUSTS

Ajaz Mr Mohammad Arshad	Eastmans Chambers, Reading	0118 966 9094
Ameen Mr Danish	18 St John Street, Manchester	0161 278 1800
Andre Mr Roger Louis	Sovereign Chambers, Leeds	0113 245 1841
Apthorp Mr George Charles	5 Essex Court, London	020 7410 2000
Artesi Miss Desiree Allison Ann	Thomas More Chambers, London	020 7404 7000
Arthur Mr Stephen Joseph	Temple Tax Chambers, London	020 7353 7884
Ash Mr Edward William	Chambers of Mr Edward Ash, Elsworth	01954 267674
Asprey Mr Nicholas	Clock Chambers, Wolverhampton	01902 313444
	Serle Court, London	020 7242 6105
Atkinson Mr Jody Roy	St John's Chambers, Bristol	0117 923 4700
Austin Mr Ian	Holborn Chambers, London	020 7242 6060
Azhar Mr Ali Mohammad	9 King's Bench Walk, London	020 7353 9564
Bailey Mr Thomas Iain	Chambers of Mr Thomas Bailey, Milton Keynes	07983 447117
Barnes Mr Luke Clive	3 Dr Johnson's Buildings, London	020 7353 4854
Beaumont Mr Dean Andrew	KCH Garden Square, Nottingham	0115 941 8851
Beaumont Mr Marc Clifford	9 Stone Buildings, London	020 7404 5055
	Windsor Barristers' Chambers, Windsor	01753 839321
Becker Mr Timothy George Christie	Chambers of Mr Timothy Becker, Liverpool	0151 703 0319
	Clerksroom (London), London	0845 083 3000
Bennion-Pedley Mr Edward	13 KBW, Oxford	01865 311066
	13 King's Bench Walk, London	020 7353 7204
Bishop Mr Stephen Anthony	Goldsmith Chambers, London	020 7353 6802
Bleasdale Miss Marie-Claire	Radcliffe Chambers, London	020 7831 0081
Blohm Mr Leslie Adrian	St John's Chambers, Bristol	0117 923 4700
Bojarski Mr Andrzej Leonard	36 Bedford Row, London	020 7421 8000
Bolton Mr Robert John	2 King's Bench Walk, London	020 7353 1746
Boyd Mr Stephen James Harvey	Selborne Chambers, London	020 7420 9500
Bragge Mr Thomas Hereward	Stour Chambers, Canterbury	01227 764899
Bragiel Mr Edward Bronislaw Henryk	Hogarth Chambers, London	020 7404 0404
Braithwaite Mr Thomas James	Serle Court, London	020 7242 6105
Bredemear Mr Zachary Charles	1 Chancery Lane, London	0845 634 6666
Brook Mr Paul Antony	Park Lane Plowden, Leeds	0113 228 5049
	Park Lane Plowden, Newcastle Upon Tyne	0191 211 4087
Brown Miss Susan Margaret	One Essex Court, London	020 7936 3030
Brown Mr Philip Stephen	9 Stone Buildings, London	020 7404 5055
Bryden Mr Christopher James Yuen Kang	4 King's Bench Walk, London	020 7822 7000

Buchan Miss Caroline Venetia	Chambers of Miss C Buchan, Haywards Heath	01444 482222
Buck Mr John	Tanfield Chambers, London	020 7421 5300
Buckhaven Mr Simon	Hardwicke, London	020 7242 2523
Buckle Mr Jonathan	Regency Chambers, Cambridge	01223 301517
	Regency Chambers, Peterborough	01733 315215
Bullock Mr Robert Gustaf	The Chambers of Mr Bullock, Brighton	01273 321050
Buswell Mr Richard Thomas	Hardwicke, London	020 7242 2523
Buttimore Mr Gabriel	13 KBW, Oxford	01865 311066
	13 King's Bench Walk, London	020 7353 7204
Calhaem Mr Simon Malcolm	29 Bedford Row Chambers, London	020 7404 1044
Cant Mr Christopher Ian	9 Stone Buildings, London	020 7404 5055
Capon Mr Philip Christopher William	East Anglian Chambers, Chelmsford	01473 214481
	East Anglian Chambers, Ipswich	01473 214481
	East Anglian Chambers, Norwich	01473 214481
	St Philips Chambers, Birmingham	0121 246 7000
Carr Mr Christopher Sean	36 Bedford Row, London	020 7421 8000
Castle Mr Peter Bolton	13 Old Square Chambers, London	020 7831 4445
Chaffin-Laird Miss Olivia Carolyn	No5 Chambers, Birmingham	0845 210 5555
	No5 Chambers, Bristol	0845 210 5555
	No5 Chambers, London	0845 210 5555
Choudhury Miss Sadiya Asghar	Pump Court Tax Chambers, London	020 7414 8080
Chowdhary Mr Islamuddin	Cassian Chambers, Ilford	07796 262641
Christensen Mr Carlton	10 King's Bench Walk, London	020 7353 7742
Clark Mr Andrew Richard	9 St John Street, Manchester	0161 955 9000
Clarke Mr Timothy John	Cornwall Street Chambers, Birmingham	0121 233 7500
Coates Mr George Alexander Nigel	Guildford Chambers, Guildford	01483 539131
Colbey Mr Richard	Guildhall Chambers Portsmouth, Portsmouth	023 9275 2400
	Lamb Chambers, London	020 7797 8300
Conolly Dr Oliver Stephen	Pump Court Tax Chambers, London	020 7414 8080
Cooper Miss Samantha Ann	Outer Temple Chambers, London	020 7353 6381
Coster Mr Ronald David	42 Bedford Row, London	020 7831 0222
Counsell Mr Edward Frederick	Unity Street Chambers, Bristol	0117 906 9789
Crew Miss Gillian Mary	Ely Place Chambers, London	020 7400 9600
Croskell Mr Marcus James	East Anglian Chambers, Chelmsford	01473 214481
	East Anglian Chambers, Colchester	01473 214481
	East Anglian Chambers, Ipswich	01473 214481
	East Anglian Chambers, Norwich	01473 214481
Daniels Miss Philippa Catherine	36 Bedford Row, London	020 7421 8000
Davies Miss Carol Elizabeth	College Chambers, Southampton	023 8023 0338
Davies Ms Samantha Teresa	Chambers of Ms Samantha Davies, Milton Keynes	0845 123 1234
	Warwick House Chambers, London	020 7430 2323
Dean Mr Peter Thomas	36 Bedford Row, London	020 7421 8000
Demachkie Mr Jamal	3 PB Barristers, London	020 7583 8055
Devereux-Cooke Mr Richard Charles	13 Old Square Chambers, London	020 7831 4445
Dickinson Mr John Finch Heneage	St John's Chambers, Bristol	0117 923 4700
Dowell Mr Gregory Hamilton	Principal Chambers, Sevenoaks	0845 209 8080
Earle Mr James Christopher Reginald St John	Fenners Chambers, Cambridge	01223 368761
Egleton Mr Richard Wildman	Pallant Chambers, Chichester	01243 784538
Eldergill Mr Edmund Malcolm	1 Pump Court, London	020 7842 7070
Fairbank Mr Nicholas James	4 Paper Buildings, London	020 7427 5200
Fawcett Mr Neil	St Ive's Chambers, Birmingham	0121 236 0863
Fellows Mr Philip David Andrew	Hardwicke, London	020 7242 2523
Finlay Mr Darren	Sovereign Chambers, Leeds	0113 245 1841
Fowles Mr Jonathan James	Serle Court, London	020 7242 6105
Francis Mr Richard Maurice	9 Park Place, Cardiff	029 2038 2731
Gainer Mr Richard St Clair	St Margaret's Chambers, Twickenham	020 8241 3516
Gair Mr Christopher	King's Bench Chambers, Bournemouth	01202 250025
Gallivan Mr Terence John	Five Paper, London	020 7815 3200

Gasztowicz Mr Steven	Cornerstone Barristers, London	020 7242 4986
	New Street Chambers, Leicester	0116 262 5906
George Mr Michael David Roberts	St Philips Chambers, Birmingham	0121 246 7000
Godfrey Mr Lauren John	Crown Office Row Chambers, Brighton	01273 625625
Gold Mr Richard David	St John's Chambers, Bristol	0117 923 4700
Goldberg Mr Simon Ian	Trinity Chambers, Middlesbrough	01642 247569
	Trinity Chambers, Newcastle Upon Tyne	0191 232 1927
Goldstein Mr Wayne Nathan	18 St John Street, Manchester	0161 278 1800
Goodfellow Mr Giles William Jeremy	Pump Court Tax Chambers, London	020 7414 8080
Goodison Mr Adam Henry	South Square, London	020 7696 9900
Gordon Mr Jeremy	Chambers of Mr Ami Feder, London	020 7797 7788
	Chambers of Mr Ami Feder, London	020 7797 7788
	Lamb Building, Brighton	01273 820490
Gore Mr Andrew Roger	Fenners Chambers, Cambridge	01223 368761
Graham Mrs Alana Nicole	Chambers of Alana Graham, Halesowen	01384 894560
	9 Stone Buildings, London	020 7404 5055
Graham-Wells Miss Alison Christine	Exchange Chambers, Leeds	0113 203 1970
	Exchange Chambers, Liverpool	0151 236 7747
	Exchange Chambers, Manchester	0161 833 2722
Grant Mr David Ericson	Outer Temple Chambers, London	020 7353 6381
Greenan Miss Sarah Octavia	Zenith Chambers, Leeds	0113 245 5438
Gunstone Mr Robert Giles	KCH Garden Square, Nottingham	0115 941 8851
Guy Mr Richard Perran	Chambers of Mr Ami Feder, London	020 7797 7788
	King's Bench and Godolphin (KBG)Chambers, Plymouth	01752 221551
	Southernhay Chambers, Exeter	01392 255777
Hall Mr James Edward	Cornwall Street Chambers, Birmingham	0121 233 7500
Harris Mr David Robert	St Albans Chambers, St Albans	01727 843383
Harris Mr Melvyn	5 Essex Court, London	020 7410 2000
Haughty Mr Jeremy Nicholas	Chambers of Mr Ami Feder, London	020 7797 7788
	Chambers of Mr Ami Feder, London	020 7797 7788
	Rougemont Chambers, Exeter	01392 208484
Haywood Dr Jennifer Margaret	Serle Court, London	020 7242 6105
Henderson Mr James Thomas	Kings Chambers, Leeds	0845 034 3444
	Kings Chambers, Manchester	0845 034 3444
	Pump Court Tax Chambers, London	020 7414 8080
Hicks Mr Edward Gordon David	Radcliffe Chambers, London	020 7831 0081
Hill Mr Piers Nicholas	37 Park Square Chambers, Leeds	0113 243 9422
Hillier Mr William	New Street Chambers, Leicester	0116 262 5906
Hilton Ms Saisampan	Holborn Chambers, London	020 7242 6060
Hirst Mr William Timothy John	Park Lane Plowden, Leeds	0113 228 5049
Hodson Mr Matthew Paul	Farrar's Building, London	020 7583 9241
Holbech Mr Charles Edward	New Square Chambers, London	020 7419 8000
Holmes-Milner Mr James Neil	The Chambers of Grahame Aldous QC, London	020 7832 0500
Hood Mr Nigel Anthony	New Square Chambers, London	020 7419 8000
Hornett Mr Stuart Ian	Selborne Chambers, London	020 7420 9500
Horton Mr Michael John Edward	Coram Chambers, London	020 7092 3700
Howling Mr Rex Andrew	4 Paper Buildings, London	020 7427 5200
Hubbard Mr Mark Iain	New Square Chambers, London	020 7419 8000
Huggins Mr Toby James	Unity Street Chambers, Bristol	0117 906 9789
Hughes-Deane Ms Charlotte Barbara	Atlantic Chambers, Liverpool	0151 236 4421
Hunt Mr Stephen	4 Stone Buildings, London	020 7242 5524
Jones Mr Christopher David Harries	St John's Chambers, Bristol	0117 923 4700
Jones Mr Geraint Anthony	New Walk Chambers, Leicester	0871 200 1298/0116 255 9144
	9 St John Street, Manchester	0161 955 9000
	Tanfield Chambers, London	020 7421 5300
Jones Mr Geraint Martyn	Fenners Chambers, Cambridge	01223 368761
Jones Mr Mark Simeon	3 Dr Johnson's Buildings, London	020 7353 4854
Jones Mr Richard Frederick Thomas	Heavenwood Chambers, Stroud	01453 873444
Joseph Mr Charles Henry	Tanfield Chambers, London	020 7421 5300

C

Kamal Mr Setu	St James's Chambers, Manchester	0161 834 7000
	Taxchambers, London	020 7242 2744
Kelly Mr Sean	Chancery House Chambers, Leeds	0113 244 6691
Kelly Mrs Amy Louise	12 College Place, Southampton	023 8032 0320
Kemp Mr James Rupert	Trinity Chambers, Middlesbrough	01642 247569
	Trinity Chambers, Newcastle Upon Tyne	0191 232 1927
Kessler Mr James Richard	Taxchambers, London	020 7242 2744
Khan Dr Alexander	Coral House, Manchester	
Khan Mr Abdul Aleem	Gray's Chambers, Newbury	020 8518 2525
Kilvington Miss Sarah Elizabeth	18 St John Street, Manchester	0161 278 1800
Knight Mr Keith Leslie Francis	4 King's Bench Walk, London	020 7822 7000
Kramer Mr Philip Anthony	Park Lane Plowden, Newcastle Upon Tyne	0191 211 4087
Kynoch Mr Duncan Stuart Sanderson	Selborne Chambers, London	020 7420 9500
Lane Mr Simon Charles	Rougemont Chambers, Exeter	01392 208484
Le Poidevin Mr Nicholas Peter	New Square Chambers, London	020 7419 8000
Learmonth Mr Alexander Robert Magnus	New Square Chambers, London	020 7419 8000
Leonard Mr Charles Robert Weston	Hardwicke, London	020 7242 2523
Lewis Mr Wayne Anthony	Access Lawyers, London	020 8801 2345
Lonsdale Miss Marion Mary	Academy Chambers, London	020 8455 2503
Lowe Mr Mungo James	13 Old Square Chambers, London	020 7831 4445
Lyon Mrs Shane Valerie	King's Bench and Godolphin (KBG)Chambers, Plymouth	01752 221551
Lyons Mr Timothy John	4-5 Gray's Inn Square, London	020 7404 5252
	St James's Chambers, Manchester	0161 834 7000
Machell Mr John William	Serle Court, London	020 7242 6105
Mann Mr Christopher	13 KBW, Oxford	01865 311066
	13 King's Bench Walk, London	020 7353 7204
Marcus Mr Peter	Zenith Chambers, Leeds	0113 245 5438
Marsden Mr Andrew Guy	East Anglian Chambers, Chelmsford	01473 214481
	East Anglian Chambers, Colchester	01473 214481
	East Anglian Chambers, Ipswich	01473 214481
	East Anglian Chambers, Norwich	01473 214481
Marshall Mr Derek Stanley	College Chambers, Southampton	023 8023 0338
Matthias Mr David Huw	Francis Taylor Building, London	020 7353 8415
Maynard Mr Christopher Howard	Tanfield Chambers, London	020 7421 5300
McCann Miss Katie	Atlantic Chambers, Liverpool	0151 236 4421
McCarthy Mr William	Bridgewater Chambers, Manchester	0161 3877127
	1 Mitre Court Buildings, London	020 7452 8900
McCormack Mr Alan	Staple Inn Chambers, London	020 7242 5240
McCue Mr Donald	11 Stone Buildings, London	020 7831 6381
McDonnell Mr John Beresford William	13 Old Square Chambers, London	020 7831 4445
McKay Mr Christopher Alexander	Cathedral Chambers, Newport	01633 215112
McLinden Mr John Vincent Barry	Field Court Chambers, London	020 7405 6114
Meager Mrs Rowena Elisabeth	No5 Chambers, Birmingham	0845 210 5555
	No5 Chambers, Bristol	0845 210 5555
	No5 Chambers, London	0845 210 5555
Meares Mr Nigel Leslie Vellacott	11 Stone Buildings, London	020 7831 6381
Mehta Miss Anita Roxane	Crown Office Row Chambers, Brighton	01273 625625
Menon Mr Harigovind	New Court Chambers, Newcastle Upon Tyne	0191 232 1980
	Park Lane Plowden, Newcastle Upon Tyne	0191 211 4087
Miah Mr Anawar Babul	Great James Street Chambers, London	020 7440 4949
Miller Mr Ian Robertson	Broadway House Chambers, Bradford	01274 722560
	Broadway House Chambers, Leeds	0113 246 2600
Mitchell Mr David John	No5 Chambers, Birmingham	0845 210 5555
	No5 Chambers, Bristol	0845 210 5555
	No5 Chambers, London	0845 210 5555

C

Modgill Mr Alexander Jeffrey	Broadway House Chambers, Bradford	01274 722560
	Broadway House Chambers, Leeds	0113 246 2600
Monnington Mr Bruce Gilbert	Fenners Chambers, Cambridge	01223 368761
Moore Mr Jonathan Guy	Cathedral Chambers, Cardiff	02920 660129
	Cathedral Chambers, Newport	01633 215112
Morris Mr Phillip John	9 Park Place, Cardiff	029 2038 2731
Mullen Mr Mark Robert	Radcliffe Chambers, London	020 7831 0081
Newsom Mr George Lucien	Guildhall Chambers, Bristol	0117 930 9000
Nickless Mr Jason Alan	College Chambers, Southampton	023 8023 0338
Normington Mr James Adam	Park Court Chambers, Leeds	0113 243 3277
Norton Mr Giles	Enigma Chambers, Sheffield	07779 576499
	Holborn Chambers, London	020 7242 6060
Nurse Mr Gordon Bramwell William	Radcliffe Chambers, London	020 7831 0081
O'Brien Mr Nicholas William Wattebot	10 King's Bench Walk, London	020 7353 7742
O'Donoghue Mr Hugh Vincent	Carmelite Chambers, London	020 7936 6300
Ohrenstein Mr Dov	Radcliffe Chambers, London	020 7831 0081
Oliver Mr David Keightley Rideal	13 Old Square Chambers, London	020 7831 4445
Oommen Mr Jacob	Chambers of Mr Jacob Oommen, East Barnet	07958 680272
Osborne Mr James Robert	Clerksroom (London), London	0845 083 3000
O'Sullivan Mr Richard John	1215 Chambers, London	020 3291 1215
Otwal Mr Mukhtiar Singh	42 Bedford Row, London	020 7831 0222
Paget Mr Michael Rodborough	Garden Court Chambers, London	020 7993 7600
Panton Mr Alastair Howard	10 King's Bench Walk, London	020 7353 7742
Paraskos Mr Paraskevakis Christakis	11 Gray's Inn Square Chambers, London	020 7405 6879
Parker Mrs Karen Lesley	Guildhall Chambers Portsmouth, Portsmouth	023 9275 2400
Parsons Mr Andrew James	Portsmouth Barristers'Chambers, Portsmouth	023 9283 1292
Paton Mr Ewan William	Guildhall Chambers, Bristol	0117 930 9000
Payton Mr Clifford Coningsby	Alpha Court Chambers, Leamington Spa	01926 886412
Pearce Mr Robert Edgar	Radcliffe Chambers, London	020 7831 0081
Pennock Mr Ian	Park Lane Plowden, Leeds	0113 228 5049
Pettitt Mr Robert	Northampton Chambers, Northampton	01604 636271
Pithers Mr Clive Robert	Fenners Chambers, Cambridge	01223 368761
Polli Mr Timothy James	Tanfield Chambers, London	020 7421 5300
Poots Miss Laura Jill	Pump Court Tax Chambers, London	020 7414 8080
Preston Mrs Nicola	No5 Chambers, Birmingham	0845 210 5555
	No5 Chambers, Bristol	0845 210 5555
	No5 Chambers, London	0845 210 5555
Pryke Mr Stuart	Fiduciary Legal, London	07814 495366
Quirke Mr Gerard Martin	Citadel Chambers, Birmingham	0121 233 8500
Quirke Mr James Keiron	St Philips Chambers, Birmingham	0121 246 7000
Reed Mr Julian Winn	9 Park Place, Cardiff	029 2038 2731
Richman Mrs Helene Pines	Eighteen Carlton Crescent, Southampton	023 8063 9001
	9 Stone Buildings, London	020 7404 5055
	Stour Chambers, Canterbury	01227 764899
Rifat Mr Maurice Alan	1 Gray's Inn Square, London	020 7405 0001
Rinker Mr Andrew Stuart D'Artois	Chambers of Mr Andrew Rinker, London	020 7584 1091
Ritchie Mr Richard Bulkeley	XXIV Old Buildings, London	020 7691 2424
Rivalland Mr Marc-Edouard	1 Chancery Lane, London	0845 634 6666
Roberts Mr Huw Eifion	Linenhall Chambers, Chester	01244 348282
Roberts Mr Michael Charles	Chambers of Michael Roberts, Henley-On-Thames	01844 355 655
Ross Mr Sidney David	11 Stone Buildings, London	020 7831 6381
Rowntree Mr Edward John Pickering	Hardwicke, London	020 7242 2523
Ryan Mr William	Corsham Barristers Chambers, Corsham	01225 582582
	Farringdon Chambers, London	020 7089 5700

Sagar Mr Leigh	New Square Chambers, London	020 7419 8000
Samuels Mr Leslie John	Pump Court Chambers, London	020 7353 0711
	Pump Court Chambers, Winchester	01962 868 161
	Riverview Chambers, London	0844 225 3999
Sandham Mr James Andrew	Arden Chambers, London	020 7242 4244
Saunders Miss Zoe Alice	St John's Chambers, Bristol	0117 923 4700
Sefi Mr Benedict John	Harcourt Chambers, London	0844 561 7135
	Harcourt Chambers, Oxford	0844 561 7135
Sefton Mr Nicholas Edward	Linenhall Chambers, Chester	01244 348282
	Pendragon Chambers, Swansea	01792 411188
Sefton-Smith Mr Lloyd	Lamb Chambers, London	020 7797 8300
Sellers Mr Graham	Atlantic Chambers, Liverpool	0151 236 4421
Shuman Miss Karen Ann Elizabeth	1 Chancery Lane, London	0845 634 6666
	No 8 Chambers, Birmingham	0121 236 5514
Simon Mr Philipp Arnold Heinrich	4 KBW, London	020 7822 8822
Sinclair Miss Lisa Anne	Chambers of Miss Lisa Sinclair, London	020 8946 7201
Sinclair Mr Graham Kelso	East Anglian Chambers, Colchester	01473 214481
	East Anglian Chambers, Ipswich	01473 214481
	East Anglian Chambers, Norwich	01473 214481
Sisley Mr Timothy Julian Crispin	9 Stone Buildings, London	020 7404 5055
Sjostrand Miss Ekaterina	13 Old Square Chambers, London	020 7831 4445
Smith Mr Roger Hugh Traylen	No5 Chambers, Birmingham	0845 210 5555
	No5 Chambers, Bristol	0845 210 5555
	No5 Chambers, London	0845 210 5555
Sokol Mr Christopher John Francis	Deans Court Chambers, Manchester	0161 214 6000
	Taxchambers, London	020 7242 2744
	Temple Tax Chambers, London	020 7353 7884
Sowler Mr Thomas Richard Holland	The Tax Chambers of Mr Richard Sowler TD, Douglas	07624 235000
Spratt-Dawson Miss Josephine Margery	Trinity Chambers, Chelmsford	01245 605040
Stenhouse Mr John Alexander	Nightingale Chambers, Wolverley	01562 851350
Sterling Mr Robert Alan	St James's Chambers, Manchester	0161 834 7000
	Zenith Chambers, Leeds	0113 245 5438
Stevens-Hoare Miss Michelle	Hardwicke, London	020 7242 2523
Stevenson Mr Paul Anthony	Tanfield Chambers, London	020 7421 5300
Stewart Mr Nicholas John Cameron	Ely Place Chambers, London	020 7400 9600
Stirling Mr Christopher William	Field Court Chambers, London	020 7405 6114
Styles Mr Clive Richard	Becket Chambers, Canterbury	01227 786331
Taylor Miss Araba Arba Kurankyiwa	Fenners Chambers, Cambridge	01223 368761
Terry Mr Robert Jeffrey	Kings Chambers, Birmingham	0845 034 3444
	Kings Chambers, Leeds	0845 034 3444
	Kings Chambers, Manchester	0845 034 3444
	Lamb Chambers, London	020 7797 8300
Thomson Mr Martin Haldane Ahmad	Wynne Chambers, London	020 3239 6964
Trompeter Mr Nicholas Simeon	Selborne Chambers, London	020 7420 9500
Troup Mr Alexander William	St John's Chambers, Bristol	0117 923 4700
Twist Mr Stephen John	Dere Street Barristers, Newcastle Upon Tyne	0844 3351551
Upton Mr Jonathan Michael	Tanfield Chambers, London	020 7421 5300
Vallat Mr Richard Justin	Pump Court Tax Chambers, London	020 7414 8080
Van Tonder Mr Gerard Dirk	New Square Chambers, London	020 7419 8000
Warner Mr David Alexander	St Philips Chambers, Birmingham	0121 246 7000
Watson Mr Duncan Allen	Westgate Chambers, Lewes	01273 480510
Watson Mr Ian David	3 Stone Buildings, London	020 7242 4937
Whitehouse Mr Stuart Colin	Goldsmith Chambers, London	020 7353 6802
Wilkinson Mr Marc Ashley	No5 Chambers, Birmingham	0845 210 5555
	No5 Chambers, Bristol	0845 210 5555
	No5 Chambers, London	0845 210 5555
Wilson Mr Gerald Simon John	Tanfield Chambers, London	020 7421 5300
Wilton Mr Simon Daniel	Hailsham Chambers, London	020 7643 5000
Woolf The Hon Jeremy Richard George	Pump Court Tax Chambers, London	020 7414 8080

Worthley Mr Andrew Mark	Rougemont Chambers, Exeter	01392 208484
Wrottesley Miss Angela Jane	Bank House Chambers, Sheffield	0114 275 1223
Wynne Mr Ashley John	No5 Chambers, Birmingham	0845 210 5555
	No5 Chambers, Bristol	0845 210 5555
	No5 Chambers, London	0845 210 5555

FAMILY

Abasheikh Mr Omar Said Imam	Paragon Chambers, London	020 3318 9988
Abbasi Miss Nylah Naz	9 King's Bench Walk, London	020 7353 9564
Adams Ms Lindsay Eveline	1 Pump Court, London	020 7842 7070
Adamson Miss Lilias Louisa	Becket Chambers, Canterbury	01227 786331
Adler Mr Jonathan	1 Pump Court, London	020 7842 7070
Afzal Mr Fayyaz	No5 Chambers, Birmingham	0845 210 5555
	No5 Chambers, Bristol	0845 210 5555
	No5 Chambers, London	0845 210 5555
Ager Mr Richard Lawrence	Crown Office Row Chambers, Brighton	01273 625625
Ahern Mr Eugene Christopher	Trinity Chambers, Chelmsford	01245 605040
Ahmed Miss Amina	Renaissance Chambers, London	020 7404 1111
Ahmed Mr Saleem	Perivale Chambers, Perivale	020 8998 1935
Ailes Mr John Ashley	Eighteen Carlton Crescent, Southampton	023 8063 9001
Ajaz Mr Mohammad Arshad	Eastmans Chambers, Reading	0118 966 9094
Akinbolu Miss Sandra Adwoa Anifa	Chambers of Mr Ami Feder, London	020 7797 7788
	Chambers of Mr Ami Feder, London	020 7797 7788
Akman Miss Mercy Louise	36 Bedford Row, London	020 7421 8000
Akther Miss Tahina Sultana	Cobden House Chambers, Manchester	0161 833 6000
	Southernhay Chambers, Exeter	01392 255777
Alexander Miss Josephine Anne	Principal Chambers, Sevenoaks	0845 209 8080
Ali Mrs Shamim	Chambers of Mrs Shamim Ali, Hatfield	01707 276737
Allen Miss Sylvia Delores	1 Mitre Court Buildings, London	020 7452 8900
Allen Mr Douglas Stephen	Harcourt Chambers, London	0844 561 7135
Allman Miss Marisa Nichole	Zenith Chambers, Leeds	0113 245 5438
Allston Mr Anthony Stanley	3 Dr Johnson's Buildings, London	020 7353 4854
Allwood Mrs Gina Louisa	Seven Bedford Row, London	020 7242 3555
Ameen Mr Danish	18 St John Street, Manchester	0161 278 1800
Amiraftabi Miss Roshanak	Renaissance Chambers, London	020 7404 1111
Andrews Miss Melanie Alexandra	Becket Chambers, Canterbury	01227 786331
Armbrister Mr Allan Ramsay	39 Park Square, Leeds	0113 245 6633
Arshad Miss Raffia	St Mary's Family Law Chambers, Nottingham	0115 950 3503
Atkinson Mr Jody Roy	St John's Chambers, Bristol	0117 923 4700
Austin Mr Ian	Holborn Chambers, London	020 7242 6060
Austins Mr Christopher John	Chambers of Mr Christopher Austins, Bristol	01761 221 208
	Clerksroom (Taunton), Taunton	0845 083 3000
	King's Lynn Chambers, King's Lynn	01553 672 085
Awodele Mr Olufemi Adetunji	Great James Street Chambers, London	020 7440 4949
Azhar Mr Ali Mohammad	9 King's Bench Walk, London	020 7353 9564
Azmi Mr Mohammad Javed	No 8 Chambers, Birmingham	0121 236 5514
Bagchi Mr Andrew Kumar	1 Garden Court Family Law Chambers, London	020 7797 7900
Baker Mr Nicholas Michael Bridgman	Hardwicke, London	020 7242 2523
Balchin Mr Richard Alexander	New Court, London	020 7583 5123
Ballard Ms Appa	Cornwall Street Chambers, Birmingham	0121 233 7500
Banks Miss Rachael Eda	Atlantic Chambers, Liverpool	0151 236 4421
Banks Mr Francis Andrew	Atlantic Chambers, Liverpool	0151 236 4421
Barnes Mr Luke Clive	3 Dr Johnson's Buildings, London	020 7353 4854
Barnett Miss Adrienne Elise	1 Pump Court, London	020 7842 7070
Barnett Miss Sally Louise	New Street Chambers, Leicester	0116 262 5906
Barraclough Miss Lisa Ann	Colleton Chambers, Exeter	01392 274898
Barran Miss Tabitha Jane Gabriel	Renaissance Chambers, London	020 7404 1111

Barratt Mr Dominic Anthony	East Anglian Chambers, Chelmsford	01473 214481
	East Anglian Chambers, Colchester	01473 214481
	East Anglian Chambers, Ipswich	01473 214481
	East Anglian Chambers, Norwich	01473 214481
Barrett Mr Robert Scott	2 Pump Court, London	020 7353 5597
Bassiri-Dezfouli Miss Sorour	Temple Court Chambers, London	020 7353 7888
Batey Mr David Michael	Stour Chambers, Canterbury	01227 764899
Bath Mrs Baljinder Kaur	College Chambers, Southampton	023 8023 0338
Beattie Ms Annabel Dorothy	Park Court Chambers, Leeds	0113 243 3277
Beaumont Mrs Sally	Sovereign Chambers, Leeds	0113 245 1841
Becker Mr Timothy George Christie	Chambers of Mr Timothy Becker, Liverpool	0151 703 0319
	Clerksroom (London), London	0845 083 3000
Beer Miss Emily Charlotte Lemay	3 Dr Johnson's Buildings, London	020 7353 4854
Bell Miss Anne Margaret	Holborn Chambers, London	020 7242 6060
	Rougemont Chambers, Exeter	01392 208484
Bennet Ms Pauline Agnes	Regency Chambers, Peterborough	01733 315215
Bennett Miss Angela Michelle	3 Dr Johnson's Buildings, London	020 7353 4854
Beswick Miss Kirstin Wendy	Central Chambers, Manchester	0161 236 1133
Bezzam Miss Jayashree	Hampton Court Chambers, West Molesey	020 8979 0381
Bhachu Miss Sharanjeet Kaur	4 Brick Court, London	020 7832 3200
Bhanji Mr Shiraz Musa	4 Bingham Place, London	020 7486 5347
	1 Gray's Inn Square, London	020 7405 0001
Bhattacharyya Mr Ardhendu	Slough Barristers Chamber, Slough	01753 553806
Bhutta Miss Ayeesha Clare	Field Court Chambers, London	020 7405 6114
Binnion Ms Carol Anne	St Ive's Chambers, Birmingham	0121 236 0863
Bisarya Mr Neil	Number 7 Harrington Street Chambers, Liverpool	0151 242 0707
Bisbey Miss Gayle Yvette Dawn	2 Dr Johnson's Buildings, London	020 7936 2613
Bishop Mr Malcolm Leslie	Argent Chambers, London	020 7556 5500
	Equity Chambers, Birmingham	0121 236 5007
	30 Park Place, Cardiff	029 2039 8421
Blackmore Miss Sarah Elizabeth	37 Park Square Chambers, Leeds	0113 243 9422
Blake Ms Penelope Natasha	1 Gray's Inn Square, London	020 7405 0001
Bloom-Davis Mr Desmond Niall Laurence	Pump Court Chambers, London	020 7353 0711
	Pump Court Chambers, Swindon	01793 539899
	Pump Court Chambers, Winchester	01962 868 161
Bogle Mr James Stewart Lockhart	10 King's Bench Walk, London	020 7353 7742
Bojarski Mr Andrzej Leonard	36 Bedford Row, London	020 7421 8000
Borkowski Miss Gemma Francesca	Albion Chambers, Bristol	0117 927 2144
Bowe Mr Patrick Joseph	KCH Garden Square, Nottingham	0115 941 8851
Bowers Mr Rupert John	Doughty Street Chambers, London	020 7404 1313
Boyd Miss Kerstin Margaret	Tanfield Chambers, London	020 7421 5300
Bradley Ms Sally Christina	4 Paper Buildings, London	020 7427 5200
Bradley Ms Sally Frances	Sovereign Chambers, Leeds	0113 245 1841
	18 St John Street, Manchester	0161 278 1800
	Trinity Chambers, Middlesbrough	01642 247569
	Trinity Chambers, Newcastle Upon Tyne	0191 232 1927
Bramwell Mr Christopher Paul	Regency Chambers, Cambridge	01223 301517
	Regency Chambers, Peterborough	01733 315215
Breen-Lawton Miss Denise	St Paul's Chambers, Leeds	0113 245 5866
Brereton Miss Joy	4 Paper Buildings, London	020 7427 5200
Briden Ms Sarah Louise	KCH Garden Square, Nottingham	0115 941 8851
Brooke-Smith Mr John	East Anglian Chambers, Colchester	01473 214481
	East Anglian Chambers, Ipswich	01473 214481
Brown Ms Grace	Tooks Chambers, London	020 7842 7575
Bryden Mr Christopher James Yuen Kang	4 King's Bench Walk, London	020 7822 7000
Buchan Miss Caroline Venetia	Chambers of Miss C Buchan, Haywards Heath	01444 482222
Buck Mr John	Tanfield Chambers, London	020 7421 5300

C

Buckhaven Mr Simon	Hardwicke, London	020 7242 2523
Buckle Mr Jonathan	Regency Chambers, Cambridge	01223 301517
	Regency Chambers, Peterborough	01733 315215
Buckley Mr Peter Evered	Cobden House Chambers, Manchester	0161 833 6000
Bullen Mrs Mary	The Chambers Of Mary Bullen, Wilton	01722 742204
Bundell Miss Katharine Michelle	Octagon House, Norwich	01603 623186
Burdon Mr Michael Stewart	37 Park Square Chambers, Leeds	0113 243 9422
Buswell Mr Richard Thomas	Hardwicke, London	020 7242 2523
Butler Miss Judith Jane Scott	29 Bedford Row Chambers, London	020 7404 1044
Butler Mr George Victor	4 Brick Court, London	020 7832 3200
Butters Mr Richard John	37 Park Square Chambers, Leeds	0113 243 9422
Cabeza Miss Ruth Roberta Elizabeth	Field Court Chambers, London	020 7405 6114
Cade Mrs Diana	Trinity Chambers, Chelmsford	01245 605040
Cade-Davies Miss Lynsey Nicola	29 Bedford Row Chambers, London	020 7404 1044
Cairns Ms Sally	No 8 Chambers, Birmingham	0121 236 5514
Cala Dr Guiseppe	New Court, London	020 7583 5123
Calhaem Mr Simon Malcolm	29 Bedford Row Chambers, London	020 7404 1044
Campbell Mr Stafford Graham	Westgate Chambers, Lewes	01273 480510
Carney Miss Caroline Mary	QEB Hollis Whiteman, London	020 7933 8855
Carr Mr Christopher Sean	36 Bedford Row, London	020 7421 8000
Carron Mr Richard Byron	Queen Square Chambers, Bristol	0117 921 1966
Carter Miss Holly Eugenie Sophia	3 Dr Johnson's Buildings, London	020 7353 4854
Cayford Mr Philip John Berkeley	29 Bedford Row Chambers, London	020 7404 1044
Chadwick Miss Joanna Ceridwen	No5 Chambers, Birmingham	0845 210 5555
	No5 Chambers, Bristol	0845 210 5555
	No5 Chambers, London	0845 210 5555
Chan Miss Rachel Siu Yee	Stour Chambers, Canterbury	01227 764899
Chandler Mr Alexander Charles Ross	1 Garden Court Family Law Chambers, London	020 7797 7900
Chatterjee Miss Adreeja Julia	No5 Chambers, Birmingham	0845 210 5555
	No5 Chambers, Bristol	0845 210 5555
	No5 Chambers, London	0845 210 5555
Chatterjee Miss Mira	4 Brick Court, London	020 7832 3200
Chaudhry Miss Sabuhi Ashfaq	Coram Chambers, London	020 7092 3700
Chidgey Mr David Gareth	Albion Chambers, Bristol	0117 927 2144
Chippeck Mr Stephen	5 King's Bench Walk, London	020 7353 5638
Chippendale Miss Emma Lorraine	37 Park Square Chambers, Leeds	0113 243 9422
Chodha Mr Tejpal Singh	Chambers of Mr T Chodha, Gravesend	01474 326666
Choudhuri Miss Gulshanah	Sen Barristers, Eastleigh	07706 936045
Christie Miss Michelle Elaine	Northampton Chambers, Northampton	01604 636271
Christie Mr Richard Hamish	2 Pump Court, London	020 7353 5597
Church Mr John Stephen	Field Court Chambers, London	020 7405 6114
Claridge Miss Rachael Sarah	Crown Office Row Chambers, Brighton	01273 625625
Clark Mr Dingle	Goldsmith Chambers, London	020 7353 6802
Clarke Mrs Amanda Lesley	Westgate Chambers, Lewes	01273 480510
Clegg Mr Adam Gordon	Stour Chambers, Canterbury	01227 764899
Clifford Miss Victoria Louise	No5 Chambers, Birmingham	0845 210 5555
	No5 Chambers, Bristol	0845 210 5555
	No5 Chambers, London	0845 210 5555
Coates Mr George Alexander Nigel	Guildford Chambers, Guildford	01483 539131
Cohen Mr Jonathan Lionel	4 Paper Buildings, London	020 7427 5200
Colbey Mr Richard	Guildhall Chambers Portsmouth, Portsmouth	023 9275 2400
	Lamb Chambers, London	020 7797 8300
Coleclough Mrs Suzanne Maria	St Philips Chambers, Birmingham	0121 246 7000
Collins Mr Peter Richard	4 King's Bench Walk, London	020 7822 7000
Conlon Mr Michael John Patrick	Harcourt Chambers, Milton Keynes	0845 123 1234
Connolly Mrs Barbara Winifred	Seven Bedford Row, London	020 7242 3555
Conrath Mr Philip Bernard	Tanfield Chambers, London	020 7421 5300
Cook Miss Alison Noele	St Philips Chambers, Birmingham	0121 246 7000
Cotterill Miss Suzannah	Field Court Chambers, London	020 7405 6114
Counsell Mr Edward Frederick	Unity Street Chambers, Bristol	0117 906 9789
Cox Ms Sita	Stour Chambers, Canterbury	01227 764899
Crossley Ms Joanne	St Paul's Chambers, Leeds	0113 245 5866

Culverhouse Miss Emily Anna Louise	Chambers of Miss E Culverhouse, Chesham	07813 007503
Da Costa-Waldman Mrs Elissa Josephine	Clerksroom (London), London	0845 083 3000
	Clerksroom (Taunton), Taunton	0845 083 3000
	King's Lynn Chambers, King's Lynn	01553 672 085
Dalal Mr Rajen Charles James	Cobden House Chambers, Manchester	0161 833 6000
	Derwent Chambers, Derby	01332 242425
Dale Miss Lucy-Ann Georgia	4 Brick Court, London	020 7832 3200
Daniels Mr David William	Rowchester Chambers, Birmingham	0121 233 2327
Dassa Miss Regine	9 King's Bench Walk, London	020 7353 9564
Davenport Mr Richard Ian	Citadel Chambers, Birmingham	0121 233 8500
Davies Miss Lindsay Jane	Fenners Chambers, Cambridge	01223 368761
Davies Miss Rebecca Lucinda	Westgate Chambers, Lewes	01273 480510
Davies Miss Sarah Jeannette	1 Pump Court, London	020 7842 7070
Davies Mr Max James	30 Park Place, Cardiff	029 2039 8421
Davies Ms Samantha Teresa	Chambers of Ms Samantha Davies, Milton Keynes	0845 123 1234
	Warwick House Chambers, London	020 7430 2323
Davis Miss Lucy-Victoria	Pump Court Chambers, London	020 7353 0711
	Pump Court Chambers, Swindon	01793 539899
	Pump Court Chambers, Winchester	01962 868 161
De Zonie Miss Jane	14 Gray's Inn Square, London	020 7242 0858
Dean Mr James Patrick	Goldsmith Chambers, London	020 7353 6802
Dean Mr Peter Thomas	36 Bedford Row, London	020 7421 8000
Dean Mrs Christine Jacqueline	1 Pump Court, London	020 7842 7070
Deegan Mr Lawrence Jeffrey	Fenners Chambers, Cambridge	01223 368761
Degun Mr Jasvir Singh	One Essex Court, London	020 7936 3030
Deschampsneufs Miss Alice Nora	4 King's Bench Walk, London	020 7822 7000
Dhadli Mrs Perminder	KCH Garden Square, Nottingham	0115 941 8851
Dillon Ms Anne Veronica	13 KBW, Oxford	01865 311066
	13 King's Bench Walk, London	020 7353 7204
Dinan-Hayward Miss Deborah Louise	Albion Chambers, Bristol	0117 927 2144
Dipré Mr Paul Nicholas Amadeus	Chambers of Mr P N Dipré, Address withheld	0845 123 1234
	MK Family Law Chambers, Milton Keynes	0845 123 1234
Dodson Miss Joanna	Park Court Chambers, Leeds	0113 243 3277
	Renaissance Chambers, London	020 7404 1111
Dooley Ms Christine	2 Pump Court, London	020 7353 5597
Douglass Mr Paul Stephen	9 King's Bench Walk, London	020 7353 9564
Dove Mr James Francis	The Chambers of Grahame Aldous QC, London	020 7832 0500
Dowell Mr Gregory Hamilton	Principal Chambers, Sevenoaks	0845 209 8080
Dsane Miss Victoria Tsotsoo	Chambers of Miss Victoria Dsane, Sutton	020 8722 0990
Duckworth Mr Peter	29 Bedford Row Chambers, London	020 7404 1044
Dugdale Mr Jeremy Keith	Octagon House, Norwich	01603 623186
Earley Miss Sarah Jane	Pallant Chambers, Chichester	01243 784538
Edington Mrs Fiona Anne Rider	Thomas More Chambers, London	020 7404 7000
Edwards Mr Nigel Royston	St Paul's Chambers, Leeds	0113 245 5866
Edwards Mr Paul	37 Park Square Chambers, Leeds	0113 243 9422
Elcombe Mr Nicholas John	East Anglian Chambers, Chelmsford	01473 214481
	East Anglian Chambers, Colchester	01473 214481
	East Anglian Chambers, Ipswich	01473 214481
	East Anglian Chambers, Norwich	01473 214481
Eldergill Mr Edmund Malcolm	1 Pump Court, London	020 7842 7070
Elliott Mr Colin Douglas	King's Bench and Godolphin (KBG)Chambers, Plymouth	01752 221551
Elliott Mr Edward Anthony John	Garden Court Chambers, London	020 7993 7600

C

Elliott Mr Mark Daniel	3 PB Barristers, Bournemouth	01202 292102
	3 PB Barristers, Bristol	0117 928 1520
	3 PB Barristers, London	020 7583 8055
	3 PB Barristers, Oxford	01865 793 736
	3 PB Barristers, Winchester	01962 868884
Enright Ms Johanne	Chambers of Ms Johanne Enright, London	020 7287 7557
Ephraim-Adejumo Mrs Hilda Ekpo	12 Old Square Chambers, London	020 7404 0875
Espley Miss Susan	Fenners Chambers, Cambridge	01223 368761
Fairbank Mr Nicholas James	4 Paper Buildings, London	020 7427 5200
Fairburn Mr George Edward Henry	Cornwall Street Chambers, Birmingham	0121 233 7500
	Cornwall Street Chambers, Shrewsbury	01743 363 611/0121 233 7500
Fairclough Miss Lucy Helen	Northampton Chambers, Northampton	01604 636271
Fama Mrs Gudrun Hildegard	Middle Temple Lane Chambers, London	020 7583 4352
Fawcett Mr Neil	St Ive's Chambers, Birmingham	0121 236 0863
Fender Mr Carl David	Regency Chambers, Cambridge	01223 301517
	Regency Chambers, Peterborough	01733 315215
Ferguson Mr Christopher Mark	Court Yard Chambers, London	020 7936 2710
	Sovereign Chambers, Leeds	0113 245 1841
	Unity Street Chambers, Bristol	0117 906 9789
Ferguson Mrs Katharine Ann	Fenners Chambers, Cambridge	01223 368761
Ferm Mr Rodney Eric	Broadway House Chambers, Bradford	01274 722560
	Broadway House Chambers, Leeds	0113 246 2600
Flattery Ms Amanda Nichole	Kenworthy's Chambers, Manchester	0161 832 4036
Fletcher Mr Christopher Michael	Octagon House, Norwich	01603 623186
Flexman Mrs Carla Ann	Albion Chambers, Bristol	0117 927 2144
Flood Mr Edward Albert	1 Garden Court Family Law Chambers, London	020 7797 7900
Fordham Mrs Margaret Allison	Principal Chambers, Sevenoaks	0845 209 8080
Forster Ms Sarah Judith	14 Gray's Inn Square, London	020 7242 0858
	Westgate Chambers, Lewes	01273 480510
Fortune Mr Peter Carl Michael	Guildhall Chambers Portsmouth, Portsmouth	023 9275 2400
	4 King's Bench Walk, London	020 7822 7000
Foster Mr Julien Andrew Stewart	1 Garden Court Family Law Chambers, London	020 7797 7900
Francis Mr Nicholas	29 Bedford Row Chambers, London	020 7404 1044
Francis Mr Richard Maurice	9 Park Place, Cardiff	029 2038 2731
Frank Mr Ivor Richard Bainton	7 Bell Yard, London	020 7831 0636
Frantzis Miss Roxanne	KBW, Leeds	0113 297 1200
Fry Mr Neil John	Coram Chambers, London	020 7092 3700
Galway-Cooper Dr Philip Anthony	Five St Andrew's Hill, London	020 7332 5400
Geadah Mr Anthony Edward	29 Bedford Row Chambers, London	020 7404 1044
George Miss Susan Deborah	Coram Chambers, London	020 7092 3700
George Mr Michael David Roberts	St Philips Chambers, Birmingham	0121 246 7000
German Miss Kelly Anne	Eastbourne Chambers, Eastbourne	01323 642102
Gerry Miss Felicity Ruth	36 Bedford Row, London	020 7421 8000
Gilbertson Mrs Helen Alison	Octagon House, Norwich	01603 623186
Gill Miss Baljinder	10 King's Bench Walk, London	020 7353 7742
Gill Miss Pamilla	Goldsmith Chambers, London	020 7353 6802
Gillan Mrs Dominique Lye-Ping	Guildford Chambers, Guildford	01483 539131
Gillman Miss Rachel Mary	1 Garden Court Family Law Chambers, London	020 7797 7900
Gillott Mr Paul Alan Ashley	15 Winckley Square, Preston	01772 252828
Giz Miss Alev Ayse	1 Garden Court Family Law Chambers, London	020 7797 7900
Glaser Mr Michael Samson	14 Gray's Inn Square, London	020 7242 0858
Gold Miss Debra Anne	Fenners Chambers, Cambridge	01223 368761
Goldie Miss Katie Jane	Albion Chambers, Bristol	0117 927 2144
Goldrein Mr Iain Saville	7 Bell Yard, London	020 7831 0636
	Number 7 Harrington Street Chambers, Liverpool	0151 242 0707

Goodall Miss Rachael Jane	3 PB Barristers, Bournemouth	01202 292102
	3 PB Barristers, Bristol	0117 928 1520
	3 PB Barristers, London	020 7583 8055
	3 PB Barristers, Oxford	01865 793 736
	3 PB Barristers, Winchester	01962 868884
Gooderham Miss Elizabeth Ann	Northampton Chambers, Northampton	01604 636271
Gore Mr Andrew Julian Mark	37 Park Square Chambers, Leeds	0113 243 9422
Gore Ms Sally Elizabeth	14 Gray's Inn Square, London	020 7242 0858
Grant-Garwood Mr Joshua Dahren	1 Pump Court, London	020 7842 7070
Gray Mr Justin Henry Walford	Trinity Chambers, Middlesbrough	01642 247569
	Trinity Chambers, Newcastle Upon Tyne	0191 232 1927
Gray Mr Roger Anderson	5 Pump Court, London	020 7353 2532
Green Miss Victoria Louise	1 KBW Chambers, London	020 7936 1500
	King's Bench Chambers, Lewes	01273 402600
Greenan Miss Sarah Octavia	Zenith Chambers, Leeds	0113 245 5438
Greenfield Mr Peter Charles	King's Bench Chambers, Bournemouth	01202 250025
Gregory Ms Ann Marie	St Paul's Chambers, Leeds	0113 245 5866
Grieve Miss Kate Makepeace	36 Bedford Row, London	020 7421 8000
Grundy Ms Clare	St Johns Buildings, Manchester	0161 214 1500
	St Johns Buildings Liverpool, Liverpool	0151 243 6000
	16 Winckley Square, Preston	01772 256100
Hale Mr Charles Stanley	4 Paper Buildings, London	020 7427 5200
Hall Mr Jeremy John	Becket Chambers, Canterbury	01227 786331
Hall Mr Richard Andrew	Pump Court Chambers, London	020 7353 0711
	Pump Court Chambers, Swindon	01793 539899
	Pump Court Chambers, Winchester	01962 868 161
Halstead Mr Robin Bernard	One Essex Court, London	020 7936 3030
Hames Mr Christopher William	4 Paper Buildings, London	020 7427 5200
Hamilton Mr John Conrad	Field Court Chambers, London	020 7405 6114
Hannant Miss Lisa Diane	5 Pump Court, London	020 7353 2532
Haque Mr Gazi Mosta Gawsal	Dollis Hill Chambers, London	020 8208 1663
Harding Mr Christopher James	Thomas More Chambers, London	020 7404 7000
Harper Miss Helen Catherine	Renaissance Chambers, London	020 7404 1111
Harrington Miss Tina Amanda	Trinity Chambers, Chelmsford	01245 605040
Harris Miss Katie Anne	Octagon House, Norwich	01603 623186
Harris Mr Wilbert Arthurlyn	Rowchester Chambers, Birmingham	0121 233 2327
Harrison Dr Graeme	12 College Place, Southampton	023 8032 0320
Hasan Miss Ayesha	3 Dr Johnson's Buildings, London	020 7353 4854
Hassall Mr Craig Jonathan	Sovereign Chambers, Leeds	0113 245 1841
Hay Mr Malcolm John Marshall	3 Dr Johnson's Buildings, London	020 7353 4854
Hayford Miss Jane Helene	New Court, London	020 7583 5123
Haywood Miss Janet	Guildford Chambers, Guildford	01483 539131
Heaton Miss Laura Jane	29 Bedford Row Chambers, London	020 7404 1044
Hellens Mr Matthew James	3 Dr Johnson's Buildings, London	020 7353 4854
Hendron Mr Henry Joseph Christopher	Strand Chambers, London	020 7117 6920
Henstock-Turner Mrs Sarah Elizabeth	College Chambers, Southampton	023 8023 0338
Henthorn Miss Kate Marie	7 Bell Yard, London	020 7831 0636
	18 St John Street, Manchester	0161 278 1800
Hepher Mr Paul Arthur Richard	4 Paper Buildings, London	020 7427 5200
Heppenstall Miss Claire Norah	1 Garden Court Family Law Chambers, London	020 7797 7900
Hewitt Miss Alexandra Helen	Linenhall Chambers, Chester	01244 348282
Hill Mr Simon Michael	33 Bedford Row, London	020 7242 6476
Hillas Miss Samantha	Atlantic Chambers, Liverpool	0151 236 4421
Hillier Mr William	New Street Chambers, Leicester	0116 262 5906
Hine Mr Charles Roderick John	King's Bench Chambers, Bournemouth	01202 250025
Hinton Mr Neil Pearse	King's Bench Chambers, Bournemouth	01202 250025
Hobbs Ms Naomi Josephine	No 8 Chambers, Birmingham	0121 236 5514
Holland Mr William	1 Gray's Inn Square, London	020 7405 0001
Hollow Mr Paul John	Fenners Chambers, Cambridge	01223 368761
Holt Mrs Jane Rosemary	KCH Garden Square, Nottingham	0115 941 8851

Barrister	Chambers	Telephone
Hookway Mr Richard Aelred	Zenith Chambers, Leeds	0113 245 5438
Hornblower Mrs Sarah Patience	Rougemont Chambers, Exeter	01392 208484
Horne-Roberts Mrs Jennifer	Goldsmith Chambers, London	020 7353 6802
Horton Mr Mark Varney	Colleton Chambers, Exeter	01392 274898
Horton Mr Michael John Edward	Coram Chambers, London	020 7092 3700
Howard Miss Amanda Jayne	Atlantic Chambers, Liverpool	0151 236 4421
	37 Park Square Chambers, Leeds	0113 243 9422
Howard Mr Steven James	3 PB Barristers, Bournemouth	01202 292102
	3 PB Barristers, London	020 7583 8055
Howe Mr Darren Francis	1 Garden Court Family Law Chambers, London	020 7797 7900
Howe Mr Gavin Paul	Crown Office Row Chambers, Brighton	01273 625625
Howling Mr Rex Andrew	4 Paper Buildings, London	020 7427 5200
Hudd Miss Anne Marguerita Jane	29 Bedford Row Chambers, London	020 7404 1044
Hudson Mr John Edward Gerard	Zenith Chambers, Leeds	0113 245 5438
Hughes Dr Constance Mary	1 Pump Court, London	020 7842 7070
Hughes Miss Meryl Elizabeth	Fenners Chambers, Cambridge	01223 368761
Hughes Mrs Kathryn Sally	Chavasse Court Chambers, Liverpool	0151 229 2030
Hunt Miss Alison Lorna	Regency Chambers, Cambridge	01223 301517
	Regency Chambers, Peterborough	01733 315215
Hussain Mr Basharat	Cornwall Street Chambers, Birmingham	0121 233 7500
Hussain Mr Muhammad Altaf	Chambers of Mr M A Hussain, London	020 8679 2398
Hussein Mr Timur	1 Pump Court, London	020 7842 7070
Hypolite-De-Souza Mrs Josephine Claudia	12 Old Square Chambers, London	020 7404 0875
Iqbal Mr Mashood	London View Chambers, Sawbridgeworth	07788 912493
Irving Miss Gillian	Linenhall Chambers, Chester	01244 348282
	9 St John Street, Manchester	0161 955 9000
	15 Winckley Square, Preston	01772 252828
Islam Mr Saiful	3 Dr Johnson's Buildings, London	020 7353 4854
Ismail Miss Nazmun Nisha	Central Chambers, Manchester	0161 236 1133
	No5 Chambers, Birmingham	0845 210 5555
	No5 Chambers, Bristol	0845 210 5555
	No5 Chambers, London	0845 210 5555
Iten Miss Corinne Beatrice	Pump Court Chambers, London	020 7353 0711
Jack Mr Nicholas Robert	Octagon House, Norwich	01603 623186
Jacques Mr Gareth Edward	Regency Chambers, Peterborough	01733 315215
Jagutpal Mr Previn Sing	4 Brick Court, London	020 7832 3200
James Mr George Christopher Mohun	No5 Chambers, Birmingham	0845 210 5555
	No5 Chambers, Bristol	0845 210 5555
	No5 Chambers, London	0845 210 5555
James Mrs Venice Imogen	No 8 Chambers, Birmingham	0121 236 5514
Japheth Miss Bethan	Linenhall Chambers, Chester	01244 348282
Jarman Mr Mark Christopher	4 Paper Buildings, London	020 7427 5200
Jay Mr Grenville Richard	Regent Chambers, Stoke On Trent	01782 286666
Jenkins Mr David Crofton	2 King's Bench Walk, London	020 7353 1746
Johnson Miss Melanie Jane	1 Pump Court, London	020 7842 7070
Johnson Miss Sarah Susan	Kenworthy's Chambers, Manchester	0161 832 4036
Johnson Mr Simon Nicholas	Stour Chambers, Canterbury	01227 764899
Johnson Mrs Carolyn Ann	Cobden House Chambers, Manchester	0161 833 6000
Johnstone Mr Mark Anthony	4 Paper Buildings, London	020 7427 5200
Jones Mr Rhys Charles Mansel	14 Gray's Inn Square, London	020 7242 0858
Jones Mrs Hettie Georgia	Liberty Chambers, Tenby	01834 844458
Joseph Mr Sellappah Job	Chambers of Mr S J Joseph, London	020 8809 3083/020 8802 9889
Joshi Mr Pramod Kumar	One Essex Court, London	020 7936 3030
Judge Miss Parveen	1 Mitre Court Buildings, London	020 7452 8900
Kabweru-Namulemu Miss Karen Hasasha	KCH Garden Square, Nottingham	0115 941 8851
Kansal Miss Seema	12 Old Square Chambers, London	020 7404 0875

Name	Chambers	Telephone
Kelly Mr Geoffrey Robert	Pump Court Chambers, London	020 7353 0711
	Pump Court Chambers, Swindon	01793 539899
	Pump Court Chambers, Winchester	01962 868 161
Kerr Mr Neil Forsyth	3 Dr Johnson's Buildings, London	020 7353 4854
Ker-Reid Mr John	Pump Court Chambers, London	020 7353 0711
	Pump Court Chambers, Swindon	01793 539899
	Pump Court Chambers, Winchester	01962 868 161
Khalid Mr James	Goulds Green Chambers, Uxbridge	01895 422574
	Goulds Green Chambers, Uxbridge	01895 422574
Khan Mr Abdul Aleem	Gray's Chambers, Newbury	020 8518 2525
Khan Mr Ayoub	Chambers of Mr Ayoub Khan, Birmingham	07930 987202
Khan Mr Forz	Chambers of Mr F Khan, London	07854 109584
	6 King's Bench Walk, London	020 7353 4931
Khan Mr Imran	St Albans Chambers, St Albans	01727 843383
Khan Mr Mahmood Shafi	Luton Chambers, Luton	01582 598394
	Willesden Chambers, London	020 3273 1042
Khan Mr Tariq Ali	Chambers of Mr T A Khan, Coventry	02476 666 400
Kidd Mr Peter William	Number 7 Harrington Street Chambers, Liverpool	0151 242 0707
Kilvington Miss Sarah Elizabeth	18 St John Street, Manchester	0161 278 1800
King Miss Samantha Leonie	4 Paper Buildings, London	020 7427 5200
King Mr Charles Granville	Chambers of Mr C G King, Stroud	07949 461717
Kinnear Miss Elise	Field Court Chambers, London	020 7405 6114
Kirby Miss Ruth Mary Anthony	4 Paper Buildings, London	020 7427 5200
Knight Mr Benjamin James	Central Chambers, Manchester	0161 236 1133
Knowles Miss Linsey	Albion Chambers, Bristol	0117 927 2144
	6 Pump Court, London	020 7797 8400
	6 Pump Court Chambers, Maidstone	01622 688094
Krushner Mr Damian Mark	Oakwood Chambers, London	07789 435485
Lanson Miss Lauren Elizabeth	1 Gray's Inn Square, London	020 7405 0001
Larizadeh Mr Cyrus Rais	4 Paper Buildings, London	020 7427 5200
Lau Miss Vanessa Hoi Chun	18 St John Street, Manchester	0161 278 1800
Lawrence Miss Pamela Avril	Nexus Chambers, London	020 7404 1147/020 7831 8309
Lawrence Miss Samantha Dionne	3 Dr Johnson's Buildings, London	020 7353 4854
Le Fort Mr Michael Cameron Raoul	King's Bench Chambers, Bournemouth	01202 250025
Lear Miss Estelle Christine	Tanfield Chambers, London	020 7421 5300
Lee Miss Taryn Jane	37 Park Square Chambers, Leeds	0113 243 9422
Lenaghan Mr Anthony	Dyers Chambers, London	020 7404 1881
Lewis Mr Stuart John	New Walk Chambers, Leicester	0871 200 1298/0116 255 9144
Lewis Mr Wayne Anthony	Access Lawyers, London	020 8801 2345
Limbrey Mr Bernard Martin	3 Dr Johnson's Buildings, London	020 7353 4854
Lindsay Mr Jeremy Mark Henry	37 Park Square Chambers, Leeds	0113 243 9422
Littlewood Miss Rebecca Mae	1 Pump Court, London	020 7842 7070
Lloyd Ms Rhiannon	4 Paper Buildings, London	020 7427 5200
Loeb Miss Dinah Yolande	Westgate Chambers, Lewes	01273 480510
Longhurst-Woods Ms Lesley	2 Louisa Close, London	020 8985 8716
Lopez Mr Paul Anthony	St Ive's Chambers, Birmingham	0121 236 0863
Lorenzo Ms Claudia	Pump Court Chambers, London	020 7353 0711
	Pump Court Chambers, Swindon	01793 539899
	Pump Court Chambers, Winchester	01962 868 161
Love Miss Sharon Ann	Garden Court Chambers, London	020 7993 7600
Lugsdin Mr Martin	Kenworthy's Chambers, Manchester	0161 832 4036
Lule Miss Jacqueline	1 Mitre Court Buildings, London	020 7452 8900
Lyon Mr Gavin	Northampton Chambers, Northampton	01604 636271
Lyons Miss Tara Yasmin	Pump Court Chambers, London	020 7353 0711
	Pump Court Chambers, Winchester	01962 868 161
	Riverview Chambers, London	0844 225 3999
Lyons Mr David Wakefield	King's Bench Chambers, Bournemouth	01202 250025
	2 Pump Court, London	020 7353 5597
MacKenzie Miss Julie Fiona	Pump Court Chambers, London	020 7353 0711
	Pump Court Chambers, Swindon	01793 539899
	Pump Court Chambers, Winchester	01962 868 161
Mackley Mr David John	18 St John Street, Manchester	0161 278 1800

C

Maddison Mr David Thomas James	Cobden House Chambers, Manchester	0161 833 6000
Magee Miss Rosein Moira	Pallant Chambers, Chichester	01243 784538
Mahmood Mr Abid	Central Chambers, Manchester	0161 236 1133
	No5 Chambers, Birmingham	0845 210 5555
	No5 Chambers, Bristol	0845 210 5555
	No5 Chambers, London	0845 210 5555
Mahtab Miss Sumita Laila-Al	7 Bell Yard, London	020 7831 0636
Maitland Jones Mr Mark Griffith	13 KBW, Oxford	01865 311066
	13 King's Bench Walk, London	020 7353 7204
Malone Mr David John	1 Gray's Inn Square, London	020 7405 0001
Mandalia Mr Vinesh Lalji	St Philips Chambers, Birmingham	0121 246 7000
Manley Miss Lesley Patrica	Chambers of Marion Smullen and Kerim Fuad QC, London	020 7427 4400
Mannan Mr Charles Madani Fuad	Temple Court Chambers, London	020 7353 7888
Mansfield Mr Benjamin Elliot	KCH Garden Square, Nottingham	0115 941 8851
Marks Miss Gillian	14 Gray's Inn Square, London	020 7242 0858
Marks Miss Jacqueline Stephanie	Coram Chambers, London	020 7092 3700
Marks Mr Jonathan Clive	4 Pump Court, London	020 7842 5555
Marley Miss Sarah Anne	Coram Chambers, London	020 7092 3700
Marsden Mr Andrew Guy	East Anglian Chambers, Chelmsford	01473 214481
	East Anglian Chambers, Colchester	01473 214481
	East Anglian Chambers, Ipswich	01473 214481
	East Anglian Chambers, Norwich	01473 214481
Marshall Mr Derek Stanley	College Chambers, Southampton	023 8023 0338
Martignetti Mr Ian	Regency Chambers, Cambridge	01223 301517
	Regency Chambers, Peterborough	01733 315215
Martin Mr Piers James	4 King's Bench Walk, London	020 7822 7000
Martin Mrs Dianne Joan Abegail	St John's Chambers, Bristol	0117 923 4700
Maselli Mr Mauro	Chambers of Mr M Maselli, Peterborough	07786 320064
	Priestgate Chambers, Peterborough	01733 865 042
Mashembo Mrs Carol	St John's Chambers, Bristol	0117 923 4700
Massey Miss Stella Maria	Central Chambers, Manchester	0161 236 1133
Mather Miss Kate	1 Garden Court Family Law Chambers, London	020 7797 7900
Mather Mr Brian Howard	Trinity Chambers, Middlesbrough	01642 247569
	Trinity Chambers, Newcastle Upon Tyne	0191 232 1927
Maton Mr Neil Foster	Pallant Chambers, Chichester	01243 784538
Max Miss Sally Ann	29 Bedford Row Chambers, London	020 7404 1044
Mayhew Miss Judith	3 Dr Johnson's Buildings, London	020 7353 4854
Maynard Mr Matthew David	St Ive's Chambers, Birmingham	0121 236 0863
McCabe Miss Louise Anne	St Philips Chambers, Birmingham	0121 246 7000
McCann Miss Katie	Atlantic Chambers, Liverpool	0151 236 4421
McCormack Mr Alan	Staple Inn Chambers, London	020 7242 5240
McCrae Miss Fiona	Trinity Chambers, Middlesbrough	01642 247569
	Trinity Chambers, Newcastle Upon Tyne	0191 232 1927
McCullough Miss Louise Clare	Chambers of Mr Ami Feder, London	020 7797 7788
	Chambers of Mr Ami Feder, London	020 7797 7788
	Lamb Building, Brighton	01273 820490
McGhee Mr Stuart Edward	College Chambers, Southampton	023 8023 0338
McGowan Miss Maura Patricia	2 Bedford Row, London	020 7440 8888
	Lincoln House Chambers, Manchester	0161 832 5701
McKay Mr Christopher Alexander	Cathedral Chambers, Newport	01633 215112
McMillan Mrs Carol Ann	Westgate Chambers, Lewes	01273 480510
McMullan Ms Laura Christina	Coram Chambers, London	020 7092 3700
McWatters Mr Christopher George	Garden Court Chambers, London	020 7993 7600
Meachin Miss Vanessa Veronica	St Philips Chambers, Birmingham	0121 246 7000
Mehta Miss Anita Roxane	Crown Office Row Chambers, Brighton	01273 625625
Meichen Mr Jonathan Brian	St Philips Chambers, Birmingham	0121 246 7000

C

Barrister	Chambers	Telephone
Mendes Da Costa Mr David	Chambers of Mr D Mendes Da Costa, London	020 8747 4633
	MK Family Law Chambers, Milton Keynes	0845 123 1234
	No. 3 Fleet Street Chambers, London	020 7936 4474
Merry Mr Hugh Gairns	12 College Place, Southampton	023 8032 0320
Miah Mr Anawar Babul	Great James Street Chambers, London	020 7440 4949
Miller Miss Catherine	East Anglian Chambers, Chelmsford	01473 214481
	East Anglian Chambers, Ipswich	01473 214481
	East Anglian Chambers, Norwich	01473 214481
Miller Mr Christopher Albert	14 Gray's Inn Square, London	020 7242 0858
Mills Miss Barbara	4 Paper Buildings, London	020 7427 5200
Milne Mrs Arlene Joan	Cobden House Chambers, Manchester	0161 833 6000
Milsom Mrs Catherine Mary	Argent Chambers, London	020 7556 5500
Mitropoulos Mr Christos	5 Pump Court, London	020 7353 2532
Modgill Mr Alexander Jeffrey	Broadway House Chambers, Bradford	01274 722560
	Broadway House Chambers, Leeds	0113 246 2600
Mohammad Mr Nazar	Legis Chambers, Aylesbury	01296 431125
	No. 3 Fleet Street Chambers, London	020 7936 4474
Moore Mr Jonathan Guy	Cathedral Chambers, Cardiff	02920 660129
	Cathedral Chambers, Newport	01633 215112
Moran Mr Christopher John	39 Park Square, Leeds	0113 245 6633
Morgan Mr Colin Thomas Patrick	Pallant Chambers, Chichester	01243 784538
Morris Miss Brenda Alison	14 Gray's Inn Square, London	020 7242 0858
Morris Ms Christina Gaye	Coram Chambers, London	020 7092 3700
Morrison Mr Christopher Quintin	Old Court Chambers, Middlesbrough	01642 232523
Murkin Mrs Sandria	Becket Chambers, Canterbury	01227 786331
Murray Miss Judith Rowena	4 Paper Buildings, London	020 7427 5200
Murray Mr Lance John Mole	Nexus Chambers, London	020 7404 1147/020 7831 8309
Mustafa Ms Hala Mohamed Kamel	1 Crown Office Row, London	020 7797 7500
	Crown Office Row Chambers, Brighton	01273 625625
Mustakim Mr Abdul Yunus Al	Chambers of Mr Mustakim, London	
Mylvaganam Ms Tanoo	1 Gray's Inn Square, London	020 7405 0001
Newport Mr Ian Alun	College Chambers, Southampton	023 8023 0338
Nichols Mr Stuart Richard	1 Garden Court Family Law Chambers, London	020 7797 7900
Nickless Mr Jason Alan	College Chambers, Southampton	023 8023 0338
Noble Mr Philip Robert	Thomas More Chambers, London	020 7404 7000
Norton Mr Andrew David	1 Garden Court Family Law Chambers, London	020 7797 7900
Nosworthy Mr Jonathan Alex	St Philips Chambers, Birmingham	0121 246 7000
Obuka Ms Obijuo Agwu	Chambers of Miss O A Obuka, London	020 7936 4474
Ojutiku Mrs Fadekemi Omotayo	4 King's Bench Walk, London	020 7822 7000
Okine Miss Julie Anne	Goldsmith Chambers, London	020 7353 6802
Okoye Miss Joy Nwamala	Chambers of Joy Okoye, London	07976 426871/020 7405 7011
Oldham Mrs Frances Mary Theresa	36 Bedford Row, London	020 7421 8000
	37 Park Square Chambers, Leeds	0113 243 9422
O'Leary Ms Michele Ann	1 Pump Court, London	020 7842 7070
Ong Miss Grace Yu Mae	Argent Chambers, London	020 7556 5500
Oommen Mr Jacob	Chambers of Mr Jacob Oommen, East Barnet	07958 680272
Orchover Ms Frances Rachel	Coram Chambers, London	020 7092 3700
Osborne Mr David Thomas	Chambers of Mr D T Osborne, Taunton	01823 400 705
O'Sullivan Mr Bernard Anthony	Henderson Chambers, London	020 7583 9020
O'Toole Mr Bartholomew Vincent	5 King's Bench Walk, London	020 7353 5638
Pallo Mr Simon Russel	Bank House Chambers, Sheffield	0114 275 1223
Palmer Mr Edward James	Regent Chambers, Stoke On Trent	01782 286666
Panagiotopoulou Miss Sophie Thalia	Staple Inn Chambers, London	020 7242 5240
Papazian Miss Cliona Concepta	4 Paper Buildings, London	020 7427 5200
Parnell Mrs Cherie Eileen	East Anglian Chambers, Colchester	01473 214481
	East Anglian Chambers, Ipswich	01473 214481
	East Anglian Chambers, Norwich	01473 214481

Parsons Mr Andrew James	Portsmouth Barristers'Chambers, Portsmouth	023 9283 1292
Pascoe Ms Soraya	1 Gray's Inn Square, London	020 7405 0001
Patel Mr Yasin Ahmed	25 Bedford Row, London	020 7067 1500
Payne Mr David James	No 8 Chambers, Birmingham	0121 236 5514
Peacock Miss Lisa Jayne	3 Dr Johnson's Buildings, London	020 7353 4854
Pearman Mr Lee Charles	4 Brick Court, London	020 7832 3200
Pears Mr Derrick Allan	Tanfield Chambers, London	020 7421 5300
Peddie Mr Ian James Crofton	Garden Court Chambers, London	020 7993 7600
	St Johns Buildings Liverpool, Liverpool	0151 243 6000
	Westgate Chambers, Lewes	01273 480510
Peel Mr Robert Roger	29 Bedford Row Chambers, London	020 7404 1044
Pemberton Miss Yolanda Erica	St Philips Chambers, Birmingham	0121 246 7000
Persaud Dr Marcia Chitroutie	1 Gray's Inn Square, London	020 7405 0001
Pettitt Mr Robert	Northampton Chambers, Northampton	01604 636271
Pickering Mr Simon Toby	Wilberforce Chambers, Hull	01482 323264
Pithers Mr Clive Robert	Fenners Chambers, Cambridge	01223 368761
Pitt-Lewis Mrs Janet Rebecca	Cornwall Street Chambers, Birmingham	0121 233 7500
	Cornwall Street Chambers, Shrewsbury	01743 363 611/0121 233 7500
Pitts Miss Charlotte Frances	Albion Chambers, Bristol	0117 927 2144
Pope Miss Anna	Linenhall Chambers, Chester	01244 348282
Popley Miss Heather Louise	New Street Chambers, Leicester	0116 262 5906
Posner Miss Gabrielle Jan	Renaissance Chambers, London	020 7404 1111
Posta Mr Adrian Mark	Albion Chambers, Bristol	0117 927 2144
Potter Miss Louise	Harcourt Chambers, London	0844 561 7135
	Harcourt Chambers, Oxford	0844 561 7135
Powell Mr Robin Edward	Tanfield Chambers, London	020 7421 5300
Preston Miss Kim Deborah	4 King's Bench Walk, London	020 7822 7000
Price Mrs Huma Sabih	St Andrews Chambers, London	020 8368 3686
Procter Mr Alfred George Haydn	1 Garden Court Family Law Chambers, London	020 7797 7900
Pye Miss Margaret Jayne	Zenith Chambers, Leeds	0113 245 5438
Quinn Miss Victoria Kathleen	Thomas More Chambers, London	020 7404 7000
Quirke Mr Gerard Martin	Citadel Chambers, Birmingham	0121 233 8500
Qureshi Miss Dilruba	Temple Court Chambers, London	020 7353 7888
Rai Miss Puneet Kaur	Thomas More Chambers, London	020 7404 7000
Ramdas-Harsia Mr Rohan Mukesh	1 Pump Court, London	020 7842 7070
Ramzan Mr Mohammed Anwar	Great James Street Chambers, London	020 7440 4949
Rana Mr Mohammed Akram	Clapham Law Chambers, London	020 7978 8482
Ratcliffe Miss Frances Anne	Radcliffe Chambers, London	020 7831 0081
Rawal Miss Anita	Chambers of Mr Ami Feder, London	020 7797 7788
	Chambers of Mr Ami Feder, London	020 7797 7788
	Lamb Building, Brighton	01273 820490
Record Mrs Celia Saint Claire	Chambers of Lawrence Jones, London	020 7831 1444
Reed Ms Lucy Emma	St John's Chambers, Bristol	0117 923 4700
Rees Mr Robert Charles David	New Walk Chambers, Leicester	0871 200 1298/0116 255 9144
Reid Miss Claudette Patricia	Chambers of Miss Claudette Reid, London	
Reid Mr Sebastian Peter Scott	Tanfield Chambers, London	020 7421 5300
Renton The Hon Mrs Clare Olivia	29 Bedford Row Chambers, London	020 7404 1044
Reynolds Mr John Adam	King's Bench Chambers, Bournemouth	01202 250025
Rhodes Miss Amanda Louise	Unity Street Chambers, Bristol	0117 906 9789
Rippon Mr Simon John	Citadel Chambers, Birmingham	0121 233 8500
Riza Mr Alper Ali	Goldsmith Chambers, London	020 7353 6802
Roberts Mr Huw Eifion	Linenhall Chambers, Chester	01244 348282
Roberts Mr James Mcclintock	1 KBW Chambers, London	020 7936 1500
	King's Bench Chambers, Lewes	01273 402600
Rosenblatt Mr Jeremy George	42 Bedford Row, London	020 7831 0222
Ross Ms Jennifer	King's Bench Chambers, Bournemouth	01202 250025
Rothwell Mrs Joanne Lesley	No5 Chambers, Birmingham	0845 210 5555
	No5 Chambers, Bristol	0845 210 5555
	No5 Chambers, London	0845 210 5555

Rowe Miss Freya Emily Beatrice	Thomas More Chambers, London	020 7404 7000
Rowland Mr Robin Frank	No5 Chambers, Birmingham	0845 210 5555
	No5 Chambers, Bristol	0845 210 5555
	No5 Chambers, London	0845 210 5555
Rowlinson Miss Wendy Julia	Pallant Chambers, Chichester	01243 784538
Roy Mr Stefan Alexander Hiren	5 Pump Court, London	020 7353 2532
Rudd Miss Zoe Ann	College Chambers, Southampton	023 8023 0338
Russell Mr Guy Jonothon	Westgate Chambers, Lewes	01273 480510
Samra Miss Sharn	Broadway House Chambers, Bradford	01274 722560
	Broadway House Chambers, Leeds	0113 246 2600
Samuels Mr Leslie John	Pump Court Chambers, London	020 7353 0711
	Pump Court Chambers, Winchester	01962 868 161
	Riverview Chambers, London	0844 225 3999
Sandford Mr Simon John Austin	5 King's Bench Walk, London	020 7353 5638
Sapstead Miss Louise Anne	KCH Garden Square, Nottingham	0115 941 8851
Saunders Miss Zoe Alice	St John's Chambers, Bristol	0117 923 4700
Savvides Miss Maria	Northampton Chambers, Northampton	01604 636271
Sawtell Mr David Robert Fraser	4 King's Bench Walk, London	020 7822 7000
Sayed Miss Ruby	1 Pump Court, London	020 7842 7070
Scott Mr Stuart	1 Pump Court, London	020 7842 7070
Scott Ms Laura Louise	14 Gray's Inn Square, London	020 7242 0858
Seeboruth Mr Royln Jean-Paul	Chambers of Royln Seeboruth, Aylesbury	01296 393329
Sefi Mr Benedict John	Harcourt Chambers, London	0844 561 7135
	Harcourt Chambers, Oxford	0844 561 7135
Sefton Mr Nicholas Edward	Linenhall Chambers, Chester	01244 348282
	Pendragon Chambers, Swansea	01792 411188
Seguss Miss Penelope Marie	The Chambers of Penelope Seguss, London	020 8877 0707
Self Mr Gary Peter	College Chambers, Southampton	023 8023 0338
	St David's Chambers, Swansea	01792 559924
Shamim Mr Mohammed	Clapham Law Chambers, London	020 7978 8482
Sharma Mr Sanjeev Mohan	Equity Chambers, Birmingham	0121 236 5007
Sharp Mr Christopher Francis	Harcourt Chambers, London	0844 561 7135
	Harcourt Chambers, Oxford	0844 561 7135
	St John's Chambers, Bristol	0117 923 4700
Shaw Miss Joanna Elizabeth	One Essex Court, London	020 7936 3030
Shaw Mr Julian	St Johns Buildings, Chester	01244 323070
	St Johns Buildings, Manchester	0161 214 1500
	St Johns Buildings Liverpool, Liverpool	0151 243 6000
Shaw Ms Nicola Jane Duckworth	Trinity Chambers, Middlesbrough	01642 247569
	Trinity Chambers, Newcastle Upon Tyne	0191 232 1927
	15 Winckley Square, Preston	01772 252828
Shield Miss Deborah	42 Bedford Row, London	020 7831 0222
Short Ms Mandy Lisa	14 Gray's Inn Square, London	020 7242 0858
Shuttleworth Mr Timothy William	Tanfield Chambers, London	020 7421 5300
Silverton Miss Catherine Anne	Sovereign Chambers, Leeds	0113 245 1841
Simpson Miss Carol Monica	Amethyst Chambers, London	020 7936 4966
Singh-Hayer Mr Bansa	Deans Court Chambers, Manchester	0161 214 6000
	Deans Court Chambers, Preston	01772 565 600
Sleight Mr Nigel	Regency Chambers, Cambridge	01223 301517
	Regency Chambers, Peterborough	01733 315215
Small Mrs Arlene Annmarie	Clerksroom (London), London	0845 083 3000
	Clerksroom (Taunton), Taunton	0845 083 3000
	King's Lynn Chambers, King's Lynn	01553 672 085
Smallwood Miss Anne Elizabeth	No5 Chambers, Birmingham	0845 210 5555
	No5 Chambers, Bristol	0845 210 5555
	No5 Chambers, London	0845 210 5555
Smith Mr Adam John	Crown Office Row Chambers, Brighton	01273 625625
Smith Mr Julian Robert	Lincoln's Inn Fields Chambers, London	0845 123 1234
Smith Mr Roger Gavin Abbey	1 Hare Court, London	020 7797 7070

C

Sofaer Miss Moira	Goldsmith Chambers, London	020 7353 6802
Soni Miss Bansi	Garden Court Chambers, London	020 7993 7600
Sood Mrs Usha Rani	Trent Chambers, Nottingham	0115 941 9596
Southern Miss Emma Catherine	12 College Place, Southampton	023 8032 0320
Spain Mr Timothy Harrisson	Trinity Chambers, Middlesbrough	01642 247569
	Trinity Chambers, Newcastle Upon Tyne	0191 232 1927
Sparrow Mrs Marie-Claire	Holborn Chambers, London	020 7242 6060
Spencer Mr Shaun Anthony	St Johns Buildings, Chester	01244 323070
	St Johns Buildings, Manchester	0161 214 1500
	16 Winckley Square, Preston	01772 256100
Spratt-Dawson Miss Josephine Margery	Trinity Chambers, Chelmsford	01245 605040
Sproull Mr Nicholas	Albion Chambers, Bristol	0117 927 2144
Squire Mr Philip Denby	3 Dr Johnson's Buildings, London	020 7353 4854
Stanley Mrs Gillian Frances	1 Garden Court Family Law Chambers, London	020 7797 7900
Starr Mrs Teresa Margaret	Great James Street Chambers, London	020 7440 4949
Stevens Mrs Hazel Ann	East Anglian Chambers, Chelmsford	01473 214481
	East Anglian Chambers, Ipswich	01473 214481
	East Anglian Chambers, Norwich	01473 214481
Stringer Mr Leon Peter	15 Winckley Square, Preston	01772 252828
Strongman Mrs Carol Ann	No 8 Chambers, Birmingham	0121 236 5514
Styles Mr Clive Richard	Becket Chambers, Canterbury	01227 786331
Styles Mrs Kay Margaret	Harcourt Chambers, London	0844 561 7135
	Harcourt Chambers, Oxford	0844 561 7135
Sugar Mr Simon Gareth	1 Garden Court Family Law Chambers, London	020 7797 7900
Sutton Mr Clive Raymond	Chambers of Mr Clive Sutton, Bruerne	07973 386702
Swift Mr Jonathan Peter	29 Bedford Row Chambers, London	020 7404 1044
Symms Miss Kathryn Ann	Number 7 Harrington Street Chambers, Liverpool	0151 242 0707
Tambling Mr Richard	1 Garden Court Family Law Chambers, London	020 7797 7900
Tansey Miss Anouska	2-3 Hind Court Chambers, London	020 7822 2150
Targett-Parker Miss Leanne Susan	No. 3 Fleet Street Chambers, London	020 7936 4474
	The Chambers of Miss Leanne Targett-Parker, London	020 8674 6694
Tautz Mr William Henry	Tooks Chambers, London	020 7842 7575
Taylor Miss Linda Kathryn	Westgate Chambers, Lewes	01273 480510
Taylor Mr Alex Geoffrey	Park Court Chambers, Leeds	0113 243 3277
	Park Lane Plowden, Leeds	0113 228 5049
Taylor Mr Rhys Steadman	30 Park Place, Cardiff	029 2039 8421
Taylor Mrs Susan	Trinity Chambers, Middlesbrough	01642 247569
	Trinity Chambers, Newcastle Upon Tyne	0191 232 1927
Taylor Mrs Yvonne Marie	Trinity Chambers, Middlesbrough	01642 247569
	Trinity Chambers, Newcastle Upon Tyne	0191 232 1927
Taylor Ms Mary-Jane	Coram Chambers, London	020 7092 3700
Thind Miss Anita	Regency Chambers, Cambridge	01223 301517
	Regency Chambers, Peterborough	01733 315215
Thomas Miss Jacqueline Louise	37 Park Square Chambers, Leeds	0113 243 9422
Thomas Mr Gareth	Atlantic Chambers, Liverpool	0151 236 4421
Thomas Mrs Felicity	Westgate Chambers, Lewes	01273 480510
Thornton Mr John Robert	Stour Chambers, Canterbury	01227 764899
Toch Miss Joanna Patricia	Chambers of Miss J P Toch, Tonbridge	01892 833 005
	Chambers of Mr Ami Feder, London	020 7797 7788
	Chambers of Mr Ami Feder, London	020 7797 7788
Tompkins Miss Kate	36 Bedford Row, London	020 7421 8000
Tregidgo Mr Marc Gordon	4 King's Bench Walk, London	020 7822 7000
Tresman Mr Lewis Robert Simon	Staple Inn Chambers, London	020 7242 5240

C

Trotter Miss Helen Claire	Pump Court Chambers, London	020 7353 0711
	Pump Court Chambers, Swindon	01793 539899
	Pump Court Chambers, Winchester	01962 868 161
Tucker Mr James William Richard	Teucro Chambers, Epsom	
Turnbull Mrs Linda Angela	1 Gray's Inn Square, London	020 7405 0001
Twist Mr Stephen John	Dere Street Barristers, Newcastle Upon Tyne	0844 3351551
Twydell Miss Cherry Louisa	Trinity Chambers, Chelmsford	01245 605040
Tyler Mr Thomas Geoffrey	3 PB Barristers, Bournemouth	01202 292102
	3 PB Barristers, Bristol	0117 928 1520
	3 PB Barristers, London	020 7583 8055
	3 PB Barristers, Oxford	01865 793 736
	3 PB Barristers, Winchester	01962 868884
Tyler Mr William John	36 Bedford Row, London	020 7421 8000
Van Der Leij Dr Martina	Field Court Chambers, London	020 7405 6114
Van Spall Ms Penelope-Jane	Chartlands Chambers, Northampton	01604 603322
Vavrecka Mr David Paul Frank	Coram Chambers, London	020 7092 3700
Vencatachellum Ms Glenda Roxande	Rowchester Chambers, Birmingham	0121 233 2327
Verdan Mr Alexander	4 Paper Buildings, London	020 7427 5200
Villarosa Miss Annunziata	Clerksroom (London), London	0845 083 3000
	Clerksroom (Taunton), Taunton	0845 083 3000
Vollenweider Mr Amiot Marcus Ellerton	Thomas More Chambers, London	020 7404 7000
Wade Miss Rebecca Lucy	Northampton Chambers, Northampton	01604 636271
Wagstaff Mr Andrew Martin Nicholas	Westgate Chambers, Lewes	01273 480510
Walden-Smith Mr David Edward	29 Bedford Row Chambers, London	020 7404 1044
Waley Mr Eric Richard Thomas	Assize Court Chambers, Bristol	0117 926 4587
Walji Miss Shabnam	Regency Chambers, Cambridge	01223 301517
	Regency Chambers, Peterborough	01733 315215
Wall Mr Christopher James Lynton	Becket Chambers, Canterbury	01227 786331
Ward Miss Kelly Jane	Pallant Chambers, Chichester	01243 784538
Ward Mr Martin Stuart	14 Gray's Inn Square, London	020 7242 0858
Wastall Mr Andrew James Frederick	Park Court Chambers, Leeds	0113 243 3277
Watkins Miss Rachel Claire	Chartlands Chambers, Northampton	01604 603322
Watson Mr Duncan Allen	Westgate Chambers, Lewes	01273 480510
Watson Ms Claire	East Anglian Chambers, Chelmsford	01473 214481
	East Anglian Chambers, Ipswich	01473 214481
	East Anglian Chambers, Norwich	01473 214481
Webster Miss Sarah Mary	Staple Inn Chambers, London	020 7242 5240
Welch Mr David William	Alexander Chambers, London	0845 652 0451/0854 652 0451
	Warwick House Chambers, London	020 7430 2323
Welch Mr Robert William	Unity Street Chambers, Bristol	0117 906 9789
Wheaton Mr Ian Malcolm James	Eighteen Carlton Crescent, Southampton	023 8063 9001
Whitehouse Mr Stuart Colin	Goldsmith Chambers, London	020 7353 6802
Whyatt Mr Michael George	15 Winckley Square, Preston	01772 252828
Widdison-Thom Mrs Stacey Jane	Kingsley Chambers, Barkingside	07891 441 445
Wilkinson Mr Francis John	Field Court Chambers, London	020 7405 6114
Wilkinson Ms Tiffany Jodie	Trinity Chambers, Chelmsford	01245 605040
Williams Miss Anna	Trinity Chambers, Chelmsford	01245 605040
Williams Miss June Cleo	No 8 Chambers, Birmingham	0121 236 5514
Williams Miss Micaila Teresa	Optimus Chambers, Braintree	01376 691 885/07736 283873
Wills Miss Alexandra Itari	Christ Church Chambers, London	020 7409 5278/07788 512787
Wills-Goldingham Miss Claire Louise Margaret	Albion Chambers, Bristol	0117 927 2144
Wilson Mr Gerald Simon John	Tanfield Chambers, London	020 7421 5300
Wilson Ms Charmaine Kimberley	Westgate Chambers, Lewes	01273 480510
Wingert Miss Rachel Thomas	Renaissance Chambers, London	020 7404 1111
Winslett Mr Frank	Westgate Chambers, Lewes	01273 480510
Wood Miss Joanna Rachel	1 Pump Court, London	020 7842 7070
Wood Miss Katherine Anne	Trinity Chambers, Middlesbrough	01642 247569
	Trinity Chambers, Newcastle Upon Tyne	0191 232 1927

Wood Ms Katie Anne	4 Paper Buildings, London	020 7427 5200
Wright Mrs Yasmin Tajdin	Cobden House Chambers, Manchester	0161 833 6000
Wrottesley Miss Angela Jane	Bank House Chambers, Sheffield	0114 275 1223
Wynne Mr Ashley John	No5 Chambers, Birmingham	0845 210 5555
	No5 Chambers, Bristol	0845 210 5555
	No5 Chambers, London	0845 210 5555
Yeung Mr Stuart Roy	Northampton Chambers, Northampton	01604 636271

FAMILY PROVISION

Abasheikh Mr Omar Said Imam	Paragon Chambers, London	020 3318 9988
Adamson Miss Lilias Louisa	Becket Chambers, Canterbury	01227 786331
Adler Mr Jonathan	1 Pump Court, London	020 7842 7070
Afzal Mr Fayyaz	No5 Chambers, Birmingham	0845 210 5555
	No5 Chambers, Bristol	0845 210 5555
	No5 Chambers, London	0845 210 5555
Ailes Mr John Ashley	Eighteen Carlton Crescent, Southampton	023 8063 9001
Ajaz Mr Mohammad Arshad	Eastmans Chambers, Reading	0118 966 9094
Akman Miss Mercy Louise	36 Bedford Row, London	020 7421 8000
Allen Mr Douglas Stephen	Harcourt Chambers, London	0844 561 7135
Allman Miss Marisa Nichole	Zenith Chambers, Leeds	0113 245 5438
Alloway Mr Tor Hugh	Talloway Chambers, London	020 7419 5047
Allwood Mrs Gina Louisa	Seven Bedford Row, London	020 7242 3555
Anderson Mr Nicholas Guy	1 KBW Chambers, London	020 7936 1500
	King's Bench Chambers, Lewes	01273 402600
Argent Mr Gavin Richard	Westgate Chambers, Lewes	01273 480510
Arshad Miss Raffia	St Mary's Family Law Chambers, Nottingham	0115 950 3503
Asprey Mr Nicholas	Clock Chambers, Wolverhampton	01902 313444
	Serle Court, London	020 7242 6105
Atkinson Mr Jody Roy	St John's Chambers, Bristol	0117 923 4700
Bagchi Mr Andrew Kumar	1 Garden Court Family Law Chambers, London	020 7797 7900
Bailey Mr Charles Andrew Stuart	Trinity Chambers, Chelmsford	01245 605040
Baker Mr Nicholas Michael Bridgman	Hardwicke, London	020 7242 2523
Balchin Mr Richard Alexander	New Court, London	020 7583 5123
Ballard Ms Appa	Cornwall Street Chambers, Birmingham	0121 233 7500
Banks Miss Rachael Eda	Atlantic Chambers, Liverpool	0151 236 4421
Banks Mr Francis Andrew	Atlantic Chambers, Liverpool	0151 236 4421
Barnes Mr Luke Clive	3 Dr Johnson's Buildings, London	020 7353 4854
Barratt Mr Dominic Anthony	East Anglian Chambers, Chelmsford	01473 214481
	East Anglian Chambers, Colchester	01473 214481
	East Anglian Chambers, Ipswich	01473 214481
	East Anglian Chambers, Norwich	01473 214481
Barrett Mr Robert Scott	2 Pump Court, London	020 7353 5597
Bassiri-Dezfouli Miss Sorour	Temple Court Chambers, London	020 7353 7888
Batey Mr David Michael	Stour Chambers, Canterbury	01227 764899
Beaumont Mr Marc Clifford	9 Stone Buildings, London	020 7404 5055
	Windsor Barristers' Chambers, Windsor	01753 839321
Becker Mr Timothy George Christie	Chambers of Mr Timothy Becker, Liverpool	0151 703 0319
	Clerksroom (London), London	0845 083 3000
Beer Miss Emily Charlotte Lemay	3 Dr Johnson's Buildings, London	020 7353 4854
Bennett Miss Angela Michelle	3 Dr Johnson's Buildings, London	020 7353 4854
Bhutta Miss Ayeesha Clare	Field Court Chambers, London	020 7405 6114
Bishop Mr Malcolm Leslie	Argent Chambers, London	020 7556 5500
	Equity Chambers, Birmingham	0121 236 5007
	30 Park Place, Cardiff	029 2039 8421
Bleasdale Miss Marie-Claire	Radcliffe Chambers, London	020 7831 0081
Bojarski Mr Andrzej Leonard	36 Bedford Row, London	020 7421 8000
Boyd Miss Kerstin Margaret	Tanfield Chambers, London	020 7421 5300

Bragiel Mr Edward Bronislaw Henryk	Hogarth Chambers, London	020 7404 0404
Bray Miss Helen Lorna	Walnut House, Exeter	01392 279751
Brereton Miss Joy	4 Paper Buildings, London	020 7427 5200
Brown Miss Stephanie Amanda	No5 Chambers, Birmingham	0845 210 5555
	No5 Chambers, Bristol	0845 210 5555
	No5 Chambers, London	0845 210 5555
Bryden Mr Christopher James Yuen Kang	4 King's Bench Walk, London	020 7822 7000
Buck Mr John	Tanfield Chambers, London	020 7421 5300
Buckhaven Mr Simon	Hardwicke, London	020 7242 2523
Buckle Mr Jonathan	Regency Chambers, Cambridge	01223 301517
	Regency Chambers, Peterborough	01733 315215
Buckley Mr Peter Evered	Cobden House Chambers, Manchester	0161 833 6000
Bullock Mrs Sally	New Court, London	020 7583 5123
Burdon Mr Michael Stewart	37 Park Square Chambers, Leeds	0113 243 9422
Buswell Mr Richard Thomas	Hardwicke, London	020 7242 2523
Butler Miss Judith Jane Scott	29 Bedford Row Chambers, London	020 7404 1044
Butters Mr Richard John	37 Park Square Chambers, Leeds	0113 243 9422
Buttimore Mr Gabriel	13 KBW, Oxford	01865 311066
	13 King's Bench Walk, London	020 7353 7204
Cabeza Miss Ruth Roberta Elizabeth	Field Court Chambers, London	020 7405 6114
Cade-Davies Miss Lynsey Nicola	29 Bedford Row Chambers, London	020 7404 1044
Calhaem Mr Simon Malcolm	29 Bedford Row Chambers, London	020 7404 1044
Campbell Mr Stafford Graham	Westgate Chambers, Lewes	01273 480510
Capon Mr Philip Christopher William	East Anglian Chambers, Chelmsford	01473 214481
	East Anglian Chambers, Ipswich	01473 214481
	East Anglian Chambers, Norwich	01473 214481
	St Philips Chambers, Birmingham	0121 246 7000
Carr Mr Adrian James Selden	Tanfield Chambers, London	020 7421 5300
Carr Mr Christopher Sean	36 Bedford Row, London	020 7421 8000
Carron Mr Richard Byron	Queen Square Chambers, Bristol	0117 921 1966
Carter Miss Holly Eugenie Sophia	3 Dr Johnson's Buildings, London	020 7353 4854
Cayford Mr Philip John Berkeley	29 Bedford Row Chambers, London	020 7404 1044
Chadwick Miss Joanna Ceridwen	No5 Chambers, Birmingham	0845 210 5555
	No5 Chambers, Bristol	0845 210 5555
	No5 Chambers, London	0845 210 5555
Chapman Mr Nicholas John	29 Bedford Row Chambers, London	020 7404 1044
Chatterjee Miss Adreeja Julia	No5 Chambers, Birmingham	0845 210 5555
	No5 Chambers, Bristol	0845 210 5555
	No5 Chambers, London	0845 210 5555
Chaudhry Miss Sabuhi Ashfaq	Coram Chambers, London	020 7092 3700
Cherrett Mr Darryl Joseph	Carmelite Chambers, London	020 7936 6300
Chippeck Mr Stephen	5 King's Bench Walk, London	020 7353 5638
Chippendale Miss Emma Lorraine	37 Park Square Chambers, Leeds	0113 243 9422
Christie Mr Richard Hamish	2 Pump Court, London	020 7353 5597
Clark Mr Andrew Richard	9 St John Street, Manchester	0161 955 9000
Clark Mr Dingle	Goldsmith Chambers, London	020 7353 6802
Clarke Mrs Amanda Lesley	Westgate Chambers, Lewes	01273 480510
Clegg Mr Adam Gordon	Stour Chambers, Canterbury	01227 764899
Clifford Miss Victoria Louise	No5 Chambers, Birmingham	0845 210 5555
	No5 Chambers, Bristol	0845 210 5555
	No5 Chambers, London	0845 210 5555
Cohen Mr Jonathan Lionel	4 Paper Buildings, London	020 7427 5200
Colbey Mr Richard	Guildhall Chambers Portsmouth, Portsmouth	023 9275 2400
	Lamb Chambers, London	020 7797 8300
Conlon Mr Michael John Patrick	Harcourt Chambers, Milton Keynes	0845 123 1234
Connolly Mrs Barbara Winifred	Seven Bedford Row, London	020 7242 3555
Conrath Mr Philip Bernard	Tanfield Chambers, London	020 7421 5300
Cook Miss Alison Noele	St Philips Chambers, Birmingham	0121 246 7000
Cotterill Miss Suzannah	Field Court Chambers, London	020 7405 6114
Counsell Mr Edward Frederick	Unity Street Chambers, Bristol	0117 906 9789
Cox Ms Sita	Stour Chambers, Canterbury	01227 764899
Crossley Ms Joanne	St Paul's Chambers, Leeds	0113 245 5866

Da Costa-Waldman Mrs Elissa Josephine	Clerksroom (London), London	0845 083 3000
	Clerksroom (Taunton), Taunton	0845 083 3000
	King's Lynn Chambers, King's Lynn	01553 672 085
Dale Miss Lucy-Ann Georgia	4 Brick Court, London	020 7832 3200
Daly Mr David	Heathway Chambers, London	020 8293 0509
Daniels Mr David William	Rowchester Chambers, Birmingham	0121 233 2327
Davies Miss Carol Elizabeth	College Chambers, Southampton	023 8023 0338
Davies Miss Lindsay Jane	Fenners Chambers, Cambridge	01223 368761
Davies Miss Sarah Jeannette	1 Pump Court, London	020 7842 7070
Davies Mr Max James	30 Park Place, Cardiff	029 2039 8421
Davies Ms Samantha Teresa	Chambers of Ms Samantha Davies, Milton Keynes	0845 123 1234
	Warwick House Chambers, London	020 7430 2323
De Jehan Mr David	Park Lane Plowden, Leeds	0113 228 5049
De Zonie Miss Jane	14 Gray's Inn Square, London	020 7242 0858
Dean Mrs Christine Jacqueline	1 Pump Court, London	020 7842 7070
Deegan Mr Lawrence Jeffrey	Fenners Chambers, Cambridge	01223 368761
Degun Mr Jasvir Singh	One Essex Court, London	020 7936 3030
Devereux-Cooke Mr Richard Charles	13 Old Square Chambers, London	020 7831 4445
Dhaliwal Miss Davinder Kaur	No 8 Chambers, Birmingham	0121 236 5514
Dickinson Mr John Finch Heneage	St John's Chambers, Bristol	0117 923 4700
Dipré Mr Paul Nicholas Amadeus	Chambers of Mr P N Dipré, Address withheld	0845 123 1234
	MK Family Law Chambers, Milton Keynes	0845 123 1234
Dove Mr James Francis	The Chambers of Grahame Aldous QC, London	020 7832 0500
Dowell Mr Gregory Hamilton	Principal Chambers, Sevenoaks	0845 209 8080
Dunlop Mr Hamish Michael	3 PB Barristers, Bournemouth	01202 292102
	3 PB Barristers, Bristol	0117 928 1520
	3 PB Barristers, London	020 7583 8055
	3 PB Barristers, Oxford	01865 793 736
	3 PB Barristers, Winchester	01962 868884
Edington Mrs Fiona Anne Rider	Thomas More Chambers, London	020 7404 7000
Egleton Mr Richard Wildman	Pallant Chambers, Chichester	01243 784538
Elliott Mr Colin Douglas	King's Bench and Godolphin (KBG)Chambers, Plymouth	01752 221551
Elliott Mr Edward Anthony John	Garden Court Chambers, London	020 7993 7600
Ephraim-Adejumo Mrs Hilda Ekpo	12 Old Square Chambers, London	020 7404 0875
Fairbank Mr Nicholas James	4 Paper Buildings, London	020 7427 5200
Fama Mrs Gudrun Hildegard	Middle Temple Lane Chambers, London	020 7583 4352
Fawcett Mr Neil	St Ive's Chambers, Birmingham	0121 236 0863
Fender Mr Carl David	Regency Chambers, Cambridge	01223 301517
	Regency Chambers, Peterborough	01733 315215
Ferguson Mrs Katharine Ann	Fenners Chambers, Cambridge	01223 368761
Ferm Mr Rodney Eric	Broadway House Chambers, Bradford	01274 722560
	Broadway House Chambers, Leeds	0113 246 2600
Flattery Ms Amanda Nichole	Kenworthy's Chambers, Manchester	0161 832 4036
Fletcher Mr Christopher Michael	Octagon House, Norwich	01603 623186
Flood Mr Edward Albert	1 Garden Court Family Law Chambers, London	020 7797 7900
Fordham Mrs Margaret Allison	Principal Chambers, Sevenoaks	0845 209 8080
Francis Mr Nicholas	29 Bedford Row Chambers, London	020 7404 1044
Francis Mr Richard Maurice	9 Park Place, Cardiff	029 2038 2731
Geadah Mr Anthony Edward	29 Bedford Row Chambers, London	020 7404 1044
George Mr Michael David Roberts	St Philips Chambers, Birmingham	0121 246 7000
George Mr Nicholas Frank Raymond	New Walk Chambers, Leicester	0871 200 1298/0116 255 9144
German Miss Kelly Anne	Eastbourne Chambers, Eastbourne	01323 642102
Gilbertson Mrs Helen Alison	Octagon House, Norwich	01603 623186
Gillan Mrs Dominique Lye-Ping	Guildford Chambers, Guildford	01483 539131
Gillman Miss Rachel Mary	1 Garden Court Family Law Chambers, London	020 7797 7900

Glaser Mr Michael Samson	14 Gray's Inn Square, London	020 7242 0858
Glover Mr Stephen Julian	37 Park Square Chambers, Leeds	0113 243 9422
Gold Mr Richard David	St John's Chambers, Bristol	0117 923 4700
Goldstein Mr Wayne Nathan	18 St John Street, Manchester	0161 278 1800
Goodall Miss Rachael Jane	3 PB Barristers, Bournemouth	01202 292102
	3 PB Barristers, Bristol	0117 928 1520
	3 PB Barristers, London	020 7583 8055
	3 PB Barristers, Oxford	01865 793 736
	3 PB Barristers, Winchester	01962 868884
Gooderham Miss Elizabeth Ann	Northampton Chambers, Northampton	01604 636271
Gordon Mr Jeremy	Chambers of Mr Ami Feder, London	020 7797 7788
	Chambers of Mr Ami Feder, London	020 7797 7788
	Lamb Building, Brighton	01273 820490
Gore Mr Andrew Julian Mark	37 Park Square Chambers, Leeds	0113 243 9422
Gore Ms Sally Elizabeth	14 Gray's Inn Square, London	020 7242 0858
Grant-Garwood Mr Joshua Dahren	1 Pump Court, London	020 7842 7070
Gray Mr Justin Henry Walford	Trinity Chambers, Middlesbrough	01642 247569
	Trinity Chambers, Newcastle Upon Tyne	0191 232 1927
Gray Mr Roger Anderson	5 Pump Court, London	020 7353 2532
Green Miss Victoria Louise	1 KBW Chambers, London	020 7936 1500
	King's Bench Chambers, Lewes	01273 402600
Greenan Miss Sarah Octavia	Zenith Chambers, Leeds	0113 245 5438
Greenfield Mr Peter Charles	King's Bench Chambers, Bournemouth	01202 250025
Gregory Ms Ann Marie	St Paul's Chambers, Leeds	0113 245 5866
Grey Ms Sharon Monica	Octagon House, Norwich	01603 623186
Grundy Ms Clare	St Johns Buildings, Manchester	0161 214 1500
	St Johns Buildings Liverpool, Liverpool	0151 243 6000
	16 Winckley Square, Preston	01772 256100
Guy Mr Richard Perran	Chambers of Mr Ami Feder, London	020 7797 7788
	King's Bench and Godolphin (KBG)Chambers, Plymouth	01752 221551
	Southernhay Chambers, Exeter	01392 255777
Hale Mr Charles Stanley	4 Paper Buildings, London	020 7427 5200
Hall Mr Jeremy John	Becket Chambers, Canterbury	01227 786331
Hall Mr Richard Andrew	Pump Court Chambers, London	020 7353 0711
	Pump Court Chambers, Swindon	01793 539899
	Pump Court Chambers, Winchester	01962 868 161
Hamilton Mr John Conrad	Field Court Chambers, London	020 7405 6114
Harrington Miss Tina Amanda	Trinity Chambers, Chelmsford	01245 605040
Harris Mr Wilbert Arthurlyn	Rowchester Chambers, Birmingham	0121 233 2327
Harrison Dr Graeme	12 College Place, Southampton	023 8032 0320
Hasan Miss Ayesha	3 Dr Johnson's Buildings, London	020 7353 4854
Hay Mr Malcolm John Marshall	3 Dr Johnson's Buildings, London	020 7353 4854
Heaton Miss Laura Jane	29 Bedford Row Chambers, London	020 7404 1044
Heppenstall Miss Claire Norah	1 Garden Court Family Law Chambers, London	020 7797 7900
Hillas Miss Samantha	Atlantic Chambers, Liverpool	0151 236 4421
Hillier Mr William	New Street Chambers, Leicester	0116 262 5906
Hine Mr Charles Roderick John	King's Bench Chambers, Bournemouth	01202 250025
Hobbs Ms Naomi Josephine	No 8 Chambers, Birmingham	0121 236 5514
Holbech Mr Charles Edward	New Square Chambers, London	020 7419 8000
Holland Mr William	1 Gray's Inn Square, London	020 7405 0001
Hollow Mr Paul John	Fenners Chambers, Cambridge	01223 368761
Holt Mrs Jane Rosemary	KCH Garden Square, Nottingham	0115 941 8851
Hookway Mr Richard Aelred	Zenith Chambers, Leeds	0113 245 5438
Horne-Roberts Mrs Jennifer	Goldsmith Chambers, London	020 7353 6802
Horton Mr Michael John Edward	Coram Chambers, London	020 7092 3700
Howard Miss Amanda Jayne	Atlantic Chambers, Liverpool	0151 236 4421
	37 Park Square Chambers, Leeds	0113 243 9422
Howling Mr Rex Andrew	4 Paper Buildings, London	020 7427 5200
Hudd Miss Anne Marguerita Jane	29 Bedford Row Chambers, London	020 7404 1044
Hudson Mr John Edward Gerard	Zenith Chambers, Leeds	0113 245 5438

Barrister	Chambers	Telephone
Hughes-Deane Ms Charlotte Barbara	Atlantic Chambers, Liverpool	0151 236 4421
Hunt Mr Stephen	4 Stone Buildings, London	020 7242 5524
Hussain Mr Muhammad Altaf	Chambers of Mr M A Hussain, London	020 8679 2398
Hussein Mr Timur	1 Pump Court, London	020 7842 7070
Jacques Mr Gareth Edward	Regency Chambers, Peterborough	01733 315215
Jagutpal Mr Previn Sing	4 Brick Court, London	020 7832 3200
Jarman Mr Mark Christopher	4 Paper Buildings, London	020 7427 5200
Jenkins Mr David Crofton	2 King's Bench Walk, London	020 7353 1746
Johnstone Mr Mark Anthony	4 Paper Buildings, London	020 7427 5200
Jones Mr Christopher David Harries	St John's Chambers, Bristol	0117 923 4700
Jones Mr Rhys Charles Mansel	14 Gray's Inn Square, London	020 7242 0858
Joseph Mr Sellappah Job	Chambers of Mr S J Joseph, London	020 8809 3083/020 8802 9889
Joshi Mr Pramod Kumar	One Essex Court, London	020 7936 3030
Josty Mr David Stephen	College Chambers, Southampton	023 8023 0338
Jowett Mr Timothy David Christian	9 Park Place, Cardiff	029 2038 2731
Kabweru-Namulemu Miss Karen Hasasha	KCH Garden Square, Nottingham	0115 941 8851
Kelly Mr Geoffrey Robert	Pump Court Chambers, London	020 7353 0711
	Pump Court Chambers, Swindon	01793 539899
	Pump Court Chambers, Winchester	01962 868 161
Kelly Mr Sean	Chancery House Chambers, Leeds	0113 244 6691
Kerr Mr Neil Forsyth	3 Dr Johnson's Buildings, London	020 7353 4854
Ker-Reid Mr John	Pump Court Chambers, London	020 7353 0711
	Pump Court Chambers, Swindon	01793 539899
	Pump Court Chambers, Winchester	01962 868 161
Khalid Mr James	Goulds Green Chambers, Uxbridge	01895 422574
	Goulds Green Chambers, Uxbridge	01895 422574
Khan Dr Alexander	Coral House, Manchester	
Khan Mr Abdul Aleem	Gray's Chambers, Newbury	020 8518 2525
Khan Mr Shaukat Ali	Chambers of Mr S A Khan, Kingston Upon Thames	020 8541 3875
Kidd Mr Peter William	Number 7 Harrington Street Chambers, Liverpool	0151 242 0707
Kilvington Miss Sarah Elizabeth	18 St John Street, Manchester	0161 278 1800
King Mr Charles Granville	Chambers of Mr C G King, Stroud	07949 461717
Kirby Miss Ruth Mary Anthony	4 Paper Buildings, London	020 7427 5200
Kramer Mr Philip Anthony	Park Lane Plowden, Newcastle Upon Tyne	0191 211 4087
Lamb Mr Edward Charles	The Chambers of Grahame Aldous QC, London	020 7832 0500
Lane Mr Simon Charles	Rougemont Chambers, Exeter	01392 208484
Lawrence Miss Pamela Avril	Nexus Chambers, London	020 7404 1147/020 7831 8309
Le Fort Mr Michael Cameron Raoul	King's Bench Chambers, Bournemouth	01202 250025
Learmonth Mr Alexander Robert Magnus	New Square Chambers, London	020 7419 8000
Lee Miss Taryn Jane	37 Park Square Chambers, Leeds	0113 243 9422
Leslie Miss Marie Rita	Albion Chambers, Bristol	0117 927 2144
Lewis Mr Stuart John	New Walk Chambers, Leicester	0871 200 1298/0116 255 9144
Limbrey Mr Bernard Martin	3 Dr Johnson's Buildings, London	020 7353 4854
Littlewood Miss Rebecca Mae	1 Pump Court, London	020 7842 7070
Loeb Miss Dinah Yolande	Westgate Chambers, Lewes	01273 480510
Lonsdale Miss Marion Mary	Academy Chambers, London	020 8455 2503
Lopez Mr Paul Anthony	St Ive's Chambers, Birmingham	0121 236 0863
Lorenzo Ms Claudia	Pump Court Chambers, London	020 7353 0711
	Pump Court Chambers, Swindon	01793 539899
	Pump Court Chambers, Winchester	01962 868 161
Love Miss Sharon Ann	Garden Court Chambers, London	020 7993 7600
Lyon Mr Gavin	Northampton Chambers, Northampton	01604 636271
Lyons Miss Tara Yasmin	Pump Court Chambers, London	020 7353 0711
	Pump Court Chambers, Winchester	01962 868 161
	Riverview Chambers, London	0844 225 3999

C

MacKenzie Miss Julie Fiona	Pump Court Chambers, London	020 7353 0711
	Pump Court Chambers, Swindon	01793 539899
	Pump Court Chambers, Winchester	01962 868 161
MacLynn Miss Claire Louise	4 Brick Court, London	020 7832 3200
Maddison Mr David Thomas James	Cobden House Chambers, Manchester	0161 833 6000
Magee Miss Rosein Moira	Pallant Chambers, Chichester	01243 784538
Mahmood Mr Abid	Central Chambers, Manchester	0161 236 1133
	No5 Chambers, Birmingham	0845 210 5555
	No5 Chambers, Bristol	0845 210 5555
	No5 Chambers, London	0845 210 5555
Marks Miss Gillian	14 Gray's Inn Square, London	020 7242 0858
Marley Miss Sarah Anne	Coram Chambers, London	020 7092 3700
Marsden Mr Andrew Guy	East Anglian Chambers, Chelmsford	01473 214481
	East Anglian Chambers, Colchester	01473 214481
	East Anglian Chambers, Ipswich	01473 214481
	East Anglian Chambers, Norwich	01473 214481
Marshall Mr Derek Stanley	College Chambers, Southampton	023 8023 0338
Martignetti Mr Ian	Regency Chambers, Cambridge	01223 301517
	Regency Chambers, Peterborough	01733 315215
Martin Mrs Dianne Joan Abegail	St John's Chambers, Bristol	0117 923 4700
Mashembo Mrs Carol	St John's Chambers, Bristol	0117 923 4700
Mather Miss Kate	1 Garden Court Family Law Chambers, London	020 7797 7900
Mather Mr Brian Howard	Trinity Chambers, Middlesbrough	01642 247569
	Trinity Chambers, Newcastle Upon Tyne	0191 232 1927
Maton Mr Neil Foster	Pallant Chambers, Chichester	01243 784538
Matthias Mr David Huw	Francis Taylor Building, London	020 7353 8415
Maynard Mr Matthew David	St Ive's Chambers, Birmingham	0121 236 0863
McCabe Miss Louise Anne	St Philips Chambers, Birmingham	0121 246 7000
McCann Miss Katie	Atlantic Chambers, Liverpool	0151 236 4421
McCormack Mr Alan	Staple Inn Chambers, London	020 7242 5240
McCrae Miss Fiona	Trinity Chambers, Middlesbrough	01642 247569
	Trinity Chambers, Newcastle Upon Tyne	0191 232 1927
McDonnell Mr John Beresford William	13 Old Square Chambers, London	020 7831 4445
McGhee Mr Stuart Edward	College Chambers, Southampton	023 8023 0338
McMullan Ms Laura Christina	Coram Chambers, London	020 7092 3700
Meachin Miss Vanessa Veronica	St Philips Chambers, Birmingham	0121 246 7000
Meares Mr Nigel Leslie Vellacott	11 Stone Buildings, London	020 7831 6381
Mehta Miss Anita Roxane	Crown Office Row Chambers, Brighton	01273 625625
Meichen Mr Jonathan Brian	St Philips Chambers, Birmingham	0121 246 7000
Melville-Shreeve Mr Michael David	Walnut House, Exeter	01392 279751
Miller Miss Catherine	East Anglian Chambers, Chelmsford	01473 214481
	East Anglian Chambers, Ipswich	01473 214481
	East Anglian Chambers, Norwich	01473 214481
Miller Mr Christopher Albert	14 Gray's Inn Square, London	020 7242 0858
Miller Mr Ian Robertson	Broadway House Chambers, Bradford	01274 722560
	Broadway House Chambers, Leeds	0113 246 2600
Mills Miss Barbara	4 Paper Buildings, London	020 7427 5200
Milne Mrs Arlene Joan	Cobden House Chambers, Manchester	0161 833 6000
Mitchell Mr David John	No5 Chambers, Birmingham	0845 210 5555
	No5 Chambers, Bristol	0845 210 5555
	No5 Chambers, London	0845 210 5555
Mitropoulos Mr Christos	5 Pump Court, London	020 7353 2532
Modgill Mr Alexander Jeffrey	Broadway House Chambers, Bradford	01274 722560
	Broadway House Chambers, Leeds	0113 246 2600
Moore Mr Jonathan Guy	Cathedral Chambers, Cardiff	02920 660129
	Cathedral Chambers, Newport	01633 215112
Moore Mrs Therese Finola	4 Brick Court, London	020 7832 3200
Morris Miss Brenda Alison	14 Gray's Inn Square, London	020 7242 0858
Morris Ms Christina Gaye	Coram Chambers, London	020 7092 3700
Mullen Miss Jayne Alison	St Ive's Chambers, Birmingham	0121 236 0863

Name	Chambers	Telephone
Mullen Mr Mark Robert	Radcliffe Chambers, London	020 7831 0081
Murkin Mrs Sandria	Becket Chambers, Canterbury	01227 786331
Murray Miss Judith Rowena	4 Paper Buildings, London	020 7427 5200
Newman Mrs Veronica	Chambers of Mrs V Newman, Cardiff	029 2048 8797
Newport Mr Ian Alun	College Chambers, Southampton	023 8023 0338
Newsom Mr George Lucien	Guildhall Chambers, Bristol	0117 930 9000
Nichols Mr Stuart Richard	1 Garden Court Family Law Chambers, London	020 7797 7900
Nickless Mr Jason Alan	College Chambers, Southampton	023 8023 0338
Noble Mr Philip Robert	Thomas More Chambers, London	020 7404 7000
Norman Mr Michael Charles	3 PB Barristers, Bournemouth	01202 292102
	3 PB Barristers, Bristol	0117 928 1520
	3 PB Barristers, London	020 7583 8055
	3 PB Barristers, Oxford	01865 793 736
	3 PB Barristers, Winchester	01962 868884
Norton Mr Andrew David	1 Garden Court Family Law Chambers, London	020 7797 7900
Nosworthy Mr Jonathan Alex	St Philips Chambers, Birmingham	0121 246 7000
Obuka Ms Obijuo Agwu	Chambers of Miss O A Obuka, London	020 7936 4474
O'Donovan Mr Ronan Daniel James	14 Gray's Inn Square, London	020 7242 0858
Okine Miss Julie Anne	Goldsmith Chambers, London	020 7353 6802
Okoye Miss Joy Nwamala	Chambers of Joy Okoye, London	07976 426871/020 7405 7011
Oldham Mrs Frances Mary Theresa	36 Bedford Row, London	020 7421 8000
	37 Park Square Chambers, Leeds	0113 243 9422
O'Leary Ms Michele Ann	1 Pump Court, London	020 7842 7070
Ong Miss Grace Yu Mae	Argent Chambers, London	020 7556 5500
Osborne Mr James Robert	Clerksroom (London), London	0845 083 3000
O'Sullivan Mr Bernard Anthony	Henderson Chambers, London	020 7583 9020
O'Toole Mr Bartholomew Vincent	5 King's Bench Walk, London	020 7353 5638
Parnell Mrs Cherie Eileen	East Anglian Chambers, Colchester	01473 214481
	East Anglian Chambers, Ipswich	01473 214481
	East Anglian Chambers, Norwich	01473 214481
Peacock Miss Lisa Jayne	3 Dr Johnson's Buildings, London	020 7353 4854
Pearce Mr Robert Edgar	Radcliffe Chambers, London	020 7831 0081
Pearman Mr Lee Charles	4 Brick Court, London	020 7832 3200
Pears Mr Derrick Allan	Tanfield Chambers, London	020 7421 5300
Peat Mr Charlie Andrew	1 Pump Court, London	020 7842 7070
Peckham Ms Jane Louise	1 Crown Office Row, London	020 7797 7500
	Crown Office Row Chambers, Brighton	01273 625625
Pettitt Mr Robert	Northampton Chambers, Northampton	01604 636271
Pithers Mr Clive Robert	Fenners Chambers, Cambridge	01223 368761
Procter Mr Alfred George Haydn	1 Garden Court Family Law Chambers, London	020 7797 7900
Pye Miss Margaret Jayne	Zenith Chambers, Leeds	0113 245 5438
Quirke Mr Gerard Martin	Citadel Chambers, Birmingham	0121 233 8500
Rai Miss Puneet Kaur	Thomas More Chambers, London	020 7404 7000
Ratcliffe Miss Frances Anne	Radcliffe Chambers, London	020 7831 0081
Reed Mr Julian Winn	9 Park Place, Cardiff	029 2038 2731
Reed Ms Lucy Emma	St John's Chambers, Bristol	0117 923 4700
Rhodes Miss Amanda Louise	Unity Street Chambers, Bristol	0117 906 9789
Roberts Mr Huw Eifion	Linenhall Chambers, Chester	01244 348282
Roberts Mr James Mcclintock	1 KBW Chambers, London	020 7936 1500
	King's Bench Chambers, Lewes	01273 402600
Roberts Mr Michael Charles	Chambers of Michael Roberts, Henley-On-Thames	01844 355 655
Rosenblatt Mr Jeremy George	42 Bedford Row, London	020 7831 0222
Ross Mr Sidney David	11 Stone Buildings, London	020 7831 6381
Row Mr Charles Philip	Queen Square Chambers, Bristol	0117 921 1966
Rowe Miss Freya Emily Beatrice	Thomas More Chambers, London	020 7404 7000
Rowland Mr Robin Frank	No5 Chambers, Birmingham	0845 210 5555
	No5 Chambers, Bristol	0845 210 5555
	No5 Chambers, London	0845 210 5555
Rudd Miss Zoe Ann	College Chambers, Southampton	023 8023 0338

C

Name	Chambers	Telephone
Sagar Mr Leigh	New Square Chambers, London	020 7419 8000
Samuels Mr Leslie John	Pump Court Chambers, London	020 7353 0711
	Pump Court Chambers, Winchester	01962 868 161
	Riverview Chambers, London	0844 225 3999
Sapstead Miss Louise Anne	KCH Garden Square, Nottingham	0115 941 8851
Saunders Miss Zoe Alice	St John's Chambers, Bristol	0117 923 4700
Savvides Miss Maria	Northampton Chambers, Northampton	01604 636271
Saxton Miss Nicola Helen	St Paul's Chambers, Leeds	0113 245 5866
Scott Mr Stuart	1 Pump Court, London	020 7842 7070
Sefi Mr Benedict John	Harcourt Chambers, London	0844 561 7135
	Harcourt Chambers, Oxford	0844 561 7135
Self Mr Gary Peter	College Chambers, Southampton	023 8023 0338
	St David's Chambers, Swansea	01792 559924
Sellers Mr Graham	Atlantic Chambers, Liverpool	0151 236 4421
Sharp Mr David Ian	Tanfield Chambers, London	020 7421 5300
Shaw Mr Julian	St Johns Buildings, Chester	01244 323070
	St Johns Buildings, Manchester	0161 214 1500
	St Johns Buildings Liverpool, Liverpool	0151 243 6000
Shield Miss Deborah	42 Bedford Row, London	020 7831 0222
Short Ms Mandy Lisa	14 Gray's Inn Square, London	020 7242 0858
Shuman Miss Karen Ann Elizabeth	1 Chancery Lane, London	0845 634 6666
	No 8 Chambers, Birmingham	0121 236 5514
Shuttleworth Mr Timothy William	Tanfield Chambers, London	020 7421 5300
Sinclair Mr Graham Kelso	East Anglian Chambers, Colchester	01473 214481
	East Anglian Chambers, Ipswich	01473 214481
	East Anglian Chambers, Norwich	01473 214481
Singh-Hayer Mr Bansa	Deans Court Chambers, Manchester	0161 214 6000
	Deans Court Chambers, Preston	01772 565 600
Sleight Mr Nigel	Regency Chambers, Cambridge	01223 301517
	Regency Chambers, Peterborough	01733 315215
Small Mrs Arlene Annmarie	Clerksroom (London), London	0845 083 3000
	Clerksroom (Taunton), Taunton	0845 083 3000
	King's Lynn Chambers, King's Lynn	01553 672 085
Smith Mr Matthew Robert	Sovereign Chambers, Leeds	0113 245 1841
Smith Mr Robert Clive	1 Paper Buildings, London	020 7353 3728
	RCS Chambers, Stainton	01709 814 147
Smout Mr William Kingsley	Guildford Chambers, Guildford	01483 539131
Sofaer Miss Moira	Goldsmith Chambers, London	020 7353 6802
Sood Mrs Usha Rani	Trent Chambers, Nottingham	0115 941 9596
Spratt-Dawson Miss Josephine Margery	Trinity Chambers, Chelmsford	01245 605040
Stanley Mrs Gillian Frances	1 Garden Court Family Law Chambers, London	020 7797 7900
Starr Mrs Teresa Margaret	Great James Street Chambers, London	020 7440 4949
Stenhouse Mr John Alexander	Nightingale Chambers, Wolverley	01562 851350
Sterling Mr Robert Alan	St James's Chambers, Manchester	0161 834 7000
	Zenith Chambers, Leeds	0113 245 5438
Stevens Mrs Hazel Ann	East Anglian Chambers, Chelmsford	01473 214481
	East Anglian Chambers, Ipswich	01473 214481
	East Anglian Chambers, Norwich	01473 214481
Stewart Mr Nicholas John Cameron	Ely Place Chambers, London	020 7400 9600
Stirling Mr Christopher William	Field Court Chambers, London	020 7405 6114
Stringer Mr Leon Peter	15 Winckley Square, Preston	01772 252828
Styles Mr Clive Richard	Becket Chambers, Canterbury	01227 786331
Styles Mrs Kay Margaret	Harcourt Chambers, London	0844 561 7135
	Harcourt Chambers, Oxford	0844 561 7135
Sugar Mr Simon Gareth	1 Garden Court Family Law Chambers, London	020 7797 7900
Sutton Mr Clive Raymond	Chambers of Mr Clive Sutton, Bruerne	07973 386702
Swift Mr Jonathan Peter	29 Bedford Row Chambers, London	020 7404 1044
Symms Miss Kathryn Ann	Number 7 Harrington Street Chambers, Liverpool	0151 242 0707

C

Tambling Mr Richard	1 Garden Court Family Law Chambers, London	020 7797 7900
Tansey Miss Anouska	2-3 Hind Court Chambers, London	020 7822 2150
Targett-Parker Miss Leanne Susan	No. 3 Fleet Street Chambers, London	020 7936 4474
	The Chambers of Miss Leanne Targett-Parker, London	020 8674 6694
Taylor Miss Araba Arba Kurankyiwa	Fenners Chambers, Cambridge	01223 368761
Taylor Mr Rhys Steadman	30 Park Place, Cardiff	029 2039 8421
Taylor Mrs Susan	Trinity Chambers, Middlesbrough	01642 247569
	Trinity Chambers, Newcastle Upon Tyne	0191 232 1927
Taylor Mrs Yvonne Marie	Trinity Chambers, Middlesbrough	01642 247569
	Trinity Chambers, Newcastle Upon Tyne	0191 232 1927
Taylor Ms Mary-Jane	Coram Chambers, London	020 7092 3700
Terry Mr Robert Jeffrey	Kings Chambers, Birmingham	0845 034 3444
	Kings Chambers, Leeds	0845 034 3444
	Kings Chambers, Manchester	0845 034 3444
	Lamb Chambers, London	020 7797 8300
Thind Miss Anita	Regency Chambers, Cambridge	01223 301517
	Regency Chambers, Peterborough	01733 315215
Thomas Miss Jacqueline Louise	37 Park Square Chambers, Leeds	0113 243 9422
Thomas Mrs Felicity	Westgate Chambers, Lewes	01273 480510
Thornton Mr John Robert	Stour Chambers, Canterbury	01227 764899
Toch Miss Joanna Patricia	Chambers of Miss J P Toch, Tonbridge	01892 833 005
	Chambers of Mr Ami Feder, London	020 7797 7788
	Chambers of Mr Ami Feder, London	020 7797 7788
Tregidgo Mr Marc Gordon	4 King's Bench Walk, London	020 7822 7000
Tucker Mr James William Richard	Teucro Chambers, Epsom	
Turnbull Mrs Linda Angela	1 Gray's Inn Square, London	020 7405 0001
Twist Mr Stephen John	Dere Street Barristers, Newcastle Upon Tyne	0844 3351551
Tyler Mr Thomas Geoffrey	3 PB Barristers, Bournemouth	01202 292102
	3 PB Barristers, Bristol	0117 928 1520
	3 PB Barristers, London	020 7583 8055
	3 PB Barristers, Oxford	01865 793 736
	3 PB Barristers, Winchester	01962 868884
Tyler Mr William John	36 Bedford Row, London	020 7421 8000
Van Spall Ms Penelope-Jane	Chartlands Chambers, Northampton	01604 603322
Vane The Hon Christopher John Fletcher	Trinity Chambers, Middlesbrough	01642 247569
	Trinity Chambers, Newcastle Upon Tyne	0191 232 1927
Vernon Mr Elliot Curt	No. 3 Fleet Street Chambers, London	020 7936 4474
Villarosa Miss Annunziata	Clerksroom (London), London	0845 083 3000
	Clerksroom (Taunton), Taunton	0845 083 3000
Vollenweider Mr Amiot Marcus Ellerton	Thomas More Chambers, London	020 7404 7000
Wade Miss Rebecca Lucy	Northampton Chambers, Northampton	01604 636271
Walden-Smith Mr David Edward	29 Bedford Row Chambers, London	020 7404 1044
Wales Mr Matthew James	Guildhall Chambers, Bristol	0117 930 9000
Wall Mr Christopher James Lynton	Becket Chambers, Canterbury	01227 786331
Warner Mr David Alexander	St Philips Chambers, Birmingham	0121 246 7000
Watkins Miss Rachel Claire	Chartlands Chambers, Northampton	01604 603322
Watson Mr Duncan Allen	Westgate Chambers, Lewes	01273 480510
Whitehouse Mr Stuart Colin	Goldsmith Chambers, London	020 7353 6802
Whyatt Mr Michael George	15 Winckley Square, Preston	01772 252828
Wilkinson Ms Tiffany Jodie	Trinity Chambers, Chelmsford	01245 605040
Wilson Mr Gerald Simon John	Tanfield Chambers, London	020 7421 5300

Wynne Mr Ashley John	No5 Chambers, Birmingham	0845 210 5555
	No5 Chambers, Bristol	0845 210 5555
	No5 Chambers, London	0845 210 5555

FILM, CABLE & TV

Abrahams Mr James	8 New Square, London	020 7405 4321
Akinsanya Mr Stephen Olubunmi	Old Bailey Chambers, London	020 3008 6404
Algazy Mr Jacques Max	Cloisters, London	020 7827 4000
Andrews Mr Paul Leslie	Great James Street Chambers, London	020 7440 4949
Bate Mr Stephen Robert De Breteuil	5RB, London	020 7242 2902
Beloff Mr Rupert Joseph Alexei	No5 Chambers, Birmingham	0845 210 5555
	No5 Chambers, Bristol	0845 210 5555
	No5 Chambers, London	0845 210 5555
Bowhill Miss Jessie Kate	8 New Square, London	020 7405 4321
Bragiel Mr Edward Bronislaw Henryk	Hogarth Chambers, London	020 7404 0404
Bullock Mr Robert Gustaf	The Chambers of Mr Bullock, Brighton	01273 321050
Caplan Mr Jonathan Michael	Five Paper Buildings, London	020 7583 6117
	Riverview Chambers, London	0844 225 3999
Christie Mr Iain Robert	5RB, London	020 7242 2902
Coulter Mr Barry John	Clerksroom (London), London	0845 083 3000
	Clerksroom (Taunton), Taunton	0845 083 3000
	King's Lynn Chambers, King's Lynn	01553 672 085
De Mounteney Mr Jonathan Patrick	Chambers of Mr J P De Mounteney, Reading	0118 934 6822
Dillon Mr Thomas William Matthew	Chambers of Thomas Dillon, London	020 7692 2722
Drummond Mr Bruce Jonathon Hutcheon	Cornwall Street Chambers, Birmingham	0121 233 7500
	Palmyra Chambers, Warrington	01925 444919
Edwards Mr Jonathan William	Westgate Chambers, Lewes	01273 480510
Edwards Mr Nigel Royston	St Paul's Chambers, Leeds	0113 245 5866
Engelman Mr Mark Trevor	Hardwicke, London	020 7242 2523
Engelman Mr Philip	Cloisters, London	020 7827 4000
	Trinity Chambers, Middlesbrough	01642 247569
	Trinity Chambers, Newcastle Upon Tyne	0191 232 1927
Fern Mr Gary	7 Stones IP, London	020 7193 4033
Fitzgerald Mr John Vincent	Ingenuity IP Chambers, Petts Wood	
Gerasimidis Mr Nicolas	Guildhall Chambers, Bristol	0117 930 9000
Heal Mrs Madeleine	New Square Chambers, London	020 7419 8000
Higginson Mr Timothy Nicholas Bennett	Littleton Chambers, London	020 7797 8600
	St John's Chambers, Bristol	0117 923 4700
Iyer Miss Shobana	Swan Chambers, Richmond	0845 123 1234
Johnson Mr Phillip Michael	Chambers of Mr P Johnson, London	020 7288 2256
Jones Mr Kelvin Mcallister	Templis Chambers, London	020 7649 9808
Kime Mr Matthew Jonathan	Cobden House Chambers, Manchester	0161 833 6000
	Ingenuity IP Chambers, Petts Wood	
	No. 3 Fleet Street Chambers, London	020 7936 4474
Lamb Mr Jeffrey Thomas	Westgate Chambers, Lewes	01273 480510
Lane Ms Lindsay Ruth Busfield	8 New Square, London	020 7405 4321
Lenaghan Mr Anthony	Dyers Chambers, London	020 7404 1881
Lewis Mr Wayne Anthony	Access Lawyers, London	020 8801 2345
Mahmood Mr Abid	Central Chambers, Manchester	0161 236 1133
	No5 Chambers, Birmingham	0845 210 5555
	No5 Chambers, Bristol	0845 210 5555
	No5 Chambers, London	0845 210 5555
Mather Mr Nicholas Ian Stewart	Furnival Chambers, London	020 7405 3232
Matthias Mr David Huw	Francis Taylor Building, London	020 7353 8415
Maxwell Lewis Mr Cameron	Lamb Chambers, London	020 7797 8300
Michalos Miss Christina Antigone Diana	5RB, London	020 7242 2902
Onslow Mr Robert Denzil	8 New Square, London	020 7405 4321
Osborne Mr James Robert	Clerksroom (London), London	0845 083 3000

Perry Miss Jacqueline Anne	2 Temple Gardens, London	020 7822 1200
Platts-Mills Mr Mark Fortescue	8 New Square, London	020 7405 4321
Reed Mr Jeremy Nigel	Hogarth Chambers, London	020 7404 0404
Rinker Mr Andrew Stuart D'Artois	Chambers of Mr Andrew Rinker, London	020 7584 1091
Rogers Miss Christy Abigail	Ingenuity IP Chambers, Petts Wood	
	No. 3 Fleet Street Chambers, London	020 7936 4474
Roughton Mr Ashley Wentworth	Hogarth Chambers, London	020 7404 0404
Shirley Mr James Patrick	Stone Chambers, London	020 7440 6900
Silverton Miss Catherine Anne	Sovereign Chambers, Leeds	0113 245 1841
Singarajah Mr Frederico	1 Gray's Inn Square, London	020 7405 0001
Stanford Mr Tony James	Old Bailey Chambers, London	020 3008 6404
Stebbings Mr Ian Anthony	1 Gray's Inn Square, London	020 7405 0001
Stevenson Mr Daniel Keith	9-12 Bell Yard, London	020 7400 1800
Storey Mr Richard Alexander	3 Temple Gardens, London	020 7353 3102
Tarbitt Mr Nicholas Edward Henry	Cornwall Street Chambers, Birmingham	0121 233 7500
Ward Mr Robin Henry	8 New Square, London	020 7405 4321

FINANCIAL SERVICES

Ajaz Mr Mohammad Arshad	Eastmans Chambers, Reading	0118 966 9094
Aliker Mr Phillip Bliss	Tanfield Chambers, London	020 7421 5300
Allerhand Mr Ludwik Edmund	Chambers of Mr Ludwik Allerhand, London	020 8291 4356
Antell Mr John Jason	King's Bench and Godolphin (KBG)Chambers, Plymouth	01752 221551
Ashley-Norman Mr Jonathan Charles	3 Raymond Buildings, London	020 7400 6400
Banham Mr Matthew Ian	Nine Bedford Row, London	020 7489 2727
Barnard Mr James Philip	11 Stone Buildings, London	020 7831 6381
Barnett Mr Jeremy Victor	2 Bedford Row, London	020 7440 8888
	St Paul's Chambers, Leeds	0113 245 5866
Beaumont Mr Benjamin	Chambers of Dr Michael Arnheim, London	020 7833 5093
	Middle Temple Lane Chambers, London	020 7583 4352
Beaumont Mr Marc Clifford	9 Stone Buildings, London	020 7404 5055
	Windsor Barristers' Chambers, Windsor	01753 839321
Bell Mr Thomas Capel	Hardwicke, London	020 7242 2523
Berriman Mr Trevor St John	43 Temple Row Chambers, Birmingham	0121 237 6035
Bishop Mr Malcolm Leslie	Argent Chambers, London	020 7556 5500
	Equity Chambers, Birmingham	0121 236 5007
	30 Park Place, Cardiff	029 2039 8421
Bowes Mr Michael Anthony	Cobden House Chambers, Manchester	0161 833 6000
	Outer Temple Chambers, London	020 7353 6381
Buchan Miss Caroline Venetia	Chambers of Miss C Buchan, Haywards Heath	01444 482222
Budworth Mr Martin James	Kings Chambers, Birmingham	0845 034 3444
	Kings Chambers, Leeds	0845 034 3444
	Kings Chambers, Manchester	0845 034 3444
Bullock Mr Robert Gustaf	The Chambers of Mr Bullock, Brighton	01273 321050
Buttimore Mr Gabriel	13 KBW, Oxford	01865 311066
	13 King's Bench Walk, London	020 7353 7204
Buxton Mr Thomas Justin	Charter Chambers, London	020 7618 4400
Carlisle Mr Timothy St John Ogilvie	Field Court Chambers, London	020 7405 6114
Chawla Mr Neil	No5 Chambers, Birmingham	0845 210 5555
	No5 Chambers, Bristol	0845 210 5555
	No5 Chambers, London	0845 210 5555
Chowdhary Mr Islamuddin	Cassian Chambers, Ilford	07796 262641
Clark Miss Geraldine	Serle Court, London	020 7242 6105
Clarke Mr Nicholas Patrick James	18 St John Street, Manchester	0161 278 1800

Cockings Mr Giles Francis Sacheveral	Furnival Chambers, London	020 7405 3232
Corsellis Mr Nicholas Robert Alexander	3 Temple Gardens, London	020 7353 3102
Dalby Mr Joseph Francis	4-5 Gray's Inn Square, London	020 7404 5252
Deacon Mr Robert Murray	11 Stone Buildings, London	020 7831 6381
Doran Mr Gerard Patrick	Lincoln House Chambers, Manchester	0161 832 5701
Du Toit Sc Mr Johan Ignatius	Selborne Chambers, London	020 7420 9500
	St Philips Chambers, Birmingham	0121 246 7000
Egan Mr Patrick Manus Dermot	Thomas More Chambers, London	020 7404 7000
Engelman Mr Philip	Cloisters, London	020 7827 4000
	Trinity Chambers, Middlesbrough	01642 247569
	Trinity Chambers, Newcastle Upon Tyne	0191 232 1927
Farrell Mr Simon Henry	3 Raymond Buildings, London	020 7400 6400
Fawcett Mr Neil	St Ive's Chambers, Birmingham	0121 236 0863
Ferry-Swainson Mr Richard Joseph	2 Bedford Row, London	020 7440 8888
Finucane Mr Brendan Godfrey Eamonn	Outer Temple Chambers, London	020 7353 6381
Freeman Miss Lisa Claire	Furnival Chambers, London	020 7405 3232
Gibbons Miss Mary Regina	Stone Chambers, London	020 7440 6900
Gledhill Mr Lee Andre	Alexander Chambers, London	0845 652 0451/0854 652 0451
	Trident Barristers Chambers, Manchester	0161 663 3123
Godfrey Mr Howard Anthony	2 Bedford Row, London	020 7440 8888
Godfrey Mr Lauren John	Crown Office Row Chambers, Brighton	01273 625625
Goodison Mr Adam Henry	South Square, London	020 7696 9900
Grant Mr David Ericson	Outer Temple Chambers, London	020 7353 6381
Guy Mr John David Colin	Tanfield Chambers, London	020 7421 5300
Hackett Mr Philip George	Argent Chambers, London	020 7556 5500
Hall Mr James Edward	Cornwall Street Chambers, Birmingham	0121 233 7500
Hamilton Mr Peter Bernard	4 Pump Court, London	020 7842 5555
Hanif Miss Saima Naz	4-5 Gray's Inn Square, London	020 7404 5252
Henderson Mr Neil John	Stone Chambers, London	020 7440 6900
Higginson Mr Timothy Nicholas Bennett	Littleton Chambers, London	020 7797 8600
	St John's Chambers, Bristol	0117 923 4700
Hill Mr Michael Gordon	Trinity Chambers, Middlesbrough	01642 247569
	Trinity Chambers, Newcastle Upon Tyne	0191 232 1927
Hood Mr David	Prince of Wales Chambers, London	020 7622 7415
Hood Mr Nigel Anthony	New Square Chambers, London	020 7419 8000
Hurst Mr Brian	39 Park Square, Leeds	0113 245 6633
Jayakrishnan Mr Harry Sisubalan	Trent Chambers, Nottingham	0115 941 9596
Joseph Dr Sandradee Theresa	13 Old Square Chambers, London	020 7831 4445
Keel Mr Douglas Vincent	11 Stone Buildings, London	020 7831 6381
Kelly Mr Sean	Chancery House Chambers, Leeds	0113 244 6691
Lavin Miss Mary Mandie Jane	196 Temple Chamber, London	020 7099 9257
Lawrence Sir Ivan John	5 Pump Court, London	020 7353 2532
Lenon Mr Andrew Ralph Fitzmaurice	One Essex Court, London	020 7583 2000
Leonard Mr James Alexander	Outer Temple Chambers, London	020 7353 6381
Lewiecki Miss Marie	Old Bailey Chambers, London	020 3008 6404
Lewis Mr Dominic	Five Paper Buildings, London	020 7583 6117
Lissack Mr Richard Anthony	Outer Temple Chambers, London	020 7353 6381
	Riverview Chambers, London	0844 225 3999
MacEvilly Mr Conn Jeremy	9 Stone Buildings, London	020 7404 5055
Maguire Mr Andrew James	Exchange Chambers, Liverpool	0151 236 7747
	Exchange Chambers, Manchester	0161 833 2722
	St Philips Chambers, Birmingham	0121 246 7000
Mansell Mr Jason Francis Guy	Seven Bedford Row, London	020 7242 3555
Marquand Mr Charles Nicholas Hilary	4 Stone Buildings, London	020 7242 5524
Mawrey Mr Richard Brooks	Henderson Chambers, London	020 7583 9020

Name	Chambers	Telephone
McDonnell Mr John Beresford William	13 Old Square Chambers, London	020 7831 4445
Medcroft Mr Nicholas Julian	Outer Temple Chambers, London	020 7353 6381
Meredith Mr Christopher William	Furnival Chambers, London	020 7405 3232
Milne Mr Richard James	23 Essex Street, London	020 7413 0353
Newbold Dr Anne Lorraine Elsie	Minerva Chambers, Ocean Village	00 350 20042779
Padfield Mr Nicholas David	Chambers of Nicholas Padfield QC, London	020 7351 1961
Parsons Mr Andrew James	Portsmouth Barristers'Chambers, Portsmouth	023 9283 1292
Peat Mr Richard Colin	13 Old Square Chambers, London	020 7831 4445
Picarda Mr Hubert Alistair Paul	Chambers of Mr Hubert Picarda QC, London	020 7242 3566
Pinto Miss Amanda Eve	Five Paper Buildings, London	020 7583 6117
Pugh Mr John Bishop	John Pugh's Chambers, Liverpool	0151 236 5415
Quirke Mr Gerard Martin	Citadel Chambers, Birmingham	0121 233 8500
Rana Mr Mohammed Akram	Clapham Law Chambers, London	020 7978 8482
Rees Prof William Michael	1 Gray's Inn Square, London	020 7405 0001
Reffin Miss Clare Alyson	One Essex Court, London	020 7583 2000
Rhodes Mr Robert Elliott	Outer Temple Chambers, London	020 7353 6381
	Principal Chambers, Sevenoaks	0845 209 8080
	St Philips Chambers, Birmingham	0121 246 7000
Richman Mrs Helene Pines	Eighteen Carlton Crescent, Southampton	023 8063 9001
	9 Stone Buildings, London	020 7404 5055
	Stour Chambers, Canterbury	01227 764899
Rinker Mr Andrew Stuart D'Artois	Chambers of Mr Andrew Rinker, London	020 7584 1091
Ritchie Mr Richard Bulkeley	XXIV Old Buildings, London	020 7691 2424
Rivalland Mr Marc-Edouard	1 Chancery Lane, London	0845 634 6666
Seeboruth Mr Royln Jean-Paul	Chambers of Royln Seeboruth, Aylesbury	01296 393329
Sheridan Mr Iain Douglas	London Scottish, Stratford Upon Avon	07971 681724
Simpson Mr David Joseph	196 Temple Chamber, London	020 7099 9257
Smith Mr Ian Alfio	11 Stone Buildings, London	020 7831 6381
Solley Mr Stephen Malcolm	Charter Chambers, London	020 7618 4400
Sowler Mr Thomas Richard Holland	The Tax Chambers of Mr Richard Sowler TD, Douglas	07624 235000
Spalton Mr George David John	Four New Square, London	020 7822 2000
Speaight Mr Anthony Hugh	4 Pump Court, London	020 7842 5555
Sterling Mr Robert Alan	St James's Chambers, Manchester	0161 834 7000
	Zenith Chambers, Leeds	0113 245 5438
Stewart Mr Nicholas John Cameron	Ely Place Chambers, London	020 7400 9600
Summers Mr Benjamin Dylan James	3 Raymond Buildings, London	020 7400 6400
Tabari Mr Ali-Reza	St Philips Chambers, Birmingham	0121 246 7000
Taylor Mr Simon	Chambers of Andrew Mitchell QC, London	020 7440 9950
Taylor Ms Karen Anne	Themis Chambers, London	07967 418976
Temmink Mr Robert-Jan	Quadrant Chambers, London	020 7583 4444
Todd Mr Michael Alan	Erskine Chambers, London	020 7242 5532
Treverton-Jones Mr Gregory Dennis	39 Essex Street, London	020 7832 1111
	82 King Street, Manchester	0161 870 9969
Trompeter Mr Nicholas Simeon	Selborne Chambers, London	020 7420 9500
Vineall Mr Nicholas Edward John	4 Pump Court, London	020 7842 5555
Von Pommern-Peglow Dr Michael Alfred Herman Pr.	Brunswick Chambers, London	020 7353 1987
Walker Mr Adam Nigel	Seven Bedford Row, London	020 7242 3555
Ward Miss Alexandra	9-12 Bell Yard, London	020 7400 1800
Waters Mr Malcolm Ian	Radcliffe Chambers, London	020 7831 0081
Watson Mr Benjamin Turquand	3 Raymond Buildings, London	020 7400 6400
Watson-Gandy Prof Mark	13 Old Square Chambers, London	020 7831 4445
Watthey Mr James Robertson	Hardwicke, London	020 7242 2523
Wheaton Mr Ian Malcolm James	Eighteen Carlton Crescent, Southampton	023 8063 9001

Wiktorowski-Solecki Miss Tamara	Middle Temple Lane Chambers, London	020 7583 4352
Wilkinson Mr Marc Ashley	No5 Chambers, Birmingham	0845 210 5555
	No5 Chambers, Bristol	0845 210 5555
	No5 Chambers, London	0845 210 5555
Williams Mr Mark John	Queen Square Chambers, Bristol	0117 921 1966
Willmer Mr Stephen James	Argent Chambers, London	020 7556 5500
Wills Miss Alexandra Itari	Christ Church Chambers, London	020 7409 5278/07788 512787
Wolman Mr Clive Richard	11 Stone Buildings, London	020 7831 6381

FOREIGN LAW

Abasheikh Mr Omar Said Imam	Paragon Chambers, London	020 3318 9988
Ajaz Mr Mohammad Arshad	Eastmans Chambers, Reading	0118 966 9094
Alexandra Miss Sebastiane	Holborn Chambers, London	020 7242 6060
Allwood Mrs Gina Louisa	Seven Bedford Row, London	020 7242 3555
Almihdar Mr Ali Hamed	Outer Temple Chambers, London	020 7353 6381
Artesi Miss Desiree Allison Ann	Thomas More Chambers, London	020 7404 7000
Azhar Mr Ali Mohammad	9 King's Bench Walk, London	020 7353 9564
Bezzam Miss Jayashree	Hampton Court Chambers, West Molesey	020 8979 0381
Cala Dr Guiseppe	New Court, London	020 7583 5123
Caldwell Mr Peter Hugh Coyles	Dyers Chambers, London	020 7404 1881
Coulter Mr Barry John	Clerksroom (London), London	0845 083 3000
	Clerksroom (Taunton), Taunton	0845 083 3000
	King's Lynn Chambers, King's Lynn	01553 672 085
Culmer Miss Gabrielle Fiona	2 King's Bench Walk, London	020 7353 1746
Davies Mr Henry Olusola	Trinity Chambers, Birmingham	0121 346 4672
Del Fabbro Mr Oscar	23 Essex Street, London	020 7413 0353
Devine Mr Michael Buxton	Rougemont Chambers, Exeter	01392 208484
Drummond Mr Bruce Jonathon Hutcheon	Cornwall Street Chambers, Birmingham	0121 233 7500
	Palmyra Chambers, Warrington	01925 444919
Edwards Mr Nigel Royston	St Paul's Chambers, Leeds	0113 245 5866
Fordham Mrs Margaret Allison	Principal Chambers, Sevenoaks	0845 209 8080
Forlin Mr Gerard Emlyn	Cornerstone Barristers, London	020 7242 4986
Gayan Mr Anil Kumarsingh	Clapham Law Chambers, London	020 7978 8482
Gersch Mr Adam Nissen	Argent Chambers, London	020 7556 5500
Godwin Mr William George Henry	3 Hare Court, London	020 7415 7800
	St John's Chambers, Bristol	0117 923 4700
Hall Mr Nicholas	Westgate Chambers, Lewes	01273 480510
Harris Mr Paul	Doughty Street Chambers, Bristol	01179 058 717
	Doughty Street Chambers, London	020 7404 1313
	Doughty Street Chambers, Manchester	0161 618 1066
Heal Mrs Madeleine	New Square Chambers, London	020 7419 8000
Hewson Ms Barbara Mary	Hardwicke, London	020 7242 2523
Hilton Ms Saisampan	Holborn Chambers, London	020 7242 6060
Hossain Mr Ajmalul	Selborne Chambers, London	020 7420 9500
	St Philips Chambers, Birmingham	0121 246 7000
Iqbal Mr Mashood	London View Chambers, Sawbridgeworth	07788 912493
Jafar Mr Abdurahman Akhtar	Chambers of Mr Abdurahman Jafar, Ilford	07828 937338
Kelly Mr Matthias John	39 Essex Street, London	020 7832 1111
Khan Mr Abdul Aleem	Gray's Chambers, Newbury	020 8518 2525
Kwiatkowski Mr Feliks Jerzy	Kew Chambers, Kew	0844 8099991
Lewiecki Miss Marie	Old Bailey Chambers, London	020 3008 6404
MacEvilly Mr Conn Jeremy	9 Stone Buildings, London	020 7404 5055
Mahmood Mr Abid	Central Chambers, Manchester	0161 236 1133
	No5 Chambers, Birmingham	0845 210 5555
	No5 Chambers, Bristol	0845 210 5555
	No5 Chambers, London	0845 210 5555
McKinney Miss Nicola Alexandra	4 KBW, London	020 7822 8822
McLinden Mr John Vincent Barry	Field Court Chambers, London	020 7405 6114

C

Metzger Mr Kevin Albert	11 Gray's Inn Square Chambers, London	020 7405 6879
Miah Mr Anawar Babul	Great James Street Chambers, London	020 7440 4949
Moll Mr Christiaan Eric	Blackfriars Chambers, London	020 7353 7400
Mustakim Mr Abdul Yunus Al	Chambers of Mr Mustakim, London	
Mylvaganam Ms Tanoo	1 Gray's Inn Square, London	020 7405 0001
Nsugbe Mr Oba Eric	Pump Court Chambers, London	020 7353 0711
	Pump Court Chambers, Swindon	01793 539899
	Pump Court Chambers, Winchester	01962 868 161
O'Connor Mr Patrick Michael Joseph	Doughty Street Chambers, Bristol	01179 058 717
	Doughty Street Chambers, London	020 7404 1313
	Doughty Street Chambers, Manchester	0161 618 1066
Ogunbusola Mr Victor Olaniyi	Chambers of Victor Ogumbusola, Basildon	07413 634231
Okoye Miss Joy Nwamala	Chambers of Joy Okoye, London	07976 426871/020 7405 7011
O'Sullivan Mr Richard John	1215 Chambers, London	020 3291 1215
Qureshi Mr Asif Hasan	Quadrant Chambers, London	020 7583 4444
Rana Mr Mohammed Akram	Clapham Law Chambers, London	020 7978 8482
Reeds Mr Gareth David	Canary Wharf Chambers, London	020 7183 8011
Richman Mrs Helene Pines	Eighteen Carlton Crescent, Southampton	023 8063 9001
	9 Stone Buildings, London	020 7404 5055
	Stour Chambers, Canterbury	01227 764899
Rinker Mr Andrew Stuart D'Artois	Chambers of Mr Andrew Rinker, London	020 7584 1091
Rosemarine Mr Andrew Marc	Chambers of Mr A M Rosemarine, Manchester	0161 740 3861
Rosenblatt Mr Jeremy George	42 Bedford Row, London	020 7831 0222
Saini Mr Parminder Paul Singh	12 Old Square Chambers, London	020 7404 0875
Shirley Mr James Patrick	Stone Chambers, London	020 7440 6900
Sood Mrs Usha Rani	Trent Chambers, Nottingham	0115 941 9596
Sparrow Mrs Marie-Claire	Holborn Chambers, London	020 7242 6060
Stanzel Mrs Sarah Astrid	Tanfield Chambers, London	020 7421 5300
Stevens Mr Stuart Standish	Holborn Chambers, London	020 7242 6060
Stuart Mr Bruce Ian	Lombard Chambers, London	020 7107 2100
Taylor Mr Simon	Chambers of Andrew Mitchell QC, London	020 7440 9950
Thomson Mr Martin Haldane Ahmad	Wynne Chambers, London	020 3239 6964
Twydell Miss Cherry Louisa	Trinity Chambers, Chelmsford	01245 605040
Ume Mr Cyril Obiora	12 Old Square Chambers, London	020 7404 0875
Von Pommern-Peglow Dr Michael Alfred Herman Pr.	Brunswick Chambers, London	020 7353 1987
Watson Mr Benjamin Turquand	3 Raymond Buildings, London	020 7400 6400
Watson Mr Ian David	3 Stone Buildings, London	020 7242 4937
Wills Miss Alexandra Itari	Christ Church Chambers, London	020 7409 5278/07788 512787

FRANCHISING

Abrahams Mr James	8 New Square, London	020 7405 4321
Beaumont Mr Marc Clifford	9 Stone Buildings, London	020 7404 5055
	Windsor Barristers' Chambers, Windsor	01753 839321
Berkley Mr Michael Stuart	Rougemont Chambers, Exeter	01392 208484
Blackwood Mr Clive David	Lamb Chambers, London	020 7797 8300
Bowhill Miss Jessie Kate	8 New Square, London	020 7405 4321
Boyd Mr Stephen James Harvey	Selborne Chambers, London	020 7420 9500
Bredemear Mr Zachary Charles	1 Chancery Lane, London	0845 634 6666
Budworth Mr Martin James	Kings Chambers, Birmingham	0845 034 3444
	Kings Chambers, Leeds	0845 034 3444
	Kings Chambers, Manchester	0845 034 3444
Coulter Mr Barry John	Clerksroom (London), London	0845 083 3000
	Clerksroom (Taunton), Taunton	0845 083 3000
	King's Lynn Chambers, King's Lynn	01553 672 085
Cunningham Mr Graham Taylor	Hardwicke, London	020 7242 2523

C

Davies Mr James Edwin	3 PB Barristers, Bournemouth	01202 292102
	3 PB Barristers, Bristol	0117 928 1520
	3 PB Barristers, London	020 7583 8055
	3 PB Barristers, Oxford	01865 793 736
	3 PB Barristers, Winchester	01962 868884
di Mambro Mr David Jesse Andrew	Pallant Chambers, Chichester	01243 784538
	Radcliffe Chambers, London	020 7831 0081
Engelman Mr Mark Trevor	Hardwicke, London	020 7242 2523
Fern Mr Gary	7 Stones IP, London	020 7193 4033
Garvie Mr Carl Peter	St Philips Chambers, Birmingham	0121 246 7000
Godfrey Mr Lauren John	Crown Office Row Chambers, Brighton	01273 625625
Goodman Mr Andrew David	1 Chancery Lane, London	0845 634 6666
Hamer Mr George Clemens	8 New Square, London	020 7405 4321
Hill Mr Jonathan	8 New Square, London	020 7405 4321
Hussain Mr Muhammad Altaf	Chambers of Mr M A Hussain, London	020 8679 2398
Lane Ms Lindsay Ruth Busfield	8 New Square, London	020 7405 4321
Marshall Mr Derek Stanley	College Chambers, Southampton	023 8023 0338
McCarthy Mr William	Bridgewater Chambers, Manchester	0161 3877127
	1 Mitre Court Buildings, London	020 7452 8900
Nath Mr Rakesh	Strand Chambers, London	020 7117 6920
Onslow Mr Robert Denzil	8 New Square, London	020 7405 4321
Panton Mr Alastair Howard	10 King's Bench Walk, London	020 7353 7742
Purves Mr Gavin Bowman	Swan House, London	020 8998 3035
Rosenblatt Mr Jeremy George	42 Bedford Row, London	020 7831 0222
Staddon Mr Paul	Tanfield Chambers, London	020 7421 5300
Stevens-Hoare Miss Michelle	Hardwicke, London	020 7242 2523
Tritton Mr Robert Guy Henton	Hogarth Chambers, London	020 7404 0404
Warner Mr David Alexander	St Philips Chambers, Birmingham	0121 246 7000

HEALTH & SAFETY

Abu-Mustafa Mr Jehad	1 Paper Buildings, London	020 7353 3728
Alam Ms Jan	Ropewalk Chambers, Nottingham	0115 947 2581
Allwood Mrs Gina Louisa	Seven Bedford Row, London	020 7242 3555
Andrews Mr Paul Leslie	Great James Street Chambers, London	020 7440 4949
Ashley-Norman Mr Jonathan Charles	3 Raymond Buildings, London	020 7400 6400
Askey Mr Robert John	Palmyra Chambers, Warrington	01925 444919
Bagley Miss Louisa Ellen	1 Paper Buildings, London	020 7353 3728
Baird Mr James Stevenson	Bank House Chambers, Sheffield	0114 275 1223
Bajwa Mr Ali Naseem	Garden Court Chambers, London	020 7993 7600
Berriman Mr Trevor St John	43 Temple Row Chambers, Birmingham	0121 237 6035
Birch Mr Roger Allen	Five St Andrew's Hill, London	020 7332 5400
	Sovereign Chambers, Leeds	0113 245 1841
Birkby Mr Richard Adam	Park Court Chambers, Leeds	0113 243 3277
Blair Mr Peter Michael	Guildhall Chambers, Bristol	0117 930 9000
	6 King's Bench Walk, London	020 7583 0410
Bond Mr Richard Ian Winsor	Citadel Chambers, Birmingham	0121 233 8500
Bourne Mr Ian Maclean	Charter Chambers, London	020 7618 4400
Bourne-Arton Mr Simon Nicholas	Park Court Chambers, Leeds	0113 243 3277
Bowers Mr Rupert John	Doughty Street Chambers, London	020 7404 1313
Bowes Mr Michael Anthony	Cobden House Chambers, Manchester	0161 833 6000
	Outer Temple Chambers, London	020 7353 6381
Brady Mr Scott	3 Temple Gardens, London	020 7353 3102
Breen-Lawton Miss Denise	St Paul's Chambers, Leeds	0113 245 5866
Bridge Mr Giles	Broadway House Chambers, Bradford	01274 722560
	Broadway House Chambers, Leeds	0113 246 2600
Brown Mr Roger Charles Arthur	Kenworthy's Chambers, Manchester	0161 832 4036
Brunner Ms Catherine Jane	Albion Chambers, Bristol	0117 927 2144
	36 Bedford Row, London	020 7421 8000
Bryan Mr Robert John	1 Paper Buildings, London	020 7353 3728
Bryden Mr Christopher James Yuen Kang	4 King's Bench Walk, London	020 7822 7000

Buchan Miss Caroline Venetia	Chambers of Miss C Buchan, Haywards Heath	01444 482222
Buchanan Mr James Ian Charles	2 Hare Court, London	020 7353 3982
Buckle Mr Jonathan	Regency Chambers, Cambridge	01223 301517
	Regency Chambers, Peterborough	01733 315215
Byrne Mr Garrett Thomas	4-5 Gray's Inn Square, London	020 7404 5252
Callery Mr Martin	Cobden House Chambers, Manchester	0161 833 6000
Campbell Mr Oliver Edward Wilhelm	Henderson Chambers, London	020 7583 9020
Canby Miss Fiona Jane	Temple Garden Chambers, London	020 7583 1315
Caplan Mr Jonathan Michael	Five Paper Buildings, London	020 7583 6117
	Riverview Chambers, London	0844 225 3999
Carrasco Mr Glenn Lawrence	9-12 Bell Yard, London	020 7400 1800
Carter Miss Nathalie Veronique	1 Gray's Inn Square, London	020 7405 0001
Cartwright Mr Ivan Matthew	KCH Garden Square, Nottingham	0115 941 8851
Cassidy Mr Patrick Stephen	Kenworthy's Chambers, Manchester	0161 832 4036
Cattermull Miss Emma Jayne	East Anglian Chambers, Chelmsford	01473 214481
	East Anglian Chambers, Ipswich	01473 214481
	East Anglian Chambers, Norwich	01473 214481
Chalk Mr Alexander John Gervase	6 King's Bench Walk, London	020 7583 0410
Chawla Mr Mukul	9-12 Bell Yard, London	020 7400 1800
Chawla Mr Neil	No5 Chambers, Birmingham	0845 210 5555
	No5 Chambers, Bristol	0845 210 5555
	No5 Chambers, London	0845 210 5555
Clarke Mr Jamie Roy	Hardwicke, London	020 7242 2523
Clegg Mr William	2 Bedford Row, London	020 7440 8888
Climie Mr Roger Stephen	King's Bench and Godolphin (KBG)Chambers, Plymouth	01752 221551
	Outer Temple Chambers, London	020 7353 6381
Compton Mr Benjamin Edward Welstead	Outer Temple Chambers, London	020 7353 6381
Conlon Mr Michael John Patrick	Harcourt Chambers, Milton Keynes	0845 123 1234
Cooper Mr John Michael	Crown Office Chambers, London	020 7797 8100
Coster Mr Ronald David	42 Bedford Row, London	020 7831 0222
Coulter Mr Barry John	Clerksroom (London), London	0845 083 3000
	Clerksroom (Taunton), Taunton	0845 083 3000
	King's Lynn Chambers, King's Lynn	01553 672 085
Cox Mr Jonathan Edward	KCH Garden Square, Nottingham	0115 941 8851
Darbishire Mr Adrian Munro	QEB Hollis Whiteman, London	020 7933 8855
Del Fabbro Mr Oscar	23 Essex Street, London	020 7413 0353
Dempsey Miss Karen Marie	3 Temple Gardens, London	020 7353 3102
Denney Mr Stuart Henry Macdonald	Deans Court Chambers, Manchester	0161 214 6000
	Deans Court Chambers, Preston	01772 565 600
	Thomas More Chambers, London	020 7404 7000
Dennis Mr Mark Jonathan	6 King's Bench Walk, London	020 7583 0410
Dixey Mr Ian Roger	Guildhall Chambers, Bristol	0117 930 9000
Donne Mr Jeremy Nigel	QEB Hollis Whiteman, London	020 7933 8855
Doran Mr Gerard Patrick	Lincoln House Chambers, Manchester	0161 832 5701
Dos Santos Mr Alexander	Charter Chambers, London	020 7618 4400
Douglass Mr Paul Stephen	9 King's Bench Walk, London	020 7353 9564
Dowell Mr Gregory Hamilton	Principal Chambers, Sevenoaks	0845 209 8080
Duffy Mr Derek James	St Paul's Chambers, Leeds	0113 245 5866
Eastwood Miss Philippa Clemency Anne	Doughty Street Chambers, London	020 7404 1313
Edwards Mr Jonathan William	Westgate Chambers, Lewes	01273 480510
Edwards Mr Nigel Royston	St Paul's Chambers, Leeds	0113 245 5866
Enoch Mr Dafydd Huw	Apex, Cardiff	02920 232 032
	23 Essex Street, London	020 7413 0353
Ferry-Swainson Mr Richard Joseph	2 Bedford Row, London	020 7440 8888
Fetto Mr Niazi Peter	2 Temple Gardens, London	020 7822 1200
Finlay Mr Darren	Sovereign Chambers, Leeds	0113 245 1841
Finucane Mr Brendan Godfrey Eamonn	Outer Temple Chambers, London	020 7353 6381

Name	Chambers	Telephone
Fish Mr David Thomas	Deans Court Chambers, Manchester	0161 214 6000
	Deans Court Chambers, Preston	01772 565 600
	Goldsmith Chambers, London	020 7353 6802
Fisher Mr Jervis Andrew	Citadel Chambers, Birmingham	0121 233 8500
Fitzgibbon Mr Neil Kevin	Carmelite Chambers, London	020 7936 6300
Follon Mr Daniel Richard Thomas	1 Gray's Inn Square, London	020 7405 0001
Forlin Mr Gerard Emlyn	Cornerstone Barristers, London	020 7242 4986
Frame Mr Stuart James	Staple Inn Chambers, London	020 7242 5240
Fryer Mr Nigel Mccrae	Queen Square Chambers, Bristol	0117 921 1966
Fuller Mr Alan Peter	Albion Chambers, Bristol	0117 927 2144
Gadd Mr Adam Brian	Pump Court Chambers, London	020 7353 0711
	Pump Court Chambers, Winchester	01962 868 161
	Riverview Chambers, London	0844 225 3999
Gair Mr Christopher	King's Bench Chambers, Bournemouth	01202 250025
Ganesan Mr Muthupandi Peter	Furnival Chambers, London	020 7405 3232
Garlick Mr Paul Richard	Furnival Chambers, London	020 7405 3232
German Miss Kelly Anne	Eastbourne Chambers, Eastbourne	01323 642102
Gerry Miss Felicity Ruth	36 Bedford Row, London	020 7421 8000
Gilchrist Miss Naomi Roberta	St Philips Chambers, Birmingham	0121 246 7000
Gladwell Mr Simon Mark	East Anglian Chambers, Ipswich	01473 214481
Gledhill Mr Lee Andre	Alexander Chambers, London	0845 652 0451/0854 652 0451
	Trident Barristers Chambers, Manchester	0161 663 3123
Glyn Mr Caspar Hilary Gordon	Cloisters, London	020 7827 4000
Gobir Mr Nuhu Garba	9 Park Place, Cardiff	029 2038 2731
Goddard Miss Suzanne Hazel	Lincoln House Chambers, Manchester	0161 832 5701
Godfrey Mr Lauren John	Crown Office Row Chambers, Brighton	01273 625625
Goldrein Mr Iain Saville	7 Bell Yard, London	020 7831 0636
	Number 7 Harrington Street Chambers, Liverpool	0151 242 0707
Goodfellow Mr Stephen John	East Anglian Chambers, Chelmsford	01473 214481
	East Anglian Chambers, Ipswich	01473 214481
	East Anglian Chambers, Norwich	01473 214481
Goose Mr Julian Nicholas	2 Hare Court, London	020 7353 3982
	Zenith Chambers, Leeds	0113 245 5438
Goudie Mr William Martin Phillip	Charter Chambers, London	020 7618 4400
Grant Mr Chudi Paul	Kenworthy's Chambers, Manchester	0161 832 4036
Green Mr Timothy Sinclair	St Philips Chambers, Birmingham	0121 246 7000
Griffiths Mr Peter	2 Bedford Row, London	020 7440 8888
	30 Park Place, Cardiff	029 2039 8421
Hackett Mr Philip George	Argent Chambers, London	020 7556 5500
Hadrill Mr Keith Paul	Furnival Chambers, London	020 7405 3232
Hall Mr Nicholas	Westgate Chambers, Lewes	01273 480510
Ham Mr Nicholas Treharne	Dyers Chambers, London	020 7404 1881
Hamilton Mr Nigel	Broadway House Chambers, Bradford	01274 722560
	Broadway House Chambers, Leeds	0113 246 2600
Hanlon Mr James Tobias	Old Bailey Chambers, London	020 3008 6404
Harris Mr James	Five St Andrew's Hill, London	020 7332 5400
Harrison Dr Graeme	12 College Place, Southampton	023 8032 0320
Harrison Mr John Foster	St Paul's Chambers, Leeds	0113 245 5866
Harrison Mr Peter John	6 Pump Court, London	020 7797 8400
	6 Pump Court Chambers, Maidstone	01622 688094
Harvey Mr Stephen Frank	18 Red Lion Court, London	020 7520 6000
	18 Red Lion Court (Annexe), Chelmsford	01245 280880
Hassall Mr Craig Jonathan	Sovereign Chambers, Leeds	0113 245 1841
Haukeland Mr Martin Jonathan	42 Bedford Row, London	020 7831 0222
Hegarty Mr Kevin John	St Philips Chambers, Birmingham	0121 246 7000
Henley Mr Andrew Michael	Furnival Chambers, London	020 7405 3232
Henson Miss Christine Ruth	Crown Office Row Chambers, Brighton	01273 625625
Higgins Mr Adrian John	13 KBW, Oxford	01865 311066
	13 King's Bench Walk, London	020 7353 7204

Hill Mr Michael Gordon	Trinity Chambers, Middlesbrough	01642 247569
	Trinity Chambers, Newcastle Upon Tyne	0191 232 1927
Hine Mr Charles Roderick John	King's Bench Chambers, Bournemouth	01202 250025
Hinton Mr Neil Pearse	King's Bench Chambers, Bournemouth	01202 250025
Hirst Miss Rebecca Elisabeth	Cobden House Chambers, Manchester	0161 833 6000
Hirst Mr Karl Douglas	No5 Chambers, Birmingham	0845 210 5555
	No5 Chambers, Bristol	0845 210 5555
	No5 Chambers, London	0845 210 5555
Hobson Miss Sally Anne	1 Paper Buildings, London	020 7353 3728
Hodgkiss Ms Suzanne Jane	43 Temple Row Chambers, Birmingham	0121 237 6035
Hood Mr David	Prince of Wales Chambers, London	020 7622 7415
Hussain Miss Frida Khanam	Furnival Chambers, London	020 7405 3232
Hutchinson Mr Colin Thomas	Garden Court Chambers, London	020 7993 7600
Inyundo Mr Richard Kwame Swaka	6 King's Bench Walk, London	020 7583 0410
Jackson Mr Andrew Fraser	5 Pump Court, London	020 7353 2532
Jackson Mr Mark Joseph	No 8 Chambers, Birmingham	0121 236 5514
Janner The Hon Daniel Joseph Mitchell	23 Essex Street, London	020 7413 0353
	Exchange Chambers, Manchester	0161 833 2722
	St Philips Chambers, Birmingham	0121 246 7000
Jarratt Miss Alice Cordelia Betchworth	Carmelite Chambers, London	020 7936 6300
Jenkins Mr Edward Nicholas	Five Paper Buildings, London	020 7583 6117
Jones Mr Alun	St Paul's Chambers, Leeds	0113 245 5866
Jowett Mr Timothy David Christian	9 Park Place, Cardiff	029 2038 2731
Keeling Mr Adrian Francis	No5 Chambers, Birmingham	0845 210 5555
	No5 Chambers, Bristol	0845 210 5555
	No5 Chambers, London	0845 210 5555
Keith Mr Benjamin Charles Andrew	Five St Andrew's Hill, London	020 7332 5400
Kelly Mr Richard Bernard	East Anglian Chambers, Chelmsford	01473 214481
	East Anglian Chambers, Colchester	01473 214481
	East Anglian Chambers, Ipswich	01473 214481
	East Anglian Chambers, Norwich	01473 214481
Kennedy Miss Lucy Julia	QEB Hollis Whiteman, London	020 7933 8855
Kessling Mr Christopher David	Chambers of Mr Christopher Kessling, Leicester	01509 890690
Khan Mr Forz	Chambers of Mr F Khan, London	07854 109584
	6 King's Bench Walk, London	020 7353 4931
Lane Mr Christopher Paul	No 8 Chambers, Birmingham	0121 236 5514
Larkin Mr Sean	QEB Hollis Whiteman, London	020 7933 8855
Le Fevre Miss Sarah Margaret	3 Raymond Buildings, London	020 7400 6400
Leonard Mr James Alexander	Outer Temple Chambers, London	020 7353 6381
Levett Miss Francesca Anna	Five St Andrew's Hill, London	020 7332 5400
Lewiecki Miss Marie	Old Bailey Chambers, London	020 3008 6404
Liddiard Mr Martin Thomas	No5 Chambers, Birmingham	0845 210 5555
	No5 Chambers, Bristol	0845 210 5555
	No5 Chambers, London	0845 210 5555
Linehan Mr Stephen John	St Philips Chambers, Birmingham	0121 246 7000
Lissack Mr Richard Anthony	Outer Temple Chambers, London	020 7353 6381
	Riverview Chambers, London	0844 225 3999
Lopez Mr Juan Nemesio	Francis Taylor Building, London	020 7353 8415
Lowe Mr Rupert William Manley	Guildhall Chambers, Bristol	0117 930 9000
Lule Miss Jacqueline	1 Mitre Court Buildings, London	020 7452 8900
Malone Mr David John	1 Gray's Inn Square, London	020 7405 0001
Mannion Mr John Dennis	Tolzey Chambers, Bristol	
Marcus Mr Peter	Zenith Chambers, Leeds	0113 245 5438
Marshall Mr Derek Stanley	College Chambers, Southampton	023 8023 0338
Matthias Mr David Huw	Francis Taylor Building, London	020 7353 8415
McCulloch Miss Fiona Catharine Jane	Middle Temple Lane Chambers, London	020 7583 4352

Barrister	Chambers	Telephone
McDonald Ms Melanie Sharon	No5 Chambers, Birmingham	0845 210 5555
	No5 Chambers, Bristol	0845 210 5555
	No5 Chambers, London	0845 210 5555
McLoughlin Mr Kevin	Temple Garden Chambers, London	020 7583 1315
McTague Miss Meghann Rose	2 Temple Gardens, London	020 7822 1200
Meeke Mr Robert Martin James	Colleton Chambers, Exeter	01392 274898
Melville-Shreeve Mr Michael David	Walnut House, Exeter	01392 279751
Mendelle Mr Paul Michael	25 Bedford Row, London	020 7067 1500
Midgley Miss Anna Victoria Jane	Albion Chambers, Bristol	0117 927 2144
Miller Mr Peter Owen Michael	Cornerstone Barristers, London	020 7242 4986
Mills Mr Kristian Anthony	Trinity Chambers, Middlesbrough	01642 247569
	Trinity Chambers, Newcastle Upon Tyne	0191 232 1927
Monaghan Ms Susan Mary	No5 Chambers, Birmingham	0845 210 5555
	No5 Chambers, Bristol	0845 210 5555
	No5 Chambers, London	0845 210 5555
Mooney Mr Stephen John	Albion Chambers, Bristol	0117 927 2144
Moran Mr Patrick Michael	15 New Bridge Street, London	020 7842 1900
Morris Ms Johanna	Chambers of Marion Smullen and Kerim Fuad QC, London	020 7427 4400
Mousley Mr William Howard	2 King's Bench Walk, London	020 7353 1746
Newman Mr Timothy John	No5 Chambers, Birmingham	0845 210 5555
	No5 Chambers, Bristol	0845 210 5555
	No5 Chambers, London	0845 210 5555
Norton Mr Giles	Enigma Chambers, Sheffield	07779 576499
	Holborn Chambers, London	020 7242 6060
Nuttall Mr Andrew Peter	Lincoln House Chambers, Manchester	0161 832 5701
Oakley Miss Louise Michelle	2 Bedford Row, London	020 7440 8888
O'Connor Mr Patrick Michael Joseph	Doughty Street Chambers, Bristol	01179 058 717
	Doughty Street Chambers, London	020 7404 1313
	Doughty Street Chambers, Manchester	0161 618 1066
Offer Mr Alexander	Garden Court Chambers, London	020 7993 7600
	Park Court Chambers, Leeds	0113 243 3277
O'Neill Mr Brian Patrick	2 Hare Court, London	020 7353 3982
Oommen Mr Jacob	Chambers of Mr Jacob Oommen, East Barnet	07958 680272
Osborne Mr James Robert	Clerksroom (London), London	0845 083 3000
Parker Mrs Karen Lesley	Guildhall Chambers Portsmouth, Portsmouth	023 9275 2400
Parry Mr Charles Robert	Pump Court Chambers, London	020 7353 0711
	Pump Court Chambers, Swindon	01793 539899
	Pump Court Chambers, Winchester	01962 868 161
Penny Miss Abigail Sarah Prudence	4 Breams Buildings, London	020 7092 1900
Perrins Mr Gregory Lloyd	1 Paper Buildings, London	020 7353 3728
Phillips Mr Simon Benjamin	Francis Taylor Building, London	020 7353 8415
	Park Court Chambers, Leeds	0113 243 3277
Pickering Mr Simon Toby	Wilberforce Chambers, Hull	01482 323264
Prior Mr Paul Stephen	36 Bedford Row, London	020 7421 8000
Puar Mr Mikhael	30 Park Place, Cardiff	029 2039 8421
Quirke Mr Gerard Martin	Citadel Chambers, Birmingham	0121 233 8500
Raggatt Mr Timothy Walter Harold	4 King's Bench Walk, London	020 7822 7000
	St Philips Chambers, Birmingham	0121 246 7000
Rhodes Mr Robert Elliott	Outer Temple Chambers, London	020 7353 6381
	Principal Chambers, Sevenoaks	0845 209 8080
	St Philips Chambers, Birmingham	0121 246 7000
Richardson Mr Garth Douglas Anthony	Devon Chambers, Plymouth	01752 661659
	Rougemont Chambers, Exeter	01392 208484
Ritchie Miss Shauna	2 Bedford Row, London	020 7440 8888
Ritchie Mr Andrew George	The Chambers of Grahame Aldous QC, London	020 7832 0500
Roberts Miss Lisa	Lincoln House Chambers, Manchester	0161 832 5701
Roberts Mr Richard Vaughan	Henderson Chambers, London	020 7583 9020

Name	Chambers	Telephone
Ruffell Mr Mark Beresford	Pump Court Chambers, London	020 7353 0711
	Pump Court Chambers, Swindon	01793 539899
	Pump Court Chambers, Winchester	01962 868 161
Rule Mr Philip David	Castle Chambers, Harrow-on-the-Hill	020 8423 6579
Rush Mr Craig Peter	2 Bedford Row, London	020 7440 8888
Russell Mr Graham Alexander	Citadel Chambers, Birmingham	0121 233 8500
Russell Mr Guy Jonothon	Westgate Chambers, Lewes	01273 480510
Salmon Mr Jonathan Carl	St Philips Chambers, Birmingham	0121 246 7000
Sekhon Mr Narinder Singh	Sovereign Chambers, Leeds	0113 245 1841
Sharma Miss Sunyana	3 PB Barristers, Bournemouth	01202 292102
	3 PB Barristers, London	020 7583 8055
Sharpe Mr Timothy James	Temple Garden Chambers, London	020 7583 1315
Silverton Miss Catherine Anne	Sovereign Chambers, Leeds	0113 245 1841
Skinner Mr Samuel Richard Edward	KCH Garden Square, Nottingham	0115 941 8851
Smith Miss Eileen Joan	Trinity Chambers, Middlesbrough	01642 247569
	Trinity Chambers, Newcastle Upon Tyne	0191 232 1927
Smith Mr Robert Ian	St Paul's Chambers, Leeds	0113 245 5866
Snow Mr Darren Mark	Charter Chambers, London	020 7618 4400
Spencer Mr Paul Anthony	3 Serjeants Inn, London	020 7427 5000
Stanford Mr Tony James	Old Bailey Chambers, London	020 3008 6404
Stead Mr Richard James	St John's Chambers, Bristol	0117 923 4700
Stebbings Mr Ian Anthony	1 Gray's Inn Square, London	020 7405 0001
Stein Mr Daniel Alexander	No5 Chambers, Birmingham	0845 210 5555
	No5 Chambers, Bristol	0845 210 5555
	No5 Chambers, London	0845 210 5555
Stemp Mr Scott	12 College Place, Southampton	023 8032 0320
Stephens Mr Michael Allen	Design Chambers, London	020 7353 0747
	St Ive's Chambers, Birmingham	0121 236 0863
Stevenson Mr Daniel Keith	9-12 Bell Yard, London	020 7400 1800
Stubbs Mr Andrew James	St Paul's Chambers, Leeds	0113 245 5866
Thomas Mr Andrew Martin	Lincoln House Chambers, Manchester	0161 832 5701
	Linenhall Chambers, Chester	01244 348282
Tomassi Mr Mark David	Charter Chambers, London	020 7618 4400
Treverton-Jones Mr Gregory Dennis	39 Essex Street, London	020 7832 1111
	82 King Street, Manchester	0161 870 9969
Udom Miss Nancy Ini	Five St Andrew's Hill, London	020 7332 5400
Upton Mr John Stewart	4 King's Bench Walk, London	020 7822 7000
Van Overdijk Miss Claire Orit	No5 Chambers, Birmingham	0845 210 5555
	No5 Chambers, Bristol	0845 210 5555
	No5 Chambers, London	0845 210 5555
Ward Miss Alexandra	9-12 Bell Yard, London	020 7400 1800
Watson Mr Benjamin Turquand	3 Raymond Buildings, London	020 7400 6400
Webster Mr Alistair Stevenson	Chambers of Andrew Mitchell QC, London	020 7440 9950
	Lincoln House Chambers, Manchester	0161 832 5701
Weekes Mr Mark Vincent	6 King's Bench Walk, London	020 7583 0410
Wells Mr Caspar John Mowlem	Goldsmith Chambers, London	020 7353 6802
Wheaton Mr Ian Malcolm James	Eighteen Carlton Crescent, Southampton	023 8063 9001
Whitehouse Mr Stuart Colin	Goldsmith Chambers, London	020 7353 6802
Wightwick Mr Iain	Riverview Chambers, London	0844 225 3999
	Unity Street Chambers, Bristol	0117 906 9789
Wilcox Mr Jerome Carl Jean	Alexander Chambers, London	0845 652 0451/0854 652 0451
Williams Mr Ben Dylan	Kings Chambers, Birmingham	0845 034 3444
	Kings Chambers, Leeds	0845 034 3444
	Kings Chambers, Manchester	0845 034 3444
Wraith Mr Nigel Patrick	Colleton Chambers, Exeter	01392 274898
Wrottesley Miss Angela Jane	Bank House Chambers, Sheffield	0114 275 1223

HEALTHCARE

Name	Chambers	Telephone
Alam Ms Jan	Ropewalk Chambers, Nottingham	0115 947 2581
Apthorp Mr George Charles	5 Essex Court, London	020 7410 2000
Auburn Mr Jonathan Walter	4-5 Gray's Inn Square, London	020 7404 5252

C

Barrister	Chambers	Telephone
Baldwin Dr Timothy John	Garden Court Chambers, London	020 7993 7600
Bowen Mr Nicholas James Hugh	Doughty Street Chambers, Bristol	01179 058 717
	Doughty Street Chambers, London	020 7404 1313
	Doughty Street Chambers, Manchester	0161 618 1066
Bowsher Mr Michael Frederick Thomas	Monckton Chambers, London	020 7405 7211
Butler Mr Simon David	The Chambers of Grahame Aldous QC, London	020 7832 0500
Del Fabbro Mr Oscar	23 Essex Street, London	020 7413 0353
Dempsey Miss Karen Marie	3 Temple Gardens, London	020 7353 3102
Dolan Dr Bridget Maura	3 Serjeants Inn, London	020 7427 5000
Duffy Mr Derek James	St Paul's Chambers, Leeds	0113 245 5866
Engelman Mr Philip	Cloisters, London	020 7827 4000
	Trinity Chambers, Middlesbrough	01642 247569
	Trinity Chambers, Newcastle Upon Tyne	0191 232 1927
Enoch Mr Dafydd Huw	Apex, Cardiff	02920 232 032
	23 Essex Street, London	020 7413 0353
Finucane Mr Brendan Godfrey Eamonn	Outer Temple Chambers, London	020 7353 6381
Foster Mr Charles Andrew	Outer Temple Chambers, London	020 7353 6381
Fullwood Mr Adam Garrett	Kings Chambers, Birmingham	0845 034 3444
	Kings Chambers, Leeds	0845 034 3444
	Kings Chambers, Manchester	0845 034 3444
Gledhill Mr Lee Andre	Alexander Chambers, London	0845 652 0451/0854 652 0451
	Trident Barristers Chambers, Manchester	0161 663 3123
Goldrein Mr Iain Saville	7 Bell Yard, London	020 7831 0636
	Number 7 Harrington Street Chambers, Liverpool	0151 242 0707
Guy Mr Richard Perran	Chambers of Mr Ami Feder, London	020 7797 7788
	King's Bench and Godolphin (KBG)Chambers, Plymouth	01752 221551
	Southernhay Chambers, Exeter	01392 255777
Harris Mr Wilbert Arthurlyn	Rowchester Chambers, Birmingham	0121 233 2327
Islam-Choudhury Mr Mugni	No5 Chambers, Birmingham	0845 210 5555
	No5 Chambers, Bristol	0845 210 5555
	No5 Chambers, London	0845 210 5555
Jones Mr Alun	St Paul's Chambers, Leeds	0113 245 5866
Lavin Miss Mary Mandie Jane	196 Temple Chamber, London	020 7099 9257
Markus Ms Kate	Doughty Street Chambers, Bristol	01179 058 717
	Doughty Street Chambers, London	020 7404 1313
	Doughty Street Chambers, Manchester	0161 618 1066
Marshall Miss Vanessa Juliette	Seven Bedford Row, London	020 7242 3555
Matthias Mr David Huw	Francis Taylor Building, London	020 7353 8415
McDonald Ms Melanie Sharon	No5 Chambers, Birmingham	0845 210 5555
	No5 Chambers, Bristol	0845 210 5555
	No5 Chambers, London	0845 210 5555
Millin Mrs Leslie Marilyn	The Chambers of Mrs Leslie Millin, Wokingham	0118 978 8026
Monaghan Ms Susan Mary	No5 Chambers, Birmingham	0845 210 5555
	No5 Chambers, Bristol	0845 210 5555
	No5 Chambers, London	0845 210 5555
Nicol Mr Nicholas Keith	1 Pump Court, London	020 7842 7070
Parker Mrs Karen Lesley	Guildhall Chambers Portsmouth, Portsmouth	023 9275 2400
Persaud Dr Marcia Chitroutie	1 Gray's Inn Square, London	020 7405 0001
Plimmer Miss Melanie Ann	Kings Chambers, Birmingham	0845 034 3444
	Kings Chambers, Leeds	0845 034 3444
	Kings Chambers, Manchester	0845 034 3444
Ritchie Mr Andrew George	The Chambers of Grahame Aldous QC, London	020 7832 0500
Scott Mr Andrew David Peter	Park Lane Plowden, Leeds	0113 228 5049
Silverton Miss Catherine Anne	Sovereign Chambers, Leeds	0113 245 1841

Sood Mrs Usha Rani	Trent Chambers, Nottingham	0115 941 9596
Spencer Mr Paul Anthony	3 Serjeants Inn, London	020 7427 5000
Stanford Mr Tony James	Old Bailey Chambers, London	020 3008 6404
Stebbings Mr Ian Anthony	1 Gray's Inn Square, London	020 7405 0001
Van Overdijk Miss Claire Orit	No5 Chambers, Birmingham	0845 210 5555
	No5 Chambers, Bristol	0845 210 5555
	No5 Chambers, London	0845 210 5555
Williams Mr Ben Dylan	Kings Chambers, Birmingham	0845 034 3444
	Kings Chambers, Leeds	0845 034 3444
	Kings Chambers, Manchester	0845 034 3444

HOUSING

Adewale Mr Remi Adetokunbo Sanni	Chambers of G. D. Tetteh, London	020 7353 7095
	Chambers of Mr R. A. Adewale, Address withheld	020 7231 2814
Agnihotri Mr Naveen	12 College Place, Southampton	023 8032 0320
Akther Miss Tahina Sultana	Cobden House Chambers, Manchester	0161 833 6000
	Southernhay Chambers, Exeter	01392 255777
Alam Ms Jan	Ropewalk Chambers, Nottingham	0115 947 2581
Ali Mrs Shamim	Chambers of Mrs Shamim Ali, Hatfield	01707 276737
Allison Mr Simon Robert	Hardwicke, London	020 7242 2523
Amraoui Mr Thomas	4-5 Gray's Inn Square, London	020 7404 5252
Angammana Mr Gamini Bertram	Chambers of Gamini Angammana, London	020 8771 5205
Artesi Miss Desiree Allison Ann	Thomas More Chambers, London	020 7404 7000
Askey Mr Robert John	Palmyra Chambers, Warrington	01925 444919
Auburn Mr Jonathan Walter	4-5 Gray's Inn Square, London	020 7404 5252
Awodele Mr Olufemi Adetunji	Great James Street Chambers, London	020 7440 4949
Azhar Mr Ali Mohammad	9 King's Bench Walk, London	020 7353 9564
Badejo Mr Abimbola Rafiu	5 Pump Court, London	020 7353 2532
Bailey Miss Rosana Henrietta	10 King's Bench Walk, London	020 7353 7742
Baldwin Dr Timothy John	Garden Court Chambers, London	020 7993 7600
Barber Mr Phillip Arthur	Zenith Chambers, Leeds	0113 245 5438
Bastin Mr Alexander Charles	Hardwicke, London	020 7242 2523
Bath Mrs Baljinder Kaur	College Chambers, Southampton	023 8023 0338
Baumohl Mr Mark Christopher	Field Court Chambers, London	020 7405 6114
Beaumont Mr Dean Andrew	KCH Garden Square, Nottingham	0115 941 8851
Beaumont Mr Marc Clifford	9 Stone Buildings, London	020 7404 5055
	Windsor Barristers' Chambers, Windsor	01753 839321
Beckley Mr John Mark	Garden Court Chambers, London	020 7993 7600
Bedloe Mr Giles Robert	Dyers Chambers, London	020 7404 1881
Berry Mr Adrian Christopher	Garden Court Chambers, London	020 7993 7600
Bezzam Miss Jayashree	Hampton Court Chambers, West Molesey	020 8979 0381
Bhakar Mr Surinder Singh	4 King's Bench Walk, London	020 7822 7000
Bogle Mr James Stewart Lockhart	10 King's Bench Walk, London	020 7353 7742
Bourke Ms Sarah Victoria Norma	Tooks Chambers, London	020 7842 7575
Braier Mr Jason Dean	Field Court Chambers, London	020 7405 6114
Bredemear Mr Zachary Charles	1 Chancery Lane, London	0845 634 6666
Broatch Mr Donald	Five Paper, London	020 7815 3200
Brockley Mr Nigel Simon	No5 Chambers, Birmingham	0845 210 5555
	No5 Chambers, Bristol	0845 210 5555
	No5 Chambers, London	0845 210 5555
Brown Miss Susan Margaret	One Essex Court, London	020 7936 3030
Browne Mr James William	Lamb Chambers, London	020 7797 8300
Bryden Mr Christopher James Yuen Kang	4 King's Bench Walk, London	020 7822 7000
Buckle Mr Jonathan	Regency Chambers, Cambridge	01223 301517
	Regency Chambers, Peterborough	01733 315215
Budworth Mr Richard Dutton	2-3 Hind Court Chambers, London	020 7822 2150
Butler Mr Simon David	The Chambers of Grahame Aldous QC, London	020 7832 0500
Campbell Mr Stafford Graham	Westgate Chambers, Lewes	01273 480510

Carrington Mr Dominic	Chambers of Martin Burr, London	0845 123 1234
Cartwright Mr Ivan Matthew	KCH Garden Square, Nottingham	0115 941 8851
Cattermole Miss Rebecca Elke	Tanfield Chambers, London	020 7421 5300
Cattermull Miss Emma Jayne	East Anglian Chambers, Chelmsford	01473 214481
	East Anglian Chambers, Ipswich	01473 214481
	East Anglian Chambers, Norwich	01473 214481
Chaffin-Laird Miss Olivia Carolyn	No5 Chambers, Birmingham	0845 210 5555
	No5 Chambers, Bristol	0845 210 5555
	No5 Chambers, London	0845 210 5555
Charalambides Mr Leonidas	Francis Taylor Building, London	020 7353 8415
Christensen Mr Carlton	10 King's Bench Walk, London	020 7353 7742
Chute Ms Andrea Alexandra	Rougemont Chambers, Exeter	01392 208484
	Tooks Chambers, London	020 7842 7575
Clarke Miss Lisa Tarin	Staple Inn Chambers, London	020 7242 5240
Clarke Mr George Robert Ivan	5 Pump Court, London	020 7353 2532
Clifton Miss Jane April	Lamb Chambers, London	020 7797 8300
Cooper Miss Christine	Field Court Chambers, London	020 7405 6114
Coster Mr Ronald David	42 Bedford Row, London	020 7831 0222
Crew Miss Gillian Mary	Ely Place Chambers, London	020 7400 9600
Croskell Mr Marcus James	East Anglian Chambers, Chelmsford	01473 214481
	East Anglian Chambers, Colchester	01473 214481
	East Anglian Chambers, Ipswich	01473 214481
	East Anglian Chambers, Norwich	01473 214481
Daly Mr David	Heathway Chambers, London	020 8293 0509
Datta Mr Shomik	42 Bedford Row, London	020 7831 0222
Davies Ms Elizabeth Mary	Garden Court Chambers, London	020 7993 7600
Davies Ms Samantha Teresa	Chambers of Ms Samantha Davies, Milton Keynes	0845 123 1234
	Warwick House Chambers, London	020 7430 2323
De Mello Mr Rembert Joseph Julius	No5 Chambers, Birmingham	0845 210 5555
	No5 Chambers, Bristol	0845 210 5555
	No5 Chambers, London	0845 210 5555
Demachkie Mr Jamal	3 PB Barristers, London	020 7583 8055
Denbin Mr Jack Arnold	Greenway, Sonning-on-Thames	0118 969 2484
Devereux-Cooke Mr Richard Charles	13 Old Square Chambers, London	020 7831 4445
Dhaliwal Miss Davinder Kaur	No 8 Chambers, Birmingham	0121 236 5514
Diamond Mr Paul	Chambers of Mr Paul Diamond, Cambridge	01223 264544
Dipré Mr Paul Nicholas Amadeus	Chambers of Mr P N Dipré, Address withheld	0845 123 1234
	MK Family Law Chambers, Milton Keynes	0845 123 1234
Dovar Mr Daniel	Tanfield Chambers, London	020 7421 5300
Dowell Mr Gregory Hamilton	Principal Chambers, Sevenoaks	0845 209 8080
Dsane Miss Victoria Tsotsoo	Chambers of Miss Victoria Dsane, Sutton	020 8722 0990
Dubin Mr Joshua Charles	1 Pump Court, London	020 7842 7070
Earle Mr James Christopher Reginald St John	Fenners Chambers, Cambridge	01223 368761
Eaton Mr Tobias Barnaby	Staple Inn Chambers, London	020 7242 5240
Edwards Mr Martin Richard	39 Essex Street, London	020 7832 1111
	82 King Street, Manchester	0161 870 9969
Egleton Mr Richard Wildman	Pallant Chambers, Chichester	01243 784538
Elliott Mr Colin Douglas	King's Bench and Godolphin (KBG)Chambers, Plymouth	01752 221551
Elliott Mr Edward Anthony John	Garden Court Chambers, London	020 7993 7600
Ephraim-Adejumo Mrs Hilda Ekpo	12 Old Square Chambers, London	020 7404 0875
Esprit Mr Benoit	Barristers Chambers, London	020 3417 6461
	Legis Chambers, Aylesbury	01296 431125
Fagborun Bennett Ms Morayo Abosede	Hardwicke, London	020 7242 2523
Fain Mr Carl Ian	Tanfield Chambers, London	020 7421 5300
Falkowski Mr Damian	4-5 Gray's Inn Square, London	020 7404 5252

Name	Chambers	Telephone
Fama Mrs Gudrun Hildegard	Middle Temple Lane Chambers, London	020 7583 4352
Feldman Mr Matthew Richard Bankes	42 Bedford Row, London	020 7831 0222
Ferber Ms Iris	42 Bedford Row, London	020 7831 0222
Finlay Mr Darren	Sovereign Chambers, Leeds	0113 245 1841
Foulkes Miss Rebecca	5 Pump Court, London	020 7353 2532
Frank Mr Ivor Richard Bainton	7 Bell Yard, London	020 7831 0636
Fullwood Mr Adam Garrett	Kings Chambers, Birmingham	0845 034 3444
	Kings Chambers, Leeds	0845 034 3444
	Kings Chambers, Manchester	0845 034 3444
Gallivan Mr Terence John	Five Paper, London	020 7815 3200
Galway-Cooper Dr Philip Anthony	Five St Andrew's Hill, London	020 7332 5400
Gannon Mr Kevin Francis	1 Pump Court, London	020 7842 7070
Gelbart Mr Geoff Alan	1 Gray's Inn Square, London	020 7405 0001
German Miss Kelly Anne	Eastbourne Chambers, Eastbourne	01323 642102
Gibbons Ms Ellodie	Tanfield Chambers, London	020 7421 5300
Godfrey Mr Lauren John	Crown Office Row Chambers, Brighton	01273 625625
Gofur Mr Abdul	Thomas More Chambers, London	020 7404 7000
Gold Mr Richard David	St John's Chambers, Bristol	0117 923 4700
Goodfellow Mr Stephen John	East Anglian Chambers, Chelmsford	01473 214481
	East Anglian Chambers, Ipswich	01473 214481
	East Anglian Chambers, Norwich	01473 214481
Gore Mrs Harriet Nkechi Adimora	Kensington Chambers, London	020 7373 2217
Granville Stafford Mr Andrew	4 King's Bench Walk, London	020 7822 7000
Greenan Miss Sarah Octavia	Zenith Chambers, Leeds	0113 245 5438
Griffiths Mr David	St Philips Chambers, Birmingham	0121 246 7000
Ground Mr Patrick	Chambers of Mr Patrick Ground QC, London	020 7736 0131
Gunstone Mr Robert Giles	KCH Garden Square, Nottingham	0115 941 8851
Ham Mr Nicholas Treharne	Dyers Chambers, London	020 7404 1881
Hammond Mr Tim Mark	Tanfield Chambers, London	020 7421 5300
Hanif Miss Saima Naz	4-5 Gray's Inn Square, London	020 7404 5252
Harrap Mr Robert Philip	Five Paper, London	020 7815 3200
Harris Mr James	Five St Andrew's Hill, London	020 7332 5400
Harris Mr Paul	Doughty Street Chambers, Bristol	01179 058 717
	Doughty Street Chambers, London	020 7404 1313
	Doughty Street Chambers, Manchester	0161 618 1066
Harrison Dr Graeme	12 College Place, Southampton	023 8032 0320
Haughty Mr Jeremy Nicholas	Chambers of Mr Ami Feder, London	020 7797 7788
	Chambers of Mr Ami Feder, London	020 7797 7788
	Rougemont Chambers, Exeter	01392 208484
Hendron Mr Henry Joseph Christopher	Strand Chambers, London	020 7117 6920
Heppinstall Mr Adam John	Henderson Chambers, London	020 7583 9020
Hicks Mr Edward Gordon David	Radcliffe Chambers, London	020 7831 0081
Hill Mr Michael Gordon	Trinity Chambers, Middlesbrough	01642 247569
	Trinity Chambers, Newcastle Upon Tyne	0191 232 1927
Hill Mr Piers Nicholas	37 Park Square Chambers, Leeds	0113 243 9422
Hillier Mr William	New Street Chambers, Leicester	0116 262 5906
Hobson Mr John Graham	4-5 Gray's Inn Square, London	020 7404 5252
Hodgson Mrs Jane Lee	Five Paper, London	020 7815 3200
Hodson Mr Matthew Paul	Farrar's Building, London	020 7583 9241
Hodson Mr Peter David	Chambers of Ian Macdonald QC, Manchester	0161 236 1840
Holland Mr Charles Christopher	Francis Taylor Building, London	020 7353 8415
	Trinity Chambers, Middlesbrough	01642 247569
	Trinity Chambers, Newcastle Upon Tyne	0191 232 1927
Holland Mr Rowan Guy	Five Paper, London	020 7815 3200
Huggins Mr Toby James	Unity Street Chambers, Bristol	0117 906 9789
Hughes-Deane Ms Charlotte Barbara	Atlantic Chambers, Liverpool	0151 236 4421

Name	Chambers	Telephone
Hussain Mr Muhammad Altaf	Chambers of Mr M A Hussain, London	020 8679 2398
Jafar Mr Abdurahman Akhtar	Chambers of Mr Abdurahman Jafar, Ilford	07828 937338
Jones Mr Alun	St Paul's Chambers, Leeds	0113 245 5866
Jones Mr Ian Harvey	Holbrook Chambers, Leicester	07771 961962
Jones Mr Mark Andrew	St Ive's Chambers, Birmingham	0121 236 0863
Joseph Mr Sellappah Job	Chambers of Mr S J Joseph, London	020 8809 3083/020 8802 9889
Josling Mr William Henry Charles	37 Park Square Chambers, Leeds	0113 243 9422
Jowett Mr Timothy David Christian	9 Park Place, Cardiff	029 2038 2731
Kansal Miss Seema	12 Old Square Chambers, London	020 7404 0875
Kelly Mr Shaw Martin	Staple Inn Chambers, London	020 7242 5240
Kelly Mrs Amy Louise	12 College Place, Southampton	023 8032 0320
Kemp Mr James Rupert	Trinity Chambers, Middlesbrough	01642 247569
	Trinity Chambers, Newcastle Upon Tyne	0191 232 1927
Khalid Mr James	Goulds Green Chambers, Uxbridge	01895 422574
	Goulds Green Chambers, Uxbridge	01895 422574
Khan Mr Abdul Aleem	Gray's Chambers, Newbury	020 8518 2525
Khan Mr Shaukat Ali	Chambers of Mr S A Khan, Kingston Upon Thames	020 8541 3875
Kilcoyne Mr Patrick Desmond Oliver	42 Bedford Row, London	020 7831 0222
King Mr Charles Granville	Chambers of Mr C G King, Stroud	07949 461717
Kirk Mr Thomas Sean Robinson	12 College Place, Southampton	023 8032 0320
Kohli Mr Ryan Singh	Cornerstone Barristers, London	020 7242 4986
Kramer Mr Philip Anthony	Park Lane Plowden, Newcastle Upon Tyne	0191 211 4087
Kwiatkowski Mr Feliks Jerzy	Kew Chambers, Kew	0844 8099991
Kynoch Mr Duncan Stuart Sanderson	Selborne Chambers, London	020 7420 9500
Lam Mr Chuen Fat	Chambers of Martin Burr, London	0845 123 1234
Lamb Mr Jeffrey Thomas	Westgate Chambers, Lewes	01273 480510
Lane Mr Christopher Paul	No 8 Chambers, Birmingham	0121 236 5514
Lane Mr Simon Charles	Rougemont Chambers, Exeter	01392 208484
Lawrence Miss Anne Mary	Atlas Chambers, London	020 7269 7980
Lawrence Miss Pamela Avril	Nexus Chambers, London	020 7404 1147/020 7831 8309
Lewis Mr Wayne Anthony	Access Lawyers, London	020 8801 2345
Lloyd Mr John Nesbitt	Rougemont Chambers, Exeter	01392 208484
Lo Mr Bernard Norman	Field Court Chambers, London	020 7405 6114
Lock Mr David Anthony	No5 Chambers, Birmingham	0845 210 5555
	No5 Chambers, Bristol	0845 210 5555
	No5 Chambers, London	0845 210 5555
Lofthouse Mr James	1 Gray's Inn Square, London	020 7405 0001
Longhurst-Woods Ms Lesley	2 Louisa Close, London	020 8985 8716
Lopez Mr Juan Nemesio	Francis Taylor Building, London	020 7353 8415
Lowe Mr Mungo James	13 Old Square Chambers, London	020 7831 4445
Luh Miss Shu Shin	Garden Court Chambers, London	020 7993 7600
MacBean Mr Andrew Hamish	Queen Square Chambers, Bristol	0117 921 1966
Mahmood Mr Abid	Central Chambers, Manchester	0161 236 1133
	No5 Chambers, Birmingham	0845 210 5555
	No5 Chambers, Bristol	0845 210 5555
	No5 Chambers, London	0845 210 5555
Mahmood Mr Imran Waseem	5 Pump Court, London	020 7353 2532
Mainwaring Mr Robert Paul Clason	Portal Chambers, Llandysul	01559 395 292
Maltz Mr Ben Daniel	Five Paper, London	020 7815 3200
Marcus Mr Peter	Zenith Chambers, Leeds	0113 245 5438
Mason Mr Ian Douglas	Amethyst Chambers, London	020 7936 4966
Matthias Mr David Huw	Francis Taylor Building, London	020 7353 8415
McCarthy Mr William	Bridgewater Chambers, Manchester	0161 3877127
	1 Mitre Court Buildings, London	020 7452 8900
McCormack Mr Alan	Staple Inn Chambers, London	020 7242 5240
McCulloch Miss Fiona Catharine Jane	Middle Temple Lane Chambers, London	020 7583 4352
Miller Mr Ian Daukes Douglas	1 Chancery Lane, London	0845 634 6666

Miller Mr Peter Owen Michael	Cornerstone Barristers, London	020 7242 4986
Modgill Mr Alexander Jeffrey	Broadway House Chambers, Bradford	01274 722560
	Broadway House Chambers, Leeds	0113 246 2600
Moffat Mr Russell Dean	Linenhall Chambers, Chester	01244 348282
Moll Mr Christiaan Eric	Blackfriars Chambers, London	020 7353 7400
Monnington Mr Bruce Gilbert	Fenners Chambers, Cambridge	01223 368761
Moran Mr Christopher John	39 Park Square, Leeds	0113 245 6633
Morgan Dr Austen Jude	33 Bedford Row, London	020 7242 6476
Morris Ms Johanna	Chambers of Marion Smullen and Kerim Fuad QC, London	020 7427 4400
Morton Miss Rowan Frances	Alexander Chambers, London	0845 652 0451/0854 652 0451
	Guildford Chambers, Guildford	01483 539131
Moss Mr Christopher Stephen	St Johns Buildings, Manchester	0161 214 1500
	St Johns Buildings Liverpool, Liverpool	0151 243 6000
	16 Winckley Square, Preston	01772 256100
Moulder Mr Paul John	Alexander Chambers, London	0845 652 0451/0854 652 0451
	Guildford Chambers, Guildford	01483 539131
Muir Miss Nicola Jane	Hardwicke, London	020 7242 2523
Mullee Mr Brendan Paul	Hardwicke, London	020 7242 2523
Munir Dr Ashley Edward	Five St Andrew's Hill, London	020 7332 5400
Murray Mr Charles Humphrey Stewart	Rougemont Chambers, Exeter	01392 208484
Nall-Cain The Hon Richard Christopher Philip	St Albans Chambers, St Albans	01727 843383
Newman Mr James Andrew	Ely Place Chambers, London	020 7400 9600
Nickless Mr Jason Alan	College Chambers, Southampton	023 8023 0338
Nicol Mr Nicholas Keith	1 Pump Court, London	020 7842 7070
Norman Mr Jared Simon Gregory	Field Court Chambers, London	020 7405 6114
O'Brien Mr Nicholas William Wattebot	10 King's Bench Walk, London	020 7353 7742
Offer Mr Alexander	Garden Court Chambers, London	020 7993 7600
	Park Court Chambers, Leeds	0113 243 3277
Okoya Mr William Ebikise	Arden Chambers, London	020 7242 4244
Onipede Dr Victor Olusegun	Chambers of Dr V O Onipede, London	07956 207159
Oommen Mr Jacob	Chambers of Mr Jacob Oommen, East Barnet	07958 680272
Orme Miss Emily Charlotte	Arden Chambers, London	020 7242 4244
Osborne Mr James Robert	Clerksroom (London), London	0845 083 3000
O'Sullivan Mr Richard John	1215 Chambers, London	020 3291 1215
O'Toole Mr Bartholomew Vincent	5 King's Bench Walk, London	020 7353 5638
Paget Mr Michael Rodborough	Garden Court Chambers, London	020 7993 7600
Palmer Mr Edward James	Regent Chambers, Stoke On Trent	01782 286666
Panton Mr Alastair Howard	10 King's Bench Walk, London	020 7353 7742
Parker Mrs Karen Lesley	Guildhall Chambers Portsmouth, Portsmouth	023 9275 2400
Pascall Mr Matthew Stephen	Alexander Chambers, London	0845 652 0451/0854 652 0451
	Guildford Chambers, Guildford	01483 539131
Payne Mr David James	No 8 Chambers, Birmingham	0121 236 5514
Peckham Ms Jane Louise	1 Crown Office Row, London	020 7797 7500
	Crown Office Row Chambers, Brighton	01273 625625
Pennington-Legh Mr Jonathan Piers	Field Court Chambers, London	020 7405 6114
Persaud Dr Marcia Chitroutie	1 Gray's Inn Square, London	020 7405 0001
Phillips Miss Emma Louise	1 Pump Court, London	020 7842 7070
Pickering Mr Simon Toby	Wilberforce Chambers, Hull	01482 323264
Pithers Mr Clive Robert	Fenners Chambers, Cambridge	01223 368761
Puar Mr Mikhael	30 Park Place, Cardiff	029 2039 8421
Quirke Mr Gerard Martin	Citadel Chambers, Birmingham	0121 233 8500
Rahman Mr Anis	12 Old Square Chambers, London	020 7404 0875
Rai Mr Amarjit Singh	St Philips Chambers, Birmingham	0121 246 7000
Rainey Mr Philip Carslake	Tanfield Chambers, London	020 7421 5300
Rana Mr Mohammed Akram	Clapham Law Chambers, London	020 7978 8482
Ratcliffe Miss Frances Anne	Radcliffe Chambers, London	020 7831 0081
Read Mr Simon Eric	Zenith Chambers, Leeds	0113 245 5438

Reid Miss Claudette Patricia	Chambers of Miss Claudette Reid, London	
Reid Mr Sebastian Peter Scott	Tanfield Chambers, London	020 7421 5300
Rhodes Miss Amanda Louise	Unity Street Chambers, Bristol	0117 906 9789
Roberts Mr Richard Vaughan	Henderson Chambers, London	020 7583 9020
Rogers Mr Michael Peter	Chambers of Mr Ami Feder, London	020 7797 7788
	Chambers of Mr Ami Feder, London	020 7797 7788
Roy Mr Stefan Alexander Hiren	5 Pump Court, London	020 7353 2532
Rushton Mr Jonathon Barker	36 Bedford Row, London	020 7421 8000
Russell Mr Thomas Charles Welldon	KCH Garden Square, Nottingham	0115 941 8851
Sadiq Mr Muhammad Faisel	Ely Place Chambers, London	020 7400 9600
Saifee Mr Faisal Aftaab	Thomas More Chambers, London	020 7404 7000
Sandham Mr James Andrew	Arden Chambers, London	020 7242 4244
Scolding Miss Fiona Kate	Hardwicke, London	020 7242 2523
Seal Mr Julius Damien	Chambers of Mr Julius Seal, London	020 7328 0158
Seeboruth Mr Royln Jean-Paul	Chambers of Royln Seeboruth, Aylesbury	01296 393329
Sefton-Smith Mr Lloyd	Lamb Chambers, London	020 7797 8300
Sellers Mr Graham	Atlantic Chambers, Liverpool	0151 236 4421
Shaw Miss Joanna Elizabeth	One Essex Court, London	020 7936 3030
Sheftel Mr Andrew Lawson Baylies	Tanfield Chambers, London	020 7421 5300
Shuman Miss Karen Ann Elizabeth	1 Chancery Lane, London	0845 634 6666
	No 8 Chambers, Birmingham	0121 236 5514
Silverton Miss Catherine Anne	Sovereign Chambers, Leeds	0113 245 1841
Sinclair Mr Graham Kelso	East Anglian Chambers, Colchester	01473 214481
	East Anglian Chambers, Ipswich	01473 214481
	East Anglian Chambers, Norwich	01473 214481
Skelly Mr Andrew Jon	Hardwicke, London	020 7242 2523
Smith Miss Eileen Joan	Trinity Chambers, Middlesbrough	01642 247569
	Trinity Chambers, Newcastle Upon Tyne	0191 232 1927
Sonaike Mr Kolarele Oladele Obafemi	One Essex Court, London	020 7936 3030
Sood Mrs Usha Rani	Trent Chambers, Nottingham	0115 941 9596
Southern Miss Emma Catherine	12 College Place, Southampton	023 8032 0320
Speller Mr Bruce Christopher Norman	The White House, Battle	01424 777944
Spratt Mr Christopher David Richard Dean	9 Stone Buildings, London	020 7404 5055
Stagg Mr Paul Andrew	1 Chancery Lane, London	0845 634 6666
Stanford Mr Tony James	Old Bailey Chambers, London	020 3008 6404
Stenhouse Mr John Alexander	Nightingale Chambers, Wolverley	01562 851350
Stephenson Mr David Matthew	1 Mitre Court Buildings, London	020 7452 8900
Stinchcombe Mr Paul David	4-5 Gray's Inn Square, London	020 7404 5252
Tapsell Mr Paul Richard	Becket Chambers, Canterbury	01227 786331
Taussig Mr Gurion	The Chambers of Grahame Aldous QC, London	020 7832 0500
Tee Mr Gregory James	Guildford Chambers, Guildford	01483 539131
Tempest Mr Alistair Mark	Field Court Chambers, London	020 7405 6114
Thomas Dr David Keith	1 Gray's Inn Square, London	020 7405 0001
	Rougemont Chambers, Exeter	01392 208484
Thomas Mrs Felicity	Westgate Chambers, Lewes	01273 480510
Topal Mr Erol	Lamb Chambers, London	020 7797 8300
Trumpington Mr John Henry	Staple Inn Chambers, London	020 7242 5240
Tueje Miss Patricia	1 Pump Court, London	020 7842 7070
Turnbull Miss Helen Mary	Lamb Chambers, London	020 7797 8300
Ume Mr Cyril Obiora	12 Old Square Chambers, London	020 7404 0875
Van Overdijk Miss Claire Orit	No5 Chambers, Birmingham	0845 210 5555
	No5 Chambers, Bristol	0845 210 5555
	No5 Chambers, London	0845 210 5555
Vanhegan Mr Toby Bartholomew	Arden Chambers, London	020 7242 4244
Vasilescu Mr Andrei Constantin	Chambers of Martin Burr, London	0845 123 1234
Verduyn Dr Anthony James	St Philips Chambers, Birmingham	0121 246 7000
Vernon Mr Elliot Curt	No. 3 Fleet Street Chambers, London	020 7936 4474

Name	Chambers	Telephone
Wagstaff Mr Andrew Martin Nicholas	Westgate Chambers, Lewes	01273 480510
Wald Mr Richard Daniel	39 Essex Street, London	020 7832 1111
	82 King Street, Manchester	0161 870 9969
	Riverview Chambers, London	0844 225 3999
Walsh Mr Michael Patrick	Tanfield Chambers, London	020 7421 5300
Waritay Mr Samuel	Chambers of Mr Samuel Waritay, London	0845 803 7767
Warner Mr David Alexander	St Philips Chambers, Birmingham	0121 246 7000
Watson Mr Duncan Allen	Westgate Chambers, Lewes	01273 480510
Watterson Ms Anna Elizabeth	1 Mitre Court Buildings, London	020 7452 8900
Welch Mr Robert William	Unity Street Chambers, Bristol	0117 906 9789
Wenban-Smith Mr Mungo William	4-5 Gray's Inn Square, London	020 7404 5252
Whitehouse Mr Stuart Colin	Goldsmith Chambers, London	020 7353 6802
Wightwick Mr Iain	Riverview Chambers, London	0844 225 3999
	Unity Street Chambers, Bristol	0117 906 9789
Wiktorowski-Solecki Miss Tamara	Middle Temple Lane Chambers, London	020 7583 4352
Wilkinson Mr Marc Ashley	No5 Chambers, Birmingham	0845 210 5555
	No5 Chambers, Bristol	0845 210 5555
	No5 Chambers, London	0845 210 5555
Williams Miss June Cleo	No 8 Chambers, Birmingham	0121 236 5514
Wills Miss Alexandra Itari	Christ Church Chambers, London	020 7409 5278/07788 512787
Winslett Mr Frank	Westgate Chambers, Lewes	01273 480510
Wragg Mr Jonathan Robert	Highgate Chambers, London	020 8340 6031
Wrottesley Miss Angela Jane	Bank House Chambers, Sheffield	0114 275 1223
Wylie Mr Neil Richard	KCH Garden Square, Nottingham	0115 941 8851
Young Mr Martin Ford	9 Stone Buildings, London	020 7404 5055
Zeitler Miss Barbara	3 Dr Johnson's Buildings, London	020 7353 4854

HUMAN RIGHTS

Name	Chambers	Telephone
Abasheikh Mr Omar Said Imam	Paragon Chambers, London	020 3318 9988
Adler Mr Jonathan	1 Pump Court, London	020 7842 7070
Ahluwalia Mr Navtej Singh	Garden Court Chambers, London	020 7993 7600
Ahmed Mr Nazir	Centurion Chambers, West Bromwich	0121 553 4613
Ajaz Mr Mohammad Arshad	Eastmans Chambers, Reading	0118 966 9094
Albutt Mr Ian Leslie	Cornerstone Barristers, London	020 7242 4986
	Heavenwood Chambers, Stroud	01453 873444
Algazy Mr Jacques Max	Cloisters, London	020 7827 4000
Ali Mr Ishtiyaq	Chartlands Chambers, Northampton	01604 603322
Allwood Mrs Gina Louisa	Seven Bedford Row, London	020 7242 3555
Amraoui Mr Thomas	4-5 Gray's Inn Square, London	020 7404 5252
Arkhurst Mr Reginald Leon	4 King's Bench Walk, London	020 7822 7000
Arnold Mr Graham John	Farringdon Chambers, London	020 7089 5700
Askey Mr Robert John	Palmyra Chambers, Warrington	01925 444919
Auburn Mr Jonathan Walter	4-5 Gray's Inn Square, London	020 7404 5252
Austin Mr Ian	Holborn Chambers, London	020 7242 6060
Aylett Mr Kenneth George	4 Breams Buildings, London	020 7092 1900
	15 New Bridge Street, London	020 7842 1900
Azhar Mr Ali Mohammad	9 King's Bench Walk, London	020 7353 9564
Azmi Mr Mohammad Javed	No 8 Chambers, Birmingham	0121 236 5514
Bajwa Mr Ali Naseem	Garden Court Chambers, London	020 7993 7600
Banks Miss Fiona Jane	Monckton Chambers, London	020 7405 7211
Barber Mr Phillip Arthur	Zenith Chambers, Leeds	0113 245 5438
Barnes Ms Rachel Ann	3 Raymond Buildings, London	020 7400 6400
Barraclough Mr Nicholas Maylin	187 Fleet Street, London	020 7430 7430
Beharrylal Mr Satyanand Sarju	15 New Bridge Street, London	020 7842 1900
Beloff Mr Rupert Joseph Alexei	No5 Chambers, Birmingham	0845 210 5555
	No5 Chambers, Bristol	0845 210 5555
	No5 Chambers, London	0845 210 5555
Berry Mr Adrian Christopher	Garden Court Chambers, London	020 7993 7600
Bertham Mr Anthony Christopher	3 Temple Gardens, London	020 7353 3102
Bezzam Miss Jayashree	Hampton Court Chambers, West Molesey	020 8979 0381

Bhanji Mr Shiraz Musa	4 Bingham Place, London	020 7486 5347
	1 Gray's Inn Square, London	020 7405 0001
Birnbaum Mr Michael Ian	9-12 Bell Yard, London	020 7400 1800
Bishop Mr Malcolm Leslie	Argent Chambers, London	020 7556 5500
	Equity Chambers, Birmingham	0121 236 5007
	30 Park Place, Cardiff	029 2039 8421
Bowen Mr Nicholas James Hugh	Doughty Street Chambers, Bristol	01179 058 717
	Doughty Street Chambers, London	020 7404 1313
	Doughty Street Chambers, Manchester	0161 618 1066
Bowers Mr Rupert John	Doughty Street Chambers, London	020 7404 1313
Bradshaw Mr Mark Kieran	No5 Chambers, Birmingham	0845 210 5555
	No5 Chambers, Bristol	0845 210 5555
	No5 Chambers, London	0845 210 5555
Bramwell Miss Corinne Victoria	Nine Bedford Row, London	020 7489 2727
Brehan Ms Daire	Chambers of Ms D Brehan, London	07808 726877
Broatch Mr Donald	Five Paper, London	020 7815 3200
Brown Mr Sam Clement	Atkinson Bevan Chambers, London	020 7353 2112
Brown Ms Grace	Tooks Chambers, London	020 7842 7575
Browne Mr Desmond John Michael	5RB, London	020 7242 2902
Bryden Mr Christopher James Yuen Kang	4 King's Bench Walk, London	020 7822 7000
Buchan Miss Caroline Venetia	Chambers of Miss C Buchan, Haywards Heath	01444 482222
Bunting Mr Daniel Alexander James	2 Dr Johnson's Buildings, London	020 7936 2613
Bunting Mr Jude James	Tooks Chambers, London	020 7842 7575
Burnett Mr Iain	4 King's Bench Walk, London	020 7822 7000
Burrett Mr Alex	1 Gray's Inn Square, London	020 7405 0001
Byrne Mr Garrett Thomas	4-5 Gray's Inn Square, London	020 7404 5252
Byrnes Miss Aisling Alice Elizabeth	25 Bedford Row, London	020 7067 1500
Callery Mr Martin	Cobden House Chambers, Manchester	0161 833 6000
Carr Mr Christopher Sean	36 Bedford Row, London	020 7421 8000
Casey Mr Paul Joseph	Chambers of Marion Smullen and Kerim Fuad QC, London	020 7427 4400
Cassidy Mr Patrick Stephen	Kenworthy's Chambers, Manchester	0161 832 4036
Cattermull Miss Emma Jayne	East Anglian Chambers, Chelmsford	01473 214481
	East Anglian Chambers, Ipswich	01473 214481
	East Anglian Chambers, Norwich	01473 214481
Cecil Miss Joanne Michelle	1 Pump Court, London	020 7842 7070
Chalk Mr Alexander John Gervase	6 King's Bench Walk, London	020 7583 0410
Chambers Ms Rachel Elizabeth	Cloisters, London	020 7827 4000
Chelvan Mr S	No5 Chambers, Birmingham	0845 210 5555
	No5 Chambers, Bristol	0845 210 5555
	No5 Chambers, London	0845 210 5555
	Trent Chambers, Nottingham	0115 941 9596
Chippeck Mr Stephen	5 King's Bench Walk, London	020 7353 5638
Chipperfield Mr Jeremy Steven	Cranford Chambers, London	020 7404 7454
Chodha Mr Tejpal Singh	Chambers of Mr T Chodha, Gravesend	01474 326666
Chute Ms Andrea Alexandra	Rougemont Chambers, Exeter	01392 208484
	Tooks Chambers, London	020 7842 7575
Clay Mr Jonathan Roger	Cornerstone Barristers, London	020 7242 4986
Coleman Mr Daniel Gerald Mayow	1 Gray's Inn Square, London	020 7405 0001
Comb Mr David William	Trinity Chambers, Middlesbrough	01642 247569
	Trinity Chambers, Newcastle Upon Tyne	0191 232 1927
Connolly Mr Dominic Regan	Five St Andrew's Hill, London	020 7332 5400
Costello Mr Paul James	Chambers of Mr Paul J Costello, Biggleswade	07846 016 399
Coster Mr Ronald David	42 Bedford Row, London	020 7831 0222
Critchley Mr John Stephen	Field Court Chambers, London	020 7405 6114
Crosfill Mr John	Field Court Chambers, London	020 7405 6114
Darroch Miss Fiona Culverwell	Clerksroom (London), London	0845 083 3000
	Clerksroom (Taunton), Taunton	0845 083 3000
	King's Lynn Chambers, King's Lynn	01553 672 085
Dassa Miss Regine	9 King's Bench Walk, London	020 7353 9564

C

Name	Chambers	Telephone
Davey Mr Charles	64 Bridge Street, Manchester	0845 083 3000
	Chambers of Mr C Davey, Bishop's Stortford	01279 506412
	Clerksroom (Taunton), Taunton	0845 083 3000
Davies Mr Henry Olusola	Trinity Chambers, Birmingham	0121 346 4672
Davies Ms Samantha Teresa	Chambers of Ms Samantha Davies, Milton Keynes	0845 123 1234
	Warwick House Chambers, London	020 7430 2323
Del Fabbro Mr Oscar	23 Essex Street, London	020 7413 0353
Delany Ms Francesca	1 Mitre Court Buildings, London	020 7452 8900
Dhaliwal Miss Davinder Kaur	No 8 Chambers, Birmingham	0121 236 5514
Doerfel Mr Jan Hendrik Jamison	1215 Chambers, London	020 3291 1215
	Chambers of Mr J H Doerfel, Richmond	0845 123 1234
Dos Santos Mr Alexander	Charter Chambers, London	020 7618 4400
Dubin Mr Joshua Charles	1 Pump Court, London	020 7842 7070
Eastwood Miss Philippa Clemency Anne	Doughty Street Chambers, London	020 7404 1313
Edington Mrs Fiona Anne Rider	Thomas More Chambers, London	020 7404 7000
Edwards Mr Denis	Francis Taylor Building, London	020 7353 8415
Edwards Mr Nigel Royston	St Paul's Chambers, Leeds	0113 245 5866
Engelman Mr Philip	Cloisters, London	020 7827 4000
	Trinity Chambers, Middlesbrough	01642 247569
	Trinity Chambers, Newcastle Upon Tyne	0191 232 1927
Ephraim-Adejumo Mrs Hilda Ekpo	12 Old Square Chambers, London	020 7404 0875
Facenna Mr Gerald Carlo	Monckton Chambers, London	020 7405 7211
Fagborun Bennett Ms Morayo Abosede	Hardwicke, London	020 7242 2523
Fama Mrs Gudrun Hildegard	Middle Temple Lane Chambers, London	020 7583 4352
Farrell Mr Simon Henry	3 Raymond Buildings, London	020 7400 6400
Faryl Miss Alaha Begum	Central Chambers, Manchester	0161 236 1133
Ferry-Swainson Mr Richard Joseph	2 Bedford Row, London	020 7440 8888
Fetto Mr Niazi Peter	2 Temple Gardens, London	020 7822 1200
Fielden Dr Christa Maria	1 Mitre Court Buildings, London	020 7452 8900
Fitzmaurice Mr Guy Edward Christian	Staple Inn Chambers, London	020 7242 5240
Frantzis Miss Roxanne	KBW, Leeds	0113 297 1200
Fraser Mr Mark-Anthony	Dyers Chambers, London	020 7404 1881
Fullwood Mr Adam Garrett	Kings Chambers, Birmingham	0845 034 3444
	Kings Chambers, Leeds	0845 034 3444
	Kings Chambers, Manchester	0845 034 3444
Gadd Mr Adam Brian	Pump Court Chambers, London	020 7353 0711
	Pump Court Chambers, Winchester	01962 868 161
	Riverview Chambers, London	0844 225 3999
Gallagher Ms Caoilfhionn Anna	Doughty Street Chambers, Bristol	01179 058 717
	Doughty Street Chambers, London	020 7404 1313
	Doughty Street Chambers, Manchester	0161 618 1066
Gallivan Mr Terence John	Five Paper, London	020 7815 3200
Ganesan Mr Muthupandi Peter	Furnival Chambers, London	020 7405 3232
Gardner Mr James Piers	Monckton Chambers, London	020 7405 7211
Garlick Mr Paul Richard	Furnival Chambers, London	020 7405 3232
Gaskin Mr Francis John Gerald	4 Breams Buildings, London	020 7092 1900
Gelbart Mr Geoff Alan	1 Gray's Inn Square, London	020 7405 0001
German Miss Kelly Anne	Eastbourne Chambers, Eastbourne	01323 642102
Gerry Miss Felicity Ruth	36 Bedford Row, London	020 7421 8000
Gill Miss Baljinder	10 King's Bench Walk, London	020 7353 7742
Gill Mr Manjit Singh	No5 Chambers, Birmingham	0845 210 5555
	No5 Chambers, Bristol	0845 210 5555
	No5 Chambers, London	0845 210 5555
Gledhill Mr Lee Andre	Alexander Chambers, London	0845 652 0451/0854 652 0451
	Trident Barristers Chambers, Manchester	0161 663 3123

C

Glyn Mr Caspar Hilary Gordon	Cloisters, London	020 7827 4000
Godfrey Mr Lauren John	Crown Office Row Chambers, Brighton	01273 625625
Goldrein Mr Iain Saville	7 Bell Yard, London	020 7831 0636
	Number 7 Harrington Street Chambers, Liverpool	0151 242 0707
Goodman Mr Alexander David Edmund	Atlas Chambers, London	020 7269 7980
	4-5 Gray's Inn Square, London	020 7404 5252
Goudie Mr William Martin Phillip	Charter Chambers, London	020 7618 4400
Grennan Mr Barry Edward	Kenworthy's Chambers, Manchester	0161 832 4036
Grunwald Mr Henry Cyril	Charter Chambers, London	020 7618 4400
Gurden Miss Alison Louise	1 Gray's Inn Square, London	020 7405 0001
Guy Mr Richard Perran	Chambers of Mr Ami Feder, London	020 7797 7788
	King's Bench and Godolphin (KBG)Chambers, Plymouth	01752 221551
	Southernhay Chambers, Exeter	01392 255777
Hamilton Mr John Conrad	Field Court Chambers, London	020 7405 6114
Hanlon Mr James Tobias	Old Bailey Chambers, London	020 3008 6404
Harris Mr Paul	Doughty Street Chambers, Bristol	01179 058 717
	Doughty Street Chambers, London	020 7404 1313
	Doughty Street Chambers, Manchester	0161 618 1066
Harris Mr Wilbert Arthurlyn	Rowchester Chambers, Birmingham	0121 233 2327
Harrison Dr Graeme	12 College Place, Southampton	023 8032 0320
Hawkin Mr Benjamin	1 Mitre Court Buildings, London	020 7452 8900
Hendron Mr Henry Joseph Christopher	Strand Chambers, London	020 7117 6920
Hill Ms Eleanor Mary Henrietta	Doughty Street Chambers, Bristol	01179 058 717
	Doughty Street Chambers, London	020 7404 1313
	Doughty Street Chambers, Manchester	0161 618 1066
Hirst Miss Rebecca Elisabeth	Cobden House Chambers, Manchester	0161 833 6000
Hollis Mrs Kim	25 Bedford Row, London	020 7067 1500
Hood Mr David	Prince of Wales Chambers, London	020 7622 7415
Hossain Mr Mohammed Monwar	No. 3 Fleet Street Chambers, London	020 7936 4474
Hussain Miss Frida Khanam	Furnival Chambers, London	020 7405 3232
Hussain Mr Tasaddat	Broadway House Chambers, Bradford	01274 722560
	Broadway House Chambers, Leeds	0113 246 2600
Hutchinson Mr Colin Thomas	Garden Court Chambers, London	020 7993 7600
Inyundo Mr Richard Kwame Swaka	6 King's Bench Walk, London	020 7583 0410
Iqbal Miss Samina	Renaissance Chambers, London	020 7404 1111
Iqbal Mr Mashood	London View Chambers, Sawbridgeworth	07788 912493
Irwin Mr Gavin David	Dyers Chambers, London	020 7404 1881
Jafferji Mr Zainulabedin Hatim	Chambers of Mr Jafferji, Leicester	07957 198777
Jarvis Mr Paul	6 King's Bench Walk, London	020 7583 0410
Jayakrishnan Mr Harry Sisubalan	Trent Chambers, Nottingham	0115 941 9596
Jones Miss Jacinta Elizabeth Barrett	1 Mitre Court Buildings, London	020 7452 8900
Jones Mr John Richard William	Doughty Street Chambers, Bristol	01179 058 717
	Doughty Street Chambers, London	020 7404 1313
	Doughty Street Chambers, Manchester	0161 618 1066
Jones Mr Mark Andrew	St Ive's Chambers, Birmingham	0121 236 0863
Joshi Mr Rajendra Jugatray	18 Red Lion Court, London	020 7520 6000
	18 Red Lion Court (Annexe), Chelmsford	01245 280880
Juss Prof Satvinder Singh	3 Hare Court, London	020 7415 7800
Keith Mr Benjamin Charles Andrew	Five St Andrew's Hill, London	020 7332 5400
Khalid Mr James	Goulds Green Chambers, Uxbridge	01895 422574
	Goulds Green Chambers, Uxbridge	01895 422574
Khalique Miss Nageena	No5 Chambers, Birmingham	0845 210 5555
	No5 Chambers, Bristol	0845 210 5555
	No5 Chambers, London	0845 210 5555
Khan Mr Abdul Aleem	Gray's Chambers, Newbury	020 8518 2525
Khan Mr Arfan	Field Court Chambers, London	020 7405 6114
Khan Mr Ayoub	Chambers of Mr Ayoub Khan, Birmingham	07930 987202

Khan Mr Forz	Chambers of Mr F Khan, London	07854 109584
	6 King's Bench Walk, London	020 7353 4931
Khan Mr Mahmood Shafi	Luton Chambers, Luton	01582 598394
	Willesden Chambers, London	020 3273 1042
Khan Mr Shahnawaz Zulfiquar	1 Gray's Inn Square, London	020 7405 0001
Khan Mr Zarif	Dyers Chambers, London	020 7404 1881
King Mr John Patrick	Nine Bedford Row, London	020 7489 2727
Knight Mr Benjamin James	Central Chambers, Manchester	0161 236 1133
Knight Mr Graeme Edward Verdon	7 Bell Yard, London	020 7831 0636
	Carmelite Chambers, London	020 7936 6300
	The Barristers Chambers, Address withheld	07966 056368
Kohli Mr Ryan Singh	Cornerstone Barristers, London	020 7242 4986
Kramer Mr Philip Anthony	Park Lane Plowden, Newcastle Upon Tyne	0191 211 4087
Lahiffe Mr Martin Patrick Joseph	3 Temple Gardens, London	020 7353 3102
Lal Mr Sanjay	4 King's Bench Walk, London	020 7822 7000
Lams Mr Barnabas Jeffrey	4 Brick Court, London	020 7832 3200
Lane Mr Christopher Paul	No 8 Chambers, Birmingham	0121 236 5514
Lawrence Sir Ivan John	5 Pump Court, London	020 7353 2532
Lemer Mr David James	Doughty Street Chambers, London	020 7404 1313
Lenaghan Mr Anthony	Dyers Chambers, London	020 7404 1881
Levinson Miss Jemma	1 Mitre Court Buildings, London	020 7452 8900
Lewiecki Miss Marie	Old Bailey Chambers, London	020 3008 6404
Lewis Mr Dominic	Five Paper Buildings, London	020 7583 6117
Lewis Mr Wayne Anthony	Access Lawyers, London	020 8801 2345
Lloyd Mr Benjamin John	6 King's Bench Walk, London	020 7583 0410
Lock Mr David Anthony	No5 Chambers, Birmingham	0845 210 5555
	No5 Chambers, Bristol	0845 210 5555
	No5 Chambers, London	0845 210 5555
Lofthouse Mr James	1 Gray's Inn Square, London	020 7405 0001
Luh Miss Shu Shin	Garden Court Chambers, London	020 7993 7600
Lule Miss Jacqueline	1 Mitre Court Buildings, London	020 7452 8900
MacKenzie Smith Mrs Catherine Joanna	10 King's Bench Walk, London	020 7353 7742
Mahmood Mr Abid	Central Chambers, Manchester	0161 236 1133
	No5 Chambers, Birmingham	0845 210 5555
	No5 Chambers, Bristol	0845 210 5555
	No5 Chambers, London	0845 210 5555
Maka Mr Isaac	Chambers of Mr Isaac Maka, Ilford	07973 308 301
	4 King's Bench Walk, London	020 7822 7000
Malone Mr David John	1 Gray's Inn Square, London	020 7405 0001
Mandalia Mr Vinesh Lalji	St Philips Chambers, Birmingham	0121 246 7000
Mannion Ms Amy Elisabeth	9-12 Bell Yard, London	020 7400 1800
	1 Crown Office Row, London	020 7797 7500
Markus Ms Kate	Doughty Street Chambers, Bristol	01179 058 717
	Doughty Street Chambers, London	020 7404 1313
	Doughty Street Chambers, Manchester	0161 618 1066
Marler Lieutenant Colonel Lee Gary	Bretton Woods Law, London	
	18 Red Lion Court, London	020 7520 6000
Martin Mr Jonathan David	10 King's Bench Walk, London	020 7353 7742
Masters Mr Alan Bruce Raymond	1 Pump Court, London	020 7842 7070
Mather Mr Nicholas Ian Stewart	Furnival Chambers, London	020 7405 3232
Matthias Mr David Huw	Francis Taylor Building, London	020 7353 8415
McBride Mr Martin Jeremy	Monckton Chambers, London	020 7405 7211
McDonald Ms Melanie Sharon	No5 Chambers, Birmingham	0845 210 5555
	No5 Chambers, Bristol	0845 210 5555
	No5 Chambers, London	0845 210 5555
McGowan Miss Maura Patricia	2 Bedford Row, London	020 7440 8888
	Lincoln House Chambers, Manchester	0161 832 5701
McLinden Mr John Vincent Barry	Field Court Chambers, London	020 7405 6114
McNicholas Mr Christopher John	Goresbrook Chambers, Milton Keynes	0845 123 1234
Medhurst Mr David Charles	4 Brick Court, London	020 7832 3200
Menon Mr Rajiv	Garden Court Chambers, London	020 7993 7600

Metcalfe Dr Eric William	Monckton Chambers, London	020 7405 7211
Miah Mr Anawar Babul	Great James Street Chambers, London	020 7440 4949
Michalos Miss Christina Antigone Diana	5RB, London	020 7242 2902
Moffett Mr Jonathan Keith	4-5 Gray's Inn Square, London	020 7404 5252
Moll Mr Christiaan Eric	Blackfriars Chambers, London	020 7353 7400
Moran Mr Christopher John	39 Park Square, Leeds	0113 245 6633
Moran Mr Patrick Michael	15 New Bridge Street, London	020 7842 1900
Morgan Dr Austen Jude	33 Bedford Row, London	020 7242 6476
Morris Mr Ben	Chavasse Court Chambers, Liverpool	0151 229 2030
Morris Ms Johanna	Chambers of Marion Smullen and Kerim Fuad QC, London	020 7427 4400
Mousley Mr William Howard	2 King's Bench Walk, London	020 7353 1746
Muller Mr Antonie Sean	Citadel Chambers, Birmingham	0121 233 8500
Muman Mr Vijay Kumar	43 Temple Row Chambers, Birmingham	0121 237 6035
Muquit Mr Mohammed Shuyeb	1 Mitre Court Buildings, London	020 7452 8900
Murphy Mr Michael Patrick	Central Chambers, Manchester	0161 236 1133
	10 King's Bench Walk, London	020 7353 7742
Mustakim Mr Abdul Yunus Al	Chambers of Mr Mustakim, London	
Myers Mr Benjamin John	Exchange Chambers, Liverpool	0151 236 7747
	Exchange Chambers, Manchester	0161 833 2722
Mylvaganam Ms Tanoo	1 Gray's Inn Square, London	020 7405 0001
Neville Mr Joseph Richard	43 Temple Row Chambers, Birmingham	0121 237 6035
Nicholls Mr Colin Alfred Arthur	3 Raymond Buildings, London	020 7400 6400
Nicol Mr Nicholas Keith	1 Pump Court, London	020 7842 7070
O'Brien Mr Nicholas William Wattebot	10 King's Bench Walk, London	020 7353 7742
O'Connor Mr Patrick Michael Joseph	Doughty Street Chambers, Bristol	01179 058 717
	Doughty Street Chambers, London	020 7404 1313
	Doughty Street Chambers, Manchester	0161 618 1066
Offer Mr Alexander	Garden Court Chambers, London	020 7993 7600
	Park Court Chambers, Leeds	0113 243 3277
Onalaja Mr James Oluwatosin	2 Pump Court, London	020 7353 5597
O'Neill Mr Brian Patrick	2 Hare Court, London	020 7353 3982
Oommen Mr Jacob	Chambers of Mr Jacob Oommen, East Barnet	07958 680272
Owen Mr Timothy Wynn	Matrix Chambers, London	020 7404 3447
Owusu-Yianoma Mr David Kwasi Dartey	1 Mitre Court Buildings, London	020 7452 8900
Palmer Mr Iain Franklyn	Renaissance Chambers, London	020 7404 1111
Paraskos Mr Paraskevakis Christakis	11 Gray's Inn Square Chambers, London	020 7405 6879
Parnell Mrs Cherie Eileen	East Anglian Chambers, Colchester	01473 214481
	East Anglian Chambers, Ipswich	01473 214481
	East Anglian Chambers, Norwich	01473 214481
Pascoe Ms Soraya	1 Gray's Inn Square, London	020 7405 0001
Patel Miss Gita	Kenworthy's Chambers, Manchester	0161 832 4036
Patel Mr Yasin Ahmed	25 Bedford Row, London	020 7067 1500
Penny Miss Abigail Sarah Prudence	4 Breams Buildings, London	020 7092 1900
Peretz Mr George Michael John	Monckton Chambers, London	020 7405 7211
Perian Mr Steven	3 Temple Gardens, London	020 7353 3102
Persaud Dr Marcia Chitroutie	1 Gray's Inn Square, London	020 7405 0001
Physsas Miss Claire	Renaissance Chambers, London	020 7404 1111
Pipe Mr Adam	No 8 Chambers, Birmingham	0121 236 5514
Plimmer Miss Melanie Ann	Kings Chambers, Birmingham	0845 034 3444
	Kings Chambers, Leeds	0845 034 3444
	Kings Chambers, Manchester	0845 034 3444
Plowright Mr Joseph Edward	1 Gray's Inn Square, London	020 7405 0001
Prior Mr Paul Stephen	36 Bedford Row, London	020 7421 8000
Prior Mrs Mary	36 Bedford Row, London	020 7421 8000
Quinn Miss Victoria Kathleen	Thomas More Chambers, London	020 7404 7000
Qureshi Mr Asif Hasan	Quadrant Chambers, London	020 7583 4444

C

Ahmed Mr Nazir	Centurion Chambers, West Bromwich	0121 553 4613
Ajaz Mr Mohammad Arshad	Eastmans Chambers, Reading	0118 966 9094
Akinbolu Miss Sandra Adwoa Anifa	Chambers of Mr Ami Feder, London	020 7797 7788
	Chambers of Mr Ami Feder, London	020 7797 7788
Alakija Mr Ayodele Hugh	No 8 Chambers, Birmingham	0121 236 5514
Alexander Miss Josephine Anne	Principal Chambers, Sevenoaks	0845 209 8080
Ali Mr Ishtiyaq	Chartlands Chambers, Northampton	01604 603322
Ali Mrs Shamim	Chambers of Mrs Shamim Ali, Hatfield	01707 276737
Allen Ms Frances	Renaissance Chambers, London	020 7404 1111
Allwood Mrs Gina Louisa	Seven Bedford Row, London	020 7242 3555
Ameen Mr Danish	18 St John Street, Manchester	0161 278 1800
Amraoui Mr Thomas	4-5 Gray's Inn Square, London	020 7404 5252
Appiah Miss Linda	Guildford Chambers, Guildford	01483 539131
Arkhurst Mr Reginald Leon	4 King's Bench Walk, London	020 7822 7000
Arnold Mr Graham John	Farringdon Chambers, London	020 7089 5700
Auburn Mr Jonathan Walter	4-5 Gray's Inn Square, London	020 7404 5252
Austin Mr Ian	Holborn Chambers, London	020 7242 6060
Awodele Mr Olufemi Adetunji	Great James Street Chambers, London	020 7440 4949
Azhar Mr Ali Mohammad	9 King's Bench Walk, London	020 7353 9564
Azmi Mr Mohammad Javed	No 8 Chambers, Birmingham	0121 236 5514
Bagral Miss Ravinder	No5 Chambers, Birmingham	0845 210 5555
	No5 Chambers, Bristol	0845 210 5555
	No5 Chambers, London	0845 210 5555
Bajwa Mr Ali Naseem	Garden Court Chambers, London	020 7993 7600
Bassiri-Dezfouli Miss Sorour	Temple Court Chambers, London	020 7353 7888
Beloff Mr Rupert Joseph Alexei	No5 Chambers, Birmingham	0845 210 5555
	No5 Chambers, Bristol	0845 210 5555
	No5 Chambers, London	0845 210 5555
Berry Mr Adrian Christopher	Garden Court Chambers, London	020 7993 7600
Bezzam Miss Jayashree	Hampton Court Chambers, West Molesey	020 8979 0381
Bhanji Mr Shiraz Musa	4 Bingham Place, London	020 7486 5347
	1 Gray's Inn Square, London	020 7405 0001
Bhatti Miss Balvinder	Citadel Chambers, Birmingham	0121 233 8500
Birkby Mr Richard Adam	Park Court Chambers, Leeds	0113 243 3277
Bisarya Mr Neil	Number 7 Harrington Street Chambers, Liverpool	0151 242 0707
Bradshaw Mr Mark Kieran	No5 Chambers, Birmingham	0845 210 5555
	No5 Chambers, Bristol	0845 210 5555
	No5 Chambers, London	0845 210 5555
Brown Ms Grace	Tooks Chambers, London	020 7842 7575
Buchan Miss Caroline Venetia	Chambers of Miss C Buchan, Haywards Heath	01444 482222
Bunting Mr Daniel Alexander James	2 Dr Johnson's Buildings, London	020 7936 2613
Burnett Mr Iain	4 King's Bench Walk, London	020 7822 7000
Burrett Mr Alex	1 Gray's Inn Square, London	020 7405 0001
Cairns Ms Sally	No 8 Chambers, Birmingham	0121 236 5514
Canter Mr Simon Alexander	Richmond Canter Immigration Barristers, London	020 3440 5820
Carrington Mr Dominic	Chambers of Martin Burr, London	0845 123 1234
Cattermull Miss Emma Jayne	East Anglian Chambers, Chelmsford	01473 214481
	East Anglian Chambers, Ipswich	01473 214481
	East Anglian Chambers, Norwich	01473 214481
Chelvan Mr S	No5 Chambers, Birmingham	0845 210 5555
	No5 Chambers, Bristol	0845 210 5555
	No5 Chambers, London	0845 210 5555
	Trent Chambers, Nottingham	0115 941 9596
Chipperfield Mr Jeremy Steven	Cranford Chambers, London	020 7404 7454
Chodha Mr Tejpal Singh	Chambers of Mr T Chodha, Gravesend	01474 326666
Clark Mr Dingle	Goldsmith Chambers, London	020 7353 6802
Coleman Mr Daniel Gerald Mayow	1 Gray's Inn Square, London	020 7405 0001
Collins Mr Peter Richard	4 King's Bench Walk, London	020 7822 7000

C

Name	Chambers	Telephone
Comb Mr David William	Trinity Chambers, Middlesbrough	01642 247569
	Trinity Chambers, Newcastle Upon Tyne	0191 232 1927
Conlon Mr Michael John Patrick	Harcourt Chambers, Milton Keynes	0845 123 1234
Costello Mr Paul James	Chambers of Mr Paul J Costello, Biggleswade	07846 016 399
Culverhouse Miss Emily Anna Louise	Chambers of Miss E Culverhouse, Chesham	07813 007503
Dassa Miss Regine	9 King's Bench Walk, London	020 7353 9564
Davies Mr Henry Olusola	Trinity Chambers, Birmingham	0121 346 4672
Davison Mr Guy Dixon	1 Gray's Inn Square, London	020 7405 0001
Dean Mr James Patrick	Goldsmith Chambers, London	020 7353 6802
Dean Mr Peter Thomas	36 Bedford Row, London	020 7421 8000
Del Fabbro Mr Oscar	23 Essex Street, London	020 7413 0353
Delany Ms Francesca	1 Mitre Court Buildings, London	020 7452 8900
Dhaliwal Miss Davinder Kaur	No 8 Chambers, Birmingham	0121 236 5514
Dipré Mr Paul Nicholas Amadeus	Chambers of Mr P N Dipré, Address withheld	0845 123 1234
	MK Family Law Chambers, Milton Keynes	0845 123 1234
Doerfel Mr Jan Hendrik Jamison	1215 Chambers, London	020 3291 1215
	Chambers of Mr J H Doerfel, Richmond	0845 123 1234
Douglass Mr Paul Stephen	9 King's Bench Walk, London	020 7353 9564
Dunne Mr Anthony James	KBW, Leeds	0113 297 1200
Edwards Mr Denis	Francis Taylor Building, London	020 7353 8415
Edwards Mr Paul	37 Park Square Chambers, Leeds	0113 243 9422
Ephraim-Adejumo Mrs Hilda Ekpo	12 Old Square Chambers, London	020 7404 0875
Fama Mrs Gudrun Hildegard	Middle Temple Lane Chambers, London	020 7583 4352
Farbey Miss Judith Sarah	Doughty Street Chambers, Bristol	01179 058 717
	Doughty Street Chambers, London	020 7404 1313
	Doughty Street Chambers, Manchester	0161 618 1066
Faryl Miss Alaha Begum	Central Chambers, Manchester	0161 236 1133
Fetto Mr Niazi Peter	2 Temple Gardens, London	020 7822 1200
Fielden Dr Christa Maria	1 Mitre Court Buildings, London	020 7452 8900
Frantzis Miss Roxanne	KBW, Leeds	0113 297 1200
Ganesan Mr Muthupandi Peter	Furnival Chambers, London	020 7405 3232
Garcha Mr Gurdeep Singh	Citadel Chambers, Birmingham	0121 233 8500
Gaskin Mr Francis John Gerald	4 Breams Buildings, London	020 7092 1900
Gill Miss Baljinder	10 King's Bench Walk, London	020 7353 7742
Gill Mr Manjit Singh	No5 Chambers, Birmingham	0845 210 5555
	No5 Chambers, Bristol	0845 210 5555
	No5 Chambers, London	0845 210 5555
Gill Mr Satinderjit Singh	Five Paper, London	020 7815 3200
Gobir Mr Nuhu Garba	9 Park Place, Cardiff	029 2038 2731
Goodman Mr Alexander David Edmund	Atlas Chambers, London	020 7269 7980
	4-5 Gray's Inn Square, London	020 7404 5252
Hafiz Mr Mohammed Ghulam	Chambers of Mr M G Hafiz, London	020 8677 5778
Hamilton Mr John Conrad	Field Court Chambers, London	020 7405 6114
Haque Mr Gazi Mosta Gawsal	Dollis Hill Chambers, London	020 8208 1663
Harris Mr Michael Peter	10 King's Bench Walk, London	020 7353 7742
Harris Mr Paul	Doughty Street Chambers, Bristol	01179 058 717
	Doughty Street Chambers, London	020 7404 1313
	Doughty Street Chambers, Manchester	0161 618 1066
Harris Mr Wilbert Arthurlyn	Rowchester Chambers, Birmingham	0121 233 2327
Hartman Mr Michael	One Essex Court, London	020 7936 3030
Hashim Mr Mu'Min Iran Muhammad	Chambers of Marion Smullen and Kerim Fuad QC, London	020 7427 4400
	Paragon Chambers, London	020 3318 9988
Hawkin Mr Benjamin	1 Mitre Court Buildings, London	020 7452 8900
Heller Mrs Anne	10 King's Bench Walk, London	020 7353 7742

Name	Chambers	Telephone
Hendron Mr Henry Joseph Christopher	Strand Chambers, London	020 7117 6920
Hill Mr Simon Michael	33 Bedford Row, London	020 7242 6476
Hobbs Ms Naomi Josephine	No 8 Chambers, Birmingham	0121 236 5514
Hossain Mr Mohammed Monwar	No. 3 Fleet Street Chambers, London	020 7936 4474
Hussain Mr Mukhtar	Lincoln House Chambers, Manchester	0161 832 5701
Hussain Mr Tasaddat	Broadway House Chambers, Bradford	01274 722560
	Broadway House Chambers, Leeds	0113 246 2600
Hypolite-De-Souza Mrs Josephine Claudia	12 Old Square Chambers, London	020 7404 0875
Iqbal Miss Samina	Renaissance Chambers, London	020 7404 1111
Iqbal Mr Mashood	London View Chambers, Sawbridgeworth	07788 912493
Islam Mr Aminul Ruhul	Chambers of Mr Aminul R. Islam, London	020 7247 1977
Jafar Mr Abdurahman Akhtar	Chambers of Mr Abdurahman Jafar, Ilford	07828 937338
Jafferji Mr Zainulabedin Hatim	Chambers of Mr Jafferji, Leicester	07957 198777
Jaisri Mr Shashi Satyendra	1 Mitre Court Buildings, London	020 7452 8900
James Mrs Venice Imogen	No 8 Chambers, Birmingham	0121 236 5514
Jones Miss Jacinta Elizabeth Barrett	1 Mitre Court Buildings, London	020 7452 8900
Jones Mr Mark Andrew	St Ive's Chambers, Birmingham	0121 236 0863
Jorro Mr Peter Antonio Raimo	Garden Court Chambers, London	020 7993 7600
Joseph Mr Sellappah Job	Chambers of Mr S J Joseph, London	020 8809 3083/020 8802 9889
Jowett Mr Timothy David Christian	9 Park Place, Cardiff	029 2038 2731
Judge Miss Parveen	1 Mitre Court Buildings, London	020 7452 8900
Juss Prof Satvinder Singh	3 Hare Court, London	020 7415 7800
Kannangara Mr Harshaka Hemantha	Temple Court Chambers, London	020 7353 7888
Kansal Miss Seema	12 Old Square Chambers, London	020 7404 0875
Keith Mr Benjamin Charles Andrew	Five St Andrew's Hill, London	020 7332 5400
Kelly Mr Shaw Martin	Staple Inn Chambers, London	020 7242 5240
Khalid Mr James	Goulds Green Chambers, Uxbridge	01895 422574
	Goulds Green Chambers, Uxbridge	01895 422574
Khan Mr Abdul Aleem	Gray's Chambers, Newbury	020 8518 2525
Khan Mr Ayoub	Chambers of Mr Ayoub Khan, Birmingham	07930 987202
Khan Mr Forz	Chambers of Mr F Khan, London	07854 109584
	6 King's Bench Walk, London	020 7353 4931
Khan Mr Mahmood Shafi	Luton Chambers, Luton	01582 598394
	Willesden Chambers, London	020 3273 1042
Khan Mr Shahnawaz Zulfiquar	1 Gray's Inn Square, London	020 7405 0001
Khan Mr Tariq Ali	Chambers of Mr T A Khan, Coventry	02476 666 400
Khan Mr Zarif	Dyers Chambers, London	020 7404 1881
Knight Mr Graeme Edward Verdon	7 Bell Yard, London	020 7831 0636
	Carmelite Chambers, London	020 7936 6300
	The Barristers Chambers, Address withheld	07966 056368
Krushner Mr Damian Mark	Oakwood Chambers, London	07789 435485
Lal Mr Sanjay	4 King's Bench Walk, London	020 7822 7000
Lams Mr Barnabas Jeffrey	4 Brick Court, London	020 7832 3200
Lane Mr Christopher Paul	No 8 Chambers, Birmingham	0121 236 5514
Langley Mr Charles Howard	2 Bedford Row, London	020 7440 8888
Lawrence Miss Samantha Dionne	3 Dr Johnson's Buildings, London	020 7353 4854
Lemer Mr David James	Doughty Street Chambers, London	020 7404 1313
Lenaghan Mr Anthony	Dyers Chambers, London	020 7404 1881
Lewis Mr Wayne Anthony	Access Lawyers, London	020 8801 2345
Logan Mr Graeme Alexander	4 Breams Buildings, London	020 7092 1900
	15 New Bridge Street, London	020 7842 1900
Longhurst-Woods Ms Lesley	2 Louisa Close, London	020 8985 8716
Luh Miss Shu Shin	Garden Court Chambers, London	020 7993 7600
Lule Miss Jacqueline	1 Mitre Court Buildings, London	020 7452 8900

Name	Chambers	Telephone
MacDonald Mr Ian Alexander	Chambers of Ian Macdonald QC, Manchester	0161 236 1840
	Garden Court Chambers, London	020 7993 7600
	Kings Court Chambers, Birmingham	07967 910864
MacKenzie Smith Mrs Catherine Joanna	10 King's Bench Walk, London	020 7353 7742
Mahmood Mr Abid	Central Chambers, Manchester	0161 236 1133
	No5 Chambers, Birmingham	0845 210 5555
	No5 Chambers, Bristol	0845 210 5555
	No5 Chambers, London	0845 210 5555
Maka Mr Isaac	Chambers of Mr Isaac Maka, Ilford	07973 308 301
	4 King's Bench Walk, London	020 7822 7000
Mandalia Mr Vinesh Lalji	St Philips Chambers, Birmingham	0121 246 7000
Mann Mr Jasvir Singh	No5 Chambers, Birmingham	0845 210 5555
	No5 Chambers, Bristol	0845 210 5555
	No5 Chambers, London	0845 210 5555
Mannan Mr Charles Madani Fuad	Temple Court Chambers, London	020 7353 7888
Martin Mr James Stephen	5 King's Bench Walk, London	020 7353 5638
Martin Mr Jonathan David	10 King's Bench Walk, London	020 7353 7742
Mason Mr Ian Douglas	Amethyst Chambers, London	020 7936 4966
Matthias Mr David Huw	Francis Taylor Building, London	020 7353 8415
McCrae Miss Fiona	Trinity Chambers, Middlesbrough	01642 247569
	Trinity Chambers, Newcastle Upon Tyne	0191 232 1927
McKinney Miss Nicola Alexandra	4 KBW, London	020 7822 8822
McNicholas Mr Christopher John	Goresbrook Chambers, Milton Keynes	0845 123 1234
Medhurst Mr David Charles	4 Brick Court, London	020 7832 3200
Metcalfe Dr Eric William	Monckton Chambers, London	020 7405 7211
Miah Mr Anawar Babul	Great James Street Chambers, London	020 7440 4949
Middleton Mr Joseph	Doughty Street Chambers, Bristol	01179 058 717
	Doughty Street Chambers, London	020 7404 1313
	Doughty Street Chambers, Manchester	0161 618 1066
Mitchell Mr Jonathan	1 Gray's Inn Square, London	020 7405 0001
	Holborn Chambers, London	020 7242 6060
Mohammad Mr Nazar	Legis Chambers, Aylesbury	01296 431125
	No. 3 Fleet Street Chambers, London	020 7936 4474
Morgan Dr Austen Jude	33 Bedford Row, London	020 7242 6476
Mullins Mr Mark Lovel Rupert	Five St Andrew's Hill, London	020 7332 5400
Muman Mr Vijay Kumar	43 Temple Row Chambers, Birmingham	0121 237 6035
Munir Dr Ashley Edward	Five St Andrew's Hill, London	020 7332 5400
Muquit Mr Mohammed Shuyeb	1 Mitre Court Buildings, London	020 7452 8900
Murphy Mr Michael Patrick	Central Chambers, Manchester	0161 236 1133
	10 King's Bench Walk, London	020 7353 7742
Nasim Mr Zia-Ul-Mustafa	Milestone Chambers, London	
Nassar Miss Victoria Katie	Fortis Green Chambers, Wilmslow	0161 439 5804
Neville Mr Joseph Richard	43 Temple Row Chambers, Birmingham	0121 237 6035
O'Brien Mr Nicholas William Wattebot	10 King's Bench Walk, London	020 7353 7742
Obuka Ms Obijuo Agwu	Chambers of Miss O A Obuka, London	020 7936 4474
Ogunbusola Mr Victor Olaniyi	Chambers of Victor Ogumbusola, Basildon	07413 634231
Ojutiku Mrs Fadekemi Omotayo	4 King's Bench Walk, London	020 7822 7000
Onipede Dr Victor Olusegun	Chambers of Dr V O Onipede, London	07956 207159
Oommen Mr Jacob	Chambers of Mr Jacob Oommen, East Barnet	07958 680272
Otchie Mr Andrew Akuafo	12 Old Square Chambers, London	020 7404 0875
O'Toole Mr Bartholomew Vincent	5 King's Bench Walk, London	020 7353 5638
Palmer Mr Iain Franklyn	Renaissance Chambers, London	020 7404 1111
Panagiotopoulou Miss Sophie Thalia	Staple Inn Chambers, London	020 7242 5240
Pande Miss Kakoly	2 Dr Johnson's Buildings, London	020 7936 2613

Name	Chambers	Telephone
Paraskos Mr Paraskevakis Christakis	11 Gray's Inn Square Chambers, London	020 7405 6879
Parker Mrs Karen Lesley	Guildhall Chambers Portsmouth, Portsmouth	023 9275 2400
Patel Miss Gita	Kenworthy's Chambers, Manchester	0161 832 4036
Perry Mr Lewis Kenneth	Rowchester Chambers, Birmingham	0121 233 2327
Persaud Dr Marcia Chitroutie	1 Gray's Inn Square, London	020 7405 0001
Physsas Miss Claire	Renaissance Chambers, London	020 7404 1111
Pipe Mr Adam	No 8 Chambers, Birmingham	0121 236 5514
Plimmer Miss Melanie Ann	Kings Chambers, Birmingham	0845 034 3444
	Kings Chambers, Leeds	0845 034 3444
	Kings Chambers, Manchester	0845 034 3444
Plowright Mr Joseph Edward	1 Gray's Inn Square, London	020 7405 0001
Pope Miss Anna	Linenhall Chambers, Chester	01244 348282
Powis Miss Samantha Inez	Citadel Chambers, Birmingham	0121 233 8500
Price Mr Charles John	No5 Chambers, Birmingham	0845 210 5555
	No5 Chambers, Bristol	0845 210 5555
	No5 Chambers, London	0845 210 5555
Price Mrs Huma Sabih	St Andrews Chambers, London	020 8368 3686
Puar Mr Mikhael	30 Park Place, Cardiff	029 2039 8421
Quinn Miss Victoria Kathleen	Thomas More Chambers, London	020 7404 7000
Qureshi Miss Dilruba	Temple Court Chambers, London	020 7353 7888
Qureshi Mr Abdul Saleem	Barclay Chambers, London	020 8558 2289
Rahman Mr Anis	12 Old Square Chambers, London	020 7404 0875
Rahman Mr Leo Ferhanur	Chambers of Leo Rahman, Brighton	07814 004 790
Rahman Mr Luthfur	Chambers of Mr L Rahman, Rochester	07947 588362
Rai Mr Rajesh Kumar	1 Mitre Court Buildings, London	020 7452 8900
Ramzan Mr Mohammed Anwar	Great James Street Chambers, London	020 7440 4949
Rana Mr Mohammed Akram	Clapham Law Chambers, London	020 7978 8482
Rasoul Miss Miriam Hamean	Trinity Chambers, Middlesbrough	01642 247569
	Trinity Chambers, Newcastle Upon Tyne	0191 232 1927
Raw Mr Edward	Tanfield Chambers, London	020 7421 5300
Rees Prof William Michael	1 Gray's Inn Square, London	020 7405 0001
Reid Miss Claudette Patricia	Chambers of Miss Claudette Reid, London	
Rendle Mr Jeremy Mark	9 King's Bench Walk, London	020 7353 9564
Rene Mr Jacques Mario	Chambers of Mr J M Rene, London	07768 854321
Richards Mr Duncan James	Chambers of Mr Ami Feder, London	020 7797 7788
	Chambers of Mr Ami Feder, London	020 7797 7788
	Principal Chambers, Sevenoaks	0845 209 8080
Richardson Mr Paul Andrew	1 Gray's Inn Square, London	020 7405 0001
Richmond Mr Paul Anthony Oliffe	Richmond Canter Immigration Barristers, London	020 3440 5820
Riza Mr Alper Ali	Goldsmith Chambers, London	020 7353 6802
Rudd Mr Michael	36 Bedford Row, London	020 7421 8000
Rutherford Miss Emma Victoria	No 8 Chambers, Birmingham	0121 236 5514
Saini Mr Parminder Paul Singh	12 Old Square Chambers, London	020 7404 0875
Santamera Miss Louise Alexandria	New Bailey Chambers, Liverpool	0151 236 9402
Scally Miss Josephine Theresa Sarah	Palmyra Chambers, Warrington	01925 444919
Seeboruth Mr Royln Jean-Paul	Chambers of Royln Seeboruth, Aylesbury	01296 393329
Sekhon Mr Narinder Singh	Sovereign Chambers, Leeds	0113 245 1841
Shamim Mr Mohammed	Clapham Law Chambers, London	020 7978 8482
Sher Miss Shamim Akhtar	Chambers of Miss Shamim Sher, Ilford	07581 201823
Silverton Miss Catherine Anne	Sovereign Chambers, Leeds	0113 245 1841
Simpson Miss Carol Monica	Amethyst Chambers, London	020 7936 4966
Singarajah Mr Frederico	1 Gray's Inn Square, London	020 7405 0001
Singer Mr Richard Adam	1 Gray's Inn Square, London	020 7405 0001
Sinker Mr Andrew Tennant	New Bailey Chambers, Liverpool	0151 236 9402
Slatter Mr Alexis Andrew Mallatratt	Tooks Chambers, London	020 7842 7575
Smith Mr Mark William	Aegis Chambers, Wembley	

C

Name	Chambers	Telephone
Solomon Mr Reuben	12 Old Square Chambers, London	020 7404 0875
Sood Mrs Usha Rani	Trent Chambers, Nottingham	0115 941 9596
Southey Mr David Hugh	Tooks Chambers, London	020 7842 7575
Sowerby Mr Matthew Giles	1 Gray's Inn Square, London	020 7405 0001
Spooner Mr Henry Neville	Tolzey Chambers, Bristol	
	Westgate Chambers, Lewes	01273 480510
Stanage Mr Nick Sean	Doughty Street Chambers, Bristol	01179 058 717
	Doughty Street Chambers, London	020 7404 1313
	Doughty Street Chambers, Manchester	0161 618 1066
Symes Mr Mark Adrian	Garden Court Chambers, London	020 7993 7600
Targett-Parker Miss Leanne Susan	No. 3 Fleet Street Chambers, London	020 7936 4474
	The Chambers of Miss Leanne Targett-Parker, London	020 8674 6694
Tregidgo Mr Marc Gordon	4 King's Bench Walk, London	020 7822 7000
Treharne Mr Neil Simon	Dingle Chambers, Bristol	07818 827754
Trumpington Mr John Henry	Staple Inn Chambers, London	020 7242 5240
Turnbull Mrs Linda Angela	1 Gray's Inn Square, London	020 7405 0001
Unigwe Mr Sylvester Emefiona	Essex House Chambers, London	020 7692 0677
	11 Gray's Inn Square Chambers, London	020 7405 6879
Vanhegan Mr Toby Bartholomew	Arden Chambers, London	020 7242 4244
Vaughan Mr Anthony	Garden Court Chambers, London	020 7993 7600
Vencatachellum Ms Glenda Roxande	Rowchester Chambers, Birmingham	0121 233 2327
Victor-Mazeli Miss Jacqueline	Bell Yard Chambers, London	020 7306 9292
	Chambers of Martin Burr, London	0845 123 1234
Vokes Mr Stephen John	No 8 Chambers, Birmingham	0121 236 5514
Waldman Mr Amos	Doughty Street Chambers, Bristol	01179 058 717
	Doughty Street Chambers, London	020 7404 1313
	Doughty Street Chambers, Manchester	0161 618 1066
Watkinson Mr Howard	9-12 Bell Yard, London	020 7400 1800
Watterson Ms Anna Elizabeth	1 Mitre Court Buildings, London	020 7452 8900
Widdison-Thom Mrs Stacey Jane	Kingsley Chambers, Barkingside	07891 441 445
Williams Mr Simon Christopher	12 Old Square Chambers, London	020 7404 0875
Wood Miss Joanna Rachel	1 Pump Court, London	020 7842 7070
Wright Mrs Yasmin Tajdin	Cobden House Chambers, Manchester	0161 833 6000
Yeo Mr Colin Anthony	Renaissance Chambers, London	020 7404 1111
Zeitler Miss Barbara	3 Dr Johnson's Buildings, London	020 7353 4854

INDUSTRIAL DISEASES

Name	Chambers	Telephone
Campbell Mr Oliver Edward Wilhelm	Henderson Chambers, London	020 7583 9020
Coster Mr Ronald David	42 Bedford Row, London	020 7831 0222
De Berry Mr Philip John	18 St John Street, Manchester	0161 278 1800
Dowell Mr Gregory Hamilton	Principal Chambers, Sevenoaks	0845 209 8080
Finlay Mr Darren	Sovereign Chambers, Leeds	0113 245 1841
Kramer Mr Philip Anthony	Park Lane Plowden, Newcastle Upon Tyne	0191 211 4087
Matthias Mr David Huw	Francis Taylor Building, London	020 7353 8415
Nickless Mr Jason Alan	College Chambers, Southampton	023 8023 0338
Smith Mr Michael David	Kenworthy's Chambers, Manchester	0161 832 4036
Treharne Mr Neil Simon	Dingle Chambers, Bristol	07818 827754
Walker Mr Adam Nigel	Seven Bedford Row, London	020 7242 3555

INFORMATION TECHNOLOGY

Name	Chambers	Telephone
Abrahams Mr James	8 New Square, London	020 7405 4321
Ajaz Mr Mohammad Arshad	Eastmans Chambers, Reading	0118 966 9094
Algazy Mr Jacques Max	Cloisters, London	020 7827 4000
Antell Mr John Jason	King's Bench and Godolphin (KBG)Chambers, Plymouth	01752 221551
Barnett Mr Jeremy Victor	2 Bedford Row, London	020 7440 8888
	St Paul's Chambers, Leeds	0113 245 5866
Barwise Miss Stephanie Nicola	Atkin Chambers, London	020 7404 0102
Beaumont Mr Marc Clifford	9 Stone Buildings, London	020 7404 5055
	Windsor Barristers' Chambers, Windsor	01753 839321

C

Boulding Mr Philip Vincent	Keating Chambers, London	020 7544 2600
Bowling Mr James Stuart	4 Pump Court, London	020 7842 5555
Bowsher Mr Michael Frederick Thomas	Monckton Chambers, London	020 7405 7211
Burr Mr Andrew Charles	Atkin Chambers, London	020 7404 0102
Charlton Mr Alexander Murray	4 Pump Court, London	020 7842 5555
Coster Mr Ronald David	42 Bedford Row, London	020 7831 0222
Crangle Mr Thomas Peter	4 Pump Court, London	020 7842 5555
Crawshaw Mr Simon Richard	Atkin Chambers, London	020 7404 0102
Cunningham Mr Graham Taylor	Hardwicke, London	020 7242 2523
Dillon Mr Thomas William Matthew	Chambers of Thomas Dillon, London	020 7692 2722
Doerries Miss Chantal-Aimée Renee Aemelia An	Atkin Chambers, London	020 7404 0102
Engelman Mr Mark Trevor	Hardwicke, London	020 7242 2523
Facenna Mr Gerald Carlo	Monckton Chambers, London	020 7405 7211
Fern Mr Gary	7 Stones IP, London	020 7193 4033
Fitzgerald Mr John Vincent	Ingenuity IP Chambers, Petts Wood	
Friedman Mr David Peter	4 Pump Court, London	020 7842 5555
Garrett Miss Lucy Margaret	Keating Chambers, London	020 7544 2600
Gatty Mr Daniel Simon	Hardwicke, London	020 7242 2523
Gillies Miss Jennie	4 Pump Court, London	020 7842 5555
Godfrey Mr Lauren John	Crown Office Row Chambers, Brighton	01273 625625
Green Mr Jonathan Paul	Dyers Chambers, London	020 7404 1881
Guy Mr John David Colin	Tanfield Chambers, London	020 7421 5300
Hamer Mr George Clemens	8 New Square, London	020 7405 4321
Hargreaves Mr Simon John Robert	Keating Chambers, London	020 7544 2600
Heal Mrs Madeleine	New Square Chambers, London	020 7419 8000
Iyer Miss Shobana	Swan Chambers, Richmond	0845 123 1234
Jafar Mr Abdurahman Akhtar	Chambers of Mr Abdurahman Jafar, Ilford	07828 937338
Jinadu Mr Abdul-Lateef Abodurin Olayinka	Keating Chambers, London	020 7544 2600
Johnson Mr Phillip Michael	Chambers of Mr P Johnson, London	020 7288 2256
Jones Mr Kelvin Mcallister	Templis Chambers, London	020 7649 9808
Jones Mr Richard Frederick Thomas	Heavenwood Chambers, Stroud	01453 873444
Keane Mr Owen Ashley	Design Chambers, London	020 7353 0747
Kime Mr Matthew Jonathan	Cobden House Chambers, Manchester	0161 833 6000
	Ingenuity IP Chambers, Petts Wood	
	No. 3 Fleet Street Chambers, London	020 7936 4474
Knight Mr Benjamin James	Central Chambers, Manchester	0161 236 1133
Kwiatkowski Mr Feliks Jerzy	Kew Chambers, Kew	0844 8099991
Lambert Miss Jane Elizabeth	NIPC, Huddersfield	0800 862 0055
Lane Ms Lindsay Ruth Busfield	8 New Square, London	020 7405 4321
Lawrence Dr Heather Bunting Elizabeth	11 South Square, London	020 7405 1222
Lenaghan Mr Anthony	Dyers Chambers, London	020 7404 1881
Ludbrook Mr Timothy Vivian	13 Old Square Chambers, London	020 7831 4445
Mason Mr Stephen Charles Winston	Chambers of Mr S C W Mason, Biggleswade	01462 701 036
Matthias Mr David Huw	Francis Taylor Building, London	020 7353 8415
Mawrey Mr Richard Brooks	Henderson Chambers, London	020 7583 9020
McCafferty Miss Lynne	4 Pump Court, London	020 7842 5555
Murphy Mr Damian	Enterprise Chambers, Leeds	0113 246 0391
	Enterprise Chambers, London	020 7405 9471
	Enterprise Chambers, Newcastle Upon Tyne	0191 222 3344
Onslow Mr Robert Denzil	8 New Square, London	020 7405 4321
Osborne Mr James Robert	Clerksroom (London), London	0845 083 3000
Panton Mr Alastair Howard	10 King's Bench Walk, London	020 7353 7742
Pennicott Mr Ian	Keating Chambers, London	020 7544 2600
Penny Mr Timothy Charles	11 Stone Buildings, London	020 7831 6381
Platts-Mills Mr Mark Fortescue	8 New Square, London	020 7405 4321
Power Mr Lawrence Imam	4 KBW, London	020 7822 8822
Purves Mr Gavin Bowman	Swan House, London	020 8998 3035

Reed Mr Jeremy Nigel	Hogarth Chambers, London	020 7404 0404
Roberts Mr Philip Duncan	One Essex Court, London	020 7583 2000
Rogers Miss Christy Abigail	Ingenuity IP Chambers, Petts Wood	
	No. 3 Fleet Street Chambers, London	020 7936 4474
Roughton Mr Ashley Wentworth	Hogarth Chambers, London	020 7404 0404
Royce Mr Darryl Fraser	Atkin Chambers, London	020 7404 0102
Sampson Dr Timothy Michael George	One Essex Court, London	020 7936 3030
Scott Holland Mr Gideon Silas	Keating Chambers, London	020 7544 2600
Sears Mr Robert David Murray	Four New Square, London	020 7822 2000
Sefton-Smith Mr Lloyd	Lamb Chambers, London	020 7797 8300
Shirley Mr James Patrick	Stone Chambers, London	020 7440 6900
Silcock Mr Ian Peter	Hardwicke, London	020 7242 2523
Singarajah Mr Frederico	1 Gray's Inn Square, London	020 7405 0001
Speaight Mr Anthony Hugh	4 Pump Court, London	020 7842 5555
Stansfield Mr Piers Alistair	Keating Chambers, London	020 7544 2600
Stein Mr Daniel Alexander	No5 Chambers, Birmingham	0845 210 5555
	No5 Chambers, Bristol	0845 210 5555
	No5 Chambers, London	0845 210 5555
Stephens Miss Jessica	Keating Chambers, London	020 7544 2600
Stewart Mr Nicholas John Cameron	Ely Place Chambers, London	020 7400 9600
Taylor Mr Michael Joseph Fitz	4 Pump Court, London	020 7842 5555
Temmink Mr Robert-Jan	Quadrant Chambers, London	020 7583 4444
Townend Mr Samuel John	Keating Chambers, London	020 7544 2600
Tritton Mr Robert Guy Henton	Hogarth Chambers, London	020 7404 0404
Vitiello Mr Fabio Angelo-Giuseppe	Staple Inn Chambers, London	020 7242 5240
Zoest Ms Jacqueline Amy	Carmelite Chambers, London	020 7936 6300

INQUESTS

Andre Mr Roger Louis	Sovereign Chambers, Leeds	0113 245 1841
Askey Mr Robert John	Palmyra Chambers, Warrington	01925 444919
Bourke Ms Sarah Victoria Norma	Tooks Chambers, London	020 7842 7575
Bowden Mr Guy Robert	4 Breams Buildings, London	020 7092 1900
Bryan Mr Robert John	1 Paper Buildings, London	020 7353 3728
Cartwright Mr Ivan Matthew	KCH Garden Square, Nottingham	0115 941 8851
Casey Mr Paul Joseph	Chambers of Marion Smullen and Kerim Fuad QC, London	020 7427 4400
Claridge Miss Rachael Sarah	Crown Office Row Chambers, Brighton	01273 625625
Clements Miss Paula Kate	Alexander Chambers, London	0845 652 0451/0854 652 0451
	Guildford Chambers, Guildford	01483 539131
Climie Mr Roger Stephen	King's Bench and Godolphin (KBG)Chambers, Plymouth	01752 221551
	Outer Temple Chambers, London	020 7353 6381
Coster Mr Ronald David	42 Bedford Row, London	020 7831 0222
Crew Miss Gillian Mary	Ely Place Chambers, London	020 7400 9600
Dixon Mr David Steven	Sovereign Chambers, Leeds	0113 245 1841
Doherty Mr Nicholas Brudenell	4 King's Bench Walk, London	020 7822 7000
Dolan Dr Bridget Maura	3 Serjeants Inn, London	020 7427 5000
Dos Santos Mr Alexander	Charter Chambers, London	020 7618 4400
Dowden Mr Andrew Philip	Castle Chambers, Harrow-on-the-Hill	020 8423 6579
	Melbury House, Leicester	07801 037802
Draycott Mr Simon Douglas	Citadel Chambers, Birmingham	0121 233 8500
	Five St Andrew's Hill, London	020 7332 5400
Duffy Mr Derek James	St Paul's Chambers, Leeds	0113 245 5866
Edington Mrs Fiona Anne Rider	Thomas More Chambers, London	020 7404 7000
Edwards Mr Nigel Royston	St Paul's Chambers, Leeds	0113 245 5866
Foulkes Miss Rebecca	5 Pump Court, London	020 7353 2532
Gallagher Ms Caoilfhionn Anna	Doughty Street Chambers, Bristol	01179 058 717
	Doughty Street Chambers, London	020 7404 1313
	Doughty Street Chambers, Manchester	0161 618 1066
Gersch Mr Adam Nissen	Argent Chambers, London	020 7556 5500
Gledhill Mr Lee Andre	Alexander Chambers, London	0845 652 0451/0854 652 0451
	Trident Barristers Chambers, Manchester	0161 663 3123

C

Name	Chambers	Telephone
Goodlad Mr Grant David	Farrar's Building, London	020 7583 9241
Granville Stafford Mr Andrew	4 King's Bench Walk, London	020 7822 7000
Griffin Mr Nicholas John	Five Paper Buildings, London	020 7583 6117
Gurden Miss Alison Louise	1 Gray's Inn Square, London	020 7405 0001
Hanlon Mr James Tobias	Old Bailey Chambers, London	020 3008 6404
Harrison Dr Graeme	12 College Place, Southampton	023 8032 0320
Harrison Mr John Foster	St Paul's Chambers, Leeds	0113 245 5866
Henson Miss Christine Ruth	Crown Office Row Chambers, Brighton	01273 625625
Hill Ms Eleanor Mary Henrietta	Doughty Street Chambers, Bristol	01179 058 717
	Doughty Street Chambers, London	020 7404 1313
	Doughty Street Chambers, Manchester	0161 618 1066
Hinton Mr Neil Pearse	King's Bench Chambers, Bournemouth	01202 250025
Hood Mr David	Prince of Wales Chambers, London	020 7622 7415
Jackson Mr Andrew Fraser	5 Pump Court, London	020 7353 2532
Jarratt Miss Alice Cordelia Betchworth	Carmelite Chambers, London	020 7936 6300
Jones Mr Mark Andrew	St Ive's Chambers, Birmingham	0121 236 0863
Kramer Mr Philip Anthony	Park Lane Plowden, Newcastle Upon Tyne	0191 211 4087
Krushner Mr Damian Mark	Oakwood Chambers, London	07789 435485
Marshall Miss Vanessa Juliette	Seven Bedford Row, London	020 7242 3555
Matthias Mr David Huw	Francis Taylor Building, London	020 7353 8415
May Mr Christopher John	Five St Andrew's Hill, London	020 7332 5400
McCulloch Miss Fiona Catharine Jane	Middle Temple Lane Chambers, London	020 7583 4352
McNally Mr John Joseph	Dyers Chambers, London	020 7404 1881
Melville-Shreeve Mr Michael David	Walnut House, Exeter	01392 279751
Menon Mr Rajiv	Garden Court Chambers, London	020 7993 7600
Milne Mr Alexander Hugh	18 Red Lion Court, London	020 7520 6000
	18 Red Lion Court (Annexe), Chelmsford	01245 280880
Monaghan Ms Susan Mary	No5 Chambers, Birmingham	0845 210 5555
	No5 Chambers, Bristol	0845 210 5555
	No5 Chambers, London	0845 210 5555
Mustakim Mr Abdul Yunus Al	Chambers of Mr Mustakim, London	
O'Neill Miss Sally Jane	Furnival Chambers, London	020 7405 3232
Owen Mr Timothy Wynn	Matrix Chambers, London	020 7404 3447
Perry Mr Christopher Edward	Palmyra Chambers, Warrington	01925 444919
Real Miss Kirsty Nichola	Albion Chambers, Bristol	0117 927 2144
Reed Mr Simon John	New Walk Chambers, Leicester	0871 200 1298/0116 255 9144
Ritchie Miss Shauna	2 Bedford Row, London	020 7440 8888
Rooke Mr Alexander John Giles	Argent Chambers, London	020 7556 5500
Rule Mr Philip David	Castle Chambers, Harrow-on-the-Hill	020 8423 6579
Rustom Mr Shiraz Sam	1215 Chambers, London	020 3291 1215
	Cranford Chambers, London	020 7404 7454
	1 Mitre Court Buildings, London	020 7452 8900
Scott Mr Andrew David Peter	Park Lane Plowden, Leeds	0113 228 5049
Sefton-Smith Mr Lloyd	Lamb Chambers, London	020 7797 8300
Skelt Mr Ian Stuart	KBW, Leeds	0113 297 1200
Smith Mr Michael David	Kenworthy's Chambers, Manchester	0161 832 4036
Stead Mr Richard James	St John's Chambers, Bristol	0117 923 4700
Stebbings Mr Ian Anthony	1 Gray's Inn Square, London	020 7405 0001
Stevenson Mr Robert Lloyd	Sovereign Chambers, Leeds	0113 245 1841
Tresman Mr Lewis Robert Simon	Staple Inn Chambers, London	020 7242 5240
Walker Mr Adam Nigel	Seven Bedford Row, London	020 7242 3555
Williams Mr Ben Dylan	Kings Chambers, Birmingham	0845 034 3444
	Kings Chambers, Leeds	0845 034 3444
	Kings Chambers, Manchester	0845 034 3444

INSOLVENCY

Name	Chambers	Telephone
Adewale Mr Remi Adetokunbo Sanni	Chambers of G. D. Tetteh, London	020 7353 7095
	Chambers of Mr R. A. Adewale, Address withheld	020 7231 2814
Ajaz Mr Mohammad Arshad	Eastmans Chambers, Reading	0118 966 9094

C

Name	Chambers	Telephone
Allison Mr Simon Robert	Hardwicke, London	020 7242 2523
Anderson Mr Richard Neil Macdiarmid	Arbitration Chambers, London	020 7267 2137
Angammana Mr Gamini Bertram	Chambers of Gamini Angammana, London	020 8771 5205
Apthorp Mr George Charles	5 Essex Court, London	020 7410 2000
Ascroft Mr Richard Geoffrey	Guildhall Chambers, Bristol	0117 930 9000
Askey Mr Robert John	Palmyra Chambers, Warrington	01925 444919
Aswani Mr Ravi Girdharilal	Stone Chambers, London	020 7440 6900
Atkin Mrs Clare Catherine	Erimus Chambers, Bedford	01234 720952
Bailey Miss Rosana Henrietta	10 King's Bench Walk, London	020 7353 7742
Barnard Mr James Philip	11 Stone Buildings, London	020 7831 6381
Beaumont Mr Marc Clifford	9 Stone Buildings, London	020 7404 5055
	Windsor Barristers' Chambers, Windsor	01753 839321
Becker Mr Timothy George Christie	Chambers of Mr Timothy Becker, Liverpool	0151 703 0319
	Clerksroom (London), London	0845 083 3000
Beloff Mr Rupert Joseph Alexei	No5 Chambers, Birmingham	0845 210 5555
	No5 Chambers, Bristol	0845 210 5555
	No5 Chambers, London	0845 210 5555
Berkley Mr Michael Stuart	Rougemont Chambers, Exeter	01392 208484
Birch Mr Roger Allen	Five St Andrew's Hill, London	020 7332 5400
	Sovereign Chambers, Leeds	0113 245 1841
Blackwood Mr Clive David	Lamb Chambers, London	020 7797 8300
Bleasdale Miss Marie-Claire	Radcliffe Chambers, London	020 7831 0081
Blohm Mr Leslie Adrian	St John's Chambers, Bristol	0117 923 4700
Bogle Mr James Stewart Lockhart	10 King's Bench Walk, London	020 7353 7742
Bourne Mr Geoffrey Robert	13 Old Square Chambers, London	020 7831 4445
Bowling Mr James Stuart	4 Pump Court, London	020 7842 5555
Boyd Mr Stephen James Harvey	Selborne Chambers, London	020 7420 9500
Bragge Mr Thomas Hereward	Stour Chambers, Canterbury	01227 764899
Bragiel Mr Edward Bronislaw Henryk	Hogarth Chambers, London	020 7404 0404
Bredemear Mr Zachary Charles	1 Chancery Lane, London	0845 634 6666
Brook Mr Paul Antony	Park Lane Plowden, Leeds	0113 228 5049
	Park Lane Plowden, Newcastle Upon Tyne	0191 211 4087
Brown Miss Susan Margaret	One Essex Court, London	020 7936 3030
Browne Mr James William	Lamb Chambers, London	020 7797 8300
Bryden Mr Christopher James Yuen Kang	4 King's Bench Walk, London	020 7822 7000
Buchan Miss Caroline Venetia	Chambers of Miss C Buchan, Haywards Heath	01444 482222
Budworth Mr Martin James	Kings Chambers, Birmingham	0845 034 3444
	Kings Chambers, Leeds	0845 034 3444
	Kings Chambers, Manchester	0845 034 3444
Bullock Mr Robert Gustaf	The Chambers of Mr Bullock, Brighton	01273 321050
Butler Mr Andrew	Tanfield Chambers, London	020 7421 5300
Butler Mr Rupert James	3 Hare Court, London	020 7415 7800
Buttimore Mr Gabriel	13 KBW, Oxford	01865 311066
	13 King's Bench Walk, London	020 7353 7204
Capon Mr Philip Christopher William	East Anglian Chambers, Chelmsford	01473 214481
	East Anglian Chambers, Ipswich	01473 214481
	East Anglian Chambers, Norwich	01473 214481
	St Philips Chambers, Birmingham	0121 246 7000
Carlisle Mr Timothy St John Ogilvie	Field Court Chambers, London	020 7405 6114
Castle Mr Peter Bolton	13 Old Square Chambers, London	020 7831 4445
Cattermull Miss Emma Jayne	East Anglian Chambers, Chelmsford	01473 214481
	East Anglian Chambers, Ipswich	01473 214481
	East Anglian Chambers, Norwich	01473 214481
Cawsey Mr Barry Donald	Clerksroom (London), London	0845 083 3000
	Clerksroom (Taunton), Taunton	0845 083 3000
Chesner Mr Howard Michael	One Essex Court, London	020 7936 3030

Barrister	Chambers	Telephone
Chowdhary Mr Islamuddin	Cassian Chambers, Ilford	07796 262641
Christensen Mr Carlton	10 King's Bench Walk, London	020 7353 7742
Christie Mr David Henderson	Seven Bedford Row, London	020 7242 3555
Clark Mr Andrew Richard	9 St John Street, Manchester	0161 955 9000
Clark Ms Julia Elisabeth	Hogarth Chambers, London	020 7404 0404
Clarke Mr Nicholas Patrick James	18 St John Street, Manchester	0161 278 1800
Clegg Mr Simon Robert Jonathan	St Philips Chambers, Birmingham	0121 246 7000
Cohen Mr Edward Mervyn	11 Stone Buildings, London	020 7831 6381
Colbey Mr Richard	Guildhall Chambers Portsmouth, Portsmouth	023 9275 2400
	Lamb Chambers, London	020 7797 8300
Coster Mr Ronald David	42 Bedford Row, London	020 7831 0222
Coulter Mr Barry John	Clerksroom (London), London	0845 083 3000
	Clerksroom (Taunton), Taunton	0845 083 3000
	King's Lynn Chambers, King's Lynn	01553 672 085
Crawley Mr Ross Alexander	Middle Temple Lane Chambers, London	020 7583 4352
Crew Miss Gillian Mary	Ely Place Chambers, London	020 7400 9600
Culmer Miss Gabrielle Fiona	2 King's Bench Walk, London	020 7353 1746
Daniels Miss Philippa Catherine	36 Bedford Row, London	020 7421 8000
Davey Mr Charles	64 Bridge Street, Manchester	0845 083 3000
	Chambers of Mr C Davey, Bishop's Stortford	01279 506412
	Clerksroom (Taunton), Taunton	0845 083 3000
Davies Mr James Edwin	3 PB Barristers, Bournemouth	01202 292102
	3 PB Barristers, Bristol	0117 928 1520
	3 PB Barristers, London	020 7583 8055
	3 PB Barristers, Oxford	01865 793 736
	3 PB Barristers, Winchester	01962 868884
Devlin Mr Bernard Joseph	Five St Andrew's Hill, London	020 7332 5400
Dipré Mr Paul Nicholas Amadeus	Chambers of Mr P N Dipré, Address withheld	0845 123 1234
	MK Family Law Chambers, Milton Keynes	0845 123 1234
Earle Mr James Christopher Reginald St John	Fenners Chambers, Cambridge	01223 368761
Egleton Mr Richard Wildman	Pallant Chambers, Chichester	01243 784538
Eilledge Miss Amanda Gail Caroline	11 Stone Buildings, London	020 7831 6381
Fawcett Mr Neil	St Ive's Chambers, Birmingham	0121 236 0863
Finlay Mr Darren	Sovereign Chambers, Leeds	0113 245 1841
Fisher Mr David	New Square Chambers, London	020 7419 8000
Fowles Mr Jonathan James	Serle Court, London	020 7242 6105
French Mr Paul Beckinton	Guildhall Chambers, Bristol	0117 930 9000
Gainer Mr Richard St Clair	St Margaret's Chambers, Twickenham	020 8241 3516
Galway-Cooper Dr Philip Anthony	Five St Andrew's Hill, London	020 7332 5400
Garvie Mr Carl Peter	St Philips Chambers, Birmingham	0121 246 7000
Gasztowicz Mr Steven	Cornerstone Barristers, London	020 7242 4986
	New Street Chambers, Leicester	0116 262 5906
Gibbons Miss Mary Regina	Stone Chambers, London	020 7440 6900
Glover Mr Marc Philip	Tanfield Chambers, London	020 7421 5300
Godfrey Mr Lauren John	Crown Office Row Chambers, Brighton	01273 625625
Goldstein Mr Wayne Nathan	18 St John Street, Manchester	0161 278 1800
Goodison Mr Adam Henry	South Square, London	020 7696 9900
Graham Mr Thomas Patrick Henry	New Square Chambers, London	020 7419 8000
Graham Mrs Alana Nicole	Chambers of Alana Graham, Halesowen	01384 894560
	9 Stone Buildings, London	020 7404 5055
Graham-Wells Miss Alison Christine	Exchange Chambers, Leeds	0113 203 1970
	Exchange Chambers, Liverpool	0151 236 7747
	Exchange Chambers, Manchester	0161 833 2722
Grant Mr David Ericson	Outer Temple Chambers, London	020 7353 6381
Griffiths Mr David	St Philips Chambers, Birmingham	0121 246 7000
Gunstone Mr Robert Giles	KCH Garden Square, Nottingham	0115 941 8851
Gupta Mr Amit	St Philips Chambers, Birmingham	0121 246 7000

Guy Mr Richard Perran	Chambers of Mr Ami Feder, London	020 7797 7788
	King's Bench and Godolphin (KBG)Chambers, Plymouth	01752 221551
	Southernhay Chambers, Exeter	01392 255777
Hallett Miss Katherine Elizabeth	13 Old Square Chambers, London	020 7831 4445
Hammond Mr Tim Mark	Tanfield Chambers, London	020 7421 5300
Harris Mr David Robert	St Albans Chambers, St Albans	01727 843383
Harris Mr Melvyn	5 Essex Court, London	020 7410 2000
Hartman Mr Michael	One Essex Court, London	020 7936 3030
Hayes Mr Richard James	Lamb Chambers, London	020 7797 8300
Haywood Dr Jennifer Margaret	Serle Court, London	020 7242 6105
Henderson Mr Neil John	Stone Chambers, London	020 7440 6900
Hendron Mr Henry Joseph Christopher	Strand Chambers, London	020 7117 6920
Hicks Mr Edward Gordon David	Radcliffe Chambers, London	020 7831 0081
Hill Mr Michael Gordon	Trinity Chambers, Middlesbrough	01642 247569
	Trinity Chambers, Newcastle Upon Tyne	0191 232 1927
Hillier Mr William	New Street Chambers, Leicester	0116 262 5906
Hirst Mr Martin Lewis	13 KBW, Oxford	01865 311066
	13 King's Bench Walk, London	020 7353 7204
Hodgkiss Ms Suzanne Jane	43 Temple Row Chambers, Birmingham	0121 237 6035
Holland Mr Charles Christopher	Francis Taylor Building, London	020 7353 8415
	Trinity Chambers, Middlesbrough	01642 247569
	Trinity Chambers, Newcastle Upon Tyne	0191 232 1927
Holmes-Milner Mr James Neil	The Chambers of Grahame Aldous QC, London	020 7832 0500
Hood Mr Nigel Anthony	New Square Chambers, London	020 7419 8000
Hornett Mr Stuart Ian	Selborne Chambers, London	020 7420 9500
Horton Mr Michael John Edward	Coram Chambers, London	020 7092 3700
Hossain Mr Ajmalul	Selborne Chambers, London	020 7420 9500
	St Philips Chambers, Birmingham	0121 246 7000
Howard Mr Robin William John	Fenners Chambers, Cambridge	01223 368761
Hubbard Mr Mark Iain	New Square Chambers, London	020 7419 8000
Huggins Mr Toby James	Unity Street Chambers, Bristol	0117 906 9789
Hunt Mr Stephen	4 Stone Buildings, London	020 7242 5524
Hussain Mr Muhammad Altaf	Chambers of Mr M A Hussain, London	020 8679 2398
Jones Mr Christopher David Harries	St John's Chambers, Bristol	0117 923 4700
Jones Mr Lawrence Victor	Chambers of Lawrence Jones, London	020 7831 1444
Jones Ms Cheryl Stephanie	No5 Chambers, Birmingham	0845 210 5555
	No5 Chambers, Bristol	0845 210 5555
	No5 Chambers, London	0845 210 5555
Joseph Dr Sandradee Theresa	13 Old Square Chambers, London	020 7831 4445
Joseph Mr Charles Henry	Tanfield Chambers, London	020 7421 5300
Joseph Mr Paul Wolfe	No5 Chambers, Birmingham	0845 210 5555
	No5 Chambers, Bristol	0845 210 5555
	No5 Chambers, London	0845 210 5555
Keel Mr Douglas Vincent	11 Stone Buildings, London	020 7831 6381
Kelly Mr Sean	Chancery House Chambers, Leeds	0113 244 6691
Khan Dr Alexander	Coral House, Manchester	
Khan Mr Abdul Aleem	Gray's Chambers, Newbury	020 8518 2525
Khan Mr Arfan	Field Court Chambers, London	020 7405 6114
Kidd Mr Peter William	Number 7 Harrington Street Chambers, Liverpool	0151 242 0707
King Mr Charles Granville	Chambers of Mr C G King, Stroud	07949 461717
Kramer Mr Philip Anthony	Park Lane Plowden, Newcastle Upon Tyne	0191 211 4087
Kynoch Mr Duncan Stuart Sanderson	Selborne Chambers, London	020 7420 9500
Lane Mr Simon Charles	Rougemont Chambers, Exeter	01392 208484
Lee Miss Krista Chui Lan	Keating Chambers, London	020 7544 2600

Barrister	Chambers	Telephone
Leonard Mr Charles Robert Weston	Hardwicke, London	020 7242 2523
Lewiecki Miss Marie	Old Bailey Chambers, London	020 3008 6404
Littman Mr Jeffrey James	Chambers of Mr Jeffrey Littman, London	020 8922 6844
	9 Park Place, Cardiff	029 2038 2731
Lonsdale Miss Marion Mary	Academy Chambers, London	020 8455 2503
Lowe Mr Mungo James	13 Old Square Chambers, London	020 7831 4445
MacEvilly Mr Conn Jeremy	9 Stone Buildings, London	020 7404 5055
Macpherson Mr Duncan Charles Stewart	One Essex Court, London	020 7936 3030
Macro Miss Morwenna Margaret	Five Paper, London	020 7815 3200
Maher Ms Martha Johanna Dorothy	St John's Chambers, Bristol	0117 923 4700
Mann Mr Christopher	13 KBW, Oxford	01865 311066
	13 King's Bench Walk, London	020 7353 7204
Marshall Mr Derek Stanley	College Chambers, Southampton	023 8023 0338
Mason Mr Ian Douglas	Amethyst Chambers, London	020 7936 4966
Matthias Mr David Huw	Francis Taylor Building, London	020 7353 8415
McCombie Mr Fergus Alexander Paul	1 Gray's Inn Square, London	020 7405 0001
McDonnell Mr John Beresford William	13 Old Square Chambers, London	020 7831 4445
McLinden Mr John Vincent Barry	Field Court Chambers, London	020 7405 6114
McNae Mr Jonathan James	Selborne Chambers, London	020 7420 9500
Meager Mrs Rowena Elisabeth	No5 Chambers, Birmingham	0845 210 5555
	No5 Chambers, Bristol	0845 210 5555
	No5 Chambers, London	0845 210 5555
Michael Mr Nicholas	East Anglian Chambers, Chelmsford	01473 214481
	East Anglian Chambers, Colchester	01473 214481
	East Anglian Chambers, Ipswich	01473 214481
	East Anglian Chambers, Norwich	01473 214481
Mills Mr Kristian Anthony	Trinity Chambers, Middlesbrough	01642 247569
	Trinity Chambers, Newcastle Upon Tyne	0191 232 1927
Mills Mr Simon Thomas	Five Paper, London	020 7815 3200
Morgan Dr Austen Jude	33 Bedford Row, London	020 7242 6476
Mullen Mr Mark Robert	Radcliffe Chambers, London	020 7831 0081
Newman Mrs Veronica	Chambers of Mrs V Newman, Cardiff	029 2048 8797
Nicholls Mr David James	11 Stone Buildings, London	020 7831 6381
Nickless Mr Jason Alan	College Chambers, Southampton	023 8023 0338
Noble Mr Andrew	Enterprise Chambers, Leeds	0113 246 0391
Normington Mr James Adam	Park Court Chambers, Leeds	0113 243 3277
Norton Mr Giles	Enigma Chambers, Sheffield	07779 576499
	Holborn Chambers, London	020 7242 6060
O'Brien Mr Nicholas William Wattebot	10 King's Bench Walk, London	020 7353 7742
Ohrenstein Mr Dov	Radcliffe Chambers, London	020 7831 0081
Oliver Dr Peter James Robert	4 Pump Court, London	020 7842 5555
Oliver Mr David Keightley Rideal	13 Old Square Chambers, London	020 7831 4445
O'Mahony Mr Jonathan Solomon	9 Stone Buildings, London	020 7404 5055
Oommen Mr Jacob	Chambers of Mr Jacob Oommen, East Barnet	07958 680272
O'Sullivan Mr Richard John	1215 Chambers, London	020 3291 1215
Parker Miss Wendy	Hardwicke, London	020 7242 2523
Parsons Mr Andrew James	Portsmouth Barristers'Chambers, Portsmouth	023 9283 1292
Payton Mr Clifford Coningsby	Alpha Court Chambers, Leamington Spa	01926 886412
Peat Mr Richard Colin	13 Old Square Chambers, London	020 7831 4445
Pennington-Legh Mr Jonathan Piers	Field Court Chambers, London	020 7405 6114
Plant Mr James Richard	Farrar's Building, London	020 7583 9241
Powell Mr Oliver Jonathan	3 PB Barristers, London	020 7583 8055
Power Mr Lawrence Imam	4 KBW, London	020 7822 8822
Preston Mr Nicholas John Holman	Clerksroom (Taunton), Taunton	0845 083 3000
Quirke Mr Gerard Martin	Citadel Chambers, Birmingham	0121 233 8500
Rainey Mr Philip Carslake	Tanfield Chambers, London	020 7421 5300

Rana Mr Mohammed Akram	Clapham Law Chambers, London	020 7978 8482
Reed Mr Simon John	New Walk Chambers, Leicester	0871 200 1298/0116 255 9144
Reeds Mr Gareth David	Canary Wharf Chambers, London	020 7183 8011
Rifat Mr Maurice Alan	1 Gray's Inn Square, London	020 7405 0001
Ritchie Mr Richard Bulkeley	XXIV Old Buildings, London	020 7691 2424
Rivalland Mr Marc-Edouard	1 Chancery Lane, London	0845 634 6666
Riza Mr Alper Ali	Goldsmith Chambers, London	020 7353 6802
Roberts Mr Michael Charles	Chambers of Michael Roberts, Henley-On-Thames	01844 355 655
Rowntree Mr Edward John Pickering	Hardwicke, London	020 7242 2523
Seal Mr Julius Damien	Chambers of Mr Julius Seal, London	020 7328 0158
Sellers Mr Graham	Atlantic Chambers, Liverpool	0151 236 4421
Sinclair Miss Lisa Anne	Chambers of Miss Lisa Sinclair, London	020 8946 7201
Singarajah Mr Frederico	1 Gray's Inn Square, London	020 7405 0001
Sisley Mr Timothy Julian Crispin	9 Stone Buildings, London	020 7404 5055
Sjostrand Miss Ekaterina	13 Old Square Chambers, London	020 7831 4445
Smith Mr Robert Clive	1 Paper Buildings, London	020 7353 3728
	RCS Chambers, Stainton	01709 814 147
Smithers Dr Roger Howard	Alexander Chambers, London	0845 652 0451/0854 652 0451
	Clerksroom (Taunton), Taunton	0845 083 3000
	Guildford Chambers, Guildford	01483 539131
Stenhouse Mr John Alexander	Nightingale Chambers, Wolverley	01562 851350
Sterling Mr Robert Alan	St James's Chambers, Manchester	0161 834 7000
	Zenith Chambers, Leeds	0113 245 5438
Stirling Mr Christopher William	Field Court Chambers, London	020 7405 6114
Stubbs Mr Richard John Morris	Trinity Chambers, Middlesbrough	01642 247569
	Trinity Chambers, Newcastle Upon Tyne	0191 232 1927
Sugarman Mr Jason Ashley	9-12 Bell Yard, London	020 7400 1800
Tabari Mr Ali-Reza	St Philips Chambers, Birmingham	0121 246 7000
Temmink Mr Robert-Jan	Quadrant Chambers, London	020 7583 4444
Temple Ms Eleanor Louise	Kings Chambers, Birmingham	0845 034 3444
	Kings Chambers, Leeds	0845 034 3444
	Kings Chambers, Manchester	0845 034 3444
Terry Mr Robert Jeffrey	Kings Chambers, Birmingham	0845 034 3444
	Kings Chambers, Leeds	0845 034 3444
	Kings Chambers, Manchester	0845 034 3444
	Lamb Chambers, London	020 7797 8300
Thornley Miss Hannah Elise	South Square, London	020 7696 9900
Todd Mr Michael Alan	Erskine Chambers, London	020 7242 5532
Treharne Mr Neil Simon	Dingle Chambers, Bristol	07818 827754
Trompeter Mr Nicholas Simeon	Selborne Chambers, London	020 7420 9500
Trumpington Mr John Henry	Staple Inn Chambers, London	020 7242 5240
Tucker Mr James William Richard	Teucro Chambers, Epsom	
Turnbull Miss Helen Mary	Lamb Chambers, London	020 7797 8300
Van Tonder Mr Gerard Dirk	New Square Chambers, London	020 7419 8000
Vasilescu Mr Andrei Constantin	Chambers of Martin Burr, London	0845 123 1234
Vaughan-Williams Mr Arthur Laurence	13 Old Square Chambers, London	020 7831 4445
Vernon Mr Elliot Curt	No. 3 Fleet Street Chambers, London	020 7936 4474
Walford Mr Richard Henry Howard	Serle Court, London	020 7242 6105
Walsh Mr Michael Patrick	Tanfield Chambers, London	020 7421 5300
Warner Mr David Alexander	St Philips Chambers, Birmingham	0121 246 7000
Watson Mr Alaric	11 Stone Buildings, London	020 7831 6381
Watson Mr Duncan Allen	Westgate Chambers, Lewes	01273 480510
Watson-Gandy Prof Mark	13 Old Square Chambers, London	020 7831 4445
Wheaton Mr Ian Malcolm James	Eighteen Carlton Crescent, Southampton	023 8063 9001
Wiktorowski-Solecki Miss Tamara	Middle Temple Lane Chambers, London	020 7583 4352
Wilkinson Mr Marc Ashley	No5 Chambers, Birmingham	0845 210 5555
	No5 Chambers, Bristol	0845 210 5555
	No5 Chambers, London	0845 210 5555

Barrister	Chambers	Telephone
Williams Miss June Cleo	No 8 Chambers, Birmingham	0121 236 5514
Williams Mr Simon Paul	Radcliffe Chambers, London	020 7831 0081
Wills Miss Alexandra Itari	Christ Church Chambers, London	020 7409 5278/07788 512787
Wise Mr Leslie Michael	10 King's Bench Walk, London	020 7353 7742
Wolman Mr Clive Richard	11 Stone Buildings, London	020 7831 6381
Yell Mr Nicholas Anthony	1 Chancery Lane, London	0845 634 6666

INSURANCE

Barrister	Chambers	Telephone
Ackland Miss Sacha Marie	Temple Garden Chambers, London	020 7583 1315
Ahmed Mr Ishfaq	Stone Chambers, London	020 7440 6900
Ajaz Mr Mohammad Arshad	Eastmans Chambers, Reading	0118 966 9094
Aliker Mr Phillip Bliss	Tanfield Chambers, London	020 7421 5300
Alliott Mr George Beckles	Temple Garden Chambers, London	020 7583 1315
Alloway Mr Tor Hugh	Talloway Chambers, London	020 7419 5047
Andre Mr Roger Louis	Sovereign Chambers, Leeds	0113 245 1841
Ansell Miss Rachel Louise	4 Pump Court, London	020 7842 5555
Antell Mr John Jason	King's Bench and Godolphin (KBG)Chambers, Plymouth	01752 221551
Aswani Mr Ravi Girdharilal	Stone Chambers, London	020 7440 6900
Barnard Mr James Philip	11 Stone Buildings, London	020 7831 6381
Beaumont Mr Marc Clifford	9 Stone Buildings, London	020 7404 5055
	Windsor Barristers' Chambers, Windsor	01753 839321
Becker Mr Timothy George Christie	Chambers of Mr Timothy Becker, Liverpool	0151 703 0319
	Clerksroom (London), London	0845 083 3000
Bellamy Mr Jonathan Mark	39 Essex Street, London	020 7832 1111
	82 King Street, Manchester	0161 870 9969
Benson Mr Imran Michael Jafarey	Hailsham Chambers, London	020 7643 5000
Bishop Mr Alan Richard	11 Stone Buildings, London	020 7831 6381
Blackwood Mr Clive David	Lamb Chambers, London	020 7797 8300
Bourne Mr Geoffrey Robert	13 Old Square Chambers, London	020 7831 4445
Bowling Mr James Stuart	4 Pump Court, London	020 7842 5555
Brittain Mr Marc John	1 Gray's Inn Square, London	020 7405 0001
Buchan Miss Caroline Venetia	Chambers of Miss C Buchan, Haywards Heath	01444 482222
Budworth Mr Martin James	Kings Chambers, Birmingham	0845 034 3444
	Kings Chambers, Leeds	0845 034 3444
	Kings Chambers, Manchester	0845 034 3444
Cattermull Miss Emma Jayne	East Anglian Chambers, Chelmsford	01473 214481
	East Anglian Chambers, Ipswich	01473 214481
	East Anglian Chambers, Norwich	01473 214481
Cawsey Mr Barry Donald	Clerksroom (London), London	0845 083 3000
	Clerksroom (Taunton), Taunton	0845 083 3000
Charkham Mr Graham Harold	20 Essex Street, London	020 7842 1200
Clark Miss Geraldine	Serle Court, London	020 7242 6105
Clarke Mr Jamie Roy	Hardwicke, London	020 7242 2523
Cohen Mr Edward Mervyn	11 Stone Buildings, London	020 7831 6381
Colbey Mr Richard	Guildhall Chambers Portsmouth, Portsmouth	023 9275 2400
	Lamb Chambers, London	020 7797 8300
Constable Mr Adam Michael	Keating Chambers, London	020 7544 2600
Coster Mr Ronald David	42 Bedford Row, London	020 7831 0222
Coulter Mr Barry John	Clerksroom (London), London	0845 083 3000
	Clerksroom (Taunton), Taunton	0845 083 3000
	King's Lynn Chambers, King's Lynn	01553 672 085
Crangle Mr Thomas Peter	4 Pump Court, London	020 7842 5555
Crowley Mr Daniel John	2 Temple Gardens, London	020 7822 1200
Curtis Mr Michael Alexander	Crown Office Chambers, London	020 7797 8100
Davis Mr Andrew Paul	Crown Office Chambers, London	020 7797 8100
De Jehan Mr David	Park Lane Plowden, Leeds	0113 228 5049
Deacon Mr Robert Murray	11 Stone Buildings, London	020 7831 6381

Name	Chambers	Telephone
Dipré Mr Paul Nicholas Amadeus	Chambers of Mr P N Dipré, Address withheld	0845 123 1234
	MK Family Law Chambers, Milton Keynes	0845 123 1234
Douthwaite Mr Charles Philip	Four New Square, London	020 7822 2000
Dyer Mr Allen Gordon	4 Pump Court, London	020 7842 5555
Engelman Mr Philip	Cloisters, London	020 7827 4000
	Trinity Chambers, Middlesbrough	01642 247569
	Trinity Chambers, Newcastle Upon Tyne	0191 232 1927
Fetto Mr Niazi Peter	2 Temple Gardens, London	020 7822 1200
Field Mr Julian Nigel	Crown Office Chambers, London	020 7797 8100
Finlay Mr Darren	Sovereign Chambers, Leeds	0113 245 1841
Fisher Mr David	New Square Chambers, London	020 7419 8000
Friedman Mr David Peter	4 Pump Court, London	020 7842 5555
Fullerton Mr Michael Andrew	7 Bell Yard, London	020 7831 0636
	Chambers of Mr Michael Fullerton, Hove	01273 772050
Gainer Mr Richard St Clair	St Margaret's Chambers, Twickenham	020 8241 3516
Gayan Mr Anil Kumarsingh	Clapham Law Chambers, London	020 7978 8482
Gee Mr Steven Mark	Stone Chambers, London	020 7440 6900
Gibbons Miss Mary Regina	Stone Chambers, London	020 7440 6900
Gillies Miss Jennie	4 Pump Court, London	020 7842 5555
Gilmore Miss Mary Seanin	Four New Square, London	020 7822 2000
Godfrey Mr Lauren John	Crown Office Row Chambers, Brighton	01273 625625
Godwin Mr William George Henry	3 Hare Court, London	020 7415 7800
	St John's Chambers, Bristol	0117 923 4700
Goldrein Mr Iain Saville	7 Bell Yard, London	020 7831 0636
	Number 7 Harrington Street Chambers, Liverpool	0151 242 0707
Goldstein Mr Wayne Nathan	18 St John Street, Manchester	0161 278 1800
Graham Mrs Alana Nicole	Chambers of Alana Graham, Halesowen	01384 894560
	9 Stone Buildings, London	020 7404 5055
Grant Mr Marcus H James	Temple Garden Chambers, London	020 7583 1315
Green Miss Alison Anne	2 Temple Gardens, London	020 7822 1200
Hall Mr James Edward	Cornwall Street Chambers, Birmingham	0121 233 7500
Hamilton Mr Peter Bernard	4 Pump Court, London	020 7842 5555
Hammerton Mr Alastair Rolf	1 Chancery Lane, London	0845 634 6666
Hayes Mr Richard James	Lamb Chambers, London	020 7797 8300
Higginson Mr Timothy Nicholas Bennett	Littleton Chambers, London	020 7797 8600
	St John's Chambers, Bristol	0117 923 4700
Hirst Mr Martin Lewis	13 KBW, Oxford	01865 311066
	13 King's Bench Walk, London	020 7353 7204
Holdsworth Mr James Arthur	Temple Garden Chambers, London	020 7583 1315
Hood Mr Nigel Anthony	New Square Chambers, London	020 7419 8000
Howells Mr Stephen John	Stone Chambers, London	020 7440 6900
Hughes Mr Adrian Warwick	39 Essex Street, London	020 7832 1111
	82 King Street, Manchester	0161 870 9969
Hunt Mr Stephen	4 Stone Buildings, London	020 7242 5524
Hurst Mr Brian	39 Park Square, Leeds	0113 245 6633
Hutchin Mr Edward Alister David	Temple Garden Chambers, London	020 7583 1315
Jarman Mr Samuel James Guthrie	4 KBW, London	020 7822 8822
	Lombard Chambers, London	020 7107 2100
Jayakrishnan Mr Harry Sisubalan	Trent Chambers, Nottingham	0115 941 9596
Johnson Miss Laura Wendy	1 Chancery Lane, London	0845 634 6666
Jones Mr Geraint Anthony	New Walk Chambers, Leicester	0871 200 1298/0116 255 9144
	9 St John Street, Manchester	0161 955 9000
	Tanfield Chambers, London	020 7421 5300
Joseph Dr Sandradee Theresa	13 Old Square Chambers, London	020 7831 4445

Joseph Mr Paul Wolfe	No5 Chambers, Birmingham	0845 210 5555
	No5 Chambers, Bristol	0845 210 5555
	No5 Chambers, London	0845 210 5555
Kramer Mr Philip Anthony	Park Lane Plowden, Newcastle Upon Tyne	0191 211 4087
Lawrence The Hon Patrick John Tristram	Four New Square, London	020 7822 2000
Lee Miss Krista Chui Lan	Keating Chambers, London	020 7544 2600
Macpherson Mr Duncan Charles Stewart	One Essex Court, London	020 7936 3030
Matthias Mr David Huw	Francis Taylor Building, London	020 7353 8415
McDonald Mr John William	2 Temple Gardens, London	020 7822 1200
Medd Mr James Powys	Crown Office Chambers, London	020 7797 8100
Meredith-Hardy Mr John Octavian	Farrar's Building, London	020 7583 9241
Miller Mr Andrew	2 Temple Gardens, London	020 7822 1200
Moulder Mr Paul John	Alexander Chambers, London	0845 652 0451/0854 652 0451
	Guildford Chambers, Guildford	01483 539131
Nicholson Mr Jeremy Mark	4 Pump Court, London	020 7842 5555
Noble Mr Andrew	Enterprise Chambers, Leeds	0113 246 0391
Norton Mr Giles	Enigma Chambers, Sheffield	07779 576499
	Holborn Chambers, London	020 7242 6060
Oliver Dr Peter James Robert	4 Pump Court, London	020 7842 5555
Oommen Mr Jacob	Chambers of Mr Jacob Oommen, East Barnet	07958 680272
Osborne Mr James Robert	Clerksroom (London), London	0845 083 3000
Osborne Mr Richard	4 Pump Court, London	020 7842 5555
O'Sullivan Mr Thomas Sean Patrick	4 Pump Court, London	020 7842 5555
Owens Miss Elspeth Eluned	4 Pump Court, London	020 7842 5555
Palmer Mr Howard William Arthur	2 Temple Gardens, London	020 7822 1200
Palmer Mr James Savill	Henderson Chambers, London	020 7583 9020
Parker Mrs Karen Lesley	Guildhall Chambers Portsmouth, Portsmouth	023 9275 2400
Phillips Mr Andrew Charles	Crown Office Chambers, London	020 7797 8100
Plant Mr James Richard	Farrar's Building, London	020 7583 9241
Purchas Mr James Alexander Francis	4 Pump Court, London	020 7842 5555
Quiney Mr Charles Benedictus Alexander	Crown Office Chambers, London	020 7797 8100
Rigney Mr Andrew James	Crown Office Chambers, London	020 7797 8100
Ritchie Mr Andrew George	The Chambers of Grahame Aldous QC, London	020 7832 0500
Rivalland Mr Marc-Edouard	1 Chancery Lane, London	0845 634 6666
Roberts Mr Michael Charles	Chambers of Michael Roberts, Henley-On-Thames	01844 355 655
Rogers Mr Ian Paul	Monckton Chambers, London	020 7405 7211
Sefton-Smith Mr Lloyd	Lamb Chambers, London	020 7797 8300
Sellers Mr Graham	Atlantic Chambers, Liverpool	0151 236 4421
Selvaratnam Miss Vasanti Emily Indrani	Stone Chambers, London	020 7440 6900
Shapiro Mr Daniel Jonathan	Crown Office Chambers, London	020 7797 8100
Shirley Mr James Patrick	Stone Chambers, London	020 7440 6900
Singarajah Mr Frederico	1 Gray's Inn Square, London	020 7405 0001
Singer Mr Andrew Michael	Kings Chambers, Birmingham	0845 034 3444
	Kings Chambers, Leeds	0845 034 3444
	Kings Chambers, Manchester	0845 034 3444
Sisley Mr Timothy Julian Crispin	9 Stone Buildings, London	020 7404 5055
Snow Mr Darren Mark	Charter Chambers, London	020 7618 4400
Spalton Mr George David John	Four New Square, London	020 7822 2000
Speaight Mr Anthony Hugh	4 Pump Court, London	020 7842 5555
Speller Mr Bruce Christopher Norman	The White House, Battle	01424 777944
Spencer Mr Martin Benedict	Hailsham Chambers, London	020 7643 5000
Stansfield Mr Piers Alistair	Keating Chambers, London	020 7544 2600
Starcevic Mr Petar	St Philips Chambers, Birmingham	0121 246 7000

Name	Chambers	Telephone
Stead Mr Richard James	St John's Chambers, Bristol	0117 923 4700
Stern Mr David Patrick Julian	King's Bench Chambers, Bournemouth	01202 250025
	11 Stone Buildings, London	020 7831 6381
Stevenson Mr Paul Anthony	Tanfield Chambers, London	020 7421 5300
Stevenson Mr Robert Lloyd	Sovereign Chambers, Leeds	0113 245 1841
Stride Mr Lionel Alexander	Temple Garden Chambers, London	020 7583 1315
Temmink Mr Robert-Jan	Quadrant Chambers, London	020 7583 4444
Terry Mr Robert Jeffrey	Kings Chambers, Birmingham	0845 034 3444
	Kings Chambers, Leeds	0845 034 3444
	Kings Chambers, Manchester	0845 034 3444
	Lamb Chambers, London	020 7797 8300
Ticciati Mr Oliver	4 Pump Court, London	020 7842 5555
Tozzi Mr Nigel Kenneth	4 Pump Court, London	020 7842 5555
Vaughan-Williams Mr Arthur Laurence	13 Old Square Chambers, London	020 7831 4445
Vineall Mr Nicholas Edward John	4 Pump Court, London	020 7842 5555
Vonberg Mr Thomas Charles	Devereux Chambers, London	020 7353 7534
Walker Mr Adam Nigel	Seven Bedford Row, London	020 7242 3555
Watthey Mr James Robertson	Hardwicke, London	020 7242 2523
Wilkinson Mr Marc Ashley	No5 Chambers, Birmingham	0845 210 5555
	No5 Chambers, Bristol	0845 210 5555
	No5 Chambers, London	0845 210 5555
Williams Mr Mark John	Queen Square Chambers, Bristol	0117 921 1966
Wills Miss Alexandra Itari	Christ Church Chambers, London	020 7409 5278/07788 512787
Winser Mr Crispin David Richard	Crown Office Chambers, London	020 7797 8100
Wolman Mr Clive Richard	11 Stone Buildings, London	020 7831 6381

INSURANCE/REINSURANCE

Name	Chambers	Telephone
Ackland Miss Sacha Marie	Temple Garden Chambers, London	020 7583 1315
Ajaz Mr Mohammad Arshad	Eastmans Chambers, Reading	0118 966 9094
Alloway Mr Tor Hugh	Talloway Chambers, London	020 7419 5047
Antell Mr John Jason	King's Bench and Godolphin (KBG)Chambers, Plymouth	01752 221551
Aswani Mr Ravi Girdharilal	Stone Chambers, London	020 7440 6900
Beaumont Mr Benjamin	Chambers of Dr Michael Arnheim, London	020 7833 5093
	Middle Temple Lane Chambers, London	020 7583 4352
Buchan Miss Caroline Venetia	Chambers of Miss C Buchan, Haywards Heath	01444 482222
Bullock Mr Robert Gustaf	The Chambers of Mr Bullock, Brighton	01273 321050
Charkham Mr Graham Harold	20 Essex Street, London	020 7842 1200
Clark Miss Geraldine	Serle Court, London	020 7242 6105
Coster Mr Ronald David	42 Bedford Row, London	020 7831 0222
Crowley Mr Daniel John	2 Temple Gardens, London	020 7822 1200
Engelman Mr Philip	Cloisters, London	020 7827 4000
	Trinity Chambers, Middlesbrough	01642 247569
	Trinity Chambers, Newcastle Upon Tyne	0191 232 1927
Falkowski Mr Damian	4-5 Gray's Inn Square, London	020 7404 5252
Field Mr Julian Nigel	Crown Office Chambers, London	020 7797 8100
Gee Mr Steven Mark	Stone Chambers, London	020 7440 6900
Gibbons Miss Mary Regina	Stone Chambers, London	020 7440 6900
Godfrey Mr Lauren John	Crown Office Row Chambers, Brighton	01273 625625
Godwin Mr William George Henry	3 Hare Court, London	020 7415 7800
	St John's Chambers, Bristol	0117 923 4700
Green Miss Alison Anne	2 Temple Gardens, London	020 7822 1200
Hamilton Mr Gavin	3 PB Barristers, Bournemouth	01202 292102
	3 PB Barristers, Bristol	0117 928 1520
	3 PB Barristers, London	020 7583 8055
	3 PB Barristers, Oxford	01865 793 736
	3 PB Barristers, Winchester	01962 868884
Irvin Mr Peter	Brick Court Chambers, London	020 7379 3550

Name	Chambers	Telephone
Iyer Miss Shobana	Swan Chambers, Richmond	0845 123 1234
Jarman Mr Samuel James Guthrie	4 KBW, London	020 7822 8822
	Lombard Chambers, London	020 7107 2100
Jones Mr Geraint Anthony	New Walk Chambers, Leicester	0871 200 1298/0116 255 9144
	9 St John Street, Manchester	0161 955 9000
	Tanfield Chambers, London	020 7421 5300
Jones Mr Lawrence Victor	Chambers of Lawrence Jones, London	020 7831 1444
Kent Mr Michael Harcourt	Crown Office Chambers, London	020 7797 8100
Leabeater Mr James Ferguson	4 Pump Court, London	020 7842 5555
Lenon Mr Andrew Ralph Fitzmaurice	One Essex Court, London	020 7583 2000
MacKenzie Smith Mrs Catherine Joanna	10 King's Bench Walk, London	020 7353 7742
Matthias Mr David Huw	Francis Taylor Building, London	020 7353 8415
Miller Mr Andrew	2 Temple Gardens, London	020 7822 1200
Nolten Miss Sonia Jayne	2 Temple Gardens, London	020 7822 1200
Norton Mr Giles	Enigma Chambers, Sheffield	07779 576499
	Holborn Chambers, London	020 7242 6060
O'Sullivan Mr Thomas Sean Patrick	4 Pump Court, London	020 7842 5555
O'Toole Mr Simon Gerard	5 Pump Court, London	020 7353 2532
	Riverview Chambers, London	0844 225 3999
Palmer Mr Howard William Arthur	2 Temple Gardens, London	020 7822 1200
Pettican Mr Kevin	11 Stone Buildings, London	020 7831 6381
Phillips Mr Andrew Charles	Crown Office Chambers, London	020 7797 8100
Quiney Mr Charles Benedictus Alexander	Crown Office Chambers, London	020 7797 8100
Reffin Miss Clare Alyson	One Essex Court, London	020 7583 2000
Rigney Mr Andrew James	Crown Office Chambers, London	020 7797 8100
Rinker Mr Andrew Stuart D'Artois	Chambers of Mr Andrew Rinker, London	020 7584 1091
Selvaratnam Miss Vasanti Emily Indrani	Stone Chambers, London	020 7440 6900
Shapiro Mr Daniel Jonathan	Crown Office Chambers, London	020 7797 8100
Shirley Mr James Patrick	Stone Chambers, London	020 7440 6900
Singarajah Mr Frederico	1 Gray's Inn Square, London	020 7405 0001
Snow Mr Darren Mark	Charter Chambers, London	020 7618 4400
Soto-Miranda Mr Diego Fernando	One Essex Court, London	020 7936 3030
Spencer Mr Martin Benedict	Hailsham Chambers, London	020 7643 5000
Stevenson Mr Paul Anthony	Tanfield Chambers, London	020 7421 5300
Temmink Mr Robert-Jan	Quadrant Chambers, London	020 7583 4444
Tompkinson Miss Deborah Ann	Clerksroom (London), London	0845 083 3000
	Clerksroom (Taunton), Taunton	0845 083 3000
Tozzi Mr Nigel Kenneth	4 Pump Court, London	020 7842 5555
Unigwe Mr Sylvester Emefiona	Essex House Chambers, London	020 7692 0677
	11 Gray's Inn Square Chambers, London	020 7405 6879
Vaughan-Williams Mr Arthur Laurence	13 Old Square Chambers, London	020 7831 4445
Von Pommern-Peglow Dr Michael Alfred Herman Pr.	Brunswick Chambers, London	020 7353 1987
Watthey Mr James Robertson	Hardwicke, London	020 7242 2523
Williams Mr Mark John	Queen Square Chambers, Bristol	0117 921 1966
Wills Miss Alexandra Itari	Christ Church Chambers, London	020 7409 5278/07788 512787
Winser Mr Crispin David Richard	Crown Office Chambers, London	020 7797 8100
Wright Mr Alexander Paul	4 Pump Court, London	020 7842 5555

INTELLECTUAL PROPERTY

Name	Chambers	Telephone
Abrahams Mr James	8 New Square, London	020 7405 4321
Afeeva Mr Mark Kudzo Dzitosi	Matrix Chambers, London	020 7404 3447
Andrews Mr Paul Leslie	Great James Street Chambers, London	020 7440 4949
Bailey Miss Rosana Henrietta	10 King's Bench Walk, London	020 7353 7742
Beaumont Mr Marc Clifford	9 Stone Buildings, London	020 7404 5055
	Windsor Barristers' Chambers, Windsor	01753 839321

Bezzam Miss Jayashree	Hampton Court Chambers, West Molesey	020 8979 0381
Bowhill Miss Jessie Kate	8 New Square, London	020 7405 4321
Bragiel Mr Edward Bronislaw Henryk	Hogarth Chambers, London	020 7404 0404
Browne Mr Desmond John Michael	5RB, London	020 7242 2902
Buchan Miss Caroline Venetia	Chambers of Miss C Buchan, Haywards Heath	01444 482222
Budworth Mr Richard Dutton	2-3 Hind Court Chambers, London	020 7822 2150
Christie Mr Iain Robert	5RB, London	020 7242 2902
Clark Ms Julia Elisabeth	Hogarth Chambers, London	020 7404 0404
Cohen Mr Edward Mervyn	11 Stone Buildings, London	020 7831 6381
Colbey Mr Richard	Guildhall Chambers Portsmouth, Portsmouth	023 9275 2400
	Lamb Chambers, London	020 7797 8300
Coulter Mr Barry John	Clerksroom (London), London	0845 083 3000
	Clerksroom (Taunton), Taunton	0845 083 3000
	King's Lynn Chambers, King's Lynn	01553 672 085
Craig Mr Aubrey John	Chancery House Chambers, Leeds	0113 244 6691
	St Philips Chambers, Birmingham	0121 246 7000
Critchley Mr John Stephen	Field Court Chambers, London	020 7405 6114
Crowe Mr Cameron	36 Bedford Row, London	020 7421 8000
Cunningham Mr Graham Taylor	Hardwicke, London	020 7242 2523
De Jehan Mr David	Park Lane Plowden, Leeds	0113 228 5049
De Mounteney Mr Jonathan Patrick	Chambers of Mr J P De Mounteney, Reading	0118 934 6822
Deacon Mr Robert Murray	11 Stone Buildings, London	020 7831 6381
Devlin Mr Bernard Joseph	Five St Andrew's Hill, London	020 7332 5400
di Mambro Mr David Jesse Andrew	Pallant Chambers, Chichester	01243 784538
	Radcliffe Chambers, London	020 7831 0081
Dillon Mr Thomas William Matthew	Chambers of Thomas Dillon, London	020 7692 2722
Drummond Mr Bruce Jonathon Hutcheon	Cornwall Street Chambers, Birmingham	0121 233 7500
	Palmyra Chambers, Warrington	01925 444919
Engelman Mr Mark Trevor	Hardwicke, London	020 7242 2523
Fairpo Ms Catherine Anne	Atlas Chambers, London	020 7269 7980
Fern Mr Gary	7 Stones IP, London	020 7193 4033
Fitzgerald Mr John Vincent	Ingenuity IP Chambers, Petts Wood	
Gerasimidis Mr Nicolas	Guildhall Chambers, Bristol	0117 930 9000
Hamer Mr George Clemens	8 New Square, London	020 7405 4321
Heal Mrs Madeleine	New Square Chambers, London	020 7419 8000
Hill Mr Jonathan	8 New Square, London	020 7405 4321
Himsworth Miss Emma Katherine	One Essex Court, London	020 7583 2000
Hobbs Mr Geoffrey William	One Essex Court, London	020 7583 2000
Iqbal Mr Mashood	London View Chambers, Sawbridgeworth	07788 912493
Iyer Miss Shobana	Swan Chambers, Richmond	0845 123 1234
Jenkins Mr Edward Nicholas	Five Paper Buildings, London	020 7583 6117
Johnson Mr Phillip Michael	Chambers of Mr P Johnson, London	020 7288 2256
Jolliffe Mrs Victoria Esther Jean	5RB, London	020 7242 2902
Jones Mr Christopher David Harries	St John's Chambers, Bristol	0117 923 4700
Jones Mr Kelvin Mcallister	Templis Chambers, London	020 7649 9808
Keane Mr Owen Ashley	Design Chambers, London	020 7353 0747
Khan Dr Alexander	Coral House, Manchester	
Kime Mr Matthew Jonathan	Cobden House Chambers, Manchester	0161 833 6000
	Ingenuity IP Chambers, Petts Wood	
	No. 3 Fleet Street Chambers, London	020 7936 4474
Knight Mr Benjamin James	Central Chambers, Manchester	0161 236 1133
Lambert Miss Jane Elizabeth	NIPC, Huddersfield	0800 862 0055
Lane Ms Lindsay Ruth Busfield	8 New Square, London	020 7405 4321
Lawrence Dr Heather Bunting Elizabeth	11 South Square, London	020 7405 1222
Levett Miss Francesca Anna	Five St Andrew's Hill, London	020 7332 5400
Lewis Mr Dominic	Five Paper Buildings, London	020 7583 6117
Lewis Mr Wayne Anthony	Access Lawyers, London	020 8801 2345

Name	Chambers	Telephone
Ludbrook Mr Timothy Vivian	13 Old Square Chambers, London	020 7831 4445
Mainwaring Mr Robert Paul Clason	Portal Chambers, Llandysul	01559 395 292
Matthias Mr David Huw	Francis Taylor Building, London	020 7353 8415
Maxwell Lewis Mr Cameron	Lamb Chambers, London	020 7797 8300
McDonnell Mr John Beresford William	13 Old Square Chambers, London	020 7831 4445
Michalos Miss Christina Antigone Diana	5RB, London	020 7242 2902
Munden Mr Richard Alexander John	5RB, London	020 7242 2902
Murphy Mr Damian	Enterprise Chambers, Leeds	0113 246 0391
	Enterprise Chambers, London	020 7405 9471
	Enterprise Chambers, Newcastle Upon Tyne	0191 222 3344
Nath Mr Rakesh	Strand Chambers, London	020 7117 6920
Norton Mr Giles	Enigma Chambers, Sheffield	07779 576499
	Holborn Chambers, London	020 7242 6060
Onslow Mr Robert Denzil	8 New Square, London	020 7405 4321
Paley Ms Ruth Theresa Elizabeth	23 Essex Street, London	020 7413 0353
Paraskos Mr Paraskevakis Christakis	11 Gray's Inn Square Chambers, London	020 7405 6879
Parsons Mr Andrew James	Portsmouth Barristers'Chambers, Portsmouth	023 9283 1292
Pearson Mr Christopher	Lamb Chambers, London	020 7797 8300
Penny Mr Timothy Charles	11 Stone Buildings, London	020 7831 6381
Platts-Mills Mr Mark Fortescue	8 New Square, London	020 7405 4321
Powell Mr William Rhys	Regency Chambers, Cambridge	01223 301517
	Regency Chambers, Peterborough	01733 315215
Prokofiev Mr Sergey	Lincoln House Chambers, Manchester	0161 832 5701
Purves Mr Gavin Bowman	Swan House, London	020 8998 3035
Quirke Mr Gerard Martin	Citadel Chambers, Birmingham	0121 233 8500
Reed Mr Jeremy Nigel	Hogarth Chambers, London	020 7404 0404
Rinker Mr Andrew Stuart D'Artois	Chambers of Mr Andrew Rinker, London	020 7584 1091
Roberts Mr Michael Charles	Chambers of Michael Roberts, Henley-On-Thames	01844 355 655
Roberts Mr Philip Duncan	One Essex Court, London	020 7583 2000
Rogers Miss Christy Abigail	Ingenuity IP Chambers, Petts Wood	
	No. 3 Fleet Street Chambers, London	020 7936 4474
Roughton Mr Ashley Wentworth	Hogarth Chambers, London	020 7404 0404
Saini Mr Parminder Paul Singh	12 Old Square Chambers, London	020 7404 0875
Sampson Dr Timothy Michael George	One Essex Court, London	020 7936 3030
Seeboruth Mr Royln Jean-Paul	Chambers of Royln Seeboruth, Aylesbury	01296 393329
Silcock Mr Ian Peter	Hardwicke, London	020 7242 2523
Singarajah Mr Frederico	1 Gray's Inn Square, London	020 7405 0001
Smithers Dr Roger Howard	Alexander Chambers, London	0845 652 0451/0854 652 0451
	Clerksroom (Taunton), Taunton	0845 083 3000
	Guildford Chambers, Guildford	01483 539131
Speker Mr Adam Samuel Edward	5RB, London	020 7242 2902
Staddon Mr Paul	Tanfield Chambers, London	020 7421 5300
Stein Mr Daniel Alexander	No5 Chambers, Birmingham	0845 210 5555
	No5 Chambers, Bristol	0845 210 5555
	No5 Chambers, London	0845 210 5555
Stevenson Dr Simon John	Park Lane Plowden, Leeds	0113 228 5049
Tarbitt Mr Nicholas Edward Henry	Cornwall Street Chambers, Birmingham	0121 233 7500
Thomas Mr James Austin	KCH Garden Square, Nottingham	0115 941 8851
Tritton Mr Robert Guy Henton	Hogarth Chambers, London	020 7404 0404
Vitiello Mr Fabio Angelo-Giuseppe	Staple Inn Chambers, London	020 7242 5240
Warby Mr Mark David John	5RB, London	020 7242 2902
Ward Mr Robin Henry	8 New Square, London	020 7405 4321

C

Whyatt Mr Bernard Anthony	Chambers of Mr Bernard Whyatt, Ardley	01869 346160

INTERNATIONAL TRADE

Abasheikh Mr Omar Said Imam	Paragon Chambers, London	020 3318 9988
Ahmed Mr Ishfaq	Stone Chambers, London	020 7440 6900
Algazy Mr Jacques Max	Cloisters, London	020 7827 4000
Aliker Mr Phillip Bliss	Tanfield Chambers, London	020 7421 5300
Allerhand Mr Ludwik Edmund	Chambers of Mr Ludwik Allerhand, London	020 8291 4356
Arkhurst Mr Reginald Leon	4 King's Bench Walk, London	020 7822 7000
Aswani Mr Ravi Girdharilal	Stone Chambers, London	020 7440 6900
Blackwood Mr Clive David	Lamb Chambers, London	020 7797 8300
Bueno Mr Antonio De Padua Jose Maria	Clerksroom (Taunton), Taunton	0845 083 3000
Bullock Mr Robert Gustaf	The Chambers of Mr Bullock, Brighton	01273 321050
Buttimore Mr Gabriel	13 KBW, Oxford	01865 311066
	13 King's Bench Walk, London	020 7353 7204
Charkham Mr Graham Harold	20 Essex Street, London	020 7842 1200
Chern Mr Cyril	Crown Office Chambers, London	020 7797 8100
Clark Miss Geraldine	Serle Court, London	020 7242 6105
Coster Mr Ronald David	42 Bedford Row, London	020 7831 0222
Coulter Mr Barry John	Clerksroom (London), London	0845 083 3000
	Clerksroom (Taunton), Taunton	0845 083 3000
	King's Lynn Chambers, King's Lynn	01553 672 085
Devine Mr Michael Buxton	Rougemont Chambers, Exeter	01392 208484
Engelman Mr Philip	Cloisters, London	020 7827 4000
	Trinity Chambers, Middlesbrough	01642 247569
	Trinity Chambers, Newcastle Upon Tyne	0191 232 1927
Falkowski Mr Damian	4-5 Gray's Inn Square, London	020 7404 5252
Finlay Mr Darren	Sovereign Chambers, Leeds	0113 245 1841
Gee Mr Steven Mark	Stone Chambers, London	020 7440 6900
Gibbons Miss Mary Regina	Stone Chambers, London	020 7440 6900
Godwin Mr William George Henry	3 Hare Court, London	020 7415 7800
	St John's Chambers, Bristol	0117 923 4700
Goodison Mr Adam Henry	South Square, London	020 7696 9900
Henderson Mr Neil John	Stone Chambers, London	020 7440 6900
Hossain Mr Ajmalul	Selborne Chambers, London	020 7420 9500
	St Philips Chambers, Birmingham	0121 246 7000
Hughes Mr Adrian Warwick	39 Essex Street, London	020 7832 1111
	82 King Street, Manchester	0161 870 9969
Irvin Mr Peter	Brick Court Chambers, London	020 7379 3550
Iyer Miss Shobana	Swan Chambers, Richmond	0845 123 1234
Keel Mr Douglas Vincent	11 Stone Buildings, London	020 7831 6381
Kime Mr Matthew Jonathan	Cobden House Chambers, Manchester	0161 833 6000
	Ingenuity IP Chambers, Petts Wood	
	No. 3 Fleet Street Chambers, London	020 7936 4474
Lenon Mr Andrew Ralph Fitzmaurice	One Essex Court, London	020 7583 2000
Lewis Mr Wayne Anthony	Access Lawyers, London	020 8801 2345
Mahmood Mr Abid	Central Chambers, Manchester	0161 236 1133
	No5 Chambers, Birmingham	0845 210 5555
	No5 Chambers, Bristol	0845 210 5555
	No5 Chambers, London	0845 210 5555
Matthias Mr David Huw	Francis Taylor Building, London	020 7353 8415
Maxwell Lewis Mr Cameron	Lamb Chambers, London	020 7797 8300
Nath Mr Rakesh	Strand Chambers, London	020 7117 6920
Ogunbusola Mr Victor Olaniyi	Chambers of Victor Ogumbusola, Basildon	07413 634231
Osborne Mr James Robert	Clerksroom (London), London	0845 083 3000
Paraskos Mr Paraskevakis Christakis	11 Gray's Inn Square Chambers, London	020 7405 6879

Parsons Mr Andrew James	Portsmouth Barristers'Chambers, Portsmouth	023 9283 1292
Payton Mr Clifford Coningsby	Alpha Court Chambers, Leamington Spa	01926 886412
Qureshi Mr Asif Hasan	Quadrant Chambers, London	020 7583 4444
Reffin Miss Clare Alyson	One Essex Court, London	020 7583 2000
Rigney Mr Andrew James	Crown Office Chambers, London	020 7797 8100
Rinker Mr Andrew Stuart D'Artois	Chambers of Mr Andrew Rinker, London	020 7584 1091
Seeboruth Mr Royln Jean-Paul	Chambers of Royln Seeboruth, Aylesbury	01296 393329
Selvaratnam Miss Vasanti Emily Indrani	Stone Chambers, London	020 7440 6900
Shirley Mr James Patrick	Stone Chambers, London	020 7440 6900
Simon Mr Philipp Arnold Heinrich	4 KBW, London	020 7822 8822
Singarajah Mr Frederico	1 Gray's Inn Square, London	020 7405 0001
Soto-Miranda Mr Diego Fernando	One Essex Court, London	020 7936 3030
Sowler Mr Thomas Richard Holland	The Tax Chambers of Mr Richard Sowler TD, Douglas	07624 235000
Spalton Mr George David John	Four New Square, London	020 7822 2000
Vitiello Mr Fabio Angelo-Giuseppe	Staple Inn Chambers, London	020 7242 5240
Von Pommern-Peglow Dr Michael Alfred Herman Pr.	Brunswick Chambers, London	020 7353 1987
Walford Mr Richard Henry Howard	Serle Court, London	020 7242 6105
Watthey Mr James Robertson	Hardwicke, London	020 7242 2523
Wills Miss Alexandra Itari	Christ Church Chambers, London	020 7409 5278/07788 512787

ISLAMIC SHARIA LAW

Abasheikh Mr Omar Said Imam	Paragon Chambers, London	020 3318 9988
Ajaz Mr Mohammad Arshad	Eastmans Chambers, Reading	0118 966 9094
Almihdar Mr Ali Hamed	Outer Temple Chambers, London	020 7353 6381
Ameen Mr Danish	18 St John Street, Manchester	0161 278 1800
Arshad Miss Raffia	St Mary's Family Law Chambers, Nottingham	0115 950 3503
Azhar Mr Ali Mohammad	9 King's Bench Walk, London	020 7353 9564
Brewin Mr Carl Patrick	3 PB Barristers, London	020 7583 8055
Habib Miss Shysta	Kenworthy's Chambers, Manchester	0161 832 4036
Hasan Miss Ayesha	3 Dr Johnson's Buildings, London	020 7353 4854
Iqbal Mr Mashood	London View Chambers, Sawbridgeworth	07788 912493
Khan Mr Ayoub	Chambers of Mr Ayoub Khan, Birmingham	07930 987202
Khan Mr Mahmood Shafi	Luton Chambers, Luton	01582 598394
	Willesden Chambers, London	020 3273 1042
Khan Mr Zarif	Dyers Chambers, London	020 7404 1881
Mahmood Mr Abid	Central Chambers, Manchester	0161 236 1133
	No5 Chambers, Birmingham	0845 210 5555
	No5 Chambers, Bristol	0845 210 5555
	No5 Chambers, London	0845 210 5555
Mustakim Mr Abdul Yunus Al	Chambers of Mr Mustakim, London	
Nasim Mr Zia-Ul-Mustafa	Milestone Chambers, London	
Rahman Mr Anis	12 Old Square Chambers, London	020 7404 0875
Thomson Mr Martin Haldane Ahmad	Wynne Chambers, London	020 3239 6964

LAND

Ailes Mr John Ashley	Eighteen Carlton Crescent, Southampton	023 8063 9001
Albutt Mr Ian Leslie	Cornerstone Barristers, London	020 7242 4986
	Heavenwood Chambers, Stroud	01453 873444
Allison Mr Simon Robert	Hardwicke, London	020 7242 2523
Allwood Mrs Gina Louisa	Seven Bedford Row, London	020 7242 3555
Antell Mr John Jason	King's Bench and Godolphin (KBG)Chambers, Plymouth	01752 221551
Askey Mr Robert John	Palmyra Chambers, Warrington	01925 444919

C

Asprey Mr Nicholas	Clock Chambers, Wolverhampton	01902 313444
	Serle Court, London	020 7242 6105
Bailey Mr Michael Robert	Tanfield Chambers, London	020 7421 5300
Braithwaite Mr Thomas James	Serle Court, London	020 7242 6105
Branchflower Mr George	Zenith Chambers, Leeds	0113 245 5438
Bredemear Mr Zachary Charles	1 Chancery Lane, London	0845 634 6666
Brown Miss Susan Margaret	One Essex Court, London	020 7936 3030
Bruce Mr Andrew Jonathan	Serle Court, London	020 7242 6105
Buchan Miss Caroline Venetia	Chambers of Miss C Buchan, Haywards Heath	01444 482222
Buckhaven Mr Simon	Hardwicke, London	020 7242 2523
Butler Mr Simon David	The Chambers of Grahame Aldous QC, London	020 7832 0500
Buttimore Mr Gabriel	13 KBW, Oxford	01865 311066
	13 King's Bench Walk, London	020 7353 7204
Caun Mr Lawrence	Lamb Chambers, London	020 7797 8300
Coster Mr Ronald David	42 Bedford Row, London	020 7831 0222
Crew Miss Gillian Mary	Ely Place Chambers, London	020 7400 9600
di Mambro Mr David Jesse Andrew	Pallant Chambers, Chichester	01243 784538
	Radcliffe Chambers, London	020 7831 0081
Dovar Mr Daniel	Tanfield Chambers, London	020 7421 5300
Dowell Mr Gregory Hamilton	Principal Chambers, Sevenoaks	0845 209 8080
Esprit Mr Benoit	Barristers Chambers, London	020 3417 6461
	Legis Chambers, Aylesbury	01296 431125
Fairbank Mr Nicholas James	4 Paper Buildings, London	020 7427 5200
Falkowski Mr Damian	4-5 Gray's Inn Square, London	020 7404 5252
Fellows Mr Philip David Andrew	Hardwicke, London	020 7242 2523
Gillott Mr Paul Alan Ashley	15 Winckley Square, Preston	01772 252828
Glaser Mr Michael Samson	14 Gray's Inn Square, London	020 7242 0858
Goodall Mr Charles Vernon Machin-	Queen Square Chambers, Bristol	0117 921 1966
Graham-Wells Miss Alison Christine	Exchange Chambers, Leeds	0113 203 1970
	Exchange Chambers, Liverpool	0151 236 7747
	Exchange Chambers, Manchester	0161 833 2722
Harris Mr David Robert	St Albans Chambers, St Albans	01727 843383
Harris Mr James	Five St Andrew's Hill, London	020 7332 5400
Hillier Mr William	New Street Chambers, Leicester	0116 262 5906
Hoar Mr Francis John Patrick	Field Court Chambers, London	020 7405 6114
Holland Mr Charles Christopher	Francis Taylor Building, London	020 7353 8415
	Trinity Chambers, Middlesbrough	01642 247569
	Trinity Chambers, Newcastle Upon Tyne	0191 232 1927
Horton Mr Matthew Bethell	39 Essex Street, London	020 7832 1111
	82 King Street, Manchester	0161 870 9969
Hughes-Deane Ms Charlotte Barbara	Atlantic Chambers, Liverpool	0151 236 4421
Jones Mr Emyr Gweirydd	9 Park Place, Cardiff	029 2038 2731
Kirk Mr Graeme Charles	One Essex Court, London	020 7936 3030
Kramer Mr Philip Anthony	Park Lane Plowden, Newcastle Upon Tyne	0191 211 4087
Lane Mr Simon Charles	Rougemont Chambers, Exeter	01392 208484
Lopez Mr Juan Nemesio	Francis Taylor Building, London	020 7353 8415
Loveday Mr Mark Alan	Tanfield Chambers, London	020 7421 5300
MacEvilly Mr Conn Jeremy	9 Stone Buildings, London	020 7404 5055
Marsden Mr Andrew Guy	East Anglian Chambers, Chelmsford	01473 214481
	East Anglian Chambers, Colchester	01473 214481
	East Anglian Chambers, Ipswich	01473 214481
	East Anglian Chambers, Norwich	01473 214481
Matthias Mr David Huw	Francis Taylor Building, London	020 7353 8415
McCombie Mr Fergus Alexander Paul	1 Gray's Inn Square, London	020 7405 0001
McCormack Mr Alan	Staple Inn Chambers, London	020 7242 5240
McKay Mr Christopher Alexander	Cathedral Chambers, Newport	01633 215112
McNae Mr Jonathan James	Selborne Chambers, London	020 7420 9500
Moffat Mr Russell Dean	Linenhall Chambers, Chester	01244 348282
Mullen Mr Mark Robert	Radcliffe Chambers, London	020 7831 0081
Nickless Mr Jason Alan	College Chambers, Southampton	023 8023 0338

Name	Chambers	Telephone
Norton Mr Giles	Enigma Chambers, Sheffield	07779 576499
	Holborn Chambers, London	020 7242 6060
O'Brien Mr Nicholas William Wattebot	10 King's Bench Walk, London	020 7353 7742
O'Sullivan Mr Richard John	1215 Chambers, London	020 3291 1215
Paton Mr Ewan William	Guildhall Chambers, Bristol	0117 930 9000
Polli Mr Timothy James	Tanfield Chambers, London	020 7421 5300
Rifat Mr Maurice Alan	1 Gray's Inn Square, London	020 7405 0001
Roberts Mr Huw Eifion	Linenhall Chambers, Chester	01244 348282
Sefton-Smith Mr Lloyd	Lamb Chambers, London	020 7797 8300
Sharples Mr John Edmund	St John's Chambers, Bristol	0117 923 4700
Shaw Mr Julian	St Johns Buildings, Chester	01244 323070
	St Johns Buildings, Manchester	0161 214 1500
	St Johns Buildings Liverpool, Liverpool	0151 243 6000
Sinclair Miss Lisa Anne	Chambers of Miss Lisa Sinclair, London	020 8946 7201
Stephens Mr Michael Allen	Design Chambers, London	020 7353 0747
	St Ive's Chambers, Birmingham	0121 236 0863
Stevens-Hoare Miss Michelle	Hardwicke, London	020 7242 2523
Stirling Mr Christopher William	Field Court Chambers, London	020 7405 6114
Swirsky Mr Adam Abraham Burl Bradbury	Lamb Chambers, London	020 7797 8300
Trumpington Mr John Henry	Staple Inn Chambers, London	020 7242 5240
Turnbull Miss Helen Mary	Lamb Chambers, London	020 7797 8300
Upton Mr Jonathan Michael	Tanfield Chambers, London	020 7421 5300
Van Tonder Mr Gerard Dirk	New Square Chambers, London	020 7419 8000
Vickery Mr Neil Michael	13 KBW, Oxford	01865 311066
	13 King's Bench Walk, London	020 7353 7204
Walsh Mr Michael Patrick	Tanfield Chambers, London	020 7421 5300
Wheaton Mr Ian Malcolm James	Eighteen Carlton Crescent, Southampton	023 8063 9001
Wightwick Mr Iain	Riverview Chambers, London	0844 225 3999
	Unity Street Chambers, Bristol	0117 906 9789
Wilcox Mr Jerome Carl Jean	Alexander Chambers, London	0845 652 0451/0854 652 0451
Wilkins Mr Christopher John	Pallant Chambers, Chichester	01243 784538
Wills Miss Alexandra Itari	Christ Church Chambers, London	020 7409 5278/07788 512787
Zeitler Miss Barbara	3 Dr Johnson's Buildings, London	020 7353 4854

LANDLORD & TENANT

Name	Chambers	Telephone
Abbasi Miss Nylah Naz	9 King's Bench Walk, London	020 7353 9564
Adewale Mr Remi Adetokunbo Sanni	Chambers of G. D. Tetteh, London	020 7353 7095
	Chambers of Mr R. A. Adewale, Address withheld	020 7231 2814
Afzal Mr Fayyaz	No5 Chambers, Birmingham	0845 210 5555
	No5 Chambers, Bristol	0845 210 5555
	No5 Chambers, London	0845 210 5555
Agnihotri Mr Naveen	12 College Place, Southampton	023 8032 0320
Ahmed Mr Saleem	Perivale Chambers, Perivale	020 8998 1935
Ailes Mr John Ashley	Eighteen Carlton Crescent, Southampton	023 8063 9001
Ajaz Mr Mohammad Arshad	Eastmans Chambers, Reading	0118 966 9094
Akther Miss Tahina Sultana	Cobden House Chambers, Manchester	0161 833 6000
	Southernhay Chambers, Exeter	01392 255777
Alam Ms Jan	Ropewalk Chambers, Nottingham	0115 947 2581
Aliker Mr Phillip Bliss	Tanfield Chambers, London	020 7421 5300
Allison Mr Simon Robert	Hardwicke, London	020 7242 2523
Allston Mr Anthony Stanley	3 Dr Johnson's Buildings, London	020 7353 4854
Aly Miss Sheila	Warwick House Chambers, London	020 7430 2323
Ameen Mr Danish	18 St John Street, Manchester	0161 278 1800
Andre Mr Roger Louis	Sovereign Chambers, Leeds	0113 245 1841
Andrews Mr Paul Leslie	Great James Street Chambers, London	020 7440 4949
Angammana Mr Gamini Bertram	Chambers of Gamini Angammana, London	020 8771 5205

Armstrong Mr Stuart David	Arden Chambers, London	020 7242 4244
Arnheim Dr Michael Thomas Walter	Chambers of Dr Michael Arnheim, London	020 7833 5093
	Holborn Chambers, London	020 7242 6060
	Principal Chambers, Sevenoaks	0845 209 8080
Artesi Miss Desiree Allison Ann	Thomas More Chambers, London	020 7404 7000
Ash Mr Edward William	Chambers of Mr Edward Ash, Elsworth	01954 267674
Asprey Mr Nicholas	Clock Chambers, Wolverhampton	01902 313444
	Serle Court, London	020 7242 6105
Aswani Mr Ravi Girdharilal	Stone Chambers, London	020 7440 6900
Awodele Mr Olufemi Adetunji	Great James Street Chambers, London	020 7440 4949
Azhar Mr Ali Mohammad	9 King's Bench Walk, London	020 7353 9564
Badejo Mr Abimbola Rafiu	5 Pump Court, London	020 7353 2532
Bailey Miss Rosana Henrietta	10 King's Bench Walk, London	020 7353 7742
Bailey Mr Thomas Iain	Chambers of Mr Thomas Bailey, Milton Keynes	07983 447117
Baldwin Dr Timothy John	Garden Court Chambers, London	020 7993 7600
Barber Mr Phillip Arthur	Zenith Chambers, Leeds	0113 245 5438
Barnes Mr Luke Clive	3 Dr Johnson's Buildings, London	020 7353 4854
Bassiri-Dezfouli Miss Sorour	Temple Court Chambers, London	020 7353 7888
Bastin Mr Alexander Charles	Hardwicke, London	020 7242 2523
Bath Mrs Baljinder Kaur	College Chambers, Southampton	023 8023 0338
Baumohl Mr Mark Christopher	Field Court Chambers, London	020 7405 6114
Beaumont Mr Dean Andrew	KCH Garden Square, Nottingham	0115 941 8851
Beaumont Mr Marc Clifford	9 Stone Buildings, London	020 7404 5055
	Windsor Barristers' Chambers, Windsor	01753 839321
Becker Mr Timothy George Christie	Chambers of Mr Timothy Becker, Liverpool	0151 703 0319
	Clerksroom (London), London	0845 083 3000
Bedloe Mr Giles Robert	Dyers Chambers, London	020 7404 1881
Beloff Mr Rupert Joseph Alexei	No5 Chambers, Birmingham	0845 210 5555
	No5 Chambers, Bristol	0845 210 5555
	No5 Chambers, London	0845 210 5555
Bennett Mr David Laurence	Liverpool Civil Law, Liverpool	0151 242 0500
Bennion-Pedley Mr Edward	13 KBW, Oxford	01865 311066
	13 King's Bench Walk, London	020 7353 7204
Berkley Mr David Nahum	1 Gray's Inn Square, London	020 7405 0001
	St Johns Buildings, Chester	01244 323070
	St Johns Buildings, Manchester	0161 214 1500
	St Johns Buildings Liverpool, Liverpool	0151 243 6000
Berkley Mr Michael Stuart	Rougemont Chambers, Exeter	01392 208484
Berry Mr Nicholas Michael	Rougemont Chambers, Exeter	01392 208484
Bhakar Mr Surinder Singh	4 King's Bench Walk, London	020 7822 7000
Bhattacharyya Mr Ardhendu	Slough Barristers Chamber, Slough	01753 553806
Bishop Mr Stephen Anthony	Goldsmith Chambers, London	020 7353 6802
Blaker Mr Gary Mark	Selborne Chambers, London	020 7420 9500
Bleasdale Miss Marie-Claire	Radcliffe Chambers, London	020 7831 0081
Blohm Mr Leslie Adrian	St John's Chambers, Bristol	0117 923 4700
Bogle Mr James Stewart Lockhart	10 King's Bench Walk, London	020 7353 7742
Boyd Mr Stephen James Harvey	Selborne Chambers, London	020 7420 9500
Bragge Mr Thomas Hereward	Stour Chambers, Canterbury	01227 764899
Bragiel Mr Edward Bronislaw Henryk	Hogarth Chambers, London	020 7404 0404
Braier Mr Jason Dean	Field Court Chambers, London	020 7405 6114
Bredemear Mr Zachary Charles	1 Chancery Lane, London	0845 634 6666
Brewin Mr Carl Patrick	3 PB Barristers, London	020 7583 8055
Brilliant Mr Simon Howard	Lamb Chambers, London	020 7797 8300
Broatch Mr Donald	Five Paper, London	020 7815 3200
Brockley Mr Nigel Simon	No5 Chambers, Birmingham	0845 210 5555
	No5 Chambers, Bristol	0845 210 5555
	No5 Chambers, London	0845 210 5555

Name	Chambers	Telephone
Brook Mr Paul Antony	Park Lane Plowden, Leeds	0113 228 5049
	Park Lane Plowden, Newcastle Upon Tyne	0191 211 4087
Brown Miss Susan Margaret	One Essex Court, London	020 7936 3030
Brown Mr Philip Stephen	9 Stone Buildings, London	020 7404 5055
Browne Mr James William	Lamb Chambers, London	020 7797 8300
Bruce Mr Andrew Jonathan	Serle Court, London	020 7242 6105
Bryden Mr Christopher James Yuen Kang	4 King's Bench Walk, London	020 7822 7000
Buchan Miss Caroline Venetia	Chambers of Miss C Buchan, Haywards Heath	01444 482222
Buck Mr John	Tanfield Chambers, London	020 7421 5300
Buckle Mr Jonathan	Regency Chambers, Cambridge	01223 301517
	Regency Chambers, Peterborough	01733 315215
Buckpitt Mr Michael David	Tanfield Chambers, London	020 7421 5300
Budworth Mr Richard Dutton	2-3 Hind Court Chambers, London	020 7822 2150
Bullock Mr Robert Gustaf	The Chambers of Mr Bullock, Brighton	01273 321050
Burns Mr Jeremy Stuart	12 College Place, Southampton	023 8032 0320
Butler Mr Andrew	Tanfield Chambers, London	020 7421 5300
Butler Mr Simon David	The Chambers of Grahame Aldous QC, London	020 7832 0500
Buttimore Mr Gabriel	13 KBW, Oxford	01865 311066
	13 King's Bench Walk, London	020 7353 7204
Campbell Mr Stafford Graham	Westgate Chambers, Lewes	01273 480510
Candlin Miss Naomi Helen	St Philips Chambers, Birmingham	0121 246 7000
Cant Mr Christopher Ian	9 Stone Buildings, London	020 7404 5055
Capon Mr Philip Christopher William	East Anglian Chambers, Chelmsford	01473 214481
	East Anglian Chambers, Ipswich	01473 214481
	East Anglian Chambers, Norwich	01473 214481
	St Philips Chambers, Birmingham	0121 246 7000
Carr Mr Adrian James Selden	Tanfield Chambers, London	020 7421 5300
Carr Mr Christopher Sean	36 Bedford Row, London	020 7421 8000
Carrington Mr Dominic	Chambers of Martin Burr, London	0845 123 1234
Cartwright Mr Ivan Matthew	KCH Garden Square, Nottingham	0115 941 8851
Cattermole Miss Rebecca Elke	Tanfield Chambers, London	020 7421 5300
Cattermull Miss Emma Jayne	East Anglian Chambers, Chelmsford	01473 214481
	East Anglian Chambers, Ipswich	01473 214481
	East Anglian Chambers, Norwich	01473 214481
Cawsey Mr Barry Donald	Clerksroom (London), London	0845 083 3000
	Clerksroom (Taunton), Taunton	0845 083 3000
Chaffin-Laird Miss Olivia Carolyn	No5 Chambers, Birmingham	0845 210 5555
	No5 Chambers, Bristol	0845 210 5555
	No5 Chambers, London	0845 210 5555
Challinor Mr Thomas Michael	Citadel Chambers, Birmingham	0121 233 8500
Charalambides Mr Leonidas	Francis Taylor Building, London	020 7353 8415
Chesner Mr Howard Michael	One Essex Court, London	020 7936 3030
Christensen Mr Carlton	10 King's Bench Walk, London	020 7353 7742
Chute Ms Andrea Alexandra	Rougemont Chambers, Exeter	01392 208484
	Tooks Chambers, London	020 7842 7575
Clark Mr Andrew Richard	9 St John Street, Manchester	0161 955 9000
Clarke Miss Lisa Tarin	Staple Inn Chambers, London	020 7242 5240
Clarke Mr George Robert Ivan	5 Pump Court, London	020 7353 2532
Clarke Mr Timothy John	Cornwall Street Chambers, Birmingham	0121 233 7500
Clayton Mr Nigel Garvin	Kings Chambers, Birmingham	0845 034 3444
	Kings Chambers, Leeds	0845 034 3444
	Kings Chambers, Manchester	0845 034 3444
Clegg Mr Adam Gordon	Stour Chambers, Canterbury	01227 764899
Clifton Miss Jane April	Lamb Chambers, London	020 7797 8300
Colbey Mr Richard	Guildhall Chambers Portsmouth, Portsmouth	023 9275 2400
	Lamb Chambers, London	020 7797 8300
Collard Mr Michael David	5 Pump Court, London	020 7353 2532

Name	Chambers	Telephone
Collett Mr Gavin Charles	Rougemont Chambers, Exeter	01392 208484
Comerton Miss Julie Anne	4 KBW, London	020 7822 8822
Cooper Miss Christine	Field Court Chambers, London	020 7405 6114
Coster Mr Ronald David	42 Bedford Row, London	020 7831 0222
Cotterell Mr David William	Albion Chambers, Bristol	0117 927 2144
Crawley Mr Ross Alexander	Middle Temple Lane Chambers, London	020 7583 4352
Crew Miss Gillian Mary	Ely Place Chambers, London	020 7400 9600
Croskell Mr Marcus James	East Anglian Chambers, Chelmsford	01473 214481
	East Anglian Chambers, Colchester	01473 214481
	East Anglian Chambers, Ipswich	01473 214481
	East Anglian Chambers, Norwich	01473 214481
Daly Mr David	Heathway Chambers, London	020 8293 0509
Daniels Miss Philippa Catherine	36 Bedford Row, London	020 7421 8000
Datta Mr Shomik	42 Bedford Row, London	020 7831 0222
Davey Mr Charles	64 Bridge Street, Manchester	0845 083 3000
	Chambers of Mr C Davey, Bishop's Stortford	01279 506412
	Clerksroom (Taunton), Taunton	0845 083 3000
Davies Miss Carol Elizabeth	College Chambers, Southampton	023 8023 0338
Davies Mr James Edwin	3 PB Barristers, Bournemouth	01202 292102
	3 PB Barristers, Bristol	0117 928 1520
	3 PB Barristers, London	020 7583 8055
	3 PB Barristers, Oxford	01865 793 736
	3 PB Barristers, Winchester	01962 868884
Davies Mr Max James	30 Park Place, Cardiff	029 2039 8421
Davies Ms Elizabeth Mary	Garden Court Chambers, London	020 7993 7600
Davies Ms Samantha Teresa	Chambers of Ms Samantha Davies, Milton Keynes	0845 123 1234
	Warwick House Chambers, London	020 7430 2323
De Mello Mr Rembert Joseph Julius	No5 Chambers, Birmingham	0845 210 5555
	No5 Chambers, Bristol	0845 210 5555
	No5 Chambers, London	0845 210 5555
De Mounteney Mr Jonathan Patrick	Chambers of Mr J P De Mounteney, Reading	0118 934 6822
De Waal Mr John Henry Lowndes	Hardwicke, London	020 7242 2523
Deacon Mr Robert Murray	11 Stone Buildings, London	020 7831 6381
Dean Mr James Patrick	Goldsmith Chambers, London	020 7353 6802
Dean Mr Peter Thomas	36 Bedford Row, London	020 7421 8000
Degun Mr Jasvir Singh	One Essex Court, London	020 7936 3030
Demachkie Mr Jamal	3 PB Barristers, London	020 7583 8055
Denbin Mr Jack Arnold	Greenway, Sonning-on-Thames	0118 969 2484
Devereux-Cooke Mr Richard Charles	13 Old Square Chambers, London	020 7831 4445
Devlin Mr Bernard Joseph	Five St Andrew's Hill, London	020 7332 5400
di Mambro Mr David Jesse Andrew	Pallant Chambers, Chichester	01243 784538
	Radcliffe Chambers, London	020 7831 0081
Dipré Mr Paul Nicholas Amadeus	Chambers of Mr P N Dipré, Address withheld	0845 123 1234
	MK Family Law Chambers, Milton Keynes	0845 123 1234
Doran Mr Gerard Patrick	Lincoln House Chambers, Manchester	0161 832 5701
Douthwaite Mr Charles Philip	Four New Square, London	020 7822 2000
Dovar Mr Daniel	Tanfield Chambers, London	020 7421 5300
Dowell Mr Gregory Hamilton	Principal Chambers, Sevenoaks	0845 209 8080
Dsane Miss Victoria Tsotsoo	Chambers of Miss Victoria Dsane, Sutton	020 8722 0990
Dubin Mr Joshua Charles	1 Pump Court, London	020 7842 7070
Earle Mr James Christopher Reginald St John	Fenners Chambers, Cambridge	01223 368761
Eaton Mr Tobias Barnaby	Staple Inn Chambers, London	020 7242 5240
Egleton Mr Richard Wildman	Pallant Chambers, Chichester	01243 784538
Eilledge Miss Amanda Gail Caroline	11 Stone Buildings, London	020 7831 6381
Elliott Mr Colin Douglas	King's Bench and Godolphin (KBG)Chambers, Plymouth	01752 221551

Name	Chambers	Telephone
Elliott Mr Edward Anthony John	Garden Court Chambers, London	020 7993 7600
England Mrs Lisa Johanna Louise	Guildhall Chambers Portsmouth, Portsmouth	023 9275 2400
Ephraim-Adejumo Mrs Hilda Ekpo	12 Old Square Chambers, London	020 7404 0875
Esprit Mr Benoit	Barristers Chambers, London	020 3417 6461
	Legis Chambers, Aylesbury	01296 431125
Fagborun Bennett Ms Morayo Abosede	Hardwicke, London	020 7242 2523
Fain Mr Carl Ian	Tanfield Chambers, London	020 7421 5300
Falkowski Mr Damian	4-5 Gray's Inn Square, London	020 7404 5252
Fawcett Mr Neil	St Ive's Chambers, Birmingham	0121 236 0863
Feldman Mr Matthew Richard Bankes	42 Bedford Row, London	020 7831 0222
Fellows Mr Philip David Andrew	Hardwicke, London	020 7242 2523
Felton Mr Timothy John Fowler	Rougemont Chambers, Exeter	01392 208484
Ferber Ms Iris	42 Bedford Row, London	020 7831 0222
Fieldsend Mr James William	Tanfield Chambers, London	020 7421 5300
Finlay Mr Darren	Sovereign Chambers, Leeds	0113 245 1841
Follon Mr Daniel Richard Thomas	1 Gray's Inn Square, London	020 7405 0001
Foulkes Miss Rebecca	5 Pump Court, London	020 7353 2532
Fowles Mr Jonathan James	Serle Court, London	020 7242 6105
Fox Mr John Harvey	Chambers of Mr Ami Feder, London	020 7797 7788
	Chambers of Mr Ami Feder, London	020 7797 7788
	Lamb Building, Brighton	01273 820490
Francis Mr Richard Maurice	9 Park Place, Cardiff	029 2038 2731
Gadd Mr Adam Brian	Pump Court Chambers, London	020 7353 0711
	Pump Court Chambers, Winchester	01962 868 161
	Riverview Chambers, London	0844 225 3999
Gainer Mr Richard St Clair	St Margaret's Chambers, Twickenham	020 8241 3516
Gair Mr Christopher	King's Bench Chambers, Bournemouth	01202 250025
Gallagher Mr Stanley Harold	Tanfield Chambers, London	020 7421 5300
Gallivan Mr Terence John	Five Paper, London	020 7815 3200
Galway-Cooper Dr Philip Anthony	Five St Andrew's Hill, London	020 7332 5400
Gatty Mr Daniel Simon	Hardwicke, London	020 7242 2523
Gelbart Mr Geoff Alan	1 Gray's Inn Square, London	020 7405 0001
George Mr Nicholas Frank Raymond	New Walk Chambers, Leicester	0871 200 1298/0116 255 9144
German Miss Kelly Anne	Eastbourne Chambers, Eastbourne	01323 642102
Gibbons Ms Ellodie	Tanfield Chambers, London	020 7421 5300
Giles Mr David William	1 Gray's Inn Square, London	020 7405 0001
Gill Miss Baljinder	10 King's Bench Walk, London	020 7353 7742
Glover Mr Marc Philip	Tanfield Chambers, London	020 7421 5300
Godfrey Mr Lauren John	Crown Office Row Chambers, Brighton	01273 625625
Gofur Mr Abdul	Thomas More Chambers, London	020 7404 7000
Gold Mr Richard David	St John's Chambers, Bristol	0117 923 4700
Goldberg Mr Simon Ian	Trinity Chambers, Middlesbrough	01642 247569
	Trinity Chambers, Newcastle Upon Tyne	0191 232 1927
Goldstein Mr Wayne Nathan	18 St John Street, Manchester	0161 278 1800
Goodall Mr Charles Vernon Machin-	Queen Square Chambers, Bristol	0117 921 1966
Goodfellow Mr Stephen John	East Anglian Chambers, Chelmsford	01473 214481
	East Anglian Chambers, Ipswich	01473 214481
	East Anglian Chambers, Norwich	01473 214481
Gore Mr Andrew Roger	Fenners Chambers, Cambridge	01223 368761
Gore Mrs Harriet Nkechi Adimora	Kensington Chambers, London	020 7373 2217
Gourlay Miss Amanda Kirsten	Tanfield Chambers, London	020 7421 5300
Graham-Wells Miss Alison Christine	Exchange Chambers, Leeds	0113 203 1970
	Exchange Chambers, Liverpool	0151 236 7747
	Exchange Chambers, Manchester	0161 833 2722
Granville Stafford Mr Andrew	4 King's Bench Walk, London	020 7822 7000
Greenan Miss Sarah Octavia	Zenith Chambers, Leeds	0113 245 5438
Greenfield Mr Peter Charles	King's Bench Chambers, Bournemouth	01202 250025
Griffiths Mr David	St Philips Chambers, Birmingham	0121 246 7000
Ground Mr Patrick	Chambers of Mr Patrick Ground QC, London	020 7736 0131

Gunstone Mr Robert Giles	KCH Garden Square, Nottingham	0115 941 8851
Gupta Mr Amit	St Philips Chambers, Birmingham	0121 246 7000
Hall Mr James Edward	Cornwall Street Chambers, Birmingham	0121 233 7500
Hallett Miss Katherine Elizabeth	13 Old Square Chambers, London	020 7831 4445
Halstead Mr Robin Bernard	One Essex Court, London	020 7936 3030
Ham Mr Nicholas Treharne	Dyers Chambers, London	020 7404 1881
Hamilton Mr Gavin	3 PB Barristers, Bournemouth	01202 292102
	3 PB Barristers, Bristol	0117 928 1520
	3 PB Barristers, London	020 7583 8055
	3 PB Barristers, Oxford	01865 793 736
	3 PB Barristers, Winchester	01962 868884
Hammond Mr Tim Mark	Tanfield Chambers, London	020 7421 5300
Hanif Miss Saima Naz	4-5 Gray's Inn Square, London	020 7404 5252
Hansen Mr William Joseph	No5 Chambers, Birmingham	0845 210 5555
	No5 Chambers, Bristol	0845 210 5555
	No5 Chambers, London	0845 210 5555
Harrap Mr Robert Philip	Five Paper, London	020 7815 3200
Harris Mr David Robert	St Albans Chambers, St Albans	01727 843383
Harris Mr James	Five St Andrew's Hill, London	020 7332 5400
Harris Mr Melvyn	5 Essex Court, London	020 7410 2000
Harrison Dr Graeme	12 College Place, Southampton	023 8032 0320
Harrison Mr Piers William Benedict	Tanfield Chambers, London	020 7421 5300
Haughty Mr Jeremy Nicholas	Chambers of Mr Ami Feder, London	020 7797 7788
	Chambers of Mr Ami Feder, London	020 7797 7788
	Rougemont Chambers, Exeter	01392 208484
Hayes Mr Richard James	Lamb Chambers, London	020 7797 8300
Henderson Miss Josephine	Five Paper, London	020 7815 3200
Hendron Mr Henry Joseph Christopher	Strand Chambers, London	020 7117 6920
Heppinstall Mr Adam John	Henderson Chambers, London	020 7583 9020
Hicks Mr Edward Gordon David	Radcliffe Chambers, London	020 7831 0081
Higginson Mr Timothy Nicholas Bennett	Littleton Chambers, London	020 7797 8600
	St John's Chambers, Bristol	0117 923 4700
Hill Mr Michael Gordon	Trinity Chambers, Middlesbrough	01642 247569
	Trinity Chambers, Newcastle Upon Tyne	0191 232 1927
Hill Mr Piers Nicholas	37 Park Square Chambers, Leeds	0113 243 9422
Hill Mr Simon Michael	33 Bedford Row, London	020 7242 6476
Hillier Mr William	New Street Chambers, Leicester	0116 262 5906
Hillman Mr Gerard Paul	Carmelite Chambers, London	020 7936 6300
Hobson Mr John Graham	4-5 Gray's Inn Square, London	020 7404 5252
Hodgkiss Ms Suzanne Jane	43 Temple Row Chambers, Birmingham	0121 237 6035
Hodgson Mrs Jane Lee	Five Paper, London	020 7815 3200
Hodson Mr Matthew Paul	Farrar's Building, London	020 7583 9241
Hogben Mrs Helen Jane	Fountain Chambers, Middlesbrough	01642 804040
Holbech Mr Charles Edward	New Square Chambers, London	020 7419 8000
Holland Mr Rowan Guy	Five Paper, London	020 7815 3200
Holmes-Milner Mr James Neil	The Chambers of Grahame Aldous QC, London	020 7832 0500
Holroyd Mr John James	Zenith Chambers, Leeds	0113 245 5438
Hormaeche Miss Alejandra	Tanfield Chambers, London	020 7421 5300
Horne Mr Charles Hugh Wilson	Kings Chambers, Birmingham	0845 034 3444
	Kings Chambers, Leeds	0845 034 3444
	Kings Chambers, Manchester	0845 034 3444
Hornett Mr Stuart Ian	Selborne Chambers, London	020 7420 9500
Howlett Mr James Anthony	KCH Garden Square, Nottingham	0115 941 8851
Huggins Mr Toby James	Unity Street Chambers, Bristol	0117 906 9789
Hughes-Deane Ms Charlotte Barbara	Atlantic Chambers, Liverpool	0151 236 4421
Hunt Mr Stephen	4 Stone Buildings, London	020 7242 5524
Hussain Mr Muhammad Altaf	Chambers of Mr M A Hussain, London	020 8679 2398

Name	Chambers	Telephone
Hutchin Mr Edward Alister David	Temple Garden Chambers, London	020 7583 1315
Isaac Mr Nicholas Dudley	Tanfield Chambers, London	020 7421 5300
Iyer Miss Shobana	Swan Chambers, Richmond	0845 123 1234
Jacques Mr Gareth Edward	Regency Chambers, Peterborough	01733 315215
Jafar Mr Abdurahman Akhtar	Chambers of Mr Abdurahman Jafar, Ilford	07828 937338
Jaisri Mr Shashi Satyendra	1 Mitre Court Buildings, London	020 7452 8900
Jefferies Mr Thomas Robert	Landmark Chambers, London	020 7430 1221
Jones Mr Alun	St Paul's Chambers, Leeds	0113 245 5866
Jones Mr Christopher David Harries	St John's Chambers, Bristol	0117 923 4700
Jones Mr Emyr Gweirydd	9 Park Place, Cardiff	029 2038 2731
Jones Mr Geraint Martyn	Fenners Chambers, Cambridge	01223 368761
Jones Mr Mark Simeon	3 Dr Johnson's Buildings, London	020 7353 4854
Jones Mr Rhys Charles Mansel	14 Gray's Inn Square, London	020 7242 0858
Joseph Mr Charles Henry	Tanfield Chambers, London	020 7421 5300
Joseph Mr Sellappah Job	Chambers of Mr S J Joseph, London	020 8809 3083/020 8802 9889
Josling Mr William Henry Charles	37 Park Square Chambers, Leeds	0113 243 9422
Jowett Mr Timothy David Christian	9 Park Place, Cardiff	029 2038 2731
Kee Mr Peter William	Becket Chambers, Canterbury	01227 786331
Keel Mr Douglas Vincent	11 Stone Buildings, London	020 7831 6381
Kelly Mr Sean	Chancery House Chambers, Leeds	0113 244 6691
Kelly Mr Shaw Martin	Staple Inn Chambers, London	020 7242 5240
Kelly Mrs Amy Louise	12 College Place, Southampton	023 8032 0320
Kemp Mr James Rupert	Trinity Chambers, Middlesbrough	01642 247569
	Trinity Chambers, Newcastle Upon Tyne	0191 232 1927
Kerr Mr Derek William	Lamb Chambers, London	020 7797 8300
Khalid Mr James	Goulds Green Chambers, Uxbridge	01895 422574
	Goulds Green Chambers, Uxbridge	01895 422574
Khan Dr Alexander	Coral House, Manchester	
Khan Mr Abdul Aleem	Gray's Chambers, Newbury	020 8518 2525
Khan Mr Mahmood Shafi	Luton Chambers, Luton	01582 598394
	Willesden Chambers, London	020 3273 1042
Khan Mr Shahnawaz Zulfiquar	1 Gray's Inn Square, London	020 7405 0001
Khan Mr Shaukat Ali	Chambers of Mr S A Khan, Kingston Upon Thames	020 8541 3875
Kidd Mr Peter William	Number 7 Harrington Street Chambers, Liverpool	0151 242 0707
Kilcoyne Mr Patrick Desmond Oliver	42 Bedford Row, London	020 7831 0222
King Mr Charles Granville	Chambers of Mr C G King, Stroud	07949 461717
Kirk Mr Graeme Charles	One Essex Court, London	020 7936 3030
Kirk Mr Thomas Sean Robinson	12 College Place, Southampton	023 8032 0320
Kitzing Miss Susanna Loraine	Park Court Chambers, Leeds	0113 243 3277
Knight Mr Keith Leslie Francis	4 King's Bench Walk, London	020 7822 7000
Kohli Mr Ryan Singh	Cornerstone Barristers, London	020 7242 4986
Kramer Mr Philip Anthony	Park Lane Plowden, Newcastle Upon Tyne	0191 211 4087
Kwiatkowski Mr Feliks Jerzy	Kew Chambers, Kew	0844 8099991
Kynoch Mr Duncan Stuart Sanderson	Selborne Chambers, London	020 7420 9500
Lamb Mr Jeffrey Thomas	Westgate Chambers, Lewes	01273 480510
Lambert Mrs Alison Janet	Trinity Chambers, Chelmsford	01245 605040
Lane Mr Christopher Paul	No 8 Chambers, Birmingham	0121 236 5514
Law Mr John Edward	The Chambers of Grahame Aldous QC, London	020 7832 0500
Lawrence Miss Pamela Avril	Nexus Chambers, London	020 7404 1147/020 7831 8309
Lee Mr Rosslyn Alexander	Dere Street Barristers, York	0844 3351551
	York Chambers, Newcastle Upon Tyne	0191 206 4677
Leighton Mr Peter Leonard	4 King's Bench Walk, London	020 7822 7000
Leonard Mr Charles Robert Weston	Hardwicke, London	020 7242 2523
Lewis Mr Wayne Anthony	Access Lawyers, London	020 8801 2345
Lippold Ms Sarah Ida Louise	13 KBW, Oxford	01865 311066
	13 King's Bench Walk, London	020 7353 7204

Littman Mr Jeffrey James	Chambers of Mr Jeffrey Littman, London	020 8922 6844
	9 Park Place, Cardiff	029 2038 2731
Livingstone Mr Simon John	Thomas More Chambers, London	020 7404 7000
Lloyd Mr John Nesbitt	Rougemont Chambers, Exeter	01392 208484
Lo Mr Bernard Norman	Field Court Chambers, London	020 7405 6114
Lofthouse Mr James	1 Gray's Inn Square, London	020 7405 0001
Longhurst-Woods Ms Lesley	2 Louisa Close, London	020 8985 8716
Lonsdale Miss Marion Mary	Academy Chambers, London	020 8455 2503
Lonsdale Mr David James	33 Bedford Row, London	020 7242 6476
Lopez Mr Juan Nemesio	Francis Taylor Building, London	020 7353 8415
Loveday Mr Mark Alan	Tanfield Chambers, London	020 7421 5300
Lowe Mr Mungo James	13 Old Square Chambers, London	020 7831 4445
Macpherson Mr Duncan Charles Stewart	One Essex Court, London	020 7936 3030
Maguire Mr Andrew James	Exchange Chambers, Liverpool	0151 236 7747
	Exchange Chambers, Manchester	0161 833 2722
	St Philips Chambers, Birmingham	0121 246 7000
Mahmood Mr Abid	Central Chambers, Manchester	0161 236 1133
	No5 Chambers, Birmingham	0845 210 5555
	No5 Chambers, Bristol	0845 210 5555
	No5 Chambers, London	0845 210 5555
Mahmood Mr Imran Waseem	5 Pump Court, London	020 7353 2532
Mainwaring Mr Robert Paul Clason	Portal Chambers, Llandysul	01559 395 292
Maltz Mr Ben Daniel	Five Paper, London	020 7815 3200
Mankau Mrs Louise	Tanfield Chambers, London	020 7421 5300
Mann Mr Christopher	13 KBW, Oxford	01865 311066
	13 King's Bench Walk, London	020 7353 7204
Marcus Mr Peter	Zenith Chambers, Leeds	0113 245 5438
Marshall Mr Derek Stanley	College Chambers, Southampton	023 8023 0338
Mason Mr Ian Douglas	Amethyst Chambers, London	020 7936 4966
Matthias Mr David Huw	Francis Taylor Building, London	020 7353 8415
Maynard Mr Christopher Howard	Tanfield Chambers, London	020 7421 5300
McCarthy Mr William	Bridgewater Chambers, Manchester	0161 3877127
	1 Mitre Court Buildings, London	020 7452 8900
McCombie Mr Fergus Alexander Paul	1 Gray's Inn Square, London	020 7405 0001
McCormack Mr Alan	Staple Inn Chambers, London	020 7242 5240
McCulloch Miss Fiona Catharine Jane	Middle Temple Lane Chambers, London	020 7583 4352
McDonald Mr John William	2 Temple Gardens, London	020 7822 1200
McDonnell Mr John Beresford William	13 Old Square Chambers, London	020 7831 4445
McKay Mr Christopher Alexander	Cathedral Chambers, Newport	01633 215112
McKinney Miss Nicola Alexandra	4 KBW, London	020 7822 8822
McMorrow Mr Patrick Joseph	4 King's Bench Walk, London	020 7822 7000
McNae Mr Jonathan James	Selborne Chambers, London	020 7420 9500
McNeill Mr David Martin	Five St Andrew's Hill, London	020 7332 5400
Meager Mrs Rowena Elisabeth	No5 Chambers, Birmingham	0845 210 5555
	No5 Chambers, Bristol	0845 210 5555
	No5 Chambers, London	0845 210 5555
Meares Mr Nigel Leslie Vellacott	11 Stone Buildings, London	020 7831 6381
Mendes Da Costa Mr David	Chambers of Mr D Mendes Da Costa, London	020 8747 4633
	MK Family Law Chambers, Milton Keynes	0845 123 1234
	No. 3 Fleet Street Chambers, London	020 7936 4474
Menon Mr Harigovind	New Court Chambers, Newcastle Upon Tyne	0191 232 1980
	Park Lane Plowden, Newcastle Upon Tyne	0191 211 4087
Michael Mr Nicholas	East Anglian Chambers, Chelmsford	01473 214481
	East Anglian Chambers, Colchester	01473 214481
	East Anglian Chambers, Ipswich	01473 214481
	East Anglian Chambers, Norwich	01473 214481

Name	Chambers	Telephone
Miller Mr Ian Daukes Douglas	1 Chancery Lane, London	0845 634 6666
Mitchell Mr David John	No5 Chambers, Birmingham	0845 210 5555
	No5 Chambers, Bristol	0845 210 5555
	No5 Chambers, London	0845 210 5555
Modgill Mr Alexander Jeffrey	Broadway House Chambers, Bradford	01274 722560
	Broadway House Chambers, Leeds	0113 246 2600
Moffat Mr Russell Dean	Linenhall Chambers, Chester	01244 348282
Mohammad Mr Nazar	Legis Chambers, Aylesbury	01296 431125
	No. 3 Fleet Street Chambers, London	020 7936 4474
Monnington Mr Bruce Gilbert	Fenners Chambers, Cambridge	01223 368761
Moran Mr Christopher John	39 Park Square, Leeds	0113 245 6633
Morris Mr Phillip John	9 Park Place, Cardiff	029 2038 2731
Morris Ms Johanna	Chambers of Marion Smullen and Kerim Fuad QC, London	020 7427 4400
Moss Mr Christopher Stephen	St Johns Buildings, Manchester	0161 214 1500
	St Johns Buildings Liverpool, Liverpool	0151 243 6000
	16 Winckley Square, Preston	01772 256100
Moulder Mr Paul John	Alexander Chambers, London	0845 652 0451/0854 652 0451
	Guildford Chambers, Guildford	01483 539131
Muir Miss Nicola Jane	Hardwicke, London	020 7242 2523
Mullee Mr Brendan Paul	Hardwicke, London	020 7242 2523
Mullen Mr Mark Robert	Radcliffe Chambers, London	020 7831 0081
Muman Mr Vijay Kumar	43 Temple Row Chambers, Birmingham	0121 237 6035
Munir Dr Ashley Edward	Five St Andrew's Hill, London	020 7332 5400
Munro Mr Joshua Neil	Hailsham Chambers, London	020 7643 5000
Murphy Mr Damian	Enterprise Chambers, Leeds	0113 246 0391
	Enterprise Chambers, London	020 7405 9471
	Enterprise Chambers, Newcastle Upon Tyne	0191 222 3344
Murray Mr Charles Humphrey Stewart	Rougemont Chambers, Exeter	01392 208484
Nabi Mr Sajjad	5 Pump Court, London	020 7353 2532
Nall-Cain The Hon Richard Christopher Philip	St Albans Chambers, St Albans	01727 843383
Newman Miss Rebecca Jane	Clerksroom (Taunton), Taunton	0845 083 3000
	King's Lynn Chambers, King's Lynn	01553 672 085
Newman Mr James Andrew	Ely Place Chambers, London	020 7400 9600
Newsom Mr George Lucien	Guildhall Chambers, Bristol	0117 930 9000
Nicholls Mr David James	11 Stone Buildings, London	020 7831 6381
Nickless Mr Jason Alan	College Chambers, Southampton	023 8023 0338
Nicol Mr Nicholas Keith	1 Pump Court, London	020 7842 7070
Noble Mr Andrew	Enterprise Chambers, Leeds	0113 246 0391
Noble Mr Philip Robert	Thomas More Chambers, London	020 7404 7000
Norman Mr Jared Simon Gregory	Field Court Chambers, London	020 7405 6114
Normington Mr James Adam	Park Court Chambers, Leeds	0113 243 3277
Norton Mr Giles	Enigma Chambers, Sheffield	07779 576499
	Holborn Chambers, London	020 7242 6060
Nurse Mr Gordon Bramwell William	Radcliffe Chambers, London	020 7831 0081
O'Brien Mr Nicholas William Wattebot	10 King's Bench Walk, London	020 7353 7742
O'Brien Mr Sean Timothy	St Philips Chambers, Birmingham	0121 246 7000
Offer Mr Alexander	Garden Court Chambers, London	020 7993 7600
	Park Court Chambers, Leeds	0113 243 3277
Ohrenstein Mr Dov	Radcliffe Chambers, London	020 7831 0081
Okoya Mr William Ebikise	Arden Chambers, London	020 7242 4244
O'Mahony Mr Jonathan Solomon	9 Stone Buildings, London	020 7404 5055
O'Neill Mr Jonathan Norman	Rougemont Chambers, Exeter	01392 208484
Onipede Dr Victor Olusegun	Chambers of Dr V O Onipede, London	07956 207159
Oommen Mr Jacob	Chambers of Mr Jacob Oommen, East Barnet	07958 680272
Orme Miss Emily Charlotte	Arden Chambers, London	020 7242 4244
Osborne Mr James Robert	Clerksroom (London), London	0845 083 3000

Name	Chambers	Telephone
O'Sullivan Mr Richard John	1215 Chambers, London	020 3291 1215
O'Toole Mr Bartholomew Vincent	5 King's Bench Walk, London	020 7353 5638
O'Toole Mr Simon Gerard	5 Pump Court, London	020 7353 2532
	Riverview Chambers, London	0844 225 3999
Otwal Mr Mukhtiar Singh	42 Bedford Row, London	020 7831 0222
Oulton Mr Richard Arthur Courtenay	5 Essex Court, London	020 7410 2000
Paget Mr Michael Rodborough	Garden Court Chambers, London	020 7993 7600
Palmer Miss Suzanne Elizabeth Josephine	4 King's Bench Walk, London	020 7822 7000
Palmer Mr Edward James	Regent Chambers, Stoke On Trent	01782 286666
Panton Mr Alastair Howard	10 King's Bench Walk, London	020 7353 7742
Paraskos Mr Paraskevakis Christakis	11 Gray's Inn Square Chambers, London	020 7405 6879
Parker Mrs Karen Lesley	Guildhall Chambers Portsmouth, Portsmouth	023 9275 2400
Parsons Mr Andrew James	Portsmouth Barristers'Chambers, Portsmouth	023 9283 1292
Pascall Mr Matthew Stephen	Alexander Chambers, London	0845 652 0451/0854 652 0451
	Guildford Chambers, Guildford	01483 539131
Paton Mr Ewan William	Guildhall Chambers, Bristol	0117 930 9000
Payne Mr David James	No 8 Chambers, Birmingham	0121 236 5514
Payton Mr Clifford Coningsby	Alpha Court Chambers, Leamington Spa	01926 886412
Pearce Mr Robert Edgar	Radcliffe Chambers, London	020 7831 0081
Peckham Ms Jane Louise	1 Crown Office Row, London	020 7797 7500
	Crown Office Row Chambers, Brighton	01273 625625
Pennington-Legh Mr Jonathan Piers	Field Court Chambers, London	020 7405 6114
Pennock Mr Ian	Park Lane Plowden, Leeds	0113 228 5049
Persaud Dr Marcia Chitroutie	1 Gray's Inn Square, London	020 7405 0001
Petersen Mr Thomas James	Goldsmith Chambers, London	020 7353 6802
Phillips Miss Emma Louise	1 Pump Court, London	020 7842 7070
Philpott Mr Anthony Luke	12 Old Square Chambers, London	020 7404 0875
Pithers Mr Clive Robert	Fenners Chambers, Cambridge	01223 368761
Plant Mr James Richard	Farrar's Building, London	020 7583 9241
Platt Miss Heather Louise	Pump Court Chambers, London	020 7353 0711
	Pump Court Chambers, Swindon	01793 539899
	Riverview Chambers, London	0844 225 3999
Polli Mr Timothy James	Tanfield Chambers, London	020 7421 5300
Powell Mr William Rhys	Regency Chambers, Cambridge	01223 301517
	Regency Chambers, Peterborough	01733 315215
Puar Mr Mikhael	30 Park Place, Cardiff	029 2039 8421
Quirke Mr Gerard Martin	Citadel Chambers, Birmingham	0121 233 8500
Rahman Mr Anis	12 Old Square Chambers, London	020 7404 0875
Rai Mr Amarjit Singh	St Philips Chambers, Birmingham	0121 246 7000
Rainey Mr Philip Carslake	Tanfield Chambers, London	020 7421 5300
Ramzan Mr Mohammed Anwar	Great James Street Chambers, London	020 7440 4949
Rana Mr Mohammed Akram	Clapham Law Chambers, London	020 7978 8482
Randolph Mr Paul Leslie	Field Court Chambers, London	020 7405 6114
Ratcliffe Miss Frances Anne	Radcliffe Chambers, London	020 7831 0081
Read Mr Simon Eric	Zenith Chambers, Leeds	0113 245 5438
Record Mrs Celia Saint Claire	Chambers of Lawrence Jones, London	020 7831 1444
Reeds Mr Gareth David	Canary Wharf Chambers, London	020 7183 8011
Reid Miss Cheryl Louise Pegg	Temple Court Chambers, London	020 7353 7888
Reid Miss Claudette Patricia	Chambers of Miss Claudette Reid, London	
Reid Mr Sebastian Peter Scott	Tanfield Chambers, London	020 7421 5300
Ridd Mr David Ian Mcgregor	Farrar's Building, London	020 7583 9241
Rifat Mr Maurice Alan	1 Gray's Inn Square, London	020 7405 0001
Risso-Gill Mr Edward David Charles	Thomas More Chambers, London	020 7404 7000
Roberts Mr Huw Eifion	Linenhall Chambers, Chester	01244 348282
Roberts Mr Michael Charles	Chambers of Michael Roberts, Henley-On-Thames	01844 355 655
Roberts Mr Richard Vaughan	Henderson Chambers, London	020 7583 9020
Robinson Miss Laura	Tanfield Chambers, London	020 7421 5300

Barrister	Chambers	Telephone
Rogers Mr Daniel James	Number 7 Harrington Street Chambers, Liverpool	0151 242 0707
Rogers Mr Michael Peter	Chambers of Mr Ami Feder, London	020 7797 7788
	Chambers of Mr Ami Feder, London	020 7797 7788
Rowntree Mr Edward John Pickering	Hardwicke, London	020 7242 2523
Roy Mr Stefan Alexander Hiren	5 Pump Court, London	020 7353 2532
Rubens Miss Jacqueline Ann	1 Pump Court, London	020 7842 7070
Rudd Mr Michael	36 Bedford Row, London	020 7421 8000
Russell Mr Thomas Charles Welldon	KCH Garden Square, Nottingham	0115 941 8851
Sadiq Mr Muhammad Faisel	Ely Place Chambers, London	020 7400 9600
Saifee Mr Faisal Aftaab	Thomas More Chambers, London	020 7404 7000
Sandham Mr James Andrew	Arden Chambers, London	020 7242 4244
Sawtell Mr David Robert Fraser	4 King's Bench Walk, London	020 7822 7000
Seal Mr Julius Damien	Chambers of Mr Julius Seal, London	020 7328 0158
Seeboruth Mr Royln Jean-Paul	Chambers of Royln Seeboruth, Aylesbury	01296 393329
Sefi Mr Benedict John	Harcourt Chambers, London	0844 561 7135
	Harcourt Chambers, Oxford	0844 561 7135
Sefton-Smith Mr Lloyd	Lamb Chambers, London	020 7797 8300
Sellers Mr Graham	Atlantic Chambers, Liverpool	0151 236 4421
Sen Mr Aditya Kumar	Coram Chambers, London	020 7092 3700
Shamim Mr Mohammed	Clapham Law Chambers, London	020 7978 8482
Sharples Mr John Edmund	St John's Chambers, Bristol	0117 923 4700
Shaw Miss Joanna Elizabeth	One Essex Court, London	020 7936 3030
Shaw Mr Julian	St Johns Buildings, Chester	01244 323070
	St Johns Buildings, Manchester	0161 214 1500
	St Johns Buildings Liverpool, Liverpool	0151 243 6000
Sheftel Mr Andrew Lawson Baylies	Tanfield Chambers, London	020 7421 5300
Shuman Miss Karen Ann Elizabeth	1 Chancery Lane, London	0845 634 6666
	No 8 Chambers, Birmingham	0121 236 5514
Sinclair Miss Lisa Anne	Chambers of Miss Lisa Sinclair, London	020 8946 7201
Sinclair Mr Graham Kelso	East Anglian Chambers, Colchester	01473 214481
	East Anglian Chambers, Ipswich	01473 214481
	East Anglian Chambers, Norwich	01473 214481
Singarajah Mr Frederico	1 Gray's Inn Square, London	020 7405 0001
Sisley Mr Timothy Julian Crispin	9 Stone Buildings, London	020 7404 5055
Skelly Mr Andrew Jon	Hardwicke, London	020 7242 2523
Smith Mr Julian Robert	Lincoln's Inn Fields Chambers, London	0845 123 1234
Smith Mr Matthew Robert	Sovereign Chambers, Leeds	0113 245 1841
Smith Mr Robert Clive	1 Paper Buildings, London	020 7353 3728
	RCS Chambers, Stainton	01709 814 147
Smith Mr Roger Hugh Traylen	No5 Chambers, Birmingham	0845 210 5555
	No5 Chambers, Bristol	0845 210 5555
	No5 Chambers, London	0845 210 5555
Smithers Dr Roger Howard	Alexander Chambers, London	0845 652 0451/0854 652 0451
	Clerksroom (Taunton), Taunton	0845 083 3000
	Guildford Chambers, Guildford	01483 539131
Smyth Mr Christopher Julian Worsley	Queen Square Chambers, Bristol	0117 921 1966
Speller Mr Bruce Christopher Norman	The White House, Battle	01424 777944
Staddon Mr Paul	Tanfield Chambers, London	020 7421 5300
Stagg Mr Paul Andrew	1 Chancery Lane, London	0845 634 6666
Starr Mrs Teresa Margaret	Great James Street Chambers, London	020 7440 4949
Stenhouse Mr John Alexander	Nightingale Chambers, Wolverley	01562 851350
Stephens Mr Michael Allen	Design Chambers, London	020 7353 0747
	St Ive's Chambers, Birmingham	0121 236 0863
Sterling Mr Robert Alan	St James's Chambers, Manchester	0161 834 7000
	Zenith Chambers, Leeds	0113 245 5438
Stevenson Dr Simon John	Park Lane Plowden, Leeds	0113 228 5049
Stevenson Mr Paul Anthony	Tanfield Chambers, London	020 7421 5300

Name	Chambers	Telephone
Steynor Mr Alan Charles	Keating Chambers, London	020 7544 2600
Stubbs Mr Richard John Morris	Trinity Chambers, Middlesbrough	01642 247569
	Trinity Chambers, Newcastle Upon Tyne	0191 232 1927
Swirsky Mr Adam Abraham Burl Bradbury	Lamb Chambers, London	020 7797 8300
Tapsell Mr Paul Richard	Becket Chambers, Canterbury	01227 786331
Tee Mr Gregory James	Guildford Chambers, Guildford	01483 539131
Tempest Mr Alistair Mark	Field Court Chambers, London	020 7405 6114
Thomas Mrs Felicity	Westgate Chambers, Lewes	01273 480510
Thrower Mr James Simeon	Chambers of Simeon Thrower, London	020 8878 7374
Tinnion Mr Antoine	Trinity Chambers, Middlesbrough	01642 247569
	Trinity Chambers, Newcastle Upon Tyne	0191 232 1927
Topal Mr Erol	Lamb Chambers, London	020 7797 8300
Treharne Mr Neil Simon	Dingle Chambers, Bristol	07818 827754
Trompeter Mr Nicholas Simeon	Selborne Chambers, London	020 7420 9500
Troup Mr Alexander William	St John's Chambers, Bristol	0117 923 4700
Trumpington Mr John Henry	Staple Inn Chambers, London	020 7242 5240
Tucker Mr James William Richard	Teucro Chambers, Epsom	
Tueje Miss Patricia	1 Pump Court, London	020 7842 7070
Turnbull Miss Helen Mary	Lamb Chambers, London	020 7797 8300
Twine Miss Nicola	Park Lane Plowden, Leeds	0113 228 5049
Ume Mr Cyril Obiora	12 Old Square Chambers, London	020 7404 0875
Upton Mr Jonathan Michael	Tanfield Chambers, London	020 7421 5300
Valentine Mr Justin Simon	Atlantic Chambers, Liverpool	0151 236 4421
Van Der Leij Dr Martina	Field Court Chambers, London	020 7405 6114
Van Overdijk Miss Claire Orit	No5 Chambers, Birmingham	0845 210 5555
	No5 Chambers, Bristol	0845 210 5555
	No5 Chambers, London	0845 210 5555
Van Tonder Mr Gerard Dirk	New Square Chambers, London	020 7419 8000
Vane The Hon Christopher John Fletcher	Trinity Chambers, Middlesbrough	01642 247569
	Trinity Chambers, Newcastle Upon Tyne	0191 232 1927
Vanhegan Mr Toby Bartholomew	Arden Chambers, London	020 7242 4244
Vaughan-Williams Mr Arthur Laurence	13 Old Square Chambers, London	020 7831 4445
Verduyn Dr Anthony James	St Philips Chambers, Birmingham	0121 246 7000
Vernon Mr Elliot Curt	No. 3 Fleet Street Chambers, London	020 7936 4474
Vickery Mr Neil Michael	13 KBW, Oxford	01865 311066
	13 King's Bench Walk, London	020 7353 7204
Vitiello Mr Fabio Angelo-Giuseppe	Staple Inn Chambers, London	020 7242 5240
Wagstaff Mr Andrew Martin Nicholas	Westgate Chambers, Lewes	01273 480510
Wales Mr Matthew James	Guildhall Chambers, Bristol	0117 930 9000
Walker Mr Adam Nigel	Seven Bedford Row, London	020 7242 3555
Walker-Nolan Mr Benjamin	Thomas More Chambers, London	020 7404 7000
Walsh Mr Michael Patrick	Tanfield Chambers, London	020 7421 5300
Ward Mr Peter Mark	The Chambers of Peter Ward, London	020 3402 2152
Waritay Mr Samuel	Chambers of Mr Samuel Waritay, London	0845 803 7767
Warner Mr David Alexander	St Philips Chambers, Birmingham	0121 246 7000
Watson Mr Duncan Allen	Westgate Chambers, Lewes	01273 480510
Watterson Ms Anna Elizabeth	1 Mitre Court Buildings, London	020 7452 8900
Welch Mr Robert William	Unity Street Chambers, Bristol	0117 906 9789
Wenban-Smith Mr Mungo William	4-5 Gray's Inn Square, London	020 7404 5252
Wheatley Mr Geraint Rhys	Kings Chambers, Birmingham	0845 034 3444
	Kings Chambers, Leeds	0845 034 3444
	Kings Chambers, Manchester	0845 034 3444
Wheaton Mr Ian Malcolm James	Eighteen Carlton Crescent, Southampton	023 8063 9001
White Mr Peter-John Spencer	Great Barford Chambers, Bedford	012134 870004
White Mr Steven James	Park Court Chambers, Leeds	0113 243 3277

Whitehouse Mr Stuart Colin	Goldsmith Chambers, London	020 7353 6802
Widdett Ms Ceri Louise	Park Court Chambers, Leeds	0113 243 3277
Wightwick Mr Iain	Riverview Chambers, London	0844 225 3999
	Unity Street Chambers, Bristol	0117 906 9789
Wiktorowski-Solecki Miss Tamara	Middle Temple Lane Chambers, London	020 7583 4352
Wilkins Mr Christopher John	Pallant Chambers, Chichester	01243 784538
Wilkinson Mr Marc Ashley	No5 Chambers, Birmingham	0845 210 5555
	No5 Chambers, Bristol	0845 210 5555
	No5 Chambers, London	0845 210 5555
Williams Miss June Cleo	No 8 Chambers, Birmingham	0121 236 5514
Williams Mr Simon Paul	Radcliffe Chambers, London	020 7831 0081
Wills Miss Alexandra Itari	Christ Church Chambers, London	020 7409 5278/07788 512787
Winn-Smith Mr Matthew	Lamb Chambers, London	020 7797 8300
Winslett Mr Frank	Westgate Chambers, Lewes	01273 480510
Wolman Mr Clive Richard	11 Stone Buildings, London	020 7831 6381
Wolstenholme Miss Janine	Sovereign Chambers, Leeds	0113 245 1841
Wragg Mr Jonathan Robert	Highgate Chambers, London	020 8340 6031
Wright Mr Stuart Graham	Crown Office Row Chambers, Brighton	01273 625625
Wrottesley Miss Angela Jane	Bank House Chambers, Sheffield	0114 275 1223
Wylie Mr Neil Richard	KCH Garden Square, Nottingham	0115 941 8851
Young Mr Lee Terence	Eighteen Carlton Crescent, Southampton	023 8063 9001
Young Mr Martin Ford	9 Stone Buildings, London	020 7404 5055
Zeitler Miss Barbara	3 Dr Johnson's Buildings, London	020 7353 4854

LICENSING

Afeeva Mr Mark Kudzo Dzitosi	Matrix Chambers, London	020 7404 3447
Alam Ms Jan	Ropewalk Chambers, Nottingham	0115 947 2581
Algazy Mr Jacques Max	Cloisters, London	020 7827 4000
Andre Mr Roger Louis	Sovereign Chambers, Leeds	0113 245 1841
Atkins Mr Richard Paul	St Philips Chambers, Birmingham	0121 246 7000
Austin Mr Ian	Holborn Chambers, London	020 7242 6060
Bahra Miss Narita	9-12 Bell Yard, London	020 7400 1800
	2 Hare Court, London	020 7353 3982
Ball Mr Steven James	Number 7 Harrington Street Chambers, Liverpool	0151 242 0707
Barker Mr Kerry	Guildhall Chambers, Bristol	0117 930 9000
Bartfeld Mr Jason Maurice	187 Fleet Street, London	020 7430 7430
Bates Mr Alan Twan	Monckton Chambers, London	020 7405 7211
Bedloe Mr Giles Robert	Dyers Chambers, London	020 7404 1881
Birkby Mr Richard Adam	Park Court Chambers, Leeds	0113 243 3277
Bishop Mr Malcolm Leslie	Argent Chambers, London	020 7556 5500
	Equity Chambers, Birmingham	0121 236 5007
	30 Park Place, Cardiff	029 2039 8421
Bleaney Mr Nicholas Simon	Atkinson Bevan Chambers, London	020 7353 2112
Booth Mr Alexander Henry Spencer	Francis Taylor Building, London	020 7353 8415
Boswell Mr Andrew Timothy	13 KBW, Oxford	01865 311066
	13 King's Bench Walk, London	020 7353 7204
Bourne-Arton Mr James Luke	St Paul's Chambers, Leeds	0113 245 5866
Bowes Mr Michael Anthony	Cobden House Chambers, Manchester	0161 833 6000
	Outer Temple Chambers, London	020 7353 6381
Brady Mr Scott	3 Temple Gardens, London	020 7353 3102
Bridge Mr Giles	Broadway House Chambers, Bradford	01274 722560
	Broadway House Chambers, Leeds	0113 246 2600
Brown Mr Roger Charles Arthur	Kenworthy's Chambers, Manchester	0161 832 4036
Bryan Mr Robert John	1 Paper Buildings, London	020 7353 3728
Bryden Mr Christopher James Yuen Kang	4 King's Bench Walk, London	020 7822 7000
Buchan Miss Caroline Venetia	Chambers of Miss C Buchan, Haywards Heath	01444 482222
Callery Mr Martin	Cobden House Chambers, Manchester	0161 833 6000
Carrasco Mr Glenn Lawrence	9-12 Bell Yard, London	020 7400 1800
Cavender Ms Susan Penelope	Guildhall Chambers, Bristol	0117 930 9000

Name	Chambers	Telephone
Chalk Mr Alexander John Gervase	6 King's Bench Walk, London	020 7583 0410
Challinor Mr Jonathan Gerald	Cornwall Street Chambers, Birmingham	0121 233 7500
Challinor Mr Thomas Michael	Citadel Chambers, Birmingham	0121 233 8500
Charalambides Mr Leonidas	Francis Taylor Building, London	020 7353 8415
Clarke Mr Rory James	Cornerstone Barristers, London	020 7242 4986
Clover Miss Sarah	Kings Chambers, Leeds	0845 034 3444
	Kings Chambers, Manchester	0845 034 3444
Collard Mr Michael David	5 Pump Court, London	020 7353 2532
Collett Mr Gavin Charles	Rougemont Chambers, Exeter	01392 208484
Comerton Miss Julie Anne	4 KBW, London	020 7822 8822
Cooper Mr Paul Andrew	Portal Chambers, Llandysul	01559 395 292
Corsellis Mr Nicholas Robert Alexander	3 Temple Gardens, London	020 7353 3102
Coster Mr Ronald David	42 Bedford Row, London	020 7831 0222
Cox Mr Jonathan Edward	KCH Garden Square, Nottingham	0115 941 8851
Crew Miss Gillian Mary	Ely Place Chambers, London	020 7400 9600
Croskell Mr Marcus James	East Anglian Chambers, Chelmsford	01473 214481
	East Anglian Chambers, Colchester	01473 214481
	East Anglian Chambers, Ipswich	01473 214481
	East Anglian Chambers, Norwich	01473 214481
Crouch Mr Stephen William Michael	The Chambers of S W M Crouch, Badby	01327 315 742
Culver Mr Edward James	4 King's Bench Walk, London	020 7822 7000
Dagg Mr John Douglas	Trinity Chambers, Chelmsford	01245 605040
Dassa Miss Regine	9 King's Bench Walk, London	020 7353 9564
Davey Mr Neil Martin	Old Court Chambers, Middlesbrough	01642 232523
	39 Park Square, Leeds	0113 245 6633
	3 Temple Gardens, London	020 7353 3102
Davidson Mr Andrew Edward	Citadel Chambers, Birmingham	0121 233 8500
Davies Mr Jonathan Norval	9-12 Bell Yard, London	020 7400 1800
Davis Mr Simon John	St Philips Chambers, Birmingham	0121 246 7000
Dawson Mr Richard Jon Foster	Lincoln House Chambers, Manchester	0161 832 5701
De Haan Mr Kevin Charles	Francis Taylor Building, London	020 7353 8415
Dempsey Miss Karen Marie	3 Temple Gardens, London	020 7353 3102
Dixon Mr James Malcolm	No5 Chambers, Birmingham	0845 210 5555
	No5 Chambers, Bristol	0845 210 5555
	No5 Chambers, London	0845 210 5555
Doherty Mr Nicholas Brudenell	4 King's Bench Walk, London	020 7822 7000
Doran Mr Gerard Patrick	Lincoln House Chambers, Manchester	0161 832 5701
Earle Mr James Christopher Reginald St John	Fenners Chambers, Cambridge	01223 368761
Eastwood Miss Philippa Clemency Anne	Doughty Street Chambers, London	020 7404 1313
Edwards Mr Martin Richard	39 Essex Street, London	020 7832 1111
	82 King Street, Manchester	0161 870 9969
Edwards Mr Nigel Royston	St Paul's Chambers, Leeds	0113 245 5866
Engelman Mr Philip	Cloisters, London	020 7827 4000
	Trinity Chambers, Middlesbrough	01642 247569
	Trinity Chambers, Newcastle Upon Tyne	0191 232 1927
Evans Mr Andrew David	St Philips Chambers, Birmingham	0121 246 7000
Evans Mr Philip	QEB Hollis Whiteman, London	020 7933 8855
Facenna Mr Gerald Carlo	Monckton Chambers, London	020 7405 7211
Falk Mr Charles Morton James	3 PB Barristers, London	020 7583 8055
Fama Mrs Gudrun Hildegard	Middle Temple Lane Chambers, London	020 7583 4352
Fernandes Miss Sue-Ellen Cassiana	No5 Chambers, Birmingham	0845 210 5555
	No5 Chambers, Bristol	0845 210 5555
	No5 Chambers, London	0845 210 5555
Fish Mr David Thomas	Deans Court Chambers, Manchester	0161 214 6000
	Deans Court Chambers, Preston	01772 565 600
	Goldsmith Chambers, London	020 7353 6802
Fisher Mr Jervis Andrew	Citadel Chambers, Birmingham	0121 233 8500

Barrister	Chambers	Telephone
Follon Mr Daniel Richard Thomas	1 Gray's Inn Square, London	020 7405 0001
Foulkes Miss Rebecca	5 Pump Court, London	020 7353 2532
Gent Mr Matthew Thomas	Sovereign Chambers, Leeds	0113 245 1841
Gersch Mr Adam Nissen	Argent Chambers, London	020 7556 5500
Gilchrist Miss Naomi Roberta	St Philips Chambers, Birmingham	0121 246 7000
Gladwell Mr Simon Mark	East Anglian Chambers, Ipswich	01473 214481
Gledhill Mr Lee Andre	Alexander Chambers, London	0845 652 0451/0854 652 0451
	Trident Barristers Chambers, Manchester	0161 663 3123
Glenser Mr Peter Heath	Nine Bedford Row, London	020 7489 2727
Gofur Mr Abdul	Thomas More Chambers, London	020 7404 7000
Goodfellow Mr Stephen John	East Anglian Chambers, Chelmsford	01473 214481
	East Anglian Chambers, Ipswich	01473 214481
	East Anglian Chambers, Norwich	01473 214481
Goodman Mr Alexander David Edmund	Atlas Chambers, London	020 7269 7980
	4-5 Gray's Inn Square, London	020 7404 5252
Goodwin Mr Michael	Old Bailey Chambers, London	020 3008 6404
Gouriet Mr Gerald William	Francis Taylor Building, London	020 7353 8415
Grant Mr Gary Steven	Francis Taylor Building, London	020 7353 8415
Greenfield Mr Peter Charles	King's Bench Chambers, Bournemouth	01202 250025
Griffin Mr Nicholas John	Five Paper Buildings, London	020 7583 6117
Griffiths Mr Hugh Robert James	Furnival Chambers, London	020 7405 3232
Guest Mr Peter Liam	187 Fleet Street, London	020 7430 7430
Hadrill Mr Keith Paul	Furnival Chambers, London	020 7405 3232
Halden Mr Angus Robert	Queen Square Chambers, Bristol	0117 921 1966
Hall Mr Nicholas	Westgate Chambers, Lewes	01273 480510
Ham Mr Nicholas Treharne	Dyers Chambers, London	020 7404 1881
Hamblin Mr Nicholas Howard	Westgate Chambers, Lewes	01273 480510
Hamilton Mr Nigel	Broadway House Chambers, Bradford	01274 722560
	Broadway House Chambers, Leeds	0113 246 2600
Hanlon Mr James Tobias	Old Bailey Chambers, London	020 3008 6404
Hannam Mr Timothy James	Citadel Chambers, Birmingham	0121 233 8500
Hardy Mr Maximilian John Lee	Nine Bedford Row, London	020 7489 2727
Hargreaves Mr Benjamin Thomas	Carmelite Chambers, London	020 7936 6300
Harrison Mr Peter John	6 Pump Court, London	020 7797 8400
	6 Pump Court Chambers, Maidstone	01622 688094
Harvey Mr John Gilbert	No5 Chambers, Birmingham	0845 210 5555
	No5 Chambers, Bristol	0845 210 5555
	No5 Chambers, London	0845 210 5555
Hassall Mr Craig Jonathan	Sovereign Chambers, Leeds	0113 245 1841
Haughty Mr Jeremy Nicholas	Chambers of Mr Ami Feder, London	020 7797 7788
	Chambers of Mr Ami Feder, London	020 7797 7788
	Rougemont Chambers, Exeter	01392 208484
Heeley Miss Michelle Louise	No5 Chambers, Birmingham	0845 210 5555
	No5 Chambers, Bristol	0845 210 5555
	No5 Chambers, London	0845 210 5555
Henley Mr Andrew Michael	Furnival Chambers, London	020 7405 3232
Higgins Mr Daniel Malcolm Buhlea	Nine Bedford Row, London	020 7489 2727
Hill Mr Simon Michael	33 Bedford Row, London	020 7242 6476
Hines Mr James Philip	3 Raymond Buildings, London	020 7400 6400
Hinton Mr Neil Pearse	King's Bench Chambers, Bournemouth	01202 250025
Hirst Miss Rebecca Elisabeth	Cobden House Chambers, Manchester	0161 833 6000
Hobson Miss Laura Elise	Citadel Chambers, Birmingham	0121 233 8500
Holland Mr Charles Christopher	Francis Taylor Building, London	020 7353 8415
	Trinity Chambers, Middlesbrough	01642 247569
	Trinity Chambers, Newcastle Upon Tyne	0191 232 1927
Hunter Mr Timothy Charles	Atkinson Bevan Chambers, London	020 7353 2112
Hussain Mr Ghulam	Crown Office Row Chambers, Brighton	01273 625625
Hussain Mr Muhammad Altaf	Chambers of Mr M A Hussain, London	020 8679 2398
Hypolite-De-Souza Mrs Josephine Claudia	12 Old Square Chambers, London	020 7404 0875

C

Jackson Mr Andrew Fraser	5 Pump Court, London	020 7353 2532
Jackson Mr Christopher Marshall	Liverpool Civil Law, Liverpool	0151 242 0500
Jackson Mr Mark Joseph	No 8 Chambers, Birmingham	0121 236 5514
Jafar Mr Abdurahman Akhtar	Chambers of Mr Abdurahman Jafar, Ilford	07828 937338
Jarratt Miss Alice Cordelia Betchworth	Carmelite Chambers, London	020 7936 6300
Jayakrishnan Mr Harry Sisubalan	Trent Chambers, Nottingham	0115 941 9596
Jenkins Mr Edward Nicholas	Five Paper Buildings, London	020 7583 6117
Johnson Miss Zoe Elisabeth	QEB Hollis Whiteman, London	020 7933 8855
Jones Mr Ian Harvey	Holbrook Chambers, Leicester	07771 961962
Jory Mr Richard Norman	9-12 Bell Yard, London	020 7400 1800
Kapila Miss Rachel Prakash	3 Raymond Buildings, London	020 7400 6400
Keith Mr Benjamin Charles Andrew	Five St Andrew's Hill, London	020 7332 5400
Kent Mr Michael Harcourt	Crown Office Chambers, London	020 7797 8100
Keogh Mr Richard Thomas	Farringdon Chambers, London	020 7089 5700
Khan Mr Zarif	Dyers Chambers, London	020 7404 1881
Kirk Mr Thomas Sean Robinson	12 College Place, Southampton	023 8032 0320
Knight Mr Benjamin James	Central Chambers, Manchester	0161 236 1133
Knight Mr Graeme Edward Verdon	7 Bell Yard, London	020 7831 0636
	Carmelite Chambers, London	020 7936 6300
	The Barristers Chambers, Address withheld	07966 056368
Kohli Mr Ryan Singh	Cornerstone Barristers, London	020 7242 4986
Kolvin Mr Philip Alan	Cornerstone Barristers, London	020 7242 4986
	Kings Chambers, Leeds	0845 034 3444
	Kings Chambers, Manchester	0845 034 3444
Kramer Mr Philip Anthony	Park Lane Plowden, Newcastle Upon Tyne	0191 211 4087
Ladenburg Mr Guy Alexander	3 Raymond Buildings, London	020 7400 6400
Law Mr John Edward	The Chambers of Grahame Aldous QC, London	020 7832 0500
Lawrence Dr Heather Bunting Elizabeth	11 South Square, London	020 7405 1222
Lawrence Sir Ivan John	5 Pump Court, London	020 7353 2532
Le Fevre Miss Sarah Margaret	3 Raymond Buildings, London	020 7400 6400
Leigh Mr Kevin	No5 Chambers, Birmingham	0845 210 5555
	No5 Chambers, Bristol	0845 210 5555
	No5 Chambers, London	0845 210 5555
Lenaghan Mr Anthony	Dyers Chambers, London	020 7404 1881
Levett Miss Francesca Anna	Five St Andrew's Hill, London	020 7332 5400
Lewiecki Miss Marie	Old Bailey Chambers, London	020 3008 6404
Liddiard Mr Martin Thomas	No5 Chambers, Birmingham	0845 210 5555
	No5 Chambers, Bristol	0845 210 5555
	No5 Chambers, London	0845 210 5555
Light Prof Roy Alan	St John's Chambers, Bristol	0117 923 4700
Linehan Mr Stephen John	St Philips Chambers, Birmingham	0121 246 7000
Lodge Mr Hugo Daniel Paul	Atkinson Bevan Chambers, London	020 7353 2112
Lopez Mr Juan Nemesio	Francis Taylor Building, London	020 7353 8415
Lowe Mr Christopher John	KCH Garden Square, Nottingham	0115 941 8851
Lowe Mr Mungo James	13 Old Square Chambers, London	020 7831 4445
Lyons Mr David Wakefield	King's Bench Chambers, Bournemouth	01202 250025
	2 Pump Court, London	020 7353 5597
Mahtab Miss Sumita Laila-Al	7 Bell Yard, London	020 7831 0636
Maitland Mr Marc Claude	King's Bench Chambers, Bournemouth	01202 250025
Maka Mr Isaac	Chambers of Mr Isaac Maka, Ilford	07973 308 301
	4 King's Bench Walk, London	020 7822 7000
Malone Mr David John	1 Gray's Inn Square, London	020 7405 0001
Marcus Mr Peter	Zenith Chambers, Leeds	0113 245 5438
Marshall Mr Derek Stanley	College Chambers, Southampton	023 8023 0338
Martignetti Mr Ian	Regency Chambers, Cambridge	01223 301517
	Regency Chambers, Peterborough	01733 315215
Matthias Mr David Huw	Francis Taylor Building, London	020 7353 8415
McCormack Mr Alan	Staple Inn Chambers, London	020 7242 5240

C

Name	Chambers	Telephone
McGowan Miss Maura Patricia	2 Bedford Row, London	020 7440 8888
	Lincoln House Chambers, Manchester	0161 832 5701
McKinney Miss Nicola Alexandra	4 KBW, London	020 7822 8822
McNeill Mr David Martin	Five St Andrew's Hill, London	020 7332 5400
Meegan Mr Trevor Leo	Citadel Chambers, Birmingham	0121 233 8500
Miah Mr Anawar Babul	Great James Street Chambers, London	020 7440 4949
Michael Mr Nicholas	East Anglian Chambers, Chelmsford	01473 214481
	East Anglian Chambers, Colchester	01473 214481
	East Anglian Chambers, Ipswich	01473 214481
	East Anglian Chambers, Norwich	01473 214481
Miller Miss Wendy Anne May	Citadel Chambers, Birmingham	0121 233 8500
Miller Mr Peter Owen Michael	Cornerstone Barristers, London	020 7242 4986
Mitchell Mr Christian Richard	Alexander Chambers, London	0845 652 0451/0854 652 0451
	Guildford Chambers, Guildford	01483 539131
Monkcom Mr Stephen Philip	Tanfield Chambers, London	020 7421 5300
Moran Mr Patrick Michael	15 New Bridge Street, London	020 7842 1900
Morris Mr Ieuan John	9 Park Place, Cardiff	029 2038 2731
Morris Ms Johanna	Chambers of Marion Smullen and Kerim Fuad QC, London	020 7427 4400
Moulder Mr Paul John	Alexander Chambers, London	0845 652 0451/0854 652 0451
	Guildford Chambers, Guildford	01483 539131
Mousley Mr William Howard	2 King's Bench Walk, London	020 7353 1746
Muller Mr Antonie Sean	Citadel Chambers, Birmingham	0121 233 8500
Muman Mr Vijay Kumar	43 Temple Row Chambers, Birmingham	0121 237 6035
Newbold Mr Michael Paul	9-12 Bell Yard, London	020 7400 1800
Newman Mr James Andrew	Ely Place Chambers, London	020 7400 9600
Newport Mr Ian Alun	College Chambers, Southampton	023 8023 0338
Norton Mr Giles	Enigma Chambers, Sheffield	07779 576499
	Holborn Chambers, London	020 7242 6060
Oakley Miss Louise Michelle	2 Bedford Row, London	020 7440 8888
O'Brien Mr Nicholas William Wattebot	10 King's Bench Walk, London	020 7353 7742
Onipede Dr Victor Olusegun	Chambers of Dr V O Onipede, London	07956 207159
Oommen Mr Jacob	Chambers of Mr Jacob Oommen, East Barnet	07958 680272
Osborne Mr David Thomas	Chambers of Mr D T Osborne, Taunton	01823 400 705
Osborne Mr James Robert	Clerksroom (London), London	0845 083 3000
O'Toole Mr Bartholomew Vincent	5 King's Bench Walk, London	020 7353 5638
Panagiotopoulou Miss Tania	Staple Inn Chambers, London	020 7242 5240
Paraskos Mr Paraskevakis Christakis	11 Gray's Inn Square Chambers, London	020 7405 6879
Parker Miss Wendy	Hardwicke, London	020 7242 2523
Parker Mrs Karen Lesley	Guildhall Chambers Portsmouth, Portsmouth	023 9275 2400
Pascall Mr Matthew Stephen	Alexander Chambers, London	0845 652 0451/0854 652 0451
	Guildford Chambers, Guildford	01483 539131
Penni Miss Sally Selorm-Juliet	Kenworthy's Chambers, Manchester	0161 832 4036
Penny Miss Abigail Sarah Prudence	4 Breams Buildings, London	020 7092 1900
Perry Mr Lewis Kenneth	Rowchester Chambers, Birmingham	0121 233 2327
Persaud Dr Marcia Chitroutie	1 Gray's Inn Square, London	020 7405 0001
Phillips Mr Jeremy Gavin	Francis Taylor Building, London	020 7353 8415
Phillips Mr Simon Benjamin	Francis Taylor Building, London	020 7353 8415
	Park Court Chambers, Leeds	0113 243 3277
Pickup Mr James Kenneth	2 Hare Court, London	020 7353 3982
	Lincoln House Chambers, Manchester	0161 832 5701
Power Mr Archangelo Carlo	2 Bedford Row, London	020 7440 8888
Quirke Mr Gerard Martin	Citadel Chambers, Birmingham	0121 233 8500
Ramasamy Mr Selvaraju	QEB Hollis Whiteman, London	020 7933 8855
Ramzan Mr Mohammed Anwar	Great James Street Chambers, London	020 7440 4949
Rana Mr Mohammed Akram	Clapham Law Chambers, London	020 7978 8482

Name	Chambers	Telephone
Richards Mr David James Martin	3 PB Barristers, Bournemouth	01202 292102
	3 PB Barristers, Bristol	0117 928 1520
	3 PB Barristers, London	020 7583 8055
	3 PB Barristers, Oxford	01865 793 736
	3 PB Barristers, Winchester	01962 868884
Richardson Mr Garth Douglas Anthony	Devon Chambers, Plymouth	01752 661659
	Rougemont Chambers, Exeter	01392 208484
Rooke Mr Alexander John Giles	Argent Chambers, London	020 7556 5500
Roy Mr Stefan Alexander Hiren	5 Pump Court, London	020 7353 2532
Rudd Mr Michael	36 Bedford Row, London	020 7421 8000
Ruffell Mr Mark Beresford	Pump Court Chambers, London	020 7353 0711
	Pump Court Chambers, Swindon	01793 539899
	Pump Court Chambers, Winchester	01962 868 161
Rule Mr Philip David	Castle Chambers, Harrow-on-the-Hill	020 8423 6579
Russell Mr Guy Jonothon	Westgate Chambers, Lewes	01273 480510
Ryle Ms Kate Frances	5 Pump Court, London	020 7353 2532
Sadiq Mr Muhammad Faisel	Ely Place Chambers, London	020 7400 9600
Salmon Mr Jonathan Carl	St Philips Chambers, Birmingham	0121 246 7000
Salter Mr Michael Richard	Ely Place Chambers, London	020 7400 9600
Scott Bell Mrs Rosalind Sara	Trinity Chambers, Middlesbrough	01642 247569
	Trinity Chambers, Newcastle Upon Tyne	0191 232 1927
Seeboruth Mr Royln Jean-Paul	Chambers of Royln Seeboruth, Aylesbury	01296 393329
Seymour Mr Mark William	9-12 Bell Yard, London	020 7400 1800
Shapiro Mr Selwyn	2 King's Bench Walk, London	020 7353 1746
Sharma Miss Sunyana	3 PB Barristers, Bournemouth	01202 292102
	3 PB Barristers, London	020 7583 8055
Silverton Miss Catherine Anne	Sovereign Chambers, Leeds	0113 245 1841
Skinner Mr Samuel Richard Edward	KCH Garden Square, Nottingham	0115 941 8851
Smith Miss Eileen Joan	Trinity Chambers, Middlesbrough	01642 247569
	Trinity Chambers, Newcastle Upon Tyne	0191 232 1927
Smith Mr James Alastair	9-12 Bell Yard, London	020 7400 1800
Smith Ms Rachel Catherine	Lincoln House Chambers, Manchester	0161 832 5701
Smoker Miss Kathleen Mary	Heavenwood Chambers, Stroud	01453 873444
Smyth Mr Christopher Julian Worsley	Queen Square Chambers, Bristol	0117 921 1966
Sonaike Mr Kolarele Oladele Obafemi	One Essex Court, London	020 7936 3030
Spears Miss Katharine Sarah	Carmelite Chambers, London	020 7936 6300
Spence Mr Simon Peter	18 Red Lion Court, London	020 7520 6000
	18 Red Lion Court (Annexe), Chelmsford	01245 280880
Stanford Mr Tony James	Old Bailey Chambers, London	020 3008 6404
Starr Mrs Teresa Margaret	Great James Street Chambers, London	020 7440 4949
Stebbings Mr Ian Anthony	1 Gray's Inn Square, London	020 7405 0001
Steel Mr John Brychan	4-5 Gray's Inn Square, London	020 7404 5252
Stevenson Mr Daniel Keith	9-12 Bell Yard, London	020 7400 1800
Stevenson Mr Robert Lloyd	Sovereign Chambers, Leeds	0113 245 1841
Storey Mr Richard Alexander	3 Temple Gardens, London	020 7353 3102
Stork Mr Brian Raymond	3 Temple Gardens, London	020 7353 3102
Sugarman Mr Jason Ashley	9-12 Bell Yard, London	020 7400 1800
Sullivan Mr Geoffrey Charles Alexander	36 Bedford Row, London	020 7421 8000
Sumnall Miss Charlene Emma Louise	Five Paper Buildings, London	020 7583 6117
Tapsell Mr Paul Richard	Becket Chambers, Canterbury	01227 786331
Targett-Parker Miss Leanne Susan	No. 3 Fleet Street Chambers, London	020 7936 4474
	The Chambers of Miss Leanne Targett-Parker, London	020 8674 6694
Taylor Mr Phillip Brian	Richmond Green Chambers, Richmond	020 8948 4801
Taylor Ms Karen Anne	Themis Chambers, London	07967 418976

Tetlow Mr Bernard Geoffrey	Charter Chambers, London	020 7618 4400
Thomas Mr Mark David	5 Essex Court, London	020 7410 2000
Thompson Mr Ryan Jerome	Dyers Chambers, London	020 7404 1881
Tresman Mr Lewis Robert Simon	Staple Inn Chambers, London	020 7242 5240
Trumpington Mr John Henry	Staple Inn Chambers, London	020 7242 5240
Twist Mr Stephen John	Dere Street Barristers, Newcastle Upon Tyne	0844 3351551
Upton Mr John Stewart	4 King's Bench Walk, London	020 7822 7000
Van Der Leij Dr Martina	Field Court Chambers, London	020 7405 6114
Vasilescu Mr Andrei Constantin	Chambers of Martin Burr, London	0845 123 1234
Vernon Mr Elliot Curt	No. 3 Fleet Street Chambers, London	020 7936 4474
Wadsley Mr Peter John Campbell	St John's Chambers, Bristol	0117 923 4700
Wagstaff Mr Andrew Martin Nicholas	Westgate Chambers, Lewes	01273 480510
Watson Mr Benjamin Turquand	3 Raymond Buildings, London	020 7400 6400
Watson Mr Graham	Colleton Chambers, Exeter	01392 274898
Weekes Mr Mark Vincent	6 King's Bench Walk, London	020 7583 0410
Whale Mr Stephen John	4-5 Gray's Inn Square, London	020 7404 5252
White Mr Daniel Edward Mills	Citadel Chambers, Birmingham	0121 233 8500
Widdison-Thom Mrs Stacey Jane	Kingsley Chambers, Barkingside	07891 441 445
Wilcox Mr Jerome Carl Jean	Alexander Chambers, London	0845 652 0451/0854 652 0451
Williams Mr Ben Dylan	Kings Chambers, Birmingham	0845 034 3444
	Kings Chambers, Leeds	0845 034 3444
	Kings Chambers, Manchester	0845 034 3444
Williams Mr Owen David Parker	9 Park Place, Cardiff	029 2038 2731
Willmer Mr Stephen James	Argent Chambers, London	020 7556 5500
Woods Mr Terence Mccartan	187 Fleet Street, London	020 7430 7430
Yeo Mr Nicholas	3 Raymond Buildings, London	020 7400 6400
Young Mr Martin Ford	9 Stone Buildings, London	020 7404 5055
Zwart Mr Auberon Christiaan Conrad	39 Essex Street, London	020 7832 1111
	82 King Street, Manchester	0161 870 9969

LOCAL GOVERNMENT

Abu-Mustafa Mr Jehad	1 Paper Buildings, London	020 7353 3728
Adewale Mr Remi Adetokunbo Sanni	Chambers of G. D. Tetteh, London	020 7353 7095
	Chambers of Mr R. A. Adewale, Address withheld	020 7231 2814
Ajaz Mr Mohammad Arshad	Eastmans Chambers, Reading	0118 966 9094
Akers Mr Robert Matthew Harry	St Johns Buildings, Chester	01244 323070
	St Johns Buildings, Manchester	0161 214 1500
	16 Winckley Square, Preston	01772 256100
Albutt Mr Ian Leslie	Cornerstone Barristers, London	020 7242 4986
	Heavenwood Chambers, Stroud	01453 873444
Algazy Mr Jacques Max	Cloisters, London	020 7827 4000
Alliott Mr George Beckles	Temple Garden Chambers, London	020 7583 1315
Altaras Mr David Maurice	36 Bedford Row, London	020 7421 8000
Amraoui Mr Thomas	4-5 Gray's Inn Square, London	020 7404 5252
Anderson Mr Jack Duthie	4-5 Gray's Inn Square, London	020 7404 5252
Angammana Mr Gamini Bertram	Chambers of Gamini Angammana, London	020 8771 5205
Artesi Miss Desiree Allison Ann	Thomas More Chambers, London	020 7404 7000
Auburn Mr Jonathan Walter	4-5 Gray's Inn Square, London	020 7404 5252
Baldwin Dr Timothy John	Garden Court Chambers, London	020 7993 7600
Bates Mr Alan Twan	Monckton Chambers, London	020 7405 7211
Bates Mr John Hayward	Old Square Chambers, Bristol	0117 930 5100
	Old Square Chambers, London	020 7269 0300
Beaumont Mr Marc Clifford	9 Stone Buildings, London	020 7404 5055
	Windsor Barristers' Chambers, Windsor	01753 839321
Berry Mr Adrian Christopher	Garden Court Chambers, London	020 7993 7600
Bhattacharyya Mr Ardhendu	Slough Barristers Chamber, Slough	01753 553806
Bishop Mr Malcolm Leslie	Argent Chambers, London	020 7556 5500
	Equity Chambers, Birmingham	0121 236 5007
	30 Park Place, Cardiff	029 2039 8421

Blair Mr Peter Michael	Guildhall Chambers, Bristol	0117 930 9000
	6 King's Bench Walk, London	020 7583 0410
Booth Mr Alexander Henry Spencer	Francis Taylor Building, London	020 7353 8415
Boswell Mr Andrew Timothy	13 KBW, Oxford	01865 311066
	13 King's Bench Walk, London	020 7353 7204
Bourne Mr Charles Gregory	4-5 Gray's Inn Square, London	020 7404 5252
Bowsher Mr Michael Frederick Thomas	Monckton Chambers, London	020 7405 7211
Broatch Mr Donald	Five Paper, London	020 7815 3200
Brown Mr Roger Charles Arthur	Kenworthy's Chambers, Manchester	0161 832 4036
Bryden Mr Christopher James Yuen Kang	4 King's Bench Walk, London	020 7822 7000
Burton Mr James William	39 Essex Street, London	020 7832 1111
	82 King Street, Manchester	0161 870 9969
Butler Mr Simon David	The Chambers of Grahame Aldous QC, London	020 7832 0500
Byrne Mr Garrett Thomas	4-5 Gray's Inn Square, London	020 7404 5252
Cartwright Mr Ivan Matthew	KCH Garden Square, Nottingham	0115 941 8851
Cattermole Miss Rebecca Elke	Tanfield Chambers, London	020 7421 5300
Chaffin-Laird Miss Olivia Carolyn	No5 Chambers, Birmingham	0845 210 5555
	No5 Chambers, Bristol	0845 210 5555
	No5 Chambers, London	0845 210 5555
Charalambides Mr Leonidas	Francis Taylor Building, London	020 7353 8415
Christensen Mr Carlton	10 King's Bench Walk, London	020 7353 7742
Christie Mr Iain Robert	5RB, London	020 7242 2902
Clarke Mr Rory James	Cornerstone Barristers, London	020 7242 4986
Clay Mr Jonathan Roger	Cornerstone Barristers, London	020 7242 4986
Collard Mr Michael David	5 Pump Court, London	020 7353 2532
Comerton Miss Julie Anne	4 KBW, London	020 7822 8822
Cooper Miss Christine	Field Court Chambers, London	020 7405 6114
Cooper Mr Paul Andrew	Portal Chambers, Llandysul	01559 395 292
Coyle Mr Anthony Noel	Zenith Chambers, Leeds	0113 245 5438
Crawford Mr Lincoln Santo	12 King's Bench Walk, London	020 7583 0811
Crew Miss Gillian Mary	Ely Place Chambers, London	020 7400 9600
Dagg Mr John Douglas	Trinity Chambers, Chelmsford	01245 605040
Dalby Mr Joseph Francis	4-5 Gray's Inn Square, London	020 7404 5252
Daly Mr David	Heathway Chambers, London	020 8293 0509
Davies Mr Jonathan Norval	9-12 Bell Yard, London	020 7400 1800
Davies Ms Elizabeth Mary	Garden Court Chambers, London	020 7993 7600
De Mello Mr Rembert Joseph Julius	No5 Chambers, Birmingham	0845 210 5555
	No5 Chambers, Bristol	0845 210 5555
	No5 Chambers, London	0845 210 5555
Doran Mr Gerard Patrick	Lincoln House Chambers, Manchester	0161 832 5701
Dos Santos Mr Alexander	Charter Chambers, London	020 7618 4400
Dubin Mr Joshua Charles	1 Pump Court, London	020 7842 7070
Dyble Mr Steven John	18 Red Lion Court, London	020 7520 6000
	18 Red Lion Court (Annexe), Chelmsford	01245 280880
Earle Mr James Christopher Reginald St John	Fenners Chambers, Cambridge	01223 368761
Eastwood Miss Philippa Clemency Anne	Doughty Street Chambers, London	020 7404 1313
Eaton Mr Tobias Barnaby	Staple Inn Chambers, London	020 7242 5240
Edwards Mr Denis	Francis Taylor Building, London	020 7353 8415
Edwards Mr Martin Richard	39 Essex Street, London	020 7832 1111
	82 King Street, Manchester	0161 870 9969
Egleton Mr Richard Wildman	Pallant Chambers, Chichester	01243 784538
Elliott Mr Jason	Dere Street Barristers, Newcastle Upon Tyne	0844 3351551
Engelman Mr Philip	Cloisters, London	020 7827 4000
	Trinity Chambers, Middlesbrough	01642 247569
	Trinity Chambers, Newcastle Upon Tyne	0191 232 1927
Facenna Mr Gerald Carlo	Monckton Chambers, London	020 7405 7211

Fagborun Bennett Ms Morayo Abosede	Hardwicke, London	020 7242 2523
Falkowski Mr Damian	4-5 Gray's Inn Square, London	020 7404 5252
Fender Mr Carl David	Regency Chambers, Cambridge	01223 301517
	Regency Chambers, Peterborough	01733 315215
Fraser-Urquhart Mr Andrew	4-5 Gray's Inn Square, London	020 7404 5252
Fullwood Mr Adam Garrett	Kings Chambers, Birmingham	0845 034 3444
	Kings Chambers, Leeds	0845 034 3444
	Kings Chambers, Manchester	0845 034 3444
Gallagher Ms Caoilfhionn Anna	Doughty Street Chambers, Bristol	01179 058 717
	Doughty Street Chambers, London	020 7404 1313
	Doughty Street Chambers, Manchester	0161 618 1066
Gallivan Mr Terence John	Five Paper, London	020 7815 3200
Gardiner Mr William David Hugh	Holborn Chambers, London	020 7242 6060
Gasztowicz Mr Steven	Cornerstone Barristers, London	020 7242 4986
	New Street Chambers, Leicester	0116 262 5906
Gill Mr Manjit Singh	No5 Chambers, Birmingham	0845 210 5555
	No5 Chambers, Bristol	0845 210 5555
	No5 Chambers, London	0845 210 5555
Godfrey Mr Lauren John	Crown Office Row Chambers, Brighton	01273 625625
Goodman Mr Alexander David Edmund	Atlas Chambers, London	020 7269 7980
	4-5 Gray's Inn Square, London	020 7404 5252
Gore Mr Andrew Roger	Fenners Chambers, Cambridge	01223 368761
Grant Mr Chudi Paul	Kenworthy's Chambers, Manchester	0161 832 4036
Greatorex Mr Paul	4-5 Gray's Inn Square, London	020 7404 5252
Green Mr Jonathan Paul	Dyers Chambers, London	020 7404 1881
Greenan Miss Sarah Octavia	Zenith Chambers, Leeds	0113 245 5438
Ground Mr Patrick	Chambers of Mr Patrick Ground QC, London	020 7736 0131
Guy Mr Richard Perran	Chambers of Mr Ami Feder, London	020 7797 7788
	King's Bench and Godolphin (KBG)Chambers, Plymouth	01752 221551
	Southernhay Chambers, Exeter	01392 255777
Ham Mr Nicholas Treharne	Dyers Chambers, London	020 7404 1881
Hanif Miss Saima Naz	4-5 Gray's Inn Square, London	020 7404 5252
Hanlon Mr James Tobias	Old Bailey Chambers, London	020 3008 6404
Harris Mr Julian Gilbert Vaughan	Citadel Chambers, Birmingham	0121 233 8500
Harrison Mr Peter John	6 Pump Court, London	020 7797 8400
	6 Pump Court Chambers, Maidstone	01622 688094
Harwood Mr Richard John	39 Essex Street, London	020 7832 1111
	82 King Street, Manchester	0161 870 9969
Hearnden Mr Richard Christopher	Furnival Chambers, London	020 7405 3232
Henderson Miss Josephine	Five Paper, London	020 7815 3200
Hill Mr Piers Nicholas	37 Park Square Chambers, Leeds	0113 243 9422
Hobson Mr John Graham	4-5 Gray's Inn Square, London	020 7404 5252
Hodgson Mrs Jane Lee	Five Paper, London	020 7815 3200
Holland Mr Charles Christopher	Francis Taylor Building, London	020 7353 8415
	Trinity Chambers, Middlesbrough	01642 247569
	Trinity Chambers, Newcastle Upon Tyne	0191 232 1927
Horton Mr Matthew Bethell	39 Essex Street, London	020 7832 1111
	82 King Street, Manchester	0161 870 9969
Howlett Mr James Anthony	KCH Garden Square, Nottingham	0115 941 8851
Huggins Mr Toby James	Unity Street Chambers, Bristol	0117 906 9789
Hughes Mr William Lloyd	9-12 Bell Yard, London	020 7400 1800
Humphreys Mr Richard William	Francis Taylor Building, London	020 7353 8415
	No5 Chambers, Birmingham	0845 210 5555
	No5 Chambers, Bristol	0845 210 5555
	No5 Chambers, London	0845 210 5555
Hussain Mr Ghulam	Crown Office Row Chambers, Brighton	01273 625625
Hussain Mr Muhammad Altaf	Chambers of Mr M A Hussain, London	020 8679 2398
Hutchinson Mr Colin Thomas	Garden Court Chambers, London	020 7993 7600

Name	Chambers	Telephone
Irwin Mr Gavin David	Dyers Chambers, London	020 7404 1881
Jackson Mr Mark Joseph	No 8 Chambers, Birmingham	0121 236 5514
Jafar Mr Abdurahman Akhtar	Chambers of Mr Abdurahman Jafar, Ilford	07828 937338
Jayakrishnan Mr Harry Sisubalan	Trent Chambers, Nottingham	0115 941 9596
Joffe Ms Natasha Juliet Louise	Outer Temple Chambers, London	020 7353 6381
Johnson Miss Laura Wendy	1 Chancery Lane, London	0845 634 6666
Jones Mr Emyr Gweirydd	9 Park Place, Cardiff	029 2038 2731
Jones Mr Ian Harvey	Holbrook Chambers, Leicester	07771 961962
Jones Mr Richard Frederick Thomas	Heavenwood Chambers, Stroud	01453 873444
Kelly Mrs Amy Louise	12 College Place, Southampton	023 8032 0320
Kennedy Mr Christopher Laurence Paul	9 St John Street, Manchester	0161 955 9000
Kent Mr Michael Harcourt	Crown Office Chambers, London	020 7797 8100
Khalique Miss Nageena	No5 Chambers, Birmingham	0845 210 5555
	No5 Chambers, Bristol	0845 210 5555
	No5 Chambers, London	0845 210 5555
Khan Mr Ayoub	Chambers of Mr Ayoub Khan, Birmingham	07930 987202
Kohli Mr Ryan Singh	Cornerstone Barristers, London	020 7242 4986
Lambert Mrs Alison Janet	Trinity Chambers, Chelmsford	01245 605040
Lane Mr Michael John	East Anglian Chambers, Colchester	01473 214481
	East Anglian Chambers, Ipswich	01473 214481
	East Anglian Chambers, Norwich	01473 214481
Lenaghan Mr Anthony	Dyers Chambers, London	020 7404 1881
Levett Miss Francesca Anna	Five St Andrew's Hill, London	020 7332 5400
Lewiecki Miss Marie	Old Bailey Chambers, London	020 3008 6404
Lloyd Mr John Nesbitt	Rougemont Chambers, Exeter	01392 208484
Lock Mr David Anthony	No5 Chambers, Birmingham	0845 210 5555
	No5 Chambers, Bristol	0845 210 5555
	No5 Chambers, London	0845 210 5555
Lopez Mr Juan Nemesio	Francis Taylor Building, London	020 7353 8415
Loveday Mr David Robert	4-5 Gray's Inn Square, London	020 7404 5252
Lowe Mr Mungo James	13 Old Square Chambers, London	020 7831 4445
Mainwaring Mr Robert Paul Clason	Portal Chambers, Llandysul	01559 395 292
Malone Mr David John	1 Gray's Inn Square, London	020 7405 0001
Mandalia Mr Vinesh Lalji	St Philips Chambers, Birmingham	0121 246 7000
Marcus Mr Peter	Zenith Chambers, Leeds	0113 245 5438
Markus Ms Kate	Doughty Street Chambers, Bristol	01179 058 717
	Doughty Street Chambers, London	020 7404 1313
	Doughty Street Chambers, Manchester	0161 618 1066
Matthias Mr David Huw	Francis Taylor Building, London	020 7353 8415
Mawrey Mr Richard Brooks	Henderson Chambers, London	020 7583 9020
McCombie Mr Fergus Alexander Paul	1 Gray's Inn Square, London	020 7405 0001
McDonald Ms Melanie Sharon	No5 Chambers, Birmingham	0845 210 5555
	No5 Chambers, Bristol	0845 210 5555
	No5 Chambers, London	0845 210 5555
McKiernan Mr Edward Joseph	Farringdon Chambers, London	020 7089 5700
McNeill Mr David Martin	Five St Andrew's Hill, London	020 7332 5400
Miller Mr Peter Owen Michael	Cornerstone Barristers, London	020 7242 4986
Moffett Mr Jonathan Keith	4-5 Gray's Inn Square, London	020 7404 5252
Mustakim Mr Abdul Yunus Al	Chambers of Mr Mustakim, London	
Mynors Dr Charles Baskerville	Francis Taylor Building, London	020 7353 8415
Newsom Mr George Lucien	Guildhall Chambers, Bristol	0117 930 9000
Norman Mr Jared Simon Gregory	Field Court Chambers, London	020 7405 6114
Okoya Mr William Ebikise	Arden Chambers, London	020 7242 4244
Orme Miss Emily Charlotte	Arden Chambers, London	020 7242 4244
Ornsby Miss Suzanne Doreen	Francis Taylor Building, London	020 7353 8415
	St John's Chambers, Bristol	0117 923 4700
O'Sullivan Mr Richard John	1215 Chambers, London	020 3291 1215
Paget Mr Michael Rodborough	Garden Court Chambers, London	020 7993 7600
Pascoe Ms Soraya	1 Gray's Inn Square, London	020 7405 0001
Payne Mr David James	No 8 Chambers, Birmingham	0121 236 5514
Perry Mr Christopher Edward	Palmyra Chambers, Warrington	01925 444919

Plimmer Miss Melanie Ann	Kings Chambers, Birmingham	0845 034 3444
	Kings Chambers, Leeds	0845 034 3444
	Kings Chambers, Manchester	0845 034 3444
Pointing Mr John Eric	Chambers of Mr John Pointing, London	020 8997 2285
Powell Mr William Rhys	Regency Chambers, Cambridge	01223 301517
	Regency Chambers, Peterborough	01733 315215
Price Mr Andrew Robert	Dyers Chambers, London	020 7404 1881
Read Mr Simon Eric	Zenith Chambers, Leeds	0113 245 5438
Reid Mr Sebastian Peter Scott	Tanfield Chambers, London	020 7421 5300
Roberts Mr Richard Vaughan	Henderson Chambers, London	020 7583 9020
Roy Mr Stefan Alexander Hiren	5 Pump Court, London	020 7353 2532
Royce Mr Darryl Fraser	Atkin Chambers, London	020 7404 0102
Rubens Miss Jacqueline Ann	1 Pump Court, London	020 7842 7070
Rudd Mr Michael	36 Bedford Row, London	020 7421 8000
Ruffell Mr Mark Beresford	Pump Court Chambers, London	020 7353 0711
	Pump Court Chambers, Swindon	01793 539899
	Pump Court Chambers, Winchester	01962 868 161
Rule Mr Philip David	Castle Chambers, Harrow-on-the-Hill	020 8423 6579
Rushton Mr Jonathon Barker	36 Bedford Row, London	020 7421 8000
Russell-Mitra Miss Jessica Suparna	1 Mitre Court Buildings, London	020 7452 8900
Sadiq Mr Muhammad Faisel	Ely Place Chambers, London	020 7400 9600
Saifee Mr Faisal Aftaab	Thomas More Chambers, London	020 7404 7000
Salmon Mr Jonathan Carl	St Philips Chambers, Birmingham	0121 246 7000
Sandham Mr James Andrew	Arden Chambers, London	020 7242 4244
Scally Miss Josephine Theresa Sarah	Palmyra Chambers, Warrington	01925 444919
Scolding Miss Fiona Kate	Hardwicke, London	020 7242 2523
Sears Mr Robert David Murray	Four New Square, London	020 7822 2000
Seymour Mr Mark William	9-12 Bell Yard, London	020 7400 1800
Shapiro Mr Selwyn	2 King's Bench Walk, London	020 7353 1746
Sheikh Ms Saira Kabir	Francis Taylor Building, London	020 7353 8415
Silverton Miss Catherine Anne	Sovereign Chambers, Leeds	0113 245 1841
Sinclair Mr Graham Kelso	East Anglian Chambers, Colchester	01473 214481
	East Anglian Chambers, Ipswich	01473 214481
	East Anglian Chambers, Norwich	01473 214481
Smith Miss Eileen Joan	Trinity Chambers, Middlesbrough	01642 247569
	Trinity Chambers, Newcastle Upon Tyne	0191 232 1927
Smith Mr James Alastair	9-12 Bell Yard, London	020 7400 1800
Smoker Miss Kathleen Mary	Heavenwood Chambers, Stroud	01453 873444
Sonaike Mr Kolarele Oladele Obafemi	One Essex Court, London	020 7936 3030
Spencer Mr Paul Anthony	3 Serjeants Inn, London	020 7427 5000
Stagg Mr Paul Andrew	1 Chancery Lane, London	0845 634 6666
Stanford Mr Tony James	Old Bailey Chambers, London	020 3008 6404
Stebbings Mr Ian Anthony	1 Gray's Inn Square, London	020 7405 0001
Steel Mr John Brychan	4-5 Gray's Inn Square, London	020 7404 5252
Stemp Mr Scott	12 College Place, Southampton	023 8032 0320
Stevenson Mr Daniel Keith	9-12 Bell Yard, London	020 7400 1800
Stinchcombe Mr Paul David	4-5 Gray's Inn Square, London	020 7404 5252
Storey Mr Richard Alexander	3 Temple Gardens, London	020 7353 3102
Storrie Mr Timothy James	Lincoln House Chambers, Manchester	0161 832 5701
Sugarman Mr Jason Ashley	9-12 Bell Yard, London	020 7400 1800
Tapsell Mr Paul Richard	Becket Chambers, Canterbury	01227 786331
Tatford Mr Warwick Henry Patrick	9-12 Bell Yard, London	020 7400 1800
Taylor Mrs Yvonne Marie	Trinity Chambers, Middlesbrough	01642 247569
	Trinity Chambers, Newcastle Upon Tyne	0191 232 1927
Taylor Ms Karen Anne	Themis Chambers, London	07967 418976
Thomas Miss Megan Moira	6 Pump Court, London	020 7797 8400
	6 Pump Court Chambers, Maidstone	01622 688094
Thomas Mr Mark David	5 Essex Court, London	020 7410 2000
Thomas Mrs Felicity	Westgate Chambers, Lewes	01273 480510

Thompson Mr Andrew Edward Courtney	Tanfield Chambers, London	020 7421 5300
Townsend Mrs Harriet Caroline Jane	Cornerstone Barristers, London	020 7242 4986
Twist Mr Stephen John	Dere Street Barristers, Newcastle Upon Tyne	0844 3351551
Udom Miss Nancy Ini	Five St Andrew's Hill, London	020 7332 5400
Upton Mr John Stewart	4 King's Bench Walk, London	020 7822 7000
Van Overdijk Miss Claire Orit	No5 Chambers, Birmingham	0845 210 5555
	No5 Chambers, Bristol	0845 210 5555
	No5 Chambers, London	0845 210 5555
Vanhegan Mr Toby Bartholomew	Arden Chambers, London	020 7242 4244
Vaughan-Williams Mr Arthur Laurence	13 Old Square Chambers, London	020 7831 4445
Wadsley Mr Peter John Campbell	St John's Chambers, Bristol	0117 923 4700
Wald Mr Richard Daniel	39 Essex Street, London	020 7832 1111
	82 King Street, Manchester	0161 870 9969
	Riverview Chambers, London	0844 225 3999
Ward Miss Alexandra	9-12 Bell Yard, London	020 7400 1800
Warner Mr David Alexander	St Philips Chambers, Birmingham	0121 246 7000
Warnock Mr Andrew Ronald	1 Chancery Lane, London	0845 634 6666
Wenban-Smith Mr Mungo William	4-5 Gray's Inn Square, London	020 7404 5252
Whale Mr Stephen John	4-5 Gray's Inn Square, London	020 7404 5252
Wightwick Mr Iain	Riverview Chambers, London	0844 225 3999
	Unity Street Chambers, Bristol	0117 906 9789
Wigley Miss Jenny	No5 Chambers, Birmingham	0845 210 5555
	No5 Chambers, Bristol	0845 210 5555
	No5 Chambers, London	0845 210 5555
Wignall Mr Edward Gordon	No5 Chambers, Birmingham	0845 210 5555
	No5 Chambers, Bristol	0845 210 5555
	No5 Chambers, London	0845 210 5555
Williams Mr Ben Dylan	Kings Chambers, Birmingham	0845 034 3444
	Kings Chambers, Leeds	0845 034 3444
	Kings Chambers, Manchester	0845 034 3444
Williams Mr Rhodri John	Henderson Chambers, London	020 7583 9020
	30 Park Place, Cardiff	029 2039 8421
Wise Mr Ian	Doughty Street Chambers, Bristol	01179 058 717
	Doughty Street Chambers, London	020 7404 1313
	Doughty Street Chambers, Manchester	0161 618 1066
Wolstenholme Miss Janine	Sovereign Chambers, Leeds	0113 245 1841
Wragg Mr Jonathan Robert	Highgate Chambers, London	020 8340 6031
Young Mr Martin Ford	9 Stone Buildings, London	020 7404 5055
Zeitler Miss Barbara	3 Dr Johnson's Buildings, London	020 7353 4854

C

MEDICAL NEGLIGENCE

Abasheikh Mr Omar Said Imam	Paragon Chambers, London	020 3318 9988
Ajaz Mr Mohammad Arshad	Eastmans Chambers, Reading	0118 966 9094
Alam Ms Jan	Ropewalk Chambers, Nottingham	0115 947 2581
Alliott Mr George Beckles	Temple Garden Chambers, London	020 7583 1315
Allston Mr Anthony Stanley	3 Dr Johnson's Buildings, London	020 7353 4854
Andre Mr Roger Louis	Sovereign Chambers, Leeds	0113 245 1841
Angammana Mr Gamini Bertram	Chambers of Gamini Angammana, London	020 8771 5205
Arnheim Dr Michael Thomas Walter	Chambers of Dr Michael Arnheim, London	020 7833 5093
	Holborn Chambers, London	020 7242 6060
	Principal Chambers, Sevenoaks	0845 209 8080
Ashworth Miss Fiona Katherine Anne	Kings Chambers, Birmingham	0845 034 3444
	Kings Chambers, Leeds	0845 034 3444
	Kings Chambers, Manchester	0845 034 3444
Baldwin Dr Timothy John	Garden Court Chambers, London	020 7993 7600
Beaumont Mr Marc Clifford	9 Stone Buildings, London	020 7404 5055
	Windsor Barristers' Chambers, Windsor	01753 839321

Name	Chambers	Telephone
Beloff Mr Rupert Joseph Alexei	No5 Chambers, Birmingham	0845 210 5555
	No5 Chambers, Bristol	0845 210 5555
	No5 Chambers, London	0845 210 5555
Bennett Miss Emma Louise	Exchange Chambers, Leeds	0113 203 1970
	Exchange Chambers, Liverpool	0151 236 7747
	Exchange Chambers, Manchester	0161 833 2722
Bhattacharyya Mr Ardhendu	Slough Barristers Chamber, Slough	01753 553806
Birch Mr Roger Allen	Five St Andrew's Hill, London	020 7332 5400
	Sovereign Chambers, Leeds	0113 245 1841
Bloom Dr Margaret	Hardwicke, London	020 7242 2523
Bogle Mr James Stewart Lockhart	10 King's Bench Walk, London	020 7353 7742
Bonehill Mr Nicholas Benjamin	4 Breams Buildings, London	020 7092 1900
Boyd Miss Kerstin Margaret	Tanfield Chambers, London	020 7421 5300
Buchan Miss Caroline Venetia	Chambers of Miss C Buchan, Haywards Heath	01444 482222
Buchan Mr Andrew	Cloisters, London	020 7827 4000
Buckhaven Mr Simon	Hardwicke, London	020 7242 2523
Buckle Mr Jonathan	Regency Chambers, Cambridge	01223 301517
	Regency Chambers, Peterborough	01733 315215
Buckley Mr Peter Evered	Cobden House Chambers, Manchester	0161 833 6000
Butler Mr Simon David	The Chambers of Grahame Aldous QC, London	020 7832 0500
Carlisle Mr Timothy St John Ogilvie	Field Court Chambers, London	020 7405 6114
Cartwright Mr Ivan Matthew	KCH Garden Square, Nottingham	0115 941 8851
Cattermull Miss Emma Jayne	East Anglian Chambers, Chelmsford	01473 214481
	East Anglian Chambers, Ipswich	01473 214481
	East Anglian Chambers, Norwich	01473 214481
Challenger Mr Colin Westcott	Lamb Chambers, London	020 7797 8300
Chippeck Mr Stephen	5 King's Bench Walk, London	020 7353 5638
Clarke Mr Jamie Roy	Hardwicke, London	020 7242 2523
Climie Mr Roger Stephen	King's Bench and Godolphin (KBG)Chambers, Plymouth	01752 221551
	Outer Temple Chambers, London	020 7353 6381
Colbey Mr Richard	Guildhall Chambers Portsmouth, Portsmouth	023 9275 2400
	Lamb Chambers, London	020 7797 8300
Compton Mr Benjamin Edward Welstead	Outer Temple Chambers, London	020 7353 6381
Corsellis Mr Nicholas Robert Alexander	3 Temple Gardens, London	020 7353 3102
Coster Mr Ronald David	42 Bedford Row, London	020 7831 0222
Coulter Mr Barry John	Clerksroom (London), London	0845 083 3000
	Clerksroom (Taunton), Taunton	0845 083 3000
	King's Lynn Chambers, King's Lynn	01553 672 085
Counsell Mr James Henry	Outer Temple Chambers, London	020 7353 6381
Crawford Mr Lincoln Santo	12 King's Bench Walk, London	020 7583 0811
Culverhouse Miss Emily Anna Louise	Chambers of Miss E Culverhouse, Chesham	07813 007503
Davis Mr Andrew Paul	Crown Office Chambers, London	020 7797 8100
De Jehan Mr David	Park Lane Plowden, Leeds	0113 228 5049
Dean Mr James Patrick	Goldsmith Chambers, London	020 7353 6802
Dean Mr Paul Benjamin	Crown Office Chambers, London	020 7797 8100
Edwards Mr Daniel Hugh	Dere Street Barristers, York	0844 3351551
	York Chambers, Newcastle Upon Tyne	0191 206 4677
Edwards Mr Jonathan William	Westgate Chambers, Lewes	01273 480510
Ellis Dr Peter Simon	Seven Bedford Row, London	020 7242 3555
Feldschreiber Dr Peter	Four New Square, London	020 7822 2000
Ferm Mr Rodney Eric	Broadway House Chambers, Bradford	01274 722560
	Broadway House Chambers, Leeds	0113 246 2600
Fetto Mr Niazi Peter	2 Temple Gardens, London	020 7822 1200
Formby Ms Emily Jane	39 Essex Street, London	020 7832 1111
Foster Mr Charles Andrew	Outer Temple Chambers, London	020 7353 6381
Foulkes Miss Rebecca	5 Pump Court, London	020 7353 2532

Barrister	Chambers	Telephone
Fox Mr John Harvey	Chambers of Mr Ami Feder, London	020 7797 7788
	Chambers of Mr Ami Feder, London	020 7797 7788
	Lamb Building, Brighton	01273 820490
Gadd Mr Adam Brian	Pump Court Chambers, London	020 7353 0711
	Pump Court Chambers, Winchester	01962 868 161
	Riverview Chambers, London	0844 225 3999
Galway-Cooper Dr Philip Anthony	Five St Andrew's Hill, London	020 7332 5400
Gamble Mrs Esther Ruth	No5 Chambers, Birmingham	0845 210 5555
	No5 Chambers, Bristol	0845 210 5555
	No5 Chambers, London	0845 210 5555
	St Philips Chambers, Birmingham	0121 246 7000
George Mr Nicholas Frank Raymond	New Walk Chambers, Leicester	0871 200 1298/0116 255 9144
Gledhill Mr Lee Andre	Alexander Chambers, London	0845 652 0451/0854 652 0451
	Trident Barristers Chambers, Manchester	0161 663 3123
Glover Mr Stephen Julian	37 Park Square Chambers, Leeds	0113 243 9422
Goldman Mrs Linda	Henderson Chambers, London	020 7583 9020
Goldrein Mr Iain Saville	7 Bell Yard, London	020 7831 0636
	Number 7 Harrington Street Chambers, Liverpool	0151 242 0707
Goldstein Mr Wayne Nathan	18 St John Street, Manchester	0161 278 1800
Goodfellow Mr Stephen John	East Anglian Chambers, Chelmsford	01473 214481
	East Anglian Chambers, Ipswich	01473 214481
	East Anglian Chambers, Norwich	01473 214481
Granville Stafford Mr Andrew	4 King's Bench Walk, London	020 7822 7000
Halstead Mr Robin Bernard	One Essex Court, London	020 7936 3030
Harrison Dr Graeme	12 College Place, Southampton	023 8032 0320
Harrison Mr John Foster	St Paul's Chambers, Leeds	0113 245 5866
Hartman Mr Michael	One Essex Court, London	020 7936 3030
Harvey Mr John Gilbert	No5 Chambers, Birmingham	0845 210 5555
	No5 Chambers, Bristol	0845 210 5555
	No5 Chambers, London	0845 210 5555
Hendron Mr Henry Joseph Christopher	Strand Chambers, London	020 7117 6920
Hewson Ms Barbara Mary	Hardwicke, London	020 7242 2523
Hill Mr Michael Gordon	Trinity Chambers, Middlesbrough	01642 247569
	Trinity Chambers, Newcastle Upon Tyne	0191 232 1927
Hill Mr Nicholas Mark	Pump Court Chambers, London	020 7353 0711
	Pump Court Chambers, Swindon	01793 539899
	St Philips Chambers, Birmingham	0121 246 7000
Hirst Mr Karl Douglas	No5 Chambers, Birmingham	0845 210 5555
	No5 Chambers, Bristol	0845 210 5555
	No5 Chambers, London	0845 210 5555
Hodgkiss Ms Suzanne Jane	43 Temple Row Chambers, Birmingham	0121 237 6035
Hodson Mr Peter David	Chambers of Ian Macdonald QC, Manchester	0161 236 1840
Holdsworth Mr James Arthur	Temple Garden Chambers, London	020 7583 1315
Holt Miss Abigail Claire	Lincoln House Chambers, Manchester	0161 832 5701
Hussain Mr Muhammad Altaf	Chambers of Mr M A Hussain, London	020 8679 2398
Hutchin Mr Edward Alister David	Temple Garden Chambers, London	020 7583 1315
Hutchinson Mr Colin Thomas	Garden Court Chambers, London	020 7993 7600
Jackson Mr Christopher Marshall	Liverpool Civil Law, Liverpool	0151 242 0500
Jenkins Mr Hywel Iestyn	Outer Temple Chambers, London	020 7353 6381
John Mr Thomas Huw	Goresbrook Chambers, Milton Keynes	0845 123 1234
Johnson Miss Laura Wendy	1 Chancery Lane, London	0845 634 6666
Jones Mr Alun	St Paul's Chambers, Leeds	0113 245 5866
Jones Mr Geraint Anthony	New Walk Chambers, Leicester	0871 200 1298/0116 255 9144
	9 St John Street, Manchester	0161 955 9000
	Tanfield Chambers, London	020 7421 5300
Jones Mr Richard Frederick Thomas	Heavenwood Chambers, Stroud	01453 873444
Kelly Mr Matthias John	39 Essex Street, London	020 7832 1111

Barrister	Chambers	Telephone
Kennedy Mr Christopher Laurence Paul	9 St John Street, Manchester	0161 955 9000
Kent Mr Michael Harcourt	Crown Office Chambers, London	020 7797 8100
Khalique Miss Nageena	No5 Chambers, Birmingham	0845 210 5555
	No5 Chambers, Bristol	0845 210 5555
	No5 Chambers, London	0845 210 5555
Khan Mr Ayoub	Chambers of Mr Ayoub Khan, Birmingham	07930 987202
Kirtley Mr Paul George	Exchange Chambers, Leeds	0113 203 1970
	Exchange Chambers, Liverpool	0151 236 7747
	Littleton Chambers, London	020 7797 8600
Knight Mr Keith Leslie Francis	4 King's Bench Walk, London	020 7822 7000
Kramer Mr Philip Anthony	Park Lane Plowden, Newcastle Upon Tyne	0191 211 4087
Lavin Miss Mary Mandie Jane	196 Temple Chamber, London	020 7099 9257
Ley Mr Spencer	Farrar's Building, London	020 7583 9241
Lissack Mr Richard Anthony	Outer Temple Chambers, London	020 7353 6381
	Riverview Chambers, London	0844 225 3999
Livingstone Mr Simon John	Thomas More Chambers, London	020 7404 7000
Lock Mr David Anthony	No5 Chambers, Birmingham	0845 210 5555
	No5 Chambers, Bristol	0845 210 5555
	No5 Chambers, London	0845 210 5555
Lyons Miss Tara Yasmin	Pump Court Chambers, London	020 7353 0711
	Pump Court Chambers, Winchester	01962 868 161
	Riverview Chambers, London	0844 225 3999
Marks Mr Jonathan Clive	4 Pump Court, London	020 7842 5555
Marshall Miss Vanessa Juliette	Seven Bedford Row, London	020 7242 3555
Marshall Mr Derek Stanley	College Chambers, Southampton	023 8023 0338
Martignetti Mr Ian	Regency Chambers, Cambridge	01223 301517
	Regency Chambers, Peterborough	01733 315215
Martin Mr Bradley David	2 Temple Gardens, London	020 7822 1200
Matthias Mr David Huw	Francis Taylor Building, London	020 7353 8415
McDonald Ms Melanie Sharon	No5 Chambers, Birmingham	0845 210 5555
	No5 Chambers, Bristol	0845 210 5555
	No5 Chambers, London	0845 210 5555
Menzies Mr Richard Mark	Lamb Chambers, London	020 7797 8300
Meredith-Hardy Mr John Octavian	Farrar's Building, London	020 7583 9241
Michalos Miss Christina Antigone Diana	5RB, London	020 7242 2902
Miles Mr Edward Napier Tremayne	Lamb Chambers, London	020 7797 8300
Mills Mr Kristian Anthony	Trinity Chambers, Middlesbrough	01642 247569
	Trinity Chambers, Newcastle Upon Tyne	0191 232 1927
Morton Miss Rowan Frances	Alexander Chambers, London	0845 652 0451/0854 652 0451
	Guildford Chambers, Guildford	01483 539131
Newman Mr Timothy John	No5 Chambers, Birmingham	0845 210 5555
	No5 Chambers, Bristol	0845 210 5555
	No5 Chambers, London	0845 210 5555
Nickless Mr Jason Alan	College Chambers, Southampton	023 8023 0338
Norton Mr Giles	Enigma Chambers, Sheffield	07779 576499
	Holborn Chambers, London	020 7242 6060
Osborne Mr James Robert	Clerksroom (London), London	0845 083 3000
Paige Mr Richard Mark	Sovereign Chambers, Leeds	0113 245 1841
Palmer Mr James Savill	Henderson Chambers, London	020 7583 9020
Parker Mrs Karen Lesley	Guildhall Chambers Portsmouth, Portsmouth	023 9275 2400
Pascall Mr Matthew Stephen	Alexander Chambers, London	0845 652 0451/0854 652 0451
	Guildford Chambers, Guildford	01483 539131
Persaud Dr Marcia Chitroutie	1 Gray's Inn Square, London	020 7405 0001
Pickup Mr James Kenneth	2 Hare Court, London	020 7353 3982
	Lincoln House Chambers, Manchester	0161 832 5701
Power Mr Richard Michael Arthur	Lamb Chambers, London	020 7797 8300
Randolph Mr Paul Leslie	Field Court Chambers, London	020 7405 6114
Read Mr Daniel James	Farrar's Building, London	020 7583 9241

Barrister	Chambers	Telephone
Reed Mr Simon John	New Walk Chambers, Leicester	0871 200 1298/0116 255 9144
Ritchie Mr Andrew George	The Chambers of Grahame Aldous QC, London	020 7832 0500
Rivalland Mr Marc-Edouard	1 Chancery Lane, London	0845 634 6666
Russell Mr Thomas Charles Welldon	KCH Garden Square, Nottingham	0115 941 8851
Sharp Mr Christopher Francis	Harcourt Chambers, London	0844 561 7135
	Harcourt Chambers, Oxford	0844 561 7135
	St John's Chambers, Bristol	0117 923 4700
Shaw Mr Julian	St Johns Buildings, Chester	01244 323070
	St Johns Buildings, Manchester	0161 214 1500
	St Johns Buildings Liverpool, Liverpool	0151 243 6000
Silverton Miss Catherine Anne	Sovereign Chambers, Leeds	0113 245 1841
Singarajah Mr Frederico	1 Gray's Inn Square, London	020 7405 0001
Smith Mr Matthew Robert	Sovereign Chambers, Leeds	0113 245 1841
Smith Mr Michael David	Kenworthy's Chambers, Manchester	0161 832 4036
Smith Mr Robert Ian	St Paul's Chambers, Leeds	0113 245 5866
Sood Mrs Usha Rani	Trent Chambers, Nottingham	0115 941 9596
Spencer Mr Martin Benedict	Hailsham Chambers, London	020 7643 5000
Spooner Mr Henry Neville	Tolzey Chambers, Bristol	
	Westgate Chambers, Lewes	01273 480510
Stanford Mr Tony James	Old Bailey Chambers, London	020 3008 6404
Starcevic Mr Petar	St Philips Chambers, Birmingham	0121 246 7000
Stephens Mr Michael Allen	Design Chambers, London	020 7353 0747
	St Ive's Chambers, Birmingham	0121 236 0863
Stevenson Mr Daniel Keith	9-12 Bell Yard, London	020 7400 1800
Stewart Mr Richard Paul	Lamb Chambers, London	020 7797 8300
Syril Mr George Carmel	Luton Chambers, Luton	01582 598394
	Willesden Chambers, London	020 3273 1042
Tavares Mr Nathan Warren	Outer Temple Chambers, London	020 7353 6381
Taylor Miss Eve Rebecca	St John's Chambers, Bristol	0117 923 4700
Thomas Mr Andrew Martin	Lincoln House Chambers, Manchester	0161 832 5701
	Linenhall Chambers, Chester	01244 348282
Trusted Mr James Harry	Outer Temple Chambers, London	020 7353 6381
Waley Mr Eric Richard Thomas	Assize Court Chambers, Bristol	0117 926 4587
Wheaton Mr Ian Malcolm James	Eighteen Carlton Crescent, Southampton	023 8063 9001
Widdett Ms Ceri Louise	Park Court Chambers, Leeds	0113 243 3277
Wightwick Mr Iain	Riverview Chambers, London	0844 225 3999
	Unity Street Chambers, Bristol	0117 906 9789
Willer Mr Robert Michael	Ely Place Chambers, London	020 7400 9600
Wills Miss Alexandra Itari	Christ Church Chambers, London	020 7409 5278/07788 512787

MENTAL HEALTH

Barrister	Chambers	Telephone
Alam Ms Jan	Ropewalk Chambers, Nottingham	0115 947 2581
Allwood Mrs Gina Louisa	Seven Bedford Row, London	020 7242 3555
Amraoui Mr Thomas	4-5 Gray's Inn Square, London	020 7404 5252
Bagley Miss Louisa Ellen	1 Paper Buildings, London	020 7353 3728
Bahra Miss Narita	9-12 Bell Yard, London	020 7400 1800
	2 Hare Court, London	020 7353 3982
Baldwin Dr Timothy John	Garden Court Chambers, London	020 7993 7600
Barber Mr Phillip Arthur	Zenith Chambers, Leeds	0113 245 5438
Bell Mr Dominic Michael St. John	Chambers of Marion Smullen and Kerim Fuad QC, London	020 7427 4400
Bennett Mr Ieuan Gereint	9 Park Place, Cardiff	029 2038 2731
Berriman Mr Trevor St John	43 Temple Row Chambers, Birmingham	0121 237 6035
Beyts Mr Chester Andoe Michael	25 Bedford Row, London	020 7067 1500
Birkby Mr Richard Adam	Park Court Chambers, Leeds	0113 243 3277
Bisarya Mr Neil	Number 7 Harrington Street Chambers, Liverpool	0151 242 0707
Bogle Mr James Stewart Lockhart	10 King's Bench Walk, London	020 7353 7742

Name	Chambers	Telephone
Bowen Mr Nicholas James Hugh	Doughty Street Chambers, Bristol	01179 058 717
	Doughty Street Chambers, London	020 7404 1313
	Doughty Street Chambers, Manchester	0161 618 1066
Brehan Ms Daire	Chambers of Ms D Brehan, London	07808 726877
Brereton Miss Joy	4 Paper Buildings, London	020 7427 5200
Brown Mr Sam Clement	Atkinson Bevan Chambers, London	020 7353 2112
Brown Ms Grace	Tooks Chambers, London	020 7842 7575
Buchan Mr Andrew	Cloisters, London	020 7827 4000
Butler Mr George Victor	4 Brick Court, London	020 7832 3200
Caddle Miss Sherrie Loretta	Charter Chambers, London	020 7618 4400
Carney Miss Caroline Mary	QEB Hollis Whiteman, London	020 7933 8855
Carrion Benitez Ms Miriam	36 Bedford Row, London	020 7421 8000
Casey Mr Paul Joseph	Chambers of Marion Smullen and Kerim Fuad QC, London	020 7427 4400
Cattermull Miss Emma Jayne	East Anglian Chambers, Chelmsford	01473 214481
	East Anglian Chambers, Ipswich	01473 214481
	East Anglian Chambers, Norwich	01473 214481
Chipperfield Mr Jeremy Steven	Cranford Chambers, London	020 7404 7454
Clarke Mr Nicholas Patrick James	18 St John Street, Manchester	0161 278 1800
Colbey Mr Richard	Guildhall Chambers Portsmouth, Portsmouth	023 9275 2400
	Lamb Chambers, London	020 7797 8300
Coyle Mr Anthony Noel	Zenith Chambers, Leeds	0113 245 5438
Culverhouse Miss Emily Anna Louise	Chambers of Miss E Culverhouse, Chesham	07813 007503
Davies Miss Claire Suzanne	Farringdon Chambers, London	020 7089 5700
De Burgos Mr Jamie Michael Abulafia	36 Bedford Row, London	020 7421 8000
De Mello Mr Rembert Joseph Julius	No5 Chambers, Birmingham	0845 210 5555
	No5 Chambers, Bristol	0845 210 5555
	No5 Chambers, London	0845 210 5555
Dean Mr James Patrick	Goldsmith Chambers, London	020 7353 6802
Dipré Mr Paul Nicholas Amadeus	Chambers of Mr P N Dipré, Address withheld	0845 123 1234
	MK Family Law Chambers, Milton Keynes	0845 123 1234
Dolan Dr Bridget Maura	3 Serjeants Inn, London	020 7427 5000
Dowell Mr Gregory Hamilton	Principal Chambers, Sevenoaks	0845 209 8080
Dugdale Mr Jeremy Keith	Octagon House, Norwich	01603 623186
Dunn Miss Katherine Louise	Trinity Chambers, Middlesbrough	01642 247569
	Trinity Chambers, Newcastle Upon Tyne	0191 232 1927
Earle Mr James Christopher Reginald St John	Fenners Chambers, Cambridge	01223 368761
Eastwood Miss Philippa Clemency Anne	Doughty Street Chambers, London	020 7404 1313
Edwards Mr Denis	Francis Taylor Building, London	020 7353 8415
Ellis Dr Peter Simon	Seven Bedford Row, London	020 7242 3555
Ephraim-Adejumo Mrs Hilda Ekpo	12 Old Square Chambers, London	020 7404 0875
Fishwick Mr Gregory David Philip Kyle	187 Fleet Street, London	020 7430 7430
Forster Ms Sarah Judith	14 Gray's Inn Square, London	020 7242 0858
	Westgate Chambers, Lewes	01273 480510
Fullwood Mr Adam Garrett	Kings Chambers, Birmingham	0845 034 3444
	Kings Chambers, Leeds	0845 034 3444
	Kings Chambers, Manchester	0845 034 3444
Gallivan Mr Terence John	Five Paper, London	020 7815 3200
Gaskin Miss Leila	Charter Chambers, London	020 7618 4400
Gerry Miss Felicity Ruth	36 Bedford Row, London	020 7421 8000
Gledhill Mr Lee Andre	Alexander Chambers, London	0845 652 0451/0854 652 0451
	Trident Barristers Chambers, Manchester	0161 663 3123
Gore Ms Sally Elizabeth	14 Gray's Inn Square, London	020 7242 0858
Goudie Mr William Martin Phillip	Charter Chambers, London	020 7618 4400

C

Grant Mr Chudi Paul	Kenworthy's Chambers, Manchester	0161 832 4036
Grundy Ms Clare	St Johns Buildings, Manchester	0161 214 1500
	St Johns Buildings Liverpool, Liverpool	0151 243 6000
	16 Winckley Square, Preston	01772 256100
Hamilton Mr John Conrad	Field Court Chambers, London	020 7405 6114
Hamilton Mr Nigel	Broadway House Chambers, Bradford	01274 722560
	Broadway House Chambers, Leeds	0113 246 2600
Hancock Ms Maria	Westgate Chambers, Lewes	01273 480510
Harding Mr Matthew Austin	39 Park Square, Leeds	0113 245 6633
Harris Miss Stella Cassandra Methven	Tooks Chambers, London	020 7842 7575
Harris Mr Wilbert Arthurlyn	Rowchester Chambers, Birmingham	0121 233 2327
Harrison Dr Graeme	12 College Place, Southampton	023 8032 0320
Hewson Ms Barbara Mary	Hardwicke, London	020 7242 2523
Hirst Miss Kathryn Anne	Furnival Chambers, London	020 7405 3232
Holbech Mr Charles Edward	New Square Chambers, London	020 7419 8000
Horton Mr Mark Varney	Colleton Chambers, Exeter	01392 274898
Hunt Mr Stephen	4 Stone Buildings, London	020 7242 5524
Hussain Mr Muhammad Altaf	Chambers of Mr M A Hussain, London	020 8679 2398
Irving Miss Gillian	Linenhall Chambers, Chester	01244 348282
	9 St John Street, Manchester	0161 955 9000
	15 Winckley Square, Preston	01772 252828
John Mr Thomas Huw	Goresbrook Chambers, Milton Keynes	0845 123 1234
Jones Mr Alun	St Paul's Chambers, Leeds	0113 245 5866
Kent Mr Michael Harcourt	Crown Office Chambers, London	020 7797 8100
Khalique Miss Nageena	No5 Chambers, Birmingham	0845 210 5555
	No5 Chambers, Bristol	0845 210 5555
	No5 Chambers, London	0845 210 5555
King Mr Graham Anthony	1 Gray's Inn Square, London	020 7405 0001
Knight Mr Graeme Edward Verdon	7 Bell Yard, London	020 7831 0636
	Carmelite Chambers, London	020 7936 6300
	The Barristers Chambers, Address withheld	07966 056368
Lal Mr Sanjay	4 King's Bench Walk, London	020 7822 7000
Lane Mr Christopher Paul	No 8 Chambers, Birmingham	0121 236 5514
Learmonth Mr Alexander Robert Magnus	New Square Chambers, London	020 7419 8000
Lee Miss Taryn Jane	37 Park Square Chambers, Leeds	0113 243 9422
Lenaghan Mr Anthony	Dyers Chambers, London	020 7404 1881
Lewis Mr Andrew Simon	4 Breams Buildings, London	020 7092 1900
Lock Mr David Anthony	No5 Chambers, Birmingham	0845 210 5555
	No5 Chambers, Bristol	0845 210 5555
	No5 Chambers, London	0845 210 5555
Lopez Mr Paul Anthony	St Ive's Chambers, Birmingham	0121 236 0863
Luh Miss Shu Shin	Garden Court Chambers, London	020 7993 7600
Malone Mr David John	1 Gray's Inn Square, London	020 7405 0001
Mann Mr Jonathan Simon	25 Bedford Row, London	020 7067 1500
Markus Ms Kate	Doughty Street Chambers, Bristol	01179 058 717
	Doughty Street Chambers, London	020 7404 1313
	Doughty Street Chambers, Manchester	0161 618 1066
Matthias Mr David Huw	Francis Taylor Building, London	020 7353 8415
McDonald Ms Melanie Sharon	No5 Chambers, Birmingham	0845 210 5555
	No5 Chambers, Bristol	0845 210 5555
	No5 Chambers, London	0845 210 5555
Milsom Mrs Catherine Mary	Argent Chambers, London	020 7556 5500
Moll Mr Christiaan Eric	Blackfriars Chambers, London	020 7353 7400
Morris Ms Johanna	Chambers of Marion Smullen and Kerim Fuad QC, London	020 7427 4400
Murkin Mrs Sandria	Becket Chambers, Canterbury	01227 786331
Murray Mr Charles Humphrey Stewart	Rougemont Chambers, Exeter	01392 208484
Oakley Miss Louise Michelle	2 Bedford Row, London	020 7440 8888

Barrister	Chambers	Telephone
Oldham Mrs Frances Mary Theresa	36 Bedford Row, London	020 7421 8000
	37 Park Square Chambers, Leeds	0113 243 9422
Owen Mr Timothy Wynn	Matrix Chambers, London	020 7404 3447
Paget Mr Michael Rodborough	Garden Court Chambers, London	020 7993 7600
Paraskos Mr Paraskevakis Christakis	11 Gray's Inn Square Chambers, London	020 7405 6879
Pearce Mr Robert Edgar	Radcliffe Chambers, London	020 7831 0081
Peddie Mr Ian James Crofton	Garden Court Chambers, London	020 7993 7600
	St Johns Buildings Liverpool, Liverpool	0151 243 6000
	Westgate Chambers, Lewes	01273 480510
Penny Miss Abigail Sarah Prudence	4 Breams Buildings, London	020 7092 1900
Perian Mr Steven	3 Temple Gardens, London	020 7353 3102
Persaud Dr Marcia Chitroutie	1 Gray's Inn Square, London	020 7405 0001
Rahman Mr Luthfur	Chambers of Mr L Rahman, Rochester	07947 588362
Real Miss Kirsty Nichola	Albion Chambers, Bristol	0117 927 2144
Rudd Miss Zoe Ann	College Chambers, Southampton	023 8023 0338
Rustom Mr Shiraz Sam	1215 Chambers, London	020 3291 1215
	Cranford Chambers, London	020 7404 7454
	1 Mitre Court Buildings, London	020 7452 8900
Scally Miss Josephine Theresa Sarah	Palmyra Chambers, Warrington	01925 444919
Scolding Miss Fiona Kate	Hardwicke, London	020 7242 2523
Singh-Hayer Mr Bansa	Deans Court Chambers, Manchester	0161 214 6000
	Deans Court Chambers, Preston	01772 565 600
Smith Miss Eileen Joan	Trinity Chambers, Middlesbrough	01642 247569
	Trinity Chambers, Newcastle Upon Tyne	0191 232 1927
Sood Mrs Usha Rani	Trent Chambers, Nottingham	0115 941 9596
Southey Mr David Hugh	Tooks Chambers, London	020 7842 7575
Spain Mr Timothy Harrisson	Trinity Chambers, Middlesbrough	01642 247569
	Trinity Chambers, Newcastle Upon Tyne	0191 232 1927
Spears Miss Katharine Sarah	Carmelite Chambers, London	020 7936 6300
Spencer Mr Martin Benedict	Hailsham Chambers, London	020 7643 5000
Stanford Mr Tony James	Old Bailey Chambers, London	020 3008 6404
Stelling Mr Nigel Roy	Citadel Chambers, Birmingham	0121 233 8500
Stone Mr Joseph	Doughty Street Chambers, Bristol	01179 058 717
	Doughty Street Chambers, London	020 7404 1313
	Doughty Street Chambers, Manchester	0161 618 1066
Tambling Mr Richard	1 Garden Court Family Law Chambers, London	020 7797 7900
Taylor Miss Araba Arba Kurankyiwa	Fenners Chambers, Cambridge	01223 368761
Taylor Mrs Susan	Trinity Chambers, Middlesbrough	01642 247569
	Trinity Chambers, Newcastle Upon Tyne	0191 232 1927
Thomas Mrs Felicity	Westgate Chambers, Lewes	01273 480510
Tizzano Mr Franco Salvatore	Old Bailey Chambers, London	020 3008 6404
Tyler Mr William John	36 Bedford Row, London	020 7421 8000
Upton Mr John Stewart	4 King's Bench Walk, London	020 7822 7000
Van Overdijk Miss Claire Orit	No5 Chambers, Birmingham	0845 210 5555
	No5 Chambers, Bristol	0845 210 5555
	No5 Chambers, London	0845 210 5555
Vollenweider Mr Amiot Marcus Ellerton	Thomas More Chambers, London	020 7404 7000
Waley Mr Eric Richard Thomas	Assize Court Chambers, Bristol	0117 926 4587
Walton Miss Karen Tanya	Dyers Chambers, London	020 7404 1881
Watson Mr Tom Bradley	Chavasse Court Chambers, Liverpool	0151 229 2030
Whitfield Mr Jonathan	Doughty Street Chambers, London	020 7404 1313
Whyatt Mr Michael George	15 Winckley Square, Preston	01772 252828

PARLIAMENTARY

Barrister	Chambers	Telephone
Amraoui Mr Thomas	4-5 Gray's Inn Square, London	020 7404 5252

C

Asprey Mr Nicholas	Clock Chambers, Wolverhampton	01902 313444
	Serle Court, London	020 7242 6105
Bowers Mr Rupert John	Doughty Street Chambers, London	020 7404 1313
Brown Mr Edward Francis Trevenen	QEB Hollis Whiteman, London	020 7933 8855
Chalk Mr Alexander John Gervase	6 King's Bench Walk, London	020 7583 0410
Christie Mr Iain Robert	5RB, London	020 7242 2902
Coyle Mr Anthony Noel	Zenith Chambers, Leeds	0113 245 5438
Devlin Mr Timothy Robert	Furnival Chambers, London	020 7405 3232
Facenna Mr Gerald Carlo	Monckton Chambers, London	020 7405 7211
Gallagher Ms Caoilfhionn Anna	Doughty Street Chambers, Bristol	01179 058 717
	Doughty Street Chambers, London	020 7404 1313
	Doughty Street Chambers, Manchester	0161 618 1066
Goldrein Mr Iain Saville	7 Bell Yard, London	020 7831 0636
	Number 7 Harrington Street Chambers, Liverpool	0151 242 0707
Goodman Mr Alexander David Edmund	Atlas Chambers, London	020 7269 7980
	4-5 Gray's Inn Square, London	020 7404 5252
Harwood Mr Richard John	39 Essex Street, London	020 7832 1111
	82 King Street, Manchester	0161 870 9969
Hendron Mr Henry Joseph Christopher	Strand Chambers, London	020 7117 6920
Hobson Mr John Graham	4-5 Gray's Inn Square, London	020 7404 5252
Honey Mr Richard Arthur	Francis Taylor Building, London	020 7353 8415
Horton Mr Matthew Bethell	39 Essex Street, London	020 7832 1111
	82 King Street, Manchester	0161 870 9969
John Miss Laura Elizabeth	Monckton Chambers, London	020 7405 7211
Juss Prof Satvinder Singh	3 Hare Court, London	020 7415 7800
Lewiecki Miss Marie	Old Bailey Chambers, London	020 3008 6404
Lock Mr David Anthony	No5 Chambers, Birmingham	0845 210 5555
	No5 Chambers, Bristol	0845 210 5555
	No5 Chambers, London	0845 210 5555
Malone Mr David John	1 Gray's Inn Square, London	020 7405 0001
Mather Mr Nicholas Ian Stewart	Furnival Chambers, London	020 7405 3232
Matthias Mr David Huw	Francis Taylor Building, London	020 7353 8415
Metcalfe Dr Eric William	Monckton Chambers, London	020 7405 7211
Nardell Mr Gordon Lawrence	39 Essex Street, London	020 7832 1111
	82 King Street, Manchester	0161 870 9969
Owen Mr Timothy Wynn	Matrix Chambers, London	020 7404 3447
Roche Mr Patrick Richard Redmond	Tooks Chambers, London	020 7842 7575
Rosemarine Mr Andrew Marc	Chambers of Mr A M Rosemarine, Manchester	0161 740 3861
Skinner Mr Samuel Richard Edward	KCH Garden Square, Nottingham	0115 941 8851
Stebbings Mr Ian Anthony	1 Gray's Inn Square, London	020 7405 0001
Stinchcombe Mr Paul David	4-5 Gray's Inn Square, London	020 7404 5252
Thomas Miss Megan Moira	6 Pump Court, London	020 7797 8400
	6 Pump Court Chambers, Maidstone	01622 688094
Thomas Mr Mark David	5 Essex Court, London	020 7410 2000
Webster Mr Alistair Stevenson	Chambers of Andrew Mitchell QC, London	020 7440 9950
	Lincoln House Chambers, Manchester	0161 832 5701

PARTNERSHIP

Ajaz Mr Mohammad Arshad	Eastmans Chambers, Reading	0118 966 9094
Algazy Mr Jacques Max	Cloisters, London	020 7827 4000
Apthorp Mr George Charles	5 Essex Court, London	020 7410 2000
Arthur Mr Stephen Joseph	Temple Tax Chambers, London	020 7353 7884
Askey Mr Robert John	Palmyra Chambers, Warrington	01925 444919
Asprey Mr Nicholas	Clock Chambers, Wolverhampton	01902 313444
	Serle Court, London	020 7242 6105
Bailey Miss Rosana Henrietta	10 King's Bench Walk, London	020 7353 7742
Banks Mr Roderick Charles I'Anson	48 Bedford Row, London	020 7430 2005
Bax Mr James Alexander	Rougemont Chambers, Exeter	01392 208484

C

Beaumont Mr Marc Clifford	9 Stone Buildings, London	020 7404 5055
	Windsor Barristers' Chambers, Windsor	01753 839321
Bennion-Pedley Mr Edward	13 KBW, Oxford	01865 311066
	13 King's Bench Walk, London	020 7353 7204
Berkley Mr Michael Stuart	Rougemont Chambers, Exeter	01392 208484
Blackmore Mr John Hugh	St John's Chambers, Bristol	0117 923 4700
Blackwood Mr Clive David	Lamb Chambers, London	020 7797 8300
Bleasdale Miss Marie-Claire	Radcliffe Chambers, London	020 7831 0081
Blohm Mr Leslie Adrian	St John's Chambers, Bristol	0117 923 4700
Bogle Mr James Stewart Lockhart	10 King's Bench Walk, London	020 7353 7742
Bourne Mr Geoffrey Robert	13 Old Square Chambers, London	020 7831 4445
Boyd Mr Stephen James Harvey	Selborne Chambers, London	020 7420 9500
Bragiel Mr Edward Bronislaw Henryk	Hogarth Chambers, London	020 7404 0404
Braithwaite Mr Thomas James	Serle Court, London	020 7242 6105
Bredemear Mr Zachary Charles	1 Chancery Lane, London	0845 634 6666
Brook Mr Paul Antony	Park Lane Plowden, Leeds	0113 228 5049
	Park Lane Plowden, Newcastle Upon Tyne	0191 211 4087
Brown Miss Susan Margaret	One Essex Court, London	020 7936 3030
Bryden Mr Christopher James Yuen Kang	4 King's Bench Walk, London	020 7822 7000
Buchan Miss Caroline Venetia	Chambers of Miss C Buchan, Haywards Heath	01444 482222
Buckhaven Mr Simon	Hardwicke, London	020 7242 2523
Bullock Mr Robert Gustaf	The Chambers of Mr Bullock, Brighton	01273 321050
Butler Mr Andrew	Tanfield Chambers, London	020 7421 5300
Buttimore Mr Gabriel	13 KBW, Oxford	01865 311066
	13 King's Bench Walk, London	020 7353 7204
Cant Mr Christopher Ian	9 Stone Buildings, London	020 7404 5055
Capon Mr Philip Christopher William	East Anglian Chambers, Chelmsford	01473 214481
	East Anglian Chambers, Ipswich	01473 214481
	East Anglian Chambers, Norwich	01473 214481
	St Philips Chambers, Birmingham	0121 246 7000
Carr Mr Adrian James Selden	Tanfield Chambers, London	020 7421 5300
Castle Mr Peter Bolton	13 Old Square Chambers, London	020 7831 4445
Cawsey Mr Barry Donald	Clerksroom (London), London	0845 083 3000
	Clerksroom (Taunton), Taunton	0845 083 3000
Chesner Mr Howard Michael	One Essex Court, London	020 7936 3030
Chowdhary Mr Islamuddin	Cassian Chambers, Ilford	07796 262641
Christensen Mr Carlton	10 King's Bench Walk, London	020 7353 7742
Christie Mr David Henderson	Seven Bedford Row, London	020 7242 3555
Clark Mr Andrew Richard	9 St John Street, Manchester	0161 955 9000
Clegg Mr Simon Robert Jonathan	St Philips Chambers, Birmingham	0121 246 7000
Cohen Mr Edward Mervyn	11 Stone Buildings, London	020 7831 6381
Colbey Mr Richard	Guildhall Chambers Portsmouth, Portsmouth	023 9275 2400
	Lamb Chambers, London	020 7797 8300
Coster Mr Ronald David	42 Bedford Row, London	020 7831 0222
Coulter Mr Barry John	Clerksroom (London), London	0845 083 3000
	Clerksroom (Taunton), Taunton	0845 083 3000
	King's Lynn Chambers, King's Lynn	01553 672 085
Critchley Mr John Stephen	Field Court Chambers, London	020 7405 6114
Davies Ms Samantha Teresa	Chambers of Ms Samantha Davies, Milton Keynes	0845 123 1234
	Warwick House Chambers, London	020 7430 2323
De Jehan Mr David	Park Lane Plowden, Leeds	0113 228 5049
Deacon Mr Robert Murray	11 Stone Buildings, London	020 7831 6381
Devereux-Cooke Mr Richard Charles	13 Old Square Chambers, London	020 7831 4445
Devlin Mr Bernard Joseph	Five St Andrew's Hill, London	020 7332 5400
di Mambro Mr David Jesse Andrew	Pallant Chambers, Chichester	01243 784538
	Radcliffe Chambers, London	020 7831 0081
Dickinson Mr John Finch Heneage	St John's Chambers, Bristol	0117 923 4700

Name	Chambers	Telephone
Du Toit Sc Mr Johan Ignatius	Selborne Chambers, London	020 7420 9500
	St Philips Chambers, Birmingham	0121 246 7000
Earle Mr James Christopher Reginald St John	Fenners Chambers, Cambridge	01223 368761
Egleton Mr Richard Wildman	Pallant Chambers, Chichester	01243 784538
Eilledge Miss Amanda Gail Caroline	11 Stone Buildings, London	020 7831 6381
Eldergill Mr Edmund Malcolm	1 Pump Court, London	020 7842 7070
Engelman Mr Philip	Cloisters, London	020 7827 4000
	Trinity Chambers, Middlesbrough	01642 247569
	Trinity Chambers, Newcastle Upon Tyne	0191 232 1927
Fellows Mr Philip David Andrew	Hardwicke, London	020 7242 2523
Ferm Mr Rodney Eric	Broadway House Chambers, Bradford	01274 722560
	Broadway House Chambers, Leeds	0113 246 2600
Finlay Mr Darren	Sovereign Chambers, Leeds	0113 245 1841
Fisher Mr David	New Square Chambers, London	020 7419 8000
Fowles Mr Jonathan James	Serle Court, London	020 7242 6105
Francis Mr Richard Maurice	9 Park Place, Cardiff	029 2038 2731
Gallivan Mr Terence John	Five Paper, London	020 7815 3200
Garvie Mr Carl Peter	St Philips Chambers, Birmingham	0121 246 7000
Gatty Mr Daniel Simon	Hardwicke, London	020 7242 2523
Gelbart Mr Geoff Alan	1 Gray's Inn Square, London	020 7405 0001
Glaser Mr Michael Samson	14 Gray's Inn Square, London	020 7242 0858
Gledhill Mr Lee Andre	Alexander Chambers, London	0845 652 0451/0854 652 0451
	Trident Barristers Chambers, Manchester	0161 663 3123
Godfrey Mr Lauren John	Crown Office Row Chambers, Brighton	01273 625625
Goldberg Mr Simon Ian	Trinity Chambers, Middlesbrough	01642 247569
	Trinity Chambers, Newcastle Upon Tyne	0191 232 1927
Goodfellow Mr Stephen John	East Anglian Chambers, Chelmsford	01473 214481
	East Anglian Chambers, Ipswich	01473 214481
	East Anglian Chambers, Norwich	01473 214481
Goodman Mr Andrew David	1 Chancery Lane, London	0845 634 6666
Graham Mr Thomas Patrick Henry	New Square Chambers, London	020 7419 8000
Graham Mrs Alana Nicole	Chambers of Alana Graham, Halesowen	01384 894560
	9 Stone Buildings, London	020 7404 5055
Granville Stafford Mr Andrew	4 King's Bench Walk, London	020 7822 7000
Greenan Miss Sarah Octavia	Zenith Chambers, Leeds	0113 245 5438
Hansen Mr William Joseph	No5 Chambers, Birmingham	0845 210 5555
	No5 Chambers, Bristol	0845 210 5555
	No5 Chambers, London	0845 210 5555
Harris Mr Melvyn	5 Essex Court, London	020 7410 2000
Haughty Mr Jeremy Nicholas	Chambers of Mr Ami Feder, London	020 7797 7788
	Chambers of Mr Ami Feder, London	020 7797 7788
	Rougemont Chambers, Exeter	01392 208484
Haywood Dr Jennifer Margaret	Serle Court, London	020 7242 6105
Higginson Mr Timothy Nicholas Bennett	Littleton Chambers, London	020 7797 8600
	St John's Chambers, Bristol	0117 923 4700
Hodgkiss Ms Suzanne Jane	43 Temple Row Chambers, Birmingham	0121 237 6035
Hodson Mr Matthew Paul	Farrar's Building, London	020 7583 9241
Holland Mr Charles Christopher	Francis Taylor Building, London	020 7353 8415
	Trinity Chambers, Middlesbrough	01642 247569
	Trinity Chambers, Newcastle Upon Tyne	0191 232 1927
Hood Mr Nigel Anthony	New Square Chambers, London	020 7419 8000
Hornett Mr Stuart Ian	Selborne Chambers, London	020 7420 9500
Huggins Mr Toby James	Unity Street Chambers, Bristol	0117 906 9789
Hunt Mr Stephen	4 Stone Buildings, London	020 7242 5524
Hussain Mr Muhammad Altaf	Chambers of Mr M A Hussain, London	020 8679 2398

Name	Chambers	Telephone
Irvin Mr Peter	Brick Court Chambers, London	020 7379 3550
Iyer Miss Shobana	Swan Chambers, Richmond	0845 123 1234
Jacobson Mr Lawrence	Five Paper, London	020 7815 3200
Jelf Mr Simon Edward	48 Bedford Row, London	020 7430 2005
Jones Mr Christopher David Harries	St John's Chambers, Bristol	0117 923 4700
Jones Mr Geraint Anthony	New Walk Chambers, Leicester	0871 200 1298/0116 255 9144
	9 St John Street, Manchester	0161 955 9000
	Tanfield Chambers, London	020 7421 5300
Joseph Mr Charles Henry	Tanfield Chambers, London	020 7421 5300
Joseph Mr Paul Wolfe	No5 Chambers, Birmingham	0845 210 5555
	No5 Chambers, Bristol	0845 210 5555
	No5 Chambers, London	0845 210 5555
Keel Mr Douglas Vincent	11 Stone Buildings, London	020 7831 6381
Kelly Mr Sean	Chancery House Chambers, Leeds	0113 244 6691
Khan Dr Alexander	Coral House, Manchester	
Khan Mr Abdul Aleem	Gray's Chambers, Newbury	020 8518 2525
Kramer Mr Philip Anthony	Park Lane Plowden, Newcastle Upon Tyne	0191 211 4087
Kynoch Mr Duncan Stuart Sanderson	Selborne Chambers, London	020 7420 9500
Lane Mr Simon Charles	Rougemont Chambers, Exeter	01392 208484
Le Poidevin Mr Nicholas Peter	New Square Chambers, London	020 7419 8000
Lenon Mr Andrew Ralph Fitzmaurice	One Essex Court, London	020 7583 2000
Leonard Mr Charles Robert Weston	Hardwicke, London	020 7242 2523
Lewiecki Miss Marie	Old Bailey Chambers, London	020 3008 6404
Lonsdale Mr David James	33 Bedford Row, London	020 7242 6476
Lowe Mr Mungo James	13 Old Square Chambers, London	020 7831 4445
Machell Mr John William	Serle Court, London	020 7242 6105
Macpherson Mr Duncan Charles Stewart	One Essex Court, London	020 7936 3030
Maguire Mr Andrew James	Exchange Chambers, Liverpool	0151 236 7747
	Exchange Chambers, Manchester	0161 833 2722
	St Philips Chambers, Birmingham	0121 246 7000
Maher Ms Martha Johanna Dorothy	St John's Chambers, Bristol	0117 923 4700
Marsden Mr Andrew Charles	St John's Chambers, Bristol	0117 923 4700
Marsden Mr Andrew Guy	East Anglian Chambers, Chelmsford	01473 214481
	East Anglian Chambers, Colchester	01473 214481
	East Anglian Chambers, Ipswich	01473 214481
	East Anglian Chambers, Norwich	01473 214481
Marshall Mr Derek Stanley	College Chambers, Southampton	023 8023 0338
Matthias Mr David Huw	Francis Taylor Building, London	020 7353 8415
Maxwell Lewis Mr Cameron	Lamb Chambers, London	020 7797 8300
Maynard Mr Christopher Howard	Tanfield Chambers, London	020 7421 5300
McCracken Mr James	Cornwall Street Chambers, Birmingham	0121 233 7500
McCue Mr Donald	11 Stone Buildings, London	020 7831 6381
McDonnell Mr John Beresford William	13 Old Square Chambers, London	020 7831 4445
McLinden Mr John Vincent Barry	Field Court Chambers, London	020 7405 6114
Melville-Shreeve Mr Michael David	Walnut House, Exeter	01392 279751
Michael Mr Nicholas	East Anglian Chambers, Chelmsford	01473 214481
	East Anglian Chambers, Colchester	01473 214481
	East Anglian Chambers, Ipswich	01473 214481
	East Anglian Chambers, Norwich	01473 214481
Miles Mr Richard Iain	One Essex Court, London	020 7936 3030
Mills Mr Simon Thomas	Five Paper, London	020 7815 3200
Mitchell Mr David John	No5 Chambers, Birmingham	0845 210 5555
	No5 Chambers, Bristol	0845 210 5555
	No5 Chambers, London	0845 210 5555
Monnington Mr Bruce Gilbert	Fenners Chambers, Cambridge	01223 368761
Murphy Mr Damian	Enterprise Chambers, Leeds	0113 246 0391
	Enterprise Chambers, London	020 7405 9471
	Enterprise Chambers, Newcastle Upon Tyne	0191 222 3344

C

Name	Chambers	Telephone
Murray Mr Charles Humphrey Stewart	Rougemont Chambers, Exeter	01392 208484
Newsom Mr George Lucien	Guildhall Chambers, Bristol	0117 930 9000
Nickless Mr Jason Alan	College Chambers, Southampton	023 8023 0338
Noble Mr Andrew	Enterprise Chambers, Leeds	0113 246 0391
Normington Mr James Adam	Park Court Chambers, Leeds	0113 243 3277
O'Brien Mr Nicholas William Wattebot	10 King's Bench Walk, London	020 7353 7742
Ohrenstein Mr Dov	Radcliffe Chambers, London	020 7831 0081
O'Mahony Mr Jonathan Solomon	9 Stone Buildings, London	020 7404 5055
Oommen Mr Jacob	Chambers of Mr Jacob Oommen, East Barnet	07958 680272
Osborne Mr James Robert	Clerksroom (London), London	0845 083 3000
Otwal Mr Mukhtiar Singh	42 Bedford Row, London	020 7831 0222
Parker Miss Wendy	Hardwicke, London	020 7242 2523
Parker Mrs Karen Lesley	Guildhall Chambers Portsmouth, Portsmouth	023 9275 2400
Pearce Mr Robert Edgar	Radcliffe Chambers, London	020 7831 0081
Pennock Mr Ian	Park Lane Plowden, Leeds	0113 228 5049
Penny Mr Timothy Charles	11 Stone Buildings, London	020 7831 6381
Platford Mr Graham Roy	Five Paper, London	020 7815 3200
Polli Mr Timothy James	Tanfield Chambers, London	020 7421 5300
Purves Mr Gavin Bowman	Swan House, London	020 8998 3035
Quirke Mr Gerard Martin	Citadel Chambers, Birmingham	0121 233 8500
Rahman Mr Anis	12 Old Square Chambers, London	020 7404 0875
Ratcliffe Miss Frances Anne	Radcliffe Chambers, London	020 7831 0081
Rifat Mr Maurice Alan	1 Gray's Inn Square, London	020 7405 0001
Rinker Mr Andrew Stuart D'Artois	Chambers of Mr Andrew Rinker, London	020 7584 1091
Ritchie Mr Richard Bulkeley	XXIV Old Buildings, London	020 7691 2424
Rivalland Mr Marc-Edouard	1 Chancery Lane, London	0845 634 6666
Roberts Mr Michael Charles	Chambers of Michael Roberts, Henley-On-Thames	01844 355 655
Russell Mr Thomas Charles Welldon	KCH Garden Square, Nottingham	0115 941 8851
Sellers Mr Graham	Atlantic Chambers, Liverpool	0151 236 4421
Sen Mr Aditya Kumar	Coram Chambers, London	020 7092 3700
Sinclair Miss Lisa Anne	Chambers of Miss Lisa Sinclair, London	020 8946 7201
Sinclair Mr Graham Kelso	East Anglian Chambers, Colchester	01473 214481
	East Anglian Chambers, Ipswich	01473 214481
	East Anglian Chambers, Norwich	01473 214481
Singarajah Mr Frederico	1 Gray's Inn Square, London	020 7405 0001
Sisley Mr Timothy Julian Crispin	9 Stone Buildings, London	020 7404 5055
Sjostrand Miss Ekaterina	13 Old Square Chambers, London	020 7831 4445
Smith Mr Matthew Robert	Sovereign Chambers, Leeds	0113 245 1841
Smith Mr Robert Clive	1 Paper Buildings, London	020 7353 3728
	RCS Chambers, Stainton	01709 814 147
Spencer Mr Martin Benedict	Hailsham Chambers, London	020 7643 5000
Stenhouse Mr John Alexander	Nightingale Chambers, Wolverley	01562 851350
Sterling Mr Robert Alan	St James's Chambers, Manchester	0161 834 7000
	Zenith Chambers, Leeds	0113 245 5438
Stevenson Dr Simon John	Park Lane Plowden, Leeds	0113 228 5049
Stewart Mr Nicholas John Cameron	Ely Place Chambers, London	020 7400 9600
Stirling Mr Christopher William	Field Court Chambers, London	020 7405 6114
Stuart Mr James William	Lamb Chambers, London	020 7797 8300
Swirsky Mr Adam Abraham Burl Bradbury	Lamb Chambers, London	020 7797 8300
Taylor Miss Araba Arba Kurankyiwa	Fenners Chambers, Cambridge	01223 368761
Temmink Mr Robert-Jan	Quadrant Chambers, London	020 7583 4444
Temple Ms Eleanor Louise	Kings Chambers, Birmingham	0845 034 3444
	Kings Chambers, Leeds	0845 034 3444
	Kings Chambers, Manchester	0845 034 3444

Name	Chambers	Telephone
Terry Mr Robert Jeffrey	Kings Chambers, Birmingham	0845 034 3444
	Kings Chambers, Leeds	0845 034 3444
	Kings Chambers, Manchester	0845 034 3444
	Lamb Chambers, London	020 7797 8300
Thornley Miss Hannah Elise	South Square, London	020 7696 9900
Topal Mr Erol	Lamb Chambers, London	020 7797 8300
Treverton-Jones Mr Gregory Dennis	39 Essex Street, London	020 7832 1111
	82 King Street, Manchester	0161 870 9969
Trompeter Mr Nicholas Simeon	Selborne Chambers, London	020 7420 9500
Trumpington Mr John Henry	Staple Inn Chambers, London	020 7242 5240
Upton Mr Jonathan Michael	Tanfield Chambers, London	020 7421 5300
Van Tonder Mr Gerard Dirk	New Square Chambers, London	020 7419 8000
Vane The Hon Christopher John Fletcher	Trinity Chambers, Middlesbrough	01642 247569
	Trinity Chambers, Newcastle Upon Tyne	0191 232 1927
Vaughan-Williams Mr Arthur Laurence	13 Old Square Chambers, London	020 7831 4445
Vernon Mr Elliot Curt	No. 3 Fleet Street Chambers, London	020 7936 4474
Warner Mr David Alexander	St Philips Chambers, Birmingham	0121 246 7000
Watson-Gandy Prof Mark	13 Old Square Chambers, London	020 7831 4445
White Mr Oliver Zachary	Littleton Chambers, London	020 7797 8600
Wilcox Mr Jerome Carl Jean	Alexander Chambers, London	0845 652 0451/0854 652 0451
Wilkinson Mr Marc Ashley	No5 Chambers, Birmingham	0845 210 5555
	No5 Chambers, Bristol	0845 210 5555
	No5 Chambers, London	0845 210 5555
Williams Mr Simon Paul	Radcliffe Chambers, London	020 7831 0081
Wills Miss Alexandra Itari	Christ Church Chambers, London	020 7409 5278/07788 512787
Wise Mr Leslie Michael	10 King's Bench Walk, London	020 7353 7742
Young Mr Martin Ford	9 Stone Buildings, London	020 7404 5055

PATENTS

Name	Chambers	Telephone
Abrahams Mr James	8 New Square, London	020 7405 4321
Andrews Mr Paul Leslie	Great James Street Chambers, London	020 7440 4949
Bowhill Miss Jessie Kate	8 New Square, London	020 7405 4321
Craig Mr Aubrey John	Chancery House Chambers, Leeds	0113 244 6691
	St Philips Chambers, Birmingham	0121 246 7000
De Mounteney Mr Jonathan Patrick	Chambers of Mr J P De Mounteney, Reading	0118 934 6822
Engelman Mr Mark Trevor	Hardwicke, London	020 7242 2523
Fern Mr Gary	7 Stones IP, London	020 7193 4033
Fitzgerald Mr John Vincent	Ingenuity IP Chambers, Petts Wood	
Hamer Mr George Clemens	8 New Square, London	020 7405 4321
Heal Mrs Madeleine	New Square Chambers, London	020 7419 8000
Hill Mr Jonathan	8 New Square, London	020 7405 4321
Himsworth Miss Emma Katherine	One Essex Court, London	020 7583 2000
Hobbs Mr Geoffrey William	One Essex Court, London	020 7583 2000
Hussain Mr Muhammad Altaf	Chambers of Mr M A Hussain, London	020 8679 2398
Iyer Miss Shobana	Swan Chambers, Richmond	0845 123 1234
Johnson Mr Phillip Michael	Chambers of Mr P Johnson, London	020 7288 2256
Jones Mr Kelvin Mcallister	Templis Chambers, London	020 7649 9808
Khan Dr Alexander	Coral House, Manchester	
Kime Mr Matthew Jonathan	Cobden House Chambers, Manchester	0161 833 6000
	Ingenuity IP Chambers, Petts Wood	
	No. 3 Fleet Street Chambers, London	020 7936 4474
Lambert Miss Jane Elizabeth	NIPC, Huddersfield	0800 862 0055
Lane Ms Lindsay Ruth Busfield	8 New Square, London	020 7405 4321
Lawrence Dr Heather Bunting Elizabeth	11 South Square, London	020 7405 1222
Nicol Mr Stuart Henry David	13 King's Bench Walk, London	020 7353 7204
Norton Mr Giles	Enigma Chambers, Sheffield	07779 576499
	Holborn Chambers, London	020 7242 6060
Onslow Mr Robert Denzil	8 New Square, London	020 7405 4321

C

Barrister	Chambers	Telephone
Pearson Mr Christopher	Lamb Chambers, London	020 7797 8300
Platts-Mills Mr Mark Fortescue	8 New Square, London	020 7405 4321
Powell Mr William Rhys	Regency Chambers, Cambridge	01223 301517
	Regency Chambers, Peterborough	01733 315215
Reed Mr Jeremy Nigel	Hogarth Chambers, London	020 7404 0404
Roberts Mr Philip Duncan	One Essex Court, London	020 7583 2000
Rogers Miss Christy Abigail	Ingenuity IP Chambers, Petts Wood	
	No. 3 Fleet Street Chambers, London	020 7936 4474
Roughton Mr Ashley Wentworth	Hogarth Chambers, London	020 7404 0404
Sampson Dr Timothy Michael George	One Essex Court, London	020 7936 3030
Seeboruth Mr Royln Jean-Paul	Chambers of Royln Seeboruth, Aylesbury	01296 393329
Singarajah Mr Frederico	1 Gray's Inn Square, London	020 7405 0001
Tritton Mr Robert Guy Henton	Hogarth Chambers, London	020 7404 0404
Ward Mr Robin Henry	8 New Square, London	020 7405 4321

PENSIONS

Barrister	Chambers	Telephone
Ajaz Mr Mohammad Arshad	Eastmans Chambers, Reading	0118 966 9094
Arthur Mr Stephen Joseph	Temple Tax Chambers, London	020 7353 7884
Ashley Mr Neil Martin	East Anglian Chambers, Chelmsford	01473 214481
	East Anglian Chambers, Ipswich	01473 214481
	East Anglian Chambers, Norwich	01473 214481
Buchan Miss Caroline Venetia	Chambers of Miss C Buchan, Haywards Heath	01444 482222
Buchan Mr Andrew	Cloisters, London	020 7827 4000
De Mello Mr Rembert Joseph Julius	No5 Chambers, Birmingham	0845 210 5555
	No5 Chambers, Bristol	0845 210 5555
	No5 Chambers, London	0845 210 5555
Ginniff Mr Nigel Thomas	Atlantic Chambers, Liverpool	0151 236 4421
Godfrey Mr Lauren John	Crown Office Row Chambers, Brighton	01273 625625
Grant Mr David Ericson	Outer Temple Chambers, London	020 7353 6381
Hamilton Mr Peter Bernard	4 Pump Court, London	020 7842 5555
Hussain Mr Muhammad Altaf	Chambers of Mr M A Hussain, London	020 8679 2398
Jones Mr Christopher David Harries	St John's Chambers, Bristol	0117 923 4700
Lamb Mr Jeffrey Thomas	Westgate Chambers, Lewes	01273 480510
Lenon Mr Andrew Ralph Fitzmaurice	One Essex Court, London	020 7583 2000
Ling Ms Naomi	Outer Temple Chambers, London	020 7353 6381
Margo Mr Saul Nicholas	Outer Temple Chambers, London	020 7353 6381
McLinden Mr John Vincent Barry	Field Court Chambers, London	020 7405 6114
O'Donovan Mr Kevin John	No5 Chambers, Birmingham	0845 210 5555
	No5 Chambers, Bristol	0845 210 5555
	No5 Chambers, London	0845 210 5555
Parsons Mr Andrew James	Portsmouth Barristers'Chambers, Portsmouth	023 9283 1292
Ratcliffe Miss Frances Anne	Radcliffe Chambers, London	020 7831 0081
Rickards Mr James	Outer Temple Chambers, London	020 7353 6381
Saxton Miss Nicola Helen	St Paul's Chambers, Leeds	0113 245 5866
Short Mr Andrew John	Outer Temple Chambers, London	020 7353 6381
	Riverview Chambers, London	0844 225 3999
Spink Mr Andrew John Murray	Outer Temple Chambers, London	020 7353 6381
	Riverview Chambers, London	0844 225 3999
Trotter Miss Helen Claire	Pump Court Chambers, London	020 7353 0711
	Pump Court Chambers, Swindon	01793 539899
	Pump Court Chambers, Winchester	01962 868 161

PERSONAL INJURY

Barrister	Chambers	Telephone
Ackland Miss Sacha Marie	Temple Garden Chambers, London	020 7583 1315
Adamson Mr Alan	Kew Chambers, Kew	0844 8099991
Afzal Mr Fayyaz	No5 Chambers, Birmingham	0845 210 5555
	No5 Chambers, Bristol	0845 210 5555
	No5 Chambers, London	0845 210 5555
Ahmed Mr Ishfaq	Stone Chambers, London	020 7440 6900

Barrister	Chambers	Telephone
Ailes Mr John Ashley	Eighteen Carlton Crescent, Southampton	023 8063 9001
Akers Mr Robert Matthew Harry	St Johns Buildings, Chester	01244 323070
	St Johns Buildings, Manchester	0161 214 1500
	16 Winckley Square, Preston	01772 256100
Akin-Olugbade Mr Oluwajeminipe Babarinsade	Nexus Chambers, London	020 7404 1147/020 7831 8309
Ali Mr Ishtiyaq	Chartlands Chambers, Northampton	01604 603322
Alliott Mr George Beckles	Temple Garden Chambers, London	020 7583 1315
Alloway Mr Tor Hugh	Talloway Chambers, London	020 7419 5047
Allston Mr Anthony Stanley	3 Dr Johnson's Buildings, London	020 7353 4854
Aly Miss Sheila	Warwick House Chambers, London	020 7430 2323
Ameen Mr Danish	18 St John Street, Manchester	0161 278 1800
Anderson Mr Simon Peter Bede	Park Court Chambers, Leeds	0113 243 3277
Andre Mr Roger Louis	Sovereign Chambers, Leeds	0113 245 1841
Andrews Miss Melanie Alexandra	Becket Chambers, Canterbury	01227 786331
Angammana Mr Gamini Bertram	Chambers of Gamini Angammana, London	020 8771 5205
Antell Mr John Jason	King's Bench and Godolphin (KBG)Chambers, Plymouth	01752 221551
Argent Mr Gavin Richard	Westgate Chambers, Lewes	01273 480510
Arnheim Dr Michael Thomas Walter	Chambers of Dr Michael Arnheim, London	020 7833 5093
	Holborn Chambers, London	020 7242 6060
	Principal Chambers, Sevenoaks	0845 209 8080
Ashford-Thom Mr Ian	3 PB Barristers, London	020 7583 8055
	Temple Garden Chambers, London	020 7583 1315
Ashworth Miss Fiona Katherine Anne	Kings Chambers, Birmingham	0845 034 3444
	Kings Chambers, Leeds	0845 034 3444
	Kings Chambers, Manchester	0845 034 3444
Askey Mr Robert John	Palmyra Chambers, Warrington	01925 444919
Austins Mr Christopher John	Chambers of Mr Christopher Austins, Bristol	01761 221 208
	Clerksroom (Taunton), Taunton	0845 083 3000
	King's Lynn Chambers, King's Lynn	01553 672 085
Azhar Mr Ali Mohammad	9 King's Bench Walk, London	020 7353 9564
Azib Ms Rehana	2 Temple Gardens, London	020 7822 1200
Bailey Mr Michael Robert	Tanfield Chambers, London	020 7421 5300
Bailey Mr Russell Stuart	No5 Chambers, Birmingham	0845 210 5555
	No5 Chambers, Bristol	0845 210 5555
	No5 Chambers, London	0845 210 5555
Baldwin Dr Timothy John	Garden Court Chambers, London	020 7993 7600
Ball Mr Steven James	Number 7 Harrington Street Chambers, Liverpool	0151 242 0707
Barnes Miss Andrea Lynda	Clerksroom (Taunton), Taunton	0845 083 3000
	King's Lynn Chambers, King's Lynn	01553 672 085
Bashir Mr Mohammed Issrar	Chambers of M I Bashir, London	07932 948487
	12 Old Square Chambers, London	020 7404 0875
Batey Mr David Michael	Stour Chambers, Canterbury	01227 764899
Baumohl Mr Mark Christopher	Field Court Chambers, London	020 7405 6114
Bax Mr James Alexander	Rougemont Chambers, Exeter	01392 208484
Beaumont Mrs Sally	Sovereign Chambers, Leeds	0113 245 1841
Becker Mr Timothy George Christie	Chambers of Mr Timothy Becker, Liverpool	0151 703 0319
	Clerksroom (London), London	0845 083 3000
Beloff Mr Rupert Joseph Alexei	No5 Chambers, Birmingham	0845 210 5555
	No5 Chambers, Bristol	0845 210 5555
	No5 Chambers, London	0845 210 5555
Bennett Miss Emma Louise	Exchange Chambers, Leeds	0113 203 1970
	Exchange Chambers, Liverpool	0151 236 7747
	Exchange Chambers, Manchester	0161 833 2722
Bhattacharyya Mr Ardhendu	Slough Barristers Chamber, Slough	01753 553806
Birch Mr Roger Allen	Five St Andrew's Hill, London	020 7332 5400
	Sovereign Chambers, Leeds	0113 245 1841

C

Birkby Mr Richard Adam	Park Court Chambers, Leeds	0113 243 3277
Bishop Mr Stephen Anthony	Goldsmith Chambers, London	020 7353 6802
Bloom Dr Margaret	Hardwicke, London	020 7242 2523
Bogle Mr James Stewart Lockhart	10 King's Bench Walk, London	020 7353 7742
Borkowski Miss Gemma Francesca	Albion Chambers, Bristol	0117 927 2144
Boyd Miss Kerstin Margaret	Tanfield Chambers, London	020 7421 5300
Bragge Mr Thomas Hereward	Stour Chambers, Canterbury	01227 764899
Brittain Mr Marc John	1 Gray's Inn Square, London	020 7405 0001
Brockley Mr Nigel Simon	No5 Chambers, Birmingham	0845 210 5555
	No5 Chambers, Bristol	0845 210 5555
	No5 Chambers, London	0845 210 5555
Brooke-Smith Mr John	East Anglian Chambers, Colchester	01473 214481
	East Anglian Chambers, Ipswich	01473 214481
Brown Mr Cameron Kennedy Duncan	9-12 Bell Yard, London	020 7400 1800
Brunning Mr Matthew David George	No5 Chambers, Birmingham	0845 210 5555
	No5 Chambers, Bristol	0845 210 5555
	No5 Chambers, London	0845 210 5555
Bryden Mr Christopher James Yuen Kang	4 King's Bench Walk, London	020 7822 7000
Buchan Miss Caroline Venetia	Chambers of Miss C Buchan, Haywards Heath	01444 482222
Buchan Mr Andrew	Cloisters, London	020 7827 4000
Buckle Mr Jonathan	Regency Chambers, Cambridge	01223 301517
	Regency Chambers, Peterborough	01733 315215
Buckley Mr Peter Evered	Cobden House Chambers, Manchester	0161 833 6000
Budworth Mr Richard Dutton	2-3 Hind Court Chambers, London	020 7822 2150
Burnett Mr Iain	4 King's Bench Walk, London	020 7822 7000
Butler Mr Rupert James	3 Hare Court, London	020 7415 7800
Butler Mr Simon David	The Chambers of Grahame Aldous QC, London	020 7832 0500
Calvert Mr David Edward	12 King's Bench Walk, London	020 7583 0811
	St James's Chambers, Manchester	0161 834 7000
Campbell Mr Oliver Edward Wilhelm	Henderson Chambers, London	020 7583 9020
Canby Miss Fiona Jane	Temple Garden Chambers, London	020 7583 1315
Carlisle Mr Timothy St John Ogilvie	Field Court Chambers, London	020 7405 6114
Carr Mr Christopher Sean	36 Bedford Row, London	020 7421 8000
Cartwright Mr Ivan Matthew	KCH Garden Square, Nottingham	0115 941 8851
Cattermull Miss Emma Jayne	East Anglian Chambers, Chelmsford	01473 214481
	East Anglian Chambers, Ipswich	01473 214481
	East Anglian Chambers, Norwich	01473 214481
Caun Mr Lawrence	Lamb Chambers, London	020 7797 8300
Cawsey Mr Barry Donald	Clerksroom (London), London	0845 083 3000
	Clerksroom (Taunton), Taunton	0845 083 3000
Chadwick Miss Joanna Ceridwen	No5 Chambers, Birmingham	0845 210 5555
	No5 Chambers, Bristol	0845 210 5555
	No5 Chambers, London	0845 210 5555
Challenger Mr Colin Westcott	Lamb Chambers, London	020 7797 8300
Challinor Mr Thomas Michael	Citadel Chambers, Birmingham	0121 233 8500
Chan Miss Susan	13 KBW, Oxford	01865 311066
	13 King's Bench Walk, London	020 7353 7204
Checa-Dover Miss Olivia	KBW, Leeds	0113 297 1200
Chesner Mr Howard Michael	One Essex Court, London	020 7936 3030
Chippeck Mr Stephen	5 King's Bench Walk, London	020 7353 5638
Christensen Mr Carlton	10 King's Bench Walk, London	020 7353 7742
Clarke Miss Lisa Tarin	Staple Inn Chambers, London	020 7242 5240
Clarke Mr Jamie Roy	Hardwicke, London	020 7242 2523
Clarke Mr Nikolas Michael	Field Court Chambers, London	020 7405 6114
Clegg Mr Adam Gordon	Stour Chambers, Canterbury	01227 764899
Clifton Miss Jane April	Lamb Chambers, London	020 7797 8300
Climie Mr Roger Stephen	King's Bench and Godolphin (KBG)Chambers, Plymouth	01752 221551
	Outer Temple Chambers, London	020 7353 6381
Cline Mr Robert James	Atlantic Chambers, Liverpool	0151 236 4421

C

Barrister	Chambers	Telephone
Coates Mr George Alexander Nigel	Guildford Chambers, Guildford	01483 539131
Cofie Mr Edmund Kpakpo	Nexus Chambers, London	020 7404 1147/020 7831 8309
Colbey Mr Richard	Guildhall Chambers Portsmouth, Portsmouth	023 9275 2400
	Lamb Chambers, London	020 7797 8300
Collins Mr Peter Richard	4 King's Bench Walk, London	020 7822 7000
Comerton Miss Julie Anne	4 KBW, London	020 7822 8822
Compton Mr Benjamin Edward Welstead	Outer Temple Chambers, London	020 7353 6381
Conlon Mr Michael John Patrick	Harcourt Chambers, Milton Keynes	0845 123 1234
Cooksey Mr Nicholas	River Chambers, Shrewsbury	01743 350505
Coster Mr Ronald David	42 Bedford Row, London	020 7831 0222
Coulter Mr Barry John	Clerksroom (London), London	0845 083 3000
	Clerksroom (Taunton), Taunton	0845 083 3000
	King's Lynn Chambers, King's Lynn	01553 672 085
Counsell Mr James Henry	Outer Temple Chambers, London	020 7353 6381
Cox Miss Kerry Amanda	Park Lane Plowden, Newcastle Upon Tyne	0191 211 4087
Cox Miss Olivia Rodrigues	Atlantic Chambers, Liverpool	0151 236 4421
Cox Ms Sita	Stour Chambers, Canterbury	01227 764899
Coyle Mr Anthony Noel	Zenith Chambers, Leeds	0113 245 5438
Crawford Mr Lincoln Santo	12 King's Bench Walk, London	020 7583 0811
Crawley Mr Ross Alexander	Middle Temple Lane Chambers, London	020 7583 4352
Crew Miss Gillian Mary	Ely Place Chambers, London	020 7400 9600
Croskell Mr Marcus James	East Anglian Chambers, Chelmsford	01473 214481
	East Anglian Chambers, Colchester	01473 214481
	East Anglian Chambers, Ipswich	01473 214481
	East Anglian Chambers, Norwich	01473 214481
Crow Mr Charles Duncan Timothy	No5 Chambers, Birmingham	0845 210 5555
	No5 Chambers, Bristol	0845 210 5555
	No5 Chambers, London	0845 210 5555
Culley Miss Laura Joan	Citadel Chambers, Birmingham	0121 233 8500
Culverhouse Miss Emily Anna Louise	Chambers of Miss E Culverhouse, Chesham	07813 007503
Currie Mr Fergus Hugh	Unity Street Chambers, Bristol	0117 906 9789
Curwen Mr David Christian	Unity Street Chambers, Bristol	0117 906 9789
Dalal Mr Rajen Charles James	Cobden House Chambers, Manchester	0161 833 6000
	Derwent Chambers, Derby	01332 242425
Daniels Mr David William	Rowchester Chambers, Birmingham	0121 233 2327
Darlington Miss Elizabeth	5 Pump Court, London	020 7353 2532
	Zenith Chambers, Leeds	0113 245 5438
Davey Mr Charles	64 Bridge Street, Manchester	0845 083 3000
	Chambers of Mr C Davey, Bishop's Stortford	01279 506412
	Clerksroom (Taunton), Taunton	0845 083 3000
Davies Mr Henry Olusola	Trinity Chambers, Birmingham	0121 346 4672
Davis Mr Andrew Paul	Crown Office Chambers, London	020 7797 8100
De Berry Mr Philip John	18 St John Street, Manchester	0161 278 1800
De Jehan Mr David	Park Lane Plowden, Leeds	0113 228 5049
Dean Mr James Patrick	Goldsmith Chambers, London	020 7353 6802
Dean Mr Paul Benjamin	Crown Office Chambers, London	020 7797 8100
Deegan Mr Lawrence Jeffrey	Fenners Chambers, Cambridge	01223 368761
Dennis Miss Rebecca Louise	Queen Square Chambers, Bristol	0117 921 1966
Devereux-Cooke Mr Richard Charles	13 Old Square Chambers, London	020 7831 4445
Devlin Mr Bernard Joseph	Five St Andrew's Hill, London	020 7332 5400
Dipré Mr Paul Nicholas Amadeus	Chambers of Mr P N Dipré, Address withheld	0845 123 1234
	MK Family Law Chambers, Milton Keynes	0845 123 1234
Douthwaite Mr Charles Philip	Four New Square, London	020 7822 2000
Dowden Mr Andrew Philip	Castle Chambers, Harrow-on-the-Hill	020 8423 6579
	Melbury House, Leicester	07801 037802
Dowell Mr Gregory Hamilton	Principal Chambers, Sevenoaks	0845 209 8080

Downey Mr Neil James	Atlantic Chambers, Liverpool	0151 236 4421
Dracass Mr Timothy William	Pump Court Chambers, London	020 7353 0711
	Pump Court Chambers, Winchester	01962 868 161
	Riverview Chambers, London	0844 225 3999
Dunlop Mr Hamish Michael	3 PB Barristers, Bournemouth	01202 292102
	3 PB Barristers, Bristol	0117 928 1520
	3 PB Barristers, London	020 7583 8055
	3 PB Barristers, Oxford	01865 793 736
	3 PB Barristers, Winchester	01962 868884
Dunne Mr Anthony James	KBW, Leeds	0113 297 1200
Earle Mr James Christopher Reginald St John	Fenners Chambers, Cambridge	01223 368761
Edge Mr Timothy Richard	Deans Court Chambers, Manchester	0161 214 6000
	Deans Court Chambers, Preston	01772 565 600
Edwards Mr Daniel Hugh	Dere Street Barristers, York	0844 3351551
	York Chambers, Newcastle Upon Tyne	0191 206 4677
Edwards Mr Dickon Harrison	5 Pump Court, London	020 7353 2532
Egleton Mr Richard Wildman	Pallant Chambers, Chichester	01243 784538
Elfield Miss Laura Elaine	The Chambers of Grahame Aldous QC, London	020 7832 0500
Elliott Mr Edward Anthony John	Garden Court Chambers, London	020 7993 7600
Ellis Dr Peter Simon	Seven Bedford Row, London	020 7242 3555
England Mrs Lisa Johanna Louise	Guildhall Chambers Portsmouth, Portsmouth	023 9275 2400
Ephraim-Adejumo Mrs Hilda Ekpo	12 Old Square Chambers, London	020 7404 0875
Feldschreiber Dr Peter	Four New Square, London	020 7822 2000
Fender Mr Carl David	Regency Chambers, Cambridge	01223 301517
	Regency Chambers, Peterborough	01733 315215
Ferm Mr Rodney Eric	Broadway House Chambers, Bradford	01274 722560
	Broadway House Chambers, Leeds	0113 246 2600
Fetto Mr Niazi Peter	2 Temple Gardens, London	020 7822 1200
Finlay Mr Darren	Sovereign Chambers, Leeds	0113 245 1841
Fletcher Mr James Watford	Five St Andrew's Hill, London	020 7332 5400
Flexman Mrs Carla Ann	Albion Chambers, Bristol	0117 927 2144
Follon Mr Daniel Richard Thomas	1 Gray's Inn Square, London	020 7405 0001
Fordham Mrs Margaret Allison	Principal Chambers, Sevenoaks	0845 209 8080
Formby Ms Emily Jane	39 Essex Street, London	020 7832 1111
Forte Mr Timothy Axel	Dyers Chambers, London	020 7404 1881
Fortune Mr Peter Carl Michael	Guildhall Chambers Portsmouth, Portsmouth	023 9275 2400
	4 King's Bench Walk, London	020 7822 7000
Foulkes Miss Rebecca	5 Pump Court, London	020 7353 2532
Found Mr Timothy Paul	Farrar's Building, London	020 7583 9241
Fox Mr John Harvey	Chambers of Mr Ami Feder, London	020 7797 7788
	Chambers of Mr Ami Feder, London	020 7797 7788
	Lamb Building, Brighton	01273 820490
Francis Mr Richard Maurice	9 Park Place, Cardiff	029 2038 2731
Frantzis Miss Roxanne	KBW, Leeds	0113 297 1200
Fraser Mr Mark-Anthony	Dyers Chambers, London	020 7404 1881
Freeman Mr Peter Mark	Farrar's Building, London	020 7583 9241
Fullerton Mr Michael Andrew	7 Bell Yard, London	020 7831 0636
	Chambers of Mr Michael Fullerton, Hove	01273 772050
Gadd Mr Adam Brian	Pump Court Chambers, London	020 7353 0711
	Pump Court Chambers, Winchester	01962 868 161
	Riverview Chambers, London	0844 225 3999
Gair Mr Christopher	King's Bench Chambers, Bournemouth	01202 250025
Galway-Cooper Dr Philip Anthony	Five St Andrew's Hill, London	020 7332 5400
Gamble Mrs Esther Ruth	No5 Chambers, Birmingham	0845 210 5555
	No5 Chambers, Bristol	0845 210 5555
	No5 Chambers, London	0845 210 5555
	St Philips Chambers, Birmingham	0121 246 7000
Gelbart Mr Geoff Alan	1 Gray's Inn Square, London	020 7405 0001
George Mr Michael David Roberts	St Philips Chambers, Birmingham	0121 246 7000

C

Name	Chambers	Telephone
George Mr Nicholas Frank Raymond	New Walk Chambers, Leicester	0871 200 1298/0116 255 9144
Giles Mr David William	1 Gray's Inn Square, London	020 7405 0001
Gill Miss Baljinder	10 King's Bench Walk, London	020 7353 7742
Gledhill Mr Lee Andre	Alexander Chambers, London	0845 652 0451/0854 652 0451
	Trident Barristers Chambers, Manchester	0161 663 3123
Glover Mr Stephen Julian	37 Park Square Chambers, Leeds	0113 243 9422
Glyn Mr Caspar Hilary Gordon	Cloisters, London	020 7827 4000
Godfrey Mr Lauren John	Crown Office Row Chambers, Brighton	01273 625625
Goldman Mrs Linda	Henderson Chambers, London	020 7583 9020
Goldrein Mr Iain Saville	7 Bell Yard, London	020 7831 0636
	Number 7 Harrington Street Chambers, Liverpool	0151 242 0707
Goode Mr Julian Leigh Alexander	St Johns Buildings, Manchester	0161 214 1500
	St Johns Buildings Liverpool, Liverpool	0151 243 6000
	16 Winckley Square, Preston	01772 256100
Goodfellow Mr Stephen John	East Anglian Chambers, Chelmsford	01473 214481
	East Anglian Chambers, Ipswich	01473 214481
	East Anglian Chambers, Norwich	01473 214481
Goodlad Mr Grant David	Farrar's Building, London	020 7583 9241
Gore Mr Andrew Julian Mark	37 Park Square Chambers, Leeds	0113 243 9422
Gow Mr Henry	New Bailey Chambers, Liverpool	0151 236 9402
Graham Mrs Alana Nicole	Chambers of Alana Graham, Halesowen	01384 894560
	9 Stone Buildings, London	020 7404 5055
Grant Mr Marcus H James	Temple Garden Chambers, London	020 7583 1315
Grant Mr Murray Ross	13 KBW, Oxford	01865 311066
	13 King's Bench Walk, London	020 7353 7204
Granville Stafford Mr Andrew	4 King's Bench Walk, London	020 7822 7000
Griffiths Miss Alison Clare	4 King's Bench Walk, London	020 7822 7000
Griffiths Mr David	St Philips Chambers, Birmingham	0121 246 7000
Habib Miss Shysta	Kenworthy's Chambers, Manchester	0161 832 4036
Hadgill Mr Clinton Alexander	St Albans Chambers, St Albans	01727 843383
Hall Mr Jeremy John	Becket Chambers, Canterbury	01227 786331
Halliwell Mr Toby George	Unity Street Chambers, Bristol	0117 906 9789
Halstead Mr Robin Bernard	One Essex Court, London	020 7936 3030
Hamblin Mr Nicholas Howard	Westgate Chambers, Lewes	01273 480510
Hammerton Mr Alastair Rolf	1 Chancery Lane, London	0845 634 6666
Hammond Mr Tim Mark	Tanfield Chambers, London	020 7421 5300
Harrington Miss Clare Stephanie	13 KBW, Oxford	01865 311066
	13 King's Bench Walk, London	020 7353 7204
Harris Mr David Robert	St Albans Chambers, St Albans	01727 843383
Harris Mr Melvyn	5 Essex Court, London	020 7410 2000
Harrison Dr Graeme	12 College Place, Southampton	023 8032 0320
Hartley Mr Richard Anthony	Cobden House Chambers, Manchester	0161 833 6000
Hartman Mr Michael	One Essex Court, London	020 7936 3030
Harvey Mr John Gilbert	No5 Chambers, Birmingham	0845 210 5555
	No5 Chambers, Bristol	0845 210 5555
	No5 Chambers, London	0845 210 5555
Hatch Miss Lisa Sharmila	One Essex Court, London	020 7936 3030
Haughty Mr Jeremy Nicholas	Chambers of Mr Ami Feder, London	020 7797 7788
	Chambers of Mr Ami Feder, London	020 7797 7788
	Rougemont Chambers, Exeter	01392 208484
Haukeland Mr Martin Jonathan	42 Bedford Row, London	020 7831 0222
Havenhand Mr John Barry	Clerksroom (London), London	0845 083 3000
	Clerksroom (Taunton), Taunton	0845 083 3000
	King's Lynn Chambers, King's Lynn	01553 672 085
Hawkes Mr Malcolm Alexander	Dyers Chambers, London	020 7404 1881
Hendron Mr Henry Joseph Christopher	Strand Chambers, London	020 7117 6920
Heppinstall Mr Adam John	Henderson Chambers, London	020 7583 9020
Higgins Mr Adrian John	13 KBW, Oxford	01865 311066
	13 King's Bench Walk, London	020 7353 7204

C

Barrister	Chambers	Telephone
Hill Mr Michael Gordon	Trinity Chambers, Middlesbrough	01642 247569
	Trinity Chambers, Newcastle Upon Tyne	0191 232 1927
Hill Mr Nicholas Mark	Pump Court Chambers, London	020 7353 0711
	Pump Court Chambers, Swindon	01793 539899
	St Philips Chambers, Birmingham	0121 246 7000
Hillier Mr William	New Street Chambers, Leicester	0116 262 5906
Hirst Miss Rebecca Elisabeth	Cobden House Chambers, Manchester	0161 833 6000
Hirst Mr Karl Douglas	No5 Chambers, Birmingham	0845 210 5555
	No5 Chambers, Bristol	0845 210 5555
	No5 Chambers, London	0845 210 5555
Hirst Mr Martin Lewis	13 KBW, Oxford	01865 311066
	13 King's Bench Walk, London	020 7353 7204
Hirst Mr William Timothy John	Park Lane Plowden, Leeds	0113 228 5049
Hoar Mr Francis John Patrick	Field Court Chambers, London	020 7405 6114
Hobson Miss Laura Elise	Citadel Chambers, Birmingham	0121 233 8500
Hodder Mr Philip James	Clerksroom (Taunton), Taunton	0845 083 3000
	King's Lynn Chambers, King's Lynn	01553 672 085
Hodgkiss Ms Suzanne Jane	43 Temple Row Chambers, Birmingham	0121 237 6035
Hodson Mr Matthew Paul	Farrar's Building, London	020 7583 9241
Hodson Mr Peter David	Chambers of Ian Macdonald QC, Manchester	0161 236 1840
Holdsworth Mr James Arthur	Temple Garden Chambers, London	020 7583 1315
Hollow Mr Paul John	Fenners Chambers, Cambridge	01223 368761
Holmes-Milner Mr James Neil	The Chambers of Grahame Aldous QC, London	020 7832 0500
Holt Miss Abigail Claire	Lincoln House Chambers, Manchester	0161 832 5701
Hormaeche Miss Alejandra	Tanfield Chambers, London	020 7421 5300
Horne-Roberts Mrs Jennifer	Goldsmith Chambers, London	020 7353 6802
Howard Miss Amanda Jayne	Atlantic Chambers, Liverpool	0151 236 4421
	37 Park Square Chambers, Leeds	0113 243 9422
Howard Mr Robin William John	Fenners Chambers, Cambridge	01223 368761
Hussain Mr Muhammad Altaf	Chambers of Mr M A Hussain, London	020 8679 2398
Hussain Mr Tasaddat	Broadway House Chambers, Bradford	01274 722560
	Broadway House Chambers, Leeds	0113 246 2600
Hutchin Mr Edward Alister David	Temple Garden Chambers, London	020 7583 1315
Hutchinson Mr Colin Thomas	Garden Court Chambers, London	020 7993 7600
Hymanson Miss Deanna Susan	Cobden House Chambers, Manchester	0161 833 6000
Ismail Miss Nazmun Nisha	Central Chambers, Manchester	0161 236 1133
	No5 Chambers, Birmingham	0845 210 5555
	No5 Chambers, Bristol	0845 210 5555
	No5 Chambers, London	0845 210 5555
Jackson Mr Christopher Marshall	Liverpool Civil Law, Liverpool	0151 242 0500
Jafar Mr Abdurahman Akhtar	Chambers of Mr Abdurahman Jafar, Ilford	07828 937338
Jayakrishnan Mr Harry Sisubalan	Trent Chambers, Nottingham	0115 941 9596
Jefferies Mr Andrew	Dyers Chambers, London	020 7404 1881
	Westgate Chambers, Lewes	01273 480510
Jenkins Mr David Crofton	2 King's Bench Walk, London	020 7353 1746
Jenkins Mr Hywel Iestyn	Outer Temple Chambers, London	020 7353 6381
Joffe Ms Natasha Juliet Louise	Outer Temple Chambers, London	020 7353 6381
John Mr Thomas Huw	Goresbrook Chambers, Milton Keynes	0845 123 1234
Johnson Miss Laura Wendy	1 Chancery Lane, London	0845 634 6666
Jones Mr Alun	St Paul's Chambers, Leeds	0113 245 5866
Jones Mr Geraint Anthony	New Walk Chambers, Leicester	0871 200 1298/0116 255 9144
	9 St John Street, Manchester	0161 955 9000
	Tanfield Chambers, London	020 7421 5300
Jones Mr Ian Harvey	Holbrook Chambers, Leicester	07771 961962
Jones Mrs Hettie Georgia	Liberty Chambers, Tenby	01834 844458
Joshi Mr Pramod Kumar	One Essex Court, London	020 7936 3030
Josling Mr William Henry Charles	37 Park Square Chambers, Leeds	0113 243 9422
Jowett Mr Timothy David Christian	9 Park Place, Cardiff	029 2038 2731

Barrister	Chambers	Telephone
Kee Mr Peter William	Becket Chambers, Canterbury	01227 786331
Kelly Mr Matthias John	39 Essex Street, London	020 7832 1111
Kemp Mr James Rupert	Trinity Chambers, Middlesbrough	01642 247569
	Trinity Chambers, Newcastle Upon Tyne	0191 232 1927
Kennedy Mr Christopher Laurence Paul	9 St John Street, Manchester	0161 955 9000
Kent Mr Michael Harcourt	Crown Office Chambers, London	020 7797 8100
Khalid Mr James	Goulds Green Chambers, Uxbridge	01895 422574
	Goulds Green Chambers, Uxbridge	01895 422574
Khan Dr Alexander	Coral House, Manchester	
Khan Mr Abdul Aleem	Gray's Chambers, Newbury	020 8518 2525
Khan Mr Ayoub	Chambers of Mr Ayoub Khan, Birmingham	07930 987202
Khan Mr Imran	St Albans Chambers, St Albans	01727 843383
Khan Mr Tariq Ali	Chambers of Mr T A Khan, Coventry	02476 666 400
Kidd Mr Peter William	Number 7 Harrington Street Chambers, Liverpool	0151 242 0707
Kirk Mr Thomas Sean Robinson	12 College Place, Southampton	023 8032 0320
Kirtley Mr Paul George	Exchange Chambers, Leeds	0113 203 1970
	Exchange Chambers, Liverpool	0151 236 7747
	Littleton Chambers, London	020 7797 8600
Kitzing Miss Susanna Loraine	Park Court Chambers, Leeds	0113 243 3277
Knight Mr Keith Leslie Francis	4 King's Bench Walk, London	020 7822 7000
Kramer Mr Philip Anthony	Park Lane Plowden, Newcastle Upon Tyne	0191 211 4087
Kwiatkowski Mr Feliks Jerzy	Kew Chambers, Kew	0844 8099991
Lamb Mr Jeffrey Thomas	Westgate Chambers, Lewes	01273 480510
Lane Mr Christopher Paul	No 8 Chambers, Birmingham	0121 236 5514
Laughland Mr James Russell	Temple Garden Chambers, London	020 7583 1315
Lawrence Miss Pamela Avril	Nexus Chambers, London	020 7404 1147/020 7831 8309
Lawson Mr Andrew Charles	St Johns Buildings, Manchester	0161 214 1500
	St Johns Buildings Liverpool, Liverpool	0151 243 6000
	16 Winckley Square, Preston	01772 256100
Lee Mr Rosslyn Alexander	Dere Street Barristers, York	0844 3351551
	York Chambers, Newcastle Upon Tyne	0191 206 4677
Lenaghan Mr Anthony	Dyers Chambers, London	020 7404 1881
Lewis Mr Wayne Anthony	Access Lawyers, London	020 8801 2345
Ley Mr Spencer	Farrar's Building, London	020 7583 9241
Lippold Ms Sarah Ida Louise	13 KBW, Oxford	01865 311066
	13 King's Bench Walk, London	020 7353 7204
Livesey Mr John William Allan	Albion Chambers, Bristol	0117 927 2144
Livingstone Mr Simon John	Thomas More Chambers, London	020 7404 7000
Lloyd Mr John Nesbitt	Rougemont Chambers, Exeter	01392 208484
Lofthouse Mr James	1 Gray's Inn Square, London	020 7405 0001
Lopez Mr Paul Anthony	St Ive's Chambers, Birmingham	0121 236 0863
Lyons Miss Tara Yasmin	Pump Court Chambers, London	020 7353 0711
	Pump Court Chambers, Winchester	01962 868 161
	Riverview Chambers, London	0844 225 3999
Mahmood Mr Abid	Central Chambers, Manchester	0161 236 1133
	No5 Chambers, Birmingham	0845 210 5555
	No5 Chambers, Bristol	0845 210 5555
	No5 Chambers, London	0845 210 5555
Mahmood Mr Imran Waseem	5 Pump Court, London	020 7353 2532
Mahtab Miss Sumita Laila-Al	7 Bell Yard, London	020 7831 0636
Maitland Jones Mr Mark Griffith	13 KBW, Oxford	01865 311066
	13 King's Bench Walk, London	020 7353 7204
Maitland Mr Marc Claude	King's Bench Chambers, Bournemouth	01202 250025
Malik Miss Sarah	Hardwicke, London	020 7242 2523
Mallett Mr Simon Jeremy	KBW, Leeds	0113 297 1200
Mankau Mrs Louise	Tanfield Chambers, London	020 7421 5300
Mann Mr Christopher	13 KBW, Oxford	01865 311066
	13 King's Bench Walk, London	020 7353 7204

Margo Mr Saul Nicholas	Outer Temple Chambers, London	020 7353 6381
Marks Mr Jonathan Clive	4 Pump Court, London	020 7842 5555
Marshall Miss Vanessa Juliette	Seven Bedford Row, London	020 7242 3555
Marshall Mr Derek Stanley	College Chambers, Southampton	023 8023 0338
Martignetti Mr Ian	Regency Chambers, Cambridge	01223 301517
	Regency Chambers, Peterborough	01733 315215
Martin Mr Bradley David	2 Temple Gardens, London	020 7822 1200
Mason Mr Ian Douglas	Amethyst Chambers, London	020 7936 4966
Matthias Mr David Huw	Francis Taylor Building, London	020 7353 8415
McCormack Mr Alan	Staple Inn Chambers, London	020 7242 5240
McCormick Mr William Thomas	Ely Place Chambers, London	020 7400 9600
McCulloch Miss Fiona Catharine Jane	Middle Temple Lane Chambers, London	020 7583 4352
McDonald Mr Brent Andrew	Old Square Chambers, Bristol	0117 930 5100
McDonald Mr John William	2 Temple Gardens, London	020 7822 1200
McGee Dr Tristan Paul	Foxhill Chambers, Penrith	01768 482710
McMorrow Mr Patrick Joseph	4 King's Bench Walk, London	020 7822 7000
McNeill Mr David Martin	Five St Andrew's Hill, London	020 7332 5400
McTague Miss Meghann Rose	2 Temple Gardens, London	020 7822 1200
Medd Mr James Powys	Crown Office Chambers, London	020 7797 8100
Mellor Miss Rachel Elizabeth	Broadway House Chambers, Bradford	01274 722560
	Broadway House Chambers, Leeds	0113 246 2600
Melville-Shreeve Mr Michael David	Walnut House, Exeter	01392 279751
Menary Mr Alexander William Christopher	KBW, Leeds	0113 297 1200
Menzies Mr Richard Mark	Lamb Chambers, London	020 7797 8300
Meredith-Hardy Mr John Octavian	Farrar's Building, London	020 7583 9241
Metzer Mr Anthony David Erwin	Argent Chambers, London	020 7556 5500
Michael Mr Nicholas	East Anglian Chambers, Chelmsford	01473 214481
	East Anglian Chambers, Colchester	01473 214481
	East Anglian Chambers, Ipswich	01473 214481
	East Anglian Chambers, Norwich	01473 214481
Michalos Miss Christina Antigone Diana	5RB, London	020 7242 2902
Miles Mr Edward Napier Tremayne	Lamb Chambers, London	020 7797 8300
Miles Mr Richard Iain	One Essex Court, London	020 7936 3030
Miller Mr Andrew	2 Temple Gardens, London	020 7822 1200
Miller Mr Ian Daukes Douglas	1 Chancery Lane, London	0845 634 6666
Mills Mr Kristian Anthony	Trinity Chambers, Middlesbrough	01642 247569
	Trinity Chambers, Newcastle Upon Tyne	0191 232 1927
Milne Mrs Arlene Joan	Cobden House Chambers, Manchester	0161 833 6000
Mitchell Mr Alistair Stephen Fabian	49 Chambers, Bridgnorth	01746 761545
Modgill Mr Alexander Jeffrey	Broadway House Chambers, Bradford	01274 722560
	Broadway House Chambers, Leeds	0113 246 2600
Moffat Mr Russell Dean	Linenhall Chambers, Chester	01244 348282
Mohammad Mr Nazar	Legis Chambers, Aylesbury	01296 431125
	No. 3 Fleet Street Chambers, London	020 7936 4474
Moore Mr James Anthony	Goldsmith Chambers, London	020 7353 6802
	39 Park Square, Leeds	0113 245 6633
Morris Mr Phillip John	9 Park Place, Cardiff	029 2038 2731
Morris Ms Johanna	Chambers of Marion Smullen and Kerim Fuad QC, London	020 7427 4400
Morton Miss Rowan Frances	Alexander Chambers, London	0845 652 0451/0854 652 0451
	Guildford Chambers, Guildford	01483 539131
Moss Mr Christopher Stephen	St Johns Buildings, Manchester	0161 214 1500
	St Johns Buildings Liverpool, Liverpool	0151 243 6000
	16 Winckley Square, Preston	01772 256100
Moss Mr Richard John	4 King's Bench Walk, London	020 7822 7000
Moulder Mr Paul John	Alexander Chambers, London	0845 652 0451/0854 652 0451
	Guildford Chambers, Guildford	01483 539131
Munir Dr Ashley Edward	Five St Andrew's Hill, London	020 7332 5400
Munro Mr Joshua Neil	Hailsham Chambers, London	020 7643 5000

Murray Mr Charles Humphrey Stewart	Rougemont Chambers, Exeter	01392 208484
Mutch Mr Iain Richard Alistair	Palmyra Chambers, Warrington	01925 444919
Nall-Cain The Hon Richard Christopher Philip	St Albans Chambers, St Albans	01727 843383
Newman Miss Rebecca Jane	Clerksroom (Taunton), Taunton	0845 083 3000
	King's Lynn Chambers, King's Lynn	01553 672 085
Newman Mr James Andrew	Ely Place Chambers, London	020 7400 9600
Newman Mr Paul	3 PB Barristers, Bournemouth	01202 292102
	3 PB Barristers, Bristol	0117 928 1520
	3 PB Barristers, London	020 7583 8055
	3 PB Barristers, Oxford	01865 793 736
	3 PB Barristers, Winchester	01962 868884
Newman Mr Timothy John	No5 Chambers, Birmingham	0845 210 5555
	No5 Chambers, Bristol	0845 210 5555
	No5 Chambers, London	0845 210 5555
Newman Mrs Veronica	Chambers of Mrs V Newman, Cardiff	029 2048 8797
Nickless Mr Jason Alan	College Chambers, Southampton	023 8023 0338
Noble Mr Philip Robert	Thomas More Chambers, London	020 7404 7000
Norman Mr Jared Simon Gregory	Field Court Chambers, London	020 7405 6114
Norton Mr Giles	Enigma Chambers, Sheffield	07779 576499
	Holborn Chambers, London	020 7242 6060
O'Brien Mr Nicholas William Wattebot	10 King's Bench Walk, London	020 7353 7742
O'Donovan Mr Kevin John	No5 Chambers, Birmingham	0845 210 5555
	No5 Chambers, Bristol	0845 210 5555
	No5 Chambers, London	0845 210 5555
Ogunbusola Mr Victor Olaniyi	Chambers of Victor Ogumbusola, Basildon	07413 634231
O'Neill Mr Jonathan Norman	Rougemont Chambers, Exeter	01392 208484
Oommen Mr Jacob	Chambers of Mr Jacob Oommen, East Barnet	07958 680272
Osborne Mr David Thomas	Chambers of Mr D T Osborne, Taunton	01823 400 705
Osborne Mr James Robert	Clerksroom (London), London	0845 083 3000
O'Toole Mr Bartholomew Vincent	5 King's Bench Walk, London	020 7353 5638
Oulton Mr Richard Arthur Courtenay	5 Essex Court, London	020 7410 2000
Owen-Thomas Mr Richard Matthew	13 KBW, Oxford	01865 311066
	13 King's Bench Walk, London	020 7353 7204
Paige Mr Richard Mark	Sovereign Chambers, Leeds	0113 245 1841
Pallo Mr Simon Russel	Bank House Chambers, Sheffield	0114 275 1223
Palmer Miss Suzanne Elizabeth Josephine	4 King's Bench Walk, London	020 7822 7000
Palmer Mr James Savill	Henderson Chambers, London	020 7583 9020
Pardoe Mr Matthew James	Dyers Chambers, London	020 7404 1881
Parker Mrs Karen Lesley	Guildhall Chambers Portsmouth, Portsmouth	023 9275 2400
Parr Mr John Edward	Cobden House Chambers, Manchester	0161 833 6000
Parry Mr Charles Robert	Pump Court Chambers, London	020 7353 0711
	Pump Court Chambers, Swindon	01793 539899
	Pump Court Chambers, Winchester	01962 868 161
Parsons Mr Andrew James	Portsmouth Barristers'Chambers, Portsmouth	023 9283 1292
Pascall Mr Matthew Stephen	Alexander Chambers, London	0845 652 0451/0854 652 0451
	Guildford Chambers, Guildford	01483 539131
Pascoe Ms Soraya	1 Gray's Inn Square, London	020 7405 0001
Pennington-Legh Mr Jonathan Piers	Field Court Chambers, London	020 7405 6114
Perry Miss Jacqueline Anne	2 Temple Gardens, London	020 7822 1200
Perry Mr Christopher Edward	Palmyra Chambers, Warrington	01925 444919
Persaud Dr Marcia Chitroutie	1 Gray's Inn Square, London	020 7405 0001
Petersen Mr Thomas James	Goldsmith Chambers, London	020 7353 6802
Pettitt Mr Robert	Northampton Chambers, Northampton	01604 636271
Philipson Miss Amy Victoria	Sovereign Chambers, Leeds	0113 245 1841
Phillips Mr Andrew Charles	Crown Office Chambers, London	020 7797 8100

Philpott Mr Anthony Luke	12 Old Square Chambers, London	020 7404 0875
Pickering Mr Simon Toby	Wilberforce Chambers, Hull	01482 323264
Pickup Mr James Kenneth	2 Hare Court, London	020 7353 3982
	Lincoln House Chambers, Manchester	0161 832 5701
Pigram Mr Christopher Stuart	East Anglian Chambers, Chelmsford	01473 214481
	East Anglian Chambers, Colchester	01473 214481
	East Anglian Chambers, Ipswich	01473 214481
Plant Mr James Richard	Farrar's Building, London	020 7583 9241
Platt Miss Heather Louise	Pump Court Chambers, London	020 7353 0711
	Pump Court Chambers, Swindon	01793 539899
	Riverview Chambers, London	0844 225 3999
Posta Mr Adrian Mark	Albion Chambers, Bristol	0117 927 2144
Powell Mr William Rhys	Regency Chambers, Cambridge	01223 301517
	Regency Chambers, Peterborough	01733 315215
Power Mr Richard Michael Arthur	Lamb Chambers, London	020 7797 8300
Quickfall Mr Roger Mark	Park Lane Plowden, Leeds	0113 228 5049
Quinn Miss Victoria Kathleen	Thomas More Chambers, London	020 7404 7000
Quirke Mr Gerard Martin	Citadel Chambers, Birmingham	0121 233 8500
Rai Miss Puneet Kaur	Thomas More Chambers, London	020 7404 7000
Rai Mr Amarjit Singh	St Philips Chambers, Birmingham	0121 246 7000
Randolph Mr Paul Leslie	Field Court Chambers, London	020 7405 6114
Read Mr Daniel James	Farrar's Building, London	020 7583 9241
Record Mrs Celia Saint Claire	Chambers of Lawrence Jones, London	020 7831 1444
Reed Mr Julian Winn	9 Park Place, Cardiff	029 2038 2731
Reed Mr Simon John	New Walk Chambers, Leicester	0871 200 1298/0116 255 9144
Rees Mr Hefin Ednyfed	39 Essex Street, London	020 7832 1111
Reevell Mr Simon Justin	39 Park Square, Leeds	0113 245 6633
Regan Mr David Robert	St John's Chambers, Bristol	0117 923 4700
Reid Miss Cheryl Louise Pegg	Temple Court Chambers, London	020 7353 7888
Reid Mr Sebastian Peter Scott	Tanfield Chambers, London	020 7421 5300
Reiff-Musgrove Miss Kaja	Dyers Chambers, London	020 7404 1881
Richards Mr Duncan James	Chambers of Mr Ami Feder, London	020 7797 7788
	Chambers of Mr Ami Feder, London	020 7797 7788
	Principal Chambers, Sevenoaks	0845 209 8080
Richardson Mr Garth Douglas Anthony	Devon Chambers, Plymouth	01752 661659
	Rougemont Chambers, Exeter	01392 208484
Rifat Mr Maurice Alan	1 Gray's Inn Square, London	020 7405 0001
Rippon Mr Simon John	Citadel Chambers, Birmingham	0121 233 8500
Ritchie Mr Andrew George	The Chambers of Grahame Aldous QC, London	020 7832 0500
Rivalland Mr Marc-Edouard	1 Chancery Lane, London	0845 634 6666
Roberts Mr Richard Vaughan	Henderson Chambers, London	020 7583 9020
Rogers Mr Daniel James	Number 7 Harrington Street Chambers, Liverpool	0151 242 0707
Rogers Mr Michael Peter	Chambers of Mr Ami Feder, London	020 7797 7788
	Chambers of Mr Ami Feder, London	020 7797 7788
Ross Mr Simon Hadleigh	Zenith Chambers, Leeds	0113 245 5438
Roy Mr Stefan Alexander Hiren	5 Pump Court, London	020 7353 2532
Rudd Mr Michael	36 Bedford Row, London	020 7421 8000
Russell Mr Graham Alexander	Citadel Chambers, Birmingham	0121 233 8500
Russell Mr Guy Jonothon	Westgate Chambers, Lewes	01273 480510
Russell Mr Thomas Charles Welldon	KCH Garden Square, Nottingham	0115 941 8851
Saifee Mr Faisal Aftaab	Thomas More Chambers, London	020 7404 7000
Salter Mr Michael Richard	Ely Place Chambers, London	020 7400 9600
Samra Miss Sharn	Broadway House Chambers, Bradford	01274 722560
	Broadway House Chambers, Leeds	0113 246 2600
Sawtell Mr David Robert Fraser	4 King's Bench Walk, London	020 7822 7000
Scally Miss Josephine Theresa Sarah	Palmyra Chambers, Warrington	01925 444919
Scott Mr Andrew David Peter	Park Lane Plowden, Leeds	0113 228 5049
Seal Mr Julius Damien	Chambers of Mr Julius Seal, London	020 7328 0158
Seeboruth Mr Royln Jean-Paul	Chambers of Royln Seeboruth, Aylesbury	01296 393329

Shamim Mr Mohammed	Clapham Law Chambers, London	020 7978 8482
Sharp Mr Christopher Francis	Harcourt Chambers, London	0844 561 7135
	Harcourt Chambers, Oxford	0844 561 7135
	St John's Chambers, Bristol	0117 923 4700
Sharpe Mr Timothy James	Temple Garden Chambers, London	020 7583 1315
Shaw Miss Joanna Elizabeth	One Essex Court, London	020 7936 3030
Shaw Mr Julian	St Johns Buildings, Chester	01244 323070
	St Johns Buildings, Manchester	0161 214 1500
	St Johns Buildings Liverpool, Liverpool	0151 243 6000
Shepherd Mr Richard Andrew John	Albion Chambers, Bristol	0117 927 2144
Shield Miss Deborah	42 Bedford Row, London	020 7831 0222
Silverton Miss Catherine Anne	Sovereign Chambers, Leeds	0113 245 1841
Skelly Mr Andrew Jon	Hardwicke, London	020 7242 2523
Skelt Mr Ian Stuart	KBW, Leeds	0113 297 1200
Skinner Mr Samuel Richard Edward	KCH Garden Square, Nottingham	0115 941 8851
Skyner Mr Robert Stephen	39 Park Square, Leeds	0113 245 6633
Small Mr John Robert	36 Bedford Row, London	020 7421 8000
Smith Mr Mark William	Aegis Chambers, Wembley	
Smith Mr Matthew Robert	Sovereign Chambers, Leeds	0113 245 1841
Smith Mr Michael David	Kenworthy's Chambers, Manchester	0161 832 4036
Smith Mr Robert Clive	1 Paper Buildings, London	020 7353 3728
	RCS Chambers, Stainton	01709 814 147
Smith Mr Robert Ian	St Paul's Chambers, Leeds	0113 245 5866
Smith Mr Roger Hugh Traylen	No5 Chambers, Birmingham	0845 210 5555
	No5 Chambers, Bristol	0845 210 5555
	No5 Chambers, London	0845 210 5555
Snook Mr Harry Benedick	St Albans Chambers, St Albans	01727 843383
Sood Mrs Usha Rani	Trent Chambers, Nottingham	0115 941 9596
Sparrow Mrs Marie-Claire	Holborn Chambers, London	020 7242 6060
Spencer Mr Martin Benedict	Hailsham Chambers, London	020 7643 5000
Spicer Mr Robert Haden	Frederick Place Chambers, Bristol	0117 946 7059
Sproull Mr Nicholas	Albion Chambers, Bristol	0117 927 2144
Stagg Mr Paul Andrew	1 Chancery Lane, London	0845 634 6666
Starcevic Mr Petar	St Philips Chambers, Birmingham	0121 246 7000
Starr Mrs Teresa Margaret	Great James Street Chambers, London	020 7440 4949
Stead Mr Richard James	St John's Chambers, Bristol	0117 923 4700
Stebbings Mr Ian Anthony	1 Gray's Inn Square, London	020 7405 0001
Stephens Mr Michael Allen	Design Chambers, London	020 7353 0747
	St Ive's Chambers, Birmingham	0121 236 0863
Stephenson Mr David Matthew	1 Mitre Court Buildings, London	020 7452 8900
Stevenson Mr Robert Lloyd	Sovereign Chambers, Leeds	0113 245 1841
Stewart Mr Richard Paul	Lamb Chambers, London	020 7797 8300
Strelitz Mr Paul Stephen	East Anglian Chambers, Chelmsford	01473 214481
	East Anglian Chambers, Colchester	01473 214481
	East Anglian Chambers, Ipswich	01473 214481
Stride Mr Lionel Alexander	Temple Garden Chambers, London	020 7583 1315
Sutherland Mr James More	Nexus Chambers, London	020 7404 1147/020 7831 8309
Syril Mr George Carmel	Luton Chambers, Luton	01582 598394
	Willesden Chambers, London	020 3273 1042
Taft Mr Christopher Heiton	St James's Chambers, Manchester	0161 834 7000
Talbot Mr Jack Richard	Dyers Chambers, London	020 7404 1881
Tarbitt Mr Nicholas Edward Henry	Cornwall Street Chambers, Birmingham	0121 233 7500
Taussig Mr Gurion	The Chambers of Grahame Aldous QC, London	020 7832 0500
Tavares Mr Nathan Warren	Outer Temple Chambers, London	020 7353 6381
Taylor Miss Eve Rebecca	St John's Chambers, Bristol	0117 923 4700
Taylor Mr Phillip Brian	Richmond Green Chambers, Richmond	020 8948 4801
Thomas Mr Andrew Martin	Lincoln House Chambers, Manchester	0161 832 5701
	Linenhall Chambers, Chester	01244 348282
Thomas Mr Gareth	Atlantic Chambers, Liverpool	0151 236 4421
Thomas Mr Mark David	5 Essex Court, London	020 7410 2000

Name	Chambers	Telephone
Thompson Mr Ryan Jerome	Dyers Chambers, London	020 7404 1881
Ticciati Mr Oliver	4 Pump Court, London	020 7842 5555
Tomlinson Mr Michael James	3 PB Barristers, Bournemouth	01202 292102
	3 PB Barristers, Bristol	0117 928 1520
	3 PB Barristers, London	020 7583 8055
	3 PB Barristers, Oxford	01865 793 736
	3 PB Barristers, Winchester	01962 868884
Tompkinson Miss Deborah Ann	Clerksroom (London), London	0845 083 3000
	Clerksroom (Taunton), Taunton	0845 083 3000
Treharne Mr Neil Simon	Dingle Chambers, Bristol	07818 827754
Tresman Mr Lewis Robert Simon	Staple Inn Chambers, London	020 7242 5240
Treverton-Jones Mr Gregory Dennis	39 Essex Street, London	020 7832 1111
	82 King Street, Manchester	0161 870 9969
Trumpington Mr John Henry	Staple Inn Chambers, London	020 7242 5240
Trusted Mr James Harry	Outer Temple Chambers, London	020 7353 6381
Tucker Mr James William Richard	Teucro Chambers, Epsom	
Tunley Mr James Christopher Gordon	4 KBW, London	020 7822 8822
Turner Mr Justyn Robert Surtees	4 King's Bench Walk, London	020 7822 7000
Twine Miss Nicola	Park Lane Plowden, Leeds	0113 228 5049
Vaitilingam Mr Adam Skanda	Albion Chambers, Bristol	0117 927 2144
Van Der Leij Dr Martina	Field Court Chambers, London	020 7405 6114
Vasilescu Mr Andrei Constantin	Chambers of Martin Burr, London	0845 123 1234
Vaughan Mr Terence Paul	Fenners Chambers, Cambridge	01223 368761
Vollenweider Mr Amiot Marcus Ellerton	Thomas More Chambers, London	020 7404 7000
Wagstaff Mr Andrew Martin Nicholas	Westgate Chambers, Lewes	01273 480510
Waley Mr Eric Richard Thomas	Assize Court Chambers, Bristol	0117 926 4587
Walji Miss Shabnam	Regency Chambers, Cambridge	01223 301517
	Regency Chambers, Peterborough	01733 315215
Walker Mr Adam Nigel	Seven Bedford Row, London	020 7242 3555
Walker-Nolan Mr Benjamin	Thomas More Chambers, London	020 7404 7000
Wastall Mr Andrew James Frederick	Park Court Chambers, Leeds	0113 243 3277
Watson Mr Duncan Allen	Westgate Chambers, Lewes	01273 480510
Webster Mr Keith	4 King's Bench Walk, London	020 7822 7000
Welch Mr Robert William	Unity Street Chambers, Bristol	0117 906 9789
Wells Mr Caspar John Mowlem	Goldsmith Chambers, London	020 7353 6802
Wheaton Mr Ian Malcolm James	Eighteen Carlton Crescent, Southampton	023 8063 9001
White Mr Matthew James	St John's Chambers, Bristol	0117 923 4700
White Mr Peter-John Spencer	Great Barford Chambers, Bedford	012134 870004
Whitehouse Mr Stuart Colin	Goldsmith Chambers, London	020 7353 6802
Whyatt Mr Michael George	15 Winckley Square, Preston	01772 252828
Whyte Miss Monica Patricia	42 Bedford Row, London	020 7831 0222
Widdett Ms Ceri Louise	Park Court Chambers, Leeds	0113 243 3277
Wightwick Mr Iain	Riverview Chambers, London	0844 225 3999
	Unity Street Chambers, Bristol	0117 906 9789
Willer Mr Robert Michael	Ely Place Chambers, London	020 7400 9600
Willetts Mr Andrew Philip	King's Bench and Godolphin (KBG)Chambers, Plymouth	01752 221551
	New Walk Chambers, Leicester	0871 200 1298/0116 255 9144
Williams Miss June Cleo	No 8 Chambers, Birmingham	0121 236 5514
Williams Mr Mark John	Queen Square Chambers, Bristol	0117 921 1966
Wills Miss Alexandra Itari	Christ Church Chambers, London	020 7409 5278/07788 512787
Wilson Mr Richard Carver	36 Bedford Row, London	020 7421 8000
Wilton Mr Simon Daniel	Hailsham Chambers, London	020 7643 5000
Winn-Smith Mr Matthew	Lamb Chambers, London	020 7797 8300
Winstone The Hon Anne Hilary Welch	Old Square Chambers, Bristol	0117 930 5100
	Old Square Chambers, London	020 7269 0300
Wood Miss Caroline Sarah	Sovereign Chambers, Leeds	0113 245 1841

Wood Mr Richard Michael	East Anglian Chambers, Chelmsford	01473 214481
	East Anglian Chambers, Ipswich	01473 214481
	East Anglian Chambers, Norwich	01473 214481
Worrall Mr Philip George	Kew Chambers, Kew	0844 8099991
Wrottesley Miss Angela Jane	Bank House Chambers, Sheffield	0114 275 1223
Wylie Mr Neil Richard	KCH Garden Square, Nottingham	0115 941 8851
Yell Mr Nicholas Anthony	1 Chancery Lane, London	0845 634 6666
Young Mr Lee Terence	Eighteen Carlton Crescent, Southampton	023 8063 9001
Young Mr Martin Ford	9 Stone Buildings, London	020 7404 5055

PRIVATE INTERNATIONAL

Abasheikh Mr Omar Said Imam	Paragon Chambers, London	020 3318 9988
Ahmed Mr Ishfaq	Stone Chambers, London	020 7440 6900
Ajaz Mr Mohammad Arshad	Eastmans Chambers, Reading	0118 966 9094
Algazy Mr Jacques Max	Cloisters, London	020 7827 4000
Aliker Mr Phillip Bliss	Tanfield Chambers, London	020 7421 5300
Arkhurst Mr Reginald Leon	4 King's Bench Walk, London	020 7822 7000
Artesi Miss Desiree Allison Ann	Thomas More Chambers, London	020 7404 7000
Arthur Mr Stephen Joseph	Temple Tax Chambers, London	020 7353 7884
Aswani Mr Ravi Girdharilal	Stone Chambers, London	020 7440 6900
Azhar Mr Ali Mohammad	9 King's Bench Walk, London	020 7353 9564
Berkin Mr Martyn David Maurice	Crown Office Chambers, London	020 7797 8100
Bezzam Miss Jayashree	Hampton Court Chambers, West Molesey	020 8979 0381
Bowsher Mr Michael Frederick Thomas	Monckton Chambers, London	020 7405 7211
Brunner Mr Peter Roland	Brick Court Chambers, London	020 7379 3550
Buchan Miss Caroline Venetia	Chambers of Miss C Buchan, Haywards Heath	01444 482222
Butler Mr Rupert James	3 Hare Court, London	020 7415 7800
Buttimore Mr Gabriel	13 KBW, Oxford	01865 311066
	13 King's Bench Walk, London	020 7353 7204
Cala Dr Guiseppe	New Court, London	020 7583 5123
Carney Miss Caroline Mary	QEB Hollis Whiteman, London	020 7933 8855
Castle Mr Peter Bolton	13 Old Square Chambers, London	020 7831 4445
Chern Mr Cyril	Crown Office Chambers, London	020 7797 8100
Chowdhary Mr Islamuddin	Cassian Chambers, Ilford	07796 262641
Chute Ms Andrea Alexandra	Rougemont Chambers, Exeter	01392 208484
	Tooks Chambers, London	020 7842 7575
Clark Miss Geraldine	Serle Court, London	020 7242 6105
Colbey Mr Richard	Guildhall Chambers Portsmouth, Portsmouth	023 9275 2400
	Lamb Chambers, London	020 7797 8300
Coster Mr Ronald David	42 Bedford Row, London	020 7831 0222
Crowley Mr Daniel John	2 Temple Gardens, London	020 7822 1200
Dalby Mr Joseph Francis	4-5 Gray's Inn Square, London	020 7404 5252
Davies Ms Samantha Teresa	Chambers of Ms Samantha Davies, Milton Keynes	0845 123 1234
	Warwick House Chambers, London	020 7430 2323
Devine Mr Michael Buxton	Rougemont Chambers, Exeter	01392 208484
Dillon Mr Thomas William Matthew	Chambers of Thomas Dillon, London	020 7692 2722
Dipré Mr Paul Nicholas Amadeus	Chambers of Mr P N Dipré, Address withheld	0845 123 1234
	MK Family Law Chambers, Milton Keynes	0845 123 1234
Fowles Mr Jonathan James	Serle Court, London	020 7242 6105
Gibbons Miss Mary Regina	Stone Chambers, London	020 7440 6900
Gill Mr Manjit Singh	No5 Chambers, Birmingham	0845 210 5555
	No5 Chambers, Bristol	0845 210 5555
	No5 Chambers, London	0845 210 5555
Green Miss Alison Anne	2 Temple Gardens, London	020 7822 1200
Green Mr Patrick Curtis	Henderson Chambers, London	020 7583 9020
Hackett Mr Philip George	Argent Chambers, London	020 7556 5500

C

Harris Mr Wilbert Arthurlyn	Rowchester Chambers, Birmingham	0121 233 2327
Hilton Ms Saisampan	Holborn Chambers, London	020 7242 6060
Hossain Mr Ajmalul	Selborne Chambers, London	020 7420 9500
	St Philips Chambers, Birmingham	0121 246 7000
Howells Mr Stephen John	Stone Chambers, London	020 7440 6900
Hunt Mr Stephen	4 Stone Buildings, London	020 7242 5524
Hussain Mr Muhammad Altaf	Chambers of Mr M A Hussain, London	020 8679 2398
Iyer Miss Shobana	Swan Chambers, Richmond	0845 123 1234
Johnson Mr Phillip Michael	Chambers of Mr P Johnson, London	020 7288 2256
Keel Mr Douglas Vincent	11 Stone Buildings, London	020 7831 6381
Khalil Mr Karim Shakir	Octagon House, Norwich	01603 623186
	1 Paper Buildings, London	020 7353 3728
King Mr Gelaga Perry	2 Bedford Row, London	020 7440 8888
Kwiatkowski Mr Feliks Jerzy	Kew Chambers, Kew	0844 8099991
Latymer Mr Tam	Chambers of Tam Latymer, London	020 7353 2795
Le Poidevin Mr Nicholas Peter	New Square Chambers, London	020 7419 8000
Lenon Mr Andrew Ralph Fitzmaurice	One Essex Court, London	020 7583 2000
Lewiecki Miss Marie	Old Bailey Chambers, London	020 3008 6404
Lodge Mr Hugo Daniel Paul	Atkinson Bevan Chambers, London	020 7353 2112
MacKenzie Smith Mrs Catherine Joanna	10 King's Bench Walk, London	020 7353 7742
Matthias Mr David Huw	Francis Taylor Building, London	020 7353 8415
McDonnell Mr John Beresford William	13 Old Square Chambers, London	020 7831 4445
McLinden Mr John Vincent Barry	Field Court Chambers, London	020 7405 6114
Metcalfe Dr Eric William	Monckton Chambers, London	020 7405 7211
Morgan Dr Austen Jude	33 Bedford Row, London	020 7242 6476
Normington Mr James Adam	Park Court Chambers, Leeds	0113 243 3277
O'Connor Mr Patrick Michael Joseph	Doughty Street Chambers, Bristol	01179 058 717
	Doughty Street Chambers, London	020 7404 1313
	Doughty Street Chambers, Manchester	0161 618 1066
Ogunbusola Mr Victor Olaniyi	Chambers of Victor Ogumbusola, Basildon	07413 634231
O'Sullivan Mr Richard John	1215 Chambers, London	020 3291 1215
Padfield Mr Nicholas David	Chambers of Nicholas Padfield QC, London	020 7351 1961
Palmer Mr Howard William Arthur	2 Temple Gardens, London	020 7822 1200
Palmer Mr James Savill	Henderson Chambers, London	020 7583 9020
Payton Mr Clifford Coningsby	Alpha Court Chambers, Leamington Spa	01926 886412
Pearce Mr Robert Edgar	Radcliffe Chambers, London	020 7831 0081
Pryke Mr Stuart	Fiduciary Legal, London	07814 495366
Quiney Mr Charles Benedictus Alexander	Crown Office Chambers, London	020 7797 8100
Reeds Mr Gareth David	Canary Wharf Chambers, London	020 7183 8011
Reffin Miss Clare Alyson	One Essex Court, London	020 7583 2000
Richman Mrs Helene Pines	Eighteen Carlton Crescent, Southampton	023 8063 9001
	9 Stone Buildings, London	020 7404 5055
	Stour Chambers, Canterbury	01227 764899
Rigney Mr Andrew James	Crown Office Chambers, London	020 7797 8100
Rinker Mr Andrew Stuart D'Artois	Chambers of Mr Andrew Rinker, London	020 7584 1091
Ritchie Mr Richard Bulkeley	XXIV Old Buildings, London	020 7691 2424
Rosemarine Mr Andrew Marc	Chambers of Mr A M Rosemarine, Manchester	0161 740 3861
Sagar Mr Leigh	New Square Chambers, London	020 7419 8000
Seeboruth Mr Royln Jean-Paul	Chambers of Royln Seeboruth, Aylesbury	01296 393329
Selvaratnam Miss Vasanti Emily Indrani	Stone Chambers, London	020 7440 6900
Sen Mr Aditya Kumar	Coram Chambers, London	020 7092 3700
Shirley Mr James Patrick	Stone Chambers, London	020 7440 6900

Simon Mr Philipp Arnold Heinrich	4 KBW, London	020 7822 8822
Singarajah Mr Frederico	1 Gray's Inn Square, London	020 7405 0001
Sjostrand Miss Ekaterina	13 Old Square Chambers, London	020 7831 4445
Sood Mrs Usha Rani	Trent Chambers, Nottingham	0115 941 9596
Sowler Mr Thomas Richard Holland	The Tax Chambers of Mr Richard Sowler TD, Douglas	07624 235000
Spalton Mr George David John	Four New Square, London	020 7822 2000
Stewart Mr Nicholas John Cameron	Ely Place Chambers, London	020 7400 9600
Tivadar Mr Daniel	3 Hare Court, London	020 7415 7800
Vaughan-Williams Mr Arthur Laurence	13 Old Square Chambers, London	020 7831 4445
Von Pommern-Peglow Dr Michael Alfred Herman Pr.	Brunswick Chambers, London	020 7353 1987
Watson-Gandy Prof Mark	13 Old Square Chambers, London	020 7831 4445
Watthey Mr James Robertson	Hardwicke, London	020 7242 2523
Wills Miss Alexandra Itari	Christ Church Chambers, London	020 7409 5278/07788 512787

PROBATE & ADMINISTRATION

Ailes Mr John Ashley	Eighteen Carlton Crescent, Southampton	023 8063 9001
Ajaz Mr Mohammad Arshad	Eastmans Chambers, Reading	0118 966 9094
Allston Mr Anthony Stanley	3 Dr Johnson's Buildings, London	020 7353 4854
Andre Mr Roger Louis	Sovereign Chambers, Leeds	0113 245 1841
Asprey Mr Nicholas	Clock Chambers, Wolverhampton	01902 313444
	Serle Court, London	020 7242 6105
Azhar Mr Ali Mohammad	9 King's Bench Walk, London	020 7353 9564
Bailey Miss Rosana Henrietta	10 King's Bench Walk, London	020 7353 7742
Bailey Mr Michael Robert	Tanfield Chambers, London	020 7421 5300
Barnes Mr Luke Clive	3 Dr Johnson's Buildings, London	020 7353 4854
Beaumont Mr Marc Clifford	9 Stone Buildings, London	020 7404 5055
	Windsor Barristers' Chambers, Windsor	01753 839321
Bleasdale Miss Marie-Claire	Radcliffe Chambers, London	020 7831 0081
Blohm Mr Leslie Adrian	St John's Chambers, Bristol	0117 923 4700
Bojarski Mr Andrzej Leonard	36 Bedford Row, London	020 7421 8000
Boyd Mr Stephen James Harvey	Selborne Chambers, London	020 7420 9500
Bragiel Mr Edward Bronislaw Henryk	Hogarth Chambers, London	020 7404 0404
Bredemear Mr Zachary Charles	1 Chancery Lane, London	0845 634 6666
Brown Mr Philip Stephen	9 Stone Buildings, London	020 7404 5055
Bryden Mr Christopher James Yuen Kang	4 King's Bench Walk, London	020 7822 7000
Buchan Miss Caroline Venetia	Chambers of Miss C Buchan, Haywards Heath	01444 482222
Buckhaven Mr Simon	Hardwicke, London	020 7242 2523
Buckle Mr Jonathan	Regency Chambers, Cambridge	01223 301517
	Regency Chambers, Peterborough	01733 315215
Buttimore Mr Gabriel	13 KBW, Oxford	01865 311066
	13 King's Bench Walk, London	020 7353 7204
Calhaem Mr Simon Malcolm	29 Bedford Row Chambers, London	020 7404 1044
Capon Mr Philip Christopher William	East Anglian Chambers, Chelmsford	01473 214481
	East Anglian Chambers, Ipswich	01473 214481
	East Anglian Chambers, Norwich	01473 214481
	St Philips Chambers, Birmingham	0121 246 7000
Carr Mr Adrian James Selden	Tanfield Chambers, London	020 7421 5300
Castle Mr Peter Bolton	13 Old Square Chambers, London	020 7831 4445
Chowdhary Mr Islamuddin	Cassian Chambers, Ilford	07796 262641
Christensen Mr Carlton	10 King's Bench Walk, London	020 7353 7742
Clarke Mr Timothy John	Cornwall Street Chambers, Birmingham	0121 233 7500
Cohen Mr Edward Mervyn	11 Stone Buildings, London	020 7831 6381
Coster Mr Ronald David	42 Bedford Row, London	020 7831 0222
Daly Mr David	Heathway Chambers, London	020 8293 0509

C

Davies Ms Samantha Teresa	Chambers of Ms Samantha Davies, Milton Keynes	0845 123 1234
	Warwick House Chambers, London	020 7430 2323
Denbin Mr Jack Arnold	Greenway, Sonning-on-Thames	0118 969 2484
Devlin Mr Bernard Joseph	Five St Andrew's Hill, London	020 7332 5400
Dickinson Mr John Finch Heneage	St John's Chambers, Bristol	0117 923 4700
Dinan-Hayward Miss Deborah Louise	Albion Chambers, Bristol	0117 927 2144
Dipré Mr Paul Nicholas Amadeus	Chambers of Mr P N Dipré, Address withheld	0845 123 1234
	MK Family Law Chambers, Milton Keynes	0845 123 1234
Dowell Mr Gregory Hamilton	Principal Chambers, Sevenoaks	0845 209 8080
Egleton Mr Richard Wildman	Pallant Chambers, Chichester	01243 784538
Eldergill Mr Edmund Malcolm	1 Pump Court, London	020 7842 7070
Esprit Mr Benoit	Barristers Chambers, London	020 3417 6461
	Legis Chambers, Aylesbury	01296 431125
Finlay Mr Darren	Sovereign Chambers, Leeds	0113 245 1841
Fitzmaurice Mr Guy Edward Christian	Staple Inn Chambers, London	020 7242 5240
Fowles Mr Jonathan James	Serle Court, London	020 7242 6105
Francis Mr Andrew James	Serle Court, London	020 7242 6105
	Zenith Chambers, Leeds	0113 245 5438
Francis Mr Richard Maurice	9 Park Place, Cardiff	029 2038 2731
Gardiner Mr William David Hugh	Holborn Chambers, London	020 7242 6060
Gold Mr Richard David	St John's Chambers, Bristol	0117 923 4700
Goldstein Mr Wayne Nathan	18 St John Street, Manchester	0161 278 1800
Gordon Mr Jeremy	Chambers of Mr Ami Feder, London	020 7797 7788
	Chambers of Mr Ami Feder, London	020 7797 7788
	Lamb Building, Brighton	01273 820490
Gore Mr Andrew Roger	Fenners Chambers, Cambridge	01223 368761
Graham Mrs Alana Nicole	Chambers of Alana Graham, Halesowen	01384 894560
	9 Stone Buildings, London	020 7404 5055
Graham-Wells Miss Alison Christine	Exchange Chambers, Leeds	0113 203 1970
	Exchange Chambers, Liverpool	0151 236 7747
	Exchange Chambers, Manchester	0161 833 2722
Greenan Miss Sarah Octavia	Zenith Chambers, Leeds	0113 245 5438
Guy Mr Richard Perran	Chambers of Mr Ami Feder, London	020 7797 7788
	King's Bench and Godolphin (KBG)Chambers, Plymouth	01752 221551
	Southernhay Chambers, Exeter	01392 255777
Hallett Miss Katherine Elizabeth	13 Old Square Chambers, London	020 7831 4445
Harris Mr David Robert	St Albans Chambers, St Albans	01727 843383
Harris Mr Melvyn	5 Essex Court, London	020 7410 2000
Haywood Dr Jennifer Margaret	Serle Court, London	020 7242 6105
Hicks Mr Edward Gordon David	Radcliffe Chambers, London	020 7831 0081
Hill Mr Piers Nicholas	37 Park Square Chambers, Leeds	0113 243 9422
Holbech Mr Charles Edward	New Square Chambers, London	020 7419 8000
Huggins Mr Toby James	Unity Street Chambers, Bristol	0117 906 9789
Hughes-Deane Ms Charlotte Barbara	Atlantic Chambers, Liverpool	0151 236 4421
Hunt Mr Stephen	4 Stone Buildings, London	020 7242 5524
Jacobson Mr Lawrence	Five Paper, London	020 7815 3200
Jones Mr Christopher David Harries	St John's Chambers, Bristol	0117 923 4700
Jones Mr Emyr Gweirydd	9 Park Place, Cardiff	029 2038 2731
Jones Mr Mark Simeon	3 Dr Johnson's Buildings, London	020 7353 4854
Jones Mr Rhys Charles Mansel	14 Gray's Inn Square, London	020 7242 0858
Joseph Mr Charles Henry	Tanfield Chambers, London	020 7421 5300
Kelly Mr Sean	Chancery House Chambers, Leeds	0113 244 6691
Kelly Mrs Amy Louise	12 College Place, Southampton	023 8032 0320
Khan Dr Alexander	Coral House, Manchester	
Khan Mr Abdul Aleem	Gray's Chambers, Newbury	020 8518 2525
Kramer Mr Philip Anthony	Park Lane Plowden, Newcastle Upon Tyne	0191 211 4087

Kynoch Mr Duncan Stuart Sanderson	Selborne Chambers, London	020 7420 9500
Le Poidevin Mr Nicholas Peter	New Square Chambers, London	020 7419 8000
Learmonth Mr Alexander Robert Magnus	New Square Chambers, London	020 7419 8000
Leslie Miss Marie Rita	Albion Chambers, Bristol	0117 927 2144
Lonsdale Miss Marion Mary	Academy Chambers, London	020 8455 2503
Lowe Mr Mungo James	13 Old Square Chambers, London	020 7831 4445
Machell Mr John William	Serle Court, London	020 7242 6105
Marsden Mr Andrew Guy	East Anglian Chambers, Chelmsford	01473 214481
	East Anglian Chambers, Colchester	01473 214481
	East Anglian Chambers, Ipswich	01473 214481
	East Anglian Chambers, Norwich	01473 214481
Marshall Mr Derek Stanley	College Chambers, Southampton	023 8023 0338
Matthias Mr David Huw	Francis Taylor Building, London	020 7353 8415
McDonnell Mr John Beresford William	13 Old Square Chambers, London	020 7831 4445
McLinden Mr John Vincent Barry	Field Court Chambers, London	020 7405 6114
Meager Mrs Rowena Elisabeth	No5 Chambers, Birmingham	0845 210 5555
	No5 Chambers, Bristol	0845 210 5555
	No5 Chambers, London	0845 210 5555
Meares Mr Nigel Leslie Vellacott	11 Stone Buildings, London	020 7831 6381
Menon Mr Harigovind	New Court Chambers, Newcastle Upon Tyne	0191 232 1980
	Park Lane Plowden, Newcastle Upon Tyne	0191 211 4087
Mitchell Mr David John	No5 Chambers, Birmingham	0845 210 5555
	No5 Chambers, Bristol	0845 210 5555
	No5 Chambers, London	0845 210 5555
Monnington Mr Bruce Gilbert	Fenners Chambers, Cambridge	01223 368761
Mullen Mr Mark Robert	Radcliffe Chambers, London	020 7831 0081
Newsom Mr George Lucien	Guildhall Chambers, Bristol	0117 930 9000
Nickless Mr Jason Alan	College Chambers, Southampton	023 8023 0338
Noble Mr Philip Robert	Thomas More Chambers, London	020 7404 7000
Norman Mr Michael Charles	3 PB Barristers, Bournemouth	01202 292102
	3 PB Barristers, Bristol	0117 928 1520
	3 PB Barristers, London	020 7583 8055
	3 PB Barristers, Oxford	01865 793 736
	3 PB Barristers, Winchester	01962 868884
Normington Mr James Adam	Park Court Chambers, Leeds	0113 243 3277
Nurse Mr Gordon Bramwell William	Radcliffe Chambers, London	020 7831 0081
Ohrenstein Mr Dov	Radcliffe Chambers, London	020 7831 0081
Oommen Mr Jacob	Chambers of Mr Jacob Oommen, East Barnet	07958 680272
Osborne Mr James Robert	Clerksroom (London), London	0845 083 3000
O'Sullivan Mr Richard John	1215 Chambers, London	020 3291 1215
Panton Mr Alastair Howard	10 King's Bench Walk, London	020 7353 7742
Paton Mr Ewan William	Guildhall Chambers, Bristol	0117 930 9000
Payton Mr Clifford Coningsby	Alpha Court Chambers, Leamington Spa	01926 886412
Pearce Mr Robert Edgar	Radcliffe Chambers, London	020 7831 0081
Pithers Mr Clive Robert	Fenners Chambers, Cambridge	01223 368761
Purves Mr Gavin Bowman	Swan House, London	020 8998 3035
Quirke Mr Gerard Martin	Citadel Chambers, Birmingham	0121 233 8500
Quirke Mr James Keiron	St Philips Chambers, Birmingham	0121 246 7000
Ratcliffe Miss Frances Anne	Radcliffe Chambers, London	020 7831 0081
Richman Mrs Helene Pines	Eighteen Carlton Crescent, Southampton	023 8063 9001
	9 Stone Buildings, London	020 7404 5055
	Stour Chambers, Canterbury	01227 764899
Rinker Mr Andrew Stuart D'Artois	Chambers of Mr Andrew Rinker, London	020 7584 1091
Roberts Mr Michael Charles	Chambers of Michael Roberts, Henley-On-Thames	01844 355 655

Ross Mr Sidney David	11 Stone Buildings, London	020 7831 6381
Sagar Mr Leigh	New Square Chambers, London	020 7419 8000
Samuels Mr Leslie John	Pump Court Chambers, London	020 7353 0711
	Pump Court Chambers, Winchester	01962 868 161
	Riverview Chambers, London	0844 225 3999
Sandham Mr James Andrew	Arden Chambers, London	020 7242 4244
Saunders Miss Zoe Alice	St John's Chambers, Bristol	0117 923 4700
Sefi Mr Benedict John	Harcourt Chambers, London	0844 561 7135
	Harcourt Chambers, Oxford	0844 561 7135
Sellers Mr Graham	Atlantic Chambers, Liverpool	0151 236 4421
Sharples Mr John Edmund	St John's Chambers, Bristol	0117 923 4700
Simon Mr Philipp Arnold Heinrich	4 KBW, London	020 7822 8822
Sinclair Miss Lisa Anne	Chambers of Miss Lisa Sinclair, London	020 8946 7201
Sinclair Mr Graham Kelso	East Anglian Chambers, Colchester	01473 214481
	East Anglian Chambers, Ipswich	01473 214481
	East Anglian Chambers, Norwich	01473 214481
Sisley Mr Timothy Julian Crispin	9 Stone Buildings, London	020 7404 5055
Sjostrand Miss Ekaterina	13 Old Square Chambers, London	020 7831 4445
Smith Mr Roger Hugh Traylen	No5 Chambers, Birmingham	0845 210 5555
	No5 Chambers, Bristol	0845 210 5555
	No5 Chambers, London	0845 210 5555
Smithers Dr Roger Howard	Alexander Chambers, London	0845 652 0451/0854 652 0451
	Clerksroom (Taunton), Taunton	0845 083 3000
	Guildford Chambers, Guildford	01483 539131
Spratt-Dawson Miss Josephine Margery	Trinity Chambers, Chelmsford	01245 605040
Stenhouse Mr John Alexander	Nightingale Chambers, Wolverley	01562 851350
Sterling Mr Robert Alan	St James's Chambers, Manchester	0161 834 7000
	Zenith Chambers, Leeds	0113 245 5438
Stevens-Hoare Miss Michelle	Hardwicke, London	020 7242 2523
Stirling Mr Christopher William	Field Court Chambers, London	020 7405 6114
Styles Mr Clive Richard	Becket Chambers, Canterbury	01227 786331
Sugar Mr Simon Gareth	1 Garden Court Family Law Chambers, London	020 7797 7900
Swirsky Mr Adam Abraham Burl Bradbury	Lamb Chambers, London	020 7797 8300
Taylor Miss Araba Arba Kurankyiwa	Fenners Chambers, Cambridge	01223 368761
Tucker Mr Ashley Russell	Park Court Chambers, Leeds	0113 243 3277
Vane The Hon Christopher John Fletcher	Trinity Chambers, Middlesbrough	01642 247569
	Trinity Chambers, Newcastle Upon Tyne	0191 232 1927
Vaughan-Williams Mr Arthur Laurence	13 Old Square Chambers, London	020 7831 4445
Vernon Mr Elliot Curt	No. 3 Fleet Street Chambers, London	020 7936 4474
Wales Mr Matthew James	Guildhall Chambers, Bristol	0117 930 9000
Warner Mr David Alexander	St Philips Chambers, Birmingham	0121 246 7000
Watson Mr Ian David	3 Stone Buildings, London	020 7242 4937
Wills Miss Alexandra Itari	Christ Church Chambers, London	020 7409 5278/07788 512787
Wills-Goldingham Miss Claire Louise Margaret	Albion Chambers, Bristol	0117 927 2144

PROFESSIONAL NEGLIGENCE

Aeberli Mr Peter Dolph	3 PB Barristers, Bournemouth	01202 292102
	3 PB Barristers, Bristol	0117 928 1520
	3 PB Barristers, London	020 7583 8055
	3 PB Barristers, Oxford	01865 793 736
	3 PB Barristers, Winchester	01962 868884
Afzal Mr Fayyaz	No5 Chambers, Birmingham	0845 210 5555
	No5 Chambers, Bristol	0845 210 5555
	No5 Chambers, London	0845 210 5555
Ailes Mr John Ashley	Eighteen Carlton Crescent, Southampton	023 8063 9001

Barrister	Chambers	Telephone
Ajaz Mr Mohammad Arshad	Eastmans Chambers, Reading	0118 966 9094
Alam Ms Jan	Ropewalk Chambers, Nottingham	0115 947 2581
Alliott Mr George Beckles	Temple Garden Chambers, London	020 7583 1315
Allison Mr Simon Robert	Hardwicke, London	020 7242 2523
Aly Miss Sheila	Warwick House Chambers, London	020 7430 2323
Andre Mr Roger Louis	Sovereign Chambers, Leeds	0113 245 1841
Angammana Mr Gamini Bertram	Chambers of Gamini Angammana, London	020 8771 5205
Ansell Miss Rachel Louise	4 Pump Court, London	020 7842 5555
Arnheim Dr Michael Thomas Walter	Chambers of Dr Michael Arnheim, London	020 7833 5093
	Holborn Chambers, London	020 7242 6060
	Principal Chambers, Sevenoaks	0845 209 8080
Ash Mr Edward William	Chambers of Mr Edward Ash, Elsworth	01954 267674
Ashford-Thom Mr Ian	3 PB Barristers, London	020 7583 8055
	Temple Garden Chambers, London	020 7583 1315
Askey Mr Robert John	Palmyra Chambers, Warrington	01925 444919
Asprey Mr Nicholas	Clock Chambers, Wolverhampton	01902 313444
	Serle Court, London	020 7242 6105
Aswani Mr Ravi Girdharilal	Stone Chambers, London	020 7440 6900
Badejo Mr Abimbola Rafiu	5 Pump Court, London	020 7353 2532
Bailey Mr Russell Stuart	No5 Chambers, Birmingham	0845 210 5555
	No5 Chambers, Bristol	0845 210 5555
	No5 Chambers, London	0845 210 5555
Bailey Mr Thomas Iain	Chambers of Mr Thomas Bailey, Milton Keynes	07983 447117
Baldwin Dr Timothy John	Garden Court Chambers, London	020 7993 7600
Barnard Mr James Philip	11 Stone Buildings, London	020 7831 6381
Barwise Miss Stephanie Nicola	Atkin Chambers, London	020 7404 0102
Beaumont Mr Marc Clifford	9 Stone Buildings, London	020 7404 5055
	Windsor Barristers' Chambers, Windsor	01753 839321
Becker Mr Timothy George Christie	Chambers of Mr Timothy Becker, Liverpool	0151 703 0319
	Clerksroom (London), London	0845 083 3000
Bell Mr Thomas Capel	Hardwicke, London	020 7242 2523
Bellamy Mr Jonathan Mark	39 Essex Street, London	020 7832 1111
	82 King Street, Manchester	0161 870 9969
Bennett Miss Emma Louise	Exchange Chambers, Leeds	0113 203 1970
	Exchange Chambers, Liverpool	0151 236 7747
	Exchange Chambers, Manchester	0161 833 2722
Bennion-Pedley Mr Edward	13 KBW, Oxford	01865 311066
	13 King's Bench Walk, London	020 7353 7204
Benson Mr Imran Michael Jafarey	Hailsham Chambers, London	020 7643 5000
Berkley Mr David Nahum	1 Gray's Inn Square, London	020 7405 0001
	St Johns Buildings, Chester	01244 323070
	St Johns Buildings, Manchester	0161 214 1500
	St Johns Buildings Liverpool, Liverpool	0151 243 6000
Berkley Mr Michael Stuart	Rougemont Chambers, Exeter	01392 208484
Bhattacharyya Mr Ardhendu	Slough Barristers Chamber, Slough	01753 553806
Birch Mr Roger Allen	Five St Andrew's Hill, London	020 7332 5400
	Sovereign Chambers, Leeds	0113 245 1841
Bishop Mr Malcolm Leslie	Argent Chambers, London	020 7556 5500
	Equity Chambers, Birmingham	0121 236 5007
	30 Park Place, Cardiff	029 2039 8421
Blackmore Mr John Hugh	St John's Chambers, Bristol	0117 923 4700
Bleasdale Miss Marie-Claire	Radcliffe Chambers, London	020 7831 0081
Blohm Mr Leslie Adrian	St John's Chambers, Bristol	0117 923 4700
Bloom Dr Margaret	Hardwicke, London	020 7242 2523
Bogle Mr James Stewart Lockhart	10 King's Bench Walk, London	020 7353 7742
Boulding Mr Philip Vincent	Keating Chambers, London	020 7544 2600
Bourne Mr Charles Gregory	4-5 Gray's Inn Square, London	020 7404 5252

Bourne Mr Geoffrey Robert	13 Old Square Chambers, London	020 7831 4445
Bowen Mr Nicholas James Hugh	Doughty Street Chambers, Bristol	01179 058 717
	Doughty Street Chambers, London	020 7404 1313
	Doughty Street Chambers, Manchester	0161 618 1066
Bowling Mr James Stuart	4 Pump Court, London	020 7842 5555
Boyd Mr Stephen James Harvey	Selborne Chambers, London	020 7420 9500
Bragge Mr Thomas Hereward	Stour Chambers, Canterbury	01227 764899
Bragiel Mr Edward Bronislaw Henryk	Hogarth Chambers, London	020 7404 0404
Branchflower Mr George	Zenith Chambers, Leeds	0113 245 5438
Bredemear Mr Zachary Charles	1 Chancery Lane, London	0845 634 6666
Brittain Mr Marc John	1 Gray's Inn Square, London	020 7405 0001
Brown Mr Simon Jonathan	Crown Office Chambers, London	020 7797 8100
Bruce Mr Andrew Jonathan	Serle Court, London	020 7242 6105
Brunner Mr Peter Roland	Brick Court Chambers, London	020 7379 3550
Bryant Mr Keith	Outer Temple Chambers, London	020 7353 6381
Bryden Mr Christopher James Yuen Kang	4 King's Bench Walk, London	020 7822 7000
Buchan Miss Caroline Venetia	Chambers of Miss C Buchan, Haywards Heath	01444 482222
Buchan Mr Andrew	Cloisters, London	020 7827 4000
Buckhaven Mr Simon	Hardwicke, London	020 7242 2523
Buckley Mr Peter Evered	Cobden House Chambers, Manchester	0161 833 6000
Budworth Mr Martin James	Kings Chambers, Birmingham	0845 034 3444
	Kings Chambers, Leeds	0845 034 3444
	Kings Chambers, Manchester	0845 034 3444
Budworth Mr Richard Dutton	2-3 Hind Court Chambers, London	020 7822 2150
Bullock Mr Robert Gustaf	The Chambers of Mr Bullock, Brighton	01273 321050
Burns Mr Jeremy Stuart	12 College Place, Southampton	023 8032 0320
Burr Mr Andrew Charles	Atkin Chambers, London	020 7404 0102
Busuttil Mr Godwin John Antoine	5RB, London	020 7242 2902
Buswell Mr Richard Thomas	Hardwicke, London	020 7242 2523
Butler Mr Rupert James	3 Hare Court, London	020 7415 7800
Buttimore Mr Gabriel	13 KBW, Oxford	01865 311066
	13 King's Bench Walk, London	020 7353 7204
Campbell Mr Oliver Edward Wilhelm	Henderson Chambers, London	020 7583 9020
Cant Mr Christopher Ian	9 Stone Buildings, London	020 7404 5055
Capon Mr Philip Christopher William	East Anglian Chambers, Chelmsford	01473 214481
	East Anglian Chambers, Ipswich	01473 214481
	East Anglian Chambers, Norwich	01473 214481
	St Philips Chambers, Birmingham	0121 246 7000
Carney Miss Caroline Mary	QEB Hollis Whiteman, London	020 7933 8855
Castle Mr Peter Bolton	13 Old Square Chambers, London	020 7831 4445
Cattermull Miss Emma Jayne	East Anglian Chambers, Chelmsford	01473 214481
	East Anglian Chambers, Ipswich	01473 214481
	East Anglian Chambers, Norwich	01473 214481
Caun Mr Lawrence	Lamb Chambers, London	020 7797 8300
Cawsey Mr Barry Donald	Clerksroom (London), London	0845 083 3000
	Clerksroom (Taunton), Taunton	0845 083 3000
Challenger Mr Colin Westcott	Lamb Chambers, London	020 7797 8300
Chambers Miss Gaynor Marie	Keating Chambers, London	020 7544 2600
Chowdhary Mr Islamuddin	Cassian Chambers, Ilford	07796 262641
Christensen Mr Carlton	10 King's Bench Walk, London	020 7353 7742
Christie Mr David Henderson	Seven Bedford Row, London	020 7242 3555
Chute Ms Andrea Alexandra	Rougemont Chambers, Exeter	01392 208484
	Tooks Chambers, London	020 7842 7575
Clark Miss Geraldine	Serle Court, London	020 7242 6105
Clark Mr Andrew Richard	9 St John Street, Manchester	0161 955 9000
Clarke Mr George Robert Ivan	5 Pump Court, London	020 7353 2532
Clarke Mr Jamie Roy	Hardwicke, London	020 7242 2523
Clement Mr Ryan Wayne	Conference Chambers, Harrow	020 8144 0134
Climie Mr Roger Stephen	King's Bench and Godolphin (KBG)Chambers, Plymouth	01752 221551
	Outer Temple Chambers, London	020 7353 6381

Barrister	Chambers	Telephone
Coates Mr George Alexander Nigel	Guildford Chambers, Guildford	01483 539131
Cohen Mr Edward Mervyn	11 Stone Buildings, London	020 7831 6381
Cohen Mr Jonathan Lionel	4 Paper Buildings, London	020 7427 5200
Collard Mr Michael David	5 Pump Court, London	020 7353 2532
Constable Mr Adam Michael	Keating Chambers, London	020 7544 2600
Corsellis Mr Nicholas Robert Alexander	3 Temple Gardens, London	020 7353 3102
Costello Mr Paul James	Chambers of Mr Paul J Costello, Biggleswade	07846 016 399
Coster Mr Ronald David	42 Bedford Row, London	020 7831 0222
Coulter Mr Barry John	Clerksroom (London), London	0845 083 3000
	Clerksroom (Taunton), Taunton	0845 083 3000
	King's Lynn Chambers, King's Lynn	01553 672 085
Counsell Mr James Henry	Outer Temple Chambers, London	020 7353 6381
Cox Miss Olivia Rodrigues	Atlantic Chambers, Liverpool	0151 236 4421
Cramsie Mr James Sinclair Beresford	13 KBW, Oxford	01865 311066
	13 King's Bench Walk, London	020 7353 7204
Crangle Mr Thomas Peter	4 Pump Court, London	020 7842 5555
Crawshaw Mr Simon Richard	Atkin Chambers, London	020 7404 0102
Crowe Mr Cameron	36 Bedford Row, London	020 7421 8000
Crowley Mr Daniel John	2 Temple Gardens, London	020 7822 1200
Curtis Mr Michael Alexander	Crown Office Chambers, London	020 7797 8100
Darling Mr Paul Antony	Keating Chambers, London	020 7544 2600
Davey Mr Charles	64 Bridge Street, Manchester	0845 083 3000
	Chambers of Mr C Davey, Bishop's Stortford	01279 506412
	Clerksroom (Taunton), Taunton	0845 083 3000
Davies Miss Carol Elizabeth	College Chambers, Southampton	023 8023 0338
Davies Mr James Edwin	3 PB Barristers, Bournemouth	01202 292102
	3 PB Barristers, Bristol	0117 928 1520
	3 PB Barristers, London	020 7583 8055
	3 PB Barristers, Oxford	01865 793 736
	3 PB Barristers, Winchester	01962 868884
Davis Mr Andrew Paul	Crown Office Chambers, London	020 7797 8100
De Berry Mr Philip John	18 St John Street, Manchester	0161 278 1800
De Jehan Mr David	Park Lane Plowden, Leeds	0113 228 5049
De Waal Mr John Henry Lowndes	Hardwicke, London	020 7242 2523
Deacon Mr Robert Murray	11 Stone Buildings, London	020 7831 6381
Dean Mr James Patrick	Goldsmith Chambers, London	020 7353 6802
Dean Mr Paul Benjamin	Crown Office Chambers, London	020 7797 8100
Dean Mr Peter Thomas	36 Bedford Row, London	020 7421 8000
Demachkie Mr Jamal	3 PB Barristers, London	020 7583 8055
Devlin Mr Bernard Joseph	Five St Andrew's Hill, London	020 7332 5400
Doerries Miss Chantal-Aimée Renee Aemelia An	Atkin Chambers, London	020 7404 0102
Douthwaite Mr Charles Philip	Four New Square, London	020 7822 2000
Dovar Mr Daniel	Tanfield Chambers, London	020 7421 5300
Du Toit Sc Mr Johan Ignatius	Selborne Chambers, London	020 7420 9500
	St Philips Chambers, Birmingham	0121 246 7000
Dyer Mr Allen Gordon	4 Pump Court, London	020 7842 5555
Earle Mr James Christopher Reginald St John	Fenners Chambers, Cambridge	01223 368761
Eastwood Miss Philippa Clemency Anne	Doughty Street Chambers, London	020 7404 1313
Edwards Mr Nigel Royston	St Paul's Chambers, Leeds	0113 245 5866
Egleton Mr Richard Wildman	Pallant Chambers, Chichester	01243 784538
Eilledge Miss Amanda Gail Caroline	11 Stone Buildings, London	020 7831 6381
Elliott Mr Timothy Stanley	Keating Chambers, London	020 7544 2600
Engelman Mr Philip	Cloisters, London	020 7827 4000
	Trinity Chambers, Middlesbrough	01642 247569
	Trinity Chambers, Newcastle Upon Tyne	0191 232 1927

Ensaff Mr Omar Sherif	No5 Chambers, Birmingham	0845 210 5555
	No5 Chambers, Bristol	0845 210 5555
	No5 Chambers, London	0845 210 5555
Evans Mr Robert Jonathan	Keating Chambers, London	020 7544 2600
Fairbank Mr Nicholas James	4 Paper Buildings, London	020 7427 5200
Falkowski Mr Damian	4-5 Gray's Inn Square, London	020 7404 5252
Farrell Mr Simon Henry	3 Raymond Buildings, London	020 7400 6400
Fellows Mr Philip David Andrew	Hardwicke, London	020 7242 2523
Ferber Ms Iris	42 Bedford Row, London	020 7831 0222
Ferm Mr Rodney Eric	Broadway House Chambers, Bradford	01274 722560
	Broadway House Chambers, Leeds	0113 246 2600
Fetto Mr Niazi Peter	2 Temple Gardens, London	020 7822 1200
Field Mr Julian Nigel	Crown Office Chambers, London	020 7797 8100
Finlay Mr Darren	Sovereign Chambers, Leeds	0113 245 1841
Fisher Mr David	New Square Chambers, London	020 7419 8000
Follon Mr Daniel Richard Thomas	1 Gray's Inn Square, London	020 7405 0001
Formby Ms Emily Jane	39 Essex Street, London	020 7832 1111
Foster Mr Charles Andrew	Outer Temple Chambers, London	020 7353 6381
Found Mr Timothy Paul	Farrar's Building, London	020 7583 9241
Francis Mr Andrew James	Serle Court, London	020 7242 6105
	Zenith Chambers, Leeds	0113 245 5438
Franklin Miss Kim	Crown Office Chambers, London	020 7797 8100
Fullerton Mr Michael Andrew	7 Bell Yard, London	020 7831 0636
	Chambers of Mr Michael Fullerton, Hove	01273 772050
Furst Mr Stephen Andrew	Keating Chambers, London	020 7544 2600
Gadd Mr Adam Brian	Pump Court Chambers, London	020 7353 0711
	Pump Court Chambers, Winchester	01962 868 161
	Riverview Chambers, London	0844 225 3999
Gallivan Mr Terence John	Five Paper, London	020 7815 3200
Galway-Cooper Dr Philip Anthony	Five St Andrew's Hill, London	020 7332 5400
Garrett Miss Lucy Margaret	Keating Chambers, London	020 7544 2600
Garvie Mr Carl Peter	St Philips Chambers, Birmingham	0121 246 7000
Gasztowicz Mr Steven	Cornerstone Barristers, London	020 7242 4986
	New Street Chambers, Leicester	0116 262 5906
Gatty Mr Daniel Simon	Hardwicke, London	020 7242 2523
Gee Mr Steven Mark	Stone Chambers, London	020 7440 6900
George Mr Nicholas Frank Raymond	New Walk Chambers, Leicester	0871 200 1298/0116 255 9144
Gersch Mr Adam Nissen	Argent Chambers, London	020 7556 5500
Giles Mr David William	1 Gray's Inn Square, London	020 7405 0001
Gillies Miss Jennie	4 Pump Court, London	020 7842 5555
Gilmore Miss Mary Seanin	Four New Square, London	020 7822 2000
Gledhill Mr Lee Andre	Alexander Chambers, London	0845 652 0451/0854 652 0451
	Trident Barristers Chambers, Manchester	0161 663 3123
Glover Mr Stephen Julian	37 Park Square Chambers, Leeds	0113 243 9422
Godfrey Mr Lauren John	Crown Office Row Chambers, Brighton	01273 625625
Godwin Mr William George Henry	3 Hare Court, London	020 7415 7800
	St John's Chambers, Bristol	0117 923 4700
Goldberg Mr Simon Ian	Trinity Chambers, Middlesbrough	01642 247569
	Trinity Chambers, Newcastle Upon Tyne	0191 232 1927
Goldstone Mr Simon Lewis	4 Pump Court, London	020 7842 5555
Goodfellow Mr Giles William Jeremy	Pump Court Tax Chambers, London	020 7414 8080
Goodfellow Mr Stephen John	East Anglian Chambers, Chelmsford	01473 214481
	East Anglian Chambers, Ipswich	01473 214481
	East Anglian Chambers, Norwich	01473 214481
Goodman Mr Andrew David	1 Chancery Lane, London	0845 634 6666
Gordon Mr Jeremy	Chambers of Mr Ami Feder, London	020 7797 7788
	Chambers of Mr Ami Feder, London	020 7797 7788
	Lamb Building, Brighton	01273 820490
Gore Mr Andrew Roger	Fenners Chambers, Cambridge	01223 368761

Gough Miss Karen Louise	Arbitration Chambers, London	020 7267 2137
	39 Essex Street, London	020 7832 1111
	82 King Street, Manchester	0161 870 9969
Graham Mrs Alana Nicole	Chambers of Alana Graham, Halesowen	01384 894560
	9 Stone Buildings, London	020 7404 5055
Grant Mr David Ericson	Outer Temple Chambers, London	020 7353 6381
Granville Stafford Mr Andrew	4 King's Bench Walk, London	020 7822 7000
Greatorex Mr Paul	4-5 Gray's Inn Square, London	020 7404 5252
Greenan Miss Sarah Octavia	Zenith Chambers, Leeds	0113 245 5438
Ground Mr Patrick	Chambers of Mr Patrick Ground QC, London	020 7736 0131
Grundy Ms Clare	St Johns Buildings, Manchester	0161 214 1500
	St Johns Buildings Liverpool, Liverpool	0151 243 6000
	16 Winckley Square, Preston	01772 256100
Gun Cuninghame Mr Julian Arthur	Gough Square Chambers, London	020 7353 0924
Gupta Mr Amit	St Philips Chambers, Birmingham	0121 246 7000
Guy Mr Richard Perran	Chambers of Mr Ami Feder, London	020 7797 7788
	King's Bench and Godolphin (KBG)Chambers, Plymouth	01752 221551
	Southernhay Chambers, Exeter	01392 255777
Hackett Mr Philip George	Argent Chambers, London	020 7556 5500
Halden Mr Angus Robert	Queen Square Chambers, Bristol	0117 921 1966
Hall Mr James Edward	Cornwall Street Chambers, Birmingham	0121 233 7500
Hamer Mr George Clemens	8 New Square, London	020 7405 4321
Hamilton Mr Gavin	3 PB Barristers, Bournemouth	01202 292102
	3 PB Barristers, Bristol	0117 928 1520
	3 PB Barristers, London	020 7583 8055
	3 PB Barristers, Oxford	01865 793 736
	3 PB Barristers, Winchester	01962 868884
Hamilton Mr Nigel	Broadway House Chambers, Bradford	01274 722560
	Broadway House Chambers, Leeds	0113 246 2600
Hamilton Mr Peter Bernard	4 Pump Court, London	020 7842 5555
Hammerton Mr Alastair Rolf	1 Chancery Lane, London	0845 634 6666
Hannaford Miss Sarah Jane	Keating Chambers, London	020 7544 2600
Hansen Mr William Joseph	No5 Chambers, Birmingham	0845 210 5555
	No5 Chambers, Bristol	0845 210 5555
	No5 Chambers, London	0845 210 5555
Hargreaves Mr Simon John Robert	Keating Chambers, London	020 7544 2600
Harris Mr James	Five St Andrew's Hill, London	020 7332 5400
Harris Mr Melvyn	5 Essex Court, London	020 7410 2000
Harrison Dr Graeme	12 College Place, Southampton	023 8032 0320
Harrison Mr John Foster	St Paul's Chambers, Leeds	0113 245 5866
Harvey Mr John Gilbert	No5 Chambers, Birmingham	0845 210 5555
	No5 Chambers, Bristol	0845 210 5555
	No5 Chambers, London	0845 210 5555
Hendron Mr Henry Joseph Christopher	Strand Chambers, London	020 7117 6920
Hewson Ms Barbara Mary	Hardwicke, London	020 7242 2523
Higginson Mr Timothy Nicholas Bennett	Littleton Chambers, London	020 7797 8600
	St John's Chambers, Bristol	0117 923 4700
Hill Mr Michael Gordon	Trinity Chambers, Middlesbrough	01642 247569
	Trinity Chambers, Newcastle Upon Tyne	0191 232 1927
Hill Mr Nicholas Mark	Pump Court Chambers, London	020 7353 0711
	Pump Court Chambers, Swindon	01793 539899
	St Philips Chambers, Birmingham	0121 246 7000
Hirst Mr Karl Douglas	No5 Chambers, Birmingham	0845 210 5555
	No5 Chambers, Bristol	0845 210 5555
	No5 Chambers, London	0845 210 5555
Hirst Mr William Timothy John	Park Lane Plowden, Leeds	0113 228 5049

Hodder Mr Philip James	Clerksroom (Taunton), Taunton	0845 083 3000
	King's Lynn Chambers, King's Lynn	01553 672 085
Hodgkiss Ms Suzanne Jane	43 Temple Row Chambers, Birmingham	0121 237 6035
Hodson Mr Matthew Paul	Farrar's Building, London	020 7583 9241
Hodson Mr Peter David	Chambers of Ian Macdonald QC, Manchester	0161 236 1840
Holbech Mr Charles Edward	New Square Chambers, London	020 7419 8000
Holdsworth Mr James Arthur	Temple Garden Chambers, London	020 7583 1315
Holland Mr Charles Christopher	Francis Taylor Building, London	020 7353 8415
	Trinity Chambers, Middlesbrough	01642 247569
	Trinity Chambers, Newcastle Upon Tyne	0191 232 1927
Holland Mr Rowan Guy	Five Paper, London	020 7815 3200
Holmes-Milner Mr James Neil	The Chambers of Grahame Aldous QC, London	020 7832 0500
Holroyd Mr John James	Zenith Chambers, Leeds	0113 245 5438
Hood Mr Nigel Anthony	New Square Chambers, London	020 7419 8000
Hornett Mr Stuart Ian	Selborne Chambers, London	020 7420 9500
Horton Mr Matthew Bethell	39 Essex Street, London	020 7832 1111
	82 King Street, Manchester	0161 870 9969
Howard Mr Robin William John	Fenners Chambers, Cambridge	01223 368761
Hubbard Mr Mark Iain	New Square Chambers, London	020 7419 8000
Hughes Mr Adrian Warwick	39 Essex Street, London	020 7832 1111
	82 King Street, Manchester	0161 870 9969
Hunt Mr Stephen	4 Stone Buildings, London	020 7242 5524
Hurst Mr Brian	39 Park Square, Leeds	0113 245 6633
Hutchinson Mr Colin Thomas	Garden Court Chambers, London	020 7993 7600
Irvin Mr Peter	Brick Court Chambers, London	020 7379 3550
Isaac Mr Nicholas Dudley	Tanfield Chambers, London	020 7421 5300
Iyer Miss Shobana	Swan Chambers, Richmond	0845 123 1234
Jackson Miss Rosemary Elizabeth	Keating Chambers, London	020 7544 2600
Jacobson Mr Lawrence	Five Paper, London	020 7815 3200
Jinadu Mr Abdul-Lateef Abodurin Olayinka	Keating Chambers, London	020 7544 2600
Joffe Ms Natasha Juliet Louise	Outer Temple Chambers, London	020 7353 6381
Johnson Miss Laura Wendy	1 Chancery Lane, London	0845 634 6666
Jones Mr Alun	St Paul's Chambers, Leeds	0113 245 5866
Jones Mr Christopher David Harries	St John's Chambers, Bristol	0117 923 4700
Jones Mr Geraint Anthony	New Walk Chambers, Leicester	0871 200 1298/0116 255 9144
	9 St John Street, Manchester	0161 955 9000
	Tanfield Chambers, London	020 7421 5300
Jones Mr Geraint Martyn	Fenners Chambers, Cambridge	01223 368761
Jones Mr Lawrence Victor	Chambers of Lawrence Jones, London	020 7831 1444
Jones Mr Richard Frederick Thomas	Heavenwood Chambers, Stroud	01453 873444
Joseph Mr Charles Henry	Tanfield Chambers, London	020 7421 5300
Joseph Mr Paul Wolfe	No5 Chambers, Birmingham	0845 210 5555
	No5 Chambers, Bristol	0845 210 5555
	No5 Chambers, London	0845 210 5555
Keel Mr Douglas Vincent	11 Stone Buildings, London	020 7831 6381
Kelly Mr Sean	Chancery House Chambers, Leeds	0113 244 6691
Kemp Mr James Rupert	Trinity Chambers, Middlesbrough	01642 247569
	Trinity Chambers, Newcastle Upon Tyne	0191 232 1927
Kennedy Mr Christopher Laurence Paul	9 St John Street, Manchester	0161 955 9000
Kenny Mr Martin William	Walnut House, Exeter	01392 279751
Kent Mr Michael Harcourt	Crown Office Chambers, London	020 7797 8100
Khan Mr Abdul Aleem	Gray's Chambers, Newbury	020 8518 2525
Kirk Mr Thomas Sean Robinson	12 College Place, Southampton	023 8032 0320
Kirtley Mr Paul George	Exchange Chambers, Leeds	0113 203 1970
	Exchange Chambers, Liverpool	0151 236 7747
	Littleton Chambers, London	020 7797 8600
Knight Mr Keith Leslie Francis	4 King's Bench Walk, London	020 7822 7000

Kramer Mr Philip Anthony	Park Lane Plowden, Newcastle Upon Tyne	0191 211 4087
Kwiatkowski Mr Feliks Jerzy	Kew Chambers, Kew	0844 8099991
Kynoch Mr Duncan Stuart Sanderson	Selborne Chambers, London	020 7420 9500
Lamb Mr Edward Charles	The Chambers of Grahame Aldous QC, London	020 7832 0500
Lamont Mr Calum	Keating Chambers, London	020 7544 2600
Lane Mr Simon Charles	Rougemont Chambers, Exeter	01392 208484
Lavin Miss Mary Mandie Jane	196 Temple Chamber, London	020 7099 9257
Lawrence The Hon Patrick John Tristram	Four New Square, London	020 7822 2000
Le Poidevin Mr Nicholas Peter	New Square Chambers, London	020 7419 8000
Leabeater Mr James Ferguson	4 Pump Court, London	020 7842 5555
Lee Miss Krista Chui Lan	Keating Chambers, London	020 7544 2600
Lemon Miss Jane Katherine	Keating Chambers, London	020 7544 2600
Lennard Mr Stephen Charles	Hardwicke, London	020 7242 2523
Lenon Mr Andrew Ralph Fitzmaurice	One Essex Court, London	020 7583 2000
Leonard Mr Charles Robert Weston	Hardwicke, London	020 7242 2523
Ley Mr Spencer	Farrar's Building, London	020 7583 9241
Lindsey Ms Susan	Crown Office Chambers, London	020 7797 8100
Lissack Mr Richard Anthony	Outer Temple Chambers, London	020 7353 6381
	Riverview Chambers, London	0844 225 3999
Littman Mr Jeffrey James	Chambers of Mr Jeffrey Littman, London	020 8922 6844
	9 Park Place, Cardiff	029 2038 2731
Livingstone Mr Simon John	Thomas More Chambers, London	020 7404 7000
Lloyd Mr John Nesbitt	Rougemont Chambers, Exeter	01392 208484
Lonsdale Miss Marion Mary	Academy Chambers, London	020 8455 2503
Lonsdale Mr David James	33 Bedford Row, London	020 7242 6476
Lord Mr Wayne Edward	Construction Chambers, Derby	01332 617 917
Lowe Mr Mungo James	13 Old Square Chambers, London	020 7831 4445
Lule Miss Jacqueline	1 Mitre Court Buildings, London	020 7452 8900
Lyons Miss Tara Yasmin	Pump Court Chambers, London	020 7353 0711
	Pump Court Chambers, Winchester	01962 868 161
	Riverview Chambers, London	0844 225 3999
Macpherson Mr Duncan Charles Stewart	One Essex Court, London	020 7936 3030
Maher Ms Martha Johanna Dorothy	St John's Chambers, Bristol	0117 923 4700
Mahmood Mr Abid	Central Chambers, Manchester	0161 236 1133
	No5 Chambers, Birmingham	0845 210 5555
	No5 Chambers, Bristol	0845 210 5555
	No5 Chambers, London	0845 210 5555
Malone Mr David John	1 Gray's Inn Square, London	020 7405 0001
Mann Mr Christopher	13 KBW, Oxford	01865 311066
	13 King's Bench Walk, London	020 7353 7204
Mantle Mr Peter John	Monckton Chambers, London	020 7405 7211
Marks Mr Jonathan Clive	4 Pump Court, London	020 7842 5555
Marsden Mr Andrew Guy	East Anglian Chambers, Chelmsford	01473 214481
	East Anglian Chambers, Colchester	01473 214481
	East Anglian Chambers, Ipswich	01473 214481
	East Anglian Chambers, Norwich	01473 214481
Marshall Miss Vanessa Juliette	Seven Bedford Row, London	020 7242 3555
Marshall Mr Derek Stanley	College Chambers, Southampton	023 8023 0338
Martin Mr Bradley David	2 Temple Gardens, London	020 7822 1200
Matthias Mr David Huw	Francis Taylor Building, London	020 7353 8415
Maugham Mr Jolyon Toby Dennis	11 New Square, London	020 7242 4017
McCann Miss Katie	Atlantic Chambers, Liverpool	0151 236 4421
McCombie Mr Fergus Alexander Paul	1 Gray's Inn Square, London	020 7405 0001
McCormick Mr William Thomas	Ely Place Chambers, London	020 7400 9600
McCue Mr Donald	11 Stone Buildings, London	020 7831 6381
McDonald Mr John William	2 Temple Gardens, London	020 7822 1200

McDonald Ms Melanie Sharon	No5 Chambers, Birmingham	0845 210 5555
	No5 Chambers, Bristol	0845 210 5555
	No5 Chambers, London	0845 210 5555
McDonnell Mr John Beresford William	13 Old Square Chambers, London	020 7831 4445
McKiernan Mr Edward Joseph	Farringdon Chambers, London	020 7089 5700
McKinney Miss Nicola Alexandra	4 KBW, London	020 7822 8822
McLinden Mr John Vincent Barry	Field Court Chambers, London	020 7405 6114
McNae Mr Jonathan James	Selborne Chambers, London	020 7420 9500
Meager Mrs Rowena Elisabeth	No5 Chambers, Birmingham	0845 210 5555
	No5 Chambers, Bristol	0845 210 5555
	No5 Chambers, London	0845 210 5555
Meares Mr Nigel Leslie Vellacott	11 Stone Buildings, London	020 7831 6381
Medd Mr James Powys	Crown Office Chambers, London	020 7797 8100
Melville-Shreeve Mr Michael David	Walnut House, Exeter	01392 279751
Menon Mr Harigovind	New Court Chambers, Newcastle Upon Tyne	0191 232 1980
	Park Lane Plowden, Newcastle Upon Tyne	0191 211 4087
Menzies Mr Richard Mark	Lamb Chambers, London	020 7797 8300
Meredith-Hardy Mr John Octavian	Farrar's Building, London	020 7583 9241
Metzer Mr Anthony David Erwin	Argent Chambers, London	020 7556 5500
Michalos Miss Christina Antigone Diana	5RB, London	020 7242 2902
Miles Mr Richard Iain	One Essex Court, London	020 7936 3030
Miller Mr Andrew	2 Temple Gardens, London	020 7822 1200
Miller Mr Ian Daukes Douglas	1 Chancery Lane, London	0845 634 6666
Milne Mrs Arlene Joan	Cobden House Chambers, Manchester	0161 833 6000
Monnington Mr Bruce Gilbert	Fenners Chambers, Cambridge	01223 368761
Mort Mr Justin John Glasbrook	Keating Chambers, London	020 7544 2600
Morton Miss Rowan Frances	Alexander Chambers, London	0845 652 0451/0854 652 0451
	Guildford Chambers, Guildford	01483 539131
Muir Miss Nicola Jane	Hardwicke, London	020 7242 2523
Munro Mr Joshua Neil	Hailsham Chambers, London	020 7643 5000
Murray Mr Charles Humphrey Stewart	Rougemont Chambers, Exeter	01392 208484
Nabi Mr Sajjad	5 Pump Court, London	020 7353 2532
Newman Mr James Andrew	Ely Place Chambers, London	020 7400 9600
Newman Mr Paul	3 PB Barristers, Bournemouth	01202 292102
	3 PB Barristers, Bristol	0117 928 1520
	3 PB Barristers, London	020 7583 8055
	3 PB Barristers, Oxford	01865 793 736
	3 PB Barristers, Winchester	01962 868884
Newman Mr Timothy John	No5 Chambers, Birmingham	0845 210 5555
	No5 Chambers, Bristol	0845 210 5555
	No5 Chambers, London	0845 210 5555
Nicholson Mr Jeremy Mark	4 Pump Court, London	020 7842 5555
Nickless Mr Jason Alan	College Chambers, Southampton	023 8023 0338
Nissen Mr Alexander David	Keating Chambers, London	020 7544 2600
Noble Mr Andrew	Enterprise Chambers, Leeds	0113 246 0391
Noble Mr Philip Robert	Thomas More Chambers, London	020 7404 7000
Nolten Miss Sonia Jayne	2 Temple Gardens, London	020 7822 1200
Norton Mr Giles	Enigma Chambers, Sheffield	07779 576499
	Holborn Chambers, London	020 7242 6060
Nurse Mr Gordon Bramwell William	Radcliffe Chambers, London	020 7831 0081
O'Brien Mr Nicholas William Wattebot	10 King's Bench Walk, London	020 7353 7742
O'Connor Mr Patrick Michael Joseph	Doughty Street Chambers, Bristol	01179 058 717
	Doughty Street Chambers, London	020 7404 1313
	Doughty Street Chambers, Manchester	0161 618 1066
Ohrenstein Mr Dov	Radcliffe Chambers, London	020 7831 0081
Oliver Dr Peter James Robert	4 Pump Court, London	020 7842 5555
Ornsby Miss Suzanne Doreen	Francis Taylor Building, London	020 7353 8415
	St John's Chambers, Bristol	0117 923 4700

Osborne Mr James Robert	Clerksroom (London), London	0845 083 3000
Osborne Mr Richard	4 Pump Court, London	020 7842 5555
O'Sullivan Mr Thomas Sean Patrick	4 Pump Court, London	020 7842 5555
O'Toole Mr Bartholomew Vincent	5 King's Bench Walk, London	020 7353 5638
O'Toole Mr Simon Gerard	5 Pump Court, London	020 7353 2532
	Riverview Chambers, London	0844 225 3999
Otwal Mr Mukhtiar Singh	42 Bedford Row, London	020 7831 0222
Oulton Mr Richard Arthur Courtenay	5 Essex Court, London	020 7410 2000
Owens Miss Elspeth Eluned	4 Pump Court, London	020 7842 5555
Padfield Mr Nicholas David	Chambers of Nicholas Padfield QC, London	020 7351 1961
Palmer Mr James Savill	Henderson Chambers, London	020 7583 9020
Panton Mr Alastair Howard	10 King's Bench Walk, London	020 7353 7742
Parker Miss Wendy	Hardwicke, London	020 7242 2523
Parker Mrs Karen Lesley	Guildhall Chambers Portsmouth, Portsmouth	023 9275 2400
Parsons Mr Andrew James	Portsmouth Barristers'Chambers, Portsmouth	023 9283 1292
Pascall Mr Matthew Stephen	Alexander Chambers, London	0845 652 0451/0854 652 0451
	Guildford Chambers, Guildford	01483 539131
Payton Mr Clifford Coningsby	Alpha Court Chambers, Leamington Spa	01926 886412
Pearce Mr Robert Edgar	Radcliffe Chambers, London	020 7831 0081
Pennicott Mr Ian	Keating Chambers, London	020 7544 2600
Pennock Mr Ian	Park Lane Plowden, Leeds	0113 228 5049
Penny Mr Timothy Charles	11 Stone Buildings, London	020 7831 6381
Perry Mr Christopher Edward	Palmyra Chambers, Warrington	01925 444919
Phillips Mr Andrew Charles	Crown Office Chambers, London	020 7797 8100
Pickup Mr James Kenneth	2 Hare Court, London	020 7353 3982
	Lincoln House Chambers, Manchester	0161 832 5701
Platford Mr Graham Roy	Five Paper, London	020 7815 3200
Polli Mr Timothy James	Tanfield Chambers, London	020 7421 5300
Potter Miss Alison Lisa	4 Pump Court, London	020 7842 5555
Power Mr Richard Michael Arthur	Lamb Chambers, London	020 7797 8300
Pretsell Mr James Davidson	Farrar's Building, London	020 7583 9241
Prior Mr Paul Stephen	36 Bedford Row, London	020 7421 8000
Prior Mrs Mary	36 Bedford Row, London	020 7421 8000
Purchas Mr James Alexander Francis	4 Pump Court, London	020 7842 5555
Quiney Mr Charles Benedictus Alexander	Crown Office Chambers, London	020 7797 8100
Quirke Mr Gerard Martin	Citadel Chambers, Birmingham	0121 233 8500
Quirke Mr James Keiron	St Philips Chambers, Birmingham	0121 246 7000
Rai Miss Puneet Kaur	Thomas More Chambers, London	020 7404 7000
Rai Mr Amarjit Singh	St Philips Chambers, Birmingham	0121 246 7000
Rainey Mr Philip Carslake	Tanfield Chambers, London	020 7421 5300
Randolph Mr Paul Leslie	Field Court Chambers, London	020 7405 6114
Ratcliffe Miss Frances Anne	Radcliffe Chambers, London	020 7831 0081
Rawat Miss Houzla Bibi Mahmad	Carmelite Chambers, London	020 7936 6300
Reed Mr Simon John	New Walk Chambers, Leicester	0871 200 1298/0116 255 9144
Rees Mr Hefin Ednyfed	39 Essex Street, London	020 7832 1111
Reffin Miss Clare Alyson	One Essex Court, London	020 7583 2000
Regan Mr David Robert	St John's Chambers, Bristol	0117 923 4700
Richman Mrs Helene Pines	Eighteen Carlton Crescent, Southampton	023 8063 9001
	9 Stone Buildings, London	020 7404 5055
	Stour Chambers, Canterbury	01227 764899
Ridd Mr David Ian Mcgregor	Farrar's Building, London	020 7583 9241
Rifat Mr Maurice Alan	1 Gray's Inn Square, London	020 7405 0001
Rigney Mr Andrew James	Crown Office Chambers, London	020 7797 8100
Ritchie Mr Andrew George	The Chambers of Grahame Aldous QC, London	020 7832 0500
Rivalland Mr Marc-Edouard	1 Chancery Lane, London	0845 634 6666

Roberts Mr Michael Charles	Chambers of Michael Roberts, Henley-On-Thames	01844 355 655
Roberts Mr Richard Vaughan	Henderson Chambers, London	020 7583 9020
Rogers Mr Daniel James	Number 7 Harrington Street Chambers, Liverpool	0151 242 0707
Rogers Mr Ian Paul	Monckton Chambers, London	020 7405 7211
Rosemarine Mr Andrew Marc	Chambers of Mr A M Rosemarine, Manchester	0161 740 3861
Ross Mr Sidney David	11 Stone Buildings, London	020 7831 6381
Ross Mr Simon Hadleigh	Zenith Chambers, Leeds	0113 245 5438
Rowntree Mr Edward John Pickering	Hardwicke, London	020 7242 2523
Roy Mr Stefan Alexander Hiren	5 Pump Court, London	020 7353 2532
Royce Mr Darryl Fraser	Atkin Chambers, London	020 7404 0102
Rushton Ms Nicola Jane	Five Paper, London	020 7815 3200
Russell Mr Thomas Charles Welldon	KCH Garden Square, Nottingham	0115 941 8851
Sampson Mr Graeme William	3 PB Barristers, Bournemouth	01202 292102
	3 PB Barristers, Bristol	0117 928 1520
	3 PB Barristers, London	020 7583 8055
	3 PB Barristers, Oxford	01865 793 736
	3 PB Barristers, Winchester	01962 868884
Scott Holland Mr Gideon Silas	Keating Chambers, London	020 7544 2600
Seal Mr Julius Damien	Chambers of Mr Julius Seal, London	020 7328 0158
Sears Mr Robert David Murray	Four New Square, London	020 7822 2000
Seeboruth Mr Royln Jean-Paul	Chambers of Royln Seeboruth, Aylesbury	01296 393329
Sefton-Smith Mr Lloyd	Lamb Chambers, London	020 7797 8300
Selby Mr Jonathan Lee	Keating Chambers, London	020 7544 2600
Sellers Mr Graham	Atlantic Chambers, Liverpool	0151 236 4421
Shapiro Mr Daniel Jonathan	Crown Office Chambers, London	020 7797 8100
Sharp Mr Christopher Francis	Harcourt Chambers, London	0844 561 7135
	Harcourt Chambers, Oxford	0844 561 7135
	St John's Chambers, Bristol	0117 923 4700
Shaw Mr Jonathan Paul	No5 Chambers, Birmingham	0845 210 5555
	No5 Chambers, Bristol	0845 210 5555
	No5 Chambers, London	0845 210 5555
	Zenith Chambers, Leeds	0113 245 5438
Shaw Mr Julian	St Johns Buildings, Chester	01244 323070
	St Johns Buildings, Manchester	0161 214 1500
	St Johns Buildings Liverpool, Liverpool	0151 243 6000
Shirley Mr James Patrick	Stone Chambers, London	020 7440 6900
Shuman Miss Karen Ann Elizabeth	1 Chancery Lane, London	0845 634 6666
	No 8 Chambers, Birmingham	0121 236 5514
Silverton Miss Catherine Anne	Sovereign Chambers, Leeds	0113 245 1841
Simpson Mr David Joseph	196 Temple Chamber, London	020 7099 9257
Sinclair Miss Lisa Anne	Chambers of Miss Lisa Sinclair, London	020 8946 7201
Sinclair Mr Graham Kelso	East Anglian Chambers, Colchester	01473 214481
	East Anglian Chambers, Ipswich	01473 214481
	East Anglian Chambers, Norwich	01473 214481
Singarajah Mr Frederico	1 Gray's Inn Square, London	020 7405 0001
Singer Mr Andrew Michael	Kings Chambers, Birmingham	0845 034 3444
	Kings Chambers, Leeds	0845 034 3444
	Kings Chambers, Manchester	0845 034 3444
Sisley Mr Timothy Julian Crispin	9 Stone Buildings, London	020 7404 5055
Sjostrand Miss Ekaterina	13 Old Square Chambers, London	020 7831 4445
Skelly Mr Andrew Jon	Hardwicke, London	020 7242 2523
Skelt Mr Ian Stuart	KBW, Leeds	0113 297 1200
Sliwinski Mr Robert Andrew	SWL Chambers, Loudwater	01494 616007
Smith Mr Robert Clive	1 Paper Buildings, London	020 7353 3728
	RCS Chambers, Stainton	01709 814 147
Smith Mr Robert Ian	St Paul's Chambers, Leeds	0113 245 5866

Name	Chambers	Telephone
Smith Mr Roger Hugh Traylen	No5 Chambers, Birmingham	0845 210 5555
	No5 Chambers, Bristol	0845 210 5555
	No5 Chambers, London	0845 210 5555
Smithers Dr Roger Howard	Alexander Chambers, London	0845 652 0451/0854 652 0451
	Clerksroom (Taunton), Taunton	0845 083 3000
	Guildford Chambers, Guildford	01483 539131
Snow Mr Darren Mark	Charter Chambers, London	020 7618 4400
Spalton Mr George David John	Four New Square, London	020 7822 2000
Spencer Mr Martin Benedict	Hailsham Chambers, London	020 7643 5000
Spicer Mr Robert Haden	Frederick Place Chambers, Bristol	0117 946 7059
Staddon Mr Paul	Tanfield Chambers, London	020 7421 5300
Stagg Mr Paul Andrew	1 Chancery Lane, London	0845 634 6666
Stanford Mr Tony James	Old Bailey Chambers, London	020 3008 6404
Stansfield Mr Piers Alistair	Keating Chambers, London	020 7544 2600
Starcevic Mr Petar	St Philips Chambers, Birmingham	0121 246 7000
Stead Mr Richard James	St John's Chambers, Bristol	0117 923 4700
Stebbings Mr Ian Anthony	1 Gray's Inn Square, London	020 7405 0001
Stenhouse Mr John Alexander	Nightingale Chambers, Wolverley	01562 851350
Stephens Miss Jessica	Keating Chambers, London	020 7544 2600
Stephens Mr Michael Allen	Design Chambers, London	020 7353 0747
	St Ive's Chambers, Birmingham	0121 236 0863
Sterling Mr Robert Alan	St James's Chambers, Manchester	0161 834 7000
	Zenith Chambers, Leeds	0113 245 5438
Stevens-Hoare Miss Michelle	Hardwicke, London	020 7242 2523
Stevenson Mr Paul Anthony	Tanfield Chambers, London	020 7421 5300
Stewart Mr Richard Paul	Lamb Chambers, London	020 7797 8300
Steynor Mr Alan Charles	Keating Chambers, London	020 7544 2600
Stirling Mr Christopher William	Field Court Chambers, London	020 7405 6114
Stride Mr Lionel Alexander	Temple Garden Chambers, London	020 7583 1315
Stuart Mr James William	Lamb Chambers, London	020 7797 8300
Swirsky Mr Adam Abraham Burl Bradbury	Lamb Chambers, London	020 7797 8300
Tavares Mr Nathan Warren	Outer Temple Chambers, London	020 7353 6381
Taylor Miss Araba Arba Kurankyiwa	Fenners Chambers, Cambridge	01223 368761
Temmink Mr Robert-Jan	Quadrant Chambers, London	020 7583 4444
Temple Ms Eleanor Louise	Kings Chambers, Birmingham	0845 034 3444
	Kings Chambers, Leeds	0845 034 3444
	Kings Chambers, Manchester	0845 034 3444
Thomas Mr Andrew Martin	Lincoln House Chambers, Manchester	0161 832 5701
	Linenhall Chambers, Chester	01244 348282
Thompson Mr Andrew Edward Courtney	Tanfield Chambers, London	020 7421 5300
Thompson Mr Michael James	Keating Chambers, London	020 7544 2600
Thornley Miss Hannah Elise	South Square, London	020 7696 9900
Ticciati Mr Oliver	4 Pump Court, London	020 7842 5555
Tompkinson Miss Deborah Ann	Clerksroom (London), London	0845 083 3000
	Clerksroom (Taunton), Taunton	0845 083 3000
Townend Mr Samuel John	Keating Chambers, London	020 7544 2600
Tozzi Mr Nigel Kenneth	4 Pump Court, London	020 7842 5555
Treverton-Jones Mr Gregory Dennis	39 Essex Street, London	020 7832 1111
	82 King Street, Manchester	0161 870 9969
Trompeter Mr Nicholas Simeon	Selborne Chambers, London	020 7420 9500
Troup Mr Alexander William	St John's Chambers, Bristol	0117 923 4700
Trumpington Mr John Henry	Staple Inn Chambers, London	020 7242 5240
Tucker Mr Ashley Russell	Park Court Chambers, Leeds	0113 243 3277
Turnbull Miss Helen Mary	Lamb Chambers, London	020 7797 8300
Vallat Mr Richard Justin	Pump Court Tax Chambers, London	020 7414 8080
Van Der Leij Dr Martina	Field Court Chambers, London	020 7405 6114
Van Tonder Mr Gerard Dirk	New Square Chambers, London	020 7419 8000
Vaughan Mr Terence Paul	Fenners Chambers, Cambridge	01223 368761
Vaughan-Williams Mr Arthur Laurence	13 Old Square Chambers, London	020 7831 4445
Vernon Mr Elliot Curt	No. 3 Fleet Street Chambers, London	020 7936 4474
Vineall Mr Nicholas Edward John	4 Pump Court, London	020 7842 5555

Vonberg Mr Thomas Charles	Devereux Chambers, London	020 7353 7534
Walford Mr Richard Henry Howard	Serle Court, London	020 7242 6105
Walker Mr Adam Nigel	Seven Bedford Row, London	020 7242 3555
Walsh Mr Michael Patrick	Tanfield Chambers, London	020 7421 5300
Warner Mr David Alexander	St Philips Chambers, Birmingham	0121 246 7000
Warnock Mr Andrew Ronald	1 Chancery Lane, London	0845 634 6666
Watson Mr Alaric	11 Stone Buildings, London	020 7831 6381
Watthey Mr James Robertson	Hardwicke, London	020 7242 2523
Wells Mr Caspar John Mowlem	Goldsmith Chambers, London	020 7353 6802
Wheaton Mr Ian Malcolm James	Eighteen Carlton Crescent, Southampton	023 8063 9001
White Mr Matthew James	St John's Chambers, Bristol	0117 923 4700
White Mr Oliver Zachary	Littleton Chambers, London	020 7797 8600
White Mr Peter-John Spencer	Great Barford Chambers, Bedford	012134 870004
White Mr Steven James	Park Court Chambers, Leeds	0113 243 3277
Widdett Ms Ceri Louise	Park Court Chambers, Leeds	0113 243 3277
Wightwick Mr Iain	Riverview Chambers, London	0844 225 3999
	Unity Street Chambers, Bristol	0117 906 9789
Wilkins Mr Christopher John	Pallant Chambers, Chichester	01243 784538
Wilkinson Mr Marc Ashley	No5 Chambers, Birmingham	0845 210 5555
	No5 Chambers, Bristol	0845 210 5555
	No5 Chambers, London	0845 210 5555
Willer Mr Robert Michael	Ely Place Chambers, London	020 7400 9600
Williams Mr Mark John	Queen Square Chambers, Bristol	0117 921 1966
Williams Mr Simon Paul	Radcliffe Chambers, London	020 7831 0081
Williamson Mr Adrian John Gerard Hughes	Keating Chambers, London	020 7544 2600
Wills Miss Alexandra Itari	Christ Church Chambers, London	020 7409 5278/07788 512787
Wilson Mr Richard Carver	36 Bedford Row, London	020 7421 8000
Wilton Mr Simon Daniel	Hailsham Chambers, London	020 7643 5000
Winser Mr Crispin David Richard	Crown Office Chambers, London	020 7797 8100
Wolman Mr Clive Richard	11 Stone Buildings, London	020 7831 6381
Woodward Mr Jeremy Paul	Pallant Chambers, Chichester	01243 784538
Woolf The Hon Jeremy Richard George	Pump Court Tax Chambers, London	020 7414 8080
Wright Mr Alexander Paul	4 Pump Court, London	020 7842 5555
Wright Mr Frederick George Ian	Crown Office Chambers, London	020 7797 8100
Wynne Mr Ashley John	No5 Chambers, Birmingham	0845 210 5555
	No5 Chambers, Bristol	0845 210 5555
	No5 Chambers, London	0845 210 5555
Yell Mr Nicholas Anthony	1 Chancery Lane, London	0845 634 6666
Young Mr Martin Ford	9 Stone Buildings, London	020 7404 5055

C

PUBLIC INTERNATIONAL

Abasheikh Mr Omar Said Imam	Paragon Chambers, London	020 3318 9988
Ajaz Mr Mohammad Arshad	Eastmans Chambers, Reading	0118 966 9094
Alexandra Miss Sebastiane	Holborn Chambers, London	020 7242 6060
Arkhurst Mr Reginald Leon	4 King's Bench Walk, London	020 7822 7000
Arnold Mr Graham John	Farringdon Chambers, London	020 7089 5700
Artesi Miss Desiree Allison Ann	Thomas More Chambers, London	020 7404 7000
Bajwa Mr Ali Naseem	Garden Court Chambers, London	020 7993 7600
Barnes Ms Rachel Ann	3 Raymond Buildings, London	020 7400 6400
Beaumont Mr Benjamin	Chambers of Dr Michael Arnheim, London	020 7833 5093
	Middle Temple Lane Chambers, London	020 7583 4352
Birnbaum Mr Michael Ian	9-12 Bell Yard, London	020 7400 1800
Bunting Mr Daniel Alexander James	2 Dr Johnson's Buildings, London	020 7936 2613
Caldwell Mr Peter Hugh Coyles	Dyers Chambers, London	020 7404 1881
Carrion Benitez Ms Miriam	36 Bedford Row, London	020 7421 8000
Cecil Miss Joanne Michelle	1 Pump Court, London	020 7842 7070
Chowdhary Mr Islamuddin	Cassian Chambers, Ilford	07796 262641
Christie Mr Iain Robert	5RB, London	020 7242 2902
Dalby Mr Joseph Francis	4-5 Gray's Inn Square, London	020 7404 5252

Name	Chambers	Telephone
Darroch Miss Fiona Culverwell	Clerksroom (London), London	0845 083 3000
	Clerksroom (Taunton), Taunton	0845 083 3000
	King's Lynn Chambers, King's Lynn	01553 672 085
Davies Mr Henry Olusola	Trinity Chambers, Birmingham	0121 346 4672
Dillon Mr Thomas William Matthew	Chambers of Thomas Dillon, London	020 7692 2722
Facenna Mr Gerald Carlo	Monckton Chambers, London	020 7405 7211
Forlin Mr Gerard Emlyn	Cornerstone Barristers, London	020 7242 4986
Gardner Mr James Piers	Monckton Chambers, London	020 7405 7211
Gill Mr Manjit Singh	No5 Chambers, Birmingham	0845 210 5555
	No5 Chambers, Bristol	0845 210 5555
	No5 Chambers, London	0845 210 5555
Greatorex Mr Paul	4-5 Gray's Inn Square, London	020 7404 5252
Hackett Mr Philip George	Argent Chambers, London	020 7556 5500
Harris Mr Wilbert Arthurlyn	Rowchester Chambers, Birmingham	0121 233 2327
Hossain Mr Ajmalul	Selborne Chambers, London	020 7420 9500
	St Philips Chambers, Birmingham	0121 246 7000
Iyer Miss Shobana	Swan Chambers, Richmond	0845 123 1234
Jafar Mr Abdurahman Akhtar	Chambers of Mr Abdurahman Jafar, Ilford	07828 937338
John Miss Laura Elizabeth	Monckton Chambers, London	020 7405 7211
Jones Mr Mark Andrew	St Ive's Chambers, Birmingham	0121 236 0863
Keith Mr Benjamin Charles Andrew	Five St Andrew's Hill, London	020 7332 5400
Khan Mr Arfan	Field Court Chambers, London	020 7405 6114
Lewiecki Miss Marie	Old Bailey Chambers, London	020 3008 6404
Mahmood Mr Abid	Central Chambers, Manchester	0161 236 1133
	No5 Chambers, Birmingham	0845 210 5555
	No5 Chambers, Bristol	0845 210 5555
	No5 Chambers, London	0845 210 5555
Maka Mr Isaac	Chambers of Mr Isaac Maka, Ilford	07973 308 301
	4 King's Bench Walk, London	020 7822 7000
Malone Mr David John	1 Gray's Inn Square, London	020 7405 0001
Marler Lieutenant Colonel Lee Gary	Bretton Woods Law, London	
	18 Red Lion Court, London	020 7520 6000
Matthias Mr David Huw	Francis Taylor Building, London	020 7353 8415
McBride Mr Martin Jeremy	Monckton Chambers, London	020 7405 7211
McNally Mr John Joseph	Dyers Chambers, London	020 7404 1881
Metcalfe Dr Eric William	Monckton Chambers, London	020 7405 7211
Miah Mr Anawar Babul	Great James Street Chambers, London	020 7440 4949
Morgan Dr Austen Jude	33 Bedford Row, London	020 7242 6476
Muquit Mr Mohammed Shuyeb	1 Mitre Court Buildings, London	020 7452 8900
Nardell Mr Gordon Lawrence	39 Essex Street, London	020 7832 1111
	82 King Street, Manchester	0161 870 9969
Nasim Mr Zia-Ul-Mustafa	Milestone Chambers, London	
O'Connor Mr Patrick Michael Joseph	Doughty Street Chambers, Bristol	01179 058 717
	Doughty Street Chambers, London	020 7404 1313
	Doughty Street Chambers, Manchester	0161 618 1066
Owusu-Yianoma Mr David Kwasi Dartey	1 Mitre Court Buildings, London	020 7452 8900
Padfield Mr Nicholas David	Chambers of Nicholas Padfield QC, London	020 7351 1961
Plimmer Miss Melanie Ann	Kings Chambers, Birmingham	0845 034 3444
	Kings Chambers, Leeds	0845 034 3444
	Kings Chambers, Manchester	0845 034 3444
Quirke Mr James Keiron	St Philips Chambers, Birmingham	0121 246 7000
Qureshi Mr Asif Hasan	Quadrant Chambers, London	020 7583 4444
Rosemarine Mr Andrew Marc	Chambers of Mr A M Rosemarine, Manchester	0161 740 3861
Russell Miss Marguerite	Garden Court Chambers, London	020 7993 7600
Seeboruth Mr Royln Jean-Paul	Chambers of Royln Seeboruth, Aylesbury	01296 393329
Simon Mr Philipp Arnold Heinrich	4 KBW, London	020 7822 8822
Singarajah Mr Frederico	1 Gray's Inn Square, London	020 7405 0001
Skinner Mr Samuel Richard Edward	KCH Garden Square, Nottingham	0115 941 8851
Sood Mrs Usha Rani	Trent Chambers, Nottingham	0115 941 9596

C

Soto-Miranda Mr Diego Fernando	One Essex Court, London	020 7936 3030
Sparrow Mrs Marie-Claire	Holborn Chambers, London	020 7242 6060
Van Overdijk Miss Claire Orit	No5 Chambers, Birmingham	0845 210 5555
	No5 Chambers, Bristol	0845 210 5555
	No5 Chambers, London	0845 210 5555
Von Pommern-Peglow Dr Michael Alfred Herman Pr.	Brunswick Chambers, London	020 7353 1987
Watson Mr Benjamin Turquand	3 Raymond Buildings, London	020 7400 6400
Watson-Gandy Prof Mark	13 Old Square Chambers, London	020 7831 4445
Wills Miss Alexandra Itari	Christ Church Chambers, London	020 7409 5278/07788 512787
Wood Mr James Alexander Douglas	Doughty Street Chambers, Bristol	01179 058 717
	Doughty Street Chambers, London	020 7404 1313
	Doughty Street Chambers, Manchester	0161 618 1066

PUBLIC LAW

Ahluwalia Mr Navtej Singh	Garden Court Chambers, London	020 7993 7600
Ajaz Mr Mohammad Arshad	Eastmans Chambers, Reading	0118 966 9094
Akers Mr Robert Matthew Harry	St Johns Buildings, Chester	01244 323070
	St Johns Buildings, Manchester	0161 214 1500
	16 Winckley Square, Preston	01772 256100
Albutt Mr Ian Leslie	Cornerstone Barristers, London	020 7242 4986
	Heavenwood Chambers, Stroud	01453 873444
Alexandra Miss Sebastiane	Holborn Chambers, London	020 7242 6060
Algazy Mr Jacques Max	Cloisters, London	020 7827 4000
Allwood Mrs Gina Louisa	Seven Bedford Row, London	020 7242 3555
Askey Mr Robert John	Palmyra Chambers, Warrington	01925 444919
Bhanji Mr Shiraz Musa	4 Bingham Place, London	020 7486 5347
	1 Gray's Inn Square, London	020 7405 0001
Bradshaw Mr Mark Kieran	No5 Chambers, Birmingham	0845 210 5555
	No5 Chambers, Bristol	0845 210 5555
	No5 Chambers, London	0845 210 5555
Bunting Mr Daniel Alexander James	2 Dr Johnson's Buildings, London	020 7936 2613
Butler Mr Simon David	The Chambers of Grahame Aldous QC, London	020 7832 0500
Carrasco Mr Glenn Lawrence	9-12 Bell Yard, London	020 7400 1800
Dalby Mr Joseph Francis	4-5 Gray's Inn Square, London	020 7404 5252
Darroch Miss Fiona Culverwell	Clerksroom (London), London	0845 083 3000
	Clerksroom (Taunton), Taunton	0845 083 3000
	King's Lynn Chambers, King's Lynn	01553 672 085
Davies Mr Henry Olusola	Trinity Chambers, Birmingham	0121 346 4672
Dean Mr James Patrick	Goldsmith Chambers, London	020 7353 6802
Dos Santos Mr Alexander	Charter Chambers, London	020 7618 4400
Edwards Mr Denis	Francis Taylor Building, London	020 7353 8415
Engelman Mr Philip	Cloisters, London	020 7827 4000
	Trinity Chambers, Middlesbrough	01642 247569
	Trinity Chambers, Newcastle Upon Tyne	0191 232 1927
Facenna Mr Gerald Carlo	Monckton Chambers, London	020 7405 7211
Fellows Mr Philip David Andrew	Hardwicke, London	020 7242 2523
Frawley Ms Lyndsey Anne	Quorum Chambers, St Albans	01727 884516
	Quorum Tax Chambers, London	020 7043 5189
Gallagher Ms Caoilfhionn Anna	Doughty Street Chambers, Bristol	01179 058 717
	Doughty Street Chambers, London	020 7404 1313
	Doughty Street Chambers, Manchester	0161 618 1066
Gardner Mr James Piers	Monckton Chambers, London	020 7405 7211
Gillman Miss Rachel Mary	1 Garden Court Family Law Chambers, London	020 7797 7900
Gledhill Mr Lee Andre	Alexander Chambers, London	0845 652 0451/0854 652 0451
	Trident Barristers Chambers, Manchester	0161 663 3123
Griffin Mr Nicholas John	Five Paper Buildings, London	020 7583 6117
Gurden Miss Alison Louise	1 Gray's Inn Square, London	020 7405 0001
Hanlon Mr James Tobias	Old Bailey Chambers, London	020 3008 6404
Henderson Miss Josephine	Five Paper, London	020 7815 3200

Holmes Ms Elisa	Monckton Chambers, London	020 7405 7211
Hood Mr David	Prince of Wales Chambers, London	020 7622 7415
Horton Mr Matthew Bethell	39 Essex Street, London	020 7832 1111
	82 King Street, Manchester	0161 870 9969
Ismail Miss Nazmun Nisha	Central Chambers, Manchester	0161 236 1133
	No5 Chambers, Birmingham	0845 210 5555
	No5 Chambers, Bristol	0845 210 5555
	No5 Chambers, London	0845 210 5555
Iyer Miss Shobana	Swan Chambers, Richmond	0845 123 1234
Jarratt Miss Alice Cordelia Betchworth	Carmelite Chambers, London	020 7936 6300
Jones Miss Emily Louise	Temple Garden Chambers, London	020 7583 1315
Jones Miss Jacinta Elizabeth Barrett	1 Mitre Court Buildings, London	020 7452 8900
Jones Mr Emyr Gweirydd	9 Park Place, Cardiff	029 2038 2731
Jones Mr Mark Andrew	St Ive's Chambers, Birmingham	0121 236 0863
Kansal Miss Seema	12 Old Square Chambers, London	020 7404 0875
Keith Mr Benjamin Charles Andrew	Five St Andrew's Hill, London	020 7332 5400
Kramer Mr Philip Anthony	Park Lane Plowden, Newcastle Upon Tyne	0191 211 4087
Lawrence Miss Samantha Dionne	3 Dr Johnson's Buildings, London	020 7353 4854
Lopez Mr Juan Nemesio	Francis Taylor Building, London	020 7353 8415
Maka Mr Isaac	Chambers of Mr Isaac Maka, Ilford	07973 308 301
	4 King's Bench Walk, London	020 7822 7000
Mannion Ms Amy Elisabeth	9-12 Bell Yard, London	020 7400 1800
	1 Crown Office Row, London	020 7797 7500
Matthias Mr David Huw	Francis Taylor Building, London	020 7353 8415
McBride Mr Martin Jeremy	Monckton Chambers, London	020 7405 7211
McCombie Mr Fergus Alexander Paul	1 Gray's Inn Square, London	020 7405 0001
McNally Mr John Joseph	Dyers Chambers, London	020 7404 1881
Moffett Mr Jonathan Keith	4-5 Gray's Inn Square, London	020 7404 5252
Muman Mr Vijay Kumar	43 Temple Row Chambers, Birmingham	0121 237 6035
Mustakim Mr Abdul Yunus Al	Chambers of Mr Mustakim, London	
O'Brien Mr Nicholas William Wattebot	10 King's Bench Walk, London	020 7353 7742
O'Connor Miss Hilda Ann	Kidby Chambers, Woodbridge	
Oommen Mr Jacob	Chambers of Mr Jacob Oommen, East Barnet	07958 680272
O'Sullivan Mr Richard John	1215 Chambers, London	020 3291 1215
Owen Mr Timothy Wynn	Matrix Chambers, London	020 7404 3447
Pawson-Pounds Mr Daniel James	6 King's Bench Walk, London	020 7583 0410
Pedro Mr Terry Adebisi	1 Pump Court, London	020 7842 7070
Peretz Mr George Michael John	Monckton Chambers, London	020 7405 7211
Purchas Mr Robin Michael	Francis Taylor Building, London	020 7353 8415
Rana Mr Mohammed Akram	Clapham Law Chambers, London	020 7978 8482
Read Mr Simon Eric	Zenith Chambers, Leeds	0113 245 5438
Richman Mrs Helene Pines	Eighteen Carlton Crescent, Southampton	023 8063 9001
	9 Stone Buildings, London	020 7404 5055
	Stour Chambers, Canterbury	01227 764899
Rinker Mr Andrew Stuart D'Artois	Chambers of Mr Andrew Rinker, London	020 7584 1091
Rule Mr Philip David	Castle Chambers, Harrow-on-the-Hill	020 8423 6579
Santamera Miss Louise Alexandria	New Bailey Chambers, Liverpool	0151 236 9402
Skelt Mr Ian Stuart	KBW, Leeds	0113 297 1200
Southey Mr David Hugh	Tooks Chambers, London	020 7842 7575
Thomas Mr Gareth	Atlantic Chambers, Liverpool	0151 236 4421
Wadsley Mr Peter John Campbell	St John's Chambers, Bristol	0117 923 4700
Watterson Ms Anna Elizabeth	1 Mitre Court Buildings, London	020 7452 8900
West Dr Ewan Donald	Monckton Chambers, London	020 7405 7211
Williams Mr Ben Dylan	Kings Chambers, Birmingham	0845 034 3444
	Kings Chambers, Leeds	0845 034 3444
	Kings Chambers, Manchester	0845 034 3444

Williams Ms Sandra Alessandra Caroline	The Chambers Of Alessandra Williams, Tadworth	07941 944950
Wills Miss Alexandra Itari	Christ Church Chambers, London	020 7409 5278/07788 512787
Wragg Mr Jonathan Robert	Highgate Chambers, London	020 8340 6031

REGULATORY LAW

Abu-Mustafa Mr Jehad	1 Paper Buildings, London	020 7353 3728
Afzal Mr Fayyaz	No5 Chambers, Birmingham	0845 210 5555
	No5 Chambers, Bristol	0845 210 5555
	No5 Chambers, London	0845 210 5555
Aina Mr Benjamin Adejowon Olufemi	Old Bailey Chambers, London	020 3008 6404
Ajaz Mr Mohammad Arshad	Eastmans Chambers, Reading	0118 966 9094
Akers Mr Robert Matthew Harry	St Johns Buildings, Chester	01244 323070
	St Johns Buildings, Manchester	0161 214 1500
	16 Winckley Square, Preston	01772 256100
Alam Ms Jan	Ropewalk Chambers, Nottingham	0115 947 2581
Aleeson Mr Warwick Lan Grieg	187 Fleet Street, London	020 7430 7430
Alexandra Miss Sebastiane	Holborn Chambers, London	020 7242 6060
Algazy Mr Jacques Max	Cloisters, London	020 7827 4000
Andrews Mr Paul Leslie	Great James Street Chambers, London	020 7440 4949
Archer Miss Audrey Sybil Dorothy	3 PB Barristers, Bournemouth	01202 292102
	3 PB Barristers, Bristol	0117 928 1520
	3 PB Barristers, London	020 7583 8055
	3 PB Barristers, Oxford	01865 793 736
	3 PB Barristers, Winchester	01962 868884
Arnold Mr Peter Matthew Miller	No5 Chambers, Birmingham	0845 210 5555
	No5 Chambers, Bristol	0845 210 5555
	No5 Chambers, London	0845 210 5555
Artesi Miss Desiree Allison Ann	Thomas More Chambers, London	020 7404 7000
Ashley-Norman Mr Jonathan Charles	3 Raymond Buildings, London	020 7400 6400
Badenoch Mr Tony David	6 King's Bench Walk, London	020 7583 0410
Bagley Miss Louisa Ellen	1 Paper Buildings, London	020 7353 3728
Baird Mr James Stevenson	Bank House Chambers, Sheffield	0114 275 1223
Baker Miss Maureen Anne	Seven Bedford Row, London	020 7242 3555
Ball Mr Ian David	Cornwall Street Chambers, Birmingham	0121 233 7500
Banham Mr Matthew Ian	Nine Bedford Row, London	020 7489 2727
Barclay Mr Robin Nicholas John	2 Hare Court, London	020 7353 3982
Barker Mr Kerry	Guildhall Chambers, Bristol	0117 930 9000
Barnes Ms Rachel Ann	3 Raymond Buildings, London	020 7400 6400
Barnett Mr Jeremy Victor	2 Bedford Row, London	020 7440 8888
	St Paul's Chambers, Leeds	0113 245 5866
Barraclough Mr Nicholas Maylin	187 Fleet Street, London	020 7430 7430
Barry Mr Denis Fintan Patrick	Five Paper Buildings, London	020 7583 6117
Barry Mr Kevin James	36 Bedford Row, London	020 7421 8000
Bates Mr Alan Twan	Monckton Chambers, London	020 7405 7211
Beaumont Mr Marc Clifford	9 Stone Buildings, London	020 7404 5055
	Windsor Barristers' Chambers, Windsor	01753 839321
Beharrylal Mr Satyanand Sarju	15 New Bridge Street, London	020 7842 1900
Bennett Miss Emma Louise	Exchange Chambers, Leeds	0113 203 1970
	Exchange Chambers, Liverpool	0151 236 7747
	Exchange Chambers, Manchester	0161 833 2722
Bennett Mr Ieuan Gereint	9 Park Place, Cardiff	029 2038 2731
Bennett Mr Miles Alexander Fordham	Five Paper Buildings, London	020 7583 6117
Benson Mr Jeremy Keith	18 Red Lion Court, London	020 7520 6000
Berriman Mr Trevor St John	43 Temple Row Chambers, Birmingham	0121 237 6035
Bertham Mr Anthony Christopher	3 Temple Gardens, London	020 7353 3102
Bex Miss Kate	2 Hare Court, London	020 7353 3982
Bickler Mr Simon Lloyd	St Paul's Chambers, Leeds	0113 245 5866
Birch Mr Roger Allen	Five St Andrew's Hill, London	020 7332 5400
	Sovereign Chambers, Leeds	0113 245 1841
Birkby Mr Richard Adam	Park Court Chambers, Leeds	0113 243 3277

Name	Chambers	Telephone
Birnbaum Mr Michael Ian	9-12 Bell Yard, London	020 7400 1800
Bisarya Mr Neil	Number 7 Harrington Street Chambers, Liverpool	0151 242 0707
Blackburn Mr Luke Sebastian	Seven Bedford Row, London	020 7242 3555
Blair Mr Peter Michael	Guildhall Chambers, Bristol	0117 930 9000
	6 King's Bench Walk, London	020 7583 0410
Bond Mr Richard Ian Winsor	Citadel Chambers, Birmingham	0121 233 8500
Bonehill Mr Nicholas Benjamin	4 Breams Buildings, London	020 7092 1900
Bourne Mr Charles Gregory	4-5 Gray's Inn Square, London	020 7404 5252
Bourne-Arton Mr James Luke	St Paul's Chambers, Leeds	0113 245 5866
Bowers Mr Rupert John	Doughty Street Chambers, London	020 7404 1313
Boyd Mr Phillip Joseph George	Lincoln House Chambers, Manchester	0161 832 5701
Braamskamp Ms Christine Jolanda	3 Raymond Buildings, London	020 7400 6400
Bradly Mr David Lawrence	39 Essex Street, London	020 7832 1111
Bradnock Mr Thomas Philip	Colleton Chambers, Exeter	01392 274898
Brady Mr Scott	3 Temple Gardens, London	020 7353 3102
Branston Mr Gareth Philip	23 Essex Street, London	020 7413 0353
Brassington Mr Stephen David	2 Hare Court, London	020 7353 3982
Brehan Ms Daire	Chambers of Ms D Brehan, London	07808 726877
Bridge Mr Giles	Broadway House Chambers, Bradford	01274 722560
	Broadway House Chambers, Leeds	0113 246 2600
Broadley Mr John	Cobden House Chambers, Manchester	0161 833 6000
Brown Mr Roger Charles Arthur	Kenworthy's Chambers, Manchester	0161 832 4036
Brown Mr Simon Jonathan	Crown Office Chambers, London	020 7797 8100
Brunner Ms Catherine Jane	Albion Chambers, Bristol	0117 927 2144
	36 Bedford Row, London	020 7421 8000
Bryan Mr Robert John	1 Paper Buildings, London	020 7353 3728
Buchan Miss Caroline Venetia	Chambers of Miss C Buchan, Haywards Heath	01444 482222
Buchanan Mr James Ian Charles	2 Hare Court, London	020 7353 3982
Buckle Mr Jonathan	Regency Chambers, Cambridge	01223 301517
	Regency Chambers, Peterborough	01733 315215
Bullock Mr Robert Gustaf	The Chambers of Mr Bullock, Brighton	01273 321050
Burnett Mr Iain	4 King's Bench Walk, London	020 7822 7000
Burton Mr John Malcolm	3 Temple Gardens, London	020 7353 3102
Butler Mr Simon David	The Chambers of Grahame Aldous QC, London	020 7832 0500
Buxton Mr Thomas Justin	Charter Chambers, London	020 7618 4400
Byrne Mr Garrett Thomas	4-5 Gray's Inn Square, London	020 7404 5252
Byrnes Miss Aisling Alice Elizabeth	25 Bedford Row, London	020 7067 1500
Callery Mr Martin	Cobden House Chambers, Manchester	0161 833 6000
Cammerman Mr Gideon Saul	187 Fleet Street, London	020 7430 7430
Campbell Mr Alasdair James	St Paul's Chambers, Leeds	0113 245 5866
Campbell Mr Oliver Edward Wilhelm	Henderson Chambers, London	020 7583 9020
Caplan Mr Jonathan Michael	Five Paper Buildings, London	020 7583 6117
	Riverview Chambers, London	0844 225 3999
Carr Mr Christopher Sean	36 Bedford Row, London	020 7421 8000
Carter Miss Nathalie Veronique	1 Gray's Inn Square, London	020 7405 0001
Cassidy Mr Patrick Stephen	Kenworthy's Chambers, Manchester	0161 832 4036
Chalk Mr Alexander John Gervase	6 King's Bench Walk, London	020 7583 0410
Challinor Mr Jonathan Gerald	Cornwall Street Chambers, Birmingham	0121 233 7500
Chawla Mr Mukul	9-12 Bell Yard, London	020 7400 1800
Chawla Mr Neil	No5 Chambers, Birmingham	0845 210 5555
	No5 Chambers, Bristol	0845 210 5555
	No5 Chambers, London	0845 210 5555
Clegg Mr William	2 Bedford Row, London	020 7440 8888
Clements Miss Paula Kate	Alexander Chambers, London	0845 652 0451/0854 652 0451
	Guildford Chambers, Guildford	01483 539131
Climie Mr Roger Stephen	King's Bench and Godolphin (KBG)Chambers, Plymouth	01752 221551
	Outer Temple Chambers, London	020 7353 6381

C

Cockings Mr Giles Francis Sacheveral	Furnival Chambers, London	020 7405 3232
Coltart Mr Christopher Mccallum	2 Hare Court, London	020 7353 3982
Comb Mr David William	Trinity Chambers, Middlesbrough	01642 247569
	Trinity Chambers, Newcastle Upon Tyne	0191 232 1927
Compton Mr Benjamin Edward Welstead	Outer Temple Chambers, London	020 7353 6381
Conlon Mr Michael John Patrick	Harcourt Chambers, Milton Keynes	0845 123 1234
Connolly Mr Dominic Regan	Five St Andrew's Hill, London	020 7332 5400
Corsellis Mr Nicholas Robert Alexander	3 Temple Gardens, London	020 7353 3102
Cotter Mr Nicholas Andrew James Horlor	1 Paper Buildings, London	020 7353 3728
Counsell Mr James Henry	Outer Temple Chambers, London	020 7353 6381
Cox Mr Jonathan Edward	KCH Garden Square, Nottingham	0115 941 8851
Crabb Miss Samantha Jill	Citadel Chambers, Birmingham	0121 233 8500
Crawley Mr Ross Alexander	Middle Temple Lane Chambers, London	020 7583 4352
Crosfill Mr John	Field Court Chambers, London	020 7405 6114
Crowe Mr Cameron	36 Bedford Row, London	020 7421 8000
Crowther Ms Lucy Ellen	Apex, Cardiff	02920 232 032
Dalby Mr Joseph Francis	4-5 Gray's Inn Square, London	020 7404 5252
Darbishire Mr Adrian Munro	QEB Hollis Whiteman, London	020 7933 8855
Davidge Miss Justine Marie	4 King's Bench Walk, London	020 7822 7000
Davidson Mr Andrew Edward	Citadel Chambers, Birmingham	0121 233 8500
Davis Mr Simon John	St Philips Chambers, Birmingham	0121 246 7000
Del Fabbro Mr Oscar	23 Essex Street, London	020 7413 0353
Delamere Miss Isabel Sarah	4 Breams Buildings, London	020 7092 1900
Dempsey Miss Karen Marie	3 Temple Gardens, London	020 7353 3102
Denney Mr Stuart Henry Macdonald	Deans Court Chambers, Manchester	0161 214 6000
	Deans Court Chambers, Preston	01772 565 600
	Thomas More Chambers, London	020 7404 7000
Desmond Mr Denis John	Cornwall Street Chambers, Birmingham	0121 233 7500
Devlin Mr Timothy Robert	Furnival Chambers, London	020 7405 3232
Dillon Mr Thomas William Matthew	Chambers of Thomas Dillon, London	020 7692 2722
Dixon Mr David Steven	Sovereign Chambers, Leeds	0113 245 1841
Donne Mr Jeremy Nigel	QEB Hollis Whiteman, London	020 7933 8855
Donnelly Mr Stephen John	Dyers Chambers, London	020 7404 1881
Dos Santos Mr Alexander	Charter Chambers, London	020 7618 4400
Douglass Mr Paul Stephen	9 King's Bench Walk, London	020 7353 9564
Drew Mr Simon Patrick	No5 Chambers, Birmingham	0845 210 5555
	No5 Chambers, Bristol	0845 210 5555
	No5 Chambers, London	0845 210 5555
Duck Mr Michael Charles	No5 Chambers, Birmingham	0845 210 5555
	No5 Chambers, Bristol	0845 210 5555
	No5 Chambers, London	0845 210 5555
Duffy Mr Derek James	St Paul's Chambers, Leeds	0113 245 5866
Dunn Miss Katherine Louise	Trinity Chambers, Middlesbrough	01642 247569
	Trinity Chambers, Newcastle Upon Tyne	0191 232 1927
Dutt Miss Nisha	Middle Temple Lane Chambers, London	020 7583 4352
Eastwood Miss Philippa Clemency Anne	Doughty Street Chambers, London	020 7404 1313
Edwards Mr Denis	Francis Taylor Building, London	020 7353 8415
Edwards Mr Nigel Royston	St Paul's Chambers, Leeds	0113 245 5866
Elias Mr David	9 Park Place, Cardiff	029 2038 2731
Elliott Mr Eric Alan	Sovereign Chambers, Leeds	0113 245 1841
	Trinity Chambers, Middlesbrough	01642 247569
	Trinity Chambers, Newcastle Upon Tyne	0191 232 1927
	York Chambers, Newcastle Upon Tyne	0191 206 4677

Ellis Miss Sarah Louise	9-12 Bell Yard, London	020 7400 1800
Engelman Mr Philip	Cloisters, London	020 7827 4000
	Trinity Chambers, Middlesbrough	01642 247569
	Trinity Chambers, Newcastle Upon Tyne	0191 232 1927
Enoch Mr Dafydd Huw	Apex, Cardiff	02920 232 032
	23 Essex Street, London	020 7413 0353
Evans Mr Philip	QEB Hollis Whiteman, London	020 7933 8855
Facenna Mr Gerald Carlo	Monckton Chambers, London	020 7405 7211
Farrell Mr Simon Henry	3 Raymond Buildings, London	020 7400 6400
Faure Walker Miss Julia Frances	2 Hare Court, London	020 7353 3982
Ferguson Mr Craig Charles	2 Hare Court, London	020 7353 3982
Ferguson Mr Stephen Michael	2 Bedford Row, London	020 7440 8888
Ferm Mr Rodney Eric	Broadway House Chambers, Bradford	01274 722560
	Broadway House Chambers, Leeds	0113 246 2600
Ferry-Swainson Mr Richard Joseph	2 Bedford Row, London	020 7440 8888
Field Mr Stephen Anthony	1 Pump Court, London	020 7842 7070
Finnigan Mr Peter Anthony	QEB Hollis Whiteman, London	020 7933 8855
Finucane Mr Brendan Godfrey Eamonn	Outer Temple Chambers, London	020 7353 6381
Fish Mr David Thomas	Deans Court Chambers, Manchester	0161 214 6000
	Deans Court Chambers, Preston	01772 565 600
	Goldsmith Chambers, London	020 7353 6802
Fisher Mr Jervis Andrew	Citadel Chambers, Birmingham	0121 233 8500
Fisher Mr Jonathan Simon	Devereux Chambers, London	020 7353 7534
Fitzmaurice Mr Guy Edward Christian	Staple Inn Chambers, London	020 7242 5240
Follon Mr Daniel Richard Thomas	1 Gray's Inn Square, London	020 7405 0001
Forlin Mr Gerard Emlyn	Cornerstone Barristers, London	020 7242 4986
Forsyth Miss Samantha	No5 Chambers, Birmingham	0845 210 5555
	No5 Chambers, Bristol	0845 210 5555
	No5 Chambers, London	0845 210 5555
Foulkes Miss Rebecca	5 Pump Court, London	020 7353 2532
Foulkes Mr Christopher David	2 Hare Court, London	020 7353 3982
Frame Mr Stuart James	Staple Inn Chambers, London	020 7242 5240
Freeman Miss Lisa Claire	Furnival Chambers, London	020 7405 3232
Fryer Mr Nigel Mccrae	Queen Square Chambers, Bristol	0117 921 1966
Frymann Mr Andrew Philip	187 Fleet Street, London	020 7430 7430
Fuller Mr Alan Peter	Albion Chambers, Bristol	0117 927 2144
Gadd Mr Adam Brian	Pump Court Chambers, London	020 7353 0711
	Pump Court Chambers, Winchester	01962 868 161
	Riverview Chambers, London	0844 225 3999
Galbraith-Marten Mr Jason Nicholas	Cloisters, London	020 7827 4000
Ganesan Mr Muthupandi Peter	Furnival Chambers, London	020 7405 3232
Gardner Mr James Piers	Monckton Chambers, London	020 7405 7211
Garlick Mr Paul Richard	Furnival Chambers, London	020 7405 3232
Gau Mr Justin Charles	Pump Court Chambers, London	020 7353 0711
	Pump Court Chambers, Swindon	01793 539899
	Pump Court Chambers, Winchester	01962 868 161
Gent Mr Matthew Thomas	Sovereign Chambers, Leeds	0113 245 1841
Gerasimidis Mr Nicolas	Guildhall Chambers, Bristol	0117 930 9000
German Miss Kelly Anne	Eastbourne Chambers, Eastbourne	01323 642102
Gersch Mr Adam Nissen	Argent Chambers, London	020 7556 5500
Gibbons Miss Mary Regina	Stone Chambers, London	020 7440 6900
Gibbs Mr Philip Mark	KCH Garden Square, Nottingham	0115 941 8851
Gilchrist Miss Naomi Roberta	St Philips Chambers, Birmingham	0121 246 7000
Gill Mr Manjit Singh	No5 Chambers, Birmingham	0845 210 5555
	No5 Chambers, Bristol	0845 210 5555
	No5 Chambers, London	0845 210 5555
Gill Mr Rajinder Singh	Charter Chambers, London	020 7618 4400
Gillespie Mr Christopher Michael	2 Hare Court, London	020 7353 3982
Gillet Ms Gemma Louise	Dyers Chambers, London	020 7404 1881
Gladwell Mr Simon Mark	East Anglian Chambers, Ipswich	01473 214481
Glasgow Mr Oliver Edwin James	2 Hare Court, London	020 7353 3982

C

Gledhill Mr Lee Andre	Alexander Chambers, London	0845 652 0451/0854 652 0451
	Trident Barristers Chambers, Manchester	0161 663 3123
Glyn Mr Caspar Hilary Gordon	Cloisters, London	020 7827 4000
Gobir Mr Nuhu Garba	9 Park Place, Cardiff	029 2038 2731
Goddard Miss Suzanne Hazel	Lincoln House Chambers, Manchester	0161 832 5701
Godfrey Mr Howard Anthony	2 Bedford Row, London	020 7440 8888
Godfrey Mr Lauren John	Crown Office Row Chambers, Brighton	01273 625625
Godfrey Mr Thomas William Netherton	23 Essex Street, London	020 7413 0353
Gofur Mr Abdul	Thomas More Chambers, London	020 7404 7000
Goldstone Mr Simon Lewis	4 Pump Court, London	020 7842 5555
Goodwin Mr Michael	Old Bailey Chambers, London	020 3008 6404
Goudie Mr William Martin Phillip	Charter Chambers, London	020 7618 4400
Graham Mr Michael John Geoffrey	Trinity Chambers, Middlesbrough	01642 247569
	Trinity Chambers, Newcastle Upon Tyne	0191 232 1927
Grant Mr Chudi Paul	Kenworthy's Chambers, Manchester	0161 832 4036
Granville Stafford Mr Andrew	4 King's Bench Walk, London	020 7822 7000
Green Mr Timothy Sinclair	St Philips Chambers, Birmingham	0121 246 7000
Grego Mr Kevin Christopher	Citadel Chambers, Birmingham	0121 233 8500
Griffin Mr Nicholas John	Five Paper Buildings, London	020 7583 6117
Griffiths Mr Peter	2 Bedford Row, London	020 7440 8888
	30 Park Place, Cardiff	029 2039 8421
Guest Mr Peter Liam	187 Fleet Street, London	020 7430 7430
Hackett Mr Philip George	Argent Chambers, London	020 7556 5500
Hadrill Mr Keith Paul	Furnival Chambers, London	020 7405 3232
Hamer Mr Charles Henry	Citadel Chambers, Birmingham	0121 233 8500
Hamilton Miss Amanda Jean	Furnival Chambers, London	020 7405 3232
Hamilton Mr Nigel	Broadway House Chambers, Bradford	01274 722560
	Broadway House Chambers, Leeds	0113 246 2600
Hammerton Mr Alastair Rolf	1 Chancery Lane, London	0845 634 6666
Hanlon Mr James Tobias	Old Bailey Chambers, London	020 3008 6404
Hannam Mr Timothy James	Citadel Chambers, Birmingham	0121 233 8500
Harbage Mr William John Hirons	36 Bedford Row, London	020 7421 8000
	37 Park Square Chambers, Leeds	0113 243 9422
Harding Mr Christopher James	Thomas More Chambers, London	020 7404 7000
Hardy Mr Maximilian John Lee	Nine Bedford Row, London	020 7489 2727
Harris Mr Adrian David	23 Essex Street, London	020 7413 0353
Harris Mr Julian Gilbert Vaughan	Citadel Chambers, Birmingham	0121 233 8500
Harris Ms Rebecca Elizabeth	QEB Hollis Whiteman, London	020 7933 8855
Harrison Mr John Foster	St Paul's Chambers, Leeds	0113 245 5866
Harrison Mr Peter John	6 Pump Court, London	020 7797 8400
	6 Pump Court Chambers, Maidstone	01622 688094
Harvey Mr Stephen Frank	18 Red Lion Court, London	020 7520 6000
	18 Red Lion Court (Annexe), Chelmsford	01245 280880
Hassall Mr Craig Jonathan	Sovereign Chambers, Leeds	0113 245 1841
Hawkes Mr Malcolm Alexander	Dyers Chambers, London	020 7404 1881
Hearnden Miss Alexis Katrina	39 Essex Street, London	020 7832 1111
	82 King Street, Manchester	0161 870 9969
Hearnden Mr Richard Christopher	Furnival Chambers, London	020 7405 3232
Heeley Miss Michelle Louise	No5 Chambers, Birmingham	0845 210 5555
	No5 Chambers, Bristol	0845 210 5555
	No5 Chambers, London	0845 210 5555
Hendron Mr Henry Joseph Christopher	Strand Chambers, London	020 7117 6920
Henley Mr Andrew Michael	Furnival Chambers, London	020 7405 3232
Henson Miss Christine Ruth	Crown Office Row Chambers, Brighton	01273 625625
Higgins Mr Daniel Malcolm Buhlea	Nine Bedford Row, London	020 7489 2727
Higginson Mr Timothy Nicholas Bennett	Littleton Chambers, London	020 7797 8600
	St John's Chambers, Bristol	0117 923 4700

C

Barrister	Chambers	Telephone
Hill Mr Michael Gordon	Trinity Chambers, Middlesbrough	01642 247569
	Trinity Chambers, Newcastle Upon Tyne	0191 232 1927
Himsworth Mr Mark Stephen	Dyers Chambers, London	020 7404 1881
Hine Mr Charles Roderick John	King's Bench Chambers, Bournemouth	01202 250025
Hines Mr James Philip	3 Raymond Buildings, London	020 7400 6400
Hirst Miss Kathryn Anne	Furnival Chambers, London	020 7405 3232
Hirst Miss Rebecca Elisabeth	Cobden House Chambers, Manchester	0161 833 6000
Hislop Mr David Seymour	Doughty Street Chambers, Bristol	01179 058 717
	Doughty Street Chambers, London	020 7404 1313
	Doughty Street Chambers, Manchester	0161 618 1066
Hobson Miss Laura Elise	Citadel Chambers, Birmingham	0121 233 8500
Hogg The Right Hon Douglas Martin	Carmelite Chambers, London	020 7936 6300
	Hailsham Chambers, London	020 7643 5000
	37 Park Square Chambers, Leeds	0113 243 9422
Holland Mr Charles Christopher	Francis Taylor Building, London	020 7353 8415
	Trinity Chambers, Middlesbrough	01642 247569
	Trinity Chambers, Newcastle Upon Tyne	0191 232 1927
Holt Miss Abigail Claire	Lincoln House Chambers, Manchester	0161 832 5701
Hood Mr David	Prince of Wales Chambers, London	020 7622 7415
Hopper Mr Stephen John	Five Paper Buildings, London	020 7583 6117
Howell Ms Claire Elizabeth Siobhan	36 Bedford Row, London	020 7421 8000
Hughes Mr William Lloyd	9-12 Bell Yard, London	020 7400 1800
Hussain Miss Frida Khanam	Furnival Chambers, London	020 7405 3232
Hussain Mr Ghulam	Crown Office Row Chambers, Brighton	01273 625625
Iqbal Mr Mashood	London View Chambers, Sawbridgeworth	07788 912493
Irwin Mr Gavin David	Dyers Chambers, London	020 7404 1881
Islam Mr Mohammad Fakrul	18 Red Lion Court, London	020 7520 6000
Iyer Miss Shobana	Swan Chambers, Richmond	0845 123 1234
Jackson Mr Mark Joseph	No 8 Chambers, Birmingham	0121 236 5514
James Mr Roderick Ian	Charter Chambers, London	020 7618 4400
Jarratt Miss Alice Cordelia Betchworth	Carmelite Chambers, London	020 7936 6300
Jayakrishnan Mr Harry Sisubalan	Trent Chambers, Nottingham	0115 941 9596
Jenkins Mr Edward Nicholas	Five Paper Buildings, London	020 7583 6117
John Miss Laura Elizabeth	Monckton Chambers, London	020 7405 7211
Johnson Miss Zoe Elisabeth	QEB Hollis Whiteman, London	020 7933 8855
Johnston Miss Anne-Marie	Carmelite Chambers, London	020 7936 6300
Jones Mr Alun	St Paul's Chambers, Leeds	0113 245 5866
Jones Mr Mark Andrew	St Ive's Chambers, Birmingham	0121 236 0863
Jones Mr Richard Frederick Thomas	Heavenwood Chambers, Stroud	01453 873444
Joseph Dr Sandradee Theresa	13 Old Square Chambers, London	020 7831 4445
Joshi Mr Rajendra Jugatray	18 Red Lion Court, London	020 7520 6000
	18 Red Lion Court (Annexe), Chelmsford	01245 280880
Jowett Mr Timothy David Christian	9 Park Place, Cardiff	029 2038 2731
Kapila Miss Rachel Prakash	3 Raymond Buildings, London	020 7400 6400
Keeling Mr Adrian Francis	No5 Chambers, Birmingham	0845 210 5555
	No5 Chambers, Bristol	0845 210 5555
	No5 Chambers, London	0845 210 5555
Keith Mr Benjamin Charles Andrew	Five St Andrew's Hill, London	020 7332 5400
Kelly Mr Richard Bernard	East Anglian Chambers, Chelmsford	01473 214481
	East Anglian Chambers, Colchester	01473 214481
	East Anglian Chambers, Ipswich	01473 214481
	East Anglian Chambers, Norwich	01473 214481
Kennedy Miss Lucy Julia	QEB Hollis Whiteman, London	020 7933 8855
Kennedy Mr Peter Nicholas Dodgson	15 Winckley Square, Preston	01772 252828
Kessling Mr Christopher David	Chambers of Mr Christopher Kessling, Leicester	01509 890690
Khalique Miss Nageena	No5 Chambers, Birmingham	0845 210 5555
	No5 Chambers, Bristol	0845 210 5555
	No5 Chambers, London	0845 210 5555

Name	Chambers	Telephone
Khan Mr Ayoub	Chambers of Mr Ayoub Khan, Birmingham	07930 987202
Khan Mr Forz	Chambers of Mr F Khan, London	07854 109584
	6 King's Bench Walk, London	020 7353 4931
King Mr Gelaga Perry	2 Bedford Row, London	020 7440 8888
King Mr John Patrick	Nine Bedford Row, London	020 7489 2727
Kinnear Mr Jonathan Shea	9-12 Bell Yard, London	020 7400 1800
Kirtley Mr Paul George	Exchange Chambers, Leeds	0113 203 1970
	Exchange Chambers, Liverpool	0151 236 7747
	Littleton Chambers, London	020 7797 8600
Knight Mr Graeme Edward Verdon	7 Bell Yard, London	020 7831 0636
	Carmelite Chambers, London	020 7936 6300
	The Barristers Chambers, Address withheld	07966 056368
Kohli Mr Ryan Singh	Cornerstone Barristers, London	020 7242 4986
Lahiffe Mr Martin Patrick Joseph	3 Temple Gardens, London	020 7353 3102
Lake Mr James Edward	St Paul's Chambers, Leeds	0113 245 5866
Lakha Mr Abbas	Nine Bedford Row, London	020 7489 2727
Lal Mr Sanjay	4 King's Bench Walk, London	020 7822 7000
Lambert Mrs Alison Janet	Trinity Chambers, Chelmsford	01245 605040
Larkin Mr Sean	QEB Hollis Whiteman, London	020 7933 8855
Lavin Miss Mary Mandie Jane	196 Temple Chamber, London	020 7099 9257
Lawrence Sir Ivan John	5 Pump Court, London	020 7353 2532
Lawton Mr Paul Anthony	Lincoln House Chambers, Manchester	0161 832 5701
	18 Red Lion Court, London	020 7520 6000
Le Fevre Miss Sarah Margaret	3 Raymond Buildings, London	020 7400 6400
Leake Mr Stephen	Carmelite Chambers, London	020 7936 6300
Ledward Miss Jocelyn Victoria	QEB Hollis Whiteman, London	020 7933 8855
Lennon Mr John Francis	23 Essex Street, London	020 7413 0353
Leonard Mr James Alexander	Outer Temple Chambers, London	020 7353 6381
Levett Miss Francesca Anna	Five St Andrew's Hill, London	020 7332 5400
Lewiecki Miss Marie	Old Bailey Chambers, London	020 3008 6404
Lewington Miss Francesca Anna	Crown Office Row Chambers, Brighton	01273 625625
Lewis Mr Dominic	Five Paper Buildings, London	020 7583 6117
Lewis Mr Jonathan Simon	Henderson Chambers, London	020 7583 9020
Liddiard Mr Martin Thomas	No5 Chambers, Birmingham	0845 210 5555
	No5 Chambers, Bristol	0845 210 5555
	No5 Chambers, London	0845 210 5555
Linehan Mr Stephen John	St Philips Chambers, Birmingham	0121 246 7000
Lissack Mr Richard Anthony	Outer Temple Chambers, London	020 7353 6381
	Riverview Chambers, London	0844 225 3999
Lithman Mr Nigel Lloyd	2 Bedford Row, London	020 7440 8888
Lopez Mr Juan Nemesio	Francis Taylor Building, London	020 7353 8415
Lowe Mr Rupert William Manley	Guildhall Chambers, Bristol	0117 930 9000
Lule Miss Jacqueline	1 Mitre Court Buildings, London	020 7452 8900
Lynch Mr Jerome	Charter Chambers, London	020 7618 4400
Magee Mr Samuel Cairns	2 Bedford Row, London	020 7440 8888
Mahmood Mr Abid	Central Chambers, Manchester	0161 236 1133
	No5 Chambers, Birmingham	0845 210 5555
	No5 Chambers, Bristol	0845 210 5555
	No5 Chambers, London	0845 210 5555
Maka Mr Isaac	Chambers of Mr Isaac Maka, Ilford	07973 308 301
	4 King's Bench Walk, London	020 7822 7000
Malcolm Miss Helen Katharine Lucy	3 Raymond Buildings, London	020 7400 6400
Malone Mr David John	1 Gray's Inn Square, London	020 7405 0001
Mansell Mr Jason Francis Guy	Seven Bedford Row, London	020 7242 3555
Marcus Mr Peter	Zenith Chambers, Leeds	0113 245 5438
Margo Mr Saul Nicholas	Outer Temple Chambers, London	020 7353 6381
Markus Ms Kate	Doughty Street Chambers, Bristol	01179 058 717
	Doughty Street Chambers, London	020 7404 1313
	Doughty Street Chambers, Manchester	0161 618 1066
Martin Mr Bradley David	2 Temple Gardens, London	020 7822 1200
Martin Mr James Stephen	5 King's Bench Walk, London	020 7353 5638
Mather Mr Nicholas Ian Stewart	Furnival Chambers, London	020 7405 3232

Name	Chambers	Telephone
Matthias Mr David Huw	Francis Taylor Building, London	020 7353 8415
Maxwell Mr Adrian Robert John	St John's Chambers, Bristol	0117 923 4700
May Mr Christopher John	Five St Andrew's Hill, London	020 7332 5400
Mayo Mr Simon Peter	187 Fleet Street, London	020 7430 7430
McDonald Ms Melanie Sharon	No5 Chambers, Birmingham	0845 210 5555
	No5 Chambers, Bristol	0845 210 5555
	No5 Chambers, London	0845 210 5555
McGhee Mr Philip James	QEB Hollis Whiteman, London	020 7933 8855
McGowan Miss Maura Patricia	2 Bedford Row, London	020 7440 8888
	Lincoln House Chambers, Manchester	0161 832 5701
Medcroft Mr Nicholas Julian	Outer Temple Chambers, London	020 7353 6381
Mendelle Mr Paul Michael	25 Bedford Row, London	020 7067 1500
Metzer Mr Anthony David Erwin	Argent Chambers, London	020 7556 5500
Midgley Miss Anna Victoria Jane	Albion Chambers, Bristol	0117 927 2144
Miller Mr David Robin	Furnival Chambers, London	020 7405 3232
Miller Mr Peter Owen Michael	Cornerstone Barristers, London	020 7242 4986
Mills Mr Kristian Anthony	Trinity Chambers, Middlesbrough	01642 247569
	Trinity Chambers, Newcastle Upon Tyne	0191 232 1927
Mitchell Mr Christian Richard	Alexander Chambers, London	0845 652 0451/0854 652 0451
	Guildford Chambers, Guildford	01483 539131
Moller Ms Alice Christina	Alexander Chambers, London	0845 652 0451/0854 652 0451
	Chambers of Ms A C Moller, Address withheld	07966 448572
Monaghan Ms Susan Mary	No5 Chambers, Birmingham	0845 210 5555
	No5 Chambers, Bristol	0845 210 5555
	No5 Chambers, London	0845 210 5555
Mooney Mr Stephen John	Albion Chambers, Bristol	0117 927 2144
Moorhouse Mr Brendon Scott	Guildhall Chambers, Bristol	0117 930 9000
Moran Mr Patrick Michael	15 New Bridge Street, London	020 7842 1900
Morris Mr David Paul	Outer Temple Chambers, London	020 7353 6381
Morris Ms Johanna	Chambers of Marion Smullen and Kerim Fuad QC, London	020 7427 4400
Morton Miss Rowan Frances	Alexander Chambers, London	0845 652 0451/0854 652 0451
	Guildford Chambers, Guildford	01483 539131
Mousley Mr William Howard	2 King's Bench Walk, London	020 7353 1746
Muller Mr Antonie Sean	Citadel Chambers, Birmingham	0121 233 8500
Muman Mr Vijay Kumar	43 Temple Row Chambers, Birmingham	0121 237 6035
Mylvaganam Ms Tanoo	1 Gray's Inn Square, London	020 7405 0001
Newbold Mr Michael Paul	9-12 Bell Yard, London	020 7400 1800
Newcomb Mr Quinton John	1 Paper Buildings, London	020 7353 3728
Newman Mr Alan Ronald Harvey	Argent Chambers, London	020 7556 5500
Newton-Price Mr James Edward	Pump Court Chambers, London	020 7353 0711
	Pump Court Chambers, Swindon	01793 539899
	Pump Court Chambers, Winchester	01962 868 161
Nicholls Mr Christopher Benjamin	Citadel Chambers, Birmingham	0121 233 8500
Nicholson Mr Thomas Edward Cyril	Atkinson Bevan Chambers, London	020 7353 2112
Norman Mr Jared Simon Gregory	Field Court Chambers, London	020 7405 6114
Nuttall Mr Andrew Peter	Lincoln House Chambers, Manchester	0161 832 5701
Oakley Miss Louise Michelle	2 Bedford Row, London	020 7440 8888
O'Connor Mr Patrick Michael Joseph	Doughty Street Chambers, Bristol	01179 058 717
	Doughty Street Chambers, London	020 7404 1313
	Doughty Street Chambers, Manchester	0161 618 1066
Offer Mr Alexander	Garden Court Chambers, London	020 7993 7600
	Park Court Chambers, Leeds	0113 243 3277
Ogunbusola Mr Victor Olaniyi	Chambers of Victor Ogumbusola, Basildon	07413 634231
Omideyi Miss Anuoluwapo Iyanu	Furnival Chambers, London	020 7405 3232
O'Neill Miss Sally Jane	Furnival Chambers, London	020 7405 3232
O'Neill Mr Brian Patrick	2 Hare Court, London	020 7353 3982
Oommen Mr Jacob	Chambers of Mr Jacob Oommen, East Barnet	07958 680272
Ossack Mrs Tanya Rachelle Elise	3 Temple Gardens, London	020 7353 3102

Name	Chambers	Telephone
Owen Miss Carys	18 Red Lion Court, London	020 7520 6000
	18 Red Lion Court (Annexe), Chelmsford	01245 280880
Owen Mr Timothy Wynn	Matrix Chambers, London	020 7404 3447
Owen Ms Elen Mai	Linenhall Chambers, Chester	01244 348282
Ozin Mr Paul David	23 Essex Street, London	020 7413 0353
Page Mr Jonathan Rowland Thomas	Carmelite Chambers, London	020 7936 6300
Paley Ms Ruth Theresa Elizabeth	23 Essex Street, London	020 7413 0353
Palmer Miss Claire Louise	Thomas More Chambers, London	020 7404 7000
Palmer Miss Suzanne Elizabeth Josephine	4 King's Bench Walk, London	020 7822 7000
Palmer Mr Robert Henry	Monckton Chambers, London	020 7405 7211
Pardoe Mr Rupert Adam Corin	23 Essex Street, London	020 7413 0353
Pascoe Ms Soraya	1 Gray's Inn Square, London	020 7405 0001
Patterson Mr Stewart	Pump Court Chambers, London	020 7353 0711
	Pump Court Chambers, Swindon	01793 539899
	Pump Court Chambers, Winchester	01962 868 161
Pawson-Pounds Mr Daniel James	6 King's Bench Walk, London	020 7583 0410
Paxton Mr Christopher	18 Red Lion Court, London	020 7520 6000
	18 Red Lion Court (Annexe), Chelmsford	01245 280880
Peat Mr Richard Colin	13 Old Square Chambers, London	020 7831 4445
Peet Mr Andrew Geraint	Chambers of Mr Andrew Peet, Leicester	07966 238437
Penni Miss Sally Selorm-Juliet	Kenworthy's Chambers, Manchester	0161 832 4036
Penny Miss Abigail Sarah Prudence	4 Breams Buildings, London	020 7092 1900
Peretz Mr George Michael John	Monckton Chambers, London	020 7405 7211
Perrins Mr Gregory Lloyd	1 Paper Buildings, London	020 7353 3728
Phillips Mr Simon Benjamin	Francis Taylor Building, London	020 7353 8415
	Park Court Chambers, Leeds	0113 243 3277
Pierpoint Miss Katherine Anne	Lincoln House Chambers, Manchester	0161 832 5701
Pinto Miss Amanda Eve	Five Paper Buildings, London	020 7583 6117
Pointing Mr John Eric	Chambers of Mr John Pointing, London	020 8997 2285
Pople Miss Alison Ruth	2 Bedford Row, London	020 7440 8888
Powell Mr Oliver Jonathan	3 PB Barristers, London	020 7583 8055
Pownall Mr Stephen Orlando Fletcher	2 Hare Court, London	020 7353 3982
Pretsell Mr James Davidson	Farrar's Building, London	020 7583 9241
Price Mr Andrew Robert	Dyers Chambers, London	020 7404 1881
Prior Mr Paul Stephen	36 Bedford Row, London	020 7421 8000
Prior Mrs Mary	36 Bedford Row, London	020 7421 8000
Puar Mr Mikhael	30 Park Place, Cardiff	029 2039 8421
Pugh Mr John Bishop	John Pugh's Chambers, Liverpool	0151 236 5415
Purnell Mr Paul Oliver	Farringdon Chambers, London	020 7089 5700
Quinn Mr Tomas Anthony	4 King's Bench Walk, London	020 7822 7000
Quirke Mr Gerard Martin	Citadel Chambers, Birmingham	0121 233 8500
Quirke Mr James Keiron	St Philips Chambers, Birmingham	0121 246 7000
Qureshi Mr Tanveer Aftab	25 Bedford Row, London	020 7067 1500
Raggatt Mr Timothy Walter Harold	4 King's Bench Walk, London	020 7822 7000
	St Philips Chambers, Birmingham	0121 246 7000
Ramasamy Mr Selvaraju	QEB Hollis Whiteman, London	020 7933 8855
Rawat Miss Houzla Bibi Mahmad	Carmelite Chambers, London	020 7936 6300
Rees Mr Jonathan Elystan	Apex, Cardiff	02920 232 032
Reiff-Musgrove Miss Kaja	Dyers Chambers, London	020 7404 1881
Rhodes Mr Nicholas Piers	Charter Chambers, London	020 7618 4400
Rhodes Mr Robert Elliott	Outer Temple Chambers, London	020 7353 6381
	Principal Chambers, Sevenoaks	0845 209 8080
	St Philips Chambers, Birmingham	0121 246 7000
Richards Mr David James Martin	3 PB Barristers, Bournemouth	01202 292102
	3 PB Barristers, Bristol	0117 928 1520
	3 PB Barristers, London	020 7583 8055
	3 PB Barristers, Oxford	01865 793 736
	3 PB Barristers, Winchester	01962 868884

Richardson Mr Alistair Paul George	6 King's Bench Walk, London	020 7583 0410
Richardson Mr Garth Douglas Anthony	Devon Chambers, Plymouth	01752 661659
	Rougemont Chambers, Exeter	01392 208484
Rickarby Mr William Edmund	Cornwall Street Chambers, Birmingham	0121 233 7500
Riggs Miss Samantha	25 Bedford Row, London	020 7067 1500
Rimmer Mr Anthony Michael	187 Fleet Street, London	020 7430 7430
Roberts Miss Lisa	Lincoln House Chambers, Manchester	0161 832 5701
Roberts Mr Timothy David	Fountain Chambers, Middlesbrough	01642 804040
	QEB Hollis Whiteman, London	020 7933 8855
Robinson Mr Nicholas James Lansdale	3 PB Barristers, Bournemouth	01202 292102
	3 PB Barristers, Bristol	0117 928 1520
	3 PB Barristers, London	020 7583 8055
	3 PB Barristers, Oxford	01865 793 736
	3 PB Barristers, Winchester	01962 868884
Rooney Mr Paul	New Court Chambers, Newcastle Upon Tyne	0191 232 1980
	QEB Hollis Whiteman, London	020 7933 8855
Row Mr Charles Philip	Queen Square Chambers, Bristol	0117 921 1966
Rudd Mr Michael	36 Bedford Row, London	020 7421 8000
Ruffell Mr Mark Beresford	Pump Court Chambers, London	020 7353 0711
	Pump Court Chambers, Swindon	01793 539899
	Pump Court Chambers, Winchester	01962 868 161
Rule Mr Philip David	Castle Chambers, Harrow-on-the-Hill	020 8423 6579
Russell Mr Graham Alexander	Citadel Chambers, Birmingham	0121 233 8500
Russell-Mitra Miss Jessica Suparna	1 Mitre Court Buildings, London	020 7452 8900
Salmon Mr Jonathan Carl	St Philips Chambers, Birmingham	0121 246 7000
Salter Mr Michael Richard	Ely Place Chambers, London	020 7400 9600
Sandford Mr Robert Stanley	Bank House Chambers, Sheffield	0114 275 1223
Sangster Mr Nigel	25 Bedford Row, London	020 7067 1500
Scott Bell Mrs Rosalind Sara	Trinity Chambers, Middlesbrough	01642 247569
	Trinity Chambers, Newcastle Upon Tyne	0191 232 1927
Scott Mr Andrew David Peter	Park Lane Plowden, Leeds	0113 228 5049
Scott Mr Matthew John	Pump Court Chambers, London	020 7353 0711
	Pump Court Chambers, Swindon	01793 539899
	Pump Court Chambers, Winchester	01962 868 161
Sear Miss Joanne	13 KBW, Oxford	01865 311066
	13 King's Bench Walk, London	020 7353 7204
Sharma Miss Sunyana	3 PB Barristers, Bournemouth	01202 292102
	3 PB Barristers, London	020 7583 8055
Sharma Mr Jamie	187 Fleet Street, London	020 7430 7430
Sharpe Mr Martin Laurence	Park Court Chambers, Leeds	0113 243 3277
Sheikh Mr Irshad Ahmed	187 Fleet Street, London	020 7430 7430
Shepherd Mr Richard Andrew John	Albion Chambers, Bristol	0117 927 2144
Silverton Miss Catherine Anne	Sovereign Chambers, Leeds	0113 245 1841
Simpson Mr David Joseph	196 Temple Chamber, London	020 7099 9257
Simpson Mr Graeme Michael	Citadel Chambers, Birmingham	0121 233 8500
Sinclair Miss Lisa Anne	Chambers of Miss Lisa Sinclair, London	020 8946 7201
Singarajah Mr Frederico	1 Gray's Inn Square, London	020 7405 0001
Singh Mr Dapinderpaul	23 Essex Street, London	020 7413 0353
	Park Court Chambers, Leeds	0113 243 3277
Sjolin Ms Catarina Marianne	36 Bedford Row, London	020 7421 8000
Skinner Mr Samuel Richard Edward	KCH Garden Square, Nottingham	0115 941 8851
Smith Miss Eileen Joan	Trinity Chambers, Middlesbrough	01642 247569
	Trinity Chambers, Newcastle Upon Tyne	0191 232 1927
Smith Mr Alisdair Robert Macsorley	9-12 Bell Yard, London	020 7400 1800
Smith Mr Clive Francis	Chambers of Marion Smullen and Kerim Fuad QC, London	020 7427 4400
Smith Mr Robert Ian	St Paul's Chambers, Leeds	0113 245 5866

C

Name	Chambers	Telephone
Snow Mr Darren Mark	Charter Chambers, London	020 7618 4400
Solley Mr Stephen Malcolm	Charter Chambers, London	020 7618 4400
Sowler Mr Thomas Richard Holland	The Tax Chambers of Mr Richard Sowler TD, Douglas	07624 235000
Spears Miss Katharine Sarah	Carmelite Chambers, London	020 7936 6300
Spencer Mr Paul Anthony	3 Serjeants Inn, London	020 7427 5000
Spencer Mr Shaun Anthony	St Johns Buildings, Chester	01244 323070
	St Johns Buildings, Manchester	0161 214 1500
	16 Winckley Square, Preston	01772 256100
Squirrell Mr Benjamin	Nine Bedford Row, London	020 7489 2727
Standfast Mr Philip Arthur	St Paul's Chambers, Leeds	0113 245 5866
Stanford Mr Tony James	Old Bailey Chambers, London	020 3008 6404
Stebbings Mr Ian Anthony	1 Gray's Inn Square, London	020 7405 0001
Stein Mr Daniel Alexander	No5 Chambers, Birmingham	0845 210 5555
	No5 Chambers, Bristol	0845 210 5555
	No5 Chambers, London	0845 210 5555
Stelling Mr Nigel Roy	Citadel Chambers, Birmingham	0121 233 8500
Stevenson Mr Daniel Keith	9-12 Bell Yard, London	020 7400 1800
Stevenson Mr Robert Lloyd	Sovereign Chambers, Leeds	0113 245 1841
Storey Mr Richard Alexander	3 Temple Gardens, London	020 7353 3102
Storrie Mr Timothy James	Lincoln House Chambers, Manchester	0161 832 5701
Stott Mr Philip Geoffrey	QEB Hollis Whiteman, London	020 7933 8855
Stranex Mr Andrew John	St Paul's Chambers, Leeds	0113 245 5866
Stuart Mr Bruce Ian	Lombard Chambers, London	020 7107 2100
Stubbs Mr Andrew James	St Paul's Chambers, Leeds	0113 245 5866
Sugarman Mr Jason Ashley	9-12 Bell Yard, London	020 7400 1800
Sullivan Mr Geoffrey Charles Alexander	36 Bedford Row, London	020 7421 8000
Summers Miss Allison	36 Bedford Row, London	020 7421 8000
Sumnall Miss Charlene Emma Louise	Five Paper Buildings, London	020 7583 6117
Talbot Mr Jack Richard	Dyers Chambers, London	020 7404 1881
Tatford Mr Warwick Henry Patrick	9-12 Bell Yard, London	020 7400 1800
Taylor Mr Jason	Albion Chambers, Bristol	0117 927 2144
Taylor Mrs Susan	Trinity Chambers, Middlesbrough	01642 247569
	Trinity Chambers, Newcastle Upon Tyne	0191 232 1927
Taylor Ms Karen Anne	Themis Chambers, London	07967 418976
Tetlow Mr Bernard Geoffrey	Charter Chambers, London	020 7618 4400
Thomas Mr James Austin	KCH Garden Square, Nottingham	0115 941 8851
Thomas Mr Mark David	5 Essex Court, London	020 7410 2000
Thompson Mr Patrick Miles	KBW, Leeds	0113 297 1200
	St Johns Buildings, Manchester	0161 214 1500
	St Johns Buildings Liverpool, Liverpool	0151 243 6000
	16 Winckley Square, Preston	01772 256100
Thompson Mr Ryan Jerome	Dyers Chambers, London	020 7404 1881
Tomassi Mr Mark David	Charter Chambers, London	020 7618 4400
Tompkins Miss Kate	36 Bedford Row, London	020 7421 8000
Toomey Mr Kevin Ian	2 Bedford Row, London	020 7440 8888
Treharne Mr Neil Simon	Dingle Chambers, Bristol	07818 827754
Treverton-Jones Mr Gregory Dennis	39 Essex Street, London	020 7832 1111
	82 King Street, Manchester	0161 870 9969
Tucker Mr James Eckhord	Queen Square Chambers, Bristol	0117 921 1966
Udom Miss Nancy Ini	Five St Andrew's Hill, London	020 7332 5400
Upton Mr John Stewart	4 King's Bench Walk, London	020 7822 7000
Vaitilingam Mr Adam Skanda	Albion Chambers, Bristol	0117 927 2144
Van Overdijk Miss Claire Orit	No5 Chambers, Birmingham	0845 210 5555
	No5 Chambers, Bristol	0845 210 5555
	No5 Chambers, London	0845 210 5555
Walters Miss Vivian Irene Elizabeth	Five St Andrew's Hill, London	020 7332 5400
Ward Miss Alexandra	9-12 Bell Yard, London	020 7400 1800
Warrington Mr John Edward Lawrence	Five St Andrew's Hill, London	020 7332 5400

Watkinson Mr Howard	9-12 Bell Yard, London	020 7400 1800
Watson Mr Anthony Dennis	Lincoln House Chambers, Manchester	0161 832 5701
Webster Miss Shelley Anne	Carmelite Chambers, London	020 7936 6300
Weekes Miss Anesta Glendora	23 Essex Street, London	020 7413 0353
Wells Mr Colin John	25 Bedford Row, London	020 7067 1500
West Dr Ewan Donald	Monckton Chambers, London	020 7405 7211
Whitfield Mr Jonathan	Doughty Street Chambers, London	020 7404 1313
Wiktorowski-Solecki Miss Tamara	Middle Temple Lane Chambers, London	020 7583 4352
Wilcox Mr Jerome Carl Jean	Alexander Chambers, London	0845 652 0451/0854 652 0451
Williams Mr Ben Dylan	Kings Chambers, Birmingham	0845 034 3444
	Kings Chambers, Leeds	0845 034 3444
	Kings Chambers, Manchester	0845 034 3444
Williams Mr Simon Christopher	12 Old Square Chambers, London	020 7404 0875
Williams Ms Sandra Alessandra Caroline	The Chambers Of Alessandra Williams, Tadworth	07941 944950
Willmer Mr Stephen James	Argent Chambers, London	020 7556 5500
Wills Miss Alexandra Itari	Christ Church Chambers, London	020 7409 5278/07788 512787
Wilson Mr Scott	Themis Chambers, London	07967 418976
Woods Mr Terence Mccartan	187 Fleet Street, London	020 7430 7430
Yeo Mr Nicholas	3 Raymond Buildings, London	020 7400 6400

ROAD TRAFFIC AND HIGHWAYS

Ajaz Mr Mohammad Arshad	Eastmans Chambers, Reading	0118 966 9094
Akers Mr Robert Matthew Harry	St Johns Buildings, Chester	01244 323070
	St Johns Buildings, Manchester	0161 214 1500
	16 Winckley Square, Preston	01772 256100
Arnold Mr Peter Matthew Miller	No5 Chambers, Birmingham	0845 210 5555
	No5 Chambers, Bristol	0845 210 5555
	No5 Chambers, London	0845 210 5555
Askey Mr Robert John	Palmyra Chambers, Warrington	01925 444919
Barnes Mr Ashley James	Chambers of Mr Ashley Barnes, St Helens	01744 814072
	New Bailey Chambers, Liverpool	0151 236 9402
Becker Mr Paul Antony	Chavasse Court Chambers, Liverpool	0151 229 2030
Beeson Mr Nigel Adrian Laurence	New Bailey Chambers, Liverpool	0151 236 9402
Bergenthal Mr Ronnie Mark	Old Bailey Chambers, London	020 3008 6404
Broadley Mr John	Cobden House Chambers, Manchester	0161 833 6000
Bryan Mr Robert John	1 Paper Buildings, London	020 7353 3728
Butterworth Mr Martin Frank	Citadel Chambers, Birmingham	0121 233 8500
Campbell Mr Alasdair James	St Paul's Chambers, Leeds	0113 245 5866
Cherrett Mr Darryl Joseph	Carmelite Chambers, London	020 7936 6300
Clark Mr Dingle	Goldsmith Chambers, London	020 7353 6802
Conlon Mr Michael John Patrick	Harcourt Chambers, Milton Keynes	0845 123 1234
Connell Mr Edward Samuel	Five St Andrew's Hill, London	020 7332 5400
Corre Mr Neil Bernard	Redbourne Chambers, London	020 8346 8524
Coster Mr Ronald David	42 Bedford Row, London	020 7831 0222
Croskell Mr Marcus James	East Anglian Chambers, Chelmsford	01473 214481
	East Anglian Chambers, Colchester	01473 214481
	East Anglian Chambers, Ipswich	01473 214481
	East Anglian Chambers, Norwich	01473 214481
Davenport Mr Richard Ian	Citadel Chambers, Birmingham	0121 233 8500
Davies Mr Henry Olusola	Trinity Chambers, Birmingham	0121 346 4672
Dean Mr James Patrick	Goldsmith Chambers, London	020 7353 6802
Dempsey Miss Karen Marie	3 Temple Gardens, London	020 7353 3102
Dennis Mr Mark Jonathan	6 King's Bench Walk, London	020 7583 0410
Desmond Mr Denis John	Cornwall Street Chambers, Birmingham	0121 233 7500
Doherty Mr Nicholas Brudenell	4 King's Bench Walk, London	020 7822 7000
Douglass Miss Geraldine Maisie	Portal Chambers, Llandysul	01559 395 292
Draycott Mr Simon Douglas	Citadel Chambers, Birmingham	0121 233 8500
	Five St Andrew's Hill, London	020 7332 5400
Duffy Mr Derek James	St Paul's Chambers, Leeds	0113 245 5866

C

Name	Chambers	Telephone
Dyble Mr Steven John	18 Red Lion Court, London	020 7520 6000
	18 Red Lion Court (Annexe), Chelmsford	01245 280880
Esprit Mr Benoit	Barristers Chambers, London	020 3417 6461
	Legis Chambers, Aylesbury	01296 431125
Falkowski Mr Damian	4-5 Gray's Inn Square, London	020 7404 5252
Fenny Mr Ian Charles	Guildhall Chambers, Bristol	0117 930 9000
Finlay Mr Darren	Sovereign Chambers, Leeds	0113 245 1841
Fitzgibbon Mr Neil Kevin	Carmelite Chambers, London	020 7936 6300
Fortune Mr Peter Carl Michael	Guildhall Chambers Portsmouth, Portsmouth	023 9275 2400
	4 King's Bench Walk, London	020 7822 7000
Foulkes Miss Rebecca	5 Pump Court, London	020 7353 2532
Gilchrist Miss Naomi Roberta	St Philips Chambers, Birmingham	0121 246 7000
Goodall Miss Emma	Dyers Chambers, London	020 7404 1881
Grego Mr Kevin Christopher	Citadel Chambers, Birmingham	0121 233 8500
Gurden Miss Alison Louise	1 Gray's Inn Square, London	020 7405 0001
Hamer Mr Charles Henry	Citadel Chambers, Birmingham	0121 233 8500
Hammett Mr Michael Greville	9 Park Place, Cardiff	029 2038 2731
Harris Mr David Robert	St Albans Chambers, St Albans	01727 843383
Harris Mr James	Five St Andrew's Hill, London	020 7332 5400
Harrison Mr Paul John	13 KBW, Oxford	01865 311066
	13 King's Bench Walk, London	020 7353 7204
Henson Miss Christine Ruth	Crown Office Row Chambers, Brighton	01273 625625
Hillier Mr William	New Street Chambers, Leicester	0116 262 5906
Hinton Mr Neil Pearse	King's Bench Chambers, Bournemouth	01202 250025
Hobson Miss Laura Elise	Citadel Chambers, Birmingham	0121 233 8500
Hood Mr David	Prince of Wales Chambers, London	020 7622 7415
Horton Mr Matthew Bethell	39 Essex Street, London	020 7832 1111
	82 King Street, Manchester	0161 870 9969
Jackson Mr Andrew Fraser	5 Pump Court, London	020 7353 2532
Janner The Hon Daniel Joseph Mitchell	23 Essex Street, London	020 7413 0353
	Exchange Chambers, Manchester	0161 833 2722
	St Philips Chambers, Birmingham	0121 246 7000
Jones Mr Richard Frederick Thomas	Heavenwood Chambers, Stroud	01453 873444
Joseph Mr Sellappah Job	Chambers of Mr S J Joseph, London	020 8809 3083/020 8802 9889
Khalid Mr James	Goulds Green Chambers, Uxbridge	01895 422574
	Goulds Green Chambers, Uxbridge	01895 422574
Knight Mr Keith Leslie Francis	4 King's Bench Walk, London	020 7822 7000
Lycourgou Miss Olive	4 King's Bench Walk, London	020 7822 7000
Matthias Mr David Huw	Francis Taylor Building, London	020 7353 8415
McCulloch Miss Fiona Catharine Jane	Middle Temple Lane Chambers, London	020 7583 4352
McKone Mr Mark Desmond	Sovereign Chambers, Leeds	0113 245 1841
Mitchell Mr Alistair Stephen Fabian	49 Chambers, Bridgnorth	01746 761545
Moffat Mr Russell Dean	Linenhall Chambers, Chester	01244 348282
Norton Mr Giles	Enigma Chambers, Sheffield	07779 576499
	Holborn Chambers, London	020 7242 6060
Oommen Mr Jacob	Chambers of Mr Jacob Oommen, East Barnet	07958 680272
Osborne Mr James Robert	Clerksroom (London), London	0845 083 3000
Owen Ms Elen Mai	Linenhall Chambers, Chester	01244 348282
Perian Mr Steven	3 Temple Gardens, London	020 7353 3102
Powis Miss Samantha Inez	Citadel Chambers, Birmingham	0121 233 8500
Pyne Mr Russell David	2 King's Bench Walk, London	020 7353 1746
Rahman Mr Anis	12 Old Square Chambers, London	020 7404 0875
Reed Mr Simon John	New Walk Chambers, Leicester	0871 200 1298/0116 255 9144
Reynolds Mr John Adam	King's Bench Chambers, Bournemouth	01202 250025
Rimmer Mr Nicholas Patrick Edward	23 Essex Street, London	020 7413 0353
Ritchie Miss Shauna	2 Bedford Row, London	020 7440 8888
Rooke Mr Alexander John Giles	Argent Chambers, London	020 7556 5500
Ross Mr Gordon Macrae	3 Temple Gardens, London	020 7353 3102
Rupasinha Mr Sunil Jayantha	Old Bailey Chambers, London	020 3008 6404

Russell Mr Thomas Charles Welldon | KCH Garden Square, Nottingham | 0115 941 8851
Shamim Mr Mohammed | Clapham Law Chambers, London | 020 7978 8482
Shaw Mr Julian | St Johns Buildings, Chester | 01244 323070
St Johns Buildings, Manchester | 0161 214 1500
St Johns Buildings Liverpool, Liverpool | 0151 243 6000
Shellard Mr Robin James Spencer | Queen Square Chambers, Bristol | 0117 921 1966
Smith Mr Michael David | Kenworthy's Chambers, Manchester | 0161 832 4036
Stebbings Mr Ian Anthony | 1 Gray's Inn Square, London | 020 7405 0001
Stemp Mr Scott | 12 College Place, Southampton | 023 8032 0320
Stuart Mr Bruce Ian | Lombard Chambers, London | 020 7107 2100
Treharne Mr Neil Simon | Dingle Chambers, Bristol | 07818 827754
Trumpington Mr John Henry | Staple Inn Chambers, London | 020 7242 5240
Turner Mr Jonathan James | Argent Chambers, London | 020 7556 5500
Walker Mr Adam Nigel | Seven Bedford Row, London | 020 7242 3555
Walters Miss Vivian Irene Elizabeth | Five St Andrew's Hill, London | 020 7332 5400
Walton Miss Karen Tanya | Dyers Chambers, London | 020 7404 1881
Warner Mr Anthony Charles Broughton | Citadel Chambers, Birmingham | 0121 233 8500
Wightwick Mr Iain | Riverview Chambers, London | 0844 225 3999
Unity Street Chambers, Bristol | 0117 906 9789
Wilcox Mr Jerome Carl Jean | Alexander Chambers, London | 0845 652 0451/0854 652 0451
Wilkins Mr Andrew Lewis | Cornwall Street Chambers, Birmingham | 0121 233 7500
Williams Mr Ben Dylan | Kings Chambers, Birmingham | 0845 034 3444
Kings Chambers, Leeds | 0845 034 3444
Kings Chambers, Manchester | 0845 034 3444
Williams Ms Sandra Alessandra Caroline | The Chambers Of Alessandra Williams, Tadworth | 07941 944950
Winslett Mr Frank | Westgate Chambers, Lewes | 01273 480510

SALE & CARRIAGE OF GOODS

Ahmed Mr Ishfaq | Stone Chambers, London | 020 7440 6900
Aliker Mr Phillip Bliss | Tanfield Chambers, London | 020 7421 5300
Alliott Mr George Beckles | Temple Garden Chambers, London | 020 7583 1315
Alloway Mr Tor Hugh | Talloway Chambers, London | 020 7419 5047
Allwood Mrs Gina Louisa | Seven Bedford Row, London | 020 7242 3555
Andre Mr Roger Louis | Sovereign Chambers, Leeds | 0113 245 1841
Antell Mr John Jason | King's Bench and Godolphin (KBG)Chambers, Plymouth | 01752 221551
Argent Mr Gavin Richard | Westgate Chambers, Lewes | 01273 480510
Askey Mr Robert John | Palmyra Chambers, Warrington | 01925 444919
Aswani Mr Ravi Girdharilal | Stone Chambers, London | 020 7440 6900
Bailey Miss Rosana Henrietta | 10 King's Bench Walk, London | 020 7353 7742
Bailey Mr Russell Stuart | No5 Chambers, Birmingham | 0845 210 5555
No5 Chambers, Bristol | 0845 210 5555
No5 Chambers, London | 0845 210 5555
Barnard Mr James Philip | 11 Stone Buildings, London | 020 7831 6381
Beaumont Mr Marc Clifford | 9 Stone Buildings, London | 020 7404 5055
Windsor Barristers' Chambers, Windsor | 01753 839321
Bedloe Mr Giles Robert | Dyers Chambers, London | 020 7404 1881
Bell Mr Thomas Capel | Hardwicke, London | 020 7242 2523
Beloff Mr Rupert Joseph Alexei | No5 Chambers, Birmingham | 0845 210 5555
No5 Chambers, Bristol | 0845 210 5555
No5 Chambers, London | 0845 210 5555
Berkley Mr Michael Stuart | Rougemont Chambers, Exeter | 01392 208484
Berriman Mr Trevor St John | 43 Temple Row Chambers, Birmingham | 0121 237 6035
Bishop Mr Stephen Anthony | Goldsmith Chambers, London | 020 7353 6802
Blackwood Mr Clive David | Lamb Chambers, London | 020 7797 8300
Bogle Mr James Stewart Lockhart | 10 King's Bench Walk, London | 020 7353 7742
Boyd Mr Stephen James Harvey | Selborne Chambers, London | 020 7420 9500
Brunner Mr Peter Roland | Brick Court Chambers, London | 020 7379 3550

C

Bryden Mr Christopher James Yuen Kang	4 King's Bench Walk, London	020 7822 7000
Buchan Miss Caroline Venetia	Chambers of Miss C Buchan, Haywards Heath	01444 482222
Budworth Mr Martin James	Kings Chambers, Birmingham	0845 034 3444
	Kings Chambers, Leeds	0845 034 3444
	Kings Chambers, Manchester	0845 034 3444
Budworth Mr Richard Dutton	2-3 Hind Court Chambers, London	020 7822 2150
Bueno Mr Antonio De Padua Jose Maria	Clerksroom (Taunton), Taunton	0845 083 3000
Bullock Mr Robert Gustaf	The Chambers of Mr Bullock, Brighton	01273 321050
Butler Mr Andrew	Tanfield Chambers, London	020 7421 5300
Butler Mr Rupert James	3 Hare Court, London	020 7415 7800
Buttimore Mr Gabriel	13 KBW, Oxford	01865 311066
	13 King's Bench Walk, London	020 7353 7204
Capon Mr Philip Christopher William	East Anglian Chambers, Chelmsford	01473 214481
	East Anglian Chambers, Ipswich	01473 214481
	East Anglian Chambers, Norwich	01473 214481
	St Philips Chambers, Birmingham	0121 246 7000
Cawsey Mr Barry Donald	Clerksroom (London), London	0845 083 3000
	Clerksroom (Taunton), Taunton	0845 083 3000
Challinor Mr Thomas Michael	Citadel Chambers, Birmingham	0121 233 8500
Charkham Mr Graham Harold	20 Essex Street, London	020 7842 1200
Christensen Mr Carlton	10 King's Bench Walk, London	020 7353 7742
Clark Miss Geraldine	Serle Court, London	020 7242 6105
Clegg Mr Simon Robert Jonathan	St Philips Chambers, Birmingham	0121 246 7000
Clifton Miss Jane April	Lamb Chambers, London	020 7797 8300
Coates Mr George Alexander Nigel	Guildford Chambers, Guildford	01483 539131
Cohen Mr Edward Mervyn	11 Stone Buildings, London	020 7831 6381
Colbey Mr Richard	Guildhall Chambers Portsmouth, Portsmouth	023 9275 2400
	Lamb Chambers, London	020 7797 8300
Coster Mr Ronald David	42 Bedford Row, London	020 7831 0222
Coulter Mr Barry John	Clerksroom (London), London	0845 083 3000
	Clerksroom (Taunton), Taunton	0845 083 3000
	King's Lynn Chambers, King's Lynn	01553 672 085
Cox Miss Olivia Rodrigues	Atlantic Chambers, Liverpool	0151 236 4421
Crangle Mr Thomas Peter	4 Pump Court, London	020 7842 5555
Crowley Mr Daniel John	2 Temple Gardens, London	020 7822 1200
Cunningham Mr Graham Taylor	Hardwicke, London	020 7242 2523
Daniels Miss Philippa Catherine	36 Bedford Row, London	020 7421 8000
Davis Mr Andrew Paul	Crown Office Chambers, London	020 7797 8100
Dean Mr Peter Thomas	36 Bedford Row, London	020 7421 8000
Denbin Mr Jack Arnold	Greenway, Sonning-on-Thames	0118 969 2484
Devine Mr Michael Buxton	Rougemont Chambers, Exeter	01392 208484
Devlin Mr Bernard Joseph	Five St Andrew's Hill, London	020 7332 5400
Dipré Mr Paul Nicholas Amadeus	Chambers of Mr P N Dipré, Address withheld	0845 123 1234
	MK Family Law Chambers, Milton Keynes	0845 123 1234
Edwards Mr Nigel Royston	St Paul's Chambers, Leeds	0113 245 5866
Engelman Mr Philip	Cloisters, London	020 7827 4000
	Trinity Chambers, Middlesbrough	01642 247569
	Trinity Chambers, Newcastle Upon Tyne	0191 232 1927
Falkowski Mr Damian	4-5 Gray's Inn Square, London	020 7404 5252
Fawcett Mr Neil	St Ive's Chambers, Birmingham	0121 236 0863
Ferm Mr Rodney Eric	Broadway House Chambers, Bradford	01274 722560
	Broadway House Chambers, Leeds	0113 246 2600
Fetto Mr Niazi Peter	2 Temple Gardens, London	020 7822 1200
Field Mr Julian Nigel	Crown Office Chambers, London	020 7797 8100
Finlay Mr Darren	Sovereign Chambers, Leeds	0113 245 1841
Fisher Mr David	New Square Chambers, London	020 7419 8000

Barrister	Chambers	Telephone
Gadd Mr Adam Brian	Pump Court Chambers, London	020 7353 0711
	Pump Court Chambers, Winchester	01962 868 161
	Riverview Chambers, London	0844 225 3999
Gatty Mr Daniel Simon	Hardwicke, London	020 7242 2523
Gee Mr Steven Mark	Stone Chambers, London	020 7440 6900
Gelbart Mr Geoff Alan	1 Gray's Inn Square, London	020 7405 0001
Godfrey Mr Lauren John	Crown Office Row Chambers, Brighton	01273 625625
Godwin Mr William George Henry	3 Hare Court, London	020 7415 7800
	St John's Chambers, Bristol	0117 923 4700
Gold Mr Richard David	St John's Chambers, Bristol	0117 923 4700
Goldberg Mr Simon Ian	Trinity Chambers, Middlesbrough	01642 247569
	Trinity Chambers, Newcastle Upon Tyne	0191 232 1927
Goodfellow Mr Stephen John	East Anglian Chambers, Chelmsford	01473 214481
	East Anglian Chambers, Ipswich	01473 214481
	East Anglian Chambers, Norwich	01473 214481
Goodison Mr Adam Henry	South Square, London	020 7696 9900
Graham Mr Thomas Patrick Henry	New Square Chambers, London	020 7419 8000
Graham Mrs Alana Nicole	Chambers of Alana Graham, Halesowen	01384 894560
	9 Stone Buildings, London	020 7404 5055
Hallett Miss Katherine Elizabeth	13 Old Square Chambers, London	020 7831 4445
Ham Mr Nicholas Treharne	Dyers Chambers, London	020 7404 1881
Harris Mr Melvyn	5 Essex Court, London	020 7410 2000
Haughty Mr Jeremy Nicholas	Chambers of Mr Ami Feder, London	020 7797 7788
	Chambers of Mr Ami Feder, London	020 7797 7788
	Rougemont Chambers, Exeter	01392 208484
Hayes Mr Richard James	Lamb Chambers, London	020 7797 8300
Henderson Mr Neil John	Stone Chambers, London	020 7440 6900
Hendron Mr Henry Joseph Christopher	Strand Chambers, London	020 7117 6920
Hill Mr Michael Gordon	Trinity Chambers, Middlesbrough	01642 247569
	Trinity Chambers, Newcastle Upon Tyne	0191 232 1927
Hirst Mr Martin Lewis	13 KBW, Oxford	01865 311066
	13 King's Bench Walk, London	020 7353 7204
Hodgkiss Ms Suzanne Jane	43 Temple Row Chambers, Birmingham	0121 237 6035
Hodson Mr Matthew Paul	Farrar's Building, London	020 7583 9241
Huggins Mr Toby James	Unity Street Chambers, Bristol	0117 906 9789
Hussain Miss Frida Khanam	Furnival Chambers, London	020 7405 3232
Irvin Mr Peter	Brick Court Chambers, London	020 7379 3550
Iyer Miss Shobana	Swan Chambers, Richmond	0845 123 1234
Jayakrishnan Mr Harry Sisubalan	Trent Chambers, Nottingham	0115 941 9596
Jones Mr Christopher David Harries	St John's Chambers, Bristol	0117 923 4700
Jones Mr Geraint Anthony	New Walk Chambers, Leicester	0871 200 1298/0116 255 9144
	9 St John Street, Manchester	0161 955 9000
	Tanfield Chambers, London	020 7421 5300
Jones Mr Richard Frederick Thomas	Heavenwood Chambers, Stroud	01453 873444
Jowett Mr Timothy David Christian	9 Park Place, Cardiff	029 2038 2731
Kelly Mr Sean	Chancery House Chambers, Leeds	0113 244 6691
Kelly Mrs Amy Louise	12 College Place, Southampton	023 8032 0320
Kent Mr Michael Harcourt	Crown Office Chambers, London	020 7797 8100
Khalid Mr James	Goulds Green Chambers, Uxbridge	01895 422574
	Goulds Green Chambers, Uxbridge	01895 422574
Knight Mr Keith Leslie Francis	4 King's Bench Walk, London	020 7822 7000
Kramer Mr Philip Anthony	Park Lane Plowden, Newcastle Upon Tyne	0191 211 4087
Kwiatkowski Mr Feliks Jerzy	Kew Chambers, Kew	0844 8099991
Kynoch Mr Duncan Stuart Sanderson	Selborne Chambers, London	020 7420 9500
Lane Mr Christopher Paul	No 8 Chambers, Birmingham	0121 236 5514
Lane Mr Simon Charles	Rougemont Chambers, Exeter	01392 208484
Leabeater Mr James Ferguson	4 Pump Court, London	020 7842 5555

C

Lennard Mr Stephen Charles	Hardwicke, London	020 7242 2523
Lenon Mr Andrew Ralph Fitzmaurice	One Essex Court, London	020 7583 2000
Limbrey Mr Bernard Martin	3 Dr Johnson's Buildings, London	020 7353 4854
Lippold Ms Sarah Ida Louise	13 KBW, Oxford	01865 311066
	13 King's Bench Walk, London	020 7353 7204
Lofthouse Mr James	1 Gray's Inn Square, London	020 7405 0001
Lyons Miss Tara Yasmin	Pump Court Chambers, London	020 7353 0711
	Pump Court Chambers, Winchester	01962 868 161
	Riverview Chambers, London	0844 225 3999
Maguire Mr Andrew James	Exchange Chambers, Liverpool	0151 236 7747
	Exchange Chambers, Manchester	0161 833 2722
	St Philips Chambers, Birmingham	0121 246 7000
Mann Mr Christopher	13 KBW, Oxford	01865 311066
	13 King's Bench Walk, London	020 7353 7204
Marsden Mr Andrew Charles	St John's Chambers, Bristol	0117 923 4700
Marsden Mr Andrew Guy	East Anglian Chambers, Chelmsford	01473 214481
	East Anglian Chambers, Colchester	01473 214481
	East Anglian Chambers, Ipswich	01473 214481
	East Anglian Chambers, Norwich	01473 214481
Marshall Mr Derek Stanley	College Chambers, Southampton	023 8023 0338
Matthias Mr David Huw	Francis Taylor Building, London	020 7353 8415
Mawrey Mr Richard Brooks	Henderson Chambers, London	020 7583 9020
Maxwell Lewis Mr Cameron	Lamb Chambers, London	020 7797 8300
McCue Mr Donald	11 Stone Buildings, London	020 7831 6381
McCulloch Miss Fiona Catharine Jane	Middle Temple Lane Chambers, London	020 7583 4352
Medd Mr James Powys	Crown Office Chambers, London	020 7797 8100
Mendelle Mr Paul Michael	25 Bedford Row, London	020 7067 1500
Michael Mr Nicholas	East Anglian Chambers, Chelmsford	01473 214481
	East Anglian Chambers, Colchester	01473 214481
	East Anglian Chambers, Ipswich	01473 214481
	East Anglian Chambers, Norwich	01473 214481
Miles Mr Richard Iain	One Essex Court, London	020 7936 3030
Miller Mr Andrew	2 Temple Gardens, London	020 7822 1200
Mills Mr Kristian Anthony	Trinity Chambers, Middlesbrough	01642 247569
	Trinity Chambers, Newcastle Upon Tyne	0191 232 1927
Mills Mr Simon Thomas	Five Paper, London	020 7815 3200
Modgill Mr Alexander Jeffrey	Broadway House Chambers, Bradford	01274 722560
	Broadway House Chambers, Leeds	0113 246 2600
Moffat Mr Russell Dean	Linenhall Chambers, Chester	01244 348282
Moulder Mr Paul John	Alexander Chambers, London	0845 652 0451/0854 652 0451
	Guildford Chambers, Guildford	01483 539131
Murphy Mr Damian	Enterprise Chambers, Leeds	0113 246 0391
	Enterprise Chambers, London	020 7405 9471
	Enterprise Chambers, Newcastle Upon Tyne	0191 222 3344
Neville Mr Joseph Richard	43 Temple Row Chambers, Birmingham	0121 237 6035
Newman Mr Paul	3 PB Barristers, Bournemouth	01202 292102
	3 PB Barristers, Bristol	0117 928 1520
	3 PB Barristers, London	020 7583 8055
	3 PB Barristers, Oxford	01865 793 736
	3 PB Barristers, Winchester	01962 868884
Noble Mr Andrew	Enterprise Chambers, Leeds	0113 246 0391
Norman Mr Jared Simon Gregory	Field Court Chambers, London	020 7405 6114
Norman Mr Michael Charles	3 PB Barristers, Bournemouth	01202 292102
	3 PB Barristers, Bristol	0117 928 1520
	3 PB Barristers, London	020 7583 8055
	3 PB Barristers, Oxford	01865 793 736
	3 PB Barristers, Winchester	01962 868884
Normington Mr James Adam	Park Court Chambers, Leeds	0113 243 3277
Norton Mr Giles	Enigma Chambers, Sheffield	07779 576499
	Holborn Chambers, London	020 7242 6060

Name	Chambers	Telephone
O'Brien Mr Nicholas William Wattebot	10 King's Bench Walk, London	020 7353 7742
Oommen Mr Jacob	Chambers of Mr Jacob Oommen, East Barnet	07958 680272
Osborne Mr James Robert	Clerksroom (London), London	0845 083 3000
O'Sullivan Mr Thomas Sean Patrick	4 Pump Court, London	020 7842 5555
O'Toole Mr Bartholomew Vincent	5 King's Bench Walk, London	020 7353 5638
Owens Miss Elspeth Eluned	4 Pump Court, London	020 7842 5555
Palmer Mr James Savill	Henderson Chambers, London	020 7583 9020
Panton Mr Alastair Howard	10 King's Bench Walk, London	020 7353 7742
Paraskos Mr Paraskevakis Christakis	11 Gray's Inn Square Chambers, London	020 7405 6879
Parsons Mr Andrew James	Portsmouth Barristers'Chambers, Portsmouth	023 9283 1292
Pascall Mr Matthew Stephen	Alexander Chambers, London	0845 652 0451/0854 652 0451
	Guildford Chambers, Guildford	01483 539131
Payton Mr Clifford Coningsby	Alpha Court Chambers, Leamington Spa	01926 886412
Pennock Mr Ian	Park Lane Plowden, Leeds	0113 228 5049
Phillips Mr Andrew Charles	Crown Office Chambers, London	020 7797 8100
Plant Mr James Richard	Farrar's Building, London	020 7583 9241
Platford Mr Graham Roy	Five Paper, London	020 7815 3200
Pugh Mr John Bishop	John Pugh's Chambers, Liverpool	0151 236 5415
Quiney Mr Charles Benedictus Alexander	Crown Office Chambers, London	020 7797 8100
Quirke Mr Gerard Martin	Citadel Chambers, Birmingham	0121 233 8500
Randolph Mr Paul Leslie	Field Court Chambers, London	020 7405 6114
Reffin Miss Clare Alyson	One Essex Court, London	020 7583 2000
Ridd Mr David Ian Mcgregor	Farrar's Building, London	020 7583 9241
Rigney Mr Andrew James	Crown Office Chambers, London	020 7797 8100
Roberts Mr Allan Calvin	Guildhall Chambers, Bristol	0117 930 9000
	Guildhall Chambers, Bristol	0117 930 9000
Roberts Mr Michael Charles	Chambers of Michael Roberts, Henley-On-Thames	01844 355 655
Roberts Mr Richard Vaughan	Henderson Chambers, London	020 7583 9020
Rogers Mr Daniel James	Number 7 Harrington Street Chambers, Liverpool	0151 242 0707
Rogers Mr Ian Paul	Monckton Chambers, London	020 7405 7211
Roy Mr Stefan Alexander Hiren	5 Pump Court, London	020 7353 2532
Sawtell Mr David Robert Fraser	4 King's Bench Walk, London	020 7822 7000
Seeboruth Mr Royln Jean-Paul	Chambers of Royln Seeboruth, Aylesbury	01296 393329
Sellers Mr Graham	Atlantic Chambers, Liverpool	0151 236 4421
Selvaratnam Miss Vasanti Emily Indrani	Stone Chambers, London	020 7440 6900
Sen Mr Aditya Kumar	Coram Chambers, London	020 7092 3700
Shamim Mr Mohammed	Clapham Law Chambers, London	020 7978 8482
Shapiro Mr Daniel Jonathan	Crown Office Chambers, London	020 7797 8100
Shirley Mr James Patrick	Stone Chambers, London	020 7440 6900
Simon Mr Philipp Arnold Heinrich	4 KBW, London	020 7822 8822
Sinclair Mr Graham Kelso	East Anglian Chambers, Colchester	01473 214481
	East Anglian Chambers, Ipswich	01473 214481
	East Anglian Chambers, Norwich	01473 214481
Singarajah Mr Frederico	1 Gray's Inn Square, London	020 7405 0001
Sisley Mr Timothy Julian Crispin	9 Stone Buildings, London	020 7404 5055
Sjostrand Miss Ekaterina	13 Old Square Chambers, London	020 7831 4445
Smith Mr Robert Clive	1 Paper Buildings, London	020 7353 3728
	RCS Chambers, Stainton	01709 814 147
Smith Mr Robert Ian	St Paul's Chambers, Leeds	0113 245 5866
Snow Mr Darren Mark	Charter Chambers, London	020 7618 4400
Soto-Miranda Mr Diego Fernando	One Essex Court, London	020 7936 3030
Staddon Mr Paul	Tanfield Chambers, London	020 7421 5300
Stead Mr Richard James	St John's Chambers, Bristol	0117 923 4700
Stenhouse Mr John Alexander	Nightingale Chambers, Wolverley	01562 851350

Stephens Mr Michael Allen	Design Chambers, London	020 7353 0747
	St Ive's Chambers, Birmingham	0121 236 0863
Stevenson Mr Paul Anthony	Tanfield Chambers, London	020 7421 5300
Taylor Ms Karen Anne	Themis Chambers, London	07967 418976
Temple Ms Eleanor Louise	Kings Chambers, Birmingham	0845 034 3444
	Kings Chambers, Leeds	0845 034 3444
	Kings Chambers, Manchester	0845 034 3444
Thomas Mr Mark David	5 Essex Court, London	020 7410 2000
Ticciati Mr Oliver	4 Pump Court, London	020 7842 5555
Tompkinson Miss Deborah Ann	Clerksroom (London), London	0845 083 3000
	Clerksroom (Taunton), Taunton	0845 083 3000
Topal Mr Erol	Lamb Chambers, London	020 7797 8300
Tozzi Mr Nigel Kenneth	4 Pump Court, London	020 7842 5555
Treharne Mr Neil Simon	Dingle Chambers, Bristol	07818 827754
Trumpington Mr John Henry	Staple Inn Chambers, London	020 7242 5240
Vaughan Mr Terence Paul	Fenners Chambers, Cambridge	01223 368761
Vernon Mr Elliot Curt	No. 3 Fleet Street Chambers, London	020 7936 4474
Vitiello Mr Fabio Angelo-Giuseppe	Staple Inn Chambers, London	020 7242 5240
Watson Mr Alaric	11 Stone Buildings, London	020 7831 6381
Watthey Mr James Robertson	Hardwicke, London	020 7242 2523
Wells Mr Caspar John Mowlem	Goldsmith Chambers, London	020 7353 6802
Wheatley Mr Geraint Rhys	Kings Chambers, Birmingham	0845 034 3444
	Kings Chambers, Leeds	0845 034 3444
	Kings Chambers, Manchester	0845 034 3444
Wightwick Mr Iain	Riverview Chambers, London	0844 225 3999
	Unity Street Chambers, Bristol	0117 906 9789
Wilkinson Mr Marc Ashley	No5 Chambers, Birmingham	0845 210 5555
	No5 Chambers, Bristol	0845 210 5555
	No5 Chambers, London	0845 210 5555
Williamson Mr Adrian John Gerard Hughes	Keating Chambers, London	020 7544 2600
Wills Miss Alexandra Itari	Christ Church Chambers, London	020 7409 5278/07788 512787
Young Mr Martin Ford	9 Stone Buildings, London	020 7404 5055

SHARE OPTIONS

Arthur Mr Stephen Joseph	Temple Tax Chambers, London	020 7353 7884
Beaumont Mr Marc Clifford	9 Stone Buildings, London	020 7404 5055
	Windsor Barristers' Chambers, Windsor	01753 839321
Buchan Miss Caroline Venetia	Chambers of Miss C Buchan, Haywards Heath	01444 482222
Glyn Mr Caspar Hilary Gordon	Cloisters, London	020 7827 4000
Godfrey Mr Lauren John	Crown Office Row Chambers, Brighton	01273 625625
Graham Mrs Alana Nicole	Chambers of Alana Graham, Halesowen	01384 894560
	9 Stone Buildings, London	020 7404 5055
Iqbal Mr Mashood	London View Chambers, Sawbridgeworth	07788 912493
Iyer Miss Shobana	Swan Chambers, Richmond	0845 123 1234
Keel Mr Douglas Vincent	11 Stone Buildings, London	020 7831 6381
Lall Mr Tarlochan	Monckton Chambers, London	020 7405 7211
Meredith Mr Christopher William	Furnival Chambers, London	020 7405 3232
Miller Mr Andrew	2 Temple Gardens, London	020 7822 1200
Newbold Dr Anne Lorraine Elsie	Minerva Chambers, Ocean Village	00 350 20042779
Parsons Mr Andrew James	Portsmouth Barristers'Chambers, Portsmouth	023 9283 1292
Roberts Mr Michael Charles	Chambers of Michael Roberts, Henley-On-Thames	01844 355 655
Singarajah Mr Frederico	1 Gray's Inn Square, London	020 7405 0001
Sowler Mr Thomas Richard Holland	The Tax Chambers of Mr Richard Sowler TD, Douglas	07624 235000
Sterling Mr Robert Alan	St James's Chambers, Manchester	0161 834 7000
	Zenith Chambers, Leeds	0113 245 5438
Todd Mr Michael Alan	Erskine Chambers, London	020 7242 5532

Name	Chambers	Telephone
Van Tonder Mr Gerard Dirk	New Square Chambers, London	020 7419 8000

SHIPPING/ADMIRALTY

Name	Chambers	Telephone
Ahmed Mr Ishfaq	Stone Chambers, London	020 7440 6900
Alexandra Miss Sebastiane	Holborn Chambers, London	020 7242 6060
Aswani Mr Ravi Girdharilal	Stone Chambers, London	020 7440 6900
Bullock Mr Robert Gustaf	The Chambers of Mr Bullock, Brighton	01273 321050
Charkham Mr Graham Harold	20 Essex Street, London	020 7842 1200
Clark Miss Geraldine	Serle Court, London	020 7242 6105
Coster Mr Ronald David	42 Bedford Row, London	020 7831 0222
Coulter Mr Barry John	Clerksroom (London), London	0845 083 3000
	Clerksroom (Taunton), Taunton	0845 083 3000
	King's Lynn Chambers, King's Lynn	01553 672 085
Devine Mr Michael Buxton	Rougemont Chambers, Exeter	01392 208484
Gibbons Miss Mary Regina	Stone Chambers, London	020 7440 6900
Godwin Mr William George Henry	3 Hare Court, London	020 7415 7800
	St John's Chambers, Bristol	0117 923 4700
Henderson Mr Neil John	Stone Chambers, London	020 7440 6900
Hendron Mr Henry Joseph Christopher	Strand Chambers, London	020 7117 6920
Irvin Mr Peter	Brick Court Chambers, London	020 7379 3550
Leabeater Mr James Ferguson	4 Pump Court, London	020 7842 5555
Ogunbusola Mr Victor Olaniyi	Chambers of Victor Ogumbusola, Basildon	07413 634231
O'Sullivan Mr Thomas Sean Patrick	4 Pump Court, London	020 7842 5555
Owens Miss Elspeth Eluned	4 Pump Court, London	020 7842 5555
Paraskos Mr Paraskevakis Christakis	11 Gray's Inn Square Chambers, London	020 7405 6879
Parsons Mr Andrew James	Portsmouth Barristers'Chambers, Portsmouth	023 9283 1292
Rahman Mr Anis	12 Old Square Chambers, London	020 7404 0875
Rinker Mr Andrew Stuart D'Artois	Chambers of Mr Andrew Rinker, London	020 7584 1091
Selvaratnam Miss Vasanti Emily Indrani	Stone Chambers, London	020 7440 6900
Shirley Mr James Patrick	Stone Chambers, London	020 7440 6900
Singarajah Mr Frederico	1 Gray's Inn Square, London	020 7405 0001
Soto-Miranda Mr Diego Fernando	One Essex Court, London	020 7936 3030
Temmink Mr Robert-Jan	Quadrant Chambers, London	020 7583 4444
Vitiello Mr Fabio Angelo-Giuseppe	Staple Inn Chambers, London	020 7242 5240
Watthey Mr James Robertson	Hardwicke, London	020 7242 2523
Wills Miss Alexandra Itari	Christ Church Chambers, London	020 7409 5278/07788 512787
Wright Mr Alexander Paul	4 Pump Court, London	020 7842 5555

SPORTS

Name	Chambers	Telephone
Abrahams Mr James	8 New Square, London	020 7405 4321
Abu-Mustafa Mr Jehad	1 Paper Buildings, London	020 7353 3728
Afeeva Mr Mark Kudzo Dzitosi	Matrix Chambers, London	020 7404 3447
Akinsanya Mr Stephen Olubunmi	Old Bailey Chambers, London	020 3008 6404
Algazy Mr Jacques Max	Cloisters, London	020 7827 4000
Allwood Mrs Gina Louisa	Seven Bedford Row, London	020 7242 3555
Ameen Mr Danish	18 St John Street, Manchester	0161 278 1800
Andrews Mr Paul Leslie	Great James Street Chambers, London	020 7440 4949
Arnheim Dr Michael Thomas Walter	Chambers of Dr Michael Arnheim, London	020 7833 5093
	Holborn Chambers, London	020 7242 6060
	Principal Chambers, Sevenoaks	0845 209 8080
Austin Mr Ian	Holborn Chambers, London	020 7242 6060
Bajwa Mr Ali Naseem	Garden Court Chambers, London	020 7993 7600
Ball Mr Steven James	Number 7 Harrington Street Chambers, Liverpool	0151 242 0707
Banks Miss Fiona Jane	Monckton Chambers, London	020 7405 7211
Barker Mr Kerry	Guildhall Chambers, Bristol	0117 930 9000

C

Barrister	Chambers	Telephone
Bate Mr Stephen Robert De Breteuil	5RB, London	020 7242 2902
Beaumont Mr Marc Clifford	9 Stone Buildings, London	020 7404 5055
	Windsor Barristers' Chambers, Windsor	01753 839321
Beharrylal Mr Satyanand Sarju	15 New Bridge Street, London	020 7842 1900
Bellamy Mr Jonathan Mark	39 Essex Street, London	020 7832 1111
	82 King Street, Manchester	0161 870 9969
Beloff Mr Rupert Joseph Alexei	No5 Chambers, Birmingham	0845 210 5555
	No5 Chambers, Bristol	0845 210 5555
	No5 Chambers, London	0845 210 5555
Blakey Mr Michael Charles	St Johns Buildings, Manchester	0161 214 1500
	St Johns Buildings Liverpool, Liverpool	0151 243 6000
	16 Winckley Square, Preston	01772 256100
Bourne-Arton Mr Simon Nicholas	Park Court Chambers, Leeds	0113 243 3277
Bowers Mr Rupert John	Doughty Street Chambers, London	020 7404 1313
Bowhill Miss Jessie Kate	8 New Square, London	020 7405 4321
Boyd Mr Stephen James Harvey	Selborne Chambers, London	020 7420 9500
Brady Mr Scott	3 Temple Gardens, London	020 7353 3102
Bragiel Mr Edward Bronislaw Henryk	Hogarth Chambers, London	020 7404 0404
Bryan Mr Robert John	1 Paper Buildings, London	020 7353 3728
Budworth Mr Martin James	Kings Chambers, Birmingham	0845 034 3444
	Kings Chambers, Leeds	0845 034 3444
	Kings Chambers, Manchester	0845 034 3444
Busuttil Mr Godwin John Antoine	5RB, London	020 7242 2902
Butler Mr Rupert James	3 Hare Court, London	020 7415 7800
Byrnes Miss Aisling Alice Elizabeth	25 Bedford Row, London	020 7067 1500
Callery Mr Martin	Cobden House Chambers, Manchester	0161 833 6000
Campbell Mr Oliver Edward Wilhelm	Henderson Chambers, London	020 7583 9020
Caplan Mr Jonathan Michael	Five Paper Buildings, London	020 7583 6117
	Riverview Chambers, London	0844 225 3999
Chodha Mr Tejpal Singh	Chambers of Mr T Chodha, Gravesend	01474 326666
Clark Mr Dingle	Goldsmith Chambers, London	020 7353 6802
Claxton Mr Elroy Geraldo	23 Essex Street, London	020 7413 0353
	Old Bailey Chambers, London	020 3008 6404
Colbey Mr Richard	Guildhall Chambers Portsmouth, Portsmouth	023 9275 2400
	Lamb Chambers, London	020 7797 8300
Connell Mr Edward Samuel	Five St Andrew's Hill, London	020 7332 5400
Corsellis Mr Nicholas Robert Alexander	3 Temple Gardens, London	020 7353 3102
Costello Mr Paul James	Chambers of Mr Paul J Costello, Biggleswade	07846 016 399
Cotter Mr Mark James	Five St Andrew's Hill, London	020 7332 5400
Cotter Mr Nicholas Andrew James Horlor	1 Paper Buildings, London	020 7353 3728
Coulter Mr Barry John	Clerksroom (London), London	0845 083 3000
	Clerksroom (Taunton), Taunton	0845 083 3000
	King's Lynn Chambers, King's Lynn	01553 672 085
Crawford Mr Lincoln Santo	12 King's Bench Walk, London	020 7583 0811
Crinion Mr Charles Edward	1 Mitre Court Buildings, London	020 7452 8900
Critchley Mr John Stephen	Field Court Chambers, London	020 7405 6114
Cross Mr Anthony Maurice	Lincoln House Chambers, Manchester	0161 832 5701
Crouch Mr Stephen William Michael	The Chambers of S W M Crouch, Badby	01327 315 742
Crowe Mr Cameron	36 Bedford Row, London	020 7421 8000
Crystal Mr Jonathan	Argent Chambers, London	020 7556 5500
Davis Mr Adam David	Dyers Chambers, London	020 7404 1881
Dawson Mr Richard Jon Foster	Lincoln House Chambers, Manchester	0161 832 5701
Deacon Mr Robert Murray	11 Stone Buildings, London	020 7831 6381
Dean Mr Jacob	5RB, London	020 7242 2902
Del Fabbro Mr Oscar	23 Essex Street, London	020 7413 0353
Dempsey Miss Karen Marie	3 Temple Gardens, London	020 7353 3102

Barrister	Chambers	Telephone
Denney Mr Stuart Henry Macdonald	Deans Court Chambers, Manchester	0161 214 6000
	Deans Court Chambers, Preston	01772 565 600
	Thomas More Chambers, London	020 7404 7000
Dixey Mr Ian Roger	Guildhall Chambers, Bristol	0117 930 9000
Donnelly Mr Stephen John	Dyers Chambers, London	020 7404 1881
Dos Santos Mr Alexander	Charter Chambers, London	020 7618 4400
Eaton Mr Tobias Barnaby	Staple Inn Chambers, London	020 7242 5240
Edwards Mr Nigel Royston	St Paul's Chambers, Leeds	0113 245 5866
Elliott Mr Eric Alan	Sovereign Chambers, Leeds	0113 245 1841
	Trinity Chambers, Middlesbrough	01642 247569
	Trinity Chambers, Newcastle Upon Tyne	0191 232 1927
	York Chambers, Newcastle Upon Tyne	0191 206 4677
Engelman Mr Mark Trevor	Hardwicke, London	020 7242 2523
Engelman Mr Philip	Cloisters, London	020 7827 4000
	Trinity Chambers, Middlesbrough	01642 247569
	Trinity Chambers, Newcastle Upon Tyne	0191 232 1927
Enoch Mr Dafydd Huw	Apex, Cardiff	02920 232 032
	23 Essex Street, London	020 7413 0353
Evans Mr Philip	QEB Hollis Whiteman, London	020 7933 8855
Evans Mr Simeon Vaughan	St Johns Buildings, Manchester	0161 214 1500
	St Johns Buildings Liverpool, Liverpool	0151 243 6000
	16 Winckley Square, Preston	01772 256100
Farley Mr David Dunbar	St Johns Buildings, Manchester	0161 214 1500
	St Johns Buildings Liverpool, Liverpool	0151 243 6000
	16 Winckley Square, Preston	01772 256100
Ferm Mr Rodney Eric	Broadway House Chambers, Bradford	01274 722560
	Broadway House Chambers, Leeds	0113 246 2600
Fern Mr Gary	7 Stones IP, London	020 7193 4033
Fielding Mr Janick Raphael Alexander	4 King's Bench Walk, London	020 7822 7000
Finn Mr Terence	Erimus Chambers, Bedford	01234 720952
	Forest Chambers, Boston	01775 840827
Finnigan Mr Peter Anthony	QEB Hollis Whiteman, London	020 7933 8855
Fisher Mr David	New Square Chambers, London	020 7419 8000
Fisher Mr Jervis Andrew	Citadel Chambers, Birmingham	0121 233 8500
Ford Mr Mark Steven	Lincoln House Chambers, Manchester	0161 832 5701
Freeman Mr Peter Mark	Farrar's Building, London	020 7583 9241
Friend Mr Mark Owen	Lincoln House Chambers, Manchester	0161 832 5701
Garvie Mr Carl Peter	St Philips Chambers, Birmingham	0121 246 7000
Gent Mr Matthew Thomas	Sovereign Chambers, Leeds	0113 245 1841
Gibbs Mr Philip Mark	KCH Garden Square, Nottingham	0115 941 8851
Gill Mr Manjit Singh	No5 Chambers, Birmingham	0845 210 5555
	No5 Chambers, Bristol	0845 210 5555
	No5 Chambers, London	0845 210 5555
Gilroy Mr Paul	Old Square Chambers, London	020 7269 0300
	9 St John Street, Manchester	0161 955 9000
Glasgow Mr Oliver Edwin James	2 Hare Court, London	020 7353 3982
Gledhill Mr Lee Andre	Alexander Chambers, London	0845 652 0451/0854 652 0451
	Trident Barristers Chambers, Manchester	0161 663 3123
Glyn Mr Caspar Hilary Gordon	Cloisters, London	020 7827 4000
Goldberg Mr Simon Ian	Trinity Chambers, Middlesbrough	01642 247569
	Trinity Chambers, Newcastle Upon Tyne	0191 232 1927
Goldrein Mr Iain Saville	7 Bell Yard, London	020 7831 0636
	Number 7 Harrington Street Chambers, Liverpool	0151 242 0707
Green Mr Patrick Curtis	Henderson Chambers, London	020 7583 9020
Griffiths Mr David	St Philips Chambers, Birmingham	0121 246 7000

Name	Chambers	Telephone
Griffiths Mr Peter	2 Bedford Row, London	020 7440 8888
	30 Park Place, Cardiff	029 2039 8421
Hadrill Mr Keith Paul	Furnival Chambers, London	020 7405 3232
Hamer Mr George Clemens	8 New Square, London	020 7405 4321
Hamilton Mr Nigel	Broadway House Chambers, Bradford	01274 722560
	Broadway House Chambers, Leeds	0113 246 2600
Hanlon Mr James Tobias	Old Bailey Chambers, London	020 3008 6404
Hartley Mr Richard Anthony	Cobden House Chambers, Manchester	0161 833 6000
Heal Mrs Madeleine	New Square Chambers, London	020 7419 8000
Henderson Mr Neil John	Stone Chambers, London	020 7440 6900
Hendron Mr Henry Joseph Christopher	Strand Chambers, London	020 7117 6920
Henthorn Miss Kate Marie	7 Bell Yard, London	020 7831 0636
	18 St John Street, Manchester	0161 278 1800
Higgins Mr Daniel Malcolm Buhlea	Nine Bedford Row, London	020 7489 2727
Higginson Mr Timothy Nicholas Bennett	Littleton Chambers, London	020 7797 8600
	St John's Chambers, Bristol	0117 923 4700
Hill Mr Jonathan	8 New Square, London	020 7405 4321
Hislop Mr David Seymour	Doughty Street Chambers, Bristol	01179 058 717
	Doughty Street Chambers, London	020 7404 1313
	Doughty Street Chambers, Manchester	0161 618 1066
Hobson Miss Laura Elise	Citadel Chambers, Birmingham	0121 233 8500
Hodkinson Mr Gary Stephen	Chambers of Mr Ami Feder, London	020 7797 7788
	Chambers of Mr Ami Feder, London	020 7797 7788
Holmes Ms Elisa	Monckton Chambers, London	020 7405 7211
Hood Mr David	Prince of Wales Chambers, London	020 7622 7415
Iyer Miss Shobana	Swan Chambers, Richmond	0845 123 1234
Jackson Mr Andrew Fraser	5 Pump Court, London	020 7353 2532
Jacobson Mr Lawrence	Five Paper, London	020 7815 3200
Jarratt Miss Alice Cordelia Betchworth	Carmelite Chambers, London	020 7936 6300
Johnson Miss Amanda	Exchange Chambers, Leeds	0113 203 1970
	Exchange Chambers, Liverpool	0151 236 7747
	Exchange Chambers, Manchester	0161 833 2722
Johnson Mr Phillip Michael	Chambers of Mr P Johnson, London	020 7288 2256
Jolliffe Mrs Victoria Esther Jean	5RB, London	020 7242 2902
Jones Mr Geraint Anthony	New Walk Chambers, Leicester	0871 200 1298/0116 255 9144
	9 St John Street, Manchester	0161 955 9000
	Tanfield Chambers, London	020 7421 5300
Kapila Miss Rachel Prakash	3 Raymond Buildings, London	020 7400 6400
Keeling Mr Adrian Francis	No5 Chambers, Birmingham	0845 210 5555
	No5 Chambers, Bristol	0845 210 5555
	No5 Chambers, London	0845 210 5555
Kelly Mr Matthias John	39 Essex Street, London	020 7832 1111
King Mr Gelaga Perry	2 Bedford Row, London	020 7440 8888
King Mr Graham Anthony	1 Gray's Inn Square, London	020 7405 0001
Kinnear Mr Jonathan Shea	9-12 Bell Yard, London	020 7400 1800
Knight Mr Benjamin James	Central Chambers, Manchester	0161 236 1133
Knight Mr Keith Leslie Francis	4 King's Bench Walk, London	020 7822 7000
Lahiffe Mr Martin Patrick Joseph	3 Temple Gardens, London	020 7353 3102
Lal Mr Sanjay	4 King's Bench Walk, London	020 7822 7000
Lamb Mr Jeffrey Thomas	Westgate Chambers, Lewes	01273 480510
Lane Ms Lindsay Ruth Busfield	8 New Square, London	020 7405 4321
Langley Mr Charles Howard	2 Bedford Row, London	020 7440 8888
Lawrence The Hon Patrick John Tristram	Four New Square, London	020 7822 2000
Lennard Mr Stephen Charles	Hardwicke, London	020 7242 2523
Lewis Mr Wayne Anthony	Access Lawyers, London	020 8801 2345
Lissack Mr Richard Anthony	Outer Temple Chambers, London	020 7353 6381
	Riverview Chambers, London	0844 225 3999
Magee Mr Samuel Cairns	2 Bedford Row, London	020 7440 8888
Maher Ms Martha Johanna Dorothy	St John's Chambers, Bristol	0117 923 4700

Name	Chambers	Telephone
Mahmood Mr Abid	Central Chambers, Manchester	0161 236 1133
	No5 Chambers, Birmingham	0845 210 5555
	No5 Chambers, Bristol	0845 210 5555
	No5 Chambers, London	0845 210 5555
Malone Mr David John	1 Gray's Inn Square, London	020 7405 0001
Mansell Mr Jason Francis Guy	Seven Bedford Row, London	020 7242 3555
Mather Mr Nicholas Ian Stewart	Furnival Chambers, London	020 7405 3232
Matthias Mr David Huw	Francis Taylor Building, London	020 7353 8415
Maxwell Lewis Mr Cameron	Lamb Chambers, London	020 7797 8300
McCombie Mr Fergus Alexander Paul	1 Gray's Inn Square, London	020 7405 0001
McCormick Mr William Thomas	Ely Place Chambers, London	020 7400 9600
McKone Mr Mark Desmond	Sovereign Chambers, Leeds	0113 245 1841
Melville-Shreeve Mr Michael David	Walnut House, Exeter	01392 279751
Meredith Mr Christopher William	Furnival Chambers, London	020 7405 3232
Michalos Miss Christina Antigone Diana	5RB, London	020 7242 2902
Miller Mr Andrew	2 Temple Gardens, London	020 7822 1200
Mousley Mr William Howard	2 King's Bench Walk, London	020 7353 1746
Munden Mr Richard Alexander John	5RB, London	020 7242 2902
Murphy Mr Damian	Enterprise Chambers, Leeds	0113 246 0391
	Enterprise Chambers, London	020 7405 9471
	Enterprise Chambers, Newcastle Upon Tyne	0191 222 3344
Murray Mr Daniel Evan Duncan	Old Bailey Chambers, London	020 3008 6404
Newcomb Mr Quinton John	1 Paper Buildings, London	020 7353 3728
Nurse Mr Gordon Bramwell William	Radcliffe Chambers, London	020 7831 0081
O'Gorman Mr Christopher Francis	Cornwall Street Chambers, Birmingham	0121 233 7500
Onslow Mr Robert Denzil	8 New Square, London	020 7405 4321
Osborne Mr James Robert	Clerksroom (London), London	0845 083 3000
O'Toole Mr Bartholomew Vincent	5 King's Bench Walk, London	020 7353 5638
Owen Mr Timothy Wynn	Matrix Chambers, London	020 7404 3447
Palmer Mr James Savill	Henderson Chambers, London	020 7583 9020
Paraskos Mr Paraskevakis Christakis	11 Gray's Inn Square Chambers, London	020 7405 6879
Pascoe Ms Soraya	1 Gray's Inn Square, London	020 7405 0001
Patel Mr Yasin Ahmed	25 Bedford Row, London	020 7067 1500
Penny Mr Timothy Charles	11 Stone Buildings, London	020 7831 6381
Phillips Mr Simon Benjamin	Francis Taylor Building, London	020 7353 8415
	Park Court Chambers, Leeds	0113 243 3277
Pickup Mr James Kenneth	2 Hare Court, London	020 7353 3982
	Lincoln House Chambers, Manchester	0161 832 5701
Platts-Mills Mr Mark Fortescue	8 New Square, London	020 7405 4321
Plimmer Miss Melanie Ann	Kings Chambers, Birmingham	0845 034 3444
	Kings Chambers, Leeds	0845 034 3444
	Kings Chambers, Manchester	0845 034 3444
Prior Mr Paul Stephen	36 Bedford Row, London	020 7421 8000
Prior Mrs Mary	36 Bedford Row, London	020 7421 8000
Quinlan Mr Christopher John	Guildhall Chambers, Bristol	0117 930 9000
Rees Mr Jonathan Elystan	Apex, Cardiff	02920 232 032
Rees Prof William Michael	1 Gray's Inn Square, London	020 7405 0001
Reiz Mr Stanley	Carmelite Chambers, London	020 7936 6300
Rhodes Mr Nicholas Piers	Charter Chambers, London	020 7618 4400
Roberts Mr Michael Charles	Chambers of Michael Roberts, Henley-On-Thames	01844 355 655
Seeboruth Mr Royln Jean-Paul	Chambers of Royln Seeboruth, Aylesbury	01296 393329
Selby Mr Lawrence Julian Catello	Nine Bedford Row, London	020 7489 2727
Shirley Mr James Patrick	Stone Chambers, London	020 7440 6900
Silverton Miss Catherine Anne	Sovereign Chambers, Leeds	0113 245 1841
Singarajah Mr Frederico	1 Gray's Inn Square, London	020 7405 0001
Skinner Mr Samuel Richard Edward	KCH Garden Square, Nottingham	0115 941 8851
Smith Mr Alisdair Robert Macsorley	9-12 Bell Yard, London	020 7400 1800

Smith Mr Clive Francis	Chambers of Marion Smullen and Kerim Fuad QC, London	020 7427 4400
Smith Mr Robert Ian	St Paul's Chambers, Leeds	0113 245 5866
Sood Mrs Usha Rani	Trent Chambers, Nottingham	0115 941 9596
Soto-Miranda Mr Diego Fernando	One Essex Court, London	020 7936 3030
Spalton Mr George David John	Four New Square, London	020 7822 2000
Stead Mr Richard James	St John's Chambers, Bristol	0117 923 4700
Stebbings Mr Ian Anthony	1 Gray's Inn Square, London	020 7405 0001
Stelling Mr Nigel Roy	Citadel Chambers, Birmingham	0121 233 8500
Stevenson Mr Paul Anthony	Tanfield Chambers, London	020 7421 5300
Stevenson Mr Robert Lloyd	Sovereign Chambers, Leeds	0113 245 1841
Stewart Mr Nicholas John Cameron	Ely Place Chambers, London	020 7400 9600
Stinchcombe Mr Paul David	4-5 Gray's Inn Square, London	020 7404 5252
Storey Mr Richard Alexander	3 Temple Gardens, London	020 7353 3102
Stork Mr Brian Raymond	3 Temple Gardens, London	020 7353 3102
Stott Mr Philip Geoffrey	QEB Hollis Whiteman, London	020 7933 8855
Stride Mr Lionel Alexander	Temple Garden Chambers, London	020 7583 1315
Sutton-Mattocks Mr Christopher John	5 King's Bench Walk, London	020 7353 5638
Tarbitt Mr Nicholas Edward Henry	Cornwall Street Chambers, Birmingham	0121 233 7500
Taylor Mrs Susan	Trinity Chambers, Middlesbrough	01642 247569
	Trinity Chambers, Newcastle Upon Tyne	0191 232 1927
Thomas Mr James Austin	KCH Garden Square, Nottingham	0115 941 8851
Thomas Mr Mark David	5 Essex Court, London	020 7410 2000
Tozzi Mr Nigel Kenneth	4 Pump Court, London	020 7842 5555
Treharne Mr Neil Simon	Dingle Chambers, Bristol	07818 827754
Treverton-Jones Mr Gregory Dennis	39 Essex Street, London	020 7832 1111
	82 King Street, Manchester	0161 870 9969
Waldman Mr Amos	Doughty Street Chambers, Bristol	01179 058 717
	Doughty Street Chambers, London	020 7404 1313
	Doughty Street Chambers, Manchester	0161 618 1066
Walker Mr Adam Nigel	Seven Bedford Row, London	020 7242 3555
Wall Mr Mark Arthur	Citadel Chambers, Birmingham	0121 233 8500
Warby Mr Mark David John	5RB, London	020 7242 2902
Ward Mr Robin Henry	8 New Square, London	020 7405 4321
Webster Mr Alistair Stevenson	Chambers of Andrew Mitchell QC, London	020 7440 9950
	Lincoln House Chambers, Manchester	0161 832 5701
Wells Mr Colin John	25 Bedford Row, London	020 7067 1500
West Dr Ewan Donald	Monckton Chambers, London	020 7405 7211
White Mr Daniel Edward Mills	Citadel Chambers, Birmingham	0121 233 8500
Williams Mr Ben Dylan	Kings Chambers, Birmingham	0845 034 3444
	Kings Chambers, Leeds	0845 034 3444
	Kings Chambers, Manchester	0845 034 3444
Wilson Mr Scott	Themis Chambers, London	07967 418976
Woods Mr Terence Mccartan	187 Fleet Street, London	020 7430 7430

TAX (CAPITAL & INCOME)

Ajaz Mr Mohammad Arshad	Eastmans Chambers, Reading	0118 966 9094
Akin Mr Barrie Simon	Gray's Inn Tax Chambers, London	020 7242 2642
	No 8 Chambers, Birmingham	0121 236 5514
Anderson Mr Richard Neil Macdiarmid	Arbitration Chambers, London	020 7267 2137
Arthur Mr Stephen Joseph	Temple Tax Chambers, London	020 7353 7884
Choudhury Miss Sadiya Asghar	Pump Court Tax Chambers, London	020 7414 8080
Clarke Mr Nicholas Patrick James	18 St John Street, Manchester	0161 278 1800
Colbey Mr Richard	Guildhall Chambers Portsmouth, Portsmouth	023 9275 2400
	Lamb Chambers, London	020 7797 8300
Conolly Dr Oliver Stephen	Pump Court Tax Chambers, London	020 7414 8080
Davies Mr Jonathan Huw	Old Square Chambers, Bristol	0117 930 5100
	Old Square Chambers, London	020 7269 0300

Edwards Mr Nigel Royston	St Paul's Chambers, Leeds	0113 245 5866
Eldergill Mr Edmund Malcolm	1 Pump Court, London	020 7842 7070
Facenna Mr Gerald Carlo	Monckton Chambers, London	020 7405 7211
Fairpo Ms Catherine Anne	Atlas Chambers, London	020 7269 7980
Frawley Ms Lyndsey Anne	Quorum Chambers, St Albans	01727 884516
	Quorum Tax Chambers, London	020 7043 5189
Ginniff Mr Nigel Thomas	Atlantic Chambers, Liverpool	0151 236 4421
Godfrey Mr Lauren John	Crown Office Row Chambers, Brighton	01273 625625
Goodfellow Mr Giles William Jeremy	Pump Court Tax Chambers, London	020 7414 8080
Graham Mrs Alana Nicole	Chambers of Alana Graham, Halesowen	01384 894560
	9 Stone Buildings, London	020 7404 5055
Graham-Wells Miss Alison Christine	Exchange Chambers, Leeds	0113 203 1970
	Exchange Chambers, Liverpool	0151 236 7747
	Exchange Chambers, Manchester	0161 833 2722
Hanlon Mr James Tobias	Old Bailey Chambers, London	020 3008 6404
Henderson Mr James Thomas	Kings Chambers, Leeds	0845 034 3444
	Kings Chambers, Manchester	0845 034 3444
	Pump Court Tax Chambers, London	020 7414 8080
Holbech Mr Charles Edward	New Square Chambers, London	020 7419 8000
Hunt Mr Stephen	4 Stone Buildings, London	020 7242 5524
Kamal Mr Setu	St James's Chambers, Manchester	0161 834 7000
	Taxchambers, London	020 7242 2744
Keel Mr Douglas Vincent	11 Stone Buildings, London	020 7831 6381
Kessler Mr James Richard	Taxchambers, London	020 7242 2744
Kinnear Mr Jonathan Shea	9-12 Bell Yard, London	020 7400 1800
Lall Mr Tarlochan	Monckton Chambers, London	020 7405 7211
Lewiecki Miss Marie	Old Bailey Chambers, London	020 3008 6404
Lonsdale Miss Marion Mary	Academy Chambers, London	020 8455 2503
Lyons Mr Timothy John	4-5 Gray's Inn Square, London	020 7404 5252
	St James's Chambers, Manchester	0161 834 7000
MacKenzie Mr Robert Sutherland	Middle Temple Lane Chambers, London	020 7583 4352
Maugham Mr Jolyon Toby Dennis	11 New Square, London	020 7242 4017
Norton Mr Giles	Enigma Chambers, Sheffield	07779 576499
	Holborn Chambers, London	020 7242 6060
Poots Miss Laura Jill	Pump Court Tax Chambers, London	020 7414 8080
Pryke Mr Stuart	Fiduciary Legal, London	07814 495366
Rinker Mr Andrew Stuart D'Artois	Chambers of Mr Andrew Rinker, London	020 7584 1091
Rowell Mr George Edward	St John's Chambers, Bristol	0117 923 4700
Sagar Mr Leigh	New Square Chambers, London	020 7419 8000
Seeboruth Mr Royln Jean-Paul	Chambers of Royln Seeboruth, Aylesbury	01296 393329
Singh Mr Dapinderpaul	23 Essex Street, London	020 7413 0353
	Park Court Chambers, Leeds	0113 243 3277
Singh-Tiwana Mr Ekwall	No5 Chambers, Birmingham	0845 210 5555
	No5 Chambers, Bristol	0845 210 5555
	No5 Chambers, London	0845 210 5555
Sokol Mr Christopher John Francis	Deans Court Chambers, Manchester	0161 214 6000
	Taxchambers, London	020 7242 2744
	Temple Tax Chambers, London	020 7353 7884
Sowler Mr Thomas Richard Holland	The Tax Chambers of Mr Richard Sowler TD, Douglas	07624 235000
Tallon Mr John Mark	Pump Court Tax Chambers, London	020 7414 8080
Vallat Mr Richard Justin	Pump Court Tax Chambers, London	020 7414 8080
Vaughan-Williams Mr Arthur Laurence	13 Old Square Chambers, London	020 7831 4445
Watson Mr Ian David	3 Stone Buildings, London	020 7242 4937
Wiktorowski-Solecki Miss Tamara	Middle Temple Lane Chambers, London	020 7583 4352
Wills Miss Alexandra Itari	Christ Church Chambers, London	020 7409 5278/07788 512787

Woolf The Hon Jeremy Richard George	Pump Court Tax Chambers, London	020 7414 8080

TAX (CORPORATE)

Ajaz Mr Mohammad Arshad	Eastmans Chambers, Reading	0118 966 9094
Akin Mr Barrie Simon	Gray's Inn Tax Chambers, London	020 7242 2642
	No 8 Chambers, Birmingham	0121 236 5514
Anderson Mr Richard Neil Macdiarmid	Arbitration Chambers, London	020 7267 2137
Arthur Mr Stephen Joseph	Temple Tax Chambers, London	020 7353 7884
Choudhury Miss Sadiya Asghar	Pump Court Tax Chambers, London	020 7414 8080
Clarke Mr Nicholas Patrick James	18 St John Street, Manchester	0161 278 1800
Conolly Dr Oliver Stephen	Pump Court Tax Chambers, London	020 7414 8080
Edwards Mr Nigel Royston	St Paul's Chambers, Leeds	0113 245 5866
Fairpo Ms Catherine Anne	Atlas Chambers, London	020 7269 7980
Frawley Ms Lyndsey Anne	Quorum Chambers, St Albans	01727 884516
	Quorum Tax Chambers, London	020 7043 5189
Ginniff Mr Nigel Thomas	Atlantic Chambers, Liverpool	0151 236 4421
Godfrey Mr Lauren John	Crown Office Row Chambers, Brighton	01273 625625
Goodfellow Mr Giles William Jeremy	Pump Court Tax Chambers, London	020 7414 8080
Graham Mrs Alana Nicole	Chambers of Alana Graham, Halesowen	01384 894560
	9 Stone Buildings, London	020 7404 5055
Graham-Wells Miss Alison Christine	Exchange Chambers, Leeds	0113 203 1970
	Exchange Chambers, Liverpool	0151 236 7747
	Exchange Chambers, Manchester	0161 833 2722
Hamilton Mrs Penelope Ann	Pump Court Tax Chambers, London	020 7414 8080
Hanlon Mr James Tobias	Old Bailey Chambers, London	020 3008 6404
Henderson Mr James Thomas	Kings Chambers, Leeds	0845 034 3444
	Kings Chambers, Manchester	0845 034 3444
	Pump Court Tax Chambers, London	020 7414 8080
Kamal Mr Setu	St James's Chambers, Manchester	0161 834 7000
	Taxchambers, London	020 7242 2744
Keel Mr Douglas Vincent	11 Stone Buildings, London	020 7831 6381
Kessler Mr James Richard	Taxchambers, London	020 7242 2744
Khan Mr Arfan	Field Court Chambers, London	020 7405 6114
Lall Mr Tarlochan	Monckton Chambers, London	020 7405 7211
Lewiecki Miss Marie	Old Bailey Chambers, London	020 3008 6404
Lyons Mr Timothy John	4-5 Gray's Inn Square, London	020 7404 5252
	St James's Chambers, Manchester	0161 834 7000
Mantle Mr Peter John	Monckton Chambers, London	020 7405 7211
Maugham Mr Jolyon Toby Dennis	11 New Square, London	020 7242 4017
Norton Mr Giles	Enigma Chambers, Sheffield	07779 576499
	Holborn Chambers, London	020 7242 6060
Poots Miss Laura Jill	Pump Court Tax Chambers, London	020 7414 8080
Rinker Mr Andrew Stuart D'Artois	Chambers of Mr Andrew Rinker, London	020 7584 1091
Rowell Mr George Edward	St John's Chambers, Bristol	0117 923 4700
Seeboruth Mr Royln Jean-Paul	Chambers of Royln Seeboruth, Aylesbury	01296 393329
Sheridan Mr Iain Douglas	London Scottish, Stratford Upon Avon	07971 681724
Singarajah Mr Frederico	1 Gray's Inn Square, London	020 7405 0001
Singh Mr Dapinderpaul	23 Essex Street, London	020 7413 0353
	Park Court Chambers, Leeds	0113 243 3277
Singh-Tiwana Mr Ekwall	No5 Chambers, Birmingham	0845 210 5555
	No5 Chambers, Bristol	0845 210 5555
	No5 Chambers, London	0845 210 5555
Sloane Miss Valentina	Monckton Chambers, London	020 7405 7211
Sokol Mr Christopher John Francis	Deans Court Chambers, Manchester	0161 214 6000
	Taxchambers, London	020 7242 2744
	Temple Tax Chambers, London	020 7353 7884
Sowler Mr Thomas Richard Holland	The Tax Chambers of Mr Richard Sowler TD, Douglas	07624 235000
Tallon Mr John Mark	Pump Court Tax Chambers, London	020 7414 8080

C

Barrister	Chambers	Telephone
Vallat Mr Richard Justin	Pump Court Tax Chambers, London	020 7414 8080
Vaughan-Williams Mr Arthur Laurence	13 Old Square Chambers, London	020 7831 4445
Wiktorowski-Solecki Miss Tamara	Middle Temple Lane Chambers, London	020 7583 4352
Woolf The Hon Jeremy Richard George	Pump Court Tax Chambers, London	020 7414 8080

TELECOMMUNICATIONS

Barrister	Chambers	Telephone
Abrahams Mr James	8 New Square, London	020 7405 4321
Ajaz Mr Mohammad Arshad	Eastmans Chambers, Reading	0118 966 9094
Antell Mr John Jason	King's Bench and Godolphin (KBG)Chambers, Plymouth	01752 221551
Banks Miss Fiona Jane	Monckton Chambers, London	020 7405 7211
Bate Mr Stephen Robert De Breteuil	5RB, London	020 7242 2902
Bates Mr Alan Twan	Monckton Chambers, London	020 7405 7211
Beaumont Mr Marc Clifford	9 Stone Buildings, London	020 7404 5055
	Windsor Barristers' Chambers, Windsor	01753 839321
Bullock Mr Robert Gustaf	The Chambers of Mr Bullock, Brighton	01273 321050
Burr Mr Andrew Charles	Atkin Chambers, London	020 7404 0102
Charlton Mr Alexander Murray	4 Pump Court, London	020 7842 5555
Cunningham Mr Graham Taylor	Hardwicke, London	020 7242 2523
Engelman Mr Mark Trevor	Hardwicke, London	020 7242 2523
Facenna Mr Gerald Carlo	Monckton Chambers, London	020 7405 7211
Fern Mr Gary	7 Stones IP, London	020 7193 4033
Fitzgerald Mr John Vincent	Ingenuity IP Chambers, Petts Wood	
Hamer Mr George Clemens	8 New Square, London	020 7405 4321
Harwood Mr Richard John	39 Essex Street, London	020 7832 1111
	82 King Street, Manchester	0161 870 9969
Higginson Mr Timothy Nicholas Bennett	Littleton Chambers, London	020 7797 8600
	St John's Chambers, Bristol	0117 923 4700
Iyer Miss Shobana	Swan Chambers, Richmond	0845 123 1234
John Miss Laura Elizabeth	Monckton Chambers, London	020 7405 7211
Keane Mr Owen Ashley	Design Chambers, London	020 7353 0747
Kime Mr Matthew Jonathan	Cobden House Chambers, Manchester	0161 833 6000
	Ingenuity IP Chambers, Petts Wood	
	No. 3 Fleet Street Chambers, London	020 7936 4474
Lambert Miss Jane Elizabeth	NIPC, Huddersfield	0800 862 0055
Lane Ms Lindsay Ruth Busfield	8 New Square, London	020 7405 4321
Levy Miss Juliette	Selborne Chambers, London	020 7420 9500
Matthias Mr David Huw	Francis Taylor Building, London	020 7353 8415
McLinden Mr John Vincent Barry	Field Court Chambers, London	020 7405 6114
Miller Mr Andrew	2 Temple Gardens, London	020 7822 1200
Murphy Mr Damian	Enterprise Chambers, Leeds	0113 246 0391
	Enterprise Chambers, London	020 7405 9471
	Enterprise Chambers, Newcastle Upon Tyne	0191 222 3344
Onslow Mr Robert Denzil	8 New Square, London	020 7405 4321
Osborne Mr James Robert	Clerksroom (London), London	0845 083 3000
Palmer Mr Robert Henry	Monckton Chambers, London	020 7405 7211
Penny Mr Timothy Charles	11 Stone Buildings, London	020 7831 6381
Peretz Mr George Michael John	Monckton Chambers, London	020 7405 7211
Purves Mr Gavin Bowman	Swan House, London	020 8998 3035
Rayment Mr Benedick Michael	Monckton Chambers, London	020 7405 7211
Rogers Miss Christy Abigail	Ingenuity IP Chambers, Petts Wood	
	No. 3 Fleet Street Chambers, London	020 7936 4474
Rogers Mr Ian Paul	Monckton Chambers, London	020 7405 7211
Roughton Mr Ashley Wentworth	Hogarth Chambers, London	020 7404 0404
Royce Mr Darryl Fraser	Atkin Chambers, London	020 7404 0102
Sears Mr Robert David Murray	Four New Square, London	020 7822 2000
Silverton Miss Catherine Anne	Sovereign Chambers, Leeds	0113 245 1841

Name	Chambers	Telephone
Singarajah Mr Frederico	1 Gray's Inn Square, London	020 7405 0001
West Dr Ewan Donald	Monckton Chambers, London	020 7405 7211
Wilkinson Mr Marc Ashley	No5 Chambers, Birmingham	0845 210 5555
	No5 Chambers, Bristol	0845 210 5555
	No5 Chambers, London	0845 210 5555

TOWN & COUNTRY PLANNING

Name	Chambers	Telephone
Albutt Mr Ian Leslie	Cornerstone Barristers, London	020 7242 4986
	Heavenwood Chambers, Stroud	01453 873444
Altaras Mr David Maurice	36 Bedford Row, London	020 7421 8000
Amraoui Mr Thomas	4-5 Gray's Inn Square, London	020 7404 5252
Anderson Mr Jack Duthie	4-5 Gray's Inn Square, London	020 7404 5252
Andrews Mr Paul Leslie	Great James Street Chambers, London	020 7440 4949
Atkinson Mr Giles Matthew Quintus	6 Pump Court, London	020 7797 8400
	6 Pump Court Chambers, Maidstone	01622 688094
Auburn Mr Jonathan Walter	4-5 Gray's Inn Square, London	020 7404 5252
Bates Mr John Hayward	Old Square Chambers, Bristol	0117 930 5100
	Old Square Chambers, London	020 7269 0300
Beaumont Mr Marc Clifford	9 Stone Buildings, London	020 7404 5055
	Windsor Barristers' Chambers, Windsor	01753 839321
Bhanji Mr Shiraz Musa	4 Bingham Place, London	020 7486 5347
	1 Gray's Inn Square, London	020 7405 0001
Blohm Mr Leslie Adrian	St John's Chambers, Bristol	0117 923 4700
Booth Mr Alexander Henry Spencer	Francis Taylor Building, London	020 7353 8415
Bourne Mr Charles Gregory	4-5 Gray's Inn Square, London	020 7404 5252
Brady Mr Scott	3 Temple Gardens, London	020 7353 3102
Brunt Mr Philip Edwin	No 8 Chambers, Birmingham	0121 236 5514
Burns Mr Jeremy Stuart	12 College Place, Southampton	023 8032 0320
Burton Mr James William	39 Essex Street, London	020 7832 1111
	82 King Street, Manchester	0161 870 9969
Byrd Miss Noemi Csilla Maria	6 Pump Court, London	020 7797 8400
	6 Pump Court Chambers, Maidstone	01622 688094
Cahill Mr Paul Jeremy	No5 Chambers, Birmingham	0845 210 5555
	No5 Chambers, Bristol	0845 210 5555
	No5 Chambers, London	0845 210 5555
Cairnes Mr Simon Paul Steven	No5 Chambers, Birmingham	0845 210 5555
	No5 Chambers, Bristol	0845 210 5555
	No5 Chambers, London	0845 210 5555
	3 PB Barristers, Winchester	01962 868884
Candlin Miss Naomi Helen	St Philips Chambers, Birmingham	0121 246 7000
Charalambides Mr Leonidas	Francis Taylor Building, London	020 7353 8415
Choongh Mr Satnam Singh	No5 Chambers, Birmingham	0845 210 5555
	No5 Chambers, Bristol	0845 210 5555
	No5 Chambers, London	0845 210 5555
Clarke Mr Rory James	Cornerstone Barristers, London	020 7242 4986
Clay Mr Jonathan Roger	Cornerstone Barristers, London	020 7242 4986
Cocks Mr David John	18 Red Lion Court, London	020 7520 6000
	18 Red Lion Court (Annexe), Chelmsford	01245 280880
Collett Mr Gavin Charles	Rougemont Chambers, Exeter	01392 208484
Cooper Mr Paul Andrew	Portal Chambers, Llandysul	01559 395 292
Cotterell Mr David William	Albion Chambers, Bristol	0117 927 2144
Crowe Mr Cameron	36 Bedford Row, London	020 7421 8000
Dagg Mr John Douglas	Trinity Chambers, Chelmsford	01245 605040
Darroch Miss Fiona Culverwell	Clerksroom (London), London	0845 083 3000
	Clerksroom (Taunton), Taunton	0845 083 3000
	King's Lynn Chambers, King's Lynn	01553 672 085
De Mello Mr Rembert Joseph Julius	No5 Chambers, Birmingham	0845 210 5555
	No5 Chambers, Bristol	0845 210 5555
	No5 Chambers, London	0845 210 5555
Dempsey Miss Karen Marie	3 Temple Gardens, London	020 7353 3102
di Mambro Mr David Jesse Andrew	Pallant Chambers, Chichester	01243 784538
	Radcliffe Chambers, London	020 7831 0081

C

Barrister	Chambers	Telephone
Dipré Mr Paul Nicholas Amadeus	Chambers of Mr P N Dipré, Address withheld	0845 123 1234
	MK Family Law Chambers, Milton Keynes	0845 123 1234
Douglass Miss Geraldine Maisie	Portal Chambers, Llandysul	01559 395 292
Druce Mr Michael James	Cornerstone Barristers, London	020 7242 4986
Earle Mr James Christopher Reginald St John	Fenners Chambers, Cambridge	01223 368761
Edwards Mr Denis	Francis Taylor Building, London	020 7353 8415
Edwards Mr Jonathan William	Westgate Chambers, Lewes	01273 480510
Edwards Mr Martin Richard	39 Essex Street, London	020 7832 1111
	82 King Street, Manchester	0161 870 9969
Egleton Mr Richard Wildman	Pallant Chambers, Chichester	01243 784538
Falkowski Mr Damian	4-5 Gray's Inn Square, London	020 7404 5252
Foulkes Miss Rebecca	5 Pump Court, London	020 7353 2532
Fraser-Urquhart Mr Andrew	4-5 Gray's Inn Square, London	020 7404 5252
Galway-Cooper Dr Philip Anthony	Five St Andrew's Hill, London	020 7332 5400
Gasztowicz Mr Steven	Cornerstone Barristers, London	020 7242 4986
	New Street Chambers, Leicester	0116 262 5906
George Mr Charles Richard	Francis Taylor Building, London	020 7353 8415
Goodman Mr Alexander David Edmund	Atlas Chambers, London	020 7269 7980
	4-5 Gray's Inn Square, London	020 7404 5252
Gore Mr Andrew Roger	Fenners Chambers, Cambridge	01223 368761
Greatorex Mr Paul	4-5 Gray's Inn Square, London	020 7404 5252
Ground Mr Patrick	Chambers of Mr Patrick Ground QC, London	020 7736 0131
Guy Mr Richard Perran	Chambers of Mr Ami Feder, London	020 7797 7788
	King's Bench and Godolphin (KBG)Chambers, Plymouth	01752 221551
	Southernhay Chambers, Exeter	01392 255777
Ham Mr Nicholas Treharne	Dyers Chambers, London	020 7404 1881
Hamilton Mr Nigel	Broadway House Chambers, Bradford	01274 722560
	Broadway House Chambers, Leeds	0113 246 2600
Hanif Miss Saima Naz	4-5 Gray's Inn Square, London	020 7404 5252
Harrison Mr Peter John	6 Pump Court, London	020 7797 8400
	6 Pump Court Chambers, Maidstone	01622 688094
Harvey Mr John Gilbert	No5 Chambers, Birmingham	0845 210 5555
	No5 Chambers, Bristol	0845 210 5555
	No5 Chambers, London	0845 210 5555
Harwood Mr Richard John	39 Essex Street, London	020 7832 1111
	82 King Street, Manchester	0161 870 9969
Hill Mr Nicholas Mark	Pump Court Chambers, London	020 7353 0711
	Pump Court Chambers, Swindon	01793 539899
	St Philips Chambers, Birmingham	0121 246 7000
Hill Mr Piers Nicholas	37 Park Square Chambers, Leeds	0113 243 9422
Hobson Mr John Graham	4-5 Gray's Inn Square, London	020 7404 5252
Hodgkiss Ms Suzanne Jane	43 Temple Row Chambers, Birmingham	0121 237 6035
Holroyd Mr John James	Zenith Chambers, Leeds	0113 245 5438
Honey Mr Richard Arthur	Francis Taylor Building, London	020 7353 8415
Horton Mr Matthew Bethell	39 Essex Street, London	020 7832 1111
	82 King Street, Manchester	0161 870 9969
Howlett Mr James Anthony	KCH Garden Square, Nottingham	0115 941 8851
Humphreys Mr Richard William	Francis Taylor Building, London	020 7353 8415
	No5 Chambers, Birmingham	0845 210 5555
	No5 Chambers, Bristol	0845 210 5555
	No5 Chambers, London	0845 210 5555
Jackson Mr Mark Joseph	No 8 Chambers, Birmingham	0121 236 5514
Jayakrishnan Mr Harry Sisubalan	Trent Chambers, Nottingham	0115 941 9596
Jones Mr Alun	St Paul's Chambers, Leeds	0113 245 5866
Jones Mr Emyr Gweirydd	9 Park Place, Cardiff	029 2038 2731
Jones Mr Richard Frederick Thomas	Heavenwood Chambers, Stroud	01453 873444

Barrister	Chambers	Telephone
Jones Mr Timothy Arthur	No5 Chambers, Birmingham	0845 210 5555
	No5 Chambers, Bristol	0845 210 5555
	No5 Chambers, London	0845 210 5555
Kolvin Mr Philip Alan	Cornerstone Barristers, London	020 7242 4986
	Kings Chambers, Leeds	0845 034 3444
	Kings Chambers, Manchester	0845 034 3444
Lane Mr Michael John	East Anglian Chambers, Colchester	01473 214481
	East Anglian Chambers, Ipswich	01473 214481
	East Anglian Chambers, Norwich	01473 214481
Lane Mr Simon Charles	Rougemont Chambers, Exeter	01392 208484
Leigh Mr Kevin	No5 Chambers, Birmingham	0845 210 5555
	No5 Chambers, Bristol	0845 210 5555
	No5 Chambers, London	0845 210 5555
Levett Miss Francesca Anna	Five St Andrew's Hill, London	020 7332 5400
Lewis Mr Meyric	Francis Taylor Building, London	020 7353 8415
Lloyd Mr John Nesbitt	Rougemont Chambers, Exeter	01392 208484
Lopez Mr Juan Nemesio	Francis Taylor Building, London	020 7353 8415
Loveday Mr David Robert	4-5 Gray's Inn Square, London	020 7404 5252
Mainwaring Mr Robert Paul Clason	Portal Chambers, Llandysul	01559 395 292
Marcus Mr Peter	Zenith Chambers, Leeds	0113 245 5438
Marsden Mr Andrew Guy	East Anglian Chambers, Chelmsford	01473 214481
	East Anglian Chambers, Colchester	01473 214481
	East Anglian Chambers, Ipswich	01473 214481
	East Anglian Chambers, Norwich	01473 214481
Masters Mr Alan Bruce Raymond	1 Pump Court, London	020 7842 7070
Matthias Mr David Huw	Francis Taylor Building, London	020 7353 8415
McCracken Mr Robert Henry Joy	Francis Taylor Building, London	020 7353 8415
McGee Dr Tristan Paul	Foxhill Chambers, Penrith	01768 482710
McGrath Mr Andrew John	No5 Chambers, Birmingham	0845 210 5555
	No5 Chambers, Bristol	0845 210 5555
	No5 Chambers, London	0845 210 5555
McKay Mr Christopher Alexander	Cathedral Chambers, Newport	01633 215112
Meager Mrs Rowena Elisabeth	No5 Chambers, Birmingham	0845 210 5555
	No5 Chambers, Bristol	0845 210 5555
	No5 Chambers, London	0845 210 5555
Miah Mr Anawar Babul	Great James Street Chambers, London	020 7440 4949
Miller Mr Peter Owen Michael	Cornerstone Barristers, London	020 7242 4986
Mitchell Mr Alistair Stephen Fabian	49 Chambers, Bridgnorth	01746 761545
Moffett Mr Jonathan Keith	4-5 Gray's Inn Square, London	020 7404 5252
Moll Mr Christiaan Eric	Blackfriars Chambers, London	020 7353 7400
Monnington Mr Bruce Gilbert	Fenners Chambers, Cambridge	01223 368761
Montague Mrs Susan	Weald Chambers, Address withheld	01424 882 876
Morris Mr Ieuan John	9 Park Place, Cardiff	029 2038 2731
Mynors Dr Charles Baskerville	Francis Taylor Building, London	020 7353 8415
Nardell Mr Gordon Lawrence	39 Essex Street, London	020 7832 1111
	82 King Street, Manchester	0161 870 9969
Newport Mr Ian Alun	College Chambers, Southampton	023 8023 0338
Newsom Mr George Lucien	Guildhall Chambers, Bristol	0117 930 9000
Normington Mr James Adam	Park Court Chambers, Leeds	0113 243 3277
O'Neill Mr Jonathan Norman	Rougemont Chambers, Exeter	01392 208484
Ornsby Miss Suzanne Doreen	Francis Taylor Building, London	020 7353 8415
	St John's Chambers, Bristol	0117 923 4700
Osborne Mr James Robert	Clerksroom (London), London	0845 083 3000
Parker Mrs Karen Lesley	Guildhall Chambers Portsmouth, Portsmouth	023 9275 2400
Petersen Mr Thomas James	Goldsmith Chambers, London	020 7353 6802
Phillips Mr Jeremy Gavin	Francis Taylor Building, London	020 7353 8415
Phillips Mr Simon Benjamin	Francis Taylor Building, London	020 7353 8415
	Park Court Chambers, Leeds	0113 243 3277
Potter Miss Alison Lisa	4 Pump Court, London	020 7842 5555
Powell Mr Jonathan David	Atlas Chambers, London	020 7269 7980
Powell Mr William Rhys	Regency Chambers, Cambridge	01223 301517
	Regency Chambers, Peterborough	01733 315215
Price Mr Andrew Robert	Dyers Chambers, London	020 7404 1881

Barrister	Chambers	Telephone
Purchas Mr Robin Michael	Francis Taylor Building, London	020 7353 8415
Purves Mr Gavin Bowman	Swan House, London	020 8998 3035
Quirke Mr Gerard Martin	Citadel Chambers, Birmingham	0121 233 8500
Rana Mr Mohammed Akram	Clapham Law Chambers, London	020 7978 8482
Richardson Mr Garth Douglas Anthony	Devon Chambers, Plymouth	01752 661659
	Rougemont Chambers, Exeter	01392 208484
Rubens Miss Jacqueline Ann	1 Pump Court, London	020 7842 7070
Rudd Mr Michael	36 Bedford Row, London	020 7421 8000
Rushton Mr Jonathon Barker	36 Bedford Row, London	020 7421 8000
Russell Mr Guy Jonothon	Westgate Chambers, Lewes	01273 480510
Sampson Mr Graeme William	3 PB Barristers, Bournemouth	01202 292102
	3 PB Barristers, Bristol	0117 928 1520
	3 PB Barristers, London	020 7583 8055
	3 PB Barristers, Oxford	01865 793 736
	3 PB Barristers, Winchester	01962 868884
Seeboruth Mr Royln Jean-Paul	Chambers of Royln Seeboruth, Aylesbury	01296 393329
Sellers Mr Graham	Atlantic Chambers, Liverpool	0151 236 4421
Shapiro Mr Selwyn	2 King's Bench Walk, London	020 7353 1746
Sheikh Ms Saira Kabir	Francis Taylor Building, London	020 7353 8415
Sheppard Mr Timothy Derie	No5 Chambers, Birmingham	0845 210 5555
	No5 Chambers, Bristol	0845 210 5555
	No5 Chambers, London	0845 210 5555
Skelly Mr Andrew Jon	Hardwicke, London	020 7242 2523
Skinner Mr Samuel Richard Edward	KCH Garden Square, Nottingham	0115 941 8851
Smith Mr Robert Clive	1 Paper Buildings, London	020 7353 3728
	RCS Chambers, Stainton	01709 814 147
Sood Mrs Usha Rani	Trent Chambers, Nottingham	0115 941 9596
Sowler Mr Thomas Richard Holland	The Tax Chambers of Mr Richard Sowler TD, Douglas	07624 235000
Steel Mr John Brychan	4-5 Gray's Inn Square, London	020 7404 5252
Stemp Mr Scott	12 College Place, Southampton	023 8032 0320
Stenhouse Mr John Alexander	Nightingale Chambers, Wolverley	01562 851350
Stinchcombe Mr Paul David	4-5 Gray's Inn Square, London	020 7404 5252
Sugarman Mr Jason Ashley	9-12 Bell Yard, London	020 7400 1800
Tapsell Mr Paul Richard	Becket Chambers, Canterbury	01227 786331
Taylor Ms Karen Anne	Themis Chambers, London	07967 418976
Thomas Miss Megan Moira	6 Pump Court, London	020 7797 8400
	6 Pump Court Chambers, Maidstone	01622 688094
Townsend Mrs Harriet Caroline Jane	Cornerstone Barristers, London	020 7242 4986
Treharne Mr Neil Simon	Dingle Chambers, Bristol	07818 827754
Vaughan-Williams Mr Arthur Laurence	13 Old Square Chambers, London	020 7831 4445
Wadsley Mr Peter John Campbell	St John's Chambers, Bristol	0117 923 4700
Wald Mr Richard Daniel	39 Essex Street, London	020 7832 1111
	82 King Street, Manchester	0161 870 9969
	Riverview Chambers, London	0844 225 3999
Walsh Mr Michael Patrick	Tanfield Chambers, London	020 7421 5300
Ward Mr Peter Mark	The Chambers of Peter Ward, London	020 3402 2152
Whale Mr Stephen John	4-5 Gray's Inn Square, London	020 7404 5252
Wigley Miss Jenny	No5 Chambers, Birmingham	0845 210 5555
	No5 Chambers, Bristol	0845 210 5555
	No5 Chambers, London	0845 210 5555
Williams Miss Anne Margaret	6 Pump Court, London	020 7797 8400
	6 Pump Court Chambers, Maidstone	01622 688094
Zwart Mr Auberon Christiaan Conrad	39 Essex Street, London	020 7832 1111
	82 King Street, Manchester	0161 870 9969

TRADEMARKS

Barrister	Chambers	Telephone
Abrahams Mr James	8 New Square, London	020 7405 4321
Andrews Mr Paul Leslie	Great James Street Chambers, London	020 7440 4949
Bagley Miss Louisa Ellen	1 Paper Buildings, London	020 7353 3728
Bailey Miss Rosana Henrietta	10 King's Bench Walk, London	020 7353 7742

Name	Chambers	Telephone
Blackmore Mr John Hugh	St John's Chambers, Bristol	0117 923 4700
Bowhill Miss Jessie Kate	8 New Square, London	020 7405 4321
Bragiel Mr Edward Bronislaw Henryk	Hogarth Chambers, London	020 7404 0404
Buchan Miss Caroline Venetia	Chambers of Miss C Buchan, Haywards Heath	01444 482222
Budworth Mr Martin James	Kings Chambers, Birmingham	0845 034 3444
	Kings Chambers, Leeds	0845 034 3444
	Kings Chambers, Manchester	0845 034 3444
Clark Ms Julia Elisabeth	Hogarth Chambers, London	020 7404 0404
Craig Mr Aubrey John	Chancery House Chambers, Leeds	0113 244 6691
	St Philips Chambers, Birmingham	0121 246 7000
Critchley Mr John Stephen	Field Court Chambers, London	020 7405 6114
Cunningham Mr Graham Taylor	Hardwicke, London	020 7242 2523
De Mounteney Mr Jonathan Patrick	Chambers of Mr J P De Mounteney, Reading	0118 934 6822
Deacon Mr Robert Murray	11 Stone Buildings, London	020 7831 6381
Devlin Mr Bernard Joseph	Five St Andrew's Hill, London	020 7332 5400
Dillon Mr Thomas William Matthew	Chambers of Thomas Dillon, London	020 7692 2722
Edwards Mr Nigel Royston	St Paul's Chambers, Leeds	0113 245 5866
Engelman Mr Mark Trevor	Hardwicke, London	020 7242 2523
Fern Mr Gary	7 Stones IP, London	020 7193 4033
Fitzgerald Mr John Vincent	Ingenuity IP Chambers, Petts Wood	
Gersch Mr Adam Nissen	Argent Chambers, London	020 7556 5500
Grant Mr Chudi Paul	Kenworthy's Chambers, Manchester	0161 832 4036
Griffin Miss Lynn Myfanwy	23 Essex Street, London	020 7413 0353
Ham Mr Nicholas Treharne	Dyers Chambers, London	020 7404 1881
Hamer Mr George Clemens	8 New Square, London	020 7405 4321
Heal Mrs Madeleine	New Square Chambers, London	020 7419 8000
Hendron Mr Henry Joseph Christopher	Strand Chambers, London	020 7117 6920
Hill Mr Jonathan	8 New Square, London	020 7405 4321
Himsworth Miss Emma Katherine	One Essex Court, London	020 7583 2000
Himsworth Mr Mark Stephen	Dyers Chambers, London	020 7404 1881
Hobbs Mr Geoffrey William	One Essex Court, London	020 7583 2000
Irwin Mr Gavin David	Dyers Chambers, London	020 7404 1881
Iyer Miss Shobana	Swan Chambers, Richmond	0845 123 1234
Jenkins Mr Edward Nicholas	Five Paper Buildings, London	020 7583 6117
Johnson Mr Phillip Michael	Chambers of Mr P Johnson, London	020 7288 2256
Jones Mr Christopher David Harries	St John's Chambers, Bristol	0117 923 4700
Jones Mr Kelvin Mcallister	Templis Chambers, London	020 7649 9808
Khan Dr Alexander	Coral House, Manchester	
Kime Mr Matthew Jonathan	Cobden House Chambers, Manchester	0161 833 6000
	Ingenuity IP Chambers, Petts Wood	
	No. 3 Fleet Street Chambers, London	020 7936 4474
Lambert Miss Jane Elizabeth	NIPC, Huddersfield	0800 862 0055
Lane Ms Lindsay Ruth Busfield	8 New Square, London	020 7405 4321
Lawrence Dr Heather Bunting Elizabeth	11 South Square, London	020 7405 1222
Le Fevre Miss Sarah Margaret	3 Raymond Buildings, London	020 7400 6400
Levett Miss Francesca Anna	Five St Andrew's Hill, London	020 7332 5400
Michalos Miss Christina Antigone Diana	5RB, London	020 7242 2902
Nicol Mr Stuart Henry David	13 King's Bench Walk, London	020 7353 7204
Norton Mr Giles	Enigma Chambers, Sheffield	07779 576499
	Holborn Chambers, London	020 7242 6060
Onslow Mr Robert Denzil	8 New Square, London	020 7405 4321
Paraskos Mr Paraskevakis Christakis	11 Gray's Inn Square Chambers, London	020 7405 6879
Parsons Mr Andrew James	Portsmouth Barristers'Chambers, Portsmouth	023 9283 1292
Pearson Mr Christopher	Lamb Chambers, London	020 7797 8300
Penny Mr Timothy Charles	11 Stone Buildings, London	020 7831 6381
Platts-Mills Mr Mark Fortescue	8 New Square, London	020 7405 4321
Purves Mr Gavin Bowman	Swan House, London	020 8998 3035

Reed Mr Jeremy Nigel	Hogarth Chambers, London	020 7404 0404
Roberts Mr Philip Duncan	One Essex Court, London	020 7583 2000
Rogers Miss Christy Abigail	Ingenuity IP Chambers, Petts Wood	
	No. 3 Fleet Street Chambers, London	020 7936 4474
Roughton Mr Ashley Wentworth	Hogarth Chambers, London	020 7404 0404
Sampson Dr Timothy Michael George	One Essex Court, London	020 7936 3030
Seeboruth Mr Royln Jean-Paul	Chambers of Royln Seeboruth, Aylesbury	01296 393329
Singarajah Mr Frederico	1 Gray's Inn Square, London	020 7405 0001
Smith Miss Eileen Joan	Trinity Chambers, Middlesbrough	01642 247569
	Trinity Chambers, Newcastle Upon Tyne	0191 232 1927
Stein Mr Daniel Alexander	No5 Chambers, Birmingham	0845 210 5555
	No5 Chambers, Bristol	0845 210 5555
	No5 Chambers, London	0845 210 5555
Sumnall Miss Charlene Emma Louise	Five Paper Buildings, London	020 7583 6117
Taylor Ms Karen Anne	Themis Chambers, London	07967 418976
Tritton Mr Robert Guy Henton	Hogarth Chambers, London	020 7404 0404
Ward Mr Robin Henry	8 New Square, London	020 7405 4321

UNIT TRUSTS

Pryke Mr Stuart	Fiduciary Legal, London	07814 495366
Rinker Mr Andrew Stuart D'Artois	Chambers of Mr Andrew Rinker, London	020 7584 1091
Seeboruth Mr Royln Jean-Paul	Chambers of Royln Seeboruth, Aylesbury	01296 393329
Singarajah Mr Frederico	1 Gray's Inn Square, London	020 7405 0001
Wolman Mr Clive Richard	11 Stone Buildings, London	020 7831 6381

AARONBERG MR DAVID JEFFREY QC (2010)

15 New Bridge Street
London EC4V 6AU ☎020 7842 1900
✉clerks@15nbs.com
Call Date: Jul 1981, Inner Temple
Pupil Supervisor, Recorder

ABASHEIKH MR OMAR SAID IMAM

Paragon Chambers
8 Creed Lane, St. Paul, London EC4V 5BR
☎020 3318 9988
✉contact@paragonchambers.com
Call Date: Jul 2006, Gray's Inn

Practising Areas: Administrative, Arbitration, Commercial Litigation, Company & Commercial, Crime, Crime (Corporate/Fraud), Employment, Family, Family Provision, Foreign Law, Human Rights, Immigration, International Trade, Islamic Sharia Law, Medical Negligence, Private International, Public International

ABBASI MISS NYLAH NAZ

9 King's Bench Walk
Lower Ground Floor South, 9 King's Bench Walk, Temple, London EC4Y 7DX
☎020 7353 9564 ✉9kbw@btconnect.com
Call Date: Mar 2001, Lincoln's Inn

Practising Areas: Family, Immigration, Landlord & Tenant

ABRAHAMS MR JAMES

8 New Square
8 New Square, Lincoln's Inn, London WC2A 3QP ☎020 7405 4321 ✉clerks@8newsquare.co.uk
Call Date: Oct 1997, Gray's Inn
Pupil Supervisor

Practising Areas: Copyright, EC & Competition Law, Entertainment, Film, Cable & TV, Franchising, Information Technology, Intellectual Property, Patents, Sports, Telecommunications, Trademarks

ABU-MUSTAFA MR JEHAD

1 Paper Buildings
1st Floor, 1 Paper Buildings, Temple, London EC4Y 7EP ☎020 7353 3728
✉clerks@onepaper.co.uk
Call Date: Nov 2007, Middle Temple

Practising Areas: Courts Martial, Crime, Crime (Corporate/Fraud), Health & Safety, Local Government, Regulatory Law, Sports

ACKERLEY MISS REBECCA ELIZABETH

New Bailey Chambers
4th Floor, Corn Exchange, Fenwick Street, Liverpool, Merseyside L2 7QS
☎0151 236 9402 ✉clerks@newbailey.com
Call Date: Nov 2004, Lincoln's Inn

ACKLAND MISS SACHA MARIE

Temple Garden Chambers
1 Harcourt Buildings, Temple, London EC4Y 9DA ☎020 7583 1315 ✉clerks@tgchambers.com
Call Date: Oct 1998, Inner Temple

Practising Areas: Insurance, Insurance/Reinsurance, Personal Injury

ADAMS MS LINDSAY EVELINE

1 Pump Court
Elm Court, Temple, London EC4Y 7AB
☎020 7842 7070 ✉(name)@pumpcourt.co.uk
Call Date: Nov 1987, Middle Temple
Pupil Supervisor

Practising Areas: Family

ADAMS MR RICHARD JAMES THOMAS

St Philips Chambers
55 Temple Row, Birmingham B2 5LS
☎0121 246 7000 ✉clerks@st-philips.com
Call Date: Oct 1999, Gray's Inn

ADAMS MR ROBERT GEORGE SETON

Trinity Chambers
The Custom House, 39 Quayside, Newcastle Upon Tyne NE1 3DE ☎0191 232 1927
✉info@trinitychambers.co.uk
Trinity Chambers
Multi Media Exchange, 72-80 Corporation Road, Middlesbrough TS1 2RF
☎01642 247569 ✉info@trinitychambers.co.uk
Call Date: Oct 1993, Inner Temple
Pupil Supervisor, Recorder

ADAMSON MR ALAN

Kew Chambers
354 Kew Road, Kew, Surrey TW9 3DU
☎0844 8099991 ✉admin@kewchambers.co.uk
Call Date: Oct 1997, Inner Temple

Practising Areas: Common Law (General), Personal Injury

ADAMSON MISS LILIAS LOUISA

Becket Chambers
17 New Dover Road, Canterbury, Kent CT1 3AS ☎01227 786331
✉clerks@becket-chambers.co.uk
Call Date: Nov 1994, Gray's Inn

Practising Areas: Care Proceedings, Family, Family Provision

ADDISON MR KENNETH PAUL

5 Pump Court
Ground Floor, 5 Pump Court, Temple, London EC4Y 7AP ☎020 7353 2532
✉clerks@5pumpcourt.com
Call Date: Jul 1988, Middle Temple

Practising Areas: Crime, Crime (Corporate/Fraud)

ADDY MISS LAURA REBECCA

Sovereign Chambers
46 Park Place, Leeds LS1 2RY
☎0113 245 1841
✉clerks@sovereignchambers.co.uk
Call Date: Jul 2004, Middle Temple

ADEWALE MR REMI ADETOKUNBO SANNI

Chambers of Mr R. A. Adewale
Address withheld ☎020 7231 2814
Chambers of G. D. Tetteh
Ground Floor, 2 Middle Temple Lane, Temple, London EC4Y 9AA ☎020 7353 7095
Call Date: Oct 1995, Middle Temple

Practising Areas: Administrative, Chancery (General), Chancery (Land Law), Civil Liberties, Commercial Litigation, Commercial Property, Common Law (General), Discrimination, Education, Employment, Housing, Insolvency, Landlord & Tenant, Local Government

ADJEI MR CYRIL JOHN

Five Paper
Ground Floor, 5 Paper Buildings, Temple, London EC4Y 7HB ☎020 7815 3200
Call Date: Oct 1995, Inner Temple
Pupil Supervisor

Practising Areas: Employment

ADKIN MR TIMOTHY CLIVE

42 Bedford Row
London WC1R 4LL ☎020 7831 0222
✉clerks@42br.com
Call Date: Nov 2004, Lincoln's Inn

Practising Areas: Employment

ADLER MR JONATHAN

1 Pump Court
Elm Court, Temple, London EC4Y 7AB
☎020 7842 7070 ✉(name)@pumpcourt.co.uk
Call Date: Oct 1999, Inner Temple

Practising Areas: Care Proceedings, Family, Family Provision, Human Rights, Immigration

AEBERLI MR PETER DOLPH

3 PB Barristers
3 Paper Buildings, Temple, London EC4Y 7EU
☎020 7583 8055
3 PB Barristers
Royal Talbot House, 2 Victoria Street, Bristol, Avon BS1 6BB ☎0117 928 1520
3 PB Barristers
30 Christchurch Road, Bournemouth, Dorset BH1 3PD ☎01202 292102 ✉clerks.bournemouth@3paper.co.uk
3 PB Barristers
4 St Peter Street, Winchester SO23 8BW
☎01962 868884 ✉clerks.winchester@3paper.co.uk
3 PB Barristers
23 Beaumont Street, Oxford OX1 2NP
☎01865 793 736
Call Date: Nov 1990, Middle Temple

Practising Areas: Arbitration, Commercial Litigation, Common Law (General), Construction, Professional Negligence

AFEEVA MR MARK KUDZO DZITOSI

Matrix Chambers
Griffin Building, Gray's Inn, London WC1R 5LN ☎020 7404 3447 ✉matrix@matrixlaw.co.uk/lscott@matrixlaw.co.uk
Call Date: Oct 1997, Inner Temple

Practising Areas: Defamation, Discrimination, Employment, Entertainment, Intellectual Property, Licensing, Sports

AFZAL MR FAYYAZ OBE

No5 Chambers
Fountain Court, Steelhouse Lane, Birmingham B4 6DR ☎0845 210 5555 ✉info@no5.com
No5 Chambers
Greenwood House, 4-7 Salisbury Court, London EC4Y 8AA ☎0845 210 5555
No5 Chambers
38 Queen Square, Bristol BS1 4QS
☎0845 210 5555
Call Date: Oct 1999, Lincoln's Inn
Pupil Supervisor

Practising Areas: Crime, Crime (Corporate/Fraud), Family, Family Provision, Immigration, Landlord & Tenant, Personal Injury, Professional Negligence, Regulatory Law

C

AFZAL MR ZAHEER

St Philips Chambers
55 Temple Row, Birmingham B2 5LS
☎0121 246 7000 ✉clerks@st-philips.com
Call Date: Jul 2000, Gray's Inn

AGER MR RICHARD LAWRENCE

Crown Office Row Chambers
119 Church Street, Brighton, Sussex BN1 1UD ☎01273 625625 ✉clerks@1cor.com
Call Date: Nov 2004, Middle Temple

Practising Areas: Care Proceedings, Family

AGEROS MR DAVID KEITH JUSTIN

4 Paper Buildings
1st Floor, 4 Paper Buildings, Temple, London EC4Y 7EX ☎020 7427 5200 ✉clerks@4pb.com
Call Date: Nov 1993, Inner Temple

AGGREY-ORLEANS MR BERTRAND-LESLIE KWEKU

12 King's Bench Walk
12 King's Bench Walk, Temple, London EC4Y 7EL ☎020 7583 0811
Call Date: Oct 1998, Inner Temple

AGNIHOTRI MR NAVEEN

12 College Place
Fauvelle Buildings, 12 College Place, Southampton SO15 2FE ☎023 8032 0320 ✉clerks@12cp.co.uk
Call Date: Jul 2001, Gray's Inn

Practising Areas: Chancery (General), Chancery (Land Law), Civil Litigation, Common Law (General), Construction, Discrimination, Employment, Housing, Landlord & Tenant

C

AHERN MR EUGENE CHRISTOPHER

Trinity Chambers
Highfield House, Moulsham Street, Chelmsford, Essex CM2 9AH
☎01245 605040 ✉clerks@trinitychambers.com
Call Date: Jul 2007, Middle Temple

Practising Areas: Care Proceedings, Family

AHLUWALIA MR NAVTEJ SINGH

Garden Court Chambers
57-60 Lincoln's Inn Fields, London WC2A 3LJ
☎020 7993 7600 ✉info@gclaw.co.uk
Call Date: Mar 2001, Middle Temple

Practising Areas: Administrative, Civil Litigation, Human Rights, Immigration, Public Law

AHMAD MS AYSHA

42 Bedford Row
London WC1R 4LL ☎020 7831 0222
✉clerks@42br.com
Call Date: Oct 1996, Middle Temple

Practising Areas: Discrimination, Employment

AHMAD MR KASHIF ZUBAIR

Blenheim Chambers
605 Blenheim Centre, Hounslow, Middlesex TW3 1ND ☎07588 608288 ✉kashif.ahmad786@yahoo.co.uk
Call Date: Jul 1999, Lincoln's Inn

Practising Areas: Administrative, Common Law (General), Immigration

AHMAD DR MIRZA FARAKH NAVID

St Philips Chambers
55 Temple Row, Birmingham B2 5LS
☎0121 246 7000 ✉clerks@st-philips.com
Call Date: Jul 1984, Gray's Inn
Pupil Supervisor

AHMED MISS AMINA

Renaissance Chambers
5th Floor, Gray's Inn Chambers, Gray's Inn, London WC1R 5JA ☎020 7404 1111
✉clerks@renaissancechambers.co.uk
Call Date: Feb 1995, Middle Temple

Practising Areas: Care Proceedings, Family

AHMED MR GULAM MORTUZA

Chambers of Marion Smullen and Kerim Fuad QC
1 Inner Temple Lane, London EC4Y 1AF
☎020 7427 4400 ✉clerks@1itl.com
Call Date: Oct 1997, Lincoln's Inn
Pupil Supervisor

AHMED MR ISHFAQ

Stone Chambers
4 Field Court, Gray's Inn, London WC1R 5EF
☎020 7440 6900 ✉clerks@stonechambers.com
Call Date: Oct 1999, Lincoln's Inn

Practising Areas: Admiralty, Arbitration, Aviation, Banking, Commercial Litigation, Common Law (General), Company & Commercial, Employment, Insurance, International Trade, Personal Injury, Private International, Sale & Carriage of Goods, Shipping/Admiralty

AHMED MR MOBIN UDDIN

Chambers of Mobin U Ahmed
36 Chase Road, London N14 4EU
☎ 020 8886 2015 ✉ mobinuahmed@hotmail.co.uk
Call Date: Nov 1969, Lincoln's Inn

AHMED MR NAZIR

Centurion Chambers
Chambers of Mer Nazir Ahmed, 1st Floor Paragon House, 79 Birmingham Road, West Bromwich B70 6PX ☎ 0121 553 4613
✉ clerks@centurionchambers.com
Call Date: May 1992, Inner Temple

Practising Areas: Administrative, Human Rights, Immigration

AHMED MR SALEEM

Perivale Chambers
Ground Floor, 15 Colwyn Avenue, Perivale, Middlesex UB6 8JX ☎ 020 8998 1935
✉ naushadahmed@hotmail.com
Call Date: Feb 1971, Inner Temple
Pupil Supervisor

Practising Areas: Employment, Family, Landlord & Tenant

AHMED MR SIRAJ ISSAP

St Johns Buildings Liverpool
8th Floor India Buildings, Water Street, Liverpool L2 0XG ☎ 0151 243 6000
✉ clerk@stjohnsbuildings.co.uk
St Johns Buildings
21 White Friars, Chester CH1 1NZ
☎ 01244 323070 ✉ clerk@stjohnsbuildings.co.uk
St Johns Buildings
24a - 28 St John Street, Manchester M3 4DJ
☎ 0161 214 1500 ✉ clerk@stjohnsbuildings.co.uk
Call Date: Mar 2001, Middle Temple

AHYA MISS SONAL

KCH Garden Square
1 Oxford Street, Nottingham NG1 5BH
☎ 0115 941 8851 ✉ clerks@kchgardensquare.co.uk
Call Date: Nov 1995, Lincoln's Inn

AILES MR JOHN ASHLEY

Eighteen Carlton Crescent
Rownhams House, Rownhams, Southampton SO16 8LF ☎ 023 8063 9001
✉ clerks@18carltoncrescent.co.uk
Call Date: Jul 1975, Middle Temple
Pupil Supervisor

Practising Areas: Care Proceedings, Chancery (General), Chancery (Land Law), Children's Law, Civil Litigation, Common Law (General), Costs, Crime, Family, Family Provision, Land, Landlord & Tenant, Personal Injury, Probate & Administration, Professional Negligence

AINA MR BENJAMIN ADEJOWON OLUFEMI QC (2009)

Old Bailey Chambers
15 Old Bailey, London EC4M 7EF
☎ 020 3008 6404
✉ clerks@15oldbaileychambers.com
Call Date: Jul 1987, Lincoln's Inn

Practising Areas: Administrative, Crime (Corporate/Fraud), Regulatory Law

AJAZ MR MOHAMMAD ARSHAD

Eastmans Chambers
41 St Bartholomew's Road, Reading, Berkshire RG1 3QA ☎ 0118 966 9094
✉ eastmans@hotmail.co.uk
Call Date: Jul 2011, Lincoln's Inn

Practising Areas: Ancillary Relief, Asset Finance, Banking, Bankruptcy, Care Proceedings, Chancery (General), Chancery (Land Law), Charities, Children's Law, Civil Litigation, Commercial Litigation, Common Law (General), Company & Commercial, Construction, Consumer, Coroners Inquests, Corporate Finance, Costs, Crime (Corporate/Fraud), Data Protection, Disciplinary Tribunals, EC & Competition Law, Education, Energy, Equity, Wills & Trusts, Family, Family Provision, Financial Services, Foreign Law, Human Rights, Immigration, Information Technology, Insolvency, Insurance, Insurance/Reinsurance, Islamic Sharia Law, Landlord & Tenant, Local Government, Medical Negligence, Partnership, Pensions, Private International, Probate & Administration, Professional Negligence, Public International, Public Law, Regulatory Law, Road Traffic And Highways, Tax (Capital & Income), Tax (Corporate), Telecommunications

AKERS MR ROBERT MATTHEW HARRY

St Johns Buildings
24a - 28 St John Street, Manchester M3 4DJ
☎ 0161 214 1500 ✉ clerk@stjohnsbuildings.co.uk
St Johns Buildings
21 White Friars, Chester CH1 1NZ
☎ 01244 323070 ✉ clerk@stjohnsbuildings.co.uk
16 Winckley Square
Preston PR1 3JJ ☎ 01772 256100
Call Date: Nov 2003, Inner Temple

Practising Areas: Civil Litigation, Crime, Discrimination, Education, Environment, Local

Government, Personal Injury, Public Law, Regulatory Law, Road Traffic And Highways

AKIN MR BARRIE SIMON

Gray's Inn Tax Chambers
3rd Floor, Gray's Inn Chambers, Gray's Inn, London WC1R 5JA ☎ 020 7242 2642
✉ clerks@taxbar.com
No 8 Chambers
8 Fountain Court, Steelhouse Lane, Birmingham B4 6DR ☎ 0121 236 5514
✉ clerks@no8chambers.co.uk
Call Date: Jul 1976, Middle Temple

Practising Areas: Tax (Capital & Income), Tax (Corporate)

AKINBOLU MISS SANDRA ADWOA ANIFA

Chambers of Mr Ami Feder
Ground Floor, Lamb Building, Temple, London EC4Y 7AS ☎ 020 7797 7788
✉ clerks@lambbuilding.co.uk
Chambers of Mr Ami Feder
Ground Floor, Lamb Building, Temple, London EC4Y 7AS ☎ 020 7797 7788
✉ clerks@lambbuilding.co.uk
Call Date: Oct 2002, Middle Temple

Practising Areas: Children's Law, Civil Liberties, Family, Immigration

AKIN-OLUGBADE MR OLUWAJEMINIPE BABARINSADE

Nexus Chambers
7 New Square, Lincolns Inn, London WC2A 3QS ☎ 020 7404 1147 / 020 7831 8309
✉ info@nexuschambers.com
Call Date: Oct 1998, Lincoln's Inn

Practising Areas: Crime, Crime (Corporate/Fraud), Personal Injury

AKINSANYA MR STEPHEN OLUBUNMI

Old Bailey Chambers
15 Old Bailey, London EC4M 7EF
☎ 020 3008 6404
✉ clerks@15oldbaileychambers.com
Call Date: Nov 1993, Inner Temple

Practising Areas: Arbitration, Common Law (General), Courts Martial, Crime, Crime (Corporate/Fraud), Film, Cable & TV, Sports

AKMAN MISS MERCY LOUISE

36 Bedford Row
London WC1R 4JH ☎ 020 7421 8000
✉ chambers@36bedfordrow.co.uk
Call Date: Nov 1982, Gray's Inn

Practising Areas: Ancillary Relief, Arbitration, Care Proceedings, Children's Law, Family, Family Provision

AKTHER MISS RIPON

Renaissance Chambers
5th Floor, Gray's Inn Chambers, Gray's Inn, London WC1R 5JA ☎ 020 7404 1111
✉ clerks@renaissancechambers.co.uk
Call Date: Mar 2003, Lincoln's Inn

AKTHER MISS TAHINA SULTANA

Cobden House Chambers
19 Quay Street, Manchester M3 3HN
☎ 0161 833 6000 ✉ Clerks@Cobden.co.uk
Southernhay Chambers
33 Southernhay East, Exeter EX1 1NX
☎ 01392 255777
✉ clerks@southernhaychambers.co.uk
Call Date: Oct 2003, Lincoln's Inn

Practising Areas: Family, Housing, Landlord & Tenant

AKUDOLU MISS NNEKA VERONICA ANASTESIA

2 Pump Court
1st Floor, 2 Pump Court, Temple, London EC4Y 7AH ☎ 020 7353 5597
✉ clerks@2pumpcourt.co.uk
Call Date: Oct 2002, Middle Temple

Practising Areas: Courts Martial, Crime, Employment

AKWAGYIRAM MR SAMUEL MANTEAW

12 Old Square Chambers
1st Floor, 12 Old Square, Lincoln's Inn, London WC2A 3TX ☎ 020 7404 0875
✉ clerks@12oldsquare.com
Call Date: Nov 1985, Inner Temple

ALAKIJA MR AYODELE HUGH

No 8 Chambers
8 Fountain Court, Steelhouse Lane, Birmingham B4 6DR ☎ 0121 236 5514
✉ clerks@no8chambers.co.uk
Call Date: Oct 1996, Gray's Inn

Practising Areas: Common Law (General), Crime, Immigration

ALAM MS JAN

Ropewalk Chambers
24 The Ropewalk, Nottingham NG1 5EF
☎ 0115 947 2581 ✉ clerks@ropewalk.co.uk
Call Date: Jul 2003, Gray's Inn

Practising Areas: Common Law (General), Education, Employment, Health & Safety, Healthcare, Housing, Landlord & Tenant, Licensing, Medical Negligence, Mental Health, Professional Negligence, Regulatory Law

ALBUTT MR IAN LESLIE

Cornerstone Barristers
2-3 Gray's Inn Square, Gray's Inn, London WC1R 5JH ☎ 020 7242 4986
✉ chambers@2-3gis.co.uk
Heavenwood Chambers
Heavenwood Chambers, Heavenwood House, 71 Bownham Park, Rodborough Common, Stroud, Gloucestershire GL5 5BZ
☎ 01453 873444 ✉ kms@heavenwood.co.uk
Call Date: Jul 1981, Gray's Inn
Pupil Supervisor

Practising Areas: Administrative, Environment, Human Rights, Land, Local Government, Public Law, Town & Country Planning

ALDRED MR MARK STEVEN

QEB Hollis Whiteman
1-2 Laurence Pountney Hill, London EC4R 0EU ☎ 020 7933 8855 ✉ barristers@qebhw.co.uk
Call Date: Mar 1996, Middle Temple

ALEESON MR WARWICK LAN GRIEG

187 Fleet Street
London EC4A 2AT ☎ 020 7430 7430
✉ chambers@187fleetstreet.com
Call Date: Nov 1994, Gray's Inn
Pupil Supervisor

Practising Areas: Crime, Crime (Corporate/Fraud), Regulatory Law

ALEXANDER MISS JOSEPHINE ANNE

Principal Chambers
15 Lime Tree Walk, Sevenoaks, Kent TN13 1YH ☎ 0845 209 8080
Call Date: Feb 1994, Middle Temple

Practising Areas: Family, Immigration

ALEXANDRA MISS SEBASTIANE

Holborn Chambers
6 Gate Street, Lincoln's Inn Fields, London WC2A 3HP ☎ 020 7242 6060
Call Date: Nov 2002, Inner Temple

Practising Areas: Aviation, Banking, Chancery (General), Commercial Litigation, Common Law (General), Company & Commercial, Courts Martial, Entertainment, Foreign Law, Public International, Public Law, Regulatory Law, Shipping/Admiralty

ALGAZY MR JACQUES MAX QC (2012)

Cloisters
1 Pump Court, Temple, London EC4Y 7AA
☎ 020 7827 4000 ✉ clerks@cloisters.com
Call Date: Nov 1980, Gray's Inn
Pupil Supervisor

Practising Areas: Administrative, Civil Liberties, Civil Litigation, Commercial Litigation, Common Law (General), Defamation, Disciplinary Tribunals, Discrimination, EC & Competition Law, Employment, Entertainment, Film, Cable & TV, Human Rights, Information Technology, International Trade, Licensing, Local Government, Partnership, Private International, Public Law, Regulatory Law, Sports

ALI MR ISHTIYAQ

Chartlands Chambers
3 St Giles Terrace, Northampton NN1 2BN
☎ 01604 603322
✉ enquiries@chartlands-chambers.co.uk
Call Date: Nov 1996, Lincoln's Inn

Practising Areas: Common Law (General), Human Rights, Immigration, Personal Injury

ALI MRS SHAMIM

Chambers of Mrs Shamim Ali
19 Flamingo Close, Salisbury Village, Hatfield, Hertfordshire AL10 9LU ☎ 01707 276737
✉ a2a_herts@hotmail.com
Call Date: Jul 1998, Lincoln's Inn

Practising Areas: Arbitration, Civil Liberties, Family, Housing, Immigration

ALI MR ZAFAR QC (2012)

23 Essex Street
London WC2R 3AA ☎ 020 7413 0353
✉ clerks@23es.com
Call Date: Nov 1994, Middle Temple
Pupil Supervisor

Practising Areas: Crime, Crime (Corporate/Fraud)

ALIBHAI MR ARI KARIM

QEB Hollis Whiteman
1-2 Laurence Pountney Hill, London EC4R 0EU ☎ 020 7933 8855 ✉ barristers@qebhw.co.uk
Call Date: Oct 2003, Gray's Inn

ALIKER MR PHILLIP BLISS

Tanfield Chambers
2-5 Warwick Court, London WC1R 5DJ
☎ 020 7421 5300 ✉ clerks@tanfieldchambers.co.uk
Call Date: Oct 1990, Inner Temple
Pupil Supervisor

Practising Areas: Arbitration, Banking, Chancery (Land Law), Commercial Litigation, Commercial Property, Financial Services, Insurance, International Trade, Landlord & Tenant, Private International, Sale & Carriage of Goods

ALLEN MR DOUGLAS STEPHEN

Harcourt Chambers
1st Floor, 2 Harcourt Buildings, Temple, London EC4Y 9DB ☎ 0844 561 7135
Call Date: Oct 1995, Lincoln's Inn

Practising Areas: Care Proceedings, Family, Family Provision

ALLEN MS FRANCES

Renaissance Chambers
5th Floor, Gray's Inn Chambers, Gray's Inn, London WC1R 5JA ☎ 020 7404 1111
✉ clerks@renaissancechambers.co.uk
Call Date: Oct 1995, Inner Temple

Practising Areas: Immigration

C

ALLEN MR NEIL

39 Essex Street
London WC2R 3AT ☎ 020 7832 1111
✉ clerks@39essex.com
Call Date: Oct 1999, Middle Temple

ALLEN MISS SYLVIA DELORES

1 Mitre Court Buildings
1 Mitre Court Buildings, Temple, London EC4Y 7BS ☎ 020 7452 8900 ✉ clerks@1mcb.com
Call Date: Jul 1983, Gray's Inn

Practising Areas: Children's Law, Family

ALLERHAND MR LUDWIK EDMUND

Chambers of Mr Ludwik Allerhand
38 Dunoon Road, Forest Hill, London SE23 3TF ☎ 020 8291 4356
✉ ludwikallerhand@btinternet.com
Call Date: Nov 2001, Inner Temple

Practising Areas: Commodities, Company & Commercial, Financial Services, International Trade

ALLIOTT MR GEORGE BECKLES

Temple Garden Chambers
1 Harcourt Buildings, Temple, London EC4Y 9DA ☎ 020 7583 1315 ✉ clerks@tgchambers.com
Call Date: Jul 1981, Inner Temple
Pupil Supervisor

Practising Areas: Commercial Litigation, Common Law (General), Construction, Courts Martial, Employment, Insurance, Local Government, Medical Negligence, Personal Injury, Professional Negligence, Sale & Carriage of Goods

ALLISON MR SIMON ROBERT

Hardwicke
New Square, Lincoln's Inn, London WC2A 3SB ☎ 020 7242 2523
✉ enquiries@hardwicke.co.uk
Call Date: Oct 2005, Lincoln's Inn

Practising Areas: Bankruptcy, Chancery (Land Law), Civil Litigation, Commercial Litigation, Commercial Property, Housing, Insolvency, Land, Landlord & Tenant, Professional Negligence

ALLMAN MISS MARISA NICHOLE

Zenith Chambers
10 Park Square, Leeds LS1 2LH
☎ 0113 245 5438 ✉ clerks@zenithchambers.co.uk
Call Date: Oct 1998, Lincoln's Inn

Practising Areas: Family, Family Provision

ALLOWAY MR TOR HUGH

Talloway Chambers
Rivington House, 82 Great Eastern Street, London EC2A 3JF ☎ 020 7419 5047
✉ tor@talloway.com
Call Date: Jul 1985, Lincoln's Inn
Pupil Supervisor

Practising Areas: Common Law (General), Employment, Family Provision, Insurance, Insurance/Reinsurance, Personal Injury, Sale & Carriage of Goods

ALLSOP MR JULIAN ELISEO

Guildhall Chambers
23 Broad Street, Bristol BS1 2HG
☎ 0117 930 9000 ✉ hoc@guildhallchambers.co.uk
Call Date: Oct 1999, Lincoln's Inn

Practising Areas: Construction, Employment

ALLSTON MR ANTHONY STANLEY

3 Dr Johnson's Buildings
Ground Floor, 3 Dr Johnson's Buildings, Temple, London EC4Y 7BA ☎ 020 7353 4854
✉ clerks@3djb.co.uk
Call Date: Jul 1975, Gray's Inn
Pupil Supervisor

Practising Areas: Chancery (Land Law), Common Law (General), Family, Landlord & Tenant, Medical Negligence, Personal Injury, Probate & Administration

ALLWOOD MRS GINA LOUISA

Seven Bedford Row
7 Bedford Row, London WC1R 4BS
☎ 020 7242 3555 ✉ clerks@7br.co.uk
Call Date: Jul 2002, Gray's Inn

Practising Areas: Administrative, Care Proceedings, Children's Law, Civil Liberties, Civil Litigation, Commercial Property, Commodities, Costs, Disciplinary Tribunals, Education, Employment, Family, Family Provision, Foreign Law, Health & Safety, Human Rights, Immigration, Land, Mental Health, Public Law, Sale & Carriage of Goods, Sports

ALMIHDAR MR ALI HAMED

Outer Temple Chambers
The Outer Temple, 222 Strand, London WC2R 1BA ☎ 020 7353 6381
✉ clerks@outertemple.com
Call Date: Nov 2003, Middle Temple

Practising Areas: Arbitration, Commercial Litigation, Commodities, Energy, Environment, Foreign Law, Islamic Sharia Law

ALOMO MR RICHARD OLUSOJI

14 Gray's Inn Square
14 Gray's Inn Square, Gray's Inn, London WC1R 5JP ☎ 020 7242 0858 ✉ clerks@14gis.co.uk
Call Date: Nov 1990, Inner Temple
Pupil Supervisor

Practising Areas: Administrative, Arbitration, Chancery (Land Law), Civil Liberties, Common Land, Discrimination, Employment

ALTARAS MR DAVID MAURICE

36 Bedford Row
London WC1R 4JH ☎ 020 7421 8000
✉ chambers@36bedfordrow.co.uk
Call Date: Nov 1969, Lincoln's Inn
Pupil Supervisor, Recorder

Practising Areas: Administrative, Arbitration, Chancery (General), Chancery (Land Law), Civil Liberties, Commercial Litigation, Common Law (General), Environment, Local Government, Town & Country Planning

ALY MISS SHEILA

Warwick House Chambers
8 Warwick Court, Warwick House Chambers, Gray's Inn, London WC1R 5DJ
☎ 020 7430 2323
✉ clerks@warwickhousechambers.com
Call Date: Oct 2002, Lincoln's Inn

Practising Areas: Common Law (General), Defamation, Discrimination, Employment, Entertainment, Landlord & Tenant, Personal Injury, Professional Negligence

AMARASINHA MR REVANTHA ARJUNA

9-12 Bell Yard
London WC2A 2JR ☎ 020 7400 1800
✉ clerks@9-12bellyard.com
Call Date: Oct 1996, Middle Temple

AMEEN MR DANISH

18 St John Street
Manchester M3 4EA ☎ 0161 278 1800
✉ clerks@18sjs.com
Call Date: Mar 2006, Lincoln's Inn

Practising Areas: Care Proceedings, Chancery (Land Law), Common Law (General), Equity, Wills & Trusts, Family, Immigration, Islamic Sharia Law, Landlord & Tenant, Personal Injury, Sports

AMIN MISS FARAH

4 King's Bench Walk
2nd Floor, 4 King's Bench Walk, Temple, London EC4Y 7DL ☎ 020 7822 7000
✉ clerks@4kbw.co.uk
Call Date: Jul 1991, Lincoln's Inn

AMIRAFTABI MISS ROSHANAK

Renaissance Chambers
5th Floor, Gray's Inn Chambers, Gray's Inn, London WC1R 5JA ☎020 7404 1111
✉clerks@renaissancechambers.co.uk
Call Date: Feb 1993, Gray's Inn
Pupil Supervisor

Practising Areas: Family

AMIS MR CHRISTOPHER JOCELYN

23 Essex Street
London WC2R 3AA ☎020 7413 0353
✉clerks@23es.com
Call Date: Nov 1991, Gray's Inn
Pupil Supervisor

Practising Areas: Crime

AMRAOUI MR THOMAS

4-5 Gray's Inn Square
Gray's Inn, London WC1R 5AH
☎020 7404 5252 ✉clerks@4-5.co.uk
Call Date: Nov 2007, Gray's Inn

Practising Areas: Administrative, Civil Liberties, Common Law (General), Discrimination, Education, Employment, Environment, Housing, Human Rights, Immigration, Local Government, Mental Health, Parliamentary, Town & Country Planning

ANDERS MR JONATHAN JAMES

Chambers of Marion Smullen and Kerim Fuad QC
1 Inner Temple Lane, London EC4Y 1AF
☎020 7427 4400 ✉clerks@1itl.com
Call Date: Feb 1990, Inner Temple

ANDERSON MR JACK DUTHIE

4-5 Gray's Inn Square
Gray's Inn, London WC1R 5AH
☎020 7404 5252 ✉clerks@4-5.co.uk
Call Date: Nov 2006, Inner Temple

Practising Areas: Administrative, Common Law (General), Employment, Local Government, Town & Country Planning

ANDERSON MR JAMIE HENRIE

Trinity Chambers
The Custom House, 39 Quayside, Newcastle Upon Tyne NE1 3DE ☎0191 232 1927
✉info@trinitychambers.co.uk
Trinity Chambers
Multi Media Exchange, 72-80 Corporation Road, Middlesbrough TS1 2RF
☎01642 247569 ✉info@trinitychambers.co.uk
Call Date: Jul 2004, Lincoln's Inn

Practising Areas: Discrimination, Employment

ANDERSON MR MARK ROGER QC (2010)

No5 Chambers
Fountain Court, Steelhouse Lane, Birmingham B4 6DR ☎0845 210 5555 ✉info@no5.com
No5 Chambers
Greenwood House, 4-7 Salisbury Court, London EC4Y 8AA ☎0845 210 5555
No5 Chambers
38 Queen Square, Bristol BS1 4QS
☎0845 210 5555
Call Date: Jul 1983, Middle Temple
Pupil Supervisor, Recorder

Practising Areas: Commercial Litigation

ANDERSON MR NICHOLAS GUY

1 KBW Chambers
1 King's Bench Walk, Temple, London EC4Y 7DB ☎020 7936 1500 ✉clerks@1kbw.co.uk
King's Bench Chambers
174 High Street, Lewes BN7 1YE
☎01273 402600
Call Date: Oct 1995, Gray's Inn
Pupil Supervisor

Practising Areas: Ancillary Relief, Children's Law, Family Provision

ANDERSON MR RICHARD NEIL MACDIARMID

Arbitration Chambers
22 Willes Road, London NW5 3DS
☎020 7267 2137 ✉john.tackaberry@39essex.com
Call Date: Apr 1991, Gray's Inn

Practising Areas: Admiralty, Arbitration, Company & Commercial, Construction, Crime, Crime (Corporate/Fraud), Defamation, Insolvency, Tax (Capital & Income), Tax (Corporate)

ANDERSON MR SIMON PETER BEDE

Park Court Chambers
16 Park Place, Leeds LS1 2SJ
☎0113 243 3277
✉clerks@parkcourtchambers.co.uk
Call Date: Nov 1997, Lincoln's Inn

Practising Areas: Commercial Litigation, Common Law (General), Employment, Personal Injury

C

ANDRE MR ROGER LOUIS

Sovereign Chambers
46 Park Place, Leeds LS1 2RY
☎ 0113 245 1841
✉ clerks@sovereignchambers.co.uk
Call Date: Oct 1999, Middle Temple

Practising Areas: Administrative, Civil Litigation, Common Law (General), Company & Commercial, Defamation, Education, Equity, Wills & Trusts, Inquests, Insurance, Landlord & Tenant, Licensing, Medical Negligence, Personal Injury, Probate & Administration, Professional Negligence, Sale & Carriage of Goods

ANDRESS MR COLIN MICHAEL

33 Bedford Row
London WC1R 4JH ☎ 020 7242 6476
✉ clerks@33bedfordrow.co.uk
Call Date: Jul 2002, Gray's Inn

ANDREWS MISS MELANIE ALEXANDRA

Becket Chambers
17 New Dover Road, Canterbury, Kent CT1 3AS ☎ 01227 786331
✉ clerks@becket-chambers.co.uk
Call Date: Oct 2005, Middle Temple

Practising Areas: Care Proceedings, Family, Personal Injury

ANDREWS MR PAUL LESLIE

Great James Street Chambers
37 Great James Street, London WC1N 3HB
☎ 020 7440 4949 ✉ chambers@greatjames.co.uk
Call Date: Nov 2003, Inner Temple

Practising Areas: Agriculture, Common Law (General), Construction, Copyright, Courts Martial, Crime, Crime (Corporate/Fraud), Defamation, Entertainment, Environment, Film, Cable & TV, Health & Safety, Intellectual Property, Landlord & Tenant, Patents, Regulatory Law, Sports, Town & Country Planning, Trademarks

ANGAMMANA MR GAMINI BERTRAM

Chambers of Gamini Angammana
'Woodcroft', 13 Woodend, Upper Norwood, London SE19 3NU ☎ 020 8771 5205
✉ woodcroftchambers@btconnect.com
Call Date: Nov 1983, Lincoln's Inn

Practising Areas: Common Law (General), Defamation, Housing, Insolvency, Landlord & Tenant, Local Government, Medical Negligence, Personal Injury, Professional Negligence

ANNING MISS SARA ELIZABETH

Park Lane Plowden
19 Westgate, Leeds LS1 2RD
☎ 0113 228 5049 ✉ clerks@parklaneplowden.co.uk
Call Date: Oct 1995, Inner Temple

ANSELL MISS RACHEL LOUISE

4 Pump Court
4 Pump Court, Temple, London EC4Y 7AN
☎ 020 7842 5555 ✉ chambers@4pumpcourt.com
Call Date: Oct 1995, Middle Temple
Pupil Supervisor

Practising Areas: Commercial Litigation, Construction, Insurance, Professional Negligence

ANSTEY MRS EVE ALEXANDRA SORREL

Pallant Chambers
12 North Pallant, Chichester, West Sussex PO19 1TQ ☎ 01243 784538
✉ clerks@pallantchambers.co.uk
Call Date: Nov 2005, Middle Temple

ANTELL MR JOHN JASON

King's Bench and Godolphin (KBG)Chambers
115 North Hill, Plymouth, Devon PL4 8JY
☎ 01752 221551 ✉ clerks@kbgchambers.co.uk
Call Date: Oct 1992, Middle Temple

Practising Areas: Banking, Chancery (General), Chancery (Land Law), Civil Litigation, Commercial Litigation, Common Law (General), Company & Commercial, Construction, Consumer, Data Protection, Discrimination, Employment, Financial Services, Information Technology, Insurance, Insurance/Reinsurance, Land, Personal Injury, Sale & Carriage of Goods, Telecommunications

APFEL MR FREDDY

37 Park Square Chambers
37 Park Square, Leeds LS1 2NY
☎ 0113 243 9422 ✉ chambers@no37.co.uk
Call Date: Jul 1986, Middle Temple
Pupil Supervisor

Practising Areas: Courts Martial, Crime, Crime (Corporate/Fraud)

APPIAH MISS LINDA

Guildford Chambers
Stoke House, Leapale Lane, Guildford, Surrey GU1 4LY ☎01483 539131
✉clerks@guildfordchambers.co.uk
Call Date: Nov 2001, Middle Temple

Practising Areas: Common Law (General), Crime, Immigration

APTHORP MR GEORGE CHARLES

5 Essex Court
1st Floor, 5 Essex Court, Temple, London EC4Y 9AH ☎020 7410 2000
✉clerks@5essexcourt.co.uk
Call Date: Feb 1983, Inner Temple
Pupil Supervisor

Practising Areas: Civil Litigation, Common Law (General), Disciplinary Tribunals, Discrimination, Equity, Wills & Trusts, Healthcare, Insolvency, Partnership

ARCHER MISS AUDREY SYBIL DOROTHY

3 PB Barristers
3 Paper Buildings, Temple, London EC4Y 7EU ☎020 7583 8055
3 PB Barristers
Royal Talbot House, 2 Victoria Street, Bristol, Avon BS1 6BB ☎0117 928 1520
3 PB Barristers
30 Christchurch Road, Bournemouth, Dorset BH1 3PD ☎01202 292102 ✉clerks.bournemouth@3paper.co.uk
3 PB Barristers
4 St Peter Street, Winchester SO23 8BW ☎01962 868884 ✉clerks.winchester@3paper.co.uk
3 PB Barristers
23 Beaumont Street, Oxford OX1 2NP ☎01865 793 736
Call Date: Oct 2004, Middle Temple

Practising Areas: Courts Martial, Crime, Crime (Corporate/Fraud), Regulatory Law

ARCHER MS LORNA HELEN

1 Pump Court
Elm Court, Temple, London EC4Y 7AB ☎020 7842 7070 ✉(name)@pumpcourt.co.uk
Call Date: Nov 1986, Gray's Inn

ARCHER MR TREVOR JON

18 Red Lion Court
London EC4A 3EB ☎020 7520 6000
✉chambers@18rlc.co.uk
Call Date: Jul 2005, Inner Temple

ARGENT MR GAVIN RICHARD

Westgate Chambers
64 High Street, Lewes, East Sussex BN7 1XG ☎01273 480510
✉clerks@westgate-chambers.co.uk
Call Date: Jul 1978, Middle Temple

Practising Areas: Common Law (General), Crime, Family Provision, Personal Injury, Sale & Carriage of Goods

ARGYLE MR BRIAN JOHN

187 Fleet Street
London EC4A 2AT ☎020 7430 7430
✉chambers@187fleetstreet.com
Chambers of K A Williams-Howes
148 Lower Richmond Road, Putney, London SW15 1LU ☎020 8704 1010
✉katie@williams-howes.com
Call Date: Jul 1972, Gray's Inn
Pupil Supervisor, Recorder

Practising Areas: Crime, Crime (Corporate/Fraud)

ARGYROPOULOS MR KYRIAKOS

15 New Bridge Street
London EC4V 6AU ☎020 7842 1900
✉clerks@15nbs.com
Call Date: Nov 1991, Inner Temple
Pupil Supervisor

ARIS MR JASON MARK

Citadel Chambers
The Citadel, 190 Corporation Street, Birmingham B4 6QD ☎0121 233 8500
✉clerks@citadelchambers.com
Call Date: Oct 1998, Inner Temple

Practising Areas: Common Law (General), Crime

ARKHURST MR REGINALD LEON

4 King's Bench Walk
2nd Floor, 4 King's Bench Walk, Temple, London EC4Y 7DL ☎020 7822 7000
✉clerks@4kbw.co.uk
Call Date: Jul 1984, Middle Temple

Practising Areas: Administrative, Arbitration, Human Rights, Immigration, International Trade, Private International, Public International

C

ARMBRISTER MR ALLAN RAMSAY

39 Park Square
Leeds LS1 2NU ☎0113 245 6633
✉seniorclerk@39parksquarechambers.co.uk
Call Date: Nov 1984, Inner Temple

Practising Areas: Care Proceedings, Crime, Crime (Corporate/Fraud), Family

ARMSTRONG MR DEAN PAUL

2 Bedford Row
London WC1R 4BU ☎020 7440 8888
✉clerks@2bedfordrow.co.uk
Call Date: Jul 1985, Gray's Inn
Pupil Supervisor

Practising Areas: Courts Martial, Crime, Crime (Corporate/Fraud)

ARMSTRONG MR STUART DAVID

Arden Chambers
20 Bloomsbury Square, London WC1A 2NS
☎020 7242 4244 ✉clerks@ardenchambers.com
Call Date: Oct 1995, Gray's Inn

Practising Areas: Common Law (General), Landlord & Tenant

ARNHEIM DR MICHAEL THOMAS WALTER

Chambers of Dr Michael Arnheim
101 Queen Alexandra Mansions, Judd Street, London WC1H 9DP ☎020 7833 5093
✉arnheim.law@gmail.com
Holborn Chambers
6 Gate Street, Lincoln's Inn Fields, London WC2A 3HP ☎020 7242 6060
Principal Chambers
15 Lime Tree Walk, Sevenoaks, Kent TN13 1YH ☎0845 209 8080
Call Date: Jul 1988, Lincoln's Inn
Pupil Supervisor

Practising Areas: Civil Liberties, Common Law (General), Defamation, Entertainment, Landlord & Tenant, Medical Negligence, Personal Injury, Professional Negligence, Sports

ARNOLD MR GRAHAM JOHN

Farringdon Chambers
180 Bermondsey Street, London SE1 3TQ
☎020 7089 5700
Call Date: Nov 2002, Lincoln's Inn

Practising Areas: Administrative, Civil Liberties, Crime, Employment, Human Rights, Immigration, Public International

ARNOLD MR JAMES MATTHEW

Outer Temple Chambers
The Outer Temple, 222 Strand, London WC2R 1BA ☎020 7353 6381
✉clerks@outertemple.com
Call Date: Oct 2000, Middle Temple
Pupil Supervisor

Practising Areas: Commercial Litigation, Employment

ARNOLD MR PETER MATTHEW MILLER

No5 Chambers
Fountain Court, Steelhouse Lane, Birmingham B4 6DR ☎0845 210 5555 ✉info@no5.com
No5 Chambers
Greenwood House, 4-7 Salisbury Court, London EC4Y 8AA ☎0845 210 5555
No5 Chambers
38 Queen Square, Bristol BS1 4QS
☎0845 210 5555
Call Date: Jul 1972, Lincoln's Inn
Pupil Supervisor

Practising Areas: Civil Litigation, Crime, Crime (Corporate/Fraud), Regulatory Law, Road Traffic And Highways

ARNONE MS ANNA

Eastbourne Chambers
5 Chiswick Place, Eastbourne, East Sussex BN21 4NH ☎01323 642102
✉clerks@eastbournechambers.co.uk
Call Date: Jul 2002, Middle Temple

ARSHAD MISS FARRHAT

Doughty Street Chambers
53-54 Doughty Street, London WC1N 2LS
☎020 7404 1313 ✉enquiries@doughtystreet.co.uk
Doughty Street Chambers
Pall Mall Court, 61-67 King Street, Manchester M2 4PD ☎0161 618 1066
Doughty Street Chambers
5th Floor, Broad Quay House, Prince Street, Bristol BS1 4DJ ☎01179 058 717
Call Date: Nov 1998, Inner Temple

Practising Areas: Administrative, Civil Liberties, Crime

ARSHAD MISS RAFFIA

St Mary's Family Law Chambers
26-28 High Pavement, The Lace Market, Nottingham NG1 1HN ☎0115 950 3503
✉clerks@stmarysflc.co.uk
Call Date: Jul 2002, Middle Temple

Practising Areas: Family, Family Provision, Islamic Sharia Law

ARTESI MISS DESIREE ALLISON ANN

Thomas More Chambers
7 Lincoln's Inn Fields, London WC2A 3BP
☎020 7404 7000 ✉clerks@thomasmore.co.uk
Call Date: Oct 1998, Inner Temple

Practising Areas: Administrative, Arbitration, Chancery (General), Commercial Litigation, Commercial Property, Common Law (General), Equity, Wills & Trusts, Foreign Law, Housing, Landlord & Tenant, Local Government, Private International, Public International, Regulatory Law

ARTHUR MRS HELEN FRANCES CATHERINE

No5 Chambers
Fountain Court, Steelhouse Lane, Birmingham B4 6DR ☎0845 210 5555 ✉info@no5.com
No5 Chambers
Greenwood House, 4-7 Salisbury Court, London EC4Y 8AA ☎0845 210 5555
No5 Chambers
38 Queen Square, Bristol BS1 4QS
☎0845 210 5555
Call Date: Oct 2003, Middle Temple

ARTHUR MR STEPHEN JOSEPH

Temple Tax Chambers
1st Floor, 3 Temple Gardens, Temple, London EC4Y 9AU ☎020 7353 7884
✉clerks@templetax.com
Call Date: Nov 2002, Middle Temple

Practising Areas: Asset Finance, Company & Commercial, Equity, Wills & Trusts, Partnership, Pensions, Private International, Share Options, Tax (Capital & Income), Tax (Corporate)

C

ASCHERSON MISS ISOBEL RUTH

23 Essex Street
London WC2R 3AA ☎020 7413 0353
✉clerks@23es.com
Call Date: Feb 1991, Gray's Inn

ASCROFT MR RICHARD GEOFFREY

Guildhall Chambers
23 Broad Street, Bristol BS1 2HG
☎0117 930 9000 ✉hoc@guildhallchambers.co.uk
Call Date: Nov 1995, Lincoln's Inn
Pupil Supervisor

Practising Areas: Bankruptcy, Commercial Litigation, Company & Commercial, Insolvency

ASGHAR MR TAZAFAR

Brompton Chambers
1st Floor, 353A Station Road, Harrow, Middlesex HA1 1LN ☎0560 3685647
✉bromptonchamber@aol.com
Call Date: Nov 2001, Lincoln's Inn

ASH MR EDWARD WILLIAM

Chambers of Mr Edward Ash
23 Rogers Close, Elsworth, Cambridgeshire CB23 4JJ ☎01954 267674
Call Date: Oct 1993, Middle Temple

Practising Areas: Chancery (General), Chancery (Land Law), Commercial Property, Common Law (General), Conveyancing, Equity, Wills & Trusts, Landlord & Tenant, Professional Negligence

ASHFORD-THOM MR IAN

Temple Garden Chambers
1 Harcourt Buildings, Temple, London EC4Y 9DA ☎020 7583 1315 ✉clerks@tgchambers.com
3 PB Barristers
3 Paper Buildings, Temple, London EC4Y 7EU
☎020 7583 8055
Call Date: Jul 1977, Gray's Inn
Pupil Supervisor

Practising Areas: Administrative, Common Law (General), Employment, Personal Injury, Professional Negligence

ASHIQ MR RIZWAN

1 Gray's Inn Square
Ground Floor, 1 Gray's Inn Square, London WC1R 5AA ☎020 7405 0001
Call Date: Jul 2001, Lincoln's Inn

ASHLEY MR MARK ROBERT

Pump Court Chambers
31 Southgate Street, Winchester, Hampshire SO23 9EB ☎01962 868 161
✉clerks@3pumpcourt.com
Pump Court Chambers
Upper Ground Floor, 3 Pump Court, Temple, London EC4Y 7AJ ☎020 7353 0711
✉clerks@3pumpcourt.com
Pump Court Chambers
5 Temple Chambers, Temple Street, Swindon SN1 1SQ ☎01793 539899
✉clerks@3pumpcourt.com
Call Date: Nov 1993, Lincoln's Inn

ASHLEY MR NEIL MARTIN

East Anglian Chambers
15 The Close, Norwich, Norfolk NR1 4DZ
☎ 01473 214481 ✉ norwich@ealaw.co.uk
East Anglian Chambers
Gresham House, 5 Museum Street, Ipswich, Suffolk IP1 1HQ ☎ 01473 214481
✉ ipswich@ealaw.co.uk
East Anglian Chambers
140 New London Road, Chelmsford, Essex CM2 0AW ☎ 01473 214481
✉ chelmsford@ealaw.co.uk
Call Date: Mar 1999, Lincoln's Inn
Pupil Supervisor

Practising Areas: Commercial Litigation, Company & Commercial, Discrimination, Employment, Pensions

ASHLEY-NORMAN MR JONATHAN CHARLES

3 Raymond Buildings
3 Raymond Buildings, Gray's Inn, London WC1R 5BH ☎ 020 7400 6400
✉ clerks@3rblaw.com
Call Date: Jul 1989, Middle Temple
Pupil Supervisor

Practising Areas: Crime, Crime (Corporate/Fraud), Financial Services, Health & Safety, Regulatory Law

ASHTON DR RAYMOND KEIGHLEY

9 Stone Buildings
Lincoln's Inn, London WC2A 3NN
☎ 020 7404 5055 ✉ clerks@9stonebuildings.com
Call Date: Jul 1979, Lincoln's Inn

ASHWORTH MISS FIONA KATHERINE ANNE

Kings Chambers
36 Young Street, Manchester M3 3FT
☎ 0845 034 3444 ✉ clerks@kingschambers.com
Kings Chambers
5 Park Square East, Leeds LS1 2NE
☎ 0845 034 3444 ✉ clerks@kingschambers.com
Kings Chambers
Embassy House, 60 Church Street, Birmingham B3 2DJ ☎ 0845 034 3444
✉ clerks@kingschambers.com
Call Date: Jul 1988, Lincoln's Inn
Pupil Supervisor, Recorder

Practising Areas: Medical Negligence, Personal Injury

ASKEY MR ROBERT JOHN

Palmyra Chambers
Royal House, 46 Legh Street, Warrington WA1 1UJ ☎ 01925 444919
✉ clerk@palmyrachambers.com
Call Date: Jul 1998, Lincoln's Inn
Pupil Supervisor

Practising Areas: Administrative, Asset Finance, Banking, Bankruptcy, Chancery (General), Chancery (Land Law), Civil Litigation, Commercial Litigation, Commercial Property, Common Law (General), Company & Commercial, Construction, Consumer, Conveyancing, Coroners Inquests, Costs, Crime (Corporate/Fraud), Data Protection, Disciplinary Tribunals, Discrimination, Education, Employment, Health & Safety, Housing, Human Rights, Inquests, Insolvency, Land, Partnership, Personal Injury, Professional Negligence, Public Law, Road Traffic And Highways, Sale & Carriage of Goods

ASPREY MR NICHOLAS

Serle Court
6 New Square, Lincoln's Inn, London WC2A 3QS ☎ 020 7242 6105 ✉ clerks@serlecourt.co.uk
Clock Chambers
18 Waterloo Road, Wolverhampton WV1 4BL
☎ 01902 313444
✉ clockchambers@btconnect.com
Call Date: Jul 1969, Inner Temple
Pupil Supervisor

Practising Areas: Arbitration, Chancery (General), Chancery (Land Law), Charities, Civil Litigation, Commercial Litigation, Commercial Property, Common Land, Company & Commercial, Conveyancing, Costs, Equity, Wills & Trusts, Family Provision, Land, Landlord & Tenant, Parliamentary, Partnership, Probate & Administration, Professional Negligence

ASTERIS MR PETER DAVID

Pump Court Chambers
31 Southgate Street, Winchester, Hampshire SO23 9EB ☎ 01962 868 161
✉ clerks@3pumpcourt.com
Pump Court Chambers
Upper Ground Floor, 3 Pump Court, Temple, London EC4Y 7AJ ☎ 020 7353 0711
✉ clerks@3pumpcourt.com
Pump Court Chambers
5 Temple Chambers, Temple Street, Swindon SN1 1SQ ☎ 01793 539899
✉ clerks@3pumpcourt.com
Call Date: Oct 1996, Lincoln's Inn
Pupil Supervisor

ASWANI MR RAVI GIRDHARILAL

Stone Chambers
4 Field Court, Gray's Inn, London WC1R 5EF
☎020 7440 6900 ✉clerks@stonechambers.com
Call Date: Jul 2000, Lincoln's Inn

Practising Areas: Admiralty, Arbitration, Banking, Bankruptcy, Chancery (General), Commercial Litigation, Commodities, Common Law (General), Company & Commercial, Energy, Insolvency, Insurance, Insurance/Reinsurance, International Trade, Landlord & Tenant, Private International, Professional Negligence, Sale & Carriage of Goods, Shipping/Admiralty

ATKIN MRS CLARE CATHERINE

Erimus Chambers
PO Box 1440, Bedford MK43 6AJ
☎01234 720952 ✉clerks@erimuschambers.com
Call Date: Jul 2001, Middle Temple

Practising Areas: Bankruptcy, Common Law (General), Insolvency

ATKINS MR RICHARD PAUL QC (2011)

St Philips Chambers
55 Temple Row, Birmingham B2 5LS
☎0121 246 7000 ✉clerks@st-philips.com
Call Date: Jul 1989, Gray's Inn
Pupil Supervisor, Recorder

Practising Areas: Crime, Crime (Corporate/Fraud), Licensing

ATKINSON MR GILES MATTHEW QUINTUS

6 Pump Court
1st Floor, 6 Pump Court, Temple, London EC4Y 7AR ☎020 7797 8400
✉richardconstable@6pumpcourt.co.uk
6 Pump Court Chambers
6-8 Mill Street, Maidstone, Kent ME15 6XH
☎01622 688094 ✉annexe@6pumpcourt.co.uk
Call Date: Jul 2002, Middle Temple

Practising Areas: Town & Country Planning

ATKINSON MR JODY ROY

St John's Chambers
101 Victoria Street, Bristol BS1 6PU
☎0117 923 4700 ✉clerks@stjohnschambers.co.uk
Call Date: Jul 2005, Inner Temple

Practising Areas: Ancillary Relief, Care Proceedings, Chancery (General), Children's Law, Discrimination, Employment, Equity, Wills & Trusts, Family, Family Provision

ATKINSON MR NICHOLAS JEREMY QC (1991)

Atkinson Bevan Chambers
1st Floor, 2 Harcourt Buildings, Temple, London EC4Y 9DB ☎020 7353 2112
✉clerks@2hb.co.uk
Staple Inn Chambers
1st Floor, 9 Staple Inn, Holborn Bars, London WC1V 7QH ☎020 7242 5240
✉clerks@stapleinn.co.uk
Call Date: Nov 1971, Inner Temple
Recorder

Practising Areas: Courts Martial, Crime, Crime (Corporate/Fraud), Ecclesiastical

ATKINSON MR RICHARD DUNCAN

6 King's Bench Walk
Ground Floor, 6 King's Bench Walk, Temple, London EC4Y 7DR ☎020 7583 0410
✉clerks@6kbw.com
Call Date: Oct 1995, Gray's Inn
Pupil Supervisor

ATTRIDGE MR DANIEL JAMES MACKENZIE

Trinity Chambers
Highfield House, Moulsham Street, Chelmsford, Essex CM2 9AH
☎01245 605040 ✉clerks@trinitychambers.com
Call Date: Nov 2000, Middle Temple

ATTWOOLL MR CHRISTOPHER BENJAMIN

KBW
The Engine House, No 1 Foundry Square, Leeds LS11 5DL ☎0113 297 1200
✉clerks@kbwchambers.com
Call Date: Jul 1980, Middle Temple
Pupil Supervisor, Recorder

AUBURN MR JONATHAN WALTER

4-5 Gray's Inn Square
Gray's Inn, London WC1R 5AH
☎020 7404 5252 ✉clerks@4-5.co.uk
Call Date: Nov 1999, Middle Temple
Pupil Supervisor

Practising Areas: Administrative, Civil Liberties, Discrimination, Education, Healthcare, Housing, Human Rights, Immigration, Local Government, Town & Country Planning

AUSTIN MR IAN

Holborn Chambers
6 Gate Street, Lincoln's Inn Fields, London WC2A 3HP ☎ 020 7242 6060
Call Date: Nov 2003, Middle Temple

Practising Areas: Bankruptcy, Care Proceedings, Common Law (General), Conveyancing, Crime, Crime (Corporate/Fraud), Employment, Equity, Wills & Trusts, Family, Human Rights, Immigration, Licensing, Sports

AUSTIN MR JONATHAN EDWARD NEWNS

Linenhall Chambers
1 Stanley Place, Chester CH1 2LU
☎ 01244 348282
✉ clerks@linenhallchambers.co.uk
Call Date: Oct 1991, Middle Temple
Pupil Supervisor

Practising Areas: Crime, Crime (Corporate/Fraud)

AUSTIN MISS REBECCA LOUISE

2 King's Bench Walk
2 King's Bench Walk, Temple, London EC4Y 7DE ☎ 020 7353 1746 ✉ clerks@2kbw.com
Call Date: Oct 2002, Middle Temple

AUSTINS MR CHRISTOPHER JOHN

Chambers of Mr Christopher Austins
Rookwood House, East Harptree, Bristol BS40 6AQ ☎ 01761 221 208
Clerksroom (Taunton)
Equity House, Administration Centre, Blackbrook Park Avenue, Taunton, Somerset TA1 2PX ☎ 0845 083 3000
✉ mail@clerksroom.com
King's Lynn Chambers
26 The Birches, South Wootton, King's Lynn, Norfolk PE30 3JG ☎ 01553 672 085
✉ timothy.leader@tesco.net
Call Date: Jul 1988, Gray's Inn

Practising Areas: Aviation, Common Law (General), Crime, Family, Personal Injury

AWODELE MR OLUFEMI ADETUNJI

Great James Street Chambers
37 Great James Street, London WC1N 3HB
☎ 020 7440 4949 ✉ chambers@greatjames.co.uk
Call Date: Jul 2002, Gray's Inn

Practising Areas: Children's Law, Civil Litigation, Crime, Defamation, Discrimination, Employment, Entertainment, Family, Housing, Immigration, Landlord & Tenant

AYLETT MR KENNETH GEORGE

15 New Bridge Street
London EC4V 6AU ☎ 020 7842 1900
✉ clerks@15nbs.com
4 Breams Buildings
Chancery Lane, London EC4A 1HP
☎ 020 7092 1900 ✉ clerks@4bb.co.uk
Call Date: Jul 1972, Inner Temple

Practising Areas: Crime, Crime (Corporate/Fraud), Human Rights

AYLOTT MR COLIN CHRISTOPHER

Carmelite Chambers
9 Carmelite Street, London EC4Y 0DR
☎ 020 7936 6300
✉ clerks@carmelitechambers.co.uk
Call Date: Nov 1989, Inner Temple
Pupil Supervisor

Practising Areas: Crime, Crime (Corporate/Fraud), Disciplinary Tribunals

AZAM MR AJMAL

Hardwicke
New Square, Lincoln's Inn, London WC2A 3SB ☎ 020 7242 2523
✉ enquiries@hardwicke.co.uk
Call Date: Jul 2006, Gray's Inn

AZHAR MR ALI MOHAMMAD

9 King's Bench Walk
Lower Ground Floor South, 9 King's Bench Walk, Temple, London EC4Y 7DX
☎ 020 7353 9564 ✉ 9kbw@btconnect.com
Call Date: Jul 1962, Gray's Inn
Pupil Supervisor

Practising Areas: Crime, Defamation, Equity, Wills & Trusts, Family, Foreign Law, Housing, Human Rights, Immigration, Islamic Sharia Law, Landlord & Tenant, Personal Injury, Private International, Probate & Administration

AZHAR MISS MARINA

4 Brick Court
4 Brick Court, Temple, London EC4Y 9AD
☎ 020 7832 3200 ✉ clerks@4bc.co.uk
Call Date: Nov 1990, Lincoln's Inn

AZIB MS REHANA

2 Temple Gardens
2 Temple Gardens, Temple, London EC4Y 9AY ☎ 020 7822 1200 ✉ clerks@2tg.co.uk
Call Date: Nov 2003, Inner Temple

Practising Areas: Employment, Personal Injury

C

AZIZ MR SHIRAZ

Garden Court Chambers
57-60 Lincoln's Inn Fields, London WC2A 3LJ
☎020 7993 7600 ✉info@gclaw.co.uk
Call Date: Nov 2006, Middle Temple

AZMI MR MOHAMMAD JAVED

No 8 Chambers
8 Fountain Court, Steelhouse Lane, Birmingham B4 6DR ☎0121 236 5514
✉clerks@no8chambers.co.uk
Call Date: Mar 1998, Middle Temple

Practising Areas: Family, Human Rights, Immigration

BADEJO MR ABIMBOLA RAFIU

5 Pump Court
Ground Floor, 5 Pump Court, Temple, London EC4Y 7AP ☎020 7353 2532
✉clerks@5pumpcourt.com
Call Date: Nov 1993, Lincoln's Inn

Practising Areas: Commercial Property, Common Law (General), Disciplinary Tribunals, Housing, Landlord & Tenant, Professional Negligence

BADENOCH MR TONY DAVID

6 King's Bench Walk
Ground Floor, 6 King's Bench Walk, Temple, London EC4Y 7DR ☎020 7583 0410
✉clerks@6kbw.com
Call Date: Nov 1996, Middle Temple

Practising Areas: Civil Liberties, Crime, Crime (Corporate/Fraud), Regulatory Law

BADGER MR CHRISTOPHER JAMES

23 Essex Street
London WC2R 3AA ☎020 7413 0353
✉clerks@23es.com
Call Date: Nov 2002, Middle Temple

Practising Areas: Crime, Crime (Corporate/Fraud)

BAGCHI MR ANDREW KUMAR

1 Garden Court Family Law Chambers
Ground Floor, One Garden Court, Temple, London EC4Y 9BJ ☎020 7797 7900
✉clerks@1gc.com
Call Date: Jul 1989, Middle Temple
Pupil Supervisor

Practising Areas: Administrative, Care Proceedings, Family, Family Provision

BAGLEY MISS LOUISA ELLEN

1 Paper Buildings
1st Floor, 1 Paper Buildings, Temple, London EC4Y 7EP ☎020 7353 3728
✉clerks@onepaper.co.uk
Call Date: Oct 2000, Middle Temple

Practising Areas: Courts Martial, Crime, Crime (Corporate/Fraud), Disciplinary Tribunals, Health & Safety, Mental Health, Regulatory Law, Trademarks

BAGRAL MISS RAVINDER

No5 Chambers
Greenwood House, 4-7 Salisbury Court, London EC4Y 8AA ☎0845 210 5555
No5 Chambers
38 Queen Square, Bristol BS1 4QS
☎0845 210 5555
No5 Chambers
Fountain Court, Steelhouse Lane, Birmingham B4 6DR ☎0845 210 5555 ✉info@no5.com
Call Date: Oct 1996, Inner Temple

Practising Areas: Immigration

BAHRA MISS NARITA

2 Hare Court
Lower Ground, Ground, 1st & 2nd Floor, 2 Hare Court, Temple, London EC4Y 7BH
☎020 7353 3982 ✉clerks@2harecourt.com
9-12 Bell Yard
London WC2A 2JR ☎020 7400 1800
✉clerks@9-12bellyard.com
Call Date: Nov 1997, Lincoln's Inn
Pupil Supervisor

Practising Areas: Courts Martial, Crime, Crime (Corporate/Fraud), Licensing, Mental Health

BAILEY MR ANTHONY REGINALD

2 King's Bench Walk
2 King's Bench Walk, Temple, London EC4Y 7DE ☎020 7353 1746 ✉clerks@2kbw.com
Call Date: Nov 1972, Inner Temple
Pupil Supervisor

BAILEY MR CHARLES ANDREW STUART

Trinity Chambers
Highfield House, Moulsham Street, Chelmsford, Essex CM2 9AH
☎01245 605040 ✉clerks@trinitychambers.com
Call Date: Oct 1993, Lincoln's Inn
Pupil Supervisor

Practising Areas: Ancillary Relief, Care Proceedings, Chancery (Land Law), Employment, Family Provision

BAILEY MR JAMES THOMAS

New Square Chambers
12 New Square, Lincoln's Inn, London WC2A 3SW ☎ 020 7419 8000 ✉ robin.hollington@newsquarechambers.co.uk
Call Date: Oct 1999, Gray's Inn
Pupil Supervisor

BAILEY MR MICHAEL ROBERT

Tanfield Chambers
2-5 Warwick Court, London WC1R 5DJ
☎ 020 7421 5300 ✉ clerks@tanfieldchambers.co.uk
Call Date: Nov 1986, Gray's Inn
Pupil Supervisor

Practising Areas: Ancillary Relief, Care Proceedings, Children's Law, Land, Personal Injury, Probate & Administration

BAILEY MISS ROSANA HENRIETTA

10 King's Bench Walk
Ground Floor, 10 King's Bench Walk, Temple, London EC4Y 7EB ☎ 020 7353 7742
✉ Chambers@10kingsbenchwalk.co.uk
Call Date: Oct 1994, Gray's Inn

Practising Areas: Chancery (General), Chancery (Land Law), Commercial Litigation, Commercial Property, Company & Commercial, Copyright, Housing, Insolvency, Intellectual Property, Landlord & Tenant, Partnership, Probate & Administration, Sale & Carriage of Goods, Trademarks

BAILEY MR RUSSELL STUART

No5 Chambers
Greenwood House, 4-7 Salisbury Court, London EC4Y 8AA ☎ 0845 210 5555
No5 Chambers
38 Queen Square, Bristol BS1 4QS
☎ 0845 210 5555
No5 Chambers
Fountain Court, Steelhouse Lane, Birmingham B4 6DR ☎ 0845 210 5555 ✉ info@no5.com
Call Date: Nov 1985, Inner Temple
Pupil Supervisor

Practising Areas: Commercial Litigation, Commercial Property, Common Law (General), Employment, Personal Injury, Professional Negligence, Sale & Carriage of Goods

BAILEY MISS SASHA

2 Pump Court
1st Floor, 2 Pump Court, Temple, London EC4Y 7AH ☎ 020 7353 5597
✉ clerks@2pumpcourt.co.uk
Call Date: Jul 2002, Lincoln's Inn

Practising Areas: Crime

BAILEY MR STEPHEN JOHN

33 Bedford Row
London WC1R 4JH ☎ 020 7242 6476
✉ clerks@33bedfordrow.co.uk
Call Date: Jul 1991, Gray's Inn

BAILEY MR STEVEN WILLIAM

No5 Chambers
Fountain Court, Steelhouse Lane, Birmingham B4 6DR ☎ 0845 210 5555 ✉ info@no5.com
No5 Chambers
Greenwood House, 4-7 Salisbury Court, London EC4Y 8AA ☎ 0845 210 5555
No5 Chambers
38 Queen Square, Bristol BS1 4QS
☎ 0845 210 5555
Call Date: Oct 1992, Middle Temple

BAILEY MR THOMAS IAIN

Chambers of Mr Thomas Bailey
Eaton Place, 90 Mill Road, Water Eaton, Milton Keynes MK2 2UZ ☎ 07983 447117
✉ tombailey888@yahoo.co.uk
Call Date: Jul 1984, Gray's Inn

Practising Areas: Chancery (Land Law), Common Land, Common Law (General), Conveyancing, Equity, Wills & Trusts, Landlord & Tenant, Professional Negligence

BAINS MR SATNAM

1 Mitre Court Buildings
1 Mitre Court Buildings, Temple, London EC4Y 7BS ☎ 020 7452 8900 ✉ clerks@1mcb.com
Call Date: Mar 2002, Middle Temple

BAIRD MR JAMES STEVENSON

Bank House Chambers
Old Bank House, Hartshead, Sheffield S1 2EL
☎ 0114 275 1223 ✉ w.digby@bankhousechambers.co.uk
Call Date: Nov 1977, Middle Temple
Pupil Supervisor, Recorder

Practising Areas: Crime, Crime (Corporate/Fraud), Health & Safety, Regulatory Law

BAJWA MR ALI NASEEM QC (2011)

Garden Court Chambers
57-60 Lincoln's Inn Fields, London WC2A 3LJ
☎ 020 7993 7600 ✉ info@gclaw.co.uk
Call Date: Nov 1993, Gray's Inn
Pupil Supervisor

Practising Areas: Civil Liberties, Courts Martial, Crime, Crime (Corporate/Fraud), Health & Safety, Human Rights, Immigration, Public International, Sports

BAKER MR ANDREW JAMES

No5 Chambers
Fountain Court, Steelhouse Lane, Birmingham B4 6DR ☎0845 210 5555 ✉info@no5.com
No5 Chambers
Greenwood House, 4-7 Salisbury Court, London EC4Y 8AA ☎0845 210 5555
No5 Chambers
38 Queen Square, Bristol BS1 4QS ☎0845 210 5555
Call Date: Oct 1990, Middle Temple

BAKER MISS MAUREEN ANNE QC (2009)

Seven Bedford Row
7 Bedford Row, London WC1R 4BS ☎020 7242 3555 ✉clerks@7br.co.uk
Call Date: Jul 1984, Gray's Inn
Recorder

Practising Areas: Crime, Regulatory Law

BAKER MR NICHOLAS MICHAEL BRIDGMAN

Hardwicke
New Square, Lincoln's Inn, London WC2A 3SB ☎020 7242 2523 ✉enquiries@hardwicke.co.uk
Call Date: Jul 1980, Gray's Inn
Pupil Supervisor

Practising Areas: Care Proceedings, Family, Family Provision

BAKER MR SIMON ARTHUR

Argent Chambers
5 Bell Yard, London WC2A 2JR ☎020 7556 5500 ✉briefsin@argentchambers.co.uk
Call Date: Oct 1998, Inner Temple
Pupil Supervisor

BAKER MR THOMAS MATTHEW

QEB Hollis Whiteman
1-2 Laurence Pountney Hill, London EC4R 0EU ☎020 7933 8855 ✉barristers@qebhw.co.uk
Call Date: Nov 2004, Middle Temple

BAKI MR NEIL FARRES

25 Bedford Row
London WC1R 4HD ☎020 7067 1500 ✉clerks@25bedfordrow.com
Call Date: Jul 2003, Middle Temple

Practising Areas: Crime, Crime (Corporate/Fraud)

BALCHIN MR RICHARD ALEXANDER

New Court
Ground Floor, New Court, Temple, London EC4Y 9BE ☎020 7583 5123 ✉clerks@newcourtchambers.com
Call Date: Oct 1997, Inner Temple
Pupil Supervisor

Practising Areas: Common Law (General), Family, Family Provision

BALDRY MR RUPERT PATRICK CRAIG QC (2010)

Pump Court Tax Chambers
16 Bedford Row, London WC1R 4EF ☎020 7414 8080 ✉clerks@pumptax.com
Call Date: Feb 1987, Middle Temple
Pupil Supervisor

BALDWIN DR TIMOTHY JOHN

Garden Court Chambers
57-60 Lincoln's Inn Fields, London WC2A 3LJ ☎020 7993 7600 ✉info@gclaw.co.uk
Call Date: Nov 2001, Lincoln's Inn

Practising Areas: Administrative, Chancery (General), Chancery (Land Law), Civil Liberties, Common Law (General), Environment, Healthcare, Housing, Landlord & Tenant, Local Government, Medical Negligence, Mental Health, Personal Injury, Professional Negligence

BALL MR IAN DAVID

Cornwall Street Chambers
85-87 Cornwall Street, Birmingham B3 3BY ☎0121 233 7500 ✉clerks@cornwallstreet.co.uk
Call Date: Oct 1992, Middle Temple

Practising Areas: Crime, Environment, Regulatory Law

BALL MR STEVEN JAMES

Number 7 Harrington Street Chambers
7 Harrington Street, Liverpool L2 9YH ☎0151 242 0707 ✉clerks@7hs.co.uk
Call Date: Oct 1996, Inner Temple

Practising Areas: Common Law (General), Courts Martial, Crime, Licensing, Personal Injury, Sports

BALLARD MS APPA

Cornwall Street Chambers
85-87 Cornwall Street, Birmingham B3 3BY
☎0121 233 7500 ✉clerks@cornwallstreet.co.uk
Call Date: Jul 2006, Lincoln's Inn

Practising Areas: Chancery (General), Chancery (Land Law), Family, Family Provision

BANERJEE MR SUBHANKAR

Atkinson Bevan Chambers
1st Floor, 2 Harcourt Buildings, Temple, London EC4Y 9DB ☎020 7353 2112
✉clerks@2hb.co.uk
Call Date: Nov 2000, Inner Temple

Practising Areas: Crime

BANHAM MR MATTHEW IAN

Nine Bedford Row
9 Bedford Row, London WC1R 4AZ
☎020 7489 2727 ✉clerks@9bedfordrow.co.uk
Call Date: Oct 1999, Inner Temple

Practising Areas: Courts Martial, Crime, Crime (Corporate/Fraud), Financial Services, Regulatory Law

BANKOLE MRS MARGARET

Chambers of Mrs Margaret Bankole
6 Macarathur Close, Wyatt Road, Forest Gate, London E7 9NT ☎07983 302695
✉margaretmcf1996@yahoo.co.uk
Call Date: Jul 1988, Middle Temple
Pupil Supervisor

BANKS MISS FIONA JANE

Monckton Chambers
1 & 2 Raymond Buildings, Gray's Inn, London WC1R 5NR ☎020 7405 7211
✉chambers@monckton.com
Call Date: Oct 2006, Inner Temple

Practising Areas: Administrative, Commercial Litigation, Competition, EC & Competition Law, Human Rights, Sports, Telecommunications

BANKS MR FRANCIS ANDREW

Atlantic Chambers
4-6 Cook Street, Liverpool L2 9QU
☎0151 236 4421 ✉info@atlanticchambers.co.uk
Call Date: Jul 1995, Gray's Inn

Practising Areas: Ancillary Relief, Family, Family Provision

BANKS MISS RACHAEL EDA

Atlantic Chambers
4-6 Cook Street, Liverpool L2 9QU
☎0151 236 4421 ✉info@atlanticchambers.co.uk
Call Date: Nov 1993, Inner Temple
Pupil Supervisor

Practising Areas: Family, Family Provision

BANKS MR RODERICK CHARLES I'ANSON

48 Bedford Row
London WC1R 4LR ☎020 7430 2005
✉tyroon@partnershipcounsel.co.uk
Call Date: Jul 1974, Lincoln's Inn
Pupil Supervisor

Practising Areas: Partnership

BANKS MR TIMOTHY JAMES

15 New Bridge Street
London EC4V 6AU ☎020 7842 1900
✉clerks@15nbs.com
Call Date: Nov 1983, Inner Temple
Pupil Supervisor

Practising Areas: Crime

BANNOCKS MR DAVID GEORGE

4 Brick Court
4 Brick Court, Temple, London EC4Y 9AD
☎020 7832 3200 ✉clerks@4bc.co.uk
Call Date: Jul 2002, Middle Temple

BARBER MR PHILLIP ARTHUR

Zenith Chambers
10 Park Square, Leeds LS1 2LH
☎0113 245 5438 ✉clerks@zenithchambers.co.uk
Call Date: Nov 1991, Gray's Inn

Practising Areas: Commercial Property, Housing, Human Rights, Landlord & Tenant, Mental Health

BARBOUR MISS LAURA

Lincoln House Chambers
Tower 12, The Avenue North, Spinningfields, 18-22 Bridge Street, Manchester M3 3BZ
☎0161 832 5701
✉info@lincolnhousechambers.com
Call Date: Oct 2006, Gray's Inn

BARCLAY MR ROBIN NICHOLAS JOHN

2 Hare Court
Lower Ground, Ground, 1st & 2nd Floor, 2 Hare Court, Temple, London EC4Y 7BH
☎ 020 7353 3982 ✉ clerks@2harecourt.com
Call Date: Jul 1999, Middle Temple

Practising Areas: Crime, Crime (Corporate/Fraud), Regulatory Law

BARKER MR KERRY

Guildhall Chambers
23 Broad Street, Bristol BS1 2HG
☎ 0117 930 9000 ✉ hoc@guildhallchambers.co.uk
Call Date: Jul 1972, Gray's Inn
Pupil Supervisor

Practising Areas: Administrative, Crime, Crime (Corporate/Fraud), Licensing, Regulatory Law, Sports

BARNARD MR JAMES PHILIP

11 Stone Buildings
11 Stone Buildings, Lincoln's Inn, London WC2A 3TG ☎ 020 7831 6381 ✉ clerks@11sb.com
Call Date: Oct 1993, Middle Temple

Practising Areas: Banking, Bankruptcy, Chancery (General), Commercial Litigation, Common Law (General), Financial Services, Insolvency, Insurance, Professional Negligence, Sale & Carriage of Goods

BARNES MISS ANDREA LYNDA

Clerksroom (Taunton)
Equity House, Administration Centre, Blackbrook Park Avenue, Taunton, Somerset TA1 2PX ☎ 0845 083 3000
✉ mail@clerksroom.com
King's Lynn Chambers
26 The Birches, South Wootton, King's Lynn, Norfolk PE30 3JG ☎ 01553 672 085
✉ timothy.leader@tesco.net
Call Date: Nov 1999, Lincoln's Inn

Practising Areas: Commercial Litigation, Common Law (General), Personal Injury

BARNES MR ASHLEY JAMES

Chambers of Mr Ashley Barnes
1 The Beeches, Suttonleach, St Helens, Merseyside WA9 4SU ☎ 01744 814072
✉ ashleyjamesbarnes@live.com
New Bailey Chambers
4th Floor, Corn Exchange, Fenwick Street, Liverpool, Merseyside L2 7QS
☎ 0151 236 9402 ✉ clerks@newbailey.com
Call Date: Oct 1990, Inner Temple
Pupil Supervisor

Practising Areas: Crime, Road Traffic And Highways

BARNES MR DAVID JONATHAN

3 Temple Gardens
Lower Ground Floor, 3 Temple Gardens, Temple, London EC4Y 9AU ☎ 020 7353 3102
✉ clerks@3tg.co.uk
Call Date: Nov 1981, Gray's Inn
Pupil Supervisor

Practising Areas: Crime

BARNES MR LUKE CLIVE

3 Dr Johnson's Buildings
Ground Floor, 3 Dr Johnson's Buildings, Temple, London EC4Y 7BA ☎ 020 7353 4854
✉ clerks@3djb.co.uk
Call Date: Nov 1996, Gray's Inn
Pupil Supervisor

Practising Areas: Chancery (Land Law), Common Law (General), Equity, Wills & Trusts, Family, Family Provision, Landlord & Tenant, Probate & Administration

BARNES MS RACHEL ANN

3 Raymond Buildings
3 Raymond Buildings, Gray's Inn, London WC1R 5BH ☎ 020 7400 6400
✉ clerks@3rblaw.com
Call Date: Nov 2004, Gray's Inn

Practising Areas: Administrative, Crime, Crime (Corporate/Fraud), Human Rights, Public International, Regulatory Law

BARNETT MISS ADRIENNE ELISE

1 Pump Court
Elm Court, Temple, London EC4Y 7AB
☎ 020 7842 7070 ✉ (name)@pumpcourt.co.uk
Call Date: Jul 1981, Middle Temple

Practising Areas: Care Proceedings, Family

BARNETT MR JEREMY VICTOR

St Paul's Chambers
5th Floor, St Paul's House, 23 Park Square South, Leeds LS1 2ND ☎ 0113 245 5866
2 Bedford Row
London WC1R 4BU ☎ 020 7440 8888
✉ clerks@2bedfordrow.co.uk
Call Date: Jul 1980, Gray's Inn
Pupil Supervisor, Recorder

Practising Areas: Commercial Litigation, Company & Commercial, Crime, Crime (Corporate/Fraud), Energy, Environment, Financial Services, Information Technology, Regulatory Law

BARNETT MISS SALLY LOUISE

New Street Chambers
2 New Street, Leicester LE1 5NA
☎ 0116 262 5906 ✉ clerks@2newstreet.co.uk
Call Date: Nov 1987, Middle Temple
Pupil Supervisor

Practising Areas: Family

BARNEY MS HELEN

No5 Chambers
Fountain Court, Steelhouse Lane, Birmingham B4 6DR ☎ 0845 210 5555 ✉ info@no5.com
No5 Chambers
Greenwood House, 4-7 Salisbury Court, London EC4Y 8AA ☎ 0845 210 5555
No5 Chambers
38 Queen Square, Bristol BS1 4QS
☎ 0845 210 5555
Call Date: Oct 1999, Lincoln's Inn

Practising Areas: Common Law (General), Employment

BARRACLOUGH MISS LISA ANN

Colleton Chambers
Colleton Crescent, Exeter, Devon EX2 4DG
☎ 01392 274898 ✉ clerks@colletonchambers.co.uk
Call Date: Oct 1999, Lincoln's Inn

Practising Areas: Care Proceedings, Family

BARRACLOUGH MR NICHOLAS MAYLIN

187 Fleet Street
London EC4A 2AT ☎ 020 7430 7430
✉ chambers@187fleetstreet.com
Call Date: Nov 1990, Inner Temple
Pupil Supervisor

Practising Areas: Courts Martial, Crime, Crime (Corporate/Fraud), Human Rights, Regulatory Law

BARRAN MISS TABITHA JANE GABRIEL

Renaissance Chambers
5th Floor, Gray's Inn Chambers, Gray's Inn, London WC1R 5JA ☎ 020 7404 1111
✉ clerks@renaissancechambers.co.uk
Call Date: Oct 1998, Inner Temple
Pupil Supervisor

Practising Areas: Family

BARRATT MR DOMINIC ANTHONY

East Anglian Chambers
140 New London Road, Chelmsford, Essex CM2 0AW ☎ 01473 214481
✉ chelmsford@ealaw.co.uk
East Anglian Chambers
53 North Hill, Colchester, Essex CO1 1QA
☎ 01473 214481 ✉ colchester@ealaw.co.uk
East Anglian Chambers
15 The Close, Norwich, Norfolk NR1 4DZ
☎ 01473 214481 ✉ norwich@ealaw.co.uk
East Anglian Chambers
Gresham House, 5 Museum Street, Ipswich, Suffolk IP1 1HQ ☎ 01473 214481
✉ ipswich@ealaw.co.uk
Call Date: Nov 1992, Gray's Inn
Pupil Supervisor

Practising Areas: Ancillary Relief, Care Proceedings, Children's Law, Family, Family Provision

BARRETT MR KEVIN JOHN

No5 Chambers
Fountain Court, Steelhouse Lane, Birmingham B4 6DR ☎ 0845 210 5555 ✉ info@no5.com
No5 Chambers
Greenwood House, 4-7 Salisbury Court, London EC4Y 8AA ☎ 0845 210 5555
No5 Chambers
38 Queen Square, Bristol BS1 4QS
☎ 0845 210 5555
Call Date: Nov 2008, Middle Temple

Practising Areas: Arbitration, Construction

BARRETT MR ROBERT SCOTT

2 Pump Court
1st Floor, 2 Pump Court, Temple, London EC4Y 7AH ☎ 020 7353 5597
✉ clerks@2pumpcourt.co.uk
Call Date: Jul 1978, Gray's Inn
Pupil Supervisor

Practising Areas: Common Law (General), Crime, Crime (Corporate/Fraud), Family, Family Provision

BARRY MR DENIS FINTAN PATRICK

Five Paper Buildings
1st Floor, Five Paper Buildings, Temple, London EC4Y 7HB ☎ 020 7583 6117
✉ clerks@5pb.co.uk
Call Date: Oct 1996, Inner Temple
Pupil Supervisor

Practising Areas: Consumer, Crime (Corporate/Fraud), EC & Competition Law, Environment, Regulatory Law

BARRY MR KEVIN JAMES

36 Bedford Row
London WC1R 4JH ☎ 020 7421 8000
✉ chambers@36bedfordrow.co.uk
Call Date: Nov 1997, Lincoln's Inn
Pupil Supervisor

Practising Areas: Crime, Crime (Corporate/Fraud), Regulatory Law

BARTFELD MR JASON MAURICE

187 Fleet Street
London EC4A 2AT ☎ 020 7430 7430
✉ chambers@187fleetstreet.com
Call Date: Oct 1995, Middle Temple

Practising Areas: Civil Liberties, Crime, Crime (Corporate/Fraud), Licensing

BARTLET-JONES MR STEPHEN WILLIAM

1 Pump Court
Elm Court, Temple, London EC4Y 7AB
☎ 020 7842 7070 ✉ (name)@pumpcourt.co.uk
Call Date: Oct 2004, Lincoln's Inn

BARTON MS CHLOE LOUISE

Charter Chambers
33 John Street, London WC1N 2AT
☎ 020 7618 4400 ✉ clerks@charterchambers.com
Call Date: Jul 2006, Inner Temple

Practising Areas: Crime

BARTON MR HUGH GEOFFREY

Lincoln House Chambers
Tower 12, The Avenue North, Spinningfields, 18-22 Bridge Street, Manchester M3 3BZ
☎ 0161 832 5701
✉ info@lincolnhousechambers.com
Call Date: Nov 1989, Middle Temple
Pupil Supervisor

Practising Areas: Civil Liberties, Crime, Crime (Corporate/Fraud)

BARTON MR JEREMY CHARLES

2 King's Bench Walk
2 King's Bench Walk, Temple, London EC4Y 7DE ☎ 020 7353 1746 ✉ clerks@2kbw.com
Call Date: Jul 2004, Middle Temple

BARUAH MISS RIMA

Thomas More Chambers
7 Lincoln's Inn Fields, London WC2A 3BP
☎ 020 7404 7000 ✉ clerks@thomasmore.co.uk
Call Date: Feb 1994, Inner Temple

Practising Areas: Civil Liberties, Common Law (General)

BARWISE MISS STEPHANIE NICOLA QC (2006)

Atkin Chambers
1 Atkin Building, Gray's Inn, London WC1R 5AT ☎ 020 7404 0102
✉ clerks@atkinchambers.com
Call Date: Jul 1988, Middle Temple

Practising Areas: Arbitration, Commercial Litigation, Construction, Information Technology, Professional Negligence

BASHIR MR MOHAMMED ISSRAR

12 Old Square Chambers
1st Floor, 12 Old Square, Lincoln's Inn, London WC2A 3TX ☎ 020 7404 0875
✉ clerks@12oldsquare.com
Chambers of M I Bashir
2 Elmcroft Gardens, Kingsbury, London NW9 9QP ☎ 07932 948487
✉ mibachambers@gmail.com
Call Date: Nov 2002, Inner Temple

Practising Areas: Crime, Personal Injury

BASS MR TIMOTHY JAMES

Farringdon Chambers
180 Bermondsey Street, London SE1 3TQ
☎ 020 7089 5700
Call Date: Nov 1999, Middle Temple

Practising Areas: Crime

BASSIRI-DEZFOULI MISS SOROUR

Temple Court Chambers
2nd Floor, 2 Dr Johnson's Building, Temple, London EC4Y 7AY ☎ 020 7353 7888
✉ clerks@templecourt.co.uk
Call Date: Oct 1996, Lincoln's Inn

Practising Areas: Family, Family Provision, Immigration, Landlord & Tenant

BASTIN MR ALEXANDER CHARLES

Hardwicke
New Square, Lincoln's Inn, London WC2A 3SB ☎ 020 7242 2523
✉ enquiries@hardwicke.co.uk
Call Date: Oct 1995, Middle Temple
Pupil Supervisor

Practising Areas: Chancery (Land Law), Commercial Property, Common Law (General), Housing, Landlord & Tenant

BATCUP MR DAVID JOHN

Charter Chambers
33 John Street, London WC1N 2AT
☎ 020 7618 4400 ✉ clerks@charterchambers.com
Call Date: Jul 1974, Gray's Inn
Pupil Supervisor, Recorder

Practising Areas: Crime, Crime (Corporate/Fraud)

BATE MR STEPHEN ROBERT DE BRETEUIL

5RB
1st Floor, 5 Raymond Buildings, Gray's Inn, London WC1R 5BP ☎ 020 7242 2902
✉ clerks@5rb.com
Call Date: Jul 1981, Middle Temple

Practising Areas: Copyright, Entertainment, Film, Cable & TV, Sports, Telecommunications

BATES MR ALAN TWAN

Monckton Chambers
1 & 2 Raymond Buildings, Gray's Inn, London WC1R 5NR ☎ 020 7405 7211
✉ chambers@monckton.com
Call Date: Oct 2003, Middle Temple

Practising Areas: Administrative, Competition, EC & Competition Law, Education, Environment, Licensing, Local Government, Regulatory Law, Telecommunications

BATES MR JOHN HAYWARD

Old Square Chambers
10-11 Bedford Row, London WC1R 4BU
☎ 020 7269 0300 ✉ clerks@oldsquare.co.uk
Old Square Chambers
3 Orchard Court, St Augustine's Yard, Bristol BS1 5DP ☎ 0117 930 5100
✉ clerks@oldsquare.co.uk
Call Date: Jul 1973, Middle Temple
Pupil Supervisor

Practising Areas: Environment, Local Government, Town & Country Planning

BATEY MR DAVID MICHAEL

Stour Chambers
Mill Studio, 17a Stour Street, Canterbury, Kent CT1 2NR ☎ 01227 764899
✉ clerks@stourchambers.co.uk
Call Date: Jul 1989, Gray's Inn

Practising Areas: Care Proceedings, Civil Litigation, Common Law (General), Family, Family Provision, Personal Injury

BATH MRS BALJINDER KAUR

College Chambers
19 Carlton Crescent, Southampton, Hampshire SO15 2ET ☎ 023 8023 0338
✉ clerks@college-chambers.co.uk
Call Date: Oct 1996, Lincoln's Inn

Practising Areas: Common Law (General), Family, Housing, Landlord & Tenant

BATISTE MR SIMON ANTHONY

No.6 Park Square
Leeds LS1 2LW ☎ 0113 245 9763
✉ Tim@no6.co.uk
Call Date: Oct 1995, Lincoln's Inn

BATSTONE MR WILLIAM HAROLD FITZHERBERT

Guildhall Chambers
23 Broad Street, Bristol BS1 2HG
☎ 0117 930 9000 ✉ hoc@guildhallchambers.co.uk
Call Date: Jul 1982, Middle Temple

Practising Areas: Agriculture

BATTIE MISS ELEANOR HARRIET

Crown Office Row Chambers
119 Church Street, Brighton, Sussex BN1 1UD ☎ 01273 625625 ✉ clerks@1cor.com
Call Date: Jul 2004, Lincoln's Inn

BAUMOHL MR MARK CHRISTOPHER

Field Court Chambers
5 Field Court, Gray's Inn, London WC1R 5EF
☎ 020 7405 6114 ✉ clerks@fieldcourt.co.uk
Call Date: Oct 2001, Middle Temple

Practising Areas: Housing, Landlord & Tenant, Personal Injury

BAUR MR CHRISTOPHER THOMAS

Furnival Chambers
32 Furnival Street, London EC4A 1JQ
☎ 020 7405 3232
Call Date: Jul 1972, Middle Temple
Pupil Supervisor

Practising Areas: Crime, Crime (Corporate/Fraud)

BAX MR JAMES ALEXANDER

Rougemont Chambers
Victory House, Dean Clarke Gardens, Southernhay East, Exeter EX2 4AA
☎ 01392 208484
✉ clerks@rougemontchambers.co.uk
Call Date: Oct 1999, Lincoln's Inn

Practising Areas: Commercial Litigation, Common Law (General), Employment, Partnership, Personal Injury

BAXTER MISS BERNADETTE

Lincoln House Chambers
Tower 12, The Avenue North, Spinningfields, 18-22 Bridge Street, Manchester M3 3BZ
☎ 0161 832 5701
✉ info@lincolnhousechambers.com
Call Date: Jul 1987, Middle Temple
Pupil Supervisor, Recorder

Practising Areas: Crime, Crime (Corporate/Fraud)

BAYLIS MR CHRISTOPHER LLOYD GERSHWIN

Riverview Chambers
Hamilton House, 1 Temple Avenue, London EC4Y 0HA ☎ 0844 225 3999
✉ chrisbaylis@riverviewchambers.com
Call Date: Nov 1986, Inner Temple

BAYLISS MR THOMAS WILLIAM MAXWELL QC (2003)

Park Court Chambers
16 Park Place, Leeds LS1 2SJ
☎ 0113 243 3277
✉ clerks@parkcourtchambers.co.uk
5 King's Bench Walk
5 King's Bench Walk, Temple, London EC4Y 7DN ☎ 020 7353 5638 ✉ clerks@5kbw.co.uk
Call Date: Jul 1977, Inner Temple
Recorder

BAZINI MR DANIEL

No5 Chambers
Greenwood House, 4-7 Salisbury Court, London EC4Y 8AA ☎ 0845 210 5555
No5 Chambers
38 Queen Square, Bristol BS1 4QS
☎ 0845 210 5555
No5 Chambers
Fountain Court, Steelhouse Lane, Birmingham B4 6DR ☎ 0845 210 5555 ✉ info@no5.com
Call Date: Nov 1992, Gray's Inn

BEAN MR MATTHEW ALLEN

KBW
The Engine House, No 1 Foundry Square, Leeds LS11 5DL ☎ 0113 297 1200
✉ clerks@kbwchambers.com
Call Date: Oct 1997, Middle Temple

Practising Areas: Employment

BEARDMORE MR WILLIAM EDWARD

Chavasse Court Chambers
18 Queen Avenue, Liverpool L2 4TX
☎ 0151 229 2030
✉ clerks@chavassechambers.co.uk
Call Date: Jul 2005, Gray's Inn

BEASLEY MR THOMAS HUMPHREY CLOVIS

Radcliffe Chambers
Ground Floor, 11 New Square, Lincoln's Inn, London WC2A 3QB ☎ 020 7831 0081
✉ clerks@radcliffechambers.com
Call Date: Jul 2003, Middle Temple

BEATTIE MS ANNABEL DOROTHY

Park Court Chambers
16 Park Place, Leeds LS1 2SJ
☎ 0113 243 3277
✉ clerks@parkcourtchambers.co.uk
Call Date: Jul 2005, Inner Temple

Practising Areas: Ancillary Relief, Children's Law, Civil Litigation, Family

BEAUMONT MR BENJAMIN

Chambers of Dr Michael Arnheim
101 Queen Alexandra Mansions, Judd Street, London WC1H 9DP ☎ 020 7833 5093
✉ arnheim.law@gmail.com
Middle Temple Lane Chambers
2nd Floor South, 1 Middle Temple Lane, London EC4Y 9AA ☎ 020 7583 4352
✉ chambers@mtlchambers.com
Call Date: Jul 1978, Inner Temple

Practising Areas: Arbitration, Banking, Commercial Litigation, Commercial Property, Construction, Financial Services, Insurance/Reinsurance, Public International

BEAUMONT MR DEAN ANDREW

KCH Garden Square
1 Oxford Street, Nottingham NG1 5BH
☎0115 941 8851 ✉clerks@kchgardensquare.co.uk
Call Date: Jul 1999, Lincoln's Inn

Practising Areas: Chancery (Land Law), Commercial Litigation, Employment, Equity, Wills & Trusts, Housing, Landlord & Tenant

BEAUMONT MR MARC CLIFFORD

Windsor Barristers' Chambers
Windsor Chambers, Castle Hill House, 12 Castle Hill, Windsor, Berkshire SL4 1PD
☎01753 839321 ✉mcb@windsorchambers.com
9 Stone Buildings
Lincoln's Inn, London WC2A 3NN
☎020 7404 5055 ✉clerks@9stonebuildings.com
Call Date: Jul 1985, Gray's Inn
Pupil Supervisor

Practising Areas: Administrative, Arbitration, Asset Finance, Banking, Bankruptcy, Chancery (General), Chancery (Land Law), Commercial Litigation, Commercial Property, Common Law (General), Company & Commercial, Competition, Construction, Conveyancing, Defamation, Discrimination, Education, Employment, Environment, Equity, Wills & Trusts, Family Provision, Financial Services, Franchising, Housing, Information Technology, Insolvency, Insurance, Intellectual Property, Landlord & Tenant, Local Government, Medical Negligence, Partnership, Probate & Administration, Professional Negligence, Regulatory Law, Sale & Carriage of Goods, Share Options, Sports, Telecommunications, Town & Country Planning

BEAUMONT MRS SALLY

Sovereign Chambers
46 Park Place, Leeds LS1 2RY
☎0113 245 1841
✉clerks@sovereignchambers.co.uk
Call Date: Oct 1999, Lincoln's Inn
Pupil Supervisor

Practising Areas: Family, Personal Injury

BEBB MR GORDON MONTFORT QC (2002)

Outer Temple Chambers
The Outer Temple, 222 Strand, London WC2R 1BA ☎020 7353 6381
✉clerks@outertemple.com
Call Date: Nov 1975, Middle Temple
Recorder

BECKER MR PAUL ANTONY

Chavasse Court Chambers
18 Queen Avenue, Liverpool L2 4TX
☎0151 229 2030
✉clerks@chavassechambers.co.uk
Call Date: Nov 1990, Gray's Inn
Pupil Supervisor

Practising Areas: Crime, Crime (Corporate/Fraud), Road Traffic And Highways

BECKER MR TIMOTHY GEORGE CHRISTIE

Clerksroom (London)
3rd Floor, 218 Strand, London WC2R 1AT
☎0845 083 3000 ✉mail@clerksroom.com
Chambers of Mr Timothy Becker
53 Rodney Street, Liverpool L1 9ER
☎0151 703 0319
Call Date: Jul 1992, Middle Temple

Practising Areas: Bankruptcy, Chancery (Land Law), Commercial Litigation, Common Law (General), Company & Commercial, Consumer, Conveyancing, Costs, Employment, Entertainment, Equity, Wills & Trusts, Family, Family Provision, Insolvency, Insurance, Landlord & Tenant, Personal Injury, Professional Negligence

BECKLEY MR JOHN MARK

Garden Court Chambers
57-60 Lincoln's Inn Fields, London WC2A 3LJ
☎020 7993 7600 ✉info@gclaw.co.uk
Call Date: Jul 2003, Middle Temple

Practising Areas: Housing

BEDENHAM MR DAVID

4-5 Gray's Inn Square
Gray's Inn, London WC1R 5AH
☎020 7404 5252 ✉clerks@4-5.co.uk
Call Date: Jul 2005, Gray's Inn

BEDFORD MR BECKET NATHANIEL

No5 Chambers
Fountain Court, Steelhouse Lane, Birmingham B4 6DR ☎0845 210 5555 ✉info@no5.com
No5 Chambers
Greenwood House, 4-7 Salisbury Court, London EC4Y 8AA ☎0845 210 5555
No5 Chambers
38 Queen Square, Bristol BS1 4QS
☎0845 210 5555
Call Date: Nov 1989, Middle Temple

BEDLOE MR GILES ROBERT

Dyers Chambers
35 Bedford Row, London WC1R 4JH
☎020 7404 1881 ✉admin@dyerschambers.com
Call Date: Nov 2001, Middle Temple

Practising Areas: Administrative, Bankruptcy, Chancery (General), Chancery (Land Law), Common Law (General), Employment, Housing, Landlord & Tenant, Licensing, Sale & Carriage of Goods

BEECHEY MR NICHOLAS CHARLES

Old Bailey Chambers
15 Old Bailey, London EC4M 7EF
☎020 3008 6404
✉clerks@15oldbaileychambers.com
Call Date: Jul 2002, Middle Temple

BEER MISS EMILY CHARLOTTE LEMAY

3 Dr Johnson's Buildings
Ground Floor, 3 Dr Johnson's Buildings, Temple, London EC4Y 7BA ☎020 7353 4854
✉clerks@3djb.co.uk
Call Date: Oct 2004, Gray's Inn

Practising Areas: Family, Family Provision

BEESON MR NIGEL ADRIAN LAURENCE

New Bailey Chambers
4th Floor, Corn Exchange, Fenwick Street, Liverpool, Merseyside L2 7QS
☎0151 236 9402 ✉clerks@newbailey.com
Call Date: Jul 1983, Lincoln's Inn
Pupil Supervisor

Practising Areas: Crime, Road Traffic And Highways

BEGGS MR JOHN PETER QC (2009)

3 Serjeants Inn
London EC4Y 1BQ ☎020 7427 5000
✉clerks@3serjeantsinn.com
Call Date: Nov 1989, Gray's Inn
Pupil Supervisor

BEHARRYLAL MR SATYANAND SARJU

15 New Bridge Street
London EC4V 6AU ☎020 7842 1900
✉clerks@15nbs.com
Call Date: Oct 1997, Lincoln's Inn
Pupil Supervisor

Practising Areas: Chancery (General), Civil Liberties, Common Law (General), Courts Martial, Crime, Crime (Corporate/Fraud), Human Rights, Regulatory Law, Sports

BELL MISS ANNE MARGARET OBE

Rougemont Chambers
Victory House, Dean Clarke Gardens, Southernhay East, Exeter EX2 4AA
☎01392 208484
✉clerks@rougemontchambers.co.uk
Holborn Chambers
6 Gate Street, Lincoln's Inn Fields, London WC2A 3HP ☎020 7242 6060
Call Date: Nov 1975, Gray's Inn
Pupil Supervisor

Practising Areas: Chancery (Land Law), Family

BELL MR DOMINIC MICHAEL ST. JOHN

Chambers of Marion Smullen and Kerim Fuad QC
1 Inner Temple Lane, London EC4Y 1AF
☎020 7427 4400 ✉clerks@1itl.com
Call Date: Nov 1992, Inner Temple

Practising Areas: Civil Liberties, Crime, Crime (Corporate/Fraud), Mental Health

BELL MR THOMAS CAPEL

Hardwicke
New Square, Lincoln's Inn, London WC2A 3SB ☎020 7242 2523
✉enquiries@hardwicke.co.uk
Call Date: Oct 2006, Lincoln's Inn

Practising Areas: Asset Finance, Banking, Commercial Litigation, Financial Services, Professional Negligence, Sale & Carriage of Goods

C

BELLAMY MR JONATHAN MARK

39 Essex Street
London WC2R 3AT ☎020 7832 1111
✉clerks@39essex.com
82 King Street
Manchester M2 4WQ ☎0161 870 9969
Call Date: Nov 1986, Lincoln's Inn
Pupil Supervisor

Practising Areas: Arbitration, Commercial Litigation, Common Law (General), Construction, Insurance, Professional Negligence, Sports

BELOFF MR RUPERT JOSEPH ALEXEI

No5 Chambers
Greenwood House, 4-7 Salisbury Court, London EC4Y 8AA ☎0845 210 5555
No5 Chambers
38 Queen Square, Bristol BS1 4QS
☎0845 210 5555
No5 Chambers
Fountain Court, Steelhouse Lane, Birmingham B4 6DR ☎0845 210 5555 ✉info@no5.com
Call Date: Oct 2001, Gray's Inn

Practising Areas: Administrative, Bankruptcy, Commercial Litigation, Common Law (General), Entertainment, Film, Cable & TV, Human Rights, Immigration, Insolvency, Landlord & Tenant, Medical Negligence, Personal Injury, Sale & Carriage of Goods, Sports

BENDALL MR RICHARD GILES

Furnival Chambers
32 Furnival Street, London EC4A 1JQ
☎020 7405 3232
Call Date: Jul 1979, Lincoln's Inn
Pupil Supervisor

Practising Areas: Courts Martial, Crime, Crime (Corporate/Fraud)

BENJAMIN MR DANIEL ROBERT

2 Dr Johnson's Buildings
2 Dr Johnson's Buildings, Temple, London EC4Y 7AY ☎020 7936 2613 ✉clerks@2drj.com
Call Date: Jul 2006, Middle Temple

Practising Areas: Courts Martial, Crime, Crime (Corporate/Fraud)

BENNET MS PAULINE AGNES

Regency Chambers
45 Priestgate, Peterborough PE1 1LB
☎01733 315215 ✉clerks@regencychambers.law.co.uk
Call Date: Oct 1991, Lincoln's Inn
Pupil Supervisor

Practising Areas: Ancillary Relief, Children's Law, Family

BENNETT MISS ANGELA MICHELLE

3 Dr Johnson's Buildings
Ground Floor, 3 Dr Johnson's Buildings, Temple, London EC4Y 7BA ☎020 7353 4854
✉clerks@3djb.co.uk
Call Date: Jul 2005, Lincoln's Inn

Practising Areas: Care Proceedings, Family, Family Provision

BENNETT MR DAVID LAURENCE

Liverpool Civil Law
3rd Floor, 1 Old Hall Street, Liverpool L3 9HF
☎0151 242 0500 ✉clerks@liverpoolcivillaw.com
Call Date: Nov 1977, Middle Temple
Pupil Supervisor

Practising Areas: Landlord & Tenant

BENNETT MISS EMMA LOUISE

Exchange Chambers
Oxford House, Oxford Row, Leeds LS1 3BE
☎0113 203 1970
✉spencer@exchangechambers.co.uk
Exchange Chambers
One Derby Square, Derby Square, Liverpool L2 9XX ☎0151 236 7747
✉info@exchangechambers.co.uk
Exchange Chambers
7 Ralli Courts, West Riverside, Manchester M3 5FT ☎0161 833 2722
Call Date: Oct 2004, Lincoln's Inn

Practising Areas: Commercial Litigation, Common Law (General), Crime, Crime (Corporate/Fraud), Medical Negligence, Personal Injury, Professional Negligence, Regulatory Law

BENNETT MR IEUAN GEREINT

9 Park Place
Cardiff, South Glamorgan CF10 3DP
☎029 2038 2731 ✉clerks@9parkplace.co.uk
Call Date: Jul 1989, Middle Temple

Practising Areas: Courts Martial, Crime, Crime (Corporate/Fraud), Mental Health, Regulatory Law

BENNETT MR MILES ALEXANDER FORDHAM

Five Paper Buildings
1st Floor, Five Paper Buildings, Temple, London EC4Y 7HB ☎ 020 7583 6117
✉ clerks@5pb.co.uk
Call Date: Nov 1986, Inner Temple
Pupil Supervisor

Practising Areas: Copyright, Crime, Regulatory Law

BENNION-PEDLEY MR EDWARD

13 King's Bench Walk
13 King's Bench Walk, Temple, London EC4Y 7EN ☎ 020 7353 7204 ✉ clerks@13kbw.co.uk
13 KBW
32 Beaumont Street, Oxford OX1 2NP
☎ 01865 311066 ✉ clerks@13kbw.co.uk
Call Date: Nov 2004, Middle Temple

Practising Areas: Chancery (General), Chancery (Land Law), Charities, Commercial Litigation, Commercial Property, Construction, Conveyancing, Equity, Wills & Trusts, Landlord & Tenant, Partnership, Professional Negligence

BENSON MR IMRAN MICHAEL JAFAREY

Hailsham Chambers
Ground Floor, 4 Paper Buildings, Temple, London EC4Y 7EX ☎ 020 7643 5000
✉ clerks@hailshamchambers.com
Call Date: Oct 2005, Middle Temple

Practising Areas: Banking, Commercial Litigation, Insurance, Professional Negligence

BENSON MR JEREMY KEITH QC (2001)

18 Red Lion Court
London EC4A 3EB ☎ 020 7520 6000
✉ chambers@18rlc.co.uk
Call Date: Jul 1978, Middle Temple
Recorder

Practising Areas: Crime, Crime (Corporate/Fraud), Regulatory Law

BENTHALL MR DOMINIC GABRIEL MENUHIN

15 New Bridge Street
London EC4V 6AU ☎ 020 7842 1900
✉ clerks@15nbs.com
Call Date: Nov 2002, Middle Temple

BENTLEY MR DAVID NEIL

Doughty Street Chambers
53-54 Doughty Street, London WC1N 2LS
☎ 020 7404 1313 ✉ enquiries@doughtystreet.co.uk
Doughty Street Chambers
Pall Mall Court, 61-67 King Street, Manchester M2 4PD ☎ 0161 618 1066
Doughty Street Chambers
5th Floor, Broad Quay House, Prince Street, Bristol BS1 4DJ ☎ 01179 058 717
Call Date: Feb 1984, Gray's Inn
Pupil Supervisor

Practising Areas: Crime, Crime (Corporate/Fraud)

BENTLEY MR DAVID PAUL

St Johns Buildings
24a - 28 St John Street, Manchester M3 4DJ
☎ 0161 214 1500 ✉ clerk@stjohnsbuildings.co.uk
St Johns Buildings
21 White Friars, Chester CH1 1NZ
☎ 01244 323070 ✉ clerk@stjohnsbuildings.co.uk
16 Winckley Square
Preston PR1 3JJ ☎ 01772 256100
Call Date: Oct 1998, Lincoln's Inn

BENZYNIE MR ROBERT JOSEPH

Charter Chambers
33 John Street, London WC1N 2AT
☎ 020 7618 4400 ✉ clerks@charterchambers.com
Call Date: Nov 1992, Gray's Inn

BERGENTHAL MR RONNIE MARK

Old Bailey Chambers
15 Old Bailey, London EC4M 7EF
☎ 020 3008 6404
✉ clerks@15oldbaileychambers.com
Call Date: Oct 1993, Middle Temple
Pupil Supervisor

Practising Areas: Courts Martial, Crime, Crime (Corporate/Fraud), Road Traffic And Highways

BERGIN MR TIMOTHY WILLIAM

1 Crown Office Row
1 Crown Office Row, Temple, London EC4Y 7HH ☎ 020 7797 7500 ✉ mail@1cor.com
Crown Office Row Chambers
119 Church Street, Brighton, Sussex BN1 1UD ☎ 01273 625625 ✉ clerks@1cor.com
Call Date: Jul 1987, Middle Temple
Pupil Supervisor

BERKIN MR MARTYN DAVID MAURICE

Crown Office Chambers
2 Crown Office Row, Temple, London EC4Y 7HJ ☎020 7797 8100
✉mail@crownofficechambers.com
Call Date: Jul 1966, Inner Temple
Pupil Supervisor

Practising Areas: Commercial Litigation, Company & Commercial, Private International

BERKLEY MR DAVID NAHUM QC (1999)

1 Gray's Inn Square
Ground Floor, 1 Gray's Inn Square, London WC1R 5AA ☎020 7405 0001
St Johns Buildings
24a - 28 St John Street, Manchester M3 4DJ ☎0161 214 1500 ✉clerk@stjohnsbuildings.co.uk
St Johns Buildings Liverpool
8th Floor India Buildings, Water Street, Liverpool L2 0XG ☎0151 243 6000
✉clerk@stjohnsbuildings.co.uk
St Johns Buildings
21 White Friars, Chester CH1 1NZ
☎01244 323070 ✉clerk@stjohnsbuildings.co.uk
Call Date: May 1979, Middle Temple
Recorder

Practising Areas: Chancery (General), Commercial Litigation, Commercial Property, Employment, Entertainment, Landlord & Tenant, Professional Negligence

BERKLEY MR MICHAEL STUART

Rougemont Chambers
Victory House, Dean Clarke Gardens, Southernhay East, Exeter EX2 4AA
☎01392 208484
✉clerks@rougemontchambers.co.uk
Call Date: Jul 1989, Middle Temple
Pupil Supervisor, Recorder

Practising Areas: Banking, Chancery (Land Law), Commercial Litigation, Commercial Property, Common Law (General), Company & Commercial, Franchising, Insolvency, Landlord & Tenant, Partnership, Professional Negligence, Sale & Carriage of Goods

BERMINGHAM MR GERALD EDWARD

No5 Chambers
Fountain Court, Steelhouse Lane, Birmingham B4 6DR ☎0845 210 5555 ✉info@no5.com
No5 Chambers
Greenwood House, 4-7 Salisbury Court, London EC4Y 8AA ☎0845 210 5555
No5 Chambers
38 Queen Square, Bristol BS1 4QS
☎0845 210 5555
Call Date: Feb 1985, Gray's Inn
Pupil Supervisor

BERRIMAN MR TREVOR ST JOHN

43 Temple Row Chambers
6th Floor, 43 Temple Row, Birmingham B2 5LS ☎0121 237 6035 ✉clerks@43templerow.co.uk
Call Date: Nov 1988, Inner Temple
Pupil Supervisor

Practising Areas: Asset Finance, Courts Martial, Crime, Crime (Corporate/Fraud), Financial Services, Health & Safety, Mental Health, Regulatory Law, Sale & Carriage of Goods

BERRY MR ADRIAN CHRISTOPHER

Garden Court Chambers
57-60 Lincoln's Inn Fields, London WC2A 3LJ
☎020 7993 7600 ✉info@gclaw.co.uk
Call Date: Oct 1998, Inner Temple

Practising Areas: Administrative, Civil Liberties, Discrimination, EC & Competition Law, Education, Housing, Human Rights, Immigration, Local Government

BERRY MR NICHOLAS

Citadel Chambers
The Citadel, 190 Corporation Street, Birmingham B4 6QD ☎0121 233 8500
✉clerks@citadelchambers.com
Call Date: Oct 2004, Lincoln's Inn

Practising Areas: Crime, Crime (Corporate/Fraud)

BERRY MR NICHOLAS MICHAEL

Rougemont Chambers
Victory House, Dean Clarke Gardens, Southernhay East, Exeter EX2 4AA
☎01392 208484
✉clerks@rougemontchambers.co.uk
Call Date: Nov 1988, Inner Temple
Pupil Supervisor

Practising Areas: Banking, Bankruptcy, Chancery (General), Chancery (Land Law), Commercial Litigation, Commercial Property, Common Land, Common Law (General), Company & Commercial, Construction, Conveyancing, Landlord & Tenant

BERTHAM MR ANTHONY CHRISTOPHER

3 Temple Gardens
Lower Ground Floor, 3 Temple Gardens, Temple, London EC4Y 9AU ☎ 020 7353 3102
✉ clerks@3tg.co.uk
Call Date: Oct 1993, Lincoln's Inn

Practising Areas: Crime, Crime (Corporate/Fraud), Human Rights, Regulatory Law

BERTRAM MR JONATHAN PETER

Seven Bedford Row
7 Bedford Row, London WC1R 4BS
☎ 020 7242 3555 ✉ clerks@7br.co.uk
Call Date: Oct 2003, Lincoln's Inn

Practising Areas: Commercial Litigation, Crime (Corporate/Fraud), Discrimination, Employment

BESWICK MISS KIRSTIN WENDY

Central Chambers
89 Princess Street, Manchester M1 4HT
☎ 0161 236 1133 ✉ clerks@centralchambers.co.uk
Call Date: Oct 2001, Middle Temple

Practising Areas: Crime, Crime (Corporate/Fraud), Family

BETTS MR STEPHEN

Chambers of Mr S Betts
Sundern, 8 Southview Road, Marlow, Buckinghamshire SL7 3JP ☎ 07739 892093
✉ admin@cslassociates.co.uk
Call Date: Nov 2008, Lincoln's Inn

Practising Areas: Crime

BEVAN MISS MIRANDA JANE

2 Hare Court
Lower Ground, Ground, 1st & 2nd Floor, 2 Hare Court, Temple, London EC4Y 7BH
☎ 020 7353 3982 ✉ clerks@2harecourt.com
Call Date: Oct 2000, Inner Temple

BEWLEY MISS SUHAYLA

East Anglian Chambers
53 North Hill, Colchester, Essex CO1 1QA
☎ 01473 214481 ✉ colchester@ealaw.co.uk
East Anglian Chambers
Gresham House, 5 Museum Street, Ipswich, Suffolk IP1 1HQ ☎ 01473 214481
✉ ipswich@ealaw.co.uk
East Anglian Chambers
140 New London Road, Chelmsford, Essex CM2 0AW ☎ 01473 214481
✉ chelmsford@ealaw.co.uk
Call Date: Jul 2007, Lincoln's Inn

Practising Areas: Employment

BEWSEY MISS JANE QC (2010)

18 Red Lion Court
London EC4A 3EB ☎ 020 7520 6000
✉ chambers@18rlc.co.uk
18 Red Lion Court (Annexe)
Thornwood House, 102 New London Road, Chelmsford, Essex CM2 0RG
☎ 01245 280880
Call Date: Jul 1986, Inner Temple
Pupil Supervisor

BEX MISS KATE

2 Hare Court
Lower Ground, Ground, 1st & 2nd Floor, 2 Hare Court, Temple, London EC4Y 7BH
☎ 020 7353 3982 ✉ clerks@2harecourt.com
Call Date: Nov 1992, Inner Temple
Pupil Supervisor

Practising Areas: Crime, Crime (Corporate/Fraud), Regulatory Law

BEYTS MR CHESTER ANDOE MICHAEL

25 Bedford Row
London WC1R 4HD ☎ 020 7067 1500
✉ clerks@25bedfordrow.com
Call Date: Nov 1978, Inner Temple
Pupil Supervisor

Practising Areas: Crime, Crime (Corporate/Fraud), Environment, Mental Health

BEZZAM MISS JAYASHREE

Hampton Court Chambers
28 Bedster Gardens, Hurst Park, West Molesey, Surrey KT8 1SZ ☎ 020 8979 0381
Call Date: Jul 1997, Lincoln's Inn

Practising Areas: Ancillary Relief, Arbitration, Aviation, Bankruptcy, Chancery (General), Chancery (Land Law), Civil Litigation, Common Law (General), Company & Commercial, Employment, Family, Foreign Law, Housing, Human Rights, Immigration, Intellectual Property, Private International

BHACHU MISS SHARANJEET KAUR

4 Brick Court
4 Brick Court, Temple, London EC4Y 9AD
☎ 020 7832 3200 ✉ clerks@4bc.co.uk
Call Date: Mar 1999, Lincoln's Inn

Practising Areas: Ancillary Relief, Family

BHAKAR MR SURINDER SINGH

4 King's Bench Walk
2nd Floor, 4 King's Bench Walk, Temple, London EC4Y 7DL ☎ 020 7822 7000
✉ clerks@4kbw.co.uk
Call Date: Nov 1986, Gray's Inn

Practising Areas: Commercial Property, Common Law (General), Housing, Landlord & Tenant

BHANJI MR SHIRAZ MUSA

1 Gray's Inn Square
Ground Floor, 1 Gray's Inn Square, London WC1R 5AA ☎ 020 7405 0001
4 Bingham Place
London W1U 5AT ☎ 020 7486 5347
✉ bhanji@regencyhotelwestend.co.uk
Call Date: Jul 1979, Gray's Inn

Practising Areas: Administrative, Ancillary Relief, Arbitration, Civil Liberties, Courts Martial, Discrimination, Education, Family, Human Rights, Immigration, Public Law, Town & Country Planning

BHATTACHARYYA MR ARDHENDU

Slough Barristers Chamber
11 St. Bernards Road, Slough, Berkshire SL3 7NT ☎ 01753 553806
✉ arden_bhattacharya2000@yahoo.co.uk
Call Date: Nov 1974, Inner Temple

Practising Areas: Arbitration, Common Law (General), Crime, Education, Employment, Family, Landlord & Tenant, Local Government, Medical Negligence, Personal Injury, Professional Negligence

BHATTI MISS BALVINDER

Citadel Chambers
The Citadel, 190 Corporation Street, Birmingham B4 6QD ☎ 0121 233 8500
✉ clerks@citadelchambers.com
Call Date: Oct 2003, Lincoln's Inn

Practising Areas: Civil Liberties, Crime, Employment, Immigration

BHUTTA MISS AYEESHA CLARE

Field Court Chambers
5 Field Court, Gray's Inn, London WC1R 5EF
☎ 020 7405 6114 ✉ clerks@fieldcourt.co.uk
Call Date: Oct 2006, Middle Temple

Practising Areas: Care Proceedings, Children's Law, Family, Family Provision

BICARREGUI MISS ANNA CLAIRE VICTORIA

4-5 Gray's Inn Square
Gray's Inn, London WC1R 5AH
☎ 020 7404 5252 ✉ clerks@4-5.co.uk
Call Date: Jul 2004, Lincoln's Inn

Practising Areas: Civil Liberties, Data Protection, Disciplinary Tribunals, Education, Employment

BICKERSTAFF MISS DEBORAH JANE QC (2012)

Nine Bedford Row
9 Bedford Row, London WC1R 4AZ
☎ 020 7489 2727 ✉ clerks@9bedfordrow.co.uk
Call Date: Nov 1989, Inner Temple
Pupil Supervisor

BICKLER MR SIMON LLOYD QC (2011)

St Paul's Chambers
5th Floor, St Paul's House, 23 Park Square South, Leeds LS1 2ND ☎ 0113 245 5866
Call Date: Nov 1988, Inner Temple
Pupil Supervisor

Practising Areas: Care Proceedings, Crime, Crime (Corporate/Fraud), Regulatory Law

BIGGS MR STUART

9-12 Bell Yard
London WC2A 2JR ☎ 020 7400 1800
✉ clerks@9-12bellyard.com
Call Date: Nov 1999, Middle Temple

BILSLAND MISS ALISAN MARGARET

St James's Chambers
68 Quay Street, Manchester M3 3EJ
☎ 0161 834 7000 ✉ clerks@stjameschambers.com
Call Date: Nov 2000, Lincoln's Inn

Practising Areas: Civil Litigation, Disciplinary Tribunals, Employment

BINGHAM MR ANTHONY WILLIAM

3 PB Barristers
3 Paper Buildings, Temple, London EC4Y 7EU
☎ 020 7583 8055
3 PB Barristers
30 Christchurch Road, Bournemouth, Dorset BH1 3PD ☎ 01202 292102 ✉ clerks.bournemouth@3paper.co.uk

3 PB Barristers
4 St Peter Street, Winchester SO23 8BW
☎01962 868884 ✉clerks.winchester@3paper.co.uk
3 PB Barristers
Royal Talbot House, 2 Victoria Street, Bristol, Avon BS1 6BB ☎0117 928 1520
3 PB Barristers
23 Beaumont Street, Oxford OX1 2NP
☎01865 793 736
Call Date: Nov 1992, Lincoln's Inn

Practising Areas: Construction

BINNION MS CAROL ANNE

St Ive's Chambers
Whittall Street, Birmingham B4 6DH
☎0121 236 0863 ✉clerks@stiveschambers.co.uk
Call Date: Jul 2010, Middle Temple

Practising Areas: Family

BIRBECK MR ALAN GILES

Dyers Chambers
35 Bedford Row, London WC1R 4JH
☎020 7404 1881 ✉admin@dyerschambers.com
Call Date: Jul 2006, Inner Temple

Practising Areas: Crime, Crime (Corporate/Fraud)

BIRCH MR ROGER ALLEN

Five St Andrew's Hill
5 St Andrew's Hill, London EC4V 5BZ
☎020 7332 5400 ✉Clerks@5sah.co.uk
Sovereign Chambers
46 Park Place, Leeds LS1 2RY
☎0113 245 1841
✉clerks@sovereignchambers.co.uk
Call Date: Nov 1979, Gray's Inn

Practising Areas: Bankruptcy, Charities, Health & Safety, Insolvency, Medical Negligence, Personal Injury, Professional Negligence, Regulatory Law

BIRKBY MR RICHARD ADAM

Park Court Chambers
16 Park Place, Leeds LS1 2SJ
☎0113 243 3277
✉clerks@parkcourtchambers.co.uk
Call Date: Oct 2006, Middle Temple

Practising Areas: Civil Liberties, Crime, Crime (Corporate/Fraud), Defamation, Education, Environment, Health & Safety, Immigration, Licensing, Mental Health, Personal Injury, Regulatory Law

BIRNBAUM MR MICHAEL IAN QC (1992)

9-12 Bell Yard
London WC2A 2JR ☎020 7400 1800
✉clerks@9-12bellyard.com
Call Date: Nov 1969, Middle Temple
Recorder

Practising Areas: Administrative, Civil Liberties, Courts Martial, Crime, Crime (Corporate/Fraud), Human Rights, Public International, Regulatory Law

BISARYA MR NEIL

Number 7 Harrington Street Chambers
7 Harrington Street, Liverpool L2 9YH
☎0151 242 0707 ✉clerks@7hs.co.uk
Call Date: Nov 1998, Lincoln's Inn

Practising Areas: Care Proceedings, Civil Liberties, Common Law (General), Crime, Crime (Corporate/Fraud), Education, Employment, Family, Immigration, Mental Health, Regulatory Law

BISBEY MISS GAYLE YVETTE DAWN

2 Dr Johnson's Buildings
2 Dr Johnson's Buildings, Temple, London EC4Y 7AY ☎020 7936 2613 ✉clerks@2drj.com
Call Date: Oct 2002, Lincoln's Inn

Practising Areas: Crime, Family

BISGROVE MR MICHAEL JOHN

6 King's Bench Walk
Ground Floor, 6 King's Bench Walk, Temple, London EC4Y 7DR ☎020 7583 0410
✉clerks@6kbw.com
Call Date: Oct 2006, Middle Temple

BISHOP MR ALAN RICHARD

11 Stone Buildings
11 Stone Buildings, Lincoln's Inn, London WC2A 3TG ☎020 7831 6381 ✉clerks@11sb.com
Call Date: Jul 1973, Middle Temple
Pupil Supervisor

Practising Areas: Commercial Litigation, Common Law (General), Employment, Insurance

BISHOP MR GORDON WILLIAM

Chambers of Gordon Bishop
Brook House, Rough Road, Woking, Surrey GU22 0RB ☎01483 486 730
✉gordonbishop@gmail.com
Call Date: Nov 1968, Middle Temple
Pupil Supervisor

Practising Areas: Commercial Litigation, Common Law (General), Copyright, Defamation

BISHOP MR JOHN MICHAEL

No. 3 Fleet Street Chambers
3 Fleet Street, London EC4Y 1DP
☎020 7936 4474 ✉clerks@3fleetstreet.com
Call Date: Nov 1970, Middle Temple
Pupil Supervisor

BISHOP MR MALCOLM LESLIE QC (1993)

Argent Chambers
5 Bell Yard, London WC2A 2JR
☎020 7556 5500
✉briefsin@argentchambers.co.uk
30 Park Place
Cardiff CF10 3BS ☎029 2039 8421
✉clerks@30parkplace.law.co.uk
Equity Chambers
First Floor, McLaren Building, 46 Priory Queensway, Birmingham B4 7LR
☎0121 236 5007 ✉clerks@equitychambers.org.uk
Call Date: Jul 1968, Inner Temple
Recorder

Practising Areas: Administrative, Arbitration, Banking, Care Proceedings, Civil Liberties, Commercial Litigation, Common Law (General), Company & Commercial, Courts Martial, Crime, Defamation, Education, Employment, Family, Family Provision, Financial Services, Human Rights, Licensing, Local Government, Professional Negligence

BISHOP MR STEPHEN ANTHONY

Goldsmith Chambers
Ground Floor, Goldsmith Building, Temple, London EC4Y 7BL ☎020 7353 6802
✉clerks@goldsmithchambers.com
Call Date: Jul 2006, Inner Temple

Practising Areas: Chancery (General), Common Law (General), Crime, Employment, Equity, Wills & Trusts, Landlord & Tenant, Personal Injury, Sale & Carriage of Goods

BISWAS MISS NISHA SUJATA

Chavasse Court Chambers
18 Queen Avenue, Liverpool L2 4TX
☎0151 229 2030
✉clerks@chavassechambers.co.uk
Call Date: Oct 1996, Lincoln's Inn

BLACKBURN MR LUKE SEBASTIAN

Seven Bedford Row
7 Bedford Row, London WC1R 4BS
☎020 7242 3555 ✉clerks@7br.co.uk
Call Date: Nov 1993, Middle Temple
Pupil Supervisor

Practising Areas: Regulatory Law

BLACKMORE MR JOHN HUGH

St John's Chambers
101 Victoria Street, Bristol BS1 6PU
☎0117 923 4700 ✉clerks@stjohnschambers.co.uk
Call Date: May 1983, Inner Temple
Pupil Supervisor

Practising Areas: Chancery (General), Commercial Litigation, Company & Commercial, Competition, Copyright, Partnership, Professional Negligence, Trademarks

BLACKMORE MISS SARAH ELIZABETH

37 Park Square Chambers
37 Park Square, Leeds LS1 2NY
☎0113 243 9422 ✉chambers@no37.co.uk
Call Date: Oct 1993, Inner Temple
Pupil Supervisor

Practising Areas: Care Proceedings, Family

BLACKSHAW MR HENRY WILLIAM RANDLE

St Johns Buildings
24a - 28 St John Street, Manchester M3 4DJ
☎0161 214 1500 ✉clerk@stjohnsbuildings.co.uk
St Johns Buildings
21 White Friars, Chester CH1 1NZ
☎01244 323070 ✉clerk@stjohnsbuildings.co.uk
16 Winckley Square
Preston PR1 3JJ ☎01772 256100
Call Date: Oct 1993, Middle Temple

BLACKWOOD MR CLIVE DAVID

Lamb Chambers
Lamb Building, Elm Court, Temple, London EC4Y 7AS ☎ 020 7797 8300
✉ info@lambchambers.co.uk
Call Date: Nov 1986, Inner Temple
Pupil Supervisor

Practising Areas: Banking, Bankruptcy, Chancery (General), Civil Liberties, Commercial Litigation, Common Law (General), Company & Commercial, Construction, EC & Competition Law, Employment, Franchising, Insolvency, Insurance, International Trade, Partnership, Sale & Carriage of Goods

BLAIN MR RODERICK GRAHAM

12 College Place
Fauvelle Buildings, 12 College Place, Southampton SO15 2FE ☎ 023 8032 0320
✉ clerks@12cp.co.uk
Call Date: Oct 1991, Middle Temple

Practising Areas: Courts Martial, Crime, Crime (Corporate/Fraud)

BLAIR MR PETER MICHAEL QC (2006)

Guildhall Chambers
23 Broad Street, Bristol BS1 2HG
☎ 0117 930 9000 ✉ hoc@guildhallchambers.co.uk
6 King's Bench Walk
Ground Floor, 6 King's Bench Walk, Temple, London EC4Y 7DR ☎ 020 7583 0410
✉ clerks@6kbw.com
Call Date: Jul 1983, Inner Temple
Recorder

Practising Areas: Crime, Crime (Corporate/Fraud), Environment, Health & Safety, Local Government, Regulatory Law

C

BLAKE MR CHRISTOPHER IAN

5 King's Bench Walk
5 King's Bench Walk, Temple, London EC4Y 7DN ☎ 020 7353 5638 ✉ clerks@5kbw.co.uk
Call Date: Nov 1990, Inner Temple
Pupil Supervisor

Practising Areas: Crime

BLAKE MS PENELOPE NATASHA

1 Gray's Inn Square
Ground Floor, 1 Gray's Inn Square, London WC1R 5AA ☎ 020 7405 0001
Call Date: Jul 1996, Gray's Inn

Practising Areas: Common Law (General), Crime, Family

BLAKER MR GARY MARK

Selborne Chambers
10 Essex Street, London WC2R 3AA
☎ 020 7420 9500
✉ clerks@selbornechambers.co.uk
Call Date: Oct 1993, Middle Temple
Pupil Supervisor

Practising Areas: Chancery (General), Chancery (Land Law), Commercial Property, Conveyancing, Landlord & Tenant

BLAKEY MR MICHAEL CHARLES

St Johns Buildings
24a - 28 St John Street, Manchester M3 4DJ
☎ 0161 214 1500 ✉ clerk@stjohnsbuildings.co.uk
16 Winckley Square
Preston PR1 3JJ ☎ 01772 256100
St Johns Buildings Liverpool
8th Floor India Buildings, Water Street, Liverpool L2 0XG ☎ 0151 243 6000
✉ clerk@stjohnsbuildings.co.uk
Call Date: Nov 1989, Middle Temple
Pupil Supervisor

Practising Areas: Courts Martial, Crime, Crime (Corporate/Fraud), Sports

BLAYNEY MR DAVID JAMES

Serle Court
6 New Square, Lincoln's Inn, London WC2A 3QS ☎ 020 7242 6105 ✉ clerks@serlecourt.co.uk
Call Date: Oct 1992, Lincoln's Inn
Pupil Supervisor

BLEANEY MR NICHOLAS SIMON

Atkinson Bevan Chambers
1st Floor, 2 Harcourt Buildings, Temple, London EC4Y 9DB ☎ 020 7353 2112
✉ clerks@2hb.co.uk
Call Date: Nov 1988, Lincoln's Inn
Pupil Supervisor

Practising Areas: Courts Martial, Crime, Crime (Corporate/Fraud), Licensing

BLEASDALE MISS MARIE-CLAIRE

Radcliffe Chambers
Ground Floor, 11 New Square, Lincoln's Inn, London WC2A 3QB ☎ 020 7831 0081
✉ clerks@radcliffechambers.com
Call Date: Oct 1993, Lincoln's Inn

Practising Areas: Bankruptcy, Chancery (General), Chancery (Land Law), Commercial Property, Common Law (General), Company & Commercial, Conveyancing, Equity, Wills & Trusts, Family Provision, Insolvency, Landlord

& Tenant, Partnership, Probate & Administration, Professional Negligence

BLEASDALE MR PAUL EDWARD QC (2001)

No5 Chambers
Fountain Court, Steelhouse Lane, Birmingham B4 6DR ☎0845 210 5555 ✉info@no5.com
No5 Chambers
Greenwood House, 4-7 Salisbury Court, London EC4Y 8AA ☎0845 210 5555
No5 Chambers
38 Queen Square, Bristol BS1 4QS
☎0845 210 5555
Call Date: Jul 1978, Inner Temple
Recorder

BLOHM MR LESLIE ADRIAN QC (2006)

St John's Chambers
101 Victoria Street, Bristol BS1 6PU
☎0117 923 4700 ✉clerks@stjohnschambers.co.uk
Call Date: Jul 1982, Lincoln's Inn
Recorder

Practising Areas: Agriculture, Banking, Chancery (General), Chancery (Land Law), Commercial Litigation, Commercial Property, Common Land, Company & Commercial, Equity, Wills & Trusts, Insolvency, Landlord & Tenant, Partnership, Probate & Administration, Professional Negligence, Town & Country Planning

BLOOM DR MARGARET

Hardwicke
New Square, Lincoln's Inn, London WC2A 3SB ☎020 7242 2523
✉enquiries@hardwicke.co.uk
Call Date: Oct 1994, Lincoln's Inn
Pupil Supervisor

Practising Areas: Medical Negligence, Personal Injury, Professional Negligence

BLOOM-DAVIS MR DESMOND NIALL LAURENCE

Pump Court Chambers
Upper Ground Floor, 3 Pump Court, Temple, London EC4Y 7AJ ☎020 7353 0711
✉clerks@3pumpcourt.com
Pump Court Chambers
5 Temple Chambers, Temple Street, Swindon SN1 1SQ ☎01793 539899
✉clerks@3pumpcourt.com
Pump Court Chambers
31 Southgate Street, Winchester, Hampshire SO23 9EB ☎01962 868 161
✉clerks@3pumpcourt.com
Call Date: Jul 1986, Inner Temple
Pupil Supervisor

Practising Areas: Family

BLOOMER MR CHARLES HOWARD

Lincoln House Chambers
Tower 12, The Avenue North, Spinningfields, 18-22 Bridge Street, Manchester M3 3BZ
☎0161 832 5701
✉info@lincolnhousechambers.com
Call Date: Jul 1985, Lincoln's Inn

BLOOMER MR JAMES ANDREW

Goldsmith Chambers
Ground Floor, Goldsmith Building, Temple, London EC4Y 7BL ☎020 7353 6802
✉clerks@goldsmithchambers.com
Call Date: Nov 2000, Lincoln's Inn
Pupil Supervisor

BLOOMFIELD MR RICHARD WILLIAM

Chambers of Mr Richard Bloomfield
19 Chollerford Mews, Hollywell, Whitley Bay, Tyne and Wear NE25 0TX ☎01670 360042
✉richard@richardbloomfield.co.uk
Call Date: Jul 1984, Gray's Inn
Pupil Supervisor

Practising Areas: Bankruptcy, Common Law (General), Crime, Crime (Corporate/Fraud)

BLUNT MR OLIVER SIMON PETER QC (1994)

Furnival Chambers
32 Furnival Street, London EC4A 1JQ
☎020 7405 3232
Call Date: Nov 1974, Middle Temple
Recorder

Practising Areas: Crime

BOAITEY MISS CHARLOTTE

12 Old Square Chambers
1st Floor, 12 Old Square, Lincoln's Inn, London WC2A 3TX ☎020 7404 0875
✉clerks@12oldsquare.com
Call Date: Nov 1976, Middle Temple
Pupil Supervisor

Practising Areas: Common Law (General)

BOGLE MR JAMES STEWART LOCKHART

10 King's Bench Walk
Ground Floor, 10 King's Bench Walk, Temple, London EC4Y 7EB ☎ 020 7353 7742
✉ Chambers@10kingsbenchwalk.co.uk
Call Date: Oct 1991, Middle Temple
Pupil Supervisor

Practising Areas: Banking, Bankruptcy, Chancery (General), Chancery (Land Law), Commercial Litigation, Common Law (General), Employment, Family, Housing, Insolvency, Landlord & Tenant, Medical Negligence, Mental Health, Partnership, Personal Injury, Professional Negligence, Sale & Carriage of Goods

BOJARSKI MR ANDRZEJ LEONARD

36 Bedford Row
London WC1R 4JH ☎ 020 7421 8000
✉ chambers@36bedfordrow.co.uk
Call Date: Oct 1995, Gray's Inn
Pupil Supervisor

Practising Areas: Ancillary Relief, Care Proceedings, Chancery (Land Law), Children's Law, Common Law (General), Equity, Wills & Trusts, Family, Family Provision, Probate & Administration

BOLTON MR ROBERT JOHN

2 King's Bench Walk
2 King's Bench Walk, Temple, London EC4Y 7DE ☎ 020 7353 1746 ✉ clerks@2kbw.com
Call Date: Jul 1987, Gray's Inn

Practising Areas: Equity, Wills & Trusts

BOND MISS JACQUELINE KATHRYN

1 Mitre Court Buildings
1 Mitre Court Buildings, Temple, London EC4Y 7BS ☎ 020 7452 8900 ✉ clerks@1mcb.com
4 King's Bench Walk
2nd Floor, 4 King's Bench Walk, Temple, London EC4Y 7DL ☎ 020 7822 7000
✉ clerks@4kbw.co.uk
Call Date: Oct 1994, Middle Temple

BOND MR RICHARD IAN WINSOR

Citadel Chambers
The Citadel, 190 Corporation Street, Birmingham B4 6QD ☎ 0121 233 8500
✉ clerks@citadelchambers.com
Call Date: Jul 1988, Middle Temple
Pupil Supervisor, Recorder

Practising Areas: Courts Martial, Crime, Crime (Corporate/Fraud), Health & Safety, Regulatory Law

BONEHILL MR NICHOLAS BENJAMIN

4 Breams Buildings
Chancery Lane, London EC4A 1HP
☎ 020 7092 1900 ✉ clerks@4bb.co.uk
Call Date: Jul 2006, Middle Temple

Practising Areas: Courts Martial, Crime, Crime (Corporate/Fraud), Medical Negligence, Regulatory Law

BOOTH MR ALEXANDER HENRY SPENCER

Francis Taylor Building
Inner Temple, London EC4Y 7BY
☎ 020 7353 8415 ✉ clerks@ftb.eu.com
Call Date: Nov 2000, Middle Temple

Practising Areas: Administrative, Common Land, Education, Energy, Entertainment, Environment, Licensing, Local Government, Town & Country Planning

BOOTH MR NIGEL ROBERT

Call Date: Oct 1994, Gray's Inn

BOOTH MR SIMON MARK

Atlantic Chambers
4-6 Cook Street, Liverpool L2 9QU
☎ 0151 236 4421 ✉ info@atlanticchambers.co.uk
Call Date: Nov 1985, Lincoln's Inn

BORKOWSKI MISS GEMMA FRANCESCA

Albion Chambers
Broad Street, Bristol BS1 1DR
☎ 0117 927 2144 ✉ clerks@albionchambers.co.uk
Call Date: Oct 2005, Inner Temple

Practising Areas: Employment, Family, Personal Injury

BORRELLI MR MICHAEL FRANCIS ANTONY QC (2000)

187 Fleet Street
London EC4A 2AT ☎ 020 7430 7430
✉ chambers@187fleetstreet.com
Call Date: Nov 1977, Middle Temple

Practising Areas: Crime, Crime (Corporate/Fraud)

BOSWELL MR ANDREW TIMOTHY

13 King's Bench Walk
13 King's Bench Walk, Temple, London EC4Y 7EN ☎020 7353 7204 ✉clerks@13kbw.co.uk
13 KBW
32 Beaumont Street, Oxford OX1 2NP
☎01865 311066 ✉clerks@13kbw.co.uk
Call Date: Nov 2004, Gray's Inn

Practising Areas: Courts Martial, Crime, Crime (Corporate/Fraud), Licensing, Local Government

BOTROS MR JOHN MICHAEL

Cambria Chambers
The Coal Exchange, Mount Stuart Square, Cardiff Bay, Cardiff CF10 5EB
☎0845 123 1234 ✉Info@cambriachambers.co.uk
Call Date: Feb 1992, Middle Temple

BOULDING MR PHILIP VINCENT QC (1996)

Keating Chambers
15 Essex Street, London WC2R 3AA
☎020 7544 2600 ✉clerks@keatingchambers.com
Call Date: Nov 1979, Gray's Inn

Practising Areas: Arbitration, Commercial Litigation, Construction, Energy, Environment, Information Technology, Professional Negligence

BOULTON MR RICHARD EDWARD STANLEY QC (2011)

One Essex Court
Ground Floor, One Essex Court, Temple, London EC4Y 9AR ☎020 7583 2000
✉clerks@oeclaw.co.uk
Call Date: Jul 2003, Inner Temple

BOUMPHREY MR JOHN ROSS STAVELEY

Zenith Chambers
10 Park Square, Leeds LS1 2LH
☎0113 245 5438 ✉clerks@zenithchambers.co.uk
Call Date: Nov 1992, Inner Temple
Pupil Supervisor

BOURKE MS SARAH VICTORIA NORMA

Tooks Chambers
81 Farringdon Street, London EC4A 4BL
☎020 7842 7575 ✉clerks@tooks.co.uk
Call Date: Oct 1996, Gray's Inn

Practising Areas: Discrimination, Employment, Housing, Inquests

BOURNE MR CHARLES GREGORY

4-5 Gray's Inn Square
Gray's Inn, London WC1R 5AH
☎020 7404 5252 ✉clerks@4-5.co.uk
Call Date: Oct 1991, Middle Temple
Pupil Supervisor

Practising Areas: Administrative, Civil Liberties, Common Law (General), Discrimination, Employment, Local Government, Professional Negligence, Regulatory Law, Town & Country Planning

BOURNE MR COLIN PETER

Kings Chambers
36 Young Street, Manchester M3 3FT
☎0845 034 3444 ✉clerks@kingschambers.com
Kings Chambers
5 Park Square East, Leeds LS1 2NE
☎0845 034 3444 ✉clerks@kingschambers.com
Kings Chambers
Embassy House, 60 Church Street, Birmingham B3 2DJ ☎0845 034 3444
✉clerks@kingschambers.com
Call Date: Oct 1997, Gray's Inn

Practising Areas: Discrimination, Employment

BOURNE MR GEOFFREY ROBERT

13 Old Square Chambers
Ground Floor, 14 Old Square, Lincoln's Inn, London WC2A 3UE ☎020 7831 4445
✉clerks@13oldsquare.com
Call Date: Nov 1978, Gray's Inn
Pupil Supervisor

Practising Areas: Arbitration, Banking, Chancery (General), Chancery (Land Law), Civil Litigation, Commercial Litigation, Common Law (General), Insolvency, Insurance, Partnership, Professional Negligence

BOURNE MR IAN MACLEAN QC (2006)

Charter Chambers
33 John Street, London WC1N 2AT
☎020 7618 4400 ✉clerks@charterchambers.com
Call Date: Jul 1977, Inner Temple
Recorder

Practising Areas: Courts Martial, Crime, Crime (Corporate/Fraud), Health & Safety

BOURNE-ARTON MR JAMES LUKE

St Paul's Chambers
5th Floor, St Paul's House, 23 Park Square South, Leeds LS1 2ND ☎0113 245 5866
Call Date: Oct 2001, Inner Temple

Practising Areas: Crime, Crime (Corporate/Fraud), Licensing, Regulatory Law

BOURNE-ARTON MR SIMON NICHOLAS QC (1994)

Park Court Chambers
16 Park Place, Leeds LS1 2SJ
☎0113 243 3277
✉clerks@parkcourtchambers.co.uk
Call Date: Nov 1975, Inner Temple
Recorder

Practising Areas: Courts Martial, Crime, Crime (Corporate/Fraud), Health & Safety, Sports

BOWDEN MR GUY ROBERT

4 Breams Buildings
Chancery Lane, London EC4A 1HP
☎020 7092 1900 ✉clerks@4bb.co.uk
Call Date: Oct 2003, Inner Temple

Practising Areas: Common Law (General), Coroners Inquests, Crime, Crime (Corporate/Fraud), Inquests

BOWE MR PATRICK JOSEPH

KCH Garden Square
1 Oxford Street, Nottingham NG1 5BH
☎0115 941 8851 ✉clerks@kchgardensquare.co.uk
Call Date: Jul 2000, Lincoln's Inn

Practising Areas: Ancillary Relief, Family

C

BOWEN MR JAMES FRANCIS

Garden Court Chambers
57-60 Lincoln's Inn Fields, London WC2A 3LJ
☎020 7993 7600 ✉info@gclaw.co.uk
Call Date: Nov 1979, Gray's Inn
Pupil Supervisor

BOWEN MR NICHOLAS JAMES HUGH QC (2009)

Doughty Street Chambers
53-54 Doughty Street, London WC1N 2LS
☎020 7404 1313 ✉enquiries@doughtystreet.co.uk
Doughty Street Chambers
Pall Mall Court, 61-67 King Street, Manchester M2 4PD ☎0161 618 1066
Doughty Street Chambers
5th Floor, Broad Quay House, Prince Street, Bristol BS1 4DJ ☎01179 058 717
Call Date: Nov 1984, Gray's Inn

Practising Areas: Administrative, Care Proceedings, Children's Law, Civil Liberties, Civil Litigation, Commercial Litigation, Common Law (General), Construction, Coroners Inquests, Data Protection, Disciplinary Tribunals, Education, Healthcare, Human Rights, Mental Health, Professional Negligence

BOWERS MR RUPERT JOHN

Doughty Street Chambers
53-54 Doughty Street, London WC1N 2LS
☎020 7404 1313 ✉enquiries@doughtystreet.co.uk
Call Date: Oct 1995, Gray's Inn
Pupil Supervisor

Practising Areas: Administrative, Care Proceedings, Civil Liberties, Crime, Crime (Corporate/Fraud), Family, Health & Safety, Human Rights, Parliamentary, Regulatory Law, Sports

BOWES MR MICHAEL ANTHONY QC (2001)

Outer Temple Chambers
The Outer Temple, 222 Strand, London WC2R 1BA ☎020 7353 6381
✉clerks@outertemple.com
Cobden House Chambers
19 Quay Street, Manchester M3 3HN
☎0161 833 6000 ✉Clerks@Cobden.co.uk
Call Date: Jul 1980, Middle Temple
Recorder

Practising Areas: Courts Martial, Crime, Crime (Corporate/Fraud), Financial Services, Health & Safety, Licensing

BOWHILL MISS JESSIE KATE

8 New Square
8 New Square, Lincoln's Inn, London WC2A 3QP ☎020 7405 4321 ✉clerks@8newsquare.co.uk
Call Date: Oct 2003, Gray's Inn

Practising Areas: Copyright, Entertainment, Film, Cable & TV, Franchising, Intellectual Property, Patents, Sports, Trademarks

BOWKER MR ROBERT JAMES

Tanfield Chambers
2-5 Warwick Court, London WC1R 5DJ
☎020 7421 5300 ✉clerks@tanfieldchambers.co.uk
Call Date: Nov 1995, Lincoln's Inn

BOWLING MR JAMES STUART

4 Pump Court
4 Pump Court, Temple, London EC4Y 7AN
☎ 020 7842 5555 ✉ chambers@4pumpcourt.com
Call Date: Nov 1999, Middle Temple

Practising Areas: Asset Finance, Banking, Bankruptcy, Commercial Litigation, Construction, Corporate Finance, Information Technology, Insolvency, Insurance, Professional Negligence

BOWSHER MR MICHAEL FREDERICK THOMAS QC (2006)

Monckton Chambers
1 & 2 Raymond Buildings, Gray's Inn, London WC1R 5NR ☎ 020 7405 7211
✉ chambers@monckton.com
Call Date: Nov 1985, Middle Temple

Practising Areas: Administrative, Arbitration, Commercial Litigation, Competition, Construction, EC & Competition Law, Healthcare, Information Technology, Local Government, Private International

BOYCE MR WILLIAM QC (2001)

QEB Hollis Whiteman
1-2 Laurence Pountney Hill, London EC4R 0EU ☎ 020 7933 8855 ✉ barristers@qebhw.co.uk
Call Date: Jul 1976, Gray's Inn
Recorder

BOYD MISS KERSTIN MARGARET

Tanfield Chambers
2-5 Warwick Court, London WC1R 5DJ
☎ 020 7421 5300 ✉ clerks@tanfieldchambers.co.uk
Call Date: Jul 1979, Gray's Inn
Pupil Supervisor

Practising Areas: Family, Family Provision, Medical Negligence, Personal Injury

BOYD MR PHILLIP JOSEPH GEORGE

Lincoln House Chambers
Tower 12, The Avenue North, Spinningfields, 18-22 Bridge Street, Manchester M3 3BZ
☎ 0161 832 5701
✉ info@lincolnhousechambers.com
Call Date: Nov 1993, Gray's Inn
Pupil Supervisor

Practising Areas: Crime, Crime (Corporate/Fraud), Regulatory Law

BOYD MR STEPHEN JAMES HARVEY

Selborne Chambers
10 Essex Street, London WC2R 3AA
☎ 020 7420 9500
✉ clerks@selbornechambers.co.uk
Call Date: Jul 1977, Gray's Inn
Pupil Supervisor

Practising Areas: Banking, Bankruptcy, Chancery (General), Chancery (Land Law), Commercial Litigation, Commercial Property, Common Law (General), Conveyancing, Employment, Equity, Wills & Trusts, Franchising, Insolvency, Landlord & Tenant, Partnership, Probate & Administration, Professional Negligence, Sale & Carriage of Goods, Sports

BOYES MR IAN DAVID

3 Temple Gardens
Lower Ground Floor, 3 Temple Gardens, Temple, London EC4Y 9AU ☎ 020 7353 3102
✉ clerks@3tg.co.uk
Call Date: Nov 2003, Lincoln's Inn

BOYLE MISS KAREN

St James's Chambers
68 Quay Street, Manchester M3 3EJ
☎ 0161 834 7000 ✉ clerks@stjameschambers.com
12 King's Bench Walk
12 King's Bench Walk, Temple, London EC4Y 7EL ☎ 020 7583 0811
Call Date: Jul 2000, Lincoln's Inn

BRAAMSKAMP MS CHRISTINE JOLANDA

3 Raymond Buildings
3 Raymond Buildings, Gray's Inn, London WC1R 5BH ☎ 020 7400 6400
✉ clerks@3rblaw.com
Call Date: Jul 2000, Gray's Inn

Practising Areas: Crime, Crime (Corporate/Fraud), Regulatory Law

BRADLEY MISS CAROLINE

23 Essex Street
London WC2R 3AA ☎ 020 7413 0353
✉ clerks@23es.com
Call Date: Nov 1985, Middle Temple
Pupil Supervisor

BRADLEY MS SALLY CHRISTINA

4 Paper Buildings
1st Floor, 4 Paper Buildings, Temple, London EC4Y 7EX ☎ 020 7427 5200 ✉ clerks@4pb.com
Call Date: Nov 1989, Inner Temple
Pupil Supervisor

Practising Areas: Family

BRADLEY MS SALLY FRANCES QC (1999)

Trinity Chambers
The Custom House, 39 Quayside, Newcastle Upon Tyne NE1 3DE ☎ 0191 232 1927 ✉ info@trinitychambers.co.uk
Sovereign Chambers
46 Park Place, Leeds LS1 2RY ☎ 0113 245 1841 ✉ clerks@sovereignchambers.co.uk
18 St John Street
Manchester M3 4EA ☎ 0161 278 1800 ✉ clerks@18sjs.com
Trinity Chambers
Multi Media Exchange, 72-80 Corporation Road, Middlesbrough TS1 2RF ☎ 01642 247569 ✉ info@trinitychambers.co.uk
Call Date: Nov 1978, Lincoln's Inn
Recorder

Practising Areas: Care Proceedings, Family

BRADLY MR DAVID LAWRENCE

39 Essex Street
London WC2R 3AT ☎ 020 7832 1111 ✉ clerks@39essex.com
Call Date: Jul 1987, Middle Temple
Pupil Supervisor

Practising Areas: Regulatory Law

BRADNOCK MR THOMAS PHILIP

Colleton Chambers
Colleton Crescent, Exeter, Devon EX2 4DG ☎ 01392 274898 ✉ clerks@colletonchambers.co.uk
Call Date: Oct 1997, Gray's Inn

Practising Areas: Crime, Environment, Regulatory Law

BRADSHAW MR MARK KIERAN

No5 Chambers
Fountain Court, Steelhouse Lane, Birmingham B4 6DR ☎ 0845 210 5555 ✉ info@no5.com
No5 Chambers
Greenwood House, 4-7 Salisbury Court, London EC4Y 8AA ☎ 0845 210 5555
No5 Chambers
38 Queen Square, Bristol BS1 4QS ☎ 0845 210 5555
Call Date: Jul 2002, Gray's Inn

Practising Areas: Administrative, Human Rights, Immigration, Public Law

BRADY MR SCOTT

3 Temple Gardens
Lower Ground Floor, 3 Temple Gardens, Temple, London EC4Y 9AU ☎ 020 7353 3102 ✉ clerks@3tg.co.uk
Call Date: Jul 1998, Middle Temple

Practising Areas: Courts Martial, Crime, Crime (Corporate/Fraud), Defamation, Health & Safety, Licensing, Regulatory Law, Sports, Town & Country Planning

BRAGGE MR THOMAS HEREWARD

Stour Chambers
Mill Studio, 17a Stour Street, Canterbury, Kent CT1 2NR ☎ 01227 764899 ✉ clerks@stourchambers.co.uk
Call Date: Oct 2000, Inner Temple

Practising Areas: Administrative, Bankruptcy, Chancery (General), Commercial Litigation, Common Law (General), Equity, Wills & Trusts, Insolvency, Landlord & Tenant, Personal Injury, Professional Negligence

BRAGIEL MR EDWARD BRONISLAW HENRYK

Hogarth Chambers
5 New Square, Lincoln's Inn, London WC2A 3RJ ☎ 020 7404 0404 ✉ barristers@hogarthchambers.com
Call Date: Jul 1977, Middle Temple
Pupil Supervisor

Practising Areas: Bankruptcy, Chancery (General), Chancery (Land Law), Charities, Commercial Litigation, Commercial Property, Company & Commercial, Conveyancing, Copyright, Entertainment, Equity, Wills & Trusts, Family Provision, Film, Cable & TV, Insolvency, Intellectual Property, Landlord & Tenant, Partnership, Probate & Administration, Professional Negligence, Sports, Trademarks

BRAIER MR JASON DEAN

Field Court Chambers
5 Field Court, Gray's Inn, London WC1R 5EF
☎ 020 7405 6114 ✉ clerks@fieldcourt.co.uk
Call Date: Jul 2002, Inner Temple

Practising Areas: Administrative, Commercial Litigation, Common Law (General), Discrimination, Employment, Housing, Landlord & Tenant

BRAIN MISS PAMELA FRANCIS

Chambers of Marion Smullen and Kerim Fuad QC
1 Inner Temple Lane, London EC4Y 1AF
☎ 020 7427 4400 ✉ clerks@1itl.com
Call Date: Nov 1985, Inner Temple
Pupil Supervisor

Practising Areas: Crime

BRAITHWAITE MR THOMAS JAMES

Serle Court
6 New Square, Lincoln's Inn, London WC2A 3QS ☎ 020 7242 6105 ✉ clerks@serlecourt.co.uk
Call Date: Oct 1998, Lincoln's Inn
Pupil Supervisor

Practising Areas: Common Land, Equity, Wills & Trusts, Land, Partnership

BRAMWELL MR CHRISTOPHER PAUL

Regency Chambers
45 Priestgate, Peterborough PE1 1LB
☎ 01733 315215 ✉ clerks@regencychambers.law.co.uk
Regency Chambers
Sheraton House, Castle Park, Cambridge CB3 0AX ☎ 01223 301517
Call Date: Nov 1996, Gray's Inn
Pupil Supervisor

Practising Areas: Care Proceedings, Family

BRAMWELL MISS CORINNE VICTORIA

Nine Bedford Row
9 Bedford Row, London WC1R 4AZ
☎ 020 7489 2727 ✉ clerks@9bedfordrow.co.uk
Call Date: Oct 2005, Inner Temple

Practising Areas: Crime, Crime (Corporate/Fraud), Human Rights

BRANCHFLOWER MR GEORGE

Zenith Chambers
10 Park Square, Leeds LS1 2LH
☎ 0113 245 5438 ✉ clerks@zenithchambers.co.uk
Call Date: Oct 1997, Lincoln's Inn
Pupil Supervisor

Practising Areas: Chancery (Land Law), Civil Litigation, Commercial Litigation, Common Law (General), Employment, Land, Professional Negligence

BRAND MISS RACHEL RENNIE VIRGINIA ANN QC (2000)

Citadel Chambers
The Citadel, 190 Corporation Street, Birmingham B4 6QD ☎ 0121 233 8500
✉ clerks@citadelchambers.com
Call Date: Jul 1981, Gray's Inn
Recorder

Practising Areas: Crime, Crime (Corporate/Fraud)

BRANSTON MR GARETH PHILIP

23 Essex Street
London WC2R 3AA ☎ 020 7413 0353
✉ clerks@23es.com
Call Date: Oct 1996, Gray's Inn
Pupil Supervisor

Practising Areas: Crime, Crime (Corporate/Fraud), Regulatory Law

BRASSINGTON MR STEPHEN DAVID

2 Hare Court
Lower Ground, Ground, 1st & 2nd Floor, 2 Hare Court, Temple, London EC4Y 7BH
☎ 020 7353 3982 ✉ clerks@2harecourt.com
Call Date: Nov 1994, Inner Temple
Pupil Supervisor

Practising Areas: Crime, Crime (Corporate/Fraud), Regulatory Law

BRAUN MS MINKA CHAYA

25 Bedford Row
London WC1R 4HD ☎ 020 7067 1500
✉ clerks@25bedfordrow.com
Call Date: Jul 2000, Inner Temple
Pupil Supervisor

Practising Areas: Crime

BRAY MISS CAROLINE JANE

36 Bedford Row
London WC1R 4JH ☎ 020 7421 8000
✉ chambers@36bedfordrow.co.uk
Call Date: Jul 2000, Lincoln's Inn

Practising Areas: Crime

BRAY MISS HELEN LORNA

Walnut House
63 St. David's Hill, Exeter, Devon EX4 4DW
☎ 01392 279751 ✉ clerks@walnuthouse.co.uk
Call Date: Jul 2004, Gray's Inn

Practising Areas: Ancillary Relief, Civil Litigation, Family Provision

BREDEMEAR MR ZACHARY CHARLES

1 Chancery Lane
London WC2A 1LF ☎ 0845 634 6666
✉ clerks@1chancerylane.com
Call Date: Oct 1996, Inner Temple
Pupil Supervisor

Practising Areas: Chancery (General), Chancery (Land Law), Civil Litigation, Commercial Litigation, Commercial Property, Common Land, Common Law (General), Construction, Conveyancing, Equity, Wills & Trusts, Franchising, Housing, Insolvency, Land, Landlord & Tenant, Partnership, Probate & Administration, Professional Negligence

BREEN-LAWTON MISS DENISE

St Paul's Chambers
5th Floor, St Paul's House, 23 Park Square South, Leeds LS1 2ND ☎ 0113 245 5866
Call Date: Jul 2000, Gray's Inn
Pupil Supervisor

Practising Areas: Care Proceedings, Crime, Crime (Corporate/Fraud), Family, Health & Safety

BREHAN MS DAIRE

Chambers of Ms D Brehan
4 Pair North, 3 Hare Court, Temple, London EC4Y 7BJ ☎ 07808 726877
✉ brennan_holahan@hotmail.com
Call Date: Jul 2002, Inner Temple

Practising Areas: Crime, Crime (Corporate/Fraud), Discrimination, Employment, Human Rights, Mental Health, Regulatory Law

BRERETON MISS JOY

4 Paper Buildings
1st Floor, 4 Paper Buildings, Temple, London EC4Y 7EX ☎ 020 7427 5200 ✉ clerks@4pb.com
Call Date: Nov 1990, Gray's Inn
Pupil Supervisor

Practising Areas: Care Proceedings, Family, Family Provision, Mental Health

BRETT MR MATTHEW CHRISTOPHER ANTHONY

Harcourt Chambers
1st Floor, 2 Harcourt Buildings, Temple, London EC4Y 9DB ☎ 0844 561 7135
Harcourt Chambers
Churchill House, 3 St Aldate's Courtyard, St Aldate's, Oxford OX1 1BN ☎ 0844 561 7135
Call Date: Nov 1987, Middle Temple

BREWIN MR CARL PATRICK

3 PB Barristers
3 Paper Buildings, Temple, London EC4Y 7EU
☎ 020 7583 8055
Call Date: Oct 2006, Middle Temple

Practising Areas: Administrative, Chancery (General), Chancery (Land Law), Commercial Litigation, Commercial Property, Common Land, Common Law (General), Conveyancing, Islamic Sharia Law, Landlord & Tenant

BRICKMAN MISS LAURA GILLIAN

Carmelite Chambers
9 Carmelite Street, London EC4Y 0DR
☎ 020 7936 6300
✉ clerks@carmelitechambers.co.uk
Call Date: Jul 1976, Inner Temple
Pupil Supervisor

Practising Areas: Crime, Crime (Corporate/Fraud)

BRIDEN MS SARAH LOUISE

KCH Garden Square
1 Oxford Street, Nottingham NG1 5BH
☎ 0115 941 8851 ✉ clerks@kchgardensquare.co.uk
Call Date: Jul 1999, Inner Temple

Practising Areas: Care Proceedings, Children's Law, Family

BRIDGE MR GILES

Broadway House Chambers
Broadway House, 9 Bank Street, Bradford, West Yorkshire BD1 1TW ☎01274 722560
✉clerks@broadwayhouse.co.uk
Broadway House Chambers
25 Park Square West, Leeds, West Yorkshire LS1 2PW ☎0113 246 2600
✉clerks@broadwayhouse.co.uk
Call Date: Jul 2000, Middle Temple
Pupil Supervisor

Practising Areas: Crime, Crime (Corporate/Fraud), Environment, Health & Safety, Licensing, Regulatory Law

BRIEGEL MR PIETER DAVID ROY

5 King's Bench Walk
5 King's Bench Walk, Temple, London EC4Y 7DN ☎020 7353 5638 ✉clerks@5kbw.co.uk
Call Date: Nov 1986, Middle Temple
Pupil Supervisor

BRIGHT MISS RACHEL ZELDA

187 Fleet Street
London EC4A 2AT ☎020 7430 7430
✉chambers@187fleetstreet.com
4 Brick Court
4 Brick Court, Temple, London EC4Y 9AD
☎020 7832 3200 ✉clerks@4bc.co.uk
Call Date: Oct 1991, Lincoln's Inn
Pupil Supervisor

Practising Areas: Crime, Crime (Corporate/Fraud)

BRILLIANT MR SIMON HOWARD

Lamb Chambers
Lamb Building, Elm Court, Temple, London EC4Y 7AS ☎020 7797 8300
✉info@lambchambers.co.uk
Call Date: Jul 1976, Middle Temple
Pupil Supervisor

Practising Areas: Chancery (Land Law), Landlord & Tenant

BRIMELOW MISS JANINE KIRSTY QC (2011)

Doughty Street Chambers
53-54 Doughty Street, London WC1N 2LS
☎020 7404 1313 ✉enquiries@doughtystreet.co.uk
Doughty Street Chambers
Pall Mall Court, 61-67 King Street, Manchester M2 4PD ☎0161 618 1066
Doughty Street Chambers
5th Floor, Broad Quay House, Prince Street, Bristol BS1 4DJ ☎01179 058 717
Call Date: Oct 1991, Gray's Inn
Pupil Supervisor

Practising Areas: Crime, Crime (Corporate/Fraud)

BRISCOE MISS CONSTANCE

9-12 Bell Yard
London WC2A 2JR ☎020 7400 1800
✉clerks@9-12bellyard.com
Call Date: Nov 1983, Inner Temple
Recorder

BRITTAIN MR MARC JOHN

1 Gray's Inn Square
Ground Floor, 1 Gray's Inn Square, London WC1R 5AA ☎020 7405 0001
Call Date: Jul 1983, Gray's Inn
Pupil Supervisor

Practising Areas: Commercial Litigation, Common Law (General), Insurance, Personal Injury, Professional Negligence

BRITTENDEN MR STUART

Old Square Chambers
10-11 Bedford Row, London WC1R 4BU
☎020 7269 0300 ✉clerks@oldsquare.co.uk
Old Square Chambers
3 Orchard Court, St Augustine's Yard, Bristol BS1 5DP ☎0117 930 5100
✉clerks@oldsquare.co.uk
Call Date: Oct 1999, Gray's Inn

BROADLEY MR JOHN

Cobden House Chambers
19 Quay Street, Manchester M3 3HN
☎0161 833 6000 ✉Clerks@Cobden.co.uk
Call Date: Jul 1973, Middle Temple
Pupil Supervisor

Practising Areas: Crime, Crime (Corporate/Fraud), Regulatory Law, Road Traffic And Highways

BROATCH MR DONALD

Five Paper
Ground Floor, 5 Paper Buildings, Temple, London EC4Y 7HB ☎020 7815 3200
Call Date: May 1971, Middle Temple
Pupil Supervisor

Practising Areas: Administrative, Housing, Human Rights, Landlord & Tenant, Local Government

BROCKLEY MR NIGEL SIMON

No5 Chambers
Greenwood House, 4-7 Salisbury Court, London EC4Y 8AA ☎0845 210 5555
No5 Chambers
38 Queen Square, Bristol BS1 4QS
☎0845 210 5555
No5 Chambers
Fountain Court, Steelhouse Lane, Birmingham B4 6DR ☎0845 210 5555 ✉info@no5.com
Call Date: Nov 1992, Lincoln's Inn

Practising Areas: Chancery (General), Commercial Property, Common Law (General), Company & Commercial, Employment, Housing, Landlord & Tenant, Personal Injury

BRODIE MR GRAHAM PAUL

Chambers of Andrew Mitchell QC
33 Chancery Lane, London WC2A 1EN
☎020 7440 9950 ✉clerks@33cllaw.com
Call Date: Jul 1989, Middle Temple

BROGDEN MR PETER CIERAN

Keating Chambers
15 Essex Street, London WC2R 3AA
☎020 7544 2600 ✉clerks@keatingchambers.com
Call Date: Jul 2006, Inner Temple

BROMLEY-MARTIN MR MICHAEL GRANVILLE QC (2002)

3 Raymond Buildings
3 Raymond Buildings, Gray's Inn, London WC1R 5BH ☎020 7400 6400
✉clerks@3rblaw.com
Call Date: Nov 1979, Gray's Inn
Recorder

BROOK MR DALE MATTHEW

15 New Bridge Street
London EC4V 6AU ☎020 7842 1900
✉clerks@15nbs.com
Call Date: Nov 2003, Inner Temple

BROOK MR PAUL ANTONY

Park Lane Plowden
19 Westgate, Leeds LS1 2RD
☎0113 228 5049 ✉clerks@parklaneplowden.co.uk
Park Lane Plowden
Lombard House, 4-8 Lombard Street, Newcastle Upon Tyne NE1 3AE
☎0191 211 4087 ✉clerks@parklaneplowden.co.uk
Call Date: Nov 1986, Inner Temple

Practising Areas: Agriculture, Arbitration, Bankruptcy, Chancery (Land Law), Company & Commercial, Conveyancing, Equity, Wills & Trusts, Insolvency, Landlord & Tenant, Partnership

BROOKE MR DAVID MICHAEL GRAHAM

KBW
The Engine House, No 1 Foundry Square, Leeds LS11 5DL ☎0113 297 1200
✉clerks@kbwchambers.com
Call Date: Nov 1990, Inner Temple
Pupil Supervisor

Practising Areas: Crime

BROOKE-SMITH MR JOHN

East Anglian Chambers
53 North Hill, Colchester, Essex CO1 1QA
☎01473 214481 ✉colchester@ealaw.co.uk
East Anglian Chambers
Gresham House, 5 Museum Street, Ipswich, Suffolk IP1 1HQ ☎01473 214481
✉ipswich@ealaw.co.uk
Call Date: Jul 1981, Gray's Inn
Pupil Supervisor, Recorder

Practising Areas: Family, Personal Injury

BROOME MISS NICOLA KERRY

QEB Hollis Whiteman
1-2 Laurence Pountney Hill, London EC4R 0EU ☎020 7933 8855 ✉barristers@qebhw.co.uk
Call Date: Oct 2003, Gray's Inn

BROUNGER MR DAVID WILLIAM JOHN

Field Court Chambers
5 Field Court, Gray's Inn, London WC1R 5EF
☎020 7405 6114 ✉clerks@fieldcourt.co.uk
Call Date: Nov 1990, Inner Temple
Pupil Supervisor

BROWN MR CAMERON KENNEDY DUNCAN

9-12 Bell Yard
London WC2A 2JR ☎020 7400 1800
✉clerks@9-12bellyard.com
Call Date: Oct 1998, Inner Temple

Practising Areas: Common Law (General), Crime, Employment, Personal Injury

BROWN MR EDWARD FRANCIS TREVENEN QC (2008)

QEB Hollis Whiteman
1-2 Laurence Pountney Hill, London EC4R 0EU ☎ 020 7933 8855 ✉ barristers@qebhw.co.uk
Call Date: Jul 1983, Gray's Inn
Recorder

Practising Areas: Courts Martial, Crime, Crime (Corporate/Fraud), Parliamentary

BROWN MS GRACE

Tooks Chambers
81 Farringdon Street, London EC4A 4BL
☎ 020 7842 7575 ✉ clerks@tooks.co.uk
Call Date: Oct 1995, Inner Temple
Pupil Supervisor

Practising Areas: Civil Liberties, Education, Family, Human Rights, Immigration, Mental Health

BROWN MR PHILIP STEPHEN

9 Stone Buildings
Lincoln's Inn, London WC2A 3NN
☎ 020 7404 5055 ✉ clerks@9stonebuildings.com
Call Date: Oct 1991, Lincoln's Inn

Practising Areas: Administrative, Chancery (General), Chancery (Land Law), Commercial Litigation, Commercial Property, Common Law (General), Company & Commercial, Employment, Equity, Wills & Trusts, Landlord & Tenant, Probate & Administration

BROWN MR ROGER CHARLES ARTHUR

Kenworthy's Chambers
Arlington House, Bloom Street, Salford, Manchester M3 6AJ ☎ 0161 832 4036
Call Date: Nov 1976, Inner Temple
Pupil Supervisor

Practising Areas: Administrative, Commercial Property, Crime, Crime (Corporate/Fraud), Environment, Health & Safety, Licensing, Local Government, Regulatory Law

BROWN MR SAM CLEMENT

Atkinson Bevan Chambers
1st Floor, 2 Harcourt Buildings, Temple, London EC4Y 9DB ☎ 020 7353 2112
✉ clerks@2hb.co.uk
Call Date: Nov 2004, Inner Temple

Practising Areas: Administrative, Civil Liberties, Courts Martial, Crime, Crime (Corporate/Fraud), Human Rights, Mental Health

BROWN MR SIMON JONATHAN

Crown Office Chambers
2 Crown Office Row, Temple, London EC4Y 7HJ ☎ 020 7797 8100
✉ mail@crownofficechambers.com
Call Date: Jul 1988, Gray's Inn
Pupil Supervisor

Practising Areas: Costs, Employment, Professional Negligence, Regulatory Law

BROWN MISS STEPHANIE AMANDA

No5 Chambers
Fountain Court, Steelhouse Lane, Birmingham B4 6DR ☎ 0845 210 5555 ✉ info@no5.com
No5 Chambers
Greenwood House, 4-7 Salisbury Court, London EC4Y 8AA ☎ 0845 210 5555
No5 Chambers
38 Queen Square, Bristol BS1 4QS
☎ 0845 210 5555
Call Date: Jul 1982, Lincoln's Inn
Pupil Supervisor

Practising Areas: Family Provision

BROWN MISS SUSAN MARGARET

One Essex Court
1st Floor, Temple, London EC4Y 9AR
☎ 020 7936 3030 ✉ clerks@1ec.co.uk
Call Date: Jul 1989, Lincoln's Inn
Pupil Supervisor

Practising Areas: Bankruptcy, Chancery (General), Chancery (Land Law), Civil Litigation, Commercial Litigation, Commercial Property, Company & Commercial, Equity, Wills & Trusts, Housing, Insolvency, Land, Landlord & Tenant, Partnership

BROWN MR TIMOTHY WILLIAM

13 King's Bench Walk
13 King's Bench Walk, Temple, London EC4Y 7EN ☎ 020 7353 7204 ✉ clerks@13kbw.co.uk
13 KBW
32 Beaumont Street, Oxford OX1 2NP
☎ 01865 311066 ✉ clerks@13kbw.co.uk
Call Date: Mar 2005, Inner Temple

Practising Areas: Commercial Litigation, Discrimination, Employment

BROWNE MR DESMOND JOHN MICHAEL QC (1990)

5RB
1st Floor, 5 Raymond Buildings, Gray's Inn, London WC1R 5BP ☎ 020 7242 2902
✉ clerks@5rb.com
Call Date: Nov 1969, Gray's Inn
Recorder

Practising Areas: Copyright, Defamation, Human Rights, Intellectual Property

BROWNE MR JAMES WILLIAM

Lamb Chambers
Lamb Building, Elm Court, Temple, London EC4Y 7AS ☎020 7797 8300
✉info@lambchambers.co.uk
Call Date: Oct 1994, Middle Temple

Practising Areas: Chancery (Land Law), Commercial Property, Housing, Insolvency, Landlord & Tenant

BRUCE MR ANDREW JONATHAN

Serle Court
6 New Square, Lincoln's Inn, London WC2A 3QS ☎020 7242 6105 ✉clerks@serlecourt.co.uk
Call Date: Oct 1992, Middle Temple
Pupil Supervisor, Recorder

Practising Areas: Chancery (General), Chancery (Land Law), Commercial Litigation, Commercial Property, Land, Landlord & Tenant, Professional Negligence

BRUNNER MS CATHERINE JANE

Albion Chambers
Broad Street, Bristol BS1 1DR
☎0117 927 2144 ✉clerks@albionchambers.co.uk
36 Bedford Row
London WC1R 4JH ☎020 7421 8000
✉chambers@36bedfordrow.co.uk
Call Date: Oct 1997, Inner Temple

Practising Areas: Crime, Crime (Corporate/Fraud), Employment, Health & Safety, Regulatory Law

C

BRUNNER MR PETER ROLAND

Brick Court Chambers
7-8 Essex Street, London WC2R 3LD
☎020 7379 3550 ✉clerks@brickcourt.co.uk
Call Date: Jul 1971, Middle Temple
Pupil Supervisor

Practising Areas: Construction, Private International, Professional Negligence, Sale & Carriage of Goods

BRUNNING MR MATTHEW DAVID GEORGE

No5 Chambers
Fountain Court, Steelhouse Lane, Birmingham B4 6DR ☎0845 210 5555 ✉info@no5.com
No5 Chambers
Greenwood House, 4-7 Salisbury Court, London EC4Y 8AA ☎0845 210 5555
No5 Chambers
38 Queen Square, Bristol BS1 4QS
☎0845 210 5555
Call Date: Nov 1997, Middle Temple

Practising Areas: Personal Injury

BRUNT MR PHILIP EDWIN

No 8 Chambers
8 Fountain Court, Steelhouse Lane, Birmingham B4 6DR ☎0121 236 5514
✉clerks@no8chambers.co.uk
Call Date: Nov 1991, Lincoln's Inn

Practising Areas: Common Law (General), Crime, Crime (Corporate/Fraud), Employment, Town & Country Planning

BRUNTON MR SEAN ALEXANDER MCKAY

Colleton Chambers
Colleton Crescent, Exeter, Devon EX2 4DG
☎01392 274898 ✉clerks@colletonchambers.co.uk
3 PB Barristers
Royal Talbot House, 2 Victoria Street, Bristol, Avon BS1 6BB ☎0117 928 1520
Call Date: Oct 1990, Middle Temple

BRYAN MR REX VICTOR

East Anglian Chambers
140 New London Road, Chelmsford, Essex CM2 0AW ☎01473 214481
✉chelmsford@ealaw.co.uk
East Anglian Chambers
Gresham House, 5 Museum Street, Ipswich, Suffolk IP1 1HQ ☎01473 214481
✉ipswich@ealaw.co.uk
East Anglian Chambers
15 The Close, Norwich, Norfolk NR1 4DZ
☎01473 214481 ✉norwich@ealaw.co.uk
Call Date: Nov 1971, Lincoln's Inn
Pupil Supervisor, Recorder

BRYAN MR ROBERT JOHN

1 Paper Buildings
1st Floor, 1 Paper Buildings, Temple, London EC4Y 7EP ☎020 7353 3728
✉clerks@onepaper.co.uk
Call Date: Oct 1992, Middle Temple
Pupil Supervisor

Practising Areas: Coroners Inquests, Courts Martial, Crime, Crime (Corporate/Fraud), Disciplinary Tribunals, Health & Safety, Inquests, Licensing, Regulatory Law, Road Traffic And Highways, Sports

BRYANT MR KEITH

Outer Temple Chambers
The Outer Temple, 222 Strand, London WC2R 1BA ☎ 020 7353 6381
✉ clerks@outertemple.com
Call Date: Oct 1991, Middle Temple
Pupil Supervisor

Practising Areas: Employment, Professional Negligence

BRYANT-HERON MR MARK NICHOLAS

9-12 Bell Yard
London WC2A 2JR ☎ 020 7400 1800
✉ clerks@9-12bellyard.com
Call Date: Nov 1986, Middle Temple
Pupil Supervisor, Recorder

Practising Areas: Crime, Crime (Corporate/Fraud), Disciplinary Tribunals

BRYDEN MR CHRISTOPHER JAMES YUEN KANG

4 King's Bench Walk
2nd Floor, 4 King's Bench Walk, Temple, London EC4Y 7DL ☎ 020 7822 7000
✉ clerks@4kbw.co.uk
Call Date: Jul 2003, Gray's Inn

Practising Areas: Administrative, Asset Finance, Banking, Bankruptcy, Chancery (General), Chancery (Land Law), Commercial Litigation, Commercial Property, Common Land, Common Law (General), Company & Commercial, Construction, Discrimination, Employment, Entertainment, Equity, Wills & Trusts, Family, Family Provision, Health & Safety, Housing, Human Rights, Insolvency, Landlord & Tenant, Licensing, Local Government, Partnership, Personal Injury, Probate & Administration, Professional Negligence, Sale & Carriage of Goods

BUCHAN MR ANDREW

Cloisters
1 Pump Court, Temple, London EC4Y 7AA
☎ 020 7827 4000 ✉ clerks@cloisters.com
Call Date: Jul 1981, Gray's Inn
Pupil Supervisor

Practising Areas: Civil Liberties, Employment, Medical Negligence, Mental Health, Pensions, Personal Injury, Professional Negligence

BUCHAN MISS CAROLINE VENETIA

Chambers of Miss C Buchan
9 Savill Road, Haywards Heath, East Sussex RH16 2NY ☎ 01444 482222
✉ carolinebuchan@yahoo.com
Call Date: Oct 2000, Middle Temple

Practising Areas: Arbitration, Bankruptcy, Charities, Commercial Litigation, Commercial Property, Common Law (General), Company & Commercial, Construction, Conveyancing, Copyright, Data Protection, Defamation, Discrimination, Education, Employment, Environment, Equity, Wills & Trusts, Family, Financial Services, Health & Safety, Human Rights, Immigration, Insolvency, Insurance, Insurance/Reinsurance, Intellectual Property, Land, Landlord & Tenant, Licensing, Medical Negligence, Partnership, Pensions, Personal Injury, Private International, Probate & Administration, Professional Negligence, Regulatory Law, Sale & Carriage of Goods, Share Options, Trademarks

BUCHANAN MR JAMES IAN CHARLES

2 Hare Court
Lower Ground, Ground, 1st & 2nd Floor, 2 Hare Court, Temple, London EC4Y 7BH
☎ 020 7353 3982 ✉ clerks@2harecourt.com
Call Date: Nov 1993, Gray's Inn

Practising Areas: Crime, Crime (Corporate/Fraud), Health & Safety, Regulatory Law

BUCK MR JOHN

Tanfield Chambers
2-5 Warwick Court, London WC1R 5DJ
☎ 020 7421 5300 ✉ clerks@tanfieldchambers.co.uk
Call Date: Nov 1987, Gray's Inn
Pupil Supervisor

Practising Areas: Ancillary Relief, Care Proceedings, Common Law (General), Equity, Wills & Trusts, Family, Family Provision, Landlord & Tenant

BUCKHAVEN MR SIMON

Hardwicke
New Square, Lincoln's Inn, London WC2A 3SB ☎ 020 7242 2523
✉ enquiries@hardwicke.co.uk
Call Date: Jul 1970, Gray's Inn
Pupil Supervisor

Practising Areas: Ancillary Relief, Chancery (General), Chancery (Land Law), Children's Law, Civil Litigation, Commercial Litigation, Common Law (General), Defamation, Equity, Wills & Trusts, Family, Family Provision, Land, Medical Negligence, Partnership, Probate & Administration, Professional Negligence

BUCKLE MR JONATHAN

Regency Chambers
45 Priestgate, Peterborough PE1 1LB
☎01733 315215 ✉clerks@regencychambers.law.co.uk
Regency Chambers
Sheraton House, Castle Park, Cambridge CB3 0AX ☎01223 301517
Call Date: Nov 1990, Lincoln's Inn
Pupil Supervisor

Practising Areas: Common Law (General), Employment, Equity, Wills & Trusts, Family, Family Provision, Health & Safety, Housing, Landlord & Tenant, Medical Negligence, Personal Injury, Probate & Administration, Regulatory Law

BUCKLEY MR PETER EVERED

Cobden House Chambers
19 Quay Street, Manchester M3 3HN
☎0161 833 6000 ✉Clerks@Cobden.co.uk
Call Date: Jul 1972, Gray's Inn
Pupil Supervisor

Practising Areas: Defamation, Family, Family Provision, Medical Negligence, Personal Injury, Professional Negligence

BUCKPITT MR MICHAEL DAVID

Tanfield Chambers
2-5 Warwick Court, London WC1R 5DJ
☎020 7421 5300 ✉clerks@tanfieldchambers.co.uk
Call Date: Feb 1988, Gray's Inn
Pupil Supervisor

Practising Areas: Chancery (Land Law), Commercial Litigation, Landlord & Tenant

C

BUDWORTH MR MARTIN JAMES

Kings Chambers
36 Young Street, Manchester M3 3FT
☎0845 034 3444 ✉clerks@kingschambers.com
Kings Chambers
5 Park Square East, Leeds LS1 2NE
☎0845 034 3444 ✉clerks@kingschambers.com
Kings Chambers
Embassy House, 60 Church Street, Birmingham B3 2DJ ☎0845 034 3444
✉clerks@kingschambers.com
Call Date: Nov 1999, Inner Temple

Practising Areas: Banking, Bankruptcy, Chancery (General), Commercial Litigation, Company & Commercial, Discrimination, Employment, Financial Services, Franchising, Insolvency, Insurance, Professional Negligence, Sale & Carriage of Goods, Sports, Trademarks

BUDWORTH MR RICHARD DUTTON

2-3 Hind Court Chambers
2-3 Hind Court, Fleet Street, London EC4A 3DL ☎020 7822 2150 ✉david@2-3hindcourt.com
Call Date: Jul 1982, Inner Temple

Practising Areas: Common Land, Common Law (General), Courts Martial, Housing, Intellectual Property, Landlord & Tenant, Personal Injury, Professional Negligence, Sale & Carriage of Goods

BUENO MR ANTONIO DE PADUA JOSE MARIA QC (1989)

Clerksroom (Taunton)
Equity House, Administration Centre, Blackbrook Park Avenue, Taunton, Somerset TA1 2PX ☎0845 083 3000
✉mail@clerksroom.com
Call Date: Jun 1964, Middle Temple
Recorder

Practising Areas: Arbitration, Banking, Commercial Litigation, Common Law (General), Corporate Finance, International Trade, Sale & Carriage of Goods

BULL MR NICHOLAS DAVID

Old Bailey Chambers
15 Old Bailey, London EC4M 7EF
☎020 3008 6404
✉clerks@15oldbaileychambers.com
Call Date: Oct 2004, Inner Temple

Practising Areas: Crime, Crime (Corporate/Fraud)

BULLEN MRS MARY

The Chambers Of Mary Bullen
7 Grovely Mews, Shaftsbury Road, Wilton SP2 0JW ☎01722 742204
✉marybullen123@btinternet.com
Call Date: Mar 2005, Inner Temple

Practising Areas: Civil Liberties, Common Law (General), Crime, Employment, Family

BULLOCK MR ROBERT GUSTAF

The Chambers of Mr Bullock
Arden Lodge, 11 Montpelier Villas, Brighton BN1 3DG ☎01273 321050
Call Date: Nov 2000, Middle Temple

Practising Areas: Admiralty, Arbitration, Banking, Chancery (General), Chancery (Land Law), Commercial Litigation, Commercial Property, Common Land, Common Law (General), Construction, Defamation, Employment, Entertainment, Equity, Wills & Trusts, Film, Cable & TV,

Financial Services, Insolvency, Insurance/Reinsurance, International Trade, Landlord & Tenant, Partnership, Professional Negligence, Regulatory Law, Sale & Carriage of Goods, Shipping/Admiralty, Telecommunications

BULLOCK MRS SALLY

New Court
Ground Floor, New Court, Temple, London EC4Y 9BE ☎ 020 7583 5123
✉ clerks@newcourtchambers.com
Call Date: Oct 1995, Middle Temple

Practising Areas: Family Provision

BUNDELL MISS KATHARINE MICHELLE

Octagon House
19 Colegate, Norwich NR3 1AT
☎ 01603 623186 ✉ clerks@octagonhouse.co.uk
Call Date: Oct 1991, Middle Temple
Pupil Supervisor

Practising Areas: Family

BUNTING MR DANIEL ALEXANDER JAMES

2 Dr Johnson's Buildings
2 Dr Johnson's Buildings, Temple, London EC4Y 7AY ☎ 020 7936 2613 ✉ clerks@2drj.com
Call Date: Nov 2001, Middle Temple

Practising Areas: Administrative, Civil Liberties, Courts Martial, Crime, Crime (Corporate/Fraud), Human Rights, Immigration, Public International, Public Law

BUNTING MR JUDE JAMES

Tooks Chambers
81 Farringdon Street, London EC4A 4BL
☎ 020 7842 7575 ✉ clerks@tooks.co.uk
Call Date: Jul 2006, Gray's Inn

Practising Areas: Administrative, Civil Liberties, Defamation, Discrimination, Employment, Human Rights

BUNYAN MR ANGUS GUY

2 Hare Court
Lower Ground, Ground, 1st & 2nd Floor, 2 Hare Court, Temple, London EC4Y 7BH
☎ 020 7353 3982 ✉ clerks@2harecourt.com
Call Date: Oct 1999, Lincoln's Inn

BURDEN MR EDWARD ANGUS

St Philips Chambers
55 Temple Row, Birmingham B2 5LS
☎ 0121 246 7000 ✉ clerks@st-philips.com
Call Date: Nov 1994, Lincoln's Inn

BURDON MR MICHAEL STEWART

37 Park Square Chambers
37 Park Square, Leeds LS1 2NY
☎ 0113 243 9422 ✉ chambers@no37.co.uk
Call Date: Nov 1993, Lincoln's Inn
Pupil Supervisor

Practising Areas: Care Proceedings, Family, Family Provision

BURGE MISS ALISON JAYNE

Pump Court Chambers
31 Southgate Street, Winchester, Hampshire SO23 9EB ☎ 01962 868 161
✉ clerks@3pumpcourt.com
Pump Court Chambers
Upper Ground Floor, 3 Pump Court, Temple, London EC4Y 7AJ ☎ 020 7353 0711
✉ clerks@3pumpcourt.com
Pump Court Chambers
5 Temple Chambers, Temple Street, Swindon SN1 1SQ ☎ 01793 539899
✉ clerks@3pumpcourt.com
Call Date: Jul 2002, Gray's Inn

BURGHER MR BENJIMIN GEORGE

Outer Temple Chambers
The Outer Temple, 222 Strand, London WC2R 1BA ☎ 020 7353 6381
✉ clerks@outertemple.com
Call Date: Nov 1995, Gray's Inn

Practising Areas: Commercial Litigation, Discrimination, Employment

BURKE MR TREVOR MICHAEL QC (2001)

3 Raymond Buildings
3 Raymond Buildings, Gray's Inn, London WC1R 5BH ☎ 020 7400 6400
✉ clerks@3rblaw.com
Call Date: Jul 1981, Middle Temple

BURNETT MR IAIN

4 King's Bench Walk
2nd Floor, 4 King's Bench Walk, Temple, London EC4Y 7DL ☎ 020 7822 7000
✉ clerks@4kbw.co.uk
Call Date: Oct 1993, Lincoln's Inn

Practising Areas: Administrative, Human Rights, Immigration, Personal Injury, Regulatory Law

BURNS MR JEREMY STUART

12 College Place
Fauvelle Buildings, 12 College Place, Southampton SO15 2FE ☎ 023 8032 0320
✉ clerks@12cp.co.uk
Call Date: Nov 1996, Lincoln's Inn

Practising Areas: Chancery (General), Chancery (Land Law), Commercial Litigation, Common Law (General), Employment, Landlord & Tenant, Professional Negligence, Town & Country Planning

BURR MR ANDREW CHARLES

Atkin Chambers
1 Atkin Building, Gray's Inn, London WC1R 5AT ☎ 020 7404 0102
✉ clerks@atkinchambers.com
Call Date: Nov 1981, Inner Temple
Pupil Supervisor

Practising Areas: Arbitration, Commercial Litigation, Construction, Energy, Information Technology, Professional Negligence, Telecommunications

BURRETT MR ALEX

1 Gray's Inn Square
Ground Floor, 1 Gray's Inn Square, London WC1R 5AA ☎ 020 7405 0001
Call Date: Jul 1999, Inner Temple

Practising Areas: Administrative, Civil Liberties, Discrimination, Education, Human Rights, Immigration

BURROWS MR SIMON PAUL

Kings Chambers
36 Young Street, Manchester M3 3FT
☎ 0845 034 3444 ✉ clerks@kingschambers.com
Kings Chambers
5 Park Square East, Leeds LS1 2NE
☎ 0845 034 3444 ✉ clerks@kingschambers.com
Kings Chambers
Embassy House, 60 Church Street, Birmingham B3 2DJ ☎ 0845 034 3444
✉ clerks@kingschambers.com
Call Date: Nov 1990, Inner Temple

BURTON MR CHARLES DOMINIC PAUL

9-12 Bell Yard
London WC2A 2JR ☎ 020 7400 1800
✉ clerks@9-12bellyard.com
Call Date: Nov 1983, Inner Temple
Pupil Supervisor

BURTON MR JAMES WILLIAM

39 Essex Street
London WC2R 3AT ☎ 020 7832 1111
✉ clerks@39essex.com
82 King Street
Manchester M2 4WQ ☎ 0161 870 9969
Call Date: Oct 2001, Lincoln's Inn

Practising Areas: Administrative, Environment, Local Government, Town & Country Planning

BURTON MR JOHN MALCOLM QC (2010)

3 Temple Gardens
Lower Ground Floor, 3 Temple Gardens, Temple, London EC4Y 9AU ☎ 020 7353 3102
✉ clerks@3tg.co.uk
Call Date: Jul 1979, Inner Temple
Pupil Supervisor

Practising Areas: Crime (Corporate/Fraud), Employment, Regulatory Law

BUSH MR DOMINIC LUKE

Castle Chambers
The Old Fire Station, 90 High Street, Harrow-on-the-Hill, Middlesex HA1 3LP
☎ 020 8423 6579 ✉ info@castlechambers.net
Call Date: Jul 1999, Middle Temple

BUSSEY-JONES MRS ELISABETH BARBARA

2 King's Bench Walk
2 King's Bench Walk, Temple, London EC4Y 7DE ☎ 020 7353 1746 ✉ clerks@2kbw.com
Call Date: Nov 1997, Inner Temple
Pupil Supervisor

BUSUTTIL MR GODWIN JOHN ANTOINE

5RB
1st Floor, 5 Raymond Buildings, Gray's Inn, London WC1R 5BP ☎ 020 7242 2902
✉ clerks@5rb.com
Call Date: Oct 1994, Lincoln's Inn
Pupil Supervisor

Practising Areas: Commercial Litigation, Data Protection, Defamation, Entertainment, Professional Negligence, Sports

BUSWELL MR RICHARD THOMAS

Hardwicke
New Square, Lincoln's Inn, London WC2A 3SB ☎ 020 7242 2523
✉ enquiries@hardwicke.co.uk
Call Date: Jul 1985, Middle Temple
Pupil Supervisor

Practising Areas: Ancillary Relief, Chancery (General), Children's Law, Equity, Wills &

C

Trusts, Family, Family Provision, Professional Negligence

BUTLER MR ANDREW

Tanfield Chambers
2-5 Warwick Court, London WC1R 5DJ
☎ 020 7421 5300 ✉ clerks@tanfieldchambers.co.uk
Call Date: Nov 1993, Middle Temple
Pupil Supervisor

Practising Areas: Bankruptcy, Chancery (Land Law), Commercial Litigation, Common Law (General), Company & Commercial, Insolvency, Landlord & Tenant, Partnership, Sale & Carriage of Goods

BUTLER MR GEORGE VICTOR

4 Brick Court
4 Brick Court, Temple, London EC4Y 9AD
☎ 020 7832 3200 ✉ clerks@4bc.co.uk
Call Date: Jul 2004, Inner Temple

Practising Areas: Family, Mental Health

BUTLER MISS JUDITH JANE SCOTT

29 Bedford Row Chambers
London WC1R 4HE ☎ 020 7404 1044
✉ clerks@29br.co.uk
Call Date: Oct 1993, Middle Temple

Practising Areas: Care Proceedings, Family, Family Provision

BUTLER MS REBECCA SOPHIE

Willingdon Chambers
Chapel Wood House, Knapp Lane, Romsey SO51 9BT ✉ rebecca@willingdonmediation.co.uk
Call Date: Jul 2001, Inner Temple

BUTLER MR RUPERT JAMES

3 Hare Court
3 Hare Court, Temple, London EC4Y 7BJ
☎ 020 7415 7800 ✉ clerks@3harecourt.com
Call Date: Jul 1988, Middle Temple

Practising Areas: Banking, Bankruptcy, Chancery (General), Chancery (Land Law), Commercial Litigation, Commercial Property, Common Law (General), Company & Commercial, Defamation, Discrimination, Employment, Insolvency, Personal Injury, Private International, Professional Negligence, Sale & Carriage of Goods, Sports

BUTLER MR SIMON DAVID

The Chambers of Grahame Aldous QC
9 Gough Square, London EC4A 3DG
☎ 020 7832 0500 ✉ clerks@9goughsquare.co.uk
Call Date: Oct 1996, Inner Temple

Practising Areas: Administrative, Chancery (General), Chancery (Land Law), Civil Litigation, Commercial Litigation, Commercial Property, Common Law (General), Company & Commercial, Costs, Environment, Healthcare, Housing, Land, Landlord & Tenant, Local Government, Medical Negligence, Personal Injury, Public Law, Regulatory Law

BUTLER-COLE MS VICTORIA

39 Essex Street
London WC2R 3AT ☎ 020 7832 1111
✉ clerks@39essex.com
82 King Street
Manchester M2 4WQ ☎ 0161 870 9969
Call Date: Jul 2005, Middle Temple

BUTT MR MATTHEW PAUL

3 Raymond Buildings
3 Raymond Buildings, Gray's Inn, London WC1R 5BH ☎ 020 7400 6400
✉ clerks@3rblaw.com
Call Date: Jul 2002, Gray's Inn

BUTTERS MR JONATHAN BRYN

Devereux Chambers
Queen Elizabeth Building, Temple, London EC4Y 9BS ☎ 020 7353 7534
✉ clerks@devchambers.co.uk
Call Date: Nov 2003, Middle Temple

BUTTERS MR RICHARD JOHN

37 Park Square Chambers
37 Park Square, Leeds LS1 2NY
☎ 0113 243 9422 ✉ chambers@no37.co.uk
Call Date: Oct 2001, Middle Temple

Practising Areas: Crime, Crime (Corporate/Fraud), Family, Family Provision

BUTTERWORTH MR MARTIN FRANK

Citadel Chambers
The Citadel, 190 Corporation Street, Birmingham B4 6QD ☎ 0121 233 8500
✉ clerks@citadelchambers.com
Call Date: Jul 1985, Lincoln's Inn
Pupil Supervisor, Recorder

Practising Areas: Crime, Crime (Corporate/Fraud), Road Traffic And Highways

BUTTIMORE MR GABRIEL

13 King's Bench Walk
13 King's Bench Walk, Temple, London EC4Y 7EN ☎ 020 7353 7204 ✉ clerks@13kbw.co.uk
13 KBW
32 Beaumont Street, Oxford OX1 2NP
☎ 01865 311066 ✉ clerks@13kbw.co.uk
Call Date: Feb 1993, Gray's Inn

Practising Areas: Bankruptcy, Chancery (General), Chancery (Land Law), Civil Litigation, Commercial Litigation, Commercial Property, Commodities, Common Land, Common Law (General), Company & Commercial, Construction, Consumer, Conveyancing, Data Protection, Equity, Wills & Trusts, Family Provision, Financial Services, Insolvency, International Trade, Land, Landlord & Tenant, Partnership, Private International, Probate & Administration, Professional Negligence, Sale & Carriage of Goods

BUXTON MR THOMAS JUSTIN

Charter Chambers
33 John Street, London WC1N 2AT
☎ 020 7618 4400 ✉ clerks@charterchambers.com
Call Date: Jul 1983, Gray's Inn

Practising Areas: Crime, Crime (Corporate/Fraud), Financial Services, Regulatory Law

BYRD MISS NOEMI CSILLA MARIA

6 Pump Court Chambers
6-8 Mill Street, Maidstone, Kent ME15 6XH
☎ 01622 688094 ✉ annexe@6pumpcourt.co.uk
6 Pump Court
1st Floor, 6 Pump Court, Temple, London EC4Y 7AR ☎ 020 7797 8400
✉ richardconstable@6pumpcourt.co.uk
Call Date: Oct 2004, Gray's Inn

Practising Areas: Town & Country Planning

BYRNE MR GARRETT THOMAS

4-5 Gray's Inn Square
Gray's Inn, London WC1R 5AH
☎ 020 7404 5252 ✉ clerks@4-5.co.uk
Call Date: Nov 1986, Gray's Inn
Pupil Supervisor

Practising Areas: Commercial Litigation, Commercial Property, Crime, Crime (Corporate/Fraud), Environment, Health & Safety, Human Rights, Local Government, Regulatory Law

BYRNE MR JAMES PAUL

The Chambers of Grahame Aldous QC
9 Gough Square, London EC4A 3DG
☎ 020 7832 0500 ✉ clerks@9goughsquare.co.uk
Call Date: Jul 2006, Lincoln's Inn

BYRNES MISS AISLING ALICE ELIZABETH

25 Bedford Row
London WC1R 4HD ☎ 020 7067 1500
✉ clerks@25bedfordrow.com
Call Date: Oct 1994, Gray's Inn
Pupil Supervisor

Practising Areas: Civil Liberties, Courts Martial, Crime, Crime (Corporate/Fraud), Human Rights, Regulatory Law, Sports

CABEZA MISS RUTH ROBERTA ELIZABETH

Field Court Chambers
5 Field Court, Gray's Inn, London WC1R 5EF
☎ 020 7405 6114 ✉ clerks@fieldcourt.co.uk
Call Date: Mar 1998, Middle Temple
Pupil Supervisor

Practising Areas: Care Proceedings, Family, Family Provision

CADDLE MISS SHERRIE LORETTA

Charter Chambers
33 John Street, London WC1N 2AT
☎ 020 7618 4400 ✉ clerks@charterchambers.com
Call Date: Nov 1983, Lincoln's Inn
Pupil Supervisor

Practising Areas: Crime, Crime (Corporate/Fraud), Mental Health

CADE MRS DIANA

Trinity Chambers
Highfield House, Moulsham Street, Chelmsford, Essex CM2 9AH
☎ 01245 605040 ✉ clerks@trinitychambers.com
Call Date: Nov 1994, Inner Temple

Practising Areas: Care Proceedings, Family

CADE-DAVIES MISS LYNSEY NICOLA

29 Bedford Row Chambers
London WC1R 4HE ☎ 020 7404 1044
✉ clerks@29br.co.uk
Call Date: Oct 2005, Inner Temple

Practising Areas: Family, Family Provision

CAFFERKEY MISS ANNETTE MARIE

Arden Chambers
20 Bloomsbury Square, London WC1A 2NS
☎ 020 7242 4244 ✉ clerks@ardenchambers.com
Call Date: Nov 1994, Inner Temple

CAHILL MR PAUL JEREMY QC (2002)

No5 Chambers
Fountain Court, Steelhouse Lane, Birmingham B4 6DR ☎ 0845 210 5555 ✉ info@no5.com
No5 Chambers
Greenwood House, 4-7 Salisbury Court, London EC4Y 8AA ☎ 0845 210 5555
No5 Chambers
38 Queen Square, Bristol BS1 4QS
☎ 0845 210 5555
Call Date: Jul 1975, Middle Temple

Practising Areas: Environment, Town & Country Planning

CAINS MS LINDA HILARY

37 Park Square Chambers
37 Park Square, Leeds LS1 2NY
☎ 0113 243 9422 ✉ chambers@no37.co.uk
Call Date: Oct 1990, Middle Temple
Pupil Supervisor

CAIRNES MR SIMON PAUL STEVEN

No5 Chambers
38 Queen Square, Bristol BS1 4QS
☎ 0845 210 5555
No5 Chambers
Greenwood House, 4-7 Salisbury Court, London EC4Y 8AA ☎ 0845 210 5555
No5 Chambers
Fountain Court, Steelhouse Lane, Birmingham B4 6DR ☎ 0845 210 5555 ✉ info@no5.com
3 PB Barristers
4 St Peter Street, Winchester SO23 8BW
☎ 01962 868884 ✉ clerks.winchester@3paper.co.uk
Call Date: Nov 1980, Gray's Inn
Pupil Supervisor

Practising Areas: Town & Country Planning

CAIRNS MS SALLY

No 8 Chambers
8 Fountain Court, Steelhouse Lane, Birmingham B4 6DR ☎ 0121 236 5514
✉ clerks@no8chambers.co.uk
Call Date: Jul 2006, Gray's Inn

Practising Areas: Crime, Family, Immigration

CALA DR GUISEPPE

New Court
Ground Floor, New Court, Temple, London EC4Y 9BE ☎ 020 7583 5123
✉ clerks@newcourtchambers.com 1971, Inner Temple

Practising Areas: Family, Foreign Law, Private International

CALDWELL MR PETER HUGH COYLES

Dyers Chambers
35 Bedford Row, London WC1R 4JH
☎ 020 7404 1881 ✉ admin@dyerschambers.com
Call Date: Oct 1995, Gray's Inn
Pupil Supervisor

Practising Areas: Administrative, Civil Liberties, Courts Martial, Crime, Crime (Corporate/Fraud), Foreign Law, Public International

CALHAEM MR SIMON MALCOLM

29 Bedford Row Chambers
London WC1R 4HE ☎ 020 7404 1044
✉ clerks@29br.co.uk
Call Date: Oct 1999, Lincoln's Inn

Practising Areas: Bankruptcy, Chancery (General), Equity, Wills & Trusts, Family, Family Provision, Probate & Administration

CALLAN MS JANE ELIZABETH

Trinity Chambers
The Custom House, 39 Quayside, Newcastle Upon Tyne NE1 3DE ☎ 0191 232 1927
✉ info@trinitychambers.co.uk
Trinity Chambers
Multi Media Exchange, 72-80 Corporation Road, Middlesbrough TS1 2RF
☎ 01642 247569 ✉ info@trinitychambers.co.uk
Call Date: Nov 1995, Middle Temple
Pupil Supervisor

Practising Areas: Discrimination, Employment

CALLERY MR MARTIN

Cobden House Chambers
19 Quay Street, Manchester M3 3HN
☎ 0161 833 6000 ✉ Clerks@Cobden.co.uk
Call Date: Mar 1997, Middle Temple

Practising Areas: Civil Liberties, Courts Martial, Crime, Crime (Corporate/Fraud), Environment, Health & Safety, Human Rights, Licensing, Regulatory Law, Sports

CALVERT MR DAVID EDWARD

St James's Chambers
68 Quay Street, Manchester M3 3EJ
☎0161 834 7000 ✉clerks@stjameschambers.com
12 King's Bench Walk
12 King's Bench Walk, Temple, London EC4Y 7EL ☎020 7583 0811
Call Date: Nov 1995, Inner Temple

Practising Areas: Employment, Personal Injury

CALWAY MR MARK EDWARD

Renaissance Chambers
5th Floor, Gray's Inn Chambers, Gray's Inn, London WC1R 5JA ☎020 7404 1111
✉clerks@renaissancechambers.co.uk
Call Date: Feb 1989, Inner Temple

CAMMEGH MR JOHN STEPHEN

Nine Bedford Row
9 Bedford Row, London WC1R 4AZ
☎020 7489 2727 ✉clerks@9bedfordrow.co.uk
Call Date: Nov 1987, Inner Temple

CAMMERMAN MR GIDEON SAUL

187 Fleet Street
London EC4A 2AT ☎020 7430 7430
✉chambers@187fleetstreet.com
Call Date: Nov 1996, Middle Temple

Practising Areas: Crime, Crime (Corporate/Fraud), Regulatory Law

CAMPBELL MR ALASDAIR JAMES

St Paul's Chambers
5th Floor, St Paul's House, 23 Park Square South, Leeds LS1 2ND ☎0113 245 5866
Call Date: Oct 1999, Lincoln's Inn

Practising Areas: Crime, Crime (Corporate/Fraud), Regulatory Law, Road Traffic And Highways

CAMPBELL MR OLIVER EDWARD WILHELM

Henderson Chambers
2 Harcourt Buildings, Temple, London EC4Y 9DB ☎020 7583 9020
✉clerks@hendersonchambers.co.uk
Call Date: Oct 1992, Middle Temple
Pupil Supervisor

Practising Areas: Civil Litigation, Commercial Litigation, Common Law (General), Coroners Inquests, Crime (Corporate/Fraud), Employment, Health & Safety, Industrial Diseases, Personal Injury, Professional Negligence, Regulatory Law, Sports

CAMPBELL MR STAFFORD GRAHAM

Westgate Chambers
64 High Street, Lewes, East Sussex BN7 1XG
☎01273 480510
✉clerks@westgate-chambers.co.uk
Call Date: Jul 1979, Gray's Inn
Pupil Supervisor

Practising Areas: Common Law (General), Family, Family Provision, Housing, Landlord & Tenant

CAMPBELL MR STEPHEN GORDON

No5 Chambers
Fountain Court, Steelhouse Lane, Birmingham B4 6DR ☎0845 210 5555 ✉info@no5.com
No5 Chambers
Greenwood House, 4-7 Salisbury Court, London EC4Y 8AA ☎0845 210 5555
No5 Chambers
38 Queen Square, Bristol BS1 4QS
☎0845 210 5555
Call Date: Jul 1982, Middle Temple
Recorder

CAMPBELL-BROWN MISS ANNE LOUISE

One Essex Court
1st Floor, Temple, London EC4Y 9AR
☎020 7936 3030 ✉clerks@1ec.co.uk
Call Date: Nov 1993, Middle Temple
Pupil Supervisor

CANBY MISS FIONA JANE

Temple Garden Chambers
1 Harcourt Buildings, Temple, London EC4Y 9DA ☎020 7583 1315 ✉clerks@tgchambers.com
Call Date: Jul 2001, Middle Temple

Practising Areas: Health & Safety, Personal Injury

CANDLIN MISS NAOMI HELEN

St Philips Chambers
55 Temple Row, Birmingham B2 5LS
☎0121 246 7000 ✉clerks@st-philips.com
Call Date: Oct 2003, Lincoln's Inn

Practising Areas: Chancery (Land Law), Commercial Property, Landlord & Tenant, Town & Country Planning

C

CANNING MR RICHARD

39 Park Square
Leeds LS1 2NU ☎0113 245 6633
✉seniorclerk@39parksquarechambers.co.uk
Call Date: Nov 2004, Lincoln's Inn

Practising Areas: Courts Martial, Crime, Crime (Corporate/Fraud)

CANT MR CHRISTOPHER IAN

9 Stone Buildings
Lincoln's Inn, London WC2A 3NN
☎020 7404 5055 ✉clerks@9stonebuildings.com
Call Date: Jul 1973, Lincoln's Inn
Pupil Supervisor

Practising Areas: Chancery (General), Chancery (Land Law), Charities, Commercial Litigation, Commercial Property, Company & Commercial, Conveyancing, Equity, Wills & Trusts, Landlord & Tenant, Partnership, Professional Negligence

CANTER MR SIMON ALEXANDER

Richmond Canter Immigration Barristers
1 Fetter Lane, London EC4A 1BR
☎020 3440 5820
✉info@immigrationbarrister.co.uk
Call Date: Oct 2000, Inner Temple
Pupil Supervisor

Practising Areas: Immigration

CAPLAN MR JONATHAN MICHAEL QC (1991)

Five Paper Buildings
1st Floor, Five Paper Buildings, Temple, London EC4Y 7HB ☎020 7583 6117
✉clerks@5pb.co.uk
Riverview Chambers
Hamilton House, 1 Temple Avenue, London EC4Y 0HA ☎0844 225 3999
✉chrisbaylis@riverviewchambers.com
Call Date: Jul 1973, Gray's Inn
Recorder

Practising Areas: Administrative, Crime (Corporate/Fraud), Defamation, Entertainment, Film, Cable & TV, Health & Safety, Regulatory Law, Sports

CAPON MR PHILIP CHRISTOPHER WILLIAM

East Anglian Chambers
Gresham House, 5 Museum Street, Ipswich, Suffolk IP1 1HQ ☎01473 214481
✉ipswich@ealaw.co.uk
East Anglian Chambers
140 New London Road, Chelmsford, Essex CM2 0AW ☎01473 214481
✉chelmsford@ealaw.co.uk
East Anglian Chambers
15 The Close, Norwich, Norfolk NR1 4DZ
☎01473 214481 ✉norwich@ealaw.co.uk
St Philips Chambers
55 Temple Row, Birmingham B2 5LS
☎0121 246 7000 ✉clerks@st-philips.com
Call Date: Oct 1990, Inner Temple
Pupil Supervisor

Practising Areas: Bankruptcy, Chancery (General), Chancery (Land Law), Commercial Litigation, Common Law (General), Company & Commercial, Equity, Wills & Trusts, Family Provision, Insolvency, Landlord & Tenant, Partnership, Probate & Administration, Professional Negligence, Sale & Carriage of Goods

CAPPS MR DEVERAL CARMICHAEL

Trinity Chambers
The Custom House, 39 Quayside, Newcastle Upon Tyne NE1 3DE ☎0191 232 1927
✉info@trinitychambers.co.uk
Trinity Chambers
Multi Media Exchange, 72-80 Corporation Road, Middlesbrough TS1 2RF
☎01642 247569 ✉info@trinitychambers.co.uk
Call Date: Oct 1995, Inner Temple

CAREY MISS JACQUELINE ANNE

2 Bedford Row
London WC1R 4BU ☎020 7440 8888
✉clerks@2bedfordrow.co.uk
Call Date: Oct 1999, Lincoln's Inn
Pupil Supervisor

Practising Areas: Crime, Crime (Corporate/Fraud)

CAREY-HUGHES MR RICHARD JOHN QC (2000)

Nine Bedford Row
9 Bedford Row, London WC1R 4AZ
☎020 7489 2727 ✉clerks@9bedfordrow.co.uk
Call Date: Jul 1977, Gray's Inn
Recorder

Practising Areas: Crime, Crime (Corporate/Fraud)

CARLISLE MR TIMOTHY ST JOHN OGILVIE

Field Court Chambers
5 Field Court, Gray's Inn, London WC1R 5EF
☎020 7405 6114 ✉clerks@fieldcourt.co.uk
Call Date: Nov 1984, Gray's Inn
Pupil Supervisor

Practising Areas: Banking, Bankruptcy, Chancery (General), Chancery (Land Law), Commercial Litigation, Common Law (General),

C

Company & Commercial, Financial Services, Insolvency, Medical Negligence, Personal Injury

CARNE MR ROGER ENYS

Nine Bedford Row
9 Bedford Row, London WC1R 4AZ
☎020 7489 2727 ✉clerks@9bedfordrow.co.uk
Call Date: Nov 1969, Inner Temple
Pupil Supervisor

Practising Areas: Crime, Crime (Corporate/Fraud)

CARNEY MISS CAROLINE MARY SC

QEB Hollis Whiteman
1-2 Laurence Pountney Hill, London EC4R 0EU ☎020 7933 8855 ✉barristers@qebhw.co.uk
Call Date: Nov 1980, Middle Temple

Practising Areas: Family, Mental Health, Private International, Professional Negligence

CARR MR ADRIAN JAMES SELDEN

Tanfield Chambers
2-5 Warwick Court, London WC1R 5DJ
☎020 7421 5300 ✉clerks@tanfieldchambers.co.uk
Call Date: Nov 1999, Inner Temple

Practising Areas: Chancery (General), Chancery (Land Law), Company & Commercial, Family Provision, Landlord & Tenant, Partnership, Probate & Administration

CARR MR CHRISTOPHER SEAN

36 Bedford Row
London WC1R 4JH ☎020 7421 8000
✉chambers@36bedfordrow.co.uk
Call Date: Oct 2002, Inner Temple

Practising Areas: Ancillary Relief, Chancery (General), Chancery (Land Law), Civil Liberties, Civil Litigation, Disciplinary Tribunals, Employment, Equity, Wills & Trusts, Family, Family Provision, Human Rights, Landlord & Tenant, Personal Injury, Regulatory Law

CARR MR JAMES CHRISTOPHER DANIEL

4 Breams Buildings
Chancery Lane, London EC4A 1HP
☎020 7092 1900 ✉clerks@4bb.co.uk
Call Date: Nov 2001, Middle Temple

Practising Areas: Crime, Crime (Corporate/Fraud)

CARRASCO MR GLENN LAWRENCE

9-12 Bell Yard
London WC2A 2JR ☎020 7400 1800
✉clerks@9-12bellyard.com
Call Date: Oct 1997, Inner Temple
Pupil Supervisor

Practising Areas: Crime, Crime (Corporate/Fraud), Health & Safety, Licensing, Public Law

CARRINGTON MR DOMINIC

Chambers of Martin Burr
15 Old Bailey, London EC4M 7EF
☎0845 123 1234 ✉clerks@barristerweb.com
Call Date: Nov 1996, Middle Temple

Practising Areas: Common Law (General), Crime, Housing, Immigration, Landlord & Tenant

CARRION BENITEZ MS MIRIAM

36 Bedford Row
London WC1R 4JH ☎020 7421 8000
✉chambers@36bedfordrow.co.uk
Call Date: Jul 2001, Gray's Inn

Practising Areas: Administrative, Civil Liberties, Discrimination, Employment, Mental Health, Public International

CARRODUS MISS GAIL CAROLINE

Huntercombe Chambers
Timbers Farmhouse, Henley-On-Thames RG9 5SY ☎01491 641934
Call Date: Nov 1978, Gray's Inn

CARRON MR RICHARD BYRON

Queen Square Chambers
56 Queen Square, Bristol BS1 4PR
☎0117 921 1966 ✉crime@qs-c.co.uk
Call Date: Oct 1992, Middle Temple

Practising Areas: Ancillary Relief, Care Proceedings, Children's Law, Family, Family Provision

CARROTT MR SYLVESTER EMANUEL

1 Pump Court
Elm Court, Temple, London EC4Y 7AB
☎020 7842 7070 ✉(name)@pumpcourt.co.uk
Call Date: Jul 1980, Gray's Inn
Pupil Supervisor

CARTER MISS HOLLY EUGENIE SOPHIA

3 Dr Johnson's Buildings
Ground Floor, 3 Dr Johnson's Buildings, Temple, London EC4Y 7BA ☎ 020 7353 4854
✉ clerks@3djb.co.uk
Call Date: Oct 1993, Inner Temple
Pupil Supervisor

Practising Areas: Family, Family Provision

CARTER MISS NATHALIE VERONIQUE

1 Gray's Inn Square
Ground Floor, 1 Gray's Inn Square, London WC1R 5AA ☎ 020 7405 0001
Call Date: Jul 2004, Inner Temple

Practising Areas: Crime, Crime (Corporate/ Fraud), Environment, Health & Safety, Regulatory Law

CARTER MR PETER QC (1995)

18 Red Lion Court
London EC4A 3EB ☎ 020 7520 6000
✉ chambers@18rlc.co.uk
Park Court Chambers
16 Park Place, Leeds LS1 2SJ
☎ 0113 243 3277
✉ clerks@parkcourtchambers.co.uk
18 Red Lion Court (Annexe)
Thornwood House, 102 New London Road, Chelmsford, Essex CM2 0RG
☎ 01245 280880
Call Date: Jul 1974, Gray's Inn
Pupil Supervisor

CARTER MR RICHARD CHARLES

St Johns Buildings
24a - 28 St John Street, Manchester M3 4DJ
☎ 0161 214 1500 ✉ clerk@stjohnsbuildings.co.uk
St Johns Buildings
21 White Friars, Chester CH1 1NZ
☎ 01244 323070 ✉ clerk@stjohnsbuildings.co.uk
16 Winckley Square
Preston PR1 3JJ ☎ 01772 256100
Call Date: Nov 1990, Inner Temple
Pupil Supervisor

CARTER-STEPHENSON MR GEORGE ANTHONY QC (1998)

25 Bedford Row
London WC1R 4HD ☎ 020 7067 1500
✉ clerks@25bedfordrow.com
Call Date: Jul 1975, Inner Temple

Practising Areas: Crime, Crime (Corporate/ Fraud)

CARTWRIGHT MR IVAN MATTHEW

KCH Garden Square
1 Oxford Street, Nottingham NG1 5BH
☎ 0115 941 8851 ✉ clerks@kchgardensquare.co.uk
Call Date: Nov 1993, Gray's Inn

Practising Areas: Administrative, Bankruptcy, Civil Litigation, Common Law (General), Costs, Discrimination, Employment, Health & Safety, Housing, Inquests, Landlord & Tenant, Local Government, Medical Negligence, Personal Injury

CASE MISS MAGDALEN MARY CLAIRE

St Johns Buildings
24a - 28 St John Street, Manchester M3 4DJ
☎ 0161 214 1500 ✉ clerk@stjohnsbuildings.co.uk
16 Winckley Square
Preston PR1 3JJ ☎ 01772 256100
St Johns Buildings Liverpool
8th Floor India Buildings, Water Street, Liverpool L2 0XG ☎ 0151 243 6000
✉ clerk@stjohnsbuildings.co.uk
Call Date: Oct 1992, Middle Temple

CASE MR RICHARD JOHN

No5 Chambers
Greenwood House, 4-7 Salisbury Court, London EC4Y 8AA ☎ 0845 210 5555
No5 Chambers
38 Queen Square, Bristol BS1 4QS
☎ 0845 210 5555
No5 Chambers
Fountain Court, Steelhouse Lane, Birmingham B4 6DR ☎ 0845 210 5555 ✉ info@no5.com
Call Date: Oct 1996, Middle Temple

Practising Areas: Employment

CASEY MR PAUL JOSEPH

Chambers of Marion Smullen and Kerim Fuad QC
1 Inner Temple Lane, London EC4Y 1AF
☎ 020 7427 4400 ✉ clerks@1itl.com
Call Date: Jul 1999, Middle Temple

Practising Areas: Civil Liberties, Common Law (General), Coroners Inquests, Courts Martial, Crime, Crime (Corporate/Fraud), Employment, Human Rights, Inquests, Mental Health

CASSEL MISS BATHSHEBA ANNA

Walnut House
63 St. David's Hill, Exeter, Devon EX4 4DW
☎ 01392 279751 ✉ clerks@walnuthouse.co.uk
Call Date: Jul 2005, Inner Temple

CASSIDY MR PATRICK STEPHEN

Kenworthy's Chambers
Arlington House, Bloom Street, Salford, Manchester M3 6AJ ☎0161 832 4036
Call Date: Jul 1982, Lincoln's Inn
Pupil Supervisor

Practising Areas: Courts Martial, Crime, Education, Health & Safety, Human Rights, Regulatory Law

CASTLE MR PETER BOLTON

13 Old Square Chambers
Ground Floor, 14 Old Square, Lincoln's Inn, London WC2A 3UE ☎020 7831 4445
✉clerks@13oldsquare.com
Call Date: Jul 1970, Middle Temple
Pupil Supervisor

Practising Areas: Agriculture, Arbitration, Banking, Bankruptcy, Chancery (General), Commercial Litigation, Commercial Property, Company & Commercial, Equity, Wills & Trusts, Insolvency, Partnership, Private International, Probate & Administration, Professional Negligence

CASWELL MR BENJAMIN CECIL

No.6 Park Square
Leeds LS1 2LW ☎0113 245 9763
✉Tim@no6.co.uk
Call Date: Oct 1993, Middle Temple

CATTERMOLE MISS REBECCA ELKE

Tanfield Chambers
2-5 Warwick Court, London WC1R 5DJ
☎020 7421 5300 ✉clerks@tanfieldchambers.co.uk
Call Date: Oct 1999, Middle Temple

Practising Areas: Chancery (Land Law), Housing, Landlord & Tenant, Local Government

C

CATTERMULL MISS EMMA JAYNE

East Anglian Chambers
Gresham House, 5 Museum Street, Ipswich, Suffolk IP1 1HQ ☎01473 214481
✉ipswich@ealaw.co.uk
East Anglian Chambers
140 New London Road, Chelmsford, Essex CM2 0AW ☎01473 214481
✉chelmsford@ealaw.co.uk
East Anglian Chambers
15 The Close, Norwich, Norfolk NR1 4DZ
☎01473 214481 ✉norwich@ealaw.co.uk
Call Date: Oct 2004, Inner Temple

Practising Areas: Bankruptcy, Chancery (General), Chancery (Land Law), Commercial Litigation, Commercial Property, Common Law (General), Company & Commercial, Conveyancing, Discrimination, Education, Employment, Health & Safety, Housing, Human Rights, Immigration, Insolvency, Insurance, Landlord & Tenant, Medical Negligence, Mental Health, Personal Injury, Professional Negligence

CAUDLE MR JOHN ARTHUR

2 Bedford Row
London WC1R 4BU ☎020 7440 8888
✉clerks@2bedfordrow.co.uk
Call Date: Nov 1976, Middle Temple
Pupil Supervisor

Practising Areas: Crime

CAUN MR LAWRENCE

Lamb Chambers
Lamb Building, Elm Court, Temple, London EC4Y 7AS ☎020 7797 8300
✉info@lambchambers.co.uk
Call Date: Nov 1977, Lincoln's Inn
Pupil Supervisor

Practising Areas: Chancery (General), Chancery (Land Law), Civil Litigation, Commercial Property, Common Law (General), Land, Personal Injury, Professional Negligence

CAVENDER MS SUSAN PENELOPE

Guildhall Chambers
23 Broad Street, Bristol BS1 2HG
☎0117 930 9000 ✉hoc@guildhallchambers.co.uk
Call Date: Oct 2004, Gray's Inn

Practising Areas: Crime, Licensing

CAWSEY MR BARRY DONALD

Clerksroom (Taunton)
Equity House, Administration Centre, Blackbrook Park Avenue, Taunton, Somerset TA1 2PX ☎0845 083 3000
✉mail@clerksroom.com
Clerksroom (London)
3rd Floor, 218 Strand, London WC2R 1AT
☎0845 083 3000 ✉mail@clerksroom.com
Call Date: Jul 2001, Inner Temple

Practising Areas: Bankruptcy, Chancery (General), Commercial Litigation, Common Law (General), Construction, Insolvency, Insurance, Landlord & Tenant, Partnership, Personal Injury, Professional Negligence, Sale & Carriage of Goods

CAWSEY MS LAURA

Chambers of Ian Macdonald QC
Garden Court North, 22 Oxford Court, Manchester M2 3WQ ☎ 0161 236 1840
✉ clerks@gcnchambers.co.uk
Call Date: Nov 2004, Lincoln's Inn

CAYFORD MR PHILIP JOHN BERKELEY QC (2002)

29 Bedford Row Chambers
London WC1R 4HE ☎ 020 7404 1044
✉ clerks@29br.co.uk
Call Date: Jul 1975, Middle Temple

Practising Areas: Family, Family Provision

CECIL MISS JOANNE MICHELLE

1 Pump Court
Elm Court, Temple, London EC4Y 7AB
☎ 020 7842 7070 ✉ (name)@pumpcourt.co.uk
Call Date: Nov 2005, Inner Temple

Practising Areas: Administrative, Civil Liberties, Crime, Crime (Corporate/Fraud), Human Rights, Public International

CELLAN-JONES MR DEINIOL JAMES

1 KBW Chambers
1 King's Bench Walk, Temple, London EC4Y 7DB ☎ 020 7936 1500 ✉ clerks@1kbw.co.uk
King's Bench Chambers
174 High Street, Lewes BN7 1YE
☎ 01273 402600
Call Date: Nov 1988, Middle Temple
Pupil Supervisor

Practising Areas: Ancillary Relief, Children's Law

CHADWICK MR DANIEL JAMES

25 Bedford Row
London WC1R 4HD ☎ 020 7067 1500
✉ clerks@25bedfordrow.com
Call Date: Oct 2006, Middle Temple

Practising Areas: Crime, Crime (Corporate/Fraud)

CHADWICK MISS JOANNA CERIDWEN

No5 Chambers
Fountain Court, Steelhouse Lane, Birmingham B4 6DR ☎ 0845 210 5555 ✉ info@no5.com
No5 Chambers
Greenwood House, 4-7 Salisbury Court, London EC4Y 8AA ☎ 0845 210 5555
No5 Chambers
38 Queen Square, Bristol BS1 4QS
☎ 0845 210 5555
Call Date: Nov 1988, Middle Temple

Practising Areas: Care Proceedings, Civil Liberties, Common Law (General), Crime, Discrimination, Employment, Family, Family Provision, Personal Injury

CHAFFIN-LAIRD MISS OLIVIA CAROLYN

No5 Chambers
Fountain Court, Steelhouse Lane, Birmingham B4 6DR ☎ 0845 210 5555 ✉ info@no5.com
No5 Chambers
Greenwood House, 4-7 Salisbury Court, London EC4Y 8AA ☎ 0845 210 5555
No5 Chambers
38 Queen Square, Bristol BS1 4QS
☎ 0845 210 5555
Call Date: Jul 2001, Gray's Inn

Practising Areas: Common Law (General), Construction, Equity, Wills & Trusts, Housing, Landlord & Tenant, Local Government

CHALK MR ALEXANDER JOHN GERVASE

6 King's Bench Walk
Ground Floor, 6 King's Bench Walk, Temple, London EC4Y 7DR ☎ 020 7583 0410
✉ clerks@6kbw.com
Call Date: Oct 2001, Middle Temple

Practising Areas: Courts Martial, Crime, Crime (Corporate/Fraud), Defamation, Health & Safety, Human Rights, Licensing, Parliamentary, Regulatory Law

CHALLENGER MR COLIN WESTCOTT

Lamb Chambers
Lamb Building, Elm Court, Temple, London EC4Y 7AS ☎ 020 7797 8300
✉ info@lambchambers.co.uk
Call Date: Nov 1970, Inner Temple
Pupil Supervisor

Practising Areas: Chancery (General), Commercial Litigation, Commercial Property, Common Law (General), Medical Negligence, Personal Injury, Professional Negligence

CHALLINOR MR JONATHAN GERALD

Cornwall Street Chambers
85-87 Cornwall Street, Birmingham B3 3BY
☎0121 233 7500 ✉clerks@cornwallstreet.co.uk
Call Date: Nov 1998, Inner Temple

Practising Areas: Courts Martial, Crime, Licensing, Regulatory Law

CHALLINOR MR THOMAS MICHAEL

Citadel Chambers
The Citadel, 190 Corporation Street, Birmingham B4 6QD ☎0121 233 8500
✉clerks@citadelchambers.com
Call Date: Jul 2004, Gray's Inn

Practising Areas: Common Law (General), Crime, Crime (Corporate/Fraud), Landlord & Tenant, Licensing, Personal Injury, Sale & Carriage of Goods

CHALMERS MISS SUZANNE FRANCES

Crown Office Chambers
2 Crown Office Row, Temple, London EC4Y 7HJ ☎020 7797 8100
✉mail@crownofficechambers.com
Call Date: Oct 1995, Gray's Inn
Pupil Supervisor

CHAMBERS MISS GAYNOR MARIE

Keating Chambers
15 Essex Street, London WC2R 3AA
☎020 7544 2600 ✉clerks@keatingchambers.com
Call Date: Nov 1998, Middle Temple
Pupil Supervisor

Practising Areas: Arbitration, Construction, Professional Negligence

CHAMBERS MS RACHEL ELIZABETH

Cloisters
1 Pump Court, Temple, London EC4Y 7AA
☎020 7827 4000 ✉clerks@cloisters.com
Call Date: Oct 2002, Inner Temple

Practising Areas: Discrimination, Employment, Human Rights

CHAN MISS RACHEL SIU YEE

Stour Chambers
Mill Studio, 17a Stour Street, Canterbury, Kent CT1 2NR ☎01227 764899
✉clerks@stourchambers.co.uk
Call Date: Jul 2004, Lincoln's Inn

Practising Areas: Care Proceedings, Crime, Family

CHAN MISS SUSAN

13 King's Bench Walk
13 King's Bench Walk, Temple, London EC4Y 7EN ☎020 7353 7204 ✉clerks@13kbw.co.uk
13 KBW
32 Beaumont Street, Oxford OX1 2NP
☎01865 311066 ✉clerks@13kbw.co.uk
Call Date: Oct 1994, Gray's Inn

Practising Areas: Common Law (General), Discrimination, Employment, Personal Injury

CHANDARANA MR YOGAIN JITENDRA

Nine Bedford Row
9 Bedford Row, London WC1R 4AZ
☎020 7489 2727 ✉clerks@9bedfordrow.co.uk
Call Date: Oct 1997, Lincoln's Inn

CHANDLER MR ALEXANDER CHARLES ROSS

1 Garden Court Family Law Chambers
Ground Floor, One Garden Court, Temple, London EC4Y 9BJ ☎020 7797 7900
✉clerks@1gc.com
Call Date: Oct 1995, Middle Temple
Pupil Supervisor

Practising Areas: Family

CHANNON MISS REBECCA ANNE

Dyers Chambers
35 Bedford Row, London WC1R 4JH
☎020 7404 1881 ✉admin@dyerschambers.com
Call Date: Jul 2007, Middle Temple

Practising Areas: Crime

CHAPLIN MR ADRIAN ROLAND

9-12 Bell Yard
London WC2A 2JR ☎020 7400 1800
✉clerks@9-12bellyard.com
Call Date: Oct 1990, Gray's Inn
Pupil Supervisor

CHAPMAN MISS GEMMA RENNAI ALICE

Regency Chambers
45 Priestgate, Peterborough PE1 1LB
☎01733 315215 ✉clerks@regencychambers.law.co.uk
Regency Chambers
Sheraton House, Castle Park, Cambridge CB3 0AX ☎01223 301517
Call Date: Mar 2002, Lincoln's Inn

CHAPMAN MISS HELEN CLARE

37 Park Square Chambers
37 Park Square, Leeds LS1 2NY
☎ 0113 243 9422 ✉ chambers@no37.co.uk
Call Date: Jul 2006, Middle Temple

CHAPMAN MR JOHN FARRAR

Pump Court Chambers
Upper Ground Floor, 3 Pump Court, Temple, London EC4Y 7AJ ☎ 020 7353 0711
✉ clerks@3pumpcourt.com
Pump Court Chambers
5 Temple Chambers, Temple Street, Swindon SN1 1SQ ☎ 01793 539899
✉ clerks@3pumpcourt.com
Pump Court Chambers
31 Southgate Street, Winchester, Hampshire SO23 9EB ☎ 01962 868 161
✉ clerks@3pumpcourt.com
Call Date: Jul 2003, Lincoln's Inn
Pupil Supervisor

CHAPMAN MR NICHOLAS JOHN

29 Bedford Row Chambers
London WC1R 4HE ☎ 020 7404 1044
✉ clerks@29br.co.uk
Call Date: Oct 1990, Inner Temple
Pupil Supervisor

Practising Areas: Family Provision

CHARALAMBIDES MR LEONIDAS

Francis Taylor Building
Inner Temple, London EC4Y 7BY
☎ 020 7353 8415 ✉ clerks@ftb.eu.com
Call Date: Jul 1998, Inner Temple

Practising Areas: Administrative, Chancery (General), Chancery (Land Law), Commercial Property, Common Land, Entertainment, Environment, Housing, Landlord & Tenant, Licensing, Local Government, Town & Country Planning

CHARKHAM MR GRAHAM HAROLD

20 Essex Street
London WC2R 3AL ☎ 020 7842 1200
✉ clerks@20essexst.com
Call Date: May 1993, Inner Temple

Practising Areas: Admiralty, Arbitration, Banking, Commercial Litigation, Commodities, Insurance, Insurance/Reinsurance, International Trade, Sale & Carriage of Goods, Shipping/Admiralty

CHARLES MS KATRINA SKEVI

Farringdon Chambers
180 Bermondsey Street, London SE1 3TQ
☎ 020 7089 5700
Call Date: Oct 1999, Inner Temple

Practising Areas: Crime

CHARLTON MR ALEXANDER MURRAY QC (2008)

4 Pump Court
4 Pump Court, Temple, London EC4Y 7AN
☎ 020 7842 5555 ✉ chambers@4pumpcourt.com
Call Date: Jul 1983, Middle Temple

Practising Areas: Information Technology, Telecommunications

CHARNLEY MISS BETHAN REBECCA

Nine Bedford Row
9 Bedford Row, London WC1R 4AZ
☎ 020 7489 2727 ✉ clerks@9bedfordrow.co.uk
Call Date: Oct 2007, Lincoln's Inn

Practising Areas: Crime

CHATTERJEE MISS ADREEJA JULIA

No5 Chambers
Fountain Court, Steelhouse Lane, Birmingham B4 6DR ☎ 0845 210 5555 ✉ info@no5.com
No5 Chambers
Greenwood House, 4-7 Salisbury Court, London EC4Y 8AA ☎ 0845 210 5555
No5 Chambers
38 Queen Square, Bristol BS1 4QS
☎ 0845 210 5555
Call Date: Nov 1997, Gray's Inn

Practising Areas: Ancillary Relief, Care Proceedings, Chancery (Land Law), Family, Family Provision

CHATTERJEE MISS MIRA

4 Brick Court
4 Brick Court, Temple, London EC4Y 9AD
☎ 020 7832 3200 ✉ clerks@4bc.co.uk
Call Date: Nov 1973, Middle Temple
Pupil Supervisor

Practising Areas: Family

CHAUDHRY MISS SABUHI ASHFAQ

Coram Chambers
9-11 Fulwood Place, London WC1V 6HG
☎ 020 7092 3700 ✉ mail@coramchambers.co.uk
Call Date: Oct 1993, Lincoln's Inn

Practising Areas: Family, Family Provision

C

CHAUDHURI MR AVIRUP

187 Fleet Street
London EC4A 2AT ☎ 020 7430 7430
✉ chambers@187fleetstreet.com
Call Date: Feb 1990, Middle Temple
Pupil Supervisor

CHAWLA MR MUKUL QC (2001)

9-12 Bell Yard
London WC2A 2JR ☎ 020 7400 1800
✉ clerks@9-12bellyard.com
Call Date: Jul 1983, Gray's Inn

Practising Areas: Crime, Crime (Corporate/Fraud), Health & Safety, Regulatory Law

CHAWLA MR NEIL

No5 Chambers
Fountain Court, Steelhouse Lane, Birmingham B4 6DR ☎ 0845 210 5555 ✉ info@no5.com
No5 Chambers
Greenwood House, 4-7 Salisbury Court, London EC4Y 8AA ☎ 0845 210 5555
No5 Chambers
38 Queen Square, Bristol BS1 4QS
☎ 0845 210 5555
Call Date: Jul 2000, Lincoln's Inn

Practising Areas: Crime (Corporate/Fraud), Employment, Financial Services, Health & Safety, Regulatory Law

CHECA-DOVER MISS OLIVIA

KBW
The Engine House, No 1 Foundry Square, Leeds LS11 5DL ☎ 0113 297 1200
✉ clerks@kbwchambers.com
Call Date: Jul 2007, Lincoln's Inn

Practising Areas: Crime, Employment, Personal Injury

CHEEMA MISS PARMJIT KAUR

2 Hare Court
Lower Ground, Ground, 1st & 2nd Floor, 2 Hare Court, Temple, London EC4Y 7BH
☎ 020 7353 3982 ✉ clerks@2harecourt.com
Call Date: Jul 1989, Gray's Inn
Pupil Supervisor, Recorder

Practising Areas: Crime, Crime (Corporate/Fraud)

CHELVAN MR S

No5 Chambers
Greenwood House, 4-7 Salisbury Court, London EC4Y 8AA ☎ 0845 210 5555
No5 Chambers
Fountain Court, Steelhouse Lane, Birmingham B4 6DR ☎ 0845 210 5555 ✉ info@no5.com
Trent Chambers
9 Regent Street, Nottingham NG1 5BS
☎ 0115 941 9596 ✉ clerks@trentchambers.co.uk
No5 Chambers
38 Queen Square, Bristol BS1 4QS
☎ 0845 210 5555
Call Date: Oct 1999, Inner Temple
Pupil Supervisor

Practising Areas: Civil Liberties, Human Rights, Immigration

CHERN MR CYRIL

Crown Office Chambers
2 Crown Office Row, Temple, London EC4Y 7HJ ☎ 020 7797 8100
✉ mail@crownofficechambers.com
Call Date: Nov 2001, Gray's Inn

Practising Areas: Construction, International Trade, Private International

CHERRETT MR DARRYL JOSEPH

Carmelite Chambers
9 Carmelite Street, London EC4Y 0DR
☎ 020 7936 6300
✉ clerks@carmelitechambers.co.uk
Call Date: Jul 2004, Middle Temple

Practising Areas: Crime, Crime (Corporate/Fraud), Family Provision, Road Traffic And Highways

CHESNER MR HOWARD MICHAEL

One Essex Court
1st Floor, Temple, London EC4Y 9AR
☎ 020 7936 3030 ✉ clerks@1ec.co.uk
Call Date: Jul 1995, Gray's Inn

Practising Areas: Bankruptcy, Chancery (General), Commercial Litigation, Common Law (General), Company & Commercial, Employment, Insolvency, Landlord & Tenant, Partnership, Personal Injury

CHEVES MR SIMON THOMSON

Tanfield Chambers
2-5 Warwick Court, London WC1R 5DJ
☎ 020 7421 5300 ✉ clerks@tanfieldchambers.co.uk
Call Date: Jul 1980, Inner Temple

CHIBAFA MR JONATHAN

18 Red Lion Court
London EC4A 3EB ☎ 020 7520 6000
✉ chambers@18rlc.co.uk
Call Date: Nov 2006, Middle Temple

CHICHESTER-CLARK MR ADAM TAMNIARN

13 Old Square Chambers
Ground Floor, 14 Old Square, Lincoln's Inn, London WC2A 3UE ☎ 020 7831 4445
✉ clerks@13oldsquare.com
Call Date: Nov 2000, Middle Temple

CHIDGEY MR DAVID GARETH

Albion Chambers
Broad Street, Bristol BS1 1DR
☎ 0117 927 2144 ✉ clerks@albionchambers.co.uk
Call Date: Oct 2000, Middle Temple

Practising Areas: Crime, Employment, Family

CHINN MR ANTONY NIGEL CATON QC (2003)

Nine Bedford Row
9 Bedford Row, London WC1R 4AZ
☎ 020 7489 2727 ✉ clerks@9bedfordrow.co.uk
Call Date: Nov 1972, Middle Temple
Recorder

CHIPPECK MR STEPHEN

5 King's Bench Walk
5 King's Bench Walk, Temple, London EC4Y 7DN ☎ 020 7353 5638 ✉ clerks@5kbw.co.uk
Call Date: Jul 1988, Lincoln's Inn

Practising Areas: Care Proceedings, Civil Liberties, Common Law (General), Crime, Employment, Family, Family Provision, Human Rights, Medical Negligence, Personal Injury

CHIPPENDALE MISS EMMA LORRAINE

37 Park Square Chambers
37 Park Square, Leeds LS1 2NY
☎ 0113 243 9422 ✉ chambers@no37.co.uk
Call Date: Jul 2002, Middle Temple

Practising Areas: Care Proceedings, Children's Law, Family, Family Provision

CHIPPERFIELD MR JEREMY STEVEN

Cranford Chambers
8 Warwick Court, London WC1R 5DJ
☎ 020 7404 7454 ✉ jemima.ivens@cranfordchambers.com
Call Date: Oct 1995, Inner Temple
Pupil Supervisor

Practising Areas: Civil Liberties, Coroners Inquests, Courts Martial, Crime, Crime (Corporate/Fraud), Disciplinary Tribunals, Human Rights, Immigration, Mental Health

CHIRICO MR DAVID DOMENICO

1 Pump Court
Elm Court, Temple, London EC4Y 7AB
☎ 020 7842 7070 ✉ (name)@pumpcourt.co.uk
Call Date: Nov 2002, Middle Temple

CHODHA MR TEJPAL SINGH

Chambers of Mr T Chodha
112 Hampton Crescent, Gravesend DA12 4HY ☎ 01474 326666
Call Date: Jul 1984, Inner Temple

Practising Areas: Crime, Family, Human Rights, Immigration, Sports

CHOLERTON MR NIGEL PHILIP

Eighteen Carlton Crescent
Rownhams House, Rownhams, Southampton SO16 8LF ☎ 023 8063 9001
✉ clerks@18carltoncrescent.co.uk
Midland Chambers
174 Blagreaves Lane, Littleover, Derby DE23 1PU ☎ 01332 749529 ✉ nglchol@aol.com
Call Date: Mar 2007, Lincoln's Inn

CHOONGH MR SATNAM SINGH

No5 Chambers
Fountain Court, Steelhouse Lane, Birmingham B4 6DR ☎ 0845 210 5555 ✉ info@no5.com
No5 Chambers
Greenwood House, 4-7 Salisbury Court, London EC4Y 8AA ☎ 0845 210 5555
No5 Chambers
38 Queen Square, Bristol BS1 4QS
☎ 0845 210 5555
Call Date: Oct 1994, Lincoln's Inn

Practising Areas: Employment, Environment, Town & Country Planning

CHOUDHURI MISS GULSHANAH

Sen Barristers
30 Sycamore Avenue, Chandlers Ford, Eastleigh, Hampshire SO53 5RH
☎ 07706 936045 ✉ info@senbarristers.co.uk
Call Date: Nov 1995, Lincoln's Inn

Practising Areas: Common Law (General), Education, Family

CHOUDHURY MISS SADIYA ASGHAR

Pump Court Tax Chambers
16 Bedford Row, London WC1R 4EF
☎ 020 7414 8080 ✉ clerks@pumptax.com
Call Date: Oct 2002, Lincoln's Inn

Practising Areas: Equity, Wills & Trusts, Tax (Capital & Income), Tax (Corporate)

CHOWDHARY MR ISLAMUDDIN

Cassian Chambers
43 Fowey Avenue, Ilford, Essex IG4 5JT
☎ 07796 262641 ✉ islam.chowdhary@ntlworld.com
Call Date: Jul 1982, Lincoln's Inn
Pupil Supervisor

Practising Areas: Administrative, Banking, Bankruptcy, Chancery (Land Law), Common Law (General), Defamation, Equity, Wills & Trusts, Financial Services, Insolvency, Partnership, Private International, Probate & Administration, Professional Negligence, Public International

CHRISTENSEN MR CARLTON

10 King's Bench Walk
Ground Floor, 10 King's Bench Walk, Temple, London EC4Y 7EB ☎ 020 7353 7742
✉ Chambers@10kingsbenchwalk.co.uk
Call Date: Jul 1977, Middle Temple
Pupil Supervisor

Practising Areas: Banking, Bankruptcy, Chancery (General), Chancery (Land Law), Civil Litigation, Commercial Litigation, Commercial Property, Common Law (General), Company & Commercial, Consumer, Costs, Equity, Wills & Trusts, Housing, Insolvency, Landlord & Tenant, Local Government, Partnership, Personal Injury, Probate & Administration, Professional Negligence, Sale & Carriage of Goods

CHRISTIAN MR NEIL CONNAN

Call Date: Oct 2005, Middle Temple

CHRISTIE MR DAVID HENDERSON

Seven Bedford Row
7 Bedford Row, London WC1R 4BS
☎ 020 7242 3555 ✉ clerks@7br.co.uk
Call Date: Jul 1973, Inner Temple
Pupil Supervisor

Practising Areas: Commercial Litigation, Company & Commercial, Employment, Insolvency, Partnership, Professional Negligence

CHRISTIE MR IAIN ROBERT

5RB
1st Floor, 5 Raymond Buildings, Gray's Inn, London WC1R 5BP ☎ 020 7242 2902
✉ clerks@5rb.com
Call Date: Jul 1989, Inner Temple

Practising Areas: Administrative, Civil Liberties, Commercial Litigation, Common Law (General), Defamation, Discrimination, Entertainment, Film, Cable & TV, Intellectual Property, Local Government, Parliamentary, Public International

CHRISTIE MISS MICHELLE ELAINE

Northampton Chambers
10 Spencer Parade, Northampton NN1 5AQ
☎ 01604 636271
✉ clerks@northampton-chambers.co.uk
Call Date: Oct 1999, Middle Temple
Pupil Supervisor

Practising Areas: Family

CHRISTIE MR RICHARD HAMISH QC (2006)

2 Pump Court
1st Floor, 2 Pump Court, Temple, London EC4Y 7AH ☎ 020 7353 5597
✉ clerks@2pumpcourt.co.uk
Call Date: Jul 1986, Inner Temple

Practising Areas: Civil Liberties, Common Law (General), Costs, Crime, Crime (Corporate/Fraud), Family, Family Provision

CHRISTIE MR SIMON PAUL WILLIAM

Chavasse Court Chambers
18 Queen Avenue, Liverpool L2 4TX
☎ 0151 229 2030
✉ clerks@chavassechambers.co.uk
Call Date: Feb 1988, Middle Temple
Pupil Supervisor

Practising Areas: Crime, Crime (Corporate/Fraud)

C

CHURCH MR JOHN STEPHEN

Field Court Chambers
5 Field Court, Gray's Inn, London WC1R 5EF
☎020 7405 6114 ✉clerks@fieldcourt.co.uk
Call Date: Nov 1984, Lincoln's Inn

Practising Areas: Family

CHUTE MS ANDREA ALEXANDRA

Tooks Chambers
81 Farringdon Street, London EC4A 4BL
☎020 7842 7575 ✉clerks@tooks.co.uk
Rougemont Chambers
Victory House, Dean Clarke Gardens, Southernhay East, Exeter EX2 4AA
☎01392 208484
✉clerks@rougemontchambers.co.uk
Call Date: Oct 1995, Middle Temple

Practising Areas: Chancery (Land Law), Common Land, Common Law (General), Discrimination, Employment, Housing, Human Rights, Landlord & Tenant, Private International, Professional Negligence

CIFONELLI MR ROSSANO GIUSEPPE

2 Dr Johnson's Buildings
2 Dr Johnson's Buildings, Temple, London EC4Y 7AY ☎020 7936 2613 ✉clerks@2drj.com
Call Date: Oct 1998, Gray's Inn

Practising Areas: Employment

CLARE MISS ALLISON JEAN

18 Red Lion Court
London EC4A 3EB ☎020 7520 6000
✉chambers@18rlc.co.uk
Call Date: Oct 1992, Gray's Inn
Pupil Supervisor

Practising Areas: Crime, Crime (Corporate/Fraud)

CLARIDGE MISS RACHAEL SARAH

Crown Office Row Chambers
119 Church Street, Brighton, Sussex BN1 1UD ☎01273 625625 ✉clerks@1cor.com
Call Date: Oct 1996, Inner Temple

Practising Areas: Family, Inquests

CLARK MR ANDREW RICHARD

9 St John Street
Manchester M3 4DN ☎0161 955 9000
✉civilclerks@9sjs.com/criminalclerks@9sjs.com
Call Date: Jul 1994, Inner Temple
Pupil Supervisor

Practising Areas: Chancery (General), Chancery (Land Law), Commercial Litigation, Equity, Wills & Trusts, Family Provision, Insolvency, Landlord & Tenant, Partnership, Professional Negligence

CLARK MR DINGLE

Goldsmith Chambers
Ground Floor, Goldsmith Building, Temple, London EC4Y 7BL ☎020 7353 6802
✉clerks@goldsmithchambers.com
Call Date: Jul 1981, Middle Temple
Pupil Supervisor

Practising Areas: Administrative, Ancillary Relief, Bankruptcy, Chancery (Land Law), Coroners Inquests, Courts Martial, Crime, Disciplinary Tribunals, Family, Family Provision, Immigration, Road Traffic And Highways, Sports

CLARK MISS GEORGINA

Field Court Chambers
5 Field Court, Gray's Inn, London WC1R 5EF
☎020 7405 6114 ✉clerks@fieldcourt.co.uk
Call Date: Oct 2003, Lincoln's Inn

CLARK MISS GERALDINE

Serle Court
6 New Square, Lincoln's Inn, London WC2A 3QS ☎020 7242 6105 ✉clerks@serlecourt.co.uk
Call Date: Jul 1988, Gray's Inn
Pupil Supervisor, Recorder

Practising Areas: Arbitration, Banking, Commercial Litigation, Commodities, Company & Commercial, Financial Services, Insurance, Insurance/Reinsurance, International Trade, Private International, Professional Negligence, Sale & Carriage of Goods, Shipping/Admiralty

CLARK MS JULIA ELISABETH

Hogarth Chambers
5 New Square, Lincoln's Inn, London WC2A 3RJ ☎020 7404 0404
✉barristers@hogarthchambers.com
Call Date: Jul 1984, Gray's Inn
Pupil Supervisor

Practising Areas: Chancery (General), Commercial Litigation, Company & Commercial, Copyright, Entertainment, Insolvency, Intellectual Property, Trademarks

CLARKE MRS AMANDA LESLEY

Westgate Chambers
64 High Street, Lewes, East Sussex BN7 1XG
☎ 01273 480510
✉ clerks@westgate-chambers.co.uk
Call Date: Jul 1998, Middle Temple
Pupil Supervisor

Practising Areas: Children's Law, Family, Family Provision

CLARKE MR GEORGE ROBERT IVAN

5 Pump Court
Ground Floor, 5 Pump Court, Temple, London EC4Y 7AP ☎ 020 7353 2532
✉ clerks@5pumpcourt.com
Call Date: Nov 1973, Gray's Inn
Pupil Supervisor

Practising Areas: Chancery (General), Chancery (Land Law), Commercial Property, Common Law (General), Construction, Housing, Landlord & Tenant, Professional Negligence

CLARKE MR JAMIE ROY

Hardwicke
New Square, Lincoln's Inn, London WC2A 3SB ☎ 020 7242 2523
✉ enquiries@hardwicke.co.uk
Call Date: Nov 1995, Gray's Inn

Practising Areas: Health & Safety, Insurance, Medical Negligence, Personal Injury, Professional Negligence

CLARKE MISS JESSICA ALICE

Westgate Chambers
64 High Street, Lewes, East Sussex BN7 1XG
☎ 01273 480510
✉ clerks@westgate-chambers.co.uk
Call Date: Oct 2006, Lincoln's Inn

Practising Areas: Crime

CLARKE MISS LISA TARIN

Staple Inn Chambers
1st Floor, 9 Staple Inn, Holborn Bars, London WC1V 7QH ☎ 020 7242 5240
✉ clerks@stapleinn.co.uk
Call Date: Oct 1995, Gray's Inn

Practising Areas: Common Law (General), Housing, Landlord & Tenant, Personal Injury

CLARKE MR NICHOLAS PATRICK JAMES

18 St John Street
Manchester M3 4EA ☎ 0161 278 1800
✉ clerks@18sjs.com
Call Date: Oct 2001, Lincoln's Inn

Practising Areas: Crime, Crime (Corporate/Fraud), Financial Services, Insolvency, Mental Health, Tax (Capital & Income), Tax (Corporate)

CLARKE MR NIKOLAS MICHAEL

Field Court Chambers
5 Field Court, Gray's Inn, London WC1R 5EF
☎ 020 7405 6114 ✉ clerks@fieldcourt.co.uk
Call Date: Jul 2000, Lincoln's Inn

Practising Areas: Common Law (General), Discrimination, Employment, Personal Injury

CLARKE MR RORY JAMES

Cornerstone Barristers
2-3 Gray's Inn Square, Gray's Inn, London WC1R 5JH ☎ 020 7242 4986
✉ chambers@2-3gis.co.uk
Call Date: Nov 1996, Inner Temple
Pupil Supervisor

Practising Areas: Administrative, Environment, Licensing, Local Government, Town & Country Planning

CLARKE MR TIMOTHY JOHN

Cornwall Street Chambers
85-87 Cornwall Street, Birmingham B3 3BY
☎ 0121 233 7500 ✉ clerks@cornwallstreet.co.uk
Call Date: Oct 1992, Middle Temple
Pupil Supervisor

Practising Areas: Chancery (Land Law), Ecclesiastical, Equity, Wills & Trusts, Landlord & Tenant, Probate & Administration

CLARKSON MR STUART JAMES MACGREGOR

St Ive's Chambers
Whittall Street, Birmingham B4 6DH
☎ 0121 236 0863 ✉ clerks@stiveschambers.co.uk
Call Date: Nov 1987, Gray's Inn

Practising Areas: Crime

CLAXTON MR ELROY GERALDO

Old Bailey Chambers
15 Old Bailey, London EC4M 7EF
☎ 020 3008 6404
✉ clerks@15oldbaileychambers.com
23 Essex Street
London WC2R 3AA ☎ 020 7413 0353
✉ clerks@23es.com
Call Date: Jul 1983, Inner Temple
Pupil Supervisor, Recorder

Practising Areas: Crime, Crime (Corporate/Fraud), Disciplinary Tribunals, Sports

CLAY MR JONATHAN ROGER

Cornerstone Barristers
2-3 Gray's Inn Square, Gray's Inn, London WC1R 5JH ☎ 020 7242 4986
✉ chambers@2-3gis.co.uk
Call Date: Oct 1990, Lincoln's Inn
Pupil Supervisor

Practising Areas: Administrative, Civil Liberties, Discrimination, Employment, Environment, Human Rights, Local Government, Town & Country Planning

CLAYTON MR NIGEL GARVIN

Kings Chambers
36 Young Street, Manchester M3 3FT
☎ 0845 034 3444 ✉ clerks@kingschambers.com
Kings Chambers
5 Park Square East, Leeds LS1 2NE
☎ 0845 034 3444 ✉ clerks@kingschambers.com
Kings Chambers
Embassy House, 60 Church Street, Birmingham B3 2DJ ☎ 0845 034 3444
✉ clerks@kingschambers.com
Call Date: Jul 1987, Inner Temple
Pupil Supervisor, Recorder

Practising Areas: Banking, Chancery (Land Law), Commercial Property, Conveyancing, Landlord & Tenant

CLEARY MR JAMES MICHAEL

KCH Garden Square
1 Oxford Street, Nottingham NG1 5BH
☎ 0115 941 8851 ✉ clerks@kchgardensquare.co.uk
Call Date: Nov 2003, Middle Temple

CLEGG MR ADAM GORDON

Stour Chambers
Mill Studio, 17a Stour Street, Canterbury, Kent CT1 2NR ☎ 01227 764899
✉ clerks@stourchambers.co.uk
Call Date: Nov 1994, Gray's Inn

Practising Areas: Care Proceedings, Common Law (General), Employment, Family, Family Provision, Landlord & Tenant, Personal Injury

CLEGG MR SIMON JOSEPH

Sovereign Chambers
46 Park Place, Leeds LS1 2RY
☎ 0113 245 1841
✉ clerks@sovereignchambers.co.uk
Call Date: Nov 2005, Inner Temple

CLEGG MR SIMON ROBERT JONATHAN

St Philips Chambers
55 Temple Row, Birmingham B2 5LS
☎ 0121 246 7000 ✉ clerks@st-philips.com
Call Date: Jul 1980, Lincoln's Inn
Pupil Supervisor

Practising Areas: Asset Finance, Banking, Bankruptcy, Chancery (General), Chancery (Land Law), Commercial Litigation, Company & Commercial, Insolvency, Partnership, Sale & Carriage of Goods

CLEGG MR WILLIAM QC (1991)

2 Bedford Row
London WC1R 4BU ☎ 020 7440 8888
✉ clerks@2bedfordrow.co.uk
Call Date: Jul 1972, Gray's Inn

Practising Areas: Crime, Crime (Corporate/Fraud), Health & Safety, Regulatory Law

CLEMENT MR RYAN WAYNE

Conference Chambers
P.O. Box 626, Harrow, Middlesex HA2 2DZ
☎ 020 8144 0134
✉ carole@conferencechambers.com
Call Date: Oct 1996, Middle Temple

Practising Areas: Commercial Litigation, Common Law (General), Construction, Employment, Professional Negligence

CLEMENTS MISS PAULA KATE

Alexander Chambers
13 Halstead Road, Wanstead, London E11 2AY ☎0845 652 0451 / 0854 652 0451
✉clerks@alexanderchambers.co.uk
Guildford Chambers
Stoke House, Leapale Lane, Guildford, Surrey GU1 4LY ☎01483 539131
✉clerks@guildfordchambers.co.uk
Call Date: Jul 1985, Inner Temple

Practising Areas: Coroners Inquests, Disciplinary Tribunals, Education, Inquests, Regulatory Law

CLEWS MR RICHARD ANTHONY

No.6 Park Square
Leeds LS1 2LW ☎0113 245 9763
✉Tim@no6.co.uk
Call Date: Jul 1986, Gray's Inn

CLIFF MR BARRY GEORGE

Regent Chambers
Regent House, 3 Pall Mall, Hanley, Stoke On Trent ST1 1HP ☎01782 286666
✉clerks@regentchambers.co.uk
Call Date: Jul 1988, Lincoln's Inn
Pupil Supervisor

CLIFFORD MISS VICTORIA LOUISE

No5 Chambers
Fountain Court, Steelhouse Lane, Birmingham B4 6DR ☎0845 210 5555 ✉info@no5.com
No5 Chambers
Greenwood House, 4-7 Salisbury Court, London EC4Y 8AA ☎0845 210 5555
No5 Chambers
38 Queen Square, Bristol BS1 4QS
☎0845 210 5555
Call Date: Jul 2002, Gray's Inn

Practising Areas: Family, Family Provision

CLIFT MISS CLAIRE TERESA

Clerksroom (Taunton)
Equity House, Administration Centre, Blackbrook Park Avenue, Taunton, Somerset TA1 2PX ☎0845 083 3000
✉mail@clerksroom.com
Call Date: Oct 2003, Middle Temple

CLIFTON MISS JANE APRIL

Lamb Chambers
Lamb Building, Elm Court, Temple, London EC4Y 7AS ☎020 7797 8300
✉info@lambchambers.co.uk
Call Date: Oct 2001, Middle Temple

Practising Areas: Chancery (General), Commercial Litigation, Common Law (General), Company & Commercial, Housing, Landlord & Tenant, Personal Injury, Sale & Carriage of Goods

CLIMIE MR ROGER STEPHEN

Outer Temple Chambers
The Outer Temple, 222 Strand, London WC2R 1BA ☎020 7353 6381
✉clerks@outertemple.com
King's Bench and Godolphin (KBG)Chambers
115 North Hill, Plymouth, Devon PL4 8JY
☎01752 221551 ✉clerks@kbgchambers.co.uk
Call Date: Jul 1982, Lincoln's Inn
Pupil Supervisor, Recorder

Practising Areas: Coroners Inquests, Crime (Corporate/Fraud), Environment, Health & Safety, Inquests, Medical Negligence, Personal Injury, Professional Negligence, Regulatory Law

CLINE MR ROBERT JAMES

Atlantic Chambers
4-6 Cook Street, Liverpool L2 9QU
☎0151 236 4421 ✉info@atlanticchambers.co.uk
Call Date: Oct 2002, Gray's Inn

Practising Areas: Common Law (General), Personal Injury

CLOVER MISS SARAH

Kings Chambers
36 Young Street, Manchester M3 3FT
☎0845 034 3444 ✉clerks@kingschambers.com
Kings Chambers
5 Park Square East, Leeds LS1 2NE
☎0845 034 3444 ✉clerks@kingschambers.com
Call Date: Nov 1993, Lincoln's Inn

Practising Areas: Licensing

COATES MR GEORGE ALEXANDER NIGEL

Guildford Chambers
Stoke House, Leapale Lane, Guildford, Surrey GU1 4LY ☎01483 539131
✉clerks@guildfordchambers.co.uk
Call Date: Nov 1990, Middle Temple
Pupil Supervisor

Practising Areas: Common Law (General), Equity, Wills & Trusts, Family, Personal Injury, Professional Negligence, Sale & Carriage of Goods

COBBE MR MATTHEW RANDALL

9 Park Place
Cardiff, South Glamorgan CF10 3DP
☎ 029 2038 2731 ✉ clerks@9parkplace.co.uk
Call Date: Nov 1998, Gray's Inn

COCKINGS MR GILES FRANCIS SACHEVERAL

Furnival Chambers
32 Furnival Street, London EC4A 1JQ
☎ 020 7405 3232
Call Date: Oct 1996, Middle Temple
Pupil Supervisor

Practising Areas: Courts Martial, Crime, Crime (Corporate/Fraud), Financial Services, Regulatory Law

COCKS MR DAVID JOHN QC (1982)

18 Red Lion Court
London EC4A 3EB ☎ 020 7520 6000
✉ chambers@18rlc.co.uk
18 Red Lion Court (Annexe)
Thornwood House, 102 New London Road, Chelmsford, Essex CM2 0RG
☎ 01245 280880
Call Date: Jun 1961, Lincoln's Inn

Practising Areas: Crime, Crime (Corporate/Fraud), Town & Country Planning

COFFEY MR JOHN JOSEPH QC (1996)

3 Temple Gardens
Lower Ground Floor, 3 Temple Gardens, Temple, London EC4Y 9AU ☎ 020 7353 3102
✉ clerks@3tg.co.uk
39 Park Square
Leeds LS1 2NU ☎ 0113 245 6633
✉ seniorclerk@39parksquarechambers.co.uk
Call Date: Nov 1970, Middle Temple
Recorder

Practising Areas: Courts Martial, Crime, Crime (Corporate/Fraud)

COFIE MR EDMUND KPAKPO

Nexus Chambers
7 New Square, Lincolns Inn, London WC2A 3QS ☎ 020 7404 1147 / 020 7831 8309
✉ info@nexuschambers.com
Call Date: Jul 1980, Middle Temple
Pupil Supervisor

Practising Areas: Personal Injury

COGHILL-SMITH MRS ABIGAIL CATHERINE

Chambers of Andrew Mitchell QC
33 Chancery Lane, London WC2A 1EN
☎ 020 7440 9950 ✉ clerks@33cllaw.com
Call Date: Nov 1997, Gray's Inn

COHEN MR EDWARD MERVYN

11 Stone Buildings
11 Stone Buildings, Lincoln's Inn, London WC2A 3TG ☎ 020 7831 6381 ✉ clerks@11sb.com
Call Date: Jul 1972, Middle Temple
Recorder

Practising Areas: Arbitration, Banking, Chancery (General), Commercial Litigation, Commercial Property, Company & Commercial, Defamation, Entertainment, Insolvency, Insurance, Intellectual Property, Partnership, Probate & Administration, Professional Negligence, Sale & Carriage of Goods

COHEN MR JONATHAN LIONEL QC (1997)

4 Paper Buildings
1st Floor, 4 Paper Buildings, Temple, London EC4Y 7EX ☎ 020 7427 5200 ✉ clerks@4pb.com
Call Date: Jul 1974, Lincoln's Inn
Recorder

Practising Areas: Care Proceedings, Family, Family Provision, Professional Negligence

COLBEY MR RICHARD

Lamb Chambers
Lamb Building, Elm Court, Temple, London EC4Y 7AS ☎ 020 7797 8300
✉ info@lambchambers.co.uk
Guildhall Chambers Portsmouth
Prudential Buildings, 16 Guildhall Walk, Portsmouth, Hampshire PO1 2DE
☎ 023 9275 2400 ✉ clerks@gcp-barristers.com
Call Date: Jul 1984, Inner Temple

Practising Areas: Arbitration, Aviation, Banking, Bankruptcy, Chancery (General), Chancery (Land Law), Commercial Litigation, Commercial Property, Construction, Conveyancing, Copyright, Employment, Equity, Wills & Trusts, Family, Family Provision, Insolvency, Insurance, Intellectual Property, Landlord & Tenant, Medical Negligence, Mental Health, Partnership, Personal Injury, Private International, Sale & Carriage of Goods, Sports, Tax (Capital & Income)

COLE MR JUSTIN MARK

Five Paper Buildings
1st Floor, Five Paper Buildings, Temple, London EC4Y 7HB ☎ 020 7583 6117
✉ clerks@5pb.co.uk
Call Date: May 1992, Inner Temple

COLECLOUGH MRS SUZANNE MARIA

St Philips Chambers
55 Temple Row, Birmingham B2 5LS
☎ 0121 246 7000 ✉ clerks@st-philips.com
Call Date: Mar 2005, Inner Temple

Practising Areas: Employment, Family

COLEMAN MR DANIEL GERALD MAYOW

1 Gray's Inn Square
Ground Floor, 1 Gray's Inn Square, London WC1R 5AA ☎ 020 7405 0001
Call Date: Nov 1994, Gray's Inn

Practising Areas: Human Rights, Immigration

COLEMAN MR GUY ROBERT

Lamb Chambers
Lamb Building, Elm Court, Temple, London EC4Y 7AS ☎ 020 7797 8300
✉ info@lambchambers.co.uk
Call Date: Oct 1998, Inner Temple

COLES MR STEVEN FREDERICK

Crown Office Chambers
2 Crown Office Row, Temple, London EC4Y 7HJ ☎ 020 7797 8100
✉ mail@crownofficechambers.com
Call Date: Jul 1983, Middle Temple
Pupil Supervisor

COLES-HARRINGTON MS FRANCES JULIA

2 Pump Court
1st Floor, 2 Pump Court, Temple, London EC4Y 7AH ☎ 020 7353 5597
✉ clerks@2pumpcourt.co.uk
Call Date: Nov 2001, Lincoln's Inn

Practising Areas: Courts Martial, Crime, Crime (Corporate/Fraud)

COLE-WILSON MS LOIS EKUNDAYO

1 Gray's Inn Square
Ground Floor, 1 Gray's Inn Square, London WC1R 5AA ☎ 020 7405 0001
NIPC
Kirklees Media Centre, 7 Northumberland Street, Huddersfield HD1 1RL
☎ 0800 862 0055 ✉ jill.hayfield@nipclaw.com
Call Date: Nov 1995, Inner Temple

COLLARD MR MICHAEL DAVID

5 Pump Court
Ground Floor, 5 Pump Court, Temple, London EC4Y 7AP ☎ 020 7353 2532
✉ clerks@5pumpcourt.com
Call Date: Jul 1986, Middle Temple
Pupil Supervisor

Practising Areas: Commercial Property, Construction, Landlord & Tenant, Licensing, Local Government, Professional Negligence

COLLETT MR GAVIN CHARLES

Rougemont Chambers
Victory House, Dean Clarke Gardens, Southernhay East, Exeter EX2 4AA
☎ 01392 208484
✉ clerks@rougemontchambers.co.uk
Call Date: Oct 1993, Inner Temple
Pupil Supervisor

Practising Areas: Agriculture, Arbitration, Chancery (Land Law), Common Law (General), Courts Martial, Environment, Landlord & Tenant, Licensing, Town & Country Planning

COLLINGS MR ANDREW SIMON JOHN

5 King's Bench Walk
5 King's Bench Walk, Temple, London EC4Y 7DN ☎ 020 7353 5638 ✉ clerks@5kbw.co.uk
Call Date: Nov 1987, Gray's Inn

COLLINS MR PETER RICHARD

4 King's Bench Walk
2nd Floor, 4 King's Bench Walk, Temple, London EC4Y 7DL ☎ 020 7822 7000
✉ clerks@4kbw.co.uk
Call Date: Oct 1993, Gray's Inn

Practising Areas: Family, Immigration, Personal Injury

COLLINS MISS SIOBHAN ELLEN

Citadel Chambers
The Citadel, 190 Corporation Street, Birmingham B4 6QD ☎0121 233 8500 ✉clerks@citadelchambers.com
Call Date: Oct 2005, Inner Temple

Practising Areas: Crime

COLMAN MR ANDREW

2 Hare Court
Lower Ground, Ground, 1st & 2nd Floor, 2 Hare Court, Temple, London EC4Y 7BH ☎020 7353 3982 ✉clerks@2harecourt.com
Call Date: Jul 1980, Lincoln's Inn
Pupil Supervisor

COLQUHOUN MISS CELINA DAPHNE MARIAN

No5 Chambers
Greenwood House, 4-7 Salisbury Court, London EC4Y 8AA ☎0845 210 5555
No5 Chambers
38 Queen Square, Bristol BS1 4QS ☎0845 210 5555
No5 Chambers
Fountain Court, Steelhouse Lane, Birmingham B4 6DR ☎0845 210 5555 ✉info@no5.com
Call Date: Oct 1990, Gray's Inn
Pupil Supervisor

COLTART MR CHRISTOPHER MCCALLUM

2 Hare Court
Lower Ground, Ground, 1st & 2nd Floor, 2 Hare Court, Temple, London EC4Y 7BH ☎020 7353 3982 ✉clerks@2harecourt.com
Call Date: Nov 1998, Inner Temple
Pupil Supervisor

Practising Areas: Courts Martial, Crime, Crime (Corporate/Fraud), Regulatory Law

COLVILLE MR IAIN DAVID

Arden Chambers
20 Bloomsbury Square, London WC1A 2NS ☎020 7242 4244 ✉clerks@ardenchambers.com
Call Date: Jul 1989, Inner Temple

COMB MR DAVID WILLIAM

Trinity Chambers
The Custom House, 39 Quayside, Newcastle Upon Tyne NE1 3DE ☎0191 232 1927 ✉info@trinitychambers.co.uk
Trinity Chambers
Multi Media Exchange, 72-80 Corporation Road, Middlesbrough TS1 2RF ☎01642 247569 ✉info@trinitychambers.co.uk
Call Date: Oct 2005, Inner Temple

Practising Areas: Civil Liberties, Crime, Crime (Corporate/Fraud), Disciplinary Tribunals, Human Rights, Immigration, Regulatory Law

COMERTON MISS JULIE ANNE

4 KBW
Ground Floor, 4 King's Bench Walk, Temple, London EC4Y 7DL ☎020 7822 8822 ✉law@4kbw.net
Call Date: Jul 2003, Gray's Inn

Practising Areas: Common Law (General), Crime, Crime (Corporate/Fraud), Employment, Landlord & Tenant, Licensing, Local Government, Personal Injury

COMMON MR HAMISH ANDREW

23 Essex Street
London WC2R 3AA ☎020 7413 0353 ✉clerks@23es.com
Call Date: Jul 2003, Lincoln's Inn

Practising Areas: Crime, Crime (Corporate/Fraud)

COMPTON MR ALLAN SPENCER

2 Bedford Row
London WC1R 4BU ☎020 7440 8888 ✉clerks@2bedfordrow.co.uk
Call Date: Nov 1994, Inner Temple
Pupil Supervisor

COMPTON MR BENJAMIN EDWARD WELSTEAD QC (2011)

Outer Temple Chambers
The Outer Temple, 222 Strand, London WC2R 1BA ☎020 7353 6381 ✉clerks@outertemple.com
Call Date: Nov 1979, Lincoln's Inn
Pupil Supervisor, Recorder

Practising Areas: Crime, Crime (Corporate/Fraud), Health & Safety, Medical Negligence, Personal Injury, Regulatory Law

COMYN MR TIMOTHY JOHN

Francis Taylor Building
Inner Temple, London EC4Y 7BY
☎020 7353 8415 ✉clerks@ftb.eu.com
Call Date: Jul 1980, Inner Temple
Pupil Supervisor

CONLON MR MICHAEL JOHN PATRICK

Harcourt Chambers
1 Isling Brook, Shenley Brook End, Milton Keynes MK1 9AP ☎0845 123 1234
✉clerks@barristerweb.com
Call Date: Nov 1984, Inner Temple

Practising Areas: Common Law (General), Consumer, Courts Martial, Crime, Crime (Corporate/Fraud), Disciplinary Tribunals, Discrimination, Employment, Family, Family Provision, Health & Safety, Immigration, Personal Injury, Regulatory Law, Road Traffic And Highways

CONNELL MR EDWARD SAMUEL

Five St Andrew's Hill
5 St Andrew's Hill, London EC4V 5BZ
☎020 7332 5400 ✉Clerks@5sah.co.uk
Call Date: Oct 1996, Middle Temple

Practising Areas: Courts Martial, Crime, Crime (Corporate/Fraud), Road Traffic And Highways, Sports

CONNERTY MR ANTHONY ROBIN

Lamb Chambers
Lamb Building, Elm Court, Temple, London EC4Y 7AS ☎020 7797 8300
✉info@lambchambers.co.uk
Zenith Chambers
10 Park Square, Leeds LS1 2LH
☎0113 245 5438 ✉clerks@zenithchambers.co.uk
Arc Chambers
PO Box 256, St Leonards-On-Sea TN38 1GL
☎01424 204779
Call Date: Jul 1974, Inner Temple
Pupil Supervisor

CONNOLLY MRS BARBARA WINIFRED QC (2011)

Seven Bedford Row
7 Bedford Row, London WC1R 4BS
☎020 7242 3555 ✉clerks@7br.co.uk
Call Date: Jul 1986, Inner Temple
Pupil Supervisor

Practising Areas: Care Proceedings, Family, Family Provision

CONNOLLY MS DEIRDRE JOAN

Old Bailey Chambers
15 Old Bailey, London EC4M 7EF
☎020 3008 6404
✉clerks@15oldbaileychambers.com
Call Date: Nov 1982, Gray's Inn
Pupil Supervisor

Practising Areas: Crime, Crime (Corporate/Fraud)

CONNOLLY MR DOMINIC REGAN

Five St Andrew's Hill
5 St Andrew's Hill, London EC4V 5BZ
☎020 7332 5400 ✉Clerks@5sah.co.uk
Call Date: Feb 1989, Middle Temple
Pupil Supervisor

Practising Areas: Civil Liberties, Courts Martial, Crime, Crime (Corporate/Fraud), Defamation, Human Rights, Regulatory Law

CONNOLLY MR SIMON JAMES

3 Temple Gardens
Lower Ground Floor, 3 Temple Gardens, Temple, London EC4Y 9AU ☎020 7353 3102
✉clerks@3tg.co.uk
Call Date: Jul 1981, Middle Temple
Pupil Supervisor

CONNOLLY MR STEPHEN JAMES

Exchange Chambers
7 Ralli Courts, West Riverside, Manchester M3 5FT ☎0161 833 2722
Exchange Chambers
One Derby Square, Derby Square, Liverpool L2 9XX ☎0151 236 7747
✉info@exchangechambers.co.uk
Exchange Chambers
Oxford House, Oxford Row, Leeds LS1 3BE
☎0113 203 1970
✉spencer@exchangechambers.co.uk
Call Date: Nov 2003, Lincoln's Inn
Pupil Supervisor

CONOLLY DR OLIVER STEPHEN

Pump Court Tax Chambers
16 Bedford Row, London WC1R 4EF
☎020 7414 8080 ✉clerks@pumptax.com
Call Date: Mar 2003, Lincoln's Inn
Pupil Supervisor

Practising Areas: Equity, Wills & Trusts, Tax (Capital & Income), Tax (Corporate)

CONRAD MR ALAN DAVID QC (1999)

Lincoln House Chambers
Tower 12, The Avenue North, Spinningfields, 18-22 Bridge Street, Manchester M3 3BZ
☎0161 832 5701
✉info@lincolnhousechambers.com
St Ive's Chambers
Whittall Street, Birmingham B4 6DH
☎0121 236 0863 ✉clerks@stiveschambers.co.uk
Call Date: Jul 1976, Middle Temple
Recorder

Practising Areas: Crime, Crime (Corporate/Fraud)

CONRATH MR PHILIP BERNARD

Tanfield Chambers
2-5 Warwick Court, London WC1R 5DJ
☎020 7421 5300 ✉clerks@tanfieldchambers.co.uk
Call Date: Jul 1972, Gray's Inn
Pupil Supervisor

Practising Areas: Family, Family Provision

CONSTABLE MR ADAM MICHAEL QC (2011)

Keating Chambers
15 Essex Street, London WC2R 3AA
☎020 7544 2600 ✉clerks@keatingchambers.com
Call Date: Oct 1995, Inner Temple
Pupil Supervisor

Practising Areas: Commercial Litigation, Construction, Insurance, Professional Negligence

COOK MISS ALISON NOELE

St Philips Chambers
55 Temple Row, Birmingham B2 5LS
☎0121 246 7000 ✉clerks@st-philips.com
Call Date: Feb 1989, Gray's Inn

Practising Areas: Family, Family Provision

COOK MR PAUL GRAHAM WHALLEY

Albion Chambers
Broad Street, Bristol BS1 1DR
☎0117 927 2144 ✉clerks@albionchambers.co.uk
Call Date: Nov 1992, Middle Temple
Pupil Supervisor

Practising Areas: Crime, Employment

COOKE MR DUNCAN MATTHEW

Atkinson Bevan Chambers
1st Floor, 2 Harcourt Buildings, Temple, London EC4Y 9DB ☎020 7353 2112
✉clerks@2hb.co.uk
Call Date: Mar 2010, Inner Temple

Practising Areas: Crime

COOKE MR PETER RAYMOND

Cornwall Street Chambers
85-87 Cornwall Street, Birmingham B3 3BY
☎0121 233 7500 ✉clerks@cornwallstreet.co.uk
Call Date: Jul 1985, Lincoln's Inn
Pupil Supervisor, Recorder

COOKSEY MR NICHOLAS

River Chambers
81 Underdale Road, Shrewsbury, Shropshire SY2 5EF ☎01743 350505
✉richard@riverchambers.com
Call Date: Nov 2000, Middle Temple

Practising Areas: Common Law (General), Discrimination, Employment, Personal Injury

COOMBES MR TIMOTHY JAMES

3 PB Barristers
3 Paper Buildings, Temple, London EC4Y 7EU
☎020 7583 8055
3 PB Barristers
23 Beaumont Street, Oxford OX1 2NP
☎01865 793 736
3 PB Barristers
30 Christchurch Road, Bournemouth, Dorset BH1 3PD ☎01202 292102 ✉clerks.bournemouth@3paper.co.uk
3 PB Barristers
Royal Talbot House, 2 Victoria Street, Bristol, Avon BS1 6BB ☎0117 928 1520
3 PB Barristers
4 St Peter Street, Winchester SO23 8BW
☎01962 868884 ✉clerks.winchester@3paper.co.uk
Call Date: Jul 1980, Inner Temple
Pupil Supervisor

COOPER MR BEN LION

Doughty Street Chambers
53-54 Doughty Street, London WC1N 2LS
☎020 7404 1313 ✉enquiries@doughtystreet.co.uk
Doughty Street Chambers
Pall Mall Court, 61-67 King Street, Manchester M2 4PD ☎0161 618 1066

Doughty Street Chambers
5th Floor, Broad Quay House, Prince Street, Bristol BS1 4DJ ☎01179 058 717
Call Date: Nov 1999, Middle Temple
Pupil Supervisor

COOPER MISS CHRISTINE

Field Court Chambers
5 Field Court, Gray's Inn, London WC1R 5EF
☎020 7405 6114 ✉clerks@fieldcourt.co.uk
Call Date: Jul 2006, Inner Temple

Practising Areas: Chancery (Land Law), Commercial Litigation, Commercial Property, Housing, Landlord & Tenant, Local Government

COOPER MISS DANIELLE SOPHIE

Tooks Chambers
81 Farringdon Street, London EC4A 4BL
☎020 7842 7575 ✉clerks@tooks.co.uk
Call Date: Oct 1999, Lincoln's Inn

Practising Areas: Crime, Crime (Corporate/Fraud)

COOPER MR IAN MARK

Call Date: Mar 1998, Middle Temple

Practising Areas: Banking, Bankruptcy, Chancery (General), Commercial Litigation, Company & Commercial, Corporate Finance, Financial Services, Insolvency, Partnership, Professional Negligence, Share Options

COOPER MR JOHN GORDON QC (2010)

25 Bedford Row
London WC1R 4HD ☎020 7067 1500
✉clerks@25bedfordrow.com
Call Date: Jul 1983, Middle Temple
Pupil Supervisor

Practising Areas: Crime, Crime (Corporate/Fraud)

COOPER MR JOHN MICHAEL

Crown Office Chambers
2 Crown Office Row, Temple, London EC4Y 7HJ ☎020 7797 8100
✉mail@crownofficechambers.com
Call Date: Jul 1985, Inner Temple

Practising Areas: Environment, Health & Safety

COOPER MR PAUL ANDREW

Portal Chambers
Blaencwm Mawr, Llandysul SA44 5NS
☎01559 395 292
Call Date: Jul 1998, Middle Temple

Practising Areas: Common Law (General), Crime, Education, Licensing, Local Government, Town & Country Planning

COOPER MISS SAMANTHA ANN

Outer Temple Chambers
The Outer Temple, 222 Strand, London WC2R 1BA ☎020 7353 6381
✉clerks@outertemple.com
Call Date: Oct 2007, Gray's Inn

Practising Areas: Chancery (General), Discrimination, Employment, Equity, Wills & Trusts

CORNWALL MISS VIRGINIA MARGARET

Albion Chambers
Broad Street, Bristol BS1 1DR
☎0117 927 2144 ✉clerks@albionchambers.co.uk
Call Date: Oct 1990, Middle Temple

Practising Areas: Crime

CORRE MR NEIL BERNARD

Redbourne Chambers
44 Redbourne Avenue, London N3 2BS
☎020 8346 8524
Call Date: Mar 2005, Lincoln's Inn

Practising Areas: Crime, Crime (Corporate/Fraud), Road Traffic And Highways

CORRIE MR MATTHEW JOHN GALLOWAY

13 King's Bench Walk
13 King's Bench Walk, Temple, London EC4Y 7EN ☎020 7353 7204 ✉clerks@13kbw.co.uk
13 KBW
32 Beaumont Street, Oxford OX1 2NP
☎01865 311066 ✉clerks@13kbw.co.uk
Call Date: Jul 2006, Middle Temple

CORSELLIS MR NICHOLAS ROBERT ALEXANDER

3 Temple Gardens
Lower Ground Floor, 3 Temple Gardens, Temple, London EC4Y 9AU ☎020 7353 3102
✉clerks@3tg.co.uk
Call Date: Jul 1993, Lincoln's Inn

Practising Areas: Crime, Crime (Corporate/Fraud), Defamation, Financial Services, Licensing, Medical Negligence, Professional Negligence, Regulatory Law, Sports

COSTELLO MR PAUL JAMES

Chambers of Mr Paul J Costello
Apartment 1, Pegasus House, High Street, Biggleswade, Bedfordshire SG18 0FB
☎07846 016 399 ✉costellochambers@gmail.com
Call Date: Nov 1998, Inner Temple

Practising Areas: Company & Commercial, Crime, Crime (Corporate/Fraud), Disciplinary Tribunals, Discrimination, EC & Competition Law, Employment, Environment, Human Rights, Immigration, Professional Negligence, Sports

COSTER MR RONALD DAVID

42 Bedford Row
London WC1R 4LL ☎020 7831 0222
✉clerks@42br.com
Call Date: Jul 1989, Lincoln's Inn

Practising Areas: Administrative, Arbitration, Bankruptcy, Chancery (General), Chancery (Land Law), Civil Litigation, Commercial Litigation, Commercial Property, Common Land, Common Law (General), Company & Commercial, Construction, Consumer, Coroners Inquests, Data Protection, Defamation, Disciplinary Tribunals, Discrimination, Education, Employment, Environment, Equity, Wills & Trusts, Health & Safety, Housing, Human Rights, Industrial Diseases, Information Technology, Inquests, Insolvency, Insurance, Insurance/Reinsurance, International Trade, Land, Landlord & Tenant, Licensing, Medical Negligence, Partnership, Personal Injury, Private International, Probate & Administration, Professional Negligence, Road Traffic And Highways, Sale & Carriage of Goods, Shipping/Admiralty

COTCHER MISS ANN LOUISE QC (2000)

Farringdon Chambers
180 Bermondsey Street, London SE1 3TQ
☎020 7089 5700
Call Date: Jul 1979, Middle Temple

Practising Areas: Crime

COTTER MR MARK JAMES

Five St Andrew's Hill
5 St Andrew's Hill, London EC4V 5BZ
☎020 7332 5400 ✉Clerks@5sah.co.uk
Call Date: Nov 1994, Middle Temple
Pupil Supervisor

Practising Areas: Courts Martial, Crime, Crime (Corporate/Fraud), Education, Employment, Sports

COTTER MR NICHOLAS ANDREW JAMES HORLOR

1 Paper Buildings
1st Floor, 1 Paper Buildings, Temple, London EC4Y 7EP ☎020 7353 3728
✉clerks@onepaper.co.uk
Call Date: Oct 1999, Lincoln's Inn

Practising Areas: Crime, Crime (Corporate/Fraud), Disciplinary Tribunals, Regulatory Law, Sports

COTTERELL MR DAVID WILLIAM

Albion Chambers
Broad Street, Bristol BS1 1DR
☎0117 927 2144 ✉clerks@albionchambers.co.uk
Call Date: Nov 2001, Lincoln's Inn

Practising Areas: Agriculture, Chancery (Land Law), Commercial Property, Common Land, Landlord & Tenant, Town & Country Planning

COTTERILL MISS SUZANNAH

Field Court Chambers
5 Field Court, Gray's Inn, London WC1R 5EF
☎020 7405 6114 ✉clerks@fieldcourt.co.uk
Call Date: Jul 1988, Lincoln's Inn
Pupil Supervisor

Practising Areas: Care Proceedings, Family, Family Provision

COTTLE MR STEPHEN CHARLES

Garden Court Chambers
57-60 Lincoln's Inn Fields, London WC2A 3LJ
☎020 7993 7600 ✉info@gclaw.co.uk
Call Date: Nov 1984, Inner Temple
Pupil Supervisor

COTTON MRS HEIDI ELIZABETH

Bank House Chambers
Old Bank House, Hartshead, Sheffield S1 2EL
☎0114 275 1223 ✉w.digby@bankhousechambers.co.uk
Call Date: Jul 1998, Lincoln's Inn

Practising Areas: Crime

COUGHLIN MR VINCENT WILLIAM QC (2003)

18 Red Lion Court
London EC4A 3EB ☎020 7520 6000
✉chambers@18rlc.co.uk
Apex
Harlech House, 20 Cathedral Road, Cardiff CF11 9LJ ☎02920 232 032
✉clerks@apexchambers.net

C

Temple Chambers
32 Park Place, Cardiff CF10 3BA
☎029 2039 7364
✉DBrinning@Temple-Chambers.co.uk
1 High Pavement
Nottingham NG1 1HF ☎0115 941 8218
✉clerks@1highpavement.co.uk
Call Date: Jul 1980, Middle Temple

COULTER MR BARRY JOHN

Clerksroom (Taunton)
Equity House, Administration Centre, Blackbrook Park Avenue, Taunton, Somerset TA1 2PX ☎0845 083 3000
✉mail@clerksroom.com
Clerksroom (London)
3rd Floor, 218 Strand, London WC2R 1AT
☎0845 083 3000 ✉mail@clerksroom.com
King's Lynn Chambers
26 The Birches, South Wootton, King's Lynn, Norfolk PE30 3JG ☎01553 672 085
✉timothy.leader@tesco.net
Call Date: Nov 1985, Inner Temple

Practising Areas: Commercial Litigation, Common Law (General), Company & Commercial, Construction, Discrimination, Employment, Energy, Entertainment, Film, Cable & TV, Foreign Law, Franchising, Health & Safety, Insolvency, Insurance, Intellectual Property, International Trade, Medical Negligence, Partnership, Personal Injury, Professional Negligence, Sale & Carriage of Goods, Shipping/Admiralty, Sports

COUNSELL MR EDWARD FREDERICK

Unity Street Chambers
5 Unity Street, College Green, Bristol BS1 5HH ☎0117 906 9789
✉chambers@unitystreetchambers.com
Call Date: Nov 1990, Inner Temple
Pupil Supervisor

Practising Areas: Chancery (General), Equity, Wills & Trusts, Family, Family Provision

COUNSELL MR JAMES HENRY

Outer Temple Chambers
The Outer Temple, 222 Strand, London WC2R 1BA ☎020 7353 6381
✉clerks@outertemple.com
Call Date: Jul 1984, Inner Temple
Pupil Supervisor

Practising Areas: Medical Negligence, Personal Injury, Professional Negligence, Regulatory Law

COURTS MR ROBERT ALEXANDER

3 PB Barristers
3 Paper Buildings, Temple, London EC4Y 7EU
☎020 7583 8055
3 PB Barristers
Royal Talbot House, 2 Victoria Street, Bristol, Avon BS1 6BB ☎0117 928 1520
3 PB Barristers
23 Beaumont Street, Oxford OX1 2NP
☎01865 793 736
3 PB Barristers
4 St Peter Street, Winchester SO23 8BW
☎01962 868884 ✉clerks.winchester@3paper.co.uk
3 PB Barristers
30 Christchurch Road, Bournemouth, Dorset BH1 3PD ☎01202 292102 ✉clerks.bournemouth@3paper.co.uk
Call Date: Jul 2003, Lincoln's Inn

COUSENS MR MICHAEL PATRICK

Carmelite Chambers
9 Carmelite Street, London EC4Y 0DR
☎020 7936 6300
✉clerks@carmelitechambers.co.uk
Call Date: Feb 1973, Lincoln's Inn
Pupil Supervisor

Practising Areas: Courts Martial

COWLEY MR ROBERT

No 8 Chambers
8 Fountain Court, Steelhouse Lane, Birmingham B4 6DR ☎0121 236 5514
✉clerks@no8chambers.co.uk
Call Date: Oct 1992, Lincoln's Inn

Practising Areas: Crime

COX MR JONATHAN EDWARD

KCH Garden Square
1 Oxford Street, Nottingham NG1 5BH
☎0115 941 8851 ✉clerks@kchgardensquare.co.uk
Call Date: Oct 2005, Lincoln's Inn

Practising Areas: Crime, Crime (Corporate/Fraud), Education, Health & Safety, Licensing, Regulatory Law

COX MISS KERRY AMANDA

Park Lane Plowden
Lombard House, 4-8 Lombard Street, Newcastle Upon Tyne NE1 3AE
☎0191 211 4087 ✉clerks@parklaneplowden.co.uk
Call Date: Oct 1990, Inner Temple
Pupil Supervisor

Practising Areas: Common Law (General), Personal Injury

COX MISS OLIVIA RODRIGUES

Atlantic Chambers
4-6 Cook Street, Liverpool L2 9QU
☎0151 236 4421 ✉info@atlanticchambers.co.uk
Call Date: Nov 2007, Middle Temple

Practising Areas: Commercial Litigation, Common Law (General), Construction, Personal Injury, Professional Negligence, Sale & Carriage of Goods

COX MS SITA

Stour Chambers
Mill Studio, 17a Stour Street, Canterbury, Kent CT1 2NR ☎01227 764899
✉clerks@stourchambers.co.uk
Call Date: Nov 1987, Middle Temple
Pupil Supervisor

Practising Areas: Care Proceedings, Common Law (General), Family, Family Provision, Personal Injury

COXHILL MR FRASER

QEB Hollis Whiteman
1-2 Laurence Pountney Hill, London EC4R 0EU ☎020 7933 8855 ✉barristers@qebhw.co.uk
Call Date: Jul 2004, Lincoln's Inn

COYLE MR ANTHONY NOEL

Zenith Chambers
10 Park Square, Leeds LS1 2LH
☎0113 245 5438 ✉clerks@zenithchambers.co.uk
Call Date: Nov 2003, Lincoln's Inn

Practising Areas: Civil Liberties, Common Law (General), Discrimination, Education, Employment, Local Government, Mental Health, Parliamentary, Personal Injury

CRABB MISS SAMANTHA JILL

Citadel Chambers
The Citadel, 190 Corporation Street, Birmingham B4 6QD ☎0121 233 8500
✉clerks@citadelchambers.com
Call Date: Nov 1996, Inner Temple

Practising Areas: Crime, Crime (Corporate/Fraud), Regulatory Law

CRAIG MR AUBREY JOHN

St Philips Chambers
55 Temple Row, Birmingham B2 5LS
☎0121 246 7000 ✉clerks@st-philips.com
Chancery House Chambers
7 Lisbon Square, Leeds, West Yorkshire LS1 4LY ☎0113 244 6691
✉clerks@chanceryhouse.co.uk
Call Date: Nov 1987, Inner Temple

Practising Areas: Competition, Copyright, Defamation, EC & Competition Law, Intellectual Property, Patents, Trademarks

CRAMSIE MR JAMES SINCLAIR BERESFORD

13 King's Bench Walk
13 King's Bench Walk, Temple, London EC4Y 7EN ☎020 7353 7204 ✉clerks@13kbw.co.uk
13 KBW
32 Beaumont Street, Oxford OX1 2NP
☎01865 311066 ✉clerks@13kbw.co.uk
Call Date: Nov 1988, Inner Temple
Pupil Supervisor

Practising Areas: Chancery (Land Law), Commercial Litigation, Employment, Professional Negligence

CRANGLE MR THOMAS PETER

4 Pump Court
4 Pump Court, Temple, London EC4Y 7AN
☎020 7842 5555 ✉chambers@4pumpcourt.com
Call Date: Jul 2002, Gray's Inn

Practising Areas: Common Law (General), Construction, Information Technology, Insurance, Professional Negligence, Sale & Carriage of Goods

CRASNOW MS RACHEL

Cloisters
1 Pump Court, Temple, London EC4Y 7AA
☎020 7827 4000 ✉clerks@cloisters.com
Call Date: Nov 1994, Middle Temple
Pupil Supervisor

Practising Areas: Discrimination, Employment

CRAWFORD MR LINCOLN SANTO

12 King's Bench Walk
12 King's Bench Walk, Temple, London EC4Y 7EL ☎020 7583 0811
Call Date: Nov 1977, Gray's Inn
Pupil Supervisor

Practising Areas: Administrative, Discrimination, Employment, Local Government, Medical Negligence, Personal Injury, Sports

CRAWLEY MR ROSS ALEXANDER

Middle Temple Lane Chambers
2nd Floor South, 1 Middle Temple Lane, London EC4Y 9AA ☎ 020 7583 4352
✉ chambers@mtlchambers.com
Call Date: Jul 2005, Middle Temple

Practising Areas: Common Law (General), Company & Commercial, Crime, Employment, Insolvency, Landlord & Tenant, Personal Injury, Regulatory Law

CRAWSHAW MR SIMON RICHARD

Atkin Chambers
1 Atkin Building, Gray's Inn, London WC1R 5AT ☎ 020 7404 0102
✉ clerks@atkinchambers.com
Call Date: Jul 2005, Lincoln's Inn

Practising Areas: Arbitration, Company & Commercial, Construction, Information Technology, Professional Negligence

CREW MISS GILLIAN MARY

Ely Place Chambers
30 Ely Place, London EC1N 6TD
☎ 020 7400 9600 ✉ admin@elyplace.com
Call Date: Oct 1998, Gray's Inn
Pupil Supervisor

Practising Areas: Chancery (General), Chancery (Land Law), Civil Litigation, Commercial Property, Common Law (General), Coroners Inquests, Costs, Discrimination, Employment, Equity, Wills & Trusts, Housing, Inquests, Insolvency, Land, Landlord & Tenant, Licensing, Local Government, Personal Injury

CRINION MR CHARLES EDWARD

1 Mitre Court Buildings
1 Mitre Court Buildings, Temple, London EC4Y 7BS ☎ 020 7452 8900 ✉ clerks@1mcb.com
Call Date: Nov 2002, Middle Temple

Practising Areas: Common Law (General), Crime, Employment, Sports

CRINNION MRS NEENA LATIFA

3 Temple Gardens
Lower Ground Floor, 3 Temple Gardens, Temple, London EC4Y 9AU ☎ 020 7353 3102
✉ clerks@3tg.co.uk
Call Date: Oct 1997, Gray's Inn
Pupil Supervisor

CRITCHLEY MR JOHN STEPHEN

Field Court Chambers
5 Field Court, Gray's Inn, London WC1R 5EF
☎ 020 7405 6114 ✉ clerks@fieldcourt.co.uk
Call Date: Jul 1985, Gray's Inn
Pupil Supervisor

Practising Areas: Chancery (General), Civil Liberties, Civil Litigation, Common Law (General), Copyright, Defamation, Entertainment, Human Rights, Intellectual Property, Partnership, Sports, Trademarks

CROALLY MR MILES JAMES

Field Court Chambers
5 Field Court, Gray's Inn, London WC1R 5EF
☎ 020 7405 6114 ✉ clerks@fieldcourt.co.uk
Call Date: Nov 1987, Middle Temple
Pupil Supervisor

CROCKER MISS ELIZABETH ALEXANDRA

15 New Bridge Street
London EC4V 6AU ☎ 020 7842 1900
✉ clerks@15nbs.com
Call Date: Nov 2006, Middle Temple

CRONIN MISS KATHRYN

Garden Court Chambers
57-60 Lincoln's Inn Fields, London WC2A 3LJ
☎ 020 7993 7600 ✉ info@gclaw.co.uk
Call Date: Jul 1980, Middle Temple

CROSFILL MR JOHN

Field Court Chambers
5 Field Court, Gray's Inn, London WC1R 5EF
☎ 020 7405 6114 ✉ clerks@fieldcourt.co.uk
Call Date: Nov 1995, Middle Temple
Pupil Supervisor

Practising Areas: Civil Liberties, Civil Litigation, Employment, Human Rights, Regulatory Law

CROSKELL MR MARCUS JAMES

East Anglian Chambers
53 North Hill, Colchester, Essex CO1 1QA
☎ 01473 214481 ✉ colchester@ealaw.co.uk
East Anglian Chambers
140 New London Road, Chelmsford, Essex CM2 0AW ☎ 01473 214481
✉ chelmsford@ealaw.co.uk
East Anglian Chambers
15 The Close, Norwich, Norfolk NR1 4DZ
☎ 01473 214481 ✉ norwich@ealaw.co.uk
East Anglian Chambers
Gresham House, 5 Museum Street, Ipswich, Suffolk IP1 1HQ ☎ 01473 214481
✉ ipswich@ealaw.co.uk
Call Date: Jul 2003, Lincoln's Inn

Practising Areas: Civil Litigation, Common Law (General), Courts Martial, Crime, Equity, Wills & Trusts, Housing, Landlord & Tenant, Licensing, Personal Injury, Road Traffic And Highways

CROSS MR ANTHONY MAURICE QC (2006)

Lincoln House Chambers
Tower 12, The Avenue North, Spinningfields, 18-22 Bridge Street, Manchester M3 3BZ
☎0161 832 5701
✉info@lincolnhousechambers.com
Call Date: Nov 1982, Middle Temple
Recorder

Practising Areas: Crime, Crime (Corporate/Fraud), Sports

CROSSFIELD MISS ANNE

Erimus Chambers
PO Box 1440, Bedford MK43 6AJ
☎01234 720952 ✉clerks@erimuschambers.com
Call Date: Jul 1993, Lincoln's Inn

CROSSLEY MS JOANNE

St Paul's Chambers
5th Floor, St Paul's House, 23 Park Square South, Leeds LS1 2ND ☎0113 245 5866
Call Date: Nov 1994, Middle Temple

Practising Areas: Care Proceedings, Family, Family Provision

CROSSLEY MR SIMON JUSTIN

Zenith Chambers
10 Park Square, Leeds LS1 2LH
☎0113 245 5438 ✉clerks@zenithchambers.co.uk
Call Date: Nov 1993, Inner Temple
Pupil Supervisor

CROUCH MR STEPHEN WILLIAM MICHAEL

The Chambers of S W M Crouch
6 The Glebe, Badby, Northamptonshire NN11 3AZ ☎01327 315 742
Call Date: Jul 1982, Inner Temple

Practising Areas: Common Law (General), Licensing, Sports

CROW MR CHARLES DUNCAN TIMOTHY

No5 Chambers
Fountain Court, Steelhouse Lane, Birmingham B4 6DR ☎0845 210 5555 ✉info@no5.com
No5 Chambers
Greenwood House, 4-7 Salisbury Court, London EC4Y 8AA ☎0845 210 5555
No5 Chambers
38 Queen Square, Bristol BS1 4QS
☎0845 210 5555
Call Date: Oct 1999, Lincoln's Inn

Practising Areas: Employment, Personal Injury

CROWE MR CAMERON

36 Bedford Row
London WC1R 4JH ☎020 7421 8000
✉chambers@36bedfordrow.co.uk
Call Date: Oct 2002, Inner Temple

Practising Areas: Common Law (General), Crime, Crime (Corporate/Fraud), Intellectual Property, Professional Negligence, Regulatory Law, Sports, Town & Country Planning

CROWLEY MR DANIEL JOHN

2 Temple Gardens
2 Temple Gardens, Temple, London EC4Y 9AY ☎020 7822 1200 ✉clerks@2tg.co.uk
Call Date: Oct 1990, Gray's Inn
Pupil Supervisor

Practising Areas: Arbitration, Commercial Litigation, Common Law (General), Company & Commercial, Construction, Environment, Insurance, Insurance/Reinsurance, Private International, Professional Negligence, Sale & Carriage of Goods

CROWLEY MISS LAURA LOUISE

4 Pump Court
4 Pump Court, Temple, London EC4Y 7AN
☎020 7842 5555 ✉chambers@4pumpcourt.com
Call Date: Jul 2005, Inner Temple

CROWTHER MS LUCY ELLEN

Apex
Harlech House, 20 Cathedral Road, Cardiff CF11 9LJ ☎02920 232 032
✉clerks@apexchambers.net
Call Date: Oct 1999, Inner Temple

Practising Areas: Crime, Crime (Corporate/Fraud), Employment, Regulatory Law

CROWTHER MR THOMAS EDWARD

Apex
Harlech House, 20 Cathedral Road, Cardiff CF11 9LJ ☎ 02920 232 032
✉ clerks@apexchambers.net
Call Date: Nov 1993, Inner Temple
Pupil Supervisor

Practising Areas: Crime

CRYSTAL MR JONATHAN

Argent Chambers
5 Bell Yard, London WC2A 2JR
☎ 020 7556 5500
✉ briefsin@argentchambers.co.uk
Call Date: Jul 1972, Middle Temple
Pupil Supervisor

Practising Areas: Commercial Litigation, Defamation, Entertainment, Sports

CUDDY MISS NATALIE LOUISE

Atlantic Chambers
4-6 Cook Street, Liverpool L2 9QU
☎ 0151 236 4421 ✉ info@atlanticchambers.co.uk
Call Date: Nov 2005, Inner Temple

CULLEN MISS GRACE CATHERINE

6 Pump Court
1st Floor, 6 Pump Court, Temple, London EC4Y 7AR ☎ 020 7797 8400
✉ richardconstable@6pumpcourt.co.uk
6 Pump Court Chambers
6-8 Mill Street, Maidstone, Kent ME15 6XH
☎ 01622 688094 ✉ annexe@6pumpcourt.co.uk
Call Date: Oct 2005, Lincoln's Inn

CULLEN MR JAMES WILLIAM CHRISTOPHER

Linenhall Chambers
1 Stanley Place, Chester CH1 2LU
☎ 01244 348282
✉ clerks@linenhallchambers.co.uk
Call Date: Jul 2003, Lincoln's Inn

CULLEN MR STUART JOHN

33 Bedford Row
London WC1R 4JH ☎ 020 7242 6476
✉ clerks@33bedfordrow.co.uk
Call Date: Oct 2006, Inner Temple

CULLEY MISS LAURA JOAN

Citadel Chambers
The Citadel, 190 Corporation Street, Birmingham B4 6QD ☎ 0121 233 8500
✉ clerks@citadelchambers.com
Call Date: Oct 2006, Lincoln's Inn

Practising Areas: Common Law (General), Crime, Crime (Corporate/Fraud), Personal Injury

CULMER MISS GABRIELLE FIONA

2 King's Bench Walk
2 King's Bench Walk, Temple, London EC4Y 7DE ☎ 020 7353 1746 ✉ clerks@2kbw.com
Call Date: Oct 1999, Gray's Inn

Practising Areas: Chancery (General), Commercial Litigation, Foreign Law, Insolvency

CULVER MR EDWARD JAMES

4 King's Bench Walk
2nd Floor, 4 King's Bench Walk, Temple, London EC4Y 7DL ☎ 020 7822 7000
✉ clerks@4kbw.co.uk
Call Date: Jul 2005, Inner Temple

Practising Areas: Courts Martial, Crime, Licensing

CULVERHOUSE MISS EMILY ANNA LOUISE

Chambers of Miss E Culverhouse
18 Upper Gladstone Road, Chesham, Buckinghamshire HP5 3AF ☎ 07813 007503
✉ e.culverhouse@sky.com
Call Date: Nov 1998, Lincoln's Inn
Pupil Supervisor

Practising Areas: Courts Martial, Crime, Employment, Family, Immigration, Medical Negligence, Mental Health, Personal Injury

CUNNINGHAM MISS ELIZABETH ALICE

Albion Chambers
Broad Street, Bristol BS1 1DR
☎ 0117 927 2144 ✉ clerks@albionchambers.co.uk
Call Date: Oct 1995, Middle Temple

Practising Areas: Employment

C

CUNNINGHAM MR GRAHAM TAYLOR

Hardwicke
New Square, Lincoln's Inn, London WC2A 3SB ☎ 020 7242 2523
✉ enquiries@hardwicke.co.uk
Call Date: Jul 1976, Gray's Inn

Practising Areas: Commercial Litigation, Company & Commercial, Competition, Copyright, EC & Competition Law, Franchising, Information Technology, Intellectual Property, Sale & Carriage of Goods, Telecommunications, Trademarks

CUNNINGHAM MS NAOMI BRIGID

Outer Temple Chambers
The Outer Temple, 222 Strand, London WC2R 1BA ☎ 020 7353 6381
✉ clerks@outertemple.com
Call Date: Feb 1994, Inner Temple
Pupil Supervisor

Practising Areas: Discrimination, Employment

CURRER MR PAUL JOSEPH

Trinity Chambers
The Custom House, 39 Quayside, Newcastle Upon Tyne NE1 3DE ☎ 0191 232 1927
✉ info@trinitychambers.co.uk
Trinity Chambers
Multi Media Exchange, 72-80 Corporation Road, Middlesbrough TS1 2RF
☎ 01642 247569 ✉ info@trinitychambers.co.uk
Call Date: Jul 2000, Middle Temple

CURRIE MR FERGUS HUGH

Unity Street Chambers
5 Unity Street, College Green, Bristol BS1 5HH ☎ 0117 906 9789
✉ chambers@unitystreetchambers.com
Call Date: Mar 1997, Gray's Inn
Pupil Supervisor

Practising Areas: Common Law (General), Discrimination, Employment, Personal Injury

CURTIS MS HELEN JANE

Garden Court Chambers
57-60 Lincoln's Inn Fields, London WC2A 3LJ
☎ 020 7993 7600 ✉ info@gclaw.co.uk
Call Date: Nov 1992, Middle Temple
Pupil Supervisor

CURTIS MR MICHAEL ALEXANDER QC (2008)

Crown Office Chambers
2 Crown Office Row, Temple, London EC4Y 7HJ ☎ 020 7797 8100
✉ mail@crownofficechambers.com
Call Date: Nov 1982, Middle Temple

Practising Areas: Administrative, Arbitration, Commercial Litigation, Common Law (General), Construction, Insurance, Professional Negligence

CURWEN MR DAVID CHRISTIAN

Unity Street Chambers
5 Unity Street, College Green, Bristol BS1 5HH ☎ 0117 906 9789
✉ chambers@unitystreetchambers.com
Call Date: Jul 1982, Gray's Inn
Pupil Supervisor

Practising Areas: Employment, Personal Injury

DA COSTA-WALDMAN MRS ELISSA JOSEPHINE

Clerksroom (Taunton)
Equity House, Administration Centre, Blackbrook Park Avenue, Taunton, Somerset TA1 2PX ☎ 0845 083 3000
✉ mail@clerksroom.com
Clerksroom (London)
3rd Floor, 218 Strand, London WC2R 1AT
☎ 0845 083 3000 ✉ mail@clerksroom.com
King's Lynn Chambers
26 The Birches, South Wootton, King's Lynn, Norfolk PE30 3JG ☎ 01553 672 085
✉ timothy.leader@tesco.net
Call Date: Oct 1990, Middle Temple

Practising Areas: Ancillary Relief, Chancery (General), Children's Law, Civil Litigation, Family, Family Provision

DACEY MR MARK

5 King's Bench Walk
5 King's Bench Walk, Temple, London EC4Y 7DN ☎ 020 7353 5638 ✉ clerks@5kbw.co.uk
Call Date: Nov 1985, Middle Temple
Pupil Supervisor

DAGG MR JOHN DOUGLAS

Trinity Chambers
Highfield House, Moulsham Street, Chelmsford, Essex CM2 9AH
☎ 01245 605040 ✉ clerks@trinitychambers.com
Call Date: Jul 1980, Middle Temple
Pupil Supervisor

Practising Areas: Administrative, Chancery (Land Law), Environment, Licensing, Local Government, Town & Country Planning

DALAL MR RAJEN CHARLES JAMES

Cobden House Chambers
19 Quay Street, Manchester M3 3HN
☎ 0161 833 6000 ✉ Clerks@Cobden.co.uk
Derwent Chambers
78 Friar Gate, Derby DE1 1FL
☎ 01332 242425
✉ admin@derwentchambers.co.uk
Call Date: Oct 1991, Lincoln's Inn

Practising Areas: Employment, Family, Personal Injury

DALBY MR JOSEPH FRANCIS

4-5 Gray's Inn Square
Gray's Inn, London WC1R 5AH
☎ 020 7404 5252 ✉ clerks@4-5.co.uk
Call Date: Jul 1988, Middle Temple

Practising Areas: Administrative, Chancery (General), Chancery (Land Law), Commercial Litigation, Common Law (General), Company & Commercial, Competition, EC & Competition Law, Financial Services, Local Government, Private International, Public International, Public Law, Regulatory Law

DALE MISS LUCY-ANN GEORGIA

4 Brick Court
4 Brick Court, Temple, London EC4Y 9AD
☎ 020 7832 3200 ✉ clerks@4bc.co.uk
Call Date: Jul 2002, Lincoln's Inn

Practising Areas: Children's Law, Family, Family Provision

C

DALY MR DAVID

Heathway Chambers
31 Heathway, London SE3 7AN
☎ 020 8293 0509 ✉ daviddaly@talktalk.net
Call Date: Jul 1979, Middle Temple

Practising Areas: Administrative, Chancery (General), Chancery (Land Law), Discrimination, Education, Employment, Environment, Family Provision, Housing, Landlord & Tenant, Local Government, Probate & Administration

DALY MISS ORLA MAIRE

5 King's Bench Walk
5 King's Bench Walk, Temple, London EC4Y 7DN ☎ 020 7353 5638 ✉ clerks@5kbw.co.uk
Call Date: Nov 2000, Gray's Inn

Practising Areas: Crime

DANIELS MR DAVID WILLIAM

Rowchester Chambers
4 Rowchester Court, Whittall Street, Birmingham B4 6DH ☎ 0121 233 2327
✉ clerks@rowchesterchambers.co.uk
Call Date: Oct 1995, Lincoln's Inn

Practising Areas: Common Law (General), Family, Family Provision, Personal Injury

DANIELS MISS PHILIPPA CATHERINE

36 Bedford Row
London WC1R 4JH ☎ 020 7421 8000
✉ chambers@36bedfordrow.co.uk
Call Date: Oct 1995, Inner Temple

Practising Areas: Banking, Bankruptcy, Chancery (General), Chancery (Land Law), Commercial Litigation, Company & Commercial, Equity, Wills & Trusts, Insolvency, Landlord & Tenant, Sale & Carriage of Goods

DARBISHIRE MR ADRIAN MUNRO QC (2012)

QEB Hollis Whiteman
1-2 Laurence Pountney Hill, London EC4R 0EU ☎ 020 7933 8855 ✉ barristers@qebhw.co.uk
Call Date: Oct 1993, Lincoln's Inn
Pupil Supervisor

Practising Areas: Competition, Crime, Crime (Corporate/Fraud), Health & Safety, Regulatory Law

DARBY MS RACHEL ZOE

Charter Chambers
33 John Street, London WC1N 2AT
☎ 020 7618 4400 ✉ clerks@charterchambers.com
Call Date: Oct 1997, Inner Temple
Pupil Supervisor

DARLING MR PAUL ANTONY QC (1999)

Keating Chambers
15 Essex Street, London WC2R 3AA
☎ 020 7544 2600 ✉ clerks@keatingchambers.com
Call Date: Jul 1983, Middle Temple

Practising Areas: Arbitration, Commercial Litigation, Construction, Energy, Environment, Professional Negligence

DARLINGTON MISS ELIZABETH

Zenith Chambers
10 Park Square, Leeds LS1 2LH
☎0113 245 5438 ✉clerks@zenithchambers.co.uk
5 Pump Court
Ground Floor, 5 Pump Court, Temple, London EC4Y 7AP ☎020 7353 2532
✉clerks@5pumpcourt.com
Call Date: Oct 1998, Middle Temple

Practising Areas: Common Law (General), Personal Injury

DARROCH MISS FIONA CULVERWELL

Clerksroom (Taunton)
Equity House, Administration Centre, Blackbrook Park Avenue, Taunton, Somerset TA1 2PX ☎0845 083 3000
✉mail@clerksroom.com
Clerksroom (London)
3rd Floor, 218 Strand, London WC2R 1AT
☎0845 083 3000 ✉mail@clerksroom.com
King's Lynn Chambers
26 The Birches, South Wootton, King's Lynn, Norfolk PE30 3JG ☎01553 672 085
✉timothy.leader@tesco.net
Call Date: Oct 1994, Inner Temple

Practising Areas: Administrative, Agriculture, Chancery (General), Civil Litigation, Common Law (General), Crime (Corporate/Fraud), EC & Competition Law, Energy, Environment, Human Rights, Public International, Public Law, Town & Country Planning

DARTON MR CLIFFORD JOHN

Pallant Chambers
12 North Pallant, Chichester, West Sussex PO19 1TQ ☎01243 784538
✉clerks@pallantchambers.co.uk
Call Date: Jul 1988, Middle Temple
Pupil Supervisor

DASHANI MISS SONAL

15 New Bridge Street
London EC4V 6AU ☎020 7842 1900
✉clerks@15nbs.com
Call Date: Nov 2002, Lincoln's Inn

Practising Areas: Courts Martial, Crime, Crime (Corporate/Fraud)

DASSA MISS REGINE

9 King's Bench Walk
Lower Ground Floor South, 9 King's Bench Walk, Temple, London EC4Y 7DX
☎020 7353 9564 ✉9kbw@btconnect.com
Call Date: Oct 1999, Lincoln's Inn

Practising Areas: Care Proceedings, Common Law (General), Crime, Family, Human Rights, Immigration, Licensing

DATTA MR SHOMIK

42 Bedford Row
London WC1R 4LL ☎020 7831 0222
✉clerks@42br.com
Call Date: Nov 2000, Gray's Inn

Practising Areas: Chancery (Land Law), Common Law (General), Housing, Landlord & Tenant

DAVE MISS PRIYA

3 Temple Gardens
Lower Ground Floor, 3 Temple Gardens, Temple, London EC4Y 9AU ☎020 7353 3102
✉clerks@3tg.co.uk
Call Date: Oct 2006, Lincoln's Inn

Practising Areas: Crime

DAVENPORT MR RICHARD IAN

Citadel Chambers
The Citadel, 190 Corporation Street, Birmingham B4 6QD ☎0121 233 8500
✉clerks@citadelchambers.com
Call Date: Oct 2002, Gray's Inn

Practising Areas: Crime, Crime (Corporate/Fraud), Family, Road Traffic And Highways

DAVEY MR CHARLES

Clerksroom (Taunton)
Equity House, Administration Centre, Blackbrook Park Avenue, Taunton, Somerset TA1 2PX ☎0845 083 3000
✉mail@clerksroom.com
64 Bridge Street
3rd Floor, 64 Bridge Street, Manchester M3 3BN ☎0845 083 3000
✉mail@64bridgestreet.com
Chambers of Mr C Davey
7 Blair Close, Bishop's Stortford CM23 4PR
☎01279 506412 ✉charlesdavey@gmx.com
Call Date: Feb 1989, Middle Temple

Practising Areas: Bankruptcy, Civil Liberties, Commercial Litigation, Common Law (General), Discrimination, Employment, Human Rights, Insolvency, Landlord & Tenant, Personal Injury, Professional Negligence

DAVEY MR NEIL MARTIN QC (2001)

39 Park Square
Leeds LS1 2NU ☎0113 245 6633
✉seniorclerk@39parksquarechambers.co.uk
3 Temple Gardens
Lower Ground Floor, 3 Temple Gardens, Temple, London EC4Y 9AU ☎020 7353 3102
✉clerks@3tg.co.uk
Old Court Chambers
Newham House, 96-98 Borough Road, Middlesbrough TS1 2HJ ☎01642 232523
✉clerks@oldcourtchambers.com
Call Date: Jul 1978, Middle Temple

Practising Areas: Courts Martial, Crime, Licensing

DAVIDGE MISS JUSTINE MARIE

4 King's Bench Walk
2nd Floor, 4 King's Bench Walk, Temple, London EC4Y 7DL ☎020 7822 7000
✉clerks@4kbw.co.uk
Call Date: Jul 2001, Gray's Inn
Pupil Supervisor

Practising Areas: Crime, Crime (Corporate/Fraud), Regulatory Law

DAVIDSON MR ANDREW EDWARD

Citadel Chambers
The Citadel, 190 Corporation Street, Birmingham B4 6QD ☎0121 233 8500
✉clerks@citadelchambers.com
Call Date: Oct 2003, Gray's Inn

Practising Areas: Courts Martial, Crime, Licensing, Regulatory Law

DAVIDSON MISS LAURA ANNE

No5 Chambers
Greenwood House, 4-7 Salisbury Court, London EC4Y 8AA ☎0845 210 5555
No5 Chambers
38 Queen Square, Bristol BS1 4QS
☎0845 210 5555
No5 Chambers
Fountain Court, Steelhouse Lane, Birmingham B4 6DR ☎0845 210 5555 ✉info@no5.com
Call Date: Oct 1996, Lincoln's Inn

DAVIE MISS SARA WOODHOUSE

Chambers of Ian Macdonald QC
Garden Court North, 22 Oxford Court, Manchester M2 3WQ ☎0161 236 1840
✉clerks@gcnchambers.co.uk
Call Date: Jul 2007, Middle Temple

DAVIES MISS CAROL ELIZABETH

College Chambers
19 Carlton Crescent, Southampton, Hampshire SO15 2ET ☎023 8023 0338
✉clerks@college-chambers.co.uk
Call Date: Oct 1995, Middle Temple
Pupil Supervisor

Practising Areas: Chancery (General), Chancery (Land Law), Civil Litigation, Commercial Litigation, Common Law (General), Equity, Wills & Trusts, Family Provision, Landlord & Tenant, Professional Negligence

DAVIES MISS CLAIRE SUZANNE

Farringdon Chambers
180 Bermondsey Street, London SE1 3TQ
☎020 7089 5700
Call Date: Jul 1999, Middle Temple

Practising Areas: Crime, Crime (Corporate/Fraud), Mental Health

DAVIES MS ELIZABETH MARY

Garden Court Chambers
57-60 Lincoln's Inn Fields, London WC2A 3LJ
☎020 7993 7600 ✉info@gclaw.co.uk
Call Date: Feb 1994, Inner Temple
Pupil Supervisor

Practising Areas: Administrative, Housing, Landlord & Tenant, Local Government

DAVIES MR HENRY OLUSOLA

Trinity Chambers
Suite 441, 27 Colmore Row, Birmingham B3 2EW ☎0121 346 4672 ✉tchambersb@aol.com
Call Date: Nov 1999, Middle Temple
Pupil Supervisor

Practising Areas: Administrative, Civil Litigation, Common Law (General), Crime, Crime (Corporate/Fraud), Employment, Foreign Law, Human Rights, Immigration, Personal Injury, Public International, Public Law, Road Traffic And Highways

DAVIES MR HUGH CURRY

3 Raymond Buildings
3 Raymond Buildings, Gray's Inn, London WC1R 5BH ☎020 7400 6400
✉clerks@3rblaw.com
Call Date: Oct 1990, Lincoln's Inn
Pupil Supervisor

DAVIES MR HUW PROTHEROE

Farrar's Building
Farrar's Building, Temple, London EC4Y 7BD
☎ 020 7583 9241
✉ Chambers@farrarsbuilding.co.uk
Call Date: Oct 1998, Gray's Inn
Pupil Supervisor

DAVIES MR JAKE SEBASTIAN HUNTER

Five Paper
Ground Floor, 5 Paper Buildings, Temple, London EC4Y 7HB ☎ 020 7815 3200
Call Date: Oct 1997, Inner Temple

Practising Areas: Commercial Litigation, Common Law (General), Employment

DAVIES MR JAMES EDWIN

3 PB Barristers
23 Beaumont Street, Oxford OX1 2NP
☎ 01865 793 736
3 PB Barristers
30 Christchurch Road, Bournemouth, Dorset BH1 3PD ☎ 01202 292102 ✉ clerks.bournemouth@3paper.co.uk
3 PB Barristers
3 Paper Buildings, Temple, London EC4Y 7EU
☎ 020 7583 8055
3 PB Barristers
Royal Talbot House, 2 Victoria Street, Bristol, Avon BS1 6BB ☎ 0117 928 1520
3 PB Barristers
4 St Peter Street, Winchester SO23 8BW
☎ 01962 868884 ✉ clerks.winchester@3paper.co.uk
Call Date: Oct 2004, Lincoln's Inn

Practising Areas: Bankruptcy, Chancery (General), Commercial Litigation, Franchising, Insolvency, Landlord & Tenant, Professional Negligence

DAVIES MR JONATHAN HUW

Old Square Chambers
10-11 Bedford Row, London WC1R 4BU
☎ 020 7269 0300 ✉ clerks@oldsquare.co.uk
Old Square Chambers
3 Orchard Court, St Augustine's Yard, Bristol BS1 5DP ☎ 0117 930 5100
✉ clerks@oldsquare.co.uk
Call Date: Jul 2003, Lincoln's Inn

Practising Areas: Common Law (General), Discrimination, Employment, Environment, Tax (Capital & Income)

DAVIES MR JONATHAN NORVAL

9-12 Bell Yard
London WC2A 2JR ☎ 020 7400 1800
✉ clerks@9-12bellyard.com
Call Date: Jul 1981, Inner Temple
Pupil Supervisor

Practising Areas: Courts Martial, Crime, Crime (Corporate/Fraud), Licensing, Local Government

DAVIES MISS LINDSAY JANE

Fenners Chambers
3 Madingley Road, Cambridge CB3 0EE
☎ 01223 368761 ✉ clerks@fennerschambers.com
Call Date: Jul 1975, Gray's Inn
Pupil Supervisor, Recorder

Practising Areas: Care Proceedings, Family, Family Provision

DAVIES MR MAX JAMES

30 Park Place
Cardiff CF10 3BS ☎ 029 2039 8421
✉ clerks@30parkplace.law.co.uk
Call Date: Oct 2005, Middle Temple

Practising Areas: Chancery (General), Chancery (Land Law), Family, Family Provision, Landlord & Tenant

DAVIES MISS REBECCA LUCINDA

Westgate Chambers
64 High Street, Lewes, East Sussex BN7 1XG
☎ 01273 480510
✉ clerks@westgate-chambers.co.uk
Call Date: Nov 1996, Lincoln's Inn

Practising Areas: Care Proceedings, Family

DAVIES MISS RHIANNON LAURA

St Ive's Chambers
Whittall Street, Birmingham B4 6DH
☎ 0121 236 0863 ✉ clerks@stiveschambers.co.uk
Call Date: Oct 2001, Gray's Inn

DAVIES MS SAMANTHA TERESA

Chambers of Ms Samantha Davies
PO Box 6017, Milton Keynes, Buckinghamshire MK1 9AP ☎ 0845 123 1234
✉ samanthatdavies@yahoo.co.uk
Warwick House Chambers
8 Warwick Court, Warwick House Chambers, Gray's Inn, London WC1R 5DJ
☎ 020 7430 2323
✉ clerks@warwickhousechambers.com
Call Date: Oct 2002, Inner Temple

Practising Areas: Administrative, Care Proceedings, Chancery (General), Chancery (Land Law), Common Land, Common Law (General), Conveyancing, Ecclesiastical, Equity, Wills & Trusts, Family, Family Provision, Housing, Human Rights, Landlord & Tenant, Partnership, Private International, Probate & Administration

DAVIES MISS SARAH JEANNETTE

1 Pump Court
Elm Court, Temple, London EC4Y 7AB
☎ 020 7842 7070 ✉ (name)@pumpcourt.co.uk
Call Date: Feb 1984, Gray's Inn
Pupil Supervisor

Practising Areas: Family, Family Provision

DAVIS MR ADAM DAVID QC (2012)

Dyers Chambers
35 Bedford Row, London WC1R 4JH
☎ 020 7404 1881 ✉ admin@dyerschambers.com
Call Date: Nov 1985, Inner Temple
Pupil Supervisor

Practising Areas: Crime, Crime (Corporate/Fraud), Sports

DAVIS MR ANDREW PAUL

Crown Office Chambers
2 Crown Office Row, Temple, London EC4Y 7HJ ☎ 020 7797 8100
✉ mail@crownofficechambers.com
Call Date: Oct 1996, Gray's Inn
Pupil Supervisor

Practising Areas: Commercial Litigation, Common Law (General), Insurance, Medical Negligence, Personal Injury, Professional Negligence, Sale & Carriage of Goods

DAVIS MISS LUCY-VICTORIA

Pump Court Chambers
31 Southgate Street, Winchester, Hampshire SO23 9EB ☎ 01962 868 161
✉ clerks@3pumpcourt.com
Pump Court Chambers
Upper Ground Floor, 3 Pump Court, Temple, London EC4Y 7AJ ☎ 020 7353 0711
✉ clerks@3pumpcourt.com
Pump Court Chambers
5 Temple Chambers, Temple Street, Swindon SN1 1SQ ☎ 01793 539899
✉ clerks@3pumpcourt.com
Call Date: Nov 2003, Gray's Inn

Practising Areas: Crime, Employment, Family

DAVIS MR SIMON JOHN

St Philips Chambers
55 Temple Row, Birmingham B2 5LS
☎ 0121 246 7000 ✉ clerks@st-philips.com
Call Date: Oct 1990, Middle Temple
Pupil Supervisor

Practising Areas: Courts Martial, Crime, Crime (Corporate/Fraud), Licensing, Regulatory Law

DAVIS MR WILLIAM NEAL

Charter Chambers
33 John Street, London WC1N 2AT
☎ 020 7618 4400 ✉ clerks@charterchambers.com
Call Date: Jul 2003, Gray's Inn

Practising Areas: Crime, Crime (Corporate/Fraud)

DAVISON MS ELEANOR LOUISE

Outer Temple Chambers
The Outer Temple, 222 Strand, London WC2R 1BA ☎ 020 7353 6381
✉ clerks@outertemple.com
Call Date: Nov 2003, Lincoln's Inn

DAVISON MR GUY DIXON

1 Gray's Inn Square
Ground Floor, 1 Gray's Inn Square, London WC1R 5AA ☎ 020 7405 0001
Call Date: Oct 1998, Lincoln's Inn
Pupil Supervisor

Practising Areas: Immigration

DAVY MISS FELICIA MARIE THERESE

Old Bailey Chambers
15 Old Bailey, London EC4M 7EF
☎ 020 3008 6404
✉ clerks@15oldbaileychambers.com
Call Date: Oct 2000, Middle Temple
Pupil Supervisor

DAWSON MR JAMES

2 Hare Court
Lower Ground, Ground, 1st & 2nd Floor, 2 Hare Court, Temple, London EC4Y 7BH
☎ 020 7353 3982 ✉ clerks@2harecourt.com
Call Date: Nov 1984, Middle Temple
Pupil Supervisor, Recorder

DAWSON MR RICHARD JON FOSTER

Lincoln House Chambers
Tower 12, The Avenue North, Spinningfields, 18-22 Bridge Street, Manchester M3 3BZ
☎0161 832 5701
✉info@lincolnhousechambers.com
Call Date: Oct 2001, Middle Temple

Practising Areas: Crime, Crime (Corporate/Fraud), Licensing, Sports

DAY MR DORIAN STEPHEN

St Philips Chambers
55 Temple Row, Birmingham B2 5LS
☎0121 246 7000 ✉clerks@st-philips.com
Call Date: Jul 1987, Middle Temple
Pupil Supervisor

DAY MR DOUGLAS HENRY QC (1989)

Farrar's Building
Farrar's Building, Temple, London EC4Y 7BD
☎020 7583 9241
✉Chambers@farrarsbuilding.co.uk
Call Date: Jul 1967, Lincoln's Inn
Recorder

Practising Areas: Crime, Crime (Corporate/Fraud)

DE BERRY MR PHILIP JOHN

18 St John Street
Manchester M3 4EA ☎0161 278 1800
✉clerks@18sjs.com
Call Date: Oct 2003, Lincoln's Inn

Practising Areas: Costs, Industrial Diseases, Personal Injury, Professional Negligence

DE BURGOS MR JAMIE MICHAEL ABULAFIA

36 Bedford Row
London WC1R 4JH ☎020 7421 8000
✉chambers@36bedfordrow.co.uk
Call Date: Jul 1973, Inner Temple
Pupil Supervisor

Practising Areas: Ancillary Relief, Care Proceedings, Crime, Crime (Corporate/Fraud), Mental Health

DE HAAN MR KEVIN CHARLES QC (2000)

Francis Taylor Building
Inner Temple, London EC4Y 7BY
☎020 7353 8415 ✉clerks@ftb.eu.com
Call Date: Jul 1976, Inner Temple

Practising Areas: Licensing

DE JEHAN MR DAVID

Park Lane Plowden
19 Westgate, Leeds LS1 2RD
☎0113 228 5049 ✉clerks@parklaneplowden.co.uk
Call Date: Feb 1988, Inner Temple
Pupil Supervisor

Practising Areas: Chancery (General), Commercial Litigation, Crime (Corporate/Fraud), Family Provision, Insurance, Intellectual Property, Medical Negligence, Partnership, Personal Injury, Professional Negligence

DE MELLO MR REMBERT JOSEPH JULIUS

No5 Chambers
Fountain Court, Steelhouse Lane, Birmingham B4 6DR ☎0845 210 5555 ✉info@no5.com
No5 Chambers
Greenwood House, 4-7 Salisbury Court, London EC4Y 8AA ☎0845 210 5555
No5 Chambers
38 Queen Square, Bristol BS1 4QS
☎0845 210 5555
Call Date: Feb 1983, Lincoln's Inn
Pupil Supervisor

Practising Areas: Administrative, Civil Liberties, Discrimination, Education, Housing, Landlord & Tenant, Local Government, Mental Health, Pensions, Town & Country Planning

DE MOUNTENEY MR JONATHAN PATRICK

Chambers of Mr J P De Mounteney
1 Whistley Court Farm, Lodge Road, Reading, Berkshire RG10 0EJ ☎0118 934 6822
✉jonathan.demounteney@virgin.net
Call Date: Nov 1994, Gray's Inn

Practising Areas: Common Law (General), Copyright, Defamation, Employment, Entertainment, Film, Cable & TV, Intellectual Property, Landlord & Tenant, Patents, Trademarks

DE NAVARRO MISS FRANCES ANNE

Call Date: Oct 2005, Inner Temple

DE NAVARRO MR MICHAEL ANTONY QC (1990)

2 Temple Gardens
2 Temple Gardens, Temple, London EC4Y 9AY ☎020 7822 1200 ✉clerks@2tg.co.uk
Call Date: Jul 1968, Inner Temple
Recorder

DE POURBAIX MR ROMAN

Warwick House Chambers
8 Warwick Court, Warwick House Chambers, Gray's Inn, London WC1R 5DJ
☎ 020 7430 2323
✉ clerks@warwickhousechambers.com
Call Date: Jul 2001, Lincoln's Inn
Pupil Supervisor

DE ROHAN MR JONATHAN STEWART

2 Temple Gardens
2 Temple Gardens, Temple, London EC4Y 9AY ☎ 020 7822 1200 ✉ clerks@2tg.co.uk
Call Date: Jul 1989, Middle Temple
Pupil Supervisor

DE WAAL MR JOHN HENRY LOWNDES

Hardwicke
New Square, Lincoln's Inn, London WC2A 3SB ☎ 020 7242 2523
✉ enquiries@hardwicke.co.uk
Call Date: Oct 1992, Middle Temple
Pupil Supervisor

Practising Areas: Arbitration, Chancery (Land Law), Commercial Litigation, Commercial Property, Landlord & Tenant, Professional Negligence

DE ZONIE MISS JANE

14 Gray's Inn Square
14 Gray's Inn Square, Gray's Inn, London WC1R 5JP ☎ 020 7242 0858 ✉ clerks@14gis.co.uk
Call Date: Nov 1993, Middle Temple

Practising Areas: Care Proceedings, Common Law (General), Family, Family Provision

C

DEACON MR ROBERT MURRAY

11 Stone Buildings
11 Stone Buildings, Lincoln's Inn, London WC2A 3TG ☎ 020 7831 6381 ✉ clerks@11sb.com
Call Date: Jul 1976, Gray's Inn
Pupil Supervisor

Practising Areas: Chancery (General), Commercial Litigation, Common Law (General), Construction, Copyright, Defamation, Entertainment, Financial Services, Insurance, Intellectual Property, Landlord & Tenant, Partnership, Professional Negligence, Sports, Trademarks

DEAKIN MR ANDREW CHARLES

39 Essex Street
London WC2R 3AT ☎ 020 7832 1111
✉ clerks@39essex.com
82 King Street
Manchester M2 4WQ ☎ 0161 870 9969
Call Date: Oct 2006, Lincoln's Inn

DEAL MR TIMOTHY JOHN

Deal Chambers
60 Moordown, Shooters Hill, London SE18 3NG ☎ 020 8856 8738
✉ clerk@dealchambers.co.uk
Call Date: Jul 1988, Gray's Inn

Practising Areas: Common Law (General)

DEAN MRS CHRISTINE JACQUELINE

1 Pump Court
Elm Court, Temple, London EC4Y 7AB
☎ 020 7842 7070 ✉ (name)@pumpcourt.co.uk
Call Date: Mar 2007, Lincoln's Inn

Practising Areas: Care Proceedings, Education, Family, Family Provision

DEAN MISS ELIZABETH CATHERINE

3 Temple Gardens
Lower Ground Floor, 3 Temple Gardens, Temple, London EC4Y 9AU ☎ 020 7353 3102
✉ clerks@3tg.co.uk
Call Date: Jul 2006, Inner Temple

Practising Areas: Crime

DEAN MR JACOB

5RB
1st Floor, 5 Raymond Buildings, Gray's Inn, London WC1R 5BP ☎ 020 7242 2902
✉ clerks@5rb.com
Call Date: Oct 1995, Inner Temple
Pupil Supervisor

Practising Areas: Defamation, Entertainment, Sports

DEAN MR JAMES PATRICK

Goldsmith Chambers
Ground Floor, Goldsmith Building, Temple, London EC4Y 7BL ☎ 020 7353 6802
✉ clerks@goldsmithchambers.com
Call Date: Nov 1977, Lincoln's Inn
Pupil Supervisor

Practising Areas: Administrative, Ancillary Relief, Care Proceedings, Children's Law, Common Law (General), Consumer, Courts Martial, Crime, Crime (Corporate/Fraud), Defamation,

Disciplinary Tribunals, Discrimination, Employment, Family, Immigration, Landlord & Tenant, Medical Negligence, Mental Health, Personal Injury, Professional Negligence, Public Law, Road Traffic And Highways

DEAN MR PAUL BENJAMIN

Crown Office Chambers
2 Crown Office Row, Temple, London EC4Y 7HJ ☎ 020 7797 8100
✉ mail@crownofficechambers.com
Call Date: Jul 1982, Inner Temple
Pupil Supervisor

Practising Areas: Aviation, Common Law (General), Employment, Medical Negligence, Personal Injury, Professional Negligence

DEAN MR PETER THOMAS

36 Bedford Row
London WC1R 4JH ☎ 020 7421 8000
✉ chambers@36bedfordrow.co.uk
Call Date: Nov 1987, Middle Temple
Pupil Supervisor

Practising Areas: Administrative, Agriculture, Common Law (General), Equity, Wills & Trusts, Family, Immigration, Landlord & Tenant, Professional Negligence, Sale & Carriage of Goods

DEEGAN MR LAWRENCE JEFFREY

Fenners Chambers
3 Madingley Road, Cambridge CB3 0EE
☎ 01223 368761 ✉ clerks@fennerschambers.com
Call Date: Jul 1989, Inner Temple
Pupil Supervisor

Practising Areas: Common Law (General), Family, Family Provision, Personal Injury

DEGUN MR JASVIR SINGH

One Essex Court
1st Floor, Temple, London EC4Y 9AR
☎ 020 7936 3030 ✉ clerks@1ec.co.uk
Call Date: Oct 2003, Middle Temple

Practising Areas: Bankruptcy, Care Proceedings, Common Law (General), Family, Family Provision, Landlord & Tenant

DEIGNAN DR MARY TERESA

Charter Chambers
33 John Street, London WC1N 2AT
☎ 020 7618 4400 ✉ clerks@charterchambers.com
Call Date: Oct 1991, Middle Temple
Pupil Supervisor

DEL FABBRO MR OSCAR

23 Essex Street
London WC2R 3AA ☎ 020 7413 0353
✉ clerks@23es.com
Call Date: Jul 1982, Gray's Inn
Pupil Supervisor, Recorder

Practising Areas: Civil Liberties, Common Law (General), Courts Martial, Crime, Crime (Corporate/Fraud), Foreign Law, Health & Safety, Healthcare, Human Rights, Immigration, Regulatory Law, Sports

DELAMERE MISS ISABEL SARAH

4 Breams Buildings
Chancery Lane, London EC4A 1HP
☎ 020 7092 1900 ✉ clerks@4bb.co.uk
Call Date: Nov 1985, Middle Temple
Pupil Supervisor

Practising Areas: Courts Martial, Crime, Crime (Corporate/Fraud), Regulatory Law

DELANY MS FRANCESCA

1 Mitre Court Buildings
1 Mitre Court Buildings, Temple, London EC4Y 7BS ☎ 020 7452 8900 ✉ clerks@1mcb.com
Call Date: Oct 2006, Middle Temple

Practising Areas: Crime, Human Rights, Immigration

DEMACHKIE MR JAMAL

3 PB Barristers
3 Paper Buildings, Temple, London EC4Y 7EU
☎ 020 7583 8055
Call Date: Nov 2004, Inner Temple

Practising Areas: Chancery (General), Chancery (Land Law), Commercial Litigation, Commercial Property, Equity, Wills & Trusts, Housing, Landlord & Tenant, Professional Negligence

DEMPSEY MISS KAREN MARIE

3 Temple Gardens
Lower Ground Floor, 3 Temple Gardens, Temple, London EC4Y 9AU ☎ 020 7353 3102
✉ clerks@3tg.co.uk
Call Date: Mar 1996, Lincoln's Inn

Practising Areas: Courts Martial, Crime, Crime (Corporate/Fraud), Education, Health & Safety, Healthcare, Licensing, Regulatory Law, Road Traffic And Highways, Sports, Town & Country Planning

DENBIN MR JACK ARNOLD

Greenway
Sonning Lane, Sonning-on-Thames, Berkshire RG4 6ST ☎0118 969 2484
✉jackdenbin@btinternet.com
Call Date: Jul 1973, Inner Temple

Practising Areas: Arbitration, Chancery (General), Chancery (Land Law), Commercial Property, Construction, Housing, Landlord & Tenant, Probate & Administration, Sale & Carriage of Goods

DENHOLM MR GRAHAM SWANSTON

1 Pump Court
Elm Court, Temple, London EC4Y 7AB
☎020 7842 7070 ✉(name)@pumpcourt.co.uk
Call Date: Jul 2001, Middle Temple
Pupil Supervisor

DENNEY MR STUART HENRY MACDONALD QC (2008)

Deans Court Chambers
24 St John Street, Manchester M3 4DF
☎0161 214 6000 ✉clerks@deanscourt.co.uk
Deans Court Chambers
101 Walker Street, Preston PR1 2RR
☎01772 565 600 ✉preston@deanscourt.co.uk
Thomas More Chambers
7 Lincoln's Inn Fields, London WC2A 3BP
☎020 7404 7000 ✉clerks@thomasmore.co.uk
Call Date: Jul 1982, Inner Temple

Practising Areas: Crime, Crime (Corporate/Fraud), Health & Safety, Regulatory Law, Sports

DENNIS MR MARK JONATHAN QC (2006)

6 King's Bench Walk
Ground Floor, 6 King's Bench Walk, Temple, London EC4Y 7DR ☎020 7583 0410
✉clerks@6kbw.com
Call Date: Jul 1977, Middle Temple
Recorder

Practising Areas: Crime, Crime (Corporate/Fraud), Health & Safety, Road Traffic And Highways

DENNIS MISS REBECCA LOUISE

Queen Square Chambers
56 Queen Square, Bristol BS1 4PR
☎0117 921 1966 ✉crime@qs-c.co.uk
Call Date: Jul 1994, Gray's Inn
Pupil Supervisor

Practising Areas: Crime (Corporate/Fraud), Employment, Personal Injury

DENT MR STEPHEN ROBERT CHARLES

Guildhall Chambers
23 Broad Street, Bristol BS1 2HG
☎0117 930 9000 ✉hoc@guildhallchambers.co.uk
Call Date: Feb 1991, Gray's Inn

Practising Areas: Crime, Crime (Corporate/Fraud)

DESCHAMPSNEUFS MISS ALICE NORA

4 King's Bench Walk
2nd Floor, 4 King's Bench Walk, Temple, London EC4Y 7DL ☎020 7822 7000
✉clerks@4kbw.co.uk
Call Date: Jul 1976, Inner Temple
Pupil Supervisor

Practising Areas: Family

DESMOND MR DENIS JOHN

Cornwall Street Chambers
85-87 Cornwall Street, Birmingham B3 3BY
☎0121 233 7500 ✉clerks@cornwallstreet.co.uk
Call Date: Nov 1974, Middle Temple
Pupil Supervisor, Recorder

Practising Areas: Crime, Crime (Corporate/Fraud), Disciplinary Tribunals, Regulatory Law, Road Traffic And Highways

DEVEREUX-COOKE MR RICHARD CHARLES

13 Old Square Chambers
Ground Floor, 14 Old Square, Lincoln's Inn, London WC2A 3UE ☎020 7831 4445
✉clerks@13oldsquare.com
Call Date: Oct 1999, Middle Temple
Pupil Supervisor

Practising Areas: Agriculture, Banking, Bankruptcy, Chancery (General), Chancery (Land Law), Common Land, Common Law (General), Company & Commercial, Environment, Equity, Wills & Trusts, Family Provision, Housing, Landlord & Tenant, Partnership, Personal Injury

C

DEVINE MR MICHAEL BUXTON

Rougemont Chambers
Victory House, Dean Clarke Gardens, Southernhay East, Exeter EX2 4AA
☎01392 208484
✉clerks@rougemontchambers.co.uk
Call Date: Jul 1995, Gray's Inn

Practising Areas: Arbitration, Commercial Litigation, EC & Competition Law, Foreign Law, International Trade, Private International, Sale & Carriage of Goods, Shipping/Admiralty

DEVLIN MR BERNARD JOSEPH

Five St Andrew's Hill
5 St Andrew's Hill, London EC4V 5BZ
☎020 7332 5400 ✉Clerks@5sah.co.uk
Call Date: Nov 1980, Gray's Inn
Pupil Supervisor

Practising Areas: Administrative, Banking, Chancery (General), Commercial Litigation, Commercial Property, Company & Commercial, Insolvency, Intellectual Property, Landlord & Tenant, Partnership, Personal Injury, Probate & Administration, Professional Negligence, Sale & Carriage of Goods, Trademarks

DEVLIN MR TIMOTHY ROBERT

Furnival Chambers
32 Furnival Street, London EC4A 1JQ
☎020 7405 3232
Call Date: Jul 1985, Lincoln's Inn
Pupil Supervisor

Practising Areas: Crime, EC & Competition Law, Parliamentary, Regulatory Law

DHADDA MISS SUKWINDER KAUR

2 King's Bench Walk
2 King's Bench Walk, Temple, London EC4Y 7DE ☎020 7353 1746 ✉clerks@2kbw.com
Call Date: Jul 2004, Lincoln's Inn

DHADLI MRS PERMINDER

KCH Garden Square
1 Oxford Street, Nottingham NG1 5BH
☎0115 941 8851 ✉clerks@kchgardensquare.co.uk
Call Date: Nov 1984, Middle Temple
Pupil Supervisor

Practising Areas: Ancillary Relief, Care Proceedings, Children's Law, Family

DHALIWAL MISS DAVINDER KAUR

No 8 Chambers
8 Fountain Court, Steelhouse Lane, Birmingham B4 6DR ☎0121 236 5514
✉clerks@no8chambers.co.uk
Call Date: Nov 1990, Middle Temple

Practising Areas: Administrative, Ancillary Relief, Care Proceedings, Children's Law, Family Provision, Housing, Human Rights, Immigration

DHAR MR ZEESHAN

Hardwicke
New Square, Lincoln's Inn, London WC2A 3SB ☎020 7242 2523
✉enquiries@hardwicke.co.uk
Call Date: Nov 1999, Gray's Inn

Practising Areas: Employment

DHILLON MISS KIRANDEEP KAUR

Broadway House Chambers
Broadway House, 9 Bank Street, Bradford, West Yorkshire BD1 1TW ☎01274 722560
✉clerks@broadwayhouse.co.uk
Call Date: Jul 2005, Inner Temple

DI MAMBRO MR DAVID JESSE ANDREW

Radcliffe Chambers
Ground Floor, 11 New Square, Lincoln's Inn, London WC2A 3QB ☎020 7831 0081
✉clerks@radcliffechambers.com
Pallant Chambers
12 North Pallant, Chichester, West Sussex PO19 1TQ ☎01243 784538
✉clerks@pallantchambers.co.uk
Call Date: Nov 1973, Middle Temple
Pupil Supervisor

Practising Areas: Arbitration, Chancery (General), Chancery (Land Law), Commercial Litigation, Commercial Property, Common Land, Copyright, Franchising, Intellectual Property, Land, Landlord & Tenant, Partnership, Town & Country Planning

DIAMOND MR PAUL

Chambers of Mr Paul Diamond
PO Box 1041, Barton, Cambridge CB23 7WY
☎01223 264544 ✉pauldiamond@btconnect.com
Call Date: Jul 1985, Middle Temple

Practising Areas: Administrative, Civil Liberties, Housing

DIAS MISS SAPPHO

5 King's Bench Walk
5 King's Bench Walk, Temple, London EC4Y 7DN ☎ 020 7353 5638 ✉ clerks@5kbw.co.uk
Call Date: Nov 1982, Gray's Inn
Pupil Supervisor

DICKINSON MR JOHN FINCH HENEAGE

St John's Chambers
101 Victoria Street, Bristol BS1 6PU
☎ 0117 923 4700 ✉ clerks@stjohnschambers.co.uk
Call Date: Oct 1995, Middle Temple
Pupil Supervisor

Practising Areas: Banking, Chancery (General), Chancery (Land Law), Commercial Litigation, Company & Commercial, Equity, Wills & Trusts, Family Provision, Partnership, Probate & Administration

DICKINSON MS ZARAH SHELLEY

5 Pump Court
Ground Floor, 5 Pump Court, Temple, London EC4Y 7AP ☎ 020 7353 2532
✉ clerks@5pumpcourt.com
No.6 Park Square
Leeds LS1 2LW ☎ 0113 245 9763
✉ Tim@no6.co.uk
Call Date: Jul 2002, Inner Temple

DILLIWAY-PARRY MR GUY WILLIAM

5 King's Bench Walk
5 King's Bench Walk, Temple, London EC4Y 7DN ☎ 020 7353 5638 ✉ clerks@5kbw.co.uk
Call Date: Jul 2002, Gray's Inn

Practising Areas: Courts Martial, Crime

C

DILLON MS ANNE VERONICA

13 King's Bench Walk
13 King's Bench Walk, Temple, London EC4Y 7EN ☎ 020 7353 7204 ✉ clerks@13kbw.co.uk
13 KBW
32 Beaumont Street, Oxford OX1 2NP
☎ 01865 311066 ✉ clerks@13kbw.co.uk
Call Date: Jul 2003, Inner Temple

Practising Areas: Family

DILLON MR THOMAS WILLIAM MATTHEW

Chambers of Thomas Dillon
25 Howitt Close, London NW3 4LX
☎ 020 7692 2722 ✉ post@contentadvice.eu
Call Date: Jul 1983, Middle Temple

Practising Areas: Arbitration, Copyright, Entertainment, Film, Cable & TV, Information Technology, Intellectual Property, Private International, Public International, Regulatory Law, Trademarks

DINAN-HAYWARD MISS DEBORAH LOUISE

Albion Chambers
Broad Street, Bristol BS1 1DR
☎ 0117 927 2144 ✉ clerks@albionchambers.co.uk
Call Date: Nov 1988, Inner Temple
Pupil Supervisor

Practising Areas: Family, Probate & Administration

DINEEN MS MARIA THERESE

2 Bedford Row
London WC1R 4BU ☎ 020 7440 8888
✉ clerks@2bedfordrow.co.uk
Call Date: Oct 1997, Inner Temple

DINES MISS SARAH ELIZABETH

1 Gray's Inn Square
Ground Floor, 1 Gray's Inn Square, London WC1R 5AA ☎ 020 7405 0001
Call Date: Jul 1988, Lincoln's Inn

DIPRé MR PAUL NICHOLAS AMADEUS

Chambers of Mr P N Dipré
Address withheld ☎ 0845 123 1234
✉ pauldipre@btinternet.com
MK Family Law Chambers
PO Box 6017, Milton Keynes MK1 9AP
☎ 0845 123 1234
Call Date: Nov 1991, Lincoln's Inn

Practising Areas: Chancery (Land Law), Commercial Litigation, Company & Commercial, Construction, Employment, Family, Family Provision, Housing, Immigration, Insolvency, Insurance, Landlord & Tenant, Mental Health, Personal Injury, Private International, Probate & Administration, Sale & Carriage of Goods, Town & Country Planning

DIX MISS REBECCA

2 Bedford Row
London WC1R 4BU ☎ 020 7440 8888
✉ clerks@2bedfordrow.co.uk
Call Date: Jul 2004, Inner Temple

Practising Areas: Crime, Crime (Corporate/Fraud)

DIXEY MR IAN ROGER

Guildhall Chambers
23 Broad Street, Bristol BS1 2HG
☎0117 930 9000 ✉hoc@guildhallchambers.co.uk
Call Date: Nov 1984, Inner Temple
Pupil Supervisor

Practising Areas: Crime, Health & Safety, Sports

DIXON MR DAVID STEVEN

Sovereign Chambers
46 Park Place, Leeds LS1 2RY
☎0113 245 1841
✉clerks@sovereignchambers.co.uk
Call Date: Oct 1992, Lincoln's Inn
Pupil Supervisor

Practising Areas: Coroners Inquests, Crime, Employment, Inquests, Regulatory Law

DIXON MR JAMES MALCOLM

No5 Chambers
Fountain Court, Steelhouse Lane, Birmingham B4 6DR ☎0845 210 5555 ✉info@no5.com
No5 Chambers
Greenwood House, 4-7 Salisbury Court, London EC4Y 8AA ☎0845 210 5555
No5 Chambers
38 Queen Square, Bristol BS1 4QS
☎0845 210 5555
Call Date: Mar 2001, Lincoln's Inn

Practising Areas: Crime, Employment, Licensing

DODD MR DANIEL ANDREW

Linenhall Chambers
1 Stanley Place, Chester CH1 2LU
☎01244 348282
✉clerks@linenhallchambers.co.uk
Call Date: Jul 2003, Lincoln's Inn

DODD MISS STEPHANIE JANE

9-12 Bell Yard
London WC2A 2JR ☎020 7400 1800
✉clerks@9-12bellyard.com
Call Date: Jul 2001, Gray's Inn

DODGE MR PETER CLIVE

Radcliffe Chambers
Ground Floor, 11 New Square, Lincoln's Inn, London WC2A 3QB ☎020 7831 0081
✉clerks@radcliffechambers.com
Call Date: Oct 1992, Lincoln's Inn
Pupil Supervisor

DODSON MISS JOANNA QC (1993)

Renaissance Chambers
5th Floor, Gray's Inn Chambers, Gray's Inn, London WC1R 5JA ☎020 7404 1111
✉clerks@renaissancechambers.co.uk
Park Court Chambers
16 Park Place, Leeds LS1 2SJ
☎0113 243 3277
✉clerks@parkcourtchambers.co.uk
Call Date: Nov 1971, Middle Temple

Practising Areas: Care Proceedings, Family

DOERFEL MR JAN HENDRIK JAMISON

Chambers of Mr J H Doerfel
Parkshot House, 5 Kew Road, Richmond, Surrey TW9 2PR ☎0845 123 1234
✉jandoerfel@yahoo.com
1215 Chambers
1 Fetter Lane, London EC4A 1BR
☎020 3291 1215 ✉admin@1215chambers.com
Call Date: Nov 2000, Inner Temple

Practising Areas: Administrative, Civil Liberties, Discrimination, Employment, Human Rights, Immigration

DOERRIES MISS CHANTAL-AIMéE RENEE AEMELIA AN QC (2008)

Atkin Chambers
1 Atkin Building, Gray's Inn, London WC1R 5AT ☎020 7404 0102
✉clerks@atkinchambers.com
Call Date: Oct 1992, Middle Temple

Practising Areas: Arbitration, Commercial Litigation, Construction, Energy, Information Technology, Professional Negligence

DOHERTY MR NICHOLAS BRUDENELL

4 King's Bench Walk
2nd Floor, 4 King's Bench Walk, Temple, London EC4Y 7DL ☎020 7822 7000
✉clerks@4kbw.co.uk
Call Date: Jul 1983, Lincoln's Inn

Practising Areas: Courts Martial, Crime, Crime (Corporate/Fraud), Disciplinary Tribunals, Entertainment, Inquests, Licensing, Road Traffic And Highways

DOLAN DR BRIDGET MAURA

3 Serjeants Inn
London EC4Y 1BQ ☎ 020 7427 5000
✉ clerks@3serjeantsinn.com
Call Date: Oct 1997, Middle Temple
Pupil Supervisor

Practising Areas: Healthcare, Inquests, Mental Health

DOMAN MR RICHARD WILLIAM

2 Dr Johnson's Buildings
2 Dr Johnson's Buildings, Temple, London EC4Y 7AY ☎ 020 7936 2613 ✉ clerks@2drj.com
Call Date: Nov 2003, Lincoln's Inn

DONNE MR JEREMY NIGEL QC (2003)

QEB Hollis Whiteman
1-2 Laurence Pountney Hill, London EC4R 0EU ☎ 020 7933 8855 ✉ barristers@qebhw.co.uk
Call Date: Nov 1978, Middle Temple
Recorder

Practising Areas: Courts Martial, Crime, Crime (Corporate/Fraud), Health & Safety, Regulatory Law

DONNELLY MR STEPHEN JOHN

Dyers Chambers
35 Bedford Row, London WC1R 4JH
☎ 020 7404 1881 ✉ admin@dyerschambers.com
Call Date: Oct 2001, Inner Temple

Practising Areas: Crime, Crime (Corporate/Fraud), Regulatory Law, Sports

C

DONOVAN MISS JULIET MARY

East Anglian Chambers
Gresham House, 5 Museum Street, Ipswich, Suffolk IP1 1HQ ☎ 01473 214481
✉ ipswich@ealaw.co.uk
East Anglian Chambers
53 North Hill, Colchester, Essex CO1 1QA
☎ 01473 214481 ✉ colchester@ealaw.co.uk
East Anglian Chambers
140 New London Road, Chelmsford, Essex CM2 0AW ☎ 01473 214481
✉ chelmsford@ealaw.co.uk
Call Date: Jul 2002, Middle Temple
Pupil Supervisor

DOOLEY MS CHRISTINE

2 Pump Court
1st Floor, 2 Pump Court, Temple, London EC4Y 7AH ☎ 020 7353 5597
✉ clerks@2pumpcourt.co.uk
Call Date: Jul 1980, Gray's Inn
Pupil Supervisor

Practising Areas: Family

DORAN MR GERARD PATRICK

Lincoln House Chambers
Tower 12, The Avenue North, Spinningfields, 18-22 Bridge Street, Manchester M3 3BZ
☎ 0161 832 5701
✉ info@lincolnhousechambers.com
Call Date: Nov 1993, Gray's Inn
Pupil Supervisor

Practising Areas: Administrative, Crime, Crime (Corporate/Fraud), Financial Services, Health & Safety, Landlord & Tenant, Licensing, Local Government

DOS SANTOS MR ALEXANDER

Charter Chambers
33 John Street, London WC1N 2AT
☎ 020 7618 4400 ✉ clerks@charterchambers.com
Call Date: Oct 1999, Lincoln's Inn
Pupil Supervisor

Practising Areas: Administrative, Civil Liberties, Commercial Litigation, Courts Martial, Crime, Crime (Corporate/Fraud), Employment, Health & Safety, Human Rights, Inquests, Local Government, Public Law, Regulatory Law, Sports

DOSWELL MR RUPERT JOHN

KBW
The Engine House, No 1 Foundry Square, Leeds LS11 5DL ☎ 0113 297 1200
✉ clerks@kbwchambers.com
Call Date: Oct 1996, Inner Temple
Pupil Supervisor

Practising Areas: Employment

DOUGHTY MR PETER

12 College Place
Fauvelle Buildings, 12 College Place, Southampton SO15 2FE ☎ 023 8032 0320
✉ clerks@12cp.co.uk
Call Date: Jul 1988, Lincoln's Inn
Pupil Supervisor

Practising Areas: Discrimination, Employment

DOUGLASS MISS GERALDINE MAISIE

Portal Chambers
Blaencwm Mawr, Llandysul SA44 5NS
☎ 01559 395 292
Call Date: Nov 1976, Middle Temple

Practising Areas: Common Land, Road Traffic And Highways, Town & Country Planning

DOUGLASS MR PAUL STEPHEN

9 King's Bench Walk
Lower Ground Floor South, 9 King's Bench Walk, Temple, London EC4Y 7DX
☎ 020 7353 9564 ✉ 9kbw@btconnect.com
Call Date: Jul 1996, Inner Temple

Practising Areas: Crime, Family, Health & Safety, Immigration, Regulatory Law

DOUTHWAITE MR CHARLES PHILIP

Four New Square
Four New Square, Lincoln's Inn, London WC2A 3RJ ☎ 020 7822 2000
✉ barristers@4newsquare.com
Call Date: Jul 1977, Gray's Inn
Pupil Supervisor

Practising Areas: Common Law (General), Construction, Insurance, Landlord & Tenant, Personal Injury, Professional Negligence

DOVAR MR DANIEL

Tanfield Chambers
2-5 Warwick Court, London WC1R 5DJ
☎ 020 7421 5300 ✉ clerks@tanfieldchambers.co.uk
Call Date: Oct 1997, Gray's Inn

Practising Areas: Chancery (General), Chancery (Land Law), Civil Litigation, Commercial Property, Common Law (General), Conveyancing, Housing, Land, Landlord & Tenant, Professional Negligence

DOVE MR IAN WILLIAM QC (2003)

No5 Chambers
Fountain Court, Steelhouse Lane, Birmingham B4 6DR ☎ 0845 210 5555 ✉ info@no5.com
No5 Chambers
Greenwood House, 4-7 Salisbury Court, London EC4Y 8AA ☎ 0845 210 5555
4-5 Gray's Inn Square
Gray's Inn, London WC1R 5AH
☎ 020 7404 5252 ✉ clerks@4-5.co.uk
No5 Chambers
38 Queen Square, Bristol BS1 4QS
☎ 0845 210 5555
Call Date: Jul 1986, Inner Temple
Recorder

DOVE MR JAMES FRANCIS

The Chambers of Grahame Aldous QC
9 Gough Square, London EC4A 3DG
☎ 020 7832 0500 ✉ clerks@9goughsquare.co.uk
Call Date: Nov 2006, Lincoln's Inn

Practising Areas: Care Proceedings, Children's Law, Family, Family Provision

DOWDEN MR ANDREW PHILIP

Castle Chambers
The Old Fire Station, 90 High Street, Harrow-on-the-Hill, Middlesex HA1 3LP
☎ 020 8423 6579 ✉ info@castlechambers.net
Melbury House
55 Manor Road, Oadby, Leicester, Leicestershire LE2 2LL ☎ 07801 037802
✉ melburyhousechambers@yahoo.co.uk
Call Date: Oct 1991, Lincoln's Inn

Practising Areas: Administrative, Common Law (General), Coroners Inquests, Crime, Crime (Corporate/Fraud), Disciplinary Tribunals, Employment, Inquests, Personal Injury

DOWELL MR GREGORY HAMILTON

Principal Chambers
15 Lime Tree Walk, Sevenoaks, Kent TN13 1YH ☎ 0845 209 8080
Call Date: Oct 1990, Middle Temple

Practising Areas: Agriculture, Care Proceedings, Children's Law, Civil Litigation, Common Land, Common Law (General), Consumer, Coroners Inquests, Employment, Equity, Wills & Trusts, Family, Family Provision, Health & Safety, Housing, Industrial Diseases, Land, Landlord & Tenant, Mental Health, Personal Injury, Probate & Administration

DOWNEY MR NEIL JAMES

Atlantic Chambers
4-6 Cook Street, Liverpool L2 9QU
☎ 0151 236 4421 ✉ info@atlanticchambers.co.uk
Call Date: Mar 1997, Middle Temple

Practising Areas: Common Law (General), Discrimination, Employment, Personal Injury

DOWSE MS CLARE OLIVIA MARY

3 Temple Gardens
Lower Ground Floor, 3 Temple Gardens, Temple, London EC4Y 9AU ☎ 020 7353 3102
✉ clerks@3tg.co.uk
Call Date: Jul 2002, Inner Temple

Practising Areas: Crime, Crime (Corporate/Fraud)

DRACASS MR TIMOTHY WILLIAM

Pump Court Chambers
31 Southgate Street, Winchester, Hampshire SO23 9EB ☎ 01962 868 161
✉ clerks@3pumpcourt.com
Pump Court Chambers
Upper Ground Floor, 3 Pump Court, Temple, London EC4Y 7AJ ☎ 020 7353 0711
✉ clerks@3pumpcourt.com
Riverview Chambers
Hamilton House, 1 Temple Avenue, London EC4Y 0HA ☎ 0844 225 3999
✉ chrisbaylis@riverviewchambers.com
Call Date: Oct 1998, Inner Temple
Pupil Supervisor

Practising Areas: Discrimination, Employment, Personal Injury

DRAKE MISS RACHEL ALEXIA

13 King's Bench Walk
13 King's Bench Walk, Temple, London EC4Y 7EN ☎ 020 7353 7204 ✉ clerks@13kbw.co.uk
Call Date: Nov 1995, Middle Temple
Pupil Supervisor

Practising Areas: Crime

DRAYCOTT MR SIMON DOUGLAS QC (2002)

Five St Andrew's Hill
5 St Andrew's Hill, London EC4V 5BZ
☎ 020 7332 5400 ✉ Clerks@5sah.co.uk
Citadel Chambers
The Citadel, 190 Corporation Street, Birmingham B4 6QD ☎ 0121 233 8500
✉ clerks@citadelchambers.com
Call Date: Jul 1977, Middle Temple
Recorder

Practising Areas: Common Law (General), Crime, Crime (Corporate/Fraud), Defamation, Disciplinary Tribunals, Entertainment, Inquests, Road Traffic And Highways

C

DREW MR SIMON PATRICK QC (2011)

No5 Chambers
Fountain Court, Steelhouse Lane, Birmingham B4 6DR ☎ 0845 210 5555 ✉ info@no5.com
No5 Chambers
Greenwood House, 4-7 Salisbury Court, London EC4Y 8AA ☎ 0845 210 5555
No5 Chambers
38 Queen Square, Bristol BS1 4QS
☎ 0845 210 5555
Call Date: Nov 1987, Lincoln's Inn
Pupil Supervisor

Practising Areas: Crime, Crime (Corporate/Fraud), Regulatory Law

DRUCE MR MICHAEL JAMES

Cornerstone Barristers
2-3 Gray's Inn Square, Gray's Inn, London WC1R 5JH ☎ 020 7242 4986
✉ chambers@2-3gis.co.uk
Call Date: Jul 1988, Inner Temple

Practising Areas: Town & Country Planning

DRUMMOND MR BRUCE JONATHON HUTCHEON

Cornwall Street Chambers
85-87 Cornwall Street, Birmingham B3 3BY
☎ 0121 233 7500 ✉ clerks@cornwallstreet.co.uk
Palmyra Chambers
Royal House, 46 Legh Street, Warrington WA1 1UJ ☎ 01925 444919
✉ clerk@palmyrachambers.com
Call Date: Oct 1992, Gray's Inn

Practising Areas: Commercial Litigation, Copyright, Corporate Finance, Entertainment, Film, Cable & TV, Foreign Law, Intellectual Property

DSANE MISS VICTORIA TSOTSOO

Chambers of Miss Victoria Dsane
61 Elm Grove, Sutton, Surrey SM1 4EX
☎ 020 8722 0990 ✉ vdsaneidown@hotmail.co.uk
Call Date: Nov 1971, Middle Temple
Pupil Supervisor

Practising Areas: Crime, Employment, Family, Housing, Landlord & Tenant

DU TOIT SC MR JOHAN IGNATIUS

Selborne Chambers
10 Essex Street, London WC2R 3AA
☎ 020 7420 9500
✉ clerks@selbornechambers.co.uk
St Philips Chambers
55 Temple Row, Birmingham B2 5LS
☎ 0121 246 7000 ✉ clerks@st-philips.com
Call Date: Nov 2008, Middle Temple

Practising Areas: Arbitration, Commercial Litigation, Company & Commercial, Financial Services, Partnership, Professional Negligence

DUBBERY MR MARK EDWARD

Pump Court Chambers
Upper Ground Floor, 3 Pump Court, Temple, London EC4Y 7AJ ☎ 020 7353 0711
✉ clerks@3pumpcourt.com
Pump Court Chambers
5 Temple Chambers, Temple Street, Swindon SN1 1SQ ☎ 01793 539899
✉ clerks@3pumpcourt.com

Pump Court Chambers
31 Southgate Street, Winchester, Hampshire SO23 9EB ☎01962 868 161 ✉clerks@3pumpcourt.com
Call Date: Oct 1996, Middle Temple
Pupil Supervisor

DUBIN MR JOSHUA CHARLES

1 Pump Court
Elm Court, Temple, London EC4Y 7AB ☎020 7842 7070 ✉(name)@pumpcourt.co.uk
Call Date: Nov 1997, Middle Temple
Pupil Supervisor

Practising Areas: Civil Liberties, Housing, Human Rights, Landlord & Tenant, Local Government

DUCK MR MICHAEL CHARLES QC (2011)

No5 Chambers
Fountain Court, Steelhouse Lane, Birmingham B4 6DR ☎0845 210 5555 ✉info@no5.com
No5 Chambers
Greenwood House, 4-7 Salisbury Court, London EC4Y 8AA ☎0845 210 5555
No5 Chambers
38 Queen Square, Bristol BS1 4QS ☎0845 210 5555
Call Date: Nov 1988, Gray's Inn
Pupil Supervisor

Practising Areas: Crime, Crime (Corporate/Fraud), Regulatory Law

DUCKWORTH MR PETER

29 Bedford Row Chambers
London WC1R 4HE ☎020 7404 1044 ✉clerks@29br.co.uk
Call Date: Jul 1971, Middle Temple
Pupil Supervisor

Practising Areas: Family

DUFFICY MR CONOR ROBERT

Seven Bedford Row
7 Bedford Row, London WC1R 4BS ☎020 7242 3555 ✉clerks@7br.co.uk
Call Date: Jul 2004, Middle Temple

DUFFY MR DEREK JAMES

St Paul's Chambers
5th Floor, St Paul's House, 23 Park Square South, Leeds LS1 2ND ☎0113 245 5866
Call Date: Mar 1997, Gray's Inn

Practising Areas: Care Proceedings, Children's Law, Coroners Inquests, Courts Martial, Crime, Crime (Corporate/Fraud), Disciplinary Tribunals, Health & Safety, Healthcare, Inquests, Regulatory Law, Road Traffic And Highways

DUGDALE MR JEREMY KEITH

Octagon House
19 Colegate, Norwich NR3 1AT ☎01603 623186 ✉clerks@octagonhouse.co.uk
Call Date: Oct 1992, Inner Temple
Pupil Supervisor

Practising Areas: Care Proceedings, Family, Mental Health

DULAY MISS RANJEET

1 Mitre Court Buildings
1 Mitre Court Buildings, Temple, London EC4Y 7BS ☎020 7452 8900 ✉clerks@1mcb.com
Call Date: Mar 1999, Inner Temple

DUNKELS MR PAUL RENTON QC (1993)

Walnut House
63 St. David's Hill, Exeter, Devon EX4 4DW ☎01392 279751 ✉clerks@walnuthouse.co.uk
Albion Chambers
Broad Street, Bristol BS1 1DR ☎0117 927 2144 ✉clerks@albionchambers.co.uk
Call Date: May 1972, Inner Temple
Recorder

DUNLOP MR HAMISH MICHAEL

3 PB Barristers
3 Paper Buildings, Temple, London EC4Y 7EU ☎020 7583 8055
3 PB Barristers
Royal Talbot House, 2 Victoria Street, Bristol, Avon BS1 6BB ☎0117 928 1520
3 PB Barristers
30 Christchurch Road, Bournemouth, Dorset BH1 3PD ☎01202 292102 ✉clerks.bournemouth@3paper.co.uk
3 PB Barristers
4 St Peter Street, Winchester SO23 8BW ☎01962 868884 ✉clerks.winchester@3paper.co.uk
3 PB Barristers
23 Beaumont Street, Oxford OX1 2NP ☎01865 793 736
Call Date: Nov 1991, Middle Temple
Pupil Supervisor

Practising Areas: Family Provision, Personal Injury

C

DUNN MISS KATHERINE LOUISE

Trinity Chambers
The Custom House, 39 Quayside, Newcastle Upon Tyne NE1 3DE ☎0191 232 1927
✉info@trinitychambers.co.uk
Trinity Chambers
Multi Media Exchange, 72-80 Corporation Road, Middlesbrough TS1 2RF
☎01642 247569 ✉info@trinitychambers.co.uk
Call Date: Oct 1993, Lincoln's Inn

Practising Areas: Courts Martial, Crime, Mental Health, Regulatory Law

DUNNE MR ANTHONY JAMES

KBW
The Engine House, No 1 Foundry Square, Leeds LS11 5DL ☎0113 297 1200
✉clerks@kbwchambers.com
Call Date: Nov 1999, Lincoln's Inn

Practising Areas: Common Law (General), Crime, Immigration, Personal Injury

DUNNING MR FRANCIS JOHN GROVE

37 Park Square Chambers
37 Park Square, Leeds LS1 2NY
☎0113 243 9422 ✉chambers@no37.co.uk
Call Date: Jul 1973, Inner Temple
Pupil Supervisor

Practising Areas: Crime, Crime (Corporate/Fraud), Education

DUNSTAN MR JAMES PETER

St Philips Chambers
55 Temple Row, Birmingham B2 5LS
☎0121 246 7000 ✉clerks@st-philips.com
Call Date: Feb 1995, Gray's Inn

Practising Areas: Crime

DUTT MISS NISHA

Middle Temple Lane Chambers
2nd Floor South, 1 Middle Temple Lane, London EC4Y 9AA ☎020 7583 4352
✉chambers@mtlchambers.com
Call Date: Jul 2007, Lincoln's Inn

Practising Areas: Civil Litigation, Common Law (General), Crime, Crime (Corporate/Fraud), Regulatory Law

DYBLE MR STEVEN JOHN

18 Red Lion Court
London EC4A 3EB ☎020 7520 6000
✉chambers@18rlc.co.uk
18 Red Lion Court (Annexe)
Thornwood House, 102 New London Road, Chelmsford, Essex CM2 0RG
☎01245 280880
Call Date: Nov 1986, Lincoln's Inn

Practising Areas: Crime, Crime (Corporate/Fraud), Local Government, Road Traffic And Highways

DYE MR JOHN GEOFFREY

Goldsmith Chambers
Ground Floor, Goldsmith Building, Temple, London EC4Y 7BL ☎020 7353 6802
✉clerks@goldsmithchambers.com
Call Date: Nov 2002, Inner Temple

Practising Areas: Crime, Crime (Corporate/Fraud), Employment

DYER MR ALLEN GORDON

4 Pump Court
4 Pump Court, Temple, London EC4Y 7AN
☎020 7842 5555 ✉chambers@4pumpcourt.com
Call Date: Jul 1976, Inner Temple
Pupil Supervisor

Practising Areas: Arbitration, Commercial Litigation, Company & Commercial, Construction, Insurance, Professional Negligence

EARLE MR JAMES CHRISTOPHER REGINALD ST JOHN

Fenners Chambers
3 Madingley Road, Cambridge CB3 0EE
☎01223 368761 ✉clerks@fennerschambers.com
Call Date: Oct 1996, Gray's Inn

Practising Areas: Administrative, Commercial Litigation, Common Law (General), Company & Commercial, Courts Martial, Crime, Equity, Wills & Trusts, Housing, Insolvency, Landlord & Tenant, Licensing, Local Government, Mental Health, Partnership, Personal Injury, Professional Negligence, Town & Country Planning

EARLEY MISS SARAH JANE

Pallant Chambers
12 North Pallant, Chichester, West Sussex PO19 1TQ ☎01243 784538
✉clerks@pallantchambers.co.uk
Call Date: Oct 1998, Inner Temple
Pupil Supervisor

Practising Areas: Children's Law, Family

EASTWOOD MISS CHARLOTTE

37 Park Square Chambers
37 Park Square, Leeds LS1 2NY
☎ 0113 243 9422 ✉ chambers@no37.co.uk
Call Date: Nov 2003, Middle Temple

EASTWOOD MISS PHILIPPA CLEMENCY ANNE

Doughty Street Chambers
53-54 Doughty Street, London WC1N 2LS
☎ 020 7404 1313 ✉ enquiries@doughtystreet.co.uk
Call Date: Oct 2003, Lincoln's Inn

Practising Areas: Civil Liberties, Courts Martial, Crime, Crime (Corporate/Fraud), Environment, Health & Safety, Human Rights, Licensing, Local Government, Mental Health, Professional Negligence, Regulatory Law

EASTY MISS VALERIE STEPHANIE

Garden Court Chambers
57-60 Lincoln's Inn Fields, London WC2A 3LJ
☎ 020 7993 7600 ✉ info@gclaw.co.uk
Call Date: Oct 1992, Middle Temple

EATON MR ANDREW ROBERT

Garden Court Chambers
57-60 Lincoln's Inn Fields, London WC2A 3LJ
☎ 020 7993 7600 ✉ info@gclaw.co.uk
Call Date: Nov 2004, Middle Temple

EATON HART MR ANDREW MICHAEL

Walnut House
63 St. David's Hill, Exeter, Devon EX4 4DW
☎ 01392 279751 ✉ clerks@walnuthouse.co.uk
Call Date: Jul 1989, Gray's Inn
Pupil Supervisor

EATON MR JAMES BERNARD

Thomas More Chambers
7 Lincoln's Inn Fields, London WC2A 3BP
☎ 020 7404 7000 ✉ clerks@thomasmore.co.uk
Call Date: Nov 1978, Middle Temple
Pupil Supervisor

Practising Areas: Crime, Crime (Corporate/Fraud), Employment

EATON MR TOBIAS BARNABY

Staple Inn Chambers
1st Floor, 9 Staple Inn, Holborn Bars, London WC1V 7QH ☎ 020 7242 5240
✉ clerks@stapleinn.co.uk
Call Date: Oct 2001, Inner Temple
Pupil Supervisor

Practising Areas: Administrative, Aviation, Common Law (General), Defamation, Discrimination, Housing, Landlord & Tenant, Local Government, Sports

ECKERSLEY MR SIMON RICHARD

1 High Pavement
Nottingham NG1 1HF ☎ 0115 941 8218
✉ clerks@1highpavement.co.uk
Call Date: Mar 1996, Lincoln's Inn

EDGE MR TIMOTHY RICHARD

Deans Court Chambers
24 St John Street, Manchester M3 4DF
☎ 0161 214 6000 ✉ clerks@deanscourt.co.uk
Deans Court Chambers
101 Walker Street, Preston PR1 2RR
☎ 01772 565 600 ✉ preston@deanscourt.co.uk
Call Date: Oct 1992, Gray's Inn
Pupil Supervisor

Practising Areas: Common Law (General), Employment, Personal Injury

EDHEM MISS EMMA

No5 Chambers
Greenwood House, 4-7 Salisbury Court, London EC4Y 8AA ☎ 0845 210 5555
No5 Chambers
38 Queen Square, Bristol BS1 4QS
☎ 0845 210 5555
No5 Chambers
Fountain Court, Steelhouse Lane, Birmingham B4 6DR ☎ 0845 210 5555 ✉ info@no5.com
Call Date: Oct 1993, Gray's Inn
Pupil Supervisor

EDINGTON MRS FIONA ANNE RIDER

Thomas More Chambers
7 Lincoln's Inn Fields, London WC2A 3BP
☎ 020 7404 7000 ✉ clerks@thomasmore.co.uk
Call Date: Oct 1998, Middle Temple

Practising Areas: Ancillary Relief, Care Proceedings, Children's Law, Coroners Inquests, Courts Martial, Crime, Family, Family Provision, Human Rights, Inquests

C

EDMONDS MR MICHAEL JONATHAN

4 Breams Buildings
Chancery Lane, London EC4A 1HP
☎ 020 7092 1900 ✉ clerks@4bb.co.uk
Call Date: Nov 2000, Inner Temple

Practising Areas: Courts Martial, Crime, Crime (Corporate/Fraud)

EDMONDS MISS VICTORIA JANE

St Philips Chambers
55 Temple Row, Birmingham B2 5LS
☎ 0121 246 7000 ✉ clerks@st-philips.com
Call Date: Jul 2004, Gray's Inn

EDWARDS MR ANTHONY

Chancery House Chambers
7 Lisbon Square, Leeds, West Yorkshire LS1 4LY ☎ 0113 244 6691
✉ clerks@chanceryhouse.co.uk
Call Date: Jul 1999, Middle Temple

Practising Areas: Arbitration, Commercial Litigation, Construction

EDWARDS MR DANIEL HUGH

Dere Street Barristers
14 Toft Green, York YO1 6JT
☎ 0844 3351551 ✉ clerks@derestreet.co.uk
York Chambers
Rotterdam House, 116 The Quayside, Newcastle Upon Tyne NE1 3DY
☎ 0191 206 4677
Call Date: Oct 1993, Lincoln's Inn
Pupil Supervisor

Practising Areas: Medical Negligence, Personal Injury

EDWARDS MR DENIS

Francis Taylor Building
Inner Temple, London EC4Y 7BY
☎ 020 7353 8415 ✉ clerks@ftb.eu.com
Call Date: Oct 2002, Middle Temple

Practising Areas: Administrative, Civil Liberties, Common Law (General), Data Protection, Discrimination, EC & Competition Law, Education, Employment, Environment, Human Rights, Immigration, Local Government, Mental Health, Public Law, Regulatory Law, Town & Country Planning

EDWARDS MR DICKON HARRISON

5 Pump Court
Ground Floor, 5 Pump Court, Temple, London EC4Y 7AP ☎ 020 7353 2532
✉ clerks@5pumpcourt.com
Call Date: Nov 2004, Inner Temple

Practising Areas: Common Law (General), Crime, Crime (Corporate/Fraud), Personal Injury

EDWARDS MR IAIN FREDERICK

1 Mitre Court Buildings
1 Mitre Court Buildings, Temple, London EC4Y 7BS ☎ 020 7452 8900 ✉ clerks@1mcb.com
Call Date: Oct 2000, Middle Temple

EDWARDS MR JACOB STEWART

1 Paper Buildings
1st Floor, 1 Paper Buildings, Temple, London EC4Y 7EP ☎ 020 7353 3728
✉ clerks@onepaper.co.uk
Call Date: Jul 2007, Lincoln's Inn

EDWARDS MISS JENNIFER MARY

13 King's Bench Walk
13 King's Bench Walk, Temple, London EC4Y 7EN ☎ 020 7353 7204 ✉ clerks@13kbw.co.uk
13 KBW
32 Beaumont Street, Oxford OX1 2NP
☎ 01865 311066 ✉ clerks@13kbw.co.uk
Call Date: Oct 1992, Gray's Inn
Pupil Supervisor

Practising Areas: Crime

EDWARDS MR JONATHAN GWYN MENDUS

Cambria Chambers
The Coal Exchange, Mount Stuart Square, Cardiff Bay, Cardiff CF10 5EB
☎ 0845 123 1234 ✉ Info@cambriachambers.co.uk
Call Date: Jul 1981, Lincoln's Inn
Pupil Supervisor

EDWARDS MR JONATHAN WILLIAM

Westgate Chambers
64 High Street, Lewes, East Sussex BN7 1XG
☎ 01273 480510
✉ clerks@westgate-chambers.co.uk
Call Date: Nov 1994, Lincoln's Inn

Practising Areas: Crime, Crime (Corporate/Fraud), Defamation, Entertainment, Film, Cable & TV, Health & Safety, Medical Negligence, Town & Country Planning

EDWARDS MR MARTIN RICHARD

39 Essex Street
London WC2R 3AT ☎020 7832 1111
✉clerks@39essex.com
82 King Street
Manchester M2 4WQ ☎0161 870 9969
Call Date: Nov 1995, Inner Temple

Practising Areas: Administrative, Commercial Property, Common Land, Common Law (General), Environment, Housing, Licensing, Local Government, Town & Country Planning

EDWARDS MR MATTHEW STUART

East Anglian Chambers
Gresham House, 5 Museum Street, Ipswich, Suffolk IP1 1HQ ☎01473 214481
✉ipswich@ealaw.co.uk
East Anglian Chambers
53 North Hill, Colchester, Essex CO1 1QA
☎01473 214481 ✉colchester@ealaw.co.uk
East Anglian Chambers
140 New London Road, Chelmsford, Essex CM2 0AW ☎01473 214481
✉chelmsford@ealaw.co.uk
Call Date: Jul 2006, Gray's Inn

Practising Areas: Courts Martial, Crime

EDWARDS MR NIGEL ROYSTON

St Paul's Chambers
5th Floor, St Paul's House, 23 Park Square South, Leeds LS1 2ND ☎0113 245 5866
Call Date: Nov 1995, Lincoln's Inn

Practising Areas: Ancillary Relief, Arbitration, Asset Finance, Bankruptcy, Care Proceedings, Children's Law, Common Law (General), Company & Commercial, Consumer, Conveyancing, Copyright, Coroners Inquests, Crime, Crime (Corporate/Fraud), Defamation, Disciplinary Tribunals, Energy, Entertainment, Environment, Family, Film, Cable & TV, Foreign Law, Health & Safety, Human Rights, Inquests, Licensing, Professional Negligence, Regulatory Law, Sale & Carriage of Goods, Sports, Tax (Capital & Income), Tax (Corporate), Trademarks

EDWARDS MR PAUL

37 Park Square Chambers
37 Park Square, Leeds LS1 2NY
☎0113 243 9422 ✉chambers@no37.co.uk
Call Date: Mar 2002, Lincoln's Inn

Practising Areas: Asset Finance, Common Law (General), Family, Immigration

EGAN MR PATRICK MANUS DERMOT

Thomas More Chambers
7 Lincoln's Inn Fields, London WC2A 3BP
☎020 7404 7000 ✉clerks@thomasmore.co.uk
Call Date: Nov 1991, Middle Temple

Practising Areas: Common Law (General), Discrimination, EC & Competition Law, Employment, Financial Services

EGERTON MISS CHRISTINE ANNE

KBW
The Engine House, No 1 Foundry Square, Leeds LS11 5DL ☎0113 297 1200
✉clerks@kbwchambers.com
Call Date: Oct 1992, Inner Temple
Pupil Supervisor

Practising Areas: Crime

EGLETON MR RICHARD WILDMAN

Pallant Chambers
12 North Pallant, Chichester, West Sussex PO19 1TQ ☎01243 784538
✉clerks@pallantchambers.co.uk
Call Date: Jul 1981, Gray's Inn
Pupil Supervisor

Practising Areas: Administrative, Bankruptcy, Chancery (General), Chancery (Land Law), Common Law (General), Discrimination, Education, Employment, Equity, Wills & Trusts, Family Provision, Housing, Insolvency, Landlord & Tenant, Local Government, Partnership, Personal Injury, Probate & Administration, Professional Negligence, Town & Country Planning

EILLEDGE MISS AMANDA GAIL CAROLINE

11 Stone Buildings
11 Stone Buildings, Lincoln's Inn, London WC2A 3TG ☎020 7831 6381 ✉clerks@11sb.com
Call Date: Oct 1991, Lincoln's Inn
Pupil Supervisor

Practising Areas: Banking, Chancery (General), Chancery (Land Law), Commercial Litigation, Commercial Property, Common Law (General), Company & Commercial, Conveyancing, Insolvency, Landlord & Tenant, Partnership, Professional Negligence

EISSA MR ADRIAN NADIR

25 Bedford Row
London WC1R 4HD ☎020 7067 1500
✉clerks@25bedfordrow.com
Call Date: Nov 1988, Inner Temple

Practising Areas: Crime, Crime (Corporate/ Fraud)

ELCOMBE MR NICHOLAS JOHN

East Anglian Chambers
53 North Hill, Colchester, Essex CO1 1QA
☎01473 214481 ✉colchester@ealaw.co.uk
East Anglian Chambers
140 New London Road, Chelmsford, Essex CM2 0AW ☎01473 214481
✉chelmsford@ealaw.co.uk
East Anglian Chambers
15 The Close, Norwich, Norfolk NR1 4DZ
☎01473 214481 ✉norwich@ealaw.co.uk
East Anglian Chambers
Gresham House, 5 Museum Street, Ipswich, Suffolk IP1 1HQ ☎01473 214481
✉ipswich@ealaw.co.uk
Call Date: Jul 1987, Inner Temple
Pupil Supervisor

Practising Areas: Ancillary Relief, Care Proceedings, Children's Law, Family

ELDER MISS FIONA ANN MORAG

Albion Chambers
Broad Street, Bristol BS1 1DR
☎0117 927 2144 ✉clerks@albionchambers.co.uk
Call Date: Jul 1988, Gray's Inn
Pupil Supervisor

Practising Areas: Crime, Crime (Corporate/ Fraud), Employment

ELDERGILL MR EDMUND MALCOLM

1 Pump Court
Elm Court, Temple, London EC4Y 7AB
☎020 7842 7070 ✉(name)@pumpcourt.co.uk
Call Date: Nov 1991, Inner Temple

Practising Areas: Equity, Wills & Trusts, Family, Partnership, Probate & Administration, Tax (Capital & Income)

ELESINNLA MR AYOADE

Igbobi Chambers
c/o Lawyers' Club, 3rd Floor, 218 Strand, London WC2R 1AT ☎0203 2867626
✉aelesinnla@igbobichambers.com
Call Date: Nov 2000, Inner Temple

Practising Areas: Discrimination, Employment

ELFIELD MISS LAURA ELAINE

The Chambers of Grahame Aldous QC
9 Gough Square, London EC4A 3DG
☎020 7832 0500 ✉clerks@9goughsquare.co.uk
Call Date: Mar 1996, Gray's Inn

Practising Areas: Employment, Personal Injury

ELIAS MR DAVID

9 Park Place
Cardiff, South Glamorgan CF10 3DP
☎029 2038 2731 ✉clerks@9parkplace.co.uk
Call Date: May 1994, Inner Temple
Pupil Supervisor

Practising Areas: Crime, Regulatory Law

ELLIOTT MR COLIN DOUGLAS

King's Bench and Godolphin (KBG)Chambers
115 North Hill, Plymouth, Devon PL4 8JY
☎01752 221551 ✉clerks@kbgchambers.co.uk
Call Date: Jul 1987, Gray's Inn

Practising Areas: Chancery (Land Law), Family, Family Provision, Housing, Landlord & Tenant

ELLIOTT MR EDWARD ANTHONY JOHN

Garden Court Chambers
57-60 Lincoln's Inn Fields, London WC2A 3LJ
☎020 7993 7600 ✉info@gclaw.co.uk
Call Date: Oct 2000, Gray's Inn

Practising Areas: Care Proceedings, Chancery (Land Law), Common Law (General), Crime, Family, Family Provision, Housing, Landlord & Tenant, Personal Injury

ELLIOTT MR ERIC ALAN QC (2006)

Trinity Chambers
The Custom House, 39 Quayside, Newcastle Upon Tyne NE1 3DE ☎0191 232 1927
✉info@trinitychambers.co.uk
Trinity Chambers
Multi Media Exchange, 72-80 Corporation Road, Middlesbrough TS1 2RF
☎01642 247569 ✉info@trinitychambers.co.uk
York Chambers
Rotterdam House, 116 The Quayside, Newcastle Upon Tyne NE1 3DY
☎0191 206 4677
Sovereign Chambers
46 Park Place, Leeds LS1 2RY
☎0113 245 1841
✉clerks@sovereignchambers.co.uk
Call Date: Jul 1974, Gray's Inn
Recorder

Practising Areas: Crime, Disciplinary Tribunals, Regulatory Law, Sports

ELLIOTT MR JASON

Dere Street Barristers
33 Broad Chare, Newcastle Upon Tyne NE1 3DQ ☎0844 3351551 ✉clerks@derestreet.co.uk
Call Date: Oct 1993, Inner Temple

Practising Areas: Civil Liberties, Crime, Local Government

ELLIOTT MISS MARGOT MARY

Regency Chambers
45 Priestgate, Peterborough PE1 1LB ☎01733 315215 ✉clerks@regencychambers.law.co.uk
Regency Chambers
Sheraton House, Castle Park, Cambridge CB3 0AX ☎01223 301517
Call Date: Nov 1989, Gray's Inn
Pupil Supervisor

ELLIOTT MR MARK DANIEL

3 PB Barristers
3 Paper Buildings, Temple, London EC4Y 7EU ☎020 7583 8055
3 PB Barristers
30 Christchurch Road, Bournemouth, Dorset BH1 3PD ☎01202 292102 ✉clerks.bournemouth@3paper.co.uk
3 PB Barristers
4 St Peter Street, Winchester SO23 8BW ☎01962 868884 ✉clerks.winchester@3paper.co.uk
3 PB Barristers
Royal Talbot House, 2 Victoria Street, Bristol, Avon BS1 6BB ☎0117 928 1520
3 PB Barristers
23 Beaumont Street, Oxford OX1 2NP ☎01865 793 736
Call Date: Jul 2007, Lincoln's Inn

Practising Areas: Ancillary Relief, Children's Law, Family

ELLIOTT MR RICHARD ANDREW

3 Temple Gardens
Lower Ground Floor, 3 Temple Gardens, Temple, London EC4Y 9AU ☎020 7353 3102 ✉clerks@3tg.co.uk
Call Date: Oct 2001, Middle Temple
Pupil Supervisor

ELLIOTT MS SARAH JULIA

Doughty Street Chambers
5th Floor, Broad Quay House, Prince Street, Bristol BS1 4DJ ☎01179 058 717
Doughty Street Chambers
Pall Mall Court, 61-67 King Street, Manchester M2 4PD ☎0161 618 1066
Doughty Street Chambers
53-54 Doughty Street, London WC1N 2LS ☎020 7404 1313 ✉enquiries@doughtystreet.co.uk
Call Date: Oct 1996, Gray's Inn

Practising Areas: Crime

ELLIOTT MR TIMOTHY STANLEY QC (1992)

Keating Chambers
15 Essex Street, London WC2R 3AA ☎020 7544 2600 ✉clerks@keatingchambers.com
Call Date: Jul 1975, Middle Temple

Practising Areas: Arbitration, Commercial Litigation, Construction, Energy, Environment, Professional Negligence

ELLIS DR PETER SIMON

Seven Bedford Row
7 Bedford Row, London WC1R 4BS ☎020 7242 3555 ✉clerks@7br.co.uk
Call Date: Nov 1997, Middle Temple
Pupil Supervisor

Practising Areas: Medical Negligence, Mental Health, Personal Injury

ELLIS MISS SARAH LOUISE

9-12 Bell Yard
London WC2A 2JR ☎020 7400 1800 ✉clerks@9-12bellyard.com
Call Date: Nov 1989, Gray's Inn

Practising Areas: Regulatory Law

ELLISON MR MARK CHRISTOPHER QC (2008)

QEB Hollis Whiteman
1-2 Laurence Pountney Hill, London EC4R 0EU ☎020 7933 8855 ✉barristers@qebhw.co.uk
Call Date: Nov 1979, Gray's Inn
Recorder

ELLISON MR ROBERT LEONARD

5 King's Bench Walk
5 King's Bench Walk, Temple, London EC4Y 7DN ☎020 7353 5638 ✉clerks@5kbw.co.uk
Call Date: Oct 1996, Middle Temple

EMANUEL MR DAVID HENRY

Garden Court Chambers
57-60 Lincoln's Inn Fields, London WC2A 3LJ
☎ 020 7993 7600 ✉ info@gclaw.co.uk
Call Date: Nov 1996, Gray's Inn

EMMANUEL MISS JOYCE CLARE

Kenworthy's Chambers
Arlington House, Bloom Street, Salford, Manchester M3 6AJ ☎ 0161 832 4036
Call Date: Oct 2001, Middle Temple

EMSLEY-SMITH MRS ROSALIND LUCY

Deans Court Chambers
24 St John Street, Manchester M3 4DF
☎ 0161 214 6000 ✉ clerks@deanscourt.co.uk
Deans Court Chambers
101 Walker Street, Preston PR1 2RR
☎ 01772 565 600 ✉ preston@deanscourt.co.uk
Call Date: Oct 2001, Gray's Inn

ENGELMAN MR MARK TREVOR

Hardwicke
New Square, Lincoln's Inn, London WC2A 3SB ☎ 020 7242 2523
✉ enquiries@hardwicke.co.uk
Call Date: Nov 1987, Gray's Inn
Pupil Supervisor

Practising Areas: Chancery (General), Competition, Copyright, Data Protection, Defamation, Entertainment, Film, Cable & TV, Franchising, Information Technology, Intellectual Property, Patents, Sports, Telecommunications, Trademarks

ENGELMAN MR PHILIP

Cloisters
1 Pump Court, Temple, London EC4Y 7AA
☎ 020 7827 4000 ✉ clerks@cloisters.com
Trinity Chambers
Multi Media Exchange, 72-80 Corporation Road, Middlesbrough TS1 2RF
☎ 01642 247569 ✉ info@trinitychambers.co.uk
Trinity Chambers
The Custom House, 39 Quayside, Newcastle Upon Tyne NE1 3DE ☎ 0191 232 1927
✉ info@trinitychambers.co.uk
Call Date: Jul 1979, Gray's Inn
Pupil Supervisor

Practising Areas: Administrative, Arbitration, Civil Liberties, Civil Litigation, Commercial Litigation, Common Law (General), Company & Commercial, Construction, Data Protection, Defamation, Disciplinary Tribunals, Discrimination, EC & Competition Law, Education, Employment, Entertainment, Film, Cable & TV, Financial Services, Healthcare, Human Rights, Insurance, Insurance/Reinsurance, International Trade, Licensing, Local Government, Partnership, Professional Negligence, Public Law, Regulatory Law, Sale & Carriage of Goods, Sports

ENGLAND MRS LISA JOHANNA LOUISE

Guildhall Chambers Portsmouth
Prudential Buildings, 16 Guildhall Walk, Portsmouth, Hampshire PO1 2DE
☎ 023 9275 2400 ✉ clerks@gcp-barristers.com
Call Date: Nov 1992, Gray's Inn
Pupil Supervisor

Practising Areas: Commercial Property, Common Law (General), Landlord & Tenant, Personal Injury

ENOCH MR DAFYDD HUW QC (2008)

23 Essex Street
London WC2R 3AA ☎ 020 7413 0353
✉ clerks@23es.com
Apex
Harlech House, 20 Cathedral Road, Cardiff CF11 9LJ ☎ 02920 232 032
✉ clerks@apexchambers.net
Call Date: Nov 1985, Gray's Inn
Recorder

Practising Areas: Crime, Crime (Corporate/Fraud), Environment, Health & Safety, Healthcare, Regulatory Law, Sports

ENRIGHT MS JOHANNE

Chambers of Ms Johanne Enright
19 William Blake House, 1 - 6 Dufour's Place, London W1F 7SQ ☎ 020 7287 7557
Call Date: Nov 1996, Lincoln's Inn

Practising Areas: Care Proceedings, Family

ENSAFF MR OMAR SHERIF

No5 Chambers
Fountain Court, Steelhouse Lane, Birmingham B4 6DR ☎ 0845 210 5555 ✉ info@no5.com
No5 Chambers
Greenwood House, 4-7 Salisbury Court, London EC4Y 8AA ☎ 0845 210 5555
No5 Chambers
38 Queen Square, Bristol BS1 4QS
☎ 0845 210 5555
Call Date: Oct 2000, Gray's Inn

Practising Areas: Commercial Litigation, Construction, Professional Negligence

EPHRAIM-ADEJUMO MRS HILDA EKPO

12 Old Square Chambers
1st Floor, 12 Old Square, Lincoln's Inn, London WC2A 3TX ☎ 020 7404 0875
✉ clerks@12oldsquare.com
Call Date: Nov 1989, Lincoln's Inn

Practising Areas: Care Proceedings, Children's Law, Civil Litigation, Commercial Litigation, Common Law (General), Company & Commercial, Consumer, Family, Family Provision, Housing, Human Rights, Immigration, Landlord & Tenant, Mental Health, Personal Injury

ESPLEY MISS SUSAN

Fenners Chambers
3 Madingley Road, Cambridge CB3 0EE
☎ 01223 368761 ✉ clerks@fennerschambers.com
Call Date: Jul 1976, Gray's Inn

Practising Areas: Family

ESPRIT MR BENOIT

Barristers Chambers
89A High Road, Wood Green, London N22 6BB ☎ 020 3417 6461
✉ clerk@barristerschambers.org
Legis Chambers
Cherat House, 32 Havelock Street, Aylesbury, Buckinghamshire HP20 2NX
☎ 01296 431125 ✉ espritbenoit@yahoo.co.uk
Call Date: Nov 1982, Inner Temple

Practising Areas: Bankruptcy, Chancery (General), Chancery (Land Law), Commercial Property, Costs, Crime, Discrimination, Employment, Housing, Land, Landlord & Tenant, Probate & Administration, Road Traffic And Highways

ETHERINGTON MR DAVID CHARLES LYNCH QC (1998)

18 Red Lion Court
London EC4A 3EB ☎ 020 7520 6000
✉ chambers@18rlc.co.uk
18 Red Lion Court (Annexe)
Thornwood House, 102 New London Road, Chelmsford, Essex CM2 0RG
☎ 01245 280880
Call Date: Nov 1979, Middle Temple
Recorder

Practising Areas: Crime, Crime (Corporate/Fraud)

EVANS MR ANDREW DAVID

St Philips Chambers
55 Temple Row, Birmingham B2 5LS
☎ 0121 246 7000 ✉ clerks@st-philips.com
Call Date: Nov 2000, Lincoln's Inn

Practising Areas: Common Law (General), Crime, Employment, Licensing

EVANS MR CHARLES HENRY FREDERICK

Furnival Chambers
32 Furnival Street, London EC4A 1JQ
☎ 020 7405 3232
Call Date: Nov 1988, Middle Temple
Pupil Supervisor

EVANS MR DAVID HOWARD QC (1991)

Chambers of Andrew Mitchell QC
33 Chancery Lane, London WC2A 1EN
☎ 020 7440 9950 ✉ clerks@33cllaw.com
Aspect Chambers
Aspect Court, 4 Temple Row, Birmingham B2 5HG ☎ 0121 222 2447
✉ clerks@aspectchambers.com
Call Date: Nov 1972, Middle Temple

Practising Areas: Crime, Crime (Corporate/Fraud)

EVANS MISS JUDI

St John's Chambers
101 Victoria Street, Bristol BS1 6PU
☎ 0117 923 4700 ✉ clerks@stjohnschambers.co.uk
Call Date: Nov 1996, Middle Temple

EVANS MR JULIAN JACOB

QEB Hollis Whiteman
1-2 Laurence Pountney Hill, London EC4R 0EU ☎ 020 7933 8855 ✉ barristers@qebhw.co.uk
Call Date: Oct 1997, Middle Temple
Pupil Supervisor

EVANS MR MARK QC (1995)

Chambers of Mr Mark Evans
Grove Farm, Wapley, Bristol BS37 8RW
☎ 01454 312150 ✉ evansmlaw@fsmail.net
Call Date: Nov 1971, Gray's Inn

EVANS MR PAUL HUGH

No5 Chambers
Fountain Court, Steelhouse Lane, Birmingham B4 6DR ☎0845 210 5555 ✉info@no5.com
No5 Chambers
Greenwood House, 4-7 Salisbury Court, London EC4Y 8AA ☎0845 210 5555
No5 Chambers
38 Queen Square, Bristol BS1 4QS ☎0845 210 5555
Call Date: Jul 2001, Inner Temple

Practising Areas: Costs

EVANS MR PHILIP

QEB Hollis Whiteman
1-2 Laurence Pountney Hill, London EC4R 0EU ☎020 7933 8855 ✉barristers@qebhw.co.uk
Call Date: Oct 1995, Lincoln's Inn
Pupil Supervisor

Practising Areas: Crime, Crime (Corporate/Fraud), Licensing, Regulatory Law, Sports

EVANS MR ROBERT JONATHAN

Keating Chambers
15 Essex Street, London WC2R 3AA ☎020 7544 2600 ✉clerks@keatingchambers.com
Call Date: Jul 1989, Gray's Inn
Pupil Supervisor

Practising Areas: Arbitration, Commercial Litigation, Construction, Energy, Professional Negligence

EVANS MR ROGER KENNETH

Harcourt Chambers
1st Floor, 2 Harcourt Buildings, Temple, London EC4Y 9DB ☎0844 561 7135
Harcourt Chambers
Churchill House, 3 St Aldate's Courtyard, St Aldate's, Oxford OX1 1BN ☎0844 561 7135
Call Date: Nov 1970, Middle Temple
Pupil Supervisor, Recorder

EVANS MR SIMEON VAUGHAN

St Johns Buildings
24a - 28 St John Street, Manchester M3 4DJ ☎0161 214 1500 ✉clerk@stjohnsbuildings.co.uk
16 Winckley Square
Preston PR1 3JJ ☎01772 256100
St Johns Buildings Liverpool
8th Floor India Buildings, Water Street, Liverpool L2 0XG ☎0151 243 6000 ✉clerk@stjohnsbuildings.co.uk
Call Date: Nov 1997, Lincoln's Inn

Practising Areas: Civil Liberties, Crime, Crime (Corporate/Fraud), Sports

FACENNA MR GERALD CARLO

Monckton Chambers
1 & 2 Raymond Buildings, Gray's Inn, London WC1R 5NR ☎020 7405 7211 ✉chambers@monckton.com
Call Date: Oct 2001, Lincoln's Inn
Pupil Supervisor

Practising Areas: Administrative, Agriculture, Civil Liberties, Civil Litigation, Commercial Litigation, Competition, Consumer, Data Protection, Discrimination, EC & Competition Law, Energy, Environment, Human Rights, Information Technology, Licensing, Local Government, Parliamentary, Public International, Public Law, Regulatory Law, Tax (Capital & Income), Telecommunications

FAGBORUN BENNETT MS MORAYO ABOSEDE

Hardwicke
New Square, Lincoln's Inn, London WC2A 3SB ☎020 7242 2523 ✉enquiries@hardwicke.co.uk
Call Date: Jul 2004, Lincoln's Inn

Practising Areas: Administrative, Common Law (General), Discrimination, Employment, Housing, Human Rights, Landlord & Tenant, Local Government

FAIN MR CARL IAN

Tanfield Chambers
2-5 Warwick Court, London WC1R 5DJ ☎020 7421 5300 ✉clerks@tanfieldchambers.co.uk
Call Date: Oct 2001, Lincoln's Inn

Practising Areas: Chancery (General), Chancery (Land Law), Commercial Litigation, Commercial Property, Common Law (General), Housing, Landlord & Tenant

FAIRBANK MR NICHOLAS JAMES

4 Paper Buildings
1st Floor, 4 Paper Buildings, Temple, London EC4Y 7EX ☎020 7427 5200 ✉clerks@4pb.com
Call Date: Nov 1996, Lincoln's Inn
Pupil Supervisor

Practising Areas: Ancillary Relief, Care Proceedings, Chancery (Land Law), Children's Law, Civil Litigation, Common Law (General), Equity, Wills & Trusts, Family, Family Provision, Land, Professional Negligence

FAIRBURN MR GEORGE EDWARD HENRY

Cornwall Street Chambers
85-87 Cornwall Street, Birmingham B3 3BY
☎0121 233 7500 ✉clerks@cornwallstreet.co.uk
Cornwall Street Chambers
Shrewsbury Annex, Rural Enterprise Centre, Stafford Drive, Battlefield Enterprise Park, Shrewsbury SY1 3FE
☎01743 363 611 / 0121 233 7500
Call Date: Oct 1995, Lincoln's Inn
Pupil Supervisor

Practising Areas: Care Proceedings, Children's Law, Family

FAIRCLOUGH MISS LUCY HELEN

Northampton Chambers
10 Spencer Parade, Northampton NN1 5AQ
☎01604 636271
✉clerks@northampton-chambers.co.uk
Call Date: Oct 2005, Gray's Inn

Practising Areas: Care Proceedings, Crime, Family

FAIRLEY MISS CHLOE ALICE

Park Court Chambers
16 Park Place, Leeds LS1 2SJ
☎0113 243 3277
✉clerks@parkcourtchambers.co.uk
Call Date: Oct 2004, Gray's Inn

FAIRPO MS CATHERINE ANNE

Atlas Chambers
3 Field Court, Gray's Inn, London WC1R 5EP
☎020 7269 7980 ✉clerks@atlaschambers.com
Call Date: Nov 2009, Gray's Inn

Practising Areas: Intellectual Property, Tax (Capital & Income), Tax (Corporate)

FALK MR CHARLES MORTON JAMES

3 PB Barristers
3 Paper Buildings, Temple, London EC4Y 7EU
☎020 7583 8055
Call Date: Oct 1994, Middle Temple

Practising Areas: Courts Martial, Crime, Crime (Corporate/Fraud), Licensing

FALKOWSKI MR DAMIAN

4-5 Gray's Inn Square
Gray's Inn, London WC1R 5AH
☎020 7404 5252 ✉clerks@4-5.co.uk
Call Date: Oct 1994, Gray's Inn
Pupil Supervisor

Practising Areas: Administrative, Arbitration, Banking, Bankruptcy, Chancery (General), Chancery (Land Law), Charities, Civil Litigation, Commercial Litigation, Commercial Property, Common Land, Common Law (General), Company & Commercial, Construction, Consumer, Conveyancing, Coroners Inquests, Data Protection, Disciplinary Tribunals, Environment, Housing, Insurance/Reinsurance, International Trade, Land, Landlord & Tenant, Local Government, Professional Negligence, Road Traffic And Highways, Sale & Carriage of Goods, Town & Country Planning

FAMA MRS GUDRUN HILDEGARD

Middle Temple Lane Chambers
2nd Floor South, 1 Middle Temple Lane, London EC4Y 9AA ☎020 7583 4352
✉chambers@mtlchambers.com
Call Date: Oct 1991, Gray's Inn
Pupil Supervisor

Practising Areas: Ancillary Relief, Care Proceedings, Children's Law, Common Law (General), Crime, Employment, Family, Family Provision, Housing, Human Rights, Immigration, Licensing

FAPOHUNDA MRS OLUKEMI

Furnival Chambers
32 Furnival Street, London EC4A 1JQ
☎020 7405 3232
Call Date: Jul 2002, Gray's Inn

Practising Areas: Crime, Employment

FARBEY MISS JUDITH SARAH QC (2011)

Doughty Street Chambers
53-54 Doughty Street, London WC1N 2LS
☎020 7404 1313 ✉enquiries@doughtystreet.co.uk
Doughty Street Chambers
Pall Mall Court, 61-67 King Street, Manchester M2 4PD ☎0161 618 1066
Doughty Street Chambers
5th Floor, Broad Quay House, Prince Street, Bristol BS1 4DJ ☎01179 058 717
Call Date: Oct 1992, Middle Temple
Pupil Supervisor

Practising Areas: Administrative, Immigration

FARLEY MR DAVID DUNBAR

St Johns Buildings
24a - 28 St John Street, Manchester M3 4DJ
☎0161 214 1500 ✉clerk@stjohnsbuildings.co.uk
16 Winckley Square
Preston PR1 3JJ ☎01772 256100
St Johns Buildings Liverpool
8th Floor India Buildings, Water Street, Liverpool L2 0XG ☎0151 243 6000
✉clerk@stjohnsbuildings.co.uk
Call Date: Oct 2001, Middle Temple

Practising Areas: Crime, Crime (Corporate/Fraud), Sports

FARR MR PHILIP EDWARD

1 Paper Buildings
1st Floor, 1 Paper Buildings, Temple, London EC4Y 7EP ☎020 7353 3728
✉clerks@onepaper.co.uk
Call Date: Nov 2001, Middle Temple

Practising Areas: Crime, Employment

FARRELL MR SIMON HENRY QC (2003)

3 Raymond Buildings
3 Raymond Buildings, Gray's Inn, London WC1R 5BH ☎020 7400 6400
✉clerks@3rblaw.com
Call Date: Nov 1983, Lincoln's Inn

Practising Areas: Commercial Litigation, Crime, Crime (Corporate/Fraud), Financial Services, Human Rights, Professional Negligence, Regulatory Law

FARRELLY MISS CATHERINE LOUISE

5 King's Bench Walk
5 King's Bench Walk, Temple, London EC4Y 7DN ☎020 7353 5638 ✉clerks@5kbw.co.uk
Call Date: Nov 1999, Middle Temple

Practising Areas: Crime

FARYL MISS ALAHA BEGUM

Central Chambers
89 Princess Street, Manchester M1 4HT
☎0161 236 1133 ✉clerks@centralchambers.co.uk
Call Date: Nov 2003, Lincoln's Inn

Practising Areas: Employment, Human Rights, Immigration

FAURE WALKER MISS JULIA FRANCES

2 Hare Court
Lower Ground, Ground, 1st & 2nd Floor, 2 Hare Court, Temple, London EC4Y 7BH
☎020 7353 3982 ✉clerks@2harecourt.com
Call Date: Jul 2004, Lincoln's Inn

Practising Areas: Crime, Crime (Corporate/Fraud), Regulatory Law

FAUX MR ANDREW JOHN

Cornwall Street Chambers
85-87 Cornwall Street, Birmingham B3 3BY
☎0121 233 7500 ✉clerks@cornwallstreet.co.uk
Call Date: Nov 1995, Inner Temple

FAWCETT MR NEIL

St Ive's Chambers
Whittall Street, Birmingham B4 6DH
☎0121 236 0863 ✉clerks@stiveschambers.co.uk
Call Date: Oct 2006, Lincoln's Inn

Practising Areas: Asset Finance, Banking, Chancery (General), Chancery (Land Law), Commercial Litigation, Commercial Property, Common Land, Common Law (General), Company & Commercial, Construction, Employment, Equity, Wills & Trusts, Family, Family Provision, Financial Services, Insolvency, Landlord & Tenant, Sale & Carriage of Goods

FEDER MR AMI

Chambers of Mr Ami Feder
Ground Floor, Lamb Building, Temple, London EC4Y 7AS ☎020 7797 7788
✉clerks@lambbuilding.co.uk
Lamb Building
22 Ship Street, Brighton BN1 1AD
☎01273 820490 ✉admin@lambbuilding.co.uk
Chambers of Mr Ami Feder
Ground Floor, Lamb Building, Temple, London EC4Y 7AS ☎020 7797 7788
✉clerks@lambbuilding.co.uk
Call Date: Jul 1965, Inner Temple

FEE MR CHARLES JONATHAN CONOR

29 Bedford Row Chambers
London WC1R 4HE ☎020 7404 1044
✉clerks@29br.co.uk
Call Date: Jul 2006, Gray's Inn

C

FEEHAN MR FRANCIS THOMAS QC (2010)

42 Bedford Row
London WC1R 4LL ☎020 7831 0222
✉clerks@42br.com
Call Date: Jul 1988, Lincoln's Inn
Pupil Supervisor

FEEST MR ADAM SEBASTIAN

3 PB Barristers
3 Paper Buildings, Temple, London EC4Y 7EU
☎020 7583 8055
3 PB Barristers
Royal Talbot House, 2 Victoria Street, Bristol, Avon BS1 6BB ☎0117 928 1520
3 PB Barristers
30 Christchurch Road, Bournemouth, Dorset BH1 3PD ☎01202 292102 ✉clerks.bournemouth@3paper.co.uk
3 PB Barristers
4 St Peter Street, Winchester SO23 8BW
☎01962 868884 ✉clerks.winchester@3paper.co.uk
3 PB Barristers
23 Beaumont Street, Oxford OX1 2NP
☎01865 793 736
Call Date: Feb 1994, Inner Temple
Pupil Supervisor

Practising Areas: Crime, Crime (Corporate/Fraud)

FELDMAN MR MATTHEW RICHARD BANKES

42 Bedford Row
London WC1R 4LL ☎020 7831 0222
✉clerks@42br.com
Call Date: Oct 1995, Inner Temple
Pupil Supervisor

Practising Areas: Chancery (Land Law), Commercial Property, Common Law (General), Housing, Landlord & Tenant

FELDSCHREIBER DR PETER

Four New Square
Four New Square, Lincoln's Inn, London WC2A 3RJ ☎020 7822 2000
✉barristers@4newsquare.com
Call Date: Nov 2000, Middle Temple

Practising Areas: Employment, Medical Negligence, Personal Injury

FELIX MISS ALEXANDRA MIRNALINI

QEB Hollis Whiteman
1-2 Laurence Pountney Hill, London EC4R 0EU ☎020 7933 8855 ✉barristers@qebhw.co.uk
Call Date: Oct 1999, Middle Temple
Pupil Supervisor

FELLOWS MR PHILIP DAVID ANDREW

Hardwicke
New Square, Lincoln's Inn, London WC2A 3SB ☎020 7242 2523
✉enquiries@hardwicke.co.uk
Call Date: Jul 2007, Lincoln's Inn

Practising Areas: Chancery (Land Law), Common Land, Common Law (General), Company & Commercial, Equity, Wills & Trusts, Land, Landlord & Tenant, Partnership, Professional Negligence, Public Law

FELTON MR TIMOTHY JOHN FOWLER

Rougemont Chambers
Victory House, Dean Clarke Gardens, Southernhay East, Exeter EX2 4AA
☎01392 208484
✉clerks@rougemontchambers.co.uk
Call Date: Jul 1977, Middle Temple

Practising Areas: Agriculture, Chancery (Land Law), Common Land, Common Law (General), Environment, Landlord & Tenant

FEMI-OLA MR ABIODUN JOHN

3 Temple Gardens
Lower Ground Floor, 3 Temple Gardens, Temple, London EC4Y 9AU ☎020 7353 3102
✉clerks@3tg.co.uk
Call Date: Nov 1985, Gray's Inn
Pupil Supervisor

FENDER MR CARL DAVID

Regency Chambers
45 Priestgate, Peterborough PE1 1LB
☎01733 315215 ✉clerks@regencychambers.law.co.uk
Regency Chambers
Sheraton House, Castle Park, Cambridge CB3 0AX ☎01223 301517
Call Date: Feb 1994, Middle Temple
Pupil Supervisor

Practising Areas: Administrative, Arbitration, Common Law (General), Discrimination, Employment, Family, Family Provision, Local Government, Personal Injury

FENHALLS MR MARK ROYDON ALLEN

23 Essex Street
London WC2R 3AA ☎020 7413 0353
✉clerks@23es.com
Call Date: Oct 1992, Gray's Inn
Pupil Supervisor

FENNY MR IAN CHARLES

Guildhall Chambers
23 Broad Street, Bristol BS1 2HG
☎0117 930 9000 ✉hoc@guildhallchambers.co.uk
Call Date: Jul 1978, Gray's Inn
Pupil Supervisor

Practising Areas: Crime, Road Traffic And Highways

FERBER MS IRIS

42 Bedford Row
London WC1R 4LL ☎020 7831 0222
✉clerks@42br.com
Call Date: Jul 2005, Inner Temple

Practising Areas: Chancery (General), Chancery (Land Law), Commercial Litigation, Discrimination, Employment, Housing, Landlord & Tenant, Professional Negligence

FERGUSON MR CHRISTOPHER MARK

Sovereign Chambers
46 Park Place, Leeds LS1 2RY
☎0113 245 1841
✉clerks@sovereignchambers.co.uk
Court Yard Chambers
Eltham Palace, P.O.370, London SE9 2RP
☎020 7936 2710
Unity Street Chambers
5 Unity Street, College Green, Bristol BS1 5HH ☎0117 906 9789
✉chambers@unitystreetchambers.com
Call Date: May 1979, Middle Temple
Pupil Supervisor

Practising Areas: Care Proceedings, Family

FERGUSON MR CRAIG CHARLES

2 Hare Court
Lower Ground, Ground, 1st & 2nd Floor, 2 Hare Court, Temple, London EC4Y 7BH
☎020 7353 3982 ✉clerks@2harecourt.com
Call Date: Feb 1992, Middle Temple
Pupil Supervisor

Practising Areas: Crime, Crime (Corporate/Fraud), Regulatory Law

FERGUSON MRS KATHARINE ANN

Fenners Chambers
3 Madingley Road, Cambridge CB3 0EE
☎01223 368761 ✉clerks@fennerschambers.com
Call Date: Feb 1995, Inner Temple

Practising Areas: Family, Family Provision

FERGUSON MR STEPHEN MICHAEL

2 Bedford Row
London WC1R 4BU ☎020 7440 8888
✉clerks@2bedfordrow.co.uk
Call Date: Nov 1991, Inner Temple

Practising Areas: Crime, Crime (Corporate/Fraud), Regulatory Law

FERM MR RODNEY ERIC

Broadway House Chambers
Broadway House, 9 Bank Street, Bradford, West Yorkshire BD1 1TW ☎01274 722560
✉clerks@broadwayhouse.co.uk
Broadway House Chambers
25 Park Square West, Leeds, West Yorkshire LS1 2PW ☎0113 246 2600
✉clerks@broadwayhouse.co.uk
Call Date: Jul 1972, Middle Temple
Pupil Supervisor

Practising Areas: Commercial Litigation, Common Law (General), Company & Commercial, Crime, Crime (Corporate/Fraud), Defamation, Family, Family Provision, Medical Negligence, Partnership, Personal Injury, Professional Negligence, Regulatory Law, Sale & Carriage of Goods, Sports

FERN MR GARY

7 Stones IP
88 Kingsway, Holborn, London WC2B 6AA
☎020 7193 4033
Call Date: Oct 1992, Lincoln's Inn
Pupil Supervisor

Practising Areas: Competition, Copyright, Data Protection, EC & Competition Law, Entertainment, Film, Cable & TV, Franchising, Information Technology, Intellectual Property, Patents, Sports, Telecommunications, Trademarks

FERNANDES MISS SUE-ELLEN CASSIANA

No5 Chambers
Greenwood House, 4-7 Salisbury Court, London EC4Y 8AA ☎0845 210 5555
No5 Chambers
38 Queen Square, Bristol BS1 4QS
☎0845 210 5555

No5 Chambers
Fountain Court, Steelhouse Lane, Birmingham B4 6DR ☎ 0845 210 5555 ✉ info@no5.com
Call Date: Oct 2005, Middle Temple

Practising Areas: Licensing

FERRY-SWAINSON MR RICHARD JOSEPH

2 Bedford Row
London WC1R 4BU ☎ 020 7440 8888
✉ clerks@2bedfordrow.co.uk
Call Date: Oct 1994, Lincoln's Inn

Practising Areas: Courts Martial, Crime, Crime (Corporate/Fraud), Financial Services, Health & Safety, Human Rights, Regulatory Law

FETTO MR NIAZI PETER

2 Temple Gardens
2 Temple Gardens, Temple, London EC4Y 9AY ☎ 020 7822 1200 ✉ clerks@2tg.co.uk
Call Date: Oct 1999, Inner Temple
Pupil Supervisor

Practising Areas: Discrimination, Employment, Health & Safety, Human Rights, Immigration, Insurance, Medical Negligence, Personal Injury, Professional Negligence, Sale & Carriage of Goods

FIELD MR JULIAN NIGEL

Crown Office Chambers
2 Crown Office Row, Temple, London EC4Y 7HJ ☎ 020 7797 8100
✉ mail@crownofficechambers.com
Call Date: Nov 1980, Gray's Inn
Pupil Supervisor

Practising Areas: Civil Litigation, Commercial Litigation, Common Law (General), Construction, Insurance, Insurance/Reinsurance, Professional Negligence, Sale & Carriage of Goods

FIELD MR STEPHEN ANTHONY

1 Pump Court
Elm Court, Temple, London EC4Y 7AB
☎ 020 7842 7070 ✉ (name)@pumpcourt.co.uk
Call Date: Nov 1993, Gray's Inn
Pupil Supervisor

Practising Areas: Crime, Regulatory Law

FIELDEN DR CHRISTA MARIA

1 Mitre Court Buildings
1 Mitre Court Buildings, Temple, London EC4Y 7BS ☎ 020 7452 8900 ✉ clerks@1mcb.com
Call Date: Nov 1982, Lincoln's Inn
Pupil Supervisor

Practising Areas: Administrative, Human Rights, Immigration

FIELDING MR JANICK RAPHAEL ALEXANDER

4 King's Bench Walk
2nd Floor, 4 King's Bench Walk, Temple, London EC4Y 7DL ☎ 020 7822 7000
✉ clerks@4kbw.co.uk
Call Date: Oct 1997, Inner Temple

Practising Areas: Crime, Crime (Corporate/Fraud), Sports

FIELDSEND MR JAMES WILLIAM

Tanfield Chambers
2-5 Warwick Court, London WC1R 5DJ
☎ 020 7421 5300 ✉ clerks@tanfieldchambers.co.uk
Call Date: Oct 1997, Lincoln's Inn

Practising Areas: Chancery (General), Chancery (Land Law), Commercial Property, Landlord & Tenant

FINLAY MR DARREN

Sovereign Chambers
46 Park Place, Leeds LS1 2RY
☎ 0113 245 1841
✉ clerks@sovereignchambers.co.uk
Call Date: Oct 1994, Gray's Inn

Practising Areas: Arbitration, Banking, Bankruptcy, Chancery (General), Chancery (Land Law), Civil Litigation, Commercial Litigation, Commercial Property, Common Law (General), Company & Commercial, Construction, Consumer, Coroners Inquests, Costs, Defamation, Disciplinary Tribunals, Discrimination, Employment, Equity, Wills & Trusts, Health & Safety, Housing, Industrial Diseases, Insolvency, Insurance, International Trade, Landlord & Tenant, Partnership, Personal Injury, Probate & Administration, Professional Negligence, Road Traffic And Highways, Sale & Carriage of Goods

FINN MR TERENCE

Forest Chambers
Chambers of Terence Finn, 13 Rutland Gardens, Gosberton, Boston, Lincolnshire PE11 4HR ☎01775 840827 ✉forestchambers@btinternet.com
Erimus Chambers
PO Box 1440, Bedford MK43 6AJ ☎01234 720952 ✉clerks@erimuschambers.com
Call Date: Oct 1995, Lincoln's Inn

Practising Areas: Employment, Sports

FINNIGAN MR PETER ANTHONY QC (2009)

QEB Hollis Whiteman
1-2 Laurence Pountney Hill, London EC4R 0EU ☎020 7933 8855 ✉barristers@qebhw.co.uk
Call Date: Jul 1978, Lincoln's Inn

Practising Areas: Crime, Crime (Corporate/Fraud), Regulatory Law, Sports

FINUCANE MR BRENDAN GODFREY EAMONN QC (2003)

Outer Temple Chambers
The Outer Temple, 222 Strand, London WC2R 1BA ☎020 7353 6381 ✉clerks@outertemple.com
Call Date: Jul 1976, Middle Temple

Practising Areas: Crime, Crime (Corporate/Fraud), Financial Services, Health & Safety, Healthcare, Regulatory Law

FISH MR DAVID THOMAS QC (1997)

Deans Court Chambers
24 St John Street, Manchester M3 4DF ☎0161 214 6000 ✉clerks@deanscourt.co.uk
Deans Court Chambers
101 Walker Street, Preston PR1 2RR ☎01772 565 600 ✉preston@deanscourt.co.uk
Goldsmith Chambers
Ground Floor, Goldsmith Building, Temple, London EC4Y 7BL ☎020 7353 6802 ✉clerks@goldsmithchambers.com
Call Date: Jul 1973, Inner Temple
Recorder

Practising Areas: Crime, Crime (Corporate/Fraud), Health & Safety, Licensing, Regulatory Law

FISHER MR DAVID

New Square Chambers
12 New Square, Lincoln's Inn, London WC2A 3SW ☎020 7419 8000 ✉robin.hollington@newsquarechambers.co.uk
Call Date: Nov 1985, Lincoln's Inn
Pupil Supervisor

Practising Areas: Bankruptcy, Commercial Litigation, Common Law (General), Company & Commercial, Construction, Insolvency, Insurance, Partnership, Professional Negligence, Sale & Carriage of Goods, Sports

FISHER MR JERVIS ANDREW QC (2009)

Citadel Chambers
The Citadel, 190 Corporation Street, Birmingham B4 6QD ☎0121 233 8500 ✉clerks@citadelchambers.com
Call Date: Jul 1980, Gray's Inn

Practising Areas: Courts Martial, Crime, Crime (Corporate/Fraud), Health & Safety, Licensing, Regulatory Law, Sports

FISHER MR JONATHAN SIMON QC (2003)

Devereux Chambers
Queen Elizabeth Building, Temple, London EC4Y 9BS ☎020 7353 7534 ✉clerks@devchambers.co.uk
Call Date: Jul 1980, Gray's Inn

Practising Areas: Administrative, Crime (Corporate/Fraud), Regulatory Law

FISHER MR RICHARD ALAN

Doughty Street Chambers
53-54 Doughty Street, London WC1N 2LS ☎020 7404 1313 ✉enquiries@doughtystreet.co.uk
Doughty Street Chambers
Pall Mall Court, 61-67 King Street, Manchester M2 4PD ☎0161 618 1066
Doughty Street Chambers
5th Floor, Broad Quay House, Prince Street, Bristol BS1 4DJ ☎01179 058 717
Call Date: Nov 1994, Lincoln's Inn
Pupil Supervisor

Practising Areas: Crime, Crime (Corporate/Fraud)

FISHER MS SANDRA

Renaissance Chambers
5th Floor, Gray's Inn Chambers, Gray's Inn, London WC1R 5JA ☎020 7404 1111 ✉clerks@renaissancechambers.co.uk
Call Date: Nov 1993, Inner Temple

FISHWICK MR GREGORY DAVID PHILIP KYLE

187 Fleet Street
London EC4A 2AT ☎020 7430 7430
✉chambers@187fleetstreet.com
Call Date: Oct 1996, Gray's Inn

Practising Areas: Civil Liberties, Courts Martial, Crime, Crime (Corporate/Fraud), Mental Health

FITTON-BROWN MISS REBECCA MARY

New Walk Chambers
27 New Walk, Leicester, Leicestershire LE1 6TE ☎0871 200 1298 / 0116 255 9144
✉clerks@newwalkchambers.co.uk
Call Date: Jul 1981, Inner Temple
Pupil Supervisor

FITZGERALD MR BENEDICT ANDREW

QEB Hollis Whiteman
1-2 Laurence Pountney Hill, London EC4R 0EU ☎020 7933 8855 ✉barristers@qebhw.co.uk
Call Date: Oct 2000, Lincoln's Inn
Pupil Supervisor

Practising Areas: Crime, Crime (Corporate/Fraud)

FITZGERALD MR JOHN VINCENT

Ingenuity IP Chambers
Chambers Legal Service, 71b Queensway, Petts Wood, Kent BR5 1DQ
✉lp@chamberslegalservice.com
Call Date: Jul 1971, Middle Temple
Pupil Supervisor

Practising Areas: Commercial Litigation, Competition, Copyright, Defamation, Entertainment, Film, Cable & TV, Information Technology, Intellectual Property, Patents, Telecommunications, Trademarks

FITZGERALD MR MICHAEL EDWARD

Monckton Chambers
1 & 2 Raymond Buildings, Gray's Inn, London WC1R 5NR ☎020 7405 7211
✉chambers@monckton.com
Call Date: May 1979, Lincoln's Inn

FITZGIBBON MR FRANCIS GEORGE HERBERT DILLON QC (2010)

Doughty Street Chambers
53-54 Doughty Street, London WC1N 2LS
☎020 7404 1313 ✉enquiries@doughtystreet.co.uk
Doughty Street Chambers
Pall Mall Court, 61-67 King Street, Manchester M2 4PD ☎0161 618 1066
Doughty Street Chambers
5th Floor, Broad Quay House, Prince Street, Bristol BS1 4DJ ☎01179 058 717
Call Date: Feb 1986, Middle Temple
Pupil Supervisor

Practising Areas: Crime, Crime (Corporate/Fraud)

FITZGIBBON MR NEIL KEVIN

Carmelite Chambers
9 Carmelite Street, London EC4Y 0DR
☎020 7936 6300
✉clerks@carmelitechambers.co.uk
Call Date: Nov 1989, Lincoln's Inn

Practising Areas: Crime, Health & Safety, Road Traffic And Highways

FITZHARRIS MISS GINNETTE

Call Date: Nov 1993, Lincoln's Inn

FITZMAURICE MR GUY EDWARD CHRISTIAN

Staple Inn Chambers
1st Floor, 9 Staple Inn, Holborn Bars, London WC1V 7QH ☎020 7242 5240
✉clerks@stapleinn.co.uk
Call Date: Jul 1999, Lincoln's Inn

Practising Areas: Administrative, Chancery (General), Civil Liberties, Commercial Litigation, Commercial Property, Common Law (General), Crime, Crime (Corporate/Fraud), Human Rights, Probate & Administration, Regulatory Law

FITZPATRICK MISS DENISE

Kenworthy's Chambers
Arlington House, Bloom Street, Salford, Manchester M3 6AJ ☎0161 832 4036
Call Date: Jul 2000, Middle Temple
Pupil Supervisor

FITZPATRICK MR EDWARD JAMES

Garden Court Chambers
57-60 Lincoln's Inn Fields, London WC2A 3LJ
☎020 7993 7600 ✉info@gclaw.co.uk
Call Date: Nov 1990, Gray's Inn
Pupil Supervisor

FITZPATRICK MR STEVEN MARK

2 Pump Court
1st Floor, 2 Pump Court, Temple, London EC4Y 7AH ☎020 7353 5597
✉clerks@2pumpcourt.co.uk
Call Date: Oct 2004, Lincoln's Inn

Practising Areas: Crime

FLANAGAN MISS JULIA MARY ALICE

Charter Chambers
33 John Street, London WC1N 2AT
☎020 7618 4400 ✉clerks@charterchambers.com
Call Date: Oct 1993, Lincoln's Inn

FLANAGAN MR NICHOLAS MARK

Cobden House Chambers
19 Quay Street, Manchester M3 3HN
☎0161 833 6000 ✉Clerks@Cobden.co.uk
Call Date: Jul 2004, Lincoln's Inn

FLATTERY MS AMANDA NICHOLE

Kenworthy's Chambers
Arlington House, Bloom Street, Salford, Manchester M3 6AJ ☎0161 832 4036
Call Date: Oct 1993, Lincoln's Inn
Pupil Supervisor

Practising Areas: Family, Family Provision

FLETCHER MR CHRISTOPHER MICHAEL

Octagon House
19 Colegate, Norwich NR3 1AT
☎01603 623186 ✉clerks@octagonhouse.co.uk
Call Date: Nov 1984, Inner Temple
Pupil Supervisor

Practising Areas: Ancillary Relief, Children's Law, Family, Family Provision

FLETCHER MR JAMES WATFORD

Five St Andrew's Hill
5 St Andrew's Hill, London EC4V 5BZ
☎020 7332 5400 ✉Clerks@5sah.co.uk
Call Date: Oct 2000, Middle Temple

Practising Areas: Common Law (General), Crime, Crime (Corporate/Fraud), Personal Injury

FLEXMAN MRS CARLA ANN

Albion Chambers
Broad Street, Bristol BS1 1DR
☎0117 927 2144 ✉clerks@albionchambers.co.uk
Call Date: Oct 2002, Inner Temple

Practising Areas: Family, Personal Injury

FLOOD MR DIARMUID BRENDAN MARTIN

Number 7 Harrington Street Chambers
7 Harrington Street, Liverpool L2 9YH
☎0151 242 0707 ✉clerks@7hs.co.uk
Call Date: Apr 1989, Lincoln's Inn
Pupil Supervisor

FLOOD MR EDWARD ALBERT

1 Garden Court Family Law Chambers
Ground Floor, One Garden Court, Temple, London EC4Y 9BJ ☎020 7797 7900
✉clerks@1gc.com
Call Date: Oct 2002, Middle Temple

Practising Areas: Care Proceedings, Family, Family Provision

FOINETTE MR IAN

Five St Andrew's Hill
5 St Andrew's Hill, London EC4V 5BZ
☎020 7332 5400 ✉Clerks@5sah.co.uk
Call Date: Nov 1986, Middle Temple
Pupil Supervisor

Practising Areas: Crime

FOLLON MR DANIEL RICHARD THOMAS

1 Gray's Inn Square
Ground Floor, 1 Gray's Inn Square, London WC1R 5AA ☎020 7405 0001
Call Date: Jul 2003, Middle Temple

Practising Areas: Chancery (General), Commercial Litigation, Common Law (General), Crime, Crime (Corporate/Fraud), Health & Safety, Landlord & Tenant, Licensing, Personal Injury, Professional Negligence, Regulatory Law

FOOKES MR ROBERT LAWRENCE

Francis Taylor Building
Inner Temple, London EC4Y 7BY
☎020 7353 8415 ✉clerks@ftb.eu.com
Call Date: Jul 1975, Lincoln's Inn
Pupil Supervisor

FORD MR MARK STEVEN

Lincoln House Chambers
Tower 12, The Avenue North, Spinningfields, 18-22 Bridge Street, Manchester M3 3BZ
☎0161 832 5701
✉info@lincolnhousechambers.com
Call Date: Nov 1991, Gray's Inn

Practising Areas: Crime, Crime (Corporate/Fraud), Sports

FORDHAM MISS CHLOE AUGUSTA

Furnival Chambers
32 Furnival Street, London EC4A 1JQ
☎020 7405 3232
Call Date: Jul 2005, Inner Temple

FORDHAM MRS MARGARET ALLISON

Principal Chambers
15 Lime Tree Walk, Sevenoaks, Kent TN13 1YH ☎0845 209 8080
Call Date: Oct 1990, Gray's Inn

Practising Areas: Family, Family Provision, Foreign Law, Personal Injury

FORLIN MR GERARD EMLYN QC (2010)

Cornerstone Barristers
2-3 Gray's Inn Square, Gray's Inn, London WC1R 5JH ☎020 7242 4986
✉chambers@2-3gis.co.uk
Call Date: Feb 1984, Lincoln's Inn
Pupil Supervisor

Practising Areas: Aviation, Courts Martial, Crime (Corporate/Fraud), Environment, Foreign Law, Health & Safety, Public International, Regulatory Law

FORMBY MS EMILY JANE

39 Essex Street
London WC2R 3AT ☎020 7832 1111
✉clerks@39essex.com
Call Date: Oct 1993, Middle Temple
Pupil Supervisor

Practising Areas: Medical Negligence, Personal Injury, Professional Negligence

FORSHALL MS ISABELLA LOUISE QC (2010)

Doughty Street Chambers
53-54 Doughty Street, London WC1N 2LS
☎020 7404 1313 ✉enquiries@doughtystreet.co.uk
Doughty Street Chambers
Pall Mall Court, 61-67 King Street, Manchester M2 4PD ☎0161 618 1066
Doughty Street Chambers
5th Floor, Broad Quay House, Prince Street, Bristol BS1 4DJ ☎01179 058 717
Call Date: Feb 1982, Gray's Inn
Pupil Supervisor

FORSHAW MISS SARAH ANNE QC (2008)

5 King's Bench Walk
5 King's Bench Walk, Temple, London EC4Y 7DN ☎020 7353 5638 ✉clerks@5kbw.co.uk
Call Date: Nov 1987, Middle Temple

Practising Areas: Crime

FORSTER MS SARAH JUDITH

14 Gray's Inn Square
14 Gray's Inn Square, Gray's Inn, London WC1R 5JP ☎020 7242 0858 ✉clerks@14gis.co.uk
Westgate Chambers
64 High Street, Lewes, East Sussex BN7 1XG
☎01273 480510
✉clerks@westgate-chambers.co.uk
Call Date: Nov 1976, Middle Temple
Pupil Supervisor

Practising Areas: Care Proceedings, Civil Liberties, Family, Mental Health

FORSYTH MR ANDREW ALLAN

15 New Bridge Street
London EC4V 6AU ☎020 7842 1900
✉clerks@15nbs.com
Call Date: Nov 1989, Inner Temple

FORSYTH MISS JULIE PATRICIA

Chavasse Court Chambers
18 Queen Avenue, Liverpool L2 4TX
☎0151 229 2030
✉clerks@chavassechambers.co.uk
Call Date: Jul 1983, Gray's Inn
Pupil Supervisor

FORSYTH MISS SAMANTHA

No5 Chambers
Fountain Court, Steelhouse Lane, Birmingham B4 6DR ☎0845 210 5555 ✉info@no5.com
No5 Chambers
Greenwood House, 4-7 Salisbury Court, London EC4Y 8AA ☎0845 210 5555
No5 Chambers
38 Queen Square, Bristol BS1 4QS
☎0845 210 5555
Call Date: Jul 1988, Inner Temple
Pupil Supervisor

Practising Areas: Crime, Crime (Corporate/Fraud), Regulatory Law

FORTE MR TIMOTHY AXEL

Dyers Chambers
35 Bedford Row, London WC1R 4JH
☎ 020 7404 1881 ✉ admin@dyerschambers.com
Call Date: Oct 1994, Gray's Inn
Pupil Supervisor

Practising Areas: Crime, Crime (Corporate/Fraud), Personal Injury

FORTUNE MR PETER CARL MICHAEL

4 King's Bench Walk
2nd Floor, 4 King's Bench Walk, Temple, London EC4Y 7DL ☎ 020 7822 7000
✉ clerks@4kbw.co.uk
Guildhall Chambers Portsmouth
Prudential Buildings, 16 Guildhall Walk, Portsmouth, Hampshire PO1 2DE
☎ 023 9275 2400 ✉ clerks@gcp-barristers.com
Call Date: Jul 1978, Inner Temple
Pupil Supervisor

Practising Areas: Care Proceedings, Common Law (General), Crime, Discrimination, Employment, Family, Personal Injury, Road Traffic And Highways

FOSTER MR CHARLES ANDREW

Outer Temple Chambers
The Outer Temple, 222 Strand, London WC2R 1BA ☎ 020 7353 6381
✉ clerks@outertemple.com
Call Date: Jul 1988, Inner Temple
Pupil Supervisor, Recorder

Practising Areas: Common Law (General), Healthcare, Medical Negligence, Professional Negligence

FOSTER MR JULIEN ANDREW STEWART

1 Garden Court Family Law Chambers
Ground Floor, One Garden Court, Temple, London EC4Y 9BJ ☎ 020 7797 7900
✉ clerks@1gc.com
Call Date: Oct 1995, Middle Temple
Pupil Supervisor

Practising Areas: Administrative, Care Proceedings, Family

FOULKES MR CHRISTOPHER DAVID

2 Hare Court
Lower Ground, Ground, 1st & 2nd Floor, 2 Hare Court, Temple, London EC4Y 7BH
☎ 020 7353 3982 ✉ clerks@2harecourt.com
Call Date: Oct 1994, Lincoln's Inn
Pupil Supervisor

Practising Areas: Crime, Crime (Corporate/Fraud), Regulatory Law

FOULKES MISS REBECCA

5 Pump Court
Ground Floor, 5 Pump Court, Temple, London EC4Y 7AP ☎ 020 7353 2532
✉ clerks@5pumpcourt.com
Call Date: Mar 2003, Lincoln's Inn

Practising Areas: Coroners Inquests, Crime, Crime (Corporate/Fraud), Education, Environment, Housing, Inquests, Landlord & Tenant, Licensing, Medical Negligence, Personal Injury, Regulatory Law, Road Traffic And Highways, Town & Country Planning

FOUND MR TIMOTHY PAUL

Farrar's Building
Farrar's Building, Temple, London EC4Y 7BD
☎ 020 7583 9241
✉ Chambers@farrarsbuilding.co.uk
Call Date: Jul 2006, Lincoln's Inn

Practising Areas: Common Law (General), Employment, Personal Injury, Professional Negligence

FOWLER MR EDMUND IAN CARLOSS

5 King's Bench Walk
5 King's Bench Walk, Temple, London EC4Y 7DN ☎ 020 7353 5638 ✉ clerks@5kbw.co.uk
Call Date: Oct 1992, Gray's Inn

FOWLES MR JONATHAN JAMES

Serle Court
6 New Square, Lincoln's Inn, London WC2A 3QS ☎ 020 7242 6105 ✉ clerks@serlecourt.co.uk
Call Date: Jul 2004, Gray's Inn

Practising Areas: Bankruptcy, Chancery (General), Chancery (Land Law), Charities, Commercial Litigation, Commercial Property, Company & Commercial, Equity, Wills & Trusts, Insolvency, Landlord & Tenant, Partnership, Private International, Probate & Administration

FOX MR JOHN HARVEY

Chambers of Mr Ami Feder
Ground Floor, Lamb Building, Temple, London EC4Y 7AS ☎ 020 7797 7788
✉ clerks@lambbuilding.co.uk
Lamb Building
22 Ship Street, Brighton BN1 1AD
☎ 01273 820490 ✉ admin@lambbuilding.co.uk
Chambers of Mr Ami Feder
Ground Floor, Lamb Building, Temple, London EC4Y 7AS ☎ 020 7797 7788
✉ clerks@lambbuilding.co.uk
Call Date: Jul 1973, Inner Temple

Practising Areas: Landlord & Tenant, Medical Negligence, Personal Injury

FOX MR PETER

Hind Court Chambers
London East, 100 Burford Wharf, 3 Cam Road, London E15 2SL ☎ 020 8534 2495
✉ peter_fox@btinternet.com
Call Date: Jul 2004, Gray's Inn

FRAIN-BELL MR WILLIAM JOHN

Hardwicke
New Square, Lincoln's Inn, London WC2A 3SB ☎ 020 7242 2523
✉ enquiries@hardwicke.co.uk
Call Date: Jul 2000, Middle Temple

FRAME MR STUART JAMES

Staple Inn Chambers
1st Floor, 9 Staple Inn, Holborn Bars, London WC1V 7QH ☎ 020 7242 5240
✉ clerks@stapleinn.co.uk
Call Date: May 1997, Gray's Inn

Practising Areas: Construction, Crime, Employment, Health & Safety, Regulatory Law

FRANCIS MR ANDREW JAMES

Serle Court
6 New Square, Lincoln's Inn, London WC2A 3QS ☎ 020 7242 6105 ✉ clerks@serlecourt.co.uk
Zenith Chambers
10 Park Square, Leeds LS1 2LH
☎ 0113 245 5438 ✉ clerks@zenithchambers.co.uk
Call Date: Nov 1977, Lincoln's Inn

Practising Areas: Chancery (General), Chancery (Land Law), Commercial Litigation, Commercial Property, Company & Commercial, Conveyancing, Probate & Administration, Professional Negligence

FRANCIS MR NICHOLAS QC (2002)

29 Bedford Row Chambers
London WC1R 4HE ☎ 020 7404 1044
✉ clerks@29br.co.uk
Call Date: Jul 1981, Middle Temple

Practising Areas: Arbitration, Family, Family Provision

FRANCIS MR RICHARD MAURICE

9 Park Place
Cardiff, South Glamorgan CF10 3DP
☎ 029 2038 2731 ✉ clerks@9parkplace.co.uk
Call Date: Nov 1974, Gray's Inn
Pupil Supervisor

Practising Areas: Care Proceedings, Chancery (General), Chancery (Land Law), Charities, Common Law (General), Equity, Wills & Trusts, Family, Family Provision, Landlord & Tenant, Partnership, Personal Injury, Probate & Administration

FRANK MR IVOR RICHARD BAINTON

7 Bell Yard
London WC2A 2JR ☎ 020 7831 0636
✉ kevintarrant@btconnect.com
Call Date: Jul 1979, Gray's Inn
Pupil Supervisor

Practising Areas: Care Proceedings, Civil Liberties, Crime, Family, Housing

FRANKLIN MISS KIM

Crown Office Chambers
2 Crown Office Row, Temple, London EC4Y 7HJ ☎ 020 7797 8100
✉ mail@crownofficechambers.com
Call Date: Nov 1984, Middle Temple
Pupil Supervisor

Practising Areas: Arbitration, Construction, Professional Negligence

FRANKLIN MISS REBECCA JANE

St Philips Chambers
55 Temple Row, Birmingham B2 5LS
☎ 0121 246 7000 ✉ clerks@st-philips.com
Call Date: Jul 2001, Lincoln's Inn

FRANTZIS MISS ROXANNE

KBW
The Engine House, No 1 Foundry Square, Leeds LS11 5DL ☎ 0113 297 1200
✉ clerks@kbwchambers.com
Call Date: Nov 2003, Middle Temple

Practising Areas: Discrimination, Employment, Family, Human Rights, Immigration, Personal Injury

FRASER MR MARK-ANTHONY

Dyers Chambers
35 Bedford Row, London WC1R 4JH
☎ 020 7404 1881 ✉ admin@dyerschambers.com
Call Date: Nov 2000, Middle Temple

Practising Areas: Crime, Crime (Corporate/Fraud), Human Rights, Personal Injury

FRASER-URQUHART MR ANDREW

4-5 Gray's Inn Square
Gray's Inn, London WC1R 5AH
☎ 020 7404 5252 ✉ clerks@4-5.co.uk
Call Date: Oct 1993, Middle Temple

Practising Areas: Administrative, Commercial Litigation, Discrimination, Employment, Environment, Local Government, Town & Country Planning

FRAWLEY MS LYNDSEY ANNE

Quorum Chambers
2 Victoria Square, Victoria Street, St Albans AL1 3TF ☎ 01727 884516
✉ clerks@quorumchambers.co.uk
Quorum Tax Chambers
25 Southampton Buildings, London WC2A 1AL ☎ 020 7043 5189
✉ clerks@quorumchambers.co.uk
Call Date: Oct 1995, Middle Temple

Practising Areas: Civil Litigation, Commercial Litigation, EC & Competition Law, Employment, Public Law, Tax (Capital & Income), Tax (Corporate)

FRAZER MS ALISON

Queen Square Chambers
56 Queen Square, Bristol BS1 4PR
☎ 0117 921 1966 ✉ crime@qs-c.co.uk
Call Date: Nov 1999, Gray's Inn

Practising Areas: Employment

FREEMAN MISS LISA CLAIRE

Furnival Chambers
32 Furnival Street, London EC4A 1JQ
☎ 020 7405 3232
Call Date: Oct 2005, Lincoln's Inn

Practising Areas: Courts Martial, Crime, Crime (Corporate/Fraud), Financial Services, Regulatory Law

FREEMAN MR PETER MARK

Farrar's Building
Farrar's Building, Temple, London EC4Y 7BD
☎ 020 7583 9241
✉ Chambers@farrarsbuilding.co.uk
Call Date: Oct 1992, Middle Temple
Pupil Supervisor

Practising Areas: Aviation, Personal Injury, Sports

FREEMANTLE MISS KATE PATRICIA

2 King's Bench Walk
2 King's Bench Walk, Temple, London EC4Y 7DE ☎ 020 7353 1746 ✉ clerks@2kbw.com
Call Date: Jul 2003, Lincoln's Inn

FRENCH MR PAUL BECKINTON

Guildhall Chambers
23 Broad Street, Bristol BS1 2HG
☎ 0117 930 9000 ✉ hoc@guildhallchambers.co.uk
Call Date: Jul 1989, Inner Temple

Practising Areas: Bankruptcy, Insolvency

FRIDD MR NICHOLAS TIMOTHY

Albion Chambers
Broad Street, Bristol BS1 1DR
☎ 0117 927 2144 ✉ clerks@albionchambers.co.uk
Bell Yard Chambers
116/118 Chancery Lane, London WC2A 1PP
☎ 020 7306 9292
✉ byclerks@bellyardchambers.co.uk
Call Date: Nov 1975, Inner Temple
Pupil Supervisor

Practising Areas: Crime, Employment

FRIEDMAN MR DAVID PETER QC (1990)

4 Pump Court
4 Pump Court, Temple, London EC4Y 7AN
☎ 020 7842 5555 ✉ chambers@4pumpcourt.com
Call Date: Jul 1968, Inner Temple
Recorder

Practising Areas: Arbitration, Commercial Litigation, Construction, Information Technology, Insurance

FRIEL MR JOHN ANTHONY

Hardwicke
New Square, Lincoln's Inn, London WC2A 3SB ☎ 020 7242 2523
✉ enquiries@hardwicke.co.uk
Call Date: Jul 1974, Gray's Inn

FRIEND MR MARK OWEN

Lincoln House Chambers
Tower 12, The Avenue North, Spinningfields, 18-22 Bridge Street, Manchester M3 3BZ
☎0161 832 5701
✉info@lincolnhousechambers.com
Call Date: Mar 2002, Lincoln's Inn

Practising Areas: Crime, Sports

FRIEZE MR DANIEL ISAAC

St Johns Buildings
24a - 28 St John Street, Manchester M3 4DJ
☎0161 214 1500 ✉clerk@stjohnsbuildings.co.uk
16 Winckley Square
Preston PR1 3JJ ☎01772 256100
St Johns Buildings Liverpool
8th Floor India Buildings, Water Street, Liverpool L2 0XG ☎0151 243 6000
✉clerk@stjohnsbuildings.co.uk
Call Date: Oct 1994, Gray's Inn
Pupil Supervisor

FRITH MR TIMOTHY GEORGE

Devereux Chambers
Queen Elizabeth Building, Temple, London EC4Y 9BS ☎020 7353 7534
✉clerks@devchambers.co.uk
Call Date: Nov 1996, Middle Temple

FRY MR NEIL JOHN

Coram Chambers
9-11 Fulwood Place, London WC1V 6HG
☎020 7092 3700 ✉mail@coramchambers.co.uk
Call Date: Feb 1992, Inner Temple

Practising Areas: Care Proceedings, Family

FRYER MR NIGEL MCCRAE

Queen Square Chambers
56 Queen Square, Bristol BS1 4PR
☎0117 921 1966 ✉crime@qs-c.co.uk
Call Date: Nov 1999, Middle Temple

Practising Areas: Chancery (Land Law), Crime, Crime (Corporate/Fraud), Environment, Health & Safety, Regulatory Law

FRYMAN MR NEIL

Lincoln House Chambers
Tower 12, The Avenue North, Spinningfields, 18-22 Bridge Street, Manchester M3 3BZ
☎0161 832 5701
✉info@lincolnhousechambers.com
Call Date: Jul 1989, Middle Temple

Practising Areas: Crime, Crime (Corporate/Fraud)

FRYMANN MR ANDREW PHILIP

187 Fleet Street
London EC4A 2AT ☎020 7430 7430
✉chambers@187fleetstreet.com
Call Date: Nov 1995, Inner Temple
Pupil Supervisor

Practising Areas: Courts Martial, Crime, Crime (Corporate/Fraud), Regulatory Law

FUAD MR KERIM QC (2010)

Chambers of Marion Smullen and Kerim Fuad QC
1 Inner Temple Lane, London EC4Y 1AF
☎020 7427 4400 ✉clerks@1itl.com
Call Date: Nov 1992, Inner Temple
Pupil Supervisor

Practising Areas: Crime, Crime (Corporate/Fraud)

FUDGE MRS SALLY RUTH

Furnival Chambers
32 Furnival Street, London EC4A 1JQ
☎020 7405 3232
Call Date: Nov 1998, Lincoln's Inn

Practising Areas: Crime

FULLER MR ALAN PETER

Albion Chambers
Broad Street, Bristol BS1 1DR
☎0117 927 2144 ✉clerks@albionchambers.co.uk
Call Date: Oct 1993, Gray's Inn

Practising Areas: Crime (Corporate/Fraud), Employment, Health & Safety, Regulatory Law

FULLERTON MR MICHAEL ANDREW

Chambers of Mr Michael Fullerton
5 Pembroke Avenue, Hove, East Sussex BN3 5DA ☎01273 772050
7 Bell Yard
London WC2A 2JR ☎020 7831 0636
✉kevintarrant@btconnect.com
Call Date: Feb 1990, Inner Temple
Pupil Supervisor

Practising Areas: Commercial Litigation, Common Law (General), Crime, Crime (Corporate/Fraud), Insurance, Personal Injury, Professional Negligence

FULLWOOD MR ADAM GARRETT

Kings Chambers
36 Young Street, Manchester M3 3FT
☎0845 034 3444 ✉clerks@kingschambers.com
Kings Chambers
5 Park Square East, Leeds LS1 2NE
☎0845 034 3444 ✉clerks@kingschambers.com
Kings Chambers
Embassy House, 60 Church Street, Birmingham B3 2DJ ☎0845 034 3444
✉clerks@kingschambers.com
Call Date: Mar 1996, Gray's Inn
Pupil Supervisor

Practising Areas: Healthcare, Housing, Human Rights, Local Government, Mental Health

FURLONG MR RICHARD CRAVEN

25 Bedford Row
London WC1R 4HD ☎020 7067 1500
✉clerks@25bedfordrow.com
Call Date: Oct 1994, Lincoln's Inn
Pupil Supervisor

Practising Areas: Crime, Crime (Corporate/Fraud)

FURNISS MR RICHARD ALEXANDER

42 Bedford Row
London WC1R 4LL ☎020 7831 0222
✉clerks@42br.com
Call Date: Oct 1991, Middle Temple
Pupil Supervisor

FURST MR STEPHEN ANDREW QC (1991)

Keating Chambers
15 Essex Street, London WC2R 3AA
☎020 7544 2600 ✉clerks@keatingchambers.com
Call Date: Jul 1975, Middle Temple
Recorder

Practising Areas: Arbitration, Construction, Professional Negligence

GADD MR ADAM BRIAN

Pump Court Chambers
Upper Ground Floor, 3 Pump Court, Temple, London EC4Y 7AJ ☎020 7353 0711
✉clerks@3pumpcourt.com
Pump Court Chambers
31 Southgate Street, Winchester, Hampshire SO23 9EB ☎01962 868 161
✉clerks@3pumpcourt.com
Riverview Chambers
Hamilton House, 1 Temple Avenue, London EC4Y 0HA ☎0844 225 3999
✉chrisbaylis@riverviewchambers.com
Call Date: Jul 2004, Gray's Inn

Practising Areas: Chancery (Land Law), Commercial Litigation, Common Law (General), Courts Martial, Crime, Crime (Corporate/Fraud), Defamation, Discrimination, Employment, Health & Safety, Human Rights, Landlord & Tenant, Medical Negligence, Personal Injury, Professional Negligence, Regulatory Law, Sale & Carriage of Goods

GAINER MR RICHARD ST CLAIR

St Margaret's Chambers
44 Sidney Road, St Margaret's, Twickenham, Middlesex TW1 1JR ☎020 8241 3516
Call Date: Nov 1983, Middle Temple

Practising Areas: Arbitration, Bankruptcy, Common Law (General), Crime, Employment, Equity, Wills & Trusts, Insolvency, Insurance, Landlord & Tenant

GAIR MR CHRISTOPHER

King's Bench Chambers
Wellington House, 175 Holdenhurst Road, Bournemouth, Dorset BH8 8DQ
☎01202 250025
Call Date: Jul 2000, Middle Temple

Practising Areas: Bankruptcy, Chancery (General), Common Law (General), Construction, Crime, Equity, Wills & Trusts, Health & Safety, Landlord & Tenant, Personal Injury

GALBRAITH-MARTEN MR JASON NICHOLAS

Cloisters
1 Pump Court, Temple, London EC4Y 7AA
☎020 7827 4000 ✉clerks@cloisters.com
Call Date: Oct 1991, Middle Temple
Pupil Supervisor

Practising Areas: Discrimination, Employment, Regulatory Law

GALLAGHER MS CAOILFHIONN ANNA

Doughty Street Chambers
53-54 Doughty Street, London WC1N 2LS
☎020 7404 1313 ✉enquiries@doughtystreet.co.uk
Doughty Street Chambers
Pall Mall Court, 61-67 King Street, Manchester M2 4PD ☎0161 618 1066

C

Doughty Street Chambers
5th Floor, Broad Quay House, Prince Street, Bristol BS1 4DJ ☎01179 058 717
Call Date: Oct 2006, Lincoln's Inn

Practising Areas: Administrative, Children's Law, Civil Liberties, Coroners Inquests, Human Rights, Inquests, Local Government, Parliamentary, Public Law

GALLAGHER MR JOHN DAVID EDMUND

Hardwicke
New Square, Lincoln's Inn, London WC2A 3SB ☎020 7242 2523
✉enquiries@hardwicke.co.uk
Call Date: Nov 1974, Gray's Inn
Pupil Supervisor, Recorder

GALLAGHER MS MARIA THERESA

Pump Court Chambers
5 Temple Chambers, Temple Street, Swindon SN1 1SQ ☎01793 539899
✉clerks@3pumpcourt.com
Pump Court Chambers
Upper Ground Floor, 3 Pump Court, Temple, London EC4Y 7AJ ☎020 7353 0711
✉clerks@3pumpcourt.com
Pump Court Chambers
31 Southgate Street, Winchester, Hampshire SO23 9EB ☎01962 868 161
✉clerks@3pumpcourt.com
Call Date: Nov 1997, Inner Temple

GALLAGHER MR STANLEY HAROLD

Tanfield Chambers
2-5 Warwick Court, London WC1R 5DJ
☎020 7421 5300 ✉clerks@tanfieldchambers.co.uk
Call Date: Feb 1994, Lincoln's Inn

Practising Areas: Chancery (Land Law), Commercial Property, Landlord & Tenant

GALLIVAN MR TERENCE JOHN

Five Paper
Ground Floor, 5 Paper Buildings, Temple, London EC4Y 7HB ☎020 7815 3200
Call Date: Jul 1981, Inner Temple

Practising Areas: Chancery (General), Chancery (Land Law), Civil Liberties, Commercial Litigation, Commercial Property, Common Law (General), Conveyancing, Education, Employment, Energy, Environment, Equity, Wills & Trusts, Housing, Human Rights, Landlord & Tenant, Local Government, Mental Health, Partnership, Professional Negligence

GALLOWAY MR MALCOLM KENNITH WILLIAM

Colleton Chambers
Colleton Crescent, Exeter, Devon EX2 4DG
☎01392 274898 ✉clerks@colletonchambers.co.uk
Call Date: Oct 1992, Inner Temple
Pupil Supervisor

GALVIN MR KIERAN JOHN MICHAEL CHRISTOPHE

2 Bedford Row
London WC1R 4BU ☎020 7440 8888
✉clerks@2bedfordrow.co.uk
Call Date: Nov 1996, Middle Temple

GALWAY-COOPER DR PHILIP ANTHONY

Five St Andrew's Hill
5 St Andrew's Hill, London EC4V 5BZ
☎020 7332 5400 ✉Clerks@5sah.co.uk
Call Date: Oct 1993, Inner Temple

Practising Areas: Administrative, Bankruptcy, Chancery (General), Chancery (Land Law), Commercial Litigation, Common Law (General), Company & Commercial, Construction, Family, Housing, Insolvency, Landlord & Tenant, Medical Negligence, Personal Injury, Professional Negligence, Town & Country Planning

GAMBLE MRS ESTHER RUTH

No5 Chambers
Fountain Court, Steelhouse Lane, Birmingham B4 6DR ☎0845 210 5555 ✉info@no5.com
No5 Chambers
Greenwood House, 4-7 Salisbury Court, London EC4Y 8AA ☎0845 210 5555
No5 Chambers
38 Queen Square, Bristol BS1 4QS
☎0845 210 5555
St Philips Chambers
55 Temple Row, Birmingham B2 5LS
☎0121 246 7000 ✉clerks@st-philips.com
Call Date: Jul 2001, Middle Temple

Practising Areas: Medical Negligence, Personal Injury

GANESAN MR MUTHUPANDI PETER

Furnival Chambers
32 Furnival Street, London EC4A 1JQ
☎020 7405 3232
Call Date: Oct 2003, Lincoln's Inn

Practising Areas: Administrative, Crime, Crime (Corporate/Fraud), Health & Safety, Human Rights, Immigration, Regulatory Law

GANNON MR KEVIN FRANCIS

1 Pump Court
Elm Court, Temple, London EC4Y 7AB
☎ 020 7842 7070 ✉ (name)@pumpcourt.co.uk
Call Date: Nov 1993, Inner Temple

Practising Areas: Housing

GARCHA MR GURDEEP SINGH

Citadel Chambers
The Citadel, 190 Corporation Street, Birmingham B4 6QD ☎ 0121 233 8500
✉ clerks@citadelchambers.com
Call Date: Nov 1997, Lincoln's Inn

Practising Areas: Crime, Employment, Immigration

GARDINER MR BRUCE DOUGLAS

2 Temple Gardens
2 Temple Gardens, Temple, London EC4Y 9AY ☎ 020 7822 1200 ✉ clerks@2tg.co.uk
Call Date: Oct 1994, Middle Temple
Pupil Supervisor

GARDINER MISS KERRY ANN

Queen Square Chambers
56 Queen Square, Bristol BS1 4PR
☎ 0117 921 1966 ✉ crime@qs-c.co.uk
Call Date: Oct 2006, Middle Temple

Practising Areas: Employment

GARDINER MR WILLIAM DAVID HUGH

Holborn Chambers
6 Gate Street, Lincoln's Inn Fields, London WC2A 3HP ☎ 020 7242 6060
Call Date: Nov 1976, Middle Temple

Practising Areas: Chancery (General), Local Government, Probate & Administration

GARDNER MR JAMES PIERS

Monckton Chambers
1 & 2 Raymond Buildings, Gray's Inn, London WC1R 5NR ☎ 020 7405 7211
✉ chambers@monckton.com
Call Date: Mar 2000, Gray's Inn

Practising Areas: Administrative, EC & Competition Law, Human Rights, Public International, Public Law, Regulatory Law

GARGAN MR MARK PATRICK

No.6 Park Square
Leeds LS1 2LW ☎ 0113 245 9763
✉ Tim@no6.co.uk
Call Date: Jul 1983, Middle Temple
Pupil Supervisor, Recorder

GARLICK MR PAUL RICHARD QC (1996)

Furnival Chambers
32 Furnival Street, London EC4A 1JQ
☎ 020 7405 3232
Call Date: Jul 1974, Middle Temple

Practising Areas: Crime, Crime (Corporate/Fraud), Health & Safety, Human Rights, Regulatory Law

GARNER MISS SOPHIE JANE

St Philips Chambers
55 Temple Row, Birmingham B2 5LS
☎ 0121 246 7000 ✉ clerks@st-philips.com
Call Date: Nov 1990, Middle Temple
Pupil Supervisor

Practising Areas: Discrimination, Employment

GARRETT MISS LUCY MARGARET

Keating Chambers
15 Essex Street, London WC2R 3AA
☎ 020 7544 2600 ✉ clerks@keatingchambers.com
Call Date: Oct 2001, Gray's Inn
Pupil Supervisor

Practising Areas: Arbitration, Commercial Litigation, Construction, Information Technology, Professional Negligence

GARRIDO MR DAMIAN ROBIN LEON

Harcourt Chambers
1st Floor, 2 Harcourt Buildings, Temple, London EC4Y 9DB ☎ 0844 561 7135
Call Date: Nov 1993, Middle Temple
Pupil Supervisor

GARTLAND MS DOROTHEA SUSAN

4 Paper Buildings
1st Floor, 4 Paper Buildings, Temple, London EC4Y 7EX ☎ 020 7427 5200 ✉ clerks@4pb.com
Call Date: Oct 2004, Inner Temple

GARVIE MR CARL PETER

St Philips Chambers
55 Temple Row, Birmingham B2 5LS
☎ 0121 246 7000 ✉ clerks@st-philips.com
Call Date: Mar 2008, Lincoln's Inn

Practising Areas: Arbitration, Bankruptcy, Chancery (General), Civil Litigation, Commercial Litigation, Common Law (General), Company & Commercial, Disciplinary Tribunals, Franchising, Insolvency, Partnership, Professional Negligence, Sports

GASKIN MR FRANCIS JOHN GERALD

4 Breams Buildings
Chancery Lane, London EC4A 1HP
☎ 020 7092 1900 ✉ clerks@4bb.co.uk
Call Date: Jul 2000, Middle Temple

Practising Areas: Courts Martial, Crime, Crime (Corporate/Fraud), Human Rights, Immigration

GASKIN MISS LEILA

Charter Chambers
33 John Street, London WC1N 2AT
☎ 020 7618 4400 ✉ clerks@charterchambers.com
Call Date: Oct 2000, Middle Temple

Practising Areas: Crime, Crime (Corporate/Fraud), Mental Health

GASPARRO MISS JULIA MARIE

Renaissance Chambers
5th Floor, Gray's Inn Chambers, Gray's Inn, London WC1R 5JA ☎ 020 7404 1111
✉ clerks@renaissancechambers.co.uk
Call Date: Jul 1999, Lincoln's Inn
Pupil Supervisor

GASZTOWICZ MR STEVEN QC (2009)

Cornerstone Barristers
2-3 Gray's Inn Square, Gray's Inn, London WC1R 5JH ☎ 020 7242 4986
✉ chambers@2-3gis.co.uk
New Street Chambers
2 New Street, Leicester LE1 5NA
☎ 0116 262 5906 ✉ clerks@2newstreet.co.uk
Call Date: Jul 1981, Gray's Inn

Practising Areas: Administrative, Chancery (General), Chancery (Land Law), Commercial Litigation, Commercial Property, Common Law (General), Company & Commercial, Employment, Equity, Wills & Trusts, Insolvency, Local Government, Professional Negligence, Town & Country Planning

GATES MR HARRY

4 Paper Buildings
1st Floor, 4 Paper Buildings, Temple, London EC4Y 7EX ☎ 020 7427 5200 ✉ clerks@4pb.com
Call Date: Nov 2001, Lincoln's Inn
Pupil Supervisor

GATES MISS SERENA JANE

Five St Andrew's Hill
5 St Andrew's Hill, London EC4V 5BZ
☎ 020 7332 5400 ✉ Clerks@5sah.co.uk
Call Date: Nov 2001, Middle Temple

GATTY MR DANIEL SIMON

Hardwicke
New Square, Lincoln's Inn, London WC2A 3SB ☎ 020 7242 2523
✉ enquiries@hardwicke.co.uk
Call Date: Oct 1990, Middle Temple
Pupil Supervisor

Practising Areas: Chancery (Land Law), Commercial Litigation, Commercial Property, Information Technology, Landlord & Tenant, Partnership, Professional Negligence, Sale & Carriage of Goods

GAU MR JUSTIN CHARLES

Pump Court Chambers
Upper Ground Floor, 3 Pump Court, Temple, London EC4Y 7AJ ☎ 020 7353 0711
✉ clerks@3pumpcourt.com
Pump Court Chambers
5 Temple Chambers, Temple Street, Swindon SN1 1SQ ☎ 01793 539899
✉ clerks@3pumpcourt.com
Pump Court Chambers
31 Southgate Street, Winchester, Hampshire SO23 9EB ☎ 01962 868 161
✉ clerks@3pumpcourt.com
Call Date: Jul 1989, Middle Temple
Pupil Supervisor

Practising Areas: Courts Martial, Crime, Crime (Corporate/Fraud), Ecclesiastical, Employment, Regulatory Law

GAUNT MISS SARAH LEVINA

36 Bedford Row
London WC1R 4JH ☎ 020 7421 8000
✉ chambers@36bedfordrow.co.uk
Call Date: Oct 1992, Lincoln's Inn

Practising Areas: Crime

C

GAYAN MR ANIL KUMARSINGH

Clapham Law Chambers
85 Landor Road, Clapham North, London
SW9 9RT ☎020 7978 8482
✉DANNY@claphamlawchambers.co.uk
Call Date: Nov 1972, Inner Temple

Practising Areas: Administrative, Company & Commercial, Foreign Law, Insurance

GEADAH MR ANTHONY EDWARD

29 Bedford Row Chambers
London WC1R 4HE ☎020 7404 1044
✉clerks@29br.co.uk
Call Date: Jul 2000, Gray's Inn

Practising Areas: Family, Family Provision

GEE MR STEVEN MARK QC (1993)

Stone Chambers
4 Field Court, Gray's Inn, London WC1R 5EF
☎020 7440 6900 ✉clerks@stonechambers.com
Call Date: Jul 1975, Middle Temple
Recorder

Practising Areas: Arbitration, Banking, Chancery (General), Commercial Litigation, Commodities, Company & Commercial, Competition, Energy, Insurance, Insurance/Reinsurance, International Trade, Professional Negligence, Sale & Carriage of Goods

GELBART MR GEOFF ALAN

1 Gray's Inn Square
Ground Floor, 1 Gray's Inn Square, London
WC1R 5AA ☎020 7405 0001
Call Date: Nov 1982, Lincoln's Inn
Pupil Supervisor

Practising Areas: Arbitration, Bankruptcy, Commercial Litigation, Common Law (General), Crime, Crime (Corporate/Fraud), Employment, Housing, Human Rights, Landlord & Tenant, Partnership, Personal Injury, Sale & Carriage of Goods

GENT MR MATTHEW THOMAS

Sovereign Chambers
46 Park Place, Leeds LS1 2RY
☎0113 245 1841
✉clerks@sovereignchambers.co.uk
Call Date: Nov 1998, Gray's Inn

Practising Areas: Crime, Employment, Licensing, Regulatory Law, Sports

GEORGE MR CHARLES RICHARD QC (1992)

Francis Taylor Building
Inner Temple, London EC4Y 7BY
☎020 7353 8415 ✉clerks@ftb.eu.com
Call Date: Jul 1974, Inner Temple
Recorder

Practising Areas: Town & Country Planning

GEORGE MR MICHAEL DAVID ROBERTS

St Philips Chambers
55 Temple Row, Birmingham B2 5LS
☎0121 246 7000 ✉clerks@st-philips.com
Call Date: Nov 1990, Gray's Inn
Pupil Supervisor

Practising Areas: Chancery (Land Law), Company & Commercial, Equity, Wills & Trusts, Family, Family Provision, Personal Injury

GEORGE MR NICHOLAS FRANK RAYMOND

New Walk Chambers
27 New Walk, Leicester, Leicestershire LE1 6TE ☎0871 200 1298 / 0116 255 9144
✉clerks@newwalkchambers.co.uk
Call Date: Jul 1983, Inner Temple

Practising Areas: Chancery (General), Chancery (Land Law), Commercial Litigation, Common Law (General), Company & Commercial, Construction, Family Provision, Landlord & Tenant, Medical Negligence, Personal Injury, Professional Negligence

GEORGE MISS SUSAN DEBORAH

Coram Chambers
9-11 Fulwood Place, London WC1V 6HG
☎020 7092 3700 ✉mail@coramchambers.co.uk
Call Date: Nov 1990, Gray's Inn

Practising Areas: Care Proceedings, Family

GERASIMIDIS MR NICOLAS

Guildhall Chambers
23 Broad Street, Bristol BS1 2HG
☎0117 930 9000 ✉hoc@guildhallchambers.co.uk
Call Date: Nov 1988, Inner Temple
Pupil Supervisor, Recorder

Practising Areas: Crime, Crime (Corporate/Fraud), Entertainment, Film, Cable & TV, Intellectual Property, Regulatory Law

GERMAIN MR RICHARD

Nine Bedford Row
9 Bedford Row, London WC1R 4AZ
☎ 020 7489 2727 ✉ clerks@9bedfordrow.co.uk
Call Date: Jul 1968, Inner Temple
Pupil Supervisor

Practising Areas: Crime

GERMAN MISS KELLY ANNE

Eastbourne Chambers
5 Chiswick Place, Eastbourne, East Sussex BN21 4NH ☎ 01323 642102
✉ clerks@eastbournechambers.co.uk
Call Date: Jul 2000, Lincoln's Inn

Practising Areas: Care Proceedings, Children's Law, Coroners Inquests, Crime, Education, Environment, Family, Family Provision, Health & Safety, Housing, Human Rights, Landlord & Tenant, Regulatory Law

GERRY MISS FELICITY RUTH

36 Bedford Row
London WC1R 4JH ☎ 020 7421 8000
✉ chambers@36bedfordrow.co.uk
Call Date: Oct 1994, Middle Temple
Pupil Supervisor

Practising Areas: Agriculture, Crime, Crime (Corporate/Fraud), Defamation, Family, Health & Safety, Human Rights, Mental Health

GERSCH MR ADAM NISSEN

Argent Chambers
5 Bell Yard, London WC2A 2JR
☎ 020 7556 5500
✉ briefsin@argentchambers.co.uk
Call Date: Oct 1993, Lincoln's Inn
Pupil Supervisor

Practising Areas: Administrative, Civil Litigation, Commercial Litigation, Common Law (General), Copyright, Costs, Courts Martial, Crime, Crime (Corporate/Fraud), Disciplinary Tribunals, Foreign Law, Inquests, Licensing, Professional Negligence, Regulatory Law, Trademarks

GIBBONS MR CHRISTOPHER CHARLES

Rowchester Chambers
4 Rowchester Court, Whittall Street, Birmingham B4 6DH ☎ 0121 233 2327
✉ clerks@rowchesterchambers.co.uk
Call Date: Jul 1977, Gray's Inn
Pupil Supervisor

GIBBONS MS ELLODIE

Tanfield Chambers
2-5 Warwick Court, London WC1R 5DJ
☎ 020 7421 5300 ✉ clerks@tanfieldchambers.co.uk
Call Date: Oct 1999, Inner Temple

Practising Areas: Chancery (General), Chancery (Land Law), Commercial Litigation, Commercial Property, Common Law (General), Housing, Landlord & Tenant

GIBBONS MISS MARY REGINA

Stone Chambers
4 Field Court, Gray's Inn, London WC1R 5EF
☎ 020 7440 6900 ✉ clerks@stonechambers.com
Call Date: Mar 1999, Lincoln's Inn

Practising Areas: Admiralty, Arbitration, Asset Finance, Banking, Bankruptcy, Chancery (General), Chancery (Land Law), Commercial Litigation, Commercial Property, Common Law (General), Company & Commercial, Competition, Corporate Finance, EC & Competition Law, Financial Services, Insolvency, Insurance, Insurance/Reinsurance, International Trade, Private International, Regulatory Law, Shipping/Admiralty

GIBBS MR PHILIP MARK

KCH Garden Square
1 Oxford Street, Nottingham NG1 5BH
☎ 0115 941 8851 ✉ clerks@kchgardensquare.co.uk
Call Date: Oct 1991, Inner Temple
Pupil Supervisor

Practising Areas: Crime, Crime (Corporate/Fraud), Disciplinary Tribunals, Regulatory Law, Sports

GIBSON MR CHARLES ANTHONY WARNEFORD QC (2001)

Henderson Chambers
2 Harcourt Buildings, Temple, London EC4Y 9DB ☎ 020 7583 9020
✉ clerks@hendersonchambers.co.uk
Call Date: Jul 1984, Inner Temple
Recorder

GILBERTSON MRS HELEN ALISON

Octagon House
19 Colegate, Norwich NR3 1AT
☎ 01603 623186 ✉ clerks@octagonhouse.co.uk
Call Date: Nov 1993, Middle Temple

Practising Areas: Care Proceedings, Family, Family Provision

GILCHRIST MISS NAOMI ROBERTA

St Philips Chambers
55 Temple Row, Birmingham B2 5LS
☎ 0121 246 7000 ✉ clerks@st-philips.com
Call Date: Jul 1996, Inner Temple

Practising Areas: Coroners Inquests, Courts Martial, Crime, Crime (Corporate/Fraud), Health & Safety, Licensing, Regulatory Law, Road Traffic And Highways

GILEAD MISS BERYL LOUISE

St Mary's Family Law Chambers
26-28 High Pavement, The Lace Market, Nottingham NG1 1HN ☎ 0115 950 3503
✉ clerks@stmarysflc.co.uk
Call Date: Feb 1989, Inner Temple
Pupil Supervisor

GILES MR DAVID WILLIAM

1 Gray's Inn Square
Ground Floor, 1 Gray's Inn Square, London WC1R 5AA ☎ 020 7405 0001
Call Date: Nov 1988, Lincoln's Inn
Pupil Supervisor

Practising Areas: Chancery (General), Chancery (Land Law), Common Law (General), Landlord & Tenant, Personal Injury, Professional Negligence

GILL MISS BALJINDER

10 King's Bench Walk
Ground Floor, 10 King's Bench Walk, Temple, London EC4Y 7EB ☎ 020 7353 7742
✉ Chambers@10kingsbenchwalk.co.uk
Call Date: Oct 1996, Inner Temple

Practising Areas: Ancillary Relief, Care Proceedings, Civil Litigation, Family, Human Rights, Immigration, Landlord & Tenant, Personal Injury

C

GILL MR MANJIT SINGH QC (2000)

No5 Chambers
Greenwood House, 4-7 Salisbury Court, London EC4Y 8AA ☎ 0845 210 5555
No5 Chambers
38 Queen Square, Bristol BS1 4QS
☎ 0845 210 5555
No5 Chambers
Fountain Court, Steelhouse Lane, Birmingham B4 6DR ☎ 0845 210 5555 ✉ info@no5.com
Call Date: Jul 1982, Gray's Inn

Practising Areas: Arbitration, Commercial Litigation, Education, Employment, Human Rights, Immigration, Local Government, Private International, Public International, Regulatory Law, Sports

GILL MISS PAMILLA

Goldsmith Chambers
Ground Floor, Goldsmith Building, Temple, London EC4Y 7BL ☎ 020 7353 6802
✉ clerks@goldsmithchambers.com
Call Date: Apr 1989, Lincoln's Inn

Practising Areas: Family

GILL MR RAJINDER SINGH

Charter Chambers
33 John Street, London WC1N 2AT
☎ 020 7618 4400 ✉ clerks@charterchambers.com
Call Date: Nov 2001, Inner Temple

Practising Areas: Crime, Environment, Regulatory Law

GILL MR SATINDERJIT SINGH

Five Paper
Ground Floor, 5 Paper Buildings, Temple, London EC4Y 7HB ☎ 020 7815 3200
Call Date: Feb 1991, Middle Temple

Practising Areas: Civil Litigation, Discrimination, Employment, Immigration

GILLAN MRS DOMINIQUE LYE-PING

Guildford Chambers
Stoke House, Leapale Lane, Guildford, Surrey GU1 4LY ☎ 01483 539131
✉ clerks@guildfordchambers.co.uk
Call Date: Oct 1998, Gray's Inn

Practising Areas: Ancillary Relief, Care Proceedings, Children's Law, Family, Family Provision

GILLESPIE MR CHRISTOPHER MICHAEL

2 Hare Court
Lower Ground, Ground, 1st & 2nd Floor, 2 Hare Court, Temple, London EC4Y 7BH
☎ 020 7353 3982 ✉ clerks@2harecourt.com
Call Date: Nov 1991, Gray's Inn

Practising Areas: Crime, Crime (Corporate/Fraud), Regulatory Law

GILLESPIE MISS JANE FRANCES

St Mary's Family Law Chambers
26-28 High Pavement, The Lace Market, Nottingham NG1 1HN ☎ 0115 950 3503
✉ clerks@stmarysflc.co.uk
Call Date: Oct 2001, Middle Temple
Pupil Supervisor

GILLET MS GEMMA LOUISE

Dyers Chambers
35 Bedford Row, London WC1R 4JH
☎ 020 7404 1881 ✉ admin@dyerschambers.com
Call Date: Jul 2003, Inner Temple

Practising Areas: Crime, Regulatory Law

GILLIATT MS JACQUELINE

4 Brick Court
4 Brick Court, Temple, London EC4Y 9AD
☎ 020 7832 3200 ✉ clerks@4bc.co.uk
Call Date: Feb 1992, Middle Temple
Pupil Supervisor

GILLIES MISS JENNIE

4 Pump Court
4 Pump Court, Temple, London EC4Y 7AN
☎ 020 7842 5555 ✉ chambers@4pumpcourt.com
Call Date: Jul 2000, Middle Temple

Practising Areas: Commercial Litigation, Common Law (General), Construction, Information Technology, Insurance, Professional Negligence

GILLMAN MISS RACHEL MARY

1 Garden Court Family Law Chambers
Ground Floor, One Garden Court, Temple, London EC4Y 9BJ ☎ 020 7797 7900
✉ clerks@1gc.com
Call Date: Jul 1988, Gray's Inn
Pupil Supervisor

Practising Areas: Ancillary Relief, Care Proceedings, Children's Law, Family, Family Provision, Public Law

GILLOTT MR PAUL ALAN ASHLEY

15 Winckley Square
Preston PR1 3JJ ☎ 01772 252828
✉ clerks@15winckleysq.co.uk
Call Date: Oct 1996, Middle Temple

Practising Areas: Ancillary Relief, Family, Land

GILMORE MISS MARY SEANIN

Four New Square
Four New Square, Lincoln's Inn, London WC2A 3RJ ☎ 020 7822 2000
✉ barristers@4newsquare.com
Call Date: Nov 1996, Gray's Inn

Practising Areas: Commercial Litigation, Common Law (General), Construction, Insurance, Professional Negligence

GILROY MR PAUL QC (2006)

9 St John Street
Manchester M3 4DN ☎ 0161 955 9000
✉ civilclerks@9sjs.com/criminalclerks@9sjs.com
Old Square Chambers
10-11 Bedford Row, London WC1R 4BU
☎ 020 7269 0300 ✉ clerks@oldsquare.co.uk
Call Date: Nov 1985, Gray's Inn

Practising Areas: Discrimination, Employment, Sports

GINNIFF MR NIGEL THOMAS

Atlantic Chambers
4-6 Cook Street, Liverpool L2 9QU
☎ 0151 236 4421 ✉ info@atlanticchambers.co.uk
Call Date: Jul 1978, Inner Temple

Practising Areas: Employment, Pensions, Tax (Capital & Income), Tax (Corporate)

GINSBURG MRS AMANDA

37 Park Square Chambers
37 Park Square, Leeds LS1 2NY
☎ 0113 243 9422 ✉ chambers@no37.co.uk
Call Date: Jul 1986, Lincoln's Inn

GIOVANNINI MRS ANGELA MICHELLE

Trinity Chambers
The Custom House, 39 Quayside, Newcastle Upon Tyne NE1 3DE ☎ 0191 232 1927
✉ info@trinitychambers.co.uk
Trinity Chambers
Multi Media Exchange, 72-80 Corporation Road, Middlesbrough TS1 2RF
☎ 01642 247569 ✉ info@trinitychambers.co.uk
Call Date: Nov 2000, Gray's Inn

GIZ MISS ALEV AYSE

1 Garden Court Family Law Chambers
Ground Floor, One Garden Court, Temple, London EC4Y 9BJ ☎ 020 7797 7900
✉ clerks@1gc.com
Call Date: Nov 1988, Gray's Inn

Practising Areas: Care Proceedings, Children's Law, Family

GLADWELL MR SIMON MARK

East Anglian Chambers
Gresham House, 5 Museum Street, Ipswich, Suffolk IP1 1HQ ☎01473 214481
✉ipswich@ealaw.co.uk
Call Date: Oct 1996, Inner Temple

Practising Areas: Commercial Litigation, Common Law (General), Courts Martial, Crime, Crime (Corporate/Fraud), Employment, Health & Safety, Licensing, Regulatory Law

GLASER MR MICHAEL SAMSON

14 Gray's Inn Square
14 Gray's Inn Square, Gray's Inn, London WC1R 5JP ☎020 7242 0858 ✉clerks@14gis.co.uk
Call Date: Nov 1998, Middle Temple
Pupil Supervisor

Practising Areas: Ancillary Relief, Chancery (General), Chancery (Land Law), Children's Law, Civil Litigation, Common Law (General), Family, Family Provision, Land, Partnership

GLASGOW MR OLIVER EDWIN JAMES

2 Hare Court
Lower Ground, Ground, 1st & 2nd Floor, 2 Hare Court, Temple, London EC4Y 7BH
☎020 7353 3982 ✉clerks@2harecourt.com
Call Date: Nov 1995, Middle Temple
Pupil Supervisor

Practising Areas: Asset Finance, Courts Martial, Crime, Crime (Corporate/Fraud), Defamation, Regulatory Law, Sports

GLASS MR ANTHONY TREVOR QC (1986)

QEB Hollis Whiteman
1-2 Laurence Pountney Hill, London EC4R 0EU ☎020 7933 8855 ✉barristers@qebhw.co.uk
Call Date: Jul 1965, Inner Temple
Recorder

Practising Areas: Courts Martial, Crime, Crime (Corporate/Fraud)

GLASS MRS MARY PATRICIA

12 Old Square Chambers
1st Floor, 12 Old Square, Lincoln's Inn, London WC2A 3TX ☎020 7404 0875
✉clerks@12oldsquare.com
Redemption Chambers
121 The Vale, Golders Green, London NW11 8TL ☎020 8458 5486 ✉home@ollennu92.freeserve.co.uk
Call Date: Nov 2000, Gray's Inn

GLASSBROOK MR ALEXANDER JAMES

Temple Garden Chambers
1 Harcourt Buildings, Temple, London EC4Y 9DA ☎020 7583 1315 ✉clerks@tgchambers.com
Call Date: Oct 1995, Middle Temple

GLEDHILL MR LEE ANDRE

Trident Barristers Chambers
Peter House, Oxford Street, Manchester M1 5AN ☎0161 663 3123
✉clerks@tridentchambers.com
Alexander Chambers
13 Halstead Road, Wanstead, London E11 2AY ☎0845 652 0451 / 0854 652 0451
✉clerks@alexanderchambers.co.uk
Call Date: Mar 1998, Lincoln's Inn

Practising Areas: Administrative, Care Proceedings, Civil Liberties, Civil Litigation, Commercial Litigation, Common Law (General), Coroners Inquests, Courts Martial, Crime, Crime (Corporate/Fraud), Data Protection, Defamation, Disciplinary Tribunals, Discrimination, Education, Employment, Financial Services, Health & Safety, Healthcare, Human Rights, Inquests, Licensing, Medical Negligence, Mental Health, Partnership, Personal Injury, Professional Negligence, Public Law, Regulatory Law, Sports

GLEDHILL MR SIMON CHRISTOPHER

Thomas More Chambers
7 Lincoln's Inn Fields, London WC2A 3BP
☎020 7404 7000 ✉clerks@thomasmore.co.uk
Call Date: Jul 2005, Middle Temple

Practising Areas: Crime

GLEESON MR MICHAEL GERARD

Field Court Chambers
5 Field Court, Gray's Inn, London WC1R 5EF
☎020 7405 6114 ✉clerks@fieldcourt.co.uk
Call Date: Jul 2004, Middle Temple

GLENSER MR PETER HEATH

Nine Bedford Row
9 Bedford Row, London WC1R 4AZ
☎020 7489 2727 ✉clerks@9bedfordrow.co.uk
Call Date: Oct 1993, Inner Temple
Pupil Supervisor

Practising Areas: Licensing

C

GLOAG MR ANGUS ROBIN

1 Gray's Inn Square
Ground Floor, 1 Gray's Inn Square, London WC1R 5AA ☎ 020 7405 0001
Rougemont Chambers
Victory House, Dean Clarke Gardens, Southernhay East, Exeter EX2 4AA
☎ 01392 208484
✉ clerks@rougemontchambers.co.uk
Call Date: Oct 1992, Inner Temple
Pupil Supervisor

Practising Areas: Chancery (General), Civil Litigation, Commercial Litigation, Common Law (General), Employment

GLOVER MR MARC PHILIP

Tanfield Chambers
2-5 Warwick Court, London WC1R 5DJ
☎ 020 7421 5300 ✉ clerks@tanfieldchambers.co.uk
Call Date: Oct 1999, Lincoln's Inn

Practising Areas: Bankruptcy, Chancery (General), Commercial Litigation, Commercial Property, Common Law (General), Insolvency, Landlord & Tenant

GLOVER MR STEPHEN JULIAN

37 Park Square Chambers
37 Park Square, Leeds LS1 2NY
☎ 0113 243 9422 ✉ chambers@no37.co.uk
Call Date: Jul 1978, Middle Temple
Pupil Supervisor

Practising Areas: Ancillary Relief, Commercial Litigation, Common Law (General), Family Provision, Medical Negligence, Personal Injury, Professional Negligence

GLYN MR CASPAR HILARY GORDON QC (2012)

Cloisters
1 Pump Court, Temple, London EC4Y 7AA
☎ 020 7827 4000 ✉ clerks@cloisters.com
Call Date: Nov 1992, Inner Temple
Pupil Supervisor

Practising Areas: Civil Liberties, Civil Litigation, Commercial Litigation, Common Law (General), Disciplinary Tribunals, Discrimination, Employment, Health & Safety, Human Rights, Personal Injury, Regulatory Law, Share Options, Sports

GOBIR MR NUHU GARBA

9 Park Place
Cardiff, South Glamorgan CF10 3DP
☎ 029 2038 2731 ✉ clerks@9parkplace.co.uk
Call Date: Oct 1998, Middle Temple

Practising Areas: Crime, Health & Safety, Immigration, Regulatory Law

GODDARD MISS SUZANNE HAZEL QC (2008)

Lincoln House Chambers
Tower 12, The Avenue North, Spinningfields, 18-22 Bridge Street, Manchester M3 3BZ
☎ 0161 832 5701
✉ info@lincolnhousechambers.com
Call Date: Nov 1986, Gray's Inn
Recorder

Practising Areas: Crime, Crime (Corporate/Fraud), Health & Safety, Regulatory Law

GODFREY MISS EMMA CHARLOTTE

Field Court Chambers
5 Field Court, Gray's Inn, London WC1R 5EF
☎ 020 7405 6114 ✉ clerks@fieldcourt.co.uk
Call Date: Nov 1995, Lincoln's Inn

GODFREY MR HOWARD ANTHONY QC (1991)

2 Bedford Row
London WC1R 4BU ☎ 020 7440 8888
✉ clerks@2bedfordrow.co.uk
Call Date: Nov 1970, Middle Temple

Practising Areas: Crime, Crime (Corporate/Fraud), Financial Services, Regulatory Law

GODFREY MR LAUREN JOHN

Crown Office Row Chambers
119 Church Street, Brighton, Sussex BN1 1UD ☎ 01273 625625 ✉ clerks@1cor.com
Call Date: Oct 2007, Inner Temple

Practising Areas: Banking, Bankruptcy, Chancery (General), Chancery (Land Law), Charities, Civil Liberties, Commercial Litigation, Commercial Property, Common Law (General), Company & Commercial, Competition, Construction, Discrimination, Employment, Equity, Wills & Trusts, Financial Services, Franchising, Health & Safety, Housing, Human Rights, Information Technology, Insolvency, Insurance, Insurance/Reinsurance, Landlord & Tenant, Local Government, Partnership, Pensions, Personal Injury, Professional Negligence, Regulatory Law, Sale & Carriage of Goods, Share Options, Tax (Capital & Income), Tax (Corporate)

GODFREY MR THOMAS WILLIAM NETHERTON

23 Essex Street
London WC2R 3AA ☎020 7413 0353
✉clerks@23es.com
Call Date: Jul 2003, Inner Temple

Practising Areas: Courts Martial, Crime, Crime (Corporate/Fraud), Regulatory Law

GODWIN MR WILLIAM GEORGE HENRY

3 Hare Court
3 Hare Court, Temple, London EC4Y 7BJ
☎020 7415 7800 ✉clerks@3harecourt.com
St John's Chambers
101 Victoria Street, Bristol BS1 6PU
☎0117 923 4700 ✉clerks@stjohnschambers.co.uk
Call Date: Nov 1986, Middle Temple

Practising Areas: Arbitration, Banking, Commercial Litigation, Commodities, Company & Commercial, Construction, Energy, Foreign Law, Insurance, Insurance/Reinsurance, International Trade, Professional Negligence, Sale & Carriage of Goods, Shipping/Admiralty

GOFUR MR ABDUL

Thomas More Chambers
7 Lincoln's Inn Fields, London WC2A 3BP
☎020 7404 7000 ✉clerks@thomasmore.co.uk
Call Date: Oct 1999, Inner Temple

Practising Areas: Common Law (General), Crime, Crime (Corporate/Fraud), Housing, Landlord & Tenant, Licensing, Regulatory Law

GOLD MISS DEBRA ANNE

Fenners Chambers
3 Madingley Road, Cambridge CB3 0EE
☎01223 368761 ✉clerks@fennerschambers.com
Call Date: Jul 1985, Middle Temple

Practising Areas: Family

GOLD MR RICHARD DAVID

St John's Chambers
101 Victoria Street, Bristol BS1 6PU
☎0117 923 4700 ✉clerks@stjohnschambers.co.uk
Call Date: Nov 2006, Inner Temple

Practising Areas: Banking, Bankruptcy, Chancery (General), Chancery (Land Law), Commercial Litigation, Commercial Property, Common Law (General), Equity, Wills & Trusts, Family Provision, Housing, Landlord & Tenant, Probate & Administration, Sale & Carriage of Goods

GOLDBERG MR JONATHAN JACOB QC (1989)

North Square Chambers
15 North Square, London NW11 7AD
☎020 8455 3735 ✉jongold@talk21.com
Cobden House Chambers
19 Quay Street, Manchester M3 3HN
☎0161 833 6000 ✉Clerks@Cobden.co.uk
Call Date: Feb 1971, Middle Temple
Recorder

Practising Areas: Civil Liberties, Commercial Litigation, Common Law (General), Courts Martial, Crime, Crime (Corporate/Fraud), Defamation

GOLDBERG MR SIMON IAN

Trinity Chambers
The Custom House, 39 Quayside, Newcastle Upon Tyne NE1 3DE ☎0191 232 1927
✉info@trinitychambers.co.uk
Trinity Chambers
Multi Media Exchange, 72-80 Corporation Road, Middlesbrough TS1 2RF
☎01642 247569 ✉info@trinitychambers.co.uk
Call Date: Jul 1999, Middle Temple
Pupil Supervisor

Practising Areas: Chancery (General), Civil Litigation, Commercial Litigation, Construction, Discrimination, Employment, Equity, Wills & Trusts, Landlord & Tenant, Partnership, Professional Negligence, Sale & Carriage of Goods, Sports

GOLDIE MISS KATIE JANE

Albion Chambers
Broad Street, Bristol BS1 1DR
☎0117 927 2144 ✉clerks@albionchambers.co.uk
Call Date: Oct 2004, Inner Temple

Practising Areas: Family

GOLDMAN MRS LINDA

Henderson Chambers
2 Harcourt Buildings, Temple, London EC4Y 9DB ☎020 7583 9020
✉clerks@hendersonchambers.co.uk
Call Date: Oct 1990, Middle Temple
Pupil Supervisor

Practising Areas: Employment, Medical Negligence, Personal Injury

GOLDREIN MR IAIN SAVILLE QC (1997)

Number 7 Harrington Street Chambers
7 Harrington Street, Liverpool L2 9YH
☎ 0151 242 0707 ✉ clerks@7hs.co.uk
7 Bell Yard
London WC2A 2JR ☎ 020 7831 0636
✉ kevintarrant@btconnect.com
Call Date: Jul 1975, Inner Temple
Recorder

Practising Areas: Commercial Litigation, Common Law (General), Entertainment, Family, Health & Safety, Healthcare, Human Rights, Insurance, Medical Negligence, Parliamentary, Personal Injury, Sports

GOLDRING MISS JENNIFER LEONIE

Five St Andrew's Hill
5 St Andrew's Hill, London EC4V 5BZ
☎ 020 7332 5400 ✉ Clerks@5sah.co.uk
Call Date: Nov 1993, Middle Temple

GOLDSACK MR IAN

Call Date: May 1997, Gray's Inn
Pupil Supervisor

GOLDSTEIN MR WAYNE NATHAN

18 St John Street
Manchester M3 4EA ☎ 0161 278 1800
✉ clerks@18sjs.com
Call Date: Nov 1999, Lincoln's Inn

Practising Areas: Chancery (General), Chancery (Land Law), Commercial Litigation, Common Law (General), Crime, Education, Equity, Wills & Trusts, Family Provision, Insolvency, Insurance, Landlord & Tenant, Medical Negligence, Probate & Administration

GOLDSTONE MR SIMON LEWIS

4 Pump Court
4 Pump Court, Temple, London EC4Y 7AN
☎ 020 7842 5555 ✉ chambers@4pumpcourt.com
Call Date: Jul 2004, Middle Temple

Practising Areas: Commercial Litigation, Commercial Property, Professional Negligence, Regulatory Law

GOMULKA MR MICHAEL SVEND

25 Bedford Row
London WC1R 4HD ☎ 020 7067 1500
✉ clerks@25bedfordrow.com
Call Date: Nov 2002, Inner Temple
Pupil Supervisor

Practising Areas: Crime, Crime (Corporate/Fraud)

GONZALEZ MERELLO MRS MARIA DOLORES

Holborn Chambers
6 Gate Street, Lincoln's Inn Fields, London WC2A 3HP ☎ 020 7242 6060
Call Date: Oct 2006, Lincoln's Inn

GOODALL MR CHARLES VERNON MACHIN-

Queen Square Chambers
56 Queen Square, Bristol BS1 4PR
☎ 0117 921 1966 ✉ crime@qs-c.co.uk
Call Date: Jul 1986, Inner Temple

Practising Areas: Chancery (General), Chancery (Land Law), Land, Landlord & Tenant

GOODALL MISS EMMA

Dyers Chambers
35 Bedford Row, London WC1R 4JH
☎ 020 7404 1881 ✉ admin@dyerschambers.com
Call Date: Nov 1996, Gray's Inn

Practising Areas: Crime, Crime (Corporate/Fraud), Road Traffic And Highways

GOODALL MISS RACHAEL JANE

3 PB Barristers
3 Paper Buildings, Temple, London EC4Y 7EU
☎ 020 7583 8055
3 PB Barristers
23 Beaumont Street, Oxford OX1 2NP
☎ 01865 793 736
3 PB Barristers
30 Christchurch Road, Bournemouth, Dorset BH1 3PD ☎ 01202 292102 ✉ clerks.bournemouth@3paper.co.uk
3 PB Barristers
Royal Talbot House, 2 Victoria Street, Bristol, Avon BS1 6BB ☎ 0117 928 1520
3 PB Barristers
4 St Peter Street, Winchester SO23 8BW
☎ 01962 868884 ✉ clerks.winchester@3paper.co.uk
Call Date: Jul 2000, Gray's Inn
Pupil Supervisor

Practising Areas: Ancillary Relief, Children's Law, Family, Family Provision

GOODE MR JULIAN LEIGH ALEXANDER

St Johns Buildings
24a - 28 St John Street, Manchester M3 4DJ
☎ 0161 214 1500 ✉ clerk@stjohnsbuildings.co.uk
16 Winckley Square
Preston PR1 3JJ ☎ 01772 256100

C

St Johns Buildings Liverpool
8th Floor India Buildings, Water Street, Liverpool L2 0XG ☎0151 243 6000
✉clerk@stjohnsbuildings.co.uk
Call Date: Nov 2006, Lincoln's Inn

Practising Areas: Crime, Crime (Corporate/Fraud), Personal Injury

GOODERHAM MISS ELIZABETH ANN

Northampton Chambers
10 Spencer Parade, Northampton NN1 5AQ
☎01604 636271
✉clerks@northampton-chambers.co.uk
Call Date: Jul 2001, Inner Temple

Practising Areas: Care Proceedings, Crime, Family, Family Provision

GOODFELLOW MR GILES WILLIAM JEREMY QC (2003)

Pump Court Tax Chambers
16 Bedford Row, London WC1R 4EF
☎020 7414 8080 ✉clerks@pumptax.com
Call Date: Jul 1983, Middle Temple

Practising Areas: Equity, Wills & Trusts, Professional Negligence, Tax (Capital & Income), Tax (Corporate)

GOODFELLOW MR STEPHEN JOHN

East Anglian Chambers
140 New London Road, Chelmsford, Essex CM2 0AW ☎01473 214481
✉chelmsford@ealaw.co.uk
East Anglian Chambers
Gresham House, 5 Museum Street, Ipswich, Suffolk IP1 1HQ ☎01473 214481
✉ipswich@ealaw.co.uk
East Anglian Chambers
15 The Close, Norwich, Norfolk NR1 4DZ
☎01473 214481 ✉norwich@ealaw.co.uk
Call Date: Nov 1997, Middle Temple

Practising Areas: Bankruptcy, Common Land, Common Law (General), Construction, Discrimination, Employment, Health & Safety, Housing, Landlord & Tenant, Licensing, Medical Negligence, Partnership, Personal Injury, Professional Negligence, Sale & Carriage of Goods

GOODISON MR ADAM HENRY

South Square
3-4 South Square, Gray's Inn, London WC1R 5HP ☎020 7696 9900
✉practicemanagers@southsquare.com
Call Date: Oct 1990, Middle Temple

Practising Areas: Banking, Bankruptcy, Chancery (General), Commercial Litigation, Company & Commercial, Corporate Finance, Equity, Wills & Trusts, Financial Services, Insolvency, International Trade, Sale & Carriage of Goods

GOODLAD MR GRANT DAVID

Farrar's Building
Farrar's Building, Temple, London EC4Y 7BD
☎020 7583 9241
✉Chambers@farrarsbuilding.co.uk
Call Date: Nov 2006, Lincoln's Inn

Practising Areas: Common Law (General), Coroners Inquests, Disciplinary Tribunals, Discrimination, Employment, Inquests, Personal Injury

GOODMAN MR ALEXANDER DAVID EDMUND

4-5 Gray's Inn Square
Gray's Inn, London WC1R 5AH
☎020 7404 5252 ✉clerks@4-5.co.uk
Atlas Chambers
3 Field Court, Gray's Inn, London WC1R 5EP
☎020 7269 7980 ✉clerks@atlaschambers.com
Call Date: Nov 2003, Lincoln's Inn

Practising Areas: Administrative, Civil Liberties, Common Land, Environment, Human Rights, Immigration, Licensing, Local Government, Parliamentary, Town & Country Planning

GOODMAN MR ANDREW DAVID

1 Chancery Lane
London WC2A 1LF ☎0845 634 6666
✉clerks@1chancerylane.com
Call Date: Jul 1978, Inner Temple
Pupil Supervisor

Practising Areas: Administrative, Commercial Litigation, Franchising, Partnership, Professional Negligence

GOODMAN MR SIMON CHARLES

Queen Square Chambers
56 Queen Square, Bristol BS1 4PR
☎0117 921 1966 ✉crime@qs-c.co.uk
Call Date: Nov 1996, Gray's Inn
Pupil Supervisor

GOODWILL MR GRAHAM

Chambers of Mr G Goodwill
Three Trees Farm, 20 Prickwillow Road, Isleham, Ely, Cambridgeshire CB7 5RG
☎07801729877
Call Date: Jul 1983, Inner Temple

C

GOODWIN MISS CAROLINE TRACY

Trinity Chambers
The Custom House, 39 Quayside, Newcastle Upon Tyne NE1 3DE ☎ 0191 232 1927
✉ info@trinitychambers.co.uk
Trinity Chambers
Multi Media Exchange, 72-80 Corporation Road, Middlesbrough TS1 2RF
☎ 01642 247569 ✉ info@trinitychambers.co.uk
Call Date: Nov 1988, Inner Temple
Pupil Supervisor, Recorder

GOODWIN MR MICHAEL

Old Bailey Chambers
15 Old Bailey, London EC4M 7EF
☎ 020 3008 6404
✉ clerks@15oldbaileychambers.com
Call Date: Oct 1996, Inner Temple
Pupil Supervisor

Practising Areas: Crime, Crime (Corporate/Fraud), Licensing, Regulatory Law

GOOSE MR JULIAN NICHOLAS QC (2002)

Zenith Chambers
10 Park Square, Leeds LS1 2LH
☎ 0113 245 5438 ✉ clerks@zenithchambers.co.uk
2 Hare Court
Lower Ground, Ground, 1st & 2nd Floor, 2 Hare Court, Temple, London EC4Y 7BH
☎ 020 7353 3982 ✉ clerks@2harecourt.com
Call Date: Jul 1984, Lincoln's Inn

Practising Areas: Crime, Crime (Corporate/Fraud), Health & Safety

GORASIA MR PARAS RAVJI

Kings Chambers
36 Young Street, Manchester M3 3FT
☎ 0845 034 3444 ✉ clerks@kingschambers.com
Kings Chambers
5 Park Square East, Leeds LS1 2NE
☎ 0845 034 3444 ✉ clerks@kingschambers.com
Kings Chambers
Embassy House, 60 Church Street, Birmingham B3 2DJ ☎ 0845 034 3444
✉ clerks@kingschambers.com
Call Date: Jul 2005, Inner Temple

Practising Areas: Chancery (General), Commercial Litigation, Discrimination, Employment

GORDON MR JAMES COSMO ALEXANDER

Atkinson Bevan Chambers
1st Floor, 2 Harcourt Buildings, Temple, London EC4Y 9DB ☎ 020 7353 2112
✉ clerks@2hb.co.uk
Call Date: Oct 2004, Middle Temple

GORDON MR JEREMY

Chambers of Mr Ami Feder
Ground Floor, Lamb Building, Temple, London EC4Y 7AS ☎ 020 7797 7788
✉ clerks@lambbuilding.co.uk
Lamb Building
22 Ship Street, Brighton BN1 1AD
☎ 01273 820490 ✉ admin@lambbuilding.co.uk
Chambers of Mr Ami Feder
Ground Floor, Lamb Building, Temple, London EC4Y 7AS ☎ 020 7797 7788
✉ clerks@lambbuilding.co.uk
Call Date: Jul 1974, Inner Temple
Pupil Supervisor

Practising Areas: Chancery (General), Chancery (Land Law), Common Law (General), Company & Commercial, Discrimination, Employment, Equity, Wills & Trusts, Family Provision, Probate & Administration, Professional Negligence

GORE MR ANDREW JULIAN MARK

37 Park Square Chambers
37 Park Square, Leeds LS1 2NY
☎ 0113 243 9422 ✉ chambers@no37.co.uk
Call Date: Nov 1994, Middle Temple
Pupil Supervisor

Practising Areas: Ancillary Relief, Care Proceedings, Family, Family Provision, Personal Injury

GORE MR ANDREW ROGER

Fenners Chambers
3 Madingley Road, Cambridge CB3 0EE
☎ 01223 368761 ✉ clerks@fennerschambers.com
Call Date: Nov 1973, Middle Temple
Pupil Supervisor

Practising Areas: Administrative, Agriculture, Arbitration, Chancery (General), Chancery (Land Law), Commercial Property, Common Land, Conveyancing, Environment, Equity, Wills & Trusts, Landlord & Tenant, Local Government, Probate & Administration, Professional Negligence, Town & Country Planning

GORE MRS HARRIET NKECHI ADIMORA

Kensington Chambers
5A Philbeach Gardens, London SW5 9DY
☎ 020 7373 2217 ✉ harrietgore.kensingtonchambers@btinternet.com
Call Date: Mar 1997, Middle Temple

Practising Areas: Administrative, Employment, Housing, Landlord & Tenant

GORE MS SALLY ELIZABETH

14 Gray's Inn Square
14 Gray's Inn Square, Gray's Inn, London WC1R 5JP ☎ 020 7242 0858 ✉ clerks@14gis.co.uk
Call Date: Jul 2006, Inner Temple

Practising Areas: Administrative, Care Proceedings, Education, Family, Family Provision, Mental Health

GOUDIE MR WILLIAM MARTIN PHILLIP

Charter Chambers
33 John Street, London WC1N 2AT
☎ 020 7618 4400 ✉ clerks@charterchambers.com
Call Date: Oct 1996, Inner Temple
Pupil Supervisor

Practising Areas: Administrative, Courts Martial, Crime, Crime (Corporate/Fraud), Health & Safety, Human Rights, Mental Health, Regulatory Law

GOUGH MISS KAREN LOUISE

39 Essex Street
London WC2R 3AT ☎ 020 7832 1111
✉ clerks@39essex.com
82 King Street
Manchester M2 4WQ ☎ 0161 870 9969
Arbitration Chambers
22 Willes Road, London NW5 3DS
☎ 020 7267 2137 ✉ john.tackaberry@39essex.com
Call Date: Jul 1983, Inner Temple
Pupil Supervisor

Practising Areas: Arbitration, Commercial Litigation, Common Law (General), Construction, Professional Negligence

GOURIET MR GERALD WILLIAM QC (2006)

Francis Taylor Building
Inner Temple, London EC4Y 7BY
☎ 020 7353 8415 ✉ clerks@ftb.eu.com
Call Date: Jul 1974, Inner Temple

Practising Areas: Licensing

GOURLAY MISS AMANDA KIRSTEN

Tanfield Chambers
2-5 Warwick Court, London WC1R 5DJ
☎ 020 7421 5300 ✉ clerks@tanfieldchambers.co.uk
Call Date: Jul 2004, Gray's Inn

Practising Areas: Chancery (Land Law), Landlord & Tenant

GOW MR HENRY

New Bailey Chambers
4th Floor, Corn Exchange, Fenwick Street, Liverpool, Merseyside L2 7QS
☎ 0151 236 9402 ✉ clerks@newbailey.com
Call Date: Oct 1995, Gray's Inn
Pupil Supervisor

Practising Areas: Civil Liberties, Civil Litigation, Courts Martial, Crime, Crime (Corporate/Fraud), Personal Injury

GOZEM MR GAIAS QC (1997)

Lincoln House Chambers
Tower 12, The Avenue North, Spinningfields, 18-22 Bridge Street, Manchester M3 3BZ
☎ 0161 832 5701
✉ info@lincolnhousechambers.com
Call Date: Nov 1972, Middle Temple

Practising Areas: Crime, Crime (Corporate/Fraud)

GRAHAM MRS ALANA NICOLE

9 Stone Buildings
Lincoln's Inn, London WC2A 3NN
☎ 020 7404 5055 ✉ clerks@9stonebuildings.com
Chambers of Alana Graham
Chemix Buildings, Maypole Fields, Cradley, Halesowen, West Midlands B63 2QB
☎ 01384 894560
Call Date: Nov 1993, Lincoln's Inn

Practising Areas: Arbitration, Chancery (General), Chancery (Land Law), Commercial Litigation, Company & Commercial, Employment, Equity, Wills & Trusts, Insolvency, Insurance, Partnership, Personal Injury, Probate & Administration, Professional Negligence, Sale & Carriage of Goods, Share Options, Tax (Capital & Income), Tax (Corporate)

GRAHAM MR MICHAEL JOHN GEOFFREY

Trinity Chambers
The Custom House, 39 Quayside, Newcastle Upon Tyne NE1 3DE ☎0191 232 1927
✉info@trinitychambers.co.uk
Trinity Chambers
Multi Media Exchange, 72-80 Corporation Road, Middlesbrough TS1 2RF
☎01642 247569 ✉info@trinitychambers.co.uk
Call Date: Mar 1999, Lincoln's Inn
Pupil Supervisor

Practising Areas: Regulatory Law

GRAHAM MR THOMAS PATRICK HENRY

New Square Chambers
12 New Square, Lincoln's Inn, London WC2A 3SW ☎020 7419 8000 ✉robin.hollington@newsquarechambers.co.uk
Call Date: Nov 1985, Middle Temple
Pupil Supervisor

Practising Areas: Bankruptcy, Commercial Litigation, Company & Commercial, Defamation, Insolvency, Partnership, Sale & Carriage of Goods

GRAHAM-WELLS MISS ALISON CHRISTINE

Exchange Chambers
7 Ralli Courts, West Riverside, Manchester M3 5FT ☎0161 833 2722
Exchange Chambers
One Derby Square, Derby Square, Liverpool L2 9XX ☎0151 236 7747
✉info@exchangechambers.co.uk
Exchange Chambers
Oxford House, Oxford Row, Leeds LS1 3BE
☎0113 203 1970
✉spencer@exchangechambers.co.uk
Call Date: Jul 1992, Inner Temple

Practising Areas: Administrative, Arbitration, Asset Finance, Chancery (General), Commercial Litigation, Consumer, Disciplinary Tribunals, Equity, Wills & Trusts, Insolvency, Land, Landlord & Tenant, Probate & Administration, Tax (Capital & Income), Tax (Corporate)

GRAINGER MR ALISTAIR JAMES GEORGE

13 King's Bench Walk
13 King's Bench Walk, Temple, London EC4Y 7EN ☎020 7353 7204 ✉clerks@13kbw.co.uk
13 KBW
32 Beaumont Street, Oxford OX1 2NP
☎01865 311066 ✉clerks@13kbw.co.uk
Call Date: Nov 1998, Inner Temple

GRANT MR CHUDI PAUL

Kenworthy's Chambers
Arlington House, Bloom Street, Salford, Manchester M3 6AJ ☎0161 832 4036
Call Date: Nov 2002, Lincoln's Inn

Practising Areas: Crime, Crime (Corporate/Fraud), Health & Safety, Local Government, Mental Health, Regulatory Law, Trademarks

GRANT MR DAVID ERICSON

Outer Temple Chambers
The Outer Temple, 222 Strand, London WC2R 1BA ☎020 7353 6381
✉clerks@outertemple.com
Call Date: Mar 1999, Inner Temple
Pupil Supervisor

Practising Areas: Chancery (General), Commercial Litigation, Company & Commercial, Employment, Equity, Wills & Trusts, Financial Services, Insolvency, Pensions, Professional Negligence

GRANT MR GARY STEVEN

Francis Taylor Building
Inner Temple, London EC4Y 7BY
☎020 7353 8415 ✉clerks@ftb.eu.com
Call Date: Oct 1994, Gray's Inn

Practising Areas: Civil Liberties, Common Law (General), Crime, Crime (Corporate/Fraud), Licensing

GRANT MR MARCUS H JAMES

Temple Garden Chambers
1 Harcourt Buildings, Temple, London EC4Y 9DA ☎020 7583 1315 ✉clerks@tgchambers.com
Call Date: Oct 1993, Lincoln's Inn
Pupil Supervisor

Practising Areas: Common Law (General), Insurance, Personal Injury

GRANT MR MURRAY ROSS

13 King's Bench Walk
13 King's Bench Walk, Temple, London EC4Y 7EN ☎020 7353 7204 ✉clerks@13kbw.co.uk
13 KBW
32 Beaumont Street, Oxford OX1 2NP
☎01865 311066 ✉clerks@13kbw.co.uk
Call Date: Oct 2003, Inner Temple

Practising Areas: Employment, Personal Injury

GRANT-GARWOOD MR JOSHUA DAHREN

1 Pump Court
Elm Court, Temple, London EC4Y 7AB
☎020 7842 7070 ✉(name)@pumpcourt.co.uk
Call Date: Nov 1992, Middle Temple

Practising Areas: Care Proceedings, Employment, Family, Family Provision

GRANVILLE STAFFORD MR ANDREW

4 King's Bench Walk
2nd Floor, 4 King's Bench Walk, Temple, London EC4Y 7DL ☎020 7822 7000
✉clerks@4kbw.co.uk
Call Date: Jul 1987, Gray's Inn
Pupil Supervisor

Practising Areas: Civil Litigation, Commercial Litigation, Common Law (General), Company & Commercial, Construction, Disciplinary Tribunals, Employment, Housing, Inquests, Landlord & Tenant, Medical Negligence, Partnership, Personal Injury, Professional Negligence, Regulatory Law

GRAY MISS JENNIFER

Chambers of Mr Ami Feder
Ground Floor, Lamb Building, Temple, London EC4Y 7AS ☎020 7797 7788
✉clerks@lambbuilding.co.uk
Lamb Building
22 Ship Street, Brighton BN1 1AD
☎01273 820490 ✉admin@lambbuilding.co.uk
Chambers of Mr Ami Feder
Ground Floor, Lamb Building, Temple, London EC4Y 7AS ☎020 7797 7788
✉clerks@lambbuilding.co.uk
Call Date: Oct 1992, Middle Temple
Pupil Supervisor

Practising Areas: Crime, Crime (Corporate/Fraud)

GRAY MR JUSTIN HENRY WALFORD

Trinity Chambers
The Custom House, 39 Quayside, Newcastle Upon Tyne NE1 3DE ☎0191 232 1927
✉info@trinitychambers.co.uk
Trinity Chambers
Multi Media Exchange, 72-80 Corporation Road, Middlesbrough TS1 2RF
☎01642 247569 ✉info@trinitychambers.co.uk
Call Date: Nov 1993, Inner Temple
Pupil Supervisor

Practising Areas: Administrative, Care Proceedings, Family, Family Provision

GRAY MR PETER HENRY ST JOHN

5 Pump Court
Ground Floor, 5 Pump Court, Temple, London EC4Y 7AP ☎020 7353 2532
✉clerks@5pumpcourt.com
Call Date: Nov 1984, Inner Temple
Pupil Supervisor

Practising Areas: Courts Martial, Crime, Crime (Corporate/Fraud), Defamation

GRAY MR RICHARD

St Johns Buildings
24a - 28 St John Street, Manchester M3 4DJ
☎0161 214 1500 ✉clerk@stjohnsbuildings.co.uk
16 Winckley Square
Preston PR1 3JJ ☎01772 256100
St Johns Buildings Liverpool
8th Floor India Buildings, Water Street, Liverpool L2 0XG ☎0151 243 6000
✉clerk@stjohnsbuildings.co.uk
Call Date: Nov 1986, Middle Temple

GRAY MR ROGER ANDERSON

5 Pump Court
Ground Floor, 5 Pump Court, Temple, London EC4Y 7AP ☎020 7353 2532
✉clerks@5pumpcourt.com
Call Date: Jul 1984, Lincoln's Inn
Pupil Supervisor

Practising Areas: Family, Family Provision

GREATOREX MR PAUL

4-5 Gray's Inn Square
Gray's Inn, London WC1R 5AH
☎020 7404 5252 ✉clerks@4-5.co.uk
Call Date: Oct 1999, Lincoln's Inn
Pupil Supervisor

Practising Areas: Administrative, Civil Liberties, Commercial Litigation, Common Law (General), Discrimination, Education, Employment, Environment, Local Government, Professional Negligence, Public International, Town & Country Planning

GREEN MISS ALISON ANNE

2 Temple Gardens
2 Temple Gardens, Temple, London EC4Y 9AY ☎020 7822 1200 ✉clerks@2tg.co.uk
Call Date: Jul 1974, Middle Temple
Pupil Supervisor

Practising Areas: Insurance, Insurance/Reinsurance, Private International

GREEN MR GARRY ANTHONY

Tooks Chambers
81 Farringdon Street, London EC4A 4BL
☎020 7842 7575 ✉clerks@tooks.co.uk
Call Date: Oct 1999, Inner Temple
Pupil Supervisor

Practising Areas: Crime

GREEN MR JONATHAN PAUL

Dyers Chambers
35 Bedford Row, London WC1R 4JH
☎020 7404 1881 ✉admin@dyerschambers.com
Call Date: Oct 1993, Gray's Inn

Practising Areas: Courts Martial, Crime, Crime (Corporate/Fraud), Information Technology, Local Government

GREEN MR NICHOLAS NIGEL QC (1998)

Brick Court Chambers
7-8 Essex Street, London WC2R 3LD
☎020 7379 3550 ✉clerks@brickcourt.co.uk
Call Date: Jul 1986, Inner Temple
Recorder

GREEN MR PATRICK CURTIS QC (2012)

Henderson Chambers
2 Harcourt Buildings, Temple, London EC4Y 9DB ☎020 7583 9020
✉clerks@hendersonchambers.co.uk
Call Date: Oct 1990, Middle Temple
Pupil Supervisor

Practising Areas: Administrative, Commercial Litigation, Common Law (General), Competition, Disciplinary Tribunals, Discrimination, Employment, Private International, Sports

GREEN MR TIMOTHY SINCLAIR

St Philips Chambers
55 Temple Row, Birmingham B2 5LS
☎0121 246 7000 ✉clerks@st-philips.com
Call Date: Oct 1996, Gray's Inn

Practising Areas: Crime (Corporate/Fraud), Environment, Health & Safety, Regulatory Law

GREEN MISS VICTORIA LOUISE

1 KBW Chambers
1 King's Bench Walk, Temple, London EC4Y 7DB ☎020 7936 1500 ✉clerks@1kbw.co.uk
King's Bench Chambers
174 High Street, Lewes BN7 1YE
☎01273 402600
Call Date: Oct 1994, Gray's Inn
Pupil Supervisor

Practising Areas: Family, Family Provision

GREENAN MISS SARAH OCTAVIA

Zenith Chambers
10 Park Square, Leeds LS1 2LH
☎0113 245 5438 ✉clerks@zenithchambers.co.uk
Call Date: Jul 1987, Gray's Inn
Pupil Supervisor

Practising Areas: Care Proceedings, Chancery (Land Law), Commercial Litigation, Common Land, Common Law (General), Equity, Wills & Trusts, Family, Family Provision, Housing, Landlord & Tenant, Local Government, Partnership, Probate & Administration, Professional Negligence

GREENFIELD MR PETER CHARLES

King's Bench Chambers
Wellington House, 175 Holdenhurst Road, Bournemouth, Dorset BH8 8DQ
☎01202 250025
Call Date: Nov 1989, Middle Temple
Pupil Supervisor

Practising Areas: Care Proceedings, Civil Liberties, Common Law (General), Crime, Crime (Corporate/Fraud), Employment, Family, Family Provision, Landlord & Tenant, Licensing

GREENHALGH MR MICHAEL

No.6 Park Square
Leeds LS1 2LW ☎0113 245 9763
✉Tim@no6.co.uk
Call Date: Oct 2004, Middle Temple

GREENWOOD MR ALEXANDER BARTON

Apex
Harlech House, 20 Cathedral Road, Cardiff CF11 9LJ ☎02920 232 032
✉clerks@apexchambers.net
Call Date: Mar 2002, Gray's Inn

Practising Areas: Crime

GREGG MR WILLIAM JONATHAN

St Paul's Chambers
5th Floor, St Paul's House, 23 Park Square South, Leeds LS1 2ND ☎0113 245 5866
Call Date: Oct 1990, Gray's Inn
Pupil Supervisor

Practising Areas: Crime

GREGO MR KEVIN CHRISTOPHER

Citadel Chambers
The Citadel, 190 Corporation Street, Birmingham B4 6QD ☎0121 233 8500
✉clerks@citadelchambers.com
Call Date: Nov 2001, Gray's Inn

Practising Areas: Courts Martial, Crime, Crime (Corporate/Fraud), Regulatory Law, Road Traffic And Highways

GREGORY MS ANN MARIE

St Paul's Chambers
5th Floor, St Paul's House, 23 Park Square South, Leeds LS1 2ND ☎0113 245 5866
Call Date: Nov 1994, Middle Temple

Practising Areas: Family, Family Provision

GRENNAN MR BARRY EDWARD

Kenworthy's Chambers
Arlington House, Bloom Street, Salford, Manchester M3 6AJ ☎0161 832 4036
Call Date: Jul 1977, Lincoln's Inn
Pupil Supervisor

Practising Areas: Crime, Crime (Corporate/Fraud), Human Rights

GREY MR MICHAEL HENRY JOHN

Citadel Chambers
The Citadel, 190 Corporation Street, Birmingham B4 6QD ☎0121 233 8500
✉clerks@citadelchambers.com
Call Date: Nov 1975, Middle Temple
Pupil Supervisor

Practising Areas: Crime, Crime (Corporate/Fraud)

C

GREY MR ROBERT WILLIAM

3 PB Barristers
3 Paper Buildings, Temple, London EC4Y 7EU
☎020 7583 8055
3 PB Barristers
Royal Talbot House, 2 Victoria Street, Bristol, Avon BS1 6BB ☎0117 928 1520
3 PB Barristers
30 Christchurch Road, Bournemouth, Dorset BH1 3PD ☎01202 292102 ✉clerks.bournemouth@3paper.co.uk
3 PB Barristers
4 St Peter Street, Winchester SO23 8BW
☎01962 868884 ✉clerks.winchester@3paper.co.uk
3 PB Barristers
23 Beaumont Street, Oxford OX1 2NP
☎01865 793 736
Call Date: Jul 1979, Gray's Inn
Pupil Supervisor

GREY MS SHARON MONICA

Octagon House
19 Colegate, Norwich NR3 1AT
☎01603 623186 ✉clerks@octagonhouse.co.uk
Call Date: Oct 2003, Inner Temple

Practising Areas: Family Provision

GRIEVE MISS KATE MAKEPEACE

36 Bedford Row
London WC1R 4JH ☎020 7421 8000
✉chambers@36bedfordrow.co.uk
Call Date: Jul 2006, Lincoln's Inn

Practising Areas: Family

GRIFFIN MR IAN ROSS

4 Brick Court
4 Brick Court, Temple, London EC4Y 9AD
☎020 7832 3200 ✉clerks@4bc.co.uk
Call Date: Nov 1997, Middle Temple

Practising Areas: Children's Law

GRIFFIN MISS LYNN MYFANWY

23 Essex Street
London WC2R 3AA ☎020 7413 0353
✉clerks@23es.com
Call Date: Oct 1991, Gray's Inn
Pupil Supervisor

Practising Areas: Copyright, Crime, Crime (Corporate/Fraud), Trademarks

GRIFFIN MISS MARGARET DELIA

Enterprise Chambers
43 Park Square, Leeds LS1 2NP
☎0113 246 0391
✉leeds@enterprisechambers.com
Enterprise Chambers
65 Quayside, Newcastle Upon Tyne NE1 3DE
☎0191 222 3344
✉newcastle@enterprisechambers.com
Call Date: Jul 2004, Gray's Inn

GRIFFIN MR NEIL PATRICK LUKE

9-12 Bell Yard
London WC2A 2JR ☎020 7400 1800
✉clerks@9-12bellyard.com
Call Date: Oct 1996, Gray's Inn

GRIFFIN MR NICHOLAS JOHN QC (2012)

Five Paper Buildings
1st Floor, Five Paper Buildings, Temple, London EC4Y 7HB ☎020 7583 6117
✉clerks@5pb.co.uk
Call Date: Oct 1992, Inner Temple
Pupil Supervisor

Practising Areas: Administrative, Coroners Inquests, Crime, Crime (Corporate/Fraud), Disciplinary Tribunals, Inquests, Licensing, Public Law, Regulatory Law

GRIFFITH MR SHELLEY RAPHAEL WALSH

Farringdon Chambers
180 Bermondsey Street, London SE1 3TQ
☎020 7089 5700
Call Date: Nov 1998, Middle Temple

GRIFFITHS MISS ALISON CLARE

4 King's Bench Walk
2nd Floor, 4 King's Bench Walk, Temple, London EC4Y 7DL ☎020 7822 7000
✉clerks@4kbw.co.uk
Call Date: Oct 2001, Inner Temple

Practising Areas: Common Law (General), Company & Commercial, Personal Injury

GRIFFITHS MR DAVID

St Philips Chambers
55 Temple Row, Birmingham B2 5LS
☎0121 246 7000 ✉clerks@st-philips.com
Call Date: Oct 2001, Inner Temple

Practising Areas: Arbitration, Bankruptcy, Chancery (General), Commercial Litigation, Commercial Property, Construction, Housing, Insolvency, Landlord & Tenant, Personal Injury, Sports

GRIFFITHS MR HUGH ROBERT JAMES

Furnival Chambers
32 Furnival Street, London EC4A 1JQ
☎020 7405 3232
Call Date: Nov 1972, Inner Temple

Practising Areas: Common Law (General), Crime, Crime (Corporate/Fraud), Licensing

GRIFFITHS MR PETER QC (1995)

2 Bedford Row
London WC1R 4BU ☎020 7440 8888
✉clerks@2bedfordrow.co.uk
30 Park Place
Cardiff CF10 3BS ☎029 2039 8421
✉clerks@30parkplace.law.co.uk
Call Date: Nov 1970, Gray's Inn

Practising Areas: Courts Martial, Crime, Crime (Corporate/Fraud), Health & Safety, Regulatory Law, Sports

GRIFFITHS MR ROBERT NORTON

12 College Place
Fauvelle Buildings, 12 College Place, Southampton SO15 2FE ☎023 8032 0320
✉clerks@12cp.co.uk
Call Date: Jul 1988, Middle Temple
Pupil Supervisor

Practising Areas: Crime

GRIME MR JOHN ANDREW

Pump Court Chambers
5 Temple Chambers, Temple Street, Swindon SN1 1SQ ☎01793 539899
✉clerks@3pumpcourt.com
Pump Court Chambers
Upper Ground Floor, 3 Pump Court, Temple, London EC4Y 7AJ ☎020 7353 0711
✉clerks@3pumpcourt.com
Pump Court Chambers
31 Southgate Street, Winchester, Hampshire SO23 9EB ☎01962 868 161
✉clerks@3pumpcourt.com
Call Date: Oct 1997, Lincoln's Inn
Pupil Supervisor

GROOM MR IAN JOHN

Call Date: Nov 1990, Middle Temple
Pupil Supervisor

GROUND MR PATRICK QC (1981)

Chambers of Mr Patrick Ground QC
13 Ranelagh Avenue, London SW6 3PJ
☎020 7736 0131 ✉post@patrickground.com
Call Date: Feb 1960, Inner Temple

Practising Areas: Administrative, Commercial Litigation, Construction, Environment, Housing, Landlord & Tenant, Local Government, Professional Negligence, Town & Country Planning

GRUNDY MS CLARE

St Johns Buildings
24a - 28 St John Street, Manchester M3 4DJ
☎0161 214 1500 ✉clerk@stjohnsbuildings.co.uk
16 Winckley Square
Preston PR1 3JJ ☎01772 256100
St Johns Buildings Liverpool
8th Floor India Buildings, Water Street, Liverpool L2 0XG ☎0151 243 6000
✉clerk@stjohnsbuildings.co.uk
Call Date: Jul 1989, Gray's Inn
Pupil Supervisor

Practising Areas: Care Proceedings, Common Law (General), Discrimination, Employment, Family, Family Provision, Mental Health, Professional Negligence

GRUNDY MR PHILIP MICHAEL DAVID

Call Date: Jul 1980, Middle Temple
Pupil Supervisor, Recorder

GRUNWALD MR HENRY CYRIL OBE QC

Charter Chambers
33 John Street, London WC1N 2AT
☎020 7618 4400 ✉clerks@charterchambers.com
Call Date: Jul 1972, Gray's Inn1999

Practising Areas: Courts Martial, Crime, Crime (Corporate/Fraud), Human Rights

GUEST MR PETER LIAM

187 Fleet Street
London EC4A 2AT ☎020 7430 7430
✉chambers@187fleetstreet.com
Call Date: Jul 1975, Inner Temple
Pupil Supervisor, Recorder

Practising Areas: Courts Martial, Crime, Crime (Corporate/Fraud), Licensing, Regulatory Law

GULRAIZ MR YASSER

Equity Chambers
First Floor, McLaren Building, 46 Priory Queensway, Birmingham B4 7LR
☎0121 236 5007 ✉clerks@equitychambers.org.uk
Call Date: Mar 2003, Lincoln's Inn

GUMBS MISS ANNETTE PATRICIA

Call Date: Oct 1994, Gray's Inn
Pupil Supervisor

GUN CUNINGHAME MR JULIAN ARTHUR

Gough Square Chambers
6-7 Gough Square, London EC4A 3DE
☎020 7353 0924 ✉gsc@goughsq.co.uk
Call Date: Nov 1989, Lincoln's Inn

Practising Areas: Banking, Consumer, Costs, Employment, Professional Negligence

GUNNING MR ALEXANDER RUPERT QC (2012)

4 Pump Court
4 Pump Court, Temple, London EC4Y 7AN
☎020 7842 5555 ✉chambers@4pumpcourt.com
Call Date: Nov 1994, Inner Temple
Pupil Supervisor

GUNSTONE MR ROBERT GILES

KCH Garden Square
1 Oxford Street, Nottingham NG1 5BH
☎0115 941 8851 ✉clerks@kchgardensquare.co.uk
Call Date: Jul 2007, Middle Temple

Practising Areas: Bankruptcy, Chancery (Land Law), Common Law (General), Discrimination, Education, Employment, Equity, Wills & Trusts, Housing, Insolvency, Landlord & Tenant

GUPTA MR AMIT

St Philips Chambers
55 Temple Row, Birmingham B2 5LS
☎0121 246 7000 ✉clerks@st-philips.com
Call Date: Jul 2006, Gray's Inn

Practising Areas: Banking, Bankruptcy, Chancery (General), Chancery (Land Law), Commercial Litigation, Commercial Property, Common Law (General), Company & Commercial, Insolvency, Landlord & Tenant, Professional Negligence

GURDEN MISS ALISON LOUISE

1 Gray's Inn Square
Ground Floor, 1 Gray's Inn Square, London WC1R 5AA ☎020 7405 0001
Call Date: Mar 2001, Lincoln's Inn

Practising Areas: Coroners Inquests, Crime, Disciplinary Tribunals, Discrimination, Employment, Human Rights, Inquests, Public Law, Road Traffic And Highways

C

GURNEY MR SIMON JAMES

Lincoln House Chambers
Tower 12, The Avenue North, Spinningfields, 18-22 Bridge Street, Manchester M3 3BZ
☎0161 832 5701
✉info@lincolnhousechambers.com
Call Date: Jul 2006, Inner Temple

GUY MR JOHN DAVID COLIN

Tanfield Chambers
2-5 Warwick Court, London WC1R 5DJ
☎020 7421 5300 ✉clerks@tanfieldchambers.co.uk
Call Date: Jul 1972, Gray's Inn
Pupil Supervisor

Practising Areas: Arbitration, Commercial Litigation, Common Law (General), Company & Commercial, Financial Services, Information Technology

GUY MR RICHARD PERRAN

Southernhay Chambers
33 Southernhay East, Exeter EX1 1NX
☎01392 255777
✉clerks@southernhaychambers.co.uk
King's Bench and Godolphin (KBG)Chambers
115 North Hill, Plymouth, Devon PL4 8JY
☎01752 221551 ✉clerks@kbgchambers.co.uk
Chambers of Mr Ami Feder
Ground Floor, Lamb Building, Temple, London EC4Y 7AS ☎020 7797 7788
✉clerks@lambbuilding.co.uk
Call Date: Nov 1970, Inner Temple
Pupil Supervisor

Practising Areas: Administrative, Bankruptcy, Chancery (General), Chancery (Land Law), Commercial Litigation, Common Land, Common Law (General), Education, Employment, Equity, Wills & Trusts, Family Provision, Healthcare, Human Rights, Insolvency, Local Government, Probate & Administration, Professional Negligence, Town & Country Planning

HABIB MISS SHYSTA

Kenworthy's Chambers
Arlington House, Bloom Street, Salford, Manchester M3 6AJ ☎0161 832 4036
Call Date: Jul 2002, Lincoln's Inn

Practising Areas: Civil Litigation, Islamic Sharia Law, Personal Injury

HACKETT MR PHILIP GEORGE QC (1999)

Argent Chambers
5 Bell Yard, London WC2A 2JR
☎020 7556 5500
✉briefsin@argentchambers.co.uk
Call Date: Nov 1978, Middle Temple
Pupil Supervisor

Practising Areas: Commercial Litigation, Crime (Corporate/Fraud), EC & Competition Law, Environment, Financial Services, Health & Safety, Private International, Professional Negligence, Public International, Regulatory Law

HADDEN MR RHYS THOMAS

Field Court Chambers
5 Field Court, Gray's Inn, London WC1R 5EF
☎020 7405 6114 ✉clerks@fieldcourt.co.uk
Call Date: Nov 2006, Middle Temple

HADFIELD MS CHARLOTTE SINCLAIR

3 PB Barristers
3 Paper Buildings, Temple, London EC4Y 7EU
☎020 7583 8055
Call Date: Nov 1999, Inner Temple

HADGILL MR CLINTON ALEXANDER

St Albans Chambers
2 - 4 St Peter's Street, St Albans, Hertfordshire AL1 3LF ☎01727 843383
✉clerks@stalbanschambers.com
Call Date: Oct 1998, Middle Temple

Practising Areas: Crime, Employment, Personal Injury

HADLEY MR RICHARD MARK ANDREW

No5 Chambers
Fountain Court, Steelhouse Lane, Birmingham B4 6DR ☎0845 210 5555 ✉info@no5.com
No5 Chambers
Greenwood House, 4-7 Salisbury Court, London EC4Y 8AA ☎0845 210 5555
No5 Chambers
38 Queen Square, Bristol BS1 4QS
☎0845 210 5555
Call Date: Oct 1997, Gray's Inn

HADRILL MR KEITH PAUL

Furnival Chambers
32 Furnival Street, London EC4A 1JQ
☎ 020 7405 3232
Call Date: Jul 1977, Lincoln's Inn
Pupil Supervisor

Practising Areas: Courts Martial, Crime, Crime (Corporate/Fraud), Health & Safety, Licensing, Regulatory Law, Sports

HAFIZ MR MOHAMMED GHULAM

Chambers of Mr M G Hafiz
8 Clairview Road, London SW16 6TU
☎ 020 8677 5778 ✉ mghafiz@hotmail.co.uk
Call Date: Nov 1970, Inner Temple

Practising Areas: Immigration

HAGGERTY MISS ELIZABETH FRANCES

Lamb Chambers
Lamb Building, Elm Court, Temple, London EC4Y 7AS ☎ 020 7797 8300
✉ info@lambchambers.co.uk
Call Date: Feb 1994, Lincoln's Inn

HALDEN MR ANGUS ROBERT

Queen Square Chambers
56 Queen Square, Bristol BS1 4PR
☎ 0117 921 1966 ✉ crime@qs-c.co.uk
Call Date: Jul 1999, Middle Temple

Practising Areas: Arbitration, Commercial Litigation, Construction, Crime (Corporate/Fraud), Ecclesiastical, Employment, Entertainment, Licensing, Professional Negligence

HALE MR CHARLES STANLEY

4 Paper Buildings
1st Floor, 4 Paper Buildings, Temple, London EC4Y 7EX ☎ 020 7427 5200 ✉ clerks@4pb.com
Call Date: Oct 1992, Middle Temple
Pupil Supervisor

Practising Areas: Ancillary Relief, Children's Law, Family, Family Provision

HALE MR SIMON MARK

Hardwicke
New Square, Lincoln's Inn, London WC2A 3SB ☎ 020 7242 2523
✉ enquiries@hardwicke.co.uk
Call Date: Oct 2006, Gray's Inn

HALL MR JAMES EDWARD

Cornwall Street Chambers
85-87 Cornwall Street, Birmingham B3 3BY
☎ 0121 233 7500 ✉ clerks@cornwallstreet.co.uk
Call Date: Oct 2000, Lincoln's Inn

Practising Areas: Banking, Chancery (General), Chancery (Land Law), Commercial Litigation, Common Law (General), Equity, Wills & Trusts, Financial Services, Insurance, Landlord & Tenant, Professional Negligence

HALL MR JEREMY JOHN

Becket Chambers
17 New Dover Road, Canterbury, Kent CT1 3AS ☎ 01227 786331
✉ clerks@becket-chambers.co.uk
Call Date: Feb 1988, Gray's Inn

Practising Areas: Care Proceedings, Common Law (General), Employment, Family, Family Provision, Personal Injury

HALL MISS JOANNA MARY

14 Gray's Inn Square
14 Gray's Inn Square, Gray's Inn, London WC1R 5JP ☎ 020 7242 0858 ✉ clerks@14gis.co.uk
Call Date: Nov 1973, Inner Temple
Pupil Supervisor

HALL MR NICHOLAS

Westgate Chambers
64 High Street, Lewes, East Sussex BN7 1XG
☎ 01273 480510
✉ clerks@westgate-chambers.co.uk
Call Date: Jul 1973, Gray's Inn
Pupil Supervisor

Practising Areas: Crime, Crime (Corporate/Fraud), Foreign Law, Health & Safety, Licensing

HALL MR RICHARD ANDREW

Pump Court Chambers
31 Southgate Street, Winchester, Hampshire SO23 9EB ☎ 01962 868 161
✉ clerks@3pumpcourt.com
Pump Court Chambers
Upper Ground Floor, 3 Pump Court, Temple, London EC4Y 7AJ ☎ 020 7353 0711
✉ clerks@3pumpcourt.com
Pump Court Chambers
5 Temple Chambers, Temple Street, Swindon SN1 1SQ ☎ 01793 539899
✉ clerks@3pumpcourt.com
Call Date: Nov 1995, Inner Temple

Practising Areas: Family, Family Provision

HALLETT MISS KATHERINE ELIZABETH

13 Old Square Chambers
Ground Floor, 14 Old Square, Lincoln's Inn, London WC2A 3UE ☎020 7831 4445
✉clerks@13oldsquare.com
Call Date: Oct 2006, Lincoln's Inn

Practising Areas: Bankruptcy, Chancery (General), Chancery (Land Law), Commercial Litigation, Commercial Property, Company & Commercial, Insolvency, Landlord & Tenant, Probate & Administration, Sale & Carriage of Goods

HALLIDAY-DAVIS MS DEBORAH LEE

Carmelite Chambers
9 Carmelite Street, London EC4Y 0DR
☎020 7936 6300
✉clerks@carmelitechambers.co.uk
Call Date: Nov 1999, Inner Temple
Pupil Supervisor

Practising Areas: Crime, Crime (Corporate/Fraud)

HALLIWELL MR TOBY GEORGE

Unity Street Chambers
5 Unity Street, College Green, Bristol BS1 5HH ☎0117 906 9789
✉chambers@unitystreetchambers.com
Call Date: Nov 1992, Middle Temple

Practising Areas: Employment, Personal Injury

HALLOWES MR RUPERT JOHN MICHAEL

3 Temple Gardens
Lower Ground Floor, 3 Temple Gardens, Temple, London EC4Y 9AU ☎020 7353 3102
✉clerks@3tg.co.uk
Call Date: Oct 1995, Inner Temple

Practising Areas: Crime, Crime (Corporate/Fraud)

HALSTEAD MR ROBIN BERNARD

One Essex Court
1st Floor, Temple, London EC4Y 9AR
☎020 7936 3030 ✉clerks@1ec.co.uk
Call Date: Oct 1996, Inner Temple

Practising Areas: Chancery (Land Law), Common Law (General), Family, Landlord & Tenant, Medical Negligence, Personal Injury

HAM MR NICHOLAS TREHARNE

Dyers Chambers
35 Bedford Row, London WC1R 4JH
☎020 7404 1881 ✉admin@dyerschambers.com
Call Date: Oct 1997, Middle Temple

Practising Areas: Common Law (General), Crime, Environment, Health & Safety, Housing, Landlord & Tenant, Licensing, Local Government, Sale & Carriage of Goods, Town & Country Planning, Trademarks

HAMBLIN MR NICHOLAS HOWARD

Westgate Chambers
64 High Street, Lewes, East Sussex BN7 1XG
☎01273 480510
✉clerks@westgate-chambers.co.uk
Call Date: Nov 1981, Lincoln's Inn
Pupil Supervisor

Practising Areas: Crime, Crime (Corporate/Fraud), Licensing, Personal Injury

HAMER MR CHARLES HENRY

Citadel Chambers
The Citadel, 190 Corporation Street, Birmingham B4 6QD ☎0121 233 8500
✉clerks@citadelchambers.com
Call Date: Mar 2007, Middle Temple

Practising Areas: Crime, Regulatory Law, Road Traffic And Highways

HAMER MR GEORGE CLEMENS

8 New Square
8 New Square, Lincoln's Inn, London WC2A 3QP ☎020 7405 4321 ✉clerks@8newsquare.co.uk
Call Date: Nov 1974, Gray's Inn
Pupil Supervisor

Practising Areas: Competition, Copyright, EC & Competition Law, Entertainment, Franchising, Information Technology, Intellectual Property, Patents, Professional Negligence, Sports, Telecommunications, Trademarks

HAMES MR CHRISTOPHER WILLIAM

4 Paper Buildings
1st Floor, 4 Paper Buildings, Temple, London EC4Y 7EX ☎020 7427 5200 ✉clerks@4pb.com
Call Date: Jul 1987, Inner Temple
Pupil Supervisor

Practising Areas: Family

HAMID MS RUBY

18 Red Lion Court
London EC4A 3EB ☎020 7520 6000
✉chambers@18rlc.co.uk
18 Red Lion Court (Annexe)
Thornwood House, 102 New London Road, Chelmsford, Essex CM2 0RG
☎01245 280880
Call Date: Oct 2002, Lincoln's Inn

HAMILTON MISS AMANDA JEAN

Furnival Chambers
32 Furnival Street, London EC4A 1JQ
☎020 7405 3232
Call Date: Oct 1995, Lincoln's Inn
Pupil Supervisor

Practising Areas: Employment, Regulatory Law

HAMILTON MR GAVIN

3 PB Barristers
3 Paper Buildings, Temple, London EC4Y 7EU
☎020 7583 8055
3 PB Barristers
Royal Talbot House, 2 Victoria Street, Bristol, Avon BS1 6BB ☎0117 928 1520
3 PB Barristers
23 Beaumont Street, Oxford OX1 2NP
☎01865 793 736
3 PB Barristers
4 St Peter Street, Winchester SO23 8BW
☎01962 868884 ✉clerks.winchester@3paper.co.uk
3 PB Barristers
30 Christchurch Road, Bournemouth, Dorset BH1 3PD ☎01202 292102 ✉clerks.bournemouth@3paper.co.uk
Call Date: Jul 1979, Gray's Inn
Pupil Supervisor

Practising Areas: Insurance/Reinsurance, Landlord & Tenant, Professional Negligence

HAMILTON MR JOHN CONRAD

Field Court Chambers
5 Field Court, Gray's Inn, London WC1R 5EF
☎020 7405 6114 ✉clerks@fieldcourt.co.uk
Call Date: Nov 1988, Gray's Inn
Pupil Supervisor

Practising Areas: Education, Family, Family Provision, Human Rights, Immigration, Mental Health

HAMILTON MR NIGEL

Broadway House Chambers
Broadway House, 9 Bank Street, Bradford, West Yorkshire BD1 1TW ☎01274 722560
✉clerks@broadwayhouse.co.uk
Broadway House Chambers
25 Park Square West, Leeds, West Yorkshire LS1 2PW ☎0113 246 2600
✉clerks@broadwayhouse.co.uk
Call Date: Oct 2004, Inner Temple

Practising Areas: Common Law (General), Crime, Crime (Corporate/Fraud), Environment, Health & Safety, Licensing, Mental Health, Professional Negligence, Regulatory Law, Sports, Town & Country Planning

HAMILTON MRS PENELOPE ANN

Pump Court Tax Chambers
16 Bedford Row, London WC1R 4EF
☎020 7414 8080 ✉clerks@pumptax.com
Call Date: Jul 1972, Gray's Inn

Practising Areas: Tax (Corporate)

HAMILTON MR PETER BERNARD

4 Pump Court
4 Pump Court, Temple, London EC4Y 7AN
☎020 7842 5555 ✉chambers@4pumpcourt.com
Call Date: Feb 1968, Inner Temple
Pupil Supervisor

Practising Areas: Commercial Litigation, Common Law (General), Construction, Financial Services, Insurance, Pensions, Professional Negligence

HAMILTON-SHIELD MISS ANNA-MARIA

Charter Chambers
33 John Street, London WC1N 2AT
☎020 7618 4400 ✉clerks@charterchambers.com
Call Date: Nov 1989, Middle Temple

Practising Areas: Courts Martial, Crime, Crime (Corporate/Fraud), Employment

HAMMERTON MR ALASTAIR ROLF

1 Chancery Lane
London WC2A 1LF ☎0845 634 6666
✉clerks@1chancerylane.com
Call Date: Jul 1983, Inner Temple
Pupil Supervisor, Recorder

Practising Areas: Commercial Litigation, Energy, Insurance, Personal Injury, Professional Negligence, Regulatory Law

C

HAMMETT MR MICHAEL GREVILLE

9 Park Place
Cardiff, South Glamorgan CF10 3DP
☎ 029 2038 2731 ✉ clerks@9parkplace.co.uk
Call Date: Jul 2001, Gray's Inn

Practising Areas: Crime, Road Traffic And Highways

HAMMOND MR TIM MARK

Tanfield Chambers
2-5 Warwick Court, London WC1R 5DJ
☎ 020 7421 5300 ✉ clerks@tanfieldchambers.co.uk
Call Date: Mar 2003, Lincoln's Inn

Practising Areas: Bankruptcy, Commercial Litigation, Common Law (General), Housing, Insolvency, Landlord & Tenant, Personal Injury

HANCOCK MS MARIA

Westgate Chambers
64 High Street, Lewes, East Sussex BN7 1XG
☎ 01273 480510
✉ clerks@westgate-chambers.co.uk
Call Date: Oct 1995, Gray's Inn
Pupil Supervisor

Practising Areas: Care Proceedings, Mental Health

HAND MR JONATHAN ELLIOTT SHEERMAN

Outer Temple Chambers
The Outer Temple, 222 Strand, London WC2R 1BA ☎ 020 7353 6381
✉ clerks@outertemple.com
Call Date: Nov 1990, Inner Temple
Pupil Supervisor

HANIF MISS SAIMA NAZ

4-5 Gray's Inn Square
Gray's Inn, London WC1R 5AH
☎ 020 7404 5252 ✉ clerks@4-5.co.uk
Call Date: Jul 2002, Lincoln's Inn
Pupil Supervisor

Practising Areas: Administrative, Civil Liberties, Company & Commercial, Discrimination, Education, Employment, Environment, Financial Services, Housing, Landlord & Tenant, Local Government, Town & Country Planning

HANLON MR JAMES TOBIAS

Old Bailey Chambers
15 Old Bailey, London EC4M 7EF
☎ 020 3008 6404
✉ clerks@15oldbaileychambers.com
Call Date: Nov 2006, Middle Temple

Practising Areas: Civil Liberties, Civil Litigation, Common Law (General), Coroners Inquests, Crime, Crime (Corporate/Fraud), Data Protection, Disciplinary Tribunals, Education, Employment, Health & Safety, Human Rights, Inquests, Licensing, Local Government, Public Law, Regulatory Law, Sports, Tax (Capital & Income), Tax (Corporate)

HANNAFORD MISS SARAH JANE QC (2008)

Keating Chambers
15 Essex Street, London WC2R 3AA
☎ 020 7544 2600 ✉ clerks@keatingchambers.com
Call Date: Jul 1989, Middle Temple
Pupil Supervisor

Practising Areas: Arbitration, Commercial Litigation, Construction, EC & Competition Law, Professional Negligence

HANNAM MR TIMOTHY JAMES

Citadel Chambers
The Citadel, 190 Corporation Street, Birmingham B4 6QD ☎ 0121 233 8500
✉ clerks@citadelchambers.com
Call Date: Oct 1995, Gray's Inn

Practising Areas: Common Law (General), Crime, Crime (Corporate/Fraud), Licensing, Regulatory Law

HANNANT MISS LISA DIANE

5 Pump Court
Ground Floor, 5 Pump Court, Temple, London EC4Y 7AP ☎ 020 7353 2532
✉ clerks@5pumpcourt.com
Call Date: Oct 2005, Lincoln's Inn

Practising Areas: Common Law (General), Crime, Family

HANNETT MS SARAH RUTH

4-5 Gray's Inn Square
Gray's Inn, London WC1R 5AH
☎ 020 7404 5252 ✉ clerks@4-5.co.uk
Call Date: Jul 2003, Lincoln's Inn

HANSEN MR WILLIAM JOSEPH

No5 Chambers
Greenwood House, 4-7 Salisbury Court, London EC4Y 8AA ☎0845 210 5555
No5 Chambers
38 Queen Square, Bristol BS1 4QS
☎0845 210 5555
No5 Chambers
Fountain Court, Steelhouse Lane, Birmingham B4 6DR ☎0845 210 5555 ✉info@no5.com
Call Date: Nov 1992, Lincoln's Inn

Practising Areas: Chancery (Land Law), Commercial Litigation, Commercial Property, Landlord & Tenant, Partnership, Professional Negligence

HAQUE MR GAZI MOSTA GAWSAL

Dollis Hill Chambers
197 Ellesmere Road, London NW10 1LG
☎020 8208 1663
Call Date: Jul 1970, Inner Temple

Practising Areas: Crime, Family, Immigration

HAQUE MR MUHAMMED LUTHFUL

Crown Office Chambers
2 Crown Office Row, Temple, London EC4Y 7HJ ☎020 7797 8100
✉mail@crownofficechambers.com
Call Date: Oct 1997, Lincoln's Inn
Pupil Supervisor

HARBAGE MR WILLIAM JOHN HIRONS QC (2003)

36 Bedford Row
London WC1R 4JH ☎020 7421 8000
✉chambers@36bedfordrow.co.uk
37 Park Square Chambers
37 Park Square, Leeds LS1 2NY
☎0113 243 9422 ✉chambers@no37.co.uk
Call Date: Jul 1983, Middle Temple
Recorder

Practising Areas: Courts Martial, Crime, Crime (Corporate/Fraud), Regulatory Law

HARBOTTLE MR GWILYM THOMAS

Hogarth Chambers
5 New Square, Lincoln's Inn, London WC2A 3RJ ☎020 7404 0404
✉barristers@hogarthchambers.com
Call Date: Nov 1987, Lincoln's Inn
Pupil Supervisor

HARDING MR CHRISTOPHER JAMES

Thomas More Chambers
7 Lincoln's Inn Fields, London WC2A 3BP
☎020 7404 7000 ✉clerks@thomasmore.co.uk
Call Date: Nov 1992, Inner Temple
Pupil Supervisor

Practising Areas: Common Law (General), Courts Martial, Crime, Crime (Corporate/Fraud), Family, Regulatory Law

HARDING MR MATTHEW AUSTIN

39 Park Square
Leeds LS1 2NU ☎0113 245 6633
✉seniorclerk@39parksquarechambers.co.uk
Call Date: Nov 2002, Lincoln's Inn

Practising Areas: Crime, Crime (Corporate/Fraud), Mental Health

HARDY MR MAXIMILIAN JOHN LEE

Nine Bedford Row
9 Bedford Row, London WC1R 4AZ
☎020 7489 2727 ✉clerks@9bedfordrow.co.uk
Call Date: Oct 2004, Gray's Inn

Practising Areas: Crime, Crime (Corporate/Fraud), Licensing, Regulatory Law

HARDYMAN MR MATTHEW JAMES

15 New Bridge Street
London EC4V 6AU ☎020 7842 1900
✉clerks@15nbs.com
Call Date: Oct 1997, Lincoln's Inn

Practising Areas: Common Law (General), Courts Martial, Crime

HARFORD-BELL MISS NERIDA

Garden Court Chambers
57-60 Lincoln's Inn Fields, London WC2A 3LJ
☎020 7993 7600 ✉info@gclaw.co.uk
Call Date: Nov 1984, Middle Temple
Pupil Supervisor

HARGREAVES MR BENJAMIN THOMAS

Carmelite Chambers
9 Carmelite Street, London EC4Y 0DR
☎020 7936 6300
✉clerks@carmelitechambers.co.uk
Call Date: Nov 1989, Lincoln's Inn
Pupil Supervisor

Practising Areas: Crime, Crime (Corporate/Fraud), Licensing

C

HARGREAVES MR SIMON JOHN ROBERT QC (2009)

Keating Chambers
15 Essex Street, London WC2R 3AA
☎ 020 7544 2600 ✉ clerks@keatingchambers.com
Call Date: Oct 1991, Inner Temple

Practising Areas: Arbitration, Commercial Litigation, Common Law (General), Construction, Energy, Information Technology, Professional Negligence

HAROUNOFF MR DAVID

9-12 Bell Yard
London WC2A 2JR ☎ 020 7400 1800
✉ clerks@9-12bellyard.com
Call Date: Nov 1984, Middle Temple
Pupil Supervisor

Practising Areas: Crime, Crime (Corporate/Fraud)

HARPER MISS HELEN CATHERINE

Renaissance Chambers
5th Floor, Gray's Inn Chambers, Gray's Inn, London WC1R 5JA ☎ 020 7404 1111
✉ clerks@renaissancechambers.co.uk
Call Date: Nov 2002, Middle Temple

Practising Areas: Children's Law, Family

HARRAP MR GILES THRESHER

Pump Court Chambers
31 Southgate Street, Winchester, Hampshire SO23 9EB ☎ 01962 868 161
✉ clerks@3pumpcourt.com
Pump Court Chambers
Upper Ground Floor, 3 Pump Court, Temple, London EC4Y 7AJ ☎ 020 7353 0711
✉ clerks@3pumpcourt.com
Pump Court Chambers
5 Temple Chambers, Temple Street, Swindon SN1 1SQ ☎ 01793 539899
✉ clerks@3pumpcourt.com
Call Date: Nov 1971, Inner Temple
Pupil Supervisor, Recorder

HARRAP MR ROBERT PHILIP

Five Paper
Ground Floor, 5 Paper Buildings, Temple, London EC4Y 7HB ☎ 020 7815 3200
Call Date: Oct 1997, Inner Temple

Practising Areas: Commercial Property, Common Law (General), Discrimination, Employment, Housing, Landlord & Tenant

HARRIES MR MARK ROBERT

Carmelite Chambers
9 Carmelite Street, London EC4Y 0DR
☎ 020 7936 6300
✉ clerks@carmelitechambers.co.uk
Call Date: Oct 1995, Lincoln's Inn

Practising Areas: Courts Martial, Crime, Crime (Corporate/Fraud)

HARRILL MISS JAYNE ANNE

4 Brick Court
4 Brick Court, Temple, London EC4Y 9AD
☎ 020 7832 3200 ✉ clerks@4bc.co.uk
Call Date: Oct 1990, Middle Temple
Pupil Supervisor

HARRINGTON MISS CLARE STEPHANIE

13 King's Bench Walk
13 King's Bench Walk, Temple, London EC4Y 7EN ☎ 020 7353 7204 ✉ clerks@13kbw.co.uk
13 KBW
32 Beaumont Street, Oxford OX1 2NP
☎ 01865 311066 ✉ clerks@13kbw.co.uk
Call Date: Oct 1998, Lincoln's Inn

Practising Areas: Common Law (General), Employment, Personal Injury

HARRINGTON MR TIMOTHY MARK

Citadel Chambers
The Citadel, 190 Corporation Street, Birmingham B4 6QD ☎ 0121 233 8500
✉ clerks@citadelchambers.com
Call Date: Mar 1997, Gray's Inn

Practising Areas: Crime

HARRINGTON MISS TINA AMANDA

Trinity Chambers
Highfield House, Moulsham Street, Chelmsford, Essex CM2 9AH
☎ 01245 605040 ✉ clerks@trinitychambers.com
Call Date: Nov 1985, Middle Temple
Pupil Supervisor

Practising Areas: Care Proceedings, Family, Family Provision

HARRIS MR ADRIAN DAVID

23 Essex Street
London WC2R 3AA ☎ 020 7413 0353
✉ clerks@23es.com
Call Date: Oct 2001, Inner Temple
Pupil Supervisor

Practising Areas: Crime, Crime (Corporate/Fraud), Disciplinary Tribunals, Regulatory Law

HARRIS MR DAVID ROBERT

St Albans Chambers
2 - 4 St Peter's Street, St Albans, Hertfordshire AL1 3LF ☎ 01727 843383
✉ clerks@stalbanschambers.com
Call Date: Oct 1997, Lincoln's Inn

Practising Areas: Ancillary Relief, Bankruptcy, Chancery (General), Chancery (Land Law), Civil Litigation, Common Law (General), Company & Commercial, Crime, Equity, Wills & Trusts, Insolvency, Land, Landlord & Tenant, Personal Injury, Probate & Administration, Road Traffic And Highways

HARRIS MR FRANCIS RICHARD

Field Court Chambers
5 Field Court, Gray's Inn, London WC1R 5EF
☎ 020 7405 6114 ✉ clerks@fieldcourt.co.uk
Call Date: Jul 1997, Inner Temple

HARRIS MR GLENN PETER

33 Bedford Row
London WC1R 4JH ☎ 020 7242 6476
✉ clerks@33bedfordrow.co.uk
Call Date: Oct 1994, Lincoln's Inn
Pupil Supervisor

HARRIS MR JAMES

Five St Andrew's Hill
5 St Andrew's Hill, London EC4V 5BZ
☎ 020 7332 5400 ✉ Clerks@5sah.co.uk
Call Date: Nov 1975, Gray's Inn
Pupil Supervisor

Practising Areas: Chancery (Land Law), Civil Litigation, Commercial Litigation, Commercial Property, Common Law (General), Company & Commercial, Construction, Crime, Environment, Health & Safety, Housing, Land, Landlord & Tenant, Professional Negligence, Road Traffic And Highways

HARRIS MR JULIAN GILBERT VAUGHAN

Citadel Chambers
The Citadel, 190 Corporation Street, Birmingham B4 6QD ☎ 0121 233 8500
✉ clerks@citadelchambers.com
Call Date: Nov 1982, Middle Temple

Practising Areas: Crime, Local Government, Regulatory Law

HARRIS MISS KATIE ANNE

Octagon House
19 Colegate, Norwich NR3 1AT
☎ 01603 623186 ✉ clerks@octagonhouse.co.uk
Call Date: Nov 2005, Inner Temple

Practising Areas: Care Proceedings, Children's Law, Family

HARRIS MR KEVIN LYN

Chambers of Mr K Harris
229 Tolcarne Drive, Pinner, Middlesex HA5 2DW ☎ 0845 123 1234
✉ kevinlynharris@gmail.com
Call Date: Oct 1999, Inner Temple

HARRIS MR MELVYN

5 Essex Court
1st Floor, 5 Essex Court, Temple, London EC4Y 9AH ☎ 020 7410 2000
✉ clerks@5essexcourt.co.uk
Call Date: Oct 1997, Lincoln's Inn

Practising Areas: Bankruptcy, Chancery (General), Chancery (Land Law), Commercial Litigation, Company & Commercial, Discrimination, Employment, Equity, Wills & Trusts, Insolvency, Landlord & Tenant, Partnership, Personal Injury, Probate & Administration, Professional Negligence, Sale & Carriage of Goods

HARRIS MR MICHAEL PETER

10 King's Bench Walk
Ground Floor, 10 King's Bench Walk, Temple, London EC4Y 7EB ☎ 020 7353 7742
✉ Chambers@10kingsbenchwalk.co.uk
Call Date: Oct 1993, Gray's Inn

Practising Areas: Immigration

HARRIS MR PAUL

Doughty Street Chambers
Pall Mall Court, 61-67 King Street, Manchester M2 4PD ☎ 0161 618 1066
Doughty Street Chambers
5th Floor, Broad Quay House, Prince Street, Bristol BS1 4DJ ☎ 01179 058 717
Doughty Street Chambers
53-54 Doughty Street, London WC1N 2LS
☎ 020 7404 1313 ✉ enquiries@doughtystreet.co.uk
Call Date: Feb 1976, Lincoln's Inn

Practising Areas: Administrative, Discrimination, Foreign Law, Housing, Human Rights, Immigration

HARRIS MS REBECCA ELIZABETH

QEB Hollis Whiteman
1-2 Laurence Pountney Hill, London EC4R 0EU ☎ 020 7933 8855 ✉ barristers@qebhw.co.uk
Call Date: Oct 1997, Inner Temple
Pupil Supervisor

Practising Areas: Crime, Crime (Corporate/Fraud), Regulatory Law

HARRIS MR ROGER CHARLES JAMES

2 Temple Gardens
2 Temple Gardens, Temple, London EC4Y 9AY ☎ 020 7822 1200 ✉ clerks@2tg.co.uk
Call Date: Oct 1996, Inner Temple
Pupil Supervisor

HARRIS MISS STELLA CASSANDRA METHVEN

Tooks Chambers
81 Farringdon Street, London EC4A 4BL ☎ 020 7842 7575 ✉ clerks@tooks.co.uk
Call Date: Nov 2002, Gray's Inn

Practising Areas: Courts Martial, Crime, Crime (Corporate/Fraud), Mental Health

HARRIS MR WILBERT ARTHURLYN

Rowchester Chambers
4 Rowchester Court, Whittall Street, Birmingham B4 6DH ☎ 0121 233 2327 ✉ clerks@rowchesterchambers.co.uk
Call Date: Nov 1973, Inner Temple
Pupil Supervisor

Practising Areas: Crime, Crime (Corporate/Fraud), Discrimination, Family, Family Provision, Healthcare, Human Rights, Immigration, Mental Health, Private International, Public International

HARRISON MS CAROLINE MARY ALICE

2 Temple Gardens
2 Temple Gardens, Temple, London EC4Y 9AY ☎ 020 7822 1200 ✉ clerks@2tg.co.uk
Call Date: Jul 1986, Lincoln's Inn
Pupil Supervisor

HARRISON DR GRAEME

12 College Place
Fauvelle Buildings, 12 College Place, Southampton SO15 2FE ☎ 023 8032 0320 ✉ clerks@12cp.co.uk
Call Date: Mar 1997, Inner Temple

Practising Areas: Children's Law, Coroners Inquests, Family, Family Provision, Health & Safety, Housing, Human Rights, Inquests, Landlord & Tenant, Medical Negligence, Mental Health, Personal Injury, Professional Negligence

HARRISON MR JOHN FOSTER

St Paul's Chambers
5th Floor, St Paul's House, 23 Park Square South, Leeds LS1 2ND ☎ 0113 245 5866
Call Date: Oct 1994, Lincoln's Inn
Pupil Supervisor

Practising Areas: Chancery (Land Law), Common Law (General), Company & Commercial, Coroners Inquests, Crime, Crime (Corporate/Fraud), Environment, Health & Safety, Inquests, Medical Negligence, Professional Negligence, Regulatory Law

HARRISON MR PAUL JOHN

13 King's Bench Walk
13 King's Bench Walk, Temple, London EC4Y 7EN ☎ 020 7353 7204 ✉ clerks@13kbw.co.uk
13 KBW
32 Beaumont Street, Oxford OX1 2NP ☎ 01865 311066 ✉ clerks@13kbw.co.uk
Call Date: Jul 2006, Lincoln's Inn

Practising Areas: Crime, Road Traffic And Highways

HARRISON MS PETA

St Johns Buildings Liverpool
8th Floor India Buildings, Water Street, Liverpool L2 0XG ☎ 0151 243 6000 ✉ clerk@stjohnsbuildings.co.uk
16 Winckley Square
Preston PR1 3JJ ☎ 01772 256100
St Johns Buildings
24a - 28 St John Street, Manchester M3 4DJ ☎ 0161 214 1500 ✉ clerk@stjohnsbuildings.co.uk
Call Date: Jul 2004, Inner Temple

HARRISON MR PETER JOHN QC (2006)

6 Pump Court
1st Floor, 6 Pump Court, Temple, London EC4Y 7AR ☎ 020 7797 8400 ✉ richardconstable@6pumpcourt.co.uk
6 Pump Court Chambers
6-8 Mill Street, Maidstone, Kent ME15 6XH ☎ 01622 688094 ✉ annexe@6pumpcourt.co.uk
Call Date: Jul 1987, Inner Temple

Practising Areas: Administrative, Common Land, Crime, Environment, Health & Safety, Licensing, Local Government, Regulatory Law, Town & Country Planning

HARRISON MR PIERS WILLIAM BENEDICT

Tanfield Chambers
2-5 Warwick Court, London WC1R 5DJ
☎ 020 7421 5300 ✉ clerks@tanfieldchambers.co.uk
Call Date: Mar 1997, Lincoln's Inn

Practising Areas: Common Law (General), Employment, Landlord & Tenant

HARRISON-HALL MR GILES ARTHUR

St Philips Chambers
55 Temple Row, Birmingham B2 5LS
☎ 0121 246 7000 ✉ clerks@st-philips.com
Call Date: Jul 1977, Gray's Inn
Pupil Supervisor

HART MISS AMANDA MARIJHE

Doughty Street Chambers
53-54 Doughty Street, London WC1N 2LS
☎ 020 7404 1313 ✉ enquiries@doughtystreet.co.uk
Doughty Street Chambers
Pall Mall Court, 61-67 King Street, Manchester M2 4PD ☎ 0161 618 1066
Doughty Street Chambers
5th Floor, Broad Quay House, Prince Street, Bristol BS1 4DJ ☎ 01179 058 717
Call Date: Jul 2001, Middle Temple

HARTE MR PATRICK DUDDY

3 Temple Gardens
Lower Ground Floor, 3 Temple Gardens, Temple, London EC4Y 9AU ☎ 020 7353 3102
✉ clerks@3tg.co.uk
Call Date: Nov 2006, Lincoln's Inn

HARTLEY MR ANTONY ARNOLD

No 8 Chambers
8 Fountain Court, Steelhouse Lane, Birmingham B4 6DR ☎ 0121 236 5514
✉ clerks@no8chambers.co.uk
Call Date: Feb 1991, Gray's Inn

HARTLEY MRS CAROLINE ANNE

Pump Court Chambers
31 Southgate Street, Winchester, Hampshire SO23 9EB ☎ 01962 868 161
✉ clerks@3pumpcourt.com
Pump Court Chambers
Upper Ground Floor, 3 Pump Court, Temple, London EC4Y 7AJ ☎ 020 7353 0711
✉ clerks@3pumpcourt.com
Pump Court Chambers
5 Temple Chambers, Temple Street, Swindon SN1 1SQ ☎ 01793 539899
✉ clerks@3pumpcourt.com
Call Date: Jul 2002, Middle Temple
Pupil Supervisor

Practising Areas: Children's Law

HARTLEY MR RICHARD ANTHONY QC (2008)

Cobden House Chambers
19 Quay Street, Manchester M3 3HN
☎ 0161 833 6000 ✉ Clerks@Cobden.co.uk
Call Date: Jul 1985, Middle Temple
Recorder

Practising Areas: Common Law (General), Personal Injury, Sports

HARTMAN MR MICHAEL

One Essex Court
1st Floor, Temple, London EC4Y 9AR
☎ 020 7936 3030 ✉ clerks@1ec.co.uk
Call Date: Nov 1975, Lincoln's Inn
Pupil Supervisor

Practising Areas: Bankruptcy, Commercial Litigation, Commercial Property, Company & Commercial, Employment, Immigration, Insolvency, Medical Negligence, Personal Injury

HARVEY MR JOHN GILBERT

No5 Chambers
Fountain Court, Steelhouse Lane, Birmingham B4 6DR ☎ 0845 210 5555 ✉ info@no5.com
No5 Chambers
Greenwood House, 4-7 Salisbury Court, London EC4Y 8AA ☎ 0845 210 5555
No5 Chambers
38 Queen Square, Bristol BS1 4QS
☎ 0845 210 5555
Call Date: Jul 1973, Gray's Inn
Recorder

Practising Areas: Arbitration, Common Law (General), Construction, Environment, Licensing, Medical Negligence, Personal Injury, Professional Negligence, Town & Country Planning

HARVEY MR STEPHEN FRANK QC (2006)

18 Red Lion Court
London EC4A 3EB ☎ 020 7520 6000
✉ chambers@18rlc.co.uk
18 Red Lion Court (Annexe)
Thornwood House, 102 New London Road, Chelmsford, Essex CM2 0RG
☎ 01245 280880
Call Date: Jul 1979, Gray's Inn

Practising Areas: Common Law (General), Courts Martial, Crime, Crime (Corporate/Fraud), Environment, Health & Safety, Regulatory Law

HARWOOD MR RICHARD JOHN

39 Essex Street
London WC2R 3AT ☎ 020 7832 1111
✉ clerks@39essex.com
82 King Street
Manchester M2 4WQ ☎ 0161 870 9969
Call Date: Nov 1993, Middle Temple
Pupil Supervisor

Practising Areas: Administrative, Agriculture, Energy, Environment, Local Government, Parliamentary, Telecommunications, Town & Country Planning

HARWOOD-GRAY MR BARRY JOHN

Kenworthy's Chambers
Arlington House, Bloom Street, Salford, Manchester M3 6AJ ☎ 0161 832 4036
Call Date: Nov 1998, Lincoln's Inn
Pupil Supervisor

Practising Areas: Discrimination, Employment

HASAN MISS AYESHA

3 Dr Johnson's Buildings
Ground Floor, 3 Dr Johnson's Buildings, Temple, London EC4Y 7BA ☎ 020 7353 4854
✉ clerks@3djb.co.uk
Call Date: Jul 1987, Gray's Inn
Pupil Supervisor

Practising Areas: Ancillary Relief, Children's Law, Family, Family Provision, Islamic Sharia Law

HASHIM MR MU'MIN IRAN MUHAMMAD

Chambers of Marion Smullen and Kerim Fuad QC
1 Inner Temple Lane, London EC4Y 1AF
☎ 020 7427 4400 ✉ clerks@1itl.com
Paragon Chambers
8 Creed Lane, St. Paul, London EC4V 5BR
☎ 020 3318 9988
✉ contact@paragonchambers.com
Call Date: Nov 2000, Middle Temple

Practising Areas: Crime, Employment, Immigration

HASSALL MR CRAIG JONATHAN

Sovereign Chambers
46 Park Place, Leeds LS1 2RY
☎ 0113 245 1841
✉ clerks@sovereignchambers.co.uk
Call Date: Nov 1999, Inner Temple
Pupil Supervisor

Practising Areas: Coroners Inquests, Crime, Crime (Corporate/Fraud), Disciplinary Tribunals, Employment, Environment, Family, Health & Safety, Licensing, Regulatory Law

HATCH MISS LISA SHARMILA

One Essex Court
1st Floor, Temple, London EC4Y 9AR
☎ 020 7936 3030 ✉ clerks@1ec.co.uk
Call Date: May 1995, Middle Temple

Practising Areas: Commercial Litigation, Common Law (General), Employment, Personal Injury

HATT MR JAMES WILLIAM REGINALD

4 Pump Court
4 Pump Court, Temple, London EC4Y 7AN
☎ 020 7842 5555 ✉ chambers@4pumpcourt.com
Call Date: Jul 2003, Lincoln's Inn

HAUGHEY MISS CAROLINE PHILIPPA

Furnival Chambers
32 Furnival Street, London EC4A 1JQ
☎ 020 7405 3232
Aspect Chambers
Aspect Court, 4 Temple Row, Birmingham B2 5HG ☎ 0121 222 2447
✉ clerks@aspectchambers.com
Call Date: Nov 1999, Middle Temple

HAUGHTY MR JEREMY NICHOLAS

Rougemont Chambers
Victory House, Dean Clarke Gardens, Southernhay East, Exeter EX2 4AA
☎ 01392 208484
✉ clerks@rougemontchambers.co.uk
Chambers of Mr Ami Feder
Ground Floor, Lamb Building, Temple, London EC4Y 7AS ☎ 020 7797 7788
✉ clerks@lambbuilding.co.uk
Chambers of Mr Ami Feder
Ground Floor, Lamb Building, Temple, London EC4Y 7AS ☎ 020 7797 7788
✉ clerks@lambbuilding.co.uk
Call Date: Nov 1989, Lincoln's Inn

C

Practising Areas: Chancery (General), Commercial Property, Common Law (General), Employment, Equity, Wills & Trusts, Housing, Landlord & Tenant, Licensing, Partnership, Personal Injury, Sale & Carriage of Goods

HAUKELAND MR MARTIN JONATHAN

42 Bedford Row
London WC1R 4LL ☎ 020 7831 0222
✉ clerks@42br.com
Call Date: Feb 1989, Middle Temple

Practising Areas: Education, Health & Safety, Personal Injury

HAVENHAND MR JOHN BARRY

Clerksroom (Taunton)
Equity House, Administration Centre, Blackbrook Park Avenue, Taunton, Somerset TA1 2PX ☎ 0845 083 3000
✉ mail@clerksroom.com
Clerksroom (London)
3rd Floor, 218 Strand, London WC2R 1AT
☎ 0845 083 3000 ✉ mail@clerksroom.com
King's Lynn Chambers
26 The Birches, South Wootton, King's Lynn, Norfolk PE30 3JG ☎ 01553 672 085
✉ timothy.leader@tesco.net
Call Date: Jul 1976, Middle Temple

Practising Areas: Commercial Litigation, Employment, Personal Injury

HAWES MR NEIL ASHLEY QC (2010)

Charter Chambers
33 John Street, London WC1N 2AT
☎ 020 7618 4400 ✉ clerks@charterchambers.com
Call Date: Nov 1989, Inner Temple

Practising Areas: Crime, Crime (Corporate/Fraud)

HAWKES MR MALCOLM ALEXANDER

Dyers Chambers
35 Bedford Row, London WC1R 4JH
☎ 020 7404 1881 ✉ admin@dyerschambers.com
Call Date: Oct 2006, Middle Temple

Practising Areas: Crime, Crime (Corporate/Fraud), Personal Injury, Regulatory Law

HAWKIN MR BENJAMIN

1 Mitre Court Buildings
1 Mitre Court Buildings, Temple, London EC4Y 7BS ☎ 020 7452 8900 ✉ clerks@1mcb.com
Call Date: Nov 1998, Middle Temple

Practising Areas: Administrative, Human Rights, Immigration

HAWORTH MR PHILIP MARTIN

33 Bedford Row
London WC1R 4JH ☎ 020 7242 6476
✉ clerks@33bedfordrow.co.uk
Call Date: Mar 2006, Lincoln's Inn

HAY MR MALCOLM JOHN MARSHALL

3 Dr Johnson's Buildings
Ground Floor, 3 Dr Johnson's Buildings, Temple, London EC4Y 7BA ☎ 020 7353 4854
✉ clerks@3djb.co.uk
Call Date: Nov 1972, Gray's Inn
Pupil Supervisor

Practising Areas: Ancillary Relief, Children's Law, Family, Family Provision

HAYCROFT MR ANTHONY MARK

Outer Temple Chambers
The Outer Temple, 222 Strand, London WC2R 1BA ☎ 020 7353 6381
✉ clerks@outertemple.com
Call Date: Nov 1982, Middle Temple
Pupil Supervisor

HAYES MRS CHRISTINE ELIZABETH

East Anglian Chambers
Gresham House, 5 Museum Street, Ipswich, Suffolk IP1 1HQ ☎ 01473 214481
✉ ipswich@ealaw.co.uk
Call Date: Nov 1999, Middle Temple

HAYES MRS KATHRYN ELIZABETH

Call Date: Oct 2000, Middle Temple

HAYES MR RICHARD JAMES

Lamb Chambers
Lamb Building, Elm Court, Temple, London EC4Y 7AS ☎ 020 7797 8300
✉ info@lambchambers.co.uk
Call Date: Oct 1995, Lincoln's Inn

Practising Areas: Banking, Chancery (General), Chancery (Land Law), Commercial Litigation, Commercial Property, Company & Commercial, Employment, Insolvency, Insurance, Landlord & Tenant, Sale & Carriage of Goods

HAYFORD MISS JANE HELENE

New Court
Ground Floor, New Court, Temple, London EC4Y 9BE ☎ 020 7583 5123
✉ clerks@newcourtchambers.com
Call Date: Oct 1997, Gray's Inn

Practising Areas: Family

HAYGARTH MR EDMUND BRUCE

Chavasse Court Chambers
18 Queen Avenue, Liverpool L2 4TX
☎ 0151 229 2030
✉ clerks@chavassechambers.co.uk
Call Date: Nov 1988, Gray's Inn

HAYHOE THE HON CRISPIN BERNARD GASCOIGNE

33 Bedford Row
London WC1R 4JH ☎ 020 7242 6476
✉ clerks@33bedfordrow.co.uk
Call Date: Nov 2004, Lincoln's Inn

HAYHURST MR BENJAMIN DAVID

2 Pump Court
1st Floor, 2 Pump Court, Temple, London EC4Y 7AH ☎ 020 7353 5597
✉ clerks@2pumpcourt.co.uk
Call Date: Jul 2004, Gray's Inn

HAYMERLE MR FRIEDRICH CHRISTIAN

Tooks Chambers
81 Farringdon Street, London EC4A 4BL
☎ 020 7842 7575 ✉ clerks@tooks.co.uk
Call Date: Oct 2000, Inner Temple

HAYNES MISS REBECCA

Monckton Chambers
1 & 2 Raymond Buildings, Gray's Inn, London WC1R 5NR ☎ 020 7405 7211
✉ chambers@monckton.com
Call Date: Nov 1994, Inner Temple

HAYS MR WILLIAM STORMONT

6 King's Bench Walk
Ground Floor, 6 King's Bench Walk, Temple, London EC4Y 7DR ☎ 020 7583 0410
✉ clerks@6kbw.com
Call Date: Nov 2006, Middle Temple

Practising Areas: Administrative, Courts Martial, Crime, Crime (Corporate/Fraud)

HAYTER MRS KATHLEEN

New Street Chambers
2 New Street, Leicester LE1 5NA
☎ 0116 262 5906 ✉ clerks@2newstreet.co.uk
Call Date: Jul 1982, Middle Temple
Pupil Supervisor

HAYTON MR MICHAEL PEARSON

Deans Court Chambers
24 St John Street, Manchester M3 4DF
☎ 0161 214 6000 ✉ clerks@deanscourt.co.uk
Deans Court Chambers
101 Walker Street, Preston PR1 2RR
☎ 01772 565 600 ✉ preston@deanscourt.co.uk
Call Date: Oct 1993, Lincoln's Inn
Pupil Supervisor

HAYTON MISS VIRGINA SUFEIYA

Deans Court Chambers
24 St John Street, Manchester M3 4DF
☎ 0161 214 6000 ✉ clerks@deanscourt.co.uk
Call Date: Oct 1999, Lincoln's Inn
Pupil Supervisor

HAYWOOD MISS JANET

Guildford Chambers
Stoke House, Leapale Lane, Guildford, Surrey GU1 4LY ☎ 01483 539131
✉ clerks@guildfordchambers.co.uk
Call Date: Jul 1985, Inner Temple

Practising Areas: Family

HAYWOOD DR JENNIFER MARGARET

Serle Court
6 New Square, Lincoln's Inn, London WC2A 3QS ☎ 020 7242 6105 ✉ clerks@serlecourt.co.uk
Call Date: Jul 2001, Lincoln's Inn
Pupil Supervisor

Practising Areas: Chancery (General), Charities, Commercial Litigation, Company & Commercial, Equity, Wills & Trusts, Insolvency, Partnership, Probate & Administration

HAYWOOD MR PHIL

Doughty Street Chambers
53-54 Doughty Street, London WC1N 2LS
☎ 020 7404 1313 ✉ enquiries@doughtystreet.co.uk
Doughty Street Chambers
Pall Mall Court, 61-67 King Street, Manchester M2 4PD ☎ 0161 618 1066

C

Doughty Street Chambers
5th Floor, Broad Quay House, Prince Street, Bristol BS1 4DJ ☎01179 058 717
Call Date: Mar 2001, Middle Temple

HEAL MRS MADELEINE

New Square Chambers
12 New Square, Lincoln's Inn, London WC2A 3SW ☎020 7419 8000 ✉robin.hollington@newsquarechambers.co.uk
Call Date: May 1996, Lincoln's Inn

Practising Areas: Commercial Litigation, Competition, Copyright, EC & Competition Law, Entertainment, Film, Cable & TV, Foreign Law, Information Technology, Intellectual Property, Patents, Sports, Trademarks

HEALY MISS ALEXANDRA QC (2011)

9-12 Bell Yard
London WC2A 2JR ☎020 7400 1800
✉clerks@9-12bellyard.com
Call Date: Oct 1992, Gray's Inn
Pupil Supervisor

Practising Areas: Common Law (General), Crime, Crime (Corporate/Fraud)

HEARNDEN MISS ALEXIS KATRINA

39 Essex Street
London WC2R 3AT ☎020 7832 1111
✉clerks@39essex.com
82 King Street
Manchester M2 4WQ ☎0161 870 9969
Call Date: Oct 2005, Inner Temple

Practising Areas: Regulatory Law

HEARNDEN MR RICHARD CHRISTOPHER

Furnival Chambers
32 Furnival Street, London EC4A 1JQ
☎020 7405 3232
Call Date: Nov 1998, Gray's Inn
Pupil Supervisor

Practising Areas: Crime, Crime (Corporate/Fraud), Local Government, Regulatory Law

HEARNE MISS JULIET AUDREY

Cornwall Street Chambers
Shrewsbury Annex, Rural Enterprise Centre, Stafford Drive, Battlefield Enterprise Park, Shrewsbury SY1 3FE
☎01743 363 611 / 0121 233 7500
Cornwall Street Chambers
85-87 Cornwall Street, Birmingham B3 3BY
☎0121 233 7500 ✉clerks@cornwallstreet.co.uk
Call Date: Nov 1989, Gray's Inn

HEATH MR STEPHEN DAVID

Tanfield Chambers
2-5 Warwick Court, London WC1R 5DJ
☎020 7421 5300 ✉clerks@tanfieldchambers.co.uk
Call Date: Feb 1992, Lincoln's Inn

Practising Areas: Employment

HEATON MISS LAURA JANE

29 Bedford Row Chambers
London WC1R 4HE ☎020 7404 1044
✉clerks@29br.co.uk
Call Date: Oct 1998, Middle Temple
Pupil Supervisor

Practising Areas: Family, Family Provision

HEDWORTH MS RACHEL CLAIRE

Trinity Chambers
The Custom House, 39 Quayside, Newcastle Upon Tyne NE1 3DE ☎0191 232 1927
✉info@trinitychambers.co.uk
Trinity Chambers
Multi Media Exchange, 72-80 Corporation Road, Middlesbrough TS1 2RF
☎01642 247569 ✉info@trinitychambers.co.uk
Call Date: Jul 1999, Inner Temple

HEELEY MISS MICHELLE LOUISE

No5 Chambers
Fountain Court, Steelhouse Lane, Birmingham B4 6DR ☎0845 210 5555 ✉info@no5.com
No5 Chambers
Greenwood House, 4-7 Salisbury Court, London EC4Y 8AA ☎0845 210 5555
No5 Chambers
38 Queen Square, Bristol BS1 4QS
☎0845 210 5555
Call Date: Jul 2001, Gray's Inn

Practising Areas: Crime, Licensing, Regulatory Law

HEGARTY MR KEVIN JOHN QC (2010)

St Philips Chambers
55 Temple Row, Birmingham B2 5LS
☎0121 246 7000 ✉clerks@st-philips.com
Call Date: Nov 1982, Middle Temple
Pupil Supervisor, Recorder

Practising Areas: Crime, Crime (Corporate/Fraud), Education, Environment, Health & Safety

C

HELLENS MR MATTHEW JAMES

3 Dr Johnson's Buildings
Ground Floor, 3 Dr Johnson's Buildings, Temple, London EC4Y 7BA ☎ 020 7353 4854
✉ clerks@3djb.co.uk
Call Date: Oct 1992, Lincoln's Inn

Practising Areas: Children's Law, Family

HELLER MRS ANNE

10 King's Bench Walk
Ground Floor, 10 King's Bench Walk, Temple, London EC4Y 7EB ☎ 020 7353 7742
✉ Chambers@10kingsbenchwalk.co.uk
Call Date: Nov 1995, Gray's Inn

Practising Areas: Immigration

HELLMAN MR STEPHEN GEOFFREY

Chambers of Andrew Mitchell QC
33 Chancery Lane, London WC2A 1EN
☎ 020 7440 9950 ✉ clerks@33cllaw.com
Call Date: Jul 1988, Inner Temple
Pupil Supervisor

Practising Areas: Crime

HENDERSON MR IAN FRANCIS

Farringdon Chambers
180 Bermondsey Street, London SE1 3TQ
☎ 020 7089 5700
Call Date: Nov 1990, Inner Temple
Pupil Supervisor

Practising Areas: Crime, Crime (Corporate/Fraud)

HENDERSON MR JAMES THOMAS

Pump Court Tax Chambers
16 Bedford Row, London WC1R 4EF
☎ 020 7414 8080 ✉ clerks@pumptax.com
Kings Chambers
36 Young Street, Manchester M3 3FT
☎ 0845 034 3444 ✉ clerks@kingschambers.com
Kings Chambers
5 Park Square East, Leeds LS1 2NE
☎ 0845 034 3444 ✉ clerks@kingschambers.com
Call Date: Nov 1997, Gray's Inn
Pupil Supervisor

Practising Areas: Equity, Wills & Trusts, Tax (Capital & Income), Tax (Corporate)

HENDERSON MISS JOSEPHINE

Five Paper
Ground Floor, 5 Paper Buildings, Temple, London EC4Y 7HB ☎ 020 7815 3200
Call Date: Nov 1990, Inner Temple

Practising Areas: Administrative, Landlord & Tenant, Local Government, Public Law

HENDERSON MR LAWRENCE MARK

9-12 Bell Yard
London WC2A 2JR ☎ 020 7400 1800
✉ clerks@9-12bellyard.com
Call Date: Nov 1990, Middle Temple
Pupil Supervisor

Practising Areas: Crime, Crime (Corporate/Fraud)

HENDERSON MR NEIL JOHN

Stone Chambers
4 Field Court, Gray's Inn, London WC1R 5EF
☎ 020 7440 6900 ✉ clerks@stonechambers.com
Call Date: Oct 2004, Inner Temple

Practising Areas: Admiralty, Arbitration, Banking, Bankruptcy, Commercial Litigation, Commodities, Common Law (General), Company & Commercial, Competition, EC & Competition Law, Financial Services, Insolvency, International Trade, Sale & Carriage of Goods, Shipping/Admiralty, Sports

HENDRON MR HENRY JOSEPH CHRISTOPHER

Strand Chambers
226 The Strand, London WC2R 1BA
☎ 020 7117 6920 ✉ Henry@lawsurgery.com
Call Date: Nov 2006, Middle Temple

Practising Areas: Arbitration, Bankruptcy, Chancery (General), Civil Liberties, Commercial Litigation, Commercial Property, Common Law (General), Company & Commercial, Construction, Copyright, Defamation, Discrimination, Employment, Family, Housing, Human Rights, Immigration, Insolvency, Landlord & Tenant, Medical Negligence, Parliamentary, Personal Injury, Professional Negligence, Regulatory Law, Sale & Carriage of Goods, Shipping/Admiralty, Sports, Trademarks

HENLEY MR ANDREW MICHAEL

Furnival Chambers
32 Furnival Street, London EC4A 1JQ
☎020 7405 3232
Call Date: Oct 1992, Middle Temple
Pupil Supervisor

Practising Areas: Crime, Crime (Corporate/Fraud), Health & Safety, Licensing, Regulatory Law

HENRY MR DELROY

Citadel Chambers
The Citadel, 190 Corporation Street, Birmingham B4 6QD ☎0121 233 8500
✉clerks@citadelchambers.com
Call Date: Oct 1999, Inner Temple

Practising Areas: Crime

HENRY MR EDWARD JOSEPH ALOYSIUS

QEB Hollis Whiteman
1-2 Laurence Pountney Hill, London EC4R 0EU ☎020 7933 8855 ✉barristers@qebhw.co.uk
Call Date: Nov 1988, Lincoln's Inn
Pupil Supervisor

HENSON MISS CHRISTINE RUTH

Crown Office Row Chambers
119 Church Street, Brighton, Sussex BN1 1UD ☎01273 625625 ✉clerks@1cor.com
Call Date: Oct 1994, Middle Temple
Pupil Supervisor

Practising Areas: Crime, Health & Safety, Inquests, Regulatory Law, Road Traffic And Highways

C

HENSTOCK-TURNER MRS SARAH ELIZABETH

College Chambers
19 Carlton Crescent, Southampton, Hampshire SO15 2ET ☎023 8023 0338
✉clerks@college-chambers.co.uk
Call Date: Oct 2004, Middle Temple

Practising Areas: Crime, Employment, Family

HENTHORN MISS KATE MARIE

18 St John Street
Manchester M3 4EA ☎0161 278 1800
✉clerks@18sjs.com
7 Bell Yard
London WC2A 2JR ☎020 7831 0636
✉kevintarrant@btconnect.com
Call Date: Mar 2005, Middle Temple

Practising Areas: Care Proceedings, Crime, Education, Family, Sports

HEPHER MR PAUL ARTHUR RICHARD

4 Paper Buildings
1st Floor, 4 Paper Buildings, Temple, London EC4Y 7EX ☎020 7427 5200 ✉clerks@4pb.com
Call Date: Oct 1994, Gray's Inn

Practising Areas: Care Proceedings, Family

HEPPENSTALL MISS CLAIRE NORAH

1 Garden Court Family Law Chambers
Ground Floor, One Garden Court, Temple, London EC4Y 9BJ ☎020 7797 7900
✉clerks@1gc.com
Call Date: Nov 1990, Inner Temple
Pupil Supervisor

Practising Areas: Family, Family Provision

HEPPINSTALL MR ADAM JOHN

Henderson Chambers
2 Harcourt Buildings, Temple, London EC4Y 9DB ☎020 7583 9020
✉clerks@hendersonchambers.co.uk
Call Date: Oct 1999, Middle Temple
Pupil Supervisor

Practising Areas: Chancery (Land Law), Common Law (General), Employment, Housing, Landlord & Tenant, Personal Injury

HERBERT MR PETER OBE

Justice House
67 Wentworth Avenue, Finchley, London N3 1YN ☎07973 794 946 ✉pherb5law@aol.com
Call Date: Nov 1982, Gray's Inn
Pupil Supervisor

HESLOP MR MARTIN SYDNEY QC (1995)

2 Hare Court
Lower Ground, Ground, 1st & 2nd Floor, 2 Hare Court, Temple, London EC4Y 7BH
☎020 7353 3982 ✉clerks@2harecourt.com
Call Date: Jul 1972, Lincoln's Inn
Recorder

HESTER MR PAUL STEPHEN

3 PB Barristers
3 Paper Buildings, Temple, London EC4Y 7EU
☎ 020 7583 8055
3 PB Barristers
Royal Talbot House, 2 Victoria Street, Bristol, Avon BS1 6BB ☎ 0117 928 1520
3 PB Barristers
30 Christchurch Road, Bournemouth, Dorset BH1 3PD ☎ 01202 292102 ✉ clerks.bournemouth@3paper.co.uk
3 PB Barristers
4 St Peter Street, Winchester SO23 8BW
☎ 01962 868884 ✉ clerks.winchester@3paper.co.uk
3 PB Barristers
23 Beaumont Street, Oxford OX1 2NP
☎ 01865 793 736
Call Date: Jul 1989, Middle Temple
Pupil Supervisor

HETT MR JAMES

The Chambers Of Mr Hett
53 Foxhill Road, Burton Joyce, Nottingham NG14 5DB ☎ 0115 9313958/07727 688337
Call Date: Nov 1991, Middle Temple
Pupil Supervisor

Practising Areas: Crime

HEWITT MISS ALEXANDRA HELEN

Linenhall Chambers
1 Stanley Place, Chester CH1 2LU
☎ 01244 348282
✉ clerks@linenhallchambers.co.uk
Call Date: Oct 1995, Middle Temple

Practising Areas: Care Proceedings, Family

HEWITT MR DAVID EDWARD MILES

Five St Andrew's Hill
5 St Andrew's Hill, London EC4V 5BZ
☎ 020 7332 5400 ✉ Clerks@5sah.co.uk
Call Date: Feb 1991, Middle Temple
Pupil Supervisor

Practising Areas: Crime, Crime (Corporate/Fraud)

HEWSON MS BARBARA MARY

Hardwicke
New Square, Lincoln's Inn, London WC2A 3SB ☎ 020 7242 2523
✉ enquiries@hardwicke.co.uk
Call Date: Nov 1985, Middle Temple
Pupil Supervisor

Practising Areas: Administrative, Chancery (General), Civil Liberties, Commercial Litigation, Discrimination, EC & Competition Law, Employment, Entertainment, Foreign Law, Medical Negligence, Mental Health, Professional Negligence

HEYWOOD MR MARK ADRIAN QC (2010)

5 King's Bench Walk
5 King's Bench Walk, Temple, London EC4Y 7DN ☎ 020 7353 5638 ✉ clerks@5kbw.co.uk
Call Date: Jul 1985, Gray's Inn
Pupil Supervisor, Recorder

HEYWOOD MR MARK STEPHEN QC (2012)

No5 Chambers
Fountain Court, Steelhouse Lane, Birmingham B4 6DR ☎ 0845 210 5555 ✉ info@no5.com
No5 Chambers
Greenwood House, 4-7 Salisbury Court, London EC4Y 8AA ☎ 0845 210 5555
No5 Chambers
38 Queen Square, Bristol BS1 4QS
☎ 0845 210 5555
Call Date: Jul 1986, Gray's Inn

HEYWORTH MR JAMES EDWARD WATSON

Lincoln House Chambers
Tower 12, The Avenue North, Spinningfields, 18-22 Bridge Street, Manchester M3 3BZ
☎ 0161 832 5701
✉ info@lincolnhousechambers.com
Call Date: Nov 2006, Gray's Inn

Practising Areas: Courts Martial, Crime

HICKINBOTTOM MISS ABIGAIL JEAN

Call Date: Nov 2004, Inner Temple

HICKS MR EDWARD GORDON DAVID

Radcliffe Chambers
Ground Floor, 11 New Square, Lincoln's Inn, London WC2A 3QB ☎ 020 7831 0081
✉ clerks@radcliffechambers.com
Call Date: Nov 2004, Middle Temple

Practising Areas: Bankruptcy, Chancery (General), Chancery (Land Law), Commercial Litigation, Common Law (General), Equity, Wills & Trusts, Housing, Insolvency, Landlord & Tenant, Probate & Administration

HICKS MR MARTIN LESLIE ARTHUR QC (2003)

2 Hare Court
Lower Ground, Ground, 1st & 2nd Floor, 2 Hare Court, Temple, London EC4Y 7BH
☎ 020 7353 3982 ✉ clerks@2harecourt.com
Call Date: May 1977, Inner Temple

Practising Areas: Crime, Crime (Corporate/Fraud)

HIDDLESTON MR ADAM WALLACE

3 PB Barristers
3 Paper Buildings, Temple, London EC4Y 7EU
☎ 020 7583 8055
3 PB Barristers
Royal Talbot House, 2 Victoria Street, Bristol, Avon BS1 6BB ☎ 0117 928 1520
3 PB Barristers
4 St Peter Street, Winchester SO23 8BW
☎ 01962 868884 ✉ clerks.winchester@3paper.co.uk
3 PB Barristers
23 Beaumont Street, Oxford OX1 2NP
☎ 01865 793 736
3 PB Barristers
30 Christchurch Road, Bournemouth, Dorset BH1 3PD ☎ 01202 292102 ✉ clerks.bournemouth@3paper.co.uk
Call Date: Oct 1990, Inner Temple
Pupil Supervisor

HIGGINS MR ADRIAN JOHN

13 King's Bench Walk
13 King's Bench Walk, Temple, London EC4Y 7EN ☎ 020 7353 7204 ✉ clerks@13kbw.co.uk
13 KBW
32 Beaumont Street, Oxford OX1 2NP
☎ 01865 311066 ✉ clerks@13kbw.co.uk
Call Date: Oct 1990, Lincoln's Inn

Practising Areas: Commercial Litigation, Common Law (General), Health & Safety, Personal Injury

HIGGINS MR DANIEL MALCOLM BUHLEA

Nine Bedford Row
9 Bedford Row, London WC1R 4AZ
☎ 020 7489 2727 ✉ clerks@9bedfordrow.co.uk
Call Date: Jul 2003, Inner Temple

Practising Areas: Courts Martial, Crime, Crime (Corporate/Fraud), Licensing, Regulatory Law, Sports

HIGGINSON MR PETER ST GEORGE

Charter Chambers
33 John Street, London WC1N 2AT
☎ 020 7618 4400 ✉ clerks@charterchambers.com
Call Date: Jul 1975, Lincoln's Inn
Pupil Supervisor

Practising Areas: Crime, Crime (Corporate/Fraud)

HIGGINSON MR TIMOTHY NICHOLAS BENNETT

Littleton Chambers
3 King's Bench Walk North, Temple, London EC4Y 7HR ☎ 020 7797 8600
✉ fschneider@littletonchambers.co.uk
St John's Chambers
101 Victoria Street, Bristol BS1 6PU
☎ 0117 923 4700 ✉ clerks@stjohnschambers.co.uk
Call Date: Nov 1977, Inner Temple

Practising Areas: Arbitration, Banking, Chancery (General), Commercial Litigation, Commercial Property, Employment, Entertainment, Film, Cable & TV, Financial Services, Insurance, Landlord & Tenant, Partnership, Professional Negligence, Regulatory Law, Sports, Telecommunications

HIGGS MR JONATHAN ALEXANDER CAMERON QC (2011)

5 King's Bench Walk
5 King's Bench Walk, Temple, London EC4Y 7DN ☎ 020 7353 5638 ✉ clerks@5kbw.co.uk
Call Date: Nov 1987, Middle Temple
Pupil Supervisor

Practising Areas: Crime

HIGNETT MR RICHARD JAMES

No5 Chambers
Greenwood House, 4-7 Salisbury Court, London EC4Y 8AA ☎ 0845 210 5555
No5 Chambers
38 Queen Square, Bristol BS1 4QS
☎ 0845 210 5555
No5 Chambers
Fountain Court, Steelhouse Lane, Birmingham B4 6DR ☎ 0845 210 5555 ✉ info@no5.com
Call Date: Nov 1995, Inner Temple
Pupil Supervisor

Practising Areas: Discrimination, Employment

HILL MR ANDREW CHARLES ROWLAND

Great James Street Chambers
37 Great James Street, London WC1N 3HB
☎020 7440 4949 ✉chambers@greatjames.co.uk
Chambers of Mr A C Hill
16 Hart Grove, London W5 3NB
☎07792 682928 ✉acrhill@yahoo.co.uk
Call Date: Nov 1982, Gray's Inn

HILL MS ELEANOR MARY HENRIETTA

Doughty Street Chambers
53-54 Doughty Street, London WC1N 2LS
☎020 7404 1313 ✉enquiries@doughtystreet.co.uk
Doughty Street Chambers
Pall Mall Court, 61-67 King Street, Manchester M2 4PD ☎0161 618 1066
Doughty Street Chambers
5th Floor, Broad Quay House, Prince Street, Bristol BS1 4DJ ☎01179 058 717
Call Date: Oct 1997, Inner Temple

Practising Areas: Administrative, Civil Liberties, Discrimination, Employment, Human Rights, Inquests

HILL MR JONATHAN

8 New Square
8 New Square, Lincoln's Inn, London WC2A 3QP ☎020 7405 4321 ✉clerks@8newsquare.co.uk
Call Date: Oct 2000, Lincoln's Inn

Practising Areas: Copyright, EC & Competition Law, Entertainment, Franchising, Intellectual Property, Patents, Sports, Trademarks

HILL MR MAX BENJAMIN ROWLAND QC (2008)

18 Red Lion Court
London EC4A 3EB ☎020 7520 6000
✉chambers@18rlc.co.uk
18 Red Lion Court (Annexe)
Thornwood House, 102 New London Road, Chelmsford, Essex CM2 0RG
☎01245 280880
Call Date: Nov 1987, Middle Temple
Recorder

Practising Areas: Crime, Crime (Corporate/Fraud)

HILL MR MICHAEL GORDON

Trinity Chambers
The Custom House, 39 Quayside, Newcastle Upon Tyne NE1 3DE ☎0191 232 1927
✉info@trinitychambers.co.uk
Trinity Chambers
Multi Media Exchange, 72-80 Corporation Road, Middlesbrough TS1 2RF
☎01642 247569 ✉info@trinitychambers.co.uk
Call Date: Jul 2004, Gray's Inn
Pupil Supervisor

Practising Areas: Agriculture, Banking, Bankruptcy, Chancery (General), Commercial Litigation, Commercial Property, Common Law (General), Crime, Crime (Corporate/Fraud), Environment, Financial Services, Health & Safety, Housing, Insolvency, Landlord & Tenant, Medical Negligence, Personal Injury, Professional Negligence, Regulatory Law, Sale & Carriage of Goods

HILL MR NICHOLAS IAN

No.6 Park Square
Leeds LS1 2LW ☎0113 245 9763
✉Tim@no6.co.uk
Call Date: Oct 1993, Lincoln's Inn

HILL MR NICHOLAS MARK QC (2009)

Pump Court Chambers
Upper Ground Floor, 3 Pump Court, Temple, London EC4Y 7AJ ☎020 7353 0711
✉clerks@3pumpcourt.com
Pump Court Chambers
5 Temple Chambers, Temple Street, Swindon SN1 1SQ ☎01793 539899
✉clerks@3pumpcourt.com
St Philips Chambers
55 Temple Row, Birmingham B2 5LS
☎0121 246 7000 ✉clerks@st-philips.com
Call Date: Jul 1987, Middle Temple
Recorder

Practising Areas: Civil Liberties, Commercial Litigation, Common Law (General), Ecclesiastical, Medical Negligence, Personal Injury, Professional Negligence, Town & Country Planning

HILL MR PIERS NICHOLAS

37 Park Square Chambers
37 Park Square, Leeds LS1 2NY
☎0113 243 9422 ✉chambers@no37.co.uk
Call Date: Jul 1987, Inner Temple
Pupil Supervisor

Practising Areas: Administrative, Chancery (General), Chancery (Land Law), Commercial Property, Conveyancing, Equity, Wills & Trusts,

Housing, Landlord & Tenant, Local Government, Probate & Administration, Town & Country Planning

HILL MR SIMON MICHAEL

33 Bedford Row
London WC1R 4JH ☎020 7242 6476
✉clerks@33bedfordrow.co.uk
Call Date: Nov 2001, Middle Temple

Practising Areas: Common Law (General), Family, Immigration, Landlord & Tenant, Licensing

HILLAS MISS SAMANTHA

Atlantic Chambers
4-6 Cook Street, Liverpool L2 9QU
☎0151 236 4421 ✉info@atlanticchambers.co.uk
Call Date: Oct 1996, Inner Temple

Practising Areas: Ancillary Relief, Care Proceedings, Chancery (General), Chancery (Land Law), Children's Law, Family, Family Provision

HILLIER MR WILLIAM

New Street Chambers
2 New Street, Leicester LE1 5NA
☎0116 262 5906 ✉clerks@2newstreet.co.uk
Call Date: Jul 2001, Inner Temple

Practising Areas: Ancillary Relief, Care Proceedings, Chancery (Land Law), Children's Law, Civil Litigation, Commercial Property, Common Law (General), Consumer, Equity, Wills & Trusts, Family, Family Provision, Housing, Insolvency, Land, Landlord & Tenant, Personal Injury, Road Traffic And Highways

HILLMAN MR BASIL

4 King's Bench Walk
2nd Floor, 4 King's Bench Walk, Temple, London EC4Y 7DL ☎020 7822 7000
✉clerks@4kbw.co.uk
Call Date: Nov 1968, Gray's Inn

Practising Areas: Courts Martial, Crime, Crime (Corporate/Fraud)

HILLMAN MR GERARD PAUL

Carmelite Chambers
9 Carmelite Street, London EC4Y 0DR
☎020 7936 6300
✉clerks@carmelitechambers.co.uk
Call Date: Oct 1999, Gray's Inn

Practising Areas: Chancery (General), Common Law (General), Crime, Landlord & Tenant

HILLS MR TIMOTHY JAMES

Albion Chambers
Broad Street, Bristol BS1 1DR
☎0117 927 2144 ✉clerks@albionchambers.co.uk
Call Date: Jul 1968, Lincoln's Inn
Pupil Supervisor

Practising Areas: Crime

HILTON MR ALAN JOHN HOWARD QC (1990)

QEB Hollis Whiteman
1-2 Laurence Pountney Hill, London EC4R 0EU ☎020 7933 8855 ✉barristers@qebhw.co.uk
Call Date: Nov 1964, Middle Temple
Recorder

Practising Areas: Crime, Crime (Corporate/Fraud)

HILTON MS SAISAMPAN

Holborn Chambers
6 Gate Street, Lincoln's Inn Fields, London WC2A 3HP ☎020 7242 6060
Call Date: Oct 1994, Gray's Inn

Practising Areas: Chancery (General), Chancery (Land Law), Commercial Property, Company & Commercial, Employment, Equity, Wills & Trusts, Foreign Law, Private International

HIMSWORTH MISS EMMA KATHERINE QC (2012)

One Essex Court
Ground Floor, One Essex Court, Temple, London EC4Y 9AR ☎020 7583 2000
✉clerks@oeclaw.co.uk
Call Date: Oct 1993, Gray's Inn
Pupil Supervisor

Practising Areas: Copyright, Intellectual Property, Patents, Trademarks

HIMSWORTH MR MARK STEPHEN

Dyers Chambers
35 Bedford Row, London WC1R 4JH
☎020 7404 1881 ✉admin@dyerschambers.com
Call Date: Oct 1999, Middle Temple

Practising Areas: Crime, Crime (Corporate/Fraud), Regulatory Law, Trademarks

HINDMARSH MR LUKE EDWARD THOMAS

9-12 Bell Yard
London WC2A 2JR ☎020 7400 1800
✉clerks@9-12bellyard.com
Call Date: Mar 2007, Middle Temple

Practising Areas: Crime

HINDS MR ORIEL GLENVERE

Clerksroom (Taunton)
Equity House, Administration Centre, Blackbrook Park Avenue, Taunton, Somerset TA1 2PX ☎0845 083 3000
✉mail@clerksroom.com
Clerksroom (London)
3rd Floor, 218 Strand, London WC2R 1AT
☎0845 083 3000 ✉mail@clerksroom.com
66 Worthington Road
66 Worthington Road, Surbiton, Kingston Upon Thames, Surrey KT6 7RX
☎020 8390 6359 ✉OrielG@aol.com
Call Date: Jul 1988, Inner Temple

HINE MR CHARLES RODERICK JOHN

King's Bench Chambers
Wellington House, 175 Holdenhurst Road, Bournemouth, Dorset BH8 8DQ
☎01202 250025
Call Date: Nov 1985, Gray's Inn
Pupil Supervisor

Practising Areas: Care Proceedings, Common Law (General), Courts Martial, Crime, Family, Family Provision, Health & Safety, Regulatory Law

HINES MR JAMES PHILIP

3 Raymond Buildings
3 Raymond Buildings, Gray's Inn, London WC1R 5BH ☎020 7400 6400
✉clerks@3rblaw.com
Call Date: Jul 1982, Gray's Inn
Pupil Supervisor

Practising Areas: Crime, Crime (Corporate/Fraud), Licensing, Regulatory Law

HINGSTON MR JOE

Carmelite Chambers
9 Carmelite Street, London EC4Y 0DR
☎020 7936 6300
✉clerks@carmelitechambers.co.uk
Call Date: Oct 2007, Lincoln's Inn

Practising Areas: Crime

HINTON MR NEIL PEARSE

King's Bench Chambers
Wellington House, 175 Holdenhurst Road, Bournemouth, Dorset BH8 8DQ
☎01202 250025
Call Date: Nov 1997, Lincoln's Inn

Practising Areas: Care Proceedings, Children's Law, Civil Litigation, Common Law (General), Consumer, Coroners Inquests, Courts Martial, Crime, Crime (Corporate/Fraud), Disciplinary Tribunals, Employment, Family, Health & Safety, Inquests, Licensing, Road Traffic And Highways

HIRST MR KARL DOUGLAS

No5 Chambers
Fountain Court, Steelhouse Lane, Birmingham B4 6DR ☎0845 210 5555 ✉info@no5.com
No5 Chambers
Greenwood House, 4-7 Salisbury Court, London EC4Y 8AA ☎0845 210 5555
No5 Chambers
38 Queen Square, Bristol BS1 4QS
☎0845 210 5555
Call Date: Oct 1997, Inner Temple
Pupil Supervisor

Practising Areas: Health & Safety, Medical Negligence, Personal Injury, Professional Negligence

HIRST MISS KATHRYN ANNE

Furnival Chambers
32 Furnival Street, London EC4A 1JQ
☎020 7405 3232
Call Date: Nov 1986, Inner Temple

Practising Areas: Crime, Mental Health, Regulatory Law

HIRST MR MARTIN LEWIS

13 King's Bench Walk
13 King's Bench Walk, Temple, London EC4Y 7EN ☎020 7353 7204 ✉clerks@13kbw.co.uk
13 KBW
32 Beaumont Street, Oxford OX1 2NP
☎01865 311066 ✉clerks@13kbw.co.uk
Call Date: Nov 1998, Lincoln's Inn

Practising Areas: Arbitration, Commercial Litigation, Common Law (General), Company & Commercial, Construction, Energy, Insolvency, Insurance, Personal Injury, Sale & Carriage of Goods

HIRST MISS REBECCA ELISABETH

Cobden House Chambers
19 Quay Street, Manchester M3 3HN
☎ 0161 833 6000 ✉ Clerks@Cobden.co.uk
Call Date: Nov 1999, Gray's Inn

Practising Areas: Crime, Crime (Corporate/Fraud), Health & Safety, Human Rights, Licensing, Personal Injury, Regulatory Law

HIRST MR WILLIAM TIMOTHY JOHN

Park Lane Plowden
19 Westgate, Leeds LS1 2RD
☎ 0113 228 5049 ✉ clerks@parklaneplowden.co.uk
Call Date: Nov 1970, Inner Temple
Recorder

Practising Areas: Banking, Chancery (General), Commercial Litigation, Common Law (General), Equity, Wills & Trusts, Personal Injury, Professional Negligence

HISLOP MR DAVID SEYMOUR QC (2010)

Doughty Street Chambers
53-54 Doughty Street, London WC1N 2LS
☎ 020 7404 1313 ✉ enquiries@doughtystreet.co.uk
Doughty Street Chambers
Pall Mall Court, 61-67 King Street, Manchester M2 4PD ☎ 0161 618 1066
Doughty Street Chambers
5th Floor, Broad Quay House, Prince Street, Bristol BS1 4DJ ☎ 01179 058 717
Call Date: Feb 1989, Gray's Inn
Pupil Supervisor

Practising Areas: Crime, Crime (Corporate/Fraud), Regulatory Law, Sports

HOAR MR FRANCIS JOHN PATRICK

Field Court Chambers
5 Field Court, Gray's Inn, London WC1R 5EF
☎ 020 7405 6114 ✉ clerks@fieldcourt.co.uk
Call Date: Nov 2001, Lincoln's Inn

Practising Areas: Administrative, Commercial Litigation, Employment, Land, Personal Injury

HOBBS MISS EMMA-JANE

Temple Garden Chambers
1 Harcourt Buildings, Temple, London EC4Y 9DA ☎ 020 7583 1315 ✉ clerks@tgchambers.com
Call Date: Oct 1996, Gray's Inn

HOBBS MR GEOFFREY WILLIAM QC (1991)

One Essex Court
Ground Floor, One Essex Court, Temple, London EC4Y 9AR ☎ 020 7583 2000
✉ clerks@oeclaw.co.uk
Call Date: Jul 1977, Inner Temple

Practising Areas: Copyright, Intellectual Property, Patents, Trademarks

HOBBS MS NAOMI JOSEPHINE

No 8 Chambers
8 Fountain Court, Steelhouse Lane, Birmingham B4 6DR ☎ 0121 236 5514
✉ clerks@no8chambers.co.uk
Call Date: Oct 1993, Gray's Inn

Practising Areas: Family, Family Provision, Immigration

HOBCRAFT MISS GEMMA KIERNAN

Doughty Street Chambers
53-54 Doughty Street, London WC1N 2LS
☎ 020 7404 1313 ✉ enquiries@doughtystreet.co.uk
Call Date: Jul 2006, Lincoln's Inn

HOBHOUSE MS HELEN ROSAMUND

Farrar's Building
Farrar's Building, Temple, London EC4Y 7BD
☎ 020 7583 9241
✉ Chambers@farrarsbuilding.co.uk
Call Date: Oct 1990, Inner Temple
Pupil Supervisor

HOBSON MR JOHN GRAHAM QC (2000)

4-5 Gray's Inn Square
Gray's Inn, London WC1R 5AH
☎ 020 7404 5252 ✉ clerks@4-5.co.uk
Call Date: Jul 1980, Inner Temple
Recorder

Practising Areas: Administrative, Common Land, Education, Environment, Housing, Landlord & Tenant, Local Government, Parliamentary, Town & Country Planning

HOBSON MISS LAURA ELISE

Citadel Chambers
The Citadel, 190 Corporation Street, Birmingham B4 6QD ☎ 0121 233 8500
✉ clerks@citadelchambers.com
Call Date: Jul 2003, Gray's Inn

Practising Areas: Common Law (General), Crime, Crime (Corporate/Fraud), Licensing, Personal Injury, Regulatory Law, Road Traffic And Highways, Sports

HOBSON MISS SALLY ANNE

1 Paper Buildings
1st Floor, 1 Paper Buildings, Temple, London EC4Y 7EP ☎ 020 7353 3728
✉ clerks@onepaper.co.uk
Call Date: Apr 1991, Inner Temple

Practising Areas: Coroners Inquests, Crime, Crime (Corporate/Fraud), Health & Safety

HODDER MR PHILIP JAMES

Clerksroom (Taunton)
Equity House, Administration Centre, Blackbrook Park Avenue, Taunton, Somerset TA1 2PX ☎ 0845 083 3000
✉ mail@clerksroom.com
King's Lynn Chambers
26 The Birches, South Wootton, King's Lynn, Norfolk PE30 3JG ☎ 01553 672 085
✉ timothy.leader@tesco.net
Call Date: Mar 2005, Lincoln's Inn

Practising Areas: Personal Injury, Professional Negligence

HODES MISS ANGELA EVE

Field Court Chambers
5 Field Court, Gray's Inn, London WC1R 5EF ☎ 020 7405 6114 ✉ clerks@fieldcourt.co.uk
Call Date: Nov 1979, Middle Temple
Pupil Supervisor

HODGKISS MS SUZANNE JANE

43 Temple Row Chambers
6th Floor, 43 Temple Row, Birmingham B2 5LS ☎ 0121 237 6035 ✉ clerks@43templerow.co.uk
Call Date: Nov 2000, Inner Temple

Practising Areas: Bankruptcy, Chancery (General), Chancery (Land Law), Commercial Litigation, Common Law (General), Crime, Employment, Environment, Health & Safety, Insolvency, Landlord & Tenant, Medical Negligence, Partnership, Personal Injury, Professional Negligence, Sale & Carriage of Goods, Town & Country Planning

HODGSON MRS JANE LEE

Five Paper
Ground Floor, 5 Paper Buildings, Temple, London EC4Y 7HB ☎ 020 7815 3200
Call Date: Oct 2000, Lincoln's Inn

Practising Areas: Housing, Landlord & Tenant, Local Government

HODIVALA MR JAMAS RUSI

2 Bedford Row
London WC1R 4BU ☎ 020 7440 8888
✉ clerks@2bedfordrow.co.uk
Call Date: Oct 1998, Lincoln's Inn
Pupil Supervisor

HODKINSON MR GARY STEPHEN

Chambers of Mr Ami Feder
Ground Floor, Lamb Building, Temple, London EC4Y 7AS ☎ 020 7797 7788
✉ clerks@lambbuilding.co.uk
Chambers of Mr Ami Feder
Ground Floor, Lamb Building, Temple, London EC4Y 7AS ☎ 020 7797 7788
✉ clerks@lambbuilding.co.uk
Call Date: Jul 2010, Middle Temple

Practising Areas: Commercial Litigation, Discrimination, Employment, Sports

HODSON MS KATHERINE

Goldsmith Chambers
Ground Floor, Goldsmith Building, Temple, London EC4Y 7BL ☎ 020 7353 6802
✉ clerks@goldsmithchambers.com
Call Date: Nov 2000, Inner Temple

HODSON MR MATTHEW PAUL

Farrar's Building
Farrar's Building, Temple, London EC4Y 7BD ☎ 020 7583 9241
✉ Chambers@farrarsbuilding.co.uk
Call Date: Nov 2004, Lincoln's Inn

Practising Areas: Chancery (General), Chancery (Land Law), Commercial Litigation, Common Land, Common Law (General), Company & Commercial, Construction, Employment, Equity, Wills & Trusts, Housing, Landlord & Tenant, Partnership, Personal Injury, Professional Negligence, Sale & Carriage of Goods

HODSON MR PETER DAVID

Chambers of Ian Macdonald QC
Garden Court North, 22 Oxford Court, Manchester M2 3WQ ☎ 0161 236 1840
✉ clerks@gcnchambers.co.uk
Call Date: Nov 1994, Inner Temple
Pupil Supervisor

Practising Areas: Housing, Medical Negligence, Personal Injury, Professional Negligence

HOGBEN MRS HELEN JANE

Fountain Chambers
Cleveland Business Centre, 1 Watson Street, Middlesbrough TS1 2RQ ☎01642 804040
✉clerks@fountainchambers.co.uk
Call Date: Jul 2006, Gray's Inn

Practising Areas: Chancery (General), Common Land, Employment, Landlord & Tenant

HOGG THE RIGHT HON DOUGLAS MARTIN QC (1990)

37 Park Square Chambers
37 Park Square, Leeds LS1 2NY
☎0113 243 9422 ✉chambers@no37.co.uk
Carmelite Chambers
9 Carmelite Street, London EC4Y 0DR
☎020 7936 6300
✉clerks@carmelitechambers.co.uk
Hailsham Chambers
Ground Floor, 4 Paper Buildings, Temple, London EC4Y 7EX ☎020 7643 5000
✉clerks@hailshamchambers.com
Call Date: Jul 1968, Lincoln's Inn

Practising Areas: Crime, Regulatory Law

HOGGETT-JONES MRS CAROLINE LOUISE

4 Breams Buildings
Chancery Lane, London EC4A 1HP
☎020 7092 1900 ✉clerks@4bb.co.uk
Call Date: Jul 2006, Gray's Inn

HOLBECH MR CHARLES EDWARD

New Square Chambers
12 New Square, Lincoln's Inn, London WC2A 3SW ☎020 7419 8000 ✉robin.hollington@newsquarechambers.co.uk
Call Date: Jul 1988, Lincoln's Inn

Practising Areas: Chancery (General), Chancery (Land Law), Charities, Commercial Property, Conveyancing, Equity, Wills & Trusts, Family Provision, Landlord & Tenant, Mental Health, Probate & Administration, Professional Negligence, Tax (Capital & Income)

HOLBORN MR DAVID REGINALD

18 Red Lion Court (Annexe)
Thornwood House, 102 New London Road, Chelmsford, Essex CM2 0RG
☎01245 280880
18 Red Lion Court
London EC4A 3EB ☎020 7520 6000
✉chambers@18rlc.co.uk
Call Date: Oct 1991, Inner Temple
Pupil Supervisor, Recorder

Practising Areas: Crime, Crime (Corporate/Fraud)

HOLDER MR TERENCE

Colleton Chambers
Colleton Crescent, Exeter, Devon EX2 4DG
☎01392 274898 ✉clerks@colletonchambers.co.uk
Call Date: Nov 1984, Gray's Inn

HOLDSWORTH MR JAMES ARTHUR

Temple Garden Chambers
1 Harcourt Buildings, Temple, London EC4Y 9DA ☎020 7583 1315 ✉clerks@tgchambers.com
Call Date: Feb 1977, Middle Temple
Pupil Supervisor

Practising Areas: Common Law (General), Insurance, Medical Negligence, Personal Injury, Professional Negligence

HOLLAND MR CHARLES CHRISTOPHER

Trinity Chambers
The Custom House, 39 Quayside, Newcastle Upon Tyne NE1 3DE ☎0191 232 1927
✉info@trinitychambers.co.uk
Trinity Chambers
Multi Media Exchange, 72-80 Corporation Road, Middlesbrough TS1 2RF
☎01642 247569 ✉info@trinitychambers.co.uk
Francis Taylor Building
Inner Temple, London EC4Y 7BY
☎020 7353 8415 ✉clerks@ftb.eu.com
Call Date: Nov 1994, Inner Temple
Pupil Supervisor

Practising Areas: Chancery (General), Chancery (Land Law), Civil Litigation, Commercial Litigation, Commercial Property, Common Land, Common Law (General), Company & Commercial, Construction, Housing, Insolvency, Land, Licensing, Local Government, Partnership, Professional Negligence, Regulatory Law

HOLLAND MISS CHARLOTTE KATE

Lincoln House Chambers
Tower 12, The Avenue North, Spinningfields, 18-22 Bridge Street, Manchester M3 3BZ
☎0161 832 5701
✉info@lincolnhousechambers.com
Call Date: Oct 1996, Lincoln's Inn
Pupil Supervisor

Practising Areas: Crime, Crime (Corporate/Fraud)

HOLLAND MR DAVID MOORE QC (2011)

Landmark Chambers
180 Fleet Street, London EC4A 2HG
☎020 7430 1221
✉clerks@landmarkchambers.co.uk
Call Date: Jul 1986, Inner Temple
Pupil Supervisor

HOLLAND MR RICKY JOHN

Lincoln House Chambers
Tower 12, The Avenue North, Spinningfields, 18-22 Bridge Street, Manchester M3 3BZ
☎0161 832 5701
✉info@lincolnhousechambers.com
Call Date: Nov 1994, Gray's Inn

Practising Areas: Crime, Crime (Corporate/Fraud)

HOLLAND MR ROWAN GUY

Five Paper
Ground Floor, 5 Paper Buildings, Temple, London EC4Y 7HB ☎020 7815 3200
Call Date: Mar 2001, Middle Temple

Practising Areas: Chancery (Land Law), Commercial Property, Housing, Landlord & Tenant, Professional Negligence

HOLLAND MR WILLIAM

1 Gray's Inn Square
Ground Floor, 1 Gray's Inn Square, London WC1R 5AA ☎020 7405 0001
Call Date: Jul 1982, Gray's Inn
Pupil Supervisor

Practising Areas: Family, Family Provision

HOLLINGWORTH MR GUY WILMER RISELEY

One Essex Court
Ground Floor, One Essex Court, Temple, London EC4Y 9AR ☎020 7583 2000
✉clerks@oeclaw.co.uk
Call Date: Oct 2001, Lincoln's Inn

HOLLIS MRS KIM QC (2002)

25 Bedford Row
London WC1R 4HD ☎020 7067 1500
✉clerks@25bedfordrow.com
Call Date: Jul 1979, Gray's Inn

Practising Areas: Administrative, Asset Finance, Courts Martial, Crime, Human Rights

HOLLOW MR PAUL JOHN

Fenners Chambers
3 Madingley Road, Cambridge CB3 0EE
☎01223 368761 ✉clerks@fennerschambers.com
Call Date: Nov 1981, Gray's Inn
Pupil Supervisor

Practising Areas: Family, Family Provision, Personal Injury

HOLMES MS ELISA

Monckton Chambers
1 & 2 Raymond Buildings, Gray's Inn, London WC1R 5NR ☎020 7405 7211
✉chambers@monckton.com
Call Date: Nov 2003, Inner Temple
Pupil Supervisor

Practising Areas: Competition, Public Law, Sports

HOLMES-MILNER MR JAMES NEIL

The Chambers of Grahame Aldous QC
9 Gough Square, London EC4A 3DG
☎020 7832 0500 ✉clerks@9goughsquare.co.uk
Call Date: Jul 1989, Middle Temple
Pupil Supervisor

Practising Areas: Bankruptcy, Chancery (General), Common Law (General), Employment, Equity, Wills & Trusts, Insolvency, Landlord & Tenant, Personal Injury, Professional Negligence

HOLROYD MR JOHN JAMES

Zenith Chambers
10 Park Square, Leeds LS1 2LH
☎0113 245 5438 ✉clerks@zenithchambers.co.uk
Call Date: Nov 1989, Gray's Inn
Pupil Supervisor

Practising Areas: Arbitration, Common Land, Construction, Environment, Landlord & Tenant, Professional Negligence, Town & Country Planning

HOLT MISS ABIGAIL CLAIRE

Lincoln House Chambers
Tower 12, The Avenue North, Spinningfields, 18-22 Bridge Street, Manchester M3 3BZ
☎0161 832 5701
✉info@lincolnhousechambers.com
Call Date: Oct 1993, Lincoln's Inn

Practising Areas: Common Law (General), Medical Negligence, Personal Injury, Regulatory Law

HOLT MR BENJAMIN RICHARD

5 King's Bench Walk
5 King's Bench Walk, Temple, London EC4Y 7DN ☎020 7353 5638 ✉clerks@5kbw.co.uk
Call Date: Oct 2006, Inner Temple

HOLT MRS JANE ROSEMARY

KCH Garden Square
1 Oxford Street, Nottingham NG1 5BH
☎0115 941 8851 ✉clerks@kchgardensquare.co.uk
Call Date: Oct 2006, Middle Temple

Practising Areas: Care Proceedings, Family, Family Provision

HONEY MR RICHARD ARTHUR

Francis Taylor Building
Inner Temple, London EC4Y 7BY
☎020 7353 8415 ✉clerks@ftb.eu.com
Call Date: Jul 2003, Inner Temple

Practising Areas: Administrative, Common Land, Environment, Parliamentary, Town & Country Planning

HOOD MR DAVID

Prince of Wales Chambers
90 Overstrand Mansions, Prince of Wales Drive, London SW11 4EU ☎020 7622 7415
✉DavidHoodEsq@aol.com
Call Date: Nov 1980, Inner Temple

Practising Areas: Arbitration, Civil Liberties, Civil Litigation, Commercial Litigation, Courts Martial, Crime, Crime (Corporate/Fraud), Defamation, Disciplinary Tribunals, Financial Services, Health & Safety, Human Rights, Inquests, Public Law, Regulatory Law, Road Traffic And Highways, Sports

HOOD MR NIGEL ANTHONY

New Square Chambers
12 New Square, Lincoln's Inn, London WC2A 3SW ☎020 7419 8000 ✉robin.hollington@newsquarechambers.co.uk
Call Date: Oct 1993, Inner Temple
Pupil Supervisor

Practising Areas: Bankruptcy, Chancery (General), Commercial Litigation, Company & Commercial, Equity, Wills & Trusts, Financial Services, Insolvency, Insurance, Partnership, Professional Negligence

HOOKWAY MR RICHARD AELRED

Zenith Chambers
10 Park Square, Leeds LS1 2LH
☎0113 245 5438 ✉clerks@zenithchambers.co.uk
Call Date: Nov 1990, Gray's Inn
Pupil Supervisor

Practising Areas: Family, Family Provision

HOOPER MR GOPAL ARTHUR JOHN

Thomas More Chambers
7 Lincoln's Inn Fields, London WC2A 3BP
☎020 7404 7000 ✉clerks@thomasmore.co.uk
Call Date: Jul 1973, Middle Temple
Pupil Supervisor

Practising Areas: Courts Martial, Crime, Crime (Corporate/Fraud)

HOOPER MR MARTIN CHARLES

5 King's Bench Walk
5 King's Bench Walk, Temple, London EC4Y 7DN ☎020 7353 5638 ✉clerks@5kbw.co.uk
Call Date: Jul 1988, Middle Temple
Pupil Supervisor

HOPE MISS HEATHER ROSALIND

Goldsmith Chambers
Ground Floor, Goldsmith Building, Temple, London EC4Y 7BL ☎020 7353 6802
✉clerks@goldsmithchambers.com
Call Date: Oct 1993, Gray's Inn

Practising Areas: Crime

HOPKIN MR WILLIAM WALTER

Rougemont Chambers
Victory House, Dean Clarke Gardens, Southernhay East, Exeter EX2 4AA
☎01392 208484
✉clerks@rougemontchambers.co.uk
St Leonards Chambers
Address withheld ☎07734 706185 ✉william.hopkin@btinternet.com
Call Date: Oct 2000, Inner Temple

HOPPER MR STEPHEN JOHN

Five Paper Buildings
1st Floor, Five Paper Buildings, Temple, London EC4Y 7HB ☎020 7583 6117
✉clerks@5pb.co.uk
Call Date: Nov 2001, Middle Temple

Practising Areas: Crime, Crime (Corporate/Fraud), Regulatory Law

HORLICK MISS FIONA

Outer Temple Chambers
The Outer Temple, 222 Strand, London WC2R 1BA ☎020 7353 6381
✉clerks@outertemple.com
Call Date: May 1992, Middle Temple
Pupil Supervisor

HORMAECHE MISS ALEJANDRA

Tanfield Chambers
2-5 Warwick Court, London WC1R 5DJ
☎020 7421 5300 ✉clerks@tanfieldchambers.co.uk
Call Date: Oct 1998, Middle Temple

Practising Areas: Chancery (General), Chancery (Land Law), Commercial Litigation, Commercial Property, Conveyancing, Landlord & Tenant, Personal Injury

HORNBLOWER MRS SARAH PATIENCE

Rougemont Chambers
Victory House, Dean Clarke Gardens, Southernhay East, Exeter EX2 4AA
☎01392 208484
✉clerks@rougemontchambers.co.uk
Call Date: Jul 2005, Gray's Inn

Practising Areas: Care Proceedings, Common Law (General), Crime, Discrimination, Employment, Family

HORNE MR CHARLES HUGH WILSON

Kings Chambers
36 Young Street, Manchester M3 3FT
☎0845 034 3444 ✉clerks@kingschambers.com
Kings Chambers
5 Park Square East, Leeds LS1 2NE
☎0845 034 3444 ✉clerks@kingschambers.com
Kings Chambers
Embassy House, 60 Church Street, Birmingham B3 2DJ ☎0845 034 3444
✉clerks@kingschambers.com
Call Date: Oct 1992, Lincoln's Inn
Pupil Supervisor

Practising Areas: Arbitration, Banking, Chancery (General), Chancery (Land Law), Commercial Property, Common Land, Conveyancing, Landlord & Tenant

HORNE MR JOSEPH MERIVS BRERETON

11 Gray's Inn Square Chambers
Chambers of Mr Ian Sen, 1st Floor South, 10/11 Gray's Inn Square, London WC1R 5JD
☎020 7405 6879 ✉clerks@11graysinnsquare.com
Call Date: Oct 1999, Lincoln's Inn

HORNE-ROBERTS MRS JENNIFER

Goldsmith Chambers
Ground Floor, Goldsmith Building, Temple, London EC4Y 7BL ☎020 7353 6802
✉clerks@goldsmithchambers.com
Call Date: Nov 1976, Middle Temple

Practising Areas: Administrative, Civil Liberties, Discrimination, Family, Family Provision, Personal Injury

HORNETT MR STUART IAN

Selborne Chambers
10 Essex Street, London WC2R 3AA
☎020 7420 9500
✉clerks@selbornechambers.co.uk
Call Date: Oct 1992, Middle Temple
Pupil Supervisor

Practising Areas: Bankruptcy, Chancery (General), Chancery (Land Law), Commercial Litigation, Commercial Property, Company & Commercial, Conveyancing, Equity, Wills & Trusts, Insolvency, Landlord & Tenant, Partnership, Professional Negligence

HORSTEAD MR SEAN KEVAN

Garden Court Chambers
57-60 Lincoln's Inn Fields, London WC2A 3LJ
☎020 7993 7600 ✉info@gclaw.co.uk
Call Date: Oct 1996, Middle Temple
Pupil Supervisor

HORTON MR MARK VARNEY

Colleton Chambers
Colleton Crescent, Exeter, Devon EX2 4DG
☎01392 274898 ✉clerks@colletonchambers.co.uk
Call Date: Jul 1981, Middle Temple
Recorder

Practising Areas: Care Proceedings, Family, Mental Health

HORTON MR MATTHEW BETHELL QC (1989)

39 Essex Street
London WC2R 3AT ☎020 7832 1111
✉clerks@39essex.com
82 King Street
Manchester M2 4WQ ☎0161 870 9969
Call Date: Jul 1969, Middle Temple

Practising Areas: Administrative, Common Land, Disciplinary Tribunals, Energy, Environment, Land, Local Government, Parliamentary, Professional Negligence, Public Law, Road Traffic And Highways, Town & Country Planning

HORTON MR MICHAEL JOHN EDWARD

Coram Chambers
9-11 Fulwood Place, London WC1V 6HG
☎020 7092 3700 ✉mail@coramchambers.co.uk
Call Date: Nov 1993, Gray's Inn
Pupil Supervisor

Practising Areas: Bankruptcy, Chancery (Land Law), Equity, Wills & Trusts, Family, Family Provision, Insolvency

HOSSAIN MR AJMALUL QC (1998)

Selborne Chambers
10 Essex Street, London WC2R 3AA
☎020 7420 9500
✉clerks@selbornechambers.co.uk
St Philips Chambers
55 Temple Row, Birmingham B2 5LS
☎0121 246 7000 ✉clerks@st-philips.com
Call Date: Nov 1976, Lincoln's Inn

Practising Areas: Arbitration, Banking, Commercial Litigation, Commercial Property, Company & Commercial, Corporate Finance, Foreign Law, Insolvency, International Trade, Private International, Public International

C

HOSSAIN MR MOHAMMAD MOZAMMEL

187 Fleet Street
London EC4A 2AT ☎020 7430 7430
✉chambers@187fleetstreet.com
Call Date: Jul 2001, Inner Temple

Practising Areas: Crime, Crime (Corporate/Fraud)

HOSSAIN MR MOHAMMED MONWAR

No. 3 Fleet Street Chambers
3 Fleet Street, London EC4Y 1DP
☎020 7936 4474 ✉clerks@3fleetstreet.com
Call Date: Jul 1998, Lincoln's Inn

Practising Areas: Administrative, Civil Liberties, Civil Litigation, Human Rights, Immigration

HOWARD MISS AMANDA JAYNE

Atlantic Chambers
4-6 Cook Street, Liverpool L2 9QU
☎0151 236 4421 ✉info@atlanticchambers.co.uk
37 Park Square Chambers
37 Park Square, Leeds LS1 2NY
☎0113 243 9422 ✉chambers@no37.co.uk
Call Date: Nov 1994, Inner Temple

Practising Areas: Care Proceedings, Common Law (General), Family, Family Provision, Personal Injury

HOWARD MISS ANNELI CLAIRE

Monckton Chambers
1 & 2 Raymond Buildings, Gray's Inn, London WC1R 5NR ☎020 7405 7211
✉chambers@monckton.com
Call Date: Jul 2002, Gray's Inn

HOWARD MISS NICOLA

25 Bedford Row
London WC1R 4HD ☎020 7067 1500
✉clerks@25bedfordrow.com
Call Date: Oct 1995, Middle Temple
Pupil Supervisor

Practising Areas: Crime, Crime (Corporate/Fraud)

HOWARD MR ROBIN WILLIAM JOHN

Fenners Chambers
3 Madingley Road, Cambridge CB3 0EE
☎01223 368761 ✉clerks@fennerschambers.com
Call Date: Feb 1986, Middle Temple
Pupil Supervisor

Practising Areas: Chancery (General), Common Law (General), Employment, Insolvency, Personal Injury, Professional Negligence

HOWARD MR STEVEN JAMES

3 PB Barristers
30 Christchurch Road, Bournemouth, Dorset BH1 3PD ☎ 01202 292102 ✉ clerks.bournemouth@3paper.co.uk
3 PB Barristers
3 Paper Buildings, Temple, London EC4Y 7EU ☎ 020 7583 8055
Call Date: Nov 2009, Inner Temple

Practising Areas: Care Proceedings, Family

HOWE MR DARREN FRANCIS

1 Garden Court Family Law Chambers
Ground Floor, One Garden Court, Temple, London EC4Y 9BJ ☎ 020 7797 7900 ✉ clerks@1gc.com
Call Date: Oct 1992, Gray's Inn
Pupil Supervisor

Practising Areas: Care Proceedings, Family

HOWE MR GAVIN PAUL

Crown Office Row Chambers
119 Church Street, Brighton, Sussex BN1 1UD ☎ 01273 625625 ✉ clerks@1cor.com
Call Date: Nov 2003, Gray's Inn

Practising Areas: Family

HOWELL MS CLAIRE ELIZABETH SIOBHAN

36 Bedford Row
London WC1R 4JH ☎ 020 7421 8000 ✉ chambers@36bedfordrow.co.uk
Call Date: Nov 2003, Inner Temple

Practising Areas: Crime, Crime (Corporate/Fraud), Regulatory Law

HOWELL WILLIAMS MR CRAIG QC (2009)

Francis Taylor Building
Inner Temple, London EC4Y 7BY ☎ 020 7353 8415 ✉ clerks@ftb.eu.com
Call Date: Jul 1983, Gray's Inn

HOWELLS MR STEPHEN JOHN

Stone Chambers
4 Field Court, Gray's Inn, London WC1R 5EF ☎ 020 7440 6900 ✉ clerks@stonechambers.com
Call Date: Jul 2006, Middle Temple

Practising Areas: Admiralty, Arbitration, Chancery (General), Commercial Litigation, Commercial Property, Common Law (General), Ecclesiastical, Employment, Entertainment, Insurance, Private International

HOWLETT MR JAMES ANTHONY

KCH Garden Square
1 Oxford Street, Nottingham NG1 5BH ☎ 0115 941 8851 ✉ clerks@kchgardensquare.co.uk
Call Date: Jul 1980, Middle Temple
Pupil Supervisor, Recorder

Practising Areas: Commercial Litigation, Employment, Environment, Landlord & Tenant, Local Government, Town & Country Planning

HOWLING MR REX ANDREW QC (2011)

4 Paper Buildings
1st Floor, 4 Paper Buildings, Temple, London EC4Y 7EX ☎ 020 7427 5200 ✉ clerks@4pb.com
Call Date: Oct 1991, Middle Temple
Pupil Supervisor

Practising Areas: Care Proceedings, Equity, Wills & Trusts, Family, Family Provision

HUBBARD MR MARK IAIN

New Square Chambers
12 New Square, Lincoln's Inn, London WC2A 3SW ☎ 020 7419 8000 ✉ robin.hollington@newsquarechambers.co.uk
Call Date: Nov 1991, Middle Temple
Pupil Supervisor

Practising Areas: Bankruptcy, Chancery (General), Chancery (Land Law), Commercial Litigation, Equity, Wills & Trusts, Insolvency, Professional Negligence

HUDD MISS ANNE MARGUERITA JANE

29 Bedford Row Chambers
London WC1R 4HE ☎ 020 7404 1044 ✉ clerks@29br.co.uk
Call Date: Oct 2000, Gray's Inn

Practising Areas: Family, Family Provision

HUDSON MISS ABIGAIL RACHEL

Call Date: Oct 2003, Gray's Inn

HUDSON MR JOHN EDWARD GERARD

Zenith Chambers
10 Park Square, Leeds LS1 2LH ☎ 0113 245 5438 ✉ clerks@zenithchambers.co.uk
Call Date: Nov 2006, Middle Temple

Practising Areas: Family, Family Provision

HUGGINS MR TOBY JAMES

Unity Street Chambers
5 Unity Street, College Green, Bristol BS1 5HH ☎0117 906 9789
✉chambers@unitystreetchambers.com
Call Date: Nov 1998, Middle Temple

Practising Areas: Bankruptcy, Chancery (General), Chancery (Land Law), Common Law (General), Company & Commercial, Equity, Wills & Trusts, Housing, Insolvency, Landlord & Tenant, Local Government, Partnership, Probate & Administration, Sale & Carriage of Goods

HUGHES MR ADRIAN WARWICK QC (2006)

39 Essex Street
London WC2R 3AT ☎020 7832 1111
✉clerks@39essex.com
82 King Street
Manchester M2 4WQ ☎0161 870 9969
Call Date: Jul 1984, Middle Temple

Practising Areas: Arbitration, Commercial Litigation, Company & Commercial, Construction, Insurance, International Trade, Professional Negligence

HUGHES DR CONSTANCE MARY

1 Pump Court
Elm Court, Temple, London EC4Y 7AB
☎020 7842 7070 ✉(name)@pumpcourt.co.uk
Call Date: Oct 1994, Inner Temple
Pupil Supervisor

Practising Areas: Care Proceedings, Education, Family

HUGHES MRS KATHRYN SALLY

Chavasse Court Chambers
18 Queen Avenue, Liverpool L2 4TX
☎0151 229 2030
✉clerks@chavassechambers.co.uk
Call Date: Mar 2003, Inner Temple

Practising Areas: Ancillary Relief, Care Proceedings, Family

HUGHES MISS MERYL ELIZABETH

Fenners Chambers
3 Madingley Road, Cambridge CB3 0EE
☎01223 368761 ✉clerks@fennerschambers.com
Call Date: Nov 1987, Gray's Inn

Practising Areas: Family

HUGHES MR WILLIAM LLOYD

9-12 Bell Yard
London WC2A 2JR ☎020 7400 1800
✉clerks@9-12bellyard.com
Call Date: Nov 1989, Gray's Inn
Pupil Supervisor, Recorder

Practising Areas: Common Law (General), Crime, Crime (Corporate/Fraud), Local Government, Regulatory Law

HUGHES-DEANE MS CHARLOTTE BARBARA

Atlantic Chambers
4-6 Cook Street, Liverpool L2 9QU
☎0151 236 4421 ✉info@atlanticchambers.co.uk
Call Date: Nov 2002, Lincoln's Inn

Practising Areas: Chancery (General), Chancery (Land Law), Civil Litigation, Commercial Litigation, Commercial Property, Equity, Wills & Trusts, Family Provision, Housing, Land, Landlord & Tenant, Probate & Administration

HUGHESTON-ROBERTS MR CHARLES JUSTIN

4 Breams Buildings
Chancery Lane, London EC4A 1HP
☎020 7092 1900 ✉clerks@4bb.co.uk
Call Date: Mar 2009, Gray's Inn

Practising Areas: Courts Martial, Crime, Crime (Corporate/Fraud)

HULSE MRS CECILIA HELEN

Chambers of Mr Ami Feder
Ground Floor, Lamb Building, Temple, London EC4Y 7AS ☎020 7797 7788
✉clerks@lambbuilding.co.uk
Chambers of Mr Ami Feder
Ground Floor, Lamb Building, Temple, London EC4Y 7AS ☎020 7797 7788
✉clerks@lambbuilding.co.uk
Call Date: Nov 1998, Middle Temple

Practising Areas: Civil Liberties, Common Law (General), Discrimination, Employment

HUMPHREYS MRS JACQUELINE LOUISE

St John's Chambers
101 Victoria Street, Bristol BS1 6PU
☎0117 923 4700 ✉clerks@stjohnschambers.co.uk
Call Date: Oct 1994, Lincoln's Inn

HUMPHREYS MR RICHARD WILLIAM QC (2006)

Francis Taylor Building
Inner Temple, London EC4Y 7BY
☎020 7353 8415 ✉clerks@ftb.eu.com
No5 Chambers
Fountain Court, Steelhouse Lane, Birmingham B4 6DR ☎0845 210 5555 ✉info@no5.com
No5 Chambers
38 Queen Square, Bristol BS1 4QS
☎0845 210 5555
No5 Chambers
Greenwood House, 4-7 Salisbury Court, London EC4Y 8AA ☎0845 210 5555
Call Date: Jul 1986, Inner Temple

Practising Areas: Administrative, Local Government, Town & Country Planning

HUMPHRIES MR MICHAEL JOHN QC (2003)

Francis Taylor Building
Inner Temple, London EC4Y 7BY
☎020 7353 8415 ✉clerks@ftb.eu.com
Call Date: Jul 1982, Inner Temple

HUNT MISS ALISON LORNA

Regency Chambers
45 Priestgate, Peterborough PE1 1LB
☎01733 315215 ✉clerks@regencychambers.law.co.uk
Regency Chambers
Sheraton House, Castle Park, Cambridge CB3 0AX ☎01223 301517
Call Date: Nov 2001, Middle Temple
Pupil Supervisor

Practising Areas: Care Proceedings, Family

HUNT MR STEPHEN

4 Stone Buildings
Ground Floor, 4 Stone Buildings, Lincoln's Inn, London WC2A 3XT ☎020 7242 5524
✉clerks@4stonebuildings.com
Call Date: Jul 1968, Lincoln's Inn
Pupil Supervisor

Practising Areas: Arbitration, Bankruptcy, Chancery (General), Chancery (Land Law), Charities, Commercial Property, Common Land, Company & Commercial, Construction, Conveyancing, Equity, Wills & Trusts, Family Provision, Insolvency, Insurance, Landlord & Tenant, Mental Health, Partnership, Private International, Probate & Administration, Professional Negligence, Tax (Capital & Income)

HUNTER MR TIMOTHY CHARLES

Atkinson Bevan Chambers
1st Floor, 2 Harcourt Buildings, Temple, London EC4Y 9DB ☎020 7353 2112
✉clerks@2hb.co.uk
Call Date: Oct 1998, Inner Temple

Practising Areas: Crime, Licensing

HUNTLEY MISS CLARE HELEN PATRICIA

9-12 Bell Yard
London WC2A 2JR ☎020 7400 1800
✉clerks@9-12bellyard.com
Call Date: Jul 2000, Gray's Inn

Practising Areas: Crime

HURLOCK MR LUGARD JOHN

2 Bedford Row
London WC1R 4BU ☎020 7440 8888
✉clerks@2bedfordrow.co.uk
Call Date: Oct 1993, Gray's Inn

HURST MR BRIAN

39 Park Square
Leeds LS1 2NU ☎0113 245 6633
✉seniorclerk@39parksquarechambers.co.uk
Call Date: Jul 1983, Middle Temple
Pupil Supervisor

Practising Areas: Banking, Commercial Litigation, Common Law (General), Crime, Crime (Corporate/Fraud), Financial Services, Insurance, Professional Negligence

HUSSAIN MR BASHARAT

Cornwall Street Chambers
85-87 Cornwall Street, Birmingham B3 3BY
☎0121 233 7500 ✉clerks@cornwallstreet.co.uk
Call Date: Nov 1997, Gray's Inn

Practising Areas: Chancery (General), Common Law (General), Employment, Family

HUSSAIN MISS FRIDA KHANAM

Furnival Chambers
32 Furnival Street, London EC4A 1JQ
☎020 7405 3232
Call Date: Oct 1995, Inner Temple

Practising Areas: Civil Liberties, Crime, Crime (Corporate/Fraud), Health & Safety, Human Rights, Regulatory Law, Sale & Carriage of Goods

HUSSAIN MR GHULAM

Crown Office Row Chambers
119 Church Street, Brighton, Sussex BN1 1UD ☎01273 625625 ✉clerks@1cor.com
Call Date: Oct 1998, Inner Temple

Practising Areas: Crime, Environment, Licensing, Local Government, Regulatory Law

HUSSAIN MR MUHAMMAD ALTAF

Chambers of Mr M A Hussain
29 Strathbrook Road, London SW16 3AT
☎020 8679 2398 ✉altafhussain06@yahoo.co.uk
Call Date: Jul 1970, Middle Temple

Practising Areas: Administrative, Bankruptcy, Care Proceedings, Chancery (General), Chancery (Land Law), Charities, Civil Liberties, Commercial Litigation, Commercial Property, Common Law (General), Company & Commercial, Conveyancing, Crime, Crime (Corporate/Fraud), Defamation, Discrimination, EC & Competition Law, Education, Employment, Environment, Family, Family Provision, Franchising, Housing, Insolvency, Landlord & Tenant, Licensing, Local Government, Medical Negligence, Mental Health, Partnership, Patents, Pensions, Personal Injury, Private International

HUSSAIN MR MUKHTAR QC (1992)

Lincoln House Chambers
Tower 12, The Avenue North, Spinningfields, 18-22 Bridge Street, Manchester M3 3BZ
☎0161 832 5701
✉info@lincolnhousechambers.com
Call Date: Jul 1971, Middle Temple
Recorder

Practising Areas: Administrative, Crime, Crime (Corporate/Fraud), Immigration

HUSSAIN MR TASADDAT

Broadway House Chambers
Broadway House, 9 Bank Street, Bradford, West Yorkshire BD1 1TW ☎01274 722560
✉clerks@broadwayhouse.co.uk
Broadway House Chambers
25 Park Square West, Leeds, West Yorkshire LS1 2PW ☎0113 246 2600
✉clerks@broadwayhouse.co.uk
Call Date: Oct 1998, Lincoln's Inn

Practising Areas: Administrative, Human Rights, Immigration, Personal Injury

C

HUSSEIN MR TIMUR

1 Pump Court
Elm Court, Temple, London EC4Y 7AB
☎020 7842 7070 ✉(name)@pumpcourt.co.uk
Call Date: Oct 1993, Inner Temple
Pupil Supervisor

Practising Areas: Family, Family Provision

HUTCHIN MR EDWARD ALISTER DAVID

Temple Garden Chambers
1 Harcourt Buildings, Temple, London EC4Y 9DA ☎020 7583 1315 ✉clerks@tgchambers.com
Call Date: Oct 1996, Middle Temple

Practising Areas: Chancery (General), Commercial Litigation, Common Law (General), Employment, Insurance, Landlord & Tenant, Medical Negligence, Personal Injury

HUTCHINGS MR RICHARD PETER MARK

Chambers of Marion Smullen and Kerim Fuad QC
1 Inner Temple Lane, London EC4Y 1AF
☎020 7427 4400 ✉clerks@1itl.com
Call Date: Nov 2001, Lincoln's Inn

Practising Areas: Courts Martial, Crime

HUTCHINSON MR COLIN THOMAS

Garden Court Chambers
57-60 Lincoln's Inn Fields, London WC2A 3LJ
☎020 7993 7600 ✉info@gclaw.co.uk
Call Date: Oct 1990, Middle Temple
Pupil Supervisor

Practising Areas: Administrative, Civil Liberties, Common Law (General), Discrimination, Employment, Health & Safety, Human Rights, Local Government, Medical Negligence, Personal Injury, Professional Negligence

HYAMS MISS NATALIE ANNE

Goresbrook Chambers
PO Box 6017, Milton Keynes MK1 9AP
☎0845 123 1234 ✉thomas.john6@btinternet.com
Call Date: Oct 1998, Lincoln's Inn

HYMANSON MISS DEANNA SUSAN

Cobden House Chambers
19 Quay Street, Manchester M3 3HN
☎0161 833 6000 ✉Clerks@Cobden.co.uk
Call Date: Feb 1988, Middle Temple

Practising Areas: Employment, Personal Injury

HYPOLITE-DE-SOUZA MRS JOSEPHINE CLAUDIA

12 Old Square Chambers
1st Floor, 12 Old Square, Lincoln's Inn, London WC2A 3TX ☎ 020 7404 0875
✉ clerks@12oldsquare.com
Call Date: Nov 1992, Lincoln's Inn

Practising Areas: Common Law (General), Family, Immigration, Licensing

IDEH MR DONALD

Chambers of Mr Donald Ideh
12 Ashburnham Tower, Edith Grove, Chelsea, London SW10 0EE
Call Date: Nov 1999, Middle Temple

INGRAM MR JONATHAN ANTONY

Five St Andrew's Hill
5 St Andrew's Hill, London EC4V 5BZ
☎ 020 7332 5400 ✉ Clerks@5sah.co.uk
Call Date: Jul 1984, Inner Temple
Pupil Supervisor

INGRAM MR NIGEL COLQUHOUN

2 Bedford Row
London WC1R 4BU ☎ 020 7440 8888
✉ clerks@2bedfordrow.co.uk
Call Date: Jul 1972, Inner Temple
Pupil Supervisor

Practising Areas: Crime, Crime (Corporate/Fraud), Entertainment

INYUNDO MR RICHARD KWAME SWAKA

6 King's Bench Walk
Ground Floor, 6 King's Bench Walk, Temple, London EC4Y 7DR ☎ 020 7583 0410
✉ clerks@6kbw.com
Call Date: Mar 1997, Gray's Inn
Pupil Supervisor

Practising Areas: Courts Martial, Crime, Crime (Corporate/Fraud), Health & Safety, Human Rights

IQBAL MR MASHOOD

London View Chambers
24 Highgate Grove, Sawbridgeworth CM21 0DD ☎ 07788 912493
Call Date: Oct 2011, Lincoln's Inn

Practising Areas: Banking, Commercial Litigation, Competition, Copyright, Corporate Finance, Defamation, EC & Competition Law, Employment, Family, Foreign Law, Human Rights, Immigration, Intellectual Property, Islamic Sharia Law, Regulatory Law, Share Options

IQBAL MISS SAMINA

Renaissance Chambers
5th Floor, Gray's Inn Chambers, Gray's Inn, London WC1R 5JA ☎ 020 7404 1111
✉ clerks@renaissancechambers.co.uk
Call Date: Oct 1999, Lincoln's Inn
Pupil Supervisor

Practising Areas: Human Rights, Immigration

IRVIN MR PETER

Brick Court Chambers
7-8 Essex Street, London WC2R 3LD
☎ 020 7379 3550 ✉ clerks@brickcourt.co.uk
Call Date: Jul 1972, Gray's Inn
Pupil Supervisor

Practising Areas: Arbitration, Banking, Commercial Litigation, Common Law (General), Discrimination, Employment, Entertainment, Insurance/Reinsurance, International Trade, Partnership, Professional Negligence, Sale & Carriage of Goods, Shipping/Admiralty

IRVING MISS GILLIAN QC (2006)

9 St John Street
Manchester M3 4DN ☎ 0161 955 9000
✉ civilclerks@9sjs.com/criminalclerks@9sjs.com
Linenhall Chambers
1 Stanley Place, Chester CH1 2LU
☎ 01244 348282
✉ clerks@linenhallchambers.co.uk
15 Winckley Square
Preston PR1 3JJ ☎ 01772 252828
✉ clerks@15winckleysq.co.uk
Call Date: Jul 1984, Inner Temple

Practising Areas: Care Proceedings, Family, Mental Health

IRWIN MR GAVIN DAVID

Dyers Chambers
35 Bedford Row, London WC1R 4JH
☎ 020 7404 1881 ✉ admin@dyerschambers.com
Call Date: Nov 1996, Gray's Inn

Practising Areas: Administrative, Civil Liberties, Courts Martial, Crime, Crime (Corporate/Fraud), Human Rights, Local Government, Regulatory Law, Trademarks

C

ISAAC MR NICHOLAS DUDLEY

Tanfield Chambers
2-5 Warwick Court, London WC1R 5DJ
☎ 020 7421 5300 ✉ clerks@tanfieldchambers.co.uk
Call Date: Oct 1993, Gray's Inn
Pupil Supervisor

Practising Areas: Chancery (General), Chancery (Land Law), Commercial Property, Common Law (General), Landlord & Tenant, Professional Negligence

ISHERWOOD MR JOHN STANLEY

Unity Street Chambers
5 Unity Street, College Green, Bristol BS1 5HH ☎ 0117 906 9789
✉ chambers@unitystreetchambers.com
Call Date: Jul 1978, Gray's Inn
Pupil Supervisor

ISHMAEL MR KHALID

Ashtead Park Chambers
15 Gaywood Road, Ashtead, Surrey KT21 1BL
☎ 01372 813053
✉ khalid@ashteadparkchambers.com/admin@ashteadparkchambers.com
Call Date: Feb 1989, Lincoln's Inn

ISLAM MR AMINUL RUHUL

Chambers of Mr Aminul R. Islam
14 Fakruddin Street, London E1 5BU
☎ 020 7247 1977 ✉ aminul2@hotmail.co.uk
Call Date: Oct 1997, Lincoln's Inn

Practising Areas: Crime, Immigration

ISLAM MR MOHAMMAD FAKRUL

18 Red Lion Court
London EC4A 3EB ☎ 020 7520 6000
✉ chambers@18rlc.co.uk
Call Date: Oct 2002, Middle Temple

Practising Areas: Crime, Crime (Corporate/Fraud), Regulatory Law

ISLAM MR SAIFUL

3 Dr Johnson's Buildings
Ground Floor, 3 Dr Johnson's Buildings, Temple, London EC4Y 7BA ☎ 020 7353 4854
✉ clerks@3djb.co.uk
Call Date: Oct 2005, Lincoln's Inn

Practising Areas: Family

ISLAM-CHOUDHURY MR MUGNI

No5 Chambers
Fountain Court, Steelhouse Lane, Birmingham B4 6DR ☎ 0845 210 5555 ✉ info@no5.com
No5 Chambers
Greenwood House, 4-7 Salisbury Court, London EC4Y 8AA ☎ 0845 210 5555
No5 Chambers
38 Queen Square, Bristol BS1 4QS
☎ 0845 210 5555
Call Date: Oct 1996, Lincoln's Inn

Practising Areas: Administrative, Discrimination, Employment, Healthcare

ISMAIL MISS NAZMUN NISHA

Central Chambers
89 Princess Street, Manchester M1 4HT
☎ 0161 236 1133 ✉ clerks@centralchambers.co.uk
No5 Chambers
Greenwood House, 4-7 Salisbury Court, London EC4Y 8AA ☎ 0845 210 5555
No5 Chambers
Fountain Court, Steelhouse Lane, Birmingham B4 6DR ☎ 0845 210 5555 ✉ info@no5.com
No5 Chambers
38 Queen Square, Bristol BS1 4QS
☎ 0845 210 5555
Call Date: Oct 1992, Lincoln's Inn

Practising Areas: Administrative, Children's Law, Civil Liberties, Civil Litigation, Family, Personal Injury, Public Law

ISRAEL MR JEFFREY ANTHONY

5 King's Bench Walk
5 King's Bench Walk, Temple, London EC4Y 7DN ☎ 020 7353 5638 ✉ clerks@5kbw.co.uk
Call Date: Oct 2000, Middle Temple

ITEN MISS CORINNE BEATRICE

Pump Court Chambers
Upper Ground Floor, 3 Pump Court, Temple, London EC4Y 7AJ ☎ 020 7353 0711
✉ clerks@3pumpcourt.com
Call Date: Oct 2006, Inner Temple

Practising Areas: Family

IVILL MR SCOTT ASHLEY

2 Hare Court
Lower Ground, Ground, 1st & 2nd Floor, 2 Hare Court, Temple, London EC4Y 7BH
☎ 020 7353 3982 ✉ clerks@2harecourt.com
Call Date: Nov 1997, Gray's Inn
Pupil Supervisor

Practising Areas: Crime, Crime (Corporate/Fraud)

IYER MISS SHOBANA

Swan Chambers
Parkshot House, 5 Kew Road, Richmond, Surrey TW9 2PR ☎ 0845 123 1234
✉ shobana@mycommercialbarrister.com
Call Date: Jul 1998, Gray's Inn

Practising Areas: Aviation, Chancery (General), Charities, Civil Litigation, Commercial Litigation, Commercial Property, Commodities, Common Law (General), Company & Commercial, Competition, Consumer, Copyright, Costs, Data Protection, Defamation, Discrimination, EC & Competition Law, Employment, Entertainment, Environment, Film, Cable & TV, Information Technology, Insurance/Reinsurance, Intellectual Property, International Trade, Landlord & Tenant, Partnership, Patents, Private International, Professional Negligence, Public International, Public Law, Regulatory Law, Sale & Carriage of Goods, Share Options, Sports, Telecommunications, Trademarks

JABATI MISS MARIA HANNAH

Holborn Chambers
6 Gate Street, Lincoln's Inn Fields, London WC2A 3HP ☎ 020 7242 6060
Call Date: Nov 1986, Lincoln's Inn

JACK MR NICHOLAS ROBERT

Octagon House
19 Colegate, Norwich NR3 1AT
☎ 01603 623186 ✉ clerks@octagonhouse.co.uk
Call Date: Oct 2002, Lincoln's Inn

Practising Areas: Family

JACKSON MR ADRIAN PHILIP

Call Date: Oct 1990, Lincoln's Inn
Pupil Supervisor

JACKSON MR ANDREW FRASER

5 Pump Court
Ground Floor, 5 Pump Court, Temple, London EC4Y 7AP ☎ 020 7353 2532
✉ clerks@5pumpcourt.com
Call Date: Oct 1990, Inner Temple

Practising Areas: Administrative, Coroners Inquests, Courts Martial, Crime, Crime (Corporate/Fraud), Disciplinary Tribunals, Health & Safety, Inquests, Licensing, Road Traffic And Highways, Sports

JACKSON MR CHRISTOPHER MARSHALL

Liverpool Civil Law
3rd Floor, 1 Old Hall Street, Liverpool L3 9HF
☎ 0151 242 0500 ✉ clerks@liverpoolcivillaw.com
Call Date: Nov 2002, Middle Temple
Pupil Supervisor

Practising Areas: Agriculture, Employment, Licensing, Medical Negligence, Personal Injury

JACKSON MISS FIONA ROSALIND

Chambers of Andrew Mitchell QC
33 Chancery Lane, London WC2A 1EN
☎ 020 7440 9950 ✉ clerks@33cllaw.com
Call Date: Nov 1998, Inner Temple

JACKSON MR KEVIN ROY

Becket Chambers
17 New Dover Road, Canterbury, Kent CT1 3AS ☎ 01227 786331
✉ clerks@becket-chambers.co.uk
Call Date: Nov 1984, Middle Temple

JACKSON MR MARK JOSEPH

No 8 Chambers
8 Fountain Court, Steelhouse Lane, Birmingham B4 6DR ☎ 0121 236 5514
✉ clerks@no8chambers.co.uk
Call Date: Oct 1997, Lincoln's Inn

Practising Areas: Crime, Crime (Corporate/Fraud), Environment, Health & Safety, Licensing, Local Government, Regulatory Law, Town & Country Planning

JACKSON MR MYLES GERALD

Chambers of Mr M G Jackson
37 Old Deer Park Gardens, Richmond, Surrey TW9 2TN ☎ 020 8251 7661
✉ mylesgjackson@hotmail.com
Call Date: Oct 1995, Lincoln's Inn

JACKSON MR PAUL

5 King's Bench Walk
5 King's Bench Walk, Temple, London EC4Y 7DN ☎ 020 7353 5638 ✉ clerks@5kbw.co.uk
Call Date: Jul 2002, Inner Temple

JACKSON MISS ROSEMARY ELIZABETH QC (2006)

Keating Chambers
15 Essex Street, London WC2R 3AA
☎ 020 7544 2600 ✉ clerks@keatingchambers.com
Call Date: Jul 1981, Middle Temple
Recorder

Practising Areas: Arbitration, Commercial Litigation, Construction, Energy, Environment, Professional Negligence

JACOBSON MR LAWRENCE

Five Paper
Ground Floor, 5 Paper Buildings, Temple, London EC4Y 7HB ☎ 020 7815 3200
Call Date: Nov 1985, Gray's Inn

Practising Areas: Commercial Litigation, Company & Commercial, Partnership, Probate & Administration, Professional Negligence, Sports

JACQUES MR GARETH EDWARD

Regency Chambers
45 Priestgate, Peterborough PE1 1LB
☎ 01733 315215 ✉ clerks@regencychambers.law.co.uk
Call Date: Oct 2007, Inner Temple

Practising Areas: Care Proceedings, Family, Family Provision, Landlord & Tenant

JAFAR MR ABDURAHMAN AKHTAR

Chambers of Mr Abdurahman Jafar
16 Madras Road, Ilford, Essex IG1 2EY
☎ 07828 937338 ✉ abdurahmanjafar@yahoo.co.uk
Call Date: Nov 1997, Lincoln's Inn

Practising Areas: Arbitration, Civil Liberties, Common Law (General), Foreign Law, Housing, Immigration, Information Technology, Landlord & Tenant, Licensing, Local Government, Personal Injury, Public International

JAFFA MR RONALD MERVYN

25 Bedford Row
London WC1R 4HD ☎ 020 7067 1500
✉ clerks@25bedfordrow.com
Call Date: Jul 1974, Gray's Inn
Pupil Supervisor

Practising Areas: Crime, Crime (Corporate/Fraud)

JAFFERJEE MR AFTAB ASGER QC (2008)

Atkinson Bevan Chambers
1st Floor, 2 Harcourt Buildings, Temple, London EC4Y 9DB ☎ 020 7353 2112
✉ clerks@2hb.co.uk
Call Date: Nov 1980, Inner Temple

Practising Areas: Courts Martial, Crime, Crime (Corporate/Fraud)

JAFFERJI MR ZAINULABEDIN HATIM

Chambers of Mr Jafferji
89 Lamborne Road, Leicester LE2 6HQ
☎ 07957 198777 ✉ zjafferji@gmail.com
Call Date: Mar 1999, Lincoln's Inn

Practising Areas: Administrative, Employment, Human Rights, Immigration

JAGUTPAL MR PREVIN SING

4 Brick Court
4 Brick Court, Temple, London EC4Y 9AD
☎ 020 7832 3200 ✉ clerks@4bc.co.uk
Call Date: Oct 2005, Middle Temple

Practising Areas: Family, Family Provision

JAISRI MR SHASHI SATYENDRA

1 Mitre Court Buildings
1 Mitre Court Buildings, Temple, London EC4Y 7BS ☎ 020 7452 8900 ✉ clerks@1mcb.com
Call Date: Nov 1995, Lincoln's Inn

Practising Areas: Common Law (General), Immigration, Landlord & Tenant

JAMES MR BYRON DENNIS

14 Gray's Inn Square
14 Gray's Inn Square, Gray's Inn, London WC1R 5JP ☎ 020 7242 0858 ✉ clerks@14gis.co.uk
Call Date: Oct 2006, Gray's Inn

JAMES MR DAVID JOHN

Call Date: Oct 1998, Inner Temple
Pupil Supervisor

JAMES MR GEORGE CHRISTOPHER MOHUN

No5 Chambers
Fountain Court, Steelhouse Lane, Birmingham B4 6DR ☎ 0845 210 5555 ✉ info@no5.com
No5 Chambers
Greenwood House, 4-7 Salisbury Court, London EC4Y 8AA ☎ 0845 210 5555

C

No5 Chambers
38 Queen Square, Bristol BS1 4QS
☎0845 210 5555
Call Date: Jul 1977, Middle Temple

Practising Areas: Ancillary Relief, Family

JAMES MR HENRY TRISTRAM

13 King's Bench Walk
13 King's Bench Walk, Temple, London EC4Y 7EN ☎020 7353 7204 ✉clerks@13kbw.co.uk
13 KBW
32 Beaumont Street, Oxford OX1 2NP
☎01865 311066 ✉clerks@13kbw.co.uk
Call Date: Nov 1999, Gray's Inn
Pupil Supervisor

JAMES MR MARK DAVID BARTON

Temple Garden Chambers
1 Harcourt Buildings, Temple, London EC4Y 9DA ☎020 7583 1315 ✉clerks@tgchambers.com
Call Date: Nov 1987, Middle Temple
Pupil Supervisor

JAMES MR MICHAEL PETER

Park Lane Plowden
Lombard House, 4-8 Lombard Street, Newcastle Upon Tyne NE1 3AE
☎0191 211 4087 ✉clerks@parklaneplowden.co.uk
Call Date: Nov 1989, Gray's Inn

JAMES MR NICHOLAS CHRISTOPHER

Argent Chambers
5 Bell Yard, London WC2A 2JR
☎020 7556 5500
✉briefsin@argentchambers.co.uk
Call Date: Jul 2001, Middle Temple

JAMES MR RODERICK IAN

Charter Chambers
33 John Street, London WC1N 2AT
☎020 7618 4400 ✉clerks@charterchambers.com
Call Date: Mar 1999, Lincoln's Inn
Pupil Supervisor

Practising Areas: Courts Martial, Crime, Crime (Corporate/Fraud), Regulatory Law

JAMES MRS VENICE IMOGEN

No 8 Chambers
8 Fountain Court, Steelhouse Lane, Birmingham B4 6DR ☎0121 236 5514
✉clerks@no8chambers.co.uk
Call Date: Jul 1983, Lincoln's Inn

Practising Areas: Family, Immigration

JAMES-MOORE MR SIWARD PATRICK JOSEPH

KCH Garden Square
1 Oxford Street, Nottingham NG1 5BH
☎0115 941 8851 ✉clerks@kchgardensquare.co.uk
Call Date: Jul 2000, Lincoln's Inn

JAMESON MR DANIEL ROBERT

Furnival Chambers
32 Furnival Street, London EC4A 1JQ
☎020 7405 3232
Call Date: Nov 2004, Middle Temple

Practising Areas: Crime, Crime (Corporate/Fraud)

JAMIL MISS YASMEEN

4 Brick Court
4 Brick Court, Temple, London EC4Y 9AD
☎020 7832 3200 ✉clerks@4bc.co.uk
Call Date: Oct 1998, Lincoln's Inn

Practising Areas: Children's Law

JANNER THE HON DANIEL JOSEPH MITCHELL QC (2002)

23 Essex Street
London WC2R 3AA ☎020 7413 0353
✉clerks@23es.com
Exchange Chambers
7 Ralli Courts, West Riverside, Manchester M3 5FT ☎0161 833 2722
St Philips Chambers
55 Temple Row, Birmingham B2 5LS
☎0121 246 7000 ✉clerks@st-philips.com
Call Date: Jul 1980, Middle Temple

Practising Areas: Crime, Crime (Corporate/Fraud), Health & Safety, Road Traffic And Highways

JAPHETH MISS BETHAN

Linenhall Chambers
1 Stanley Place, Chester CH1 2LU
☎01244 348282
✉clerks@linenhallchambers.co.uk
Call Date: Oct 1997, Gray's Inn

Practising Areas: Ancillary Relief, Care Proceedings, Family

JARMAIN MR STEPHEN ROBERT

1 Garden Court Family Law Chambers
Ground Floor, One Garden Court, Temple, London EC4Y 9BJ ☎020 7797 7900
✉clerks@1gc.com
Call Date: Jul 2005, Middle Temple

C

JARMAN MR MARK CHRISTOPHER

4 Paper Buildings
1st Floor, 4 Paper Buildings, Temple, London EC4Y 7EX ☎ 020 7427 5200 ✉ clerks@4pb.com
Call Date: Nov 1989, Inner Temple
Pupil Supervisor

Practising Areas: Care Proceedings, Children's Law, Family, Family Provision

JARMAN MR SAMUEL JAMES GUTHRIE

4 KBW
Ground Floor, 4 King's Bench Walk, Temple, London EC4Y 7DL ☎ 020 7822 8822
✉ law@4kbw.net
Lombard Chambers
1 Sekforde Street, Clerkenwell, London EC1R 0BE ☎ 020 7107 2100
Call Date: Jul 1989, Inner Temple
Pupil Supervisor

Practising Areas: Banking, Commercial Litigation, Insurance, Insurance/Reinsurance

JARRATT MISS ALICE CORDELIA BETCHWORTH

Carmelite Chambers
9 Carmelite Street, London EC4Y 0DR
☎ 020 7936 6300
✉ clerks@carmelitechambers.co.uk
Call Date: Oct 2007, Inner Temple

Practising Areas: Civil Litigation, Common Law (General), Costs, Courts Martial, Crime, Crime (Corporate/Fraud), Disciplinary Tribunals, Health & Safety, Inquests, Licensing, Public Law, Regulatory Law, Sports

JARVIS MR PAUL

6 King's Bench Walk
Ground Floor, 6 King's Bench Walk, Temple, London EC4Y 7DR ☎ 020 7583 0410
✉ clerks@6kbw.com
Call Date: Nov 2001, Lincoln's Inn
Pupil Supervisor

Practising Areas: Civil Liberties, Crime, Crime (Corporate/Fraud), Human Rights

JAY MR GRENVILLE RICHARD

Regent Chambers
Regent House, 3 Pall Mall, Hanley, Stoke On Trent ST1 1HP ☎ 01782 286666
✉ clerks@regentchambers.co.uk
Call Date: Nov 1975, Inner Temple

Practising Areas: Employment, Family

JAYAKRISHNAN MR HARRY SISUBALAN

Trent Chambers
9 Regent Street, Nottingham NG1 5BS
☎ 0115 941 9596 ✉ clerks@trentchambers.co.uk
Call Date: Nov 2000, Middle Temple

Practising Areas: Banking, Commercial Litigation, Common Law (General), Company & Commercial, Discrimination, Employment, Financial Services, Human Rights, Insurance, Licensing, Local Government, Personal Injury, Regulatory Law, Sale & Carriage of Goods, Town & Country Planning

JEFFERIES MR ANDREW QC (2009)

Dyers Chambers
35 Bedford Row, London WC1R 4JH
☎ 020 7404 1881 ✉ admin@dyerschambers.com
Westgate Chambers
64 High Street, Lewes, East Sussex BN7 1XG
☎ 01273 480510
✉ clerks@westgate-chambers.co.uk
Call Date: Oct 1990, Middle Temple

Practising Areas: Crime, Crime (Corporate/Fraud), Personal Injury

JEFFERIES MR THOMAS ROBERT

Landmark Chambers
180 Fleet Street, London EC4A 2HG
☎ 020 7430 1221
✉ clerks@landmarkchambers.co.uk
Call Date: Nov 1981, Middle Temple
Pupil Supervisor

Practising Areas: Chancery (Land Law), Commercial Property, Landlord & Tenant

JELF MR SIMON EDWARD

48 Bedford Row
London WC1R 4LR ☎ 020 7430 2005
✉ tyroon@partnershipcounsel.co.uk
Call Date: Oct 1996, Gray's Inn

Practising Areas: Partnership

JENKINS MR DAVID CROFTON

2 King's Bench Walk
2 King's Bench Walk, Temple, London EC4Y 7DE ☎ 020 7353 1746 ✉ clerks@2kbw.com
Call Date: Nov 1967, Inner Temple
Pupil Supervisor

Practising Areas: Common Law (General), Crime, Crime (Corporate/Fraud), Environment, Family, Family Provision, Personal Injury

JENKINS MR EDWARD NICHOLAS QC (2000)

Five Paper Buildings
1st Floor, Five Paper Buildings, Temple, London EC4Y 7HB ☎ 020 7583 6117
✉ clerks@5pb.co.uk
Call Date: Jul 1977, Middle Temple
Recorder

Practising Areas: Crime (Corporate/Fraud), Environment, Health & Safety, Intellectual Property, Licensing, Regulatory Law, Trademarks

JENKINS MR HYWEL IESTYN

Outer Temple Chambers
The Outer Temple, 222 Strand, London WC2R 1BA ☎ 020 7353 6381
✉ clerks@outertemple.com
Call Date: Jul 1974, Inner Temple
Pupil Supervisor

Practising Areas: Crime (Corporate/Fraud), Medical Negligence, Personal Injury

JENKINS MR THOMAS ALUN QC (1996)

Queen Square Chambers
56 Queen Square, Bristol BS1 4PR
☎ 0117 921 1966 ✉ crime@qs-c.co.uk
2 Bedford Row
London WC1R 4BU ☎ 020 7440 8888
✉ clerks@2bedfordrow.co.uk
Call Date: Jul 1972, Lincoln's Inn
Recorder

Practising Areas: Crime, Crime (Corporate/Fraud)

JEPSON MRS AMANDA JANE

1 Gray's Inn Square
Ground Floor, 1 Gray's Inn Square, London WC1R 5AA ☎ 020 7405 0001
Call Date: Oct 2005, Gray's Inn

JERAM MISS KIRTI

Park Lane Plowden
Lombard House, 4-8 Lombard Street, Newcastle Upon Tyne NE1 3AE
☎ 0191 211 4087 ✉ clerks@parklaneplowden.co.uk
Call Date: Nov 1996, Gray's Inn

Practising Areas: Employment

JEREMY MR DAVID HUGH THOMAS QC (2006)

QEB Hollis Whiteman
1-2 Laurence Pountney Hill, London EC4R 0EU ☎ 020 7933 8855 ✉ barristers@qebhw.co.uk
Call Date: Jul 1977, Middle Temple
Recorder

Practising Areas: Crime, Crime (Corporate/Fraud)

JESSOP MR STUART ANDREW

Nine Bedford Row
9 Bedford Row, London WC1R 4AZ
☎ 020 7489 2727 ✉ clerks@9bedfordrow.co.uk
Call Date: Jul 2002, Gray's Inn

JEWELL MR MATTHEW

1 Paper Buildings
1st Floor, 1 Paper Buildings, Temple, London EC4Y 7EP ☎ 020 7353 3728
✉ clerks@onepaper.co.uk
Call Date: Nov 1989, Lincoln's Inn
Pupil Supervisor

JINADU MR ABDUL-LATEEF ABODURIN OLAYINKA

Keating Chambers
15 Essex Street, London WC2R 3AA
☎ 020 7544 2600 ✉ clerks@keatingchambers.com
Call Date: Nov 1995, Middle Temple
Pupil Supervisor

Practising Areas: Arbitration, Commercial Litigation, Construction, Energy, Environment, Information Technology, Professional Negligence

JOBLING MR IAN MICHAEL THOMAS

2 Hare Court
Lower Ground, Ground, 1st & 2nd Floor, 2 Hare Court, Temple, London EC4Y 7BH
☎ 020 7353 3982 ✉ clerks@2harecourt.com
Call Date: Nov 1982, Gray's Inn
Pupil Supervisor

JOFFE MS NATASHA JULIET LOUISE

Outer Temple Chambers
The Outer Temple, 222 Strand, London WC2R 1BA ☎020 7353 6381
✉clerks@outertemple.com
Call Date: Oct 1992, Gray's Inn

Practising Areas: Administrative, Commercial Litigation, Common Law (General), Discrimination, Employment, Local Government, Personal Injury, Professional Negligence

JOHAL MISS SUKI KAUR

3 Dr Johnson's Buildings
Ground Floor, 3 Dr Johnson's Buildings, Temple, London EC4Y 7BA ☎020 7353 4854
✉clerks@3djb.co.uk
Call Date: Nov 1991, Middle Temple
Pupil Supervisor

JOHN MISS LAURA ELIZABETH

Monckton Chambers
1 & 2 Raymond Buildings, Gray's Inn, London WC1R 5NR ☎020 7405 7211
✉chambers@monckton.com
Call Date: Oct 2007, Inner Temple

Practising Areas: Administrative, Competition, EC & Competition Law, Environment, Parliamentary, Public International, Regulatory Law, Telecommunications

JOHN MR THOMAS HUW

Goresbrook Chambers
PO Box 6017, Milton Keynes MK1 9AP
☎0845 123 1234 ✉thomas.john6@btinternet.com
Call Date: Oct 1997, Middle Temple

Practising Areas: Common Law (General), Crime, Employment, Medical Negligence, Mental Health, Personal Injury

JOHNSON MISS AMANDA

Exchange Chambers
7 Ralli Courts, West Riverside, Manchester M3 5FT ☎0161 833 2722
Exchange Chambers
One Derby Square, Derby Square, Liverpool L2 9XX ☎0151 236 7747
✉info@exchangechambers.co.uk
Exchange Chambers
Oxford House, Oxford Row, Leeds LS1 3BE
☎0113 203 1970
✉spencer@exchangechambers.co.uk
Call Date: Oct 1992, Gray's Inn

Practising Areas: Crime, Crime (Corporate/Fraud), Sports

JOHNSON MRS CAROLYN ANN

Cobden House Chambers
19 Quay Street, Manchester M3 3HN
☎0161 833 6000 ✉Clerks@Cobden.co.uk
Call Date: Nov 1974, Gray's Inn
Pupil Supervisor

Practising Areas: Care Proceedings, Family

JOHNSON MS KATHRYN MARGARET

Lincoln House Chambers
Tower 12, The Avenue North, Spinningfields, 18-22 Bridge Street, Manchester M3 3BZ
☎0161 832 5701
✉info@lincolnhousechambers.com
Call Date: Jul 1989, Gray's Inn
Pupil Supervisor

Practising Areas: Crime, Crime (Corporate/Fraud)

JOHNSON MISS LAURA WENDY

1 Chancery Lane
London WC2A 1LF ☎0845 634 6666
✉clerks@1chancerylane.com
Call Date: Oct 2001, Gray's Inn
Pupil Supervisor

Practising Areas: Administrative, Common Law (General), Education, Insurance, Local Government, Medical Negligence, Personal Injury, Professional Negligence

JOHNSON MR LINDSAY CHARLES WHITLEY

Doughty Street Chambers
53-54 Doughty Street, London WC1N 2LS
☎020 7404 1313 ✉enquiries@doughtystreet.co.uk
Call Date: Oct 1997, Inner Temple

JOHNSON MISS MELANIE JANE

1 Pump Court
Elm Court, Temple, London EC4Y 7AB
☎020 7842 7070 ✉(name)@pumpcourt.co.uk
Call Date: Oct 1996, Middle Temple
Pupil Supervisor

Practising Areas: Care Proceedings, Family

JOHNSON MR PHILLIP MICHAEL

Chambers of Mr P Johnson
8 Packington Street, London N1 8QB
☎020 7288 2256
✉phill_m_johnson@hotmail.com
Call Date: Oct 1998, Inner Temple

Practising Areas: Administrative, Chancery (General), Copyright, Entertainment, Film,

Cable & TV, Information Technology, Intellectual Property, Patents, Private International, Sports, Trademarks

JOHNSON MISS SARAH SUSAN

Kenworthy's Chambers
Arlington House, Bloom Street, Salford, Manchester M3 6AJ ☎0161 832 4036
Call Date: Oct 2001, Lincoln's Inn

Practising Areas: Employment, Family

JOHNSON MR SIMON NICHOLAS

Stour Chambers
Mill Studio, 17a Stour Street, Canterbury, Kent CT1 2NR ☎01227 764899
✉clerks@stourchambers.co.uk
Call Date: Jul 1987, Gray's Inn
Pupil Supervisor

Practising Areas: Children's Law, Education, Family

JOHNSON MISS ZOE ELISABETH QC (2012)

QEB Hollis Whiteman
1-2 Laurence Pountney Hill, London EC4R 0EU ☎020 7933 8855 ✉barristers@qebhw.co.uk
Call Date: Nov 1990, Inner Temple
Pupil Supervisor

Practising Areas: Courts Martial, Crime, Licensing, Regulatory Law

JOHNSTON MISS ANNE-MARIE

Carmelite Chambers
9 Carmelite Street, London EC4Y 0DR
☎020 7936 6300
✉clerks@carmelitechambers.co.uk
Call Date: Oct 1990, Inner Temple

Practising Areas: Crime, Crime (Corporate/Fraud), Regulatory Law

JOHNSTON MISS CAREY ANN QC (2003)

18 Red Lion Court
London EC4A 3EB ☎020 7520 6000
✉chambers@18rlc.co.uk
18 Red Lion Court (Annexe)
Thornwood House, 102 New London Road, Chelmsford, Essex CM2 0RG
☎01245 280880
Queen Square Chambers
56 Queen Square, Bristol BS1 4PR
☎0117 921 1966 ✉crime@qs-c.co.uk
Call Date: Jul 1977, Middle Temple

JOHNSTON MR CHRISTOPHER MARK

Chambers of Marion Smullen and Kerim Fuad QC
1 Inner Temple Lane, London EC4Y 1AF
☎020 7427 4400 ✉clerks@1itl.com
Call Date: Nov 1983, Gray's Inn
Pupil Supervisor

JOHNSTONE MR MARK ANTHONY

4 Paper Buildings
1st Floor, 4 Paper Buildings, Temple, London EC4Y 7EX ☎020 7427 5200 ✉clerks@4pb.com
Call Date: Jul 1984, Inner Temple
Pupil Supervisor

Practising Areas: Ancillary Relief, Children's Law, Family, Family Provision

JOLLIFFE MRS VICTORIA ESTHER JEAN

5RB
1st Floor, 5 Raymond Buildings, Gray's Inn, London WC1R 5BP ☎020 7242 2902
✉clerks@5rb.com
Call Date: Nov 2005, Lincoln's Inn

Practising Areas: Copyright, Defamation, Entertainment, Intellectual Property, Sports

JONES MR ALUN

St Paul's Chambers
5th Floor, St Paul's House, 23 Park Square South, Leeds LS1 2ND ☎0113 245 5866
Call Date: Jul 2003, Lincoln's Inn

Practising Areas: Chancery (General), Chancery (Land Law), Commercial Litigation, Common Land, Common Law (General), Company & Commercial, Crime, Crime (Corporate/Fraud), Health & Safety, Healthcare, Housing, Landlord & Tenant, Medical Negligence, Mental Health, Personal Injury, Professional Negligence, Regulatory Law, Town & Country Planning

JONES MS ANIKA MARSHA

1 Mitre Court Buildings
1 Mitre Court Buildings, Temple, London EC4Y 7BS ☎020 7452 8900 ✉clerks@1mcb.com
Call Date: Mar 2002, Gray's Inn

JONES MS CHERYL STEPHANIE

No5 Chambers
Greenwood House, 4-7 Salisbury Court, London EC4Y 8AA ☎0845 210 5555
No5 Chambers
38 Queen Square, Bristol BS1 4QS
☎0845 210 5555
No5 Chambers
Fountain Court, Steelhouse Lane, Birmingham B4 6DR ☎0845 210 5555 ✉info@no5.com
Call Date: Oct 1996, Gray's Inn

Practising Areas: Bankruptcy, Chancery (Land Law), Conveyancing, Insolvency

JONES MR CHRISTOPHER DAVID HARRIES

St John's Chambers
101 Victoria Street, Bristol BS1 6PU
☎0117 923 4700 ✉clerks@stjohnschambers.co.uk
Call Date: Jul 2004, Gray's Inn

Practising Areas: Chancery (General), Chancery (Land Law), Charities, Commercial Litigation, Commercial Property, Common Law (General), Company & Commercial, Construction, Copyright, Defamation, Equity, Wills & Trusts, Family Provision, Insolvency, Intellectual Property, Landlord & Tenant, Partnership, Pensions, Probate & Administration, Professional Negligence, Sale & Carriage of Goods, Trademarks

JONES MISS CLAIRE-LOUISE

Chavasse Court Chambers
18 Queen Avenue, Liverpool L2 4TX
☎0151 229 2030
✉clerks@chavassechambers.co.uk
Call Date: Oct 1999, Lincoln's Inn

Practising Areas: Crime

C

JONES MR DAVID NICHOLAS

Broadway House Chambers
Broadway House, 9 Bank Street, Bradford, West Yorkshire BD1 1TW ☎01274 722560
✉clerks@broadwayhouse.co.uk
Broadway House Chambers
25 Park Square West, Leeds, West Yorkshire LS1 2PW ☎0113 246 2600
✉clerks@broadwayhouse.co.uk
Cloisters
1 Pump Court, Temple, London EC4Y 7AA
☎020 7827 4000 ✉clerks@cloisters.com
Call Date: Jul 1985, Gray's Inn
Pupil Supervisor

Practising Areas: Discrimination, Employment

JONES MISS EMILY LOUISE

Temple Garden Chambers
1 Harcourt Buildings, Temple, London EC4Y 9DA ☎020 7583 1315 ✉clerks@tgchambers.com
Call Date: Jul 2004, Middle Temple

Practising Areas: Employment, Public Law

JONES MR EMYR GWEIRYDD

9 Park Place
Cardiff, South Glamorgan CF10 3DP
☎029 2038 2731 ✉clerks@9parkplace.co.uk
Call Date: Oct 1999, Gray's Inn
Pupil Supervisor

Practising Areas: Chancery (General), Chancery (Land Law), Civil Litigation, Land, Landlord & Tenant, Local Government, Probate & Administration, Public Law, Town & Country Planning

JONES MR GARETH EDWARD

Lincoln House Chambers
Tower 12, The Avenue North, Spinningfields, 18-22 Bridge Street, Manchester M3 3BZ
☎0161 832 5701
✉info@lincolnhousechambers.com
Call Date: Oct 2002, Middle Temple

Practising Areas: Crime, Crime (Corporate/Fraud)

JONES MR GERAINT ANTHONY QC (2001)

Tanfield Chambers
2-5 Warwick Court, London WC1R 5DJ
☎020 7421 5300 ✉clerks@tanfieldchambers.co.uk
9 St John Street
Manchester M3 4DN ☎0161 955 9000
✉civilclerks@9sjs.com/criminalclerks@9sjs.com
New Walk Chambers
27 New Walk, Leicester, Leicestershire LE1 6TE ☎0871 200 1298 / 0116 255 9144
✉clerks@newwalkchambers.co.uk
Call Date: Jul 1976, Middle Temple

Practising Areas: Banking, Chancery (General), Chancery (Land Law), Commercial Litigation, Commercial Property, Entertainment, Environment, Equity, Wills & Trusts, Insurance, Insurance/Reinsurance, Medical Negligence, Partnership, Personal Injury, Professional Negligence, Sale & Carriage of Goods, Sports

JONES MR GERAINT MARTYN

Fenners Chambers
3 Madingley Road, Cambridge CB3 0EE
☎01223 368761 ✉clerks@fennerschambers.com
Call Date: Nov 1972, Gray's Inn
Pupil Supervisor

Practising Areas: Chancery (Land Law), Commercial Property, Equity, Wills & Trusts, Landlord & Tenant, Professional Negligence

JONES MISS GILLIAN HUNTER

18 Red Lion Court
London EC4A 3EB ☎020 7520 6000
✉chambers@18rlc.co.uk
18 Red Lion Court (Annexe)
Thornwood House, 102 New London Road, Chelmsford, Essex CM2 0RG
☎01245 280880
Call Date: Oct 1996, Lincoln's Inn
Pupil Supervisor

JONES MRS HETTIE GEORGIA

Liberty Chambers
Crackwell Farm, Penally, Tenby, Pembrokeshire SA70 7RY ☎01834 844458
✉hj@libertylaw.co.uk
Call Date: Oct 2002, Lincoln's Inn

Practising Areas: Civil Litigation, Crime, Family, Personal Injury

JONES MR IAN HARVEY

Holbrook Chambers
PO Box 9327, Leicester LE21 3EL
☎07771 961962 ✉legal@direct-barrister.com
Call Date: Oct 1993, Inner Temple
Pupil Supervisor

Practising Areas: Ecclesiastical, Education, Housing, Licensing, Local Government, Personal Injury

JONES MISS JACINTA ELIZABETH BARRETT

1 Mitre Court Buildings
1 Mitre Court Buildings, Temple, London EC4Y 7BS ☎020 7452 8900 ✉clerks@1mcb.com
Call Date: Jul 2002, Gray's Inn

Practising Areas: Civil Liberties, Crime, Crime (Corporate/Fraud), Human Rights, Immigration, Public Law

JONES MR JOHN RICHARD WILLIAM

Doughty Street Chambers
53-54 Doughty Street, London WC1N 2LS
☎020 7404 1313 ✉enquiries@doughtystreet.co.uk
Doughty Street Chambers
Pall Mall Court, 61-67 King Street, Manchester M2 4PD ☎0161 618 1066
Doughty Street Chambers
5th Floor, Broad Quay House, Prince Street, Bristol BS1 4DJ ☎01179 058 717
Call Date: Oct 1992, Lincoln's Inn
Pupil Supervisor

Practising Areas: Human Rights

JONES DR KAREN PATRICIA NIEVERGELT

Tanfield Chambers
2-5 Warwick Court, London WC1R 5DJ
☎020 7421 5300 ✉clerks@tanfieldchambers.co.uk
Call Date: Nov 1995, Middle Temple

JONES MS KATIE LAURA

Lincoln House Chambers
Tower 12, The Avenue North, Spinningfields, 18-22 Bridge Street, Manchester M3 3BZ
☎0161 832 5701
✉info@lincolnhousechambers.com
Call Date: Oct 2003, Gray's Inn

Practising Areas: Civil Liberties, Crime

JONES MISS KAY MARY

Field Court Chambers
5 Field Court, Gray's Inn, London WC1R 5EF
☎020 7405 6114 ✉clerks@fieldcourt.co.uk
Call Date: Jul 1974, Gray's Inn
Pupil Supervisor

JONES MR KELVIN MCALLISTER

Templis Chambers
3rd Floor South, 1A Middle Temple Lane, London EC4Y 9AA ☎020 7649 9808
✉templis@templis.com
Call Date: Oct 1995, Inner Temple

Practising Areas: Administrative, Chancery (General), Chancery (Land Law), Commercial Litigation, Commercial Property, Competition, Construction, Copyright, EC & Competition Law, Employment, Entertainment, Film, Cable & TV, Information Technology, Intellectual Property, Patents, Trademarks

JONES MR LAWRENCE VICTOR

Chambers of Lawrence Jones
8 Stone Buildings, Lincoln's Inn, London WC2A 3TA ☎ 020 7831 1444
✉ clerks@8stonebuildings.com
Call Date: Jul 1988, Lincoln's Inn
Pupil Supervisor

Practising Areas: Banking, Bankruptcy, Chancery (General), Company & Commercial, Defamation, Insolvency, Insurance/Reinsurance, Professional Negligence

JONES MR MARK ANDREW

St Ive's Chambers
Whittall Street, Birmingham B4 6DH
☎ 0121 236 0863 ✉ clerks@stiveschambers.co.uk
Call Date: Oct 2000, Middle Temple

Practising Areas: Civil Liberties, Coroners Inquests, Courts Martial, Crime, Crime (Corporate/Fraud), Discrimination, Education, Environment, Housing, Human Rights, Immigration, Inquests, Public International, Public Law, Regulatory Law

JONES MR MARK SIMEON

3 Dr Johnson's Buildings
Ground Floor, 3 Dr Johnson's Buildings, Temple, London EC4Y 7BA ☎ 020 7353 4854
✉ clerks@3djb.co.uk
Call Date: Jul 1997, Middle Temple

Practising Areas: Chancery (General), Chancery (Land Law), Commercial Litigation, Commercial Property, Equity, Wills & Trusts, Landlord & Tenant, Probate & Administration

JONES MR MARTIN WYNNE

Cranford Chambers
8 Warwick Court, London WC1R 5DJ
☎ 020 7404 7454 ✉ jemima.ivens@cranfordchambers.com
1 Mitre Court Buildings
1 Mitre Court Buildings, Temple, London EC4Y 7BS ☎ 020 7452 8900 ✉ clerks@1mcb.com
Call Date: Nov 1977, Inner Temple
Pupil Supervisor

JONES MISS RHIANNON

Farrar's Building
Farrar's Building, Temple, London EC4Y 7BD
☎ 020 7583 9241
✉ Chambers@farrarsbuilding.co.uk
Call Date: Nov 1993, Inner Temple

JONES MR RHYS CHARLES MANSEL

14 Gray's Inn Square
14 Gray's Inn Square, Gray's Inn, London WC1R 5JP ☎ 020 7242 0858 ✉ clerks@14gis.co.uk
Call Date: May 1990, Middle Temple

Practising Areas: Bankruptcy, Care Proceedings, Chancery (General), Chancery (Land Law), Common Land, Common Law (General), Family, Family Provision, Landlord & Tenant, Probate & Administration

JONES MR RICHARD FREDERICK THOMAS

Heavenwood Chambers
Heavenwood Chambers, Heavenwood House, 71 Bownham Park, Rodborough Common, Stroud, Gloucestershire GL5 5BZ
☎ 01453 873444 ✉ kms@heavenwood.co.uk
Call Date: Jul 1979, Gray's Inn
Pupil Supervisor

Practising Areas: Arbitration, Chancery (General), Chancery (Land Law), Civil Litigation, Commercial Litigation, Commercial Property, Common Law (General), Company & Commercial, Construction, Consumer, Costs, Disciplinary Tribunals, Employment, Equity, Wills & Trusts, Information Technology, Local Government, Medical Negligence, Professional Negligence, Regulatory Law, Road Traffic And Highways, Sale & Carriage of Goods, Town & Country Planning

JONES MR RICHARD HENRY QC (1996)

No5 Chambers
Greenwood House, 4-7 Salisbury Court, London EC4Y 8AA ☎ 0845 210 5555
No5 Chambers
38 Queen Square, Bristol BS1 4QS
☎ 0845 210 5555
No5 Chambers
Fountain Court, Steelhouse Lane, Birmingham B4 6DR ☎ 0845 210 5555 ✉ info@no5.com
Call Date: Nov 1972, Inner Temple
Recorder

JONES MISS RUTH

Nine Bedford Row
9 Bedford Row, London WC1R 4AZ
☎ 020 7489 2727 ✉ clerks@9bedfordrow.co.uk
Call Date: Jul 2004, Inner Temple

JONES MR TIMOTHY ARTHUR

No5 Chambers
Fountain Court, Steelhouse Lane, Birmingham B4 6DR ☎0845 210 5555 ✉info@no5.com
No5 Chambers
Greenwood House, 4-7 Salisbury Court, London EC4Y 8AA ☎0845 210 5555
No5 Chambers
38 Queen Square, Bristol BS1 4QS ☎0845 210 5555
Call Date: Jul 1975, Inner Temple
Pupil Supervisor

Practising Areas: Town & Country Planning

JONES MISS VICTORIA

3 PB Barristers
Royal Talbot House, 2 Victoria Street, Bristol, Avon BS1 6BB ☎0117 928 1520
3 PB Barristers
30 Christchurch Road, Bournemouth, Dorset BH1 3PD ☎01202 292102 ✉clerks.bournemouth@3paper.co.uk
3 PB Barristers
4 St Peter Street, Winchester SO23 8BW ☎01962 868884 ✉clerks.winchester@3paper.co.uk
3 PB Barristers
23 Beaumont Street, Oxford OX1 2NP ☎01865 793 736
3 PB Barristers
3 Paper Buildings, Temple, London EC4Y 7EU ☎020 7583 8055
Call Date: Oct 2003, Lincoln's Inn

JONES MR WILLIAM JOHN

2 Hare Court
Lower Ground, Ground, 1st & 2nd Floor, 2 Hare Court, Temple, London EC4Y 7BH ☎020 7353 3982 ✉clerks@2harecourt.com
Call Date: Nov 1972, Inner Temple
Pupil Supervisor, Recorder

Practising Areas: Crime, Crime (Corporate/ Fraud)

JORRO MR PETER ANTONIO RAIMO

Garden Court Chambers
57-60 Lincoln's Inn Fields, London WC2A 3LJ ☎020 7993 7600 ✉info@gclaw.co.uk
Call Date: Nov 1986, Lincoln's Inn

Practising Areas: Immigration

JORY MR RICHARD NORMAN

9-12 Bell Yard
London WC2A 2JR ☎020 7400 1800 ✉clerks@9-12bellyard.com
Call Date: Oct 1993, Middle Temple
Pupil Supervisor

Practising Areas: Crime, Licensing

JOSEPH MR CHARLES HENRY

Tanfield Chambers
2-5 Warwick Court, London WC1R 5DJ ☎020 7421 5300 ✉clerks@tanfieldchambers.co.uk
Call Date: Jul 1980, Lincoln's Inn
Pupil Supervisor

Practising Areas: Arbitration, Chancery (General), Chancery (Land Law), Commercial Litigation, Commercial Property, Company & Commercial, Construction, Conveyancing, Equity, Wills & Trusts, Insolvency, Landlord & Tenant, Partnership, Probate & Administration, Professional Negligence

JOSEPH MRS ELIZABETH ANNE AYODELE

Emmanuel Chambers
66 Daubeney Road, London E5 0EF ☎020 8985 3030 ✉AYOJOSEPH@aol.com
Call Date: Jul 1983, Gray's Inn

JOSEPH MR PAUL WOLFE

No5 Chambers
Fountain Court, Steelhouse Lane, Birmingham B4 6DR ☎0845 210 5555 ✉info@no5.com
No5 Chambers
Greenwood House, 4-7 Salisbury Court, London EC4Y 8AA ☎0845 210 5555
No5 Chambers
38 Queen Square, Bristol BS1 4QS ☎0845 210 5555
Call Date: Oct 2005, Inner Temple

Practising Areas: Arbitration, Bankruptcy, Chancery (General), Commercial Litigation, Insolvency, Insurance, Partnership, Professional Negligence

JOSEPH DR SANDRADEE THERESA

13 Old Square Chambers
Ground Floor, 14 Old Square, Lincoln's Inn, London WC2A 3UE ☎020 7831 4445 ✉clerks@13oldsquare.com
Call Date: Jul 1998, Inner Temple

Practising Areas: Bankruptcy, Chancery (General), Commercial Litigation, Company & Commercial, Financial Services, Insolvency, Insurance, Regulatory Law

JOSEPH MR SELLAPPAH JOB

Chambers of Mr S J Joseph
39 Hermitage Road, Haringey, London N4 1LU ☎020 8809 3083 / 020 8802 9889
✉sjoe333@yahoo.co.uk
Call Date: Nov 1983, Middle Temple
Pupil Supervisor

Practising Areas: Administrative, Commercial Litigation, Costs, Crime, Employment, Family, Family Provision, Housing, Immigration, Landlord & Tenant, Road Traffic And Highways

JOSEPHS MISS JENNIFER LOUISE

St Philips Chambers
55 Temple Row, Birmingham B2 5LS
☎0121 246 7000 ✉clerks@st-philips.com
Call Date: Jul 2000, Middle Temple

JOSHI MR PRAMOD KUMAR

One Essex Court
1st Floor, Temple, London EC4Y 9AR
☎020 7936 3030 ✉clerks@1ec.co.uk
Call Date: Nov 1992, Inner Temple

Practising Areas: Common Law (General), Family, Family Provision, Personal Injury

JOSHI MR RAJENDRA JUGATRAY

18 Red Lion Court
London EC4A 3EB ☎020 7520 6000
✉chambers@18rlc.co.uk
18 Red Lion Court (Annexe)
Thornwood House, 102 New London Road, Chelmsford, Essex CM2 0RG
☎01245 280880
Call Date: Nov 1983, Inner Temple
Pupil Supervisor

Practising Areas: Courts Martial, Crime, Crime (Corporate/Fraud), Discrimination, Human Rights, Regulatory Law

JOSLING MR WILLIAM HENRY CHARLES

37 Park Square Chambers
37 Park Square, Leeds LS1 2NY
☎0113 243 9422 ✉chambers@no37.co.uk
Call Date: Nov 1995, Lincoln's Inn

Practising Areas: Commercial Litigation, Employment, Housing, Landlord & Tenant, Personal Injury

JOSTY MR DAVID STEPHEN

College Chambers
19 Carlton Crescent, Southampton, Hampshire SO15 2ET ☎023 8023 0338
✉clerks@college-chambers.co.uk
Call Date: Jul 2002, Gray's Inn

Practising Areas: Ancillary Relief, Care Proceedings, Children's Law, Common Law (General), Family Provision

JOWETT MR TIMOTHY DAVID CHRISTIAN

9 Park Place
Cardiff, South Glamorgan CF10 3DP
☎029 2038 2731 ✉clerks@9parkplace.co.uk
Call Date: Oct 1999, Gray's Inn

Practising Areas: Common Law (General), Crime, Crime (Corporate/Fraud), Family Provision, Health & Safety, Housing, Immigration, Landlord & Tenant, Personal Injury, Regulatory Law, Sale & Carriage of Goods

JUBB MR BRIAN PATRICK

Renaissance Chambers
5th Floor, Gray's Inn Chambers, Gray's Inn, London WC1R 5JA ☎020 7404 1111
✉clerks@renaissancechambers.co.uk
Call Date: Nov 1971, Gray's Inn
Pupil Supervisor

JUDGE MISS LISA JANE

Deans Court Chambers
24 St John Street, Manchester M3 4DF
☎0161 214 6000 ✉clerks@deanscourt.co.uk
Deans Court Chambers
101 Walker Street, Preston PR1 2RR
☎01772 565 600 ✉preston@deanscourt.co.uk
Call Date: Oct 1993, Gray's Inn
Pupil Supervisor

JUDGE MISS PARVEEN

1 Mitre Court Buildings
1 Mitre Court Buildings, Temple, London EC4Y 7BS ☎020 7452 8900 ✉clerks@1mcb.com
Call Date: Mar 2001, Lincoln's Inn

Practising Areas: Crime, Crime (Corporate/Fraud), Employment, Family, Immigration

JUNG MISS BO-EUN

3 Raymond Buildings
3 Raymond Buildings, Gray's Inn, London WC1R 5BH ☎020 7400 6400
✉clerks@3rblaw.com
Call Date: Jul 2005, Lincoln's Inn

C

JURENKO MISS RENATA ANNA

33 Bedford Row
London WC1R 4JH ☎020 7242 6476
✉clerks@33bedfordrow.co.uk
Call Date: Oct 1993, Middle Temple

JUSS PROF SATVINDER SINGH

3 Hare Court
3 Hare Court, Temple, London EC4Y 7BJ
☎020 7415 7800 ✉clerks@3harecourt.com
Call Date: Nov 1989, Gray's Inn

Practising Areas: Administrative, Civil Liberties, Education, Human Rights, Immigration, Parliamentary

KABWERU-NAMULEMU MISS KAREN HASASHA

KCH Garden Square
1 Oxford Street, Nottingham NG1 5BH
☎0115 941 8851 ✉clerks@kchgardensquare.co.uk
Call Date: Jul 2001, Lincoln's Inn

Practising Areas: Care Proceedings, Family, Family Provision

KAGABA-MENDOZA MS ELIZABETH

Trinity Chambers
The Custom House, 39 Quayside, Newcastle Upon Tyne NE1 3DE ☎0191 232 1927
✉info@trinitychambers.co.uk
Trinity Chambers
Multi Media Exchange, 72-80 Corporation Road, Middlesbrough TS1 2RF
☎01642 247569 ✉info@trinitychambers.co.uk
Call Date: Jul 1999, Inner Temple

KAMAL MR SETU

Taxchambers
15 Old Square, Lincoln's Inn, London WC2A 3UE ☎020 7242 2744
✉taxchambers@15oldsquare.co.uk
St James's Chambers
68 Quay Street, Manchester M3 3EJ
☎0161 834 7000 ✉clerks@stjameschambers.com
Call Date: Mar 2004, Lincoln's Inn

Practising Areas: Equity, Wills & Trusts, Tax (Capital & Income), Tax (Corporate)

KAMLISH MR STEPHEN MICHAEL ADRIAN QC (2003)

Tooks Chambers
81 Farringdon Street, London EC4A 4BL
☎020 7842 7575 ✉clerks@tooks.co.uk
Call Date: Jul 1979, Gray's Inn

KANNANGARA MR HARSHAKA HEMANTHA

Temple Court Chambers
2nd Floor, 2 Dr Johnson's Building, Temple, London EC4Y 7AY ☎020 7353 7888
✉clerks@templecourt.co.uk
Call Date: Nov 2000, Lincoln's Inn
Pupil Supervisor

Practising Areas: Common Law (General), Immigration

KANSAL MISS SEEMA

12 Old Square Chambers
1st Floor, 12 Old Square, Lincoln's Inn, London WC2A 3TX ☎020 7404 0875
✉clerks@12oldsquare.com
Call Date: Mar 2007, Middle Temple

Practising Areas: Civil Litigation, Family, Housing, Immigration, Public Law

KAPILA MISS RACHEL PRAKASH

3 Raymond Buildings
3 Raymond Buildings, Gray's Inn, London WC1R 5BH ☎020 7400 6400
✉clerks@3rblaw.com
Call Date: Oct 2006, Middle Temple

Practising Areas: Crime, Crime (Corporate/Fraud), Licensing, Regulatory Law, Sports

KARAISKOS MISS MARIA

Old Bailey Chambers
15 Old Bailey, London EC4M 7EF
☎020 3008 6404
✉clerks@15oldbaileychambers.com
Call Date: Nov 2000, Middle Temple

Practising Areas: Crime, Crime (Corporate/Fraud)

KARK MR THOMAS VICTOR WILLIAM QC (2010)

QEB Hollis Whiteman
1-2 Laurence Pountney Hill, London EC4R 0EU ☎020 7933 8855 ✉barristers@qebhw.co.uk
Call Date: Jul 1982, Inner Temple
Pupil Supervisor, Recorder

KARMY-JONES MISS RIEL MEREDITH

18 Red Lion Court
London EC4A 3EB ☎020 7520 6000
✉chambers@18rlc.co.uk
Call Date: Nov 1995, Lincoln's Inn
Pupil Supervisor

C

KARSERAS MISS ANASTASIA ANDREA

2 Temple Gardens
2 Temple Gardens, Temple, London EC4Y 9AY ☎ 020 7822 1200 ✉ clerks@2tg.co.uk
Call Date: Oct 2000, Gray's Inn
Pupil Supervisor

KARU MR LEE QC (2010)

Nine Bedford Row
9 Bedford Row, London WC1R 4AZ
☎ 020 7489 2727 ✉ clerks@9bedfordrow.co.uk
Call Date: Jul 1985, Lincoln's Inn
Pupil Supervisor

KATZ MR PHILIP ALEC JACKSON QC (2000)

9-12 Bell Yard
London WC2A 2JR ☎ 020 7400 1800
✉ clerks@9-12bellyard.com
Call Date: Nov 1976, Middle Temple

Practising Areas: Crime, Crime (Corporate/Fraud)

KAUL MISS KALYANI QC (2011)

9-12 Bell Yard
London WC2A 2JR ☎ 020 7400 1800
✉ clerks@9-12bellyard.com
Call Date: Jul 1983, Middle Temple
Pupil Supervisor

Practising Areas: Crime

KAYNE MR CHARLES ADRIAN

Carmelite Chambers
9 Carmelite Street, London EC4Y 0DR
☎ 020 7936 6300
✉ clerks@carmelitechambers.co.uk
Call Date: Nov 1989, Inner Temple

Practising Areas: Crime

C

KEANE MR OWEN ASHLEY

Design Chambers
24 Arterberry Road, Wimbledon, London SW20 8AH ☎ 020 7353 0747
✉ manager@designchambers.com
Call Date: Nov 1988, Inner Temple

Practising Areas: Arbitration, Commercial Litigation, Common Law (General), Company & Commercial, Copyright, Entertainment, Information Technology, Intellectual Property, Telecommunications

KEARNEY MR JAMES MARTIN

Chambers of Mr Ami Feder
Ground Floor, Lamb Building, Temple, London EC4Y 7AS ☎ 020 7797 7788
✉ clerks@lambbuilding.co.uk
Lamb Building
22 Ship Street, Brighton BN1 1AD
☎ 01273 820490 ✉ admin@lambbuilding.co.uk
Chambers of Mr Ami Feder
Ground Floor, Lamb Building, Temple, London EC4Y 7AS ☎ 020 7797 7788
✉ clerks@lambbuilding.co.uk
Call Date: Feb 1992, Gray's Inn
Pupil Supervisor

KEARNEY MR JOHN

Furnival Chambers
32 Furnival Street, London EC4A 1JQ
☎ 020 7405 3232
Call Date: Nov 1994, Middle Temple

Practising Areas: Courts Martial, Crime, Crime (Corporate/Fraud)

KEATING MR DERMOT JOHN

25 Bedford Row
London WC1R 4HD ☎ 020 7067 1500
✉ clerks@25bedfordrow.com
Call Date: Nov 1997, Inner Temple
Pupil Supervisor

Practising Areas: Crime, Crime (Corporate/Fraud)

KEE MR PETER WILLIAM

Becket Chambers
17 New Dover Road, Canterbury, Kent CT1 3AS ☎ 01227 786331
✉ clerks@becket-chambers.co.uk
Call Date: Jul 1983, Middle Temple

Practising Areas: Common Law (General), Employment, Landlord & Tenant, Personal Injury

KEEL MR DOUGLAS VINCENT

11 Stone Buildings
11 Stone Buildings, Lincoln's Inn, London WC2A 3TG ☎ 020 7831 6381 ✉ clerks@11sb.com
Call Date: Oct 1997, Lincoln's Inn

Practising Areas: Asset Finance, Bankruptcy, Chancery (General), Company & Commercial, Corporate Finance, Financial Services, Insolvency, International Trade, Landlord & Tenant, Partnership, Private International, Professional Negligence, Share Options, Tax (Capital & Income), Tax (Corporate)

KEELING MR ADRIAN FRANCIS QC (2011)

No5 Chambers
Fountain Court, Steelhouse Lane, Birmingham B4 6DR ☎ 0845 210 5555 ✉ info@no5.com
No5 Chambers
Greenwood House, 4-7 Salisbury Court, London EC4Y 8AA ☎ 0845 210 5555
No5 Chambers
38 Queen Square, Bristol BS1 4QS
☎ 0845 210 5555
Call Date: Oct 1990, Inner Temple
Pupil Supervisor

Practising Areas: Commercial Litigation, Common Law (General), Crime, Crime (Corporate/Fraud), Health & Safety, Regulatory Law, Sports

KEEN MR SPENCER JOHN

Pump Court Chambers
31 Southgate Street, Winchester, Hampshire SO23 9EB ☎ 01962 868 161
✉ clerks@3pumpcourt.com
Pump Court Chambers
5 Temple Chambers, Temple Street, Swindon SN1 1SQ ☎ 01793 539899
✉ clerks@3pumpcourt.com
Riverview Chambers
Hamilton House, 1 Temple Avenue, London EC4Y 0HA ☎ 0844 225 3999
✉ chrisbaylis@riverviewchambers.com
Call Date: Nov 1998, Middle Temple

Practising Areas: Administrative, Employment

KEFFORD MR ANTHONY JOHN ROLAND

Octagon House
19 Colegate, Norwich NR3 1AT
☎ 01603 623186 ✉ clerks@octagonhouse.co.uk
Call Date: Nov 1980, Middle Temple

KEITH MR BENJAMIN CHARLES ANDREW

Five St Andrew's Hill
5 St Andrew's Hill, London EC4V 5BZ
☎ 020 7332 5400 ✉ Clerks@5sah.co.uk
Call Date: Oct 2004, Lincoln's Inn

Practising Areas: Civil Liberties, Common Law (General), Coroners Inquests, Courts Martial, Crime, Crime (Corporate/Fraud), Disciplinary Tribunals, Health & Safety, Human Rights, Immigration, Licensing, Public International, Public Law, Regulatory Law

KELLY MRS AMY LOUISE

12 College Place
Fauvelle Buildings, 12 College Place, Southampton SO15 2FE ☎ 023 8032 0320
✉ clerks@12cp.co.uk
Call Date: Nov 2000, Middle Temple

Practising Areas: Chancery (Land Law), Commercial Property, Common Land, Common Law (General), Education, Equity, Wills & Trusts, Housing, Landlord & Tenant, Local Government, Probate & Administration, Sale & Carriage of Goods

KELLY MISS EMMA LOUISE

St Philips Chambers
55 Temple Row, Birmingham B2 5LS
☎ 0121 246 7000 ✉ clerks@st-philips.com
Call Date: Oct 1997, Lincoln's Inn

KELLY MR GEOFFREY ROBERT

Pump Court Chambers
Upper Ground Floor, 3 Pump Court, Temple, London EC4Y 7AJ ☎ 020 7353 0711
✉ clerks@3pumpcourt.com
Pump Court Chambers
5 Temple Chambers, Temple Street, Swindon SN1 1SQ ☎ 01793 539899
✉ clerks@3pumpcourt.com
Pump Court Chambers
31 Southgate Street, Winchester, Hampshire SO23 9EB ☎ 01962 868 161
✉ clerks@3pumpcourt.com
Call Date: Feb 1992, Middle Temple
Pupil Supervisor

Practising Areas: Family, Family Provision

KELLY MR MARK

No5 Chambers
Fountain Court, Steelhouse Lane, Birmingham B4 6DR ☎ 0845 210 5555 ✉ info@no5.com
No5 Chambers
Greenwood House, 4-7 Salisbury Court, London EC4Y 8AA ☎ 0845 210 5555
No5 Chambers
38 Queen Square, Bristol BS1 4QS
☎ 0845 210 5555
Call Date: Nov 1985, Gray's Inn
Pupil Supervisor

KELLY MR MATTHIAS JOHN QC (1999)

39 Essex Street
London WC2R 3AT ☎ 020 7832 1111
✉ clerks@39essex.com
Call Date: Feb 1979, Gray's Inn

Practising Areas: Administrative, Civil Liberties, Common Law (General), Employment, Foreign

C

Law, Medical Negligence, Personal Injury, Sports

KELLY MR RICHARD BERNARD

East Anglian Chambers
140 New London Road, Chelmsford, Essex CM2 0AW ☎01473 214481
✉chelmsford@ealaw.co.uk
East Anglian Chambers
53 North Hill, Colchester, Essex CO1 1QA
☎01473 214481 ✉colchester@ealaw.co.uk
East Anglian Chambers
15 The Close, Norwich, Norfolk NR1 4DZ
☎01473 214481 ✉norwich@ealaw.co.uk
East Anglian Chambers
Gresham House, 5 Museum Street, Ipswich, Suffolk IP1 1HQ ☎01473 214481
✉ipswich@ealaw.co.uk
Call Date: Oct 1994, Gray's Inn

Practising Areas: Courts Martial, Crime, Crime (Corporate/Fraud), Health & Safety, Regulatory Law

KELLY MR SEAN

Chancery House Chambers
7 Lisbon Square, Leeds, West Yorkshire LS1 4LY ☎0113 244 6691
✉clerks@chanceryhouse.co.uk
Call Date: Oct 1990, Gray's Inn

Practising Areas: Banking, Bankruptcy, Chancery (General), Chancery (Land Law), Commercial Litigation, Commercial Property, Construction, Conveyancing, Corporate Finance, Equity, Wills & Trusts, Family Provision, Financial Services, Insolvency, Landlord & Tenant, Partnership, Probate & Administration, Professional Negligence, Sale & Carriage of Goods

KELLY MR SHAW MARTIN

Staple Inn Chambers
1st Floor, 9 Staple Inn, Holborn Bars, London WC1V 7QH ☎020 7242 5240
✉clerks@stapleinn.co.uk
Call Date: Oct 1997, Middle Temple

Practising Areas: Housing, Immigration, Landlord & Tenant

KEMP MR JAMES RUPERT

Trinity Chambers
The Custom House, 39 Quayside, Newcastle Upon Tyne NE1 3DE ☎0191 232 1927
✉info@trinitychambers.co.uk
Trinity Chambers
Multi Media Exchange, 72-80 Corporation Road, Middlesbrough TS1 2RF
☎01642 247569 ✉info@trinitychambers.co.uk
Call Date: Oct 1999, Inner Temple

Practising Areas: Chancery (General), Chancery (Land Law), Common Law (General), Equity, Wills & Trusts, Housing, Landlord & Tenant, Personal Injury, Professional Negligence

KENNEDY MR CHRISTOPHER LAURENCE PAUL QC (2010)

9 St John Street
Manchester M3 4DN ☎0161 955 9000
✉civilclerks@9sjs.com/criminalclerks@9sjs.com
Call Date: Jul 1989, Gray's Inn
Pupil Supervisor

Practising Areas: Common Law (General), Environment, Local Government, Medical Negligence, Personal Injury, Professional Negligence

KENNEDY MISS LUCY JULIA

QEB Hollis Whiteman
1-2 Laurence Pountney Hill, London EC4R 0EU ☎020 7933 8855 ✉barristers@qebhw.co.uk
Call Date: Nov 2000, Middle Temple

Practising Areas: Crime, Crime (Corporate/Fraud), Health & Safety, Regulatory Law

KENNEDY MR MICHAEL JOHN

Call Date: May 1985, Middle Temple
Pupil Supervisor

KENNEDY MR PETER NICHOLAS DODGSON

15 Winckley Square
Preston PR1 3JJ ☎01772 252828
✉clerks@15winckleysq.co.uk
Call Date: Jul 1977, Lincoln's Inn
Pupil Supervisor

Practising Areas: Common Law (General), Courts Martial, Crime, Crime (Corporate/Fraud), Regulatory Law

KENNEDY MR STUART VICTOR

3 PB Barristers
3 Paper Buildings, Temple, London EC4Y 7EU
☎020 7583 8055
3 PB Barristers
23 Beaumont Street, Oxford OX1 2NP
☎01865 793 736
3 PB Barristers
30 Christchurch Road, Bournemouth, Dorset BH1 3PD ☎01202 292102 ✉clerks.bournemouth@3paper.co.uk
3 PB Barristers
Royal Talbot House, 2 Victoria Street, Bristol, Avon BS1 6BB ☎0117 928 1520

3 PB Barristers
4 St Peter Street, Winchester SO23 8BW
☎01962 868884 ✉clerks.winchester@3paper.co.uk
Call Date: Oct 1999, Lincoln's Inn
Pupil Supervisor

Practising Areas: Arbitration, Common Law (General), Construction

KENNY MR MARTIN WILLIAM

Walnut House
63 St. David's Hill, Exeter, Devon EX4 4DW
☎01392 279751 ✉clerks@walnuthouse.co.uk
Call Date: Jul 1998, Inner Temple
Pupil Supervisor

Practising Areas: Ancillary Relief, Asset Finance, Care Proceedings, Children's Law, Civil Litigation, Commercial Litigation, Commercial Property, Common Law (General), Company & Commercial, Competition, Consumer, Coroners Inquests, Courts Martial, Crime, Crime (Corporate/Fraud), Defamation, Disciplinary Tribunals, Employment, Professional Negligence

KENT MR ALAN PETER QC (2009)

23 Essex Street
London WC2R 3AA ☎020 7413 0353
✉clerks@23es.com
Maidstone Chambers
33 Earl Street, Maidstone, Kent ME14 1PF
☎01622 688592
✉clerks@maidstonechambers.co.uk
Call Date: Nov 1986, Inner Temple

Practising Areas: Crime

KENT MR MICHAEL HARCOURT QC (1996)

Crown Office Chambers
2 Crown Office Row, Temple, London EC4Y 7HJ ☎020 7797 8100
✉mail@crownofficechambers.com
Call Date: Jul 1975, Middle Temple
Recorder

Practising Areas: Administrative, Arbitration, Civil Liberties, Commercial Litigation, Common Law (General), Construction, Insurance/Reinsurance, Licensing, Local Government, Medical Negligence, Mental Health, Personal Injury, Professional Negligence, Sale & Carriage of Goods

KEOGH MR ANDREW JOHN

No5 Chambers
Fountain Court, Steelhouse Lane, Birmingham B4 6DR ☎0845 210 5555 ✉info@no5.com
No5 Chambers
Greenwood House, 4-7 Salisbury Court, London EC4Y 8AA ☎0845 210 5555
No5 Chambers
38 Queen Square, Bristol BS1 4QS
☎0845 210 5555
Call Date: Nov 1978, Inner Temple
Pupil Supervisor

KEOGH MR RICHARD THOMAS

Farringdon Chambers
180 Bermondsey Street, London SE1 3TQ
☎020 7089 5700
Call Date: Nov 1991, Middle Temple
Pupil Supervisor

Practising Areas: Courts Martial, Crime, Crime (Corporate/Fraud), Employment, Licensing

KERR MR CHRISTOPHER RICHARD

2 Pump Court
1st Floor, 2 Pump Court, Temple, London EC4Y 7AH ☎020 7353 5597
✉clerks@2pumpcourt.co.uk
Call Date: Nov 1988, Middle Temple
Pupil Supervisor

Practising Areas: Crime, Crime (Corporate/Fraud)

KERR MR DEREK WILLIAM

Lamb Chambers
Lamb Building, Elm Court, Temple, London EC4Y 7AS ☎020 7797 8300
✉info@lambchambers.co.uk
Call Date: Oct 1994, Middle Temple
Pupil Supervisor

Practising Areas: Employment, Landlord & Tenant

KERR MR NEIL FORSYTH

3 Dr Johnson's Buildings
Ground Floor, 3 Dr Johnson's Buildings, Temple, London EC4Y 7BA ☎020 7353 4854
✉clerks@3djb.co.uk
Call Date: Nov 2001, Inner Temple

Practising Areas: Family, Family Provision

KER-REID MR JOHN

Pump Court Chambers
Upper Ground Floor, 3 Pump Court, Temple, London EC4Y 7AJ ☎020 7353 0711
✉clerks@3pumpcourt.com
Pump Court Chambers
5 Temple Chambers, Temple Street, Swindon SN1 1SQ ☎01793 539899
✉clerks@3pumpcourt.com
Pump Court Chambers
31 Southgate Street, Winchester, Hampshire SO23 9EB ☎01962 868 161
✉clerks@3pumpcourt.com
Call Date: Nov 1974, Inner Temple

Practising Areas: Care Proceedings, Family, Family Provision

KESSLER MR JAMES RICHARD QC (2003)

Taxchambers
15 Old Square, Lincoln's Inn, London WC2A 3UE ☎020 7242 2744
✉taxchambers@15oldsquare.co.uk
Call Date: Jul 1984, Gray's Inn

Practising Areas: Charities, Equity, Wills & Trusts, Tax (Capital & Income), Tax (Corporate)

KESSLING MR CHRISTOPHER DAVID

Chambers of Mr Christopher Kessling
14 Belvoir Street, Leicester LE1 6QH
☎01509 890690 ✉ck@cklaw.co.uk
Call Date: Oct 1992, Middle Temple
Pupil Supervisor

Practising Areas: Courts Martial, Crime, Crime (Corporate/Fraud), Health & Safety, Regulatory Law

KETTLE-WILLIAMS MISS ALEXANDRA MARGARET

Chambers of Marion Smullen and Kerim Fuad QC
1 Inner Temple Lane, London EC4Y 1AF
☎020 7427 4400 ✉clerks@1itl.com
Call Date: Oct 2004, Inner Temple

Practising Areas: Crime

KEYES MR GRANT ANDREW

Northampton Chambers
10 Spencer Parade, Northampton NN1 5AQ
☎01604 636271
✉clerks@northampton-chambers.co.uk
Call Date: Jul 2007, Gray's Inn

KHALID MR JAMES

Goulds Green Chambers
Room D, 2 Bakers Yard, High Street, Uxbridge UB8 1JZ ☎01895 422574
Goulds Green Chambers
48 Goulds Green, Uxbridge UB8 3DG
☎01895 422574 ✉jamkha@tiscali.co.uk
Call Date: Nov 1999, Lincoln's Inn

Practising Areas: Ancillary Relief, Consumer, Crime, Discrimination, Family, Family Provision, Housing, Human Rights, Immigration, Landlord & Tenant, Personal Injury, Road Traffic And Highways, Sale & Carriage of Goods

KHALIL MR KARIM SHAKIR QC (2003)

1 Paper Buildings
1st Floor, 1 Paper Buildings, Temple, London EC4Y 7EP ☎020 7353 3728
✉clerks@onepaper.co.uk
Octagon House
19 Colegate, Norwich NR3 1AT
☎01603 623186 ✉clerks@octagonhouse.co.uk
Call Date: Jul 1984, Lincoln's Inn
Recorder

Practising Areas: Common Law (General), Crime, Crime (Corporate/Fraud), Private International

KHALIQUE MISS NAGEENA

No5 Chambers
Fountain Court, Steelhouse Lane, Birmingham B4 6DR ☎0845 210 5555 ✉info@no5.com
No5 Chambers
Greenwood House, 4-7 Salisbury Court, London EC4Y 8AA ☎0845 210 5555
No5 Chambers
38 Queen Square, Bristol BS1 4QS
☎0845 210 5555
Call Date: Oct 1994, Gray's Inn

Practising Areas: Administrative, Common Law (General), Human Rights, Local Government, Medical Negligence, Mental Health, Regulatory Law

KHAMISA MR MOHAMMED JAFFER QC (2006)

Old Bailey Chambers
15 Old Bailey, London EC4M 7EF
☎020 3008 6404
✉clerks@15oldbaileychambers.com
Call Date: Nov 1985, Middle Temple

C

KHAN MISS ABDAH

Dyers Chambers
35 Bedford Row, London WC1R 4JH
☎ 020 7404 1881 ✉ admin@dyerschambers.com
Call Date: Oct 2000, Lincoln's Inn

Practising Areas: Crime

KHAN MR ABDUL ALEEM

Gray's Chambers
10 Heathside Close, Newbury, Essex IG2 7PD
☎ 020 8518 2525 ✉ aleem.khan@btinternet.com
Call Date: Jul 2003, Inner Temple

Practising Areas: Chancery (General), Chancery (Land Law), Charities, Commercial Property, Common Law (General), Conveyancing, Equity, Wills & Trusts, Family, Family Provision, Foreign Law, Housing, Human Rights, Immigration, Insolvency, Landlord & Tenant, Partnership, Personal Injury, Probate & Administration, Professional Negligence

KHAN DR ALEXANDER

Coral House
42 Charles Street, Manchester, Lancashire M1 7DB
Call Date: Nov 2000, Lincoln's Inn

Practising Areas: Arbitration, Bankruptcy, Chancery (General), Chancery (Land Law), Civil Litigation, Commercial Litigation, Commercial Property, Company & Commercial, Copyright, Defamation, Employment, Equity, Wills & Trusts, Family Provision, Insolvency, Intellectual Property, Landlord & Tenant, Partnership, Patents, Personal Injury, Probate & Administration, Trademarks

KHAN MR ARFAN

Field Court Chambers
5 Field Court, Gray's Inn, London WC1R 5EF
☎ 020 7405 6114 ✉ clerks@fieldcourt.co.uk
Call Date: Nov 2001, Lincoln's Inn

Practising Areas: Administrative, Arbitration, Chancery (General), Commercial Litigation, Company & Commercial, Employment, Entertainment, Human Rights, Insolvency, Public International, Tax (Corporate)

KHAN MR AYOUB

Chambers of Mr Ayoub Khan
127 Albert Road, Aston, Birmingham B6 5ND
☎ 07930 987202 ✉ ayoub_khan64@hotmail.com
Call Date: Jul 2005, Lincoln's Inn

Practising Areas: Care Proceedings, Commercial Litigation, Common Law (General), Crime, Crime (Corporate/Fraud), Employment, Family, Human Rights, Immigration, Islamic Sharia Law, Local Government, Medical Negligence, Personal Injury, Regulatory Law

KHAN MR FORZ

Chambers of Mr F Khan
19 Glenwood Road, Hounslow, London TW3 1SW ☎ 07854 109584 ✉ forzkhan@live.co.uk
6 King's Bench Walk
Ground, Third & Fourth Floors, 6 King's Bench Walk, Temple, London EC4Y 7DR
☎ 020 7353 4931 ✉ clerks@6kbw.co.uk
Call Date: Jul 1988, Middle Temple

Practising Areas: Administrative, Civil Liberties, Courts Martial, Crime, Crime (Corporate/Fraud), Employment, Family, Health & Safety, Human Rights, Immigration, Regulatory Law

KHAN MR HASSAN AHMED

4 Paper Buildings
1st Floor, 4 Paper Buildings, Temple, London EC4Y 7EX ☎ 020 7427 5200 ✉ clerks@4pb.com
Call Date: Nov 1999, Lincoln's Inn
Pupil Supervisor

KHAN MR IMRAN

St Albans Chambers
2 - 4 St Peter's Street, St Albans, Hertfordshire AL1 3LF ☎ 01727 843383
✉ clerks@stalbanschambers.com
Call Date: Nov 2001, Lincoln's Inn

Practising Areas: Ancillary Relief, Common Law (General), Crime (Corporate/Fraud), Family, Personal Injury

KHAN MS JUDITH QC (2010)

Garden Court Chambers
57-60 Lincoln's Inn Fields, London WC2A 3LJ
☎ 020 7993 7600 ✉ info@gclaw.co.uk
Call Date: Nov 1989, Middle Temple
Pupil Supervisor

KHAN MR MAHMOOD SHAFI

Willesden Chambers
5 Mora Road, London NW2 6SD
☎ 020 3273 1042 ✉ syril@btinternet.com
Luton Chambers
103 Wexham Close, Luton LU3 3TX
☎ 01582 598394 ✉ mshafikhan@hotmail.com
Call Date: Feb 1994, Lincoln's Inn

Practising Areas: Administrative, Civil Liberties, Commercial Litigation, Commercial Property, Common Law (General), Crime, Family, Human Rights, Immigration, Islamic Sharia Law, Landlord & Tenant

KHAN MR SAADALLAH FRANS HASSAN

Blackfriars Chambers
79-83 Temple Chambers, 3-7 Temple Avenue, London EC4Y 0HP ☎ 020 7353 7400
✉ clerks@blackfriarschambers.com
Call Date: Nov 1991, Lincoln's Inn
Pupil Supervisor

KHAN MR SHAHNAWAZ ZULFIQUAR

1 Gray's Inn Square
Ground Floor, 1 Gray's Inn Square, London WC1R 5AA ☎ 020 7405 0001
Call Date: Jul 2001, Lincoln's Inn

Practising Areas: Crime, Human Rights, Immigration, Landlord & Tenant

KHAN MR SHAUKAT ALI

Chambers of Mr S A Khan
1 Wolverton Avenue, Kingston Upon Thames, Surrey KT2 7QF ☎ 020 8541 3875
✉ shaukou.ali.khan73@hotmail.com
Call Date: Jul 1971, Lincoln's Inn
Pupil Supervisor

Practising Areas: Family Provision, Housing, Landlord & Tenant

KHAN MR SHOKAT

Kings Chambers
36 Young Street, Manchester M3 3FT
☎ 0845 034 3444 ✉ clerks@kingschambers.com
Kings Chambers
5 Park Square East, Leeds LS1 2NE
☎ 0845 034 3444 ✉ clerks@kingschambers.com
Kings Chambers
Embassy House, 60 Church Street, Birmingham B3 2DJ ☎ 0845 034 3444
✉ clerks@kingschambers.com
Call Date: Nov 1979, Middle Temple

C

KHAN MR TAHIR QC (2011)

Broadway House Chambers
Broadway House, 9 Bank Street, Bradford, West Yorkshire BD1 1TW ☎ 01274 722560
✉ clerks@broadwayhouse.co.uk
Broadway House Chambers
25 Park Square West, Leeds, West Yorkshire LS1 2PW ☎ 0113 246 2600
✉ clerks@broadwayhouse.co.uk
Call Date: Jul 1986, Lincoln's Inn
Pupil Supervisor, Recorder

Practising Areas: Crime, Crime (Corporate/Fraud), Environment

KHAN MR TARIQ ALI

Chambers of Mr T A Khan
St. Paulés Chambers, First Floor, 459 Foleshill Road, Coventry CV6 5AQ ☎ 02476 666 400
✉ tkhan@stpaulslaw.co.uk
Call Date: Nov 1996, Lincoln's Inn

Practising Areas: Crime, Family, Immigration, Personal Injury

KHAN MR ZARIF

Dyers Chambers
35 Bedford Row, London WC1R 4JH
☎ 020 7404 1881 ✉ admin@dyerschambers.com
Call Date: Oct 1996, Lincoln's Inn
Pupil Supervisor

Practising Areas: Arbitration, Courts Martial, Crime, Crime (Corporate/Fraud), Human Rights, Immigration, Islamic Sharia Law, Licensing

KHANNA MS PRIYADARSHANI

18 Red Lion Court
London EC4A 3EB ☎ 020 7520 6000
✉ chambers@18rlc.co.uk
18 Red Lion Court (Annexe)
Thornwood House, 102 New London Road, Chelmsford, Essex CM2 0RG
☎ 01245 280880
Call Date: Jul 2001, Middle Temple

KIDD MR PETER WILLIAM

Number 7 Harrington Street Chambers
7 Harrington Street, Liverpool L2 9YH
☎ 0151 242 0707 ✉ clerks@7hs.co.uk
Call Date: Jul 1987, Lincoln's Inn

Practising Areas: Ancillary Relief, Bankruptcy, Chancery (General), Civil Litigation, Commercial Litigation, Common Law (General), Family, Family Provision, Insolvency, Landlord & Tenant, Personal Injury

KILCOYNE MR PATRICK DESMOND OLIVER

42 Bedford Row
London WC1R 4LL ☎ 020 7831 0222
✉ clerks@42br.com
Call Date: May 1990, Inner Temple

Practising Areas: Chancery (Land Law), Commercial Property, Housing, Landlord & Tenant

KILLEEN MR ROBERT WILLIAM

Capital Fortune Chambers
Third Floor, 14 Nicholas Lane, London EC4N 7BN ☎ 0845 3630 430 ✉ rk@cfchambers.com
Call Date: Oct 1995, Middle Temple

KILVINGTON MISS SARAH ELIZABETH

18 St John Street
Manchester M3 4EA ☎0161 278 1800
✉clerks@18sjs.com
Call Date: Oct 1999, Middle Temple
Pupil Supervisor

Practising Areas: Care Proceedings, Chancery (Land Law), Equity, Wills & Trusts, Family, Family Provision

KIME MR MATTHEW JONATHAN

Ingenuity IP Chambers
Chambers Legal Service, 71b Queensway, Petts Wood, Kent BR5 1DQ
✉lp@chamberslegalservice.com
No. 3 Fleet Street Chambers
3 Fleet Street, London EC4Y 1DP
☎020 7936 4474 ✉clerks@3fleetstreet.com
Cobden House Chambers
19 Quay Street, Manchester M3 3HN
☎0161 833 6000 ✉Clerks@Cobden.co.uk
Call Date: Jul 1988, Middle Temple
Pupil Supervisor

Practising Areas: Commercial Litigation, Copyright, EC & Competition Law, Entertainment, Film, Cable & TV, Information Technology, Intellectual Property, International Trade, Patents, Telecommunications, Trademarks

KING MR ADAM HENRY PETER

QEB Hollis Whiteman
1-2 Laurence Pountney Hill, London EC4R 0EU ☎020 7933 8855 ✉barristers@qebhw.co.uk
Call Date: Nov 2005, Inner Temple

Practising Areas: Crime, Crime (Corporate/Fraud)

KING MR CHARLES GRANVILLE

Chambers of Mr C G King
6 All Saints Field, Stroud GL5 1NE
☎07949 461717 ✉ckingesq@yahoo.co.uk
Call Date: Nov 1995, Middle Temple

Practising Areas: Administrative, Commercial Litigation, Family, Family Provision, Housing, Insolvency, Landlord & Tenant

KING MS EMMA

2 Bedford Row
London WC1R 4BU ☎020 7440 8888
✉clerks@2bedfordrow.co.uk
Call Date: Nov 1999, Inner Temple

KING MR GELAGA PERRY

2 Bedford Row
London WC1R 4BU ☎020 7440 8888
✉clerks@2bedfordrow.co.uk
Call Date: Jul 1985, Gray's Inn
Pupil Supervisor

Practising Areas: Courts Martial, Crime, Crime (Corporate/Fraud), Private International, Regulatory Law, Sports

KING MR GRAHAM ANTHONY

1 Gray's Inn Square
Ground Floor, 1 Gray's Inn Square, London WC1R 5AA ☎020 7405 0001
Call Date: Jul 2007, Gray's Inn

Practising Areas: Common Law (General), Crime, Employment, Mental Health, Sports

KING MR JOHN PATRICK

Nine Bedford Row
9 Bedford Row, London WC1R 4AZ
☎020 7489 2727 ✉clerks@9bedfordrow.co.uk
Call Date: Jul 1983, Gray's Inn
Pupil Supervisor

Practising Areas: Civil Liberties, Crime, Crime (Corporate/Fraud), Human Rights, Regulatory Law

KING MISS SAMANTHA LEONIE

4 Paper Buildings
1st Floor, 4 Paper Buildings, Temple, London EC4Y 7EX ☎020 7427 5200 ✉clerks@4pb.com
Call Date: Nov 1990, Middle Temple

Practising Areas: Care Proceedings, Family

KINNEAR MISS ELISE

Field Court Chambers
5 Field Court, Gray's Inn, London WC1R 5EF
☎020 7405 6114 ✉clerks@fieldcourt.co.uk
Call Date: Oct 2003, Gray's Inn

Practising Areas: Children's Law, Family

KINNEAR MR JONATHAN SHEA QC (2012)

9-12 Bell Yard
London WC2A 2JR ☎020 7400 1800
✉clerks@9-12bellyard.com
Call Date: Oct 1994, Gray's Inn
Pupil Supervisor

Practising Areas: Crime, Crime (Corporate/Fraud), Regulatory Law, Sports, Tax (Capital & Income)

KIRBY MISS RUTH MARY ANTHONY

4 Paper Buildings
1st Floor, 4 Paper Buildings, Temple, London EC4Y 7EX ☎020 7427 5200 ✉clerks@4pb.com
Call Date: Oct 1994, Middle Temple
Pupil Supervisor

Practising Areas: Care Proceedings, Children's Law, Family, Family Provision

KIRK MR GRAEME CHARLES

One Essex Court
1st Floor, Temple, London EC4Y 9AR
☎020 7936 3030 ✉clerks@1ec.co.uk
Call Date: Nov 2001, Middle Temple

Practising Areas: Bankruptcy, Chancery (Land Law), Commercial Litigation, Commercial Property, Common Law (General), Employment, Land, Landlord & Tenant

KIRK MR THOMAS SEAN ROBINSON

12 College Place
Fauvelle Buildings, 12 College Place, Southampton SO15 2FE ☎023 8032 0320
✉clerks@12cp.co.uk
Call Date: Jul 2007, Lincoln's Inn

Practising Areas: Discrimination, Employment, Housing, Landlord & Tenant, Licensing, Personal Injury, Professional Negligence

KIRTLEY MR PAUL GEORGE

Exchange Chambers
Oxford House, Oxford Row, Leeds LS1 3BE
☎0113 203 1970
✉spencer@exchangechambers.co.uk
Exchange Chambers
One Derby Square, Derby Square, Liverpool L2 9XX ☎0151 236 7747
✉info@exchangechambers.co.uk
Littleton Chambers
3 King's Bench Walk North, Temple, London EC4Y 7HR ☎020 7797 8600
✉fschneider@littletonchambers.co.uk
Call Date: Jul 1982, Middle Temple
Pupil Supervisor, Recorder

Practising Areas: Discrimination, Employment, Medical Negligence, Personal Injury, Professional Negligence, Regulatory Law

KITCHEN MR SIMON DUGALD OWEN RALPH

Dyers Chambers
35 Bedford Row, London WC1R 4JH
☎020 7404 1881 ✉admin@dyerschambers.com
Call Date: Nov 1988, Lincoln's Inn

Practising Areas: Crime, Crime (Corporate/Fraud)

KITZING MISS SUSANNA LORAINE

Park Court Chambers
16 Park Place, Leeds LS1 2SJ
☎0113 243 3277
✉clerks@parkcourtchambers.co.uk
Call Date: Nov 2005, Middle Temple

Practising Areas: Chancery (General), Common Law (General), Landlord & Tenant, Personal Injury

KNIGHT MISS ADRIENNE

3 Temple Gardens
Lower Ground Floor, 3 Temple Gardens, Temple, London EC4Y 9AU ☎020 7353 3102
✉clerks@3tg.co.uk
Call Date: Jul 1981, Gray's Inn
Pupil Supervisor

KNIGHT MR BENJAMIN JAMES

Central Chambers
89 Princess Street, Manchester M1 4HT
☎0161 236 1133 ✉clerks@centralchambers.co.uk
Call Date: Jul 2004, Middle Temple

Practising Areas: Administrative, Civil Liberties, Common Law (General), Crime, Crime (Corporate/Fraud), Family, Human Rights, Information Technology, Intellectual Property, Licensing, Sports

KNIGHT MR GRAEME EDWARD VERDON

7 Bell Yard
London WC2A 2JR ☎020 7831 0636
✉kevintarrant@btconnect.com
The Barristers Chambers
Address withheld ☎07966 056368
✉gevknight@hotmail.com
Carmelite Chambers
9 Carmelite Street, London EC4Y 0DR
☎020 7936 6300
✉clerks@carmelitechambers.co.uk
Call Date: Oct 1999, Middle Temple
Pupil Supervisor

Practising Areas: Crime, Crime (Corporate/Fraud), Human Rights, Immigration, Licensing, Mental Health, Regulatory Law

KNIGHT MR KEITH LESLIE FRANCIS

4 King's Bench Walk
2nd Floor, 4 King's Bench Walk, Temple, London EC4Y 7DL ☎020 7822 7000
✉clerks@4kbw.co.uk
Call Date: Nov 1969, Gray's Inn
Pupil Supervisor

Practising Areas: Bankruptcy, Chancery (Land Law), Civil Litigation, Discrimination, Employment, Equity, Wills & Trusts, Landlord & Tenant, Medical Negligence, Personal Injury, Professional Negligence, Road Traffic And Highways, Sale & Carriage of Goods, Sports

KNOTTS MISS CAROL ELAINE

No5 Chambers
38 Queen Square, Bristol BS1 4QS
☎0845 210 5555
No5 Chambers
Greenwood House, 4-7 Salisbury Court, London EC4Y 8AA ☎0845 210 5555
No5 Chambers
Fountain Court, Steelhouse Lane, Birmingham B4 6DR ☎0845 210 5555 ✉info@no5.com
Call Date: Nov 1996, Inner Temple

KNOWLES MISS CATHERINE JULIA

Park Court Chambers
16 Park Place, Leeds LS1 2SJ
☎0113 243 3277
✉clerks@parkcourtchambers.co.uk
Call Date: Jul 2004, Middle Temple

KNOWLES MISS LINSEY

Albion Chambers
Broad Street, Bristol BS1 1DR
☎0117 927 2144 ✉clerks@albionchambers.co.uk
6 Pump Court
1st Floor, 6 Pump Court, Temple, London EC4Y 7AR ☎020 7797 8400
✉richardconstable@6pumpcourt.co.uk
6 Pump Court Chambers
6-8 Mill Street, Maidstone, Kent ME15 6XH
☎01622 688094 ✉annexe@6pumpcourt.co.uk
Call Date: Jul 2000, Lincoln's Inn

Practising Areas: Family

KNOWLES MR MARK DAVID

KCH Garden Square
1 Oxford Street, Nottingham NG1 5BH
☎0115 941 8851 ✉clerks@kchgardensquare.co.uk
Call Date: Nov 1989, Middle Temple
Pupil Supervisor

KNOX MR CHRISTOPHER JOHN

Trinity Chambers
The Custom House, 39 Quayside, Newcastle Upon Tyne NE1 3DE ☎0191 232 1927
✉info@trinitychambers.co.uk
Trinity Chambers
Multi Media Exchange, 72-80 Corporation Road, Middlesbrough TS1 2RF
☎01642 247569 ✉info@trinitychambers.co.uk
Call Date: Jul 1974, Inner Temple
Pupil Supervisor, Recorder

KOHLI MR RYAN SINGH

Cornerstone Barristers
2-3 Gray's Inn Square, Gray's Inn, London WC1R 5JH ☎020 7242 4986
✉chambers@2-3gis.co.uk
Call Date: Jul 2006, Inner Temple

Practising Areas: Administrative, Civil Liberties, Housing, Human Rights, Landlord & Tenant, Licensing, Local Government, Regulatory Law

KOLODYNSKI MR STEFAN RICHARD

St Philips Chambers
55 Temple Row, Birmingham B2 5LS
☎0121 246 7000 ✉clerks@st-philips.com
Call Date: Oct 1993, Lincoln's Inn

KOLVIN MR PHILIP ALAN QC (2009)

Cornerstone Barristers
2-3 Gray's Inn Square, Gray's Inn, London WC1R 5JH ☎020 7242 4986
✉chambers@2-3gis.co.uk
Kings Chambers
36 Young Street, Manchester M3 3FT
☎0845 034 3444 ✉clerks@kingschambers.com
Kings Chambers
5 Park Square East, Leeds LS1 2NE
☎0845 034 3444 ✉clerks@kingschambers.com
Call Date: Jul 1985, Inner Temple

Practising Areas: Licensing, Town & Country Planning

KORN MR ANTHONY HENRY

No5 Chambers
Greenwood House, 4-7 Salisbury Court, London EC4Y 8AA ☎0845 210 5555
No5 Chambers
38 Queen Square, Bristol BS1 4QS
☎0845 210 5555
No5 Chambers
Fountain Court, Steelhouse Lane, Birmingham B4 6DR ☎0845 210 5555 ✉info@no5.com
Call Date: Nov 1978, Gray's Inn

Practising Areas: Employment

KOTHARI MISS SIMA

Coram Chambers
9-11 Fulwood Place, London WC1V 6HG
☎020 7092 3700 ✉mail@coramchambers.co.uk
Call Date: Oct 1992, Gray's Inn
Pupil Supervisor

KRAMER MR PHILIP ANTHONY

Park Lane Plowden
Lombard House, 4-8 Lombard Street, Newcastle Upon Tyne NE1 3AE
☎0191 211 4087 ✉clerks@parklaneplowden.co.uk
Call Date: Jul 1982, Inner Temple
Pupil Supervisor, Recorder

Practising Areas: Administrative, Arbitration, Bankruptcy, Chancery (General), Chancery (Land Law), Civil Litigation, Commercial Litigation, Commercial Property, Common Law (General), Company & Commercial, Consumer, Coroners Inquests, Discrimination, Employment, Equity, Wills & Trusts, Family Provision, Housing, Human Rights, Industrial Diseases, Inquests, Insolvency, Insurance, Land, Landlord & Tenant, Licensing, Medical Negligence, Partnership, Personal Injury, Probate & Administration, Professional Negligence, Public Law, Sale & Carriage of Goods

KRAUSE MS FLORENCE

Meritz Chambers
PO Box 110, Hebben Bridge HX7 9AQ
☎0845 094 0856 ✉clerk@meritzchambers.co.uk
Call Date: Jul 1998, Lincoln's Inn
Pupil Supervisor

Practising Areas: Administrative, Civil Liberties, Common Law (General)

KREBS MR MICHAEL GORDON

Liverpool Civil Law
3rd Floor, 1 Old Hall Street, Liverpool L3 9HF
☎0151 242 0500 ✉clerks@liverpoolcivillaw.com
Call Date: Nov 1999, Gray's Inn

KRIKLER MR ALEXANDER RICHARD

4 Breams Buildings
Chancery Lane, London EC4A 1HP
☎020 7092 1900 ✉clerks@4bb.co.uk
Call Date: Nov 1995, Middle Temple

Practising Areas: Crime

KROLICK MR IVAN

Chambers of Mr Ami Feder
Ground Floor, Lamb Building, Temple, London EC4Y 7AS ☎020 7797 7788
✉clerks@lambbuilding.co.uk
Lamb Building
22 Ship Street, Brighton BN1 1AD
☎01273 820490 ✉admin@lambbuilding.co.uk
Chambers of Mr Ami Feder
Ground Floor, Lamb Building, Temple, London EC4Y 7AS ☎020 7797 7788
✉clerks@lambbuilding.co.uk
Call Date: Nov 1966, Gray's Inn
Pupil Supervisor

KRUSHNER MR DAMIAN MARK

Oakwood Chambers
46a Oakwood Court, London W14 8JY
☎07789 435485
Call Date: Nov 2001, Middle Temple

Practising Areas: Administrative, Common Law (General), Crime, Family, Immigration, Inquests

KURJI MS FATIM RAZAHUSEIN

No5 Chambers
Fountain Court, Steelhouse Lane, Birmingham B4 6DR ☎0845 210 5555 ✉info@no5.com
No5 Chambers
38 Queen Square, Bristol BS1 4QS
☎0845 210 5555
No5 Chambers
Greenwood House, 4-7 Salisbury Court, London EC4Y 8AA ☎0845 210 5555
Call Date: Jul 2003, Inner Temple

Practising Areas: Commercial Litigation, Employment

KWIATKOWSKI MR FELIKS JERZY

Kew Chambers
354 Kew Road, Kew, Surrey TW9 3DU
☎0844 8099991 ✉admin@kewchambers.co.uk
Call Date: Jul 1977, Middle Temple

Practising Areas: Civil Liberties, Commercial Litigation, Common Law (General), Discrimination, Employment, Foreign Law, Housing, Information Technology, Landlord & Tenant, Personal Injury, Private International, Professional Negligence, Sale & Carriage of Goods

KYNOCH MR DUNCAN STUART SANDERSON

Selborne Chambers
10 Essex Street, London WC2R 3AA
☎ 020 7420 9500
✉ clerks@selbornechambers.co.uk
Call Date: Nov 1994, Gray's Inn

Practising Areas: Bankruptcy, Chancery (General), Chancery (Land Law), Commercial Litigation, Commercial Property, Common Land, Common Law (General), Company & Commercial, Construction, Conveyancing, Equity, Wills & Trusts, Housing, Insolvency, Landlord & Tenant, Partnership, Probate & Administration, Professional Negligence, Sale & Carriage of Goods

LADENBURG MR GUY ALEXANDER

3 Raymond Buildings
3 Raymond Buildings, Gray's Inn, London WC1R 5BH ☎ 020 7400 6400
✉ clerks@3rblaw.com
Call Date: Nov 2000, Middle Temple

Practising Areas: Crime, Licensing

LAHIFFE MR MARTIN PATRICK JOSEPH

3 Temple Gardens
Lower Ground Floor, 3 Temple Gardens, Temple, London EC4Y 9AU ☎ 020 7353 3102
✉ clerks@3tg.co.uk
Call Date: Nov 1984, Middle Temple
Pupil Supervisor

Practising Areas: Administrative, Civil Liberties, Courts Martial, Crime, Crime (Corporate/Fraud), Entertainment, Human Rights, Regulatory Law, Sports

LAKE MR JAMES EDWARD

St Paul's Chambers
5th Floor, St Paul's House, 23 Park Square South, Leeds LS1 2ND ☎ 0113 245 5866
Call Date: Oct 2005, Inner Temple

Practising Areas: Crime, Crime (Corporate/Fraud), Regulatory Law

LAKHA MR ABBAS QC (2003)

Nine Bedford Row
9 Bedford Row, London WC1R 4AZ
☎ 020 7489 2727 ✉ clerks@9bedfordrow.co.uk
Call Date: Nov 1984, Inner Temple

Practising Areas: Crime, Regulatory Law

LAKHA MR SHABBIR

Farrar's Building
Farrar's Building, Temple, London EC4Y 7BD
☎ 020 7583 9241
✉ Chambers@farrarsbuilding.co.uk
Call Date: Jul 1989, Lincoln's Inn

Practising Areas: Common Law (General), Discrimination, Employment

LAKIN MISS TRACY

St Ive's Chambers
Whittall Street, Birmingham B4 6DH
☎ 0121 236 0863 ✉ clerks@stiveschambers.co.uk
Call Date: Oct 1993, Inner Temple

LAL MR SANJAY

4 King's Bench Walk
2nd Floor, 4 King's Bench Walk, Temple, London EC4Y 7DL ☎ 020 7822 7000
✉ clerks@4kbw.co.uk
Call Date: Oct 1993, Lincoln's Inn

Practising Areas: Administrative, Civil Liberties, Human Rights, Immigration, Mental Health, Regulatory Law, Sports

LALL MR TARLOCHAN

Monckton Chambers
1 & 2 Raymond Buildings, Gray's Inn, London WC1R 5NR ☎ 020 7405 7211
✉ chambers@monckton.com
Call Date: Nov 2010, Middle Temple

Practising Areas: Share Options, Tax (Capital & Income), Tax (Corporate)

LALLY MR HARBINDER SINGH

No5 Chambers
Fountain Court, Steelhouse Lane, Birmingham B4 6DR ☎ 0845 210 5555 ✉ info@no5.com
No5 Chambers
Greenwood House, 4-7 Salisbury Court, London EC4Y 8AA ☎ 0845 210 5555
No5 Chambers
38 Queen Square, Bristol BS1 4QS
☎ 0845 210 5555
Call Date: Oct 1997, Lincoln's Inn

LALLY MR JONATHAN MARTIN

Deans Court Chambers
24 St John Street, Manchester M3 4DF
☎ 0161 214 6000 ✉ clerks@deanscourt.co.uk
Deans Court Chambers
101 Walker Street, Preston PR1 2RR
☎ 01772 565 600 ✉ preston@deanscourt.co.uk
Call Date: Oct 2005, Inner Temple

LAM MR CHUEN FAT

Chambers of Martin Burr
15 Old Bailey, London EC4M 7EF
☎ 0845 123 1234 ✉ clerks@barristerweb.com
Call Date: Nov 1994, Lincoln's Inn

Practising Areas: Common Law (General), Employment, Housing

LAMB MR EDWARD CHARLES

The Chambers of Grahame Aldous QC
9 Gough Square, London EC4A 3DG
☎ 020 7832 0500 ✉ clerks@9goughsquare.co.uk
Call Date: Oct 2006, Lincoln's Inn

Practising Areas: Employment, Family Provision, Professional Negligence

LAMB MR JEFFREY THOMAS

Westgate Chambers
64 High Street, Lewes, East Sussex BN7 1XG
☎ 01273 480510
✉ clerks@westgate-chambers.co.uk
Call Date: Oct 1992, Middle Temple
Pupil Supervisor

Practising Areas: Commercial Litigation, Company & Commercial, Construction, Courts Martial, Crime, Crime (Corporate/Fraud), Defamation, Employment, Entertainment, Film, Cable & TV, Housing, Landlord & Tenant, Pensions, Personal Injury, Sports

LAMB MR JOHN RICHARD

1 Pump Court
Elm Court, Temple, London EC4Y 7AB
☎ 020 7842 7070 ✉ (name)@pumpcourt.co.uk
Call Date: May 1990, Middle Temple
Pupil Supervisor

Practising Areas: Crime, Crime (Corporate/Fraud)

LAMBERT MRS ALISON JANET

Trinity Chambers
Highfield House, Moulsham Street, Chelmsford, Essex CM2 9AH
☎ 01245 605040 ✉ clerks@trinitychambers.com
Call Date: Jul 2005, Middle Temple

Practising Areas: Common Law (General), Landlord & Tenant, Local Government, Regulatory Law

C

LAMBERT MISS JANE ELIZABETH

NIPC
Kirklees Media Centre, 7 Northumberland Street, Huddersfield HD1 1RL
☎ 0800 862 0055 ✉ jill.hayfield@nipclaw.com
Call Date: Jul 1977, Lincoln's Inn
Pupil Supervisor

Practising Areas: Competition, Copyright, EC & Competition Law, Entertainment, Information Technology, Intellectual Property, Patents, Telecommunications, Trademarks

LAMBERT MR NIGEL ROBERT WOOLF QC (1999)

Carmelite Chambers
9 Carmelite Street, London EC4Y 0DR
☎ 020 7936 6300
✉ clerks@carmelitechambers.co.uk
Call Date: Nov 1974, Gray's Inn
Recorder

Practising Areas: Courts Martial, Crime, Crime (Corporate/Fraud)

LAMONT MR CALUM

Keating Chambers
15 Essex Street, London WC2R 3AA
☎ 020 7544 2600 ✉ clerks@keatingchambers.com
Call Date: Oct 2004, Inner Temple
Pupil Supervisor

Practising Areas: Arbitration, Commercial Litigation, Construction, Professional Negligence

LAMS MR BARNABAS JEFFREY

4 Brick Court
4 Brick Court, Temple, London EC4Y 9AD
☎ 020 7832 3200 ✉ clerks@4bc.co.uk
Call Date: Oct 1995, Gray's Inn

Practising Areas: Human Rights, Immigration

LANCHESTER MR MARTIN JOHN

Guildhall Chambers
23 Broad Street, Bristol BS1 2HG
☎ 0117 930 9000 ✉ hoc@guildhallchambers.co.uk
Call Date: Nov 2001, Middle Temple

LANE MR CHRISTOPHER PAUL

No 8 Chambers
8 Fountain Court, Steelhouse Lane, Birmingham B4 6DR ☎ 0121 236 5514
✉ clerks@no8chambers.co.uk
Call Date: Oct 2002, Lincoln's Inn

Practising Areas: Bankruptcy, Commercial Property, Common Law (General), Discrimination, Health & Safety, Housing, Human Rights,

Immigration, Landlord & Tenant, Mental Health, Personal Injury, Sale & Carriage of Goods

LANE MS LINDSAY RUTH BUSFIELD

8 New Square
8 New Square, Lincoln's Inn, London WC2A 3QP ☎ 020 7405 4321 ✉ clerks@8newsquare.co.uk
Call Date: Oct 1996, Middle Temple

Practising Areas: Competition, Copyright, EC & Competition Law, Entertainment, Film, Cable & TV, Franchising, Information Technology, Intellectual Property, Patents, Sports, Telecommunications, Trademarks

LANE MR MICHAEL JOHN

East Anglian Chambers
53 North Hill, Colchester, Essex CO1 1QA ☎ 01473 214481 ✉ colchester@ealaw.co.uk
East Anglian Chambers
Gresham House, 5 Museum Street, Ipswich, Suffolk IP1 1HQ ☎ 01473 214481 ✉ ipswich@ealaw.co.uk
East Anglian Chambers
15 The Close, Norwich, Norfolk NR1 4DZ ☎ 01473 214481 ✉ norwich@ealaw.co.uk
Call Date: Jul 1983, Middle Temple
Pupil Supervisor

Practising Areas: Common Law (General), Discrimination, Education, Employment, Local Government, Town & Country Planning

LANE MISS RACHAEL CAROLINE

2 King's Bench Walk
2 King's Bench Walk, Temple, London EC4Y 7DE ☎ 020 7353 1746 ✉ clerks@2kbw.com
Call Date: Nov 2002, Lincoln's Inn

Practising Areas: Common Law (General), Crime

LANE MR SIMON CHARLES

Rougemont Chambers
Victory House, Dean Clarke Gardens, Southernhay East, Exeter EX2 4AA ☎ 01392 208484 ✉ clerks@rougemontchambers.co.uk
Call Date: Jul 2002, Inner Temple

Practising Areas: Bankruptcy, Chancery (General), Chancery (Land Law), Civil Litigation, Commercial Litigation, Commercial Property, Common Law (General), Construction, Conveyancing, Costs, Equity, Wills & Trusts, Family Provision, Housing, Insolvency, Land, Partnership, Professional Negligence, Sale & Carriage of Goods, Town & Country Planning

LANGEVAD MISS CLAIRE THERESA MANUELA

Chambers of Marion Smullen and Kerim Fuad QC
1 Inner Temple Lane, London EC4Y 1AF ☎ 020 7427 4400 ✉ clerks@1itl.com
Call Date: Oct 2005, Lincoln's Inn

Practising Areas: Crime

LANGFORD MISS SARAH MARGARET

3 PB Barristers
3 Paper Buildings, Temple, London EC4Y 7EU ☎ 020 7583 8055
3 PB Barristers
30 Christchurch Road, Bournemouth, Dorset BH1 3PD ☎ 01202 292102 ✉ clerks.bournemouth@3paper.co.uk
3 PB Barristers
4 St Peter Street, Winchester SO23 8BW ☎ 01962 868884 ✉ clerks.winchester@3paper.co.uk
3 PB Barristers
Royal Talbot House, 2 Victoria Street, Bristol, Avon BS1 6BB ☎ 0117 928 1520
3 PB Barristers
23 Beaumont Street, Oxford OX1 2NP ☎ 01865 793 736
Call Date: Jul 2005, Gray's Inn

LANGLEY MR CHARLES HOWARD

2 Bedford Row
London WC1R 4BU ☎ 020 7440 8888 ✉ clerks@2bedfordrow.co.uk
Call Date: Nov 1999, Middle Temple
Pupil Supervisor

Practising Areas: Crime, Crime (Corporate/Fraud), Immigration, Sports

LANGRIDGE MS NICOLA DAWN

Coram Chambers
9-11 Fulwood Place, London WC1V 6HG ☎ 020 7092 3700 ✉ mail@coramchambers.co.uk
Call Date: Nov 1993, Lincoln's Inn
Pupil Supervisor

LANSON MISS LAUREN ELIZABETH

1 Gray's Inn Square
Ground Floor, 1 Gray's Inn Square, London WC1R 5AA ☎ 020 7405 0001
Call Date: Nov 2006, Middle Temple

Practising Areas: Common Law (General), Employment, Family

LARIZADEH MR CYRUS RAIS

4 Paper Buildings
1st Floor, 4 Paper Buildings, Temple, London EC4Y 7EX ☎020 7427 5200 ✉clerks@4pb.com
Call Date: Nov 1992, Inner Temple
Pupil Supervisor

Practising Areas: Care Proceedings, Family

LARKIN MR SEAN QC (2010)

QEB Hollis Whiteman
1-2 Laurence Pountney Hill, London EC4R 0EU ☎020 7933 8855 ✉barristers@qebhw.co.uk
Call Date: Jul 1987, Inner Temple
Pupil Supervisor

Practising Areas: Crime, Crime (Corporate/Fraud), Health & Safety, Regulatory Law

LASK MR BENJAMIN BELA DAVID

Monckton Chambers
1 & 2 Raymond Buildings, Gray's Inn, London WC1R 5NR ☎020 7405 7211
✉chambers@monckton.com
Call Date: Nov 2003, Middle Temple

LASKER MR JEREMY STEWART

Lincoln House Chambers
Tower 12, The Avenue North, Spinningfields, 18-22 Bridge Street, Manchester M3 3BZ
☎0161 832 5701
✉info@lincolnhousechambers.com
Call Date: Jul 1976, Inner Temple
Pupil Supervisor, Recorder

Practising Areas: Crime, Crime (Corporate/Fraud)

C

LASOK MR KAROL PAUL EDWARD QC (1994)

Monckton Chambers
1 & 2 Raymond Buildings, Gray's Inn, London WC1R 5NR ☎020 7405 7211
✉chambers@monckton.com
Call Date: Jul 1977, Middle Temple
Recorder

LATYMER MR TAM

Chambers of Tam Latymer
144/145 Temple Chambers, Temple Avenue, London EC4Y 0DA ☎020 7353 2795
✉tlatymer@hotmail.com
Call Date: Nov 1998, Lincoln's Inn

Practising Areas: Company & Commercial, Crime, Private International

LAU MISS VANESSA HOI CHUN

18 St John Street
Manchester M3 4EA ☎0161 278 1800
✉clerks@18sjs.com
Call Date: Mar 2005, Middle Temple

Practising Areas: Care Proceedings, Crime, Family

LAUGHLAND MR JAMES RUSSELL

Temple Garden Chambers
1 Harcourt Buildings, Temple, London EC4Y 9DA ☎020 7583 1315 ✉clerks@tgchambers.com
Call Date: Nov 1991, Inner Temple
Pupil Supervisor

Practising Areas: Common Law (General), Personal Injury

LAVIN MISS MARY MANDIE JANE

196 Temple Chamber
3-7 Temple Avenue, London EC4Y 0HP
☎020 7099 9257
✉davidsimpson@lawandregulation.com
Call Date: Oct 1993, Middle Temple

Practising Areas: Common Law (General), Education, Financial Services, Healthcare, Medical Negligence, Professional Negligence, Regulatory Law

LAVY DR MATTHEW MONTAGUE

4 Pump Court
4 Pump Court, Temple, London EC4Y 7AN
☎020 7842 5555 ✉chambers@4pumpcourt.com
Call Date: Jul 2004, Lincoln's Inn

LAW MR JOHN EDWARD

The Chambers of Grahame Aldous QC
9 Gough Square, London EC4A 3DG
☎020 7832 0500 ✉clerks@9goughsquare.co.uk
Call Date: Oct 1996, Lincoln's Inn

Practising Areas: Chancery (Land Law), Commercial Litigation, Commercial Property, Common Law (General), Employment, Landlord & Tenant, Licensing

LAWRENCE MISS ANNE MARY

Atlas Chambers
3 Field Court, Gray's Inn, London WC1R 5EP
☎020 7269 7980 ✉clerks@atlaschambers.com
Call Date: Jul 2003, Lincoln's Inn

Practising Areas: Common Law (General), Education, Employment, Housing

LAWRENCE MR BENJAMIN RICHARD

St Johns Buildings
24a - 28 St John Street, Manchester M3 4DJ
☎ 0161 214 1500 ✉ clerk@stjohnsbuildings.co.uk
16 Winckley Square
Preston PR1 3JJ ☎ 01772 256100
St Johns Buildings Liverpool
8th Floor India Buildings, Water Street, Liverpool L2 0XG ☎ 0151 243 6000
✉ clerk@stjohnsbuildings.co.uk
Call Date: Mar 2003, Lincoln's Inn

LAWRENCE DR HEATHER BUNTING ELIZABETH

11 South Square
1st Floor, 11 South Square, Gray's Inn, London WC1R 5EY ☎ 020 7405 1222
✉ clerks@11southsquare.com
Call Date: Oct 1990, Middle Temple
Pupil Supervisor

Practising Areas: Copyright, Entertainment, Information Technology, Intellectual Property, Licensing, Patents, Trademarks

LAWRENCE SIR IVAN JOHN QC (1981)

5 Pump Court
Ground Floor, 5 Pump Court, Temple, London EC4Y 7AP ☎ 020 7353 2532
✉ clerks@5pumpcourt.com
Call Date: Feb 1962, Inner Temple

Practising Areas: Courts Martial, Crime, Crime (Corporate/Fraud), Financial Services, Human Rights, Licensing, Regulatory Law

LAWRENCE MISS PAMELA AVRIL

Nexus Chambers
7 New Square, Lincolns Inn, London WC2A 3QS ☎ 020 7404 1147 / 020 7831 8309
✉ info@nexuschambers.com
Call Date: Nov 1975, Inner Temple
Pupil Supervisor

Practising Areas: Family, Family Provision, Housing, Landlord & Tenant, Personal Injury

LAWRENCE THE HON PATRICK JOHN TRISTRAM QC (2002)

Four New Square
Four New Square, Lincoln's Inn, London WC2A 3RJ ☎ 020 7822 2000
✉ barristers@4newsquare.com
Call Date: Feb 1985, Inner Temple

Practising Areas: Insurance, Professional Negligence, Sports

LAWRENCE MISS SAMANTHA DIONNE

3 Dr Johnson's Buildings
Ground Floor, 3 Dr Johnson's Buildings, Temple, London EC4Y 7BA ☎ 020 7353 4854
✉ clerks@3djb.co.uk
Call Date: Jul 2005, Inner Temple

Practising Areas: Family, Immigration, Public Law

LAWRENSON MRS MARY CHRISTINE

Farringdon Chambers
180 Bermondsey Street, London SE1 3TQ
☎ 020 7089 5700
Call Date: Nov 1994, Lincoln's Inn

LAWSON MR ANDREW CHARLES

St Johns Buildings
24a - 28 St John Street, Manchester M3 4DJ
☎ 0161 214 1500 ✉ clerk@stjohnsbuildings.co.uk
16 Winckley Square
Preston PR1 3JJ ☎ 01772 256100
St Johns Buildings Liverpool
8th Floor India Buildings, Water Street, Liverpool L2 0XG ☎ 0151 243 6000
✉ clerk@stjohnsbuildings.co.uk
Call Date: Oct 1995, Inner Temple
Pupil Supervisor

Practising Areas: Personal Injury

LAWTON MR PAUL ANTHONY

Lincoln House Chambers
Tower 12, The Avenue North, Spinningfields, 18-22 Bridge Street, Manchester M3 3BZ
☎ 0161 832 5701
✉ info@lincolnhousechambers.com
18 Red Lion Court
London EC4A 3EB ☎ 020 7520 6000
✉ chambers@18rlc.co.uk
Call Date: Nov 1987, Lincoln's Inn
Pupil Supervisor, Recorder

Practising Areas: Courts Martial, Crime, Crime (Corporate/Fraud), Regulatory Law

LE FEVRE MISS SARAH MARGARET

3 Raymond Buildings
3 Raymond Buildings, Gray's Inn, London WC1R 5BH ☎ 020 7400 6400
✉ clerks@3rblaw.com
Call Date: Jul 2001, Lincoln's Inn

Practising Areas: Crime, Crime (Corporate/Fraud), Environment, Health & Safety, Licensing, Regulatory Law, Trademarks

LE FORT MR MICHAEL CAMERON RAOUL

King's Bench Chambers
Wellington House, 175 Holdenhurst Road, Bournemouth, Dorset BH8 8DQ
☎01202 250025
Call Date: Oct 2000, Middle Temple

Practising Areas: Care Proceedings, Common Law (General), Courts Martial, Crime, Family, Family Provision

LE POIDEVIN MR NICHOLAS PETER QC (2010)

New Square Chambers
12 New Square, Lincoln's Inn, London WC2A 3SW ☎020 7419 8000 ✉robin.hollington@newsquarechambers.co.uk
Call Date: Nov 1975, Middle Temple
Pupil Supervisor

Practising Areas: Chancery (General), Chancery (Land Law), Common Land, Ecclesiastical, Equity, Wills & Trusts, Partnership, Private International, Probate & Administration, Professional Negligence

LE QUESNE MS CATHERINE MARY

3 Dr Johnson's Buildings
Ground Floor, 3 Dr Johnson's Buildings, Temple, London EC4Y 7BA ☎020 7353 4854
✉clerks@3djb.co.uk
Call Date: Nov 1993, Inner Temple

LEABEATER MR JAMES FERGUSON

4 Pump Court
4 Pump Court, Temple, London EC4Y 7AN
☎020 7842 5555 ✉chambers@4pumpcourt.com
Call Date: Oct 1999, Lincoln's Inn
Pupil Supervisor

Practising Areas: Arbitration, Commercial Litigation, Construction, Insurance/Reinsurance, Professional Negligence, Sale & Carriage of Goods, Shipping/Admiralty

LEACH MR DOUGLAS COLIN

Guildhall Chambers
23 Broad Street, Bristol BS1 2HG
☎0117 930 9000 ✉hoc@guildhallchambers.co.uk
Call Date: Oct 2003, Inner Temple

Practising Areas: Employment

LEACH MR STUART ANDREW WARWICK

Pump Court Chambers
5 Temple Chambers, Temple Street, Swindon SN1 1SQ ☎01793 539899
✉clerks@3pumpcourt.com
Pump Court Chambers
Upper Ground Floor, 3 Pump Court, Temple, London EC4Y 7AJ ☎020 7353 0711
✉clerks@3pumpcourt.com
Pump Court Chambers
31 Southgate Street, Winchester, Hampshire SO23 9EB ☎01962 868 161
✉clerks@3pumpcourt.com
Call Date: Jul 2004, Gray's Inn

LEADER MR TIMOTHY JAMES

Clerksroom (Taunton)
Equity House, Administration Centre, Blackbrook Park Avenue, Taunton, Somerset TA1 2PX ☎0845 083 3000
✉mail@clerksroom.com
64 Bridge Street
3rd Floor, 64 Bridge Street, Manchester M3 3BN ☎0845 083 3000
✉mail@64bridgestreet.com
Clerksroom (London)
3rd Floor, 218 Strand, London WC2R 1AT
☎0845 083 3000 ✉mail@clerksroom.com
Call Date: Oct 1994, Middle Temple
Pupil Supervisor

LEAKE MR LABAN PHILIP

Furnival Chambers
32 Furnival Street, London EC4A 1JQ
☎020 7405 3232
Call Date: Oct 1996, Middle Temple

LEAKE MR STEPHEN

Carmelite Chambers
9 Carmelite Street, London EC4Y 0DR
☎020 7936 6300
✉clerks@carmelitechambers.co.uk
Call Date: Mar 2002, Middle Temple

Practising Areas: Civil Liberties, Courts Martial, Crime, Crime (Corporate/Fraud), Regulatory Law

LEAR MISS ESTELLE CHRISTINE

Tanfield Chambers
2-5 Warwick Court, London WC1R 5DJ
☎020 7421 5300 ✉clerks@tanfieldchambers.co.uk
Call Date: Jul 2006, Lincoln's Inn

Practising Areas: Family

LEARMONTH MR ALEXANDER ROBERT MAGNUS

New Square Chambers
12 New Square, Lincoln's Inn, London WC2A 3SW ☎020 7419 8000 ✉robin.hollington@newsquarechambers.co.uk
Call Date: Oct 2000, Lincoln's Inn
Pupil Supervisor

Practising Areas: Bankruptcy, Chancery (General), Chancery (Land Law), Equity, Wills & Trusts, Family Provision, Mental Health, Probate & Administration

LEDWARD MISS JOCELYN VICTORIA

QEB Hollis Whiteman
1-2 Laurence Pountney Hill, London EC4R 0EU ☎020 7933 8855 ✉barristers@qebhw.co.uk
Call Date: Nov 1999, Middle Temple
Pupil Supervisor

Practising Areas: Crime, Crime (Corporate/Fraud), Regulatory Law

LEE MR DAVID CHARLES

36 Bedford Row
London WC1R 4JH ☎020 7421 8000 ✉chambers@36bedfordrow.co.uk
Call Date: Jul 1973, Gray's Inn
Pupil Supervisor

LEE MISS KRISTA CHUI LAN

Keating Chambers
15 Essex Street, London WC2R 3AA ☎020 7544 2600 ✉clerks@keatingchambers.com
Call Date: Nov 1996, Lincoln's Inn
Pupil Supervisor

Practising Areas: Arbitration, Chancery (General), Commercial Litigation, Company & Commercial, Construction, Insolvency, Insurance, Professional Negligence

LEE MR ROSSLYN ALEXANDER

Dere Street Barristers
14 Toft Green, York YO1 6JT ☎0844 3351551 ✉clerks@derestreet.co.uk
York Chambers
Rotterdam House, 116 The Quayside, Newcastle Upon Tyne NE1 3DY ☎0191 206 4677
Call Date: Nov 1987, Gray's Inn

Practising Areas: Care Proceedings, Commercial Litigation, Education, Landlord & Tenant, Personal Injury

LEE MISS TARYN JANE QC (2012)

37 Park Square Chambers
37 Park Square, Leeds LS1 2NY ☎0113 243 9422 ✉chambers@no37.co.uk
Call Date: Jul 1992, Inner Temple
Pupil Supervisor, Recorder

Practising Areas: Care Proceedings, Education, Family, Family Provision, Mental Health

LEEPER MR THOMAS RICHARD GEOFFREY

St John's Chambers
101 Victoria Street, Bristol BS1 6PU ☎0117 923 4700 ✉clerks@stjohnschambers.co.uk
Outer Temple Chambers
The Outer Temple, 222 Strand, London WC2R 1BA ☎020 7353 6381 ✉clerks@outertemple.com
Call Date: Nov 1991, Middle Temple

LEGARD MR EDWARD THOMAS

Dere Street Barristers
14 Toft Green, York YO1 6JT ☎0844 3351551 ✉clerks@derestreet.co.uk
York Chambers
Rotterdam House, 116 The Quayside, Newcastle Upon Tyne NE1 3DY ☎0191 206 4677
Call Date: Oct 1996, Gray's Inn

LEIGH MR KEVIN

No5 Chambers
Greenwood House, 4-7 Salisbury Court, London EC4Y 8AA ☎0845 210 5555
No5 Chambers
38 Queen Square, Bristol BS1 4QS ☎0845 210 5555
No5 Chambers
Fountain Court, Steelhouse Lane, Birmingham B4 6DR ☎0845 210 5555 ✉info@no5.com
Call Date: Jul 1986, Lincoln's Inn
Pupil Supervisor

Practising Areas: Administrative, Chancery (Land Law), Licensing, Town & Country Planning

LEIGHTON MR PETER LEONARD

4 King's Bench Walk
2nd Floor, 4 King's Bench Walk, Temple, London EC4Y 7DL ☎020 7822 7000 ✉clerks@4kbw.co.uk
Call Date: Jul 1966, Inner Temple
Pupil Supervisor

Practising Areas: Landlord & Tenant

C

LEMER MR DAVID JAMES

Doughty Street Chambers
53-54 Doughty Street, London WC1N 2LS
☎ 020 7404 1313 ✉ enquiries@doughtystreet.co.uk
Call Date: Oct 2000, Middle Temple

Practising Areas: Civil Liberties, Common Law (General), Employment, Human Rights, Immigration

LEMON MISS JANE KATHERINE

Keating Chambers
15 Essex Street, London WC2R 3AA
☎ 020 7544 2600 ✉ clerks@keatingchambers.com
Call Date: Nov 1993, Inner Temple
Pupil Supervisor

Practising Areas: Arbitration, Construction, Professional Negligence

LENAGHAN MR ANTHONY

Dyers Chambers
35 Bedford Row, London WC1R 4JH
☎ 020 7404 1881 ✉ admin@dyerschambers.com
Call Date: Nov 1996, Middle Temple

Practising Areas: Care Proceedings, Civil Liberties, Common Law (General), Company & Commercial, Crime, Crime (Corporate/Fraud), Defamation, Employment, Entertainment, Family, Film, Cable & TV, Human Rights, Immigration, Information Technology, Licensing, Local Government, Mental Health, Personal Injury

LENNARD MR STEPHEN CHARLES

Hardwicke
New Square, Lincoln's Inn, London WC2A 3SB ☎ 020 7242 2523
✉ enquiries@hardwicke.co.uk
Call Date: Jul 1976, Gray's Inn
Pupil Supervisor

Practising Areas: Banking, Chancery (General), Chancery (Land Law), Commercial Litigation, Common Law (General), Company & Commercial, Discrimination, Employment, Professional Negligence, Sale & Carriage of Goods, Sports

LENNON MR JOHN FRANCIS

23 Essex Street
London WC2R 3AA ☎ 020 7413 0353
✉ clerks@23es.com
Call Date: Mar 1997, Lincoln's Inn
Pupil Supervisor

Practising Areas: Crime, Crime (Corporate/Fraud), Regulatory Law

LENON MR ANDREW RALPH FITZMAURICE QC (2006)

One Essex Court
Ground Floor, One Essex Court, Temple, London EC4Y 9AR ☎ 020 7583 2000
✉ clerks@oeclaw.co.uk
Call Date: Nov 1982, Lincoln's Inn

Practising Areas: Arbitration, Banking, Commercial Litigation, Company & Commercial, Energy, Financial Services, Insurance/Reinsurance, International Trade, Partnership, Pensions, Private International, Professional Negligence, Sale & Carriage of Goods

LEON MR MARC EDWARD

Chambers of Marc E. Leon Esq.
Suite 526, 275 Deansgate, Manchester M3 4EL ☎ 07875 340598 ✉ marc@eleon.fsnet.co.uk
Call Date: May 1988, Middle Temple

LEONARD MR CHARLES ROBERT WESTON

Hardwicke
New Square, Lincoln's Inn, London WC2A 3SB ☎ 020 7242 2523
✉ enquiries@hardwicke.co.uk
Call Date: Jul 1976, Inner Temple
Pupil Supervisor

Practising Areas: Ancillary Relief, Bankruptcy, Chancery (General), Chancery (Land Law), Commercial Litigation, Common Law (General), Equity, Wills & Trusts, Insolvency, Landlord & Tenant, Partnership, Professional Negligence

LEONARD MR JAMES ALEXANDER

Outer Temple Chambers
The Outer Temple, 222 Strand, London WC2R 1BA ☎ 020 7353 6381
✉ clerks@outertemple.com
Call Date: Nov 1989, Inner Temple
Pupil Supervisor

Practising Areas: Administrative, Common Law (General), Courts Martial, Crime, Crime (Corporate/Fraud), Financial Services, Health & Safety, Regulatory Law

LESLIE MISS MARIE RITA

Albion Chambers
Broad Street, Bristol BS1 1DR
☎ 0117 927 2144 ✉ clerks@albionchambers.co.uk
Call Date: Mar 2000, Inner Temple

Practising Areas: Chancery (Land Law), Family Provision, Probate & Administration

LESLIE MR STEPHEN WINDSOR QC (1993)

Furnival Chambers
32 Furnival Street, London EC4A 1JQ
☎ 020 7405 3232
Cobden House Chambers
19 Quay Street, Manchester M3 3HN
☎ 0161 833 6000 ✉ Clerks@Cobden.co.uk
Call Date: Feb 1971, Lincoln's Inn

Practising Areas: Banking

LEVETT MISS FRANCESCA ANNA

Five St Andrew's Hill
5 St Andrew's Hill, London EC4V 5BZ
☎ 020 7332 5400 ✉ Clerks@5sah.co.uk
Call Date: Oct 1997, Lincoln's Inn

Practising Areas: Copyright, Crime, Crime (Corporate/Fraud), Education, Employment, Health & Safety, Intellectual Property, Licensing, Local Government, Regulatory Law, Town & Country Planning, Trademarks

LEVINE MR STEVEN ADRIAN

Palmyra Chambers
Royal House, 46 Legh Street, Warrington WA1 1UJ ☎ 01925 444919
✉ clerk@palmyrachambers.com
Call Date: Nov 1989, Lincoln's Inn

LEVINSON MISS JEMMA

1 Mitre Court Buildings
1 Mitre Court Buildings, Temple, London EC4Y 7BS ☎ 020 7452 8900 ✉ clerks@1mcb.com
Call Date: Nov 2001, Gray's Inn

Practising Areas: Administrative, Civil Liberties, Crime, Human Rights

LEVY MISS JULIETTE

Selborne Chambers
10 Essex Street, London WC2R 3AA
☎ 020 7420 9500
✉ clerks@selbornechambers.co.uk
Call Date: Nov 1992, Middle Temple
Pupil Supervisor

Practising Areas: Chancery (General), Commercial Litigation, Telecommunications

LEVY MR NEIL HOWARD

Guildhall Chambers
23 Broad Street, Bristol BS1 2HG
☎ 0117 930 9000 ✉ hoc@guildhallchambers.co.uk
Guildhall Chambers
5-8 Broad Street, Bristol BS1 2HW
☎ 0117 930 9000
Call Date: Jul 1986, Lincoln's Inn
Pupil Supervisor

LEVY MR ROBERT STUART QC (2010)

XXIV Old Buildings
Ground Floor, 24 Old Buildings, Lincoln's Inn, London WC2A 3UP ☎ 020 7691 2424
✉ clerks@xxiv.co.uk
Queen Square Chambers
56 Queen Square, Bristol BS1 4PR
☎ 0117 921 1966 ✉ crime@qs-c.co.uk
Call Date: Nov 1988, Middle Temple
Pupil Supervisor

LEWIECKI MISS MARIE

Old Bailey Chambers
15 Old Bailey, London EC4M 7EF
☎ 020 3008 6404
✉ clerks@15oldbaileychambers.com
Call Date: Nov 2006, Middle Temple

Practising Areas: Administrative, Arbitration, Bankruptcy, Civil Liberties, Common Law (General), Company & Commercial, Corporate Finance, Courts Martial, Crime, Crime (Corporate/Fraud), Employment, Financial Services, Foreign Law, Health & Safety, Human Rights, Insolvency, Licensing, Local Government, Parliamentary, Partnership, Private International, Public International, Regulatory Law, Tax (Capital & Income), Tax (Corporate)

LEWINGTON MISS FRANCESCA ANNA

Crown Office Row Chambers
119 Church Street, Brighton, Sussex BN1 1UD ☎ 01273 625625 ✉ clerks@1cor.com
Call Date: Nov 2001, Inner Temple

Practising Areas: Common Law (General), Crime, Crime (Corporate/Fraud), Regulatory Law

LEWIS MR ANDREW SIMON

4 Breams Buildings
Chancery Lane, London EC4A 1HP
☎ 020 7092 1900 ✉ clerks@4bb.co.uk
Call Date: Nov 1986, Middle Temple
Pupil Supervisor

Practising Areas: Courts Martial, Crime, Mental Health

LEWIS MR DARREN EURWYN

St John's Chambers
101 Victoria Street, Bristol BS1 6PU
☎ 0117 923 4700 ✉ clerks@stjohnschambers.co.uk
Call Date: Oct 2004, Inner Temple

LEWIS MR DOMINIC

Five Paper Buildings
1st Floor, Five Paper Buildings, Temple, London EC4Y 7HB ☎020 7583 6117
✉clerks@5pb.co.uk
Call Date: Jul 2000, Inner Temple
Pupil Supervisor

Practising Areas: Administrative, Civil Liberties, Courts Martial, Financial Services, Human Rights, Intellectual Property, Regulatory Law

LEWIS MR JAMES THOMAS QC (2002)

3 Raymond Buildings
3 Raymond Buildings, Gray's Inn, London WC1R 5BH ☎020 7400 6400
✉clerks@3rblaw.com
Call Date: Jul 1987, Gray's Inn
Pupil Supervisor, Recorder

LEWIS MR JONATHAN SIMON

Henderson Chambers
2 Harcourt Buildings, Temple, London EC4Y 9DB ☎020 7583 9020
✉clerks@hendersonchambers.co.uk
Call Date: Nov 2007, Middle Temple

Practising Areas: Commercial Litigation, Common Law (General), Regulatory Law

LEWIS MR MEYRIC

Francis Taylor Building
Inner Temple, London EC4Y 7BY
☎020 7353 8415 ✉clerks@ftb.eu.com
Call Date: Nov 1986, Gray's Inn
Pupil Supervisor

Practising Areas: Town & Country Planning

LEWIS MR OWEN PRYS

9 Park Place
Cardiff, South Glamorgan CF10 3DP
☎029 2038 2731 ✉clerks@9parkplace.co.uk
Call Date: Jul 1985, Middle Temple
Pupil Supervisor

LEWIS MRS PAULINE GRACE

Holborn Chambers
6 Gate Street, Lincoln's Inn Fields, London WC2A 3HP ☎020 7242 6060
Call Date: Nov 1984, Lincoln's Inn

Practising Areas: Commercial Litigation, Commercial Property, Conveyancing, Employment

LEWIS MR STUART JOHN

New Walk Chambers
27 New Walk, Leicester, Leicestershire LE1 6TE ☎0871 200 1298 / 0116 255 9144
✉clerks@newwalkchambers.co.uk
Call Date: Jul 2002, Lincoln's Inn

Practising Areas: Care Proceedings, Common Law (General), Employment, Family, Family Provision

LEWIS MR WAYNE ANTHONY

Access Lawyers
800 High Road, Tottenham, London N17 0DH
☎020 8801 2345
Call Date: Nov 1982, Lincoln's Inn

Practising Areas: Bankruptcy, Chancery (General), Civil Litigation, Commercial Litigation, Common Law (General), Copyright, Corporate Finance, Disciplinary Tribunals, Discrimination, Employment, Entertainment, Equity, Wills & Trusts, Family, Film, Cable & TV, Housing, Human Rights, Immigration, Intellectual Property, International Trade, Landlord & Tenant, Personal Injury, Sports

LEWIS-MURRAY MRS REBECCA-JANE

Call Date: Nov 1990, Inner Temple

Practising Areas: Civil Liberties, Crime, Discrimination, Employment, Family, Human Rights, Immigration, Medical Negligence, Personal Injury

LEWISON MR JOSH

Radcliffe Chambers
Ground Floor, 11 New Square, Lincoln's Inn, London WC2A 3QB ☎020 7831 0081
✉clerks@radcliffechambers.com
Call Date: Jul 2005, Lincoln's Inn

Practising Areas: Charities

LEY MR SPENCER

Farrar's Building
Farrar's Building, Temple, London EC4Y 7BD
☎020 7583 9241
✉Chambers@farrarsbuilding.co.uk
Call Date: Jul 1985, Middle Temple

Practising Areas: Common Law (General), Medical Negligence, Personal Injury, Professional Negligence

C

LIDDIARD MR MARTIN THOMAS

No5 Chambers
Fountain Court, Steelhouse Lane, Birmingham B4 6DR ☎ 0845 210 5555 ✉ info@no5.com
No5 Chambers
Greenwood House, 4-7 Salisbury Court, London EC4Y 8AA ☎ 0845 210 5555
No5 Chambers
38 Queen Square, Bristol BS1 4QS
☎ 0845 210 5555
Call Date: Nov 1989, Inner Temple

Practising Areas: Corporate Finance, Courts Martial, Crime, Crime (Corporate/Fraud), Health & Safety, Licensing, Regulatory Law

LIDINGTON MR GARY MARK

11 Stone Buildings
11 Stone Buildings, Lincoln's Inn, London WC2A 3TG ☎ 020 7831 6381 ✉ clerks@11sb.com
Call Date: Oct 2000, Middle Temple

LIGHT PROF ROY ALAN

St John's Chambers
101 Victoria Street, Bristol BS1 6PU
☎ 0117 923 4700 ✉ clerks@stjohnschambers.co.uk
Call Date: Feb 1992, Gray's Inn

Practising Areas: Crime, Licensing

LIMBREY MR BERNARD MARTIN

3 Dr Johnson's Buildings
Ground Floor, 3 Dr Johnson's Buildings, Temple, London EC4Y 7BA ☎ 020 7353 4854
✉ clerks@3djb.co.uk
Call Date: Nov 1980, Middle Temple
Pupil Supervisor

Practising Areas: Care Proceedings, Common Law (General), Family, Family Provision, Sale & Carriage of Goods

LINDSAY MR ALISTAIR DAVID

Monckton Chambers
1 & 2 Raymond Buildings, Gray's Inn, London WC1R 5NR ☎ 020 7405 7211
✉ chambers@monckton.com
Call Date: Oct 1993, Inner Temple

Practising Areas: Competition, EC & Competition Law

LINDSAY MR JEREMY MARK HENRY

37 Park Square Chambers
37 Park Square, Leeds LS1 2NY
☎ 0113 243 9422 ✉ chambers@no37.co.uk
Call Date: Jul 1986, Gray's Inn
Pupil Supervisor

Practising Areas: Crime, Crime (Corporate/Fraud), Family

LINDSEY MS SUSAN

Crown Office Chambers
2 Crown Office Row, Temple, London EC4Y 7HJ ☎ 020 7797 8100
✉ mail@crownofficechambers.com
Call Date: Nov 1997, Inner Temple

Practising Areas: Arbitration, Construction, Professional Negligence

LINEHAN MR STEPHEN JOHN QC (1993)

St Philips Chambers
55 Temple Row, Birmingham B2 5LS
☎ 0121 246 7000 ✉ clerks@st-philips.com
Call Date: Feb 1970, Lincoln's Inn
Recorder

Practising Areas: Coroners Inquests, Courts Martial, Crime, Crime (Corporate/Fraud), Disciplinary Tribunals, Health & Safety, Licensing, Regulatory Law

LING MS NAOMI

Outer Temple Chambers
The Outer Temple, 222 Strand, London WC2R 1BA ☎ 020 7353 6381
✉ clerks@outertemple.com
Call Date: Nov 2001, Middle Temple

Practising Areas: Employment, Pensions

LINSTEAD MR PETER JAMES

Tanfield Chambers
2-5 Warwick Court, London WC1R 5DJ
☎ 020 7421 5300 ✉ clerks@tanfieldchambers.co.uk
Call Date: Oct 1994, Gray's Inn
Pupil Supervisor

Practising Areas: Commercial Litigation, Employment

C

LIPPOLD MS SARAH IDA LOUISE

13 King's Bench Walk
13 King's Bench Walk, Temple, London EC4Y 7EN ☎ 020 7353 7204 ✉ clerks@13kbw.co.uk
13 KBW
32 Beaumont Street, Oxford OX1 2NP
☎ 01865 311066 ✉ clerks@13kbw.co.uk
Call Date: Nov 1999, Inner Temple
Pupil Supervisor

Practising Areas: Chancery (Land Law), Common Law (General), Discrimination, Education, Employment, Landlord & Tenant, Personal Injury, Sale & Carriage of Goods

LISSACK MR RICHARD ANTHONY QC (1994)

Outer Temple Chambers
The Outer Temple, 222 Strand, London WC2R 1BA ☎ 020 7353 6381
✉ clerks@outertemple.com
Riverview Chambers
Hamilton House, 1 Temple Avenue, London EC4Y 0HA ☎ 0844 225 3999
✉ chrisbaylis@riverviewchambers.com
Call Date: Nov 1978, Inner Temple
Recorder

Practising Areas: Administrative, Arbitration, Civil Liberties, Commercial Litigation, Competition, Crime (Corporate/Fraud), Defamation, Employment, Entertainment, Financial Services, Health & Safety, Medical Negligence, Professional Negligence, Regulatory Law, Sports

LITHMAN MR NIGEL LLOYD QC (1997)

2 Bedford Row
London WC1R 4BU ☎ 020 7440 8888
✉ clerks@2bedfordrow.co.uk
Call Date: Nov 1976, Inner Temple

Practising Areas: Regulatory Law

LITTLEWOOD MISS REBECCA MAE

1 Pump Court
Elm Court, Temple, London EC4Y 7AB
☎ 020 7842 7070 ✉ (name)@pumpcourt.co.uk
Call Date: Nov 1988, Inner Temple
Pupil Supervisor

Practising Areas: Care Proceedings, Family, Family Provision

LITTMAN MR JEFFREY JAMES

9 Park Place
Cardiff, South Glamorgan CF10 3DP
☎ 029 2038 2731 ✉ clerks@9parkplace.co.uk
Chambers of Mr Jeffrey Littman
25 Heriot Road, Hendon, London NW4 2EG
☎ 020 8922 6844 ✉ jeffreylittman@aol.com
Call Date: Jul 1974, Middle Temple
Pupil Supervisor

Practising Areas: Administrative, Chancery (General), Chancery (Land Law), Insolvency, Landlord & Tenant, Professional Negligence

LIVESEY MR JOHN WILLIAM ALLAN

Albion Chambers
Broad Street, Bristol BS1 1DR
☎ 0117 927 2144 ✉ clerks@albionchambers.co.uk
Call Date: Nov 1990, Lincoln's Inn
Pupil Supervisor

Practising Areas: Discrimination, Employment, Personal Injury

LIVING MR MARC STEPHEN

Pallant Chambers
12 North Pallant, Chichester, West Sussex PO19 1TQ ☎ 01243 784538
✉ clerks@pallantchambers.co.uk
Call Date: Jul 1983, Middle Temple
Pupil Supervisor

LIVINGSTONE MR SIMON JOHN

Thomas More Chambers
7 Lincoln's Inn Fields, London WC2A 3BP
☎ 020 7404 7000 ✉ clerks@thomasmore.co.uk
Call Date: Oct 1990, Inner Temple

Practising Areas: Civil Litigation, Commercial Litigation, Common Law (General), Crime, Crime (Corporate/Fraud), Disciplinary Tribunals, Discrimination, Employment, Landlord & Tenant, Medical Negligence, Personal Injury, Professional Negligence

LLOYD MR BENJAMIN JOHN

6 King's Bench Walk
Ground Floor, 6 King's Bench Walk, Temple, London EC4Y 7DR ☎ 020 7583 0410
✉ clerks@6kbw.com
Call Date: Jul 2004, Lincoln's Inn

Practising Areas: Administrative, Civil Liberties, Crime, Crime (Corporate/Fraud), Human Rights

LLOYD MISS GAYNOR ELIZABETH

Call Date: Oct 1992, Lincoln's Inn
Pupil Supervisor

LLOYD MR JOHN NESBITT

Rougemont Chambers
Victory House, Dean Clarke Gardens, Southernhay East, Exeter EX2 4AA
☎ 01392 208484
✉ clerks@rougemontchambers.co.uk
Call Date: Nov 1988, Inner Temple
Pupil Supervisor

Practising Areas: Administrative, Charities, Common Land, Discrimination, Education, Employment, Environment, Housing, Landlord & Tenant, Local Government, Personal Injury, Professional Negligence, Town & Country Planning

LLOYD MR JULIAN ALASTAIR

St Johns Buildings
24a - 28 St John Street, Manchester M3 4DJ
☎ 0161 214 1500 ✉ clerk@stjohnsbuildings.co.uk
St Johns Buildings
21 White Friars, Chester CH1 1NZ
☎ 01244 323070 ✉ clerk@stjohnsbuildings.co.uk
16 Winckley Square
Preston PR1 3JJ ☎ 01772 256100
Call Date: Jul 1985, Gray's Inn
Pupil Supervisor

LLOYD MS RHIANNON

4 Paper Buildings
1st Floor, 4 Paper Buildings, Temple, London EC4Y 7EX ☎ 020 7427 5200 ✉ clerks@4pb.com
Call Date: Oct 2002, Inner Temple

Practising Areas: Ancillary Relief, Children's Law, Family

LLOYD-ELEY MR ANDREW JAMES QC (2010)

Old Bailey Chambers
15 Old Bailey, London EC4M 7EF
☎ 020 3008 6404
✉ clerks@15oldbaileychambers.com
Call Date: Nov 1979, Middle Temple
Pupil Supervisor

Practising Areas: Crime, Crime (Corporate/Fraud)

LLOYD-JONES MR JOHN BENEDICT

36 Bedford Row
London WC1R 4JH ☎ 020 7421 8000
✉ chambers@36bedfordrow.co.uk
Call Date: Nov 1993, Inner Temple
Pupil Supervisor

Practising Areas: Crime, Crime (Corporate/Fraud)

LO MR BERNARD NORMAN

Field Court Chambers
5 Field Court, Gray's Inn, London WC1R 5EF
☎ 020 7405 6114 ✉ clerks@fieldcourt.co.uk
Call Date: Nov 1991, Inner Temple
Pupil Supervisor

Practising Areas: Bankruptcy, Chancery (Land Law), Civil Litigation, Common Law (General), Consumer, Housing, Landlord & Tenant

LOCK MR DAVID ANTHONY QC (2011)

No5 Chambers
Fountain Court, Steelhouse Lane, Birmingham B4 6DR ☎ 0845 210 5555 ✉ info@no5.com
No5 Chambers
Greenwood House, 4-7 Salisbury Court, London EC4Y 8AA ☎ 0845 210 5555
No5 Chambers
38 Queen Square, Bristol BS1 4QS
☎ 0845 210 5555
Call Date: Nov 1985, Gray's Inn

Practising Areas: Administrative, Civil Liberties, Housing, Human Rights, Local Government, Medical Negligence, Mental Health, Parliamentary

LOCKHART MR ANDREW WILLIAM JARDINE QC (2010)

St Philips Chambers
55 Temple Row, Birmingham B2 5LS
☎ 0121 246 7000 ✉ clerks@st-philips.com
Call Date: Oct 1991, Lincoln's Inn
Pupil Supervisor, Recorder

LODGE MR HUGO DANIEL PAUL

Atkinson Bevan Chambers
1st Floor, 2 Harcourt Buildings, Temple, London EC4Y 9DB ☎ 020 7353 2112
✉ clerks@2hb.co.uk
Call Date: Oct 1998, Gray's Inn
Pupil Supervisor

Practising Areas: Administrative, Civil Liberties, Courts Martial, Crime, Crime (Corporate/Fraud), Licensing, Private International

C

LODY MR TUSTIAN STUART

KCH Garden Square
1 Oxford Street, Nottingham NG1 5BH
☎0115 941 8851 ✉clerks@kchgardensquare.co.uk
Call Date: Nov 1991, Gray's Inn
Pupil Supervisor

LOEB MISS DINAH YOLANDE

Westgate Chambers
64 High Street, Lewes, East Sussex BN7 1XG
☎01273 480510
✉clerks@westgate-chambers.co.uk
Call Date: Nov 2004, Middle Temple

Practising Areas: Ancillary Relief, Care Proceedings, Family, Family Provision

LOFTHOUSE MR JAMES

1 Gray's Inn Square
Ground Floor, 1 Gray's Inn Square, London WC1R 5AA ☎020 7405 0001
Call Date: Oct 1996, Inner Temple
Pupil Supervisor

Practising Areas: Civil Liberties, Common Law (General), Crime, Housing, Human Rights, Landlord & Tenant, Personal Injury, Sale & Carriage of Goods

LOFTHOUSE MR SIMON TIMOTHY QC (2006)

Atkin Chambers
1 Atkin Building, Gray's Inn, London WC1R 5AT ☎020 7404 0102
✉clerks@atkinchambers.com
Call Date: Nov 1988, Gray's Inn
Recorder

C

LOGAN MR GRAEME ALEXANDER

15 New Bridge Street
London EC4V 6AU ☎020 7842 1900
✉clerks@15nbs.com
4 Breams Buildings
Chancery Lane, London EC4A 1HP
☎020 7092 1900 ✉clerks@4bb.co.uk
Call Date: Oct 1998, Middle Temple

Practising Areas: Courts Martial, Crime, Immigration

LOGAN MISS MAURA

St John's House Chambers
One High Elm Drive, Hale Barns, Altrincham, Cheshire WA15 0JD ☎0161 980 7379
✉mauraloganllb@aol.com
Call Date: Jul 1971, Inner Temple

Practising Areas: Care Proceedings, Common Law (General)

LONG MR BENJAMIN NICHOLAS JAMES

5 Pump Court
Ground Floor, 5 Pump Court, Temple, London EC4Y 7AP ☎020 7353 2532
✉clerks@5pumpcourt.com
Call Date: Nov 2000, Inner Temple

LONG MR BENJAMIN PHILIP JACKSON

Pump Court Chambers
Upper Ground Floor, 3 Pump Court, Temple, London EC4Y 7AJ ☎020 7353 0711
✉clerks@3pumpcourt.com
Pump Court Chambers
5 Temple Chambers, Temple Street, Swindon SN1 1SQ ☎01793 539899
✉clerks@3pumpcourt.com
Pump Court Chambers
31 Southgate Street, Winchester, Hampshire SO23 9EB ☎01962 868 161
✉clerks@3pumpcourt.com
Call Date: Jul 2006, Middle Temple

LONG MISS MADELIENE MARIE

Kenworthy's Chambers
Arlington House, Bloom Street, Salford, Manchester M3 6AJ ☎0161 832 4036
Call Date: Nov 1999, Gray's Inn

LONGHURST-WOODS MS LESLEY

2 Louisa Close
2 Louisa Close, Wetherell Road, London E9 7BZ ☎020 8985 8716
✉lezwoo@btopenworld.com
Call Date: Nov 1992, Gray's Inn

Practising Areas: Company & Commercial, Crime, Employment, Entertainment, Family, Housing, Immigration, Landlord & Tenant

LONSDALE MR DAVID JAMES

33 Bedford Row
London WC1R 4JH ☎020 7242 6476
✉clerks@33bedfordrow.co.uk
Call Date: Nov 1988, Inner Temple

Practising Areas: Chancery (General), Commercial Litigation, Common Law (General), Landlord & Tenant, Partnership, Professional Negligence

LONSDALE MISS MARION MARY

Academy Chambers
63 Brim Hill, London N2 0HA
☎020 8455 2503 ✉marionlonsdale@gmail.com
Call Date: Jul 1984, Gray's Inn

Practising Areas: Administrative, Chancery (General), Commercial Litigation, Equity, Wills & Trusts, Family Provision, Insolvency, Landlord & Tenant, Probate & Administration, Professional Negligence, Tax (Capital & Income)

LOPEZ MR JUAN NEMESIO

Francis Taylor Building
Inner Temple, London EC4Y 7BY
☎020 7353 8415 ✉clerks@ftb.eu.com
Call Date: Oct 2002, Lincoln's Inn

Practising Areas: Administrative, Chancery (General), Chancery (Land Law), Civil Litigation, Commercial Litigation, Commercial Property, Common Land, Common Law (General), Crime, Data Protection, Environment, Health & Safety, Housing, Land, Landlord & Tenant, Licensing, Local Government, Public Law, Regulatory Law, Town & Country Planning

LOPEZ MR PAUL ANTHONY

St Ive's Chambers
Whittall Street, Birmingham B4 6DH
☎0121 236 0863 ✉clerks@stiveschambers.co.uk
Call Date: Jul 1982, Middle Temple
Pupil Supervisor, Recorder

Practising Areas: Care Proceedings, Family, Family Provision, Mental Health, Personal Injury

LORD MR WAYNE EDWARD

Construction Chambers
18 Skiddaw Drive, Mickleover, Derby DE3 9NE ☎01332 617 917 ✉wel@welord.co.uk
Call Date: Jul 1999, Middle Temple

Practising Areas: Construction, Professional Negligence

LORENZO MS CLAUDIA

Pump Court Chambers
Upper Ground Floor, 3 Pump Court, Temple, London EC4Y 7AJ ☎020 7353 0711
✉clerks@3pumpcourt.com
Pump Court Chambers
5 Temple Chambers, Temple Street, Swindon SN1 1SQ ☎01793 539899
✉clerks@3pumpcourt.com
Pump Court Chambers
31 Southgate Street, Winchester, Hampshire SO23 9EB ☎01962 868 161
✉clerks@3pumpcourt.com
Call Date: Apr 1991, Inner Temple

Practising Areas: Administrative, Care Proceedings, Family, Family Provision

LOURDES MR LOUIS JOSEPH

Chambers of Mr Louis Lourdes
69A, Chertsey Court, Lower Richmond Road, London SW14 7RD ☎020 8288 0133
✉richmondchambers@googlemail.com
Call Date: Nov 1998, Lincoln's Inn

LOVE MISS SHARON ANN

Garden Court Chambers
57-60 Lincoln's Inn Fields, London WC2A 3LJ
☎020 7993 7600 ✉info@gclaw.co.uk
Call Date: Oct 1997, Gray's Inn

Practising Areas: Care Proceedings, Family, Family Provision

LOVEDAY MR DAVID ROBERT

4-5 Gray's Inn Square
Gray's Inn, London WC1R 5AH
☎020 7404 5252 ✉clerks@4-5.co.uk
Call Date: Nov 2007, Inner Temple

Practising Areas: Administrative, Education, Environment, Local Government, Town & Country Planning

LOVEDAY MR MARK ALAN

Tanfield Chambers
2-5 Warwick Court, London WC1R 5DJ
☎020 7421 5300 ✉clerks@tanfieldchambers.co.uk
Call Date: Jul 1986, Inner Temple
Pupil Supervisor

Practising Areas: Chancery (Land Law), Commercial Property, Land, Landlord & Tenant

LOWE MR CHRISTOPHER JOHN

KCH Garden Square
1 Oxford Street, Nottingham NG1 5BH
☎0115 941 8851 ✉clerks@kchgardensquare.co.uk
Call Date: Jul 2001, Middle Temple

Practising Areas: Courts Martial, Crime, Crime (Corporate/Fraud), Licensing

LOWE MR MUNGO JAMES

13 Old Square Chambers
Ground Floor, 14 Old Square, Lincoln's Inn, London WC2A 3UE ☎ 020 7831 4445
✉ clerks@13oldsquare.com
Call Date: Jul 2003, Middle Temple

Practising Areas: Banking, Bankruptcy, Commercial Litigation, Commercial Property, Company & Commercial, Equity, Wills & Trusts, Housing, Insolvency, Landlord & Tenant, Licensing, Local Government, Partnership, Probate & Administration, Professional Negligence

LOWE MR RUPERT WILLIAM MANLEY

Guildhall Chambers
23 Broad Street, Bristol BS1 2HG
☎ 0117 930 9000 ✉ hoc@guildhallchambers.co.uk
Call Date: Nov 1998, Inner Temple
Pupil Supervisor

Practising Areas: Crime, Crime (Corporate/Fraud), Environment, Health & Safety, Regulatory Law

LOWNDS MR PETER ALEXANDER

Doughty Street Chambers
53-54 Doughty Street, London WC1N 2LS
☎ 020 7404 1313 ✉ enquiries@doughtystreet.co.uk
Doughty Street Chambers
Pall Mall Court, 61-67 King Street, Manchester M2 4PD ☎ 0161 618 1066
Doughty Street Chambers
5th Floor, Broad Quay House, Prince Street, Bristol BS1 4DJ ☎ 01179 058 717
Call Date: Nov 1998, Gray's Inn
Pupil Supervisor

Practising Areas: Crime, Crime (Corporate/Fraud)

LUCAS MR NOEL JOHN MAC QC (2008)

18 Red Lion Court
London EC4A 3EB ☎ 020 7520 6000
✉ chambers@18rlc.co.uk
Call Date: Jul 1979, Middle Temple
Recorder

LUCEY MISS ANNE MARIE

Trinity Chambers
Highfield House, Moulsham Street, Chelmsford, Essex CM2 9AH
☎ 01245 605040 ✉ clerks@trinitychambers.com
Call Date: Nov 2005, Middle Temple

LUCKING MRS ADRIENNE SIMONE

36 Bedford Row
London WC1R 4JH ☎ 020 7421 8000
✉ chambers@36bedfordrow.co.uk
Call Date: Nov 1989, Inner Temple
Pupil Supervisor, Recorder

Practising Areas: Crime

LUDBROOK MR TIMOTHY VIVIAN

13 Old Square Chambers
Ground Floor, 14 Old Square, Lincoln's Inn, London WC2A 3UE ☎ 020 7831 4445
✉ clerks@13oldsquare.com
Call Date: Oct 1996, Inner Temple

Practising Areas: Company & Commercial, Competition, Defamation, Information Technology, Intellectual Property

LUDLOW MR CRAIG DOMINIC

3 PB Barristers
3 Paper Buildings, Temple, London EC4Y 7EU
☎ 020 7583 8055
3 PB Barristers
Royal Talbot House, 2 Victoria Street, Bristol, Avon BS1 6BB ☎ 0117 928 1520
3 PB Barristers
30 Christchurch Road, Bournemouth, Dorset BH1 3PD ☎ 01202 292102 ✉ clerks.bournemouth@3paper.co.uk
3 PB Barristers
4 St Peter Street, Winchester SO23 8BW
☎ 01962 868884 ✉ clerks.winchester@3paper.co.uk
3 PB Barristers
23 Beaumont Street, Oxford OX1 2NP
☎ 01865 793 736
Call Date: Mar 2002, Lincoln's Inn

LUGSDIN MR MARTIN

Kenworthy's Chambers
Arlington House, Bloom Street, Salford, Manchester M3 6AJ ☎ 0161 832 4036
Call Date: Nov 2005, Middle Temple

Practising Areas: Care Proceedings, Children's Law, Family

LUH MISS SHU SHIN

Garden Court Chambers
57-60 Lincoln's Inn Fields, London WC2A 3LJ
☎ 020 7993 7600 ✉ info@gclaw.co.uk
Call Date: Oct 2006, Middle Temple

Practising Areas: Administrative, Children's Law, Civil Liberties, Civil Litigation, Discrimination, Education, Housing, Human Rights, Immigration, Mental Health

C

LULE MISS JACQUELINE

1 Mitre Court Buildings
1 Mitre Court Buildings, Temple, London EC4Y 7BS ☎ 020 7452 8900 ✉ clerks@1mcb.com
Call Date: Nov 1999, Middle Temple

Practising Areas: Civil Liberties, Commercial Litigation, Common Law (General), Crime, Crime (Corporate/Fraud), Discrimination, Employment, Family, Health & Safety, Human Rights, Immigration, Professional Negligence, Regulatory Law

LYCOURGOU MISS OLIVE

4 King's Bench Walk
2nd Floor, 4 King's Bench Walk, Temple, London EC4Y 7DL ☎ 020 7822 7000
✉ clerks@4kbw.co.uk
Call Date: Jul 1997, Gray's Inn

Practising Areas: Common Law (General), Road Traffic And Highways

LYNCH MR JEROME QC (2000)

Charter Chambers
33 John Street, London WC1N 2AT
☎ 020 7618 4400 ✉ clerks@charterchambers.com
Call Date: Jul 1983, Lincoln's Inn

Practising Areas: Crime, Crime (Corporate/Fraud), Regulatory Law

LYNCH MR JOHN PATRICK

QEB Hollis Whiteman
1-2 Laurence Pountney Hill, London EC4R 0EU ☎ 020 7933 8855 ✉ barristers@qebhw.co.uk
Call Date: Mar 2008, Gray's Inn

LYON MR GAVIN

Northampton Chambers
10 Spencer Parade, Northampton NN1 5AQ
☎ 01604 636271
✉ clerks@northampton-chambers.co.uk
Call Date: Oct 2006, Middle Temple

Practising Areas: Family, Family Provision

LYON MRS SHANE VALERIE

King's Bench and Godolphin (KBG)Chambers
115 North Hill, Plymouth, Devon PL4 8JY
☎ 01752 221551 ✉ clerks@kbgchambers.co.uk
Call Date: Nov 1976, Middle Temple
Pupil Supervisor

Practising Areas: Agriculture, Bankruptcy, Charities, Equity, Wills & Trusts

LYON MR STEPHEN JOHN

4 Paper Buildings
1st Floor, 4 Paper Buildings, Temple, London EC4Y 7EX ☎ 020 7427 5200 ✉ clerks@4pb.com
Call Date: Jul 1987, Inner Temple
Pupil Supervisor

LYONS MR DAVID WAKEFIELD

King's Bench Chambers
Wellington House, 175 Holdenhurst Road, Bournemouth, Dorset BH8 8DQ
☎ 01202 250025
2 Pump Court
1st Floor, 2 Pump Court, Temple, London EC4Y 7AH ☎ 020 7353 5597
✉ clerks@2pumpcourt.co.uk
Call Date: Jul 1987, Middle Temple

Practising Areas: Courts Martial, Crime, Crime (Corporate/Fraud), Family, Licensing

LYONS MISS TARA YASMIN

Pump Court Chambers
Upper Ground Floor, 3 Pump Court, Temple, London EC4Y 7AJ ☎ 020 7353 0711
✉ clerks@3pumpcourt.com
Riverview Chambers
Hamilton House, 1 Temple Avenue, London EC4Y 0HA ☎ 0844 225 3999
✉ chrisbaylis@riverviewchambers.com
Pump Court Chambers
31 Southgate Street, Winchester, Hampshire SO23 9EB ☎ 01962 868 161
✉ clerks@3pumpcourt.com
Call Date: Nov 2005, Middle Temple

Practising Areas: Chancery (General), Common Law (General), Employment, Family, Family Provision, Medical Negligence, Personal Injury, Professional Negligence, Sale & Carriage of Goods

LYONS MR TIMOTHY JOHN QC (2003)

4-5 Gray's Inn Square
Gray's Inn, London WC1R 5AH
☎ 020 7404 5252 ✉ clerks@4-5.co.uk
St James's Chambers
68 Quay Street, Manchester M3 3EJ
☎ 0161 834 7000 ✉ clerks@stjameschambers.com
Call Date: Jul 1980, Inner Temple

Practising Areas: Charities, EC & Competition Law, Equity, Wills & Trusts, Tax (Capital & Income), Tax (Corporate)

MACAULAY MR NEIL DAVID

Bretton Woods Law
New Broad Street House, 35 New Broad Street, London EC2M 1NH
Call Date: Nov 1990, Lincoln's Inn

MACBEAN MR ANDREW HAMISH

Queen Square Chambers
56 Queen Square, Bristol BS1 4PR
☎ 0117 921 1966 ✉ crime@qs-c.co.uk
Call Date: Nov 2002, Lincoln's Inn

Practising Areas: Commercial Litigation, Common Law (General), Construction, Housing

MACCABE MR IRVINE JOHN

No5 Chambers
Fountain Court, Steelhouse Lane, Birmingham B4 6DR ☎ 0845 210 5555 ✉ info@no5.com
No5 Chambers
Greenwood House, 4-7 Salisbury Court, London EC4Y 8AA ☎ 0845 210 5555
No5 Chambers
38 Queen Square, Bristol BS1 4QS
☎ 0845 210 5555
Call Date: Jul 1983, Gray's Inn

MACDONALD MR IAN ALEXANDER QC (1988)

Garden Court Chambers
57-60 Lincoln's Inn Fields, London WC2A 3LJ
☎ 020 7993 7600 ✉ info@gclaw.co.uk
Kings Court Chambers
3rd Floor, Albert House, 12-26 Albert Street, Birmingham B4 7UD ☎ 07967 910864 ✉ t.rehmanbar@talk21.com
Chambers of Ian Macdonald QC
Garden Court North, 22 Oxford Court, Manchester M2 3WQ ☎ 0161 236 1840
✉ clerks@gcnchambers.co.uk
Call Date: Feb 1963, Middle Temple

Practising Areas: Immigration

MACDONALD MR JOHN REGINALD QC (1976)

New Square Chambers
12 New Square, Lincoln's Inn, London WC2A 3SW ☎ 020 7419 8000 ✉ robin.hollington@newsquarechambers.co.uk
Call Date: Jun 1955, Lincoln's Inn

MACEVILLY MR CONN JEREMY

9 Stone Buildings
Lincoln's Inn, London WC2A 3NN
☎ 020 7404 5055 ✉ clerks@9stonebuildings.com
Call Date: Oct 1997, Inner Temple

Practising Areas: Bankruptcy, Chancery (General), Chancery (Land Law), Civil Litigation, Commercial Litigation, Company & Commercial, Discrimination, EC & Competition Law, Employment, Financial Services, Foreign Law, Insolvency, Land

MACFARLANE MR ANDREW LENNOX

Colleton Chambers
Colleton Crescent, Exeter, Devon EX2 4DG
☎ 01392 274898 ✉ clerks@colletonchambers.co.uk
Call Date: May 1995, Inner Temple

Practising Areas: Crime, Crime (Corporate/Fraud)

MACHELL MR JOHN WILLIAM QC (2012)

Serle Court
6 New Square, Lincoln's Inn, London WC2A 3QS ☎ 020 7242 6105 ✉ clerks@serlecourt.co.uk
Call Date: Oct 1993, Inner Temple
Pupil Supervisor

Practising Areas: Arbitration, Chancery (General), Commercial Litigation, Company & Commercial, Equity, Wills & Trusts, Partnership, Probate & Administration

MACKENZIE MISS JULIE FIONA

Pump Court Chambers
5 Temple Chambers, Temple Street, Swindon SN1 1SQ ☎ 01793 539899
✉ clerks@3pumpcourt.com
Pump Court Chambers
Upper Ground Floor, 3 Pump Court, Temple, London EC4Y 7AJ ☎ 020 7353 0711
✉ clerks@3pumpcourt.com
Pump Court Chambers
31 Southgate Street, Winchester, Hampshire SO23 9EB ☎ 01962 868 161
✉ clerks@3pumpcourt.com
Call Date: Nov 1978, Lincoln's Inn
Pupil Supervisor

Practising Areas: Ancillary Relief, Care Proceedings, Family, Family Provision

MACKENZIE MR ROBERT SUTHERLAND

Middle Temple Lane Chambers
2nd Floor South, 1 Middle Temple Lane, London EC4Y 9AA ☎020 7583 4352
✉chambers@mtlchambers.com
Call Date: Mar 1996, Gray's Inn

Practising Areas: Banking, Bankruptcy, Chancery (General), Civil Liberties, Tax (Capital & Income)

MACKENZIE SMITH MRS CATHERINE JOANNA

10 King's Bench Walk
Ground Floor, 10 King's Bench Walk, Temple, London EC4Y 7EB ☎020 7353 7742
✉Chambers@10kingsbenchwalk.co.uk
Call Date: Nov 1960, Inner Temple

Practising Areas: Banking, Bankruptcy, Chancery (General), Commercial Litigation, Common Law (General), Crime (Corporate/Fraud), EC & Competition Law, Human Rights, Immigration, Insurance/Reinsurance, Private International

MACKIE MS JEANNIE

Doughty Street Chambers
53-54 Doughty Street, London WC1N 2LS
☎020 7404 1313 ✉enquiries@doughtystreet.co.uk
Doughty Street Chambers
Pall Mall Court, 61-67 King Street, Manchester M2 4PD ☎0161 618 1066
Doughty Street Chambers
5th Floor, Broad Quay House, Prince Street, Bristol BS1 4DJ ☎01179 058 717
Call Date: Jul 1995, Inner Temple

Practising Areas: Civil Liberties, Crime

MACKLEY MR DAVID JOHN

18 St John Street
Manchester M3 4EA ☎0161 278 1800
✉clerks@18sjs.com
Call Date: Oct 1997, Lincoln's Inn

Practising Areas: Care Proceedings, Children's Law, Family

MACLAREN MISS CATRIONA LONGUEVILLE

Tanfield Chambers
2-5 Warwick Court, London WC1R 5DJ
☎020 7421 5300 ✉clerks@tanfieldchambers.co.uk
Call Date: Oct 1993, Inner Temple
Pupil Supervisor

Practising Areas: Discrimination, Employment

MACLEAN WATT MR HECTOR WILLIAM GRANTHAM

4 Breams Buildings
Chancery Lane, London EC4A 1HP
☎020 7092 1900 ✉clerks@4bb.co.uk
Call Date: Nov 2006, Middle Temple

Practising Areas: Crime

MACLYNN MISS CLAIRE LOUISE

4 Brick Court
4 Brick Court, Temple, London EC4Y 9AD
☎020 7832 3200 ✉clerks@4bc.co.uk
Call Date: Jul 2001, Gray's Inn

Practising Areas: Family Provision

MACPHERSON MR DUNCAN CHARLES STEWART

One Essex Court
1st Floor, Temple, London EC4Y 9AR
☎020 7936 3030 ✉clerks@1ec.co.uk
Call Date: May 1994, Middle Temple
Pupil Supervisor

Practising Areas: Administrative, Banking, Bankruptcy, Chancery (General), Company & Commercial, Competition, Insolvency, Insurance, Landlord & Tenant, Partnership, Professional Negligence

MACRO MISS MORWENNA MARGARET

Five Paper
Ground Floor, 5 Paper Buildings, Temple, London EC4Y 7HB ☎020 7815 3200
Call Date: Jul 2002, Inner Temple

Practising Areas: Commercial Litigation, Company & Commercial, Consumer, Costs, Insolvency

MADDISON MR DAVID THOMAS JAMES

Cobden House Chambers
19 Quay Street, Manchester M3 3HN
☎0161 833 6000 ✉Clerks@Cobden.co.uk
Call Date: Oct 1995, Gray's Inn

Practising Areas: Care Proceedings, Family, Family Provision

MAGEE MR MICHAEL JAMES

Fenners Chambers
3 Madingley Road, Cambridge CB3 0EE
☎01223 368761 ✉clerks@fennerschambers.com
Call Date: Oct 1997, Inner Temple
Pupil Supervisor

Practising Areas: Crime, Crime (Corporate/Fraud), Employment

MAGEE MISS ROSEIN MOIRA

Pallant Chambers
12 North Pallant, Chichester, West Sussex
PO19 1TQ ☎01243 784538
✉clerks@pallantchambers.co.uk
Call Date: Oct 1994, Gray's Inn

Practising Areas: Care Proceedings, Family, Family Provision

MAGEE MR SAMUEL CAIRNS

2 Bedford Row
London WC1R 4BU ☎020 7440 8888
✉clerks@2bedfordrow.co.uk
Call Date: Jul 2003, Inner Temple

Practising Areas: Courts Martial, Crime, Crime (Corporate/Fraud), Regulatory Law, Sports

MAGGS MR NICHOLAS PETER

Thomas More Chambers
7 Lincoln's Inn Fields, London WC2A 3BP
☎020 7404 7000 ✉clerks@thomasmore.co.uk
Call Date: Jul 2006, Middle Temple

MAGGS MR PATRICK TERENCE

15 New Bridge Street
London EC4V 6AU ☎020 7842 1900
✉clerks@15nbs.com
Call Date: Oct 1996, Inner Temple

Practising Areas: Courts Martial, Crime, Crime (Corporate/Fraud)

MAGINN MISS OLIVIA MARIA

New Walk Chambers
27 New Walk, Leicester, Leicestershire LE1 6TE ☎0871 200 1298 / 0116 255 9144
✉clerks@newwalkchambers.co.uk
Call Date: Jul 1998, Lincoln's Inn

Practising Areas: Crime, Crime (Corporate/Fraud)

MAGUIRE MR ANDREW JAMES

St Philips Chambers
55 Temple Row, Birmingham B2 5LS
☎0121 246 7000 ✉clerks@st-philips.com
Exchange Chambers
One Derby Square, Derby Square, Liverpool
L2 9XX ☎0151 236 7747
✉info@exchangechambers.co.uk
Exchange Chambers
7 Ralli Courts, West Riverside, Manchester
M3 5FT ☎0161 833 2722
Call Date: Nov 1988, Inner Temple

Practising Areas: Banking, Chancery (General), Chancery (Land Law), Commercial Litigation, Commercial Property, Construction, Financial Services, Landlord & Tenant, Partnership, Sale & Carriage of Goods

MAGUIRE MS CLODAGH MARY

Call Date: Nov 2003, Inner Temple

MAGUIRE MR MARTIN BENN

QEB Hollis Whiteman
1-2 Laurence Pountney Hill, London EC4R 0EU ☎020 7933 8855 ✉barristers@qebhw.co.uk
Call Date: Nov 1994, Inner Temple

MAGUIRE MR STEPHEN ARTHUR

Kings Chambers
36 Young Street, Manchester M3 3FT
☎0845 034 3444 ✉clerks@kingschambers.com
Kings Chambers
5 Park Square East, Leeds LS1 2NE
☎0845 034 3444 ✉clerks@kingschambers.com
Kings Chambers
Embassy House, 60 Church Street,
Birmingham B3 2DJ ☎0845 034 3444
✉clerks@kingschambers.com
Call Date: Mar 2007, Inner Temple

MAHER MS MARTHA JOHANNA DOROTHY

St John's Chambers
101 Victoria Street, Bristol BS1 6PU
☎0117 923 4700 ✉clerks@stjohnschambers.co.uk
Call Date: Nov 1987, Inner Temple

Practising Areas: Arbitration, Bankruptcy, Chancery (General), Commercial Litigation, Common Law (General), Company & Commercial, Insolvency, Partnership, Professional Negligence, Sports

MAHMOOD MR ABID

No5 Chambers
Fountain Court, Steelhouse Lane, Birmingham
B4 6DR ☎0845 210 5555 ✉info@no5.com
No5 Chambers
Greenwood House, 4-7 Salisbury Court,
London EC4Y 8AA ☎0845 210 5555
No5 Chambers
38 Queen Square, Bristol BS1 4QS
☎0845 210 5555

C

Central Chambers
89 Princess Street, Manchester M1 4HT
☎0161 236 1133 ✉clerks@centralchambers.co.uk
Call Date: Nov 1992, Inner Temple
Pupil Supervisor

Practising Areas: Administrative, Care Proceedings, Chancery (Land Law), Civil Liberties, Common Law (General), Crime, Crime (Corporate/Fraud), Discrimination, EC & Competition Law, Employment, Family, Family Provision, Film, Cable & TV, Foreign Law, Housing, Human Rights, Immigration, International Trade, Islamic Sharia Law, Landlord & Tenant, Personal Injury, Professional Negligence, Public International, Regulatory Law, Sports

MAHMOOD MR GHAZAN

St Johns Buildings
24a - 28 St John Street, Manchester M3 4DJ
☎0161 214 1500 ✉clerk@stjohnsbuildings.co.uk
16 Winckley Square
Preston PR1 3JJ ☎01772 256100
St Johns Buildings Liverpool
8th Floor India Buildings, Water Street, Liverpool L2 0XG ☎0151 243 6000
✉clerk@stjohnsbuildings.co.uk
Call Date: Oct 1997, Inner Temple

MAHMOOD MR IMRAN WASEEM

5 Pump Court
Ground Floor, 5 Pump Court, Temple, London EC4Y 7AP ☎020 7353 2532
✉clerks@5pumpcourt.com
Call Date: Jul 1992, Middle Temple
Pupil Supervisor

Practising Areas: Common Law (General), Crime, Employment, Housing, Landlord & Tenant, Personal Injury

MAHTAB MISS SUMITA LAILA-AL

7 Bell Yard
London WC2A 2JR ☎020 7831 0636
✉kevintarrant@btconnect.com
Call Date: Jul 2001, Gray's Inn
Pupil Supervisor

Practising Areas: Common Law (General), Crime, Family, Licensing, Personal Injury

MAINWARING MR HENRY

Clerksroom (Taunton)
Equity House, Administration Centre, Blackbrook Park Avenue, Taunton, Somerset TA1 2PX ☎0845 083 3000
✉mail@clerksroom.com
64 Bridge Street
3rd Floor, 64 Bridge Street, Manchester M3 3BN ☎0845 083 3000
✉mail@64bridgestreet.com
Clerksroom (London)
3rd Floor, 218 Strand, London WC2R 1AT
☎0845 083 3000 ✉mail@clerksroom.com
Call Date: Nov 2001, Lincoln's Inn

MAINWARING MR ROBERT PAUL CLASON

Portal Chambers
Blaencwm Mawr, Llandysul SA44 5NS
☎01559 395 292
Call Date: Nov 1996, Gray's Inn

Practising Areas: Agriculture, Arbitration, Chancery (General), Common Law (General), Conveyancing, Crime, Environment, Housing, Intellectual Property, Landlord & Tenant, Local Government, Town & Country Planning

MAIRS MR ROBIN GORDON JAMES

St Paul's Chambers
5th Floor, St Paul's House, 23 Park Square South, Leeds LS1 2ND ☎0113 245 5866
Call Date: Oct 1992, Gray's Inn
Pupil Supervisor

MAITLAND JONES MR MARK GRIFFITH

13 King's Bench Walk
13 King's Bench Walk, Temple, London EC4Y 7EN ☎020 7353 7204 ✉clerks@13kbw.co.uk
13 KBW
32 Beaumont Street, Oxford OX1 2NP
☎01865 311066 ✉clerks@13kbw.co.uk
Call Date: Nov 1986, Middle Temple
Pupil Supervisor

Practising Areas: Common Law (General), Employment, Family, Personal Injury

MAITLAND MR MARC CLAUDE

King's Bench Chambers
Wellington House, 175 Holdenhurst Road, Bournemouth, Dorset BH8 8DQ
☎01202 250025
Call Date: Jul 1988, Middle Temple

Practising Areas: Common Law (General), Crime, Licensing, Personal Injury

MAKA MR ISAAC

4 King's Bench Walk
2nd Floor, 4 King's Bench Walk, Temple, London EC4Y 7DL ☎ 020 7822 7000
✉ clerks@4kbw.co.uk
Chambers of Mr Isaac Maka
102 Thorold Road, Ilford, Essex IG1 4EX
☎ 07973 308 301 ✉ isaacmaka@hotmail.com
Call Date: Oct 1998, Lincoln's Inn
Pupil Supervisor

Practising Areas: Administrative, Civil Litigation, Common Law (General), Consumer, Human Rights, Immigration, Licensing, Public International, Public Law, Regulatory Law

MALAM MR JAMES THOMAS

St Johns Buildings
24a - 28 St John Street, Manchester M3 4DJ
☎ 0161 214 1500 ✉ clerk@stjohnsbuildings.co.uk
St Johns Buildings
21 White Friars, Chester CH1 1NZ
☎ 01244 323070 ✉ clerk@stjohnsbuildings.co.uk
16 Winckley Square
Preston PR1 3JJ ☎ 01772 256100
Call Date: Jul 2002, Gray's Inn

MALCOLM MR ALASTAIR RICHARD QC (1996)

1 Paper Buildings
1st Floor, 1 Paper Buildings, Temple, London EC4Y 7EP ☎ 020 7353 3728
✉ clerks@onepaper.co.uk
Call Date: Feb 1971, Inner Temple
Recorder

MALCOLM MISS HELEN KATHARINE LUCY QC (2006)

3 Raymond Buildings
3 Raymond Buildings, Gray's Inn, London WC1R 5BH ☎ 020 7400 6400
✉ clerks@3rblaw.com
Call Date: Nov 1986, Gray's Inn
Recorder

Practising Areas: Crime, Regulatory Law

MALHOTRA MISS MEHTAB ROSHAN

12 Old Square Chambers
1st Floor, 12 Old Square, Lincoln's Inn, London WC2A 3TX ☎ 020 7404 0875
✉ clerks@12oldsquare.com
Call Date: Oct 1996, Lincoln's Inn

MALIK MISS SARAH

Hardwicke
New Square, Lincoln's Inn, London WC2A 3SB ☎ 020 7242 2523
✉ enquiries@hardwicke.co.uk
Call Date: Nov 1999, Lincoln's Inn
Pupil Supervisor

Practising Areas: Common Law (General), Discrimination, Employment, Personal Injury

MALLENDER MR PAUL NIGEL

2-3 Hind Court Chambers
2-3 Hind Court, Fleet Street, London EC4A 3DL ☎ 020 7822 2150 ✉ david@2-3hindcourt.com
Call Date: Nov 1974, Lincoln's Inn
Pupil Supervisor

MALLETT MR SIMON JEREMY

KBW
The Engine House, No 1 Foundry Square, Leeds LS11 5DL ☎ 0113 297 1200
✉ clerks@kbwchambers.com
Call Date: Jul 1986, Inner Temple
Pupil Supervisor

Practising Areas: Disciplinary Tribunals, Employment, Personal Injury

MALONE MR DAVID JOHN

1 Gray's Inn Square
Ground Floor, 1 Gray's Inn Square, London WC1R 5AA ☎ 020 7405 0001
Call Date: Oct 1998, Gray's Inn
Pupil Supervisor

Practising Areas: Administrative, Care Proceedings, Civil Liberties, Common Law (General), Courts Martial, Crime, Crime (Corporate/Fraud), Environment, Family, Health & Safety, Human Rights, Licensing, Local Government, Mental Health, Parliamentary, Professional Negligence, Public International, Regulatory Law, Sports

MALONE MR GERALD FERGUS

Farringdon Chambers
180 Bermondsey Street, London SE1 3TQ
☎ 020 7089 5700
Call Date: Nov 1998, Inner Temple

Practising Areas: Employment

C

MALTZ MR BEN DANIEL

Five Paper
Ground Floor, 5 Paper Buildings, Temple, London EC4Y 7HB ☎ 020 7815 3200
Call Date: Oct 1998, Lincoln's Inn
Pupil Supervisor

Practising Areas: Chancery (Land Law), Commercial Property, Housing, Landlord & Tenant

MANDALIA MR VINESH LALJI

St Philips Chambers
55 Temple Row, Birmingham B2 5LS
☎ 0121 246 7000 ✉ clerks@st-philips.com
Call Date: Oct 1997, Inner Temple

Practising Areas: Administrative, Common Law (General), Crime, Family, Human Rights, Immigration, Local Government

MANKAU MRS LOUISE

Tanfield Chambers
2-5 Warwick Court, London WC1R 5DJ
☎ 020 7421 5300 ✉ clerks@tanfieldchambers.co.uk
Call Date: Nov 2005, Lincoln's Inn

Practising Areas: Employment, Landlord & Tenant, Personal Injury

MANLEY MS HILARY

St Paul's Chambers
5th Floor, St Paul's House, 23 Park Square South, Leeds LS1 2ND ☎ 0113 245 5866
16 Winckley Square
Preston PR1 3JJ ☎ 01772 256100
Call Date: Nov 1996, Gray's Inn

Practising Areas: Crime

MANLEY MISS LESLEY PATRICA

Chambers of Marion Smullen and Kerim Fuad QC
1 Inner Temple Lane, London EC4Y 1AF
☎ 020 7427 4400 ✉ clerks@1itl.com
Call Date: Nov 1983, Middle Temple
Pupil Supervisor

Practising Areas: Crime, Family

MANN MR CHRISTOPHER

13 King's Bench Walk
13 King's Bench Walk, Temple, London EC4Y 7EN ☎ 020 7353 7204 ✉ clerks@13kbw.co.uk
13 KBW
32 Beaumont Street, Oxford OX1 2NP
☎ 01865 311066 ✉ clerks@13kbw.co.uk
Call Date: Oct 1998, Lincoln's Inn
Pupil Supervisor

Practising Areas: Banking, Bankruptcy, Chancery (General), Chancery (Land Law), Commercial Litigation, Commercial Property, Company & Commercial, Construction, Employment, Equity, Wills & Trusts, Insolvency, Landlord & Tenant, Personal Injury, Professional Negligence, Sale & Carriage of Goods

MANN MISS DAYA LUCIENNE CATHERINE

Southernhay Chambers
33 Southernhay East, Exeter EX1 1NX
☎ 01392 255777
✉ clerks@southernhaychambers.co.uk
Call Date: Feb 1995, Lincoln's Inn

MANN MR JASVIR SINGH

No5 Chambers
Fountain Court, Steelhouse Lane, Birmingham B4 6DR ☎ 0845 210 5555 ✉ info@no5.com
No5 Chambers
Greenwood House, 4-7 Salisbury Court, London EC4Y 8AA ☎ 0845 210 5555
No5 Chambers
38 Queen Square, Bristol BS1 4QS
☎ 0845 210 5555
Call Date: Nov 2001, Middle Temple

Practising Areas: Crime, Immigration

MANN MR JONATHAN SIMON

25 Bedford Row
London WC1R 4HD ☎ 020 7067 1500
✉ clerks@25bedfordrow.com
Call Date: Nov 1989, Inner Temple

Practising Areas: Civil Liberties, Crime, Crime (Corporate/Fraud), Mental Health

MANN MISS SARA ANGELA

Call Date: Nov 1994, Middle Temple

MANNAN MR CHARLES MADANI FUAD

Temple Court Chambers
2nd Floor, 2 Dr Johnson's Building, Temple, London EC4Y 7AY ☎ 020 7353 7888
✉ clerks@templecourt.co.uk
Call Date: Nov 1993, Lincoln's Inn
Pupil Supervisor

Practising Areas: Commercial Litigation, Employment, Family, Immigration

C

MANNING MISS RUTH MARGARET HAYES

No 8 Chambers
8 Fountain Court, Steelhouse Lane, Birmingham B4 6DR ☎ 0121 236 5514
✉ clerks@no8chambers.co.uk
Call Date: Oct 1993, Gray's Inn

Practising Areas: Education

MANNION MS AMY ELISABETH

9-12 Bell Yard
London WC2A 2JR ☎ 020 7400 1800
✉ clerks@9-12bellyard.com
1 Crown Office Row
1 Crown Office Row, Temple, London EC4Y 7HH ☎ 020 7797 7500 ✉ mail@1cor.com
Call Date: Oct 2003, Inner Temple

Practising Areas: Administrative, Civil Liberties, Crime, Crime (Corporate/Fraud), Human Rights, Public Law

MANNION MR JOHN DENNIS

Tolzey Chambers
37 Rowlandson Gardens, Lockleaze, Bristol BS7 9UH
Call Date: May 1987, Middle Temple
Pupil Supervisor

Practising Areas: Crime, Employment, Health & Safety

MANSELL MR JASON FRANCIS GUY

Seven Bedford Row
7 Bedford Row, London WC1R 4BS
☎ 020 7242 3555 ✉ clerks@7br.co.uk
Call Date: Oct 1991, Lincoln's Inn

Practising Areas: Crime, Crime (Corporate/Fraud), Financial Services, Regulatory Law, Sports

C

MANSFIELD MR BENJAMIN ELLIOT

KCH Garden Square
1 Oxford Street, Nottingham NG1 5BH
☎ 0115 941 8851 ✉ clerks@kchgardensquare.co.uk
Call Date: Nov 2005, Inner Temple

Practising Areas: Family

MANSON MISS JULIANN

2-3 Hind Court Chambers
2-3 Hind Court, Fleet Street, London EC4A 3DL ☎ 020 7822 2150 ✉ david@2-3hindcourt.com
Call Date: Jul 1985, Middle Temple
Pupil Supervisor

MANTLE MR PETER JOHN

Monckton Chambers
1 & 2 Raymond Buildings, Gray's Inn, London WC1R 5NR ☎ 020 7405 7211
✉ chambers@monckton.com
Call Date: Jul 1989, Inner Temple
Pupil Supervisor

Practising Areas: Civil Liberties, Commercial Litigation, EC & Competition Law, Professional Negligence, Tax (Corporate)

MANYARARA MISS NATSAI

12 Old Square Chambers
1st Floor, 12 Old Square, Lincoln's Inn, London WC2A 3TX ☎ 020 7404 0875
✉ clerks@12oldsquare.com
Call Date: Jul 2001, Gray's Inn
Pupil Supervisor

Practising Areas: Common Law (General)

MARCUS MR PETER

Zenith Chambers
10 Park Square, Leeds LS1 2LH
☎ 0113 245 5438 ✉ clerks@zenithchambers.co.uk
Call Date: Jul 2004, Middle Temple

Practising Areas: Administrative, Chancery (Land Law), Common Law (General), Equity, Wills & Trusts, Health & Safety, Housing, Landlord & Tenant, Licensing, Local Government, Regulatory Law, Town & Country Planning

MARGO MR SAUL NICHOLAS

Outer Temple Chambers
The Outer Temple, 222 Strand, London WC2R 1BA ☎ 020 7353 6381
✉ clerks@outertemple.com
Call Date: Oct 2005, Lincoln's Inn

Practising Areas: Commercial Litigation, Employment, Pensions, Personal Injury, Regulatory Law

MARKHAM MISS HANNAH MEGAN

36 Bedford Row
London WC1R 4JH ☎ 020 7421 8000
✉ chambers@36bedfordrow.co.uk
Call Date: Jul 1998, Lincoln's Inn

MARKS MISS GILLIAN

14 Gray's Inn Square
14 Gray's Inn Square, Gray's Inn, London WC1R 5JP ☎ 020 7242 0858 ✉ clerks@14gis.co.uk
Call Date: Jul 1981, Gray's Inn
Pupil Supervisor, Recorder

Practising Areas: Ancillary Relief, Care Proceedings, Family, Family Provision

MARKS MISS JACQUELINE STEPHANIE

Coram Chambers
9-11 Fulwood Place, London WC1V 6HG
☎ 020 7092 3700 ✉ mail@coramchambers.co.uk
Call Date: Jul 1984, Middle Temple

Practising Areas: Family

MARKS MR JONATHAN CLIVE QC (1995)

4 Pump Court
4 Pump Court, Temple, London EC4Y 7AN
☎ 020 7842 5555 ✉ chambers@4pumpcourt.com
Call Date: Jul 1975, Inner Temple

Practising Areas: Chancery (General), Civil Liberties, Commercial Litigation, Common Law (General), Construction, Employment, Family, Medical Negligence, Personal Injury, Professional Negligence

MARKUS MS KATE

Doughty Street Chambers
53-54 Doughty Street, London WC1N 2LS
☎ 020 7404 1313 ✉ enquiries@doughtystreet.co.uk
Doughty Street Chambers
Pall Mall Court, 61-67 King Street, Manchester M2 4PD ☎ 0161 618 1066
Doughty Street Chambers
5th Floor, Broad Quay House, Prince Street, Bristol BS1 4DJ ☎ 01179 058 717
Call Date: Nov 1981, Gray's Inn
Pupil Supervisor

Practising Areas: Administrative, Civil Liberties, Discrimination, Education, Environment, Healthcare, Human Rights, Local Government, Mental Health, Regulatory Law

MARLER LIEUTENANT COLONEL LEE GARY

Bretton Woods Law
New Broad Street House, 35 New Broad Street, London EC2M 1NH
18 Red Lion Court
London EC4A 3EB ☎ 020 7520 6000
✉ chambers@18rlc.co.uk
Call Date: Nov 1987, Lincoln's Inn

Practising Areas: Administrative, Crime (Corporate/Fraud), Disciplinary Tribunals, Employment, Human Rights, Public International

MARLEY MISS SARAH ANNE

Coram Chambers
9-11 Fulwood Place, London WC1V 6HG
☎ 020 7092 3700 ✉ mail@coramchambers.co.uk
Call Date: Oct 1995, Lincoln's Inn

Practising Areas: Family, Family Provision

MAROOF MS LARA ANNE

Charter Chambers
33 John Street, London WC1N 2AT
☎ 020 7618 4400 ✉ clerks@charterchambers.com
Call Date: Jul 2001, Inner Temple

Practising Areas: Crime, Crime (Corporate/Fraud)

MARQUAND MR CHARLES NICHOLAS HILARY

4 Stone Buildings
Ground Floor, 4 Stone Buildings, Lincoln's Inn, London WC2A 3XT ☎ 020 7242 5524
✉ clerks@4stonebuildings.com
Call Date: Nov 1987, Inner Temple

Practising Areas: Arbitration, Financial Services

MARSDEN MR ANDREW CHARLES

St John's Chambers
101 Victoria Street, Bristol BS1 6PU
☎ 0117 923 4700 ✉ clerks@stjohnschambers.co.uk
Call Date: May 1994, Lincoln's Inn

Practising Areas: Commercial Litigation, Company & Commercial, Partnership, Sale & Carriage of Goods

MARSDEN MR ANDREW GUY

East Anglian Chambers
53 North Hill, Colchester, Essex CO1 1QA
☎ 01473 214481 ✉ colchester@ealaw.co.uk
East Anglian Chambers
140 New London Road, Chelmsford, Essex CM2 0AW ☎ 01473 214481
✉ chelmsford@ealaw.co.uk
East Anglian Chambers
15 The Close, Norwich, Norfolk NR1 4DZ
☎ 01473 214481 ✉ norwich@ealaw.co.uk
East Anglian Chambers
Gresham House, 5 Museum Street, Ipswich, Suffolk IP1 1HQ ☎ 01473 214481
✉ ipswich@ealaw.co.uk
Call Date: Jul 1975, Middle Temple
Pupil Supervisor, Recorder

Practising Areas: Agriculture, Ancillary Relief, Chancery (Land Law), Civil Litigation, Commercial Property, Common Land, Common

Law (General), Construction, Conveyancing, Environment, Equity, Wills & Trusts, Family, Family Provision, Land, Partnership, Probate & Administration, Professional Negligence, Sale & Carriage of Goods, Town & Country Planning

MARSH MR STEPHEN BRADLEY

Garden Court Chambers
57-60 Lincoln's Inn Fields, London WC2A 3LJ
☎ 020 7993 7600 ✉ info@gclaw.co.uk
Call Date: Jul 2005, Middle Temple

MARSHALL MR ANDREW DAVID MICHAEL CREAGH

3 PB Barristers
3 Paper Buildings, Temple, London EC4Y 7EU
☎ 020 7583 8055
3 PB Barristers
Royal Talbot House, 2 Victoria Street, Bristol, Avon BS1 6BB ☎ 0117 928 1520
3 PB Barristers
30 Christchurch Road, Bournemouth, Dorset BH1 3PD ☎ 01202 292102 ✉ clerks.bournemouth@3paper.co.uk
3 PB Barristers
4 St Peter Street, Winchester SO23 8BW
☎ 01962 868884 ✉ clerks.winchester@3paper.co.uk
3 PB Barristers
23 Beaumont Street, Oxford OX1 2NP
☎ 01865 793 736
Call Date: Jul 1981, Lincoln's Inn
Pupil Supervisor

MARSHALL MR DEREK STANLEY

College Chambers
19 Carlton Crescent, Southampton, Hampshire SO15 2ET ☎ 023 8023 0338
✉ clerks@college-chambers.co.uk
Call Date: Jul 1980, Inner Temple
Pupil Supervisor

Practising Areas: Arbitration, Bankruptcy, Chancery (General), Chancery (Land Law), Commercial Litigation, Common Land, Common Law (General), Company & Commercial, Construction, Employment, Equity, Wills & Trusts, Family, Family Provision, Franchising, Health & Safety, Insolvency, Landlord & Tenant, Licensing, Medical Negligence, Partnership, Personal Injury, Probate & Administration, Professional Negligence, Sale & Carriage of Goods

MARSHALL MRS ELIZABETH SUZANNE

Iscoed Chambers
86 St Helen's Road, Swansea SA1 4BQ
☎ 01792 652988 ✉ clerks@iscoedchambers.co.uk
Call Date: Oct 1995, Inner Temple

MARSHALL MISS VANESSA JULIETTE

Seven Bedford Row
7 Bedford Row, London WC1R 4BS
☎ 020 7242 3555 ✉ clerks@7br.co.uk
Call Date: Oct 1994, Gray's Inn
Pupil Supervisor

Practising Areas: Coroners Inquests, Crime, Healthcare, Inquests, Medical Negligence, Personal Injury, Professional Negligence

MARTIGNETTI MR IAN

Regency Chambers
45 Priestgate, Peterborough PE1 1LB
☎ 01733 315215 ✉ clerks@regencychambers.law.co.uk
Regency Chambers
Sheraton House, Castle Park, Cambridge CB3 0AX ☎ 01223 301517
Call Date: Nov 1990, Inner Temple
Pupil Supervisor

Practising Areas: Care Proceedings, Common Law (General), Education, Family, Family Provision, Licensing, Medical Negligence, Personal Injury

MARTIN MR BRADLEY DAVID

2 Temple Gardens
2 Temple Gardens, Temple, London EC4Y 9AY ☎ 020 7822 1200 ✉ clerks@2tg.co.uk
Call Date: Oct 1990, Lincoln's Inn
Pupil Supervisor

Practising Areas: Medical Negligence, Personal Injury, Professional Negligence, Regulatory Law

MARTIN MRS DIANNE JOAN ABEGAIL

St John's Chambers
101 Victoria Street, Bristol BS1 6PU
☎ 0117 923 4700 ✉ clerks@stjohnschambers.co.uk
Call Date: Oct 1992, Gray's Inn
Pupil Supervisor

Practising Areas: Care Proceedings, Family, Family Provision

MARTIN MR JAMES STEPHEN

5 King's Bench Walk
5 King's Bench Walk, Temple, London EC4Y 7DN ☎ 020 7353 5638 ✉ clerks@5kbw.co.uk
Call Date: Mar 2003, Lincoln's Inn

Practising Areas: Crime, Crime (Corporate/Fraud), Immigration, Regulatory Law

C

MARTIN MR JONATHAN DAVID

10 King's Bench Walk
Ground Floor, 10 King's Bench Walk, Temple, London EC4Y 7EB ☎020 7353 7742
✉Chambers@10kingsbenchwalk.co.uk
Call Date: Nov 1994, Middle Temple
Pupil Supervisor

Practising Areas: Human Rights, Immigration

MARTIN MR PETER JOHN

Chambers of Mr P J Martin
3 Anglesea Terrace, Wellesley Avenue, London W6 0UT ☎020 8746 1207
✉pmartinbar@btinternet.com
Call Date: Jul 1969, Gray's Inn
Pupil Supervisor

MARTIN MR PIERS JAMES

4 King's Bench Walk
2nd Floor, 4 King's Bench Walk, Temple, London EC4Y 7DL ☎020 7822 7000
✉clerks@4kbw.co.uk
Call Date: Oct 1997, Inner Temple

Practising Areas: Employment, Family

MARTIN MISS REBECCA JANE

1 Pump Court
Elm Court, Temple, London EC4Y 7AB
☎020 7842 7070 ✉(name)@pumpcourt.co.uk
Call Date: Jul 2002, Gray's Inn

MARZEC MS ALEXANDRA

5RB
1st Floor, 5 Raymond Buildings, Gray's Inn, London WC1R 5BP ☎020 7242 2902
✉clerks@5rb.com
Call Date: Nov 1990, Middle Temple
Pupil Supervisor

MASELLI MR MAURO

Chambers of Mr M Maselli
99 St Paul's Road, Peterborough PE1 3DR
☎07786 320064 ✉maselli@tiscali.co.uk
Priestgate Chambers
26 Priestgate, Peterborough PE1 1WG
☎01733 865 042
✉clerks@priestgatechambers.co.uk
Call Date: Mar 2007, Middle Temple

Practising Areas: Crime, Family

MASHEMBO MRS CAROL

St John's Chambers
101 Victoria Street, Bristol BS1 6PU
☎0117 923 4700 ✉clerks@stjohnschambers.co.uk
Call Date: Oct 1999, Lincoln's Inn

Practising Areas: Family, Family Provision

MASON MISS CATHERINE JANE

Sovereign Chambers
46 Park Place, Leeds LS1 2RY
☎0113 245 1841
✉clerks@sovereignchambers.co.uk
Call Date: Jul 2000, Middle Temple

MASON MR DAVID HUGH ROTHWELL

Dere Street Barristers
33 Broad Chare, Newcastle Upon Tyne NE1 3DQ ☎0844 3351551 ✉clerks@derestreet.co.uk
Call Date: Feb 1984, Middle Temple

Practising Areas: Discrimination, Employment

MASON MR IAN DOUGLAS

Amethyst Chambers
Ground Floor, 9 Kings Bench Walk, Inner Temple, London EC4Y 7DX
☎020 7936 4966 ✉info@amethystchambers.com
Call Date: Nov 1978, Lincoln's Inn
Pupil Supervisor

Practising Areas: Common Law (General), Environment, Housing, Immigration, Insolvency, Landlord & Tenant, Personal Injury

MASON MR JOHN JOSEPH

Cornwall Street Chambers
85-87 Cornwall Street, Birmingham B3 3BY
☎0121 233 7500 ✉clerks@cornwallstreet.co.uk
Call Date: Nov 1971, Inner Temple
Pupil Supervisor

MASON MR NICHOLAS ALAN

Park Court Chambers
16 Park Place, Leeds LS1 2SJ
☎0113 243 3277
✉clerks@parkcourtchambers.co.uk
Linenhall Chambers
1 Stanley Place, Chester CH1 2LU
☎01244 348282
✉clerks@linenhallchambers.co.uk
Call Date: Jul 1984, Gray's Inn
Pupil Supervisor

MASON MR PATRICK DAVID ANTHONY

Octagon Chambers
29 Park Street, Taunton, Somerset TA1 4DG
☎ 01823 331919
✉ jcload@Octagonchambers.co.uk
Call Date: Oct 1997, Inner Temple

MASON MR STEPHEN CHARLES WINSTON

Chambers of Mr S C W Mason
19a Church Street, Langford, Biggleswade, Bedfordshire SG18 9QT ☎ 01462 701 036
✉ stephenmason@stephenmason.co.uk
Call Date: Nov 1988, Middle Temple

Practising Areas: Company & Commercial, Information Technology

MASSARELLA MR DAVID PETER

Cloisters
1 Pump Court, Temple, London EC4Y 7AA
☎ 020 7827 4000 ✉ clerks@cloisters.com
Call Date: Nov 1999, Middle Temple
Pupil Supervisor

Practising Areas: Discrimination, Employment

MASSEY MISS STELLA MARIA

Central Chambers
89 Princess Street, Manchester M1 4HT
☎ 0161 236 1133 ✉ clerks@centralchambers.co.uk
Call Date: Feb 1990, Middle Temple
Pupil Supervisor

Practising Areas: Crime, Family

MASSIH MR MICHEL GEORGES ABDEL QC (1999)

Tooks Chambers
81 Farringdon Street, London EC4A 4BL
☎ 020 7842 7575 ✉ clerks@tooks.co.uk
Call Date: Nov 1979, Middle Temple

MASTERS MR ALAN BRUCE RAYMOND

1 Pump Court
Elm Court, Temple, London EC4Y 7AB
☎ 020 7842 7070 ✉ (name)@pumpcourt.co.uk
Call Date: Jul 1979, Middle Temple
Pupil Supervisor

Practising Areas: Administrative, Common Land, Courts Martial, Crime, Human Rights, Town & Country Planning

MATHER MISS ALISON ELISABETH

Kenworthy's Chambers
Arlington House, Bloom Street, Salford, Manchester M3 6AJ ☎ 0161 832 4036
Call Date: Oct 1997, Lincoln's Inn

MATHER MR BRIAN HOWARD

Trinity Chambers
The Custom House, 39 Quayside, Newcastle Upon Tyne NE1 3DE ☎ 0191 232 1927
✉ info@trinitychambers.co.uk
Trinity Chambers
Multi Media Exchange, 72-80 Corporation Road, Middlesbrough TS1 2RF
☎ 01642 247569 ✉ info@trinitychambers.co.uk
Call Date: Jul 2002, Gray's Inn

Practising Areas: Family, Family Provision

MATHER MISS KATE

1 Garden Court Family Law Chambers
Ground Floor, One Garden Court, Temple, London EC4Y 9BJ ☎ 020 7797 7900
✉ clerks@1gc.com
Call Date: Oct 1990, Gray's Inn
Pupil Supervisor

Practising Areas: Care Proceedings, Family, Family Provision

MATHER MR NICHOLAS IAN STEWART

Furnival Chambers
32 Furnival Street, London EC4A 1JQ
☎ 020 7405 3232
Call Date: Oct 1998, Middle Temple

Practising Areas: Administrative, Civil Liberties, Courts Martial, Crime, Film, Cable & TV, Human Rights, Parliamentary, Regulatory Law, Sports

MATON MR NEIL FOSTER

Pallant Chambers
12 North Pallant, Chichester, West Sussex PO19 1TQ ☎ 01243 784538
✉ clerks@pallantchambers.co.uk
Call Date: Jul 2001, Middle Temple

Practising Areas: Family, Family Provision

MATOVU MR DANIEL MBUSI SAJABI

2 Temple Gardens
2 Temple Gardens, Temple, London EC4Y 9AY ☎ 020 7822 1200 ✉ clerks@2tg.co.uk
Call Date: Nov 1985, Inner Temple
Pupil Supervisor

MATTHEWS MR JANEK PAUL

Pump Court Tax Chambers
16 Bedford Row, London WC1R 4EF
☎ 020 7414 8080 ✉ clerks@pumptax.com
Call Date: Jul 1972, Gray's Inn

MATTHIAS MR DAVID HUW QC (2006)

Francis Taylor Building
Inner Temple, London EC4Y 7BY
☎ 020 7353 8415 ✉ clerks@ftb.eu.com
Call Date: Jul 1980, Inner Temple
Pupil Supervisor

Practising Areas: Administrative, Agriculture, Arbitration, Banking, Bankruptcy, Chancery (General), Chancery (Land Law), Charities, Civil Liberties, Civil Litigation, Commercial Litigation, Commercial Property, Common Land, Common Law (General), Company & Commercial, Competition, Construction, Consumer, Copyright, Coroners Inquests, Corporate Finance, Costs, Courts Martial, Crime (Corporate/Fraud), Data Protection, Defamation, Disciplinary Tribunals, Discrimination, EC & Competition Law, Ecclesiastical, Education, Employment, Energy, Entertainment, Environment, Equity, Wills & Trusts, Family Provision, Film, Cable & TV, Health & Safety, Healthcare, Housing, Human Rights, Immigration, Industrial Diseases, Information Technology, Inquests, Insolvency, Insurance, Insurance/ Reinsurance, Intellectual Property, International Trade, Land, Landlord & Tenant, Licensing, Local Government, Medical Negligence, Mental Health, Parliamentary, Partnership, Personal Injury, Private International, Probate & Administration, Professional Negligence, Public International, Public Law, Regulatory Law, Road Traffic And Highways, Sale & Carriage of Goods, Sports, Telecommunications, Town & Country Planning

MAUDSLAY MISS DIANA ELIZABETH

Sovereign Chambers
46 Park Place, Leeds LS1 2RY
☎ 0113 245 1841
✉ clerks@sovereignchambers.co.uk
Call Date: Oct 1997, Gray's Inn
Pupil Supervisor

MAUDSLEY MRS PENELOPE KATHLEEN

Central Chambers
89 Princess Street, Manchester M1 4HT
☎ 0161 236 1133 ✉ clerks@centralchambers.co.uk
Trident Barristers Chambers
Peter House, Oxford Street, Manchester M1 5AN ☎ 0161 663 3123
✉ clerks@tridentchambers.com
Alexander Chambers
13 Halstead Road, Wanstead, London E11 2AY ☎ 0845 652 0451 / 0854 652 0451
✉ clerks@alexanderchambers.co.uk
Call Date: Oct 1998, Lincoln's Inn

MAUGHAM MR JOLYON TOBY DENNIS

11 New Square
1st Floor, 11 New Square, Lincoln's Inn, London WC2A 3QB ☎ 020 7242 4017
✉ john.moore@11newsquare.com
Call Date: Mar 1997, Middle Temple
Pupil Supervisor

Practising Areas: Professional Negligence, Tax (Capital & Income), Tax (Corporate)

MAUNDER MR DAVID JAMES

Queen Square Chambers
56 Queen Square, Bristol BS1 4PR
☎ 0117 921 1966 ✉ crime@qs-c.co.uk
Call Date: Oct 1993, Middle Temple

MAWDSLEY MR DAVID JOHN

Chambers of Mr David Mawdsley
17 Clinning Road, Southport, Merseyside PR8 4NU ☎ 01704 565 387
Call Date: Nov 1995, Gray's Inn

Practising Areas: Crime, Crime (Corporate/ Fraud), Employment

MAWDSLEY MR MATTHEW EDWARD

Call Date: Nov 1991, Inner Temple
Pupil Supervisor

MAWREY MS ELEANOR FRANCES

The Chambers of Grahame Aldous QC
9 Gough Square, London EC4A 3DG
☎ 020 7832 0500 ✉ clerks@9goughsquare.co.uk
Call Date: Jul 2001, Gray's Inn
Pupil Supervisor

Practising Areas: Crime, Crime (Corporate/ Fraud)

MAWREY MR RICHARD BROOKS QC (1986)

Henderson Chambers
2 Harcourt Buildings, Temple, London EC4Y 9DB ☎ 020 7583 9020
✉ clerks@hendersonchambers.co.uk
Call Date: Feb 1964, Gray's Inn
Recorder

C

Practising Areas: Administrative, Arbitration, Asset Finance, Banking, Chancery (General), Commercial Litigation, Common Law (General), Company & Commercial, Competition, Construction, EC & Competition Law, Financial Services, Information Technology, Local Government, Sale & Carriage of Goods

MAX MISS SALLY ANN

29 Bedford Row Chambers
London WC1R 4HE ☎020 7404 1044
✉clerks@29br.co.uk
Call Date: Oct 1991, Lincoln's Inn

Practising Areas: Family

MAXWELL MR ADRIAN ROBERT JOHN

St John's Chambers
101 Victoria Street, Bristol BS1 6PU
☎0117 923 4700 ✉clerks@stjohnschambers.co.uk
Call Date: Nov 1993, Middle Temple

Practising Areas: Crime, Crime (Corporate/Fraud), Regulatory Law

MAXWELL LEWIS MR CAMERON

Lamb Chambers
Lamb Building, Elm Court, Temple, London EC4Y 7AS ☎020 7797 8300
✉info@lambchambers.co.uk
Call Date: Jul 1974, Middle Temple

Practising Areas: Commercial Litigation, Copyright, Entertainment, Film, Cable & TV, Intellectual Property, International Trade, Partnership, Sale & Carriage of Goods, Sports

MAY MR CHRISTOPHER JOHN

Five St Andrew's Hill
5 St Andrew's Hill, London EC4V 5BZ
☎020 7332 5400 ✉Clerks@5sah.co.uk
Call Date: Nov 1983, Middle Temple

Practising Areas: Coroners Inquests, Crime, Crime (Corporate/Fraud), Inquests, Regulatory Law

MAYHEW MISS JUDITH

3 Dr Johnson's Buildings
Ground Floor, 3 Dr Johnson's Buildings, Temple, London EC4Y 7BA ☎020 7353 4854
✉clerks@3djb.co.uk
Call Date: Jul 2000, Middle Temple

Practising Areas: Ancillary Relief, Family

MAYNARD MR CHRISTOPHER HOWARD

Tanfield Chambers
2-5 Warwick Court, London WC1R 5DJ
☎020 7421 5300 ✉clerks@tanfieldchambers.co.uk
Call Date: Jul 1988, Gray's Inn
Pupil Supervisor

Practising Areas: Commercial Litigation, Commercial Property, Equity, Wills & Trusts, Landlord & Tenant, Partnership

MAYNARD MR MATTHEW DAVID

St Ive's Chambers
Whittall Street, Birmingham B4 6DH
☎0121 236 0863 ✉clerks@stiveschambers.co.uk
Call Date: Nov 2003, Inner Temple
Pupil Supervisor

Practising Areas: Care Proceedings, Family, Family Provision

MAYO MR SIMON PETER QC (2008)

187 Fleet Street
London EC4A 2AT ☎020 7430 7430
✉chambers@187fleetstreet.com
Call Date: Nov 1985, Inner Temple
Recorder

Practising Areas: Crime, Crime (Corporate/Fraud), Regulatory Law

MCAVOCK MAJOR GABRIELLE

2 King's Bench Walk
2 King's Bench Walk, Temple, London EC4Y 7DE ☎020 7353 1746 ✉clerks@2kbw.com
Call Date: Oct 1994, Lincoln's Inn

MCBRIDE MR MARTIN JEREMY

Monckton Chambers
1 & 2 Raymond Buildings, Gray's Inn, London WC1R 5NR ☎020 7405 7211
✉chambers@monckton.com
Call Date: Nov 2004, Inner Temple

Practising Areas: Human Rights, Public International, Public Law

MCCABE MISS LOUISE ANNE

St Philips Chambers
55 Temple Row, Birmingham B2 5LS
☎0121 246 7000 ✉clerks@st-philips.com
Call Date: Oct 1996, Inner Temple

Practising Areas: Ancillary Relief, Family, Family Provision

C

MCCAFFERTY MISS LYNNE

4 Pump Court
4 Pump Court, Temple, London EC4Y 7AN
☎ 020 7842 5555 ✉ chambers@4pumpcourt.com
Call Date: Oct 1997, Middle Temple
Pupil Supervisor

Practising Areas: Arbitration, Commercial Litigation, Information Technology

MCCANN MISS KATIE

Atlantic Chambers
4-6 Cook Street, Liverpool L2 9QU
☎ 0151 236 4421 ✉ info@atlanticchambers.co.uk
Call Date: Oct 2009, Lincoln's Inn

Practising Areas: Care Proceedings, Chancery (Land Law), Equity, Wills & Trusts, Family, Family Provision, Professional Negligence

MCCANN MISS SARAH JANE

Hardwicke
New Square, Lincoln's Inn, London WC2A 3SB ☎ 020 7242 2523
✉ enquiries@hardwicke.co.uk
Call Date: Oct 2001, Lincoln's Inn

MCCARTHY MR MARTIN RAYMOND

Farringdon Chambers
180 Bermondsey Street, London SE1 3TQ
☎ 020 7089 5700
Call Date: Nov 1994, Gray's Inn
Pupil Supervisor

Practising Areas: Crime, Crime (Corporate/Fraud)

MCCARTHY MISS TARA MIA INGER

Thomas More Chambers
7 Lincoln's Inn Fields, London WC2A 3BP
☎ 020 7404 7000 ✉ clerks@thomasmore.co.uk
Call Date: Oct 1997, Lincoln's Inn

Practising Areas: Crime, Crime (Corporate/Fraud)

MCCARTHY MR WILLIAM

Bridgewater Chambers
5 Bleasefell Chase, Worsley, Manchester M28 1UZ ☎ 0161 3877127
✉ info@barristers-chambers.com
1 Mitre Court Buildings
1 Mitre Court Buildings, Temple, London EC4Y 7BS ☎ 020 7452 8900 ✉ clerks@1mcb.com
Call Date: Nov 1996, Middle Temple

Practising Areas: Chancery (General), Commercial Litigation, Commercial Property, Common Law (General), Equity, Wills & Trusts, Franchising, Housing, Landlord & Tenant

MCCOMBIE MR FERGUS ALEXANDER PAUL

1 Gray's Inn Square
Ground Floor, 1 Gray's Inn Square, London WC1R 5AA ☎ 020 7405 0001
Call Date: Oct 1999, Gray's Inn

Practising Areas: Administrative, Civil Litigation, Commercial Litigation, Commercial Property, Common Law (General), Company & Commercial, Disciplinary Tribunals, Discrimination, Employment, Insolvency, Land, Landlord & Tenant, Local Government, Professional Negligence, Public Law, Sports

MCCORMACK MR ALAN

Staple Inn Chambers
1st Floor, 9 Staple Inn, Holborn Bars, London WC1V 7QH ☎ 020 7242 5240
✉ clerks@stapleinn.co.uk
Call Date: Oct 1990, Lincoln's Inn
Pupil Supervisor

Practising Areas: Care Proceedings, Chancery (General), Chancery (Land Law), Children's Law, Common Law (General), Costs, Employment, Equity, Wills & Trusts, Family, Family Provision, Housing, Land, Landlord & Tenant, Licensing, Personal Injury

MCCORMACK MISS HELEN

15 New Bridge Street
London EC4V 6AU ☎ 020 7842 1900
✉ clerks@15nbs.com
Call Date: Feb 1986, Middle Temple
Pupil Supervisor

MCCORMACK MISS THERESA MARIE

St Philips Chambers
55 Temple Row, Birmingham B2 5LS
☎ 0121 246 7000 ✉ clerks@st-philips.com
Call Date: Jul 2002, Inner Temple

MCCORMICK DR PAUL MARTIN

Hampshire Chambers
Malton House, 24 Hampshire Terrace, Portsmouth, Hampshire PO1 2QF
☎ 023 9282 6636 ✉ PMC.CLERK@BTCONNECT.COM
Call Date: Jul 1983, Middle Temple

MCCORMICK MR WILLIAM THOMAS QC (2010)

Ely Place Chambers
30 Ely Place, London EC1N 6TD
☎ 020 7400 9600 ✉ admin@elyplace.com
Call Date: Jul 1985, Gray's Inn
Pupil Supervisor

Practising Areas: Commercial Litigation, Common Law (General), Defamation, Employment, Personal Injury, Professional Negligence, Sports

MCCRACKEN MR JAMES

Cornwall Street Chambers
85-87 Cornwall Street, Birmingham B3 3BY
☎ 0121 233 7500 ✉ clerks@cornwallstreet.co.uk
Call Date: Nov 1998, Middle Temple

Practising Areas: Commercial Litigation, Disciplinary Tribunals, Employment, Partnership

MCCRACKEN MR ROBERT HENRY JOY QC (2003)

Francis Taylor Building
Inner Temple, London EC4Y 7BY
☎ 020 7353 8415 ✉ clerks@ftb.eu.com
Call Date: Jul 1973, Inner Temple

Practising Areas: Administrative, Environment, Town & Country Planning

MCCRAE MISS FIONA

Trinity Chambers
The Custom House, 39 Quayside, Newcastle Upon Tyne NE1 3DE ☎ 0191 232 1927
✉ info@trinitychambers.co.uk
Trinity Chambers
Multi Media Exchange, 72-80 Corporation Road, Middlesbrough TS1 2RF
☎ 01642 247569 ✉ info@trinitychambers.co.uk
Call Date: Jul 1986, Gray's Inn

Practising Areas: Family, Family Provision, Immigration

MCCRIMMON MISS CATHRYN JANE

4 Breams Buildings
Chancery Lane, London EC4A 1HP
☎ 020 7092 1900 ✉ clerks@4bb.co.uk
Call Date: Nov 1991, Middle Temple

MCCUE MR DONALD

11 Stone Buildings
11 Stone Buildings, Lincoln's Inn, London WC2A 3TG ☎ 020 7831 6381 ✉ clerks@11sb.com
Call Date: Jul 1974, Lincoln's Inn

Practising Areas: Arbitration, Banking, Chancery (General), Commercial Litigation, Construction, Equity, Wills & Trusts, Partnership, Professional Negligence, Sale & Carriage of Goods

MCCULLOCH MISS FIONA CATHARINE JANE

Middle Temple Lane Chambers
2nd Floor South, 1 Middle Temple Lane, London EC4Y 9AA ☎ 020 7583 4352
✉ chambers@mtlchambers.com
Call Date: Jul 2002, Middle Temple

Practising Areas: Civil Litigation, Common Law (General), Consumer, Courts Martial, Crime, Crime (Corporate/Fraud), Ecclesiastical, Health & Safety, Housing, Inquests, Landlord & Tenant, Personal Injury, Road Traffic And Highways, Sale & Carriage of Goods

MCCULLOUGH MISS LOUISE CLARE

Chambers of Mr Ami Feder
Ground Floor, Lamb Building, Temple, London EC4Y 7AS ☎ 020 7797 7788
✉ clerks@lambbuilding.co.uk
Lamb Building
22 Ship Street, Brighton BN1 1AD
☎ 01273 820490 ✉ admin@lambbuilding.co.uk
Chambers of Mr Ami Feder
Ground Floor, Lamb Building, Temple, London EC4Y 7AS ☎ 020 7797 7788
✉ clerks@lambbuilding.co.uk
Call Date: Oct 1991, Middle Temple
Pupil Supervisor

Practising Areas: Care Proceedings, Crime, Family

MCDERMOTT MR GERARD FRANCIS QC (1999)

Chambers of Gerard McDermott QC
Weir House, 7 Stamford Street, Stalybridge SK15 1JP ☎ 0161 304 4301
✉ gerard@mcdermottqc.com
9 St John Street
Manchester M3 4DN ☎ 0161 955 9000
✉ civilclerks@9sjs.com/criminalclerks@9sjs.com

C

Outer Temple Chambers
The Outer Temple, 222 Strand, London WC2R 1BA ☎020 7353 6381
✉clerks@outertemple.com
Call Date: Jul 1978, Middle Temple
Pupil Supervisor, Recorder

MCDERMOTT MR JOHN RAYMUND QC (2003)

Chavasse Court Chambers
18 Queen Avenue, Liverpool L2 4TX
☎0151 229 2030
✉clerks@chavassechambers.co.uk
Call Date: Nov 1976, Gray's Inn

MCDONALD MR BRENT ANDREW

Old Square Chambers
3 Orchard Court, St Augustine's Yard, Bristol BS1 5DP ☎0117 930 5100
✉clerks@oldsquare.co.uk
Call Date: Oct 2000, Gray's Inn

Practising Areas: Personal Injury

MCDONALD MISS JANET

9 Park Place
Cardiff, South Glamorgan CF10 3DP
☎029 2038 2731 ✉clerks@9parkplace.co.uk
Call Date: Jul 1984, Gray's Inn

Practising Areas: Crime, Crime (Corporate/Fraud)

MCDONALD MR JOHN WILLIAM

2 Temple Gardens
2 Temple Gardens, Temple, London EC4Y 9AY ☎020 7822 1200 ✉clerks@2tg.co.uk
Call Date: Nov 1981, Middle Temple
Pupil Supervisor

Practising Areas: Common Law (General), Construction, Insurance, Landlord & Tenant, Personal Injury, Professional Negligence

MCDONALD MS MELANIE SHARON

No5 Chambers
Greenwood House, 4-7 Salisbury Court, London EC4Y 8AA ☎0845 210 5555
No5 Chambers
38 Queen Square, Bristol BS1 4QS
☎0845 210 5555
No5 Chambers
Fountain Court, Steelhouse Lane, Birmingham B4 6DR ☎0845 210 5555 ✉info@no5.com
Call Date: Nov 1990, Inner Temple
Pupil Supervisor

Practising Areas: Administrative, Education, Health & Safety, Healthcare, Human Rights, Local Government, Medical Negligence, Mental Health, Professional Negligence, Regulatory Law

MCDONNELL MR JOHN BERESFORD WILLIAM QC (1984)

13 Old Square Chambers
Ground Floor, 14 Old Square, Lincoln's Inn, London WC2A 3UE ☎020 7831 4445
✉clerks@13oldsquare.com
Call Date: Jul 1968, Inner Temple

Practising Areas: Administrative, Banking, Bankruptcy, Chancery (General), Chancery (Land Law), Charities, Commercial Litigation, Commodities, Common Land, Company & Commercial, Construction, Conveyancing, Crime, Entertainment, Equity, Wills & Trusts, Family Provision, Financial Services, Insolvency, Intellectual Property, Landlord & Tenant, Partnership, Private International, Probate & Administration, Professional Negligence

MCDOWELL MR DANIEL ROBIN

36 Bedford Row
London WC1R 4JH ☎020 7421 8000
✉chambers@36bedfordrow.co.uk
Call Date: Oct 2001, Gray's Inn

MCFARLANE MISS CYNTHIA JULLIETT

10 King's Bench Walk
Ground Floor, 10 King's Bench Walk, Temple, London EC4Y 7EB ☎020 7353 7742
✉Chambers@10kingsbenchwalk.co.uk
Call Date: Nov 2003, Middle Temple

Practising Areas: Common Law (General), Crime

MCGEE DR TRISTAN PAUL

Foxhill Chambers
Matterdale, Penrith, Cumbria CA11 0SA
☎01768 482710
✉clerking@foxhillchambers.com
Call Date: Nov 1997, Middle Temple

Practising Areas: Energy, Personal Injury, Town & Country Planning

MCGHEE MR PHILIP JAMES

QEB Hollis Whiteman
1-2 Laurence Pountney Hill, London EC4R 0EU ☎020 7933 8855 ✉barristers@qebhw.co.uk
Call Date: Oct 2003, Gray's Inn

Practising Areas: Crime, Crime (Corporate/Fraud), Regulatory Law

MCGHEE MR STUART EDWARD

College Chambers
19 Carlton Crescent, Southampton, Hampshire SO15 2ET ☎ 023 8023 0338
✉ clerks@college-chambers.co.uk
Call Date: Mar 2000, Lincoln's Inn

Practising Areas: Chancery (General), Family, Family Provision

MCGONIGAL MR DAVID AMBROSE

Broadway House Chambers
Broadway House, 9 Bank Street, Bradford, West Yorkshire BD1 1TW ☎ 01274 722560
✉ clerks@broadwayhouse.co.uk
Broadway House Chambers
25 Park Square West, Leeds, West Yorkshire LS1 2PW ☎ 0113 246 2600
✉ clerks@broadwayhouse.co.uk
Call Date: Jul 1982, Gray's Inn
Pupil Supervisor

MCGOWAN MISS MAURA PATRICIA QC (2001)

2 Bedford Row
London WC1R 4BU ☎ 020 7440 8888
✉ clerks@2bedfordrow.co.uk
Lincoln House Chambers
Tower 12, The Avenue North, Spinningfields, 18-22 Bridge Street, Manchester M3 3BZ
☎ 0161 832 5701
✉ info@lincolnhousechambers.com
Call Date: Nov 1980, Middle Temple

Practising Areas: Administrative, Children's Law, Civil Liberties, Coroners Inquests, Courts Martial, Crime, Crime (Corporate/Fraud), Disciplinary Tribunals, Family, Human Rights, Licensing, Regulatory Law

MCGRATH MR ANDREW JOHN

No5 Chambers
Fountain Court, Steelhouse Lane, Birmingham B4 6DR ☎ 0845 210 5555 ✉ info@no5.com
No5 Chambers
Greenwood House, 4-7 Salisbury Court, London EC4Y 8AA ☎ 0845 210 5555
No5 Chambers
38 Queen Square, Bristol BS1 4QS
☎ 0845 210 5555
Call Date: Nov 1983, Gray's Inn

Practising Areas: Employment, Town & Country Planning

MCGUINNESS-WAY MR ANDREW JEFFREY SEBASTIAN

Holborn Chambers
6 Gate Street, Lincoln's Inn Fields, London WC2A 3HP ☎ 020 7242 6060
Call Date: Oct 1992, Middle Temple

MCGUIRE MR KENNETH

3 PB Barristers
3 Paper Buildings, Temple, London EC4Y 7EU
☎ 020 7583 8055
Call Date: Jul 2000, Inner Temple

MCINTOSH MS MELANIE

Becket Chambers
17 New Dover Road, Canterbury, Kent CT1 3AS ☎ 01227 786331
✉ clerks@becket-chambers.co.uk
Call Date: Mar 2002, Lincoln's Inn

MCINTOSH MISS NICOLA

KCH Garden Square
1 Oxford Street, Nottingham NG1 5BH
☎ 0115 941 8851 ✉ clerks@kchgardensquare.co.uk
Call Date: Nov 2007, Lincoln's Inn

MCKAY MR CHRISTOPHER ALEXANDER

Cathedral Chambers
10 Clytha Park Road, Newport NP20 4PB
☎ 01633 215112
Call Date: Nov 1976, Gray's Inn
Pupil Supervisor

Practising Areas: Ancillary Relief, Equity, Wills & Trusts, Family, Land, Landlord & Tenant, Town & Country Planning

MCKEE MR HUGH ANTHONY

16 Winckley Square
Preston PR1 3JJ ☎ 01772 256100
St Johns Buildings
21 White Friars, Chester CH1 1NZ
☎ 01244 323070 ✉ clerk@stjohnsbuildings.co.uk
St Johns Buildings Liverpool
8th Floor India Buildings, Water Street, Liverpool L2 0XG ☎ 0151 243 6000
✉ clerk@stjohnsbuildings.co.uk
Call Date: Nov 1983, Middle Temple
Pupil Supervisor

MCKENDRICK MR JOHN DEMPSTER

Outer Temple Chambers
The Outer Temple, 222 Strand, London WC2R 1BA ☎ 020 7353 6381
✉ clerks@outertemple.com
Call Date: Nov 1999, Inner Temple

Practising Areas: Administrative, Civil Liberties, Education

MCKEONE MS MARY BRENDA

Chambers of Ian Macdonald QC
Garden Court North, 22 Oxford Court, Manchester M2 3WQ ☎ 0161 236 1840
✉ clerks@gcnchambers.co.uk
Call Date: Feb 1986, Gray's Inn

MCKIERNAN MR EDWARD JOSEPH

Farringdon Chambers
180 Bermondsey Street, London SE1 3TQ
☎ 020 7089 5700
Call Date: Nov 1981, Lincoln's Inn
Pupil Supervisor

Practising Areas: Civil Liberties, Competition, Crime, Crime (Corporate/Fraud), Discrimination, EC & Competition Law, Employment, Local Government, Professional Negligence

MCKINNEY MISS NICOLA ALEXANDRA

4 KBW
Ground Floor, 4 King's Bench Walk, Temple, London EC4Y 7DL ☎ 020 7822 8822
✉ law@4kbw.net
Call Date: Oct 2004, Gray's Inn

Practising Areas: Common Law (General), Discrimination, Education, Employment, Foreign Law, Immigration, Landlord & Tenant, Licensing, Professional Negligence

MCKONE MR MARK DESMOND

Sovereign Chambers
46 Park Place, Leeds LS1 2RY
☎ 0113 245 1841
✉ clerks@sovereignchambers.co.uk
Call Date: Nov 1988, Lincoln's Inn
Pupil Supervisor

Practising Areas: Courts Martial, Crime, Crime (Corporate/Fraud), Road Traffic And Highways, Sports

MCLAUGHLIN MR ANDREW PETER

St John's Chambers
101 Victoria Street, Bristol BS1 6PU
☎ 0117 923 4700 ✉ clerks@stjohnschambers.co.uk
Call Date: Nov 1993, Middle Temple

MCLINDEN MR JOHN VINCENT BARRY QC (2011)

Field Court Chambers
5 Field Court, Gray's Inn, London WC1R 5EF
☎ 020 7405 6114 ✉ clerks@fieldcourt.co.uk
Call Date: Apr 1991, Inner Temple
Pupil Supervisor

Practising Areas: Administrative, Banking, Bankruptcy, Chancery (General), Chancery (Land Law), Civil Liberties, Commercial Litigation, Common Law (General), Company & Commercial, Crime, Crime (Corporate/Fraud), Defamation, Equity, Wills & Trusts, Foreign Law, Human Rights, Insolvency, Partnership, Pensions, Private International, Probate & Administration, Professional Negligence, Telecommunications

MCLOUGHLIN MR KEVIN

Temple Garden Chambers
1 Harcourt Buildings, Temple, London EC4Y 9DA ☎ 020 7583 1315 ✉ clerks@tgchambers.com
Call Date: May 2007, Middle Temple

Practising Areas: Health & Safety

MCMILLAN MRS CAROL ANN

Westgate Chambers
64 High Street, Lewes, East Sussex BN7 1XG
☎ 01273 480510
✉ clerks@westgate-chambers.co.uk
Call Date: Nov 1996, Middle Temple
Pupil Supervisor

Practising Areas: Care Proceedings, Family

MCMORROW MR PATRICK JOSEPH

4 King's Bench Walk
2nd Floor, 4 King's Bench Walk, Temple, London EC4Y 7DL ☎ 020 7822 7000
✉ clerks@4kbw.co.uk
Call Date: Oct 1996, Inner Temple

Practising Areas: Commercial Litigation, Construction, Landlord & Tenant, Personal Injury

MCMULLAN MS LAURA CHRISTINA

Coram Chambers
9-11 Fulwood Place, London WC1V 6HG
☎ 020 7092 3700 ✉ mail@coramchambers.co.uk
Call Date: Nov 2004, Inner Temple

Practising Areas: Care Proceedings, Family, Family Provision

MCNAE MR JONATHAN JAMES

Selborne Chambers
10 Essex Street, London WC2R 3AA
☎020 7420 9500
✉clerks@selbornechambers.co.uk
Call Date: Oct 2001, Gray's Inn
Pupil Supervisor

Practising Areas: Bankruptcy, Chancery (General), Chancery (Land Law), Civil Litigation, Commercial Litigation, Commercial Property, Company & Commercial, Insolvency, Land, Landlord & Tenant, Professional Negligence

MCNALLY MR JOHN JOSEPH

Dyers Chambers
35 Bedford Row, London WC1R 4JH
☎020 7404 1881 ✉admin@dyerschambers.com
Call Date: Nov 1996, Gray's Inn

Practising Areas: Crime, Crime (Corporate/Fraud), Inquests, Public International, Public Law

MCNEILL MR DAVID MARTIN

Five St Andrew's Hill
5 St Andrew's Hill, London EC4V 5BZ
☎020 7332 5400 ✉Clerks@5sah.co.uk
Call Date: Nov 2003, Inner Temple

Practising Areas: Chancery (Land Law), Commercial Litigation, Common Law (General), Crime, Crime (Corporate/Fraud), Landlord & Tenant, Licensing, Local Government, Personal Injury

MCNERNEY MR KEVIN JOHN

Call Date: Nov 1992, Inner Temple

MCNICHOLAS MR CHRISTOPHER JOHN

Goresbrook Chambers
PO Box 6017, Milton Keynes MK1 9AP
☎0845 123 1234 ✉thomas.john6@btinternet.com
Call Date: Nov 1995, Lincoln's Inn

Practising Areas: Banking, Commercial Litigation, Common Law (General), Crime, Ecclesiastical, Human Rights, Immigration

MCNICHOLAS MR EAMON JOHN

Temple Tax Chambers
1st Floor, 3 Temple Gardens, Temple, London EC4Y 9AU ☎020 7353 7884
✉clerks@templetax.com
Call Date: Oct 1994, Lincoln's Inn

MCTAGUE MISS MEGHANN ROSE

2 Temple Gardens
2 Temple Gardens, Temple, London EC4Y 9AY ☎020 7822 1200 ✉clerks@2tg.co.uk
Call Date: Oct 2004, Inner Temple

Practising Areas: Admiralty, Civil Liberties, Common Law (General), Health & Safety, Personal Injury

MCWATTERS MR CHRISTOPHER GEORGE

Garden Court Chambers
57-60 Lincoln's Inn Fields, London WC2A 3LJ
☎020 7993 7600 ✉info@gclaw.co.uk
Call Date: Nov 2004, Lincoln's Inn

Practising Areas: Family

MEACHIN MISS VANESSA VERONICA

St Philips Chambers
55 Temple Row, Birmingham B2 5LS
☎0121 246 7000 ✉clerks@st-philips.com
Call Date: Oct 1990, Inner Temple
Pupil Supervisor, Recorder

Practising Areas: Ancillary Relief, Care Proceedings, Children's Law, Family, Family Provision

MEAGER MRS ROWENA ELISABETH

No5 Chambers
Fountain Court, Steelhouse Lane, Birmingham B4 6DR ☎0845 210 5555 ✉info@no5.com
No5 Chambers
Greenwood House, 4-7 Salisbury Court, London EC4Y 8AA ☎0845 210 5555
No5 Chambers
38 Queen Square, Bristol BS1 4QS
☎0845 210 5555
Call Date: Jul 2007, Lincoln's Inn

Practising Areas: Chancery (General), Chancery (Land Law), Common Land, Conveyancing, Equity, Wills & Trusts, Insolvency, Landlord & Tenant, Probate & Administration, Professional Negligence, Town & Country Planning

MEARES MR NIGEL LESLIE VELLACOTT

11 Stone Buildings
11 Stone Buildings, Lincoln's Inn, London WC2A 3TG ☎020 7831 6381 ✉clerks@11sb.com
Call Date: Nov 1975, Middle Temple
Pupil Supervisor

Practising Areas: Chancery (General), Chancery (Land Law), Charities, Commercial Litigation, Commercial Property, Conveyancing,

C

Equity, Wills & Trusts, Family Provision, Landlord & Tenant, Probate & Administration, Professional Negligence

MEDCROFT MR NICHOLAS JULIAN

Outer Temple Chambers
The Outer Temple, 222 Strand, London WC2R 1BA ☎020 7353 6381
✉clerks@outertemple.com
Call Date: Oct 1998, Lincoln's Inn

Practising Areas: Banking, Civil Litigation, Financial Services, Regulatory Law

MEDD MR JAMES POWYS

Crown Office Chambers
2 Crown Office Row, Temple, London EC4Y 7HJ ☎020 7797 8100
✉mail@crownofficechambers.com
Call Date: Jul 1985, Middle Temple
Pupil Supervisor

Practising Areas: Arbitration, Commercial Litigation, Common Law (General), Construction, Insurance, Personal Injury, Professional Negligence, Sale & Carriage of Goods

MEDHURST MR DAVID CHARLES

4 Brick Court
4 Brick Court, Temple, London EC4Y 9AD
☎020 7832 3200 ✉clerks@4bc.co.uk
Call Date: Nov 1969, Gray's Inn
Pupil Supervisor

Practising Areas: Human Rights, Immigration

MEEGAN MR TREVOR LEO

Citadel Chambers
The Citadel, 190 Corporation Street, Birmingham B4 6QD ☎0121 233 8500
✉clerks@citadelchambers.com
Call Date: Jul 2000, Lincoln's Inn

Practising Areas: Crime, Licensing

MEEKE MR ROBERT MARTIN JAMES QC (2000)

Colleton Chambers
Colleton Crescent, Exeter, Devon EX2 4DG
☎01392 274898 ✉clerks@colletonchambers.co.uk
Call Date: Jul 1973, Gray's Inn
Recorder

Practising Areas: Courts Martial, Crime, Crime (Corporate/Fraud), Environment, Health & Safety

MEHTA MISS ANITA ROXANE

Crown Office Row Chambers
119 Church Street, Brighton, Sussex BN1 1UD ☎01273 625625 ✉clerks@1cor.com
Call Date: Oct 2002, Lincoln's Inn

Practising Areas: Equity, Wills & Trusts, Family, Family Provision

MEHTA MR SAILESH

18 Red Lion Court
London EC4A 3EB ☎020 7520 6000
✉chambers@18rlc.co.uk
Call Date: Jul 1986, Lincoln's Inn
Pupil Supervisor

MEICHEN MR JONATHAN BRIAN

St Philips Chambers
55 Temple Row, Birmingham B2 5LS
☎0121 246 7000 ✉clerks@st-philips.com
Call Date: Nov 2006, Inner Temple

Practising Areas: Care Proceedings, Discrimination, Employment, Family, Family Provision

MELLOR MISS RACHEL ELIZABETH

Broadway House Chambers
Broadway House, 9 Bank Street, Bradford, West Yorkshire BD1 1TW ☎01274 722560
✉clerks@broadwayhouse.co.uk
Broadway House Chambers
25 Park Square West, Leeds, West Yorkshire LS1 2PW ☎0113 246 2600
✉clerks@broadwayhouse.co.uk
Call Date: Jul 2004, Lincoln's Inn

Practising Areas: Employment, Personal Injury

MELVILLE-SHREEVE MR MICHAEL DAVID

Walnut House
63 St. David's Hill, Exeter, Devon EX4 4DW
☎01392 279751 ✉clerks@walnuthouse.co.uk
Call Date: Jul 1986, Gray's Inn
Pupil Supervisor

Practising Areas: Ancillary Relief, Chancery (Land Law), Common Law (General), Conveyancing, Environment, Family Provision, Health & Safety, Inquests, Partnership, Personal Injury, Professional Negligence, Sports

C

MENARY MR ALEXANDER WILLIAM CHRISTOPHER

KBW
The Engine House, No 1 Foundry Square, Leeds LS11 5DL ☎0113 297 1200
✉clerks@kbwchambers.com
Call Date: Jul 2004, Gray's Inn

Practising Areas: Common Law (General), Crime, Personal Injury

MENDELLE MR PAUL MICHAEL QC (2006)

25 Bedford Row
London WC1R 4HD ☎020 7067 1500
✉clerks@25bedfordrow.com
Call Date: Jul 1981, Lincoln's Inn

Practising Areas: Crime, Crime (Corporate/Fraud), Environment, Health & Safety, Regulatory Law, Sale & Carriage of Goods

MENDES DA COSTA MR DAVID

Chambers of Mr D Mendes Da Costa
4 Chesterfield Road, Chiswick, London W4 3HG ☎020 8747 4633
✉mendesdacosta@blueyonder.co.uk
MK Family Law Chambers
PO Box 6017, Milton Keynes MK1 9AP
☎0845 123 1234
No. 3 Fleet Street Chambers
3 Fleet Street, London EC4Y 1DP
☎020 7936 4474 ✉clerks@3fleetstreet.com
Call Date: Nov 1976, Inner Temple
Pupil Supervisor

Practising Areas: Bankruptcy, Common Law (General), Family, Landlord & Tenant

MENON MR HARIGOVIND

Park Lane Plowden
Lombard House, 4-8 Lombard Street, Newcastle Upon Tyne NE1 3AE
☎0191 211 4087 ✉clerks@parklaneplowden.co.uk
New Court Chambers
3 Broad Chare, Newcastle Upon Tyne NE1 3DQ ☎0191 232 1980
✉clerks@newcourt-chambers.co.uk
Call Date: Jul 1989, Gray's Inn
Pupil Supervisor

Practising Areas: Chancery (General), Chancery (Land Law), Civil Litigation, Common Land, Common Law (General), Employment, Equity, Wills & Trusts, Landlord & Tenant, Probate & Administration, Professional Negligence

MENON MR RAJIV QC (2011)

Garden Court Chambers
57-60 Lincoln's Inn Fields, London WC2A 3LJ
☎020 7993 7600 ✉info@gclaw.co.uk
Call Date: Nov 1993, Middle Temple
Pupil Supervisor

Practising Areas: Civil Liberties, Crime, Crime (Corporate/Fraud), Human Rights, Inquests

MENSAH MISS LORRAINE SONIA LOUISE

St Johns Buildings Liverpool
8th Floor India Buildings, Water Street, Liverpool L2 0XG ☎0151 243 6000
✉clerk@stjohnsbuildings.co.uk
16 Winckley Square
Preston PR1 3JJ ☎01772 256100
St Johns Buildings
24a - 28 St John Street, Manchester M3 4DJ
☎0161 214 1500 ✉clerk@stjohnsbuildings.co.uk
Call Date: Oct 1997, Gray's Inn

MENSAH MR MARTIN MINTAH

Atlantic Chambers
4-6 Cook Street, Liverpool L2 9QU
☎0151 236 4421 ✉info@atlanticchambers.co.uk
Call Date: Oct 2004, Inner Temple

Practising Areas: Employment

MENZIES MR GORDON WILLIAM

6 Pump Court
1st Floor, 6 Pump Court, Temple, London EC4Y 7AR ☎020 7797 8400
✉richardconstable@6pumpcourt.co.uk
6 Pump Court Chambers
6-8 Mill Street, Maidstone, Kent ME15 6XH
☎01622 688094 ✉annexe@6pumpcourt.co.uk
Call Date: Oct 1998, Inner Temple
Pupil Supervisor

MENZIES MRS JENNIFER MARY

St Johns Buildings Liverpool
8th Floor India Buildings, Water Street, Liverpool L2 0XG ☎0151 243 6000
✉clerk@stjohnsbuildings.co.uk
16 Winckley Square
Preston PR1 3JJ ☎01772 256100
St Johns Buildings
24a - 28 St John Street, Manchester M3 4DJ
☎0161 214 1500 ✉clerk@stjohnsbuildings.co.uk
Call Date: Oct 2002, Middle Temple

C

MENZIES MR RICHARD MARK

Lamb Chambers
Lamb Building, Elm Court, Temple, London EC4Y 7AS ☎ 020 7797 8300
✉ info@lambchambers.co.uk
Call Date: Nov 1993, Middle Temple
Pupil Supervisor

Practising Areas: Medical Negligence, Personal Injury, Professional Negligence

MERCER MR GEOFFREY MICHAEL QC (2002)

Walnut House
63 St. David's Hill, Exeter, Devon EX4 4DW
☎ 01392 279751 ✉ clerks@walnuthouse.co.uk
Call Date: Nov 1975, Inner Temple
Recorder

MEREDITH MR CHRISTOPHER WILLIAM

Furnival Chambers
32 Furnival Street, London EC4A 1JQ
☎ 020 7405 3232
Call Date: Nov 1988, Inner Temple
Pupil Supervisor

Practising Areas: Commodities, Company & Commercial, Corporate Finance, Crime, Crime (Corporate/Fraud), Financial Services, Share Options, Sports

MEREDITH-HARDY MR JOHN OCTAVIAN

Farrar's Building
Farrar's Building, Temple, London EC4Y 7BD
☎ 020 7583 9241
✉ Chambers@farrarsbuilding.co.uk
Call Date: Nov 1989, Inner Temple

Practising Areas: Common Law (General), Company & Commercial, Discrimination, Employment, Insurance, Medical Negligence, Personal Injury, Professional Negligence

MEREDITH-JONES MISS KATE

Linenhall Chambers
1 Stanley Place, Chester CH1 2LU
☎ 01244 348282
✉ clerks@linenhallchambers.co.uk
Call Date: Jul 2003, Middle Temple

MERRIGAN MR DAVID

Chambers of Mr Ami Feder
Ground Floor, Lamb Building, Temple, London EC4Y 7AS ☎ 020 7797 7788
✉ clerks@lambbuilding.co.uk
Lamb Building
22 Ship Street, Brighton BN1 1AD
☎ 01273 820490 ✉ admin@lambbuilding.co.uk
Chambers of Mr Ami Feder
Ground Floor, Lamb Building, Temple, London EC4Y 7AS ☎ 020 7797 7788
✉ clerks@lambbuilding.co.uk
Call Date: Jul 2004, Lincoln's Inn

MERRY MR HUGH GAIRNS

12 College Place
Fauvelle Buildings, 12 College Place, Southampton SO15 2FE ☎ 023 8032 0320
✉ clerks@12cp.co.uk
Call Date: Jul 1979, Inner Temple
Pupil Supervisor

Practising Areas: Family

MERZ MR RICHARD JAMES

9-12 Bell Yard
London WC2A 2JR ☎ 020 7400 1800
✉ clerks@9-12bellyard.com
Call Date: Jul 1972, Inner Temple
Pupil Supervisor, Recorder

Practising Areas: Crime, Disciplinary Tribunals

METCALFE DR ERIC WILLIAM

Monckton Chambers
1 & 2 Raymond Buildings, Gray's Inn, London WC1R 5NR ☎ 020 7405 7211
✉ chambers@monckton.com
Call Date: Nov 1999, Inner Temple

Practising Areas: Administrative, Civil Liberties, EC & Competition Law, Human Rights, Immigration, Parliamentary, Private International, Public International

METZER MR ANTHONY DAVID ERWIN

Argent Chambers
5 Bell Yard, London WC2A 2JR
☎ 020 7556 5500
✉ briefsin@argentchambers.co.uk
Call Date: Nov 1987, Middle Temple
Pupil Supervisor

Practising Areas: Civil Liberties, Common Law (General), Crime, Crime (Corporate/Fraud), Defamation, Personal Injury, Professional Negligence, Regulatory Law

METZGER MR KEVIN ALBERT

11 Gray's Inn Square Chambers
Chambers of Mr Ian Sen, 1st Floor South, 10/11 Gray's Inn Square, London WC1R 5JD
☎ 020 7405 6879 ✉ clerks@11graysinnsquare.com
Call Date: Nov 1984, Middle Temple
Pupil Supervisor

Practising Areas: Bankruptcy, Chancery (General), Civil Litigation, Crime, Disciplinary Tribunals, Foreign Law

MEUSZ MISS AMANDA JANE

Garden Court Chambers
57-60 Lincoln's Inn Fields, London WC2A 3LJ
☎ 020 7993 7600 ✉ info@gclaw.co.uk
Call Date: Jul 1986, Gray's Inn

MIAH MR AHMED

Temple Court Chambers
2nd Floor, 2 Dr Johnson's Building, Temple, London EC4Y 7AY ☎ 020 7353 7888
✉ clerks@templecourt.co.uk
Call Date: Oct 1998, Middle Temple
Pupil Supervisor

MIAH MR ANAWAR BABUL

Great James Street Chambers
37 Great James Street, London WC1N 3HB
☎ 020 7440 4949 ✉ chambers@greatjames.co.uk
Call Date: Jul 1998, Lincoln's Inn

Practising Areas: Commercial Litigation, Crime, Equity, Wills & Trusts, Family, Foreign Law, Human Rights, Immigration, Licensing, Public International, Town & Country Planning

C

MIAH MR ZACHARIAS AZAD AFZAL

Carmelite Chambers
9 Carmelite Street, London EC4Y 0DR
☎ 020 7936 6300
✉ clerks@carmelitechambers.co.uk
Call Date: Nov 1990, Inner Temple
Pupil Supervisor

MICHAEL MR NICHOLAS

East Anglian Chambers
15 The Close, Norwich, Norfolk NR1 4DZ
☎ 01473 214481 ✉ norwich@ealaw.co.uk
East Anglian Chambers
53 North Hill, Colchester, Essex CO1 1QA
☎ 01473 214481 ✉ colchester@ealaw.co.uk
East Anglian Chambers
140 New London Road, Chelmsford, Essex CM2 0AW ☎ 01473 214481
✉ chelmsford@ealaw.co.uk
East Anglian Chambers
Gresham House, 5 Museum Street, Ipswich, Suffolk IP1 1HQ ☎ 01473 214481
✉ ipswich@ealaw.co.uk
Call Date: Jul 2003, Middle Temple

Practising Areas: Bankruptcy, Chancery (General), Chancery (Land Law), Common Law (General), Company & Commercial, Construction, Employment, Insolvency, Landlord & Tenant, Licensing, Partnership, Personal Injury, Sale & Carriage of Goods

MICHALOS MISS CHRISTINA ANTIGONE DIANA

5RB
1st Floor, 5 Raymond Buildings, Gray's Inn, London WC1R 5BP ☎ 020 7242 2902
✉ clerks@5rb.com
Call Date: Oct 1994, Gray's Inn
Pupil Supervisor

Practising Areas: Commercial Litigation, Common Law (General), Copyright, Defamation, Entertainment, Film, Cable & TV, Human Rights, Intellectual Property, Medical Negligence, Personal Injury, Professional Negligence, Sports, Trademarks

MIDDLETON MR JOSEPH

Doughty Street Chambers
53-54 Doughty Street, London WC1N 2LS
☎ 020 7404 1313 ✉ enquiries@doughtystreet.co.uk
Doughty Street Chambers
Pall Mall Court, 61-67 King Street, Manchester M2 4PD ☎ 0161 618 1066
Doughty Street Chambers
5th Floor, Broad Quay House, Prince Street, Bristol BS1 4DJ ☎ 01179 058 717
Call Date: Nov 1997, Inner Temple

Practising Areas: Administrative, Civil Liberties, Immigration

MIDGLEY MISS ANNA VICTORIA JANE

Albion Chambers
Broad Street, Bristol BS1 1DR
☎ 0117 927 2144 ✉ clerks@albionchambers.co.uk
Call Date: Oct 2005, Middle Temple

Practising Areas: Crime, Crime (Corporate/Fraud), Health & Safety, Regulatory Law

MILES MR EDWARD NAPIER TREMAYNE

Lamb Chambers
Lamb Building, Elm Court, Temple, London EC4Y 7AS ☎ 020 7797 8300
✉ info@lambchambers.co.uk
Call Date: Feb 1989, Inner Temple

Practising Areas: Medical Negligence, Personal Injury

MILES MR RICHARD IAIN

One Essex Court
1st Floor, Temple, London EC4Y 9AR
☎ 020 7936 3030 ✉ clerks@1ec.co.uk
Call Date: Nov 1997, Gray's Inn
Pupil Supervisor

Practising Areas: Commercial Litigation, Common Law (General), Partnership, Personal Injury, Professional Negligence, Sale & Carriage of Goods

MILLER MR ANDREW

2 Temple Gardens
2 Temple Gardens, Temple, London EC4Y 9AY ☎ 020 7822 1200 ✉ clerks@2tg.co.uk
Call Date: Jul 1989, Inner Temple
Pupil Supervisor

Practising Areas: Arbitration, Aviation, Banking, Commercial Litigation, Common Law (General), Company & Commercial, Construction, Costs, Defamation, Education, Energy, Insurance, Insurance/Reinsurance, Personal Injury, Professional Negligence, Sale & Carriage of Goods, Share Options, Sports, Telecommunications

MILLER MISS CATHERINE

East Anglian Chambers
Gresham House, 5 Museum Street, Ipswich, Suffolk IP1 1HQ ☎ 01473 214481
✉ ipswich@ealaw.co.uk
East Anglian Chambers
140 New London Road, Chelmsford, Essex CM2 0AW ☎ 01473 214481
✉ chelmsford@ealaw.co.uk
East Anglian Chambers
15 The Close, Norwich, Norfolk NR1 4DZ
☎ 01473 214481 ✉ norwich@ealaw.co.uk
Call Date: Jul 2003, Gray's Inn
Pupil Supervisor

Practising Areas: Care Proceedings, Family, Family Provision

MILLER MR CHRISTOPHER ALBERT

14 Gray's Inn Square
14 Gray's Inn Square, Gray's Inn, London WC1R 5JP ☎ 020 7242 0858 ✉ clerks@14gis.co.uk
Call Date: Oct 1998, Lincoln's Inn

Practising Areas: Family, Family Provision

MILLER MR DAVID ROBIN

Furnival Chambers
32 Furnival Street, London EC4A 1JQ
☎ 020 7405 3232
Call Date: Oct 1998, Inner Temple
Pupil Supervisor

Practising Areas: Crime, Crime (Corporate/Fraud), Regulatory Law

MILLER MR IAN DAUKES DOUGLAS

1 Chancery Lane
London WC2A 1LF ☎ 0845 634 6666
✉ clerks@1chancerylane.com
Call Date: Oct 1999, Gray's Inn
Pupil Supervisor

Practising Areas: Common Law (General), Housing, Landlord & Tenant, Personal Injury, Professional Negligence

MILLER MR IAN ROBERTSON

Broadway House Chambers
Broadway House, 9 Bank Street, Bradford, West Yorkshire BD1 1TW ☎ 01274 722560
✉ clerks@broadwayhouse.co.uk
Broadway House Chambers
25 Park Square West, Leeds, West Yorkshire LS1 2PW ☎ 0113 246 2600
✉ clerks@broadwayhouse.co.uk
Call Date: Oct 1999, Lincoln's Inn
Pupil Supervisor

Practising Areas: Chancery (General), Chancery (Land Law), Common Law (General), Discrimination, Employment, Equity, Wills & Trusts, Family Provision

MILLER MR PETER OWEN MICHAEL

Cornerstone Barristers
2-3 Gray's Inn Square, Gray's Inn, London WC1R 5JH ☎ 020 7242 4986
✉ chambers@2-3gis.co.uk
Call Date: Oct 1993, Lincoln's Inn

Practising Areas: Administrative, Crime (Corporate/Fraud), Environment, Health & Safety, Housing, Licensing, Local Government, Regulatory Law, Town & Country Planning

MILLER MISS WENDY ANNE MAY

Citadel Chambers
The Citadel, 190 Corporation Street, Birmingham B4 6QD ☎0121 233 8500
✉clerks@citadelchambers.com
Call Date: Jul 2001, Middle Temple

Practising Areas: Crime, Licensing

MILLETT MR KENNETH JAMES

2 Hare Court
Lower Ground, Ground, 1st & 2nd Floor, 2 Hare Court, Temple, London EC4Y 7BH
☎020 7353 3982 ✉clerks@2harecourt.com
Call Date: Jul 1988, Inner Temple
Pupil Supervisor

Practising Areas: Civil Liberties, Crime, Crime (Corporate/Fraud)

MILLIKEN-SMITH MR MARK GORDON QC (2006)

2 Bedford Row
London WC1R 4BU ☎020 7440 8888
✉clerks@2bedfordrow.co.uk
Call Date: Nov 1986, Gray's Inn

MILLIN MRS LESLIE MARILYN

The Chambers of Mrs Leslie Millin
12 Folly Orchard, Wokingham, Berkshire RG41 2TU ☎0118 978 8026
✉lmmillin@gmail.com
Call Date: Nov 1988, Gray's Inn

Practising Areas: Employment, Healthcare

MILLS MISS BARBARA

4 Paper Buildings
1st Floor, 4 Paper Buildings, Temple, London EC4Y 7EX ☎020 7427 5200 ✉clerks@4pb.com
Call Date: Oct 1990, Inner Temple

Practising Areas: Care Proceedings, Family, Family Provision

MILLS MR BENEDICT JOHN

St Philips Chambers
55 Temple Row, Birmingham B2 5LS
☎0121 246 7000 ✉clerks@st-philips.com
Call Date: Oct 2000, Inner Temple

C

MILLS MR KRISTIAN ANTHONY

Trinity Chambers
The Custom House, 39 Quayside, Newcastle Upon Tyne NE1 3DE ☎0191 232 1927
✉info@trinitychambers.co.uk
Trinity Chambers
Multi Media Exchange, 72-80 Corporation Road, Middlesbrough TS1 2RF
☎01642 247569 ✉info@trinitychambers.co.uk
Call Date: Nov 1998, Middle Temple

Practising Areas: Bankruptcy, Chancery (General), Common Law (General), Employment, Health & Safety, Insolvency, Medical Negligence, Personal Injury, Regulatory Law, Sale & Carriage of Goods

MILLS MR SIMON THOMAS

Five Paper
Ground Floor, 5 Paper Buildings, Temple, London EC4Y 7HB ☎020 7815 3200
Call Date: Nov 1994, Lincoln's Inn
Pupil Supervisor

Practising Areas: Banking, Commercial Litigation, Company & Commercial, Insolvency, Partnership, Sale & Carriage of Goods

MILNE MR ALEXANDER HUGH QC (2010)

18 Red Lion Court
London EC4A 3EB ☎020 7520 6000
✉chambers@18rlc.co.uk
18 Red Lion Court (Annexe)
Thornwood House, 102 New London Road, Chelmsford, Essex CM2 0RG
☎01245 280880
Call Date: Nov 1981, Gray's Inn
Pupil Supervisor, Recorder

Practising Areas: Courts Martial, Crime, Crime (Corporate/Fraud), Inquests

MILNE MRS ARLENE JOAN

Cobden House Chambers
19 Quay Street, Manchester M3 3HN
☎0161 833 6000 ✉Clerks@Cobden.co.uk
Call Date: Oct 1999, Middle Temple

Practising Areas: Care Proceedings, Discrimination, Employment, Family, Family Provision, Personal Injury, Professional Negligence

MILNE MR RICHARD JAMES

23 Essex Street
London WC2R 3AA ☎020 7413 0353
✉clerks@23es.com
Call Date: Oct 1992, Middle Temple
Pupil Supervisor

Practising Areas: Courts Martial, Crime, Crime (Corporate/Fraud), Financial Services

MILROY MISS CAROLINE

Thomas More Chambers
7 Lincoln's Inn Fields, London WC2A 3BP
☎020 7404 7000 ✉clerks@thomasmore.co.uk
Call Date: Jul 2000, Gray's Inn

Practising Areas: Crime, Crime (Corporate/Fraud)

MILSOM MRS CATHERINE MARY

Argent Chambers
5 Bell Yard, London WC2A 2JR
☎020 7556 5500
✉briefsin@argentchambers.co.uk
Call Date: Nov 1994, Inner Temple
Pupil Supervisor

Practising Areas: Ancillary Relief, Courts Martial, Crime, Crime (Corporate/Fraud), Education, Family, Mental Health

MISHCON MR OLIVER ZEBEDEE

Chambers of Mr Oliver Mishcon
1 Fetter Lane, London EC4A 1BR
☎020 7993 8890 ✉info@mishcon.org
Call Date: Nov 1993, Gray's Inn

Practising Areas: Administrative, Commercial Litigation, Company & Commercial

MISKIN MR CHARLES JAMES MONCKTON QC (1998)

23 Essex Street
London WC2R 3AA ☎020 7413 0353
✉clerks@23es.com
Call Date: Jul 1975, Gray's Inn
Recorder

MISNER MR PHILIP LAWRENCE IAN

4 Breams Buildings
Chancery Lane, London EC4A 1HP
☎020 7092 1900 ✉clerks@4bb.co.uk
Call Date: Jul 1984, Middle Temple
Pupil Supervisor

Practising Areas: Crime, Crime (Corporate/Fraud)

MITCHELL MR ALISTAIR STEPHEN FABIAN

49 Chambers
PO Box 3956, Bridgnorth, Shropshire WV16 4NA ☎01746 761545
✉49chambers@googlemail.com
Call Date: Oct 1997, Middle Temple

Practising Areas: Chancery (General), Civil Litigation, Common Law (General), Construction, Crime, Discrimination, Employment, Personal Injury, Road Traffic And Highways, Town & Country Planning

MITCHELL MR ANDREW JONATHAN MILLS

No.6 Park Square
Leeds LS1 2LW ☎0113 245 9763
✉Tim@no6.co.uk
Call Date: Nov 1991, Lincoln's Inn
Pupil Supervisor

MITCHELL MR ANDREW ROBERT QC (1998)

Chambers of Andrew Mitchell QC
33 Chancery Lane, London WC2A 1EN
☎020 7440 9950 ✉clerks@33cllaw.com
Call Date: Jul 1976, Gray's Inn

Practising Areas: Crime, Crime (Corporate/Fraud)

MITCHELL MRS CATHERINE LOUISE

Palmyra Chambers
Royal House, 46 Legh Street, Warrington WA1 1UJ ☎01925 444919
✉clerk@palmyrachambers.com
Call Date: Jul 2008, Lincoln's Inn

MITCHELL MR CHRISTIAN RICHARD

Guildford Chambers
Stoke House, Leapale Lane, Guildford, Surrey GU1 4LY ☎01483 539131
✉clerks@guildfordchambers.co.uk
Alexander Chambers
13 Halstead Road, Wanstead, London E11 2AY ☎0845 652 0451 / 0854 652 0451
✉clerks@alexanderchambers.co.uk
Call Date: Jul 2001, Middle Temple

Practising Areas: Education, Employment, Licensing, Regulatory Law

MITCHELL MR DAVID GORDON

Ely Place Chambers
30 Ely Place, London EC1N 6TD
☎020 7400 9600 ✉admin@elyplace.com
Call Date: Nov 2004, Inner Temple

MITCHELL MR DAVID JOHN

No5 Chambers
Fountain Court, Steelhouse Lane, Birmingham B4 6DR ☎0845 210 5555 ✉info@no5.com
No5 Chambers
Greenwood House, 4-7 Salisbury Court, London EC4Y 8AA ☎0845 210 5555
No5 Chambers
38 Queen Square, Bristol BS1 4QS
☎0845 210 5555
Call Date: Oct 1995, Lincoln's Inn
Pupil Supervisor

Practising Areas: Agriculture, Chancery (General), Chancery (Land Law), Commercial Litigation, Conveyancing, Equity, Wills & Trusts, Family Provision, Landlord & Tenant, Partnership, Probate & Administration

MITCHELL MISS JANET VIVIAN

4 Brick Court
4 Brick Court, Temple, London EC4Y 9AD
☎020 7832 3200 ✉clerks@4bc.co.uk
Call Date: Feb 1978, Middle Temple

MITCHELL MR JONATHAN

1 Gray's Inn Square
Ground Floor, 1 Gray's Inn Square, London WC1R 5AA ☎020 7405 0001
Holborn Chambers
6 Gate Street, Lincoln's Inn Fields, London WC2A 3HP ☎020 7242 6060
Call Date: Mar 1998, Inner Temple

Practising Areas: Common Law (General), Crime, Employment, Immigration

MITCHELL MR JONATHAN STUART

25 Bedford Row
London WC1R 4HD ☎020 7067 1500
✉clerks@25bedfordrow.com
Call Date: Nov 1974, Middle Temple

Practising Areas: Crime, Crime (Corporate/Fraud)

MITCHELL MR KEITH ARNO

Chambers of Andrew Mitchell QC
33 Chancery Lane, London WC2A 1EN
☎020 7440 9950 ✉clerks@33cllaw.com
Call Date: Nov 1981, Inner Temple
Pupil Supervisor

Practising Areas: Crime, Crime (Corporate/Fraud)

MITROPOULOS MR CHRISTOS

5 Pump Court
Ground Floor, 5 Pump Court, Temple, London EC4Y 7AP ☎020 7353 2532
✉clerks@5pumpcourt.com
Call Date: Mar 1997, Lincoln's Inn

Practising Areas: Care Proceedings, Family, Family Provision

MODGIL MISS SANGITA

Carmelite Chambers
9 Carmelite Street, London EC4Y 0DR
☎020 7936 6300
✉clerks@carmelitechambers.co.uk
Call Date: Oct 1990, Gray's Inn

Practising Areas: Crime, Crime (Corporate/Fraud)

MODGILL MR ALEXANDER JEFFREY

Broadway House Chambers
Broadway House, 9 Bank Street, Bradford, West Yorkshire BD1 1TW ☎01274 722560
✉clerks@broadwayhouse.co.uk
Broadway House Chambers
25 Park Square West, Leeds, West Yorkshire LS1 2PW ☎0113 246 2600
✉clerks@broadwayhouse.co.uk
Call Date: Oct 2002, Lincoln's Inn

Practising Areas: Chancery (Land Law), Common Law (General), Employment, Equity, Wills & Trusts, Family, Family Provision, Housing, Landlord & Tenant, Personal Injury, Sale & Carriage of Goods

MOFFAT MR RUSSELL DEAN

Linenhall Chambers
1 Stanley Place, Chester CH1 2LU
☎01244 348282
✉clerks@linenhallchambers.co.uk
Call Date: Jul 1998, Lincoln's Inn
Pupil Supervisor

Practising Areas: Civil Litigation, Commercial Litigation, Common Law (General), Company & Commercial, Construction, Consumer, Costs, Employment, Housing, Land, Landlord & Tenant, Personal Injury, Road Traffic And Highways, Sale & Carriage of Goods

MOFFETT MR JONATHAN KEITH

4-5 Gray's Inn Square
Gray's Inn, London WC1R 5AH
☎020 7404 5252 ✉clerks@4-5.co.uk
Call Date: Oct 1996, Inner Temple
Pupil Supervisor

Practising Areas: Administrative, Education, Human Rights, Local Government, Public Law, Town & Country Planning

C

MOHAMMAD MR NAZAR

No. 3 Fleet Street Chambers
3 Fleet Street, London EC4Y 1DP
☎ 020 7936 4474 ✉ clerks@3fleetstreet.com
Legis Chambers
Cherat House, 32 Havelock Street, Aylesbury, Buckinghamshire HP20 2NX
☎ 01296 431125 ✉ espritbenoit@yahoo.co.uk
Call Date: Jul 2006, Inner Temple

Practising Areas: Administrative, Chancery (General), Family, Immigration, Landlord & Tenant, Personal Injury

MOLL MR CHRISTIAAN ERIC

Blackfriars Chambers
79-83 Temple Chambers, 3-7 Temple Avenue, London EC4Y 0HP ☎ 020 7353 7400
✉ clerks@blackfriarschambers.com
Call Date: Jul 1986, Middle Temple
Pupil Supervisor

Practising Areas: Education, Employment, Foreign Law, Housing, Human Rights, Mental Health, Town & Country Planning

MOLLER MS ALICE CHRISTINA

Alexander Chambers
13 Halstead Road, Wanstead, London E11 2AY ☎ 0845 652 0451 / 0854 652 0451
✉ clerks@alexanderchambers.co.uk
Chambers of Ms A C Moller
Address withheld ☎ 07966 448572 ✉ chris.moller@btinternet.com
Call Date: Nov 2006, Middle Temple

Practising Areas: Employment, Regulatory Law

MOLLOY MR ANDREW JOSEPH

St Ive's Chambers
Whittall Street, Birmingham B4 6DH
☎ 0121 236 0863 ✉ clerks@stiveschambers.co.uk
Call Date: Jul 2004, Gray's Inn

Practising Areas: Courts Martial, Crime

MOLLOY MISS SIOBHAN ANGELA

Chambers of Marion Smullen and Kerim Fuad QC
1 Inner Temple Lane, London EC4Y 1AF
☎ 020 7427 4400 ✉ clerks@1itl.com
Call Date: Mar 1998, Middle Temple

Practising Areas: Crime

MONAGHAN MR MARK EDWARD

Angel Chambers
Ethos Building, Kings Road, Swansea SA1 8AS
☎ 01792 464623 ✉ clerks@angelchambers.co.uk
Call Date: Oct 2002, Lincoln's Inn

MONAGHAN MS SUSAN MARY

No5 Chambers
Greenwood House, 4-7 Salisbury Court, London EC4Y 8AA ☎ 0845 210 5555
No5 Chambers
38 Queen Square, Bristol BS1 4QS
☎ 0845 210 5555
No5 Chambers
Fountain Court, Steelhouse Lane, Birmingham B4 6DR ☎ 0845 210 5555 ✉ info@no5.com
Call Date: Oct 1995, Inner Temple

Practising Areas: Disciplinary Tribunals, Education, Health & Safety, Healthcare, Inquests, Regulatory Law

MONKCOM MR STEPHEN PHILIP

Tanfield Chambers
2-5 Warwick Court, London WC1R 5DJ
☎ 020 7421 5300 ✉ clerks@tanfieldchambers.co.uk
Call Date: Nov 1974, Middle Temple
Pupil Supervisor

Practising Areas: Licensing

MONNINGTON MR BRUCE GILBERT

Fenners Chambers
3 Madingley Road, Cambridge CB3 0EE
☎ 01223 368761 ✉ clerks@fennerschambers.com
Call Date: Jul 1989, Inner Temple

Practising Areas: Administrative, Agriculture, Chancery (General), Chancery (Land Law), Charities, Common Land, Conveyancing, Environment, Equity, Wills & Trusts, Housing, Landlord & Tenant, Partnership, Probate & Administration, Professional Negligence, Town & Country Planning

MONTAGUE MRS SUSAN

Weald Chambers
Address withheld ☎ 01424 882 876
Call Date: Nov 1981, Inner Temple

Practising Areas: Common Land, Town & Country Planning

MOODY-STUART MR THOMAS

8 New Square
8 New Square, Lincoln's Inn, London WC2A 3QP ☎020 7405 4321 ✉clerks@8newsquare.co.uk
Call Date: Nov 1995, Middle Temple
Pupil Supervisor

MOONEY MR STEPHEN JOHN

Albion Chambers
Broad Street, Bristol BS1 1DR
☎0117 927 2144 ✉clerks@albionchambers.co.uk
Call Date: Nov 1987, Inner Temple
Pupil Supervisor

Practising Areas: Administrative, Courts Martial, Crime, Crime (Corporate/Fraud), Employment, Health & Safety, Regulatory Law

MOORE MR JAMES ANTHONY

39 Park Square
Leeds LS1 2NU ☎0113 245 6633
✉seniorclerk@39parksquarechambers.co.uk
Goldsmith Chambers
Ground Floor, Goldsmith Building, Temple, London EC4Y 7BL ☎020 7353 6802
✉clerks@goldsmithchambers.com
Call Date: Jul 1984, Lincoln's Inn

Practising Areas: Courts Martial, Crime, Personal Injury

MOORE MR JONATHAN GUY

Cathedral Chambers
10 Clytha Park Road, Newport NP20 4PB
☎01633 215112
Cathedral Chambers
28 Cathedral Road, Cardiff CF11 9LJ
☎02920 660129
Call Date: Jul 2006, Gray's Inn

Practising Areas: Ancillary Relief, Care Proceedings, Chancery (Land Law), Children's Law, Equity, Wills & Trusts, Family, Family Provision

MOORE MR RODERICK ANDREW MCGOWAN

Pump Court Chambers
Upper Ground Floor, 3 Pump Court, Temple, London EC4Y 7AJ ☎020 7353 0711
✉clerks@3pumpcourt.com
Call Date: Nov 1993, Inner Temple
Pupil Supervisor

MOORE MRS THERESE FINOLA

4 Brick Court
4 Brick Court, Temple, London EC4Y 9AD
☎020 7832 3200 ✉clerks@4bc.co.uk
Call Date: Jul 1988, Lincoln's Inn
Pupil Supervisor

Practising Areas: Ancillary Relief, Care Proceedings, Children's Law, Family Provision

MOORHOUSE MR BRENDON SCOTT

Guildhall Chambers
23 Broad Street, Bristol BS1 2HG
☎0117 930 9000 ✉hoc@guildhallchambers.co.uk
Call Date: Nov 1992, Middle Temple
Pupil Supervisor

Practising Areas: Crime, Crime (Corporate/Fraud), Environment, Regulatory Law

MOOTIEN MISS DAVINA POOLLAY

4 Breams Buildings
Chancery Lane, London EC4A 1HP
☎020 7092 1900 ✉clerks@4bb.co.uk
Call Date: Jul 2004, Gray's Inn

Practising Areas: Crime

MORADIFAR MR KAMBIZ

St John's Chambers
101 Victoria Street, Bristol BS1 6PU
☎0117 923 4700 ✉clerks@stjohnschambers.co.uk
Call Date: Nov 1998, Gray's Inn
Pupil Supervisor

MORAN MR CHRISTOPHER JOHN

39 Park Square
Leeds LS1 2NU ☎0113 245 6633
✉seniorclerk@39parksquarechambers.co.uk
Call Date: Oct 2007, Middle Temple

Practising Areas: Care Proceedings, Children's Law, Civil Liberties, Civil Litigation, Crime, Family, Housing, Human Rights, Landlord & Tenant

MORAN MR PATRICK MICHAEL

15 New Bridge Street
London EC4V 6AU ☎020 7842 1900
✉clerks@15nbs.com
Call Date: Oct 1997, Inner Temple

Practising Areas: Courts Martial, Crime, Crime (Corporate/Fraud), Health & Safety, Human Rights, Licensing, Regulatory Law

MORAN MR VINCENT JOHN QC (2011)

Keating Chambers
15 Essex Street, London WC2R 3AA
☎020 7544 2600 ✉clerks@keatingchambers.com
Call Date: Oct 1991, Gray's Inn
Pupil Supervisor

MORGAN MS ADRIENNE

No5 Chambers
Greenwood House, 4-7 Salisbury Court, London EC4Y 8AA ☎0845 210 5555
No5 Chambers
38 Queen Square, Bristol BS1 4QS
☎0845 210 5555
No5 Chambers
Fountain Court, Steelhouse Lane, Birmingham B4 6DR ☎0845 210 5555 ✉info@no5.com
Call Date: Nov 1988, Gray's Inn
Pupil Supervisor

MORGAN DR AUSTEN JUDE

33 Bedford Row
London WC1R 4JH ☎020 7242 6476
✉clerks@33bedfordrow.co.uk
Call Date: Oct 1995, Lincoln's Inn

Practising Areas: Administrative, Arbitration, Banking, Chancery (General), Commercial Litigation, Discrimination, EC & Competition Law, Housing, Human Rights, Immigration, Insolvency, Private International, Public International

MORGAN MR COLIN THOMAS PATRICK

Pallant Chambers
12 North Pallant, Chichester, West Sussex PO19 1TQ ☎01243 784538
✉clerks@pallantchambers.co.uk
Call Date: Nov 1989, Middle Temple

Practising Areas: Care Proceedings, Family

MORGAN MR JAMIE PETER

Trinity Chambers
The Custom House, 39 Quayside, Newcastle Upon Tyne NE1 3DE ☎0191 232 1927
✉info@trinitychambers.co.uk
Trinity Chambers
Multi Media Exchange, 72-80 Corporation Road, Middlesbrough TS1 2RF
☎01642 247569 ✉info@trinitychambers.co.uk
Call Date: Jul 2006, Inner Temple

Practising Areas: Commercial Litigation, Company & Commercial, Employment

MORGAN MR JOHN

Bedlington Chambers
7 New Square, Lincoln's Inn, London WC2A 2QS ☎020 7831 1159
✉clerks@bedlingtonchambers.com
Call Date: Jul 1999, Gray's Inn

Practising Areas: Common Law (General), Employment

MORGAN MR LLOYD JOHN

Chavasse Court Chambers
18 Queen Avenue, Liverpool L2 4TX
☎0151 229 2030
✉clerks@chavassechambers.co.uk
Call Date: Mar 1999, Middle Temple

MORLEY MISS KATE

Chavasse Court Chambers
18 Queen Avenue, Liverpool L2 4TX
☎0151 229 2030
✉clerks@chavassechambers.co.uk
Call Date: Oct 2004, Inner Temple

MORLEY MISS LAURA

4 Paper Buildings
1st Floor, 4 Paper Buildings, Temple, London EC4Y 7EX ☎020 7427 5200 ✉clerks@4pb.com
Call Date: Jul 2006, Middle Temple

MORRIS MISS ANNA CLAIRE

Garden Court Chambers
57-60 Lincoln's Inn Fields, London WC2A 3LJ
☎020 7993 7600 ✉info@gclaw.co.uk
Call Date: Mar 2006, Middle Temple

MORRIS MR BEN

Chavasse Court Chambers
18 Queen Avenue, Liverpool L2 4TX
☎0151 229 2030
✉clerks@chavassechambers.co.uk
Call Date: Oct 1996, Middle Temple

Practising Areas: Civil Liberties, Courts Martial, Crime, Crime (Corporate/Fraud), Human Rights

MORRIS MISS BRENDA ALISON

14 Gray's Inn Square
14 Gray's Inn Square, Gray's Inn, London WC1R 5JP ☎020 7242 0858 ✉clerks@14gis.co.uk
Call Date: Jul 1978, Middle Temple

Practising Areas: Family, Family Provision

MORRIS MS CHRISTINA GAYE

Coram Chambers
9-11 Fulwood Place, London WC1V 6HG
☎ 020 7092 3700 ✉ mail@coramchambers.co.uk
Call Date: Nov 1983, Gray's Inn
Pupil Supervisor

Practising Areas: Family, Family Provision

MORRIS MR DAVID PAUL

Outer Temple Chambers
The Outer Temple, 222 Strand, London WC2R 1BA ☎ 020 7353 6381
✉ clerks@outertemple.com
Call Date: Jul 1976, Inner Temple
Pupil Supervisor

Practising Areas: Regulatory Law

MORRIS MR IEUAN JOHN

9 Park Place
Cardiff, South Glamorgan CF10 3DP
☎ 029 2038 2731 ✉ clerks@9parkplace.co.uk
Call Date: Jul 1979, Gray's Inn
Pupil Supervisor

Practising Areas: Courts Martial, Crime, Crime (Corporate/Fraud), Licensing, Town & Country Planning

MORRIS MS JOHANNA

Chambers of Marion Smullen and Kerim Fuad QC
1 Inner Temple Lane, London EC4Y 1AF
☎ 020 7427 4400 ✉ clerks@1itl.com
Call Date: Nov 2003, Middle Temple

Practising Areas: Common Law (General), Courts Martial, Crime, Crime (Corporate/Fraud), Employment, Health & Safety, Housing, Human Rights, Landlord & Tenant, Licensing, Mental Health, Personal Injury, Regulatory Law

MORRIS MR PHILIP JAMES

39 Park Square
Leeds LS1 2NU ☎ 0113 245 6633
✉ seniorclerk@39parksquarechambers.co.uk
Call Date: Jul 2011, Middle Temple

Practising Areas: Common Law (General), Crime

MORRIS MR PHILLIP JOHN

9 Park Place
Cardiff, South Glamorgan CF10 3DP
☎ 029 2038 2731 ✉ clerks@9parkplace.co.uk
Call Date: Jul 2003, Gray's Inn

Practising Areas: Chancery (General), Chancery (Land Law), Common Law (General), Employment, Equity, Wills & Trusts, Landlord & Tenant, Personal Injury

MORRISON MR CHRISTOPHER QUINTIN

Old Court Chambers
Newham House, 96-98 Borough Road, Middlesbrough TS1 2HJ ☎ 01642 232523
✉ clerks@oldcourtchambers.com
Call Date: Nov 1986, Inner Temple
Pupil Supervisor

Practising Areas: Common Law (General), Courts Martial, Crime, Family

MORRISON MR GILES BENEDICT

15 New Bridge Street
London EC4V 6AU ☎ 020 7842 1900
✉ clerks@15nbs.com
Call Date: Nov 2002, Middle Temple

MORT MR JUSTIN JOHN GLASBROOK

Keating Chambers
15 Essex Street, London WC2R 3AA
☎ 020 7544 2600 ✉ clerks@keatingchambers.com
Call Date: Oct 1994, Middle Temple
Pupil Supervisor

Practising Areas: Arbitration, Construction, Professional Negligence

MORTON MR GARY DAVID

Pump Court Chambers
Upper Ground Floor, 3 Pump Court, Temple, London EC4Y 7AJ ☎ 020 7353 0711
✉ clerks@3pumpcourt.com
Pump Court Chambers
5 Temple Chambers, Temple Street, Swindon SN1 1SQ ☎ 01793 539899
✉ clerks@3pumpcourt.com
Pump Court Chambers
31 Southgate Street, Winchester, Hampshire SO23 9EB ☎ 01962 868 161
✉ clerks@3pumpcourt.com
Call Date: Nov 1993, Gray's Inn

Practising Areas: Discrimination, Employment

MORTON MISS ROWAN FRANCES

Guildford Chambers
Stoke House, Leapale Lane, Guildford, Surrey GU1 4LY ☎ 01483 539131
✉ clerks@guildfordchambers.co.uk
Alexander Chambers
13 Halstead Road, Wanstead, London E11 2AY ☎ 0845 652 0451 / 0854 652 0451
✉ clerks@alexanderchambers.co.uk
Call Date: Nov 2004, Lincoln's Inn

Practising Areas: Housing, Medical Negligence, Personal Injury, Professional Negligence, Regulatory Law

MORWOOD MR JONATHAN THOMAS BOYD

Hardwicke
New Square, Lincoln's Inn, London WC2A 3SB ☎ 020 7242 2523
✉ enquiries@hardwicke.co.uk
Call Date: Nov 1996, Middle Temple
Pupil Supervisor

MOSES MR STEPHEN COLIN

Furnival Chambers
32 Furnival Street, London EC4A 1JQ
☎ 020 7405 3232
Call Date: Nov 1997, Gray's Inn
Pupil Supervisor

Practising Areas: Crime, Crime (Corporate/Fraud)

MOSS MR CHRISTOPHER STEPHEN

St Johns Buildings
24a - 28 St John Street, Manchester M3 4DJ
☎ 0161 214 1500 ✉ clerk@stjohnsbuildings.co.uk
16 Winckley Square
Preston PR1 3JJ ☎ 01772 256100
St Johns Buildings Liverpool
8th Floor India Buildings, Water Street, Liverpool L2 0XG ☎ 0151 243 6000
✉ clerk@stjohnsbuildings.co.uk
Call Date: Oct 2002, Lincoln's Inn

Practising Areas: Chancery (General), Chancery (Land Law), Commercial Litigation, Commercial Property, Common Law (General), Housing, Landlord & Tenant, Personal Injury

MOSS MR EDWARD JOHN

Exchange Chambers
7 Ralli Courts, West Riverside, Manchester M3 5FT ☎ 0161 833 2722
Exchange Chambers
One Derby Square, Derby Square, Liverpool L2 9XX ☎ 0151 236 7747
✉ info@exchangechambers.co.uk
Exchange Chambers
Oxford House, Oxford Row, Leeds LS1 3BE
☎ 0113 203 1970
✉ spencer@exchangechambers.co.uk
Call Date: Jul 2005, Inner Temple

MOSS MR RICHARD JOHN

4 King's Bench Walk
2nd Floor, 4 King's Bench Walk, Temple, London EC4Y 7DL ☎ 020 7822 7000
✉ clerks@4kbw.co.uk
Call Date: Oct 2005, Lincoln's Inn

Practising Areas: Common Law (General), Crime, Personal Injury

MOSTAFA MISS MARGIA

2 Pump Court
1st Floor, 2 Pump Court, Temple, London EC4Y 7AH ☎ 020 7353 5597
✉ clerks@2pumpcourt.co.uk
Call Date: Oct 1999, Lincoln's Inn

Practising Areas: Crime, Crime (Corporate/Fraud)

MOULDER MR PAUL JOHN

Guildford Chambers
Stoke House, Leapale Lane, Guildford, Surrey GU1 4LY ☎ 01483 539131
✉ clerks@guildfordchambers.co.uk
Alexander Chambers
13 Halstead Road, Wanstead, London E11 2AY ☎ 0845 652 0451 / 0854 652 0451
✉ clerks@alexanderchambers.co.uk
Call Date: Oct 1997, Lincoln's Inn

Practising Areas: Common Law (General), Construction, Discrimination, Education, Housing, Insurance, Landlord & Tenant, Licensing, Personal Injury, Sale & Carriage of Goods

MOUSLEY MR WILLIAM HOWARD QC (2011)

2 King's Bench Walk
2 King's Bench Walk, Temple, London EC4Y 7DE ☎ 020 7353 1746 ✉ clerks@2kbw.com
Call Date: Jul 1986, Middle Temple
Pupil Supervisor, Recorder

Practising Areas: Courts Martial, Crime, Crime (Corporate/Fraud), Health & Safety, Human Rights, Licensing, Regulatory Law, Sports

MOXON MR NATHAN ANDREW

KBW
The Engine House, No 1 Foundry Square, Leeds LS11 5DL ☎ 0113 297 1200
✉ clerks@kbwchambers.com
Call Date: Jul 2006, Inner Temple

C

MOYS MR CLIVE JOHN

Radcliffe Chambers
Ground Floor, 11 New Square, Lincoln's Inn, London WC2A 3QB ☎ 020 7831 0081
✉ clerks@radcliffechambers.com
Pallant Chambers
12 North Pallant, Chichester, West Sussex PO19 1TQ ☎ 01243 784538
✉ clerks@pallantchambers.co.uk
Call Date: Jul 1998, Lincoln's Inn

MUIR MISS NICOLA JANE

Hardwicke
New Square, Lincoln's Inn, London WC2A 3SB ☎ 020 7242 2523
✉ enquiries@hardwicke.co.uk
Call Date: Nov 1998, Inner Temple

Practising Areas: Commercial Property, Conveyancing, Housing, Landlord & Tenant, Professional Negligence

MUKULU MR MATONDO KAMAU

Amethyst Chambers
Ground Floor, 9 Kings Bench Walk, Inner Temple, London EC4Y 7DX
☎ 020 7936 4966 ✉ info@amethystchambers.com
Call Date: Mar 2002, Lincoln's Inn

MULDERIG MR JOSEPH PAUL

St James's Chambers
68 Quay Street, Manchester M3 3EJ
☎ 0161 834 7000 ✉ clerks@stjameschambers.com
Call Date: Nov 2002, Lincoln's Inn

MULHOLLAND MR JAMES MALACHI QC (2011)

15 New Bridge Street
London EC4V 6AU ☎ 020 7842 1900
✉ clerks@15nbs.com
Call Date: Jul 1986, Inner Temple
Pupil Supervisor, Recorder

MULLA MISS MARIA JULIETTE

Palmyra Chambers
Royal House, 46 Legh Street, Warrington WA1 1UJ ☎ 01925 444919
✉ clerk@palmyrachambers.com
Call Date: Mar 2005, Lincoln's Inn

MULLARKEY MR IAN

KBW
The Engine House, No 1 Foundry Square, Leeds LS11 5DL ☎ 0113 297 1200
✉ clerks@kbwchambers.com
Call Date: Jul 2003, Inner Temple

Practising Areas: Common Law (General), Crime, Employment

MULLEE MR BRENDAN PAUL

Hardwicke
New Square, Lincoln's Inn, London WC2A 3SB ☎ 020 7242 2523
✉ enquiries@hardwicke.co.uk
Call Date: Oct 1996, Middle Temple

Practising Areas: Housing, Landlord & Tenant

MULLEN MISS JAYNE ALISON

St Ive's Chambers
Whittall Street, Birmingham B4 6DH
☎ 0121 236 0863 ✉ clerks@stiveschambers.co.uk
Call Date: Jul 1989, Gray's Inn
Pupil Supervisor

Practising Areas: Family Provision

MULLEN MR MARK ROBERT

Radcliffe Chambers
Ground Floor, 11 New Square, Lincoln's Inn, London WC2A 3QB ☎ 020 7831 0081
✉ clerks@radcliffechambers.com
Call Date: Jul 2001, Lincoln's Inn
Pupil Supervisor

Practising Areas: Bankruptcy, Chancery (General), Chancery (Land Law), Charities, Civil Litigation, Commercial Property, Company & Commercial, Equity, Wills & Trusts, Family Provision, Insolvency, Land, Landlord & Tenant, Probate & Administration

MULLER MR ANTONIE SEAN

Citadel Chambers
The Citadel, 190 Corporation Street, Birmingham B4 6QD ☎ 0121 233 8500
✉ clerks@citadelchambers.com
Call Date: Jul 1990, Middle Temple
Pupil Supervisor

Practising Areas: Civil Liberties, Common Law (General), Crime, Crime (Corporate/Fraud), Environment, Human Rights, Licensing, Regulatory Law

MULLIGAN MS ANN COLLETTE

15 New Bridge Street
London EC4V 6AU ☎ 020 7842 1900
✉ clerks@15nbs.com
Call Date: Jul 1989, Gray's Inn
Pupil Supervisor, Recorder

MULLINS MR MARK LOVEL RUPERT

Five St Andrew's Hill
5 St Andrew's Hill, London EC4V 5BZ
☎ 020 7332 5400 ✉ Clerks@5sah.co.uk
Call Date: Nov 1995, Inner Temple
Pupil Supervisor

Practising Areas: Administrative, Courts Martial, Crime, Immigration

MUMAN MR VIJAY KUMAR

43 Temple Row Chambers
6th Floor, 43 Temple Row, Birmingham B2 5LS ☎ 0121 237 6035 ✉ clerks@43templerow.co.uk
Call Date: Nov 2001, Gray's Inn

Practising Areas: Administrative, Chancery (General), Civil Liberties, Civil Litigation, Commercial Property, Consumer, Discrimination, Employment, Human Rights, Immigration, Landlord & Tenant, Licensing, Public Law, Regulatory Law

MUNDEN MR RICHARD ALEXANDER JOHN

5RB
1st Floor, 5 Raymond Buildings, Gray's Inn, London WC1R 5BP ☎ 020 7242 2902
✉ clerks@5rb.com
Call Date: Jul 2003, Lincoln's Inn

Practising Areas: Copyright, Defamation, Entertainment, Intellectual Property, Sports

MUNIR DR ASHLEY EDWARD

Five St Andrew's Hill
5 St Andrew's Hill, London EC4V 5BZ
☎ 020 7332 5400 ✉ Clerks@5sah.co.uk
Call Date: Jun 1956, Gray's Inn
Pupil Supervisor

Practising Areas: Administrative, Common Law (General), Crime, Housing, Immigration, Landlord & Tenant, Personal Injury

MUNRO MR DAVID PHILIP

St Philips Chambers
55 Temple Row, Birmingham B2 5LS
☎ 0121 246 7000 ✉ clerks@st-philips.com
Call Date: Nov 2001, Gray's Inn

Practising Areas: Crime

MUNRO MR JOSHUA NEIL

Hailsham Chambers
Ground Floor, 4 Paper Buildings, Temple, London EC4Y 7EX ☎ 020 7643 5000
✉ clerks@hailshamchambers.com
Call Date: Oct 2001, Gray's Inn
Pupil Supervisor

Practising Areas: Banking, Commercial Litigation, Common Law (General), Landlord & Tenant, Personal Injury, Professional Negligence

MUNT MR ALASTAIR HENRY MCLAREN

KCH Garden Square
1 Oxford Street, Nottingham NG1 5BH
☎ 0115 941 8851 ✉ clerks@kchgardensquare.co.uk
Call Date: Jul 1989, Gray's Inn

MUQUIT MR MOHAMMED SHUYEB

1 Mitre Court Buildings
1 Mitre Court Buildings, Temple, London EC4Y 7BS ☎ 020 7452 8900 ✉ clerks@1mcb.com
Call Date: Jul 1998, Inner Temple

Practising Areas: Administrative, Crime, Human Rights, Immigration, Public International

MURKIN MRS SANDRIA

Becket Chambers
17 New Dover Road, Canterbury, Kent CT1 3AS ☎ 01227 786331
✉ clerks@becket-chambers.co.uk
Call Date: Oct 2004, Inner Temple

Practising Areas: Care Proceedings, Common Law (General), Family, Family Provision, Mental Health

MURPHY MR DAMIAN

Enterprise Chambers
65 Quayside, Newcastle Upon Tyne NE1 3DE
☎ 0191 222 3344
✉ newcastle@enterprisechambers.com
Enterprise Chambers
43 Park Square, Leeds LS1 2NP
☎ 0113 246 0391
✉ leeds@enterprisechambers.com

Enterprise Chambers
9 Old Square, Lincoln's Inn, London WC2A 3SR ☎ 020 7405 9471
✉ london@enterprisechambers.com
Call Date: Jul 2001, Middle Temple
Pupil Supervisor

Practising Areas: Bankruptcy, Chancery (General), Commercial Litigation, Common Law (General), Company & Commercial, Information Technology, Intellectual Property, Landlord & Tenant, Partnership, Sale & Carriage of Goods, Sports, Telecommunications

MURPHY MR MICHAEL PATRICK

10 King's Bench Walk
Ground Floor, 10 King's Bench Walk, Temple, London EC4Y 7EB ☎ 020 7353 7742
✉ Chambers@10kingsbenchwalk.co.uk
Central Chambers
89 Princess Street, Manchester M1 4HT
☎ 0161 236 1133 ✉ clerks@centralchambers.co.uk
Call Date: Nov 1992, Inner Temple
Pupil Supervisor

Practising Areas: Administrative, Crime, Disciplinary Tribunals, Human Rights, Immigration

MURPHY MISS OLIVIA BRIDGET

Tanfield Chambers
2-5 Warwick Court, London WC1R 5DJ
☎ 020 7421 5300 ✉ clerks@tanfieldchambers.co.uk
Call Date: Nov 2001, Middle Temple

MURRAY MR ANIL PETER

Wilberforce Chambers
7 Bishop Lane, Hull HU1 1PA
☎ 01482 323264
Call Date: Jul 1989, Middle Temple
Pupil Supervisor

MURRAY MR CHARLES HUMPHREY STEWART

Rougemont Chambers
Victory House, Dean Clarke Gardens, Southernhay East, Exeter EX2 4AA
☎ 01392 208484
✉ clerks@rougemontchambers.co.uk
Call Date: Mar 2005, Inner Temple

Practising Areas: Arbitration, Chancery (General), Chancery (Land Law), Commercial Litigation, Common Law (General), Employment, Housing, Landlord & Tenant, Mental Health, Partnership, Personal Injury, Professional Negligence

MURRAY MR DANIEL EVAN DUNCAN

Old Bailey Chambers
15 Old Bailey, London EC4M 7EF
☎ 020 3008 6404
✉ clerks@15oldbaileychambers.com
Call Date: Nov 1996, Lincoln's Inn

Practising Areas: Crime, Crime (Corporate/Fraud), Sports

MURRAY MISS JUDITH ROWENA

4 Paper Buildings
1st Floor, 4 Paper Buildings, Temple, London EC4Y 7EX ☎ 020 7427 5200 ✉ clerks@4pb.com
Call Date: Oct 1994, Middle Temple

Practising Areas: Family, Family Provision

MURRAY MR LANCE JOHN MOLE

Nexus Chambers
7 New Square, Lincolns Inn, London WC2A 3QS ☎ 020 7404 1147 / 020 7831 8309
✉ info@nexuschambers.com
Call Date: Oct 2007, Middle Temple

Practising Areas: Crime, Family

MUSHTAQ MS ERIMNAZ

Doughty Street Chambers
Pall Mall Court, 61-67 King Street, Manchester M2 4PD ☎ 0161 618 1066
Doughty Street Chambers
5th Floor, Broad Quay House, Prince Street, Bristol BS1 4DJ ☎ 01179 058 717
Doughty Street Chambers
53-54 Doughty Street, London WC1N 2LS
☎ 020 7404 1313 ✉ enquiries@doughtystreet.co.uk
Call Date: Nov 2000, Inner Temple

MUSSA MISS AZREEN

Fenners Chambers
3 Madingley Road, Cambridge CB3 0EE
☎ 01223 368761 ✉ clerks@fennerschambers.com
Call Date: Oct 2003, Middle Temple

MUSTAFA MS HALA MOHAMED KAMEL

1 Crown Office Row
1 Crown Office Row, Temple, London EC4Y 7HH ☎ 020 7797 7500 ✉ mail@1cor.com
Crown Office Row Chambers
119 Church Street, Brighton, Sussex BN1 1UD ☎ 01273 625625 ✉ clerks@1cor.com
Call Date: Jul 2004, Middle Temple

Practising Areas: Family

C

MUSTAKIM MR ABDUL YUNUS AL

Chambers of Mr Mustakim
6 Shandy Street, London E1 4LX
Call Date: May 1997, Lincoln's Inn
Pupil Supervisor

Practising Areas: Administrative, Arbitration, Care Proceedings, Chancery (General), Charities, Children's Law, Civil Liberties, Civil Litigation, Commercial Litigation, Common Law (General), Costs, Defamation, Discrimination, Employment, Family, Foreign Law, Human Rights, Inquests, Islamic Sharia Law, Local Government, Public Law

MUTCH MR IAIN RICHARD ALISTAIR

Palmyra Chambers
Royal House, 46 Legh Street, Warrington WA1 1UJ ☎01925 444919
✉clerk@palmyrachambers.com
Call Date: Mar 2002, Lincoln's Inn

Practising Areas: Common Law (General), Crime, Personal Injury

MYDEEN MR KALANDAR

Chambers of Mr K Mydeen
3 Kempston House, The Downsway, Sutton SM2 5RE ☎020 8643 3633
✉kenmydeen@blueyonder.co.uk
Call Date: Nov 1973, Lincoln's Inn

Practising Areas: Chancery (General)

MYERS MR BENJAMIN JOHN

Exchange Chambers
7 Ralli Courts, West Riverside, Manchester M3 5FT ☎0161 833 2722
Exchange Chambers
One Derby Square, Derby Square, Liverpool L2 9XX ☎0151 236 7747
✉info@exchangechambers.co.uk
Call Date: Oct 1994, Inner Temple
Pupil Supervisor

Practising Areas: Administrative, Civil Liberties, Crime, Human Rights

MYLVAGANAM MS TANOO

1 Gray's Inn Square
Ground Floor, 1 Gray's Inn Square, London WC1R 5AA ☎020 7405 0001
Call Date: Jul 1983, Gray's Inn

Practising Areas: Care Proceedings, Civil Liberties, Common Law (General), Crime, Defamation, Discrimination, Education, Employment, Family, Foreign Law, Human Rights, Regulatory Law

MYNORS DR CHARLES BASKERVILLE

Francis Taylor Building
Inner Temple, London EC4Y 7BY
☎020 7353 8415 ✉clerks@ftb.eu.com
Call Date: Nov 1988, Middle Temple
Pupil Supervisor

Practising Areas: Common Land, Ecclesiastical, Environment, Local Government, Town & Country Planning

MYTTON MR PAUL VINCENT

St Philips Chambers
55 Temple Row, Birmingham B2 5LS
☎0121 246 7000 ✉clerks@st-philips.com
Call Date: Jul 1982, Lincoln's Inn
Pupil Supervisor

Practising Areas: Crime, Crime (Corporate/Fraud)

NABI MR SAJJAD

5 Pump Court
Ground Floor, 5 Pump Court, Temple, London EC4Y 7AP ☎020 7353 2532
✉clerks@5pumpcourt.com
Call Date: Oct 2003, Middle Temple

Practising Areas: Commercial Litigation, Defamation, Discrimination, Employment, Landlord & Tenant, Professional Negligence

NADIM MR AHMED

Lincoln House Chambers
Tower 12, The Avenue North, Spinningfields, 18-22 Bridge Street, Manchester M3 3BZ
☎0161 832 5701
✉info@lincolnhousechambers.com
Call Date: Jul 1982, Lincoln's Inn
Pupil Supervisor

Practising Areas: Crime, Crime (Corporate/Fraud)

NAIK MR TIMOTHY ANIL

4 Breams Buildings
Chancery Lane, London EC4A 1HP
☎020 7092 1900 ✉clerks@4bb.co.uk
Call Date: Nov 1994, Gray's Inn
Pupil Supervisor

NALL-CAIN THE HON RICHARD CHRISTOPHER PHILIP

St Albans Chambers
2 - 4 St Peter's Street, St Albans, Hertfordshire AL1 3LF ☎01727 843383
✉clerks@stalbanschambers.com
Call Date: Oct 1997, Inner Temple
Pupil Supervisor

Practising Areas: Ancillary Relief, Common Law (General), Housing, Landlord & Tenant, Personal Injury

NAQSHBANDI MISS SABA SHAFIQUE

3 Raymond Buildings
3 Raymond Buildings, Gray's Inn, London WC1R 5BH ☎ 020 7400 6400
✉ clerks@3rblaw.com
Call Date: Oct 1996, Middle Temple
Pupil Supervisor

NARDELL MR GORDON LAWRENCE QC (2010)

39 Essex Street
London WC2R 3AT ☎ 020 7832 1111
✉ clerks@39essex.com
82 King Street
Manchester M2 4WQ ☎ 0161 870 9969
Call Date: Nov 1995, Inner Temple

Practising Areas: Parliamentary, Public International, Town & Country Planning

NARTEY MISS ELIZABETH

Argent Chambers
5 Bell Yard, London WC2A 2JR
☎ 020 7556 5500
✉ briefsin@argentchambers.co.uk
Call Date: Mar 2003, Middle Temple

NASH MS EMMA JANE

2 Pump Court
1st Floor, 2 Pump Court, Temple, London EC4Y 7AH ☎ 020 7353 5597
✉ clerks@2pumpcourt.co.uk
Call Date: Jul 2001, Inner Temple

NASIM MR ZIA-UL-MUSTAFA

Milestone Chambers
267 High Road, London NW10 2RX
Call Date: Jul 2001, Lincoln's Inn

Practising Areas: Charities, Crime, Immigration, Islamic Sharia Law, Public International

NASSAR MISS VICTORIA KATIE

Fortis Green Chambers
Hillcroft, Wilmslow Park South, Wilmslow SK9 2AY ☎ 0161 439 5804
✉ victorianassar@yahoo.co.uk
Call Date: Feb 1994, Gray's Inn

Practising Areas: Immigration

NATH MR RAKESH

Strand Chambers
226 The Strand, London WC2R 1BA
☎ 020 7117 6920 ✉ Henry@lawsurgery.com
Call Date: Jul 1985, Inner Temple
Pupil Supervisor

Practising Areas: Common Law (General), Company & Commercial, Franchising, Intellectual Property, International Trade

NATHAN MR DAVID BRIAN QC (2002)

Zenith Chambers
10 Park Square, Leeds LS1 2LH
☎ 0113 245 5438 ✉ clerks@zenithchambers.co.uk
Argent Chambers
5 Bell Yard, London WC2A 2JR
☎ 020 7556 5500
✉ briefsin@argentchambers.co.uk
Call Date: Nov 1971, Middle Temple

NATHWANI MR RISHI NAREMDRAKUMAR

5 King's Bench Walk
5 King's Bench Walk, Temple, London EC4Y 7DN ☎ 020 7353 5638 ✉ clerks@5kbw.co.uk
Call Date: Jul 2006, Middle Temple

NEEDHAM MRS JULIA CHERRY

10 King's Bench Walk
Ground Floor, 10 King's Bench Walk, Temple, London EC4Y 7EB ☎ 020 7353 7742
✉ Chambers@10kingsbenchwalk.co.uk
Call Date: Nov 2000, Middle Temple

Practising Areas: Crime, Education

NEVILLE MR JOSEPH RICHARD

43 Temple Row Chambers
6th Floor, 43 Temple Row, Birmingham B2 5LS ☎ 0121 237 6035 ✉ clerks@43templerow.co.uk
Call Date: Nov 2007, Lincoln's Inn

Practising Areas: Commercial Litigation, Consumer, Discrimination, Employment, Human Rights, Immigration, Sale & Carriage of Goods

NEWBOLD DR ANNE LORRAINE ELSIE

Minerva Chambers
704 Grand Ocean Plaza, Ocean Village
☎ 00 350 20042779 ✉ l.newbold@minervachambers.com
Call Date: Nov 1990, Lincoln's Inn
Pupil Supervisor

Practising Areas: Asset Finance, Banking, Commodities, Corporate Finance, Energy, Financial Services, Share Options

NEWBOLD MR MICHAEL PAUL

9-12 Bell Yard
London WC2A 2JR ☎ 020 7400 1800
✉ clerks@9-12bellyard.com
Call Date: Jul 2004, Inner Temple

Practising Areas: Crime, Crime (Corporate/Fraud), Licensing, Regulatory Law

NEWCOMB MR QUINTON JOHN

1 Paper Buildings
1st Floor, 1 Paper Buildings, Temple, London EC4Y 7EP ☎ 020 7353 3728
✉ clerks@onepaper.co.uk
Call Date: Jul 2005, Middle Temple

Practising Areas: Courts Martial, Crime, Crime (Corporate/Fraud), Regulatory Law, Sports

NEWELL MISS CHARLOTTE ANNE

5 King's Bench Walk
5 King's Bench Walk, Temple, London EC4Y 7DN ☎ 020 7353 5638 ✉ clerks@5kbw.co.uk
Call Date: Oct 1994, Gray's Inn
Pupil Supervisor

NEWMAN MR ALAN RONALD HARVEY QC (1989)

Argent Chambers
5 Bell Yard, London WC2A 2JR
☎ 020 7556 5500
✉ briefsin@argentchambers.co.uk
Call Date: Nov 1968, Middle Temple

Practising Areas: Administrative, Civil Liberties, Civil Litigation, Crime, Defamation, Regulatory Law

NEWMAN MR JAMES ANDREW

Ely Place Chambers
30 Ely Place, London EC1N 6TD
☎ 020 7400 9600 ✉ admin@elyplace.com
Call Date: Jul 2000, Gray's Inn

Practising Areas: Commercial Litigation, Common Law (General), Housing, Landlord & Tenant, Licensing, Personal Injury, Professional Negligence

NEWMAN MR PAUL

3 PB Barristers
3 Paper Buildings, Temple, London EC4Y 7EU
☎ 020 7583 8055
3 PB Barristers
30 Christchurch Road, Bournemouth, Dorset BH1 3PD ☎ 01202 292102 ✉ clerks.bournemouth@3paper.co.uk
3 PB Barristers
4 St Peter Street, Winchester SO23 8BW
☎ 01962 868884 ✉ clerks.winchester@3paper.co.uk
3 PB Barristers
Royal Talbot House, 2 Victoria Street, Bristol, Avon BS1 6BB ☎ 0117 928 1520
3 PB Barristers
23 Beaumont Street, Oxford OX1 2NP
☎ 01865 793 736
Call Date: Nov 1982, Gray's Inn

Practising Areas: Arbitration, Chancery (General), Chancery (Land Law), Commercial Litigation, Common Law (General), Construction, Personal Injury, Professional Negligence, Sale & Carriage of Goods

NEWMAN MISS REBECCA JANE

Clerksroom (Taunton)
Equity House, Administration Centre, Blackbrook Park Avenue, Taunton, Somerset TA1 2PX ☎ 0845 083 3000
✉ mail@clerksroom.com
King's Lynn Chambers
26 The Birches, South Wootton, King's Lynn, Norfolk PE30 3JG ☎ 01553 672 085
✉ timothy.leader@tesco.net
Call Date: Nov 1991, Lincoln's Inn

Practising Areas: Company & Commercial, Employment, Landlord & Tenant, Personal Injury

NEWMAN MR TIMOTHY JOHN

No5 Chambers
Fountain Court, Steelhouse Lane, Birmingham B4 6DR ☎ 0845 210 5555 ✉ info@no5.com
No5 Chambers
Greenwood House, 4-7 Salisbury Court, London EC4Y 8AA ☎ 0845 210 5555
No5 Chambers
38 Queen Square, Bristol BS1 4QS
☎ 0845 210 5555
Call Date: Jul 1981, Gray's Inn

Practising Areas: Health & Safety, Medical Negligence, Personal Injury, Professional Negligence

NEWMAN MRS VERONICA

Chambers of Mrs V Newman
77 Roath Court Road, Roath, Cardiff CF24 3SF ☎ 029 2048 8797 ✉ newmanv@tiscali.co.uk
Call Date: Nov 1984, Gray's Inn

Practising Areas: Bankruptcy, Commercial Litigation, Employment, Family Provision, Insolvency, Personal Injury

NEWPORT MR IAN ALUN

College Chambers
19 Carlton Crescent, Southampton, Hampshire SO15 2ET ☎ 023 8023 0338
✉ clerks@college-chambers.co.uk
Call Date: Oct 2000, Gray's Inn
Pupil Supervisor

Practising Areas: Care Proceedings, Family, Family Provision, Licensing, Town & Country Planning

NEWSOM MR GEORGE LUCIEN

Guildhall Chambers
23 Broad Street, Bristol BS1 2HG
☎ 0117 930 9000 ✉ hoc@guildhallchambers.co.uk
Call Date: Nov 1973, Lincoln's Inn

Practising Areas: Administrative, Agriculture, Arbitration, Chancery (General), Chancery (Land Law), Charities, Commercial Property, Common Land, Construction, Conveyancing, Ecclesiastical, Environment, Equity, Wills & Trusts, Family Provision, Landlord & Tenant, Local Government, Partnership, Probate & Administration, Town & Country Planning

NEWSTEAD MS JENNIFER ELIZABETH

Call Date: Nov 2003, Gray's Inn

C

NEWTON MR ANDREW DAVID

187 Fleet Street
London EC4A 2AT ☎ 020 7430 7430
✉ chambers@187fleetstreet.com
Call Date: Nov 1989, Inner Temple

Practising Areas: Crime

NEWTON-PRICE MR JAMES EDWARD

Pump Court Chambers
31 Southgate Street, Winchester, Hampshire SO23 9EB ☎ 01962 868 161
✉ clerks@3pumpcourt.com
Pump Court Chambers
Upper Ground Floor, 3 Pump Court, Temple, London EC4Y 7AJ ☎ 020 7353 0711
✉ clerks@3pumpcourt.com
Pump Court Chambers
5 Temple Chambers, Temple Street, Swindon SN1 1SQ ☎ 01793 539899
✉ clerks@3pumpcourt.com
Call Date: Oct 1992, Middle Temple
Pupil Supervisor

Practising Areas: Courts Martial, Crime, Crime (Corporate/Fraud), Regulatory Law

NICHOL MR SIMON BEDE

Cobden House Chambers
19 Quay Street, Manchester M3 3HN
☎ 0161 833 6000 ✉ Clerks@Cobden.co.uk
Call Date: May 1994, Lincoln's Inn

NICHOLAS MS CHRISTINA MICHALINA DE WELD

Chambers of Martin Burr
15 Old Bailey, London EC4M 7EF
☎ 0845 123 1234 ✉ clerks@barristerweb.com
Call Date: Nov 1997, Inner Temple

NICHOLES MS CATHERINE MARGARET ELIZABETH

Coram Chambers
9-11 Fulwood Place, London WC1V 6HG
☎ 020 7092 3700 ✉ mail@coramchambers.co.uk
Call Date: May 1977, Inner Temple
Pupil Supervisor

NICHOLLS MR CHRISTOPHER BENJAMIN

Citadel Chambers
The Citadel, 190 Corporation Street, Birmingham B4 6QD ☎ 0121 233 8500
✉ clerks@citadelchambers.com
Call Date: Jul 1978, Gray's Inn
Recorder

Practising Areas: Crime, Crime (Corporate/Fraud), Regulatory Law

NICHOLLS MR CLIVE VICTOR QC (1982)

3 Raymond Buildings
3 Raymond Buildings, Gray's Inn, London WC1R 5BH ☎ 020 7400 6400
✉ clerks@3rblaw.com
Call Date: May 1957, Gray's Inn

Practising Areas: Crime

NICHOLLS MR COLIN ALFRED ARTHUR QC (1981)

3 Raymond Buildings
3 Raymond Buildings, Gray's Inn, London WC1R 5BH ☎ 020 7400 6400
✉ clerks@3rblaw.com
Call Date: Jul 1957, Gray's Inn

Practising Areas: Civil Liberties, Courts Martial, Crime, Crime (Corporate/Fraud), Human Rights

NICHOLLS MR DAVID JAMES

11 Stone Buildings
11 Stone Buildings, Lincoln's Inn, London WC2A 3TG ☎ 020 7831 6381 ✉ clerks@11sb.com
Call Date: Nov 2002, Lincoln's Inn

Practising Areas: Bankruptcy, Chancery (General), Chancery (Land Law), Commercial Litigation, Commercial Property, Insolvency, Landlord & Tenant

NICHOLLS MISS ELIZABETH JANE

Lincoln House Chambers
Tower 12, The Avenue North, Spinningfields, 18-22 Bridge Street, Manchester M3 3BZ
☎ 0161 832 5701
✉ info@lincolnhousechambers.com
Call Date: Jul 1984, Inner Temple
Pupil Supervisor, Recorder

NICHOLLS MR PETER JOHN

5 Pump Court
Ground Floor, 5 Pump Court, Temple, London EC4Y 7AP ☎ 020 7353 2532
✉ clerks@5pumpcourt.com
Call Date: Nov 1991, Inner Temple
Pupil Supervisor

NICHOLS MR STUART RICHARD

1 Garden Court Family Law Chambers
Ground Floor, One Garden Court, Temple, London EC4Y 9BJ ☎ 020 7797 7900
✉ clerks@1gc.com
Call Date: Nov 1989, Lincoln's Inn
Pupil Supervisor

Practising Areas: Ancillary Relief, Family, Family Provision

NICHOLSON MR JEREMY MARK QC (2000)

4 Pump Court
4 Pump Court, Temple, London EC4Y 7AN
☎ 020 7842 5555 ✉ chambers@4pumpcourt.com
Call Date: Jul 1977, Middle Temple

Practising Areas: Arbitration, Commercial Litigation, Common Law (General), Construction, Energy, Insurance, Professional Negligence

NICHOLSON PRATT MR THOMAS HYCY

15 New Bridge Street
London EC4V 6AU ☎ 020 7842 1900
✉ clerks@15nbs.com
Call Date: Jul 1986, Lincoln's Inn
Recorder

NICHOLSON MR THOMAS EDWARD CYRIL

Atkinson Bevan Chambers
1st Floor, 2 Harcourt Buildings, Temple, London EC4Y 9DB ☎ 020 7353 2112
✉ clerks@2hb.co.uk
Call Date: Jul 2001, Gray's Inn

Practising Areas: Crime, Crime (Corporate/Fraud), Regulatory Law

NICKLESS MR JASON ALAN

College Chambers
19 Carlton Crescent, Southampton, Hampshire SO15 2ET ☎ 023 8023 0338
✉ clerks@college-chambers.co.uk
Call Date: Oct 2001, Gray's Inn

Practising Areas: Ancillary Relief, Bankruptcy, Chancery (General), Chancery (Land Law), Children's Law, Civil Litigation, Commercial Litigation, Commercial Property, Common Law (General), Construction, Consumer, Coroners Inquests, Costs, Equity, Wills & Trusts, Family, Family Provision, Housing, Industrial Diseases, Insolvency, Land, Landlord & Tenant, Medical Negligence, Partnership, Personal Injury, Probate & Administration, Professional Negligence

NICKLIN MR MATTHEW JAMES

5RB
1st Floor, 5 Raymond Buildings, Gray's Inn, London WC1R 5BP ☎ 020 7242 2902
✉ clerks@5rb.com
Call Date: Oct 1993, Lincoln's Inn
Pupil Supervisor

NICOL MR NICHOLAS KEITH

1 Pump Court
Elm Court, Temple, London EC4Y 7AB
☎ 020 7842 7070 ✉ (name)@pumpcourt.co.uk
Call Date: Nov 1986, Inner Temple
Pupil Supervisor

Practising Areas: Administrative, Discrimination, Healthcare, Housing, Human Rights, Landlord & Tenant

NICOL MR STUART HENRY DAVID

13 King's Bench Walk
13 King's Bench Walk, Temple, London EC4Y 7EN ☎ 020 7353 7204 ✉ clerks@13kbw.co.uk
Call Date: Nov 1994, Lincoln's Inn

Practising Areas: Copyright, Patents, Trademarks

NIJABAT MISS SHAMA BATOOL

Call Date: Nov 1993, Middle Temple

NISSEN MR ALEXANDER DAVID QC (2006)

Keating Chambers
15 Essex Street, London WC2R 3AA
☎ 020 7544 2600 ✉ clerks@keatingchambers.com
Call Date: Jul 1985, Middle Temple
Recorder

Practising Areas: Arbitration, Construction, Professional Negligence

NIXON MISS ABIGAIL LISA BARBARA

Citadel Chambers
The Citadel, 190 Corporation Street, Birmingham B4 6QD ☎ 0121 233 8500
✉ clerks@citadelchambers.com
Call Date: Oct 1991, Inner Temple

Practising Areas: Crime

NIXON MR ANDREW IAN

St Paul's Chambers
5th Floor, St Paul's House, 23 Park Square South, Leeds LS1 2ND ☎ 0113 245 5866
Call Date: Jul 2006, Gray's Inn

NOBLE MR ANDREW

Enterprise Chambers
43 Park Square, Leeds LS1 2NP
☎ 0113 246 0391
✉ leeds@enterprisechambers.com
Call Date: Nov 1992, Lincoln's Inn

Practising Areas: Arbitration, Chancery (General), Chancery (Land Law), Commercial Litigation, Commercial Property, Company & Commercial, Construction, Energy, Insolvency, Insurance, Landlord & Tenant, Partnership, Professional Negligence, Sale & Carriage of Goods

NOBLE MR PHILIP ROBERT

Thomas More Chambers
7 Lincoln's Inn Fields, London WC2A 3BP
☎ 020 7404 7000 ✉ clerks@thomasmore.co.uk
Call Date: Jul 1978, Inner Temple
Pupil Supervisor

Practising Areas: Care Proceedings, Chancery (General), Common Law (General), Family, Family Provision, Landlord & Tenant, Personal Injury, Probate & Administration, Professional Negligence

NOLTEN MISS SONIA JAYNE

2 Temple Gardens
2 Temple Gardens, Temple, London EC4Y 9AY ☎ 020 7822 1200 ✉ clerks@2tg.co.uk
Call Date: Nov 2002, Inner Temple

Practising Areas: Banking, Commercial Litigation, Construction, Insurance/Reinsurance, Professional Negligence

NORMAN MR JARED SIMON GREGORY

Field Court Chambers
5 Field Court, Gray's Inn, London WC1R 5EF
☎ 020 7405 6114 ✉ clerks@fieldcourt.co.uk
Call Date: Nov 2001, Middle Temple

Practising Areas: Common Law (General), Housing, Landlord & Tenant, Local Government, Personal Injury, Regulatory Law, Sale & Carriage of Goods

NORMAN MS JULIAN ELIZABETH

11 Gray's Inn Square Chambers
Chambers of Mr Ian Sen, 1st Floor South, 10/11 Gray's Inn Square, London WC1R 5JD
☎ 020 7405 6879 ✉ clerks@11graysinnsquare.com
Call Date: Mar 2012, Middle Temple

NORMAN MR MICHAEL CHARLES

3 PB Barristers
3 Paper Buildings, Temple, London EC4Y 7EU
☎ 020 7583 8055
3 PB Barristers
Royal Talbot House, 2 Victoria Street, Bristol, Avon BS1 6BB ☎ 0117 928 1520
3 PB Barristers
4 St Peter Street, Winchester SO23 8BW
☎ 01962 868884 ✉ clerks.winchester@3paper.co.uk
3 PB Barristers
23 Beaumont Street, Oxford OX1 2NP
☎ 01865 793 736
3 PB Barristers
30 Christchurch Road, Bournemouth, Dorset BH1 3PD ☎ 01202 292102 ✉ clerks.bournemouth@3paper.co.uk
Call Date: Feb 1971, Gray's Inn
Pupil Supervisor, Recorder

Practising Areas: Chancery (Land Law), Commercial Litigation, Common Law (General), Family Provision, Probate & Administration, Sale & Carriage of Goods

NORMINGTON MR JAMES ADAM

Park Court Chambers
16 Park Place, Leeds LS1 2SJ
☎ 0113 243 3277
✉ clerks@parkcourtchambers.co.uk
Call Date: Nov 2005, Inner Temple

Practising Areas: Arbitration, Chancery (General), Chancery (Land Law), Commercial Litigation, Commercial Property, Common Land, Company & Commercial, Ecclesiastical, Equity, Wills & Trusts, Insolvency, Landlord & Tenant, Partnership, Private International, Probate & Administration, Sale & Carriage of Goods, Town & Country Planning

NORTON MR ANDREW DAVID

1 Garden Court Family Law Chambers
Ground Floor, One Garden Court, Temple, London EC4Y 9BJ ☎ 020 7797 7900
✉ clerks@1gc.com
Call Date: Oct 1992, Inner Temple
Pupil Supervisor

Practising Areas: Care Proceedings, Family, Family Provision

NORTON MR GILES

Enigma Chambers
Troway Hall, Troway Marsh Lane, Sheffield S21 5RU ☎ 07779 576499
✉ law@enigmachambers.co.uk
Holborn Chambers
6 Gate Street, Lincoln's Inn Fields, London WC2A 3HP ☎ 020 7242 6060
Call Date: Nov 2004, Inner Temple

Practising Areas: Chancery (General), Chancery (Land Law), Civil Litigation, Commercial Litigation, Commercial Property, Common Land, Common Law (General), Company & Commercial, Consumer, Crime, Crime (Corporate/Fraud), Defamation, Employment, Equity, Wills & Trusts, Health & Safety, Insolvency, Insurance, Insurance/Reinsurance, Intellectual Property, Land, Landlord & Tenant, Licensing, Medical Negligence, Patents, Personal Injury, Professional Negligence, Road Traffic And Highways, Sale & Carriage of Goods, Tax (Capital & Income), Tax (Corporate), Trademarks

NOSWORTHY MR JONATHAN ALEX

St Philips Chambers
55 Temple Row, Birmingham B2 5LS
☎ 0121 246 7000 ✉ clerks@st-philips.com
Call Date: Nov 2000, Middle Temple

Practising Areas: Chancery (Land Law), Family, Family Provision

NSUGBE MR OBA ERIC QC (2002)

Pump Court Chambers
Upper Ground Floor, 3 Pump Court, Temple, London EC4Y 7AJ ☎ 020 7353 0711
✉ clerks@3pumpcourt.com
Pump Court Chambers
5 Temple Chambers, Temple Street, Swindon SN1 1SQ ☎ 01793 539899
✉ clerks@3pumpcourt.com
Pump Court Chambers
31 Southgate Street, Winchester, Hampshire SO23 9EB ☎ 01962 868 161
✉ clerks@3pumpcourt.com
Call Date: Jul 1985, Gray's Inn
Pupil Supervisor, Recorder

Practising Areas: Commercial Litigation, Common Law (General), Crime, Crime (Corporate/Fraud), Foreign Law

NURSE MR GORDON BRAMWELL WILLIAM

Radcliffe Chambers
Ground Floor, 11 New Square, Lincoln's Inn, London WC2A 3QB ☎ 020 7831 0081
✉ clerks@radcliffechambers.com
Call Date: Nov 1973, Middle Temple
Pupil Supervisor

Practising Areas: Chancery (General), Chancery (Land Law), Charities, Commercial Litigation, Commercial Property, Conveyancing, Equity, Wills & Trusts, Landlord & Tenant, Probate & Administration, Professional Negligence, Sports

NUTTALL MR ANDREW PETER

Lincoln House Chambers
Tower 12, The Avenue North, Spinningfields, 18-22 Bridge Street, Manchester M3 3BZ
☎ 0161 832 5701
✉ info@lincolnhousechambers.com
Call Date: Nov 1978, Lincoln's Inn
Recorder

Practising Areas: Crime, Crime (Corporate/Fraud), Health & Safety, Regulatory Law

NWOSU MISS SHERYL ADA

4 Breams Buildings
Chancery Lane, London EC4A 1HP
☎ 020 7092 1900 ✉ clerks@4bb.co.uk
Call Date: Nov 2000, Middle Temple

Practising Areas: Crime, Crime (Corporate/Fraud)

OAKLEY MISS LOUISE MICHELLE

2 Bedford Row
London WC1R 4BU ☎ 020 7440 8888
✉ clerks@2bedfordrow.co.uk
Call Date: Jul 2001, Middle Temple

Practising Areas: Courts Martial, Crime, Health & Safety, Licensing, Mental Health, Regulatory Law

O'BRIEN MR DAVID

Trinity Chambers
Highfield House, Moulsham Street, Chelmsford, Essex CM2 9AH
☎ 01245 605040 ✉ clerks@trinitychambers.com
Call Date: Nov 1994, Middle Temple

Practising Areas: Ancillary Relief, Care Proceedings, Children's Law

O'BRIEN MR NICHOLAS WILLIAM WATTEBOT

10 King's Bench Walk
Ground Floor, 10 King's Bench Walk, Temple, London EC4Y 7EB ☎ 020 7353 7742
✉ Chambers@10kingsbenchwalk.co.uk
Call Date: Nov 1996, Lincoln's Inn

Practising Areas: Administrative, Asset Finance, Bankruptcy, Chancery (General), Chancery (Land Law), Civil Liberties, Civil Litigation, Commercial Property, Common Law (General), Company & Commercial, Construction, Consumer, Defamation, Discrimination, Employment, Equity, Wills & Trusts, Housing, Human Rights, Immigration, Insolvency, Land, Landlord & Tenant, Licensing, Partnership, Personal Injury, Professional Negligence, Public Law, Sale & Carriage of Goods

O'BRIEN MR SEAN TIMOTHY

St Philips Chambers
55 Temple Row, Birmingham B2 5LS
☎ 0121 246 7000 ✉ clerks@st-philips.com
Call Date: Oct 2001, Lincoln's Inn

Practising Areas: Common Law (General), Company & Commercial, Discrimination, Employment, Landlord & Tenant

OBUKA MS OBIJUO AGWU

Chambers of Miss O A Obuka
Suite 14502, 2nd Floor, 145-157 St John Street, London EC1V 4PW ☎ 020 7936 4474
✉ obijuo.obuka@sky.com
Call Date: Oct 1993, Inner Temple

Practising Areas: Family, Family Provision, Immigration

O'BYRNE MR ANDREW JOHN MARTIN QC (2006)

St Johns Buildings
24a - 28 St John Street, Manchester M3 4DJ
☎ 0161 214 1500 ✉ clerk@stjohnsbuildings.co.uk
16 Winckley Square
Preston PR1 3JJ ☎ 01772 256100
St Johns Buildings Liverpool
8th Floor India Buildings, Water Street, Liverpool L2 0XG ☎ 0151 243 6000
✉ clerk@stjohnsbuildings.co.uk
Call Date: Jul 1978, Gray's Inn

Practising Areas: Crime, Crime (Corporate/Fraud)

O'CONNOR MS CHARLOTTE JANE ANDREWS

Nine Bedford Row
9 Bedford Row, London WC1R 4AZ
☎ 020 7489 2727 ✉ clerks@9bedfordrow.co.uk
Call Date: Oct 1999, Inner Temple
Pupil Supervisor

Practising Areas: Crime, Crime (Corporate/Fraud)

O'CONNOR MISS HILDA ANN

Kidby Chambers
Grundisburgh Road, Woodbridge, Suffolk IP13 6QA
Call Date: Nov 1991, Gray's Inn

Practising Areas: Common Law (General), Company & Commercial, Competition, EC & Competition Law, Public Law

O'CONNOR MR PATRICK MICHAEL JOSEPH QC (1993)

Doughty Street Chambers
53-54 Doughty Street, London WC1N 2LS
☎020 7404 1313 ✉enquiries@doughtystreet.co.uk
Doughty Street Chambers
Pall Mall Court, 61-67 King Street, Manchester M2 4PD ☎0161 618 1066
Doughty Street Chambers
5th Floor, Broad Quay House, Prince Street, Bristol BS1 4DJ ☎01179 058 717
Call Date: Nov 1970, Inner Temple

Practising Areas: Administrative, Civil Liberties, Common Law (General), Courts Martial, Crime, Crime (Corporate/Fraud), Foreign Law, Health & Safety, Human Rights, Private International, Professional Negligence, Public International, Regulatory Law

O'DAIR MR DAVID RICHARD FRAZER

36 Bedford Row
London WC1R 4JH ☎020 7421 8000
✉chambers@36bedfordrow.co.uk
Call Date: Nov 1987, Gray's Inn

Practising Areas: Discrimination, Employment

O'DOHERTY MR PAUL JOSEPH

3 PB Barristers
3 Paper Buildings, Temple, London EC4Y 7EU
☎020 7583 8055
3 PB Barristers
23 Beaumont Street, Oxford OX1 2NP
☎01865 793 736
3 PB Barristers
30 Christchurch Road, Bournemouth, Dorset BH1 3PD ☎01202 292102 ✉clerks.bournemouth@3paper.co.uk
3 PB Barristers
Royal Talbot House, 2 Victoria Street, Bristol, Avon BS1 6BB ☎0117 928 1520
3 PB Barristers
4 St Peter Street, Winchester SO23 8BW
☎01962 868884 ✉clerks.winchester@3paper.co.uk
Call Date: Nov 2000, Middle Temple

O'DONNELL MR DUNCAN GERARD

1 Paper Buildings
1st Floor, 1 Paper Buildings, Temple, London EC4Y 7EP ☎020 7353 3728
✉clerks@onepaper.co.uk
Call Date: Oct 1992, Gray's Inn

O'DONOGHUE MR HUGH VINCENT

Carmelite Chambers
9 Carmelite Street, London EC4Y 0DR
☎020 7936 6300
✉clerks@carmelitechambers.co.uk
Call Date: Oct 2004, Inner Temple

Practising Areas: Administrative, Aviation, Bankruptcy, Chancery (General), Civil Liberties, Commercial Litigation, Common Law (General), Company & Commercial, Copyright, Courts Martial, Crime, Crime (Corporate/Fraud), Defamation, EC & Competition Law, Equity, Wills & Trusts

O'DONOHOE MR ANTHONY FRANCIS

Chavasse Court Chambers
18 Queen Avenue, Liverpool L2 4TX
☎0151 229 2030
✉clerks@chavassechambers.co.uk
Call Date: Jul 1983, Middle Temple
Pupil Supervisor, Recorder

O'DONOVAN MR KEVIN JOHN

No5 Chambers
Fountain Court, Steelhouse Lane, Birmingham B4 6DR ☎0845 210 5555 ✉info@no5.com
No5 Chambers
Greenwood House, 4-7 Salisbury Court, London EC4Y 8AA ☎0845 210 5555
No5 Chambers
38 Queen Square, Bristol BS1 4QS
☎0845 210 5555
Call Date: Jul 1978, Middle Temple
Pupil Supervisor

Practising Areas: Employment, Pensions, Personal Injury

O'DONOVAN MR RONAN DANIEL JAMES

14 Gray's Inn Square
14 Gray's Inn Square, Gray's Inn, London WC1R 5JP ☎020 7242 0858 ✉clerks@14gis.co.uk
Call Date: Nov 1995, Lincoln's Inn
Pupil Supervisor

Practising Areas: Children's Law, Family Provision

OFEI-KWATIA MISS DIDO ASANTEWA

12 Old Square Chambers
1st Floor, 12 Old Square, Lincoln's Inn, London WC2A 3TX ☎020 7404 0875
✉clerks@12oldsquare.com
Call Date: Jul 2002, Lincoln's Inn

OFFENBACH MR ROGER LEON

25 Bedford Row
London WC1R 4HD ☎ 020 7067 1500
✉ clerks@25bedfordrow.com
Call Date: Jul 1978, Inner Temple
Pupil Supervisor

Practising Areas: Crime, Crime (Corporate/ Fraud)

OFFER MR ALEXANDER

Park Court Chambers
16 Park Place, Leeds LS1 2SJ
☎ 0113 243 3277
✉ clerks@parkcourtchambers.co.uk
Garden Court Chambers
57-60 Lincoln's Inn Fields, London WC2A 3LJ
☎ 020 7993 7600 ✉ info@gclaw.co.uk
Call Date: Oct 1998, Middle Temple
Pupil Supervisor

Practising Areas: Administrative, Civil Liberties, Coroners Inquests, Crime, Crime (Corporate/ Fraud), Health & Safety, Housing, Human Rights, Landlord & Tenant, Regulatory Law

O'GORMAN MR CHRISTOPHER FRANCIS

Cornwall Street Chambers
85-87 Cornwall Street, Birmingham B3 3BY
☎ 0121 233 7500 ✉ clerks@cornwallstreet.co.uk
Call Date: Nov 1987, Gray's Inn

Practising Areas: Crime, Sports

OGUNBIYI MR OLUWOLE AFOLABI

Chambers of Mr O A Ogunbiyi
6 Vicarage Heights, Benfleet, Essex SS7 1QA
☎ 01268 631 618 ✉ oao@lineone.net
Call Date: Jul 1995, Lincoln's Inn

OGUNBUSOLA MR VICTOR OLANIYI

Chambers of Victor Ogumbusola
23 Cockerell Close, Burnt Mill, Basildon SS13 1QR ☎ 07413 634231
✉ victorogunbusola@hotmail.com
Call Date: Jul 2000, Lincoln's Inn

Practising Areas: Aviation, Banking, Commercial Litigation, Common Law (General), Crime, Crime (Corporate/Fraud), Energy, Foreign Law, Immigration, International Trade, Personal Injury, Private International, Regulatory Law, Shipping/Admiralty

OHRENSTEIN MR DOV

Radcliffe Chambers
Ground Floor, 11 New Square, Lincoln's Inn, London WC2A 3QB ☎ 020 7831 0081
✉ clerks@radcliffechambers.com
Call Date: Oct 1995, Gray's Inn

Practising Areas: Agriculture, Banking, Bankruptcy, Chancery (General), Chancery (Land Law), Commercial Litigation, Commercial Property, Common Land, Company & Commercial, Conveyancing, Equity, Wills & Trusts, Insolvency, Landlord & Tenant, Partnership, Probate & Administration, Professional Negligence

OJI MISS ATIM ANENE IFEOMA

Amethyst Chambers
Ground Floor, 9 Kings Bench Walk, Inner Temple, London EC4Y 7DX
☎ 020 7936 4966 ✉ info@amethystchambers.com
Call Date: Nov 1992, Inner Temple

OJUTIKU MRS FADEKEMI OMOTAYO

4 King's Bench Walk
2nd Floor, 4 King's Bench Walk, Temple, London EC4Y 7DL ☎ 020 7822 7000
✉ clerks@4kbw.co.uk
Call Date: Oct 1994, Lincoln's Inn

Practising Areas: Arbitration, Care Proceedings, Family, Immigration

OKAI MR ANTHONY SETH

12 Old Square Chambers
1st Floor, 12 Old Square, Lincoln's Inn, London WC2A 3TX ☎ 020 7404 0875
✉ clerks@12oldsquare.com
Call Date: Jul 1973, Inner Temple
Pupil Supervisor

O'KANE MISS SARAH CAROLINE

Argent Chambers
5 Bell Yard, London WC2A 2JR
☎ 020 7556 5500
✉ briefsin@argentchambers.co.uk
Call Date: Oct 2001, Middle Temple

Practising Areas: Crime, Crime (Corporate/ Fraud)

OKE MR OLANREWAJU OLADIPUPO

Kingsway Chambers
Suite 51, 95 Wilton Road, London SW1V 3BX
☎ 020 7404 2357
Call Date: Jul 1979, Lincoln's Inn

Practising Areas: Entertainment

OKINE MISS JULIE ANNE

Goldsmith Chambers
Ground Floor, Goldsmith Building, Temple, London EC4Y 7BL ☎ 020 7353 6802
✉ clerks@goldsmithchambers.com
Call Date: Oct 1996, Lincoln's Inn
Pupil Supervisor

Practising Areas: Family, Family Provision

OKOYA MR WILLIAM EBIKISE

Arden Chambers
20 Bloomsbury Square, London WC1A 2NS
☎ 020 7242 4244 ✉ clerks@ardenchambers.com
Call Date: Nov 1989, Gray's Inn
Pupil Supervisor

Practising Areas: Commercial Property, Company & Commercial, Housing, Landlord & Tenant, Local Government

OKOYE MISS JOY NWAMALA

Chambers of Joy Okoye
9 Redbourne Avenue, Finchley Church End, London N3 2BP
☎ 07976 426871 / 020 7405 7011
✉ okoyejoy@hotmail.com
Call Date: Jul 1981, Inner Temple
Pupil Supervisor

Practising Areas: Arbitration, Care Proceedings, Commercial Litigation, Common Law (General), Company & Commercial, Employment, Family, Family Provision, Foreign Law

OLDFIELD MISS JANE LISA CATHERINE

18 Red Lion Court
London EC4A 3EB ☎ 020 7520 6000
✉ chambers@18rlc.co.uk
18 Red Lion Court (Annexe)
Thornwood House, 102 New London Road, Chelmsford, Essex CM2 0RG
☎ 01245 280880
Call Date: Oct 2004, Middle Temple

Practising Areas: Crime

OLDHAM MRS FRANCES MARY THERESA QC (1994)

36 Bedford Row
London WC1R 4JH ☎ 020 7421 8000
✉ chambers@36bedfordrow.co.uk
37 Park Square Chambers
37 Park Square, Leeds LS1 2NY
☎ 0113 243 9422 ✉ chambers@no37.co.uk
Call Date: Jul 1977, Gray's Inn
Recorder

Practising Areas: Care Proceedings, Crime, Crime (Corporate/Fraud), Family, Family Provision, Mental Health

O'LEARY MS MICHELE ANN

1 Pump Court
Elm Court, Temple, London EC4Y 7AB
☎ 020 7842 7070 ✉ (name)@pumpcourt.co.uk
Call Date: Nov 1983, Gray's Inn
Pupil Supervisor

Practising Areas: Care Proceedings, Family, Family Provision

OLIVER MR DAVID KEIGHTLEY RIDEAL QC (1986)

13 Old Square Chambers
Ground Floor, 14 Old Square, Lincoln's Inn, London WC2A 3UE ☎ 020 7831 4445
✉ clerks@13oldsquare.com
Call Date: Jul 1972, Lincoln's Inn

Practising Areas: Chancery (General), Chancery (Land Law), Commercial Litigation, Company & Commercial, EC & Competition Law, Equity, Wills & Trusts, Insolvency

OLIVER MISS JULIET DIANNE

5 Pump Court
Ground Floor, 5 Pump Court, Temple, London EC4Y 7AP ☎ 020 7353 2532
✉ clerks@5pumpcourt.com
Call Date: Nov 1974, Gray's Inn

OLIVER MR MICHAEL RICHARD

15 New Bridge Street
London EC4V 6AU ☎ 020 7842 1900
✉ clerks@15nbs.com
Call Date: Jul 1977, Inner Temple
Pupil Supervisor

OLIVER DR PETER JAMES ROBERT

4 Pump Court
4 Pump Court, Temple, London EC4Y 7AN
☎ 020 7842 5555 ✉ chambers@4pumpcourt.com
Call Date: Jul 2002, Lincoln's Inn

Practising Areas: Banking, Bankruptcy, Commercial Litigation, Construction, Insolvency, Insurance, Professional Negligence

O'MAHONY MR DAVID ST JOHN

Seven Bedford Row
7 Bedford Row, London WC1R 4BS
☎ 020 7242 3555 ✉ clerks@7br.co.uk
Call Date: Oct 2000, Inner Temple
Pupil Supervisor

O'MAHONY MR JONATHAN SOLOMON

9 Stone Buildings
Lincoln's Inn, London WC2A 3NN
☎020 7404 5055 ✉clerks@9stonebuildings.com
Call Date: Nov 2000, Inner Temple
Pupil Supervisor

Practising Areas: Bankruptcy, Chancery (General), Chancery (Land Law), Commercial Property, Insolvency, Landlord & Tenant, Partnership

OMIDEYI MISS ANUOLUWAPO IYANU

Furnival Chambers
32 Furnival Street, London EC4A 1JQ
☎020 7405 3232
Call Date: Jul 2001, Lincoln's Inn

Practising Areas: Crime, Crime (Corporate/Fraud), Entertainment, Regulatory Law

ONALAJA MR JAMES OLUWATOSIN

2 Pump Court
1st Floor, 2 Pump Court, Temple, London EC4Y 7AH ☎020 7353 5597
✉clerks@2pumpcourt.co.uk
Call Date: Oct 2004, Lincoln's Inn

Practising Areas: Civil Liberties, Courts Martial, Crime, Crime (Corporate/Fraud), Human Rights

O'NEILL MR BRIAN PATRICK QC (2010)

2 Hare Court
Lower Ground, Ground, 1st & 2nd Floor, 2 Hare Court, Temple, London EC4Y 7BH
☎020 7353 3982 ✉clerks@2harecourt.com
Call Date: Nov 1987, Gray's Inn
Pupil Supervisor, Recorder

Practising Areas: Civil Liberties, Courts Martial, Crime, Crime (Corporate/Fraud), Health & Safety, Human Rights, Regulatory Law

O'NEILL MR JONATHAN NORMAN

Rougemont Chambers
Victory House, Dean Clarke Gardens, Southernhay East, Exeter EX2 4AA
☎01392 208484
✉clerks@rougemontchambers.co.uk
Call Date: Nov 2007, Inner Temple

Practising Areas: Chancery (General), Chancery (Land Law), Employment, Landlord & Tenant, Personal Injury, Town & Country Planning

O'NEILL MISS LOUISE CATHERINE

St John's Chambers
101 Victoria Street, Bristol BS1 6PU
☎0117 923 4700 ✉clerks@stjohnschambers.co.uk
Call Date: Feb 1989, Gray's Inn

O'NEILL MISS SALLY JANE QC (1997)

Furnival Chambers
32 Furnival Street, London EC4A 1JQ
☎020 7405 3232
Call Date: Nov 1976, Gray's Inn

Practising Areas: Crime, Inquests, Regulatory Law

ONG MISS GRACE YU MAE

Argent Chambers
5 Bell Yard, London WC2A 2JR
☎020 7556 5500
✉briefsin@argentchambers.co.uk
Call Date: Jul 1985, Lincoln's Inn
Pupil Supervisor

Practising Areas: Care Proceedings, Courts Martial, Crime, Crime (Corporate/Fraud), Family, Family Provision

ONIPEDE DR VICTOR OLUSEGUN

Chambers of Dr V O Onipede
34 Meeting House Lane, London SE15 2UN
☎07956 207159
Call Date: Oct 2000, Lincoln's Inn
Pupil Supervisor

Practising Areas: Administrative, Banking, Civil Litigation, Crime, Disciplinary Tribunals, Employment, Housing, Immigration, Landlord & Tenant, Licensing

ONSLOW MR ROBERT DENZIL

8 New Square
8 New Square, Lincoln's Inn, London WC2A 3QP ☎020 7405 4321 ✉clerks@8newsquare.co.uk
Call Date: Oct 1991, Lincoln's Inn
Pupil Supervisor

Practising Areas: Competition, Copyright, EC & Competition Law, Entertainment, Film, Cable & TV, Franchising, Information Technology, Intellectual Property, Patents, Sports, Telecommunications, Trademarks

C

OOMMEN MR JACOB

Chambers of Mr Jacob Oommen
1 Stuart Road, East Barnet, Hertfordshire EN4 8XG ☎07958 680272 ✉jacob.oommen@justbarrister.com
Call Date: Mar 2001, Middle Temple

Practising Areas: Administrative, Ancillary Relief, Arbitration, Bankruptcy, Chancery (General), Civil Litigation, Common Law (General), Consumer, Coroners Inquests, Crime, Disciplinary Tribunals, Discrimination, Employment, Equity, Wills & Trusts, Family, Health & Safety, Housing, Human Rights, Immigration, Insolvency, Insurance, Landlord & Tenant, Licensing, Partnership, Personal Injury, Probate & Administration, Public Law, Regulatory Law, Road Traffic And Highways, Sale & Carriage of Goods

ORCHARD MR ANTHONY EDWARD QC (2011)

Carmelite Chambers
9 Carmelite Street, London EC4Y 0DR
☎020 7936 6300
✉clerks@carmelitechambers.co.uk
Call Date: Oct 1991, Inner Temple
Pupil Supervisor

Practising Areas: Crime, Crime (Corporate/Fraud)

ORCHARD MISS CATHLYN ESTHER

Citadel Chambers
The Citadel, 190 Corporation Street, Birmingham B4 6QD ☎0121 233 8500
✉clerks@citadelchambers.com
Call Date: Oct 1999, Lincoln's Inn

Practising Areas: Crime

ORCHOVER MS FRANCES RACHEL

Coram Chambers
9-11 Fulwood Place, London WC1V 6HG
☎020 7092 3700 ✉mail@coramchambers.co.uk
Call Date: Jul 1989, Middle Temple
Pupil Supervisor

Practising Areas: Family

ORME MISS EMILY CHARLOTTE

Arden Chambers
20 Bloomsbury Square, London WC1A 2NS
☎020 7242 4244 ✉clerks@ardenchambers.com
Call Date: Jul 2003, Lincoln's Inn

Practising Areas: Administrative, Housing, Landlord & Tenant, Local Government

ORMONDROYD MR MATTHEW CAIN

Francis Taylor Building
Inner Temple, London EC4Y 7BY
☎020 7353 8415 ✉clerks@ftb.eu.com
Call Date: Oct 2007, Lincoln's Inn

ORNSBY MISS SUZANNE DOREEN QC (2012)

Francis Taylor Building
Inner Temple, London EC4Y 7BY
☎020 7353 8415 ✉clerks@ftb.eu.com
St John's Chambers
101 Victoria Street, Bristol BS1 6PU
☎0117 923 4700 ✉clerks@stjohnschambers.co.uk
Call Date: Nov 1986, Middle Temple
Pupil Supervisor

Practising Areas: Administrative, Environment, Local Government, Professional Negligence, Town & Country Planning

O'RYAN MR RORY CHARLES MARK

Chambers of Ian Macdonald QC
Garden Court North, 22 Oxford Court, Manchester M2 3WQ ☎0161 236 1840
✉clerks@gcnchambers.co.uk
Call Date: Mar 2000, Middle Temple
Pupil Supervisor

OSBORNE MR DAVID THOMAS

Chambers of Mr D T Osborne
The Granary, Preston Bowyer, Milverton, Taunton, Somerset TA4 1PQ
☎01823 400 705 ✉david@david-osborne.com
Call Date: Jul 1974, Gray's Inn

Practising Areas: Common Law (General), Crime, Family, Licensing, Personal Injury

OSBORNE MR JAMES ROBERT

Clerksroom (London)
3rd Floor, 218 Strand, London WC2R 1AT
☎0845 083 3000 ✉mail@clerksroom.com
Call Date: Jul 2006, Lincoln's Inn

Practising Areas: Agriculture, Aviation, Bankruptcy, Chancery (General), Commercial Litigation, Common Law (General), Company & Commercial, Construction, Defamation, Education, Entertainment, Environment, Equity, Wills & Trusts, Family Provision, Film, Cable & TV, Health & Safety, Housing, Information Technology, Insurance, International Trade, Landlord & Tenant, Licensing, Medical Negligence, Partnership, Personal Injury, Probate & Administration, Professional Negligence, Road Traffic And Highways, Sale & Carriage of Goods, Sports, Telecommunications, Town & Country Planning

OSBORNE MR RICHARD

4 Pump Court
4 Pump Court, Temple, London EC4Y 7AN
☎ 020 7842 5555 ✉ chambers@4pumpcourt.com
Call Date: Oct 2005, Inner Temple

Practising Areas: Construction, Insurance, Professional Negligence

OSSACK MRS TANYA RACHELLE ELISE

3 Temple Gardens
Lower Ground Floor, 3 Temple Gardens, Temple, London EC4Y 9AU ☎ 020 7353 3102
✉ clerks@3tg.co.uk
Call Date: Oct 1993, Gray's Inn

Practising Areas: Crime, Regulatory Law

O'SULLIVAN MR BERNARD ANTHONY

Henderson Chambers
2 Harcourt Buildings, Temple, London EC4Y 9DB ☎ 020 7583 9020
✉ clerks@hendersonchambers.co.uk
Call Date: Jul 1971, Inner Temple
Pupil Supervisor

Practising Areas: Common Law (General), Family, Family Provision

O'SULLIVAN MR RICHARD JOHN

1215 Chambers
1 Fetter Lane, London EC4A 1BR
☎ 020 3291 1215 ✉ admin@1215chambers.com
Call Date: Oct 1999, Inner Temple

Practising Areas: Administrative, Ancillary Relief, Arbitration, Bankruptcy, Chancery (General), Chancery (Land Law), Civil Liberties, Civil Litigation, Commercial Litigation, Commercial Property, Common Law (General), Company & Commercial, Equity, Wills & Trusts, Foreign Law, Housing, Insolvency, Land, Landlord & Tenant, Local Government, Private International, Probate & Administration, Public Law

C

O'SULLIVAN MR THOMAS SEAN PATRICK

4 Pump Court
4 Pump Court, Temple, London EC4Y 7AN
☎ 020 7842 5555 ✉ chambers@4pumpcourt.com
Call Date: Oct 1997, Middle Temple
Pupil Supervisor

Practising Areas: Arbitration, Commercial Litigation, Commodities, Energy, Insurance, Insurance/Reinsurance, Professional Negligence, Sale & Carriage of Goods, Shipping/Admiralty

OTCHIE MR ANDREW AKUAFO

12 Old Square Chambers
1st Floor, 12 Old Square, Lincoln's Inn, London WC2A 3TX ☎ 020 7404 0875
✉ clerks@12oldsquare.com
Call Date: Nov 2005, Gray's Inn

Practising Areas: Civil Litigation, Crime, Employment, Immigration

O'TOOLE MR BARTHOLOMEW VINCENT

5 King's Bench Walk
5 King's Bench Walk, Temple, London EC4Y 7DN ☎ 020 7353 5638 ✉ clerks@5kbw.co.uk
Call Date: Nov 1980, Middle Temple
Pupil Supervisor

Practising Areas: Chancery (General), Common Law (General), Crime, Discrimination, Employment, Family, Family Provision, Housing, Immigration, Landlord & Tenant, Licensing, Personal Injury, Professional Negligence, Sale & Carriage of Goods, Sports

O'TOOLE MR SIMON GERARD

5 Pump Court
Ground Floor, 5 Pump Court, Temple, London EC4Y 7AP ☎ 020 7353 2532
✉ clerks@5pumpcourt.com
Riverview Chambers
Hamilton House, 1 Temple Avenue, London EC4Y 0HA ☎ 0844 225 3999
✉ chrisbaylis@riverviewchambers.com
Call Date: Jul 1984, Inner Temple

Practising Areas: Chancery (Land Law), Commercial Litigation, Company & Commercial, Conveyancing, Employment, Insurance/Reinsurance, Landlord & Tenant, Professional Negligence

OTWAL MR MUKHTIAR SINGH

42 Bedford Row
London WC1R 4LL ☎ 020 7831 0222
✉ clerks@42br.com
Call Date: Nov 1991, Lincoln's Inn

Practising Areas: Administrative, Arbitration, Chancery (General), Chancery (Land Law), Commercial Litigation, Commercial Property, Common Law (General), Company & Commercial, Equity, Wills & Trusts, Landlord & Tenant, Partnership, Professional Negligence

OULTON MR RICHARD ARTHUR COURTENAY

5 Essex Court
1st Floor, 5 Essex Court, Temple, London EC4Y 9AH ☎020 7410 2000
✉clerks@5essexcourt.co.uk
Call Date: Nov 1995, Middle Temple
Pupil Supervisor

Practising Areas: Chancery (General), Chancery (Land Law), Commercial Property, Common Law (General), Company & Commercial, Discrimination, Employment, Landlord & Tenant, Personal Injury, Professional Negligence

OUTTERSIDE MR DAVID MICHAEL

1 High Pavement
Nottingham NG1 1HF ☎0115 941 8218
✉clerks@1highpavement.co.uk
Call Date: Jul 2004, Inner Temple

OWEN MISS CARYS

18 Red Lion Court
London EC4A 3EB ☎020 7520 6000
✉chambers@18rlc.co.uk
18 Red Lion Court (Annexe)
Thornwood House, 102 New London Road, Chelmsford, Essex CM2 0RG
☎01245 280880
Call Date: Oct 2002, Lincoln's Inn

Practising Areas: Crime, Crime (Corporate/Fraud), Regulatory Law

OWEN MS ELEN MAI

Linenhall Chambers
1 Stanley Place, Chester CH1 2LU
☎01244 348282
✉clerks@linenhallchambers.co.uk
Call Date: Nov 1985, Gray's Inn

Practising Areas: Crime, Regulatory Law, Road Traffic And Highways

OWEN MR TIMOTHY WYNN QC (2000)

Matrix Chambers
Griffin Building, Gray's Inn, London WC1R 5LN ☎020 7404 3447 ✉matrix@matrixlaw.co.uk/Iscott@matrixlaw.co.uk
Call Date: Jul 1983, Middle Temple

Practising Areas: Administrative, Asset Finance, Civil Liberties, Civil Litigation, Commercial Litigation, Common Law (General), Coroners Inquests, Courts Martial, Crime, Crime (Corporate/Fraud), Disciplinary Tribunals, Human Rights, Inquests, Mental Health, Parliamentary, Public Law, Regulatory Law, Sports

OWEN MISS WENDY JANE

Call Date: Jul 2002, Middle Temple

OWENS MISS ELSPETH ELUNED

4 Pump Court
4 Pump Court, Temple, London EC4Y 7AN
☎020 7842 5555 ✉chambers@4pumpcourt.com
Call Date: Oct 2007, Middle Temple

Practising Areas: Arbitration, Commercial Litigation, Common Law (General), Company & Commercial, Construction, Energy, Insurance, Professional Negligence, Sale & Carriage of Goods, Shipping/Admiralty

OWEN-THOMAS MR RICHARD MATTHEW

13 King's Bench Walk
13 King's Bench Walk, Temple, London EC4Y 7EN ☎020 7353 7204 ✉clerks@13kbw.co.uk
13 KBW
32 Beaumont Street, Oxford OX1 2NP
☎01865 311066 ✉clerks@13kbw.co.uk
Call Date: Nov 2000, Middle Temple
Pupil Supervisor

Practising Areas: Commercial Litigation, Common Law (General), Company & Commercial, Discrimination, Employment, Personal Injury

OWUSU-YIANOMA MR DAVID KWASI DARTEY

1 Mitre Court Buildings
1 Mitre Court Buildings, Temple, London EC4Y 7BS ☎020 7452 8900 ✉clerks@1mcb.com
Call Date: Nov 1992, Inner Temple
Pupil Supervisor

Practising Areas: Crime, Crime (Corporate/Fraud), Human Rights, Public International

OZIN MR PAUL DAVID

23 Essex Street
London WC2R 3AA ☎020 7413 0353
✉clerks@23es.com
Call Date: Nov 1987, Middle Temple
Pupil Supervisor

Practising Areas: Administrative, Crime, Crime (Corporate/Fraud), Environment, Regulatory Law

PADFIELD MR NICHOLAS DAVID QC (1991)

Chambers of Nicholas Padfield QC
2 Netherton Grove, Chelsea, London SW10 9TQ ☎020 7351 1961
✉ndp@nicholaspadfieldqc.com
Call Date: Nov 1972, Inner Temple
Pupil Supervisor

Practising Areas: Administrative, Banking, Commercial Litigation, Construction, Financial Services, Private International, Professional Negligence, Public International

PAGE MISS ADRIENNE MAY QC (1999)

5RB
1st Floor, 5 Raymond Buildings, Gray's Inn, London WC1R 5BP ☎020 7242 2902
✉clerks@5rb.com
Call Date: Jul 1974, Middle Temple

Practising Areas: Defamation

PAGE MR JONATHAN ROWLAND THOMAS

Carmelite Chambers
9 Carmelite Street, London EC4Y 0DR
☎020 7936 6300
✉clerks@carmelitechambers.co.uk
Call Date: Oct 1996, Middle Temple

Practising Areas: Crime, Crime (Corporate/Fraud), Disciplinary Tribunals, Regulatory Law

PAGET MS HENRIETTA FRANCES

9-12 Bell Yard
London WC2A 2JR ☎020 7400 1800
✉clerks@9-12bellyard.com
Call Date: Oct 1999, Inner Temple
Pupil Supervisor

PAGET MR MICHAEL RODBOROUGH

Garden Court Chambers
57-60 Lincoln's Inn Fields, London WC2A 3LJ
☎020 7993 7600 ✉info@gclaw.co.uk
Call Date: Oct 1995, Lincoln's Inn

Practising Areas: Administrative, Chancery (Land Law), Common Law (General), Equity, Wills & Trusts, Housing, Landlord & Tenant, Local Government, Mental Health

PAIGE MR RICHARD MARK

Sovereign Chambers
46 Park Place, Leeds LS1 2RY
☎0113 245 1841
✉clerks@sovereignchambers.co.uk
Call Date: Oct 1997, Middle Temple
Pupil Supervisor

Practising Areas: Common Law (General), Medical Negligence, Personal Injury

PAINES MR NICHOLAS PAUL BILLOT QC (1997)

Monckton Chambers
1 & 2 Raymond Buildings, Gray's Inn, London WC1R 5NR ☎020 7405 7211
✉chambers@monckton.com
Call Date: Apr 1978, Gray's Inn

PALEY MS RUTH THERESA ELIZABETH

23 Essex Street
London WC2R 3AA ☎020 7413 0353
✉clerks@23es.com
Call Date: Oct 2003, Gray's Inn

Practising Areas: Crime, Crime (Corporate/Fraud), Intellectual Property, Regulatory Law

PALLO MR SIMON RUSSEL

Bank House Chambers
Old Bank House, Hartshead, Sheffield S1 2EL
☎0114 275 1223 ✉w.
digby@bankhousechambers.co.uk
Call Date: Jul 2003, Gray's Inn

Practising Areas: Common Law (General), Crime, Employment, Family, Personal Injury

PALMER MISS CLAIRE LOUISE

Thomas More Chambers
7 Lincoln's Inn Fields, London WC2A 3BP
☎020 7404 7000 ✉clerks@thomasmore.co.uk
Call Date: Oct 2003, Lincoln's Inn
Pupil Supervisor

Practising Areas: Commercial Litigation, Common Law (General), Crime, Discrimination, Employment, Regulatory Law

PALMER MR EDWARD JAMES

Regent Chambers
Regent House, 3 Pall Mall, Hanley, Stoke On Trent ST1 1HP ☎01782 286666
✉clerks@regentchambers.co.uk
Call Date: Jul 2000, Lincoln's Inn

Practising Areas: Common Law (General), Crime, Family, Housing, Landlord & Tenant

PALMER MR HOWARD WILLIAM ARTHUR QC (1999)

2 Temple Gardens
2 Temple Gardens, Temple, London EC4Y 9AY ☎ 020 7822 1200 ✉ clerks@2tg.co.uk
Call Date: Jul 1977, Inner Temple
Recorder

Practising Areas: Construction, Insurance, Insurance/Reinsurance, Private International

PALMER MR IAIN FRANKLYN

Renaissance Chambers
5th Floor, Gray's Inn Chambers, Gray's Inn, London WC1R 5JA ☎ 020 7404 1111
✉ clerks@renaissancechambers.co.uk
Call Date: Nov 1999, Middle Temple

Practising Areas: Discrimination, Employment, Human Rights, Immigration

PALMER MR JAMES SAVILL

Henderson Chambers
2 Harcourt Buildings, Temple, London EC4Y 9DB ☎ 020 7583 9020
✉ clerks@hendersonchambers.co.uk
Call Date: Nov 1983, Middle Temple

Practising Areas: Commercial Litigation, Common Law (General), Employment, Insurance, Medical Negligence, Personal Injury, Private International, Professional Negligence, Sale & Carriage of Goods, Sports

PALMER MR NATHAN EMMANUEL

5 Pump Court
Ground Floor, 5 Pump Court, Temple, London EC4Y 7AP ☎ 020 7353 2532
✉ clerks@5pumpcourt.com
Call Date: Oct 1994, Middle Temple

Practising Areas: Crime

PALMER MR ROBERT HENRY

Monckton Chambers
1 & 2 Raymond Buildings, Gray's Inn, London WC1R 5NR ☎ 020 7405 7211
✉ chambers@monckton.com
Call Date: Oct 1998, Gray's Inn
Pupil Supervisor

Practising Areas: Administrative, Civil Liberties, Regulatory Law, Telecommunications

PALMER MISS SUZANNE ELIZABETH JOSEPHINE

4 King's Bench Walk
2nd Floor, 4 King's Bench Walk, Temple, London EC4Y 7DL ☎ 020 7822 7000
✉ clerks@4kbw.co.uk
Call Date: Nov 1995, Middle Temple
Pupil Supervisor

Practising Areas: Commercial Litigation, Common Law (General), Discrimination, Employment, Landlord & Tenant, Personal Injury, Regulatory Law

PANAGIOTOPOULOU MISS SOPHIE THALIA

Staple Inn Chambers
1st Floor, 9 Staple Inn, Holborn Bars, London WC1V 7QH ☎ 020 7242 5240
✉ clerks@stapleinn.co.uk
Call Date: Oct 1995, Middle Temple

Practising Areas: Family, Immigration

PANAGIOTOPOULOU MISS TANIA

Staple Inn Chambers
1st Floor, 9 Staple Inn, Holborn Bars, London WC1V 7QH ☎ 020 7242 5240
✉ clerks@stapleinn.co.uk
Call Date: Oct 1994, Middle Temple

Practising Areas: Courts Martial, Crime, Crime (Corporate/Fraud), Licensing

PANDE MISS KAKOLY

2 Dr Johnson's Buildings
2 Dr Johnson's Buildings, Temple, London EC4Y 7AY ☎ 020 7936 2613 ✉ clerks@2drj.com
Call Date: Oct 2005, Middle Temple

Practising Areas: Crime, Crime (Corporate/Fraud), Employment, Immigration

PANDYA MISS ABHA

12 King's Bench Walk
12 King's Bench Walk, Temple, London EC4Y 7EL ☎ 020 7583 0811
Call Date: Mar 2007, Middle Temple

PANTON MR ALASTAIR HOWARD

10 King's Bench Walk
Ground Floor, 10 King's Bench Walk, Temple, London EC4Y 7EB ☎ 020 7353 7742
✉ Chambers@10kingsbenchwalk.co.uk
Call Date: Oct 1996, Inner Temple

Practising Areas: Chancery (General), Chancery (Land Law), Commercial Litigation, Commercial Property, Common Law (General),

Construction, Conveyancing, Equity, Wills & Trusts, Franchising, Housing, Information Technology, Landlord & Tenant, Probate & Administration, Professional Negligence, Sale & Carriage of Goods

PANTON MR WILLIAM DWIGHT

Amethyst Chambers
Ground Floor, 9 Kings Bench Walk, Inner Temple, London EC4Y 7DX
☎ 020 7936 4966 ✉ info@amethystchambers.com
Call Date: Nov 1977, Inner Temple
Pupil Supervisor

Practising Areas: Civil Liberties, Common Law (General), Crime, Discrimination, Employment

PAPAGEORGIS MR GEORGE MICHAEL

4 Breams Buildings
Chancery Lane, London EC4A 1HP
☎ 020 7092 1900 ✉ clerks@4bb.co.uk
Call Date: Jul 1981, Middle Temple
Pupil Supervisor

PAPAZIAN MISS CLIONA CONCEPTA

4 Paper Buildings
1st Floor, 4 Paper Buildings, Temple, London EC4Y 7EX ☎ 020 7427 5200 ✉ clerks@4pb.com
Call Date: Nov 1994, Inner Temple
Pupil Supervisor

Practising Areas: Care Proceedings, Children's Law, Family

PARASKOS MR PARASKEVAKIS CHRISTAKIS

11 Gray's Inn Square Chambers
Chambers of Mr Ian Sen, 1st Floor South, 10/11 Gray's Inn Square, London WC1R 5JD
☎ 020 7405 6879 ✉ clerks@11graysinnsquare.com
Call Date: Jul 2003, Middle Temple

Practising Areas: Administrative, Chancery (General), Chancery (Land Law), Civil Liberties, Civil Litigation, Commercial Litigation, Commercial Property, Common Law (General), Construction, Consumer, Copyright, Crime, Crime (Corporate/Fraud), Defamation, Disciplinary Tribunals, Discrimination, Employment, Energy, Entertainment, Equity, Wills & Trusts, Human Rights, Immigration, Intellectual Property, International Trade, Landlord & Tenant, Licensing, Mental Health, Sale & Carriage of Goods, Shipping/Admiralty, Sports, Trademarks

PARDOE MR MATTHEW JAMES

Dyers Chambers
35 Bedford Row, London WC1R 4JH
☎ 020 7404 1881 ✉ admin@dyerschambers.com
Call Date: Feb 1992, Inner Temple

Practising Areas: Courts Martial, Crime, Crime (Corporate/Fraud), Employment, Personal Injury

PARDOE MR RUPERT ADAM CORIN

23 Essex Street
London WC2R 3AA ☎ 020 7413 0353
✉ clerks@23es.com
Call Date: Jul 1984, Inner Temple
Pupil Supervisor

Practising Areas: Crime, Crime (Corporate/Fraud), Regulatory Law

PARE MR CHRISTOPHER MICHAEL

Call Date: Jul 2006, Middle Temple

PARKER MRS KAREN LESLEY

Guildhall Chambers Portsmouth
Prudential Buildings, 16 Guildhall Walk, Portsmouth, Hampshire PO1 2DE
☎ 023 9275 2400 ✉ clerks@gcp-barristers.com
Call Date: Jul 2001, Inner Temple

Practising Areas: Chancery (General), Chancery (Land Law), Commercial Litigation, Commercial Property, Common Law (General), Company & Commercial, Construction, Defamation, Discrimination, Employment, Environment, Equity, Wills & Trusts, Health & Safety, Healthcare, Housing, Immigration, Insurance, Landlord & Tenant, Licensing, Medical Negligence, Partnership, Personal Injury, Professional Negligence, Town & Country Planning

PARKER MISS WENDY

Hardwicke
New Square, Lincoln's Inn, London WC2A 3SB ☎ 020 7242 2523
✉ enquiries@hardwicke.co.uk
Call Date: Jul 1978, Middle Temple
Pupil Supervisor

Practising Areas: Bankruptcy, Chancery (General), Common Law (General), Employment, Insolvency, Licensing, Partnership, Professional Negligence

PARNELL MRS CHERIE EILEEN

East Anglian Chambers
Gresham House, 5 Museum Street, Ipswich, Suffolk IP1 1HQ ☎01473 214481
✉ipswich@ealaw.co.uk
East Anglian Chambers
53 North Hill, Colchester, Essex CO1 1QA
☎01473 214481 ✉colchester@ealaw.co.uk
East Anglian Chambers
15 The Close, Norwich, Norfolk NR1 4DZ
☎01473 214481 ✉norwich@ealaw.co.uk
Call Date: Nov 2000, Middle Temple

Practising Areas: Care Proceedings, Family, Family Provision, Human Rights

PARR MR JOHN EDWARD

Cobden House Chambers
19 Quay Street, Manchester M3 3HN
☎0161 833 6000 ✉Clerks@Cobden.co.uk
Call Date: Jul 1989, Middle Temple

Practising Areas: Personal Injury

PARRY MR CHARLES ROBERT

Pump Court Chambers
31 Southgate Street, Winchester, Hampshire SO23 9EB ☎01962 868 161
✉clerks@3pumpcourt.com
Pump Court Chambers
Upper Ground Floor, 3 Pump Court, Temple, London EC4Y 7AJ ☎020 7353 0711
✉clerks@3pumpcourt.com
Pump Court Chambers
5 Temple Chambers, Temple Street, Swindon SN1 1SQ ☎01793 539899
✉clerks@3pumpcourt.com
Call Date: Nov 1973, Middle Temple
Pupil Supervisor

Practising Areas: Agriculture, Arbitration, Common Law (General), Employment, Health & Safety, Personal Injury

PARSONS MR ANDREW JAMES

Portsmouth Barristers'Chambers
Victory House, 7 Bellevue Terrace, Portsmouth, Hampshire PO5 3AT
☎023 9283 1292 ✉clerks@portsmouthbar.com
Call Date: Jul 1985, Inner Temple
Pupil Supervisor

Practising Areas: Admiralty, Arbitration, Chancery (General), Chancery (Land Law), Commercial Litigation, Commercial Property, Common Law (General), Company & Commercial, Construction, Copyright, Corporate Finance, Equity, Wills & Trusts, Family, Financial Services, Insolvency, Intellectual Property, International Trade, Landlord & Tenant, Pensions, Personal Injury, Professional Negligence, Sale & Carriage of Goods, Share Options, Shipping/Admiralty, Trademarks

PASCALL MR MATTHEW STEPHEN

Guildford Chambers
Stoke House, Leapale Lane, Guildford, Surrey GU1 4LY ☎01483 539131
✉clerks@guildfordchambers.co.uk
Alexander Chambers
13 Halstead Road, Wanstead, London E11 2AY ☎0845 652 0451 / 0854 652 0451
✉clerks@alexanderchambers.co.uk
Call Date: Jul 1984, Middle Temple
Pupil Supervisor

Practising Areas: Commercial Litigation, Construction, Education, Employment, Housing, Landlord & Tenant, Licensing, Medical Negligence, Personal Injury, Professional Negligence, Sale & Carriage of Goods

PASCOE MS SORAYA

1 Gray's Inn Square
Ground Floor, 1 Gray's Inn Square, London WC1R 5AA ☎020 7405 0001
Call Date: Jul 1999, Gray's Inn

Practising Areas: Administrative, Bankruptcy, Care Proceedings, Civil Liberties, Common Law (General), Crime, Education, Employment, Family, Human Rights, Local Government, Personal Injury, Regulatory Law, Sports

PATCHETT-JOYCE MR MICHAEL THURSTON

Outer Temple Chambers
The Outer Temple, 222 Strand, London WC2R 1BA ☎020 7353 6381
✉clerks@outertemple.com
Call Date: Jul 1981, Middle Temple
Pupil Supervisor

PATEL MISS GITA

Kenworthy's Chambers
Arlington House, Bloom Street, Salford, Manchester M3 6AJ ☎0161 832 4036
Call Date: Jul 1988, Inner Temple
Pupil Supervisor

Practising Areas: Administrative, Human Rights, Immigration

PATEL MR JAYANTILAL LALJI

Chambers of Mr Julius Seal
189 Randolph Avenue, Maida Vale, London W9 1DJ ☎020 7328 0158 ✉julius.seal@ntlworld.com
Call Date: Nov 1999, Inner Temple

C

PATEL MR YASIN AHMED

25 Bedford Row
London WC1R 4HD ☎ 020 7067 1500
✉ clerks@25bedfordrow.com
Call Date: Jul 2002, Gray's Inn

Practising Areas: Civil Liberties, Crime, Crime (Corporate/Fraud), Employment, Family, Human Rights, Sports

PATON MR EWAN WILLIAM

Guildhall Chambers
23 Broad Street, Bristol BS1 2HG
☎ 0117 930 9000 ✉ hoc@guildhallchambers.co.uk
Call Date: Oct 1996, Inner Temple
Pupil Supervisor

Practising Areas: Chancery (General), Chancery (Land Law), Conveyancing, Equity, Wills & Trusts, Land, Landlord & Tenant, Probate & Administration

PATON MR IAN FRANCIS

QEB Hollis Whiteman
1-2 Laurence Pountney Hill, London EC4R 0EU ☎ 020 7933 8855 ✉ barristers@qebhw.co.uk
Call Date: Apr 1975, Middle Temple
Pupil Supervisor, Recorder

Practising Areas: Courts Martial, Crime, Crime (Corporate/Fraud)

PATTERSON MR STEWART

Pump Court Chambers
31 Southgate Street, Winchester, Hampshire SO23 9EB ☎ 01962 868 161
✉ clerks@3pumpcourt.com
Pump Court Chambers
Upper Ground Floor, 3 Pump Court, Temple, London EC4Y 7AJ ☎ 020 7353 0711
✉ clerks@3pumpcourt.com
Pump Court Chambers
5 Temple Chambers, Temple Street, Swindon SN1 1SQ ☎ 01793 539899
✉ clerks@3pumpcourt.com
Call Date: Nov 1967, Middle Temple
Pupil Supervisor, Recorder

Practising Areas: Common Law (General), Company & Commercial, Construction, Courts Martial, Crime, Crime (Corporate/Fraud), Regulatory Law

PAWSON MISS TAMARA SHAHAN

KBW
The Engine House, No 1 Foundry Square, Leeds LS11 5DL ☎ 0113 297 1200
✉ clerks@kbwchambers.com
Call Date: Oct 2003, Lincoln's Inn

PAWSON-POUNDS MR DANIEL JAMES

6 King's Bench Walk
Ground Floor, 6 King's Bench Walk, Temple, London EC4Y 7DR ☎ 020 7583 0410
✉ clerks@6kbw.com
Call Date: Jul 2007, Middle Temple

Practising Areas: Courts Martial, Crime, Crime (Corporate/Fraud), Public Law, Regulatory Law

PAXTON MR CHRISTOPHER

18 Red Lion Court
London EC4A 3EB ☎ 020 7520 6000
✉ chambers@18rlc.co.uk
18 Red Lion Court (Annexe)
Thornwood House, 102 New London Road, Chelmsford, Essex CM2 0RG
☎ 01245 280880
Call Date: Nov 1991, Gray's Inn

Practising Areas: Regulatory Law

PAYNE MR DAVID JAMES

No 8 Chambers
8 Fountain Court, Steelhouse Lane, Birmingham B4 6DR ☎ 0121 236 5514
✉ clerks@no8chambers.co.uk
Call Date: Jul 2003, Gray's Inn

Practising Areas: Common Law (General), Family, Housing, Landlord & Tenant, Local Government

PAYNE MR GEOFFREY DONALD STEPHEN

25 Bedford Row
London WC1R 4HD ☎ 020 7067 1500
✉ clerks@25bedfordrow.com
Call Date: Oct 2000, Inner Temple

Practising Areas: Crime

PAYNE MR THOMAS HENRY

18 Red Lion Court
London EC4A 3EB ☎ 020 7520 6000
✉ chambers@18rlc.co.uk
Call Date: Oct 1998, Middle Temple
Pupil Supervisor

PAYTON MR CLIFFORD CONINGSBY

Alpha Court Chambers
Stuart House, Buckingham Lodge, 23 Kenilworth Road, Leamington Spa CV32 6JD
☎ 01926 886412 ✉ CP@Payton.uk.net
Call Date: Jul 1972, Inner Temple

Practising Areas: Banking, Chancery (General), Chancery (Land Law), Commercial Property,

Common Law (General), Company & Commercial, Ecclesiastical, Equity, Wills & Trusts, Insolvency, International Trade, Landlord & Tenant, Private International, Probate & Administration, Professional Negligence, Sale & Carriage of Goods

PEACOCK MISS LISA JAYNE

3 Dr Johnson's Buildings
Ground Floor, 3 Dr Johnson's Buildings, Temple, London EC4Y 7BA ☎ 020 7353 4854
✉ clerks@3djb.co.uk
Call Date: Oct 1992, Lincoln's Inn

Practising Areas: Care Proceedings, Family, Family Provision

PEARCE MR ROBERT EDGAR QC (2006)

Radcliffe Chambers
Ground Floor, 11 New Square, Lincoln's Inn, London WC2A 3QB ☎ 020 7831 0081
✉ clerks@radcliffechambers.com
Call Date: Jul 1977, Middle Temple

Practising Areas: Agriculture, Chancery (General), Chancery (Land Law), Charities, Commercial Litigation, Commercial Property, Common Land, Company & Commercial, Conveyancing, Equity, Wills & Trusts, Family Provision, Landlord & Tenant, Mental Health, Partnership, Private International, Probate & Administration, Professional Negligence

PEARMAN MR LEE CHARLES

4 Brick Court
4 Brick Court, Temple, London EC4Y 9AD
☎ 020 7832 3200 ✉ clerks@4bc.co.uk
Call Date: Jul 2003, Middle Temple

Practising Areas: Care Proceedings, Family, Family Provision

PEARMAN MR RICHARD SCOTT

Ely Place Chambers
30 Ely Place, London EC1N 6TD
☎ 020 7400 9600 ✉ admin@elyplace.com
Call Date: Oct 1999, Middle Temple
Pupil Supervisor

PEARS MR DERRICK ALLAN

Tanfield Chambers
2-5 Warwick Court, London WC1R 5DJ
☎ 020 7421 5300 ✉ clerks@tanfieldchambers.co.uk
Call Date: Jul 1975, Inner Temple
Pupil Supervisor

Practising Areas: Care Proceedings, Family, Family Provision

PEARSON MR CHRISTOPHER

Lamb Chambers
Lamb Building, Elm Court, Temple, London EC4Y 7AS ☎ 020 7797 8300
✉ info@lambchambers.co.uk
Call Date: Oct 1995, Inner Temple

Practising Areas: Commercial Litigation, Copyright, Defamation, Entertainment, Intellectual Property, Patents, Trademarks

PEAT MR CHARLIE ANDREW

1 Pump Court
Elm Court, Temple, London EC4Y 7AB
☎ 020 7842 7070 ✉ (name)@pumpcourt.co.uk
Call Date: Jul 2003, Middle Temple

Practising Areas: Family Provision

PEAT MR RICHARD COLIN

13 Old Square Chambers
Ground Floor, 14 Old Square, Lincoln's Inn, London WC2A 3UE ☎ 020 7831 4445
✉ clerks@13oldsquare.com
Call Date: Oct 1993, Gray's Inn

Practising Areas: Company & Commercial, Corporate Finance, Financial Services, Insolvency, Regulatory Law

PECKHAM MS JANE LOUISE

1 Crown Office Row
1 Crown Office Row, Temple, London EC4Y 7HH ☎ 020 7797 7500 ✉ mail@1cor.com
Crown Office Row Chambers
119 Church Street, Brighton, Sussex BN1 1UD ☎ 01273 625625 ✉ clerks@1cor.com
Call Date: Oct 1999, Inner Temple
Pupil Supervisor

Practising Areas: Common Law (General), Family Provision, Housing, Landlord & Tenant

PEDDIE MR IAN JAMES CROFTON QC (1992)

Garden Court Chambers
57-60 Lincoln's Inn Fields, London WC2A 3LJ
☎ 020 7993 7600 ✉ info@gclaw.co.uk
St Johns Buildings Liverpool
8th Floor India Buildings, Water Street, Liverpool L2 0XG ☎ 0151 243 6000
✉ clerk@stjohnsbuildings.co.uk
Westgate Chambers
64 High Street, Lewes, East Sussex BN7 1XG
☎ 01273 480510
✉ clerks@westgate-chambers.co.uk
Call Date: Jul 1971, Inner Temple

Practising Areas: Care Proceedings, Crime, Family, Mental Health

C

PEDRO MR TERRY ADEBISI

1 Pump Court
Elm Court, Temple, London EC4Y 7AB
☎ 020 7842 7070 ✉ (name)@pumpcourt.co.uk
Call Date: Oct 1996, Middle Temple

Practising Areas: Crime, Public Law

PEEL MR ROBERT ROGER QC (2010)

29 Bedford Row Chambers
London WC1R 4HE ☎ 020 7404 1044
✉ clerks@29br.co.uk
Call Date: Oct 1990, Middle Temple

Practising Areas: Family

PEET MR ANDREW GERAINT

Chambers of Mr Andrew Peet
2 Sycamore Close, Stretton Hall, Leicester LE2 4QU ☎ 07966 238437
✉ andrew@peet593.orangehome.co.uk
Call Date: Oct 1991, Inner Temple
Pupil Supervisor

Practising Areas: Crime, Crime (Corporate/Fraud), Regulatory Law

PEIRSON MR OLIVER JAMES

Pump Court Chambers
31 Southgate Street, Winchester, Hampshire SO23 9EB ☎ 01962 868 161
✉ clerks@3pumpcourt.com
Pump Court Chambers
Upper Ground Floor, 3 Pump Court, Temple, London EC4Y 7AJ ☎ 020 7353 0711
✉ clerks@3pumpcourt.com
Pump Court Chambers
5 Temple Chambers, Temple Street, Swindon SN1 1SQ ☎ 01793 539899
✉ clerks@3pumpcourt.com
Call Date: Oct 1993, Lincoln's Inn

C

PEMBERTON MISS YOLANDA ERICA

St Philips Chambers
55 Temple Row, Birmingham B2 5LS
☎ 0121 246 7000 ✉ clerks@st-philips.com
Call Date: Mar 2002, Lincoln's Inn

Practising Areas: Children's Law, Family

PENNI MISS SALLY SELORM-JULIET

Kenworthy's Chambers
Arlington House, Bloom Street, Salford, Manchester M3 6AJ ☎ 0161 832 4036
Call Date: Oct 2000, Gray's Inn
Pupil Supervisor

Practising Areas: Education, Employment, Licensing, Regulatory Law

PENNICOTT MR IAN QC (2003)

Keating Chambers
15 Essex Street, London WC2R 3AA
☎ 020 7544 2600 ✉ clerks@keatingchambers.com
Call Date: Jul 1982, Middle Temple

Practising Areas: Arbitration, Commercial Litigation, Construction, Energy, Environment, Information Technology, Professional Negligence

PENNINGTON-LEGH MR JONATHAN PIERS

Field Court Chambers
5 Field Court, Gray's Inn, London WC1R 5EF
☎ 020 7405 6114 ✉ clerks@fieldcourt.co.uk
Call Date: Oct 2000, Inner Temple

Practising Areas: Bankruptcy, Commercial Litigation, Housing, Insolvency, Landlord & Tenant, Personal Injury

PENNOCK MR IAN

Park Lane Plowden
19 Westgate, Leeds LS1 2RD
☎ 0113 228 5049 ✉ clerks@parklaneplowden.co.uk
Call Date: Jul 2001, Lincoln's Inn

Practising Areas: Chancery (General), Chancery (Land Law), Commercial Litigation, Commercial Property, Company & Commercial, Equity, Wills & Trusts, Landlord & Tenant, Partnership, Professional Negligence, Sale & Carriage of Goods

PENNY MISS ABIGAIL SARAH PRUDENCE

4 Breams Buildings
Chancery Lane, London EC4A 1HP
☎ 020 7092 1900 ✉ clerks@4bb.co.uk
Call Date: Oct 1999, Middle Temple

Practising Areas: Civil Liberties, Crime, Crime (Corporate/Fraud), Defamation, Health & Safety, Human Rights, Licensing, Mental Health, Regulatory Law

PENNY MR TIMOTHY CHARLES

11 Stone Buildings
11 Stone Buildings, Lincoln's Inn, London WC2A 3TG ☎ 020 7831 6381 ✉ clerks@11sb.com
Call Date: Jul 1988, Inner Temple
Pupil Supervisor

Practising Areas: Chancery (General), Commercial Litigation, Company & Commercial, Copyright, Entertainment, Information Technology,

Intellectual Property, Partnership, Professional Negligence, Sports, Telecommunications, Trademarks

PENTOL MR SIMON ALEX

25 Bedford Row
London WC1R 4HD ☎ 020 7067 1500
✉ clerks@25bedfordrow.com
Call Date: Nov 1982, Middle Temple
Pupil Supervisor

Practising Areas: Crime, Crime (Corporate/Fraud)

PERETZ MR GEORGE MICHAEL JOHN

Monckton Chambers
1 & 2 Raymond Buildings, Gray's Inn, London WC1R 5NR ☎ 020 7405 7211
✉ chambers@monckton.com
Call Date: Nov 1990, Middle Temple
Pupil Supervisor

Practising Areas: Administrative, Agriculture, Civil Liberties, Civil Litigation, Common Law (General), Competition, Consumer, Data Protection, Discrimination, EC & Competition Law, Human Rights, Public Law, Regulatory Law, Telecommunications

PERIAN MR STEVEN

3 Temple Gardens
Lower Ground Floor, 3 Temple Gardens, Temple, London EC4Y 9AU ☎ 020 7353 3102
✉ clerks@3tg.co.uk
Call Date: Nov 1987, Lincoln's Inn
Pupil Supervisor

Practising Areas: Civil Liberties, Copyright, Costs, Crime, Crime (Corporate/Fraud), Data Protection, Disciplinary Tribunals, Discrimination, Human Rights, Mental Health, Road Traffic And Highways

PERRINS MR GREGORY LLOYD

1 Paper Buildings
1st Floor, 1 Paper Buildings, Temple, London EC4Y 7EP ☎ 020 7353 3728
✉ clerks@onepaper.co.uk
Call Date: Oct 1997, Inner Temple
Pupil Supervisor

Practising Areas: Crime, Crime (Corporate/Fraud), Health & Safety, Regulatory Law

PERRY MR CHRISTOPHER EDWARD

Palmyra Chambers
Royal House, 46 Legh Street, Warrington WA1 1UJ ☎ 01925 444919
✉ clerk@palmyrachambers.com
Call Date: Nov 2002, Lincoln's Inn

Practising Areas: Aviation, Civil Litigation, Commercial Litigation, Common Law (General), Coroners Inquests, Costs, Inquests, Local Government, Personal Injury, Professional Negligence

PERRY MR DEREK ANEURIN

Albion Chambers
Broad Street, Bristol BS1 1DR
☎ 0117 927 2144 ✉ clerks@albionchambers.co.uk
Call Date: Nov 2006, Gray's Inn

PERRY MISS JACQUELINE ANNE QC (2006)

2 Temple Gardens
2 Temple Gardens, Temple, London EC4Y 9AY ☎ 020 7822 1200 ✉ clerks@2tg.co.uk
Call Date: Feb 1975, Gray's Inn

Practising Areas: Commercial Litigation, Common Law (General), Film, Cable & TV, Personal Injury

PERRY MR LEWIS KENNETH

Rowchester Chambers
4 Rowchester Court, Whittall Street, Birmingham B4 6DH ☎ 0121 233 2327
✉ clerks@rowchesterchambers.co.uk
Call Date: Mar 2002, Gray's Inn

Practising Areas: Crime, Crime (Corporate/Fraud), Immigration, Licensing

PERSAUD DR MARCIA CHITROUTIE

1 Gray's Inn Square
Ground Floor, 1 Gray's Inn Square, London WC1R 5AA ☎ 020 7405 0001
Call Date: Oct 2000, Middle Temple
Pupil Supervisor

Practising Areas: Care Proceedings, Crime, Discrimination, Employment, Family, Healthcare, Housing, Human Rights, Immigration, Landlord & Tenant, Licensing, Medical Negligence, Mental Health, Personal Injury

PERSSON MR MATTHEW STEPHEN

4 Paper Buildings
1st Floor, 4 Paper Buildings, Temple, London EC4Y 7EX ☎ 020 7427 5200 ✉ clerks@4pb.com
Call Date: Nov 2003, Inner Temple

PETERSEN MR THOMAS JAMES TD JP

Goldsmith Chambers
Ground Floor, Goldsmith Building, Temple, London EC4Y 7BL ☎020 7353 6802
✉clerks@goldsmithchambers.com
Call Date: Jul 2004, Lincoln's Inn

Practising Areas: Commercial Property, Common Law (General), Construction, Crime, Employment, Landlord & Tenant, Personal Injury, Town & Country Planning

PETERSON MISS GERALDINE SHELDA

Chambers of Mr Ami Feder
Ground Floor, Lamb Building, Temple, London EC4Y 7AS ☎020 7797 7788
✉clerks@lambbuilding.co.uk
Lamb Building
22 Ship Street, Brighton BN1 1AD
☎01273 820490 ✉admin@lambbuilding.co.uk
Chambers of Mr Ami Feder
Ground Floor, Lamb Building, Temple, London EC4Y 7AS ☎020 7797 7788
✉clerks@lambbuilding.co.uk
Call Date: Oct 1997, Middle Temple
Pupil Supervisor

Practising Areas: Administrative, Civil Liberties

PETTICAN MR KEVIN

11 Stone Buildings
11 Stone Buildings, Lincoln's Inn, London WC2A 3TG ☎020 7831 6381 ✉clerks@11sb.com
Call Date: Nov 1994, Inner Temple

Practising Areas: Arbitration, Banking, Commercial Litigation, Company & Commercial, Construction, Employment, Insurance/Reinsurance

PETTITT MR ROBERT

Northampton Chambers
10 Spencer Parade, Northampton NN1 5AQ
☎01604 636271
✉clerks@northampton-chambers.co.uk
Call Date: Jul 2002, Middle Temple

Practising Areas: Ancillary Relief, Care Proceedings, Equity, Wills & Trusts, Family, Family Provision, Personal Injury

PHELAN MS SARAH JANE DOROTHY

Chavasse Court Chambers
18 Queen Avenue, Liverpool L2 4TX
☎0151 229 2030
✉clerks@chavassechambers.co.uk
Call Date: Nov 1999, Inner Temple

PHILIPSON MISS AMY VICTORIA

Sovereign Chambers
46 Park Place, Leeds LS1 2RY
☎0113 245 1841
✉clerks@sovereignchambers.co.uk
Call Date: Nov 2006, Inner Temple

Practising Areas: Civil Litigation, Employment, Personal Injury

PHILLIPS MR ANDREW CHARLES

Crown Office Chambers
2 Crown Office Row, Temple, London EC4Y 7HJ ☎020 7797 8100
✉mail@crownofficechambers.com
Call Date: Jul 1978, Middle Temple
Pupil Supervisor

Practising Areas: Commercial Litigation, Common Law (General), Construction, Insurance, Insurance/Reinsurance, Personal Injury, Professional Negligence, Sale & Carriage of Goods

PHILLIPS MISS EMMA LOUISE

1 Pump Court
Elm Court, Temple, London EC4Y 7AB
☎020 7842 7070 ✉(name)@pumpcourt.co.uk
Call Date: Nov 2001, Middle Temple

Practising Areas: Common Law (General), Crime, Crime (Corporate/Fraud), Employment, Housing, Landlord & Tenant

PHILLIPS MR JEREMY GAVIN

Francis Taylor Building
Inner Temple, London EC4Y 7BY
☎020 7353 8415 ✉clerks@ftb.eu.com
Call Date: Mar 2004, Inner Temple

Practising Areas: Licensing, Town & Country Planning

PHILLIPS MR MATTHEW JAMES

Outer Temple Chambers
The Outer Temple, 222 Strand, London WC2R 1BA ☎020 7353 6381
✉clerks@outertemple.com
Call Date: Nov 1993, Lincoln's Inn

PHILLIPS MR SIMON BENJAMIN QC (2010)

Park Court Chambers
16 Park Place, Leeds LS1 2SJ
☎ 0113 243 3277
✉ clerks@parkcourtchambers.co.uk
Francis Taylor Building
Inner Temple, London EC4Y 7BY
☎ 020 7353 8415 ✉ clerks@ftb.eu.com
Call Date: Jul 1985, Inner Temple
Pupil Supervisor, Recorder

Practising Areas: Crime, Crime (Corporate/Fraud), Environment, Health & Safety, Licensing, Regulatory Law, Sports, Town & Country Planning

PHILLIPSON MISS NICOLA JANE

Zenith Chambers
10 Park Square, Leeds LS1 2LH
☎ 0113 245 5438 ✉ clerks@zenithchambers.co.uk
Call Date: Nov 1999, Lincoln's Inn

PHILPOTT MR ANTHONY LUKE

12 Old Square Chambers
1st Floor, 12 Old Square, Lincoln's Inn, London WC2A 3TX ☎ 020 7404 0875
✉ clerks@12oldsquare.com
Call Date: Nov 1987, Gray's Inn

Practising Areas: Banking, Commercial Property, Construction, Discrimination, Employment, Landlord & Tenant, Personal Injury

PHYSSAS MISS CLAIRE

Renaissance Chambers
5th Floor, Gray's Inn Chambers, Gray's Inn, London WC1R 5JA ☎ 020 7404 1111
✉ clerks@renaissancechambers.co.uk
Call Date: Oct 2004, Lincoln's Inn

Practising Areas: Human Rights, Immigration

PICARDA MR HUBERT ALISTAIR PAUL QC (1992)

Chambers of Mr Hubert Picarda QC
Third Floor North, 9 Old Square, Lincoln's Inn, London WC2A 3SR ☎ 020 7242 3566
✉ hpicarda@aol.com
Call Date: Feb 1962, Inner Temple

Practising Areas: Chancery (Land Law), Charities, Commercial Litigation, Company & Commercial, Financial Services

PICKERING MR SIMON TOBY

Wilberforce Chambers
7 Bishop Lane, Hull HU1 1PA
☎ 01482 323264
Call Date: Oct 1996, Inner Temple

Practising Areas: Care Proceedings, Chancery (General), Common Law (General), Employment, Family, Health & Safety, Housing, Personal Injury

PICKUP MR JAMES KENNETH QC (2000)

Lincoln House Chambers
Tower 12, The Avenue North, Spinningfields, 18-22 Bridge Street, Manchester M3 3BZ
☎ 0161 832 5701
✉ info@lincolnhousechambers.com
2 Hare Court
Lower Ground, Ground, 1st & 2nd Floor, 2 Hare Court, Temple, London EC4Y 7BH
☎ 020 7353 3982 ✉ clerks@2harecourt.com
Call Date: Jul 1976, Gray's Inn
Recorder

Practising Areas: Civil Liberties, Crime, Crime (Corporate/Fraud), Licensing, Medical Negligence, Personal Injury, Professional Negligence, Sports

PIERPOINT MISS KATHERINE ANNE

Lincoln House Chambers
Tower 12, The Avenue North, Spinningfields, 18-22 Bridge Street, Manchester M3 3BZ
☎ 0161 832 5701
✉ info@lincolnhousechambers.com
Call Date: Oct 1998, Lincoln's Inn
Pupil Supervisor

Practising Areas: Crime, Crime (Corporate/Fraud), Regulatory Law

PIGOT MISS DIANA MARGUERITE

2 Pump Court
1st Floor, 2 Pump Court, Temple, London EC4Y 7AH ☎ 020 7353 5597
✉ clerks@2pumpcourt.co.uk
Call Date: Nov 1978, Inner Temple

Practising Areas: Crime

PIGOTT MRS FRANCES WINIFRED

Atkin Chambers
1 Atkin Building, Gray's Inn, London WC1R 5AT ☎ 020 7404 0102
✉ clerks@atkinchambers.com
St Philips Chambers
55 Temple Row, Birmingham B2 5LS
☎ 0121 246 7000 ✉ clerks@st-philips.com
Call Date: Oct 1994, Gray's Inn

Practising Areas: Construction

PIGRAM MR CHRISTOPHER STUART

East Anglian Chambers
53 North Hill, Colchester, Essex CO1 1QA
☎01473 214481 ✉colchester@ealaw.co.uk
East Anglian Chambers
140 New London Road, Chelmsford, Essex CM2 0AW ☎01473 214481
✉chelmsford@ealaw.co.uk
East Anglian Chambers
Gresham House, 5 Museum Street, Ipswich, Suffolk IP1 1HQ ☎01473 214481
✉ipswich@ealaw.co.uk
Call Date: Jul 2000, Gray's Inn
Pupil Supervisor

Practising Areas: Chancery (Land Law), Common Law (General), Employment, Personal Injury

PIKE MR JEREMY JOHN

Francis Taylor Building
Inner Temple, London EC4Y 7BY
☎020 7353 8415 ✉clerks@ftb.eu.com
Call Date: Jul 2001, Middle Temple

PINKUS MISS MOLLY CARLA

Farringdon Chambers
180 Bermondsey Street, London SE1 3TQ
☎020 7089 5700
Call Date: Oct 1997, Middle Temple

Practising Areas: Crime

PINTO MISS AMANDA EVE QC (2006)

Five Paper Buildings
1st Floor, Five Paper Buildings, Temple, London EC4Y 7HB ☎020 7583 6117
✉clerks@5pb.co.uk
Call Date: Nov 1983, Middle Temple
Recorder

Practising Areas: Crime (Corporate/Fraud), Financial Services, Regulatory Law

PIPE MR ADAM

No 8 Chambers
8 Fountain Court, Steelhouse Lane, Birmingham B4 6DR ☎0121 236 5514
✉clerks@no8chambers.co.uk
Call Date: Oct 1999, Middle Temple

Practising Areas: Civil Liberties, Human Rights, Immigration

PITHERS MR CLIVE ROBERT

Fenners Chambers
3 Madingley Road, Cambridge CB3 0EE
☎01223 368761 ✉clerks@fennerschambers.com
Call Date: Feb 1989, Gray's Inn

Practising Areas: Chancery (General), Chancery (Land Law), Common Law (General), Equity, Wills & Trusts, Family, Family Provision, Housing, Landlord & Tenant, Probate & Administration

PITT-LEWIS MRS JANET REBECCA

Cornwall Street Chambers
85-87 Cornwall Street, Birmingham B3 3BY
☎0121 233 7500 ✉clerks@cornwallstreet.co.uk
Cornwall Street Chambers
Shrewsbury Annex, Rural Enterprise Centre, Stafford Drive, Battlefield Enterprise Park, Shrewsbury SY1 3FE
☎01743 363 611 / 0121 233 7500
Call Date: Jul 1976, Middle Temple
Pupil Supervisor

Practising Areas: Crime, Family

PITTS MISS CHARLOTTE FRANCES

Albion Chambers
Broad Street, Bristol BS1 1DR
☎0117 927 2144 ✉clerks@albionchambers.co.uk
Call Date: Oct 1999, Inner Temple

Practising Areas: Family

PITTS MISS EMILY ODETTE

Colleton Chambers
Colleton Crescent, Exeter, Devon EX2 4DG
☎01392 274898 ✉clerks@colletonchambers.co.uk
Call Date: Oct 2000, Inner Temple

Practising Areas: Crime

PLANT MR JAMES RICHARD

Farrar's Building
Farrar's Building, Temple, London EC4Y 7BD
☎020 7583 9241
✉Chambers@farrarsbuilding.co.uk
Call Date: Nov 2004, Middle Temple

Practising Areas: Commercial Litigation, Common Law (General), Employment, Insolvency, Insurance, Landlord & Tenant, Personal Injury, Sale & Carriage of Goods

PLASCHKES MS SARAH GEORGINA QC (2011)

QEB Hollis Whiteman
1-2 Laurence Pountney Hill, London EC4R 0EU ☎ 020 7933 8855 ✉ barristers@qebhw.co.uk
Call Date: Jul 1988, Inner Temple
Pupil Supervisor, Recorder

PLATFORD MR GRAHAM ROY

Five Paper
Ground Floor, 5 Paper Buildings, Temple, London EC4Y 7HB ☎ 020 7815 3200
Call Date: Nov 1970, Gray's Inn
Pupil Supervisor

Practising Areas: Arbitration, Commercial Litigation, Company & Commercial, Partnership, Professional Negligence, Sale & Carriage of Goods

PLATT MISS HEATHER LOUISE

Pump Court Chambers
Upper Ground Floor, 3 Pump Court, Temple, London EC4Y 7AJ ☎ 020 7353 0711
✉ clerks@3pumpcourt.com
Pump Court Chambers
5 Temple Chambers, Temple Street, Swindon SN1 1SQ ☎ 01793 539899
✉ clerks@3pumpcourt.com
Riverview Chambers
Hamilton House, 1 Temple Avenue, London EC4Y 0HA ☎ 0844 225 3999
✉ chrisbaylis@riverviewchambers.com
Call Date: Oct 2002, Lincoln's Inn
Pupil Supervisor

Practising Areas: Chancery (Land Law), Discrimination, Employment, Landlord & Tenant, Personal Injury

PLATTS-MILLS MR MARK FORTESCUE QC (1995)

8 New Square
8 New Square, Lincoln's Inn, London WC2A 3QP ☎ 020 7405 4321 ✉ clerks@8newsquare.co.uk
Call Date: Jul 1974, Inner Temple

Practising Areas: Copyright, Entertainment, Film, Cable & TV, Information Technology, Intellectual Property, Patents, Sports, Trademarks

PLIMMER MISS MELANIE ANN

Kings Chambers
36 Young Street, Manchester M3 3FT
☎ 0845 034 3444 ✉ clerks@kingschambers.com
Kings Chambers
5 Park Square East, Leeds LS1 2NE
☎ 0845 034 3444 ✉ clerks@kingschambers.com
Kings Chambers
Embassy House, 60 Church Street, Birmingham B3 2DJ ☎ 0845 034 3444
✉ clerks@kingschambers.com
Call Date: Mar 1996, Gray's Inn

Practising Areas: Administrative, Civil Liberties, Disciplinary Tribunals, Employment, Healthcare, Human Rights, Immigration, Local Government, Public International, Sports

PLOWRIGHT MR JOSEPH EDWARD

1 Gray's Inn Square
Ground Floor, 1 Gray's Inn Square, London WC1R 5AA ☎ 020 7405 0001
Call Date: Oct 1999, Inner Temple

Practising Areas: Crime, Human Rights, Immigration

POINTING MR JOHN ERIC

Chambers of Mr John Pointing
46 Arlington Road, Ealing, London W13 8PE
☎ 020 8997 2285 ✉ johnpointing@hotmail.com
Call Date: Oct 1992, Middle Temple

Practising Areas: Consumer, Environment, Local Government, Regulatory Law

POJUR MR DAVID ELLIOT

St Johns Buildings
24a - 28 St John Street, Manchester M3 4DJ
☎ 0161 214 1500 ✉ clerk@stjohnsbuildings.co.uk
16 Winckley Square
Preston PR1 3JJ ☎ 01772 256100
St Johns Buildings Liverpool
8th Floor India Buildings, Water Street, Liverpool L2 0XG ☎ 0151 243 6000
✉ clerk@stjohnsbuildings.co.uk
Call Date: Nov 2001, Middle Temple

POKU MISS MARY LAUREEN

9-12 Bell Yard
London WC2A 2JR ☎ 020 7400 1800
✉ clerks@9-12bellyard.com
Call Date: Nov 1993, Lincoln's Inn

POLLI MR TIMOTHY JAMES

Tanfield Chambers
2-5 Warwick Court, London WC1R 5DJ
☎ 020 7421 5300 ✉ clerks@tanfieldchambers.co.uk
Call Date: Jul 1997, Middle Temple

Practising Areas: Banking, Chancery (General), Chancery (Land Law), Civil Litigation, Commercial Litigation, Commercial Property, Common Law (General), Conveyancing, Equity, Wills & Trusts, Land, Landlord & Tenant, Partnership, Professional Negligence

POLNAY MR JONATHAN SAMUEL

5 King's Bench Walk
5 King's Bench Walk, Temple, London EC4Y 7DN ☎ 020 7353 5638 ✉ clerks@5kbw.co.uk
Call Date: Nov 2000, Middle Temple

Practising Areas: Crime, Crime (Corporate/Fraud)

PONS MR GARY STEPHEN

Five St Andrew's Hill
5 St Andrew's Hill, London EC4V 5BZ
☎ 020 7332 5400 ✉ Clerks@5sah.co.uk
Call Date: Oct 1995, Gray's Inn

POOTS MISS LAURA JILL

Pump Court Tax Chambers
16 Bedford Row, London WC1R 4EF
☎ 020 7414 8080 ✉ clerks@pumptax.com
Call Date: Oct 2007, Middle Temple

Practising Areas: Equity, Wills & Trusts, Tax (Capital & Income), Tax (Corporate)

POPE MISS ANNA

Linenhall Chambers
1 Stanley Place, Chester CH1 2LU
☎ 01244 348282
✉ clerks@linenhallchambers.co.uk
Call Date: Oct 2007, Middle Temple

Practising Areas: Crime, Family, Immigration

POPLAWSKI MR ROMAN

33 Bedford Row
London WC1R 4JH ☎ 020 7242 6476
✉ clerks@33bedfordrow.co.uk
Call Date: Nov 1989, Lincoln's Inn

POPLE MISS ALISON RUTH

2 Bedford Row
London WC1R 4BU ☎ 020 7440 8888
✉ clerks@2bedfordrow.co.uk
Call Date: Nov 1993, Middle Temple

Practising Areas: Crime, Crime (Corporate/Fraud), Regulatory Law

POPLEY MISS HEATHER LOUISE

New Street Chambers
2 New Street, Leicester LE1 5NA
☎ 0116 262 5906 ✉ clerks@2newstreet.co.uk
Call Date: Nov 2003, Gray's Inn

Practising Areas: Family

PORTER MR JAMIE ROBERT

King's Bench Chambers
Wellington House, 175 Holdenhurst Road, Bournemouth, Dorset BH8 8DQ
☎ 01202 250025
Call Date: Oct 1997, Inner Temple

Practising Areas: Crime, Employment

PORTER MR MARTIN HUGH QC (2006)

2 Temple Gardens
2 Temple Gardens, Temple, London EC4Y 9AY ☎ 020 7822 1200 ✉ clerks@2tg.co.uk
Call Date: Jul 1986, Inner Temple

PORTER-PHILLIPS MRS CLARE MARY ELIZABETH

Call Date: Mar 2001, Lincoln's Inn

POSNER MISS GABRIELLE JAN

Renaissance Chambers
5th Floor, Gray's Inn Chambers, Gray's Inn, London WC1R 5JA ☎ 020 7404 1111
✉ clerks@renaissancechambers.co.uk
Call Date: Jul 1984, Inner Temple
Pupil Supervisor

Practising Areas: Children's Law, Family

POSTA MR ADRIAN MARK

Albion Chambers
Broad Street, Bristol BS1 1DR
☎ 0117 927 2144 ✉ clerks@albionchambers.co.uk
Call Date: Oct 1996, Middle Temple

Practising Areas: Family, Personal Injury

POTE MR ANDREW THOMAS

13 King's Bench Walk
13 King's Bench Walk, Temple, London EC4Y 7EN ☎ 020 7353 7204 ✉ clerks@13kbw.co.uk
13 KBW
32 Beaumont Street, Oxford OX1 2NP
☎ 01865 311066 ✉ clerks@13kbw.co.uk
Call Date: Nov 1983, Gray's Inn
Pupil Supervisor

POTTER MISS ALISON LISA

4 Pump Court
4 Pump Court, Temple, London EC4Y 7AN
☎ 020 7842 5555 ✉ chambers@4pumpcourt.com
Call Date: Feb 1987, Middle Temple

Practising Areas: Common Law (General), Environment, Professional Negligence, Town & Country Planning

POTTER REV HARRY DRUMMOND

25 Bedford Row
London WC1R 4HD ☎ 020 7067 1500
✉ clerks@25bedfordrow.com
Call Date: Oct 1993, Gray's Inn

Practising Areas: Courts Martial, Crime

POTTER MISS LOUISE

Harcourt Chambers
1st Floor, 2 Harcourt Buildings, Temple, London EC4Y 9DB ☎ 0844 561 7135
Harcourt Chambers
Churchill House, 3 St Aldate's Courtyard, St Aldate's, Oxford OX1 1BN ☎ 0844 561 7135
Call Date: Nov 1993, Inner Temple
Pupil Supervisor

Practising Areas: Family

POTTINGER MR GAVIN JAMES

4 Breams Buildings
Chancery Lane, London EC4A 1HP
☎ 020 7092 1900 ✉ clerks@4bb.co.uk
Call Date: Oct 1991, Inner Temple

POULET MRS REBECCA MARIA QC (1995)

QEB Hollis Whiteman
1-2 Laurence Pountney Hill, London EC4R 0EU ☎ 020 7933 8855 ✉ barristers@qebhw.co.uk
Call Date: Nov 1975, Lincoln's Inn
Recorder

POWELL MR JONATHAN DAVID

Atlas Chambers
3 Field Court, Gray's Inn, London WC1R 5EP
☎ 020 7269 7980 ✉ clerks@atlaschambers.com
Call Date: Nov 1984, Inner Temple

Practising Areas: Environment, Town & Country Planning

POWELL MR OLIVER JONATHAN

3 PB Barristers
3 Paper Buildings, Temple, London EC4Y 7EU
☎ 020 7583 8055
Call Date: Jul 2006, Gray's Inn

Practising Areas: Crime, Crime (Corporate/Fraud), Environment, Insolvency, Regulatory Law

POWELL MR ROBIN EDWARD

Tanfield Chambers
2-5 Warwick Court, London WC1R 5DJ
☎ 020 7421 5300 ✉ clerks@tanfieldchambers.co.uk
Call Date: Nov 1993, Inner Temple
Pupil Supervisor

Practising Areas: Family

POWELL MR WILLIAM RHYS

Regency Chambers
45 Priestgate, Peterborough PE1 1LB
☎ 01733 315215 ✉ clerks@regencychambers.law.co.uk
Regency Chambers
Sheraton House, Castle Park, Cambridge CB3 0AX ☎ 01223 301517
Call Date: Nov 1971, Lincoln's Inn

Practising Areas: Agriculture, Common Law (General), Copyright, Education, Intellectual Property, Landlord & Tenant, Local Government, Patents, Personal Injury, Town & Country Planning

POWER MS ALEXIA CLARE

Furnival Chambers
32 Furnival Street, London EC4A 1JQ
☎ 020 7405 3232
Call Date: Oct 1992, Gray's Inn
Pupil Supervisor

Practising Areas: Crime, Crime (Corporate/Fraud)

POWER MR ARCHANGELO CARLO

2 Bedford Row
London WC1R 4BU ☎ 020 7440 8888
✉ clerks@2bedfordrow.co.uk
Call Date: Nov 2001, Middle Temple

Practising Areas: Courts Martial, Crime, Crime (Corporate/Fraud), Licensing

POWER MR LAWRENCE IMAM

4 KBW
Ground Floor, 4 King's Bench Walk, Temple, London EC4Y 7DL ☎ 020 7822 8822
✉ law@4kbw.net
Call Date: Nov 1995, Middle Temple
Pupil Supervisor

Practising Areas: Chancery (General), Commercial Litigation, Common Law (General), Crime (Corporate/Fraud), Information Technology, Insolvency

POWER MR LEWIS NIALL QC (2011)

Chambers of Mr Ami Feder
Ground Floor, Lamb Building, Temple, London EC4Y 7AS ☎ 020 7797 7788
✉ clerks@lambbuilding.co.uk
Lamb Building
22 Ship Street, Brighton BN1 1AD
☎ 01273 820490 ✉ admin@lambbuilding.co.uk
Chambers of Mr Ami Feder
Ground Floor, Lamb Building, Temple, London EC4Y 7AS ☎ 020 7797 7788
✉ clerks@lambbuilding.co.uk
Call Date: Nov 1990, Gray's Inn

POWER MR RICHARD MICHAEL ARTHUR

Lamb Chambers
Lamb Building, Elm Court, Temple, London EC4Y 7AS ☎ 020 7797 8300
✉ info@lambchambers.co.uk
Call Date: Nov 1983, Middle Temple

Practising Areas: Common Law (General), Medical Negligence, Personal Injury, Professional Negligence

POWIS MISS SAMANTHA INEZ

Citadel Chambers
The Citadel, 190 Corporation Street, Birmingham B4 6QD ☎ 0121 233 8500
✉ clerks@citadelchambers.com
Call Date: Nov 1985, Lincoln's Inn

Practising Areas: Crime, Immigration, Road Traffic And Highways

POWNALL MR STEPHEN ORLANDO FLETCHER QC (2002)

2 Hare Court
Lower Ground, Ground, 1st & 2nd Floor, 2 Hare Court, Temple, London EC4Y 7BH
☎ 020 7353 3982 ✉ clerks@2harecourt.com
Call Date: Jul 1975, Inner Temple
Recorder

Practising Areas: Crime, Regulatory Law

PRESLAND MS SAMANTHA LOUISE

Outer Temple Chambers
The Outer Temple, 222 Strand, London WC2R 1BA ☎ 020 7353 6381
✉ clerks@outertemple.com
Call Date: Mar 2001, Middle Temple

PRESTON MR DAVID HENRY

Ely Place Chambers
30 Ely Place, London EC1N 6TD
☎ 020 7400 9600 ✉ admin@elyplace.com
Call Date: Nov 1993, Lincoln's Inn
Pupil Supervisor

Practising Areas: Employment

PRESTON MISS KIM DEBORAH

4 King's Bench Walk
2nd Floor, 4 King's Bench Walk, Temple, London EC4Y 7DL ☎ 020 7822 7000
✉ clerks@4kbw.co.uk
Call Date: Nov 1991, Inner Temple
Pupil Supervisor

Practising Areas: Care Proceedings, Crime, Family

PRESTON MR NICHOLAS JOHN HOLMAN

Clerksroom (Taunton)
Equity House, Administration Centre, Blackbrook Park Avenue, Taunton, Somerset TA1 2PX ☎ 0845 083 3000
✉ mail@clerksroom.com
Call Date: Jul 1986, Gray's Inn

Practising Areas: Bankruptcy, Commercial Litigation, Common Law (General), Company & Commercial, Insolvency

PRESTON MRS NICOLA

No5 Chambers
Fountain Court, Steelhouse Lane, Birmingham B4 6DR ☎0845 210 5555 ✉info@no5.com
No5 Chambers
Greenwood House, 4-7 Salisbury Court, London EC4Y 8AA ☎0845 210 5555
No5 Chambers
38 Queen Square, Bristol BS1 4QS
☎0845 210 5555
Call Date: Nov 1992, Lincoln's Inn

Practising Areas: Equity, Wills & Trusts

PRETSELL MR JAMES DAVIDSON

Farrar's Building
Farrar's Building, Temple, London EC4Y 7BD
☎020 7583 9241
✉Chambers@farrarsbuilding.co.uk
Call Date: Nov 1998, Gray's Inn
Pupil Supervisor

Practising Areas: Common Law (General), Discrimination, Employment, Professional Negligence, Regulatory Law

PRICE MR ALBERT JOHN QC (2009)

23 Essex Street
London WC2R 3AA ☎020 7413 0353
✉clerks@23es.com
Call Date: Jul 1982, Inner Temple
Recorder

Practising Areas: Crime, Crime (Corporate/Fraud)

PRICE MR ANDREW ROBERT

Dyers Chambers
35 Bedford Row, London WC1R 4JH
☎020 7404 1881 ✉admin@dyerschambers.com
Call Date: Oct 2003, Middle Temple

Practising Areas: Crime, Crime (Corporate/Fraud), Local Government, Regulatory Law, Town & Country Planning

PRICE MR CHARLES JOHN

No5 Chambers
Fountain Court, Steelhouse Lane, Birmingham B4 6DR ☎0845 210 5555 ✉info@no5.com
No5 Chambers
Greenwood House, 4-7 Salisbury Court, London EC4Y 8AA ☎0845 210 5555
No5 Chambers
38 Queen Square, Bristol BS1 4QS
☎0845 210 5555
Call Date: Nov 1999, Middle Temple

Practising Areas: Employment, Immigration

PRICE MRS HUMA SABIH

St Andrews Chambers
St Andrews House, 52 Manor Drive, London N20 0DX ☎020 8368 3686
✉standrewschambers@live.co.uk
Call Date: Nov 1991, Inner Temple

Practising Areas: Family, Immigration

PRICE MRS LOUISE THERESE

Albion Chambers
Broad Street, Bristol BS1 1DR
☎0117 927 2144 ✉clerks@albionchambers.co.uk
Call Date: Nov 1972, Middle Temple

PRICE ROWLANDS MR GWYNN

St Ive's Chambers
Whittall Street, Birmingham B4 6DH
☎0121 236 0863 ✉clerks@stiveschambers.co.uk
Call Date: May 1985, Inner Temple
Pupil Supervisor

PRINN MISS HELEN ELIZABETH

Octagon House
19 Colegate, Norwich NR3 1AT
☎01603 623186 ✉clerks@octagonhouse.co.uk
Call Date: Oct 1993, Middle Temple

PRIOR MR CHARLES ROBERT CHRISTOPHER

Atlantic Chambers
4-6 Cook Street, Liverpool L2 9QU
☎0151 236 4421 ✉info@atlanticchambers.co.uk
Call Date: Oct 1995, Lincoln's Inn
Pupil Supervisor

PRIOR MRS MARY

36 Bedford Row
London WC1R 4JH ☎020 7421 8000
✉chambers@36bedfordrow.co.uk
Call Date: Oct 1990, Gray's Inn
Pupil Supervisor

Practising Areas: Crime, Crime (Corporate/Fraud), Human Rights, Professional Negligence, Regulatory Law, Sports

PRIOR MR PAUL STEPHEN

36 Bedford Row
London WC1R 4JH ☎020 7421 8000
✉chambers@36bedfordrow.co.uk
Call Date: Nov 2003, Lincoln's Inn

Practising Areas: Arbitration, Crime, Crime (Corporate/Fraud), Health & Safety, Human Rights, Professional Negligence, Regulatory Law, Sports

PRITCHARD MISS CECILIA MARY

Oriel Chambers
18 Ribblesdale Place, Preston PR1 3NA
☎01772 254 764 ✉clerks@oriel-chambers.co.uk
Oriel Chambers
14 Water Street, Liverpool, Merseyside L2 8TD ☎0151 236 7191
✉clerks@orielchambers.co.uk
Call Date: Jul 1998, Middle Temple

PRITCHARD MRS TERESA JULIA

5 Pump Court
Ground Floor, 5 Pump Court, Temple, London EC4Y 7AP ☎020 7353 2532
✉clerks@5pumpcourt.com
Call Date: Oct 1994, Lincoln's Inn
Pupil Supervisor

Practising Areas: Care Proceedings, Children's Law

PROCTER MR ALFRED GEORGE HAYDN

1 Garden Court Family Law Chambers
Ground Floor, One Garden Court, Temple, London EC4Y 9BJ ☎020 7797 7900
✉clerks@1gc.com
Call Date: Jul 2005, Middle Temple

Practising Areas: Ancillary Relief, Children's Law, Family, Family Provision

PROKOFIEV MR SERGEY

Lincoln House Chambers
Tower 12, The Avenue North, Spinningfields, 18-22 Bridge Street, Manchester M3 3BZ
☎0161 832 5701
✉info@lincolnhousechambers.com
Call Date: Jul 2004, Lincoln's Inn

Practising Areas: Common Law (General), Crime, Crime (Corporate/Fraud), Employment, Environment, Intellectual Property

PRYKE MR STUART

Fiduciary Legal
5 North Court, Clevedon Road, London TW1 2HS ☎07814 495366 ✉stuart.pryke@fiduciarylegal.com
Call Date: Oct 1994, Lincoln's Inn

Practising Areas: Chancery (General), Equity, Wills & Trusts, Private International, Tax (Capital & Income), Unit Trusts

PRZYBYLSKA MISS SARAH ELLEN

2 Hare Court
Lower Ground, Ground, 1st & 2nd Floor, 2 Hare Court, Temple, London EC4Y 7BH
☎020 7353 3982 ✉clerks@2harecourt.com
Call Date: Oct 2006, Middle Temple

PUAR MR MIKHAEL

30 Park Place
Cardiff CF10 3BS ☎029 2039 8421
✉clerks@30parkplace.law.co.uk
Call Date: Jul 2006, Gray's Inn

Practising Areas: Bankruptcy, Common Law (General), Crime, Employment, Health & Safety, Housing, Immigration, Landlord & Tenant, Regulatory Law

PUGH MR JOHN BISHOP

John Pugh's Chambers
707 - 709, The Corn Exchange, Fenwick Street, Liverpool L2 7RB ☎0151 236 5415
✉john@johnpughschambers.co.uk
Call Date: Jul 1972, Lincoln's Inn

Practising Areas: Arbitration, Asset Finance, Banking, Civil Litigation, Commercial Litigation, Common Law (General), Financial Services, Regulatory Law, Sale & Carriage of Goods

PULLEN MR TIMOTHY JOHN

King's Bench and Godolphin (KBG)Chambers
115 North Hill, Plymouth, Devon PL4 8JY
☎01752 221551 ✉clerks@kbgchambers.co.uk
Doughty Street Chambers
53-54 Doughty Street, London WC1N 2LS
☎020 7404 1313 ✉enquiries@doughtystreet.co.uk
Call Date: Nov 1993, Middle Temple

PURCHAS MR JAMES ALEXANDER FRANCIS

4 Pump Court
4 Pump Court, Temple, London EC4Y 7AN
☎ 020 7842 5555 ✉ chambers@4pumpcourt.com
Call Date: Oct 1997, Inner Temple
Pupil Supervisor

Practising Areas: Commercial Litigation, Insurance, Professional Negligence

PURCHAS MR ROBIN MICHAEL QC (1987)

Francis Taylor Building
Inner Temple, London EC4Y 7BY
☎ 020 7353 8415 ✉ clerks@ftb.eu.com
Call Date: Nov 1968, Inner Temple
Recorder

Practising Areas: Administrative, Environment, Public Law, Town & Country Planning

PURNELL MR PAUL OLIVER QC (1982)

Farringdon Chambers
180 Bermondsey Street, London SE1 3TQ
☎ 020 7089 5700
Call Date: Nov 1962, Inner Temple

Practising Areas: Civil Liberties, Courts Martial, Crime, Crime (Corporate/Fraud), Regulatory Law

PURVES MR GAVIN BOWMAN

Swan House
P.O.Box 8749, London W13 8ZX
☎ 020 8998 3035 ✉ swanchambers@yahoo.co.uk
Call Date: Jul 1979, Gray's Inn

Practising Areas: Banking, Chancery (General), Common Law (General), Copyright, EC & Competition Law, Entertainment, Environment, Franchising, Information Technology, Intellectual Property, Partnership, Probate & Administration, Telecommunications, Town & Country Planning, Trademarks

PUTNAM MR THOMAS DREW

Putnam
14 Keyes Road, London NW2 3XA
☎ 020 8438 2950 ✉ tom@lending_law.co.uk
Call Date: Jul 1976, Gray's Inn
Pupil Supervisor

PYE MISS MARGARET JAYNE

Zenith Chambers
10 Park Square, Leeds LS1 2LH
☎ 0113 245 5438 ✉ clerks@zenithchambers.co.uk
Call Date: May 1995, Middle Temple
Pupil Supervisor, Recorder

Practising Areas: Care Proceedings, Family, Family Provision

PYNE MR RUSSELL DAVID

2 King's Bench Walk
2 King's Bench Walk, Temple, London EC4Y 7DE ☎ 020 7353 1746 ✉ clerks@2kbw.com
Call Date: Oct 1991, Inner Temple
Pupil Supervisor

Practising Areas: Courts Martial, Crime, Road Traffic And Highways

QUICKFALL MR ROGER MARK

Park Lane Plowden
19 Westgate, Leeds LS1 2RD
☎ 0113 228 5049 ✉ clerks@parklaneplowden.co.uk
Call Date: Oct 2003, Middle Temple

Practising Areas: Employment, Personal Injury

QUIGLEY MS LOUISE

St Johns Buildings
24a - 28 St John Street, Manchester M3 4DJ
☎ 0161 214 1500 ✉ clerk@stjohnsbuildings.co.uk
16 Winckley Square
Preston PR1 3JJ ☎ 01772 256100
St Johns Buildings Liverpool
8th Floor India Buildings, Water Street, Liverpool L2 0XG ☎ 0151 243 6000
✉ clerk@stjohnsbuildings.co.uk
Call Date: Nov 2003, Inner Temple

Practising Areas: Employment

QUINEY MR CHARLES BENEDICTUS ALEXANDER

Crown Office Chambers
2 Crown Office Row, Temple, London EC4Y 7HJ ☎ 020 7797 8100
✉ mail@crownofficechambers.com
Call Date: Mar 1998, Gray's Inn
Pupil Supervisor

Practising Areas: Arbitration, Chancery (General), Commercial Litigation, Common Law (General), Company & Commercial, Construction, Insurance, Insurance/Reinsurance, Private International, Professional Negligence, Sale & Carriage of Goods

QUINLAN MR CHRISTOPHER JOHN QC (2011)

Guildhall Chambers
23 Broad Street, Bristol BS1 2HG
☎0117 930 9000 ✉hoc@guildhallchambers.co.uk
Call Date: Nov 1992, Inner Temple
Pupil Supervisor

Practising Areas: Crime, Sports

QUINN MR TOMAS ANTHONY

4 King's Bench Walk
2nd Floor, 4 King's Bench Walk, Temple, London EC4Y 7DL ☎020 7822 7000
✉clerks@4kbw.co.uk
Call Date: Jul 2006, Lincoln's Inn

Practising Areas: Courts Martial, Crime, Crime (Corporate/Fraud), Regulatory Law

QUINN MISS VICTORIA KATHLEEN

Thomas More Chambers
7 Lincoln's Inn Fields, London WC2A 3BP
☎020 7404 7000 ✉clerks@thomasmore.co.uk
Call Date: Oct 1995, Lincoln's Inn
Pupil Supervisor

Practising Areas: Family, Human Rights, Immigration, Personal Injury

QUINNEY MISS NICOLA TAMSIN

Call Date: Jul 2001, Gray's Inn

QUIRKE MR GERARD MARTIN

Citadel Chambers
The Citadel, 190 Corporation Street, Birmingham B4 6QD ☎0121 233 8500
✉clerks@citadelchambers.com
Call Date: Nov 1988, Middle Temple

Practising Areas: Arbitration, Bankruptcy, Care Proceedings, Chancery (General), Chancery (Land Law), Charities, Common Land, Common Law (General), Company & Commercial, Construction, Conveyancing, Crime, Crime (Corporate/Fraud), Equity, Wills & Trusts, Family, Family Provision, Financial Services, Health & Safety, Housing, Insolvency, Intellectual Property, Landlord & Tenant, Licensing, Partnership, Personal Injury, Probate & Administration, Professional Negligence, Regulatory Law, Sale & Carriage of Goods, Town & Country Planning

C

QUIRKE MR JAMES KEIRON

St Philips Chambers
55 Temple Row, Birmingham B2 5LS
☎0121 246 7000 ✉clerks@st-philips.com
Call Date: Nov 1974, Gray's Inn
Pupil Supervisor

Practising Areas: Equity, Wills & Trusts, Probate & Administration, Professional Negligence, Public International, Regulatory Law

QURESHI MR ABDUL SALEEM

Barclay Chambers
Ground Floor, 2a Barclay Road, Leytonstone, London E11 3DG ☎020 8558 2289
✉barqureshi@hotmail.co.uk
Call Date: Jul 1972, Middle Temple
Pupil Supervisor

Practising Areas: Immigration

QURESHI MR ASIF HASAN

Quadrant Chambers
Quadrant House, 10 Fleet Street, London EC4Y 1AU ☎020 7583 4444
✉info@quadrantchambers.com
Call Date: Nov 1978, Lincoln's Inn

Practising Areas: Discrimination, EC & Competition Law, Foreign Law, Human Rights, International Trade, Public International

QURESHI MISS DILRUBA

Temple Court Chambers
2nd Floor, 2 Dr Johnson's Building, Temple, London EC4Y 7AY ☎020 7353 7888
✉clerks@templecourt.co.uk
Call Date: Mar 2002, Lincoln's Inn

Practising Areas: Civil Litigation, Family, Immigration

QURESHI MR TANVEER AFTAB

25 Bedford Row
London WC1R 4HD ☎020 7067 1500
✉clerks@25bedfordrow.com
Call Date: Nov 2000, Lincoln's Inn

Practising Areas: Civil Liberties, Crime (Corporate/Fraud), Employment, Regulatory Law

RADFORD MRS NADINE POGGIOLI QC (1995)

187 Fleet Street
London EC4A 2AT ☎020 7430 7430
✉chambers@187fleetstreet.com
Call Date: Nov 1974, Lincoln's Inn

Practising Areas: Crime, Crime (Corporate/Fraud)

RAFFERTY MISS ANGELA MARGARET MARY

1 Paper Buildings
1st Floor, 1 Paper Buildings, Temple, London EC4Y 7EP ☎ 020 7353 3728
✉ clerks@onepaper.co.uk
Call Date: Feb 1995, Lincoln's Inn
Pupil Supervisor

Practising Areas: Crime

RAFTER MISS KATHRYN MICHELLE

KBW
The Engine House, No 1 Foundry Square, Leeds LS11 5DL ☎ 0113 297 1200
✉ clerks@kbwchambers.com
Call Date: Oct 2005, Middle Temple

Practising Areas: Crime

RAGGATT MR TIMOTHY WALTER HAROLD QC (1993)

4 King's Bench Walk
2nd Floor, 4 King's Bench Walk, Temple, London EC4Y 7DL ☎ 020 7822 7000
✉ clerks@4kbw.co.uk
St Philips Chambers
55 Temple Row, Birmingham B2 5LS
☎ 0121 246 7000 ✉ clerks@st-philips.com
Call Date: Jul 1972, Inner Temple
Recorder

Practising Areas: Courts Martial, Crime, Crime (Corporate/Fraud), Health & Safety, Regulatory Law

RAHMAN MR ANIS OBE

12 Old Square Chambers
1st Floor, 12 Old Square, Lincoln's Inn, London WC2A 3TX ☎ 020 7404 0875
✉ clerks@12oldsquare.com
Call Date: Nov 1990, Inner Temple
Pupil Supervisor

Practising Areas: Aviation, Civil Liberties, Civil Litigation, Commercial Litigation, Commercial Property, Common Law (General), Company & Commercial, Crime, Defamation, Discrimination, Employment, Housing, Human Rights, Immigration, Islamic Sharia Law, Landlord & Tenant, Partnership, Road Traffic And Highways, Shipping/Admiralty

RAHMAN MR LEO FERHANUR

Chambers of Leo Rahman
30 Balsdean Road, Brighton, Sussex BN2 6PF
☎ 07814 004 790 ✉ leorahman@aol.com
Call Date: Jul 1998, Lincoln's Inn

Practising Areas: Civil Litigation, Employment, Immigration

RAHMAN MR LUTHFUR

Chambers of Mr L Rahman
201 Maidstone Road, Rochester, Kent ME1 3ES ☎ 07947 588362 ✉ luthfur99@gmail.com
Call Date: Oct 1996, Middle Temple

Practising Areas: Discrimination, Employment, Human Rights, Immigration, Mental Health

RAHMAN MR SAMI UR

Field Court Chambers
5 Field Court, Gray's Inn, London WC1R 5EF
☎ 020 7405 6114 ✉ clerks@fieldcourt.co.uk
Call Date: Oct 1996, Lincoln's Inn

Practising Areas: Chancery (General), Chancery (Land Law), Commercial Litigation, Common Law (General), Discrimination, Employment

RAI MR AMARJIT SINGH

St Philips Chambers
55 Temple Row, Birmingham B2 5LS
☎ 0121 246 7000 ✉ clerks@st-philips.com
Call Date: Jul 1989, Middle Temple

Practising Areas: Commercial Litigation, Housing, Landlord & Tenant, Personal Injury, Professional Negligence

RAI MISS PUNEET KAUR

Thomas More Chambers
7 Lincoln's Inn Fields, London WC2A 3BP
☎ 020 7404 7000 ✉ clerks@thomasmore.co.uk
Call Date: Oct 2004, Lincoln's Inn

Practising Areas: Ancillary Relief, Children's Law, Civil Litigation, Common Law (General), Crime, Family, Family Provision, Personal Injury, Professional Negligence

RAI MR RAJESH KUMAR

1 Mitre Court Buildings
1 Mitre Court Buildings, Temple, London EC4Y 7BS ☎ 020 7452 8900 ✉ clerks@1mcb.com
Call Date: Feb 1993, Lincoln's Inn

Practising Areas: Civil Liberties, Crime (Corporate/Fraud), EC & Competition Law, Energy, Environment, Human Rights, Immigration

RAINEY MR PHILIP CARSLAKE QC (2010)

Tanfield Chambers
2-5 Warwick Court, London WC1R 5DJ
☎ 020 7421 5300 ✉ clerks@tanfieldchambers.co.uk
Call Date: Oct 1990, Middle Temple

Practising Areas: Bankruptcy, Chancery (Land Law), Commercial Litigation, Commercial Property, Common Law (General), Housing, Insolvency, Landlord & Tenant, Professional Negligence

RAINSFORD MR MARK DAVID QC (2006)

Chambers of Andrew Mitchell QC
33 Chancery Lane, London WC2A 1EN
☎ 020 7440 9950 ✉ clerks@33cllaw.com
Call Date: Nov 1985, Lincoln's Inn

RALPH MR CRAIG

Kings Chambers
36 Young Street, Manchester M3 3FT
☎ 0845 034 3444 ✉ clerks@kingschambers.com
Kings Chambers
5 Park Square East, Leeds LS1 2NE
☎ 0845 034 3444 ✉ clerks@kingschambers.com
Kings Chambers
Embassy House, 60 Church Street, Birmingham B3 2DJ ☎ 0845 034 3444
✉ clerks@kingschambers.com
Call Date: Oct 2002, Middle Temple

Practising Areas: Costs

RAMAMOORTHY MISS DIVYA

1 Gray's Inn Square
Ground Floor, 1 Gray's Inn Square, London WC1R 5AA ☎ 020 7405 0001
Call Date: Mar 2006, Middle Temple

RAMASAMY MR SELVARAJU

QEB Hollis Whiteman
1-2 Laurence Pountney Hill, London EC4R 0EU ☎ 020 7933 8855 ✉ barristers@qebhw.co.uk
Call Date: Nov 1992, Inner Temple
Pupil Supervisor

Practising Areas: Courts Martial, Crime, Licensing, Regulatory Law

RAMBLE MR DONALD ROBERT LOUIS

Five St Andrew's Hill
5 St Andrew's Hill, London EC4V 5BZ
☎ 020 7332 5400 ✉ Clerks@5sah.co.uk
Call Date: Nov 1998, Middle Temple

Practising Areas: Crime

RAMDAS-HARSIA MR ROHAN MUKESH

1 Pump Court
Elm Court, Temple, London EC4Y 7AB
☎ 020 7842 7070 ✉ (name)@pumpcourt.co.uk
Call Date: Nov 1999, Middle Temple
Pupil Supervisor

Practising Areas: Care Proceedings, Family, Human Rights

RAMZAN MR MOHAMMED ANWAR

Great James Street Chambers
37 Great James Street, London WC1N 3HB
☎ 020 7440 4949 ✉ chambers@greatjames.co.uk
Call Date: Oct 1995, Lincoln's Inn

Practising Areas: Crime, Employment, Family, Immigration, Landlord & Tenant, Licensing

RANA MR MOHAMMED AKRAM

Clapham Law Chambers
85 Landor Road, Clapham North, London SW9 9RT ☎ 020 7978 8482
✉ DANNY@claphamlawchambers.co.uk
Call Date: Nov 1995, Lincoln's Inn

Practising Areas: Administrative, Ancillary Relief, Bankruptcy, Chancery (General), Civil Liberties, Civil Litigation, Common Law (General), Crime, Employment, Family, Financial Services, Foreign Law, Housing, Human Rights, Immigration, Insolvency, Landlord & Tenant, Licensing, Public Law, Town & Country Planning

RANDALL MRS REBECCA

25 Bedford Row
London WC1R 4HD ☎ 020 7067 1500
✉ clerks@25bedfordrow.com
Call Date: Jul 2005, Gray's Inn

Practising Areas: Crime, Crime (Corporate/Fraud)

C

RANDOLPH MR PAUL LESLIE

Field Court Chambers
5 Field Court, Gray's Inn, London WC1R 5EF
☎ 020 7405 6114 ✉ clerks@fieldcourt.co.uk
Call Date: Nov 1971, Inner Temple
Pupil Supervisor

Practising Areas: Common Law (General), Employment, Landlord & Tenant, Medical Negligence, Personal Injury, Professional Negligence, Sale & Carriage of Goods

RANKIN MR JAMES ROWLAND EVELYN

Francis Taylor Building
Inner Temple, London EC4Y 7BY
☎ 020 7353 8415 ✉ clerks@ftb.eu.com
Call Date: Jul 1983, Inner Temple
Pupil Supervisor

RASOUL MISS MIRIAM HAMEAN

Trinity Chambers
The Custom House, 39 Quayside, Newcastle Upon Tyne NE1 3DE ☎ 0191 232 1927
✉ info@trinitychambers.co.uk
Trinity Chambers
Multi Media Exchange, 72-80 Corporation Road, Middlesbrough TS1 2RF
☎ 01642 247569 ✉ info@trinitychambers.co.uk
Call Date: Jul 2001, Lincoln's Inn

Practising Areas: Immigration

RATCLIFFE MISS FRANCES ANNE

Radcliffe Chambers
Ground Floor, 11 New Square, Lincoln's Inn, London WC2A 3QB ☎ 020 7831 0081
✉ clerks@radcliffechambers.com
Call Date: Oct 2002, Lincoln's Inn

Practising Areas: Chancery (General), Chancery (Land Law), Commercial Litigation, Commercial Property, Family, Family Provision, Housing, Landlord & Tenant, Partnership, Pensions, Probate & Administration, Professional Negligence

RAUDNITZ MR PAUL NIKOLAI

QEB Hollis Whiteman
1-2 Laurence Pountney Hill, London EC4R 0EU ☎ 020 7933 8855 ✉ barristers@qebhw.co.uk
Call Date: Nov 1994, Inner Temple
Pupil Supervisor

RAW MR EDWARD

Tanfield Chambers
2-5 Warwick Court, London WC1R 5DJ
☎ 020 7421 5300 ✉ clerks@tanfieldchambers.co.uk
Call Date: Jul 1963, Inner Temple
Pupil Supervisor

Practising Areas: Common Law (General), Crime, Human Rights, Immigration

RAWAL MISS ANITA

Chambers of Mr Ami Feder
Ground Floor, Lamb Building, Temple, London EC4Y 7AS ☎ 020 7797 7788
✉ clerks@lambbuilding.co.uk
Lamb Building
22 Ship Street, Brighton BN1 1AD
☎ 01273 820490 ✉ admin@lambbuilding.co.uk
Chambers of Mr Ami Feder
Ground Floor, Lamb Building, Temple, London EC4Y 7AS ☎ 020 7797 7788
✉ clerks@lambbuilding.co.uk
Call Date: Oct 2004, Middle Temple

Practising Areas: Ancillary Relief, Children's Law, Family

RAWAT MISS HOUZLA BIBI MAHMAD

Carmelite Chambers
9 Carmelite Street, London EC4Y 0DR
☎ 020 7936 6300
✉ clerks@carmelitechambers.co.uk
Call Date: Oct 2001, Middle Temple

Practising Areas: Crime, Crime (Corporate/Fraud), Professional Negligence, Regulatory Law

RAWAT MRS ISMET PARVEEN

Hermitage Court Chambers
117a-117b Inwood Road, Hounslow, Middlesex TW3 1XJ ☎ 07852 146056
✉ hermitagecourtchambers@gmx.com
Conference Chambers
P.O. Box 626, Harrow, Middlesex HA2 2DZ
☎ 020 8144 0134
✉ carole@conferencechambers.com
Call Date: Nov 1992, Inner Temple

RAWCLIFFE MR ANTHONY MARK WILSON

4 Brick Court
4 Brick Court, Temple, London EC4Y 9AD
☎ 020 7832 3200 ✉ clerks@4bc.co.uk
Call Date: Nov 1996, Middle Temple

Practising Areas: Children's Law

RAWLINGS MR CLIVE PATRICK

Hardwicke
New Square, Lincoln's Inn, London WC2A 3SB ☎ 020 7242 2523
✉ enquiries@hardwicke.co.uk
Call Date: Nov 1994, Inner Temple
Pupil Supervisor

Practising Areas: Education

RAYMENT MR BENEDICK MICHAEL

Monckton Chambers
1 & 2 Raymond Buildings, Gray's Inn, London WC1R 5NR ☎ 020 7405 7211
✉ chambers@monckton.com
Call Date: Oct 1996, Inner Temple

Practising Areas: Administrative, Civil Liberties, Commercial Litigation, Competition, EC & Competition Law, Telecommunications

READ MR DANIEL JAMES

Farrar's Building
Farrar's Building, Temple, London EC4Y 7BD
☎ 020 7583 9241
✉ Chambers@farrarsbuilding.co.uk
Call Date: Oct 2006, Gray's Inn

Practising Areas: Common Law (General), Employment, Medical Negligence, Personal Injury

READ MR SIMON ERIC

Zenith Chambers
10 Park Square, Leeds LS1 2LH
☎ 0113 245 5438 ✉ clerks@zenithchambers.co.uk
Call Date: Nov 1989, Inner Temple

Practising Areas: Administrative, Common Law (General), Housing, Landlord & Tenant, Local Government, Public Law

REAL MISS KIRSTY NICHOLA

Albion Chambers
Broad Street, Bristol BS1 1DR
☎ 0117 927 2144 ✉ clerks@albionchambers.co.uk
Call Date: Oct 1996, Inner Temple

Practising Areas: Crime, Crime (Corporate/Fraud), Inquests, Mental Health

RECORD MRS CELIA SAINT CLAIRE

Chambers of Lawrence Jones
8 Stone Buildings, Lincoln's Inn, London WC2A 3TA ☎ 020 7831 1444
✉ clerks@8stonebuildings.com
Call Date: Mar 1998, Middle Temple

Practising Areas: Administrative, Banking, Bankruptcy, Chancery (General), Commercial Litigation, Employment, Family, Landlord & Tenant, Personal Injury

REECE MR BRIAN ALFRED WILLIAM

187 Fleet Street
London EC4A 2AT ☎ 020 7430 7430
✉ chambers@187fleetstreet.com
Call Date: Jul 1974, Middle Temple
Pupil Supervisor

Practising Areas: Crime, Crime (Corporate/Fraud)

REED MR JEREMY NIGEL

Hogarth Chambers
5 New Square, Lincoln's Inn, London WC2A 3RJ ☎ 020 7404 0404
✉ barristers@hogarthchambers.com
Call Date: Oct 1997, Middle Temple
Pupil Supervisor

Practising Areas: Copyright, Entertainment, Film, Cable & TV, Information Technology, Intellectual Property, Patents, Trademarks

REED MR JULIAN WINN

9 Park Place
Cardiff, South Glamorgan CF10 3DP
☎ 029 2038 2731 ✉ clerks@9parkplace.co.uk
Call Date: Nov 1991, Inner Temple

Practising Areas: Asset Finance, Care Proceedings, Common Law (General), Equity, Wills & Trusts, Family Provision, Personal Injury

REED MS LUCY EMMA

St John's Chambers
101 Victoria Street, Bristol BS1 6PU
☎ 0117 923 4700 ✉ clerks@stjohnschambers.co.uk
Call Date: Oct 2002, Lincoln's Inn

Practising Areas: Care Proceedings, Education, Family, Family Provision

REED MR PIERS KNOWLE MOORHOUSE

3 Temple Gardens
Lower Ground Floor, 3 Temple Gardens, Temple, London EC4Y 9AU ☎020 7353 3102
✉clerks@3tg.co.uk
Call Date: Nov 1974, Lincoln's Inn
Pupil Supervisor

REED MR SIMON JOHN

New Walk Chambers
27 New Walk, Leicester, Leicestershire LE1 6TE ☎0871 200 1298 / 0116 255 9144
✉clerks@newwalkchambers.co.uk
Call Date: Mar 1998, Gray's Inn
Pupil Supervisor

Practising Areas: Bankruptcy, Chancery (General), Civil Litigation, Commercial Litigation, Common Law (General), Consumer, Coroners Inquests, Discrimination, Employment, Inquests, Insolvency, Medical Negligence, Personal Injury, Professional Negligence, Road Traffic And Highways

REEDER MR JOHN QC (1989)

Stone Chambers
4 Field Court, Gray's Inn, London WC1R 5EF
☎020 7440 6900 ✉clerks@stonechambers.com
Call Date: Jul 1971, Gray's Inn

REEDS MR GARETH DAVID

Canary Wharf Chambers
Level 33, 25 Canada Square, London E14 5LQ
☎020 7183 8011
✉admin@canarywharfchambers.com
Call Date: Oct 2001, Lincoln's Inn

Practising Areas: Arbitration, Commercial Litigation, Common Law (General), Company & Commercial, Competition, Construction, EC & Competition Law, Employment, Foreign Law, Insolvency, Landlord & Tenant, Private International

REES MR HEFIN EDNYFED

39 Essex Street
London WC2R 3AT ☎020 7832 1111
✉clerks@39essex.com
Call Date: Nov 1992, Inner Temple
Pupil Supervisor

Practising Areas: Commercial Litigation, Common Law (General), Employment, Personal Injury, Professional Negligence

REES MR JAMES WILLIAM STEWART

Southernhay Chambers
33 Southernhay East, Exeter EX1 1NX
☎01392 255777
✉clerks@southernhaychambers.co.uk
Call Date: Nov 1994, Gray's Inn
Pupil Supervisor

REES MR JONATHAN DAVID QC (2010)

2 Hare Court
Lower Ground, Ground, 1st & 2nd Floor, 2 Hare Court, Temple, London EC4Y 7BH
☎020 7353 3982 ✉clerks@2harecourt.com
Call Date: Nov 1987, Gray's Inn
Pupil Supervisor, Recorder

Practising Areas: Crime, Crime (Corporate/Fraud)

REES MR JONATHAN ELYSTAN

Apex
Harlech House, 20 Cathedral Road, Cardiff CF11 9LJ ☎02920 232 032
✉clerks@apexchambers.net
Call Date: Oct 2000, Inner Temple

Practising Areas: Crime (Corporate/Fraud), Disciplinary Tribunals, Regulatory Law, Sports

REES MISS NAOMI ANGELIQUE

3 PB Barristers
3 Paper Buildings, Temple, London EC4Y 7EU
☎020 7583 8055
3 PB Barristers
4 St Peter Street, Winchester SO23 8BW
☎01962 868884 ✉clerks.winchester@3paper.co.uk
Call Date: Jul 2006, Middle Temple

REES MR ROBERT CHARLES DAVID

New Walk Chambers
27 New Walk, Leicester, Leicestershire LE1 6TE ☎0871 200 1298 / 0116 255 9144
✉clerks@newwalkchambers.co.uk
Call Date: Feb 1978, Middle Temple
Pupil Supervisor

Practising Areas: Civil Liberties, Discrimination, Employment, Family

REES PROF WILLIAM MICHAEL

1 Gray's Inn Square
Ground Floor, 1 Gray's Inn Square, London WC1R 5AA ☎020 7405 0001
Call Date: Jul 1973, Inner Temple

Practising Areas: Civil Liberties, Company & Commercial, Discrimination, Education, Employment, Financial Services, Immigration, Sports

REEVELL MRS LOUISE MARIE

39 Park Square
Leeds LS1 2NU ☎0113 245 6633
✉seniorclerk@39parksquarechambers.co.uk
Call Date: Oct 2001, Lincoln's Inn

Practising Areas: Courts Martial, Crime

REEVELL MR SIMON JUSTIN

39 Park Square
Leeds LS1 2NU ☎0113 245 6633
✉seniorclerk@39parksquarechambers.co.uk
Call Date: Oct 1990, Lincoln's Inn
Pupil Supervisor

Practising Areas: Common Land, Courts Martial, Crime, Crime (Corporate/Fraud), Personal Injury

REFFIN MISS CLARE ALYSON

One Essex Court
Ground Floor, One Essex Court, Temple, London EC4Y 9AR ☎020 7583 2000
✉clerks@oeclaw.co.uk
Call Date: Jul 1981, Middle Temple
Pupil Supervisor

Practising Areas: Arbitration, Banking, Chancery (General), Commercial Litigation, Commodities, Company & Commercial, Employment, Financial Services, Insurance/Reinsurance, International Trade, Private International, Professional Negligence, Sale & Carriage of Goods

REGAN MR DAVID ROBERT

St John's Chambers
101 Victoria Street, Bristol BS1 6PU
☎0117 923 4700 ✉clerks@stjohnschambers.co.uk
Call Date: Nov 1994, Inner Temple

Practising Areas: Common Law (General), Employment, Personal Injury, Professional Negligence

REID MISS CHERYL LOUISE PEGG

Temple Court Chambers
2nd Floor, 2 Dr Johnson's Building, Temple, London EC4Y 7AY ☎020 7353 7888
✉clerks@templecourt.co.uk
Call Date: Jul 2003, Lincoln's Inn

Practising Areas: Commercial Litigation, Common Law (General), Energy, Landlord & Tenant, Personal Injury

REID MISS CLAUDETTE PATRICIA

Chambers of Miss Claudette Reid
C P Reid Direct Access, Barrister, PO Box 583872, London SE27 7BJ
Call Date: Oct 1990, Gray's Inn
Pupil Supervisor

Practising Areas: Ancillary Relief, Civil Litigation, Employment, Family, Housing, Immigration, Landlord & Tenant

REID MR DICKON

5 King's Bench Walk
5 King's Bench Walk, Temple, London EC4Y 7DN ☎020 7353 5638 ✉clerks@5kbw.co.uk
Call Date: Nov 2005, Inner Temple

REID MR PAUL CAMPBELL QC (2001)

Lincoln House Chambers
Tower 12, The Avenue North, Spinningfields, 18-22 Bridge Street, Manchester M3 3BZ
☎0161 832 5701
✉info@lincolnhousechambers.com
Call Date: Jul 1973, Gray's Inn
Recorder

REID MR SEBASTIAN PETER SCOTT

Tanfield Chambers
2-5 Warwick Court, London WC1R 5DJ
☎020 7421 5300 ✉clerks@tanfieldchambers.co.uk
Call Date: Jul 1982, Gray's Inn

Practising Areas: Commercial Litigation, Common Law (General), Family, Housing, Landlord & Tenant, Local Government, Personal Injury

REID-CHALMERS MISS EMMA LOUISE

Triangle Chambers
Blair Atholl, 11 The Triangle, North Ferriby, East Yorkshire HU14 3AT ☎01482 632075
✉emmarc@emmarc.karoo.co.uk
Call Date: Jul 1996, Lincoln's Inn

C

REIFF-MUSGROVE MISS KAJA

Dyers Chambers
35 Bedford Row, London WC1R 4JH
☎020 7404 1881 ✉admin@dyerschambers.com
Call Date: Nov 1992, Middle Temple

Practising Areas: Crime, Crime (Corporate/Fraud), Personal Injury, Regulatory Law

REIZ MR STANLEY

Carmelite Chambers
9 Carmelite Street, London EC4Y 0DR
☎020 7936 6300
✉clerks@carmelitechambers.co.uk
Call Date: Mar 2001, Lincoln's Inn
Pupil Supervisor

Practising Areas: Crime, Crime (Corporate/Fraud), Sports

RENDLE MR JEREMY MARK

9 King's Bench Walk
Lower Ground Floor South, 9 King's Bench Walk, Temple, London EC4Y 7DX
☎020 7353 9564 ✉9kbw@btconnect.com
Call Date: Jul 2000, Inner Temple

Practising Areas: Crime, Employment, Human Rights, Immigration

RENE MR JACQUES MARIO

Chambers of Mr J M Rene
20 Fairoak Drive, Eltham, London SE9 2QH
☎07768 854321 ✉jacques_rene30@hotmail.com
Call Date: Oct 1998, Lincoln's Inn

Practising Areas: Immigration

RENOUF MR GERARD JOHN PETER

2 Pump Court
1st Floor, 2 Pump Court, Temple, London EC4Y 7AH ☎020 7353 5597
✉clerks@2pumpcourt.co.uk
Call Date: Jul 1977, Inner Temple
Pupil Supervisor

Practising Areas: Crime

RENTON THE HON MRS CLARE OLIVIA

29 Bedford Row Chambers
London WC1R 4HE ☎020 7404 1044
✉clerks@29br.co.uk
Call Date: Nov 1972, Lincoln's Inn

Practising Areas: Family

RENVOIZE MR EDWARD PHILIP

1 Paper Buildings
1st Floor, 1 Paper Buildings, Temple, London EC4Y 7EP ☎020 7353 3728
✉clerks@onepaper.co.uk
No.6 Park Square
Leeds LS1 2LW ☎0113 245 9763
✉Tim@no6.co.uk
Call Date: Oct 2004, Lincoln's Inn

Practising Areas: Crime, Crime (Corporate/Fraud)

REVERE MS CARLA

1 Chancery Lane
London WC2A 1LF ☎0845 634 6666
✉clerks@1chancerylane.com
Call Date: Oct 2001, Inner Temple

REYNOLDS MR ADRIAN LEONARD

1 High Pavement
Nottingham NG1 1HF ☎0115 941 8218
✉clerks@1highpavement.co.uk
Call Date: Nov 1982, Gray's Inn
Pupil Supervisor, Recorder

REYNOLDS MR JOHN ADAM

King's Bench Chambers
Wellington House, 175 Holdenhurst Road, Bournemouth, Dorset BH8 8DQ
☎01202 250025
Call Date: Oct 1998, Gray's Inn

Practising Areas: Care Proceedings, Common Law (General), Crime, Family, Road Traffic And Highways

RHODES MISS AMANDA LOUISE

Unity Street Chambers
5 Unity Street, College Green, Bristol BS1 5HH ☎0117 906 9789
✉chambers@unitystreetchambers.com
Call Date: May 1990, Lincoln's Inn

Practising Areas: Ancillary Relief, Care Proceedings, Children's Law, Crime, Family, Family Provision, Housing

RHODES MR NICHOLAS PIERS QC (2008)

Charter Chambers
33 John Street, London WC1N 2AT
☎020 7618 4400 ✉clerks@charterchambers.com
Call Date: Jul 1981, Lincoln's Inn
Recorder

Practising Areas: Courts Martial, Crime, Crime (Corporate/Fraud), Regulatory Law, Sports

RHODES MR ROBERT ELLIOTT QC (1989)

Outer Temple Chambers
The Outer Temple, 222 Strand, London WC2R 1BA ☎ 020 7353 6381
✉ clerks@outertemple.com
Principal Chambers
15 Lime Tree Walk, Sevenoaks, Kent TN13 1YH ☎ 0845 209 8080
St Philips Chambers
55 Temple Row, Birmingham B2 5LS
☎ 0121 246 7000 ✉ clerks@st-philips.com
Call Date: Jul 1968, Inner Temple

Practising Areas: Administrative, Common Law (General), Crime, Crime (Corporate/Fraud), Financial Services, Health & Safety, Regulatory Law

RHYS MISS MEGAN JILL

Call Date: Nov 1994, Inner Temple

RHYS-DAVIES MR ADAM

Sovereign Chambers
46 Park Place, Leeds LS1 2RY
☎ 0113 245 1841
✉ clerks@sovereignchambers.co.uk
Call Date: Oct 1998, Middle Temple

RICE MR CHRISTOPHER DOUGLAS

Crown Office Row Chambers
119 Church Street, Brighton, Sussex BN1 1UD ☎ 01273 625625 ✉ clerks@1cor.com
Call Date: Jul 1991, Middle Temple

RICHARDS MR DAVID JAMES MARTIN

3 PB Barristers
3 Paper Buildings, Temple, London EC4Y 7EU
☎ 020 7583 8055
3 PB Barristers
Royal Talbot House, 2 Victoria Street, Bristol, Avon BS1 6BB ☎ 0117 928 1520
3 PB Barristers
30 Christchurch Road, Bournemouth, Dorset BH1 3PD ☎ 01202 292102 ✉ clerks.bournemouth@3paper.co.uk
3 PB Barristers
4 St Peter Street, Winchester SO23 8BW
☎ 01962 868884 ✉ clerks.winchester@3paper.co.uk
3 PB Barristers
23 Beaumont Street, Oxford OX1 2NP
☎ 01865 793 736
Call Date: Jul 1989, Middle Temple
Pupil Supervisor

Practising Areas: Courts Martial, Crime, Crime (Corporate/Fraud), Licensing, Regulatory Law

RICHARDS MR DUNCAN JAMES

Chambers of Mr Ami Feder
Ground Floor, Lamb Building, Temple, London EC4Y 7AS ☎ 020 7797 7788
✉ clerks@lambbuilding.co.uk
Principal Chambers
15 Lime Tree Walk, Sevenoaks, Kent TN13 1YH ☎ 0845 209 8080
Chambers of Mr Ami Feder
Ground Floor, Lamb Building, Temple, London EC4Y 7AS ☎ 020 7797 7788
✉ clerks@lambbuilding.co.uk
Call Date: Oct 2007, Inner Temple

Practising Areas: Administrative, Civil Liberties, Common Law (General), Human Rights, Immigration, Personal Injury

RICHARDS MR HUGH ALAN

No5 Chambers
Fountain Court, Steelhouse Lane, Birmingham B4 6DR ☎ 0845 210 5555 ✉ info@no5.com
No5 Chambers
Greenwood House, 4-7 Salisbury Court, London EC4Y 8AA ☎ 0845 210 5555
No5 Chambers
38 Queen Square, Bristol BS1 4QS
☎ 0845 210 5555
Call Date: Nov 1992, Inner Temple

RICHARDSON MR ALISTAIR PAUL GEORGE

6 King's Bench Walk
Ground Floor, 6 King's Bench Walk, Temple, London EC4Y 7DR ☎ 020 7583 0410
✉ clerks@6kbw.com
Call Date: Oct 2006, Inner Temple

Practising Areas: Administrative, Civil Liberties, Courts Martial, Crime, Crime (Corporate/Fraud), Disciplinary Tribunals, Entertainment, Regulatory Law

RICHARDSON MR GARTH DOUGLAS ANTHONY

Rougemont Chambers
Victory House, Dean Clarke Gardens, Southernhay East, Exeter EX2 4AA
☎ 01392 208484
✉ clerks@rougemontchambers.co.uk
Devon Chambers
3 St Andrew Street, Plymouth PL1 2AH
☎ 01752 661659 ✉ clerks@devonchambers.co.uk
Call Date: Jul 1975, Middle Temple
Pupil Supervisor

Practising Areas: Administrative, Employment, Health & Safety, Licensing, Personal Injury, Regulatory Law, Town & Country Planning

RICHARDSON MR PAUL ANDREW

1 Gray's Inn Square
Ground Floor, 1 Gray's Inn Square, London WC1R 5AA ☎ 020 7405 0001
Call Date: Feb 1993, Inner Temple

Practising Areas: Crime, Human Rights, Immigration

RICHMAN MRS HELENE PINES

9 Stone Buildings
Lincoln's Inn, London WC2A 3NN
☎ 020 7404 5055 ✉ clerks@9stonebuildings.com
Eighteen Carlton Crescent
Rownhams House, Rownhams, Southampton SO16 8LF ☎ 023 8063 9001
✉ clerks@18carltoncrescent.co.uk
Stour Chambers
Mill Studio, 17a Stour Street, Canterbury, Kent CT1 2NR ☎ 01227 764899
✉ clerks@stourchambers.co.uk
Call Date: Jul 1992, Middle Temple
Pupil Supervisor

Practising Areas: Ancillary Relief, Banking, Chancery (General), Chancery (Land Law), Charities, Civil Litigation, Company & Commercial, Equity, Wills & Trusts, Financial Services, Foreign Law, Private International, Probate & Administration, Professional Negligence, Public Law

RICHMOND MR BERNARD GRANT QC (2006)

Chambers of Mr Ami Feder
Ground Floor, Lamb Building, Temple, London EC4Y 7AS ☎ 020 7797 7788
✉ clerks@lambbuilding.co.uk
Central Chambers
89 Princess Street, Manchester M1 4HT
☎ 0161 236 1133 ✉ clerks@centralchambers.co.uk
Chambers of Mr Ami Feder
Ground Floor, Lamb Building, Temple, London EC4Y 7AS ☎ 020 7797 7788
✉ clerks@lambbuilding.co.uk
Call Date: Jul 1988, Middle Temple
Pupil Supervisor

Practising Areas: Crime

RICHMOND MR PAUL ANTHONY OLIFFE

Richmond Canter Immigration Barristers
1 Fetter Lane, London EC4A 1BR
☎ 020 3440 5820
✉ info@immigrationbarrister.co.uk
Call Date: Oct 1998, Inner Temple

Practising Areas: Immigration

RICKARBY MR WILLIAM EDMUND

Cornwall Street Chambers
85-87 Cornwall Street, Birmingham B3 3BY
☎ 0121 233 7500 ✉ clerks@cornwallstreet.co.uk
Call Date: Jul 1975, Gray's Inn

Practising Areas: Crime, Environment, Human Rights, Regulatory Law

RICKARD MR MARCUS JOHN REID

18 Red Lion Court
London EC4A 3EB ☎ 020 7520 6000
✉ chambers@18rlc.co.uk
Call Date: Jul 2000, Inner Temple

RICKARDS MR JAMES

Outer Temple Chambers
The Outer Temple, 222 Strand, London WC2R 1BA ☎ 020 7353 6381
✉ clerks@outertemple.com
Call Date: Mar 2002, Inner Temple

Practising Areas: Chancery (General), Commercial Litigation, Pensions

RIDD MR DAVID IAN MCGREGOR

Farrar's Building
Farrar's Building, Temple, London EC4Y 7BD
☎ 020 7583 9241
✉ Chambers@farrarsbuilding.co.uk
Call Date: Jul 1975, Middle Temple
Pupil Supervisor

Practising Areas: Arbitration, Banking, Chancery (General), Commercial Litigation, Commercial Property, Construction, Employment, Landlord & Tenant, Professional Negligence, Sale & Carriage of Goods

RIFAT MR MAURICE ALAN

1 Gray's Inn Square
Ground Floor, 1 Gray's Inn Square, London WC1R 5AA ☎ 020 7405 0001
Call Date: Nov 1990, Inner Temple
Pupil Supervisor

Practising Areas: Arbitration, Bankruptcy, Chancery (General), Civil Litigation, Commercial Litigation, Commercial Property, Common Law (General), Company & Commercial, Construction, Costs, Equity, Wills & Trusts, Insolvency, Land, Landlord & Tenant, Partnership, Personal Injury, Professional Negligence

RIGGS MISS SAMANTHA

25 Bedford Row
London WC1R 4HD ☎ 020 7067 1500
✉ clerks@25bedfordrow.com
Call Date: Oct 1996, Gray's Inn

Practising Areas: Crime, Crime (Corporate/Fraud), Environment, Regulatory Law

RIGNEY MR ANDREW JAMES QC (2010)

Crown Office Chambers
2 Crown Office Row, Temple, London EC4Y 7HJ ☎ 020 7797 8100
✉ mail@crownofficechambers.com
Call Date: Oct 1992, Gray's Inn
Pupil Supervisor

Practising Areas: Arbitration, Commercial Litigation, Common Law (General), Construction, Insurance, Insurance/Reinsurance, International Trade, Private International, Professional Negligence, Sale & Carriage of Goods

RILEY MS GERALDINE MARGARET

Cobden House Chambers
19 Quay Street, Manchester M3 3HN
☎ 0161 833 6000 ✉ Clerks@Cobden.co.uk
Call Date: Oct 2002, Inner Temple

RIMMER MR ANTHONY MICHAEL

187 Fleet Street
London EC4A 2AT ☎ 020 7430 7430
✉ chambers@187fleetstreet.com
Call Date: Jul 1983, Gray's Inn
Pupil Supervisor

Practising Areas: Administrative, Chancery (General), Common Law (General), Crime, Regulatory Law

RIMMER MISS CATHERINE LOUISE

Call Date: Jul 2004, Gray's Inn

RIMMER MR NICHOLAS PATRICK EDWARD

23 Essex Street
London WC2R 3AA ☎ 020 7413 0353
✉ clerks@23es.com
Call Date: Jul 2004, Lincoln's Inn

Practising Areas: Crime, Crime (Corporate/Fraud), Road Traffic And Highways

RINDER MR ROBERT MICHAEL

2 Hare Court
Lower Ground, Ground, 1st & 2nd Floor, 2 Hare Court, Temple, London EC4Y 7BH
☎ 020 7353 3982 ✉ clerks@2harecourt.com
Call Date: Oct 2001, Inner Temple

Practising Areas: Crime

RINKER MR ANDREW STUART D'ARTOIS

Chambers of Mr Andrew Rinker
3 Kensington Gate, London W8 5NA
☎ 020 7584 1091 ✉ a.rinker@btinernet.com
Call Date: Jul 2011, Middle Temple

Practising Areas: Arbitration, Asset Finance, Banking, Chancery (General), Chancery (Land Law), Civil Litigation, Commercial Litigation, Company & Commercial, Competition, Corporate Finance, Crime (Corporate/Fraud), Defamation, Energy, Equity, Wills & Trusts, Film, Cable & TV, Financial Services, Foreign Law, Insurance/Reinsurance, Intellectual Property, International Trade, Partnership, Private International, Probate & Administration, Public Law, Shipping/Admiralty, Tax (Capital & Income), Tax (Corporate), Unit Trusts

RIPPON MR SIMON JOHN

Citadel Chambers
The Citadel, 190 Corporation Street, Birmingham B4 6QD ☎ 0121 233 8500
✉ clerks@citadelchambers.com
Call Date: Nov 1996, Gray's Inn

Practising Areas: Arbitration, Care Proceedings, Civil Liberties, Common Law (General), Courts Martial, Crime, Crime (Corporate/Fraud), Defamation, Discrimination, Employment, Family, Personal Injury

RISSO-GILL MR EDWARD DAVID CHARLES

Thomas More Chambers
7 Lincoln's Inn Fields, London WC2A 3BP
☎ 020 7404 7000 ✉ clerks@thomasmore.co.uk
Call Date: Nov 1998, Inner Temple

Practising Areas: Chancery (Land Law), Commercial Property, Common Law (General), Conveyancing, Human Rights, Landlord & Tenant

C

RITCHIE MR ANDREW GEORGE QC (2009)

The Chambers of Grahame Aldous QC
9 Gough Square, London EC4A 3DG
☎020 7832 0500 ✉clerks@9goughsquare.co.uk
Call Date: Feb 1985, Inner Temple

Practising Areas: Arbitration, Common Law (General), Health & Safety, Healthcare, Insurance, Medical Negligence, Personal Injury, Professional Negligence

RITCHIE MR RICHARD BULKELEY

XXIV Old Buildings
Ground Floor, 24 Old Buildings, Lincoln's Inn, London WC2A 3UP ☎020 7691 2424
✉clerks@xxiv.co.uk
Call Date: Jul 1978, Middle Temple
Pupil Supervisor

Practising Areas: Bankruptcy, Chancery (General), Chancery (Land Law), Commercial Litigation, Company & Commercial, Equity, Wills & Trusts, Financial Services, Insolvency, Partnership, Private International

RITCHIE MISS SHAUNA

2 Bedford Row
London WC1R 4BU ☎020 7440 8888
✉clerks@2bedfordrow.co.uk
Call Date: Nov 2000, Lincoln's Inn
Pupil Supervisor

Practising Areas: Coroners Inquests, Crime, Crime (Corporate/Fraud), Disciplinary Tribunals, Health & Safety, Inquests, Road Traffic And Highways

RIVALLAND MR MARC-EDOUARD

1 Chancery Lane
London WC2A 1LF ☎0845 634 6666
✉clerks@1chancerylane.com
Call Date: Jul 1987, Middle Temple
Pupil Supervisor

Practising Areas: Administrative, Bankruptcy, Commercial Litigation, Common Law (General), Company & Commercial, Employment, Equity, Wills & Trusts, Financial Services, Insolvency, Insurance, Medical Negligence, Partnership, Personal Injury, Professional Negligence

RIZA MR ALPER ALI QC (1991)

Goldsmith Chambers
Ground Floor, Goldsmith Building, Temple, London EC4Y 7BL ☎020 7353 6802
✉clerks@goldsmithchambers.com
Call Date: Nov 1973, Gray's Inn
Recorder

Practising Areas: Administrative, Chancery (General), Common Law (General), Crime, Discrimination, Family, Human Rights, Immigration, Insolvency

ROBERTS MR ALLAN CALVIN

Guildhall Chambers
23 Broad Street, Bristol BS1 2HG
☎0117 930 9000 ✉hoc@guildhallchambers.co.uk
Guildhall Chambers
5-8 Broad Street, Bristol BS1 2HW
☎0117 930 9000
Call Date: Nov 2004, Middle Temple

Practising Areas: Commercial Litigation, Common Law (General), Employment, Sale & Carriage of Goods

ROBERTS MISS BEVERLEY JAN

4 King's Bench Walk
2nd Floor, 4 King's Bench Walk, Temple, London EC4Y 7DL ☎020 7822 7000
✉clerks@4kbw.co.uk
Call Date: Mar 1998, Middle Temple

ROBERTS MISS GEMMA VICTORIA

No5 Chambers
Fountain Court, Steelhouse Lane, Birmingham B4 6DR ☎0845 210 5555 ✉info@no5.com
No5 Chambers
Greenwood House, 4-7 Salisbury Court, London EC4Y 8AA ☎0845 210 5555
No5 Chambers
38 Queen Square, Bristol BS1 4QS
☎0845 210 5555
Call Date: Oct 2006, Gray's Inn

ROBERTS MR HUW EIFION

Linenhall Chambers
1 Stanley Place, Chester CH1 2LU
☎01244 348282
✉clerks@linenhallchambers.co.uk
Call Date: Nov 1993, Gray's Inn
Pupil Supervisor

Practising Areas: Ancillary Relief, Chancery (Land Law), Civil Litigation, Common Law (General), Equity, Wills & Trusts, Family, Family Provision, Land, Landlord & Tenant

ROBERTS MR JACK

Sheldan
Chirk Road, Gobowen, Oswestry, Shropshire SY11 3LB ☎ 01691 657635
✉ jack@roberts155560.fsnet.co.uk
Call Date: Nov 1998, Middle Temple

Practising Areas: Discrimination, Employment

ROBERTS MR JAMES MCCLINTOCK

1 KBW Chambers
1 King's Bench Walk, Temple, London EC4Y 7DB ☎ 020 7936 1500 ✉ clerks@1kbw.co.uk
King's Bench Chambers
174 High Street, Lewes BN7 1YE
☎ 01273 402600
Call Date: Oct 1993, Gray's Inn
Pupil Supervisor, Recorder

Practising Areas: Ancillary Relief, Children's Law, Family, Family Provision

ROBERTS MISS LISA

Lincoln House Chambers
Tower 12, The Avenue North, Spinningfields, 18-22 Bridge Street, Manchester M3 3BZ
☎ 0161 832 5701
✉ info@lincolnhousechambers.com
Call Date: Oct 1993, Lincoln's Inn
Pupil Supervisor

Practising Areas: Crime, Crime (Corporate/Fraud), Health & Safety, Regulatory Law

ROBERTS MR MARC ALEXANDER

4 Brick Court
4 Brick Court, Temple, London EC4Y 9AD
☎ 020 7832 3200 ✉ clerks@4bc.co.uk
Call Date: Nov 1984, Inner Temple

ROBERTS MR MICHAEL CHARLES

Chambers of Michael Roberts
Fawley House, 100A St Andrews Road, Henley-On-Thames, Oxfordshire RG9 1PL
☎ 01844 355 655
✉ mcr@michaelrobertsbarrister.co.uk
Call Date: Jul 1978, Lincoln's Inn

Practising Areas: Bankruptcy, Chancery (General), Chancery (Land Law), Charities, Commercial Litigation, Commercial Property, Common Law (General), Company & Commercial, Construction, Conveyancing, Copyright, Discrimination, Employment, Entertainment, Equity, Wills & Trusts, Family Provision, Insolvency, Insurance, Intellectual Property, Landlord & Tenant, Partnership, Probate & Administration, Professional Negligence, Sale & Carriage of Goods, Share Options, Sports

ROBERTS MR PHILIP DUNCAN

One Essex Court
Ground Floor, One Essex Court, Temple, London EC4Y 9AR ☎ 020 7583 2000
✉ clerks@oeclaw.co.uk
Call Date: Oct 1996, Inner Temple
Pupil Supervisor

Practising Areas: Copyright, Information Technology, Intellectual Property, Patents, Trademarks

ROBERTS MR RICHARD VAUGHAN

Henderson Chambers
2 Harcourt Buildings, Temple, London EC4Y 9DB ☎ 020 7583 9020
✉ clerks@hendersonchambers.co.uk
Call Date: Oct 2006, Lincoln's Inn

Practising Areas: Bankruptcy, Commercial Litigation, Commercial Property, Common Land, Common Law (General), Company & Commercial, Employment, Health & Safety, Housing, Landlord & Tenant, Local Government, Personal Injury, Professional Negligence, Sale & Carriage of Goods

ROBERTS MR STUART ROYD

Chancery House Chambers
7 Lisbon Square, Leeds, West Yorkshire LS1 4LY ☎ 0113 244 6691
✉ clerks@chanceryhouse.co.uk
Call Date: Nov 1994, Middle Temple
Pupil Supervisor

ROBERTS MR TIMOTHY DAVID QC (2003)

Fountain Chambers
Cleveland Business Centre, 1 Watson Street, Middlesbrough TS1 2RQ ☎ 01642 804040
✉ clerks@fountainchambers.co.uk
QEB Hollis Whiteman
1-2 Laurence Pountney Hill, London EC4R 0EU ☎ 020 7933 8855 ✉ barristers@qebhw.co.uk
Call Date: Jul 1978, Gray's Inn
Recorder

Practising Areas: Courts Martial, Crime, Crime (Corporate/Fraud), Environment, Regulatory Law

ROBERTSHAW MR MARTIN ANDREW

39 Park Square
Leeds LS1 2NU ☎ 0113 245 6633
✉ seniorclerk@39parksquarechambers.co.uk
Call Date: Nov 1977, Middle Temple

Practising Areas: Crime, Crime (Corporate/Fraud)

ROBERTSON MR ANGUS FREDERICK

2 King's Bench Walk
2 King's Bench Walk, Temple, London EC4Y 7DE ☎ 020 7353 1746 ✉ clerks@2kbw.com
Call Date: Jul 1978, Middle Temple
Pupil Supervisor

ROBINSON MISS ANNE-LOUISE

Clerksroom (Taunton)
Equity House, Administration Centre, Blackbrook Park Avenue, Taunton, Somerset TA1 2PX ☎ 0845 083 3000 ✉ mail@clerksroom.com
Call Date: Jul 1978, Lincoln's Inn

ROBINSON MISS CLAIRE MARIA

Charter Chambers
33 John Street, London WC1N 2AT ☎ 020 7618 4400 ✉ clerks@charterchambers.com
Call Date: Oct 1991, Gray's Inn

Practising Areas: Crime, Crime (Corporate/Fraud)

ROBINSON MR DANIEL MICHAEL

5 King's Bench Walk
5 King's Bench Walk, Temple, London EC4Y 7DN ☎ 020 7353 5638 ✉ clerks@5kbw.co.uk
Call Date: Nov 1993, Lincoln's Inn
Pupil Supervisor

ROBINSON MISS KAREN

QEB Hollis Whiteman
1-2 Laurence Pountney Hill, London EC4R 0EU ☎ 020 7933 8855 ✉ barristers@qebhw.co.uk
Call Date: Nov 2000, Lincoln's Inn

ROBINSON MISS LAURA

Tanfield Chambers
2-5 Warwick Court, London WC1R 5DJ ☎ 020 7421 5300 ✉ clerks@tanfieldchambers.co.uk
Call Date: Oct 2001, Inner Temple

Practising Areas: Chancery (General), Chancery (Land Law), Discrimination, Employment, Landlord & Tenant

ROBINSON MR NICHOLAS JAMES LANSDALE

3 PB Barristers
3 Paper Buildings, Temple, London EC4Y 7EU ☎ 020 7583 8055
3 PB Barristers
23 Beaumont Street, Oxford OX1 2NP ☎ 01865 793 736
3 PB Barristers
4 St Peter Street, Winchester SO23 8BW ☎ 01962 868884 ✉ clerks.winchester@3paper.co.uk
3 PB Barristers
Royal Talbot House, 2 Victoria Street, Bristol, Avon BS1 6BB ☎ 0117 928 1520
3 PB Barristers
30 Christchurch Road, Bournemouth, Dorset BH1 3PD ☎ 01202 292102 ✉ clerks.bournemouth@3paper.co.uk
Call Date: Jul 2006, Inner Temple

Practising Areas: Crime, Crime (Corporate/Fraud), Employment, Regulatory Law

ROBINSON MR SAM ANDREW

Tooks Chambers
81 Farringdon Street, London EC4A 4BL ☎ 020 7842 7575 ✉ clerks@tooks.co.uk
Call Date: Oct 2002, Middle Temple

ROBINSON-YOUNG MR DAVID TILLEY

Dere Street Barristers
33 Broad Chare, Newcastle Upon Tyne NE1 3DQ ☎ 0844 3351551 ✉ clerks@derestreet.co.uk
Call Date: Jul 1999, Lincoln's Inn
Pupil Supervisor

Practising Areas: Discrimination, Employment

ROBSON MR JOHN MALCOLM

Arden Chambers
20 Bloomsbury Square, London WC1A 2NS ☎ 020 7242 4244 ✉ clerks@ardenchambers.com
Call Date: Jul 1974, Inner Temple
Pupil Supervisor

ROCHE MR PATRICK RICHARD REDMOND

Tooks Chambers
81 Farringdon Street, London EC4A 4BL ☎ 020 7842 7575 ✉ clerks@tooks.co.uk
Call Date: Jul 1977, Middle Temple
Pupil Supervisor, Recorder

Practising Areas: Administrative, Civil Liberties, Common Law (General), Crime, Human Rights, Parliamentary

RODDICK MISS HELEN

9 Park Place
Cardiff, South Glamorgan CF10 3DP
☎ 029 2038 2731 ✉ clerks@9parkplace.co.uk
Call Date: Jul 2004, Gray's Inn

RODHAM MISS SUSAN ANNE

5 King's Bench Walk
5 King's Bench Walk, Temple, London EC4Y 7DN ☎ 020 7353 5638 ✉ clerks@5kbw.co.uk
Call Date: Nov 1989, Gray's Inn
Pupil Supervisor

ROGERS MR CHRISTOPHER THOMAS

Five Paper
Ground Floor, 5 Paper Buildings, Temple, London EC4Y 7HB ☎ 020 7815 3200
Call Date: Jul 2004, Middle Temple

Practising Areas: Asset Finance, Banking, Bankruptcy, Commercial Litigation, Company & Commercial

ROGERS MISS CHRISTY ABIGAIL

Ingenuity IP Chambers
Chambers Legal Service, 71b Queensway, Petts Wood, Kent BR5 1DQ
✉ lp@chamberslegalservice.com
No. 3 Fleet Street Chambers
3 Fleet Street, London EC4Y 1DP
☎ 020 7936 4474 ✉ clerks@3fleetstreet.com
Call Date: Oct 1999, Middle Temple

Practising Areas: Commercial Litigation, Competition, Copyright, Defamation, EC & Competition Law, Entertainment, Film, Cable & TV, Information Technology, Intellectual Property, Patents, Telecommunications, Trademarks

ROGERS MR DANIEL JAMES

Number 7 Harrington Street Chambers
7 Harrington Street, Liverpool L2 9YH
☎ 0151 242 0707 ✉ clerks@7hs.co.uk
Call Date: Oct 1997, Inner Temple
Pupil Supervisor

Practising Areas: Commercial Litigation, Common Law (General), Landlord & Tenant, Personal Injury, Professional Negligence, Sale & Carriage of Goods

ROGERS MR IAN PAUL

Monckton Chambers
1 & 2 Raymond Buildings, Gray's Inn, London WC1R 5NR ☎ 020 7405 7211
✉ chambers@monckton.com
Call Date: Oct 1995, Gray's Inn
Pupil Supervisor

Practising Areas: Administrative, Banking, Civil Liberties, Commercial Litigation, Common Law (General), Discrimination, EC & Competition Law, Education, Employment, Entertainment, Insurance, Professional Negligence, Sale & Carriage of Goods, Telecommunications

ROGERS MR MICHAEL PETER

Chambers of Mr Ami Feder
Ground Floor, Lamb Building, Temple, London EC4Y 7AS ☎ 020 7797 7788
✉ clerks@lambbuilding.co.uk
Chambers of Mr Ami Feder
Ground Floor, Lamb Building, Temple, London EC4Y 7AS ☎ 020 7797 7788
✉ clerks@lambbuilding.co.uk
Call Date: Jul 2002, Lincoln's Inn

Practising Areas: Common Law (General), Crime, Employment, Housing, Landlord & Tenant, Personal Injury

ROOKE MR ALEXANDER JOHN GILES

Argent Chambers
5 Bell Yard, London WC2A 2JR
☎ 020 7556 5500
✉ briefsin@argentchambers.co.uk
Call Date: Jul 2001, Lincoln's Inn

Practising Areas: Common Law (General), Coroners Inquests, Courts Martial, Crime, Crime (Corporate/Fraud), Defamation, Inquests, Licensing, Road Traffic And Highways

ROONEY MR PAUL

QEB Hollis Whiteman
1-2 Laurence Pountney Hill, London EC4R 0EU ☎ 020 7933 8855 ✉ barristers@qebhw.co.uk
New Court Chambers
3 Broad Chare, Newcastle Upon Tyne NE1 3DQ ☎ 0191 232 1980
✉ clerks@newcourt-chambers.co.uk
Call Date: Jul 2007, Inner Temple

Practising Areas: Crime, Regulatory Law

ROSE MR ALEXANDER JAMES

Garden Court Chambers
57-60 Lincoln's Inn Fields, London WC2A 3LJ
☎ 020 7993 7600 ✉ info@gclaw.co.uk
Call Date: Jul 2003, Gray's Inn

ROSE MR DAVID LESLIE

No.6 Park Square
Leeds LS1 2LW ☎0113 245 9763
✉Tim@no6.co.uk
Call Date: Jul 1977, Middle Temple
Pupil Supervisor

ROSE MISS PAMELA SUSAN

1 Mitre Court Buildings
1 Mitre Court Buildings, Temple, London EC4Y 7BS ☎020 7452 8900 ✉clerks@1mcb.com
Call Date: Jul 1980, Inner Temple
Pupil Supervisor

Practising Areas: Civil Liberties, Crime, Crime (Corporate/Fraud)

ROSEMARINE MR ANDREW MARC

Chambers of Mr A M Rosemarine
International Law Chambers, 78 Cavendish Road, Salford, Manchester M7 4WA
☎0161 740 3861 ✉help@rosemarine.co.uk
Call Date: Nov 1989, Gray's Inn

Practising Areas: Civil Liberties, EC & Competition Law, Foreign Law, Parliamentary, Private International, Professional Negligence, Public International

ROSEN MR JONATHAN LEON

1 Gray's Inn Square
Ground Floor, 1 Gray's Inn Square, London WC1R 5AA ☎020 7405 0001
Call Date: Nov 1996, Gray's Inn

Practising Areas: Courts Martial, Crime, Crime (Corporate/Fraud)

ROSENBLATT MR JEREMY GEORGE

42 Bedford Row
London WC1R 4LL ☎020 7831 0222
✉clerks@42br.com
Call Date: Jul 1985, Gray's Inn

Practising Areas: Care Proceedings, Children's Law, Family, Family Provision, Foreign Law, Franchising

ROSS MR ANTHONY JOHN

1 Pump Court
Elm Court, Temple, London EC4Y 7AB
☎020 7842 7070 ✉(name)@pumpcourt.co.uk
Call Date: Oct 1991, Lincoln's Inn

ROSS MR GORDON MACRAE

3 Temple Gardens
Lower Ground Floor, 3 Temple Gardens, Temple, London EC4Y 9AU ☎020 7353 3102
✉clerks@3tg.co.uk
Call Date: Jul 1986, Inner Temple

Practising Areas: Crime, Crime (Corporate/Fraud), Road Traffic And Highways

ROSS MS JENNIFER

King's Bench Chambers
Wellington House, 175 Holdenhurst Road, Bournemouth, Dorset BH8 8DQ
☎01202 250025
Call Date: Jul 2007, Middle Temple

Practising Areas: Family

ROSS MR SIDNEY DAVID

11 Stone Buildings
11 Stone Buildings, Lincoln's Inn, London WC2A 3TG ☎020 7831 6381 ✉clerks@11sb.com
Call Date: Jul 1983, Middle Temple
Pupil Supervisor

Practising Areas: Chancery (General), Chancery (Land Law), Conveyancing, Equity, Wills & Trusts, Family Provision, Probate & Administration, Professional Negligence

ROSS MR SIMON HADLEIGH

Zenith Chambers
10 Park Square, Leeds LS1 2LH
☎0113 245 5438 ✉clerks@zenithchambers.co.uk
Call Date: Nov 1999, Lincoln's Inn
Pupil Supervisor

Practising Areas: Common Law (General), Personal Injury, Professional Negligence

ROTHWELL MRS JOANNE LESLEY

No5 Chambers
Fountain Court, Steelhouse Lane, Birmingham B4 6DR ☎0845 210 5555 ✉info@no5.com
No5 Chambers
Greenwood House, 4-7 Salisbury Court, London EC4Y 8AA ☎0845 210 5555
No5 Chambers
38 Queen Square, Bristol BS1 4QS
☎0845 210 5555
Call Date: Oct 1993, Inner Temple

Practising Areas: Administrative, Family

ROUGHTON MR ASHLEY WENTWORTH

Hogarth Chambers
5 New Square, Lincoln's Inn, London WC2A 3RJ ☎020 7404 0404
✉barristers@hogarthchambers.com
Call Date: Oct 1992, Inner Temple
Pupil Supervisor

Practising Areas: Copyright, Crime, Crime (Corporate/Fraud), EC & Competition Law, Entertainment, Film, Cable & TV, Information Technology, Intellectual Property, Patents, Telecommunications, Trademarks

ROUSE MR JUSTIN CLIVE DOUGLAS

Nine Bedford Row
9 Bedford Row, London WC1R 4AZ
☎020 7489 2727 ✉clerks@9bedfordrow.co.uk
Call Date: Jul 1982, Lincoln's Inn
Pupil Supervisor, Recorder

Practising Areas: Courts Martial, Crime, Crime (Corporate/Fraud)

ROW MR CHARLES PHILIP

Queen Square Chambers
56 Queen Square, Bristol BS1 4PR
☎0117 921 1966 ✉crime@qs-c.co.uk
Call Date: Oct 1993, Lincoln's Inn
Pupil Supervisor

Practising Areas: Crime, Crime (Corporate/Fraud), Family Provision, Regulatory Law

ROWE MISS FREYA EMILY BEATRICE

Thomas More Chambers
7 Lincoln's Inn Fields, London WC2A 3BP
☎020 7404 7000 ✉clerks@thomasmore.co.uk
Call Date: Oct 1996, Inner Temple

Practising Areas: Common Law (General), Crime, Crime (Corporate/Fraud), Family, Family Provision

ROWELL MR GEORGE EDWARD

St John's Chambers
101 Victoria Street, Bristol BS1 6PU
☎0117 923 4700 ✉clerks@stjohnschambers.co.uk
Call Date: Nov 2004, Lincoln's Inn

Practising Areas: Chancery (General), Company & Commercial, Employment, Tax (Capital & Income), Tax (Corporate)

ROWLAND MR ROBIN FRANK

No5 Chambers
Fountain Court, Steelhouse Lane, Birmingham B4 6DR ☎0845 210 5555 ✉info@no5.com
No5 Chambers
Greenwood House, 4-7 Salisbury Court, London EC4Y 8AA ☎0845 210 5555
No5 Chambers
38 Queen Square, Bristol BS1 4QS
☎0845 210 5555
Call Date: Nov 1977, Middle Temple
Pupil Supervisor, Recorder

Practising Areas: Family, Family Provision

ROWLANDS MR PETER FRANCIS CLEVELAND

Garden Court Chambers
57-60 Lincoln's Inn Fields, London WC2A 3LJ
☎020 7993 7600 ✉info@gclaw.co.uk
Call Date: Feb 1990, Middle Temple
Pupil Supervisor

ROWLEY-FOX MS RACHAEL

Garden Court Chambers
57-60 Lincoln's Inn Fields, London WC2A 3LJ
☎020 7993 7600 ✉info@gclaw.co.uk
Call Date: Jul 1998, Gray's Inn
Pupil Supervisor

ROWLINSON MISS WENDY JULIA

Pallant Chambers
12 North Pallant, Chichester, West Sussex PO19 1TQ ☎01243 784538
✉clerks@pallantchambers.co.uk
Call Date: Jul 1981, Gray's Inn

Practising Areas: Ancillary Relief, Family

ROWNTREE MR EDWARD JOHN PICKERING

Hardwicke
New Square, Lincoln's Inn, London WC2A 3SB ☎020 7242 2523
✉enquiries@hardwicke.co.uk
Call Date: Oct 1996, Lincoln's Inn

Practising Areas: Bankruptcy, Chancery (General), Chancery (Land Law), Commercial Litigation, Commercial Property, Company & Commercial, Equity, Wills & Trusts, Insolvency, Landlord & Tenant, Professional Negligence

C

ROY MR STEFAN ALEXANDER HIREN

5 Pump Court
Ground Floor, 5 Pump Court, Temple, London EC4Y 7AP ☎ 020 7353 2532
✉ clerks@5pumpcourt.com
Call Date: May 1996, Gray's Inn

Practising Areas: Care Proceedings, Chancery (General), Commercial Litigation, Common Law (General), Crime, Crime (Corporate/Fraud), Family, Housing, Landlord & Tenant, Licensing, Local Government, Personal Injury, Professional Negligence, Sale & Carriage of Goods

ROYCE MR DARRYL FRASER

Atkin Chambers
1 Atkin Building, Gray's Inn, London WC1R 5AT ☎ 020 7404 0102
✉ clerks@atkinchambers.com
Call Date: Nov 1976, Gray's Inn
Pupil Supervisor

Practising Areas: Arbitration, Commercial Litigation, Construction, Energy, Information Technology, Local Government, Professional Negligence, Telecommunications

RUBENS MISS JACQUELINE ANN

1 Pump Court
Elm Court, Temple, London EC4Y 7AB
☎ 020 7842 7070 ✉ (name)@pumpcourt.co.uk
Call Date: Nov 1989, Inner Temple

Practising Areas: Administrative, Chancery (Land Law), Common Law (General), Discrimination, Education, Environment, Human Rights, Landlord & Tenant, Local Government, Town & Country Planning

RUDD MR MATTHEW ALLAN

Broadway House Chambers
Broadway House, 9 Bank Street, Bradford, West Yorkshire BD1 1TW ☎ 01274 722560
✉ clerks@broadwayhouse.co.uk
Broadway House Chambers
25 Park Square West, Leeds, West Yorkshire LS1 2PW ☎ 0113 246 2600
✉ clerks@broadwayhouse.co.uk
Call Date: Nov 1994, Inner Temple
Pupil Supervisor

Practising Areas: Ancillary Relief, Employment

RUDD MR MICHAEL

36 Bedford Row
London WC1R 4JH ☎ 020 7421 8000
✉ chambers@36bedfordrow.co.uk
Call Date: Oct 2002, Inner Temple

Practising Areas: Common Law (General), Crime, Crime (Corporate/Fraud), Employment, Environment, Immigration, Landlord & Tenant, Licensing, Local Government, Personal Injury, Regulatory Law, Town & Country Planning

RUDD MISS ZOE ANN

College Chambers
19 Carlton Crescent, Southampton, Hampshire SO15 2ET ☎ 023 8023 0338
✉ clerks@college-chambers.co.uk
Call Date: Jul 2003, Gray's Inn

Practising Areas: Care Proceedings, Family, Family Provision, Mental Health

RUDOLF MR NATHANIEL DAVID

25 Bedford Row
London WC1R 4HD ☎ 020 7067 1500
✉ clerks@25bedfordrow.com
Call Date: Nov 1996, Middle Temple
Pupil Supervisor

Practising Areas: Crime, Crime (Corporate/Fraud)

RUFFELL MR MARK BERESFORD

Pump Court Chambers
31 Southgate Street, Winchester, Hampshire SO23 9EB ☎ 01962 868 161
✉ clerks@3pumpcourt.com
Pump Court Chambers
Upper Ground Floor, 3 Pump Court, Temple, London EC4Y 7AJ ☎ 020 7353 0711
✉ clerks@3pumpcourt.com
Pump Court Chambers
5 Temple Chambers, Temple Street, Swindon SN1 1SQ ☎ 01793 539899
✉ clerks@3pumpcourt.com
Call Date: Nov 1992, Middle Temple

Practising Areas: Courts Martial, Crime, Crime (Corporate/Fraud), Ecclesiastical, Health & Safety, Licensing, Local Government, Regulatory Law

RULE MR JONATHAN DANIEL

Palmyra Chambers
Royal House, 46 Legh Street, Warrington WA1 1UJ ☎ 01925 444919
✉ clerk@palmyrachambers.com
Call Date: Nov 1993, Gray's Inn

RULE MR PHILIP DAVID

Castle Chambers
The Old Fire Station, 90 High Street, Harrow-on-the-Hill, Middlesex HA1 3LP
☎ 020 8423 6579 ✉ info@castlechambers.net
Call Date: Jul 2001, Lincoln's Inn
Pupil Supervisor

Practising Areas: Administrative, Civil Liberties, Common Law (General), Coroners Inquests, Courts Martial, Crime, Crime (Corporate/Fraud), Disciplinary Tribunals, Health & Safety, Human Rights, Inquests, Licensing, Local Government, Public Law, Regulatory Law

RUPASINHA MR SUNIL JAYANTHA

Old Bailey Chambers
15 Old Bailey, London EC4M 7EF
☎ 020 3008 6404
✉ clerks@15oldbaileychambers.com
Call Date: Nov 1983, Inner Temple

Practising Areas: Road Traffic And Highways

RUSH MR CRAIG PETER

2 Bedford Row
London WC1R 4BU ☎ 020 7440 8888
✉ clerks@2bedfordrow.co.uk
Call Date: Nov 1989, Inner Temple
Pupil Supervisor

Practising Areas: Crime, Crime (Corporate/Fraud), Health & Safety

RUSHTON MR JONATHON BARKER

36 Bedford Row
London WC1R 4JH ☎ 020 7421 8000
✉ chambers@36bedfordrow.co.uk
Call Date: Nov 1997, Inner Temple
Pupil Supervisor

Practising Areas: Commercial Property, Common Law (General), Environment, Housing, Local Government, Town & Country Planning

RUSHTON MS NICOLA JANE

Five Paper
Ground Floor, 5 Paper Buildings, Temple, London EC4Y 7HB ☎ 020 7815 3200
Call Date: Oct 1993, Gray's Inn
Pupil Supervisor

Practising Areas: Commercial Litigation, Company & Commercial, Professional Negligence

RUSSELL MS ALISON ELIZABETH

Pump Court Chambers
Upper Ground Floor, 3 Pump Court, Temple, London EC4Y 7AJ ☎ 020 7353 0711
✉ clerks@3pumpcourt.com
Pump Court Chambers
5 Temple Chambers, Temple Street, Swindon SN1 1SQ ☎ 01793 539899
✉ clerks@3pumpcourt.com
Pump Court Chambers
31 Southgate Street, Winchester, Hampshire SO23 9EB ☎ 01962 868 161
✉ clerks@3pumpcourt.com
Call Date: Oct 1993, Middle Temple

RUSSELL MR GRAHAM ALEXANDER

Citadel Chambers
The Citadel, 190 Corporation Street, Birmingham B4 6QD ☎ 0121 233 8500
✉ clerks@citadelchambers.com
Call Date: Nov 2004, Inner Temple

Practising Areas: Civil Liberties, Common Law (General), Crime, Crime (Corporate/Fraud), Employment, Health & Safety, Human Rights, Personal Injury, Regulatory Law

RUSSELL MR GUY JONOTHON

Westgate Chambers
64 High Street, Lewes, East Sussex BN7 1XG
☎ 01273 480510
✉ clerks@westgate-chambers.co.uk
Call Date: Nov 1985, Gray's Inn

Practising Areas: Crime, Crime (Corporate/Fraud), Family, Health & Safety, Licensing, Personal Injury, Town & Country Planning

RUSSELL MISS MARGUERITE

Garden Court Chambers
57-60 Lincoln's Inn Fields, London WC2A 3LJ
☎ 020 7993 7600 ✉ info@gclaw.co.uk
Call Date: Jul 1972, Lincoln's Inn
Pupil Supervisor

Practising Areas: Courts Martial, Crime, Crime (Corporate/Fraud), Human Rights, Public International

RUSSELL MR THOMAS CHARLES WELLDON

KCH Garden Square
1 Oxford Street, Nottingham NG1 5BH
☎ 0115 941 8851 ✉ clerks@kchgardensquare.co.uk
Call Date: Oct 2004, Inner Temple

Practising Areas: Bankruptcy, Chancery (General), Civil Litigation, Commercial Litigation, Common Law (General), Consumer, Employment, Housing, Landlord & Tenant, Medical

Negligence, Partnership, Personal Injury, Professional Negligence, Road Traffic And Highways

RUSSELL-MITRA MISS JESSICA SUPARNA

1 Mitre Court Buildings
1 Mitre Court Buildings, Temple, London EC4Y 7BS ☎020 7452 8900 ✉clerks@1mcb.com
Call Date: Oct 2003, Middle Temple

Practising Areas: Civil Liberties, Common Law (General), Crime, Crime (Corporate/Fraud), Education, Local Government, Regulatory Law

RUSTOM MR SHIRAZ SAM

1 Mitre Court Buildings
1 Mitre Court Buildings, Temple, London EC4Y 7BS ☎020 7452 8900 ✉clerks@1mcb.com
1215 Chambers
1 Fetter Lane, London EC4A 1BR
☎020 3291 1215 ✉admin@1215chambers.com
Cranford Chambers
8 Warwick Court, London WC1R 5DJ
☎020 7404 7454 ✉jemima.ivens@cranfordchambers.com
Call Date: Oct 1998, Middle Temple
Pupil Supervisor

Practising Areas: Common Law (General), Coroners Inquests, Courts Martial, Crime, Crime (Corporate/Fraud), Human Rights, Inquests, Mental Health

RUTHERFORD MISS EMMA VICTORIA

No 8 Chambers
8 Fountain Court, Steelhouse Lane, Birmingham B4 6DR ☎0121 236 5514
✉clerks@no8chambers.co.uk
Call Date: Jul 2002, Middle Temple

Practising Areas: Common Law (General), Crime, Immigration

RUTTER MR GARY MARK

Chambers of Marion Smullen and Kerim Fuad QC
1 Inner Temple Lane, London EC4Y 1AF
☎020 7427 4400 ✉clerks@1itl.com
Call Date: Nov 1997, Gray's Inn

Practising Areas: Crime

RYAN MR DAVID PATRICK

3 Temple Gardens
Lower Ground Floor, 3 Temple Gardens, Temple, London EC4Y 9AU ☎020 7353 3102
✉clerks@3tg.co.uk
Call Date: Nov 1985, Inner Temple
Pupil Supervisor

RYAN MR WILLIAM

Farringdon Chambers
180 Bermondsey Street, London SE1 3TQ
☎020 7089 5700
Corsham Barristers Chambers
New Farm House, Silver Street, Corsham SN13 9PG ☎01225 582582
✉enquiries@corshamlaw.co.uk
Call Date: Oct 1994, Gray's Inn

Practising Areas: Crime, Discrimination, Employment, Equity, Wills & Trusts

RYLE MS KATE FRANCES

5 Pump Court
Ground Floor, 5 Pump Court, Temple, London EC4Y 7AP ☎020 7353 2532
✉clerks@5pumpcourt.com
Call Date: Oct 2002, Inner Temple

Practising Areas: Crime, Licensing

SABIC MS IRENA

Garden Court Chambers
57-60 Lincoln's Inn Fields, London WC2A 3LJ
☎020 7993 7600 ✉info@gclaw.co.uk
Call Date: Oct 2002, Inner Temple

SADD MR PATRICK JAMES THOMAS

Outer Temple Chambers
The Outer Temple, 222 Strand, London WC2R 1BA ☎020 7353 6381
✉clerks@outertemple.com
Call Date: Nov 1984, Middle Temple
Pupil Supervisor

SADIQ MR MUHAMMAD FAISEL

Ely Place Chambers
30 Ely Place, London EC1N 6TD
☎020 7400 9600 ✉admin@elyplace.com
Call Date: Oct 2000, Inner Temple
Pupil Supervisor

Practising Areas: Administrative, Chancery (General), Chancery (Land Law), Commercial Litigation, Common Land, Housing, Human Rights, Landlord & Tenant, Licensing, Local Government

SADIQ MR TARIQ MAHMOOD

St Philips Chambers
55 Temple Row, Birmingham B2 5LS
☎ 0121 246 7000 ✉ clerks@st-philips.com
Call Date: Nov 1993, Gray's Inn

Practising Areas: Discrimination, Employment

SADLER MISS RHIANNON JANE

Westgate Chambers
64 High Street, Lewes, East Sussex BN7 1XG
☎ 01273 480510
✉ clerks@westgate-chambers.co.uk
Call Date: Jul 2004, Middle Temple

Practising Areas: Courts Martial, Crime, Crime (Corporate/Fraud)

SAGAR MR LEIGH

New Square Chambers
12 New Square, Lincoln's Inn, London WC2A 3SW ☎ 020 7419 8000 ✉ robin.hollington@newsquarechambers.co.uk
Call Date: Jul 1983, Lincoln's Inn
Pupil Supervisor

Practising Areas: Equity, Wills & Trusts, Family Provision, Private International, Probate & Administration, Tax (Capital & Income)

SAGOE MR FREDRICK KOJO

Villa Chambers
33 St Peters Road, Oundle, Peterborough PE8 4NU ☎ 01832 273 097
Call Date: Jul 1983, Gray's Inn

SAIFEE MR FAISAL AFTAAB

Thomas More Chambers
7 Lincoln's Inn Fields, London WC2A 3BP
☎ 020 7404 7000 ✉ clerks@thomasmore.co.uk
Call Date: Jul 2003, Middle Temple

Practising Areas: Chancery (General), Civil Liberties, Common Law (General), Discrimination, Employment, Environment, Housing, Human Rights, Landlord & Tenant, Local Government, Personal Injury

SAINI MR PARMINDER PAUL SINGH

12 Old Square Chambers
1st Floor, 12 Old Square, Lincoln's Inn, London WC2A 3TX ☎ 020 7404 0875
✉ clerks@12oldsquare.com
Call Date: Nov 2001, Gray's Inn

Practising Areas: Arbitration, Civil Litigation, Common Law (General), Copyright, Defamation, Employment, Entertainment, Foreign Law, Human Rights, Immigration, Intellectual Property

SALLON MR CHRISTOPHER ROBERT QC (1994)

Doughty Street Chambers
53-54 Doughty Street, London WC1N 2LS
☎ 020 7404 1313 ✉ enquiries@doughtystreet.co.uk
Doughty Street Chambers
Pall Mall Court, 61-67 King Street, Manchester M2 4PD ☎ 0161 618 1066
Doughty Street Chambers
5th Floor, Broad Quay House, Prince Street, Bristol BS1 4DJ ☎ 01179 058 717
Call Date: Jul 1973, Gray's Inn
Recorder

Practising Areas: Courts Martial, Crime, Crime (Corporate/Fraud)

SALMON MR JONATHAN CARL

St Philips Chambers
55 Temple Row, Birmingham B2 5LS
☎ 0121 246 7000 ✉ clerks@st-philips.com
Call Date: Nov 1987, Inner Temple
Pupil Supervisor

Practising Areas: Crime (Corporate/Fraud), Environment, Health & Safety, Licensing, Local Government, Regulatory Law

SALTER MR MICHAEL RICHARD

Ely Place Chambers
30 Ely Place, London EC1N 6TD
☎ 020 7400 9600 ✉ admin@elyplace.com
Call Date: Oct 1999, Inner Temple
Pupil Supervisor

Practising Areas: Common Law (General), Employment, Licensing, Personal Injury, Regulatory Law

SALTER MISS SIBBY ANNE VICTORIA

3 Temple Gardens
Lower Ground Floor, 3 Temple Gardens, Temple, London EC4Y 9AU ☎ 020 7353 3102
✉ clerks@3tg.co.uk
Call Date: Oct 1991, Middle Temple

Practising Areas: Crime

C

SAMPSON MR GRAEME WILLIAM

3 PB Barristers
3 Paper Buildings, Temple, London EC4Y 7EU ☎020 7583 8055
3 PB Barristers
Royal Talbot House, 2 Victoria Street, Bristol, Avon BS1 6BB ☎0117 928 1520
3 PB Barristers
4 St Peter Street, Winchester SO23 8BW ☎01962 868884 ✉clerks.winchester@3paper.co.uk
3 PB Barristers
23 Beaumont Street, Oxford OX1 2NP ☎01865 793 736
3 PB Barristers
30 Christchurch Road, Bournemouth, Dorset BH1 3PD ☎01202 292102 ✉clerks.bournemouth@3paper.co.uk
Call Date: Nov 1981, Gray's Inn
Pupil Supervisor

Practising Areas: Construction, Professional Negligence, Town & Country Planning

SAMPSON DR TIMOTHY MICHAEL GEORGE

One Essex Court
1st Floor, Temple, London EC4Y 9AR ☎020 7936 3030 ✉clerks@1ec.co.uk
Call Date: Mar 2000, Lincoln's Inn

Practising Areas: Chancery (General), Commercial Litigation, Company & Commercial, Competition, Copyright, Information Technology, Intellectual Property, Patents, Trademarks

SAMRA MISS SHARN

Broadway House Chambers
Broadway House, 9 Bank Street, Bradford, West Yorkshire BD1 1TW ☎01274 722560 ✉clerks@broadwayhouse.co.uk
Broadway House Chambers
25 Park Square West, Leeds, West Yorkshire LS1 2PW ☎0113 246 2600 ✉clerks@broadwayhouse.co.uk
Call Date: Nov 2002, Lincoln's Inn

Practising Areas: Employment, Family, Personal Injury

SAMUEL MISS ANA ELIZABETH

Call Date: Jul 2004, Inner Temple

SAMUEL MR RICHARD GEOFFREY GRAHAM

3 Hare Court
3 Hare Court, Temple, London EC4Y 7BJ ☎020 7415 7800 ✉clerks@3harecourt.com
Call Date: Nov 1996, Middle Temple
Pupil Supervisor

Practising Areas: Arbitration, Commercial Litigation, Company & Commercial, Employment

SAMUELS MR LESLIE JOHN QC (2011)

Pump Court Chambers
Upper Ground Floor, 3 Pump Court, Temple, London EC4Y 7AJ ☎020 7353 0711 ✉clerks@3pumpcourt.com
Pump Court Chambers
31 Southgate Street, Winchester, Hampshire SO23 9EB ☎01962 868 161 ✉clerks@3pumpcourt.com
Riverview Chambers
Hamilton House, 1 Temple Avenue, London EC4Y 0HA ☎0844 225 3999 ✉chrisbaylis@riverviewchambers.com
Call Date: Jul 1989, Gray's Inn
Pupil Supervisor

Practising Areas: Employment, Equity, Wills & Trusts, Family, Family Provision, Probate & Administration

SANDERSON MS ELEANOR KATHLEEN

2 Bedford Row
London WC1R 4BU ☎020 7440 8888 ✉clerks@2bedfordrow.co.uk
Call Date: Jul 2005, Inner Temple

SANDFORD MR ROBERT STANLEY

Bank House Chambers
Old Bank House, Hartshead, Sheffield S1 2EL ☎0114 275 1223 ✉w.digby@bankhousechambers.co.uk
Call Date: Nov 1999, Middle Temple

Practising Areas: Crime, Crime (Corporate/Fraud), Regulatory Law

SANDFORD MR SIMON JOHN AUSTIN

5 King's Bench Walk
5 King's Bench Walk, Temple, London EC4Y 7DN ☎020 7353 5638 ✉clerks@5kbw.co.uk
Call Date: Nov 1979, Gray's Inn
Pupil Supervisor

Practising Areas: Care Proceedings, Courts Martial, Crime, Crime (Corporate/Fraud), Family

SANDHAM MR JAMES ANDREW

Arden Chambers
20 Bloomsbury Square, London WC1A 2NS
☎ 020 7242 4244 ✉ clerks@ardenchambers.com
Call Date: Mar 2003, Lincoln's Inn

Practising Areas: Bankruptcy, Chancery (General), Chancery (Land Law), Commercial Property, Common Land, Common Law (General), Construction, Conveyancing, Discrimination, Education, Equity, Wills & Trusts, Housing, Human Rights, Landlord & Tenant, Local Government, Probate & Administration

SANDIFORD MR JONATHAN

St Paul's Chambers
5th Floor, St Paul's House, 23 Park Square South, Leeds LS1 2ND ☎ 0113 245 5866
Call Date: Oct 1992, Gray's Inn

SANGSTER MR NIGEL QC (1998)

25 Bedford Row
London WC1R 4HD ☎ 020 7067 1500
✉ clerks@25bedfordrow.com
Call Date: Nov 1976, Middle Temple
Recorder

Practising Areas: Crime (Corporate/Fraud), Regulatory Law

SANTAMERA MISS LOUISE ALEXANDRIA

New Bailey Chambers
4th Floor, Corn Exchange, Fenwick Street, Liverpool, Merseyside L2 7QS
☎ 0151 236 9402 ✉ clerks@newbailey.com
Call Date: Oct 2002, Gray's Inn

Practising Areas: Crime, Employment, Immigration, Public Law

SAPSTEAD MISS LOUISE ANNE

KCH Garden Square
1 Oxford Street, Nottingham NG1 5BH
☎ 0115 941 8851 ✉ clerks@kchgardensquare.co.uk
Call Date: Jul 2004, Lincoln's Inn

Practising Areas: Care Proceedings, Common Law (General), Family, Family Provision

SASTRY MR BOB AJAY DWARAKANATH

Call Date: Oct 1996, Inner Temple

SAUNDERS MR MARK DANIEL

No.6 Park Square
Leeds LS1 2LW ☎ 0113 245 9763
✉ Tim@no6.co.uk
Call Date: Oct 2002, Inner Temple

SAUNDERS MR NEIL

3 Raymond Buildings
3 Raymond Buildings, Gray's Inn, London WC1R 5BH ☎ 020 7400 6400
✉ clerks@3rblaw.com
Call Date: Nov 1983, Middle Temple
Pupil Supervisor, Recorder

Practising Areas: Crime, Crime (Corporate/Fraud)

SAUNDERS MISS ZOE ALICE

St John's Chambers
101 Victoria Street, Bristol BS1 6PU
☎ 0117 923 4700 ✉ clerks@stjohnschambers.co.uk
Call Date: Oct 2003, Gray's Inn

Practising Areas: Chancery (Land Law), Equity, Wills & Trusts, Family, Family Provision, Probate & Administration

SAUNT MS LINDA PATRICIA

Chambers of Andrew Mitchell QC
33 Chancery Lane, London WC2A 1EN
☎ 020 7440 9950 ✉ clerks@33cllaw.com
Call Date: Nov 1986, Inner Temple

Practising Areas: Crime (Corporate/Fraud)

SAVVIDES MISS MARIA

Northampton Chambers
10 Spencer Parade, Northampton NN1 5AQ
☎ 01604 636271
✉ clerks@northampton-chambers.co.uk
Call Date: Jul 1986, Middle Temple
Pupil Supervisor

Practising Areas: Care Proceedings, Crime, Family, Family Provision

SAWTELL MR DAVID ROBERT FRASER

4 King's Bench Walk
2nd Floor, 4 King's Bench Walk, Temple, London EC4Y 7DL ☎ 020 7822 7000
✉ clerks@4kbw.co.uk
Call Date: Nov 2005, Lincoln's Inn

Practising Areas: Commercial Litigation, Commercial Property, Common Law (General), Company & Commercial, Discrimination, Employment, Family, Landlord & Tenant, Personal Injury, Sale & Carriage of Goods

SAXBY MR OLIVER CHARLES JOHN

6 Pump Court
1st Floor, 6 Pump Court, Temple, London EC4Y 7AR ☎ 020 7797 8400
✉ richardconstable@6pumpcourt.co.uk
6 Pump Court Chambers
6-8 Mill Street, Maidstone, Kent ME15 6XH
☎ 01622 688094 ✉ annexe@6pumpcourt.co.uk
Call Date: Nov 1992, Inner Temple
Pupil Supervisor

Practising Areas: Crime, Crime (Corporate/Fraud)

SAXTON MISS NICOLA HELEN

St Paul's Chambers
5th Floor, St Paul's House, 23 Park Square South, Leeds LS1 2ND ☎ 0113 245 5866
Call Date: Nov 1992, Inner Temple
Pupil Supervisor

Practising Areas: Family Provision, Pensions

SAYED MISS NERMINE ABDEL

Old Bailey Chambers
15 Old Bailey, London EC4M 7EF
☎ 020 3008 6404
✉ clerks@15oldbaileychambers.com
Call Date: Nov 2001, Middle Temple

Practising Areas: Crime, Crime (Corporate/Fraud)

SAYED MISS RUBY

1 Pump Court
Elm Court, Temple, London EC4Y 7AB
☎ 020 7842 7070 ✉ (name)@pumpcourt.co.uk
Call Date: Mar 1999, Inner Temple

Practising Areas: Care Proceedings, Family

SCALLY MISS JOSEPHINE THERESA SARAH

Palmyra Chambers
Royal House, 46 Legh Street, Warrington WA1 1UJ ☎ 01925 444919
✉ clerk@palmyrachambers.com
Call Date: Feb 1984, Lincoln's Inn

Practising Areas: Administrative, Common Law (General), Consumer, Immigration, Local Government, Mental Health, Personal Injury

SCHAW MILLER MR STEPHEN GRANT

New Square Chambers
12 New Square, Lincoln's Inn, London WC2A 3SW ☎ 020 7419 8000 ✉ robin.hollington@newsquarechambers.co.uk
Call Date: Nov 1988, Inner Temple
Pupil Supervisor

SCHOFIELD MR THOMAS LEON

No5 Chambers
Fountain Court, Steelhouse Lane, Birmingham B4 6DR ☎ 0845 210 5555 ✉ info@no5.com
No5 Chambers
Greenwood House, 4-7 Salisbury Court, London EC4Y 8AA ☎ 0845 210 5555
No5 Chambers
38 Queen Square, Bristol BS1 4QS
☎ 0845 210 5555
Call Date: Oct 2001, Lincoln's Inn

Practising Areas: Crime, Crime (Corporate/Fraud)

SCOBIE MR JAMES TIMOTHY NORMAN QC (2010)

Garden Court Chambers
57-60 Lincoln's Inn Fields, London WC2A 3LJ
☎ 020 7993 7600 ✉ info@gclaw.co.uk
Call Date: Jul 1984, Gray's Inn
Pupil Supervisor

SCOLDING MISS FIONA KATE

Hardwicke
New Square, Lincoln's Inn, London WC2A 3SB ☎ 020 7242 2523
✉ enquiries@hardwicke.co.uk
Call Date: Nov 1996, Gray's Inn
Pupil Supervisor

Practising Areas: Administrative, Civil Liberties, Education, Housing, Local Government, Mental Health

SCOTT MR ANDREW DAVID PETER

Park Lane Plowden
19 Westgate, Leeds LS1 2RD
☎ 0113 228 5049 ✉ clerks@parklaneplowden.co.uk
Call Date: Jul 2002, Gray's Inn

Practising Areas: Civil Liberties, Common Law (General), Consumer, Data Protection, Disciplinary Tribunals, Healthcare, Human Rights, Inquests, Personal Injury, Regulatory Law

SCOTT BELL MRS ROSALIND SARA

Trinity Chambers
The Custom House, 39 Quayside, Newcastle Upon Tyne NE1 3DE ☎ 0191 232 1927
✉ info@trinitychambers.co.uk
Trinity Chambers
Multi Media Exchange, 72-80 Corporation Road, Middlesbrough TS1 2RF
☎ 01642 247569 ✉ info@trinitychambers.co.uk
Call Date: Oct 1993, Middle Temple
Pupil Supervisor

Practising Areas: Courts Martial, Crime, Crime (Corporate/Fraud), Disciplinary Tribunals, Licensing, Regulatory Law

SCOTT HOLLAND MR GIDEON SILAS

Keating Chambers
15 Essex Street, London WC2R 3AA
☎ 020 7544 2600 ✉ clerks@keatingchambers.com
Call Date: Oct 1999, Lincoln's Inn
Pupil Supervisor

Practising Areas: Arbitration, Commercial Litigation, Construction, Energy, Environment, Information Technology, Professional Negligence

SCOTT MS LAURA LOUISE

14 Gray's Inn Square
14 Gray's Inn Square, Gray's Inn, London WC1R 5JP ☎ 020 7242 0858 ✉ clerks@14gis.co.uk
Call Date: Jul 2001, Inner Temple

Practising Areas: Care Proceedings, Education, Family

C

SCOTT MR MATTHEW JOHN

Pump Court Chambers
Upper Ground Floor, 3 Pump Court, Temple, London EC4Y 7AJ ☎ 020 7353 0711
✉ clerks@3pumpcourt.com
Pump Court Chambers
5 Temple Chambers, Temple Street, Swindon SN1 1SQ ☎ 01793 539899
✉ clerks@3pumpcourt.com
Pump Court Chambers
31 Southgate Street, Winchester, Hampshire SO23 9EB ☎ 01962 868 161
✉ clerks@3pumpcourt.com
Call Date: Nov 1985, Inner Temple
Pupil Supervisor

Practising Areas: Courts Martial, Crime (Corporate/Fraud), Regulatory Law

SCOTT MR STUART

1 Pump Court
Elm Court, Temple, London EC4Y 7AB
☎ 020 7842 7070 ✉ (name)@pumpcourt.co.uk
Call Date: Nov 1998, Inner Temple

Practising Areas: Education, Family, Family Provision

SCREECHE-POWELL MISS GENEVIEVE BERNADETTE FAITH

Field Court Chambers
5 Field Court, Gray's Inn, London WC1R 5EF
☎ 020 7405 6114 ✉ clerks@fieldcourt.co.uk
Call Date: Oct 1997, Gray's Inn

SCULLY MRS JENNIFER LESLEY

St Johns Buildings Liverpool
8th Floor India Buildings, Water Street, Liverpool L2 0XG ☎ 0151 243 6000
✉ clerk@stjohnsbuildings.co.uk
16 Winckley Square
Preston PR1 3JJ ☎ 01772 256100
St Johns Buildings
24a - 28 St John Street, Manchester M3 4DJ
☎ 0161 214 1500 ✉ clerk@stjohnsbuildings.co.uk
Call Date: Jul 2006, Middle Temple

SCUTT MR DAVID ROBERT

9-12 Bell Yard
London WC2A 2JR ☎ 020 7400 1800
✉ clerks@9-12bellyard.com
Call Date: Nov 1989, Middle Temple
Pupil Supervisor

Practising Areas: Courts Martial, Crime, Crime (Corporate/Fraud), Human Rights

SEAL MR JULIUS DAMIEN

Chambers of Mr Julius Seal
189 Randolph Avenue, Maida Vale, London W9 1DJ ☎ 020 7328 0158 ✉ julius.seal@ntlworld.com
Call Date: Nov 1967, Lincoln's Inn
Pupil Supervisor

Practising Areas: Bankruptcy, Care Proceedings, Chancery (General), Commercial Litigation, Common Law (General), Company & Commercial, Housing, Insolvency, Landlord & Tenant, Personal Injury, Professional Negligence

SEAR MISS JOANNE

13 King's Bench Walk
13 King's Bench Walk, Temple, London EC4Y 7EN ☎020 7353 7204 ✉clerks@13kbw.co.uk
13 KBW
32 Beaumont Street, Oxford OX1 2NP
☎01865 311066 ✉clerks@13kbw.co.uk
Call Date: Jul 2004, Gray's Inn

Practising Areas: Crime, Crime (Corporate/ Fraud), Regulatory Law

SEARLE MISS CORINNE LOUISE TEAGUE

Walnut House
63 St. David's Hill, Exeter, Devon EX4 4DW
☎01392 279751 ✉clerks@walnuthouse.co.uk
Call Date: Jul 1982, Gray's Inn
Pupil Supervisor, Recorder

SEARLE MR JASON ARIO XAVIER

Call Date: Oct 1993, Middle Temple

SEARS MR ROBERT DAVID MURRAY QC (2003)

Four New Square
Four New Square, Lincoln's Inn, London WC2A 3RJ ☎020 7822 2000
✉barristers@4newsquare.com
Call Date: Nov 1984, Middle Temple

Practising Areas: Arbitration, Commercial Litigation, Construction, Energy, Information Technology, Local Government, Professional Negligence, Telecommunications

SEDDON MR JAMES DURAN

Garden Court Chambers
57-60 Lincoln's Inn Fields, London WC2A 3LJ
☎020 7993 7600 ✉info@gclaw.co.uk
Call Date: Feb 1994, Middle Temple

SEEBORUTH MR ROYLN JEAN-PAUL

Chambers of Royln Seeboruth
Abbotts Close Chambers, 4 Abbotts Close, Aylesbury, Bucks HP20 1HZ ☎01296 393329
✉rseeboruth@live.co.uk
Call Date: Nov 1986, Middle Temple
Pupil Supervisor

Practising Areas: Administrative, Ancillary Relief, Chancery (General), Civil Liberties, Commercial Litigation, Commodities, Common Law (General), Copyright, Crime, Discrimination, Employment, Family, Financial Services, Housing, Human Rights, Immigration, Intellectual Property, International Trade, Landlord & Tenant, Licensing, Patents, Personal Injury, Private International, Professional Negligence, Public International, Sale & Carriage of Goods, Sports, Tax (Capital & Income), Tax (Corporate), Town & Country Planning, Trademarks, Unit Trusts

SEFI MR BENEDICT JOHN

Harcourt Chambers
1st Floor, 2 Harcourt Buildings, Temple, London EC4Y 9DB ☎0844 561 7135
Harcourt Chambers
Churchill House, 3 St Aldate's Courtyard, St Aldate's, Oxford OX1 1BN ☎0844 561 7135
Call Date: Jul 1972, Inner Temple
Pupil Supervisor

Practising Areas: Chancery (Land Law), Common Land, Environment, Equity, Wills & Trusts, Family, Family Provision, Landlord & Tenant, Probate & Administration

SEFTON MR NICHOLAS EDWARD

Linenhall Chambers
1 Stanley Place, Chester CH1 2LU
☎01244 348282
✉clerks@linenhallchambers.co.uk
Pendragon Chambers
Suite 7, J Shed, Kings Road, SA1 Waterfront, Swansea SA1 8PL ☎01792 411188
✉clerks@pendragonchambers.com
Call Date: Jul 2004, Gray's Inn

Practising Areas: Care Proceedings, Crime, Equity, Wills & Trusts, Family

SEFTON-SMITH MR LLOYD

Lamb Chambers
Lamb Building, Elm Court, Temple, London EC4Y 7AS ☎020 7797 8300
✉info@lambchambers.co.uk
Call Date: Oct 1993, Lincoln's Inn
Pupil Supervisor

Practising Areas: Bankruptcy, Chancery (Land Law), Civil Litigation, Commercial Litigation, Common Law (General), Conveyancing, Ecclesiastical, Equity, Wills & Trusts, Housing, Information Technology, Inquests, Insurance, Land, Landlord & Tenant, Professional Negligence

SEGUSS MISS PENELOPE MARIE

The Chambers of Penelope Seguss
28 Burcote Road, London SW18 3LQ
☎020 8877 0707 ✉pseguss@btinternet.com
Call Date: Oct 1996, Gray's Inn

Practising Areas: Family

SEITLER MS DEBORAH

Renaissance Chambers
5th Floor, Gray's Inn Chambers, Gray's Inn, London WC1R 5JA ☎ 020 7404 1111
✉ clerks@renaissancechambers.co.uk
Call Date: Nov 1991, Inner Temple

SEKAR MR CHANDRA

Angell Park Chambers
Unit 11, Amberley Court, Angell Road, London SW9 7HL ☎ 020 7737 5957
✉ info@chandrasekar.co.uk
Call Date: Mar 1996, Gray's Inn

Practising Areas: Civil Liberties, Common Law (General), Coroners Inquests, Courts Martial, Crime, Crime (Corporate/Fraud), Disciplinary Tribunals, Discrimination, Employment

SEKHON MRS JAGDEEP KAUR

No 8 Chambers
8 Fountain Court, Steelhouse Lane, Birmingham B4 6DR ☎ 0121 236 5514
✉ clerks@no8chambers.co.uk
Call Date: Nov 1999, Gray's Inn

SEKHON MR NARINDER SINGH

Sovereign Chambers
46 Park Place, Leeds LS1 2RY
☎ 0113 245 1841
✉ clerks@sovereignchambers.co.uk
Call Date: Nov 2000, Lincoln's Inn

Practising Areas: Crime, Crime (Corporate/Fraud), Health & Safety, Human Rights, Immigration

SELBY MR ANDREW ROBERT VINCENT

Chambers of Mr Ami Feder
Ground Floor, Lamb Building, Temple, London EC4Y 7AS ☎ 020 7797 7788
✉ clerks@lambbuilding.co.uk
Lamb Building
22 Ship Street, Brighton BN1 1AD
☎ 01273 820490 ✉ admin@lambbuilding.co.uk
Chambers of Mr Ami Feder
Ground Floor, Lamb Building, Temple, London EC4Y 7AS ☎ 020 7797 7788
✉ clerks@lambbuilding.co.uk
Call Date: Nov 1997, Gray's Inn
Pupil Supervisor

SELBY MR JONATHAN LEE

Keating Chambers
15 Essex Street, London WC2R 3AA
☎ 020 7544 2600 ✉ clerks@keatingchambers.com
Call Date: Nov 1999, Gray's Inn
Pupil Supervisor

Practising Areas: Construction, Professional Negligence

SELBY MR LAWRENCE JULIAN CATELLO

Nine Bedford Row
9 Bedford Row, London WC1R 4AZ
☎ 020 7489 2727 ✉ clerks@9bedfordrow.co.uk
Call Date: Mar 1997, Gray's Inn

Practising Areas: Arbitration, Sports

SELF MR GARY PETER

College Chambers
19 Carlton Crescent, Southampton, Hampshire SO15 2ET ☎ 023 8023 0338
✉ clerks@college-chambers.co.uk
St David's Chambers
Myrtle Cottage, Norton Road, Mumbles, Swansea SA3 5TQ ☎ 01792 559924 ✉ j.vallack@ntlworld.com
Call Date: Oct 1991, Lincoln's Inn
Pupil Supervisor

Practising Areas: Care Proceedings, Common Law (General), Discrimination, Employment, Family, Family Provision

SELLERS MR GRAHAM

Atlantic Chambers
4-6 Cook Street, Liverpool L2 9QU
☎ 0151 236 4421 ✉ info@atlanticchambers.co.uk
Call Date: Oct 1990, Middle Temple

Practising Areas: Agriculture, Arbitration, Banking, Bankruptcy, Chancery (General), Chancery (Land Law), Commercial Litigation, Commercial Property, Company & Commercial, Construction, Conveyancing, Equity, Wills & Trusts, Family Provision, Housing, Insolvency, Insurance, Landlord & Tenant, Partnership, Probate & Administration, Professional Negligence, Sale & Carriage of Goods, Town & Country Planning

C

SELVARATNAM MISS VASANTI EMILY INDRANI QC (2001)

Stone Chambers
4 Field Court, Gray's Inn, London WC1R 5EF
☎ 020 7440 6900 ✉ clerks@stonechambers.com
Call Date: Jul 1983, Middle Temple
Recorder

Practising Areas: Admiralty, Arbitration, Banking, Commercial Litigation, Commodities, Insurance, Insurance/Reinsurance, International Trade, Private International, Sale & Carriage of Goods, Shipping/Admiralty

SEN MR ADITYA KUMAR

Coram Chambers
9-11 Fulwood Place, London WC1V 6HG
☎ 020 7092 3700 ✉ mail@coramchambers.co.uk
Call Date: Jul 1977, Lincoln's Inn
Pupil Supervisor

Practising Areas: Chancery (General), Commercial Litigation, Common Law (General), Company & Commercial, Crime (Corporate/Fraud), Landlord & Tenant, Partnership, Private International, Sale & Carriage of Goods

SERGIDES MS MARINA

Garden Court Chambers
57-60 Lincoln's Inn Fields, London WC2A 3LJ
☎ 020 7993 7600 ✉ info@gclaw.co.uk
Call Date: Nov 2000, Inner Temple

SERR MR ASHLEY BARRIE

Park Lane Plowden
19 Westgate, Leeds LS1 2RD
☎ 0113 228 5049 ✉ clerks@parklaneplowden.co.uk
Call Date: Nov 1996, Middle Temple
Pupil Supervisor

Practising Areas: Commercial Litigation, Common Law (General), Discrimination, Employment

SEYMOUR MR MARK WILLIAM

9-12 Bell Yard
London WC2A 2JR ☎ 020 7400 1800
✉ clerks@9-12bellyard.com
Call Date: Oct 1992, Middle Temple

Practising Areas: Crime, Crime (Corporate/Fraud), Licensing, Local Government

SHALE MR JUSTIN ANTON

King's Bench Chambers
Wellington House, 175 Holdenhurst Road, Bournemouth, Dorset BH8 8DQ
☎ 01202 250025
Call Date: Jul 1982, Inner Temple
Pupil Supervisor

SHALOM MISS MIRIAM

Field Court Chambers
5 Field Court, Gray's Inn, London WC1R 5EF
☎ 020 7405 6114 ✉ clerks@fieldcourt.co.uk
Call Date: Jul 2003, Middle Temple

SHAMIM MR MOHAMMED

Clapham Law Chambers
85 Landor Road, Clapham North, London SW9 9RT ☎ 020 7978 8482
✉ DANNY@claphamlawchambers.co.uk
Call Date: Jul 1975, Lincoln's Inn

Practising Areas: Arbitration, Civil Litigation, Commercial Litigation, Common Law (General), Corporate Finance, Family, Human Rights, Immigration, Landlord & Tenant, Personal Injury, Road Traffic And Highways, Sale & Carriage of Goods

SHANNON MR SIMON JOSEPH

3 Temple Gardens
Lower Ground Floor, 3 Temple Gardens, Temple, London EC4Y 9AU ☎ 020 7353 3102
✉ clerks@3tg.co.uk
Call Date: Mar 1999, Inner Temple

SHAPIRO MR DANIEL JONATHAN

Crown Office Chambers
2 Crown Office Row, Temple, London EC4Y 7HJ ☎ 020 7797 8100
✉ mail@crownofficechambers.com
Call Date: Oct 1999, Inner Temple
Pupil Supervisor

Practising Areas: Arbitration, Commercial Litigation, Common Law (General), Company & Commercial, Construction, Insurance, Insurance/Reinsurance, Professional Negligence, Sale & Carriage of Goods

SHAPIRO MR SELWYN

2 King's Bench Walk
2 King's Bench Walk, Temple, London EC4Y 7DE ☎ 020 7353 1746 ✉ clerks@2kbw.com
Call Date: Jul 1979, Inner Temple
Pupil Supervisor

Practising Areas: Civil Liberties, Courts Martial, Crime, Crime (Corporate/Fraud), Environment, Licensing, Local Government, Town & Country Planning

SHARLAND MR ANDREW JOHN

4-5 Gray's Inn Square
Gray's Inn, London WC1R 5AH
☎ 020 7404 5252 ✉ clerks@4-5.co.uk
Call Date: Oct 1996, Gray's Inn
Pupil Supervisor

SHARMA MR JAMIE

187 Fleet Street
London EC4A 2AT ☎ 020 7430 7430
✉ chambers@187fleetstreet.com
Call Date: Oct 2005, Inner Temple

Practising Areas: Crime, Crime (Corporate/Fraud), Regulatory Law

SHARMA MISS NEELAM

187 Fleet Street
London EC4A 2AT ☎ 020 7430 7430
✉ chambers@187fleetstreet.com
Call Date: Jul 2000, Lincoln's Inn

SHARMA MR SANJEEV MOHAN

Equity Chambers
First Floor, McLaren Building, 46 Priory Queensway, Birmingham B4 7LR
☎ 0121 236 5007 ✉ clerks@equitychambers.org.uk
Call Date: Jul 2004, Inner Temple

Practising Areas: Civil Liberties, Crime, Crime (Corporate/Fraud), Family

SHARMA MISS SUNYANA

3 PB Barristers
3 Paper Buildings, Temple, London EC4Y 7EU
☎ 020 7583 8055
3 PB Barristers
30 Christchurch Road, Bournemouth, Dorset BH1 3PD ☎ 01202 292102 ✉ clerks.bournemouth@3paper.co.uk
Call Date: Jul 2006, Inner Temple

Practising Areas: Crime, Crime (Corporate/Fraud), Health & Safety, Licensing, Regulatory Law

SHARP MR CHRISTOPHER FRANCIS QC (1999)

St John's Chambers
101 Victoria Street, Bristol BS1 6PU
☎ 0117 923 4700 ✉ clerks@stjohnschambers.co.uk
Harcourt Chambers
1st Floor, 2 Harcourt Buildings, Temple, London EC4Y 9DB ☎ 0844 561 7135
Harcourt Chambers
Churchill House, 3 St Aldate's Courtyard, St Aldate's, Oxford OX1 1BN ☎ 0844 561 7135
Call Date: Jul 1975, Inner Temple
Recorder

Practising Areas: Family, Medical Negligence, Personal Injury, Professional Negligence

SHARP MR DAVID IAN

Tanfield Chambers
2-5 Warwick Court, London WC1R 5DJ
☎ 020 7421 5300 ✉ clerks@tanfieldchambers.co.uk
Call Date: Nov 1986, Middle Temple
Pupil Supervisor

Practising Areas: Ancillary Relief, Children's Law, Family Provision

SHARPE MR MARTIN LAURENCE

Park Court Chambers
16 Park Place, Leeds LS1 2SJ
☎ 0113 243 3277
✉ clerks@parkcourtchambers.co.uk
Call Date: Nov 1989, Middle Temple
Pupil Supervisor

Practising Areas: Crime, Crime (Corporate/Fraud), Regulatory Law

SHARPE MR TIMOTHY JAMES

Temple Garden Chambers
1 Harcourt Buildings, Temple, London EC4Y 9DA ☎ 020 7583 1315 ✉ clerks@tgchambers.com
Call Date: Oct 2002, Lincoln's Inn

Practising Areas: Common Law (General), Health & Safety, Personal Injury

SHARPLES MR JOHN EDMUND

St John's Chambers
101 Victoria Street, Bristol BS1 6PU
☎ 0117 923 4700 ✉ clerks@stjohnschambers.co.uk
Call Date: Nov 1992, Middle Temple

Practising Areas: Chancery (General), Chancery (Land Law), Land, Landlord & Tenant, Probate & Administration

SHAW MR ANDREW DAVID

1 Paper Buildings
1st Floor, 1 Paper Buildings, Temple, London EC4Y 7EP ☎ 020 7353 3728
✉ clerks@onepaper.co.uk
Call Date: Mar 1998, Lincoln's Inn
Pupil Supervisor

SHAW MISS JOANNA ELIZABETH

One Essex Court
1st Floor, Temple, London EC4Y 9AR
☎ 020 7936 3030 ✉ clerks@1ec.co.uk
Call Date: Oct 2000, Middle Temple

Practising Areas: Chancery (Land Law), Civil Liberties, Common Law (General), Discrimination, Employment, Family, Housing, Landlord & Tenant, Personal Injury

SHAW MR JONATHAN PAUL

Zenith Chambers
10 Park Square, Leeds LS1 2LH
☎ 0113 245 5438 ✉ clerks@zenithchambers.co.uk
No5 Chambers
Greenwood House, 4-7 Salisbury Court, London EC4Y 8AA ☎ 0845 210 5555
No5 Chambers
38 Queen Square, Bristol BS1 4QS
☎ 0845 210 5555
No5 Chambers
Fountain Court, Steelhouse Lane, Birmingham B4 6DR ☎ 0845 210 5555 ✉ info@no5.com
Call Date: Jul 2008, Inner Temple

Practising Areas: Arbitration, Commercial Litigation, Construction, Professional Negligence

SHAW MR JULIAN

St Johns Buildings
24a - 28 St John Street, Manchester M3 4DJ
☎ 0161 214 1500 ✉ clerk@stjohnsbuildings.co.uk
St Johns Buildings
21 White Friars, Chester CH1 1NZ
☎ 01244 323070 ✉ clerk@stjohnsbuildings.co.uk
St Johns Buildings Liverpool
8th Floor India Buildings, Water Street, Liverpool L2 0XG ☎ 0151 243 6000
✉ clerk@stjohnsbuildings.co.uk
Call Date: Nov 1984, Gray's Inn
Pupil Supervisor, Recorder

Practising Areas: Care Proceedings, Children's Law, Civil Litigation, Commercial Litigation, Common Law (General), Company & Commercial, Construction, Family, Family Provision, Land, Landlord & Tenant, Medical Negligence, Personal Injury, Professional Negligence, Road Traffic And Highways

SHAW MR MICHAEL JOHN

9-12 Bell Yard
London WC2A 2JR ☎ 020 7400 1800
✉ clerks@9-12bellyard.com
Call Date: Nov 1994, Middle Temple

Practising Areas: Administrative, Crime, Crime (Corporate/Fraud)

SHAW MS NICOLA JANE DUCKWORTH

Trinity Chambers
Multi Media Exchange, 72-80 Corporation Road, Middlesbrough TS1 2RF
☎ 01642 247569 ✉ info@trinitychambers.co.uk
15 Winckley Square
Preston PR1 3JJ ☎ 01772 252828
✉ clerks@15winckleysq.co.uk
Trinity Chambers
The Custom House, 39 Quayside, Newcastle Upon Tyne NE1 3DE ☎ 0191 232 1927
✉ info@trinitychambers.co.uk
Call Date: Oct 1992, Lincoln's Inn

Practising Areas: Ancillary Relief, Chancery (Land Law), Children's Law, Family

SHEFTEL MR ANDREW LAWSON BAYLIES

Tanfield Chambers
2-5 Warwick Court, London WC1R 5DJ
☎ 020 7421 5300 ✉ clerks@tanfieldchambers.co.uk
Call Date: Nov 2004, Inner Temple

Practising Areas: Chancery (Land Law), Commercial Litigation, Commercial Property, Employment, Housing, Landlord & Tenant

SHEIKH MR IRSHAD AHMED

187 Fleet Street
London EC4A 2AT ☎ 020 7430 7430
✉ chambers@187fleetstreet.com
Call Date: Jul 1983, Lincoln's Inn
Pupil Supervisor

Practising Areas: Crime, Crime (Corporate/Fraud), Regulatory Law

SHEIKH MS SAIRA KABIR

Francis Taylor Building
Inner Temple, London EC4Y 7BY
☎ 020 7353 8415 ✉ clerks@ftb.eu.com
Call Date: Nov 2000, Inner Temple
Pupil Supervisor

Practising Areas: Administrative, Environment, Local Government, Town & Country Planning

SHELLARD MR ROBIN JAMES SPENCER

Queen Square Chambers
56 Queen Square, Bristol BS1 4PR
☎ 0117 921 1966 ✉ crime@qs-c.co.uk
Call Date: Nov 1992, Inner Temple
Pupil Supervisor

Practising Areas: Road Traffic And Highways

SHEPHERD MR JAMES MICHAEL

Castle Chambers
The Old Fire Station, 90 High Street, Harrow-on-the-Hill, Middlesex HA1 3LP
☎020 8423 6579 ✉info@castlechambers.net
Melbury House
55 Manor Road, Oadby, Leicester, Leicestershire LE2 2LL ☎07801 037802
✉melburyhousechambers@yahoo.co.uk
Call Date: Jul 2002, Gray's Inn

SHEPHERD MISS JOANNE ELIZABETH

37 Park Square Chambers
37 Park Square, Leeds LS1 2NY
☎0113 243 9422 ✉chambers@no37.co.uk
Call Date: Oct 1993, Inner Temple

SHEPHERD MISS JUDITH ELIZABETH

42 Bedford Row
London WC1R 4LL ☎020 7831 0222
✉clerks@42br.com
Call Date: Oct 1996, Lincoln's Inn

Practising Areas: Discrimination, Employment

SHEPHERD MR RICHARD ANDREW JOHN

Albion Chambers
Broad Street, Bristol BS1 1DR
☎0117 927 2144 ✉clerks@albionchambers.co.uk
Call Date: Jul 2001, Middle Temple
Pupil Supervisor

Practising Areas: Crime, Employment, Personal Injury, Regulatory Law

SHEPPARD MR TIMOTHY DERIE

No5 Chambers
Greenwood House, 4-7 Salisbury Court, London EC4Y 8AA ☎0845 210 5555
No5 Chambers
38 Queen Square, Bristol BS1 4QS
☎0845 210 5555
No5 Chambers
Fountain Court, Steelhouse Lane, Birmingham B4 6DR ☎0845 210 5555 ✉info@no5.com
Call Date: Nov 1995, Inner Temple

Practising Areas: Administrative, Discrimination, Employment, Town & Country Planning

SHEPPARD-JONES MISS VICTORIA LOUISE

Carmelite Chambers
9 Carmelite Street, London EC4Y 0DR
☎020 7936 6300
✉clerks@carmelitechambers.co.uk
Call Date: Nov 2005, Inner Temple

Practising Areas: Crime, Crime (Corporate/Fraud)

SHER MR CHRISTOPHER

Furnival Chambers
32 Furnival Street, London EC4A 1JQ
☎020 7405 3232
Call Date: Nov 1993, Gray's Inn

SHER MISS SHAMIM AKHTAR

Chambers of Miss Shamim Sher
3 Coronation Close, Ilford, Essex IG6 1DB
☎07581 201823 ✉shamim50@live.co.uk
Call Date: May 1995, Lincoln's Inn

Practising Areas: Immigration

SHERAFAT MANSOORI MISS SARA LOUISE

Matrix Chambers
Griffin Building, Gray's Inn, London WC1R 5LN ☎020 7404 3447 ✉matrix@matrixlaw.co.uk/Iscott@matrixlaw.co.uk
Call Date: Nov 1997, Lincoln's Inn

SHERBORN MISS NATALIE LOUISE

25 Bedford Row
London WC1R 4HD ☎020 7067 1500
✉clerks@25bedfordrow.com
Call Date: Nov 2000, Gray's Inn

Practising Areas: Crime, Crime (Corporate/Fraud)

SHERIDAN MR IAIN DOUGLAS

London Scottish
183 Loxley Road, Stratford Upon Avon, Warwickshire CV37 7DU ☎07971 681724
✉isheridan@londonscottishlaw.com
Call Date: Nov 1997, Inner Temple

Practising Areas: Company & Commercial, Financial Services, Tax (Corporate)

SHERRARD MR CHARLES ISAAC QC (2012)

Furnival Chambers
32 Furnival Street, London EC4A 1JQ
☎020 7405 3232
Call Date: Nov 1986, Middle Temple
Pupil Supervisor

SHERRIFF MR SIMON BRUCE

Goldsmith Chambers
Ground Floor, Goldsmith Building, Temple, London EC4Y 7BL ☎ 020 7353 6802
✉ clerks@goldsmithchambers.com
Call Date: Nov 1999, Inner Temple

Practising Areas: Crime

SHIELD MISS DEBORAH

42 Bedford Row
London WC1R 4LL ☎ 020 7831 0222
✉ clerks@42br.com
Call Date: Nov 1991, Inner Temple

Practising Areas: Care Proceedings, Common Law (General), Family, Family Provision, Personal Injury

SHIELDS MISS CAROLINE ANN

No.6 Park Square
Leeds LS1 2LW ☎ 0113 245 9763
✉ Tim@no6.co.uk
Call Date: Oct 2006, Middle Temple

SHIKDER MR KUTUB UDDIN AHMED MBE

T H Barristers Chambers
178 Whitechapel Road, London E1 1BJ
☎ 020 7377 8090 ✉ thbchambers@aol.com
Call Date: Nov 1990, Lincoln's Inn

SHIRLEY MR JAMES PATRICK

Stone Chambers
4 Field Court, Gray's Inn, London WC1R 5EF
☎ 020 7440 6900 ✉ clerks@stonechambers.com
Call Date: Nov 2002, Middle Temple

Practising Areas: Admiralty, Arbitration, Banking, Commercial Litigation, Commodities, Common Law (General), Entertainment, Film, Cable & TV, Foreign Law, Information Technology, Insurance, Insurance/Reinsurance, International Trade, Private International, Professional Negligence, Sale & Carriage of Goods, Shipping/Admiralty, Sports

SHIRLEY MISS LYNNE

East Anglian Chambers
Gresham House, 5 Museum Street, Ipswich, Suffolk IP1 1HQ ☎ 01473 214481
✉ ipswich@ealaw.co.uk
East Anglian Chambers
140 New London Road, Chelmsford, Essex CM2 0AW ☎ 01473 214481
✉ chelmsford@ealaw.co.uk
East Anglian Chambers
15 The Close, Norwich, Norfolk NR1 4DZ
☎ 01473 214481 ✉ norwich@ealaw.co.uk
Call Date: Jul 2002, Middle Temple

SHORE MISS VICTORIA LOUISE

5RB
1st Floor, 5 Raymond Buildings, Gray's Inn, London WC1R 5BP ☎ 020 7242 2902
✉ clerks@5rb.com
Call Date: Nov 2005, Lincoln's Inn

Practising Areas: Defamation, Entertainment

SHOREY MISS CARRIE LORRAE

Nine Bedford Row
9 Bedford Row, London WC1R 4AZ
☎ 020 7489 2727 ✉ clerks@9bedfordrow.co.uk
Call Date: Jul 2006, Middle Temple

Practising Areas: Crime

SHORT MR ANDREW JOHN QC (2010)

Outer Temple Chambers
The Outer Temple, 222 Strand, London WC2R 1BA ☎ 020 7353 6381
✉ clerks@outertemple.com
Riverview Chambers
Hamilton House, 1 Temple Avenue, London EC4Y 0HA ☎ 0844 225 3999
✉ chrisbaylis@riverviewchambers.com
Call Date: Nov 1990, Gray's Inn
Pupil Supervisor

Practising Areas: Discrimination, Employment, Pensions

SHORT MISS ANNA LOUISE

St James's Chambers
68 Quay Street, Manchester M3 3EJ
☎ 0161 834 7000 ✉ clerks@stjameschambers.com
12 King's Bench Walk
12 King's Bench Walk, Temple, London EC4Y 7EL ☎ 020 7583 0811
Call Date: Nov 1997, Gray's Inn

SHORT MR GARY PETER

KCH Garden Square
1 Oxford Street, Nottingham NG1 5BH
☎ 0115 941 8851 ✉ clerks@kchgardensquare.co.uk
Call Date: Nov 1996, Gray's Inn

Practising Areas: Crime, Crime (Corporate/Fraud)

C

SHORT MS MANDY LISA

14 Gray's Inn Square
14 Gray's Inn Square, Gray's Inn, London WC1R 5JP ☎ 020 7242 0858 ✉ clerks@14gis.co.uk
Call Date: Jul 2003, Middle Temple

Practising Areas: Care Proceedings, Education, Family, Family Provision

SHOTTON MS SOPHIE DIANA

15 New Bridge Street
London EC4V 6AU ☎ 020 7842 1900
✉ clerks@15nbs.com
Call Date: Oct 1999, Inner Temple

Practising Areas: Courts Martial, Crime, Crime (Corporate/Fraud), Human Rights

SHUMAN MISS KAREN ANN ELIZABETH

1 Chancery Lane
London WC2A 1LF ☎ 0845 634 6666
✉ clerks@1chancerylane.com
No 8 Chambers
8 Fountain Court, Steelhouse Lane, Birmingham B4 6DR ☎ 0121 236 5514
✉ clerks@no8chambers.co.uk
Call Date: Oct 1991, Lincoln's Inn
Pupil Supervisor

Practising Areas: Chancery (Land Law), Commercial Property, Equity, Wills & Trusts, Family Provision, Housing, Landlord & Tenant, Professional Negligence

SHUTTLEWORTH MR TIMOTHY WILLIAM

Tanfield Chambers
2-5 Warwick Court, London WC1R 5DJ
☎ 020 7421 5300 ✉ clerks@tanfieldchambers.co.uk
Call Date: Jul 1971, Gray's Inn
Pupil Supervisor

Practising Areas: Care Proceedings, Family, Family Provision

SIDHU MR NAVJOT QC (2012)

25 Bedford Row
London WC1R 4HD ☎ 020 7067 1500
✉ clerks@25bedfordrow.com
Call Date: Nov 1993, Lincoln's Inn
Pupil Supervisor

Practising Areas: Crime, Crime (Corporate/Fraud)

SIKAND MISS MAYA

Garden Court Chambers
57-60 Lincoln's Inn Fields, London WC2A 3LJ
☎ 020 7993 7600 ✉ info@gclaw.co.uk
Call Date: Nov 1997, Middle Temple
Pupil Supervisor

Practising Areas: Administrative, Civil Liberties, Crime, Human Rights

SILCOCK MR IAN PETER

Hardwicke
New Square, Lincoln's Inn, London WC2A 3SB ☎ 020 7242 2523
✉ enquiries@hardwicke.co.uk
Call Date: Oct 1997, Middle Temple

Practising Areas: Commercial Litigation, Entertainment, Information Technology, Intellectual Property

SILCOTT MR TYRONE JOHN

Charter Chambers
33 John Street, London WC1N 2AT
☎ 020 7618 4400 ✉ clerks@charterchambers.com
Call Date: Jul 2004, Middle Temple
Pupil Supervisor

Practising Areas: Crime

SILVERTON MISS CATHERINE ANNE

Sovereign Chambers
46 Park Place, Leeds LS1 2RY
☎ 0113 245 1841
✉ clerks@sovereignchambers.co.uk
Call Date: Nov 2001, Lincoln's Inn

Practising Areas: Care Proceedings, Charities, Civil Liberties, Commercial Litigation, Common Law (General), Courts Martial, Crime, Crime (Corporate/Fraud), Defamation, Discrimination, Education, Employment, Entertainment, Family, Film, Cable & TV, Health & Safety, Healthcare, Housing, Immigration, Licensing, Local Government, Medical Negligence, Personal Injury, Professional Negligence, Regulatory Law, Sports, Telecommunications

SIMON MR PHILIPP ARNOLD HEINRICH

4 KBW
Ground Floor, 4 King's Bench Walk, Temple, London EC4Y 7DL ☎ 020 7822 8822
✉ law@4kbw.net
Call Date: Oct 2004, Inner Temple

Practising Areas: Commercial Litigation, EC & Competition Law, Equity, Wills & Trusts, International Trade, Private International, Probate &

Administration, Public International, Sale & Carriage of Goods

SIMPSON MISS CAROL MONICA

Amethyst Chambers
Ground Floor, 9 Kings Bench Walk, Inner Temple, London EC4Y 7DX
☎020 7936 4966 ✉info@amethystchambers.com
Call Date: Mar 1998, Gray's Inn

Practising Areas: Employment, Family, Immigration

SIMPSON MR DAVID JOSEPH

196 Temple Chamber
3-7 Temple Avenue, London EC4Y 0HP
☎020 7099 9257
✉davidsimpson@lawandregulation.com
Call Date: Oct 1992, Gray's Inn

Practising Areas: Administrative, Commercial Litigation, Common Law (General), Financial Services, Professional Negligence, Regulatory Law

SIMPSON MR GRAEME MICHAEL

Citadel Chambers
The Citadel, 190 Corporation Street, Birmingham B4 6QD ☎0121 233 8500
✉clerks@citadelchambers.com
Call Date: Nov 1994, Middle Temple

Practising Areas: Crime, Crime (Corporate/Fraud), Human Rights, Regulatory Law

SIMS MISS ALICE ANTONIA

Keating Chambers
15 Essex Street, London WC2R 3AA
☎020 7544 2600 ✉clerks@keatingchambers.com
Call Date: Jul 2004, Inner Temple

Practising Areas: Construction, Energy

SINCLAIR MR GRAHAM KELSO

East Anglian Chambers
15 The Close, Norwich, Norfolk NR1 4DZ
☎01473 214481 ✉norwich@ealaw.co.uk
East Anglian Chambers
53 North Hill, Colchester, Essex CO1 1QA
☎01473 214481 ✉colchester@ealaw.co.uk
East Anglian Chambers
Gresham House, 5 Museum Street, Ipswich, Suffolk IP1 1HQ ☎01473 214481
✉ipswich@ealaw.co.uk
Call Date: Jul 1979, Gray's Inn
Pupil Supervisor

Practising Areas: Administrative, Chancery (General), Chancery (Land Law), Common Land, Common Law (General), Equity, Wills & Trusts, Family Provision, Housing, Landlord & Tenant, Local Government, Partnership, Probate & Administration, Professional Negligence, Sale & Carriage of Goods

SINCLAIR MISS LISA ANNE

Chambers of Miss Lisa Sinclair
Glencairn House, 70 Ridgway, London SW19 4RA ☎020 8946 7201 ✉lisaasinclair@yahoo.com
Call Date: Jul 1993, Gray's Inn

Practising Areas: Bankruptcy, Chancery (General), Chancery (Land Law), Civil Litigation, Commercial Property, Construction, Conveyancing, Equity, Wills & Trusts, Insolvency, Land, Landlord & Tenant, Partnership, Probate & Administration, Professional Negligence, Regulatory Law

SINGARAJAH MR FREDERICO

1 Gray's Inn Square
Ground Floor, 1 Gray's Inn Square, London WC1R 5AA ☎020 7405 0001
Call Date: Jul 2009, Gray's Inn

Practising Areas: Administrative, Arbitration, Aviation, Bankruptcy, Chancery (General), Civil Liberties, Commercial Litigation, Commodities, Common Law (General), Company & Commercial, Competition, Construction, Copyright, Crime (Corporate/Fraud), Defamation, EC & Competition Law, Employment, Energy, Entertainment, Environment, Film, Cable & TV, Human Rights, Immigration, Information Technology, Insolvency, Insurance, Insurance/Reinsurance, Intellectual Property, International Trade, Landlord & Tenant, Medical Negligence, Partnership, Patents, Private International, Professional Negligence, Public International, Regulatory Law, Sale & Carriage of Goods, Share Options, Shipping/Admiralty, Sports, Tax (Corporate), Telecommunications, Trademarks, Unit Trusts

SINGER MR ANDREW MICHAEL

Kings Chambers
36 Young Street, Manchester M3 3FT
☎0845 034 3444 ✉clerks@kingschambers.com
Kings Chambers
5 Park Square East, Leeds LS1 2NE
☎0845 034 3444 ✉clerks@kingschambers.com
Kings Chambers
Embassy House, 60 Church Street, Birmingham B3 2DJ ☎0845 034 3444
✉clerks@kingschambers.com
Call Date: Nov 1990, Gray's Inn
Pupil Supervisor

Practising Areas: Arbitration, Commercial Litigation, Construction, Insurance, Professional Negligence

SINGER MR NICHOLAS PAUL

42 Bedford Row
London WC1R 4LL ☎020 7831 0222
✉clerks@42br.com
Call Date: Jul 2006, Gray's Inn

Practising Areas: Employment

SINGER MR PHILIP FRANCIS QC (1994)

2 Pump Court
1st Floor, 2 Pump Court, Temple, London EC4Y 7AH ☎020 7353 5597
✉clerks@2pumpcourt.co.uk
Call Date: Feb 1964, Inner Temple
Recorder

SINGER MR RICHARD ADAM

1 Gray's Inn Square
Ground Floor, 1 Gray's Inn Square, London WC1R 5AA ☎020 7405 0001
Call Date: Oct 2001, Lincoln's Inn

Practising Areas: Common Law (General), Courts Martial, Crime, Employment, Immigration

SINGH MR DAPINDERPAUL

23 Essex Street
London WC2R 3AA ☎020 7413 0353
✉clerks@23es.com
Park Court Chambers
16 Park Place, Leeds LS1 2SJ
☎0113 243 3277
✉clerks@parkcourtchambers.co.uk
Call Date: Jul 2000, Middle Temple

Practising Areas: Copyright, Crime, Crime (Corporate/Fraud), Regulatory Law, Tax (Capital & Income), Tax (Corporate)

SINGH MR TALBIR

No5 Chambers
Fountain Court, Steelhouse Lane, Birmingham B4 6DR ☎0845 210 5555 ✉info@no5.com
No5 Chambers
Greenwood House, 4-7 Salisbury Court, London EC4Y 8AA ☎0845 210 5555
No5 Chambers
38 Queen Square, Bristol BS1 4QS
☎0845 210 5555
Call Date: Jul 1997, Gray's Inn

SINGH-HAYER MR BANSA

Deans Court Chambers
24 St John Street, Manchester M3 4DF
☎0161 214 6000 ✉clerks@deanscourt.co.uk
Deans Court Chambers
101 Walker Street, Preston PR1 2RR
☎01772 565 600 ✉preston@deanscourt.co.uk
Call Date: Nov 1988, Gray's Inn
Pupil Supervisor

Practising Areas: Family, Family Provision, Mental Health

SINGH-TIWANA MR EKWALL

No5 Chambers
Fountain Court, Steelhouse Lane, Birmingham B4 6DR ☎0845 210 5555 ✉info@no5.com
No5 Chambers
Greenwood House, 4-7 Salisbury Court, London EC4Y 8AA ☎0845 210 5555
No5 Chambers
38 Queen Square, Bristol BS1 4QS
☎0845 210 5555
Call Date: Nov 1988, Middle Temple
Pupil Supervisor

Practising Areas: Crime (Corporate/Fraud), Tax (Capital & Income), Tax (Corporate)

SINGLETON MR MICHAEL JOHN

St Ive's Chambers
Whittall Street, Birmingham B4 6DH
☎0121 236 0863 ✉clerks@stiveschambers.co.uk
Call Date: Jul 1987, Middle Temple
Pupil Supervisor

SINKER MR ANDREW TENNANT

New Bailey Chambers
4th Floor, Corn Exchange, Fenwick Street, Liverpool, Merseyside L2 7QS
☎0151 236 9402 ✉clerks@newbailey.com
Call Date: Oct 1991, Lincoln's Inn

Practising Areas: Crime, Crime (Corporate/Fraud), Immigration

SISLEY MR TIMOTHY JULIAN CRISPIN

9 Stone Buildings
Lincoln's Inn, London WC2A 3NN
☎020 7404 5055 ✉clerks@9stonebuildings.com
Call Date: Feb 1989, Middle Temple
Pupil Supervisor

Practising Areas: Banking, Bankruptcy, Chancery (General), Chancery (Land Law), Commercial Litigation, Commercial Property,

Common Law (General), Company & Commercial, Construction, Equity, Wills & Trusts, Insolvency, Insurance, Landlord & Tenant, Partnership, Probate & Administration, Professional Negligence, Sale & Carriage of Goods

SJOLIN MS CATARINA MARIANNE

36 Bedford Row
London WC1R 4JH ☎ 020 7421 8000
✉ chambers@36bedfordrow.co.uk
Call Date: Nov 1998, Gray's Inn

Practising Areas: Crime, Crime (Corporate/ Fraud), Regulatory Law

SJOSTRAND MISS EKATERINA

13 Old Square Chambers
Ground Floor, 14 Old Square, Lincoln's Inn, London WC2A 3UE ☎ 020 7831 4445
✉ clerks@13oldsquare.com
Call Date: Oct 2003, Inner Temple

Practising Areas: Arbitration, Banking, Bankruptcy, Chancery (General), Chancery (Land Law), Commercial Litigation, Commercial Property, Company & Commercial, Equity, Wills & Trusts, Insolvency, Partnership, Private International, Probate & Administration, Professional Negligence, Sale & Carriage of Goods

SKELLY MR ANDREW JON

Hardwicke
New Square, Lincoln's Inn, London WC2A 3SB ☎ 020 7242 2523
✉ enquiries@hardwicke.co.uk
Call Date: Oct 1994, Inner Temple

Practising Areas: Chancery (General), Chancery (Land Law), Commercial Litigation, Commercial Property, Common Law (General), Conveyancing, Housing, Landlord & Tenant, Personal Injury, Professional Negligence, Town & Country Planning

SKELT MR IAN STUART

KBW
The Engine House, No 1 Foundry Square, Leeds LS11 5DL ☎ 0113 297 1200
✉ clerks@kbwchambers.com
Call Date: Oct 1994, Lincoln's Inn
Pupil Supervisor

Practising Areas: Administrative, Civil Litigation, Common Law (General), Coroners Inquests, Discrimination, Employment, Human Rights, Inquests, Personal Injury, Professional Negligence, Public Law

SKINNER MR ANDREW MURRAY

College Chambers
19 Carlton Crescent, Southampton, Hampshire SO15 2ET ☎ 023 8023 0338
✉ clerks@college-chambers.co.uk
Call Date: Jul 2000, Middle Temple

SKINNER MR SAMUEL RICHARD EDWARD

KCH Garden Square
1 Oxford Street, Nottingham NG1 5BH
☎ 0115 941 8851 ✉ clerks@kchgardensquare.co.uk
Call Date: Oct 2007, Gray's Inn

Practising Areas: Administrative, Bankruptcy, Charities, Civil Liberties, Common Law (General), Courts Martial, Crime, Crime (Corporate/ Fraud), Defamation, Discrimination, Education, Employment, Environment, Health & Safety, Human Rights, Licensing, Parliamentary, Personal Injury, Public International, Regulatory Law, Sports, Town & Country Planning

SKITTRELL MISS ELAINE ANGELA

Park Court Chambers
16 Park Place, Leeds LS1 2SJ
☎ 0113 243 3277
✉ clerks@parkcourtchambers.co.uk
Call Date: Jul 1999, Middle Temple

SKYNER MR ROBERT STEPHEN

39 Park Square
Leeds LS1 2NU ☎ 0113 245 6633
✉ seniorclerk@39parksquarechambers.co.uk
Call Date: Mar 2003, Middle Temple

Practising Areas: Common Law (General), Crime, Personal Injury

SLACK MR HENRY ALEXANDER FERGUSSON

Hardwicke
New Square, Lincoln's Inn, London WC2A 3SB ☎ 020 7242 2523
✉ enquiries@hardwicke.co.uk
Call Date: Oct 1999, Lincoln's Inn

SLATTER MR ALEXIS ANDREW MALLATRATT

Tooks Chambers
81 Farringdon Street, London EC4A 4BL
☎ 020 7842 7575 ✉ clerks@tooks.co.uk
Call Date: Nov 1999, Inner Temple

Practising Areas: Immigration

SLEIGHT MR NIGEL

Regency Chambers
45 Priestgate, Peterborough PE1 1LB
☎ 01733 315215 ✉ clerks@regencychambers.law.co.uk
Regency Chambers
Sheraton House, Castle Park, Cambridge CB3 0AX ☎ 01223 301517
Call Date: Oct 1998, Lincoln's Inn
Pupil Supervisor

Practising Areas: Care Proceedings, Common Law (General), Family, Family Provision

SLIWINSKI MR ROBERT ANDREW

SWL Chambers
Aston Court, Frederick Place, Loudwater, Buckinghamshire HP11 1LA ☎ 01494 616007
✉ robert@swl-legal.co.uk
Call Date: Oct 1990, Middle Temple

Practising Areas: Arbitration, Commercial Litigation, Commercial Property, Common Law (General), Construction, Energy, Environment, Professional Negligence

SLOANE MISS VALENTINA

Monckton Chambers
1 & 2 Raymond Buildings, Gray's Inn, London WC1R 5NR ☎ 020 7405 7211
✉ chambers@monckton.com
Call Date: Oct 2000, Gray's Inn

Practising Areas: EC & Competition Law, Tax (Corporate)

SMALL MRS ARLENE ANNMARIE

Clerksroom (Taunton)
Equity House, Administration Centre, Blackbrook Park Avenue, Taunton, Somerset TA1 2PX ☎ 0845 083 3000
✉ mail@clerksroom.com
Clerksroom (London)
3rd Floor, 218 Strand, London WC2R 1AT
☎ 0845 083 3000 ✉ mail@clerksroom.com
King's Lynn Chambers
26 The Birches, South Wootton, King's Lynn, Norfolk PE30 3JG ☎ 01553 672 085
✉ timothy.leader@tesco.net
Call Date: Oct 1997, Middle Temple

Practising Areas: Care Proceedings, Family, Family Provision

SMALL MR JOHN ROBERT

36 Bedford Row
London WC1R 4JH ☎ 020 7421 8000
✉ chambers@36bedfordrow.co.uk
Call Date: Oct 2002, Inner Temple

Practising Areas: Commercial Litigation, Discrimination, Employment, Personal Injury

SMALL MISS PENELOPE SUSAN

Chambers of Andrew Mitchell QC
33 Chancery Lane, London WC2A 1EN
☎ 020 7440 9950 ✉ clerks@33cllaw.com
Call Date: Oct 1992, Inner Temple
Pupil Supervisor

Practising Areas: Crime, Crime (Corporate/Fraud)

SMALLWOOD MISS ANNE ELIZABETH

No5 Chambers
Fountain Court, Steelhouse Lane, Birmingham B4 6DR ☎ 0845 210 5555 ✉ info@no5.com
No5 Chambers
Greenwood House, 4-7 Salisbury Court, London EC4Y 8AA ☎ 0845 210 5555
No5 Chambers
38 Queen Square, Bristol BS1 4QS
☎ 0845 210 5555
Call Date: Nov 1977, Middle Temple
Pupil Supervisor

Practising Areas: Family

SMART MR ROGER BERNARD

QEB Hollis Whiteman
1-2 Laurence Pountney Hill, London EC4R 0EU ☎ 020 7933 8855 ✉ barristers@qebhw.co.uk
Call Date: Jul 1989, Inner Temple
Pupil Supervisor

SMITH MR ADAM JOHN

Crown Office Row Chambers
119 Church Street, Brighton, Sussex BN1 1UD ☎ 01273 625625 ✉ clerks@1cor.com
Call Date: Nov 1987, Inner Temple
Pupil Supervisor

Practising Areas: Family

SMITH MR ALISDAIR ROBERT MACSORLEY

9-12 Bell Yard
London WC2A 2JR ☎020 7400 1800
✉clerks@9-12bellyard.com
Call Date: Jul 1981, Gray's Inn
Pupil Supervisor

Practising Areas: Administrative, Civil Liberties, Courts Martial, Crime, Crime (Corporate/Fraud), Education, Environment, Regulatory Law, Sports

SMITH MR CLIVE FRANCIS

Chambers of Marion Smullen and Kerim Fuad QC
1 Inner Temple Lane, London EC4Y 1AF
☎020 7427 4400 ✉clerks@1itl.com
Call Date: Jul 2003, Lincoln's Inn

Practising Areas: Courts Martial, Crime, Crime (Corporate/Fraud), Regulatory Law, Sports

SMITH MR DAVID ANDREW

9-12 Bell Yard
London WC2A 2JR ☎020 7400 1800
✉clerks@9-12bellyard.com
Call Date: Jul 1988, Middle Temple
Pupil Supervisor

Practising Areas: Crime, Crime (Corporate/Fraud)

SMITH MISS EILEEN JOAN

Trinity Chambers
The Custom House, 39 Quayside, Newcastle Upon Tyne NE1 3DE ☎0191 232 1927
✉info@trinitychambers.co.uk
Trinity Chambers
Multi Media Exchange, 72-80 Corporation Road, Middlesbrough TS1 2RF
☎01642 247569 ✉info@trinitychambers.co.uk
Call Date: Oct 2002, Middle Temple

Practising Areas: Administrative, Agriculture, Copyright, Courts Martial, Crime, Crime (Corporate/Fraud), Education, Entertainment, Environment, Health & Safety, Housing, Licensing, Local Government, Mental Health, Regulatory Law, Trademarks

SMITH MR IAN ALFIO

11 Stone Buildings
11 Stone Buildings, Lincoln's Inn, London WC2A 3TG ☎020 7831 6381 ✉clerks@11sb.com
Call Date: Jul 2003, Middle Temple

Practising Areas: Commercial Litigation, Company & Commercial, Crime (Corporate/Fraud), Financial Services

SMITH MR JAMES ALASTAIR

9-12 Bell Yard
London WC2A 2JR ☎020 7400 1800
✉clerks@9-12bellyard.com
Call Date: Oct 2001, Inner Temple

Practising Areas: Crime, Crime (Corporate/Fraud), Licensing, Local Government

SMITH MRS JANE LESLEY

Southernhay Chambers
33 Southernhay East, Exeter EX1 1NX
☎01392 255777
✉clerks@southernhaychambers.co.uk
Call Date: Jul 2007, Inner Temple

SMITH MR JULIAN ROBERT

Lincoln's Inn Fields Chambers
88 Kingsway, London WC2B 6AA
☎0845 123 1234 ✉jsmith@lincolnsinnfields.com
Call Date: Mar 1998, Lincoln's Inn

Practising Areas: Common Law (General), Courts Martial, Employment, Family, Landlord & Tenant

SMITH MISS KERRY ANN

Chambers of Ian Macdonald QC
Garden Court North, 22 Oxford Court, Manchester M2 3WQ ☎0161 236 1840
✉clerks@gcnchambers.co.uk
Call Date: Jul 2002, Lincoln's Inn

SMITH MR MARK WILLIAM

Aegis Chambers
39 Mostyn Avenue, Wembley, Middlesex HA9 8AY
Call Date: Mar 1997, Gray's Inn
Pupil Supervisor

Practising Areas: Crime, Crime (Corporate/Fraud), Immigration, Personal Injury

SMITH MR MATTHEW ROBERT

Sovereign Chambers
46 Park Place, Leeds LS1 2RY
☎0113 245 1841
✉clerks@sovereignchambers.co.uk
Call Date: Nov 1996, Inner Temple
Pupil Supervisor

Practising Areas: Chancery (General), Commercial Litigation, Company & Commercial, Family Provision, Landlord & Tenant, Medical Negligence, Partnership, Personal Injury

C

SMITH MR MICHAEL DAVID

Kenworthy's Chambers
Arlington House, Bloom Street, Salford, Manchester M3 6AJ ☎0161 832 4036
Call Date: Oct 2001, Lincoln's Inn

Practising Areas: Industrial Diseases, Inquests, Medical Negligence, Personal Injury, Road Traffic And Highways

SMITH MR NICHOLAS GILBERT

Guildhall Chambers
23 Broad Street, Bristol BS1 2HG
☎0117 930 9000 ✉hoc@guildhallchambers.co.uk
Call Date: Nov 1990, Lincoln's Inn

SMITH MS RACHEL CATHERINE

Lincoln House Chambers
Tower 12, The Avenue North, Spinningfields, 18-22 Bridge Street, Manchester M3 3BZ
☎0161 832 5701
✉info@lincolnhousechambers.com
Call Date: Oct 1990, Lincoln's Inn
Pupil Supervisor, Recorder

Practising Areas: Crime, Crime (Corporate/Fraud), Licensing

SMITH MR ROBERT CLIVE

RCS Chambers
Penny Hill, Holme Hall Lane, Stainton S66 7RD ☎01709 814 147
✉robert@rcschambers.com
1 Paper Buildings
1st Floor, 1 Paper Buildings, Temple, London EC4Y 7EP ☎020 7353 3728
✉clerks@onepaper.co.uk
Call Date: Jul 1974, Middle Temple

Practising Areas: Bankruptcy, Commercial Litigation, Common Land, Common Law (General), Construction, Employment, Family Provision, Insolvency, Landlord & Tenant, Partnership, Personal Injury, Professional Negligence, Sale & Carriage of Goods, Town & Country Planning

SMITH MR ROBERT IAN

St Paul's Chambers
5th Floor, St Paul's House, 23 Park Square South, Leeds LS1 2ND ☎0113 245 5866
Call Date: Oct 1995, Lincoln's Inn
Pupil Supervisor

Practising Areas: Commercial Litigation, Common Law (General), Company & Commercial, Construction, Health & Safety, Medical Negligence, Personal Injury, Professional Negligence, Regulatory Law, Sale & Carriage of Goods, Sports

SMITH MR ROGER GAVIN ABBEY

1 Hare Court
1 Hare Court, Temple, London EC4Y 7BE
☎020 7797 7070 ✉clerks@1hc.com
Call Date: Nov 1981, Middle Temple
Pupil Supervisor

Practising Areas: Arbitration, Family

SMITH MR ROGER HUGH TRAYLEN

No5 Chambers
Fountain Court, Steelhouse Lane, Birmingham B4 6DR ☎0845 210 5555 ✉info@no5.com
No5 Chambers
Greenwood House, 4-7 Salisbury Court, London EC4Y 8AA ☎0845 210 5555
No5 Chambers
38 Queen Square, Bristol BS1 4QS
☎0845 210 5555
Call Date: Nov 1968, Gray's Inn
Pupil Supervisor

Practising Areas: Chancery (General), Chancery (Land Law), Commercial Litigation, Commercial Property, Common Law (General), Equity, Wills & Trusts, Landlord & Tenant, Personal Injury, Probate & Administration, Professional Negligence

SMITH MR SIMON NOEL

3 Temple Gardens
Lower Ground Floor, 3 Temple Gardens, Temple, London EC4Y 9AU ☎020 7353 3102
✉clerks@3tg.co.uk
Call Date: Jul 1981, Gray's Inn
Pupil Supervisor

SMITHERS DR ROGER HOWARD

Guildford Chambers
Stoke House, Leapale Lane, Guildford, Surrey GU1 4LY ☎01483 539131
✉clerks@guildfordchambers.co.uk
Clerksroom (Taunton)
Equity House, Administration Centre, Blackbrook Park Avenue, Taunton, Somerset TA1 2PX ☎0845 083 3000
✉mail@clerksroom.com
Alexander Chambers
13 Halstead Road, Wanstead, London E11 2AY ☎0845 652 0451 / 0854 652 0451
✉clerks@alexanderchambers.co.uk
Call Date: Oct 1990, Inner Temple
Pupil Supervisor

Practising Areas: Chancery (General), Chancery (Land Law), Company & Commercial, Insolvency, Intellectual Property, Landlord & Tenant, Probate & Administration, Professional Negligence

SMITTEN MR BEN JAMES

25 Bedford Row
London WC1R 4HD ☎ 020 7067 1500
✉ clerks@25bedfordrow.com
Call Date: Nov 1999, Middle Temple

Practising Areas: Crime, Crime (Corporate/Fraud)

SMOKER MISS KATHLEEN MARY

Heavenwood Chambers
Heavenwood Chambers, Heavenwood House, 71 Bownham Park, Rodborough Common, Stroud, Gloucestershire GL5 5BZ
☎ 01453 873444 ✉ kms@heavenwood.co.uk
Call Date: May 1974, Gray's Inn
Pupil Supervisor

Practising Areas: Crime, Licensing, Local Government

SMOUT MR WILLIAM KINGSLEY

Guildford Chambers
Stoke House, Leapale Lane, Guildford, Surrey GU1 4LY ☎ 01483 539131
✉ clerks@guildfordchambers.co.uk
Call Date: Oct 2005, Lincoln's Inn

Practising Areas: Ancillary Relief, Children's Law, Family Provision

SMULLEN MRS MARION

Chambers of Marion Smullen and Kerim Fuad QC
1 Inner Temple Lane, London EC4Y 1AF
☎ 020 7427 4400 ✉ clerks@1itl.com
Call Date: Jul 1985, Gray's Inn
Pupil Supervisor

Practising Areas: Crime

SMYTH MR CHRISTOPHER JULIAN WORSLEY

Queen Square Chambers
56 Queen Square, Bristol BS1 4PR
☎ 0117 921 1966 ✉ crime@qs-c.co.uk
Call Date: Mar 2006, Gray's Inn

Practising Areas: Commercial Property, Common Land, Crime, Crime (Corporate/Fraud), Landlord & Tenant, Licensing

SNELUS MR JAMES GORDON ERNEST

St Mary's Family Law Chambers
26-28 High Pavement, The Lace Market, Nottingham NG1 1HN ☎ 0115 950 3503
✉ clerks@stmarysflc.co.uk
Call Date: Oct 1999, Inner Temple

SNOOK MR HARRY BENEDICK

St Albans Chambers
2 - 4 St Peter's Street, St Albans, Hertfordshire AL1 3LF ☎ 01727 843383
✉ clerks@stalbanschambers.com
Call Date: Nov 2006, Inner Temple

Practising Areas: Crime, Employment, Personal Injury

SNOW MR DARREN MARK

Charter Chambers
33 John Street, London WC1N 2AT
☎ 020 7618 4400 ✉ clerks@charterchambers.com
Call Date: Oct 2000, Middle Temple

Practising Areas: Arbitration, Aviation, Commercial Litigation, Common Law (General), Crime, Crime (Corporate/Fraud), Environment, Health & Safety, Insurance, Insurance/Reinsurance, Professional Negligence, Regulatory Law, Sale & Carriage of Goods

SOFAER MISS MOIRA

Goldsmith Chambers
Ground Floor, Goldsmith Building, Temple, London EC4Y 7BL ☎ 020 7353 6802
✉ clerks@goldsmithchambers.com
Call Date: Jul 1975, Middle Temple

Practising Areas: Care Proceedings, Family, Family Provision

SOKOL MR CHRISTOPHER JOHN FRANCIS QC (2006)

Taxchambers
15 Old Square, Lincoln's Inn, London WC2A 3UE ☎ 020 7242 2744
✉ taxchambers@15oldsquare.co.uk
Deans Court Chambers
24 St John Street, Manchester M3 4DF
☎ 0161 214 6000 ✉ clerks@deanscourt.co.uk
Temple Tax Chambers
1st Floor, 3 Temple Gardens, Temple, London EC4Y 9AU ☎ 020 7353 7884
✉ clerks@templetax.com
Call Date: Jul 1975, Lincoln's Inn

Practising Areas: Equity, Wills & Trusts, Tax (Capital & Income), Tax (Corporate)

SOLLEY MR STEPHEN MALCOLM QC (1989)

Charter Chambers
33 John Street, London WC1N 2AT
☎ 020 7618 4400 ✉ clerks@charterchambers.com
Call Date: Nov 1969, Inner Temple
Recorder

Practising Areas: Civil Liberties, Crime (Corporate/Fraud), Environment, Financial Services, Human Rights, Regulatory Law

SOLOMON MR REUBEN

12 Old Square Chambers
1st Floor, 12 Old Square, Lincoln's Inn, London WC2A 3TX ☎ 020 7404 0875
✉ clerks@12oldsquare.com
Call Date: Oct 1993, Lincoln's Inn

Practising Areas: Human Rights, Immigration

SONAIKE MR KOLARELE OLADELE OBAFEMI

One Essex Court
1st Floor, Temple, London EC4Y 9AR
☎ 020 7936 3030 ✉ clerks@1ec.co.uk
Call Date: Oct 1998, Inner Temple

Practising Areas: Commercial Litigation, Common Law (General), Discrimination, Employment, Housing, Licensing, Local Government

SONES MR RICHARD

5 King's Bench Walk
5 King's Bench Walk, Temple, London EC4Y 7DN ☎ 020 7353 5638 ✉ clerks@5kbw.co.uk
Call Date: Nov 1969, Inner Temple
Pupil Supervisor

SONI MISS BANSI

Garden Court Chambers
57-60 Lincoln's Inn Fields, London WC2A 3LJ
☎ 020 7993 7600 ✉ info@gclaw.co.uk
Call Date: Nov 2003, Middle Temple

Practising Areas: Family

SOOD MRS USHA RANI

Trent Chambers
9 Regent Street, Nottingham NG1 5BS
☎ 0115 941 9596 ✉ clerks@trentchambers.co.uk
Call Date: Jul 1974, Gray's Inn
Pupil Supervisor

Practising Areas: Administrative, Care Proceedings, Civil Liberties, Common Land, Common Law (General), Discrimination, Education, Employment, Family, Family Provision, Foreign Law, Healthcare, Housing, Immigration, Medical Negligence, Mental Health, Personal Injury, Private International, Public International, Sports, Town & Country Planning

SOTO-MIRANDA MR DIEGO FERNANDO

One Essex Court
1st Floor, Temple, London EC4Y 9AR
☎ 020 7936 3030 ✉ clerks@1ec.co.uk
Call Date: Jul 2001, Inner Temple

Practising Areas: Administrative, Commercial Litigation, Common Law (General), Defamation, Insurance/Reinsurance, International Trade, Public International, Sale & Carriage of Goods, Shipping/Admiralty, Sports

SOUTHERN MISS EMMA CATHERINE

12 College Place
Fauvelle Buildings, 12 College Place, Southampton SO15 2FE ☎ 023 8032 0320
✉ clerks@12cp.co.uk
Call Date: Jul 2006, Lincoln's Inn

Practising Areas: Ancillary Relief, Family, Housing

SOUTHEY MR DAVID HUGH QC (2010)

Tooks Chambers
81 Farringdon Street, London EC4A 4BL
☎ 020 7842 7575 ✉ clerks@tooks.co.uk
Call Date: Nov 1996, Inner Temple
Pupil Supervisor, Recorder

Practising Areas: Administrative, Human Rights, Immigration, Mental Health, Public Law

SOWERBY MR MATTHEW GILES

1 Gray's Inn Square
Ground Floor, 1 Gray's Inn Square, London WC1R 5AA ☎ 020 7405 0001
Call Date: Jul 1987, Middle Temple

Practising Areas: Immigration

SOWLER MR THOMAS RICHARD HOLLAND TD

The Tax Chambers of Mr Richard Sowler TD
6 Church Road Marina, Douglas IM1 2HQ
☎ 07624 235000
Call Date: Jul 1974, Inner Temple

Practising Areas: Asset Finance, Banking, Charities, Commercial Litigation, Company & Commercial, Corporate Finance, Equity, Wills & Trusts, Financial Services, International Trade, Private International, Regulatory Law, Share Options, Tax (Capital & Income), Tax (Corporate), Town & Country Planning

SPAIN MR TIMOTHY HARRISSON

Trinity Chambers
The Custom House, 39 Quayside, Newcastle Upon Tyne NE1 3DE ☎0191 232 1927
✉info@trinitychambers.co.uk
Trinity Chambers
Multi Media Exchange, 72-80 Corporation Road, Middlesbrough TS1 2RF
☎01642 247569 ✉info@trinitychambers.co.uk
Call Date: Jul 1983, Gray's Inn
Pupil Supervisor

Practising Areas: Care Proceedings, Family, Mental Health

SPALTON MR GEORGE DAVID JOHN

Four New Square
Four New Square, Lincoln's Inn, London WC2A 3RJ ☎020 7822 2000
✉barristers@4newsquare.com
Call Date: Jul 2004, Lincoln's Inn

Practising Areas: Arbitration, Banking, Commercial Litigation, Commodities, Company & Commercial, Financial Services, Insurance, International Trade, Private International, Professional Negligence, Sports

SPARROW MRS MARIE-CLAIRE

Holborn Chambers
6 Gate Street, Lincoln's Inn Fields, London WC2A 3HP ☎020 7242 6060
Call Date: Nov 1977, Lincoln's Inn
Pupil Supervisor

Practising Areas: Care Proceedings, Crime, Crime (Corporate/Fraud), Discrimination, EC & Competition Law, Employment, Family, Foreign Law, Personal Injury, Public International

SPEAIGHT MR ANTHONY HUGH QC (1995)

4 Pump Court
4 Pump Court, Temple, London EC4Y 7AN
☎020 7842 5555 ✉chambers@4pumpcourt.com
Call Date: Jul 1973, Middle Temple

Practising Areas: Administrative, Arbitration, Construction, Financial Services, Information Technology, Insurance

SPEARING MS RACHEL MICHELLE

Pump Court Chambers
31 Southgate Street, Winchester, Hampshire SO23 9EB ☎01962 868 161
✉clerks@3pumpcourt.com
Pump Court Chambers
Upper Ground Floor, 3 Pump Court, Temple, London EC4Y 7AJ ☎020 7353 0711
✉clerks@3pumpcourt.com
Pump Court Chambers
5 Temple Chambers, Temple Street, Swindon SN1 1SQ ☎01793 539899
✉clerks@3pumpcourt.com
Call Date: Oct 1999, Inner Temple
Pupil Supervisor

SPEARS MISS KATHARINE SARAH

Carmelite Chambers
9 Carmelite Street, London EC4Y 0DR
☎020 7936 6300
✉clerks@carmelitechambers.co.uk
Call Date: Nov 2005, Middle Temple

Practising Areas: Civil Liberties, Courts Martial, Crime, Crime (Corporate/Fraud), Human Rights, Licensing, Mental Health, Regulatory Law

SPEKER MR ADAM SAMUEL EDWARD

5RB
1st Floor, 5 Raymond Buildings, Gray's Inn, London WC1R 5BP ☎020 7242 2902
✉clerks@5rb.com
Call Date: Oct 1999, Middle Temple
Pupil Supervisor

Practising Areas: Common Law (General), Defamation, Entertainment, Human Rights, Intellectual Property

SPELLER MR BRUCE CHRISTOPHER NORMAN

The White House
Whatlington, Battle, East Sussex TN33 0ND
☎01424 777944 ✉brucespeller@btinternet.com
Call Date: Jul 1976, Inner Temple
Pupil Supervisor

Practising Areas: Chancery (Land Law), Commercial Litigation, Employment, Housing, Insurance, Landlord & Tenant

SPENCE MR SIMON PETER QC (2009)

18 Red Lion Court
London EC4A 3EB ☎020 7520 6000
✉chambers@18rlc.co.uk
18 Red Lion Court (Annexe)
Thornwood House, 102 New London Road, Chelmsford, Essex CM2 0RG
☎01245 280880
Call Date: Jul 1985, Inner Temple
Recorder

Practising Areas: Crime, Crime (Corporate/Fraud), Human Rights, Licensing

SPENCE MR STEPHEN NICHOLAS

1 Paper Buildings
1st Floor, 1 Paper Buildings, Temple, London EC4Y 7EP ☎ 020 7353 3728
✉ clerks@onepaper.co.uk
Call Date: Jul 1983, Gray's Inn

SPENCER MR JOHN JOSEPH

KBW
The Engine House, No 1 Foundry Square, Leeds LS11 5DL ☎ 0113 297 1200
✉ clerks@kbwchambers.com
Call Date: Jul 2001, Gray's Inn

SPENCER MISS LARA SHARON

Walnut House
63 St. David's Hill, Exeter, Devon EX4 4DW
☎ 01392 279751 ✉ clerks@walnuthouse.co.uk
Call Date: Jul 2000, Lincoln's Inn

SPENCER MR MARTIN BENEDICT QC (2003)

Hailsham Chambers
Ground Floor, 4 Paper Buildings, Temple, London EC4Y 7EX ☎ 020 7643 5000
✉ clerks@hailshamchambers.com
Call Date: Jul 1979, Inner Temple
Recorder

Practising Areas: Common Law (General), Insurance, Insurance/Reinsurance, Medical Negligence, Mental Health, Partnership, Personal Injury, Professional Negligence

SPENCER MR PAUL ANTHONY

3 Serjeants Inn
London EC4Y 1BQ ☎ 020 7427 5000
✉ clerks@3serjeantsinn.com
Call Date: Nov 1988, Middle Temple
Pupil Supervisor

Practising Areas: Administrative, Civil Liberties, Common Law (General), Crime (Corporate/Fraud), Health & Safety, Healthcare, Local Government, Regulatory Law

SPENCER MR SHAUN ANTHONY

St Johns Buildings
24a - 28 St John Street, Manchester M3 4DJ
☎ 0161 214 1500 ✉ clerk@stjohnsbuildings.co.uk
St Johns Buildings
21 White Friars, Chester CH1 1NZ
☎ 01244 323070 ✉ clerk@stjohnsbuildings.co.uk
16 Winckley Square
Preston PR1 3JJ ☎ 01772 256100
Call Date: Jul 2005, Lincoln's Inn

Practising Areas: Ancillary Relief, Care Proceedings, Children's Law, Environment, Family, Regulatory Law

SPENS MR DAVID PATRICK QC (1995)

Garden Court Chambers
57-60 Lincoln's Inn Fields, London WC2A 3LJ
☎ 020 7993 7600 ✉ info@gclaw.co.uk
Call Date: Nov 1973, Inner Temple
Recorder

Practising Areas: Crime, Crime (Corporate/Fraud)

SPENWYN MS MARIE ANN

Carmelite Chambers
9 Carmelite Street, London EC4Y 0DR
☎ 020 7936 6300
✉ clerks@carmelitechambers.co.uk
Call Date: Oct 1999, Gray's Inn
Pupil Supervisor

Practising Areas: Crime, Crime (Corporate/Fraud)

SPICER MR ROBERT HADEN

Frederick Place Chambers
9 Frederick Place, Frederick Place Chambers, Clifton, Bristol BS8 1AS ☎ 0117 946 7059
✉ rsp4593558@aol.com
Call Date: Jul 1970, Inner Temple

Practising Areas: Civil Liberties, Common Law (General), Discrimination, Employment, Personal Injury, Professional Negligence

SPINK MR ANDREW JOHN MURRAY QC (2003)

Outer Temple Chambers
The Outer Temple, 222 Strand, London WC2R 1BA ☎ 020 7353 6381
✉ clerks@outertemple.com
Riverview Chambers
Hamilton House, 1 Temple Avenue, London EC4Y 0HA ☎ 0844 225 3999
✉ chrisbaylis@riverviewchambers.com
Call Date: Nov 1985, Middle Temple
Recorder

Practising Areas: Company & Commercial, Pensions

C

SPOONER MR HENRY NEVILLE

Westgate Chambers
64 High Street, Lewes, East Sussex BN7 1XG
☎ 01273 480510
✉ clerks@westgate-chambers.co.uk
Tolzey Chambers
37 Rowlandson Gardens, Lockleaze, Bristol BS7 9UH
Call Date: Nov 1971, Lincoln's Inn
Pupil Supervisor

Practising Areas: Civil Liberties, Common Law (General), Crime, Defamation, Human Rights, Immigration, Medical Negligence

SPRATLING MRS ANNE VIRGINIA

Coram Chambers
9-11 Fulwood Place, London WC1V 6HG
☎ 020 7092 3700 ✉ mail@coramchambers.co.uk
Call Date: Jul 1980, Lincoln's Inn
Pupil Supervisor

SPRATT MR CHRISTOPHER DAVID RICHARD DEAN

9 Stone Buildings
Lincoln's Inn, London WC2A 3NN
☎ 020 7404 5055 ✉ clerks@9stonebuildings.com
Call Date: Nov 1986, Gray's Inn
Pupil Supervisor

Practising Areas: Chancery (General), Civil Liberties, Commercial Litigation, Common Land, Competition, Construction, Conveyancing, Employment, Entertainment, Housing

SPRATT-DAWSON MISS JOSEPHINE MARGERY

Trinity Chambers
Highfield House, Moulsham Street, Chelmsford, Essex CM2 9AH
☎ 01245 605040 ✉ clerks@trinitychambers.com
Call Date: Oct 1993, Gray's Inn
Pupil Supervisor

Practising Areas: Chancery (General), Chancery (Land Law), Common Law (General), Equity, Wills & Trusts, Family, Family Provision, Probate & Administration

SPROSON MISS EILEEN

2 King's Bench Walk
2 King's Bench Walk, Temple, London EC4Y 7DE ☎ 020 7353 1746 ✉ clerks@2kbw.com
Call Date: Jul 2005, Gray's Inn

SPROULL MR NICHOLAS

Albion Chambers
Broad Street, Bristol BS1 1DR
☎ 0117 927 2144 ✉ clerks@albionchambers.co.uk
Call Date: Nov 1992, Gray's Inn
Pupil Supervisor

Practising Areas: Employment, Family, Personal Injury

SQUIRE MR PHILIP DENBY

3 Dr Johnson's Buildings
Ground Floor, 3 Dr Johnson's Buildings, Temple, London EC4Y 7BA ☎ 020 7353 4854
✉ clerks@3djb.co.uk
Call Date: Nov 1997, Inner Temple
Pupil Supervisor

Practising Areas: Family

SQUIRRELL MR BENJAMIN

Nine Bedford Row
9 Bedford Row, London WC1R 4AZ
☎ 020 7489 2727 ✉ clerks@9bedfordrow.co.uk
Call Date: Oct 1990, Inner Temple
Pupil Supervisor

Practising Areas: Crime, Regulatory Law

ST LOUIS MR BRIAN LLOYD

15 New Bridge Street
London EC4V 6AU ☎ 020 7842 1900
✉ clerks@15nbs.com
Call Date: Oct 1994, Middle Temple
Pupil Supervisor

Practising Areas: Civil Liberties, Courts Martial, Crime, Crime (Corporate/Fraud), Employment

STABLES MR GORDON

Call Date: Oct 1995, Lincoln's Inn
Pupil Supervisor

STADDON MR PAUL

Tanfield Chambers
2-5 Warwick Court, London WC1R 5DJ
☎ 020 7421 5300 ✉ clerks@tanfieldchambers.co.uk
Call Date: Jul 1976, Inner Temple

Practising Areas: Arbitration, Banking, Chancery (General), Chancery (Land Law), Commercial Property, Employment, Entertainment, Franchising, Intellectual Property, Landlord & Tenant, Professional Negligence, Sale & Carriage of Goods

STAGG MR PAUL ANDREW

1 Chancery Lane
London WC2A 1LF ☎0845 634 6666
✉clerks@1chancerylane.com
Call Date: Oct 1994, Gray's Inn
Pupil Supervisor

Practising Areas: Administrative, Civil Liberties, Common Law (General), Discrimination, Education, Employment, Housing, Landlord & Tenant, Local Government, Personal Injury, Professional Negligence

STANAGE MR NICK SEAN

Doughty Street Chambers
53-54 Doughty Street, London WC1N 2LS
☎020 7404 1313 ✉enquiries@doughtystreet.co.uk
Doughty Street Chambers
Pall Mall Court, 61-67 King Street, Manchester M2 4PD ☎0161 618 1066
Doughty Street Chambers
5th Floor, Broad Quay House, Prince Street, Bristol BS1 4DJ ☎01179 058 717
Call Date: Oct 1997, Inner Temple

Practising Areas: Civil Liberties, Common Law (General), Human Rights, Immigration

STANBURY MRS LOUISE EMMA

Bank House Chambers
Old Bank House, Hartshead, Sheffield S1 2EL
☎0114 275 1223 ✉w.digby@bankhousechambers.co.uk
Call Date: Oct 2004, Lincoln's Inn

STANBURY MR MATTHEW FRANCIS

Chambers of Ian Macdonald QC
Garden Court North, 22 Oxford Court, Manchester M2 3WQ ☎0161 236 1840
✉clerks@gcnchambers.co.uk
Call Date: Oct 2004, Gray's Inn

Practising Areas: Administrative, Civil Liberties, Common Law (General), Crime, Human Rights

STANDFAST MR PHILIP ARTHUR

St Paul's Chambers
5th Floor, St Paul's House, 23 Park Square South, Leeds LS1 2ND ☎0113 245 5866
Call Date: Jul 1980, Inner Temple
Pupil Supervisor

Practising Areas: Crime, Discrimination, Employment, Regulatory Law

STANFORD MR TONY JAMES

Old Bailey Chambers
15 Old Bailey, London EC4M 7EF
☎020 3008 6404
✉clerks@15oldbaileychambers.com
Call Date: Nov 1996, Lincoln's Inn

Practising Areas: Administrative, Civil Liberties, Common Law (General), Courts Martial, Crime, Crime (Corporate/Fraud), Defamation, Ecclesiastical, Education, Employment, Entertainment, Environment, Film, Cable & TV, Health & Safety, Healthcare, Housing, Human Rights, Licensing, Local Government, Medical Negligence, Mental Health, Professional Negligence, Regulatory Law

STANISTREET MISS PENELOPE

Call Date: Oct 1993, Lincoln's Inn
Pupil Supervisor

STANLEY MRS GILLIAN FRANCES

1 Garden Court Family Law Chambers
Ground Floor, One Garden Court, Temple, London EC4Y 9BJ ☎020 7797 7900
✉clerks@1gc.com
Call Date: Jul 2001, Middle Temple
Pupil Supervisor

Practising Areas: Family, Family Provision

STANSFIELD MR PIERS ALISTAIR QC (2012)

Keating Chambers
15 Essex Street, London WC2R 3AA
☎020 7544 2600 ✉clerks@keatingchambers.com
Call Date: Nov 1993, Inner Temple
Pupil Supervisor

Practising Areas: Arbitration, Construction, Energy, Information Technology, Insurance, Professional Negligence

STANZEL MRS SARAH ASTRID

Tanfield Chambers
2-5 Warwick Court, London WC1R 5DJ
☎020 7421 5300 ✉clerks@tanfieldchambers.co.uk
Call Date: Jul 1999, Inner Temple

Practising Areas: Employment, Foreign Law

C

STAPLES MISS JOANNA LIDA

Dyers Chambers
35 Bedford Row, London WC1R 4JH
☎ 020 7404 1881 ✉ admin@dyerschambers.com
Call Date: Oct 2003, Lincoln's Inn

Practising Areas: Crime

STARCEVIC MR PETAR

St Philips Chambers
55 Temple Row, Birmingham B2 5LS
☎ 0121 246 7000 ✉ clerks@st-philips.com
Call Date: Jul 1983, Inner Temple
Pupil Supervisor

Practising Areas: Common Law (General), Discrimination, Employment, Insurance, Medical Negligence, Personal Injury, Professional Negligence

STARR MRS TERESA MARGARET

Great James Street Chambers
37 Great James Street, London WC1N 3HB
☎ 020 7440 4949 ✉ chambers@greatjames.co.uk
Call Date: Oct 2000, Middle Temple

Practising Areas: Care Proceedings, Common Law (General), Crime, Family, Family Provision, Landlord & Tenant, Licensing, Personal Injury

STAVROU MISS XENIA

5 King's Bench Walk
5 King's Bench Walk, Temple, London EC4Y 7DN ☎ 020 7353 5638 ✉ clerks@5kbw.co.uk
Call Date: Nov 1998, Middle Temple

STEAD MR RICHARD JAMES

St John's Chambers
101 Victoria Street, Bristol BS1 6PU
☎ 0117 923 4700 ✉ clerks@stjohnschambers.co.uk
Call Date: Jul 1979, Middle Temple
Pupil Supervisor, Recorder

Practising Areas: Arbitration, Civil Litigation, Common Law (General), Construction, Health & Safety, Inquests, Insurance, Personal Injury, Professional Negligence, Sale & Carriage of Goods, Sports

STEBBINGS MR IAN ANTHONY

1 Gray's Inn Square
Ground Floor, 1 Gray's Inn Square, London WC1R 5AA ☎ 020 7405 0001
Call Date: Oct 2001, Lincoln's Inn

Practising Areas: Aviation, Civil Litigation, Common Law (General), Coroners Inquests, Courts Martial, Crime, Disciplinary Tribunals, Discrimination, Education, Employment, Environment, Film, Cable & TV, Health & Safety, Healthcare, Inquests, Licensing, Local Government, Parliamentary, Personal Injury, Professional Negligence, Regulatory Law, Road Traffic And Highways, Sports

STEDMAN MR ARYAN JOHN

Chambers of Mr A J Stedman
24a Palm Bay Avenue, Cliftonville, Kent CT9 3DQ ☎ 07702 870575
✉ aryanstedman@hotmail.com
Call Date: Nov 1997, Middle Temple

Practising Areas: Administrative, Employment

STEEL MR JOHN BRYCHAN QC (1993)

4-5 Gray's Inn Square
Gray's Inn, London WC1R 5AH
☎ 020 7404 5252 ✉ clerks@4-5.co.uk
Call Date: Jul 1978, Gray's Inn
Recorder

Practising Areas: Administrative, Aviation, Environment, Licensing, Local Government, Town & Country Planning

STEELE MISS JENNIFER ANNE

New Walk Chambers
27 New Walk, Leicester, Leicestershire LE1 6TE ☎ 0871 200 1298 / 0116 255 9144
✉ clerks@newwalkchambers.co.uk
Call Date: Jul 2002, Middle Temple
Pupil Supervisor

STEIN MR DANIEL ALEXANDER

No5 Chambers
Fountain Court, Steelhouse Lane, Birmingham B4 6DR ☎ 0845 210 5555 ✉ info@no5.com
No5 Chambers
Greenwood House, 4-7 Salisbury Court, London EC4Y 8AA ☎ 0845 210 5555
No5 Chambers
38 Queen Square, Bristol BS1 4QS
☎ 0845 210 5555
Call Date: Jul 1998, Gray's Inn

Practising Areas: Copyright, Crime, Crime (Corporate/Fraud), Environment, Health & Safety, Information Technology, Intellectual Property, Regulatory Law, Trademarks

STEIN MR SAMUEL QC (2009)

Dyers Chambers
35 Bedford Row, London WC1R 4JH
☎020 7404 1881 ✉admin@dyerschambers.com
Westgate Chambers
64 High Street, Lewes, East Sussex BN7 1XG
☎01273 480510
✉clerks@westgate-chambers.co.uk
Call Date: Nov 1988, Inner Temple

Practising Areas: Crime, Crime (Corporate/Fraud)

STELLING MR NIGEL ROY

Citadel Chambers
The Citadel, 190 Corporation Street, Birmingham B4 6QD ☎0121 233 8500
✉clerks@citadelchambers.com
Call Date: Jul 1987, Inner Temple

Practising Areas: Crime, Crime (Corporate/Fraud), Mental Health, Regulatory Law, Sports

STEMP MR SCOTT

12 College Place
Fauvelle Buildings, 12 College Place, Southampton SO15 2FE ☎023 8032 0320
✉clerks@12cp.co.uk
Call Date: Oct 2000, Inner Temple

Practising Areas: Common Law (General), Crime, Crime (Corporate/Fraud), Environment, Health & Safety, Local Government, Road Traffic And Highways, Town & Country Planning

STENHOUSE MR JOHN ALEXANDER

Nightingale Chambers
Nightingale Cottage, Drakelow Lane, Wolverley, Worcestershire DY11 5RU
☎01562 851350 ✉john@jasten.free-online.co.uk
Call Date: Nov 1986, Lincoln's Inn

Practising Areas: Bankruptcy, Chancery (General), Chancery (Land Law), Commercial Litigation, Commercial Property, Common Law (General), Company & Commercial, Construction, Environment, Equity, Wills & Trusts, Family Provision, Housing, Human Rights, Insolvency, Landlord & Tenant, Partnership, Probate & Administration, Professional Negligence, Sale & Carriage of Goods, Town & Country Planning

STEPHENS MISS JESSICA

Keating Chambers
15 Essex Street, London WC2R 3AA
☎020 7544 2600 ✉clerks@keatingchambers.com
Call Date: Jul 2001, Lincoln's Inn
Pupil Supervisor

Practising Areas: Arbitration, Common Law (General), Construction, Information Technology, Professional Negligence

STEPHENS MR MICHAEL ALLEN

St Ive's Chambers
Whittall Street, Birmingham B4 6DH
☎0121 236 0863 ✉clerks@stiveschambers.co.uk
Design Chambers
24 Arterberry Road, Wimbledon, London SW20 8AH ☎020 7353 0747
✉manager@designchambers.com
Call Date: Jul 1983, Middle Temple
Pupil Supervisor

Practising Areas: Arbitration, Commercial Litigation, Commercial Property, Common Law (General), Construction, Consumer, Disciplinary Tribunals, Health & Safety, Land, Landlord & Tenant, Medical Negligence, Personal Injury, Professional Negligence, Sale & Carriage of Goods

STEPHENSON MR DAVID MATTHEW

1 Mitre Court Buildings
1 Mitre Court Buildings, Temple, London EC4Y 7BS ☎020 7452 8900 ✉clerks@1mcb.com
Call Date: Oct 2005, Lincoln's Inn

Practising Areas: Discrimination, Employment, Housing, Personal Injury

STERLING MR ROBERT ALAN

St James's Chambers
68 Quay Street, Manchester M3 3EJ
☎0161 834 7000 ✉clerks@stjameschambers.com
Zenith Chambers
10 Park Square, Leeds LS1 2LH
☎0113 245 5438 ✉clerks@zenithchambers.co.uk
Call Date: Jul 1970, Gray's Inn
Pupil Supervisor

Practising Areas: Bankruptcy, Chancery (General), Chancery (Land Law), Charities, Commercial Litigation, Commercial Property, Common Land, Company & Commercial, Conveyancing, Copyright, Equity, Wills & Trusts, Family Provision, Financial Services, Insolvency, Landlord & Tenant, Partnership, Probate

C

& Administration, Professional Negligence, Share Options

STERN MR DAVID PATRICK JULIAN

King's Bench Chambers
Wellington House, 175 Holdenhurst Road, Bournemouth, Dorset BH8 8DQ
☎01202 250025
11 Stone Buildings
11 Stone Buildings, Lincoln's Inn, London WC2A 3TG ☎020 7831 6381 ✉clerks@11sb.com
Call Date: Jul 1989, Lincoln's Inn
Pupil Supervisor

Practising Areas: Arbitration, Crime, Crime (Corporate/Fraud), Insurance

STERNBERG MR MICHAEL VIVIAN QC (2008)

4 Paper Buildings
1st Floor, 4 Paper Buildings, Temple, London EC4Y 7EX ☎020 7427 5200 ✉clerks@4pb.com
Call Date: Jul 1975, Gray's Inn

STEVENS MR ANDREW JOHN CHARLES

4 Pump Court
4 Pump Court, Temple, London EC4Y 7AN
☎020 7842 5555 ✉chambers@4pumpcourt.com
Call Date: Oct 2007, Lincoln's Inn

STEVENS MRS HAZEL ANN

East Anglian Chambers
Gresham House, 5 Museum Street, Ipswich, Suffolk IP1 1HQ ☎01473 214481
✉ipswich@ealaw.co.uk
East Anglian Chambers
140 New London Road, Chelmsford, Essex CM2 0AW ☎01473 214481
✉chelmsford@ealaw.co.uk
East Anglian Chambers
15 The Close, Norwich, Norfolk NR1 4DZ
☎01473 214481 ✉norwich@ealaw.co.uk
Call Date: Jul 2001, Lincoln's Inn

Practising Areas: Common Law (General), Company & Commercial, Crime, Family, Family Provision

STEVENS MR MARK NICHOLAS

Chambers of Marion Smullen and Kerim Fuad QC
1 Inner Temple Lane, London EC4Y 1AF
☎020 7427 4400 ✉clerks@1itl.com
Call Date: Nov 1998, Inner Temple

Practising Areas: Courts Martial, Crime, Crime (Corporate/Fraud), Human Rights

STEVENS MR STUART STANDISH

Holborn Chambers
6 Gate Street, Lincoln's Inn Fields, London WC2A 3HP ☎020 7242 6060
Call Date: Jul 1970, Gray's Inn
Pupil Supervisor

Practising Areas: Civil Liberties, Common Law (General), Crime, Crime (Corporate/Fraud), Defamation, Foreign Law

STEVENS MISS SUSANNAH RACHEL

QEB Hollis Whiteman
1-2 Laurence Pountney Hill, London EC4R 0EU ☎020 7933 8855 ✉barristers@qebhw.co.uk
Call Date: Oct 1997, Middle Temple
Pupil Supervisor

STEVENS-HOARE MISS MICHELLE

Hardwicke
New Square, Lincoln's Inn, London WC2A 3SB ☎020 7242 2523
✉enquiries@hardwicke.co.uk
Call Date: Jul 1986, Middle Temple
Pupil Supervisor

Practising Areas: Chancery (Land Law), Civil Litigation, Commercial Litigation, Commercial Property, Common Law (General), Equity, Wills & Trusts, Franchising, Land, Probate & Administration, Professional Negligence

STEVENSON MR DANIEL KEITH

9-12 Bell Yard
London WC2A 2JR ☎020 7400 1800
✉clerks@9-12bellyard.com
Call Date: Oct 2002, Lincoln's Inn

Practising Areas: Crime, Employment, Environment, Film, Cable & TV, Health & Safety, Licensing, Local Government, Medical Negligence, Regulatory Law

STEVENSON MR PAUL ANTHONY

Tanfield Chambers
2-5 Warwick Court, London WC1R 5DJ
☎020 7421 5300 ✉clerks@tanfieldchambers.co.uk
Call Date: Oct 2006, Middle Temple

Practising Areas: Administrative, Chancery (General), Chancery (Land Law), Commercial Litigation, Commercial Property, Employment, Equity, Wills & Trusts, Insurance, Insurance/Reinsurance, Landlord & Tenant, Professional Negligence, Sale & Carriage of Goods, Sports

STEVENSON MR ROBERT LLOYD

Sovereign Chambers
46 Park Place, Leeds LS1 2RY
☎0113 245 1841
✉clerks@sovereignchambers.co.uk
Call Date: Jul 2003, Inner Temple

Practising Areas: Coroners Inquests, Crime, Crime (Corporate/Fraud), Disciplinary Tribunals, Employment, Environment, Inquests, Insurance, Licensing, Personal Injury, Regulatory Law, Sports

STEVENSON DR SIMON JOHN

Park Lane Plowden
19 Westgate, Leeds LS1 2RD
☎0113 228 5049 ✉clerks@parklaneplowden.co.uk
Call Date: Mar 1999, Lincoln's Inn

Practising Areas: Chancery (General), Chancery (Land Law), Charities, Commercial Litigation, Company & Commercial, Intellectual Property, Landlord & Tenant, Partnership

STEWART MR NICHOLAS JOHN CAMERON QC (1987)

Ely Place Chambers
30 Ely Place, London EC1N 6TD
☎020 7400 9600 ✉admin@elyplace.com
Call Date: Jul 1971, Inner Temple

Practising Areas: Administrative, Agriculture, Arbitration, Chancery (General), Chancery (Land Law), Charities, Civil Liberties, Commercial Litigation, Commercial Property, Common Law (General), Company & Commercial, Defamation, Education, Entertainment, Equity, Wills & Trusts, Family Provision, Financial Services, Information Technology, Partnership, Private International, Sports

STEWART MR RICHARD PAUL

Lamb Chambers
Lamb Building, Elm Court, Temple, London EC4Y 7AS ☎020 7797 8300
✉info@lambchambers.co.uk
Call Date: Jul 1975, Gray's Inn
Pupil Supervisor

Practising Areas: Discrimination, Employment, Medical Negligence, Personal Injury, Professional Negligence

STEYNOR MR ALAN CHARLES

Keating Chambers
15 Essex Street, London WC2R 3AA
☎020 7544 2600 ✉clerks@keatingchambers.com
Call Date: Jul 1975, Gray's Inn
Pupil Supervisor, Recorder

Practising Areas: Arbitration, Construction, Environment, Landlord & Tenant, Professional Negligence

STIMPSON MR CHRISTOPHER HUGH

Atkinson Bevan Chambers
1st Floor, 2 Harcourt Buildings, Temple, London EC4Y 9DB ☎020 7353 2112
✉clerks@2hb.co.uk
Call Date: Oct 1999, Middle Temple

Practising Areas: Crime, Crime (Corporate/Fraud)

STIMPSON MR MICHAEL EDWARD

Keating Chambers
15 Essex Street, London WC2R 3AA
☎020 7544 2600 ✉clerks@keatingchambers.com
Call Date: Nov 1969, Lincoln's Inn

STINCHCOMBE MR PAUL DAVID QC (2011)

4-5 Gray's Inn Square
Gray's Inn, London WC1R 5AH
☎020 7404 5252 ✉clerks@4-5.co.uk
Call Date: Jul 1985, Lincoln's Inn
Pupil Supervisor

Practising Areas: Administrative, Civil Liberties, Education, Housing, Local Government, Parliamentary, Sports, Town & Country Planning

STIRLING MR CHRISTOPHER WILLIAM

Field Court Chambers
5 Field Court, Gray's Inn, London WC1R 5EF
☎020 7405 6114 ✉clerks@fieldcourt.co.uk
Call Date: Oct 1993, Inner Temple

Practising Areas: Ancillary Relief, Bankruptcy, Chancery (Land Law), Civil Litigation, Commercial Litigation, Common Law (General), Employment, Equity, Wills & Trusts, Family Provision, Insolvency, Land, Partnership, Probate & Administration, Professional Negligence

STONE MR JOSEPH

Doughty Street Chambers
53-54 Doughty Street, London WC1N 2LS ☎ 020 7404 1313 ✉ enquiries@doughtystreet.co.uk
Doughty Street Chambers
Pall Mall Court, 61-67 King Street, Manchester M2 4PD ☎ 0161 618 1066
Doughty Street Chambers
5th Floor, Broad Quay House, Prince Street, Bristol BS1 4DJ ☎ 01179 058 717
Call Date: Jul 1989, Inner Temple
Pupil Supervisor

Practising Areas: Civil Liberties, Crime, Crime (Corporate/Fraud), Human Rights, Mental Health

STONER MR CHRISTOPHER PAUL QC (2010)

Serle Court
6 New Square, Lincoln's Inn, London WC2A 3QS ☎ 020 7242 6105 ✉ clerks@serlecourt.co.uk
Call Date: Oct 1991, Lincoln's Inn

STOPA MR CHRISTOPHER PAUL MICHAEL

2 King's Bench Walk
2 King's Bench Walk, Temple, London EC4Y 7DE ☎ 020 7353 1746 ✉ clerks@2kbw.com
Call Date: Nov 1976, Middle Temple
Pupil Supervisor

STOREY MR RICHARD ALEXANDER

3 Temple Gardens
Lower Ground Floor, 3 Temple Gardens, Temple, London EC4Y 9AU ☎ 020 7353 3102 ✉ clerks@3tg.co.uk
Call Date: Nov 2005, Lincoln's Inn

Practising Areas: Civil Liberties, Common Law (General), Courts Martial, Crime, Crime (Corporate/Fraud), Film, Cable & TV, Licensing, Local Government, Regulatory Law, Sports

STORK MR BRIAN RAYMOND

3 Temple Gardens
Lower Ground Floor, 3 Temple Gardens, Temple, London EC4Y 9AU ☎ 020 7353 3102 ✉ clerks@3tg.co.uk
Call Date: Jul 1981, Inner Temple
Pupil Supervisor

Practising Areas: Courts Martial, Crime, Crime (Corporate/Fraud), Licensing, Sports

STORRIE MR TIMOTHY JAMES

Lincoln House Chambers
Tower 12, The Avenue North, Spinningfields, 18-22 Bridge Street, Manchester M3 3BZ ☎ 0161 832 5701 ✉ info@lincolnhousechambers.com
Call Date: Oct 1993, Middle Temple
Pupil Supervisor

Practising Areas: Administrative, Civil Liberties, Courts Martial, Crime, Crime (Corporate/Fraud), Human Rights, Local Government, Regulatory Law

STOTT MR MATTHEW GLENN

Field Court Chambers
5 Field Court, Gray's Inn, London WC1R 5EF ☎ 020 7405 6114 ✉ clerks@fieldcourt.co.uk
Broadway House Chambers
Broadway House, 9 Bank Street, Bradford, West Yorkshire BD1 1TW ☎ 01274 722560 ✉ clerks@broadwayhouse.co.uk
Broadway House Chambers
25 Park Square West, Leeds, West Yorkshire LS1 2PW ☎ 0113 246 2600 ✉ clerks@broadwayhouse.co.uk
Call Date: Oct 2005, Middle Temple

STOTT MR PHILIP GEOFFREY

QEB Hollis Whiteman
1-2 Laurence Pountney Hill, London EC4R 0EU ☎ 020 7933 8855 ✉ barristers@qebhw.co.uk
Call Date: Jul 2004, Middle Temple

Practising Areas: Crime, Crime (Corporate/Fraud), Regulatory Law, Sports

STRANEX MR ANDREW JOHN

St Paul's Chambers
5th Floor, St Paul's House, 23 Park Square South, Leeds LS1 2ND ☎ 0113 245 5866
Call Date: Jul 2000, Gray's Inn

Practising Areas: Common Law (General), Courts Martial, Crime, Crime (Corporate/Fraud), Regulatory Law

STRELITZ MR PAUL STEPHEN

East Anglian Chambers
Gresham House, 5 Museum Street, Ipswich, Suffolk IP1 1HQ ☎ 01473 214481 ✉ ipswich@ealaw.co.uk
East Anglian Chambers
53 North Hill, Colchester, Essex CO1 1QA ☎ 01473 214481 ✉ colchester@ealaw.co.uk
East Anglian Chambers
140 New London Road, Chelmsford, Essex CM2 0AW ☎ 01473 214481 ✉ chelmsford@ealaw.co.uk
Call Date: Nov 2005, Lincoln's Inn

Practising Areas: Employment, Personal Injury

STRIDE MR LIONEL ALEXANDER

Temple Garden Chambers
1 Harcourt Buildings, Temple, London EC4Y 9DA ☎ 020 7583 1315 ✉ clerks@tgchambers.com
Call Date: Oct 2005, Lincoln's Inn

Practising Areas: Employment, Insurance, Personal Injury, Professional Negligence, Sports

STRINGER MR LEON PETER

15 Winckley Square
Preston PR1 3JJ ☎ 01772 252828
✉ clerks@15winckleysq.co.uk
Call Date: Oct 1996, Lincoln's Inn

Practising Areas: Care Proceedings, Company & Commercial, Employment, Family, Family Provision

STRONG MR ADRIAN PETER CIARAN

KBW
The Engine House, No 1 Foundry Square, Leeds LS11 5DL ☎ 0113 297 1200
✉ clerks@kbwchambers.com
Call Date: Jul 2001, Gray's Inn
Pupil Supervisor

Practising Areas: Administrative, Coroners Inquests, Crime, Crime (Corporate/Fraud), Data Protection

STRONGMAN MRS CAROL ANN

No 8 Chambers
8 Fountain Court, Steelhouse Lane, Birmingham B4 6DR ☎ 0121 236 5514
✉ clerks@no8chambers.co.uk
Call Date: Oct 2003, Lincoln's Inn

Practising Areas: Care Proceedings, Family

STRUDWICK MISS LINDA DIANE

QEB Hollis Whiteman
1-2 Laurence Pountney Hill, London EC4R 0EU ☎ 020 7933 8855 ✉ barristers@qebhw.co.uk
Call Date: Jul 1973, Lincoln's Inn
Pupil Supervisor

STUART MR BRUCE IAN

Lombard Chambers
1 Sekforde Street, Clerkenwell, London EC1R 0BE ☎ 020 7107 2100
Call Date: Nov 1977, Gray's Inn
Pupil Supervisor

Practising Areas: Coroners Inquests, Courts Martial, Crime, Data Protection, Disciplinary Tribunals, Foreign Law, Regulatory Law, Road Traffic And Highways

STUART MR JAMES WILLIAM

Lamb Chambers
Lamb Building, Elm Court, Temple, London EC4Y 7AS ☎ 020 7797 8300
✉ info@lambchambers.co.uk
Call Date: Oct 1990, Gray's Inn
Pupil Supervisor

Practising Areas: Civil Litigation, Commercial Litigation, Disciplinary Tribunals, Discrimination, Employment, Partnership, Professional Negligence

STUBBS MR ANDREW JAMES QC (2008)

St Paul's Chambers
5th Floor, St Paul's House, 23 Park Square South, Leeds LS1 2ND ☎ 0113 245 5866
Call Date: Jul 1988, Lincoln's Inn
Recorder

Practising Areas: Care Proceedings, Crime, Crime (Corporate/Fraud), Health & Safety, Human Rights, Regulatory Law

STUBBS MR RICHARD JOHN MORRIS

Trinity Chambers
The Custom House, 39 Quayside, Newcastle Upon Tyne NE1 3DE ☎ 0191 232 1927
✉ info@trinitychambers.co.uk
Trinity Chambers
Multi Media Exchange, 72-80 Corporation Road, Middlesbrough TS1 2RF
☎ 01642 247569 ✉ info@trinitychambers.co.uk
Call Date: Jul 2005, Lincoln's Inn

Practising Areas: Administrative, Bankruptcy, Chancery (General), Chancery (Land Law), Commercial Litigation, Employment, Insolvency, Landlord & Tenant

STYLES MR CLIVE RICHARD

Becket Chambers
17 New Dover Road, Canterbury, Kent CT1 3AS ☎ 01227 786331
✉ clerks@becket-chambers.co.uk
Call Date: Oct 1990, Gray's Inn

Practising Areas: Ancillary Relief, Care Proceedings, Children's Law, Common Law (General), Equity, Wills & Trusts, Family, Family Provision, Probate & Administration

STYLES MRS KAY MARGARET

Harcourt Chambers
1st Floor, 2 Harcourt Buildings, Temple, London EC4Y 9DB ☎ 0844 561 7135
Harcourt Chambers
Churchill House, 3 St Aldate's Courtyard, St Aldate's, Oxford OX1 1BN ☎ 0844 561 7135
Call Date: Oct 2000, Middle Temple

Practising Areas: Chancery (Land Law), Family, Family Provision

SUGAR MR SIMON GARETH

1 Garden Court Family Law Chambers
Ground Floor, One Garden Court, Temple, London EC4Y 9BJ ☎ 020 7797 7900
✉ clerks@1gc.com
Call Date: Nov 1990, Middle Temple

Practising Areas: Family, Family Provision, Probate & Administration

SUGARMAN MR JASON ASHLEY

9-12 Bell Yard
London WC2A 2JR ☎ 020 7400 1800
✉ clerks@9-12bellyard.com
Call Date: Jul 1995, Inner Temple
Pupil Supervisor

Practising Areas: Courts Martial, Crime, Crime (Corporate/Fraud), Insolvency, Licensing, Local Government, Regulatory Law, Town & Country Planning

SUGGETT MR IAIN ROBERT OTTAR

Warwick Chambers
959 Chester Road, Birmingham, Birmingham B24 0HQ ☎ 0121 382 9122
✉ warwickchambers@hotmail.com
Call Date: Nov 1989, Lincoln's Inn

Practising Areas: Crime, Crime (Corporate/Fraud)

SUKUL MR RABI SHANKAR

Balham Chambers
Basement, 82 Balham High Road, London SW12 9AG ☎ 020 8675 4609
Call Date: Jul 1988, Lincoln's Inn

Practising Areas: Crime

SULLIVAN MR GEOFFREY CHARLES ALEXANDER

36 Bedford Row
London WC1R 4JH ☎ 020 7421 8000
✉ chambers@36bedfordrow.co.uk
Call Date: Jul 2001, Inner Temple

Practising Areas: Crime, Crime (Corporate/Fraud), Licensing, Regulatory Law

SUMMERS MISS ALLISON

36 Bedford Row
London WC1R 4JH ☎ 020 7421 8000
✉ chambers@36bedfordrow.co.uk
Call Date: Nov 2000, Lincoln's Inn
Pupil Supervisor

Practising Areas: Crime, Crime (Corporate/Fraud), Regulatory Law

SUMMERS MR BENJAMIN DYLAN JAMES

3 Raymond Buildings
3 Raymond Buildings, Gray's Inn, London WC1R 5BH ☎ 020 7400 6400
✉ clerks@3rblaw.com
Call Date: Nov 1994, Inner Temple

Practising Areas: Courts Martial, Crime, Crime (Corporate/Fraud), Financial Services

SUMMERS MR GARY

23 Essex Street
London WC2R 3AA ☎ 020 7413 0353
✉ clerks@23es.com
Call Date: Nov 1985, Gray's Inn
Pupil Supervisor

SUMNALL MISS CHARLENE EMMA LOUISE

Five Paper Buildings
1st Floor, Five Paper Buildings, Temple, London EC4Y 7HB ☎ 020 7583 6117
✉ clerks@5pb.co.uk
Call Date: Jul 2003, Lincoln's Inn

Practising Areas: Copyright, Crime (Corporate/Fraud), Licensing, Regulatory Law, Trademarks

SUTER MR ERICH GEORGE BERNARD

Park Chambers
3 Park Drive, Weybridge Park, Surrey KT13 8UU ☎ 01932 820082
✉ clerks@ParkChambers.co.uk
Call Date: May 1979, Middle Temple

Practising Areas: Disciplinary Tribunals, Discrimination, Employment

SUTHERLAND MR JAMES MORE

Nexus Chambers
7 New Square, Lincolns Inn, London WC2A 3QS ☎ 020 7404 1147 / 020 7831 8309
✉ info@nexuschambers.com
Call Date: Oct 1999, Middle Temple

Practising Areas: Crime, Crime (Corporate/Fraud), Personal Injury

SUTTON MR CLIVE RAYMOND

Chambers of Mr Clive Sutton
18 Mill Lane, Stoke, Bruerne, Northamptonshire NN12 7SH
☎07973 386702
✉cs@clivesuttonbarristerdirect.co.uk
Call Date: Jul 1987, Inner Temple
Pupil Supervisor

Practising Areas: Children's Law, Family, Family Provision

SUTTON-MATTOCKS MR CHRISTOPHER JOHN

5 King's Bench Walk
5 King's Bench Walk, Temple, London EC4Y 7DN ☎020 7353 5638 ✉clerks@5kbw.co.uk
Call Date: Jul 1975, Middle Temple

Practising Areas: Courts Martial, Crime, Crime (Corporate/Fraud), Sports

SWAIN MR JON DAVID

Furnival Chambers
32 Furnival Street, London EC4A 1JQ
☎020 7405 3232
Call Date: Nov 1983, Lincoln's Inn
Pupil Supervisor

SWEENEY MR CHRISTIAN NOEL

3 PB Barristers
3 Paper Buildings, Temple, London EC4Y 7EU
☎020 7583 8055
3 PB Barristers
Royal Talbot House, 2 Victoria Street, Bristol, Avon BS1 6BB ☎0117 928 1520
3 PB Barristers
23 Beaumont Street, Oxford OX1 2NP
☎01865 793 736
3 PB Barristers
4 St Peter Street, Winchester SO23 8BW
☎01962 868884 ✉clerks.winchester@3paper.co.uk
3 PB Barristers
30 Christchurch Road, Bournemouth, Dorset BH1 3PD ☎01202 292102 ✉clerks.bournemouth@3paper.co.uk
Call Date: Oct 1992, Gray's Inn
Pupil Supervisor

SWEENEY MRS LINDA MARY

Call Date: Nov 1999, Middle Temple

SWEENEY MR NOEL CHRISTOPHER

Veritas Chambers
186 High Street, Worle, North Somerset BS22 6JD ☎01934 853 382 ✉nole@nsweeney.plus.com
Call Date: Jul 1975, Gray's Inn
Pupil Supervisor

Practising Areas: Agriculture, Crime, Crime (Corporate/Fraud), Human Rights

SWIFT MR JONATHAN PETER

29 Bedford Row Chambers
London WC1R 4HE ☎020 7404 1044
✉clerks@29br.co.uk
Call Date: Nov 1977, Inner Temple
Pupil Supervisor, Recorder

Practising Areas: Care Proceedings, Family, Family Provision

SWINNERTON MR DAVID MICHAEL

Cornwall Street Chambers
85-87 Cornwall Street, Birmingham B3 3BY
☎0121 233 7500 ✉clerks@cornwallstreet.co.uk
Call Date: Nov 1995, Lincoln's Inn

Practising Areas: Crime, Discrimination, Employment

SWIRSKY MR ADAM ABRAHAM BURL BRADBURY

Lamb Chambers
Lamb Building, Elm Court, Temple, London EC4Y 7AS ☎020 7797 8300
✉info@lambchambers.co.uk
Call Date: Nov 1989, Middle Temple
Pupil Supervisor

Practising Areas: Bankruptcy, Chancery (General), Chancery (Land Law), Civil Litigation, Commercial Litigation, Commercial Property, Common Law (General), Employment, Land, Landlord & Tenant, Partnership, Probate & Administration, Professional Negligence

SYFRET MR NICHOLAS QC (2008)

13 King's Bench Walk
13 King's Bench Walk, Temple, London EC4Y 7EN ☎020 7353 7204 ✉clerks@13kbw.co.uk
13 KBW
32 Beaumont Street, Oxford OX1 2NP
☎01865 311066 ✉clerks@13kbw.co.uk
Citadel Chambers
The Citadel, 190 Corporation Street, Birmingham B4 6QD ☎0121 233 8500
✉clerks@citadelchambers.com
Call Date: Jul 1979, Middle Temple
Recorder

Practising Areas: Crime, Crime (Corporate/ Fraud)

SYMES MR MARK ADRIAN

Garden Court Chambers
57-60 Lincoln's Inn Fields, London WC2A 3LJ
☎020 7993 7600 ✉info@gclaw.co.uk
Call Date: Nov 2004, Lincoln's Inn

Practising Areas: Administrative, Immigration

SYMMS MISS KATHRYN ANN

Number 7 Harrington Street Chambers
7 Harrington Street, Liverpool L2 9YH
☎0151 242 0707 ✉clerks@7hs.co.uk
Call Date: Oct 1990, Gray's Inn

Practising Areas: Care Proceedings, Family, Family Provision

SYRIL MR GEORGE CARMEL

Willesden Chambers
5 Mora Road, London NW2 6SD
☎020 3273 1042 ✉syril@btinternet.com
Luton Chambers
103 Wexham Close, Luton LU3 3TX
☎01582 598394 ✉mshafikhan@hotmail.com
Call Date: Jul 1980, Lincoln's Inn
Pupil Supervisor

Practising Areas: Bankruptcy, Common Law (General), Employment, Medical Negligence, Personal Injury

TABARI MR ALI-REZA

St Philips Chambers
55 Temple Row, Birmingham B2 5LS
☎0121 246 7000 ✉clerks@st-philips.com
Call Date: Nov 2006, Inner Temple

Practising Areas: Administrative, Banking, Chancery (General), Commercial Litigation, Company & Commercial, Financial Services, Insolvency

TAFT MR CHRISTOPHER HEITON

St James's Chambers
68 Quay Street, Manchester M3 3EJ
☎0161 834 7000 ✉clerks@stjameschambers.com
Call Date: Oct 1997, Middle Temple

Practising Areas: Employment, Personal Injury

TAGHDISSIAN MR JAMES ALI

Colleton Chambers
Colleton Crescent, Exeter, Devon EX2 4DG
☎01392 274898 ✉clerks@colletonchambers.co.uk
Call Date: Oct 2005, Gray's Inn

TAGON MISS TAMIA

Call Date: May 1997, Lincoln's Inn

TAHTA MISS NATASHA ALEXANDRA

QEB Hollis Whiteman
1-2 Laurence Pountney Hill, London EC4R 0EU ☎020 7933 8855 ✉barristers@qebhw.co.uk
Call Date: Oct 1998, Inner Temple

Practising Areas: Crime

TALBOT MR JACK RICHARD

Dyers Chambers
35 Bedford Row, London WC1R 4JH
☎020 7404 1881 ✉admin@dyerschambers.com
Call Date: Oct 2004, Middle Temple

Practising Areas: Crime, Crime (Corporate/ Fraud), Personal Injury, Regulatory Law

TALBOT MISS NICOLA EMMA

1 Paper Buildings
1st Floor, 1 Paper Buildings, Temple, London EC4Y 7EP ☎020 7353 3728
✉clerks@onepaper.co.uk
Call Date: Oct 2007, Lincoln's Inn

TALLON MR JOHN MARK QC (2000)

Pump Court Tax Chambers
16 Bedford Row, London WC1R 4EF
☎020 7414 8080 ✉clerks@pumptax.com
Call Date: Jul 1975, Middle Temple

Practising Areas: Tax (Capital & Income), Tax (Corporate)

TAMBLING MR RICHARD

1 Garden Court Family Law Chambers
Ground Floor, One Garden Court, Temple, London EC4Y 9BJ ☎020 7797 7900
✉clerks@1gc.com
Call Date: Oct 2005, Middle Temple

Practising Areas: Family, Family Provision, Mental Health

TANCHEL MISS VIVIENNE JOY

2 Hare Court
Lower Ground, Ground, 1st & 2nd Floor, 2 Hare Court, Temple, London EC4Y 7BH
☎020 7353 3982 ✉clerks@2harecourt.com
Call Date: Nov 2005, Middle Temple

TANSEY MISS ANOUSKA

2-3 Hind Court Chambers
2-3 Hind Court, Fleet Street, London EC4A 3DL ☎ 020 7822 2150 ✉ david@2-3hindcourt.com
Call Date: Nov 2004, Gray's Inn

Practising Areas: Care Proceedings, Family, Family Provision

TANSEY MR ROCK BENEDICT QC (1990)

25 Bedford Row
London WC1R 4HD ☎ 020 7067 1500
✉ clerks@25bedfordrow.com
Call Date: Jul 1966, Lincoln's Inn
Recorder

TAPSELL MR PAUL RICHARD

Becket Chambers
17 New Dover Road, Canterbury, Kent CT1 3AS ☎ 01227 786331
✉ clerks@becket-chambers.co.uk
Call Date: Oct 1991, Middle Temple

Practising Areas: Common Law (General), Crime, Discrimination, Employment, Housing, Landlord & Tenant, Licensing, Local Government, Town & Country Planning

TARBITT MR NICHOLAS EDWARD HENRY

Cornwall Street Chambers
85-87 Cornwall Street, Birmingham B3 3BY
☎ 0121 233 7500 ✉ clerks@cornwallstreet.co.uk
Call Date: Jul 1988, Inner Temple

Practising Areas: Film, Cable & TV, Intellectual Property, Personal Injury, Sports

TARGETT-PARKER MISS LEANNE SUSAN

The Chambers of Miss Leanne Targett-Parker
4 Romola Road, London SE24 9AZ
☎ 020 8674 6694 ✉ parkerls@yahoo.co.uk
No. 3 Fleet Street Chambers
3 Fleet Street, London EC4Y 1DP
☎ 020 7936 4474 ✉ clerks@3fleetstreet.com
Call Date: Oct 2005, Lincoln's Inn

Practising Areas: Care Proceedings, Common Law (General), Crime, Discrimination, Employment, Family, Family Provision, Human Rights, Immigration, Licensing

TATFORD MR WARWICK HENRY PATRICK

9-12 Bell Yard
London WC2A 2JR ☎ 020 7400 1800
✉ clerks@9-12bellyard.com
Call Date: Oct 1993, Lincoln's Inn
Pupil Supervisor

Practising Areas: Courts Martial, Crime, Crime (Corporate/Fraud), Local Government, Regulatory Law

TATLOW MR NICHOLAS MARK

Citadel Chambers
The Citadel, 190 Corporation Street, Birmingham B4 6QD ☎ 0121 233 8500
✉ clerks@citadelchambers.com
Call Date: May 1996, Gray's Inn

Practising Areas: Crime

TAURAH MS SHEILA DOOLARY

Clerksroom (Taunton)
Equity House, Administration Centre, Blackbrook Park Avenue, Taunton, Somerset TA1 2PX ☎ 0845 083 3000
✉ mail@clerksroom.com
Call Date: Oct 1991, Lincoln's Inn

TAUSSIG MR GURION

The Chambers of Grahame Aldous QC
9 Gough Square, London EC4A 3DG
☎ 020 7832 0500 ✉ clerks@9goughsquare.co.uk
Call Date: Jul 2001, Inner Temple

Practising Areas: Commercial Litigation, Common Law (General), Housing, Personal Injury

TAUTZ MR WILLIAM HENRY

Tooks Chambers
81 Farringdon Street, London EC4A 4BL
☎ 020 7842 7575 ✉ clerks@tooks.co.uk
Call Date: Oct 2004, Gray's Inn

Practising Areas: Education, Family

TAVARES MR NATHAN WARREN

Outer Temple Chambers
The Outer Temple, 222 Strand, London WC2R 1BA ☎ 020 7353 6381
✉ clerks@outertemple.com
Call Date: Oct 1992, Middle Temple
Pupil Supervisor

Practising Areas: Common Law (General), Medical Negligence, Personal Injury, Professional Negligence

C

TAYLOR MR ALEX GEOFFREY

Park Lane Plowden
19 Westgate, Leeds LS1 2RD
☎ 0113 228 5049 ✉ clerks@parklaneplowden.co.uk
Park Court Chambers
16 Park Place, Leeds LS1 2SJ
☎ 0113 243 3277
✉ clerks@parkcourtchambers.co.uk
Call Date: Jul 2000, Inner Temple

Practising Areas: Family

TAYLOR MR ALEXANDER RAYMOND LESLIE

Deans Court Chambers
24 St John Street, Manchester M3 4DF
☎ 0161 214 6000 ✉ clerks@deanscourt.co.uk
Deans Court Chambers
101 Walker Street, Preston PR1 2RR
☎ 01772 565 600 ✉ preston@deanscourt.co.uk
Call Date: Nov 2003, Lincoln's Inn

TAYLOR MISS ARABA ARBA KURANKYIWA

Fenners Chambers
3 Madingley Road, Cambridge CB3 0EE
☎ 01223 368761 ✉ clerks@fennerschambers.com
Call Date: Jul 1985, Middle Temple
Pupil Supervisor

Practising Areas: Bankruptcy, Chancery (General), Chancery (Land Law), Charities, Conveyancing, Ecclesiastical, Equity, Wills & Trusts, Family Provision, Mental Health, Partnership, Probate & Administration, Professional Negligence

TAYLOR MR DAVID BARTHOLOMEW

No5 Chambers
Fountain Court, Steelhouse Lane, Birmingham B4 6DR ☎ 0845 210 5555 ✉ info@no5.com
No5 Chambers
Greenwood House, 4-7 Salisbury Court, London EC4Y 8AA ☎ 0845 210 5555
No5 Chambers
38 Queen Square, Bristol BS1 4QS
☎ 0845 210 5555
Call Date: Nov 1993, Lincoln's Inn

TAYLOR MISS EVE REBECCA

St John's Chambers
101 Victoria Street, Bristol BS1 6PU
☎ 0117 923 4700 ✉ clerks@stjohnschambers.co.uk
Call Date: Nov 2003, Lincoln's Inn

Practising Areas: Arbitration, Construction, Medical Negligence, Personal Injury

TAYLOR MR JASON

Albion Chambers
Broad Street, Bristol BS1 1DR
☎ 0117 927 2144 ✉ clerks@albionchambers.co.uk
Call Date: Nov 1995, Gray's Inn

Practising Areas: Crime, Employment, Regulatory Law

TAYLOR MR JONATHAN FORD

St Johns Buildings Liverpool
8th Floor India Buildings, Water Street, Liverpool L2 0XG ☎ 0151 243 6000
✉ clerk@stjohnsbuildings.co.uk
16 Winckley Square
Preston PR1 3JJ ☎ 01772 256100
St Johns Buildings
24a - 28 St John Street, Manchester M3 4DJ
☎ 0161 214 1500 ✉ clerk@stjohnsbuildings.co.uk
Call Date: Nov 1991, Middle Temple

TAYLOR MS KAREN ANNE

Themis Chambers
Suite 14067, 145-157 St John's Street, London EC1V 4PY ☎ 07967 418976
✉ karentaylor@themischambers.co.uk
Call Date: Jul 2004, Inner Temple

Practising Areas: Commercial Litigation, Crime (Corporate/Fraud), Financial Services, Licensing, Local Government, Regulatory Law, Sale & Carriage of Goods, Town & Country Planning, Trademarks

TAYLOR MISS LINDA KATHRYN

Westgate Chambers
64 High Street, Lewes, East Sussex BN7 1XG
☎ 01273 480510
✉ clerks@westgate-chambers.co.uk
Call Date: Oct 1998, Middle Temple

Practising Areas: Family

TAYLOR MS MARY-JANE

Coram Chambers
9-11 Fulwood Place, London WC1V 6HG
☎ 020 7092 3700 ✉ mail@coramchambers.co.uk
Call Date: Oct 2003, Inner Temple

Practising Areas: Care Proceedings, Family, Family Provision

TAYLOR MR MICHAEL JOSEPH FITZ

4 Pump Court
4 Pump Court, Temple, London EC4Y 7AN
☎ 020 7842 5555 ✉ chambers@4pumpcourt.com
Call Date: Nov 1996, Middle Temple
Pupil Supervisor

Practising Areas: Commercial Litigation, Common Law (General), Construction, Information Technology

TAYLOR MR PHILLIP BRIAN MBE

Richmond Green Chambers
5 Connaught Road, Richmond, Surrey TW10 6DW ☎ 020 8948 4801
✉ richmondchambers@btconnect.com
Call Date: Nov 1991, Lincoln's Inn

Practising Areas: Bankruptcy, Commercial Litigation, Common Law (General), Licensing, Personal Injury

TAYLOR MR RHYS STEADMAN

30 Park Place
Cardiff CF10 3BS ☎ 029 2039 8421
✉ clerks@30parkplace.law.co.uk
Call Date: Nov 1996, Inner Temple
Pupil Supervisor

Practising Areas: Chancery (Land Law), Family, Family Provision

TAYLOR MR SIMON

Chambers of Andrew Mitchell QC
33 Chancery Lane, London WC2A 1EN
☎ 020 7440 9950 ✉ clerks@33cllaw.com
Call Date: Oct 1993, Inner Temple
Pupil Supervisor

Practising Areas: Commercial Litigation, Common Law (General), Company & Commercial, Financial Services, Foreign Law

TAYLOR MR STEPHEN NICHOLAS SIMON

KCH Garden Square
1 Oxford Street, Nottingham NG1 5BH
☎ 0115 941 8851 ✉ clerks@kchgardensquare.co.uk
Call Date: Jul 2002, Inner Temple

TAYLOR MRS SUSAN

Trinity Chambers
The Custom House, 39 Quayside, Newcastle Upon Tyne NE1 3DE ☎ 0191 232 1927
✉ info@trinitychambers.co.uk
Trinity Chambers
Multi Media Exchange, 72-80 Corporation Road, Middlesbrough TS1 2RF
☎ 01642 247569 ✉ info@trinitychambers.co.uk
Call Date: Nov 1987, Middle Temple
Pupil Supervisor, Recorder

Practising Areas: Agriculture, Care Proceedings, Family, Family Provision, Mental Health, Regulatory Law, Sports

TAYLOR MRS YVONNE MARIE

Trinity Chambers
The Custom House, 39 Quayside, Newcastle Upon Tyne NE1 3DE ☎ 0191 232 1927
✉ info@trinitychambers.co.uk
Trinity Chambers
Multi Media Exchange, 72-80 Corporation Road, Middlesbrough TS1 2RF
☎ 01642 247569 ✉ info@trinitychambers.co.uk
Call Date: Jul 1998, Inner Temple

Practising Areas: Care Proceedings, Common Law (General), Courts Martial, Crime, Family, Family Provision, Local Government

TEE MR GREGORY JAMES

Guildford Chambers
Stoke House, Leapale Lane, Guildford, Surrey GU1 4LY ☎ 01483 539131
✉ clerks@guildfordchambers.co.uk
Call Date: Jul 1999, Inner Temple

Practising Areas: Commercial Litigation, Housing, Landlord & Tenant

TEJI MISS USHA DEVI

1 Pump Court
Elm Court, Temple, London EC4Y 7AB
☎ 020 7842 7070 ✉ (name)@pumpcourt.co.uk
Call Date: Jul 1981, Lincoln's Inn

TELFORD MR PETER

Yealm House Chambers
88-90 Yealm Road, Plymouth PL8 1BL
☎ 01752 873227 ✉ petertelford@hotmail.co.uk
Southernhay Chambers
33 Southernhay East, Exeter EX1 1NX
☎ 01392 255777
✉ clerks@southernhaychambers.co.uk
Call Date: Jul 1985, Lincoln's Inn
Pupil Supervisor

TEMMINK MR ROBERT-JAN

Quadrant Chambers
Quadrant House, 10 Fleet Street, London EC4Y 1AU ☎ 020 7583 4444
✉ info@quadrantchambers.com
Call Date: Oct 1996, Middle Temple
Pupil Supervisor

Practising Areas: Admiralty, Arbitration, Aviation, Banking, Bankruptcy, Chancery (General), Civil Litigation, Commercial Litigation, Common Law (General), Company & Commercial, Construction, Financial Services, Information Technology, Insolvency, Insurance, Insurance/Reinsurance, Partnership, Professional Negligence, Shipping/Admiralty

TEMPEST MR ALISTAIR MARK

Field Court Chambers
5 Field Court, Gray's Inn, London WC1R 5EF
☎ 020 7405 6114 ✉ clerks@fieldcourt.co.uk
Call Date: Oct 1997, Middle Temple
Pupil Supervisor

Practising Areas: Bankruptcy, Common Law (General), Housing, Landlord & Tenant

TEMPLE MR BENJAMIN TOBY AFAMADO

5 King's Bench Walk
5 King's Bench Walk, Temple, London EC4Y 7DN ☎ 020 7353 5638 ✉ clerks@5kbw.co.uk
Call Date: Oct 1997, Inner Temple

TEMPLE MS ELEANOR LOUISE

Kings Chambers
36 Young Street, Manchester M3 3FT
☎ 0845 034 3444 ✉ clerks@kingschambers.com
Kings Chambers
5 Park Square East, Leeds LS1 2NE
☎ 0845 034 3444 ✉ clerks@kingschambers.com
Kings Chambers
Embassy House, 60 Church Street, Birmingham B3 2DJ ☎ 0845 034 3444
✉ clerks@kingschambers.com
Call Date: Jul 2000, Inner Temple

Practising Areas: Banking, Bankruptcy, Chancery (General), Commercial Litigation, Commercial Property, Company & Commercial, Insolvency, Partnership, Professional Negligence, Sale & Carriage of Goods

TERRY MR ROBERT JEFFREY

Kings Chambers
36 Young Street, Manchester M3 3FT
☎ 0845 034 3444 ✉ clerks@kingschambers.com
Kings Chambers
5 Park Square East, Leeds LS1 2NE
☎ 0845 034 3444 ✉ clerks@kingschambers.com
Kings Chambers
Embassy House, 60 Church Street, Birmingham B3 2DJ ☎ 0845 034 3444
✉ clerks@kingschambers.com
Lamb Chambers
Lamb Building, Elm Court, Temple, London EC4Y 7AS ☎ 020 7797 8300
✉ info@lambchambers.co.uk
Call Date: Jul 1976, Lincoln's Inn
Pupil Supervisor

Practising Areas: Arbitration, Banking, Bankruptcy, Chancery (General), Chancery (Land Law), Commercial Litigation, Commercial Property, Company & Commercial, Construction, Equity, Wills & Trusts, Family Provision, Insolvency, Insurance, Partnership

TETHER MS MELANIE GEORGIA KIM

Old Square Chambers
10-11 Bedford Row, London WC1R 4BU
☎ 020 7269 0300 ✉ clerks@oldsquare.co.uk
Old Square Chambers
3 Orchard Court, St Augustine's Yard, Bristol BS1 5DP ☎ 0117 930 5100
✉ clerks@oldsquare.co.uk
Call Date: Jul 1995, Inner Temple

Practising Areas: Employment

TETLOW MR BERNARD GEOFFREY QC (2011)

Charter Chambers
33 John Street, London WC1N 2AT
☎ 020 7618 4400 ✉ clerks@charterchambers.com
Call Date: Nov 1984, Middle Temple
Pupil Supervisor

Practising Areas: Crime, Crime (Corporate/Fraud), Licensing, Regulatory Law

TETTEH LADY GIFTY DEDE

Chambers of G. D. Tetteh
Ground Floor, 2 Middle Temple Lane, Temple, London EC4Y 9AA ☎ 020 7353 7095
Call Date: Nov 2000, Middle Temple
Pupil Supervisor

THAROO MRS SAFIA

42 Bedford Row
London WC1R 4LL ☎020 7831 0222
✉clerks@42br.com
Call Date: Jul 2004, Inner Temple

Practising Areas: Employment

THIND MISS ANITA

Regency Chambers
45 Priestgate, Peterborough PE1 1LB
☎01733 315215 ✉clerks@regencychambers.law.co.uk
Regency Chambers
Sheraton House, Castle Park, Cambridge CB3 0AX ☎01223 301517
Call Date: Nov 1988, Inner Temple
Pupil Supervisor

Practising Areas: Family, Family Provision

THOMAS MR ANDREW MARTIN QC (2008)

Lincoln House Chambers
Tower 12, The Avenue North, Spinningfields, 18-22 Bridge Street, Manchester M3 3BZ
☎0161 832 5701
✉info@lincolnhousechambers.com
Linenhall Chambers
1 Stanley Place, Chester CH1 2LU
☎01244 348282
✉clerks@linenhallchambers.co.uk
Call Date: Nov 1989, Gray's Inn
Recorder

Practising Areas: Administrative, Commercial Litigation, Common Law (General), Crime, Crime (Corporate/Fraud), Employment, Environment, Health & Safety, Medical Negligence, Personal Injury, Professional Negligence

THOMAS MR DANIEL JAMES

Lincoln House Chambers
Tower 12, The Avenue North, Spinningfields, 18-22 Bridge Street, Manchester M3 3BZ
☎0161 832 5701
✉info@lincolnhousechambers.com
Call Date: Jul 2005, Middle Temple

THOMAS DR DAVID KEITH

Rougemont Chambers
Victory House, Dean Clarke Gardens, Southernhay East, Exeter EX2 4AA
☎01392 208484
✉clerks@rougemontchambers.co.uk
1 Gray's Inn Square
Ground Floor, 1 Gray's Inn Square, London WC1R 5AA ☎020 7405 0001
Call Date: Jul 2003, Inner Temple

Practising Areas: Housing

THOMAS MRS FELICITY

Westgate Chambers
64 High Street, Lewes, East Sussex BN7 1XG
☎01273 480510
✉clerks@westgate-chambers.co.uk
Call Date: Nov 2005, Middle Temple

Practising Areas: Care Proceedings, Chancery (Land Law), Commercial Property, Common Land, Common Law (General), Discrimination, Employment, Family, Family Provision, Housing, Landlord & Tenant, Local Government, Mental Health

THOMAS MR GARETH

Atlantic Chambers
4-6 Cook Street, Liverpool L2 9QU
☎0151 236 4421 ✉info@atlanticchambers.co.uk
Call Date: Jul 1977, Gray's Inn
Pupil Supervisor

Practising Areas: Ancillary Relief, Disciplinary Tribunals, Employment, Family, Personal Injury, Public Law

THOMAS MISS JACQUELINE LOUISE

37 Park Square Chambers
37 Park Square, Leeds LS1 2NY
☎0113 243 9422 ✉chambers@no37.co.uk
Call Date: Oct 2000, Lincoln's Inn

Practising Areas: Care Proceedings, Family, Family Provision

THOMAS MR JAMES AUSTIN

KCH Garden Square
1 Oxford Street, Nottingham NG1 5BH
☎0115 941 8851 ✉clerks@kchgardensquare.co.uk
Call Date: Jul 1999, Middle Temple

Practising Areas: Crime, Crime (Corporate/Fraud), Intellectual Property, Regulatory Law, Sports

THOMAS MR MARK DAVID

5 Essex Court
1st Floor, 5 Essex Court, Temple, London EC4Y 9AH ☎020 7410 2000
✉clerks@5essexcourt.co.uk
Call Date: Oct 2006, Lincoln's Inn

Practising Areas: Commercial Litigation, Common Law (General), Discrimination, Education, Employment, Human Rights, Licensing, Local Government, Parliamentary, Personal Injury, Regulatory Law, Sale & Carriage of Goods, Sports

THOMAS MISS MEGAN MOIRA

6 Pump Court
1st Floor, 6 Pump Court, Temple, London EC4Y 7AR ☎ 020 7797 8400
✉ richardconstable@6pumpcourt.co.uk
6 Pump Court Chambers
6-8 Mill Street, Maidstone, Kent ME15 6XH
☎ 01622 688094 ✉ annexe@6pumpcourt.co.uk
Call Date: Jul 1987, Gray's Inn
Pupil Supervisor

Practising Areas: Administrative, Environment, Local Government, Parliamentary, Town & Country Planning

THOMAS MS REBECCA JANE

42 Bedford Row
London WC1R 4LL ☎ 020 7831 0222
✉ clerks@42br.com
Call Date: Nov 1999, Inner Temple

Practising Areas: Employment

THOMAS MR ROBERT OWAIN PHILIP QC (2011)

Quadrant Chambers
Quadrant House, 10 Fleet Street, London EC4Y 1AU ☎ 020 7583 4444
✉ info@quadrantchambers.com
Call Date: Nov 1992, Lincoln's Inn
Pupil Supervisor

THOMAS MR SIMON CHRISTOPHER

Seven Bedford Row
7 Bedford Row, London WC1R 4BS
☎ 020 7242 3555 ✉ clerks@7br.co.uk
Call Date: Oct 1995, Inner Temple
Pupil Supervisor

THOMAS MR TIMOTHY NICHOLAS

Lombard Chambers
1 Sekforde Street, Clerkenwell, London EC1R 0BE ☎ 020 7107 2100
Call Date: Oct 2002, Lincoln's Inn

Practising Areas: Crime, Crime (Corporate/Fraud)

THOMPSON MR ANDREW EDWARD COURTNEY

Tanfield Chambers
2-5 Warwick Court, London WC1R 5DJ
☎ 020 7421 5300 ✉ clerks@tanfieldchambers.co.uk
Call Date: Nov 1969, Inner Temple
Pupil Supervisor

Practising Areas: Administrative, Common Law (General), Education, Employment, Local Government, Professional Negligence

THOMPSON MR ANDREW IAN

18 Red Lion Court
London EC4A 3EB ☎ 020 7520 6000
✉ chambers@18rlc.co.uk
Call Date: Oct 1991, Gray's Inn
Pupil Supervisor

THOMPSON MR MICHAEL JAMES

Keating Chambers
15 Essex Street, London WC2R 3AA
☎ 020 7544 2600 ✉ clerks@keatingchambers.com
Call Date: Jul 2005, Middle Temple

Practising Areas: Arbitration, Commercial Litigation, Construction, EC & Competition Law, Energy, Professional Negligence

THOMPSON MR PATRICK MILES

St Johns Buildings
24a - 28 St John Street, Manchester M3 4DJ
☎ 0161 214 1500 ✉ clerk@stjohnsbuildings.co.uk
16 Winckley Square
Preston PR1 3JJ ☎ 01772 256100
St Johns Buildings Liverpool
8th Floor India Buildings, Water Street, Liverpool L2 0XG ☎ 0151 243 6000
✉ clerk@stjohnsbuildings.co.uk
KBW
The Engine House, No 1 Foundry Square, Leeds LS11 5DL ☎ 0113 297 1200
✉ clerks@kbwchambers.com
Call Date: Oct 1990, Gray's Inn
Recorder

Practising Areas: Crime, Crime (Corporate/Fraud), Regulatory Law

THOMPSON MISS PAULINE SONITA

5 King's Bench Walk
5 King's Bench Walk, Temple, London EC4Y 7DN ☎ 020 7353 5638 ✉ clerks@5kbw.co.uk
Call Date: Jul 1998, Middle Temple
Pupil Supervisor

Practising Areas: Crime, Crime (Corporate/Fraud)

THOMPSON MR RYAN JEROME

Dyers Chambers
35 Bedford Row, London WC1R 4JH
☎020 7404 1881 ✉admin@dyerschambers.com
Call Date: Mar 1999, Lincoln's Inn

Practising Areas: Crime, Crime (Corporate/Fraud), Licensing, Personal Injury, Regulatory Law

THOMSON MR MARTIN HALDANE AHMAD

Wynne Chambers
5 Kimberley Road, London NW6 7SG
☎020 3239 6964 ✉admin@wynnechambers.co.uk
Call Date: Jul 1979, Gray's Inn

Practising Areas: Charities, Civil Liberties, Discrimination, Employment, Equity, Wills & Trusts, Foreign Law, Islamic Sharia Law

THORNLEY MISS HANNAH ELISE

South Square
3-4 South Square, Gray's Inn, London WC1R 5HP ☎020 7696 9900
✉practicemanagers@southsquare.com
Call Date: Oct 2003, Middle Temple

Practising Areas: Banking, Bankruptcy, Chancery (General), Commercial Litigation, Company & Commercial, Insolvency, Partnership, Professional Negligence

THORNTON MR JOHN ROBERT

Stour Chambers
Mill Studio, 17a Stour Street, Canterbury, Kent CT1 2NR ☎01227 764899
✉clerks@stourchambers.co.uk
Call Date: Nov 2002, Gray's Inn

Practising Areas: Common Law (General), Crime, Crime (Corporate/Fraud), Education, Family, Family Provision

THROWER MR JAMES SIMEON

Chambers of Simeon Thrower
16 Langside Avenue, London SW15 5QT
☎020 8878 7374 ✉simlawhome@aol.com
Call Date: Jul 1973, Middle Temple
Pupil Supervisor

Practising Areas: Banking, Chancery (General), Chancery (Land Law), Commercial Litigation, Commercial Property, Company & Commercial, Landlord & Tenant

THYNE MR RICHARD MICHAEL

Call Date: Oct 2002, Lincoln's Inn

TICCIATI MR OLIVER

4 Pump Court
4 Pump Court, Temple, London EC4Y 7AN
☎020 7842 5555 ✉chambers@4pumpcourt.com
Call Date: Jul 1979, Inner Temple
Pupil Supervisor

Practising Areas: Commercial Litigation, Common Law (General), Construction, Insurance, Personal Injury, Professional Negligence, Sale & Carriage of Goods

TICEHURST MR JOSS EDWARD

Walnut House
63 St. David's Hill, Exeter, Devon EX4 4DW
☎01392 279751 ✉clerks@walnuthouse.co.uk
Call Date: Nov 2006, Inner Temple

TINNION MR ANTOINE

Trinity Chambers
The Custom House, 39 Quayside, Newcastle Upon Tyne NE1 3DE ☎0191 232 1927
✉info@trinitychambers.co.uk
Trinity Chambers
Multi Media Exchange, 72-80 Corporation Road, Middlesbrough TS1 2RF
☎01642 247569 ✉info@trinitychambers.co.uk
Call Date: Nov 2004, Lincoln's Inn

Practising Areas: Chancery (Land Law), Commercial Litigation, Conveyancing, Discrimination, Employment, Landlord & Tenant

TIVADAR MR DANIEL

3 Hare Court
3 Hare Court, Temple, London EC4Y 7BJ
☎020 7415 7800 ✉clerks@3harecourt.com
Call Date: Nov 2005, Middle Temple

Practising Areas: Civil Liberties, Commercial Litigation, Common Law (General), Discrimination, Employment, Private International

TIZZANO MR FRANCO SALVATORE

Old Bailey Chambers
15 Old Bailey, London EC4M 7EF
☎020 3008 6404
✉clerks@15oldbaileychambers.com
Call Date: Feb 1989, Middle Temple
Pupil Supervisor

Practising Areas: Coroners Inquests, Crime, Crime (Corporate/Fraud), Employment, Mental Health

TOCH MISS JOANNA PATRICIA

Chambers of Mr Ami Feder
Ground Floor, Lamb Building, Temple, London EC4Y 7AS ☎020 7797 7788 ✉clerks@lambbuilding.co.uk
Chambers of Mr Ami Feder
Ground Floor, Lamb Building, Temple, London EC4Y 7AS ☎020 7797 7788 ✉clerks@lambbuilding.co.uk
Chambers of Miss J P Toch
1 John Brunt VC Court, Church Road, Paddock Wood, Tonbridge, Kent TH12 6ET ☎01892 833 005 ✉j.toch@yahoo.co.uk
Call Date: Nov 1988, Middle Temple
Pupil Supervisor

Practising Areas: Family, Family Provision

TODD MR MICHAEL ALAN QC (1997)

Erskine Chambers
33 Chancery Lane, London WC2A 1EN ☎020 7242 5532 ✉clerks@erskinechambers.com
Call Date: Jul 1977, Lincoln's Inn

Practising Areas: Banking, Commercial Litigation, Company & Commercial, Corporate Finance, Financial Services, Insolvency, Share Options

TOLSON MR ROBIN STEWART QC (2001)

St John's Chambers
101 Victoria Street, Bristol BS1 6PU ☎0117 923 4700 ✉clerks@stjohnschambers.co.uk
12 College Place
Fauvelle Buildings, 12 College Place, Southampton SO15 2FE ☎023 8032 0320 ✉clerks@12cp.co.uk
Call Date: Nov 1980, Inner Temple

TOMASSI MR MARK DAVID

Charter Chambers
33 John Street, London WC1N 2AT ☎020 7618 4400 ✉clerks@charterchambers.com
Call Date: Nov 1981, Middle Temple
Pupil Supervisor

Practising Areas: Courts Martial, Crime, Health & Safety, Regulatory Law

TOMLINSON MR MICHAEL JAMES

3 PB Barristers
3 Paper Buildings, Temple, London EC4Y 7EU ☎020 7583 8055
3 PB Barristers
30 Christchurch Road, Bournemouth, Dorset BH1 3PD ☎01202 292102 ✉clerks.bournemouth@3paper.co.uk
3 PB Barristers
4 St Peter Street, Winchester SO23 8BW ☎01962 868884 ✉clerks.winchester@3paper.co.uk
3 PB Barristers
Royal Talbot House, 2 Victoria Street, Bristol, Avon BS1 6BB ☎0117 928 1520
3 PB Barristers
23 Beaumont Street, Oxford OX1 2NP ☎01865 793 736
Call Date: Nov 2002, Middle Temple

Practising Areas: Common Law (General), Personal Injury

TOMPKINS MISS KATE

36 Bedford Row
London WC1R 4JH ☎020 7421 8000 ✉chambers@36bedfordrow.co.uk
Call Date: Jul 2003, Lincoln's Inn

Practising Areas: Administrative, Care Proceedings, Crime, Family, Regulatory Law

TOMPKINSON MISS DEBORAH ANN

Clerksroom (Taunton)
Equity House, Administration Centre, Blackbrook Park Avenue, Taunton, Somerset TA1 2PX ☎0845 083 3000 ✉mail@clerksroom.com
Clerksroom (London)
3rd Floor, 218 Strand, London WC2R 1AT ☎0845 083 3000 ✉mail@clerksroom.com
Call Date: Nov 1984, Middle Temple

Practising Areas: Commercial Litigation, Common Law (General), Employment, Insurance/Reinsurance, Personal Injury, Professional Negligence, Sale & Carriage of Goods

TONGE MR CHRISTOPHER PAUL

Bank House Chambers
Old Bank House, Hartshead, Sheffield S1 2EL ☎0114 275 1223 ✉w.digby@bankhousechambers.co.uk
Call Date: Jul 1988, Inner Temple
Pupil Supervisor

Practising Areas: Crime

TOOMEY MR KEVIN IAN

2 Bedford Row
London WC1R 4BU ☎ 020 7440 8888
✉ clerks@2bedfordrow.co.uk
Call Date: Jul 2004, Gray's Inn

Practising Areas: Crime, Crime (Corporate/Fraud), Regulatory Law

TOONE MR ROBERT FRANCIS

KBW
The Engine House, No 1 Foundry Square, Leeds LS11 5DL ☎ 0113 297 1200
✉ clerks@kbwchambers.com
Call Date: Oct 1993, Inner Temple

Practising Areas: Employment

TOPAL MR EROL

Lamb Chambers
Lamb Building, Elm Court, Temple, London EC4Y 7AS ☎ 020 7797 8300
✉ info@lambchambers.co.uk
Call Date: Jul 1998, Middle Temple

Practising Areas: Arbitration, Chancery (Land Law), Commercial Litigation, Commercial Property, Common Law (General), Construction, Crime, Discrimination, Employment, Housing, Landlord & Tenant, Partnership, Sale & Carriage of Goods

TORODE MISS JOANNA DOROTHEA

Chambers of Andrew Mitchell QC
33 Chancery Lane, London WC2A 1EN
☎ 020 7440 9950 ✉ clerks@33cllaw.com
Call Date: Nov 2006, Middle Temple

TOWNEND MR SAMUEL JOHN

Keating Chambers
15 Essex Street, London WC2R 3AA
☎ 020 7544 2600 ✉ clerks@keatingchambers.com
Call Date: Oct 1999, Lincoln's Inn
Pupil Supervisor

Practising Areas: Arbitration, Commercial Litigation, Construction, Energy, Environment, Information Technology, Professional Negligence

TOWNSEND MRS HARRIET CAROLINE JANE

Cornerstone Barristers
2-3 Gray's Inn Square, Gray's Inn, London WC1R 5JH ☎ 020 7242 4986
✉ chambers@2-3gis.co.uk
Call Date: Nov 1992, Middle Temple

Practising Areas: Environment, Local Government, Town & Country Planning

TOZZI MR NIGEL KENNETH QC (2001)

4 Pump Court
4 Pump Court, Temple, London EC4Y 7AN
☎ 020 7842 5555 ✉ chambers@4pumpcourt.com
Call Date: Jul 1980, Gray's Inn

Practising Areas: Arbitration, Banking, Commercial Litigation, Construction, Employment, Entertainment, Insurance, Insurance/Reinsurance, Professional Negligence, Sale & Carriage of Goods, Sports

TRAVERS MR DAVID QC (2010)

6 Pump Court
1st Floor, 6 Pump Court, Temple, London EC4Y 7AR ☎ 020 7797 8400
✉ richardconstable@6pumpcourt.co.uk
6 Pump Court Chambers
6-8 Mill Street, Maidstone, Kent ME15 6XH
☎ 01622 688094 ✉ annexe@6pumpcourt.co.uk
Call Date: Jul 1981, Middle Temple
Pupil Supervisor

TRAVERS MR HUGH

Pump Court Chambers
Upper Ground Floor, 3 Pump Court, Temple, London EC4Y 7AJ ☎ 020 7353 0711
✉ clerks@3pumpcourt.com
Pump Court Chambers
5 Temple Chambers, Temple Street, Swindon SN1 1SQ ☎ 01793 539899
✉ clerks@3pumpcourt.com
Pump Court Chambers
31 Southgate Street, Winchester, Hampshire SO23 9EB ☎ 01962 868 161
✉ clerks@3pumpcourt.com
Call Date: Nov 1988, Middle Temple

TRAVERSI MR JOHN DAVID STEPHEN ANTONA

Nine Bedford Row
9 Bedford Row, London WC1R 4AZ
☎ 020 7489 2727 ✉ clerks@9bedfordrow.co.uk
Call Date: Jul 1977, Gray's Inn
Pupil Supervisor

Practising Areas: Administrative, Crime, Crime (Corporate/Fraud)

TREGIDGO MR MARC GORDON

4 King's Bench Walk
2nd Floor, 4 King's Bench Walk, Temple, London EC4Y 7DL ☎ 020 7822 7000
✉ clerks@4kbw.co.uk
Call Date: Jul 2002, Middle Temple

Practising Areas: Administrative, Care Proceedings, Common Law (General), Crime, Family, Family Provision, Immigration

TREHARNE MR NEIL SIMON

Dingle Chambers
1 Chardstock Avenue, Coombe Dingle, Bristol BS9 2RY ☎ 07818 827754 ✉ N.treharne@btinternet.com
Call Date: Nov 2001, Lincoln's Inn

Practising Areas: Chancery (Land Law), Civil Litigation, Common Law (General), Consumer, Coroners Inquests, Courts Martial, Crime, Crime (Corporate/Fraud), Disciplinary Tribunals, Discrimination, Employment, Entertainment, Immigration, Industrial Diseases, Insolvency, Landlord & Tenant, Personal Injury, Regulatory Law, Road Traffic And Highways, Sale & Carriage of Goods, Sports, Town & Country Planning

TRESMAN MR LEWIS ROBERT SIMON

Staple Inn Chambers
1st Floor, 9 Staple Inn, Holborn Bars, London WC1V 7QH ☎ 020 7242 5240
✉ clerks@stapleinn.co.uk
Call Date: Nov 1980, Gray's Inn
Pupil Supervisor

Practising Areas: Ancillary Relief, Care Proceedings, Children's Law, Civil Litigation, Crime, Disciplinary Tribunals, Employment, Family, Inquests, Licensing, Personal Injury

TREVERTON-JONES MR GREGORY DENNIS QC (2002)

39 Essex Street
London WC2R 3AT ☎ 020 7832 1111
✉ clerks@39essex.com
82 King Street
Manchester M2 4WQ ☎ 0161 870 9969
Call Date: Nov 1977, Inner Temple

Practising Areas: Administrative, Civil Liberties, Common Law (General), Financial Services, Health & Safety, Human Rights, Partnership, Personal Injury, Professional Negligence, Regulatory Law, Sports

TRITTON MR ROBERT GUY HENTON

Hogarth Chambers
5 New Square, Lincoln's Inn, London WC2A 3RJ ☎ 020 7404 0404
✉ barristers@hogarthchambers.com
Call Date: Jul 1987, Inner Temple
Pupil Supervisor

Practising Areas: Copyright, EC & Competition Law, Entertainment, Franchising, Information Technology, Intellectual Property, Patents, Trademarks

TROMPETER MR NICHOLAS SIMEON

Selborne Chambers
10 Essex Street, London WC2R 3AA
☎ 020 7420 9500
✉ clerks@selbornechambers.co.uk
Call Date: Jul 2006, Gray's Inn

Practising Areas: Banking, Bankruptcy, Chancery (General), Chancery (Land Law), Commercial Litigation, Commercial Property, Company & Commercial, Conveyancing, Corporate Finance, Equity, Wills & Trusts, Financial Services, Insolvency, Landlord & Tenant, Partnership, Professional Negligence

TROOP MR PAUL BENJAMIN

Tooks Chambers
81 Farringdon Street, London EC4A 4BL
☎ 020 7842 7575 ✉ clerks@tooks.co.uk
Call Date: Oct 1998, Lincoln's Inn
Pupil Supervisor

TROTTER MISS HELEN CLAIRE

Pump Court Chambers
Upper Ground Floor, 3 Pump Court, Temple, London EC4Y 7AJ ☎ 020 7353 0711
✉ clerks@3pumpcourt.com
Pump Court Chambers
5 Temple Chambers, Temple Street, Swindon SN1 1SQ ☎ 01793 539899
✉ clerks@3pumpcourt.com
Pump Court Chambers
31 Southgate Street, Winchester, Hampshire SO23 9EB ☎ 01962 868 161
✉ clerks@3pumpcourt.com
Call Date: Oct 2004, Gray's Inn

Practising Areas: Employment, Family, Pensions

TROUP MR ALEXANDER WILLIAM

St John's Chambers
101 Victoria Street, Bristol BS1 6PU
☎ 0117 923 4700 ✉ clerks@stjohnschambers.co.uk
Call Date: Nov 1998, Gray's Inn
Pupil Supervisor

Practising Areas: Chancery (General), Chancery (Land Law), Commercial Litigation, Equity, Wills & Trusts, Landlord & Tenant, Professional Negligence

TROWLER MS REBECCA QC (2012)

Doughty Street Chambers
53-54 Doughty Street, London WC1N 2LS
☎ 020 7404 1313 ✉ enquiries@doughtystreet.co.uk
Doughty Street Chambers
Pall Mall Court, 61-67 King Street, Manchester M2 4PD ☎ 0161 618 1066
Doughty Street Chambers
5th Floor, Broad Quay House, Prince Street, Bristol BS1 4DJ ☎ 01179 058 717
Call Date: Oct 1995, Gray's Inn
Pupil Supervisor

Practising Areas: Civil Liberties, Crime, Crime (Corporate/Fraud), Human Rights

TRUMPINGTON MR JOHN HENRY

Staple Inn Chambers
1st Floor, 9 Staple Inn, Holborn Bars, London WC1V 7QH ☎ 020 7242 5240
✉ clerks@stapleinn.co.uk
Call Date: Feb 1985, Middle Temple
Pupil Supervisor

Practising Areas: Administrative, Chancery (General), Chancery (Land Law), Civil Litigation, Commercial Litigation, Commercial Property, Common Law (General), Company & Commercial, Disciplinary Tribunals, Housing, Immigration, Insolvency, Land, Landlord & Tenant, Licensing, Partnership, Personal Injury, Professional Negligence, Road Traffic And Highways, Sale & Carriage of Goods

TRUSTED MR JAMES HARRY

Outer Temple Chambers
The Outer Temple, 222 Strand, London WC2R 1BA ☎ 020 7353 6381
✉ clerks@outertemple.com
Call Date: Jul 1985, Inner Temple
Pupil Supervisor

Practising Areas: Medical Negligence, Personal Injury

TUCKER MR ASHLEY RUSSELL

Park Court Chambers
16 Park Place, Leeds LS1 2SJ
☎ 0113 243 3277
✉ clerks@parkcourtchambers.co.uk
Call Date: Nov 1990, Middle Temple
Pupil Supervisor

Practising Areas: Chancery (General), Commercial Litigation, Coroners Inquests, Discrimination, Employment, Probate & Administration, Professional Negligence

TUCKER MR JAMES ECKHORD

Queen Square Chambers
56 Queen Square, Bristol BS1 4PR
☎ 0117 921 1966 ✉ crime@qs-c.co.uk
Call Date: Oct 2004, Gray's Inn

Practising Areas: Administrative, Crime, Crime (Corporate/Fraud), Regulatory Law

TUCKER MR JAMES WILLIAM RICHARD

Teucro Chambers
Global House, 1 Ashley Avenue, Epsom, Surrey KT18 5AD
Call Date: Jul 2002, Middle Temple

Practising Areas: Chancery (General), Chancery (Land Law), Common Law (General), Company & Commercial, Crime, Crime (Corporate/Fraud), Family, Family Provision, Insolvency, Landlord & Tenant, Personal Injury

TUEJE MISS PATRICIA

1 Pump Court
Elm Court, Temple, London EC4Y 7AB
☎ 020 7842 7070 ✉ (name)@pumpcourt.co.uk
Call Date: Mar 1999, Inner Temple

Practising Areas: Housing, Landlord & Tenant

TUNLEY MR JAMES CHRISTOPHER GORDON

4 KBW
Ground Floor, 4 King's Bench Walk, Temple, London EC4Y 7DL ☎ 020 7822 8822
✉ law@4kbw.net
Call Date: Jul 2005, Lincoln's Inn

Practising Areas: Discrimination, Employment, Personal Injury

C

TURNBULL MISS HELEN MARY

Lamb Chambers
Lamb Building, Elm Court, Temple, London EC4Y 7AS ☎ 020 7797 8300
✉ info@lambchambers.co.uk
Call Date: Nov 2004, Inner Temple

Practising Areas: Bankruptcy, Chancery (General), Chancery (Land Law), Civil Litigation, Commercial Litigation, Commercial Property, Common Law (General), Company & Commercial, Consumer, Costs, Housing, Insolvency, Land, Landlord & Tenant, Professional Negligence

TURNBULL MRS LINDA ANGELA

1 Gray's Inn Square
Ground Floor, 1 Gray's Inn Square, London WC1R 5AA ☎ 020 7405 0001
Call Date: Mar 1998, Lincoln's Inn
Pupil Supervisor

Practising Areas: Ancillary Relief, Children's Law, Family, Family Provision, Human Rights, Immigration

TURNER MR ALAN JOSEPH

Melbeck Chambers
86 Gospel End Road, Sedgley, Dudley, West Midlands DY3 3YU ☎ 020 7404 2166 ✉ alan.turner@melbeck.com
Call Date: Nov 1984, Gray's Inn

Practising Areas: Arbitration, Construction, Environment

TURNER MR JONATHAN CHADWICK QC (2003)

6 King's Bench Walk
Ground Floor, 6 King's Bench Walk, Temple, London EC4Y 7DR ☎ 020 7583 0410
✉ clerks@6kbw.com
Exchange Chambers
One Derby Square, Derby Square, Liverpool L2 9XX ☎ 0151 236 7747
✉ info@exchangechambers.co.uk
Exchange Chambers
7 Ralli Courts, West Riverside, Manchester M3 5FT ☎ 0161 833 2722
Call Date: Jul 1974, Gray's Inn
Recorder

TURNER MR JONATHAN JAMES

Argent Chambers
5 Bell Yard, London WC2A 2JR
☎ 020 7556 5500
✉ briefsin@argentchambers.co.uk
Call Date: Nov 1999, Inner Temple

Practising Areas: Crime, Crime (Corporate/Fraud), Road Traffic And Highways

TURNER MR JUSTYN ROBERT SURTEES

4 King's Bench Walk
2nd Floor, 4 King's Bench Walk, Temple, London EC4Y 7DL ☎ 020 7822 7000
✉ clerks@4kbw.co.uk
Call Date: Jul 2001, Inner Temple

Practising Areas: Common Law (General), Personal Injury

TURNER MR MATHEW JAMES LEYSHON

15 New Bridge Street
London EC4V 6AU ☎ 020 7842 1900
✉ clerks@15nbs.com
Call Date: Oct 2003, Gray's Inn

TURNER MR PAUL ANTONY

10 King's Bench Walk
Ground Floor, 10 King's Bench Walk, Temple, London EC4Y 7EB ☎ 020 7353 7742
✉ Chambers@10kingsbenchwalk.co.uk
Call Date: Nov 1998, Lincoln's Inn

TURNILL MR EVAN

Pallant Chambers
12 North Pallant, Chichester, West Sussex PO19 1TQ ☎ 01243 784538
✉ clerks@pallantchambers.co.uk
Call Date: Jul 2003, Gray's Inn

Practising Areas: Employment

TWEEDY MS LAURA ELIZABETH

Hardwicke
New Square, Lincoln's Inn, London WC2A 3SB ☎ 020 7242 2523
✉ enquiries@hardwicke.co.uk
Call Date: Jul 2007, Lincoln's Inn

TWINE MISS NICOLA

Park Lane Plowden
19 Westgate, Leeds LS1 2RD
☎ 0113 228 5049 ✉ clerks@parklaneplowden.co.uk
Call Date: Jul 1999, Middle Temple

Practising Areas: Commercial Litigation, Employment, Landlord & Tenant, Personal Injury

TWIST MR STEPHEN JOHN

Dere Street Barristers
33 Broad Chare, Newcastle Upon Tyne NE1 3DQ ☎0844 3351551 ✉clerks@derestreet.co.uk
Call Date: Jul 1979, Middle Temple
Pupil Supervisor

Practising Areas: Administrative, Ancillary Relief, Arbitration, Care Proceedings, Children's Law, Civil Liberties, Coroners Inquests, Disciplinary Tribunals, Discrimination, Employment, Equity, Wills & Trusts, Family, Family Provision, Licensing, Local Government

TWYDELL MISS CHERRY LOUISA

Trinity Chambers
Highfield House, Moulsham Street, Chelmsford, Essex CM2 9AH
☎01245 605040 ✉clerks@trinitychambers.com
Call Date: May 1985, Middle Temple

Practising Areas: Care Proceedings, Family, Foreign Law

TYLER MR THOMAS GEOFFREY

3 PB Barristers
3 Paper Buildings, Temple, London EC4Y 7EU
☎020 7583 8055
3 PB Barristers
Royal Talbot House, 2 Victoria Street, Bristol, Avon BS1 6BB ☎0117 928 1520
3 PB Barristers
4 St Peter Street, Winchester SO23 8BW
☎01962 868884 ✉clerks.winchester@3paper.co.uk
3 PB Barristers
23 Beaumont Street, Oxford OX1 2NP
☎01865 793 736
3 PB Barristers
30 Christchurch Road, Bournemouth, Dorset BH1 3PD ☎01202 292102 ✉clerks.bournemouth@3paper.co.uk
Call Date: Oct 1996, Lincoln's Inn

Practising Areas: Ancillary Relief, Family, Family Provision

TYLER MR WILLIAM JOHN

36 Bedford Row
London WC1R 4JH ☎020 7421 8000
✉chambers@36bedfordrow.co.uk
Call Date: Oct 1996, Inner Temple

Practising Areas: Children's Law, Family, Family Provision, Mental Health

TYTHCOTT MISS ELISABETH CLAIRE

18 St John Street
Manchester M3 4EA ☎0161 278 1800
✉clerks@18sjs.com
Call Date: Nov 1989, Inner Temple
Pupil Supervisor

UDOM MISS NANCY INI

Five St Andrew's Hill
5 St Andrew's Hill, London EC4V 5BZ
☎020 7332 5400 ✉Clerks@5sah.co.uk
Call Date: Nov 2002, Lincoln's Inn

Practising Areas: Crime, Crime (Corporate/Fraud), Education, Health & Safety, Local Government, Regulatory Law

UDUJE MR BENJAMIN ELLIOTT

42 Bedford Row
London WC1R 4LL ☎020 7831 0222
✉clerks@42br.com
Call Date: Nov 1992, Middle Temple

Practising Areas: Civil Liberties, Commercial Litigation, Common Law (General), Discrimination, Employment

UFF MR DAVID CHARLES

Call Date: Jul 1981, Gray's Inn
Pupil Supervisor

UME MR CYRIL OBIORA

12 Old Square Chambers
1st Floor, 12 Old Square, Lincoln's Inn, London WC2A 3TX ☎020 7404 0875
✉clerks@12oldsquare.com
Call Date: Jul 1972, Gray's Inn
Pupil Supervisor

Practising Areas: Bankruptcy, Care Proceedings, Education, Foreign Law, Housing, Landlord & Tenant

UNDERHILL MISS ALISON

East Anglian Chambers
53 North Hill, Colchester, Essex CO1 1QA
☎01473 214481 ✉colchester@ealaw.co.uk
East Anglian Chambers
140 New London Road, Chelmsford, Essex CM2 0AW ☎01473 214481
✉chelmsford@ealaw.co.uk
East Anglian Chambers
15 The Close, Norwich, Norfolk NR1 4DZ
☎01473 214481 ✉norwich@ealaw.co.uk

East Anglian Chambers
Gresham House, 5 Museum Street, Ipswich, Suffolk IP1 1HQ ☎01473 214481
✉ipswich@ealaw.co.uk
Call Date: Oct 1997, Gray's Inn

UNIGWE MR SYLVESTER EMEFIONA

11 Gray's Inn Square Chambers
Chambers of Mr Ian Sen, 1st Floor South, 10/11 Gray's Inn Square, London WC1R 5JD ☎020 7405 6879 ✉clerks@11graysinnsquare.com
Essex House Chambers
122-126 Kilburn High Road, Kilburn, London NW6 4HY ☎020 7692 0677
✉essexhousechambers@yahoo.co.uk
Call Date: Jul 1972, Lincoln's Inn

Practising Areas: Civil Litigation, Crime, Disciplinary Tribunals, Employment, Immigration, Insurance/Reinsurance

UPSON MR MICHAEL JAMES

Bank House Chambers
Old Bank House, Hartshead, Sheffield S1 2EL ☎0114 275 1223 ✉w.digby@bankhousechambers.co.uk
Call Date: Oct 1993, Lincoln's Inn
Pupil Supervisor

UPTON MR ALEXANDER STUART ALLEN

23 Essex Street
London WC2R 3AA ☎020 7413 0353
✉clerks@23es.com
Call Date: Oct 2004, Lincoln's Inn

Practising Areas: Crime, Crime (Corporate/Fraud)

UPTON MR JOHN STEWART

4 King's Bench Walk
2nd Floor, 4 King's Bench Walk, Temple, London EC4Y 7DL ☎020 7822 7000
✉clerks@4kbw.co.uk
Call Date: Oct 1998, Gray's Inn

Practising Areas: Administrative, Civil Liberties, Courts Martial, Crime, Crime (Corporate/Fraud), Health & Safety, Human Rights, Licensing, Local Government, Mental Health, Regulatory Law

UPTON MR JONATHAN MICHAEL

Tanfield Chambers
2-5 Warwick Court, London WC1R 5DJ
☎020 7421 5300 ✉clerks@tanfieldchambers.co.uk
Call Date: Jul 2004, Gray's Inn

Practising Areas: Chancery (Land Law), Commercial Litigation, Commercial Property, Equity, Wills & Trusts, Land, Landlord & Tenant, Partnership

USHER MR NEIL MORRIS

Lincoln House Chambers
Tower 12, The Avenue North, Spinningfields, 18-22 Bridge Street, Manchester M3 3BZ
☎0161 832 5701
✉info@lincolnhousechambers.com
Call Date: Oct 1993, Middle Temple
Pupil Supervisor

Practising Areas: Crime, Crime (Corporate/Fraud)

VAHIBOGLU MISS AYSE

Colleton Chambers
Colleton Crescent, Exeter, Devon EX2 4DG
☎01392 274898 ✉clerks@colletonchambers.co.uk
Call Date: Jul 2003, Middle Temple

VAITILINGAM MR ADAM SKANDA QC (2010)

Albion Chambers
Broad Street, Bristol BS1 1DR
☎0117 927 2144 ✉clerks@albionchambers.co.uk
Call Date: Nov 1987, Middle Temple
Pupil Supervisor, Recorder

Practising Areas: Common Law (General), Crime, Employment, Personal Injury, Regulatory Law

VALDER MR PAUL

Five St Andrew's Hill
5 St Andrew's Hill, London EC4V 5BZ
☎020 7332 5400 ✉Clerks@5sah.co.uk
Call Date: Nov 1994, Inner Temple

VALENTINE MR JUSTIN SIMON

Atlantic Chambers
4-6 Cook Street, Liverpool L2 9QU
☎0151 236 4421 ✉info@atlanticchambers.co.uk
Call Date: Oct 1999, Middle Temple

Practising Areas: Landlord & Tenant

VALIOS MR NICHOLAS PAUL QC (1991)

4 Breams Buildings
Chancery Lane, London EC4A 1HP
☎ 020 7092 1900 ✉ clerks@4bb.co.uk
No 8 Chambers
8 Fountain Court, Steelhouse Lane, Birmingham B4 6DR ☎ 0121 236 5514
✉ clerks@no8chambers.co.uk
Call Date: Jun 1964, Inner Temple
Recorder

Practising Areas: Common Law (General), Courts Martial, Crime, Crime (Corporate/Fraud)

VALLANCE MR HENRY

Old Bailey Chambers
15 Old Bailey, London EC4M 7EF
☎ 020 3008 6404
✉ clerks@15oldbaileychambers.com
Call Date: Nov 2004, Inner Temple

Practising Areas: Crime

VALLAT MR RICHARD JUSTIN

Pump Court Tax Chambers
16 Bedford Row, London WC1R 4EF
☎ 020 7414 8080 ✉ clerks@pumptax.com
Call Date: Oct 1997, Gray's Inn
Pupil Supervisor

Practising Areas: Equity, Wills & Trusts, Professional Negligence, Tax (Capital & Income), Tax (Corporate)

VALLEY MISS HELEN MARIA

25 Bedford Row
London WC1R 4HD ☎ 020 7067 1500
✉ clerks@25bedfordrow.com
Call Date: Oct 1990, Middle Temple
Pupil Supervisor

Practising Areas: Crime, Crime (Corporate/Fraud)

VALLI MR YUNUS

No.6 Park Square
Leeds LS1 2LW ☎ 0113 245 9763
✉ Tim@no6.co.uk
Call Date: Nov 1994, Lincoln's Inn

VAN DER LEIJ DR MARTINA

Field Court Chambers
5 Field Court, Gray's Inn, London WC1R 5EF
☎ 020 7405 6114 ✉ clerks@fieldcourt.co.uk
Call Date: Jul 2001, Inner Temple

Practising Areas: Commercial Litigation, Common Law (General), Family, Landlord & Tenant, Licensing, Personal Injury, Professional Negligence

VAN OVERDIJK MISS CLAIRE ORIT

No5 Chambers
Greenwood House, 4-7 Salisbury Court, London EC4Y 8AA ☎ 0845 210 5555
No5 Chambers
38 Queen Square, Bristol BS1 4QS
☎ 0845 210 5555
No5 Chambers
Fountain Court, Steelhouse Lane, Birmingham B4 6DR ☎ 0845 210 5555 ✉ info@no5.com
Call Date: Jul 2003, Lincoln's Inn

Practising Areas: Administrative, Chancery (General), Chancery (Land Law), Civil Liberties, Commercial Litigation, Commercial Property, Company & Commercial, Health & Safety, Healthcare, Housing, Human Rights, Landlord & Tenant, Local Government, Mental Health, Public International, Regulatory Law

VAN ROL MRS KATHERINE ANN

4 Paper Buildings
1st Floor, 4 Paper Buildings, Temple, London EC4Y 7EX ☎ 020 7427 5200 ✉ clerks@4pb.com
Call Date: Jul 2002, Lincoln's Inn

VAN SPALL MS PENELOPE-JANE

Chartlands Chambers
3 St Giles Terrace, Northampton NN1 2BN
☎ 01604 603322
✉ enquiries@chartlands-chambers.co.uk
Call Date: Jul 1998, Gray's Inn

Practising Areas: Care Proceedings, Education, Family, Family Provision

VAN TONDER MR GERARD DIRK

New Square Chambers
12 New Square, Lincoln's Inn, London WC2A 3SW ☎ 020 7419 8000 ✉ robin.hollington@newsquarechambers.co.uk
Call Date: Nov 1990, Middle Temple
Pupil Supervisor

Practising Areas: Banking, Bankruptcy, Chancery (General), Chancery (Land Law), Civil Litigation, Commercial Litigation, Commercial Property, Company & Commercial, Conveyancing, Costs, Equity, Wills & Trusts, Insolvency,

Land, Landlord & Tenant, Partnership, Professional Negligence, Share Options

VANE THE HON CHRISTOPHER JOHN FLETCHER

Trinity Chambers
The Custom House, 39 Quayside, Newcastle Upon Tyne NE1 3DE ☎0191 232 1927
✉info@trinitychambers.co.uk
Trinity Chambers
Multi Media Exchange, 72-80 Corporation Road, Middlesbrough TS1 2RF
☎01642 247569 ✉info@trinitychambers.co.uk
Call Date: Nov 1976, Inner Temple

Practising Areas: Chancery (General), Chancery (Land Law), Family Provision, Landlord & Tenant, Partnership, Probate & Administration

VANHEGAN MR TOBY BARTHOLOMEW

Arden Chambers
20 Bloomsbury Square, London WC1A 2NS
☎020 7242 4244 ✉clerks@ardenchambers.com
Call Date: Oct 1996, Middle Temple
Pupil Supervisor

Practising Areas: Administrative, Chancery (Land Law), Commercial Property, Housing, Human Rights, Immigration, Landlord & Tenant, Local Government

VARLEY MR JAMES ROBERT KENRICK

1 High Pavement
Nottingham NG1 1HF ☎0115 941 8218
✉clerks@1highpavement.co.uk
Call Date: Nov 1997, Lincoln's Inn

Practising Areas: Crime

VASILESCU MR ANDREI CONSTANTIN

Chambers of Martin Burr
15 Old Bailey, London EC4M 7EF
☎0845 123 1234 ✉clerks@barristerweb.com
Call Date: Nov 1993, Lincoln's Inn

Practising Areas: Bankruptcy, Chancery (Land Law), Civil Litigation, Commercial Litigation, Common Land, Company & Commercial, Copyright, Housing, Insolvency, Licensing, Personal Injury

VASSALL-ADAMS MR GUY LUKE

Doughty Street Chambers
53-54 Doughty Street, London WC1N 2LS
☎020 7404 1313 ✉enquiries@doughtystreet.co.uk
Doughty Street Chambers
Pall Mall Court, 61-67 King Street, Manchester M2 4PD ☎0161 618 1066
Doughty Street Chambers
5th Floor, Broad Quay House, Prince Street, Bristol BS1 4DJ ☎01179 058 717
Call Date: Nov 2000, Middle Temple
Pupil Supervisor

Practising Areas: Administrative, Civil Liberties, Defamation, Human Rights

VAUGHAN MR ANTHONY

Garden Court Chambers
57-60 Lincoln's Inn Fields, London WC2A 3LJ
☎020 7993 7600 ✉info@gclaw.co.uk
Call Date: Oct 2006, Inner Temple

Practising Areas: Administrative, Discrimination, Employment, Immigration

VAUGHAN MR SIMON PETER

Exchange Chambers
7 Ralli Courts, West Riverside, Manchester M3 5FT ☎0161 833 2722
Exchange Chambers
One Derby Square, Derby Square, Liverpool L2 9XX ☎0151 236 7747
✉info@exchangechambers.co.uk
Exchange Chambers
Oxford House, Oxford Row, Leeds LS1 3BE
☎0113 203 1970
✉spencer@exchangechambers.co.uk
Call Date: Nov 1989, Gray's Inn
Pupil Supervisor

VAUGHAN MR TERENCE PAUL

Fenners Chambers
3 Madingley Road, Cambridge CB3 0EE
☎01223 368761 ✉clerks@fennerschambers.com
Call Date: Oct 1996, Middle Temple

Practising Areas: Arbitration, Commercial Litigation, Common Law (General), Construction, Personal Injury, Professional Negligence, Sale & Carriage of Goods

VAUGHAN-WILLIAMS MR ARTHUR LAURENCE

13 Old Square Chambers
Ground Floor, 14 Old Square, Lincoln's Inn, London WC2A 3UE ☎ 020 7831 4445
✉ clerks@13oldsquare.com
Call Date: Nov 1988, Lincoln's Inn

Practising Areas: Arbitration, Banking, Bankruptcy, Chancery (General), Chancery (Land Law), Commercial Litigation, Commercial Property, Insolvency, Insurance, Insurance/Reinsurance, Landlord & Tenant, Local Government, Partnership, Private International, Probate & Administration, Professional Negligence, Tax (Capital & Income), Tax (Corporate), Town & Country Planning

VAVRECKA MR DAVID PAUL FRANK

Coram Chambers
9-11 Fulwood Place, London WC1V 6HG
☎ 020 7092 3700 ✉ mail@coramchambers.co.uk
Call Date: Oct 1992, Middle Temple
Pupil Supervisor

Practising Areas: Care Proceedings, Family

VENCATACHELLUM MS GLENDA ROXANDE

Rowchester Chambers
4 Rowchester Court, Whittall Street, Birmingham B4 6DH ☎ 0121 233 2327
✉ clerks@rowchesterchambers.co.uk
Call Date: Oct 1996, Middle Temple

Practising Areas: Ancillary Relief, Care Proceedings, Family, Human Rights, Immigration

VERDAN MR ALEXANDER QC (2006)

4 Paper Buildings
1st Floor, 4 Paper Buildings, Temple, London EC4Y 7EX ☎ 020 7427 5200 ✉ clerks@4pb.com
Call Date: Nov 1987, Inner Temple
Recorder

Practising Areas: Family

VERDUYN DR ANTHONY JAMES

St Philips Chambers
55 Temple Row, Birmingham B2 5LS
☎ 0121 246 7000 ✉ clerks@st-philips.com
Call Date: Oct 1993, Lincoln's Inn
Pupil Supervisor, Recorder

Practising Areas: Chancery (General), Chancery (Land Law), Commercial Litigation, Commercial Property, Housing, Landlord & Tenant

VERNON MR ELLIOT CURT

No. 3 Fleet Street Chambers
3 Fleet Street, London EC4Y 1DP
☎ 020 7936 4474 ✉ clerks@3fleetstreet.com
Call Date: Oct 2001, Lincoln's Inn

Practising Areas: Banking, Bankruptcy, Chancery (General), Chancery (Land Law), Commercial Litigation, Commercial Property, Common Law (General), Company & Commercial, Conveyancing, Family Provision, Housing, Insolvency, Landlord & Tenant, Licensing, Partnership, Probate & Administration, Professional Negligence, Sale & Carriage of Goods

VERNON MR ROBERT ANTHONY

9 Park Place
Cardiff, South Glamorgan CF10 3DP
☎ 029 2038 2731 ✉ clerks@9parkplace.co.uk
Call Date: Nov 2000, Lincoln's Inn

VICKERY MR NEIL MICHAEL

13 King's Bench Walk
13 King's Bench Walk, Temple, London EC4Y 7EN ☎ 020 7353 7204 ✉ clerks@13kbw.co.uk
13 KBW
32 Beaumont Street, Oxford OX1 2NP
☎ 01865 311066 ✉ clerks@13kbw.co.uk
Call Date: Jul 1985, Gray's Inn
Pupil Supervisor

Practising Areas: Chancery (Land Law), Commercial Litigation, Commercial Property, Disciplinary Tribunals, Employment, Land, Landlord & Tenant

VICTOR-MAZELI MISS JACQUELINE

Bell Yard Chambers
116/118 Chancery Lane, London WC2A 1PP
☎ 020 7306 9292
✉ byclerks@bellyardchambers.co.uk
Chambers of Martin Burr
15 Old Bailey, London EC4M 7EF
☎ 0845 123 1234 ✉ clerks@barristerweb.com
Call Date: Nov 1997, Middle Temple

Practising Areas: Civil Litigation, Human Rights, Immigration

VILLAROSA MISS ANNUNZIATA

Clerksroom (London)
3rd Floor, 218 Strand, London WC2R 1AT
☎ 0845 083 3000 ✉ mail@clerksroom.com
Clerksroom (Taunton)
Equity House, Administration Centre, Blackbrook Park Avenue, Taunton, Somerset TA1 2PX ☎ 0845 083 3000
✉ mail@clerksroom.com
Call Date: Jul 1995, Middle Temple

Practising Areas: Ancillary Relief, Children's Law, Family, Family Provision

VINE MR JAMES PETER STOCKMAN

Five St Andrew's Hill
5 St Andrew's Hill, London EC4V 5BZ
☎ 020 7332 5400 ✉ Clerks@5sah.co.uk
Call Date: Nov 1977, Middle Temple
Pupil Supervisor

Practising Areas: Crime, Crime (Corporate/Fraud)

VINE MS SARAH JANE

2 Pump Court
1st Floor, 2 Pump Court, Temple, London EC4Y 7AH ☎ 020 7353 5597
✉ clerks@2pumpcourt.co.uk
Call Date: Mar 1997, Inner Temple

Practising Areas: Crime

VINEALL MR NICHOLAS EDWARD JOHN QC (2006)

4 Pump Court
4 Pump Court, Temple, London EC4Y 7AN
☎ 020 7842 5555 ✉ chambers@4pumpcourt.com
Call Date: Nov 1988, Middle Temple

Practising Areas: Commercial Litigation, Construction, Financial Services, Insurance, Professional Negligence

VITIELLO MR FABIO ANGELO-GIUSEPPE

Staple Inn Chambers
1st Floor, 9 Staple Inn, Holborn Bars, London WC1V 7QH ☎ 020 7242 5240
✉ clerks@stapleinn.co.uk
Call Date: Oct 1995, Inner Temple

Practising Areas: Chancery (General), Civil Litigation, Commercial Litigation, Common Law (General), Company & Commercial, Information Technology, Intellectual Property, International Trade, Landlord & Tenant, Sale & Carriage of Goods, Shipping/Admiralty

VOKES MR STEPHEN JOHN

No 8 Chambers
8 Fountain Court, Steelhouse Lane, Birmingham B4 6DR ☎ 0121 236 5514
✉ clerks@no8chambers.co.uk
Call Date: Jul 1989, Lincoln's Inn

Practising Areas: Immigration

VOLLENWEIDER MR AMIOT MARCUS ELLERTON

Thomas More Chambers
7 Lincoln's Inn Fields, London WC2A 3BP
☎ 020 7404 7000 ✉ clerks@thomasmore.co.uk
Call Date: Oct 2000, Gray's Inn
Pupil Supervisor

Practising Areas: Ancillary Relief, Care Proceedings, Children's Law, Common Law (General), Costs, Courts Martial, Crime, Crime (Corporate/Fraud), Defamation, Family, Family Provision, Mental Health, Personal Injury

VON POMMERN-PEGLOW DR MICHAEL ALFRED HERMAN PR.

Brunswick Chambers
2 Middle Temple Lane, Temple, London EC4Y 9AA ☎ 020 7353 1987
✉ alpha@brunswickchambers.net
Call Date: Jul 1993, Middle Temple

Practising Areas: Arbitration, Banking, Commercial Litigation, Company & Commercial, Competition, Corporate Finance, EC & Competition Law, Energy, Financial Services, Foreign Law, Insurance/Reinsurance, International Trade, Private International, Public International

VON WACHTER LADY VICTORIA NORA CRESSIDA

5 Essex Court
1st Floor, 5 Essex Court, Temple, London EC4Y 9AH ☎ 020 7410 2000
✉ clerks@5essexcourt.co.uk
Call Date: Jul 1997, Gray's Inn
Pupil Supervisor

Practising Areas: Employment

VONBERG MR THOMAS CHARLES

Devereux Chambers
Queen Elizabeth Building, Temple, London EC4Y 9BS ☎ 020 7353 7534
✉ clerks@devchambers.co.uk
Call Date: Nov 2004, Middle Temple

Practising Areas: Commercial Litigation, Company & Commercial, Insurance, Professional Negligence

VOUT MR ANDREW PAUL

1 High Pavement
Nottingham NG1 1HF ☎ 0115 941 8218
✉ clerks@1highpavement.co.uk
9-12 Bell Yard
London WC2A 2JR ☎ 020 7400 1800
✉ clerks@9-12bellyard.com
Call Date: Nov 1995, Gray's Inn
Pupil Supervisor

Practising Areas: Crime, Crime (Corporate/Fraud)

WACEK MISS KIM MARIE

4 KBW
Ground Floor, 4 King's Bench Walk, Temple, London EC4Y 7DL ☎020 7822 8822
✉law@4kbw.net
Clerksroom (Taunton)
Equity House, Administration Centre, Blackbrook Park Avenue, Taunton, Somerset TA1 2PX ☎0845 083 3000
✉mail@clerksroom.com
Call Date: Nov 2003, Middle Temple

WADDINGTON MR JAMES CHARLES

9-12 Bell Yard
London WC2A 2JR ☎020 7400 1800
✉clerks@9-12bellyard.com
Call Date: Jul 1983, Gray's Inn
Pupil Supervisor

WADE MR IAN QC (2010)

Five Paper Buildings
1st Floor, Five Paper Buildings, Temple, London EC4Y 7HB ☎020 7583 6117
✉clerks@5pb.co.uk
Call Date: Nov 1977, Gray's Inn
Pupil Supervisor

Practising Areas: Crime

WADE MISS REBECCA LUCY

Northampton Chambers
10 Spencer Parade, Northampton NN1 5AQ
☎01604 636271
✉clerks@northampton-chambers.co.uk
Call Date: Jul 2003, Gray's Inn
Pupil Supervisor

Practising Areas: Care Proceedings, Crime, Family, Family Provision

WADSLEY MR PETER JOHN CAMPBELL

St John's Chambers
101 Victoria Street, Bristol BS1 6PU
☎0117 923 4700 ✉clerks@stjohnschambers.co.uk
Call Date: Jul 1984, Middle Temple
Pupil Supervisor

Practising Areas: Administrative, Licensing, Local Government, Public Law, Town & Country Planning

WAGSTAFF MR ANDREW MARTIN NICHOLAS

Westgate Chambers
64 High Street, Lewes, East Sussex BN7 1XG
☎01273 480510
✉clerks@westgate-chambers.co.uk
Call Date: Oct 2006, Gray's Inn

Practising Areas: Ancillary Relief, Common Law (General), Crime, Ecclesiastical, Employment, Family, Housing, Landlord & Tenant, Licensing, Personal Injury

WAHIWALA MR AMRIK SINGH

East Anglian Chambers
15 The Close, Norwich, Norfolk NR1 4DZ
☎01473 214481 ✉norwich@ealaw.co.uk
East Anglian Chambers
53 North Hill, Colchester, Essex CO1 1QA
☎01473 214481 ✉colchester@ealaw.co.uk
East Anglian Chambers
140 New London Road, Chelmsford, Essex CM2 0AW ☎01473 214481
✉chelmsford@ealaw.co.uk
East Anglian Chambers
Gresham House, 5 Museum Street, Ipswich, Suffolk IP1 1HQ ☎01473 214481
✉ipswich@ealaw.co.uk
Call Date: Jul 2003, Middle Temple

WAITE MR KIRIL

1 Chancery Lane
London WC2A 1LF ☎0845 634 6666
✉clerks@1chancerylane.com
Call Date: Nov 1997, Gray's Inn
Pupil Supervisor

WAKERLEY MR PAUL CHARLES MACLENNON

QEB Hollis Whiteman
1-2 Laurence Pountney Hill, London EC4R 0EU ☎020 7933 8855 ✉barristers@qebhw.co.uk
Call Date: Nov 1990, Gray's Inn
Pupil Supervisor

WALD MR RICHARD DANIEL

39 Essex Street
London WC2R 3AT ☎020 7832 1111
✉clerks@39essex.com
82 King Street
Manchester M2 4WQ ☎0161 870 9969
Riverview Chambers
Hamilton House, 1 Temple Avenue, London EC4Y 0HA ☎0844 225 3999
✉chrisbaylis@riverviewchambers.com
Call Date: Nov 1997, Gray's Inn
Pupil Supervisor

Practising Areas: Administrative, Crime, Environment, Housing, Local Government, Town & Country Planning

WALDEN-SMITH MR DAVID EDWARD

29 Bedford Row Chambers
London WC1R 4HE ☎020 7404 1044
✉clerks@29br.co.uk
Call Date: Jul 1985, Lincoln's Inn

Practising Areas: Family, Family Provision

WALDMAN MR AMOS

Doughty Street Chambers
Pall Mall Court, 61-67 King Street, Manchester M2 4PD ☎0161 618 1066
Doughty Street Chambers
5th Floor, Broad Quay House, Prince Street, Bristol BS1 4DJ ☎01179 058 717
Doughty Street Chambers
53-54 Doughty Street, London WC1N 2LS
☎020 7404 1313 ✉enquiries@doughtystreet.co.uk
Call Date: Nov 2001, Middle Temple

Practising Areas: Crime, Human Rights, Immigration, Sports

WALES MR MATTHEW JAMES

Guildhall Chambers
23 Broad Street, Bristol BS1 2HG
☎0117 930 9000 ✉hoc@guildhallchambers.co.uk
Call Date: Oct 1993, Inner Temple
Pupil Supervisor

Practising Areas: Chancery (General), Chancery (Land Law), Commercial Litigation, Commercial Property, Family Provision, Landlord & Tenant, Probate & Administration

WALEY MR ERIC RICHARD THOMAS

Assize Court Chambers
14 Small Street, Bristol BS1 1DE
☎0117 926 4587 ✉carly@assize.co.uk
Call Date: Nov 1976, Inner Temple
Pupil Supervisor

Practising Areas: Care Proceedings, Common Law (General), Crime, Crime (Corporate/Fraud), Family, Medical Negligence, Mental Health, Personal Injury

WALFORD MR RICHARD HENRY HOWARD

Serle Court
6 New Square, Lincoln's Inn, London WC2A 3QS ☎020 7242 6105 ✉clerks@serlecourt.co.uk
Call Date: Jul 1984, Middle Temple
Pupil Supervisor

Practising Areas: Chancery (General), Commercial Litigation, Company & Commercial, Insolvency, International Trade, Professional Negligence

WALJI MISS SHABNAM

Regency Chambers
45 Priestgate, Peterborough PE1 1LB
☎01733 315215 ✉clerks@regencychambers.law.co.uk
Regency Chambers
Sheraton House, Castle Park, Cambridge CB3 0AX ☎01223 301517
Call Date: Jul 2001, Gray's Inn

Practising Areas: Common Law (General), Family, Personal Injury

WALKER MR ADAM NIGEL

Seven Bedford Row
7 Bedford Row, London WC1R 4BS
☎020 7242 3555 ✉clerks@7br.co.uk
Call Date: Jul 2000, Lincoln's Inn

Practising Areas: Civil Litigation, Commercial Litigation, Consumer, Coroners Inquests, Costs, Discrimination, Employment, Financial Services, Industrial Diseases, Inquests, Insurance, Landlord & Tenant, Personal Injury, Professional Negligence, Road Traffic And Highways, Sports

WALKER MISS AMELIA POPPY

Hardwicke
New Square, Lincoln's Inn, London WC2A 3SB ☎020 7242 2523
✉enquiries@hardwicke.co.uk
Call Date: Oct 2007, Inner Temple

WALKER MR LIAM DAVID

Doughty Street Chambers
53-54 Doughty Street, London WC1N 2LS
☎020 7404 1313 ✉enquiries@doughtystreet.co.uk
Call Date: Nov 2001, Gray's Inn
Pupil Supervisor

Practising Areas: Courts Martial, Crime, Crime (Corporate/Fraud)

WALKER MR PAUL CHRISTOPHER

5 King's Bench Walk
5 King's Bench Walk, Temple, London EC4Y 7DN ☎020 7353 5638 ✉clerks@5kbw.co.uk
Call Date: Oct 1993, Lincoln's Inn
Pupil Supervisor

Practising Areas: Crime, Crime (Corporate/Fraud)

WALKER MR STEVEN PETER

4-5 Gray's Inn Square
Gray's Inn, London WC1R 5AH
☎020 7404 5252 ✉clerks@4-5.co.uk
Call Date: Mar 2008, Middle Temple

WALKER-NOLAN MR BENJAMIN

Thomas More Chambers
7 Lincoln's Inn Fields, London WC2A 3BP
☎020 7404 7000 ✉clerks@thomasmore.co.uk
Call Date: Mar 2002, Middle Temple

Practising Areas: Civil Litigation, Courts Martial, Crime, Landlord & Tenant, Personal Injury

WALL MR CHRISTOPHER JAMES LYNTON

Becket Chambers
17 New Dover Road, Canterbury, Kent CT1 3AS ☎01227 786331
✉clerks@becket-chambers.co.uk
Call Date: Nov 1987, Lincoln's Inn

Practising Areas: Care Proceedings, Family, Family Provision

WALL MR MARK ARTHUR QC (2006)

Citadel Chambers
The Citadel, 190 Corporation Street, Birmingham B4 6QD ☎0121 233 8500
✉clerks@citadelchambers.com
Call Date: Nov 1985, Lincoln's Inn
Recorder

Practising Areas: Crime, Crime (Corporate/Fraud), Sports

WALLACE MR SHAUN ANTHONY

Great James Street Chambers
37 Great James Street, London WC1N 3HB
☎020 7440 4949 ✉chambers@greatjames.co.uk
Call Date: Nov 1984, Inner Temple

Practising Areas: Crime

WALLING MR PHILIP THOMAS GEORGE

7 Bell Yard
London WC2A 2JR ☎020 7831 0636
✉kevintarrant@btconnect.com
Call Date: Nov 1986, Lincoln's Inn

WALMSLEY MR ALAN

5 King's Bench Walk
5 King's Bench Walk, Temple, London EC4Y 7DN ☎020 7353 5638 ✉clerks@5kbw.co.uk
Call Date: Nov 1991, Inner Temple

Practising Areas: Crime, Crime (Corporate/Fraud)

WALSH MR DARREN STEPHEN

Queen Square Chambers
56 Queen Square, Bristol BS1 4PR
☎0117 921 1966 ✉crime@qs-c.co.uk
Call Date: Oct 1997, Inner Temple

WALSH MR MICHAEL PATRICK

Tanfield Chambers
2-5 Warwick Court, London WC1R 5DJ
☎020 7421 5300 ✉clerks@tanfieldchambers.co.uk
Call Date: Jul 2006, Middle Temple

Practising Areas: Arbitration, Chancery (General), Chancery (Land Law), Commercial Litigation, Commercial Property, Housing, Insolvency, Land, Landlord & Tenant, Professional Negligence, Town & Country Planning

WALSH MR STEPHEN PAUL QC (2009)

3 Raymond Buildings
3 Raymond Buildings, Gray's Inn, London WC1R 5BH ☎020 7400 6400
✉clerks@3rblaw.com
Call Date: Nov 1983, Middle Temple

WALSH MR TIMOTHY EDMUND

Guildhall Chambers
23 Broad Street, Bristol BS1 2HG
☎0117 930 9000 ✉hoc@guildhallchambers.co.uk
Call Date: Oct 2000, Inner Temple
Pupil Supervisor

WALTERS MR EDMUND JOHN

13 King's Bench Walk
13 King's Bench Walk, Temple, London EC4Y 7EN ☎020 7353 7204 ✉clerks@13kbw.co.uk
Call Date: Nov 1991, Middle Temple

WALTERS MISS VIVIAN IRENE ELIZABETH

Five St Andrew's Hill
5 St Andrew's Hill, London EC4V 5BZ
☎ 020 7332 5400 ✉ Clerks@5sah.co.uk
Call Date: Nov 1991, Middle Temple
Pupil Supervisor

Practising Areas: Crime (Corporate/Fraud), Regulatory Law, Road Traffic And Highways

WALTON MISS KAREN TANYA

Dyers Chambers
35 Bedford Row, London WC1R 4JH
☎ 020 7404 1881 ✉ admin@dyerschambers.com
Call Date: Mar 1998, Middle Temple

Practising Areas: Crime, Crime (Corporate/Fraud), Mental Health, Road Traffic And Highways

WARBY MR MARK DAVID JOHN QC (2002)

5RB
1st Floor, 5 Raymond Buildings, Gray's Inn, London WC1R 5BP ☎ 020 7242 2902
✉ clerks@5rb.com
Call Date: Nov 1981, Gray's Inn

Practising Areas: Commercial Litigation, Copyright, Defamation, Entertainment, Intellectual Property, Sports

WARD MISS ALEXANDRA

9-12 Bell Yard
London WC2A 2JR ☎ 020 7400 1800
✉ clerks@9-12bellyard.com
Call Date: Jul 2000, Lincoln's Inn

Practising Areas: Crime, Crime (Corporate/Fraud), Financial Services, Health & Safety, Local Government, Regulatory Law

WARD MR ANTHONY DOUGLAS

3 PB Barristers
Royal Talbot House, 2 Victoria Street, Bristol, Avon BS1 6BB ☎ 0117 928 1520
Call Date: Jul 1971, Inner Temple
Pupil Supervisor

WARD MR JOHN DAVID

39 Park Square
Leeds LS1 2NU ☎ 0113 245 6633
✉ seniorclerk@39parksquarechambers.co.uk
Call Date: Jul 2004, Lincoln's Inn

WARD MISS KELLY JANE

Pallant Chambers
12 North Pallant, Chichester, West Sussex PO19 1TQ ☎ 01243 784538
✉ clerks@pallantchambers.co.uk
Call Date: Oct 2001, Middle Temple

Practising Areas: Care Proceedings, Children's Law, Family

WARD MR MARTIN STUART

14 Gray's Inn Square
14 Gray's Inn Square, Gray's Inn, London WC1R 5JP ☎ 020 7242 0858 ✉ clerks@14gis.co.uk
Call Date: Oct 1992, Lincoln's Inn
Pupil Supervisor

Practising Areas: Commercial Litigation, Common Law (General), Discrimination, Education, Employment, Family

WARD MR PETER MARK

The Chambers of Peter Ward
88 Kingsway, London WC2B 6AA
☎ 020 3402 2152 ✉ whurr@yahoo.com
Call Date: Oct 1996, Inner Temple

Practising Areas: Civil Liberties, Common Law (General), Crime, Discrimination, Education, Employment, Human Rights, Landlord & Tenant, Town & Country Planning

WARD MR ROBIN HENRY

8 New Square
8 New Square, Lincoln's Inn, London WC2A 3QP ☎ 020 7405 4321 ✉ clerks@8newsquare.co.uk
Call Date: Nov 2000, Middle Temple

Practising Areas: Copyright, Entertainment, Film, Cable & TV, Intellectual Property, Patents, Sports, Trademarks

WARD MR TIMOTHY JUSTIN QC (2011)

Monckton Chambers
1 & 2 Raymond Buildings, Gray's Inn, London WC1R 5NR ☎ 020 7405 7211
✉ chambers@monckton.com
Call Date: Oct 1994, Gray's Inn
Pupil Supervisor

WARITAY MR SAMUEL

Chambers of Mr Samuel Waritay
2nd Floor, 145-147 St John Street, London EC1V 4PY ☎ 0845 803 7767
✉ Waritay@onetel.com
Call Date: Nov 1993, Inner Temple

Practising Areas: Commercial Property, Common Law (General), Housing, Landlord & Tenant

WARNE MR PETER LAWRENCE

Lincoln House Chambers
Tower 12, The Avenue North, Spinningfields, 18-22 Bridge Street, Manchester M3 3BZ
☎ 0161 832 5701
✉ info@lincolnhousechambers.com
Call Date: Nov 1993, Inner Temple

WARNER MR ANTHONY CHARLES BROUGHTON

Citadel Chambers
The Citadel, 190 Corporation Street, Birmingham B4 6QD ☎ 0121 233 8500
✉ clerks@citadelchambers.com
Call Date: Jul 1979, Gray's Inn
Pupil Supervisor, Recorder

Practising Areas: Crime, Crime (Corporate/Fraud), Road Traffic And Highways

WARNER MR DAVID ALEXANDER

St Philips Chambers
55 Temple Row, Birmingham B2 5LS
☎ 0121 246 7000 ✉ clerks@st-philips.com
Call Date: Oct 1996, Gray's Inn
Pupil Supervisor

Practising Areas: Administrative, Arbitration, Bankruptcy, Chancery (General), Chancery (Land Law), Commercial Litigation, Commercial Property, Common Law (General), Company & Commercial, Equity, Wills & Trusts, Family Provision, Franchising, Housing, Insolvency, Landlord & Tenant, Local Government, Partnership, Probate & Administration, Professional Negligence

WARNOCK MR ANDREW RONALD QC (2012)

1 Chancery Lane
London WC2A 1LF ☎ 0845 634 6666
✉ clerks@1chancerylane.com
Call Date: Nov 1993, Inner Temple
Pupil Supervisor

Practising Areas: Education, Local Government, Professional Negligence

WARRINGTON MR JOHN EDWARD LAWRENCE

Five St Andrew's Hill
5 St Andrew's Hill, London EC4V 5BZ
☎ 020 7332 5400 ✉ Clerks@5sah.co.uk
Call Date: Jul 2000, Lincoln's Inn

Practising Areas: Crime, Crime (Corporate/Fraud), Regulatory Law

WARWICK MISS JOANNA LOUISE

QEB Hollis Whiteman
1-2 Laurence Pountney Hill, London EC4R 0EU ☎ 020 7933 8855 ✉ barristers@qebhw.co.uk
Call Date: Jul 2004, Lincoln's Inn

WASTALL MR ANDREW JAMES FREDERICK

Park Court Chambers
16 Park Place, Leeds LS1 2SJ
☎ 0113 243 3277
✉ clerks@parkcourtchambers.co.uk
Call Date: Oct 2005, Gray's Inn

Practising Areas: Employment, Family, Personal Injury

WASUNNA MR CHRISTIAN CHRISTOPHER PETER

2 Dr Johnson's Buildings
2 Dr Johnson's Buildings, Temple, London EC4Y 7AY ☎ 020 7936 2613 ✉ clerks@2drj.com
Call Date: Nov 2000, Gray's Inn

Practising Areas: Crime

WATERS MR DAVID EBSWORTH QC (1999)

2 Hare Court
Lower Ground, Ground, 1st & 2nd Floor, 2 Hare Court, Temple, London EC4Y 7BH
☎ 020 7353 3982 ✉ clerks@2harecourt.com
Call Date: May 1973, Middle Temple
Recorder

Practising Areas: Crime, Crime (Corporate/Fraud)

WATERS MR MALCOLM IAN QC (1997)

Radcliffe Chambers
Ground Floor, 11 New Square, Lincoln's Inn, London WC2A 3QB ☎ 020 7831 0081
✉ clerks@radcliffechambers.com
Call Date: Jul 1977, Lincoln's Inn

Practising Areas: Banking, Financial Services

WATKINS MISS RACHEL CLAIRE

Chartlands Chambers
3 St Giles Terrace, Northampton NN1 2BN
☎ 01604 603322
✉ enquiries@chartlands-chambers.co.uk
Call Date: Oct 1998, Middle Temple
Pupil Supervisor

Practising Areas: Care Proceedings, Family, Family Provision

WATKINSON MR HOWARD

9-12 Bell Yard
London WC2A 2JR ☎ 020 7400 1800
✉ clerks@9-12bellyard.com
Call Date: Oct 2006, Lincoln's Inn

Practising Areas: Crime, Crime (Corporate/ Fraud), Immigration, Regulatory Law

WATSON MR ALARIC

11 Stone Buildings
11 Stone Buildings, Lincoln's Inn, London WC2A 3TG ☎ 020 7831 6381 ✉ clerks@11sb.com
Call Date: Nov 1997, Middle Temple

Practising Areas: Bankruptcy, Chancery (General), Chancery (Land Law), Commercial Litigation, Commercial Property, Common Law (General), Employment, Insolvency, Professional Negligence, Sale & Carriage of Goods

WATSON MR ANTHONY DENNIS QC (2009)

Lincoln House Chambers
Tower 12, The Avenue North, Spinningfields, 18-22 Bridge Street, Manchester M3 3BZ
☎ 0161 832 5701
✉ info@lincolnhousechambers.com
Call Date: Jul 1985, Inner Temple
Recorder

Practising Areas: Crime, Crime (Corporate/ Fraud), Regulatory Law

WATSON MR BENJAMIN TURQUAND

3 Raymond Buildings
3 Raymond Buildings, Gray's Inn, London WC1R 5BH ☎ 020 7400 6400
✉ clerks@3rblaw.com
Call Date: Oct 2002, Lincoln's Inn

Practising Areas: Administrative, Civil Liberties, Courts Martial, Crime, Crime (Corporate/ Fraud), Financial Services, Foreign Law, Health & Safety, Human Rights, Licensing, Public International

WATSON MS CLAIRE

East Anglian Chambers
140 New London Road, Chelmsford, Essex CM2 0AW ☎ 01473 214481
✉ chelmsford@ealaw.co.uk
East Anglian Chambers
Gresham House, 5 Museum Street, Ipswich, Suffolk IP1 1HQ ☎ 01473 214481
✉ ipswich@ealaw.co.uk
East Anglian Chambers
15 The Close, Norwich, Norfolk NR1 4DZ
☎ 01473 214481 ✉ norwich@ealaw.co.uk
Call Date: Nov 1991, Lincoln's Inn
Pupil Supervisor

Practising Areas: Crime, Family

WATSON MR DUNCAN ALLEN

Westgate Chambers
64 High Street, Lewes, East Sussex BN7 1XG
☎ 01273 480510
✉ clerks@westgate-chambers.co.uk
Call Date: Oct 1997, Inner Temple

Practising Areas: Ancillary Relief, Bankruptcy, Care Proceedings, Chancery (General), Chancery (Land Law), Civil Litigation, Common Law (General), Equity, Wills & Trusts, Family, Family Provision, Housing, Insolvency, Landlord & Tenant, Personal Injury

WATSON MR GRAHAM

Colleton Chambers
Colleton Crescent, Exeter, Devon EX2 4DG
☎ 01392 274898 ✉ clerks@colletonchambers.co.uk
Call Date: Oct 1996, Lincoln's Inn
Pupil Supervisor

Practising Areas: Disciplinary Tribunals, Employment, Licensing

WATSON MR IAN DAVID

3 Stone Buildings
Ground Floor, 3 Stone Buildings, Lincoln's Inn, London WC2A 3XL ☎ 020 7242 4937
✉ clerks@3sb.law.co.uk
Call Date: Jul 2005, Lincoln's Inn

Practising Areas: Chancery (General), Equity, Wills & Trusts, Foreign Law, Probate & Administration, Tax (Capital & Income)

WATSON MISS ISABELLE MARGARET

4 Brick Court
4 Brick Court, Temple, London EC4Y 9AD
☎ 020 7832 3200 ✉ clerks@4bc.co.uk
Call Date: Oct 1991, Middle Temple
Pupil Supervisor

WATSON MR MARK ANDREW

KCH Garden Square
1 Oxford Street, Nottingham NG1 5BH
☎0115 941 8851 ✉clerks@kchgardensquare.co.uk
Call Date: Jul 1999, Gray's Inn

Practising Areas: Crime, Crime (Corporate/Fraud)

WATSON MR TOM BRADLEY

Chavasse Court Chambers
18 Queen Avenue, Liverpool L2 4TX
☎0151 229 2030
✉clerks@chavassechambers.co.uk
Call Date: Oct 1990, Inner Temple
Pupil Supervisor

Practising Areas: Courts Martial, Crime, Crime (Corporate/Fraud), Mental Health

WATSON-GANDY PROF MARK

13 Old Square Chambers
Ground Floor, 14 Old Square, Lincoln's Inn, London WC2A 3UE ☎020 7831 4445
✉clerks@13oldsquare.com
Call Date: Oct 1990, Inner Temple
Pupil Supervisor

Practising Areas: Arbitration, Banking, Corporate Finance, Financial Services, Insolvency, Partnership, Private International, Public International

WATTERSON MS ANNA ELIZABETH

1 Mitre Court Buildings
1 Mitre Court Buildings, Temple, London EC4Y 7BS ☎020 7452 8900 ✉clerks@1mcb.com
Call Date: Nov 2007, Inner Temple

Practising Areas: Civil Liberties, Civil Litigation, Common Law (General), Housing, Human Rights, Immigration, Landlord & Tenant, Public Law

WATTHEY MR JAMES ROBERTSON

Hardwicke
New Square, Lincoln's Inn, London WC2A 3SB ☎020 7242 2523
✉enquiries@hardwicke.co.uk
Call Date: Nov 2000, Gray's Inn
Pupil Supervisor

Practising Areas: Admiralty, Arbitration, Aviation, Banking, Commercial Litigation, Commodities, Energy, Financial Services, Insurance, Insurance/Reinsurance, International Trade, Private International, Professional Negligence, Sale & Carriage of Goods, Shipping/Admiralty

WAYNE MR NICHOLAS

Argent Chambers
5 Bell Yard, London WC2A 2JR
☎020 7556 5500
✉briefsin@argentchambers.co.uk
Call Date: Jul 1994, Middle Temple

Practising Areas: Common Law (General), Crime, Crime (Corporate/Fraud)

WEATHERBY MR PETER FRANCIS QC (2012)

Chambers of Ian Macdonald QC
Garden Court North, 22 Oxford Court, Manchester M2 3WQ ☎0161 236 1840
✉clerks@gcnchambers.co.uk
Garden Court Chambers
57-60 Lincoln's Inn Fields, London WC2A 3LJ
☎020 7993 7600 ✉info@gclaw.co.uk
Call Date: Nov 1992, Gray's Inn
Pupil Supervisor

Practising Areas: Administrative, Civil Liberties, Crime, Crime (Corporate/Fraud), Human Rights

WEAVER MR BRETT

6 King's Bench Walk
Ground Floor, 6 King's Bench Walk, Temple, London EC4Y 7DR ☎020 7583 0410
✉clerks@6kbw.com
Call Date: Mar 2003, Lincoln's Inn

Practising Areas: Courts Martial, Crime, Crime (Corporate/Fraud)

WEBB MISS LORRAINE ELIZABETH

Roxwell
Dukes Manor, The Street, Roxwell, Chelmsford, Essex CM1 4PE ☎01245 248341
✉lorrainewebbbarrister@yahoo.co.uk
Call Date: Jul 1980, Middle Temple

WEBB MR PAUL HAYDN COULSON

7 Bell Yard
London WC2A 2JR ☎020 7831 0636
✉kevintarrant@btconnect.com
Call Date: Jul 2003, Middle Temple

WEBBER MR DOMINIC DENZIL FERNANDEZ

5 King's Bench Walk
5 King's Bench Walk, Temple, London EC4Y 7DN ☎020 7353 5638 ✉clerks@5kbw.co.uk
Call Date: Nov 1985, Gray's Inn
Pupil Supervisor

Practising Areas: Crime

C

WEBSTER MR ALISTAIR STEVENSON QC (1995)

Lincoln House Chambers
Tower 12, The Avenue North, Spinningfields, 18-22 Bridge Street, Manchester M3 3BZ
☎ 0161 832 5701
✉ info@lincolnhousechambers.com
Chambers of Andrew Mitchell QC
33 Chancery Lane, London WC2A 1EN
☎ 020 7440 9950 ✉ clerks@33cllaw.com
Call Date: Jul 1976, Middle Temple
Recorder

Practising Areas: Civil Liberties, Crime, Crime (Corporate/Fraud), Health & Safety, Human Rights, Parliamentary, Sports

WEBSTER MR KEITH

4 King's Bench Walk
2nd Floor, 4 King's Bench Walk, Temple, London EC4Y 7DL ☎ 020 7822 7000
✉ clerks@4kbw.co.uk
Call Date: Jul 2006, Gray's Inn

Practising Areas: Commercial Litigation, Common Law (General), Crime, Employment, Personal Injury

WEBSTER MISS SARAH MARY

Staple Inn Chambers
1st Floor, 9 Staple Inn, Holborn Bars, London WC1V 7QH ☎ 020 7242 5240
✉ clerks@stapleinn.co.uk
Call Date: Jul 2006, Middle Temple

Practising Areas: Care Proceedings, Family

WEBSTER MISS SHELLEY ANNE

Carmelite Chambers
9 Carmelite Street, London EC4Y 0DR
☎ 020 7936 6300
✉ clerks@carmelitechambers.co.uk
Call Date: Oct 2002, Lincoln's Inn

Practising Areas: Costs, Crime, Crime (Corporate/Fraud), Disciplinary Tribunals, Regulatory Law

WEEKES MISS ANESTA GLENDORA QC (1999)

23 Essex Street
London WC2R 3AA ☎ 020 7413 0353
✉ clerks@23es.com
Call Date: Jul 1981, Gray's Inn
Recorder

Practising Areas: Regulatory Law

WEEKES MR MARK VINCENT

6 King's Bench Walk
Ground Floor, 6 King's Bench Walk, Temple, London EC4Y 7DR ☎ 020 7583 0410
✉ clerks@6kbw.com
Call Date: Nov 1999, Lincoln's Inn

Practising Areas: Civil Liberties, Courts Martial, Crime, Crime (Corporate/Fraud), Health & Safety, Human Rights, Licensing

WEERERATNE MS RUFINA ASWINI

Doughty Street Chambers
53-54 Doughty Street, London WC1N 2LS
☎ 020 7404 1313 ✉ enquiries@doughtystreet.co.uk
Doughty Street Chambers
Pall Mall Court, 61-67 King Street, Manchester M2 4PD ☎ 0161 618 1066
Doughty Street Chambers
5th Floor, Broad Quay House, Prince Street, Bristol BS1 4DJ ☎ 01179 058 717
Call Date: Jul 1986, Gray's Inn
Pupil Supervisor

WEETCH MR OLIVER PETER MCCALLUM

Chambers of Marion Smullen and Kerim Fuad QC
1 Inner Temple Lane, London EC4Y 1AF
☎ 020 7427 4400 ✉ clerks@1itl.com
Call Date: Oct 2001, Middle Temple

Practising Areas: Crime

WEISS MR ALFRED ANTHONY

Exchange Chambers
One Derby Square, Derby Square, Liverpool L2 9XX ☎ 0151 236 7747
✉ info@exchangechambers.co.uk
Call Date: Oct 2006, Lincoln's Inn

WELCH MR AUSTIN PETER

Lincoln House Chambers
Tower 12, The Avenue North, Spinningfields, 18-22 Bridge Street, Manchester M3 3BZ
☎ 0161 832 5701
✉ info@lincolnhousechambers.com
Call Date: Oct 2005, Middle Temple

WELCH MR DAVID WILLIAM

Warwick House Chambers
8 Warwick Court, Warwick House Chambers, Gray's Inn, London WC1R 5DJ
☎020 7430 2323
✉clerks@warwickhousechambers.com
Alexander Chambers
13 Halstead Road, Wanstead, London E11 2AY ☎0845 652 0451 / 0854 652 0451
✉clerks@alexanderchambers.co.uk
Call Date: Oct 2005, Inner Temple

Practising Areas: Civil Litigation, Employment, Family

WELCH MR ROBERT WILLIAM

Unity Street Chambers
5 Unity Street, College Green, Bristol BS1 5HH ☎0117 906 9789
✉chambers@unitystreetchambers.com
Call Date: Mar 2007, Middle Temple

Practising Areas: Crime, Family, Housing, Landlord & Tenant, Personal Injury

WELLS MR CASPAR JOHN MOWLEM

Goldsmith Chambers
Ground Floor, Goldsmith Building, Temple, London EC4Y 7BL ☎020 7353 6802
✉clerks@goldsmithchambers.com
Call Date: Oct 2000, Middle Temple

Practising Areas: Commercial Litigation, Common Law (General), Defamation, Health & Safety, Personal Injury, Professional Negligence, Sale & Carriage of Goods

WELLS MR COLIN JOHN

25 Bedford Row
London WC1R 4HD ☎020 7067 1500
✉clerks@25bedfordrow.com
Call Date: Nov 1987, Inner Temple
Pupil Supervisor

Practising Areas: Civil Liberties, Crime, Crime (Corporate/Fraud), Regulatory Law, Sports

WENBAN-SMITH MR MUNGO WILLIAM

4-5 Gray's Inn Square
Gray's Inn, London WC1R 5AH
☎020 7404 5252 ✉clerks@4-5.co.uk
Call Date: Jul 2004, Lincoln's Inn

Practising Areas: Administrative, Common Law (General), Discrimination, Education, Employment, Housing, Human Rights, Landlord & Tenant, Local Government

WEST DR EWAN DONALD

Monckton Chambers
1 & 2 Raymond Buildings, Gray's Inn, London WC1R 5NR ☎020 7405 7211
✉chambers@monckton.com
Call Date: Jul 2006, Lincoln's Inn

Practising Areas: Administrative, Competition, EC & Competition Law, Human Rights, Public Law, Regulatory Law, Sports, Telecommunications

WESTERN MR ADAM JOHN BROOKS

Citadel Chambers
The Citadel, 190 Corporation Street, Birmingham B4 6QD ☎0121 233 8500
✉clerks@citadelchambers.com
Call Date: Mar 1997, Gray's Inn

Practising Areas: Crime, Crime (Corporate/Fraud)

WESTGATE MR MARTIN TREVOR QC (2010)

Doughty Street Chambers
53-54 Doughty Street, London WC1N 2LS
☎020 7404 1313 ✉enquiries@doughtystreet.co.uk
Doughty Street Chambers
Pall Mall Court, 61-67 King Street, Manchester M2 4PD ☎0161 618 1066
Doughty Street Chambers
5th Floor, Broad Quay House, Prince Street, Bristol BS1 4DJ ☎01179 058 717
Call Date: Nov 1985, Middle Temple
Pupil Supervisor

WESTON MR LOUIS ROY PAUL

3 PB Barristers
3 Paper Buildings, Temple, London EC4Y 7EU
☎020 7583 8055
3 PB Barristers
30 Christchurch Road, Bournemouth, Dorset BH1 3PD ☎01202 292102 ✉clerks.bournemouth@3paper.co.uk
3 PB Barristers
4 St Peter Street, Winchester SO23 8BW
☎01962 868884 ✉clerks.winchester@3paper.co.uk
3 PB Barristers
Royal Talbot House, 2 Victoria Street, Bristol, Avon BS1 6BB ☎0117 928 1520
3 PB Barristers
23 Beaumont Street, Oxford OX1 2NP
☎01865 793 736
Call Date: Nov 1994, Lincoln's Inn
Pupil Supervisor

WHALE MR STEPHEN JOHN

4-5 Gray's Inn Square
Gray's Inn, London WC1R 5AH
☎ 020 7404 5252 ✉ clerks@4-5.co.uk
Call Date: Oct 1999, Gray's Inn
Pupil Supervisor

Practising Areas: Administrative, Environment, Licensing, Local Government, Town & Country Planning

WHAWELL MISS LEESHA CLAIRE

3 Temple Gardens
Lower Ground Floor, 3 Temple Gardens, Temple, London EC4Y 9AU ☎ 020 7353 3102
✉ clerks@3tg.co.uk
Call Date: Jul 2005, Lincoln's Inn

Practising Areas: Crime, Crime (Corporate/Fraud)

WHEATLEY MR GERAINT RHYS

Kings Chambers
36 Young Street, Manchester M3 3FT
☎ 0845 034 3444 ✉ clerks@kingschambers.com
Kings Chambers
5 Park Square East, Leeds LS1 2NE
☎ 0845 034 3444 ✉ clerks@kingschambers.com
Kings Chambers
Embassy House, 60 Church Street, Birmingham B3 2DJ ☎ 0845 034 3444
✉ clerks@kingschambers.com
Call Date: Oct 2001, Gray's Inn

Practising Areas: Banking, Chancery (General), Chancery (Land Law), Commercial Litigation, Commercial Property, Landlord & Tenant, Sale & Carriage of Goods

WHEATON MR IAN MALCOLM JAMES

Eighteen Carlton Crescent
Rownhams House, Rownhams, Southampton SO16 8LF ☎ 023 8063 9001
✉ clerks@18carltoncrescent.co.uk
Call Date: Jul 2002, Lincoln's Inn

Practising Areas: Ancillary Relief, Bankruptcy, Care Proceedings, Chancery (Land Law), Commercial Litigation, Construction, Defamation, Discrimination, Employment, Family, Financial Services, Health & Safety, Insolvency, Land, Landlord & Tenant, Medical Negligence, Personal Injury, Professional Negligence

WHEELER MR RICHARD GEORGE

3 PB Barristers
3 Paper Buildings, Temple, London EC4Y 7EU
☎ 020 7583 8055
3 PB Barristers
Royal Talbot House, 2 Victoria Street, Bristol, Avon BS1 6BB ☎ 0117 928 1520
3 PB Barristers
30 Christchurch Road, Bournemouth, Dorset BH1 3PD ☎ 01202 292102 ✉ clerks.bournemouth@3paper.co.uk
3 PB Barristers
4 St Peter Street, Winchester SO23 8BW
☎ 01962 868884 ✉ clerks.winchester@3paper.co.uk
3 PB Barristers
23 Beaumont Street, Oxford OX1 2NP
☎ 01865 793 736
Call Date: Jul 2004, Inner Temple

WHIPPMAN MRS CONSTANCE

33 Bedford Row
London WC1R 4JH ☎ 020 7242 6476
✉ clerks@33bedfordrow.co.uk
Call Date: Nov 1978, Gray's Inn
Pupil Supervisor

WHITE MR BARRY

Walnut House
63 St. David's Hill, Exeter, Devon EX4 4DW
☎ 01392 279751 ✉ clerks@walnuthouse.co.uk
Call Date: Jul 2004, Gray's Inn

WHITE MS CERI ANN

4 Paper Buildings
1st Floor, 4 Paper Buildings, Temple, London EC4Y 7EX ☎ 020 7427 5200 ✉ clerks@4pb.com
Call Date: Oct 2002, Gray's Inn

Practising Areas: Children's Law

WHITE MR DANIEL EDWARD MILLS

Citadel Chambers
The Citadel, 190 Corporation Street, Birmingham B4 6QD ☎ 0121 233 8500
✉ clerks@citadelchambers.com
Call Date: Oct 2003, Gray's Inn

Practising Areas: Common Law (General), Crime, Employment, Licensing, Sports

WHITE MR MATTHEW JAMES

St John's Chambers
101 Victoria Street, Bristol BS1 6PU
☎0117 923 4700 ✉clerks@stjohnschambers.co.uk
Call Date: Oct 1997, Gray's Inn
Pupil Supervisor

Practising Areas: Common Law (General), Construction, Discrimination, Employment, Personal Injury, Professional Negligence

WHITE MR OLIVER ZACHARY

Littleton Chambers
3 King's Bench Walk North, Temple, London EC4Y 7HR ☎020 7797 8600
✉fschneider@littletonchambers.co.uk
Call Date: Nov 2001, Lincoln's Inn
Pupil Supervisor

Practising Areas: Administrative, Civil Liberties, Commercial Litigation, Common Law (General), Company & Commercial, Employment, Partnership, Professional Negligence

WHITE MR PETER-JOHN SPENCER

Great Barford Chambers
Bridge Cottage, 88 Green End Road, Bedford, Bedford MK44 3HD ☎012134 870004
✉peter_johnwhite@hotmail.com
Call Date: Jul 1977, Inner Temple
Pupil Supervisor

Practising Areas: Chancery (Land Law), Common Law (General), Landlord & Tenant, Personal Injury, Professional Negligence

WHITE MR STEVEN JAMES

Park Court Chambers
16 Park Place, Leeds LS1 2SJ
☎0113 243 3277
✉clerks@parkcourtchambers.co.uk
Call Date: Nov 1998, Inner Temple

Practising Areas: Chancery (General), Commercial Litigation, Common Law (General), Employment, Landlord & Tenant, Professional Negligence

WHITE MRS TANYA

Great Barford Chambers
Bridge Cottage, 88 Green End Road, Bedford, Bedford MK44 3HD ☎012134 870004
✉peter_johnwhite@hotmail.com
Call Date: Feb 1983, Middle Temple

Practising Areas: Common Law (General)

WHITEHALL MR MARK ANTHONY

Colleton Chambers
Colleton Crescent, Exeter, Devon EX2 4DG
☎01392 274898 ✉clerks@colletonchambers.co.uk
Call Date: Jul 1983, Inner Temple
Pupil Supervisor

WHITEHOUSE MR CHRISTOPHER

Farringdon Chambers
180 Bermondsey Street, London SE1 3TQ
☎020 7089 5700
Call Date: Nov 1997, Gray's Inn

WHITEHOUSE MRS SARAH ALICE

6 King's Bench Walk
Ground Floor, 6 King's Bench Walk, Temple, London EC4Y 7DR ☎020 7583 0410
✉clerks@6kbw.com
Call Date: Oct 1993, Lincoln's Inn
Pupil Supervisor

WHITEHOUSE MR STUART COLIN

Goldsmith Chambers
Ground Floor, Goldsmith Building, Temple, London EC4Y 7BL ☎020 7353 6802
✉clerks@goldsmithchambers.com
Call Date: Jul 1987, Middle Temple
Pupil Supervisor

Practising Areas: Care Proceedings, Common Law (General), Equity, Wills & Trusts, Family, Family Provision, Health & Safety, Housing, Human Rights, Landlord & Tenant, Personal Injury

WHITFIELD MR JONATHAN QC (2010)

Doughty Street Chambers
53-54 Doughty Street, London WC1N 2LS
☎020 7404 1313 ✉enquiries@doughtystreet.co.uk
Call Date: Jul 1985, Middle Temple
Pupil Supervisor

Practising Areas: Civil Liberties, Courts Martial, Crime, Crime (Corporate/Fraud), Human Rights, Mental Health, Regulatory Law

WHITLEY MR JONATHAN DENTON

Castle Chambers
The Old Fire Station, 90 High Street, Harrow-on-the-Hill, Middlesex HA1 3LP
☎020 8423 6579 ✉info@castlechambers.net
Call Date: Nov 1993, Inner Temple

WHITTAM MS SAMANTHA ABIGAIL

14 Gray's Inn Square
14 Gray's Inn Square, Gray's Inn, London WC1R 5JP ☎020 7242 0858 ✉clerks@14gis.co.uk
Call Date: Nov 1995, Middle Temple

WHYATT MR BERNARD ANTHONY

Chambers of Mr Bernard Whyatt
Stonecroft, Somerton Road, Ardley, Oxfordshire OX27 7PF ☎01869 346160 ✉bernard.whyatt@bptm.co.uk
Call Date: Oct 1996, Middle Temple

Practising Areas: Intellectual Property

WHYATT MR MICHAEL GEORGE

15 Winckley Square
Preston PR1 3JJ ☎01772 252828 ✉clerks@15winckleysq.co.uk
Call Date: Feb 1992, Gray's Inn
Pupil Supervisor

Practising Areas: Ancillary Relief, Civil Litigation, Family, Family Provision, Mental Health, Personal Injury

WHYTE MISS ANNE LYNNE QC (2010)

Atlantic Chambers
4-6 Cook Street, Liverpool L2 9QU ☎0151 236 4421 ✉info@atlanticchambers.co.uk
Call Date: Feb 1993, Lincoln's Inn
Pupil Supervisor

WHYTE MISS MONICA PATRICIA

42 Bedford Row
London WC1R 4LL ☎020 7831 0222 ✉clerks@42br.com
Call Date: Oct 1996, Inner Temple

Practising Areas: Civil Litigation, Common Law (General), Employment, Personal Injury

WICKINS MISS STEFANIE LORRAINE

Trinity Chambers
Highfield House, Moulsham Street, Chelmsford, Essex CM2 9AH ☎01245 605040 ✉clerks@trinitychambers.com
Call Date: Nov 1994, Lincoln's Inn

WICKS MR DAVID CHARLES

Pump Court Chambers
Upper Ground Floor, 3 Pump Court, Temple, London EC4Y 7AJ ☎020 7353 0711 ✉clerks@3pumpcourt.com
Pump Court Chambers
5 Temple Chambers, Temple Street, Swindon SN1 1SQ ☎01793 539899 ✉clerks@3pumpcourt.com
Pump Court Chambers
31 Southgate Street, Winchester, Hampshire SO23 9EB ☎01962 868 161 ✉clerks@3pumpcourt.com
Call Date: Jul 1989, Middle Temple

WIDDETT MS CERI LOUISE

Park Court Chambers
16 Park Place, Leeds LS1 2SJ ☎0113 243 3277 ✉clerks@parkcourtchambers.co.uk
Call Date: Oct 1994, Gray's Inn
Pupil Supervisor

Practising Areas: Commercial Litigation, Common Law (General), Defamation, Employment, Landlord & Tenant, Medical Negligence, Personal Injury, Professional Negligence

WIDDISON-THOM MRS STACEY JANE

Kingsley Chambers
104 Tanners Lane, Barkingside, Essex IG6 1QE ☎07891 441 445 ✉s.widdison@kingsleychambers.com
Call Date: Oct 2000, Inner Temple

Practising Areas: Family, Immigration, Licensing

WIGHTWICK MR IAIN

Unity Street Chambers
5 Unity Street, College Green, Bristol BS1 5HH ☎0117 906 9789 ✉chambers@unitystreetchambers.com
Riverview Chambers
Hamilton House, 1 Temple Avenue, London EC4Y 0HA ☎0844 225 3999 ✉chrisbaylis@riverviewchambers.com
Call Date: Nov 1985, Inner Temple
Pupil Supervisor

Practising Areas: Chancery (General), Chancery (Land Law), Civil Litigation, Commercial Litigation, Common Land, Common Law (General), Construction, Consumer, Health & Safety, Housing, Human Rights, Land, Landlord & Tenant, Local Government, Medical Negligence, Personal Injury, Professional Negligence, Road Traffic And Highways, Sale & Carriage of Goods

WIGLEY MISS JENNY

No5 Chambers
Greenwood House, 4-7 Salisbury Court, London EC4Y 8AA ☎0845 210 5555
No5 Chambers
38 Queen Square, Bristol BS1 4QS
☎0845 210 5555
No5 Chambers
Fountain Court, Steelhouse Lane, Birmingham B4 6DR ☎0845 210 5555 ✉info@no5.com
Call Date: Nov 2000, Middle Temple

Practising Areas: Administrative, Environment, Local Government, Town & Country Planning

WIGNALL MR EDWARD GORDON

No5 Chambers
Greenwood House, 4-7 Salisbury Court, London EC4Y 8AA ☎0845 210 5555
No5 Chambers
38 Queen Square, Bristol BS1 4QS
☎0845 210 5555
No5 Chambers
Fountain Court, Steelhouse Lane, Birmingham B4 6DR ☎0845 210 5555 ✉info@no5.com
Call Date: Jul 1987, Gray's Inn

Practising Areas: Agriculture, Commercial Litigation, Common Law (General), Employment, Environment, Local Government

WIKTOROWSKI-SOLECKI MISS TAMARA

Middle Temple Lane Chambers
2nd Floor South, 1 Middle Temple Lane, London EC4Y 9AA ☎020 7583 4352
✉chambers@mtlchambers.com
Call Date: Oct 1999, Lincoln's Inn

Practising Areas: Administrative, Banking, Bankruptcy, Chancery (General), Civil Liberties, Commercial Litigation, Commercial Property, Company & Commercial, Crime (Corporate/Fraud), Defamation, EC & Competition Law, Financial Services, Housing, Human Rights, Insolvency, Landlord & Tenant, Regulatory Law, Tax (Capital & Income), Tax (Corporate)

WILCKEN MR ANTHONY DAVID FELIX

QEB Hollis Whiteman
1-2 Laurence Pountney Hill, London EC4R 0EU ☎020 7933 8855 ✉barristers@qebhw.co.uk
Call Date: Nov 1966, Middle Temple
Pupil Supervisor, Recorder

WILCOX MR JEROME CARL JEAN

Alexander Chambers
13 Halstead Road, Wanstead, London E11 2AY ☎0845 652 0451 / 0854 652 0451
✉clerks@alexanderchambers.co.uk
Call Date: Nov 1988, Middle Temple

Practising Areas: Arbitration, Chancery (General), Civil Litigation, Commercial Litigation, Commercial Property, Common Law (General), Company & Commercial, Consumer, Crime, Crime (Corporate/Fraud), Disciplinary Tribunals, Health & Safety, Land, Licensing, Partnership, Regulatory Law, Road Traffic And Highways

WILCOX MR LAWRENCE GAYWOOD

Octagon Chambers
29 Park Street, Taunton, Somerset TA1 4DG
☎01823 331919
✉jcload@Octagonchambers.co.uk
Call Date: Oct 1996, Lincoln's Inn

WILD MR SIMON PETER

9-12 Bell Yard
London WC2A 2JR ☎020 7400 1800
✉clerks@9-12bellyard.com
Call Date: Jul 1977, Inner Temple
Pupil Supervisor

Practising Areas: Crime, Crime (Corporate/Fraud)

WILDE MISS CARMEL JOAN-MARIE

Chavasse Court Chambers
18 Queen Avenue, Liverpool L2 4TX
☎0151 229 2030
✉clerks@chavassechambers.co.uk
Call Date: Oct 2004, Inner Temple

WILDING MR KEITH

Principal Chambers
15 Lime Tree Walk, Sevenoaks, Kent TN13 1YH ☎0845 209 8080
Call Date: Oct 1990, Inner Temple
Pupil Supervisor

WILDING MISS LISA MARIE

Old Bailey Chambers
15 Old Bailey, London EC4M 7EF
☎020 3008 6404
✉clerks@15oldbaileychambers.com
Call Date: Nov 1993, Inner Temple
Pupil Supervisor

WILKES MISS ALISON VICTORIA

5 King's Bench Walk
5 King's Bench Walk, Temple, London EC4Y 7DN ☎020 7353 5638 ✉clerks@5kbw.co.uk
Call Date: Oct 2005, Middle Temple

WILKINS MR ANDREW LEWIS

Cornwall Street Chambers
85-87 Cornwall Street, Birmingham B3 3BY ☎0121 233 7500 ✉clerks@cornwallstreet.co.uk
Call Date: Oct 1995, Lincoln's Inn

Practising Areas: Crime, Environment, Road Traffic And Highways

WILKINS MR CHRISTOPHER JOHN

Pallant Chambers
12 North Pallant, Chichester, West Sussex PO19 1TQ ☎01243 784538 ✉clerks@pallantchambers.co.uk
Call Date: May 1993, Lincoln's Inn

Practising Areas: Chancery (General), Company & Commercial, Land, Landlord & Tenant, Professional Negligence

WILKINS MR THOMAS ALEXANDER

Atkinson Bevan Chambers
1st Floor, 2 Harcourt Buildings, Temple, London EC4Y 9DB ☎020 7353 2112 ✉clerks@2hb.co.uk
Call Date: Oct 1993, Middle Temple
Pupil Supervisor

Practising Areas: Crime

WILKINSON MR FRANCIS JOHN

Field Court Chambers
5 Field Court, Gray's Inn, London WC1R 5EF ☎020 7405 6114 ✉clerks@fieldcourt.co.uk
Call Date: Oct 2001, Middle Temple
Pupil Supervisor

Practising Areas: Care Proceedings, Family

WILKINSON MISS KATIE

43 Temple Row Chambers
6th Floor, 43 Temple Row, Birmingham B2 5LS ☎0121 237 6035 ✉clerks@43templerow.co.uk
Call Date: Oct 2003, Lincoln's Inn

Practising Areas: Civil Litigation, Common Law (General), Consumer

WILKINSON MR MARC ASHLEY

No5 Chambers
Fountain Court, Steelhouse Lane, Birmingham B4 6DR ☎0845 210 5555 ✉info@no5.com
No5 Chambers
Greenwood House, 4-7 Salisbury Court, London EC4Y 8AA ☎0845 210 5555
No5 Chambers
38 Queen Square, Bristol BS1 4QS ☎0845 210 5555
Call Date: Nov 1992, Lincoln's Inn

Practising Areas: Agriculture, Asset Finance, Banking, Bankruptcy, Chancery (General), Chancery (Land Law), Commercial Litigation, Commercial Property, Common Land, Common Law (General), Company & Commercial, Conveyancing, Equity, Wills & Trusts, Financial Services, Housing, Insolvency, Insurance, Landlord & Tenant, Partnership, Professional Negligence, Sale & Carriage of Goods, Telecommunications

WILKINSON MR MICHAEL DAVID BARTHOLOMEW

18 St John Street
Manchester M3 4EA ☎0161 278 1800 ✉clerks@18sjs.com
Call Date: Oct 2006, Inner Temple

WILKINSON MS TIFFANY JODIE

Trinity Chambers
Highfield House, Moulsham Street, Chelmsford, Essex CM2 9AH ☎01245 605040 ✉clerks@trinitychambers.com
Call Date: Nov 2003, Inner Temple

Practising Areas: Care Proceedings, Family, Family Provision

WILLANS MR DAVID

Northampton Chambers
10 Spencer Parade, Northampton NN1 5AQ ☎01604 636271 ✉clerks@northampton-chambers.co.uk
Call Date: Oct 1995, Lincoln's Inn

WILLER MR ROBERT MICHAEL

Ely Place Chambers
30 Ely Place, London EC1N 6TD ☎020 7400 9600 ✉admin@elyplace.com
Call Date: Jul 1970, Middle Temple
Pupil Supervisor

Practising Areas: Commercial Litigation, Medical Negligence, Personal Injury, Professional Negligence

WILLETTS MR ANDREW PHILIP

King's Bench and Godolphin (KBG)Chambers
115 North Hill, Plymouth, Devon PL4 8JY
☎01752 221551 ✉clerks@kbgchambers.co.uk
New Walk Chambers
27 New Walk, Leicester, Leicestershire LE1 6TE ☎0871 200 1298 / 0116 255 9144
✉clerks@newwalkchambers.co.uk
Call Date: Nov 1997, Inner Temple
Pupil Supervisor, Recorder

Practising Areas: Chancery (General), Commercial Litigation, Common Law (General), Personal Injury

WILLIAMS MR ALEXANDER JAMES HYATT

3 Temple Gardens
Lower Ground Floor, 3 Temple Gardens, Temple, London EC4Y 9AU ☎020 7353 3102
✉clerks@3tg.co.uk
Call Date: Nov 1995, Middle Temple
Pupil Supervisor

WILLIAMS MR ANDREW ARTHUR

Atlantic Chambers
4-6 Cook Street, Liverpool L2 9QU
☎0151 236 4421 ✉info@atlanticchambers.co.uk
Call Date: Oct 1994, Gray's Inn
Pupil Supervisor

WILLIAMS MISS ANNA

Trinity Chambers
Highfield House, Moulsham Street, Chelmsford, Essex CM2 9AH
☎01245 605040 ✉clerks@trinitychambers.com
Call Date: Nov 1990, Gray's Inn

Practising Areas: Ancillary Relief, Children's Law, Family

WILLIAMS MISS ANNE MARGARET

6 Pump Court
1st Floor, 6 Pump Court, Temple, London EC4Y 7AR ☎020 7797 8400
✉richardconstable@6pumpcourt.co.uk
6 Pump Court Chambers
6-8 Mill Street, Maidstone, Kent ME15 6XH
☎01622 688094 ✉annexe@6pumpcourt.co.uk
Call Date: Nov 1980, Gray's Inn
Pupil Supervisor

Practising Areas: Town & Country Planning

WILLIAMS MR BEN DYLAN

Kings Chambers
36 Young Street, Manchester M3 3FT
☎0845 034 3444 ✉clerks@kingschambers.com
Kings Chambers
5 Park Square East, Leeds LS1 2NE
☎0845 034 3444 ✉clerks@kingschambers.com
Kings Chambers
Embassy House, 60 Church Street, Birmingham B3 2DJ ☎0845 034 3444
✉clerks@kingschambers.com
Call Date: Jul 2001, Middle Temple

Practising Areas: Administrative, Coroners Inquests, Courts Martial, Crime (Corporate/Fraud), Disciplinary Tribunals, Discrimination, Education, Employment, Environment, Health & Safety, Healthcare, Human Rights, Inquests, Licensing, Local Government, Public Law, Regulatory Law, Road Traffic And Highways, Sports

WILLIAMS MS CERYS LOUISE

St Johns Buildings Liverpool
8th Floor India Buildings, Water Street, Liverpool L2 0XG ☎0151 243 6000
✉clerk@stjohnsbuildings.co.uk
16 Winckley Square
Preston PR1 3JJ ☎01772 256100
St Johns Buildings
24a - 28 St John Street, Manchester M3 4DJ
☎0161 214 1500 ✉clerk@stjohnsbuildings.co.uk
Call Date: Jul 2008, Gray's Inn

WILLIAMS MR CHRISTOPHER PAUL

Tooks Chambers
81 Farringdon Street, London EC4A 4BL
☎020 7842 7575 ✉clerks@tooks.co.uk
Call Date: Feb 1988, Inner Temple
Pupil Supervisor

WILLIAMS MISS JUNE CLEO

No 8 Chambers
8 Fountain Court, Steelhouse Lane, Birmingham B4 6DR ☎0121 236 5514
✉clerks@no8chambers.co.uk
Call Date: Nov 1999, Inner Temple

Practising Areas: Bankruptcy, Children's Law, Civil Litigation, Commercial Litigation, Common Law (General), Costs, Family, Housing, Insolvency, Landlord & Tenant, Personal Injury

WILLIAMS MR MARK JOHN

Queen Square Chambers
56 Queen Square, Bristol BS1 4PR
☎ 0117 921 1966 ✉ crime@qs-c.co.uk
Call Date: Oct 1998, Gray's Inn

Practising Areas: Commercial Litigation, Common Law (General), Employment, Financial Services, Insurance, Insurance/Reinsurance, Personal Injury, Professional Negligence

WILLIAMS MR MEYRICK JOHNS

Argent Chambers
5 Bell Yard, London WC2A 2JR
☎ 020 7556 5500
✉ briefsin@argentchambers.co.uk
Call Date: Oct 2003, Inner Temple

WILLIAMS MISS MICAILA TERESA

Optimus Chambers
The Chambers of Miss Micaila Williams, Po Box 11193, Braintree, Essex CM7 0HQ
☎ 01376 691 885/07736 283873
Call Date: Jul 2004, Inner Temple

Practising Areas: Care Proceedings, Courts Martial, Crime, Employment, Family

WILLIAMS MR OWEN DAVID PARKER

9 Park Place
Cardiff, South Glamorgan CF10 3DP
☎ 029 2038 2731 ✉ clerks@9parkplace.co.uk
Call Date: Oct 2000, Gray's Inn

Practising Areas: Crime, Licensing

WILLIAMS MR PAUL KENNETH

Old Bailey Chambers
15 Old Bailey, London EC4M 7EF
☎ 020 3008 6404
✉ clerks@15oldbaileychambers.com
Call Date: Jul 1990, Inner Temple
Pupil Supervisor

WILLIAMS MR RHODRI JOHN QC (2010)

30 Park Place
Cardiff CF10 3BS ☎ 029 2039 8421
✉ clerks@30parkplace.law.co.uk
Henderson Chambers
2 Harcourt Buildings, Temple, London EC4Y 9DB ☎ 020 7583 9020
✉ clerks@hendersonchambers.co.uk
Call Date: Jul 1987, Gray's Inn
Pupil Supervisor

Practising Areas: Administrative, EC & Competition Law, Local Government

WILLIAMS MS SANDRA ALESSANDRA CAROLINE

The Chambers Of Alessandra Williams
P O Box 363, Tadworth KT20 9EJ
☎ 07941 944950 ✉ alessandra.williams@yahoo.co.uk
Call Date: Nov 2003, Lincoln's Inn

Practising Areas: Crime, Disciplinary Tribunals, Employment, Public Law, Regulatory Law, Road Traffic And Highways

WILLIAMS MR SIMON CHRISTOPHER

12 Old Square Chambers
1st Floor, 12 Old Square, Lincoln's Inn, London WC2A 3TX ☎ 020 7404 0875
✉ clerks@12oldsquare.com
Call Date: Nov 1999, Inner Temple

Practising Areas: Crime, Immigration, Regulatory Law

WILLIAMS MR SIMON PAUL

Radcliffe Chambers
Ground Floor, 11 New Square, Lincoln's Inn, London WC2A 3QB ☎ 020 7831 0081
✉ clerks@radcliffechambers.com
Call Date: Nov 1984, Inner Temple
Pupil Supervisor

Practising Areas: Chancery (Land Law), Commercial Litigation, Commercial Property, Company & Commercial, Construction, Conveyancing, Insolvency, Landlord & Tenant, Partnership, Professional Negligence

WILLIAMS-HOWES MRS KATIE ANTOINETTE

Chambers of K A Williams-Howes
148 Lower Richmond Road, Putney, London SW15 1LU ☎ 020 8704 1010
✉ katie@williams-howes.com
Call Date: Nov 1993, Middle Temple

WILLIAMSON MR ADRIAN JOHN GERARD HUGHES QC (2002)

Keating Chambers
15 Essex Street, London WC2R 3AA
☎ 020 7544 2600 ✉ clerks@keatingchambers.com
Call Date: Nov 1983, Middle Temple
Recorder

Practising Areas: Arbitration, Commercial Litigation, Construction, Professional Negligence, Sale & Carriage of Goods

WILLIAMSON MR ALISDAIR GEORGE JAMES

3 Raymond Buildings
3 Raymond Buildings, Gray's Inn, London WC1R 5BH ☎ 020 7400 6400
✉ clerks@3rblaw.com
Call Date: Nov 1994, Middle Temple
Pupil Supervisor

WILLMER MR STEPHEN JAMES

Argent Chambers
5 Bell Yard, London WC2A 2JR
☎ 020 7556 5500
✉ briefsin@argentchambers.co.uk
Call Date: Nov 2004, Middle Temple

Practising Areas: Crime, Crime (Corporate/ Fraud), Financial Services, Licensing, Regulatory Law

WILLS MISS ALEXANDRA ITARI

Christ Church Chambers
Mayfair Point, 34 South Molton Street, London W1K 5RG ☎ 020 7409 5278/07788 512787
Call Date: Nov 2000, Inner Temple

Practising Areas: Administrative, Admiralty, Ancillary Relief, Arbitration, Asset Finance, Banking, Bankruptcy, Chancery (General), Civil Liberties, Civil Litigation, Commercial Litigation, Commercial Property, Common Law (General), Company & Commercial, Construction, Conveyancing, Corporate Finance, Costs, Disciplinary Tribunals, Education, Energy, Environment, Family, Financial Services, Foreign Law, Housing, Human Rights, Insolvency, Insurance, Insurance/Reinsurance, International Trade, Land, Landlord & Tenant, Medical Negligence, Partnership, Personal Injury, Private International, Probate & Administration, Professional Negligence, Public International, Public Law, Regulatory Law, Sale & Carriage of Goods, Shipping/Admiralty, Tax (Capital & Income)

WILLS-GOLDINGHAM MISS CLAIRE LOUISE MARGARET QC (2012)

Albion Chambers
Broad Street, Bristol BS1 1DR
☎ 0117 927 2144 ✉ clerks@albionchambers.co.uk
Call Date: Jul 1988, Inner Temple
Pupil Supervisor

Practising Areas: Family, Probate & Administration

WILSON MR ALAN ANTHONY

Kenworthy's Chambers
Arlington House, Bloom Street, Salford, Manchester M3 6AJ ☎ 0161 832 4036
Call Date: Nov 2005, Inner Temple

WILSON MS CHARMAINE KIMBERLEY

Westgate Chambers
64 High Street, Lewes, East Sussex BN7 1XG
☎ 01273 480510
✉ clerks@westgate-chambers.co.uk
Call Date: Jul 2003, Inner Temple

Practising Areas: Common Law (General), Crime, Family

WILSON MR GERALD SIMON JOHN

Tanfield Chambers
2-5 Warwick Court, London WC1R 5DJ
☎ 020 7421 5300 ✉ clerks@tanfieldchambers.co.uk
Call Date: Nov 1989, Gray's Inn

Practising Areas: Equity, Wills & Trusts, Family, Family Provision

WILSON MISS HELEN TRACY

Call Date: Oct 2004, Gray's Inn

WILSON MR JONATHAN CHARLES

37 Park Square Chambers
37 Park Square, Leeds LS1 2NY
☎ 0113 243 9422 ✉ chambers@no37.co.uk
Call Date: Mar 2005, Lincoln's Inn

WILSON MR PAUL RICHARD

Broadway House Chambers
Broadway House, 9 Bank Street, Bradford, West Yorkshire BD1 1TW ☎ 01274 722560
✉ clerks@broadwayhouse.co.uk
Call Date: Nov 1989, Lincoln's Inn
Pupil Supervisor

Practising Areas: Discrimination, Employment

WILSON MR RICHARD CARVER QC (2003)

36 Bedford Row
London WC1R 4JH ☎ 020 7421 8000
✉ chambers@36bedfordrow.co.uk
Call Date: Nov 1981, Lincoln's Inn
Recorder

Practising Areas: Agriculture, Commercial Litigation, Common Law (General), Discrimination, Employment, Personal Injury, Professional Negligence

WILSON MR SCOTT

Themis Chambers
Suite 14067, 145-157 St John's Street, London EC1V 4PY ☎ 07967 418976
✉ karentaylor@themischambers.co.uk
Call Date: Nov 1993, Lincoln's Inn

Practising Areas: Crime (Corporate/Fraud), Employment, Regulatory Law, Sports

WILSON-BARNES MISS LUCY EMMA

St James's Chambers
68 Quay Street, Manchester M3 3EJ
☎ 0161 834 7000 ✉ clerks@stjameschambers.com
Zenith Chambers
10 Park Square, Leeds LS1 2LH
☎ 0113 245 5438 ✉ clerks@zenithchambers.co.uk
Call Date: Jul 1989, Inner Temple
Pupil Supervisor

WILSON-SMITH MR CHRISTOPHER QC (1986)

Outer Temple Chambers
The Outer Temple, 222 Strand, London WC2R 1BA ☎ 020 7353 6381
✉ clerks@outertemple.com
St John's Chambers
101 Victoria Street, Bristol BS1 6PU
☎ 0117 923 4700 ✉ clerks@stjohnschambers.co.uk
Call Date: Nov 1965, Gray's Inn
Recorder

WILTON MR SIMON DANIEL

Hailsham Chambers
Ground Floor, 4 Paper Buildings, Temple, London EC4Y 7EX ☎ 020 7643 5000
✉ clerks@hailshamchambers.com
Call Date: Oct 1993, Gray's Inn
Pupil Supervisor

Practising Areas: Common Law (General), Equity, Wills & Trusts, Personal Injury, Professional Negligence

WING MR CHRISTOPHER JOHN

1 Paper Buildings
1st Floor, 1 Paper Buildings, Temple, London EC4Y 7EP ☎ 020 7353 3728
✉ clerks@onepaper.co.uk
Call Date: Jul 1985, Gray's Inn
Pupil Supervisor

WING MR JAMES

3 Temple Gardens
Lower Ground Floor, 3 Temple Gardens, Temple, London EC4Y 9AU ☎ 020 7353 3102
✉ clerks@3tg.co.uk
Call Date: Oct 2003, Lincoln's Inn

WINGERT MISS RACHEL THOMAS

Renaissance Chambers
5th Floor, Gray's Inn Chambers, Gray's Inn, London WC1R 5JA ☎ 020 7404 1111
✉ clerks@renaissancechambers.co.uk
Call Date: Jul 1980, Middle Temple

Practising Areas: Care Proceedings, Family

WINN-SMITH MR MATTHEW

Lamb Chambers
Lamb Building, Elm Court, Temple, London EC4Y 7AS ☎ 020 7797 8300
✉ info@lambchambers.co.uk
Call Date: Mar 2003, Lincoln's Inn

Practising Areas: Commercial Litigation, Common Law (General), Landlord & Tenant, Personal Injury

WINSER MR CRISPIN DAVID RICHARD

Crown Office Chambers
2 Crown Office Row, Temple, London EC4Y 7HJ ☎ 020 7797 8100
✉ mail@crownofficechambers.com
Call Date: Oct 2003, Inner Temple

Practising Areas: Arbitration, Commercial Litigation, Common Law (General), Construction, Insurance, Insurance/Reinsurance, Professional Negligence

WINSHIP MR JULIAN ABDULLA

Furnival Chambers
32 Furnival Street, London EC4A 1JQ
☎ 020 7405 3232
Call Date: Oct 1995, Gray's Inn
Pupil Supervisor

Practising Areas: Crime

WINSLETT MR FRANK

Westgate Chambers
64 High Street, Lewes, East Sussex BN7 1XG
☎ 01273 480510
✉ clerks@westgate-chambers.co.uk
Call Date: Mar 2004, Middle Temple
Pupil Supervisor

Practising Areas: Ancillary Relief, Care Proceedings, Children's Law, Civil Litigation, Common

Law (General), Coroners Inquests, Crime, Family, Housing, Landlord & Tenant, Road Traffic And Highways

WINSTANLEY MISS ALICE BRYONY

St Philips Chambers
55 Temple Row, Birmingham B2 5LS
☎0121 246 7000 ✉clerks@st-philips.com
Call Date: Oct 2006, Lincoln's Inn

WINSTONE THE HON ANNE HILARY WELCH

Old Square Chambers
3 Orchard Court, St Augustine's Yard, Bristol BS1 5DP ☎0117 930 5100
✉clerks@oldsquare.co.uk
Old Square Chambers
10-11 Bedford Row, London WC1R 4BU
☎020 7269 0300 ✉clerks@oldsquare.co.uk
Call Date: Oct 1998, Lincoln's Inn

Practising Areas: Employment, Personal Injury

WISE MR IAN QC (2010)

Doughty Street Chambers
53-54 Doughty Street, London WC1N 2LS
☎020 7404 1313 ✉enquiries@doughtystreet.co.uk
Doughty Street Chambers
Pall Mall Court, 61-67 King Street, Manchester M2 4PD ☎0161 618 1066
Doughty Street Chambers
5th Floor, Broad Quay House, Prince Street, Bristol BS1 4DJ ☎01179 058 717
Call Date: Oct 1992, Gray's Inn
Pupil Supervisor

Practising Areas: Administrative, Civil Liberties, Education, Human Rights, Local Government

WISE MR LESLIE MICHAEL

10 King's Bench Walk
Ground Floor, 10 King's Bench Walk, Temple, London EC4Y 7EB ☎020 7353 7742
✉Chambers@10kingsbenchwalk.co.uk
Call Date: Nov 1985, Middle Temple
Pupil Supervisor

Practising Areas: Arbitration, Bankruptcy, Commercial Litigation, Company & Commercial, Crime, Crime (Corporate/Fraud), Insolvency, Partnership

WISEMAN MR ADAM PHILIP PASTERNAK

18 Red Lion Court
London EC4A 3EB ☎020 7520 6000
✉chambers@18rlc.co.uk
18 Red Lion Court (Annexe)
Thornwood House, 102 New London Road, Chelmsford, Essex CM2 0RG
☎01245 280880
Call Date: Nov 1994, Inner Temple
Pupil Supervisor

Practising Areas: Crime, Crime (Corporate/Fraud)

WITCOMBE MR RICHARD JOSHUA

Chambers of Marion Smullen and Kerim Fuad QC
1 Inner Temple Lane, London EC4Y 1AF
☎020 7427 4400 ✉clerks@1itl.com
Call Date: Oct 1997, Lincoln's Inn
Pupil Supervisor

WOLFE MISS MADELEINE LOUISE

Chambers of Marion Smullen and Kerim Fuad QC
1 Inner Temple Lane, London EC4Y 1AF
☎020 7427 4400 ✉clerks@1itl.com
Call Date: Oct 1998, Inner Temple

WOLMAN MR CLIVE RICHARD

11 Stone Buildings
11 Stone Buildings, Lincoln's Inn, London WC2A 3TG ☎020 7831 6381 ✉clerks@11sb.com
Call Date: Jul 2003, Middle Temple

Practising Areas: Banking, Bankruptcy, Chancery (General), Commercial Litigation, Company & Commercial, Corporate Finance, Defamation, EC & Competition Law, Financial Services, Insolvency, Insurance, Landlord & Tenant, Professional Negligence, Unit Trusts

WOLSTENHOLME MISS JANINE

Sovereign Chambers
46 Park Place, Leeds LS1 2RY
☎0113 245 1841
✉clerks@sovereignchambers.co.uk
Call Date: Jul 2002, Middle Temple

Practising Areas: Chancery (General), Chancery (Land Law), Civil Litigation, Commercial Litigation, Common Law (General), Education, Landlord & Tenant, Local Government

WONG MISS NATASHA PUI-WAI

187 Fleet Street
London EC4A 2AT ☎020 7430 7430
✉chambers@187fleetstreet.com
Call Date: Nov 1993, Middle Temple
Pupil Supervisor

Practising Areas: Crime (Corporate/Fraud)

WOOD MISS CAROLINE SARAH

Sovereign Chambers
46 Park Place, Leeds LS1 2RY
☎0113 245 1841
✉clerks@sovereignchambers.co.uk
Call Date: Mar 1998, Gray's Inn

Practising Areas: Common Law (General), Personal Injury

WOOD MISS HANNAH LOUISE

Call Date: Jul 2007, Lincoln's Inn

WOOD MR JAMES ALEXANDER DOUGLAS QC (1999)

Doughty Street Chambers
53-54 Doughty Street, London WC1N 2LS
☎020 7404 1313 ✉enquiries@doughtystreet.co.uk
Doughty Street Chambers
Pall Mall Court, 61-67 King Street, Manchester M2 4PD ☎0161 618 1066
Doughty Street Chambers
5th Floor, Broad Quay House, Prince Street, Bristol BS1 4DJ ☎01179 058 717
Call Date: Nov 1975, Middle Temple
Recorder

Practising Areas: Civil Liberties, Common Law (General), Courts Martial, Crime, Crime (Corporate/Fraud), Human Rights, Public International

WOOD MISS JOANNA RACHEL

1 Pump Court
Elm Court, Temple, London EC4Y 7AB
☎020 7842 7070 ✉(name)@pumpcourt.co.uk
Call Date: Oct 1996, Inner Temple

Practising Areas: Care Proceedings, Family, Human Rights, Immigration

WOOD MISS KATHERINE ANNE

Trinity Chambers
The Custom House, 39 Quayside, Newcastle Upon Tyne NE1 3DE ☎0191 232 1927
✉info@trinitychambers.co.uk
Trinity Chambers
Multi Media Exchange, 72-80 Corporation Road, Middlesbrough TS1 2RF
☎01642 247569 ✉info@trinitychambers.co.uk
Call Date: Jul 2002, Middle Temple
Pupil Supervisor

Practising Areas: Common Law (General), Family

WOOD MS KATIE ANNE

4 Paper Buildings
1st Floor, 4 Paper Buildings, Temple, London EC4Y 7EX ☎020 7427 5200 ✉clerks@4pb.com
Call Date: Jul 2001, Inner Temple

Practising Areas: Ancillary Relief, Children's Law, Family

WOOD MR MICHAEL MURE QC (1999)

Chambers of Mr Michael Wood QC
21 Tonsley Place, Wandsworth, London SW18 1BH ☎020 8874 3474 ✉mwoodqc@hotmail.com
Call Date: Jul 1976, Middle Temple

Practising Areas: Coroners Inquests, Crime, Crime (Corporate/Fraud), Disciplinary Tribunals

WOOD MISS NATALIE RACHAEL

2 King's Bench Walk
2 King's Bench Walk, Temple, London EC4Y 7DE ☎020 7353 1746 ✉clerks@2kbw.com
Call Date: Jul 2001, Middle Temple

WOOD MR RICHARD JAMES

9 King's Bench Walk
Lower Ground Floor South, 9 King's Bench Walk, Temple, London EC4Y 7DX
☎020 7353 9564 ✉9kbw@btconnect.com
Call Date: Nov 2001, Middle Temple
Pupil Supervisor

Practising Areas: Crime

C

WOOD MR RICHARD MICHAEL

East Anglian Chambers
Gresham House, 5 Museum Street, Ipswich, Suffolk IP1 1HQ ☎01473 214481
✉ipswich@ealaw.co.uk
East Anglian Chambers
140 New London Road, Chelmsford, Essex CM2 0AW ☎01473 214481
✉chelmsford@ealaw.co.uk
East Anglian Chambers
15 The Close, Norwich, Norfolk NR1 4DZ
☎01473 214481 ✉norwich@ealaw.co.uk
Call Date: Nov 1995, Gray's Inn
Pupil Supervisor

Practising Areas: Crime, Crime (Corporate/Fraud), Discrimination, Employment, Personal Injury

WOOD MR STEPHEN

Broadway House Chambers
Broadway House, 9 Bank Street, Bradford, West Yorkshire BD1 1TW ☎01274 722560
✉clerks@broadwayhouse.co.uk
Broadway House Chambers
25 Park Square West, Leeds, West Yorkshire LS1 2PW ☎0113 246 2600
✉clerks@broadwayhouse.co.uk
Call Date: Nov 1991, Inner Temple
Pupil Supervisor

Practising Areas: Crime

WOODCOCK MR JONATHAN

3 Temple Gardens
Lower Ground Floor, 3 Temple Gardens, Temple, London EC4Y 9AU ☎020 7353 3102
✉clerks@3tg.co.uk
Call Date: Nov 1981, Middle Temple
Pupil Supervisor

WOODS MR GEORGE ROBERT

4 Pump Court
4 Pump Court, Temple, London EC4Y 7AN
☎020 7842 5555 ✉chambers@4pumpcourt.com
Call Date: Mar 2003, Middle Temple

WOODS MR TERENCE MCCARTAN

187 Fleet Street
London EC4A 2AT ☎020 7430 7430
✉chambers@187fleetstreet.com
Call Date: Nov 1989, Middle Temple
Pupil Supervisor

Practising Areas: Courts Martial, Crime, Crime (Corporate/Fraud), Human Rights, Licensing, Regulatory Law, Sports

WOODWARD MR JEREMY PAUL

Pallant Chambers
12 North Pallant, Chichester, West Sussex PO19 1TQ ☎01243 784538
✉clerks@pallantchambers.co.uk
Call Date: Oct 1996, Inner Temple

Practising Areas: Commercial Property, Common Law (General), Construction, Professional Negligence

WOODWARD MISS JOANNE CLAIRE

9 St John Street
Manchester M3 4DN ☎0161 955 9000
✉civilclerks@9sjs.com/criminalclerks@9sjs.com
Call Date: Nov 1989, Gray's Inn
Pupil Supervisor

Practising Areas: Civil Litigation, Disciplinary Tribunals, Employment

WOOLF THE HON JEREMY RICHARD GEORGE

Pump Court Tax Chambers
16 Bedford Row, London WC1R 4EF
☎020 7414 8080 ✉clerks@pumptax.com
Call Date: Jul 1986, Inner Temple
Pupil Supervisor

Practising Areas: Administrative, Equity, Wills & Trusts, Professional Negligence, Tax (Capital & Income), Tax (Corporate)

WOOSEY MISS ELIZABETH JANE

Linenhall Chambers
1 Stanley Place, Chester CH1 2LU
☎01244 348282
✉clerks@linenhallchambers.co.uk
Call Date: Jul 1993, Lincoln's Inn
Pupil Supervisor

WORRALL MR JOHN RAYMOND GUY

Zenith Chambers
10 Park Square, Leeds LS1 2LH
☎0113 245 5438 ✉clerks@zenithchambers.co.uk
Call Date: Jul 1984, Gray's Inn

WORRALL MR PHILIP GEORGE

Kew Chambers
354 Kew Road, Kew, Surrey TW9 3DU
☎0844 8099991 ✉admin@kewchambers.co.uk
Call Date: Jul 2001, Gray's Inn

Practising Areas: Common Law (General), Personal Injury

WORSLEY MISS CHARLOTTE HELEN GRACE

No.6 Park Square
Leeds LS1 2LW ☎0113 245 9763
✉Tim@no6.co.uk
Call Date: Oct 2002, Middle Temple

WORTHLEY MR ANDREW MARK

Rougemont Chambers
Victory House, Dean Clarke Gardens, Southernhay East, Exeter EX2 4AA
☎01392 208484
✉clerks@rougemontchambers.co.uk
Call Date: Oct 2004, Lincoln's Inn

Practising Areas: Chancery (Land Law), Employment, Equity, Wills & Trusts

WRAGG MR JONATHAN ROBERT

Highgate Chambers
62A Great North Road, Highgate, London N6 4LT ☎020 8340 6031
✉enquiries@highgatechambers.co.uk
Call Date: Nov 1995, Gray's Inn

Practising Areas: Administrative, Civil Litigation, Common Land, Housing, Landlord & Tenant, Local Government, Public Law

WRAITH MR NIGEL PATRICK

Colleton Chambers
Colleton Crescent, Exeter, Devon EX2 4DG
☎01392 274898 ✉clerks@colletonchambers.co.uk
Call Date: Jul 2004, Middle Temple

Practising Areas: Crime, Environment, Health & Safety

WREN MR ANDREW JOHN

St Mary's Family Law Chambers
26-28 High Pavement, The Lace Market, Nottingham NG1 1HN ☎0115 950 3503
✉clerks@stmarysflc.co.uk
Call Date: Jul 2005, Middle Temple

WRIGHT MR ALASTAIR DAVID

St Johns Buildings
24a - 28 St John Street, Manchester M3 4DJ
☎0161 214 1500 ✉clerk@stjohnsbuildings.co.uk
16 Winckley Square
Preston PR1 3JJ ☎01772 256100
St Johns Buildings Liverpool
8th Floor India Buildings, Water Street, Liverpool L2 0XG ☎0151 243 6000
✉clerk@stjohnsbuildings.co.uk
Call Date: Oct 1991, Lincoln's Inn
Pupil Supervisor

WRIGHT MR ALEXANDER PAUL

4 Pump Court
4 Pump Court, Temple, London EC4Y 7AN
☎020 7842 5555 ✉chambers@4pumpcourt.com
Call Date: Jul 2007, Middle Temple

Practising Areas: Arbitration, Commercial Litigation, Commodities, Construction, Insurance/Reinsurance, Professional Negligence, Shipping/Admiralty

WRIGHT MR FREDERICK GEORGE IAN

Crown Office Chambers
2 Crown Office Row, Temple, London EC4Y 7HJ ☎020 7797 8100
✉mail@crownofficechambers.com
Call Date: Jul 1989, Inner Temple

Practising Areas: Arbitration, Commercial Litigation, Construction, Professional Negligence

WRIGHT MR IAN

Five Paper
Ground Floor, 5 Paper Buildings, Temple, London EC4Y 7HB ☎020 7815 3200
Call Date: Nov 1983, Middle Temple
Pupil Supervisor

Practising Areas: Discrimination, Employment

WRIGHT MR JEREMY JOHN

2 King's Bench Walk
2 King's Bench Walk, Temple, London EC4Y 7DE ☎020 7353 1746 ✉clerks@2kbw.com
Call Date: Jul 1970, Inner Temple
Pupil Supervisor, Recorder

WRIGHT MR STUART GRAHAM

Crown Office Row Chambers
119 Church Street, Brighton, Sussex BN1 1UD ☎01273 625625 ✉clerks@1cor.com
Call Date: Jul 2000, Inner Temple
Pupil Supervisor

Practising Areas: Common Law (General), Landlord & Tenant

WRIGHT MRS YASMIN TAJDIN

Cobden House Chambers
19 Quay Street, Manchester M3 3HN
☎0161 833 6000 ✉Clerks@Cobden.co.uk
Call Date: Nov 1990, Inner Temple

Practising Areas: Care Proceedings, Family, Immigration

WROTTESLEY MISS ANGELA JANE

Bank House Chambers
Old Bank House, Hartshead, Sheffield S1 2EL
☎0114 275 1223 ✉w.
digby@bankhousechambers.co.uk
Call Date: Oct 1999, Inner Temple
Pupil Supervisor

Practising Areas: Common Law (General), Crime, Education, Environment, Equity, Wills & Trusts, Family, Health & Safety, Housing, Landlord & Tenant, Personal Injury

WYGAS MR LUKE

4 Pump Court
4 Pump Court, Temple, London EC4Y 7AN
☎020 7842 5555 ✉chambers@4pumpcourt.com
Call Date: Nov 2004, Middle Temple

WYLIE MR NEIL RICHARD

KCH Garden Square
1 Oxford Street, Nottingham NG1 5BH
☎0115 941 8851 ✉clerks@kchgardensquare.co.uk
Call Date: Nov 1996, Gray's Inn
Pupil Supervisor

Practising Areas: Commercial Litigation, Common Law (General), Employment, Housing, Landlord & Tenant, Personal Injury

WYNN MR TOBY

KBW
The Engine House, No 1 Foundry Square, Leeds LS11 5DL ☎0113 297 1200
✉clerks@kbwchambers.com
Call Date: Jul 1982, Gray's Inn
Pupil Supervisor, Recorder

Practising Areas: Employment

WYNNE MR ANDREW MARK

Call Date: Oct 2001, Lincoln's Inn

WYNNE MR ASHLEY JOHN

No5 Chambers
Fountain Court, Steelhouse Lane, Birmingham B4 6DR ☎0845 210 5555 ✉info@no5.com
No5 Chambers
Greenwood House, 4-7 Salisbury Court, London EC4Y 8AA ☎0845 210 5555
No5 Chambers
38 Queen Square, Bristol BS1 4QS
☎0845 210 5555
Call Date: Nov 1990, Gray's Inn

Practising Areas: Equity, Wills & Trusts, Family, Family Provision, Professional Negligence

YELL MR NICHOLAS ANTHONY

1 Chancery Lane
London WC2A 1LF ☎0845 634 6666
✉clerks@1chancerylane.com
Call Date: Jul 1979, Middle Temple
Pupil Supervisor

Practising Areas: Banking, Bankruptcy, Chancery (General), Commercial Litigation, Common Law (General), Company & Commercial, Employment, Insolvency, Personal Injury, Professional Negligence

YEO MR COLIN ANTHONY

Renaissance Chambers
5th Floor, Gray's Inn Chambers, Gray's Inn, London WC1R 5JA ☎020 7404 1111
✉clerks@renaissancechambers.co.uk
Call Date: Mar 2002, Middle Temple

Practising Areas: Immigration

YEO MR NICHOLAS

3 Raymond Buildings
3 Raymond Buildings, Gray's Inn, London WC1R 5BH ☎020 7400 6400
✉clerks@3rblaw.com
Call Date: Nov 1999, Inner Temple
Pupil Supervisor

Practising Areas: Administrative, Crime, Crime (Corporate/Fraud), Licensing, Regulatory Law

YEUNG MR STUART ROY

Northampton Chambers
10 Spencer Parade, Northampton NN1 5AQ
☎01604 636271
✉clerks@northampton-chambers.co.uk
Call Date: Nov 1989, Inner Temple
Pupil Supervisor

Practising Areas: Commercial Litigation, Common Law (General), Crime, Family

YOUNG MR LEE TERENCE

Eighteen Carlton Crescent
Rownhams House, Rownhams, Southampton SO16 8LF ☎023 8063 9001
✉clerks@18carltoncrescent.co.uk
Call Date: Oct 1991, Middle Temple
Pupil Supervisor

Practising Areas: Arbitration, Company & Commercial, Landlord & Tenant, Personal Injury

YOUNG MR MARTIN FORD

9 Stone Buildings
Lincoln's Inn, London WC2A 3NN
☎020 7404 5055 ✉clerks@9stonebuildings.com
Call Date: Nov 1984, Middle Temple
Pupil Supervisor

Practising Areas: Chancery (General), Chancery (Land Law), Commercial Litigation, Commercial Property, Company & Commercial, Discrimination, Employment, Housing, Landlord & Tenant, Licensing, Local Government, Partnership, Personal Injury, Professional Negligence, Sale & Carriage of Goods

YOUNGER-BANKS MRS BRYNN LEADBITTER

Zenith Chambers
10 Park Square, Leeds LS1 2LH
☎0113 245 5438 ✉clerks@zenithchambers.co.uk
Call Date: Nov 1994, Gray's Inn

ZAFFUTO MISS ROSA

The Chambers Of Ms Rosa Zaffuto
10 Walnut Tree Close, Cheshunt, Hertfordshire EN8 8NH ☎01992 633474
Lombard Chambers
1 Sekforde Street, Clerkenwell, London EC1R 0BE ☎020 7107 2100
Call Date: Nov 2001, Middle Temple

ZAMAN MISS SHAZMA NAZ

37 Park Square Chambers
37 Park Square, Leeds LS1 2NY
☎0113 243 9422 ✉chambers@no37.co.uk
Call Date: Nov 2003, Middle Temple

ZEITLER MISS BARBARA

3 Dr Johnson's Buildings
Ground Floor, 3 Dr Johnson's Buildings, Temple, London EC4Y 7BA ☎020 7353 4854
✉clerks@3djb.co.uk
Call Date: Nov 2001, Lincoln's Inn

Practising Areas: Common Law (General), Disciplinary Tribunals, Employment, Housing, Immigration, Land, Landlord & Tenant, Local Government

ZEITLIN MR DEREK JAMES

Nine Bedford Row
9 Bedford Row, London WC1R 4AZ
☎020 7489 2727 ✉clerks@9bedfordrow.co.uk
Call Date: Jul 1974, Lincoln's Inn
Pupil Supervisor

ZOEST MS JACQUELINE AMY

Carmelite Chambers
9 Carmelite Street, London EC4Y 0DR
☎020 7936 6300
✉clerks@carmelitechambers.co.uk
Call Date: Oct 1995, Gray's Inn

Practising Areas: Crime (Corporate/Fraud), Information Technology

ZWART MR AUBERON CHRISTIAAN CONRAD

39 Essex Street
London WC2R 3AT ☎020 7832 1111
✉clerks@39essex.com
82 King Street
Manchester M2 4WQ ☎0161 870 9969
Call Date: Oct 1997, Inner Temple

Practising Areas: Environment, Licensing, Town & Country Planning

C

C

Chambers by Location

This section lists chambers in England and Wales by the town or city in which they are located. The town/city names are in alphabetical order and under those main headings chambers are listed alphabetically, thus 7 King's Bench Walk would be listed before 4 Pump Court under London.

Information for each set of chambers includes full contact details. Some chambers have opted to include additional information about themselves in this part of the Directory. Additional information includes the names of barristers practising from that chambers, date chambers were established, opening times, chambers' facilities, languages spoken, details regarding fees and a list of the types of work undertaken. Please note that details of the types of work undertaken by those chambers which have chosen not to include this information in Part D may be found in *Part A Types of Work by Chambers.*

Note: For those chambers listed in this section, information has been supplied by the Bar Council and supplemented with information from chambers.

The following symbols indicate that barristers are:

† Recorders
* Door Tenants/Associate Member

CHAMBERS OF MR R. A. ADEWALE

Address withheld

Chambers of: Mr R A S Adewale

THE BARRISTERS CHAMBERS

Address withheld
07966 056368
Fax: 020 7691 7337
E-mail: gevknight@hotmail.com

Chambers of: Mr G E V Knight

CHAMBERS OF MR P N DIPRÉ

Address withheld
0845 123 1234
Fax: 0845 430 4321; DX: 31412 Milton Keynes

Chambers of: Mr P N A Dipré

CHAMBERS OF MRS V HARPER

Address withheld

Chambers of: Mrs V Harper

CHAMBERS OF MS LEONORA KLEIN

Address withheld
020 7419 7841
E-mail: leoklein7@hotmail.com

Chambers of: Ms L J Klein

CHAMBERS OF MS A C MOLLER

Address withheld
07966 448572
E-mail: chris.moller@btinternet.com

Chambers of: Ms A C Moller

CHAMBERS OF MRS SUE MONTAGUE

Address withheld
01424 882 876; mobile 07999 583630

Chambers of: Mrs S Montague

MUSAALA & CO

Address withheld

Chambers of: Miss C R M Musaala Mukasa

CHAMBERS OF MISS DANIELLE O'DONOVAN

Address withheld
E-mail: danielodonovan@hotmail.co.uk

Chambers of: Ms D M O'Donovan

CHAMBERS OF MR JOHN SIMMONS

Address withheld

Chambers of: Mr J P Simmons

ST LEONARDS CHAMBERS

Address withheld
07734 706185
E-mail: william.hopkin@btinternet.com

Chambers of: Mr W W Hopkin

CHAMBERS OF MR A VEEN •

Address withheld

Chambers of: Mr A T Veen

INNER TEMPLE CHAMBERS

P.O.Box 1677 Aba, 58 Pound Road, Abia State
70 3189 9078
E-mail: chimaumez@msn.com

Chambers of: Mr C N Umezuruike

ST JOHN'S HOUSE CHAMBERS

One High Elm Drive, Hale Barns, Altrincham, Cheshire WA15 0JD
0161 980 7379
Fax: 0161 980 7379
E-mail: mauraloganllb@aol.com

Chambers of: Miss M Logan

Disability access
Wheelchair access, Disabled parking available

CHAMBERS OF MR BERNARD WHYATT

Stonecroft, Somerton Road, Ardley, Oxfordshire OX27 7PF
01869 346160
Fax: 01869 346148
E-mail: bernard.whyatt@bptm.co.uk

Chambers of: Mr B A Whyatt

†Recorder *Door Tenant/Associate Member

D

20 COURSE ROAD

20 Course Road, Ascot, Berks SL5 7HL
07932 671509; DX: 36403 Ascot
E-mail: pamelaradcliffe@estl.demon.co.uk

Chambers of: Ms P J Radcliffe

ASHTEAD PARK CHAMBERS

15 Gaywood Road, Ashtead, Surrey KT21 1BL
01372 813053
Fax: 01372 351212; DX: 30715 Epsom
E-mail: khalid@ashteadparkchambers.com/ admin@ashteadparkchambers.com

Chambers of: Mr K Ishmael

CHAMBERS OF MR PAUL DAVID

P.O. Box 4472, Shortland Street, Auckland 1140
0064 9 379 5589
Fax: 0064 9 379 5590
E-mail: paul@pauldavid.co.nz

Chambers of: Mr P W David

Disability access
Staff briefed or trained on duties under the disability legislation, Wheelchair access, Disabled parking available

LEGIS CHAMBERS

Cherat House, 32 Havelock Street, Aylesbury, Buckinghamshire HP20 2NX
01296 431125
Fax: 01296 431129
E-mail: espritbenoit@yahoo.co.uk

Chambers of: Mr B Esprit

CHAMBERS OF ROYLN SEEBORUTH

Abbotts Close Chambers, 4 Abbotts Close, Aylesbury, Bucks HP20 1HZ
01296 393329
Fax: 01296 393329
E-mail: rseeboruth@live.co.uk

Chambers of: Mr R J P Seeboruth

Disability access
Staff briefed or trained on duties under the disability legislation, Wheelchair access, Disabled parking available

HARVEST CHAMBERS

83 Cork Street, Eccles, Aylesford, Kent ME20 7HQ
01622 790070
Fax: 01622 790070
E-mail: harvestchambers@btinternet.com

Chambers of: Mr D E Clarke

THE CHAMBERS OF S W M CROUCH

6 The Glebe, Badby, Northamptonshire NN11 3AZ
01327 315 742

KINGSLEY CHAMBERS

104 Tanners Lane, Barkingside, Essex IG6 1QE
07891 441 445
Fax: 020 8252 6971
E-mail: s.widdison@kingsleychambers.com

Chambers of: Mrs S J Widdison-Thom

CHAMBERS OF ISHAN KOLHATKAR

76 Cedar Lawn Avenue, Barnet, Hertfordshire EN5 2LN
07703 441010
E-mail: ishan@kolhatkar.co.uk

Chambers of: Mr I K Kolhatkar

CHAMBERS OF VICTOR OGUMBUSOLA

23 Cockerell Close, Burnt Mill, Basildon SS13 1QR
07413 634231
Fax: 01268 470508
E-mail: victorogunbusola@hotmail.com

Chambers of: Mr V O Ogunbusola

THE CHAMBERS OF JOAO ARSENIO

8 Windsor Gardens, Basingstoke RG22 4XW
01256 346435
Fax: 01256 346435

Chambers of: Dr J Arsenio

BRUNEL CHAMBERS

24 Magdalen Ave, Bath BA2 4QB
01225 447730
Fax: 01225 447730
E-mail: richardjnicholls@btinternet.com

Chambers of: Mr R J Nicholls

THE WHITE HOUSE

Whatlington, Battle, East Sussex TN33 0ND
01424 777944
E-mail: brucespeller@btinternet.com

Chambers of: Mr B C N Speller

CHAMBERS OF MR A BURDIS-SMITH

43 Mill Lane, Clophill, Bedford MK45 4BX
07766 014583
E-mail: burdissmith.alan@gmail.com

Chambers of: Mr A Burdis-Smith

ERIMUS CHAMBERS

PO Box 1440, Bedford MK43 6AJ
01234 720952
Fax: 01234 721397
E-mail: clerks@erimuschambers.com

Chambers of: Miss K R Boyes

GREAT BARFORD CHAMBERS

Bridge Cottage, 88 Green End Road, Bedford, Bedford MK44 3HD
012134 870004
Fax: 01234 870009
E-mail: peter_johnwhite@hotmail.com

Chambers of: Mrs T White, Mr P J S White

Disability access
Wheelchair access, Disabled parking available

CHAMBERS OF DR CORA VIALS

152 Ulsterville Avenue, Lisburn Road, Belfast BT9 7AR

CRESCENT CHAMBERS

14 The Crescent, Belmont, Surrey SM2 6BJ
020 8643 4286; DX: 200608 Cheam
E-mail: douglivingstone@btinternet.com

Chambers of: Mr T D Livingstone

Disability access
Staff briefed or trained on duties under the disability legislation, Wheelchair access, Disabled parking available

CHAMBERS OF MR O A OGUNBIYI

6 Vicarage Heights, Benfleet, Essex SS7 1QA
01268 631 618
E-mail: oao@lineone.net

Chambers of: Mr O A Ogunbiyi

NORTHEASTERN LAW CHAMBERS

69 Minster Moorgate, Beverley, East Yorkshire HU17 8HP
E-mail: thelma@northeastern.wanadoo.co.uk

Chambers of: Mrs T E Osborne-Halsey

OSTERLEY COURT CHAMBERS

124 Penhill Road, Bexley, Kent DA5 3EL
07956 655265/07825 959604

Chambers of: Miss N Sharma

Disability access
Disabled parking available

CHAMBERS OF MR PAUL J COSTELLO

Apartment 1, Pegasus House, High Street, Biggleswade, Bedfordshire SG18 0FB
07846 016 399
E-mail: costellochambers@gmail.com

Chambers of: Mr P J Costello

Disability access
Staff briefed or trained on duties under the disability legislation, Wheelchair access, Disabled parking available

D

CHAMBERS OF MR S C W MASON

19a Church Street, Langford, Biggleswade, Bedfordshire SG18 9QT
01462 701 036
E-mail: stephenmason@stephenmason.co.uk

Chambers of: Mr S C W Mason

Disability access
Staff briefed or trained on duties under the disability legislation, Disabled parking available

ASPECT CHAMBERS

Aspect Court, 4 Temple Row, Birmingham B2 5HG
0121 222 2447
Fax: 0121 222 2448
E-mail: clerks@aspectchambers.com

Chambers of: Mr D H Evans QC

KINGS COURT CHAMBERS

3rd Floor, Albert House, 12-26 Albert Street, Birmingham B4 7UD
07967 910864
E-mail: t.rehmanbar@talk21.com

Chambers of: Mr I A MacDonald QC, Mr T Rehman

CITADEL CHAMBERS

The Citadel, 190 Corporation Street, Birmingham B4 6QD
0121 233 8500
Fax: 0121 233 8501; DX: 23503 Birmingham 3
E-mail: clerks@citadelchambers.com
URL: clerks@citadelchambers.com

Chambers of: Mr J A Fisher QC
Clerks: Rodney Neeld, David Dobson, Matthew Fleming, Richard Cornes; Practice Manager: W B Maynard; Administrator: R Ellison; S Gates

Fisher, Andrew QC *1980*
Andreae-Jones, William QC *1965†*
Benson, Richard QC *1974†*
Brand, Rachel QC *1981†*
Wall, Mark QC *1985†*
Grey, Michael *1975*
Redmond, Steven *1975*
Nicholls, Benjamin *1978†*
Warner, Anthony *1979†*
Harris, Julian *1982*
Masters, Lee *1984*
Butterworth, Martin *1985†*
Powis, Samantha *1985*
Aspinall, Michael *1986*
Stelling, Nigel *1987*
Bond, Richard *1988†*
Quirke, Gerard *1988*
Watts, Lawrence *1988*
Kenning, Thomas *1989*
Muller, Antonie *1990*
Nixon, Abigail *1991*
Sidhu-Brar, Sean *1991*
Simpson, Graeme *1994*
Hannam, Timothy *1995*
Crabb, Samantha *1996*
Rippon, Simon *1996*
Tatlow, Nicholas *1996*
Garcha, Gurdeep Singh *1997*
Harrington, Timothy *1997*
Western, Adam *1997*
Aris, Jason *1998*
Henry, Delroy *1999*
Orchard, Cathlyn *1999*
Meegan, Trevor *2000*
Grego, Kevin *2001*
Miller, Wendy *2001*
Davenport, Richard *2002*
Bhatti, Balvinder *2003*
Davidson, Andrew *2003*
Hobson, Laura *2003*
White, Daniel *2003*
Berry, Nicholas *2004*
Challinor, Thomas *2004*
Russell, Graham *2004*
Collins, Siobhan *2005*
Culley, Laura *2006*
Lomas, Sophie *2006*
Hamer, Charles *2007*
Close, Benjamin *2009*
Redgrave, Adrian QC *1968**
Draycott, Simon QC *1977†**
Syfret, Nicholas QC *1979†**

Types of work
Accountancy • Anti-social Behaviour Orders • Assessment of costs • Asset forfeiture • Asset recovery • Care proceedings • Civil actions against the police • Common law (general) • Confiscation • Coroners • Coroner's inquests • Corporate fraud • Costs • Courts martial • Crime • Crime and criminal due process • Employment • Family law • Firearms • Forfeiture • Fraud • Homicide • Immigration • Licensing • Malicious prosecution • Mental health • Money laundering • Motor vehicles • Personal injury • Police • Police discipline • Prison law • Prisoners' rights • Professional negligence • Regulatory and disciplinary law • Road haulage • Road traffic • Road traffic offences • Serial crime • Serious fraud

Disability access
Staff briefed or trained on duties under the disability legislation, Wheelchair access

COMMONWEALTH CHAMBERS

354 Moseley Road, Birmingham B12 9AZ
0121 446 5732
E-mail: mirzarashid786@hotmail.com

Chambers of: Mr M A Rashid

†Recorder *Door Tenant/Associate Member

CORNWALL STREET CHAMBERS

85-87 Cornwall Street, Birmingham B3 3BY
0121 233 7500
Fax: 0121 233 7501; DX: 741120 Birmingham70
E-mail: clerks@cornwallstreet.co.uk
URL: www.cornwallstreet.co.uk

Chambers of: Mr R D H Smith QC

Also at: Cornwall Street Chambers, Shrewsbury Annex, Rural Enterprise Centre, Stafford Drive, Battlefield Enterprise Park, Shrewsbury SY1 3FE

Smith, Roger QC *1972*
Mason, John *1971*
Desmond, Denis *1974†*
Seddon, Dorothy *1974*
Rickarby, William *1975*
Lowe, Anthony *1976†*
Pitt-Lewis, Janet *1976*
Tucker, Andrew *1977*
Pittaway, Amanda *1980*
Somerville, Bryce *1980*
Davis, Jonathan *1983*
Cooke, Peter *1985†*
O'Gorman, Christopher *1987*
Slater, Julie *1988*
Tarbitt, Nicholas *1988*
Hearne, Juliet *1989*
Ball, Ian *1992*
Cadwaladr, Stephen *1992*
Clarke, Timothy *1992*
Drummond, Bruce *1992*
Shakoor, Tariq *1992*
Griffiths, Michael *1993*
Brotherton, John *1994*
Fairburn, George *1995*
Faux, Andrew *1995*
Swinnerton, David *1995*
Wilkins, Andrew *1995*
Woolhouse, Oliver *1996*
Bugeja, Evelyn *1997*
Hussain, Basharat *1997*
Sapwell, Timothy *1997*
Challinor, Jonathan *1998*
McCracken, James *1998*
Hall, James *2000*
Kasasian, Laura *2002*
Plunkett, Raymond *2004*
Sharman, Mark *2004*
Virk, Sundeep *2004*
Giles, Molly *2005*
Veasey-Pugh, Jonathan *2005*
Ballard, Appa *2006*
Hancox, Lisa *2006*
Keith, Patrick *2006*
Shoker, Chavir *2006*
Langdon, Katie *2007*
Dyal, Mandeep *2008*
Jacques, Timothy *2008*
Rank, Christopher *2008*
Bradshaw, Simon *2009*
Hall, Nigel *2001**

Types of work
Care proceedings · Children · Commercial law · Common law (general) · Crime · Employment · Family law · Immigration · Insolvency · Licensing · Media and entertainment · Mental health · Pensions · Personal injury · Police · Regulatory and disciplinary law · Trusts · Wills

EQUITY CHAMBERS

First Floor, McLaren Building, 46 Priory Queensway, Birmingham B4 7LR
0121 236 5007
Fax: 0121 448 8756; DX: 23531 Birmingham B3
E-mail: clerks@equitychambers.org.uk
URL: www.equitychambers.org.uk
Out of hours telephone: 07807 009381

Chambers of: Mr B Singh
Clerks: Daisy Hulme, Ashley Brunt (Junior), Claire Barnes; Alma Walker (Senior Administration); Ashley Brunt (Junior Clerk/Administration)

Singh, Balbir *1984*
Sandhu, Sunit *1990*
Daneshyar, Osama *1996*
Dubb, Tarlowchan *1997*
Lallie, Ranjit *1997*
Gulraiz, Yasser *2003*
Jutla, Charnjit *2003*
Sharma, Sanjeev *2004*
Sidhu, Akaal *2008*
Bishop, Malcolm QC *1968†**
Thomas, Roger QC *1969†**
Lewis, Paul QC *1981†**

Types of work
Common law (general) · Corporate fraud · Crime · Employment · Family law · Fraud · Human rights · Immigration · Judicial review · Licensing · Personal injury

Disability access
Staff briefed or trained on duties under the disability legislation, Disabled parking available

†Recorder *Door Tenant/Associate Member

D

NO 8 CHAMBERS

8 Fountain Court, Steelhouse Lane, Birmingham B4 6DR
0121 236 5514
Fax: 0121 236 8225; DX: 16078 Birmingham Ftn Court
E-mail: clerks@no8chambers.co.uk
URL: www.no8chambers.co.uk

Chambers of: Mr M J Jackson
Clerks: Christina Maloney, Rosemarie Maloney

Jackson, Mark *1997*
White, Amanda *1976*
James, Venice *1983*
Cook, Gary *1989*
Vokes, Stephen *1989*
Dhaliwal, Davinder *1990*
Brunt, Philip *1991*
Hartley, Antony *1991*
Scott-Jones, Alison *1991*
Chaggar, Maninder *1992*
Cowley, Robert *1992*
Hobbs, Naomi *1993*
Manning, Ruth *1993*
Alakija, Dele *1996*
Azmi, Mohammad *1998*
Pipe, Adam *1999*
Williams, June *1999*
De Oliveira, Liz *2000*
O'Shea, Joanne *2000*
Lane, Christopher *2002*
Rutherford, Emma *2002*
Payne, David *2003*
Strongman, Carol *2003*
Cairns, Sally *2006*
Barnfield, Alexander *2007*
Valios, Nicholas QC *1964†**
Thomas of Gresford, Lord QC OBE *1967†**
Hevingham, Paul *2006**

Types of work
Arbitration · Capital tax · Care proceedings · Chancery (land law) · Clinical negligence · Commercial law · Commercial property · Common law (general) · Consumer law · Corporate fraud · Courts martial · Crime · Defamation · Discrimination · Employment · Equity · Family law · Family provision · Foreign law · Health and safety · Housing · Human rights · Immigration · Income tax · Insolvency · Insurance · Landlord and tenant · Licensing · Medical negligence · Pensions · Personal injury · Personal insolvency · Road haulage · Sale and carriage of goods · Trusts · Wills

Disability access
Staff briefed or trained on duties under the disability legislation, Wheelchair access, Disabled parking available

CHAMBERS OF MR AYOUB KHAN

127 Albert Road, Aston, Birmingham B6 5ND
07930 987202
E-mail: ayoub_khan64@hotmail.com

Chambers of: Mr A Khan

KINGS CHAMBERS

Embassy House, 60 Church Street, Birmingham B3 2DJ
0845 034 3444
Fax: 0845 034 3445; DX: 13023 Birmingham
E-mail: clerks@kingschambers.com

NO5 CHAMBERS

Fountain Court, Steelhouse Lane, Birmingham B4 6DR
0845 210 5555
Fax: 0121 606 1501; DX: 16075 Birmingham Ftn Court
E-mail: info@no5.com
URL: www.no5.com
Out of hours telephone: 07774 298047

Chambers of: Mr P E Bleasdale QC
Practice Director: Tony McDaid; Practice Managers: Patrick Hawkins, Robert Woods, Andrew Trotter, James Parks, Abdul Hafeez, Martin Hulbert, Zoe Owen, Samantha Maguire-Thompson, Andrew Bisbey; Finance Manager: Ian Tullett

Also at: No5 Chambers, Greenwood House, 4-7 Salisbury Court, London EC4Y 8AA Tel: +44 (0) 845 210 5555, Fax: +44 (0)20 7900 1582

Also at: No5 Chambers, 38 Queen Square, Bristol BS1 4QS Tel: +44 (0)845 210 5555 Fax: +44 (0)117 917 8501

†Recorder *Door Tenant/Associate Member

Bleasdale, Paul QC *1978*†
Smith, Tony QC *1958*†
Kingston, Martin QC *1972*
Tedd, Rex QC *1970*†
Hotten, Christopher QC *1972*†
Evans, Gareth QC *1973*†
Jones, Richard QC *1972*†
Gill, Manjit QC *1982*
Cahill, Jeremy QC *1975*
Howker, David QC *1982*
Hunjan, Satinder QC *1984*†
Dove, Ian QC *1986*†
Meyer, Lorna QC *1986*
Burrows, Michael QC *1979*†
Bright, Christopher QC *1985*†
Anderson, Mark QC *1983*†
Mason, David QC *1986*†
Lock, David QC *1985*
Drew, Simon QC *1987*
Duck, Michael QC *1988*
Keeling, Adrian QC *1990*
Heywood, Mark QC *1986*
Bell, Gary QC *1989*
West, John *1965*
Smith, Roger *1968*
Whitaker, Stephen *1970*
Arnold, Peter *1972*
Cliff, Graham *1973*†
Harvey, John *1973*†
Jones, Timothy *1975*
Bealby, Walter *1976*
Giles, Roger *1976*
Henson, Graham *1976*
Iles, David *1977*
James, Christopher *1977*
Pusey, William *1977*
Rowland, Robin *1977*†
Smallwood, Anne *1977*
Keogh, Andrew *1978*
Korn, Anthony *1978*
Michael, Simon *1978*
O'Donovan, Kevin *1978*
Cairnes, Paul *1980*
Newman, Timothy *1981*
Brown, Stephanie *1982*
Campbell, Stephen *1982*†
Thompson, Neil *1982*
De Mello, Ramby *1983*
Maccabe, Irvine *1983*
McGrath, Andrew *1983*
Newdick, Christopher *1983*
Bailey, Russell *1985*
Bell, Anthony *1985*
Bermingham, Gerald *1985*
Doyle, James *1985*
Kelly, Mark *1985*
Moat, Richard *1985*
Sharif, Nadia *1985*
Leigh, Kevin *1986*
Thorogood, Bernard *1986*†
Wignall, Gordon *1987*
Baker, Caroline *1988*
Birk, Dewinder *1988*
Bridge, Ian *1988*
Chadwick, Joanna *1988*
Forsyth, Samantha *1988*
Morgan, Adrienne *1988*
Singh-Tiwana, Ekwall *1988*
Wallace, Andrew *1988*
Attwood, John *1989*
Bedford, Becket *1989*
Duthie, Malcolm *1989*
Liddiard, Martin *1989*
Anning, Michael *1990*
Baker, Andrew *1990*
Boora, Jinder *1990*
Colquhoun, Celina *1990*
McDonald, Melanie *1990*
Wynne, Ashley *1990*
Al-Rashid, Mahmud *1991*
Buckingham, Sarah *1991*
Dooley, Allan *1991*†
Friel, Michele *1991*
Marshall, Paul *1991*
Radburn, Mark *1991*
Bailey, Steven *1992*
Bazini, Danny *1992*
Brockley, Nigel *1992*
Farrer, Adam *1992*
Goatley, Peter *1992*
Hansen, William *1992*
Ismail, Nazmun Nisha *1992*
Mahmood, Abid *1992*
Mallick, Nabila *1992*
Preston, Nicola *1992*
Richards, Hugh *1992*
Wilkinson, Marc *1992*
Xydias, Nicholas *1992*
Bradley, Phillip *1993*
Campbell, Rhona *1993*
Dutta, Nandini *1993*
Edhem, Emma *1993*
Nicholson, Edward *1993*
Rothwell, Joanne *1993*
Sumeray, Caroline *1993*
Taylor, David *1993*
Choongh, Satnam *1994*
Dean, Brian *1994*
Fox, Simon *1994*
Jones, Jonathan *1994*
Khalique, Nageena *1994*
Nuvoloni, Stefano *1994*
Potter, Anthony *1994*
Smallwood, Robert *1994*
Stoll, James *1994*
Tyack, David *1994*
Butterfield, John *1995*†
Diamond, Anna *1995*
Hignett, Richard *1995*
Kershaw, Dean *1995*†
Mitchell, David *1995*
Monaghan, Susan *1995*
Sheppard, Tim *1995*
Bagral, Ravinder *1996*
Case, Richard *1996*
Davidson, Laura *1996*
Hancox, Sally *1996*†
Holloway, David *1996*
Islam-Choudhury, Mugni *1996*
Jones, Cheryl *1996*
Knotts, Carol *1996*
Pitchers, Henry *1996*
Power, Elizabeth *1996*
Brunning, Matthew *1997*
Chatterjee, Adreeja *1997*
Compton, Gareth *1997*
Hadley, Richard *1997*
Hirst, Karl *1997*
Lally, Harbinder Singh *1997*
Rowley, Rachel *1997*
Singh, Talbir *1997*
Young, Christopher *1997*
Brown, Kristina *1998*
Derrington, Jonathan *1998*
Kimblin, Richard *1998*
Stein, Alexander *1998*
Afzal, Fayyaz OBE *1999*
Barney, Helen *1999*
Brook, Matthew *1999*
Butt, Nassera *1999*
Chelvan, S *1999*
Coughlan, John *1999*
Crow, Charles *1999*
Denning, Louisa *1999*
Gamble, Jamie *1999*
Hargreaves, Teresa *1999*
Price, Charles *1999*
Abberley, Stephen *2000*
Chawla, Neil *2000*
Ensaff, Omar *2000*
Wigley, Jenny *2000*
Willetts, Glenn *2000*
Adkinson, Richard *2001*
Bains, Param *2001*
Beloff, Rupert *2001*
Brown, Emma *2001*
Chaffin-Laird, Olivia *2001*
Dixon, James *2001*
Evans, Paul *2001*
Forster, Bridget *2001*
Gamble, Esther *2001*
Heeley, Michelle *2001*
Mann, Jasvir *2001*
Pole, Tim *2001*
Schofield, Thomas *2001*
Wingrave, Michael *2001*
Worlock, Simon *2001*
Bradshaw, Mark *2002*
Clifford, Victoria *2002*
Mantle, Philip *2002*
McClement, Lynette *2002*
Arthur, Helen *2003*
Cobill, Nicholas *2003*
Oscroft, Daniel *2003*
Owen, Denise *2003*
Pinnock, Earl *2003*
Van Overdijk, Claire *2003*
Davies, Rhys *2004*
Gupta, Mamta *2004*
Leslie, James *2004*
Allen, Juliet *2005*
Allen, Sarah *2005*
Cooke, Richard *2005*
Feeney, Katie *2005*
Feeny, Jack *2005*
Fernandes, Suella *2005*
Grant, Orla *2005*
Joseph, Paul *2005*
Punt, Dr Jonathan *2005*
Reed, Steven *2005*
Sandhu, Harpreet *2005*
Taylor, Kathryn *2005*
Williams, Philip *2005*
Yasseri, Yasmin *2005*
Enonchong, Nelson *2006*
Gallacher, Kirsty *2006*
Roberts, Gemma *2006*
Yates, Victoria *2006*
Boyden, Matthew *2007*
Hunka, Simon *2007*
Meager, Rowena *2007*
Oakes, Richard *2007*
Smyth, Jack *2007*
Barrett, Kevin *2008*
Corfield, Louise *2008*
Pye, Derek *2008*
Shaw, Jonathan *2008*
Williams, Hermione *2008*
Grimshaw, Richard *2010*
Jennings, Caroline *2010*
Osmund-Smith, Thea *2010*
O'Brien, Michael QC *2011*
Humphreys, Richard QC *1986**
Hanson, Timothy *1989**
Murray, Carole *1989**
Phillips, Moira *1989**
Grant, Edward *1991**
Renouf, Mark *1994**
Armstrong, Douglas *1999**
Kurji, Fatim *2003**
Tyers-Smith, Peter *2005**

D

†Recorder *Door Tenant/Associate Member

D

Types of work
Administrative law · Agriculture · Alternative dispute resolution · Arbitration · Asset finance · Banking · Capital tax · Clinical negligence · Commercial law · Commercial litigation · Commercial property · Company, commercial and competition · Confiscation of the proceeds of crime · Construction law · Conveyancing · Copyright · Corporate finance · Corporate fraud · Corporation tax · Costs · Court of Protection · Crime · Employment · Energy · Engineering disputes · Environment · Equity · Family law · Family provision · Financial services · Fraud · Human rights · Immigration · Income tax · Industrial diseases · Information technology · Insolvency · Insurance · Intellectual property · International arbitration · International trade · Judicial review · Landlord and tenant · Licensing · Partnerships · Patents · Personal injury · Personal insolvency · Planning · Police discipline · Prison law · Professional negligence · Property · Public law · Regulatory and disciplinary law · Serious fraud · Sport · Succession · Tax · Trademarks · Travel law · Trusts · Wills

Opening times: 7.30am - 6.30pm Monday - Friday (24-hour mobile answerphone)

Chambers' facilities
Conference Rooms, Disks Accepted, Video Conference

Disability access
Disabled parking available, Staff briefed or trained on duties under the disability legislation, Wheelchair access, Induction loop or infra red system

Languages spoken
Bengali, Chinese (Mandarin), French, German, Hindi, Hungarian, Irish, Italian, Japanese, Kashmiri, Mirpuri, Portuguese, Punjabi, Spanish, Swahili, Turkish, Urdu, Welsh

Fees policy
Chambers operates a flexible charging policy regularly agreeing pre-fixed budgets prior to work being undertaken for both advisory and court work.

Additional Information

No5 Chambers offers a comprehensive across the board service.

Throughout its 100-year history, No5 Chambers has developed a reputation for breaking new ground and continues to be regarded as a progressive and forward-thinking set, maintaining its success in traditional sectors of law whilst offering specialist advice and representation at the cutting edge of newly evolving areas. Having grown to over 200 barristers, including 26 silks, Chambers provides a first class service from its offices in Birmingham, London and Bristol.

In recent years Chambers has made significant inroads into the South West and Wales from its office in Bristol whilst its London office continues to go from strength to strength housing more than 50 tenants. Chambers continues to attract high quality work in all disciplines, combining excellent service standards with a progressive, modern and flexible approach to clients' needs.

No5 prides itself on forming partnerships with solicitor clients and other professionals. It is a member of the Turkish British Chambers of Commerce and Industry and is increasing its links with Turkey taking further steps in its objective to provide its services to the global markets. Chambers has associate tenants in Dubai, Spain, Cayman, Hong Kong, Singapore and India and is keen to develop further links particularly in the fields of construction, international arbitration, commercial work and environmental.

Dedicated specialist clerking teams based throughout the country have detailed knowledge of the individuals and groups they manage and support and are available to advise clients on the most suitable Counsel for a particular case. Chambers organises a structured training and induction programme for clerks and members alike.

A highly respected set, No5 Chambers remains a well-reputed provider of informative and topical seminars, allowing the latest issues and developments to be discussed with highly qualified speakers and sector experts. Many members of Chambers write or contribute to legal textbooks and specialist journals.

No5 Chambers has a wide-ranging practice and has for many years modelled itself as a top end one stop shopping service without diluting the quality, service and experience it offers to clients. Further details on No5 and its members can be found on its website www.no5.com.

ROWCHESTER CHAMBERS

4 Rowchester Court, Whittall Street, Birmingham B4 6DH
0121 233 2327
Fax: 0121 236 7645; DX: 16080
Birmingham Ftn Court
E-mail: clerks@rowchesterchambers.co.uk

Chambers of: Mr W A Harris

Disability access
Staff briefed or trained on duties under the disability legislation, Wheelchair access, Disabled parking available

ST IVE'S CHAMBERS

Whittall Street, Birmingham B4 6DH
0121 236 0863
Fax: 0121 236 6961; DX: 16072 Fountain Court Birmingham
E-mail: clerks@stiveschambers.co.uk
URL: www.stiveschambers.co.uk
Out of hours telephone: 0121 236 0863

Chambers of: Mr M J Keehan QC
Clerks: Sarah Robinson (Practice Manager Family), Nick Burden (Practice Manager Family), Clare Radburn (Practice Manager Civil), Philip Hidson (Practice Manager Crime), Natalie Feakes (Assistant Practice Manager Family), Ross Hands (Assistant Practice Manager Civil), Jake Connell (Assistant Practice Manager Crime); Practice Manager: Jackie Maskew (Chambers Director)

Keehan, Michael QC *1982†*
Andrews, Peter QC *1970†*
Crowley, Jane QC *1976†*
Conrad, Alan QC *1976†*
Tillyard, James QC *1978†*
Geekie, Charles QC *1985*
Delahunty, Jo QC *1986*
Weston, Jeremy QC *1991*
Chavasse, Ann *1971*
Hodgson, *1975*
Coke, Edward *1976†*
Anthony, Peter *1981*
Lopez, Paul *1982†*
Stephens, Michael *1983*
Price Rowlands, Gwynn *1985*
Jackson, David *1986*
Clarkson, Stuart *1987*
Singleton, Michael *1987*
Preen, Catherine *1988*
Mullen, Jayne *1989*
Starks, Nicholas *1989*
Haynes, Matthew *1991*
Brown, Michelle *1992*
Dewsbery, Richard *1992*
Lattimer, Justine *1992*
Rogers, Gregory *1992*
Cole, Nicholas *1993*
Lakin, Tracy *1993*
Hawkins, Lucy *1994*
Cooper, Peter *1996*
Jacobs, Alexander *1997*
Pritchard, Sarah *1997*
Isaacs, Elizabeth *1998*
Watkin, Tony *1998*
Coughtrie, Scott *2000*
Howell-Jones, Nicholas *2000*
Jones, Mark A *2000*
Singh, Karamjit *2000*
Bache, Nina Marie *2001*
Chapman, *2001*
Davies, Rhiannon *2001*
Thomas, Roger *2001*
Bowe, Timothy *2003*
Day, Andrew *2003*
Maynard, Matthew *2003*
Saunders, Kevin *2003*
Caney, Michelle *2004*
Molloy, Andrew *2004*
Picken, James *2004*
Briggs, Claire *2005*
Cheetham, Gareth *2005*
Jacobs, Amy *2005*
Lohmus, Michael *2005*
Fawcett, Neil *2006*
Mian, Najma *2006*
Gammon, Charmian *2007*
Muzaffer, Adem *2007*
Newman, Anya *2007*
Raji-Lawal, Tom *2008*
Fahy, Sarah *2009*
Hamilton, Annabel *2009*
Howells, Dympna *2009*
Jackson, Amy *2009*
Jarmola, Justin *2009*
Binnion, Carol *2010*
Bond, Julia *2010*
Hadden, Jason *2011*

Types of work
Adoption · Ancillary relief · Animals · Anti-social Behaviour Orders · Asbestos-related diseases · Asylum · Banking and Finance · Boundaries · Care proceedings · Chancery · Chancery (commercial) · Chancery (general) · Chancery (land law) · Child abduction · Child abuse · Child care law · Child support · Children · Civil fraud · Civil law · Civil litigation · Civil partnerships · Clinical negligence · Cohabitation · Commercial contracts · Commercial litigation · Commercial property · Common land · Common law (general) · Company law · Company winding up applications · Computer crime · Confiscation of the proceeds of crime · Consumer credit · Consumer law · Contracts · Court of Protection · Courts martial · Crime · Customs · Directors' disqualification · Disability discrimination · Disciplinary procedures · Disciplinary tribunals · Discrimination · Divorce · Domestic violence injunctions · Drink driving · Education · Environment · Excise · Family law · Family provision · Financial provision · Financial provision for children · Firearms · Food law · Forced Marriage · Forfeiture · Fostering · Fraud · Freezing orders · Guarantees · Homicide · Housing · Industrial deafness · Industrial diseases · Inheritance · Inheritance and cohabitees · Insolvency · Internet crime · Judicial review · Landlord and tenant · Lands Tribunal · Leave to remove · Licensing · Limited partnerships · Local authorities · Matrimonial · Matrimonial finance · Mediation · Mental health · Military law · Motor vehicles · Partnerships · Personal injury · Planning · Police · Prison law · Prisoners' rights · Private children law · Product liability · Product safety · Professional negligence · Property · Public access · Real property · Regulatory and disciplinary law · Regulatory crime · Rights of way · Road haulage · Road traffic · Road traffic offences · School sites · Serial crime · Serious fraud · Sexual Offences · Special Guardianship · Speeding · Succession ·

Terrorism · Torts · Trade Descriptions Act · Trademarks · Trading standards · Trusts · Unmarried couples · Wardship · Wills

Disability access
Wheelchair access, Disabled parking available

D

ST PHILIPS CHAMBERS

55 Temple Row, Birmingham B2 5LS
0121 246 7000
Fax: 0121 246 7001; DX: 723240 Birmingham 56
E-mail: jwilson@st-philips.com
URL: www.st-philips.com
Out of hours telephone: 0121 246 7000

Chambers of: Mr K J Hegarty QC
Clerks: Joe Wilson (Chief Clerk); Senior Clerks: Justin Luckman (Civil); Mark Mansell (Family); James Turner (Crime); Finance Manager: Hafiz Arslan

Hegarty, Kevin QC *1982†*
Crigman, David QC *1969†*
Linehan, Stephen QC *1970†*
Raggatt, Timothy QC *1972†*
Randall, John QC *1978†*
Millington, Christopher QC *1976†*
Khangure, Avtar QC *1985†*
Ashworth, Lance QC *1987†*
Haynes, Peter QC *1983*
Zaman, Mohammed QC *1985*
Hill, Mark QC *1987†*
Lockhart, Andrew QC *1991†*
Laird, Francis QC *1986†*
Atkins, Richard QC *1989†*
MacDonald, Alistair QC *1995†*
Smith, Andrew QC *1997†*
Garrett, Michael *1967*
Morse, Malcolm *1967†*
Hodgkinson, Robert *1968*
Readings, Douglas *1972†*
Dillon, Clare *1974*
Quirke, James *1974*
Spollon, Guy *1976*
Harrison-Hall, Giles *1977*
Neaves, Andrew *1977*
Darby, Patrick *1978*
Clegg, Simon *1980*
Kushner, Martine *1980†*
Linnemann, Bernard *1980*
Thomas, Stephen *1980†*
Berlin, Barry *1981†*
Eyre, Stephen *1981†*
Mathew, Nergis-Anne *1981*
Shoker, Makhan *1981*
Mytton, Paul *1982*
Edwards, John *1983†*
Evans, John *1983*
Messling, Lawrence *1983*
Starcevic, Petar *1983*
Ahmad, Mirza *1984*
Rochford, Thomas *1984†*
Stockill, David *1985*
Adams, Christopher *1986†*
Cartwright, Nicolas *1986†*
Jackson, Andrew *1986*
Ward, Simon *1986†*
Craig, Aubrey *1987*
Day, Dorian *1987*
McGrath, Elizabeth *1987*
Salmon, Jonathan *1987*
Thompson, Blondel *1987*
Buxton, Sarah *1988*
Maguire, Andrew *1988*
Rumney, Conrad *1988*
Bristoll, Sandra *1989†*
Cook, Alison *1989*
Pepperall, Edward *1989†*
Rai, Amarjit *1989*
Beever, Edmund *1990*
Davis, Simon *1990*
Garner, Sophie *1990*
George, Michael *1990*
Meachin, Vanessa *1990†*
Puzey, James *1990*
George, Sarah *1991*
Gidney, Jonathan *1991*
Lewis, Robin *1991*
Samuel, Glyn *1991*
Todd, Susan *1991*
Baker, William *1992*
Barnes, Matthew *1992*
Moseley, Julie *1992*
Sparrow, Julie *1992*
Johnston, Anthony *1993*
Kolodynski, Stefan *1993*
Kubik, Heidi *1993*
Marklew, Lee *1993*
Montgomery, Kristina *1993†*
Sadiq, Tariq *1993*
Verduyn, Anthony *1993†*
Burden, Angus *1994*
Carter, Rosalyn *1994*
Charman, Andrew *1994*
Hankin, Jonas *1994*
Maxwell, David *1994*
Smith, Nicholas *1994*
Wainwright, Patrick *1994*
Walker, Elizabeth *1994*
Dunstan, James *1995*
Jones, Carolyn *1995*
Whitehead, Darron *1995*
Brennan, John *1996*
Crawford, Shane *1996*
Gilchrist, Naomi *1996*
Green, Timothy *1996*
McCabe, Louise *1996*
Morgan, James *1996†*
Phillips, Simon *1996*
Warner, David *1996*
Ali, Huma *1997*
Jones, Huw *1997*
Kelly, Emma *1997*
Mandalia, Vinesh *1997*
Hodgetts, Elizabeth *1998*
Hussain, Zira *1998*
Adams, Richard *1999*
Bond, Leisha *1999*
Caulfield, Barbara *1999*
Najib, Shakil *1999*
Punia, Raj *1999*
Williams, Heledd *1999*
Afzal, Zaheer *2000*
Bahia, Sharonjit *2000*
Evans, Andrew *2000*
Howell-Jones, Nicholas *2000*
Josephs, Jennifer *2000*
Mills, Benedict *2000*
Nosworthy, Jonathan *2000*
Sarginson, Jane *2000*
Speed, Ian *2000*
Dean, Paul J *2001*
Franklin, Rebecca *2001*
Griffiths, David *2001*
Munro, David *2001*
O'Brien, Sean *2001*
Richards, Elizabeth *2001*
Walkling, Thomas *2001*
McCormack, Theresa *2002*
Pemberton, Yolanda *2002*
Tindal, James *2002*
Weaver, Matthew *2002*
Baran, Colin *2003*
Candlin, Naomi *2003*
Watson, Christopher *2003*
Brown, Marc *2004*
Edmonds, Victoria *2004*
Parathalingam, Amrisha *2004*
Riley, Davina *2004*
Brown, Nicholas *2005*
Coleclough, Suzanne *2005*
Barker, Jonathan *2006*
Dickinson, Rosa *2006*
Gupta, Amit *2006*
Meichen, Jonathan *2006*
Pemberton, Lydia *2006*
Tabari, Ali Reza *2006*
Williams, Benjamin *2006*
Winstanley, Alice *2006*
Bush, Hannah *2007*
Collins, Deborah *2007*
Mohammed, Iqbal *2007*
French, Charlotte *2008*
Garvie, Carl *2008*
Mundy, Robert *2008*
Millington, Joseph *2009*
Redmond, Jack *2009*
Rogers, Kate *2009*
Vernon-Asimeng, Kathryn *2009*
Roberts, Dominic *2011*
Rhodes, Robert QC *1968**
Matthews, Martin *1970**
Corbett, James QC *1975†**
Hossain, Ajmalul QC *1976**
Cousins, Jeremy QC *1977†**

 †Recorder *Door Tenant/Associate Member

Martin, Gerard QC *1978*†*
Mousley, Timothy QC *1979*†*
Dyer, Roger *1980**
Janner, Daniel QC *1980**
Cobb, Stephen QC *1985*†*
Harrison, Sarah *1989**
Capon, Philip *1990**
Powell, Richard *1991**
Roberts, Stuart *1994**
Buck, William *2001**
Cherry, Peter *2003**
Brown, Harriet *2005**
Crossley, Dominic *2006**
Harris, Jonathan *2006**
Gardiner, Helen *2007**
Du Toit Sc, Johan *2008**

Types of work

Administrative law · Adoption · Alternative dispute resolution · Arbitration · Asset recovery · Banking · Banking and Finance · Capital tax · Care proceedings · Chancery · Chancery (general) · Chancery (land law) · Charities · Children · Commercial litigation · Commercial property · Common law (general) · Company, commercial and competition · Construction law · Consumer law · Conveyancing · Coroners · Corporate fraud · Corporation tax · Courts martial · Crime · Crime and criminal due process · Discrimination · EC competition law · Education · Employment · Environment · Equity · Family law · Family provision · Financial services · Franchising · Fraud · Health and safety · Housing · Human rights · Immigration · Income tax · Insolvency · Insurance · Intellectual property · Landlord and tenant · Licensing · Litigation · Local government and public services · Matrimonial finance · Medical negligence · Mental health · Money laundering · Partnerships · Pensions · Personal injury · Personal insolvency · Planning · Police · Prison law · Professional negligence · Property · Regulatory and disciplinary law · Road traffic · Sale and carriage of goods · Sport · Succession · Taxation and duties · Torts · Trading standards · Travel law · Trusts

Chambers Established 1998
Opening times: 8.00am - 6.00pm

Chambers' facilities

Multi-media presentation and video conferencing suites

Disability access

Staff briefed or trained on duties under the disability legislation, Wheelchair access, Disabled parking available

Languages spoken

Bengali, French, German, Hindi, Italian, Punjabi, Russian, Spanish, Urdu, Welsh

Fees policy

St Philips operates a competitive and flexible charging policy. Our clerks are happy to discuss fees and fee structures on an individual basis.

43 TEMPLE ROW CHAMBERS

6th Floor, 43 Temple Row, Birmingham B2 5LS
0121 237 6035
Fax: 0121 237 6113; DX: 13001 Birmingham
E-mail: clerks@43templerow.co.uk

Chambers of: Mr T S J Berriman

Disability access

Staff briefed or trained on duties under the disability legislation, Wheelchair access, Disabled parking available

TRINITY CHAMBERS

Suite 441, 27 Colmore Row, Birmingham B3 2EW
0121 346 4672
Fax: 0121 434 5662
E-mail: tchambersb@aol.com

Chambers of: Mr H O Davies

WARWICK CHAMBERS

959 Chester Road, Birmingham, Birmingham B24 0HQ
0121 382 9122
Fax: 0121 350 3367
E-mail: warwickchambers@hotmail.com

Chambers of: Mr I R O Suggett

Disability access

Staff briefed or trained on duties under the disability legislation, Disabled parking available

CHAMBERS OF MR C DAVEY

7 Blair Close, Bishop's Stortford CM23 4PR
01279 506412
E-mail: charlesdavey@gmx.com

Chambers of: Mr C Davey

†Recorder *Door Tenant/Associate Member

CHAMBERS OF MR THOMAS SWEENEY

4 Parkway, Daisy Hill, Westoughton, Bolton BL5 2RY
01942 819206
E-mail: Tasjas5@hotmail.co.uk

Chambers of: Mr T G Sweeney

D

CHAMBERS OF MISS ONUZO

38 Gateshead Road, Borehamwood WD6 4NQ

FOREST CHAMBERS

Chambers of Terence Finn, 13 Rutland Gardens, Gosberton, Boston, Lincolnshire PE11 4HR
01775 840827
E-mail: forestchambers@btinternet.com

Chambers of: Mr T Finn

Disability access
Staff briefed or trained on duties under the disability legislation, Wheelchair access, Disabled parking available

KING'S BENCH CHAMBERS

Wellington House, 175 Holdenhurst Road, Bournemouth, Dorset BH8 8DQ
01202 250025
Fax: 0870 1231 783; DX: 145960 Bournemouth 19

Chambers of: Mr C R J Hine

Disability access
Staff briefed or trained on duties under the disability legislation, Wheelchair access, Disabled parking available

3 PB BARRISTERS

30 Christchurch Road, Bournemouth, Dorset BH1 3PD
01202 292102
Fax: 01202 298498; DX: 7612 Bournemouth
E-mail: clerks.bournemouth@3paper.co.uk
URL: www.3pb.co.uk
Out of hours telephone: 07836 607159 (Stephen Clark - Mobile)

Chambers of: Mr Ian Lawrie QC
Clerks: Stephen Clark (Senior Clerk), Robert Leonard, Suzy Martin (Fees), Katie Sidaway, Sian Constant; Lisa Wilson, Marketing Manager; Finance Manager: Head of Business Admin and Finance, Neil Monro

Also at: London, Oxford, Winchester and Bristol

Lawrie, Ian QC *1985*†
Parroy, Michael QC *1969*†
Vere-Hodge, Michael QC *1970*
Farley, Roger QC *1974*†
Jones, Stewart QC *1972*†
Braslavsky, Nicholas QC *1983*†
Bromley-Davenport, John QC *1972*
Lickley, Nigel QC *1983*†
Parker, Christopher QC *1986*†
Parrish, Samuel *1962*
Solomon, Susan *1967*
Aylwin, Christopher *1970*
Swinstead, David *1970*
Norman, Michael *1971*†
Curran, Leo *1972*
Jennings, Peter *1972*
Coleman, Anthony *1973*†
Stephenson, Ben *1973*
Bartlett, David *1975*†
Tyson, Richard *1975*†
Kent, Peter *1978*
Mitchell, Nigel *1978*
Grey, Robert *1979*
Hamilton, Gavin *1979*
Leach, Robin *1979*
Leviseur, Nicholas *1979*
Partridge, Ian *1979*
Coombes, Timothy *1980*
Edge, Ian *1981*
Marshall, David *1981*
Sampson, Graeme *1981*
Strutt, Martin *1981*
Martin, Nicola *1982*
Newman, Paul *1982*
Onslow, Richard *1982*
Lomas, Mark *1983*
Stancombe, Barry *1983*
O'Hara, Sarah *1984*
Palfrey, Monty *1985*
Whittle-Martin, Lucia *1985*
Clark, Tonia *1986*
Hudson, Elisabeth *1987*
Hendry, Lucy *1988*
Rowland, Nicholas *1988*†
Zabihi, Tanya *1988*
Bradbury, Timothy *1989*
Hester, Paul *1989*
Richards, David *1989*
Aeberli, Peter *1990*
Griffiths, Hayley *1990*
Hiddleston, Adam *1990*
Knapp, Sophie *1990*
Buckley-Clarke, Amanda *1991*
Dunlop, Hamish *1991*
Katrak, Cyrus *1991*
Robins, Imogen *1991*
Ross, Iain *1991*
Bingham, Tony *1992*
Sweeney, Noel *1992*
Clargo, John *1994*
Dawson, James *1994*
Earle, Judy *1994*
Feest, Adam *1994*
Mitchell, Jack *1994*
Reid, David *1994*
Topliss, Megan *1994*
Weston, Louis *1994*
De Freitas, Melanie *1995*
McDevitt, Colin *1995*
McIlroy, David *1995*
Strachan, Elaine *1995*
Davison, James *1996*
Lorie, Andrew *1996*
Tyler, Thomas *1996*
Wilson, Lachlan *1996*
Purdy, Catherine *1997*
Sullivan, Mark *1997*
Griffiths, Emma *1998*
Taylor, Rufus *1998*
Horner, Robert *1999*
Kennedy, Stuart *1999*
Goodall, Rachael *2000*
Isaacs, Oliver *2000*
O'Doherty, Paul *2000*
Sheriff, Andrew *2000*
Worton, Louise *2000*
Cassidy, Sheena *2001*
Whelan, Christopher *2001*
Ludlow, Craig *2002*
Moss, Karen *2002*
Shillingford, Julia *2002*
Tomlinson, Michael *2002*
Courts, Robert *2003*
Gullick, Mathew *2003*
Jones, Victoria *2003*
Archer, Audrey *2004*
Davies, James *2004*
Hepworth, Elizabeth *2004*
Horder, Tom *2004*
Wheeler, Richard *2004*
Anderson, Katherine *2005*
Clarke, Sarah *2005*
Langford, Sarah *2005*
Musgrave, Anarkali *2005*
Cannings, Matthew *2006*
Da Costa, Francisca *2006*
Davies, Nick *2006*
Green, Mark *2006*
Robinson, Nick *2006*
Sharma, Sunyana *2006*
Davies, Harriet *2007*
Elliott, Mark *2007*
Jones, Ximena *2007*
MacPhail, Andrew *2007*
Paulin, Michael *2007*
Perfect, Andrew *2007*

Chegwidden, James *2008*
Dunseath, Katherine *2008*
Edwards, Christopher *2008*
Alleyne, Ebony *2009*
Ashkar, Natalie *2009*
Borrett, Richard *2009*
Bowes, Gemma *2009*
Currie, Philip *2009*
Howard, Steven *2009*
Sanghera, Sharandish *2009*
Webb, Thomas *2010*
Wyeth, Stephen *2010*
Davies, Eleanor *1998**

Types of work

Accountancy · Adjudication · Administrative law · Adoption · Alternative dispute resolution · Ancillary relief · Animals · Arab commercial law · Arab law · Arbitration · Asbestos-related diseases · Asset forfeiture · Asset recovery · Banking · Bills of exchange · Boundaries · Building · Care proceedings · Chancery (commercial) · Chancery (general) · Chancery (land law) · Child care law · Children · Civil actions against the police · Civil partnerships · Clinical negligence · Cohabitation · Commercial contracts · Commercial fraud · Commercial law · Commercial litigation · Commercial property · Common land · Common law (general) · Company, commercial and competition · Computer contracts · Computer crime · Computer litigation · Confiscation · Conflict of laws · Construction law · Consumer credit · Consumer law · Contracts · Copyright · Corporate finance · Corporate fraud · Corporate governance · Corporate insolvency · Corporate liability · Corporate manslaughter · Corporate recovery · Costs · Court of Protection · Courts martial · Crime · Crime and criminal due process · Criminal judicial review · Cross-border litigation and remedies · Damages · Disability discrimination · Disasters · Disciplinary procedures · Disciplinary tribunals · Discrimination · Divorce · Domestic violence injunctions · Ecclesiastical law · Economic torts · Education · Election law · Employment · Engineering disputes · Equine law · Equity · Factoring · Family law · Family provision · Financial provision · Financial services · Firearms · Foreign law · Franchising · Fraud · Freezing orders · Guarantees · Health and safety · Holiday injury and damages · Homicide · Housing · Industrial deafness · Industrial diseases · Information technology · Inheritance · Inquests · Insolvency · Insurance · Intellectual property · International arbitration · International commercial arbitration · International fraud and asset tracing · Islamic family law · Islamic law · Judicial review · Landlord and tenant · Lands Tribunal · Licensing · Matrimonial finance · Mediation · Medical negligence · Middle Eastern law · Military law · Multi-party litigation · Occupational diseases · Partnerships · Passing off · Personal injury · Personal insolvency · Planning · Police · Product liability · Professional negligence · Public law · Real property · Regulatory and disciplinary law · Rights of light · Rights of way · Road traffic · Sale and carriage of goods · Serial crime · Serious fraud · Shareholder agreements · Succession · Tax · Technology and Construction Court · Torts · Trust litigation · Trusts · Wardship · Wills

Disability access

Induction loop or infra red system

BROADWAY HOUSE CHAMBERS

Broadway House, 9 Bank Street, Bradford, West Yorkshire BD1 1TW
01274 722560
Fax: 01274 370708; DX: 729860 Bradford 22
E-mail: clerks@broadwayhouse.co.uk
URL: www.broadwayhouse.co.uk

Chambers of: Mr D N Jones
Clerks: David Rhodes, Robin Slade; Administrator: Helen Craven

Also at: Broadway House Chambers, 25 Park Square West, Leeds LS1 2PW. Tel: 0113 246 2600; Fax: 0113 246 2609

Hyland, Graham QC *1978†*
Jones, David *1985*
Hill, James QC *1984†*
Mansell, Richard QC *1991†*
Colborne, Michelle QC *1993*
Khan, Tahir QC *1986†*
Topham, John *1970*
Ferm, Rodney *1972*
Wood, Martin *1973*
Isaacs, Paul *1974†*
Kershaw, Andrew *1975†*
Cohen, Raphael *1981*
Shelton, Gordon *1981†*
McGonigal, David *1982*
Howard, Ian *1987*
Myers, Simon *1987*
Askins, Nicholas *1989*
Wilson, Paul *1989*
Drake, Sophie *1990†*
Cole, Robert *1991*
Wood, Stephen *1991*
Hendron, Gerald *1992*
Barlow, Sarah *1993*
Crosland, Ben *1993*
Rudd, Matthew *1994*
Walker-Kane, Jonathan *1994*
Beckett, Jayne *1995*
Morland, Camille *1996*
Peers, Nicola *1996*
Hussain, Tasaddat *1998*
Miller, Ian *1999*
Bridge, Giles *2000*
Brown, Christopher *2001*
Green, Kenneth *2001*
Downing, Emma *2002*
Modgill, Alexander *2002*
Samra, Sharn *2002*
Shaikh, Semaab *2002*
Hampton, Peter *2003*
Azmi, Louise *2004*
Hamilton, Nigel *2004*
Mellor, Rachel *2004*
Power, Nick *2004*
Dhillon, Kirandeep *2005*
Langford, Abigail *2005*
Larton, Claire *2005*
Stott, Matthew *2005*
Smith, Joseph *2008*
Walsh, Kathryn *2008*
Benson, Clare *2009*

†Recorder *Door Tenant/Associate Member

Carlin, Niall *2009*
Durham Hall, Christian *2009*
Ward, Emily *2011*

Types of work
Capital tax · Care proceedings · Commercial litigation · Common law (general) · Corporation tax · Crime · Discrimination · Employment · Environment · Equity · Family law · Family provision · Housing · Immigration · Income tax · Landlord and tenant · Licensing · Medical negligence · Mental health · Partnerships · Personal injury · Personal insolvency · Professional negligence · Sale and carriage of goods · Trusts · Wills

Disability access
Staff briefed or trained on duties under the disability legislation, Disabled parking available

OPTIMUS CHAMBERS

The Chambers of Miss Micaila Williams, Po Box 11193, Braintree, Essex CM7 0HQ
01376 691 885/07736 283873
Fax: 01376 691 885

CHAMBERS OF LESLEY MITCHELL

Stapleton Lodge, 71 Hamilton Road, Brentford, Middlesex TW8 0QF
020 8568 2164
Fax: 020 8560 2798
E-mail: lesley@mitchellsegal.co.uk

Chambers of: Ms L Mitchell

THE CHAMBERS OF MR JONATHAN TRUSSLER

3 York Parade, Great West Road, Brentford, Middlesex TW8 9AA

49 CHAMBERS

PO Box 3956, Bridgnorth, Shropshire WV16 4NA
01746 761545
Fax: 01746 767968; DX: 23205 Bridgnorth
E-mail: 49chambers@googlemail.com

Chambers of: Mr A S F Mitchell

Disability access
Staff briefed or trained on duties under the disability legislation, Disabled parking available

THE CHAMBERS OF MR BULLOCK

Arden Lodge, 11 Montpelier Villas, Brighton BN1 3DG
01273 321050

Chambers of: Mr R G Bullock

CROWN OFFICE ROW CHAMBERS

119 Church Street, Brighton, Sussex BN1 1UD
01273 625625
Fax: 01273 698888; DX: 36670 Brighton 2
E-mail: clerks@1cor.com
URL: www.lcor.com
Out of hours telephone: 07799 040 352

Chambers of: The Hon P N Havers QC
Clerks: David Bingham (Senior Clerk, Brighton), James Hart, Stuart Taylor, Mark Worsley, Laura Ketchum, Thomas Lawrance; Chambers Director: Bob Wilson

Havers, Philip QC *1974*
King-Smith, James *1980*
Ashwell, Paul *1977*
Booth, Roger TD *1966*
Morris-Coole, Christopher *1974*†
McLaughlin, Karen *1982*
Stevenson-Watt, Neville *1985*
Smith, Adam *1987*
Bergin, Timothy *1987*
Le Prevost, Aviva *1990*
Rice, Christopher *1991*
Grant, Jules *1991*
Cave, Jeremy *1992*
Sinnatt, Simon *1993*
Taylor, Nigel *1993*
Morelli, Luisa *1993*
Jenkins, Rowan *1994*
Henson, Christine *1994*
Healey, Susan *1995*
Claridge, Rachael *1996*
Roach, Jacqueline *1996*
Sharghy, Pegah *1998*
Wells, Camilla *1998*
Hussain, Ghulam *1998*
Peckham, Jane *1999*
Wright, Stuart *2000*
Cogin, Leo *2000*
Lewington, Francesca *2001*
Mehta, Anita *2002*
Howe, Gavin *2003*
Ager, Richard *2004*
Battie, Eleanor *2004*
Mustafa, Hala *2004*
Miller, Daniel *2005*
Knott, Samantha *2005*
Godfrey, Lauren *2007*
John, Charlotte *2008*
Tregoning, Bruce *2009*
Ciborowska, Clare *2009*
Saunders, Denise *2008*
Walker, Michael *2008*
Murdoch, Catriona *2009**

Types of work
Animals · Care proceedings · Children · Common law (general) · Corporate fraud ·

†Recorder *Door Tenant/Associate Member

Crime · Employment · Environment · Family law · Family provision · Housing · Insolvency · Landlord and tenant · Licensing · Matrimonial · Mediation · Personal injury · Personal insolvency · Planning · Professional negligence · Real property · Road traffic · Trusts

Disability access
Staff briefed or trained on duties under the disability legislation, Wheelchair access, Disabled parking available

CHAMBERS OF DOMINIC DUDKOWSKI

7 White Street, Brighton, East Sussex BN2 0JH
07905 365189

Chambers of: Mr D C Dudkowski

Disability access
Staff briefed or trained on duties under the disability legislation

LAMB BUILDING

22 Ship Street, Brighton BN1 1AD
01273 820490
E-mail: admin@lambbuilding.co.uk

Chambers of: Mr A Feder

CHAMBERS OF LEO RAHMAN

30 Balsdean Road, Brighton, Sussex BN2 6PF
07814 004 790
Fax: 01775 718 036
E-mail: leorahman@aol.com

ALBION CHAMBERS

Broad Street, Bristol BS1 1DR
0117 927 2144
Fax: 0117 926 2569; DX: 7822 Bristol
E-mail: clerks@albionchambers.co.uk
URL: www.albionchambers.co.uk
Out of hours telephone: 0117 927 2144

Chambers of: Mr M D G Fitton QC
Clerks: Bonnie Colbeck (Crime), Nicholas Jeanes (Crime), Michael Harding (Family/Civil), Julie Hathway (Family/Civil), Theresa Lyne; Chambers Director: Paul Fletcher; Chambers Manager: Ian Woodward, Billing Clerk: Dominic Farrell; Fees Clerk: Sarah Attwood; Finance Administrator: Lesley Carpenter

Fitton, Michael QC *1991†*
Hughes, Ignatius QC *1986†*
Vaitilingam, Adam QC *1987†*
Ekaney, Nkumbe QC *1990*
Wills-Goldingham, Claire QC *1988*
Jervis, *1966*
Hills, Timothy *1968*
O'Brien, Nicholas *1968*
Price, Louise *1972*
Grumbar, Paul *1974†*
Fridd, Nicholas *1975*
Steen, Martin *1976*
Duval, Robert *1979*
Norris, John Geraint *1980*
Mooney, Stephen *1987*
Tait, Don *1987†*
Dinan-Hayward, Deborah *1988*
Elder, Fiona *1988*
Cornwall, Virginia *1990*
Livesey, John *1990*
Rowsell, Claire *1991*
Burns, Simon *1992*
Cook, Paul *1992*
Sproull, Nicholas *1992*
Burgess, Edward *1993†*
Fuller, Alan *1993*
Stanniland, Jonathan *1993*
Cunningham, Elizabeth *1995*
Nelson, Giles *1995*
Taylor, Jason *1995*
Leafe, Daniel *1996*
Posta, Adrian *1996*
Real, Kirsty *1996*
Siva, Kannan *1996*
Brunner, Kate *1997*
Wiltshire, Hannah *1998*
Pitts, Charlotte *1999*
Chidgey, David *2000*
Knowles, Linsey *2000*
Leslie, Marie *2000*
Regan, Sarah *2000*
Cotterell, David *2001*
Shepherd, Richard *2001*
Cranfield, James *2002*
Flexman, Carla *2002*
Goldie, Katie *2004*
Jenkins, Benjamin *2004*
Borkowski, Gemma *2005*
Khandker, Monisha *2005*
Midgley, Anna *2005*
Heckscher, William *2006*
Perry, Derek *2006*
Emslie, Simon *2007*
Fuller, Stuart *2007*
Baggley, Phillip *2009*
Brazenall, Emily *2009*
Thornhill, Andrew QC *1969**
Dunkels, Paul QC *1972†**
Mehigan, Simon QC *1980**
Storey, Paul QC *1982†**
Branigan, Kate QC *1984**

Types of work
Care proceedings · Chancery (land law) · Common law (general) · Courts martial · Crime · Discrimination · Employment · Equity · Family law · Family provision · Inquests · Landlord and tenant · Local authorities · Mental health · Personal injury · Professional negligence · Succession · Trusts · Wills

Disability access
Staff briefed or trained on duties under the disability legislation, Wheelchair access

ASSIZE COURT CHAMBERS

14 Small Street, Bristol BS1 1DE
0117 926 4587
Fax: 0117 922 6835; DX: 78134 Bristol
E-mail: carly@assize.co.uk

Chambers of: Mr T A Evans

Disability access
Staff briefed or trained on duties under the disability legislation, Wheelchair access

D

CHAMBERS OF MR CHRISTOPHER AUSTINS

Rookwood House, East Harptree, Bristol BS40 6AQ
01761 221 208
Fax: 0870 166 0529

Chambers of: Mr C J Austins

BRISTOL FAMILY JUSTICE CHAMBERS

1 Friary, Temple Quay, Bristol BS1 6EA
01453 834437

DINGLE CHAMBERS

1 Chardstock Avenue, Coombe Dingle, Bristol BS9 2RY
07818 827754
E-mail: N.treharne@btinternet.com

Chambers of: Mr N S Treharne

DOUGHTY STREET CHAMBERS

5th Floor, Broad Quay House, Prince Street, Bristol BS1 4DJ
01179 058 717
Fax: 020 7404 2283; DX: 7871 Bristol

CHAMBERS OF MR MARK EVANS

Grove Farm, Wapley, Bristol BS37 8RW
01454 312150
Fax: 01454 312150
E-mail: evansmlaw@fsmail.net

Chambers of: Mr M Evans QC

FOSTERS CHAMBERS

17 Small Street, Bristol BS1 1DE
0117927 9604
Fax: 0117 925 0609; DX: 78206 Bristol
E-mail: tabmac@fastmail.fm

Chambers of: Miss T L MacFarlane

FREDERICK PLACE CHAMBERS

9 Frederick Place, Frederick Place Chambers, Clifton, Bristol BS8 1AS
0117 946 7059
E-mail: rsp4593558@aol.com

Chambers of: Mr R H Spicer

Disability access
Staff briefed or trained on duties under the disability legislation, Disabled parking available

GUILDHALL CHAMBERS

5-8 Broad Street, Bristol BS1 2HW
0117 930 9000
Fax: 0117 930 3898

GUILDHALL CHAMBERS

23 Broad Street, Bristol BS1 2HG
0117 930 9000
Fax: 0117 9303800; DX: 7823 Bristol
E-mail: hoc@guildhallchambers.co.uk

Chambers of: Mr P M Blair QC

Disability access
Wheelchair access, Disabled parking available

NO5 CHAMBERS

38 Queen Square, Bristol BS1 4QS
0845 210 5555
Fax: 0117 917 8501; DX: 7838 Bristol
URL: www.no5.com
Out of hours telephone: 07774 298047

Chambers of: Mr P E Bleasdale QC
Practice Director: Tony McDaid: Practice Managers: Patrick Hawkins, Andrew Bisbey, Robert Woods, Andrew Trotter, James Parks, Abdul Hafeez, Martin Hulbert, Zoe Owen, Robert Woods, Samantha Maguire-Thompson; Finance Manager: Ian Tullett

Also at: No5 Chambers, Fountain Court, Steelhouse Lane, Birmingham B4 6DR Tel: +44 (0) 845 210 5555, Fax: +44 (0) 121 606 1501.

Also at: No5 Chambers, Greenwood House, 4-7 Salisbury Court, London EC4Y 8AA, Tel: +44 (0) 845 210 5555, Fax: +44 (0) 20 7900 1582

Bleasdale, Paul QC *1978*†
Smith, Tony QC *1958*†
Kingston, Martin QC *1972*
Tedd, Rex QC *1970*†
Hotten, Christopher QC *1972*†
Evans, Gareth QC *1973*†
Jones, Richard QC *1972*†
Gill, Manjit QC *1982*
Cahill, Jeremy QC *1975*
Howker, David QC *1982*
Hunjan, Satinder QC *1984*†
Dove, Ian QC *1986*†
Meyer, Lorna QC *1986*
Burrows, Michael QC *1979*†
Bright, Christopher QC *1985*†
Anderson, Mark QC *1983*†
Mason, David QC *1986*†
Lock, David QC *1985*
Drew, Simon QC *1987*
Duck, Michael QC *1988*
Keeling, Adrian QC *1990*
Heywood, Mark QC *1986*
Bell, Gary QC *1989*
West, John *1965*
Smith, Roger *1968*
Whitaker, Stephen *1970*
Arnold, Peter *1972*
Cliff, Graham *1973*†
Harvey, John *1973*†
Jones, Timothy *1975*
Bealby, Walter *1976*
Giles, Roger *1976*
Henson, Graham *1976*
Iles, David *1977*
James, Christopher *1977*
Pusey, William *1977*
Rowland, Robin *1977*†
Smallwood, Anne *1977*
Keogh, Andrew *1978*
Korn, Anthony *1978*
Michael, Simon *1978*
O'Donovan, Kevin *1978*
Cairnes, Paul *1980*
Newman, Timothy *1981*
Brown, Stephanie *1982*
Campbell, Stephen *1982*†
Thompson, Neil *1982*
De Mello, Ramby *1983*
Maccabe, Irvine *1983*
McGrath, Andrew *1983*
Newdick, Christopher *1983*
Bailey, Russell *1985*
Bell, Anthony *1985*
Bermingham, Gerald *1985*
Doyle, James *1985*
Kelly, Mark *1985*
Moat, Richard *1985*
Sharif, Nadia *1985*
Leigh, Kevin *1986*
Thorogood, Bernard *1986*†
Wignall, Gordon *1987*
Baker, Caroline *1988*
Birk, Dewinder *1988*
Bridge, Ian *1988*
Chadwick, Joanna *1988*
Forsyth, Samantha *1988*
Morgan, Adrienne *1988*
Singh-Tiwana, Ekwall *1988*
Wallace, Andrew *1988*
Attwood, John *1989*
Bedford, Becket *1989*
Duthie, Malcolm *1989*
Liddiard, Martin *1989*
Murray, Carole *1989*
Anning, Michael *1990*
Baker, Andrew *1990*
Boora, Jinder *1990*
Colquhoun, Celina *1990*
McDonald, Melanie *1990*
Wynne, Ashley *1990*
Al-Rashid, Mahmud *1991*
Buckingham, Sarah *1991*
Dooley, Allan *1991*†
Friel, Michele *1991*
Marshall, Paul *1991*
Radburn, Mark *1991*
Bailey, Steven *1992*
Bazini, Danny *1992*
Brockley, Nigel *1992*
Farrer, Adam *1992*
Goatley, Peter *1992*
Hansen, William *1992*
Ismail, Nazmun Nisha *1992*
Mahmood, Abid *1992*
Mallick, Nabila *1992*
Preston, Nicola *1992*
Richards, Hugh *1992*
Wilkinson, Marc *1992*
Xydias, Nicholas *1992*
Bradley, Phillip *1993*
Campbell, Rhona *1993*
Dutta, Nandini *1993*
Edhem, Emma *1993*
Nicholson, Edward *1993*
Rothwell, Joanne *1993*
Sumeray, Caroline *1993*
Taylor, David *1993*
Choongh, Satnam *1994*
Dean, Brian *1994*
Fox, Simon *1994*
Jones, Jonathan *1994*
Khalique, Nageena *1994*
Nuvoloni, Stefano *1994*
Potter, Anthony *1994*
Smallwood, Robert *1994*
Stoll, James *1994*
Tyack, David *1994*
Butterfield, John *1995*†
Diamond, Anna *1995*
Hignett, Richard *1995*
Kershaw, Dean *1995*†
Mitchell, David *1995*
Monaghan, Susan *1995*
Sheppard, Tim *1995*
Bagral, Ravinder *1996*
Case, Richard *1996*
Davidson, Laura *1996*
Hancox, Sally *1996*†
Holloway, David *1996*
Islam-Choudhury, Mugni *1996*
Jones, Cheryl *1996*
Knotts, Carol *1996*
Pitchers, Henry *1996*
Power, Elizabeth *1996*
Brunning, Matthew *1997*
Chatterjee, Adreeja *1997*
Compton, Gareth *1997*
Hadley, Richard *1997*
Hirst, Karl *1997*
Lally, Harbinder Singh *1997*
Rowley, Rachel *1997*
Singh, Talbir *1997*
Young, Christopher *1997*
Brown, Kristina *1998*
Derrington, Jonathan *1998*
Kimblin, Richard *1998*
Stein, Alexander *1998*
Afzal, Fayyaz OBE *1999*
Armstrong, Douglas *1999*
Barney, Helen *1999*
Brook, Matthew *1999*
Butt, Nassera *1999*
Chelvan, S *1999*
Coughlan, John *1999*
Crow, Charles *1999*
Denning, Louisa *1999*
Gamble, Jamie *1999*
Hargreaves, Teresa *1999*
Price, Charles *1999*
Abberley, Stephen *2000*
Chawla, Neil *2000*
Ensaff, Omar *2000*
Wigley, Jenny *2000*
Willetts, Glenn *2000*
Adkinson, Richard *2001*
Bains, Param *2001*
Beloff, Rupert *2001*
Brown, Emma *2001*
Chaffin-Laird, Olivia *2001*
Dixon, James *2001*
Evans, Paul *2001*
Forster, Bridget *2001*
Gamble, Esther *2001*
Heeley, Michelle *2001*
Mann, Jasvir *2001*
Pole, Tim *2001*
Schofield, Thomas *2001*
Wingrave, Michael *2001*
Worlock, Simon *2001*
Bradshaw, Mark *2002*
Clifford, Victoria *2002*
Mantle, Philip *2002*
McClement, Lynette *2002*
Arthur, Helen *2003*
Cobill, Nicholas *2003*
Oscroft, Daniel *2003*
Owen, Denise *2003*
Pinnock, Earl *2003*
Van Overdijk, Claire *2003*
Davies, Rhys *2004*
Gupta, Mamta *2004*
Leslie, James *2004*
Allen, Juliet *2005*
Allen, Sarah *2005*
Cooke, Richard *2005*
Feeney, Katie *2005*
Feeny, Jack *2005*
Fernandes, Suella *2005*
Grant, Orla *2005*
Joseph, Paul *2005*
Punt, Dr Jonathan *2005*
Reed, Steven *2005*
Sandhu, Harpreet *2005*
Taylor, Kathryn *2005*
Williams, Philip *2005*
Yasseri, Yasmin *2005*
Enonchong, Nelson *2006*
Gallacher, Kirsty *2006*
Roberts, Gemma *2006*
Yates, Victoria *2006*
Boyden, Matthew *2007*
Hunka, Simon *2007*
Meager, Rowena *2007*
Oakes, Richard *2007*
Smyth, Jack *2007*
Barrett, Kevin *2008*
Corfield, Louise *2008*
Pye, Derek *2008*
Shaw, Jonathan *2008*
Williams, Hermione *2008*
Grimshaw, Richard *2010*
Jennings, Caroline *2010*
Osmund-Smith, Thea *2010*
O'Brien, Michael QC *2011*
Humphreys, Richard QC *1986**
Hanson, Timothy *1989**
Phillips, Moira *1989**
Grant, Edward *1991**
Renouf, Mark *1994**
Kurji, Fatim *2003**
Tyers-Smith, Peter *2005**

Types of work

Administrative law · Agriculture · Arbitration · Asset finance · Banking · Capital tax · Clinical negligence ·

Commercial law · Commercial litigation · Commercial property · Company, commercial and competition · Construction law · Conveyancing · Copyright · Corporate finance · Corporate fraud · Corporation tax · Court of Protection · Crime · Employment · Energy · Environment · Equity · Family law · Family provision · Financial services · Human rights · Immigration · Income tax · Industrial diseases · Information technology · Insolvency · Insurance · Intellectual property · International arbitration · International trade · Judicial review · Landlord and tenant · Licensing · Partnerships · Patents · Personal injury · Personal insolvency · Planning · Prison law · Property · Public law · Sport · Succession · Trademarks · Trusts · Wills

Disability access
Disabled parking available, Staff briefed or trained on duties under the disability legislation, Wheelchair access, Induction loop or infra red system

D

OLD SQUARE CHAMBERS

3 Orchard Court, St Augustine's Yard, Bristol BS1 5DP
0117 930 5100
Fax: 0117 927 3478; DX: 78229 Bristol
E-mail: clerks@oldsquare.co.uk

Chambers of: Mr N J Cooksley QC, Miss E J McNeill QC

Disability access
Staff briefed or trained on duties under the disability legislation, Wheelchair access, Disabled parking available, Induction loop or infra red system

3 PB BARRISTERS

Royal Talbot House, 2 Victoria Street, Bristol, Avon BS1 6BB
0117 928 1520
Fax: 0117 928 1525
URL: www.3pb.co.uk
Out of hours telephone: 07855 377452 (Mark Heath - Mobile)

Chambers of: Mr Ian Lawrie QC
Clerks: Mark Heath (Senior Clerk), Tom Cox, Phillipa Caine; Lisa Wilson, Marketing Manager; Finance Manager: Head of Business Admin and Finance: Neil Monro

Also at: London, Bournemouth, Oxford, Winchester

Lawrie, Ian QC *1985*†
Parroy, Michael QC *1969*†
Vere-Hodge, Michael QC *1970*
Farley, Roger QC *1974*†
Jones, Stewart QC *1972*†
Braslavsky, Nicholas QC *1983*†
Bromley-Davenport, John QC *1972*
Lickley, Nigel QC *1983*†
Parker, Christopher QC *1986*†
Parrish, Samuel *1962*
Solomon, Susan *1967*
Aylwin, Christopher *1970*
Swinstead, David *1970*
Norman, Michael *1971*†
Ward, Anthony *1971*
Curran, Leo *1972*
Jennings, Peter *1972*
Coleman, Anthony *1973*†
Stephenson, Ben *1973*
Bartlett, David *1975*†
Tyson, Richard *1975*†
Kent, Peter *1978*
Mitchell, Nigel *1978*
Grey, Robert *1979*
Hamilton, Gavin *1979*
Leach, Robin *1979*
Leviseur, Nicholas *1979*
Partridge, Ian *1979*
Coombes, Timothy *1980*
Edge, Ian *1981*
Marshall, David *1981*
Sampson, Graeme *1981*
Strutt, Martin *1981*
Martin, Nicola *1982*
Newman, Paul *1982*
Onslow, Richard *1982*
Lomas, Mark *1983*
Stancombe, Barry *1983*
O'Hara, Sarah *1984*
Palfrey, Monty *1985*
Whittle-Martin, Lucia *1985*
Clark, Tonia *1986*
Hudson, Elisabeth *1987*
Hendry, Lucy *1988*
Rowland, Nicholas *1988*†
Zabihi, Tanya *1988*
Bradbury, Timothy *1989*
Hester, Paul *1989*
Richards, David *1989*
Aeberli, Peter *1990*
Brunton, Sean *1990*
Griffiths, Hayley *1990*
Hiddleston, Adam *1990*
Knapp, Sophie *1990*
Buckley-Clarke, Amanda *1991*
Dunlop, Hamish *1991*
Katrak, Cyrus *1991*
Robins, Imogen *1991*
Ross, Iain *1991*
Bingham, Tony *1992*
Sweeney, Noel *1992*
Clargo, John *1994*
Dawson, James *1994*
Earle, Judy *1994*
Feest, Adam *1994*
Mitchell, Jack *1994*
Reid, David *1994*
Topliss, Megan *1994*
Weston, Louis *1994*
De Freitas, Melanie *1995*
McDevitt, Colin *1995*
McIlroy, David *1995*
Strachan, Elaine *1995*
Davison, James *1996*
Lorie, Andrew *1996*
Tyler, Thomas *1996*
Wilson, Lachlan *1996*
Purdy, Catherine *1997*
Sullivan, Mark *1997*
Davies, Eleanor *1998*
Griffiths, Emma *1998*
Taylor, Rufus *1998*
Horner, Robert *1999*
Kennedy, Stuart *1999*
Goodall, Rachael *2000*
Isaacs, Oliver *2000*
O'Doherty, Paul *2000*
Sheriff, Andrew *2000*
Worton, Louise *2000*
Cassidy, Sheena *2001*
Whelan, Christopher *2001*
Ludlow, Craig *2002*
Moss, Karen *2002*
Shillingford, Julia *2002*
Tomlinson, Michael *2002*
Courts, Robert *2003*
Gullick, Mathew *2003*
Jones, Victoria *2003*
Archer, Audrey *2004*
Davies, James *2004*
Hepworth, Elizabeth *2004*
Horder, Tom *2004*
Wheeler, Richard *2004*
Anderson, Katherine *2005*
Clarke, Sarah *2005*
Langford, Sarah *2005*
Musgrave, Anarkali *2005*
Cannings, Matthew *2006*
Da Costa, Francisca *2006*
Davies, Nick *2006*
Green, Mark *2006*
Robinson, Nick *2006*
Davies, Harriet *2007*
Elliott, Mark *2007*
Jones, Ximena *2007*
MacPhail, Andrew *2007*
Paulin, Michael *2007*
Perfect, Andrew *2007*
Chegwidden, James *2008*
Dunseath, Katherine *2008*
Edwards, Christopher *2008*

Alleyne, Ebony *2009*
Ashkar, Natalie *2009*
Bowes, Gemma *2009*
Currie, Philip *2009*
Frost, Nicola *2009*
Sanghera, Sharandish *2009*
Webb, Thomas *2010*
Wyeth, Stephen *2010*
Kean, Graham *2012*

Types of work

Accountancy · Adjudication · Administrative law · Adoption · Alternative dispute resolution · Ancillary relief · Animals · Arab commercial law · Arab law · Arbitration · Asbestos-related diseases · Asset forfeiture · Asset recovery · Banking · Bills of exchange · Boundaries · Building · Chancery (commercial) · Chancery (general) · Chancery (land law) · Child care law · Children · Civil actions against the police · Civil partnerships · Clinical negligence · Cohabitation · Commercial contracts · Commercial fraud · Commercial law · Commercial litigation · Commercial property · Common land · Common law (general) · Company, commercial and competition · Computer contracts · Computer crime · Computer litigation · Confiscation · Conflict of laws · Construction law · Consumer credit · Consumer law · Contracts · Copyright · Corporate finance · Corporate fraud · Corporate governance · Corporate insolvency · Corporate liability · Corporate manslaughter · Corporate recovery · Costs · Court of Protection · Courts martial · Crime · Crime and criminal due process · Criminal judicial review · Cross-border litigation and remedies · Damages · Disability discrimination · Disasters · Disciplinary procedures · Disciplinary tribunals · Discrimination · Divorce · Domestic violence injunctions · Ecclesiastical law · Economic torts · Education · Election law · Employment · Engineering disputes · Equine law · Equity · Factoring · Family law · Family provision · Financial provision · Financial services · Firearms · Foreign law · Franchising · Fraud · Freezing orders · Guarantees · Health and safety · Holiday injury and damages · Homicide · Housing · Industrial deafness · Industrial diseases · Information technology · Inheritance and cohabitees · Inquests · Insolvency · Insurance · Intellectual property · International arbitration · International commercial arbitration · International fraud and asset tracing · Islamic family law · Islamic law · Judicial review · Landlord and tenant · Lands Tribunal · Licensing · Matrimonial finance · Mediation · Medical negligence · Middle Eastern law · Military law · Multi-party litigation · Occupational diseases · Partnerships · Passing off · Personal injury · Personal insolvency · Planning · Police · Product liability · Professional negligence · Public law · Real property · Regulatory and disciplinary law · Rights of light · Rights of way · Road traffic · Sale and carriage of goods · Serial crime · Serious fraud · Shareholder agreements · Succession · Tax · Technology and Construction Court · Torts · Trust litigation · Trusts · Wardship · Wills

Disability access

Staff briefed or trained on duties under the disability legislation, Wheelchair access, Disabled parking available

D

QUEEN SQUARE CHAMBERS

56 Queen Square, Bristol BS1 4PR
0117 921 1966
Fax: 0117 927 6493; DX: 7870 Bristol
E-mail: crime@qs-c.co.uk
URL: www.queensquarechambers.co.uk

Chambers of: Mr C J Taylor
Clerks: James Dowse (Civil), Gary Brown (Crime); Practice Manager: Chief Executive: Steve Freeman; Administrator: John Dummer

Also at: Castle Court, 6 Cathedral Road, Cardiff, CF11 9LJ. DX: 141861 Cardiff 28
Tel: 02920 501750. Fax: 020920 647652

Taylor, Christopher *1982*
Jenkins, Alun QC *1972*†
Levy, Robert QC *1988*
Martin, David *1969*
Threlfall, George *1972*
Darian, Ann *1974*
Rea, Karen *1980*
Goodall, Charles *1986*
Warren, Philip *1988*
Rowley, Jane *1988*
Halliday, Ian *1989*
Barlow, Melissa *1991*
Carron, Richard *1992*
Shellard, Robin *1992*
Maunder, David *1993*
Row, Charles *1993*
Dennis, Rebecca *1994*
Goodman, Simon *1996*
Walsh, Darren *1997*
Williams, Mark *1998*
Frazer, Alison *1999*
Fryer, Nigel *1999*
Halden, Angus *1999*
Gohil, Pushpanjali *2000*
Elford, Caroline *2002*
Farquhar, Fiona *2002*
MacBean, Andrew *2002*
Roberts, Stephen *2002*
Willmott, Oliver *2002*
McNair, Duncan *2003*
Heard, Jonathan *2004*
Lewis, Joanna *2004*
Lucas, Joanna *2004*
Tucker, James *2004*
Gardiner, Kerry *2006*
Graham, Gareth *2006*
Houshyari-Darian, Alice *2006*
Smyth, Christopher *2006*
Tibbitts, Simon *2006*
Walsh, Rosie *2006*
Clayton, Lucy *2009*
Jennings, Sarah *2009*
Pascoe, Nigel QC *1966*†*
Bromige, James *2010*
McCabe, Imogen *2010*
Donne, Anthony QC *1973**
Johnston, Carey QC *1977**
Keehan, Michael QC *1982*†*
Chute, Andrea *1995**

†Recorder *Door Tenant/Associate Member

D

Types of work

Adjudication · Adoption · Ancillary relief · Anti-social Behaviour Orders · Arbitration · Asbestos-related diseases · Asset forfeiture · Asset recovery · Boundaries · Building · Care proceedings · Chancery · Chancery (commercial) · Chancery (general) · Chancery (land law) · Child abduction · Child abuse · Child care law · Child support · Children · Civil actions against the police · Civil fraud · Civil litigation · Civil partnerships · Clinical negligence · Cohabitation · Commercial fraud · Commercial property · Common land · Common law (general) · Computer crime · Confiscation of the proceeds of crime · Construction law · Consumer law · Contaminated land · Coroner's inquests · Coroners · Corporate fraud · Corporate manslaughter · Crime · Crime and criminal due process · Criminal judicial review · Defamation · Disability discrimination · Disciplinary procedures · Disciplinary tribunals · Discrimination · Divorce · Domestic violence injunctions · Drink driving · Engineering disputes · Environment · Extradition · Family law · Financial provision · Financial provision for children · Fire and other property damage claims · Firearms · Food law · Forced Marriage · Forfeiture · Fostering · Fraud · Health and safety · Healthcare law · Holiday injury and damages · Homicide · Housing · Industrial deafness · Industrial diseases · Industrial relations law · Inheritance · Inquests · International criminal law · International fraud and asset tracing · Internet crime · Landlord and tenant · Leasehold enfranchisement · Leave to remove · Licensing · Litigation · Local authority claims · Local authority liability · Malicious falsehood · Malicious prosecution · Matrimonial · Matrimonial finance · Mediation · Medical negligence · Money laundering · Motor vehicles · Occupational diseases · Pensions · Personal injury · Police · Police discipline · Pollution · Prison law · Prisoners' rights · Private children law · Product liability · Product safety · Professional negligence · Public access · Regulatory and disciplinary law · Regulatory crime · Remedies · Rights of light · Rights of way · Road haulage · Road traffic · Road traffic offences · Serial crime · Serious fraud · Sexual Offences · Special Guardianship · Speeding · Sports medicine · Terrorism · Title to land · Torts · Trade Descriptions Act · Trading standards · Unmarried couples · Wardship

Disability access

Wheelchair access, Disabled parking available

ST JOHN'S CHAMBERS

101 Victoria Street, Bristol BS1 6PU
0117 923 4700
Fax: 0117 929 4821; DX: 743350 Bristol 36
E-mail: clerks@stjohnschambers.co.uk
URL: www.stjohnschambers.co.uk
Out of hours telephone: 07947 702506

Chambers of: Mr R J Stead
Practice Manager: Robert Bocock (Commercial and Chancery Practice Group); Annette Bushell (Personal Injury and Clinical Negligence Practice Group), Luke Hodgson (Family Practice Manager), Derek Jenkins (Chief Executive); Isabelle Mills (Office Manager), Sarah Tune (Marketing Manager)

Stead, Richard *1979*†
Wilson-Smith, Christopher QC *1965*†*
Sharp, Christopher QC *1975*†
Tolson, Robin QC *1980*
Jacklin, Susan QC *1980*†
Blohm, Leslie QC *1982*†
Pressdee, Piers QC *1991*
Ornsby, Suzanne QC *1986**
Dawson, Alexander *1969*†*
Fletcher, David *1971*
Bullock, Ian *1975*
Corfield, Sheelagh *1975*
Das, Kamala *1975*
Grice, Timothy *1975*†
Higginson, Tim *1977**
Mawhinney, Richard *1977**
Neill, Robin *1979*
Auld, Charles TD *1980*
Duthie, Catriona *1981*
Blackmore, John *1983*
Wadsley, Peter *1984*
Hunter, Susan *1985*
Godwin, William *1986**
Edwards, Glyn *1987*
Maher, Martha *1987*
Morgan, Simon *1988*
Adams, Guy *1989*
O'Neill, Louise *1989*
O'Sullivan, Derek *1990**
Leeper, Thomas *1991*
Harris, Elizabeth *1992*
Light, Roy *1992*
Martin, Dianne *1992*
Sharples, John *1992*
Maxwell, Adrian *1993*
McLaughlin, Andrew *1993*
Skellorn, Kathryn *1993*
Humphreys, Jacqueline *1994**
Marsden, Andrew *1994*
Miller, Nicholas *1994*
Phillimore, Sarah *1994*
Regan, David *1994*
Dickinson, John *1995*
Evans, Judi *1996*
White, Matthew *1997*
Horne, Julian *1998*
Moradifar, Kambiz *1998*
Troup, Alex *1998*
Bond, Abigail *1999*
Mashembo, Carol *1999*
Thornton, Delia *1999*
McKinlay, Vanessa *2000*
Hussain, Zahid *2001*
Russell, Rachel *2001*
Pearce-Smith, James *2002*
Reed, Lucy *2002*
Symington, Anna *2002*
Belyavin, Julia *2003*
Jenkins, Philip *2003*
Saunders, Zoë *2003*
Taylor, Rebecca *2003*
Commins, Andrew *2004*
Jones, Christopher *2004*
Lewis, Darren *2004*
Rowell, George *2004*
Atkinson, Jody *2005*
Gold, Richard *2006*
Coventry, Charles *2007*
Kearney, Andrew *2007*
Knapton, Sarah *2007*
Lewis, Paul *2007**

 †Recorder *Door Tenant/Associate Member

West, Patrick *2007*
Hooper, Katie *2008**
Clarke, Michael *2009*
Leonard, Claire *2009*
Norman, Richard *2009*
Wooding, Oliver *2009*
Pointon, Nicholas *2010*
Harrowing, Peter *2011*
Judd, Frances QC *1984**

Types of work

Administrative law · Agriculture · Arbitration · Banking · Capital tax · Care proceedings · Chancery (general) · Chancery (land law) · Charities · Civil fraud · Civil liberties · Clinical negligence · Commercial law · Commercial litigation · Commercial property · Common land · Common law (general) · Company, commercial and competition · Competition law · Construction law · Consumer law · Copyright · Corporate fraud · Corporation tax · Courts martial · Crime · Defamation · Discrimination · EC competition law · Ecclesiastical law · Education · Employment · Energy · Environment · Equity · Family law · Family provision · Financial services · Franchising · Housing · Income tax · Insolvency · Insurance · Intellectual property · Landlord and tenant · Licensing · Local authorities · Medical negligence · Mental health · Partnerships · Patents · Pensions · Personal injury · Personal insolvency · Planning · Professional negligence · Sale and carriage of goods · Sport · Succession · Trademarks · Trusts · Wills

Disability access

Staff briefed or trained on duties under the disability legislation, Wheelchair access, Disabled parking available

TOLZEY CHAMBERS

37 Rowlandson Gardens, Lockleaze, Bristol BS7 9UH

Chambers of: Mr J D Mannion

UNITY STREET CHAMBERS

5 Unity Street, College Green, Bristol BS1 5HH
0117 906 9789
Fax: 0117 906 9799; DX: 7868 Bristol
E-mail: chambers@unitystreetchambers.com
URL: www.unitystreetchambers.com

Chambers of: Mr J S Isherwood
Clerks: Clair Wadden, Kate Brunton

Isherwood, John *1978*
Curwen, David *1982*
Wightwick, Iain *1985*
Counsell, Edward *1990*
Rhodes, Amanda *1990*
Halliwell, Toby *1992*
Currie, Fergus *1997*
Huggins, Toby *1998*
Welch, Robert *2007*
Ferguson, Christopher *1979**
Dawson, Judy *1993**
Marven, Robert *1994**

Types of work

Care proceedings · Chancery (general) · Chancery (land law) · Clinical negligence · Commercial law · Commercial litigation · Commercial property · Common law (general) · Company, commercial and competition · Construction law · Consumer law · Crime · Employment · Equity · Family law · Family provision · Health and safety · Housing · Human rights · Information technology · Landlord and tenant · Local authorities · Medical negligence · Partnerships · Personal injury · Professional negligence · Sale and carriage of goods · Trusts · Wills

Disability access

Staff briefed or trained on duties under the disability legislation

CHAMBERS OF MICHAEL FURMINGER

4 Marcent Row, St Mary's Hill, Brixham, Devon TQ5 9GQ
01803 414 545
E-mail: michaelfurminger@live.com

PRINCESS COURT CHAMBERS

122 Princess Court, Bromley Hill, Bromley BR1 4JU
020 8460 2046

Chambers of: Mrs E O Boateng

SUNDRIDGE CHAMBERS

10 Sundridge House, Burnt Ash Lane, Bromley, Kent BR1 5AE
020 8464 9772
Fax: 020 8460 3603
E-mail: sundridgechambers@sky.com

Chambers of: Mrs V J Weaver

Disability access

Staff briefed or trained on duties under the disability legislation, Disabled parking available

CHAMBERS OF MR CLIVE SUTTON

18 Mill Lane, Stoke, Bruerne, Northamptonshire NN12 7SH
07973 386702
E-mail: cs@clivesuttonbarristerdirect.co.uk

†Recorder *Door Tenant/Associate Member

D

CHAMBERS OF MR IZZET SINAN

Floor 8, 7 Rue Guimard, Brussels B-1040
00 32 2 507 7522
Fax: 00 32 2 507 7555

Chambers of: Mr I M Sinan

Disability access
Staff briefed or trained on duties under the disability legislation, Wheelchair access, Disabled parking available

CHAMBERS OF MRS CAROLE ANNE HENRY

78 Moorhen Way, Buckingham, Buckinghamshire MK18 1GU
01280 824520
Fax: 01280 814964
E-mail: caroleahenry@aol.com

Chambers of: Mrs C A Henry

RYE GREEN CHAMBERS

Rye Green Farm, Burwash, East Sussex TN19 7HP
01435 882577
Fax: 01435 882545
E-mail: law@banksr.com

Chambers of: Mr R J Banks

Disability access
Staff briefed or trained on duties under the disability legislation, Wheelchair access, Disabled parking available

25 SPRINGWATER AVENUE

25 Springwater Avenue, Holcombe Brook, Bury, Lancashire BL0 9RH
01204 883 630
Fax: 01204 883 630
E-mail: dr.f.chaudhry@hotmail.co.uk

Chambers of: Dr F A Chaudhry

Disability access
Staff briefed or trained on duties under the disability legislation, Disabled parking available

CHAMBERS OF MR C J G PARKER

22 Crowstones, Buxton SK17 6NZ
01298 212439
E-mail: cjgparker@hotmail.co.uk

CHAMBERS OF IAN C THOMPSON TD

Spirthill Farm, Spirthill, Calne, Wiltshire SN11 9HP
07714 758579
E-mail: ian.c.thompson@btinternet.com

Chambers of: Mr I C Thompson TD

CHAMBERS OF MR PAUL DIAMOND

PO Box 1041, Barton, Cambridge CB23 7WY
01223 264544
E-mail: pauldiamond@btconnect.com

Chambers of: Mr P Diamond

FENNERS CHAMBERS

3 Madingley Road, Cambridge CB3 0EE
01223 368761
Fax: 01223 313007; DX: 5809 Cambridge
E-mail: clerks@fennerschambers.com

Chambers of: Mr M M Collier

Disability access
Staff briefed or trained on duties under the disability legislation, Wheelchair access, Disabled parking available

REGENCY CHAMBERS

Sheraton House, Castle Park, Cambridge CB3 0AX
01223 301517
Fax: 01223 359267; DX: 12349 Peterborough

Chambers of: Mr I R Martignetti

BECKET CHAMBERS

17 New Dover Road, Canterbury, Kent CT1 3AS
01227 786331
Fax: 01227 786329; DX: 5330 Canterbury
E-mail: clerks@becket-chambers.co.uk
URL: www.becket-chambers.co.uk
Out of hours telephone: 07738 305404
Clerks: Paul Eaton (Senior Clerk), Arron Smith

Also at: Kent House, Romney Place, Maidstone, Kent ME15 6LH Tel: 01622 230957 Fax: 08444 432686 DX: 4803 Maidstone

Kee, Peter *1983*
Edginton, Horace Ronald *1984*
Jackson, Kevin Roy *1984*
Newton, Philip *1984*
Mills, Corey *1987*
Wall, Christopher *1987*
Hall, Jeremy John *1988*
Styles, Clive Richard *1990*
Tapsell, Paul *1991*
Adamson, Lilias Louisa *1994*
Fairbank, Nicholas *1996*
McIntosh, Melanie *2002*
Murkin, Sandria *2004*
Andrews, Melanie *2005*
Coates, Holly *2008*
Reynolds, Victoria *2008*
Kenny, Edward *2009*
Thistle, Dean *2010*
Bartlett, Andrew QC *1974*†*

Types of work
Care proceedings · Commercial law · Common law (general) · Crime · Employment · Environment · Family law · Family provision · Human rights · Landlord and tenant · Licensing · Local authorities · Mediation · Partnerships · Personal injury · Personal insolvency · Planning · Professional negligence

Disability access
Staff briefed or trained on duties under the disability legislation, Wheelchair access, Disabled parking available

STOUR CHAMBERS

Mill Studio, 17a Stour Street, Canterbury, Kent CT1 2NR
01227 764899
Fax: 01227 764941; DX: 5342 Canterbury
E-mail: clerks@stourchambers.co.uk

Chambers of: Ms S Cox

Disability access
Staff briefed or trained on duties under the disability legislation, Wheelchair access, Disabled parking available

APEX

Harlech House, 20 Cathedral Road, Cardiff CF11 9LJ
02920 232 032
Fax: 02920 233 636; DX: 141874 Cardiff 28
E-mail: clerks@apexchambers.net

Chambers of: Mr D V Williams

Disability access
Staff briefed or trained on duties under the disability legislation, Disabled parking available

CAMBRIA CHAMBERS

The Coal Exchange, Mount Stuart Square, Cardiff Bay, Cardiff CF10 5EB
0845 123 1234
Fax: 02920 482522; DX: 200763 Cardiff
E-mail: Info@cambriachambers.co.uk

Chambers of: Mr J G M Edwards

CATHEDRAL CHAMBERS

28 Cathedral Road, Cardiff CF11 9LJ
02920 660129

CENTURION CHAMBERS

Suite 9, Temple Court, Cathedral Road, Cardiff CF11 9HA
029 2078 6472
Fax: 029 2078 6471

Chambers of: Mr G S Sukul

Disability access
Staff briefed or trained on duties under the disability legislation, Wheelchair access, Disabled parking available

CIVITAS CHAMBERS

Global Reach, Celtic Gateway, Cardiff Bay, Cardiff CF11 0SN
0845 0713 007
Fax: 0845 0713 008; DX: 50750 Cardiff 2
E-mail: clerks@civitaslaw.com

Disability access
Staff briefed or trained on duties under the disability legislation, Wheelchair access, Disabled parking available

2-3 GRAY'S INN SQUARE

One Caspian Point, Pierhead Street, Cardiff Bay, Cardiff CF10 4DQ
02920 444022
Fax: 02920 444023
E-mail: Cardiff@2-3gis.co.uk

†Recorder *Door Tenant/Associate Member

D

CHAMBERS OF MRS V NEWMAN

77 Roath Court Road, Roath, Cardiff CF24 3SF
029 2048 8797
Fax: 029 2048 8797; DX: 122155 Roath Cardiff
E-mail: newmanv@tiscali.co.uk

Chambers of: Mrs V Newman

9 PARK PLACE

9 Park Place, Cardiff, South Glamorgan CF10 3DP
029 2038 2731
Fax: 029 2022 2542; DX: 50751 Cardiff 2
E-mail: clerks@9parkplace.co.uk

Disability access
Staff briefed or trained on duties under the disability legislation, Wheelchair access, Disabled parking available, Induction loop or infra red system

30 PARK PLACE

30 Park Place, Cardiff CF10 3BS
029 2039 8421
Fax: 029 2039 8725; DX: 50756 Cardiff 2
E-mail: clerks@30parkplace.law.co.uk

Chambers of: Mr J H H Tillyard QC, Mr J Furness QC

Disability access
Staff briefed or trained on duties under the disability legislation, Wheelchair access, Disabled parking available, Induction loop or infra red system

REDLAND CHAMBERS

Redland House, Bonvilston, Cardiff, Vale of Glamorgan CF5 6TT
01446 781060
E-mail: jacquelinearcher@btinternet.com

Chambers of: Mrs J A Archer

Disability access
Wheelchair access, Disabled parking available

CHAMBERS OF MR J C REES QC

Sophia House, 28 Cathedral Road, Cardiff CF11 9LJ
02920 233 313
Fax: 02920 660 247
E-mail: clerks@jcrqc.com

Chambers of: Mr J C Rees QC

Disability access
Wheelchair access, Disabled parking available

CHAMBERS OF RICHARD STEER

Haywood House North, Dumfries Place, Cardiff CF10 3GA
07950 401818; DX: 33093 Cardiff
E-mail: law@richardsteer.com

Chambers of: Mr L R Steer

TEMPLE CHAMBERS

32 Park Place, Cardiff CF10 3BA
029 2039 7364
Fax: 029 2023 8423; DX: 50769 Cardiff 2
E-mail: DBrinning@Temple-Chambers.co.uk

Chambers of: Mr H L A Roberts

Disability access
Staff briefed or trained on duties under the disability legislation, Wheelchair access, Disabled parking available

CHAMBERS OF MISS A WHALLEY

18 Mulcaster Crescent, Stanwix, Carlisle, Cumbria CA3 9EA
07759 520140; DX: 63000 Carlisle
E-mail: acwabroad@yahoo.com

Chambers of: Miss A C Whalley

CARMARTHEN CHAMBERS

30 Spilman Street, Carmarthen, Dyfed SA31 1LQ
01267 234410
Fax: 01994 240817
E-mail: richard@griffiths2833.freeserve.co.uk

Chambers of: Mr R S Griffiths

Disability access
Wheelchair access, Disabled parking available

VICTORY CHAMBERS

Dan-Y-Coed, New Mill, St Clears, Carmarthen SA33 4HS
01994 231704
Fax: 01994 231689
E-mail: legaleyes@btinternet.com

Chambers of: Mr D J Folland

TUPWOOD CHAMBERS

Pilgrims Lodge, Tupwood Scrubbs Road, Caterham, Surrey CR3 6TH
01883 720959; DX: 36807 Caterham

Chambers of: Ms W Levy

CHAMBERS OF MR C AMOR

2 Eastcliff, Boundary Lane, The Warren, Caversham, Berkshire RG4 7TH
01189 472298

Chambers of: Mr C L Amor

CLIFFORD CHAMBERS

26 Clifford Road, Chafford Hundred, Essex RM16 6NY
07961 556294
E-mail: igraham745@btinternet.com

Chambers of: Mr I B Graham

CRYSTAL CHAMBERS

Chambers of Miss L A Carter, PO Box 7502, Chelmsford CM2 0WR
01245 496515
Fax: 01245 496514; DX: 89705 Chelmsford 2
E-mail: lesley@crystalchambers.co.uk

Chambers of: Miss L A Carter

EAST ANGLIAN CHAMBERS

140 New London Road, Chelmsford, Essex CM2 0AW
01473 214481
Fax: 01245 215661; DX: 89714 Chelmsford 2
E-mail: chelmsford@ealaw.co.uk

Chambers of: Mr G K Sinclair

Disability access
Staff briefed or trained on duties under the disability legislation, Wheelchair access, Disabled parking available

18 RED LION COURT (ANNEXE)

Thornwood House, 102 New London Road, Chelmsford, Essex CM2 0RG
01245 280880
Fax: 01245 280882; DX: 139165 Chelmsford 11

Chambers of: Mr D C L Etherington QC

Disability access
Staff briefed or trained on duties under the disability legislation, Wheelchair access

ROXWELL

Dukes Manor, The Street, Roxwell, Chelmsford, Essex CM1 4PE
01245 248341
Fax: 01245 248085
E-mail: lorrainewebbbarrister@yahoo.co.uk

Chambers of: Miss L E Webb

Disability access
Wheelchair access, Disabled parking available

TRINITY CHAMBERS

Highfield House, Moulsham Street, Chelmsford, Essex CM2 9AH
01245 605040
Fax: 01245 605041; DX: 89725 Chelmsford 2
E-mail: clerks@trinitychambers.com
URL: www.trinitychambers.com
Out of hours telephone: 07981 195851

Chambers of: Miss T A Harrington
Clerks: Keith Willmore (Chief Clerk), Tony Sleigh (Senior Clerk)

Harrington, Tina *1985*
Dagg, John *1980*
Twydell, Cherry *1985*
Williams, Anna *1990*
Bailey, Andrew *1993*
Simison, Jeremy *1993*
Spratt-Dawson, Josephine *1993*
Cade, Diana *1994*
O'Brien, David *1994*
Wickins, Stefanie *1994*
Green, William *1998*
Attridge, Daniel *2000*
Richardson, Grahame *2001*
Wilkinson, Tiffany *2003*
Lambert, Alison *2005*
Lucey, Anne-Marie *2005*
Yule, Stephanie *2005*
Ahern, Eugene *2007*
Vickers, Craig *2008*
Catton-Newell, Sally *2009*
Sullivan, Liam *2009*
Taylor, Mark *2010*
Harper, Joseph QC *1970*

Types of work
Care proceedings · Chancery (general) · Clinical negligence · Commercial law · Commercial litigation · Common land · Common law (general) · Company, commercial and competition · Corporate

fraud · Education · Employment · Environment · Equity · Family law · Family provision · Human rights · Immigration · Insolvency · Landlord and tenant · Licensing · Local authorities · Medical negligence · Mental health · Personal injury · Personal insolvency · Planning · Professional negligence · Sale and carriage of goods · Trusts · Wills

Disability access
Staff briefed or trained on duties under the disability legislation, Wheelchair access, Disabled parking available

CHAMBERS OF MISS E CULVERHOUSE

18 Upper Gladstone Road, Chesham, Buckinghamshire HP5 3AF
07813 007503
Fax: 01494 778050; DX: 50306 Chesham
E-mail: e.culverhouse@sky.com

Chambers of: Miss E A L Culverhouse

THE CHAMBERS OF MS ROSA ZAFFUTO

10 Walnut Tree Close, Cheshunt, Hertfordshire EN8 8NH
01992 633474
Fax: 01992 633474

LINENHALL CHAMBERS

1 Stanley Place, Chester CH1 2LU
01244 348282
Fax: 01244 342336; DX: 19984 Chester1
E-mail: clerks@linenhallchambers.co.uk
URL: www.linenhallchambers.co.uk

Chambers of: Mr A J O'Toole
Clerk: Robert King (Director of Clerking); Practice Manager: Angela Malcolmson LLB (Hons)

O'Toole, Anthony *1993*
Jones, Wyn Lloyd *1979*†
Carlile of Berriew, Lord QC *1970*†*
Medland, Simon QC *1991*
Lewis-Jones, Meirion *1971*
France-Hayhurst, Jeannie *1972*
Scholz, Karl *1973*
Jamieson, Anthony *1974*
Somerville, Thomas *1979*
Moss, Peter *1980*
Halsall, Kim *1982*
Hennell, Gordon *1982*
Le Brocq, Mark *1982*
Bould, Duncan *1984*
Anderson, Brendan *1985*
Owen, Elen *1985*
Mills, Simon *1986*
Hornby, Robert *1990*†
Philpotts, John *1990*
Austin, Jonathan *1991*
Morris, Shân *1991*
Sammon, Sarah *1991*
Dunford, Matthew *1992*
Edwards, Owen *1992*
Williams, John Wyn *1992*
Erwood, Heather *1993*
Roberts, Huw *1993*
Woosey, Jane *1993*
Abberton, David *1994*
Mullan, Richard *1994*
Williams, Nicholas *1994*
Hewitt, Alexandra *1995*
Japheth, Bethan *1997*
Masselis, Maria *1997*
Waller, *1997*
Ap Mihangel, Sion *1998*
Lovelady, John *1998*
Moffat, Russell *1998*
Roberts, Dafydd *1998*
Blythin, David *1999*
Corbett-Jones, Matthew *1999*
Roberts, Gareth *1999*
Williamson, Brett *2000*
Harris, Caroline *2001*
Lloyd, Trefor *2001*
Jamieson, Fiona *2002*
Mihangel, Mair *2002*
Rogers, Simon *2002*
Cullen, James *2003*
Dodd, Daniel *2003*
Meredith-Jones, Kate *2003*
Barnes, Paulinus *2004*
La Grua, Jayne *2004*
Sefton, Nicholas *2004*
Anslow, Kathryn *2005*
Barrington-Badrawy, Sarah *2005*
Whitty, Michael *2005*
Curtis, Matthew *2006*
Jones, Clare *2006*
Bureau, Tom *2007*
Clemo, Philip *2007*
Coutts, James *2007*
McInnes, Andrew *2007*
Pope, Anna *2007*
Jenkins, James *2008*
McGivern, Aidan *2008*
Willmott, Frances *2008*
Morgan, Sarah-Jayne *2009*
Barrow, Michael *2010*
Thomas of Gresford, Lord QC OBE *1967*†*
Thomas, Nigel *1976*†*
Ganner, Joseph *1983**
Irving, Gillian QC *1984**
Mason, Nicholas *1984**
Henke, Ruth QC *1987**
Thomas, Andrew QC *1989*†*
Williams, Heledd *1999**
Kerruish-Jones, Matthew *2003**

Types of work
Agriculture · Arbitration · Care proceedings · Chancery (general) · Civil actions against the police · Commercial law · Common land · Common law (general) · Company, commercial and competition · Consumer law · Corporate fraud · Courts martial · Crime · Defamation · Discrimination · Ecclesiastical law · Education · Employment · Environment · Equity · Family law · Family provision · Housing · Landlord and tenant · Licensing · Local authorities · Medical negligence · Partnerships · Personal injury · Planning · Professional negligence · Sale and carriage of goods · Succession · Trademarks · Trusts · Wills

Disability access
Wheelchair access, Disabled parking available

ST JOHNS BUILDINGS

21 White Friars, Chester CH1 1NZ
01244 323070
Fax: 01244 342930; DX: 19979 Chester
E-mail: clerk@stjohnsbuildings.co.uk

Chambers of: Mr A Hayden QC

Disability access
Staff briefed or trained on duties under the disability legislation

26 MORLEY AVENUE

26 Morley Avenue, Ashgate, Chesterfield, Derbyshire S40 4DA
01246 234 790

Chambers of: Mr N R Grainger

Disability access
Staff briefed or trained on duties under the disability legislation, Wheelchair access, Disabled parking available

PALLANT CHAMBERS

12 North Pallant, Chichester, West Sussex PO19 1TQ
01243 784538
Fax: 01243 780861; DX: 30303 Chichester
E-mail: clerks@pallantchambers.co.uk
URL: www.pallantchambers.co.uk
Out of hours telephone: 07720 713 660

Chambers of: Miss L J Davis
Clerks: Alister Williams (Senior Clerk), Sarah Sweatman, Danny Hazell, Ashley Clark, Tamsin Harwood; Administrator: Librarian: Julia Smith; Administration: Sarah Linford

Davis, Lucinda *1981*†
di Mambro, David *1973*
Taylor, Charles *1974*
Egleton, *1981*
Rowlinson, Wendy *1981*
Gibbons, Orlando *1982*
Haven, Kevin *1982*
Living, Marc *1983*
Mullis, Roger *1987*
Darton, Clifford *1988*
Morgan, Colin *1989*
Emerson, William *1992*
Geser, Anita *1992*
Loosemore, Mary *1992*
Wilkins, Christopher *1993*
Holmes, Justin *1994*
Magee, Rosein *1994*
Pain, Kevin *1995*
Woodward, Jeremy *1996*
Earley, Sarah *1998*
Moys, Clive *1998*
Maton, Neil *2001*
Ward, Kelly *2001*
Tai, Farzana *2003*
Turnill, Evan *2003*
Anstey, Eve *2005*
Cooke, Thomas *2006*
Worthen, Tom *2007*
Dewhurst, Eleanor *2008*
Hoile, Elinor *2008*
Brookes, Christopher *2010*
Tawfik, Nadia *2010*
Weatherill, Bernard QC *1974*†*

Types of work
Administrative law · Building · Care proceedings · Chancery (general) · Chancery (land law) · Clinical negligence · Commercial law · Common law (general) · Construction law · Crime · Employment · Equity · Family law · Family provision · Housing · Insolvency · Insurance · Landlord and tenant · Licensing · Medical negligence · Partnerships · Personal injury · Personal insolvency · Professional negligence · Property · Sale and carriage of goods · Trusts · Wills

Disability access
Staff briefed or trained on duties under the disability legislation, Wheelchair access, Disabled parking available

CHAMBERS OF MR A. DON GREEN

32 Durham Avenue, Cleveleys, Lancashire FY5 2DP
01253 866307
Fax: 01253 866307
E-mail: dongreenccbb@hotmail.com

Chambers of: Mr A D Green

CHAMBERS OF MR A J STEDMAN

24a Palm Bay Avenue, Cliftonville, Kent CT9 3DQ
07702 870575
E-mail: aryanstedman@hotmail.com

Chambers of: Mr A J Stedman

THE LAW OFFICE OF CAMPBELL ROBOTHAM LLC

C/O Po Box 1618, Md 20735, Clinton
E-mail: jrobotham4@gmail.com

D

EAST ANGLIAN CHAMBERS

53 North Hill, Colchester, Essex CO1 1QA
01473 214481
Fax: 01206 245850; DX: 3611 Colchester
E-mail: colchester@ealaw.co.uk

Chambers of: Mr G K Sinclair

Disability access
Staff briefed or trained on duties under the disability legislation, Wheelchair access, Disabled parking available

CORSHAM BARRISTERS CHAMBERS

New Farm House, Silver Street, Corsham SN13 9PG
01225 582582
Fax: 01225 585899
E-mail: enquiries@corshamlaw.co.uk

Chambers of: Mr W Ryan

CHAMBERS OF MR T A KHAN

St. Paulés Chambers, First Floor, 459 Foleshill Road, Coventry CV6 5AQ
02476 666 400
Fax: 02476 665 995
E-mail: tkhan@stpaulslaw.co.uk

Chambers of: Mr T A Khan

THE CHAMBERS OF MR GERALD PRICE QC

Ivy House, 25 Westgate, Cowbridge, Vale of Glamorgan CF71 7AQ
01446 774029
Fax: 01446 774029
E-mail: ytnop@hotmail.co.uk

Chambers of: Mr G A Price QC

CHAMBERS OF MS SUSAN COHEN

17 John Street, Cronulla 2230
00 61 612 9527 9488
Fax: 00 61 612 9527 9489
E-mail: suecohen@bigpond.com

Chambers of: Ms S E Cohen

ADVOLEX CHAMBERS

70 Coulsdon Road, Coulsdon, Croydon, Surrey CR5 2LB
0871 951 9000
Fax: 0871 951 9500

Chambers of: Mr G A Leech

Disability access
Staff briefed or trained on duties under the disability legislation

CONSTRUCTION CHAMBERS

18 Skiddaw Drive, Mickleover, Derby DE3 9NE
01332 617 917
E-mail: wel@welord.co.uk

Chambers of: Mr W E Lord

DERWENT CHAMBERS

78 Friar Gate, Derby DE1 1FL
01332 242425
Fax: 01332 242420; DX: 11507 Derby
E-mail: admin@derwentchambers.co.uk

Chambers of: Mr P J McCandless

Disability access
Staff briefed or trained on duties under the disability legislation, Wheelchair access, Disabled parking available

MIDLAND CHAMBERS

174 Blagreaves Lane, Littleover, Derby DE23 1PU
01332 749529
E-mail: nglchol@aol.com

Chambers of: Mr N P Cholerton

PHOENIX CHAMBERS

106 Normanton Lane, Littleover, Derby DE23 6GR
07939 545788
Fax: 01332 271639
E-mail: sharongibbons@email.com

Chambers of: Miss S L Gibbons

VERNON STREET CHAMBERS

3 Vernon Street, Derby DE1 1FR
01332 343 932; DX: 11510 Derby
E-mail: clerks@vernonstreetchambers.com

Chambers of: Mr H S Johal

CHAMBERS OF RT HON VISCOUNT DILHORNE

The Dower House, Minterne Parva, Dorchester, Dorset DT2 7AP
01300 341392
Fax: 01300 341152
E-mail: dilhorne@thelegalguru.co.uk

Chambers of: The Right Hon Viscount Dilhorne

THE TAX CHAMBERS OF MR RICHARD SOWLER TD

6 Church Road Marina, Douglas IM1 2HQ
07624 235000

CLONTARF CHAMBERS

13 Seapark Drive, Clontarf, Dublin
00 353 861 73 9529
Fax: 00353 185 35 471
E-mail: mstimpson@lawlibrary.ie

Chambers of: Mr M E Stimpson

MELBECK CHAMBERS

86 Gospel End Road, Sedgley, Dudley, West Midlands DY3 3YU
020 7404 2166
Fax: 020 7404 2177
E-mail: alan.turner@melbeck.com

Chambers of: Mr A J Turner

Disability access
Staff briefed or trained on duties under the disability legislation, Wheelchair access, Disabled parking available

CHAMBERS OF MRS H. FLETCHER-ROGERS

5 Furlong Lane, Totternhoe, Dunstable, Bedfordshire LU6 1QR
01582 472300
Fax: 01582 472300
E-mail: hfrogers@dial.pipex.com

Chambers of: Mrs H S Fletcher Rogers

CHAMBERS OF MR JACOB OOMMEN

1 Stuart Road, East Barnet, Hertfordshire EN4 8XG
07958 680272
Fax: 020 8361 5171
E-mail: jacob.oommen@justbarrister.com

Chambers of: Mr J Oommen

RIDGEWAY CHAMBERS

3a Ridgeway Avenue, East Barnet, Hertfordshire EN4 8TR
020 8440 0904
Fax: 020 8440 0904
E-mail: cmwilliams@ukonline.co.uk

Chambers of: Miss C M Williams

THE CHAMBERS OF ROBINA OMAR

Safari, Lake View Road, Furnace Wood, Feldbridge, East Grinstead, West Sussex RH19 2QE
01342 712326
Fax: 01342 712326
E-mail: robina.omar@hotmail.co.uk

Chambers of: Miss R Omar

EASTBOURNE CHAMBERS

5 Chiswick Place, Eastbourne, East Sussex BN21 4NH
01323 642102
Fax: 01323 641402; DX: 6925 Eastbourne
E-mail: clerks@eastbournechambers.co.uk

Chambers of: Mr J C R Dale

Disability access
Staff briefed or trained on duties under the disability legislation

THE CHAMBERS OF ADRIAN TURNER

4 Charleston Road, Eastbourne BN21 1SF
01323 737388
Fax: 01323 737388

Chambers of: Mr A J Turner

Disability access
Disabled parking available

D

SEN BARRISTERS

30 Sycamore Avenue, Chandlers Ford, Eastleigh, Hampshire SO53 5RH
07706 936045
E-mail: info@senbarristers.co.uk

Chambers of: Miss G Choudhuri

THE CHAMBERS OF ALAN MELVIN-CARR

Po Box 23961, Edinburgh EH3 1BD

CHAMBERS OF MR EDWARD ASH

23 Rogers Close, Elsworth, Cambridgeshire CB23 4JJ
01954 267674
Fax: 01954 267674; DX: 46408 St Ives (Cambridge)

Chambers of: Mr E W Ash

CATHEDRAL CHAMBERS

3 Lion Court, Haddenham, Ely, Cambridgeshire CB6 3XL
07800 851813
E-mail: michaelduffy@orange.net

Chambers of: Mr M Duffy

Disability access
Staff briefed or trained on duties under the disability legislation, Wheelchair access, Disabled parking available

CHAMBERS OF MR G GOODWILL

Three Trees Farm, 20 Prickwillow Road, Isleham, Ely, Cambridgeshire CB7 5RG
07801729877
Fax: 01353 664966

Chambers of: Mr G Goodwill

Disability access
Disabled parking available

CHAMBERS OF MR N J JOSS

8 Albert Road, Epsom, Surrey KT17 4EH
07734 104551
E-mail: normjoss@btinternet.com

Chambers of: Mr N J Joss

TEUCRO CHAMBERS

Global House, 1 Ashley Avenue, Epsom, Surrey KT18 5AD

Chambers of: Mr J W R Tucker, Mr J W R Tucker

CHAMBERS OF ROBERT FISCHEL QC

2é Molino, Camino La Lobilla, Estepona 29680
0034 95280 4346
Fax: 0034 95280 4346
E-mail: rgfischel@gmail.com

Chambers of: Mr R G Fischel QC

COLLETON CHAMBERS

Colleton Crescent, Exeter, Devon EX2 4DG
01392 274898
Fax: 01392 412368; DX: 8330 Exeter
E-mail: clerks@colletonchambers.co.uk

Chambers of: Mr R M J Meeke QC

Disability access
Wheelchair access, Disabled parking available

ROUGEMONT CHAMBERS

Victory House, Dean Clarke Gardens, Southernhay East, Exeter EX2 4AA
01392 208484
Fax: 01392 208204; DX: 8396 Exeter 1
E-mail: clerks@rougemontchambers.co.uk
URL: www.rougemontchambers.co.uk
Out of hours telephone: 01392 208484

Chambers of: Mr M S Berkley
Clerks: Harry Turner, Lisa Glithero, Sam Morgan

Berkley, Michael *1989*†
Bell, Anne OBE *1975*
Moore, Nigel *1978*
Berry, Nicholas *1988*
Lloyd, John *1988*
Haughty, Jeremy *1989*
Bryan, Carmel *1993*
Collett, Gavin *1993*
Ball, Steven *1995*
Bax, James *1999*
Hopkin, William *2000*
Lane, Simon *2002*
Thomas, David *2003*
Hornblower, Sarah *2005*
Hammond, Tim *2007*
O'Neill, Jonathan *2007*
Richardson, Garth *1975**
Felton, Timothy *1977**
Gloag, Angus *1992**
Devine, Michael *1995**
Brady, Ann *2001**
Worthley, Andrew *2004**
Ferrari, Nicholas *2005**
Murray, Charles *2005**
Rozier, James *2007**
Herbert, Jane *2008**

†Recorder *Door Tenant/Associate Member

Types of work

Administrative law · Adoption · Agriculture · Alternative dispute resolution · American law · Ancillary relief · Arbitration · Asylum · Banking · Boundaries · Building · Care proceedings · Chancery (commercial) · Chancery (general) · Chancery (land law) · Charities · Child abduction · Child care law · Children · Civil law · Clinical negligence · Cohabitation · Commercial contracts · Commercial law · Commercial litigation · Commercial property · Common land · Common law (general) · Company law · Company, commercial and competition · Confiscation · Constitutional and administrative law · Construction law · Consumer credit · Consumer law · Contracts · Conveyancing · Coroner's inquests · Corporate finance · Corporate fraud · Courts martial · Crime · Criminal judicial review · Directors' disqualification · Disability and health · Discrimination · Divorce · Domestic violence injunctions · ECHR · Education · Employment · Environment · Equity · Family law · Family provision · Financial provision · Firearms · Foreign law · Franchising · Fraud · Health and safety · Housing · Human rights · Immigration · Industrial relations law · Inheritance and cohabitees · Inquests · Insolvency · International trade · Judicial review · Landlord and tenant · Lands Tribunal · Licensing · Local authorities · Matrimonial · Matrimonial finance · Mediation · Medical law · Medical negligence · Mental health · Parliamentary · Partnerships · Personal injury · Personal insolvency · Planning · Prison law · Private children law · Professional negligence · Public law · Real property · Rights of way · Road traffic · Sale of business · Succession · Torts · Trusts · Unmarried couples · Wardship · Wills

Disability access

Staff briefed or trained on duties under the disability legislation, Disabled parking available

SOUTHERNHAY CHAMBERS

33 Southernhay East, Exeter EX1 1NX
01392 255777
Fax: 01392 412021; DX: 8353 Exeter
E-mail: clerks@southernhaychambers.co.uk

Chambers of: Mr C J Naish

Disability access

Staff briefed or trained on duties under the disability legislation, Disabled parking available

D

WALNUT HOUSE

63 St. David's Hill, Exeter, Devon EX4 4DW
01392 279751
Fax: 01392 412080; DX: 115582 Exeter
E-mail: clerks@walnuthouse.co.uk
URL: www.walnuthouse.co.uk
Out of hours telephone: 07876 652758

Chambers of: Mr S R Laws QC
Clerk: Bernard Haynard (Senior Clerk)

Laws, Simon QC *1991*
Mercer, Geoffrey QC *1975*†
Dunkels, Paul QC *1972*†
Barnes, Jonathan *1970*†
Searle, Corinne *1982*†
Melville-Shreeve, Michael *1986*
Treneer, Mark *1987*
Eaton Hart, Andrew *1989*
McCarthy, Mary *1994*
Evans, David *1996*
Kenny, Martin *1998*
Spencer, Lara *2000*
Bremridge, Lee *2003*
Bray, Helen *2004*
White, Barry *2004*
Cassel, Bathsheba *2005*
Ticehurst, Joss *2006*
Asprey, Louise *2007*
Fitzherbert, Brian *2008*
Payne, Felicity *2010*
Ekaney, Nkumbe QC *1990**

Types of work

Agriculture · Animals · Anti-social Behaviour Orders · Asset recovery · Asylum · Banking and Finance · Care proceedings · Chancery · Chancery (commercial) · Chancery (general) · Chancery (land law) · Children · Civil fraud · Civil law · Civil litigation · Civil partnerships · Commercial fraud · Commercial law · Commercial litigation · Common land · Common law (general) · Company law · Company, commercial and competition · Competition law · Computer crime · Confidential information · Constitutional and administrative law · Consumer law · Contracts · Coroners · Corporate fraud · Corporate manslaughter · Council tax · Courts martial · Crime · Crime and criminal due process · Criminal judicial review · Disciplinary procedures · Discrimination · Dispute resolution · Dispute resolution and arbitration · Domestic violence injunctions · Education · Employee benefit trusts ·

†Recorder *Door Tenant/Associate Member

D

Employment · Environment · European law · European, Foreign and International law · Extradition · Family law · Family provision · Financial services · Firearms · Foreign law · Fraud · Health and safety · Healthcare law · Highways · Homicide · Housing · Industrial relations law · Insolvency · Intellectual property · International criminal law · Landlord and tenant · Licensing · Litigation · Local authorities · Local government and public services · Malicious prosecution · Matrimonial · Medical negligence · Mental health · Military law · Partnerships · Pensions · Personal injury · Personal injury and torts · Planning · Police · Prison law · Private client · Professional negligence · Property · Public access · Public health · Real property · Regulatory and disciplinary law · Regulatory crime · Road traffic · Serial crime · Sexual Offences · Shipping · Social welfare · Special Guardianship · Succession · Tax · Taxation and duties · Torts · Trademarks · Travel law · Trusts · Unmarried couples · VAT

Disability access
Wheelchair access, Disabled parking available

FARINGDON CHAMBERS

First Floor, Marlborough House, Bromsgrove, Faringdon, Oxfordshire SN7 7QJ
01367 240598
Fax: 01367 240256; DX: 81010 Faringdon
URL: www.faringdonchambers.co.uk
Out of hours telephone: 07770 594456

Chambers of: Mr R A J Purdie
Practice Manager: Jayne Richards

Purdie, Robert *1979*

Types of work
Adoption · Ancillary relief · Care proceedings · Chancery (general) · Child abduction · Child abuse · Child care law · Child support · Civil partnerships · Cohabitation · Divorce · Domestic violence injunctions · Ecclesiastical law · Family law · Family provision · Financial provision · Financial provision for children · Forced Marriage · Fostering · Inheritance · Inheritance and cohabitees · Leave to remove · Matrimonial · Matrimonial finance · Private children law · Special Guardianship · Succession · Trusts · Unmarried couples · Wills

Disability access
Staff briefed or trained on duties under the disability legislation, Disabled parking available

AGRI-LAW CHAMBERS

Briery Lodge, Briery Hill Lane, Gloucester, Gloucestershire GL18 1NH
07989 720675
E-mail: serena@agri-law.co.uk

Chambers of: Mrs S M Gowling

CHAMBERS OF MR T CHODHA

112 Hampton Crescent, Gravesend DA12 4HY
01474 326666
Fax: 01474 328989

Chambers of: Mr T S Chodha

GUILDFORD CHAMBERS

Stoke House, Leapale Lane, Guildford, Surrey GU1 4LY
01483 539131
Fax: 01483 300542; DX: 97863 Guildford 5
E-mail: clerks@guildfordchambers.co.uk

Chambers of: Mr G A N Coates

Disability access
Staff briefed or trained on duties under the disability legislation, Wheelchair access, Disabled parking available

CHAMBERS OF MR ANDREW HENLEY

8 St Mildred's Road, Guildford, Surrey GU1 1TX
01483 570430
Fax: 01483 570430

CHAMBERS OF ALANA GRAHAM

Chemix Buildings, Maypole Fields, Cradley, Halesowen, West Midlands B63 2QB
01384 894560
Fax: 01384 895217

Chambers of: Mrs A N Graham

Disability access
Staff briefed or trained on duties under the disability legislation, Wheelchair access, Disabled parking available

HARROGATE CHAMBERS

5 The Grove, Harrogate HG1 5NN
01423 520771
Fax: 01423 520771

CHAMBERS OF MR AKINJIDE

The Cedars, The Common, Stanmore, Harrow, Middlesex HA7 3HR
020 8950 9508

Chambers of: Chief R Akinjide

BROMPTON CHAMBERS

1st Floor, 353A Station Road, Harrow, Middlesex HA1 1LN
0560 3685647; DX: 4224 Harrow
E-mail: bromptonchamber@aol.com

Chambers of: Miss L Neenan

Disability access
Staff briefed or trained on duties under the disability legislation, Wheelchair access, Disabled parking available

CONFERENCE CHAMBERS

P.O. Box 626, Harrow, Middlesex HA2 2DZ
020 8144 0134
Fax: 0800 242 5323
E-mail: carole@conferencechambers.com

Chambers of: Mr R W Clement

CHAMBERS OF MR HORACE REID

136 Regal Way, Kenton, Harrow, Middlesex HA3 0SQ
020 8907 4880
E-mail: horacereid@ymail.com

Chambers of: Mr H D Reid

CASTLE CHAMBERS

The Old Fire Station, 90 High Street, Harrow-on-the-Hill, Middlesex HA1 3LP
020 8423 6579
Fax: 020 8423 2926; DX: 4211 Harrow
E-mail: info@castlechambers.net

Chambers of: Mr M F Kimsey

Disability access
Staff briefed or trained on duties under the disability legislation, Disabled parking available

CHAMBERS OF MRS SHAMIM ALI

19 Flamingo Close, Salisbury Village, Hatfield, Hertfordshire AL10 9LU
01707 276737
Fax: 01707 262979
E-mail: a2a_herts@hotmail.com

Chambers of: Mrs S Ali

BALMORAL CHAMBERS

10 Nield Road, Hayes, Middlesex UB3 1SE
07904 144 405
Fax: 020 8573 4301
E-mail: nicolabrissette@googlemail.com

Chambers of: Miss N L Brissett

CHAMBERS OF MISS C BUCHAN

9 Savill Road, Haywards Heath, East Sussex RH16 2NY
01444 482222
E-mail: carolinebuchan@yahoo.com

Chambers of: Miss C V Buchan

MERITZ CHAMBERS

PO Box 110, Hebben Bridge HX7 9AQ
0845 094 0856
Fax: 0871 433 4759
E-mail: clerk@meritzchambers.co.uk

Chambers of: Ms F Krause

HUNTERCOMBE CHAMBERS

Timbers Farmhouse, Henley-On-Thames RG9 5SY
01491 641934; DX: 80516 Henley-On-Thames

Chambers of: Miss G C Carrodus

Disability access
Staff briefed or trained on duties under the disability legislation, Wheelchair access, Disabled parking available

D

CHAMBERS OF MICHAEL ROBERTS

Fawley House, 100A St Andrews Road, Henley-On-Thames, Oxfordshire RG9 1PL
01844 355 655
Fax: 01491 577118; DX: 137640 Henley On Thames
E-mail: mcr@michaelrobertsbarrister.co.uk

Chambers of: Mr M C Roberts

MIDDLESEX CHAMBERS

89 Easton Street, High Wycombe HP11 1LT
0203 1764186
Fax: 0203 1764182; DX: 42259 Slough West
E-mail: middlesexchambers@googlemail.com

Chambers of: Mr S Rashid

JUSTICE COURT CHAMBERS

23 Wykin Road, Hinckley, Leicestershire LE10 0HU
02476 325859
Fax: 02476 320708/020 7060 5786
E-mail: blessedseat@yahoo.co.uk

Chambers of: Mr F A Siddiqi

Disability access
Staff briefed or trained on duties under the disability legislation, Disabled parking available

CHAMBERS OF MR C INGHAM

4 Arch Road, Great Wymondley, Hitchin, Hertfordshire SG4 7EP
01438 727 814
Fax: 01438 727 814
E-mail: charlesningham@btinternet.com

Chambers of: Mr C N Ingham

CHAMBERS OF MR ROBERT LEWIS

Brekun House, Westmill Lane, Ickleford, Hitchin, Hertfordshire SG5 3RN

CHAMBERS OF MRS AUDREY CAMPBELL-MOFFAT

3102 Tower One, Admiralty Centre, 18 Harcourt Road, Hong Kong
00 852 2810 8222
Fax: 00 852 2810 0777
E-mail: campmoff@libertychambers.com

Chambers of: Mrs A P Campbell-Moffat

Disability access
Wheelchair access, Disabled parking available

BLENHEIM CHAMBERS

605 Blenheim Centre, Hounslow, Middlesex TW3 1ND
07588 608288
E-mail: kashif.ahmad786@yahoo.co.uk

Chambers of: Mr K Z Ahmad

HERMITAGE COURT CHAMBERS

117a-117b Inwood Road, Hounslow, Middlesex TW3 1XJ
07852 146056
Fax: 020 8814 2415
E-mail: hermitagecourtchambers@gmx.com

Chambers of: Mrs I P Rawat

Disability access
Staff briefed or trained on duties under the disability legislation, Wheelchair access, Disabled parking available

CHAMBERS OF MR MICHAEL FULLERTON

5 Pembroke Avenue, Hove, East Sussex BN3 5DA
01273 772050
Fax: 01273 739930; DX: 59272 Hove

Chambers of: Mr M A Fullerton

Disability access
Wheelchair access, Disabled parking available

NIPC

Kirklees Media Centre, 7 Northumberland Street, Huddersfield HD1 1RL
0800 862 0055
Fax: 0870 990 5082
E-mail: jill.hayfield@nipclaw.com

Chambers of: Miss J E Lambert

Disability access
Staff briefed or trained on duties under the disability legislation, Wheelchair access, Disabled parking available, Induction loop or infra red system

SCULCOATES CHAMBERS

46 Abbey Way, Hull, East Yorkshire HU5 1DA
07760 201578
E-mail: tonycoyle27@live.co.uk

WILBERFORCE CHAMBERS

7 Bishop Lane, Hull HU1 1PA
01482 323264
Fax: 01482 325533; DX: 11940 Hull
URL: www.wilberforcechambershull.co.uk

Chambers of: Mr A P Murray
Practice Manager: Phillip Paxton

Murray, Anil *1989*
Swift, Malcolm QC *1970*
Gateshill, Bernard *1972*†
Miller, Paul *1974*†
Genney, Paul *1976*
Garth, Steven *1983*
Cameron, Neil *1984*
Godfrey, John *1985*
Comaish, Andrew *1989*
Hirst, Simon *1993*
Trimmer, Carol *1993*
Thackray, John *1994*
Pickering, Simon *1996*
Clive, Nigel P T *1998*
Robinson, Stephen *1999*
Baines, Charlotte *2000*
Fearon, Sarah *2000*
Scott, January *2000*
Collins, Sally *2002*
Foster, Wendy *2005*
Wilson, Andrew *2005*
Carnie, Alan *2006*
Thompson, Richard *2007*
Baggs, Julia *2008*
Holmes, Claire *2009*
Jenkins, Joanne *2009*
Ledden, Thomas *2009*

Types of work
Care proceedings · Chancery (general) · Common law (general) · Crime · Employment · Family law · Family provision · Health and safety · Landlord and tenant · Personal injury · Professional negligence

Disability access
Staff briefed or trained on duties under the disability legislation, Wheelchair access, Disabled parking available

CHAMBERS OF MR N J SAUNDERS

Cottage Farm, Hamerton, Huntingdon, Cambridgeshire PE28 5QW
01832 293689
Fax: 01832 293079
E-mail: nicholasjsaunders@hotmail.com

Chambers of: Mr N J Saunders

Disability access
Wheelchair access, Disabled parking available

CASSIAN CHAMBERS

43 Fowey Avenue, Ilford, Essex IG4 5JT
07796 262641
E-mail: islam.chowdhary@ntlworld.com

Chambers of: Mr I Chowdhary

CHAMBERS OF MR ABDURAHMAN JAFAR

16 Madras Road, Ilford, Essex IG1 2EY
07828 937338
Fax: 0871 714 3889
E-mail: abdurahmanjafar@yahoo.co.uk

Chambers of: Mr A A Jafar

Disability access
Disabled parking available

CHAMBERS OF MR ISAAC MAKA

102 Thorold Road, Ilford, Essex IG1 4EX
07973 308 301
Fax: 020 8220 3621
E-mail: isaacmaka@hotmail.com

Chambers of: Mr I Maka

Disability access
Wheelchair access, Disabled parking available

CHAMBERS OF MISS SHAMIM SHER

3 Coronation Close, Ilford, Essex IG6 1DB
07581 201823
Fax: 020 8550 5323
E-mail: shamim50@live.co.uk

Chambers of: Miss S A Sher

D

†Recorder *Door Tenant/Associate Member

D

EAST ANGLIAN CHAMBERS

Gresham House, 5 Museum Street, Ipswich, Suffolk IP1 1HQ
01473 214481
Fax: 01473 231388; DX: 3227 Ipswich
E-mail: ipswich@ealaw.co.uk
URL: www.ealaw.co.uk
Out of hours telephone: 01473 214481

Chambers of: Mr G K Sinclair
Clerks: Fraser McLaren (Senior Clerk), Alison Scanes (Deputy Senior Clerk); Administrator: Head of Administration: Carol Bull (01603 751407); Fees Clerk: Theresa Mathias (01603 75142)

Also at: 15 The Close, Norwich NR1 4DZ Tel: 01603 617351 Fax: 01603 751400

Also at: 140 New London Road, Chelmsford CM2 0AW Tel: 01245 215660 Fax: 01245 215661

Also at: 53 North Hill, Colchester, CO1 1QA Tel: 01206 572756 Fax: 01206 245850

Sinclair, Graham *1979*
Akast, John *1968*†
Bryan, Rex *1971*†
Wardlow, John *1971*
Waters, John *1974*
Marsden, Andrew *1975*†
Bryant, Caroline *1976*
Hamey, John *1979*
Brooke-Smith, John *1981*†
Redmayne, Simon *1982*
Lane, Michael *1983*
Bettle, Janet *1985*
Elcombe, Nicholas *1987*
Capon, Philip *1990*
Watson, Claire *1991*
Barratt, Dominic *1992*
Butcher, Russell *1992*
Parry-Jones, Carole *1992*
Walsh, Patricia *1993*
Kelly, Richard *1994*
Freeman, Sally *1995*
Wheetman, Alan *1995*
Wood, Richard *1995*
Gladwell, Simon M *1996*
Goodfellow, Stephen *1997*
Underhill, Alison *1997*
Akram, Farzana *1999*
Ashley, Neil *1999*
Bradbury, Joanna *1999*
Harvey, Shona *1999*
Hayes, Christine *1999*
Korniej, Rebekah *1999*
Brown, Luke *2000*
O'Sullivan, Richard *2000*
Parnell, Cherie *2000*
Pigram, Christopher *2000*
Stevens, Hazel *2001*
Donovan, Juliet *2002*
Plant, April *2002*
Shirley, Lynne *2002*
Brightman, Justina *2003*
Croskell, Marcus *2003*
Martin, Jade *2003*
Michael, Nicholas *2003*
Miller, Kate *2003*
Voelcker, Harriet *2003*
Wahiwala, Amrik *2003*
Cattermull, Emma *2004*
Strelitz, Paul *2005*
Connell, Amy *2006*
White, Elizabeth *2006*
Bewley, Suhayla *2007*
Pine, Mika *2007*
Spence, Gemma-Louise *2007*
Myers, Rupert *2008*
Newton, Alice *2009*
Slaughter, Jessica *2009*
Sorel-Cameron, Matthew *2009*
Williams, Fiona *2009*
Duxbury, Sarah *2010*
Nicklin, Andrew *2010*
Sheehan, Michael *2010*
Pugh-Smith, John *1977**
Walters, John QC *1977**
Dyer, Shereen *2003**

Types of work
Agriculture · Care proceedings · Charities · Clinical negligence · Commercial law · Commercial litigation · Common law (general) · Construction law · Consumer law · Corporate fraud · Courts martial · Crime · Discrimination · Employment · Family law · Family provision · Insolvency · Landlord and tenant · Licensing · Local authorities · Medical negligence · Mental health · Personal injury · Planning · Professional negligence · Trusts · Wills

Disability access
Staff briefed or trained on duties under the disability legislation, Wheelchair access, Disabled parking available

2 KBW IPSWICH

1st Floor, Fisons House, 159 Princes Street, Ipswich, Suffolk IP1 1QH
01473 287518
Fax: 01473 280518; DX: 3237 Ipswich
E-mail: kbwipswich@btconnect.com

Disability access
Staff briefed or trained on duties under the disability legislation, Wheelchair access, Disabled parking available

TRINITY CHAMBERS

36 Museum Street, Ipswich, Suffolk IP1 1JQ
01473 282020
Fax: 01473 282021; DX: 3219 Ipswich
E-mail: clerks@trinity-ipswich.law.co.uk

KEW CHAMBERS

354 Kew Road, Kew, Surrey TW9 3DU
0844 8099991
Fax: 020 8332 7152; DX: 90354 Brentford
E-mail: admin@kewchambers.co.uk
URL: www.kewchambers.co.uk

Chambers of: Mr S D Fisher
Clerk: Caroline Prior (Chief Clerk); Practice Manager: Caroline Prior (Chief Clerk)

Fisher, Steve *2000*
Graham, Roger *1973*
Kwiatkowski, Feliks *1977*
Adamson, Alan *1997*
Brooke, Johan *1997*
Worrall, Philip *2001*
Whittock, Robert *2006*

Types of work
Company, commercial and competition · Employment · Personal injury

 †Recorder *Door Tenant/Associate Member

Disability access
Staff briefed or trained on duties under the disability legislation, Wheelchair access, Disabled parking available

KING'S LYNN CHAMBERS

26 The Birches, South Wootton, King's Lynn, Norfolk PE30 3JG
01553 672 085
E-mail: timothy.leader@tesco.net

Chambers of: The Head of Chambers

HEADLAND CHAMBERS

275 Richmond Road, Kingston Upon Thames, Surrey KT2 5DJ
07725 028108
E-mail: sebastian.head@headlandchambers.com

Chambers of: Mr J S Head

CHAMBERS OF MR S A KHAN

1 Wolverton Avenue, Kingston Upon Thames, Surrey KT2 7QF
020 8541 3875
Fax: 020 8541 3875
E-mail: shaukou.ali.khan73@hotmail.com

Chambers of: Mr S A Khan

Disability access
Disabled parking available

CHAMBERS OF SIAN SPIER

8 Upper Park Road, Kingston Upon Thames, Surrey KT2 5LD
020 8546 7868
E-mail: sianhines@me.com

Chambers of: Miss S Spier

66 WORTHINGTON ROAD

66 Worthington Road, Surbiton, Kingston Upon Thames, Surrey KT6 7RX
020 8390 6359
Fax: 020 8390 6359
E-mail: OrielG@aol.com

Chambers of: Mr O G Hinds

Disability access
Staff briefed or trained on duties under the disability legislation, Disabled parking available

CHAMBERS OF SARAH BREACH

The Old Farm House, Brook Farm, Marthall Lane, Marthall, Knutsford, Cheshire WA16 7ST
01565 880272
Fax: 01565 880095
E-mail: sbreach@btconnect.com

Chambers of: Miss S L Breach

WESTLEIGH CHAMBERS

4 Vickery Close, Curry Rivel, Langport, Somerset TA10 0PY
01458 251261
Fax: 01458 251261
E-mail: JHLLECKIE@AOL.COM

Chambers of: Mr J H Leckie

Disability access
Wheelchair access, Disabled parking available

TREMAINE CHAMBERS

Balmain, Launceston, Cornwall PL15 8UD
01566 781557
E-mail: tremainelegal@gmail.com

Chambers of: Mr D J West

LAVENHAM CHAMBERS

Rookery Farm, Lavenham (near Sudbury), Suffolk CO10 0BJ
01787 248247
Fax: 01787 247846; DX: 41311 Sudbury
E-mail: susangratwicke@yahoo.co.uk

Chambers of: Miss S A Gratwicke

Disability access
Staff briefed or trained on duties under the disability legislation, Wheelchair access, Disabled parking available

ALPHA COURT CHAMBERS

Stuart House, Buckingham Lodge, 23 Kenilworth Road, Leamington Spa CV32 6JD
01926 886412
E-mail: CP@Payton.uk.net

Chambers of: Mr C C Payton

Disability access
Staff briefed or trained on duties under the disability legislation, Disabled parking available

CHRISTOPHER WILLIAM DICKSON

Forelands House, Givons Grove, Leatherhead, Surrey KT22 8LY

BROADWAY HOUSE CHAMBERS

25 Park Square West, Leeds, West Yorkshire LS1 2PW
0113 246 2600
Fax: 0113 246 2609; DX: 26403 Leeds Park Square
E-mail: clerks@broadwayhouse.co.uk
URL: www.broadwayhouse.co.uk

Chambers of: Mr J G K Hyland QC
Clerks: David Rhodes, Robin Slade; Administrator: Helen Craven

Also at: Broadway House Chambers, 9 Bank Street, Bradford BD1 1TW Tel: 01274 722560 Fax: 01274 370708

Hyland, Graham QC *1978†*
Mansell, Richard QC *1991†*
Colborne, Michelle QC *1993*
Khan, Tahir QC *1986†*
Topham, John *1970*
Ferm, Rodney *1972*
Wood, Martin *1973*
Isaacs, Paul *1974†*
Kershaw, Andrew *1975†*
Cohen, Raphael *1981*
Shelton, Gordon *1981†*
McGonigal, David *1982*
Jones, David *1985*
Howard, Ian *1987*
Myers, Simon *1987*
Askins, Nicholas *1989*
Wilson, Paul *1989*
Drake, Sophie *1990†*
Cole, Robert *1991*
Wood, Stephen *1991*
Hendron, Gerald *1992*
Barlow, Sarah *1993*
Crosland, Ben *1993*
Rudd, Matthew *1994*
Walker-Kane, Jonathan *1994*
Beckett, Jayne *1995*
Morland, Camille *1996*
Peers, Nicola *1996*
Hussain, Tasaddat *1998*
Miller, Ian *1999*
Bridge, Giles *2000*
Brown, Christopher *2001*
Green, Kenneth *2001*
Downing, Emma *2002*
Modgill, Alexander *2002*
Samra, Sharn *2002*
Shaikh, Semaab *2002*
Hampton, Peter *2003*
Azmi, Louise *2004*
Hamilton, Nigel *2004*
Mellor, Rachel *2004*
Power, Nick *2004*
Langford, Abigail *2005*
Larton, Claire *2005*
Stott, Matthew *2005*
Walsh, Kathryn *2008*
Benson, Clare *2009*
Durham Hall, Christian *2009*
Hill, James QC *1984†**

Types of work
Capital tax · Care proceedings · Commercial litigation · Common law (general) · Corporation tax · Crime · Discrimination · Employment · Environment · Equity · Family law · Family provision · Housing · Immigration · Income tax · Landlord and tenant · Licensing · Medical negligence · Mental health · Partnerships · Personal injury · Personal insolvency · Professional negligence · Sale and carriage of goods · Trusts · Wills

CHANCERY HOUSE CHAMBERS

CHANCERY HOUSE CHAMBERS Commercial & Chancery Law

7 Lisbon Square, Leeds, West Yorkshire LS1 4LY
0113 244 6691
Fax: 0113 244 6766; DX: 26421 Leeds Park Square
E-mail: clerks@chanceryhouse.co.uk
URL: www.chanceryhouse.co.uk
Out of hours telephone: 07770 624448

Chambers of: Mr G S Pipe
Clerks: Colin Hedley (Senior Clerk), Claire Fulthorpe (1st Junior)

Pipe, Gregory *1995*
Craig, Aubrey *1987*
Harrison, Sarah *1989*
Kelly, Sean *1990*
Lloyd, Marisa *1994*
Roberts, Stuart *1994*
Edwards, Anthony *1999*
Still, *1999*
Buck, William *2001*
Cherry, Peter *2003*
Crossley, Dominic *2006*
Gardiner, Helen *2007*
Gale, Jonathan *2009*
Stubley, Anna *2010*

Types of work
Agriculture · Banking · Capital tax · Chancery (general) · Chancery (land law) · Clinical negligence · Commercial law · Commercial litigation · Commercial property · Common law (general) · Company, commercial and competition · Competition law · Conflict of laws · Construction law · Consumer law · Conveyancing · Copyright · Corporate finance · Corporation tax · Discrimination · EC competition law · Education · Employment · Environment · Equity · Financial services · Foreign law · Franchising · Health and safety · Housing · Human rights · Immigration · Income tax · Information technology · Insolvency · Insurance · Intellectual property · International law · International trade · Landlord and tenant · Medical negligence · Partnerships · Patents · Personal injury · Personal insolvency · Planning · Professional negligence · Sale and carriage of goods · Share options · Succession · Trademarks · Trusts · Wills

Disability access
Staff briefed or trained on duties under the disability legislation, Wheelchair access, Disabled parking available

 †Recorder *Door Tenant/Associate Member

ENTERPRISE CHAMBERS

43 Park Square, Leeds LS1 2NP
0113 246 0391
Fax: 0113 242 4802; DX: 26448 Leeds Park Square
E-mail: leeds@enterprisechambers.com
URL: www.enterprisechambers.com
Out of hours telephone: 07780 671478

Chambers of: Mr B R Weatherill QC
Clerks: Antony Armstrong (Senior Clerk), Joanne Caunt, Ellen Cockcroft; Accounts Manager: Hannah Steininger-Nath

Weatherill, Bernard QC *1974*†
Arden, Peter QC *1983*
Bhaloo, Zia QC *1990*
James, Michael *1976*
Morgan, Charles *1978*
Hutton, Caroline *1979*
Groves, Hugo *1980*
Ife, Linden *1982*
Barker, James *1984*
Zelin, Geoffrey *1984*
Jack, Adrian *1986*†
Jarron, Stephanie *1990*
Pickering, James *1991*
Duddridge, Robert *1992*
Jory, Hugh *1992*
Klein, Jonathan *1992*
Noble, Andrew *1992*
Williamson, Bridget *1993*
Francis, Edward *1995*
Mauger, Shanti *1996*
Ilyas, Shaiba *1998*
Calland, Timothy *1999*
Rodger, Jonathan *1999*
Johnson, Simon *2000*
McCulloch, Niall *2000*
West, Matthew *2000*
Murphy, Damian *2001*
Page, Rebecca *2001*
Jackson, Claire *2002*
Beswetherick, Anthony *2003*
Kalfon, Olivier *2003*
Griffin, Margaret *2004*
Gunaratna, Kavan *2004*
Toman, Cristin *2004*
Markandya, Susannah *2005*
Bond, Kelly *2007*
Burslem, Sarah *2008*
Gale, Phillip *2008*
Meech, Jennifer *2008*
Maddison, Matthew *2010*

Types of work
Agriculture · Arbitration · Banking · Chancery (commercial) · Chancery (general) · Commercial law · Commercial litigation · Commercial property · Company law · Conveyancing · Environment · Equity · Housing · Insolvency · Landlord and tenant · Licensing · Mediation · Partnerships · Personal insolvency · Professional negligence · Real property · Succession · Trusts · Wills

Disability access
Staff briefed or trained on duties under the disability legislation

EXCHANGE CHAMBERS

Oxford House, Oxford Row, Leeds LS1 3BE
0113 203 1970
Fax: 0113 345 3326; DX: 26406 Leeds Park Square
E-mail: spencer@exchangechambers.co.uk

Chambers of: Mr W T S Braithwaite QC

KBW

The Engine House, No 1 Foundry Square, Leeds LS11 5DL
0113 297 1200
Fax: 0113 297 1201; DX: 26433 Leeds Park Square
E-mail: clerks@kbwchambers.com
URL: www.kbwchambers.com
Out of hours telephone: 07952 070485

Chambers of: Mr A J Robertson QC
Clerks: Lee Baines, James Morrow, Daniel Ward, Jayne Turner; Fees Clerk: Jo Fox, Ama Asomaning

Robertson, Andrew QC *1975*
Robson, David QC *1965*†
Campbell, Nicholas QC *1978*†
Waterman, Adrian QC *1988*†
Woodcock, Robert QC *1978*
Radcliffe, Francis *1962*
Attwooll, Christopher *1980*†
Wynn, Toby *1982*†
Mallett, Simon *1986*
Mallett, Sarah *1988*
Barradell, Richard *1990*
Brooke, David *1990*
Dodds, Shaun *1990*
Thompson, Patrick *1990*†
Egerton, Christine *1992*
Denton, Amanda *1993*
Toone, Robert *1993*
Cleasby, Paul *1994*
Skelt, Ian *1994*
Doswell, Rupert *1996*
Bean, Matthew *1997*
Dempster, Tina *1997*
Dunne, Anthony *1999*
Stevens, Rebecca *1999*
Spencer, Joseph *2001*
Strong, Adrian *2001*
Frantzis, Roxanne *2003*
Mullarkey, Ian *2003*
Pawson, Tamara *2003*
Thorne, Oliver *2003*
Menary, Alexander *2004*
Rafter, Kathryn *2005*
Moxon, Nathan *2006*
Checa-Dover, Olivia *2007*
Quinn, Conor *2007*
Dawes, Beverley *2008*
Smithies, Deborah *2008*
Abrantes-Stanworth, Carla *2009*
Singh, Manisha *2009*
Wynn, Joseph *2011*

Types of work
Anti-social Behaviour Orders · Arbitration · Care proceedings · Chancery (general) · Chancery (land law) · Civil actions against the police · Commercial litigation · Common law (general) · Company, commercial and competition · Confiscation · Corporate finance · Corporate fraud · Courts martial · Crime · Defamation · Employment · Environment · Equity · Family law · Family provision · Immigration · Inquests · Insolvency ·

D

†Recorder *Door Tenant/Associate Member

Landlord and tenant · Licensing · Medical negligence · Occupational diseases · Partnerships · Pensions · Personal injury · Professional negligence · Succession · Trusts · VAT · Wills

Disability access

Staff briefed or trained on duties under the disability legislation, Wheelchair access, Disabled parking available

D

KINGS CHAMBERS

5 Park Square East, Leeds LS1 2NE
0845 034 3444
Fax: 0845 034 3445; DX: 713113 Leeds Park Square
E-mail: clerks@kingschambers.com
URL: www.kingschambers.com
Out of hours telephone: 07836 589842

Chambers of: Dr Nicholas J Braslavsky

Clerks: Andrew Reeves, Rory Davis, Gary Young, Paul Clarke, Harry Young, Mark Ronson, Scott Leach, Gary Smith, Jake Brooke; Senior Clerks: William Brown, Colin Griffin, Stephen Loxton; Administrator: Alison Brereton; Chambers Director: Debra Andrés

Also at: Kings Chambers, 36 Young Street, Manchester M3 3FT Tel: 0845 034 3444 Fax: 0845 034 3445; Embassy House, 60 Church Street, Birmingham, B3 2DJ, DX: 13023 Birmingham Tel: 0845 034 3444 Fax No: 0845 034 3445

Braslavsky, Nicholas QC *1983†*
Sauvain, Stephen QC *1977†*
Booth, Michael QC *1981*
Fraser, Vincent QC *1981†*
Chaisty, Paul QC *1982†*
Manley, David QC *1981†*
Crean, Anthony QC *1987*
Anderson, Lesley QC *1989†*
Casement, David QC *1992*
Rawlinson, Michael QC *1991*
Tucker, Paul QC *1990*
Poole, Nigel QC *1989†*
Owen, Eric *1969*
Terry, Jeffrey *1976*
Evans, Alan *1978*
Khan, Shokat *1979*
Barrett, John *1982†*
Berragan, Neil *1982*
Halliwell, Mark *1985†*
Clayton, Nigel *1987†*
Hilton, Simon *1987†*
Ashworth, Fiona *1988†*
Stockley, Ruth *1988*
Burrows, Simon *1990*
Singer, Andrew *1990*
Grantham, Andrew *1991*
Smith, Matthew *1991*
Carter, Martin *1992*
Horne, Wilson *1992*
Powis, Lucy *1992*
Clover, Sarah *1993*
Ditchfield, Michael *1993*
Harper, Mark *1993*
Lander, Richard *1993*
Ponter, Ian *1993*
Pritchard, Sarah *1993*
Boyd, James *1994*
Pennifer, Kelly *1994*
Latimer, Andrew *1995*
Doyle, Louis *1996*
Easton, Jonathan *1996*
Fullwood, Adam *1996*
McBride, Gavin *1996*
Plimmer, Melanie *1996*
Roussak, Jeremy *1996*
Bourne, Colin *1997*
Friston, Mark *1997*
Plaut, Simon *1997*
Siddall, Nicholas *1997*
Cannock, Giles *1998*
McGee, Andrew *1998*
Young, Simon *1998*
Brown, Catherine *1999*
Budworth, Martin *1999*
Griffiths, Brian *1999*
Hall, Matthew *1999*
Mulholland, Helen *1999*
Ranales-Cotos, Tina *1999*
Lakin, Paul *2000*
Temple, Eleanor *2000*
Walmisley, Lisa *2000*
Hughes, Paul *2001*
Wheatley, Geraint *2001*
Williams, Ben *2001*
Hunter, John *2002*
Karim, Sam *2002*
Lancaster, Roger *2002*
Ralph, Craig *2002*
Duckworth, Emily *2003*
Mayoh, Michelle *2003*
Rowan, Gregg *2003*
Galloway, Rachel *2004*
Gardner, Francesca *2004*
Gorasia, Paras *2005*
Harding, Ben *2005*
Law, Charlotte *2005*
Dainty, Cheryl *2006*
Johnson, Paul *2006*
Lieberman, Gemma *2006*
Livingston, Richard *2006*
Latham, Kevin *2007*
Maguire, Stephen *2007*
Smith, Nathan *2007*
Ward, Johnny *2007*
D'Arcy, Eleanor *2008*
Gill, Anthony *2008*
McNamara, Stephen *2008*
Daniels, Laura *2009*
Taylor, Ruth *2010*
Freedman, Clive QC *1978†**
Kolvin, Philip QC *1985**
Crawford, Colin *1997**
Henderson, James *1997**
Keay, Andrew *2010**

Types of work

Administrative law · Arbitration · Banking · Capital tax · Chancery (general) · Chancery (land law) · Charities · Clinical negligence · Commercial law · Commercial litigation · Commercial property · Common land · Common law (general) · Company, commercial and competition · Competition law · Construction law · Consumer law · Conveyancing · Copyright · Corporate finance · Corporate fraud · Corporation tax · Costs · Discrimination · EC competition law · Education · Employment · Entertainment · Environment · Equity · Financial services · Franchising · Health and safety · Housing · Immigration · Income tax · Information technology · Insolvency · Insurance · Intellectual property · International trade · Landlord and tenant · Licensing · Local authorities · Medical

 †Recorder *Door Tenant/Associate Member

negligence · Parliamentary · Partnerships · Patents · Pensions · Personal injury · Personal insolvency · Planning · Professional negligence · Regulatory and disciplinary law · Sale and carriage of goods · Share options · Sport · Succession · Trademarks · Trusts · Wills

Disability access
Staff briefed or trained on duties under the disability legislation, Wheelchair access, Disabled parking available

NO.6 PARK SQUARE

No.6 Park Square, Leeds LS1 2LW
0113 245 9763
Fax: 0113 242 4395; DX: 26402 Leeds Park Square
E-mail: Tim@no6.co.uk

Chambers of: Mr R M M Jameson QC

PARK COURT CHAMBERS

16 Park Place, Leeds LS1 2SJ
0113 243 3277
Fax: 0113 242 1285; DX: 26401 Leeds Park Square
E-mail: clerks@parkcourtchambers.co.uk
URL: www.parkcourtchambers.co.uk

Chambers of: Mr R S Smith QC
Clerk: Moira Paxton; Practice Manager: Chief Executive: Michael Meeson; Administrator: Karen Wade

Also at: 3 Broad Chare, Quayside, Newcastle NE1 3QD Tel: 0191 232 1980 Fax: 0191 232 3730 DX: 61012 Newcastle-upon-Tyne Email: clearks@npc-n.co.uk Web: to be confirmed Contact: Michael Meeson (Chief Executive) Clerk: Frank Hughes

Smith, Robert QC *1971*
Lodge, Anton QC *1966†*
Dodson, Joanna QC *1971*
Bourne-Arton, Simon QC *1975†*
Carter, Peter QC *1974*
Price, Richard OBE QC *1969†*
Hatton, David QC *1976†*
MacDonald, Alistair QC *1983†*
Bayliss, Thomas QC *1977†*
Jackson, Simon QC *1982†*
Cox, Bryan QC *1979†*
Phillips, Simon QC *1985†*
Greaney, Paul QC *1993*
Lumley, Nicholas QC *1992*
Hartley, Timothy *1970*
Reid, Paul *1975†*
Sterling, Valerie *1981*
Brook, Ian *1983*
Mason, Nicholas *1984*
Wigin, Caroline *1984†*
Beattie, Sharon *1986*
Taylor, Alan *1986*
Uttley, Stephen *1986*
Young, David *1986*
Bashir, Nadim *1988*
Sharpe, Martin *1989*
Tehrani, Christopher *1990*
Tucker, Ashley *1990*
Turner, Taryn *1990†*
Patel, Elyas *1991*
Cross, Joanna *1992*
Pitter, Jason *1994*
Widdett, Ceri Louise *1994*
Williams, Paul *1994*
Amesu, Sharon *1997*
Anderson, Simon *1997*
Blatchford, *1997*
Terris, Sally *1997*
Green, Samuel *1998*
Offer, Alex *1998*
White, Steven *1998*
Batts, Gillian *1999*
Parsons, Glenn *1999*
Skittrell, Elaine *1999*
Hussain, Nawaz *2000*
Singh, Dapinder *2000*
Taylor, Alex *2000*
Cranidge, Ruth *2001*
Escoriza, Natalia *2002*
De La Poer, Nicholas *2003*
Hudson, Chloe *2003*
Fairley, Chloe *2004*
Knowles, Catherine *2004*
Beattie, Annabel *2005*
Hashmi, Afshan *2005*
Kitzing, Susanna *2005*
Normington, James *2005*
Wastall, Andrew *2005*
Birkby, Adam *2006*
Mercer, Kirsten *2006*
Fry, Eleanor *2007*
Aspinall, Christopher *2008*
Campbell, Benjamin *2008*
Alistari, Nicoleta *2009*
Thomas, *2010*

Types of work
Administrative law · Arbitration · Care proceedings · Chancery (general) · Civil liberties · Clinical negligence · Commercial law · Commercial litigation · Commercial property · Common law (general) · Company, commercial and competition · Competition law · Consumer law · Corporate fraud · Courts martial · Crime · Discrimination · Education · Employment · Environment · Equity · Family law · Family provision · Financial services · Health and safety · Housing · Human rights · Immigration · Insolvency · Insurance · Intellectual property · Landlord and tenant · Licensing · Local authorities · Medical negligence · Mental health · Partnerships · Personal injury · Personal insolvency · Planning · Professional negligence · Succession · Trusts · Wills

Disability access
Staff briefed or trained on duties under the disability legislation, Wheelchair access, Disabled parking available

PARK LANE PLOWDEN

19 Westgate, Leeds LS1 2RD
0113 228 5049
Fax: 0113 228 1500; DX: 26404 Leeds Park Square
E-mail: clerks@parklaneplowden.co.uk

Chambers of: Mr S C Brown QC

Disability access
Staff briefed or trained on duties under the disability legislation, Wheelchair access, Induction loop or infra red system

†Recorder *Door Tenant/Associate Member

D

37 PARK SQUARE CHAMBERS

37 Park Square, Leeds LS1 2NY
0113 243 9422
Fax: 0113 242 4229; DX: 26405 Leeds Park Square
E-mail: chambers@no37.co.uk
URL: www.no37.co.uk
Out of hours telephone: 07976 397802

Chambers of: Mr S J Glover, Miss T J Lee QC
Clerks: Leigh Royall (Senior Clerk), Donna Gaughan, Jennifer Wright, Matthew Taylor; Administrator: Colin Philpott; Finance Manager: Colin Philpott

Glover, Stephen *1978*
Lee, Taryn QC *1992*†
Marshall-Andrews, Robert QC *1967*†*
Hogg, Douglas QC *1968**
Hockman, Stephen QC *1970**
Oldham, Frances QC *1977*†*
Harbage, William QC *1983*†*
Dunning, John *1973*
Sleightholme, John *1982*
Fleming, Paul *1983*
Apfel, Freddy *1986*
Ginsburg, Amanda *1986*
Lindsay, Jeremy *1986*
Shaw, Elizabeth *1986*
Hill, Piers *1987*
Cains, Linda *1990*
Frith, Nicholas *1992*
Blackmore, Sarah *1993*
Burdon, Michael *1993*
Shepherd, Joanne *1993*
Gore, Mark *1994*
Howard, Amanda *1994*
Josling, William *1995*
Taylor, David *1995*
Thomas, Jacqueline *2000*
Butters, Richard *2001*
Chippendale, Emma *2002*
Edwards, Paul *2002*
Brook, Dale *2003*
Eastwood, Charlotte *2003*
Madderson, Naomi *2003*
Zaman, Shazma *2003*
Wilson, Jonathan *2005*
Chapman, Helen *2006*
Grant, Giles *2006*
Goodwin, James *2008*
Bruce, Zoe *2009*
Phillips, David *2010*
Watterson, Mark *2011*
Leslie, Stephen QC *1971**

Types of work
Care proceedings · Chancery (general) · Civil law · Clinical negligence · Contracts · Coroner's inquests · Courts martial · Crime · Ecclesiastical law · Education · Employment · Equity · Family law · Family provision · Firearms · Health and safety · Immigration · Industrial diseases · Judicial review · Landlord and tenant · Licensing · Matrimonial finance · Medical negligence · Occupational diseases · Partnerships · Personal injury · Personal insolvency · Planning · Professional negligence · Serious fraud · Trusts · Wills

Disability access
Staff briefed or trained on duties under the disability legislation, Disabled parking available

39 PARK SQUARE

39 Park Square, Leeds LS1 2NU
0113 245 6633
Fax: 0113 242 1567; DX: 26407 Leeds Park Square
E-mail: seniorclerk@39parksquarechambers.co.uk

Chambers of: Mr N M Davey QC

SOVEREIGN CHAMBERS

SovereignChambers

46 Park Place, Leeds LS1 2RY
0113 245 1841
Fax: 0113 242 0194; DX: 26408 Leeds Park Square
E-mail: clerks@sovereignchambers.co.uk
URL: www.sovereignchambers.co.uk

Chambers of: Mr D M Gordon
Clerks: Claudine Cooper (Family), Francine Kirk (Civil), Yvonne Crosbie (Criminal), Zoe Malir (Regulatory and Disciplinary), Fees Clerk: Kirsty Bentley; Practice Manager: Chambers Director: Shelagh Kirkby; Administration Assistant: Surjit Bharj, Liz Twohey

Gordon, David *1984*†
Bradley, Sally QC *1978*†
Elliott, Eric QC *1974*†
Lewis, Andrew QC *1985*†
Haigh, Martin *1970*
Orbaum, David *1978*
Palmer, Patrick *1978*†
Birch, Roger *1979*
Ferguson, Christopher *1979*

†Recorder *Door Tenant/Associate Member

Davies, Felicity *1980*†
Haring, Simon *1982*
Partington, David *1987*
Fricker, Susan *1988*
Hill, Louise *1988*
McKone, Mark *1988*
Hargan, James *1990*
Marson, Denise *1990*†
Dixon, David *1992*
Geddes, Joanna *1992*
Shiels, Ian *1992*
Woolfall, Richard *1992*†
Dawson, Judy *1993*
Keeley, James *1993*
Semple, Andrew Blair *1993*
Finlay, Darren *1994*
Wilson, Peter Julian *1995*
Withyman, Elizabeth *1995*
Dunn, Christopher *1996*
Smith, Matthew *1996*
Maudslay, Diana *1997*
Paige, Richard *1997*
Gent, Matthew Thomas *1998*
Rhys-Davies, Adam *1998*
Wood, Caroline *1998*
Andre, Roger *1999*
Beaumont, Sally *1999*
Hassall, Craig *1999*
Murden, Claire *1999*
Doherty, Patrizia *2000*
Mason, Catherine Jane *2000*
Sekhon, Narinder *2000*
Elliott, Julie-Ann *2001*
Hercock, David *2001*
Silverton, Catherine *2001*
Wolstenholme, Janine *2002*
Stevenson, Robert *2003*
Addy, Laura *2004*
Brown, Stephen *2004*
Ross, Fiona *2004*
Clegg, Simon *2005*
Wilson, Andrew *2005*
Philipson, Amy *2006*
Sampson, Helen *2006*
Coupe, Toby *2007*
Wilkinson, Anna *2007*
Harrow, Julia *2009*
Young, Stuart *2009*
Lippiatt, Huw *2010*

Types of work

Arbitration · Care proceedings · Chancery (general) · Civil fraud · Civil liberties · Company, commercial and competition · Construction law · Copyright · Corporate fraud · Crime · EC competition law · Employment · Environment · Equity · Family law · Family provision · Housing · Immigration · Insolvency · Intellectual property · Landlord and tenant · Licensing · Local authorities · Medical negligence · Partnerships · Patents · Personal injury · Planning · Police discipline · Prison law · Professional negligence · Regulatory and disciplinary law · Trademarks · Trusts · Wills

Chambers Established 1925
Opening times: 8.45am - 5.45pm

Chambers' facilities

Conference Rooms, Disks Accepted, Work received and returned via e-mail

Disability access

Staff briefed or trained on duties under the disability legislation, Wheelchair access, Disabled parking available

Languages spoken

Chinese (Mandarin), French, German, Hebrew, Italian, Punjabi, Spanish, Urdu

ST PAUL'S CHAMBERS

5th Floor, St Paul's House, 23 Park Square South, Leeds LS1 2ND
0113 245 5866
Fax: 0113 245 5807; DX: 26410 Leeds Park Square

Disability access

Staff briefed or trained on duties under the disability legislation, Wheelchair access, Disabled parking available

ZENITH CHAMBERS

10 Park Square, Leeds LS1 2LH
0113 245 5438
Fax: 0113 242 3515; DX: 26412 Leeds Park Square
E-mail: clerks@zenithchambers.co.uk
URL: www.zenithchambers.co.uk
Out of hours telephone: 0113 252 1047

Chambers of: Mr J N Goose QC

Clerks: Liz Gage, Clive Taylor, Rebecca Hartley, Hayley Sanderson, Stephen Render, Hannah Dempsey, Laura Myers, Stephnie Jaryckyj; Chief Executive: Andrew Argyle; Fees Administrators: Erica Newby, Veronica Cliff, Adele Collins; Marketing Assistant: Fay Cuthbert; Reception: Val Finn, Kath Birch; Finance: Angela Battle

Goose, Julian QC *1984*
Campbell, Andrew QC *1972*†
Corbett, James QC *1975*†
Nathan, David QC *1971*
Collins, John *1956*
Sterling, Robert *1970*
Connerty, Anthony *1974*
Bradshaw, David *1975*†
Francis, Andrew *1977*
Hall, David *1980*†
Hajimitsis, Anthony *1984*
Worrall, John *1984*
Bickerdike, Roger *1986*
Greenan, Sarah *1987*
Newman, Austin *1987*
Holroyd, John *1989*
Howd, Stephen *1989*
Read, Simon *1989*
Wilson-Barnes, Lucy *1989*
Hookway, Aelred *1990*
Barber, Philip *1991*
Exall, Gordon *1991*
Kealey, Simon *1991*†
Boumphrey, John *1992*
Hayes, John *1992*
Bindloss, Edward *1993*†
Crossley, Justin *1993*
Storey, Tom *1993*
Henley, Mark *1994*
Pema, Anesh *1994*
Younger-Banks, Brynn *1994*
Browne, Gerald *1995*
Potts, Warren *1995*
Pye, Jayne *1995*†
Tyson, Thomas *1995*
Wilson, Andrew *1995*
Wordsworth, Philippa *1995*
Kelly, Geraldine *1996*
Branchflower, George *1997*
Greatorex, Helen *1997*
Smith, Chris *1997*
Allman, Marisa *1998*
Darlington, Elizabeth *1998*
Worsley, Nicholas *1998*
McCallum, Louise *1999*†
Perkins, Simon *1999*
Phillipson, Nicola *1999*
Ross, Simon *1999*
Shaw, Howard *1999*
Bell, Jillian *2000*
McKinlay, Kate *2000*
Hartshorn, Sabrina *2001*
Stuart-Lofthouse, Michele *2001*
Down, Lisa *2002*

†Recorder *Door Tenant/Associate Member

Vodanovic, Vilma *2002*
Coyle, Anthony *2003*
Duffy, Catherine *2003*
Lawrenson, Sarah *2003*
Strange, Jessica *2003*
Donkin, Matthew *2004*
Marcus, Peter *2004*
Garnham, Clare *2005*
Khan, Ruwena *2005*
Hartley, Bronia *2006*
Pratt, Ashley *2006*
Ahmed, Sobia *2007*
Lawley, Frances *2007*
Myers, John *2007*
Donnelly, Lewis *2008*
Shaw, Jonathan *2008*
Cross, Jane QC *1982**
Hudson, John *2006**
Sowden, Lucy *2006**
Pye, Derek *2008**

Types of work
Agriculture · Arbitration · Capital tax · Care proceedings · Chancery (general) · Chancery (land law) · Charities · Clinical negligence · Commercial law · Commercial litigation · Common law (general) · Company, commercial and competition · Construction law · Copyright · Courts martial · Crime · Ecclesiastical law · Employment · Environment · Equity · Family law · Family provision · Health and safety · Housing · Income tax · Industrial diseases · Intellectual property · Landlord and tenant · Licensing · Medical negligence · Mental health · Partnerships · Personal injury · Personal insolvency · Planning · Professional negligence · Property · Sale and carriage of goods · Succession · Trusts · Wills

Disability access
Staff briefed or trained on duties under the disability legislation, Wheelchair access, Disabled parking available

HOLBROOK CHAMBERS

PO Box 9327, Leicester LE21 3EL
07771 961962
Fax: 0116 312 0180
E-mail: legal@direct-barrister.com

Chambers of: Mr I H Jones

CHAMBERS OF MR JAFFERJI

89 Lamborne Road, Leicester LE2 6HQ
07957 198777
Fax: 0116 290 2038
E-mail: zjafferji@gmail.com

Chambers of: Mr Z H Jafferji

CHAMBERS OF MR CHRISTOPHER KESSLING

14 Belvoir Street, Leicester LE1 6QH
01509 890690
E-mail: ck@cklaw.co.uk

Chambers of: Mr C D Kessling

MELBURY HOUSE

55 Manor Road, Oadby, Leicester, Leicestershire LE2 2LL
07801 037802
E-mail: melburyhousechambers@yahoo.co.uk

Chambers of: Mr M T Khan

Disability access
Staff briefed or trained on duties under the disability legislation, Wheelchair access, Disabled parking available

NEW STREET CHAMBERS

2 New Street, Leicester LE1 5NA
0116 262 5906
Fax: 0116 251 2023; DX: 10849 Leicester
E-mail: clerks@2newstreet.co.uk

Chambers of: Mr M Wyatt

NEW WALK CHAMBERS

27 New Walk, Leicester, Leicestershire LE1 6TE
0871 200 1298/0116 255 9144
Fax: 0871 200 1288/0116 255 9084; DX: 72390 Leicester 22
E-mail: clerks@newwalkchambers.co.uk

Chambers of: Mr J Snell

Disability access
Staff briefed or trained on duties under the disability legislation, Disabled parking available

CHAMBERS OF MR ANDREW PEET

2 Sycamore Close, Stretton Hall, Leicester LE2 4QU
07966 238437
Fax: 0116 271 2388
E-mail: andrew@peet593.orangehome.co.uk

Chambers of: Mr A G Peet

KING'S BENCH CHAMBERS

174 High Street, Lewes BN7 1YE
01273 402600
Fax: 01273 402609

WESTGATE CHAMBERS

64 High Street, Lewes, East Sussex BN7 1XG
01273 480510
Fax: 01273 483179; DX: 50250 Lewes 4
E-mail: clerks@westgate-chambers.co.uk
URL: www.westgate-chambers.co.uk
Out of hours telephone: Available upon request

Chambers of: Mr P G Meredith
Clerks: Jason Britcher (Senior Clerk), Paul Tuffs (Deputy Senior Clerk), Penny Wadsworth (Family and Civil Clerk), James Still (Crime Clerk); Administrator: Financial - K Haynes, N Field

Meredith, Philip *1979*
Trembath, Graham QC *1978*
Stein, Sam QC *1988*
Jefferies, Andrew QC *1990*
Cherrill, Richard *1965*
Spooner, Henry *1971*
Hall, Nicholas *1973*
Forster, Sarah *1976*
Argent, Gavin *1978*
Campbell, Graham *1979*
Rowling, Fiona *1980*
Hamblin, Nicholas *1981*
Russell, Guy *1985*
Judge, Andrew *1986*
Adebayo, Tayo *1989*
Lindop, Sarah *1989*
Ray-Crosby, Irena *1990*
Lamb, Jeffrey *1992*
Frith, Alexandra *1993*
Howe, Sara-Lisa *1993*
Edwards, Jonathan *1994*
Hancock, Maria *1995*
Barnes, Nicholas *1996*
Cherrill, Beverley *1996*
Davies, Rebecca *1996*
McMillan, Carol *1996*
Watson, Duncan *1997*
Clarke, Amanda *1998*
Taylor, Linda *1998*
Bayley, Laura *1999*
Down, Barbara *1999*
Walsh, Martha *2000*
Addison, Yolanda *2003*
Kavanagh, Dennis *2003*
Wilson, Charmaine *2003*
Loeb, Dinah *2004*
Sadler, Rhiannon *2004*
Stephens, Andrew *2004*
Winslett, Frank *2004*
Thomas, Felicity *2005*
Burrows, Gareth *2006*
Clarke, Jessica *2006*
Wagstaff, Andrew *2006*
Atkinson, Jonathan *2007*
Barrett, Charlotte *2007*
Prior, Christopher *2007*
Pryor, Alison *2008*
Taite, Sarah *2008*
Little, Trina *2010*
Peddie, Ian QC *1971**

Types of work

Care proceedings · Civil liberties · Common law (general) · Crime · Employment · Family law · Housing · Landlord and tenant · Medical negligence · Personal injury

Disability access

Staff briefed or trained on duties under the disability legislation, Wheelchair access, Disabled parking available

ATLANTIC CHAMBERS

4-6 Cook Street, Liverpool L2 9QU
0151 236 4421
Fax: 0151 236 1559; DX: 14176 Liverpool
E-mail: info@atlanticchambers.co.uk
URL: www.atlanticchambers.co.uk

Chambers of: Mr A F S Donovan
Clerks: Lee Cadwallader (Head Clerk), Gary Quinn (Deputy Head Clerk); Administrator: Julie Evans

Donovan, Scott *1975†*
Tedd, Rex QC *1970†*
Edis, Andrew QC *1980†*
Benson, John QC *1978†*
Cobb, Stephen QC *1985†*
Driver, Stuart QC *1988†*
Whyte, Anne QC *1993*
Gorton, Simon QC *1988*
Knowles, Gwynneth QC *1993*
Haselhurst, Ian *1976*
Thomas, Gareth *1977*
Ginniff, Nigel *1978*
Sellars, Michael *1980*
Howe, Ruth *1983*
Corless, John *1984†*
Ryan, Nicholas *1984*
Booth, Simon *1985*
Woolfenden, Ivan *1985*
Pickering, Andrew *1987*
Lund, Celia *1988*
Beattie, Ann *1989*
Hunt, Nicola *1989*
Sharpe, Malcolm *1989†*
Dawes, Simon *1990*
Sellers, Graham *1990*
Johnson, Christine *1991*
Jackson, Nicholas *1992*
Banks, Rachael *1993*
Brandon, Helen *1993*
Davey, Michelle *1993*
Grace, Timothy *1993*
Green, David *1993*
Howard, Amanda *1994*
Williams, Andrew *1994*
Banks, Andrew *1995*
Grundy, Liam *1995*
Prior, Charles *1995*
Delaney, Kenneth *1996*
Hillas, Samantha *1996*
Horne, Kenderik *1996*
McDonald, Lawrence *1996*
Downey, Neil *1997*
Bennett, Abigail *1998*
Gorton, Carl *1999*
Smith, Sophie *1999*
Valentine, Justin *1999*
Bonner, Lee *2000*
Livesley, Rhian *2000*
Armstrong, Michael *2002*
Chester, Mark *2002*
Cline, Robert James *2002*
Hughes-Deane, Charlotte *2002*
Sigee, Peter *2002*
Fraser, Donald *2003*
Derbyshire, Hugh *2004*
Mensah, Martin *2004*
Sumner, Daian *2004*
Tinkler, David *2004*
Wale, Elizabeth *2004*
Cuddy, Natalie *2005*
Cox, Olivia *2007*
Eastwood, Shannon *2007*
Kohanzad, Rad *2007*
Patience, James *2007*
Bar, Monika *2008*
Berthelsen, Eleonore *2009*
France-Hayhurst, Lucinda *2009*
McCann, Katie *2009*
Fazackerley, Thomas *2010*

Types of work

Agriculture · Arbitration · Banking · Capital tax · Care proceedings · Chancery (general) · Chancery (land law) · Civil liberties · Clinical negligence · Commercial litigation · Commercial property · Common land · Company, commercial and competition · Confiscation · Confiscation of the proceeds of crime · Conveyancing · Copyright · Corporate fraud · Corporation tax · Courts martial · Crime · Defamation · Discrimination · Ecclesiastical law ·

†Recorder *Door Tenant/Associate Member

D

Education · Employment · Equity · Family law · Family provision · Housing · Immigration · Income tax · Insolvency · Insurance · Intellectual property · Judicial review · Landlord and tenant · Licensing · Medical negligence · Mental health · Partnerships · Pensions · Personal injury · Personal insolvency · Planning · Professional negligence · Public law · Sale and carriage of goods · Succession · Trusts · Wills

Disability access
Staff briefed or trained on duties under the disability legislation, Wheelchair access

CHAMBERS OF MR TIMOTHY BECKER

53 Rodney Street, Liverpool L1 9ER
0151 703 0319
Fax: 0151 703 0322

Chambers of: Mr T G C Becker

CHAVASSE COURT CHAMBERS

18 Queen Avenue, Liverpool L2 4TX
0151 229 2030
Fax: 0151 229 2039; DX: 14223 Liverpool
E-mail: clerks@chavassechambers.co.uk
URL: www.chavassechambers.co.uk

Chambers of: Mr J R McDermott QC
Clerks: Colin Cubley (Senior Clerk), Sandra McConnell (Clerk), Alan Harvey (Criminal Clerk), Christopher Jones (Criminal Clerk), Mark Shannon (Family Clerk)

McDermott, John QC *1976*
Baxter, Gerald *1971*
Pepper, Theresa *1973*†
Pickavance, Graham *1973*
Cliff, Elizabeth *1975*
Barraclough, Anthony *1978*
Rose, Anthony *1978*
Forsyth, Julie *1983*
O'Donohoe, Anthony *1983*†
Bagley, Michael *1984*
Christie, Simon *1988*
Haygarth, Edmund *1988*
Becker, Paul *1990*
Watson, Tom *1990*
Williams, David *1990*†
Greenwood, Celestine *1991**
Lander, Charles *1993*
Sherman, Susan *1993*
Gatenby, James *1994*
Bannon, Tammi *1994*
Biswas, Nisha *1996*
Morris, Ben *1996*
Povoas, Simon *1996*
Deans, Jacqueline *1997*
Jones, Claire *1999*
Machin, Susan *1999*
Morgan, Lloyd *1999*
Phelan, Sarah Jane *1999*
Steward, Mark *2002*
Hawks, James *2003*
Hughes, Kathryn *2003*
Robinson, Kirsty *2003*
Cook, Oliver *2004*
Gosling, Deborah *2004*
Morley, Kate *2004*
Temple, Rachel *2004*
Wilde, Carmel *2004*
Beardmore, William *2005*
Redmond, Christine *2006*
Wint, Earl *2007*
Badman, Kyra *2011*
Noble, Arthur *1965**
Mercer, Ian *2001**

Types of work
Care proceedings · Common law (general) · Crime · Family law · Family provision

Disability access
Staff briefed or trained on duties under the disability legislation, Wheelchair access

EXCHANGE CHAMBERS

One Derby Square, Derby Square, Liverpool L2 9XX
0151 236 7747
Fax: 0151 236 3433; DX: 14207 Liverpool
E-mail: info@exchangechambers.co.uk

Chambers of: Mr W T S Braithwaite QC

Disability access
Staff briefed or trained on duties under the disability legislation, Wheelchair access, Disabled parking available

NUMBER 7 HARRINGTON STREET CHAMBERS

7 Harrington Street, Liverpool L2 9YH
0151 242 0707
Fax: 0151 236 2800; DX: 14221 Liverpool
E-mail: clerks@7hs.co.uk
URL: www.7hs.co.uk

Chambers of: Mr R J Pratt QC
Clerks: Claire Smith (Criminal Clerk), Sarah Gleaves (Civil Clerk), Jennifer Mogan (Family Clerk), Faye Woods (Civil Clerk), Hannah Gilligan (Family Clerk), Amy Chadwick (Criminal Clerk), John Kilgallon (Senior Clerk), Nick Roberts (Senior Civil Clerk), Carolyn Cregeen (Senior Family Clerk), Rachel Kehoe (Senior Criminal Clerk); Administrator: Pauline Haines/Claire Tumilty; Practice Director: John Kilgallon; Assistant Practice Directors: Nick Roberts

Pratt, Richard QC *1980*†
Riordan, Stephen QC *1972*
Lawson Rogers, Stuart QC *1969*†
Moran, Andrew QC *1976*
Goldrein, Iain QC *1975*†
Flewitt, Neil QC *1981*†
Menary, Andrew QC *1982*†
Johnson, Nicholas QC *1987*

†Recorder *Door Tenant/Associate Member

Power, Nigel QC *1992*
Unsworth, Ian QC *1992*
Wolff, Michael *1964*
Geey, David *1970*†
McDonald, Andrew *1971*
Bellis, Gordon *1972*
Compton-Rickett, Mary *1972*
Halligan, Rodney *1972*
Biddle, Neville *1974*
Pickavance, Michael *1974*
Rae, James *1976*
Grice, Kevin *1977*†
Davies, Michael *1979*
Nutter, Julian *1979**
Carville, Brendan *1980*
Gibson, Arthur *1980*
Lazarus, Grant *1981*
Owen, David *1981*
Riding, Henry *1981*
Gregory, Peter *1982*†
McKeon, James *1982*
Byrne, James *1983*
Chatterton, Mark *1983*
Loveridge, Andrew *1983*†
McGuire, Deirdre *1983*
Reade, Kevin *1983*
Killeen, Simon *1984*†
Khan, Jamil *1986*
Knapp, Stephen *1986*
Lennon, Desmond *1986*
Kenward, Tim *1987*
Kidd, Peter *1987*
Parker, Steven *1987*
Reaney, Janet *1987*
Lawrence, Nigel *1988*
Sutton, Keith *1988*
Flood, Diarmuid *1989*
Downie, Andrew *1990*
Symms, Kate *1990*
Bispham, Christine *1991*
Driver, Simon *1991*
Grover, Tim *1991*
Seed, Stephen *1991*
Alty, Andrew *1992*
Parry-Jones, Trevor *1992*
Whitehurst, Ian *1994*
Wrenn, Helen *1994*
Baker, Clive *1995*
Burke, Brendan *1995*
Carney, Andrew *1995*
Greenfield, Jeremy *1995*
Jones, Gerald *1995*
Loftus, Teresa *1995*
Turner, Nicola *1995*
Ball, Steven J *1996*
Mallon, Joanna *1996*
McLachlan, David *1996*
Ford, Andrew *1997*
Rogers, Daniel *1997*
Bisarya, Neil *1998*
Brennan, Elizabeth *1998*
Grant, Kenneth *1998*
Swain, Jacqueline *1998*
Holt, Sarah *1999*
Jones, Michael *1999*
Miles, Nicola *1999*
Naughton, Lianne *1999*
Ralston, William *2000*
Tully, Philip *2000*
Whalley, *2000*
Wood, Daniel *2000*
Hertzog, Frances *2001*
Jenkinson, Lee *2001*
Langley, Sarah *2001*
Roberts, Mark *2001*
Duffy, Jonathan *2002*
Edmunds, Lisa *2002*
Freeman, Emma *2002*
Reid, Martin *2003*
Wright, Paul *2003*
Fisher, Craig *2004*
Dunne, David *2005*
Knagg, Christopher *2005*
Roberts, Victoria *2005*
Webster, Barbara *2005*
Birkett, Lianne *2006*
Lindsay, Fraser *2006*
O'Donohue, Katherine *2006*
Treadwell, Brian *2006*
Woerner, Steven *2006*
Ashley, Julie *2007*
Paton, Danielle *2007*
Watters, Sarah *2007*
Handy, Benjamin *2008*
O'Leary, John *2010*
Thomas, Gemma *2010*
Berry, Anthony QC *1976**

Types of work
Commercial law · Commercial litigation · Corporate fraud · Employment · Family law · Insolvency · Licensing · Medical negligence · Personal injury · Planning

Chambers Established 1999
Opening times: 8.30am - 6.00pm

Disability access
Staff briefed or trained on duties under the disability legislation, Wheelchair access

Languages spoken
French, German, Greek, Russian, Urdu

ST JOHNS BUILDINGS LIVERPOOL

8th Floor India Buildings, Water Street, Liverpool L2 0XG
0151 243 6000
Fax: 0151 243 6040; DX: 14227 Liverpool
E-mail: clerk@stjohnsbuildings.co.uk
URL: www.stjohnsbuildings.co.uk
Out of hours telephone: 07850 193895; 07870 657202

Chambers of: Mr A Hayden QC
Clerks: Stuart Jones (Senior Clerk), Alastair Webster (Diary Clerk - Crime), Gail Curran (Diary Clerk - Family), Claire Odiam (Diary Clerk - Civil), Emma Wall (Diary Clerk - Family); Administrator: Helen Southworth, Greg Brooker

Also at: 24a-28 St John Street, Manchester M3 4DJ. Tel: 0161 214 1500; Fax: 0161 835 3929. DX 728861 Manchester 4

Also at: 21 White Friars, Chester CH1 1NZ. Tel: 01244 323 070; Fax: 01244 323 930; DX 19979 Chester.

Also at: 16 Winckley Square, Preston PR1 3JJ. Tel: 01772 256100; Fax: 01772 251101; DX 714582 Preston 14.

Also at: 26 Paradise Square, Sheffield S1 2DE. Tel: 0114 273 8951; Fax: 0114 276 0848; DX 10565 Sheffield 1.

Hayden, Anthony QC *1987*†
Watson, Paul QC *1978*†
Redfern, Michael QC *1970*†
Berkley, David QC *1979*†
O'Byrne, Andrew QC *1978*
Samuels, Jeffrey QC *1988*
Harrison, Sally QC *1992*
Thomas, Keith *1969*
Phillips, Bernard *1970*†
Green, Roger *1972*
Hedgecoe, John *1972*
Herman, Raymond *1972*†
Neale, Nicholas L *1972*
Bedford, Stephen *1974*†
McNeill, John *1974*
Shannon, Eric *1974*
Lowe, Geoffrey *1975*†
Andrews, Philip *1977*
Feeny, Charles *1977*
Longworth, Antony *1978*
Grundy, Philip *1980*†
Mercer, David *1980*
Owen, Gail *1980*†
Long, Andrew *1981*
Uff, David *1981*
Bruce, David *1982*
Gal, Sonia *1982*†
Garside, David *1982*
Holt, Julian *1982*
Harrison, Keith *1983*
Harrison, Peter *1983*
Khawar, Aftab *1983*
McKee, Hugh *1983*
McKenna, Brian *1983*
Slater, Michael *1983*†
Pickup, David *1984*
Shaw, Julian *1984*†
Wright, Sarah *1984*
Kennedy, Michael *1985*
Lloyd, Julian *1985*
Dickinson, Jonathan *1986*
Gray, Richard *1986*
Taylor, Julian *1986*†
Brennand, Timothy *1987*
Dagnall, Jane M *1987*
Oates, John *1987*
Walker, Jane *1987*
Batra, Bunty *1988*

D

Crabtree, Simon *1988*
Davitt, Paula *1988*
Eastwood, Charles *1988*
Sanders, Damian *1988*
Blakey, Michael *1989*
Britcliffe, Anne *1989*
Grundy, Clare *1989*
Holder, Simon *1989*
O'Brien, Joseph *1989*
Partington, Lisa *1989*
Carter, Richard *1990*
Groom, Ian *1990*
Jackson, Adrian *1990*
Rosario, Desmond *1990*
Thompson, Jonathan *1990*
Thompson, Patrick *1990*†
Watson, David *1990*
Chaudhry, Zia *1991*
Edwards, Mererid *1991*†
Mawdsley, Matthew *1991*
Roberts, Mark *1991*
Savage, Timothy *1991*
Taylor, Jonathan *1991*
Wright, Alastair *1991*
Ashmole, Timothy *1992*
Case, Magdalen *1992*
Green, Andrew *1992*
Lloyd, Gaynor *1992*
McNerney, Kevin *1992*
Norton, Richard *1992*
Blackshaw, Henry *1993*
Fitzharris, Ginnette *1993*
Ford, Caroline *1993*
Gibson, John *1993*†
Harrison, Rachael *1993*
Harrison, Leona *1993*†
Hughes, Dermot *1993*
Jones, Ben *1993*
Kloss, Alexander W *1993*
Mathieson, Guy A D *1993*†
Newton, Stuart *1993*
Nijabat, Shama *1993*
Orme, Richard *1993*
Polglase, David *1993*
Rodikis, Joanna *1993*
Searle, Jason *1993*
Stanistreet, Penelope *1993*
Wilson, Myles *1993*
Booth, Nigel *1994*
Chukwuemeka, John *1994*
Connor, Mark *1994*
Douglas, Stephen *1994*
Frieze, Daniel *1994*
Gumbs, Annette P *1994*
Houghton, Lisa *1994*
Lowe, Craig *1994*
Mann, Sara *1994*
Reynolds, Gary *1994*
Rhys, Megan Jill *1994*
Rowley, Karl *1994*†
Wild, Steven *1994*
Hargan, Carl *1995*
Kelly, Siobhan *1995*
Lawson, Andrew *1995*
McHugh, Pauline M *1995*
Parry, Philip *1995*
Simkin, Iain *1995*
Stables, Gordon *1995*
Aslett, Pepin *1996*
Crilley, Darrel *1996*
Mintz, Simon *1996*
Sastry, Bob *1996*
Bailey, Andrew *1997*
Denton, Douglas *1997*
Evans, Simeon *1997*
Goldsack, Ian *1997*
Mahmood, Ghazan *1997*
Mensah, Lorraine *1997*
Parry, Simon *1997*
Tyler, Paula *1997*
Williams, Zillah *1997*
Zentar, Remy *1997*
Bentley, David *1998*
Buckley, Patrick *1998*
Burnell, Kate *1998*
Edwards, Susan *1998*
James, David *1998*
Murdin, Liam *1998*
Muth, Susanne *1998*
Simmonds, Alexandra *1998*
Stockwell, Matthew *1998*
Taylor, David *1998*
Thomas, Clare *1998*
Astbury, Philip *1999*
Deas, Susan *1999*
Holsgrove, Lara *1999*
Lord, Andrew *1999*
Ratledge, John *1999*
Sweeney, Linda *1999*
Cavanagh, Lorraine *2000*
Hayes, Kathryn *2000*
Leach, Natasha *2000*
Ahmed, Siraj *2001*
Blewitt, Jennifer *2001*
Bridgman, Andrew *2001*
Farley, David *2001*
King, Oliver *2001*
Marshall, Laura Jane *2001*
Pojur, David *2001*
Porter-Phillips, Clare *2001*
Quinney, Nicola *2001*
Van-Der-Haer, Audrey *2001*
Vir Singh, Sylvia *2001*
Wynne, Andrew *2001*
Hodgkinson, Paul *2002*
Malam, James *2002*
McCloskey, Louise *2002*
Menzies, Jennifer *2002*
Montaldo, Neil *2002*
Moss, Christopher *2002*
Mottram, Cheryl *2002*
Owen, Wendy *2002*
Rawlinson, Michael J *2002*
Senior, Mark *2002*
Smith, Paul *2002*
Smith, Rebecca *2002*
Thyne, Richard *2002*
Akers, Robert *2003*
Ali, Kashif *2003*
Hudson, Abigail *2003*
Lawrence, Benjamin *2003*
Maguire, Clodagh *2003*
Newstead, *2003*
Quigley, Louise *2003*
Abraham, Jade *2004*
Connolly, Timothy *2004*
Cooper, Douglas *2004*
Greenhalgh, Jane *2004*
Harrison, Peta *2004*
Hickinbottom, Abigail *2004*
Murphy, Paul *2004*
Poole, William *2004*
Rimmer, Catherine *2004*
Samuel, Ana *2004*
Sutton, Rebecca *2004*
Waddell, Philippa *2004*
Watkins, Adam *2004*
Wilson, Helen *2004*
Christian, Neil *2005*
De Navarro, Frances *2005*
Marshall, Lucy *2005*
McGarry, Steven *2005*
Spencer, Shaun *2005*
Thompson, Gareth *2005*
White, Debra *2005*
Bower, Laurinda *2006*
Flynn, Steven *2006*
Goode, Julian *2006*
Kelly, Ben *2006*
Pare, Christopher *2006*
Rae, Louise *2006*
Rook, Rachael *2006*
Scully, Jenny *2006*
Wilkinson, Timothy *2006*
Allen, Fergal *2007*
Erlen, Nicole *2007*
Haggis, Andrew *2007*
Owen-Casey, Neil *2007*
Pemberton, Jessica *2007*
Vanderpump, Henry *2007*
Wood, Hannah *2007*
Bellamy, Jonathan *2008*
Cooper, Elisabeth *2008*
England, Laura *2008*
Garcha, Sukhdev *2008*
Gomer, Elis *2008*
Maddison, Simon *2008*
Metcalfe, Daniel *2008*
Murray, Simon *2008*
Walker, Hannah *2008*
Williams, Cerys *2008*
Baines, David *2009*
Edwards, Thomas *2009*
Nash, Laura *2009*
Roberts, Elliw *2009*

Types of work

Administrative law • Agriculture • Animals • Anti-social Behaviour Orders • Arbitration • Asset recovery • Asylum • Banking • Building societies • Capital tax • Care proceedings • Chancery • Chancery (general) • Charities • Children • Civil fraud • Civil law • Civil liberties • Civil litigation • Civil partnerships • Civil recovery • Cohabitation • Commercial fraud • Commercial law • Commercial litigation • Commodities • Common law (general) • Company law • Company, commercial and competition • Competition law • Computer crime • Confidential information • Conflict of laws • Constitutional law • Construction law • Consumer credit • Consumer law • Contracts • Copyright • Coroners • Corporate finance • Corporate fraud • Corporate manslaughter • Costs • Council tax • Crime • Crime and criminal due process • Criminal judicial review • Cross-border litigation and remedies • Customs • Data protection • Design • Disasters • Disciplinary procedures • Discrimination • Dispute resolution •

†Recorder *Door Tenant/Associate Member

Domestic violence injunctions • EC competition law • ECHR • Education • Employee benefit trusts • Employment • Energy • Entertainment • Environment • Equity • Excise • Extradition • Family law • Family provision • Financial instruments • Financial services • Fire and other property damage claims • Firearms • Fraud • Freedom of expression • Freezing orders • Funding arrangements • Gaming and lotteries • Group litigation • Guarantees • Health and safety • Healthcare law • Highways • Homicide • Housing • Income tax • Industrial relations law • Information technology • Insolvency • Insurance (long term) • International criminal law • Internet law • Investments • Labour arbitration • Landlord and tenant • Legal advice • Licensing • Local authorities • Malicious prosecution • Markets and fairs • Matrimonial • Media • Media and entertainment • Medical negligence • Mental health • Military law • Mining • Money laundering • Multi-party litigation • National Insurance • Off-shore trust litigation • Parliamentary • Partnerships • Passing off • Patents • Pensions • Personal injury • Personal insolvency • Planning • Police • Prison law • Privacy • Procurement • Professional negligence • Public access • Public health • Public law • Publishing • Rating and CPO • Real property • Regulatory and disciplinary law • Regulatory crime • Remedies • Road traffic • Securities law and regulation • Serial crime • Sexual Offences • Social welfare • Society of Lloyd's • Special Guardianship • Stamp duty • Succession • Tax • Telecommunications • Terrorism • Torts • Trade secrets • Trademarks • Travel law • Trust litigation • Trusts • Unincorporated associations • Unmarried couples • Utilities • VAT • Water

Disability access

Wheelchair access, Disabled parking available

JOHN PUGH'S CHAMBERS

707 - 709, The Corn Exchange, Fenwick Street, Liverpool L2 7RB

0151 236 5415

Fax: 0151 227 5468; DX: 14182 Liverpool

E-mail: john@johnpughschambers.co.uk

Chambers of: Mr J B Pugh

Disability access

Staff briefed or trained on duties under the disability legislation, Wheelchair access, Disabled parking available

LIVERPOOL CIVIL LAW

3rd Floor, 1 Old Hall Street, Liverpool L3 9HF

0151 242 0500

Fax: 0151 242 0505; DX: 14169 Liverpool

E-mail: clerks@liverpoolcivillaw.com

Disability access

Staff briefed or trained on duties under the disability legislation

MARINER'S WHARF CHAMBERS

26 Barchester Drive, Aigburth, Liverpool L17 5BZ

0151 727 0983

E-mail: johnmitc@live.co.uk

Chambers of: Mr J H E Harris

NEW BAILEY CHAMBERS

4th Floor, Corn Exchange, Fenwick Street, Liverpool, Merseyside L2 7QS

0151 236 9402

Fax: 0151 231 1296; DX: 14193 Liverpool

E-mail: clerks@newbailey.com

Chambers of: Mr D A Ackerley

Disability access

Staff briefed or trained on duties under the disability legislation, Wheelchair access, Disabled parking available

ORIEL CHAMBERS

14 Water Street, Liverpool, Merseyside L2 8TD

0151 236 7191

Fax: 0151 227 5909; DX: 14106 Liverpool

E-mail: clerks@orielchambers.co.uk

URL: www.orielchambers.co.uk

Chambers of: Mr R Bradley

Clerks: Andrew Hampton, John Newsham, Julie Konarski (Preston), Paul Gotham, Sarah Stephenson, Tom Craig; Chambers Director/Senior Clerk: Sarah Cavanagh, Chambers Manager: Paul Thompson, Fees Administration: Cheryl Allen, Zara Magee, Vicky McGregor

Also at: 18 Ribblesdale Place, Preston, Lancashire PR1 3NA

Bradley, Richard *1978*
Bennett, Martyn *1969*
Alldis, Christopher *1970†*
Hind, Kenneth CBE *1973*
Murray, Ashley *1974†*
Cowan, Peter *1980†*
Bundred, Gillian *1982*
Wells, Graham *1982†*
O'Keeffe, Darren *1984*
Evans, Suzanne *1985*
Fox, Anna *1986*
Goodbody, Peter *1986*
Ellis, Catherine *1987*
Baldwin, John *1990*
Garden, Ian *1989*
Nicholls, Jane *1989*
Lewthwaite, Joanne *1990*
Holloway, Timothy *1991*
Rahman, Yaqub *1991†*
Belbin, Heather *1992*
Foster, Peter *1992*
Gruffydd, John *1992*
Mills, Stuart *1992*
Brant, Paul *1993*
Dawson, James *1994*
Rankin, William K *1994*
Benson, James *1995*
Hughes, Rachel *1995*
Clarke, Susan *1996*
Cottrell, Matthew *1996*
Frodsham, Alexander *1996*
Hennessy, Shirley *1997*
Pritchard, Cecilia *1998*
Stanger, Mark *1998*
Berry, Karl *1999*
Clarke, Lindsay *1999*
Purcell, Deirdre *2000*
Burns, Judith *2001*
Gray, John *2001*
Howe, Andrew P *2002*
Sholicar, Ann *2001*
Middleton, Christopher *2002*
Williams, Graham *2002*
McMurtrie, Christopher *2003*
Bartlett, Catherine *2004*
Gosling, Tom *2004*
Williams, Alexander *2004*
Champion, Karina *2005*
Cooper, Mark *2005*
Wolfenden, Peter *2007*
Emery, Philip *2008*
Parr, Margaret *2008*
Cummings, Stephanie *2010*

Types of work
Ancillary relief · Asset finance · Banking · Care proceedings · Chancery (general) · Clinical negligence · Commercial litigation · Common law (general) · Construction law · Crime · Discrimination · Employment · Environment · Factoring · Family law · Housing · Insolvency · Insurance · Judicial review · Landlord and tenant · Personal injury · Personal insolvency · Professional negligence · Sale and carriage of goods

Chambers Established 1965
Opening times: 8.30am - 6.00pm

Chambers' facilities
Conference Rooms, Video Conference, Limited disabled access, E-mail

Disability access
Staff briefed or trained on duties under the disability legislation, Wheelchair access, Disabled parking available

Languages spoken
Afrikaans, French, Spanish

Fees policy
Fee information and structuring can be obtained through the clerks. Conditional fee agreements accepted.

CHAMBERS OF MR VINCENT YIP

4 Westbury Close, Liverpool L17 5BD
0151 324 0880
E-mail: clerks@vincentyip.co.uk

Chambers of: Mr V Yip

PENLAN CHAMBERS

The Coach House, Penlan, Croeslan, Llandysul, Ceredigion SA44 4SL
01559 363333
Fax: 01559 362814
E-mail: georgiahay@btconnect.com

Chambers of: Ms G S Hay

Disability access
Staff briefed or trained on duties under the disability legislation, Wheelchair access, Disabled parking available

PORTAL CHAMBERS

Blaencwm Mawr, Llandysul SA44 5NS
01559 395 292
Fax: 01559 395 292
URL: www.portalchambers.com
Out of hours telephone: 01559 395292

Chambers of: Miss G M Douglass
Clerk: Abbie Ball

Douglass, Tina *1976*
Jennings, Peter *1972*
Mainwaring, Paul *1996*
Cooper, Paul *1998*
Lloyd, Trefor *2001*

Disability access
Staff briefed or trained on duties under the disability legislation, Wheelchair access, Disabled parking available

1215 CHAMBERS

1 Fetter Lane, London EC4A 1BR
020 3291 1215
Fax: 020 3291 1216; DX: 372 Chancery Lane
E-mail: admin@1215chambers.com

Chambers of: Mr R J O'Sullivan

ACADEMY CHAMBERS

63 Brim Hill, London N2 0HA
020 8455 2503
Fax: 0870 705 2837
E-mail: marionlonsdale@gmail.com

Chambers of: Miss M M Lonsdale

†Recorder *Door Tenant/Associate Member

ACCESS LAWYERS

800 High Road, Tottenham, London N17 0DH
020 8801 2345
Fax: 020 8801 2555

Chambers of: Mr W A Lewis

AGNUS CHAMBERS

PO Box 64196, London WC1A 9FE
020 7637 9670
Fax: 020 7637 9670

Chambers of: Miss M E Candilio

CHAMBERS OF MOBIN U AHMED

36 Chase Road, London N14 4EU
020 8886 2015
Fax: 020 8886 2015
E-mail: mobinuahmed@hotmail.co.uk

Chambers of: Mr M U Ahmed

A J CHAMBERS

12 Sperling Road, Bruce Grove, London N17 6UH
020 8885 5775
Fax: 020 8493 8292; DX: 121 London Chancery Lane

Chambers of: Miss A J Armour

ALEXANDER CHAMBERS

13 Halstead Road, Wanstead, London E11 2AY
0845 652 0451/0854 652 0451
Fax: 0845 652 0499/0854 652 0451; DX: 52554 Wanstead London
E-mail: clerks@alexanderchambers.co.uk

Chambers of: Mr L A Gledhill

Disability access
Staff briefed or trained on duties under the disability legislation, Wheelchair access, Disabled parking available, Induction loop or infra red system

CHAMBERS OF MS M ALI

24 Camden High Street, London NW1 0JH
020 7387 2032
Fax: 020 7388 6575; DX: 57056 Camden Town

CHAMBERS OF MR LUDWIK ALLERHAND

38 Dunoon Road, Forest Hill, London SE23 3TF
020 8291 4356
E-mail: ludwikallerhand@btinternet.com

Chambers of: Mr L E Allerhand

AMETHYST CHAMBERS

Ground Floor, 9 Kings Bench Walk, Inner Temple, London EC4Y 7DX
020 7936 4966
Fax: 020 7936 3489
E-mail: info@amethystchambers.com

CHAMBERS OF ANWOBO AMIHERE

1st Floor, 20 Sewardstone Gardens, Chingford, London E4 7QE
020 8524 3054
Fax: 020 8524 3054
E-mail: aamihere@aol.com

Chambers of: Mr A Amihere

CHAMBERS OF GAMINI ANGAMMANA

'Woodcroft', 13 Woodend, Upper Norwood, London SE19 3NU
020 8771 5205
Fax: 020 8771 5205
E-mail: woodcroftchambers@btconnect.com

Chambers of: Mr G B Angammana

Disability access
Disabled parking available

ANGELL PARK CHAMBERS

Unit 11, Amberley Court, Angell Road, London SW9 7HL
020 7737 5957
Fax: 020 7978 8226
E-mail: info@chandrasekar.co.uk

Chambers of: Mr C Sekar

Disability access
Staff briefed or trained on duties under the disability legislation, Disabled parking available

D

ARBITRATION CHAMBERS

22 Willes Road, London NW5 3DS
020 7267 2137
Fax: 020 7482 1018; DX: 298 Lde
E-mail: john.tackaberry@39essex.com

Chambers of: Mr J A Tackaberry QC

Disability access
Wheelchair access, Disabled parking available

ARDEN CHAMBERS

20 Bloomsbury Square, London WC1A 2NS
020 7242 4244
Fax: 020 7242 3224
E-mail: clerks@ardenchambers.com
URL: www.ardenchambers.com and www.housinglawdirect.com

Chambers of: Mr A P R Arden QC
Clerks: Mike Alexander (Clerk to Chambers), Neil Goodwright (Clerk), Martin Cornwell (Fees Clerk); Administrator: Anita Heartfield

Arden, Andrew QC *1974*
Robson, John *1974*
Baker, Christopher *1984*
Roberts, Clare *1988*
Colville, Iain *1989*
Manning, Jonathan *1989*
Okoya, William *1989*
Dymond, Andrew *1991*
Cafferkey, Annette *1994*
Armstrong, Stuart *1995*
Vanhegan, Toby *1996*
McKeown, Sarah *1998*
McCafferty, John *2000*
Ackland-Vincent, Gillian *2001*
Loveland, Ian *2001*
Bates, Justin *2003*
Orme, Emily *2003*
Sandham, James *2003*
Smith, Stephanie *2004*
Chan, Rebecca *2006*
Cowan, David *2006*
West, Laura *2006*
Salmon, Sarah *2007*
Brown, Robert *2008*
Madge-Wyld, Samuel *2008*
Cullen, Clare *2009*

Types of work
Administrative law · Boundaries · Chancery (land law) · Commercial contracts · Commercial property · Community care · Compulsory Purchase · Constitutional and administrative law · Discrimination · Environment · Housing · Human rights · Judicial review · Land compensation · Landlord and tenant · Local authorities · Local authority claims · Mental health · Mortgages · Planning · Procurement · Public law · Rating and CPO · Real property · Social security · Social services · Trading standards · Trusts · Wills

Chambers Established 1993
Opening times: 8.30am - 6.30pm

Chambers' facilities
Conference Rooms

Disability access
Staff briefed or trained on duties under the disability legislation, Wheelchair access (by appointment)

Languages spoken
French, Italian

ARGENT CHAMBERS

5 Bell Yard, London WC2A 2JR
020 7556 5500
Fax: 020 7556 5565; DX: 494 Lde
E-mail: briefsin@argentchambers.co.uk
URL: www.argentchambers.co.uk
Out of hours telephone: 020 7556 5500

Chambers of: Mr H A D De Silva QC
Clerks: Billy Harris, Lynn Pilkington, Will Taborn, Alex King, Senior Clerk: Michael Martin; Practice Manager: Chambers Manager: John Holland; Business Development Manager: Laura Piercey; Fees/Billing Team: Carole Gavin, Mark Spalding, Hannah Sparkes

De Silva, Harendra QC *1970†*
De Silva, Desmond QC *1964*
Newman, Alan QC *1968*
Bishop, Malcolm QC *1968†*
Hackett, Philip QC *1978*
Nathan, David QC *1971*
Johnson, Roderick QC *1975*
Lett, Brian QC *1971†*
Zorbas, Panos *1964*
Mullen, Patrick *1967*

 †Recorder *Door Tenant/Associate Member

Crystal, Jonathan *1972*
Hoon, Notu *1975*
Hayes, Jerry *1977*
Blower, Graham *1980*
Bolton, Frances *1981*
Horgan, Timothy *1982*
Ward, Simon *1984*
Ong, Grace *1985*
Metzer, Anthony *1987*
Fitch-Holland, Andrew *1990*
Lawrence, Rachel *1992*
Gatley, Mark *1993*
Gersch, Adam *1993*
D'Souza, Dominic *1993*
Mylvaganam, Paul *1993*
Bentwood, Richard *1994*
Cox, Dominic *1994*
Milsom, Catherine *1994*
Wayne, Nicholas *1994*
Mansoor, Parveen *1996*
Morgan, Adam *1996*
Williams, Mark *1996*
Wright, Alex *1997*
Baker, Simon *1998*
Gregory, Rupert *1998*
Page, Philippa *1999*
Lowe, Elizabeth *1999*
Turner, Jonathan *1999*
Goudie, Alexander *2000*
Paul, Matthew *2000*
James, Nicholas *2001*
O'Kane, Sarah *2001*
Rooke, Alexander *2001*
Van Duyvenbode, Damian *2001*
Marney, Nicholas *2002*
Jones, Daniel *2002*
O'Toole, Francis *2002*
Holmes, Jessica *2003*
Nartey, Elizabeth *2003*
Williams, Meyrick *2003*
Collins, Louisa *2004*
Lill, Stuart *2004*
Willmer, Stephen *2004*
Scott, Christopher *2005*
Edge, Alan *2006*
Hale, Victoria *2006*
Forbes, Victoria *2007*
Hassall, David *2011*
Brotherton, Matthew *1995**
Hikmet, Berin *2000**

Types of work

Banking · Civil actions against the police · Commercial law · Company law · Competition law · Constitutional and administrative law · Corporate fraud · Courts martial · Crime · European law · Family law · Foreign law · Human rights · Immigration · International law · Judicial review · Licensing · Litigation · Local government and public services · Media · Personal injury · Prison law · Sport

Opening times: 8.30am - 6.30pm

Disability access

Staff briefed or trained on duties under the disability legislation, Wheelchair access, Disabled parking available

Languages spoken

Chinese (Cantonese), Chinese (Mandarin), French, German, Greek, Gujarati, Hindi, Hungarian, Ibo, Italian, Japanese, Malay, Spanish, Tamil, Urdu, Welsh

CHAMBERS OF DR MICHAEL ARNHEIM

101 Queen Alexandra Mansions, Judd Street, London WC1H 9DP
020 7833 5093
Fax: 020 7916 0962; DX: 330 London Chancery Lane
E-mail: arnheim.law@gmail.com

Chambers of: Dr M T W Arnheim

ARTESIAN LAW

3 Bolt Court, Fleet Street, London EC4A 3DQ
02 0361 77738; DX: 275 Lde
E-mail: contact@artesianlaw.com

CHAMBERS OF MR M J ASHER

86 Kensington Park Road, London W11 2PL
020 7727 0271
E-mail: michael@asher.demon.co.uk

Chambers of: Mr M J Asher

ATKIN CHAMBERS

AtkinChambers Barristers

1 Atkin Building, Gray's Inn, London WC1R 5AT
020 7404 0102
Fax: 020 7405 7456; DX: 1033 London Chancery Lane
E-mail: clerks@atkinchambers.com
URL: www.atkinchambers.com
Out of hours telephone: 07799 844018

Chambers of: Mr A White QC
Clerks: Simon Slattery, Justin Wilson; Practice Manager: Natasha Willicombe (Practice Manager), Andrew Burrows (Assistant Practice Manager), Ryan Walker (Practice Manager), James Ingham (Assistant Practice Manager)

White, Andrew QC *1980*
Dennys, Nicholas QC *1975*
Acton Davis, Jonathan QC *1977†*
Baatz, Nicholas QC *1978*
Bowdery, Martin QC *1980†*
Dennison, Stephen QC *1985*
Streatfeild-James, David QC *1986*
Raeside, Mark QC *1982*
Goddard, Andrew QC *1985*
Barwise, Stephanie QC *1988*
Lofthouse, Simon QC *1988†*
Doerries, Chantal-Aimée QC *1992*
Fraser, Peter D QC *1989†*
McMullan, Manus QC *1994*
Parkin, Fiona QC *1993*
Rawley, Dominique QC *1991*
Walker, Steven QC *1993*
Royce, Darryl *1976*
Burr, Andrew *1981*
Clay, Robert *1989*
Pigott, Frances *1994*
Howells, James *1995*
Clarke, Patrick *1997*
Collings, Nicholas *1997*
Lewis, Christopher *1998*
Cheng, Serena *2000*
Hussain, Riaz *2001*
Chennells, Mark *2002*
Slow, Camille *2002*
Jones, Jennifer *2003*
Briggs, Lucie *2004*
Crawshaw, Simon *2005*
Lixenberg, Marc *2005*
Hanna, Ronan *2006*
Khayum, Zulfikar *2006*
Fenn, Andrew *2007*
Land, Peter *2007*
Neuberger, Edmund *2008*
Eljadi, Omar *2009*
Johnson, David *2010*
Reese, Colin QC *1973**

Types of work
Adjudication · Alternative dispute resolution · Arbitration · Commercial law · Commercial litigation · Construction law · Dry shipping · Energy · Environment · Information technology · Insurance · International commercial arbitration · Procurement · Professional negligence · Telecommunications

Disability access
Staff briefed or trained on duties under the disability legislation, Disabled parking available

ATLAS CHAMBERS

3 Field Court, Gray's Inn, London WC1R 5EP
020 7269 7980
Fax: 020 7269 7981; DX: 82 London Chancery Lane
E-mail: clerks@atlaschambers.com
URL: www.atlaschambers.com
Out of hours telephone: 07967 029543

Chambers of: Mr S P Randle
Clerk: John Lister; Practice Manager: John Lister; Administrator: Polly Rothera; Stephen Marshall

Randle, Simon *1982*
Jefferis, Michael *1976*
Powell, Jonathan *1984*
Forsyth, Christopher *1987*
Gordon, Keith *2003*
Lawrence, Anne *2003*
Montes Manzano, Ximena *2004*
Howard, Joseph *2006*
Fairpo, Anne *2009*
Lewis, Robert *1996**
Hoffman, David *1997**
Goodman, Alexander *2003**

Types of work
Administrative law · Capital tax · Chancery (general) · Education · Energy · Environment · Housing · Human rights · Income tax · Local authorities · Partnerships · Planning · Professional negligence

AVONDALE CHAMBERS

134 Engel Park, Mill Hill East, London NW7 2HP
020 8346 1126

Chambers of: Eur.Ing. C Shaikh

Disability access
Staff briefed or trained on duties under the disability legislation, Wheelchair access, Disabled parking available

CHAMBERS OF MR A H AWAN

326 Ada Court, 10-16 Maida Vale, St John's Wood, London W9 1TE
07884 372954

Chambers of: Mr A H Awan

CHAMBERS OF HARBINDER BAHIA

115 Gordon Road, South Woodford, London E18 1DT
07930 364727
E-mail: harbinder.bahia@googlemail.com

Chambers of: Miss H Bahia

BALHAM CHAMBERS

Basement, 82 Balham High Road, London SW12 9AG
020 8675 4609
Fax: 020 8675 3415; DX: 34002 Tooting North

Chambers of: Mr R S Sukul

Disability access
Disabled parking available

CHAMBERS OF MRS MARGARET BANKOLE

6 Macarathur Close, Wyatt Road, Forest Gate, London E7 9NT
07983 302695
Fax: 020 8552 0813
E-mail: margaretmcf1996@yahoo.co.uk

Chambers of: Mrs M Bankole

BARCLAY CHAMBERS

Ground Floor, 2a Barclay Road, Leytonstone, London E11 3DG
020 8558 2289
Fax: 020 8558 3849
E-mail: barqureshi@hotmail.co.uk

Chambers of: Mr A S Qureshi

CHAMBERS OF MR D BARNARD

Third Floor South, 6 Raymond Buildings, Grays Inn, London WC1R 5BN
020 7242 1873
E-mail: dbar1873@aol.com

Chambers of: Mr D N Barnard

BARRISTERS CHAMBERS

89A High Road, Wood Green, London N22 6BB
020 3417 6461
Fax: 020 3417 6463
E-mail: clerk@barristerschambers.org

Chambers of: Mr B Esprit

CHAMBERS OF M I BASHIR

2 Elmcroft Gardens, Kingsbury, London NW9 9QP
07932 948487
E-mail: mibachambers@gmail.com

Chambers of: Mr M I Bashir

2 BEDFORD ROW

2 Bedford Row, London WC1R 4BU
020 7440 8888
Fax: 020 7242 1738; DX: 17 London Chancery Lane
E-mail: clerks@2bedfordrow.co.uk
URL: www.2bedfordrow.co.uk
Out of hours telephone: 07792 730 823

Chambers of: Mr W Clegg QC
Clerk: John Grimmer; Administrator: Marion Ohlson

Clegg, William QC *1972*
Godfrey, Howard QC *1970*
Griffiths, Peter QC *1970*
Munday, Andrew QC *1973*
Lithman, Nigel QC *1976*
Wolkind, Michael QC *1976*
McGowan, Maura QC *1980*
Lodder, Peter QC *1981*
Sturman, James QC *1982*
Kovalevsky, Richard QC *1983*
Dodd, John QC *1979*
Ayling, Tracy QC *1983*
Stern, Ian QC *1983*
Milliken-Smith, Mark QC *1986*
Altman, Brian QC *1981*
Whittam, William QC *1983*
Matthews, Richard QC *1989*
Conway, Charles *1969*
Champion, Deborah *1970*
Ingram, Nigel *1972*
Halsey, Mark *1974*
Caudle, John *1976*
Abell, Anthony *1977*
Gilbert, Barry *1978*
Haynes, Michael *1979*
Levy, Michael *1979*
Livingston, Richard *1980*
Donnelly, John *1983*
Armstrong, Dean *1985*
Kendal, Timothy *1985*
King, Gelaga *1985*
Rush, Craig *1989*
Ferguson, Stephen *1991*
Hammond, Sean *1991*
Agnew, Christine *1992*
Budworth, Adam *1992*
Charbit, Valerie *1992*
Epstein, Michael *1992*
Hurlock, Lugard *1993*
Pople, Alison *1993*
Compton, Allan *1994*
Ferry-Swainson, Richard *1994*
Vullo, Stephen *1996*
Dineen, Maria *1997*
Hodivala, Jamas *1998*
Carey, Jacqueline *1999*
Khan, Ashraf *1999*
King, Emma *1999*
Langley, Charles *1999*
McGee, Andrew *1999*
Hunt, Quentin *2000*
Llewellyn-Waters, Hanna *2000*
Ritchie, Shauna *2000*
Oakley, Lousie *2001*
Power, Archangelo *2001*
George, Dean *2002*
Harrison, James *2002*
Wyatt, Anthony *2002*
Magee, Samuel *2003*
Dix, Rebecca *2004*
Singh, Sandesh *2004*
Toomey, Kevin *2004*
Sanderson, Eleanor *2005*
Jamieson, Katrina *2007*
Stoton, Austin Dr *2007*
Hogman, Timothy *2008*
Martin, Christopher *2008*
Milner, Jonas *2008*
Pehar, Vedrana *2008*
Daniel, Thomas *2009*
Patience, David *2009*
Jenkins, Alun QC *1972*†*
Dodd, Margaret *1979**
Barnett, Jeremy *1980*†*
McMeekin, Ian *1987**
Garson, Robert *1999**

Types of work
Administrative law · Asset forfeiture · Asset recovery · Computer crime · Confiscation · Coroner's inquests · Coroners · Corporate fraud · Corporate liability · Corporate manslaughter · Courts martial · Crime and criminal due process · Criminal judicial review · ECHR · Environment · Extradition · Financial services · Firearms · Forfeiture · Fraud · Health and safety · Homicide · Inquests · International criminal law · International fraud and asset tracing · International human rights law · Internet crime · Judicial review · Money laundering · Police discipline · Privy Council Appeals · Public inquiries · Regulatory and disciplinary law · Road traffic offences · Serial crime · Serious fraud · Sport · Trading standards · War crimes tribunals

Opening times: 8.00am - 7.00pm

Disability access
Staff briefed or trained on duties under the disability legislation, Disabled parking available

Languages spoken
Arabic, Dutch, French, German, Hebrew, Italian, Krio (Sierra Leone), Russian, Serbo-Croat

Chambers Profile

Clients of 2 Bedford Row benefit from the knowledge, expertise and support of one of the country's leading criminal and regula-

†Recorder *Door Tenant/Associate Member

D

tory sets. Committed to all aspects of criminal law, we advise and represent clients in a wide variety of proceedings and investigations, from high-profile fraud and murder cases, to health and safety and professional disciplinary proceedings. Our members have appeared in the ICTY in The Hague, the ECHR, Privy Council, Supreme Court (House of Lords), Court of Appeal, Administrative Court and all courts and tribunals of first instance, as well as public inquiries. An increasing volume of our work is international and our members attend hearings around the globe.

The set

We serve a variety of clients, spanning national governments, international companies, local authorities and other public bodies, regulators, trade unions, and professional and sporting authorities, as well as individuals. We can call upon the combined expertise of 18 Queen's Counsel and 58 juniors, including the former Attorney-General, a Deputy High Court Judge, first senior treasury counsel, standing counsel to the Health and Safety Executive, a number of recorders and currently the Vice-Chair of the Bar Council and past Chairman of the Bar Council and the Criminal Bar Association.

Types of work undertaken.

Crime: As one of the acknowledged 'magic circle' criminal sets, we have an outstanding track record in high-profile trials, including corporate crimes and war crimes. Examples include Corporal Lee Clegg; the Hillsborough Football Stadium disaster; the Hatfield, Potters Bar and Tebay rail disasters; David Copeland (Brixton nail bomber); Michael Stone; Colin Stagg; Barry George; Levi Bellfield (Milly Dowler murder), Vincent Tabak (Joanna Yeates murder), Tony Martin; Paul Burrell; Stephen Lawrence; and Kenneth Noye (M25 murder), The Liquid Bomb Plot.

Fraud: Criminal fraud is an important part of our workload. Our members have appeared in complex, high-profile cases, from Brent Walker to Levitt, WSTC, Cheney Pensions, Izodia plc, Asil Nadir, BAE, Jubilee Line, Pharmaceuticals, Torex, Robinsons (solicitors), Imperial Consolidated, Derby FC Collapse.

Health and safety: We have particular expertise in health and safety enforcement work, including corporate and involuntary manslaughter, particularly in the construction and transport industries, and one of our members has written the leading textbook on the subject.

Professional and disciplinary tribunals: Over the years our members have developed an intuitive understanding of how professional bodies think, which allows them to tailor their advocacy for the greatest effect. We represent professionals before the GMC, GDC, AOP, GSCC, PTD, RPS, SRA among others, as well as acting for professional bodies themselves.

Financial services regulation: The team has considerable experience in SFO, FSA, DTI, and HM Revenue & Customs investigations, prosecutions and appeals.

Inquests and public inquiries: Our regulatory group assists clients before coroners' inquests and public inquiries, providing high-quality advice and representation. Examples include De Menezes, Marc Blanco, Stephen Lawrence, Victoria Climbié, Shipman and Ashwood Special Hospital inquiries.

Sports law: Members also frequently appear before professional sporting tribunals, particularly football, rugby and cricket, boxing and represent many premiership clubs and individual players.

International work: Our members have undertaken work in the US, West Indies, Middle East, Gibraltar, Hong Kong and most of mainland Europe and Russia in particular. For more details please see our website.

SEVEN BEDFORD ROW

7 Bedford Row, London WC1R 4BS
020 7242 3555
Fax: 020 7242 2511; DX: 347 London Chancery Lane
E-mail: clerks@7br.co.uk

Disability access

Staff briefed or trained on duties under the disability legislation, Wheelchair access, Disabled parking available, Induction loop or infra red system

NINE BEDFORD ROW

9 Bedford Row, London WC1R 4AZ
020 7489 2727
Fax: 020 7489 2828; DX: 453 London Chancery Lane
E-mail: clerks@9bedfordrow.co.uk
URL: www.9bedfordrow.co.uk
Out of hours telephone: 07971 153192

Chambers of: Mr A C Berry QC
Clerks: Michael Eves (Senior Clerk), Paul Outen (1st Junior Clerk), Trevor Austin, Russell Good, Elliot Styles, Matthew Corner (Junior Clerk); Administrator: Julian Bradley; Fees Clerk: Helen Davey

Berry, Anthony QC *1976*
Garside, Charles QC *1971†*
Kay, Steven QC *1977†*
Marsh, Elizabeth QC *1979*
Carey-Hughes, Richard QC *1977†*
Watson, Paul QC *1978†*
Chinn, Antony QC *1972†*
Fortune, Robert QC *1976*
Lakha, Abbas QC *1984*
Hughes, Ignatius QC *1986†*
Karu, Lee QC *1985*
Bickerstaff, Jane QC *1989*
May, Patricia *1965†*
Germain, Richard *1968*
Carne, Roger *1969*
Lockyer, Jane *1970*
Mirwitch, Jane *1974*
Zeitlin, Derek *1974*
Burgess, David *1975*
Traversi, John *1977*
French, Louis *1979*
Hughes, David *1980*
Rouse, Justin *1982†*
King, John *1983*
Amer, Adrian *1984*
Cleaver, Wayne *1986*
Whittaker, David *1986†*
Young, David *1986*
Cammegh, John *1987*
Stirling, Simon *1989*
Squirrell, Benjamin *1990*
Akinsanya, Jonathan *1993*
Glenser, Peter *1993*
Vickers, Edmund *1993*
Arora, Anita *1994*
Welsh, James *1994*
Cohen, Samantha *1995*
Faul, Anne *1996*
Chandarana, Yogain *1997*
Higgins, Gillian Kay *1997*
Selby, Lawrence *1997*
Banham, Matthew *1999*
O'Connor, Charlotte *1999*
Darling, Polly *2000*
Hakme, Mustapha *2000*
Noble, Will *2000*
Cadman, Toby *2001*
Jessop, Stuart *2002*
Khan, Aisha *2002*
Benlamkadem, Fayza *2003*
Higgins, Daniel *2003*
Hardy, Maximilian *2004*
Jones, Ruth *2004*
Paton-Philip, Richard *2004*
Sullivan, Sean *2004*
Bramwell, Corinne *2005*
Shorey, Carrie *2006*
Bentley, Harry *2007*
Charnley, Bethan *2007*
Brewer, Aneurin *2008*
Bafadhel, *2009*
Binding, Chloe *2009*
Shroff, Tessa *2009*
Parker, Kate *2010*
Maher, Michael *1995**

Types of work
Child abuse · Commercial fraud · Confiscation · Corporate fraud · Corporate manslaughter · Crime · Regulatory and disciplinary law · Serial crime · Serious fraud

Opening times: 8.30am - 6.30pm

Chambers' facilities
Conference Rooms, Disks Accepted, Library, telephone conferencing, video conferencing, video/DVD/CD playing facilities, E-mail, website, direct dial telephone with voicemail, computer access and legal research facility

Disability access
Wheelchair access, Disabled parking available

Languages spoken
Arabic, French, German, Gujarati, Hindi, Italian, Punjabi, Spanish, Swahili

Additional information
Nine Bedford Row has been long established in the vanguard of leading criminal sets with an enviable reputation for commitment and service to the cause of its clients.

Headed by 12 QCs, acknowledged within the profession as heavyweights in the field, backed by an array of notable juniors, Nine Bedford Row offers extensive experience of involvement in the prosecution and defence of allegations of serious and complex crime.

Nine Bedford Row prides itself on the quality, diversity, and depth of its members, who are highly experienced in mainstream criminal work, and in the areas of regulatory and confiscation practice. Chambers has a substantial presence in the area of international law.

The history of Nine Bedford Row goes back over half a century. Chambers was established at 4 Brick Court in the Temple, in rooms formerly occupied by the great Lord Denning and moved into their elegant Georgian premises in Bedford Row in 2000, where

†Recorder *Door Tenant/Associate Member

D

they have steadily expanded into one of London's largest and most powerful sets. Within this impressive building, they provide modern facilities, including designated consultation rooms and the supporting services of an experienced, friendly and helpful clerks' room headed by Michael Eves, doyen of barristers' clerks.

Members and former members have served not only their clients but also their profession with distinction. Chambers has provided leadership within the Criminal Bar Association, including the first female Chair of that organisation and no fewer than four of the association's past Secretaries. The present Head of Chambers, Anthony Berry QC, is the Chair of the influential Heads of Chambers committee. Former members of chambers have accepted judicial appointments to the High Court, Central Criminal Court and Crown Court benches.

On an academic front chambers has provided lectures on all aspects of practice and legislation, and we have held series of lectures well received by members of the Bar, solicitors and academics, recently extending to cover international work.

Chambers is justifiably proud of its long record of implementing an equal opportunity policy, which has resulted in a diverse and committed team of highly professional men and women.

Types of work undertaken:
Our 63 members including 11 QCs practising exclusively in the criminal courts, we can justifiably claim to offer expertise in every aspect of criminal litigation.

We are regularly instructed to defend in cases ranging from serious commercial fraud to murder, drugs and armed robberies and the ensuing confiscation hearings. Over the years members of our chambers have been prominent in numerous high-profile defence cases.

We are also instructed to prosecute at all levels by the Serious Fraud Office, the Department of Trade and Industry, Customs and Excise, the Inland Revenue and the Crown Prosecution Service.

Nine Bedford Row is recognised as a set, and through individual members as a leader in the field of advice and representation in criminal law.

25 BEDFORD ROW

25 Bedford Row, London WC1R 4HD
020 7067 1500
Fax: 020 7067 1507; DX: 1043 London Chancery Lane
E-mail: clerks@25bedfordrow.com
URL: www.25bedfordrow.com
Out of hours telephone: 07843 470731

Chambers of: Mr G A Carter-Stephenson QC, Mr P M Mendelle QC
Senior Clerks: Guy Williams, Emma Makepeace, John Carson; Administrator: Jacky Chase

Carter-Stephenson, George QC *1975*
Mendelle, Paul QC *1981*
Tansey, Rock QC *1966*†
Salmon, Charles QC *1972*
Sangster, Nigel QC *1976*†
Ellis, Diana QC *1978*†
Doyle, Peter QC *1975*
Hollis, Kim QC *1979*
Dein, Jeremy QC *1982*†
Keleher, Paul QC *1980*
Hooper, David QC *1971*
Fortson, Rudi QC *1976*
Cooper, John QC *1983*
Price, Tom QC *1985*
Hynes, Paul QC *1987*
Sidhu, Jo QC *1993*
Jaffa, Ronald *1974*
Mitchell, Jonathan *1974*
Beyts, Chester *1978*
Offenbach, Roger *1978*
Maley, Bill *1982*
Pentol, Simon *1982*
Redhead, Leroy *1982*
Wells, Colin *1987*
Eissa, Adrian *1988*
Mann, Jonathan *1989*
Piercy, Arlette *1990*
Valley, Helen *1990*
Akuwudike, Emma *1992*
Daw, Christopher *1993*
Potter, Harry *1993*
Byrnes, Aisling *1994*
Furlong, Richard *1994*
Smith, Tyrone *1994*
Howard, Nicola *1995*
Osman, Osman *1995*
Guiloff, Carolina *1996*
Riggs, Samantha *1996*
Rudolf, Nathaniel *1996*
Gardiner, Sebastian *1997*
Keating, Dermot *1997*
Evans, Joanna *1998*
Simpson, Melanie *1998*
O'Reilly, Beth Melissa *1999*
Smitten, Ben *1999*
Braun, Minka *2000*
Payne, Geoffrey *2000*
Qureshi, Tanveer *2000*
Sherborn, Natalie *2000*
Cook, Emily *2002*

†Recorder *Door Tenant/Associate Member

Gomulka, Michael *2002*
Patel, Yasin *2002*
Baki, Neil *2003*
Stevenson, Monica *2004*
Breger, Daniel *2005*
Ledgister, Roy *2005*
Radstone, Matthew *2005*
Randall, Rebecca *2005*
Blom-Cooper, Sam *2006*
Chadwick, Daniel *2006*
Malhotra, Priya *2007*
Arnot Drummond, Kathryn *2008*
Shaw, Robert *2008*
Stuart-Smith, Emma *2009*

Types of work

Civil liberties · Confiscation · Corporate fraud · Crime · Criminal judicial review · ECHR · European law · Extradition · Firearms · Foreign law · Homicide · Human rights · Inquests · International criminal law · International human rights law · Police · Prison law · Serial crime · Serious fraud · Tax · VAT

Disability access

Staff briefed or trained on duties under the disability legislation, Disabled parking available

29 BEDFORD ROW CHAMBERS

29 Bedford Row Chambers, London WC1R 4HE
020 7404 1044
Fax: 020 7831 0626; DX: 1044 London Chancery Lane
E-mail: clerks@29br.co.uk
URL: www.2br.co.uk

Chambers of: Mr N Francis QC
Clerk: James Shortall (Senior Clerk); Administrator: Nicola Kessell

Francis, Nicholas QC *1981*
Scott, Timothy QC *1975*†
Storey, Paul QC *1982*†
Cayford, Philip QC *1975*
Peel, Robert QC *1990*
Pressdee, Piers QC *1991*
Chamberlayne, Patrick QC *1992*
Shaw, Howard QC *1973*
Wagstaffe, Christopher QC *1992*
Duckworth, Peter *1971*
Renton, Clare *1972*
Swift, Jonathan *1977*†
Ramsahoye, Indira *1980*
Wehrle, Jacqueline *1984*
Emanuel, Mark *1985*
Walden-Smith, David *1985*
Reynolds, Stephen *1987*
Arnot, Lee *1990*
Campbell, Alexis *1990*
Chapman, Nicholas *1990*
Storey-Rea, Alexa *1990*
Tod, Jonathan *1990*
Wentworth, Annabel *1990*
Max, Sally *1991*
Bates, Richard *1992*
Southgate, Jonathan *1992*
Butler, Judith *1993*
Domenge, Victoria *1993*
Molyneux, Brent *1994*
Allen, Nicholas *1995*
Amaouche, Sassa-Ann *1996*
Collins, Ken *1996*
Mitchell, Peter *1996*
Griffiths, Dafydd *1997*
Owens, Lucy *1997*
Heaton, Laura *1998*
Black, Georgina *1999*
Calhaem, Simon *1999*
Geadah, Anthony *2000*
Hudd, Anne *2000*
Willins, Andrew *2000*
Fearnley, Ben *2001*
Francis, Victoria *2001*
Lewis, Max *2002*
Butterfield, Christopher *2004*
Cade-Davies, Lynsey *2005*
Fee, Conor *2006*
Teacher, Petra *2006*
Williams, Helen *2007*
Sheridan, Amber *2008*
Eriera, Anton *2010*

Types of work

Adoption · Ancillary relief · Care proceedings · Child abduction · Child support · Children · Cohabitation · Common law (general) · Divorce · Domestic violence injunctions · Family law · Family provision · Financial provision · Matrimonial · Matrimonial finance · Pensions · Professional negligence · Unmarried couples · Wardship

Chambers Established 1965
Opening times: 8.30am - 7.00pm

Chambers' facilities

Conference Rooms

Disability access

Wheelchair access, Disabled parking available

Languages spoken

French, German, Hebrew, Spanish

Fees policy

Refer to clerks.

33 BEDFORD ROW

33 Bedford Row, London WC1R 4JH
020 7242 6476
Fax: 020 7831 6065; DX: 75 London Chancery Lane
E-mail: clerks@33bedfordrow.co.uk

Chambers of: Mrs C Whippman

Disability access

Staff briefed or trained on duties under the disability legislation, Wheelchair access, Disabled parking available, Induction loop or infra red system

D

36 BEDFORD ROW

36 Bedford Row, London WC1R 4JH
020 7421 8000
Fax: 020 7421 8035/020 7421 8080; DX: 360 Lde
E-mail: chambers@36bedfordrow.co.uk

Disability access
Staff briefed or trained on duties under the disability legislation, Wheelchair access, Induction loop or infra red system

42 BEDFORD ROW

London WC1R 4LL
020 7831 0222
Fax: 020 7831 2239; DX: 201 London Chancery Lane
E-mail: clerks@42br.com
URL: www.42br.com
Out of hours telephone: Steve Sheridan: 07850 484 244

Chambers of: Mr Frank Feehan QC
Clerks: Alan Brewer (Senior Clerk), Steve Sheridan, James Tidnam, Joe Shepherd; Administrator: Commercial Manager: Tony Charlick

Also at: Byrom Street Chambers, 12 Byrom Street, Manchester M3 4PP Tel: 0161 829 2100 Fax: 0161 8292101

Feehan, Frank QC *1988*
Cook, Tina QC *1988*
Hamlin, Patrick *1970*
Batchelor, Mark *1971*
Daiches, Michael *1977*
Newman, Philip *1977*
Utley, Charles *1979*
Treasure, Francis *1980*
Lederman, Howard *1982*
Azim, Rehna *1984*
Dabbs, David *1984*
Bennett, Jonathan *1985*
Rosenblatt, Jeremy *1985*
King, Fawzia *1985*
Braithwaite, Garfield *1987*
Taylor, Gemma *1988*
Phil-Ebosie, Sheila *1988*
Coster, Ronald *1989*
Jerman, Anthony *1989*
Haukeland, Martin *1989*
Kilcoyne, Desmond *1990*
Furniss, Richard *1991*
Lazarus, Mary *1991*
Todman, Deborah *1991*
Shield, Deborah *1991*
Murch, Stephen *1991*
Otwal, Mukhtiar *1991*
Uduje, Benjamin *1992*
Hawkes, Naomi *1994*
McKenna, Anna *1994*
McCormack, Philip *1994*
Woodward-Carlton, Damian *1995*
Choudhury, Fareha *1995*
Feldman, Matthew *1995*
Matthewson, Scott *1996*
Shepherd, Jude *1996*
Ahmad, Aysha *1996*
Whyte, Monica *1996*
Gardner, Eilidh *1997*
Thomas, Rebecca *1999*
Naughton, Sebastian *1999*
Gregory, Richard *2000*
Datta, Shomik *2000*
Little, Richard *2000*
Cassidy, Francis *2000*
Lee, Jessica *2000*
Holmes, Andrew *2000*
Stather, Julie *2000*
Ganteaume, Natalie *2001*
Ormond-Walshe, Sarah *2001*
Wood, Thomas *2002*
Phillips, Katie *2002*
Chaloner, Mark *2002*
Cameron, Robert *2003*
Walker, Maria-Amália *2003*
Tharoo, Safia *2004*
Holloway, Orlando *2004*
Adkin, Timothy *2004*
Robertson, Mary *2005*
Ferber, Iris *2005*
Webber, Ruth *2006*
Singer, Nicholas *2006*
Oganah, Janet *2007*
Clark, Neil *2007*
Minoprio, Delia *2007*
Barnes, Christopher *2008*
Testar, Philippa *2009*
Buckingham, Christopher *2009*
Newman, Jonathan *2009*
Conn, Francesca *2010*
Chakravarty, Anushka *2010*
Troy, Pauline *2011*
Kotilaine, Jennifer *2011*
Maxwell, Patrick *2011*

Types of work
Administrative law · Care proceedings · Chancery (general) · Chancery (land law) · Common law (general) · Company, commercial and competition · Construction law · Conveyancing · Education · Employment · Environment · Family law · Family provision · Housing · Insolvency · Insurance · Landlord and tenant · Licensing · Local authorities · Medical negligence · Mental health · Partnerships · Personal injury · Personal insolvency · Planning · Professional negligence · Sale and carriage of goods

Disability access
Staff briefed or trained on duties under the disability legislation, Wheelchair access, Disabled parking available

48 BEDFORD ROW

48 Bedford Row, London WC1R 4LR
020 7430 2005
Fax: 020 7831 4885; DX: 284 London Chancery Lane
E-mail: tyroon@partnershipcounsel.co.uk
URL: www.partnershipcounsel.co.uk
Out of hours telephone: 07751 022 914 (mobile)

Chambers of: Mr Roderick I'Anson Banks
Practice Manager: Mr Tyroon Win

Banks, Roderick I'Anson *1974*
Jelf, Simon Edward *1996*

Types of work
Limited Liability Partnerships · Limited Partnerships · Partnerships

Disability access
Staff briefed or trained on duties under the disability legislation, Wheelchair access

BEDLINGTON CHAMBERS

7 New Square, Lincoln's Inn, London WC2A 2QS
020 7831 1159
Fax: 020 7242 9744; DX: 149 Lde
E-mail: clerks@bedlingtonchambers.com

Chambers of: Mr J Morgan

7 BELL YARD

7 Bell Yard, London WC2A 2JR
020 7831 0636
Fax: 020 7831 0719; DX: 98 London Chancery Lane
E-mail: kevintarrant@btconnect.com

Chambers of: Mr C S N Van Hagen

9-12 BELL YARD

9-12 Bell Yard, London WC2A 2JR
020 7400 1800
Fax: 020 7404 1405; DX: 390 London Chancery Lane
E-mail: clerks@9-12bellyard.com
URL: www.9-12bellyard.com
Out of hours telephone: 07976 239064 (A May); 07813 001194 (S Parr)

Chambers of: Mr M Chawla QC
Clerks: Angela May (Senior Clerk), Steven Parr (First Junior Clerk), David Selsdon (Second Junior Clerk), Dean Begley (Third Junior Clerk), Fred Cross (Junior Clerk); Administration: Keith Secker; Senior Fees Clerk: Marc Jennings

Criminal Defence Service

Community Legal Service

Chawla, Mukul QC *1983*
Katz, Philip QC *1976*
Carlile of Berriew, Lord QC *1970*†
Birnbaum, Michael QC *1969*†
McGuinness, John QC *1980*†
Holland, Michael QC *1984*
Kaul, Kaly QC *1983*
Healy, Alexandra QC *1992*
Kinnear, Jonathan QC *1994*
Merz, Richard *1972*†
Barker, Alison *1973*
Heaton-Armstrong, Anthony *1973*
Wild, Simon *1977*
Orsulik, Michael *1978*
Chan, Dianne *1979*
Davies, Jonathan N *1981*
Smith, Alisdair *1981*
Briscoe, Constance *1983*†
Burton, Charles *1983*
Waddington, James *1983*
Harounoff, David *1984*
Bryant-Heron, Mark *1986*†
Hadley, Steven *1987*
Smith, David *1988*
Ellis, Sarah *1989*
Hughes, William *1989*†
Scutt, David *1989*
Chaplin, Adrian *1990*
Henderson, Lawrence *1990*
Seymour, Mark *1992*
Jory, Richard *1993*
Poku, Mary *1993*
Tatford, Warwick *1993*

Smaller, Elizabeth *1995*
Sugarman, Jason *1995*
Amarasinha, Revantha *1996*
Griffin, Neil *1996*
Carrasco, Glenn *1997*
Brown, Cameron *1998*
Selby, Sarah *1998*
Biggs, Stuart *1999*
Dunham, Nicholas *1999*
Paget, Henrietta *1999*
Huntley, Clare *2000*
Sharkey, Paul *2000*
Ward, Alexandra *2000*
Chapman, Nicholas *2001*
Dodd, Stephanie *2001*
Smith, Alastair *2001*
Stevenson, Daniel *2002*
Mannion, Amy *2003*
Newbold, Michael *2004*
Sternberg, Daniel *2006*
Watkinson, Howard *2006*
Hindmarsh, Luke *2007*
Hoskins, Thomas *2007*
Mackinnon, Laura *2007*
Sayer, Sebastian *2007*
Tyler, Katherine *2007*
Duncan, Katherine *2008*
Sareen, Ellis *2008*
Barnes, Natasha *2010*
Martin, William *2010*
Lawson Rogers, Stuart QC *1969*†*
Kerrigan, Herbert *1990**
Al-Yunusi, Abdullah *1994**
Watson, Hal *2003**

Types of work
Administrative law · Civil liberties · Commercial litigation · Common law (general) · Corporate fraud · Courts martial · Crime · Employment · Extradition · Inquests · Licensing · Local authorities · Mental health · Personal injury · Planning · Professional negligence · Regulatory and disciplinary law · Sport

Chambers Established 1965
Opening times: 8.30am - 6.30pm

Chambers' facilities
Chambers is fully computerised and work can be accepted in any digital format either on disk or by e-mail. We have dedicated conference rooms and can arrange video conferencing.

Disability access
Staff briefed or trained on duties under the disability legislation

Languages spoken
French, German, Gujarati, Hebrew, Hindi, Italian, Punjabi, Russian, Spanish, Urdu

Fees policy
Chambers endeavours to offer a fair and flexible pricing policy. If you wish to discuss fees please speak to the clerks who will be happy to help.

Additional information
9-12 Bell Yard is a leading set of barristers' chambers specialising in criminal law. All members of Chambers have experience and expertise in criminal litigation, both prosecuting and defending, and many individuals possess specialist knowledge in other fields, including common law, administrative law, licensing and the regulatory sector.

Advocacy and advisory work are undertaken for solicitors in City law firms and High Street practices. Other professional clients include the Crown Prosecution Service, Government departments, legal departments of major companies, and local authorities.

9-12 Bell Yard is committed to equal opportunities in all aspects of work, and has been awarded the Legal Services Commission's 'Quality Mark'.

9-12 Bell Yard has a long-established reputation in cases concerning fraud, corruption, murder and serious and organised crime. Nowadays we apply our criminal expertise to all types of proceeding. Professional disciplinary proceedings, Judicial Review, and all types of civil/criminal cross-over work are catered for by members of Chambers.

Our expertise is broadly based and extends to cases concerning:
— Serious fraud
— Money laundering
— Sexual offences
— Offences involving vulnerable witnesses, including children and the mentally disordered
— Murder and all offences against the person
— Property-related crime
— Drugs offences
— Confiscation and forfeiture proceedings
— Extradition and mutual legal assistance
— Professional disciplinary proceedings.

Advocacy and advisory work are undertaken for solicitors in City law firms as well as High Street practices around the UK. Other professional clients include the Crown Prosecution Service, Her Majesty's Revenue & Customs, the Serious Fraud Office, BERR (Department for Business, Enterprise and Regulatory Reform) legal departments.

BELL YARD CHAMBERS

116/118 Chancery Lane, London WC2A 1PP
020 7306 9292
Fax: 020 7404 5143; DX: 0075 London Chancery Lane
E-mail: byclerks@bellyardchambers.co.uk
URL: www.bellyardchambers.co.uk
Out of hours telephone: 020 8290 5129

Chambers of: Mr P J Sutton
Clerk: Mrs Karen Bardens

†Recorder *Door Tenant/Associate Member

Sutton, Philip *1971*
Gibson-Lee, David *1970*
Victor-Mazeli, Jacqueline *1997*
Bowen, Nicola *2003*
Dick, James *2003*
Mardner, Sharn *2003*
Kerner, Angela *1965**
Fridd, Nicholas *1975**
Hussain, Rafaquat *1996**

Types of work
Adoption · Alternative dispute resolution · Ancillary relief · Anti-social Behaviour Orders · Arbitration · Asylum · Breach of confidence · Care proceedings · Child care law · Children · Civil actions against the police · Civil law · Common law (general) · Computer crime · Conciliation · Confidential information · Confiscation of the proceeds of crime · Corporate fraud · Corporate manslaughter · Crime · Crime and criminal due process · Criminal judicial review · Disability discrimination · Disciplinary procedures · Disciplinary tribunals · Discrimination · Dispute resolution · Dispute resolution and arbitration · Divorce · Employment · Extradition · Family law · Firearms · Forfeiture · Fraud · Homicide · Immigration · International criminal law · Internet crime · Litigation · Malicious prosecution · Matrimonial · Matrimonial finance · Mediation · Motor vehicles · Police · Prison law · Private children law · Regulatory and disciplinary law · Road traffic · Road traffic offences · Serial crime · Serious fraud · Sexual Offences · Terrorism

Disability access
Staff briefed or trained on duties under the disability legislation, Wheelchair access

CHAMBERS OF MISS M BHAMRA

Victoria, London
07880 600 192
E-mail: mkbhamra@yahoo.co.uk

Chambers of: Miss M K Bhamra

4 BINGHAM PLACE

4 Bingham Place, London W1U 5AT
020 7486 5347
Fax: 020 7224 2077
E-mail: bhanji@regencyhotelwestend.co.uk

Disability access
Staff briefed or trained on duties under the disability legislation

177 BITTACY HILL

177 Bittacy Hill, London NW7 1RT
07775 535738
E-mail: rdaniellaw@aol.com

Chambers of: Mr R Daniel

Disability access
Staff briefed or trained on duties under the disability legislation, Disabled parking available

BLACKFRIARS CHAMBERS

79-83 Temple Chambers, 3-7 Temple Avenue, London EC4Y 0HP
020 7353 7400
Fax: 020 7353 7100; DX: 260 London Chancery Lane
E-mail: clerks@blackfriarschambers.com

Chambers of: Mr C E Moll

Disability access
Wheelchair access, Disabled parking available

BLACKSTONE CHAMBERS

Blackstone House, Temple, London EC4Y 9BW
020 7583 1770
Fax: 020 7822 7350; DX: 281 London Chancery Lane
E-mail: clerks@blackstonechambers.com
URL: www.blackstonechambers.com
Out of hours telephone: 020 7822 7272

Chambers of: Miss M G C Carss-Frisk QC, Mr A N G Peto QC
Senior Clerk: Gary Oliver; Chambers Director: Julia Hornor MA (Hons) (Oxon); Communications and Marketing Manager: Lesley Goodlet

Carss-Frisk, Monica QC *1985*
Peto, Anthony QC *1985*
Brodie, Stanley QC *1954*
Lester of Herne Hill, Lord QC *1963*
Beloff, Michael QC *1967†*
Donaldson, David QC *1968†*
Englehart, Robert QC *1969†*
Hunt, David QC *1969†*
Dohmann, Barbara QC *1971†*
Mendelson, Maurice QC *1965*
Harvie, Jonathan QC *1973†*
Pannick, Lord QC *1979†*
Jowell, Sir Jeffrey QC *1965*
Nathan, Stephen QC *1969†*
Howell, John QC *1979†*
Flint, Charles QC *1975*
Mill, Ian QC *1981*
Goulding, Paul QC *1984*
Beazley, Thomas QC *1979*
Page, Hugo QC *1977*
Shaw, Mark QC *1987*
Anderson, Robert QC *1986*

†Recorder *Door Tenant/Associate Member

Rose, Dinah QC *1989*
Fordham, Michael QC *1990*
Otty, Timothy QC *1990*
Eadie, James QC *1984*
Howe, Robert QC *1988*
Saini, Pushpinder QC *1991*
Lewis, Adam QC *1985*
Green, Andrew QC *1988*
Herberg, Javan QC *1992*
Hunter, Andrew QC *1993*
Beal, Kieron QC *1995*
De La Mare, Thomas QC *1995*
Goodwin-Gill, Guy *1971*
Clarke, Gerard *1986*
Whittaker, Simon *1987*
Briggs, Adrian *1989*
Hare, Ivan *1991*
Croxford, Thomas *1992*
Gledhill, Andreas *1992*
Pollard, Joanna *1993*
Collier, Jane *1994*
Dixon, Emma *1994*
White, Gemma *1994*
Mulcahy, Jane *1995*
Weisselberg, Tom *1995*
McCrudden, Christopher *1996*
Gallafent, Kate *1997*
George, Andrew *1997*
Weir, Claire *1998*
Callaghan, Catherine *1999*
Jaffey, Ben *1999*
Kennelly, Brian *1999*
Palmer, Stephanie *2000*
Powell, Leona *2000*
Sen Gupta, Diya *2000*
De Marco, Nicholas *2001*
Fatima, Shaheed *2001*
Pievsky, David *2001*
Windle, Victoria *2001*
Vinall, Mark *2002*
Donnelly, Catherine *2003*
Hickman, Tom *2003*
Weekes, Robert *2003*
Wilkinson, Sarah *2003*
Segan, James *2004*
Patel, Naina *2005*
Steele, Iain *2005*
Jones, Tristan *2006*
Richards, Tom *2006*
Boyd, Jessica *2007*
Mussa, Hanif *2007*
Pritchard, Simon *2007*
Lowe, David *2008*
Neill, Emily *2008*
Cleaver, Thomas *2009*
Luckhurst, Paul *2009*
Mountford, Thomas *2009*
Campbell, Fraser *2010*
Scott, Andrew *2010*
Sibbel, Shane *2010*

Types of work
Administrative law · Alternative dispute resolution · Arbitration · Asylum · Aviation · Banking · Chancery (general) · Civil fraud · Civil liberties · Commercial fraud · Commercial law · Commercial litigation · Commercial regulation · Commodities · Company law · Competition law · Confidential information · Conflict of laws · Constitutional law · Copyright · Corporate finance · Data protection · Defamation · Discrimination · Dispute resolution · EC competition law · ECHR · Education · Election law · Employment · Entertainment · Environment · European law · Financial services · Freedom of information · Freezing orders · Gaming and lotteries · Human rights · Immigration · Insolvency · Insurance · Intellectual property · International arbitration · International commercial arbitration · International human rights law · International law · International trade · Judicial review · Local authorities · Media and entertainment · Mediation · Partnerships · Passing off · Planning · Police · Prison law · Privacy · Procurement · Professional negligence · Public inquiries · Public law · Regulatory and disciplinary law · Restraint of trade · Sale and carriage of goods · Sport · State aid · Telecommunications

Disability access
Staff briefed or trained on duties under the disability legislation, Wheelchair access, Disabled parking available, Induction loop or infra red system

BOSTON MANOR CHAMBERS

69-75 Boston Manor Road, London TW8 9JJ
020 8567 5963
Fax: 020 8812 0781; DX: 159063 Ealing 7
E-mail: chambers@edriver.plus.com

Chambers of: Ms E R Driver

Disability access
Staff briefed or trained on duties under the disability legislation, Wheelchair access, Disabled parking available

4 BREAMS BUILDINGS

Chancery Lane, London EC4A 1HP
020 7092 1900
Fax: 020 7092 1999; DX: 441 London Chancery Lane
E-mail: clerks@4bb.co.uk

Chambers of: Mr S A Trimmer QC

Disability access
Wheelchair access, Induction loop or infra red system

CHAMBERS OF MS D BREHAN

4 Pair North, 3 Hare Court, Temple, London EC4Y 7BJ
07808 726877
E-mail: brennan_holahan@hotmail.com

Chambers of: Ms D Brehan

BRETTON WOODS LAW

New Broad Street House, 35 New Broad Street, London EC2M 1NH

ONE BRICK COURT

1st Floor, One Brick Court, Temple, London EC4Y 9BY
020 7353 8845
Fax: 020 7583 9144; DX: 468 London Chancery Lane
E-mail: clerks@onebrickcourt.com
URL: www.onebrickcourt.com
Out of hours telephone: 020 7353 8845

Chambers of: Mr A H Caldecott QC
Clerks: D Mace, M Warner; Administrator: Emma Billimore

Caldecott, Andrew QC *1975*
Rampton, Richard QC *1965*
Barca, Manuel QC *1986*
Starte, Harvey *1985*
Atkinson, Timothy *1988*
Phillips, Jane *1989*
Addy, Caroline *1991*
Evans, Catrin *1994*
Palin, Sarah *1999*
Eardley, Aidan *2002*
Glen, David *2002*
Helme, Ian *2005*
Wilson, Katharine *2005*
Kissin, Clare *2009*
Ready, Hannah *2010*
Scherbel-Ball, Jonathan *2010*
Garnier, Edward QC MP *1976**

Types of work
Defamation

Disability access
Staff briefed or trained on duties under the disability legislation, Disabled parking available

4 BRICK COURT

4 Brick Court, Temple, London EC4Y 9AD
020 7832 3200
Fax: 020 7797 8929; DX: 491 London Chancery Lane
E-mail: clerks@4bc.co.uk
URL: www.4bc.co.uk
Out of hours telephone: 07970 712955

Chambers of: Miss J V Mitchell
Clerks: Clive Barrett, Kevin McCarthy; Practice Manager: Mary Callaghan

Mitchell, Janet *1978*
Arlidge, Anthony QC *1962*
Knowles, Gwynneth QC *1993*
Medhurst, David *1969*
Chatterjee, Mira *1973*
Quinn, Susan *1983*
Davey, Helen *1984*
O'Brien, Haylee *1984*
Roberts, Marc *1984*
Whelan, Roma *1984*
Lynch, Peter *1985*
Moore, Finola *1988*
Azhar, Marina *1990*
Harrill, Jayne *1990*
Bright, Rachel *1991*
Watson, Isabelle *1991*
Gilliatt, Jacqueline *1992*
Pavlou, Paul *1993*
Lams, Barnabas *1995*
Morton, Rachael *1995*
Rawcliffe, Mark *1996*
Griffin, Ian *1997*
Jamil, Yasmeen *1998*
Bhachu, Sharan *1999*
Pepper, Judith *1999*
Purss, Nairn *1999*
MacLynn, Louise *2001*
Rahman, Tahmina *2001*
Bannocks, David *2002*
Dale, Lucy-Ann *2002*
Knott, Helen *2002*
Pearman, Lee *2003*
Butler, George Victor *2004*
Badejo, Bibi *2005*
Barrie, Laura *2005*
Davies, Gregory *2005*
Jagutpal, Previn *2005*
Potter, Timothy *2005*
Haworth, Sarah *2006*
Mason, Marc *2006*
Pugh, Kieran *2006*
Shaw, Ella *2006*
March, Natasha *2008*
Norman, James *2008*

Types of work
Civil law · Crime · Family law · Immigration

Disability access
Staff briefed or trained on duties under the disability legislation, Disabled parking available

BRICK COURT CHAMBERS

7-8 Essex Street, London WC2R 3LD
020 7379 3550
Fax: 020 7379 3558; DX: 302 London Chancery Lane
E-mail: clerks@brickcourt.co.uk
URL: www.brickcourt.co.uk
Out of hours telephone: 07768 614183 J Hawes and 07768 614193 I Moyler

Chambers of: Mr J W Hirst QC, Mr N N Green QC
Senior Clerks: Julian Hawes, Ian Moyler; Lyana Peniston (Pupillage)

Also at: 36 Avenue d'Auderghem, B 1040 Brussels Tel: +32 2 230 3161 Fax: +32 2 230 3347

Green, Nicholas QC *1986†*
Hirst, Jonathan QC *1975†*
Vaughan, David QC CBE *1963†*
Kentridge, Sydney QC *1977*
Heilbron, Hilary QC *1971*
Cran, Mark QC *1973†*
Charlton, Timothy QC *1974*
Gordon, Richard QC *1972†*
Hapgood, Mark QC *1979*
Howard, Mark QC *1980*
Ruttle, Stephen QC *1976*
Leggatt, George QC *1983†*
Wood, William QC *1980*
Hollander, Charles QC *1978†*
Anderson, David QC *1985†*
Otton-Goulder, Catharine QC *1983†*
Lord, Richard QC *1981*
Brealey, Mark QC *1984*
Swainston, Michael QC *1985*
Flynn, James QC *1978*
Lydiard, Andrew QC *1980†*
Calver, Neil QC *1987†*
Adam, Tom QC *1991*
Davies, Helen QC *1991*
Lord, Tim QC *1992*
Randolph, Fergus QC *1985*
Hoskins, Mark QC *1991*
MacLean, Alan QC *1993*
Robertson, Aidan QC *1995*
Slade, Richard QC *1987*
Matovu, Harry QC *1988*
Stratford, Jemima QC *1993*
Jowell, Daniel QC *1995*
Salzedo, Simon QC *1995*
Bools, Michael QC *1991*

†Recorder *Door Tenant/Associate Member

Demetriou, Marie QC *1995*
Brunner, Peter *1971*
Irvin, Peter *1972*
Lee, Sarah *1990*
Wright, Paul *1990*
Roxburgh, Alan *1992*
Haydon, Alec *1993*
Masefield, Roger *1994*
Dhillon, Jasbir *1996*
O'Donoghue, Robert *1996*
Reichert, Klaus SC *1996*
Thomas, Andrew *1996*
Chamberlain, Martin *1997*
Bacon, Kelyn *1998*
Birt, Simon *1998*
Gray, Margaret *1998*
West, Colin *1999*
Henshaw, Andrew *2000*
Lester, Maya *2000*
Pilbrow, Fionn *2001*
Saunders, Nicholas *2001*
Ford, Sarah *2002*
Midwinter, Stephen *2002*
Scannell, David *2003*
Wakefield, Victoria *2003*
Willis, Antony *2004*
Dawid, Jonathan *2005*
Hobson, Fred *2005*
Rothschild, Gerard *2005*
Abram, Sarah *2006*
Love, Sarah *2006*
Blakeley, Richard *2007*
Singla, Tony *2007*
Eschwege, Richard *2008*
Harrison, Edward *2008*
Morrison, Craig *2008*
Jones, Oliver *2009*
Plewman, Thomas *2009*
Piccinin, Daniel *2010*
Birdling, Malcolm *2011*
Sutton, Alastair *1972**
Wyatt, Derrick QC *1972**
MacRory, Richard CBE QC *1974**
Muchlinski, Peter *1981**
Woloniecki, Jan *1983**
Le Sueur, Andrew *1987**
Andenas, Mads *1997**

Types of work
Administrative law · Admiralty · Agriculture · Arbitration · Asset finance · Banking · Chancery (general) · Commercial litigation · Commodities · Common law (general) · Company, commercial and competition · Competition law · Conflict of laws · Construction law · Defamation · EC competition law · Employment · Entertainment · Environment · Financial services · Foreign law · Information technology · Insurance · International law · International trade · Local authorities · Media and entertainment · Professional negligence · Sale and carriage of goods · Shipping · Sport · Telecommunications

Disability access
Wheelchair access, Disabled parking available

30 BROOKSBY STREET

30 Brooksby Street, London N1 1HA
020 7607 3854
E-mail: peter.hayward@orange.net

Chambers of: Mr P M Hayward

Disability access
Disabled parking available

BRUNSWICK CHAMBERS

2 Middle Temple Lane, Temple, London EC4Y 9AA
020 7353 1987
Fax: 020 7583 1558
E-mail: alpha@brunswickchambers.net

Chambers of: Dr M A H P Von Pommern-Peglow

CHAMBERS OF MARTIN BURR

15 Old Bailey, London EC4M 7EF
0845 123 1234
Fax: 0845 430 4321
E-mail: clerks@barristerweb.com

Chambers of: Mr D M Kemp

Disability access
Staff briefed or trained on duties under the disability legislation, Wheelchair access, Disabled parking available

THE CHAMBERS OF NAVAZ BUSTANI

5 St John's Lane, London EC1M 4BH
07957 394258/020 7060 9760
Fax: 020 70609740
E-mail: navaz13@yahoo.co.uk

Chambers of: Ms N Bustani

CANARY WHARF CHAMBERS

Level 33, 25 Canada Square, London E14 5LQ
020 7183 8011
Fax: 020 7183 8830; DX: 42659 Isle Of Dogs
E-mail: admin@canarywharfchambers.com

Chambers of: Mr G D Reeds

CAPITAL FORTUNE CHAMBERS

Third Floor, 14 Nicholas Lane, London EC4N 7BN
0845 3630 430
Fax: 0845 3630 431
E-mail: rk@cfchambers.com

Chambers of: Mr R W Killeen

†Recorder *Door Tenant/Associate Member

CARMELITE CHAMBERS

9 Carmelite Street, London EC4Y 0DR
020 7936 6300
Fax: 020 7936 6301; DX: 226 Chancery Lane
E-mail: clerks@carmelitechambers.co.uk
URL: www.carmelitechambers.co.uk
Out of hours telephone: 07760 26195

Chambers of: Mr N R W Lambert QC
Clerks: Marc King, Matthew Butchard, Chris Mitchell, Dean Allen, Tom Barnes, Sophie Walsh, Lois Hayes; Administrator: Orla O'Sullivan; Fees Clerk: Norman Brooks, Sian Marsh

Lambert, Nigel QC *1974*†
Marshall-Andrews, Robert QC *1967*†
Lederman, David QC *1966*†
Hogg, Douglas QC *1968*
Taylor, William QC *1990*
Jones, John QC *1981*†
Bott, Charles QC *1979*
Csoka, Simon QC *1991*
Smith, Leonard QC *1991*
Orchard, Anthony QC *1991*
Corrigan, Peter *1972*
Cousens, Michael *1973*
Kogan, Barry *1973*
Brickman, Laura *1976*
Shields, Sonja *1977*
Gillard, Isabelle *1980*
Woodall, Peter *1983*
Molyneux, Simon *1986*
Clark, Peter *1988*
Taylor, Martin *1988*
Aylott, Colin *1989*
Fitzgibbon, Neil *1989*
Hargreaves, Ben *1989*
Henley, Christopher *1989*
James, Grahame *1989*
Kayne, Adrian *1989*
Johnston, Annie *1990*
Miah, Zac *1990*
Modgil, Sangita *1990*
Binder, Peter *1991*
England, William *1991*
Ventham, Tony *1991*
Jones, Howard *1992*
Button, Richard *1993*
Gruchy, Simon *1993*
Kane, Adam *1993*
Qazi, Ayaz *1993*
Sherratt, Mathew *1994*
Sweet, Louise *1994*
Walker, James *1994*
Bell, Alphege *1995*
Edwards, Nigel R *1995*
Harries, Mark *1995*
Lawson, Matthew *1995*
Panayi, Pavlos *1995*
Zoest, Jacqueline *1995*
Fosuhene, Amelia *1996*
Haeems, David *1996*
Morrell, Roxanne *1996*
Page, Jonathan *1996*
Tilbury, James *1996*
Stapleton, Elaine *1997*
Buckland, Matthew *1998*
Johnson, Gregory *1998*
Halliday-Davis, Lee *1999*
Hillman, Gerard *1999*
Knight, Graeme *1999*
Lawrence, Soraya *1999*
Mahmood, Saleema *1999*
Muir-Wilson, Louise *1999*
Spenwyn, Marie *1999*
Power, Laurie-Anne *2000*
Rawat, Houzla *2001*
Reiz, Stan *2001*
Hallworth, Andrew *2002*
King-Underwood, Gregory *2002*
Leake, Stephen *2002*
Webster, Shelley *2002*
Page, Douglas *2003*
Titus, Francesca *2003*
Cherrett, Darryl *2004*
O'Donoghue, Hugh *2004*
Rollin, Aron *2004*
Hendron, Ashley *2005*
Hocknell, Laura *2005*
Sheppard-Jones, Victoria *2005*
Spears, Katharine *2005*
McGowan, Laura *2006*
Hingston, Joe *2007*
Jarratt, Alice *2007*
Oborne, Jennifer *2007*
MacManus, Sabha *2008*

Types of work
Corporate fraud · Courts martial · Crime · Fraud · Health and safety

Disability access
Staff briefed or trained on duties under the disability legislation, Disabled parking available, Induction loop or infra red system

1 CHANCERY LANE

1 Chancery Lane, London WC2A 1LF
0845 634 6666
Fax: 0845 634 6667; DX: 364 London Chancery Lane
E-mail: clerks@1chancerylane.com
URL: www.1chancerylane.com
Out of hours telephone: 0845 634 6666

Chambers of: Mr J G Ross QC
Clerks: David Barrow, Clark Chessis; Administrator: Jenny Fensham; Business Manager: Genevieve Quierin, Fees: Audrey Cockram

Ross, John QC *1971*†
Faulks, Lord QC *1973*
Readhead, Simon QC *1979*†
Bishop, Edward QC *1985*
Warnock, Andrew QC *1993*
Hunter, William *1972*
Walmsley, Keith *1973*
Bryant, John *1976*
Goodman, Andrew *1978*
Norman, John *1979*
Yell, Nicholas *1979*
Hammerton, Alastair *1983*†
Waters, Julian *1986*
Rivalland, Marc *1987*
Althaus, Justin *1988*
Weddell, Geoffrey *1989*
Piper, Angus *1991*
Shuman, Karen *1991*
Chapman, Matthew *1994*
Stagg, Paul *1994*
Thomson, David *1994*
Collett, Ivor *1995*
Bredemear, Zachary *1996*
Jackson, Samantha *1996*
Mortimer, Sophie *1996*
Prager, Sarah *1997*
Waite, Kiril *1997*
Miller, Ian *1999*
Murray, Simon *2000*
Trigger, Simon *2000*
Hicks, Ben *2001*
Johnson, Laura *2001*
Khalid, Saleem *2001*
Revere, Carla *2001*
Harding, Jack *2004*
Spencer, Andrew *2004*
Clarke, Ian *2005*
Abbott, Roderick *2006*
Dobie, Lisa *2006*
Grant, Rebecca *2008*
Crockett, Thomas *2009*
McClenaghan, Frances *2009*

Types of work
Administrative law · Chancery (land law) · Civil liberties · Commercial litigation · Common law (general) · Conflict of laws · Construction law · Consumer law · Cross-border litigation and remedies · Discrimination · Education · Environment · Fire and other property damage claims · Franchising · Healthcare law · Highways · Housing · Human rights · Insurance · Landlord and tenant · Local authority claims · Medical negligence · Mental health · Personal injury · Police · Professional negligence · Real property · Social welfare · Sport · Travel law

D

Disability access
Wheelchair access, Disabled parking available

CHARTER CHAMBERS

D

charter

33 John Street, London WC1N 2AT
020 7618 4400
Fax: 020 7618 4401; DX: 429 London Chancery Lane
E-mail: clerks@charterchambers.com
URL: www.charterchambers.com
Out of hours telephone: 07184 597597

Chambers of: Mr J Lynch QC
Clerks: Lloyd Richards, Ian Sheridan, James Hall, Sam Kennett, Patrick Duane (Senior Clerk); Practice Manager: Chambers Director: Ian Payn; Fees Clerk: Chris Blake; Billing Clerk: Sandeep Bhandal

Lynch, Jerome QC *1983*
Solley, Stephen QC *1969*†
Greenberg, Joanna QC *1972*
Grunwald, Henry OBE QC *1972*
Bourne, Ian QC *1977*†
Rhodes, Nicholas QC *1981*†
Hawes, Neil QC *1989*
Tetlow, Bernard QC *1984*
Martin-Sperry, David *1971*
Batcup, David *1974*†
Higginson, Peter *1975*
Jackson, Calvin *1975*
Tomassi, Mark *1981*
Buxton, Thomas *1983*
Caddle, Sherrie *1983*
Taylor, David *1986*
Hamilton-Shield, Anna *1989*
Lavers, Michael *1990*
Deignan, Mary-Teresa *1991*
Phillips, Paul *1991*
Robinson, Claire *1991*
Adkin, Tana *1992*
Benzynie, Robert *1992*
Flanagan, Julia *1993*
Simpson, Jonathan *1993*
Chand, Ragveer *1994*
Goudie, Martin *1996*
Mohabir, Gerry *1996*
Darby, Rachel *1997*
Cross, Jason *1998*
Dos Santos, Alexander *1999*
James, Roderick *1999*
Gaskin, Leila *2000*
Snow, Darren *2000*
Gill, Rajinder *2001*
Mansfield, Kathrine *2001*
Maroof, Lara *2001*
Welsh, Abigail *2001*
Davis, William *2003*
Silcott, Tyrone *2004*
Esposito, Vincenzo *2005*
Barton, Chloe *2006*
Jamieson, Alexander *2007*
Weston, Craig *2007*
Wood, David *2007*
Renton, Oliver *2008*
Ewings, David *2009*
Bayley, Laura *2010*
Melleney, Peter *2010*

Types of work
Chancery (general) · Common law (general) · Courts martial · Crime · Family law · Family provision · Inquests · Insolvency · Local authorities · Malicious prosecution · Medical negligence · Personal injury · Professional negligence · Public access · Regulatory and disciplinary law

Opening times: 8.30am - 6.30pm

Chambers' facilities
Conference Rooms, Disks Accepted

Disability access
Staff briefed or trained on duties under the disability legislation

Languages spoken
French, German, Indonesian, Italian, Malay, Romanian, Spanish

CHL CHAMBERS

50 Colney Hatch Lane, Muswell Hill, London N10 1EA
020 8883 7706
Fax: 020 8883 7706
E-mail: acesreill@aol.com

Chambers of: Mrs L D Ponnampalam Reilly

Disability access
Wheelchair access, Disabled parking available

CLABENZ CHAMBERS

Palladia, Central Court, 25 Southampton Buildings, London WC2A 1AL
020 7129 1428

CLAPHAM LAW CHAMBERS

85 Landor Road, Clapham North, London SW9 9RT
020 7978 8482
Fax: 020 7642 5888; DX: 53263 Clapham Common
E-mail: DANNY@claphamlawchambers.co.uk

Disability access
Staff briefed or trained on duties under the disability legislation, Wheelchair access, Disabled parking available

CLERKSROOM (LONDON)

3rd Floor, 218 Strand, London WC2R 1AT
0845 083 3000
Fax: 0845 083 3001; DX: 232 London Chancery Lane
E-mail: mail@clerksroom.com

Disability access
Staff briefed or trained on duties under the disability legislation, Wheelchair access

CLOISTERS

1 Pump Court, Temple, London EC4Y 7AA
020 7827 4000
Fax: 020 7827 4100; DX: 452 London Chancery Lane
E-mail: clerks@cloisters.com

Chambers of: Mr R G B Allen QC

Disability access
Staff briefed or trained on duties under the disability legislation, Wheelchair access, Disabled parking available

CLOTH FAIR CHAMBERS

39-40 Cloth Fair, London EC1A 7NT
020 7710 6444
Fax: 020 7710 6446; DX: 321 London Chancery Lane
E-mail: email@clothfairchambers.com

Chambers of: Mr N R Purnell QC

Disability access
Staff briefed or trained on duties under the disability legislation, Wheelchair access, Disabled parking available

CORAM CHAMBERS

9-11 Fulwood Place, London WC1V 6HG
020 7092 3700
Fax: 020 7092 3777; DX: 404 London Chancery Lane
E-mail: mail@coramchambers.co.uk

Chambers of: Miss M J Cover

Disability access
Staff briefed or trained on duties under the disability legislation, Wheelchair access, Disabled parking available

CORNERSTONE BARRISTERS

cornerstone barristers

2-3 Gray's Inn Square, Gray's Inn, London WC1R 5JH
020 7242 4986
Fax: 020 7405 1166; DX: 316 London Chancery Lane
E-mail: chambers@2-3gis.co.uk
URL: www.cornerstonebarristers.com
Out of hours telephone: 07831 106972

Chambers of: Miss M J Cook, Mr J D C Findlay QC
Clerks: Martin Hart, Elliot Langdorf, Jason Savage, Paul Cray, Alex Hill, Taryn Butler; Practice Manager: Chief Executive: Warren Foot; Administrator: Rose Vance; Marketing Executive: Phil Desmondez

Also at: 2-3 Gray's Inn Square, One Caspian Point, Pierhead Street, Cardiff Bay, Cardiff CF10 4DQ

Cook, Mary *1982*
Findlay, James QC *1984*
Dinkin, Anthony QC *1968*†
Sauvain, Stephen QC *1977*†
Lowe, Mark QC *1972*†
Fraser, Vincent QC *1981*†
Ellis, Morag QC *1984*
Gasztowicz, Steven QC *1981*
Bird, Simon QC *1987*
McGuire, Bryan QC *1983*
Forlin, Gerard QC *1984*
Bhose, Ranjit QC *1989*
Stephenson, Geoffrey *1971*
Lamming, David *1972*
Alesbury, Alun *1974*
Thomas, Adrian Trevelyan *1974*
Stoker, Graham *1977*
Albutt, Ian *1981*
Shadarevian, Paul *1984*
Bedford, Michael *1985*
Druce, Michael *1988*
Rutledge, Kelvin *1989*
Clay, Jonathan *1990*
Holbrook, Jon *1991*
Green, Robin *1992*
Rowlands, Catherine *1992*
Townsend, Harriet *1992*
Hutchings, Matthew *1993*
Miller, Peter *1993*
Cosgrove, Thomas *1994*
Ground, Richard *1994*
Beglan, Wayne *1996*
Clarke, Rory *1996*
Lintott, David *1996*
Bhogal, Kuljit *1998*
Davies, Sian *1999*
Etiebet, Peggy *2001*
Murphy, Melissa *2001*
Ranatunga, Asitha *2001*
Welfare, Damien *2001*
Cannon, Josef *2002*
Parry, Clare *2005*
Weller, Sophie *2005*
King, Sinead *2006*
Kohli, Ryan *2006*
Oscroft, Jennifer *2006*
Flanagan, Hugh *2008*
Williams, Robert *2008*
Dring, Emma *2009*
Ponter, Ian *1993**
Easton, Jonathan *1996**

Types of work
Administrative law · Alternative dispute resolution · Anti-social Behaviour Orders · Arbitration · Boundaries · Chancery

†Recorder *Door Tenant/Associate Member

D

(commercial) · Chancery (general) · Chancery (land law) · Civil fraud · Civil law · Clinical negligence · Commercial planning · Commercial property · Compulsory Purchase · Constitutional and administrative law · Consumer credit · Consumer law · Contaminated land · Contracts · Coroner's inquests · Coroners · Corporate fraud · Corporate manslaughter · Courts martial · Crime · Criminal judicial review · Customs · Data protection · Defamation · Disability and health · Disasters · Disciplinary tribunals · Education · Election law · Employment · Environment · Food law · Fraud · Gaming and lotteries · Health and safety · Highways · Housing · Human rights · Immigration · Industrial deafness · Industrial diseases · Industrial relations law · Inquests · Internet gaming and licensing · Judicial review · Land compensation · Landlord and tenant · Lands Tribunal · Leasehold enfranchisement · Licensing · Local authorities · Local authority claims · Local authority liability · Local government finance · Mineral rights · Mining · Overseas accidents · Parliamentary · Personal injury · Planning · Pollution · Privy Council · Privy Council Appeals · Procurement · Product safety · Professional negligence · Public inquiries · Public law · Railways · Rating and CPO · Real property · Regulatory and disciplinary law · Rights of way · Road traffic · Serious fraud · Social security · Social services · Sport · Trade Descriptions Act · Trading standards · Transport and Works Act inquiries · Unincorporated associations · Utilities · Water

Opening times: 8.00am - 6.30pm

Chambers' facilities
Conference Rooms, Disks Accepted, Skype Conferencing, Direct-dial telephone, Voice-mail, Individual E-mail boxes, Website

Disability access
Staff briefed or trained on duties under the disability legislation, Wheelchair access, Disabled parking available

Languages spoken
Afrikaans, French, German, Greek, Italian, Spanish, Welsh

Fees policy
Fees will be negotiated with the clerks depending on the case and the seniority and experience of the selected counsel. The clerks will always strive to accommodate the particular requirements of each client, and flexible terms, including all-in fees, fixed rates and bulk billing can be arranged.

CORNERSTONE CHAMBERS

15 Old Bailey, London EC4M 7EF
020 3008 8392
Fax: 020 7371 6071
E-mail: anntayo7@gmail.com/anntayo@cornerstonechambrers.co/anntayo@cornerstonechambrers.com

Chambers of: Miss A I Tayo

COURT YARD CHAMBERS

Eltham Palace, P.O.370, London SE9 2RP
020 7936 2710
Fax: 020 7936 4004; DX: 32508 Eltham

Chambers of: Mr C M Ferguson

CHAMBERS OF MS M COUTINO

136 De Beauvoir Road, London N1 4DJ
07958 202997
E-mail: mlcoutino@googlemail.com

CHAMBERS OF MR A CRAIG

95 Court Lane, Dulwich, London SE21 7EF
020 8265 2290
E-mail: alistaircraig@btinternet.com

Chambers of: Mr A T Craig

CRANFORD CHAMBERS

8 Warwick Court, London WC1R 5DJ
020 7404 7454
E-mail: jemima.ivens@cranfordchambers.com

CROMWELL-AYEH-KUMI CHAMBERS

25 Taylors Green, London W3 7PF
020 8740 6982
Fax: 020 8740 6982
E-mail: ishmaelkumi@gmail.com

Chambers of: Mr I J Kumi

CROWN OFFICE CHAMBERS

2 Crown Office Row, Temple, London EC4Y 7HJ
020 7797 8100
Fax: 020 7797 8101; DX: 80 London Chancery Lane
E-mail: mail@crownofficechambers.com
URL: www.crownofficechambers.com
Out of hours telephone: 07931 328751 (Andy Flanagan)

Chambers of: Mr R D Lynagh QC
Clerk: Andy Flanagan (Senior Managing Clerk)

Bartlett, Andrew QC *1974*†
Lynagh, Richard QC *1975*†
Harvey, Michael QC *1966*†
Machell, Raymond QC *1973*†
Spencer, Michael QC *1970*†
Purchas, Christopher QC *1966*†
Tattersall, Geoffrey QC *1970*†
Allan, David QC *1974*†
Kent, Michael QC *1975*†
Turner, Mark QC *1981*†
Hunter, Winston QC *1985*†
Melton, Christopher QC *1982*†
Waite, Jonathan QC *1978*
Bickford-Smith, Margaret QC *1973*†
Rowley, James QC *1987*†
Curtis, Michael QC *1982*
Heaton, David QC *1983*†
Rigney, Andrew QC *1992*
Platt, David QC *1987*
Berkin, Martyn *1966*
Matthews, Dennis *1973*
Nixon, Colin *1973*
Davies, Nicholas *1975*
Stevenson, John *1975*
Greenbourne, John *1978*
Phillips, Andrew *1978*
Catford, Gordon *1980*
Field, Julian *1980*
Dean, Paul *1982*
Jones, Charlotte *1982*†
Coles, Steven *1983*
Williams, A John *1983*
Franklin, Kim *1984*
Cooper, John *1985*
Ferris, Shaun *1985*
Medd, James *1985*
Pearce, Richard *1985*†
Foster, Catherine *1986*
Brown, Simon J *1988*
Hatfield, Sally *1988*†
Morton, Peter *1988*
Vandyck, William *1988*
Woolgar, Dermot *1988*
Snowden, Steven *1989*
Wright, Ian *1989*
Ageros, James *1990*
Evans-Tovey, Jason *1990*
Power, Erica *1990*
Howarth, Simon *1991*
Gee, Toby *1992*
Hitching, Isabel *1992*
Antelme, Alexander *1993*
Blakesley, Patrick *1993*
Burns, Peter *1993*
Ruck, Mary *1993*
Tyrrell, Richard *1993*
Allen, Darryl *1995*
Antrobus, Simon *1995*
Balysz, Mark *1995*
Chalmers, Suzanne *1995*
Maxwell-Scott, James *1995*
Stokell, Robert *1995*
Toogood, Claire *1995*
Broome, Edward *1996*
Davis, Andrew *1996*
Haque, Muhammed *1997*
Kay, Dominic *1997*
Lindsey, Susan *1997*
Ferro, Jack *1998*
Horne, Julian *1998*
Laney, Anna *1998*
Quiney, Ben *1998*
Woodbridge, Victoria *1998*
Armitage, Mark *1999*
Mauladad, Farrah *1999*
Shapiro, Daniel *1999*
Boyle, Matthew *2000*
MacPherson, Alexander *2000*
Chern, Cyril *2001*
Pimlott, Charles *2001*
Taylor, Rebecca *2001*
Davis, Justin *2003*
De Gregorio, Michele *2003*
Vann, Harry *2003*
Winser, Crispin *2003*
Hellebronth, Rosanna *2004*
Houghton, Peter *2005*
Kendrick, Julia *2005*
Atkins, Michael *2006*
Boon, Elizabeth *2006*
Myhill, David *2006*
Sage, Richard *2006*
Smith, Andrew QC *2006*
Lambertsen, Siobhan *2007*
Whittaker, Nadia *2007*
Pagett, Helen *2008*
Holmes, Rory *2009*
MacAulay, Jack *2009*
Parratt, David *2009*
McColgan, Caroline *2010*
Taczalski, Carlo *2010*

Types of work
Adjudication · Arbitration · Chancery · Clinical negligence · Commercial law · Costs · Engineering disputes · Healthcare law · Industrial diseases · Mediation · Personal injury · Product liability · Professional negligence · Regulatory and disciplinary law

Opening times: 8.00am - 7.00pm

Chambers' facilities
Conference Rooms, Video Conference, Fully administered ADR service available

Disability access
Staff briefed or trained on duties under the disability legislation, Wheelchair access, Disabled parking available

Languages spoken
French, German, Italian

Fees policy
Crown Office Chambers is committed to a realistic and flexible approach. Hourly rates are available upon application. Estimates of likely total fees will be provided if requested. Conditional fee work is undertaken as well as direct access work.

†Recorder *Door Tenant/Associate Member

D

1 CROWN OFFICE ROW

1 Crown Office Row, Temple, London EC4Y 7HH
020 7797 7500
Fax: 020 7797 7550; DX: 1020 London Chancery Lane
E-mail: mail@1cor.com
URL: www.1cor.com
Out of hours telephone: 07808 583447

Chambers of: The Hon P N Havers QC
Clerks: Matthew Phipps (Senior Clerk), Andrew Tull, John McLaren, Thomas Lawrance; Chambers Director: Bob Wilson

Also at: Crown Office Row Chambers, 119 Church Street, Brighton, Sussex BN1 1UD

Havers, Philip QC *1974*
Seabrook, Robert QC *1964*†
Badenoch, James QC *1968*†
Miller, Stephen QC *1971*†
Coonan, Kieran QC *1971*†
Coghlan, Terence QC *1968*†
Mansfield, Guy QC *1972*†
Smith, Sally QC *1977*
Gumbel, Elizabeth-Anne QC *1974*
Rees, Paul QC *1980*
Bowron, Margaret QC *1978*†
Garnham, Neil QC *1982*†
Balcombe, David QC *1980*†
Glynn, Joanna QC *1983*
Hart, David QC *1982*
Forde, Martin QC *1984*
Edis, William QC *1985*†
Lambert, Christina QC *1988*
McCullough, Angus QC *1990*
Whipple, Philippa QC *1994*
Whitting, John QC *1991*
Evans, David QC *1988*
King-Smith, James *1980*
Gimlette, John *1986*
Wheeler, Marina *1987*
Witcomb, Henry *1989*
Kennedy, Andrew *1989*
Downs, Martin *1990*
Cave, Jeremy *1992*
Booth, Richard *1993*
Colin, Giles *1994*
Chawatama, Sydney *1994*
Lambert, Sarah *1994*
Levinson, Justin *1994*
Thomas, Owain *1995*
Hyam, Jeremy *1995*
Sanders, Oliver *1995*
Rahman, Shaheen *1996*
Bradley, Clodagh *1996*
Skelton, Peter *1997*
Taylor, Zoe *1998*
Sheldon, Neil *1998*
Neenan, Caroline *1999*
Smith, Richard *1999*
Mellor, Christopher *1999*
Kellar, Robert *1999*
Barnes, Matthew *2000*
O'Donnell, Iain *2000*
Singh, Sarabjit *2001*
Manknell, David *2001*
Lambert, Suzanne *2002*
Rogerson, Judith *2003*
Strugo, Andrea Lindsay *2003*
Mannion, Amy *2003*
Wastell, Robert *2004*
Mumford, Richard *2004*
Jolliffe, John *2005*
Marcus, Rachel *2005*
Rathod, Pritesh *2006*
Cross, Caroline *2006*
Donmall, Matthew *2006*
Beattie, Kate *2007*
Wagner, Adam *2007*
McArdle, Isabel *2008*
Hill, Matthew *2009*
Henderson, Alasdair *2009*
Flinn, Matthew *2010*
Roche, Maria *2010*
Eskerie, Karwan *2010*

Types of work
Administrative law · Asylum · Clinical negligence · Common law (general) · Construction law · Coroners · Costs · Crime · Discrimination · Divorce · Employment · Environment · Health and safety · Healthcare law · Human rights · Immigration · Judicial review · Matrimonial finance · Mediation · Medical law · Mental health · Military law · Personal injury · Prison law · Professional negligence · Public law · Regulatory and disciplinary law · Road traffic · Sale and carriage of goods · Sport · VAT

Disability access
Staff briefed or trained on duties under the disability legislation, Wheelchair access, Disabled parking available

CHAMBERS OF DENIS DALY

6 Maresfield Gardens, Hampstead, London NW3 5SU
07809 465658
E-mail: den.daly@gmail.com

Chambers of: Mr D M P S Daly

CHAMBERS OF FRANCIS DAVEY

Flat 8, Manor Lea, 295 Green Lanes, London N4 2EU
020 8442 8099
Fax: 020 7788 3404; DX: 57451 Finsbury Park
E-mail: fjmdla@gmail.com

Chambers of: Mr F J M Davey

CHAMBERS OF MR KARL DAVIES

17 Burnhill House, Norman Street, London EC1V 3PQ
07932 044635
E-mail: karlldavies@hotmail.com

Chambers of: Mr K L Davies

 †Recorder *Door Tenant/Associate Member

DEAL CHAMBERS

60 Moordown, Shooters Hill, London SE18 3NG
020 8856 8738
Fax: 0871 7146140
E-mail: clerk@dealchambers.co.uk

Chambers of: Mr T J Deal

Disability access
Staff briefed or trained on duties under the disability legislation, Disabled parking available

DEKOVEN CHAMBERS

8 Stone Buildings, Lincoln's Inn, London WC2A 3TA
020 7831 9521
E-mail: rdk@dekovenchambers.com

Chambers of: Mr R M Dekoven

DESIGN CHAMBERS

24 Arterberry Road, Wimbledon, London SW20 8AH
020 7353 0747
Fax: 020 8947 3869
E-mail: manager@designchambers.com

Chambers of: Mr R A Hodgson

Disability access
Staff briefed or trained on duties under the disability legislation, Disabled parking available

DEVEREUX CHAMBERS

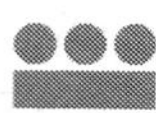

devereux

Queen Elizabeth Building, Temple, London EC4Y 9BS
020 7353 7534
Fax: 020 7583 5150; DX: 349 London Chancery Lane
E-mail: clerks@devchambers.co.uk
URL: www.devereuxchambers.co.uk
Out of hours telephone: 07825 331123

Chambers of: Miss I A Simler QC
Clerks: Vince Plant (Head of Clerking Services), Glenn Billenness (Deputy Senior Clerk); Practice Manager: Cheri Tidman, Will Jackman (Senior Clerks), Lisa Happe (Business Development Manager); Administrator: Mark Noble (Office and Facilities Manager); Chief Executive Officer: Beverly Landais; Finance Manager: Susan Murray (Senior Accounts Manager)

Simler, Ingrid QC *1987*†
Edelman, Colin QC *1977*†
Glancy, Robert QC *1972*†
Brennan, Timothy QC *1981*†
Fisher, Jonathan QC *1980*
Read, Graham QC *1981*
Killalea, Stephen QC *1981*
Wynter, Colin QC *1984*
Carr, Bruce QC *1986*†
Weir, Robert QC *1992*
Bard, Nicholas *1979*
Mendoza, Colin *1983*
Silvester, Bruce *1983*
Hyams, Oliver *1989*
Randall, Nicholas *1990*
Harrison, Richard *1991*
Edwards, Peter *1992*
Padfield, Alison *1992*
Burns, Andrew *1993*†
Cartwright, Richard *1994*
Sethi, Mohinderpal *1996*
Cottrell, Stephen *1998*
Nawbatt, Akash *1999*
Catherwood, Shaen *2000*
Hunter, Robert *2000*
Belgrove, Sophie *2001*
Lynch, Ben *2001*
Mayhew, Alice *2001*
Watson, Sarah *2002*
Butters, Jonathan *2003*
Bell, Laura *2004*
Harris, Lucinda *2004*
Vonberg, Thomas *2004*
Barsam, Talia *2006*
Cordrey, Thomas *2006*
Nicholls, Samuel *2006*
Stone, Christopher *2007*
Carse, Alice *2008*
Balmer, Kate *2009*
Crozier, Jesse *2009*
Hirsch, Georgina *2009*
Royle, Richard *1983**
Frith, Timothy *1996**

Types of work
Administrative law · Arbitration · Capital tax · Civil liberties · Commercial litigation · Commercial property · Common law (general) · Company, commercial and competition · Construction law · Consumer law · Corporate fraud · Discrimination · Education · Employment · Entertainment · Environment · Health and safety · Human rights · Income tax · Information technology · Insurance · Local authorities · Medical negligence · Mental health ·

†Recorder *Door Tenant/Associate Member

D

Pensions · Personal injury · Professional negligence · Sale and carriage of goods · Sport · Telecommunications

Chambers Established 1948
Opening times: 8.00am - 7.00pm (24-hr answering service available)

Chambers' facilities
Conference Rooms, Disks Accepted, Video Conference, Disabled access and facilities, Law Society accredited seminar programme Fully networked IT system, e-mail, voicemail, Instructions accepted on a conditional fee basis in accordance with recommended conditional fee agreements

Disability access
Staff briefed or trained on duties under the disability legislation, Wheelchair access, Disabled parking available, Induction loop or infra red system

Languages spoken
French, Spanish

Fees policy
Devereux aims to offer competitive rates which the clerks will be happy to discuss. Estimates of fees will be given on request.

CHAMBERS OF THOMAS DILLON

25 Howitt Close, London NW3 4LX
020 7692 2722
E-mail: post@contentadvice.eu

Chambers of: Mr T W M Dillon

THE CHAMBERS OF J DINGLE & H HODGKIN

3rd Floor, 218 Strand, London WC2R 1DR
0845 083 3000
Fax: 0845 083 3001; DX: 232 London Chancery Lane
E-mail: mail@clerksroom.com

Chambers of: Mr H J Hodgkin, Mr J C Dingle

Disability access
Staff briefed or trained on duties under the disability legislation, Wheelchair access

DOLLIS HILL CHAMBERS

197 Ellesmere Road, London NW10 1LG
020 8208 1663
Fax: 020 8208 1663

Chambers of: Mr G M G Haque

Disability access
Staff briefed or trained on duties under the disability legislation, Disabled parking available

DOUGHTY STREET CHAMBERS

53-54 Doughty Street, London WC1N 2LS
020 7404 1313
Fax: 020 7404 2283; DX: 223 London Chancery Lane
E-mail: enquiries@doughtystreet.co.uk
URL: www.doughtystreet.co.uk
Out of hours telephone: 020 7404 1313 (24 hours with emergency numbers)

Chambers of: Mr E H Fitzgerald QC CBE, Mr G R Robertson QC
Clerks: Chris Errity, Richard Bayliss, Mark Byrne, Arsineh Gaspariance, Richard Goodman, Emily Martin, Rob Joyce, Eresha Reid, Paul Read, Sian Wilkins, Anthony Ward, Dan Sullivan, Rachel Finch, Callum Stebbing, Graham Briggs (Criminal), Paul Friend (Civil); Head of Facilities: Sarah Earl; Business Development Coordinator: Sean Collum; Finance Manager: Andreas Michaelidies

Also at: Doughty Street Chambers, Pall Mall Court, 61-67 King Street, Manchester, M2 4PD Tel: 0161 618 1066 Fax: 020 7404 2283/84

Also at: Doughty Street Chambers, 5th Floor, Broad Quay House, Prince Street, Bristol, BS1 4DJ Tel: 01179 058 717 Fax: 020 7404 2283/84

Fitzgerald, Edward QC CBE *1978*
Robertson, Geoffrey QC *1973†*
Kennedy of the Shaws, Helena QC *1972*
O'Connor, Patrick QC *1970*
Sallon, Christopher QC *1973†*
Gibson, Christopher QC *1976†*
Rees, Edward QC *1973*
Wood, James QC *1975†*
Millar, Gavin QC *1981†*
Hall, Andrew QC *1991*
Rogers, Heather QC *1983†*
Williams, Heather QC *1985*
Oppenheim, Robin QC *1988†*
Bowen, Nicholas QC *1984*
Hermer, Richard QC *1993*
Forshall, Isabella QC *1982*
Westgate, Martin QC *1985*
Whitfield, Jonathan QC *1985*
Fitzgibbon, Francis QC *1986*

Hislop, David QC *1989*
Wise, Ian QC *1992*
Brimelow, Kirsty QC *1991*
Kaufmann, Phillippa QC *1991*
Farbey, Judith QC *1992*
Bowen, Paul QC *1993*
Trowler, Rebecca QC *1995*
Cayley, Andrew QC *2007*
Carter, David *1971*
Latham, Robert *1976*
Paul, Nicholas *1980*
Hough, Christopher *1981*
Markus, Kate *1981*
Bentley, David *1984*
Bloom, Tracey *1984*
Evans, Jill *1986*
Samuel, Gerwyn *1986*
Weereratne, Aswini *1986*
Soertsz, Lauren *1987*
Hatfield, Sally *1988*†
Brown, Nicholas *1989*
Stone, Joseph *1989*
Taylor, Paul *1989*
Reeder, Stephen *1991*
Whitaker, Quincy *1991*
Cooper, Jonathan *1992*
Cox, Simon *1992*
Jones, John R W D *1992*
Pullen, Tim *1993*
Walsh, John *1993*
Draycott, Paul *1994*
Fisher, Richard *1994*
Grey, Siobhan *1994*
Henderson, Mark *1994*
Sparks, Paula *1994*
Bowers, Rupert *1995*
Brown, Althea *1995*
Chataway, Benjamin *1995*
Jordash, Wayne *1995*
MacKie, Jeannie *1995*
Preston, Dominic *1995*
Cragg, Stephen *1996*
Elliott, Sarah *1996*
Hudson, Anthony *1996*
Mukherjee, Tublu *1996*
Toms, Nick *1996*
Burnham, Ulele *1997*
Durance, Alex *1997*
Hill, Henrietta *1997*
Johnson, Lindsay *1997*
Middleton, Joseph *1997*
Powles, Steven *1997*
Stanage, Nick *1997*
Arshad, Farrhat *1998*
Lownds, Peter *1998*
Shepherd, Jim *1998*
Burton, Jamie *1999*
Cooper, Ben *1999*
Hobson, John *1999*
Kilroy, Charlotte *1999*
Narain, Benjamin *1999*
Bennett, Daniel *2000*
Lemer, David *2000*
Mushtaq, *2000*
Vassall-Adams, Guy *2000*
Brander, Ruth *2001*
Hart, Amanda *2001*
Haywood, Phil *2001*
Marquis, Piers *2001*
Sleeman, Susan *2001*
Waldman, Amos *2001*
Walker, Liam *2001*
Dubinsky, Laura *2002*
Power, Eloise *2002*
Rhodes, David *2002*
Thomas, Richard *2002*
Eastwood, Philippa *2003*
Gerry, Alison *2003*
MacKenzie, Alasdair *2004*
Newton, Ben *2004*
Suterwalla, Azeem *2004*
Haines, David *2005*
Higgins, Nichola *2005*
Gallagher, Caoilfhionn *2006*
Hobcraft, Gemma *2006*
Price, Louise *2006*
Annand, Kate *2007*
Grady, Kate *2007*
Okewale, Tunde *2007*
Pickup, Alison *2007*
Timan, Annabel *2007*
Broach, Stephen *2008*
Gask, Alexander *2008*
Knorr, Michelle *2008*
Lambert, Harry *2008*
Meredith, Catherine *2008*
Stevens, Thomas *2008*
Brownhill, Ian *2009*
Peevers, Charlotte *2009*
Silverstone, Benjamin *2009*
Alamuddin, Amal *2010*
Grubeck, Nikolaus *2010*
Pilkington, Andrew *2010*
Scott-Mason, Holly *2010*
Harris, Paul *1976**
Kadri, Sadakat *1989**
Grief, Nicholas *1996**

Types of work

Administrative law · Civil actions against the police · Civil liberties · Common law (general) · Copyright · Corporate fraud · Crime · Defamation · Discrimination · Education · Employment · Environment · Extradition · Housing · Human rights · Immigration · Intellectual property · International law · Landlord and tenant · Local authorities · Media and entertainment · Medical negligence · Mental health · Personal injury · Prisoners' rights · Professional negligence · Public law · Regulatory and disciplinary law

Disability access

Staff briefed or trained on duties under the disability legislation, Wheelchair access, Disabled parking available, Induction loop or infra red system

D

2 DR JOHNSON'S BUILDINGS

2 Dr Johnson's Buildings, Temple, London EC4Y 7AY
020 7936 2613
Fax: 020 7353 9439; DX: 210 London Chancery Lane
E-mail: clerks@2drj.com

Chambers of: Mr D M Love

Disability access

Staff briefed or trained on duties under the disability legislation, Disabled parking available

3 DR JOHNSON'S BUILDINGS

Three Dr Johnson's Buildings

Ground Floor, 3 Dr Johnson's Buildings, Temple, London EC4Y 7BA
020 7353 4854
Fax: 020 7583 8784; DX: 1009 London Chancery Lane
E-mail: clerks@3djb.co.uk
URL: www.3djb.co.uk

Chambers of: Mr A M Szerard
Clerk: J E Hubbard

Szerard, Andrei *1986*
Hay, Malcolm *1972*
Allston, Anthony *1975*
Harris, Annmarie *1975*
Sabido, John *1976*
Limbrey, Bernard *1980*
Birks, Simon *1981*
Hasan, Ayesha *1987*
Maxwell, Judith *1988*
Moss, Norman *1990*
Teggin, Victoria *1990*
Glanville, Susan *1991*
Johal, Sukhjinder *1991*
Hellens, Matthew *1992*
Peacock, Lisa *1992*
Carter, Holly *1993*
Cronshaw, Michael *1993*
Le Quesne, Catherine *1993*
Redford, Jessica *1994*

†Recorder *Door Tenant/Associate Member

Steadman, Russell *1995*
Barnes, Luke *1996*
Jones, Mark *1997*
Squire, Philip *1997*
Davies, Adrian *1998*
Mayhew, Judith *2000*
Kerr, Neil *2001*
Lashbrook, Kellie *2001*
Zeitler, Barbara *2001*
Piskolti, Catherine *2003*
Wilkinson, Peter *2003*
Beer, Emily *2004*
Bennett, Angela *2005*
Islam, Saiful *2005*
Lawrence, Samantha *2005*
Birtchnell, Benjamin *2009*
Brindle, Jessica *2009*
Palmer, Briony *2009*
Erwood, Heather *1993**
Ellis, Catherine *2003**

Types of work
Care proceedings · Chancery (general) · Common law (general) · Education · Employment · Entertainment · Family law · Family provision · Foreign law · Housing · Judicial review · Landlord and tenant · Personal injury

Chambers Established 1944
Opening times: 8.45am - 6.15pm

Chambers' facilities
Telephone Conferencing

Disability access
Staff briefed or trained on duties under the disability legislation, Disabled parking available

Languages spoken
Croatian, Farsi, French, Urdu

DYERS CHAMBERS

35 Bedford Row, London WC1R 4JH
020 7404 1881
Fax: 020 7404 1991; DX: 175 London Chancery Lane
E-mail: admin@dyerschambers.com

Chambers of: Mr Andrew Campbell-Tiech QC

Disability access
Staff briefed or trained on duties under the disability legislation, Wheelchair access, Disabled parking available

EDULAW CHAMBERS

127 Abbots Gardens, London N2 0JJ

ELY PLACE CHAMBERS

30 Ely Place, London EC1N 6TD
020 7400 9600
Fax: 020 7400 9630; DX: 291 London Chancery Lane
E-mail: admin@elyplace.com
URL: www.elyplace.com
Out of hours telephone: 07885 469845/ 07736 288055/07870 128617

Chambers of: Mr William McCormick
Senior Clerk: Christopher Drury; Practice Manager: Christopher Drury (Chambers Director); Administrator: Richard Sheehan; Kevin Morrow, Carol Belford, Dave Lovitt

McCormick, William QC *1985*
Thwaites, Ronald QC *1970*
Stewart, Nicholas QC *1971*
Willer, Robert *1970*
Evans, William *1977†*
Daniels, Iain *1992*
Barlow, Craig *1992*
Stone, Russell *1992*
Preston, David *1993*
Sinai, Ali *1997*
Perhar, Simon *1997*
Crew, Gillian *1998*
Salter, Michael *1999*
Newman, James *2000*
Sadiq, Faisel *2000*
Ahmed, Bushra *2001*
Samson, John *2001*
Blackmore, Sally *2003*
Mitchell, David *2004*
Price, Jonathan *2004*
Stroud, Amy *2004*
Ryan, Liam *2007*
Briggs, Aidan *2009*
Powlesland, Paul *2009*
Urquhart, Catherine *2010*
Cole, Max *2011*
Friston, Mark *1997**
Pearman, Scott *1999**
Hughes, Paul *2001**

Disability access
Staff briefed or trained on duties under the disability legislation, Wheelchair access, Disabled parking available

EMMANUEL CHAMBERS

66 Daubeney Road, London E5 0EF
020 8985 3030
Fax: 020 8985 3030
E-mail: AYOJOSEPH@aol.com

Chambers of: Mrs E A A Joseph

ENFIELD CHAMBERS

21 Natal Road, Bounds Green, London N11 2HU
07973 910880

CHAMBERS OF MS JOHANNE ENRIGHT

19 William Blake House, 1 - 6 Dufour's Place, London W1F 7SQ
020 7287 7557; DX: 37202 Piccadilly

Chambers of: Ms J Enright

ENTERPRISE CHAMBERS

9 Old Square, Lincoln's Inn, London WC2A 3SR
020 7405 9471
Fax: 020 7242 1447; DX: 301 London Chancery Lane
E-mail: london@enterprisechambers.com
URL: www.enterprisechambers.com
Out of hours telephone: 07780 671478

Chambers of: Mr B R Weatherill QC
Clerks: Antony Armstrong (Senior Clerk), Mark Belford, Michael Ireland, Charlotte Temple, Luke Daws; Accounts Manager: Hannah Steininger-Nath

Also at: Enterprise Chambers, 43 Park Square, Leeds LS1 2NP

Also at: Enterprise Chambers, 65 Quayside, Newcastle Upon Tyne NE1 3DE

Weatherill, Bernard QC *1974†*
Arden, Peter QC *1983*
Bhaloo, Zia QC *1990*
James, Michael *1976*
Morgan, Charles *1978*
Hutton, Caroline *1979*
Groves, Hugo *1980*
Ife, Linden *1982*
Barker, James *1984*
Zelin, Geoffrey *1984*
Jack, Adrian *1986†*
Jarron, Stephanie *1990*
Pickering, James *1991*
Duddridge, Robert *1992*
Jory, Hugh *1992*
Klein, Jonathan *1992*
Noble, Andrew *1992*
Williamson, Bridget *1993*
Francis, Edward *1995*
Mauger, Shanti *1996*
Ilyas, Shaiba *1998*
Calland, Timothy *1999*
Rodger, Jonathan *1999*
Johnson, Simon *2000*
McCulloch, Niall *2000*
West, Matthew *2000*
Murphy, Damian *2001*
Page, Rebecca *2001*
Jackson, Claire *2002*
Beswetherick, Anthony *2003*
Kalfon, Olivier *2003*
Griffin, Margaret *2004*
Gunaratna, Kavan *2004*
Toman, Cristin *2004*
Markandya, Susannah *2005*
Bond, Kelly *2007*
Heath, Duncan *2007*
Burslem, Sarah *2008*
Gale, Phillip *2008*
Meech, Jennifer *2008*
Davies, James *2009*
Maddison, Matthew *2010*

Types of work
Agriculture · Arbitration · Banking · Chancery (commercial) · Chancery (general) · Commercial law · Commercial litigation · Commercial property · Company law · Conveyancing · Environment · Equity · Housing · Insolvency · Landlord and tenant · Licensing · Mediation · Partnerships · Personal insolvency · Professional negligence · Real property · Succession · Trusts · Wills

Disability access
Staff briefed or trained on duties under the disability legislation, Wheelchair access, Disabled parking available

EQUITY COURT CHAMBERS

3 Rectory Close, London SW20 9DQ
07890 994550
Fax: 0191 209 6195
E-mail: m_a_hay@yahoo.co.uk

Chambers of: Mr M A Hay

ERSKINE CHAMBERS

33 Chancery Lane, London WC2A 1EN
020 7242 5532
Fax: 020 7831 0125; DX: 308 London Chancery Lane
E-mail: clerks@erskinechambers.com
URL: www.erskinechambers.com
Out of hours telephone: Emergency numbers available on answerphone via main number

Chambers of: Mr M A Todd QC
Clerk: Mike Hannibal; Administrator: Monika Graczykowska

Todd, Michael QC *1977*
Mabb, David QC *1979*
Moore, Martin QC *1982*
Chivers, David QC *1983*
Snowden, Richard QC *1986*
Bryant, Ceri QC *1984*
Cone, John *1975*
Prentice, Daniel *1982*
Roberts, Catherine *1986*
Gillyon, Philip *1988*
Stokes, Mary *1989*
Thompson, Andrew *1991*
Dougherty, Nigel *1993*
Potts, James *1994*
Thornton, Andrew *1994*
Davies, Edward *1998*
Horan, Stephen *2002*
Shaw, Benjamin *2002*
Griffiths, Ben *2004*
Barden, Alexander *2005*
Parfitt, Matthew *2005*
Harty, Patrick *2008*
Rivett, Jack *2010*
Nolan, Richard *1999**

Types of work
Accountancy · Arbitration · Asset finance · Banking · Capital markets · Chancery (commercial) · Commercial fraud · Commercial law · Commercial litigation · Company law · Corporate finance · Corporate governance · Corporate insolvency · Corporate liability · Corporate recovery · Cross-border litigation and

†Recorder *Door Tenant/Associate Member

remedies · Directors' disqualification · Dispute resolution · Employee benefit trusts · Financial instruments · Financial services · Freezing orders · Fund management · Gambling · Gaming and lotteries · Guarantees · Insolvency · Insurance (long term) · Investments · Limited partnerships · Mergers and acquisitions · Offshore finance · Offshore investment · Partnerships · Privy Council · Privy Council Appeals · Professional negligence · Sale of business · Securities law and regulation · Share options · Shareholder agreements · Unincorporated associations · Unit trusts · Warranty claims

Disability access
Staff briefed or trained on duties under the disability legislation, Wheelchair access, Disabled parking available

ONE ESSEX COURT

First Floor, One Essex Court, Temple, London EC4Y 9AR
020 7556 5500
Fax: 020 7583 5500

Disability access
Disabled parking available

ONE ESSEX COURT

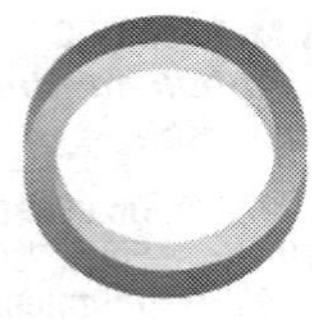

ONE ESSEX COURT

Ground Floor, One Essex Court, Temple, London EC4Y 9AR
020 7583 2000
Fax: 020 7583 0118; DX: 430 London Chancery Lane
E-mail: clerks@oeclaw.co.uk
URL: www.oeclaw.co.uk
Out of hours telephone: See website

Chambers of: Lord A S Grabiner QC
Clerk: Darren Burrows; Administrator: Joanne Huxley; Assistant Administrator: Sally Henry

Grabiner, A S QC *1968*†
Strauss, Nicholas QC *1965*†
Leaver, Peter QC *1967*†
Glick, Ian QC *1970*†
Hobbs, Geoffrey QC *1977*
Sharpe, Thomas QC *1976*
Onions, Jeffery QC *1981*
Fitzgerald, Susanna QC *1973*
Auld, Stephen QC *1979*
Davies, Rhodri QC *1979*
MacLean, Kenneth QC *1985*
Rabinowitz, Laurence QC *1987*
Gammie, Malcolm QC *1997*
McCaughran, John QC *1982*
Graham, Charles QC *1986*
Gillis, Richard QC *1982*
Lenon, Andrew QC *1982*
Orr, Craig QC *1986*
De Garr Robinson, Anthony QC *1987*
Sullivan, Michael QC *1983*
Kitchener, Neil QC *1991*
Choo Choy, Alain QC *1991*
Wolfson, David QC *1992*
Toledano, Daniel QC *1993*
Cavender, David QC *1993*
Boulton, Richard QC *2003*
Himsworth, Emma QC *1993*
Malone, Michael *1975*
Griffiths, *1981*
Reffin, Clare *1981*
Brown, Hannah *1992*
O'Sullivan, Zoë *1993*
Nourse, Edmund *1994*
Hossain, Sa'ad *1995*
Redfern, Alan *1995*
Bingham, Camilla *1996*
Roberts, Philip *1996*
Fealy, Michael *1997*
Gledhill, Orlando *1998*
Colton, Simon *1999*
Cook, Matthew *1999*
Elliott, Steven *2001*
Hollingworth, Guy *2001*
Spitz, Derek *2001*
Strong, Ben *2001*
Boase, Anna *2002*
Goldsmith, James *2002*
Nadin, James *2002*
Hubbard, Daniel *2003*
Menashy, Michelle *2003*
Emmett, Laurence *2004*
Patton, Conall *2004*
Smith, Henry Forbes *2004*
Campbell, Eleanor *2005*
Clark, Michael *2005*
Dracos, Marcos *2005*
Isaac, Sebastian *2005*
Polley, Alexander *2005*
Caplan, David *2006*
Foyle, Andrew *2006*
Mott, Richard *2006*
Oakeshott, Rachel *2006*
Lemer, Saul *2007*
O'Leary, Sam *2007*
Sloboda, Nicholas *2007*
Bompas, Abra *2008*
D'Arcy, Michael *2008*
Shah, Nehali *2008*
Baiou, Mehdi *2009*
Brown, Alexander *2009*
Paine, Douglas *2009*
Petkovic, James *2009*
Watkins, Michael *2009*
Butler, Oliver *2010*
Jones, Emma *2010*
Rushworth, Adam *2010*
Lodder, Andrew *2012*

Types of work
Accountancy · Administrative law · Alternative dispute resolution · Arbitration · Auditing · Banking · Bills of exchange · Civil law · Commercial law · Commodities · Company law · Competition law · Conflict of laws · Derivatives · Directors' disqualification · Economic torts · Employment · Energy · Entertainment · European law · European Union · Financial services · Fraud · Fund management · Gambling · Guarantees · Information technology · Insolvency · Insurance · Intellectual property · Letters of credit · Licensing · Media · Mediation · Mergers and acquisitions · Partnerships · Pensions · Performance bonds · Professional negligence · Public law · Restitution ·

Restraint of trade · Sale and carriage of goods · Sale of business · Shareholder agreements · Sport · Strategic alliances · Tax · Telecommunications · Utilities · Warranty claims

Chambers Established 1966
Opening times: 8.00am - 9.00pm

Disability access
Wheelchair access, Disabled parking available

Fees policy
Advisory work at One Essex Court is in most cases time costed. Current hourly charge rates for individuals or groups of individuals will be sent on request.

ONE ESSEX COURT

1st Floor, Temple, London EC4Y 9AR
020 7936 3030
Fax: 020 7583 1606; DX: 371 London Chancery Lane
E-mail: clerks@1ec.co.uk
URL: www.1ec.co.uk
Out of hours telephone: 07721 866858

Chambers of: Sir A B Baldry MP
Clerks: Ian Hogg (Senior Clerk), Lloyd Parker (First Junior Clerk)

Baldry, Tony MP *1975*
Hartman, Michael *1975*
Brown, Susan *1989*
Joshi, Pramod *1992*
Campbell-Brown, Louise *1993*
Macpherson, Duncan *1994*
Chesner, Howard *1995*
Hatch, Lisa *1995*
Oakley, Paul *1995*
Halstead, Robin *1996*
Miller, Jonathan *1996*
Miles, Richard *1997*
Sonaike, Kolarele *1998*
Sampson, Tim *2000*
Shaw, Joanna *2000*
Hyde, Sarah-Jane *2001*
Kirk, Graeme *2001*
Soto-Miranda, Diego *2001*
Van Heck, Dirk *2001*
Freedman, Michelle *2002*
Degun, Jasvir *2003*
O'Callaghan, Louise *2006*
Parke, Genevieve *2006*
Read, Emma *2006*
Williams, Jamie *2006*
Waterworth, Caroline *2008*
Wilson, Andrew *2010*

5 ESSEX COURT

1st Floor, 5 Essex Court, Temple, London EC4Y 9AH
020 7410 2000
Fax: 020 7410 2010; DX: 1048 London Chancery Lane
E-mail: clerks@5essexcourt.co.uk

Chambers of: Miss F Barton QC

Disability access
Disabled parking available

ESSEX COURT CHAMBERS

24 Lincoln's Inn Fields, London WC2A 3EG
020 7813 8000
Fax: 020 7813 8080; DX: 320 London Chancery Lane
E-mail: clerksroom@essexcourt.net
URL: www.essexcourt.net
Out of hours telephone: 020 7813 8000

Chambers of: Mr A G S Pollock QC
Clerks: David Grief (Senior Clerk), Joe Ferrigno (Deputy Senior Clerk), Sam Biggerstaff, Ben Perry; Administrator: Lisa Young

Pollock, Gordon QC *1968*
Thomas, Michael CMG QC *1955*
Hunter, Ian QC *1967†*
Boyd, Stewart QC *1967†*
Veeder, VV QC *1971†*
Siberry, Richard QC *1974†*
Gilman, Jonathan QC *1965*
Berman, Franklin QC KCMG *1966*
Cordara, Roderick QC *1975*
Crookenden, Simon QC *1975*
Gruder, Jeffrey QC *1977*
Hochhauser, Andrew QC *1977*
Jacobs, Richard QC *1979*
Mildon, David QC *1980*
Andrews, Geraldine QC *1981†*
Dunning, Graham QC *1982*
Berry, Steven QC *1984*
Shaw, Malcolm QC *1988*
Templeman, Mark QC *1981*
Joseph, David QC *1984*
Millett, Richard QC *1985*
Smouha, Joe QC *1986*
Davies, Huw QC *1985*
Griffiths, Martin QC *1986*
Lockey, John QC *1987*
Bryan, Simon QC *1988*
Foxton, David QC *1989*
Mercer, Hugh QC *1985*
Flynn, Vernon QC *1991*
Landau, Toby QC *1993*
Lowe, Vaughan QC *1993*
Smith, Christopher QC *1989*
Blanchard, Claire QC *1992*
Stanley, Paul QC *1993*
Cockerill, Sara QC *1990*
Eicke, Tim QC *1993*
McGrath, Paul QC *1994*
Collins, James QC *1995*
Dicks, Anthony *1961*
Boyle, Alan *1977*
Smith, Mark *1981*
Snider, John *1982*
Watson, Philippa *1988*
Ciumei, Charles *1991*
Dye, Brian *1991*
Eaton, Nigel *1991*
Hopkins, Philippa *1994*
Hunter, Martin *1994*
Houseman, Stephen *1995*
Lau, Martin *1996*
Craig, David *1997*
Key, Paul *1997*
Pillow, Nathan *1997*
Scorey, David *1997*
Wordsworth, Sam *1997*
Diwan, Ricky *1998*
Hart, Neil *1998*
Moollan, Salim *1998*
King, Edmund *1999*
Doyle, Shane *2001*
Brown, Edward *2002*
Ng, Jern-Fei *2002*
Quirk, Iain *2002*
Williams, QC *2003*
Brier, Jeremy *2004*
Davies, David *2004*
Russell, Jane *2004*
Wells, Jessica *2004*
Dhar, Siddharth *2005*
Peters, David *2005*
Sarooshi, Dan *2005*
Sander, Amy *2006*
Walker, Damien *2006*
Willan, James *2006*
Wood, Emily *2006*
Dilnot, Anna *2008*
Dudnikov, Anton *2008*
Ford, Thomas *2008*
Board, Adam *2010*
Jung, Catherine *2010*
Legg, Andrew *2010*
Griffith, Gavin QC *1969**
Ong, Colin *1991**

†Recorder *Door Tenant/Associate Member

D

Types of work
Administrative law · Agriculture · Arbitration · Asset recovery · Aviation · Banking · Chinese law · Civil liberties · Commercial fraud · Commodities · Company law · Computer litigation · Conflict of laws · Construction law · Corporate recovery · Derivatives · E-commerce · Employment · Energy · Engineering disputes · Entertainment · Environment · European law · Financial services · Hong Kong law · Human rights · Immigration · Insolvency · Insurance · Intellectual property · International commercial arbitration · International law · International trade · Internet crime · Islamic law · Media · Product liability · Professional negligence · Railways · Road traffic · Sale and carriage of goods · Securities law and regulation · Shipping · South Asian law · South East Asian law · Sport · Taxation and duties · Utilities

Disability access
Staff briefed or trained on duties under the disability legislation, Wheelchair access

ESSEX HOUSE CHAMBERS

122-126 Kilburn High Road, Kilburn, London NW6 4HY
020 7692 0677
Fax: 020 7328 7091
E-mail: essexhousechambers@yahoo.co.uk

Chambers of: Mr Y N K S Serugo-Lugo

Disability access
Staff briefed or trained on duties under the disability legislation, Disabled parking available

20 ESSEX STREET

BARRISTERS

20 Essex Street, London WC2R 3AL
020 7842 1200
Fax: 020 7842 1270; DX: 0009 London Chancery Lane
E-mail: clerks@20essexst.com
URL: www.20essexst.com
Out of hours telephone: 020 7842 1200

Chambers of: Mr I A Milligan QC
Clerks: Neil Palmer, Brian Lee, Mathew Kesbey, Arron Zitver, Christopher Theobald; Chambers Manager: Daniel Clark

Also at: Maxwell Chambers, #02-09 32 Maxwell Road, Singapore 069115 Tel: +65 6225 7230, Fax: +65 6224 9462

Milligan, Iain QC *1973*
Neill of Bladen, QC *1951*
Lauterpacht, Elihu QC CBE *1950*
Layton, Alexander QC *1976*†
Young, Timothy QC *1977*
Males, Stephen QC *1978*†
Hancock, Christopher QC *1983*†
Morris, Stephen QC *1981*†
Matthews, Duncan QC *1986*
Bethlehem, Daniel QC *1988*
Tselentis, Michael QC *1995*
Owen, David QC *1983*
Baker, Andrew QC *1988*
Atherton, Stephen QC *1989*
Morpuss, Guy QC *1991*
Edey, Philip QC *1994*
Coburn, Michael QC *1990*
Kimmins, Charles QC *1994*
Ashcroft, Michael QC *1997*
Akka, Lawrence QC *1991*
Masters, Sara QC *1993*
Wood, Michael KCMG *1968*
Lew, Julian QC *1970*
Broadbent, Edmund *1980*
Ambrose, Clare *1992*
Anderson, Julie *1993*
Charkham, Graham *1993*
Collett, Michael *1995*
Kenny, Julian *1997*
Swaroop, Sudhanshu *1997*
Jarvis, Malcolm *1998*
Fulton, Andrew *1999*
Jones, Susannah *1999*
Lewis, David *1999*
Raphael, Thomas *1999*
Byam-Cook, Henry *2000*
Snook, Sean *2000*
Leahy, Blair *2001*
Lee, Michael *2001*

†Recorder *Door Tenant/Associate Member

Papadopoulos, Socrates *2001*
Sutton, David *2001*
Parry, Angharad *2002*
Thompson, Antony SC *2002*
Olbourne, Benjamin *2003*
Bovensiepen, Daniel *2004*
Milnes, Simon *2005*
Davies, Josephine *2006*
Edwards, Patricia *2006*
Verdirame, Guglielmo *2006*
Pearce, Luke *2007*
Talmon, Stefan *2007*
Tan, Charlotte *2008*
Tresman, Sarah *2008*
Caron, David *2009*
Ho, Edward *2009*
Hamilton, Rupert *2010*
Nevill, Penelope *2010*

Types of work

Administrative law · Admiralty · Arbitration · Aviation · Banking · Civil liberties · Commercial law · Commercial litigation · Commodities · Competition law · Conflict of laws · Construction law · EC competition law · Energy · Environment · Financial services · Human rights · Immigration · Insolvency · Insurance · Intellectual property · International law · International trade · Professional negligence · Sale and carriage of goods · Shipping

Disability access

Staff briefed or trained on duties under the disability legislation, Disabled parking available, Induction loop or infra red system

23 ESSEX STREET

23 essex street

23 Essex Street, London WC2R 3AA
020 7413 0353
Fax: 020 7413 0374; DX: 148 London Chancery Lane
E-mail: clerks@23es.com
URL: www.23es.com
Out of hours telephone: On answerphone

Chambers of: Mr S C Russell Flint QC

Clerks: Richard Fowler (Senior Clerk), Sean Gould, Robert Mayes, Sarah Reynolds, Jamie Clack, Adam Chapman, Joe Wheeler, Ben O'Neill, Liam Kitcher, Richard Fowler; Finance Manager: Jonathan Page

Also at: City Gate East, Toll House Hill, Nottingham, NG1 5FS

Also at: 82 King Street, 82 King Street, Manchester M2 4WQ

Russell Flint, Simon QC *1980†*
Purnell, Nicholas QC *1968*
Miskin, Charles QC *1975†*
Weekes, Anesta QC *1981†*
Janner, Daniel QC *1980*
Rees, Gareth QC *1981*
Shant, Nirmal QC *1984†*
Enoch, Dafydd QC *1985†*
Price, John QC *1982†*
Kent, Alan QC *1986*
Morley, Iain QC *1988*
Nelson, Cairns QC *1987†*
Bogan, Paul QC *1983*
Ali, Zafar QC *1994*
Causer, John *1979*
Harrison, Michael *1979*
Del Fabbro, Oscar *1982†*
Brown, Roy *1983*
Claxton, Elroy *1983†*
Riley, John *1983*
Pardoe, Rupert *1984*
Bradley, Caroline *1985*
Summers, Gary *1985*
Cranston-Morris, Wayne *1986*
Moore, Neil *1986*
Holt, Karen *1987†*
Ozin, Paul *1987*
Forgan, Hugh *1989*
Easteal, Andrew *1990†*
Amis, Christopher *1991*
Ascherson, Isobel *1991*
Griffin, Lynn *1991*
Acheson, Ian *1992*
Curtis-Raleigh, Giles *1992*
Fenhalls, Mark *1992*
Hurst, Andrew *1992†*
Milne, Richard *1992*
Trafford, Mark *1992*
Clark, Timothy *1993†*
Lumsdon, Kate *1993*
O'Connor, Gerard *1993*
Marshall, Eloise *1994*
McDonagh, Matthew *1994†*
Platt, Stephen *1994*
Sellers, Robin *1994*
Casella, Bart *1995*
Durran, Alexia *1995†*
McGrath, Francis *1995*
Raynor, Keith *1995*
Aiolfi, Laurence *1996*
Branston, Gareth *1996*
Hope, Ian *1996*
Hossain, Ahmed *1996*
Campbell, Sarah *1997*
Lennon, Jonathan *1997*
Allan, David *1998*
Salako-Olorunfemi, Toyin *1998*
Sandys, Neil *1998*
Scamardella, Rossano *1998*
Turkson, Tetteh *1998*
Bates, Lesley *1999*
Dunkin, Oliver *1999*
Fugallo, Daniel *1999*
Khan, Ashraf *1999*
Smith, Graham *1999*
Husbands, Abigail *2000*
Povall, David *2000*
Singh, Dapinder *2000*
Eaglestone, William *2001*
Harris, Adrian *2001*
Badger, Christopher *2002*
Saul, Sonya *2002*
Sharpe, Richard *2002*
Common, Hamish *2003*
Godfrey, Tom *2003*
Paley, Ruth *2003*
Mills, Alexander *2004*
Mohammed, Rashad *2004*
Rimmer, Nicholas *2004*
Upton, Alexander *2004*
Culleton, Louise *2005*
Kinch, Hannah *2006*
Templeton, *2006*
Vanstone, Rebecca *2006*
Webb, Holly *2006*
Duffy, Patrick *2007*
Pulle, Roshani *2007*
Rasiah, Nathan *2007*
Devlin, Thomas *2009*
Elia, Elena *2009*
Lister, Daniel *2009*
Acker, Lizzy *2010*
Elagab, Yousif *2010*
Scott, Cameron *2012*

Types of work

Anti-social Behaviour Orders · Asset forfeiture · Asset recovery · Aviation · Child abduction · Child abuse · Civil actions against the police · Computer crime · Confiscation · Contaminated land · Copyright theft · Copyright Tribunal · Coroner's inquests · Coroners · Corporate fraud · Corporate manslaughter ·

Councillors and standards · Courts martial · Crime and criminal due process · Criminal judicial review · Disciplinary tribunals · Extradition · Financial services · Firearms · Forfeiture · Fraud · Freezing orders · Homicide · Inquests · International fraud and asset tracing · Internet crime · Judicial review · Licensing · Malicious prosecution · Media · Military law · Money laundering · Motor vehicles · Pharmaceuticals · Police · Police discipline · Pollution · Prison law · Prisoners' rights · Public inquiries · Regulatory and disciplinary law · Road haulage · Road traffic · Road traffic offences · Serial crime · Serious fraud · Tax · Trademarks · Trading standards · VAT

Chambers Established 1934
Opening times: 9.00am - 6.00pm

Chambers' facilities
3 Conference Rooms, Grand Board/Dining room, conference call facilities, Wireless connectivity, Modern reference library, Fully equipped kitchen, Seminar suite. Also available for private hire. Contact reception@23es.com to discuss your requirements.

Disability access
Staff briefed or trained on duties under the disability legislation, Wheelchair access, Induction loop or infra red system

Languages spoken
Afrikaans, French, German, Greek, Hindi, Italian, Punjabi, Russian, Spanish, Urdu

Fees policy
We aim to ensure we can provide counsel to meet the needs of all our clients. Our senior clerks will always take into account the level of expertise of counsel and the time required in and out of court when discussing fees.

39 ESSEX STREET

ThirtyNine
ESSEX STREET

39 Essex Street, London WC2R 3AT
020 7832 1111
Fax: 020 7353 3978; DX: 298 London Chancery Lane
E-mail: clerks@39essex.com
URL: www.39essex.com

Chambers of: Mr R M Jay QC, Mr S R Tromans QC
Clerks: Alastair Davidson (Senior Clerk), Sheraton Doyle, Ben Sundborg, Andrew Poyser, Luke Diebelius, Owen Lawrence, Nathan Hitchman, Peter Campbell, Niki Merison, Gemma Goodwin, Thomas Neale, Oliver Duane; Chief Executive and Director of Clerking: David Barnes

Also at: 82 King Street, Manchester M2 4WQ Tel: 0161 870 0333

Jay, Robert QC *1981*†
Tromans, Stephen QC *1999*
Goldblatt, Simon QC *1953*
Tackaberry, John QC *1967*
Glasgow, Edwin QC CBE *1969*
Horton, Matthew QC *1969*
Ullstein, Augustus QC *1970*†
Pleming, Nigel QC *1971*
Wilmot-Smith, Richard QC *1978*†
Norris, William QC *1974*
Kelly, Matthias QC *1979*
Nelson, Vincent QC *1980*
Melville, David QC *1975*
Treverton-Jones, Gregory QC *1977*
Block, Neil QC *1980*
Rodway, Susan QC *1981*
Foster, Alison QC *1984*
Catchpole, Stuart QC *1987*†
McCaul, Colin QC *1978*
Morgan, Jeremy QC *1989*
Cory-Wright, Charles QC *1984*
Hughes, Adrian QC *1984*
Manzoni, Charles QC *1988*
Kovats, Steven QC *1989*
Wilken, Sean QC *1991*
Nardell, Gordon QC *1995*
Giovannetti, Lisa QC *1990*
Grey, Eleanor QC *1990*
Pershad, Rohan QC *1991*
Richards, Jenni QC *1991*
Morris, Fenella QC *1990*
Tonna, John *1974*
Noble, Roderick *1977*
Pugh-Smith, John *1977*
Edwards, Simon *1978*
Brown, Geoffrey *1981*
Smith, Marion *1981*
Du Cann, Christian *1982*
Gough, Karen *1983*
Bellamy, Jonathan *1986*
Bradly, David *1987*
Doherty, Bernard *1990*
O'Sullivan, Derek *1990*
Todd, James *1990*
Rees, Hefin *1992*
Brodie, Bruce *1993*
Formby, Emily *1993*
Harwood, Richard *1993*
Marven, Robert *1994*
Thornton, Justine *1994*
Williams, Benjamin *1994*
Edwards, Martin *1995*
Robb, Adam *1995*
Patel, Parishil *1996*
Sinclair, Duncan *1996*
Wald, Richard Daniel *1997*
Zwart, Christiaan *1997*
Ayling, Judith *1998*
Church, Camilla *1998*
Denis-Smith, John *1998*
Grange, Kate *1998*

Sachdeva, Vikram *1998*
Truscott, Caroline *1998*
Allen, Neil *1999*
Greaney, Nicola *1999*
Thomann, Colin *1999*
Connors, Jess *2000*
Scott, Katharine *2000*
Burton, James *2001*
Ghaly, Karim *2001*
Dunlop, Rory *2002*
Ruck Keene, Alexander *2002*
Staker, Christopher *2003*
Bodnar, Alexandra *2004*
Crapper, Sadie *2004*
Lazarus, Robert *2004*
Allen, Caroline *2005*
Butler-Cole, Victoria *2005*
Hearnden, Alexis *2005*
Deakin, Andrew *2006*
Fraser, Quintin *2006*
Mant, Peter *2006*
O'Hagan, Rachael *2006*
Drake, Rebecca *2007*
Wiles, Ellen *2007*
Holborn, Jack *2008*
Norris, Josephine *2008*
Dobson, Catherine *2009*
Simons, Zack *2009*
Brown, Anthony *2010*
Grogan, Rose *2010*
Hennessey, Patrick *2010*
Rainey, Angela *2010*
Mayhew, David *2011*
Thomas, David Brynmor *2011*
Stern, Kristina *1996**
Lane, Patrick *1997**

Types of work
Administrative law · Arbitration · Civil liberties · Clinical negligence · Commercial litigation · Common law (general) · Community care · Construction law · Costs · Discrimination · Dispute resolution · EC competition law · Education · Employment · Energy · Entertainment · Environment · Fire and other property damage claims · Health and safety · Human rights · Immigration · Industrial diseases · Insurance · International arbitration · Judicial review · Local authorities · Media and entertainment · Mediation · Medical negligence · Mental health · Parliamentary · Personal injury · Planning · Product liability · Professional negligence · Regulatory and disciplinary law · Sale and carriage of goods · Sport · Taxation and duties · Utilities

Chambers Established 1896
Opening times: 8.00am - 6.30pm

Chambers' facilities
Conference Rooms, Disks Accepted, Video Conference, E-mail

Disability access
Staff briefed or trained on duties under the disability legislation, Wheelchair access

Languages spoken
Arabic, French, German, Gujarati, Italian, Spanish

Fees policy
Fees on application to the Clerks Room or the Chambers Director.

EUROLAWYER CHAMBERS

PO Box 3621, London N7 0BQ
020 7607 0075
E-mail: OLav@eurolawyer.plus.com

Chambers of: Mr O G Ernstzen

Disability access
Staff briefed or trained on duties under the disability legislation, Disabled parking available

FALCON CHAMBERS

Falcon Court, London EC4Y 1AA
020 7353 2484; Fax: 020 7353 1261; DX: 408 London Chancery Lane
E-mail: clerks@falcon-chambers.com
URL: www.falcon-chambers.com
Out of hours telephone: 07507 638 536

Chambers of: Mr J R Gaunt QC, Mr G C C Fetherstonhaugh QC
Clerk: Steven Francis; Chambers Director: Edith A Robertson

Fetherstonhaugh, Guy QC *1983*
Gaunt, Jonathan QC *1972*
Wood, Derek QC CBE *1964†*
Reynolds, Kirk QC *1974*
Dowding, Nicholas QC *1979*
Fancourt, Timothy QC *1987†*
Rodger, Martin QC *1986*
Small, Jonathan QC *1990*
Jourdan, Stephen QC *1989*
Denyer-Green, Barry *1972*
Harpum, Charles *1976*
Moss, Joanne R *1976*
Radevsky, Anthony *1978*
Cole, Edward *1980*
Clark, Wayne *1982*
Cowen, Gary *1990*
Bignell, Janet *1992†*
Dray, Martin *1992*
Shea, Caroline *1994*
Tanney, Anthony *1994*
Taskis, Catherine *1995*
Windsor, Emily *1995*
Sefton, Mark *1996*
Tozer, Stephanie *1996*
Peters, Edward *1998*
Rosenthal, Adam *1999*
Fitzgerald, Elizabeth *2001*
Duckworth, Nathaniel *2002*
Healey, Greville *2002*
Radley-Gardner, Oliver *2003*
Summers, John *2004*
Cox, Tamsin *2005*
Sissons, Philip *2005*
Ollech, Joseph *2006*
Robinson, Daniel *2008*
Lees, Kester *2010*
Sutherland, Jamie *2010*
Fairley, Ciara *2011*

Types of work
Agriculture · Arbitration · Chancery (land law) · Commercial property · Common land · Conveyancing · EC competition law · Housing · Insolvency · Landlord and tenant · Planning · Professional negligence · Real property

Disability access
Wheelchair access, Disabled parking available

†Recorder *Door Tenant/Associate Member

FARRAR'S BUILDING

D

Farrar's Building, Temple, London EC4Y 7BD
020 7583 9241
Fax: 020 7583 0090; DX: 406 London Chancery Lane
E-mail: Chambers@farrarsbuilding.co.uk
URL: www.farrarsbuilding.co.uk
Out of hours telephone: Home: 01245 601710, Mobile: 07768 366558

Chambers of: Mr P J Harrington QC
Clerk: Alan Kilbey MBE (Senior Clerk and Practice Manager); Administrator: Janet Eades

Harrington, Patrick QC *1973†*
Elias, Gerard QC *1968†*
Williams, John Leighton QC *1964†*
Day, Douglas QC *1967†*
Murphy, Ian QC *1972†*
Jeffreys, Alan QC *1970*
Lewis, Paul QC *1981†*
Murphy, Peter *1980*
Watt-Pringle, Jonathan QC *1987*
Unsworth, Ian QC *1992*
Nussey, Richard *1971*
Ridd, Ian *1975*
Keene, Gillian *1980*
David, Paul *1981*
Ley, Nigel Spencer *1985*
Peebles, Andrew *1987*
Lakha, Shabbir *1989*
Meredith-Hardy, John *1989*
Hobhouse, Helen *1990*
Potter, David *1990*
Freeman, Peter *1992*
Jones, Rhiannon *1993*
Pack, Melissa *1995*
Evans, Lee *1996*
Davies, Huw P *1998*
Pretsell, James *1998*
Tozzi, Sarah *1998*
Wille, Andrew *1998*
Cohen, Howard *1999*
Rodger, Senay *1999*
Watkins, Guy *1999*
Cox, Carwyn *2002*
Kerruish-Jones, Matthew *2003*
Hodson, Matthew *2004*
Plant, James *2004*
Bourne-Arton, Tom *2005*
Roderick, David *2005*
Sole, Emma *2005*
Thomas, Clive *2005*
Crawford, Georgina *2006*
Found, Timothy *2006*
Goodlad, Grant *2006*
Read, Daniel *2006*
Townsend, Edmund *2006*
Erinle, Bonike *2008*
Khan, Changez *2008*
Saxena, Hannah *2010*
Lewis, Marian *1977**
Evans, Elwen QC *1980†**
Hughes, David *1997**

Types of work
Administrative law · Chancery (general) · Civil liberties · Clinical negligence · Commercial litigation · Common law (general) · Costs · Crime · Employment · Health and safety · Landlord and tenant · Personal injury · Professional negligence · Sale and carriage of goods · Sport

Chambers' facilities
Conference Rooms

Disability access
Disabled parking available

Languages spoken
French

Fees policy
Up to five years call £60-85. Up to ten years call £85-150. Over ten years call £125-400. Fees are assessed to take account of a number of factors and are not charged purely on an hourly rate basis. The Senior Clerk Alan Kilbey is happy to give an indication as to the likely fee range on inquiry.

Additional Information
Farrar's Building is a long-established set of Chambers with particular expertise in the following five main areas of practice: personal injury; employment; serious and white collar crime; health and safety; and inquiries and disciplinary tribunals.

Members also specialise in clinical negligence, professional negligence, insurance, product liability and commercial. Personal injury is the largest area; Chambers is involved in the whole spectrum of cases from very serious catastrophic injury claims to straightforward small track claims.

The health and safety team works closely with the PI team and has been involved in a number of high profile cases. Employment law is a major area of practice for Chambers. We have a growing reputation, specialising in all aspects of this field. Chambers has a specialist criminal team, involved in major fraud and serious crime cases. It has close links with Wales where it remains a dominant force.

Chambers has a long history of involvement in public inquiries. Our practitioners have substantial experience both of appearing in them, and of chairing and/or appearing before a range of regulatory and disciplinary tribunals.

Members of Chambers also offer expertise in contract and commercial litigation, covering sale of goods and consumer credit and commercial fraud, insurance matters and product liability. We also offer practitioners in clinical negligence and all areas of professional negligence. Costs and taxation matters include solicitors' bills of costs and counsel's fees, legal aid costs and costs in matrimonial matters. Sports and competition cases include

†Recorder *Door Tenant/Associate Member

contracts, advertising and sponsorship, restraint of trade.

FARRINGDON CHAMBERS

180 Bermondsey Street, London SE1 3TQ
020 7089 5700
Fax: 020 7089 5701; DX: 80707 Bermondsey
URL: www.farringdon-law.co.uk
Out of hours telephone: 07506 116 194

Chambers of: Mr P O Purnell QC
Clerks: Robert Minns (Fees Clerk), Reece Hassan, James Coppin, Robert Archer (Senior Clerk)

Purnell, Paul QC *1962*
Cotcher, Ann QC *1979*
McKiernan, Edward *1981*
Morley, Gareth *1982*
John-Jules, Charles *1983*
Lynn, Jeremy *1983*
Dunn, Alexander *1985*
Henderson, Ian *1990*
Keogh, Richard *1991*
Simms, Sonia *1993*
Lawrenson, Mary *1994*
McCarthy, Martin *1994*
Ryan, William *1994*
Gordon, Clare *1995*
Pinkus, Molly *1997*
Whitehouse, Christopher *1997*
Griffith, Shelley *1998*
Malone, Fergus Gerald *1998*
Bass, Timothy *1999*
Charles, Katrina *1999*
Davies, Claire *1999*
Arnold, Abbe *2000*
Ahluwalia, Paramjit *2002*
Arnold, Graham *2002*
Krieger, Gregory *2005*
Rogers, Bethan *2007*
Azmeh, Umar *2009*

Types of work
Administrative law · Commercial litigation · Common law (general) · Confiscation · Corporate fraud · Crime · Discrimination · Employment · Human rights · Inquests · Licensing · Mental health · Prison law · Professional negligence · Restraint of trade

Disability access
Wheelchair access, Disabled parking available

FIDUCIARY LEGAL

5 North Court, Clevedon Road, London TW1 2HS
07814 495366
E-mail: stuart.pryke@fiduciarylegal.com

Chambers of: Mr S Pryke

FIELD COURT CHAMBERS

5 Field Court, Gray's Inn, London WC1R 5EF
020 7405 6114
Fax: 020 7831 6112; DX: 457 London Chancery Lane
E-mail: clerks@fieldcourt.co.uk

Chambers of: Miss L K Tapson, Mr J S Critchley

Disability access
Staff briefed or trained on duties under the disability legislation, Disabled parking available

FIVE PAPER

Ground Floor, 5 Paper Buildings, Temple, London EC4Y 7HB
020 7815 3200
Fax: 020 7815 3201; DX: 415 London Chancery Lane
E-mail: clerks@fivepaper.com
URL: www.fivepaper.com
Out of hours telephone: 07930 463737

Chambers of: Mr N J Grundy
Clerks: David Portch, Sarah Beale, Colin Bunyan, Alan Stammers

Grundy, Nicholas *1993*
Norris, Paul *1963*
Walsh, Steven *1965*
Platford, Graham *1970*
Broatch, Donald *1971*
Percival, Robert *1971*
Bull, Roger *1974*
Gallivan, Terry *1981*
Lyne, Mark *1981*
Wright, Ian *1983*
Jacobson, Lawrence *1985*
John, Peter *1989*
Rich, Jonathan *1989*
Henderson, Josephine *1990*
Gill, Satinder *1991*
Evans, Stephen *1992*
Rushton, Nicola *1993*
Mills, Simon *1994*
Adjei, Cyril *1995*
Sleeman, Rachel *1996*
Brownhill, Joanna *1997*
Davies, Jake *1997*
Harrap, Robert *1997*
Maltz, Ben *1998*
Rai, Sonia *1998*
Beecham, Sara *1999*
Jack, Angela *1999*
Hall, Angela *2000*
Hodgson, Jane *2000*
Leivesley, Julie *2000*
Glass, Mary *2001*
Holland, Guy *2001*
Osler, Victoria *2001*

D

Conlan, Tina *2002*
Macro, Morwenna *2002*
Christopher-Chambers, Gillian *2003*
Rogers, Christopher *2004*
Ter Haar, Camilla *2005*
Moate, Jennifer *2006*
Preston, Lewis *2007*
Williams, Rhys *2007*
Adams, Brynmor *2008*
Britton, Byron *2008*
Roche, Juanita *2004**

Types of work
Administrative law · Agency · Agriculture · Alternative dispute resolution · Ancillary relief · Anti-social Behaviour Orders · Assessment of costs · Asset finance · Asset recovery · Banking · Bills of exchange · Boundaries · Chancery · Chancery (commercial) · Chancery (general) · Chancery (land law) · Children · Civil fraud · Civil law · Civil litigation · Civil partnerships · Civil recovery · Cohabitation · Commercial contracts · Commercial fraud · Commercial law · Commercial litigation · Commercial property · Common land · Common law (general) · Community care · Company law · Company winding up applications · Conciliation · Confiscation · Consumer credit · Contaminated land · Contracts · Conveyancing · Corporate governance · Corporate insolvency · Corporate liability · Corporate recovery · Costs · Council tax · Councillors and standards · Court of Protection · Damages · Derivatives · Directors' disqualification · Disability discrimination · Disciplinary procedures · Disciplinary tribunals · Discrimination · Dispute resolution · Divorce · ECHR · Economic torts · Employment · Environment · Equity · Factoring · Family law · Family provision · Financial instruments · Financial provision · Financial provision for children · Forfeiture · Freedom of information · Freezing orders · Funding arrangements · Group litigation · Guarantees · Health and safety · Housing · Inheritance · Inheritance and cohabitees · Insolvency · International trade · Judicial review · Landlord and tenant · Lands Tribunal · Leasehold enfranchisement · Legal advice · Legal aid costs · Letters of credit · Licensing · Limited partnerships · Local authorities · Local authority claims · Local authority liability · Local government finance · Matrimonial · Matrimonial finance · Mediation · Mental health · Mortgages · Multi-party litigation · Ombudsman · Partnerships · Pensions · Personal insolvency · Pollution · Private children law · Privy Council · Privy Council Appeals · Professional negligence · Public access · Public inquiries · Real property · Regulatory and disciplinary law · Remedies · Restitution · Restraint of trade · Rights of light · Rights of way · Sale and carriage of goods · Sale of business · Shareholder agreements · Social welfare · Succession · Timeshare · Title to land · Torts · Trust litigation · Trusts · Unmarried couples · Warranty claims · Wills

Disability access
Staff briefed or trained on duties under the disability legislation, Disabled parking available

187 FLEET STREET

Fleet Street

187 Fleet Street, London EC4A 2AT
020 7430 7430
Fax: 020 7430 7431; DX: 464 London Chancery Lane
E-mail: chambers@187fleetstreet.com
URL: www.187fleetstreet.com
Out of hours telephone: 07976 281902

Chambers of: Mr A D H Trollope QC
Clerks: John Pyne (Senior Clerk), Richard Willicombe, Theresa Tyler, Tom Parker, Jack Parry, Akash Bharadia; Practice Manager: John Pyne; Administrator: Emma Gluckstein

Trollope, Andrew QC *1971†*
Radford, Nadine QC *1974*
Borrelli, Michael QC *1977*
King, Philip QC *1974*
Fuller, Jonathan QC *1977†*
Mayo, Simon QC *1985†*
Price, Roderick *1971*
Argyle, Brian *1972†*
Reece, Brian *1974*
Guest, Peter *1975†*
Reynolds, Stella *1983*
Rimmer, Anthony *1983*
Sheikh, Irshad *1983*
Lachkovic, James *1987*
Van Stone, Grant *1988*
Newton, Andrew *1989*
Woods, Terence *1989*
Barraclough, Nicholas *1990*
Chaudhuri, Avirup *1990*
Graffius, Mark *1990*
Bright, Rachel *1991*
Wong, Natasha *1993*
Aleeson, Warwick *1994*
Bartfeld, Jason *1995*
Frymann, Andrew *1995*
Cammerman, Gideon *1996*
Fishwick, Gregory *1996*
Butler, Adam *1997*
Madden, John *1997*
Kazakos, Leon *1999*
Kurzner, Emma *1999*
Punjani, Yasmin *2000*
Sharma, Neelam *2000*
Hossain, Mozammel *2001*
Eadie, Charlotte *2002*
Baird, David *2003*
Hughes, Henry *2003*

 †Recorder *Door Tenant/Associate Member

Ellis, Rachel *2004*
Lee, Rebecca *2004*
Sharma, Jamie *2005*
Keighley, Mary *2006*
Bewley, James *2007*
Woods, Alexander *2007*
Chotalia, Satya *2008*
Lawler, Donal *2008*
Osman, Nabeel *2008*
Unwin, Gregory *2008*
Dewji, Ali *2010*
Williams, Mair *2010*
Butcher, Richard *1985**
Korda, Anthony *1988**
Jones, Robert *1993**
Rouse, James *2000**
Smiles, Sarah-Jane *2008**

Types of work

Anti-social Behaviour Orders · Asset forfeiture · Asset recovery · Civil actions against the police · Civil fraud · Computer crime · Confiscation · Coroner's inquests · Coroners · Corporate fraud · Corporate manslaughter · Crime · Crime and criminal due process · Criminal judicial review · Extradition · Firearms · Forfeiture · Fraud · Homicide · Inquests · International criminal law · International fraud and asset tracing · Internet crime · Malicious prosecution · Motor vehicles · Police · Police discipline · Prison law · Prisoners' rights · Public access · Regulatory crime · Road traffic · Road traffic offences · Serial crime · Serious fraud · Sexual Offences · Sport · Terrorism · VAT

Chambers Established 1976
Opening times: 8.30am - 6.30pm

Chambers' facilities

Fully networked building, Disabled access, Parking, Direct dial telephones with voicemail, Individual e-mail, Website, Lift to all floors

Disability access

Staff briefed or trained on duties under the disability legislation, Wheelchair access, Disabled parking available

Languages spoken

Bengali, French, German, Hindi, Italian

Additional Information

187 Fleet Street is a leading set of chambers specialising in criminal and regulatory work, providing representation at every level, for both publicly and privately funded instructions. The set has gained a reputation for excellence in its advocacy and advisory work, offering a first-class service to professional and lay clients alike. Chambers is regularly instructed in high-profile and leading cases and is well equipped to deal with all types of criminal and regulatory matters, in this country and abroad. We have particular expertise in serious fraud and white-collar crime, as well as homicide, terrorism, revenue cases, money laundering and all forms of serious organised crime. Chambers additionally offers a wealth of experience in many other areas related to the criminal law, including disciplinary and tribunal hearings and provides specialist representation in the following areas: VAT tribunals, police discipline, Courts Martial and parole board hearings, mental health reviews, prison law, health and safety and human rights.

A key strength of Chambers lies in the breadth and depth of experience of its members who have conducted many high-profile cases across a wide spectrum. We have particular expertise in the following areas: serious fraud, including market rigging in share issues and takeovers, cartels and price-fixing, advance fee, high yield investment/ponzi and 'boiler-room' frauds, fraudulent trading/Phoenix, money laundering/confiscation, MTIC, VAT/excise evasion and revenue cases; drugs offences and ancillary matters arising under the Drug Trafficking Offences Act and Proceeds of Crime Act; terrorism offences; murder; serious sexual offences, offences against the person and sports law.

For further details, including the notable cases conducted by members of Chambers, please see our website: www.187fleetstreet.com.

NO. 3 FLEET STREET CHAMBERS

3 Fleet Street, London EC4Y 1DP
020 7936 4474
Fax: 020 7936 4473; DX: 398 London Chancery Lane
E-mail: clerks@3fleetstreet.com

CHAMBERS OF WILFRED FORSTER-JONES

79 Grays Inn Road, London WC1X 8TT
020 7831 0037
Fax: 020 7404 9707; DX: 0008 Chancery Lane
E-mail: chambers_79graysinnroad@yahoo.co.uk

Chambers of: Mr W J E Forster-Jones

FOUNTAIN COURT CHAMBERS

D

Fountain Court, Temple, London EC4Y 9DH
020 7583 3335
Fax: 020 7353 0329; DX: 5 Lde
E-mail: chambers@fountaincourt.co.uk
URL: www.fountaincourt.co.uk
Out of hours telephone: 07920 475415

Chambers of: Mr T J Dutton QC
Clerks: Alex Taylor (Director of Clerking), Richard Gittins, Paul Martenstyn, Oliver Miney; Administrator: Prue Woodbridge; Marketing and Pupillage Assistant: Javan Abass; Finance Manager: Nicola McCardle

Dutton, Timothy QC *1979*
Dehn, Conrad QC *1952*
Boswood, Anthony QC *1970*
Brindle, Michael QC *1975*†
Crane, Michael QC *1975*
Railton, David QC *1979*†
Browne-Wilkinson, Simon QC *1981*†
Moriarty, Stephen QC *1986*
Doctor, Brian QC *1991*
Rubin, Stephen QC *1977*†
McLaren, Michael QC *1981*
Brook Smith, Philip QC *1982*†
Cox, Raymond QC *1982*
Philipps, Guy QC *1986*
Béar, Charles QC *1986*
Thanki, Bankim QC *1988*
Robertson, Patricia QC *1988*
Howe, Timothy QC *1987*
Simpson, Mark QC *1992*
Green, Michael QC *1987*
Handyside, Richard QC *1993*
Chapman, Jeffrey QC *1989*
Dale, Derrick QC *1990*
Shah, Akhil QC *1990*
Smith, Marcus QC *1991*
Mitchell, Andrew QC *1992*
Gott, Paul QC *1991*
Coleman, Richard QC *1994*
Lucas, Bridget *1989*
Taylor, John *1993*
Tolley, Adam *1994*
Sinclair, Paul *1997*
Goodall, Patrick *1998*
King, Henry *1998*
Nambisan, Deepak *1998*
Phelps, Rosalind *1998*
Wheeler, Giles *1998*
Levey, Edward *1999*
Cutress, James *2000*
Yeo, Nik *2000*
Zellick, Adam *2000*
Carpenter, Chloe *2001*
Casey, Paul *2002*
Oppenheimer, Tamara *2002*
Watt, Katherine *2002*
Butler, Marianne Jane *2003*
McClelland, James *2004*
Murray, David *2004*
Allen, Rupert *2005*
Atrill, Simon *2005*
Duffy, James *2005*
Milner, Alexander *2006*
Jones-Fenleigh, Harriet *2007*
Power, Richard *2007*
Sher, Adam *2007*
Ulyatt, Craig *2008*
Bennett, Natasha *2009*
Edmonds, Daniel *2010*
Horowitz, Deborah *2010*
Leslie, Nico *2010*
Jacobs, Francis QC *1964**
Wormington, Timothy *1977**
Burrows, Andrew QC *1985**
Hamilton, Philippa *1996**

Types of work
Administrative law · Admiralty · Arbitration · Asset finance · Aviation · Banking · Chancery (general) · Clinical negligence · Commercial law · Commercial litigation · Common law (general) · Company, commercial and competition · Competition law · Construction law · Copyright · Corporate finance · Defamation · EC competition law · Employment · Energy · Entertainment · Financial services · Information technology · Insolvency · Insurance · Intellectual property · International arbitration · International trade · Media and entertainment · Medical negligence · Patents · Personal insolvency · Professional negligence · Sale and carriage of goods · Shipping · Sport · Telecommunications

Disability access
Staff briefed or trained on duties under the disability legislation, Wheelchair access, Disabled parking available

FRANCIS TAYLOR BUILDING

Inner Temple, London EC4Y 7BY
020 7353 8415
Fax: 020 7353 7622; DX: 402 Lde
E-mail: clerks@ftb.eu.com
URL: www.FTB.eu.com

Chambers of: Mr R M Purchas QC
Clerks: Paul Coveney (Senior Clerk), Andrew Briton (Principal Clerk), James Kemp (Principal Clerk); Practice Manager: Chambers Manager: Vicki Cousins

Purchas, Robin QC *1968*†
Roots, Guy QC *1969*
Phillips, Richard QC *1970*
George, Charles QC *1974*†
Newberry, Clive QC *1978*
Mehigan, Simon QC *1980*
De Haan, Kevin QC *1976*
McCracken, Robert QC *1973*
Tait, Andrew QC *1981*
Humphries, Michael QC *1982*
Gouriet, Gerald QC *1974*
Matthias, David QC *1980*
Humphreys, Richard QC *1986*
Howell Williams, Craig QC *1983*
Glover, Richard QC *1984*
Phillips, Simon QC *1985*†
Newcombe, Andrew QC *1987*
Edwards, Douglas QC *1992*
Jones, Gregory QC *1991*
Ornsby, Suzanne QC *1986*
Fookes, Robert *1975*
Petchey, Philip *1976*
Milner, Jonathan *1977*
Comyn, Timothy *1980*
Rankin, James *1983*
Lewis, Meyric *1986*
Mynors, Charles *1988*
Grant, Gary *1994*
Holland, Charles *1994*
Pereira, James *1996*
Phillpot, Hereward *1997*
Charalambides, Leo *1998*
Booth, Alexander *2000*
Sheikh, Saira Kabir *2000*
Pike, Jeremy *2001*
Edwards, Denis *2002*
Lopez, Juan *2002*
Honey, Richard *2003*
Phillips, Jeremy *2004*

†Recorder *Door Tenant/Associate Member

Eleftheriadis, Pavlos *2006*
Smith, Mark *2006*
Ormondroyd, Cain *2007*
Clutten, Rebecca *2008*
Graham Paul, Annabel *2008*
Sackman, Sarah *2008*
Tafur, Isabella *2009*
Westaway, Ned *2009*
Graham, David *2010*
Abrahams, Darren *1999**

Types of work

Administrative law · Common land · Compulsory Purchase · Consumer law · Contaminated land · Ecclesiastical law · Education · Employment · Energy · Environment · European law · Gaming and lotteries · Health and safety · Highways · Housing · Human rights · Immigration · Judicial review · Land compensation · Landlord and tenant · Lands Tribunal · Licensing · Local authorities · Parliamentary · Planning · Pollution · Procurement · Public inquiries · Public law · Railways · Rating and CPO · Regulatory crime · Restitution · Rights of light · Road traffic · Utilities

Disability access

Staff briefed or trained on duties under the disability legislation, Wheelchair access, Disabled parking available, Induction loop or infra red system

FURNIVAL CHAMBERS

32 Furnival Street, London EC4A 1JQ
020 7405 3232
Fax: 020 7405 3322; DX: 72 London Chancery Lane
Out of hours telephone: 020 7405 3232

Chambers of: Mr O S P Blunt QC, Miss S J O'Neill QC
Clerks: Stephen Ball (Senior Clerk), Joel Mason

Blunt, Oliver QC *1974*†
O'Neill, Sally QC *1976*
Evans, Anthony QC *1965*
Lodge, Anton QC *1966*†
Rees, John Charles QC *1972*
Leslie, Stephen QC *1971*
Carter-Manning, Jeremy QC *1975*
Woodley, Sonia QC *1968*
Garlick, Paul QC *1974*
Menary, Andrew QC *1982*†
McAtasney, Philippa QC *1985*
Rafferty, Stuart QC *1975*†
Sherrard, Charles QC *1986*
Lewis, Raymond *1971*
Baur, Christopher *1972*
Connor, Gino *1974*
Matthews, Lisa *1974*
May, Nigel *1974*†
Winberg, Stephen *1974*
Latham, Michael *1975*
Hadrill, Keith *1977*
Bendall, Richard *1979*
Romans, Philip *1982*
Ganner, Joseph *1983*
Headlam, Roy *1983*
Merrick, Nicola *1983*
Swain, Jon *1983*
Brock, David *1984*
Devlin, Tim *1985*
Henry, Annette *1984*
Boulter, Terence *1986*
Hirst, Kathryn *1986*
Gregory, Barry *1987*
Wilson, Graeme *1987*
Evans, Charles *1988*
Meredith, Chris *1988*
English, Caroline *1989*
Forster, Timothy *1990*
Rutherford, Martin *1990*
Patel, Sandip *1991*
Power, Alexia *1992*
Siddle, Trevor *1991*
Fawcett, Michelle *1993*
Sher, Christopher *1993*
Kearney, John *1994*
Smith, Emma *1994*
Hamilton, Amanda *1995*
Hussain, Frida *1995*
Winship, Julian *1995*
Cockings, Giles *1996*
Durose, David *1996*
Leake, Laban *1996*
Meek, Susan *1997*
Moses, Stephen *1997*
Chinner, Fer *1998*
Fudge, Sally *1998*
Hearnden, Richard *1998*
Mather, Nicholas *1998*
Miller, David *1998*
Haughey, Caroline *1999*
Grattage, Stephen *2000*
Norrman, Edith *2000*
Cohen, Ross *2001*
Omideyi, Anu *2001*
Fapohunda, Kemi *2002*
Smith, Joel *2002*
Spreadborough, Paul *2002*
Ganesan, Muthupandi *2003*
Jameson, Daniel *2004*
Brown, Catherine *2005*
Fordham, Chloe *2005*
Freeman, Lisa *2005*
Gordon, Ben *2005*
Powell, Charlotte *2005*
Harris, Craig *2006*
Jordan, Andrew *2006*
Wilson, Lisa *2006*
Hearn, Nicholas *2007*
Bostock, Amanda *2008*
Chidley, Matthew *2008*
Draper, Guy *2008*
Ibekwe, Frances *2008*
Bald, Lisa *2009*
Boulton, Clementine *2009*
Hayden, Stella *2009*
Wade, Nathaniel *2009*
Molyneux, Briony *2009*
Shafton, Emma *2011*
Garson, Robert *1999**
Reynolds, Lee *2002**

Types of work

Asset forfeiture · Confiscation · Copyright · Corporate fraud · Courts martial · Crime · Money laundering

Chambers Established 1985
Opening times: 8.15am - 6.45pm

Chambers' facilities

Conference Rooms, Video Conference, Disks Accepted, E-mail

Disability access

Staff briefed or trained on duties under the disability legislation, Wheelchair access, Disabled parking available

†Recorder *Door Tenant/Associate Member

D

THE CHAMBERS OF LAURA GARCIA-MILLER

116 Loudoun Road, London NW8 0ND
020 7722 9855
Fax: 020 7722 4155
E-mail: laura.garcia.miller@me.com

Chambers of: Ms L Garcia-Miller

1 GARDEN COURT FAMILY LAW CHAMBERS

Ground Floor, One Garden Court, Temple, London EC4Y 9BJ
020 7797 7900
Fax: 020 7797 7929; DX: 1034 London Chancery Lane
E-mail: clerks@1gc.com
URL: www.1gc.com
Out of hours telephone: As above

Chambers of: Miss J C Bazley QC, Mr S W S Cobb QC

Clerks: Howard Rayner (Senior Clerk), Chris Ferrison (Senior Clerking Manager), Paul Harris, Danny Chapman (Clerking Managers), Greg Goodman, Charlie Samuel-Hill (Junior Clerk), Lewis Foley (Junior Clerk), George Clark, Bradley Spong, Harry Smith; Administrator: PA to Chambers Manager: Harvinder Kaur

Bazley, Janet QC *1980*†
Cobb, Stephen QC *1985*†
Platt, Eleanor QC *1960*†
Ball, Alison QC *1972*†
Crowley, Jane QC *1976*†
Geekie, Charles QC *1985*
Russell, Alison H QC *1983*†
Morgan, Sarah QC *1988*
Willbourne, Caroline *1970*
Coleman, Bruce *1972*†
Shenton, Suzanne *1973*
Szwed, Elizabeth *1974*
Horrocks, Peter *1977*
McEwan, Vera JP *1979*
Halkyard, Kay *1980*
Burles, David *1984*
McIlwain, Sylvester *1985*
Pyle, Susan *1985*
Stocker, John *1985*
Crawley, Gary *1988*
Daniels, Nicholas *1988*
Gillman, Rachel *1988*
Giz, Alev *1988*
Bagchi, Andrew *1989*
Chisholm, Malcolm *1989*
Liebrecht, Michael *1989*
Nichols, Stuart *1989*
Heppenstall, Claire *1990*
Jenkins, Catherine *1990*
Mather, Kate *1990*
Sugar, Simon *1990*
Krishnadasan, Doushka *1991*
Robbins, Ian *1991*
Bugg, Ian *1992*
Howe, Darren *1992*
Norton, Andrew *1992*
Downham, Gillian *1993*
Hurworth, Jillian *1993*
Moore, Alison *1994*
Stone, Sally *1994*
Chandler, Alexander *1995*
Foster, Julien *1995*
Hudson, Emma *1995*
Momtaz, Sam *1995*
Fox, Nicola *1996*
Wiley, Francesca *1996*
Black-Branch, Jonathan *1998*
McEleavy, Peter *1999*
Mitchell, Rebecca *2000*
Segal, Sharon *2000*
Stanley, Gillian *2001*
Flood, Edward *2002*
Middleton, Caroline *2002*
Perrins, Philip *2002*
Jones, Richard *2003*
Evans, Sarah *2004*
Jarmain, Stephen *2005*
Procter, Alfred *2005*
Tambling, Richard *2005*
Clapham, Penelope *2007*
Cole, Georgina *2007*
MacLeod, Elena *2007*
Dudley, Thomas *2008*
Sprinz, Lucy *2008*
Jones, Eleri *2009*

Types of work
Care proceedings · Education · Family law · Family provision · Local authorities · Mental health

Disability access
Staff briefed or trained on duties under the disability legislation, Disabled parking available, Induction loop or infra red system

GARDEN COURT CHAMBERS

57-60 Lincoln's Inn Fields, London WC2A 3LJ
020 7993 7600
Fax: 020 7993 7700; DX: 34 London Chancery Lane
E-mail: info@gclaw.co.uk

Chambers of: Mr D R Watkinson, Mr C H Blaxland QC

Disability access
Staff briefed or trained on duties under the disability legislation, Wheelchair access, Disabled parking available, Induction loop or infra red system

HOLBORN CHAMBERS

6 Gate Street, Lincoln's Inn Fields, London WC2A 3HP
020 7242 6060
Fax: 020 7242 2777; DX: 159 London Chancery Lane

Chambers of: Mr S S Stevens

Disability access
Staff briefed or trained on duties under the disability legislation

 †Recorder *Door Tenant/Associate Member

GOLDSMITH CHAMBERS

Ground Floor, Goldsmith Building, Temple, London EC4Y 7BL
020 7353 6802
Fax: 020 7583 5255; DX: 376 London Chancery Lane
E-mail: clerks@goldsmithchambers.com
URL: www.goldsmithchambers.com
Out of hours telephone: 07732 233058

Chambers of: Lord D M Thomas of Gresford QC OBE

Clerks: Timothy McBennett, Alex Nunn, John Francis (Diary Team Manager); Administrator: Ashley Perkins

Thomas of Gresford, Lord QC OBE *1967†*
Riza, Alper QC *1973†*
Mason, James *1969*
Meikle, Robert *1970*
Harkus, George *1975*
Sofaer, Moira *1975*
Dean, James *1977*
Routley, Patrick *1979*
Clark, Dingle *1981*
Jenkins, Alun *1981*
Morris, Michael *1984*
Mailer, Clifford *1987*
Whitehouse, Stuart *1987*
Gill, Pamilla *1989*
Fane, Angela *1992*
Hope, Heather *1993*
Kavanagh, Jennifer *1993*
Pollock, Hilary *1993*
Sheehan, Anne-Marie *1994*
Lucas, Phillip *1995*
Nott, Emma *1995*
Okine, Julie *1996*
Royle, Charles *1997*
Millin, Melissa *1999*
Sherriff, Simon *1999*
Bloomer, James *2000*
Hodson, Katherine *2000*
McCune, Rodney *2000*
Wells, Caspar *2000*
Cunliffe, Alexander *2001*
Dye, John *2002*
Hill, Rina-Marie *2002*
Jubb, David *2002*
Wilson, Victoria *2002*
Petersen, Tom TD JP *2004*
Wacey, Nicola *2004*
Barrie, Laura *2005*
Gilmore, Alexandra *2005*
Bishop, Stephen *2006*
Hall, Nicola *2006*
Lue, Stephen *2006*
Davis, Alan *2007*
Irvine, Celeste *2007*
Khokhani, Erika *2007*
Sutherland-Mack, Jessica *2007*
Murphy, Diana *2010*
Colvin, Andrew *1972**
Fish, David QC *1973†**
Horne-Roberts, Jennifer *1976**
Moore, Anthony *1984**
Shipman, Anthony *1992**

Types of work

Administrative law · Adoption · Arbitration · Care proceedings · Chancery (general) · Chancery (land law) · Child care law · Civil liberties · Clinical negligence · Commercial litigation · Common law (general) · Company, commercial and competition · Conflict of laws · Construction law · Consumer law · Corporate fraud · Courts martial · Crime · Discrimination · Dispute resolution · Drink driving · Education · Employment · Equity · Family law · Family provision · Foreign law · Fostering · Housing · Immigration · Insolvency · Landlord and tenant · Licensing · Local authorities · Mental health · Parliamentary · Partnerships · Pensions · Personal injury · Personal insolvency · Prison law · Professional negligence · Real property · Sale and carriage of goods · Speeding · Succession · Trusts · War crimes tribunals · Wills

Chambers Established 1986
Opening times: 8.30am - 6.00pm

Chambers' facilities

Conference Rooms, Disks Accepted, Pleadings/Documents by e-mail, Telephone conferences

Disability access

Staff briefed or trained on duties under the disability legislation, Disabled parking available

Languages spoken

Afrikaans, French, German, Italian, Punjabi, Spanish, Urdu

Fees policy

The clerks will gladly provide fee estimates and guideline hourly rates for different counsel. See our website for further details.

THE CHAMBERS OF GRAHAME ALDOUS QC

9 Gough Square, London EC4A 3DG
020 7832 0500
Fax: 020 7353 1344; DX: 439 London Chancery Lane
E-mail: clerks@9goughsquare.co.uk
URL: www.9goughsquare.co.uk

Chambers of: Mr G L Aldous QC

Clerks: Garry Farrow (Family), Michael Goodridge (Civil), Ian Collins (Crime); Practice Manager: Chief Executive: Fiona Robb

†Recorder *Door Tenant/Associate Member

D

Aldous, Grahame QC *1979*†
Foy, John QC *1969*†
Baillie, Andrew QC *1970*†
Ritchie, Andrew QC *1985*
Giret, Joseph QC *1985*
Cottage, Rosina QC *1988*
Goddard, Christopher *1973*
Eyre, Giles *1974*†
Davies, Trevor *1978*
Wilson, Christopher *1980*†
Pinfold, Martin *1981*
Hillier, Nicolas *1982*
Hiorns, Roger *1983*
Naik, Gaurang *1985*
Williams, Vincent *1985*
Levy, Jacob *1986*
Loades, Jonathan *1986*
Buckett, Edwin *1988*
Whalan, Mark *1988*
Belgrave, Susan *1989*
Holmes-Milner, James *1989*
Glynn, Stephen *1990*
Jones, Philip *1990*
Crowther, Jeremy *1991*
Downey, Aileen *1991*†
Lucas, Edward *1991*
Begley, Laura *1993*
Lawson, Daniel *1994*
Stephenson, Christopher *1994*
Parker, Timothy *1995*
Butler, Simon *1996*
Elfield, Laura *1996*
Ford, Jeremy *1996*
Shetty, Rajeev *1996*†
Vindis, Tara *1996*
Walsh, Michael *1996*
Winter, Melanie *1996*
Godfrey, Timothy *1997*
Little, Tom *1997*
McKechnie, Stuart *1997*
Payne, Johnathan *1997*
Brindle, Simon *1998*
Gibbons, Perrin *1998*
Mooney, Giles *1998*
Cobb, Joanna *1999*
Dawson, Adam *2000*
Harden, Claire *2000*
Munday, Gareth *2000*
Nelson, Linda *2000*
Sharghy, Shahram *2000*
Adair, Emma-Jane *2001*
Briggs, Laura *2001*
Mawrey, Eleanor *2001*
Taussig, Gurion *2001*
Thacker, James *2001*
McAllister, Robert *2002*
Millington, Oliver *2003*
Pounder, Esther *2003*
Verity, Emily *2003*
Hogarth, Alastair *2005*
MacLachlan, Esther *2005*
Atkinson, Catherine *2006*
Byrne, James *2006*
Dove, James *2006*
Lamb, Edward *2006*
Newcomb, Jennifer *2006*
Lamont, Kate *2007*
Restall, Thomas *2007*
Rodgers, Benedict *2007*
Bumpus, Laura *2008*
Parker, Lycia *2010*
Tibbitts, Holly *2010*
Zurawel, Benjamin *2010*

Types of work
Ancillary relief · Animal rights law · Animals · Anti-social Behaviour Orders · Asbestos-related diseases · Asset forfeiture · Asylum · Bloodstock · Boundaries · Care proceedings · Child abduction · Child abuse · Child care law · Child support · Children · Civil actions against the police · Civil fraud · Clinical negligence · Commercial contracts · Commercial property · Common law (general) · Computer crime · Confiscation · Corporate fraud · Corporate manslaughter · Court of Protection · Courts martial · Crime · Crime and criminal due process · Criminal judicial review · Disability and health · Disability discrimination · Disasters · Disciplinary procedures · Disciplinary tribunals · Discrimination · Economic torts · Employment · Equine law · Extradition · Family law · Firearms · Food law · Forfeiture · Fraud · Health and safety · Highways · Holiday injury and damages · Homicide · Housing · Industrial deafness · Industrial diseases · Industrial relations law · Inquests · International fraud and asset tracing · Internet crime · Landlord and tenant · Local authority liability · Malicious prosecution · Matrimonial finance · Mediation · Medical negligence · Medicines Act · Motor vehicles · NHS inquiries · Occupational diseases · Overseas accidents · Personal injury · Police discipline · Private children law · Product liability · Product safety · Professional negligence · Public inquiries · Regulatory and disciplinary law · Road haulage · Road traffic offences · Serial crime · Serious fraud · Sports medicine · Technical contracts · Torts · Trusts · Wardship

Disability access
Staff briefed or trained on duties under the disability legislation, Wheelchair access

GOUGH SQUARE CHAMBERS

6-7 Gough Square, London EC4A 3DE
020 7353 0924
Fax: 020 7353 2221; DX: 476 London Chancery Lane
E-mail: gsc@goughsq.co.uk
URL: www.goughsq.co.uk
Out of hours telephone: 07860 219162

Chambers of: Miss C M Andrews
Clerk: Bob Weekes (Senior Clerk)

Andrews, Claire *1979*
Kirk, Jonathan QC *1995*
Philpott, Fred *1974*
Sayer, Peter *1975*
Hayes, Josephine *1980*
Goulding, Jonathan *1984*
Neville, Stephen *1986*
Gun Cuninghame, Julian *1989*
Say, Bradley *1993*
MacDonald, Iain *1996*
Popplewell, Simon *2000*
Howells, Geraint *2002*
Urell, Katherine *2002*
Bala, Ruth *2006*
Ross, James *2006*
Samuels, Thomas *2009*
Finch, Lee *2010*

†Recorder *Door Tenant/Associate Member

Types of work

Administrative law · Banking · Capital tax · Chancery (general) · Chancery (land law) · Civil fraud · Commercial contracts · Commercial fraud · Commercial litigation · Commercial regulation · Company, commercial and competition · Confiscation · Consumer credit · Consumer law · Corporate fraud · Environment · Equity · Food law · Franchising · Health and safety · Insolvency · Landlord and tenant · Licensing · Pensions · Product safety · Professional negligence · Regulatory and disciplinary law · Road haulage · Sale and carriage of goods · Timeshare · Trade Descriptions Act · Trademarks · Trading standards · Trusts · Wills

Disability access

Staff briefed or trained on duties under the disability legislation, Wheelchair access, Disabled parking available

1 GRAY'S INN SQUARE

Ground Floor, 1 Gray's Inn Square, London WC1R 5AA

020 7405 0001

Fax: 020 7405 0002; DX: 1013 London Chancery Lane

Chambers of: Mr D J Malone

Disability access

Staff briefed or trained on duties under the disability legislation, Wheelchair access, Disabled parking available

4-5 GRAY'S INN SQUARE

Gray's Inn, London WC1R 5AH

020 7404 5252

Fax: 020 7242 7803; DX: 1029 London Chancery Lane

E-mail: clerks@4-5.co.uk

URL: www.4-5.co.uk

Chambers of: Mr R Spearman QC

Clerks: Mark Regan, Daniel Perry; Senior Clerk: Michael Kaplan; Practice Manager: Tracey Jones

Spearman, Richard QC *1977*†
Straker, Timothy QC *1977*
Griffiths, Robert QC *1974*
Ash, Brian QC *1975*
Steel, John QC *1978*†
McManus, Richard QC *1982*
Malek, Hodge QC *1983*†
Hobson, John QC *1980*†
Clayton, Richard QC *1977*
Corner, Timothy QC *1981*†
Village, Peter QC *1983*
Lyons, Timothy QC *1980*
Hill, Thomas QC *1988*
Brown, Paul QC *1991*
Coppel, Philip QC *1994*
Stinchcombe, Paul QC *1985*
Campbell, John SC *2009*
Davey, Toby *1977*
Carnes, Andrew *1984*
Byrne, Garrett *1986*
Ramsden, James *1987*
Bourne, Charles *1991*
Tabachnik, Andrew *1991*
Fraser-Urquhart, Andrew *1993*
White, Robert *1993*
Falkowski, Damian *1994*
Davies, Sarah-Jane *1996*
Moffett, Jonathan *1996*
Sharland, Andrew *1996*
Strachan, James *1996*
Bolton, Caroline *1998*
Dearing, Anthony *1998*
Auburn, Jonathan *1999*
Greatorex, Paul *1999*
Whale, Stephen *1999*
Busch, Lisa *2000*
Hanif, Saima *2002*
Goodman, Alexander *2003*
Hannett, Sarah *2003*
Bicarregui, Anna *2004*
Buttler, Christopher *2004*
Wenban-Smith, Mungo *2004*
Bedenham, David *2005*
Anderson, Jack *2006*
Dehon, Estelle *2006*
Helme, Edward *2006*
Pratley, Michelle *2006*
Amraoui, Thomas *2007*
Loveday, David *2007*
Thelen, Jennifer *2007*
Jackson, Philippa *2008*
Walker, Steven *2008**
Campbell, John *2009*
Emmerson, Heather *2009*
Tankel, Benjamin *2009*
Dove, Ian QC *1986*†*
Dalby, Joseph *1988**
Barav, Ami *1993**
Peter, Natasha *2001**
Lee, Annabel *2010**

Types of work

Administrative law · Admiralty · Arbitration · Aviation · Banking · Civil liberties ·

Commercial law · Competition law · Corporate fraud · Defamation · Discrimination · EC competition law · Education · Employment · Environment · Financial services · Housing · Immigration · Insurance · International law · Landlord and tenant · Local authorities · Parliamentary · Planning · Professional negligence · Shipping · Sport · Telecommunications

Chambers Established 1936
Opening times: 8.30am - 7.00pm

Chambers' facilities
Conference Rooms, Disks Accepted, E-mail, Facilities for the disabled

Disability access
Staff briefed or trained on duties under the disability legislation, Wheelchair access, Disabled parking available

Languages spoken
French, German, Greek, Spanish

Fees policy
Clerk will quote fees on request.

Additional Information

The Chambers:
4-5 Gray's Inn Square is one of the leading sets of chambers in London. Its pre-eminence has been recognised for many years in various independent legal publications.

Members of chambers possess expertise and experience of the highest quality in the fields of public law and judicial review, planning and environmental law, commercial law, European Community law, human rights, employment law and sports law. The intersection of these specialisations within chambers allows collaboration between members on complex litigation.

Many members hold part-time judicial appointments in England, as well as overseas. The Head of Chambers is Richard Spearman QC. Several of the present juniors are on the Treasury Panels of Counsel instructed on behalf of the Crown.

Foreign Connections:
Members of chambers have appeared in the Privy Council, the European Court of Justice and of Human Rights, international arbitration tribunals and other courts worldwide, including the Far East, the Caribbean, Cyprus, Gibraltar, Belfast and Bermuda. Members have been admitted to the Bars of Trinidad & Tobago, New South Wales, Belfast, Dublin and other jurisdictions.

Recent Publications: Chapters and Articles
All members have written or contributed to leading legal publications, ranging from Halsbury's Laws of England to textbooks on human rights, the Encyclopaedia of Planning and the Encyclopaedia of Local Government.

Former Members:
The Right Honourable Sir Konrad Schiemann; the Right Honourable Sir David Keene; the Honourable Sir Andrew Collins; the Right Honourable Sir Alan Moses; The Honourable Sir Duncan Ouseley; Richard Yorke QC (1956) (QC - 1971); The Right Honorable Sir Jeremy Sullivan; Sir Douglas Frank QC, former President of the Lands Tribunal; His Honour Bernard Marder QC, President of the Lands Tribunal; His Honour Judge Barratt QC; Victor Wellings QC, former President of the Lands Tribunal; His Honour Judge Gregory Stone QC; His Honour Judge Mole QC, His Honour Judge Huskinson, His Honour Judge Shanks.

Associate Tenants:
Professor G H Treitel QC; Patrick Patelin; John Sacker QC (NSW); Mansoor Jamal Malik (Oman); Dr Ami Barav; Richard Halsall; Nuno Santos-Costa; Jahangir Baglari; Thierry Marembert; Ian Dove QC; Natasha Peter; Joseph Dalby; Greg Laughton SC; Sir David Keene (Arbitrator); Peter Gribble; Caroline Kenny SC; Steven Walker.

11 GRAY'S INN SQUARE CHAMBERS

Chambers of Mr Ian Sen, 1st Floor South, 10/11 Gray's Inn Square, London WC1R 5JD
020 7405 6879
Fax: 020 7430 0502; DX: 161 London Ch Lane
E-mail: clerks@11graysinnsquare.com

Chambers of: Mr D I Sen

Disability access
Staff briefed or trained on duties under the disability legislation, Disabled parking available

12 GRAY'S INN SQUARE

Gray's Inn, London WC1R 5JP
020 7067 1960
Fax: 020 7183 6443
E-mail: almqc@12graysinn.com

Chambers of: Mr A L Marriott QC

14 GRAY'S INN SQUARE

14 Gray's Inn Square, Gray's Inn, London WC1R 5JP
020 7242 0858
Fax: 020 7242 5434; DX: 399 London Chancery Lane
E-mail: clerks@14gis.co.uk
URL: www.14graysinnsquare.co.uk
Out of hours telephone: 07778 068332

Chambers of: Ms S J Forster
Clerk: Geoffrey Carr BA

Forster, Sarah *1976*
Hall, Joanna *1973*
McNab, Mhairi *1974*
Slomnicka, Barbara *1976*
Kingsley, Richard *1977*
Morris, Brenda *1978*
Marks, Gillian *1981†*
Ford, Monica *1984*
Connell, Joan *1985*
Habboo, Camille *1987*
Roberts, Patricia *1987*
Spooner, Judith *1987*
Evans, Dylan *1989*
Sinclair, Jean-Paul *1989*
Alomo, Richard *1990*
Jones, Rhys *1990*
Pearson, Carolyn *1990*
James, Rachael *1992*
Ward, Martin *1992*
De Zonie, Jane *1993*
O'Donovan, Ronan *1995*
Whittam, Samantha *1995*
Glaser, Michael *1998*
Miller, Christopher *1998*
Savage, Mai-Ling *1998*
Bhari, Poonam *1999*
Scott, Laura *2001*
Cameron, Gillon *2002*
Short, Mandy *2003*
Lamb, Henry *2004*
Spencer, Anna *2004*
Gore, Sally *2006*
James, Byron *2006*
Pope, Sarah *2006*
Walker-Mckevitt, Emma *2006*
Wilkinson, Jonathan *2006*
Calnan, Eleanor *2007*
Blatchly, Phillip *2008*
Murray, Ewan *2008*
Bainham, Andrew *2009*
Hammond, Sara *2009*
Shaw, Jenna *2009*
Stevenson, Christopher *2009*

Types of work
Care proceedings · Common law (general) · Family law · Family provision · Housing · Landlord and tenant · Mental health · Personal injury

Disability access
Staff briefed or trained on duties under the disability legislation, Wheelchair access, Disabled parking available

GRAY'S INN TAX CHAMBERS

3rd Floor, Gray's Inn Chambers, Gray's Inn, London WC1R 5JA
020 7242 2642
Fax: 020 7831 9017; DX: 352 London Chancery Lane
E-mail: clerks@taxbar.com

Chambers of: Mr J M Grundy

Disability access
Staff briefed or trained on duties under the disability legislation, Wheelchair access, Disabled parking available

GREAT JAMES STREET CHAMBERS

37 Great James Street, London WC1N 3HB
020 7440 4949
Fax: 020 7440 4950; DX: 440 London Chancery Lane
E-mail: chambers@greatjames.co.uk
URL: www.greatjames.co.uk
Out of hours telephone: 07968 444401

Chambers of: Mr R A Jones QC
Clerks: Joel Michaels, Michael Bailey, Nicole Couse

Jones, Alun QC *1972†*
Hill, Andrew *1982*
Lanlehin, Olajide *1994*
Ramzan, Anwar *1995*
Miah, Anawar *1998*
Starr, Teresa *2000*
Jones, Amanda *2001*
Lange, Peter *2001*
Awodele, Olufemi *2002*
Andrews, Paul *2003*
Henley, Martin *2004*
Bhatt, Unnati *2007*
Dyke, Thomas *2007*
Stansfeld, James *2008*

Types of work
Administrative law · Commercial law · Conflict of laws · Corporate fraud · Courts martial · Crime · Extradition · Human rights · Immigration · Licensing

GREAT RUSSELL STREET CHAMBERS

265, 10 Great Russell Street, London WC1B 3BQ
020 3239 0650/07581 248366

GREEN LANE CHAMBERS

272 Green Lane, London SW16 3BA
020 8623 1654
Fax: 020 8623 1654
E-mail: a_sharda@hotmail.com

Chambers of: Mr A K Sharda

†Recorder *Door Tenant/Associate Member

D

CHAMBERS OF MR PETER GRIBBLE

Flat D, 2 Surrendale Place, London W9 2QW
020 7289 2744
E-mail: petergribble@compuserve.com

Chambers of: Mr P J Gribble

CHAMBERS OF MR PATRICK GROUND QC

13 Ranelagh Avenue, London SW6 3PJ
020 7736 0131
Fax: 020 7371 9649
E-mail: post@patrickground.com

Chambers of: Mr P Ground QC

Also at: Cornerstone Barristers 2-3 Gray's Inn SquareLondon WC1R 5JH

Ground, Patrick QC *1960**

Types of work
Administrative law · Building · Commercial contracts · Disciplinary tribunals · Education · Landlord and tenant · Local authorities · Planning · Professional negligence

CHAMBERS OF MR M G HAFIZ

8 Clairview Road, London SW16 6TU
020 8677 5778
Fax: 020 8677 5778
E-mail: mghafiz@hotmail.co.uk

Chambers of: Mr M G Hafiz

HAILSHAM CHAMBERS

Ground Floor, 4 Paper Buildings, Temple, London EC4Y 7EX
020 7643 5000
Fax: 020 7353 5778; DX: 1036 London Chancery Lane
E-mail: clerks@hailshamchambers.com
URL: www.hailshamchambers.com
Out of hours telephone: 07836 324917

Chambers of: Mr M B Spencer QC
Clerks: Stephen Smith (Senior Clerk), Michael Kilbey (First Junior Clerk)

Spencer, Martin QC *1979†*
McGregor, Harvey QC *1955*
Livesey, Bernard QC *1969*
Pooles, Michael QC *1978†*
Pittaway, David QC *1977†*
West-Knights, L J QC *1977†*
Flenley, William QC *1988*
Picton, Julian QC *1988*
Post, Andrew QC *1988*
Hutton, Alexander QC *1992*
De Freitas, Anthony *1971†*
Tracy Forster, Jane *1975*
Mishcon, Jane *1979*
Neale, Fiona *1981*
Holwill, Derek *1982*
Campbell, Glenn *1985*
Jackson, Matthew *1986*
Bacon, Francis *1988†*
Price, Clare *1988*
Mangat, Tejina *1990*
Howarth, Simon *1991*
Pollock, Evelyn *1991*
Axon, Andrew *1992*
Peacock, Nicholas *1992*
Wilton, Simon *1993*
Charlwood, Spike *1994*
Christie-Brown, Sarah *1994*
Ewins, Catherine *1995*
Sawyer, Katrine *1996*
Stacey, Dan *1996*
Ferguson, Eva *1999*
McMahon, Heather *1999*
Mitchell, Paul *1999*
Carpenter, Jamie *2000*
Munro, Joshua *2001*
Gilberthorpe, James *2002*
MacKinnon, Lucy *2003*
Bankes-Jones, Henry *2004*
Bennett, David *2005*
Benson, Imran *2005*
Bailey, Stephen *2006*
Nash, Alice *2006*
Simpson, Jacqueline *2006*
O'Reilly, Niamh *2007*
Juckes, David *2008*
Pilsbury, Nicholas *2008*
Curtis-Rouse, Alice *2009*
Meiland, Justin *2010*
Marshall-Andrews, Robert QC *1967†**
Hogg, Douglas QC *1968**

Types of work
Administrative law · Agriculture · Arbitration · Civil liberties · Clinical negligence · Commercial law · Commodities · Conflict of laws · Construction law · Consumer law · Costs · Damages · Disciplinary tribunals · Employment · Foreign law · Housing · Information technology · Insurance · Landlord and tenant · Licensing · Medical law · Medical negligence · Mental health · Partnerships · Personal injury · Professional negligence · Sale and carriage of goods · Sport · Trusts

Disability access
Staff briefed or trained on duties under the disability legislation, Wheelchair access, Disabled parking available

THE CHAMBERS OF SHAHEEN HAJI

89F Philbeach Gardens, London SW5 9EU
07553 867153
E-mail: sheni1@hotmail.com

 †Recorder *Door Tenant/Associate Member

HARCOURT CHAMBERS

HARCOURT
CHAMBERS

LONDON OXFORD

1st Floor, 2 Harcourt Buildings, Temple, London EC4Y 9DB
0844 561 7135
Fax: 020 7353 6968; DX: 373 London Chancery Lane
E-mail: sboutwood@harcourtchambers.co.uk
URL: www.harcourtchambers.co.uk

Chambers of: Miss F J Judd QC
Practice Manager: Judith Partington; Chambers Director: Simon Boutwood

Also at: Harcourt Chambers, Churchill House, 3 St Aldate's Courtyard, St Aldate's, Oxford OX1 1BN

Judd, Frances QC *1984*
Vater, John QC *1995*
Evans, Roger *1970†*
Rodgers, June *1971†*
Sefi, Benedict *1972*
Collinson, Alicia *1982*
Brett, Matthew *1987*
Gibbons, Sarah *1987*
Hay, Fiona *1989†*
Granshaw, Sara *1991*
Garrido, Damian *1993*
Potter, Louise *1993*
Allen, Douglas *1995*
Goodwin, Nicholas *1995†*
Vine, Aidan *1995*
Miller, Simon *1996*
Sampson, Jonathan *1997*
Brookes-Baker, Matthew *1998*
Leong, Andrew *1998*
Wraight, Oliver *1998*
Kirkwood, Edward *1999*
Little, Helen *1999*
Jeakings, Craig *2000*
Styles, Margaret *2000*
Devereux, Edward *2001*
Green, Jason *2001*
Turner, James *2001*
Forbes, Alex *2003*
Tomlinson, Elizabeth *2004*
Williams, Alison *2004*
Wilkins, Chloe *2006*
Hylton, Nasstassia *2007*
Perry, Alex *2007*
Wilkinson, Helen *2007*
Cox, Sian *2008*
Crispin, Stephen *2008*
Marusza, David *2009*
Rayner, Emily *2009*
Ramsden, Justine *2010*
Sharp, Christopher QC *1975†**
Jacklin, Susan QC *1980†**
Higgins, Mark *2005**

Types of work
Administrative law · Care proceedings · Chancery (land law) · Company, commercial and competition · Ecclesiastical law · Education · Employment · Equity · Family law · Family provision · Local authorities · Medical negligence · Personal injury · Planning · Professional negligence · Trusts · Wills

Disability access
Wheelchair access, Disabled parking available

ATKINSON BEVAN CHAMBERS

1st Floor, 2 Harcourt Buildings, Temple, London EC4Y 9DB
020 7353 2112
Fax: 020 7353 8339; DX: 489 London Chancery Lane
E-mail: clerks@2hb.co.uk
URL: www.2hb.co.uk

Chambers of: Mr N J Atkinson QC
Clerks: Simon Butler, David Fardon, Ben Cressey, Ross Chapman, Tom Tracy; Administrator: Vicky Beasley

Atkinson, Nicholas QC *1971†*
Shorrock, Michael QC *1966†*
Howes, Sally M QC *1983*
Jafferjee, Aftab QC *1980*
Etherton, Gillian QC *1988*
Clayton, Stephen *1973*
Williams, John *1973†*
Smyth, Stephen *1974†*
Paltenghi, Mark *1979*
Gadsden, Mark *1980*
Carpenter, Jane *1984*
Farmer, Matthew *1987*
Bleaney, Nicholas *1988*
Clement, Peter *1988*
Dawes, James *1993*
Fitzgerald, Toby *1993*
Wilkins, Thomas *1993*
Halkerston, Sally *1994*
Kelleher, Benedict *1994*
Thompson, Sally *1994*
Cavin, Paul *1995*
Alexander, Nicholas *1996*
Knight, Jennifer *1996*
Hunter, Timothy *1998*
Lodge, Hugo Dan *1998*
Blumgart, Kate *1999*
Brown, James *1999*
Giddens, Sarah *1999*
Stimpson, Christopher *1999*
Banerjee, Subhankar *2000*
Osborne, Jane *2000*
Nicholson, Thomas *2001*
Stangoe, Heather *2001*
Duncan, Hannah *2002*
Brown, Sam *2004*
French, Hugh *2004*
Gordon, James *2004*
Fleck, Nicola *2006*
Franklin, Edward *2006*
Kent, Rupert *2006*
Seelig, Leo *2007*
Burgess, Jenny *2008*
Cooke, Duncan *2010*

Types of work
Confiscation · Corporate fraud · Courts martial · Crime · Licensing · Mental health

Disability access
Staff briefed or trained on duties under the disability legislation, Disabled parking available

D

HARDWICKE

New Square, Lincoln's Inn, London WC2A 3SB
020 7242 2523
Fax: 020 7691 1234; DX: 393 London Chancery Lane
E-mail: enquiries@hardwicke.co.uk

Chambers of: Mr N D Jones QC, Mr P S M Reed QC

Disability access
Staff briefed or trained on duties under the disability legislation, Wheelchair access, Disabled parking available

1 HARE COURT

1 Hare Court, Temple, London EC4Y 7BE
020 7797 7070
Fax: 020 7797 7435; DX: 342 London Chancery Lane
E-mail: clerks@1hc.com

Chambers of: Mr N N G Cusworth QC

Disability access
Staff briefed or trained on duties under the disability legislation, Wheelchair access, Disabled parking available

2 HARE COURT

Lower Ground, Ground, 1st & 2nd Floor, 2 Hare Court, Temple, London EC4Y 7BH
020 7353 3982
Fax: 020 7353 0667; DX: 444 London Chancery Lane
E-mail: clerks@2harecourt.com

Chambers of: Mr S O F Pownall QC

Disability access
Staff briefed or trained on duties under the disability legislation, Wheelchair access, Disabled parking available

3 HARE COURT

3 Hare Court, Temple, London EC4Y 7BJ
020 7415 7800
Fax: 020 7415 7811; DX: 212 London Chancery Lane
E-mail: clerks@3harecourt.com
URL: www.3harecourt.com
Out of hours telephone: 020 7415 7800

Chambers of: Mr J M Dingemans QC
Clerks: Toby Eales, Darren Whitbread, Simon Hamilton, Duane Hitchman, Catherine Farmiloe, James Donovan; Practice Manager: Marketing Manager: Mika Thom; Administrator: Michael Oliver; Fees Clerk: Susan Johnson

Dingemans, James QC *1987*
Strachan, Mark QC *1969*
Guthrie, James QC *1975*†
Knox, Peter QC *1983*
Davenport, Simon QC *1987*
Stevens, Howard QC *1990*
McLeod, Iain *1969*†
Neville-Clarke, Sebastian *1973*
Young, Andrew *1977*
Janusz, Pierre *1979*
Godwin, William *1986*
Letman, Paul *1987*
Butler, Rupert *1988*
Juss, Satvinder *1989*
Casey, Aidan *1992*
Happold, Matthew *1995*
Roe, Thomas *1995*
Samuel, Richard *1996*
Deal, Katherine *1997*
Crowther, Sarah *1999*
Saxby, Dan *2000*
Poole, Tom *2001*
Atwal, Navjot *2002*
Hawkins, James Peter *2003*
Lewis, Daniel *2003*
Strang, Robert *2003*
Clarke, Daniel *2005*
Johnson, Clara *2005*
Tivadar, Daniel *2005*
Ibrahim, Sara *2006*
Masood, Hafsah *2006*
Pennington-Benton, Rowan *2008*
Pugh, Helen *2008*
Wijeyaratne, Asela *2008*
Ajmone-Marsan, Cosimo *2009*
Halban, Alexander *2009*

Types of work
Civil fraud · Commercial law · Constitutional and administrative law · Employment · Insolvency · Professional negligence · Public law · Travel law

Disability access
Staff briefed or trained on duties under the disability legislation, Disabled parking available

CHAMBERS OF MR G F HAWKER

3rd Floor, Flat North, 2 Raymond Buildings, Gray's Inn, London WC1R 5BH
020 7405 1953
Fax: 020 7405 7553
E-mail: geoffreyhawker@cuthbertlake.co.uk

Chambers of: Mr G F Hawker TD

HEATHWAY CHAMBERS

31 Heathway, London SE3 7AN
020 8293 0509
E-mail: daviddaly@talktalk.net

Chambers of: Mr D Daly

HENDERSON CHAMBERS

2 Harcourt Buildings, Temple, London EC4Y 9DB
020 7583 9020
Fax: 020 7583 2686; DX: 1039 London Chancery Lane
E-mail: clerks@hendersonchambers.co.uk
URL: www.hendersonchambers.co.uk
Out of hours telephone: J White 01344 621838; H Gilson mobile 07841 344040

Chambers of: Mr C A W Gibson QC
Clerk: John White (Chief Clerk); Practice Manager: Harry Gilson (Senior Practice Manager); Administrator: Helen Ghalem (Administration Manager)

Gibson, Charles QC *1984*†
Mawrey, Richard QC *1964*†
Susman, Peter QC *1966*†
West, Lawrence QC *1979*†
Popat, Prashant QC *1992*
Dashwood, Alan CBE QC *1969*
Williams, Rhodri QC *1987*
Green, Patrick QC *1990*
O'Sullivan, Bernard *1971*
Harvey, Jonathan *1974*
Hamer, Kenneth *1975*†
Hibbert, William *1979*
Palmer, James *1983*
Steinert, Jonathan *1986*
Brook, David *1988*
Davies, Andrew *1988*
Smith, Julia *1988*
Goldman, Linda *1990*
Campbell, Oliver *1992*
Sheehan, Malcolm *1993*
Riley-Smith, Toby *1995*
Webb, Geraint *1995*
Withington, Angus *1995*
Kinnier, Andrew *1996*
Heppinstall, Adam *1999*
Dilworth, Noel *2001*
Sethi, Natasha *2001*
Chowdhury, Nazeer *2002*
Purnell, James *2002*
Bradley, Matthew *2004*
Cohen, Abigail *2005*
Donnelly, Kathleen *2005*
Wilson, Hannah *2005*
Richardson, Matthew *2006*
Roberts, Richard *2006*
Lewis, Jonathan *2007*
Robertson, Nicole *2007*
Warwick, Henry *2007*
Evans, Thomas *2008*
Humphreys, Elizabeth *2009*
Rosenthal, Dennis *2009*
Curtain, Hannah *2010*
Skinner, Paul *2010*
Williams, James *2010*
Bentley, Philip QC *1970**
Stanbrook, Clive QC OBE *1972**
Ratliff, John *1980**
Scudamore, Jeremy *1982**
Garner, Adrian *1985**
Ashworth, Lance QC *1987*†*
Schoneveld, Frank *1992**

Types of work
Administrative law · Alternative dispute resolution · Arbitration · Asbestos-related diseases · Boundaries · Civil actions against the police · Clinical negligence · Commercial fraud · Commercial law · Commercial litigation · Commercial property · Commercial regulation · Common law (general) · Competition law · Compulsory Purchase · Computer contracts · Computer crime · Computer litigation · Constitutional and administrative law · Construction law · Consumer credit · Consumer law · Contaminated land · Coroner's inquests · Corporate finance · Corporate liability · Corporate manslaughter · Cross-border litigation and remedies · Data protection · Directors' disqualification · Disability discrimination · Disasters · Disciplinary procedures · Disciplinary tribunals · Discrimination · Dispute resolution · E-commerce · EC competition law · Election law · Employment · Environment · European law · European Union · Financial services · Fire and other property damage claims · Food law · Freedom of information · Freezing orders · Group litigation · Health and safety · Healthcare law · Holiday injury and damages · Housing · Human rights · Immigration · Industrial diseases · Industrial relations law · Information technology · Inquests · Insurance · Internet law · Judicial review · Labour arbitration · Land compensation · Landlord and tenant · Lands Tribunal · Local authorities · Local authority claims · Local authority liability · Local government finance · Mediation · Medical law · Medical negligence · Medicines Act · Mortgages · Motor vehicles · Multi-party litigation · NHS inquiries · Occupational diseases · Oil and gas law · Ombudsman · Overseas accidents · Parliamentary · Personal injury · Pharmaceuticals · Police · Pollution · Privy Council · Procurement · Product liability · Product safety · Professional negligence · Public health · Public inquiries · Public law · Railways · Real property · Regulatory and disciplinary law · Rights of light · Rights of way · Road haulage · Road traffic · Road traffic offences · Sale and carriage of goods · Scientific cases · Shareholder agreements · Society of Lloyd's · Solicitor's indemnity · Sport · Sports medicine · Telecommunications · Trade Descriptions Act · Trading standards · Travel law · Utilities · Warranty claims · Water

Chambers Established 1954

†Recorder *Door Tenant/Associate Member

D

Opening times: 8.00am - 7.00pm and outside these hours by arrangement (see out of hours tel nos)

Chambers' facilities
Conference Rooms, Disks Accepted, E-mail, Wi-Fi, Multi-point Video Conferencing

Disability access
Staff briefed or trained on duties under the disability legislation, Wheelchair access, Disabled parking available

Languages spoken
Afrikaans, French, German, Japanese, Spanish, Welsh

Fees policy
Fees are negotiated with the Chief Clerk: our aim is that fees will be reasonable and competitive, depending on the importance and nature of the work and the expertise and seniority of counsel.

HIGHGATE CHAMBERS

81 Cheverton Road, London N19 3BA
020 7272 2245
Fax: 020 7272 2245

Chambers of: Mrs J Horne-Roberts

HIGHGATE CHAMBERS

62A Great North Road, Highgate, London N6 4LT
020 8340 6031
Fax: 020 8348 3830; DX: 51901 Highgate
E-mail: enquiries@highgatechambers.co.uk

Chambers of: Mr J R Wragg

10 HIGHLEVER ROAD

10 Highlever Road, North Kensington, London W10 6PS
020 8969 8514
Fax: 020 8969 8514
E-mail: znsayeed@uk2.net

Chambers of: Mr M A Sayeed

Disability access
Staff briefed or trained on duties under the disability legislation, Disabled parking available

CHAMBERS OF MR A C HILL

16 Hart Grove, London W5 3NB
07792 682928
E-mail: acrhill@yahoo.co.uk

Chambers of: Mr A C R Hill

HIND COURT CHAMBERS

London East, 100 Burford Wharf, 3 Cam Road, London E15 2SL
020 8534 2495
Fax: 020 8534 2495
E-mail: peter_fox@btinternet.com

Chambers of: Mr P Fox

2-3 HIND COURT CHAMBERS

2-3 Hind Court, Fleet Street, London EC4A 3DL
020 7822 2150
Fax: 020 7822 2155; DX: 102 London Chancery Lane
E-mail: david@2-3hindcourt.com

Chambers of: Mr P N Mallender

HOGARTH CHAMBERS

5 New Square, Lincoln's Inn, London WC2A 3RJ
020 7404 0404
Fax: 020 7404 0505; DX: 16 London Chancery Lane
E-mail: barristers@hogarthchambers.com

Chambers of: Mr R N L Wyand QC, Mr A J D Wilson QC

CHAMBERS OF MR M M HOSSAIN

Hossain Law Associates, 113 New Road, London E1 1HJ
020 7539 3401
Fax: 020 7539 3402
E-mail: monwar27@yahoo.co.uk

Chambers of: Mr M M Hossain

CHAMBERS OF MR M A HUSSAIN

29 Strathbrook Road, London SW16 3AT
020 8679 2398
Fax: 020 8679 2398
E-mail: altafhussain06@yahoo.co.uk

Chambers of: Mr M A Hussain

CHAMBERS OF MR DONALD IDEH

12 Ashburnham Tower, Edith Grove, Chelsea, London SW10 0EE

Chambers of: Mr D Ideh

IGBOBI CHAMBERS

c/o Lawyers' Club, 3rd Floor, 218 Strand, London WC2R 1AT
0203 2867626
Fax: 020 7583 5921; DX: 232 London Chancery Lane
E-mail: aelesinnla@igbobichambers.com

Chambers of: Mr A Elesinnla

CHAMBERS OF MARION SMULLEN AND KERIM FUAD QC

1 Inner Temple Lane, London EC4Y 1AF
020 7427 4400
Fax: 020 7427 4427; DX: 286 London Chancery Lane
E-mail: clerks@1itl.com
URL: www.1itl.com
Out of hours telephone: 020 7427 4400

Chambers of: Mrs M Smullen, Mr K Fuad QC
Clerks: Simon Duggan (Senior Clerk), Neil Jackson

Fuad, Kerim QC *1992*
Smullen, Marion *1985*
Adonis, George *1973*
Johnston, Christopher *1983*
Manley, Lesley *1983*
Brain, Pamela *1985*
Anders, Jon *1990*
Bell, Dominic *1992*
Morris, Sarah *1996*
Ahmed, Gulam *1997*
Rutter, Gary *1997*
Witcombe, Richard *1997*
Molloy, Siobhan *1998*
Stevens, Mark *1998*
Wolfe, Madeleine *1998*
Blackman, Edmund *1999*
Casey, Paul *1999*
Molloy, Kevin *1999*
Hashim, Mu'Min *2000*
Hutchings, Richard *2001*
Weetch, Oliver *2001*
Walklate, Andrew *2002*
Hope, Andrew *2003*
Morris, Johanna *2003*
Smith, Clive *2003*
Kettle-Williams, Alexandra *2004*
Langevad, Claire *2005*
Elliott, Simon *2007*
Cahill, Rowena *2008*
Pollard, Eliza *2008*
Hardy, Joanna *2010*
Witcher, Colin *2010*

Types of work
Courts martial · Crime · Inquests · Mental health · Prison law · Regulatory and disciplinary law

Disability access
Staff briefed or trained on duties under the disability legislation, Disabled parking available

INVICTUS CHAMBERS LONDON

First Floor, 1 Mitre Court Buildings, Temple, London EC4Y 7BS DX: 106 London Chancery Lane
E-mail: admin@invictuschamberslondon.co.uk

Chambers of: Mr K E Rogers

CHAMBERS OF MR AMINUL R. ISLAM

14 Fakruddin Street, London E1 5BU
020 7247 1977
E-mail: aminul2@hotmail.co.uk

Chambers of: Mr A R Islam

CHAMBERS OF MR RICHARD JOB

16 Aberdeen Court, Aberdeen Park, London N5 2BH
020 7226 3811
E-mail: richardjob11@gmail.com

Chambers of: Mr R L Job

CHAMBERS OF MR P JOHNSON

8 Packington Street, London N1 8QB
020 7288 2256
E-mail: phill_m_johnson@hotmail.com

Chambers of: Mr P M Johnson

CHAMBERS OF LAWRENCE JONES

8 Stone Buildings, Lincoln's Inn, London WC2A 3TA
020 7831 1444
Fax: 020 7900 2416; DX: 277 London Chancery Lane
E-mail: clerks@8stonebuildings.com

Chambers of: Mr L V Jones

D

JUSTICE HOUSE

67 Wentworth Avenue, Finchley, London N3 1YN
07973 794 946
E-mail: pherb5law@aol.com

Chambers of: Mr P Herbert OBE

KEATING CHAMBERS

15 Essex Street, London WC2R 3AA
020 7544 2600
Fax: 020 7544 2700; DX: 1045 London Chancery Lane
E-mail: clerks@keatingchambers.com
URL: www.keatingchambers.com

Chambers of: Mr P A Darling QC
Clerks: Nick Child (Senior Clerk), Barry Bridgman (Consultant Senior Clerk), Chris Sunderland, Rob Bryant, William Shrubsall, Rob Cowup, Gareth Davies, Anthony Carroll, James Luxmoore, Shabana Moliko; Administrator: Nicola Humphreys; Richard Murch, Anna Dairion, Nina Khan; Finance Manager: Nicola Humphreys

Darling, Paul QC *1983*
Uff, John QC CBE *1970*†
Thomas, Christopher QC *1973*†
Marrin, John QC *1974*†
Furst, Stephen QC *1975*†
Elliott, Timothy QC *1975*
Gaitskell, Robert QC *1978*†
Boulding, Philip QC *1979*
Taverner, Marcus QC *1981*
Thomas, David QC *1982*
O'Farrell, Finola QC *1983*†
Williamson, Adrian QC *1983*†
Jackson, Rosemary QC *1981*†
Nissen, Alexander QC *1985*†
Jefford, Nerys QC *1986*†
Hannaford, Sarah QC *1989*
Hargreaves, Simon QC *1991*
Harding, Richard QC *1992*
Buehrlen, Veronique QC *1991*
Moran, Vincent QC *1991*
Constable, Adam QC *1995*
Hughes, Simon QC *1995*
Rowlands, Marc QC *1990*
Stansfield, Piers QC *1993*
Steynor, Alan *1975*†
Randall, Louise *1988*
Evans, Robert *1989*
McCredie, Fionnuala *1992*
Lee, Jonathan *1993*
Lemon, Jane *1993*
Mort, Justin *1994*
Buckingham, Paul *1995*
Jinadu, Abdul-Lateef *1995*
Lee, Krista *1996*
Coplin, Richard *1997*
Chambers, Gaynor *1998*
Scott Holland, Gideon *1999*
Selby, Jonathan *1999*
Townend, Samuel *1999*
Garrett, Lucy *2001*
Stephens, Jessica *2001*
Repper, Elizabeth *2002*
Lamont, Calum *2004*
Sims, Alice *2004*
Lazur, Thomas *2005*
Thompson, James *2005*
Webb, William *2005*
Brogden, Peter *2006*
Bury, Paul *2008*
Sareen, Ben *2008*
Williams, Sarah *2008*
Gollancz, David *2010*
Sheard, David *2010*
Owen, Tom *2011*
Stimpson, Michael *1969**
Pennicott, Ian QC *1982**

Types of work
Adjudication · Alternative dispute resolution · Arbitration · Boundaries · Building · Commercial contracts · Commercial litigation · Computer contracts · Computer litigation · Construction law · Contracts · Energy · Engineering disputes · Fire and other property damage claims · Information technology · Insurance · International arbitration · International commercial arbitration · Lands Tribunal · Local authorities · Performance bonds · Procurement · Professional negligence · Railways · Ship building · Technical contracts · Telecommunications · Utilities

Disability access
Wheelchair access, Disabled parking available

CHAMBERS OF MR BRIAN JAMES KENNEDY

72 Linzee Road, London N8 7RE
07891 747 342
Fax: 020 8348 2979

KENSINGTON CHAMBERS

5A Philbeach Gardens, London SW5 9DY
020 7373 2217
Fax: 020 7373 2217
E-mail: harrietgore.kensingtonchambers@btinternet.com

Chambers of: Mrs H N A Gore

CHAMBERS OF MR F KHAN

19 Glenwood Road, Hounslow, London TW3 1SW
07854 109584
E-mail: forzkhan@live.co.uk

Chambers of: Mr F Khan

†Recorder *Door Tenant/Associate Member

1 KBW CHAMBERS

1 King's Bench Walk, Temple, London EC4Y 7DB
020 7936 1500
Fax: 020 7936 1590; DX: 20 London Chancery Lane
E-mail: clerks@1kbw.co.uk
URL: www.1kbw.co.uk
Out of hours telephone: 07831 339391

Chambers of: Mr R A Anelay QC
Clerks: David Dear, Nicola Cade, Tim Madden, Mark Betts, Joe Lamb, Jed Watson; Administrator: Sue Gray (Director), Gary Feltham (Fees Clerk), Ruvimbo Mapika (Administration Assistant), Ann Martin (Typist), Jaqui Shiel (Reception)

Also at: 1 King's Bench Walk at Lewes, 174 High Street, Lewes, East Sussex BN7 1YE Tel: 01273 402600 Fax: 01273 402609

Anelay, Richard QC *1970*†
Singleton, Barry QC *1968*
Pratt, Camden QC *1970*†
Scriven, Pamela QC *1970*†
Bellamy, Stephen QC *1974*†
Turner, James QC *1976*
Howard, Charles QC *1975*
Kirk, Anthony QC *1981*
Newton, Clive QC *1968*
Eaton, Deborah QC *1985*†
Pocock, Christopher QC *1984*
Marshall, Philip QC *1989*
Harrison, Richard QC *1993*
Warren, Michael *1971*†
Budden, Caroline *1977*†
Harding, Cherry *1978*
Hornsby, Walton *1980*
Lister, Caroline *1980*†
Woodbridge, Julian *1981*
Cudby, Markanza *1983*†
Shay, Stephen *1984*
Cellan-Jones, Deiniol *1988*
Selman, Elizabeth *1989*
Barton, Richard *1990*
Fletcher, Marcus *1990*
McCourt, Christopher *1993*
Roberts, James *1993*†
Baughan, Andrew *1994*
Cook, Ian *1994*
Green, Victoria *1994*
Anderson, Nicholas *1995*
Brazil, Dominic *1995*
Crosthwaite, Graham *1995*
Hamilton, Carolyn *1996*
Thain, Ashley *1996*
Gardner, Alan *1997*
Castle, Richard *1998*
Rogers, Shona *1998*
Oliver, Harry *1999*
Reardon, Madeleine *2001*
Nagpal, Deepak *2002*
Holmes, Martha *2003*
Kelsey, Katherine *2003*
Harris, Caroline *2004*
Perrins, Jennifer *2004*
Wilkins, Susan *2004*
Newman, Peter *2005*
Watts, Andrea *2006*
McHugh, Kelan *2007*
Ozwell, Katherine *2007*
Tatton-Bennett, Alexander *2007*
Moys, Laura *2008*
Hartley, Charlotte *2009*
Ridley, Samantha *2009*
Grice, Jo *1991**

Types of work
Administrative law · Adoption · Alternative dispute resolution · Ancillary relief · Anti-social Behaviour Orders · Asset forfeiture · Asset recovery · Care proceedings · Child abduction · Child abuse · Child care law · Child support · Children · Civil actions against the police · Civil partnerships · Cohabitation · Confiscation of the proceeds of crime · Coroner's inquests · Coroners · Corporate fraud · Corporate manslaughter · Crime · Crime and criminal due process · Criminal judicial review · Divorce · Domestic violence injunctions · Equity · Family law · Family provision · Financial provision · Firearms · Forfeiture · Fraud · Homicide · Inquests · International criminal law · International fraud and asset tracing · Landlord and tenant · Licensing · Local authorities · Malicious prosecution · Matrimonial · Matrimonial finance · Mediation · Medical negligence · Mental health · Parliamentary · Personal injury · Personal insolvency · Police · Police discipline · Prison law · Prisoners' rights · Private children law · Professional negligence · Serial crime · Serious fraud · Sexual Offences · Special Guardianship · Trusts · Unmarried couples · Wardship

Opening times: 8.30am - 7.00pm

Chambers' facilities
Conference Rooms, Video Conference, E-mail, Telephone conferences

Disability access
Staff briefed or trained on duties under the disability legislation, Disabled parking available

Languages spoken
French, German, Portuguese, Spanish

†Recorder *Door Tenant/Associate Member

D

2 KING'S BENCH WALK

2 King's Bench Walk, Temple, London EC4Y 7DE
020 7353 1746
Fax: 020 7583 2051; DX: 1032 London Chancery Lane
E-mail: clerks@2kbw.com
URL: www.2kbw.com

Chambers of: Mr T J Mousley QC
Clerk: Daren Milton; Administrator: Chambers Administration Assistant: Alex Smith; Chambers Manager: Tracey McCarthy

Mousley, Timothy QC *1979*†
Mousley, William QC *1986*†
Selfe, Michael *1965*†
Parish, Stephen *1966*†
Jenkins, David *1967*
Wright, Jeremy *1970*†
Bailey, Anthony *1972*
Stopa, Christopher *1976*
Cochand, Charles *1978*
Robertson, Angus *1978*
Lofthouse, John *1979*
Shapiro, Selwyn *1979*
Foster, Simon *1982*
Bolton, Robert *1987*
Clarke, Michelle *1988*
Fleming, Adrian *1991*
Pyne, Russell *1991*
McAvock, Gabrielle *1994*
Russell, Fern *1994*
Britton, James *1996*
Venturi, Gary *1996*
Bussey-Jones, Elisabeth *1997*
Wellings, Oliver *2001*
Wood, Natalie *2001*
Austin, Rebecca *2002*
Lane, Rachael *2002*
McElduff, Barry *2002*
Freemantle, Kate *2003*
Barton, Jeremy *2004*
Dhadda, Sukwinder *2004*
Sharman, Brian *2004*
Sproson, Eileen *2005*
Williams, Michael *2005*
Fairley, Paul *2007*
Forrest, Robert *2007*
Foster, Erica *2007*
Hewertson, Christopher *2007*
Hollingsworth, Edward *2007*
Mulvanny, Berenice *2009*
Brocklehurst, Kelly *2010*
Culmer, Gabrielle *1999**
Williams, Jonathan *2007**

Types of work
Administrative law · Common law (general) · Crime · Education · Employment · Family law · Human rights

Disability access
Disabled parking available

4 KBW

Ground Floor, 4 King's Bench Walk, Temple, London EC4Y 7DL
020 7822 8822
Fax: 020 7822 8844; DX: 422 London Chancery Lane
E-mail: law@4kbw.net
URL: www.4kbw.net
Out of hours telephone: 07923 079 333

Chambers of: Mr L I Power
Clerks: Stephanie Tickner; Senior Clerk: Jason Roukin; Finance Manager: Sallie Berriff

Power, Lawrence *1995*
Beckman, Michael QC *1954*
Jarman, Samuel *1989*
Toogood, Katherine *1998*
McKinney, Nicola *2004*
Simon, Philipp *2004*
Tunley, James *2005*
Zoubir, Adam *2005*
Dann, Jared *2007*
Ditchburn, John *2007*
Barber, Jimmy *2008*
Owen, Naomi *2008*
Loxton, Christopher *2009*
McClymont, Greg *2010*

Types of work
Arbitration · Banking · Chancery · Commercial litigation · Employment · Information technology · Insolvency

Disability access
Wheelchair access, Disabled parking available

4 KING'S BENCH WALK

2nd Floor, 4 King's Bench Walk, Temple, London EC4Y 7DL
020 7822 7000
Fax: 0871 288 5693; DX: 1050 London Chancery Lane
E-mail: clerks@4kbw.co.uk
URL: www.4kbw.co.uk

Chambers of: Mr T W H Raggatt QC
Clerk: Lee Cook (Principal Clerk)

Raggatt, Timothy QC *1972*†
Thomas, Roger QC *1969*†
Leighton, Peter *1966*
Hillman, Basil *1968*
Knight, Keith *1969*
Spencer Bernard, Robert *1969*†
Mallison, Kate *1974*
Perry, Naomi *1974*
Deschampsneufs, Alice *1976*
Fortune, Peter *1978*
McConnell, Christopher *1979*
Purdie, Robert *1979*
Doherty, Nicholas *1983*
Arkhurst, Reginald *1984*
Bhakar, Surinder *1986*
Granville Stafford, Andrew *1987*

†Recorder *Door Tenant/Associate Member

Amin, Farah *1991*
Preston, *1991*
Burnett, Iain *1993*
Collins, Peter *1993*
Lal, Sanjay *1993*
Bond, Jackie *1994*
Ojutiku, Kemi *1994*
Palmer, Suzanne *1995*
Chbat, Nadia *1996*
McMorrow, Patrick *1996*
Fielding, Janick *1997*
Lycourgou, Olive *1997*
Martin, Piers *1997*
Maka, Issac *1998*
Roberts, Beverly *1998*
Upton, John *1998*
Critchley, Anne-Marie *1999*
Harris, Lee *1999*
Holme, Gavin *1999*
Salis, Robert *1999*
Roques, Michael *2000*
Davidge, Justine *2001*
Griffiths, Alison *2001*
Silva, David *2001*
Turner, Justyn *2001*
Tregidgo, Marc *2002*
Bryden, Christopher *2003*
Jacobs, Michaella *2003*
Carpenter, Naomi *2004*
Brown, John *2005*
Culver, Edward *2005*
Durber, Joanna *2005*
Moss, Richard *2005*
Sawtell, *2005*
Quinn, Tomas *2006*
Vooght, Abigail *2006*
Webster, Keith *2006*
Williams, Greg *2006*
Chaplin, Sophie *2007*
Wright, Lisa *2007*
Bonavero, Philippe *2008*
Dobby, Helen *2008*
Marsh, Nancy *2008*
John, Katherine *2010*
Rudman, Sara *1992**
Morton, Elizabeth *1999**

Types of work
Common law (general) · Contracts · Crime · Defamation · Education · Employment · Family law · Immigration · Landlord and tenant · Media · Personal injury · Professional negligence · Public law · Real property · Torts

Disability access
Staff briefed or trained on duties under the disability legislation, Disabled parking available

5 KING'S BENCH WALK

5 King's Bench Walk, Temple, London EC4Y 7DN
020 7353 5638
Fax: 020 7353 6166; DX: 367 London Chancery Lane
E-mail: clerks@5kbw.co.uk

Chambers of: Mr M A Heywood QC, Miss S A Forshaw QC

Disability access
Staff briefed or trained on duties under the disability legislation, Disabled parking available

6 KING'S BENCH WALK

Ground Floor, 6 King's Bench Walk, Temple, London EC4Y 7DR
020 7583 0410
Fax: 020 7353 8791
E-mail: clerks@6kbw.com

Chambers of: Mr D P Fisher QC, Mr D Perry QC

Disability access
Staff briefed or trained on duties under the disability legislation, Wheelchair access, Disabled parking available

6 KING'S BENCH WALK

Ground, Third & Fourth Floors, 6 King's Bench Walk, Temple, London EC4Y 7DR
020 7353 4931
Fax: 020 7353 1726
E-mail: clerks@6kbw.co.uk

Chambers of: Mr S Kadri QC

Disability access
Staff briefed or trained on duties under the disability legislation, Wheelchair access, Disabled parking available

7 KING'S BENCH WALK

Ground Floor, 7 King's Bench Walk, Temple, London EC4Y 7DS
020 7910 8300
Fax: 020 7910 8400; DX: 239 London Chancery Lane
E-mail: clerks@7kbw.co.uk

Chambers of: Mr G S J Kealey QC

Disability access
Disabled parking available

9 KING'S BENCH WALK

Lower Ground Floor South, 9 King's Bench Walk, Temple, London EC4Y 7DX
020 7353 9564
Fax: 020 7353 7943; DX: 118 London Chancery Lane
E-mail: 9kbw@btconnect.com

Chambers of: Mr A M Azhar

Disability access
Staff briefed or trained on duties under the disability legislation, Disabled parking available

D

D

10 KING'S BENCH WALK

Ground Floor, 10 King's Bench Walk, Temple, London EC4Y 7EB
020 7353 7742
Fax: 020 7583 0579; DX: 24 London Chancery Lane
E-mail: Chambers@10kingsbenchwalk.co.uk

Chambers of: Mr C J Algar

11 KING'S BENCH WALK

11 King's Bench Walk, Temple, London EC4Y 7EQ
020 7632 8500
Fax: 020 7583 9123; DX: 368 London Chancery Lane
E-mail: clerksteam@11kbu.com
URL: www.11kbw.com
Out of hours telephone: 07831 304 714

Chambers of: Mr J Goudie QC
Clerks: Mark Dann, Darren Bacon, John Davitt, Michael Smith, Martin Pownall, Faye Burfoot; Senior Clerks: Philip Monham, Lucy Barbet; Chief Executive: David Stead; Administrator: Claire Halas; Other Admin: Charlotte Robertson

Goudie, James QC *1970*
McGregor, Alistair J QC *1974*
Jeans, Christopher QC *1980*
Lynch, Adrian QC *1983*†
Kerr, Tim QC *1983*†
Cavanagh, John QC *1985*†
Giffin, Nigel QC *1986*
Lewis, Clive QC *1987*†
Laing, Elisabeth QC *1980*†
Wallington, Peter QC *1987*
Devonshire, Simon QC *1988*
Pitt-Payne, Timothy QC *1989*
Swift, Jonathan QC *1989*†
Oldham, Peter QC *1990*
Oudkerk, Daniel QC *1992*
Stilitz, Daniel QC *1992*
Sheldon, Clive QC *1991*
Jones, Seán QC *1991*
Nicholls, Paul QC *1992*
Moore, George *1970*
Oldham, Jane *1985*
Moore, Sarah *1990*
Choudhury, Akhlaq *1992*†
Coppel, Jason *1994*
Porter, Nigel *1994*
Steyn, Karen *1995*
Leiper, Richard *1996*
Wilson, Julian *1997*
McCafferty, Jane *1998*
Proops, *1998*
Rhee, Deok-Joo *1998*
Iyengar, *1999*
Blake, Andrew *2000*
Hooper, Ben *2000*
Milford, Julian *2000*
Clement, Joanne *2002*
Cornwell, James *2002*
Pilgerstorfer, Marcus *2002*
Edge, Andrew *2003*
Stone, Judith *2003*
Stout, Holly *2003*
Forshaw, Simon *2004*
Halliday, Patrick *2005*
Kamm, Rachel *2006*
Cross, Thomas *2007*
Rogers, Amy *2007*
Hopkins, Robin *2008*
Knight, Christopher *2008*
Barrett, *2009*
Capewell, Edward *2009*
Eddy, Katherine *2009*
Lee, Michael *2009*
Dennis, Ronnie *2010*
Slarks, Hannah *2011*
Moore, George *1970**

Types of work
Administrative law · Arbitration · Commercial law · Commercial litigation · Data protection · Employment · European law · Freedom of information · Healthcare law · Human rights · Immigration · Litigation · Local government and public services · Restraint of trade · Sport

Disability access
Staff briefed or trained on duties under the disability legislation, Disabled parking available

12 KING'S BENCH WALK

12
King's Bench Walk

12 King's Bench Walk, Temple, London EC4Y 7EL
020 7583 0811
Fax: 020 7583 7228; DX: 1037 London Chancery Lane
URL: www.12kbw.co.uk
Out of hours telephone: John Cooper: 07930 392 866; Graham Johnson: 07960 657 118

Chambers of: Mr A A Hogarth QC
Clerks: Graham Johnson, John Cooper; Practice Manager: Kevin McCourt, Lekie Johnson, Laura Wells, Tristan Wrigham, Phillip Austin; Jason Rowley

Also at: Royal Talbot House, 2 Victoria Street, Bristol, BSI 6BN

Hogarth, Andrew QC *1974*
Walker, Ronald QC *1962*†
Methuen, Richard QC *1972*†
Burton, Frank QC *1982*†
Martin, Gerard QC *1978*†
Williams, Nicholas QC *1976*†
Worthington, Stephen QC *1976*†
Featherby, William QC *1978*†
Rawlinson, Michael QC *1991*
Russell, Paul QC *1984*
Spencer-Lewis, Neville *1970*
King, John *1973*
Gallagher, Brian *1975*
Crawford, Lincoln *1977*
Levene, Simon *1977*†
Tudor-Evans, Quintin *1977*
Davison, Richard *1982*
Sanderson, David *1985*
Lewers, Nigel *1986*
Newbery, Freya *1986*†
Charles, Henry *1987*

†Recorder *Door Tenant/Associate Member

Pickering, Andrew *1987*
Hamill, Hugh *1988*
Chambers, Adam *1989*
Brown, Catherine *1990†*
Chandler, Kate *1990*
Candlin, James *1991*
Thornett, Gary *1991*
Audland, William *1992*
Jackson, Stephanie *1992*
Spears, Portia *1992*
Vincent, Patrick *1992*
Katyar, Arun *1993*
Kendall, Joel *1993*
D'Souza, Carolyn *1994*
Dignum, Marcus *1994*
Tobin, Daniel *1994*
Viney, Richard *1994*
Calvert, David *1995*
Peck, Catherine *1995*
John, Simon *1996*
Petts, Timothy *1996†*
Thomson, Louise *1996*
Leech, Ben *1997*
Madan, Pankaj *1997*
Short, Anna *1997*
Steinberg, Harry *1997*
Aggrey-Orleans, Kweku *1998*
Callow, David *1998*
Payton, Alexander *1998*
Boyle, Karen *2000*
Frost, Angela *2001*
Roy, Andrew *2002*
Newnham, Mary *2003*
Sharpe, David *2004*
Kemp, Edward *2005*
Scott, Gemma *2005*
Sullivan, James *2005*
Youshani, Elahe *2005*
Carington, Alexander *2006*
Kennedy, Roisin *2006*
Kerr, Patrick *2006*
Swoboda, John-Paul *2006*
Gordon Walker, Emily *2007*
O'Neill, Michael *2007*
Pandya, Abha *2007*
Read, Emily *2007*
Robertshaw, Charles *2007*
Aldred, Lois *2008*
Holland, Russell *2008*
MacLean, Niall *2008*
Pacey, Thomas *2008*
Wilson, Thea *2008*
Boyle, Lucy *2009*
Cashman, Vanessa *2009*
Rudd, Oliver *2009*

Types of work
Clinical negligence · Discrimination · Employment · Industrial diseases · Insurance · Personal injury · Professional negligence · Property · Sport

Disability access
Staff briefed or trained on duties under the disability legislation, Wheelchair access, Disabled parking available

13 KING'S BENCH WALK

13 King's Bench Walk, Temple, London EC4Y 7EN
020 7353 7204
Fax: 020 7583 0252; DX: 359 London Chancery Lane
E-mail: clerks@13kbw.co.uk
URL: www.13kbw.co.uk

Chambers of: Mr N Syfret QC
Clerk: Kevin Kelly; Administrator: Penny McFall

Also at: 13 KBW, 32 Beaumont Street, Oxford OX1 2NP

Syfret, Nicholas QC *1979†*
Redgrave, Adrian QC *1968*
Dawson, Alexander *1969†*
McGeorge, Anthony *1969*
Lamb, Robert *1973*
Goodwin, Deirdre *1974*
Bright, David *1976†*
Higgins, Anthony *1978*
Daly, Nigel *1979†*
Scott, Charles *1980*
Pote, Andrew *1983*
Sime, Stuart *1983*
Coode, Jonathan *1984*
Vickery, Neil *1985*
Maitland Jones, Mark *1986*
Blake, Arthur *1988*
Cramsie, Sinclair *1988*
Higgins, Adrian *1990*
Walters, Edmund *1991*
Edwards, Jennifer *1992*
Williams, Hugh *1992*
Buttimore, Gabriel *1993*
Chan, Susan *1994*
Nicol, Stuart *1994*
Woodhouse, Nigel *1997*
Grainger, Alistair *1998*
Harrington, Clare *1998*
Hirst, Martin *1998*
Hobbs, Daniel *1998*
Mann, Christopher *1998*
James, Henry *1999*
Lippold, Sarah *1999*
Dillon, Anne *2003*
Grant, Murray *2003*
Bennion-Pedley, Edward *2004*
Boswell, Timothy *2004*
Gurnham, Paul *2004*
Brown, Tim *2005*
Corrie, Matthew *2006*
Harrison, Paul *2006*
Yeatman, Trudi *2006*
McCormick, Lucy *2008*
Molloy, Steven *2008*
Lynch, Julian *2009*
Spanier, Samson *2009*
Stimmler, Benjamin *2009*
Williams, Richard *2009*
Reid, Paul *1975†**

Types of work
Administrative law · Banking · Chancery (general) · Clinical negligence · Common law (general) · Company, commercial and competition · Corporate fraud · Crime · Employment · Environment · Family law · Immigration · Insurance · Intellectual property · Landlord and tenant · Licensing · Local authorities · Medical law · Partnerships · Personal injury · Prison law · Professional negligence · Public law · Real property · Unincorporated associations

Disability access
Disabled parking available

KINGSWAY CHAMBERS

Suite 51, 95 Wilton Road, London SW1V 3BX
020 7404 2357
Fax: 020 7404 2357

Chambers of: Mr O O Oke

Disability access
Staff briefed or trained on duties under the disability legislation, Disabled parking available

†Recorder *Door Tenant/Associate Member

D

CHAMBERS OF MR R W KIRK

20 Redcliffe Square, London SW10 9JZ
020 7373 7364
Fax: 020 7373 2314
E-mail: robert.kirk@btinternet.com

Chambers of: Mr R W Kirk

CHAMBERS OF MR AMI FEDER

Ground Floor, Lamb Building, Temple, London EC4Y 7AS
020 7797 7788; Fax: 020 7353 0535, DX: 1038 London Chancery Lane
E-mail: clerks@lambbuilding.co.uk
URL: www.lambbuilding.co.uk
Out of hours telephone: 07721 339232

Chambers of: Mr A Feder
Clerks: Gary Goodger, David Corne, Paul Hammond, Philip Silverman, David O'Sullivan, Harry Butcher, Luke Clark; Administrator: Maxine Kinghorn

Also at: Lamb Building (Brighton), 22 Ship Street, Brighton, East Sussex BN1 1AD

Feder, Ami *1965*
Worrall, Anna QC *1959*†
Richmond, Bernard QC *1988*
Power, Lewis QC *1990*
Krolick, Ivan *1966*
Guy, Richard *1970*
Fox, John *1973*
Gordon, Jeremy *1974*
Sherman, Robert *1977*
Brennan, Janice *1980*
Gilbert, Francis *1980*
Phillips, Michael *1980*
O'Malley, Julie *1983*
Caldwell, Andrew *1984*
Toch, Joanna *1988*
Haughty, Jeremy *1989*
Wainwright, Jeremy *1990*
McCullough, Louise *1991*
Crampin, Paul *1992*
Gray, Jennifer *1992*
Kearney, Seamus *1992*
Fisher, Justine *1994*
Fripp, Eric *1994*
Dykers, Joy *1995*
Sahu, Mark *1995*
Peterson, Geraldine *1997*
Pretzell, Andreas *1997*
Selby, Andrew *1997*
Shannon, Nicola *1997*
Hulse, Cecilia *1998*
Laughton, Victoria *1998*
Lee, Gordon *1998*
Rhone-Adrien, Paula *1998*
Alexander, Andrew *1999*
Collins, Deirdre *1999*
Newport, Michael *1999*
Pease, Alexandra *1999*
Asanovic, Bojana *2000*
Briddock, Allan *2000*
Kelleher, Katherine *2000*
Syed, Safora *2000*
Chapman, Dawn *2001*
Powell, Michelle *2001*
Ahluwalia, Paramjit *2002*
Akinbolu, Sandra *2002*
James, Rhodri *2002*
Leslie, Clare *2002*
Rogers, Michael *2002*
Harrison, Jon *2003*
Loke, Siew Ying *2003*
Merrigan, David *2004*
Rawal, Anita *2004*
Reeve, Veronica *2004*
Daykin, Emma *2005*
Darnbrough, Daniel *2006*
Hyde, Michael *2006*
Jesurum, Raphael *2006*
Wilford, Ellis *2006*
Abzarian, Arash *2007*
Goudarzi, Sarah *2007*
McCarthy, Keelin *2007*
Mobbs, Richard *2007*
Richards, Duncan *2007*
Di Francesco, Alessandro *2008*
Ul-Haq, Yasmeen *2008*
Stephanou, Sarah *2008*
Chapman, Juliet *2009*
Holmes, Joseph *2009*
Moffatt, Rowena *2009*
Radford, Althea *2009*
Stevens, Heather *2009*
Fletcher, Eleanor *2010*
Hodkinson, Gary *2010*
Patton, Robin *1983**
Shamji, Rahim *2000**

Types of work
Arbitration · Care proceedings · Chancery (general) · Chancery (land law) · Clinical negligence · Common law (general) · Company, commercial and competition · Construction law · Consumer law · Corporate fraud · Courts martial · Crime · Discrimination · Employment · Equity · Family law · Family provision · Foreign law · German law · Housing · Human rights · Immigration · Insolvency · Israeli law · Landlord and tenant · Licensing · Local authorities · Mediation · Medical negligence · Mental health · Partnerships · Personal insolvency · Planning · Privy Council Appeals · Professional negligence · Public law · Sale and carriage of goods · Sport · Succession · Trusts · Wills

Chambers Established 1954
Opening times: 8.30am - 6.30pm

Chambers' facilities
Conference Rooms, Disks Accepted, Video Conference

Languages spoken
Dutch, French, German, Hebrew, Italian, Punjabi, Spanish

Fees policy
The clerks will be happy to advise on fees on a case by case basis, including if appropriate hourly rates.

†Recorder *Door Tenant/Associate Member

LAMB CHAMBERS

Lamb Building, Elm Court, Temple, London EC4Y 7AS
020 7797 8300
Fax: 020 7797 8308; DX: 418 Lde
E-mail: info@lambchambers.co.uk
URL: www.lambchambers.co.uk
Out of hours telephone: 07944 896383

Chambers of: Mr J M Cherry QC
Clerks: John Kelly (Senior Clerk), Paul O'Mullane, Adrian Hawes, Clifford Alderson; Administrator: Duncan Venables

Cherry, John QC *1961*
Hay, Robin *1964*
Challenger, Colin *1970*
West, Mark *1973*†
Connerty, Anthony *1974*
Maxwell Lewis, Cameron *1974*
Stewart, Paul *1975*
Briden, Timothy *1976*
Brilliant, Simon *1976*
Terry, Jeffrey *1976*
Caun, Lawrence *1977*
Mayall, David *1979*
Power, Richard *1983*
Colbey, Richard *1984*
Emerson, Paul *1984*
Blackwood, Clive *1986*
Miles, Napier *1989*
Swirsky, Adam *1989*
Stuart, James *1990*
Menzies, Richard *1993*
Sefton-Smith, Lloyd *1993*
Browne, James *1994*
Haggerty, Elizabeth *1994*
Kerr, Derek *1994*
Hayes, Richard *1995*
Pearson, Christopher *1995*
Prand, Annette *1995*
Richards, Jonathan *1995*
Daley, Howard *1997*
King, Mark *1997*
Coleman, Guy *1998*
O'Brien, Niamh *1998*
Topal, Erol *1998*
Davies, Emily *2000*
Wright, Abigail *2000*
Clifton, Jane *2001*
Kerr, Joanna *2001*
Seifert, Victoria *2002*
Winchester, Allyn *2002*
Winn-Smith, Matthew *2003*
Gist, *2004*
John, Morgan *2004*
Pressman, Bernard *2004*
Turnbull, Helen *2004*
Willink, David *2004*
Dwomoh, Elizabeth *2005*
Jacob, Winston *2005*
Dippenaar, Daniel *2007*
Evans, Leanne *2007*
Varma, Rahul *2007*
Seal, Philippa *2008*
Jacob, Vaughan *2009*
Bridgeman, James *2010*
Hassall, David *2011*
Shaw, Stephen *1975**
Coombes Davies, Mair *1988**
Walpole, Sean *2008**

Types of work
Administrative law · Arbitration · Banking · Chancery (general) · Chancery (land law) · Commercial litigation · Commercial property · Common land · Common law (general) · Company, commercial and competition · Competition law · Construction law · Consumer law · Copyright · Discrimination · EC competition law · Employment · Environment · Equity · Financial services · Housing · Information technology · Insolvency · Insurance · Intellectual property · International trade · Landlord and tenant · Local authorities · Medical negligence · Mental health · Partnerships · Personal injury · Personal insolvency · Planning · Professional negligence · Sale and carriage of goods · Trademarks · Trusts · Wills

Disability access
Staff briefed or trained on duties under the disability legislation, Wheelchair access, Disabled parking available

D

LANDMARK CHAMBERS

180 Fleet Street, London EC4A 2HG
020 7430 1221
Fax: 020 7421 6060; DX: 1042 London Chancery Lane
E-mail: clerks@landmarkchambers.co.uk
URL: www.landmarkchambers.co.uk

Chambers of: Mr D J Holgate QC, Mr T J Mould QC
Clerks: Jay Fullilove (Senior Clerk), Tom Grove, Bill King; Chambers Director: Holly Gavaghan; Finance Manager: Neil Dunlop

Holgate, David QC *1978*
Mould, Timothy QC *1987*
Woolley, David QC *1962*
Lockhart-Mummery, Christopher QC *1971*†
Clarkson, Patrick QC *1972*†
Harper, Joseph QC *1970*
Drabble, Richard QC *1975*
Hicks, William QC *1975*
Katkowski, Christopher QC *1982*
Male, John QC *1976*
King, Neil QC *1980*
Elvin, David QC *1983*
Price Lewis, Rhodri QC *1975*
Harris, Russell QC *1986*
Holland, David QC *1986*
Lieven, Nathalie QC *1989*
Cameron, Neil QC *1982*
Holland, Katharine QC *1989*
Litton, John QC *1989*
Morshead, Timothy QC *1995*
Warren, Rupert QC *1994*
Bickford-Smith, Stephen *1972*
Caws, Eian *1974*
Lewsley, Christopher *1976*
Pickles, Simon *1978*
Smith, David *1980*
Jefferies, Thomas *1981*
Morgan, Stephen *1983*
Langham, Richard *1986*
Taylor, Reuben *1990*
Taggart, Nicholas *1991*
White, Sasha *1991*
Forsdick, David *1993*
Boyle, Christopher *1994*
Jacobs, Christopher *1994*
Keen, Graeme *1995*
Lamont, Camilla *1995*
O'Callaghan, Declan *1995*
Reed, Matthew *1995*
Weekes, Tom *1995*
Lyness, Scott *1996*
Maurici, James *1996*
Nathan, Philip *1996*
Watkin, Toby *1996*
Broadfoot, Samantha *1997*
Kolinsky, Daniel *1998*
Stacey, Myriam *1998*
Olley, Katherine *1999*
Patry Hoskins, Carine *1999*
Walton, Robert *1999*
Buley, Tim *2000*
Ward, Galina *2000*
Williams, Guy *2000*
Blundell, David *2001*
Walder, Aaron *2002*
Leventhal, Zoe *2002*

†Recorder *Door Tenant/Associate Member

Banner, Charles *2004*
Blackmore, Sasha *2005*
Lewis, Gwion *2005*
Moules, Richard *2005*
Wills, Jonathan *2006*
Yates, Katrina *2006*
Lean, Jacqueline *2007*
Nye, Louisa *2007*
Turney, Richard *2007*
Harling-Phillips, Emma *2009*
Helmore, Katherine *2009*
Byass, Andrew *2010*
Parkinson, Andrew *2010*

D

Types of work
Environment · Planning · Property · Public law

Disability access
Staff briefed or trained on duties under the disability legislation, Wheelchair access, Disabled parking available, Induction loop or infra red system

CHAMBERS OF MISS ELIZABETH LANLEHIN

60 Woodhouse Road, Leytonstone, London E11 3NA
0793 941039

Chambers of: Miss E Lanlehin

CHAMBERS OF TAM LATYMER

144/145 Temple Chambers, Temple Avenue, London EC4Y 0DA
020 7353 2795
Fax: 020 7353 8331; DX: 213 London Chancery Lane
E-mail: tlatymer@hotmail.com

Chambers of: Mr T Latymer

Disability access
Wheelchair access, Disabled parking available

LINCOLN'S INN FIELDS CHAMBERS

88 Kingsway, London WC2B 6AA
0845 123 1234
E-mail: jsmith@lincolnsinnfields.com

Chambers of: Mr J R Smith

Disability access
Wheelchair access, Disabled parking available

LITTLETON CHAMBERS

3 King's Bench Walk North, Temple, London EC4Y 7HR
020 7797 8600
Fax: 020 7797 8699; DX: 1047 London Chancery Lane
E-mail: fschneider@littletonchambers.co.uk

Chambers of: Mr A B Clarke QC, Mr B C Freedman QC

Disability access
Staff briefed or trained on duties under the disability legislation, Wheelchair access, Disabled parking available

CHAMBERS OF MR JEFFREY LITTMAN

25 Heriot Road, Hendon, London NW4 2EG
020 8922 6844
Fax: 020 8632 9099
E-mail: jeffreylittman@aol.com

Chambers of: Mr J J Littman

CHAMBERS OF MR E M LIXANDRU

5 Ebbett Court, Victoria Road, London W3 6BW
07580 885314
E-mail: e.m.lixandru@live.co.uk

Chambers of: Mr E M Lixandru

CHAMBERS OF L LLOYD

3 Archery Fields House, Wharton Street, London WC1X 9PN
020 7837 4727
E-mail: lloyd.lloyd@cantab.net

Chambers of: Mr L Lloyd

LOMBARD CHAMBERS

1 Sekforde Street, Clerkenwell, London EC1R 0BE
020 7107 2100
Fax: 020 7107 2101; DX: 53332 Clerkenwell
URL: www.lombardchambers.com
Out of hours telephone: 07765 454323

Chambers of: Mr B I Stuart
Clerk: Ian Lee

Stuart, Bruce *1977*
Bull, Gregory QC *1976*
Davis, Greville *1976*
Stafford-Michael, Simon *1982*
McGuire, Donal *1983*

Butcher, Richard *1985*
Sharma, Pavan *1993*
Alfred, Stephan *1996*
Zaffuto, Rosa *2001*
Thomas, Timothy *2002*
Mohindru, Anurag *2004*
Panesar, Rishy *2004*
Cole, Gordon QC *1979**
Pratt, Richard QC *1980†**
Jarman, Samuel *1989**

Types of work

Corporate fraud · Crime · Financial services

Disability access

Wheelchair access, Disabled parking available

2 LOUISA CLOSE

2 Louisa Close, Wetherell Road, London E9 7BZ
020 8985 8716
Fax: 020 8985 8716
E-mail: lezwoo@btopenworld.com

Chambers of: Ms L Longhurst-Woods

Disability access

Staff briefed or trained on duties under the disability legislation, Wheelchair access, Disabled parking available, Induction loop or infra red system

CHAMBERS OF MR LOUIS LOURDES

69A, Chertsey Court, Lower Richmond Road, London SW14 7RD
020 8288 0133
Fax: 020 8288 2596
E-mail: richmondchambers@googlemail.com

Chambers of: Mr L J Lourdes

CHAMBERS OF THANDI LUBIMBI

46A Cannon Hill, Southgate, London N14 6LH
07857 034494; DX: 34304 Southgate
E-mail: thandi.lubimbi@gmail.com

Chambers of: Miss T B Lubimbi

CHAMBERS OF MR MACLEOD-JAMES

105 Chanctonbury Way, Woodside Park, London N12 7AA
07789 697477; DX: 57255 Finchley 2
E-mail: nmj.clientrecall@gmail.com

Chambers of: Mr N M MacLeod-James

THE CHAMBERS OF MISS NAYYERA MAHMOOD HASHMI

Suite 162, 4 Montpelier Street, Knightsbridge, London SW7 1EE

MAITLAND CHAMBERS

7 Stone Buildings, Lincoln's Inn, London WC2A 3SZ
020 7406 1200
Fax: 020 7406 1300; DX: 326 London Chancery Lane
E-mail: clerks@maitlandchambers.com
URL: www.maitlandchambers.com
Out of hours telephone: 07767 487537

Chambers of: Mr C H Pymont QC
Clerks: Colin Dawson, Danny Wilkinson, Rob Penson, Daniel Woodbridge, Danielle Jerome, Sam Dempsey, Senior Clerks: Lee Cutler, John Wiggs; Practice Manager: Stewart Thompson; Administrator: Valerie Piper; Finance Manager: Rumi Serafimova

Pymont, Christopher QC *1979†*
McCall, Christopher QC *1966*
Driscoll, Michael QC *1970*
Jackson, Judith QC *1975*
Newman, Catherine QC *1979†*
Trace, Anthony QC *1981*
Cunningham, Mark QC *1980*
Girolami, Paul QC *1983*
McGhee, John QC *1984*
Collings, Matthew QC *1985*
Nicholls, John QC *1986*
Johnson, Edwin QC *1987*
Parker, Christopher R QC *1984*
Chambers, Dominic QC *1987*
Peacock, Nicholas QC *1989*
Russen, Jonathan QC *1986*
Leech, Thomas QC *1988*
Morgan, Richard QC *1988*
Tipples, Amanda QC *1991†*
Walker, Andrew QC *1991*
Gibbon, Michael QC *1993*
Cullen, Edmund QC *1990*
Stubbs, Rebecca QC *1994*
Thomas, Nigel *1976†*
Walton, Alastair *1977*
Evans, Timothy *1979*
Walton, Carolyn *1980*
Dagnall, John *1983*
Harry, Timothy *1983*
Clifford, James *1984*
Dutton, Timothy C *1985*
Harrison, Philomena *1985*
Banner, Gregory *1989*
Wonnacott, Mark *1989*
Pryor, Michael *1992*
Grant, Thomas *1993*
Aldridge, James *1994*
Johns, Alan *1994*
Westwood, Andrew *1994*
Atkins, Siward *1995*
Margolin, Daniel *1995*
Ayres, Andrew *1996*
Hanham, James *1996*
Clarke, Paul *1997*
Addy, Catherine *1998*
Hayman, George *1998*
Hutton, Louise *1998*
Mumford, David *2000*
Smith, Adam *2001*
Smith, Matthew *2001*
Higgins, Gabrielle *2002*
John, Benjamin *2002*
Fowler, Richard *2003*
Winter, Alexander *2003*
Keller, Ciaran *2004*
Dewar, Fiona *2005*
McCluskey, Alec *2005*
Munby, Thomas *2006*
Allcock, Jonathan *2007*
Foskett, Rosanna *2008*

†Recorder *Door Tenant/Associate Member

D

Scher, Laurie *2008*
Sheehan, James *2008*
Ballance, James *2009*
Phillips, Oliver *2009*
Carr, Christopher *2010*
Jhittay, Narinder *2010*
Shankardass, Vijay *1972**
Randall, John QC *1978†**
Courtenay, Charles *1999**
Smith, Charles *2002**
Fox, David *2005**

Types of work
Administrative law · Agriculture · Alternative dispute resolution · Arbitration · Asset recovery · Banking · Boundaries · Breach of confidence · Capital tax · Chancery (commercial) · Chancery (general) · Chancery (land law) · Charities · Civil fraud · Commercial contracts · Commercial fraud · Commercial law · Commercial litigation · Commercial property · Common land · Company, commercial and competition · Competition law · Compulsory Purchase · Conflict of laws · Contaminated land · Contracts · Conveyancing · Corporate finance · Corporate insolvency · Corporate recovery · Corporation tax · Customs · Directors' disqualification · Dispute resolution · EC competition law · Education · Energy · Entertainment · Equity · Family provision · Financial services · Freezing orders · Housing · Income tax · Insolvency · Insurance · Intellectual property · International arbitration · International fraud and asset tracing · International law · International trade · Land compensation · Landlord and tenant · Lands Tribunal · Leasehold enfranchisement · Licensing · Limited partnerships · Local authorities · Media · Media and entertainment · Mining · Mortgages · Offshore finance · Offshore investment · Offshore trust litigation · Partnerships · Passing off · Pensions · Personal insolvency · Private client · Privy Council Appeals · Professional negligence · Public inquiries · Real property · Sale and carriage of goods · Share options · Shareholder agreements · Sport · Succession · Taxation and duties · Telecommunications · Trademarks · Trust litigation · Trusts · Warranty claims · Wills

Chambers Established 1870
Opening times: 8.00am - 7.00pm

Chambers' facilities
E-mail

Disability access
Staff briefed or trained on duties under the disability legislation, Wheelchair access, Disabled parking available

Languages spoken
French, Spanish

Fees policy
Fees will be negotiated with the clerk depending on the case.

CHAMBERS OF DR MARY MALECKA

Box 365, 43 Bedford Street, Westminster, London WC2E 9HA
07973 425313
E-mail: DRMARYM@TALK21.COM

Chambers of: Dr M M Malecka

Disability access
Staff briefed or trained on duties under the disability legislation

CHAMBERS OF AHMED A MALIK

243a Whitechapel Road, London E1 1DB
020 7978 8482/020 7642 5777
Fax: 020 7642 5888

Chambers of: Mr A A Malik

MALINS CHAMBERS

115 Temple Chambers, Temple Avenue, London EC4Y 0DA
020 7353 8868
E-mail: malins@btinternet.com

Chambers of: Mr J H Malins QC

Disability access
Staff briefed or trained on duties under the disability legislation, Wheelchair access, Disabled parking available

CHAMBERS OF PETER MARKS

1 Maxted Road, London SE15 4LL
07885 163086

Chambers of: Dr P Marks

CHAMBERS OF MR P J MARTIN

3 Anglesea Terrace, Wellesley Avenue, London W6 0UT
020 8746 1207
Fax: 020 8746 1207
E-mail: pmartinbar@btinternet.com

Chambers of: Mr P J Martin

†Recorder *Door Tenant/Associate Member

MATRIX CHAMBERS

Griffin Building, Gray's Inn, London WC1R 5LN
020 7404 3447
Fax: 020 7404 3448; DX: 400 London Chancery Lane
E-mail: matrix@matrixlaw.co.uk/lscott@matrixlaw.co.uk
URL: www.matrixlaw.co.uk

Chambers of: Mr T D Linden QC
Practice Managers: Cliff Holland, Jason Housden, Paul Venables; Chair of Management Committee: Thomas Linden QC; Chief Executive: Lindsay Scott; Chief Operating Officer: Kevin Hooper

Linden, Thomas QC *1989*†
Tomlinson, Hugh QC *1983*
Brennan, Daniel QC *1967*†
Booth, Cherie QC *1976*†
Montgomery, Clare QC *1980*†
MacDonald, Kenneth QC *1978*
Owen, Timothy QC *1983*
Emmerson, Ben QC *1986*
White, Antony QC *1983*
Thompson, Rhodri QC *1989*
Sands, Philippe QC *1985*
Monaghan, Karon QC *1989*
Hermer, Richard QC *1993*
Mountfield, Helen QC *1991*
Ryder, Matthew QC *1992*
Husain, Raza QC *1993*
Bailin, Alex QC *1995*
Knowles, Julian QC *1994*
Grodzinski, Sam QC *1996*
Wolfe, David QC *1992*
Laddie, James QC *1995*
Sheridan, Maurice *1984*
Cook, Kate *1990*
Kibling, Thomas *1990*
Marks, Jonathan *1992*
Simor, Jessica *1992*
Bodnar, Andrew *1995*
Gearty, Conor *1995*
Friedman, Daniel *1996*
Glasson, Jonathan *1996*
Knights, Samantha *1996*
O'Neill, Aidan QC (Scotland) *1996*
Summers, Mark *1996*
Afeeva, Mark *1997*
Morris, Gillian *1997*
Mansoori, Sara *1997*
Skinner, Lorna *1997*
Squires, Daniel *1998*
Crawford, James SC *1999*
Kentridge, Janet *1999*
Mitrophanous, Eleni *1999*
MacDonald, Alison *2000*
Tridimas, Takis *2000*
Armstrong, Nicholas *2001*
McColgan, Aileen *2001*
Brown, Christopher *2002*
Choo, Andrew *2002*
Purchase, Mathew *2002*
Chinkin, Christine *2003*
Prince, Laura *2003*
Hetherington, Tessa *2004*
Darwin, Claire *2005*
Law, Helen *2005*
Ni Ghralaigh, Blinne *2005*
Douglas, Zachary *2006*
Watkins, Aaron *2006*
Butler, Michelle *2007*
Craven, Edward *2007*
McNair-Wilson, Laura *2007*
Prochaska, Elizabeth *2007*
Logan, Rachel *2008*
Sandell, Adam *2008*
Smith, Andrew *2008*
Gibson, Nicholas *2009*
Desai, Rajendra *2010*
Buckley, Joanna *2011*

Types of work
Administrative law · Arbitration · Civil actions against the police · Civil liberties · Commercial law · Commercial litigation · Community care · Competition law · Corporate fraud · Crime · Data protection · Defamation · Discrimination · EC competition law · Education · Election law · Employment · Environment · European Union · Extradition · Freedom of expression · Healthcare law · Human rights · Immigration · International law · Local authorities · Local government and public services · Media · Mediation · Mental health · Prison law · Sport · Tax

Disability access
Staff briefed or trained on duties under the disability legislation, Wheelchair access, Disabled parking available

CHAMBERS OF MR K L MAY

24 Eliot Place, London SE3 0QL
020 8297 2579
Fax: 020 8297 9539
E-mail: Kieranlmay@aol.com

Chambers of: Mr K L May

Disability access
Wheelchair access, Disabled parking available

CHAMBERS OF MR ALEX MCBRIDE

14 Walden Street, London E1 2AN
07779 604 777

CHAMBERS OF MR D MENDES DA COSTA

4 Chesterfield Road, Chiswick, London W4 3HG
020 8747 4633
Fax: 020 8711 3167
E-mail: mendesdacosta@blueyonder.co.uk

Chambers of: Mr D Mendes Da Costa

CHAMBERS OF MISS SHARON MICHAELS

c/o 5 King Street Cloisters, Clifton Walk, King Street, Hammersmith, London W6 0GY
07877 681003
E-mail: sharonmichaels@btinternet.com

Chambers of: Miss S L Michaels

D

MIDDLE TEMPLE LANE CHAMBERS

2nd Floor South, 1 Middle Temple Lane, London EC4Y 9AA
020 7583 4352
Fax: 020 7353 5547; DX: 74 Chancery Lane
E-mail: chambers@mtlchambers.com
URL: www.mtlchambers.com
Out of hours telephone: 07901 553396

Chambers of: Mr R S MacKenzie
Clerk: Brenda Anderson (Senior Clerk)

MacKenzie, Robert *1996*
Beaumont, Ben *1978*
Armour, Alison *1979*
Fama, Gudrun *1991*
Patel, Bhavin *1991*
Newton, Claire *1992*
Crane, Suzanne *1995*
Donelon, Anne *1995*
Culling, Maria *1997*
Hughes, Jumoke *1999*
Wiktorowski-Solecki, Tamara *1999*
Schofield, Elizabeth *2000*
McCulloch, Cathy *2002*
Crawley, Ross *2005*
McKenna, Joseph *2005*
Dutt, Nisha *2007*
Mulchrone, Rory *2009*

Types of work
Civil law · Commercial law · Confiscation of the proceeds of crime · Consumer credit · Crime · Employment · Equine law · Family law · Fraud · Human rights · Immigration · Landlord and tenant · Money laundering · Personal injury · Prison law · Property · Road traffic · Tax

MILESTONE CHAMBERS

267 High Road, London NW10 2RX

CHAMBERS OF MR OLIVER MISHCON

1 Fetter Lane, London EC4A 1BR
020 7993 8890
Fax: 020 7692 4667
E-mail: info@mishcon.org

Chambers of: Mr O Z Mishcon

CHAMBERS OF ANDREW MITCHELL QC

33 Chancery Lane, London WC2A 1EN
020 7440 9950
Fax: 020 7430 2818; DX: 33 Chancery Lane
E-mail: clerks@33cllaw.com

Chambers of: Mr A R Mitchell QC

Disability access
Staff briefed or trained on duties under the disability legislation, Wheelchair access, Disabled parking available

1 MITRE COURT BUILDINGS

1 Mitre Court Buildings, Temple, London EC4Y 7BS
020 7452 8900
Fax: 020 7452 8999; DX: 195 Lde
E-mail: clerks@1mcb.com

Chambers of: Lord A M Gifford QC

Disability access
Staff briefed or trained on duties under the disability legislation

CHAMBERS OF MR AMI FEDER

Ground Floor, Lamb Building, Temple, London EC4Y 7AS
020 7797 7788; DX: 1038 London Chancery Lane
E-mail: clerks@lambbuilding.co.uk

Chambers of: Mr A Feder

Disability access
Staff briefed or trained on duties under the disability legislation, Wheelchair access, Disabled parking available

MOATLANDS CHAMBERS

2 Moarlands House, Cromer Street, London WC1H 8DF
07813 828697
E-mail: sjw976@googlemail.com

Chambers of: Mr S J Walker

MONCKTON CHAMBERS

1 & 2 Raymond Buildings, Gray's Inn, London WC1R 5NR
020 7405 7211
Fax: 020 7405 2084; DX: 257 London Chancery Lane
E-mail: chambers@monckton.com
URL: www.monckton.com
Out of hours telephone: 020 7405 7211

Chambers of: Mr K P E Lasok QC
Clerks: David Hockney, Tony Burgess, John Keegan, Steven Duffett, Sam Fullilove, Tom Tanner; Practice Manager: Marketing Co-ordinator: Simon Spence;

Administrator: Jolanta Luroseviciene; Chambers Director: Ann Langford; Finance Manager: Caroline Gowan

Lasok, Paul QC *1977†*
Swift, John Anthony QC *1965*
Paines, Nicholas QC *1978*
Vajda, Christopher QC *1979*
Hall, Melanie QC *1982*
Bowsher, Michael QC *1985*
Turner, Jonathan QC *1988*
Harris, Paul QC *1994*
Ward, Tim QC *1994*
Beard, Daniel QC *1996*
Moser, Philip QC *1992*
Fitzgerald, Michael *1979*
MacNab, Andrew *1986*
Mantle, Peter *1989*
Peretz, George *1990*
Skilbeck, Jennifer *1991*
Hill, Raymond *1992*
Lindsay, Alistair *1993*
Haynes, Rebecca *1994*
Rogers, Ian *1995*
Smith, Kassie *1995*
Rayment, Benedick *1996*
Holmes, Josh *1997*
Palmer, Robert *1998*
Kreisberger, Ronit *1999*
Metcalfe, Eric *1999*
Pickford, Meredith *1999*
Gardner, James Piers *2000*
Gregory, Julian *2000*
Sloane, Valentina *2000*
Williams, Robert *2000*
Facenna, Gerry *2001*
Howard, Anneli *2002*
Bates, Alan *2003*
Holmes, Elisa *2003*
Lask, Benjamin *2003*
McBride, Jeremy *2004*
McGurk, Brendan *2004*
Woolfe, Philip *2004*
Holiner, Drew *2005*
Banks, Fiona *2006*
West, Ewan *2006*
Blackwood, Anneliese *2007*
John, Laura Elizabeth *2007*
Draper, Owain *2008*
Osepciu, Ligia-Maria *2008*
Unterhalter, David SC *2009*
Lall, Tarlochan *2010*
Mitchell, Frank *2010*
Berridge, Alison *2011*
Collins, Michael *1978**
Currie, Heriot *1979**

Types of work
Administrative law · Agriculture · Arbitration · Civil liberties · Commercial law · Commercial litigation · Company, commercial and competition · Competition law · Conflict of laws · Construction law · Customs · ECHR · Employment · Environment · European law · Human rights · Intellectual property · International law · International trade · Procurement · Public law · Sport · Telecommunications · VAT

Chambers Established 1940
Opening times: 8.00am - 7.00pm Monday to Friday

Chambers' facilities
Conference Rooms, Disks Accepted, E-mail

Disability access
Staff briefed or trained on duties under the disability legislation, Wheelchair access, Disabled parking available

Languages spoken
Dutch, French, German, Italian, Russian, Spanish

Fees policy
As a general guide chambers' fees are charged on an hourly rate basis agreed in advance. Hourly rates for each member of chambers are available upon request. The clerks are happy to discuss other bases for calculating fees and will always try and accommodate the clients' requirements.

CHAMBERS OF BRIKENA MUHAREMI-MLINAKU

9a Bulwer Road, London E11 1DE
020 8279 2247

Chambers of: Mrs B Muharemi-Mlinaku

CHAMBERS OF MISS P MUQIT

149 Riverside Mansions, Milk Yard, Wapping, London E1W 3SU
07888 606866
E-mail: piyamuqit@gmail.com

Chambers of: Miss P D Muqit

CHAMBERS OF MR MUSTAKIM

6 Shandy Street, London E1 4LX

Chambers of: Mr A Y A Mustakim

NEVERN MANSIONS

Flat 8, 27A Nevern Square, London SW5 9TH
07973 320654
Fax: 020 7681 1556
E-mail: tony@cottle.demon.co.uk

Chambers of: Mr M A H Cottle

15 NEVERN PLACE

PO Box 42611, London SW5 9XZ
020 7193 2921
Fax: 0845 345 2713
E-mail: david@davidhyde.net

Chambers of: Mr D A Hyde

†Recorder *Door Tenant/Associate Member

D

15 NEW BRIDGE STREET

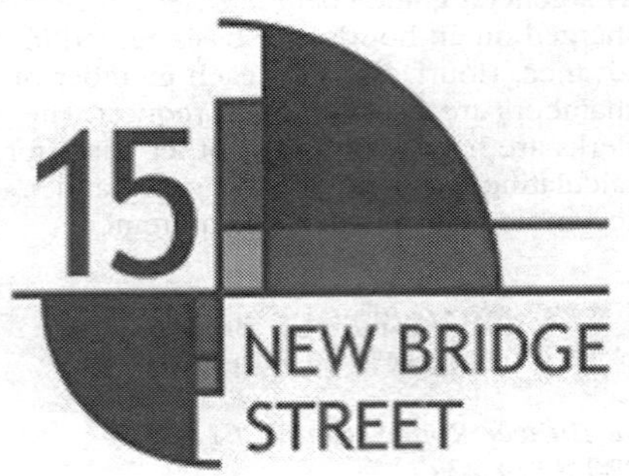

15 New Bridge Street, London EC4V 6AU
020 7842 1900
Fax: 020 7842 1901; DX: 162 London Chancery Lane
E-mail: clerks@15nbs.com
URL: www.15nbs.com
Out of hours telephone: Please refer to our website

Chambers of: Mr D J Aaronberg QC, Mr J M Mulholland QC
Clerks: Robert Mayes, First Junior; Joe Wheeler, Second Junior, Senior Clerk: Sean Gould; Receptionist and Admin: Katie Cameron; Finance Manager: Joe Barrett

Aaronberg, David QC *1981*†
Mulholland, James QC *1986*†
Oliver, Michael *1977*
Walsh, Peter *1978*
Field, Rory *1980*
Amakye, Grace *1983*†
Banks, Timothy *1983*
Greenan, John *1984*
McCormack, Helen *1986*
Nicholson Pratt, Tom *1986*†
Lloyd, Francis *1987*
Forsyth, Andrew *1989*
Mulligan, Ann *1989*†
Argyropoulos, Kyri *1991*
St Louis, Brian *1994*
Maggs, Patrick *1996*
Beharrylal, Anand *1997*
Gillett, Tonia *1997*
Hardyman, Matthew *1997*
Moran, Patrick *1997*
Shotton, Sophie *1999*
Edenborough, James *2001*
Rollinson, Darryn *2001*
Benthall, Dominic *2002*
Dashani, Sonal *2002*
Morrison, Giles *2002*
Brook, Dale *2003*
Turner, Mathew *2003*
Collis, Michael *2004*
Zentler-Munro, Ruth *2004*
Stark, Samantha *2005*
Crocker, Elizabeth *2006*
O'Gunleye, Marisha *2006*
Ross, Neil *2006*
Callinan, Clodaghmuire *2007*
Grout, Christopher *2007*
Ridout, Frances *2007*
Ward, Robert *2007*
Hartley, Louise *2008*
Lloyd, Douglas *2008*

Types of work
Anti-social Behaviour Orders · Asset forfeiture · Asset recovery · Child abuse · Civil actions against the police · Civil liberties · Commercial fraud · Computer crime · Confiscation · Coroner's inquests · Coroners · Corporate fraud · Corporate manslaughter · Courts martial · Crime · Crime and criminal due process · Criminal judicial review · Customs · ECHR · Extradition · Firearms · Forfeiture · Fraud · Freezing orders · Homicide · Immigration · Inquests · International criminal law · International fraud and asset tracing · International human rights law · Internet crime · Judicial review · Malicious prosecution · Military law · Money laundering · Motor vehicles · Police · Police discipline · Prison law · Prisoners' rights · Privacy · Road haulage · Road traffic · Road traffic offences · Serial crime · Serious fraud · Sexual Offences · Terrorism

Disability access
Staff briefed or trained on duties under the disability legislation, Induction loop or infra red system

NEW COURT

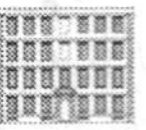

NEW COURT CHAMBERS

Ground Floor, New Court, Temple, London EC4Y 9BE
020 7583 5123
Fax: 020 7353 3383; DX: 0018 London Chancery Lane
E-mail: clerks@newcourtchambers.com
URL: www.newcourtchambers.com
Out of hours telephone: 07721 830320 (Paul Bloomfield, Senior Clerk); 07939 215684 (James Stammers, First Junior)

Chambers of: Dr G Cala
Clerks: James Stammers, Adam Grant, Senior Clerk: Paul Bloomfield, Lloyd Smith (Fees Clerk); Administrator: J Clark

Also at: 283 Via Dei Gracchi, 00192 Rome, Italy Tel: 0039 06 322 3893 Fax: 0039 06 323 0312

Cala, Guiseppe *1971*
Courtney, Ann *1987*
Soffa, Helen *1990*
Charlton, Judith *1991*
Bain, Giles *1993*
Bullock, Sally *1995*
Poole, Christopher *1996*
Balchin, Richard *1997*
Hayford, Jane *1997*
McMeechan, Sarah *2000*
Nanayakkara, Dinali *2000*
Banerji, Jay *2001*
Michaels, Tali *2001*
Shaw, Andrew *2001*
Chan, Wing *2002*
Hine, Stephanie *2003*
Hefford, Anna *2004*
Wallace, Sam Christopher *2004*
Jackson, Sally *2006*
Lefteri, Kyriacos *2006*
Singh, Ranjit *2007*
Wilkinson, Robert *2007*
Jenkins, Philippa *2008*
Saley, Raisa *2008*
Richardson, Matthew *2009*
Stuart, Damian *2009*

†Recorder *Door Tenant/Associate Member

Types of work
Adoption, Ancillary Relief · Care proceedings · Child Abuse, Children · Family law · Family provision · Mental Health, Unmarried Couples

Chambers Established 1981
Opening times: 8.30am - 6.30pm

Chambers' facilities
Conference Rooms, Disks Accepted, E-mail, Parking, Telephone Conferences, Seminar Room

Disability access
Staff briefed or trained on duties under the disability legislation, Wheelchair access, Disabled parking available

Languages spoken
Italian

Fees policy
Fees can be negotiated with the clerk depending on the estimated time required for preparation, estimated time to be in court, case complexity, issues at stake, seniority of the barrister.

THREE NEW SQUARE IP

3 New Square, Lincoln's Inn, London WC2A 3RS
020 7405 1111
Fax: 020 7405 7800; DX: 454 London Chancery Lane
E-mail: clerks@3newsquare.co.uk
URL: www.3newsquare.co.uk
Out of hours telephone: 07733 111221

Chambers of: Mr S J Thorley QC
Clerks: Tim Fairburn, David Court; Senior Clerk: Nicholas Hill; Administrator: Zena Dodd

Thorley, Simon QC *1972*	**Mitcheson,** Thomas *1996*
Watson, Antony QC *1968*	**Hinchliffe,** Tom *1997*
Miller, Richard QC *1976*	**Malynicz,** Simon *1997*
Waugh, Andrew QC *1982*	**Pritchard,** Geoffrey *1998*
Burkill, Guy QC *1981*	**Hughes,** Dominic *2001*
Turner, Justin QC *1992*	**Copeland,** Miles *2004*
McFarland, Denise *1987*	**Delaney,** Joe *2006*
Campbell, Douglas *1993*	**Heald,** Jeremy *2010*

Types of work
Arbitration · Copyright · EC competition law · Entertainment · Environment · Franchising · Information technology · Intellectual property · Licensing · Media and entertainment · Patents · Professional negligence · Sale and carriage of goods · Telecommunications · Trademarks

Chambers Established 1940
Opening times: 8.45am - 7.30pm

Chambers' facilities
Conference Rooms

Disability access
Staff briefed or trained on duties under the disability legislation, Disabled parking available

Languages spoken
French, Japanese, Swahili

Three New Square Chambers of Simon Thorley QC

This set specialises in all aspects of intellectual property, including patents, trademarks, passing off, copyright and designs. Other areas of expertise include information technology, breach of confidence and malicious falsehood.

The Set: Chambers has specialised in intellectual property litigation for more than 50 years and its 16 tenants including six QCs, are all leading practitioners in this area. The set was located at 6 Pump Court, Temple, until April 1995.

All members appear frequently in the High Court, Patents County Court and Appellate Courts. They also engage regularly in arbitration work both as advocates and arbitrators, and hearings before the Trade Marks Registry, the European and UK Patent Offices and the European Court of Justice.

Simon Thorley QC is a Deputy High Court Judge, Richard Miller QC is a past Chairman of the Intellectual Property Bar Association and Douglas Campbell is a Civil Recorder. Chambers won the Chambers & Partners IP/IT Chambers of the Year Award in 2010, with Andrew Waugh QC picking up the IP Silk of the Year Award for 2010. Denise McFarland is a CEDR accredited mediator. Douglas Campbell and Simon Malynicz are on the Attorney General's 'B' Panel and Tom Mitcheson is standing counsel for the Comptroller General of Patents, Design and Trade Marks. Since his retirement from the Court of Appeal, Sir William Aldous is available to accept instructions to act as an arbitrator in appropriate matters, as are other members of Chambers.

Members of chambers receive instructions from solicitors, patent and trade mark attorneys, in-house lawyers and lawyers practising overseas.

The majority of members are scientifically literate - as useful background for the many disputes handled that involve technical subject matter. Senior members also edit *Terrell on the Law of Patents*, the leading textbook in this area. Simon Malynicz is co-author of 'Gurry on Breach of Confidence'.

Types of work undertaken: Patent disputes form a large proportion of chambers' work, mainly involving infringement or revocation proceedings. Much of the work is leading edge, embracing all major areas of technology mechanical patents.

All members are involved in trade mark litigation, mainly in the High Court concerning proceedings to determine infringement and validity. Members also appear before the Registrar of Trade Marks, notably in opposition and revocation matters. Passing off is a particular specialism.

All areas of copyright and design right law are handled. Cases include literary, musical and artistic copyright in the fields of fashion, music, entertainment and literature as well as industrial designs.

Members also practise in the areas of breach of confidence, malicious falsehood, entertainment and media, restrictive covenants, franchising and the licensing of all intellectual property rights, as well as related areas of competition law.

Finally chambers has a strong practice in information technology matters, not only those involving intellectual property rights such as copyright but also contractual disputes with a technical subject matter.

FOUR NEW SQUARE

Four New Square, Lincoln's Inn, London WC2A 3RJ
020 7822 2000
Fax: 020 7822 2001; DX: 1041 London Chancery Lane
E-mail: barristers@4newsquare.com

Chambers of: Miss S L Carr QC

Disability access
Staff briefed or trained on duties under the disability legislation, Wheelchair access, Disabled parking available, Induction loop or infra red system

8 NEW SQUARE

8 NEW SQUARE
INTELLECTUAL PROPERTY

8 New Square, Lincoln's Inn, London WC2A 3QP
020 7405 4321
Fax: 020 7405 9955; DX: 379 London Chancery Lane
E-mail: clerks@8newsquare.co.uk
URL: www.8newsquare.co.uk
Out of hours telephone: 07887 763993

Chambers of: Mr M F Platts-Mills QC
Clerks: John Call (Senior Clerk), Tony Liddon (Deputy Senior Clerk), Ben Newham, Paul Worrall, Jack Joselyn; Practice Manager: Nicholas Wise, Martin Williams; Business Development and Administration Manager: Harri Gibson

Platts-Mills, Mark QC *1974*
Baldwin, John QC *1977*
Howe, Martin QC *1978*
Alexander, Daniel QC *1988*
Mellor, James QC *1986*
Meade, Richard QC *1991*
Tappin, Michael QC *1991*
Speck, Adrian QC *1993*
Hamer, George *1974*
Clark, Fiona *1982*
Onslow, Robert *1991*
May, Charlotte *1995*
Moody-Stuart, Thomas *1995*
St Ville, James *1995*
Lane, Lindsay *1996*
Abrahams, James *1997*
Berkeley, Iona *1999*
Chacksfield, Mark *1999*
Hill, Jonathan *2000*
Ward, Henry *2000*
Bowhill, Jessie *2003*
Lykiardopoulos, Andrew *2004*
Whyte, James *2005*
Jamal, Isabel *2008*

Types of work
Breach of confidence · Competition law · Computer contracts · Computer litigation · Confidential information · Copyright · Data protection · E-commerce · EC competition law · Entertainment · Information technology · Intellectual property · Malicious falsehood · Media and entertainment · Passing off · Patents · Publishing · Registered designs · Sport · Telecommunications · Trade secrets · Trademarks · Unregistered designs

Opening times: 8.30am - 7.00pm

Chambers' facilities
Email: All members and clerks may be contacted using the address construction '[name.surname]@8newsquare.co.uk', eg. john.baldwin@8newsquare.co.uk

Disability access
Staff briefed or trained on duties under the disability legislation, Disabled parking available

Additional Information

8 New Square is the largest set in the UK specialising entirely in intellectual property and related fields of law. Members of Chambers have a very wide range of legal, technical, and strategic expertise covering every aspect of intellectual property and a wide variety of other cases, especially those where technical knowledge is of importance. Cases undertaken by members cover five principal areas:

Intellectual Property
Work includes patent, trade and service marks, copyright (industrial, artistic and software), registered and unregistered designs, passing off, counterfeiting and trade libel, confidential information and trade secrets, technology transfer and licensing, plant breeders' rights, merchandising and franchising.

High technology and information technology
This covers biotechnology, data protection and privacy (information technology, computer contracts), technical commercial disputes, pharmaceutical regulation, public inquiries, Internet and domain name law.

Media and entertainment
Work undertaken includes performers' rights, television (including cable and satellite), broadcasting, film, literary, musical and artistic copyright litigation, publishing and entertainment contracts and disputes, advertising and marketing.

Communications
Areas covered include computer litigation, Internet law, Internet gaming and licensing, publishing telecommunications.

Competition and EU law
This includes competition aspects of intellectual property, EU competition law and free movement of goods and services and EU regulatory law in pharmaceutical and other technical fields.

Several members have written, or are editors of, leading intellectual property textbooks and encyclopaedias. These include *Kerly on Trade Marks and Trade Names*, *The Modern Law of Copyright and Designs* and *Russell-Clarke & Howe on Industrial Designs*, *The Reports of Patent Cases* and *The Fleet Street Reports*.

Clients are invited to visit our website www.8newsquare.co.uk for more information on cases and Chambers services.

11 NEW SQUARE

1st Floor, 11 New Square, Lincoln's Inn, London WC2A 3QB
020 7242 4017
Fax: 020 7831 2391; DX: 315 London Chancery Lane
E-mail: john.moore@11newsquare.com

Chambers of: Mr J R Gardiner QC

Disability access
Staff briefed or trained on duties under the disability legislation, Disabled parking available

NEW SQUARE CHAMBERS

NEW SQUARE CHAMBERS

12 New Square, Lincoln's Inn, London WC2A 3SW
020 7419 8000
Fax: 020 7419 8050; DX: 1056 London Chancery Lane
E-mail: robin.hollington@newsquarechambers.co.uk
URL: www.newsquarechambers.co.uk
Out of hours telephone: Answerphone/ 07831 320288

Chambers of: Mr R F Hollington QC
Clerks: Clive Petchey (Senior Clerk), Neil Garrett, Phil Reeves, Michelle Greene, Daniel Westerman; Chambers Manager: Kerry McLean; Marketing Manager: Paula Fox

Hollington, Robin QC *1979*†
MacDonald, John QC *1955*
Laurence, George QC *1972*
Mathew, Robin QC *1974*
Smith, Stephen QC *1983*†
Thom, James QC *1974*†
Le Poidevin, Nicholas QC *1975*
Stewart Smith, Rodney *1964*
Ross Martyn, John *1969*
Tucker, Lynton *1971*
Munro, Kenneth *1973*
Bennett, Gordon *1974*
Chapple, Malcolm *1975*
Semken, Christopher *1977*
Hill-Smith, Alexander *1978*†
Sagar, Leigh *1983*
Eaton Turner, David *1984*
Fisher, David *1985*
Graham, Thomas *1985*
Staddon, Claire *1985*
Crail, Ross *1986*
Holbech, Charles *1988*
Schaw Miller, Stephen *1988*
Peacock, Ian *1990*
Simpson, Edwin *1990*
Van Tonder, Gerard *1990*
Adamyk, Simon *1991*
Hubbard, Mark *1991*
Eidinow, John *1992*
Evans-Gordon, Jane *1992*
Hood, Nigel *1993*
Heal, Madeleine *1996*
Prentis, Sebastian *1996*
Pryce, Gary *1997*
Bailey, James *1999*
Pay, Adrian *1999*
Brightwell, James *2000*
Learmonth, Alexander *2000*

†Recorder *Door Tenant/Associate Member

Allsop, Nicola *2002*
Akkouh, Tim *2004*
Gillett, Emily *2005*
Pringle, Watson *2005*
Ford, Charlotte *2007*
Littler, Anna *2008*
Wright, Caley *2008*
Fletcher, Thomas *2009*

Types of work

Administrative law · Arbitration · Banking · Capital tax · Chancery (general) · Chancery (land law) · Charities · Civil liberties · Commercial litigation · Commercial property · Common land · Common law (general) · Company, commercial and competition · Conflict of laws · Conveyancing · Corporate finance · Corporate fraud · Corporation tax · Employment · Entertainment · Equity · Family provision · Financial services · Foreign law · Housing · Income tax · Insolvency · Intellectual property · International law · Landlord and tenant · Local authorities · Medical negligence · Mental health · Parliamentary · Partnerships · Pensions · Personal insolvency · Planning · Professional negligence · Sale and carriage of goods · Share options · Succession · Trusts · Wills

Disability access

Staff briefed or trained on duties under the disability legislation, Wheelchair access, Disabled parking available

NEXUS CHAMBERS

7 New Square, Lincolns Inn, London WC2A 3QS
020 7404 1147/020 7831 8309
Fax: 020 7 242 9744; DX: 391 Lde
E-mail: info@nexuschambers.com

Chambers of: The Head of Chambers

NO5 CHAMBERS

Greenwood House, 4-7 Salisbury Court, London EC4Y 8AA
0845 210 5555
Fax: 020 7900 1582; DX: 449 London Chancery Lane
URL: www.no5.com
Out of hours telephone: 07774 298047

Chambers of: Mr P E Bleasdale QC
Practice Director: Tony McDaid; Practice Managers: Patrick Hawkins, Robert Woods, Andrew Bisbey, Andrew Trotter, James Parks, Abdul Hafeez, Martin Hulbert, Zoe Owen, Samantha Maguire-Thompson; Finance Manager: Ian Tullett

Also at: No5 Chambers, Fountain Court, Steelhouse Lane, Birmingham B4 6DR Tel: +44 (0) 845 210 5555, Fax: +44 (0) 121 606 1501

Also at: No5 Chambers, 38 Queen Square, Bristol BS1 4QS Tel: +44 (0)845 210 5555 Fax: +44 (0)117 917 8502

Bleasdale, Paul QC *1978*†
Smith, Tony QC *1958*†
Kingston, Martin QC *1972*
Tedd, Rex QC *1970*†
Hotten, Christopher QC *1972*†
Evans, Gareth QC *1973*†
Jones, Richard QC *1972*†
Gill, Manjit QC *1982*
Cahill, Jeremy QC *1975*
Howker, David QC *1982*
Hunjan, Satinder QC *1984*†
Dove, Ian QC *1986*†
Meyer, Lorna QC *1986*
Burrows, Michael QC *1979*†
Bright, Christopher QC *1985*†
Anderson, Mark QC *1983*†
Mason, David QC *1986*†
Lock, David QC *1985*
Drew, Simon QC *1987*
Duck, Michael QC *1988*
Keeling, Adrian QC *1990*
Heywood, Mark QC *1986*
Bell, Gary QC *1989*
West, John *1965*
Smith, Roger *1968*
Whitaker, Stephen *1970*
Arnold, Peter *1972*
Cliff, Graham *1973*†
Harvey, John *1973*†
Jones, Timothy *1975*
Bealby, Walter *1976*
Giles, Roger *1976*
Henson, Graham *1976*
Iles, David *1977*
James, Christopher *1977*
Pusey, William *1977*
Rowland, Robin *1977*†
Smallwood, Anne *1977*
Keogh, Andrew *1978*
Korn, Anthony *1978*
Michael, Simon *1978*
O'Donovan, Kevin *1978*
Cairnes, Paul *1980*
Newman, Timothy *1981*
Brown, Stephanie *1982*
Campbell, Stephen *1982*†
Thompson, Neil *1982*
De Mello, Ramby *1983*
Maccabe, Irvine *1983*
McGrath, Andrew *1983*
Newdick, Christopher *1983*
Bailey, Russell *1985*
Bell, Anthony *1985*
Bermingham, Gerald *1985*
Doyle, James *1985*
Kelly, Mark *1985*
Moat, Richard *1985*
Sharif, Nadia *1985*
Leigh, Kevin *1986*
Thorogood, Bernard *1986*†
Wignall, Gordon *1987*
Baker, Caroline *1988*
Birk, Dewinder *1988*
Bridge, Ian *1988*
Chadwick, Joanna *1988*
Forsyth, Samantha *1988*
Morgan, Adrienne *1988*
Singh-Tiwana, Ekwall *1988*
Wallace, Andrew *1988*
Attwood, John *1989*
Bedford, Becket *1989*
Duthie, Malcolm *1989*
Liddiard, Martin *1989*
Murray, Carole *1989*
Anning, Michael *1990*
Baker, Andrew *1990*
Boora, Jinder *1990*
Colquhoun, Celina *1990*
McDonald, Melanie *1990*
Wynne, Ashley *1990*
Al-Rashid, Mahmud *1991*
Buckingham, Sarah *1991*
Dooley, Allan *1991*†
Friel, Michele *1991*
Marshall, Paul *1991*
Radburn, Mark *1991*
Bailey, Steven *1992*
Bazini, Danny *1992*
Brockley, Nigel *1992*
Farrer, Adam *1992*
Goatley, Peter *1992*
Hansen, William *1992*
Ismail, Nazmun Nisha *1992*
Mahmood, Abid *1992*
Mallick, Nabila *1992*
Preston, Nicola *1992*
Richards, Hugh *1992*
Wilkinson, Marc *1992*
Xydias, Nicholas *1992*
Bradley, Phillip *1993*

Campbell, Rhona *1993*
Dutta, Nandini *1993*
Edhem, Emma *1993*
Nicholson, Edward *1993*
Rothwell, Joanne *1993*
Sumeray, Caroline *1993*
Taylor, David *1993*
Choongh, Satnam *1994*
Dean, Brian *1994*
Fox, Simon *1994*
Jones, Jonathan *1994*
Khalique, Nageena *1994*
Nuvoloni, Stefano *1994*
Potter, Anthony *1994*
Smallwood, Robert *1994*
Stoll, James *1994*
Tyack, David *1994*
Butterfield, John *1995*†
Diamond, Anna *1995*
Hignett, Richard *1995*
Kershaw, Dean *1995*†
Mitchell, David *1995*
Monaghan, Susan *1995*
Sheppard, Tim *1995*
Bagral, Ravinder *1996*
Case, Richard *1996*
Davidson, Laura *1996*
Hancox, Sally *1996*†
Holloway, David *1996*
Islam-Choudhury, Mugni *1996*
Jones, Cheryl *1996*
Knotts, Carol *1996*
Pitchers, Henry *1996*
Power, Elizabeth *1996*
Brunning, Matthew *1997*
Chatterjee, Adreeja *1997*
Compton, Gareth *1997*
Hadley, Richard *1997*
Hirst, Karl *1997*
Lally, Harbinder Singh *1997*
Rowley, Rachel *1997*
Singh, Talbir *1997*
Young, Christopher *1997*
Brown, Kristina *1998*
Derrington, Jonathan *1998*
Kimblin, Richard *1998*
Stein, Alexander *1998*
Afzal, Fayyaz OBE *1999*
Barney, Helen *1999*
Brook, Matthew *1999*
Butt, Nassera *1999*
Chelvan, S *1999*
Coughlan, John *1999*
Crow, Charles *1999*
Denning, Louisa *1999*
Gamble, Jamie *1999*
Hargreaves, Teresa *1999*
Price, Charles *1999*
Abberley, Stephen *2000*
Chawla, Neil *2000*
Ensaff, Omar *2000*
Wigley, Jenny *2000*
Willetts, Glenn *2000*
Adkinson, Richard *2001*
Bains, Param *2001*
Beloff, Rupert *2001*
Brown, Emma *2001*
Chaffin-Laird, Olivia *2001*
Dixon, James *2001*
Evans, Paul *2001*
Forster, Bridget *2001*
Gamble, Esther *2001*
Heeley, Michelle *2001*
Mann, Jasvir *2001*
Pole, Tim *2001*
Schofield, Thomas *2001*
Wingrave, Michael *2001*
Worlock, Simon *2001*
Bradshaw, Mark *2002*
Clifford, Victoria *2002*
Mantle, Philip *2002*
McClement, Lynette *2002*
Arthur, Helen *2003*
Cobill, Nicholas *2003*
Oscroft, Daniel *2003*
Owen, Denise *2003*
Pinnock, Earl *2003*
Van Overdijk, Claire *2003*
Davies, Rhys *2004*
Gupta, Mamta *2004*
Leslie, James *2004*
Allen, Juliet *2005*
Allen, Sarah *2005*
Cooke, Richard *2005*
Feeney, Katie *2005*
Feeny, Jack *2005*
Fernandes, Suella *2005*
Grant, Orla *2005*
Joseph, Paul *2005*
Punt, Dr Jonathan *2005*
Reed, Steven *2005*
Sandhu, Harpreet *2005*
Taylor, Kathryn *2005*
Williams, Philip *2005*
Yasseri, Yasmin *2005*
Enonchong, Nelson *2006*
Gallacher, Kirsty *2006*
Roberts, Gemma *2006*
Yates, Victoria *2006*
Boyden, Matthew *2007*
Hunka, Simon *2007*
Meager, Rowena *2007*
Oakes, Richard *2007*
Smyth, Jack *2007*
Barrett, Kevin *2008*
Corfield, Louise *2008*
Pye, Derek *2008*
Shaw, Jonathan *2008*
Williams, Hermione *2008*
Grimshaw, Richard *2010*
Jennings, Caroline *2010*
Osmund-Smith, Thea *2010*
O'Brien, Michael QC *2011*
Humphreys, Richard QC *1986**
Hanson, Timothy *1989**
Phillips, Moira *1989**
Grant, Edward *1991**
Renouf, Mark *1994**
Armstrong, Douglas *1999**
Kurji, Fatim *2003**
Tyers-Smith, Peter *2005**

Types of work
Administrative law · Agriculture · Arbitration · Asset finance · Banking · Capital tax · Clinical negligence · Commercial law · Commercial litigation · Commercial property · Company, commercial and competition · Construction law · Conveyancing · Copyright · Corporate finance · Corporate fraud · Corporation tax · Court of Protection · Crime · Employment · Energy · Environment · Equity · Family law · Family provision · Financial services · Human rights · Immigration · Income tax · Industrial diseases · Information technology · Insolvency · Insurance · Intellectual property · International arbitration · International trade · Judicial review · Landlord and tenant · Licensing · Partnerships · Patents · Personal injury · Personal insolvency · Planning · Prison law · Property · Public law · Sport · Succession · Trademarks · Trusts · Wills

Disability access
Staff briefed or trained on duties under the disability legislation, Wheelchair access, Induction loop or infra red system

NORTH SQUARE CHAMBERS

15 North Square, London NW11 7AD
020 8455 3735
Fax: 020 8458 8043
E-mail: jongold@talk21.com

Chambers of: Mr J J Goldberg QC

OAKWOOD CHAMBERS

46a Oakwood Court, London W14 8JY
07789 435485

Chambers of: Mr D M Krushner

CHAMBERS OF MISS O A OBUKA

Suite 14502, 2nd Floor, 145-157 St John Street, London EC1V 4PW
020 7936 4474
Fax: 020 7936 4473
E-mail: obijuo.obuka@sky.com

Chambers of: Ms O A Obuka

†Recorder *Door Tenant/Associate Member

D

CHAMBERS OF JOY OKOYE

9 Redbourne Avenue, Finchley Church End, London N3 2BP
07976 426871/020 7405 7011
Fax: 020 8349 0265
E-mail: okoyejoy@hotmail.com

Chambers of: Miss J N Okoye

Disability access
Wheelchair access

OLD BAILEY CHAMBERS

15 Old Bailey, London EC4M 7EF
020 3008 6404
Fax: 020 3008 6405; DX: 157380 Old Bailey 5
E-mail: clerks@15oldbaileychambers.com

Chambers of: Mr M J Khamisa QC, Mr B A O Aina QC

Disability access
Staff briefed or trained on duties under the disability legislation, Wheelchair access, Disabled parking available, Induction loop or infra red system

XXIV OLD BUILDINGS

Ground Floor, 24 Old Buildings, Lincoln's Inn, London WC2A 3UP
020 7691 2424
Fax: 0870 460 2178; DX: 307 London Chancery Lane
E-mail: clerks@xxiv.co.uk
URL: www.xxiv.co.uk
Out of hours telephone: 07774 240112

Chambers of: Mr M E Mann QC, Mr A G Steinfeld QC
Clerks: Daniel Wilson, Paul Matthews, Martyn Nicholls, James Ladbrook; Practice Manager: Practice Director: Nicholas Luckman; Administrator: Kathryn Paterson

Mann, Martin QC *1968*
Steinfeld, Alan QC *1968*
Black, Michael QC *1978*
Moverley Smith, Stephen QC *1985*
Shepherd, Philip QC *1975*
Tregear, Francis QC *1980*
Brownbill, David QC *1989*
Talbot Rice, Elspeth QC *1990*
Levy, Robert QC *1988*
King, Michael *1971*
Stephens, John *1975*
Ritchie, Richard *1978*
Gadd, Michael *1981*
Weaver, Elizabeth *1982*
Galley, Helen *1987*
Harington, Amanda *1989*
Ghaffar, Arshad *1991*
Meakin, Ian *1991*
Staff, Marcus *1994*
Adair, Stuart *1995*
Pelling, Alexander *1995*
Shah, Bajul *1996*
Thompson, Steven *1996*
Hughes, Jessica *1997*
De Mestre, Lyndsey *1999*
Knight, Edward *1999*
Montagu-Smith, Thomas *2001*
Bayliss, Sarah *2002*
McLarnon, Neil *2004*
Cloherty, Adam *2005*
Cumming, Edward *2006*
Hitchens, Erin *2006*
Holden, Andrew *2007*
Langlois, Nicole *2008*
Curry, Owen *2009*
Murphy, Heather *2009*
Warents, Daniel *2009*
Sharpe, Harry *2010*
Virgo, Graham *1989**

Types of work
Alternative dispute resolution · Arbitration · Aviation · Bahamas law · Banking · Banking and Finance · British Virgin Islands law · Capital markets · Chancery (commercial) · Chancery (general) · Chancery (land law) · Charities · Civil fraud · Civil litigation · Commercial contracts · Commercial fraud · Commercial law · Commercial litigation · Commercial property · Common land · Company law · Company, commercial and competition · Conflict of laws · Construction law · Contracts · Corporate finance · Corporate liability · Cross-border litigation and remedies · Directors' disqualification · Dispute resolution · Ecclesiastical law · Energy · Equity · European law · Family provision · Financial instruments · Financial services · Foreign law · Freezing orders · Group litigation · Insolvency · International law · International trade · Investments · Landlord and tenant · Mediation · Money laundering · Multi-party litigation · Offshore finance · Offshore investment · Offshore trust litigation · Partnerships · Pensions · Personal insolvency · Private client · Privy Council · Professional negligence · Property · Remedies · Share options · Succession · Travel law · Trust litigation · Trusts · Wills

Disability access
Staff briefed or trained on duties under the disability legislation, Wheelchair access, Induction loop or infra red system

TEN OLD SQUARE

Ground Floor, Ten Old Square, Lincoln's Inn, London WC2A 3SU
020 7405 0758
Fax: 020 7831 8237; DX: 306 London Chancery Lane
E-mail: clerks@tenoldsquare.com
URL: www.tenoldsquare.com

Chambers of: Mr L Price QC CBE
Clerk: Keith Plowman

Barlow, Francis QC *1965*
Taube, Simon QC *1980*
Rajah, Eason QC *1989*
Hill, Gregory *1972*
Wallington, Richard *1972*
Schmitz, David *1976*
Stafford, Paul *1987*
Meadway, Susannah *1988*
Callman, Jeremy *1991*
Gavaghan, Jonathan *1992*
Farrelly, Kevin *1993*
Laughton, Samuel *1993*
Waterworth, Michael *1994*
Arnfield, Robert *1996*
Price, Evan *1997*
Dew, Richard *1999*
Bedworth, Georgia *2001*
Beer, Julia *2003*
Boutle, Toby *2004*
Winston, Naomi *2006*
Roseman, Gideon *2007*
Waterworth, Caroline *2008*
Pickering, Leon *2010*

Types of work
Banking · Capital tax · Chancery (general) · Chancery (land law) · Charities · Commercial litigation · Commercial property · Company, commercial and competition · Conflict of laws · Construction law · Conveyancing · Corporate finance · Corporation tax · Education · Equity · Family provision · Financial services · Insolvency · Landlord and tenant · Partnerships · Pensions · Personal insolvency · Professional negligence · Property · Sale and carriage of goods · Succession · Trusts · Wills

Disability access
Staff briefed or trained on duties under the disability legislation, Disabled parking available

11 OLD SQUARE

11 Old Square, Lincoln's Inn, London WC2A 3TS
020 7242 5022
Fax: 020 7404 0445

13 OLD SQUARE CHAMBERS

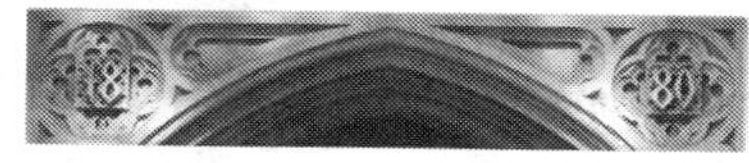

THIRTEEN OLD SQUARE CHAMBERS

Ground Floor, 14 Old Square, Lincoln's Inn, London WC2A 3UE
020 7831 4445
Fax: 020 7841 5825; DX: 52 London Chancery Lane
E-mail: clerks@13oldsquare.com
URL: www.13oldsquare.com
Out of hours telephone: 07775 781995

Chambers of: Mr J B W McDonnell QC
Clerks: Justin Brown (Senior Clerk), Steve Anten, Haydn Powell, Frank Lee

McDonnell, John QC *1968*
Lowe, David QC *1965*
Oliver, David QC *1972*
Jones, Edward Bartley QC *1975*†
Booth, Michael QC *1981*
Castle, Peter *1970*
Lloyd, Stephen *1971*
Jefferis, Michael *1976*
Detter De Lupis Frankopan, Ingrid *1977*
Bourne, Robert *1978*
Turner, Jonathan D C *1982*
Vaughan-Williams, Laurence *1988*
Watson-Gandy, Mark *1990*
Maynard-Connor, Giles *1992*
Peat, Richard *1993*
Ludbrook, Tim *1996*
Joseph, Sandradee *1998*
Devereux-Cooke, Richard *1999*
Mohyuddin, David *1999*
Chichester-Clark, Adam *2000*
Couser, James *2000*
Olleson, Simon *2002*
Lowe, Mungo *2003*
Sjostrand, Ekaterina *2003*
Kokelaar, Sebastian *2004*
Hallett, Katherine *2006*
Burkitt, Daniel *2008*
Knight, Emma *2008*
Smith, Michael *2008*
Fairpo, Anne *2009*
Hunter, Simon *2009*
Miall, Hugh *2009*

Types of work
Accountancy · Administrative law · Agriculture · Arbitration · Banking · Breach of confidence · Chancery (general) · Chancery (land law) · Charities · Civil fraud · Commercial law · Commercial litigation · Commercial property · Common land · Common law (general) · Company, commercial and competition · Conflict of laws · Conveyancing · Corporate finance · Court of Protection · Directors' disqualification · Disciplinary tribunals · Employment · Entertainment · Equity · Family provision · Financial services · Hong Kong law · Housing · Human rights · Insolvency · Insurance · Intellectual property · Landlord and tenant · Mediation · Partnerships · Passing off · Personal insolvency · Planning · Professional

D

†Recorder *Door Tenant/Associate Member

negligence · Sport · Succession · Trusts · Wills

Chambers Established 2004
Opening times: 8.30am - 6.30pm

Disability access
Wheelchair access

Languages spoken
French, Russian, Spanish

Additional information
13 Old Square Chambers is the newest set of chancery chambers. It was formed in 2004 by John McDonnell QC. The clerks are an established team who worked together in John McDonnell's original chambers. Members specialise in a variety of fields practised by the modern Chancery Bar.

12 OLD SQUARE CHAMBERS

1st Floor, 12 Old Square, Lincoln's Inn, London WC2A 3TX
020 7404 0875
Fax: 020 7404 8377; DX: 130 London Chancery Lane
E-mail: clerks@12oldsquare.com
URL: www.12oldsquare.com
Out of hours telephone: 07985 212358

Chambers of: Miss C Boaitey
Clerks: Akash Bharadia, Ishaq Botchway; Practice Manager: Steven Russell

Boaitey, Charlotte *1976*
Offeh, John *1969*
Ume, Cyril *1972*
Waithe, John *1972*
Okai, Anthony *1973*
Alesbury, Alun *1974*
Sheikh, Raana *1977*
Ndlovu, Lazarus *1979*
Marshall, Ita *1980*
Westmaas, Derek *1984*
Akwagyiram, Samuel *1985*
Philpott, Anthony *1987*
Adams, Derek *1988*
Ephraim-Adejumo, Hilda *1989*
Rahman, Anis OBE *1990*
Hypolite-De-Souza, Josephine *1992*
Layne, Ronald *1992*
Kodagoda, Fritz *1993*
Solomon, Reuben *1993*
Miszkiel, Ursula *1994*
Bustani, Navaz *1995*
Waheed, Erum *1995*
Malhotra, Mehtab *1996*
Lalani, Salma *1998*
Ankrah, Alexandra *1999*
Anyene, Eleazar *1999*
Williams, Simon *1999*
Bonsu, Michaela *2000*
Glass, Patricia *2000*
Manyarara, Natsai *2001*
Saini, Parminder *2001*
Bashir, Mohammed *2002*
Ofei-Kwatia, Dido *2002*
Ukachi-Lois, Onye *2003*
Cantor, Esther *2004*
Klear, Najinder *2004*
Balroop, Darryl *2005*
Otchie, Andrew *2005*
Dave, Ishanraj *2006*
Kansal, Seema *2007*
Malik, Zulqarnain *2007*
Karim, Shahadoth *2008*
Biggs, Michael *2010*

Types of work
Crime · Education · Employment · Family law · Housing · Immigration · Intellectual property · Landlord and tenant · Licensing · Medical negligence · Personal injury

Disability access
Staff briefed or trained on duties under the disability legislation

OLD SQUARE CHAMBERS

10-11 Bedford Row, London WC1R 4BU
020 7269 0300
Fax: 020 7405 1387; DX: 1046 London Chancery Lane
E-mail: clerks@oldsquare.co.uk

Chambers of: Mr N J Cooksley QC, Miss E J McNeill QC

Disability access
Staff briefed or trained on duties under the disability legislation, Wheelchair access, Disabled parking available, Induction loop or infra red system

CHAMBERS OF DR V O ONIPEDE

34 Meeting House Lane, London SE15 2UN
07956 207159
Fax: 020 7732 9551

Chambers of: Dr V O Onipede

CHAMBERS OF MR JOHN R ORME

71 Breton House, Barbican, London EC2Y 8DQ
020 7628 0755
Fax: 020 7628 0755
E-mail: jrolaw@ronague.plus.com

Chambers of: Mr J R Orme

OUTER TEMPLE CHAMBERS

The Outer Temple, 222 Strand, London WC2R 1BA
020 7353 6381
Fax: 020 7583 1786; DX: 351 London
E-mail: clerks@outertemple.com
URL: www.outertemple.com

Chambers of: Mr P C Mott QC
Clerks: Graham Woods, Stephen Somerville, David Smith; Practice Manager: Steve Graham (Business Development Director); Christine Kings (Commercial Director); Finance Manager: Andrew Dinkenor

Also at: Manchester, St James's Building, 61-95 Oxford Street, Manchester, M1 6FQ

Mott, Philip QC *1970*†
Rawley, Alan QC *1958*†
Wilson-Smith, Christopher QC *1965*†
Rhodes, Robert QC *1968*
Lissack, Richard QC *1978*†
Gibson, Christopher QC *1976*†
McDermott, Gerard QC *1978*†
Bowes, Michael QC *1980*†
Bebb, Gordon QC *1975*†
Finucane, Brendan QC *1976*
Westcott, David QC *1982*
Spink, Andrew QC *1985*†
Short, Andrew QC *1990*
Compton, Ben QC *1979*†
Stallworthy, Nicolas QC *1993*
Jenkins, Hywel *1974*
Morris, David *1976*
Mawhinney, Richard *1977*
Patchett-Joyce, Michael *1981*
Climie, Stephen *1982*†
Haycroft, Anthony *1982*
Counsell, James *1984*
Jenkins, Alan *1984*
Kemp, Christopher *1984*†
Sadd, Patrick *1984*
Trusted, Harry *1985*
Aldridge, James *1987*
Foster, Charles *1988*†
McCormick, Alison *1988*
Mullins, Mark *1988*
Hitchcock, Richard *1989*
Leonard, James *1989*
Hallissey, Caroline *1990*
Hand, Jonathan *1990*
Bryant, Keith *1991*
Nesbitt, Tim *1991*
Horlick, Fiona *1992*
Joffe, Natasha *1992*
Tavares, Nathan *1992*
Vickers, Rachel *1992*
Barnett, Daniel *1993*
Phillips, Matthew *1993*
Woolf, Eliot *1993*
Cunningham, Naomi *1994*
Allen, Andrew *1995*
Burgher, Benjimin *1995*
Seymour, Lydia *1997*
Jerram, Harriet *1998*
Medcroft, Nicholas *1998*
Grant, David E *1999*
McKendrick, John *1999*
Arnold, James *2000*
Guthrie, Cara *2000*
Ling, Naomi *2001*
Presland, Samantha *2001*
Rickards, James *2002*
Almihdar, Ali Hamed *2003*
Assersohn, Oliver *2003*
Davison, Eleanor *2003*
Uberoi, Michael *2004*
Khan, Farhaz *2005*
Margo, Saul *2005*
Edwards, Kate *2006*
Baker, Clare *2007*
Bradley, Ben *2007*
Cooper, Samantha *2007*
Dickason, Robert *2007*
Gore, Keira *2008*
Hill, Nicholas *2008*
Young, William *2008*
Moffatt, Jonathan *2009*
Oakes, Simon *2010*
Haggan, Nicholas QC *1977*†*
Leeper, Thomas *1991**

Types of work

Arbitration · Asset recovery · Care proceedings · Clinical negligence · Commercial law · Commercial litigation · Common law (general) · Corporate fraud · Corporate manslaughter · Crime · Disciplinary tribunals · Dispute resolution · Employment · Financial services · Health and safety · Islamic law · Local authorities · Money laundering · Partnerships · Pensions · Personal injury · Professional negligence · Public inquiries · Travel law · Trusts

Disability access

Wheelchair access, Disabled parking available

CHAMBERS OF NICHOLAS PADFIELD QC

2 Netherton Grove, Chelsea, London SW10 9TQ
020 7351 1961
Fax: 020 7351 4084
E-mail: ndp@nicholaspadfieldqc.com

Chambers of: Mr N D Padfield QC

1 PAPER BUILDINGS

1st Floor, 1 Paper Buildings, Temple, London EC4Y 7EP
020 7353 3728
Fax: 020 7353 2911; DX: 332 London Chancery Lane
E-mail: clerks@onepaper.co.uk
URL: www.onepaper.co.uk
Out of hours telephone: 07834 765688

Chambers of: Mr M J Hubbard QC
Clerks: Mark Cornell, Steve McCarthy, Neil Martin, Justin Callaghan, Danielle McGee, Peter Sheffield (Fees); Marketing Director: Brett Carver

Hubbard, Michael QC *1972*†
Malcolm, Alastair QC *1971*†
Khalil, Karim QC *1984*†
Harvey, Stephen *1979*
Farmer, John *1970*
Harrison, Roger *1970*†
Kellett, Charles *1971*
Spence, Stephen *1983*
Vass, Hugh *1983*
Cox, Lindsay *1984*
Lamb, Maria *1984*†
Wing, Christopher *1985*
Buckley, William *1987*
Morgan, Christopher *1987*
Seely, Jonathan *1987*
Carter, William *1989*
Jewell, Matthew *1989*
Hobson, Sally *1991*
Bryan, Robert *1992*
McNiff, Matthew *1992*
O'Donnell, Duncan *1992*
Myatt, Charles *1993*
Falk, Charles *1994*
Rafferty, Angela *1995*
Shaw, Barnaby *1996*
Eley, Joanne *1997*
Perrins, Gregory *1997*
Matthews, Claire *1998*
Shaw, Andrew *1998*
Cotter, Nicholas *1999*
Bagley, Louisa *2000*
Fairbairn, Rebecca *2000*
Brown, Azza *2001*
Farr, Philip *2001*
Devas, Nicola *2003*
Howard, Louise *2004*
Renvoize, Edward *2004*
Newcomb, Quinton *2005*
Davies, Unyime *2006*
Hone, Barnaby *2006*
Abu-Mustafa, Jehad *2007*
Edwards, Jacob *2007*
Compton, Charlotte *2008*
Smith, Robert *1974**

Types of work
Aviation · Confiscation · Corporate fraud · Courts martial · Crime · Family law · Health and safety · Regulatory and disciplinary law · Sport

Chambers Established 1954
Opening times: 9.00am - 6.00pm

Chambers' facilities
Conference Rooms

Disability access
Staff briefed or trained on duties under the disability legislation, Disabled parking available

Languages spoken
Arabic, British Sign Language, French, German, Norwegian

3 PB BARRISTERS

3 Paper Buildings, Temple, London EC4Y 7EU
020 7583 8055
Fax: 020 7353 6271; DX: 1024 London Chancery Lane
URL: www.3pb.co.uk
Out of hours telephone: (David Phillips - Mobile 07808 137904)

Chambers of: Mr Ian Lawrie QC
Clerks: J C Charlick (Consultant Clerk), Stephen Evers (Practice Development Clerk), Craig Brown, Simon Lyons, Jay Carter, Chris O'Brien, Sam Watson, David Phillips; Lisa Wilson, Marketing Manager; Finance Manager: Head of Business Admin and Finance: Neil Monro

Also at: 3 PB Barristers, 23 Beaumont Street, Oxford OX1 2NP

Also at: 3 PB Barristers, 30 Christchurch Road, Bournemouth, Dorset BH1 3PD

Also at: 3 PB Barristers, 4 St Peter Street, Winchester SO23 8BW

Also at: 3 PB Barristers, Royal Talbot House, 2 Victoria Street, Bristol, Avon BS1 6BB

Lawrie, Ian QC *1985*†
Parroy, Michael QC *1969*†
Vere-Hodge, Michael QC *1970*
Farley, Roger QC *1974*†
Jones, Stewart QC *1972*†
Braslavsky, Nicholas QC *1983*†
Bromley-Davenport, John QC *1972*
Lickley, Nigel QC *1983*†
Parker, Christopher QC *1986*†
Parrish, Samuel *1962*
Solomon, Susan *1967*
Aylwin, Christopher *1970*
Brown, *1970*
Swinstead, David *1970*
Norman, Michael *1971*†
Curran, Leo *1972*
Jennings, Peter *1972*
Coleman, Anthony *1973*†
Stephenson, Ben *1973*
Bartlett, David *1975*†
Tyson, Richard *1975*†
Ashford-Thom, Ian *1977*
Kent, Peter *1978*
Mitchell, Nigel *1978*
Grey, Robert *1979*
Hamilton, Gavin *1979*
Leach, Robin *1979*
Leviseur, Nicholas *1979*
Partridge, Ian *1979*
Coombes, Timothy *1980*
Edge, Ian *1981*
Marshall, David *1981*
Sampson, Graeme *1981*
Strutt, Martin *1981*
Martin, Nicola *1982*
Newman, Paul *1982*
Onslow, Richard *1982*
Lomas, Mark *1983*
Stancombe, Barry *1983*
O'Hara, Sarah *1984*
Palfrey, Monty *1985*
Whittle-Martin, Lucia *1985*
Clark, Tonia *1986*
Hudson, Elisabeth *1987*
Hendry, Lucy *1988*
Rowland, Nicholas *1988*†
Zabihi, Tanya *1988*
Bradbury, Timothy *1989*
Hester, Paul *1989*
Richards, David *1989*
Aeberli, Peter *1990*
Griffiths, Hayley *1990*
Hiddleston, Adam *1990*
Knapp, Sophie *1990*
Buckley-Clarke, Amanda *1991*
Dunlop, Hamish *1991*
Katrak, Cyrus *1991*
Robins, Imogen *1991*
Ross, Iain *1991*
Bingham, Tony *1992*
Sweeney, Noel *1992*
Clargo, John *1994*
Dawson, James *1994*
Earle, Judy *1994*
Falk, Charles *1994*
Feest, Adam *1994*
Mitchell, Jack *1994*
Reid, David *1994*
Topliss, Megan *1994*
Weston, Louis *1994*
De Freitas, Melanie *1995*
McDevitt, Colin *1995*
McIlroy, David *1995*
Strachan, Elaine *1995*
Davison, James *1996*
Lorie, Andrew *1996*
Tyler, Thomas *1996*
Wilson, Lachlan *1996*
Purdy, Catherine *1997*
Sullivan, Mark *1997*
Griffiths, Emma *1998*
Taylor, Rufus *1998*
Hadfield, Charlotte *1999*
Horner, Robert *1999*
Kennedy, Stuart *1999*
Goodall, Rachael *2000*
Isaacs, Oliver *2000*
McGuire, Kenneth *2000*
O'Doherty, Paul *2000*
Sheriff, Andrew *2000*
Worton, Louise *2000*
Cassidy, Sheena *2001*
Whelan, Christopher *2001*
Ludlow, Craig *2002*
Moss, Karen *2002*
Tomlinson, Michael *2002*
Courts, Robert *2003*
Gullick, Mathew *2003*
Jones, Victoria *2003*
Rimmer, Hugh *2003*
Archer, Audrey *2004*
Davies, James *2004*
Demachkie, Jamal *2004*
Hepworth, Elizabeth *2004*
Horder, Tom *2004*
Wheeler, Richard *2004*
Anderson, Katherine *2005*
Clarke, Sarah *2005*
Langford, Sarah *2005*
Musgrave, Anarkali *2005*
Stone, Caroline *2005*
Brewin, Carl *2006*
Cannings, Matthew *2006*
Da Costa, Francisca *2006*
Davies, Nick *2006*
Green, Mark *2006*
MacWhannell, Iain *2006*
Powell, Oliver *2006*
Rees, Naomi *2006*
Robinson, Nick *2006*
Sharma, Sunyana *2006*
Davies, Harriet *2007*

†Recorder *Door Tenant/Associate Member

Elliott, Mark *2007*
Jones, Ximena *2007*
MacPhail, Andrew *2007*
O'Donohoe, *2007*
Oram, Sebastian *2007*
Paulin, Michael *2007*
Perfect, Andrew *2007*
Dunseath, Katherine *2008*
Edwards, Christopher *2008*
Alleyne, Ebony *2009*
Ashkar, Natalie *2009*
Bowes, Gemma *2009*
Currie, Philip *2009*
Howard, Steven *2009*
Line, Alex *2009*
Sanghera, Sharandish *2009*
Webb, Thomas *2010*
Wyeth, Stephen *2010*
Talbot-Ponsonby, Thomas *2011*
Davies, Eleanor *1998**
Helmi, Hala *2000**
Shillingford, Julia *2002**

Types of work

Accountancy · Adjudication · Administrative law · Adoption · Alternative dispute resolution · Ancillary relief · Animals · Arab commercial law · Arab law · Arbitration · Asbestos-related diseases · Asset forfeiture · Asset recovery · Banking · Bills of exchange · Boundaries · Building · Care proceedings · Chancery (commercial) · Chancery (general) · Chancery (land law) · Child care law · Children · Civil actions against the police · Civil partnerships · Clinical negligence · Cohabitation · Commercial contracts · Commercial fraud · Commercial law · Commercial litigation · Commercial property · Common land · Common law (general) · Company, commercial and competition · Computer contracts · Computer crime · Computer litigation · Confiscation · Conflict of laws · Construction law · Consumer credit · Consumer law · Contracts · Copyright · Corporate finance · Corporate fraud · Corporate governance · Corporate insolvency · Corporate liability · Corporate manslaughter · Corporate recovery · Costs · Court of Protection · Courts martial · Crime · Crime and criminal due process · Criminal judicial review · Cross-border litigation and remedies · Damages · Disability discrimination · Disasters · Disciplinary procedures · Disciplinary tribunals · Discrimination · Divorce · Domestic violence injunctions · Ecclesiastical law · Economic torts · Education · Election law · Employment · Engineering disputes · Equine law · Equity · Factoring · Family law · Family provision · Financial provision · Financial services · Firearms · Foreign law · Franchising · Fraud · Freezing orders · Guarantees · Health and safety · Holiday injury and damages · Homicide · Housing · Industrial deafness · Industrial diseases · Information technology · Inheritance and cohabitees · Inquests · Insolvency · Insurance · Intellectual property · International arbitration · International commercial arbitration · International fraud and asset tracing · Islamic family law · Islamic law · Judicial review · Landlord and tenant · Lands Tribunal · Licensing · Matrimonial finance · Mediation · Medical negligence · Middle Eastern law · Military law · Multi-party litigation · Occupational diseases · Partnerships · Passing off · Personal injury · Personal insolvency · Planning · Police · Product liability · Professional negligence · Public law · Real property · Regulatory and disciplinary law · Rights of light · Rights of way · Road traffic · Sale and carriage of goods · Serial crime · Serious fraud · Shareholder agreements · Succession · Tax · Technology and Construction Court · Torts · Trust litigation · Trusts · Wardship · Wills

Disability access

Staff briefed or trained on duties under the disability legislation, Disabled parking available

4 PAPER BUILDINGS

1st Floor, 4 Paper Buildings, Temple, London EC4Y 7EX
020 7427 5200
Fax: 020 7353 4979; DX: 1035 London Chancery Lane
E-mail: clerks@4pb.com
URL: www.4pb.com
Out of hours telephone: 07810 482828

Chambers of: Mr Alex Verdan QC

Clerk: Michael Reeves; Practice Manager: Clare Bello

Verdan, Alexander QC *1987†*
Scotland of Asthal, Baroness QC *1977*
Cohen, Jonathan QC *1974†*
Setright, Henry QC *1979†*
Scott-Manderson, Marcus QC *1980*
Branigan, Kate QC *1984*
Delahunty, Jo QC *1986*
Sternberg, Michael QC *1975*
Wood, Catherine QC *1985†*
Howling, Rex QC *1991*
Gupta, Teertha QC *1990†*
Barrington-Smyth, Amanda *1972*
Barda, Robin *1975*
Rayson, Jane *1982*
Johnstone, Mark *1984*
Coleman, Elizabeth *1985*
Perkins, Alistair *1986*
Hames, Christopher *1987*
Lyon, Stephen *1987*
Probyn, Jane *1988†*
Shaw, James *1988*
Bradley, Sally *1989*
Jarman, Mark *1989*
Brereton, Joy *1990*
Brown, Joanne *1990*
Grief, Alison *1990†*
King, Samantha *1990*

Mills, Barbara *1990*
Williams, David *1990*
Bedingfield, David *1991*†
Tughan, John *1991*
Hale, Charles *1992*
Larizadeh, Cyrus *1992*
Simon, Michael *1992*
Ageros, Justin *1993*
Littlewood, Robert *1993*
Hepher, Paul *1994*
Kirby, Ruth *1994*
Murray, Judith *1994*
Papazian, Cliona *1994*
Lewis, Sarah *1995*
Aber, Gordon *1996*
Fairbank, Nicholas *1996*
Copley, James *1997*
Johnston, Justine *1997*
Jones, Oliver *1998*
Cheetham, Lucy *1999*
Khan, Hassan *1999*
Perry, Cleo *2000*
Foulkes, Rebecca *2001*
Gates, Harry *2001*
Wood, Katie *2001*
Lloyd, Rhiannon *2002*
Van Rol, Katherine *2002*
White, Ceri *2002*
Persson, Matthew *2003*
Gartland, Dorothea Susan *2004*
Morley, Laura *2006*
Wallace, Nicola *2006*
Woodham, Samantha *2006*
Clayton, Henry *2007*
Gration, Michael *2007*
Renton, Jacqueline *2007*
Baird-Murray, Jasper *2008*
Powell, Andrew *2008*
Connors, Sophie *2009*
Edwards, Michael *2010*
Nosworthy, Harry *2010*

Types of work
Adoption · Ancillary relief · Child abduction · Child abuse · Child care law · Child support · Children · Family law · Family provision · Forced Marriage · Leave to remove · Partnerships · Unmarried couples

Opening times: 8.30am - 6.30pm

Chambers' facilities
Conference Rooms, Disks Accepted, Car parking facilities available on request

Disability access
Staff briefed or trained on duties under the disability legislation, Disabled parking available, Induction loop or infra red system

Languages spoken
French, German, Spanish

FIVE PAPER BUILDINGS

1st Floor, Five Paper Buildings, Temple, London EC4Y 7HB
020 7583 6117
Fax: 020 7353 0075; DX: 365 London Chancery Lane
E-mail: clerks@5pb.co.uk

Chambers of: Mr M J Brompton QC, Mr J M Caplan QC

Disability access
Wheelchair access, Disabled parking available

PARAGON CHAMBERS

8 Creed Lane, St. Paul, London EC4V 5BR
020 3318 9988
Fax: 020 3318 9958; DX: 42610 Cheapside
E-mail: contact@paragonchambers.com

Chambers of: Mr M C Usher, Mr O S I Abasheikh

CHAMBERS OF MISS J PATEL

77 Chesterfield Road, London E10 6EN
020 8539 7147
E-mail: jaya.patel1@btinternet.com

Chambers of: Miss J Patel

THE CHAMBERS OF MR S PATEL

35 Ravenscroft Avenue, London NW11 8BH
020 8458 7501
Fax: 020 8458 7501

Chambers of: Mr S Patel

CHAMBERS OF MR LIAM PEPPER

65L Warwick Square, London SW1V 2AL
07889 172288
E-mail: liamgeorgepepper@gmail.com

Chambers of: Mr L G Pepper

CHAMBERS OF MR HUBERT PICARDA QC

Third Floor North, 9 Old Square, Lincoln's Inn, London WC2A 3SR
020 7242 3566
Fax: 020 7831 3584
E-mail: hpicarda@aol.com

Chambers of: Mr H A P Picarda QC

CHAMBERS OF MR JOHN POINTING

46 Arlington Road, Ealing, London W13 8PE
020 8997 2285
E-mail: johnpointing@hotmail.com

Chambers of: Mr J E Pointing

Disability access
Wheelchair access, Disabled parking available

D

PRINCE HENRY'S CHAMBERS

2 Tamar House, 12 Tavistock Place, London WC1H 9RD
020 7837 1645
Fax: 020 7713 0377
E-mail: d.harris4@btconnect.com
Out of hours telephone: 020 7837 1645

Chambers of: Mr D R Harris

Also at: Little Firs, The Avenue, Ascot, Berkshire SL5 7LY

Also at: 23 Ellesmere Road, Berkhamsted, Herts HP4 2EX

Harris, David *1973*
Young, Andrew *1992*
Wicks, Raymond *1997*

Types of work
Arbitration · Capital tax · Construction law · Corporation tax · Customs · Income tax · Landlord and tenant · National Insurance · Professional negligence · Social security · VAT

PRINCE OF WALES CHAMBERS

90 Overstrand Mansions, Prince of Wales Drive, London SW11 4EU
020 7622 7415
Fax: 020 7622 7415
E-mail: DavidHoodEsq@aol.com

Chambers of: Mr D Hood

1 PUMP COURT

Elm Court, Temple, London EC4Y 7AH
020 7842 7070
Fax: 020 7842 7088; DX: 109 London Chancery Lane
E-mail: clerks@pumpcourt.co.uk
URL: www.1pumpcourt.co.uk
Out of hours telephone: 07774 238444
Clerks: Mycal Thomas, Scott Haley, John Collins, Clare Sabido, Sarah Bowyer, Lucy Adams, Mayani Weeriman, Tazmin Wilson, Marc Gilby, Andy Williams; Senior Clerk: Ian Burrow; Administrator: Jeannine Lewis; Receptionist: Deborah Gardner-Wood

Hayden, Anthony QC *1987†*
Hoyal, Jane *1976*
Bickler, Simon QC *1987*
Masters, Alan *1979*
Carrott, Sylvester *1980*
Hodgson, Martin *1980*
Barnett, Adrienne *1981*
Teji, Usha *1981*
O'Leary, Michele *1983*
Higham, James *1982*
Davies, Sarah *1984*
Presland, James *1985*
Archer, Lorna *1986*
Ladak, Tahera *1986*
Nicol, Nicholas *1986*
Adams, Lindsay *1987*
Littlewood, Rebecca *1988*
Dent, Sally *1989*
Huda, Abida *1989*
Polson, Alistair *1989*
Rubens, Jacqueline *1989*
Lamb, John *1990*
Breese-Laughran, Eleanore *1991*
Dixon, Anne *1991*
Eldergill, Edmund *1991*
Nabi, Zia *1991*
Ross, Anthony *1991*
Grant-Garwood, Joshua *1992*
Field, Stephen *1993*
Gannon, Kevin *1993*
Hussein, Timur *1993*
Kaler, Manjeet *1993*
McCrindell, James *1993*
Hilken, Alice *1994*
Hughes, Mary *1994*
Holloway, Sharon *1994*
Khubber, Ranjiv *1994*
English, Robert *1996*
Johnson, Melanie *1996*
Monah, Helen *1996*
Pedro, Terry *1996*
Wood, Joanna *1996*
Chandran, Parosha *1997*
Adedeji, Yinka *1997*
Dubin, Joshua *1997*
McDonald, Mark *1997*
Blum, Doron *1998*
Kaza, Ajanta *1998*
Scott, Stuart *1998*
Adler, Jonathan *1999*
Butcher, Helen *1999*
Ramdas-Harsia, Rohan *1999*
Sayed, Ruby *1999*
Tueje, Patricia *1999*
Barker, Jennifer *2000*
Harris, Michelle *2000*
Kotak, Raggi *2000*
Parham, Sam *2000*
Denholm, Graham *2001*
Phillips, Emma *2001*
Chirico, David *2002*
Martin, Rebecca *2002*
Peat, Charlie *2003*
Bartlet-Jones, Stephen *2004*
Kiai, Gilda *2004*
Waldron, Lorraine *2004*
Cecil, Joanne *2005*
Compton, Justine *2005*
King, Emma *2005*
Sinclair, Caroline *2005*
Wibberley, Lucie *2005*
Sammy, Natasha *2006*
Dean, Christine *2007*
Hutchison, Eleanor *2007*
Short, Harriet *2007*
Elgadhy, Amean *2008*
Hall, Toby *2008*
Loughran, Gemma *2008*
Gilbert, Andrew *2009*
Hemery, Philippa *2009*
Cohen, Marisa *2010*
Wheeler, Rupert *2010*
Dowd, Christopher *2012*
O'Ceallaigh, Greagoir *2006**

Types of work
Administrative law · Care proceedings · Chancery (general) · Chancery (land law) · Civil liberties · Common law (general) · Corporate fraud · Crime · Discrimination · Education · Employment · Environment · Equity · Family law · Family provision · Housing · Human rights · Immigration · Landlord and tenant · Licensing · Local authorities · Mental health · Personal injury · Professional negligence · Trusts · Wills

Disability access
Staff briefed or trained on duties under the disability legislation, Wheelchair access, Disabled parking available

2 PUMP COURT

1st Floor, 2 Pump Court, Temple, London EC4Y 7AH
020 7353 5597
Fax: 020 7583 2122; DX: 290 London

†Recorder *Door Tenant/Associate Member

Chancery Lane
E-mail: clerks@2pumpcourt.co.uk

Chambers of: Mr R H Christie QC

Disability access
Staff briefed or trained on duties under the disability legislation, Wheelchair access, Disabled parking available

D

4 PUMP COURT

4 Pump Court, Temple, London EC4Y 7AN
020 7842 5555
Fax: 020 7583 2036; DX: 303 London Chancery Lane
E-mail: chambers@4pumpcourt.com
URL: www.4pumpcourt.com
Out of hours telephone: Available on answerphone

Chambers of: Mr J B Storey QC, Mr N K Tozzi QC
Clerks: Jon Robinson, Carl Wall, Stewart Gibbs; Practice Manager: Carolyn McCombe

Storey, Jeremy QC *1974†*
Tozzi, Nigel QC *1980*
Temple, Anthony QC *1968*
Friedman, David QC *1968†*
Blunt, David QC *1967†*
Moger, Christopher QC *1972†*
Speaight, Anthony QC *1973*
Marks, Jonathan QC *1975*
Douglas, Michael QC *1974†*
Nicholson, Jeremy QC *1977*
Cross, James QC *1985*
Vineall, Nicholas QC *1988*
Charlton, Alexander QC *1983*
Christie, Aidan QC *1988*
McCall, Duncan QC *1988*
Neish, Andrew QC *1988*
Brannigan, Sean QC *1994*
Davie, Michael QC *1993*
Gunning, Alexander QC *1994*
Hamilton, Peter *1968*
Dyer, Allen *1976*
Ticciati, Oliver *1979*
Bergin, Terence *1985*
Potter, Alison *1987*
Henderson, Simon *1993*
Vaughan-Neil, Kate *1994*
Ansell, Rachel *1995*
Hickey, Alexander *1995*
Lewis, Jonathan *1996*
Packman, Claire *1996*
Taylor, Michael *1996*
McCafferty, Lynne *1997*
O'Sullivan, Sean *1997*
Pilling, Ben *1997*
Purchas, James *1997*
Bowling, James *1999*
Leabeater, James *1999*
Gillies, Jennie *2000*
Livesey, Kate *2001*
Crangle, Thomas *2002*
Oliver, Peter *2002*
Hatt, James *2003*
Woods, George *2003*
Chatterjee, Rangan *2004*
Goldstone, Simon *2004*
Lavy, Matthew *2004*
Wygas, Luke *2004*
Crowley, Laura *2005*
Osborne, Richard *2005*
Owens, Elspeth *2007*
Stevens, Andrew *2007*
Wright, Alexander *2007*
Goodkin, Daniel *2008*
Temple, Adam *2008*
Munro, Iain *2009*
Naylor, Martyn *2009*
Coleman, Russell SC *1986**

Types of work
Arbitration · Banking · Chancery (general) · Commercial law · Commercial litigation · Common law (general) · Construction law · Consumer law · Dispute resolution and arbitration · Employment · Entertainment · Family provision · Financial services · Information technology · Insurance · International trade · Landlord and tenant · Licensing · Medical negligence · Personal injury · Professional negligence · Sale and carriage of goods · Sport · Telecommunications

Disability access
Staff briefed or trained on duties under the disability legislation, Wheelchair access, Disabled parking available

5 PUMP COURT

Ground Floor, 5 Pump Court, Temple, London EC4Y 7AP
020 7353 2532
Fax: 020 7353 5321; DX: 497 London Chancery Lane
E-mail: clerks@5pumpcourt.com
URL: www.5pumpcourt.com
Out of hours telephone: 07976 368031

Chambers of: Mr M D Collard
Clerks: Tim Markham (Senior Clerk), John Wooloughan, Jay Dorton, Sam Thompson, Rupinder Chana; Fees & Accounts Manager: Dee Taylor-Nelson

Collard, Michael *1986*
Lawrence, Sir Ivan QC *1962*
Dow, Kenneth *1970*
Boothby, Jo *1972†*
Clarke, Ivan *1973*
Evison, John *1974*
Keith, Alistair *1974*
Oliver, Juliet *1974*

†Recorder *Door Tenant/Associate Member

Cartwright, Crispian *1976*†
Chaize, Tristan *1977*
Corben, Paul *1979*
Ratcliffe, Anne *1981*
Eldridge, Mark *1982*
Gray, Roger *1984*
Gray, Peter *1984*
O'Toole, Simon *1984*
Cleaver, Henry *1985*
Wauchope, Piers *1985*
Addison, Paul *1988*
Hall, Adrian *1989*
Jackson, Andrew Fraser *1990*
Nicholls, Jack *1991*
Mahmood, Imran *1992*
Solari, Yolanda *1992*
Badejo, Abimbola *1993*
Hogben, Paul *1993*
Maddan, Archie *1993*
Palmer, Nathan *1994*
Pritchard, Teresa *1994*
Scott-Phillips, Alexander *1995*
Roy, Stefan *1996*
Mitropoulos, Chris *1997*
James, Emily *1999*
Long, Benjamin *2000*
Soora, Brinder *2000*
Kasriel, Andrew *2001*
Dickinson, Zarah *2002*
Hepburn, Katrina *2002*
Ryle, Kate *2002*
Choudhury, Nawazish *2003*
Foulkes, Rebecca *2003*
Hill, Sophie *2003*
Nabi, Sajjad *2003*
Sparks, Catherine *2003*
Edwards, Dickon *2004*
Hannant, Lisa *2005*
Hartnett, Elizabeth *2005*
Magennis, Olivia *2005*
Round, Kate *2005*
Ashworth, Steven *2006*
Calas-Prolingheuer, Sophie *2006*
Conway, Simon *2006*
Croxford, Kerrie *2007*
Gordon, Henry *2007*
Channer, Benjamin *2008*
McDermott, Mathew *2008*
Davey, Roger *1978**
Johal, Devinder *1995**
Darlington, Elizabeth *1998**

Types of work
Administrative law · Arbitration · Boundaries · Care proceedings · Chancery (general) · Chancery (land law) · Commercial law · Commercial litigation · Common law (general) · Construction law · Consumer credit · Coroner's inquests · Crime · Education · Employment · Family law · Family provision · Housing · Immigration · Landlord and tenant · Licensing · Litigation · Mediation · Mental health · Partnerships · Personal injury · Personal insolvency · Prison law · Professional negligence · Real property · Regulatory and disciplinary law

Chambers Established 1870
Opening times: 8.30am - 7.00pm

Chambers' facilities
Seminars CPD accredited, electronic library. E-mail, Free parking by arrangement, Video playback facilities

Disability access
Staff briefed or trained on duties under the disability legislation, Disabled parking available

Fees policy
No set rates for paperwork, although fees can be agreed in advance on sight of the papers, or guidance given as to appropriate hourly rates.

Types of work undertaken
Five Pump Court Chambers is a long-established common law set with three specialist practice groups focusing on civil, criminal and family law. Conditional fee and public access work is undertaken. Chambers has dedicated conference rooms with video facilities, and free parking is available. Conferences can be arranged out of London. Chambers has been awarded Quality Mark for the Bar status.

Principal areas of practice

Civil: Business and Commercial, Construction, Professional Negligence and Liability, Employment and Discrimination, Personal Injury, Property, Landlord and Tenant.

Criminal: Fraud, sexual offences, DTI, serious violence, car ringing and importation of drugs.

Family: Financial provision and children.

6 PUMP COURT

1st Floor, 6 Pump Court, Temple, London EC4Y 7AR
020 7797 8400
Fax: 020 7797 8401; DX: 293 London Chancery Lane
E-mail: richardconstable@6pumpcourt.co.uk
URL: www.6pumpcourt.co.uk

Chambers of: Mr S A Hockman QC, Mr P J Harrison QC
Senior Clerk: Richard Constable

Also at: 6-8 Mill Street, Maidstone, Kent ME15 6XH

Hockman, Stephen QC *1970*
Harrison, Peter QC *1987*
Barraclough, Richard QC *1980*
Gower, Peter QC *1985*†
Martin, Roy QC *1990*
Travers, David QC *1981*
Laws, Eleanor QC *1990*
Armstrong, Grant *1978*
Harris, Mark *1980*
Williams, Anne *1980*
Baldock, Nicholas *1983*
Topping, Caroline *1984*
Taylor, Paul *1985*
Thomas, Megan *1987*
Campbell, Jane *1990*
Forbes, Peter *1990*
O'Higgins, John *1990*
Upton, William *1990*
Saxby, Oliver *1992*
Espley, Andrew *1993*
Bates, Pascal *1994*
Ellin, Nina *1994*
Grant, Edward *1994*
Moore, Danny *1994*
Watson, Mark *1994*
Alcock, Peter *1995*
Beard, Mark *1996*
Charles, Deborah *1996*†
Donnelly, Catherine *1997*
Robinson, Tanya *1997*
Taylor, Simon *1997*
Banwell, Richard *1998*
Bennett, Lee *1998*
Menzies, Gordon *1998*
Luttman, Lucy *2001*
Oragwu, Adaku *2001*
Atkinson, Giles *2002*
Lambert, Emmaline *2003*

†Recorder *Door Tenant/Associate Member

Tahir, Perican *2004*
Cullen, Grace *2005*
Crowdy, Isabella *2007*
Dobbie, Alice *2007*
Ostrowski, Nicholas *2009*
Phillips, Ian Rees *2009*
Phillips, Laura *2009*
Knowles, Linsey *2000**
Byrd, Noemi *2004**

Types of work

Administrative law · Care proceedings · Commercial law · Commercial litigation · Common law (general) · Consumer law · Corporate fraud · Crime · Employment · Energy · Environment · Family law · Family provision · Food law · Fraud · Health and safety · Human rights · Inquests · Judicial review · Landlord and tenant · Licensing · Local authorities · Mediation · Medical negligence · Natural resources · Parliamentary · Personal injury · Planning · Professional negligence · Public inquiries · Trading standards

Disability access

Disabled parking available

PUMP COURT CHAMBERS

Upper Ground Floor, 3 Pump Court, Temple, London EC4Y 7AJ
020 7353 0711
Fax: 0845 259 3241; DX: 362 London Chancery Lane
E-mail: clerks@3pumpcourt.com
URL: www.pumpcourtchambers.com
Out of hours telephone: 07515 334453

Chambers of: Mr O E Nsugbe QC
Clerks: David Barber, Jonathan Cue, Tony Atkins, Charlotte Horn, David Fielder, Tim Dockrill; Administrator: Andrea Cheshire; Fee Collection: Holly Bell (Swindon)

Also at: 31 Southgate Street, Winchester SO23 9EE Tel: 01962 868161 Fax: 01962 867645; 5 Temple Chambers, Swindon SN1 1SQ Tel: 01793 539899 Fax: 01793 539866

Nsugbe, Oba QC *1985*†
Pascoe, Nigel QC *1966*†
Donne, Anthony QC *1973*
Campbell, Susan QC *1986*
Hill, Mark QC *1987*†
Samuels, Leslie QC *1989*
Patterson, Stewart *1967*†
Harrap, Giles *1971*†
Abbott, Frank *1972*†
Parry, Charles *1973*
Butt, Michael *1974*
Ker-Reid, John *1974*
Gabb, Charles *1975*
Jones, Stephen *1978*
MacKenzie, Julie *1978*
Allardice, Miranda *1982*
Blount, Martin *1982*
Scott, Matthew *1985*
Bloom-Davis, Desmond *1986*
Travers, Hugh *1988*
Boydell, Edward *1989*†
Gau, Justin *1989*
Houston, Andrew *1989*
Wicks, David *1989*
Breslin, Catherine *1990*
Khan, Helen *1990*
Howe, Penny *1991*
Lorenzo, Claudia *1991*
Kelly, Geoffrey *1992*
Newton-Price, James *1992*
Ruffell, Mark *1992*
Ashley, Mark *1993*
Gunther, Elizabeth *1993*
Moore, Roderick *1993*
Morton, Gary *1993*
Peirson, Oliver *1993*
Russell, Alison *1993*
Smith, Leonorah *1993*
Tregilgas-Davey, Marcus *1993*
Pawson, Robert *1994*
Hall, Richard *1995*
Asteris, Peter *1996*
Dubbery, Mark *1996*
Hall, Michael *1996*
Jones, Sarah *1996*
Ephgrave, Amy *1997*
Gallagher, Maria *1997*
Grime, Andrew *1997*
Ward, Anne *1997*
Dracass, Timothy *1998*
Keen, Spencer *1998*
Bond, Andrew *1999*
Spearing, Rachel *1999*
Brown, Anne *2000*
Islam, Naznin *2000*
Ramadhan, Lubeya *2000*
Tutt, Richard *2000*
Burge, Alison *2002*
Hartley, Caroline *2002*
Platt, Heather *2002*
Shravat, Neelo *2002*
Berry, Amy *2003*
Chapman, John *2003*
Davis, Lucy-Victoria *2003*
Street, Charlotte *2003*
Gadd, Adam *2004*
Leach, Stuart *2004*
Trotter, Helen *2004*
Lyons, Tara *2005*
Troup, Rachel *2005*
Connors, Hannah *2006*
Iten, Corinne *2006*
Long, Benjamin *2006*
O'Driscoll, Patricia *2006*
Gilbert, Daniella *2007*
Lee, Jennifer *2007*
Bruce, Eleanor *2008*
Purkis, Simon *2008*
Williamson, Nicholas *2009*

Types of work

Arbitration · Care proceedings · Chancery (land law) · Civil liberties · Commercial law · Commercial litigation · Commercial property · Company, commercial and competition · Construction law · Corporate fraud · Courts martial · Crime · Ecclesiastical law · Employment · Environment · Family law · Family provision · Foreign law · Inheritance and cohabitees · Landlord and tenant · Licensing · Medical negligence · Personal injury · Planning · Professional negligence · Sport · Succession · War crimes tribunals

Opening times: 8.00am - 6.00pm

Chambers' facilities

Conference Rooms, Disks Accepted, E-mail, Disabled Parking

Disability access

Staff briefed or trained on duties under the disability legislation, Disabled parking available

 †Recorder *Door Tenant/Associate Member

Languages spoken
French, German

Fees policy
Fees are negotiated with the clerks who are happy to discuss hourly rates and provide estimates.

PUMP COURT TAX CHAMBERS

PUMP COURT
TAX CHAMBERS

16 Bedford Row, London WC1R 4EF
020 7414 8080
Fax: 020 7414 8099; DX: 312 London Chancery Lane
E-mail: clerks@pumptax.com
URL: www.pumptax.com
Out of hours telephone: 07887 992575/ 07921 772162

Chambers of: Mr A R Thornhill QC
Senior Clerk: Nigel Jones; Administrator: Pia Giles

Thornhill, Andrew QC *1969*
Aaronson, Graham QC *1966*
Milne, David QC *1970*
Massey, William QC *1977*
Prosser, Kevin QC *1982*
Tallon, John QC *1975*
Goodfellow, Giles QC *1983*
Ewart, David QC *1987*
Ghosh, Julian QC *1993*
Baldry, Rupert QC *1987*
Richards, Ian *1971*
Hamilton, Penelope *1972*
Matthews, Jan *1972*
White, Jeremy *1976*
Thomas, Roger *1979*
Woolf, Jeremy *1986*
Hitchmough, Andrew *1991*
Wilson, Elizabeth *1995*
Henderson, James *1997*
Vallat, Richard *1997*
Chamberlain, Emma *1998*
Dunn, Sarah *1998*
Choudhury, Sadiya *2002*
Conolly, Oliver *2003*
Rivett, James *2004*
Yates, David *2004*
Bremner, Jonathan *2005*
Chacko, Thomas *2007*
Poots, Laura *2007*
Yang, Zizhen *2009*
Bradley, Charles *2010*

Types of work
Alternative dispute resolution · Capital tax · Corporation tax · Customs · Employee benefit trusts · European Union · Income tax · Mediation · National Insurance · Private client · Professional negligence · Stamp duty · Trusts · VAT · Wills

Opening times: 8.30am - 6.30pm

Disability access
Staff briefed or trained on duties under the disability legislation, Wheelchair access, Disabled parking available

PUTNAM

14 Keyes Road, London NW2 3XA
020 8438 2950
Fax: 020 8452 3912; DX: 35354 Cricklewood
E-mail: tom@lending_law.co.uk

Chambers of: Mr T D Putnam

CHAMBERS OF MR K QADRI

84 Augustus Road, London SW19 6EL
07956 205798
Fax: 020 8788 9930
E-mail: kkadri1993@yahoo.co.uk

Chambers of: Mr K Qadri

Disability access
Staff briefed or trained on duties under the disability legislation, Disabled parking available

QEB HOLLIS WHITEMAN

1-2 Laurence Pountney Hill, London EC4R 0EU
020 7933 8855
Fax: 020 7929 3732; DX: 858 London City
E-mail: barristers@qebhw.co.uk
URL: www.qebholliswhiteman.co.uk
Out of hours telephone: Duty Clerk 24 hour 07855 099271

Chambers of: Mr M C Ellison QC
Clerks: Martin Secrett, Chris Emmings; Administrator: Sarah Finlayson

Ellison, Mark QC *1979†*
Poulet, Rebecca QC *1975†*
Whiteman, Peter QC *1967†*
Grey, Robin QC *1957*
Glass, Anthony QC *1965†*
Hilton, John QC *1964†*
Kyte, Peter QC *1970†*
Boyce, William QC *1976†*
Donne, Jeremy QC *1978†*
Roberts, Timothy QC *1978†*
Jeremy, David QC *1977†*
Brown, Edward QC *1983†*
Aylett, Crispin QC *1985*
Finnigan, Peter QC *1978*
Kark, Thomas QC *1982†*
Larkin, Sean QC *1987*
Plaschkes, Sarah QC *1988†*
Johnson, Zoe QC *1990*
Darbishire, Adrian QC *1993*
Wilcken, Anthony *1966†*
Strudwick, Linda *1973*
Paton, Ian *1975†*
Bagge, *1979*
Carney, Caroline SC *1980*
Groome, David *1987*
Henry, Edward *1988*
Smart, Roger *1989*
Wakerley, Paul *1990*
Barnfather, Lydia *1992*
Ramasamy, Selva *1992*
Maguire, Benn *1994*
Raudnitz, Paul *1994*
Evans, Philip *1995*
Aldred, Mark *1996*
Evans, Julian *1997*
Harris, Rebecca *1997*
Stevens, Susannah *1997*
Tahta, Natasha *1998*
Felix, Alexandra *1999*
Ledward, Jocelyn *1999*
Fitzgerald, Ben *2000*
Kennedy, Lucy *2000*
Robinson, Karen *2000*
Alibhai, Ari *2003*
Broome, Kerry *2003*
McGhee, Philip *2003*
Baker, Tom *2004*
Coxhill, Fraser *2004*
Stott, Philip *2004*
Warwick, Joanna *2004*
Daly, Caoimhe *2005*
King, Adam *2005*
Gokani, Rachna *2006*
Broomfield, Tom *2007*
Rooney, Paul *2007*
Alexis, Fallon *2008*
Lynch, John *2008*
Léél, Robin *2009*
Meggy, Rhys *2009*
Dyer, Polly *2010*
Naylor, Tim *2010*

Types of work
Confiscation · Copyright theft · Corporate fraud · Courts martial · Crime · Extradition · Fraud · Health and safety · Licensing · Regulatory and disciplinary law · Serious fraud · Sport

Opening times: 8.30am - 6:30pm

Chambers' facilities
Conference Rooms

Disability access
Staff briefed or trained on duties under the disability legislation, Wheelchair access, Disabled parking available

Languages spoken
French, German, Greek, Italian, Russian, Spanish, Swedish, Welsh

Fees policy
Fees will be negotiated with the clerk.

QUADRANT CHAMBERS

Quadrant House, 10 Fleet Street, London EC4Y 1AU
020 7583 4444
Fax: 020 7583 4455; DX: 292 London Chancery Lane
E-mail: info@quadrantchambers.com

Chambers of: Mr S P N Rainey QC, Mr L E Persey QC

Disability access
Staff briefed or trained on duties under the disability legislation, Wheelchair access, Disabled parking available

QUEEN ELIZABETH BUILDING

QEB

3rd Floor, Queen Elizabeth Building, Temple, London EC4Y 9BS
020 7797 7837
Fax: 020 7353 5422; DX: 339 London Chancery Lane
E-mail: clerks@qeb.co.uk
URL: www.qeb.co.uk
Out of hours telephone: 01245 442331/07802 179670

Chambers of: Mr L Marks QC
Clerks: Ivor Treherne, Stephen Morley

Marks, Lewis QC *1984*
Stone, Lucy QC *1983*
Hyde, Charles QC *1988†*
Amos, Tim QC *1987†*
Roberts, Jennifer QC *1988†*
Leech, Stewart QC *1992*
Hosford-Tanner, Michael *1974*
Tidbury, Andrew *1976†*
Brudenell, Thomas *1977*
Wise, Oliver *1981*
Edwards, Sarah *1990*
Firth, Matthew *1991*
Clarke, Elizabeth *1991*
Cowton, Catherine *1995*
Thorpe, Alexander *1995*
Ewins, James *1996*
Phipps, Sarah *1997*
Lazarides, Marcus *1999*
Brooks, Duncan *2000*
Bentham, Daniel *2000*
Harvey, Tristan *2002*
Sirikanda, Morgan *2002*
Batt, Charanjit *2004*
Budden, Rosemary *2003*
Singer, Samantha *2004*
Westley, Nicholas *2005*
Faggionato, Marina *2006*
Tyzack, William *2007*
Younis, Saima *2008*
Kisser, Amy *2009*
Headley, Fitzrene *2011*
Baker, Hannah *2005**
Wiseman, Naomi *2011**

Types of work
Care proceedings · Clinical negligence ·

†Recorder *Door Tenant/Associate Member

Family law · Family provision · Professional negligence

Disability access
Staff briefed or trained on duties under the disability legislation, Wheelchair access, Disabled parking available

QUEEN'S GATE CHAMBERS

Flat 2, 27 Stanhope Gardens, London SW7 5QX
07765 404650

Chambers of: Ms P H G Van Der Craats

QUORUM TAX CHAMBERS

25 Southampton Buildings, London WC2A 1AL
020 7043 5189
E-mail: clerks@quorumchambers.co.uk

Chambers of: Ms L A Frawley

RADCLIFFE CHAMBERS

Radcliffe Chambers

Ground Floor, 11 New Square, Lincoln's Inn, London WC2A 3QB
020 7831 0081
Fax: 020 7405 2560; DX: 319 London Chancery Lane
E-mail: clerks@radcliffechambers.com
URL: www.radcliffechambers.com
Out of hours telephone: See website

Chambers of: Mr K Rowley QC
Clerks: Keith Nagle (Senior Clerk), John Clark (Senior Clerk); Administrator: Claire Hewitt; Director of Client Care & Marketing: Catherine Calder

Rowley, Keith QC *1979*
Marten, Hedley *1966*
Crampin, Peter QC *1976*†
Waters, Malcolm QC *1977*
Pearce, Robert QC *1977*
Quint, Francesca *1970*
di Mambro, David *1973*
Nurse, Gordon *1973*
Crawford, Grant *1974*
Heywood, Michael *1975*
Acton, Stephen *1977*
Ovey, Elizabeth *1978*
Dumont, Thomas *1979*
Staunton, Ulick *1984*
Williams, Simon *1984*
Feltham, Piers *1985*
Smith, Howard *1986*
Mullis, Roger *1987*
West, Mark *1987*
McQuail, Katherine *1989*
Dodge, Peter *1992*
Majumdar, Shantanu *1992*
Bleasdale, Marie-Claire *1993*
Smith, Peter *1993*
Holmes, Justin *1994*
Ohrenstein, Dov *1995*
Selway, Kate *1995*
Moys, Clive *1998*
Moffett, William *2000*
Wells, Nathan *2000*
Flavin, Marcus *2001*
Mullen, Mark *2001*
Winfield, Joshua *2001*
Ratcliffe, Frances *2002*
Barrett, Steven *2003*
Beasley, Thomas *2003*
Buckley, Christopher *2004*
Fell, Mark *2004*
Hicks, Edward *2004*
Lewison, Josh *2005*
Mathers, Wendy *2005*
Doran, Catherine *2008*
Brown, Natalie *2009*
Burton, Daniel *2009*
Moollan, Iqbal *1998**

Types of work
Agriculture · Arbitration · Bahamas law · Banking · Capital tax · Chancery (general) · Chancery (land law) · Charities · Commercial law · Commercial litigation · Commercial property · Common land · Common law (general) · Company, commercial and competition · Conveyancing · Court of Protection · Ecclesiastical law · Education · Employment · Environment · Equity · Family provision · Financial services · Housing · Income tax · Insolvency · Landlord and tenant · Licensing · Local authorities · Mining · Partnerships · Pensions · Personal insolvency · Planning · Professional negligence · Rights of light · Succession · Trusts · Wills

Disability access
Staff briefed or trained on duties under the disability legislation, Disabled parking available

CHAMBERS OF MR JULIUS SEAL

189 Randolph Avenue, Maida Vale, London W9 1DJ
020 7328 0158
Fax: 020 7328 0158
E-mail: julius.seal@ntlworld.com

Chambers of: Mr J D Seal

5RB

1st Floor, 5 Raymond Buildings, Gray's Inn, London WC1R 5BP
020 7242 2902
Fax: 020 7831 2686; DX: 1054 London Chancery Lane
E-mail: clerks@5rb.com

Chambers of: Mr D J M Browne QC, Mr M D J Warby QC

Disability access
Disabled parking available

†Recorder *Door Tenant/Associate Member

D

18 RED LION COURT

18 Red Lion Court, London EC4A 3EB
020 7520 6000
Fax: 020 7520 6248; DX: 478 London Chancery Lane
E-mail: chambers@18rlc.co.uk
URL: www.18rlc.co.uk
Out of hours telephone: 07710 077419

Chambers of: Mr Max Hill QC
Practice Manager: Practice Director: Mark Bennett

Also at: 18 Red Lion Court (Annexe), Thornwood House, 102 New London Road, Chelmsford, Essex CM2 0RG

Hill, Max QC *1987†*
Spencer, Derek QC *1961*
Arlidge, Anthony QC *1962*
Cocks, David QC *1961*
Parkins, Graham QC *1972*
Sutton, Richard QC *1969†*
Shaw, Antony QC *1975*
Carter, Peter QC *1974*
Etherington, David QC *1979†*
Lynch, Patricia QC *1979†*
Benson, Jeremy QC *1978†*
Johnston, Carey QC *1977*
Coughlin, Vincent QC *1980*
Lucas, Noel QC *1979†*
Spence, Simon QC *1985†*
Milne, Alexander QC *1981†*
Bewsey, Jane QC *1986*
Hales, Sally-Ann QC *1988†*
Levett, Martyn *1978†*
Pounder, Gerard *1980†*
Tucker, Lorraine *1982*
Joshi, Rajendra *1983*
Sheff, Janine *1983*
Shroff, Cyrus *1983*
Du Preez, Robin *1985*
Morris, Brendan *1985*
Dyble, Steven *1986*
Lyons, John *1986*
Marshall, Andrew *1986†*
Mehta, Sailesh *1986*
Walbank, David *1987*
Collery, Shane *1988†*
Beynon, Richard *1990*
Lawson, Sara *1990*
Gursoy, Ramiz *1991*
Holborn, David *1991†*
Paxton, Christopher *1991*
Skelley, Michael *1991*
Thompson, Andrew *1991*
Clare, Allison *1992*
Gowen, Matthew *1992*
D'Cruz, Rufus *1993*
Dempster, Jennifer *1993*
Forster, Tom *1993*
Jameson, Barnaby *1993*
May, Nicola *1993*
Fell, Alistair *1994*
Nelson, Michelle *1994*
Wiseman, Adam *1994*
Casey, Noel *1995*
Karmy-Jones, Riel *1995*
Leigh, Samantha *1995†*
Rose, Stephen *1995*
Jones, Gillian *1996*
Wilson, David *1996*
Requena, Stephen *1997*
Atkins, Victoria *1998*
Moll, Louis-Peter *1998*
Payne, Thomas *1998*
Chalkley, Rebecca *1999*
Rickard, Marcus *2000*
Dance, Matthew *2001*
Khanna, Priyadarshani *2001*
Willcocks, Hannah *2001*
Hamid, Ruby *2002*
Islam, Mohammad *2002*
Owen, Carys *2002*
Gargitter, Emma *2003*
Sawyer, Jamie *2003*
Eales, Hannah *2004*
Oldfield, Jane *2004*
Archer, Trevor *2005*
Baines, Max *2005*
Mahmutaj, Klentiana *2005*
Lewis, Sarah *2006*
Claxton, David *2008*
Dite, Alexis *2008*
Kingswell, Gemma *2008*
Parsons, Naomi *2008*
Hall, Aja *2009*
Kenyon, Laura *2009*
Robinson, Daniel *2010*
Garlick, Helen *1974**
Lawton, Paul *1987†**
Williams, David Huw QC *1988**
Pacifico, Adam *1991**
Jonson, Lydia *2000**
Brown, Emma *2002**
Farrant, James *2007**
Mansingh, Urmilla *2009**

Types of work
Anti-social Behaviour Orders · Asset forfeiture · Asset recovery · Child abuse · Civil liberties · Commercial fraud · Confiscation · Coroner's inquests · Coroners · Corporate fraud · Corporate manslaughter · Courts martial · Crime · Crime and criminal due process · Criminal judicial review · Disciplinary procedures · Disciplinary tribunals · ECHR · Extradition · Firearms · Forfeiture · Fraud · Health and safety · Homicide · Human rights · Inquests · International criminal law · International fraud and asset tracing · International human rights law · Police · Prison law · Prisoners' rights · Privy Council Appeals · Public inquiries · Regulatory and disciplinary law · Road traffic offences · Serial crime · Serious fraud · Sexual Offences · Taxation and duties · Terrorism

Disability access
Staff briefed or trained on duties under the disability legislation, Wheelchair access

REDBOURNE CHAMBERS

44 Redbourne Avenue, London N3 2BS
020 8346 8524
Fax: 020 8346 8524; DX: 57272 Finchley 2

Chambers of: Mr N B Corre

REDEMPTION CHAMBERS

121 The Vale, Golders Green, London NW11 8TL
020 8458 5486
E-mail: home@ollennu92.freeserve.co.uk

Chambers of: Mr A K N A Ollennu

†Recorder *Door Tenant/Associate Member

CHAMBERS OF MISS CLAUDETTE REID

C P Reid Direct Access, Barrister, PO Box 583872, London SE27 7BJ

Chambers of: Miss C P Reid

RENAISSANCE CHAMBERS

renaissance chambers

5th Floor, Gray's Inn Chambers, Gray's Inn, London WC1R 5JA
020 7404 1111
Fax: 020 7430 1522; DX: 0074 London Chancery Lane
E-mail: clerks@renaissancechambers.co.uk
URL: www.renaissancechambers.co.uk
Out of hours telephone: 07525 967 266

Chambers of: Mr B P Jubb
Clerks: Danny Jones, Mark Venables; Practice Manager: Elaine Cheeseman; Rob Andrews (Fees Clerk); Finance Manager: Elaine Cheeseman

Jubb, Brian *1971*
Dodson, Joanna QC *1971*
Clough, Richard *1971*
Haywood, Janette *1977*
Thompson, Dermot Main *1977*
Wingert, Rachel *1980*
Plange, Janet *1981*
More O'Ferrall, Geraldine *1983*
Nazareth, Melanie *1984*
Posner, Gabrielle Jan *1984*
Weiniger, Noah *1984*
Boye-Anawomah, Margo *1989*
Calway, Mark *1989*
Cregan, Paul *1990*
Ancliffe, Shiva *1991*
Seitler, Deborah *1991*
Gilling, Denise *1992*
Amiraftabi, Roshi *1993*
Fisher, Sandra *1993*
Jegarajah, Shivani *1993*
Yong, Pearl *1993*
Parr, Judith *1994*
Ahmed, Amina *1995*
Allen, Frances *1995*
Bayati, Charlotte *1995*
Gandhi, Paulene *1995*
Metaxa, William *1995*
Archer, Christopher *1996*
Barran, Tabitha *1998*
Coyle, Stephen *1998*
Gasparro, Julia Marie *1999*
Iqbal, Samina *1999*
Palmer, Iain *1999*
Paramjorthy, Nishan *1999*
Saifolahi, Sanaz *2000*
Benneh, Adelaide *2001*
Harper, Helen *2002*
Yeo, Colin *2002*
Akther, Ripon *2003*
Chokowry, Katy *2003*
Fletcher, Matthew *2003*
Fox, Claire *2003*
Physsas, Claire *2004*
Train, Sophie *2005*
Pinder, Sarah *2006*
Chaudhry, Mehvish *2008*
Swan, Jennifer *2009*
Tobin, Kezia *2010*
Lillington, Simon *1980**
Compton, Timothy *1984**
Thompson, Polly *1990**

Types of work
Adoption · Ancillary relief · Care proceedings · Child abduction · Children · Community care · Family law · Family provision · Human rights · Immigration · Mental health · Personal insolvency · Unmarried couples · Wardship

Disability access
Staff briefed or trained on duties under the disability legislation, Wheelchair access, Disabled parking available

CHAMBERS OF MR J M RENE

20 Fairoak Drive, Eltham, London SE9 2QH
07768 854321
Fax: 020 8859 4104
E-mail: jacques_rene30@hotmail.com

RICHMOND CANTER IMMIGRATION BARRISTERS

1 Fetter Lane, London EC4A 1BR
020 3440 5820
Fax: 020 3440 5401
E-mail: info@immigrationbarrister.co.uk

Chambers of: Mr P A O Richmond, Mr S A Canter

CHAMBERS OF MR ANDREW RINKER

3 Kensington Gate, London W8 5NA
020 7584 1091
Fax: 020 7584 1091
E-mail: a.rinker@btinernet.com

RIVERVIEW CHAMBERS

Hamilton House, 1 Temple Avenue, London EC4Y 0HA
0844 225 3999
E-mail: chrisbaylis@riverviewchambers.com

Chambers of: Mr C L G Baylis

D

ROEHAMPTON CHAMBERS

30 Stoughton Close, Roehampton, London SW15 4LS
020 8788 1238
Fax: 020 8788 1238

Chambers of: Mr P G Proghoulis

CHAMBERS OF YETUNDE RUBAN

9 Grenaby Road, Croydon, London CR0 2EJ
020 8665 5834
Fax: 020 8665 5834
E-mail: yetruban@yahoo.co.uk

Chambers of: Ms Y Olupitan-Ruban

CHAMBERS OF MR S J JOSEPH

39 Hermitage Road, Haringey, London N4 1LU
020 8809 3083/020 8802 9889
Fax: 020 8809 3083/020 8800 5845
E-mail: sjoe333@yahoo.co.uk

Chambers of: Mr S J Joseph

THE CHAMBERS OF PENELOPE SEGUSS

28 Burcote Road, London SW18 3LQ
020 8877 0707
E-mail: pseguss@btinternet.com

SELBORNE CHAMBERS

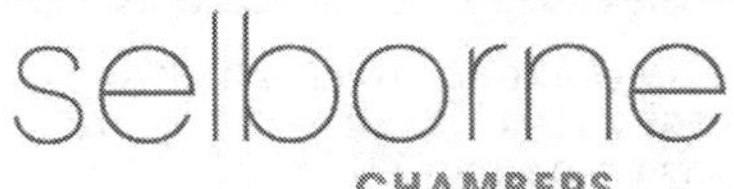

10 Essex Street, London WC2R 3AA
020 7420 9500
Fax: 020 7420 9555; DX: 185 London Chancery Lane
E-mail: clerks@selbornechambers.co.uk
URL: www.selbornechambers.co.uk
Out of hours telephone: 07967 752967

Chambers of: Mr R Tager QC
Clerks: Greg Piner (Senior Clerk), Paul Bunting (1st Junior Clerk); Administrator: Angela Wiggett

Tager, Romie QC *1970*
Hossain, Ajmalul QC *1976*
Warwick, Mark *1974*
Kremen, Philip *1975*
Boyd, Stephen *1977*
Cakebread, Stuart *1978*
Jackson, Hugh *1981*
Mendoza, Neil *1982*
Bojczuk, William *1983*
Francis, Adrian *1988*
Clarke, Ian *1990*
Hornett, Stuart *1992*
Levy, Juliette *1992*
Blaker, Gary *1993*
Charman, Andrew *1994*
Goold, Alexander *1994*
Kynoch, Duncan *1994*
Clegg, Richard *1999*
Kitson, Justin *2000*
McNae, Jonathan *2001*
Barton, Zoe *2003*
Webb, Henry *2005*
De La Piquerie, Paul *2006*
Trompeter, Nicholas *2006*
Chorfi, Camilla *2008*
Du Toit Sc, Johan *2008*
McLoughlin, Simon *2009*
Welford, David *2010*

Types of work
Arbitration · Banking · Chancery (general) · Chancery (land law) · Commercial law · Commercial litigation · Commercial property · Common land · Common law (general) · Company, commercial and competition · Conflict of laws · Consumer law · Conveyancing · Entertainment · Environment · Equity · Financial services · Franchising · Information technology · Insolvency · Insurance · International trade · Landlord and tenant · Partnerships · Pensions · Personal insolvency · Professional negligence · Sale and carriage of goods · Share options · Sport · Succession · Trusts · Wills

Disability access
Staff briefed or trained on duties under the disability legislation, Wheelchair access

3 SERJEANTS INN

3 Serjeants Inn, London EC4Y 1BQ
020 7427 5000
Fax: 020 7353 0425; DX: 421 London Chancery Lane
E-mail: clerks@3serjeantsinn.com

Chambers of: Mr J P Beggs QC, Mr P C A Moon QC

Disability access
Staff briefed or trained on duties under the disability legislation, Wheelchair access, Disabled parking available, Induction loop or infra red system

SERLE COURT

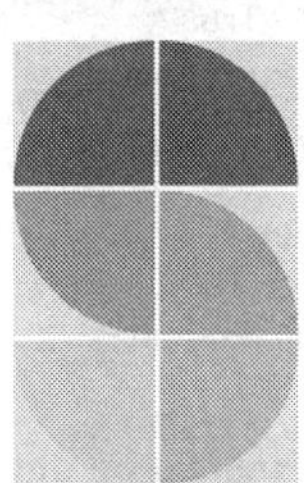

serle court

6 New Square, Lincoln's Inn, London WC2A 3QS
020 7242 6105
Fax: 020 7405 4004; DX: 1025 London Chancery Lane
E-mail: clerks@serlecourt.co.uk
URL: www.serlecourt.co.uk
Out of hours telephone: 07714 853642

Chambers of: Mr A G Boyle QC
Clerks: Steven Whitaker (Head Clerk), Nick Hockney, Paul Reece; Chief Executive: Nicola Sawford

Boyle, Alan QC *1972*
Talbot, Patrick QC *1969†*
Singh, Kuldip QC *1975†*
Hinks, Frank QC *1973*
Jones, Elizabeth QC *1984*
Joffe, QC *1975*
Chaisty, Paul QC *1982†*
Dowley, Dominic QC *1983*
Quigley, Conor QC *1985*
Marshall, Philip QC *1987†*
Jones, Philip QC *1985*
Ashworth, Lance QC *1987†*
Qureshi, Khawar QC *1990*
Lavender, Nicholas QC *1989*
Casement, David QC *1992*
Stoner, Christopher QC *1991*
Edenborough, Michael QC *1992*
Machell, John QC *1993*
Norbury, Hugh QC *1995*
Asprey, Nicholas *1969*
Burling, Julian *1976*
Ballantyne, William *1977*
Francis, Andrew *1977*
Henderson, William *1978*
Rogers, Beverly-Ann *1978*
Walford, Richard *1984*
Clark, Geraldine *1988†*
Harrison, Nicholas *1988*
Lindner, Brigitte *1988*
Moran, Andrew *1989*
Grantham, Andrew *1991*
Blayney, David *1992*
Bruce, Andrew *1992†*
Drake, David *1994*
Higgo, Justin *1995*
Lightman, Daniel *1995*
Collingwood, Timothy *1996*
Adkin, Jonathan *1997*
Richardson, Giles *1997*
Braithwaite, Thomas *1998*
Hattan, Simon *1999*
Den Besten, Ruth *2001*
Haywood, Jennifer *2001*
Jordan, Ruth *2001*
Hagen, Dakis *2002*
Fowles, Jonathan *2004*
Morrison, Matthew *2004*
Palmer, Michael *2004*
Harris, Jonathan *2006*
Mather, James *2006*
Rathmell, Robin *2006*
McCourt Fritz, Dan *2007*
Tilley, Gareth *2007*
Adams, Paul *2008*
Elias, Thomas *2008*
Holcombe, Sophie *2009*
Corbett, James QC *1975†**

Types of work
Administrative law · Arab commercial law · Arab law · Arbitration · Art · Banking · Chancery (general) · Charities · Chinese law · Civil fraud · Commercial law · Commercial litigation · Commercial property · Company, commercial and competition · Copyright · Corporate fraud · Ecclesiastical law · Energy · Equity · Financial services · Human rights · Insolvency · Insurance · Intellectual property · International law · Landlord and tenant · Media and entertainment · Mediation · Parliamentary · Partnerships · Professional negligence · Property · Regulatory and disciplinary law · Shipping · Sport · Tax · Telecommunications · Trusts · Wills

Disability access
Staff briefed or trained on duties under the disability legislation, Wheelchair access, Disabled parking available

CHAMBERS OF MISS LISA SINCLAIR

Glencairn House, 70 Ridgway, London SW19 4RA
020 8946 7201
E-mail: lisaasinclair@yahoo.com

Chambers of: Miss L A Sinclair

CHAMBERS OF MR MALCOLM SINCLAIR

First Floor, Holborn Gate, 330, High Holborn, London WC1V 7QT
020 7242 0644
Fax: 020 8958 1328
E-mail: malcolmsinclair@gmail.com

Chambers of: Mr M D Sinclair

Disability access
Wheelchair access

SNARESBROOK CHAMBERS

45 Empress Avenue, London E12 5ET
020 8989 7765
Fax: 020 8989 7765
E-mail: info@snaresbrookchambers.com

Chambers of: Mr J M Barry

†Recorder *Door Tenant/Associate Member

SOUTH SQUARE

SOUTH SQUARE

3-4 South Square, Gray's Inn, London WC1R 5HP
020 7696 9900
Fax: 020 7696 9911; DX: 338 London Chancery Lane
E-mail: practicemanagers@southsquare.com
URL: www.southsquare.com

Chambers of: Mr W S P Trower QC
Practice Manager: Michael Killick, Jim Costa, Dylan Playfoot, Marco Malatesta; Other Admin: Marketing and Communications Manager: Niti Sidpra; Support Services Manager: Paul Edwards; Finance Manager: Christopher Brinklow

Trower, William QC *1983*
Crystal, Michael QC *1970*
Brougham, Christopher QC *1969*
Moss, Gabriel QC *1974*
Mortimore, Simon QC *1972*
Adkins, Richard QC *1982*
Sheldon, Richard QC *1979*
Hacker, Richard QC *1977*
Knowles, Robin QC CBE *1982†*
Phillips, Mark QC *1984†*
Dicker, Robin QC *1986*
Pascoe, Martin QC *1977*
Oditah, Fidelis QC *1992*
Alexander, David QC *1987*
Zacaroli, Antony James QC *1987*
Marks, David QC *1974*
Davis, Glen QC *1992*
Isaacs, Barry QC *1994*
Toube, Felicity QC *1995*
Fletcher, Ian *1971*
Briggs, John *1973*
Arnold, Mark *1988*
Bristoll, Sandra *1989†*
Goodison, Adam *1990*
Stonefrost, Hilary *1991*
Tamlyn, Lloyd *1991*
Valentin, Ben *1995*
Frazer, Lucy *1996*
Goldring, Jeremy *1996*
Allison, David *1998*
Bayfield, Daniel *1998*
Smith, Tom *1999*
Fisher, Richard *2000*
Perkins, Joanna *2001*
Robins, Stephen *2001*
Haywood, Marcus *2002*
Thornley, Hannah *2003*
Peters, Georgina *2005*
Worthington, QC *2005*
Willson, William *2006*
Al-Attar, Adam *2007*
Cooke, Charlotte *2008*
Phillips, Henry *2008*
Shandro, Sandy *2008*
De Koven, Ronald *2009*

Types of work
Arbitration · Asset finance · Banking · Chancery · Chancery (general) · Civil fraud · Commercial law · Commercial litigation · Commodities · Company law · Company, commercial and competition · Contracts · Corporate finance · Corporate insolvency · Corporate recovery · Cross-border litigation and remedies · European law · Financial services · German law · Guarantees · Insolvency · Insurance · International trade · Partnerships · Pensions · Personal insolvency · Privy Council · Professional negligence · Securities law and regulation · Share options · Sport · Trusts

Opening times: 7.30am - 7.00pm. Reception open from 8:00 am until 8.00pm.

Chambers' facilities
Large conference rooms for meetings, arbitrations and seminars

Disability access
Staff briefed or trained on duties under the disability legislation, Wheelchair access, Disabled parking available

Languages spoken
French, German, Italian, Spanish

Fees policy
Details will be provided on request.

11 SOUTH SQUARE

1st Floor, 11 South Square, Gray's Inn, London WC1R 5EY
020 7405 1222
Fax: 020 7242 4282; DX: 433 London Chancery Lane
E-mail: clerks@11southsquare.com
URL: www.11southsquare.com

Chambers of: Mr A M Silverleaf QC
Clerks: Ashley Carr, Ben Connor, Gareth Edwards, Michelle Carter, Jordan Foley; Administrator: Eileen Whitbread

Silverleaf, Michael QC *1980*
Carr, Henry QC *1982*
Purvis, Iain QC *1986*
Vanhegan, Mark QC *1990*
Acland, Piers QC *1993*
Hacon, Richard *1979*
Lawrence, Heather *1990*
Reid, Jacqueline *1992*
Cuddigan, Hugo *1995*
Fernando, Giles *1998*
Brandreth, Benet *1999*
Nicholson, Brian *2000*
Pickard, Kathryn *2001*
Edwards-Stuart, Anna *2002*
Aikens, Christopher *2005*
Alkin, Thomas *2006*
Hall, Christopher *2010*
Bently, Lionel *2009**

Types of work
Copyright · Information technology · Intellectual property · Patents · Trademarks

Disability access
Staff briefed or trained on duties under the disability legislation, Wheelchair access, Disabled parking available

†Recorder *Door Tenant/Associate Member

ST ANDREWS CHAMBERS

St Andrews House, 52 Manor Drive, London N20 0DX
020 8368 3686
Fax: 020 8368 3686; DX: 132893 Whetstone 2
E-mail: standrewschambers@live.co.uk

Chambers of: Mrs H S Price

FIVE ST ANDREW'S HILL

5 St Andrew's Hill, London EC4V 5BZ
020 7332 5400
Fax: 020 7489 7847; DX: 417 London
E-mail: Clerks@5sah.co.uk

Disability access
Staff briefed or trained on duties under the disability legislation, Wheelchair access, Disabled parking available

STANHOPE CHAMBERS

60 Stanhope Avenue, London N3 3NA
020 8343 1277
E-mail: andrewcohenbarrister@gmail.com

Chambers of: Mr A R Cohen

STAPLE INN CHAMBERS

1st Floor, 9 Staple Inn, Holborn Bars, London WC1V 7QH
020 7242 5240
Fax: 020 7405 9495; DX: 132 London Chancery Lane
E-mail: clerks@stapleinn.co.uk

Disability access
Staff briefed or trained on duties under the disability legislation, Wheelchair access, Disabled parking available

CHAMBERS OF MR A K STONE

97 River Avenue, Palmers Green, London N13 5RP
07956 360101
Fax: 020 8882 3283
E-mail: anwarkstone@yahoo.co.uk

Chambers of: Mr A K Stone

3 STONE BUILDINGS

Ground Floor, 3 Stone Buildings, Lincoln's Inn, London WC2A 3XL
020 7242 4937
Fax: 020 7405 3896; DX: 317 London Chancery Lane
E-mail: clerks@3sb.law.co.uk
URL: www.3sb.law.co.uk

Chambers of: Mr A Twigger QC
Clerk: Andrew Palmer

Also at: 10 Rockefeller Plaza, 16th Floor, New York, NY 10020-1903 Tel: 001 212 713 7636 Fax: 001 212 713 7679

Twigger, Andrew QC *1994*
Cooper, Gilead QC *1983*
Lord, David QC *1987*
Cosedge, Andrew *1972*
Palmer, Norman QC *1973*
Gibbons, James *1974*
Tunkel, Alan *1976*
Da Silva, David *1978*
Hantusch, Robert *1982*
Peacocke, Teresa Rosen *1982*
Collaco Moraes, Francis *1985*
Moeran, Fenner *1996*
Wilson, Richard *1996*
Child, Andrew *1997*
Burton, Paul *1998*
Bornman, Kerry *1999*
McDonnell, Constance *2000*
Harris, Luke *2001*
Hilton, Oliver *2002*
Carney, Joseph *2004*
Slater, Matthew *2005*
Watson, Ian *2005*
Seaman, Jennifer *2007*
Weale, James *2007*
Cumming, Seth *2010*

Types of work
Arbitration · Banking · Capital tax · Chancery (general) · Chancery (land law) · Charities · Commercial litigation · Commercial property · Company, commercial and competition · Conflict of laws · Conveyancing · Copyright · Corporation tax · Cultural property law · Entertainment · Equity · Family provision · Financial services · Income tax · Insolvency · Insurance · Landlord and tenant · Media and entertainment · Mediation · Partnerships · Pensions · Personal insolvency · Professional negligence · Sport · Succession · Trusts · Wills

Disability access
Staff briefed or trained on duties under the disability legislation, Wheelchair access, Disabled parking available

D

D

4 STONE BUILDINGS

Ground Floor, 4 Stone Buildings, Lincoln's Inn, London WC2A 3XT
020 7242 5524
Fax: 020 7831 7907; DX: 385 London Chancery Lane
E-mail: clerks@4stonebuildings.com
URL: www.4stonebuildings.com
Out of hours telephone: 07595 294 754 (Senior Clerk)

Chambers of: Mr A G Bompas QC
Clerk: David Goddard

Bompas, George QC *1975*
Brisby, John QC *1978*
Miles, Robert QC *1987*
Davis-White, Malcolm QC *1984*
Crow, Jonathan QC *1981*
Hill, Richard QC *1993*
Hunt, Stephen *1968*
Griffiths, Peter *1977*
Harman, Sarah *1987*
Marquand, Charles *1987*
Brettler, Jonathan *1988*
Harrison, Christopher *1988*
Greenwood, Paul *1991*
Clutterbuck, Andrew *1992*
Cox, Nicholas *1992*
Fraser, Orlando *1994*
Boeddinghaus, Hermann *1996*
Markham, Anna *1996*
De Mestre, Andrew Etienne *1998*
Denton-Cox, Gregory *2000*
Shivji, Sharif *2001*
Nersessian, Tiran *2002*
Tomson, Alastair *2004*
Gentleman, Tom *2005*
Holliman, Adam *2005*
Lilly, William *2006*
Cook, Alexander *2008*
Knott, James *2008*
Patterson, Phillip *2008*
Timmins, Nicola *2008*
Holland, Eleanor *2010*
Wigley, Joseph *2010*

Types of work
Banking · Civil fraud · Commercial litigation · Company, commercial and competition · Corporate finance · Equity · Financial services · Insolvency · Insurance · Partnerships · Personal insolvency · Professional negligence · Trusts · Wills

Disability access
Disabled parking available

5 STONE BUILDINGS

5 Stone Buildings, Lincoln's Inn, London WC2A 3XT
020 7242 6201
Fax: 020 7831 8102; DX: 304 London Chancery Lane
E-mail: clerks@5sblaw.com

Chambers of: Mr H M Harrod

Disability access
Staff briefed or trained on duties under the disability legislation, Disabled parking available

7 STONES IP

88 Kingsway, Holborn, London WC2B 6AA
020 7193 4033
Fax: 020 7788 2945

Chambers of: Mr G Fern

9 STONE BUILDINGS

9 STONE BUILDINGS
Barristers' Chambers

Lincoln's Inn, London WC2A 3NN
020 7404 5055
Fax: 020 7405 1551; DX: 314 London Chancery Lane
E-mail: clerks@9stonebuildings.com
URL: www.9stonebuildings.com
Out of hours telephone: 01702 232529
Mobile 07774 989964

Chambers of: Mr C I Cant
Clerk: Alan Austin

Cant, Christopher *1973*
Chapman, Vivian QC *1970*
Ashe, Michael QC *1971†*
Jacob, Isaac *1963*
Rowell, David *1972*
Denehan, Edward *1981*
Young, Martin *1984*
Counsell, Lynne *1986*
Spratt, Christopher *1986*
Sisley, Timothy *1989*
Flower, Philip *1979*
Brown, Philip *1991*
Richman, Helene *1992*
Wood, Lana *1993*
Graham, Alana *1993*
Shaw, Peter *1995*
Bromilow, Daniel *1996*
Palser, Elaine *2002*
O'Mahony, Jonathan *2000*
Curl, Joseph *2007*
Hewitt, Edward *2007*
MacEvilly, Conn *1997*
Brown, Rory *2009*
Deb, Shuvra *2007*
Arumugam, Raj *2008*
Ashton, Raymond *1979**
Beaumont, Raymond *1985**
Critelli, Nicholas *1991**
Watson, Craig *2001**

Types of work
Agriculture · Arbitration · Banking · Capital tax · Chancery (general) · Chancery (land law) · Charities · Commercial litigation · Commercial property · Common land · Company, commercial and competition · Conflict of laws · Conveyancing · Copyright · Corporate finance · Corporate fraud · Corporation tax · Employment · Entertainment · Equity · Family provision · Financial services · Foreign law · Housing · Income tax · Information technology · Insolvency · Insurance · Intellectual property · International trade · Landlord and tenant · Media and entertainment · Medical negligence · Partnerships · Personal injury · Personal insolvency · Planning ·

†Recorder *Door Tenant/Associate Member

Professional negligence · Share options · Succession · Trusts · Wills

Chambers Established 1900
Opening times: 8.30am - 6.30pm

Chambers' facilities
E-mail

Disability access
Staff briefed or trained on duties under the disability legislation, Wheelchair access, Disabled parking available

Fees policy
There is no fixed fee policy to enable all clients access to members of chambers irrespective of the financial worth of the lay client. The senior clerk would be delighted to discuss fee levels as and when required.

11 STONE BUILDINGS

11 Stone Buildings, Lincoln's Inn, London WC2A 3TG
020 7831 6381
Fax: 020 7831 2575; DX: 1022 London Chancery Lane
E-mail: clerks@11sb.com
URL: www.11sb.com
Out of hours telephone: Matthew Curness, Mobile: 07776 235906

Chambers of: Mr E M Cohen
Clerks: Michael Couling (Chambers Director), Matthew Curness, Gary Collins, Richard Powell, Lee Wright, Lisa Cottrell, Justin Yoong, Harrison Killick, Frances Collins, Bianca Elliott; Administrator: Nilam Shah

Cohen, Edward *1972†*
Cousins, Jeremy QC *1977†*
Gourgey, Alan QC *1984*
Agnello, Raquel QC *1986*
Hilliard, Lexa QC *1987*
Bishop, Alan *1973*
Salter, Adrian *1973*
McCue, Donald *1974*
Meares, Nigel *1975*
Deacon, Robert *1976*
Arkush, Jonathan *1977*
Ross, Sidney *1983*
Kyriakides, Tina *1984*
Shekerdemian, Marcia *1987*
Penny, Tim *1988*
Kennedy-Mcgregor, Marilyn *1989*
Deacock, Adam *1991*
Eilledge, Amanda *1991*
Meyer, Birgitta *1992*
Barnard, James *1993*
Cowen, Timothy *1993*
Mallin, Max *1993*
Lopian, Jonathan *1994*
Pettican, Kevin *1994*
Boardman, Christopher *1995*
Riley, Jamie *1995*
Watson, Alaric *1997*
Pester, Iain *1999*
Lidington, Gary *2000*
Comiskey, Reuben *2002*
Nicholls, David *2002*
Clarke, Sarah *2003*
Robinson, Thomas *2003*
Smith, Ian *2003*
Wolman, Clive *2003*
McCambley, Dawn *2005*
Head, Peter *2008*
Hinks, Philip *2008*
Shepherd, Thomas *2008*
Newton, Laura *2009*
Stern, David *1989**
Keel, Douglas *1997**

Types of work
Arbitration · Banking and Finance · Chancery (general) · Civil fraud · Commercial law · Commercial litigation · Commercial property · Company, commercial and competition · Corporate fraud · Employment · Entertainment · Information technology · Insolvency · Insurance · Intellectual property · Media · Mortgages · Professional negligence · Sport · Succession · Trusts · Wills

Disability access
Staff briefed or trained on duties under the disability legislation, Wheelchair access, Disabled parking available

STONE CHAMBERS

4 Field Court, Gray's Inn, London WC1R 5EF
020 7440 6900
Fax: 020 7242 0197; DX: 483 London Chancery Lane
E-mail: clerks@stonechambers.com

Chambers of: Mr S M Gee QC

Disability access
Staff briefed or trained on duties under the disability legislation, Wheelchair access, Disabled parking available, Induction loop or infra red system

STONE CHAMBERS

Ground Floor, 67 Queens Road, Leytonstone, London E11 1BA
020 8518 7416
Fax: 020 8518 7416
E-mail: prinsgunaskara@yahoo.com

Chambers of: Mr P Gunasekara

Disability access
Staff briefed or trained on duties under the disability legislation, Disabled parking available

CHAMBERS OF MR DAVID STOTESBURY

21 Redmore Road, London W6 0HZ
020 8748 2447
E-mail: d.c.stotesbury@btinternet.com

Chambers of: Mr D C Stotesbury

†Recorder *Door Tenant/Associate Member

D

STRAND CHAMBERS

226 The Strand, London WC2R 1BA
020 7117 6920
Fax: 020 7112 6806
E-mail: Henry@lawsurgery.com

Chambers of: Mr H J C Hendron

CHAMBERS OF MR JOHN SUDDABY

29 Rhodes Avenue, London NN22 7UR
020 8888 7185
E-mail: john@suddaby.com

Chambers of: Mr J A Suddaby

SWAN HOUSE

P.O.Box 8749, London W13 8ZX
020 8998 3035
Fax: 020 8998 3055
E-mail: swanchambers@yahoo.co.uk

Chambers of: Mr G B Purves

Disability access
Staff briefed or trained on duties under the disability legislation, Wheelchair access, Disabled parking available

T H BARRISTERS CHAMBERS

178 Whitechapel Road, London E1 1BJ
020 7377 8090
Fax: 020 7377 6322
E-mail: thbchambers@aol.com

Chambers of: Mr K U A Shikder MBE

Disability access
Staff briefed or trained on duties under the disability legislation

TALLOWAY CHAMBERS

Rivington House, 82 Great Eastern Street, London EC2A 3JF
020 7419 5047
Fax: 020 7657 4537
E-mail: tor@talloway.com

Chambers of: Mr T H Alloway

TANFIELD CHAMBERS

2-5 Warwick Court, London WC1R 5DJ
020 7421 5300
Fax: 020 7421 5333; DX: 46 London Chancery Lane
E-mail: clerks@tanfieldchambers.co.uk
URL: www.tanfieldchambers.co.uk

Chambers of: Mr G A Jones QC
Clerks: David Wright, Joanne Meah, Jan Campbell (Fees Clerk), Zoe Bluck; Assistant Clerks: Nick Chuter, Luke Faulkner; Junior Clerks: Alice Hunt, Jack Skingle, Kevin Moore (Senior Clerk); Administrator: Eamonn Kelly

Jones, Geraint QC *1976*
Rainey, Philip QC *1990*
Raw, Edward *1963*
Merrylees, Gavin *1964*
Thompson, Andrew E C *1969*
Shuttleworth, Timothy *1971*
Conrath, Philip *1972*
Guy, David *1972*
Monkcom, Stephen *1974*
Pears, D A *1975*
Staddon, Paul *1976*
Nowinski, Richard *1977*
Dencer, Mark *1978*
Boyd, Kerstin *1979*
Coney, Christopher *1979*
Cheves, Simon *1980*
Joseph, Charles *1980*
Reid, Sebastian *1982*
Bailey, Michael *1986*
Loveday, Mark *1986*
Sharp, David *1986*
Bamford, Christopher *1987*
Buck, John *1987*
Buckpitt, Michael *1988*
Maynard, Christopher *1988*
Wilson, Gerald *1989*
Aliker, Phillip *1990*
Bretherton, Kerry *1992*
Heath, Stephen *1992*
Butler, Andrew *1993*
Isaac, Nicholas *1993*
MacLaren, Catriona *1993*
Powell, Robin *1993*
Gallagher, Stan *1994*
Linstead, Peter *1994*
Marnham, Michelle *1994*
Bowker, Robert *1995*
Heather, Christopher *1995*
Jones, Karen *1995*
Dovar, Daniel *1997*
Fieldsend, James *1997*
Harrison, Piers *1997*
Polli, Timothy *1997*
Hormaeche, Alejandra *1998*
Carr, Adrian *1999*
Cattermole, Rebecca *1999*
Gibbons, Ellodie *1999*
Glover, Marc *1999*
Stanzel, Sarah *1999*
Fain, Carl *2001*
Murphy, Olivia *2001*
Robinson, Laura *2001*
Carpenter-Leitch, Tom *2002*
Hammond, Tim *2003*
Gourlay, Amanda *2004*
Sheftel, Andrew *2004*
Upton, Jonathan *2004*
Mankau, Louise *2005*
De Cordova, Gemma *2006*
Lear, Estelle *2006*
Stevenson, Paul *2006*
Walsh, Michael *2006*
Evans, Gwyn *2007*
Lewis, Sara *2007*
Crampin, Cecily *2008*
Modha, Niraj *2010*
Cohen, Hélène *2001**
Subedi, Surya OBE *2007**
Mitchell, Iain QC *2012**

Types of work
Administrative law · Adoption · Alternative dispute resolution · Ancillary relief · Arab law · Arbitration · Asbestos-related diseases · Banking · Boundaries · British Virgin Islands law · Care proceedings · Chancery (general) · Chancery (land law) · Civil actions against the police · Clinical negligence · Commercial law · Commercial litigation · Commercial property · Commodities · Common land · Common law (general) · Company, commercial and competition · Computer litigation · Conciliation · Conflict of laws · Construction law · Consumer law · Cross-border litigation and remedies · Directors' disqualification · Disciplinary procedures · Disciplinary tribunals · Discrimination · EC competition law · Education · Employment · European law · Family law · Family provision · Franchising · Freezing orders · Gambling · Gaming and lotteries · Hindu law · Holiday injury and damages · Housing · Industrial relations law · Information technology · Insolvency · Insurance · International arbitration · International commercial arbitration · Internet gaming and licensing · Islamic law · Landlord and tenant · Lands Tribunal · Leasehold enfranchisement · Licensing · Local authorities · Mediation · Medical negligence · Middle Eastern law · Mortgages · Nepalese law · Niger law · Oil and gas law · Partnerships · Passing off · Personal injury · Personal insolvency · Private children law · Professional negligence · Real property · Rights of light · Rights of way · Sale and carriage of goods · Shareholder agreements · Succession · Technology and Construction Court · Trusts

Opening times: 8.30am - 6.30pm

Chambers' facilities
Conference Rooms

Disability access
Staff briefed or trained on duties under the disability legislation, Wheelchair access, Disabled parking available

Languages spoken
French, German, Hebrew, Italian, Portuguese, Russian, Spanish

Fees policy
Fees vary according to the complexity of the case, and the expertise and seniority of counsel: refer for details to clerks.

THE CHAMBERS OF MISS LEANNE TARGETT-PARKER

4 Romola Road, London SE24 9AZ
020 8674 6694
E-mail: parkerls@yahoo.co.uk

TAXCHAMBERS

15 Old Square, Lincoln's Inn, London WC2A 3UE
020 7242 2744
Fax: 020 7831 8095; DX: 386 London Chancery Lane
E-mail: taxchambers@15oldsquare.co.uk
URL: www.taxchambers.com

Chambers of: Mr Stephen Brandon QC
Senior Clerk: Anthony Hall

Brandon, Stephen QC *1978*
Venables, Robert QC *1973*
Kessler, James QC *1984*
Hardy, Amanda *1993*
Mullan, Rory *2000*
Cannon, Patrick *2003*
Kamal, Setu *2004*
Brown, Harriet *2005*
Marre, Oliver *2011*

Types of work
Capital tax · Charities · Corporate finance · Corporation tax · Income tax · International tax · Pensions · Stamp duty · Trusts · Wills

Disability access
Staff briefed or trained on duties under the disability legislation, Disabled parking available

TEMPLE CHAMBERS

29 Forest Hill Road, East Dulwich, London SE22 0SG
020 8299 0959
Fax: 020 8299 0959/020 7353 4469
E-mail: latiff95@hotmail.com

Chambers of: Mr L A Adenekan

196 TEMPLE CHAMBER

3-7 Temple Avenue, London EC4Y 0HP
020 7099 9257
Fax: 020 7099 2454
E-mail: davidsimpson@lawandregulation.com

Chambers of: Mr D J Simpson

TEMPLE COURT CHAMBERS

2nd Floor, 2 Dr Johnson's Building, Temple, London EC4Y 7AY
020 7353 7888
Fax: 020 7353 7885; DX: 425 London Chancery Lane
E-mail: clerks@templecourt.co.uk

Chambers of: Mr C M F Mannan

Disability access
Staff briefed or trained on duties under the disability legislation

D

TEMPLE GARDEN CHAMBERS

temple garden chambers

1 Harcourt Buildings, Temple, London EC4Y 9DA
020 7583 1315
Fax: 020 7353 3969; DX: 382 London Chancery Lane
E-mail: clerks@tgchambers.com
URL: www.tgchambers.com
Out of hours telephone: 020 8943 2507

Chambers of: Mr R Tam QC
Clerks: Dean Norton (Senior Clerk), Nancy Rice (First Junior Clerk), Keith Sharman (First Junior Clerk); Administrator: Gaye Spencer-King

Tam, Robin QC *1986*
Nice, Sir Geoffrey QC *1971*†
Wilkinson, Nigel QC *1972*†
Prynne, Andrew QC *1975*
Jackson, Simon QC *1982*†
Grieve, Dominic MP QC *1980*
Browne, Simon P QC *1982*
Morton, Keith QC *1990*
Khan, Karim A.A. QC *1992*
Bate-Williams, John *1976*†
Ashford-Thom, Ian *1977*
Holdsworth, James *1977*
MacPherson, Angus *1977*
Hoskins, William *1980*
Alliott, George *1981*
Kilcoyne, Paul *1985*
McFarlane, Alastair *1985*
Bell, James *1987*
James, Mark *1987*
Astor, Philip *1989*
McGahey, Cathryn *1990*
Laughland, James *1991*
Arney, James *1992*
Curtis, Charles *1992*
Wilkinson, Richard *1992*
Barr, David *1993*
Grant, Marcus *1993*
Glassbrook, Alexander *1995*
Moss, Nicholas *1995*
Pack, Melissa *1995*
Hobbs, Emma-Jane *1996*
Hutchin, Edward *1996*
O'Connor, Andrew *1996*
Smyth, Julia *1996*
Adamson, Dominic *1997*
McGrath, Paul *1997*
Ackland, Sacha *1998*
Davies, George *1998*
Kapoor, Shaman *1999*
Casey, Benjamin *2000*
Dardis, Heather *2000*
Dixon, Rodney *2000*
Canby, Fiona *2001*
Rapp, Michael *2002*
Sharpe, Timothy *2002*
Sweeney, Lydia *2002*
Hay, Benjamin *2004*
Jones, Louise *2004*
Ellis, Aidan *2005*
Stride, Lionel *2005*
Johnson, Anthony *2006*
Reeves, Sian *2006*
Hughes, Joanna *2007*
McLoughlin, Kevin *2007*
Price, Emma *2007*
Northey, Emma *2009*
White, David R. *2009*
Irwin, William *2010*
MacLeod, Murdo SC *2011*

Types of work
Administrative law · Clinical negligence · Commercial litigation · Common law (general) · Consumer law · Coroners · Costs · Employment · Health and safety · Human rights · Immigration · Insurance · Landlord and tenant · Personal injury · Professional negligence · Public law

Chambers Established 1952
Opening times: 8.30am - 6.30pm

Chambers' facilities
Conference Rooms, Disks Accepted, E-mail

Disability access
Staff briefed or trained on duties under the disability legislation, Wheelchair access, Disabled parking available

Languages spoken
French, German, Punjabi, Spanish, Welsh

Fees policy
Refer to the senior clerk. Estimate of fees and conditional fees available.

Additional Information
Temple Garden Chambers is a highly regarded set both in the UK and internationally. With 10 silks and 50 juniors chambers covers most aspects of civil common law. Traditionally our core areas are professional and clinical negligence, personal injury, health and safety, costs litigation, employment law, immigration, public and administrative law and judicial review. Chambers also leads the field in public and judicial inquiries and inquests (Princess Diana, Leveson, Baha Mousa, Bloody Sunday) and international public law (Former Yugoslavia, Sudan, Lebanon, Libya). TGC is a set of chambers committed to providing a professional, efficient and friendly service to all our clients. The well regarded clerking team is willing to provide guidance on any matter and prides itself on its open and friendly approach.

2 TEMPLE GARDENS

2 Temple Gardens, Temple, London EC4Y 9AY
020 7822 1200
Fax: 020 7822 1300; DX: 134 London Chancery Lane
E-mail: clerks@2tg.co.uk

Chambers of: Mr B J Browne QC

Disability access
Staff briefed or trained on duties under the disability legislation, Disabled parking available

3 TEMPLE GARDENS

Lower Ground Floor, 3 Temple Gardens, Temple, London EC4Y 9AU
020 7353 3102
Fax: 020 7353 0960; DX: 485 London Chancery Lane
E-mail: clerks@3tg.co.uk

Disability access
Staff briefed or trained on duties under the disability legislation, Disabled parking available

TEMPLE TAX CHAMBERS

1st Floor, 3 Temple Gardens, Temple, London EC4Y 9AU
020 7353 7884
Fax: 020 7583 2044
E-mail: clerks@templetax.com

Chambers of: Mr M G Sherry
Clerks: Anne de Rose, Claire James, Lucy Campbell

Bramwell, Richard QC *1967*
Sokol, Christopher QC *1975*
Sherry, Michael *1978*
Southern, David *1982*
James, Alun *1986*
Ridgway, Philip *1986*
McNicholas, Eamon *1994*
Redpath, Scott *1996*
Schwarz, Jonathan *1998*
Brown, Timothy *2001*
Murray, Rebecca *2001*
Arthur, Stephen *2002*
Collins, Michael *2003*
Redston, Anne *2009*

Types of work
Capital tax · Corporation tax · Customs · Employee benefit trusts · Income tax · Pensions · Stamp duty · Tax · Tax investigations · Taxation and duties · Trusts · VAT

TEMPLIS CHAMBERS

3rd Floor South, 1A Middle Temple Lane, London EC4Y 9AA
020 7649 9808
Fax: 020 7649 9432
E-mail: templis@templis.com

CHAMBERS OF G. D. TETTEH

Ground Floor, 2 Middle Temple Lane, Temple, London EC4Y 9AA
020 7353 7095
Fax: 020 7353 7098; DX: 435 London Chancery Lane

Chambers of: Lady G D Tetteh

THEMIS CHAMBERS

Suite 14067, 145-157 St John's Street, London EC1V 4PY
07967 418976
Fax: 0872 1553293
E-mail: karentaylor@themischambers.co.uk

Chambers of: Ms K A Taylor

THOMAS MORE CHAMBERS

7 Lincoln's Inn Fields, London WC2A 3BP
020 7404 7000
Fax: 020 7831 4606; DX: 90 London Chancery Lane
E-mail: clerks@thomasmore.co.uk

Chambers of: Mr C G Cox QC

Disability access
Staff briefed or trained on duties under the disability legislation, Wheelchair access, Disabled parking available

D

3 RAYMOND BUILDINGS

THREE RAYMOND BUILDINGS

BARRISTERS

3 Raymond Buildings, Gray's Inn, London WC1R 5BH
020 7400 6400
Fax: 020 7400 6464; DX: 237 London Chancery Lane
E-mail: clerks@3rblaw.com
URL: www.3rblaw.com
Out of hours telephone: 020 7400 6400

Chambers of: Mr A A Cameron QC
Clerk: Eddie Holland; Practice Manager: Alison Marshall

Cameron, Alexander QC *1986*
Nicholls, Colin QC *1957*
Nicholls, Clive QC *1957*
Batten, Stephen QC *1968*†
Burke, Trevor QC *1981*
Bromley-Martin, Michael QC *1979*†
Lewis, James QC *1987*†
Farrell, Simon QC *1983*
Humphryes, Jane QC *1983*†
Horwell, Richard QC *1976*
Gibbs, Patrick QC *1986*
Malcolm, Helen QC *1986*†
Hardy, John QC *1988*†
Walsh, Stephen QC *1983*
Keith, Hugo QC *1989*
Atchley, Richard *1977*†
Hines, James *1982*
Saunders, Neil *1983*†
Ashley-Norman, Jonathan *1989*
Davies, Hugh *1990*
Brandon, Ben *1991*
Wormald, Richard *1993*
Agha, Siza *1994*
Summers, Ben *1994*
Williamson, Alisdair *1994*
Emlyn Jones, William *1996*
Naqshbandi, Saba *1996*
Gritt, Edmund *1997*
Williamson, Ailsa *1997*
Baumber, Kevin *1998*
Dobbin, Clair *1999*
Yeo, Nicholas *1999*
Braamskamp, Christine *2000*
Ladenburg, Guy *2000*
Le Fevre, Sarah *2001*
Butt, Matthew *2002*
Watson, Benjamin *2002*
Ponte, Luke *2003*
Barnes, Rachel *2004*
Scott, Rachel *2004*
Jung, Bo-Eun *2005*
Kapila, Rachel *2006*
Collins, Emma *2008*
Morris, Robert *2008*
Hill, Patrick *2010*
Oliver, Heather *2010*

Types of work
Administrative law · Asset forfeiture · Asset recovery · Civil liberties · Common law (general) · Confiscation of the proceeds of crime · Coroner's inquests · Corporate fraud · Corporate manslaughter · Courts martial · Crime · Criminal judicial review · ECHR · Environment · Extradition · Fraud · Health and safety · Homicide · International criminal law · International fraud and asset tracing · International human rights law · Judicial review · Licensing · Money laundering · Police discipline · Public inquiries · Regulatory and disciplinary law · Regulatory crime · Road traffic · Sexual Offences · Sport · Terrorism · Trading standards · War crimes tribunals

Chambers Established 1926
Opening times: 8.30am - 6.30pm Monday - Friday

Chambers' facilities
Conference Rooms, Disks Accepted, E-mail

Disability access
Wheelchair access, Disabled parking available

Languages spoken
Arabic, Dutch, French, German, Italian, Korean, Spanish, Urdu

CHAMBERS OF SIMEON THROWER

16 Langside Avenue, London SW15 5QT
020 8878 7374
E-mail: simlawhome@aol.com

Chambers of: Mr J S Thrower

TOOKS CHAMBERS

81 Farringdon Street, London EC4A 4BL
020 7842 7575
Fax: 020 7842 7576; DX: 68 London Chancery Lane
E-mail: clerks@tooks.co.uk
URL: www.tooks.co.uk
Out of hours telephone: 07850 823676
Clerks: Carol Thomas (Executive Clerk), Martin Parker (Senior Clerk), Simon Gardner (Deputy Senior Clerk), Sumaya Gilmore (Civil Clerk), Lynsey Waugh (Family Clerk), Alistair Roberts (Crime Clerk), Kieran McCool (Junior), Carol Basulwa (Junior), Lennox Lees (Junior); Lee Wakeling (Fees Clerk/Administrator); Sandra Joseph; Yvonne Esson

Mansfield, Michael QC *1967*
Roche, Patrick *1977*†
Aspinall, John QC *1971*
Massih, Michel QC *1979*
Baird, Vera QC *1975*
Kamlish, Stephen QC *1979*
Bennathan, Joel QC *1985*†
Waterman, Adrian QC *1988*†
Southey, Hugh QC *1996*†
Magarian, Michael QC *1988*
Wilcock, Peter QC *1988*
Montrose, Stuart *1972*
Woodcraft, Elizabeth *1980*
Boswell, Jenny *1982*
McNulty, Lawrence *1985*

Farnon, Patricia *1986*
Huseyin, Martin *1988*
Rayner, Catherine *1988*
Williams, Chris *1988*
Mostyn, Piers *1989*
Chapman, Rebecca *1990*
Hawley, Carol *1990*
Wade, Clare *1990*
Braganza, Nicola *1992*
Munroe, Allison *1992*
Drew, Sandhya *1993*
Thorne, Katy *1994*
Brown, Grace *1995*
Chute, Andrea *1995*
Hodgetts, Glen *1995*
Weston, Amanda *1995*
Bourke, Sarah *1996*
Vallejo, Jacqui *1997*
Wrack, Nick *1997*
Troop, Paul Benjamin *1998*
Wilson, Rebekah *1998*
Cooper, Danielle *1999*
Green, Garry *1999*
Rought-Brooks, Hannah *1999*
Slatter, Alexis *1999*
Bovey, Mungo *2000*
Haymerle, Friedrich *2000*
Hussain, Nawaz *2000*
Sethi, Rita *2000*
Williams, Felicity *2000*
Choudhry, *2001*
Harris, Stella *2002*
Meads, Victoria *2002*
Mian, Naeem *2002*
Robinson, Sam *2002*
Smith, Abigail *2003*
Harrison, Anthony *2004*
Straw, Adam *2004*
Tautz, William *2004*
Tafadar, Sultana *2005*
Ali, Khadija *2006*
Bunting, Jude *2006*
Hirst, Leonie *2006*
Burton, Katherine *2007*
Ekeledo, Peggy *2007*
Nereshraaj, Srikantharajah *2007*
Newell, Giles *2007*
Reynolds, Richard *2007*
Lumsdaine, Naomi *2008*
Mehigan, James *2008*
Obi-Ezekpazu, Maureen *2008*
Jones, Bronwen *2009*
Lloyd, Siobhan *2010*
Nicholls, Jesse *2010*
Redley, Clive *2010*

Types of work

Administrative law · Care proceedings · Civil liberties · Crime · Discrimination · Education · Employment · Family law · Immigration · Prison law

TRINITY HOUSE

11 Spratt Hall Road, Wanstead, London E11 2RQ
020 8989 1331
Fax: 020 8989 1331
E-mail: trinity_house@yahoo.com

3 VERULAM BUILDINGS

3 Verulam Buildings, London WC1R 5NT
020 7831 8441
Fax: 020 7831 8479; DX: 331 London Chancery Lane
E-mail: chambers@3vb.com
URL: www.3vb.com

Chambers of: Mr A Malek QC
Senior Practice Manager: Nicholas Hill, Paul Cooklin; Practice Managers: Richard Ansell, Stephen Penson, Raj Lamba, Robert Croke, Andrew Monks, Billy Forecast, Ashleigh Shaw, Stuart Pullum, Harry Freeman

Malek, Ali QC *1980*†
Jarvis, John QC *1970*†
Symons, Christopher QC *1972*†
Elliott, Nicholas QC *1972*
Salter, Richard QC *1975*†
Blair, Michael QC *1965*
Mitchell, Gregory QC *1979*†
Sutcliffe, Andrew QC *1983*†
Onslow, Andrew QC *1982*
Phillips, Stephen QC *1984*†
Phillips, Rory QC *1984*
Weitzman, Thomas QC *1984*
McQuater, Ewan QC *1985*
Fletcher, Andrew QC *1980*
Nash, Jonathan QC *1986*
Beltrami, Adrian QC *1989*
Lowenstein, Paul QC *1988*
Kinsky, Cyril QC *1988*
Tolaney, Sonia QC *1995*
Odgers, John QC *1990*
Freedman, Clive *1975*
Birch, Elizabeth *1978*
Cranfield, Peter *1982*
Lazarus, Michael *1987*
Start, Angharad *1988*
Evans, James *1991*
Phillips, Jonathan Mark *1991*
Edwards, Richard *1993*
Quest, David *1993*
Davies-Jones, Jonathan *1994*
Hardwick, Matthew *1994*
Brent, Richard *1995*
Wilson, Ian *1995*
Gibaud, Catherine *1996*
Head, David *1997*
Parker, Matthew *1997*
Craig, Nicholas *1998*
De Verneuil Smith, Peter *1998*
McKendrick, Ewan *1998*
Ratcliffe, Peter *1998*
Mallinckrodt, Sophie *1999*
John, Laura *2001*
Edwards, William *2002*
Harris, Christopher *2002*
Pillai, Rajesh *2002*
McPherson, George *2003*
Simpson, David *2003*
Eborall, Charlotte *2004*
Kramer, Adam *2004*
Lacob, Lisa *2004*
MacDonald, James *2005*
Hanke, Richard *2006*
Knight, Alexia *2007*
Purves, Robert *2007*
Bond, Christopher *2008*
Holderness, Kate *2008*
Jeavons, Anne *2008*
Phipps, Sandy *2008*
De Vecchi, Thomas *2009*
Van Sante-Kenley, Theodor *2009*
Burdin, *2010*
Onabanjo, *2010*
Schmelzer, *2010*
Wee, *2010*
Ralston, Scott *2012*

Types of work

Administrative law · Agriculture · Arbitration · Banking · Commercial fraud · Commercial litigation · Commercial property · Commodities · Common law (general) · Company, commercial and competition · Conflict of laws ·

†Recorder *Door Tenant/Associate Member

Construction law · EC competition law · Entertainment · Financial services · Gaming and lotteries · Information technology · Insolvency · Insurance · Intellectual property · International law · International trade · Partnerships · Pensions · Professional negligence · Sale and carriage of goods · Shipping · Sport · Telecommunications

Disability access
Staff briefed or trained on duties under the disability legislation, Wheelchair access, Disabled parking available

THE CHAMBERS OF GHEORGHE VIRTOPEANU

10 Clifford Road, London E17 4JE
020 8711 6822
E-mail: gheorghe.virtopeanu@gmail.com

CHAMBERS OF MR WALKER-SMITH

32 Westbourne Park Villas, London W2 5EA
020 7229 6128; DX: 35806 Queensway

Chambers of: Sir J J Walker-Smith

THE CHAMBERS OF PETER WARD

88 Kingsway, London WC2B 6AA
020 3402 2152
Fax: 020 7841 1001
E-mail: whurr@yahoo.com

Chambers of: Mr P M Ward

Disability access
Staff briefed or trained on duties under the disability legislation, Wheelchair access, Disabled parking available

CHAMBERS OF MR SAMUEL WARITAY

2nd Floor, 145-147 St John Street, London EC1V 4PY
0845 803 7767
Fax: 0870 762 7472
E-mail: Waritay@onetel.com

Chambers of: Mr S Waritay

WARWICK HOUSE CHAMBERS

8 Warwick Court, Warwick House Chambers, Gray's Inn, London WC1R 5DJ
020 7430 2323
Fax: 020 7430 9171; DX: 1001 London Chancery Lane
E-mail: clerks@warwickhousechambers.com

Chambers of: Mrs C Drew, Mr C T Drew

Disability access
Staff briefed or trained on duties under the disability legislation, Wheelchair access, Disabled parking available

WESTBOURNE CHAMBERS

62 Westbourne Park Villas, London W2 5EB
07956 950350
E-mail: DeborahBarrister@aol.com

Chambers of: Miss D A Morris

Disability access
Disabled parking available

WILBERFORCE CHAMBERS

8 New Square, Lincoln's Inn, London WC2A 3QP
020 7306 0102
Fax: 020 7306 0095; DX: 311 London Chancery Lane
E-mail: chambers@wilberforce.co.uk
URL: www.wilberforce.co.uk

Chambers of: Mr J V Martin QC
Clerks: First Junior Clerks: Danny Smillie, Mark Rushton; Assistant Clerks: Fraser Geddes, Robert Johnstone, Declan Redmond; Practice Manager: Deputy Chief Executive: John Treacy; Fees Clerk: Ceri Wilkins, Financial Adminstrator: Laura Coban, Marketing & Events: Naomi Shogbola; Finance Manager: James Salisbury

Martin, John QC *1972*
Nugee, Edward TD QC *1955*†
Barnes, Michael QC *1965*†
Cohen, Lawrence QC *1974*
Croxford, Ian QC *1976*
Ham, Robert QC *1973*
Furber, John QC *1973*
Mowschenson, Terence QC *1977*†
Phillips, David QC *1976*†
Green, Brian QC *1980*
Bloch, Michael QC *1979*
Nugee, Christopher QC *1983*†

Furness, Michael QC *1982*
Wardell, John QC *1979*
Seitler, Jonathan QC *1985*
Tennet, Michael QC *1985*
Karas, Jonathan QC *1986*
Lowe, Thomas QC *1985*
Ayliffe, James QC *1987*
Smith, Joanna QC *1990*
Newman, Paul QC *1991*
Wicks, Joanne QC *1990*
Hutchings, Martin QC *1986*
Child, John *1966*
Seymour, Thomas *1975*
Studer, Mark *1976*
Hughes, Gabriel *1978*
Hochberg, Daniel *1982*
Bryant, Judith *1987*
Fadipe, Gabriel *1991*
Evans, Jonathan *1994*
Halkerston, Graeme *1994*
Stanley, Clare *1994*
Campbell, Emily *1995*
Reed, Rupert *1996*
Greenhill, Julian *1997*
Scott, Tiffany *1998*
Singla, Nikki *2000*
Sawyer, Edward *2001*
Davey, Jonathan *2003*
Hilliard, Jonathan *2003*
Mold, Andrew *2003*
McKechnie, Emily *2005*
Allen, Sebastian *2006*
Bor, Harris *2006*
Walmsley, James *2007*
Faulkner, Benjamin *2008*
McCreath, James *2009*
Murphy, Emer *2009*
Chew, Jonathan *2010*
Roscoe, Thomas *2010*
Davies, Stephen QC *1983**
Furze, Caroline *1992**

Types of work
Banking · Capital tax · Chancery (general) · Chancery (land law) · Charities · Commercial law · Commercial litigation · Commercial property · Company, commercial and competition · Ecclesiastical law · Employment · Energy · Equity · Family provision · Financial services · Income tax · Insolvency · Intellectual property · Landlord and tenant · Local authorities · Pensions · Planning · Professional negligence · Sport · Succession · Trusts · Wills

Opening times: 8.30am - 6.30pm (Monday - Friday)

Chambers' facilities
Conference Rooms, Disks Accepted, Video Conference, Purpose-built seminar room

Disability access
Staff briefed or trained on duties under the disability legislation, Wheelchair access, Disabled parking available

Languages spoken
Arabic, French, German, Italian, Spanish

Fees policy
Chambers' recognition of the rapidly changing market for legal services is reflected in its approach to setting fees. Hence our clerks can offer hourly rates, fixed fees, brief fees, refreshers, stage repayments and conditional fee agreements or some combination for each piece of work or for groups of cases. Our clerks aim to charge a realistic and reasonable fee having regard to the barrister's experience, the time expended and the value of the work to the client. Our wish is to develop and maintain long-term and professional working relationships with all our clients and to foster that relationship by our approach to fees. Declan Redmond, Senior Clerk will be happy to discuss fees and fee structures with you.

WILLESDEN CHAMBERS

5 Mora Road, London NW2 6SD
020 3273 1042
Fax: 020 8450 2964
E-mail: syril@btinternet.com

Chambers of: Mr G C Syril

Disability access
Staff briefed or trained on duties under the disability legislation, Wheelchair access

CHAMBERS OF K A WILLIAMS-HOWES

148 Lower Richmond Road, Putney, London SW15 1LU
020 8704 1010
E-mail: katie@williams-howes.com

Chambers of: Mrs K A Williams-Howes

Disability access
Staff briefed or trained on duties under the disability legislation, Disabled parking available

CHAMBERS OF JOHN ALBAN WILLIAMS

53 Wilmington Avenue, London W4 3HA
07956 235232
Fax: 020 8580 5859
E-mail: jalbanwilliams@aol.com

Chambers of: Mr J A Williams

CHRIST CHURCH CHAMBERS

Mayfair Point, 34 South Molton Street, London W1K 5RG
020 7409 5278/07788 512787

Chambers of: Miss A I Wills

D

CHAMBERS OF MR MICHAEL WOOD QC

21 Tonsley Place, Wandsworth, London SW18 1BH
020 8874 3474
Fax: 0870 141 5036; DX: 297 London Chancery Lane
E-mail: mwoodqc@hotmail.com

Chambers of: Mr M M Wood QC

Disability access
Disabled parking available

CHAMBERS OF MISS R WOOD

Flat 12, 237a Long Lane, London SE1 4PX

WYNNE CHAMBERS

5 Kimberley Road, London NW6 7SG
020 3239 6964
Fax: 020 3014 8839
E-mail: admin@wynnechambers.co.uk
URL: www.wynnechambers.co.uk
Out of hours telephone: 020 3239 6946

Chambers of: Mr M H A Thomson

Thomson, Ahmad *1979*

Types of work
Charities · Discrimination · Employment · Islamic law · Trusts · Wills

Disability access
Staff briefed or trained on duties under the disability legislation

SWL CHAMBERS

Aston Court, Frederick Place, Loudwater, Buckinghamshire HP11 1LA
01494 616007
Fax: 01494 616189
E-mail: robert@swl-legal.co.uk

Chambers of: Mr R A Sliwinski

SAPPHIRE CHAMBERS

The Gatehouse, 43B Churchgate, Loughborough, Leicestershire LE11 1UE
07805 852724; DX: 19610 Loughborough

Chambers of: Miss J Kumar

CHAMBERS OF MR N M B KHAN

452 Dunstable Road, Luton, Bedfordshire LU4 8DJ
07508 876022
Fax: 020 8709 2058
E-mail: chambers.nbk@gmx.com

Chambers of: Mr N M B Khan

LUTON CHAMBERS

103 Wexham Close, Luton LU3 3TX
01582 598394
Fax: 01582 618335
E-mail: mshafikhan@hotmail.com

Chambers of: Mr M S Khan

Disability access
Staff briefed or trained on duties under the disability legislation, Wheelchair access, Disabled parking available

CHAMBERS OF MR I C CASSIE

Brackens, Captains Row, Lymington, Hampshire SO41 9RP
020 7243 0316/07785 394253
Fax: 020 7243 0316

Chambers of: Mr I C Cassie

CHAMBERS OF MR CLIFFORD JOSEPH

Tiggers, Hall Place Lane, Burchetts Green, Maidenhead, Berkshire SL6 6QY
01628 822267
Fax: 01628 822267
E-mail: planning.cliffordjoseph@tinyworld.co.uk

Chambers of: Mr C D Joseph

Disability access
Wheelchair access, Disabled parking available

BECKET CHAMBERS

Romney Place, Maidstone ME15 6LH
01622 230957
Fax: 0844 443 2686; DX: 4803 Maidstone

BEDLINGTON CHAMBERS

20 Staffa Road, Maidstone ME15 9ST
01622 744 015
E-mail: clerks@bedlingtonchambers.com

Chambers of: Mr J Morgan

MAIDSTONE CHAMBERS

maidstone chambers

33 Earl Street, Maidstone, Kent ME14 1PF
01622 688592
Fax: 01622 683305; DX: 51982 Maidstone 2
E-mail: clerks@maidstonechambers.co.uk
URL: www.maidstonechambers.co.uk
Out of hours telephone: 07767 351682

Chambers of: Mr P J Sinclair
Clerks: Danielle Dixon, Kay Burford

Sinclair, Philip *1995*
Jacobson, Mary *1992*
Wright, Trevor RD *1992*
Zimbler, Alexia *1993*
Greene, Paul *1994*
Stern, Thomas *1995*
Burt, Joanna *1998*
Dunn, Tom *1998*
Fitzgerald, John *1998*
Wickens, Simon *1998*
De Banzie, Robert *2000*
Ross, James *2001*
King, Judith *2002*
Calder, Lynette *2003*
Brand, Kieran *2007*
Lewis, Katherine *2009*
Kent, Alan QC *1986**
Luckhurst, John *2006**

Types of work
Commercial contracts · Commercial law · Construction law · Crime · Employment · Family law · Landlord and tenant · Litigation · Personal injury · Real property

Disability access
Staff briefed or trained on duties under the disability legislation, Wheelchair access, Disabled parking available

6 PUMP COURT CHAMBERS

6-8 Mill Street, Maidstone, Kent ME15 6XH
01622 688094
Fax: 01622 688096; DX: 51967 Maidstone
E-mail: annexe@6pumpcourt.co.uk
URL: www.6pumpcourt.co.uk

Chambers of: Mr S A Hockman QC, Mr P J Harrison QC
Senior Clerk: Richard Constable; Administrator: Angela Fullex

Also at: 1st Floor, 6 Pump Court, Temple, London EC4Y 7AR

Hockman, Stephen QC *1970*
Harrison, Peter QC *1987*
Barraclough, Richard QC *1980*
Gower, Peter QC *1985†*
Martin, Roy QC *1990*
Travers, David QC *1981*
Laws, Eleanor QC *1990*
Armstrong, Grant *1978*
Harris, Mark *1980*
Williams, Anne *1980*
Baldock, Nicholas *1983*
Topping, Caroline *1984*
Taylor, Paul *1985*
Thomas, Megan *1987*
Campbell, Jane *1990*
Forbes, Peter *1990*
O'Higgins, John *1990*
Upton, William *1990*
Saxby, Oliver *1992*
Espley, Andrew *1993*
Bates, Pascal *1994*
Ellin, Nina *1994*
Grant, Edward *1994*
Moore, Danny *1994*
Watson, Mark *1994*
Alcock, Peter *1995*
Beard, Mark *1996*
Charles, Deborah *1996†*
Donnelly, Catherine *1997*
Robinson, Tanya *1997*
Taylor, Simon *1997*
Banwell, Richard *1998*
Bennett, Lee *1998*
Menzies, Gordon *1998*
Luttman, Lucy *2001*
Oragwu, Adaku *2001*
Atkinson, Giles *2002*
Lambert, Emmaline *2003*
Tahir, Perican *2004*
Cullen, Grace *2005*
Crowdy, Isabella *2007*
Dobbie, Alice *2007*
Ostrowski, Nicholas *2009*
Phillips, Ian Rees *2009*
Phillips, Laura *2009*
Knowles, Linsey *2000**
Byrd, Noemi *2004**

Types of work
Administrative law · Care proceedings · Commercial law · Commercial litigation · Common law (general) · Consumer law · Corporate fraud · Crime · Employment · Energy · Environment · Family law · Family provision · Food law · Fraud · Health and safety · Human rights · Inquests · Judicial review · Landlord and tenant · Licensing · Local authorities · Mediation · Medical negligence · Natural resources · Parliamentary · Personal injury · Planning · Professional negligence · Public inquiries · Trading standards

D

†Recorder *Door Tenant/Associate Member

D

CHAMBERS OF MRS CHRISTINA BENNETT

Castlecor, Mallow, Co Cork
00 353 224 8545
E-mail: mscbennett@eircom.net

Chambers of: Mrs C Bennett

CHAMBERS OF MICHAEL FORWARD

1 Outer Silk Mills, Malmesbury SN16 9LP
01666 510639
E-mail: mforwardlawyer@yahoo.com

Chambers of: Mr M E Forward

RESOLUTION CHAMBERS

The Old School House, Walwyn Road, Colwall, Malvern, Worcestershire WR13 6PL
01684 541008
Fax: 01684 541008
E-mail: mmilne@milne-arbitration.co.uk

Chambers of: Mr M Milne

Disability access
Staff briefed or trained on duties under the disability legislation, Wheelchair access, Disabled parking available

64 BRIDGE STREET

3rd Floor, 64 Bridge Street, Manchester M3 3BN
0845 083 3000
Fax: 0845 083 3001; DX: 14349 Manchester
E-mail: mail@64bridgestreet.com

Disability access
Staff briefed or trained on duties under the disability legislation, Wheelchair access

BRIDGEWATER CHAMBERS

5 Bleasefell Chase, Worsley, Manchester M28 1UZ
0161 3877127; DX: 706993 Walkden
E-mail: info@barristers-chambers.com

Chambers of: Mr W McCarthy

Disability access
Wheelchair access, Disabled parking available

BYROM STREET CHAMBERS

12 Byrom Street, Manchester M3 4PP
0161 829 2100
Fax: 0161 829 2101; DX: 718156 Manchester 3
E-mail: clerks@byromstreet.com
URL: www.byromstreet.com
Out of hours telephone: 07899 816403/ 07949 958205

Chambers of: Mr R D Machell QC
Clerks: Mrs Terry Creathorn (Senior Clerk), Steve Price (Deputy Senior Clerk); Administrator: Michelle Seaton, Emma Rogers, Lucy Smith; Accounts: Colin Harrison

Also at: Crown Office Chambers, 2 Crown Office Row, Temple, London, EC4Y 7JH Tel: 0207 797 8100

Machell, Raymond QC *1973*†
Tattersall, Geoffrey QC *1970*†
Allan, David QC *1974*†
Hunter, Winston QC *1985*†
Melton, Christopher QC *1982*†
Myerson, Simon QC *1986*†
Rowley, James QC *1987*†
Heaton, David QC *1983*†
Lewis, Andrew QC *1985*†
Pearce, Richard *1985*†
Hatfield, Sally *1988*†
Burns, Peter *1993*
Ruck, Mary *1993*
Allen, Darryl *1995*

Types of work
Arbitration · Asbestos-related diseases · Commercial litigation · Common law (general) · Constitutional and administrative law · Ecclesiastical law · Employment · Environment · Health and safety · Human rights · Industrial diseases · Insurance · Local authorities · Mediation · Medical law · Medical negligence · Mental health · Personal injury · Professional negligence · Regulatory and disciplinary law · Sale and carriage of goods · Sport

Disability access
Staff briefed or trained on duties under the disability legislation, Wheelchair access, Disabled parking available

CENTRAL CHAMBERS

CENTRAL CHAMBERS

89 Princess Street, Manchester M1 4HT
0161 236 1133
Fax: 0161 236 1177; DX: 14467 Manchester 2
E-mail: clerks@centralchambers.co.uk
URL: www.centralchambers.co.uk
Out of hours telephone: 07950 953158

Chambers of: Miss S Massey
Clerks: Alisha Street, Fees Clerk: Jayne Lever, Neil Vickers

Massey, Stella *1990*
Richmond, Bernard QC *1988*
Staunton, William *1986*
Ismail, Nazmun Nisha *1992*
Thorndike, Tony *1994*
Maudsley, Penelope *1998*
Patrick, Caroline *1999*
Henshaw, Gwen *2000*
Beswick, Kirstin *2001*
Hartley, Richard *2001*
Faryl, Alaha *2003*
Knight, Benjamin *2004*
Lomax, Emily *2004*
Karnik, Mikhil *2005*
Lynch, Joseph *2007*
Holt, Jonathan *2009*
Jones, Keith *2009*
Mahmood, Abid *1992**
Murphy, Michael *1992**
Collins, James *1997**

Types of work
Administrative law · Care proceedings · Civil liberties · Clinical negligence · Commercial law · Corporate fraud · Crime · Disability and health · Discrimination · Education · Employment · Environment · Family law · Family provision · Health and safety · Housing · Human rights · Immigration · Insolvency · Judicial review · Landlord and tenant · Mental health · Personal injury · Prisoners' rights · Professional negligence · Public access · Regulatory and disciplinary law · Road traffic

Disability access
Staff briefed or trained on duties under the disability legislation, Disabled parking available

COBDEN HOUSE CHAMBERS

Cobden House
CHAMBERS

19 Quay Street, Manchester M3 3HN
0161 833 6000
Fax: 0161 833 6001; DX: 14327 Manchester
E-mail: Clerks@Cobden.co.uk
URL: www.cobden.co.uk
Out of hours telephone: 0751 537 1105

Chambers of: Mr R B Farley QC
Clerks: Mr Neil McHugh (Senior Clerk), David Hewitt (Senior Criminal Clerk), Daniel Monaghan (Senior Civil Clerk), Christina Crook (Deputy Senior Clerk & Family Clerk); Administrator: Jackie Morton

Criminal Defence Service

Community Legal Service

Farley, Roger QC *1974†*
Goldberg, Jonathan QC *1971†*
Leslie, Stephen QC *1971*
Blackwell, Louise QC *1985*
Hartley, Richard QC *1985†*
Narayan, Harry *1970*
Buckley, Peter *1972*
Broadley, John *1973*
Johnson, Carolyn *1974*
Goldwater, Michael *1977*
Oughton, Richard *1978*
White, Timothy *1978*
Brereton, Fiorella *1979*
Fallows, Paula *1981*
Green, Colin *1982*
Kenny, David *1982*
Sheridan, Paul *1984*
Metcalfe, Ian *1985*
Hymanson, Deanna *1988*
Oultram, Jonathan *1988*
Littler, Martin *1989*
Parr, John *1989*
Willitts, Timothy *1989*
Musaheb, Kevin *1990*
Willems, Marc *1990*
Wright, Yasmin *1990*
Dalal, Rajen *1991*
Hodgson, Timothy *1991*
Nichol, Simon *1994*
Maddison, David *1995*
Orr, Julian *1995*
Sandiford, David *1995*
Mazzag, Anthony *1996*
Callery, Martin *1997*
Georgiou, Angela *1997*
Nowland, Lee *1997*
Jones, Michael *1998*
Goddard, Richard *1999*
Hirst, Rebecca *1999*
MacGregor, Craig *1999*
Milne, Arlene *1999*
Knowles, Michael *2000*
Piears, Angela *2001*
Riley, Geraldine *2002*
Whatley, Paul *2002*
Akther, Tahina *2003*
Gregg, Rebecca *2003*
Marriott, Jamie *2003*
Parmar, Chetna *2003*

†Recorder *Door Tenant/Associate Member

Flanagan, Nicholas *2004*
Mirza, Mussadak *2004*
Boyle, Jonathan *2005*
Keeling-Roberts, Sam *2005*
Openshaw, Samantha *2005*
Walthall, Arron *2005*
Ballinger, Katherine *2008*
Cochrane, Stefanie *2008*
Stevens, Richard *2008*
Lewis, Gary *2010*
McCubbin, Ian *2010*
Rutherford, Helen *2010*
Bowes, Michael QC *1980*†*
Kime, Matthew *1988**

D

Types of work

Administrative law · Agriculture · Arbitration · Banking · Capital tax · Care proceedings · Chancery (general) · Chancery (land law) · Charities · Commercial litigation · Commercial property · Common land · Common law (general) · Company, commercial and competition · Competition law · Conveyancing · Copyright · Corporate fraud · Courts martial · Crime · Defamation · Employment · Environment · Equity · Family law · Family provision · Housing · Income tax · Information technology · Insolvency · Intellectual property · Landlord and tenant · Licensing · Medical negligence · Partnerships · Patents · Pensions · Personal injury · Personal insolvency · Professional negligence · Regulatory and disciplinary law · Sale and carriage of goods · Succession · Trademarks · Trusts · Wills

Opening times: 8.30am - 6.30pm

Chambers' facilities

Conference Rooms, Disks Accepted, Video Conference, Facilities for seminars and arbitrations

Disability access

Wheelchair access, Disabled parking available

Languages spoken

French, Gujarati

The Chambers

Cobden House Chambers is able to offer a wide range of expertise by means of specialist departments in the area of chancery, commercial law, crime, employment law, family housing and personal injury. Individual members are able to offer additional specialisms and full details can be obtained from the clerks. Chambers provide a fast and efficient service and a timetable for the completion of instructions can be given on delivery. In addition, chambers provide services for alternative dispute resolution and mediation. The senior clerks will be happy to discuss fee levels and tailor quotations to meet most budgets. Further details can be found on the website and in chambers' brochure which can be obtained from the clerking team.

CORAL HOUSE

42 Charles Street, Manchester, Lancashire M1 7DB

Chambers of: Dr A Khan

DEANS COURT CHAMBERS

24 St John Street, Manchester M3 4DF
0161 214 6000
Fax: 0161 214 6001; DX: 718155 Manchester 3
E-mail: clerks@deanscourt.co.uk
URL: www.deanscourt.co.uk

Chambers of: Mr M G Turner QC
Clerk: Matthew Gibbons (Senior Clerk)

Also at: Deans Court Chambers, 101 Walker Street, Preston PR1 2RR

Turner, Mark QC *1981*†
Grime, Stephen QC *1970*
Fish, David QC *1973*†
Horlock, Timothy QC *1981*
Field, Patrick QC *1981*†
Sephton, Craig QC *1981*
Bromley-Davenport, John QC *1972*
Sokol, Christopher QC *1975*
Denney, Stuart QC *1982*
Grocott, Susan QC *1986*†
Cross, Jane QC *1982*
Heaton, Frances QC *1985*†
Atherton, Peter *1975*†
Eccles, David *1976*
Ryder, Timothy *1977*†
Trippier, Ruth *1978*
Davies, Hugh *1982*
Smith, Timothy *1982*†
Davies, Russell *1983*
Trotman, Timothy *1983*
Jackson, Wayne *1984*
Bancroft, Louise *1985*
Campbell, Glenn *1985*
Brody, Karen *1986*†
Humphries, Paul *1986*
Hobson, Heather *1987*
Hudson, Christopher *1987*†
Grimshaw, Nicholas *1988*
Rankin, Ciaran *1988*
Singh-Hayer, Bansa *1988*
Smith, Peter *1988*
Grace, Jonathan *1989*
Kitching, Robin *1989*
Smith, Michael *1989*
Cheetham, Julia *1990*
Courtney, Nicholas *1990*
Butler, Jonathan *1992*
Edge, Timothy *1992*
Ironfield, Janet *1992*
Livesey, Fraser *1992*
Woodward, Alison *1992*
Hayton, Michael *1993*

 †Recorder *Door Tenant/Associate Member

Horgan, Peter *1993*
Judge, Lisa *1993*
Savill, Mark *1993*
Clegg, Sebastian *1994*
Fothergill, Francesca *1994*
Rothery, Peter *1994*
Bland, Carolyn *1995*
Boyle, David *1996*
Dawar, Archna *1996*
Higgins, Paul *1996*
McCann, Simon *1996*
Dudley-Jones, Elizabeth *1997*
Cartwright, Sophie *1998*
Moody, Joanna *1998*
Paul, Daniel *1998*
Watkinson, Sasha *1998*
Whitehall, Richard *1998*
Booth, Sarah *1999*
Hayton, Virginia *1999*
Hicks, Pascale *1999*
Morton, Elizabeth *1999*
Olson, Ross *1999*
Hart, Joseph *2000*
Earnshaw, Zoe *2001*
Emsley-Smith, Ros *2001*
McMaster, Robert *2001*
Singh, Anthony *2001*
Poole, Alex *2002*
Heyworth, Victoria *2003*
Taylor, Alexander *2003*
Tyler, William *2003*
Bentley, Anna *2004*
Brown, Michelle *2005*
Lally, Jonathan *2005*
Walters, Carly *2005*
Harrison, Victoria *2006*
Meredith Davies, Gemma *2007*
Greenwood, Rachel *2008*
Burke, Samuel *2009*
King, Jonathan *2009*
Sharron, Eliza *2009*
Paterson, James *2010*

Types of work

Arbitration · Banking · Care proceedings · Chancery (general) · Chancery (land law) · Clinical negligence · Commercial litigation · Common law (general) · Construction law · Corporate fraud · Crime · Employment · Environment · Equity · Family law · Family provision · Health and safety · Information technology · Insolvency · Insurance · Landlord and tenant · Licensing · Medical negligence · Personal injury · Personal insolvency · Professional negligence · Sale and carriage of goods · Trusts · Wills

Disability access

Staff briefed or trained on duties under the disability legislation, Wheelchair access, Disabled parking available

DOUGHTY STREET CHAMBERS

Pall Mall Court, 61-67 King Street, Manchester M2 4PD
0161 618 1066
Fax: 020 7404 2283; DX: 14446 Manchester 2

EXCHANGE CHAMBERS

7 Ralli Courts, West Riverside, Manchester M3 5FT
0161 833 2722
Fax: 0161 833 2789; DX: 14330 Manchester

Chambers of: Mr W T S Braithwaite QC

CHAMBERS OF IAN MACDONALD QC

CHAMBERS of IAN MACDONALD QC

Garden Court North, 22 Oxford Court, Manchester M2 3WQ
0161 236 1840
Fax: 0161 236 0929; DX: 715637 Manchester 2
E-mail: clerks@gcnchambers.co.uk
URL: www.gcnchambers.co.uk
Out of hours telephone: 07970 721337

Chambers of: Mr I A MacDonald QC
Clerks: Sarah Wright (Senior Clerk), Annmarie Nightingale (First Junior Clerk)

MacDonald, Ian QC *1963*
George, Mark QC *1976*
Weatherby, Pete QC *1992*
McKeone, Mary *1986*
Barlow, Mark *1992*
Grahame, Nina *1993*
Hodson, Peter *1994*
Firth, Georgina *1995*
Stark, James *1998*
O'Ryan, Rory *2000*
Smith, Kerry *2002*
Byles, Andrew *2003*
Fitzpatrick, Andrew *2003*
McLeish, Philip *2003*
Birdee, Sonia *2004*
Cawsey, Laura *2004*
Jagadesham, Vijay *2004*
Stanbury, Matthew *2004*
Stone, Kate *2004*
McCormack, Benjamin *2005*
Baillie, Brigid *2007*
Davie, Sara *2007*
Ficklin, Jared *2007*
Ayres, Katy *2008*
Warren, Camille *2008*

Types of work

Administrative law · Anti-social Behaviour Orders · Asbestos-related diseases · Asset forfeiture · Asset recovery · Asylum · Civil actions against the police · Civil law · Civil liberties · Common law (general) ·

Community care · Computer crime · Confiscation · Constitutional and administrative law · Coroner's inquests · Coroners · Corporate fraud · Corporate manslaughter · Court of Protection · Courts martial · Crime · Crime and criminal due process · Criminal judicial review · Disability discrimination · Disciplinary procedures · Disciplinary tribunals · Discrimination · ECHR · Education · Employee benefit trusts · Employment · Extradition · Family law · Firearms · Forfeiture · Fraud · Freedom of information · Health and safety · Homicide · Housing · Human rights · Immigration · Industrial diseases · Industrial relations law · Inquests · International criminal law · International fraud and asset tracing · International human rights law · Internet crime · Judicial review · Labour arbitration · Landlord and tenant · Litigation · Local government and public services · Malicious prosecution · Mental health · Military law · Mortgages · Motor vehicles · Ombudsman · Pensions · Personal injury · Police · Police discipline · Prison law · Privacy · Property · Public inquiries · Public law · Regulatory and disciplinary law · Road haulage · Road traffic · Road traffic offences · Serial crime · Serious fraud · Social security · Social services · Social welfare

Disability access

Staff briefed or trained on duties under the disability legislation, Wheelchair access, Disabled parking available

KENWORTHY'S CHAMBERS

Arlington House, Bloom Street, Salford, Manchester M3 6AJ
0161 832 4036
Fax: 0161 832 0370; DX: 718200 Manchester 3
URL: www.kenworthysbarristers.co.uk
Out of hours telephone: 07971 564 644

Chambers of: Mr F J Burns

Clerks: Paul Mander (Senior Criminal Clerk), Rachel Campbell (Civil Clerk), Thomas Harrington (Criminal Clerk), Courtney Soden (Immigration Clerk) Jamie Conwell (Junior Clerk); Practice Manager: Maria Rushworth; Administrator: Sue Barlow

Burns, Francis *1971*
Nolan, Benjamin QC *1971†*
Woodcock, Robert QC *1978*
Brown, Roger *1976*
Grennan, Barry *1977*
Marsh, John *1977*
Donnelly, William *1981*
Cassidy, Patrick *1982*
Morris, Anthony J *1986*
Patel, Gita *1988*
Edusei, Francis *1989*
Williamson, Patrick *1989*
Flattery, Amanda *1993*
Timson, Corin *1994*
Marrs, Andrew *1995*
Whelan, Geoff *1996*
Mather, Alison *1997*
Harwood-Gray, Barry *1998*
Asquith, Marc *1999*
Long, Madeliene *1999*
Morton, David *1999*
Fitzpatrick, Denise *2000*
Haque, Sara *2000*
Khan, Shazia *2000*
McDonald, Margaret *2000*
Penni, Sally *2000*
White, Rachel *2000*
Emmanuel, Joyce Clare *2001*
Johnson, Sarah *2001*
Schwenk, Mark *2001*
Smith, Michael *2001*
Brown, George *2002*
Buckle, Colin *2002*
Grant, Chudi *2002*
Habib, Shysta *2002*
Sin, Fung *2003*
Niaz, Anisa *2004*
Nicholson, John *2004*
Cragg, Janet *2005*
Lugsdin, Martin *2005*
Wilson, Alan *2005*
Luck, Julie-Anne *2006*
Pickering, Rebecca *2007*
Micah, Carol *2009*
Quegan, Peter QVRM TD *2010*
Tettey, Stephen *2010*
Blakebrough, Simon *2011*
Lister, Kevin *2012*

Types of work

Administrative law · Anti-social Behaviour Orders · Asylum · Care proceedings · Children · Civil actions against the police · Commercial law · Common law (general) · Corporate fraud · Costs · Crime · Defamation · Employment · Family law · Family provision · Health and safety · Housing · Human rights · Immigration ·

†Recorder *Door Tenant/Associate Member

Inquests · Judicial review · Landlord and tenant · Licensing · Mental health · Personal injury · Prison law · Professional negligence · Public access · Sexual Offences

Disability access
Staff briefed or trained on duties under the disability legislation, Wheelchair access, Disabled parking available

82 KING STREET

82 King Street, Manchester M2 4WQ
0161 870 9969

KINGS CHAMBERS

36 Young Street, Manchester M3 3FT
0845 034 3444
Fax: 0845 034 3445; DX: 718188 Manchester 3
E-mail: clerks@kingschambers.com
URL: www.kingschambers.com
Out of hours telephone: 07836 589842

Chambers of: Dr Nicholas J Braslavsky QC
Clerks: Gary Young, Paul Clarke, Harry Young, Mark Ronson, Scott Leach, Andrew Reeves, Rory Davis, Gary Smith, Jake Brooke; Senior Clerks: William Brown, Colin Griffin, Stephen Loxton; Chambers Director: Debra Andrés

Also at: 5 Park Square East, Leeds LS1 2NE Tel: 0845 034 3444 Fax: 0845 034 3445 DX: 713113 (Leeds Pk Sq); Embassy House, 60 Church Street, Birmingham, B3 2DJ, DX: 13023 Birmingham Tel: 0845 034 3444 Fax No: 0845 034 3445

Braslavsky, Nicholas QC *1983†*
Sauvain, Stephen QC *1977†*
Booth, Michael QC *1981*
Fraser, Vincent QC *1981†*
Chaisty, Paul QC *1982†*
Manley, David QC *1981†*
Crean, Anthony QC *1987*
Anderson, Lesley QC *1989†*
Casement, David QC *1992*
Rawlinson, Michael QC *1991*
Tucker, Paul QC *1990*
Poole, Nigel QC *1989†*
Owen, Eric *1969*
Terry, Jeffrey *1976*
Evans, Alan *1978*
Khan, Shokat *1979*
Barrett, John *1982†*
Berragan, Neil *1982*
Halliwell, Mark *1985†*
Clayton, Nigel *1987†*
Hilton, Simon *1987†*
Ashworth, Fiona *1988†*
Stockley, Ruth *1988*
Burrows, Simon *1990*
Singer, Andrew *1990*
Grantham, Andrew *1991*
Smith, Matthew *1991*
Carter, Martin *1992*
Horne, Wilson *1992*
Powis, Lucy *1992*
Clover, Sarah *1993*
Ditchfield, Michael *1993*
Harper, Mark *1993*
Lander, Richard *1993*
Ponter, Ian *1993*
Pritchard, Sarah *1993*
Boyd, James *1994*
Pennifer, Kelly *1994*
Latimer, Andrew *1995*
Doyle, Louis *1996*
Easton, Jonathan *1996*
Fullwood, Adam *1996*
McBride, Gavin *1996*
Plimmer, Melanie *1996*
Roussak, Jeremy *1996*
Bourne, Colin *1997*
Friston, Mark *1997*
Plaut, Simon *1997*
Siddall, Nicholas *1997*
Wright, Jonathan *1997*
Cannock, Giles *1998*
McGee, Andrew *1998*
Young, Simon *1998*
Brown, Catherine *1999*
Budworth, Martin *1999*
Griffiths, Brian *1999*
Hall, Matthew *1999*
Mulholland, Helen *1999*
Ranales-Cotos, Tina *1999*
Lakin, Paul *2000*
Temple, Eleanor *2000*
Walmisley, Lisa *2000*
Hughes, Paul *2001*
Wheatley, Geraint *2001*
Williams, Ben *2001*
Hunter, John *2002*
Karim, Sam *2002*
Lancaster, Roger *2002*
Ralph, Craig *2002*
Duckworth, Emily *2003*
Mayoh, Michelle *2003*
Galloway, Rachel *2004*
Gardner, Francesca *2004*
Reid, Sarah *2004*
Gorasia, Paras *2005*
Harding, Ben *2005*
Law, Charlotte *2005*
Dainty, Cheryl *2006*
Johnson, Paul *2006*
Lieberman, Gemma *2006*
Livingston, Richard *2006*
Latham, Kevin *2007*
Maguire, Stephen *2007*
Smith, Nathan *2007*
Ward, Johnny *2007*
D'Arcy, Eleanor *2008*
Gill, Anthony *2008*
McNamara, Stephen *2008*
Daniels, Laura *2009*
Taylor, Ruth *2010*
Freedman, Clive QC *1978†**
Kolvin, Philip QC *1985**
Crawford, Colin *1997**
Henderson, James *1997**
Keay, Andrew *2010**

Types of work
Administrative law · Arbitration · Banking · Capital tax · Chancery (general) · Chancery (land law) · Charities · Clinical negligence · Commercial law · Commercial litigation · Commercial property · Common land · Common law (general) · Company, commercial and competition · Competition law · Construction law · Consumer law · Conveyancing · Copyright · Corporate finance · Corporate fraud · Corporation

tax · Costs · Discrimination · EC competition law · Education · Employment · Entertainment · Environment · Equity · Financial services · Franchising · Health and safety · Housing · Immigration · Income tax · Information technology · Insolvency · Insurance · Intellectual property · International trade · Landlord and tenant · Licensing · Local authorities · Medical negligence · Parliamentary · Partnerships · Patents · Pensions · Personal injury · Personal insolvency · Planning · Professional negligence · Regulatory and disciplinary law · Sale and carriage of goods · Share options · Sport · Succession · Trademarks · Trusts · Wills

Disability access
Staff briefed or trained on duties under the disability legislation, Wheelchair access, Disabled parking available

CHAMBERS OF MARC E. LEON ESQ.

Suite 526, 275 Deansgate, Manchester M3 4EL
07875 340598
E-mail: marc@eleon.fsnet.co.uk

Chambers of: Mr M E Leon

LINCOLN HOUSE CHAMBERS

LINCOLN HOUSE CHAMBERS

Tower 12, The Avenue North, Spinningfields, 18-22 Bridge Street, Manchester M3 3BZ
0161 832 5701
Fax: 0161 832 0839; DX: 14338 Manchester
E-mail: info@lincolnhousechambers.com
URL: www.lincolnhousechambers.com
Out of hours telephone: 07733 371255

Chambers of: Mr A S Webster QC, Mr G Gozem QC
Clerks: David Wright (Director of Clerking), Andy McGuinness, David Gibbons, Lucy Rock, Mathew Tudor, Richard Smith, Ty Price, Kieran Trafford; Administrator: Bernadette Duggan

Gozem, Gaias QC *1972*
Webster, Alistair QC *1976†*
Hussain, Mukhtar QC *1971†*
Conrad, Alan QC *1976†*
Wright, Peter QC *1981†*
Pickup, James QC *1976†*
Reid, Paul C QC *1973†*
McGowan, Maura QC *1980*
Cross, Anthony QC *1982†*
Goddard, Suzanne QC *1986†*
Thomas, Andrew QC *1989†*
Csoka, Simon QC *1991*
Blackwell, Kate QC *1992†*
Gregory, James *1970*
Lasker, Jeremy *1976†*
Nuttall, Andrew *1978†*
Curran, Philip *1979†*
Elias, Robert *1979*
Nadim, Ahmed *1982*
Nicholls, Elizabeth *1984†*
Bloomer, Charles *1985*
Butcher, Richard *1985*
Stuart, Mark *1985*
Baxter, Bernadette *1987†*
Lawton, Paul *1987†*
McMeekin, Ian *1987*
Barton, Hugh *1989*
Fryman, Neil *1989*
Johnson, Kathryn *1989*
Bowley, Ivan *1990*
Smith, Rachel *1990†*
Donnelly, Kevin *1991*
Ford, Mark *1991*
Simons, Richard *1991*
Boyd, Joe *1993*
Daw, Christopher *1993*
Doran, Gerard *1993*

Holt, Abigail *1993*
Roberts, Lisa *1993*
Storrie, Timothy *1993*
Usher, Neil *1993*
Warne, Peter *1993*
Holden, Philip *1994*
Holland, Rick *1994*
Hackett, Martin *1995*
Nawaz, Mohammed *1995*
Holland, Charlotte *1996*
Kearney, Robert *1996*
Priestley, Roderick *1996*
Kitchin, Louise *1998*
Nield, Zoe *1998*
Pierpoint, Katherine *1998*
Dawson, Richard *2001*
Leach, Alexander *2001*
Friend, Mark *2002*
Jones, Gareth *2002*
English, Richard *2003*
Jones, Katie *2003*
Prokofiev, Sergey *2004*
Thomas, Daniel *2005*
Welch, Austin *2005*
Barbour, Laura *2006*
Gurney, Simon *2006*
Heyworth, James *2006*
Cooper, Rachel *2007*
Cowen, Louise *2010*

Types of work
Asbestos-related diseases · Civil actions against the police · Clinical negligence · Commercial law · Commercial litigation · Common law (general) · Company, commercial and competition · Confiscation · Corporate fraud · Corporate manslaughter · Crime · Customs · Disciplinary tribunals · EC competition law · Environment · Fraud · Health and safety · Housing · Human rights · Immigration · Industrial deafness · Industrial diseases · Inquests · Judicial review · Licensing · Local authorities · Medical negligence · Mental health · Personal injury · Pollution · Professional negligence · Public inquiries · Road traffic · VAT

Chambers Established 1978
Opening times: 8.30am - 6.00pm

Chambers' facilities
Disks Accepted, Video Conference, Individual email and voicemail, Telephone conferences

Disability access
Staff briefed or trained on duties under the disability legislation, Wheelchair access, Disabled parking available

Languages spoken
Arabic, French, Gujarati, Hindi, Persian, Punjabi, Russian, Spanish, Urdu

Fees policy
Fees are negotiated with the Senior Clerk. We aim to provide realistic rates or brief fees/refreshers that take into account the type of case, the seniority of Counsel, the size of case and its complexity. Chambers will advise potential clients of any fees upon request. We accept pro bono work (on a discretionary basis) and conditional fee agreements. We are always willing to adapt to assist in any way possible and all queries should be referred to the Senior Clerk.

THE CHAMBERS OF W. MASSEY

5 Allenby Road, Cadishead, Manchester M44 5EA
0161 775 6948

Chambers of: Mr W R Massey

CHAMBERS OF MR A M ROSEMARINE

International Law Chambers, 78 Cavendish Road, Salford, Manchester M7 4WA
0161 740 3861
Fax: 0161 740 3861
E-mail: help@rosemarine.co.uk

Chambers of: Mr A M Rosemarine

ST JAMES'S CHAMBERS

St. James's
CHAMBERS

68 Quay Street, Manchester M3 3EJ
0161 834 7000
Fax: 0161 834 2341; DX: 14350 Manchester1
E-mail: clerks@stjameschambers.com
URL: www.stjameschambers.co.uk
Out of hours telephone: 07976 484008

Chambers of: Mr R A Sterling
Clerk: Paul Morecroft (Senior Clerk)

Sterling, Robert *1970*
Lyons, Timothy QC *1980*
MacHin, Charles *1973*
Searle, Barrie *1975*†
Mulholland, Michael *1976*
Porter, David *1980*
Binns, David *1983*
Selwyn Sharpe, Richard *1985*
Wilson-Barnes, Lucy *1989*
Stephenson, Paul *1990*
Smith, Jonathan *1991*
Moore, Richard *1992*
Hurd, James *1994*
Calvert, David *1995*
Potts, Warren *1995*
Short, Anna *1997*
Taft, Christopher *1997*
Taskeen, Wasim *1998*
Hammond, Fayaz *1999*
Rashid, Haroon *1999*
Tindall, Paul *1999*
Bilsland, Alisan *2000*
Boyle, Karen *2000*
Mulderig, Joseph *2002*
Banks, Nathan *2003*
Hammond, Claire *2003*
Lawrenson, Sarah *2003*
Kamal, Setu *2004*
Pomfret, Bradley *2004*
Youshani, Elahe *2005*
Bunbury, Claire *2006*
Hogg, James *2006*
O'Neill, Michael *2007*
Green, Louise *2009*
Mansfield, Suzanne *2010*

†Recorder *Door Tenant/Associate Member

D

Types of work
Administrative law · Agriculture · Arbitration · Banking · Capital tax · Chancery (general) · Chancery (land law) · Charities · Civil liberties · Commercial property · Common land · Common law (general) · Company, commercial and competition · Construction law · Conveyancing · Copyright · Corporation tax · Defamation · Discrimination · Education · Employment · Environment · Equity · Family provision · Financial services · Franchising · Housing · Income tax · Information technology · Insolvency · Insurance · Intellectual property · Landlord and tenant · Licensing · Medical negligence · Mental health · Partnerships · Patents · Pensions · Personal injury · Personal insolvency · Professional negligence · Sale and carriage of goods · Share options · Succession · Telecommunications · Trademarks · Trusts · Wills

Disability access
Disabled parking available

9 ST JOHN STREET

NINESTJOHNSTREET

9 St John Street, Manchester M3 4DN
0161 955 9000
Fax: 0161 955 9001; DX: 14326 Manchester
E-mail: civilclerks@9sjs.com/criminalclerks@9sjs.com
URL: www.9sjs.com
Out of hours telephone: Tony Morrissey 07780 995995; Chris Swan 07997 490340

Chambers of: Mr C R Garside QC
Clerks: Tony Morrissey (Senior Civil Clerk), Chris Swann (Senior Criminal Clerk), Jane Slingsby, Julia Lanza, Peadar McKinstry, Andy Leech, Anthony Brown, Joseph Turner; Administrator: Ruth Bailey; Finance Manager: Ruth Bailey

Garside, Charles QC *1971†*
Carus, Roderick QC *1971†*
McDermott, Gerard QC *1978†*
Hinchliffe, Nicholas QC *1980†*
Jones, Geraint QC *1976*
Jackson, Simon QC *1982†*
Clarke, Nicholas QC *1981†*
Irving, Gillian QC *1984*
Gilroy, Paul QC *1985*
Kennedy, Christopher QC *1989*
Rigby, Terence *1971†*
Cadwallader, Peter *1973*
Riley, Christine *1974*
McDonald, Paul *1975*
Grundy, Nigel *1983†*
Bower, Alistair *1986*
Breen, Carlo *1987*
Gatto, Nicola *1987*
Gilchrist, David *1987*
Monaghan, Mark *1987*
Fitzpatrick, Thomas *1988*
Barnett, Joanne *1989*
Little, Ian *1989*
Morgan, Edward *1989*
Woodward, Joanne *1989*
Preston, Darren *1991*
Connolly, Joanne *1992*
Howard, Anthony *1992*
Sabry, Karim *1992*
Bailey, Graham *1993*
Barry, Kirsten *1993*
Hamilton, Jaime *1993*
Wedderspoon, Rachel *1993*
Clark, Andrew *1994*
Fryer-Spedding, James *1994*
Lemmy, Michael *1994*
Brochwicz-Lewinski, Stefan *1995*
Darbyshire, Robert *1995*
McCluggage, Brian *1995*
Lewis, Sara *1996*
Nowell, Katie *1996*
Woodhall, Gary *1997*
Del Priore, Assunta *1998*
Mabon, Jane *1998*
Mallory, Kathrine *1998*
Thomson, Vanessa *1998*
Haisley, Matthew *1999*
Leeming, Lucy *1999*
Redmond, Helen *1999*
Thompson, Zoë *1999*
Rigby, Victoria *2000*
Eeley, Rebecca *2001*
Heyworth, Alison *2001*
McKinlay, Kirsty *2001*
Snarr, Matthew *2001*
Thomas, Dawn *2001*
Dickinson, Russell *2002*
Brandon, Louise *2003*
Curry, Caroline *2003*
Denham, Ian *2003*
Gilbart, Thomas *2003*
Savage, Jonathan *2003*
Vicary, Joanna *2003*
Morris, Benjamin *2004*
Northall, Daniel *2004*
Haines, Hannah *2005*
Hardy, Stephen *2005*
Smith, Robert *2005*
D'Cruz, Laura *2006*
Levene, Rachael *2006*
Lewis, Rachael *2006*
Amartey, Lena *2008*
Hamilton, William *2008*
Samuel, Zimran *2008*
Robinson, Graham *2009*
Greenhalgh, Emma *2010*
Langhorn, Alexander *2010*
Price, Richard *2010*
Cundy, Catherine *2011*

Types of work
Banking · Care proceedings · Chancery (general) · Civil liberties · Commercial law · Commercial litigation · Commercial property · Common law (general) · Company, commercial and competition · Construction law · Consumer law · Conveyancing · Corporate finance · Corporate fraud · Crime · Discrimination · Employment · Environment · Equity · Family law · Family provision · Financial services · Health and safety · Housing · Information technology · Insolvency · Insurance · Intellectual property · Landlord and tenant · Licensing · Medical negligence · Mental health · Personal injury · Planning · Professional negligence · Sale and carriage of goods · Succession · Trusts · Wills

Disability access
Staff briefed or trained on duties under the disability legislation, Wheelchair access, Disabled parking available

18 ST JOHN STREET

ST JOHN STREET CHAMBERS

18 St John Street, Manchester M3 4EA
0161 278 1800
Fax: 0161 835 2051; DX: 728854
Manchester 4
E-mail: clerks@18sjs.com
URL: www.18sjs.com
Out of hours telephone: 07831 660252

Chambers of: Mr P V Birkett QC
Clerk: John Hammond; Chambers Manager: Elizabeth Sheen

Birkett, Peter QC *1972*†
Brennan, Daniel QC *1967*†*
Wigglesworth, Raymond QC *1974*†
Bradley, Sally QC *1978*†*
Forrest, Alastair *1972*
Dockery, Paul *1973*
Rylands, Elizabeth *1973*
O'Brien, Paul *1974*†
Diamond, Christopher *1975*
Limb, Christopher *1975*
Fewtrell, Nicholas *1977*†
Huffer, Ian *1979*
Laprell, Mark *1979*†
Murray, Michael *1979*
Stansby, Alexandra *1985*
Vardon, Richard *1985*
Murray, Stephen *1986*
Healing, Yvonne *1987*
Sasse, Toby *1988*
Birtles, Samantha *1989*
Holloran, Fiona *1989*
Tythcott, Elisabeth *1989*
Simpson, Raquel *1990*
Dale, Jonathan *1991*
Wills, Janice *1991*
Booth, Joy *1992*
Brady, Michael *1992*
Harrison, Susan *1993*
Shenton, Rachel *1993*
Manasse, Paul *1995*
Brody, Saul *1996*
Lodge, Adam *1996*
Moore, Andrew *1996*
Faux, Rachel *1997*
Hoffman, David *1997*
Mackley, David *1997*
Chapman, Richard *1998*
Bramall, Kate *1999*
Goldstein, Wayne Nathan *1999*
Grierson, Jonathan *1999*
Kilvington, Sarah *1999*
Kaur, Lukhvinder *2000*
Markham, Andrea *2000*
Norman, Benjamin *2000*
Scott, John *2000*
Caplan, Leonie *2001*
Clarke, Nicholas *2001*
Kajue, Soria *2001*
De Berry, Philip *2003*
Denham, Ian *2003*
Donaldson, Sarah *2003*
Rimmer, Hugh *2003*
Thomas, Laura *2003*
Begum, Rehana *2004*
Charles, Simon *2004*
Chaudhry, Saiqa *2005*
Firbank, Kit *2005*
Henthorn, Kate *2005*
Lau, Vanessa *2005*
McNall, Christopher *2005*
Murray, Elizabeth *2005*
Thomas, Arron *2005*
Ameen, Danish *2006*
Chan, Evonnie *2006*
Wilkinson, Michael *2006*
Caplan, Oliver *2007*
Davies, Rupert *2007*
Evans, Andrew *2007*
Martin, Stuart *2007*
O'Leary, Brendan *2007*
Simons, Kane *2007*
Wells, Jason *2007*
Calder, Daniel *2008*
Patterson, Hollie *2008*
Pope, Sandra *2008*
Ke, Lisi *2009*
McEwan, Malcolm *1976**
Briggs, Laura *2001**

Types of work
Accountancy · Adjudication · Administrative law · Adoption · Agriculture · Alternative dispute resolution · Ancillary relief · Animal rights law · Animals · Anti-dumping · Anti-social Behaviour Orders · Arbitration · Asbestos-related diseases · Assessment of costs · Asset finance · Asset forfeiture · Asset recovery · Asylum · Auditing · Banking · Bloodstock · Boundaries · Breach of confidence · Building · Capital tax · Care proceedings · Chancery · Chancery (commercial) · Chancery (general) · Chancery (land law) · Charities · Child abduction · Child abuse · Child care law · Child support · Children · Civil actions against the police · Civil fraud · Civil law · Civil partnerships · Clinical negligence · Cohabitation · Commercial contracts · Commercial fraud · Commercial law · Commercial litigation · Commercial planning · Commercial property · Commercial regulation · Commodities · Common land · Common law (general) · Community care · Company law · Competition law · Compulsory Purchase · Computer contracts · Computer crime · Computer litigation · Conciliation · Confidential information · Confiscation · Conflict of laws · Constitutional law · Construction law · Consumer credit · Consumer law · Contaminated land · Contracts · Conveyancing · Copyright · Copyright theft · Copyright Tribunal · Coroners · Corporate finance · Corporate fraud · Corporate governance · Corporate insolvency · Corporate liability · Corporate manslaughter · Corporate recovery · Corporation tax · Costs · Councillors and standards · Court of Protection · Courts martial · Crime · Crime and criminal due process · Criminal judicial review · Customs · Damages · Data protection · Defamation · Design · Disability and health · Disability discrimination · Disciplinary procedures · Disciplinary tribunals ·

†Recorder *Door Tenant/Associate Member

D

Discrimination · Dispute resolution · Divorce · Domestic violence injunctions · E-commerce · EC competition law · Economic torts · Education · Election law · Employee benefit trusts · Employment · Engineering disputes · Entertainment · Environment · Equine law · Equity · Extradition · Family law · Family provision · Financial provision · Fire and other property damage claims · Fire precautions · Firearms · Food law · Forfeiture · Fraud · Freedom of information · Freezing orders · Funding arrangements · Gambling · Gaming and lotteries · Group litigation · Guarantees · Health and safety · Healthcare law · Highways · Holiday injury and damages · Holiday law · Homicide · Housing · Immigration · Income tax · Industrial deafness · Industrial diseases · Industrial relations law · Information technology · Inheritance and cohabitees · Inquests · Insolvency · Intellectual property · International criminal law · International fraud and asset tracing · Internet crime · Judicial review · Labour arbitration · Land compensation · Landlord and tenant · Lands Tribunal · Leasehold enfranchisement · Legal advice · Legal aid costs · Licensing · Limited partnerships · Local authorities · Local authority claims · Local authority liability · Local government finance · Malicious falsehood · Malicious prosecution · Matrimonial · Matrimonial finance · Media · Media and entertainment · Mediation · Medical law · Medical negligence · Medicines Act · Mental health · Mergers and acquisitions · Military law · Money laundering · Mortgages · Motor vehicles · Multi-party litigation · NHS inquiries · Occupational diseases · Ombudsman · Overseas accidents · Partnerships · Passing off · Patents · Pensions · Performance bonds · Personal injury · Personal insolvency · Planning · Police · Police discipline · Pollution · Prison law · Private children law · Product liability · Product safety · Professional negligence · Public inquiries · Public law · Publishing · Real property · Registered designs · Regulatory and disciplinary law · Remedies · Restitution · Restraint of trade · Rights of light · Rights of way · Road haulage · Road traffic · Road traffic offences · Sale of business · Securities law and regulation · Serial crime · Serious fraud · Share options · Shareholder agreements · Social security · Social services · Social welfare · State aid · Strategic alliances · Succession · Tax · Tax investigations · Technical contracts · Technology and Construction Court · Telecommunications · Timeshare · Title to land · Torts · Trade Descriptions Act · Trademarks · Trading standards · Transport and Works Act inquiries · Travel law · Trust litigation · Trusts · Unincorporated associations · Unmarried couples · Unregistered designs · VAT · Wardship · Water · Wills

Disability access
Staff briefed or trained on duties under the disability legislation, Disabled parking available, Induction loop or infra red system

ST JOHNS BUILDINGS

24a - 28 St John Street, Manchester M3 4DJ
0161 214 1500
Fax: 0161 835 3929; DX: 728861 Manchester 4
E-mail: clerk@stjohnsbuildings.co.uk
URL: www.stjohnsbuildings.co.uk
Out of hours telephone: 07850 193895; 07870 657202

Chambers of: Mr A P Hayden QC
Clerks: Christopher Ronan (Chief Clerk), Sean Hulston (Senior Criminal Clerk), Teresa Thiele (Senior Civil Clerk), Paul Laverty (Senior Family Clerk); Development and Support Services Manager: David Anderson; HR & Facilities Manager: Mary Berry; Finance Manager: Paula Blackshaw

Also at: 21 White Friars, Chester CH1 1NZ. Tel: 01244 323 070; Fax: 01244 323 930; DX: 19979 Chester.

Also at: 16 Winckley Square, Preston PR1 3JJ. Tel: 01772 256100; Fax: 01772 251101; DX: 714582 Preston 14.

Also at: 26 Paradise Square, Sheffield S1 2DE. Tel: 0114 273 8951; Fax: 0114 276 0848; DX: 10565 Sheffield 1.

Also at: 8th Floor India Buildings, Water Street, Liverpool L2 0XG. Tel: 0151 243 6000; Fax: 0151 243 6040; DX: 14227 Liverpool.

Hayden, Anthony QC *1987*†
Watson, Paul QC *1978*†
Redfern, Michael QC *1970*†
Berkley, David QC *1979*†
O'Byrne, Andrew QC *1978*
Samuels, Jeffrey QC *1988*
Harrison, Sally QC *1992*
Thomas, Keith *1969*
Phillips, Bernard *1970*†
Green, Roger *1972*
Hedgecoe, John *1972*
Herman, Raymond *1972*†
Neale, Nicholas L *1972*
Bedford, Stephen *1974*†
McNeill, John *1974*
Shannon, Eric *1974*
Lowe, Geoffrey *1975*†
Andrews, Philip *1977*
Feeny, Charles *1977*
Longworth, Antony *1978*
Grundy, Philip *1980*†
Mercer, David *1980*
Owen, Gail *1980*†
Long, Andrew *1981*
Uff, David *1981*
Bruce, David *1982*
Gal, Sonia *1982*†
Garside, David *1982*
Holt, Julian *1982*
Harrison, Keith *1983*
Harrison, Peter *1983*
Khawar, Aftab *1983*
McKee, Hugh *1983*
McKenna, Brian *1983*
Slater, Michael *1983*†
Pickup, David *1984*
Shaw, Julian *1984*†
Wright, Sarah *1984*
Kennedy, Michael *1985*
Lloyd, Julian *1985*
Dickinson, Jonathan *1986*
Gray, Richard *1986*
Taylor, Julian *1986*†
Brennand, Timothy *1987*
Dagnall, Jane M *1987*
Oates, John *1987*
Walker, Jane *1987*
Batra, Bunty *1988*
Crabtree, Simon *1988*
Davitt, Paula *1988*
Eastwood, Charles *1988*
Sanders, Damian *1988*
Blakey, Michael *1989*
Britcliffe, Anne *1989*
Grundy, Clare *1989*
Holder, Simon *1989*
O'Brien, Joseph *1989*
Partington, Lisa *1989*
Carter, Richard *1990*
Groom, Ian *1990*
Jackson, Adrian *1990*
Rosario, Desmond *1990*
Thompson, Jonathan *1990*
Thompson, Patrick *1990*†
Watson, David *1990*
Chaudhry, Zia *1991*
Edwards, Mererid *1991*†
Mawdsley, Matthew *1991*
Roberts, Mark *1991*
Savage, Timothy *1991*
Taylor, Jonathan *1991*
Wright, Alastair *1991*
Ashmole, Timothy *1992*
Case, Magdalen *1992*
Green, Andrew *1992*
Lloyd, Gaynor *1992*
McNerney, Kevin *1992*
Norton, Richard *1992*
Blackshaw, Henry *1993*
Fitzharris, Ginnette *1993*
Ford, Caroline *1993*
Gibson, John *1993*†
Harrison, Rachael *1993*
Harrison, Leona *1993*†
Hughes, Dermot *1993*
Jones, Ben *1993*
Kloss, Alexander W *1993*
Mathieson, Guy A D *1993*†
Newton, Stuart *1993*
Nijabat, Shama *1993*
Orme, Richard *1993*
Polglase, David *1993*
Rodikis, Joanna *1993*
Searle, Jason *1993*
Stanistreet, Penelope *1993*
Wilson, Myles *1993*
Booth, Nigel *1994*
Chukwuemeka, John *1994*
Connor, Mark *1994*
Douglas, Stephen *1994*
Frieze, Daniel *1994*
Gumbs, Annette P *1994*
Houghton, Lisa *1994*
Lowe, Craig *1994*
Mann, Sara *1994*
Reynolds, Gary *1994*
Rhys, Megan Jill *1994*
Rowley, Karl *1994*†
Wild, Steven *1994*
Hargan, Carl *1995*
Kelly, Siobhan *1995*
Lawson, Andrew *1995*
McHugh, Pauline M *1995*
Parry, Philip *1995*
Simkin, Iain *1995*
Stables, Gordon *1995*
Aslett, Pepin *1996*
Crilley, Darrel *1996*
Mintz, Simon *1996*
Sastry, Bob *1996*
Bailey, Andrew *1997*
Denton, Douglas *1997*
Evans, Simeon *1997*
Goldsack, Ian *1997*
Mahmood, Ghazan *1997*
Mensah, Lorraine *1997*
Parry, Simon *1997*
Tyler, Paula *1997*
Williams, Zillah *1997*
Zentar, Remy *1997*
Bentley, David *1998*
Buckley, Patrick *1998*
Burnell, Kate *1998*
Edwards, Susan *1998*
James, David *1998*
Murdin, Liam *1998*
Muth, Susanne *1998*
Simmonds, Alexandra *1998*
Stockwell, Matthew *1998*
Taylor, David *1998*
Thomas, Clare *1998*
Astbury, Philip *1999*
Deas, Susan *1999*
Holsgrove, Lara *1999*
Lord, Andrew *1999*
Ratledge, John *1999*
Sweeney, Linda *1999*
Cavanagh, Lorraine *2000*
Hayes, Kathryn *2000*
Leach, Natasha *2000*
Ahmed, Siraj *2001*
Blewitt, Jennifer *2001*
Bridgman, Andrew *2001*
Farley, David *2001*
King, Oliver *2001*
Marshall, Laura Jane *2001*
Pojur, David *2001*
Porter-Phillips, Clare *2001*
Quinney, Nicola *2001*
Van-Der-Haer, Audrey *2001*
Vir Singh, Sylvia *2001*
Wynne, Andrew *2001*
Hodgkinson, Paul *2002*
Malam, James *2002*
McCloskey, Louise *2002*
Menzies, Jennifer *2002*
Montaldo, Neil *2002*
Moss, Christopher *2002*
Mottram, Cheryl *2002*
Owen, Wendy *2002*
Rawlinson, Michael J *2002*
Senior, Mark *2002*
Smith, Paul *2002*
Smith, Rebecca *2002*
Thyne, Richard *2002*
Akers, Robert *2003*
Ali, Kashif *2003*
Hudson, Abigail *2003*
Lawrence, Benjamin *2003*
Maguire, Clodagh *2003*
Newstead, Jennifer *2003*
Quigley, Louise *2003*
Abraham, Jade *2004*
Connolly, Timothy *2004*
Cooper, Douglas *2004*
Greenhalgh, Jane *2004*
Harrison, Peta *2004*
Hickinbottom, Abigail *2004*
Murphy, Paul *2004*
Poole, William *2004*
Rimmer, Catherine *2004*
Samuel, Ana *2004*
Sutton, Rebecca *2004*
Waddell, Philippa *2004*
Watkins, Adam *2004*
Wilson, Helen *2004*
Christian, Neil *2005*
De Navarro, Frances *2005*
Marshall, Lucy *2005*
McGarry, Steven *2005*
Spencer, Shaun *2005*
Thompson, Gareth *2005*
White, Debra *2005*
Bower, Laurinda *2006*
Flynn, Steven *2006*
Goode, Julian *2006*
Kelly, Ben *2006*
Pare, Christopher *2006*
Rae, Louise *2006*
Rook, Rachael *2006*
Scully, Jenny *2006*
Wilkinson, Timothy *2006*
Allen, Fergal *2007*
Erlen, Nicole *2007*
Haggis, Andrew *2007*
Owen-Casey, Neil *2007*
Pemberton, Jessica *2007*
Vanderpump, Henry *2007*
Wood, Hannah *2007*
Bellamy, Jonathan *2008*
Cooper, Elisabeth *2008*
England, Laura *2008*
Garcha, Sukhdev *2008*
Gomer, Elis *2008*
Maddison, Simon *2008*
Metcalfe, Daniel *2008*
Murray, Simon *2008*
Walker, Hannah *2008*
Williams, Cerys *2008*
Edwards, Thomas *2009*
Baines, David *2009*
Nash, Laura *2009*
Roberts, Elliw *2009*

Types of work

Administrative law · Agriculture · Animals · Anti-social Behaviour Orders · Arbitration · Asset recovery · Asylum · Banking · Building

D

†Recorder *Door Tenant/Associate Member

D

societies · Capital tax · Care proceedings · Chancery · Chancery (general) · Charities · Children · Civil fraud · Civil law · Civil liberties · Civil litigation · Civil partnerships · Civil recovery · Cohabitation · Commercial fraud · Commercial law · Commercial litigation · Commodities · Common law (general) · Company law · Company, commercial and competition · Competition law · Computer crime · Confidential information · Conflict of laws · Constitutional law · Construction law · Consumer credit · Consumer law · Contracts · Copyright · Coroners · Corporate finance · Corporate fraud · Corporate manslaughter · Costs · Council tax · Crime · Crime and criminal due process · Criminal judicial review · Cross-border litigation and remedies · Customs · Data protection · Design · Disasters · Disciplinary procedures · Discrimination · Dispute resolution · Domestic violence injunctions · EC competition law · ECHR · Education · Employee benefit trusts · Employment · Energy · Entertainment · Environment · Equity · Excise · Extradition · Family law · Family provision · Financial instruments · Financial services · Fire and other property damage claims · Firearms · Fraud · Freedom of expression · Freezing orders · Funding arrangements · Gaming and lotteries · Group litigation · Guarantees · Health and safety · Healthcare law · Highways · Homicide · Housing · Income tax · Industrial relations law · Information technology · Insolvency · Insurance (long term) · International criminal law · Internet law · Investments · Labour arbitration · Landlord and tenant · Legal advice · Licensing · Local authorities · Malicious prosecution · Markets and fairs · Matrimonial · Media · Media and entertainment · Medical negligence · Mental health · Military law · Mining · Money laundering · Multi-party litigation · National Insurance · Offshore trust litigation · Parliamentary · Partnerships · Passing off · Patents · Pensions · Personal injury · Personal insolvency · Planning · Police · Prison law · Privacy · Procurement · Professional negligence · Public access · Public health · Public law · Publishing · Rating and CPO · Real property · Regulatory and disciplinary law · Regulatory crime · Remedies · Road traffic · Securities law and regulation · Serial crime · Sexual Offences · Social welfare · Society of Lloyd's · Special Guardianship · Stamp duty · Succession · Tax · Telecommunications · Terrorism · Torts · Trade secrets · Trademarks · Travel law · Trust litigation · Trusts · Unincorporated associations · Unmarried couples · Utilities · VAT · Water

Chambers Established 2002
Opening times: 8.30am - 6.00pm

Chambers' facilities
WiFi

Disability access
Staff briefed or trained on duties under the disability legislation, Wheelchair access, Disabled parking available

Fees policy
Details of fees and/or hourly rates will be provided upon inquiry and will vary depending upon the seniority of counsel.

SULBY HOUSE CHAMBERS

2 Ranford Road, Burnage, Manchester M19 2GL
0161 224 3266
Fax: 0161 224 3266
E-mail: adam.roxborough@sulbyhouse.com

Chambers of: Mr A B Roxborough

TRIDENT BARRISTERS CHAMBERS

Peter House, Oxford Street, Manchester M1 5AN
0161 663 3123
E-mail: clerks@tridentchambers.com

Chambers of: Mr L A Gledhill

CHAMBERS OF MR S BETTS

Sundern, 8 Southview Road, Marlow, Buckinghamshire SL7 3JP
07739 892093
Fax: 01753 245547
E-mail: admin@cslassociates.co.uk

Chambers of: Mr S Betts

CHAMBERS OF MISS J STATHER

Flat 1, Wards House, 153 Smedley Street, Matlock, Derbyshire DE4 3JG
0115 931 3958
E-mail: juliestanther@hotmail.com

Chambers of: Miss J Stather

BATH CHAMBERS

PO Box 2046, Melksham, Wiltshire SN12 8EX
01225 702347
Fax: 01225 702320; DX: 43920 Melksham
E-mail: Bathchambers@btinternet.com

Chambers of: Mr J E Brooke

HUNTWYCK CHAMBERS

The Huntwyck, Hamilton Place, Melton Mowbray LE13 0LX
07843 620473
E-mail: craig@qualitysolicitors.com

AMICUS CHAMBERS

Queens Court, Newport Road, Middlesbrough TS1 5EH
01642 876334
Fax: 01642 881300; DX: 60540 Middlesbrough
E-mail: amicus.clerk@amicuschambers.co.uk
URL: www.amicuschambers.co.uk

Chambers of: Mr D Hall
Clerk: Carol Thornton; Fees Clerk: Melissa Knapper

Hall, Derek *1994*
McKie, Jackie *1995*
Robinson, Helen *1998*
Averis, Elaine *2000*
Webster, Lindsay *2005*
Stokes-Herbst, Rebecca *2006*
McReddie, Fiona *2010*

Types of work
Adoption · Ancillary relief · Care proceedings · Child abduction · Child abuse · Child care law · Child support · Cohabitation · Divorce · Domestic violence injunctions · Family law · Financial provision · Immigration · Private children law · Special Guardianship · Wardship

Disability access
Staff briefed or trained on duties under the disability legislation, Wheelchair access, Disabled parking available

FOUNTAIN CHAMBERS

Cleveland Business Centre, 1 Watson Street, Middlesbrough TS1 2RQ
01642 804040
Fax: 01642 804060; DX: 711700 Middlesbrough 11
E-mail: clerks@fountainchambers.co.uk
URL: www.fountainchambers.co.uk
Out of hours telephone: 07796 217202

Chambers of: Mr J M Hill QC
Clerks: Amanda Mallett, Janet Place, Emma Anderson, Samantha Rumins, Ryan Holden, Russell Ayles

Hill, James QC *1984*†
Bethel, Martin QC *1965*†
Roberts, Timothy QC *1978*†
Miller, Keith *1973*†
Dent, Adrian *1974*
Pinkney, Giles *1978*
Sherwin, Deborah *1979*†
West, Ian *1985*
Gilbert, Robert *1986*
Burke, Patricia *1990*
Gaston, Graeme *1991*
Kidd, Joanne *1995*
Taylor, Teresa *1994*
Mitchell, Tom *1995*
Bennett, Richard *1996*
Haugstad, Annelise *1996*
Towers, Martin *1996*
Turton, Robin *1996*
Faulks, Samuel *1997*
Price, Collette *1997*
Walker, Jonathan J *1997*
Gamble, Helen *1998*
Dodds, Kathryn *2000*
Kane, Gillian *2002*
Smith, Scott *2003*
Boucher-Giles, Benjamin *2004*
Murray, Harvey *2004*
Rainey, Kieran *2004*
Bottomley, Penny *2006*
Hogben, Helen *2006*
Brown, Rebecca *2007*
Medd, David *2011*

Types of work
Care proceedings · Clinical negligence · Commercial litigation · Common law (general) · Consumer law · Corporate fraud · Courts martial · Crime · Discrimination · Education · Employment · Environment · Equity · Family law · Family provision · Health and safety · Housing · Human rights · Landlord and tenant · Licensing · Medical negligence · Mental health · Personal injury · Personal insolvency · Professional negligence · Trusts · Wills

Disability access
Staff briefed or trained on duties under the disability legislation, Wheelchair access, Disabled parking available

104 GYPSY LANE

104 Gypsy Lane, Nunthorpe, Middlesbrough, Cleveland TS7 0DR
01642 316018
E-mail: annecmitchell@msn.com

OLD COURT CHAMBERS

Newham House, 96-98 Borough Road, Middlesbrough TS1 2HJ
01642 232523
Fax: 01642 232896; DX: 60591 Middlesbrough
E-mail: clerks@oldcourtchambers.com
URL: www.oldcourtchambers.com

Chambers of: Mr S A Constantine, Mr N Soppitt
Clerks: Daniel Foulger, Barbara Hudson; Administrator: Claire Gibson; Natalie Wilson

Constantine, Stephen *1992*
Soppitt, Nigel *1996*
Davey, Neil QC *1978*
Constable, John *1972*
Ford, Gerard *1986*
Morrison, Christopher *1986*
Gillette, John *1990*
Newcombe, Paul *1991*
Bradshaw, Ian *1992*
Sabiston, Peter *1992*
Fagan, Catherine *1993*
Baker, Christopher *1994*
Dryden, Shaun *1994*
Abrahams, Paul *2002*
Lamballe, Victoria *2002*
Borgen, Inga *2004*
O'Brien, Liam *2007*
Landin, Rachael *2008*

Types of work
Administrative law · Arbitration · Care proceedings · Civil liberties · Common law (general) · Courts martial · Crime · Discrimination · Education · Employment · Family law · Family provision · Housing · Immigration · Landlord and tenant · Licensing · Local authorities · Medical negligence · Mental health · Personal injury · Professional negligence · Sale and carriage of goods

Disability access
Staff briefed or trained on duties under the disability legislation

TRINITY CHAMBERS

Multi Media Exchange, 72-80 Corporation Road, Middlesbrough TS1 2RF
01642 247569
Fax: 01642 249897; DX: 60537 Middlesbrough
E-mail: info@trinitychambers.co.uk
URL: www.trinitychambers.co.uk
Out of hours telephone: 07842 019666
Clerks: Alison Dickason (Senior Clerk), Chris Gibbin (Teesside Clerk), Peter Finkill (Criminal Clerk), David Knight (Criminal Clerk), Tracie Rutter (Criminal Clerk), Rebecca Dixon (Civil & Family Clerk), Richard Embley (Civil & Family Clerk), Kirsty Hart (Civil & Family Clerk), Ken McLafferty (Civil & Family Clerk), Steve Preen (Civil & Family Clerk); Practice Manager: Simon Stewart OBE (Practice Director); Administrator: Chris Lucarelli (Business Development Manager); Fiona Bullock (Teesside Co-ordinator); Finance Manager: Ailsa Charlton, David Robinson (Fees Administrator)

Also at: Trinity Chambers, The Custom House, Quayside, Newcastle upon Tyne NE1 3DE Tel: 0191 232 1927 Fax: 0191 232 7975 E-mail: info@trinitychambers.co.uk URL: www.trinitychambers.co.uk

INVESTOR IN PEOPLE

Criminal Defence Service

Community Legal Service

Hedworth, Alan QC *1975*†
Bradley, Sally QC *1978*†
Elliott, Eric QC *1974*†
Duffield, Stephen *1969*
Knox, Christopher *1974*†
Hawks, Anthony *1975*†
Vane, Christopher *1976*
Callan, David *1979*
Engelman, Philip *1979*
Wilkinson, John *1979*
Smart, Jacqueline *1981*
Richardson, James *1982*

 †Recorder *Door Tenant/Associate Member

Walsh, Peter *1982*
McKenzie, Lesley *1983*
Spain, Timothy *1983*
McCrae, Fiona *1986*
Taylor, Susan *1987*†
Goodwin, Caroline *1988*†
Routledge, Shaun *1988*
Gittins, Timothy *1990*†
Rutter, Andrew *1990*
Shaw, Nicola *1992*
Smith, Rachel *1992*
Adams, Robert *1993*†
Dunn, Katherine *1993*
Gray, Justin *1993*
Scott Bell, Rosalind *1993*
Stonor, Nicholas *1993*
Holland, Charles *1994*
Callan, Jane *1995*
Sweeting, Margaret *1996*
Crawley, Kevin *1998*
Mills, Kristian *1998*
Taylor, Yvonne *1998*
Walker, Fiona *1998*
Allan, Nicola *1999*
Goldberg, Simon *1999*
Graham, Michael *1999*
Hedworth, Rachel *1999*
Kagaba-Mendoza, Elizabeth *1999*
Kemp, James *1999*
Kitching, Kossar *1999*
Currer, Paul *2000*
Giovannini, Angela *2000*
Mitford, Christopher *2001*
Phillips, Ruth *2001*
Rasoul, Miriam *2001*
Mather, Brian *2002*
Smith, Joan *2002*
Wood, Katherine *2002*
Foley, Jane *2003*
Anderson, Jamie *2004*
Brissenden, Claire *2004*
Hill, Michael *2004*
Tinnion, Antoine *2004*
Comb, David *2005*
Stubbs, Richard *2005*
Byrne, Will *2006*
Morgan, Jamie *2006*
Darby, Johanna *2007*
Crammond, Andrew *2008*
Marwick, James *2008*
Sehat, Amanda *2009*
Stafford, Andrew QC *1980**
Cobb, Stephen QC *1985*†*
Capps, Deveral *1995**

Types of work

Agriculture · Anti-social Behaviour Orders · Arbitration · Asset forfeiture · Asset recovery · Care proceedings · Chancery (commercial) · Chancery (general) · Chancery (land law) · Charities · Commercial contracts · Commercial fraud · Commercial law · Commercial litigation · Commercial planning · Commercial property · Commercial regulation · Common land · Common law (general) · Company, commercial and competition · Confiscation · Consumer law · Conveyancing · Corporate fraud · Corporate manslaughter · Courts martial · Crime · Crime and criminal due process · Criminal judicial review · Damages · Defamation · Employment · Environment · Equity · Extradition · Family law · Family provision · Firearms · Fraud · Freezing orders · Health and safety · Homicide · Housing · Immigration · Insolvency · International criminal law · Landlord and tenant · Licensing · Local authorities · Mediation · Medical law · Medical negligence · Medicines Act · Mental health · Money laundering · Partnerships · Personal injury · Personal insolvency · Planning · Prison law · Professional negligence · Public health · Road traffic · Sale and carriage of goods · Serial crime · Serious fraud · Shipping · Social security · Social welfare · Succession · Torts · Trusts · War crimes tribunals · Wills

Chambers Established 1954
Opening times: 8.30am - 6.00pm

Chambers' facilities

Conference rooms in Newcastle and Middlesbrough, Video and audio conferencing, secure e-mail

Disability access

Staff briefed or trained on duties under the disability legislation, Wheelchair access, Disabled parking available, Induction loop or infra red system

Languages spoken

French

CHAMBERS OF MR K HARRIS

229 Tolcarne Drive, Pinner, Middlesex HA5 2DW
0845 123 1234
Fax: 0845 430 4321; DX: 35601 Pinner
E-mail: kevinlynharris@gmail.com

Chambers of: Mr K L Harris

Disability access

Staff briefed or trained on duties under the disability legislation

STUDIO LEGALE COBBS

Via G.B.Morgagni 2, Milan 20129
0039 022 953 2531
E-mail: lcobbs@alice.it

Chambers of: Miss L S Cobbs

Disability access

Wheelchair access, Disabled parking available

CHAMBERS OF MR THOMAS BAILEY

Eaton Place, 90 Mill Road, Water Eaton, Milton Keynes MK2 2UZ
07983 447117; DX: 16990 Brackley
E-mail: tombailey888@yahoo.co.uk

Chambers of: Mr T I Bailey

Disability access

Wheelchair access, Disabled parking available

D

CHAMBERS OF MS SAMANTHA DAVIES

PO Box 6017, Milton Keynes, Buckinghamshire MK1 9AP
0845 123 1234
Fax: 0845 430 4321; DX: 31412 Milton Keynes
E-mail: samanthatdavies@yahoo.co.uk

Chambers of: Ms S T Davies

CHAMBERS OF JOAN GANDOLFI

47 Shackleton Place, Oldbrook, Milton Keynes MK6 2PT
0845 123 1234
E-mail: joangandolfi@sky.com

Chambers of: Mrs J Gandolfi

GORESBROOK CHAMBERS

PO Box 6017, Milton Keynes MK1 9AP
0845 123 1234
Fax: 0845 430 4321; DX: 31412 Milton Keynes
E-mail: thomas.john6@btinternet.com

Chambers of: Mr T H John

Disability access
Staff briefed or trained on duties under the disability legislation

HARCOURT CHAMBERS

1 Isling Brook, Shenley Brook End, Milton Keynes MK1 9AP
0845 123 1234
E-mail: clerks@barristerweb.com

Chambers of: Mr M J P Conlon

Disability access
Staff briefed or trained on duties under the disability legislation, Disabled parking available

CHAMBERS OF MISS Z LANE-SMITH

PO Box 6017, Milton Keynes DX: 31412 Milton Keynes

MK FAMILY LAW CHAMBERS

PO Box 6017, Milton Keynes MK1 9AP
0845 123 1234
Fax: 0845 430 4321; DX: 31412 Milton Keynes

Chambers of: Miss A J Armour

CHAMBERS OF MS M NEUFELD

PO Box 6017, Milton Keynes MK1 9AP
01908 330 134
E-mail: clerks@barristerweb.com

Chambers of: Miss M Neufeld

CHAMBERS OF MRS SUSAN J L GARNETT

Widenmayerstrasse 44, Lehel, Munich
0892 4218798
Fax: 0892 4218799
E-mail: susanjlgarnett@aol.com

Chambers of: Mrs S J L Garnett

Disability access
Staff briefed or trained on duties under the disability legislation, Wheelchair access

5 BARNSBURY CLOSE

5 Barnsbury Close, New Malden, Surrey KT3 5BP
020 8949 7748
Fax: 020 8949 7748
E-mail: emyakubu@aol.com

Chambers of: Mr E M Yakubu

CHAMBERS OF MISS KHADIJA RAHMAN

55 The Crescent, New Malden, Surrey KT3 3LE
020 7737 9330
Fax: 020 7737 9331

Chambers of: Ms K U Rahman

GRAY'S CHAMBERS

10 Heathside Close, Newbury, Essex IG2 7PD
020 8518 2525
Fax: 020 8252 7072
E-mail: aleem.khan@btinternet.com

Chambers of: Mr A A Khan

DERE STREET BARRISTERS

33 Broad Chare, Newcastle Upon Tyne NE1 3DQ
0844 3351551
Fax: 0191 261 0043; DX: 61001 Newcastle Upon Tyne
E-mail: clerks@derestreet.co.uk
URL: www.derestreet.co.uk

Also at: 14 Toft Green, York YO1 6JT
Tel: 0844 3351551, Fax: 01904 610056; DX: 65517 York 7

Chambers of: Mr B Nolan QC, Mr J C Elvidge QC
Senior Clerk: Kevin Beaumont; Practice Manager: Simon Coatsworth; Finance Manager: Julie Barrett

Elvidge, John QC *1988*
Nolan, Benjamin QC *1971*†
Lowe, William QC *1972*†
Woodcock, Robert QC *1978*
Denny, Robin *1969*
Duff, Euan DL *1973*†
Harmer, Christine *1973*
Harvey, Colin *1975*
Horner, Robin *1975*
Devlin, Jonathan *1978*
Smith, Duncan *1979*
Hunter, Geoff *1979*
Bosomworth, Michael *1979*
Twist, Stephen *1979*
Dorman-O'Gowan, Christopher *1979*
Hunt, Roderick *1981*
Finch, Thomas *1981*
Armstrong, Kester *1982*
Moulder, Pauline *1983*
Mason, David *1984*
Davis, Anthony *1986*
Proops, Helen *1986*
Richardson, Anne *1986*
Morris, Paul *1986*
Fletcher, Stephen *1987*
Price, Nicholas *1988*
Lamb, David *1987*
Lee, Ross *1987*
Makepeace, Peter *1988*
Rowlands, David *1988*
Styles, Mark *1988*
Boothroyd, Susan *1990*
Oliver, Crispin *1990*
Brown, James *1990*†
Carr, Jonathan *1990*
Choudhury, Nafeesa *1990*
Cordey, Daniel *1990*
Middleton, Claire *1991*
Clemitson, Julie *1991*
Todd, Martin *1991*
Robinson, James *1992*
Elliott, Jason *1993*
Edwards, Daniel *1993*
Lugg, Elizabeth *1994*
Wadoodi, Aisha *1994*
Woolrich, Sarah *1994*
Campbell, Diane *1995*
Randhawa, Ravinder *1995*
Newcombe, Robert *1995*
Legard, Edward *1996*
Callaghan, Elizabeth *1998*
Walker, Andrew *1998*
MacFaul, Donald *1998*
Healy, Samuel *1999*
Withyman, Jim *1999*
Buckley, Sophie *1999*
Holmes-Willis, Sarah *1999*
Mustard, Lorraine *1999*
Robinson-Young, David *1999*
Smoult-Hawtree, Karen *2000*
Gray, Ruth *2000*
Ainsley, Stephen *2001*
Wilkinson, Paul *2001*
Senior, Anthony *2002*
McCain, Charles *2002*
Smith, Jennie *2002*
Donnelly, Timothy *2003*
Henley, Carly *2003*
Lennon, Karen *2003*
Thornton, Stephen *2003*
Trory, Henry *2003*
Watson, Hal *2003*
Adams, Nathan *2004*
McDermott, Frazer *2004*
Gibson, Claire *2004*
Herrmann, Richard *2004*
Gough, Emma *2004*
Frew, Bruce *2005*
Miller, Amanda *2005*
Adcock, Deborah *2005*
Willoughby, James *2005*
Dawson, Beatrice *2006*
Rook, Stuart *2006*
Davies, Angharad *2006*
Wigglesworth, Timothy *2007*
Upton, Shona *2007*
Mugliston, Adam *2008*
Armstrong, Katherine *2009*
Holt, Kerry *2009*
Long, Kayleigh *2009*
Morgan, Philip *2010*

Types of work

Administrative law · Adoption · Agency · Agriculture · Ancillary relief · Animal rights law · Animals · Anti-social Behaviour Orders · Arbitration · Asbestos-related diseases · Assessment of costs · Asset forfeiture · Asset recovery · Asylum · Bloodstock · Boundaries · Building · Canon law (RC) · Capital tax · Care proceedings · Chancery (commercial) · Chancery (general) · Chancery (land law) · Charities · Child abduction · Child abuse · Child care law · Child support · Children · Civil actions against the police · Civil fraud · Civil law · Civil liberties · Civil partnerships · Clinical negligence · Cohabitation · Commercial contracts · Commercial fraud · Commercial law · Commercial litigation · Commercial property · Common land · Common law (general) · Community care · Company law · Compulsory Purchase · Computer crime · Confiscation · Confiscation of the proceeds of crime · Conflict of laws · Construction law · Consumer credit · Consumer law · Contaminated land · Contracts · Conveyancing · Copyright · Copyright theft · Coroner's inquests · Coroners · Corporate fraud · Corporate governance · Corporate insolvency · Corporate liability · Corporate manslaughter · Corporate recovery · Corporation tax · Costs · Councillors and standards · Court of Protection · Courts martial · Crime · Crime and criminal due process · Criminal judicial review · Cross-border litigation and remedies · Damages · Data protection · Defamation · Directors' disqualification · Disability discrimination · Disciplinary procedures · Disciplinary tribunals · Discrimination · Dispute resolution · Divorce · Domestic violence injunctions · Ecclesiastical law · ECHR · Economic torts · Education · Employee benefit trusts · Employment · Engineering disputes · Environment · Equine law · Equity · Family law · Family provision · Financial provision · Fire and other property damage claims · Firearms · Forfeiture · Fraud · Freedom of information · Funding arrangements · Group litigation · Health and safety · Highways · Holiday injury and damages · Holiday law · Homicide · Housing · Income tax ·

†Recorder *Door Tenant/Associate Member

D

Industrial deafness · Industrial diseases · Industrial relations law · Inheritance and cohabitees · Inquests · Insolvency · International fraud and asset tracing · Internet crime · Judicial review · Labour arbitration · Land compensation · Landlord and tenant · Lands Tribunal · Leasehold enfranchisement · Legal advice · Legal aid costs · Licensing · Limited partnerships · Local authorities · Local authority claims · Local authority liability · Local government finance · Malicious falsehood · Malicious prosecution · Markets and fairs · Matrimonial · Matrimonial finance · Medical negligence · Mental health · Military law · Mineral rights · Mining · Mortgages · Motor vehicles · Multi-party litigation · Occupational diseases · Offshore trust litigation · Ombudsman · Overseas accidents · Partnerships · Passing off · Pensions · Personal injury · Personal insolvency · Planning · Police · Police discipline · Pollution · Prison law · Private children law · Procurement · Professional negligence · Public health · Public inquiries · Public law · Rating and CPO · Real property · Regulatory and disciplinary law · Remedies · Restitution · Rights of light · Rights of way · Road haulage · Road traffic · Road traffic offences · Sale and carriage of goods · Sale of business · School sites · Scientific cases · Serial crime · Serious fraud · Sexual Offences · Shareholder agreements · Social security · Social services · Social welfare · Solicitor's indemnity · Special Guardianship · Sports medicine · Succession · Tax · Tax investigations · Technical contracts · Technology and Construction Court · Terrorism · Timeshare · Title to land · Torts · Trading standards · Transport and Works Act inquiries · Travel law · Trust litigation · Trusts · Unmarried couples · VAT · Wardship · Water · Wills

Disability access
Staff briefed or trained on duties under the disability legislation, Wheelchair access, Disabled parking available

CATHEDRAL CHAMBERS

First Floor, 17 Queen Street, Newcastle Upon Tyne NE1 3UG
0191 232 1311
Fax: 0191 232 1422; DX: 61277 Newcastle Upon Tyne
E-mail: mail@cathedralchambers.com
URL: www.cathedralchambers.com
Out of hours telephone: 0191 232 1311

Chambers of: Mr C G Knowles
Clerk: Dawn Kipling

Knowles, Geoffrey *1998*
Rich, Stephen *1972*
Weatherall, Julia *1985*
Hewitt, Catherine *2001*
Hedworth, Joseph *2002*
Cornberg, Antony *2003*
McIlwain, Amber *2005*

Types of work
Administrative law · Care proceedings · Chancery (general) · Common law (general) · Courts martial · Crime · Employment · Family law · Family provision · Housing · Human rights · Immigration · Insolvency · Landlord and tenant · Personal injury · Succession

Disability access
Staff briefed or trained on duties under the disability legislation, Disabled parking available

ENTERPRISE CHAMBERS

65 Quayside, Newcastle Upon Tyne NE1 3DE
0191 222 3344
Fax: 0191 222 3340; DX: 61134 Newcastle Upon Tyne
E-mail: newcastle@enterprisechambers.com
URL: www.enterprisechambers.com
Out of hours telephone: 07780 671478

Chambers of: Mr B R Weatherill QC
Clerks: Antony Armstrong (Senior Clerk), Stephen Walker; Accounts Manager: Hannah Steininger-Nath

Weatherill, Bernard QC *1974†*
Arden, Peter QC *1983*
Bhaloo, Zia QC *1990*
James, Michael *1976*
Morgan, Charles *1978*
Hutton, Caroline *1979*
Groves, Hugo *1980*
Ife, Linden *1982*
Barker, James *1984*
Zelin, Geoffrey *1984*
Jack, Adrian *1986†*
Jarron, Stephanie *1990*
Pickering, James *1991*
Duddridge, Robert *1992*
Jory, Hugh *1992*
Klein, Jonathan *1992*
Noble, Andrew *1992*
Williamson, Bridget *1993*
Francis, Edward *1995*
Mauger, Shanti *1996*
Ilyas, Shaiba *1998*
Calland, Timothy *1999*
Rodger, Jonathan *1999*
Johnson, Simon *2000*
McCulloch, Niall *2000*
West, Matthew *2000*
Murphy, Damian *2001*
Page, Rebecca *2001*
Jackson, Claire *2002*
Beswetherick, Anthony *2003*
Kalfon, Olivier *2003*
Griffin, Margaret *2004*
Gunaratna, Kavan *2004*
Toman, Cristin *2004*
Markandya, Susannah *2005*
Bond, Kelly *2007*
Burslem, Sarah *2008*
Gale, Phillip *2008*
Meech, Jennifer *2008*
Maddison, Matthew *2010*

Types of work
Agriculture · Arbitration · Banking · Chancery (commercial) · Chancery (general) · Commercial law · Commercial litigation · Commercial property · Company law · Conveyancing · Environment · Equity · Housing · Insolvency · Landlord and tenant · Licensing · Mediation · Partnerships · Personal insolvency · Professional negligence · Real property · Succession · Trusts · Wills

Disability access
Staff briefed or trained on duties under the disability legislation

CHAMBERS OF JOHN FALKENSTEIN

204 Jesmond Dene Road, Jesmond, Newcastle Upon Tyne NE2 2NL
0191 265 7999
Fax: 0191 265 7111; DX: 62560 Jesmond
E-mail: johnfalkenstein204@googlemail.com

NEW COURT CHAMBERS

3 Broad Chare, Newcastle Upon Tyne NE1 3DQ
0191 232 1980
Fax: 0191 232 3730; DX: 61012 Newcastle Upon Tyne
E-mail: clerks@newcourt-chambers.co.uk

Chambers of: Mr J W Smith

Disability access
Staff briefed or trained on duties under the disability legislation, Wheelchair access, Disabled parking available

PARK LANE PLOWDEN

Lombard House, 4-8 Lombard Street, Newcastle Upon Tyne NE1 3AE
0191 211 4087
Fax: 0191 221 2122; DX: 61062 Newcastle Upon Tyne
E-mail: clerks@parklaneplowden.co.uk

Chambers of: Mr S C Brown QC

Disability access
Staff briefed or trained on duties under the disability legislation, Wheelchair access

D

†Recorder *Door Tenant/Associate Member

TRINITY CHAMBERS

The Custom House, 39 Quayside,
Newcastle Upon Tyne NE1 3DE
0191 232 1927
Fax: 0191 232 7975; DX: 61185 Newcastle Upon Tyne
E-mail: info@trinitychambers.co.uk
URL: www.trinitychambers.co.uk
Out of hours telephone: 07842 019666

Chambers of: Mr A T Hedworth QC
Clerks: Alison Dickason (Senior Clerk), Chris Gibbin (Teesside Clerk), Peter Finkill (Criminal Clerk), David Knight (Criminal Clerk), Tracie Rutter (Criminal Clerk), Rebecca Dixon (Civil & Family Clerk), Richard Embley (Civil & Family Clerk), Kirsty Hart (Civil & Family Clerk), Ken McLafferty (Civil & Family Clerk), Steven Preen (Civil & Family Clerk); Practice Manager: Simon Stewart OBE (Practice Director); Administrator: Chris Lucarelli (Business Development Manager); Fiona Bullock (Teesside Co-ordinator); Finance Manager: Ailsa Charlton, David Robinson (Fees Administrator)

Also at: Multi Media Exchange, 72-80 Corporation Street, Middlesbrough, TS1 2RF, Tel: 01642 247569, Fax: 01642 249897
E-mail: info@trinitychambers.co.uk URL: www.trinitychambers.co.uk

BARMARK

INVESTOR IN PEOPLE

Hedworth, Alan QC *1975†*
Bradley, Sally QC *1978†*
Elliott, Eric QC *1974†*
Duffield, Stephen *1969*
Knox, Christopher *1974†*
Hawks, Anthony *1975†*
Vane, Christopher *1976*
Callan, David *1979*
Engelman, Philip *1979*
Wilkinson, John *1979*
Smart, Jacqueline *1981*
Richardson, James *1982*
Walsh, Peter *1982*
McKenzie, Lesley *1983*
Spain, Timothy *1983*
O'Sullivan, John *1984*
McCrae, Fiona *1986*
Taylor, Susan *1987†*
Goodwin, Caroline *1988†*
Routledge, Shaun *1988*
Gittins, Timothy *1990†*
Rutter, Andrew *1990*
Shaw, Nicola *1992*
Smith, Rachel *1992*
Temple, Michelle *1992*
Adams, Robert *1993†*
Dunn, Katherine *1993*
Gray, Justin *1993*
Scott Bell, Rosalind *1993*
Stonor, Nicholas *1993*
Holland, Charles *1994*
Callan, Jane *1995*
Sweeting, Margaret *1996*
Crawley, Kevin *1998*
Mills, Kristian *1998*
Taylor, Yvonne *1998*
Walker, Fiona *1998*
Allan, Nicola *1999*
Goldberg, Simon *1999*
Graham, Michael *1999*
Hedworth, Rachel *1999*
Kagaba-Mendoza, Elizabeth *1999*
Kemp, James *1999*
Kitching, Kossar *1999*
Currer, Paul *2000*
Giovannini, Angela *2000*
Mitford, Christopher *2001*
Phillips, Ruth *2001*
Rasoul, Miriam *2001*
Mather, Brian *2002*
Smith, Joan *2002*
Wood, Katherine *2002*
Foley, Jane *2003*
Spragg, Robert *2003*
Anderson, Jamie *2004*
Brissenden, Claire *2004*
Hill, Michael *2004*
Tinnion, Antoine *2004*
Comb, David *2005*
Stubbs, Richard *2005*
Byrne, Will *2006*
Morgan, Jamie *2006*
Darby, Johanna *2007*
Crammond, Andrew *2008*
Marwick, James *2008*
Sehat, Amanda *2009*
Stafford, Andrew QC *1980**
Cobb, Stephen QC *1985†**
Capps, Deveral *1995**

Types of work
Agriculture · Anti-social Behaviour Orders · Arbitration · Asset forfeiture · Asset recovery · Care proceedings · Chancery (commercial) · Chancery (general) · Chancery (land law) · Charities · Commercial contracts · Commercial fraud · Commercial law · Commercial litigation · Commercial planning · Commercial property · Commercial regulation · Common land · Common law (general) · Company, commercial and competition · Confiscation · Consumer law · Conveyancing · Corporate fraud · Corporate manslaughter · Courts martial · Crime · Crime and criminal due process · Criminal judicial review · Damages · Defamation · Employment · Environment · Equity · Extradition · Family law · Family provision · Firearms · Fraud · Freezing orders · Health and safety · Homicide · Housing · Immigration · Insolvency · International criminal law · Landlord and tenant · Licensing · Local authorities · Medical law · Medical negligence · Medicines Act · Mental health · Money laundering · Partnerships · Personal injury · Personal insolvency · Planning · Prison law · Professional negligence · Public health · Road traffic · Sale and carriage of goods · Serial crime ·

†Recorder *Door Tenant/Associate Member

Serious fraud · Shipping · Social security · Social welfare · Succession · Torts · Trusts · War crimes tribunals · Wills

Chambers Established 1954
Opening times: 8.30am - 6.00pm

Chambers' facilities
Conference rooms in Newcastle and Middlesbrough, Video and audio conferencing, Secure e-mail.

Disability access
Staff briefed or trained on duties under the disability legislation, Wheelchair access, Disabled parking available, Induction loop or infra red system

Languages spoken
French

YORK CHAMBERS

Rotterdam House, 116 The Quayside, Newcastle Upon Tyne NE1 3DY
0191 206 4677
Fax: 0191 206 4172; DX: 716754 Newcastle 20

Chambers of: Mr J C Elvidge QC

Disability access
Staff briefed or trained on duties under the disability legislation, Wheelchair access, Disabled parking available

CHAMBERS OF MR HAROLD BAKER

33C Stow Hill, Newport NP20 1JH
07966 872648; DX: 33206 Newport
E-mail: hb21@live.co.uk

Chambers of: Mr H W Baker

CATHEDRAL CHAMBERS

10 Clytha Park Road, Newport NP20 4PB
01633 215112

TEMPLE CHAMBERS

12 Clytha Park Road, Newport, Gwent NP20 4PB
01633 267403
Fax: 01633 253441; DX: 33208 Newport (Gwent)
E-mail: dbrinning@temple-chambers.co.uk

Chambers of: Mr H L Roberts

Disability access
Staff briefed or trained on duties under the disability legislation, Disabled parking available

EC CHAMBERS

PO Box 825, Bungay, Norfolk NR35 9AR
01508 483931

TRIANGLE CHAMBERS

Blair Atholl, 11 The Triangle, North Ferriby, East Yorkshire HU14 3AT
01482 632075
Fax: 01482 632075
E-mail: emmarc@emmarc.karoo.co.uk

Chambers of: Miss E L Reid-Chalmers

Disability access
Staff briefed or trained on duties under the disability legislation, Wheelchair access, Disabled parking available

CHAMBERS OF MS T THORNHILL

Crowell Brook Mill Cottage, Forthay, North Nibley GL11 6EA
07887 490554
E-mail: tthornhill@childcarelegal.co.uk

Chambers of: Ms T Thornhill

THE CHAMBERS OF RICHARD HICKMET

The Chantry, Rhode, North Petherton, Somerset TA5 2AD
01278 663388
Fax: 01278 663981; DX: 32131 Taunton
E-mail: law@richardhickmet.co.uk

Chambers of: Mr R S Hickmet

Disability access
Wheelchair access, Disabled parking available

D

CHAMBERS OF MS HART

The Old Rectory, North Tawton, Devon EX20 2EX

CHARTLANDS CHAMBERS

Chartlands Chambers Northampton

3 St Giles Terrace, Northampton NN1 2BN
01604 603322
Fax: 01604 603388; DX: 12408 Northampton
E-mail: enquiries@chartlands-chambers.co.uk
URL: www.chartlands-chambers.co.uk
Out of hours telephone: 01536 790 548

Chambers of: Mrs J E Page, Mrs J E Pinkham
Clerk: Andrew Davies

Page, Jane *1982*
Pinkham, Joy *1993*
Van Besouw, Eufron *1988*
Burns, Terence *1990*
Tapper, Paul *1991*
Robinson, Matthew *1994*
Ali, Ishtiyaq *1996*
Van Spall, Penny *1998*
Watkins, Rachel *1998*
Vissian, Hena *2002*
Rashid, Waqas *2006*
Dawson, Rachael *2007*
Lince, Elizabeth *2007*
Cowen, Jonathan *1983**
Slade Jones, Robin *1993**

Types of work
Arbitration · Asylum · Care proceedings · Common law (general) · Family law · Family provision · Immigration · Landlord and tenant · Licensing · Mental health · Partnerships · Personal injury · Professional negligence · Sale and carriage of goods

Disability access
Wheelchair access, Disabled parking available

NORTHAMPTON CHAMBERS

10 Spencer Parade, Northampton NN1 5AQ
01604 636271
Fax: 01604 232931; DX: 12464 Northampton
E-mail: clerks@northampton-chambers.co.uk
URL: www.northampton-chambers.co.uk

Chambers of: Miss M Savvides
Senior Clerk: Stuart Hall

Also at: Central Business Exchange II, West Wing, 382-390 Midsummer Boulevard, Milton Keynes MK9 2RGTel: 01604 636271 Fax: 01604 232931

Savvides, Maria *1986*
Yeung, Stuart *1989*
Smith, Nicola *1994*
Willans, David *1995*
Brookes-Baker, Matthew *1998*
Christie, Michelle *1999*
Gooderham, Elizabeth *2001*
Murphy, Lianne *2001*
Pettitt, Robert *2002*
Maynard, Matthew *2003*
Wade, Rebecca *2003*
Fairclough, Lucy *2005*
Lyon, Gavin *2006*
McCluskey, Ella *2006*
Mettam, Hannah *2006*
Turner, Abigail *2006*
Keyes, Grant *2007*
McLernon, James *2007*
O'Malley, Laura *2007*
Henderson, Charlene *2009*

Types of work
Ancillary relief · Care proceedings · Cohabitation · Common law (general) · Crime · Divorce · Domestic violence injunctions · Employment · Family law · Family provision · Inheritance and cohabitees · Litigation · Mental health · Personal injury · Private children law · Public access · Public law · Road traffic · Road traffic offences

Disability access
Disabled parking available

EAST ANGLIAN CHAMBERS

15 The Close, Norwich, Norfolk NR1 4DZ
01473 214481
Fax: 01603 751400; DX: 5213 Norwich
E-mail: norwich@ealaw.co.uk

Chambers of: Mr G K Sinclair

Disability access
Staff briefed or trained on duties under the disability legislation, Wheelchair access, Disabled parking available

OCTAGON HOUSE

19 Colegate, Norwich NR3 1AT
01603 623186
Fax: 01603 760519; DX: 5249 Norwich 1
E-mail: clerks@octagonhouse.co.uk
URL: www.octagonhouse.co.uk

Chambers of: Mr C M Fletcher
Clerks: Stephen Unsworth (Senior Clerk), Daniel Twite, Robert Gibson, Sara Webb

Fletcher, Christopher *1984*
Khalil, Karim QC *1984*†
Caddick, Nicholas QC *1986*
Lindqvist, Andrew *1968*
Ross Martyn, John *1969*
Farmer, John *1970*
Harrison, Roger *1970*†
Kellett, Charles *1971*
Ayers, Guy *1979*†
Kefford, Anthony *1980*
Shackleford, Susan *1980*
James, Ian *1981*
Butterworth, Paul *1982*
Aldous, Robert *1985*
Clare, Michael *1986*
Bell, Marika *1991*
Bundell, Katharine *1991*
Dugdale, Jeremy *1992*
Gilbertson, Helen *1993*
Oliver, Andrew *1993*
Prinn, Helen *1993*
Durr, Jude *1995*
Moore, Katharine *1995*
Baruah, Fiona *1996*
Morgans, John *1996*
Jones, Susannah Lucy *1997*
Goodman, Jonathan *1999*
Jack, Nicholas *2002*
Grey, Sharon *2003*
Harris, Katie *2005*

Types of work
Arbitration · Care proceedings · Chancery (general) · Common law (general) · Crime · Employment · Family law · Family provision · Landlord and tenant · Licensing · Personal injury

Disability access
Staff briefed or trained on duties under the disability legislation, Wheelchair access, Disabled parking available

SCOTT FARNSWORTH ASSOCIATES

Biocity Nottingham, Pennyfoot Street, Nottingham NG1 1GF
0115 974 8226
E-mail: scott@scottfarnsworthassociates.com

Chambers of: Mr S A Farnsworth

CHAMBERS OF SHEILA HAMILTON MACDONALD

1 Hanley Street, Nottingham NG1 5BL
07986 575399
E-mail: shm@familyproperty.org.uk

Chambers of: Miss S H MacDonald

THE CHAMBERS OF MR HETT

53 Foxhill Road, Burton Joyce, Nottingham NG14 5DB
0115 9313958/07727 688337

Chambers of: Mr J Hett

INVICTUS CHAMBERS

Foxhall BC, 2 King Street, Nottingham NG1 2AS
0115 845 6554
Fax: 0115 845 6554
E-mail: azeb@invictuschambers.co.uk

Chambers of: Mr A Zeb

KCH GARDEN SQUARE

K | C | H
GARDEN SQ
BARRISTERS

1 Oxford Street, Nottingham NG1 5BH
0115 941 8851
Fax: 0115 941 4169; DX: 10042 Nottingham
E-mail: clerks@kchgardensquare.co.uk
URL: www.kchgardensquare.co.uk
Out of hours telephone: 07917 860 192

Chambers of: Mr S M Lowne
Clerk: Russell Hobbs (Senior Clerk); Practice Manager: Kristina Baumgarten - Chief Executive; Administrator: Hannah Wood

Also at: 96a New Walk, Leicester, LE1 7EA, Tel: 0116 298 7500, Fax: 0116 296 7501, DX: 17003 Leicester 2

Lowne, Stephen *1981*†
Riordan, Stephen QC *1992*
Steer, David QC *1993*
Lawsin-Rogers, Stuart QC *1975*
Morgan, Andrew QC *1994*
Oldham, Frances QC *1994*
Goldrein, Ian QC *1997*
Flewitt, Neil QC *2003*
Menary, Andrew QC *2003*
Johnson, Nicholas QC *2006*
Meyer, Lorna QC *2006*
Pratt, Richard QC *2006*
Power, Nigel QC *2010*
Unsworth, Ian QC *2010*
Philo, Noel *1975*
Howlett, James *1980*†
Cranny, Amanda *1984*
Dhadli, Perminder *1984*
Gallagher, Patrick *1984*

†Recorder *Door Tenant/Associate Member

D

Cranmer-Brown, Michael *1986*
Eley, Jonathan *1987*
Van Der Zwart, Mark *1988*
Way, Ian *1988*
Dee, Jonathon *1989*
Knowles, Mark *1989*
Munt, Alastair *1989*
Taylor, Andrew *1989*
Gibbs, Philip *1991*
Lody, Stuart *1991*
Janes, Jeremy *1992*
Leonard, Edna *1992*
Straw, Jonathan *1992*
Cartwright, Ivan *1993*
Holloway, Richard *1993*
Moore, Nicola *1993*
Warburton, Julie *1993*
Gow, Ben *1994*
Ahya, Sonal *1995*
Stobart, Tracey *1995*
Short, Gary *1996*
Wylie, Neil *1996*
Ewing, Harald *1997*
Hale, Grace *1998*
Beaumont, Andrew *1999*
Briden, Sarah *1999*
Thomas, James *1999*
Watson, Mark *1999*
Bowe, Patrick *2000*
George, Timothy *2000*
James-Moore, Siward *2000*
Walsh, Moira *2000*
Kabweru-Namulemu, Karen *2001*
Lowe, Christopher *2001*
Taylor, Stephen *2002*
Cleary, James *2003*
Hallissey, John-James *2003*
Russell, Thomas *2004*
Sapstead, Louise *2004*
Bide-Thomas, James *2005*
Cox, Jonathan *2005*
Mansfield, Ben *2005*
Mellor, Faye *2005*
Williams, Anne *2005*
Holt, Jane *2006*
Mansfield, Nadia *2006*
Downes, Julie *2007*
Gunstone, Giles *2007*
McIntosh, Nicola *2007*
Skinner, Samuel *2007*
Veitch, Steven *2007*
Wells, Christopher *2007*
Davies, Alexander *2008*
Harry, Marcus *2008*
Bevan, Christopher *2009*
McCarthy, Sara *2009*
Carter, James *2010*
Plummer, Katherine *2010*
Henry, Zoe *2012*
Corbett, James QC *1975†**
Robson, Jeremy *1999**

Types of work

Care proceedings · Chancery (general) · Commercial litigation · Commercial property · Common law (general) · Copyright · Courts martial · Crime · Discrimination · Employment · Equity · Family law · Family provision · Housing · Insolvency · Intellectual property · Landlord and tenant · Licensing · Mediation · Medical negligence · Mental health · Partnerships · Personal injury · Personal insolvency · Planning · Professional negligence · Public access · Sale and carriage of goods · Succession · Trusts · Wills

Disability access

Staff briefed or trained on duties under the disability legislation, Disabled parking available

LENTON CHAMBERS

Unit 47, Lenton Business Centre, Lenton Boulevard, Nottingham NG7 2BY
0115 9701484
Fax: 0115 970 1020
E-mail: amjad@lentonchambers.com

1 HIGH PAVEMENT

1 High Pavement, Nottingham NG1 1HF
0115 941 8218
Fax: 0115 941 8240; DX: 10168 Nottingham 19
E-mail: clerks@1highpavement.co.uk
URL: www.1highpavement.co.uk

Chambers of: Mr S Smith QC and Mr G Dickinson QC
Senior Clerk: David Duric

Dickinson, Gregory QC *1981†*
Smith, Shaun QC *1981*
Joyce, Peter QC *1968†*
Mann, Paul QC *1980†*
Rafferty, Stuart QC *1975†*
Wigoder, Lewis *1977†*
Napthine, Guy *1979*
Elwick, Martin *1981*
Bhatia, Balraj *1982*
Reynolds, Adrian *1982†*
Ballentyne, Errol *1983*
Hurst, Martin *1985*
Egbuna, Robert *1988*
Evans, Michael *1988*
Stockwell, Clive *1988*
Geeson, Christopher *1989*
Thatcher, Richard *1989*
Auty, Michael *1990*
McNamara, James *1990*
Mukherjee, Avik *1990*
Munro, Sarah *1990*
Coupland, Steven *1993*
Kemp, Stephen *1995*
Vout, Andrew *1995*
Achurch, Mark *1996*
Eckersley, Simon *1996*
Knight, Sarah *1996*
Purcell, Gregor *1997*
Varley, James *1997*
Joyce, Abigail *1998*
King, Julia *1998*
Pitman, Laura *2000*
Harrison, Esther *2002*
Shelley, Dominic *2003*
Chasemore, Catherine *2004*
Outterside, David *2004*
Lloyd, Sarah *2005*
Wilson, Katrina *2007*
Gabbitas, Christopher *2009*
Hardy, Lisa *2011*
Coughlin, Vincent QC *1980**

Types of work

Corporate fraud · Crime · Licensing

Disability access

Staff briefed or trained on duties under the disability legislation, Wheelchair access, Disabled parking available

ROPEWALK CHAMBERS

24 The Ropewalk, Nottingham NG1 5EF
0115 947 2581
Fax: 0115 947 6532; DX: 10060 Nottingham 17
E-mail: clerks@ropewalk.co.uk

Disability access

Staff briefed or trained on duties under the disability legislation, Wheelchair access, Disabled parking available, Induction loop or infra red system

ST MARY'S FAMILY LAW CHAMBERS

26-28 High Pavement, The Lace Market, Nottingham NG1 1HN
0115 950 3503
Fax: 0115 958 3060; DX: 10036 Nottingham
E-mail: clerks@stmarysflc.co.uk

Chambers of: Mr N B Page

Disability access
Staff briefed or trained on duties under the disability legislation, Wheelchair access

TRENT CHAMBERS

9 Regent Street, Nottingham NG1 5BS
0115 941 9596
Fax: 0115 950 7173; DX: 10016 Nottingham
E-mail: clerks@trentchambers.co.uk

Chambers of: Mrs U R Sood

Disability access
Staff briefed or trained on duties under the disability legislation, Wheelchair access, Disabled parking available

UNICORN CHAMBERS

P.O.Box 7696, Nottingham NG3 5WZ
0115 985 6602
Fax: 0115 962 3389; DX: 702152 Nottingham 6
E-mail: sjt@unicornchambers.co.uk

Chambers of: Mr S J Taylor

CHAMBERS OF MR J C GILL

Baytree House, 2 Lampeter Close, Oakwood, Derby DE21 2RB
01332 666 135
Fax: 01332 666135
E-mail: julian.gill1@googlemail.com

Chambers of: Mr J C Gill

MINERVA CHAMBERS

704 Grand Ocean Plaza, Ocean Village
00 350 20042779
E-mail: l.newbold@minervachambers.com

Chambers of: Dr A L E Newbold

CHAMBERS OF MR JULIAN LYNCH

Mill Barn Cottage, Spring Lane, Old Oxted, Surrey RH8 9PB
01883 732 103; DX: 39353 Oxted
E-mail: bpjlynch@btinternet.com

Chambers of: Mr J Lynch

SHELDAN

Chirk Road, Gobowen, Oswestry, Shropshire SY11 3LB
01691 657635
E-mail: jack@roberts155560.fsnet.co.uk

Chambers of: Mr J Roberts

VILLA CHAMBERS

33 St Peters Road, Oundle, Peterborough PE8 4NU
01832 273 097

Chambers of: Mr F K Sagoe

CHAMBERS OF MR P DU FEU

11 Alma Place, Oxford OX4 1JW
0781 080 5224
E-mail: peterdufeu@yahoo.co.uk

Chambers of: Mr P Du Feu

CHAMBERS OF MR P GODDARD

Couching House, Oxford, Oxford OX49 5PX
01608 811550; DX: 40658 Summertown
E-mail: pdgevil@tiscali.co.uk

Chambers of: Mr P D Goddard

Disability access
Disabled parking available

D

HARCOURT CHAMBERS

HARCOURT
CHAMBERS
LONDON OXFORD

Churchill House, 3 St Aldate's Courtyard, St Aldate's, Oxford OX1 1BN
0844 561 7135
Fax: 01865 791585; DX: 96453 Oxford 4
E-mail: sboutwood@harcourtchambers.co.uk
URL: www.harcourtchambers.co.uk

Chambers of: Miss F J Judd QC
Practice Manager: Judith Partington; Chambers Director: Simon Boutwood

Judd, Frances QC *1984*
Vater, John QC *1995*
Evans, Roger *1970*†
Rodgers, June *1971*†
Sefi, Benedict *1972*
Collinson, Alicia *1982*
Brett, Matthew *1987*
Granshaw, Sara *1991*
Potter, Louise *1993*
Goodwin, Nicholas *1995*†
Vine, Aidan *1995*
Miller, Simon *1996*
Sampson, Jonathan *1997*
Brookes-Baker, Matthew *1998*
Leong, Andrew *1998*
Wraight, Oliver *1998*
Kirkwood, Edward *1999*
Little, Helen *1999*
Jeakings, Craig *2000*
Styles, Margaret *2000*
Green, Jason *2001*
Turner, James *2001*
Brightman, Justina *2003*
Forbes, Alex *2003*
Tomlinson, *2004*
Williams, Alison *2004*
Wilkins, Chloe *2006*
Hylton, Nasstassia *2007*
Cox, Sian *2008*
Crispin, Stephen *2008*
Rayner, Emily *2009*
Sharp, Christopher QC *1975*†*
Jacklin, Susan QC *1980*†*
Higgins, Mark *2005**

Types of work
Administrative law · Care proceedings · Chancery (land law) · Company, commercial and competition · Ecclesiastical law · Education · Employment · Equity · Family law · Family provision · Local authorities · Medical negligence · Personal injury · Planning · Professional negligence · Trusts · Wills

Disability access
Disabled parking available

13 KBW

32 Beaumont Street, Oxford OX1 2NP
01865 311066
Fax: 01865 311077; DX: 145842 Oxford 6
E-mail: clerks@13kbw.co.uk

Chambers of: Mr J J Baughan QC

Disability access
Disabled parking available

CHAMBERS OF DR K LAHHAM

6 Leckford Place, Oxford OX2 6JB
07876 441513
E-mail: kl@littmanchambers.com

Chambers of: Dr K Lahham

CHAMBERS OF MISS P LLOYD

53 St John's Road, Grove, Wantage, Oxford, Oxford OX12 7NP
01235 762 312
Fax: 01235 762 312

Chambers of: Miss P Lloyd

3 PB BARRISTERS

23 Beaumont Street, Oxford OX1 2NP
01865 793 736
Fax: 01865 790 760; DX: 4302 Oxford
URL: www.3pb.co.uk
Out of hours telephone: 07808 137904 (Russell Porter - Mobile)

Chambers of: Mr Ian Lawrie QC
Clerks: David Snook, James Newman, Patrick Steptoe, Russell Porter; Lisa Wilson, Marketing Manager; Finance Manager: Head of Business Admin and Finance, Neil Monro

Also at: Bournemouth, Winchester and Bristol

Lawrie, Ian QC *1985*†
Parroy, Michael QC *1969*†
Vere-Hodge, Michael QC *1970*
Farley, Roger QC *1974*†
Jones, Stewart QC *1972*†
Braslavsky, Nicholas QC *1983*†
Bromley-Davenport, John QC *1972*
Lickley, Nigel QC *1983*†
Parker, Christopher QC *1986*†
Parrish, Samuel *1962*
Solomon, Susan *1967*
Aylwin, Christopher *1970*
Swinstead, David *1970*
Norman, Michael *1971*†
Curran, Leo *1972*
Jennings, Peter *1972*

†Recorder *Door Tenant/Associate Member

Coleman, Anthony *1973*†
Stephenson, Ben *1973*
Bartlett, David *1975*†
Tyson, Richard *1975*†
Kent, Peter *1978*
Mitchell, Nigel *1978*
Grey, Robert *1979*
Hamilton, Gavin *1979*
Leach, Robin *1979*
Leviseur, Nicholas *1979*
Partridge, Ian *1979*
Coombes, Timothy *1980*
Edge, Ian *1981*
Marshall, David *1981*
Sampson, Graeme *1981*
Strutt, Martin *1981*
Martin, Nicola *1982*
Newman, Paul *1982*
Onslow, Richard *1982*
Lomas, Mark *1983*
Stancombe, Barry *1983*
O'Hara, Sarah *1984*
Palfrey, Monty *1985*
Whittle-Martin, Lucia *1985*
Clark, Tonia *1986*
Hudson, Elisabeth *1987*
Hendry, Lucy *1988*
Rowland, Nicholas *1988*†
Zabihi, Tanya *1988*
Bradbury, Timothy *1989*
Hester, Paul *1989*
Richards, David *1989*
Aeberli, Peter *1990*
Griffiths, Hayley *1990*
Hiddleston, Adam *1990*
Knapp, Sophie *1990*
Buckley-Clarke, Amanda *1991*
Dunlop, Hamish *1991*
Katrak, Cyrus *1991*
Robins, Imogen *1991*
Ross, Iain *1991*
Bingham, Tony *1992*
Sweeney, Noel *1992*
Clargo, John *1994*
Dawson, James *1994*
Earle, Judy *1994*
Feest, Adam *1994*
Mitchell, Jack *1994*
Reid, David *1994*
Topliss, Megan *1994*
Weston, Louis *1994*
De Freitas, Melanie *1995*
McDevitt, Colin *1995*
McIlroy, David *1995*
Strachan, Elaine *1995*
Davison, James *1996*
Lorie, Andrew *1996*
Tyler, Thomas *1996*
Wilson, Lachlan *1996*
Purdy, Catherine *1997*
Sullivan, Mark *1997*
Davies, Eleanor *1998*
Griffiths, Emma *1998*
Taylor, Rufus *1998*
Horner, Robert *1999*
Kennedy, Stuart *1999*
Goodall, Rachael *2000*
Isaacs, Oliver *2000*
Jones, Rupert *2000*
O'Doherty, Paul *2000*
Sheriff, Andrew *2000*
Worton, Louise *2000*
Cassidy, Sheena *2001*
Whelan, Christopher *2001*
Wood, Catherine *2001*
Ludlow, Craig *2002*
Moss, Karen *2002*
Shillingford, Julia *2002*
Tomlinson, Michael *2002*
Courts, Robert *2003*
Gullick, Mathew *2003*
Jones, Victoria *2003*
Archer, Audrey *2004*
Davies, James *2004*
Hepworth, Elizabeth *2004*
Horder, Tom *2004*
Wheeler, Richard *2004*
Anderson, Katherine *2005*
Clarke, Sarah *2005*
Langford, Sarah *2005*
Musgrave, Anarkali *2005*
Cannings, Matthew *2006*
Da Costa, Francisca *2006*
Davies, Nick *2006*
Green, Mark *2006*
Robinson, Nick *2006*
Davies, Harriet *2007*
Elliott, Mark *2007*
Jones, Ximena *2007*
MacPhail, Andrew *2007*
Paulin, Michael *2007*
Perfect, Andrew *2007*
Dunseath, Katherine *2008*
Edwards, Christopher *2008*
Alleyne, Ebony *2009*
Ashkar, Natalie *2009*
Bowes, Gemma *2009*
Currie, Philip *2009*
Sanghera, Sharandish *2009*
Webb, Thomas *2010*
Wyeth, Stephen *2010*
Talbot-Ponsonby, Thomas *2011*

Types of work

Accountancy · Adjudication · Administrative law · Adoption · Alternative dispute resolution · Ancillary relief · Animals · Arab commercial law · Arab law · Arbitration · Asbestos-related diseases · Asset forfeiture · Asset recovery · Banking · Bills of exchange · Boundaries · Building · Care proceedings · Chancery (commercial) · Chancery (general) · Chancery (land law) · Child care law · Children · Civil actions against the police · Civil partnerships · Clinical negligence · Cohabitation · Commercial contracts · Commercial fraud · Commercial law · Commercial litigation · Commercial property · Common land · Common law (general) · Company, commercial and competition · Computer contracts · Computer crime · Computer litigation · Confiscation · Conflict of laws · Construction law · Consumer credit · Consumer law · Contracts · Copyright · Corporate finance · Corporate fraud · Corporate governance · Corporate insolvency · Corporate liability · Corporate manslaughter · Corporate recovery · Costs · Court of Protection · Courts martial · Crime · Crime and criminal due process · Criminal judicial review · Cross-border litigation and remedies · Damages · Disability discrimination · Disasters · Disciplinary procedures · Disciplinary tribunals · Discrimination · Divorce · Domestic violence injunctions · Ecclesiastical law · Economic torts · Education · Election law · Employment · Engineering disputes · Equine law · Equity · Factoring · Family law · Family provision · Financial provision · Financial services · Firearms · Foreign law · Franchising · Fraud · Freezing orders · Guarantees · Health and safety · Holiday injury and damages · Homicide · Housing · Industrial deafness · Industrial diseases · Information technology · Inheritance and cohabitees · Inquests · Insolvency · Insurance · Intellectual property · International arbitration · International commercial arbitration · International fraud and asset tracing · Islamic family law · Islamic law · Judicial review · Landlord and tenant · Lands Tribunal · Licensing · Matrimonial finance · Mediation · Medical negligence · Middle Eastern law · Military law · Multi-party litigation · Occupational diseases · Partnerships · Passing off · Personal injury · Personal insolvency · Planning · Police · Product liability · Professional negligence · Public law · Real property · Regulatory and disciplinary law · Rights of light · Rights of way · Road traffic · Sale and carriage of goods · Serial crime · Serious fraud · Shareholder agreements · Succession · Tax · Technology and Construction Court · Torts · Trust litigation · Trusts · Wardship · Wills

PANGBOURNE CHAMBERS

22 Reading Road, Pangbourne RG8 7LY
07710 348055; DX: 54652 Pangbourne

Chambers of: Mr P H M Binder

CHAMBERS OF MRS HATFIELD-HADJIIOANNOU

Office 105, 1st Floor, Nicolaou Court, Corner of Eleftheriou, Venizelou & Kaningos, Paphos 8021
E-mail: harisruth@cytanet.com.cy

Chambers of: Mrs R E Hatfield-Hadjiioannou

FOXHILL CHAMBERS

Matterdale, Penrith, Cumbria CA11 0SA
01768 482710
Fax: 01768 482032
E-mail: clerking@foxhillchambers.com

Chambers of: Dr T P McGee

Disability access
Staff briefed or trained on duties under the disability legislation, Wheelchair access, Disabled parking available

PERIVALE CHAMBERS

Ground Floor, 15 Colwyn Avenue, Perivale, Middlesex UB6 8JX
020 8998 1935
E-mail: naushadahmed@hotmail.com

Chambers of: Mr S Ahmed

CHAMBERS OF MR M MASELLI

99 St Paul's Road, Peterborough PE1 3DR
07786 320064
E-mail: maselli@tiscali.co.uk

Chambers of: Mr M Maselli

PRIESTGATE CHAMBERS

26 Priestgate, Peterborough PE1 1WG
01733 865 042
Fax: 01733 865 038; DX: 12317 Peterborough
E-mail: clerks@priestgatechambers.co.uk

Chambers of: Miss F Akram

REGENCY CHAMBERS

45 Priestgate, Peterborough PE1 1LB
01733 315215
Fax: 01733 565 967; DX: 12349 Peterborough1
E-mail: clerks@regencychambers.law.co.uk

Chambers of: Mr I R Martignetti

Disability access
Wheelchair access, Disabled parking available

INGENUITY IP CHAMBERS

Chambers Legal Service, 71b Queensway, Petts Wood, Kent BR5 1DQ DX: 398 London Chancery Lane
E-mail: lp@chamberslegalservice.com

Chambers of: Mr J V Fitzgerald

VICTOR HOUSE CHAMBERS

Victor House, Westfied Road, Pitstone, Bedfordshire LU7 9GW
01296 664043
Fax: 01296 662852; DX: 90813 Leighton Buzzard
E-mail: clerks@victorhouse.co.uk

Flatt, Catherine *2002*

Types of work
Civil litigation · Commercial contracts · Coroners · Family law · Landlord and tenant · Personal injury · Road traffic

DEVON CHAMBERS

3 St Andrew Street, Plymouth PL1 2AH
01752 661659
Fax: 01752 601346; DX: 8290 Plymouth 2
E-mail: clerks@devonchambers.co.uk
URL: www.devonchambers.co.uk

Chambers of: Mr R F Linford
Clerk: Hollie Gilbery

Linford, Robert Frank *1987*†
Rowsell, Paul *1971*
Richardson, Garth *1975*
Van Den Berg, Barrie *1978*
Howard, Graham *1987*
Bailey, Edward *1990*
Taylor, Rupert *1990*
Beal, Jason *1993*
Quaife, Ramsay *1995*
Bitmead, Paul *1996*
Frampton, Stuart *1998*
James, Russell *2001*
Norsworthy, Piers *2001*
Scrivener, Kelly *2001*
Dors, Matthew *2004*
Martin, Joanna *2005*
Cox, Julia *2006*
Vince, Sarah *2007*
Daulton, Sally *2009*
Lickley, Nigel QC *1983*†*

Types of work
Admiralty · Agriculture · Arbitration · Care proceedings · Civil liberties · Common land · Common law (general) · Construction law · Corporate fraud · Courts martial · Crime · Education · Employment · Environment · Family law · Family provision · Health and safety · Housing · Immigration · Information technology · Insolvency · Landlord and tenant · Licensing · Local authorities · Medical negligence · Mental health · Personal injury · Personal insolvency · Planning · Professional negligence · Sale and carriage of goods · Shipping · Sport · Utilities

Disability access
Staff briefed or trained on duties under the disability legislation, Wheelchair access

KING'S BENCH AND GODOLPHIN (KBG)CHAMBERS

115 North Hill, Plymouth, Devon PL4 8JY
01752 221551
Fax: 01752 664379; DX: 8237 Plymouth 1
E-mail: clerks@kbgchambers.co.uk

Chambers of: Mr C D Elliott, Miss G L Small

Disability access
Staff briefed or trained on duties under the disability legislation, Disabled parking available

YEALM HOUSE CHAMBERS

88-90 Yealm Road, Plymouth PL8 1BL
01752 873227
E-mail: petertelford@hotmail.co.uk

Chambers of: Mr P Telford

THE CHAMBERS OF MR VAUGHAN-WILLIAMS

Manxonia House, Bay View Road, Port St Mary IM9 4AE
01624 836 757
Fax: 01624 836 758
E-mail: barrister@manx.net

Chambers of: Mr A L Vaughan-Williams

GUILDHALL CHAMBERS PORTSMOUTH

Prudential Buildings, 16 Guildhall Walk, Portsmouth, Hampshire PO1 2DE
023 9275 2400
Fax: 023 9275 3100; DX: 2225 Portsmouth
E-mail: clerks@gcp-barristers.com
URL: www.gcp-barristers.com
Out of hours telephone: 023 9275 2400
Clerk: Tristan Thwaites (Senior Clerk); Administrator: Stephanie Mezulis

Fortune, Peter *1978*
Colbey, Richard *1984*
Brookes, Lincoln *1992*
England, Lisa *1992*
Concannon, Timothy *1993*
Hall, Yasmin *1993*
Jenking-Rees, Laura *2002*
Marchesi, Camilla *2004*
Uddin, Taj *2010*

Types of work
Adoption · Ancillary relief · Anti-social Behaviour Orders · Arbitration · Boundaries · Care proceedings · Chancery (commercial) · Chancery (general) · Child abduction · Child abuse · Child care law · Children · Civil actions against the police · Civil fraud · Civil liberties · Clinical negligence · Cohabitation · Commercial law · Commercial litigation · Commercial property · Common law (general) · Company, commercial and competition · Confiscation · Consumer credit · Contracts · Coroner's inquests · Corporate manslaughter · Court of Protection · Crime · Criminal judicial review · Customs · Damages · Disciplinary procedures · Disciplinary tribunals · Divorce · Domestic violence injunctions · Employment · Family law · Family provision · Fraud · Freezing orders · Health and safety · Inquests · Insolvency · Insurance · Intellectual property · Judicial review · Landlord and tenant · Licensing · Matrimonial ·

†Recorder *Door Tenant/Associate Member

Matrimonial finance · Medical negligence · Motor vehicles · Partnerships · Personal injury · Personal insolvency · Planning · Private children law · Professional negligence · Public inquiries · Public law · Real property · Road haulage · Road traffic · Road traffic offences · Sale and carriage of goods · Torts · Unmarried couples · Wardship

Disability access
Staff briefed or trained on duties under the disability legislation, Wheelchair access, Disabled parking available

HAMPSHIRE CHAMBERS

Malton House, 24 Hampshire Terrace, Portsmouth, Hampshire PO1 2QF
023 9282 6636
Fax: 023 9229 7101; DX: 2270 Portsmouth
E-mail: PMC.CLERK@BTCONNECT.COM

Chambers of: Dr P M McCormick

Disability access
Staff briefed or trained on duties under the disability legislation, Disabled parking available

PORTSMOUTH BARRISTERS'CHAMBERS

Victory House, 7 Bellevue Terrace, Portsmouth, Hampshire PO5 3AT
023 9283 1292
Fax: 023 9229 1262; DX: 2239 Portsmouth
E-mail: clerks@portsmouthbar.com
URL: www.portsmouthbar.com
Out of hours telephone: 07970 779671

Chambers of: Mr A J Parsons
Clerk: Jackie Morrison

Parsons, Andrew *1985*

Types of work
Admiralty · Agency · Alternative dispute resolution · Ancillary relief · Arbitration · Banking · Boating · Boundaries · Breach of confidence · Building · Chancery (commercial) · Chancery (general) · Chancery (land law) · Civil fraud · Civil partnerships · Clinical negligence · Cohabitation · Commercial contracts · Commercial fraud · Commercial law · Commercial litigation · Commercial property · Common law (general) · Company, commercial and competition · Conciliation · Confidential information · Construction law · Contracts · Copyright · Corporate finance · Design · Dispute resolution · Dry shipping · Economic torts · Engineering disputes · Equity · Family law · Family provision · Financial provision · Financial services · Franchising · Freezing orders · Guarantees · Inheritance and cohabitees · Insolvency · Intellectual property · International trade · Landlord and tenant · Matrimonial · Matrimonial finance · Mediation · Medical negligence · Mortgages · Multi-party litigation · Partnerships · Passing off · Pensions · Personal injury · Professional negligence · Real property · Registered designs · Remedies · Restraint of trade · Rights of light · Rights of way · Sale and carriage of goods · Sale of business · Share options · Shareholder agreements · Shipping · Solicitor's indemnity · Technical contracts · Technology and Construction Court · Title to land · Torts · Trade secrets · Trademarks · Trust litigation · Unincorporated associations · Unmarried couples · Unregistered designs · Warranty claims · Wills

CHAMBERS OF MR J WARD-PROWSE

317 Havant Road, Farlington, Portsmouth, Hampshire PO6 1DD
0239 237 9708
Fax: 0239 234 6859; DX: 94955 Cosham (Portsmouth)
E-mail: j.wp@hotmail.com

Chambers of: Mr J Ward-Prowse

DEANS COURT CHAMBERS

101 Walker Street, Preston PR1 2RR
01772 565 600
Fax: 01772 565 601
E-mail: preston@deanscourt.co.uk
URL: www.deanscourt.co.uk

Chambers of: Mr M G Turner QC
Clerk: Matthew Gibbons (Senior Clerk)

Turner, Mark QC *1981*†
Grime, Stephen QC *1970*
Fish, David QC *1973*†
Horlock, Timothy QC *1981*
Field, Patrick QC *1981*†
Sephton, Craig QC *1981*
Bromley-Davenport, John QC *1972*
Denney, Stuart QC *1982*
Grocott, Susan QC *1986*†
Cross, Jane QC *1982*
Heaton, Frances QC *1985*†
Atherton, Peter *1975*†
Eccles, David *1976*
Ryder, Timothy *1977*†
Trippier, Ruth *1978*
Davies, Hugh *1982*
Smith, Timothy *1982*†
Davies, Russell *1983*
Trotman, Timothy *1983*
Jackson, Wayne *1984*
Bancroft, Louise *1985*
Campbell, Glenn *1985*
Brody, Karen *1986*†
Humphries, Paul *1986*
Hobson, Heather *1987*
Hudson, Christopher *1987*†
Grimshaw, Nicholas *1988*

Rankin, Ciaran *1988*
Singh-Hayer, Bansa *1988*
Grace, Jonathan *1989*
Kitching, Robin *1989*
Smith, Michael *1989*
Cheetham, Julia *1990*
Courtney, Nicholas *1990*
Alty, Andrew *1992*
Edge, Timothy *1992*
Ironfield, Janet *1992*
Livesey, Fraser *1992*
Woodward, Alison *1992*
Hayton, Michael *1993*
Horgan, Peter *1993*
Judge, Lisa *1993*
Savill, Mark *1993*
Clegg, Sebastian *1994*
Fothergill, Francesca *1994*
Rothery, Peter *1994*
Bland, Carolyn *1995*
Boyle, David *1996*
Higgins, Paul *1996*
McCann, Simon *1996*
Dudley-Jones, Elizabeth *1997*
Cartwright, Sophie *1998*
Moody, Joanna *1998*
Paul, Daniel *1998*
Watkinson, Sasha *1998*
Whitehall, Richard *1998*
Booth, Sarah *1999*
Hicks, Pascale *1999*
Morton, Elizabeth *1999*
Olson, Ross *1999*
Hart, Joseph *2000*
Earnshaw, Zoe *2001*
Emsley-Smith, Ros *2001*
McMaster, Robert *2001*
Singh, Anthony *2001*
Poole, Alex *2002*
Heyworth, Victoria *2003*
Taylor, Alexander *2003*
Tyler, William *2003*
Bentley, Anna *2004*
Brown, Michelle *2005*
Lally, Jonathan *2005*
Walters, Carly *2005*
Harrison, Victoria *2006*
Greenwood, Rachel *2008*
Burke, Samuel *2009*
King, Jonathan *2009*
Sharron, Eliza *2009*

Types of work
Arbitration · Banking · Care proceedings · Chancery (general) · Chancery (land law) · Clinical negligence · Commercial litigation · Common law (general) · Construction law · Corporate fraud · Crime · Employment · Environment · Equity · Family law · Family provision · Health and safety · Information technology · Insolvency · Insurance · Landlord and tenant · Licensing · Medical negligence · Personal injury · Personal insolvency · Professional negligence · Sale and carriage of goods · Trusts · Wills

NEW BAILEY CHAMBERS

3 The Light Buildings, 99 Walker Street, Preston PR1 2RR
01772 258 087
Fax: 01772 880100; DX: 710050 Preston 10
E-mail: clerks@newbailey.com

Chambers of: Mr K S Thomas

Disability access
Staff briefed or trained on duties under the disability legislation, Wheelchair access, Disabled parking available

ORIEL CHAMBERS

18 Ribblesdale Place, Preston PR1 3NA
01772 254 764
Fax: 01772 554 910; DX: 714583 Preston 14
E-mail: clerks@oriel-chambers.co.uk

Chambers of: Mr R Bradley

Disability access
Staff briefed or trained on duties under the disability legislation, Wheelchair access

16 WINCKLEY SQUARE

16 Winckley Square, Preston PR1 3JJ
01772 256100
Fax: 01772 251101; DX: 714582 Preston 14

Chambers of: Mr M H Redfern QC

CHAMBERS OF MR KEVIN TALBOT

Highfield House, Whittingham Lane, Haighton, Preston, Lancashire PR2 5SL
01772 652102
Fax: 01772 652102
E-mail: kevin.talbot@hotmail.co,uk

Chambers of: Mr R K Talbot

Disability access
Staff briefed or trained on duties under the disability legislation, Wheelchair access, Disabled parking available

15 WINCKLEY SQUARE

15 Winckley Square, Preston PR1 3JJ
01772 252828
Fax: 01772 258520; DX: 17110 Preston1
E-mail: clerks@15winckleysq.co.uk

Disability access
Wheelchair access, Disabled parking available

CHAMBERS OF MR GARY CUMBERLAND

26919 Whitestone Road, Rancho Palos Verdes, California 90275
001 310 377 0220
E-mail: glcrpv@yahoo.com

Chambers of: Mr G L Cumberland

D

D

EASTMANS CHAMBERS

41 St Bartholomew's Road, Reading, Berkshire RG1 3QA
0118 966 9094
Fax: 0118 966 9094
E-mail: eastmans@hotmail.co.uk

Chambers of: Mr M A Ajaz

THE CHAMBERS OF MR J GIRET QC

Portobello, 3 Hollycross, Crazies Hill, Reading, Berkshire RG10 8QB
07850 101062
Fax: 01189 401500
E-mail: joseph@giret.co.uk

Chambers of: Mr J J B L Giret QC

CHAMBERS OF MR J P DE MOUNTENEY

1 Whistley Court Farm, Lodge Road, Hurst, Reading, Berkshire RG10 0EJ
0118 934 6822
E-mail: jonathan.demounteney@virgin.net

Chambers of: Mr J P De Mounteney

CHAMBERS OF MICHAEL PHILLIPS

24 Green Road, Earley, Reading RG6 7BS
01189 260 880
E-mail: michaelbertramphillips@yahoo.com

Chambers of: Mr M B Phillips

CHAMBERS OF MRS S THOMSON

Marron Remise, Hennerton, Reading, Berkshire RG10 8PD
01189 406387
Fax: 01189 406387
E-mail: sallythomson.law@googlemail.com

Chambers of: Mrs S M Thomson

WARRENSIDE CHAMBERS

Blew Garth, The Warren, Caversham, Reading RG4 7TH
00 353 87631 2205; DX: 818222 Dublin

Chambers of: Mr A P Dowling-Hussey

3 WAYSIDE GREEN

3 Wayside Green, Woodcote, Reading, South Oxfordshire RG8 0PR
01491 680722
E-mail: cathy@cathygordon.co.uk

Chambers of: Miss C A Gordon

CHAMBERS OF MR GEORGE SPEED

25 Northfield Way, Hallcroft, Retford, Nottinghamshire DN22 7LJ
07968 986926
E-mail: geo_speed@hotmail.com

Chambers of: Mr G C Speed

CHAMBERS OF MR R H BRUCE

P.O. Box 748, Richmond TW9 2WU
020 8940 5895
Fax: 020 8255 4170; DX: 100253 Richmond 2
E-mail: richardhbruce@aol.com

Chambers of: Mr R H Bruce

Disability access
Disabled parking available

CHAMBERS OF MR J H DOERFEL

Parkshot House, 5 Kew Road, Richmond, Surrey TW9 2PR
0845 123 1234
Fax: 0845 430 4321
E-mail: jandoerfel@yahoo.com

Chambers of: Mr J H J Doerfel

CHAMBERS OF MR M G JACKSON

37 Old Deer Park Gardens, Richmond, Surrey TW9 2TN
020 8251 7661
Fax: 020 8251 7661
E-mail: mylesgjackson@hotmail.com

Chambers of: Mr M G Jackson

RICHMOND GREEN CHAMBERS

5 Connaught Road, Richmond, Surrey TW10 6DW
020 8948 4801
E-mail: richmondchambers@btconnect.com

Chambers of: Mr P B Taylor MBE

Disability access
Staff briefed or trained on duties under the disability legislation, Disabled parking available

SURREY CHAMBERS RICHMOND

Argyle House, 1 Dee Road, Richmond, Surrey TW9 2JN
020 8322 7785

Chambers of: Mr J W Melvin

SWAN CHAMBERS

Parkshot House, 5 Kew Road, Richmond, Surrey TW9 2PR
0845 123 1234
Fax: 0845 430 4321
E-mail: shobana@mycommercialbarrister.com

Chambers of: Miss S Iyer

TWEEDDALE CHAMBERS

3 Atwood Avenue, Kew, Richmond, Surrey TW9 4HF
020 8940 9896
E-mail: tweeddale@blueyonder.co.uk

Chambers of: Mrs K D Tweeddale

CHAMBERS OF MR L RAHMAN

201 Maidstone Road, Rochester, Kent ME1 3ES
07947 588362
E-mail: luthfur99@gmail.com

Chambers of: Mr L Rahman

WILLINGDON CHAMBERS

Chapel Wood House, Knapp Lane, Ampfield, Romsey SO51 9BT
E-mail: rebecca@willingdonmediation.co.uk

CHAMBERS OF MR J D S WISHART

7 Lower Cribden Avenue, Rawtenstall, Rossendale, Lancashire BB4 6SW
01706 220495
Fax: 01706 220495
E-mail: johnwishart@fsmail.net

Chambers of: Mr J D S Wishart

6 NEWMAN AVENUE

6 Newman Avenue, Royston, Hertfordshire SG8 7LE
01763 221993
E-mail: peter.masniuk-bar@ntlworld.com

Chambers of: Mr P Masniuk

OVERSEAS CHAMBERS

Chestnut Farm, Le Mont du Ouaisne, Saint Brelade, Jersey JE3 8AW
01534 625879
Fax: 01534 491195
E-mail: peter.harris@overseaschambers.com

Chambers of: Mr R P Harris

Disability access
Wheelchair access, Disabled parking available

LONDON VIEW CHAMBERS

24 Highgate Grove, Sawbridgeworth CM21 0DD
07788 912493
Fax: 020 8711 2196

Chambers of: Mr M Iqbal

PRINCIPAL CHAMBERS

15 Lime Tree Walk, Sevenoaks, Kent TN13 1YH
0845 209 8080
Fax: 0845 208 8282; DX: 30030 Sevenoaks

D

BANK HOUSE CHAMBERS

Old Bank House, Hartshead, Sheffield S1 2EL
0114 275 1223
Fax: 0114 276 8439; DX: 10522 Sheffield
E-mail: w.digby@bankhousechambers.co.uk
URL: www.bankhousechambers.co.uk
Out of hours telephone: 07712 577235

Chambers of: Mr J S Baird
Clerks: Mr Wayne Digby, Mr David Harrison, Miss Chantelle Bedworth; Administrator: Karen Davis

Baird, James *1977†*
Carus, Roderick QC *1971†*
Garside, Charles QC *1971†*
Aspinall, John QC *1971*
Clarke, Nicholas QC *1981†*
Smith, Shaun QC *1981*
Cranfield, Tony *1975*
Mason, David *1979*
Hillis, John *1982*
Syed, Gulzar *1983*
Sheldon, Richard *1984†*
Goddard, Katherine *1987*
Tonge, Christopher *1988*
O'Shea, Paul *1989*
Singh, Gurdial *1989*
Tighe, Dawn *1989*
Hawkins, David *1991*
Pimm, Peter *1991†*
Smith, Andrew MBE *1991*
Dorrell, Alison *1992*
Walker, Fiona *1992*
Upson, Michael *1993*
Cole, Justine *1994*
McGinty, Robert *1994*
Weir, Olivia *1995*
West, Ian *1996*
Cane-Soothill, Michael *1997*
Gould, James *1997*
Alam, Zaiban *1998*
Cotton, Heidi *1998*
Webster, David *1998*
Sandford, Robert *1999*
Wrottesley, Angela *1999*
Hussain, Nawaz *2000*
Clark, Robert *2002*
Jones, Kevin *2003*
Pallo, Simon *2003*
Horne, James *2004*
Huggins, Bianca *2004*
Stanbury, Louise *2004*
Bhatty, Farah *2005*
Morley, Kate *2006*
Chu, Josephine *2007*
Dodgson, Lance *2007*
Wheatley, Jane *2007*
Horne, David *2009*
Holsgrove, Jonathan *2011*

Types of work
Ancillary relief · Arbitration · Care proceedings · Chancery (general) · Civil law · Common law (general) · Corporate fraud · Courts martial · Crime · Employment · Family law · Health and safety · Housing · Immigration · Landlord and tenant · Matrimonial · Personal injury · Personal insolvency · Prison law · Public law

Disability access
Staff briefed or trained on duties under the disability legislation, Wheelchair access, Disabled parking available

ENIGMA CHAMBERS

Troway Hall, Troway Marsh Lane, Sheffield S21 5RU
07779 576499
Fax: 01246 413809
E-mail: law@enigmachambers.co.uk

Chambers of: Mr G Norton

Disability access
Staff briefed or trained on duties under the disability legislation, Wheelchair access, Disabled parking available

THE CHAMBERS OF MR M A IQBAL

111 West Street, Sheffield S1 4EQ
0114 201 4321
Fax: 0114 220 3805
E-mail: maziqbal@hotmail.com

Chambers of: Mr M A Iqbal

ST JOHNS BUILDINGS

26 Paradise Square, Sheffield, South Yorkshire S1 2DE
0114 273 8951
Fax: 0114 276 0848; DX: 10565 Sheffield
E-mail: clerks@paradise-sq.co.uk
URL: www.stjohnsbuildings.com
Out of hours telephone: 07850 193895; 07870 657202
Clerk: Timothy Booth

Chambers of: Mr A P Hayden QC

Also at: 24a–28 St John Street, Manchester M3 4DJ. Tel: 0161 214 1500; Fax: 0161 835 3929. DX: 728861 Manchester 4

Also at: 21 White Friars, Chester CH1 1NZ. Tel: 01244 323 070; Fax: 01244 323 930; DX: 19979 Chester.

Also at: 16 Winckley Square, Preston PR1 3JJ. Tel: 01772 256100; Fax: 01772 251101; DX: 714582 Preston 14.

Also at: 8th Floor India Buildings, Water Street, Liverpool L2 0XG. Tel: 0151 243 6000; Fax: 0151 243 6040; DX: 14227 Liverpool.

Hayden, Anthony QC *1987†*
Watson, Paul QC *1978†*
Redfern, Michael QC *1970†*
Berkley, David QC *1979†*
O'Byrne, Andrew QC *1978*
Samuels, Jeffrey QC *1988*
Harrison, Sally QC *1992*
Thomas, Keith *1969*
Phillips, Bernard *1970†*
Green, Roger *1972*
Hedgecoe, John *1972*
Herman, Raymond *1972†*
Neale, Nicholas L *1972*
Bedford, Stephen *1974†*

McNeill, John *1974*
Shannon, Eric *1974*
Lowe, Geoffrey *1975*†
Andrews, Philip *1977*
Feeny, Charles *1977*
Longworth, Antony *1978*
Grundy, Philip *1980*†
Mercer, David *1980*
Owen, Gail *1980*†
Long, Andrew *1981*
Uff, David *1981*
Bruce, David *1982*
Gal, Sonia *1982*†
Garside, David *1982*
Holt, Julian *1982*
Harrison, Keith *1983*
Harrison, Peter *1983*
Khawar, Aftab *1983*
McKee, Hugh *1983*
McKenna, Brian *1983*
Slater, Michael *1983*†
Pickup, David *1984*
Shaw, Julian *1984*†
Wright, Sarah *1984*
Kennedy, Michael *1985*
Lloyd, Julian *1985*
Dickinson, Jonathan *1986*
Gray, Richard *1986*
Taylor, Julian *1986*†
Brennand, Timothy *1987*
Dagnall, Jane M *1987*
Oates, John *1987*
Walker, Jane *1987*
Batra, Bunty *1988*
Crabtree, Simon *1988*
Davitt, Paula *1988*
Eastwood, Charles *1988*
Sanders, Damian *1988*
Blakey, Michael *1989*
Britcliffe, Anne *1989*
Grundy, Clare *1989*
Holder, Simon *1989*
O'Brien, Joseph *1989*
Partington, Lisa *1989*
Carter, Richard *1990*
Groom, Ian *1990*
Jackson, Adrian *1990*
Rosario, Desmond *1990*
Thompson, Jonathan *1990*
Thompson, Patrick *1990*†
Watson, David *1990*
Chaudhry, Zia *1991*
Edwards, Mererid *1991*†
Mawdsley, Matthew *1991*
Roberts, Mark *1991*
Savage, Timothy *1991*
Taylor, Jonathan *1991*
Wright, Alastair *1991*
Ashmole, Timothy *1992*
Case, Magdalen *1992*
Green, Andrew *1992*
Lloyd, Gaynor *1992*
McNerney, Kevin *1992*
Norton, Richard *1992*
Blackshaw, Henry *1993*
Fitzharris, Ginnette *1993*
Ford, Caroline *1993*
Gibson, John *1993*†
Harrison, Rachael *1993*
Harrison, Leona *1993*†
Hughes, Dermot *1993*
Jones, Ben *1993*
Kloss, Alexander W *1993*
Mathieson, Guy A D *1993*†
Newton, Stuart *1993*
Nijabat, Shama *1993*
Orme, Richard *1993*
Polglase, David *1993*
Rodikis, Joanna *1993*
Searle, Jason *1993*
Stanistreet, Penelope *1993*
Wilson, Myles *1993*
Booth, Nigel *1994*
Chukwuemeka, John *1994*
Connor, Mark *1994*
Douglas, Stephen *1994*
Frieze, Daniel *1994*
Gumbs, Annette P *1994*
Houghton, Lisa *1994*
Lowe, Craig *1994*
Mann, Sara *1994*
Reynolds, Gary *1994*
Rhys, Megan Jill *1994*
Rowley, Karl *1994*†
Wild, Steven *1994*
Hargan, Carl *1995*
Kelly, Siobhan *1995*
Lawson, Andrew *1995*
McHugh, Pauline M *1995*
Parry, Philip *1995*
Simkin, Iain *1995*
Stables, Gordon *1995*
Aslett, Pepin *1996*
Crilley, Darrel *1996*
Mintz, Simon *1996*
Sastry, Bob *1996*
Bailey, Andrew *1997*
Denton, Douglas *1997*
Evans, Simeon *1997*
Goldsack, Ian *1997*
Mahmood, Ghazan *1997*
Mensah, Lorraine *1997*
Parry, Simon *1997*
Tyler, Paula *1997*
Williams, Zillah *1997*
Zentar, Remy *1997*
Bentley, David *1998*
Buckley, Patrick *1998*
Burnell, Kate *1998*
Edwards, Susan *1998*
James, David *1998*
Murdin, Liam *1998*
Muth, Susanne *1998*
Simmonds, Alexandra *1998*
Stockwell, Matthew *1998*
Taylor, David *1998*
Thomas, Clare *1998*
Astbury, Philip *1999*
Deas, Susan *1999*
Holsgrove, Lara *1999*
Lord, Andrew *1999*
Ratledge, John *1999*
Sweeney, Linda *1999*
Cavanagh, Lorraine *2000*
Hayes, Kathryn *2000*
Leach, Natasha *2000*
Ahmed, Siraj *2001*
Blewitt, Jennifer *2001*
Bridgman, Andrew *2001*
Farley, David *2001*
King, Oliver *2001*
Marshall, Laura Jane *2001*
Pojur, David *2001*
Porter-Phillips, Clare *2001*
Quinney, Nicola *2001*
Van-Der-Haer, Audrey *2001*
Vir Singh, Sylvia *2001*
Wynne, Andrew *2001*
Hodgkinson, Paul *2002*
Malam, James *2002*
McCloskey, Louise *2002*
Menzies, Jennifer *2002*
Montaldo, Neil *2002*
Moss, Christopher *2002*
Mottram, Cheryl *2002*
Owen, Wendy *2002*
Rawlinson, Michael J *2002*
Senior, Mark *2002*
Smith, Paul *2002*
Smith, Rebecca *2002*
Thyne, Richard *2002*
Akers, Robert *2003*
Ali, Kashif *2003*
Hudson, Abigail *2003*
Lawrence, Benjamin *2003*
Maguire, Clodagh *2003*
Newstead, Jennifer *2003*
Quigley, Louise *2003*
Abraham, Jade *2004*
Connolly, Timothy *2004*
Cooper, Douglas *2004*
Greenhalgh, Jane *2004*
Harrison, Peta *2004*
Hickinbottom, Abigail *2004*
Murphy, Paul *2004*
Poole, William *2004*
Rimmer, Catherine *2004*
Samuel, Ana *2004*
Sutton, Rebecca *2004*
Waddell, Philippa *2004*
Watkins, Adam *2004*
Wilson, Helen *2004*
Christian, Neil *2005*
De Navarro, Frances *2005*
Marshall, Lucy *2005*
McGarry, Steven *2005*
Spencer, Shaun *2005*
Thompson, Gareth *2005*
White, Debra *2005*
Bower, Laurinda *2006*
Flynn, Steven *2006*
Goode, Julian *2006*
Kelly, Ben *2006*
Pare, Christopher *2006*
Rae, Louise *2006*
Rook, Rachael *2006*
Scully, Jenny *2006*
Wilkinson, Timothy *2006*
Allen, Fergal *2007*
Erlen, Nicole *2007*
Haggis, Andrew *2007*
Owen-Casey, Neil *2007*
Pemberton, Jessica *2007*
Vanderpump, Henry *2007*
Wood, Hannah *2007*
Bellamy, Jonathan *2008*
Cooper, Elisabeth *2008*
England, Laura *2008*
Garcha, Sukhdev *2008*
Gomer, Elis *2008*
Maddison, Simon *2008*
Metcalfe, Daniel *2008*
Murray, Simon *2008*
Walker, Hannah *2008*
Williams, Cerys *2008*
Baines, David *2009*
Edwards, Thomas *2009*
Nash, Laura *2009*
Roberts, Elliw *2009*

Types of work

Administrative law · Agriculture · Animals · Anti-social Behaviour Orders · Arbitration · Asset recovery · Asylum · Banking · Building societies · Capital tax · Care proceedings · Chancery · Chancery (general) · Charities · Children · Civil fraud · Civil law · Civil liberties · Civil litigation · Civil partnerships · Civil recovery · Cohabitation · Commercial fraud · Commercial law · Commercial litigation ·

†Recorder *Door Tenant/Associate Member

D

Commodities · Common law (general) · Company law · Company, commercial and competition · Competition law · Computer crime · Confidential information · Conflict of laws · Constitutional law · Construction law · Consumer credit · Consumer law · Contracts · Copyright · Coroners · Corporate finance · Corporate fraud · Corporate manslaughter · Costs · Council tax · Crime · Crime and criminal due process · Criminal judicial review · Cross-border litigation and remedies · Customs · Data protection · Design · Disasters · Disciplinary procedures · Discrimination · Dispute resolution · Domestic violence injunctions · EC competition law · ECHR · Education · Employee benefit trusts · Employment · Energy · Entertainment · Environment · Equity · Excise · Extradition · Family law · Family provision · Financial instruments · Financial services · Fire and other property damage claims · Firearms · Fraud · Freedom of expression · Freezing orders · Funding arrangements · Gaming and lotteries · Group litigation · Guarantees · Health and safety · Healthcare law · Highways · Homicide · Housing · Income tax · Industrial relations law · Information technology · Insolvency · Insurance (long term) · International criminal law · Internet law · Investments · Labour arbitration · Landlord and tenant · Legal advice · Licensing · Local authorities · Malicious prosecution · Markets and fairs · Matrimonial · Media · Media and entertainment · Medical negligence · Mental health · Military law · Mining · Money laundering · Multi-party litigation · National Insurance · Offshore trust litigation · Parliamentary · Partnerships · Passing off · Patents · Pensions · Personal injury · Personal insolvency · Planning · Police · Prison law · Privacy · Procurement · Professional negligence · Public access · Public health · Public law · Publishing · Rating and CPO · Real property · Regulatory and disciplinary law · Regulatory crime · Remedies · Road traffic · Securities law and regulation · Serial crime · Sexual Offences · Social welfare · Society of Lloyd's · Special Guardianship · Stamp duty · Succession · Tax · Telecommunications · Terrorism · Torts · Trade secrets · Trademarks · Travel law · Trust litigation · Trusts · Unincorporated associations · Unmarried couples · Utilities · VAT · Water

Disability access

Staff briefed or trained on duties under the disability legislation, Wheelchair access, Disabled parking available

SHERIDAN CHAMBERS

Knaresbrook, King Edward Road, Shenley, Herts WD7 9BY

01923 856 345

E-mail: norman.sheridan@gmail.com

Chambers of: Mr N P Sheridan

Disability access

Staff briefed or trained on duties under the disability legislation, Disabled parking available

ABBEY CHAMBERS

PO Box 47, 47 Ashurst Drive, Shepperton, Middlesex TW17 0LD

01932 560913

Fax: 01932 567764

E-mail: arthurjames27@btinternet.com

Chambers of: Mr A R James

Disability access

Staff briefed or trained on duties under the disability legislation, Disabled parking available

RIVER CHAMBERS

81 Underdale Road, Shrewsbury, Shropshire SY2 5EF

01743 350505

Fax: 01743 350505

E-mail: richard@riverchambers.com

Chambers of: Mr R F Powell

Disability access

Staff briefed or trained on duties under the disability legislation, Disabled parking available

CORNWALL STREET CHAMBERS

Shrewsbury Annex, Rural Enterprise Centre, Stafford Drive, Battlefield Enterprise Park, Shrewsbury SY1 3FE

01743 363 611/0121 233 7500

Fax: 01743 363 622/0121 233 7501

HILLWOOD CHAMBERS

Hillwood, Stockers Hill Road, Rodmersham Green, Sittingbourne, Kent ME9 0PJ
01795 472741; DX: 42700 Oxford Circus North

THE CHAMBERS OF MRS MAGARET HODGSON

1 Court Crescent, Slough, Berkshire SL1 3JP
01753 539260
Fax: 01753 539260
E-mail: r.andm.hodgson@talk21.com

Chambers of: Mrs M A Hodgson

SLOUGH BARRISTERS CHAMBER

11 St. Bernards Road, Slough, Berkshire SL3 7NT
01753 553806
Fax: 01753 553806
E-mail: arden_bhattacharya2000@yahoo.co.uk

Chambers of: Mr A Bhattacharyya

Disability access
Staff briefed or trained on duties under the disability legislation, Wheelchair access, Disabled parking available

GREENWAY

Sonning Lane, Sonning-on-Thames, Berkshire RG4 6ST
0118 969 2484
Fax: 0118 969 2484
E-mail: jackdenbin@btinternet.com

Chambers of: Mr J A Denbin

Disability access
Staff briefed or trained on duties under the disability legislation

EIGHTEEN CARLTON CRESCENT

Rownhams House, Rownhams, Southampton SO16 8LF
023 8063 9001; DX: 96877 Southampton 10
E-mail: clerks@18carltoncrescent.co.uk

Chambers of: Mr H R A Martineau

Disability access
Staff briefed or trained on duties under the disability legislation, Disabled parking available

COLLEGE CHAMBERS

19 Carlton Crescent, Southampton, Hampshire SO15 2ET
023 8023 0338
Fax: 023 8023 0376; DX: 38533 Southampton3
E-mail: clerks@college-chambers.co.uk
URL: www.college-chambers.co.uk
Out of hours telephone: 07748 984852

Chambers of: Mr R W Belben, Mr D S Marshall
Clerks: Mark Windebank (First Junior Clerk), Natalie Alani (Junior Clerk), Sophie Lanzoni (Junior Clerk), Sofala Stokes (Fees Clerk), Wayne Effeny (Senior Clerk); Administrator: Clare Evans; Aisha Gentles

Belben, Robin *1969*†
Marshall, Derek *1980*
Lillington, Simon *1980*
Taylor, Douglas *1981*
Hand, Anthony *1989*
Self, Gary *1991*
Nother, Daniel *1994*
Davies, Carol *1995*
Bath, Baljinder *1996*
Cotton, Stephen *1998*
Gillett, Amanda *1998*
Ballingall, Joanne *1999*
Harvey, Louise *2000*
Newport, Ian *2000*
Nickless, Jason *2001*
Josty, David *2002*
Gough, Sian *2003*
Grasso, Antonietta *2004*
Carroll, Grant *2005*
Gayford, Justine *2005*
Bower, Gemma *2006*
Curtis, Matthew *2006*
Davidson, Sally *2006*
Harby, David *2006*
Langrish, Adam *2006*
Piddington, Daniel *2008*
Pugh, David *2008*
Hughes, Jason *2009*

Types of work
Administrative law · Adoption · Agency · Ancillary relief · Asbestos-related diseases · Assessment of costs · Boundaries · Building · Care proceedings · Chancery (general) · Charities · Child abduction · Child abuse · Child care law · Child support · Children · Civil law · Civil partnerships · Clinical negligence · Cohabitation · Commercial contracts · Commercial law · Commercial litigation · Commercial property · Common land · Common law (general) · Community care · Company law · Company, commercial and competition · Confiscation · Construction law · Contracts · Corporate insolvency · Corporate recovery · Costs · Court of Protection · Crime · Damages · Defamation · Directors' disqualification · Disability discrimination · Disciplinary procedures · Disciplinary tribunals · Discrimination · Dispute resolution and arbitration · Divorce · Domestic violence injunctions · Economic torts · Education · Employment · Engineering disputes · Environment · Family law · Financial provision · Freedom of information · Gambling · Gaming and lotteries · Health and safety · Healthcare law · Highways · Holiday injury and

damages · Housing · Immigration · Industrial deafness · Industrial diseases · Industrial relations law · Insolvency · Intellectual property · Judicial review · Landlord and tenant · Lands Tribunal · Leasehold enfranchisement · Legal aid costs · Licensing · Limited partnerships · Litigation · Local authorities · Local government and public services · Malicious falsehood · Matrimonial · Matrimonial finance · Mediation · Medical law · Medical negligence · Mental health · Mortgages · Occupational diseases · Offshore trust litigation · Ombudsman · Overseas accidents · Partnerships · Personal injury · Personal insolvency · Planning · Private children law · Professional negligence · Public inquiries · Regulatory and disciplinary law · Remedies · Restitution · Rights of light · Rights of way · Sale and carriage of goods · School sites · Social security · Social services · Solicitor's indemnity · Special Guardianship · Sports medicine · Timeshare · Title to land · Torts · Transport and Works Act inquiries · Trust litigation · Trusts · Unmarried couples · Wardship

Chambers Established 1989
Opening times: 08:00 - 18:00

Disability access
Staff briefed or trained on duties under the disability legislation, Disabled parking available

Languages spoken
Dutch (Flemish), French, German, Hebrew, Italian, Punjabi, Spanish, Welsh

12 COLLEGE PLACE

Fauvelle Buildings, 12 College Place, Southampton SO15 2FE
023 8032 0320
Fax: 023 8032 0321; DX: 96875 Southampton 10
E-mail: clerks@12cp.co.uk

Chambers of: Mr N S Haggan QC

Disability access
Staff briefed or trained on duties under the disability legislation, Wheelchair access, Disabled parking available

THE CHAMBERS OF LEON FERNANDO DEL CANTO GONZALEZ

29 Carlton Crescent, Southampton SO15 2EW

Chambers of: Mr L F Del Canto Gonzalez

CHAMBERS OF MR DAVID MAWDSLEY

17 Clinning Road, Southport, Merseyside PR8 4NU
01704 565 387
Fax: 01704 565 387

Chambers of: Mr D J Mawdsley

ALBAN ABBEY CHAMBERS

16 Albert Street, St Albans, Hertfordshire AL1 1RU
01727 830 704
Fax: 01727 839 562
E-mail: ejmessuk@yahoo.co.uk

Chambers of: Miss E J Messenger

MOUNT PLEASANT CHAMBERS

2 Mount Pleasant Lane, Bricket Wood, St Albans AL2 3UZ
01923 678938
Fax: 01923 678938

Chambers of: Mr O O A O Jibowu

QUORUM CHAMBERS

2 Victoria Square, Victoria Street, St Albans AL1 3TF
01727 884516
E-mail: clerks@quorumchambers.co.uk

Chambers of: Ms L A Frawley

ST ALBANS CHAMBERS

2 - 4 St Peter's Street, St Albans, Hertfordshire AL1 3LF
01727 843383
Fax: 01727 842820; DX: 6116 St Albans
E-mail: clerks@stalbanschambers.com

Disability access
Staff briefed or trained on duties under the disability legislation

AGRI-LAW CHAMBERS

Penterry Farm, St Arvans NP16 6HG
01989 720675

Chambers of: Mr C N Gowling

TYDDEWI CHAMBERS

Felin Isaf, St David's, Pembrokeshire SA62 6QB
01437 720 853
Fax: 01437 720 080; DX: 98289 Haverfordwest
E-mail: dgill@btinternet.com

Chambers of: Mr D G B Lloyd

CHAMBERS OF MR ASHLEY BARNES

1 The Beeches, Suttonleach, St Helens, Merseyside WA9 4SU
01744 814072
E-mail: ashleyjamesbarnes@live.com

HANSON RENOUF

Regency House, Regent Road, Hill Street, St Helier, Jersey JE2 4UZ
01534 767764
Fax: 01534 767725
E-mail: enquiries@hansonrenouf.com

Chambers of: Mr T V R Hanson

Disability access
Staff briefed or trained on duties under the disability legislation, Wheelchair access, Disabled parking available

ARC CHAMBERS

PO Box 256, St Leonards-On-Sea TN38 1GL
01424 204779

Chambers of: Mr A R Connerty

THE CHAMBERS OF MR ALAN ROBERTSHAW

Ashtree Cottage, Shepards Farm, Fiddlers' Green, St Newlyn East, Cornwall TR8 5NW
01872 245974/07973 825348
Fax: 07973 825348

Chambers of: Mr A S Robertshaw

RCS CHAMBERS

Penny Hill, Holme Hall Lane, Stainton S66 7RD
01709 814 147
Fax: 01709 818793
E-mail: robert@rcschambers.com

Chambers of: Mr R C Smith

Disability access
Staff briefed or trained on duties under the disability legislation, Wheelchair access, Disabled parking available

CHAMBERS OF GERARD MCDERMOTT QC

Weir House, 7 Stamford Street, Stalybridge SK15 1JP
0161 304 4301
E-mail: gerard@mcdermottqc.com

Chambers of: Mr G F McDermott QC

THE CHAMBERS OF MR GRAHAM CAMPBELL

8, Rosedale Road, Heaton Chapel, Stockport, Cheshire SK4 2QU
0161 442 4454
E-mail: graham.campbell100@yahoo.co.uk

Chambers of: Mr G J Campbell

CHAMBERS OF JANINA PASIUK

7 Marlborough Drive, Heaton Chapel, Stockport, Cheshire SK4 2QZ
0161 442 5576
Fax: 0161 442 5576
E-mail: janinapasiuk@hotmail.co.uk

Chambers of: Ms J S Pasiuk

REGENT CHAMBERS

Regent House, 3 Pall Mall, Hanley, Stoke On Trent ST1 1HP
01782 286666
Fax: 01782 201866; DX: 20720 Hanley
E-mail: clerks@regentchambers.co.uk
URL: www.regentchambers.co.uk
Out of hours telephone: 07989 457084

Chambers of: Mr B G Cliff
Clerk: Nicola Dobson/Nikki Towle

Cliff, Barry *1988*
Jay, Grenville *1975*
Cliff, Paul *1992*
Johnson, John *1993*
Moore, Kirstie *1994*
O'Hagan, Sophia *1996*
Ali, Anis *1997*
Wallbanks, Joanne *1997*
O'Reilly, Catherine *1998*
Powell, Frederick *1999*
Palmer, Edward *2000*

D

Types of work
Care proceedings · Chancery (general) · Common law (general) · Corporate fraud · Crime · Employment · Family law · Family provision · Health and safety · Housing · Immigration · Landlord and tenant · Licensing · Personal injury

Disability access
Staff briefed or trained on duties under the disability legislation, Disabled parking available

MOSSFIELD CHAMBERS

90 Glenagoorland Road, Strabane, Co. Tyrone BT82 0ST
07970 154902
E-mail: dianenixonni@aol.com

Chambers of: Miss D E Nixon

LONDON SCOTTISH

183 Loxley Road, Stratford Upon Avon, Warwickshire CV37 7DU
07971 681724
E-mail: isheridan@londonscottishlaw.com

Chambers of: Mr I D Sheridan

HEAVENWOOD CHAMBERS

Heavenwood Chambers, Heavenwood House, 71 Bownham Park, Rodborough Common, Stroud, Gloucestershire GL5 5BZ
01453 873444
Fax: 01453 872877; DX: 58805 Stroud Phoenix
E-mail: kms@heavenwood.co.uk

Chambers of: Miss K M Smoker

CHAMBERS OF MISS ELIZABETH HINDMARSH

Over Court, Bisley, Stroud, Gloucestershire GL6 7BE
01452 770170
Fax: 01452 770840
E-mail: john.cowen@virgin.net

Chambers of: Miss E Hindmarsh

CHAMBERS OF MR C G KING

6 All Saints Field, Stroud GL5 1NE
07949 461717
E-mail: ckingesq@yahoo.co.uk

Chambers of: Mr C G King

POOL CHAMBERS

West Court, Greenhill Farm, Moreton Bagot, Studley, Warwickshire B80 7EL
07976 160802
E-mail: langton@poolchambers.co.uk

Chambers of: Mr S R Langton

CHAMBERS OF JENNIFER BRIDGE

10 The Mall, Surbiton, Surrey KT6 4EQ
020 8891 1718

Chambers of: Mrs J B Bridge

WESTFIELD CHAMBERS

10 Westfield Avenue, South Croydon, Surrey CR2 9JU
020 8657 1072
Fax: 020 8657 1072
E-mail: westfieldchambers@gmx.com

Chambers of: Mr A N Omezie

CHEAM CHAMBERS

59 Cornwall Road, Cheam, Sutton, Surrey SM2 6DU
020 8642 4210
Fax: 020 8642 4210; DX: 200605 Cheam
E-mail: janewallace@itpmail.co.uk

Chambers of: Mrs J S Wallace

Disability access
Staff briefed or trained on duties under the disability legislation, Disabled parking available

CHAMBERS OF MISS VICTORIA DSANE

61 Elm Grove, Sutton, Surrey SM1 4EX
020 8722 0990
Fax: 020 8722 0990
E-mail: vdsaneidown@hotmail.co.uk

Chambers of: Miss V T Dsane

CHAMBERS OF MR LAMACRAFT

93 Pine Walk, Charlshalton Beeches, Sutton, Surrey SM5 4HL
020 8643 1593
E-mail: ianlamacraft@gicham.co.uk

Chambers of: Mr I R Lamacraft

CHAMBERS OF MR K MYDEEN

3 Kempston House, The Downsway, Sutton SM2 5RE
020 8643 3633
Fax: 020 8406 0814
E-mail: kenmydeen@blueyonder.co.uk

Chambers of: Mr K Mydeen

CHAMBERS OF MR R J GRIERSON

2 Kenilworth Close, Four Oaks, Sutton Coldfield, West Midlands B74 2SE
0121 343 1460
Fax: 0121 308 5456
E-mail: linkrgstps@btinternet.com

Chambers of: Mr R J Grierson

Disability access
Wheelchair access, Disabled parking available

ANGEL CHAMBERS

Ethos Building, Kings Road, Swansea SA1 8AS
01792 464623
Fax: 01792 648501; DX: 743460 Swansea 21
E-mail: clerks@angelchambers.co.uk

Chambers of: Mr G W Walters

Disability access
Staff briefed or trained on duties under the disability legislation, Wheelchair access, Disabled parking available

CHAMBERS OF DOMINIC BOOTHROYD

5 Church Close, Llansamlet, Swansea SA7 9RJ
01792 799885
Fax: 01792 799825; DX: 56757 Morriston

CHAMBERS OF MR J M FORD

30 Glan Yr Afon Gardens, Swansea, Wales SA2 9HY
07855 389459
E-mail: martyn.ford3@ntlworld.com

Chambers of: Mr J M Ford

ISCOED CHAMBERS

86 St Helen's Road, Swansea SA1 4BQ
01792 652988
Fax: 01792 458089; DX: 39554 Swansea
E-mail: clerks@iscoedchambers.co.uk
URL: www.iscoedchambers.co.uk

Chambers of: Miss E M Evans QC
Clerks: Donna Williams, Julie Snary; Chambers Director: Avril Llewellyn

Evans, Elwen QC *1980*†
Rouch, Peter QC *1972*†
Griffiths, Patrick *1972*
Phillips, Frank *1972*
Jenkins, James *1974*
Craven, Robert *1979*†
Rees, Stephen *1979*
Jones, Francis *1980*
Sandbrook-Hughes, Stewert *1980*
Roblin, Laraine *1981*
Rees, Huw *1983*†
Spackman, Mark *1986*
Daycock, *1987*
Hipkin, John *1989*
Harris, David *1990*
Wright, Ian *1994*
Davies, Iwan *1995*
Marshall, Elizabeth *1995*
Rouch, Robin *1999*
Anthony, Rachel *2000*
Ashworth, Philippa *2000*
Collins, Catherine *2000*
Hobson, Paul *2000*
Richards, Catherine *2000*
Jones, Craig *2003*
Blakemore, Benjamin *2004*
Gill, Ned *2004*
Pratt, Jake *2004*
Preece, Nicola *2006*
Buckley, Georgina *2007*
Moran, Natasha *2007*
Eccles, Sarah *2008*
Scapens, Thomas *2008*
Thomas, Rhys Ab Owen *2009*
Randall, Helen *2010*

Types of work
Agriculture · Chancery (general) · Civil liberties · Commercial property · Common land · Common law (general) · Construction law · Corporate fraud · Crime · Employment · Energy · Environment · Equity · Family law · Family provision · Financial services · Franchising · Housing · Insolvency · Landlord and tenant · Licensing · Local authorities · Medical negligence · Partnerships · Personal injury · Personal insolvency · Planning · Professional negligence · Sale and carriage of goods · Succession · Trusts · Wills

Disability access
Wheelchair access, Disabled parking available

D

PENDRAGON CHAMBERS

Suite 7, J Shed, Kings Road, SA1 Waterfront, Swansea SA1 8PL
01792 411188
Fax: 01792 411189; DX: 743464 Swansea 21
E-mail: clerks@pendragonchambers.com

Chambers of: Miss S A Rudman

Disability access
Staff briefed or trained on duties under the disability legislation, Wheelchair access, Disabled parking available

ST DAVID'S CHAMBERS

Myrtle Cottage, Norton Road, Mumbles, Swansea SA3 5TQ
01792 559924; DX: 52956 Swansea
E-mail: j.vallack@ntlworld.com

Chambers of: Miss J A Vallack

Disability access
Staff briefed or trained on duties under the disability legislation, Disabled parking available

PUMP COURT CHAMBERS

5 Temple Chambers, Temple Street, Swindon SN1 1SQ
01793 539899
Fax: 0845 259 3242/0870 762 5451; DX: 38639 Swindon 2
E-mail: clerks@3pumpcourt.com
URL: www.pumpcourtchambers.com
Out of hours telephone: 07515 334453

Chambers of: Mr O E Nsugbe QC
Clerks: David Barber, Holly Bell

Also at: 3 Pump Court, Upper Ground Floor, London EC4Y 7AJ Tel: 020 7353 0711 Fax: 020 7353 3319 and at 31 Southgate Street, Winchester SO23 9EE Tel: 01962 868161 Fax: 01962 867645

Nsugbe, Oba QC *1985*†
Pascoe, Nigel QC *1966*†
Donne, Anthony QC *1973*
Hill, Mark QC *1987*†
Samuels, Leslie QC *1989*
Patterson, Stewart *1967*†
Harrap, Giles *1971*†
Abbott, Frank *1972*†
Parry, Charles *1973*
Butt, Michael *1974*
Ker-Reid, John *1974*
Gabb, Charles *1975*
Jones, Stephen *1978*
MacKenzie, Julie *1978*
Allardice, Miranda *1982*
Blount, Martin *1982*
Scott, Matthew *1985*
Bloom-Davis, Desmond *1986*
Travers, Hugh *1988*
Boydell, Edward *1989*†
Gau, Justin *1989*
Houston, Andrew *1989*
Wicks, David *1989*
Breslin, Catherine *1990*
Khan, Helen *1990*
Howe, Penny *1991*
Lorenzo, Claudia *1991*
Kelly, Geoffrey *1992*
Newton-Price, James *1992*
Ruffell, Mark *1992*
Ashley, Mark *1993*
Gunther, Elizabeth *1993*
Moore, Roderick *1993*
Morton, Gary *1993*
Peirson, Oliver *1993*
Russell, Alison *1993*
Smith, Leonorah *1993*
Tregilgas-Davey, Marcus *1993*
Pawson, Robert *1994*
Hall, Richard *1995*
Asteris, Peter *1996*
Dubbery, Mark *1996*
Hall, Michael *1996*
Jones, Sarah *1996*
Ephgrave, Amy *1997*
Gallagher, Maria *1997*
Grime, Andrew *1997*
Ward, Anne *1997*
Dracass, Timothy *1998*
Keen, Spencer *1998*
Bond, Andrew *1999*
Spearing, Rachel *1999*
Brown, Anne *2000*
Islam, Naznin *2000*
Ramadhan, Lubeya *2000*
Tutt, Richard *2000*
Burge, Alison *2002*
Hartley, Caroline *2002*
Platt, Heather *2002*
Shravat, Neelo *2002*
Berry, Amy *2003*
Chapman, John *2003*
Davis, Lucy-Victoria *2003*
Street, Charlotte *2003*
Gadd, Adam *2004*
Leach, Stuart *2004*
Trotter, Helen *2004*
Lyons, Tara *2005*
Troup, Rachel *2005*
Connors, Hannah *2006*
Iten, Corinne *2006*
Long, Benjamin *2006*
O'Driscoll, Patricia *2006*
Lee, Jennifer *2007*
Bruce, Eleanor *2008*
Purkis, Simon *2008*
Williamson, Nicholas *2009*

Types of work
Arbitration · Care proceedings · Chancery (land law) · Civil liberties · Commercial law · Commercial litigation · Commercial property · Company, commercial and competition · Construction law · Corporate fraud · Courts martial · Crime · Ecclesiastical law · Employment · Environment · Family law · Family provision · Foreign law · Inheritance and cohabitees · Landlord and tenant · Licensing · Medical negligence · Personal injury · Planning · Professional negligence · Sport · Succession · War crimes tribunals

Disability access
Staff briefed or trained on duties under the disability legislation, Disabled parking available

SELBORNE CHAMBERS

9th Floor, 174 Phillip Street, Sydney

THE CHAMBERS OF ALESSANDRA WILLIAMS

P O Box 363, Tadworth KT20 9EJ
07941 944950
E-mail: alessandra.williams@yahoo.co.uk

Chambers of: Ms S A C Williams

CLERKSROOM (TAUNTON)

Equity House, Administration Centre, Blackbrook Park Avenue, Taunton, Somerset TA1 2PX
0845 083 3000
Fax: 0845 083 3001; DX: 97188 Taunton Blackbrook
E-mail: mail@clerksroom.com

Disability access
Staff briefed or trained on duties under the disability legislation, Wheelchair access, Disabled parking available

OCTAGON CHAMBERS

29 Park Street, Taunton, Somerset TA1 4DG
01823 331919
Fax: 01823 330553; DX: 32146 Taunton
E-mail: jcload@Octagonchambers.co.uk
Out of hours telephone: 01823 331919

Chambers of: Miss R Bradberry
Clerks: Joanna Cload, Amy Clatworthy

Bradberry, Rebecca *1996*
Askham, Nigel *1973*
McVay, Bridget *1990*
Wilcox, Lawrence *1996*
Mason, Patrick *1997*
Ahuja, Harry *2001*
Cooper, Simon *2012*

Types of work
Care proceedings · Common law (general) · Corporate fraud · Courts martial · Crime · Employment · Family law · Licensing · Medical negligence · Mental health · Personal injury · Planning · Professional negligence

Disability access
Staff briefed or trained on duties under the disability legislation, Disabled parking available

CHAMBERS OF MR D T OSBORNE

The Granary, Preston Bowyer, Milverton, Taunton, Somerset TA4 1PQ
01823 400 705
Fax: 01823 400105
E-mail: david@david-osborne.com

Chambers of: Mr D T Osborne

CHAMBERS OF JONATHAN TECKS

Green Gables, Curload, Stoke St Gregory, Taunton, Somerset TA3 6JA
01823 491268
E-mail: jo@jotecks.com

Chambers of: Mr J H Tecks

LIBERTY CHAMBERS

Crackwell Farm, Penally, Tenby, Pembrokeshire SA70 7RY
01834 844458
Fax: 08717 333962
E-mail: hj@libertylaw.co.uk

Chambers of: Mrs H G Jones

THE CHAMBERS OF MR K F PITTS

'Tussocks', The Causeway, Therfield, Hertfordshire SG8 9PP
01763 287 760
Fax: 01763 287 434; DX: 37311 Royston
E-mail: keithpitts@keithpitts.f2s.com

Chambers of: Mr K F Pitts

CHAMBERS OF MISS J P TOCH

1 John Brunt VC Court, Church Road, Paddock Wood, Tonbridge, Kent TH12 6ET
01892 833 005
E-mail: j.toch@yahoo.co.uk

Chambers of: Miss J P Toch

INSTITUTE FOR HUMAN RIGHTS

Abo Akademi University, Biskopsgaton 19, Turku 20500
E-mail: dlewis@abo.fi

Chambers of: Mr D A G Lewis

D

D

ST MARGARET'S CHAMBERS

44 Sidney Road, St Margaret's, Twickenham, Middlesex TW1 1JR
020 8241 3516

Chambers of: Mr R S C Gainer

GOULDS GREEN CHAMBERS

48 Goulds Green, Uxbridge UB8 3DG
01895 422574
Fax: 01895 422574
E-mail: jamkha@tiscali.co.uk

Chambers of: Mr J Khalid

GOULDS GREEN CHAMBERS

Room D, 2 Bakers Yard, High Street, Uxbridge UB8 1JZ
01895 422574
Fax: 01895 422574

Chambers of: Mr J Khalid

INDEPENDENT CHAMBERS

Rivendale, 6 Gorse Hill Lane, The Wentworth Estate, Virgina Water, Surrey GU25 4AJ
01344 845315
Fax: 01344 849255
E-mail: admin@independentchambers.co.uk

Chambers of: Mr J McLanachan

CHAMBERS OF MR STEPHEN HOURIGAN

2 Harrison Road, Waltham Abbey, Essex EN9 3YE
01992 700845
Fax: 01992 700845
E-mail: stevehourigan@aol.com

Chambers of: Mr S D Hourigan

CHAMBERS OF MR T OXTON

Alexander Chambers, 13 Halstead Road, Wanstead E11 2AY
07833 901226

Chambers of: Mr T J E Oxton

PALMYRA CHAMBERS

Royal House, 46 Legh Street, Warrington WA1 1UJ
01925 444919
Fax: 08708 112670; DX: 17774 Warrington
E-mail: clerk@palmyrachambers.com

Chambers of: Mr J D Rule

Disability access
Staff briefed or trained on duties under the disability legislation, Wheelchair access, Disabled parking available

CHAMBERS OF MISS L SAYERS

45 Orford Green, Warrington WA2 8PQ
07850 366366
E-mail: lynnesayers@hotmail.com

Chambers of: Miss L Sayers

HARBOUR COURT CHAMBERS

140 Warsash Road, Warsash, Hampshire SO31 9JD
01489 557999
Fax: 023 8000 1809; DX: 45255 Park Gate
E-mail: peter_renfree@harbourcourt.co.uk

Chambers of: Mr P G S Renfree

Disability access
Staff briefed or trained on duties under the disability legislation, Wheelchair access, Disabled parking available

AEGIS CHAMBERS

39 Mostyn Avenue, Wembley, Middlesex HA9 8AY

Chambers of: Mr M W Smith

CHAMBERS OF MICHAEL SHRIMPTON

8 Jusons Glebe, Wendover, Buckinghamshire HP22 6PF
01296 291564
Fax: 01296 291564
E-mail: michael@mshrimpton.co.uk

Chambers of: Mr M Shrimpton

CENTURION CHAMBERS

Chambers of Mer Nazir Ahmed, 1st Floor Paragon House, 79 Birmingham Road, West Bromwich B70 6PX
0121 553 4613
Fax: 0121 553 5087
E-mail: clerks@centurionchambers.com

Chambers of: Mr N Ahmed

HAMPTON COURT CHAMBERS

28 Bedster Gardens, Hurst Park, West Molesey, Surrey KT8 1SZ
020 8979 0381
Fax: 020 8979 0381

Chambers of: Miss J Bezzam

PHYDEAUX CHAMBERS

Maison Phydeaux, 44a The Grove, Biggin Hill, Westerham, Kent TN16 3TB
01209 821442
Fax: 01209 821442
E-mail: arjo_1@tiscali.co.uk

Chambers of: Mr A R Jopling

CHAMBERS OF ANDREW REID

Westport Farm, Ruskway Lane, Westport TA10 0BN
01460 281046
E-mail: andrewreid443@me.com

PARK CHAMBERS

3 Park Drive, Weybridge Park, Surrey KT13 8UU
01932 820082
Fax: 01932 857977
E-mail: clerks@ParkChambers.co.uk

Chambers of: Mr E G B Suter

CHAMBERS OF MR EDMOND MCGOVERN

Frans Landrainstraat 27-3, Wezembeek-Oppem 1970
00 32 2 731 6171
E-mail: edmond.mcgovern@globefield.com

Chambers of: Mr E T McGovern

CHAMBERS OF MR T M HEY

Folly Hall Farm, Tranmire, Whitby, North Yorkshire YO21 2BW
07771 665397
E-mail: terencehey@hotmail.co.uk

Chambers of: Mr T M Hey

CHAMBERS OF MR RICHARD BLOOMFIELD

19 Chollerford Mews, Hollywell, Whitley Bay, Tyne and Wear NE25 0TX
01670 360042
Fax: 0191 247 8144; DX: 62607 Blyth
E-mail: richard@richardbloomfield.co.uk

Chambers of: Mr R W Bloomfield

Disability access
Staff briefed or trained on duties under the disability legislation, Disabled parking available

CHAMBERS OF MR JOHN BISHOP

Greenfields, Pean Hill, Whitstable, Kent CT5 3BH
01227 479665
E-mail: jmb@barristerbishop.co.uk

Chambers of: Mr J M Bishop

CHAMBERS OF MR WILLIAM PARKINSON

St Andrews, 3a Mort Street, Wigan, Lancashire WN6 7AU
0845 083 3000

Chambers of: Mr W H Parkinson

CHAMBERS OF MR T BALLANTINE DYKES

Ewe Close, Arkleby, Wigton, Cumbria CA7 2DS
01697 321917
Fax: 01697 322895
E-mail: t.ballantinedykes@btinternet.com

Chambers of: Mr T L Ballantine Dykes

D

D

FORTIS GREEN CHAMBERS

Hillcroft, Wilmslow Park South, Wilmslow SK9 2AY
0161 439 5804
E-mail: victorianassar@yahoo.co.uk

Chambers of: Miss V K Nassar

Disability access
Wheelchair access, Disabled parking available

THE CHAMBERS OF MARY BULLEN

7 Grovely Mews, Shaftsbury Road, Wilton SP2 0JW
01722 742204
E-mail: marybullen123@btinternet.com

Chambers of: Mrs M Bullen

THE CHAMBERS OF MR R L DAVEY

70 Belgarum Place, Winchester, Hampshire SO23 8SL
01962 865728
Fax: 01962 865679; DX: 2518 Winchester
E-mail: rldavey@ntlworld.com

Chambers of: Mr R L Davey

CHAMBERS OF MR P HERRITY

75 Provene Gardens, Waltham Chase, Winchester, Hampshire SO32 2RW
01489 894408
Fax: 01489 808034
E-mail: peter.herrity@talktalk.net

Chambers of: Mr P Herrity

3 PB BARRISTERS

4 St Peter Street, Winchester SO23 8BW
01962 868884
Fax: 01962 868644; DX: 2507 Winchester
E-mail: clerks.winchester@3paper.co.uk
URL: www.3pb.co.uk
Out of hours telephone: Mobile: 07808 137904 (Stuart Pringle)

Chambers of: Mr Ian Lawrie QC
Clerks: Lee Giles, Stephen Arnold, Tom Wood, Thomas McComb, Stuart Pringle; Administrator: Michael Corrigan, Credit Controller; Lisa Wilson, Marketing Manager; Finance Manager: Head of Business Admin and Finance, Neil Monro

Also at: 3 PB (Bournemouth), 30 Christchurch Road, Bournemouth BH1 3PD

Also at: 3 PB (Oxford), 23 Beaumont Street, Oxford OX1 2NP

Also at: 3 PB (Bristol), Royal Talbot House, 2 Victoria Street, Bristol BS1 6BN

Lawrie, Ian QC *1985*†
Parroy, Michael QC *1969*†
Vere-Hodge, Michael QC *1970*
Farley, Roger QC *1974*†
Jones, Stewart QC *1972*†
Braslavsky, Nicholas QC *1983*†
Bromley-Davenport, John QC *1972*
Lickley, Nigel QC *1983*†
Parker, Christopher QC *1986*†
Parrish, Samuel *1962*
Solomon, Susan *1967*
Aylwin, Christopher *1970*
Swinstead, David *1970*
Norman, Michael *1971*†
Curran, Leo *1972*
Jennings, Peter *1972*
Coleman, Anthony *1973*†
Stephenson, Ben *1973*
Bartlett, David *1975*†
Tyson, Richard *1975*†
Kent, Peter *1978*
Mitchell, Nigel *1978*
Grey, Robert *1979*
Hamilton, Gavin *1979*
Leach, Robin *1979*
Leviseur, Nicholas *1979*
Partridge, Ian *1979*
Cairnes, Paul *1980*
Coombes, Timothy *1980*
Edge, Ian *1981*
Marshall, David *1981*
Sampson, Graeme *1981*
Strutt, Martin *1981*
Martin, Nicola *1982*
Newman, Paul *1982*
Onslow, Richard *1982*
Lomas, Mark *1983*
Stancombe, Barry *1983*
O'Hara, Sarah *1984*
Palfrey, Monty *1985*
Whittle-Martin, Lucia *1985*
Clark, Tonia *1986*
Hudson, Elisabeth *1987*
Hendry, Lucy *1988*
Rowland, Nicholas *1988*†
Zabihi, Tanya *1988*
Bradbury, Timothy *1989*
Hester, Paul *1989*
Richards, David *1989*
Aeberli, Peter *1990*
Griffiths, Hayley *1990*
Hiddleston, Adam *1990*
Knapp, Sophie *1990*
Buckley-Clarke, Amanda *1991*
Dunlop, Hamish *1991*
Katrak, Cyrus *1991*
Robins, Imogen *1991*
Ross, Iain *1991*
Bingham, Tony *1992*
Sweeney, Noel *1992*
Clargo, John *1994*
Dawson, James *1994*
Earle, Judy *1994*
Feest, Adam *1994*
Mitchell, Jack *1994*
Reid, David *1994*
Topliss, Megan *1994*
Weston, Louis *1994*

De Freitas, Melanie *1995*
McDevitt, Colin *1995*
McIlroy, David *1995*
Strachan, Elaine *1995*
Davison, James *1996*
Lorie, Andrew *1996*
Tyler, Thomas *1996*
Wilson, Lachlan *1996*
Purdy, Catherine *1997*
Sullivan, Mark *1997*
Griffiths, Emma *1998*
Taylor, Rufus *1998*
Horner, Robert *1999*
Kennedy, Stuart *1999*
Goodall, Rachael *2000*
Isaacs, Oliver *2000*
O'Doherty, Paul *2000*
Sheriff, Andrew *2000*
Worton, Louise *2000*
Cassidy, Sheena *2001*
Whelan, Christopher *2001*
Ludlow, Craig *2002*
Moss, Karen *2002*
Shillingford, Julia *2002*
Tomlinson, Michael *2002*
Courts, Robert *2003*
Gullick, Mathew *2003*
Jones, Victoria *2003*
Archer, Audrey *2004*
Davies, James *2004*
Hepworth, Elizabeth *2004*
Horder, Tom *2004*
Wheeler, Richard *2004*
Anderson, Katherine *2005*
Clarke, Sarah *2005*
Langford, Sarah *2005*
Musgrave, Anarkali *2005*
Cannings, Matthew *2006*
Da Costa, Francisca *2006*
Davies, Nick *2006*
Green, Mark *2006*
Rees, Naomi *2006*
Robinson, Nick *2006*
Davies, Harriet *2007*
Elliott, Mark *2007*
Jones, Ximena *2007*
MacPhail, Andrew *2007*
Paulin, Michael *2007*
Perfect, Andrew *2007*
Chegwidden, James *2008*
Dunseath, Katherine *2008*
Edwards, Christopher *2008*
Alleyne, Ebony *2009*
Ashkar, Natalie *2009*
Bowes, Gemma *2009*
Currie, Philip *2009*
Sanghera, Sharandish *2009*
Webb, Thomas *2010*
Wyeth, Stephen *2010*
Davies, Eleanor *1998**

Types of work

Accountancy · Adjudication · Administrative law · Adoption · Alternative dispute resolution · Ancillary relief · Animals · Arab commercial law · Arab law · Arbitration · Asbestos-related diseases · Asset forfeiture · Asset recovery · Banking · Bills of exchange · Boundaries · Building · Care proceedings · Chancery (commercial) · Chancery (general) · Chancery (land law) · Child care law · Children · Civil actions against the police · Civil partnerships · Clinical negligence · Cohabitation · Commercial contracts · Commercial fraud · Commercial law · Commercial litigation · Commercial property · Common law (general) · Company, commercial and competition · Computer contracts · Computer crime · Computer litigation · Confiscation · Conflict of laws · Construction law · Consumer credit · Consumer law · Contracts · Copyright · Corporate finance · Corporate fraud · Corporate governance · Corporate insolvency · Corporate liability · Corporate manslaughter · Corporate recovery · Costs · Court of Protection · Courts martial · Crime · Crime and criminal due process · Criminal judicial review · Cross-border litigation and remedies · Damages · Disability discrimination · Disasters · Disciplinary procedures · Disciplinary tribunals · Discrimination · Divorce · Domestic violence injunctions · Ecclesiastical law · Economic torts · Education · Election law · Employment · Engineering disputes · Equine law · Equity · Factoring · Family law · Family provision · Financial provision · Financial services · Firearms · Foreign law · Franchising · Fraud · Freezing orders · Guarantees · Health and safety · Holiday injury and damages · Homicide · Housing · Industrial deafness · Industrial diseases · Information technology · Inheritance and cohabitees · Inquests · Insolvency · Insurance · Intellectual property · International arbitration · International commercial arbitration · International fraud and asset tracing · Islamic family law · Islamic law · Judicial review · Landlord and tenant · Lands Tribunal · Licensing · Matrimonial finance · Mediation · Medical negligence · Middle Eastern law · Military law · Multi-party litigation · Occupational diseases · Partnerships · Passing off · Personal injury · Personal insolvency · Planning · Police · Product liability · Professional negligence · Public law · Real property · Regulatory and disciplinary law · Rights of light · Rights of way · Road traffic · Sale and carriage of goods · Serial crime · Serious fraud · Shareholder agreements · Succession · Tax · Technology and Construction Court · Torts · Trust litigation · Trusts · Wardship · Wills

Disability access

Staff briefed or trained on duties under the disability legislation, Disabled parking available

PUMP COURT CHAMBERS

31 Southgate Street, Winchester, Hampshire SO23 9EB
01962 868 161
Fax: 0845 259 3240; DX: 2514 Winchester
E-mail: clerks@3pumpcourt.com
URL: www.pumpcourtchambers.com
Out of hours telephone: 07515 334453

Chambers of: Mr O E Nsugbe QC
Clerks: David Barber, Tony George; Administrator: Andrea Cheshire

Also at: 3 Pump Court, Upper Ground Floor, London EC4Y 7AY Tel: 020 7353 0711 Fax: 0845 259 3241; 5 Temple Chambers, Swindon SN1 1SQ Tel: 01793 539899 Fax: 01793 539866

†Recorder *Door Tenant/Associate Member

Nsugbe, Oba QC *1985*†
Pascoe, Nigel QC *1966*†
Donne, Anthony QC *1973*
Campbell, Susan QC *1986*
Hill, Mark QC *1987*†
Samuels, Leslie QC *1989*
Patterson, Stewart *1967*†
Harrap, Giles *1971*†
Abbott, Frank *1972*†
Parry, Charles *1973*
Butt, Michael *1974*
Ker-Reid, John *1974*
Gabb, Charles *1975*
Jones, Stephen *1978*
MacKenzie, Julie *1978*
Allardice, Miranda *1982*
Blount, Martin *1982*
Scott, Matthew *1985*
Bloom-Davis, Desmond *1986*
Travers, Hugh *1988*
Boydell, Edward *1989*†
Gau, Justin *1989*
Houston, Andrew *1989*
Wicks, David *1989*
Breslin, Catherine *1990*
Khan, Helen *1990*
Howe, Penny *1991*
Lorenzo, Claudia *1991*
Kelly, Geoffrey *1992*
Newton-Price, James *1992*
Ruffell, Mark *1992*
Ashley, Mark *1993*
Gunther, Elizabeth *1993*
Moore, Roderick *1993*
Morton, Gary *1993*
Peirson, Oliver *1993*
Russell, Alison *1993*
Smith, Leonorah *1993*
Tregilgas-Davey, Marcus *1993*
Pawson, Robert *1994*
Hall, Richard *1995*
Asteris, Peter *1996*
Dubbery, Mark *1996*
Hall, Michael *1996*
Jones, Sarah *1996*
Ephgrave, Amy *1997*
Gallagher, Maria *1997*
Grime, Andrew *1997*
Ward, Anne *1997*
Dracass, Timothy *1998*
Keen, Spencer *1998*
Bond, Andrew *1999*
Spearing, Rachel *1999*
Brown, Anne *2000*
Islam, Naznin *2000*
Ramadhan, Lubeya *2000*
Tutt, Richard *2000*
Burge, Alison *2002*
Hartley, Caroline *2002*
Platt, Heather *2002*
Shravat, Neelo *2002*
Berry, Amy *2003*
Chapman, John *2003*
Davis, Lucy-Victoria *2003*
Street, Charlotte *2003*
Gadd, Adam *2004*
Leach, Stuart *2004*
Trotter, Helen *2004*
Lyons, Tara *2005*
Troup, Rachel *2005*
Connors, Hannah *2006*
Iten, Corinne *2006*
Long, Benjamin *2006*
O'Driscoll, Patricia *2006*
Gilbert, Daniella *2007*
Lee, Jennifer *2007*
Bruce, Eleanor *2008*
Purkis, Simon *2008*
Williamson, Nicholas *2009*

Types of work
Arbitration · Care proceedings · Chancery (land law) · Civil liberties · Commercial law · Commercial litigation · Commercial property · Company, commercial and competition · Construction law · Corporate fraud · Courts martial · Crime · Ecclesiastical law · Employment · Environment · Family law · Family provision · Foreign law · Inheritance and cohabitees · Landlord and tenant · Licensing · Medical negligence · Personal injury · Planning · Professional negligence · Sport · Succession · War crimes tribunals

Disability access
Staff briefed or trained on duties under the disability legislation, Wheelchair access, Disabled parking available

QUARRY CHAMBERS

64 Quarry Road, Winchester, Hants S023 0JS
01962 622202

Chambers of: Mr D G George

WINDSOR BARRISTERS' CHAMBERS

Windsor Chambers, Castle Hill House, 12 Castle Hill, Windsor, Berkshire SL4 1PD
01753 839321
Fax: 01344 621545
E-mail: mcb@windsorchambers.com

Chambers of: Mr M C Beaumont

Disability access
Staff briefed or trained on duties under the disability legislation, Wheelchair access

BARNSTAPLE CHAMBERS

Glebe Cottage, Broadwoodkelly, Winkleigh, Devon EX19 8ED
01837 83763
Fax: 01837 83763

Chambers of: Mr S P Best

CHAMBERS OF MISS C GIANOTA

10 Lake Road, Hoylake, Wirral CH47 2BX
0151 632 5805
Fax: 0151 553 0051
E-mail: gianota@gmail.co.uk

Chambers of: Miss C Gianota

CHAMBERS OF MR GORDON HARRISON

Manor Farm, Witton, Norfolk NR28 9TU
020 7556 5500
Fax: 020 7556 5565

Chambers of: Mr G W Harrison

CHAMBERS OF GORDON BISHOP

Brook House, Rough Road, Woking, Surrey GU22 0RB
01483 486 730
E-mail: gordonbishop@gmail.com

†Recorder *Door Tenant/Associate Member

CHAMBERS OF NIGEL LEY

23 Vale Farm Road, Woking, Surrey GU21 6DE
07947 221077

Disability access
Wheelchair access, Disabled parking available

THE CHAMBERS OF MRS LESLIE MILLIN

12 Folly Orchard, Wokingham, Berkshire RG41 2TU
0118 978 8026
Fax: 0118 978 8026
E-mail: lmmillin@gmail.com

Chambers of: Mrs L M Millin

CHAMBERS OF MR AUSTIN-WILLIAMS

70 Owen Road, Chapel Ash, Wolverhampton, West Midlands WV3 0AL
07900 933143

Chambers of: Mr R A Austin-Williams

CLOCK CHAMBERS

18 Waterloo Road, Wolverhampton WV1 4BL
01902 313444
Fax: 01902 421110
E-mail: clockchambers@btconnect.com

Chambers of: Prof J Ritson

Disability access
Staff briefed or trained on duties under the disability legislation, Wheelchair access, Disabled parking available

NIGHTINGALE CHAMBERS

Nightingale Cottage, Drakelow Lane, Wolverley, Worcestershire DY11 5RU
01562 851350
Fax: 01562 852547; DX: 721540 Kidderminster 5
E-mail: john@jasten.free-online.co.uk

Chambers of: Mr J A Stenhouse

CHAMBERS OF MR ALAN BRYSON

Hatherley House, Grundisburgh Road, Burgh, Woodbridge, Suffolk IP13 6QA
01473 735266
E-mail: alan.bryson@btinternet.com

Chambers of: Mr A D Bryson

CHAMBERS OF MR CHRISTOPHER CUTTING

Pansy Cottage, Goram's Mill Lane, Laxfield, Woodbridge, Suffolk IP13 8DW
01986 798499
Fax: 01986 798499
E-mail: chcutting@btinternet.com

Chambers of: Mr C H Cutting

KIDBY CHAMBERS

Grundisburgh Road, Woodbridge, Suffolk IP13 6QA

Chambers of: Miss H A O'Connor

VERITAS CHAMBERS

186 High Street, Worle, North Somerset BS22 6JD
01934 853 382
Fax: 01934 853382; DX: 47303 Worle
E-mail: nole@nsweeney.plus.com

Chambers of: Mr N C Sweeney

Disability access
Staff briefed or trained on duties under the disability legislation, Disabled parking available

CHAMBERS OF STUART LIGHTWING

8 Thirsk Road, Yarm, Stockton-on-Tees TS15 9HE
01642 650550
Fax: 01642 650550; DX: 60524 Middlesbrough
E-mail: stuartlightwing@yahoo.co.uk

Chambers of: Mr S W Lightwing

Disability access
Staff briefed or trained on duties under the disability legislation

CHAMBERS OF MR T BRENNAN

38 Sparrow Road, Yeovil BA21 4BY
07773 322748

DERE STREET BARRISTERS

14 Toft Green, York YO1 6JT
0844 3351551
Fax: 01904 610056; DX: 65517 York 7
E-mail: clerks@derestreet.co.uk

Chambers of: Mr J C Elvidge QC

Disability access
Staff briefed or trained on duties under the disability legislation, Wheelchair access, Disabled parking available

PART E

Individual Barristers Self-Employed

This section lists Barristers in private practice. Individuals are listed alphabetically by surname and details include the chambers at which they practice, year of call to the Bar, Inn of Court and academic qualifications.

Some individuals have opted to include additional information about themselves in this part of the Directory, such as other qualifications, membership of foreign bars, other professional experience, languages spoken, publications, reported cases and a list of the types of work undertaken.

Note: For those barristers listed in this section, information has been supplied by the Bar Council in the first instance and supplemented with information provided by individual barristers.

E

AARONBERG MR DAVID JEFFREY QC (2010)

15 New Bridge Street
London EC4V 6AU, ☎020 7842 1900
✉clerks@15nbs.com
Call Date: July 1981, Inner Temple
Pupil Supervisor, Recorder
Qualifications: [BA]
david.aaronberg@15nbs.com

AARONSON MR GRAHAM RAPHAEL QC (1982)

Pump Court Tax Chambers
16 Bedford Row, London WC1R 4EF,
☎020 7414 8080 ✉clerks@pumptax.com
Call Date: Nov 1966, Middle Temple
Qualifications: [MA (Cantab)]
gaaronson@pumptax.com

Types of work: Capital tax, Corporation tax, Income tax, National Insurance

ABADOO MR JOSEPH KWAME

2 Pump Court
1st Floor, 2 Pump Court, Temple, London EC4Y 7AH, ☎020 7353 5597
✉clerks@2pumpcourt.co.uk
Call Date: Nov 2004, Middle Temple
Qualifications: [LLB (Hons)]

ABASHEIKH MR OMAR SAID IMAM

Paragon Chambers
8 Creed Lane, St. Paul, London EC4V 5BR,
☎020 3318 9988
✉contact@paragonchambers.com
Call Date: July 2006, Gray's Inn
Qualifications: [LLB (Coventry)]
osiabasheikh@paragonchambers.com

ABBAS MR NIGEL

5RB
1st Floor, 5 Raymond Buildings, Gray's Inn, London WC1R 5BP, ☎020 7242 2902
✉clerks@5rb.com
Call Date: Nov 1995, Lincoln's Inn
Qualifications: [BA (Hons)]

ABBASI MISS NYLAH NAZ

9 King's Bench Walk
Lower Ground Floor South, 9 King's Bench Walk, Temple, London EC4Y 7DX,
☎020 7353 9564 ✉9kbw@btconnect.com
Call Date: Mar 2001, Lincoln's Inn
Qualifications: [BA (Hons) Dip Law]
9kbw@btconnect.com

ABBERLEY MR STEPHEN DAVID

No5 Chambers
Fountain Court, Steelhouse Lane, Birmingham B4 6DR, ☎0845 210 5555 ✉info@no5.com
No5 Chambers
Greenwood House, 4-7 Salisbury Court, London EC4Y 8AA, ☎0845 210 5555
No5 Chambers
38 Queen Square, Bristol BS1 4QS,
☎0845 210 5555
Call Date: Nov 2000, Middle Temple
Qualifications: [LLB (Hons) (Nott'm)]
sa@no5.com

ABBERTON MR DAVID EDWARD

Linenhall Chambers
1 Stanley Place, Chester CH1 2LU,
☎01244 348282
✉clerks@linenhallchambers.co.uk
Call Date: Nov 1994, Middle Temple
Pupil Supervisor
Qualifications: [BA (Hons)]

ABBOTT MISS CHRISTINE MARY

Temple Chambers
12 Clytha Park Road, Newport, Gwent NP20 4PB, ☎01633 267403
✉dbrinning@temple-chambers.co.uk
Temple Chambers
32 Park Place, Cardiff CF10 3BA,
☎029 2039 7364
✉DBrinning@Temple-Chambers.co.uk
Cathedral Chambers
28 Cathedral Road, Cardiff CF11 9LJ,
☎02920 660129
Cathedral Chambers
10 Clytha Park Road, Newport NP20 4PB,
☎01633 215112
Call Date: Oct 1999, Middle Temple
Qualifications: [LLB (Hons)(Wales)]

ABBOTT MR FRANCIS ARTHUR

Pump Court Chambers
31 Southgate Street, Winchester, Hampshire SO23 9EB, ☎01962 868 161
✉clerks@3pumpcourt.com
Pump Court Chambers
Upper Ground Floor, 3 Pump Court, Temple, London EC4Y 7AJ, ☎020 7353 0711
✉clerks@3pumpcourt.com
Pump Court Chambers
5 Temple Chambers, Temple Street, Swindon SN1 1SQ, ☎01793 539899
✉clerks@3pumpcourt.com
Call Date: Nov 1972, Lincoln's Inn
Pupil Supervisor, Recorder
Qualifications: [BA (Nott'm)]
fa@3pumpcourt.com

E

ABBOTT MRS MARY MACCONNACHIE

36 Bedford Row
London WC1R 4JH, ☎ 020 7421 8000
✉ chambers@36bedfordrow.co.uk
Call Date: Oct 1994, Gray's Inn
Qualifications: [BA (Hons)]

ABBOTT MR RODERICK JOHN

1 Chancery Lane
London WC2A 1LF, ☎ 0845 634 6666
✉ clerks@1chancerylane.com
Call Date: Oct 2006, Middle Temple
Qualifications: [BA (Hons) (Oxon)]
rabbott@1chancerylane.com

ABEL MISS ANN PETRINA

Blackfriars Chambers
79-83 Temple Chambers, 3-7 Temple Avenue, London EC4Y 0HP, ☎ 020 7353 7400
✉ clerks@blackfriarschambers.com
Call Date: Mar 1998, Lincoln's Inn
Qualifications: [LLB (Hons)(B'ham) BA (Hons)(Warw)]
ann.abel@blackfriarschambers.com

E

ABELL MR ANTHONY ROGER

2 Bedford Row
London WC1R 4BU, ☎ 020 7440 8888
✉ clerks@2bedfordrow.co.uk
Call Date: July 1977, Gray's Inn
Pupil Supervisor
Qualifications: [LLB (Lond)]
aabell@2bedfordrow.co.uk

ABENGOWE MR JULIAN CHIMA

Call Date: Nov 2002, Inner Temple
Qualifications: [BSc (Bath) CPE (Leeds)]
JAbengowe@zenithchambers.co.uk

ABER MR GORDON

4 Paper Buildings
1st Floor, 4 Paper Buildings, Temple, London EC4Y 7EX, ☎ 020 7427 5200
✉ clerks@4pb.com
Call Date: Mar 1996, Lincoln's Inn
Qualifications: [BA LLM (Lond) LLM]

ABRAHAM DR CHAKALAMANNIL MATHEW

Warwick House Chambers
8 Warwick Court, Warwick House Chambers, Gray's Inn, London WC1R 5DJ,
☎ 020 7430 2323
✉ clerks@warwickhousechambers.com
Call Date: July 1996, Lincoln's Inn
Qualifications: [BA PhD (Lond) LLM LLB]

ABRAHAM MISS JOANNE JADE

St Johns Buildings Liverpool
8th Floor India Buildings, Water Street, Liverpool L2 0XG, ☎ 0151 243 6000
✉ clerk@stjohnsbuildings.co.uk
St Johns Buildings
21 White Friars, Chester CH1 1NZ,
☎ 01244 323070
✉ clerk@stjohnsbuildings.co.uk
16 Winckley Square
Preston PR1 3JJ, ☎ 01772 256100
Call Date: Nov 2004, Gray's Inn
Qualifications: [LLB]
jabrhm@aol.com

ABRAHAMS MR JAMES

8 New Square
8 New Square, Lincoln's Inn, London WC2A 3QP, ☎ 020 7405 4321
✉ clerks@8newsquare.co.uk
Call Date: Oct 1997, Gray's Inn
Pupil Supervisor
Qualifications: [BA BCL (Oxon)]
james.abrahams@8newsquare.co.uk

Types of work: Breach of confidence, Competition law, Copyright, Copyright theft, Copyright Tribunal, Data protection, Design, E-commerce, EC competition law, Entertainment, Franchising, Information technology, Intellectual property, Malicious falsehood, Media, Media and entertainment, Passing off, Patents, Pharmaceuticals, Scientific and technical disputes, Trade secrets, Trademarks

ABRAHAMS MR PAUL JOHN

Old Court Chambers
Newham House, 96-98 Borough Road, Middlesbrough TS1 2HJ, ☎ 01642 232523
✉ clerks@oldcourtchambers.com
Call Date: Nov 2002, Gray's Inn
Qualifications: [LLB(Hons)(Sheff)]
clerks@oldcourtchambers.com

ABRAM MISS SARAH KATHERINE

Brick Court Chambers
7-8 Essex Street, London WC2R 3LD,
☎ 020 7379 3550 ✉ clerks@brickcourt.co.uk
Call Date: Oct 2006, Inner Temple
Qualifications: [LLB (Bris) BCL (Oxon)]
sarah.abram@brickcourt.co.uk

ABRANTES-STANWORTH MISS CARLA JAYNE

KBW
The Engine House, No 1 Foundry Square, Leeds LS11 5DL, ☎0113 297 1200
✉clerks@kbwchambers.com
Call Date: July 2009, Middle Temple
Qualifications: [LLB (Hons) (B'ham) LLM (B'ham)]

ABU-MUSTAFA MR JEHAD

1 Paper Buildings
1st Floor, 1 Paper Buildings, Temple, London EC4Y 7EP, ☎020 7353 3728
✉clerks@onepaper.co.uk
Call Date: Nov 2007, Middle Temple
Qualifications: [BA (Hons) (Nott'm) PgDL (Lond)]
jehadmustafa@onepaper.co.uk

ABZARIAN MR ARASH

Chambers of Mr Ami Feder
Ground Floor, Lamb Building, Temple, London EC4Y 7AS, ☎020 7797 7788
✉clerks@lambbuilding.co.uk
Lamb Building
22 Ship Street, Brighton BN1 1AD, ☎01273 820490
✉admin@lambbuilding.co.uk
Chambers of Mr Ami Feder
Ground Floor, Lamb Building, Temple, London EC4Y 7AS, ☎020 7797 7788
✉clerks@lambbuilding.co.uk
Call Date: Mar 2007, Lincoln's Inn
Qualifications: [BSc (Lond) MSc (Lond)]

ACE MR RICHARD WILLIAM

9 Park Place
9 Park Place, Cardiff, South Glamorgan CF10 3DP, ☎029 2038 2731
✉clerks@9parkplace.co.uk
Call Date: Oct 1993, Lincoln's Inn
Qualifications: [BSc (Hons)(Reading) Dip Law (Lond)]
clerks@9parkplace.co.uk

ACHESON MR ROBERT IAN

23 Essex Street
London WC2R 3AA, ☎020 7413 0353
✉clerks@23es.com
Call Date: Feb 1992, Gray's Inn
Pupil Supervisor
Qualifications: [BA (Oxon)]
ianacheson@23es.com

ACHURCH MR TIMOTHY MARK

1 High Pavement
Nottingham NG1 1HF, ☎0115 941 8218
✉clerks@1highpavement.co.uk
Call Date: Oct 1996, Middle Temple
Qualifications: [LLB (Hons)(Manc)]
markachurch@1highpavement.co.uk

ACKER MISS ELISABETH FLORENCE LEONA

23 Essex Street
London WC2R 3AA, ☎020 7413 0353
✉clerks@23es.com
Call Date: July 2010, Middle Temple
Qualifications: [BA (Hons) (Oxon)]

ACKERLEY MR DAVID ALBERT

New Bailey Chambers
4th Floor, Corn Exchange, Fenwick Street, Liverpool, Merseyside L2 7QS, ☎0151 236 9402 ✉clerks@newbailey.com
Call Date: Nov 1992, Inner Temple
Qualifications: [LLB]
clerks@newbailey.com

ACKERLEY MISS REBECCA ELIZABETH

New Bailey Chambers
4th Floor, Corn Exchange, Fenwick Street, Liverpool, Merseyside L2 7QS, ☎0151 236 9402 ✉clerks@newbailey.com
Call Date: Nov 2004, Lincoln's Inn
Qualifications: [BA (Hons) (Manch)]
Clerks@newbailey.com

ACKLAND MISS SACHA MARIE

Temple Garden Chambers
1 Harcourt Buildings, Temple, London EC4Y 9DA, ☎020 7583 1315
✉clerks@tgchambers.com
Call Date: Oct 1998, Inner Temple
Qualifications: [BA (Lond) CPE (Lond)]
sackland@tgchambers.com

ACKLAND-VINCENT MISS GILLIAN STELLA

Arden Chambers
20 Bloomsbury Square, London WC1A 2NS, ☎020 7242 4244
✉clerks@ardenchambers.com
Call Date: July 2001, Middle Temple
Qualifications: [LLB (Hons)]

E

ACLAND DR PIERS DYKE QC (2010)

11 South Square
1st Floor, 11 South Square, Gray's Inn, London WC1R 5EY, ☎020 7405 1222
✉clerks@11southsquare.com
Riverview Chambers
Hamilton House, 1 Temple Avenue, London EC4Y 0HA, ☎0844 225 3999
✉chrisbaylis@riverviewchambers.com
Call Date: Nov 1993, Lincoln's Inn
Pupil Supervisor
Qualifications: [BSc (Hons) PhD (Lond)]
pacland@11southsquare.com

ACTON MISS JAYNE

Exchange Chambers
7 Ralli Courts, West Riverside, Manchester M3 5FT, ☎0161 833 2722
Exchange Chambers
One Derby Square, Derby Square, Liverpool L2 9XX, ☎0151 236 7747
✉info@exchangechambers.co.uk
Exchange Chambers
Oxford House, Oxford Row, Leeds LS1 3BE, ☎0113 203 1970
✉spencer@exchangechambers.co.uk
Call Date: Mar 1996, Lincoln's Inn
Qualifications: [LLB (Hons) (Sheff)]
acton@exchangechambers.co.uk

ACTON MR STEPHEN NEIL

Radcliffe Chambers
Ground Floor, 11 New Square, Lincoln's Inn, London WC2A 3QB, ☎020 7831 0081
✉clerks@radcliffechambers.com
Call Date: July 1977, Inner Temple
Pupil Supervisor
Qualifications: [MA (Cantab)]
sacton@radcliffechambers.com

Fax: 020 7405 2560;
Out of hours telephone: 0790 0423 294

Types of work: Banking, Chancery (general), Chancery (land law), Commercial litigation, Commercial property, Common land, Company, commercial and competition, Conveyancing, Equity, Family provision, Insolvency, Insurance, Landlord and tenant, Partnerships, Personal insolvency, Professional negligence, Sale and carriage of goods, Succession, Trusts, Wills

ACTON DAVIS MR JONATHAN JAMES QC (1996)

Atkin Chambers
1 Atkin Building, Gray's Inn, London WC1R 5AT, ☎020 7404 0102
✉clerks@atkinchambers.com
Call Date: July 1977, Inner Temple
Recorder
Qualifications: [LLB (Lond)]
jadavis@atkinchambers.com

ADAIR MRS EMMA-JANE

The Chambers of Grahame Aldous QC
9 Gough Square, London EC4A 3DG, ☎020 7832 0500
✉clerks@9goughsquare.co.uk
Call Date: July 2001, Gray's Inn
Qualifications: [LLB (Hons)]
emahood@9goughsquare.co.uk

ADAIR MR STUART ANTHONY

XXIV Old Buildings
Ground Floor, 24 Old Buildings, Lincoln's Inn, London WC2A 3UP, ☎020 7691 2424
✉clerks@xxiv.co.uk
Call Date: Oct 1995, Inner Temple
Pupil Supervisor
Qualifications: [LLB (Exon)]
stuart.adair@xxiv.co.uk

ADAM MR THOMAS NOBLE QC (2008)

Brick Court Chambers
7-8 Essex Street, London WC2R 3LD, ☎020 7379 3550 ✉clerks@brickcourt.co.uk
Call Date: Nov 1991, Inner Temple
Pupil Supervisor
Qualifications: [MA (Cantab)]
tom.adam@brickcourt.co.uk

ADAMS MR BRYNMOR PAUL

Five Paper
Ground Floor, 5 Paper Buildings, Temple, London EC4Y 7HB, ☎020 7815 3200
Call Date: July 2008, Lincoln's Inn
Qualifications: [BA (Oxon)]
Brynmoradams@fivepaper.com

ADAMS MR CHRISTOPHER ALAN

St Philips Chambers
55 Temple Row, Birmingham B2 5LS, ☎0121 246 7000 ✉clerks@st-philips.com
Call Date: July 1986, Lincoln's Inn
Recorder
Qualifications: [LLB (Lond)]
cadams@st-philips.co.uk

ADAMS MR DEREK ADAMA

12 Old Square Chambers
1st Floor, 12 Old Square, Lincoln's Inn, London WC2A 3TX, ☎020 7404 0875
✉clerks@12oldsquare.com
Call Date: Nov 1988, Middle Temple
Qualifications: [BA LLM (LSE) MCIArb Dip Law]
✉clerks@12oldsquare.com

ADAMS MR GUY LAIRD

St John's Chambers
101 Victoria Street, Bristol BS1 6PU, ☎0117 923 4700
✉clerks@stjohnschambers.co.uk
Call Date: July 1989, Middle Temple
Pupil Supervisor
Qualifications: [MA (Cantab)]
✉guy.adams@stjohnschambers.co.uk

ADAMS MR JAMES ROBERT

New Court Chambers
3 Broad Chare, Newcastle Upon Tyne NE1 3DQ, ☎0191 232 1980
✉clerks@newcourt-chambers.co.uk
Call Date: July 1978, Gray's Inn
Pupil Supervisor
Qualifications: [LLB (Newc)]
✉jamie.adams@newcourt-chambers.co.uk

ADAMS MISS JAYNE MARGARET

Ropewalk Chambers
24 The Ropewalk, Nottingham NG1 5EF, ☎0115 947 2581 ✉clerks@ropewalk.co.uk
Call Date: July 1982, Gray's Inn
Pupil Supervisor
Qualifications: [LLB]
✉jayneadams@ropewalk.co.uk

ADAMS MS LINDSAY EVELINE

1 Pump Court
Elm Court, Temple, London EC4Y 7AB, ☎020 7842 7070
✉(name)@pumpcourt.co.uk
Call Date: Nov 1987, Middle Temple
Pupil Supervisor
Qualifications: [LLB(Hons)]
✉la@1pumpcourt.co.uk

ADAMS MR NATHAN JOHN

Dere Street Barristers
14 Toft Green, York YO1 6JT, ☎0844 3351551
✉clerks@derestreet.co.uk
Call Date: July 2004, Inner Temple
✉clerks@yorkchambers.co.uk, nadams@yorkchambers.co.uk

ADAMS MR PAUL CHRISTOPHER

Serle Court
6 New Square, Lincoln's Inn, London WC2A 3QS, ☎020 7242 6105
✉clerks@serlecourt.co.uk
Call Date: July 2008, Lincoln's Inn
Qualifications: [BA (Oxon) BCL (Oxon)]
✉padams@serlecourt.co.uk

ADAMS MR RICHARD JAMES THOMAS

St Philips Chambers
55 Temple Row, Birmingham B2 5LS, ☎0121 246 7000 ✉clerks@st-philips.com
Call Date: Oct 1999, Gray's Inn
Qualifications: [LLB (Nott'm)]
✉radams@st-philips.com

ADAMS MR ROBERT GEORGE SETON

Trinity Chambers
The Custom House, 39 Quayside, Newcastle Upon Tyne NE1 3DE, ☎0191 232 1927
✉info@trinitychambers.co.uk
Trinity Chambers
Multi Media Exchange, 72-80 Corporation Road, Middlesbrough TS1 2RF, ☎01642 247569
✉info@trinitychambers.co.uk
Call Date: Oct 1993, Inner Temple
Pupil Supervisor, Recorder
Qualifications: [MA (Cantab)]
✉r.adams@trinitychambers.co.uk

ADAMSON MR ALAN

Kew Chambers
354 Kew Road, Kew, Surrey TW9 3DU, ☎0844 8099991
✉admin@kewchambers.co.uk
Call Date: Oct 1997, Inner Temple
Qualifications: [BA (Leic) CPE (Nott'm)]
✉adamlaw100@btopenworld.com

ADAMSON MR DOMINIC JAMES

Temple Garden Chambers
1 Harcourt Buildings, Temple, London EC4Y 9DA, ☎020 7583 1315
✉clerks@tgchambers.com
Call Date: Oct 1997, Lincoln's Inn
Pupil Supervisor
Qualifications: [LLB (Newc)]
✉dominicadamson@tgchambers.com

ADAMSON MISS LILIAS LOUISA

Becket Chambers
17 New Dover Road, Canterbury, Kent
CT1 3AS, ☎01227 786331
✉clerks@becket-chambers.co.uk
Call Date: Nov 1994, Gray's Inn
Qualifications: [BA (Hons) (Keele)]
ladamson@becket-chambers.co.uk

ADAMYK MR SIMON CHARLES

New Square Chambers
12 New Square, Lincoln's Inn, London
WC2A 3SW, ☎020 7419 8000
✉robin.hollington@newsquarechambers.co.uk
Call Date: Nov 1991, Lincoln's Inn
Pupil Supervisor
Qualifications: [BA (Hons) (Camb) LLM (Harvard)]
simon.adamyk@newsquarechambers.co.uk

ADCOCK MISS DEBORAH JANE

Dere Street Barristers
14 Toft Green, York YO1 6JT, ☎0844 3351551
✉clerks@derestreet.co.uk
York Chambers
Rotterdam House, 116 The Quayside,
Newcastle Upon Tyne NE1 3DY,
☎0191 206 4677
Call Date: July 2005, Lincoln's Inn
Qualifications: [LLB (Hons)]
clerks@yorkchambers.co.uk, dadcock@yorkchambers.co.uk

ADDISON MR KENNETH PAUL

5 Pump Court
Ground Floor, 5 Pump Court, Temple, London
EC4Y 7AP, ☎020 7353 2532
✉clerks@5pumpcourt.com
Call Date: July 1988, Middle Temple
Qualifications: [LLB (Hons)]
pauladdison@5pumpcourt.com

ADDISON MR NEIL PATRICK

Palmyra Chambers
Royal House, 46 Legh Street, Warrington
WA1 1UJ, ☎01925 444919
✉clerk@palmyrachambers.com
Call Date: Nov 1976, Gray's Inn
Pupil Supervisor
Qualifications: [BA]

ADDISON MS YOLANDA KRISTEN

Westgate Chambers
64 High Street, Lewes, East Sussex BN7 1XG,
☎01273 480510
✉clerks@westgate-chambers.co.uk
Call Date: Oct 2003, Inner Temple
Qualifications: [LLB (Lancs)]
ya@westgate-chambers.co.uk

ADDO MR JONATHAN KOFI

Five St Andrew's Hill
5 St Andrew's Hill, London EC4V 5BZ,
☎020 7332 5400 ✉Clerks@5sah.co.uk
Call Date: Oct 2006, Inner Temple
Qualifications: [LLB LLM (Exon)]

ADDY MISS CAROLINE KORDAI

One Brick Court
1st Floor, One Brick Court, Temple, London
EC4Y 9BY, ☎020 7353 8845
✉clerks@onebrickcourt.com
Call Date: Nov 1991, Inner Temple
Pupil Supervisor
Qualifications: [LLB (Exon)]
ca@onebrickcourt.com

ADDY MISS CATHERINE JOANNE

Maitland Chambers
7 Stone Buildings, Lincoln's Inn, London
WC2A 3SZ, ☎020 7406 1200
✉clerks@maitlandchambers.com
Call Date: Nov 1998, Middle Temple
Pupil Supervisor
Qualifications: [MA (Cantab) LLM (Cantab)]
cjaddy@maitlandchambers.com

ADDY MISS LAURA REBECCA

Sovereign Chambers
46 Park Place, Leeds LS1 2RY,
☎0113 245 1841
✉clerks@sovereignchambers.co.uk
Call Date: July 2004, Middle Temple
Qualifications: [LLB Hons (Dunelm)]
laura.addy@sovereignchambers.co.uk

ADEBAYO MR IBITAYO ALADE

Westgate Chambers
64 High Street, Lewes, East Sussex BN7 1XG,
☎01273 480510
✉clerks@westgate-chambers.co.uk
Call Date: Nov 1989, Inner Temple
Qualifications: [BA (Hons)(Bris) DipLaw (Bris)]

ADENEKAN MR LATIFF AREMU

Temple Chambers
29 Forest Hill Road, East Dulwich, London SE22 0SG, ☎ 020 8299 0959
✉ latiff95@hotmail.com
Call Date: Nov 1970, Inner Temple
Qualifications: [LLB (Lond)]
✉ latiff95@hotmail.com

ADEREMI MR ADEDAMOLA OLASUPO

Chambers of G. D. Tetteh
Ground Floor, 2 Middle Temple Lane, Temple, London EC4Y 9AA, ☎ 020 7353 7095
Call Date: Feb 1992, Inner Temple
Pupil Supervisor
Qualifications: [LLB (Nigeria) LLM (Nigeria)]

ADEWALE MR REMI ADETOKUNBO SANNI

Chambers of Mr R. A. Adewale
Address withheld ☎ 020 7231 2814
Chambers of G. D. Tetteh
Ground Floor, 2 Middle Temple Lane, Temple, London EC4Y 9AA, ☎ 020 7353 7095
Call Date: Oct 1995, Middle Temple
Qualifications: [LLB(Hons) LLM (Lond)]

ADEYEMI MISS TOPE

5 Pump Court
Ground Floor, 5 Pump Court, Temple, London EC4Y 7AP, ☎ 020 7353 2532
✉ clerks@5pumpcourt.com
Call Date: Nov 2008, Middle Temple
Qualifications: [LLB]

ADJEI MR CYRIL JOHN

Five Paper
Ground Floor, 5 Paper Buildings, Temple, London EC4Y 7HB, ☎ 020 7815 3200
Call Date: Oct 1995, Inner Temple
Pupil Supervisor
Qualifications: [LLB (Lond) LLM (Cantab) LLD (Italy)]
✉ cyriladjei@fivepaper.com

ADKIN MR JAMES SIMON

New Court Chambers
3 Broad Chare, Newcastle Upon Tyne NE1 3DQ, ☎ 0191 232 1980
✉ clerks@newcourt-chambers.co.uk
Call Date: Oct 1992, Lincoln's Inn
Pupil Supervisor
Qualifications: [LLB(Hons)(Newc)]
✉ james.adkin@newcourt-chambers.co.uk

ADKIN MR JONATHAN WILLIAM

Serle Court
6 New Square, Lincoln's Inn, London WC2A 3QS, ☎ 020 7242 6105
✉ clerks@serlecourt.co.uk
Call Date: Oct 1997, Gray's Inn
Pupil Supervisor
Qualifications: [MA (Oxon)]
✉ jadkin@serlecourt.co.uk

ADKIN MS TANA MARIE THERESE

Charter Chambers
33 John Street, London WC1N 2AT, ☎ 020 7618 4400
✉ clerks@charterchambers.com
Call Date: Nov 1992, Inner Temple
Qualifications: [BA (Hons)(Leics) Dip Law (Lond)]
✉ tana.adkin@charterchambers.com

ADKIN MR TIMOTHY CLIVE

42 Bedford Row
London WC1R 4LL, ☎ 020 7831 0222
✉ clerks@42br.com
Call Date: Nov 2004, Lincoln's Inn
Qualifications: [BSc (Hons)]
✉ Tim.adkin@42br.com

ADKINS MR RICHARD DAVID QC (1995)

South Square
3-4 South Square, Gray's Inn, London WC1R 5HP, ☎ 020 7696 9900
✉ practicemanagers@southsquare.com
Call Date: July 1982, Middle Temple
Qualifications: [MA (Oxon)]
✉ richardadkins@southsquare.com

ADKINSON MR RICHARD JAMES

No5 Chambers
Fountain Court, Steelhouse Lane, Birmingham B4 6DR, ☎ 0845 210 5555 ✉ info@no5.com
No5 Chambers
Greenwood House, 4-7 Salisbury Court, London EC4Y 8AA, ☎ 0845 210 5555
No5 Chambers
38 Queen Square, Bristol BS1 4QS, ☎ 0845 210 5555
Call Date: July 2001, Middle Temple
Qualifications: [MEng (Hons) Dip Law]
✉ ra@no5.com

E

ADLER MR JONATHAN

1 Pump Court
Elm Court, Temple, London EC4Y 7AB,
☎ 020 7842 7070
✉ (name)@pumpcourt.co.uk
Call Date: Oct 1999, Inner Temple
Qualifications: [BA (Warw)]
jonathan.adler@4bc.co.uk

ADONIS MR GEORGIOS

Chambers of Marion Smullen and Kerim Fuad QC
1 Inner Temple Lane, London EC4Y 1AF,
☎ 020 7427 4400 ✉ clerks@1itl.com
Call Date: July 1973, Lincoln's Inn

AEBERLI MR PETER DOLPH

3 PB Barristers
3 Paper Buildings, Temple, London EC4Y 7EU,
☎ 020 7583 8055
3 PB Barristers
Royal Talbot House, 2 Victoria Street, Bristol, Avon BS1 6BB, ☎ 0117 928 1520
3 PB Barristers
30 Christchurch Road, Bournemouth, Dorset BH1 3PD, ☎ 01202 292102
✉ clerks.bournemouth@3paper.co.uk
3 PB Barristers
4 St Peter Street, Winchester SO23 8BW,
☎ 01962 868884
✉ clerks.winchester@3paper.co.uk
3 PB Barristers
23 Beaumont Street, Oxford OX1 2NP,
☎ 01865 793 736
Call Date: Nov 1990, Middle Temple
Qualifications: [MA (Edin) Dip Arch ARIAS FCIArb CEDR RIBA BA (Oxon)]
peter.aeberli@3paper.co.uk

AFEEVA MR MARK KUDZO DZITOSI

Matrix Chambers
Griffin Building, Gray's Inn, London WC1R 5LN, ☎ 020 7404 3447
✉ matrix@matrixlaw.co.uk / Iscott@ matrixlaw.co.uk
Call Date: Oct 1997, Inner Temple
Qualifications: [LLB (Lond) LLM (Lond)]
markafeeva@matrixlaw.co.uk

E

AFZAL MR FAYYAZ

No5 Chambers
Fountain Court, Steelhouse Lane, Birmingham B4 6DR, ☎ 0845 210 5555 ✉ info@no5.com
No5 Chambers
Greenwood House, 4-7 Salisbury Court, London EC4Y 8AA, ☎ 0845 210 5555
No5 Chambers
38 Queen Square, Bristol BS1 4QS,
☎ 0845 210 5555
Call Date: Oct 1999, Lincoln's Inn
Pupil Supervisor
Qualifications: [LLB (Hons)(Staffs) Pg Dip]

AFZAL MR IMRAN SHAZAD

Gray's Inn Tax Chambers
3rd Floor, Gray's Inn Chambers, Gray's Inn, London WC1R 5JA, ☎ 020 7242 2642
✉ clerks@taxbar.com
Call Date: Oct 2008, Lincoln's Inn
Qualifications: [BA (Oxon) BCL (Oxon)]
ia@taxbar.com

AFZAL MR ZAHEER

St Philips Chambers
55 Temple Row, Birmingham B2 5LS,
☎ 0121 246 7000 ✉ clerks@st-philips.com
Call Date: July 2000, Gray's Inn
Qualifications: [B.Sc (Lond)]
zafzal@st-philips.com

AGER MR RICHARD LAWRENCE

Crown Office Row Chambers
119 Church Street, Brighton, Sussex BN1 1UD, ☎ 01273 625625
✉ clerks@1cor.com
Call Date: Nov 2004, Middle Temple
richard.ager@1cor.com

AGEROS MR DAVID KEITH JUSTIN

4 Paper Buildings
1st Floor, 4 Paper Buildings, Temple, London EC4Y 7EX, ☎ 020 7427 5200
✉ clerks@4pb.com
Call Date: Nov 1993, Inner Temple
Qualifications: [BA (Hons)(Cantab) Dip Law (Lond)]
ja@4pb.com

AGEROS MR JAMES HUGH PAUL

Crown Office Chambers
2 Crown Office Row, Temple, London EC4Y 7HJ, ☎ 020 7797 8100
✉ mail@crownofficechambers.com
Call Date: May 1990, Inner Temple
Pupil Supervisor
Qualifications: [BA (So'ton) Dip Law]

AGGREY-ORLEANS MR BERTRAND-LESLIE KWEKU

12 King's Bench Walk
12 King's Bench Walk, Temple, London EC4Y 7EL, ☎ 020 7583 0811
Call Date: Oct 1998, Inner Temple
Qualifications: [LLB (Lond)]
aggrey-orleans@12kbw.co.uk

AGHA MR SIZA

3 Raymond Buildings
3 Raymond Buildings, Gray's Inn, London WC1R 5BH, ☎ 020 7400 6400
clerks@3rblaw.com
Call Date: Feb 1994, Lincoln's Inn
Qualifications: [LLB (Hons) (Wales)]
siza.agha@3raymondbuildings.com

AGNELLO MISS RAQUEL QC (2009)

11 Stone Buildings
11 Stone Buildings, Lincoln's Inn, London WC2A 3TG, ☎ 020 7831 6381
clerks@11sb.com
Call Date: Nov 1986, Inner Temple
Qualifications: [BA (Hons) (Sussex) Dip D'Etudes ACI Arb]

AGNEW MISS CHRISTINE

2 Bedford Row
London WC1R 4BU, ☎ 020 7440 8888
clerks@2bedfordrow.co.uk
Call Date: Nov 1992, Inner Temple
Pupil Supervisor
Qualifications: [LLB]
cagnew@2bedfordrow.co.uk

AGNIHOTRI MR NAVEEN

12 College Place
Fauvelle Buildings, 12 College Place, Southampton SO15 2FE, ☎ 023 8032 0320
clerks@12cp.co.uk
Call Date: July 2001, Gray's Inn
Qualifications: [LLB (Hons) LLM]

AGYEMAN-RAWLINGS MISS AMINA

Chambers of G. D. Tetteh
Ground Floor, 2 Middle Temple Lane, Temple, London EC4Y 9AA, ☎ 020 7353 7095
Call Date: July 2007, Lincoln's Inn
Qualifications: [LLB (Notts)]

AHERN MR EUGENE CHRISTOPHER

Trinity Chambers
Highfield House, Moulsham Street, Chelmsford, Essex CM2 9AH, ☎ 01245 605040
clerks@trinitychambers.com
Call Date: July 2007, Middle Temple
Qualifications: [LLB (Hons)]
eahern@trinitychambers.com

AHLUWALIA MR NAVTEJ SINGH

Garden Court Chambers
57-60 Lincoln's Inn Fields, London WC2A 3LJ, ☎ 020 7993 7600 info@gclaw.co.uk
Call Date: Mar 2001, Middle Temple
Qualifications: [LLB (Hons) (LSE) LLM (LSE)]
navteja@gclaw.co.uk

AHMAD MS AYSHA

42 Bedford Row
London WC1R 4LL, ☎ 020 7831 0222
clerks@42br.com
Call Date: Oct 1996, Middle Temple
Qualifications: [LLM (Lond) BA (Hons)(Lond)]

AHMAD MR KASHIF ZUBAIR

Blenheim Chambers
605 Blenheim Centre, Hounslow, Middlesex TW3 1ND, ☎ 07588 608288
kashif.ahmad786@yahoo.co.uk
Call Date: July 1999, Lincoln's Inn
Qualifications: [BSc LLB MA LLM CPE]

AHMAD DR MIRZA FARAKH NAVID

St Philips Chambers
55 Temple Row, Birmingham B2 5LS, ☎ 0121 246 7000 clerks@st-philips.com
Call Date: July 1984, Gray's Inn
Pupil Supervisor
Qualifications: [BSoc Sci (Keele) MBA LLM LLD]

AHMAD MR ZUBAIR

2 Hare Court
Lower Ground, Ground, 1st & 2nd Floor, 2 Hare Court, Temple, London EC4Y 7BH, ☎ 020 7353 3982 clerks@2harecourt.com
Call Date: Oct 1995, Lincoln's Inn
Pupil Supervisor
Qualifications: [LLB (Hons)(Lond)]
zubairahmad@2harecourt.com

AHMED MISS AMINA

Renaissance Chambers
5th Floor, Gray's Inn Chambers, Gray's Inn, London WC1R 5JA, ☎020 7404 1111
✉clerks@renaissancechambers.co.uk
Call Date: Feb 1995, Middle Temple
Qualifications: [BSc (Hons)(Lond) CPE (Lond)]
aa1@renaissancechambers.co.uk

AHMED MISS BUSHRA

Ely Place Chambers
30 Ely Place, London EC1N 6TD,
☎020 7400 9600 ✉admin@elyplace.com
Call Date: Nov 2001, Middle Temple
Qualifications: [LLB (Hons)]
bahmed@elyplace.com

AHMED MR FAROOQ TAHIR

Seven Bedford Row
7 Bedford Row, London WC1R 4BS,
☎020 7242 3555 ✉clerks@7br.co.uk
Call Date: Nov 1983, Inner Temple
Recorder
Qualifications: [LLB (Hons) (Lond)]
fahmed@7br.co.uk

AHMED MR GULAM MORTUZA

Chambers of Marion Smullen and Kerim Fuad QC
1 Inner Temple Lane, London EC4Y 1AF,
☎020 7427 4400 ✉clerks@1itl.com
Call Date: Oct 1997, Lincoln's Inn
Pupil Supervisor
Qualifications: [LLB (Hons)(B'ham) LLM (B'ham)]
gulam.ahmed@1itl.com

AHMED MR ISHFAQ

Stone Chambers
4 Field Court, Gray's Inn, London WC1R 5EF,
☎020 7440 6900
✉clerks@stonechambers.com
Call Date: Oct 1999, Lincoln's Inn
Qualifications: [LLB (Hons)(Bris)]
ishfaq.ahmed@stonechambers.com

AHMED MISS JACQUELINE MICHELLE

Southernhay Chambers
33 Southernhay East, Exeter EX1 1NX,
☎01392 255777
✉clerks@southernhaychambers.co.uk
Call Date: July 1988, Inner Temple
Qualifications: [LLB (City)]
j.ahmed@southernhaychambers.co.uk, hlmjack@freeuk.com

AHMED MR MOBIN UDDIN

Chambers of Mobin U Ahmed
36 Chase Road, London N14 4EU,
☎020 8886 2015
✉mobinuahmed@hotmail.co.uk
Call Date: Nov 1969, Lincoln's Inn
Qualifications: [B.Com (Dhaka)]
mobinuahmed@hotmail.co.uk

AHMED MR NAZIR

Centurion Chambers
Chambers of Mer Nazir Ahmed, 1st Floor Paragon House, 79 Birmingham Road, West Bromwich B70 6PX, ☎0121 553 4613
✉clerks@centurionchambers.com
Call Date: May 1992, Inner Temple
Qualifications: [BSc (Hons)]

AHMED MR RASHID

6 King's Bench Walk
Ground, Third & Fourth Floors, 6 King's Bench Walk, Temple, London EC4Y 7DR,
☎020 7353 4931 ✉clerks@6kbw.co.uk
Call Date: July 2003, Lincoln's Inn
Qualifications: [LLB (Hons) (Lanc)]
rashid.ahmed@6kbw.co.uk

AHMED MR SALEEM

Perivale Chambers
Ground Floor, 15 Colwyn Avenue, Perivale, Middlesex UB6 8JX, ☎020 8998 1935
✉naushadahmed@hotmail.com
Call Date: Feb 1971, Inner Temple
Pupil Supervisor
Qualifications: [BA]

AHMED MR SIRAJ ISSAP

St Johns Buildings Liverpool
8th Floor India Buildings, Water Street, Liverpool L2 0XG, ☎0151 243 6000
✉clerk@stjohnsbuildings.co.uk
St Johns Buildings
21 White Friars, Chester CH1 1NZ,
☎01244 323070
✉clerk@stjohnsbuildings.co.uk
St Johns Buildings
24a - 28 St John Street, Manchester M3 4DJ,
☎0161 214 1500
✉clerk@stjohnsbuildings.co.uk
Call Date: Mar 2001, Middle Temple
Qualifications: [LLB (Hons) (Bris)]

AHMED MISS SOBIA

Zenith Chambers
10 Park Square, Leeds LS1 2LH,
☎0113 245 5438
✉clerks@zenithchambers.co.uk
Call Date: Oct 2007, Lincoln's Inn
Qualifications: [LLB (Hons) (Lond)]

AHMED MR USMAN

Old Square Chambers
10-11 Bedford Row, London WC1R 4BU, ☎020 7269 0300 ✉clerks@oldsquare.co.uk
Call Date: Nov 2008, Lincoln's Inn
Qualifications: [BSc (Bris) CPE UCU]
✉ahmed@oldsquare.co.uk

AHUJA MR HARPREET SINGH

Octagon Chambers
29 Park Street, Taunton, Somerset TA1 4DG, ☎01823 331919
✉jcload@Octagonchambers.co.uk
Call Date: Oct 2001, Inner Temple
Qualifications: [LLB (Lond) LLM (Manch)]
✉Hahuja@octagonchambers.co.uk

AHYA MISS SONAL

KCH Garden Square
1 Oxford Street, Nottingham NG1 5BH, ☎0115 941 8851
✉clerks@kchgardensquare.co.uk
Call Date: Nov 1995, Lincoln's Inn
Qualifications: [LLB (Hons)(Leic)]
✉sahya@kch.co.uk

AIKENS MR CHRISTOPHER ANTHONY EDWARD

11 South Square
1st Floor, 11 South Square, Gray's Inn, London WC1R 5EY, ☎020 7405 1222
✉clerks@11southsquare.com
Call Date: Oct 2005, Middle Temple
Qualifications: [BA (Hons)]
✉caikens@11southsquare.com

AILES MR JOHN ASHLEY

Eighteen Carlton Crescent
Rownhams House, Rownhams, Southampton SO16 8LF, ☎023 8063 9001
✉clerks@18carltoncrescent.co.uk
Call Date: July 1975, Middle Temple
Pupil Supervisor
Qualifications: [BA MPhil]
✉ashleyalies@18carltoncrescent.co.uk

AILES MISS VICTORIA LOUIE ELLEN

6 King's Bench Walk
Ground Floor, 6 King's Bench Walk, Temple, London EC4Y 7DR, ☎020 7583 0410
✉clerks@6kbw.com
Call Date: Oct 2005, Lincoln's Inn
Qualifications: [BA (Hons) Oxon]
✉victoria.ailes@6kbw.com

AINA MR BENJAMIN ADEJOWON OLUFEMI QC (2009)

Old Bailey Chambers
15 Old Bailey, London EC4M 7EF, ☎020 3008 6404
✉clerks@15oldbaileychambers.com
Call Date: July 1987, Lincoln's Inn
Qualifications: [LLB LLM (Lond)]
✉b.aina@15oldbaileychambers.com

AINSLEY MR STEPHEN PAUL

Dere Street Barristers
33 Broad Chare, Newcastle Upon Tyne NE1 3DQ, ☎0844 3351551
✉clerks@derestreet.co.uk
Call Date: July 2001, Middle Temple
Qualifications: [BSc (Hons) MBA CPE]
✉clerks@broadcharechambers.co.uk

AINSWORTH MR MARK JUSTIN SIMON

Exchange Chambers
7 Ralli Courts, West Riverside, Manchester M3 5FT, ☎0161 833 2722
Exchange Chambers
One Derby Square, Derby Square, Liverpool L2 9XX, ☎0151 236 7747
✉info@exchangechambers.co.uk
Exchange Chambers
Oxford House, Oxford Row, Leeds LS1 3BE, ☎0113 203 1970
✉spencer@exchangechambers.co.uk
Call Date: Oct 1992, Lincoln's Inn
Pupil Supervisor
Qualifications: [BA(Hons)(L'pool) Dip Law]
✉ainsworth@exchangechambers.co.uk

AIOLFI MR LAURENCE

23 Essex Street
London WC2R 3AA, ☎020 7413 0353
✉clerks@23es.com
Call Date: Oct 1996, Inner Temple
Qualifications: [LLB (Bris)]
✉laurenceaiolfi@23es.com

AJAZ MR MOHAMMAD ARSHAD

Eastmans Chambers
41 St Bartholomew's Road, Reading, Berkshire RG1 3QA, ☎0118 966 9094
✉eastmans@hotmail.co.uk
Call Date: July 2011, Lincoln's Inn
Qualifications: [BSc LLB (Pakistan)]

AJMONE-MARSAN MR COSIMO MARCO

3 Hare Court
3 Hare Court, Temple, London EC4Y 7BJ,
☎020 7415 7800 ✉clerks@3harecourt.com
Call Date: July 2009, Lincoln's Inn
Qualifications: [Bmus (Guildhall) BA (Oxon)]
✉cmarsan@3harecourt.com

AKAST MR JOHN FRANCIS

East Anglian Chambers
15 The Close, Norwich, Norfolk NR1 4DZ,
☎01473 214481 ✉norwich@ealaw.co.uk
East Anglian Chambers
53 North Hill, Colchester, Essex CO1 1QA,
☎01473 214481 ✉colchester@ealaw.co.uk
St David's Chambers
Myrtle Cottage, Norton Road, Mumbles,
Swansea SA3 5TQ, ☎01792 559924
✉j.vallack@ntlworld.com
East Anglian Chambers
Gresham House, 5 Museum Street, Ipswich,
Suffolk IP1 1HQ, ☎01473 214481
✉ipswich@ealaw.co.uk
Call Date: Nov 1968, Inner Temple
Pupil Supervisor, Recorder
Qualifications: [LLB]
✉johnakast@ealaw.co.uk

AKERMAN MISS KATE LOUISE

15 Winckley Square
Preston PR1 3JJ, ☎01772 252828
✉clerks@15winckleysq.co.uk
Call Date: Oct 1994, Middle Temple
Qualifications: [LLB (Hons)(Lond)]

AKERS MR ROBERT MATTHEW HARRY

St Johns Buildings
24a - 28 St John Street, Manchester M3 4DJ,
☎0161 214 1500
✉clerk@stjohnsbuildings.co.uk
St Johns Buildings
21 White Friars, Chester CH1 1NZ,
☎01244 323070
✉clerk@stjohnsbuildings.co.uk
16 Winckley Square
Preston PR1 3JJ, ☎01772 256100
Call Date: Nov 2003, Inner Temple
Qualifications: [LLB (Sheffield Hallam)]

AKHTAR MISS SHAZIA MARIAM

Hardwicke
New Square, Lincoln's Inn, London
WC2A 3SB, ☎020 7242 2523
✉enquiries@hardwicke.co.uk
Call Date: Nov 2001, Middle Temple
Qualifications: [BA (Hons)(Manch)]
✉shazia.akhtar@harwicke.co.uk

AKIN MR BARRIE SIMON

Gray's Inn Tax Chambers
3rd Floor, Gray's Inn Chambers, Gray's Inn,
London WC1R 5JA, ☎020 7242 2642
✉clerks@taxbar.com
No 8 Chambers
8 Fountain Court, Steelhouse Lane,
Birmingham B4 6DR, ☎0121 236 5514
✉clerks@no8chambers.co.uk
Call Date: July 1976, Middle Temple
Qualifications: [LLB FCA]

AKINBOLU MISS SANDRA ADWOA ANIFA

Chambers of Mr Ami Feder
Ground Floor, Lamb Building, Temple, London
EC4Y 7AS, ☎020 7797 7788
✉clerks@lambbuilding.co.uk
Chambers of Mr Ami Feder
Ground Floor, Lamb Building, Temple, London
EC4Y 7AS, ☎020 7797 7788
✉clerks@lambbuilding.co.uk
Call Date: Oct 2002, Middle Temple
Qualifications: [LLB (Essex) LLM (Essex)]

AKIN-OLUGBADE MR OLUWAJEMINIPE BABARINSADE

Nexus Chambers
7 New Square, Lincolns Inn, London
WC2A 3QS,
☎020 7404 1147 / 020 7831 8309
✉info@nexuschambers.com
Call Date: Oct 1998, Lincoln's Inn
Qualifications: [LLB (Hons)(Wales)]
✉j.akin-olugbade@nexuschambers.com

AKINSANYA MR JONATHAN

Nine Bedford Row
9 Bedford Row, London WC1R 4AZ,
☎020 7489 2727
✉clerks@9bedfordrow.co.uk
Call Date: Nov 1993, Inner Temple
Pupil Supervisor
Qualifications: [LLB (Lond)]
✉jonathan.akinsanya@9bedfordrow.co.uk

AKINSANYA MR STEPHEN OLUBUNMI

Old Bailey Chambers
15 Old Bailey, London EC4M 7EF,
☎020 3008 6404
✉clerks@15oldbaileychambers.com
Call Date: Nov 1993, Inner Temple
Qualifications: [LLB (Hons)(Bucks) BVC]

E

AKKA MR LAWRENCE MARK QC (2012)

20 Essex Street
London WC2R 3AL, ☎ 020 7842 1200
✉ clerks@20essexst.com
Call Date: Oct 1991, Lincoln's Inn
Pupil Supervisor
Qualifications: [BA (Hons) (Oxon)]
✉ clerks@20essexst.com

AKKOUH MR TIMOTHY OSMAN

New Square Chambers
12 New Square, Lincoln's Inn, London WC2A 3SW, ☎ 020 7419 8000
✉ robin.hollington@newsquarechambers.co.uk
Call Date: July 2004, Lincoln's Inn
Qualifications: [LLB Hons (Lond) LLM (Lond)]
✉ tim.akkouh@newsquarechambers.co.uk

AKMAN MISS MERCY LOUISE

36 Bedford Row
London WC1R 4JH, ☎ 020 7421 8000
✉ chambers@36bedfordrow.co.uk
Call Date: Nov 1982, Gray's Inn
Qualifications: [LLB (Hons) (Wales) DICArb (Lond)]
✉ makman@36bedfordrow.co.uk

AKRAM MISS FARZANA

Priestgate Chambers
26 Priestgate, Peterborough PE1 1WG, ☎ 01733 865 042
✉ clerks@priestgatechambers.co.uk
Call Date: July 1998, Middle Temple
Qualifications: [LLB (Hons)(Middx)]

AKTHER MISS RIPON

Renaissance Chambers
5th Floor, Gray's Inn Chambers, Gray's Inn, London WC1R 5JA, ☎ 020 7404 1111
✉ clerks@renaissancechambers.co.uk
Call Date: Mar 2003, Lincoln's Inn
Qualifications: [BA (Hons) (Lond)]
✉ ra1@renaissancechambers.co.uk

AKTHER MISS TAHINA SULTANA

Cobden House Chambers
19 Quay Street, Manchester M3 3HN, ☎ 0161 833 6000 ✉ Clerks@Cobden.co.uk
Southernhay Chambers
33 Southernhay East, Exeter EX1 1NX, ☎ 01392 255777
✉ clerks@southernhaychambers.co.uk
Call Date: Oct 2003, Lincoln's Inn
Qualifications: [LLB (Hons) (Lond)]
✉ tahina.akther@cobden.co.uk

AKUDOLU MISS NNEKA VERONICA ANASTESIA

2 Pump Court
1st Floor, 2 Pump Court, Temple, London EC4Y 7AH, ☎ 020 7353 5597
✉ clerks@2pumpcourt.co.uk
Call Date: Oct 2002, Middle Temple
Qualifications: [LLB (Wales)]
✉ nakudolu@2pumpcourt.co.uk

AKUWUDIKE MISS EMMA CHIAWUOTU

25 Bedford Row
London WC1R 4HD, ☎ 020 7067 1500
✉ clerks@25bedfordrow.com
Call Date: Nov 1992, Inner Temple
Qualifications: [LLB (Hons)]
✉ eakuwudike@25bedfordrow.com

AKWAGYIRAM MR SAMUEL MANTEAW

12 Old Square Chambers
1st Floor, 12 Old Square, Lincoln's Inn, London WC2A 3TX, ☎ 020 7404 0875
✉ clerks@12oldsquare.com
Call Date: Nov 1985, Inner Temple
Qualifications: [BA (Hons)]
✉ clerks@12oldsquare.com

AL TAI MISS ZAHRA WRIGHT

1 Gray's Inn Square
Ground Floor, 1 Gray's Inn Square, London WC1R 5AA, ☎ 020 7405 0001
Call Date: Nov 2007, Gray's Inn
Qualifications: [BA (USA)]
✉ zaltai@1gis.co.uk

ALAKIJA MR AYODELE HUGH

No 8 Chambers
8 Fountain Court, Steelhouse Lane, Birmingham B4 6DR, ☎ 0121 236 5514
✉ clerks@no8chambers.co.uk
Call Date: Oct 1996, Gray's Inn
Qualifications: [LLB (Hons)]

ALAM MS JAN

Ropewalk Chambers
24 The Ropewalk, Nottingham NG1 5EF, ☎ 0115 947 2581 ✉ clerks@ropewalk.co.uk
Call Date: July 2003, Gray's Inn
Qualifications: [LLB (Nott'm)]

E

ALAM MISS ZAIBAN NASSA

Bank House Chambers
Old Bank House, Hartshead, Sheffield S1 2EL,
☎0114 275 1223
✉w.digby@bankhousechambers.co.uk
Call Date: Mar 1998, Lincoln's Inn
Qualifications: [LLB (Hons)(Sheff)]
✉z.alam@bankhousechambers.co.uk

ALAMUDDIN MISS AMAL RAMZI

Doughty Street Chambers
53-54 Doughty Street, London WC1N 2LS,
☎020 7404 1313
✉enquiries@doughtystreet.co.uk
Call Date: Nov 2010, Inner Temple
Qualifications: [BA (Oxon) LLM (USA)]

AL-ASADY MISS JANAN

Chambers of Lawrence Jones
8 Stone Buildings, Lincoln's Inn, London
WC2A 3TA, ☎020 7831 1444
✉clerks@8stonebuildings.com
Call Date: July 2004, Middle Temple
Qualifications: [LLB Hons LLM (Lond)]

AL-ATTAR MR ADAM

South Square
3-4 South Square, Gray's Inn, London
WC1R 5HP, ☎020 7696 9900
✉practicemanagers@southsquare.com
Call Date: Nov 2007, Lincoln's Inn
Qualifications: [BA (Oxon) BCL (Oxon)]
✉adamalattar@southsquare.com

ALBA MR IAIN ANDREW

Pendragon Chambers
Suite 7, J Shed, Kings Road, SA1 Waterfront,
Swansea SA1 8PL, ☎01792 411188
✉clerks@pendragonchambers.com
Call Date: Oct 2006, Inner Temple
Qualifications: [LLB (Wales)]

ALBUTT MR IAN LESLIE

Cornerstone Barristers
2-3 Gray's Inn Square, Gray's Inn, London
WC1R 5JH, ☎020 7242 4986
✉chambers@2-3gis.co.uk
Heavenwood Chambers
Heavenwood Chambers, Heavenwood House,
71 Bownham Park, Rodborough Common,
Stroud, Gloucestershire GL5 5BZ,
☎01453 873444 ✉kms@heavenwood.co.uk
Call Date: July 1981, Gray's Inn
Pupil Supervisor
✉ialbutt@2-3gis.co.uk

ALCOCK MR PETER MICHAEL

6 Pump Court
1st Floor, 6 Pump Court, Temple, London
EC4Y 7AR, ☎020 7797 8400
✉richardconstable@6pumpcourt.co.uk
6 Pump Court Chambers
6-8 Mill Street, Maidstone, Kent ME15 6XH,
☎01622 688094
✉annexe@6pumpcourt.co.uk
Call Date: Oct 1995, Gray's Inn
Qualifications: [BA (Hons) Dip Law]
✉peteralcock@6pumpcourt.co.uk

ALDOUS MR GRAHAME LINLEY QC (2008)

The Chambers of Grahame Aldous QC
9 Gough Square, London EC4A 3DG,
☎020 7832 0500
✉clerks@9goughsquare.co.uk
Phydeaux Chambers
Maison Phydeaux, 44a The Grove, Biggin Hill,
Westerham, Kent TN16 3TB, ☎01209 821442
✉arjo_1@tiscali.co.uk
Call Date: July 1979, Inner Temple
Pupil Supervisor, Recorder
Qualifications: [LLB (Exon)]

ALDOUS MR ROBERT JOHN

Octagon House
19 Colegate, Norwich NR3 1AT,
☎01603 623186
✉clerks@octagonhouse.co.uk
Call Date: July 1985, Inner Temple
Qualifications: [BA (Cantab)]
✉clerks@octagonhouse.co.uk

ALDRED MISS LOIS

12 King's Bench Walk
12 King's Bench Walk, Temple, London
EC4Y 7EL, ☎020 7583 0811
Call Date: July 2008, Inner Temple
Qualifications: [LLB (UEA)]
✉aldred@12kbw.co.uk

ALDRED MR MARK STEVEN

QEB Hollis Whiteman
1-2 Laurence Pountney Hill, London
EC4R 0EU, ☎020 7933 8855
✉barristers@qebhw.co.uk
Call Date: Mar 1996, Middle Temple
Qualifications: [LLB (Hons)]
✉mark.aldred@qebhw.co.uk

ALDRIDGE MR JAMES HUGH

Maitland Chambers
7 Stone Buildings, Lincoln's Inn, London
WC2A 3SZ, ☎ 020 7406 1200
✉ clerks@maitlandchambers.com
Call Date: Oct 1994, Lincoln's Inn
Pupil Supervisor
Qualifications: [MA (Hons)]
✉ jaldridge@maitlandchambers.com

ALDRIDGE MR JAMES WILLIAM

Outer Temple Chambers
The Outer Temple, 222 Strand, London
WC2R 1BA, ☎ 020 7353 6381
✉ clerks@outertemple.com
Call Date: July 1987, Inner Temple
Qualifications: [BA (Lond) Dip Law]
✉ james.aldridge@outertemple.com

ALEESON MR WARWICK LAN GRIEG

187 Fleet Street
London EC4A 2AT, ☎ 020 7430 7430
✉ chambers@187fleetstreet.com
Call Date: Nov 1994, Gray's Inn
Pupil Supervisor
Qualifications: [LLB (Hons)(Wales)]
✉ warwickaleeson@187fleetstreet.com

ALESBURY MR ALUN

Cornerstone Barristers
2-3 Gray's Inn Square, Gray's Inn, London
WC1R 5JH, ☎ 020 7242 4986
✉ chambers@2-3gis.co.uk
12 Old Square Chambers
1st Floor, 12 Old Square, Lincoln's Inn,
London WC2A 3TX, ☎ 020 7404 0875
✉ clerks@12oldsquare.com
Call Date: July 1974, Inner Temple
Qualifications: [MA (Cantab)]
✉ aluna@cornerstonebarristers.com

Fax: 020 7405 1166
URL: www.cornerstonebarristers.com

Types of work: Administrative law, Common land, Compulsory Purchase, Energy, Environment, Highways, Land compensation, Licensing, Local authorities, Parliamentary, Planning, Rating and CPO, Transport and Works Act inquiries

ALEXANDER MR ANDREW MATHEW

Chambers of Mr Ami Feder
Ground Floor, Lamb Building, Temple, London
EC4Y 7AS, ☎ 020 7797 7788
✉ clerks@lambbuilding.co.uk
Lamb Building
22 Ship Street, Brighton BN1 1AD,
☎ 01273 820490
✉ admin@lambbuilding.co.uk
Chambers of Mr Ami Feder
Ground Floor, Lamb Building, Temple, London
EC4Y 7AS, ☎ 020 7797 7788
✉ clerks@lambbuilding.co.uk
Call Date: July 1999, Lincoln's Inn
Qualifications: [BA (Hons) Dip in Law]
✉ clerks@lambbuilding.co.uk

ALEXANDER MR DANIEL SAKYI QC (2003)

8 New Square
8 New Square, Lincoln's Inn, London
WC2A 3QP, ☎ 020 7405 4321
✉ clerks@8newsquare.co.uk
Call Date: July 1988, Middle Temple
Qualifications: [BA (Hons) (Oxon) LLM (USA) Dip Law]
✉ daniel.alexander@8newsquare.co.uk

Types of work: Breach of confidence, Competition law, Computer litigation, Conflict of laws, Copyright, Copyright theft, Copyright Tribunal, Data protection, Design, E-commerce, EC competition law, Entertainment, Information technology, Intellectual property, Malicious falsehood, Media, Media and entertainment, Passing off, Patents, Pharmaceuticals, Privacy, Scientific and technical disputes, Telecommunications, Trade Descriptions Act, Trade secrets, Trademarks

ALEXANDER MR DAVID ROBERT JAMES QC (2006)

South Square
3-4 South Square, Gray's Inn, London
WC1R 5HP, ☎ 020 7696 9900
✉ practicemanagers@southsquare.com
Call Date: Nov 1987, Middle Temple
Qualifications: [BA (Cantab)]
✉ davidalexander@southsquare.com

ALEXANDER MISS JOSEPHINE ANNE

Principal Chambers
15 Lime Tree Walk, Sevenoaks, Kent
TN13 1YH, ☎ 0845 209 8080
Call Date: Feb 1994, Middle Temple
Qualifications: [LLB (Hons)(Lond)]

E

ALEXANDER MR NICHOLAS

Atkinson Bevan Chambers
1st Floor, 2 Harcourt Buildings, Temple, London EC4Y 9DB, ☎ 020 7353 2112
✉ clerks@2hb.co.uk
Call Date: Oct 1996, Middle Temple
Qualifications: [LLB (Hons) LLM (Bucks)]
nalexander@2hb.co.uk

ALEXANDRA MISS SEBASTIANE

Holborn Chambers
6 Gate Street, Lincoln's Inn Fields, London WC2A 3HP, ☎ 020 7242 6060
Call Date: Nov 2002, Inner Temple
Qualifications: [ALCM LLB (Hons) LLM]

ALEXIS MISS FALLON

QEB Hollis Whiteman
1-2 Laurence Pountney Hill, London EC4R 0EU, ☎ 020 7933 8855
✉ barristers@qebhw.co.uk
Call Date: July 2008, Inner Temple
Qualifications: [LLB (Brunel)]

ALFRED MR STEPHAN HONNORAT

Lombard Chambers
1 Sekforde Street, Clerkenwell, London EC1R 0BE, ☎ 020 7107 2100
Call Date: Oct 1996, Inner Temple
Pupil Supervisor
Qualifications: [LLB (Hons)]
s.alfred@lombardchambers.com

ALGAZY MR JACQUES MAX QC (2012)

Cloisters
1 Pump Court, Temple, London EC4Y 7AA, ☎ 020 7827 4000 ✉ clerks@cloisters.com
Call Date: Nov 1980, Gray's Inn
Pupil Supervisor
Qualifications: [LLB (Reading) DESEu (France)]
ja@cloisters.com

AL'HASSAN MR KHADIM

No.6 Park Square
Leeds LS1 2LW, ☎ 0113 245 9763
✉ Tim@no6.co.uk
Call Date: Nov 1993, Inner Temple
Qualifications: [LLB (Leics)]
al'hassan@no6.co.uk

ALI MISS HUMA

St Philips Chambers
55 Temple Row, Birmingham B2 5LS, ☎ 0121 246 7000 ✉ clerks@st-philips.com
Call Date: Mar 1997, Gray's Inn
Qualifications: [LLB (L'pool)]
hali@st-philips.com

ALI MR ISHTIYAQ

Chartlands Chambers
3 St Giles Terrace, Northampton NN1 2BN, ☎ 01604 603322
✉ enquiries@chartlands-chambers.co.uk
Call Date: Nov 1996, Lincoln's Inn
Qualifications: [LLB (Hons)]

ALI MR KASHIF

Call Date: July 2003, Lincoln's Inn
Qualifications: [BA Hons (Oxon) LLM (Cantab)]
clerk@stjohnsbuildings.co.uk

ALI MISS KHADIJA

Tooks Chambers
81 Farringdon Street, London EC4A 4BL, ☎ 020 7842 7575 ✉ clerks@tooks.co.uk
Call Date: Nov 2006, Lincoln's Inn
Qualifications: [BA (Lond)]

ALI MISS MISBAH

Chambers of Ms M Ali
24 Camden High Street, London NW1 0JH, ☎ 020 7387 2032
Call Date: Oct 2001, Lincoln's Inn
Qualifications: [BSc (Hons)(Manch) LLB (Hons)]

ALI MR MOHAMMED ANIS

Regent Chambers
Regent House, 3 Pall Mall, Hanley, Stoke On Trent ST1 1HP, ☎ 01782 286666
✉ clerks@regentchambers.co.uk
Call Date: Mar 1997, Lincoln's Inn
Qualifications: [LLB (Hons)(Lond)]

ALI MR MOHAMMED AZEEM

Clock Chambers
18 Waterloo Road, Wolverhampton WV1 4BL, ☎ 01902 313444
✉ clockchambers@btconnect.com
Call Date: May 1997, Lincoln's Inn
Qualifications: [LLB (Hons)(L'pool)]

ALI MRS SHAMIM

Chambers of Mrs Shamim Ali
19 Flamingo Close, Salisbury Village, Hatfield, Hertfordshire AL10 9LU, ☎ 01707 276737
✉ a2a_herts@hotmail.com
Call Date: July 1998, Lincoln's Inn
Qualifications: [LLB (Hons)]

ALI MR ZAFAR QC (2012)

23 Essex Street
London WC2R 3AA, ☎020 7413 0353
✉clerks@23es.com
Call Date: Nov 1994, Middle Temple
Pupil Supervisor
Qualifications: [BA (Hons) (Warw) Dip Law]
✉zafarali@23es.com

ALIBHAI MR ARI KARIM

QEB Hollis Whiteman
1-2 Laurence Pountney Hill, London
EC4R 0EU, ☎020 7933 8855
✉barristers@qebhw.co.uk
Call Date: Oct 2003, Gray's Inn
Qualifications: [MA (Edin)]
✉barristers@qebhw.co.uk

ALIKER MR PHILLIP BLISS

Tanfield Chambers
2-5 Warwick Court, London WC1R 5DJ,
☎020 7421 5300
✉clerks@tanfieldchambers.co.uk
Call Date: Oct 1990, Inner Temple
Pupil Supervisor
Qualifications: [BA (USA) LLB (Hons) (Leeds) MCIArb Dip ICA (Lond)]

ALISTARI MS NICOLETA

Park Court Chambers
16 Park Place, Leeds LS1 2SJ,
☎0113 243 3277
✉clerks@parkcourtchambers.co.uk
Call Date: Oct 2009, Middle Temple
Qualifications: [LLB (Hons)]
✉nalistari@parkcourtchambers.co.uk

AL-KHAYAT MR JOSEPH

30 Park Place
Cardiff CF10 3BS, ☎029 2039 8421
✉clerks@30parkplace.law.co.uk
Call Date: July 2008, Inner Temple
Qualifications: [LLB (Cardiff)]
✉jak@30parkplace.co.uk

ALKIN MR THOMAS GUY

11 South Square
1st Floor, 11 South Square, Gray's Inn,
London WC1R 5EY, ☎020 7405 1222
✉clerks@11southsquare.com
Call Date: Nov 2006, Middle Temple
Qualifications: [BA (Hons) (Oxon)]
✉talkin@11southsquare.com

ALLAN MR CHRISTOPHER DAVID QC (1995)

Byrom Street Chambers
12 Byrom Street, Manchester M3 4PP,
☎0161 829 2100 ✉clerks@byromstreet.com
15 Winckley Square
Preston PR1 3JJ, ☎01772 252828
✉clerks@15winckleysq.co.uk
Crown Office Chambers
2 Crown Office Row, Temple, London
EC4Y 7HJ, ☎020 7797 8100
✉mail@crownofficechambers.com
42 Bedford Row
London WC1R 4LL, ☎020 7831 0222
✉clerks@42br.com
Call Date: July 1974, Gray's Inn
Recorder
Qualifications: [LLB]
✉david.allan@byromstreet.com

ALLAN MR DAVID ALEXANDER

23 Essex Street
London WC2R 3AA, ☎020 7413 0353
✉clerks@23es.com
Call Date: July 1998, Lincoln's Inn
Qualifications: [MA (Hons)]
✉davidallan@23es.com

ALLAN MS NICOLA MARGARET

Trinity Chambers
The Custom House, 39 Quayside, Newcastle
Upon Tyne NE1 3DE, ☎0191 232 1927
✉info@trinitychambers.co.uk
Trinity Chambers
Multi Media Exchange, 72-80 Corporation
Road, Middlesbrough TS1 2RF,
☎01642 247569
✉info@trinitychambers.co.uk
Call Date: July 1999, Gray's Inn
Qualifications: [BA (Hons)(N'Castle) DipLaw, MRTPI]
✉n.allan@trinitychambers.co.uk

ALLARDICE MISS MIRANDA JANE

Pump Court Chambers
Upper Ground Floor, 3 Pump Court, Temple,
London EC4Y 7AJ, ☎020 7353 0711
✉clerks@3pumpcourt.com
Pump Court Chambers
5 Temple Chambers, Temple Street, Swindon
SN1 1SQ, ☎01793 539899
✉clerks@3pumpcourt.com
Pump Court Chambers
31 Southgate Street, Winchester, Hampshire
SO23 9EB, ☎01962 868 161
✉clerks@3pumpcourt.com

E

Richmond Green Chambers
5 Connaught Road, Richmond, Surrey
TW10 6DW, ☎ 020 8948 4801
✉ richmondchambers@btconnect.com
Call Date: July 1982, Lincoln's Inn
Pupil Supervisor
Qualifications: [BA (Oxon)]

ALLCOCK MR JONATHAN CHARLES

Maitland Chambers
7 Stone Buildings, Lincoln's Inn, London
WC2A 3SZ, ☎ 020 7406 1200
✉ clerks@maitlandchambers.com
Call Date: July 2007, Middle Temple
Qualifications: [BA (Hons) (Oxon) PgDL (Lond)]
jallcock@maitlandchambers.com

ALLDIS MR CHRISTOPHER JOHN

Oriel Chambers
14 Water Street, Liverpool, Merseyside
L2 8TD, ☎ 0151 236 7191
✉ clerks@orielchambers.co.uk
Oriel Chambers
18 Ribblesdale Place, Preston PR1 3NA,
☎ 01772 254 764
✉ clerks@oriel-chambers.co.uk
Call Date: Nov 1970, Gray's Inn
Pupil Supervisor, Recorder
Qualifications: [MA LLB (Cantab)]
christopher.alldis@orielchambers.co.uk

ALLEN MR ANDREW

Outer Temple Chambers
The Outer Temple, 222 Strand, London
WC2R 1BA, ☎ 020 7353 6381
✉ clerks@outertemple.com
Call Date: Oct 1995, Inner Temple
Pupil Supervisor
Qualifications: [MA (Cantab) LLM (Lond)]

ALLEN MISS CAROLINE MARY

39 Essex Street
London WC2R 3AT, ☎ 020 7832 1111
✉ clerks@39essex.com
82 King Street
Manchester M2 4WQ, ☎ 0161 870 9969
Call Date: Oct 2005, Lincoln's Inn
Qualifications: [BA (Hons) (Oxon)]
caroline.allen@39essex.com

ALLEN MR CHRISTOPHER JOHN

Exchange Chambers
One Derby Square, Derby Square, Liverpool
L2 9XX, ☎ 0151 236 7747
✉ info@exchangechambers.co.uk
Call Date: Mar 2012, Lincoln's Inn
allen@exchangechambers.co.uk

ALLEN MR CHRISTOPHER ROY

New Walk Chambers
27 New Walk, Leicester, Leicestershire
LE1 6TE, ☎ 0871 200 1298 / 0116 255 9144
✉ clerks@newwalkchambers.co.uk
Call Date: July 2002, Gray's Inn

ALLEN MR DARRYL JOHN

Byrom Street Chambers
12 Byrom Street, Manchester M3 4PP,
☎ 0161 829 2100 ✉ clerks@byromstreet.com
Crown Office Chambers
2 Crown Office Row, Temple, London
EC4Y 7HJ, ☎ 020 7797 8100
✉ mail@crownofficechambers.com
42 Bedford Row
London WC1R 4LL, ☎ 020 7831 0222
✉ clerks@42br.com
Call Date: Oct 1995, Lincoln's Inn
Pupil Supervisor
Qualifications: [LLB (Hons)(Leeds)]
darryl.allen@byromstreet.com

ALLEN MR DOUGLAS STEPHEN

Harcourt Chambers
1st Floor, 2 Harcourt Buildings, Temple,
London EC4Y 9DB, ☎ 0844 561 7135
Call Date: Oct 1995, Lincoln's Inn
Qualifications: [BA (Hons)(B'ham)]
dallen@harcourtchambers.law.co.uk

ALLEN MR FERGAL

Call Date: Oct 2007, Lincoln's Inn
Qualifications: [LLB (L'pool)]
Fergal.Allen@stjohnsbuildings.co.uk

ALLEN MS FRANCES

Renaissance Chambers
5th Floor, Gray's Inn Chambers, Gray's Inn,
London WC1R 5JA, ☎ 020 7404 1111
✉ clerks@renaissancechambers.co.uk
Call Date: Oct 1995, Inner Temple
Qualifications: [BSc (Lond) CPE (Lond)]
fa@renaissancechambers.co.uk

ALLEN MISS JUDITH RACHEL LUCY

1 Hare Court
1 Hare Court, Temple, London EC4Y 7BE,
☎ 020 7797 7070 ✉ clerks@1hc.com
Call Date: Oct 2004, Inner Temple
Qualifications: [BA (Oxon) CPE (Lond)]
allen@1hc.com

ALLEN MISS JULIET LUCY

No5 Chambers
Fountain Court, Steelhouse Lane, Birmingham B4 6DR, ☎ 0845 210 5555 ✉ info@no5.com
No5 Chambers
Greenwood House, 4-7 Salisbury Court, London EC4Y 8AA, ☎ 0845 210 5555
No5 Chambers
38 Queen Square, Bristol BS1 4QS, ☎ 0845 210 5555
Call Date: Nov 2005, Gray's Inn
Qualifications: [LLB]

ALLEN MR MARK GRAHAM

30 Park Place
Cardiff CF10 3BS, ☎ 029 2039 8421
✉ clerks@30parkplace.law.co.uk
Call Date: July 1981, Middle Temple
Pupil Supervisor
Qualifications: [LLB (Cardiff)]
✉ mgca@30parkplace.co.uk

ALLEN MR MICHAEL DAVID PRIOR QC (2008)

7 King's Bench Walk
Ground Floor, 7 King's Bench Walk, Temple, London EC4Y 7DS, ☎ 020 7910 8300
✉ clerks@7kbw.co.uk
Call Date: Oct 1990, Gray's Inn
Qualifications: [BSc LLB LLM FRICS FCIArb]
✉ dallen@7kbw.co.uk

ALLEN MR NEIL

39 Essex Street
London WC2R 3AT, ☎ 020 7832 1111
✉ clerks@39essex.com
Call Date: Oct 1999, Middle Temple
Qualifications: [LLB (Hons)(Manch)]

ALLEN MR NICHOLAS PAUL

29 Bedford Row Chambers
London WC1R 4HE, ☎ 020 7404 1044
✉ clerks@29br.co.uk
Call Date: Oct 1995, Middle Temple
Pupil Supervisor
Qualifications: [MA (Cantab) LLM (Cantab)]
✉ nallen@29br.co.uk

ALLEN MR ROBIN GEOFFREY BRUERE QC (1995)

Cloisters
1 Pump Court, Temple, London EC4Y 7AA, ☎ 020 7827 4000 ✉ clerks@cloisters.com
Call Date: Nov 1974, Middle Temple
Recorder
Qualifications: [MA (Oxon)]
✉ clerks@cloisters.com, ra@cloisters.com, ra@cloisters.com

ALLEN MR RUPERT ALEXANDER DENDY

Fountain Court Chambers
Fountain Court, Temple, London EC4Y 9DH, ☎ 020 7583 3335
✉ chambers@fountaincourt.co.uk
Call Date: July 2005, Lincoln's Inn
Qualifications: [BA (Hons)]
✉ ra@fountaincourt.co.uk

ALLEN MISS SARAH LOUISE

No5 Chambers
Fountain Court, Steelhouse Lane, Birmingham B4 6DR, ☎ 0845 210 5555 ✉ info@no5.com
No5 Chambers
Greenwood House, 4-7 Salisbury Court, London EC4Y 8AA, ☎ 0845 210 5555
No5 Chambers
38 Queen Square, Bristol BS1 4QS, ☎ 0845 210 5555
Call Date: Nov 2005, Gray's Inn
Qualifications: [BA (Wales)]
✉ sal@no5.com

ALLEN MR SCOTT JAMIE

Four New Square
Four New Square, Lincoln's Inn, London WC2A 3RJ, ☎ 020 7822 2000
✉ barristers@4newsquare.com
Call Date: Nov 2000, Inner Temple
Qualifications: [BA (Oxon)]
✉ s.allen@4newsquare.com

ALLEN MR SEBASTIAN ALEXANDER PAYARD

Wilberforce Chambers
8 New Square, Lincoln's Inn, London WC2A 3QP, ☎ 020 7306 0102
✉ chambers@wilberforce.co.uk
Call Date: Oct 2006, Lincoln's Inn
Qualifications: [BA (Oxon) BA Law BCL]
✉ sallen@wilberforce.co.uk

ALLEN MISS SYLVIA DELORES

1 Mitre Court Buildings
1 Mitre Court Buildings, Temple, London EC4Y 7BS, ☎ 020 7452 8900
✉ clerks@1mcb.com
Call Date: July 1983, Gray's Inn
Qualifications: [LLB (Lond)]
✉ sylvia.allen@1mcb.com

E

ALLEN MR THOMAS MICHAEL CHARD

Five Paper Buildings
1st Floor, Five Paper Buildings, Temple, London EC4Y 7HB, ☎ 020 7583 6117
✉ clerks@5pb.co.uk
Call Date: Feb 1994, Middle Temple
Pupil Supervisor
Qualifications: [BA (Hons)(Dunelm) Dip Law (Lond)]
ta@5pb.co.uk

ALLERHAND MR LUDWIK EDMUND

Chambers of Mr Ludwik Allerhand
38 Dunoon Road, Forest Hill, London SE23 3TF, ☎ 020 8291 4356
✉ ludwikallerhand@btinternet.com
Call Date: Nov 2001, Inner Temple
Qualifications: [BA LLM]

ALLEYNE MS EBONY COLETTE

3 PB Barristers
3 Paper Buildings, Temple, London EC4Y 7EU, ☎ 020 7583 8055
3 PB Barristers
Royal Talbot House, 2 Victoria Street, Bristol, Avon BS1 6BB, ☎ 0117 928 1520
3 PB Barristers
4 St Peter Street, Winchester SO23 8BW, ☎ 01962 868884
✉ clerks.winchester@3paper.co.uk
3 PB Barristers
23 Beaumont Street, Oxford OX1 2NP, ☎ 01865 793 736
3 PB Barristers
30 Christchurch Road, Bournemouth, Dorset BH1 3PD, ☎ 01202 292102
✉ clerks.bournemouth@3paper.co.uk
Call Date: Oct 2009, Inner Temple
Qualifications: [BA (Cantab) LLB (Oxon)]
ebony.alleyne@3pb.co.uk

ALLEYNE-BROWN MR NATHAN

6 King's Bench Walk
Ground, Third & Fourth Floors, 6 King's Bench Walk, Temple, London EC4Y 7DR, ☎ 020 7353 4931 ✉ clerks@6kbw.co.uk
Call Date: July 2006, Inner Temple
Qualifications: [LLB (Westminster)]

ALLINGHAM-NICHOLSON MRS ELIZABETH SARAH

New Street Chambers
2 New Street, Leicester LE1 5NA, ☎ 0116 262 5906 ✉ clerks@2newstreet.co.uk
Call Date: Oct 1995, Lincoln's Inn
Qualifications: [LLB (Hons)(Lond) BA (Hons) (USA)]

ALLIOTT MR GEORGE BECKLES

Temple Garden Chambers
1 Harcourt Buildings, Temple, London EC4Y 9DA, ☎ 020 7583 1315
✉ clerks@tgchambers.com
Call Date: July 1981, Inner Temple
Pupil Supervisor
Qualifications: [LLB (Warw)]

ALLISON MISS CAROLINE FIONA

Fenners Chambers
3 Madingley Road, Cambridge CB3 0EE, ☎ 01223 368761
✉ clerks@fennerschambers.com
Call Date: July 2002, Lincoln's Inn
Qualifications: [LLB (Hons) (Leic)]
caroline.allison@fennerschambers.com

ALLISON MR DAVID WILLIAM

South Square
3-4 South Square, Gray's Inn, London WC1R 5HP, ☎ 020 7696 9900
✉ practicemanagers@southsquare.com
Call Date: Nov 1998, Middle Temple
Pupil Supervisor
Qualifications: [BA (Hons)(Cantab) MA (Cantab)]
davidallison@southsquare.com

ALLISON MR SIMON ROBERT

Hardwicke
New Square, Lincoln's Inn, London WC2A 3SB, ☎ 020 7242 2523
✉ enquiries@hardwicke.co.uk
Call Date: Oct 2005, Lincoln's Inn
Qualifications: [LLB (Hons)]
simon.allison@hardwicke.co.uk

ALLMAN MISS MARISA NICHOLE

Zenith Chambers
10 Park Square, Leeds LS1 2LH, ☎ 0113 245 5438
✉ clerks@zenithchambers.co.uk
Call Date: Oct 1998, Lincoln's Inn
Qualifications: [LLB (Hons)(B'ham)]
mallman@zenithchambers.co.uk

ALLOWAY MR TOR HUGH

Talloway Chambers
Rivington House, 82 Great Eastern Street, London EC2A 3JF, ☎ 020 7419 5047
✉ tor@talloway.com
Call Date: July 1985, Lincoln's Inn
Pupil Supervisor
Qualifications: [BSc ACII BA]
tor@talloway.com

E

ALLSOP MR JULIAN ELISEO

Guildhall Chambers
23 Broad Street, Bristol BS1 2HG,
☎0117 930 9000
✉hoc@guildhallchambers.co.uk
Call Date: Oct 1999, Lincoln's Inn
Qualifications: [LLB (Hons)(Lond) LLM (Bris)]
✉Julian.Allsop@guildhallchambers.co.uk

ALLSOP MISS NICOLA ELIZABETH

New Square Chambers
12 New Square, Lincoln's Inn, London WC2A 3SW, ☎020 7419 8000
✉robin.hollington@newsquarechambers.co.uk
Call Date: July 2002, Lincoln's Inn
Qualifications: [LLB (Hons)(Bris)]
✉nicola.allsop@newsquarechambers.co.uk

ALLSTON MR ANTHONY STANLEY

3 Dr Johnson's Buildings
Ground Floor, 3 Dr Johnson's Buildings, Temple, London EC4Y 7BA, ☎020 7353 4854
✉clerks@3djb.co.uk
Call Date: July 1975, Gray's Inn
Pupil Supervisor
Qualifications: [BA]
✉aallston@3djb.co.uk

ALLWOOD MRS GINA LOUISA

Seven Bedford Row
7 Bedford Row, London WC1R 4BS,
☎020 7242 3555 ✉clerks@7br.co.uk
Call Date: July 2002, Gray's Inn
Qualifications: [LLB (Nott'm)]
✉gallwood@7br.co.uk

ALMIHDAR MR ALI HAMED

Outer Temple Chambers
The Outer Temple, 222 Strand, London WC2R 1BA, ☎020 7353 6381
✉clerks@outertemple.com
Call Date: Nov 2003, Middle Temple
Qualifications: [LLM (Cantab) BA (Hons) (Cantab) MA Hons (Cantab) DiP Law]
✉ali.almihdar@outertemple.com

ALOMO MR RICHARD OLUSOJI

14 Gray's Inn Square
14 Gray's Inn Square, Gray's Inn, London WC1R 5JP, ☎020 7242 0858
✉clerks@14gis.co.uk
Call Date: Nov 1990, Inner Temple
Pupil Supervisor
Qualifications: [LLB (Lond) LLM (London) PG Dip ICA MCI Arb]
✉clerks@14graysinnsquare.co.uk

AL-RASHID MR MAHMUD

No5 Chambers
Greenwood House, 4-7 Salisbury Court, London EC4Y 8AA, ☎0845 210 5555
No5 Chambers
38 Queen Square, Bristol BS1 4QS,
☎0845 210 5555
No5 Chambers
Fountain Court, Steelhouse Lane, Birmingham B4 6DR, ☎0845 210 5555 ✉info@no5.com
Call Date: Oct 1991, Gray's Inn
Qualifications: [LLB (Leics)]
✉mar@no5.com

ALTARAS MR DAVID MAURICE

36 Bedford Row
London WC1R 4JH, ☎020 7421 8000
✉chambers@36bedfordrow.co.uk
Call Date: Nov 1969, Lincoln's Inn
Pupil Supervisor, Recorder
Qualifications: [MA (TCD) Dip Crim (Cantab) FCIArb Dip ICC Arb (Lond)]
✉clerks@36bedfordrow.co.uk

ALTHAUS MR ANTONY JUSTIN

1 Chancery Lane
London WC2A 1LF, ☎0845 634 6666
✉clerks@1chancerylane.com
Call Date: July 1988, Inner Temple
Pupil Supervisor
Qualifications: [BA (Oxon) Dip Law (Lond)]
✉jalthaus@1chancerylane.com

ALTMAN MR BRIAN QC (2008)

2 Bedford Row
London WC1R 4BU, ☎020 7440 8888
✉clerks@2bedfordrow.co.uk
Call Date: July 1981, Middle Temple
Qualifications: [LLB (Lond) Dip Eur Int (Amsterdam)]
✉baltman@2bedfordrow.co.uk

Fax: 020 7242 1738;
Out of hours telephone: 020 7440 8843;
DX: 17 London, Chancery Lane

Other professional qualifications: Junior Treasury Counsel at CCC 1997-2002; Senior Treasury Counsel 2002; First Senior Treasury Counsel 2010

Types of work: Corporate fraud, Crime

Circuit: South Eastern

Awards and memberships: Member CBA

Other professional experience: Recorder 2003; Bencher Middle Temple 2010

Reported Cases: *R v Gnango*, [2011] UKSC 59; [2012] 2 WLR 17; [2012] 2 All ER 129 (Supreme Court), 2011. Murder - killing of bystander by

other party in gunfight - foreseeability - nature of joint enterprise for affray - common or opposite purpose - case on appeal from Court of Appeal (see [2012] 2 Cr. App. R. 345)
R v Boggild and others, [2011] EWCA Crim 1928 (Court of Appeal), 2011. Admissibility - expert evidence - hearsay evidence - hearsay notices - murder - no case to answer.
R v Beesley and Coyle, [2011] EWCA Crim 1021 (Court of Appeal), 2010. Dangerous offenders - challenge to assessment of dangerousness on appeal - admissibility of new reports or assessments.
R v Stewart, [2009] 2 Cr App R 500 (Court of Appeal), 2009. Diminished responsibility - appellant with alcohol dependency syndrome killing victim when intoxicated - guidance on directions to jury - Homicide Act 1957.
Gian and another v CPS, [2009] EWCA Crim 2553 (Court of Appeal), 2009. Admissibility - expert evidence - hearsay evidence - hearsay notices - murder - no case to answer.

ALTY MR ANDREW STEPHEN JOHN

Number 7 Harrington Street Chambers
7 Harrington Street, Liverpool L2 9YH,
☎0151 242 0707 ✉clerks@7hs.co.uk
Call Date: Feb 1992, Inner Temple
Qualifications: [LLB (Hons)]

E

ALY MISS SHEILA

Warwick House Chambers
8 Warwick Court, Warwick House Chambers, Gray's Inn, London WC1R 5DJ,
☎020 7430 2323
✉clerks@warwickhousechambers.com
Call Date: Oct 2002, Lincoln's Inn
Qualifications: [LLB (Lond)]

AMAKYE MISS GRACE TINA

15 New Bridge Street
London EC4V 6AU, ☎020 7842 1900
✉clerks@15nbs.com
Call Date: Nov 1983, Gray's Inn
Recorder
Qualifications: [LLB (Lond)]
✉grace.amakye@15nbs.com

AMAN MS ROSINA

Coram Chambers
9-11 Fulwood Place, London WC1V 6HG,
☎020 7092 3700
✉mail@coramchambers.co.uk
Call Date: July 2005, Gray's Inn
Qualifications: [BA (Hons) (Lond)]
✉rosina.aman@coramchambers.co.uk

AMAOUCHE MISS SASSA-ANN

29 Bedford Row Chambers
London WC1R 4HE, ☎020 7404 1044
✉clerks@29br.co.uk
Call Date: Oct 1996, Inner Temple
Pupil Supervisor
Qualifications: [LLB (Lond)]
✉samaouche@29br.co.uk

Types of work: Family law, Family provision

AMARASINHA MR REVANTHA ARJUNA

9-12 Bell Yard
London WC2A 2JR, ☎020 7400 1800
✉clerks@9-12bellyard.com
Call Date: Oct 1996, Middle Temple
Qualifications: [LLB (Hons)(Lond)]
✉r.amarasinha@9-12bellyard.com

AMARTEY MISS LENA AHINEE

9 St John Street
Manchester M3 4DN, ☎0161 955 9000
✉civilclerks@9sjs.com / criminalclerks@9sjs.com
Call Date: Oct 2008, Lincoln's Inn
Qualifications: [LLB (Sheff)]
✉lamartey@9sjs.com

AMBROSE MISS CLARE MARY GENESTE

20 Essex Street
London WC2R 3AL, ☎020 7842 1200
✉clerks@20essexst.com
Call Date: Nov 1992, Gray's Inn
Pupil Supervisor
Qualifications: [BA (Oxon) LLM (Cantab)]
✉cambrose@20essexst.com

AMEEN MR DANISH

18 St John Street
Manchester M3 4EA, ☎0161 278 1800
✉clerks@18sjs.com
Call Date: Mar 2006, Lincoln's Inn
Qualifications: [LLB (Hons) (Manch)]

AMER MR ADRIAN CHARLES

Nine Bedford Row
9 Bedford Row, London WC1R 4AZ,
☎020 7489 2727
✉clerks@9bedfordrow.co.uk
Call Date: Nov 1984, Gray's Inn
Pupil Supervisor
Qualifications: [LLB (Brunel)]
✉adrian.amer@9bedfordrow.co.uk

AMESBURY MR RYAN ROBERT

Civitas Chambers
Global Reach, Celtic Gateway, Cardiff Bay, Cardiff CF11 0SN, ☎0845 0713 007
✉clerks@civitaslaw.com
Call Date: Nov 2007, Gray's Inn
Qualifications: [BA (Oxon)]
✉ryan.amesbury@civitaslaw.com

AMESU MRS SHARON ROSE

Park Court Chambers
16 Park Place, Leeds LS1 2SJ,
☎0113 243 3277
✉clerks@parkcourtchambers.co.uk
Call Date: Oct 1997, Middle Temple
Qualifications: [BA Hons (UCE) CPE (Manc)]

AMIN MISS FARAH

4 King's Bench Walk
2nd Floor, 4 King's Bench Walk, Temple, London EC4Y 7DL, ☎020 7822 7000
✉clerks@4kbw.co.uk
Call Date: July 1991, Lincoln's Inn
Qualifications: [LLB (Hons) (Lond)]

AMIRAFTABI MISS ROSHANAK

Renaissance Chambers
5th Floor, Gray's Inn Chambers, Gray's Inn, London WC1R 5JA, ☎020 7404 1111
✉clerks@renaissancechambers.co.uk
Call Date: Feb 1993, Gray's Inn
Pupil Supervisor
Qualifications: [BA]
✉ra@renaissancechambers.co.uk

AMIS MR CHRISTOPHER JOCELYN

23 Essex Street
London WC2R 3AA, ☎020 7413 0353
✉clerks@23es.com
Call Date: Nov 1991, Gray's Inn
Pupil Supervisor
Qualifications: [LLB (Lond)]

AMOR MR CHRISTOPHER LEWIS

Chambers of Mr C Amor
2 Eastcliff, Boundary Lane, The Warren, Caversham, Berkshire RG4 7TH,
☎01189 472298
Call Date: May 1984, Gray's Inn
Qualifications: [MA (Oxon)]

AMOS MR JUSTIN EDWARD

9 Park Place
9 Park Place, Cardiff, South Glamorgan CF10 3DP, ☎029 2038 2731
✉clerks@9parkplace.co.uk
Call Date: Mar 2005, Gray's Inn
Qualifications: [BA (Hons)(Oxon)]
✉jamos@9parkplace.co.uk

AMOS MR TIMOTHY ROBERT QC (2008)

Queen Elizabeth Building
3rd Floor, Queen Elizabeth Building, Temple, London EC4Y 9BS, ☎020 7797 7837
✉clerks@qeb.co.uk
Call Date: July 1987, Lincoln's Inn
Recorder
Qualifications: [MA (Oxon) Dip Law]
✉t.amos@qeb.co.uk

AMRAOUI MR THOMAS

4-5 Gray's Inn Square
Gray's Inn, London WC1R 5AH,
☎020 7404 5252 ✉clerks@4-5.co.uk
Call Date: Nov 2007, Gray's Inn
Qualifications: [BA (Oxon)]
✉tamraoui@4-5.co.uk

ANANDA MISS SUSHMA

7 King's Bench Walk
Ground Floor, 7 King's Bench Walk, Temple, London EC4Y 7DS, ☎020 7910 8300
✉clerks@7kbw.co.uk
Call Date: Nov 2007, Lincoln's Inn
Qualifications: [MA (Cantab)]
✉sananda@7kbw.co.uk

ANATO-DUMELO MISS ESTHER

Chambers of G. D. Tetteh
Ground Floor, 2 Middle Temple Lane, Temple, London EC4Y 9AA, ☎020 7353 7095
Call Date: Oct 2005, Middle Temple
Qualifications: [LLB (Hons) Wales]
✉e.anato-dumelo@gdtettehchambers.com

ANCLIFFE MRS SHIVA EDWINA

Renaissance Chambers
5th Floor, Gray's Inn Chambers, Gray's Inn, London WC1R 5JA, ☎020 7404 1111
✉clerks@renaissancechambers.co.uk
Call Date: Nov 1991, Lincoln's Inn
Pupil Supervisor
Qualifications: [LLB (Hons)]
✉sa@renaissancechambers.co.uk

E

ANDENAS PROF MADS

Brick Court Chambers
7-8 Essex Street, London WC2R 3LD,
☎ 020 7379 3550 ✉ clerks@brickcourt.co.uk
Call Date: July 1997, Middle Temple
Qualifications: [PhD (Cantab) MA DPhil]

ANDERS MR JONATHAN JAMES

Chambers of Marion Smullen and Kerim Fuad QC
1 Inner Temple Lane, London EC4Y 1AF,
☎ 020 7427 4400 ✉ clerks@1itl.com
Call Date: Feb 1990, Inner Temple
Qualifications: [LLB]
clerks@1itl.com, jonanderswork@gmail.com

ANDERSON MR BRENDAN JOSEPH

Linenhall Chambers
1 Stanley Place, Chester CH1 2LU,
☎ 01244 348282
✉ clerks@linenhallchambers.co.uk
Call Date: July 1985, Gray's Inn
Pupil Supervisor
Qualifications: [LLB (Leeds)]

ANDERSON MR COLIN JAMES DOUGLAS

St Mary's Family Law Chambers
26-28 High Pavement, The Lace Market, Nottingham NG1 1HN, ☎ 0115 950 3503
✉ clerks@stmarysflc.co.uk
Call Date: Nov 1973, Gray's Inn
Pupil Supervisor
Qualifications: [MA (Cantab)]
colin.anderson@stmarysflc.co.uk

ANDERSON MR DAVID WILLIAM KINLOCH QC (1999)

Brick Court Chambers
7-8 Essex Street, London WC2R 3LD,
☎ 020 7379 3550 ✉ clerks@brickcourt.co.uk
Call Date: July 1985, Middle Temple
Recorder
Qualifications: [MA (Oxon) BA (Cantab)]
David.Anderson@Brickcourt.co.uk

ANDERSON MR JACK DUTHIE

4-5 Gray's Inn Square
Gray's Inn, London WC1R 5AH,
☎ 020 7404 5252 ✉ clerks@4-5.co.uk
Call Date: Nov 2006, Inner Temple
Qualifications: [BA (Cantab) BCL (Oxon)]
janderson@4-5.co.uk

ANDERSON MR JAMIE HENRIE

Trinity Chambers
The Custom House, 39 Quayside, Newcastle Upon Tyne NE1 3DE, ☎ 0191 232 1927
✉ info@trinitychambers.co.uk
Trinity Chambers
Multi Media Exchange, 72-80 Corporation Road, Middlesbrough TS1 2RF,
☎ 01642 247569
✉ info@trinitychambers.co.uk
Call Date: July 2004, Lincoln's Inn
Qualifications: [LLB (Hons) LLM]

ANDERSON MISS JULIE

20 Essex Street
London WC2R 3AL, ☎ 020 7842 1200
✉ clerks@20essexst.com
Call Date: Nov 1993, Gray's Inn
Qualifications: [BA (Hons) (Oxon) Dip Law]
clerks@20essexst.com

ANDERSON MS KATHERINE ELIZABETH

3 PB Barristers
3 Paper Buildings, Temple, London EC4Y 7EU,
☎ 020 7583 8055
3 PB Barristers
23 Beaumont Street, Oxford OX1 2NP,
☎ 01865 793 736
3 PB Barristers
4 St Peter Street, Winchester SO23 8BW,
☎ 01962 868884
✉ clerks.winchester@3paper.co.uk
3 PB Barristers
Royal Talbot House, 2 Victoria Street, Bristol, Avon BS1 6BB, ☎ 0117 928 1520
3 PB Barristers
30 Christchurch Road, Bournemouth, Dorset BH1 3PD, ☎ 01202 292102
✉ clerks.bournemouth@3paper.co.uk
Call Date: Oct 2005, Inner Temple
Qualifications: [BA Emmanuel College University of Cambridge]
katherine.anderson@3paper.co.uk

ANDERSON MRS KATHLEEN BERNADETTE

King's Bench Chambers
Wellington House, 175 Holdenhurst Road, Bournemouth, Dorset BH8 8DQ,
☎ 01202 250025
Call Date: Nov 1997, Lincoln's Inn
Qualifications: [LLB (Hons)]

E

ANDERSON MS LESLEY JANE QC (2006)

Kings Chambers
36 Young Street, Manchester M3 3FT,
☎0845 034 3444
✉clerks@kingschambers.com
Kings Chambers
5 Park Square East, Leeds LS1 2NE,
☎0845 034 3444
✉clerks@kingschambers.com
Kings Chambers
Embassy House, 60 Church Street, Birmingham B3 2DJ, ☎0845 034 3444
✉clerks@kingschambers.com
Call Date: Nov 1989, Middle Temple
Recorder
Qualifications: [LLB (Manch)]

ANDERSON MR MARK ROGER QC (2010)

No5 Chambers
Fountain Court, Steelhouse Lane, Birmingham B4 6DR, ☎0845 210 5555 ✉info@no5.com
No5 Chambers
Greenwood House, 4-7 Salisbury Court, London EC4Y 8AA, ☎0845 210 5555
No5 Chambers
38 Queen Square, Bristol BS1 4QS,
☎0845 210 5555
Call Date: July 1983, Middle Temple
Pupil Supervisor, Recorder
Qualifications: [BA (Oxon)]
man@no5.com

ANDERSON MR NICHOLAS GUY

1 KBW Chambers
1 King's Bench Walk, Temple, London EC4Y 7DB, ☎020 7936 1500
✉clerks@1kbw.co.uk
King's Bench Chambers
174 High Street, Lewes BN7 1YE,
☎01273 402600
Call Date: Oct 1995, Gray's Inn
Pupil Supervisor
Qualifications: [LLB]

ANDERSON MR PETER JOHN

15 Winckley Square
Preston PR1 3JJ, ☎01772 252828
✉clerks@15winckleysq.co.uk
Call Date: July 1988, Inner Temple
Qualifications: [LLB]

ANDERSON MR RICHARD NEIL MACDIARMID

Arbitration Chambers
22 Willes Road, London NW5 3DS,
☎020 7267 2137
✉john.tackaberry@39essex.com
Call Date: Apr 1991, Gray's Inn
Qualifications: [LLB (Hons) CA FCIArB]

ANDERSON MR ROBERT EDWARD QC (2006)

Blackstone Chambers
Blackstone House, Temple, London EC4Y 9BW, ☎020 7583 1770
✉clerks@blackstonechambers.com
Call Date: Nov 1986, Middle Temple
Qualifications: [BA(Cantab)]
robertanderson@blackstonechambers.com

ANDERSON MRS SARAH IRENE

Clock Chambers
18 Waterloo Road, Wolverhampton WV1 4BL,
☎01902 313444
✉clockchambers@btconnect.com
Call Date: July 2006, Middle Temple
Qualifications: [LLB (Hons) (Wolves)]

ANDERSON MR SIMON PETER BEDE

Park Court Chambers
16 Park Place, Leeds LS1 2SJ,
☎0113 243 3277
✉clerks@parkcourtchambers.co.uk
Call Date: Nov 1997, Lincoln's Inn
Qualifications: [LLB (Hons)(Leeds)]
anderson@parkcourtchambers.co.uk

ANDRE MR ROGER LOUIS

Sovereign Chambers
46 Park Place, Leeds LS1 2RY,
☎0113 245 1841
✉clerks@sovereignchambers.co.uk
Call Date: Oct 1999, Middle Temple
Qualifications: [LLB (Hons)]
roger.andre@sovereignchambers.co.uk

ANDREAE-JONES MR WILLIAM PEARCE QC (1984)

Citadel Chambers
The Citadel, 190 Corporation Street, Birmingham B4 6QD, ☎0121 233 8500
✉clerks@citadelchambers.com
King's Bench Chambers
Wellington House, 175 Holdenhurst Road, Bournemouth, Dorset BH8 8DQ,
☎01202 250025
Call Date: Nov 1965, Inner Temple
Recorder
Qualifications: [BA (Cantab)]
clerks@citadelchambers.com

E

ANDRESS MR COLIN MICHAEL

33 Bedford Row
London WC1R 4JH, ☎020 7242 6476
✉clerks@33bedfordrow.co.uk
Call Date: July 2002, Gray's Inn
Qualifications: [BA (Oxon) MA (Oxon)]

ANDREWS MISS CLAIRE MARGUERITE

Gough Square Chambers
6-7 Gough Square, London EC4A 3DE,
☎020 7353 0924 ✉gsc@goughsq.co.uk
Call Date: Nov 1979, Gray's Inn
Pupil Supervisor
Qualifications: [FCIArb LLB (Manch)]

ANDREWS MISS GERALDINE MARY QC (2001)

Essex Court Chambers
24 Lincoln's Inn Fields, London WC2A 3EG,
☎020 7813 8000
✉clerksroom@essexcourt.net
Call Date: Nov 1981, Gray's Inn
Recorder
Qualifications: [LLB AKC (Lond) LLM]
gandrews@essexcourt.net

E

ANDREWS MISS KATHERINE ELLEN

Coram Chambers
9-11 Fulwood Place, London WC1V 6HG,
☎020 7092 3700
✉mail@coramchambers.co.uk
Call Date: July 2006, Gray's Inn
Qualifications: [BA (Leeds)]
katherine.andrews@coramchambers.co.uk

ANDREWS MISS MELANIE ALEXANDRA

Becket Chambers
17 New Dover Road, Canterbury, Kent
CT1 3AS, ☎01227 786331
✉clerks@becket-chambers.co.uk
Call Date: Oct 2005, Middle Temple
Qualifications: [BA (Hons) (York) Dip in Law]
mandrews@becket-chambers.co.uk

ANDREWS MR PAUL LESLIE

Great James Street Chambers
37 Great James Street, London WC1N 3HB,
☎020 7440 4949
✉chambers@greatjames.co.uk
Call Date: Nov 2003, Inner Temple
Qualifications: [BSc (Kingston)]

ANDREWS MR PETER JOHN QC (1991)

Seven Bedford Row
7 Bedford Row, London WC1R 4BS,
☎020 7242 3555 ✉clerks@7br.co.uk
St Ive's Chambers
Whittall Street, Birmingham B4 6DH,
☎0121 236 0863
✉clerks@stiveschambers.co.uk
Call Date: July 1970, Lincoln's Inn
Recorder
Qualifications: [LLB (Bris) D Crim (Cantab)]

ANDREWS MR PHILIP BRYAN

Call Date: Feb 1977, Inner Temple
Pupil Supervisor
Qualifications: [LLB (Hons)]

ANDREWS MR SAMUEL JAMES

39 Park Square
Leeds LS1 2NU, ☎0113 245 6633
✉seniorclerk@39parksquarechambers.co.uk
Call Date: Nov 1991, Gray's Inn
Pupil Supervisor
Qualifications: [LLB (Sheff)]
sam-andrews@sky.com

ANELAY MR RICHARD ALFRED QC (1993)

1 KBW Chambers
1 King's Bench Walk, Temple, London
EC4Y 7DB, ☎020 7936 1500
✉clerks@1kbw.co.uk
King's Bench Chambers
174 High Street, Lewes BN7 1YE,
☎01273 402600
Call Date: July 1970, Middle Temple
Recorder
Qualifications: [BA (Bris)]

ANGAMMANA MR GAMINI BERTRAM

Chambers of Gamini Angammana
'Woodcroft', 13 Woodend, Upper Norwood,
London SE19 3NU, ☎020 8771 5205
✉woodcroftchambers@btconnect.com
Call Date: Nov 1983, Lincoln's Inn
Qualifications: [LLB (Lond) LLM (Lond) PGCE]
woodcroftchambers@btconnect.com

ANGELIDES MR HARRY

Chambers of Martin Burr
15 Old Bailey, London EC4M 7EF,
☎0845 123 1234 ✉clerks@barristerweb.com
Call Date: July 1987, Lincoln's Inn
Qualifications: [LLB]

ANGUS MISS TRACEY ANNE QC (2012)

5 Stone Buildings
5 Stone Buildings, Lincoln's Inn, London WC2A 3XT, ☎020 7242 6201
✉clerks@5sblaw.com
Call Date: Nov 1991, Inner Temple
Pupil Supervisor
Qualifications: [MA (Edin) Dip Law]
✉tangus@5sblaw.com

ANKRAH MS ALEXANDRA ADUWAH

12 Old Square Chambers
1st Floor, 12 Old Square, Lincoln's Inn, London WC2A 3TX, ☎020 7404 0875
✉clerks@12oldsquare.com
Call Date: July 1999, Middle Temple
Qualifications: [BA (Hons)(Kent) DipLaw]

ANNAND MS KATE

Doughty Street Chambers
53-54 Doughty Street, London WC1N 2LS, ☎020 7404 1313
✉enquiries@doughtystreet.co.uk
Doughty Street Chambers
Pall Mall Court, 61-67 King Street, Manchester M2 4PD, ☎0161 618 1066
Doughty Street Chambers
5th Floor, Broad Quay House, Prince Street, Bristol BS1 4DJ, ☎01179 058 717
Call Date: July 2007, Middle Temple
Qualifications: [LLB (Hons) (Lond) MA (Lond)]
✉k.annand@doughtystreet.co.uk

ANNING MR MICHAEL

No5 Chambers
Fountain Court, Steelhouse Lane, Birmingham B4 6DR, ☎0845 210 5555 ✉info@no5.com
No5 Chambers
Greenwood House, 4-7 Salisbury Court, London EC4Y 8AA, ☎0845 210 5555
No5 Chambers
38 Queen Square, Bristol BS1 4QS, ☎0845 210 5555
Call Date: Nov 1990, Inner Temple
Qualifications: [BA (Dunelm) LLB (Lond)]
✉ma@no5.com

ANNING MISS SARA ELIZABETH

Park Lane Plowden
19 Westgate, Leeds LS1 2RD, ☎0113 228 5049
✉clerks@parklaneplowden.co.uk
Call Date: Oct 1995, Inner Temple
Qualifications: [BA (Newc) CPE (Hudds)]

ANSELL MISS RACHEL LOUISE

4 Pump Court
4 Pump Court, Temple, London EC4Y 7AN, ☎020 7842 5555
✉chambers@4pumpcourt.com
Call Date: Oct 1995, Middle Temple
Pupil Supervisor
Qualifications: [BA (Hons)]
✉ransell@4pumpcourt.com

ANSLOW MISS KATHRYN MAY

Linenhall Chambers
1 Stanley Place, Chester CH1 2LU, ☎01244 348282
✉clerks@linenhallchambers.co.uk
Call Date: Nov 2005, Lincoln's Inn
Qualifications: [LLB (Hons)]
✉kathryn.anslow@linenhallchambers.co.uk

ANSTEY MRS EVE ALEXANDRA SORREL

Pallant Chambers
12 North Pallant, Chichester, West Sussex PO19 1TQ, ☎01243 784538
✉clerks@pallantchambers.co.uk
Call Date: Nov 2005, Middle Temple
Qualifications: [BA (Hons) (Sussex) PGDL (Lond)]
✉eanstey@pallantchambers.co.uk

ANTELL MR JOHN JASON

King's Bench and Godolphin (KBG)Chambers
115 North Hill, Plymouth, Devon PL4 8JY, ☎01752 221551
✉clerks@kbgchambers.co.uk
Call Date: Oct 1992, Middle Temple
Qualifications: [LLB (Lond) CEng MBCS CITP]
✉mail@johnantell.co.uk

ANTELME MR ALEXANDER JOHN

Crown Office Chambers
2 Crown Office Row, Temple, London EC4Y 7HJ, ☎020 7797 8100
✉mail@crownofficechambers.com
Call Date: Oct 1993, Gray's Inn
Pupil Supervisor
Qualifications: [MA (Hons)(Oxon)]
✉antelme@crownofficechambers.com

ANTHONY MR PETER FRANCIS

St Ive's Chambers
Whittall Street, Birmingham B4 6DH, ☎0121 236 0863
✉clerks@stiveschambers.co.uk
Call Date: July 1981, Gray's Inn
Qualifications: [LLB (Hons) (Warw)]
✉peter.anthony@stiveschambers.co.uk

E

ANTHONY MRS RACHEL JANE

Iscoed Chambers
86 St Helen's Road, Swansea SA1 4BQ,
☎01792 652988
✉clerks@iscoedchambers.co.uk
Call Date: Nov 2000, Middle Temple
Qualifications: [LLB (Hons) (Manch)]
✉clerks@iscoedchambers.co.uk, ra@iscoedchambers.co.uk

ANTROBUS MR SIMON JAMES

Crown Office Chambers
2 Crown Office Row, Temple, London EC4Y 7HJ, ☎020 7797 8100
✉mail@crownofficechambers.com
Call Date: Oct 1995, Inner Temple
Qualifications: [LLB (Sheff)]
✉antrobus@crownofficechambers.com

ANYADIKE-DANES MS MONYA NNENNA MARY

2 Temple Gardens
2 Temple Gardens, Temple, London EC4Y 9AY, ☎020 7822 1200
✉clerks@2tg.co.uk
Call Date: July 1980, Gray's Inn
Qualifications: [BA (Bris) MPhil (Cantab)]

E

ANYENE MR CHUDDY UZO ELEAZAR

12 Old Square Chambers
1st Floor, 12 Old Square, Lincoln's Inn, London WC2A 3TX, ☎020 7404 0875
✉clerks@12oldsquare.com
Call Date: Oct 1999, Lincoln's Inn
Qualifications: [Dip in Law (Wolves) BSc (Hons) LLM (Lond)]
✉clerks@12oldsquare.com

ANZANI MISS SARA CLAIRE

10 King's Bench Walk
Ground Floor, 10 King's Bench Walk, Temple, London EC4Y 7EB, ☎020 7353 7742
✉Chambers@10kingsbenchwalk.co.uk
Call Date: July 2008, Inner Temple
Qualifications: [LLB (L'pool)]
✉chambers@10kingsbenchwalk.co.uk

AP MIHANGEL MR SION

Linenhall Chambers
1 Stanley Place, Chester CH1 2LU,
☎01244 348282
✉clerks@linenhallchambers.co.uk
Call Date: Nov 1998, Gray's Inn
Qualifications: [LLB (Exon)]
✉clerks@1stanleyplace.co.uk

APFEL MR FREDDY

37 Park Square Chambers
37 Park Square, Leeds LS1 2NY,
☎0113 243 9422 ✉chambers@no37.co.uk
Call Date: July 1986, Middle Temple
Pupil Supervisor
Qualifications: [LLB LLM]
✉chambers@no37.co.uk

APPIAH MISS LINDA

Guildford Chambers
Stoke House, Leapale Lane, Guildford, Surrey GU1 4LY, ☎01483 539131
✉clerks@guildfordchambers.co.uk
Call Date: Nov 2001, Middle Temple
Qualifications: [LLB (Hons)]
✉lappiah@guildfordchambers.com

APPLEBY MISS CLAIRE ELIZABETH

King's Bench and Godolphin (KBG)Chambers
115 North Hill, Plymouth, Devon PL4 8JY,
☎01752 221551
✉clerks@kbgchambers.co.uk
Call Date: Oct 2002, Lincoln's Inn
Qualifications: [LLB (L'pool)]
✉claire.appleby@kingsbenchchambers.co.uk

APPS MISS KATHERINE MARIE CLARE

Littleton Chambers
3 King's Bench Walk North, Temple, London EC4Y 7HR, ☎020 7797 8600
✉fschneider@littletonchambers.co.uk
Call Date: July 2006, Gray's Inn
Qualifications: [MA (Cantab) LLM]
✉KatherineApps@littletonchambers.co.uk

APTHORP MR GEORGE CHARLES

5 Essex Court
1st Floor, 5 Essex Court, Temple, London EC4Y 9AH, ☎020 7410 2000
✉clerks@5essexcourt.co.uk
Call Date: Feb 1983, Inner Temple
Pupil Supervisor
Qualifications: [BA]
✉apthorp@5essexcourt.co.uk

ARCHER MISS AUDREY SYBIL DOROTHY

3 PB Barristers
3 Paper Buildings, Temple, London EC4Y 7EU,
☎020 7583 8055
3 PB Barristers
Royal Talbot House, 2 Victoria Street, Bristol, Avon BS1 6BB, ☎0117 928 1520

3 PB Barristers
30 Christchurch Road, Bournemouth, Dorset BH1 3PD, ☎01202 292102
✉clerks.bournemouth@3paper.co.uk
3 PB Barristers
4 St Peter Street, Winchester SO23 8BW, ☎01962 868884
✉clerks.winchester@3paper.co.uk
3 PB Barristers
23 Beaumont Street, Oxford OX1 2NP, ☎01865 793 736
Call Date: Oct 2004, Middle Temple
Qualifications: [LLB (Hons) (So'ton) LLM (So'ton)]
✉archer3pb@yahoo.co.uk

ARCHER MISS DEBORAH ELIZABETH

Southernhay Chambers
33 Southernhay East, Exeter EX1 1NX, ☎01392 255777
✉clerks@southernhaychambers.co.uk
Call Date: Nov 1989, Inner Temple
Pupil Supervisor
Qualifications: [LLB]
✉d.archer@southernhaychambers.co.uk

ARCHER MRS JACQUELINE ANN

Redland Chambers
Redland House, Bonvilston, Cardiff, Vale of Glamorgan CF5 6TT, ☎01446 781060
✉jacquelinearcher@btinternet.com
Call Date: Feb 1988, Gray's Inn
Qualifications: [BA(Hons)]

ARCHER MR JAMES CHRISTOPHER

Renaissance Chambers
5th Floor, Gray's Inn Chambers, Gray's Inn, London WC1R 5JA, ☎020 7404 1111
✉clerks@renaissancechambers.co.uk
Call Date: Nov 1996, Gray's Inn
Qualifications: [LLB (Leeds)]
✉ca@renaissancechambers.co.uk

ARCHER MS LORNA HELEN

1 Pump Court
Elm Court, Temple, London EC4Y 7AB, ☎020 7842 7070
✉(name)@pumpcourt.co.uk
Call Date: Nov 1986, Gray's Inn
Qualifications: [BA (Hons)]

ARCHER MR RICHARD MICHAEL

15 Winckley Square
Preston PR1 3JJ, ☎01772 252828
✉clerks@15winckleysq.co.uk
Call Date: July 2007, Middle Temple
Qualifications: [LLB (Hons) (L'Pool)]

ARCHER MR STEPHEN KENDRAY

2 Temple Gardens
2 Temple Gardens, Temple, London EC4Y 9AY, ☎020 7822 1200
✉clerks@2tg.co.uk
Call Date: Nov 1979, Inner Temple
Pupil Supervisor
Qualifications: [MA (Oxon)]
✉sarcher@2tg.co.uk

ARCHER MR TREVOR JON

18 Red Lion Court
London EC4A 3EB, ☎020 7520 6000
✉chambers@18rlc.co.uk
Call Date: July 2005, Inner Temple
Qualifications: [BA CPE]
✉trevor.archer@18rlc.co.uk

ARDEN MR ANDREW PAUL RUSSEL QC (1991)

Arden Chambers
20 Bloomsbury Square, London WC1A 2NS, ☎020 7242 4244
✉clerks@ardenchambers.com
Call Date: Feb 1974, Gray's Inn
Qualifications: [LLB (Lond)]
✉andrew.arden@ardenchambers.com

ARDEN MISS KARINA JANICE

4 Breams Buildings
Chancery Lane, London EC4A 1HP, ☎020 7092 1900 ✉clerks@4bb.co.uk
Call Date: Nov 1970, Inner Temple
Pupil Supervisor
Qualifications: [LLB (Lond)]

ARDEN MR PETER LEONARD QC (2006)

Enterprise Chambers
9 Old Square, Lincoln's Inn, London WC2A 3SR, ☎020 7405 9471
✉london@enterprisechambers.com
Enterprise Chambers
65 Quayside, Newcastle Upon Tyne NE1 3DE, ☎0191 222 3344
✉newcastle@enterprisechambers.com
Enterprise Chambers
43 Park Square, Leeds LS1 2NP, ☎0113 246 0391
✉leeds@enterprisechambers.com
Call Date: July 1983, Gray's Inn
Qualifications: [LLB (Lond) LLB (Cantab)]
✉peterarden@enterprisechambers.com

E

ARENTSEN MR ANDREW NICHOLAS

Civitas Chambers
Global Reach, Celtic Gateway, Cardiff Bay, Cardiff CF11 0SN, ☎0845 0713 007
✉clerks@civitaslaw.com
Call Date: Oct 1995, Gray's Inn
Qualifications: [MA (Cantab)]
andrew.arentsen@civitaslaw.com

ARGENT MR GAVIN RICHARD

Westgate Chambers
64 High Street, Lewes, East Sussex BN7 1XG, ☎01273 480510
✉clerks@westgate-chambers.co.uk
Call Date: July 1978, Middle Temple
Qualifications: [BA (Warw)]

ARGYLE MR BRIAN JOHN

187 Fleet Street
London EC4A 2AT, ☎020 7430 7430
✉chambers@187fleetstreet.com
Chambers of K A Williams-Howes
148 Lower Richmond Road, Putney, London SW15 1LU, ☎020 8704 1010
✉katie@williams-howes.com
Call Date: July 1972, Gray's Inn
Pupil Supervisor, Recorder

ARGYROPOULOS MR KYRIAKOS

15 New Bridge Street
London EC4V 6AU, ☎020 7842 1900
✉clerks@15nbs.com
Call Date: Nov 1991, Inner Temple
Pupil Supervisor
Qualifications: [BA (York) Dip Law]
kyri.argyropoulos@15nbs.com

ARIS MR JASON MARK

Citadel Chambers
The Citadel, 190 Corporation Street, Birmingham B4 6QD, ☎0121 233 8500
✉clerks@citadelchambers.com
Call Date: Oct 1998, Inner Temple
Qualifications: [LLB (Wolves)]
clerks@citadelchambers.com

ARKHURST MR REGINALD LEON

4 King's Bench Walk
2nd Floor, 4 King's Bench Walk, Temple, London EC4Y 7DL, ☎020 7822 7000
✉clerks@4kbw.co.uk
Call Date: July 1984, Middle Temple
Qualifications: [BA (Hons)(Newcastle)]
ra@4kbw.co.uk

ARKUSH MR JONATHAN HARRY SAMUEL

11 Stone Buildings
11 Stone Buildings, Lincoln's Inn, London WC2A 3TG, ☎020 7831 6381
✉clerks@11sb.com
New Street Chambers
2 New Street, Leicester LE1 5NA, ☎0116 262 5906 ✉clerks@2newstreet.co.uk
Call Date: Nov 1977, Middle Temple
Pupil Supervisor
Qualifications: [MA (Oxon)]

ARLIDGE MR ANTHONY JOHN QC (1981)

18 Red Lion Court
London EC4A 3EB, ☎020 7520 6000
✉chambers@18rlc.co.uk
4 Brick Court
4 Brick Court, Temple, London EC4Y 9AD, ☎020 7832 3200 ✉clerks@4bc.co.uk
18 Red Lion Court (Annexe)
Thornwood House, 102 New London Road, Chelmsford, Essex CM2 0RG, ☎01245 280880
Call Date: Feb 1962, Middle Temple
Qualifications: [MA (Cantab)]
anthony.arlidge@18rlc.co.uk

ARMBRISTER MR ALLAN RAMSAY

39 Park Square
Leeds LS1 2NU, ☎0113 245 6633
✉seniorclerk@39parksquarechambers.co.uk
Call Date: Nov 1984, Inner Temple
Qualifications: [BA DML DMS]
Ararmbrister@aol.com

ARMITAGE MRS LINDY ELIZABETH

Park Lane Plowden
19 Westgate, Leeds LS1 2RD, ☎0113 228 5049
✉clerks@parklaneplowden.co.uk
Call Date: July 1985, Lincoln's Inn
Pupil Supervisor, Recorder
Qualifications: [LLB (Hons)(Leeds)]
lindy.armitage@parklaneplowden.co.uk

ARMITAGE MR MARK

Crown Office Chambers
2 Crown Office Row, Temple, London EC4Y 7HJ, ☎020 7797 8100
✉mail@crownofficechambers.com
Call Date: July 1999, Middle Temple
Qualifications: [BA (Hons) LLM (Cantab)]

ARMOUR MISS ALISON JANE

A J Chambers
12 Sperling Road, Bruce Grove, London N17 6UH, ☎ 020 8885 5775
Middle Temple Lane Chambers
2nd Floor South, 1 Middle Temple Lane, London EC4Y 9AA, ☎ 020 7583 4352
✉ chambers@mtlchambers.com
MK Family Law Chambers
PO Box 6017, Milton Keynes MK1 9AP, ☎ 0845 123 1234
Call Date: July 1979, Lincoln's Inn
Pupil Supervisor
Qualifications: [MA BA (Hons)(Newc)]

ARMSTRONG MR DEAN PAUL

2 Bedford Row
London WC1R 4BU, ☎ 020 7440 8888
✉ clerks@2bedfordrow.co.uk
Call Date: July 1985, Gray's Inn
Pupil Supervisor
Qualifications: [MA (Cantab)]
🖂 darmstrong@2bedfordrow.co.uk

ARMSTRONG MR GRANT BRUCE

6 Pump Court
1st Floor, 6 Pump Court, Temple, London EC4Y 7AR, ☎ 020 7797 8400
✉ richardconstable@6pumpcourt.co.uk
6 Pump Court Chambers
6-8 Mill Street, Maidstone, Kent ME15 6XH, ☎ 01622 688094
✉ annexe@6pumpcourt.co.uk
Carmelite Chambers
9 Carmelite Street, London EC4Y 0DR, ☎ 020 7936 6300
✉ clerks@carmelitechambers.co.uk
Call Date: July 1978, Lincoln's Inn
Qualifications: [LLB (Lond)]
🖂 grantarmstrong@6pumpcourt.co.uk

ARMSTRONG MISS KATHERINE AMANDA

Dere Street Barristers
14 Toft Green, York YO1 6JT, ☎ 0844 3351551
✉ clerks@derestreet.co.uk
Call Date: July 2009, Lincoln's Inn
Qualifications: [BA(Dunelm) CPE COLY]
🖂 kraitt@yorkchambers.co.uk

ARMSTRONG MR KESTER IDRIS SCOBELL

Dere Street Barristers
33 Broad Chare, Newcastle Upon Tyne NE1 3DQ, ☎ 0844 3351551
✉ clerks@derestreet.co.uk
Chambers of Mr L Rahman
201 Maidstone Road, Rochester, Kent ME1 3ES, ☎ 07947 588362
✉ luthfur99@gmail.com
Call Date: Nov 1982, Inner Temple
Pupil Supervisor
Qualifications: [BA (York)]
🖂 clerks@broadcharechambers.co.uk

ARMSTRONG MR MICHAEL STEPHEN

Atlantic Chambers
4-6 Cook Street, Liverpool L2 9QU, ☎ 0151 236 4421
✉ info@atlanticchambers.co.uk
Call Date: Oct 2002, Inner Temple
Qualifications: [LLB (Hons)(Manch)]
🖂 michaelarmstrong@atlanticchambers.co.uk

ARMSTRONG DR NICHOLAS JAMES BUCHANAN

Matrix Chambers
Griffin Building, Gray's Inn, London WC1R 5LN, ☎ 020 7404 3447
✉ matrix@matrixlaw.co.uk / lscott@matrixlaw.co.uk
Call Date: July 2001, Inner Temple
Pupil Supervisor
Qualifications: [LLB (Nott'm) PHd (Nott'm)]
🖂 nickarmstrong@matrixlaw.co.uk

ARMSTRONG MR ROBERT DOUGLAS

No5 Chambers
Fountain Court, Steelhouse Lane, Birmingham B4 6DR, ☎ 0845 210 5555 ✉ info@no5.com
No5 Chambers
38 Queen Square, Bristol BS1 4QS, ☎ 0845 210 5555
No5 Chambers
Greenwood House, 4-7 Salisbury Court, London EC4Y 8AA, ☎ 0845 210 5555
Call Date: Nov 1999, Inner Temple
Qualifications: [LLB]
🖂 planning@no5.com

E

ARMSTRONG MR ROBERT HYLTON

Park Lane Plowden
19 Westgate, Leeds LS1 2RD,
☎ 0113 228 5049
✉ clerks@parklaneplowden.co.uk
Call Date: July 2008, Inner Temple
Qualifications: [LLB (Newc)]
hylton.armstrong@parklaneplowden.co.uk

ARMSTRONG MR STUART DAVID

Arden Chambers
20 Bloomsbury Square, London WC1A 2NS,
☎ 020 7242 4244
✉ clerks@ardenchambers.com
Call Date: Oct 1995, Gray's Inn
Qualifications: [LLM LLB]

ARNEY MR JAMES EDWARD

Temple Garden Chambers
1 Harcourt Buildings, Temple, London
EC4Y 9DA, ☎ 020 7583 1315
✉ clerks@tgchambers.com
Call Date: Oct 1992, Lincoln's Inn
Pupil Supervisor
Qualifications: [LLB(Hons)]
jarney@tgchambers.com

ARNFIELD MR ROBERT JOHN

Ten Old Square
Ground Floor, Ten Old Square, Lincoln's Inn,
London WC2A 3SU, ☎ 020 7405 0758
✉ clerks@tenoldsquare.com
Call Date: Oct 1996, Inner Temple
Qualifications: [BA (Oxon) CPE]
clerks@tenoldsquare.com

ARNHEIM DR MICHAEL THOMAS WALTER

Chambers of Dr Michael Arnheim
101 Queen Alexandra Mansions, Judd Street,
London WC1H 9DP, ☎ 020 7833 5093
✉ arnheim.law@gmail.com
Holborn Chambers
6 Gate Street, Lincoln's Inn Fields, London
WC2A 3HP, ☎ 020 7242 6060
Principal Chambers
15 Lime Tree Walk, Sevenoaks, Kent
TN13 1YH, ☎ 0845 209 8080
Call Date: July 1988, Lincoln's Inn
Pupil Supervisor
Qualifications: [MA (South Africa) LLB (Hons) (Lond) PhD (Cantab)]

ARNOLD MR GRAHAM JOHN

Farringdon Chambers
180 Bermondsey Street, London SE1 3TQ,
☎ 020 7089 5700
Call Date: Nov 2002, Lincoln's Inn
Qualifications: [MA (Dub)]
grahamarnold@farringdon-law.co.uk

ARNOLD MR JAMES MATTHEW

Outer Temple Chambers
The Outer Temple, 222 Strand, London
WC2R 1BA, ☎ 020 7353 6381
✉ clerks@outertemple.com
Call Date: Oct 2000, Middle Temple
Pupil Supervisor
Qualifications: [LLB (Hons) (Leic)]
james.arnold@outertemple.com

ARNOLD MR MARK GRAHAM

South Square
3-4 South Square, Gray's Inn, London
WC1R 5HP, ☎ 020 7696 9900
✉ practicemanagers@southsquare.com
Call Date: July 1988, Middle Temple
Pupil Supervisor
Qualifications: [MA (Hons) (Cantab)]
markarnold@southsquare.com

ARNOLD MR PETER MATTHEW MILLER

No5 Chambers
Fountain Court, Steelhouse Lane, Birmingham
B4 6DR, ☎ 0845 210 5555 ✉ info@no5.com
No5 Chambers
Greenwood House, 4-7 Salisbury Court,
London EC4Y 8AA, ☎ 0845 210 5555
No5 Chambers
38 Queen Square, Bristol BS1 4QS,
☎ 0845 210 5555
Call Date: July 1972, Lincoln's Inn
Pupil Supervisor
Qualifications: [LLB]
pmma@blueyonder.co.uk

ARNONE MS ANNA

Eastbourne Chambers
5 Chiswick Place, Eastbourne, East Sussex
BN21 4NH, ☎ 01323 642102
✉ clerks@eastbournechambers.co.uk
Call Date: July 2002, Middle Temple
Qualifications: [BA (Hons) LLB (Hons)]

E

ARNOT MR LEE ALEXANDER

29 Bedford Row Chambers
London WC1R 4HE, ☎020 7404 1044
✉clerks@29br.co.uk
Call Date: Oct 1990, Lincoln's Inn
Pupil Supervisor
Qualifications: [BA (Cantab)]
✉larnot@29br.co.uk

ARNOT DRUMMOND MISS KATHRYN

25 Bedford Row
London WC1R 4HD, ☎020 7067 1500
✉clerks@25bedfordrow.com
Call Date: July 2008, Inner Temple
Qualifications: [MA (Edin)]

ARORA MISS ANITA

Nine Bedford Row
9 Bedford Row, London WC1R 4AZ,
☎020 7489 2727
✉clerks@9bedfordrow.co.uk
Call Date: Oct 1994, Lincoln's Inn
Qualifications: [LLB (Hons)(Coventry)]
✉anita.arora@9bedfordrow.co.uk

ARSENIO DR JOAO

The Chambers of Joao Arsenio
8 Windsor Gardens, Basingstoke RG22 4XW,
☎01256 346435
Call Date: July 2009, Middle Temple

ARSHAD MISS FARRHAT

Doughty Street Chambers
53-54 Doughty Street, London WC1N 2LS,
☎020 7404 1313
✉enquiries@doughtystreet.co.uk
Doughty Street Chambers
Pall Mall Court, 61-67 King Street, Manchester M2 4PD, ☎0161 618 1066
Doughty Street Chambers
5th Floor, Broad Quay House, Prince Street, Bristol BS1 4DJ, ☎01179 058 717
Call Date: Nov 1998, Inner Temple
Qualifications: [BA (Oxon) LLM (LSE)]
✉f.arshad@doughtystreet.co.uk

ARSHAD MISS RAFFIA

St Mary's Family Law Chambers
26-28 High Pavement, The Lace Market, Nottingham NG1 1HN, ☎0115 950 3503
✉clerks@stmarysflc.co.uk
Call Date: July 2002, Middle Temple
Qualifications: [LLM BA (Hons)]
✉raffia.arshard@stmarysflc.co.uk

ARTESI MISS DESIREE ALLISON ANN

Thomas More Chambers
7 Lincoln's Inn Fields, London WC2A 3BP,
☎020 7404 7000
✉clerks@thomasmore.co.uk
Call Date: Oct 1998, Inner Temple
Qualifications: [BSc (West Indies) LLB (Lond)]

ARTHUR MRS HELEN FRANCES CATHERINE

No5 Chambers
Fountain Court, Steelhouse Lane, Birmingham B4 6DR, ☎0845 210 5555 ✉info@no5.com
No5 Chambers
Greenwood House, 4-7 Salisbury Court, London EC4Y 8AA, ☎0845 210 5555
No5 Chambers
38 Queen Square, Bristol BS1 4QS,
☎0845 210 5555
Call Date: Oct 2003, Middle Temple
Qualifications: [LLB (Hons)(Lond)]
✉ha@no5.com, helenarthur@blueyonder.co.uk

ARTHUR MR STEPHEN JOSEPH

Temple Tax Chambers
1st Floor, 3 Temple Gardens, Temple, London EC4Y 9AU, ☎020 7353 7884
✉clerks@templetax.com
Call Date: Nov 2002, Middle Temple
Qualifications: [LLB (Hons)(Lond) CTA TEP]

ARUMUGAM MR RAJ KUMAR

9 Stone Buildings
Lincoln's Inn, London WC2A 3NN,
☎020 7404 5055
✉clerks@9stonebuildings.com
Call Date: Oct 2008, Lincoln's Inn
Qualifications: [BA (Cantab) MA (Hons) (Cantab)]
✉rarumugam@9stonebuildings.com

ASANOVIC MS BOJANA

Chambers of Mr Ami Feder
Ground Floor, Lamb Building, Temple, London EC4Y 7AS, ☎020 7797 7788
✉clerks@lambbuilding.co.uk
Chambers of Mr Ami Feder
Ground Floor, Lamb Building, Temple, London EC4Y 7AS, ☎020 7797 7788
✉clerks@lambbuilding.co.uk
Call Date: July 2000, Middle Temple
Qualifications: [BA(Hons) CPE]

E

ASCHERSON MISS ISOBEL RUTH

23 Essex Street
London WC2R 3AA, ☎ 020 7413 0353
✉ clerks@23es.com
Call Date: Feb 1991, Gray's Inn
Qualifications: [LLB (Lond)]
✉ isobelascherson@23es.com

ASCROFT MR RICHARD GEOFFREY

Guildhall Chambers
23 Broad Street, Bristol BS1 2HG,
☎ 0117 930 9000
✉ hoc@guildhallchambers.co.uk
Call Date: Nov 1995, Lincoln's Inn
Pupil Supervisor
Qualifications: [LLB (Hons) BCL (Oxon)]
✉ richard.ascroft@guildhallchambers.co.uk

ASGHAR MR TAZAFAR

Brompton Chambers
1st Floor, 353A Station Road, Harrow, Middlesex HA1 1LN, ☎ 0560 3685647
✉ bromptonchamber@aol.com
Call Date: Nov 2001, Lincoln's Inn
Qualifications: [LLB (Hons)]

ASH MR BRIAN MAXWELL QC (1990)

4-5 Gray's Inn Square
Gray's Inn, London WC1R 5AH,
☎ 020 7404 5252 ✉ clerks@4-5.co.uk
Call Date: Nov 1975, Gray's Inn
Qualifications: [BA (Oxon)]
✉ bash@4-5.co.uk

ASH MR EDWARD WILLIAM

Chambers of Mr Edward Ash
23 Rogers Close, Elsworth, Cambridgeshire CB23 4JJ, ☎ 01954 267674
Call Date: Oct 1993, Middle Temple
Qualifications: [BA (Hons)(B'ham) M Phil (Cantab) LLM (London)]

ASH MR SIMON

36 Bedford Row
London WC1R 4JH, ☎ 020 7421 8000
✉ chambers@36bedfordrow.co.uk
Call Date: Mar 1999, Gray's Inn
Qualifications: [BA]
✉ sash@36bedfordrow.co.uk

ASHCROFT MR MICHAEL JAMES QC (2011)

20 Essex Street
London WC2R 3AL, ☎ 020 7842 1200
✉ clerks@20essexst.com
Call Date: Mar 1997, Gray's Inn
Pupil Supervisor
Qualifications: [BA BCL (Oxon)]
✉ clerks@20essexst.com

ASHE MR THOMAS MICHAEL QC (1994)

9 Stone Buildings
Lincoln's Inn, London WC2A 3NN,
☎ 020 7404 5055
✉ clerks@9stonebuildings.com
Call Date: July 1971, Middle Temple
Recorder
✉ masheqc@9stonebuildings.com

ASHER MR MICHAEL JAMES

Chambers of Mr M J Asher
86 Kensington Park Road, London W11 2PL,
☎ 020 7727 0271
✉ michael@asher.demon.co.uk
Call Date: July 2000, Lincoln's Inn
Qualifications: [BA(Hons) MA (Cantab)]

ASHFORD-THOM MR IAN

Temple Garden Chambers
1 Harcourt Buildings, Temple, London EC4Y 9DA, ☎ 020 7583 1315
✉ clerks@tgchambers.com
3 PB Barristers
3 Paper Buildings, Temple, London EC4Y 7EU,
☎ 020 7583 8055
Call Date: July 1977, Gray's Inn
Pupil Supervisor
Qualifications: [LLB (Exeter)]

ASHIQ MR RIZWAN

1 Gray's Inn Square
Ground Floor, 1 Gray's Inn Square, London WC1R 5AA, ☎ 020 7405 0001
Call Date: July 2001, Lincoln's Inn
Qualifications: [LLB (Hons) (Lond)]
✉ rashiq@1gis.co.uk

ASHLEY MRS JULIE ANN

Number 7 Harrington Street Chambers
7 Harrington Street, Liverpool L2 9YH,
☎ 0151 242 0707 ✉ clerks@7hs.co.uk
Call Date: Mar 2007, Lincoln's Inn
Qualifications: [BA (Hudds) LLB (L'pool)]
✉ julie.ashley@7hs.co.uk

E

ASHLEY MR MARK ROBERT

Pump Court Chambers
31 Southgate Street, Winchester, Hampshire SO23 9EB, ☎ 01962 868 161
✉ clerks@3pumpcourt.com
Pump Court Chambers
Upper Ground Floor, 3 Pump Court, Temple, London EC4Y 7AJ, ☎ 020 7353 0711
✉ clerks@3pumpcourt.com
Pump Court Chambers
5 Temple Chambers, Temple Street, Swindon SN1 1SQ, ☎ 01793 539899
✉ clerks@3pumpcourt.com
Call Date: Nov 1993, Lincoln's Inn
Qualifications: [LLB (Hons)]

ASHLEY MR NEIL MARTIN

East Anglian Chambers
15 The Close, Norwich, Norfolk NR1 4DZ, ☎ 01473 214481 ✉ norwich@ealaw.co.uk
East Anglian Chambers
Gresham House, 5 Museum Street, Ipswich, Suffolk IP1 1HQ, ☎ 01473 214481
✉ ipswich@ealaw.co.uk
East Anglian Chambers
140 New London Road, Chelmsford, Essex CM2 0AW, ☎ 01473 214481
✉ chelmsford@ealaw.co.uk
Call Date: Mar 1999, Lincoln's Inn
Pupil Supervisor
Qualifications: [LLB (Hons)(Essex)]
🖃 neilashley@ealaw.co.uk

ASHLEY-NORMAN MR JONATHAN CHARLES

3 Raymond Buildings
3 Raymond Buildings, Gray's Inn, London WC1R 5BH, ☎ 020 7400 6400
✉ clerks@3rblaw.com
Call Date: July 1989, Middle Temple
Pupil Supervisor
Qualifications: [LLB (Exon)]
🖃 jonathan.ashley-norman@3raymondbuildings.com

ASHMOLE MR TIMOTHY MICHAEL

St Johns Buildings
24a - 28 St John Street, Manchester M3 4DJ, ☎ 0161 214 1500
✉ clerk@stjohnsbuildings.co.uk
St Johns Buildings
21 White Friars, Chester CH1 1NZ, ☎ 01244 323070
✉ clerk@stjohnsbuildings.co.uk
16 Winckley Square
Preston PR1 3JJ, ☎ 01772 256100
Call Date: Oct 1992, Inner Temple
Qualifications: [LLB (UEA)]

ASHRAPH MS SARETA JANE

Garden Court Chambers
57-60 Lincoln's Inn Fields, London WC2A 3LJ, ☎ 020 7993 7600 ✉ info@gclaw.co.uk
Call Date: Oct 2002, Inner Temple
Qualifications: [BA (Oxon) LLM]
🖃 saretaa@gclaw.co.uk

ASHTON DR RAYMOND KEIGHLEY

9 Stone Buildings
Lincoln's Inn, London WC2A 3NN, ☎ 020 7404 5055
✉ clerks@9stonebuildings.com
Call Date: July 1979, Lincoln's Inn
Qualifications: [BSC (Lond) FCA LLM PHD (Lond) MSc (Lond) PLD (Lond) FTII ACMA ACIS (Lond) AFCA PLD]

ASHWELL MR PAUL MARTYN

Crown Office Row Chambers
119 Church Street, Brighton, Sussex BN1 1UD, ☎ 01273 625625
✉ clerks@1cor.com
Call Date: July 1977, Inner Temple
Pupil Supervisor
Qualifications: [BA]
🖃 paul.ashwell@1cor.com

ASHWORTH MISS FIONA KATHERINE ANNE

Kings Chambers
36 Young Street, Manchester M3 3FT, ☎ 0845 034 3444
✉ clerks@kingschambers.com
Kings Chambers
5 Park Square East, Leeds LS1 2NE, ☎ 0845 034 3444
✉ clerks@kingschambers.com
Kings Chambers
Embassy House, 60 Church Street, Birmingham B3 2DJ, ☎ 0845 034 3444
✉ clerks@kingschambers.com
Call Date: July 1988, Lincoln's Inn
Pupil Supervisor, Recorder
Qualifications: [LLB (Hons)(Leeds)]
🖃 fashworth@kingschambers.com

ASHWORTH MR LANCE DOMINIC PIERS QC (2006)

Serle Court
6 New Square, Lincoln's Inn, London WC2A 3QS, ☎ 020 7242 6105
✉ clerks@serlecourt.co.uk
St Philips Chambers
55 Temple Row, Birmingham B2 5LS, ☎ 0121 246 7000 ✉ clerks@st-philips.com

Henderson Chambers
2 Harcourt Buildings, Temple, London
EC4Y 9DB, ☎ 020 7583 9020
✉ clerks@hendersonchambers.co.uk
Call Date: Nov 1987, Middle Temple
Recorder
Qualifications: [MA (Cantab)]

ASHWORTH MISS PHILIPPA

Iscoed Chambers
86 St Helen's Road, Swansea SA1 4BQ,
☎ 01792 652988
✉ clerks@iscoedchambers.co.uk
Call Date: Oct 2000, Gray's Inn
Pupil Supervisor
Qualifications: [BSc Hons(St Andrews) PG Dip Law]
pa@iscoedchambers.co.uk

ASHWORTH MR STEVEN DAVID

5 Pump Court
Ground Floor, 5 Pump Court, Temple, London
EC4Y 7AP, ☎ 020 7353 2532
✉ clerks@5pumpcourt.com
Call Date: July 2006, Inner Temple
Qualifications: [LLB (Leeds)]
stevenashworth@5pumpcourt.com

ASKEY MR ROBERT JOHN

Palmyra Chambers
Royal House, 46 Legh Street, Warrington
WA1 1UJ, ☎ 01925 444919
✉ clerk@palmyrachambers.com
Call Date: July 1998, Lincoln's Inn
Pupil Supervisor
Qualifications: [LLB (Hons)(Wales)]

ASKHAM MR NIGEL HEAL

Octagon Chambers
29 Park Street, Taunton, Somerset TA1 4DG,
☎ 01823 331919
✉ jcload@Octagonchambers.co.uk
Call Date: Feb 1973, Inner Temple
Qualifications: [LLB]
naskham@octagonchambers.co.uk

ASKINS MR NICHOLAS PETER

Broadway House Chambers
Broadway House, 9 Bank Street, Bradford,
West Yorkshire BD1 1TW, ☎ 01274 722560
✉ clerks@broadwayhouse.co.uk
Broadway House Chambers
25 Park Square West, Leeds, West Yorkshire
LS1 2PW, ☎ 0113 246 2600
✉ clerks@broadwayhouse.co.uk
Call Date: Nov 1989, Gray's Inn
Pupil Supervisor
Qualifications: [LLB (Lond)]
npa@broadwayhouse.co.uk

ASLAM MR QAZI MAHMUD

Staple Inn Chambers
1st Floor, 9 Staple Inn, Holborn Bars, London
WC1V 7QH, ☎ 020 7242 5240
✉ clerks@stapleinn.co.uk
Call Date: Nov 1983, Gray's Inn
Pupil Supervisor
Qualifications: [BA (Hons) (Leics)]
qma@stapleinn.co.uk

ASLETT MR PEPIN CHARLES MAGUIRE

Call Date: Nov 1996, Lincoln's Inn
Pupil Supervisor
Qualifications: [LLB (Hons)(Bucks)]
daniel.metcalfe@stjohnsbuildings.co.uk, pepin@6internet.com

ASPDEN MR GORDON JAMES

Seven Bedford Row
7 Bedford Row, London WC1R 4BS,
☎ 020 7242 3555 ✉ clerks@7br.co.uk
Call Date: Nov 1988, Gray's Inn
Pupil Supervisor
Qualifications: [LLB (Hull)]
gaspden@7br.co.uk

ASPINALL MR CHRISTOPHER JOHN

Park Court Chambers
16 Park Place, Leeds LS1 2SJ,
☎ 0113 243 3277
✉ clerks@parkcourtchambers.co.uk
Call Date: Mar 2008, Middle Temple
Qualifications: [BA (Hons) (York)]
chris.aspinall@parkcourtchambers.co.uk

ASPINALL MR JOHN MICHAEL QC (1995)

Tooks Chambers
81 Farringdon Street, London EC4A 4BL,
☎ 020 7842 7575 ✉ clerks@tooks.co.uk
Bank House Chambers
Old Bank House, Hartshead, Sheffield S1 2EL,
☎ 0114 275 1223
✉ w.digby@bankhousechambers.co.uk
Call Date: Nov 1971, Inner Temple
Qualifications: [LLB]
john.aspinall@tooks.co.uk

ASPINALL MR MICHAEL

Citadel Chambers
The Citadel, 190 Corporation Street,
Birmingham B4 6QD, ☎ 0121 233 8500
✉ clerks@citadelchambers.com
Call Date: Nov 1986, Gray's Inn
Qualifications: [BSocSci MA (Keele)]
clerks@citadelchambers.com

ASPINALL-MILES MISS MARY JACQUELINE CECILE

12 College Place
Fauvelle Buildings, 12 College Place, Southampton SO15 2FE, ☎ 023 8032 0320
✉ clerks@12cp.co.uk
Call Date: Oct 1999, Lincoln's Inn
Qualifications: [MA (Oxon) Dip in Law]
✉ maspinall-miles@12cp.co.uk

ASPLIN MISS SARAH JANE QC (2002)

3 Stone Buildings
Ground Floor, 3 Stone Buildings, Lincoln's Inn, London WC2A 3XL, ☎ 020 7242 4937
✉ clerks@3sb.law.co.uk
Call Date: July 1984, Gray's Inn
Qualifications: [MA(Cantab) BCL(Oxon)]
✉ sasplin@3sb.law.co.uk

Fax: 020 7405 3896;
Out of hours telephone: 020 7242 4937;
DX: 317 London;
Other comms: E-mail: clerks@3sb.law.co.uk

Types of work: Chancery (general), Equity, Pensions, Professional negligence, Trusts, Wills

Awards and memberships: Association Pension Lawyers; Chancery Bar Association

Other professional experience: Deputy High Court Judge

Reported Cases: *Capita Atl Pension Trustees Ltd v Gallately,* [2011] EWHC 485 (Ch) (Chancery Division High Court), 2011. Trial of issues of construction of pension solvence documentation.
Capita Atl Pension Trustees Ltd v Zurkinskas, [2010] EWHC 3365 (Chancery Division High Court), 2010. Compromised of equalisation issues involving PPF.
Aon Pension Trustees Ltd v MCP Pension Trustees Ltd, [2010] EWCA (Civ) 377 (Court of Appeal (Civ)), 2010. Concerned an important issue as to the true construction and application of s27 Trustee Act 1925 and the meaning of 'notice' in that context.
PNPF Trust Co Ltd v Taylor & Ors, [2010] EWHC 1573 (Ch), [2010] PLR 261 (Chancery Division High Court), 2010. Considered to be the most important case in the field of Pensions for a generation. Concerns construction of trust documents, administration of trust including issue of £285million deficit funds.
BT Pension Scheme Trustees Ltd v British Telecommunications plc & Ors, [2010 EWHC 2642 (Ch) (Chancery Division High Court), 2010. Considered to be the most important case in the field of Pensions for a generation. Concerns construction of trust documents, administration of trust including issue of £285million deficit funds.

ASPREY MISS LOUISE ANGELA JOAN

Walnut House
63 St. David's Hill, Exeter, Devon EX4 4DW, ☎ 01392 279751
✉ clerks@walnuthouse.co.uk
Call Date: Oct 2007, Lincoln's Inn
Qualifications: [LLB (Exon)]

ASPREY MR NICHOLAS

Serle Court
6 New Square, Lincoln's Inn, London WC2A 3QS, ☎ 020 7242 6105
✉ clerks@serlecourt.co.uk
Clock Chambers
18 Waterloo Road, Wolverhampton WV1 4BL, ☎ 01902 313444
✉ clockchambers@btconnect.com
Call Date: July 1969, Inner Temple
Pupil Supervisor
Qualifications: [LLB (Edin)]
✉ nasprey@serlecourt.co.uk

ASQUITH MR MARC NIGEL

Kenworthy's Chambers
Arlington House, Bloom Street, Salford, Manchester M3 6AJ, ☎ 0161 832 4036
Call Date: Oct 1999, Middle Temple
Qualifications: [LLB (Hons) (Wales)]

ASQUITH MR THOMAS MARK

Four New Square
Four New Square, Lincoln's Inn, London WC2A 3RJ, ☎ 020 7822 2000
✉ barristers@4newsquare.com
Call Date: Oct 2007, Lincoln's Inn
Qualifications: [BA (Oxon)]

ASSERSOHN MR OLIVER PAUL

Outer Temple Chambers
The Outer Temple, 222 Strand, London WC2R 1BA, ☎ 020 7353 6381
✉ clerks@outertemple.com
Call Date: July 2003, Middle Temple
Qualifications: [BA Hons (Warw) CPE (Lond)]
✉ oliver.assersohn@outertemple.com

E

ASTBURY MRS JOANNE

Park Lane Plowden
19 Westgate, Leeds LS1 2RD,
☎0113 228 5049
✉clerks@parklaneplowden.co.uk
Call Date: July 1989, Lincoln's Inn
Pupil Supervisor
Qualifications: [LLB (Nott'm)]
joanne.astbury@parklaneplowden.co.uk

ASTBURY MR PHILIP IAN

Call Date: Oct 1999, Gray's Inn
Qualifications: [LLB (L'pool)]
philip@astbury.wanadoo.co.uk

ASTERIS MR PETER DAVID

Pump Court Chambers
31 Southgate Street, Winchester, Hampshire
SO23 9EB, ☎01962 868 161
✉clerks@3pumpcourt.com
Pump Court Chambers
Upper Ground Floor, 3 Pump Court, Temple,
London EC4Y 7AJ, ☎020 7353 0711
✉clerks@3pumpcourt.com
Pump Court Chambers
5 Temple Chambers, Temple Street, Swindon
SN1 1SQ, ☎01793 539899
✉clerks@3pumpcourt.com
Call Date: Oct 1996, Lincoln's Inn
Pupil Supervisor
Qualifications: [LLB (Hons)(Leic)]
pa@3pumpcourt.com

ASTON MR MAURICE CHARLES

Five Paper Buildings
1st Floor, Five Paper Buildings, Temple,
London EC4Y 7HB, ☎020 7583 6117
✉clerks@5pb.co.uk
Agri-Law Chambers
Penterry Farm, St Arvans NP16 6HG,
☎01989 720675
Call Date: July 1982, Inner Temple
Pupil Supervisor
Qualifications: [LLB (So'ton)]
ma@5pb.co.uk

ASTON-CHERAIF MS EVA

7 Stones IP
88 Kingsway, Holborn, London WC2B 6AA,
☎020 7193 4033
Call Date: July 2003, Lincoln's Inn
Qualifications: [BA Hons (Lond) MA]
astoncheraif18@hotmail.co.uk

ASTOR MR PHILIP DOUGLAS PAUL

Temple Garden Chambers
1 Harcourt Buildings, Temple, London
EC4Y 9DA, ☎020 7583 1315
✉clerks@tgchambers.com
Call Date: Nov 1989, Inner Temple
Qualifications: [MA (Oxon) Dip Law (Lond)]
philipastor@tgchambers.com

ASWANI MR RAVI GIRDHARILAL

Stone Chambers
4 Field Court, Gray's Inn, London WC1R 5EF,
☎020 7440 6900
✉clerks@stonechambers.com
Call Date: July 2000, Lincoln's Inn
Qualifications: [LLB(Hons) (Lond)]

ATCHLEY MR RICHARD WALDEGRAVE

3 Raymond Buildings
3 Raymond Buildings, Gray's Inn, London
WC1R 5BH, ☎020 7400 6400
✉clerks@3rblaw.com
Zenith Chambers
10 Park Square, Leeds LS1 2LH,
☎0113 245 5438
✉clerks@zenithchambers.co.uk
Call Date: Nov 1977, Middle Temple
Pupil Supervisor, Recorder

ATHERTON MISS CHARLOTTE BESS

Exchange Chambers
One Derby Square, Derby Square, Liverpool
L2 9XX, ☎0151 236 7747
✉info@exchangechambers.co.uk
Exchange Chambers
7 Ralli Courts, West Riverside, Manchester
M3 5FT, ☎0161 833 2722
Exchange Chambers
Oxford House, Oxford Row, Leeds LS1 3BE,
☎0113 203 1970
✉spencer@exchangechambers.co.uk
Call Date: July 2003, Gray's Inn
Qualifications: [LLB (Sheff)]
atherton@exchangechambers.co.uk

ATHERTON MR PETER

Deans Court Chambers
24 St John Street, Manchester M3 4DF,
☎0161 214 6000 ✉clerks@deanscourt.co.uk
Deans Court Chambers
101 Walker Street, Preston PR1 2RR,
☎01772 565 600
✉preston@deanscourt.co.uk
Call Date: July 1975, Gray's Inn
Recorder
Qualifications: [LLB (Hons) (B'ham)]

E

ATHERTON MR STEPHEN NICHOLAS QC (2006)

20 Essex Street
London WC2R 3AL, ☎ 020 7842 1200
✉ clerks@20essexst.com
Call Date: July 1989, Middle Temple
Qualifications: [LLB (Lancs) LLM (Cantab)]

ATKIN MRS CLARE CATHERINE

Erimus Chambers
PO Box 1440, Bedford MK43 6AJ,
☎ 01234 720952
✉ clerks@erimuschambers.com
Call Date: July 2001, Middle Temple
Qualifications: [BSc LLB (Hons)]

ATKINS MR MICHAEL JONATHAN

Crown Office Chambers
2 Crown Office Row, Temple, London
EC4Y 7HJ, ☎ 020 7797 8100
✉ mail@crownofficechambers.com
Call Date: Oct 2006, Middle Temple
Qualifications: [BA (Hons) (Cantab)]
✉ atkins@crownofficechambers.com

ATKINS MR RICHARD PAUL QC (2011)

St Philips Chambers
55 Temple Row, Birmingham B2 5LS,
☎ 0121 246 7000 ✉ clerks@st-philips.com
Call Date: July 1989, Gray's Inn
Pupil Supervisor, Recorder
Qualifications: [MA (Oxon)]
✉ rpatkins@st-philips.com

ATKINS MISS VICTORIA MARY

18 Red Lion Court
London EC4A 3EB, ☎ 020 7520 6000
✉ chambers@18rlc.co.uk
Call Date: Nov 1998, Middle Temple
Qualifications: [BA (Hons)(Cantab)]
✉ victoria.atkins@18rlc.co.uk

ATKINS MR WILLIAM SIWARD

Maitland Chambers
7 Stone Buildings, Lincoln's Inn, London
WC2A 3SZ, ☎ 020 7406 1200
✉ clerks@maitlandchambers.com
Call Date: Oct 1995, Inner Temple
Pupil Supervisor
Qualifications: [MA (Edin) PHD (Cantab)]
✉ satkins@maitlandchambers.com

ATKINSON MS CATHERINE HELEN

The Chambers of Grahame Aldous QC
9 Gough Square, London EC4A 3DG,
☎ 020 7832 0500
✉ clerks@9goughsquare.co.uk
Call Date: Oct 2006, Lincoln's Inn
Qualifications: [MA (Edin)]
✉ catkinson@9goughsquare.co.uk

ATKINSON MR GILES MATTHEW QUINTUS

6 Pump Court
1st Floor, 6 Pump Court, Temple, London
EC4Y 7AR, ☎ 020 7797 8400
✉ richardconstable@6pumpcourt.co.uk
6 Pump Court Chambers
6-8 Mill Street, Maidstone, Kent ME15 6XH,
☎ 01622 688094
✉ annexe@6pumpcourt.co.uk
Call Date: July 2002, Middle Temple
Qualifications: [BA (Hons) (Oxon) MA (Nott'm) DipLaw (Lond)]
✉ Clerks@6PumpCourt.co.uk, gilesatkinson@6pumpcourt.co.uk

ATKINSON MS JESSICA JANE SINTON

1 Gray's Inn Square
Ground Floor, 1 Gray's Inn Square, London
WC1R 5AA, ☎ 020 7405 0001
Call Date: July 2006, Inner Temple
Qualifications: [BA (Herts)]
✉ jatkinson@1gis.co.uk

ATKINSON MR JODY ROY

St John's Chambers
101 Victoria Street, Bristol BS1 6PU,
☎ 0117 923 4700
✉ clerks@stjohnschambers.co.uk
Call Date: July 2005, Inner Temple
Qualifications: [BA University of Bristol MA University of York]

ATKINSON MR JONATHAN RICHARD SANDS

Westgate Chambers
64 High Street, Lewes, East Sussex BN7 1XG,
☎ 01273 480510
✉ clerks@westgate-chambers.co.uk
Call Date: Nov 2007, Middle Temple
Qualifications: [BA (Hons) (Bris) PgDL (Sussex)]
✉ JA@westgate-chambers.co.uk

E

ATKINSON MR NICHOLAS JEREMY QC (1991)

Atkinson Bevan Chambers
1st Floor, 2 Harcourt Buildings, Temple, London EC4Y 9DB, ☎ 020 7353 2112
✉ clerks@2hb.co.uk
Staple Inn Chambers
1st Floor, 9 Staple Inn, Holborn Bars, London WC1V 7QH, ☎ 020 7242 5240
✉ clerks@stapleinn.co.uk
Call Date: Nov 1971, Inner Temple
Recorder
nic_atkinson_qc@hotmail.com

ATKINSON MR RICHARD DUNCAN

6 King's Bench Walk
Ground Floor, 6 King's Bench Walk, Temple, London EC4Y 7DR, ☎ 020 7583 0410
✉ clerks@6kbw.com
Call Date: Oct 1995, Gray's Inn
Pupil Supervisor
Qualifications: [LLB (Bris)]
duncan.atkinson@6kbw.com

ATKINSON MR TIMOTHY GEORGE BRYANT

One Brick Court
1st Floor, One Brick Court, Temple, London EC4Y 9BY, ☎ 020 7353 8845
✉ clerks@onebrickcourt.com
Call Date: July 1988, Inner Temple
Pupil Supervisor
Qualifications: [BA (Oxon) Dip Law (Lond)]
ta@onebrickcourt.com

ATREYA MS NAVITA

Garden Court Chambers
57-60 Lincoln's Inn Fields, London WC2A 3LJ, ☎ 020 7993 7600 ✉ info@gclaw.co.uk
Call Date: Oct 1994, Lincoln's Inn
Qualifications: [BSc (Hons)(Lond)]
navitaa@gclaw.co.uk

ATRILL MR SIMON PAUL

Fountain Court Chambers
Fountain Court, Temple, London EC4Y 9DH, ☎ 020 7583 3335
✉ chambers@fountaincourt.co.uk
Call Date: July 2005, Inner Temple
Qualifications: [BA St Catharines College University of Cambridge BCL (Oxon) LLM (Pennyslyvania)]
sa@fountaincourt.co.uk

ATTENBOROUGH MR MICHAEL JAMES

Five Paper Buildings
1st Floor, Five Paper Buildings, Temple, London EC4Y 7HB, ☎ 020 7583 6117
✉ clerks@5pb.co.uk
Call Date: July 2008, Inner Temple
Qualifications: [LLB (Lond)]
mja@5pb.co.uk

ATTRIDGE MR DANIEL JAMES MACKENZIE

Trinity Chambers
Highfield House, Moulsham Street, Chelmsford, Essex CM2 9AH, ☎ 01245 605040
✉ clerks@trinitychambers.com
Call Date: Nov 2000, Middle Temple
Qualifications: [BA (Hons) (Sheff) LLM (Sheff)]

ATTRIDGE MR STEVEN JEFFREY

1 Gray's Inn Square
Ground Floor, 1 Gray's Inn Square, London WC1R 5AA, ☎ 020 7405 0001
Call Date: Nov 1991, Inner Temple
Qualifications: [LLB]
clerks@1gis.co.uk

ATTWOOD MR JOHN JULIAN

No5 Chambers
Fountain Court, Steelhouse Lane, Birmingham B4 6DR, ☎ 0845 210 5555 ✉ info@no5.com
No5 Chambers
Greenwood House, 4-7 Salisbury Court, London EC4Y 8AA, ☎ 0845 210 5555
No5 Chambers
38 Queen Square, Bristol BS1 4QS, ☎ 0845 210 5555
Call Date: Nov 1989, Gray's Inn
Pupil Supervisor
Qualifications: [LLB (B'ham)]
jat@no5.com

ATTWOOLL MR CHRISTOPHER BENJAMIN

KBW
The Engine House, No 1 Foundry Square, Leeds LS11 5DL, ☎ 0113 297 1200
✉ clerks@kbwchambers.com
Call Date: July 1980, Middle Temple
Pupil Supervisor, Recorder
Qualifications: [BA (Keele)]
ca@kbwchambers.com

ATWAL MR NAVJOT

3 Hare Court
3 Hare Court, Temple, London EC4Y 7BJ,
☎ 020 7415 7800 ✉ clerks@3harecourt.com
Call Date: Mar 2002, Lincoln's Inn
Qualifications: [LLB (Hons) LLM]
✉ navjotatwal@3harecourt.com

AUBREY-JOHNSON MS KATE

Garden Court Chambers
57-60 Lincoln's Inn Fields, London WC2A 3LJ,
☎ 020 7993 7600 ✉ info@gclaw.co.uk
Call Date: Oct 2001, Inner Temple
Qualifications: [BA (Hons) (Sussex) CPE (Lond)]
✉ kateaj@gclaw.co.uk

AUBURN MR JONATHAN WALTER

4-5 Gray's Inn Square
Gray's Inn, London WC1R 5AH,
☎ 020 7404 5252 ✉ clerks@4-5.co.uk
Call Date: Nov 1999, Middle Temple
Pupil Supervisor
Qualifications: [LLB (Hons) BCL (Oxon) DPhil (Oxon)]
✉ jauburn@4-5.co.uk

AUDLAND MR WILLIAM GRANT

12 King's Bench Walk
12 King's Bench Walk, Temple, London EC4Y 7EL, ☎ 020 7583 0811
Call Date: Nov 1992, Gray's Inn
Pupil Supervisor
Qualifications: [MA (Oxon) Dip Law]
✉ audland@12kbw.co.uk

AULD MR CHARLES JOHN DENHAM

St John's Chambers
101 Victoria Street, Bristol BS1 6PU,
☎ 0117 923 4700
✉ clerks@stjohnschambers.co.uk
Call Date: July 1980, Middle Temple
Pupil Supervisor
Qualifications: [BA (Dunelm)]
✉ charles.auld@stjohnschambers.co.uk

AULD MR STEPHEN ROBERT QC (1999)

One Essex Court
Ground Floor, One Essex Court, Temple, London EC4Y 9AR, ☎ 020 7583 2000
✉ clerks@oeclaw.co.uk
Call Date: July 1979, Gray's Inn
Qualifications: [BA (Cantab)]
✉ sauld@oeclaw.co.uk

AULLYBOCUS MR MOHAMMAD NADEEM

Assize Court Chambers
14 Small Street, Bristol BS1 1DE,
☎ 0117 926 4587 ✉ carly@assize.co.uk
Call Date: Oct 2001, Inner Temple
Pupil Supervisor
Qualifications: [LLB (Bris) PG Dip Law]
✉ Nadeem.Aullybocus@assize.co.uk

AUSTIN MR IAN

Holborn Chambers
6 Gate Street, Lincoln's Inn Fields, London WC2A 3HP, ☎ 020 7242 6060
Call Date: Nov 2003, Middle Temple
Qualifications: [LLB (Hons)]
✉ ianaustin@holbornchambers.co.uk

AUSTIN MR JONATHAN EDWARD NEWNS

Linenhall Chambers
1 Stanley Place, Chester CH1 2LU,
☎ 01244 348282
✉ clerks@linenhallchambers.co.uk
Call Date: Oct 1991, Middle Temple
Pupil Supervisor
Qualifications: [BA (Hons) LLB (Hons)]
✉ jaustin@1stanleyplace.co.uk

AUSTIN MISS REBECCA LOUISE

2 King's Bench Walk
2 King's Bench Walk, Temple, London EC4Y 7DE, ☎ 020 7353 1746
✉ clerks@2kbw.com
Call Date: Oct 2002, Middle Temple
Qualifications: [LLB (Newc)]
✉ raustin@2kbw.com

AUSTIN-JONES MR JONATHAN

Call Date: Oct 2001, Inner Temple
Qualifications: [LLB (Lond) LLM (Kent)]
✉ jajcounsel@gmail.com

AUSTINS MR CHRISTOPHER JOHN

Chambers of Mr Christopher Austins
Rookwood House, East Harptree, Bristol BS40 6AQ, ☎ 01761 221 208
Clerksroom (Taunton)
Equity House, Administration Centre, Blackbrook Park Avenue, Taunton, Somerset TA1 2PX, ☎ 0845 083 3000
✉ mail@clerksroom.com
King's Lynn Chambers
26 The Birches, South Wootton, King's Lynn, Norfolk PE30 3JG, ☎ 01553 672 085
✉ timothy.leader@tesco.net
Call Date: July 1988, Gray's Inn
Qualifications: [LLB (Hons)]

AUTY MR MICHAEL ROY

1 High Pavement
Nottingham NG1 1HF, ☎0115 941 8218
✉clerks@1highpavement.co.uk
Call Date: Nov 1990, Inner Temple
Qualifications: [BA]
✉michaelauty@1highpavement.co.uk

AVERIS MRS ELAINE

Amicus Chambers
Queens Court, Newport Road, Middlesbrough TS1 5EH, ☎01642 876334
✉amicus.clerk@amicuschambers.co.uk
Call Date: Mar 2000, Middle Temple
Qualifications: [BA (Hons) (Sheff)]

AWAN MR AKHTAR HUSSAIN

Chambers of Mr A H Awan
326 Ada Court, 10-16 Maida Vale, St John's Wood, London W9 1TE, ☎07884 372954
Call Date: Nov 1978, Gray's Inn
Qualifications: [LLM (Lond) BSC LLB (Punjab)]
✉akhtawHawan@gmail.com

AWODELE MR OLUFEMI ADETUNJI

Great James Street Chambers
37 Great James Street, London WC1N 3HB, ☎020 7440 4949
✉chambers@greatjames.co.uk
Call Date: July 2002, Gray's Inn
Qualifications: [LLB (Lond) LLM (Lond)]

AXON MR ANDREW ELIOT

Park Lane Plowden
19 Westgate, Leeds LS1 2RD, ☎0113 228 5049
✉clerks@parklaneplowden.co.uk
Hailsham Chambers
Ground Floor, 4 Paper Buildings, Temple, London EC4Y 7EX, ☎020 7643 5000
✉clerks@hailshamchambers.com
Call Date: Oct 1992, Middle Temple
Qualifications: [BA (Hons)]

AYERS MR GUY RUSSELL

Octagon House
19 Colegate, Norwich NR3 1AT, ☎01603 623186
✉clerks@octagonhouse.co.uk
Call Date: July 1979, Inner Temple
Pupil Supervisor, Recorder
Qualifications: [LLB (So'ton)]

AYLETT MR CRISPIN DAVID WILLIAM QC (2008)

QEB Hollis Whiteman
1-2 Laurence Pountney Hill, London EC4R 0EU, ☎020 7933 8855
✉barristers@qebhw.co.uk
Call Date: July 1985, Inner Temple
Qualifications: [BA (Hons)(Bris) Dip Law]

AYLETT MR KENNETH GEORGE

15 New Bridge Street
London EC4V 6AU, ☎020 7842 1900
✉clerks@15nbs.com
4 Breams Buildings
Chancery Lane, London EC4A 1HP, ☎020 7092 1900 ✉clerks@4bb.co.uk
Call Date: July 1972, Inner Temple
Qualifications: [BA BL]

AYLIFFE MR JAMES JUSTIN BARNETT QC (2008)

Wilberforce Chambers
8 New Square, Lincoln's Inn, London WC2A 3QP, ☎020 7306 0102
✉chambers@wilberforce.co.uk
Call Date: Nov 1987, Lincoln's Inn
Qualifications: [BA (Oxon) Dip Law (Lond)]
✉jayliffe@wilberforce.co.uk

AYLING MISS JUDITH ANN

39 Essex Street
London WC2R 3AT, ☎020 7832 1111
✉clerks@39essex.com
82 King Street
Manchester M2 4WQ, ☎0161 870 9969
Call Date: Oct 1998, Middle Temple
Pupil Supervisor
Qualifications: [MA (Hons)(Cantab) CPE (Lond)]
✉judith.ayling@39essex.com

AYLING MISS TRACY JANE QC (2006)

2 Bedford Row
London WC1R 4BU, ☎020 7440 8888
✉clerks@2bedfordrow.co.uk
Call Date: July 1983, Inner Temple
Qualifications: [BA (Hons) (Dunelm)]
✉tayling@2bedfordrow.co.uk

AYLOTT MR COLIN CHRISTOPHER

Carmelite Chambers
9 Carmelite Street, London EC4Y 0DR, ☎020 7936 6300
✉clerks@carmelitechambers.co.uk
Call Date: Nov 1989, Inner Temple
Pupil Supervisor
Qualifications: [LLB (B'ham)]

AYLWIN MR CHRISTOPHER GRANVILLE ANGUS

3 PB Barristers
3 Paper Buildings, Temple, London EC4Y 7EU, ☎020 7583 8055
3 PB Barristers
23 Beaumont Street, Oxford OX1 2NP, ☎01865 793 736
3 PB Barristers
4 St Peter Street, Winchester SO23 8BW, ☎01962 868884
✉clerks.winchester@3paper.co.uk
3 PB Barristers
Royal Talbot House, 2 Victoria Street, Bristol, Avon BS1 6BB, ☎0117 928 1520
3 PB Barristers
30 Christchurch Road, Bournemouth, Dorset BH1 3PD, ☎01202 292102
✉clerks.bournemouth@3paper.co.uk
Call Date: Nov 1970, Inner Temple
Pupil Supervisor
Qualifications: [MA (Cantab)]

AYRES MR ANDREW JOHN WILLIAM

Maitland Chambers
7 Stone Buildings, Lincoln's Inn, London WC2A 3SZ, ☎020 7406 1200
✉clerks@maitlandchambers.com
Call Date: Oct 1996, Gray's Inn
Pupil Supervisor
Qualifications: [MA (Oxon)]
✉aayres@maitlandchambers.com

AYRES MISS KATY

Chambers of Ian Macdonald QC
Garden Court North, 22 Oxford Court, Manchester M2 3WQ, ☎0161 236 1840
✉clerks@gcnchambers.co.uk
Call Date: July 2008, Middle Temple
Qualifications: [BA (Hons) (Notts)]

AZAM MR AJMAL

Hardwicke
New Square, Lincoln's Inn, London WC2A 3SB, ☎020 7242 2523
✉enquiries@hardwicke.co.uk
Call Date: July 2006, Gray's Inn
Qualifications: [LLB (Lond)]
✉ajam.azam@harwicke.co.uk, ajmal_azam@yahoo.co.uk

AZHAR MR ALI MOHAMMAD

9 King's Bench Walk
Lower Ground Floor South, 9 King's Bench Walk, Temple, London EC4Y 7DX, ☎020 7353 9564 ✉9kbw@btconnect.com
Call Date: July 1962, Gray's Inn
Pupil Supervisor
Qualifications: [MA]
✉9kbw@btconnect.com

AZHAR MISS MARINA

4 Brick Court
4 Brick Court, Temple, London EC4Y 9AD, ☎020 7832 3200 ✉clerks@4bc.co.uk
Call Date: Nov 1990, Lincoln's Inn
Qualifications: [LLB]
✉marina.azhar@4bc.co.uk

AZHAR MS SHABEENA

9 King's Bench Walk
Lower Ground Floor South, 9 King's Bench Walk, Temple, London EC4Y 7DX, ☎020 7353 9564 ✉9kbw@btconnect.com
Call Date: Nov 1995, Inner Temple
Qualifications: [BA CPE (Sussex)]

AZIB MS REHANA

2 Temple Gardens
2 Temple Gardens, Temple, London EC4Y 9AY, ☎020 7822 1200
✉clerks@2tg.co.uk
Call Date: Nov 2003, Inner Temple
Qualifications: [BA (Oxon)]
✉razib@2tg.co.uk

AZIM MISS TABSUM REHNA

42 Bedford Row
London WC1R 4LL, ☎020 7831 0222
✉clerks@42br.com
Call Date: July 1984, Middle Temple
Qualifications: [LLB]
✉rehna.azim@42br.com

AZIZ MR SHIRAZ

Garden Court Chambers
57-60 Lincoln's Inn Fields, London WC2A 3LJ, ☎020 7993 7600 ✉info@gclaw.co.uk
Call Date: Nov 2006, Middle Temple
Qualifications: [LLB (Hons) (Lond) LLM (Lond) LEC]
✉shiraz@gclaw.co.uk

E

AZMEH MR UMAR

Farringdon Chambers
180 Bermondsey Street, London SE1 3TQ,
☎ 020 7089 5700
Call Date: July 2009, Middle Temple
Qualifications: [LLB (Hons) (Lond)]
umarazmeh@farringdon-law.co.uk

AZMI MRS LOUISE JACQUELINE

Broadway House Chambers
Broadway House, 9 Bank Street, Bradford, West Yorkshire BD1 1TW, ☎ 01274 722560
clerks@broadwayhouse.co.uk
Broadway House Chambers
25 Park Square West, Leeds, West Yorkshire LS1 2PW, ☎ 0113 246 2600
clerks@broadwayhouse.co.uk
Call Date: July 2004, Lincoln's Inn
Qualifications: [BA Hons (York) CPE BVC]
clerks@broadwayhouse.co.uk

AZMI MR MOHAMMAD JAVED

No 8 Chambers
8 Fountain Court, Steelhouse Lane, Birmingham B4 6DR, ☎ 0121 236 5514
clerks@no8chambers.co.uk
Call Date: Mar 1998, Middle Temple
Qualifications: [LLB (Hons)(Luton)]
mohammadazmi@no8chambers.co.uk

AZMI MR RAZIF

Park Lane Plowden
19 Westgate, Leeds LS1 2RD,
☎ 0113 228 5049
clerks@parklaneplowden.co.uk
Call Date: Mar 2005, Middle Temple
Qualifications: [BA (Hons) PgDip Law]
Razif.azmi@parklaneplowden.co.uk

BAATZ MR NICHOLAS STEPHEN QC (1998)

Atkin Chambers
1 Atkin Building, Gray's Inn, London WC1R 5AT, ☎ 020 7404 0102
clerks@atkinchambers.com
Call Date: Nov 1978, Gray's Inn
Qualifications: [MA FCIArb BCL (Oxon)]
clerks@atkinchambers.com

BABINGTON MISS VANESSA FRANCES

Arden Chambers
20 Bloomsbury Square, London WC1A 2NS,
☎ 020 7242 4244
clerks@ardenchambers.com
Call Date: July 2008, Gray's Inn
Qualifications: [BA (Cantab)]
vanessa.babington@ardenchambers.com

BACHE MISS ABIGAIL LOUISE

Garden Court Chambers
57-60 Lincoln's Inn Fields, London WC2A 3LJ,
☎ 020 7993 7600 info@gclaw.co.uk
Call Date: Mar 2004, Middle Temple
Qualifications: [LLB (Hons) (Kent)]

BACHE MISS NINA MARIE

St Ive's Chambers
Whittall Street, Birmingham B4 6DH,
☎ 0121 236 0863
clerks@stiveschambers.co.uk
Call Date: July 2001, Middle Temple
Qualifications: [LLB (Hons)]
nina.bache@stiveschambers.co.uk

BACON MR FRANCIS MICHAEL

Hailsham Chambers
Ground Floor, 4 Paper Buildings, Temple, London EC4Y 7EX, ☎ 020 7643 5000
clerks@hailshamchambers.com
Call Date: July 1988, Gray's Inn
Pupil Supervisor, Recorder
Qualifications: [BA (Keele) MSc (Loughborough)]
francis.bacon@hailshamchambers.com

BACON MRS JANE PATRICIA

36 Bedford Row
London WC1R 4JH, ☎ 020 7421 8000
chambers@36bedfordrow.co.uk
Call Date: July 1999, Middle Temple
Qualifications: [LLB (Hons) RGN RM ADM]

BACON MR JEFFREY DAVID

Littleton Chambers
3 King's Bench Walk North, Temple, London EC4Y 7HR, ☎ 020 7797 8600
fschneider@littletonchambers.co.uk
Call Date: Nov 1989, Middle Temple
Qualifications: [BA (Hons) (Sussex) Dip EEC (Belgium)]
jbacon@littletonchambers.co.uk

BACON MISS KELYN MEHER

Brick Court Chambers
7-8 Essex Street, London WC2R 3LD,
☎ 020 7379 3550 clerks@brickcourt.co.uk
Call Date: Oct 1998, Inner Temple
Pupil Supervisor
Qualifications: [MA (Oxon) LLM (Florence)]
Kelyn.Bacon@Brickcourt.co.uk

E

BACON MR NICHOLAS MICHAEL QC (2010)

Four New Square
Four New Square, Lincoln's Inn, London WC2A 3RJ, ☎ 020 7822 2000
✉ barristers@4newsquare.com
Call Date: Oct 1992, Inner Temple
Qualifications: [LLB (Essex)(Hons)]
✉ n.bacon@4newsquare.com

Fax: 020 822 2001;
DX: 1041 London, Chancery Lane

Types of work: Chancery (commercial), Costs, Insurance, Professional negligence

Awards and memberships: Two Inner Temple scholarships awarded; PNBA; COMBAR

Other professional experience: Civil Procedure Rules committee Member 2010 - present.

Publications: Contributing Editor to *Halsbury's Laws of England*, 2002 - present day; Contributing Editor to *Green Book*, 2000 - present day; *Assessment of Costs Under CPR*, 2001; *Butterworths Civil Court Precedents*, 2000 - present day; *The Bar Handbook 2010/11*, 2010

Reported Cases: *Callery v Gray*, [2002] 1 WLR 2000 (Court of Appeal/House of Lords), 2002. Leading case on discounted fee agreements.
Garratt v Halton Borough Council, [2007] 1 All ER 147 (Court of Appeal), 2006. Leading case on enforceability of conditional fee agreements.
Hawksford Trustees Jersey Ltd (trustee of the Bald Eagle Trust) v Stella Global UK Ltd & Anor, [2012] EWCA Civ 987 (Court of Appeal), 2012. A trial and an appeal from that trial were seperate proceedings for the purpose of the Access to Justice Act 1999 s.29. Therefore a premium for after the event insurance, taken out shortly before an appeal, covering the costs of the appear and the costs of them at first instance, was not recoverable in full.
Cawdery Kaye Fireman & Taylor (A Firm) v Gary Minkin, [2012] EWCA Civ 546; [2012] 19 EG 94 (CS); (2012) 162 NJL 681; (2012) 156 (18) SJLB 31 (Court of Appeal (Civil Division)), 2012. When assessing a solicitor's bill of costs, the costs judge had erred in ruling that the solicitor was not entitled to any of its fees on the basis that it had wrongly terminated the retainer with the client before litigation had come to an end. The retainer had been suspended due to the client refusing to pay and the client had no reasonable justification for refusing to pay.
Tim Martin Interiors Ltd v Akin Gump LLP, [2011] EWCA Civ 1574; [2012] 2 All ER 1058; [2012] CP Rep 16; [2012] 2 Costs LR 325 [2012] 1 EGLR 153; (2012) 162 CA (Civ Div) (Court of Appeal (Civil Division)), 2012. A third party assessment of cousts under the Solicitors Act 1974 s.71 was of limited use to a third party, since it only allowed the costs judge to eliminated items which ought not to be laid at the door of the third party because it was outside the scope of its liability.

BADEJO MR ABIMBOLA RAFIU

5 Pump Court
Ground Floor, 5 Pump Court, Temple, London EC4Y 7AP, ☎ 020 7353 2532
✉ clerks@5pumpcourt.com
Call Date: Nov 1993, Lincoln's Inn
Qualifications: [LLB (Hons)]

BADEJO MISS BIBI MOBOLAJI

4 Brick Court
4 Brick Court, Temple, London EC4Y 9AD, ☎ 020 7832 3200 ✉ clerks@4bc.co.uk
Call Date: July 2005, Inner Temple
Qualifications: [BA LLB]

BADENOCH MR JAMES FORSTER QC (1989)

1 Crown Office Row
1 Crown Office Row, Temple, London EC4Y 7HH, ☎ 020 7797 7500
✉ mail@1cor.com
Call Date: Nov 1968, Lincoln's Inn
Recorder
Qualifications: [MA (Oxon)]
✉ james.badenoch@1cor.com

Fax: 020 7797 7550;
DX: 1020 LDE;
Other comms: E-mail: jb@jbadenoch.com

Types of work: Clinical negligence, Disciplinary procedures, Human rights, Mental health, Personal injury, Professional negligence, Public inquiries

Membership of foreign bars: Admitted to the Hong Kong Bar (*ad eundem*)

Circuit: South Eastern

Awards and memberships: Bencher of Lincoln's Inn; Fellow of the Royal Society of Medicine

Other professional experience: Deputy High Court Judge (1994 to date); Chairman of the Expert Witness Institute; Accredited Mediator; President of the Mental Health Review Tribunal (2000 to date)

E

Languages spoken: French, Italian

Publications: *Clinical Negligence* (Powers and Harris; contributor), 1990, 1994, 2000, 2008; *Urology and the Law* (Informa Healthcare), 2007

Reported Cases: *Penney and Others v East Kent HA*, [2000] Lloyd's Rep Med 41 (Court of Appeal), 2000. Medical negligence (cervical smear test): application and limits of 'Bolam Test'.
Heil v Rankin, [2000] 2 WLR 1173 (Court of Appeal), 2000. Landmark case on general damages.
Preiss v General Dental Council, [2001] Lloyd's Rep Med 491 (Privy Council), 2001. Defining 'serious professional misconduct'. Human rights in disciplinary proceedings.
Lillywhite v UCL Hospitals' Trust, [2006] Lloyd's Rep Med 268 (Court of Appeal), 2006. Clinical negligence; standard of care; burden of proof.
Birch v UCLH Hospital NHS Trust, [2008] EWHC 2237 ((Q.B.)), 2008. Patient Consent, duty of treating clinicians

BADENOCH MR TONY DAVID

6 King's Bench Walk
Ground Floor, 6 King's Bench Walk, Temple, London EC4Y 7DR, ☎ 020 7583 0410
✉ clerks@6kbw.com
Call Date: Nov 1996, Middle Temple
Qualifications: [BSc (Hons) Dip Law]
✉ tony.badenoch@6kbw.com

BADGER MR CHRISTOPHER JAMES

23 Essex Street
London WC2R 3AA, ☎ 020 7413 0353
✉ clerks@23es.com
Call Date: Nov 2002, Middle Temple
Qualifications: [BA (Hons)(Oxon)]
✉ chrisbadger@23es.com

BADMAN MISS KYRA

Chavasse Court Chambers
18 Queen Avenue, Liverpool L2 4TX,
☎ 0151 229 2030
✉ clerks@chavassechambers.co.uk
Call Date: July 2011, Inner Temple
Qualifications: [LLB (Sheff)]

BAFADHEL MISS SARAH

Nine Bedford Row
9 Bedford Row, London WC1R 4AZ,
☎ 020 7489 2727
✉ clerks@9bedfordrow.co.uk
Call Date: Oct 2009, Inner Temple
Qualifications: [LLB (B'ham) LLM (Lond)]

E

BAGCHI MR ANDREW KUMAR

1 Garden Court Family Law Chambers
Ground Floor, One Garden Court, Temple, London EC4Y 9BJ, ☎ 020 7797 7900
✉ clerks@1gc.com
Call Date: July 1989, Middle Temple
Pupil Supervisor
Qualifications: [LLB (Lond)]
✉ bagchi@1gc.com

BAGGE MR ALFRED JAMES STEPHEN

QEB Hollis Whiteman
1-2 Laurence Pountney Hill, London EC4R 0EU, ☎ 020 7933 8855
✉ barristers@qebhw.co.uk
Call Date: July 1979, Lincoln's Inn

BAGGLEY MR PHILIP JAMES

Albion Chambers
Broad Street, Bristol BS1 1DR,
☎ 0117 927 2144
✉ clerks@albionchambers.co.uk
Call Date: July 2009, Gray's Inn
Qualifications: [BA]
✉ philip.baggley@albionchambers.co.uk

BAGGS MISS JULIA CLAIRE

Wilberforce Chambers
7 Bishop Lane, Hull HU1 1PA,
☎ 01482 323264
Call Date: Mar 2008, Inner Temple
Qualifications: [BA (Dunelm)]

BAGLEY MISS LOUISA ELLEN

1 Paper Buildings
1st Floor, 1 Paper Buildings, Temple, London EC4Y 7EP, ☎ 020 7353 3728
✉ clerks@onepaper.co.uk
Call Date: Oct 2000, Middle Temple
Qualifications: [LLB (Hons) (Nott'm)]
✉ louisabagley@onepaper.co.uk

BAGLEY MR MICHAEL WALLACE WELSBY

Chavasse Court Chambers
18 Queen Avenue, Liverpool L2 4TX,
☎ 0151 229 2030
✉ clerks@chavassechambers.co.uk
Call Date: Nov 1984, Gray's Inn
Pupil Supervisor
Qualifications: [BSc (Bris)]
✉ michael.bagley@chavassechambers.co.uk

BAGNALL MR MATTHEW PHILIP COOPER

2 Pump Court
1st Floor, 2 Pump Court, Temple, London EC4Y 7AH, ☎ 020 7353 5597
✉ clerks@2pumpcourt.co.uk
Call Date: Oct 1993, Middle Temple
Qualifications: [LLB (Hons)]
✉ mbagnall@2pumpcourt.co.uk

BAGOT MR CHARLES RICHARD MILO

Hardwicke
New Square, Lincoln's Inn, London WC2A 3SB, ☎ 020 7242 2523
✉ enquiries@hardwicke.co.uk
Call Date: Oct 1997, Inner Temple
Pupil Supervisor
Qualifications: [LLB (Leic)]
✉ charles.bagot@hardwicke.co.uk

BAGRAL MISS RAVINDER

No5 Chambers
Greenwood House, 4-7 Salisbury Court, London EC4Y 8AA, ☎ 0845 210 5555
No5 Chambers
38 Queen Square, Bristol BS1 4QS, ☎ 0845 210 5555
No5 Chambers
Fountain Court, Steelhouse Lane, Birmingham B4 6DR, ☎ 0845 210 5555 ✉ info@no5.com
Call Date: Oct 1996, Inner Temple
Qualifications: [BA (Keele)]
✉ rba@no5.com

BAHIA MISS HARBINDER

Chambers of Harbinder Bahia
115 Gordon Road, South Woodford, London E18 1DT, ☎ 07930 364727
✉ harbinder.bahia@googlemail.com
Call Date: Nov 1999, Lincoln's Inn
Qualifications: [BA (Hons)(Leics)]

BAHIA MISS SHARONJIT

St Philips Chambers
55 Temple Row, Birmingham B2 5LS, ☎ 0121 246 7000 ✉ clerks@st-philips.com
Temple Chambers
32 Park Place, Cardiff CF10 3BA, ☎ 029 2039 7364
✉ DBrinning@Temple-Chambers.co.uk
Temple Chambers
12 Clytha Park Road, Newport, Gwent NP20 4PB, ☎ 01633 267403
✉ dbrinning@temple-chambers.co.uk
Call Date: Oct 2000, Gray's Inn
Qualifications: [LLB (Wolves)]
✉ sbahia@st-philips.com

BAHJA MR TOMOR

Barristers Chambers
89A High Road, Wood Green, London N22 6BB, ☎ 020 3417 6461
✉ clerk@barristerschambers.org
Call Date: Nov 2006, Lincoln's Inn
Qualifications: [LLB (Lond)]

BAHRA MISS NARITA

2 Hare Court
Lower Ground, Ground, 1st & 2nd Floor, 2 Hare Court, Temple, London EC4Y 7BH, ☎ 020 7353 3982 ✉ clerks@2harecourt.com
9-12 Bell Yard
London WC2A 2JR, ☎ 020 7400 1800
✉ clerks@9-12bellyard.com
Call Date: Nov 1997, Lincoln's Inn
Pupil Supervisor
Qualifications: [LLB (Hons)(Lond)]

BAILEY MS ALLISON ELAINE

Garden Court Chambers
57-60 Lincoln's Inn Fields, London WC2A 3LJ, ☎ 020 7993 7600 ✉ info@gclaw.co.uk
Call Date: July 2001, Middle Temple
Qualifications: [B Soc Sci (Hons) Pgdl CPE]
✉ allisonb@gclaw.co.uk

BAILEY MR ANDREW

Call Date: Oct 1997, Lincoln's Inn
Qualifications: [LLB (Hons)]
✉ bailey@paradise-sq.co.uk

BAILEY MR ANTHONY REGINALD

2 King's Bench Walk
2 King's Bench Walk, Temple, London EC4Y 7DE, ☎ 020 7353 1746
✉ clerks@2kbw.com
Call Date: Nov 1972, Inner Temple
Pupil Supervisor
✉ clerks@2kbw.com

BAILEY MR CHARLES ANDREW STUART

Trinity Chambers
Highfield House, Moulsham Street, Chelmsford, Essex CM2 9AH, ☎ 01245 605040
✉ clerks@trinitychambers.com
Call Date: Oct 1993, Lincoln's Inn
Pupil Supervisor
Qualifications: [BA (Hons) LLB (Lond)]

E

BAILEY MR DAVID JOHN QC (2006)

7 King's Bench Walk
Ground Floor, 7 King's Bench Walk, Temple, London EC4Y 7DS, ☎020 7910 8300
✉clerks@7kbw.co.uk
Call Date: July 1989, Gray's Inn
Qualifications: [BA (Oxon) LLM (USA)]
✉dbailey@7kbw.co.uk

BAILEY MR EDWARD GRENFELL

Devon Chambers
3 St Andrew Street, Plymouth PL1 2AH, ☎01752 661659
✉clerks@devonchambers.co.uk
Call Date: July 1990, Gray's Inn
Qualifications: [MA (Hons) (Edin) Dip Law (Lond)]

BAILEY MR GRAHAM ROBERT

9 St John Street
Manchester M3 4DN, ☎0161 955 9000
✉civilclerks@9sjs.com / criminalclerks@9sjs.com
Call Date: Feb 1993, Inner Temple
Qualifications: [LLB (Brunel) (Hons)]

BAILEY MR JAMES THOMAS

New Square Chambers
12 New Square, Lincoln's Inn, London WC2A 3SW, ☎020 7419 8000
✉robin.hollington@newsquarechambers.co.uk
Call Date: Oct 1999, Gray's Inn
Pupil Supervisor
Qualifications: [BA, BCL (Oxon)]
✉james.bailey@newsquarechambers.co.uk

BAILEY MR MICHAEL ROBERT

Tanfield Chambers
2-5 Warwick Court, London WC1R 5DJ, ☎020 7421 5300
✉clerks@tanfieldchambers.co.uk
Call Date: Nov 1986, Gray's Inn
Pupil Supervisor
Qualifications: [BA (Essex) LLM]

BAILEY MISS ROSANA HENRIETTA

10 King's Bench Walk
Ground Floor, 10 King's Bench Walk, Temple, London EC4Y 7EB, ☎020 7353 7742
✉Chambers@10kingsbenchwalk.co.uk
Call Date: Oct 1994, Gray's Inn
Qualifications: [LLB]
✉chambers@10kingsbenchwalk.co.uk

BAILEY MR RUSSELL STUART

No5 Chambers
Greenwood House, 4-7 Salisbury Court, London EC4Y 8AA, ☎0845 210 5555
No5 Chambers
38 Queen Square, Bristol BS1 4QS, ☎0845 210 5555
No5 Chambers
Fountain Court, Steelhouse Lane, Birmingham B4 6DR, ☎0845 210 5555 ✉info@no5.com
Call Date: Nov 1985, Inner Temple
Pupil Supervisor
Qualifications: [LLB (Lond)]

BAILEY MISS SASHA

2 Pump Court
1st Floor, 2 Pump Court, Temple, London EC4Y 7AH, ☎020 7353 5597
✉clerks@2pumpcourt.co.uk
Call Date: July 2002, Lincoln's Inn
Qualifications: [LLB (Hons)]
✉sbailey@2pumpcourt.co.uk

BAILEY MR STEPHEN JOHN

33 Bedford Row
London WC1R 4JH, ☎020 7242 6476
✉clerks@33bedfordrow.co.uk
Call Date: July 1991, Gray's Inn
Qualifications: [LLB (Hons)]
✉stevebaileybar@btinternet.com, stephenbailey@33bedfordrow.co.uk

BAILEY MR STEPHEN MERRYN JAMES

Hailsham Chambers
Ground Floor, 4 Paper Buildings, Temple, London EC4Y 7EX, ☎020 7643 5000
✉clerks@hailshamchambers.com
Call Date: July 2006, Inner Temple
Qualifications: [LLB lmm (Lond)]
✉stephen.bailey@hailshamchambers.com

BAILEY MR STEVEN WILLIAM

No5 Chambers
Fountain Court, Steelhouse Lane, Birmingham B4 6DR, ☎0845 210 5555 ✉info@no5.com
No5 Chambers
Greenwood House, 4-7 Salisbury Court, London EC4Y 8AA, ☎0845 210 5555
No5 Chambers
38 Queen Square, Bristol BS1 4QS, ☎0845 210 5555
Call Date: Oct 1992, Middle Temple
Qualifications: [BA (Hons) (Oxon) M Phil (Cantab)]
✉swb@no5.com

E

BAILEY MR THOMAS IAIN

Chambers of Mr Thomas Bailey
Eaton Place, 90 Mill Road, Water Eaton, Milton Keynes MK2 2UZ, ☎07983 447117
✉tombailey888@yahoo.co.uk
Call Date: July 1984, Gray's Inn
Qualifications: [BA (Oxon)]
tombailey888@yahoo.co.uk

BAILEY-HARRIS PROF REBECCA JANE

1 Hare Court
1 Hare Court, Temple, London EC4Y 7BE, ☎020 7797 7070 ✉clerks@1hc.com
Call Date: Mar 2000, Inner Temple
Qualifications: [BA BA (Oxon) BCL]
bailey-harris@1hc.com

BAILIN MR ALEXANDER QC (2010)

Matrix Chambers
Griffin Building, Gray's Inn, London WC1R 5LN, ☎020 7404 3447
✉matrix@matrixlaw.co.uk / lscott@matrixlaw.co.uk
Call Date: Nov 1995, Lincoln's Inn
Pupil Supervisor
Qualifications: [MA (Hons)]
alexbailin@matrixlaw.co.uk

BAILLIE MR ANDREW BRUCE QC (2001)

The Chambers of Grahame Aldous QC
9 Gough Square, London EC4A 3DG, ☎020 7832 0500
✉clerks@9goughsquare.co.uk
Call Date: Nov 1970, Inner Temple
Recorder
Qualifications: [BA]
abaillie@9goughsquare.co.uk

BAILLIE MS BRIGID MARY

Chambers of Ian Macdonald QC
Garden Court North, 22 Oxford Court, Manchester M2 3WQ, ☎0161 236 1840
✉clerks@gcnchambers.co.uk
Call Date: July 2007, Inner Temple
Qualifications: [BA (Manch) MA (Keele)]

BAIN MR GILES DAVID

New Court
Ground Floor, New Court, Temple, London EC4Y 9BE, ☎020 7583 5123
✉clerks@newcourtchambers.com
Call Date: Nov 1993, Lincoln's Inn
Pupil Supervisor
Qualifications: [LLB (Hons) (Hull)]
gbain@newcourtchambers.net

BAIN MR IAIN JAMES

Fenners Chambers
3 Madingley Road, Cambridge CB3 0EE, ☎01223 368761
✉clerks@fennerschambers.com
Call Date: July 2007, Middle Temple
Qualifications: [BA PG Dip Law]
iain.bain@fennerschambers.com

BAINES MISS CHARLOTTE LOUISE

Wilberforce Chambers
7 Bishop Lane, Hull HU1 1PA, ☎01482 323264
Call Date: Oct 2000, Lincoln's Inn
Pupil Supervisor
Qualifications: [LLB (Hons) (Hull)]

BAINES MR CHRISTOPHER MAXIMILIAN FITZROY TALBOT

18 Red Lion Court
London EC4A 3EB, ☎020 7520 6000
✉chambers@18rlc.co.uk
Call Date: Mar 2005, Lincoln's Inn
Qualifications: [BA (Hons) Oxon]
max.baines@18rlc.co.uk

BAINES MR DAVID CHRISTOPHER

Call Date: Oct 2009, Middle Temple
Qualifications: [BA (Hons) (Lancs) MA (Sheff)]
baines@paradise-sq.co.uk

BAINES MISS LAURA ANNE

Temple Court Chambers
2nd Floor, 2 Dr Johnson's Building, Temple, London EC4Y 7AY, ☎020 7353 7888
✉clerks@templecourt.co.uk
Call Date: July 2007, Lincoln's Inn
Qualifications: [LLB LLM]
clerks@templecourtchambers.co.uk

BAINHAM MR ANDREW WILLIAM ERNEST

14 Gray's Inn Square
14 Gray's Inn Square, Gray's Inn, London WC1R 5JP, ☎020 7242 0858
✉clerks@14gis.co.uk
Call Date: Mar 2009, Middle Temple
Qualifications: [LLB (Wales) LLM (Cantab) Ph.D (Cantab)]

E

BAINS MS PARAMJIT KAUR

No5 Chambers
Fountain Court, Steelhouse Lane, Birmingham B4 6DR, ☎0845 210 5555 ✉info@no5.com
No5 Chambers
Greenwood House, 4-7 Salisbury Court, London EC4Y 8AA, ☎0845 210 5555
No5 Chambers
38 Queen Square, Bristol BS1 4QS, ☎0845 210 5555
Call Date: Mar 2001, Inner Temple
Qualifications: [LLB (Brunel)]
pkb@no5.com

BAINS MR SATNAM

1 Mitre Court Buildings
1 Mitre Court Buildings, Temple, London EC4Y 7BS, ☎020 7452 8900
✉clerks@1mcb.com
Call Date: Mar 2002, Middle Temple
Qualifications: [LLB (Hons)]
satnam.bains@1mcb.com

BAIOU MR MEHDI

One Essex Court
Ground Floor, One Essex Court, Temple, London EC4Y 9AR, ☎020 7583 2000
✉clerks@oeclaw.co.uk
Call Date: July 2009, Middle Temple
Qualifications: [Grad Dip Law (Lond)]
mbaiou@oeclaw.co.uk

BAIRD MR DAVID ANTONY

187 Fleet Street
London EC4A 2AT, ☎020 7430 7430
✉chambers@187fleetstreet.com
Call Date: July 2003, Middle Temple
Qualifications: [LLB Hons]
davidbaird@187fleetstreet.com

BAIRD MR JAMES STEVENSON

Bank House Chambers
Old Bank House, Hartshead, Sheffield S1 2EL, ☎0114 275 1223
✉w.digby@bankhousechambers.co.uk
Call Date: Nov 1977, Middle Temple
Pupil Supervisor, Recorder
Qualifications: [LLB]
j.baird@bankhousechambers.co.uk

BAIRD MRS VERA QC (2000)

Tooks Chambers
81 Farringdon Street, London EC4A 4BL, ☎020 7842 7575 ✉clerks@tooks.co.uk
Call Date: Nov 1975, Gray's Inn
Qualifications: [BA LARTPI LLB]

BAIRD-MURRAY MR JASPER JAMES

4 Paper Buildings
1st Floor, 4 Paper Buildings, Temple, London EC4Y 7EX, ☎020 7427 5200
✉clerks@4pb.com
Call Date: Nov 2008, Middle Temple
Qualifications: [MA (Hons)(Edin)]
jbm@4pb.com

BAIRSTOW MISS LUCY ELIZABETH

Park Lane Plowden
Lombard House, 4-8 Lombard Street, Newcastle Upon Tyne NE1 3AE, ☎0191 211 4087
✉clerks@parklaneplowden.co.uk
Call Date: July 2006, Gray's Inn
Qualifications: [LLB (Hons) (Bris)]
lucy.bairstow@parklaneplowden.co.uk

BAJWA MR ALI NASEEM QC (2011)

Garden Court Chambers
57-60 Lincoln's Inn Fields, London WC2A 3LJ, ☎020 7993 7600 ✉info@gclaw.co.uk
Call Date: Nov 1993, Gray's Inn
Pupil Supervisor
Qualifications: [LLB]

BAKER MR ANDREW JAMES

No5 Chambers
Fountain Court, Steelhouse Lane, Birmingham B4 6DR, ☎0845 210 5555 ✉info@no5.com
No5 Chambers
Greenwood House, 4-7 Salisbury Court, London EC4Y 8AA, ☎0845 210 5555
No5 Chambers
38 Queen Square, Bristol BS1 4QS, ☎0845 210 5555
Call Date: Oct 1990, Middle Temple
Qualifications: [BSc Dip Law (Lond) MRPharmS]
ajb@no5.com

BAKER MR ANDREW WILLIAM QC (2006)

20 Essex Street
London WC2R 3AL, ☎020 7842 1200
✉clerks@20essexst.com
Call Date: July 1988, Lincoln's Inn
Qualifications: [MA (Hons) (Oxon) Dip Law (Lond)]
clerks@20essexst.com

E

BAKER MRS CAROLINE FRANCES

No5 Chambers
Fountain Court, Steelhouse Lane, Birmingham B4 6DR, ☎0845 210 5555 ✉info@no5.com
No5 Chambers
Greenwood House, 4-7 Salisbury Court, London EC4Y 8AA, ☎0845 210 5555
No5 Chambers
38 Queen Square, Bristol BS1 4QS, ☎0845 210 5555
Call Date: July 1988, Gray's Inn
Pupil Supervisor
Qualifications: [BSc (Lancs) MA (Bris)]
cb@no5.com

BAKER MR CHRISTOPHER FRANCIS JOHN

Arden Chambers
20 Bloomsbury Square, London WC1A 2NS, ☎020 7242 4244
✉clerks@ardenchambers.com
Call Date: July 1984, Middle Temple
Pupil Supervisor
Qualifications: [MA (Cantab) LLM (Lond)]
christopher.baker@ardenchambers.com

BAKER MR CHRISTOPHER MICHAEL

Old Court Chambers
Newham House, 96-98 Borough Road, Middlesbrough TS1 2HJ, ☎01642 232523
✉clerks@oldcourtchambers.com
Call Date: Oct 1994, Middle Temple
Qualifications: [LLB (Hons)(Manch)]
clerks@oldcourtchambers.com

BAKER MISS CLARE LOUISE

Outer Temple Chambers
The Outer Temple, 222 Strand, London WC2R 1BA, ☎020 7353 6381
✉clerks@outertemple.com
Call Date: Oct 2007, Middle Temple
Qualifications: [MA (Hons) (Cantab)]
clare.baker@outertemple.com

BAKER MR CLIVE ADRIAN

Number 7 Harrington Street Chambers
7 Harrington Street, Liverpool L2 9YH, ☎0151 242 0707 ✉clerks@7hs.co.uk
Call Date: Oct 1995, Gray's Inn
Qualifications: [LLB]
clive.baker@7hs.co.uk

BAKER MS FAY ELIZABETH

2 Dr Johnson's Buildings
2 Dr Johnson's Buildings, Temple, London EC4Y 7AY, ☎020 7936 2613
✉clerks@2drj.com
Call Date: Nov 1994, Gray's Inn
Qualifications: [BSc Econ]
clerks@2drj.com

BAKER MR HAROLD WILLIAM

Chambers of Mr Harold Baker
33C Stow Hill, Newport NP20 1JH, ☎07966 872648 ✉hb21@live.co.uk
Call Date: Nov 1992, Middle Temple
Qualifications: [LLB (Hons)]
hb21@live.co.uk

BAKER MISS MAUREEN ANNE QC (2009)

Seven Bedford Row
7 Bedford Row, London WC1R 4BS, ☎020 7242 3555 ✉clerks@7br.co.uk
Call Date: July 1984, Gray's Inn
Recorder
Qualifications: [BA]
mbaker@7br.co.uk

BAKER MR NICHOLAS MICHAEL BRIDGMAN

Hardwicke
New Square, Lincoln's Inn, London WC2A 3SB, ☎020 7242 2523
✉enquiries@hardwicke.co.uk
Call Date: July 1980, Gray's Inn
Pupil Supervisor
Qualifications: [BA (Oxon)]
nicholas.baker@hardwicke.co.uk

BAKER MR PHILIP WOOLF QC (2002)

Gray's Inn Tax Chambers
3rd Floor, Gray's Inn Chambers, Gray's Inn, London WC1R 5JA, ☎020 7242 2642
✉clerks@taxbar.com
Call Date: July 1979, Gray's Inn
Qualifications: [MA (Cantab) BCL (Oxon) LLM (Lond) MBA CTA (Fellow) PhD]
pb@taxbar.com, pb@taxbar.com

BAKER MR RICHARD

Seven Bedford Row
7 Bedford Row, London WC1R 4BS, ☎020 7242 3555 ✉clerks@7br.co.uk
Call Date: Nov 2000, Middle Temple
Pupil Supervisor
Qualifications: [LLB (Hons) (Newc)]
clerks@7br.co.uk

E

BAKER MR SIMON ARTHUR

Argent Chambers
5 Bell Yard, London WC2A 2JR,
☎ 020 7556 5500
✉ briefsin@argentchambers.co.uk
Call Date: Oct 1998, Inner Temple
Pupil Supervisor
Qualifications: [BA (Oxon)]
sb3@argentchambers.co.uk

BAKER MR STEPHEN MARK

Seven Bedford Row
7 Bedford Row, London WC1R 4BS,
☎ 020 7242 3555 ✉ clerks@7br.co.uk
Call Date: July 1989, Middle Temple
Qualifications: [LLB (Manch) LLM (Cantab)]

BAKER MR THOMAS MATTHEW

QEB Hollis Whiteman
1-2 Laurence Pountney Hill, London
EC4R 0EU, ☎ 020 7933 8855
✉ barristers@qebhw.co.uk
Call Date: Nov 2004, Middle Temple
Qualifications: [BA (Hons)]
barristers@qebhw.co.uk

E

BAKER MR WILLIAM DAVID

St Philips Chambers
55 Temple Row, Birmingham B2 5LS,
☎ 0121 246 7000 ✉ clerks@st-philips.com
Call Date: Oct 1992, Inner Temple
Qualifications: [LLB]
wbaker@st-philips.co.uk

BAKI MR NEIL FARRES

25 Bedford Row
London WC1R 4HD, ☎ 020 7067 1500
✉ clerks@25bedfordrow.com
Call Date: July 2003, Middle Temple
Qualifications: [LLB Hons (Lond) LLM (Lond)]
nbaki@25bedfordrow.com

BALA MISS RUTH ELIZABETH

Gough Square Chambers
6-7 Gough Square, London EC4A 3DE,
☎ 020 7353 0924 ✉ gsc@goughsq.co.uk
Call Date: July 2006, Lincoln's Inn
Qualifications: [BA (Oxon) LLM GDL]
ruth.bala@goughsq.co.uk

BALANCY MR JACQUES ALEX VIVIAN

7 Bell Yard
London WC2A 2JR, ☎ 020 7831 0636
✉ kevintarrant@btconnect.com
Call Date: July 1992, Inner Temple
Qualifications: [LLB (Lond) MBA]
ab@7bellyard.co.uk, abalancy@7bellyard.co.uk

BALCHIN MR RICHARD ALEXANDER

New Court
Ground Floor, New Court, Temple, London
EC4Y 9BE, ☎ 020 7583 5123
✉ clerks@newcourtchambers.com
Call Date: Oct 1997, Inner Temple
Pupil Supervisor
Qualifications: [BA (Hons)(Sussex) Dip Law]
rbalchin@newcourtchambers.net

BALCOMBE MR DAVID JULIAN QC (2002)

1 Crown Office Row
1 Crown Office Row, Temple, London
EC4Y 7HH, ☎ 020 7797 7500
✉ mail@1cor.com
Call Date: Nov 1980, Lincoln's Inn
Recorder
Qualifications: [BA (Kent)]
david.balcombe@1cor.com

BALD MISS LISA HELEN

Furnival Chambers
32 Furnival Street, London EC4A 1JQ,
☎ 020 7405 3232
Call Date: Oct 2009, Lincoln's Inn
Qualifications: [LLB (Lond)]
clerks@furnival.co.uk

BALDOCK MR NICHOLAS JOHN

6 Pump Court
1st Floor, 6 Pump Court, Temple, London
EC4Y 7AR, ☎ 020 7797 8400
✉ richardconstable@6pumpcourt.co.uk
6 Pump Court Chambers
6-8 Mill Street, Maidstone, Kent ME15 6XH,
☎ 01622 688094
✉ annexe@6pumpcourt.co.uk
Call Date: Nov 1983, Lincoln's Inn
Pupil Supervisor
Qualifications: [MA (Cantab)]
nicholasbaldock@6pumpcourt.co.uk

BALDRY SIR ANTONY BRIAN

One Essex Court
1st Floor, Temple, London EC4Y 9AR,
☎ 020 7936 3030 ✉ clerks@1ec.co.uk
Call Date: Nov 1975, Lincoln's Inn
Qualifications: [BA (Sussex) LLB (Sussex)]
✉ clerks@1ec.co.uk

BALDRY MR RUPERT PATRICK CRAIG QC (2010)

Pump Court Tax Chambers
16 Bedford Row, London WC1R 4EF,
☎ 020 7414 8080 ✉ clerks@pumptax.com
Call Date: Feb 1987, Middle Temple
Pupil Supervisor
Qualifications: [BA (Lond) Dip Law (Lond)]
✉ rbaldry@pumptax.com

Types of work: Capital tax, Corporation tax, Employee benefit trusts, Income tax, National Insurance, Private client, Stamp duty, VAT

BALDWIN MR JOHN GRANT

Oriel Chambers
14 Water Street, Liverpool, Merseyside
L2 8TD, ☎ 0151 236 7191
✉ clerks@orielchambers.co.uk
Oriel Chambers
18 Ribblesdale Place, Preston PR1 3NA,
☎ 01772 254 764
✉ clerks@oriel-chambers.co.uk
Call Date: Oct 1990, Gray's Inn
Pupil Supervisor
Qualifications: [MA (Cantab)]
✉ john.baldwin@orielchambers.co.uk

BALDWIN MR JOHN PAUL QC (1991)

8 New Square
8 New Square, Lincoln's Inn, London
WC2A 3QP, ☎ 020 7405 4321
✉ clerks@8newsquare.co.uk
Call Date: July 1977, Gray's Inn
Qualifications: [BSc DPhil (Oxon)]
✉ john.baldwin@8newsquare.co.uk

Types of work: Breach of confidence, Competition law, Computer litigation, Copyright, Copyright theft, Copyright Tribunal, Data protection, Design, E-commerce, EC competition law, Entertainment, Information technology, Intellectual property, Malicious falsehood, Media, Media and entertainment, Passing off, Patents, Pharmaceuticals, Product liability, Scientific and technical disputes, Telecommunications, Trade Descriptions Act, Trade secrets, Trademarks

BALDWIN MR ROGER MILES

15 Winckley Square
Preston PR1 3JJ, ☎ 01772 252828
✉ clerks@15winckleysq.co.uk
Call Date: July 1969, Gray's Inn
Qualifications: [LLB]

BALDWIN DR TIMOTHY JOHN

Garden Court Chambers
57-60 Lincoln's Inn Fields, London WC2A 3LJ,
☎ 020 7993 7600 ✉ info@gclaw.co.uk
Call Date: Nov 2001, Lincoln's Inn
Qualifications: [BSc (Hons)(Lond) PhD (Lond) LLB (Hons) (Lond) MA (Lond)]
✉ timothyb@gclaw.co.uk

BALL MISS ALISON QC (1995)

1 Garden Court Family Law Chambers
Ground Floor, One Garden Court, Temple,
London EC4Y 9BJ, ☎ 020 7797 7900
✉ clerks@1gc.com
Call Date: Nov 1972, Middle Temple
Recorder
Qualifications: [LLB (Lond)]
✉ ball@1gc.com

BALL MR DAVID JAMES

36 Bedford Row
London WC1R 4JH, ☎ 020 7421 8000
✉ chambers@36bedfordrow.co.uk
Call Date: Mar 2008, Middle Temple
Qualifications: [BA (Hons) (Dunelm) PgDL (Lond) LLM (Lond)]
✉ dball@36bedfordrow.co.uk

BALL MR IAN DAVID

Cornwall Street Chambers
85-87 Cornwall Street, Birmingham B3 3BY,
☎ 0121 233 7500
✉ clerks@cornwallstreet.co.uk
Call Date: Oct 1992, Middle Temple
Qualifications: [LLB (Hons)(B'ham)]
✉ ian.ball@cornwallstreet.co.uk

BALL MR STEVEN

Rougemont Chambers
Victory House, Dean Clarke Gardens,
Southernhay East, Exeter EX2 4AA,
☎ 01392 208484
✉ clerks@rougemontchambers.co.uk
Call Date: Oct 1995, Inner Temple
Qualifications: [BSc (Reading) LLB (Herts)]
✉ sball@rougemontchambers.co.uk

E

BALL MR STEVEN JAMES

Number 7 Harrington Street Chambers
7 Harrington Street, Liverpool L2 9YH, ☎ 0151 242 0707 ✉ clerks@7hs.co.uk
Call Date: Oct 1996, Inner Temple
Qualifications: [LLB (Hull) (Hons)]
steven.ball@7hs.co.uk

BALLANCE MR JAMES CONRAD

Maitland Chambers
7 Stone Buildings, Lincoln's Inn, London WC2A 3SZ, ☎ 020 7406 1200
✉ clerks@maitlandchambers.com
Call Date: July 2009, Gray's Inn
Qualifications: [BA BCL MPhil]
jballance@maitlandchambers.com

BALLANTYNE PROF WILLIAM MORRIS

Serle Court
6 New Square, Lincoln's Inn, London WC2A 3QS, ☎ 020 7242 6105
✉ clerks@serlecourt.co.uk
Call Date: Nov 1977, Inner Temple
Qualifications: [MA (Cantab)]
wballantyne@serlecourt.co.uk

E

BALLARD MS APPA

Cornwall Street Chambers
85-87 Cornwall Street, Birmingham B3 3BY, ☎ 0121 233 7500
✉ clerks@cornwallstreet.co.uk
Call Date: July 2006, Lincoln's Inn
Qualifications: [MA (Edin) LLB (B'ham)]
appa.ballard@cornwallstreet.co.uk

BALLARD MISS BRIONY ELIZABETH

3 Serjeants Inn
London EC4Y 1BQ, ☎ 020 7427 5000
✉ clerks@3serjeantsinn.com
Call Date: Nov 2000, Middle Temple
Qualifications: [BSc (Hons) (B'Ham) CPE]
bballard@3serjeantsinn.com

BALLENTYNE MR ERROL STANLEY

1 High Pavement
Nottingham NG1 1HF, ☎ 0115 941 8218
✉ clerks@1highpavement.co.uk
Call Date: Nov 1983, Gray's Inn
Qualifications: [BA]
errolballentyne@1highpavement.co.uk

BALLINGALL MS JOANNE

College Chambers
19 Carlton Crescent, Southampton, Hampshire SO15 2ET, ☎ 023 8023 0338
✉ clerks@college-chambers.co.uk
Call Date: Nov 1999, Inner Temple
Qualifications: [LLB]
jballingall@college-chambers.co.uk

BALLINGER MISS KATHERINE HELEN

Cobden House Chambers
19 Quay Street, Manchester M3 3HN, ☎ 0161 833 6000 ✉ Clerks@Cobden.co.uk
Call Date: July 2008, Inner Temple
Qualifications: [LLB (Bris)]

BALMER MISS KATY JOANNA MAY

Devereux Chambers
Queen Elizabeth Building, Temple, London EC4Y 9BS, ☎ 020 7353 7534
✉ clerks@devchambers.co.uk
Call Date: July 2009, Middle Temple
Qualifications: [BA (Sydney) Post Grad Dip Law (Lond)]
balmer@devchambers.co.uk

BALOCH MR FARAS SHAHNAWAZ

4 Breams Buildings
Chancery Lane, London EC4A 1HP, ☎ 020 7092 1900 ✉ clerks@4bb.co.uk
Call Date: July 2003, Middle Temple
Qualifications: [LLB Hons (Nott'm)]

BALROOP MR DARRYL

12 Old Square Chambers
1st Floor, 12 Old Square, Lincoln's Inn, London WC2A 3TX, ☎ 020 7404 0875
✉ clerks@12oldsquare.com
Call Date: Nov 2005, Inner Temple
Qualifications: [LLB University of London (External) LLM Univers]

BALYSZ MR MARK ALEXANDER

Crown Office Chambers
2 Crown Office Row, Temple, London EC4Y 7HJ, ☎ 020 7797 8100
✉ mail@crownofficechambers.com
Call Date: Nov 1995, Gray's Inn
Qualifications: [LLB]

BAMFORD MR CHRISTOPHER DAVID

Tanfield Chambers
2-5 Warwick Court, London WC1R 5DJ,
☎ 020 7421 5300
✉ clerks@tanfieldchambers.co.uk
Call Date: Nov 1987, Inner Temple
Pupil Supervisor
Qualifications: [LLB (Hons)(Hull)]
✉ cbamford@tanfieldchambers.co.uk

BAMFORD MR JEREMY RICHARD

Guildhall Chambers
23 Broad Street, Bristol BS1 2HG,
☎ 0117 930 9000
✉ hoc@guildhallchambers.co.uk
Call Date: Nov 1989, Lincoln's Inn
Pupil Supervisor
Qualifications: [BA (Oxon)]
✉ jeremy.bamford@guildhallchambers.co.uk

BANCROFT MISS ANNA LOUISE

Deans Court Chambers
24 St John Street, Manchester M3 4DF,
☎ 0161 214 6000 ✉ clerks@deanscourt.co.uk
Deans Court Chambers
101 Walker Street, Preston PR1 2RR,
☎ 01772 565 600
✉ preston@deanscourt.co.uk
Call Date: July 1985, Inner Temple
Pupil Supervisor
Qualifications: [MA (Oxon)]
✉ bancroft@deanscourt.co.uk

Fax: 0161 214 6001
URL: www.deanscourt.co.uk

Types of work: Family law

BANERJEE MRS LYDIA ELIZABETH

Littleton Chambers
3 King's Bench Walk North, Temple, London EC4Y 7HR, ☎ 020 7797 8600
✉ fschneider@littletonchambers.co.uk
Call Date: Nov 2007, Middle Temple
Qualifications: [BA (Hons) (Cantab)]
✉ LBanerjee@littletonchambers.co.uk

BANERJEE MR SUBHANKAR

Atkinson Bevan Chambers
1st Floor, 2 Harcourt Buildings, Temple, London EC4Y 9DB, ☎ 020 7353 2112
✉ clerks@2hb.co.uk
Call Date: Nov 2000, Inner Temple
Qualifications: [BA (Notts) CPE BA (Hons)]
✉ sbanerjee@2hb.co.uk

BANERJI MR JAY

New Court
Ground Floor, New Court, Temple, London EC4Y 9BE, ☎ 020 7583 5123
✉ clerks@newcourtchambers.com
Call Date: Oct 2001, Inner Temple
Qualifications: [LLM (Hons)]
✉ jbanerji@newcourtchambers.net

BANGAY MISS DEBORAH JOANNA JANET QC (2006)

1 Hare Court
1 Hare Court, Temple, London EC4Y 7BE,
☎ 020 7797 7070 ✉ clerks@1hc.com
Riverview Chambers
Hamilton House, 1 Temple Avenue, London EC4Y 0HA, ☎ 0844 225 3999
✉ chrisbaylis@riverviewchambers.com
Call Date: Feb 1981, Gray's Inn
Qualifications: [LLB (Exon) (Hons)]
✉ bangay@1hc.com

BANHAM MR COLIN

4 Breams Buildings
Chancery Lane, London EC4A 1HP,
☎ 020 7092 1900 ✉ clerks@4bb.co.uk
Call Date: Oct 1999, Lincoln's Inn
Qualifications: [LLB (Hons)(Notts)]
✉ colinbanham@hotmail.com

BANHAM MR MATTHEW IAN

Nine Bedford Row
9 Bedford Row, London WC1R 4AZ,
☎ 020 7489 2727
✉ clerks@9bedfordrow.co.uk
Call Date: Oct 1999, Inner Temple
Qualifications: [LLB (Herts)]
✉ matthew.banham@9bedfordrow.co.uk

BANKES-JONES MR JOHN HENRY MYDDLETON

Hailsham Chambers
Ground Floor, 4 Paper Buildings, Temple, London EC4Y 7EX, ☎ 020 7643 5000
✉ clerks@hailshamchambers.com
Call Date: Nov 2004, Lincoln's Inn
Qualifications: [BA (Hons) (Dunelm)]
✉ henry.bankes-jones@hailshamchambers.com

E

BANKOLE MRS MARGARET

Chambers of Mrs Margaret Bankole
6 Macarathur Close, Wyatt Road, Forest Gate, London E7 9NT, ☎ 07983 302695
✉ margaretmcf1996@yahoo.co.uk
Call Date: July 1988, Middle Temple
Pupil Supervisor
Qualifications: [LLB (Hons)]

BANKS MISS FIONA JANE

Monckton Chambers
1 & 2 Raymond Buildings, Gray's Inn, London WC1R 5NR, ☎ 020 7405 7211
✉ chambers@monckton.com
Call Date: Oct 2006, Inner Temple
Qualifications: [MA (Cantab)]
✉ fbanks@monckton.com

BANKS MR FRANCIS ANDREW

Atlantic Chambers
4-6 Cook Street, Liverpool L2 9QU,
☎ 0151 236 4421
✉ info@atlanticchambers.co.uk
Call Date: July 1995, Gray's Inn
Qualifications: [BA]
✉ andrewbanks@atlanticchambers.co.uk

E

BANKS MR NATHAN MARK

St James's Chambers
68 Quay Street, Manchester M3 3EJ,
☎ 0161 834 7000
✉ clerks@stjameschambers.com
Call Date: July 2003, Lincoln's Inn
Qualifications: [LLB Hons (B'ham)]
✉ nathan.banks@stjameschambers.com

BANKS MISS RACHAEL EDA

Atlantic Chambers
4-6 Cook Street, Liverpool L2 9QU,
☎ 0151 236 4421
✉ info@atlanticchambers.co.uk
Call Date: Nov 1993, Inner Temple
Pupil Supervisor
Qualifications: [LLB (Manch)]
✉ rachaelbanks@atlanticchambers.co.uk

BANKS MR ROBERT JAMES

Rye Green Chambers
Rye Green Farm, Burwash, East Sussex TN19 7HP, ☎ 01435 882577
✉ law@banksr.com
Call Date: July 1978, Inner Temple
Qualifications: [BSc (Econ) (Hons)]

BANKS MR RODERICK CHARLES I'ANSON

48 Bedford Row
London WC1R 4LR, ☎ 020 7430 2005
✉ tyroon@partnershipcounsel.co.uk
Call Date: July 1974, Lincoln's Inn
Pupil Supervisor
Qualifications: [LLB]
✉ rciab@partnershipcounsel.co.uk

Fax: 020 7831 4885;
Out of hours telephone: 07751 022 914;
DX: 284 LDE;
URL: www.partnershipcounsel.co.uk

Types of work: Limited Liability Partnerships, Limited partnerships, Partnerships

Awards and memberships: Founder member of the Association of Partnership Practitioners

Other professional experience: CEDR accredited mediator (1993); Consultant to the Law Commission on the Review of Partnership and Limited Partnership Law.

Publications: *Lindley on Partnership* (Sweet & Maxwell), Co-Editor; 14th edn (1979), 15th edn (1984); *Lindley & Banks on Partnership* (Sweet & Maxwell) Editor; 16th edn (1990), 17th edn (1995), 18 edn (2002), 19th edn (2010), supplement (2011); *Encyclopedia of Professional Partnerships* (Sweet & Maxwell), 1987

BANKS MR TIMOTHY JAMES

15 New Bridge Street
London EC4V 6AU, ☎ 020 7842 1900
✉ clerks@15nbs.com
Call Date: Nov 1983, Inner Temple
Pupil Supervisor
Qualifications: [BA]
✉ tim.banks@15nbs.com

BANNER MR CHARLES EDWARD RAYMOND

Landmark Chambers
180 Fleet Street, London EC4A 2HG,
☎ 020 7430 1221
✉ clerks@landmarkchambers.co.uk
Call Date: Oct 2004, Lincoln's Inn
Qualifications: [BA (Hons) MA (Oxon)]
✉ cbanner@landmarkchambers.co.uk

BANNER MR GREGORY STUART

Maitland Chambers
7 Stone Buildings, Lincoln's Inn, London WC2A 3SZ, ☎ 020 7406 1200
✉ clerks@maitlandchambers.com
Call Date: July 1989, Gray's Inn
Pupil Supervisor
Qualifications: [MA (Cantab)]
✉ gbanner@maitlandchambers.com

BANNOCKS MR DAVID GEORGE

4 Brick Court
4 Brick Court, Temple, London EC4Y 9AD,
☎ 020 7832 3200 ✉ clerks@4bc.co.uk
Call Date: July 2002, Middle Temple
Qualifications: [BA (Hons) (Lond) MA (Dunelm) Dip in Law]

BANWELL MR RICHARD JOHN

6 Pump Court
1st Floor, 6 Pump Court, Temple, London EC4Y 7AR, ☎ 020 7797 8400
✉ richardconstable@6pumpcourt.co.uk
6 Pump Court Chambers
6-8 Mill Street, Maidstone, Kent ME15 6XH,
☎ 01622 688094
✉ annexe@6pumpcourt.co.uk
Call Date: Oct 1998, Lincoln's Inn
Qualifications: [LLB (Hons)(L'Pool)]
🖃 richardbanwell@6pumpcourt.co.uk

BéAR MR CHARLES QC (2003)

Fountain Court Chambers
Fountain Court, Temple, London EC4Y 9DH,
☎ 020 7583 3335
✉ chambers@fountaincourt.co.uk
Call Date: Nov 1986, Lincoln's Inn
Qualifications: [BA(Oxon)]
🖃 cbr@fountaincourt.co.uk

BAR MISS MONIKA

Atlantic Chambers
4-6 Cook Street, Liverpool L2 9QU,
☎ 0151 236 4421
✉ info@atlanticchambers.co.uk
Call Date: Oct 2008, Inner Temple
Qualifications: [BA (York) LLB (Bris)]
🖃 info@atlanticchambers.co.uk

BARAN MR COLIN JAMES

St Philips Chambers
55 Temple Row, Birmingham B2 5LS,
☎ 0121 246 7000 ✉ clerks@st-philips.com
Call Date: Oct 2003, Middle Temple
Qualifications: [BA (Hons) (Oxon)]
🖃 cbaran@st-philips.co.uk

BARAV DR AMIHUD

4-5 Gray's Inn Square
Gray's Inn, London WC1R 5AH,
☎ 020 7404 5252 ✉ clerks@4-5.co.uk
Call Date: Oct 1993, Gray's Inn
Qualifications: [MSc (Econ) LLM (Lond) Doctorate (Germany)]

BARBER MR JIMMY

4 King's Bench Walk
2nd Floor, 4 King's Bench Walk, Temple, London EC4Y 7DL, ☎ 020 7822 7000
✉ clerks@4kbw.co.uk
4 KBW
Ground Floor, 4 King's Bench Walk, Temple, London EC4Y 7DL, ☎ 020 7822 8822
✉ law@4kbw.net
Call Date: July 2008, Lincoln's Inn
Qualifications: [LLB (Exon)]

BARBER MR PHILLIP ARTHUR

Zenith Chambers
10 Park Square, Leeds LS1 2LH,
☎ 0113 245 5438
✉ clerks@zenithchambers.co.uk
Call Date: Nov 1991, Gray's Inn
Qualifications: [LLB (Leics) LLB (Hull)]
🖃 pbarber@zenithchambers.co.uk

BARBOUR MISS LAURA

Lincoln House Chambers
Tower 12, The Avenue North, Spinningfields, 18-22 Bridge Street, Manchester M3 3BZ,
☎ 0161 832 5701
✉ info@lincolnhousechambers.com
Call Date: Oct 2006, Gray's Inn
Qualifications: [BA]
🖃 laura.barbour@lincolnhousechambers.com

BARCA MR MANUEL DAVID QC (2011)

One Brick Court
1st Floor, One Brick Court, Temple, London EC4Y 9BY, ☎ 020 7353 8845
✉ clerks@onebrickcourt.com
Call Date: Nov 1986, Lincoln's Inn
Pupil Supervisor
Qualifications: [MA (Cantab)]
🖃 mb@onebrickcourt.com

BARCELLO MR ANDREW DANIEL

9 Park Place
9 Park Place, Cardiff, South Glamorgan CF10 3DP, ☎ 029 2038 2731
✉ clerks@9parkplace.co.uk
Call Date: Mar 2001, Lincoln's Inn
Qualifications: [LLB (Hons)]

E

BARCLAY MR ROBIN NICHOLAS JOHN

2 Hare Court
Lower Ground, Ground, 1st & 2nd Floor, 2 Hare Court, Temple, London EC4Y 7BH, ☎ 020 7353 3982 ✉ clerks@2harecourt.com
Call Date: July 1999, Middle Temple
Qualifications: [BA (Hons)(Dunelm) Dip Law CPE]
robinbarclay@2harecourt.com

BARD MR NICHOLAS JAMES

Devereux Chambers
Queen Elizabeth Building, Temple, London EC4Y 9BS, ☎ 020 7353 7534
✉ clerks@devchambers.co.uk
Call Date: July 1979, Gray's Inn
Pupil Supervisor
Qualifications: [MA (Oxon)]
bard@devchambers.co.uk

BARDA MR ROBIN JOHN BLACKMORE

4 Paper Buildings
1st Floor, 4 Paper Buildings, Temple, London EC4Y 7EX, ☎ 020 7427 5200
✉ clerks@4pb.com
Call Date: July 1975, Gray's Inn
Pupil Supervisor
Qualifications: [BA (Hons)(Oxon)]
rb@4pb.com

BARDEN MR ALEXANDER ROBERT

Erskine Chambers
33 Chancery Lane, London WC2A 1EN, ☎ 020 7242 5532
✉ clerks@erskinechambers.com
Call Date: Oct 2005, Inner Temple
Qualifications: [BA St John's College University of Cambridge LL]
abarden@erskine-chambers.co.uk

BARHAM MR JONATHAN

64 Bridge Street
3rd Floor, 64 Bridge Street, Manchester M3 3BN, ☎ 0845 083 3000
✉ mail@64bridgestreet.com
Clerksroom (Taunton)
Equity House, Administration Centre, Blackbrook Park Avenue, Taunton, Somerset TA1 2PX, ☎ 0845 083 3000
✉ mail@clerksroom.com
Call Date: Oct 2002, Lincoln's Inn
Qualifications: [LLB (Exon)]
barham@clerksroom.com

BARKER MISS ALISON

9-12 Bell Yard
London WC2A 2JR, ☎ 020 7400 1800
✉ clerks@9-12bellyard.com
Call Date: July 1973, Middle Temple
Qualifications: [LLB (Hons)]
a.barker@9-12bellyard.com

BARKER MR JAMES SEBASTIAN

Enterprise Chambers
9 Old Square, Lincoln's Inn, London WC2A 3SR, ☎ 020 7405 9471
✉ london@enterprisechambers.com
Enterprise Chambers
65 Quayside, Newcastle Upon Tyne NE1 3DE, ☎ 0191 222 3344
✉ newcastle@enterprisechambers.com
Enterprise Chambers
43 Park Square, Leeds LS1 2NP, ☎ 0113 246 0391
✉ leeds@enterprisechambers.com
Call Date: July 1984, Gray's Inn
Pupil Supervisor
Qualifications: [LLB (B'Ham)]
jamesbarker@enterprisechambers.com

BARKER MS JENNIFER REBEKAH

1 Pump Court
Elm Court, Temple, London EC4Y 7AB, ☎ 020 7842 7070
✉ (name)@pumpcourt.co.uk
Call Date: July 2000, Inner Temple
Qualifications: [LLB(Hons) (Staffs)]

BARKER MR JONATHAN JAMES LEIGH

St Philips Chambers
55 Temple Row, Birmingham B2 5LS, ☎ 0121 246 7000 ✉ clerks@st-philips.com
Call Date: July 2006, Middle Temple
Qualifications: [LLB (Hons) (Lond)]
jbarker@st-philips.com

BARKER MR KERRY

Guildhall Chambers
23 Broad Street, Bristol BS1 2HG, ☎ 0117 930 9000
✉ hoc@guildhallchambers.co.uk
Call Date: July 1972, Gray's Inn
Pupil Supervisor
Qualifications: [LLB (Lond)]

BARKER MR NICHOLAS

No.6 Park Square
Leeds LS1 2LW, ☎ 0113 245 9763
✉ Tim@no6.co.uk
Call Date: Oct 1994, Gray's Inn
Qualifications: [BA]
barker@no6.co.uk

BARKLEM MR MARTYN STEPHEN

Littleton Chambers
3 King's Bench Walk North, Temple, London EC4Y 7HR, ☎ 020 7797 8600
✉ fschneider@littletonchambers.co.uk
Call Date: July 1989, Middle Temple
Pupil Supervisor, Recorder
Qualifications: [LLB (Lond)]
✉ mbarklem@littletonchambers.co.uk

BARLOW MR CRAIG MARTIN

Ely Place Chambers
30 Ely Place, London EC1N 6TD,
☎ 020 7400 9600 ✉ admin@elyplace.com
Call Date: Oct 1992, Gray's Inn
Qualifications: [LLB (Hons)]
✉ cbarlow@elyplace.com

BARLOW MR MARK DAVID

Chambers of Ian Macdonald QC
Garden Court North, 22 Oxford Court, Manchester M2 3WQ, ☎ 0161 236 1840
✉ clerks@gcnchambers.co.uk
Call Date: Oct 1992, Middle Temple
Qualifications: [LLB (Hons)]

BARLOW MISS MELISSA EMMA BENSON

Queen Square Chambers
56 Queen Square, Bristol BS1 4PR,
☎ 0117 921 1966 ✉ crime@qs-c.co.uk
Call Date: Oct 1991, Middle Temple
Pupil Supervisor
Qualifications: [BA (Hons) (Exon)]
✉ mb@qs-c.co.uk

BARLOW MR RICHARD FRANCIS DUDLEY QC (2006)

Ten Old Square
Ground Floor, Ten Old Square, Lincoln's Inn, London WC2A 3SU, ☎ 020 7405 0758
✉ clerks@tenoldsquare.com
Call Date: Feb 1965, Inner Temple
Qualifications: [MA (Oxon)]
✉ francisbarlow@tenoldsquare.com

BARLOW MISS SARAH HELEN

Broadway House Chambers
Broadway House, 9 Bank Street, Bradford, West Yorkshire BD1 1TW, ☎ 01274 722560
✉ clerks@broadwayhouse.co.uk
Broadway House Chambers
25 Park Square West, Leeds, West Yorkshire LS1 2PW, ☎ 0113 246 2600
✉ clerks@broadwayhouse.co.uk
Call Date: Oct 1993, Gray's Inn
Qualifications: [LLB (Hons)]
✉ clerks@broadwayhouse.co.uk

BARNARD MR DAVID NOWELL

Chambers of Mr D Barnard
Third Floor South, 6 Raymond Buildings, Grays Inn, London WC1R 5BN,
☎ 020 7242 1873 ✉ dbar1873@aol.com
Call Date: July 1967, Gray's Inn
Pupil Supervisor
Qualifications: [BA (Cantab)]

BARNARD MR JAMES PHILIP

11 Stone Buildings
11 Stone Buildings, Lincoln's Inn, London WC2A 3TG, ☎ 020 7831 6381
✉ clerks@11sb.com
Call Date: Oct 1993, Middle Temple
Qualifications: [BA (Hons)(Bris) CPE (Lond)]
✉ barnard@11sb.com

BARNARD MR JONATHAN JAMES

Cloth Fair Chambers
39-40 Cloth Fair, London EC1A 7NT,
☎ 020 7710 6444
✉ email@clothfairchambers.com
Call Date: Oct 1997, Middle Temple
Pupil Supervisor
Qualifications: [MA (Edin) MA (Sussex) CPE]
✉ jonathanbarnard@clothfairchambers.com

BARNES MISS ANDREA LYNDA

Clerksroom (Taunton)
Equity House, Administration Centre, Blackbrook Park Avenue, Taunton, Somerset TA1 2PX, ☎ 0845 083 3000
✉ mail@clerksroom.com
King's Lynn Chambers
26 The Birches, South Wootton, King's Lynn, Norfolk PE30 3JG, ☎ 01553 672 085
✉ timothy.leader@tesco.net
Call Date: Nov 1999, Lincoln's Inn
Qualifications: [LLB (Hons)]

BARNES MR ASHLEY JAMES

Chambers of Mr Ashley Barnes
1 The Beeches, Suttonleach, St Helens, Merseyside WA9 4SU, ☎ 01744 814072
✉ ashleyjamesbarnes@live.com
New Bailey Chambers
4th Floor, Corn Exchange, Fenwick Street, Liverpool, Merseyside L2 7QS,
☎ 0151 236 9402 ✉ clerks@newbailey.com
Call Date: Oct 1990, Inner Temple
Pupil Supervisor
Qualifications: [LLB]
✉ hemsleys@btconnect.com

E

BARNES MR CHRISTOPHER MICHAEL DOUGLAS

42 Bedford Row
London WC1R 4LL, ☎ 020 7831 0222
✉ clerks@42br.com
Call Date: Oct 2008, Gray's Inn
Qualifications: [BA]
✉ chris.barnes@42br.com

BARNES MR CHRISTOPHER PAUL

Exchange Chambers
One Derby Square, Derby Square, Liverpool L2 9XX, ☎ 0151 236 7747
✉ info@exchangechambers.co.uk
Exchange Chambers
7 Ralli Courts, West Riverside, Manchester M3 5FT, ☎ 0161 833 2722
Exchange Chambers
Oxford House, Oxford Row, Leeds LS1 3BE, ☎ 0113 203 1970
✉ spencer@exchangechambers.co.uk
Call Date: July 2000, Gray's Inn
Qualifications: [BA (Nott'm)]
✉ barnes@exchangechambers.co.uk

BARNES MR DAVID JONATHAN

3 Temple Gardens
Lower Ground Floor, 3 Temple Gardens, Temple, London EC4Y 9AU, ☎ 020 7353 3102
✉ clerks@3tg.co.uk
Call Date: Nov 1981, Gray's Inn
Pupil Supervisor
Qualifications: [BSc (Econ)]
✉ djb@3tg.co.uk

BARNES MR HENRY JONATHAN

Walnut House
63 St. David's Hill, Exeter, Devon EX4 4DW, ☎ 01392 279751
✉ clerks@walnuthouse.co.uk
Call Date: July 1970, Gray's Inn
Pupil Supervisor, Recorder
Qualifications: [LLB (So'ton)]

BARNES MR JONATHAN FRANCIS

5RB
1st Floor, 5 Raymond Buildings, Gray's Inn, London WC1R 5BP, ☎ 020 7242 2902
✉ clerks@5rb.com
Call Date: Nov 1999, Lincoln's Inn
Pupil Supervisor
Qualifications: [BA (Hons)(Oxon)]
✉ jonathanbarnes@5rb.com

BARNES MR LUKE CLIVE

3 Dr Johnson's Buildings
Ground Floor, 3 Dr Johnson's Buildings, Temple, London EC4Y 7BA, ☎ 020 7353 4854
✉ clerks@3djb.co.uk
Call Date: Nov 1996, Gray's Inn
Pupil Supervisor
Qualifications: [MA (Oxon) MA (Lond) Dip Law]
✉ lbarnes@3djb.co.uk

BARNES MR MATTHEW JOHN CAMPBELL

St Philips Chambers
55 Temple Row, Birmingham B2 5LS, ☎ 0121 246 7000 ✉ clerks@st-philips.com
Call Date: July 1992, Middle Temple
Pupil Supervisor
Qualifications: [MA (Cantab)]
✉ mbarnes@st-philips.com

BARNES MR MATTHEW PETER

1 Crown Office Row
1 Crown Office Row, Temple, London EC4Y 7HH, ☎ 020 7797 7500
✉ mail@1cor.com
Call Date: Nov 2000, Middle Temple
Qualifications: [BA (Hons) (Bris) MA]
✉ matthew.barnes@1cor.com

BARNES MR MICHAEL QC (1981)

Wilberforce Chambers
8 New Square, Lincoln's Inn, London WC2A 3QP, ☎ 020 7306 0102
✉ chambers@wilberforce.co.uk
Call Date: July 1965, Middle Temple
Recorder
Qualifications: [BA]
✉ mbarnes@wilberforce.co.uk

Types of work: Commercial property, Compulsory Purchase, Land compensation, Landlord and tenant, Local authorities, Planning

BARNES MISS NATASHA LUCY

9-12 Bell Yard
London WC2A 2JR, ☎ 020 7400 1800
✉ clerks@9-12bellyard.com
Call Date: July 2010, Gray's Inn
Qualifications: [BA]
✉ n.barnes@9-12bellyard.com

BARNES MR NICHOLAS GERARD HUGH

Westgate Chambers
64 High Street, Lewes, East Sussex BN7 1XG,
☎01273 480510
✉clerks@westgate-chambers.co.uk
Call Date: Oct 1996, Inner Temple
Qualifications: [LLB (Westminster)]

BARNES MR PAULINUS

Linenhall Chambers
1 Stanley Place, Chester CH1 2LU,
☎01244 348282
✉clerks@linenhallchambers.co.uk
Call Date: July 2004, Inner Temple
Qualifications: [BA (Hons)]
✉paulinusbarnes@hotmail.com

BARNES MS RACHEL ANN

3 Raymond Buildings
3 Raymond Buildings, Gray's Inn, London WC1R 5BH, ☎020 7400 6400
✉clerks@3rblaw.com
Call Date: Nov 2004, Gray's Inn
Qualifications: [MA LLM]

BARNES MR TIMOTHY PAUL QC (1986)

Seven Bedford Row
7 Bedford Row, London WC1R 4BS,
☎020 7242 3555 ✉clerks@7br.co.uk
Call Date: July 1968, Gray's Inn
Recorder
Qualifications: [MA (Cantab)]
✉tbarnes@7br.co.uk

BARNES MR WAYNE

3 Temple Gardens
Lower Ground Floor, 3 Temple Gardens, Temple, London EC4Y 9AU, ☎020 7353 3102
✉clerks@3tg.co.uk
Call Date: Oct 2002, Lincoln's Inn
Qualifications: [LLB]

BARNETT MISS ADRIENNE ELISE

1 Pump Court
Elm Court, Temple, London EC4Y 7AB,
☎020 7842 7070
✉(name)@pumpcourt.co.uk
Call Date: July 1981, Middle Temple
Qualifications: [BA (South Africa) LLM]
✉ab@1pumpcourt.co.uk

BARNETT MR DANIEL ALEXANDER

Outer Temple Chambers
The Outer Temple, 222 Strand, London WC2R 1BA, ☎020 7353 6381
✉clerks@outertemple.com
Call Date: Oct 1993, Lincoln's Inn
Pupil Supervisor
Qualifications: [LLB (Hons)(Leeds)]

BARNETT MR JEREMY VICTOR

St Paul's Chambers
5th Floor, St Paul's House, 23 Park Square South, Leeds LS1 2ND, ☎0113 245 5866
2 Bedford Row
London WC1R 4BU, ☎020 7440 8888
✉clerks@2bedfordrow.co.uk
Call Date: July 1980, Gray's Inn
Pupil Supervisor, Recorder
Qualifications: [LLB (L'pool)]

BARNETT MISS JOANNE KAREN

9 St John Street
Manchester M3 4DN, ☎0161 955 9000
✉civilclerks@9sjs.com /
criminalclerks@9sjs.com
Call Date: Nov 1989, Middle Temple
Pupil Supervisor
Qualifications: [LLB (Wales)]

BARNETT MISS SALLY LOUISE

New Street Chambers
2 New Street, Leicester LE1 5NA,
☎0116 262 5906 ✉clerks@2newstreet.co.uk
Call Date: Nov 1987, Middle Temple
Pupil Supervisor
Qualifications: [LLB]

BARNEY MS HELEN

No5 Chambers
Fountain Court, Steelhouse Lane, Birmingham B4 6DR, ☎0845 210 5555 ✉info@no5.com
No5 Chambers
Greenwood House, 4-7 Salisbury Court, London EC4Y 8AA, ☎0845 210 5555
No5 Chambers
38 Queen Square, Bristol BS1 4QS,
☎0845 210 5555
Call Date: Oct 1999, Lincoln's Inn
Qualifications: [LLB (Hons)(Manc)]
✉hb@no5.com

E

BARNFATHER MISS LYDIA HELEN

QEB Hollis Whiteman
1-2 Laurence Pountney Hill, London
EC4R 0EU, ☎020 7933 8855
✉barristers@qebhw.co.uk
Call Date: Oct 1992, Middle Temple
Pupil Supervisor
Qualifications: [BA (Hons)]
✉lydia.barnfather@qebhw.co.uk

BARNFIELD MR ALEXANDER JAMES

No 8 Chambers
8 Fountain Court, Steelhouse Lane,
Birmingham B4 6DR, ☎0121 236 5514
✉clerks@no8chambers.co.uk
Call Date: July 2007, Middle Temple
Qualifications: [LLB (Hons) (Lond)]
✉clerks@no8chambers.co.uk

BARR MR CHARLES DAVID

Temple Garden Chambers
1 Harcourt Buildings, Temple, London
EC4Y 9DA, ☎020 7583 1315
✉clerks@tgchambers.com
Call Date: Nov 1993, Gray's Inn
Pupil Supervisor
Qualifications: [MA (Cantab)]
✉davidbarr@tgchambers.com

BARRACLOUGH MR ANTHONY ROGER

Chavasse Court Chambers
18 Queen Avenue, Liverpool L2 4TX,
☎0151 229 2030
✉clerks@chavassechambers.co.uk
Call Date: Nov 1978, Inner Temple
Pupil Supervisor
Qualifications: [BA (Dunelm) BL]
✉barrister@barraclough.co.uk

BARRACLOUGH MISS LISA ANN

Colleton Chambers
Colleton Crescent, Exeter, Devon EX2 4DG,
☎01392 274898
✉clerks@colletonchambers.co.uk
Call Date: Oct 1999, Lincoln's Inn
Qualifications: [LLB (Hons)(B'ham)]
✉lisabarraclough@colletonchambers.co.uk

BARRACLOUGH MR NICHOLAS MAYLIN

187 Fleet Street
London EC4A 2AT, ☎020 7430 7430
✉chambers@187fleetstreet.com
Call Date: Nov 1990, Inner Temple
Pupil Supervisor
Qualifications: [LLB (Hons)]

BARRACLOUGH MR RICHARD MICHAEL QC (2003)

6 Pump Court
1st Floor, 6 Pump Court, Temple, London
EC4Y 7AR, ☎020 7797 8400
✉richardconstable@6pumpcourt.co.uk
6 Pump Court Chambers
6-8 Mill Street, Maidstone, Kent ME15 6XH,
☎01622 688094
✉annexe@6pumpcourt.co.uk
Call Date: Nov 1980, Inner Temple
Qualifications: [MA (Oxon)]
✉richardbarraclough@6pumpcourt.co.uk

BARRADELL MR RICHARD MARK

KBW
The Engine House, No 1 Foundry Square,
Leeds LS11 5DL, ☎0113 297 1200
✉clerks@kbwchambers.com
Call Date: Oct 1990, Inner Temple
Pupil Supervisor
Qualifications: [LLB]
✉rb@kbwchambers.com

BARRAN MISS TABITHA JANE GABRIEL

Renaissance Chambers
5th Floor, Gray's Inn Chambers, Gray's Inn,
London WC1R 5JA, ☎020 7404 1111
✉clerks@renaissancechambers.co.uk
Call Date: Oct 1998, Inner Temple
Pupil Supervisor
Qualifications: [BA (Bris) CPE]
✉tb@renaissancechambers.co.uk

BARRATT MR DOMINIC ANTHONY

East Anglian Chambers
140 New London Road, Chelmsford, Essex
CM2 0AW, ☎01473 214481
✉chelmsford@ealaw.co.uk
East Anglian Chambers
53 North Hill, Colchester, Essex CO1 1QA,
☎01473 214481 ✉colchester@ealaw.co.uk
East Anglian Chambers
15 The Close, Norwich, Norfolk NR1 4DZ,
☎01473 214481 ✉norwich@ealaw.co.uk
East Anglian Chambers
Gresham House, 5 Museum Street, Ipswich,
Suffolk IP1 1HQ, ☎01473 214481
✉ipswich@ealaw.co.uk
Call Date: Nov 1992, Gray's Inn
Pupil Supervisor
Qualifications: [BA (Hons)(Leeds)]
✉dominicbarratt@ealaw.co.uk

BARRETT MISS CHARLOTTE LOUISE

Westgate Chambers
64 High Street, Lewes, East Sussex BN7 1XG, ☎01273 480510
✉clerks@westgate-chambers.co.uk
Call Date: Nov 2007, Middle Temple
Qualifications: [LLB (Hons) (Surrey)]
cb@westgate-chambers.co.uk

BARRETT MR JOHN MICHAEL PAUL GOWRAN

Kings Chambers
36 Young Street, Manchester M3 3FT, ☎0845 034 3444
✉clerks@kingschambers.com
Kings Chambers
5 Park Square East, Leeds LS1 2NE, ☎0845 034 3444
✉clerks@kingschambers.com
Kings Chambers
Embassy House, 60 Church Street, Birmingham B3 2DJ, ☎0845 034 3444
✉clerks@kingschambers.com
Call Date: May 1982, Gray's Inn
Pupil Supervisor, Recorder
Qualifications: [BA]
jbarrett@kingschambers.com

BARRETT MR JOSEPH VINCENT

11 King's Bench Walk
11 King's Bench Walk, Temple, London EC4Y 7EQ, ☎020 7632 8500
✉clerksroom@11kbw.com
Call Date: Nov 2009, Lincoln's Inn
Qualifications: [LLB (Glas)]

BARRETT MR KEVIN JOHN

No5 Chambers
Fountain Court, Steelhouse Lane, Birmingham B4 6DR, ☎0845 210 5555 ✉info@no5.com
No5 Chambers
Greenwood House, 4-7 Salisbury Court, London EC4Y 8AA, ☎0845 210 5555
No5 Chambers
38 Queen Square, Bristol BS1 4QS, ☎0845 210 5555
Call Date: Nov 2008, Middle Temple
Qualifications: [LLB (Hons) (Sheff)]
kb@no5.com

BARRETT MR ROBERT SCOTT

2 Pump Court
1st Floor, 2 Pump Court, Temple, London EC4Y 7AH, ☎020 7353 5597
✉clerks@2pumpcourt.co.uk
Call Date: July 1978, Gray's Inn
Pupil Supervisor
Qualifications: [MA (Cantab)]
rbarrett@2pumpcourt.co.uk

BARRETT MISS STEPHANIE

Quadrant Chambers
Quadrant House, 10 Fleet Street, London EC4Y 1AU, ☎020 7583 4444
✉info@quadrantchambers.com
Call Date: July 2008, Middle Temple
Qualifications: [BA (Hons) (Oxon) BCL (Oxon)]

BARRETT MR STEVEN JAMES MICHAEL

Radcliffe Chambers
Ground Floor, 11 New Square, Lincoln's Inn, London WC2A 3QB, ☎020 7831 0081
✉clerks@radcliffechambers.com
Call Date: Oct 2003, Gray's Inn
Qualifications: [BA (Oxon)]

BARRIE MISS LAURA

Goldsmith Chambers
Ground Floor, Goldsmith Building, Temple, London EC4Y 7BL, ☎020 7353 6802
✉clerks@goldsmithchambers.com
4 Brick Court
4 Brick Court, Temple, London EC4Y 9AD, ☎020 7832 3200 ✉clerks@4bc.co.uk
Call Date: July 2005, Lincoln's Inn
Qualifications: [LLB (Hons) LLM]
L.Barrie@goldsmithchambers.law.co.uk

BARRINGTON-BADRAWY MISS SARAH LOUISE

Linenhall Chambers
1 Stanley Place, Chester CH1 2LU, ☎01244 348282
✉clerks@linenhallchambers.co.uk
Call Date: Oct 2005, Lincoln's Inn
Qualifications: [BA (Hons) PgDl]
sbb@nicholasstreet.com

BARRINGTON-SMYTH MISS AMANDA ROWENA

4 Paper Buildings
1st Floor, 4 Paper Buildings, Temple, London EC4Y 7EX, ☎020 7427 5200
✉clerks@4pb.com
Call Date: Nov 1972, Middle Temple
Pupil Supervisor
Qualifications: [LLB (Lond)]
abs@4pb.com

BARRON-EAVES MRS EMMA LORRAINE

15 Winckley Square
Preston PR1 3JJ, ☎01772 252828
✉clerks@15winckleysq.co.uk
Call Date: July 1998, Lincoln's Inn
Qualifications: [LLB (Hons)]

E

BARROW MR MICHAEL FRANK

Linenhall Chambers
1 Stanley Place, Chester CH1 2LU,
☎01244 348282
✉clerks@linenhallchambers.co.uk
Call Date: July 2010, Lincoln's Inn
Qualifications: [LLB (Manch)]
✉michael.barrow@linenhallchambers.co.uk

BARRY MR DENIS FINTAN PATRICK

Five Paper Buildings
1st Floor, Five Paper Buildings, Temple, London EC4Y 7HB, ☎020 7583 6117
✉clerks@5pb.co.uk
Call Date: Oct 1996, Inner Temple
Pupil Supervisor
Qualifications: [LLB (B'ham) LLM (Warw)]
✉dab@5pb.co.uk

BARRY MR JOSEPH MICHAEL

Snaresbrook Chambers
45 Empress Avenue, London E12 5ET,
☎020 8989 7765
✉info@snaresbrookchambers.com
Call Date: Nov 1987, Lincoln's Inn
Qualifications: [BA (Hons)]
✉joebarry@snaresbrookchambers.com, J.Barry@city.ac.uk

BARRY MR KEVIN JAMES

36 Bedford Row
London WC1R 4JH, ☎020 7421 8000
✉chambers@36bedfordrow.co.uk
Call Date: Nov 1997, Lincoln's Inn
Pupil Supervisor
Qualifications: [LLB (Hons)(B'ham)]
✉kbarry@36bedfordrow.co.uk

BARRY MISS KIRSTEN LESLEY

9 St John Street
Manchester M3 4DN, ☎0161 955 9000
✉civilclerks@9sjs.com / criminalclerks@9sjs.com
Call Date: Nov 1993, Lincoln's Inn
Qualifications: [LLB (Hons) (Sheff)]

BARRY MR MATTHEW JAMES

9 Park Place
9 Park Place, Cardiff, South Glamorgan CF10 3DP, ☎029 2038 2731
✉clerks@9parkplace.co.uk
Call Date: Oct 2002, Gray's Inn
Qualifications: [MA (Cantab)]
✉mbarry@9parkplace.co.uk

BARSAM MS TALIA

Devereux Chambers
Queen Elizabeth Building, Temple, London EC4Y 9BS, ☎020 7353 7534
✉clerks@devchambers.co.uk
Call Date: Nov 2006, Inner Temple
Qualifications: [BA (B'ham) BA (Cantab) LLM (USA)]

BARTER MS ISABEL CLARE

2 Temple Gardens
2 Temple Gardens, Temple, London EC4Y 9AY, ☎020 7822 1200
✉clerks@2tg.co.uk
Call Date: July 2010, Inner Temple
Qualifications: [BA (Hons) (Cantab)]
✉ib@2tg.co.uk

BARTFELD MR JASON MAURICE

187 Fleet Street
London EC4A 2AT, ☎020 7430 7430
✉chambers@187fleetstreet.com
Call Date: Oct 1995, Middle Temple
Qualifications: [BA (Hons)]
✉jasonbartfeld@187fleetstreet.com

BARTLET-JONES MR STEPHEN WILLIAM

1 Pump Court
Elm Court, Temple, London EC4Y 7AB,
☎020 7842 7070
✉(name)@pumpcourt.co.uk
Call Date: Oct 2004, Lincoln's Inn
Qualifications: [BA (Hons)]
✉sbj@1pumpcourt.co.uk

BARTLETT MR ANDREW VINCENT BRAMWELL QC (1993)

Crown Office Chambers
2 Crown Office Row, Temple, London EC4Y 7HJ, ☎020 7797 8100
✉mail@crownofficechambers.com
Becket Chambers
17 New Dover Road, Canterbury, Kent CT1 3AS, ☎01227 786331
✉clerks@becket-chambers.co.uk
Call Date: July 1974, Middle Temple
Recorder
Qualifications: [BA (Oxon) FCIArb]
✉abartlett@crownofficechambers.com

E

BARTLETT MRS CATHERINE ELIZABETH

Oriel Chambers
14 Water Street, Liverpool, Merseyside L2 8TD, ☎ 0151 236 7191
✉ clerks@orielchambers.co.uk
Oriel Chambers
18 Ribblesdale Place, Preston PR1 3NA, ☎ 01772 254 764
✉ clerks@oriel-chambers.co.uk
Call Date: July 2004, Inner Temple
✉ catherine.bartlett@orielchambers.co.uk

BARTLETT MR DARREN

King's Bench Chambers
Wellington House, 175 Holdenhurst Road, Bournemouth, Dorset BH8 8DQ,
☎ 01202 250025
Call Date: July 2009, Middle Temple
Qualifications: [BEng (Hons)]

BARTLETT MR DAVID ALAN

3 PB Barristers
3 Paper Buildings, Temple, London EC4Y 7EU, ☎ 020 7583 8055
3 PB Barristers
23 Beaumont Street, Oxford OX1 2NP, ☎ 01865 793 736
3 PB Barristers
30 Christchurch Road, Bournemouth, Dorset BH1 3PD, ☎ 01202 292102
✉ clerks.bournemouth@3paper.co.uk
3 PB Barristers
Royal Talbot House, 2 Victoria Street, Bristol, Avon BS1 6BB, ☎ 0117 928 1520
3 PB Barristers
4 St Peter Street, Winchester SO23 8BW, ☎ 01962 868884
✉ clerks.winchester@3paper.co.uk
Call Date: July 1975, Gray's Inn
Pupil Supervisor, Recorder
Qualifications: [BA (Oxon)]

BARTLETT MR ROGER JAMES LAURENCE

Five St Andrew's Hill
5 St Andrew's Hill, London EC4V 5BZ,
☎ 020 7332 5400 ✉ Clerks@5sah.co.uk
Call Date: July 1968, Middle Temple
Pupil Supervisor
Qualifications: [BA]
✉ rogerbartlett@5sah.co.uk

BARTON MS CHLOE LOUISE

Charter Chambers
33 John Street, London WC1N 2AT,
☎ 020 7618 4400
✉ clerks@charterchambers.com
Call Date: July 2006, Inner Temple
Qualifications: [LLB (Leic)]
✉ chloe.barton@charterchambers.com

BARTON MISS FIONA QC (2011)

5 Essex Court
1st Floor, 5 Essex Court, Temple, London EC4Y 9AH, ☎ 020 7410 2000
✉ clerks@5essexcourt.co.uk
Call Date: Nov 1986, Middle Temple
Pupil Supervisor
Qualifications: [LLB(Lond)]
✉ barton@5essexcourt.co.uk
URL: http://www.5essexcourt.co.uk

Types of work: Civil actions against the police, Inquests, Judicial review, Police, Police discipline, Public inquiries

BARTON MR HUGH GEOFFREY

Lincoln House Chambers
Tower 12, The Avenue North, Spinningfields, 18-22 Bridge Street, Manchester M3 3BZ,
☎ 0161 832 5701
✉ info@lincolnhousechambers.com
Call Date: Nov 1989, Middle Temple
Pupil Supervisor
Qualifications: [BA (Hons) Dip Law]
✉ hugh.barton@lincolnhousechambers.com

BARTON MR JEREMY CHARLES

2 King's Bench Walk
2 King's Bench Walk, Temple, London EC4Y 7DE, ☎ 020 7353 1746
✉ clerks@2kbw.com
Call Date: July 2004, Middle Temple
Qualifications: [LLB]
✉ jbarton@2kbw.com

BARTON MISS LORRAINE SABINE

Palmyra Chambers
Royal House, 46 Legh Street, Warrington WA1 1UJ, ☎ 01925 444919
✉ clerk@palmyrachambers.com
Call Date: Oct 2000, Lincoln's Inn
Qualifications: [LLB (Hons) (L'Pool)]

E

BARTON MR RICHARD JAMES

1 KBW Chambers
1 King's Bench Walk, Temple, London
EC4Y 7DB, ☎ 020 7936 1500
✉ clerks@1kbw.co.uk
King's Bench Chambers
174 High Street, Lewes BN7 1YE,
☎ 01273 402600
Call Date: Oct 1990, Lincoln's Inn
Pupil Supervisor
Qualifications: [BA BCL (Oxon)]
✉ rbarton@1kbw.co.uk

BARTON MISS ZOE MARIA MARSDEN

Selborne Chambers
10 Essex Street, London WC2R 3AA,
☎ 020 7420 9500
✉ clerks@selbornechambers.co.uk
Call Date: July 2003, Gray's Inn
Pupil Supervisor
Qualifications: [MA Hons (Edin) Dip Law (City)]
✉ zoe.barton@selbornechambers.co.uk

BARUAH MISS FIONA CAROLINE

Octagon House
19 Colegate, Norwich NR3 1AT,
☎ 01603 623186
✉ clerks@octagonhouse.co.uk
Call Date: Oct 1996, Inner Temple
Qualifications: [LLB (L'pool)]
✉ fionabaruah@octagonhouse.co.uk

BARUAH MISS RIMA

Thomas More Chambers
7 Lincoln's Inn Fields, London WC2A 3BP,
☎ 020 7404 7000
✉ clerks@thomasmore.co.uk
Call Date: Feb 1994, Inner Temple
Qualifications: [BSc]
✉ rbaruah@thomasmore.co.uk

BARWISE MISS STEPHANIE NICOLA QC (2006)

Atkin Chambers
1 Atkin Building, Gray's Inn, London
WC1R 5AT, ☎ 020 7404 0102
✉ clerks@atkinchambers.com
Call Date: July 1988, Middle Temple
Qualifications: [MA LLM (Cantab)]
✉ clerks@atkinchambers.com

BASHIR MR MOHAMMED ISSRAR

12 Old Square Chambers
1st Floor, 12 Old Square, Lincoln's Inn,
London WC2A 3TX, ☎ 020 7404 0875
✉ clerks@12oldsquare.com
Chambers of M I Bashir
2 Elmcroft Gardens, Kingsbury, London
NW9 9QP, ☎ 07932 948487
✉ mibachambers@gmail.com
Call Date: Nov 2002, Inner Temple
Qualifications: [LLB (Hons)]
✉ clerks@12oldsquare.com

BASHIR MR NADIM

Park Court Chambers
16 Park Place, Leeds LS1 2SJ,
☎ 0113 243 3277
✉ clerks@parkcourtchambers.co.uk
Call Date: Nov 1988, Middle Temple
Qualifications: [Pg Dip LLB (Hons)]
✉ nbashir@parkcourtchambers.co.uk

BASS MR TIMOTHY JAMES

Farringdon Chambers
180 Bermondsey Street, London SE1 3TQ,
☎ 020 7089 5700
Call Date: Nov 1999, Middle Temple
Qualifications: [LLB (Hons)]
✉ timbass@farringdon-law.co.uk

BASSANO MR ALARIC JULIAN

Exchange Chambers
7 Ralli Courts, West Riverside, Manchester
M3 5FT, ☎ 0161 833 2722
Exchange Chambers
One Derby Square, Derby Square, Liverpool
L2 9XX, ☎ 0151 236 7747
✉ info@exchangechambers.co.uk
Exchange Chambers
Oxford House, Oxford Row, Leeds LS1 3BE,
☎ 0113 203 1970
✉ spencer@exchangechambers.co.uk
Call Date: Nov 1993, Gray's Inn
Pupil Supervisor
Qualifications: [BA (Oxon)]

BASSETT MR JOHN STEWART BRITTEN

5 Essex Court
1st Floor, 5 Essex Court, Temple, London
EC4Y 9AH, ☎ 020 7410 2000
✉ clerks@5essexcourt.co.uk
Call Date: July 1975, Inner Temple
Pupil Supervisor
Qualifications: [LLB (Leeds)]
✉ bassett@5essexcourt.co.uk

Types of work: Civil actions against the police, Civil liberties, Common law (general), Data protection, Inquests, Personal injury, Police, Police discipline, Professional negligence

BASSIRI-DEZFOULI MISS SOROUR

Temple Court Chambers
2nd Floor, 2 Dr Johnson's Building, Temple, London EC4Y 7AY, ☎ 020 7353 7888
✉ clerks@templecourt.co.uk
Call Date: Oct 1996, Lincoln's Inn
Qualifications: [LLB (Hons)(UCE)]
✉ clerks@templecourt.co.uk

BASSRA MR SUKHBIR SINGH

No.6 Park Square
Leeds LS1 2LW, ☎ 0113 245 9763
✉ Tim@no6.co.uk
Call Date: May 1993, Middle Temple
✉ bassra@no6.co.uk

BASTIN MR ALEXANDER CHARLES

Hardwicke
New Square, Lincoln's Inn, London WC2A 3SB, ☎ 020 7242 2523
✉ enquiries@hardwicke.co.uk
Call Date: Oct 1995, Middle Temple
Pupil Supervisor
Qualifications: [BA (Hons) LLB (Hons)]
✉ alexander.bastin@hardwicke.co.uk

BASU DR DIJENDRA BHUSHAN

5 Essex Court
1st Floor, 5 Essex Court, Temple, London EC4Y 9AH, ☎ 020 7410 2000
✉ clerks@5essexcourt.co.uk
Call Date: Oct 1994, Lincoln's Inn
Pupil Supervisor
Qualifications: [MB BS]
✉ basu@5essexcourt.co.uk

BATCHELOR MR MARK ALFRED LOWE

42 Bedford Row
London WC1R 4LL, ☎ 020 7831 0222
✉ clerks@42br.com
Call Date: Nov 1971, Inner Temple
Pupil Supervisor
✉ mark.batchelor@42br.com

BATCUP MR DAVID JOHN

Charter Chambers
33 John Street, London WC1N 2AT, ☎ 020 7618 4400
✉ clerks@charterchambers.com
Call Date: July 1974, Gray's Inn
Pupil Supervisor, Recorder
Qualifications: [LLB (Lond)]
✉ david.batcup@charterchambers.com

BATE MR STEPHEN ROBERT DE BRETEUIL

5RB
1st Floor, 5 Raymond Buildings, Gray's Inn, London WC1R 5BP, ☎ 020 7242 2902
✉ clerks@5rb.com
Call Date: July 1981, Middle Temple
Qualifications: [MA (Cantab) Dip Law (Lond)]

BATES MR ALAN TWAN

Monckton Chambers
1 & 2 Raymond Buildings, Gray's Inn, London WC1R 5NR, ☎ 020 7405 7211
✉ chambers@monckton.com
Call Date: Oct 2003, Middle Temple
Qualifications: [BA (Hons) (Cantab)]
✉ abates@monckton.com

BATES MR JOHN HAYWARD

Old Square Chambers
10-11 Bedford Row, London WC1R 4BU, ☎ 020 7269 0300 ✉ clerks@oldsquare.co.uk
Old Square Chambers
3 Orchard Court, St Augustine's Yard, Bristol BS1 5DP, ☎ 0117 930 5100
✉ clerks@oldsquare.co.uk
Call Date: July 1973, Middle Temple
Pupil Supervisor
✉ bates@oldsquare.co.uk

BATES MR JUSTIN EDWARD

Arden Chambers
20 Bloomsbury Square, London WC1A 2NS, ☎ 020 7242 4244
✉ clerks@ardenchambers.com
Call Date: July 2003, Gray's Inn
Qualifications: [BA (Oxon) LLM (Toronto)]
✉ justin.bates@ardenchambers.com

BATES MS LESLEY

23 Essex Street
London WC2R 3AA, ☎ 020 7413 0353
✉ clerks@23es.com
Call Date: Nov 1999, Inner Temple
Pupil Supervisor
Qualifications: [LLB (Kingston)]
✉ lesleybates@23es.com

BATES MR PASCAL

6 Pump Court
1st Floor, 6 Pump Court, Temple, London EC4Y 7AR, ☎ 020 7797 8400
✉ richardconstable@6pumpcourt.co.uk
6 Pump Court Chambers
6-8 Mill Street, Maidstone, Kent ME15 6XH, ☎ 01622 688094
✉ annexe@6pumpcourt.co.uk
Call Date: Nov 1994, Middle Temple
Qualifications: [BA (Hons)]

E

BATES MR RICHARD GRAHAM

29 Bedford Row Chambers
London WC1R 4HE, ☎020 7404 1044
✉clerks@29br.co.uk
Call Date: Oct 1992, Middle Temple
Qualifications: [BA (Hons) (Dunelm) CPA]
rbates@29br.co.uk

BATE-WILLIAMS MR JOHN ROBERT ALEXANDER

Temple Garden Chambers
1 Harcourt Buildings, Temple, London EC4Y 9DA, ☎020 7583 1315
✉clerks@tgchambers.com
Call Date: Nov 1976, Inner Temple
Pupil Supervisor, Recorder
Qualifications: [LLB (Wales)]
jbw@tgchambers.com

BATEY MR DAVID MICHAEL

Stour Chambers
Mill Studio, 17a Stour Street, Canterbury, Kent CT1 2NR, ☎01227 764899
✉clerks@stourchambers.co.uk
Call Date: July 1989, Gray's Inn
Qualifications: [BA (Keele)]
clerks@stourchambers.co.uk

BATH MRS BALJINDER KAUR

College Chambers
19 Carlton Crescent, Southampton, Hampshire SO15 2ET, ☎023 8023 0338
✉clerks@college-chambers.co.uk
Call Date: Oct 1996, Lincoln's Inn
Qualifications: [LLB (Hons)(Warw)]
bbath@College-Chambers.co.uk

BATISTE MR SIMON ANTHONY

No.6 Park Square
Leeds LS1 2LW, ☎0113 245 9763
✉Tim@no6.co.uk
Call Date: Oct 1995, Lincoln's Inn
Qualifications: [LLB (Hons)(Newc)]
batiste@no6.co.uk

BATRA MR BUNTY LALIT

Call Date: Feb 1988, Gray's Inn
Qualifications: [LLB]
clerk@stjohnsbuildings.co.uk

BATSTONE MR WILLIAM HAROLD FITZHERBERT

Guildhall Chambers
23 Broad Street, Bristol BS1 2HG, ☎0117 930 9000
✉hoc@guildhallchambers.co.uk
Call Date: July 1982, Middle Temple
Qualifications: [BA (York)]
william.batstone@guildhallchambers.co.uk

BATT MISS CHARANJIT KAUR

Queen Elizabeth Building
3rd Floor, Queen Elizabeth Building, Temple, London EC4Y 9BS, ☎020 7797 7837
✉clerks@qeb.co.uk
Call Date: Mar 2003, Lincoln's Inn
Qualifications: [LLB (Hons) (B'ham) LLM (Lond)]
c.batt@qeb.co.uk

BATTEN MR STEPHEN DUVAL QC (1989)

3 Raymond Buildings
3 Raymond Buildings, Gray's Inn, London WC1R 5BH, ☎020 7400 6400
✉clerks@3rblaw.com
Call Date: Nov 1968, Middle Temple
Recorder
Qualifications: [BA (Oxon)]

BATTIE MISS ELEANOR HARRIET

Crown Office Row Chambers
119 Church Street, Brighton, Sussex BN1 1UD, ☎01273 625625
✉clerks@1cor.com
Call Date: July 2004, Lincoln's Inn
Qualifications: [BA Hons (Leeds) PGDip Law]
eleanor.battie@1cor.com, wewew

BATTS MISS GILLIAN

Park Court Chambers
16 Park Place, Leeds LS1 2SJ, ☎0113 243 3277
✉clerks@parkcourtchambers.co.uk
Call Date: Nov 1999, Lincoln's Inn
Pupil Supervisor
Qualifications: [LLB (Hons)(Leics)]
clerks@parkcourtchambers.co.uk

BATTY MRS KATE MARTHA

No.6 Park Square
Leeds LS1 2LW, ☎0113 245 9763
✉Tim@no6.co.uk
Call Date: July 2011, Middle Temple
Qualifications: [LLB (Hons) (Northumbria)]
batty@no6.co.uk

BAUGHAN MR ANDREW ROBERT

1 KBW Chambers
1 King's Bench Walk, Temple, London EC4Y 7DB, ☎020 7936 1500
✉clerks@1kbw.co.uk
King's Bench Chambers
174 High Street, Lewes BN7 1YE, ☎01273 402600
Call Date: Nov 1994, Middle Temple
Pupil Supervisor
Qualifications: [BA (Hons)(Lond) Dip Law]
✉abaughan@1kbw.co.uk

BAUMBER MR KEVIN JOHN

3 Raymond Buildings
3 Raymond Buildings, Gray's Inn, London WC1R 5BH, ☎020 7400 6400
✉clerks@3rblaw.com
Call Date: Oct 1998, Lincoln's Inn
Pupil Supervisor
Qualifications: [LLB (Hons)(Essex) BCL (Oxon)]
✉kevin.baumber@3raymondbuildings.com

BAUMOHL MR MARK CHRISTOPHER

Field Court Chambers
5 Field Court, Gray's Inn, London WC1R 5EF, ☎020 7405 6114 ✉clerks@fieldcourt.co.uk
Call Date: Oct 2001, Middle Temple
Qualifications: [LLB (Hons)]
✉mark.baumohl@fieldcourt.co.uk

BAUR MR CHRISTOPHER THOMAS

Furnival Chambers
32 Furnival Street, London EC4A 1JQ, ☎020 7405 3232
Call Date: July 1972, Middle Temple
Pupil Supervisor
✉cbaur@furnivallaw.co.uk

BAX MR JAMES ALEXANDER

Rougemont Chambers
Victory House, Dean Clarke Gardens, Southernhay East, Exeter EX2 4AA, ☎01392 208484
✉clerks@rougemontchambers.co.uk
Call Date: Oct 1999, Lincoln's Inn
Qualifications: [LLB (Hons)(Lancs)]
✉jbax@rougemontchambers.co.uk

BAXTER MISS BERNADETTE

Lincoln House Chambers
Tower 12, The Avenue North, Spinningfields, 18-22 Bridge Street, Manchester M3 3BZ, ☎0161 832 5701
✉info@lincolnhousechambers.com
Call Date: July 1987, Middle Temple
Pupil Supervisor, Recorder
Qualifications: [LLB (LSE)]
✉bernadette.baxter@lincolnhousechambers.com

BAXTER MR GERALD PEARSON

Chavasse Court Chambers
18 Queen Avenue, Liverpool L2 4TX, ☎0151 229 2030
✉clerks@chavassechambers.co.uk
Call Date: July 1971, Lincoln's Inn
Pupil Supervisor
Qualifications: [LLB (Sheff) LLM]
✉geraldbxt@aol.com

BAXTER MR MARK

5 Stone Buildings
5 Stone Buildings, Lincoln's Inn, London WC2A 3XT, ☎020 7242 6201
✉clerks@5sblaw.com
Call Date: July 2006, Lincoln's Inn
Qualifications: [LLB (Bris)]
✉mbaxter@5sblaw.com

BAYATI MS CHARLOTTE ELIZABETH

Renaissance Chambers
5th Floor, Gray's Inn Chambers, Gray's Inn, London WC1R 5JA, ☎020 7404 1111
✉clerks@renaissancechambers.co.uk
Call Date: Nov 1995, Gray's Inn
Qualifications: [LLB LLM]
✉cb@renaissancechambers.co.uk

BAYFIELD MR DANIEL

South Square
3-4 South Square, Gray's Inn, London WC1R 5HP, ☎020 7696 9900
✉practicemanagers@southsquare.com
Call Date: Oct 1998, Inner Temple
Pupil Supervisor
Qualifications: [MA (Cantab)]
✉danielbayfield@southsquare.com

BAYLEY MS LAURA

Westgate Chambers
64 High Street, Lewes, East Sussex BN7 1XG, ☎01273 480510
✉clerks@westgate-chambers.co.uk
Call Date: Oct 1999, Gray's Inn
Qualifications: [LLB (LSE)]

E

BAYLEY MRS LAURA JANE

Charter Chambers
33 John Street, London WC1N 2AT,
☎ 020 7618 4400
✉ clerks@charterchambers.com
Call Date: Mar 2010, Lincoln's Inn
Qualifications: [LLB (Surrey)]
✉ laura.bayley@charterchambers.com

BAYLIS MR CHRISTOPHER LLOYD GERSHWIN

Riverview Chambers
Hamilton House, 1 Temple Avenue, London
EC4Y 0HA, ☎ 0844 225 3999
✉ chrisbaylis@riverviewchambers.com
Call Date: Nov 1986, Inner Temple
Qualifications: [BA (Hons) MBA (Cantab) MPhil (Cantab) LLM MTh]
✉ chrisbaylis@riverviewchambers.com

BAYLISS MISS SARAH JOANNE EMMA

XXIV Old Buildings
Ground Floor, 24 Old Buildings, Lincoln's Inn,
London WC2A 3UP, ☎ 020 7691 2424
✉ clerks@xxiv.co.uk
Call Date: Oct 2002, Middle Temple
Pupil Supervisor
Qualifications: [BA (Cantab) CPE]
✉ sarah.bayliss@xxiv.co.uk

BAYLISS MR THOMAS WILLIAM MAXWELL QC (2003)

Park Court Chambers
16 Park Place, Leeds LS1 2SJ,
☎ 0113 243 3277
✉ clerks@parkcourtchambers.co.uk
5 King's Bench Walk
5 King's Bench Walk, Temple, London
EC4Y 7DN, ☎ 020 7353 5638
✉ clerks@5kbw.co.uk
Call Date: July 1977, Inner Temple
Recorder
Qualifications: [LLB (Hons)]
✉ tbayliss@parkcourtchambers.co.uk

BAYNE MR DOMINIC RICHARD NOEL

Park Lane Plowden
Lombard House, 4-8 Lombard Street,
Newcastle Upon Tyne NE1 3AE,
☎ 0191 211 4087
✉ clerks@parklaneplowden.co.uk
Call Date: Oct 1997, Middle Temple
Pupil Supervisor
Qualifications: [BSc (Hons)(Dunelm)]
✉ dominic.bayne@parklaneplowden.co.uk

BAYOUMI MISS MONA MOHAMED

Civitas Chambers
Global Reach, Celtic Gateway, Cardiff Bay,
Cardiff CF11 0SN, ☎ 0845 0713 007
✉ clerks@civitaslaw.com
Call Date: Nov 2004, Middle Temple
Qualifications: [LLB (Hons) (Wales)]
✉ mona.bayoumi@civitaslaw.com

BAZINI MR DANIEL

No5 Chambers
Greenwood House, 4-7 Salisbury Court,
London EC4Y 8AA, ☎ 0845 210 5555
No5 Chambers
38 Queen Square, Bristol BS1 4QS,
☎ 0845 210 5555
No5 Chambers
Fountain Court, Steelhouse Lane, Birmingham
B4 6DR, ☎ 0845 210 5555 ✉ info@no5.com
Call Date: Nov 1992, Gray's Inn
Qualifications: [BA (Econ) BA (Law)]
✉ dba@no5.com, danny@bazini.co.uk

BAZLEY MISS JANET CLARE QC (2006)

1 Garden Court Family Law Chambers
Ground Floor, One Garden Court, Temple,
London EC4Y 9BJ, ☎ 020 7797 7900
✉ clerks@1gc.com
Call Date: July 1980, Lincoln's Inn
Recorder
Qualifications: [LLB (Lond)]
✉ bazley@1gc.com

BEACH MISS FIONA JEAN

Stour Chambers
Mill Studio, 17a Stour Street, Canterbury, Kent
CT1 2NR, ☎ 01227 764899
✉ clerks@stourchambers.co.uk
Call Date: Mar 2001, Lincoln's Inn
Qualifications: [BA (Hons) (Sussex) CPE]
✉ clerks@stourchambers.co.uk

BEAL MR JASON PHILIP MARCUS

Devon Chambers
3 St Andrew Street, Plymouth PL1 2AH,
☎ 01752 661659
✉ clerks@devonchambers.co.uk
Call Date: Oct 1993, Gray's Inn
Pupil Supervisor
Qualifications: [BA Dip Law]
✉ jasonbeal@devonchambers.co.uk

BEAL MR KIERON CONRAD QC (2012)

Blackstone Chambers
Blackstone House, Temple, London EC4Y 9BW, ☎ 020 7583 1770
✉ clerks@blackstonechambers.com
Call Date: Nov 1995, Inner Temple
Pupil Supervisor
Qualifications: [MA (Cantab) LLM (USA) BA (Cantab)]
✉ kieronbeal@blackstonechambers.com

BEALBY MR WALTER

No5 Chambers
Fountain Court, Steelhouse Lane, Birmingham B4 6DR, ☎ 0845 210 5555 ✉ info@no5.com
No5 Chambers
Greenwood House, 4-7 Salisbury Court, London EC4Y 8AA, ☎ 0845 210 5555
No5 Chambers
38 Queen Square, Bristol BS1 4QS, ☎ 0845 210 5555
Call Date: July 1976, Middle Temple
Pupil Supervisor
Qualifications: [BA (Bris)]
✉ wb@no5.com

BEALE MISS ANNA CLAIRE

Cloisters
1 Pump Court, Temple, London EC4Y 7AA, ☎ 020 7827 4000 ✉ clerks@cloisters.com
Call Date: Oct 2001, Gray's Inn
Pupil Supervisor
Qualifications: [BA (Oxon)]
✉ abe@cloisters.com

BEAN MR MATTHEW ALLEN

KBW
The Engine House, No 1 Foundry Square, Leeds LS11 5DL, ☎ 0113 297 1200
✉ clerks@kbwchambers.com
Call Date: Oct 1997, Middle Temple
Qualifications: [BA (Hons)(Dunelm) CPE]
✉ matthewbean@kbwchambers.com

BEARD MR DANIEL MATTHEW QC (2011)

Monckton Chambers
1 & 2 Raymond Buildings, Gray's Inn, London WC1R 5NR, ☎ 020 7405 7211
✉ chambers@monckton.com
Call Date: Nov 1996, Middle Temple
Pupil Supervisor
Qualifications: [MA (Hons)(Cantab) BCL]
✉ dbeard@monckton.com

BEARD MR DAVID JOHN

Holborn Chambers
6 Gate Street, Lincoln's Inn Fields, London WC2A 3HP, ☎ 020 7242 6060
Call Date: Oct 1990, Lincoln's Inn
Qualifications: [LLB]
✉ david.beard@holbornchambers.com

BEARD MR MARK CHRISTOPHER

6 Pump Court Chambers
6-8 Mill Street, Maidstone, Kent ME15 6XH, ☎ 01622 688094
✉ annexe@6pumpcourt.co.uk
6 Pump Court
1st Floor, 6 Pump Court, Temple, London EC4Y 7AR, ☎ 020 7797 8400
✉ richardconstable@6pumpcourt.co.uk
Call Date: Oct 1996, Gray's Inn
Pupil Supervisor
Qualifications: [LLB (Lond) LLM]
✉ markbeard@6pumpcourt.co.uk

Types of work: Administrative law, Environment, Local authorities, Planning

BEARD MR SIMON

Ropewalk Chambers
24 The Ropewalk, Nottingham NG1 5EF, ☎ 0115 947 2581 ✉ clerks@ropewalk.co.uk
Call Date: Nov 1980, Gray's Inn
Pupil Supervisor
Qualifications: [MA (Oxon)]
✉ simonbeard@ropewalk.co.uk

BEARDMORE MR WILLIAM EDWARD

Chavasse Court Chambers
18 Queen Avenue, Liverpool L2 4TX, ☎ 0151 229 2030
✉ clerks@chavassechambers.co.uk
Call Date: July 2005, Gray's Inn
Qualifications: [LLB]

BEARMAN MR JUSTIN IAN

Castle Chambers
The Old Fire Station, 90 High Street, Harrow-on-the-Hill, Middlesex HA1 3LP, ☎ 020 8423 6579 ✉ info@castlechambers.net
Call Date: Nov 1992, Inner Temple
Pupil Supervisor
Qualifications: [LLB (Hull) (Hons)]

BEASLEY MR THOMAS HUMPHREY CLOVIS

Radcliffe Chambers
Ground Floor, 11 New Square, Lincoln's Inn, London WC2A 3QB, ☎ 020 7831 0081
✉ clerks@radcliffechambers.com
Call Date: July 2003, Middle Temple
Qualifications: [BA Hons (Bris) CPE]
✉ tombeasley@33bedfordrow.co.uk

BEATTIE MISS ANN LOUISE

Atlantic Chambers
4-6 Cook Street, Liverpool L2 9QU,
☎ 0151 236 4421
✉ info@atlanticchambers.co.uk
Call Date: July 1989, Middle Temple
Qualifications: [BSc (Hons) Dip Law]
✉ annbeattie@atlanticchambers.co.uk

BEATTIE MS ANNABEL DOROTHY

Park Court Chambers
16 Park Place, Leeds LS1 2SJ,
☎ 0113 243 3277
✉ clerks@parkcourtchambers.co.uk
Call Date: July 2005, Inner Temple
Qualifications: [BA (Leics) CPE]
✉ annabelbeattie231@gmail.com

BEATTIE MS KATHARINE ELEANOR

1 Crown Office Row
1 Crown Office Row, Temple, London EC4Y 7HH, ☎ 020 7797 7500
✉ mail@1cor.com
Call Date: July 2007, Lincoln's Inn
Qualifications: [BA LLB (Australia)]
✉ Kate.Beattie@1cor.com

BEATTIE MISS SHARON MICHELLE

Park Court Chambers
16 Park Place, Leeds LS1 2SJ,
☎ 0113 243 3277
✉ clerks@parkcourtchambers.co.uk
Call Date: Nov 1986, Inner Temple
Pupil Supervisor
Qualifications: [LLB (Hons)(Leeds)]
✉ sbeattie@parkcourtchambers.co.uk

BEAUMONT MR ADAM PAUL

Old Bailey Chambers
15 Old Bailey, London EC4M 7EF,
☎ 020 3008 6404
✉ clerks@15oldbaileychambers.com
Call Date: July 2009, Lincoln's Inn
Qualifications: [LLB (Leeds)]

BEAUMONT MR BENJAMIN

Chambers of Dr Michael Arnheim
101 Queen Alexandra Mansions, Judd Street, London WC1H 9DP, ☎ 020 7833 5093
✉ arnheim.law@gmail.com
Middle Temple Lane Chambers
2nd Floor South, 1 Middle Temple Lane, London EC4Y 9AA, ☎ 020 7583 4352
✉ chambers@mtlchambers.com
Call Date: July 1978, Inner Temple
Qualifications: [BSC FCI FRICS ARB]
✉ bbeaumont@ficacic.com

BEAUMONT MR DEAN ANDREW

KCH Garden Square
1 Oxford Street, Nottingham NG1 5BH,
☎ 0115 941 8851
✉ clerks@kchgardensquare.co.uk
Call Date: July 1999, Lincoln's Inn
Qualifications: [BSc (Hons)(Nott'm)]
✉ a.beaumont@kch.co.uk

BEAUMONT MR MARC CLIFFORD

Windsor Barristers' Chambers
Windsor Chambers, Castle Hill House, 12 Castle Hill, Windsor, Berkshire SL4 1PD,
☎ 01753 839321
✉ mcb@windsorchambers.com
9 Stone Buildings
Lincoln's Inn, London WC2A 3NN,
☎ 020 7404 5055
✉ clerks@9stonebuildings.com
Call Date: July 1985, Gray's Inn
Pupil Supervisor
Qualifications: [LLB (Manch)]
✉ mcb@windsorchambers.com

BEAUMONT MRS SALLY

Sovereign Chambers
46 Park Place, Leeds LS1 2RY,
☎ 0113 245 1841
✉ clerks@sovereignchambers.co.uk
Call Date: Oct 1999, Lincoln's Inn
Pupil Supervisor
Qualifications: [LLB (Hons)(Keele)]
✉ sally.beaumont@sovereignchambers.co.uk

BEAZLEY MR THOMAS ALAN GEORGE QC (2001)

Blackstone Chambers
Blackstone House, Temple, London EC4Y 9BW, ☎ 020 7583 1770
✉ clerks@blackstonechambers.com
Call Date: July 1979, Middle Temple
Qualifications: [BA LLB(Cantab)]
✉ thomasbeazley@blackstonechambers.com

BEBB MR GORDON MONTFORT QC (2002)

Outer Temple Chambers
The Outer Temple, 222 Strand, London WC2R 1BA, ☎ 020 7353 6381
✉ clerks@outertemple.com
Call Date: Nov 1975, Middle Temple
Recorder
Qualifications: [BA (Oxon)]

BECKER MR PAUL ANTONY

Chavasse Court Chambers
18 Queen Avenue, Liverpool L2 4TX,
☎ 0151 229 2030
✉ clerks@chavassechambers.co.uk
Call Date: Nov 1990, Gray's Inn
Pupil Supervisor
Qualifications: [LLB (Hons)(Leeds)]
✉ paul.becker@chavassechambers.co.uk

BECKER MR TIMOTHY GEORGE CHRISTIE

Clerksroom (London)
3rd Floor, 218 Strand, London WC2R 1AT,
☎ 0845 083 3000 ✉ mail@clerksroom.com
Chambers of Mr Timothy Becker
53 Rodney Street, Liverpool L1 9ER,
☎ 0151 703 0319
Call Date: July 1992, Middle Temple
Qualifications: [BA (Hons) (Lond) DipLaw AKC]
✉ becker@clerksroom.com

BECKETT MRS JAYNE LOUISE

Broadway House Chambers
Broadway House, 9 Bank Street, Bradford, West Yorkshire BD1 1TW, ☎ 01274 722560
✉ clerks@broadwayhouse.co.uk
Broadway House Chambers
25 Park Square West, Leeds, West Yorkshire LS1 2PW, ☎ 0113 246 2600
✉ clerks@broadwayhouse.co.uk
Call Date: Nov 1995, Middle Temple
Qualifications: [MA (Hons)(Cantab)]
✉ clerks@broadwayhouse.co.uk

BECKLEY MR JOHN MARK

Garden Court Chambers
57-60 Lincoln's Inn Fields, London WC2A 3LJ,
☎ 020 7993 7600 ✉ info@gclaw.co.uk
Call Date: July 2003, Middle Temple
Qualifications: [BA Hons (Oxon) PG Dip Law (Lond)]
✉ johnb@gclaw.co.uk

BEDDOE MR RICHARD MARTIN

Coram Chambers
9-11 Fulwood Place, London WC1V 6HG,
☎ 020 7092 3700
✉ mail@coramchambers.co.uk
Call Date: Oct 1999, Gray's Inn
Qualifications: [BSc (Wales)]
✉ richard.beddoe@coramchambers.co.uk

BEDENHAM MR DAVID

4-5 Gray's Inn Square
Gray's Inn, London WC1R 5AH,
☎ 020 7404 5252 ✉ clerks@4-5.co.uk
Call Date: July 2005, Gray's Inn
Qualifications: [LLB (Lond) LLM]
✉ clerks@4-5.co.uk

BEDFORD MR BECKET NATHANIEL

No5 Chambers
Fountain Court, Steelhouse Lane, Birmingham B4 6DR, ☎ 0845 210 5555 ✉ info@no5.com
No5 Chambers
Greenwood House, 4-7 Salisbury Court, London EC4Y 8AA, ☎ 0845 210 5555
No5 Chambers
38 Queen Square, Bristol BS1 4QS,
☎ 0845 210 5555
Call Date: Nov 1989, Middle Temple
Qualifications: [LLB (Hons)(Wales) Deug 1 (France)]
✉ bb@no5.com

BEDFORD MISS ERICA LOUISE

Call Date: Mar 2012, Inner Temple
✉ ebedford@kingschambers.com

BEDFORD MR MICHAEL CHARLES ANTHONY

Cornerstone Barristers
2-3 Gray's Inn Square, Gray's Inn, London WC1R 5JH, ☎ 020 7242 4986
✉ chambers@2-3gis.co.uk
Call Date: July 1985, Gray's Inn
Pupil Supervisor
Qualifications: [LLB (Lond)]
✉ mbedford@2-3gis.co.uk

E

BEDFORD MR STEPHEN JOHN

St Johns Buildings Liverpool
8th Floor India Buildings, Water Street, Liverpool L2 0XG, ☎0151 243 6000
✉clerk@stjohnsbuildings.co.uk
16 Winckley Square
Preston PR1 3JJ, ☎01772 256100
St Johns Buildings
24a - 28 St John Street, Manchester M3 4DJ, ☎0161 214 1500
✉clerk@stjohnsbuildings.co.uk
Call Date: July 1974, Gray's Inn
Recorder
Qualifications: [BA (Oxon)]
✉steve_bedford@btopenworld.com

BEDINGFIELD MR DAVID HERBERT

4 Paper Buildings
1st Floor, 4 Paper Buildings, Temple, London EC4Y 7EX, ☎020 7427 5200
✉clerks@4pb.com
Call Date: Nov 1991, Gray's Inn
Pupil Supervisor, Recorder
Qualifications: [BA (USA) JD (USA)]
✉db@4pb.com

BEDLOE MR GILES ROBERT

Dyers Chambers
35 Bedford Row, London WC1R 4JH, ☎020 7404 1881
✉admin@dyerschambers.com
Call Date: Nov 2001, Middle Temple
Qualifications: [BA (Hons)(Oxon) CPE]

BEDWORTH MISS GEORGIA SELINA

Ten Old Square
Ground Floor, Ten Old Square, Lincoln's Inn, London WC2A 3SU, ☎020 7405 0758
✉clerks@tenoldsquare.com
Call Date: July 2001, Middle Temple
Pupil Supervisor
Qualifications: [BA (Hons) BCL]
✉georgiabedworth@tenoldsquare.com

BEEBY MR CHRISTOPHER GABRIEL

Guildhall Chambers
23 Broad Street, Bristol BS1 2HG, ☎0117 930 9000
✉hoc@guildhallchambers.co.uk
Call Date: Nov 2006, Lincoln's Inn
Qualifications: [BA (Nott'm)]

BEECHAM MISS SARA ELISABETH

Five Paper
Ground Floor, 5 Paper Buildings, Temple, London EC4Y 7HB, ☎020 7815 3200
Call Date: Nov 1999, Middle Temple
Qualifications: [BA (Hons)(Oxon)]
✉sarabeecham@fivepaper.com

BEECHEY MISS HILARY JANE

King's Bench and Godolphin (KBG)Chambers
115 North Hill, Plymouth, Devon PL4 8JY, ☎01752 221551
✉clerks@kbgchambers.co.uk
Call Date: Nov 1987, Middle Temple
Qualifications: [BA (Hons) Dip Law (Lond)]
✉hb@kbgchambers.co.uk, theclerks@godolphinchambers.co.uk

BEECHEY MR NICHOLAS CHARLES

Old Bailey Chambers
15 Old Bailey, London EC4M 7EF, ☎020 3008 6404
✉clerks@15oldbaileychambers.com
Call Date: July 2002, Middle Temple
Qualifications: [LLB (Hons) (Sussex) BA (Hons) Sussex]
✉n.beechey@15oldbaileychambers.com

BEER MISS EMILY CHARLOTTE LEMAY

3 Dr Johnson's Buildings
Ground Floor, 3 Dr Johnson's Buildings, Temple, London EC4Y 7BA, ☎020 7353 4854
✉clerks@3djb.co.uk
Call Date: Oct 2004, Gray's Inn
Qualifications: [BA (Hons)]
✉ebeer@3djb.co.uk

BEER MR JASON BARRINGTON QC (2011)

5 Essex Court
1st Floor, 5 Essex Court, Temple, London EC4Y 9AH, ☎020 7410 2000
✉clerks@5essexcourt.co.uk
Call Date: Oct 1992, Inner Temple
Pupil Supervisor, Recorder
Qualifications: [LLB (Warw)]
✉beer@5essexcourt.co.uk

BEER MISS JULIA HELEN

Ten Old Square
Ground Floor, Ten Old Square, Lincoln's Inn, London WC2A 3SU, ☎020 7405 0758
✉clerks@tenoldsquare.com
Call Date: July 2003, Gray's Inn
Qualifications: [MA]

BEESE MISS NICOLA HELEN

St Mary's Family Law Chambers
26-28 High Pavement, The Lace Market, Nottingham NG1 1HN, ☎0115 950 3503
✉clerks@stmarysflc.co.uk
Call Date: Mar 1998, Lincoln's Inn
Qualifications: [LLB (Hons)(Sheff)]
✉nicola.beese@stmarysflc.co.uk

E

BEESON MR NIGEL ADRIAN LAURENCE

New Bailey Chambers
4th Floor, Corn Exchange, Fenwick Street, Liverpool, Merseyside L2 7QS,
☎0151 236 9402 ✉clerks@newbailey.com
Call Date: July 1983, Lincoln's Inn
Pupil Supervisor
Qualifications: [LLB (Hons)]

BEEVER MR EDMUND DAMIAN

St Philips Chambers
55 Temple Row, Birmingham B2 5LS,
☎0121 246 7000 ✉clerks@st-philips.com
Call Date: Oct 1990, Lincoln's Inn
Pupil Supervisor
Qualifications: [BA (Oxon)]
✉ebeever@st-philips.co.uk

BEEVER MISS PRUDENCE MARY

15 Winckley Square
Preston PR1 3JJ, ☎01772 252828
✉clerks@15winckleysq.co.uk
Call Date: July 2000, Middle Temple
Qualifications: [LLB(Hons) (Manc)]

BEGGS MR JOHN PETER QC (2009)

3 Serjeants Inn
London EC4Y 1BQ, ☎020 7427 5000
✉clerks@3serjeantsinn.com
Call Date: Nov 1989, Gray's Inn
Pupil Supervisor
Qualifications: [LLB (Brunel)]
✉jb@3serjeantsinn.com

BEGLAN MR WAYNE STUART

Cornerstone Barristers
2-3 Gray's Inn Square, Gray's Inn, London WC1R 5JH, ☎020 7242 4986
✉chambers@2-3gis.co.uk
Call Date: Oct 1996, Lincoln's Inn
Pupil Supervisor
Qualifications: [BA (Hons)(Keele)]
✉wbeglan@2-3gis.co.uk

BEGLEY MISS LAURA ANNE

The Chambers of Grahame Aldous QC
9 Gough Square, London EC4A 3DG,
☎020 7832 0500
✉clerks@9goughsquare.co.uk
Call Date: Nov 1993, Lincoln's Inn
Qualifications: [LLB (Hons) (Leeds)]
✉lbegley@9goughsquare.co.uk

BEGUM MISS MONWARA SHAH

1 Mitre Court Buildings
1 Mitre Court Buildings, Temple, London EC4Y 7BS, ☎020 7452 8900
✉clerks@1mcb.com
Call Date: Mar 2004, Lincoln's Inn
Qualifications: [LLB (Hons) (Nott'm)]
✉monwara.shah@1mcb.com

BEGUM MISS REHANA

18 St John Street
Manchester M3 4EA, ☎0161 278 1800
✉clerks@18sjs.com
Call Date: July 2004, Lincoln's Inn
Qualifications: [BA Hons (Leeds)]
✉clerks@18sjs.com

BEGUM MISS SHAHIDA

Garden Court Chambers
57-60 Lincoln's Inn Fields, London WC2A 3LJ,
☎020 7993 7600 ✉info@gclaw.co.uk
Call Date: Nov 2008, Inner Temple
Qualifications: [BA (Cantab) LLM (Lond) CPE]
✉shahidab@gclaw.co.uk

BEHARRYLAL MR SATYANAND SARJU

15 New Bridge Street
London EC4V 6AU, ☎020 7842 1900
✉clerks@15nbs.com
Call Date: Oct 1997, Lincoln's Inn
Pupil Supervisor
Qualifications: [LLB (Hons)(Herts) LLM (Lond)]
✉anand.beharrylal@15nbs.com

BELBEN MR ROBIN WILLIAM

College Chambers
19 Carlton Crescent, Southampton, Hampshire SO15 2ET, ☎023 8023 0338
✉clerks@college-chambers.co.uk
Call Date: Nov 1969, Lincoln's Inn
Pupil Supervisor, Recorder
Qualifications: [LLB (Hons)(Lond)]
✉rbelben@College-Chambers.co.uk

BELBIN MISS HEATHER PATRICIA

Oriel Chambers
14 Water Street, Liverpool, Merseyside L2 8TD, ☎0151 236 7191
✉clerks@orielchambers.co.uk
Oriel Chambers
18 Ribblesdale Place, Preston PR1 3NA,
☎01772 254 764
✉clerks@oriel-chambers.co.uk
Call Date: Oct 1992, Lincoln's Inn
Qualifications: [LLB(Hons)(Sheff)]
✉heather.belbin@orielchambers.co.uk

E

BELFORD MISS DORA JOY

3 Temple Gardens
Lower Ground Floor, 3 Temple Gardens, Temple, London EC4Y 9AU, ☎ 020 7353 3102
✉ clerks@3tg.co.uk
Call Date: July 1977, Middle Temple
Pupil Supervisor

BELGER MR TYRONE

2 Hare Court
Lower Ground, Ground, 1st & 2nd Floor, 2 Hare Court, Temple, London EC4Y 7BH, ☎ 020 7353 3982 ✉ clerks@2harecourt.com
Call Date: July 1984, Inner Temple
Pupil Supervisor
Qualifications: [LLB (Lond)]
tyronebelger@2harecourt.com

BELGRAVE MISS SUSAN LORRAINE

The Chambers of Grahame Aldous QC
9 Gough Square, London EC4A 3DG, ☎ 020 7832 0500
✉ clerks@9goughsquare.co.uk
Call Date: July 1989, Inner Temple
Qualifications: [BA (Hons) MSc (Econ) Lic Spec En Droit Eur LLB (Hons)]
sbelgrave@9goughsquare.co.uk

BELGROVE MISS SOPHIE DAWN

Devereux Chambers
Queen Elizabeth Building, Temple, London EC4Y 9BS, ☎ 020 7353 7534
✉ clerks@devchambers.co.uk
Call Date: Oct 2001, Middle Temple
Qualifications: [BA (Hons) (Oxon)]
belgrove@devchambers.co.uk

BELL MR ALPHEGE

Carmelite Chambers
9 Carmelite Street, London EC4Y 0DR, ☎ 020 7936 6300
✉ clerks@carmelitechambers.co.uk
Call Date: Oct 1995, Inner Temple
Qualifications: [BA (Oxon)]
abell@carmelitechambers.co.uk

BELL MISS ANNE MARGARET

Rougemont Chambers
Victory House, Dean Clarke Gardens, Southernhay East, Exeter EX2 4AA, ☎ 01392 208484
✉ clerks@rougemontchambers.co.uk
Holborn Chambers
6 Gate Street, Lincoln's Inn Fields, London WC2A 3HP, ☎ 020 7242 6060
Call Date: Nov 1975, Gray's Inn
Pupil Supervisor
Qualifications: [BA (Hons)]

BELL MR ANTHONY JOHN

No5 Chambers
Greenwood House, 4-7 Salisbury Court, London EC4Y 8AA, ☎ 0845 210 5555
No5 Chambers
38 Queen Square, Bristol BS1 4QS, ☎ 0845 210 5555
No5 Chambers
Fountain Court, Steelhouse Lane, Birmingham B4 6DR, ☎ 0845 210 5555 ✉ info@no5.com
Call Date: Nov 1985, Inner Temple
Pupil Supervisor
Qualifications: [BA (Hons)]

BELL MR DOMINIC MICHAEL ST. JOHN

Chambers of Marion Smullen and Kerim Fuad QC
1 Inner Temple Lane, London EC4Y 1AF, ☎ 020 7427 4400 ✉ clerks@1itl.com
Call Date: Nov 1992, Inner Temple
Qualifications: [LLB (Lond)]
Dominic.Bell@1ITL.com

BELL MR GARY TERENCE QC (2012)

No5 Chambers
Fountain Court, Steelhouse Lane, Birmingham B4 6DR, ☎ 0845 210 5555 ✉ info@no5.com
No5 Chambers
Greenwood House, 4-7 Salisbury Court, London EC4Y 8AA, ☎ 0845 210 5555
No5 Chambers
38 Queen Square, Bristol BS1 4QS, ☎ 0845 210 5555
Call Date: Feb 1989, Inner Temple
Qualifications: [LLB (Bris)]
gb@no5.com

BELL MISS HELEN LOUISE

2 Temple Gardens
2 Temple Gardens, Temple, London EC4Y 9AY, ☎ 020 7822 1200
✉ clerks@2tg.co.uk
Call Date: July 2002, Middle Temple
Qualifications: [BA (Hons) (Oxon)]

BELL MR JAMES

Temple Garden Chambers
1 Harcourt Buildings, Temple, London EC4Y 9DA, ☎ 020 7583 1315
✉ clerks@tgchambers.com
Chambers of Gerard McDermott QC
Weir House, 7 Stamford Street, Stalybridge SK15 1JP, ☎ 0161 304 4301
✉ gerard@mcdermottqc.com
Call Date: Nov 1987, Middle Temple
Pupil Supervisor
Qualifications: [LLB(Hons) (Wales)]

BELL MISS JILLIAN LESLEY

Zenith Chambers
10 Park Square, Leeds LS1 2LH,
☎0113 245 5438
✉clerks@zenithchambers.co.uk
Call Date: Mar 2000, Inner Temple
Qualifications: [LLB (LSE)]
jmyers@zenithchambers.co.uk

BELL MISS LAURA PATIENCE

Devereux Chambers
Queen Elizabeth Building, Temple, London EC4Y 9BS, ☎020 7353 7534
✉clerks@devchambers.co.uk
Call Date: July 2004, Lincoln's Inn
Qualifications: [Bmus Hons (Manch) PGDip Law (Manch)]
bell@devchambers.co.uk

BELL MISS MARIKA PAMELA TRACEY

Octagon House
19 Colegate, Norwich NR3 1AT,
☎01603 623186
✉clerks@octagonhouse.co.uk
Call Date: Nov 1991, Gray's Inn
Qualifications: [LLB (B'ham)]

BELL MR THOMAS CAPEL

Hardwicke
New Square, Lincoln's Inn, London WC2A 3SB, ☎020 7242 2523
✉enquiries@hardwicke.co.uk
Call Date: Oct 2006, Lincoln's Inn
Qualifications: [MA (Oxon)]
thomas.bell@hardwicke.co.uk

BELLAMY MR JONATHAN CHARLES

Call Date: July 2008, Inner Temple
Qualifications: [LLB (Manch)]
bellamy@paradise-sq.co.uk

BELLAMY MR JONATHAN MARK

39 Essex Street
London WC2R 3AT, ☎020 7832 1111
✉clerks@39essex.com
82 King Street
Manchester M2 4WQ, ☎0161 870 9969
Call Date: Nov 1986, Lincoln's Inn
Pupil Supervisor
Qualifications: [MA(Oxon) FCI Arb]
clerks@39essex.com

Types of work: Arbitration, Commercial litigation, Construction law, Insurance, International commercial arbitration, Product liability, Professional negligence, Sport

BELLAMY MR STEPHEN HOWARD QC (1996)

1 KBW Chambers
1 King's Bench Walk, Temple, London EC4Y 7DB, ☎020 7936 1500
✉clerks@1kbw.co.uk
King's Bench Chambers
174 High Street, Lewes BN7 1YE,
☎01273 402600
Call Date: Nov 1974, Lincoln's Inn
Recorder
Qualifications: [MA (Cantab) ACIArb]
sbellamy@1kbw.co.uk

BELLARA MR SUSHEEL

6 King's Bench Walk
Ground, Third & Fourth Floors, 6 King's Bench Walk, Temple, London EC4Y 7DR,
☎020 7353 4931 ✉clerks@6kbw.co.uk
Call Date: Nov 2000, Inner Temple
Qualifications: [LLB (Westminster)]

BELLIS MR WILLIAM GORDON

Number 7 Harrington Street Chambers
7 Harrington Street, Liverpool L2 9YH,
☎0151 242 0707 ✉clerks@7hs.co.uk
Call Date: July 1972, Inner Temple
Qualifications: [MA (Cantab)]
gordon.bellis@7hs.co.uk

BELOFF THE HON MICHAEL JACOB QC (1981)

Blackstone Chambers
Blackstone House, Temple, London EC4Y 9BW, ☎020 7583 1770
✉clerks@blackstonechambers.com
Call Date: Nov 1967, Gray's Inn
Recorder
Qualifications: [MA (Oxon) FICPD FRSA]
michaelbeloff@blackstonechambers.com

BELOFF MR RUPERT JOSEPH ALEXEI

No5 Chambers
Greenwood House, 4-7 Salisbury Court, London EC4Y 8AA, ☎0845 210 5555
No5 Chambers
38 Queen Square, Bristol BS1 4QS,
☎0845 210 5555
No5 Chambers
Fountain Court, Steelhouse Lane, Birmingham B4 6DR, ☎0845 210 5555 ✉info@no5.com
Call Date: Oct 2001, Gray's Inn
Qualifications: [LLB BA]
rjb@no5.com

BELTON MS CHLOE-JANE

Old Bailey Chambers
15 Old Bailey, London EC4M 7EF,
☎ 020 3008 6404
✉ clerks@15oldbaileychambers.com
Call Date: Mar 2008, Lincoln's Inn
Qualifications: [LLB (Leeds)]
✉ clerks@15oldbaileychambers.com

BELTRAMI MR ADRIAN JOSEPH QC (2008)

3 Verulam Buildings
London WC1R 5NT, ☎ 020 7831 8441
✉ chambers@3vb.com
Call Date: July 1989, Lincoln's Inn
Qualifications: [BA (Cantab) LLM (USA)]
✉ abeltrami@3vb.com

BELYAVIN MISS JULIA ROSE

St John's Chambers
101 Victoria Street, Bristol BS1 6PU,
☎ 0117 923 4700
✉ clerks@stjohnschambers.co.uk
Call Date: Mar 2003, Gray's Inn
Qualifications: [BA (Cantab)]
✉ julia.belyavin@stjohnschambers.co.uk

BENBOW MISS SARA ELIZABETH

Hardwicke
New Square, Lincoln's Inn, London
WC2A 3SB, ☎ 020 7242 2523
✉ enquiries@hardwicke.co.uk
Call Date: Nov 1990, Middle Temple
Pupil Supervisor
Qualifications: [LLB (Exon)]
✉ sara.benbow@hardwicke.co.uk

BENDALL MR RICHARD GILES

Furnival Chambers
32 Furnival Street, London EC4A 1JQ,
☎ 020 7405 3232
Call Date: July 1979, Lincoln's Inn
Pupil Supervisor
Qualifications: [LLB]

BENJAMIN MR DANIEL ROBERT

2 Dr Johnson's Buildings
2 Dr Johnson's Buildings, Temple, London
EC4Y 7AY, ☎ 020 7936 2613
✉ clerks@2drj.com
Call Date: July 2006, Middle Temple
Qualifications: [LLB (Hons) (Warw) LLM (Lond)]

BENLAMKADEM MISS FAYZA

Nine Bedford Row
9 Bedford Row, London WC1R 4AZ,
☎ 020 7489 2727
✉ clerks@9bedfordrow.co.uk
Call Date: Nov 2003, Middle Temple
Qualifications: [LLB (Hons) (Reading)]
✉ fayza.benlamkadem@9bedfordrow.co.uk

BENNATHAN MR JOEL NATHAN QC (2006)

Tooks Chambers
81 Farringdon Street, London EC4A 4BL,
☎ 020 7842 7575 ✉ clerks@tooks.co.uk
Call Date: Nov 1985, Middle Temple
Recorder
Qualifications: [LLB(Lond)]
✉ joel.bennathan@tooks.co.uk

BENNEH MISS ADELAIDE MAAME YAA AMMEAH

Renaissance Chambers
5th Floor, Gray's Inn Chambers, Gray's Inn,
London WC1R 5JA, ☎ 020 7404 1111
✉ clerks@renaissancechambers.co.uk
Call Date: Oct 2001, Lincoln's Inn
Qualifications: [LLB (Hons)(Manch)]
✉ ab@renaissancechambers.co.uk

BENNET MS PAULINE AGNES

Regency Chambers
45 Priestgate, Peterborough PE1 1LB,
☎ 01733 315215
✉ clerks@regencychambers.law.co.uk
Call Date: Oct 1991, Lincoln's Inn
Pupil Supervisor
Qualifications: [BSc (Hons) (Lond) BA (Lond)]
✉ pbennet@regencychambers.law.co.uk

BENNETT MISS ABIGAIL

Atlantic Chambers
4-6 Cook Street, Liverpool L2 9QU,
☎ 0151 236 4421
✉ info@atlanticchambers.co.uk
Call Date: Nov 1998, Middle Temple
Qualifications: [LLB (Hons)(Sheff)]
✉ info@atlanticchambers.co.uk

BENNETT MISS ANGELA MICHELLE

3 Dr Johnson's Buildings
Ground Floor, 3 Dr Johnson's Buildings,
Temple, London EC4Y 7BA, ☎ 020 7353 4854
✉ clerks@3djb.co.uk
Call Date: July 2005, Lincoln's Inn
Qualifications: [LLB (Hons)]
✉ ambennett@3djb.co.uk

BENNETT MR ANTHONY DANIEL

Doughty Street Chambers
53-54 Doughty Street, London WC1N 2LS, ☎020 7404 1313
✉enquiries@doughtystreet.co.uk
Doughty Street Chambers
Pall Mall Court, 61-67 King Street, Manchester M2 4PD, ☎0161 618 1066
Doughty Street Chambers
5th Floor, Broad Quay House, Prince Street, Bristol BS1 4DJ, ☎01179 058 717
Call Date: Nov 2000, Gray's Inn
Qualifications: [BA (Oxon) LLM (Warw)]
d.bennett@doughtystreet.co.uk

BENNETT MR CHARLES HENRY

Five St Andrew's Hill
5 St Andrew's Hill, London EC4V 5BZ, ☎020 7332 5400 ✉Clerks@5sah.co.uk
Call Date: July 1972, Inner Temple
Qualifications: [BA (Oxon)]
charlesbennett@5sah.co.uk

BENNETT MR DAVID

Hailsham Chambers
Ground Floor, 4 Paper Buildings, Temple, London EC4Y 7EX, ☎020 7643 5000
✉clerks@hailshamchambers.com
Call Date: Oct 2005, Middle Temple
Qualifications: [LLB (Hons)]
david.bennett@hailshamchambers.com

BENNETT MR DAVID LAURENCE

Liverpool Civil Law
3rd Floor, 1 Old Hall Street, Liverpool L3 9HF, ☎0151 242 0500
✉clerks@liverpoolcivillaw.com
Call Date: Nov 1977, Middle Temple
Pupil Supervisor
Qualifications: [BA (Hons)]

BENNETT MISS EMMA LOUISE

Exchange Chambers
Oxford House, Oxford Row, Leeds LS1 3BE, ☎0113 203 1970
✉spencer@exchangechambers.co.uk
Exchange Chambers
One Derby Square, Derby Square, Liverpool L2 9XX, ☎0151 236 7747
✉info@exchangechambers.co.uk
Exchange Chambers
7 Ralli Courts, West Riverside, Manchester M3 5FT, ☎0161 833 2722
Call Date: Oct 2004, Lincoln's Inn
Qualifications: [LLB (Hons) LLM]
bennett@exchangechambers.co.uk

BENNETT MR GORDON IRVINE

New Square Chambers
12 New Square, Lincoln's Inn, London WC2A 3SW, ☎020 7419 8000
✉robin.hollington@newsquarechambers.co.uk
Call Date: Feb 1974, Gray's Inn
Qualifications: [LLB (USA) Dip Int Law (Cantab) LLM (USA)]
gordon.bennett@newsquarechambers.co.uk

BENNETT MS HANNAH LUCY CHRISTINE

Old Square Chambers
10-11 Bedford Row, London WC1R 4BU, ☎020 7269 0300 ✉clerks@oldsquare.co.uk
Call Date: Oct 2010, Middle Temple
Qualifications: [MA (Cantab)]
hbennett@oldsquare.co.uk

BENNETT MR IEUAN GEREINT

9 Park Place
9 Park Place, Cardiff, South Glamorgan CF10 3DP, ☎029 2038 2731
✉clerks@9parkplace.co.uk
Call Date: July 1989, Middle Temple
Qualifications: [LLB (Wales) MA (Hull)]
ieuanandnia@bbmax.co.uk, clerks@9parkplace.co.uk

BENNETT MR JAMES PAUL DEAN

Guildhall Chambers
23 Broad Street, Bristol BS1 2HG, ☎0117 930 9000
✉hoc@guildhallchambers.co.uk
Call Date: Oct 2002, Inner Temple
Qualifications: [LLB]
james.bennett@guildhallchambers.co.uk

BENNETT MISS JANE SARAH ANN

Clerksroom (Taunton)
Equity House, Administration Centre, Blackbrook Park Avenue, Taunton, Somerset TA1 2PX, ☎0845 083 3000
✉mail@clerksroom.com
Clerksroom (London)
3rd Floor, 218 Strand, London WC2R 1AT, ☎0845 083 3000 ✉mail@clerksroom.com
King's Lynn Chambers
26 The Birches, South Wootton, King's Lynn, Norfolk PE30 3JG, ☎01553 672 085
✉timothy.leader@tesco.net
Call Date: July 2000, Middle Temple
Qualifications: [BA(Hons) (Cantab) MA (Hons) (Cantab)]

E

BENNETT MR JOHN MARTYN

Oriel Chambers
14 Water Street, Liverpool, Merseyside L2 8TD, ☎0151 236 7191
✉clerks@orielchambers.co.uk
Oriel Chambers
18 Ribblesdale Place, Preston PR1 3NA, ☎01772 254 764
✉clerks@oriel-chambers.co.uk
Call Date: July 1969, Gray's Inn
Pupil Supervisor
Qualifications: [LLB]
✉martyn.bennett@orielchambers.co.uk

BENNETT MR JONATHAN CHARLES LYDDON

42 Bedford Row
London WC1R 4LL, ☎020 7831 0222
✉clerks@42br.com
Call Date: July 1985, Gray's Inn
Pupil Supervisor
Qualifications: [MA (Cantab)]
✉jonathan.bennett@42br.com

BENNETT MR LEE

6 Pump Court
1st Floor, 6 Pump Court, Temple, London EC4Y 7AR, ☎020 7797 8400
✉richardconstable@6pumpcourt.co.uk
6 Pump Court Chambers
6-8 Mill Street, Maidstone, Kent ME15 6XH, ☎01622 688094
✉annexe@6pumpcourt.co.uk
Call Date: Nov 1998, Middle Temple
Qualifications: [LLB (Hons) LLM (Cantab)]
✉leebennett@6pumpcourt.co.uk

BENNETT MS MARIANNE LINDSAY

9 Park Place
9 Park Place, Cardiff, South Glamorgan CF10 3DP, ☎029 2038 2731
✉clerks@9parkplace.co.uk
Call Date: Oct 2003, Inner Temple
Qualifications: [LLB (Bris)]
✉mbennett@9parkplace.co.uk

BENNETT MR MILES ALEXANDER FORDHAM

Five Paper Buildings
1st Floor, Five Paper Buildings, Temple, London EC4Y 7HB, ☎020 7583 6117
✉clerks@5pb.co.uk
Call Date: Nov 1986, Inner Temple
Pupil Supervisor
Qualifications: [LLB (Hull)]
✉mb@5pb.co.uk

BENNETT MISS NATASHA AUDREY-MAY

Fountain Court Chambers
Fountain Court, Temple, London EC4Y 9DH, ☎020 7583 3335
✉chambers@fountaincourt.co.uk
Call Date: Oct 2009, Lincoln's Inn
Qualifications: [BA (Cantab) BCL (Oxon)]
✉nab@fountaincourt.co.uk

BENNETT MR RICHARD ANTHONY

Fountain Chambers
Cleveland Business Centre, 1 Watson Street, Middlesbrough TS1 2RQ, ☎01642 804040
✉clerks@fountainchambers.co.uk
Call Date: Oct 1996, Inner Temple
Pupil Supervisor
Qualifications: [BSc (Hons) (Newc) CPE]
✉rbennett@fountaincourt.co.uk

BENNETT MR RICHARD JOHN

15 Winckley Square
Preston PR1 3JJ, ☎01772 252828
✉clerks@15winckleysq.co.uk
Call Date: July 1986, Middle Temple
Qualifications: [LLB]

BENNETT MR WILLIAM

5RB
1st Floor, 5 Raymond Buildings, Gray's Inn, London WC1R 5BP, ☎020 7242 2902
✉clerks@5rb.com
Call Date: Oct 1994, Inner Temple
Pupil Supervisor
Qualifications: [BA (L'pool) CPE]
✉williambennett@5rb.com

BENNETT-JENKINS MISS SALLIE ANN QC (2006)

2 Hare Court
Lower Ground, Ground, 1st & 2nd Floor, 2 Hare Court, Temple, London EC4Y 7BH, ☎020 7353 3982 ✉clerks@2harecourt.com
Call Date: July 1984, Gray's Inn
Recorder
Qualifications: [LLB (Hons)(Lond)]
✉salliebennett-jenkins@2harecourt.com

BENNINGTON MS JANE SUSAN

Fenners Chambers
3 Madingley Road, Cambridge CB3 0EE, ☎01223 368761
✉clerks@fennerschambers.com
Call Date: July 1981, Gray's Inn
Qualifications: [BA Hons]
✉jane.bennington@fennerschambers.com

BENNION-PEDLEY MR EDWARD

13 King's Bench Walk
13 King's Bench Walk, Temple, London EC4Y 7EN, ☎ 020 7353 7204
✉ clerks@13kbw.co.uk
13 KBW
32 Beaumont Street, Oxford OX1 2NP, ☎ 01865 311066 ✉ clerks@13kbw.co.uk
Call Date: Nov 2004, Middle Temple
Qualifications: [BSc (Hons) Dip in Law]
ebennion-pedley@13kbw.co.uk

BENSON MISS CLARE PHYLLIS

Broadway House Chambers
Broadway House, 9 Bank Street, Bradford, West Yorkshire BD1 1TW, ☎ 01274 722560
✉ clerks@broadwayhouse.co.uk
Call Date: July 2009, Lincoln's Inn
Qualifications: [BA (Cantab) CPE OBPP]
cb@broadwayhouse.co.uk

BENSON MR IMRAN MICHAEL JAFAREY

Hailsham Chambers
Ground Floor, 4 Paper Buildings, Temple, London EC4Y 7EX, ☎ 020 7643 5000
✉ clerks@hailshamchambers.com
Call Date: Oct 2005, Middle Temple
Qualifications: [LLB (Hons) (Bris)]
imran.benson@hailshamchambers.com

BENSON MR JAMES D'ARCY

Oriel Chambers
14 Water Street, Liverpool, Merseyside L2 8TD, ☎ 0151 236 7191
✉ clerks@orielchambers.co.uk
Oriel Chambers
18 Ribblesdale Place, Preston PR1 3NA, ☎ 01772 254 764
✉ clerks@oriel-chambers.co.uk
Call Date: Nov 1995, Gray's Inn
Qualifications: [BA]
james.benson@orielchambers.co.uk

BENSON MR JAMES EDWARD ERIC

Blackfriars Chambers
79-83 Temple Chambers, 3-7 Temple Avenue, London EC4Y 0HP, ☎ 020 7353 7400
✉ clerks@blackfriarschambers.com
Call Date: Nov 2001, Lincoln's Inn
Pupil Supervisor
Qualifications: [LLB (Hons)(Sussex)]
james.benson@blackfriarschambers.com

BENSON MR JEREMY KEITH QC (2001)

18 Red Lion Court
London EC4A 3EB, ☎ 020 7520 6000
✉ chambers@18rlc.co.uk
Call Date: July 1978, Middle Temple
Recorder
Qualifications: [BA]
jeremy.benson@18rlc.co.uk

BENSON MR JOHN TREVOR QC (2001)

Atlantic Chambers
4-6 Cook Street, Liverpool L2 9QU, ☎ 0151 236 4421
✉ info@atlanticchambers.co.uk
1 Mitre Court Buildings
1 Mitre Court Buildings, Temple, London EC4Y 7BS, ☎ 020 7452 8900
✉ clerks@1mcb.com
Call Date: July 1978, Middle Temple
Recorder
Qualifications: [LLB (Hons) (L'pool)]
johnbenson@atlanticchambers.co.uk

BENSON MR JULIAN CHRISTOPHER WOODBURN

Guildhall Chambers
23 Broad Street, Bristol BS1 2HG, ☎ 0117 930 9000
✉ hoc@guildhallchambers.co.uk
Call Date: Nov 1991, Middle Temple
Pupil Supervisor
Qualifications: [BA (Hons) (Dunelm) BA (Hons) LLM (Cantab)]
julian.benson@guildhallchambers.co.uk

BENSON MR RICHARD ANTHONY QC (1995)

Citadel Chambers
The Citadel, 190 Corporation Street, Birmingham B4 6QD, ☎ 0121 233 8500
✉ clerks@citadelchambers.com
Call Date: July 1974, Inner Temple
Recorder
rabqc@btopenworld.com

BENTHALL MR DOMINIC GABRIEL MENUHIN

15 New Bridge Street
London EC4V 6AU, ☎ 020 7842 1900
✉ clerks@15nbs.com
Call Date: Nov 2002, Middle Temple
Qualifications: [MA (Edin) CPE]
dominic.benthall@15nbs.com

E

BENTHAM MR DANIEL MARK

Queen Elizabeth Building
3rd Floor, Queen Elizabeth Building, Temple, London EC4Y 9BS, ☎ 020 7797 7837
✉ clerks@qeb.co.uk
Call Date: Nov 2000, Middle Temple
Pupil Supervisor
Qualifications: [BA (Hons) (Oxon)]
✉ d.bentham@qeb.co.uk

BENTLEY MISS ANNA LOUISE

Deans Court Chambers
24 St John Street, Manchester M3 4DF, ☎ 0161 214 6000 ✉ clerks@deanscourt.co.uk
Deans Court Chambers
101 Walker Street, Preston PR1 2RR, ☎ 01772 565 600
✉ preston@deanscourt.co.uk
Call Date: July 2004, Middle Temple
Qualifications: [MA (Cantab)]
✉ bentley@deanscourt.co.uk

BENTLEY MR ANTHONY PHILIP QC (1991)

Henderson Chambers
2 Harcourt Buildings, Temple, London EC4Y 9DB, ☎ 020 7583 9020
✉ clerks@hendersonchambers.co.uk
Call Date: Nov 1970, Lincoln's Inn
✉ pbentley@europe.mwe.com

BENTLEY MR DAVID NEIL

Doughty Street Chambers
53-54 Doughty Street, London WC1N 2LS, ☎ 020 7404 1313
✉ enquiries@doughtystreet.co.uk
Doughty Street Chambers
Pall Mall Court, 61-67 King Street, Manchester M2 4PD, ☎ 0161 618 1066
Doughty Street Chambers
5th Floor, Broad Quay House, Prince Street, Bristol BS1 4DJ, ☎ 01179 058 717
Call Date: Feb 1984, Gray's Inn
Pupil Supervisor
Qualifications: [LLB (Lond)]
✉ d.bentley@doughtystreet.co.uk

BENTLEY MR DAVID PAUL

St Johns Buildings
24a - 28 St John Street, Manchester M3 4DJ, ☎ 0161 214 1500
✉ clerk@stjohnsbuildings.co.uk
St Johns Buildings
21 White Friars, Chester CH1 1NZ, ☎ 01244 323070
✉ clerk@stjohnsbuildings.co.uk
16 Winckley Square
Preston PR1 3JJ, ☎ 01772 256100
Call Date: Oct 1998, Lincoln's Inn
Qualifications: [LLB (Hons)(Notts)]
✉ clerk@stjohnsbuildings.co.uk, david.bentley@stjohnsbuildings.co.uk

BENTLEY MR HARRY JOSEPH

Nine Bedford Row
9 Bedford Row, London WC1R 4AZ, ☎ 020 7489 2727
✉ clerks@9bedfordrow.co.uk
Call Date: July 2007, Middle Temple
Qualifications: [LLB (Hons)]
✉ harry.bentley@9bedfordrow.co.uk

BENTLY PROF LIONEL ALEXANDER FIENNES

11 South Square
1st Floor, 11 South Square, Gray's Inn, London WC1R 5EY, ☎ 020 7405 1222
✉ clerks@11southsquare.com
Call Date: Nov 2009, Inner Temple
Qualifications: [BA (Cantab)]

BENTWOOD MR RICHARD

Argent Chambers
5 Bell Yard, London WC2A 2JR, ☎ 020 7556 5500
✉ briefsin@argentchambers.co.uk
Call Date: Nov 1994, Inner Temple
Qualifications: [LLB (Notts)]
✉ r.bentwood@argentchambers.co.uk

BENYOUNES MISS LEILA INGRID

Park Lane Plowden
19 Westgate, Leeds LS1 2RD, ☎ 0113 228 5049
✉ clerks@parklaneplowden.co.uk
Call Date: Oct 2005, Lincoln's Inn
Qualifications: [BA (Hons) (Leeds) PgDl (Manch)]
✉ leila.benyounes@parklaneplowden.co.uk

BENZIE MR STUART MITCHELL

2 Temple Gardens
2 Temple Gardens, Temple, London EC4Y 9AY, ☎ 020 7822 1200
✉ clerks@2tg.co.uk
Call Date: Nov 2002, Gray's Inn
Pupil Supervisor
Qualifications: [LLB (Lond)]
✉ sbenzie@2tg.co.uk

BENZYNIE MR ROBERT JOSEPH

Charter Chambers
33 John Street, London WC1N 2AT,
☎ 020 7618 4400
✉ clerks@charterchambers.com
Call Date: Nov 1992, Gray's Inn
Qualifications: [LLB (Bucks)]
robert.benzynie@charterchambers.com

BERESFORD MR STEPHEN ROGER

Ropewalk Chambers
24 The Ropewalk, Nottingham NG1 5EF,
☎ 0115 947 2581 ✉ clerks@ropewalk.co.uk
Call Date: July 1976, Gray's Inn
Pupil Supervisor
Qualifications: [LLB (B'ham)]

BERGENTHAL MR RONNIE MARK

Old Bailey Chambers
15 Old Bailey, London EC4M 7EF,
☎ 020 3008 6404
✉ clerks@15oldbaileychambers.com
Call Date: Oct 1993, Middle Temple
Pupil Supervisor
Qualifications: [LLB (Hons)]

BERGIN MR TERENCE EDWARD

4 Pump Court
4 Pump Court, Temple, London EC4Y 7AN,
☎ 020 7842 5555
✉ chambers@4pumpcourt.com
Call Date: Nov 1985, Inner Temple
Pupil Supervisor
Qualifications: [BA(Cantab)]
Tbergin@4pumpcourt.com

BERGIN MR TIMOTHY WILLIAM

1 Crown Office Row
1 Crown Office Row, Temple, London
EC4Y 7HH, ☎ 020 7797 7500
✉ mail@1cor.com
Crown Office Row Chambers
119 Church Street, Brighton, Sussex
BN1 1UD, ☎ 01273 625625
✉ clerks@1cor.com
Call Date: July 1987, Middle Temple
Pupil Supervisor
Qualifications: [LLB M Phil (Exon)]
timothy.bergin@1cor.com

BERKELEY MISS IONA SARAH CAROLINE

8 New Square
8 New Square, Lincoln's Inn, London
WC2A 3QP, ☎ 020 7405 4321
✉ clerks@8newsquare.co.uk
Call Date: Oct 1999, Middle Temple
Pupil Supervisor
Qualifications: [MA (Hons) (Oxon)]
iona.berkeley@8newsquare.co.uk

Types of work: Breach of confidence, Confidential information, Copyright, Design, Entertainment, Information technology, Intellectual property, Patents, Registered designs, Trademarks

BERKIN MR MARTYN DAVID MAURICE

Crown Office Chambers
2 Crown Office Row, Temple, London
EC4Y 7HJ, ☎ 020 7797 8100
✉ mail@crownofficechambers.com
Call Date: July 1966, Inner Temple
Pupil Supervisor
Qualifications: [MA (Cantab)]
berkin@crownofficechambers.com

BERKLEY MR DAVID NAHUM QC (1999)

1 Gray's Inn Square
Ground Floor, 1 Gray's Inn Square, London
WC1R 5AA, ☎ 020 7405 0001
St Johns Buildings
24a - 28 St John Street, Manchester M3 4DJ,
☎ 0161 214 1500
✉ clerk@stjohnsbuildings.co.uk
St Johns Buildings Liverpool
8th Floor India Buildings, Water Street,
Liverpool L2 0XG, ☎ 0151 243 6000
✉ clerk@stjohnsbuildings.co.uk
St Johns Buildings
21 White Friars, Chester CH1 1NZ,
☎ 01244 323070
✉ clerk@stjohnsbuildings.co.uk
Call Date: May 1979, Middle Temple
Recorder
Qualifications: [LLB (Manch)]
davidberkley@mal.com

E

BERKLEY MR MICHAEL STUART

Rougemont Chambers
Victory House, Dean Clarke Gardens, Southernhay East, Exeter EX2 4AA, ☎01392 208484
✉clerks@rougemontchambers.co.uk
Call Date: July 1989, Middle Temple
Pupil Supervisor, Recorder
Qualifications: [LLB (Hons), Appointed: Civil-only Recorder 2010]
✉mberkley@rougemontchambers.co.uk

Fax: 01392 208204;
DX: 8396 Exeter 1;
URL: www.rougemontchambers.co.uk

Types of work: Chancery (general), Chancery (land law), Commercial litigation, Commercial property, Common law (general), Equity, Landlord and tenant, Partnerships, Professional negligence, Succession, Trusts, Wills

BERKSON MR SIMON NATHANIEL

Exchange Chambers
One Derby Square, Derby Square, Liverpool L2 9XX, ☎0151 236 7747
✉info@exchangechambers.co.uk
Exchange Chambers
7 Ralli Courts, West Riverside, Manchester M3 5FT, ☎0161 833 2722
Exchange Chambers
Oxford House, Oxford Row, Leeds LS1 3BE, ☎0113 203 1970
✉spencer@exchangechambers.co.uk
Call Date: July 1986, Gray's Inn
Pupil Supervisor
Qualifications: [LLB]
✉berkson@exchangechambers.co.uk

BERLEVY MR KRISTON

Dyers Chambers
35 Bedford Row, London WC1R 4JH, ☎020 7404 1881
✉admin@dyerschambers.com
Call Date: July 2002, Lincoln's Inn
Qualifications: [LLB (Hons) 1st Class]
✉kberlevy@yahoo.com

BERLIN MR BARRY ADRIAN

St Philips Chambers
55 Temple Row, Birmingham B2 5LS, ☎0121 246 7000 ✉clerks@st-philips.com
Call Date: July 1981, Gray's Inn
Pupil Supervisor, Recorder
Qualifications: [BSc (Hons)]
✉bberlin@st-philips.com

BERMAN SIR FRANKLIN DELOW QC (1992)

Essex Court Chambers
24 Lincoln's Inn Fields, London WC2A 3EG, ☎020 7813 8000
✉clerksroom@essexcourt.net
Call Date: Nov 1966, Middle Temple
Qualifications: [MA (Oxon) BA (South Africa) BSc (South Africa)]
✉fberman@essexcourt.net

BERMINGHAM MR GERALD EDWARD

No5 Chambers
Fountain Court, Steelhouse Lane, Birmingham B4 6DR, ☎0845 210 5555 ✉info@no5.com
No5 Chambers
Greenwood House, 4-7 Salisbury Court, London EC4Y 8AA, ☎0845 210 5555
No5 Chambers
38 Queen Square, Bristol BS1 4QS, ☎0845 210 5555
Call Date: Feb 1985, Gray's Inn
Pupil Supervisor
Qualifications: [LLB (Hons)(Sheff)]
✉geb@no5.com

BERRAGAN MR NEIL

Kings Chambers
36 Young Street, Manchester M3 3FT, ☎0845 034 3444
✉clerks@kingschambers.com
Kings Chambers
5 Park Square East, Leeds LS1 2NE, ☎0845 034 3444
✉clerks@kingschambers.com
Kings Chambers
Embassy House, 60 Church Street, Birmingham B3 2DJ, ☎0845 034 3444
✉clerks@kingschambers.com
Call Date: July 1982, Gray's Inn
Pupil Supervisor
Qualifications: [MA (Oxon)]
✉nberragan@kingschambers.com

BERRIDGE MS ALISON ROSE

Monckton Chambers
1 & 2 Raymond Buildings, Gray's Inn, London WC1R 5NR, ☎020 7405 7211
✉chambers@monckton.com
Call Date: July 2011, Gray's Inn
✉aberridge@monckton.com

BERRIMAN MR TREVOR ST JOHN

43 Temple Row Chambers
6th Floor, 43 Temple Row, Birmingham B2 5LS, ☎ 0121 237 6035
✉ clerks@43templerow.co.uk
Call Date: Nov 1988, Inner Temple
Pupil Supervisor
Qualifications: [LLB (Hons)]
✉ clerks@43templerow.co.uk

BERRY MR ADRIAN CHRISTOPHER

Garden Court Chambers
57-60 Lincoln's Inn Fields, London WC2A 3LJ, ☎ 020 7993 7600 ✉ info@gclaw.co.uk
Call Date: Oct 1998, Inner Temple
Qualifications: [MA CPE]
✉ adrianb@gclaw.co.uk

BERRY MISS AMY MADELAINE

Pump Court Chambers
Upper Ground Floor, 3 Pump Court, Temple, London EC4Y 7AJ, ☎ 020 7353 0711
✉ clerks@3pumpcourt.com
Pump Court Chambers
5 Temple Chambers, Temple Street, Swindon SN1 1SQ, ☎ 01793 539899
✉ clerks@3pumpcourt.com
Pump Court Chambers
31 Southgate Street, Winchester, Hampshire SO23 9EB, ☎ 01962 868 161
✉ clerks@3pumpcourt.com
Call Date: July 2003, Lincoln's Inn
Qualifications: [LLB Hons]

BERRY MR ANTHONY CHARLES QC (1994)

Nine Bedford Row
9 Bedford Row, London WC1R 4AZ,
☎ 020 7489 2727
✉ clerks@9bedfordrow.co.uk
Number 7 Harrington Street Chambers
7 Harrington Street, Liverpool L2 9YH,
☎ 0151 242 0707 ✉ clerks@7hs.co.uk
Call Date: July 1976, Gray's Inn
Qualifications: [BA (Oxon)]
✉ anthony.berryqc@9bedfordrow.co.uk

BERRY MR KARL DEREK

Oriel Chambers
14 Water Street, Liverpool, Merseyside L2 8TD, ☎ 0151 236 7191
✉ clerks@orielchambers.co.uk
Oriel Chambers
18 Ribblesdale Place, Preston PR1 3NA,
☎ 01772 254 764
✉ clerks@oriel-chambers.co.uk
Call Date: Nov 1999, Middle Temple
Qualifications: [BA (Lond)]
✉ karl.berry@orielchambers.co.uk

BERRY MR MICHAEL JAMES ELLWOOD

3 Serjeants Inn
London EC4Y 1BQ, ☎ 020 7427 5000
✉ clerks@3serjeantsinn.com
Call Date: July 2006, Lincoln's Inn
Qualifications: [LLB (Lond) LLM (Harvard)]
✉ jberry@3serjeantsinn.com

BERRY MR NICHOLAS

Citadel Chambers
The Citadel, 190 Corporation Street, Birmingham B4 6QD, ☎ 0121 233 8500
✉ clerks@citadelchambers.com
Call Date: Oct 2004, Lincoln's Inn
Qualifications: [LLB (Hons) LLM]
✉ clerks@citadelchambers.com

BERRY MR NICHOLAS MICHAEL

Rougemont Chambers
Victory House, Dean Clarke Gardens, Southernhay East, Exeter EX2 4AA,
☎ 01392 208484
✉ clerks@rougemontchambers.co.uk
Call Date: Nov 1988, Inner Temple
Pupil Supervisor
Qualifications: [BA (Hons)]
✉ nberry@rougemontchambers.co.uk

BERRY MR STEVEN JOHN QC (2002)

Essex Court Chambers
24 Lincoln's Inn Fields, London WC2A 3EG,
☎ 020 7813 8000
✉ clerksroom@essexcourt.net
Call Date: Nov 1984, Middle Temple
Qualifications: [BA BCL (Oxon)]
✉ sberry@essexcourt.net

BERTHAM MR ANTHONY CHRISTOPHER

3 Temple Gardens
Lower Ground Floor, 3 Temple Gardens, Temple, London EC4Y 9AU, ☎ 020 7353 3102
✉ clerks@3tg.co.uk
Call Date: Oct 1993, Lincoln's Inn
Qualifications: [LLB (Hons) LLM (Cantab)]

BERTHELSEN MISS ELEONORE DIANE OHSAN

Atlantic Chambers
4-6 Cook Street, Liverpool L2 9QU,
☎ 0151 236 4421
✉ info@atlanticchambers.co.uk
Call Date: Mar 2009, Middle Temple
Qualifications: [BA (Hons) (Cantab) CPE]
✉ eleonreberthelsen@atlanticchambers.co.uk

E

BERTRAM MR JONATHAN PETER

Seven Bedford Row
7 Bedford Row, London WC1R 4BS, ☎ 020 7242 3555 ✉ clerks@7br.co.uk
Call Date: Oct 2003, Lincoln's Inn
Qualifications: [LLB (Hons) (Sheff) LLM (Nott'm)]

BEST MR STANLEY PHILIP

Barnstaple Chambers
Glebe Cottage, Broadwoodkelly, Winkleigh, Devon EX19 8ED, ☎ 01837 83763
Chambers of Nigel Ley
23 Vale Farm Road, Woking, Surrey GU21 6DE, ☎ 07947 221077
Call Date: July 1989, Middle Temple

BESWETHERICK MR ANTHONY ZAID

Enterprise Chambers
9 Old Square, Lincoln's Inn, London WC2A 3SR, ☎ 020 7405 9471
✉ london@enterprisechambers.com
Enterprise Chambers
65 Quayside, Newcastle Upon Tyne NE1 3DE, ☎ 0191 222 3344
✉ newcastle@enterprisechambers.com
Enterprise Chambers
43 Park Square, Leeds LS1 2NP, ☎ 0113 246 0391
✉ leeds@enterprisechambers.com
Call Date: Mar 2003, Lincoln's Inn
Qualifications: [BA (Hons) (Oxon) PgDl]
🖃 tonybeswtherick@enterprisechambers.com

BESWICK MISS KIRSTIN WENDY

Central Chambers
89 Princess Street, Manchester M1 4HT, ☎ 0161 236 1133
✉ clerks@centralchambers.co.uk
Call Date: Oct 2001, Middle Temple
Qualifications: [BSc (Hons) Dip Law]

BETHEL MR MARTIN QC (1983)

St Paul's Chambers
5th Floor, St Paul's House, 23 Park Square South, Leeds LS1 2ND, ☎ 0113 245 5866
Fountain Chambers
Cleveland Business Centre, 1 Watson Street, Middlesbrough TS1 2RQ, ☎ 01642 804040
✉ clerks@fountainchambers.co.uk
Call Date: Nov 1965, Inner Temple
Recorder
Qualifications: [MA (Cantab) LLM (Cantab)]
🖃 mb@stpaulschambers.com

BETHLEHEM MR DANIEL LINCOLN QC (2003)

20 Essex Street
London WC2R 3AL, ☎ 020 7842 1200
✉ clerks@20essexst.com
Call Date: Nov 1988, Middle Temple
Qualifications: [BA (South Africa) LLB (Bris) LLM (Cantab)]

BETTLE MRS JANET ROSEMARY

East Anglian Chambers
53 North Hill, Colchester, Essex CO1 1QA, ☎ 01473 214481 ✉ colchester@ealaw.co.uk
East Anglian Chambers
140 New London Road, Chelmsford, Essex CM2 0AW, ☎ 01473 214481
✉ chelmsford@ealaw.co.uk
East Anglian Chambers
15 The Close, Norwich, Norfolk NR1 4DZ, ☎ 01473 214481 ✉ norwich@ealaw.co.uk
East Anglian Chambers
Gresham House, 5 Museum Street, Ipswich, Suffolk IP1 1HQ, ☎ 01473 214481
✉ ipswich@ealaw.co.uk
Call Date: July 1985, Inner Temple
Pupil Supervisor
Qualifications: [LLB (London)]
🖃 janetbettle@ealaw.co.uk

BETTS MISS EMILY CLARE

Hardwicke
New Square, Lincoln's Inn, London WC2A 3SB, ☎ 020 7242 2523
✉ enquiries@hardwicke.co.uk
Call Date: July 2009, Middle Temple
Qualifications: [BSc (Hons) (Lond)]

BETTS MR STEPHEN

Chambers of Mr S Betts
Sundern, 8 Southview Road, Marlow, Buckinghamshire SL7 3JP, ☎ 07739 892093
✉ admin@cslassociates.co.uk
Call Date: Nov 2008, Lincoln's Inn
Qualifications: [CPE LPC]
🖃 stephenbetts@btinternet.com

BEVAN MR CHRISTOPHER WILLIAM

KCH Garden Square
1 Oxford Street, Nottingham NG1 5BH, ☎ 0115 941 8851
✉ clerks@kchgardensquare.co.uk
Call Date: July 2009, Middle Temple
Qualifications: [BA (Hons) (Cantab)]
🖃 cwb@kch.co.uk

BEVAN MISS MIRANDA JANE

2 Hare Court
Lower Ground, Ground, 1st & 2nd Floor, 2 Hare Court, Temple, London EC4Y 7BH, ☎020 7353 3982 ✉clerks@2harecourt.com
Call Date: Oct 2000, Inner Temple
Qualifications: [BA (Oxon) CPE]
✉mirandabevan@2harecourt.com

BEWLEY MISS AMANDA JANE

St Mary's Family Law Chambers
26-28 High Pavement, The Lace Market, Nottingham NG1 1HN, ☎0115 950 3503
✉clerks@stmarysflc.co.uk
Call Date: Oct 2005, Inner Temple
Qualifications: [LLB University of Liverpool]

BEWLEY MR JAMES TIMOTHY

187 Fleet Street
London EC4A 2AT, ☎020 7430 7430
✉chambers@187fleetstreet.com
Call Date: July 2007, Lincoln's Inn
Qualifications: [BA (Cantab)]
✉jamesbewley@187fleetstreet.com

BEWLEY MISS SUHAYLA

East Anglian Chambers
53 North Hill, Colchester, Essex CO1 1QA, ☎01473 214481 ✉colchester@ealaw.co.uk
East Anglian Chambers
Gresham House, 5 Museum Street, Ipswich, Suffolk IP1 1HQ, ☎01473 214481
✉ipswich@ealaw.co.uk
East Anglian Chambers
140 New London Road, Chelmsford, Essex CM2 0AW, ☎01473 214481
✉chelmsford@ealaw.co.uk
Call Date: July 2007, Lincoln's Inn
Qualifications: [LLB]

BEWSEY MISS JANE QC (2010)

18 Red Lion Court
London EC4A 3EB, ☎020 7520 6000
✉chambers@18rlc.co.uk
18 Red Lion Court (Annexe)
Thornwood House, 102 New London Road, Chelmsford, Essex CM2 0RG,
☎01245 280880
Call Date: July 1986, Inner Temple
Pupil Supervisor
Qualifications: [MA (Cantab)]
✉jane.bewsey@18rlc.co.uk

BEX MISS KATE

2 Hare Court
Lower Ground, Ground, 1st & 2nd Floor, 2 Hare Court, Temple, London EC4Y 7BH, ☎020 7353 3982 ✉clerks@2harecourt.com
Call Date: Nov 1992, Inner Temple
Pupil Supervisor
Qualifications: [BA (Hons)]
✉katebex@2harecourt.com

BEXSON MISS CATHERINE HELEN

1 Gray's Inn Square
Ground Floor, 1 Gray's Inn Square, London WC1R 5AA, ☎020 7405 0001
Call Date: Oct 1999, Inner Temple
Qualifications: [LLB (Lond) MPhil (Cantab)]
✉cbexson@hotmail.com

BEYNON MR RICHARD JOHN LLEWELLYN

18 Red Lion Court
London EC4A 3EB, ☎020 7520 6000
✉chambers@18rlc.co.uk
Call Date: Oct 1990, Inner Temple
Pupil Supervisor
Qualifications: [LLB]

BEYTS MR CHESTER ANDOE MICHAEL

25 Bedford Row
London WC1R 4HD, ☎020 7067 1500
✉clerks@25bedfordrow.com
Call Date: Nov 1978, Inner Temple
Pupil Supervisor
Qualifications: [BA (Hons) (Lond)]
✉cbeyts@25bedfordrow.com

BEZZAM MISS JAYASHREE

Hampton Court Chambers
28 Bedster Gardens, Hurst Park, West Molesey, Surrey KT8 1SZ, ☎020 8979 0381
Call Date: July 1997, Lincoln's Inn
Qualifications: [BSc BL ML]

BHACHU MISS SHARANJEET KAUR

4 Brick Court
4 Brick Court, Temple, London EC4Y 9AD, ☎020 7832 3200 ✉clerks@4bc.co.uk
Call Date: Mar 1999, Lincoln's Inn
Qualifications: [LLB (Hons)]
✉sharan.bhachu@4bc.co.uk

E

BHAKAR MR SURINDER SINGH

4 King's Bench Walk
2nd Floor, 4 King's Bench Walk, Temple, London EC4Y 7DL, ☎ 020 7822 7000
✉ clerks@4kbw.co.uk
Call Date: Nov 1986, Gray's Inn
Qualifications: [LLB (Lond) LLM (Cantab)]
✉ ssb@4kbw.co.uk

BHALOO MISS ZIA KURBAN QC (2010)

Enterprise Chambers
9 Old Square, Lincoln's Inn, London WC2A 3SR, ☎ 020 7405 9471
✉ london@enterprisechambers.com
Enterprise Chambers
65 Quayside, Newcastle Upon Tyne NE1 3DE, ☎ 0191 222 3344
✉ newcastle@enterprisechambers.com
Enterprise Chambers
43 Park Square, Leeds LS1 2NP, ☎ 0113 246 0391
✉ leeds@enterprisechambers.com
Call Date: Nov 1990, Middle Temple
Pupil Supervisor
Qualifications: [LLB (Lond) LLM (Lond)]
✉ ziabhaloo@enterprisechambers.com

BHANJI MR SHIRAZ MUSA

1 Gray's Inn Square
Ground Floor, 1 Gray's Inn Square, London WC1R 5AA, ☎ 020 7405 0001
4 Bingham Place
London W1U 5AT, ☎ 020 7486 5347
✉ bhanji@regencyhotelwestend.co.uk
Call Date: July 1979, Gray's Inn
Qualifications: [CPE BSc (Wales)]
✉ clerks@1gis.co.uk

BHARDWAJ MISS UMA

Staple Inn Chambers
1st Floor, 9 Staple Inn, Holborn Bars, London WC1V 7QH, ☎ 020 7242 5240
✉ clerks@stapleinn.co.uk
Call Date: Nov 1984, Middle Temple
Qualifications: [LLB (Lond)]
✉ ub@stapleinn.co.uk

BHARI MISS POONAM

14 Gray's Inn Square
14 Gray's Inn Square, Gray's Inn, London WC1R 5JP, ☎ 020 7242 0858
✉ clerks@14gis.co.uk
Call Date: Nov 1999, Middle Temple
Qualifications: [BEd (Hons) MA (Lond)]
✉ clerks@14graysinnsquare.co.uk

BHAT MISS SAIMA

15 Winckley Square
Preston PR1 3JJ, ☎ 01772 252828
✉ clerks@15winckleysq.co.uk
Call Date: July 1999, Middle Temple
Qualifications: [LLB (Hons)(Bris) LLM (Bristol)]

BHATIA MR BALRAJ SINGH

1 High Pavement
Nottingham NG1 1HF, ☎ 0115 941 8218
✉ clerks@1highpavement.co.uk
Call Date: Nov 1982, Inner Temple
Pupil Supervisor
Qualifications: [LLB]
✉ balrajbhatia@1highpavement.co.uk

BHATIA MISS DIVYA

Coram Chambers
9-11 Fulwood Place, London WC1V 6HG, ☎ 020 7092 3700
✉ mail@coramchambers.co.uk
Call Date: July 1986, Middle Temple
Qualifications: [MA (Oxon)]
✉ divya.bhatia@coramchambers.co.uk

BHATT MISS UNNATI

Great James Street Chambers
37 Great James Street, London WC1N 3HB, ☎ 020 7440 4949
✉ chambers@greatjames.co.uk
Call Date: Oct 2007, Middle Temple
Qualifications: [LLB (Hons) (Warw)]

BHATTACHARYYA MR ARDHENDU

Slough Barristers Chamber
11 St. Bernards Road, Slough, Berkshire SL3 7NT, ☎ 01753 553806
✉ arden_bhattacharya2000@yahoo.co.uk
Call Date: Nov 1974, Inner Temple
Qualifications: [BA MCIArb SPC ADR Dip CL FCIS FCMI]

BHATTI MISS BALVINDER

Citadel Chambers
The Citadel, 190 Corporation Street, Birmingham B4 6QD, ☎ 0121 233 8500
✉ clerks@citadelchambers.com
Call Date: Oct 2003, Lincoln's Inn
Qualifications: [LLB (Hons) (Wolves)]

BHATTY MISS FARAH NAJEEB

Bank House Chambers
Old Bank House, Hartshead, Sheffield S1 2EL, ☎ 0114 275 1223
✉ w.digby@bankhousechambers.co.uk
Call Date: July 2005, Lincoln's Inn
Qualifications: [LLB (Hons)]
✉ f.bhatty@bankhousechambers.co.uk

BHOGAL MISS KULJIT KAUR

Cornerstone Barristers
2-3 Gray's Inn Square, Gray's Inn, London WC1R 5JH, ☎ 020 7242 4986
✉ chambers@2-3gis.co.uk
Call Date: Oct 1998, Lincoln's Inn
Qualifications: [LLB (Hons)(Lond)]

BHOSE MR RANJIT QC (2012)

Cornerstone Barristers
2-3 Gray's Inn Square, Gray's Inn, London WC1R 5JH, ☎ 020 7242 4986
✉ chambers@2-3gis.co.uk
Call Date: Nov 1989, Gray's Inn
Pupil Supervisor
Qualifications: [BA (Oxon)]
✉ rbhose@2-3gis.co.uk

BHULLAR MR GURPREET SINGH

Staple Inn Chambers
1st Floor, 9 Staple Inn, Holborn Bars, London WC1V 7QH, ☎ 020 7242 5240
✉ clerks@stapleinn.co.uk
Call Date: July 2008, Lincoln's Inn
Qualifications: [BSc (Lond)]

BHUTTA MISS AYEESHA CLARE

Field Court Chambers
5 Field Court, Gray's Inn, London WC1R 5EF, ☎ 020 7405 6114 ✉ clerks@fieldcourt.co.uk
Call Date: Oct 2006, Middle Temple
Qualifications: [BA (Hons) PgDL]
✉ ayeesha.bhutta@fieldcourt.co.uk

BICARREGUI MISS ANNA CLAIRE VICTORIA

4-5 Gray's Inn Square
Gray's Inn, London WC1R 5AH, ☎ 020 7404 5252 ✉ clerks@4-5.co.uk
Call Date: July 2004, Lincoln's Inn
Qualifications: [BA Hons (Oxon)]
✉ abicarregui@4-5.co.uk

BICKERDIKE MR ROGER JOHN

Zenith Chambers
10 Park Square, Leeds LS1 2LH, ☎ 0113 245 5438
✉ clerks@zenithchambers.co.uk
Call Date: Nov 1986, Lincoln's Inn
Qualifications: [LLB (Notts)]
✉ rbickerdike@zenithchambers.co.uk

BICKERSTAFF MISS DEBORAH JANE QC (2012)

Nine Bedford Row
9 Bedford Row, London WC1R 4AZ, ☎ 020 7489 2727
✉ clerks@9bedfordrow.co.uk
Call Date: Nov 1989, Inner Temple
Pupil Supervisor
Qualifications: [LLB (Manch)]
✉ jane.bickerstaff@9bedfordrow.co.uk

BICKFORD-SMITH DR JAMES WILLIAM

Littleton Chambers
3 King's Bench Walk North, Temple, London EC4Y 7HR, ☎ 020 7797 8600
✉ fschneider@littletonchambers.co.uk
Call Date: Oct 2008, Lincoln's Inn
Qualifications: [BA (Oxon)]
✉ jbs@littletonchambers.co.uk

BICKFORD-SMITH MRS MARGARET OSBORNE QC (2003)

Crown Office Chambers
2 Crown Office Row, Temple, London EC4Y 7HJ, ☎ 020 7797 8100
✉ mail@crownofficechambers.com
Call Date: July 1973, Inner Temple
Recorder
Qualifications: [MA (Oxon)]

BICKFORD-SMITH MR STEPHEN WILLIAM

Landmark Chambers
180 Fleet Street, London EC4A 2HG, ☎ 020 7430 1221
✉ clerks@landmarkchambers.co.uk
Call Date: July 1972, Inner Temple
Pupil Supervisor
Qualifications: [BA (Oxon) FCIArb]
✉ sbsmith@landmarkchambers.co.uk

BICKLER MR SIMON LLOYD QC (2011)

St Paul's Chambers
5th Floor, St Paul's House, 23 Park Square South, Leeds LS1 2ND, ☎ 0113 245 5866
Call Date: Nov 1988, Inner Temple
Pupil Supervisor
Qualifications: [BA (Hons)(Sheff)]
✉ sb@stpaulschambers.com

BIDDLE MR NEVILLE LESLIE

Number 7 Harrington Street Chambers
7 Harrington Street, Liverpool L2 9YH, ☎ 0151 242 0707 ✉ clerks@7hs.co.uk
Call Date: Nov 1974, Gray's Inn
Pupil Supervisor
Qualifications: [BSc (Wales)]
✉ neville.biddle@7hs.co.uk

E

BIDE-THOMAS MR JAMES NICHOLAS

KCH Garden Square
1 Oxford Street, Nottingham NG1 5BH,
☎0115 941 8851
✉clerks@kchgardensquare.co.uk
Call Date: Nov 2005, Middle Temple
Qualifications: [BA (Hons) (Leic)]
jbide-thomas@kchgardensquare.co.uk

BIGGS MR MICHAEL EDWARD JAMES

12 Old Square Chambers
1st Floor, 12 Old Square, Lincoln's Inn, London WC2A 3TX, ☎020 7404 0875
✉clerks@12oldsquare.com
Call Date: July 2010, Middle Temple
Qualifications: [LLB (Hons) (Sheff)]

BIGGS MR STUART

9-12 Bell Yard
London WC2A 2JR, ☎020 7400 1800
✉clerks@9-12bellyard.com
Call Date: Nov 1999, Middle Temple
Qualifications: [MA (Hons)(Cantab)]
s.biggs@9-12bellyard.com

E

BIGNALL MR JOHN FRANCIS

7 King's Bench Walk
Ground Floor, 7 King's Bench Walk, Temple, London EC4Y 7DS, ☎020 7910 8300
✉clerks@7kbw.co.uk
Call Date: Nov 1996, Lincoln's Inn
Pupil Supervisor
Qualifications: [MA (Hons)]
jbignall@7kbw.co.uk

BIGNELL MISS JANET SUSAN

Falcon Chambers
Falcon Court, London EC4Y 1AA,
☎020 7353 2484
✉clerks@falcon-chambers.com
Call Date: Oct 1992, Lincoln's Inn
Pupil Supervisor, Recorder
Qualifications: [MA (Hons) (Cantab) BCL (Hons) (Oxon)]
bignell@falcon-chambers.com

Types of work: Boundaries, Chancery (land law), Commercial property, Common land, Conveyancing, Landlord and tenant, Lands Tribunal, Litigation, Mineral rights, Mortgages, Real property, Rights of light, Rights of way, Title to land, Water

BILSLAND MISS ALISAN MARGARET

St James's Chambers
68 Quay Street, Manchester M3 3EJ,
☎0161 834 7000
✉clerks@stjameschambers.com
Call Date: Nov 2000, Lincoln's Inn
Qualifications: [BA (Hons) (Durham)]
alisan.bilsland@stjameschambers.com

BINDER MR PETER HARDWICKE MALCOLM

Pangbourne Chambers
22 Reading Road, Pangbourne RG8 7LY,
☎07710 348055
Carmelite Chambers
9 Carmelite Street, London EC4Y 0DR,
☎020 7936 6300
✉clerks@carmelitechambers.co.uk
Call Date: Apr 1991, Middle Temple
Pupil Supervisor
Qualifications: [BA (Dunelm)]
pbinder@carmelitechambers.co.uk

BINDING MISS CHLOE LOUISE

Nine Bedford Row
9 Bedford Row, London WC1R 4AZ,
☎020 7489 2727
✉clerks@9bedfordrow.co.uk
Call Date: Oct 2009, Lincoln's Inn
Qualifications: [LLB (Warw) MPHIL (Cantab)]

BINDLOSS MR EDWARD CHRISTOPHER JAMES

Zenith Chambers
10 Park Square, Leeds LS1 2LH,
☎0113 245 5438
✉clerks@zenithchambers.co.uk
Call Date: Nov 1993, Gray's Inn
Pupil Supervisor, Recorder
Qualifications: [BA (York) Dip Law (Lond)]
ebindloss@zenithchambers.co.uk

BINDMAN MR JACOB

1 Mitre Court Buildings
1 Mitre Court Buildings, Temple, London EC4Y 7BS, ☎020 7452 8900
✉clerks@1mcb.com
Call Date: Oct 2010, Lincoln's Inn
Qualifications: [BA (Manch)]
jacob.bindman@1mcb.com

BINGHAM MR ANTHONY WILLIAM

3 PB Barristers
3 Paper Buildings, Temple, London EC4Y 7EU, ☎ 020 7583 8055
3 PB Barristers
30 Christchurch Road, Bournemouth, Dorset BH1 3PD, ☎ 01202 292102
✉ clerks.bournemouth@3paper.co.uk
3 PB Barristers
4 St Peter Street, Winchester SO23 8BW, ☎ 01962 868884
✉ clerks.winchester@3paper.co.uk
3 PB Barristers
Royal Talbot House, 2 Victoria Street, Bristol, Avon BS1 6BB, ☎ 0117 928 1520
3 PB Barristers
23 Beaumont Street, Oxford OX1 2NP, ☎ 01865 793 736
Call Date: Nov 1992, Lincoln's Inn
Qualifications: [LLB (Hons) (Lond) FCIArb]
✉ tony.bingham@3paper.co.uk

BINGHAM MISS CAMILLA

One Essex Court
Ground Floor, One Essex Court, Temple, London EC4Y 9AR, ☎ 020 7583 2000
✉ clerks@oeclaw.co.uk
Call Date: Oct 1996, Inner Temple
Qualifications: [BA (Oxon) CPE (Lond)]
✉ cbingham@oeclaw.co.uk

BINNION MS CAROL ANNE

St Ive's Chambers
Whittall Street, Birmingham B4 6DH, ☎ 0121 236 0863
✉ clerks@stiveschambers.co.uk
Call Date: July 2010, Middle Temple
Qualifications: [LLB (Hons) (Nott'm)]
✉ carol.binnion@stiveschambers.co.uk

BINNS MR DAVID ANDREW

St James's Chambers
68 Quay Street, Manchester M3 3EJ, ☎ 0161 834 7000
✉ clerks@stjameschambers.com
Call Date: July 1983, Middle Temple
Qualifications: [LLB (Hons)(L'pool)]

BIRBECK MR ALAN GILES

Dyers Chambers
35 Bedford Row, London WC1R 4JH, ☎ 020 7404 1881
✉ admin@dyerschambers.com
Call Date: July 2006, Inner Temple
Qualifications: [LLB (Lond) MSc (Oxon)]

BIRCH MISS ELIZABETH BLANCHE

3 Verulam Buildings
London WC1R 5NT, ☎ 020 7831 8441
✉ chambers@3vb.com
Call Date: July 1978, Gray's Inn
Pupil Supervisor
Qualifications: [LLB (Lond)]

BIRCH MR ROGER ALLEN

Five St Andrew's Hill
5 St Andrew's Hill, London EC4V 5BZ, ☎ 020 7332 5400 ✉ Clerks@5sah.co.uk
Sovereign Chambers
46 Park Place, Leeds LS1 2RY, ☎ 0113 245 1841
✉ clerks@sovereignchambers.co.uk
Call Date: Nov 1979, Gray's Inn
Qualifications: [BA (Cantab)]
✉ rogerbirch@5sah.co.uk

BIRCH MR WILLIAM CHARLES JOSEPH

3 Temple Gardens
Lower Ground Floor, 3 Temple Gardens, Temple, London EC4Y 9AU, ☎ 020 7353 3102
✉ clerks@3tg.co.uk
Call Date: Feb 1972, Lincoln's Inn
Pupil Supervisor
Qualifications: [MA (Lond)]
✉ gb@3tg.co.uk

BIRD MR ANDREW JAMES

Five St Andrew's Hill
5 St Andrew's Hill, London EC4V 5BZ, ☎ 020 7332 5400 ✉ Clerks@5sah.co.uk
Call Date: July 1987, Inner Temple
Pupil Supervisor
Qualifications: [MA (Cantab)]
✉ andrewbird@5sah.co.uk

BIRD MR SIMON CHRISTOPHER QC (2009)

Cornerstone Barristers
2-3 Gray's Inn Square, Gray's Inn, London WC1R 5JH, ☎ 020 7242 4986
✉ chambers@2-3gis.co.uk
Call Date: July 1987, Middle Temple
Qualifications: [LLB (Reading)]
✉ sbird@2-3gis.co.uk

BIRDEE MISS SONIA

Chambers of Ian Macdonald QC
Garden Court North, 22 Oxford Court, Manchester M2 3WQ, ☎ 0161 236 1840
✉ clerks@gcnchambers.co.uk
Call Date: Mar 2004, Middle Temple
Qualifications: [BA (Hons) (Oxon)]

BIRDLING DR MALCOLM DAVID

Brick Court Chambers
7-8 Essex Street, London WC2R 3LD,
☎ 020 7379 3550 ✉ clerks@brickcourt.co.uk
Call Date: Oct 2011, Inner Temple
Qualifications: [BA (New Zealand) BCL (New Zealand) BCL (Oxon) M Phil (Oxon)]
✉ malcolm.birdling@brickcourt.co.uk

BIRK MISS DEWINDER

No5 Chambers
Fountain Court, Steelhouse Lane, Birmingham B4 6DR, ☎ 0845 210 5555 ✉ info@no5.com
No5 Chambers
Greenwood House, 4-7 Salisbury Court, London EC4Y 8AA, ☎ 0845 210 5555
No5 Chambers
38 Queen Square, Bristol BS1 4QS,
☎ 0845 210 5555
Call Date: July 1988, Lincoln's Inn
Pupil Supervisor
Qualifications: [LLB (Hons) (Essex) MA (Leic)]

BIRKBY MR RICHARD ADAM

Park Court Chambers
16 Park Place, Leeds LS1 2SJ,
☎ 0113 243 3277
✉ clerks@parkcourtchambers.co.uk
Call Date: Oct 2006, Middle Temple
Qualifications: [BA (Hons) (Lond) MSt (Cantab)]
✉ abirkby@parkcourtchambers.co.uk

BIRKETT MISS LIANNE

Number 7 Harrington Street Chambers
7 Harrington Street, Liverpool L2 9YH,
☎ 0151 242 0707 ✉ clerks@7hs.co.uk
Call Date: July 2006, Inner Temple
Qualifications: [LLB (Lond)]
✉ lianne.birkett@7hs.co.uk

BIRKETT MR PETER VIDLER QC (1989)

18 St John Street
Manchester M3 4EA, ☎ 0161 278 1800
✉ clerks@18sjs.com
Call Date: July 1972, Inner Temple
Recorder
Qualifications: [LLB]
✉ familybirkett@aol.com

BIRKS MR SIMON ALEXANDER

3 Dr Johnson's Buildings
Ground Floor, 3 Dr Johnson's Buildings, Temple, London EC4Y 7BA, ☎ 020 7353 4854
✉ clerks@3djb.co.uk
Call Date: May 1981, Middle Temple
Qualifications: [BA]

BIRNBAUM MR MICHAEL IAN QC (1992)

9-12 Bell Yard
London WC2A 2JR, ☎ 020 7400 1800
✉ clerks@9-12bellyard.com
Call Date: Nov 1969, Middle Temple
Recorder
Qualifications: [BA (Oxon)]
✉ m.birnbaum@9-12bellyard.com

BIRRELL MR DAVID JOSEPH ANTHONY

Exchange Chambers
One Derby Square, Derby Square, Liverpool L2 9XX, ☎ 0151 236 7747
✉ info@exchangechambers.co.uk
Exchange Chambers
Oxford House, Oxford Row, Leeds LS1 3BE,
☎ 0113 203 1970
✉ spencer@exchangechambers.co.uk
Call Date: Nov 2006, Inner Temple
Qualifications: [LLB (L'pool)]
✉ birrell@exchangechambers.co.uk

BIRT MISS EMMA JOSEPHINE

King's Bench and Godolphin (KBG)Chambers
115 North Hill, Plymouth, Devon PL4 8JY,
☎ 01752 221551
✉ clerks@kbgchambers.co.uk
Call Date: Oct 2000, Inner Temple
Qualifications: [BA (Cantab) CPE (Bris)]

BIRT MR SIMON CHRISTOPHER

Brick Court Chambers
7-8 Essex Street, London WC2R 3LD,
☎ 020 7379 3550 ✉ clerks@brickcourt.co.uk
Call Date: Oct 1998, Gray's Inn
Pupil Supervisor
Qualifications: [BA BCL (Oxon)]
✉ Simon.Birt@Brickcourt.co.uk

BIRTCHNELL MR BENJAMIN NICHOLAS

3 Dr Johnson's Buildings
Ground Floor, 3 Dr Johnson's Buildings, Temple, London EC4Y 7BA, ☎ 020 7353 4854
✉ clerks@3djb.co.uk
Call Date: July 2009, Lincoln's Inn
Qualifications: [BA (Oxon) CPE COLG]

BIRTLES MISS SAMANTHA JANE

18 St John Street
Manchester M3 4EA, ☎ 0161 278 1800
✉ clerks@18sjs.com
Call Date: July 1989, Lincoln's Inn
Pupil Supervisor
Qualifications: [LLB (B'ham)]

BISARYA MR NEIL

Number 7 Harrington Street Chambers
7 Harrington Street, Liverpool L2 9YH,
☎ 0151 242 0707 ✉ clerks@7hs.co.uk
Call Date: Nov 1998, Lincoln's Inn
Qualifications: [MA (Hons)(Cantab)]
✉ neil.bisarya@7hs.co.uk

BISBEY MISS GAYLE YVETTE DAWN

2 Dr Johnson's Buildings
2 Dr Johnson's Buildings, Temple, London
EC4Y 7AY, ☎ 020 7936 2613
✉ clerks@2drj.com
Call Date: Oct 2002, Lincoln's Inn
Qualifications: [LLB (England)]
✉ g.bisbey@2drj.com

BISGROVE MR MICHAEL JOHN

6 King's Bench Walk
Ground Floor, 6 King's Bench Walk, Temple,
London EC4Y 7DR, ☎ 020 7583 0410
✉ clerks@6kbw.com
Call Date: Oct 2006, Middle Temple
Qualifications: [BA (Hons) (Cantab)]
✉ michael.bisgrove@6kbw.com

BISHOP MR ALAN RICHARD

11 Stone Buildings
11 Stone Buildings, Lincoln's Inn, London
WC2A 3TG, ☎ 020 7831 6381
✉ clerks@11sb.com
Call Date: July 1973, Middle Temple
Pupil Supervisor
Qualifications: [LLB (Lond) ACII]
✉ bishop@11sb.com

BISHOP MR DANIEL JEFFREY

Seven Bedford Row
7 Bedford Row, London WC1R 4BS,
☎ 020 7242 3555 ✉ clerks@7br.co.uk
Call Date: Oct 2007, Inner Temple
Qualifications: [BA (Oxon)]

BISHOP MR EDWARD JAMES QC (2011)

1 Chancery Lane
London WC2A 1LF, ☎ 0845 634 6666
✉ clerks@1chancerylane.com
Call Date: Nov 1985, Middle Temple
Pupil Supervisor
Qualifications: [MA (Cantab) Dip Law]
✉ ebishop@1chancerylane.com

BISHOP MR GORDON WILLIAM

Chambers of Gordon Bishop
Brook House, Rough Road, Woking, Surrey
GU22 0RB, ☎ 01483 486 730
✉ gordonbishop@gmail.com
Call Date: Nov 1968, Middle Temple
Pupil Supervisor
Qualifications: [MA (Cantab)]

BISHOP MR JOHN MICHAEL

No. 3 Fleet Street Chambers
3 Fleet Street, London EC4Y 1DP,
☎ 020 7936 4474 ✉ clerks@3fleetstreet.com
Call Date: Nov 1970, Middle Temple
Pupil Supervisor
Qualifications: [LLB (Hons) (Lond)]

BISHOP MR MALCOLM LESLIE QC (1993)

Argent Chambers
5 Bell Yard, London WC2A 2JR,
☎ 020 7556 5500
✉ briefsin@argentchambers.co.uk
30 Park Place
Cardiff CF10 3BS, ☎ 029 2039 8421
✉ clerks@30parkplace.law.co.uk
Equity Chambers
First Floor, McLaren Building, 46 Priory
Queensway, Birmingham B4 7LR,
☎ 0121 236 5007
✉ clerks@equitychambers.org.uk
Call Date: July 1968, Inner Temple
Recorder
Qualifications: [MA (Oxon)]
✉ m.bishop@argentchambers.co.uk

BISHOP MR STEPHEN ANTHONY

Goldsmith Chambers
Ground Floor, Goldsmith Building, Temple,
London EC4Y 7BL, ☎ 020 7353 6802
✉ clerks@goldsmithchambers.com
Call Date: July 2006, Inner Temple
Qualifications: [BEng (Lond)]
✉ S.Bishop@goldsmithchambers.law.co.uk

BISHOP MR TIMOTHY HARPER PAUL QC (2011)

1 Hare Court
1 Hare Court, Temple, London EC4Y 7BE,
☎ 020 7797 7070 ✉ clerks@1hc.com
Call Date: Nov 1991, Inner Temple
Pupil Supervisor
Qualifications: [MA (Hons)(Cantab)]
✉ bishop@1hc.com

E

BISHOP MR TOBY NICHOLAS

Field Court Chambers
5 Field Court, Gray's Inn, London WC1R 5EF,
☎ 020 7405 6114 ✉ clerks@fieldcourt.co.uk
Call Date: Oct 2008, Middle Temple
Qualifications: [LLB (Hons)]

BISPHAM MISS CHRISTINE

Number 7 Harrington Street Chambers
7 Harrington Street, Liverpool L2 9YH,
☎ 0151 242 0707 ✉ clerks@7hs.co.uk
Call Date: Oct 1991, Lincoln's Inn
Pupil Supervisor
Qualifications: [LLB (Hons) (Leics)]
✉ christine.bispham@7hs.co.uk

BISSET MISS CATHERINE LAURA

No.6 Park Square
Leeds LS1 2LW, ☎ 0113 245 9763
✉ Tim@no6.co.uk
Call Date: July 2009, Lincoln's Inn
Qualifications: [LLB (Sheff)]
✉ bisset@no6.co.uk

BISWAS MISS NISHA SUJATA

Chavasse Court Chambers
18 Queen Avenue, Liverpool L2 4TX,
☎ 0151 229 2030
✉ clerks@chavassechambers.co.uk
Call Date: Oct 1996, Lincoln's Inn
Qualifications: [LLB (Hons)(L'pool)]
✉ nisha.biswas@chavassechambers.co.uk

BITMEAD MR PAUL GRAHAM

Devon Chambers
3 St Andrew Street, Plymouth PL1 2AH,
☎ 01752 661659
✉ clerks@devonchambers.co.uk
Call Date: Oct 1996, Middle Temple
Qualifications: [BA (Hons) (Essex) CPE]
✉ paulbitmead@devonchambers.co.uk

BLACK MISS GEORGINA

29 Bedford Row Chambers
London WC1R 4HE, ☎ 020 7404 1044
✉ clerks@29br.co.uk
Call Date: Oct 1999, Middle Temple
Qualifications: [BA (Hons)(Sydney) LLB (Hons)]
✉ gblack@29br.co.uk

BLACK MR JOHN ALEXANDER QC (1998)

Chambers of Andrew Mitchell QC
33 Chancery Lane, London WC2A 1EN,
☎ 020 7440 9950 ✉ clerks@33cllaw.com
18 Red Lion Court
London EC4A 3EB, ☎ 020 7520 6000
✉ chambers@18rlc.co.uk
Call Date: July 1975, Inner Temple
Qualifications: [LLB (Hons)]

BLACK MR MICHAEL JONATHAN QC (1995)

XXIV Old Buildings
Ground Floor, 24 Old Buildings, Lincoln's Inn, London WC2A 3UP, ☎ 020 7691 2424
✉ clerks@xxiv.co.uk
Call Date: Feb 1978, Middle Temple
Qualifications: [LLB (Lond) FCIArb]

BLACKBAND MISS LAURA KATHERINE

4 Breams Buildings
Chancery Lane, London EC4A 1HP,
☎ 020 7092 1900 ✉ clerks@4bb.co.uk
Call Date: Nov 1997, Lincoln's Inn
Qualifications: [BA (Hons)(Oxon)]

BLACK-BRANCH DR JONATHAN LEE

1 Garden Court Family Law Chambers
Ground Floor, One Garden Court, Temple, London EC4Y 9BJ, ☎ 020 7797 7900
✉ clerks@1gc.com
Call Date: Mar 1998, Lincoln's Inn
Qualifications: [PhD (Toronto) MA DPhiL BA LLB]

BLACKBURN MRS ELIZABETH QC (1998)

Stone Chambers
4 Field Court, Gray's Inn, London WC1R 5EF,
☎ 020 7440 6900
✉ clerks@stonechambers.com
Call Date: July 1978, Middle Temple
Qualifications: [BA]
✉ elizabeth.blackburn@stonechambers.com

BLACKBURN MR LUKE SEBASTIAN

Seven Bedford Row
7 Bedford Row, London WC1R 4BS,
☎ 020 7242 3555 ✉ clerks@7br.co.uk
Call Date: Nov 1993, Middle Temple
Pupil Supervisor
Qualifications: [MA (Cantab)]
✉ lblackburn@7br.co.uk

BLACKETT-ORD MR MARK

5 Stone Buildings
5 Stone Buildings, Lincoln's Inn, London WC2A 3XT, ☎ 020 7242 6201
✉ clerks@5sblaw.com
Call Date: July 1974, Lincoln's Inn
Pupil Supervisor
Qualifications: [MA (Oxon)]
✉ mblackettord@5sblaw.com

BLACKFORD MR SIMON JOHN

2 Dr Johnson's Buildings
2 Dr Johnson's Buildings, Temple, London EC4Y 7AY, ☎ 020 7936 2613
✉ clerks@2drj.com
Call Date: July 1979, Middle Temple
Recorder
Qualifications: [MA]
✉ clerks@2drj.com

BLACKMAN MR EDMUND ARTHUR WILLIAM

Chambers of Marion Smullen and Kerim Fuad QC
1 Inner Temple Lane, London EC4Y 1AF, ☎ 020 7427 4400 ✉ clerks@1itl.com
Call Date: July 1999, Middle Temple
Pupil Supervisor
Qualifications: [MA (Edin) Dip in Law]
✉ edmund.blackman@1itl.com

BLACKMORE MR JOHN HUGH

St John's Chambers
101 Victoria Street, Bristol BS1 6PU, ☎ 0117 923 4700
✉ clerks@stjohnschambers.co.uk
Call Date: May 1983, Inner Temple
Pupil Supervisor
Qualifications: [LLB (Lond)]
✉ john.blackmore@stjohnschambers.co.uk

BLACKMORE MISS SALLY ANNE

Ely Place Chambers
30 Ely Place, London EC1N 6TD, ☎ 020 7400 9600 ✉ admin@elyplace.com
Call Date: Nov 2003, Lincoln's Inn
Qualifications: [BA (Hons) (Lond) MA (Bris) CPE (City)]

BLACKMORE MISS SARAH ELIZABETH

37 Park Square Chambers
37 Park Square, Leeds LS1 2NY, ☎ 0113 243 9422 ✉ chambers@no37.co.uk
Call Date: Oct 1993, Inner Temple
Pupil Supervisor
Qualifications: [LLB]
✉ chambers@no37.co.uk, sarahblackmore@btinternet.com

BLACKMORE MS SASHA

Landmark Chambers
180 Fleet Street, London EC4A 2HG, ☎ 020 7430 1221
✉ clerks@landmarkchambers.co.uk
Call Date: Oct 2005, Lincoln's Inn
Qualifications: [BA (Hons) (Oxon) MA (Oxon) MPROF PgDl (Lond)]
✉ sblackmore@landmarkchambers.co.uk

BLACKSHAW MR HENRY WILLIAM RANDLE

St Johns Buildings
24a - 28 St John Street, Manchester M3 4DJ, ☎ 0161 214 1500
✉ clerk@stjohnsbuildings.co.uk
St Johns Buildings
21 White Friars, Chester CH1 1NZ, ☎ 01244 323070
✉ clerk@stjohnsbuildings.co.uk
16 Winckley Square
Preston PR1 3JJ, ☎ 01772 256100
Call Date: Oct 1993, Middle Temple
Qualifications: [BA (Hons)(Dunelm) CPE Dip Law]
✉ clerk@stjohnsbuildings.co.uk, henry.blackshaw@stjohnsbuildings.co.uk

BLACKWELL MISS KATHERINE ELIZABETH QC (2012)

Lincoln House Chambers
Tower 12, The Avenue North, Spinningfields, 18-22 Bridge Street, Manchester M3 3BZ, ☎ 0161 832 5701
✉ info@lincolnhousechambers.com
Call Date: Oct 1992, Lincoln's Inn
Recorder
Qualifications: [LLB(Hons)(B'ham)]
✉ katherine.blackwell@lincolnhousechambers.com

BLACKWELL MISS LOUISE MARY QC (2006)

Cobden House Chambers
19 Quay Street, Manchester M3 3HN, ☎ 0161 833 6000 ✉ Clerks@Cobden.co.uk
Call Date: July 1985, Lincoln's Inn
Qualifications: [LLB (Hons) (Leeds)]
✉ clerks@cobden.co.uk

BLACKWOOD MR ANDREW GUY

Quadrant Chambers
Quadrant House, 10 Fleet Street, London EC4Y 1AU, ☎ 020 7583 4444
✉ info@quadrantchambers.com
Call Date: Oct 1997, Inner Temple
Qualifications: [MB (Lond) LLB (Lond)]
✉ guy.blackwood@quadrantchambers.com

E

BLACKWOOD MS ANNELIESE ROSE

Monckton Chambers
1 & 2 Raymond Buildings, Gray's Inn, London WC1R 5NR, ☎ 020 7405 7211
✉ chambers@monckton.com
Call Date: July 2007, Middle Temple
Qualifications: [LLB (Hons) (Lond) BCL (Oxon)]
✉ ablackwood@monckton.com

BLACKWOOD MR CLIVE DAVID

Lamb Chambers
Lamb Building, Elm Court, Temple, London EC4Y 7AS, ☎ 020 7797 8300
✉ info@lambchambers.co.uk
Call Date: Nov 1986, Inner Temple
Pupil Supervisor
Qualifications: [BA(Cantab)]
✉ cliveblackwood@lambchambers.co.uk

BLACKWOOD MISS REBECCA JAYNE

Southernhay Chambers
33 Southernhay East, Exeter EX1 1NX, ☎ 01392 255777
✉ clerks@southernhaychambers.co.uk
Call Date: Nov 2001, Lincoln's Inn
Qualifications: [LLB (Hons) LLM]
✉ r.blackwood@southernhaychambers.co.uk

BLAIN MR RODERICK GRAHAM

12 College Place
Fauvelle Buildings, 12 College Place, Southampton SO15 2FE, ☎ 023 8032 0320
✉ clerks@12cp.co.uk
Call Date: Oct 1991, Middle Temple
Qualifications: [BA (Scotland) DipLaw (Lond)]
✉ clerks@18carltoncrescent.co.uk

BLAIR MR BRUCE GRAEME DONALD QC (1989)

1 Hare Court
1 Hare Court, Temple, London EC4Y 7BE, ☎ 020 7797 7070 ✉ clerks@1hc.com
Dere Street Barristers
33 Broad Chare, Newcastle Upon Tyne NE1 3DQ, ☎ 0844 3351551
✉ clerks@derestreet.co.uk
Call Date: July 1969, Middle Temple
Recorder
Qualifications: [MA (Cantab)]
✉ blair@1hc.com

BLAIR MR MICHAEL CAMPBELL QC (1996)

3 Verulam Buildings
London WC1R 5NT, ☎ 020 7831 8441
✉ chambers@3vb.com
Call Date: July 1965, Middle Temple
Qualifications: [MA (Cantab) MA (USA) LLM (Cantab)]
✉ mblair@3vb.com

BLAIR MR PETER MICHAEL QC (2006)

Guildhall Chambers
23 Broad Street, Bristol BS1 2HG, ☎ 0117 930 9000
✉ hoc@guildhallchambers.co.uk
6 King's Bench Walk
Ground Floor, 6 King's Bench Walk, Temple, London EC4Y 7DR, ☎ 020 7583 0410
✉ clerks@6kbw.com
Call Date: July 1983, Inner Temple
Recorder
Qualifications: [MA (Oxon)]

BLAKE MR ANDREW MARK

11 King's Bench Walk
11 King's Bench Walk, Temple, London EC4Y 7EQ, ☎ 020 7632 8500
✉ clerksroom@11kbw.com
Call Date: Oct 2000, Lincoln's Inn
Pupil Supervisor
Qualifications: [BA (Hons) (Cantab)]
✉ andrew.blake@11kbw.com

BLAKE MR ARTHUR JOSEPH

13 King's Bench Walk
13 King's Bench Walk, Temple, London EC4Y 7EN, ☎ 020 7353 7204
✉ clerks@13kbw.co.uk
13 KBW
32 Beaumont Street, Oxford OX1 2NP, ☎ 01865 311066 ✉ clerks@13kbw.co.uk
Call Date: Feb 1988, Inner Temple
Qualifications: [LLB]
✉ ablake@13kbw.co.uk

BLAKE MR CHRISTOPHER IAN

5 King's Bench Walk
5 King's Bench Walk, Temple, London EC4Y 7DN, ☎ 020 7353 5638
✉ clerks@5kbw.co.uk
Call Date: Nov 1990, Inner Temple
Pupil Supervisor
Qualifications: [LLB (Hons)]
✉ christopher.blake@5kbw.co.uk

BLAKE MR DAVID ANTHONY

Angel Chambers
Ethos Building, Kings Road, Swansea SA1 8AS, ☎01792 464623
✉clerks@angelchambers.co.uk
Call Date: Feb 1992, Lincoln's Inn
Qualifications: [BA (Hons) (Cantab)]
✉davidblake@angelchambers.co.uk

BLAKE MR JULIAN DANIEL

6 King's Bench Walk
Ground Floor, 6 King's Bench Walk, Temple, London EC4Y 7DR, ☎020 7583 0410
✉clerks@6kbw.com
Call Date: July 2006, Middle Temple
Qualifications: [BA (Hons) (Cantab) MA (Yale) PgDL]
✉julian.blake@6kbw.com

BLAKE MR NICHOLAS

36 Bedford Row
London WC1R 4JH, ☎020 7421 8000
✉chambers@36bedfordrow.co.uk
Call Date: Nov 1997, Gray's Inn
Qualifications: [BA (Wales)]
✉clerks@36bedfordrow.co.uk

BLAKE MS PENELOPE NATASHA

1 Gray's Inn Square
Ground Floor, 1 Gray's Inn Square, London WC1R 5AA, ☎020 7405 0001
Call Date: July 1996, Gray's Inn
Qualifications: [BA (Sussex)]
✉pblake@1gis.co.uk

BLAKE-BARNARD MR VINCENT

No.6 Park Square
Leeds LS1 2LW, ☎0113 245 9763
✉Tim@no6.co.uk
Call Date: Mar 2012, Gray's Inn
✉andy@no6.co.uk

BLAKEBROUGH MR SIMON

Kenworthy's Chambers
Arlington House, Bloom Street, Salford, Manchester M3 6AJ, ☎0161 832 4036
Call Date: Mar 2011, Lincoln's Inn
Qualifications: [BA (Manch)]
✉s.blakebrough@kenworthysbarristers.co.uk

BLAKELEY MR RICHARD

Brick Court Chambers
7-8 Essex Street, London WC2R 3LD, ☎020 7379 3550 ✉clerks@brickcourt.co.uk
Call Date: July 2007, Lincoln's Inn
Qualifications: [BA (Cantab) LLM (USA)]
✉richard.blakeley@brickcourt.co.uk

BLAKEMORE MR BENJAMIN ROSS

Iscoed Chambers
86 St Helen's Road, Swansea SA1 4BQ, ☎01792 652988
✉clerks@iscoedchambers.co.uk
Call Date: July 2004, Gray's Inn
Qualifications: [LLB (Hons) (Wales)]
✉bb@iscoedchambers.co.uk

BLAKER MR GARY MARK

Selborne Chambers
10 Essex Street, London WC2R 3AA, ☎020 7420 9500
✉clerks@selbornechambers.co.uk
Call Date: Oct 1993, Middle Temple
Pupil Supervisor
Qualifications: [MA (Cantab)]
✉gary.blaker@selbornechambers.co.uk

BLAKESLEY MR PATRICK JAMES

Crown Office Chambers
2 Crown Office Row, Temple, London EC4Y 7HJ, ☎020 7797 8100
✉mail@crownofficechambers.com
Call Date: Nov 1993, Inner Temple
Pupil Supervisor
Qualifications: [MA (Oxon) CPE (City)]
✉blakesley@crownofficechambers.com

BLAKEY MR LEE

15 Winckley Square
Preston PR1 3JJ, ☎01772 252828
✉clerks@15winckleysq.co.uk
Call Date: Oct 1995, Lincoln's Inn
Qualifications: [LLB (Hons)(Lanc)]
✉clerks@15winckleysq.co.uk

BLAKEY MR MICHAEL CHARLES

St Johns Buildings
24a - 28 St John Street, Manchester M3 4DJ, ☎0161 214 1500
✉clerk@stjohnsbuildings.co.uk
16 Winckley Square
Preston PR1 3JJ, ☎01772 256100
St Johns Buildings Liverpool
8th Floor India Buildings, Water Street, Liverpool L2 0XG, ☎0151 243 6000
✉clerk@stjohnsbuildings.co.uk
Call Date: Nov 1989, Middle Temple
Pupil Supervisor
Qualifications: [LLB (Hons)]

E

BLANCHARD MISS CLAIRE QC (2010)

Essex Court Chambers
24 Lincoln's Inn Fields, London WC2A 3EG,
☎ 020 7813 8000
✉ clerksroom@essexcourt.net
Call Date: Oct 1992, Gray's Inn
Pupil Supervisor
Qualifications: [LLB (Hons) (L'pool)]
✉ cblanchard@essexcourt.net

BLAND MISS CAROLYN

Deans Court Chambers
24 St John Street, Manchester M3 4DF,
☎ 0161 214 6000 ✉ clerks@deanscourt.co.uk
Deans Court Chambers
101 Walker Street, Preston PR1 2RR,
☎ 01772 565 600
✉ preston@deanscourt.co.uk
Call Date: July 1995, Inner Temple
Pupil Supervisor
Qualifications: [LLB (Reading)]
✉ bland@deanscourt.co.uk

BLATCHFORD MR CHARLES ROBERT

Park Court Chambers
16 Park Place, Leeds LS1 2SJ,
☎ 0113 243 3277
✉ clerks@parkcourtchambers.co.uk
Call Date: July 1997, Inner Temple
Qualifications: [BSc (Dunelm) Dip in Law]

BLATCHLY MR PHILLIP IAIN

14 Gray's Inn Square
14 Gray's Inn Square, Gray's Inn, London
WC1R 5JP, ☎ 020 7242 0858
✉ clerks@14gis.co.uk
Call Date: Nov 2008, Inner Temple
Qualifications: [LLB (Hons) CPE]

BLAXLAND MR CHRISTOPHER HENRY QC (2002)

Garden Court Chambers
57-60 Lincoln's Inn Fields, London WC2A 3LJ,
☎ 020 7993 7600 ✉ info@gclaw.co.uk
Call Date: Nov 1978, Middle Temple
Qualifications: [BA (York)]
✉ henryb@gclaw.co.uk

BLAYNEY MR DAVID JAMES

Serle Court
6 New Square, Lincoln's Inn, London
WC2A 3QS, ☎ 020 7242 6105
✉ clerks@serlecourt.co.uk
Call Date: Oct 1992, Lincoln's Inn
Pupil Supervisor
Qualifications: [BA (Oxon)]
✉ dblayney@serlecourt.co.uk

BLEANEY MR NICHOLAS SIMON

Atkinson Bevan Chambers
1st Floor, 2 Harcourt Buildings, Temple,
London EC4Y 9DB, ☎ 020 7353 2112
✉ clerks@2hb.co.uk
Call Date: Nov 1988, Lincoln's Inn
Pupil Supervisor
Qualifications: [LLB (Hons)(Nott'm)]
✉ nbleaney@2hb.co.uk

BLEASDALE MISS MARIE-CLAIRE

Radcliffe Chambers
Ground Floor, 11 New Square, Lincoln's Inn,
London WC2A 3QB, ☎ 020 7831 0081
✉ clerks@radcliffechambers.com
Call Date: Oct 1993, Lincoln's Inn
Qualifications: [MA (Cantab) DipLaw (Lond)]
✉ mcbleasdale@radcliffechambers.com

BLEASDALE MR PAUL EDWARD QC (2001)

No5 Chambers
Fountain Court, Steelhouse Lane, Birmingham
B4 6DR, ☎ 0845 210 5555 ✉ info@no5.com
No5 Chambers
Greenwood House, 4-7 Salisbury Court,
London EC4Y 8AA, ☎ 0845 210 5555
No5 Chambers
38 Queen Square, Bristol BS1 4QS,
☎ 0845 210 5555
Call Date: July 1978, Inner Temple
Recorder
Qualifications: [LLB (Lond)]
✉ pb@no5.com

BLEWITT MISS JENNIFER

St Johns Buildings
24a - 28 St John Street, Manchester M3 4DJ,
☎ 0161 214 1500
✉ clerk@stjohnsbuildings.co.uk
St Johns Buildings
21 White Friars, Chester CH1 1NZ,
☎ 01244 323070
✉ clerk@stjohnsbuildings.co.uk
16 Winckley Square
Preston PR1 3JJ, ☎ 01772 256100
Call Date: July 2001, Middle Temple
Qualifications: [LLB (Hons)]
✉ clerk@stjohnsbuildings.co.uk

BLOCH MR MICHAEL GORDON QC (1998)

Wilberforce Chambers
8 New Square, Lincoln's Inn, London
WC2A 3QP, ☎ 020 7306 0102
✉ chambers@wilberforce.co.uk
Call Date: July 1979, Lincoln's Inn
Qualifications: [MA (Cantab) MPhil (UEA)]
✉ mbloch@wilberforce.co.uk

Types of work: Chancery (general), Commercial law, Commercial litigation, Company, commercial and competition, Copyright, Information technology, Insolvency, Intellectual property, Patents, Sport, Trademarks

BLOCH MR SELWYN IRVING QC (2000)

Littleton Chambers
3 King's Bench Walk North, Temple, London
EC4Y 7HR, ☎ 020 7797 8600
✉ fschneider@littletonchambers.co.uk
Call Date: July 1982, Middle Temple
Qualifications: [BA LLB]
✉ sbloch@littletonchambers.co.uk

BLOCK MR NEIL SELWYN QC (2002)

39 Essex Street
London WC2R 3AT, ☎ 020 7832 1111
✉ clerks@39essex.com
82 King Street
Manchester M2 4WQ, ☎ 0161 870 9969
Call Date: July 1980, Gray's Inn
Qualifications: [BA (Hons) LLM (Exon)]
✉ neil.block@39essex.com

BLOHM MR LESLIE ADRIAN QC (2006)

St John's Chambers
101 Victoria Street, Bristol BS1 6PU,
☎ 0117 923 4700
✉ clerks@stjohnschambers.co.uk
Call Date: July 1982, Lincoln's Inn
Recorder
Qualifications: [MA (Oxon)]
✉ leslie.blohm@stjohnschambers.co.uk

BLOM-COOPER MR SAMUEL GEORGE ABBOTT

25 Bedford Row
London WC1R 4HD, ☎ 020 7067 1500
✉ clerks@25bedfordrow.com
Call Date: Oct 2006, Middle Temple
Qualifications: [BSc (Nott'm)]
✉ sblomcooper@25bedfordrow.com

BLOOM DR MARGARET

Hardwicke
New Square, Lincoln's Inn, London
WC2A 3SB, ☎ 020 7242 2523
✉ enquiries@hardwicke.co.uk
Call Date: Oct 1994, Lincoln's Inn
Pupil Supervisor
Qualifications: [B Med Sci BM BS MRCGP (Notts) CPE (Notts)]

BLOOM MS TRACEY DORA

Doughty Street Chambers
53-54 Doughty Street, London WC1N 2LS,
☎ 020 7404 1313
✉ enquiries@doughtystreet.co.uk
Doughty Street Chambers
Pall Mall Court, 61-67 King Street, Manchester
M2 4PD, ☎ 0161 618 1066
Doughty Street Chambers
5th Floor, Broad Quay House, Prince Street,
Bristol BS1 4DJ, ☎ 01179 058 717
Call Date: July 1984, Gray's Inn
Pupil Supervisor
Qualifications: [MA (Cantab)]
✉ t.bloom@doughtystreet.co.uk

BLOOM-DAVIS MR DESMOND NIALL LAURENCE

Pump Court Chambers
Upper Ground Floor, 3 Pump Court, Temple,
London EC4Y 7AJ, ☎ 020 7353 0711
✉ clerks@3pumpcourt.com
Pump Court Chambers
5 Temple Chambers, Temple Street, Swindon
SN1 1SQ, ☎ 01793 539899
✉ clerks@3pumpcourt.com
Pump Court Chambers
31 Southgate Street, Winchester, Hampshire
SO23 9EB, ☎ 01962 868 161
✉ clerks@3pumpcourt.com
Call Date: July 1986, Inner Temple
Pupil Supervisor
Qualifications: [BA (Lond)]
✉ dbd@3pumpcourt.com

BLOOMER MR CHARLES HOWARD

Lincoln House Chambers
Tower 12, The Avenue North, Spinningfields,
18-22 Bridge Street, Manchester M3 3BZ,
☎ 0161 832 5701
✉ info@lincolnhousechambers.com
Call Date: July 1985, Lincoln's Inn
Qualifications: [LLB (Nott'm)]
✉ charles.bloomer@lincolnhousechambers.com

E

BLOOMER MR JAMES ANDREW

Goldsmith Chambers
Ground Floor, Goldsmith Building, Temple, London EC4Y 7BL, ☎ 020 7353 6802
✉ clerks@goldsmithchambers.com
Call Date: Nov 2000, Lincoln's Inn
Pupil Supervisor
Qualifications: [LLB (Nott'm)]
✉ j.bloomer@goldsmithchambers.law.co.uk

BLOOMFIELD MR RICHARD WILLIAM

Chambers of Mr Richard Bloomfield
19 Chollerford Mews, Hollywell, Whitley Bay, Tyne and Wear NE25 0TX, ☎ 01670 360042
✉ richard@richardbloomfield.co.uk
Call Date: July 1984, Gray's Inn
Pupil Supervisor
Qualifications: [BA (Hons)]
✉ richard@richardbloomfield.co.uk

BLOUNT MR MARTIN JOHN

Pump Court Chambers
31 Southgate Street, Winchester, Hampshire SO23 9EB, ☎ 01962 868 161
✉ clerks@3pumpcourt.com
Pump Court Chambers
Upper Ground Floor, 3 Pump Court, Temple, London EC4Y 7AJ, ☎ 020 7353 0711
✉ clerks@3pumpcourt.com
Pump Court Chambers
5 Temple Chambers, Temple Street, Swindon SN1 1SQ, ☎ 01793 539899
✉ clerks@3pumpcourt.com
Call Date: July 1982, Gray's Inn
Pupil Supervisor
Qualifications: [LL.B (Soton)]

BLOWER MR GRAHAM ROBERT

Argent Chambers
5 Bell Yard, London WC2A 2JR, ☎ 020 7556 5500
✉ briefsin@argentchambers.co.uk
Call Date: Nov 1980, Gray's Inn
Pupil Supervisor
Qualifications: [BA (Leeds)]
✉ g.blower@argentchambers.co.uk

BLUM MR DORON ZE'EV

1 Pump Court
Elm Court, Temple, London EC4Y 7AB, ☎ 020 7842 7070
✉ (name)@pumpcourt.co.uk
Call Date: Nov 1998, Middle Temple
Pupil Supervisor
Qualifications: [LLB (Hons)(Lond) LLM (USA)]

BLUMGART MISS TRUDI KATHERINE ROSE SARA

Atkinson Bevan Chambers
1st Floor, 2 Harcourt Buildings, Temple, London EC4Y 9DB, ☎ 020 7353 2112
✉ clerks@2hb.co.uk
Call Date: Oct 1999, Middle Temple
Qualifications: [BA (Hons)(Bris)]
✉ kateblumgart@2hb.co.uk

BLUNDELL MR DAVID ANTHONY

Landmark Chambers
180 Fleet Street, London EC4A 2HG, ☎ 020 7430 1221
✉ clerks@landmarkchambers.co.uk
Call Date: Oct 2001, Inner Temple
Qualifications: [BA (Cantab) M PHil (Cantab) CPE]
✉ dblundell@landmarkchambers.co.uk

BLUNT MR DAVID JOHN QC (1991)

4 Pump Court
4 Pump Court, Temple, London EC4Y 7AN, ☎ 020 7842 5555
✉ chambers@4pumpcourt.com
Call Date: Nov 1967, Middle Temple
Recorder
Qualifications: [MA (Cantab)]
✉ dblunt@4pumpcourt.com

BLUNT MR OLIVER SIMON PETER QC (1994)

Furnival Chambers
32 Furnival Street, London EC4A 1JQ, ☎ 020 7405 3232
Call Date: Nov 1974, Middle Temple
Recorder
Qualifications: [LLB]
✉ oblunt@furnivallaw.co.uk

BLYTHIN MR DAVID ANDREW

Linenhall Chambers
1 Stanley Place, Chester CH1 2LU, ☎ 01244 348282
✉ clerks@linenhallchambers.co.uk
Call Date: Mar 1999, Lincoln's Inn
Qualifications: [BA (Hons)]
✉ clerks@1stanleyplace.co.uk

BOAITEY MISS CHARLOTTE

12 Old Square Chambers
1st Floor, 12 Old Square, Lincoln's Inn, London WC2A 3TX, ☎ 020 7404 0875
✉ clerks@12oldsquare.com
Call Date: Nov 1976, Middle Temple
Pupil Supervisor
Qualifications: [LLB (Lond) Dip Soc Anthrop (Oxon)]
✉ clerks@12oldsquare.com

BOARD MR ADAM STUART

Essex Court Chambers
24 Lincoln's Inn Fields, London WC2A 3EG, ☎ 020 7813 8000
✉ clerksroom@essexcourt.net
Call Date: Oct 2010, Lincoln's Inn
Qualifications: [BA (Oxon) LLM (Cantab)]
✉ aboard@essexcourt.net

BOARDMAN MR CHRISTOPHER LEIGH WILSON

11 Stone Buildings
11 Stone Buildings, Lincoln's Inn, London WC2A 3TG, ☎ 020 7831 6381
✉ clerks@11sb.com
Call Date: Oct 1995, Lincoln's Inn
Pupil Supervisor
Qualifications: [LLB (Hons) LLM (Lond)]
✉ boardman@11sb.com

BOARDMAN MR MICHAEL LEOPOLD

4 Breams Buildings
Chancery Lane, London EC4A 1HP, ☎ 020 7092 1900 ✉ clerks@4bb.co.uk
Call Date: July 1979, Middle Temple
Pupil Supervisor
Qualifications: [BA (Manch) LLB (Lond)]

BOASE MISS ANNA JANE

One Essex Court
Ground Floor, One Essex Court, Temple, London EC4Y 9AR, ☎ 020 7583 2000
✉ clerks@oeclaw.co.uk
Call Date: Oct 2002, Middle Temple
Qualifications: [BA (Cantab) Dip in Law]
✉ aboase@oeclaw.co.uk

BOATENG MRS ESTHER OLABISI

Princess Court Chambers
122 Princess Court, Bromley Hill, Bromley BR1 4JU, ☎ 020 8460 2046
Call Date: July 2001, Lincoln's Inn
Qualifications: [LLB (Hons) (Bris)]
✉ pcchambers77@yahoo.com

BOATENG-ADDO MR EDWARD

7 Bell Yard
London WC2A 2JR, ☎ 020 7831 0636
✉ kevintarrant@btconnect.com
Call Date: Nov 2000, Middle Temple
Pupil Supervisor
Qualifications: [LLB (Hons) (Lond)]
✉ eba@7bellyard.co.uk

BODNAR MR ANDREW

Matrix Chambers
Griffin Building, Gray's Inn, London WC1R 5LN, ☎ 020 7404 3447
✉ matrix@matrixlaw.co.uk / lscott@matrixlaw.co.uk
Call Date: Oct 1995, Lincoln's Inn
Qualifications: [BA (Hons)(Lond) Dip in Law (Lond)]

BODNAR MISS KATHARINE ALEXANDRA

39 Essex Street
London WC2R 3AT, ☎ 020 7832 1111
✉ clerks@39essex.com
Call Date: July 2004, Inner Temple
Qualifications: [LLB BVC]
✉ Alexandra.Bodnar@39essex.com

BOEDDINGHAUS MR HERMANN

4 Stone Buildings
Ground Floor, 4 Stone Buildings, Lincoln's Inn, London WC2A 3XT, ☎ 020 7242 5524
✉ clerks@4stonebuildings.com
Call Date: Nov 1996, Lincoln's Inn
Qualifications: [BSc(Cape Town) BCL, MA (Oxon)]
✉ hb@4stonebuildings.com

BOGAN MR PAUL SIMON QC (2011)

23 Essex Street
London WC2R 3AA, ☎ 020 7413 0353
✉ clerks@23es.com
Call Date: July 1983, Gray's Inn
Pupil Supervisor
Qualifications: [BA (Hons)]
✉ paulbogan@23es.com

BOGLE MR JAMES STEWART LOCKHART

10 King's Bench Walk
Ground Floor, 10 King's Bench Walk, Temple, London EC4Y 7EB, ☎ 020 7353 7742
✉ Chambers@10kingsbenchwalk.co.uk
Call Date: Oct 1991, Middle Temple
Pupil Supervisor
Qualifications: [BA ACIArb DipLaw]
✉ chambers@10kingsbenchwalk.co.uk

BOJARSKI MR ANDRZEJ LEONARD

36 Bedford Row
London WC1R 4JH, ☎ 020 7421 8000
✉ chambers@36bedfordrow.co.uk
Call Date: Oct 1995, Gray's Inn
Pupil Supervisor
Qualifications: [LLB]
✉ abojarski@36bedfordrow.co.uk

E

BOJCZUK MR WILLIAM JOHN

Selborne Chambers
10 Essex Street, London WC2R 3AA,
☎ 020 7420 9500
✉ clerks@selbornechambers.co.uk
Call Date: July 1983, Inner Temple
Qualifications: [LLB (Lond) MA]
✉ clerks@selbornechambers.co.uk

BOLTON MISS CAROLINE JAYNE

4-5 Gray's Inn Square
Gray's Inn, London WC1R 5AH,
☎ 020 7404 5252 ✉ clerks@4-5.co.uk
Call Date: Oct 1998, Middle Temple
Qualifications: [LLB hons (Soton) LLM hons (Lond)]
✉ cbolton@4-5.co.uk

BOLTON MRS FRANCES LAWJUA

Argent Chambers
5 Bell Yard, London WC2A 2JR,
☎ 020 7556 5500
✉ briefsin@argentchambers.co.uk
Call Date: July 1981, Middle Temple
Pupil Supervisor
Qualifications: [LLB (Hons)]
✉ f.bolton@argentchambers.co.uk

BOLTON MR ROBERT JOHN

2 King's Bench Walk
2 King's Bench Walk, Temple, London EC4Y 7DE, ☎ 020 7353 1746
✉ clerks@2kbw.com
Call Date: July 1987, Gray's Inn
Qualifications: [BA (Manch)]
✉ rbolton@2kbw.com

BOMPAS MISS ABRA MAE

One Essex Court
Ground Floor, One Essex Court, Temple, London EC4Y 9AR, ☎ 020 7583 2000
✉ clerks@oeclaw.co.uk
Call Date: July 2008, Lincoln's Inn
Qualifications: [BA (Hons) PgDl]
✉ abompas@oeclaw.co.uk

BOMPAS MR ANTHONY GEORGE QC (1994)

4 Stone Buildings
Ground Floor, 4 Stone Buildings, Lincoln's Inn, London WC2A 3XT, ☎ 020 7242 5524
✉ clerks@4stonebuildings.com
Call Date: July 1975, Middle Temple
Qualifications: [MA (Oxon)]
✉ clerks@4stonebuildings.com

BONAVERO MR PHILIPPE

4 King's Bench Walk
2nd Floor, 4 King's Bench Walk, Temple, London EC4Y 7DL, ☎ 020 7822 7000
✉ clerks@4kbw.co.uk
Call Date: Nov 2008, Middle Temple
Qualifications: [LLB (Hons)]
✉ pbb@4kbw.co.uk

BOND MISS ABIGAIL RACHEL

St John's Chambers
101 Victoria Street, Bristol BS1 6PU,
☎ 0117 923 4700
✉ clerks@stjohnschambers.co.uk
Call Date: Oct 1999, Middle Temple
Qualifications: [BA (Hons) (Oxon) LLM (UEA)]

BOND MR ANDREW MARK

Pump Court Chambers
31 Southgate Street, Winchester, Hampshire SO23 9EB, ☎ 01962 868 161
✉ clerks@3pumpcourt.com
Pump Court Chambers
Upper Ground Floor, 3 Pump Court, Temple, London EC4Y 7AJ, ☎ 020 7353 0711
✉ clerks@3pumpcourt.com
Pump Court Chambers
5 Temple Chambers, Temple Street, Swindon SN1 1SQ, ☎ 01793 539899
✉ clerks@3pumpcourt.com
Call Date: Oct 1999, Inner Temple
Qualifications: [LLB (Staffs) LLM (Dumelm)]
✉ abo@3pumpcourt.com

BOND MR CHRISTOPHER WILLIAM JOHN

3 Verulam Buildings
London WC1R 5NT, ☎ 020 7831 8441
✉ chambers@3vb.com
Call Date: July 2008, Inner Temple
Qualifications: [BA (Oxon) MA M Phil PhD (Yale)]
✉ cbond@3vb.com

BOND MISS JACQUELINE KATHRYN

1 Mitre Court Buildings
1 Mitre Court Buildings, Temple, London EC4Y 7BS, ☎ 020 7452 8900
✉ clerks@1mcb.com
4 King's Bench Walk
2nd Floor, 4 King's Bench Walk, Temple, London EC4Y 7DL, ☎ 020 7822 7000
✉ clerks@4kbw.co.uk
Call Date: Oct 1994, Middle Temple
Qualifications: [LLB (Hons)]
✉ jackie.bond@1mcb.com

E

BOND MISS JULIA MARGARET

St Ive's Chambers
Whittall Street, Birmingham B4 6DH,
☎ 0121 236 0863
✉ clerks@stiveschambers.co.uk
Call Date: July 2010, Lincoln's Inn
Qualifications: [LLM (Staffs)]

BOND MISS KELLY LOUISE

Enterprise Chambers
9 Old Square, Lincoln's Inn, London
WC2A 3SR, ☎ 020 7405 9471
✉ london@enterprisechambers.com
Enterprise Chambers
65 Quayside, Newcastle Upon Tyne NE1 3DE,
☎ 0191 222 3344
✉ newcastle@enterprisechambers.com
Enterprise Chambers
43 Park Square, Leeds LS1 2NP,
☎ 0113 246 0391
✉ leeds@enterprisechambers.com
Call Date: July 2007, Middle Temple
Qualifications: [BA (Hons) (Cantab)]
🖃 kellybond@enterprisechambers.com

BOND MISS LEISHA

St Philips Chambers
55 Temple Row, Birmingham B2 5LS,
☎ 0121 246 7000 ✉ clerks@st-philips.com
Call Date: Oct 1999, Middle Temple
Qualifications: [LLB (Hons)(B'ham)]
🖃 lbond@st-philips.com

BOND DR MIEKO KUCHAR

King's Bench Chambers
Wellington House, 175 Holdenhurst Road,
Bournemouth, Dorset BH8 8DQ,
☎ 01202 250025
Call Date: Mar 2008, Lincoln's Inn
Qualifications: [BA (Cantab)]

BOND MR RICHARD IAN WINSOR

Citadel Chambers
The Citadel, 190 Corporation Street,
Birmingham B4 6QD, ☎ 0121 233 8500
✉ clerks@citadelchambers.com
Call Date: July 1988, Middle Temple
Pupil Supervisor, Recorder
Qualifications: [LLB (Hons) (Manch)]
🖃 clerks@citadelchambers.com

BONE MISS LUCY CATHERINE SARA

Littleton Chambers
3 King's Bench Walk North, Temple, London
EC4Y 7HR, ☎ 020 7797 8600
✉ fschneider@littletonchambers.co.uk
Call Date: Oct 1999, Middle Temple
Pupil Supervisor
Qualifications: [LLB (Hons) LLM (Lond)]
🖃 lbone@littletonchambers.co.uk

BONEHILL MR NICHOLAS BENJAMIN

4 Breams Buildings
Chancery Lane, London EC4A 1HP,
☎ 020 7092 1900 ✉ clerks@4bb.co.uk
Call Date: July 2006, Middle Temple
Qualifications: [LLB (Hons) (Exon)]

BONNER MR LEE BRADLEY

Atlantic Chambers
4-6 Cook Street, Liverpool L2 9QU,
☎ 0151 236 4421
✉ info@atlanticchambers.co.uk
Call Date: Nov 2000, Lincoln's Inn
Qualifications: [LLB (Hons) (Sheff)]
🖃 leebonner@atlanticchambers.co.uk

BONSU MISS MICHAELA

12 Old Square Chambers
1st Floor, 12 Old Square, Lincoln's Inn,
London WC2A 3TX, ☎ 020 7404 0875
✉ clerks@12oldsquare.com
Call Date: Nov 2000, Lincoln's Inn
Qualifications: [LLB (Hons) (Hull)]
🖃 clerks@12oldsquare.com

BOOKER MRS SZILVIA ADRIENN

Argent Chambers
5 Bell Yard, London WC2A 2JR,
☎ 020 7556 5500
✉ briefsin@argentchambers.co.uk
Call Date: Nov 2005, Inner Temple
Qualifications: [BA University of Toronto CPE University of East]
🖃 s.booker@argentchambers.co.uk

BOOLS DR MICHAEL DAVID QC (2012)

Brick Court Chambers
7-8 Essex Street, London WC2R 3LD,
☎ 020 7379 3550 ✉ clerks@brickcourt.co.uk
Call Date: Oct 1991, Middle Temple
Pupil Supervisor
Qualifications: [LLB (Hons) (UEA) D Phil (Oxon)]
🖃 Michael.Bools@Brickcourt.co.uk

E

BOON MISS ELIZABETH JADE

Crown Office Chambers
2 Crown Office Row, Temple, London
EC4Y 7HJ, ☎ 020 7797 8100
✉ mail@crownofficechambers.com
Call Date: July 2006, Inner Temple
Qualifications: [BA (Oxon)]
boon@crownofficechambers.com

BOON MISS LUCINDA CAROLINE

5 Essex Court
1st Floor, 5 Essex Court, Temple, London
EC4Y 9AH, ☎ 020 7410 2000
✉ clerks@5essexcourt.co.uk
Call Date: Oct 2002, Gray's Inn
Qualifications: [LLB (Leic)]
boon@5essexcourt.co.uk, barristers@5essexcourt.co.uk

BOORA MR JINDER SINGH

No5 Chambers
Fountain Court, Steelhouse Lane, Birmingham
B4 6DR, ☎ 0845 210 5555 ✉ info@no5.com
No5 Chambers
Greenwood House, 4-7 Salisbury Court,
London EC4Y 8AA, ☎ 0845 210 5555
No5 Chambers
38 Queen Square, Bristol BS1 4QS,
☎ 0845 210 5555
Call Date: Oct 1990, Gray's Inn
Qualifications: [LLB LLM (Warw)]
jbo@no5.com

BOOTH MR ALEXANDER HENRY SPENCER

Francis Taylor Building
Inner Temple, London EC4Y 7BY,
☎ 020 7353 8415 ✉ clerks@ftb.eu.com
Call Date: Nov 2000, Middle Temple
Qualifications: [BA (Hons) (Oxon) Dip in Law]
Alexander.booth@ftb.eu.com

BOOTH MISS ANNA JANE ELIZABETH

Garden Court Chambers
57-60 Lincoln's Inn Fields, London WC2A 3LJ,
☎ 020 7993 7600 ✉ info@gclaw.co.uk
Call Date: July 2009, Inner Temple
Qualifications: [BA (Cantab)]

BOOTH MISS CHERIE QC (1995)

Matrix Chambers
Griffin Building, Gray's Inn, London
WC1R 5LN, ☎ 020 7404 3447
✉ matrix@matrixlaw.co.uk / Iscott@matrixlaw.co.uk
Call Date: July 1976, Lincoln's Inn
Recorder
Qualifications: [LLB (Lond) FRSA FJMU]

BOOTH MR MICHAEL JOHN QC (1999)

Kings Chambers
36 Young Street, Manchester M3 3FT,
☎ 0845 034 3444
✉ clerks@kingschambers.com
Kings Chambers
5 Park Square East, Leeds LS1 2NE,
☎ 0845 034 3444
✉ clerks@kingschambers.com
13 Old Square Chambers
Ground Floor, 14 Old Square, Lincoln's Inn,
London WC2A 3UE, ☎ 020 7831 4445
✉ clerks@13oldsquare.com
Call Date: Nov 1981, Lincoln's Inn
Qualifications: [MA (Cantab)]
mbooth@kingschambers.com

BOOTH MR NIGEL ROBERT

Call Date: Oct 1994, Gray's Inn
Qualifications: [LLB Dip German Law]
nigel.booth@stjohnsbuildings.co.uk, clerk@stjohnsbuildings.co.uk

BOOTH MR PHILIP ANTONY

Park Lane Plowden
19 Westgate, Leeds LS1 2RD,
☎ 0113 228 5049
✉ clerks@parklaneplowden.co.uk
Call Date: July 2004, Inner Temple
Qualifications: [BA (Southbank)]
philip.booth@parklaneplowden.co.uk

BOOTH MR RICHARD JOHN

1 Crown Office Row
1 Crown Office Row, Temple, London
EC4Y 7HH, ☎ 020 7797 7500
✉ mail@1cor.com
Call Date: Oct 1993, Middle Temple
Pupil Supervisor
Qualifications: [MA (Hons)(Cantab) Lic Spec Dr Eur (Brussels)]
richard.booth@1cor.com

BOOTH MR ROGER GEORGE

Crown Office Row Chambers
119 Church Street, Brighton, Sussex
BN1 1UD, ☎ 01273 625625
✉ clerks@1cor.com
Call Date: Nov 1966, Gray's Inn
Pupil Supervisor
Qualifications: [LLB]
roger.booth@1cor.com

BOOTH MISS SARAH JANE

Deans Court Chambers
24 St John Street, Manchester M3 4DF, ☎0161 214 6000 ✉clerks@deanscourt.co.uk
Deans Court Chambers
101 Walker Street, Preston PR1 2RR, ☎01772 565 600
✉preston@deanscourt.co.uk
Call Date: Nov 1999, Gray's Inn
Qualifications: [LLB]
sjbooth@deanscourt.co.uk

BOOTH MR SIMON MARK

Atlantic Chambers
4-6 Cook Street, Liverpool L2 9QU, ☎0151 236 4421
✉info@atlanticchambers.co.uk
Call Date: Nov 1985, Lincoln's Inn
Qualifications: [LLB (L'pool)]

BOOTH MISS SYLVIA JOY

18 St John Street
Manchester M3 4EA, ☎0161 278 1800
✉clerks@18sjs.com
Call Date: Oct 1992, Gray's Inn
Qualifications: [LLB (Sheff)]

BOOTHBY MR JOSEPH JOHN

5 Pump Court
Ground Floor, 5 Pump Court, Temple, London EC4Y 7AP, ☎020 7353 2532
✉clerks@5pumpcourt.com
Call Date: July 1972, Middle Temple
Pupil Supervisor, Recorder
Qualifications: [BA (Lond)]
joboothby@5pumpcourt.com

BOOTHROYD MR ALEC DOMINIC

Angel Chambers
Ethos Building, Kings Road, Swansea SA1 8AS, ☎01792 464623
✉clerks@angelchambers.co.uk
Call Date: Nov 1991, Inner Temple
Qualifications: [LLB]

BOOTHROYD MISS SUSAN ELIZABETH

Dere Street Barristers
33 Broad Chare, Newcastle Upon Tyne NE1 3DQ, ☎0844 3351551
✉clerks@derestreet.co.uk
Call Date: Oct 1990, Lincoln's Inn
Qualifications: [LLB (Newc)]

BOR DR HARRIS

Wilberforce Chambers
8 New Square, Lincoln's Inn, London WC2A 3QP, ☎020 7306 0102
✉chambers@wilberforce.co.uk
Call Date: July 2006, Inner Temple
Qualifications: [BA (Lond) PhD (Cantab)]

BORGEN MISS INGA

Old Court Chambers
Newham House, 96-98 Borough Road, Middlesbrough TS1 2HJ, ☎01642 232523
✉clerks@oldcourtchambers.com
Call Date: Oct 2004, Inner Temple
Qualifications: [BA CPE]

BORKOWSKI MISS GEMMA FRANCESCA

Albion Chambers
Broad Street, Bristol BS1 1DR, ☎0117 927 2144
✉clerks@albionchambers.co.uk
Call Date: Oct 2005, Inner Temple
Qualifications: [LLB University of Bristol]
gemma.borkowski@albionchambers.co.uk

BORNMAN MISS KERRY

3 Stone Buildings
Ground Floor, 3 Stone Buildings, Lincoln's Inn, London WC2A 3XL, ☎020 7242 4937
✉clerks@3sb.law.co.uk
Call Date: Oct 1999, Middle Temple
Pupil Supervisor
Qualifications: [LLB (Hons)(Reading)]
kbornman@3sb.law.co.uk

Types of work: Chancery (general), Chancery (land law), Equity, Family provision, Inheritance and cohabitees, Professional negligence, Succession, Tax, Trust litigation, Trusts, Wills

BORRELLI MR MICHAEL FRANCIS ANTONY QC (2000)

187 Fleet Street
London EC4A 2AT, ☎020 7430 7430
✉chambers@187fleetstreet.com
Call Date: Nov 1977, Middle Temple
michaelborrelli@187fleetstreet.com

BORRETT MR RICHARD PETER

3 PB Barristers
30 Christchurch Road, Bournemouth, Dorset BH1 3PD, ☎01202 292102
✉clerks.bournemouth@3paper.co.uk
Call Date: July 2009, Lincoln's Inn
Qualifications: [BSc (L'pool) CPE LLB (Hons) (Lond)]

E

BOSANKO MR JONATHON

King's Bench and Godolphin (KBG)Chambers
115 North Hill, Plymouth, Devon PL4 8JY, ☎01752 221551
✉clerks@kbgchambers.co.uk
Call Date: July 2001, Middle Temple
Qualifications: [LLB (Hons)]
clerks@kingsbenchchambers.co.uk

BOSOMWORTH MR MICHAEL JOHN

Dere Street Barristers
33 Broad Chare, Newcastle Upon Tyne NE1 3DQ, ☎0844 3351551
✉clerks@derestreet.co.uk
York Chambers
Rotterdam House, 116 The Quayside, Newcastle Upon Tyne NE1 3DY, ☎0191 206 4677
Call Date: July 1979, Middle Temple
Qualifications: [BA (Nott'm)]

BOSTWICK MR RONALD ERWIN FRANCIS

Holborn Chambers
6 Gate Street, Lincoln's Inn Fields, London WC2A 3HP, ☎020 7242 6060
Call Date: Nov 1990, Inner Temple
Pupil Supervisor
Qualifications: [LLB (Lond)]

BOSWELL MR ANDREW TIMOTHY

13 King's Bench Walk
13 King's Bench Walk, Temple, London EC4Y 7EN, ☎020 7353 7204
✉clerks@13kbw.co.uk
13 KBW
32 Beaumont Street, Oxford OX1 2NP, ☎01865 311066 ✉clerks@13kbw.co.uk
Call Date: Nov 2004, Gray's Inn
Qualifications: [BA BCL]
tboswell@13kbw.co.uk

BOSWELL MISS JENNIFER MARY

Tooks Chambers
81 Farringdon Street, London EC4A 4BL, ☎020 7842 7575 ✉clerks@tooks.co.uk
Call Date: July 1982, Middle Temple
Qualifications: [BA (Hons) Sussex]
jenny.boswell@tooks.co.uk

BOSWELL MISS LINDSAY ALICE QC (1997)

Quadrant Chambers
Quadrant House, 10 Fleet Street, London EC4Y 1AU, ☎020 7583 4444
✉info@quadrantchambers.com
Call Date: July 1982, Gray's Inn
Qualifications: [BSc (London) Dip Law (Lond)]
lindsay.boswell@quadrantchambers.com

BOSWOOD MR ANTHONY RICHARD QC (1986)

Fountain Court Chambers
Fountain Court, Temple, London EC4Y 9DH, ☎020 7583 3335
✉chambers@fountaincourt.co.uk
Call Date: Nov 1970, Middle Temple
Qualifications: [MA BCL]
aboswood@fountaincourt.co.uk

BOTHROYD MISS SHIRLEY ANN

Littleton Chambers
3 King's Bench Walk North, Temple, London EC4Y 7HR, ☎020 7797 8600
✉fschneider@littletonchambers.co.uk
Call Date: July 1982, Middle Temple
Pupil Supervisor
Qualifications: [BA]
sbothroyd@littletonchambers.co.uk

BOTROS MR JOHN MICHAEL

Cambria Chambers
The Coal Exchange, Mount Stuart Square, Cardiff Bay, Cardiff CF10 5EB, ☎0845 123 1234
✉Info@cambriachambers.co.uk
Call Date: Feb 1992, Middle Temple
Qualifications: [MA (Oxon)]

BOTT MR CHARLES ADRIAN QC (2008)

Carmelite Chambers
9 Carmelite Street, London EC4Y 0DR, ☎020 7936 6300
✉clerks@carmelitechambers.co.uk
Call Date: Nov 1979, Gray's Inn
Qualifications: [MA (Cantab)]
cbott@carmelitechambers.co.uk

BOTTOMLEY MISS PENNY LYNNE

Fountain Chambers
Cleveland Business Centre, 1 Watson Street, Middlesbrough TS1 2RQ, ☎01642 804040
✉clerks@fountainchambers.co.uk
Call Date: July 2006, Lincoln's Inn
Qualifications: [LLB (Newc)]

BOUCHER-GILES MR BENJAMIN ARTHUR

Fountain Chambers
Cleveland Business Centre, 1 Watson Street, Middlesbrough TS1 2RQ, ☎ 01642 804040
✉ clerks@fountainchambers.co.uk
Call Date: Oct 2004, Lincoln's Inn
Qualifications: [BA PgDL]
✉ clerks@fountainchambers.co.uk

BOULD MR DUNCAN JOHN

Linenhall Chambers
1 Stanley Place, Chester CH1 2LU,
☎ 01244 348282
✉ clerks@linenhallchambers.co.uk
Call Date: July 1984, Gray's Inn
Pupil Supervisor
Qualifications: [BSc LLB (Lond)]

BOULDING MR PHILIP VINCENT QC (1996)

Keating Chambers
15 Essex Street, London WC2R 3AA,
☎ 020 7544 2600
✉ clerks@keatingchambers.com
Call Date: Nov 1979, Gray's Inn
Qualifications: [MA LLM (Cantab)]
✉ pboulding@keatingchambers.com

BOULTER MR TERENCE

Furnival Chambers
32 Furnival Street, London EC4A 1JQ,
☎ 020 7405 3232
Call Date: July 1986, Lincoln's Inn
Pupil Supervisor
Qualifications: [BA(Hons)]

BOULTON MISS CLEMENTINE

Furnival Chambers
32 Furnival Street, London EC4A 1JQ,
☎ 020 7405 3232
Call Date: July 2009, Inner Temple
Qualifications: [MA (St. Andrews)]

BOULTON MR RICHARD EDWARD STANLEY QC (2011)

One Essex Court
Ground Floor, One Essex Court, Temple, London EC4Y 9AR, ☎ 020 7583 2000
✉ clerks@oeclaw.co.uk
Call Date: July 2003, Inner Temple
Qualifications: [MA (Oxon) CPE FCA]
✉ rboulton@oeclaw.co.uk

BOUMPHREY MR JOHN ROSS STAVELEY

Zenith Chambers
10 Park Square, Leeds LS1 2LH,
☎ 0113 245 5438
✉ clerks@zenithchambers.co.uk
Call Date: Nov 1992, Inner Temple
Pupil Supervisor
Qualifications: [BA (Hons)(Warw) Dip in Law]
✉ jboumphrey@zenithchambers.co.uk

BOURKE MS SARAH VICTORIA NORMA

Tooks Chambers
81 Farringdon Street, London EC4A 4BL,
☎ 020 7842 7575 ✉ clerks@tooks.co.uk
Call Date: Oct 1996, Gray's Inn
Qualifications: [LLB (Lond)]
✉ clerks@tooks.co.uk

BOURNE MR CHARLES GREGORY

4-5 Gray's Inn Square
Gray's Inn, London WC1R 5AH,
☎ 020 7404 5252 ✉ clerks@4-5.co.uk
Call Date: Oct 1991, Middle Temple
Pupil Supervisor
Qualifications: [MA (Hons) (Cantab) Dip Law MA (France) Lettres Modernes (France)]
✉ cbourne@4-5.co.uk

BOURNE MR COLIN PETER

Kings Chambers
36 Young Street, Manchester M3 3FT,
☎ 0845 034 3444
✉ clerks@kingschambers.com
Kings Chambers
5 Park Square East, Leeds LS1 2NE,
☎ 0845 034 3444
✉ clerks@kingschambers.com
Kings Chambers
Embassy House, 60 Church Street, Birmingham B3 2DJ, ☎ 0845 034 3444
✉ clerks@kingschambers.com
Call Date: Oct 1997, Gray's Inn
Qualifications: [LLB (Manc)]

BOURNE MR GEOFFREY ROBERT

13 Old Square Chambers
Ground Floor, 14 Old Square, Lincoln's Inn, London WC2A 3UE, ☎ 020 7831 4445
✉ clerks@13oldsquare.com
Call Date: Nov 1978, Gray's Inn
Pupil Supervisor
Qualifications: [MA (Oxon)]

E

BOURNE MR IAN MACLEAN QC (2006)

Charter Chambers
33 John Street, London WC1N 2AT,
☎ 020 7618 4400
✉ clerks@charterchambers.com
Call Date: July 1977, Inner Temple
Recorder
Qualifications: [LLB Hons (Exon)]
✉ ian.bourne@charterchambers.com

BOURNE-ARTON MR JAMES LUKE

St Paul's Chambers
5th Floor, St Paul's House, 23 Park Square South, Leeds LS1 2ND, ☎ 0113 245 5866
Call Date: Oct 2001, Inner Temple
Qualifications: [LLB (Bris)]
✉ jba@stpaulschambers.com

BOURNE-ARTON MR SIMON NICHOLAS QC (1994)

Park Court Chambers
16 Park Place, Leeds LS1 2SJ,
☎ 0113 243 3277
✉ clerks@parkcourtchambers.co.uk
Call Date: Nov 1975, Inner Temple
Recorder
Qualifications: [LLB (Hons)]

E

BOURNE-ARTON MR THOMAS CHARLES DENBY

Farrar's Building
Farrar's Building, Temple, London EC4Y 7BD,
☎ 020 7583 9241
✉ Chambers@farrarsbuilding.co.uk
Call Date: Oct 2005, Inner Temple
Qualifications: [MA University of Edinburgh CPE City University]
✉ tbarton@farrarsbuilding.co.uk

BOUTLE MR TOBY JEFFERSON

Ten Old Square
Ground Floor, Ten Old Square, Lincoln's Inn, London WC2A 3SU, ☎ 020 7405 0758
✉ clerks@tenoldsquare.com
Call Date: July 2004, Lincoln's Inn
Qualifications: [BA Hons (Oxon)]
✉ tobyboutle@tenoldsquare.com

BOVENSIEPEN MR DANIEL JOHN

20 Essex Street
London WC2R 3AL, ☎ 020 7842 1200
✉ clerks@20essexst.com
Call Date: July 2004, Middle Temple
Qualifications: [BA Hons (Cantab) LLM (Cantab)]
✉ clerks@20essexst.com

BOVEY MR MUNGO

Tooks Chambers
81 Farringdon Street, London EC4A 4BL,
☎ 020 7842 7575 ✉ clerks@tooks.co.uk
Call Date: Nov 2000, Inner Temple
Qualifications: [LLB (Glas)]
✉ clerks@tooks.co.uk

BOWCOCK MISS SAMANTHA JANE

15 Winckley Square
Preston PR1 3JJ, ☎ 01772 252828
✉ clerks@15winckleysq.co.uk
Call Date: Oct 1990, Middle Temple
Qualifications: [LLB (Manch)]

BOWDEN MR GUY ROBERT

4 Breams Buildings
Chancery Lane, London EC4A 1HP,
☎ 020 7092 1900 ✉ clerks@4bb.co.uk
Call Date: Oct 2003, Inner Temple
Qualifications: [BSc (So'ton)]

BOWDEN MR TIMOTHY JOHN

Seven Bedford Row
7 Bedford Row, London WC1R 4BS,
☎ 020 7242 3555 ✉ clerks@7br.co.uk
Call Date: July 2003, Middle Temple
Qualifications: [LLB Hons (Sheff)]
✉ tbowden@7br.co.uk

BOWDERY MR MARTIN QC (2000)

Atkin Chambers
1 Atkin Building, Gray's Inn, London WC1R 5AT, ☎ 020 7404 0102
✉ clerks@atkinchambers.com
Call Date: July 1980, Inner Temple
Recorder
Qualifications: [BA (Oxon)]
✉ mbowdery@atkinchambers.com

BOWE MR PATRICK JOSEPH

KCH Garden Square
1 Oxford Street, Nottingham NG1 5BH,
☎ 0115 941 8851
✉ clerks@kchgardensquare.co.uk
Call Date: July 2000, Lincoln's Inn
Qualifications: [LLB(Hons) (Leic)]

BOWE MR TIMOTHY MICHAEL

St Ive's Chambers
Whittall Street, Birmingham B4 6DH,
☎ 0121 236 0863
✉ clerks@stiveschambers.co.uk
Call Date: July 2003, Inner Temple
Qualifications: [BA (Cantab) CPE]
✉ timothy.bowe@stiveschambers.co.uk

BOWEN MR JAMES FRANCIS

Garden Court Chambers
57-60 Lincoln's Inn Fields, London WC2A 3LJ,
☎020 7993 7600 ✉info@gclaw.co.uk
Call Date: Nov 1979, Gray's Inn
Pupil Supervisor
Qualifications: [LLB (Exon)]
✉jamesb@gclaw.co.uk

BOWEN MR NICHOLAS JAMES HUGH QC (2009)

Doughty Street Chambers
53-54 Doughty Street, London WC1N 2LS,
☎020 7404 1313
✉enquiries@doughtystreet.co.uk
Doughty Street Chambers
Pall Mall Court, 61-67 King Street, Manchester M2 4PD, ☎0161 618 1066
Doughty Street Chambers
5th Floor, Broad Quay House, Prince Street, Bristol BS1 4DJ, ☎01179 058 717
Call Date: Nov 1984, Gray's Inn
Qualifications: [BA (Sussex)]
✉n.bowen@doughtystreet.co.uk

BOWEN MISS NICOLA

Bell Yard Chambers
116/118 Chancery Lane, London WC2A 1PP,
☎020 7306 9292
✉byclerks@bellyardchambers.co.uk
Call Date: Nov 2003, Gray's Inn
Qualifications: [LLB (Cardiff)]
✉nbowen@bellyardchambers.co.uk

BOWEN MR PAUL EDWARD QC (2012)

Doughty Street Chambers
53-54 Doughty Street, London WC1N 2LS,
☎020 7404 1313
✉enquiries@doughtystreet.co.uk
Doughty Street Chambers
Pall Mall Court, 61-67 King Street, Manchester M2 4PD, ☎0161 618 1066
Doughty Street Chambers
5th Floor, Broad Quay House, Prince Street, Bristol BS1 4DJ, ☎01179 058 717
Call Date: Nov 1993, Inner Temple
Pupil Supervisor
Qualifications: [LLB (Exon)]
✉p.bowen@doughtystreet.co.uk

BOWEN MISS SARAH JENNIFER

New Walk Chambers
27 New Walk, Leicester, Leicestershire
LE1 6TE, ☎0871 200 1298 / 0116 255 9144
✉clerks@newwalkchambers.co.uk
Call Date: Oct 2006, Middle Temple
Qualifications: [BA (Hons) (Leic)]

BOWER MR ALISTAIR ROSS

9 St John Street
Manchester M3 4DN, ☎0161 955 9000
✉civilclerks@9sjs.com / criminalclerks@9sjs.com
Call Date: July 1986, Inner Temple
Qualifications: [LLB (Leeds)]

BOWER MISS GEMMA LOUISE

College Chambers
19 Carlton Crescent, Southampton, Hampshire SO15 2ET, ☎023 8023 0338
✉clerks@college-chambers.co.uk
Call Date: July 2006, Middle Temple
Qualifications: [LLB (Hons)]
✉gbower@College-Chambers.co.uk

BOWER MS LAURINDA

Call Date: Nov 2006, Lincoln's Inn
Qualifications: [LLB (Nott'm)]
✉bower@paradise-sq.co.uk

BOWERS MR JOHN SIMON QC (1998)

Littleton Chambers
3 King's Bench Walk North, Temple, London EC4Y 7HR, ☎020 7797 8600
✉fschneider@littletonchambers.co.uk
Call Date: Nov 1979, Middle Temple
Recorder
Qualifications: [MA BCL (Oxon)]
✉bowersjohnsimon@aol.com

BOWERS MR RUPERT JOHN

Doughty Street Chambers
53-54 Doughty Street, London WC1N 2LS,
☎020 7404 1313
✉enquiries@doughtystreet.co.uk
Call Date: Oct 1995, Gray's Inn
Pupil Supervisor
Qualifications: [BA (Hons)(Newc) Dip Law]
✉r.bowers@doughtystreet.co.uk

BOWES MISS GEMMA

3 PB Barristers
3 Paper Buildings, Temple, London EC4Y 7EU,
☎020 7583 8055
3 PB Barristers
Royal Talbot House, 2 Victoria Street, Bristol, Avon BS1 6BB, ☎0117 928 1520
3 PB Barristers
23 Beaumont Street, Oxford OX1 2NP,
☎01865 793 736
3 PB Barristers
4 St Peter Street, Winchester SO23 8BW,
☎01962 868884
✉clerks.winchester@3paper.co.uk

E

3 PB Barristers
30 Christchurch Road, Bournemouth, Dorset BH1 3PD, ☎01202 292102
✉clerks.bournemouth@3paper.co.uk
Call Date: July 2009, Middle Temple
Qualifications: [BA (Hons) (Dunelm) MSc (Oxon) LLB (Hons) (Lond)]

BOWES MR MICHAEL ANTHONY QC (2001)

Outer Temple Chambers
The Outer Temple, 222 Strand, London WC2R 1BA, ☎020 7353 6381
✉clerks@outertemple.com
Cobden House Chambers
19 Quay Street, Manchester M3 3HN, ☎0161 833 6000 ✉Clerks@Cobden.co.uk
Call Date: July 1980, Middle Temple
Recorder
Qualifications: [LLB (Manch)]
michael.bowesqc@outertemple.com

BOWHILL MISS JESSIE KATE

8 New Square
8 New Square, Lincoln's Inn, London WC2A 3QP, ☎020 7405 4321
✉clerks@8newsquare.co.uk
Call Date: Oct 2003, Gray's Inn
Qualifications: [LLB (Bris)]
jessie.bowhill@8newsquare.co.uk

Types of work: Confidential information, Copyright, Data protection, Entertainment, Intellectual property, Malicious falsehood, Media and entertainment, Patents, Trade secrets, Trademarks

BOWKER MR ROBERT JAMES

Tanfield Chambers
2-5 Warwick Court, London WC1R 5DJ, ☎020 7421 5300
✉clerks@tanfieldchambers.co.uk
Call Date: Nov 1995, Lincoln's Inn
Qualifications: [BA (Hons)(So'ton)]
robertbowker@tanfieldchambers.co.uk, www

BOWLEY MR IVAN RICHARD

Lincoln House Chambers
Tower 12, The Avenue North, Spinningfields, 18-22 Bridge Street, Manchester M3 3BZ, ☎0161 832 5701
✉info@lincolnhousechambers.com
Call Date: Nov 1990, Middle Temple
Pupil Supervisor
Qualifications: [Bsc (Newc) Dip Law]
ivan.bowley@lincolnhousechambers.com

BOWLING MR JAMES STUART

4 Pump Court
4 Pump Court, Temple, London EC4Y 7AN, ☎020 7842 5555
✉chambers@4pumpcourt.com
Call Date: Nov 1999, Middle Temple
Qualifications: [BA (Oxon) Dip Law]
jbowling@4pumpcourt.com

BOWMER MR MICHAEL PAUL

Four New Square
Four New Square, Lincoln's Inn, London WC2A 3RJ, ☎020 7822 2000
✉barristers@4newsquare.com
Call Date: Oct 1997, Middle Temple
Pupil Supervisor
Qualifications: [LLB (Hons)(Lond)]
m.bowmer@4newsquare.com

BOWRING PROF WILLIAM SCHUYLER BEAKBANE

Field Court Chambers
5 Field Court, Gray's Inn, London WC1R 5EF, ☎020 7405 6114 ✉clerks@fieldcourt.co.uk
Call Date: Nov 1974, Middle Temple
Qualifications: [BA (Kent)]

BOWRON MISS MARGARET RUTH QC (2001)

1 Crown Office Row
1 Crown Office Row, Temple, London EC4Y 7HH, ☎020 7797 7500
✉mail@1cor.com
Call Date: Nov 1978, Inner Temple
Recorder
Qualifications: [LLB (Lond)]
margaret.bowron@1cor.com

BOWSHER MR MICHAEL FREDERICK THOMAS QC (2006)

Monckton Chambers
1 & 2 Raymond Buildings, Gray's Inn, London WC1R 5NR, ☎020 7405 7211
✉chambers@monckton.com
Call Date: Nov 1985, Middle Temple
Qualifications: [FCIArb BA (Oxon)]
mbowsher@monckton.com

BOWSHER-MURRAY MISS CLAIRE JENNETTE

Old Square Chambers
10-11 Bedford Row, London WC1R 4BU,
☎ 020 7269 0300 ✉ clerks@oldsquare.co.uk
Old Square Chambers
3 Orchard Court, St Augustine's Yard, Bristol BS1 5DP, ☎ 0117 930 5100
✉ clerks@oldsquare.co.uk
Call Date: Oct 2007, Gray's Inn
Qualifications: [BA LLM MA (Cantab)]
✉ bowsher-murray@oldsquare.co.uk

BOYCE MR WILLIAM QC (2001)

QEB Hollis Whiteman
1-2 Laurence Pountney Hill, London EC4R 0EU, ☎ 020 7933 8855
✉ barristers@qebhw.co.uk
Call Date: July 1976, Gray's Inn
Recorder
Qualifications: [BA]
✉ barristers@qebholliswhiteman.co.uk

BOYD MR DAVID MARTIN

Coram Chambers
9-11 Fulwood Place, London WC1V 6HG,
☎ 020 7092 3700
✉ mail@coramchambers.co.uk
Call Date: Feb 1977, Middle Temple
Pupil Supervisor
Qualifications: [LLB (B'ham)]
✉ david.boyd@coramchambers.co.uk

BOYD MR JAMES ANDREW DONALDSON

Kings Chambers
36 Young Street, Manchester M3 3FT,
☎ 0845 034 3444
✉ clerks@kingschambers.com
Kings Chambers
5 Park Square East, Leeds LS1 2NE,
☎ 0845 034 3444
✉ clerks@kingschambers.com
Kings Chambers
Embassy House, 60 Church Street, Birmingham B3 2DJ, ☎ 0845 034 3444
✉ clerks@kingschambers.com
Call Date: Nov 1994, Inner Temple
Qualifications: [LLB (Manch) LLM (USA)]

BOYD MISS JESSICA

Blackstone Chambers
Blackstone House, Temple, London EC4Y 9BW, ☎ 020 7583 1770
✉ clerks@blackstonechambers.com
Call Date: Nov 2007, Inner Temple
Qualifications: [BA (Cantab) PhD Dip Law]
✉ jessicaboyd@blackstonechambers.com

BOYD MISS KERSTIN MARGARET

Tanfield Chambers
2-5 Warwick Court, London WC1R 5DJ,
☎ 020 7421 5300
✉ clerks@tanfieldchambers.co.uk
Call Date: July 1979, Gray's Inn
Pupil Supervisor
Qualifications: [BA (Cantab)]
✉ kerstinboyd@tanfieldchambers.co.uk

Types of work: Clinical negligence, Family law, Personal injury

BOYD MR PHILLIP JOSEPH GEORGE

Lincoln House Chambers
Tower 12, The Avenue North, Spinningfields, 18-22 Bridge Street, Manchester M3 3BZ,
☎ 0161 832 5701
✉ info@lincolnhousechambers.com
Call Date: Nov 1993, Gray's Inn
Pupil Supervisor
Qualifications: [MA (Cantab)]
✉ joe.boyd@lincolnhousechambers.com

BOYD MR STEPHEN JAMES HARVEY

Selborne Chambers
10 Essex Street, London WC2R 3AA,
☎ 020 7420 9500
✉ clerks@selbornechambers.co.uk
Call Date: July 1977, Gray's Inn
Pupil Supervisor
Qualifications: [BSc (Hons) PGCert]

Types of work: Commercial litigation, Common law (general), Employment, Franchising, Landlord and tenant, Mediation, Partnerships, Professional negligence, Real property, Sale and carriage of goods, Sport, Succession, Trusts, Wills

BOYD MR STEWART CRAUFURD QC (1981)

Essex Court Chambers
24 Lincoln's Inn Fields, London WC2A 3EG,
☎ 020 7813 8000
✉ clerksroom@essexcourt.net
Call Date: July 1967, Middle Temple
Recorder
Qualifications: [MA (Cantab)]
✉ sboyd@essexcourt.net

E

BOYDELL MR EDWARD PATRICK STIRRUP

Pump Court Chambers
Upper Ground Floor, 3 Pump Court, Temple, London EC4Y 7AJ, ☎020 7353 0711
✉clerks@3pumpcourt.com
Pump Court Chambers
5 Temple Chambers, Temple Street, Swindon SN1 1SQ, ☎01793 539899
✉clerks@3pumpcourt.com
Pump Court Chambers
31 Southgate Street, Winchester, Hampshire SO23 9EB, ☎01962 868 161
✉clerks@3pumpcourt.com
Call Date: Nov 1989, Middle Temple
Pupil Supervisor, Recorder
Qualifications: [BEd (Hons) (Cantab)]
✉epb@3pumpcourt.com

BOYDEN MR MATTHEW JOHN

No5 Chambers
Greenwood House, 4-7 Salisbury Court, London EC4Y 8AA, ☎0845 210 5555
No5 Chambers
38 Queen Square, Bristol BS1 4QS, ☎0845 210 5555
No5 Chambers
Fountain Court, Steelhouse Lane, Birmingham B4 6DR, ☎0845 210 5555 ✉info@no5.com
Call Date: July 2007, Middle Temple
Qualifications: [BSc (Hons) (Exon)]

E

BOYE-ANAWOMAH MISS MARGO CIARA

Renaissance Chambers
5th Floor, Gray's Inn Chambers, Gray's Inn, London WC1R 5JA, ☎020 7404 1111
✉clerks@renaissancechambers.co.uk
Call Date: Nov 1989, Inner Temple
Pupil Supervisor
Qualifications: [LLB]
✉mba@renaissancechambers.co.uk

BOYES MR IAN DAVID

3 Temple Gardens
Lower Ground Floor, 3 Temple Gardens, Temple, London EC4Y 9AU, ☎020 7353 3102
✉clerks@3tg.co.uk
Call Date: Nov 2003, Lincoln's Inn
Qualifications: [LLB (Hons) (L'pool) LLM (L'pool)]

BOYES MISS KAREN ROSALIE

Erimus Chambers
PO Box 1440, Bedford MK43 6AJ, ☎01234 720952
✉clerks@erimuschambers.com
Call Date: Oct 1991, Middle Temple
Qualifications: [LLB (Hons) (Newc)]
✉karenboyes@erimuschambers.com

BOYLE MR ALAN EDWARD

Essex Court Chambers
24 Lincoln's Inn Fields, London WC2A 3EG, ☎020 7813 8000
✉clerksroom@essexcourt.net
Call Date: July 1977, Middle Temple
Qualifications: [MA BCL (Oxon)]
✉aboyle@essexcourt.net

BOYLE MR ALAN GORDON QC (1991)

Serle Court
6 New Square, Lincoln's Inn, London WC2A 3QS, ☎020 7242 6105
✉clerks@serlecourt.co.uk
Call Date: Nov 1972, Lincoln's Inn
Qualifications: [BA (Oxon) MA (Oxon)]
✉aboyle@serlecourt.co.uk

Types of work: Alternative dispute resolution, Arbitration, Banking, Banking and Finance, Chancery, Chancery (commercial), Chancery (general), Chancery (land law), Civil fraud, Commercial fraud, Commercial litigation, Commercial planning, Commercial regulation, Company law, Company, commercial and competition, Conciliation, Corporate governance, Corporate insolvency, Dispute resolution, Dispute resolution and arbitration, E-commerce, Equity, Family provision, Financial services, Freezing orders, Inheritance and cohabitees, Insolvency, International arbitration, International commercial arbitration, Litigation, Mediation, Offshore trust litigation, Private client, Sale of business, Shareholder agreements, Sport, Succession, Trust litigation, Warranty claims, Wills

BOYLE MR CHRISTOPHER ALEXANDER DAVID

Landmark Chambers
180 Fleet Street, London EC4A 2HG, ☎020 7430 1221
✉clerks@landmarkchambers.co.uk
Call Date: Nov 1994, Lincoln's Inn
Pupil Supervisor
Qualifications: [BA (Hons)]
✉cboyle@landmarkchambers.co.uk

BOYLE MR DAVID STUART

Deans Court Chambers
24 St John Street, Manchester M3 4DF,
☎0161 214 6000 ✉clerks@deanscourt.co.uk
Deans Court Chambers
101 Walker Street, Preston PR1 2RR,
☎01772 565 600
✉preston@deanscourt.co.uk
Call Date: Mar 1996, Gray's Inn
Pupil Supervisor
Qualifications: [MA (Cantab)]
boyle@deanscourt.co.uk

BOYLE MR GERARD JAMES

3 Serjeants Inn
London EC4Y 1BQ, ☎020 7427 5000
✉clerks@3serjeantsinn.com
Call Date: Nov 1992, Gray's Inn
Pupil Supervisor
Qualifications: [BA (Cantab) MA (Cantab)]
gboyle@3serjeantsinn.com

BOYLE MR JONATHAN

Cobden House Chambers
19 Quay Street, Manchester M3 3HN,
☎0161 833 6000 ✉Clerks@Cobden.co.uk
Call Date: Oct 2005, Middle Temple
Qualifications: [BSc (Sheffield)]
clerks@cobden.co.uk

BOYLE MISS KAREN

St James's Chambers
68 Quay Street, Manchester M3 3EJ,
☎0161 834 7000
✉clerks@stjameschambers.com
12 King's Bench Walk
12 King's Bench Walk, Temple, London
EC4Y 7EL, ☎020 7583 0811
Call Date: July 2000, Lincoln's Inn
Qualifications: [LLB(Hons) (Warw)]
karen.boyle@stjameschambers.com

BOYLE MISS LUCY ANNABEL

12 King's Bench Walk
12 King's Bench Walk, Temple, London
EC4Y 7EL, ☎020 7583 0811
Call Date: July 2009, Middle Temple
Qualifications: [MA (Manch) LLB (Hons) (Manch)]
lboyle@12kbw.co.uk

BOYLE MR MATTHEW WILLIAM

Crown Office Chambers
2 Crown Office Row, Temple, London
EC4Y 7HJ, ☎020 7797 8100
✉mail@crownofficechambers.com
Call Date: July 2000, Gray's Inn
Qualifications: [MA (Oxon)]
boyle@crownofficechambers.com

BRAAMSKAMP MS CHRISTINE JOLANDA

3 Raymond Buildings
3 Raymond Buildings, Gray's Inn, London
WC1R 5BH, ☎020 7400 6400
✉clerks@3rblaw.com
Call Date: July 2000, Gray's Inn
Qualifications: [Criminal Law (MA) (Holland)]

BRABIN MR MICHAEL EDWARD

Colleton Chambers
Colleton Crescent, Exeter, Devon EX2 4DG,
☎01392 274898
✉clerks@colletonchambers.co.uk
Call Date: May 1976, Inner Temple
Pupil Supervisor
michaelbrabin@colletonchambers.co.uk

BRACE MR MICHAEL WESLEY

Civitas Chambers
Global Reach, Celtic Gateway, Cardiff Bay,
Cardiff CF11 0SN, ☎0845 0713 007
✉clerks@civitaslaw.com
Call Date: Apr 1991, Lincoln's Inn
Pupil Supervisor
Qualifications: [LLB (Hons)(Lond)]
michael.brace@civitaslaw.com

BRADBERRY MISS REBECCA

Octagon Chambers
29 Park Street, Taunton, Somerset TA1 4DG,
☎01823 331919
✉jcload@Octagonchambers.co.uk
Call Date: Oct 1996, Lincoln's Inn
Qualifications: [BA (Hons)(Warw) Dip in Law (Exon)]
rbradberry@octagonchambers.co.uk

BRADBURY MISS JOANNA SUSAN

East Anglian Chambers
15 The Close, Norwich, Norfolk NR1 4DZ,
☎01473 214481 ✉norwich@ealaw.co.uk
East Anglian Chambers
140 New London Road, Chelmsford, Essex
CM2 0AW, ☎01473 214481
✉chelmsford@ealaw.co.uk
East Anglian Chambers
Gresham House, 5 Museum Street, Ipswich,
Suffolk IP1 1HQ, ☎01473 214481
✉ipswich@ealaw.co.uk
Call Date: Nov 1999, Middle Temple
Qualifications: [BA (Hons)(Sussex)]
jobradbury@ealaw.co.uk

E

BRADBURY MRS SARA PATRICIA

New Bailey Chambers
4th Floor, Corn Exchange, Fenwick Street, Liverpool, Merseyside L2 7QS,
☎0151 236 9402 ✉clerks@newbailey.com
Call Date: Oct 1998, Gray's Inn
Qualifications: [LLB (Manch)]
sa.bradbury7@gmail.com

BRADBURY MR TIMOTHY BLACKBURN

3 PB Barristers
3 Paper Buildings, Temple, London EC4Y 7EU,
☎020 7583 8055
3 PB Barristers
Royal Talbot House, 2 Victoria Street, Bristol, Avon BS1 6BB, ☎0117 928 1520
3 PB Barristers
30 Christchurch Road, Bournemouth, Dorset BH1 3PD, ☎01202 292102
✉clerks.bournemouth@3paper.co.uk
3 PB Barristers
4 St Peter Street, Winchester SO23 8BW,
☎01962 868884
✉clerks.winchester@3paper.co.uk
3 PB Barristers
23 Beaumont Street, Oxford OX1 2NP,
☎01865 793 736
Call Date: July 1989, Inner Temple
Pupil Supervisor
Qualifications: [LLB (So'ton)]
timothy.bradbury@3paper.co.uk

BRADLEY MR BENJAMIN PAUL

Outer Temple Chambers
The Outer Temple, 222 Strand, London WC2R 1BA, ☎020 7353 6381
✉clerks@outertemple.com
Call Date: Oct 2007, Inner Temple
Qualifications: [BA (Oxon)]
ben.bradley@outertemple.com

BRADLEY MISS CAROLINE

23 Essex Street
London WC2R 3AA, ☎020 7413 0353
✉clerks@23es.com
Call Date: Nov 1985, Middle Temple
Pupil Supervisor
Qualifications: [BA (Hons)]
carolinebradley@23es.com

BRADLEY MR CHARLES EDWARD MAY

Pump Court Tax Chambers
16 Bedford Row, London WC1R 4EF,
☎020 7414 8080 ✉clerks@pumptax.com
Call Date: July 2010, Lincoln's Inn
Qualifications: [BA (Cantab) MPHIL (Cantab)]
ebradley@pumptax.com

Types of work: Capital tax, Corporation tax, Customs, Excise, Income tax, National Insurance, Private client, Stamp duty, Tax investigations, Tax tribunal, Trusts, VAT

BRADLEY MISS CLODAGH MARIA

1 Crown Office Row
1 Crown Office Row, Temple, London EC4Y 7HH, ☎020 7797 7500
✉mail@1cor.com
Call Date: Oct 1996, Middle Temple
Pupil Supervisor
Qualifications: [MA (Hons)(Cantab)]

BRADLEY MR DENIS ARTHUR ROBERT

Warwick House Chambers
8 Warwick Court, Warwick House Chambers, Gray's Inn, London WC1R 5DJ,
☎020 7430 2323
✉clerks@warwickhousechambers.com
Call Date: Feb 1965, Gray's Inn

BRADLEY MR MATTHEW JAMES

Henderson Chambers
2 Harcourt Buildings, Temple, London EC4Y 9DB, ☎020 7583 9020
✉clerks@hendersonchambers.co.uk
Call Date: Oct 2004, Lincoln's Inn
Qualifications: [BA (Hons) PgDL]
mbradley@hendersonchambers.co.uk

BRADLEY MR MICHAEL JAMES

1 Hare Court
1 Hare Court, Temple, London EC4Y 7BE,
☎020 7797 7070 ✉clerks@1hc.com
Call Date: Mar 1999, Gray's Inn
Pupil Supervisor
Qualifications: [BA (Oxon)]
bradley@1hc.com

E

BRADLEY MR PHILLIP JAMES

No5 Chambers
Fountain Court, Steelhouse Lane, Birmingham B4 6DR, ☎0845 210 5555 ✉info@no5.com
No5 Chambers
Greenwood House, 4-7 Salisbury Court, London EC4Y 8AA, ☎0845 210 5555
1 Pump Court
Elm Court, Temple, London EC4Y 7AB, ☎020 7842 7070
✉(name)@pumpcourt.co.uk
No5 Chambers
38 Queen Square, Bristol BS1 4QS, ☎0845 210 5555
Call Date: Nov 1993, Lincoln's Inn
Qualifications: [BA (Hons)]
pjb@no5.com

BRADLEY MR RICHARD

Oriel Chambers
14 Water Street, Liverpool, Merseyside L2 8TD, ☎0151 236 7191
✉clerks@orielchambers.co.uk
Oriel Chambers
18 Ribblesdale Place, Preston PR1 3NA, ☎01772 254 764
✉clerks@oriel-chambers.co.uk
Call Date: July 1978, Middle Temple
Pupil Supervisor
Qualifications: [LLB]
richard.bradley@orielchambers.co.uk

BRADLEY MS SALLY CHRISTINA

4 Paper Buildings
1st Floor, 4 Paper Buildings, Temple, London EC4Y 7EX, ☎020 7427 5200
✉clerks@4pb.com
Call Date: Nov 1989, Inner Temple
Pupil Supervisor
Qualifications: [BA]
sb@4pb.com

BRADLEY MS SALLY FRANCES QC (1999)

Trinity Chambers
The Custom House, 39 Quayside, Newcastle Upon Tyne NE1 3DE, ☎0191 232 1927
✉info@trinitychambers.co.uk
Sovereign Chambers
46 Park Place, Leeds LS1 2RY, ☎0113 245 1841
✉clerks@sovereignchambers.co.uk
18 St John Street
Manchester M3 4EA, ☎0161 278 1800
✉clerks@18sjs.com
Trinity Chambers
Multi Media Exchange, 72-80 Corporation Road, Middlesbrough TS1 2RF, ☎01642 247569
✉info@trinitychambers.co.uk
Call Date: Nov 1978, Lincoln's Inn
Recorder
Qualifications: [LLB]

BRADLY MR DAVID LAWRENCE

39 Essex Street
London WC2R 3AT, ☎020 7832 1111
✉clerks@39essex.com
Call Date: July 1987, Middle Temple
Pupil Supervisor
Qualifications: [LLB (Lond)]
david.bradly@39essex.com

BRADNOCK MR THOMAS PHILIP

Colleton Chambers
Colleton Crescent, Exeter, Devon EX2 4DG, ☎01392 274898
✉clerks@colletonchambers.co.uk
Call Date: Oct 1997, Gray's Inn
Qualifications: [BA]
thomasbradnock@colletonchambers.co.uk

BRADSHAW MR DAVID LAWRENCE

Zenith Chambers
10 Park Square, Leeds LS1 2LH, ☎0113 245 5438
✉clerks@zenithchambers.co.uk
Call Date: July 1975, Inner Temple
Pupil Supervisor, Recorder
Qualifications: [LLB]
dbradshaw@zenithchambers.co.uk

BRADSHAW MR IAN CHARLES

Old Court Chambers
Newham House, 96-98 Borough Road, Middlesbrough TS1 2HJ, ☎01642 232523
✉clerks@oldcourtchambers.com
Call Date: Oct 1992, Middle Temple
Pupil Supervisor
Qualifications: [LLB(Nott'm) LLM(Wales) MA(Hull)]
clerks@oldcourtchambers.com

E

BRADSHAW MR MARK KIERAN

No5 Chambers
Fountain Court, Steelhouse Lane, Birmingham B4 6DR, ☎0845 210 5555 ✉info@no5.com
No5 Chambers
Greenwood House, 4-7 Salisbury Court, London EC4Y 8AA, ☎0845 210 5555
No5 Chambers
38 Queen Square, Bristol BS1 4QS, ☎0845 210 5555
Call Date: July 2002, Gray's Inn
Qualifications: [LLB (Staffordshire)]
mbr@no5.com

BRADSHAW MR SIMON JOHN

Cornwall Street Chambers
85-87 Cornwall Street, Birmingham B3 3BY, ☎0121 233 7500
✉clerks@cornwallstreet.co.uk
Call Date: July 2009, Middle Temple
Qualifications: [MEng (Lond) LLB (Hons) LLM (Edin)]
simon.bradshaw@cornwallstreet.co.uk

BRADY DR ANN CATHERINE

Rougemont Chambers
Victory House, Dean Clarke Gardens, Southernhay East, Exeter EX2 4AA, ☎01392 208484
✉clerks@rougemontchambers.co.uk
Call Date: Mar 2001, Middle Temple
Qualifications: [LLB PGCE PhD]

BRADY MR MICHAEL ANTONY

18 St John Street
Manchester M3 4EA, ☎0161 278 1800
✉clerks@18sjs.com
Call Date: Oct 1992, Gray's Inn
Qualifications: [LLB (Hons)]

BRADY MR SCOTT

3 Temple Gardens
Lower Ground Floor, 3 Temple Gardens, Temple, London EC4Y 9AU, ☎020 7353 3102
✉clerks@3tg.co.uk
Call Date: July 1998, Middle Temple
Qualifications: [LLB (Edin)]
sb@3tg.co.uk

BRAGANZA MISS NICOLA

Tooks Chambers
81 Farringdon Street, London EC4A 4BL, ☎020 7842 7575 ✉clerks@tooks.co.uk
Call Date: Oct 1992, Middle Temple
Pupil Supervisor
Qualifications: [LL.B (Hons) (Reading)]

BRAGGE MR THOMAS HEREWARD

Stour Chambers
Mill Studio, 17a Stour Street, Canterbury, Kent CT1 2NR, ☎01227 764899
✉clerks@stourchambers.co.uk
Call Date: Oct 2000, Inner Temple
Qualifications: [BA (Lond) MA (Lond) CPE]
clerks@stourchambers.co.uk

BRAGIEL MR EDWARD BRONISLAW HENRYK

Hogarth Chambers
5 New Square, Lincoln's Inn, London WC2A 3RJ, ☎020 7404 0404
✉barristers@hogarthchambers.com
Call Date: July 1977, Middle Temple
Pupil Supervisor
Qualifications: [MA (Cantab)]
ebragiel@hogarthchambers.com

BRAID MR MARK ROBIN NYLE

2 Dr Johnson's Buildings
2 Dr Johnson's Buildings, Temple, London EC4Y 7AY, ☎020 7936 2613
✉clerks@2drj.com
Call Date: Nov 1999, Middle Temple
Qualifications: [MA (Hons)(Edin'b)]
clerks@2drj.com

BRAIER MR JASON DEAN

Field Court Chambers
5 Field Court, Gray's Inn, London WC1R 5EF, ☎020 7405 6114 ✉clerks@fieldcourt.co.uk
Call Date: July 2002, Inner Temple
Qualifications: [LLB (Lond) LLM (B'ham)]
jason.braier@fieldcourt.co.uk

BRAIN MISS PAMELA FRANCIS

Chambers of Marion Smullen and Kerim Fuad QC
1 Inner Temple Lane, London EC4Y 1AF, ☎020 7427 4400 ✉clerks@1itl.com
Call Date: Nov 1985, Inner Temple
Pupil Supervisor
Qualifications: [LLB (Lond)]
clerks@1itl.com

BRAITHWAITE MR GARFIELD ZIBEAN

42 Bedford Row
London WC1R 4LL, ☎020 7831 0222
✉clerks@42br.com
Call Date: Feb 1987, Gray's Inn
Pupil Supervisor
Qualifications: [LLB (Lanc)]
garfield.braithwaite@42br.com

BRAITHWAITE MR THOMAS JAMES

Serle Court
6 New Square, Lincoln's Inn, London WC2A 3QS, ☎020 7242 6105
✉clerks@serlecourt.co.uk
Call Date: Oct 1998, Lincoln's Inn
Pupil Supervisor
Qualifications: [BA (Hons)(Cantab)]
✉tbraithwaite@serlecourt.co.uk

BRAITHWAITE MR WILLIAM THOMAS SCATCHARD QC (1992)

Exchange Chambers
One Derby Square, Derby Square, Liverpool L2 9XX, ☎0151 236 7747
✉info@exchangechambers.co.uk
Exchange Chambers
7 Ralli Courts, West Riverside, Manchester M3 5FT, ☎0161 833 2722
Exchange Chambers
Oxford House, Oxford Row, Leeds LS1 3BE, ☎0113 203 1970
✉spencer@exchangechambers.co.uk
Call Date: Nov 1970, Gray's Inn
Qualifications: [LLB (L'pool)]

BRAMALL MS KATE LOUISE

18 St John Street
Manchester M3 4EA, ☎0161 278 1800
✉clerks@18sjs.com
Call Date: Oct 1999, Gray's Inn
Qualifications: [LLB (Hons) (L'pool)]

BRAMWELL MR CHRISTOPHER PAUL

Regency Chambers
45 Priestgate, Peterborough PE1 1LB, ☎01733 315215
✉clerks@regencychambers.law.co.uk
Regency Chambers
Sheraton House, Castle Park, Cambridge CB3 0AX, ☎01223 301517
Call Date: Nov 1996, Gray's Inn
Pupil Supervisor
Qualifications: [LLB (Lancs)]
✉cbramwell@regencychambers.law.co.uk, clerks@regencychambers.law.co.uk

BRAMWELL MISS CORINNE VICTORIA

Nine Bedford Row
9 Bedford Row, London WC1R 4AZ, ☎020 7489 2727
✉clerks@9bedfordrow.co.uk
Call Date: Oct 2005, Inner Temple
Qualifications: [LLB University of Sheffield]

BRAMWELL MR RICHARD MERVYN QC (1989)

Temple Tax Chambers
1st Floor, 3 Temple Gardens, Temple, London EC4Y 9AU, ☎020 7353 7884
✉clerks@templetax.com
Call Date: July 1967, Middle Temple
Qualifications: [LLM]
✉clerks@templetax.com, richardbramwellqc@hotmail.com

BRANCHFLOWER MR GEORGE

Zenith Chambers
10 Park Square, Leeds LS1 2LH, ☎0113 245 5438
✉clerks@zenithchambers.co.uk
Call Date: Oct 1997, Lincoln's Inn
Pupil Supervisor
Qualifications: [LLB (Hons)(Leeds)]
✉gbranchflower@zenithchambers.co.uk

BRAND MR KIERAN MATTHEW

Maidstone Chambers
33 Earl Street, Maidstone, Kent ME14 1PF, ☎01622 688592
✉clerks@maidstonechambers.co.uk
Call Date: Nov 2007, Middle Temple
Qualifications: [LLB (Hons)]

E

BRAND MISS RACHEL RENNIE VIRGINIA ANN QC (2000)

Citadel Chambers
The Citadel, 190 Corporation Street, Birmingham B4 6QD, ☎0121 233 8500
✉clerks@citadelchambers.com
Call Date: July 1981, Gray's Inn
Recorder
Qualifications: [BA]
✉clerks@citadelchambers.com

BRANDER MISS HELEN JULIA

2-3 Hind Court Chambers
2-3 Hind Court, Fleet Street, London EC4A 3DL, ☎020 7822 2150
✉david@2-3hindcourt.com
Call Date: Mar 2002, Lincoln's Inn
Qualifications: [LLB (Hons)]

BRANDER MS RUTH CLAIRE

Doughty Street Chambers
53-54 Doughty Street, London WC1N 2LS, ☎020 7404 1313
✉enquiries@doughtystreet.co.uk
Doughty Street Chambers
Pall Mall Court, 61-67 King Street, Manchester M2 4PD, ☎0161 618 1066

Doughty Street Chambers
5th Floor, Broad Quay House, Prince Street, Bristol BS1 4DJ, ☎01179 058 717
Call Date: Oct 2001, Middle Temple
Qualifications: [BA (Hons) (Cantab) CPE]
r.brander@doughtystreet.co.uk

BRANDON MR BENJAMIN PAUL

3 Raymond Buildings
3 Raymond Buildings, Gray's Inn, London WC1R 5BH, ☎020 7400 6400
clerks@3rblaw.com
Call Date: Nov 1991, Inner Temple
Pupil Supervisor
Qualifications: [BA (Warw) Dip Law LLM (Lond)]
ben.brandon@3raymondbuildings.com

BRANDON MR DAVID STEPHEN QC (1996)

Taxchambers
15 Old Square, Lincoln's Inn, London WC2A 3UE, ☎020 7242 2744
taxchambers@15oldsquare.co.uk
Call Date: July 1978, Gray's Inn
Qualifications: [BA (Nott'm) LLM (Keele)]
taxchambers@15oldsquare.co.uk

BRANDON MISS HELEN ELIZABETH

Atlantic Chambers
4-6 Cook Street, Liverpool L2 9QU, ☎0151 236 4421
info@atlanticchambers.co.uk
Call Date: Oct 1993, Middle Temple
Pupil Supervisor
Qualifications: [LLB (Hons)(Lancs)]
helen.mcloughlin3@btinternet.com

BRANDON MISS LOUISE ANN

9 St John Street
Manchester M3 4DN, ☎0161 955 9000
civilclerks@9sjs.com / criminalclerks@9sjs.com
Call Date: July 2003, Middle Temple
Qualifications: [BA Hons (Manch)]
louiseannbrandon@aol.com

BRANDRETH MR BENET XAN

11 South Square
1st Floor, 11 South Square, Gray's Inn, London WC1R 5EY, ☎020 7405 1222
clerks@11southsquare.com
Call Date: Nov 1999, Middle Temple
Pupil Supervisor
Qualifications: [MA (Cantab)]
bbrandreth@11southsquare.com

BRANIGAN MISS KATE VICTORIA QC (2006)

4 Paper Buildings
1st Floor, 4 Paper Buildings, Temple, London EC4Y 7EX, ☎020 7427 5200
clerks@4pb.com
Albion Chambers
Broad Street, Bristol BS1 1DR, ☎0117 927 2144
clerks@albionchambers.co.uk
Call Date: July 1984, Inner Temple
Qualifications: [LLB (So'ton)]
kb@4pb.com

BRANKOVIC MISS VICTORIA ANN

New Walk Chambers
27 New Walk, Leicester, Leicestershire LE1 6TE, ☎0871 200 1298 / 0116 255 9144
clerks@newwalkchambers.co.uk
Call Date: July 2008, Inner Temple
Qualifications: [LLB (Sheff)]
victoria_brankovic@hotmail.com

BRANNIGAN MR PETER JOHN SEAN QC (2009)

4 Pump Court
4 Pump Court, Temple, London EC4Y 7AN, ☎020 7842 5555
chambers@4pumpcourt.com
Call Date: Oct 1994, Gray's Inn
Qualifications: [BA]
sbrannigan@4pumpcourt.com

BRANSON MISS SARAH LOUISE

Coram Chambers
9-11 Fulwood Place, London WC1V 6HG, ☎020 7092 3700
mail@coramchambers.co.uk
Call Date: July 2001, Middle Temple
Qualifications: [BA (Hons) GDip (Law)]
Sarah.Branson@coramchambers.co.uk

BRANSTON MR BARNABAS MARTIN HENRY

5 Essex Court
1st Floor, 5 Essex Court, Temple, London EC4Y 9AH, ☎020 7410 2000
clerks@5essexcourt.co.uk
Call Date: Oct 1999, Middle Temple
Qualifications: [BA (Hons)(Oxon)]
branston@5essexcourt.co.uk

BRANSTON MR GARETH PHILIP

23 Essex Street
London WC2R 3AA, ☎020 7413 0353
✉clerks@23es.com
Call Date: Oct 1996, Gray's Inn
Pupil Supervisor
Qualifications: [MA (Hons)(Cantab)]

BRANT MR PAUL DAVID

Oriel Chambers
14 Water Street, Liverpool, Merseyside
L2 8TD, ☎0151 236 7191
✉clerks@orielchambers.co.uk
Oriel Chambers
18 Ribblesdale Place, Preston PR1 3NA,
☎01772 254 764
✉clerks@oriel-chambers.co.uk
Call Date: Oct 1993, Lincoln's Inn
Pupil Supervisor
Qualifications: [LLB (Hons)(L'pool)]
✉paul.brant@orielchambers.co.uk

BRASLAVSKY MR NICHOLAS JUSTIN QC (1999)

Kings Chambers
36 Young Street, Manchester M3 3FT,
☎0845 034 3444
✉clerks@kingschambers.com
Kings Chambers
5 Park Square East, Leeds LS1 2NE,
☎0845 034 3444
✉clerks@kingschambers.com
Kings Chambers
Embassy House, 60 Church Street,
Birmingham B3 2DJ, ☎0845 034 3444
✉clerks@kingschambers.com
3 PB Barristers
Royal Talbot House, 2 Victoria Street, Bristol,
Avon BS1 6BB, ☎0117 928 1520
3 PB Barristers
4 St Peter Street, Winchester SO23 8BW,
☎01962 868884
✉clerks.winchester@3paper.co.uk
3 PB Barristers
23 Beaumont Street, Oxford OX1 2NP,
☎01865 793 736
3 PB Barristers
3 Paper Buildings, Temple, London EC4Y 7EU,
☎020 7583 8055
3 PB Barristers
30 Christchurch Road, Bournemouth, Dorset
BH1 3PD, ☎01202 292102
✉clerks.bournemouth@3paper.co.uk
Call Date: July 1983, Inner Temple
Recorder
Qualifications: [LLB PhD(B'ham) M jur]
✉nbraslavsky@kingschambers.com

BRASSINGTON MR STEPHEN DAVID

2 Hare Court
Lower Ground, Ground, 1st & 2nd Floor, 2
Hare Court, Temple, London EC4Y 7BH,
☎020 7353 3982 ✉clerks@2harecourt.com
Call Date: Nov 1994, Inner Temple
Pupil Supervisor
Qualifications: [BSc (Hons)(Lond) CPE]
✉stephenbrassington@2harecourt.com

BRAUN MS MINKA CHAYA

25 Bedford Row
London WC1R 4HD, ☎020 7067 1500
✉clerks@25bedfordrow.com
Call Date: July 2000, Inner Temple
Pupil Supervisor
Qualifications: [LLB (Lond)]
✉mbraun@25bedfordrow.com

BRAY MISS CAROLINE JANE

36 Bedford Row
London WC1R 4JH, ☎020 7421 8000
✉chambers@36bedfordrow.co.uk
Call Date: July 2000, Lincoln's Inn
Qualifications: [LLB(Hons) (Leic)]
✉cbray@36bedfordrow.co.uk

BRAY MISS HELEN LORNA

Walnut House
63 St. David's Hill, Exeter, Devon EX4 4DW,
☎01392 279751
✉clerks@walnuthouse.co.uk
Call Date: July 2004, Gray's Inn
Qualifications: [BA (Oxon)]
✉helen.bray@walnuthouse.co.uk

BRAZENALL MISS EMILY JANE

Albion Chambers
Broad Street, Bristol BS1 1DR,
☎0117 927 2144
✉clerks@albionchambers.co.uk
Call Date: July 2009, Inner Temple
Qualifications: [BSc (Gloucestershire)]

BRAZIER MISS CHARLOTTE LOUISE

Staple Inn Chambers
1st Floor, 9 Staple Inn, Holborn Bars, London
WC1V 7QH, ☎020 7242 5240
✉clerks@stapleinn.co.uk
Call Date: Oct 2009, Lincoln's Inn
Qualifications: [BA (Hons) (Lond) CPE BPP]
✉cb@stapleinn.co.uk

E

BRAZIL MR DOMINIC THOMAS GEORGE

1 KBW Chambers
1 King's Bench Walk, Temple, London
EC4Y 7DB, ☎ 020 7936 1500
✉ clerks@1kbw.co.uk
King's Bench Chambers
174 High Street, Lewes BN7 1YE,
☎ 01273 402600
Call Date: Nov 1995, Middle Temple
Qualifications: [BA (Hons)]
✉ dbrazil@1kbw.co.uk

BREACH MISS SARAH LOUISE

Chambers of Sarah Breach
The Old Farm House, Brook Farm, Marthall
Lane, Marthall, Knutsford, Cheshire
WA16 7ST, ☎ 01565 880272
✉ sbreach@btconnect.com
Call Date: July 1969, Gray's Inn
Qualifications: [LLB (Sheff)]

BREALEY MR MARK PHILIP QC (2002)

Brick Court Chambers
7-8 Essex Street, London WC2R 3LD,
☎ 020 7379 3550 ✉ clerks@brickcourt.co.uk
Call Date: July 1984, Middle Temple
Qualifications: [LLB DEA LLM]
✉ Mark.Brealey@Brickcourt.co.uk

E

BREDEMEAR MR ZACHARY CHARLES

1 Chancery Lane
London WC2A 1LF, ☎ 0845 634 6666
✉ clerks@1chancerylane.com
Call Date: Oct 1996, Inner Temple
Pupil Supervisor
Qualifications: [LLB (Reading) LLM (Lond)]
✉ zbredemear@1chancerylane.com

BREEN MR CARLO ENRICO

9 St John Street
Manchester M3 4DN, ☎ 0161 955 9000
✉ civilclerks@9sjs.com /
criminalclerks@9sjs.com
Call Date: Nov 1987, Middle Temple
Qualifications: [LLB (Essex)]
✉ cebreen@hotmail.co.uk

BREEN-LAWTON MISS DENISE

St Paul's Chambers
5th Floor, St Paul's House, 23 Park Square
South, Leeds LS1 2ND, ☎ 0113 245 5866
Call Date: July 2000, Gray's Inn
Pupil Supervisor
Qualifications: [BA (Wales) Dip Law]
✉ db@stpaulschambers.com

BREESE-LAUGHRAN MS ELEANORE DELPHINE

1 Pump Court
Elm Court, Temple, London EC4Y 7AB,
☎ 020 7842 7070
✉ (name)@pumpcourt.co.uk
Call Date: Oct 1991, Lincoln's Inn
Qualifications: [MA (Hons) (Cantab) JD (USA)]
✉ dbl@1pumpcourt.co.uk

BREGER MR DANIEL

25 Bedford Row
London WC1R 4HD, ☎ 020 7067 1500
✉ clerks@25bedfordrow.com
Call Date: Nov 2005, Gray's Inn
Qualifications: [LLB]
✉ dbreger@25bedfordrow.com

BREHAN MS DAIRE

Chambers of Ms D Brehan
4 Pair North, 3 Hare Court, Temple, London
EC4Y 7BJ, ☎ 07808 726877
✉ brennan_holahan@hotmail.com
Call Date: July 2002, Inner Temple
Qualifications: [BA (Dub) LLDip (Wolves)]
✉ brennan_holahan@hotmail.com

BREMNER MR JONATHAN SINCLAIR GRANT

Pump Court Tax Chambers
16 Bedford Row, London WC1R 4EF,
☎ 020 7414 8080 ✉ clerks@pumptax.com
Call Date: Oct 2005, Inner Temple
Qualifications: [BA (Oxon) BCL]
✉ jbremner@pumptax.com

Types of work: Capital tax, Corporation tax, Equity, Income tax, National Insurance, Private client, Stamp duty, Trusts, VAT, Wills

BREMRIDGE MR LEE RICHARD

Walnut House
63 St. David's Hill, Exeter, Devon EX4 4DW,
☎ 01392 279751
✉ clerks@walnuthouse.co.uk
Call Date: Oct 2003, Gray's Inn
Qualifications: [LLB (Wales)]
✉ lee.bremridge@walnuthouse.co.uk

BRENNAN LORD DANIEL JOSEPH QC (1985)

Matrix Chambers
Griffin Building, Gray's Inn, London WC1R 5LN, ☎020 7404 3447
✉matrix@matrixlaw.co.uk / Iscott@matrixlaw.co.uk
18 St John Street
Manchester M3 4EA, ☎0161 278 1800
✉clerks@18sjs.com
Call Date: July 1967, Gray's Inn
Recorder
Qualifications: [LLB (Manch)]
✉danbrennan@matrixlaw.co.uk

BRENNAN MISS ELIZABETH GAIL

Number 7 Harrington Street Chambers
7 Harrington Street, Liverpool L2 9YH, ☎0151 242 0707 ✉clerks@7hs.co.uk
Call Date: Nov 1998, Lincoln's Inn
Qualifications: [LLB (Hons)]
✉elizabeth.brennan@7hs.co.uk

BRENNAN MISS JANICE LESLEY

Chambers of Mr Ami Feder
Ground Floor, Lamb Building, Temple, London EC4Y 7AS, ☎020 7797 7788
✉clerks@lambbuilding.co.uk
Chambers of Mr Ami Feder
Ground Floor, Lamb Building, Temple, London EC4Y 7AS, ☎020 7797 7788
✉clerks@lambbuilding.co.uk
Call Date: July 1980, Middle Temple
Pupil Supervisor
Qualifications: [LLB (Lond)]
✉clerks@lambbuilding.co.uk

BRENNAN MR JOHN DAVID

St Philips Chambers
55 Temple Row, Birmingham B2 5LS, ☎0121 246 7000 ✉clerks@st-philips.com
Call Date: Mar 1996, Lincoln's Inn
Pupil Supervisor
Qualifications: [BA (Hons)]
✉jbrennan@st-philips.co.uk

BRENNAN MR THOMAS FRANCIS RICHARD

Chambers of Mr T Brennan
38 Sparrow Road, Yeovil BA21 4BY, ☎07773 322748
Call Date: Oct 2002, Lincoln's Inn
Qualifications: [LLB (Exon)]

BRENNAN MR TIMOTHY ROGER QC (2001)

Devereux Chambers
Queen Elizabeth Building, Temple, London EC4Y 9BS, ☎020 7353 7534
✉clerks@devchambers.co.uk
Call Date: Nov 1981, Gray's Inn
Recorder
Qualifications: [BCL MA (Oxon)]
✉brennan@devchambers.co.uk

BRENNAND MR TIMOTHY WILLIAM

St Johns Buildings
24a - 28 St John Street, Manchester M3 4DJ, ☎0161 214 1500
✉clerk@stjohnsbuildings.co.uk
St Johns Buildings
21 White Friars, Chester CH1 1NZ, ☎01244 323070
✉clerk@stjohnsbuildings.co.uk
16 Winckley Square
Preston PR1 3JJ, ☎01772 256100
Call Date: Nov 1987, Gray's Inn
Qualifications: [LLB (Hons)]
✉clerk@stjohnsbuildings.co.uk

BRENT MR RICHARD

3 Verulam Buildings
London WC1R 5NT, ☎020 7831 8441
✉chambers@3vb.com
Call Date: July 1995, Middle Temple
Pupil Supervisor
Qualifications: [BA (Hons) (Cantab) D.Phil (Oxon)]
✉rbrent@3vb.com

BRENTON MR TIMOTHY DEANE QC (1998)

7 King's Bench Walk
Ground Floor, 7 King's Bench Walk, Temple, London EC4Y 7DS, ☎020 7910 8300
✉clerks@7kbw.co.uk
Call Date: July 1981, Middle Temple
Qualifications: [LLB]
✉tbrenton@7kbw.co.uk

BRERETON MRS FIORELLA

Cobden House Chambers
19 Quay Street, Manchester M3 3HN, ☎0161 833 6000 ✉Clerks@Cobden.co.uk
Call Date: Nov 1979, Gray's Inn
Pupil Supervisor
Qualifications: [BA (Hons)]

E

BRERETON MISS JOY

4 Paper Buildings
1st Floor, 4 Paper Buildings, Temple, London EC4Y 7EX, ☎ 020 7427 5200
✉ clerks@4pb.com
Call Date: Nov 1990, Gray's Inn
Pupil Supervisor
Qualifications: [LLB (Wales) LLM (Bris)]
✉ jb@4pb.com

BRESLIN MISS CATHERINE ELIZABETH

Pump Court Chambers
31 Southgate Street, Winchester, Hampshire SO23 9EB, ☎ 01962 868 161
✉ clerks@3pumpcourt.com
Pump Court Chambers
Upper Ground Floor, 3 Pump Court, Temple, London EC4Y 7AJ, ☎ 020 7353 0711
✉ clerks@3pumpcourt.com
Pump Court Chambers
5 Temple Chambers, Temple Street, Swindon SN1 1SQ, ☎ 01793 539899
✉ clerks@3pumpcourt.com
Call Date: Nov 1990, Inner Temple
Pupil Supervisor
Qualifications: [LLB (Hons)(Lond)]
✉ cb@3pumpcourt.com

E

BRETHERTON MS KERRY LOUISE

Tanfield Chambers
2-5 Warwick Court, London WC1R 5DJ, ☎ 020 7421 5300
✉ clerks@tanfieldchambers.co.uk
Call Date: Oct 1992, Lincoln's Inn
Pupil Supervisor
Qualifications: [BA(Hons)(B'ham) CPE(B'ham)]

BRETT MR MATTHEW CHRISTOPHER ANTHONY

Harcourt Chambers
1st Floor, 2 Harcourt Buildings, Temple, London EC4Y 9DB, ☎ 0844 561 7135
Harcourt Chambers
Churchill House, 3 St Aldate's Courtyard, St Aldate's, Oxford OX1 1BN, ☎ 0844 561 7135
Call Date: Nov 1987, Middle Temple
Qualifications: [BA (Oxon)]
✉ mbrett@harcourtchambers.law.co.uk

BRETTLER MR JONATHAN SAMUEL

4 Stone Buildings
Ground Floor, 4 Stone Buildings, Lincoln's Inn, London WC2A 3XT, ☎ 020 7242 5524
✉ clerks@4stonebuildings.com
Call Date: July 1988, Middle Temple
Pupil Supervisor
Qualifications: [LLB (Hons) (LSE) BCL (Oxon)]
✉ clerks@4stonebuildings.com

BREWER MR ANEURIN

Nine Bedford Row
9 Bedford Row, London WC1R 4AZ, ☎ 020 7489 2727
✉ clerks@9bedfordrow.co.uk
Call Date: Oct 2008, Inner Temple
Qualifications: [BA (Bris)]

BREWER MISS MICHELLE LOUISE

Garden Court Chambers
57-60 Lincoln's Inn Fields, London WC2A 3LJ, ☎ 020 7993 7600 ✉ info@gclaw.co.uk
Call Date: Mar 1999, Inner Temple
Qualifications: [LLB]
✉ michellelb@gclaw.co.uk

BREWIN MR CARL PATRICK

3 PB Barristers
3 Paper Buildings, Temple, London EC4Y 7EU, ☎ 020 7583 8055
Call Date: Oct 2006, Middle Temple
Qualifications: [BSc (Lond) PgDL]
✉ carl.brewin@3paper.co.uk

BREWIS MISS SARAH ANN

Park Lane Plowden
Lombard House, 4-8 Lombard Street, Newcastle Upon Tyne NE1 3AE, ☎ 0191 211 4087
✉ clerks@parklaneplowden.co.uk
Call Date: July 2003, Middle Temple
Qualifications: [LLB Hons (Nott'm)]
✉ sarah.brewis@parklaneplowden.co.uk

BRICKMAN MISS LAURA GILLIAN

Carmelite Chambers
9 Carmelite Street, London EC4Y 0DR, ☎ 020 7936 6300
✉ clerks@carmelitechambers.co.uk
Call Date: July 1976, Inner Temple
Pupil Supervisor
✉ lbrickman@carmelitechambers.co.uk

BRIDDOCK MR ALLAN IVAN

Chambers of Mr Ami Feder
Ground Floor, Lamb Building, Temple, London EC4Y 7AS, ☎ 020 7797 7788
✉ clerks@lambbuilding.co.uk
Chambers of Mr Ami Feder
Ground Floor, Lamb Building, Temple, London EC4Y 7AS, ☎ 020 7797 7788
✉ clerks@lambbuilding.co.uk
Call Date: Nov 2000, Inner Temple
Qualifications: [LLB (Lond) LLM]

BRIDEN MS SARAH LOUISE

KCH Garden Square
1 Oxford Street, Nottingham NG1 5BH,
☎ 0115 941 8851
✉ clerks@kchgardensquare.co.uk
Call Date: July 1999, Inner Temple
Qualifications: [LLB (Leics)]
sbriden@kch.co.uk

BRIDEN MR TIMOTHY JOHN

Lamb Chambers
Lamb Building, Elm Court, Temple, London EC4Y 7AS, ☎ 020 7797 8300
✉ info@lambchambers.co.uk
Call Date: July 1976, Inner Temple
Pupil Supervisor
Qualifications: [MA (Cantab) LLB (Cantab)]

Types of work: Clinical negligence, Ecclesiastical law, Health and safety, Insurance, Personal injury

BRIDGE MR CLAYTON LUKE

2 Dr Johnson's Buildings
2 Dr Johnson's Buildings, Temple, London EC4Y 7AY, ☎ 020 7936 2613
✉ clerks@2drj.com
Call Date: July 2005, Middle Temple
Qualifications: [B.B.S LLB (Hons)]
clerks@2drj.com

BRIDGE MR GILES

Broadway House Chambers
Broadway House, 9 Bank Street, Bradford, West Yorkshire BD1 1TW, ☎ 01274 722560
✉ clerks@broadwayhouse.co.uk
Broadway House Chambers
25 Park Square West, Leeds, West Yorkshire LS1 2PW, ☎ 0113 246 2600
✉ clerks@broadwayhouse.co.uk
Call Date: July 2000, Middle Temple
Pupil Supervisor
Qualifications: [BA(Hons) (Manc) PGCE (Hudds)]
gb@broadwayhouse.co.uk

BRIDGE MRS JENNIFER BRIDGET

Chambers of Jennifer Bridge
10 The Mall, Surbiton, Surrey KT6 4EQ,
☎ 020 8891 1718
Call Date: Nov 1990, Inner Temple
Qualifications: [LLB (Lond)]
jennybridge1@hotmail.co.uk

BRIDGEMAN MR JAMES JUDE

Lamb Chambers
Lamb Building, Elm Court, Temple, London EC4Y 7AS, ☎ 020 7797 8300
✉ info@lambchambers.co.uk
Call Date: July 2010, Middle Temple
Qualifications: [BA Mod (Dub) MA (Dub)]

BRIDGMAN MR ANDREW MICHAEL

St Johns Buildings
24a - 28 St John Street, Manchester M3 4DJ,
☎ 0161 214 1500
✉ clerk@stjohnsbuildings.co.uk
16 Winckley Square
Preston PR1 3JJ, ☎ 01772 256100
St Johns Buildings Liverpool
8th Floor India Buildings, Water Street, Liverpool L2 0XG, ☎ 0151 243 6000
✉ clerk@stjohnsbuildings.co.uk
Call Date: Oct 2001, Gray's Inn
Qualifications: [BDS (Manch) LLB (Manch) MA (Manch)]
clerk@stjohnsbuildings.co.uk

BRIEGEL MR PIETER DAVID ROY

5 King's Bench Walk
5 King's Bench Walk, Temple, London EC4Y 7DN, ☎ 020 7353 5638
✉ clerks@5kbw.co.uk
Call Date: Nov 1986, Middle Temple
Pupil Supervisor
Qualifications: [LLB (Lond) (Hons)]
pieter.briegel@5kbw.co.uk

BRIER MR JEREMY MARC

Essex Court Chambers
24 Lincoln's Inn Fields, London WC2A 3EG,
☎ 020 7813 8000
✉ clerksroom@essexcourt.net
Call Date: Oct 2004, Middle Temple
Qualifications: [BA (Hons) CPE]
jbrier@essexcourt.net

BRIGGS PROF ADRIAN

Blackstone Chambers
Blackstone House, Temple, London EC4Y 9BW, ☎ 020 7583 1770
✉ clerks@blackstonechambers.com
Call Date: Apr 1989, Middle Temple
Qualifications: [BCL MA (Oxon)]
adrianbriggs@blackstonechambers.com

BRIGGS MR AIDAN WILLIAM

Ely Place Chambers
30 Ely Place, London EC1N 6TD,
☎ 020 7400 9600 ✉ admin@elyplace.com
Call Date: July 2009, Inner Temple
Qualifications: [BA (Dunelm)]
abriggs@elyplace.com

E

BRIGGS MS CLAIRE ANNE

St Ive's Chambers
Whittall Street, Birmingham B4 6DH,
☎ 0121 236 0863
✉ clerks@stiveschambers.co.uk
Call Date: July 2005, Middle Temple
Qualifications: [BA (Hons)]
✉ claire.briggs@stiveschambers.co.uk

BRIGGS MR JOHN BONAR

South Square
3-4 South Square, Gray's Inn, London
WC1R 5HP, ☎ 020 7696 9900
✉ practicemanagers@southsquare.com
Call Date: July 1973, Gray's Inn
Pupil Supervisor
Qualifications: [LLB (Lond) Ex du Doc. d'Univ (France)]
✉ johnbriggs@southsquare.com

BRIGGS MS LAURA JUDITH

The Chambers of Grahame Aldous QC
9 Gough Square, London EC4A 3DG,
☎ 020 7832 0500
✉ clerks@9goughsquare.co.uk
18 St John Street
Manchester M3 4EA, ☎ 0161 278 1800
✉ clerks@18sjs.com
Call Date: July 2001, Inner Temple
Qualifications: [LLB (Manch)]
✉ lbriggs@9goughsquare.co.uk

E

BRIGGS MISS LUCIE RACHEL

Atkin Chambers
1 Atkin Building, Gray's Inn, London
WC1R 5AT, ☎ 020 7404 0102
✉ clerks@atkinchambers.com
Call Date: Oct 2004, Lincoln's Inn
Qualifications: [BSc (Hons) PgDI]
✉ clerks@atkinchambers.com

BRIGGS MR NICHOLAS NORMAN

Guildhall Chambers
23 Broad Street, Bristol BS1 2HG,
☎ 0117 930 9000
✉ hoc@guildhallchambers.co.uk
Call Date: Oct 1994, Lincoln's Inn
Pupil Supervisor
Qualifications: [LLM (Bris)]

BRIGHT MR CHRISTOPHER JOHN QC (2009)

No5 Chambers
Fountain Court, Steelhouse Lane, Birmingham
B4 6DR, ☎ 0845 210 5555 ✉ info@no5.com
No5 Chambers
Greenwood House, 4-7 Salisbury Court,
London EC4Y 8AA, ☎ 0845 210 5555
No5 Chambers
38 Queen Square, Bristol BS1 4QS,
☎ 0845 210 5555
Call Date: Nov 1985, Gray's Inn
Recorder
Qualifications: [BA (Dunelm)]
✉ cbr@no5.com

BRIGHT MR DAVID REGINALD

13 King's Bench Walk
13 King's Bench Walk, Temple, London
EC4Y 7EN, ☎ 020 7353 7204
✉ clerks@13kbw.co.uk
13 KBW
32 Beaumont Street, Oxford OX1 2NP,
☎ 01865 311066 ✉ clerks@13kbw.co.uk
Call Date: July 1976, Lincoln's Inn
Pupil Supervisor, Recorder
✉ dbright@13kbw.co.uk

BRIGHT MISS RACHEL ZELDA

187 Fleet Street
London EC4A 2AT, ☎ 020 7430 7430
✉ chambers@187fleetstreet.com
4 Brick Court
4 Brick Court, Temple, London EC4Y 9AD,
☎ 020 7832 3200 ✉ clerks@4bc.co.uk
Call Date: Oct 1991, Lincoln's Inn
Pupil Supervisor
Qualifications: [LLB (Hons) (Manch)]
✉ rachelbright@187fleetstreet.com

BRIGHT MR ROBERT GRAHAM QC (2006)

7 King's Bench Walk
Ground Floor, 7 King's Bench Walk, Temple,
London EC4Y 7DS, ☎ 020 7910 8300
✉ clerks@7kbw.co.uk
Call Date: Nov 1987, Gray's Inn
Qualifications: [BA BCL (Oxon)]
✉ rbright@7kbw.co.uk

BRIGHTMAN MISS JUSTINA ELISABETH RALLOU

East Anglian Chambers
15 The Close, Norwich, Norfolk NR1 4DZ,
☎ 01473 214481 ✉ norwich@ealaw.co.uk
East Anglian Chambers
140 New London Road, Chelmsford, Essex
CM2 0AW, ☎ 01473 214481
✉ chelmsford@ealaw.co.uk
Call Date: July 2003, Lincoln's Inn
Qualifications: [LLB Hons (Dunelm)]

BRIGHTWELL MR JAMES ROBERT

New Square Chambers
12 New Square, Lincoln's Inn, London WC2A 3SW, ☎ 020 7419 8000
✉ robin.hollington@newsquarechambers.co.uk
Call Date: Nov 2000, Lincoln's Inn
Pupil Supervisor
Qualifications: [BA (Hons) (Cantab) LLM (Cantab)]
✉ james.brightwell@newsquarechambers.co.uk

BRILLIANT MR SIMON HOWARD

Lamb Chambers
Lamb Building, Elm Court, Temple, London EC4Y 7AS, ☎ 020 7797 8300
✉ info@lambchambers.co.uk
Call Date: July 1976, Middle Temple
Pupil Supervisor
Qualifications: [LLB (Manch) BCL (Oxon)]
✉ simonbrilliant@lambchambers.co.uk

BRIMELOW MISS JANINE KIRSTY QC (2011)

Doughty Street Chambers
53-54 Doughty Street, London WC1N 2LS, ☎ 020 7404 1313
✉ enquiries@doughtystreet.co.uk
Doughty Street Chambers
Pall Mall Court, 61-67 King Street, Manchester M2 4PD, ☎ 0161 618 1066
Doughty Street Chambers
5th Floor, Broad Quay House, Prince Street, Bristol BS1 4DJ, ☎ 01179 058 717
Call Date: Oct 1991, Gray's Inn
Pupil Supervisor
Qualifications: [LLB (Hons)]

BRINDLE MISS JESSICA RUTH

3 Dr Johnson's Buildings
Ground Floor, 3 Dr Johnson's Buildings, Temple, London EC4Y 7BA, ☎ 020 7353 4854
✉ clerks@3djb.co.uk
Call Date: July 2009, Inner Temple
Qualifications: [LLB (Lond)]
✉ clerks@3djb.co.uk

BRINDLE MR MICHAEL JOHN QC (1992)

Fountain Court Chambers
Fountain Court, Temple, London EC4Y 9DH, ☎ 020 7583 3335
✉ chambers@fountaincourt.co.uk
Call Date: Nov 1975, Lincoln's Inn
Recorder
Qualifications: [MA (Oxon)]
✉ mbrindle@fountaincourt.co.uk

BRINDLE MR SIMON JAMES

The Chambers of Grahame Aldous QC
9 Gough Square, London EC4A 3DG, ☎ 020 7832 0500
✉ clerks@9goughsquare.co.uk
Call Date: July 1998, Gray's Inn
Qualifications: [LLB (Reading)]
✉ sbrindle@9goughsquare.co.uk

BRINSMEAD-STOCKHAM MR JOHN

11 New Square
1st Floor, 11 New Square, Lincoln's Inn, London WC2A 3QB, ☎ 020 7242 4017
✉ john.moore@11newsquare.com
Call Date: Oct 2005, Middle Temple
Qualifications: [BA (Hons) (Cantab)]
✉ john.moore@11newsquare.com

BRISBY MR JOHN CONSTANT SHANNON MCBURNEY QC (1996)

4 Stone Buildings
Ground Floor, 4 Stone Buildings, Lincoln's Inn, London WC2A 3XT, ☎ 020 7242 5524
✉ clerks@4stonebuildings.com
Call Date: July 1978, Lincoln's Inn
Qualifications: [MA (Oxon)]
✉ clerks@4stonebuildings.com

BRISCOE MISS CONSTANCE

9-12 Bell Yard
London WC2A 2JR, ☎ 020 7400 1800
✉ clerks@9-12bellyard.com
Call Date: Nov 1983, Inner Temple
Recorder
Qualifications: [LLB (Newc)]
✉ c.briscoe@9-12bellyard.com

BRISSENDEN MISS CLAIRE JUDITH

Trinity Chambers
The Custom House, 39 Quayside, Newcastle Upon Tyne NE1 3DE, ☎ 0191 232 1927
✉ info@trinitychambers.co.uk
Trinity Chambers
Multi Media Exchange, 72-80 Corporation Road, Middlesbrough TS1 2RF, ☎ 01642 247569
✉ info@trinitychambers.co.uk
Call Date: Nov 2004, Inner Temple
Qualifications: [LLB (Hons) (Buckingham)]

BRISSETT MISS NICOLA LUANA

Balmoral Chambers
10 Nield Road, Hayes, Middlesex UB3 1SE, ☎ 07904 144 405
✉ nicolabrissette@googlemail.com
Call Date: Feb 1995, Lincoln's Inn
Qualifications: [BA (Hons)(Lond)]
✉ nicolabrissette@googlemail.com

E

BRISTOLL MISS SANDRA JAYNE

St Philips Chambers
55 Temple Row, Birmingham B2 5LS,
☎ 0121 246 7000 ✉ clerks@st-philips.com
Call Date: July 1989, Middle Temple
Recorder
Qualifications: [MA (Cantab)]
sbristoll@st-philips.co.uk

BRITCLIFFE MISS ANNE ELIZABETH

Call Date: Apr 1989, Gray's Inn
Qualifications: [LLB (Bristol)]
clerk@stjohnsbuildings.co.uk

BRITTAIN MR MARC JOHN

1 Gray's Inn Square
Ground Floor, 1 Gray's Inn Square, London WC1R 5AA, ☎ 020 7405 0001
Call Date: July 1983, Gray's Inn
Pupil Supervisor
Qualifications: [BA]

BRITTENDEN MR STUART

Old Square Chambers
10-11 Bedford Row, London WC1R 4BU,
☎ 020 7269 0300 ✉ clerks@oldsquare.co.uk
Old Square Chambers
3 Orchard Court, St Augustine's Yard, Bristol BS1 5DP, ☎ 0117 930 5100
✉ clerks@oldsquare.co.uk
Call Date: Oct 1999, Gray's Inn
Qualifications: [LLB LLM (LSE)]
brittenden@oldsquare.co.uk

BRITTON MR BYRON DAVID JAMES

Five Paper
Ground Floor, 5 Paper Buildings, Temple, London EC4Y 7HB, ☎ 020 7815 3200
Call Date: Oct 2008, Middle Temple
Qualifications: [LLB (Hons) (Wales) LLM (Lond)]
byronbritton@fivepaper.com

BRITTON MR JAMES ROBERT

2 King's Bench Walk
2 King's Bench Walk, Temple, London EC4Y 7DE, ☎ 020 7353 1746
✉ clerks@2kbw.com
Call Date: Nov 1996, Inner Temple
Qualifications: [LLB (So'ton)]
jbritton@2kbw.com

BROACH MR STEPHEN JONATHAN

Doughty Street Chambers
53-54 Doughty Street, London WC1N 2LS,
☎ 020 7404 1313
✉ enquiries@doughtystreet.co.uk
Call Date: Oct 2008, Middle Temple
Qualifications: [MA (Hons) (Edin) Dip in Law]
s.broach@doughtystreet.co.uk

BROADBENT MR EDMUND JOHN

20 Essex Street
London WC2R 3AL, ☎ 020 7842 1200
✉ clerks@20essexst.com
Call Date: July 1980, Gray's Inn
Pupil Supervisor
Qualifications: [MA (Cantab) LLB (Cantab)]
clerks@20essexst.com

BROADFOOT MISS SAMANTHA LOUISE

Landmark Chambers
180 Fleet Street, London EC4A 2HG,
☎ 020 7430 1221
✉ clerks@landmarkchambers.co.uk
Call Date: Nov 1997, Middle Temple
Pupil Supervisor
Qualifications: [LLB (Hons)(Kent) LLM (Exon)]
sbroadfoot@landmarkchambers.co.uk

BROADHURST MISS KATHERINE ELIZABETH

9 Park Place
9 Park Place, Cardiff, South Glamorgan CF10 3DP, ☎ 029 2038 2731
✉ clerks@9parkplace.co.uk
Call Date: July 2003, Gray's Inn
Qualifications: [BA (Oxon) PgDip]
kbroadhurst@9parkplace.co.uk

BROADLEY MR JOHN

Cobden House Chambers
19 Quay Street, Manchester M3 3HN,
☎ 0161 833 6000 ✉ Clerks@Cobden.co.uk
Call Date: July 1973, Middle Temple
Pupil Supervisor
Qualifications: [LLB (Hons)]
clerks@cobden.co.uk

BROADSTOCK MR BYRON GEORGE

30 Park Place
Cardiff CF10 3BS, ☎ 029 2039 8421
✉ clerks@30parkplace.law.co.uk
Temple Chambers
32 Park Place, Cardiff CF10 3BA,
☎ 029 2039 7364
✉ DBrinning@Temple-Chambers.co.uk

Temple Chambers
12 Clytha Park Road, Newport, Gwent NP20 4PB, ☎01633 267403
✉dbrinning@temple-chambers.co.uk
Call Date: Nov 2002, Gray's Inn
Qualifications: [LLB (Hons)(L'pool) LPC]

BROATCH MR DONALD

Five Paper
Ground Floor, 5 Paper Buildings, Temple, London EC4Y 7HB, ☎020 7815 3200
Call Date: May 1971, Middle Temple
Pupil Supervisor
Qualifications: [LLB (Lond) LLM (Lond)]
donaldbroatch@fivepaper.com

BROCHWICZ-LEWINSKI MR STEFAN ANDREW

9 St John Street
Manchester M3 4DN, ☎0161 955 9000
✉civilclerks@9sjs.com / criminalclerks@9sjs.com
Call Date: Nov 1995, Gray's Inn
Pupil Supervisor
Qualifications: [LLB (Bris) LLB (Euro)]
sbl@9sjs.com

BROCK MR DAVID JAMES

Furnival Chambers
32 Furnival Street, London EC4A 1JQ, ☎020 7405 3232
Call Date: Nov 1984, Middle Temple
Pupil Supervisor
Qualifications: [BHum (Lond)]
dbrock@furnivallaw.co.uk

BROCKLEBANK MR JAMES WILLIAM

7 King's Bench Walk
Ground Floor, 7 King's Bench Walk, Temple, London EC4Y 7DS, ☎020 7910 8300
✉clerks@7kbw.co.uk
Call Date: Oct 1999, Middle Temple
Qualifications: [MA (Cantab)]
jbrocklebank@7kbw.co.uk

BROCKLEHURST MR KELLY PAUL LEWIS

2 King's Bench Walk
2 King's Bench Walk, Temple, London EC4Y 7DE, ☎020 7353 1746
✉clerks@2kbw.com
Call Date: Oct 2010, Gray's Inn
Qualifications: [BA]
kbrocklehurst@2kbw.com

BROCKLEY MR NIGEL SIMON

No5 Chambers
Greenwood House, 4-7 Salisbury Court, London EC4Y 8AA, ☎0845 210 5555
No5 Chambers
38 Queen Square, Bristol BS1 4QS, ☎0845 210 5555
No5 Chambers
Fountain Court, Steelhouse Lane, Birmingham B4 6DR, ☎0845 210 5555 ✉info@no5.com
Call Date: Nov 1992, Lincoln's Inn
Qualifications: [BA (Hons) CPE]

BROCKMAN MR CHRISTOPHER CHARLES

Guildhall Chambers
23 Broad Street, Bristol BS1 2HG, ☎0117 930 9000
✉hoc@guildhallchambers.co.uk
Call Date: Nov 1985, Middle Temple
Qualifications: [LLB]

BRODIE MR BRUCE

39 Essex Street
London WC2R 3AT, ☎020 7832 1111
✉clerks@39essex.com
82 King Street
Manchester M2 4WQ, ☎0161 870 9969
Call Date: May 1993, Inner Temple
Qualifications: [BA (Brazil) MA (Cantab)]
bruce.brodie@39essex.com

BRODIE MR GRAHAM PAUL

Chambers of Andrew Mitchell QC
33 Chancery Lane, London WC2A 1EN, ☎020 7440 9950 ✉clerks@33cllaw.com
Call Date: July 1989, Middle Temple
Qualifications: [LLB (Lond)]
gb@33cllaw.com

BRODIE MR STANLEY ERIC QC (1975)

Blackstone Chambers
Blackstone House, Temple, London EC4Y 9BW, ☎020 7583 1770
✉clerks@blackstonechambers.com
Call Date: Feb 1954, Inner Temple
Qualifications: [MA (Oxon)]
stanleybrodie@blackstonechambers.com

E

BRODY MISS KAREN RACHEL

Deans Court Chambers
24 St John Street, Manchester M3 4DF,
☎ 0161 214 6000 ✉ clerks@deanscourt.co.uk
Deans Court Chambers
101 Walker Street, Preston PR1 2RR,
☎ 01772 565 600
✉ preston@deanscourt.co.uk
Call Date: Nov 1986, Gray's Inn
Recorder
Qualifications: [LLB (Notts)]
brody@deanscourt.co.uk

BRODY MR SAUL AMOS

18 St John Street
Manchester M3 4EA, ☎ 0161 278 1800
✉ clerks@18sjs.com
Call Date: Oct 1996, Inner Temple
Qualifications: [LLB (Leeds)]

BROGDEN MR PETER CIERAN

Keating Chambers
15 Essex Street, London WC2R 3AA,
☎ 020 7544 2600
✉ clerks@keatingchambers.com
Call Date: July 2006, Inner Temple
Qualifications: [LLB (Lond) BCL (Oxon)]
pbrogden@keatingchambers.com

BROMILOW MR DANIEL JOHN

9 Stone Buildings
Lincoln's Inn, London WC2A 3NN,
☎ 020 7404 5055
✉ clerks@9stonebuildings.com
Call Date: Nov 1996, Gray's Inn
Qualifications: [BA (Cantab)]
clerks@9stonebuildings.com

BROMLEY-MARTIN MR MICHAEL GRANVILLE QC (2002)

3 Raymond Buildings
3 Raymond Buildings, Gray's Inn, London
WC1R 5BH, ☎ 020 7400 6400
✉ clerks@3rblaw.com
Call Date: Nov 1979, Gray's Inn
Recorder
Qualifications: [BSc (So'ton)]

BROMPTON MR MICHAEL JOHN QC (2003)

Five Paper Buildings
1st Floor, Five Paper Buildings, Temple,
London EC4Y 7HB, ☎ 020 7583 6117
✉ clerks@5pb.co.uk
Call Date: Nov 1973, Middle Temple
Recorder
Qualifications: [BA (Sussex)]
mjb@5pb.co.uk

BROOK MR DALE MATTHEW

15 New Bridge Street
London EC4V 6AU, ☎ 020 7842 1900
✉ clerks@15nbs.com
Call Date: Nov 2003, Inner Temple
Qualifications: [LLB (Northumbria)]
dale.brook@15nbs.com

BROOK MR DAVID LESLIE

Henderson Chambers
2 Harcourt Buildings, Temple, London
EC4Y 9DB, ☎ 020 7583 9020
✉ clerks@hendersonchambers.co.uk
Call Date: July 1988, Inner Temple
Pupil Supervisor
Qualifications: [BA (Lond) Dip Law (Lond)]
dbrook@hendersonchambers.co.uk

BROOK MR IAN STUART

Park Court Chambers
16 Park Place, Leeds LS1 2SJ,
☎ 0113 243 3277
✉ clerks@parkcourtchambers.co.uk
Call Date: July 1983, Lincoln's Inn
Qualifications: [BA(Hons)]
i.brook@parkcourtchambers.co.uk

BROOK MR MATTHEW JOHN

No5 Chambers
Fountain Court, Steelhouse Lane, Birmingham
B4 6DR, ☎ 0845 210 5555 ✉ info@no5.com
No5 Chambers
Greenwood House, 4-7 Salisbury Court,
London EC4Y 8AA, ☎ 0845 210 5555
No5 Chambers
38 Queen Square, Bristol BS1 4QS,
☎ 0845 210 5555
Call Date: Oct 1999, Gray's Inn
Qualifications: [BA (Cantab)]
mbk@no5.com

BROOK MR PAUL ANTONY

Park Lane Plowden
19 Westgate, Leeds LS1 2RD,
☎ 0113 228 5049
✉ clerks@parklaneplowden.co.uk
Park Lane Plowden
Lombard House, 4-8 Lombard Street,
Newcastle Upon Tyne NE1 3AE,
☎ 0191 211 4087
✉ clerks@parklaneplowden.co.uk
Call Date: Nov 1986, Inner Temple
Qualifications: [LLB (Leeds)]
paul.brook@parklaneplowden.co.uk

E

BROOK SMITH MR PHILIP ANDREW QC (2002)

Fountain Court Chambers
Fountain Court, Temple, London EC4Y 9DH, ☎020 7583 3335
✉chambers@fountaincourt.co.uk
Call Date: July 1982, Middle Temple
Recorder
Qualifications: [BSc MSc]
✉pbs@fountaincourt.co.uk

BROOKE MR DAVID MICHAEL GRAHAM

KBW
The Engine House, No 1 Foundry Square, Leeds LS11 5DL, ☎0113 297 1200
✉clerks@kbwchambers.com
Call Date: Nov 1990, Inner Temple
Pupil Supervisor
Qualifications: [BA (Dunelm) Dip Law (Lond)]
✉db@kbwchambers.com

BROOKE MR JOHAN ERIC

Bath Chambers
PO Box 2046, Melksham, Wiltshire SN12 8EX, ☎01225 702347
✉Bathchambers@btinternet.com
Slough Barristers Chamber
11 St. Bernards Road, Slough, Berkshire SL3 7NT, ☎01753 553806
✉arden_bhattacharya2000@yahoo.co.uk
Kew Chambers
354 Kew Road, Kew, Surrey TW9 3DU, ☎0844 8099991
✉admin@kewchambers.co.uk
Call Date: Oct 1997, Lincoln's Inn
Qualifications: [LLB (Hons)(Bris)]
✉admin@bathchambers.com

BROOKES MR CHRISTOPHER JON

Pallant Chambers
12 North Pallant, Chichester, West Sussex PO19 1TQ, ☎01243 784538
✉clerks@pallantchambers.co.uk
Call Date: July 2010, Lincoln's Inn
Qualifications: [BA (Oxon)]
✉cbrookes@pallantchambers.co.uk

BROOKES MR LINCOLN PAUL

Guildhall Chambers Portsmouth
Prudential Buildings, 16 Guildhall Walk, Portsmouth, Hampshire PO1 2DE, ☎023 9275 2400
✉clerks@gcp-barristers.com
Call Date: Nov 1992, Inner Temple
Pupil Supervisor
Qualifications: [LLB (Hons)(Lond)]
✉clerks@gcp-barristers.com

BROOKES-BAKER MR MATTHEW JAMES

Harcourt Chambers
Churchill House, 3 St Aldate's Courtyard, St Aldate's, Oxford OX1 1BN, ☎0844 561 7135
Harcourt Chambers
1st Floor, 2 Harcourt Buildings, Temple, London EC4Y 9DB, ☎0844 561 7135
Call Date: July 1998, Lincoln's Inn
Qualifications: [BA (Hons)(Exon)]
✉MBrookes-Baker@harcourtchambers.law.co.uk

BROOKE-SMITH MR JOHN

East Anglian Chambers
53 North Hill, Colchester, Essex CO1 1QA, ☎01473 214481 ✉colchester@ealaw.co.uk
East Anglian Chambers
Gresham House, 5 Museum Street, Ipswich, Suffolk IP1 1HQ, ☎01473 214481
✉ipswich@ealaw.co.uk
Call Date: July 1981, Gray's Inn
Pupil Supervisor, Recorder
Qualifications: [LLB (Exon)]
✉jbs@ealaw.co.uk

BROOKS MISS ALISON LOUISE

Staple Inn Chambers
1st Floor, 9 Staple Inn, Holborn Bars, London WC1V 7QH, ☎020 7242 5240
✉clerks@stapleinn.co.uk
Call Date: July 1989, Inner Temple
Qualifications: [LLB (Hons)]
✉ab@stapleinn.co.uk

BROOKS MR DUNCAN JOHN MACFARLANE

Queen Elizabeth Building
3rd Floor, Queen Elizabeth Building, Temple, London EC4Y 9BS, ☎020 7797 7837
✉clerks@qeb.co.uk
Call Date: Oct 2000, Gray's Inn
Pupil Supervisor
Qualifications: [LLB (Dunelm)]
✉d.brooks@qeb.co.uk

BROOKS MR JOHN DYLAN

Pendragon Chambers
Suite 7, J Shed, Kings Road, SA1 Waterfront, Swansea SA1 8PL, ☎01792 411188
✉clerks@pendragonchambers.com
Call Date: Feb 1990, Gray's Inn
Qualifications: [LLB (Wales)]
✉johnbrooks@pendragonchambers.com

BROOKS MR MATTHEW HARRY MORRISON

Garden Court Chambers
57-60 Lincoln's Inn Fields, London WC2A 3LJ,
☎ 020 7993 7600 ✉ info@gclaw.co.uk
Call Date: Oct 2005, Inner Temple
Qualifications: [BA University of Leeds CPE City University]

BROOKS MR PAUL ANTHONY

Thomas More Chambers
7 Lincoln's Inn Fields, London WC2A 3BP,
☎ 020 7404 7000
✉ clerks@thomasmore.co.uk
Call Date: July 1989, Middle Temple
Qualifications: [LLB]
pbrooks@thomasmore.co.uk

BROOKS MR PETER ANTHONY CHRISTOPHER

9 Park Place
9 Park Place, Cardiff, South Glamorgan
CF10 3DP, ☎ 029 2038 2731
✉ clerks@9parkplace.co.uk
Call Date: July 1986, Gray's Inn
Pupil Supervisor
Qualifications: [LLB (L'pool)]

E

BROOME MR CHARLES EDWARD

Crown Office Chambers
2 Crown Office Row, Temple, London
EC4Y 7HJ, ☎ 020 7797 8100
✉ mail@crownofficechambers.com
Call Date: Nov 1996, Inner Temple
Qualifications: [BA (Oxon)]

BROOME MISS NICOLA KERRY

QEB Hollis Whiteman
1-2 Laurence Pountney Hill, London
EC4R 0EU, ☎ 020 7933 8855
✉ barristers@qebhw.co.uk
Call Date: Oct 2003, Gray's Inn
Qualifications: [LLB (Manch)]
kerry.broome@qebhw.co.uk

BROOMFIELD MR NICHOLAS MARK

Four New Square
Four New Square, Lincoln's Inn, London
WC2A 3RJ, ☎ 020 7822 2000
✉ barristers@4newsquare.com
Call Date: Oct 2010, Lincoln's Inn
Qualifications: [BA (Oxon)]
n.broomfield@4newsquare.com

BROOMFIELD MR THOMAS STUART HENRY

QEB Hollis Whiteman
1-2 Laurence Pountney Hill, London
EC4R 0EU, ☎ 020 7933 8855
✉ barristers@qebhw.co.uk
Call Date: Nov 2007, Lincoln's Inn
Qualifications: [BA (Bris)]
tom.broomfield@qebhw.co.uk

BROTHERTON MR JOHN PAUL

Cornwall Street Chambers
85-87 Cornwall Street, Birmingham B3 3BY,
☎ 0121 233 7500
✉ clerks@cornwallstreet.co.uk
Call Date: Nov 1994, Lincoln's Inn
Qualifications: [BA (Hons)(Leeds) Dip Law (Chester)]
john.brotherton@cornwallstreet.co.uk

BROTHERTON MR MATTHEW SEAN DE LA HAYE BROWNE

Argent Chambers
5 Bell Yard, London WC2A 2JR,
☎ 020 7556 5500
✉ briefsin@argentchambers.co.uk
Call Date: July 1995, Lincoln's Inn
Qualifications: [MA (Cantab) PGCE]

BROUGHAM MR CHRISTOPHER JOHN QC (1988)

South Square
3-4 South Square, Gray's Inn, London
WC1R 5HP, ☎ 020 7696 9900
✉ practicemanagers@southsquare.com
Call Date: Nov 1969, Inner Temple
Qualifications: [BA (Oxon)]
christopherbrougham@southsquare.com

BROUGHTON MRS KERRIE JANE

No.6 Park Square
Leeds LS1 2LW, ☎ 0113 245 9763
✉ Tim@no6.co.uk
Call Date: Mar 2006, Inner Temple
Qualifications: [BA CPE]
Broughton@no6.co.uk

BROUNGER MR DAVID WILLIAM JOHN

Field Court Chambers
5 Field Court, Gray's Inn, London WC1R 5EF,
☎ 020 7405 6114 ✉ clerks@fieldcourt.co.uk
Call Date: Nov 1990, Inner Temple
Pupil Supervisor
Qualifications: [LLB]

BROWN MR ALEXANDER JAMES

One Essex Court
Ground Floor, One Essex Court, Temple, London EC4Y 9AR, ☎020 7583 2000
✉clerks@oeclaw.co.uk
Call Date: July 2009, Lincoln's Inn
Qualifications: [BA (Warw)]
✉abrown@oeclaw.co.uk

BROWN MISS ALTHEA SONIA

Doughty Street Chambers
53-54 Doughty Street, London WC1N 2LS, ☎020 7404 1313
✉enquiries@doughtystreet.co.uk
Doughty Street Chambers
Pall Mall Court, 61-67 King Street, Manchester M2 4PD, ☎0161 618 1066
Doughty Street Chambers
5th Floor, Broad Quay House, Prince Street, Bristol BS1 4DJ, ☎01179 058 717
Call Date: Feb 1995, Lincoln's Inn
Pupil Supervisor
Qualifications: [LLB (Hons)(Leics)]
✉a.brown@doughtystreet.co.uk

BROWN MISS ANDREA MARIE

Staple Inn Chambers
1st Floor, 9 Staple Inn, Holborn Bars, London WC1V 7QH, ☎020 7242 5240
✉clerks@stapleinn.co.uk
Call Date: Nov 1991, Lincoln's Inn
Qualifications: [LLB (Hons)]
✉amb@stapleinn.co.uk

BROWN MISS ANNE MARGARET

Pump Court Chambers
Upper Ground Floor, 3 Pump Court, Temple, London EC4Y 7AJ, ☎020 7353 0711
✉clerks@3pumpcourt.com
Pump Court Chambers
5 Temple Chambers, Temple Street, Swindon SN1 1SQ, ☎01793 539899
✉clerks@3pumpcourt.com
Pump Court Chambers
31 Southgate Street, Winchester, Hampshire SO23 9EB, ☎01962 868 161
✉clerks@3pumpcourt.com
Call Date: July 2000, Middle Temple
Pupil Supervisor
Qualifications: [BA (Hons)(Oxon)]
✉amb@3pumpcourt.com

BROWN MR ANTHONY JAMES

Dere Street Barristers
33 Broad Chare, Newcastle Upon Tyne NE1 3DQ, ☎0844 3351551
✉clerks@derestreet.co.uk
Call Date: Nov 1990, Lincoln's Inn
Pupil Supervisor, Recorder
Qualifications: [LLB (Hons)]
✉clerks@broadcharechambers.co.uk

BROWN MISS AZZA

1 Paper Buildings
1st Floor, 1 Paper Buildings, Temple, London EC4Y 7EP, ☎020 7353 3728
✉clerks@onepaper.co.uk
Call Date: July 2001, Middle Temple
Qualifications: [LLB (Hons)]
✉azzabrown@onepaper.co.uk

BROWN MR CAMERON KENNEDY DUNCAN

9-12 Bell Yard
London WC2A 2JR, ☎020 7400 1800
✉clerks@9-12bellyard.com
Call Date: Oct 1998, Inner Temple
Qualifications: [BA (Oxon)]

BROWN MS CATHERINE JOANNE

Kings Chambers
36 Young Street, Manchester M3 3FT, ☎0845 034 3444
✉clerks@kingschambers.com
Kings Chambers
5 Park Square East, Leeds LS1 2NE, ☎0845 034 3444
✉clerks@kingschambers.com
Kings Chambers
Embassy House, 60 Church Street, Birmingham B3 2DJ, ☎0845 034 3444
✉clerks@kingschambers.com
Call Date: Nov 1999, Inner Temple
Pupil Supervisor
Qualifications: [BA (Leeds)]
✉cbrown@kingschambers.com

BROWN MISS CATHERINE REBECCA

Furnival Chambers
32 Furnival Street, London EC4A 1JQ, ☎020 7405 3232
Call Date: July 2005, Middle Temple
Qualifications: [LLB (Hons) Newcastle]
✉cbrown.pupil@furnivallaw.co.uk

E

BROWN MISS CATHERINE ROBERTA

12 King's Bench Walk
12 King's Bench Walk, Temple, London
EC4Y 7EL, ☎ 020 7583 0811
Call Date: Oct 1990, Middle Temple
Pupil Supervisor, Recorder
Qualifications: [BCom (B'ham) Dip Law]
brown@12kbw.co.uk

BROWN MR CHRISTOPHER

3 PB Barristers
3 Paper Buildings, Temple, London EC4Y 7EU,
☎ 020 7583 8055
Call Date: Nov 1970, Inner Temple

BROWN MR CHRISTOPHER IAN

Broadway House Chambers
Broadway House, 9 Bank Street, Bradford,
West Yorkshire BD1 1TW, ☎ 01274 722560
clerks@broadwayhouse.co.uk
Broadway House Chambers
25 Park Square West, Leeds, West Yorkshire
LS1 2PW, ☎ 0113 246 2600
clerks@broadwayhouse.co.uk
Call Date: July 2001, Middle Temple
Qualifications: [LLB (Hons)]
clerks@broadwayhouse.co.uk, cib@broadwayhouse.co.uk

BROWN MR CHRISTOPHER MARTIN

Matrix Chambers
Griffin Building, Gray's Inn, London
WC1R 5LN, ☎ 020 7404 3447
matrix@matrixlaw.co.uk / lscott@matrixlaw.co.uk
Call Date: Nov 2002, Middle Temple
Qualifications: [LLB (Hons) (Lond) LLM]

BROWN MISS CLARE VICTORIA

2 Temple Gardens
2 Temple Gardens, Temple, London
EC4Y 9AY, ☎ 020 7822 1200
clerks@2tg.co.uk
Call Date: Oct 1993, Middle Temple
Qualifications: [MA (Cantab) BCL (Oxon)]
cbrown@2tg.co.uk

BROWN MR DAMIAN ROBERT QC (2012)

Littleton Chambers
3 King's Bench Walk North, Temple, London
EC4Y 7HR, ☎ 020 7797 8600
fschneider@littletonchambers.co.uk
Call Date: Feb 1989, Inner Temple
Pupil Supervisor
Qualifications: [BA (Lond)]
damianbrown@littletonchambers.co.uk

Fax: 020 7797 8699;
DX: 1047 London, Chancery Lane;
URL: www.littletonchambers.com

Types of work: Discrimination, Employment, Human rights, Sport

Awards and memberships: Chair, Employment Law Bar Association; Industrial Law Society; Employment Lawyers Association; Bar Standards Board Quality Assurance Committee and Professional Conduct Committee until 2011

Other professional experience: Accredited Mediator

Publications: *Blackstone's Employment Law Practice*, 2012; *Tolley's Employment Law* (Contributor), Annual; *Employment Precedents and Company Policy Documents* (Contributor), Annual; *Munkman on Employers' Liability* (Contributor), 2006; *Termination of Employment* (Contributor), 2012

Reported Cases: *QBE Management Services (UK) Ltd v Dymoke and others*, [2012] IRLR 458 (High Court), 2011. Restrictive covenant, economic torts
Kulkarni v Milton Keynes NHS Trust, [2010] ICR 101 (Court of Appeal), 2009. Article 6 and domestic tribunals.
Gate Gourmet v TGWU, [2005] IRLR 881 (High Court), 2005. Industrial action/picketing.
Botes Building Services v Fairhurst Ward Abbott, [2004] IRLR 304 (Court of Appeal), 2004. Equal pay, victimisation.
Bowden v Tuffnells Parcels, [2001] IRLR 838 (ECJ), 2001. Working time exclusions.

BROWN MR EDWARD FRANCIS TREVENEN QC (2008)

QEB Hollis Whiteman
1-2 Laurence Pountney Hill, London
EC4R 0EU, ☎ 020 7933 8855
barristers@qebhw.co.uk
Call Date: July 1983, Gray's Inn
Recorder
Qualifications: [LLB (Bucks)]
Edward.brown@qebhw.co.uk

BROWN MR EDWARD MARTIN

Essex Court Chambers
24 Lincoln's Inn Fields, London WC2A 3EG, ☎020 7813 8000
✉clerksroom@essexcourt.net
Call Date: July 2002, Lincoln's Inn
Qualifications: [BA (Hons)(Cantab)]
✉ebrown@essexcourt.net

BROWN MISS EMMA JANE

No5 Chambers
Fountain Court, Steelhouse Lane, Birmingham B4 6DR, ☎0845 210 5555 ✉info@no5.com
No5 Chambers
Greenwood House, 4-7 Salisbury Court, London EC4Y 8AA, ☎0845 210 5555
No5 Chambers
38 Queen Square, Bristol BS1 4QS, ☎0845 210 5555
Call Date: July 2001, Inner Temple
Qualifications: [LLB (Durham)]
✉eb@no5.com

BROWN MR GEOFFREY BARLOW

39 Essex Street
London WC2R 3AT, ☎020 7832 1111
✉clerks@39essex.com
82 King Street
Manchester M2 4WQ, ☎0161 870 9969
Call Date: July 1981, Inner Temple
Pupil Supervisor
Qualifications: [MA (Cantab)]
✉geoffrey.brown@39essex.com

BROWN MR GEORGE LINCOLN CLAUDE

Kenworthy's Chambers
Arlington House, Bloom Street, Salford, Manchester M3 6AJ, ☎0161 832 4036
Call Date: July 2002, Middle Temple
Qualifications: [BA (Hons)]
✉g.brown@kenworthysbarristers.co.uk

BROWN MS GRACE

Tooks Chambers
81 Farringdon Street, London EC4A 4BL, ☎020 7842 7575 ✉clerks@tooks.co.uk
Call Date: Oct 1995, Inner Temple
Pupil Supervisor
Qualifications: [BA (Hons)(Lond) CPE (Lond)]
✉grace.brown@tooks.co.uk

BROWN MISS HANNAH BEATRICE

One Essex Court
Ground Floor, One Essex Court, Temple, London EC4Y 9AR, ☎020 7583 2000
✉clerks@oeclaw.co.uk
Call Date: Oct 1992, Inner Temple
Qualifications: [BA (Cantab)]
✉hbrown@oeclaw.co.uk

BROWN MISS HARRIET ELINOR

Taxchambers
15 Old Square, Lincoln's Inn, London WC2A 3UE, ☎020 7242 2744
✉taxchambers@15oldsquare.co.uk
Call Date: Oct 2005, Middle Temple
Qualifications: [BA (Hons) (Cantab) Dip in Law MA (Hons) (Cantab)]
✉taxchambers@15oldsquare.co.uk

BROWN MR JAMES RICHARD CHARLES

Atkinson Bevan Chambers
1st Floor, 2 Harcourt Buildings, Temple, London EC4Y 9DB, ☎020 7353 2112
✉clerks@2hb.co.uk
Call Date: Oct 1999, Lincoln's Inn
Qualifications: [LLB (Hons)(Dublin) BCL (Oxon)]
✉jbrown@2hb.co.uk

BROWN MISS JOANNE

4 Paper Buildings
1st Floor, 4 Paper Buildings, Temple, London EC4Y 7EX, ☎020 7427 5200
✉clerks@4pb.com
Call Date: Nov 1990, Inner Temple
Pupil Supervisor
Qualifications: [LLB (Brunel)]
✉jb1@4pb.com

BROWN MR JOHN STEPHEN

4 King's Bench Walk
2nd Floor, 4 King's Bench Walk, Temple, London EC4Y 7DL, ☎020 7822 7000
✉clerks@4kbw.co.uk
Call Date: July 2005, Inner Temple
Qualifications: [LLB University of Bristol]
✉jb@4kbw.co.uk

E

BROWN MISS KRISTINA RACHEL

No5 Chambers
Fountain Court, Steelhouse Lane, Birmingham B4 6DR, ☎0845 210 5555 ✉info@no5.com
No5 Chambers
Greenwood House, 4-7 Salisbury Court, London EC4Y 8AA, ☎0845 210 5555
No5 Chambers
38 Queen Square, Bristol BS1 4QS, ☎0845 210 5555
Call Date: Oct 1998, Gray's Inn
Qualifications: [LLB (Hons)(Dunelm)]
kbr@no5.com

BROWN MR LUKE HENRY WILLIAM

East Anglian Chambers
15 The Close, Norwich, Norfolk NR1 4DZ, ☎01473 214481 ✉norwich@ealaw.co.uk
East Anglian Chambers
53 North Hill, Colchester, Essex CO1 1QA, ☎01473 214481 ✉colchester@ealaw.co.uk
East Anglian Chambers
Gresham House, 5 Museum Street, Ipswich, Suffolk IP1 1HQ, ☎01473 214481 ✉ipswich@ealaw.co.uk
Call Date: Oct 2000, Middle Temple
Qualifications: [BA (Hons) (Dunelm) LLB (Hons)]
lukebrown@ealaw.co.uk

E

BROWN MR MARC JEFFREY

2 Pump Court
1st Floor, 2 Pump Court, Temple, London EC4Y 7AH, ☎020 7353 5597 ✉clerks@2pumpcourt.co.uk
Call Date: Mar 2001, Lincoln's Inn
Qualifications: [LLB (Hons) (Essex)]
mbrown@2pumpcourt.co.uk

BROWN MR MARC WILLIAM

St Philips Chambers
55 Temple Row, Birmingham B2 5LS, ☎0121 246 7000 ✉clerks@st-philips.com
Call Date: Oct 2004, Gray's Inn
Qualifications: [BA (Hons) BCL]
mbrown@st-philips.co.uk

BROWN MISS MICHELLE DIANE

St Ive's Chambers
Whittall Street, Birmingham B4 6DH, ☎0121 236 0863 ✉clerks@stiveschambers.co.uk
Call Date: Feb 1992, Inner Temple
Qualifications: [LLB (Hons) (So'ton)]
michelle.brown@stiveschambers.co.uk

BROWN MISS MICHELLE KERRI

Deans Court Chambers
24 St John Street, Manchester M3 4DF, ☎0161 214 6000 ✉clerks@deanscourt.co.uk
Deans Court Chambers
101 Walker Street, Preston PR1 2RR, ☎01772 565 600 ✉preston@deanscourt.co.uk
Call Date: Nov 2005, Gray's Inn
Qualifications: [LLB]

BROWN MS NATALIE

Radcliffe Chambers
Ground Floor, 11 New Square, Lincoln's Inn, London WC2A 3QB, ☎020 7831 0081 ✉clerks@radcliffechambers.com
Call Date: Oct 2009, Gray's Inn
Qualifications: [BA]
nbrown@radcliffechambers.com

BROWN MR NICHOLAS GEOFFREY NORFOLK

St Philips Chambers
55 Temple Row, Birmingham B2 5LS, ☎0121 246 7000 ✉clerks@st-philips.com
Call Date: July 2005, Lincoln's Inn
Qualifications: [BA (Hons) MA]
mbrown@st-philips.co.uk

BROWN MR NICHOLAS ROBERT DELANO

Doughty Street Chambers
53-54 Doughty Street, London WC1N 2LS, ☎020 7404 1313 ✉enquiries@doughtystreet.co.uk
Doughty Street Chambers
Pall Mall Court, 61-67 King Street, Manchester M2 4PD, ☎0161 618 1066
Doughty Street Chambers
5th Floor, Broad Quay House, Prince Street, Bristol BS1 4DJ, ☎01179 058 717
Call Date: Nov 1989, Lincoln's Inn
Qualifications: [BA (Cantab)]
n.brown@doughtystreet.co.uk

BROWN MR PAUL MARTIN QC (2009)

4-5 Gray's Inn Square
Gray's Inn, London WC1R 5AH, ☎020 7404 5252 ✉clerks@4-5.co.uk
Call Date: Nov 1991, Inner Temple
Qualifications: [LLB (Cant) PhD (Cambs)]
pbrown@4-5.co.uk

BROWN MR PHILIP STEPHEN

9 Stone Buildings
Lincoln's Inn, London WC2A 3NN,
☎ 020 7404 5055
✉ clerks@9stonebuildings.com
Call Date: Oct 1991, Lincoln's Inn
Qualifications: [LLB (Hons) (Leeds)]

BROWN MISS REBECCA

Fountain Chambers
Cleveland Business Centre, 1 Watson Street, Middlesbrough TS1 2RQ, ☎ 01642 804040
✉ clerks@fountainchambers.co.uk
Call Date: July 2007, Lincoln's Inn
Qualifications: [LLB (Dunelm)]
🖃 rebecca_brown1985@hotmail.co.uk

BROWN MR ROBERT CHARLES WARREN

1 Gray's Inn Square
Ground Floor, 1 Gray's Inn Square, London WC1R 5AA, ☎ 020 7405 0001
Call Date: Nov 1992, Lincoln's Inn
Qualifications: [BSc (Lond) DipLaw]

BROWN MR ROBERT JAMES

Arden Chambers
20 Bloomsbury Square, London WC1A 2NS,
☎ 020 7242 4244
✉ clerks@ardenchambers.com
Call Date: Oct 2008, Lincoln's Inn
Qualifications: [BA (Lond) LLB (Lond)]
🖃 robert.brown@ardenchambers.com

BROWN MR ROBERT LORIMER

23 Essex Street
London WC2R 3AA, ☎ 020 7413 0353
✉ clerks@23es.com
Call Date: July 1983, Gray's Inn
Pupil Supervisor
Qualifications: [LLB (Leic)]
🖃 roybrown@23es.com

BROWN MR ROGER CHARLES ARTHUR

Kenworthy's Chambers
Arlington House, Bloom Street, Salford, Manchester M3 6AJ, ☎ 0161 832 4036
Call Date: Nov 1976, Inner Temple
Pupil Supervisor
Qualifications: [LLB]

BROWN DR RORY STEVEN

9 Stone Buildings
Lincoln's Inn, London WC2A 3NN,
☎ 020 7404 5055
✉ clerks@9stonebuildings.com
Call Date: Oct 2009, Inner Temple
Qualifications: [MA (Cantab) MRES PhD (Italy) EUI (Italy)]
🖃 rbrown@9stonebuildings.com

BROWN MR SAM CLEMENT

Atkinson Bevan Chambers
1st Floor, 2 Harcourt Buildings, Temple, London EC4Y 9DB, ☎ 020 7353 2112
✉ clerks@2hb.co.uk
Call Date: Nov 2004, Inner Temple
Qualifications: [BA St John's College University of Cambridge]
🖃 SBrown@2hb.co.uk

BROWN MR SIMON JONATHAN

Crown Office Chambers
2 Crown Office Row, Temple, London EC4Y 7HJ, ☎ 020 7797 8100
✉ mail@crownofficechambers.com
Call Date: July 1988, Gray's Inn
Pupil Supervisor
Qualifications: [LLB (Lond)]
🖃 brown@crownofficechambers.com

BROWN MISS STEPHANIE AMANDA

No5 Chambers
Fountain Court, Steelhouse Lane, Birmingham B4 6DR, ☎ 0845 210 5555 ✉ info@no5.com
No5 Chambers
Greenwood House, 4-7 Salisbury Court, London EC4Y 8AA, ☎ 0845 210 5555
No5 Chambers
38 Queen Square, Bristol BS1 4QS,
☎ 0845 210 5555
Call Date: July 1982, Lincoln's Inn
Pupil Supervisor
Qualifications: [LLB (Exon)]
🖃 sb@no5.com

BROWN MR STEPHEN PAUL

Sovereign Chambers
46 Park Place, Leeds LS1 2RY,
☎ 0113 245 1841
✉ clerks@sovereignchambers.co.uk
Call Date: Oct 2004, Middle Temple
Qualifications: [LLB (Hons) MA PhD]
🖃 stephen.brown@sovereignchambers.co.uk

E

BROWN MR STUART CHRISTOPHER QC (1991)

Call Date: July 1974, Inner Temple
Recorder
Qualifications: [BA BCL (Oxon)]
stuart.brown@parklaneplowden.co.uk

BROWN MISS SUSAN MARGARET

One Essex Court
1st Floor, Temple, London EC4Y 9AR,
☎ 020 7936 3030 ✉ clerks@1ec.co.uk
Call Date: July 1989, Lincoln's Inn
Pupil Supervisor
Qualifications: [BSc LLB (Lond)]

BROWN MR THOMAS ALEXANDER

Cloisters
1 Pump Court, Temple, London EC4Y 7AA,
☎ 020 7827 4000 ✉ clerks@cloisters.com
Call Date: Nov 2000, Middle Temple
Pupil Supervisor
Qualifications: [MA (Hons) (Oxon) Dip Law]
tb@cloisters.com

BROWN MR THOMAS CHRISTOPHER ELLIS

Fenners Chambers
3 Madingley Road, Cambridge CB3 0EE,
☎ 01223 368761
✉ clerks@fennerschambers.com
Call Date: Nov 1980, Gray's Inn
Qualifications: [MA (Cantab)]
tim.brown@fennerschambers.com

BROWN MR TIMOTHY DONALD

Temple Tax Chambers
1st Floor, 3 Temple Gardens, Temple, London
EC4Y 9AU, ☎ 020 7353 7884
✉ clerks@templetax.com
Call Date: July 2001, Inner Temple
Qualifications: [LLB (Nott'm)]
tim@timothybrown.co.uk

BROWN MR TIMOTHY WILLIAM

13 King's Bench Walk
13 King's Bench Walk, Temple, London
EC4Y 7EN, ☎ 020 7353 7204
✉ clerks@13kbw.co.uk
13 KBW
32 Beaumont Street, Oxford OX1 2NP,
☎ 01865 311066 ✉ clerks@13kbw.co.uk
Call Date: Mar 2005, Inner Temple
Qualifications: [MA University of Edinburgh CPE City University]
tbrown@13kbw.co.uk

BROWNBILL MR DAVID JOHN QC (2008)

XXIV Old Buildings
Ground Floor, 24 Old Buildings, Lincoln's Inn,
London WC2A 3UP, ☎ 020 7691 2424
✉ clerks@xxiv.co.uk
Call Date: July 1989, Gray's Inn
Qualifications: [LLB (Nott'm)]
djb@xxiv.co.uk

BROWNE MR BENJAMIN JAMES QC (1996)

2 Temple Gardens
2 Temple Gardens, Temple, London
EC4Y 9AY, ☎ 020 7822 1200
✉ clerks@2tg.co.uk
Call Date: July 1976, Inner Temple
Recorder
Qualifications: [MA (Oxon)]
bbrowne@2tg.co.uk

BROWNE MR DESMOND JOHN MICHAEL QC (1990)

5RB
1st Floor, 5 Raymond Buildings, Gray's Inn,
London WC1R 5BP, ☎ 020 7242 2902
✉ clerks@5rb.com
Call Date: Nov 1969, Gray's Inn
Recorder
Qualifications: [BA (Oxon)]
desmondbrowne@5rb.com

BROWNE DR GERALD ROBERT

Zenith Chambers
10 Park Square, Leeds LS1 2LH,
☎ 0113 245 5438
✉ clerks@zenithchambers.co.uk
Call Date: Nov 1995, Inner Temple
Qualifications: [MBChB (B'ham)]
gbrowne@zenithchambers.co.uk

BROWNE MR JAMES WILLIAM

Lamb Chambers
Lamb Building, Elm Court, Temple, London
EC4Y 7AS, ☎ 020 7797 8300
✉ info@lambchambers.co.uk
Call Date: Oct 1994, Middle Temple
Qualifications: [BA (Hons)(B'ham) M St (Oxon) Dip Law (Lond)]
jamesbrowne@lambchambers.co.uk

E

BROWNE MR LOUIS BARTHOLOMEW ANTHONY

Exchange Chambers
One Derby Square, Derby Square, Liverpool L2 9XX, ☎0151 236 7747
✉info@exchangechambers.co.uk
Exchange Chambers
7 Ralli Courts, West Riverside, Manchester M3 5FT, ☎0161 833 2722
Exchange Chambers
Oxford House, Oxford Row, Leeds LS1 3BE, ☎0113 203 1970
✉spencer@exchangechambers.co.uk
Call Date: Nov 1988, Lincoln's Inn
Pupil Supervisor, Recorder
Qualifications: [LLB (Hons) BCL (Oxon)]
browne@exchangechambers.co.uk

BROWNE MISS SHEREENER DONNA

Garden Court Chambers
57-60 Lincoln's Inn Fields, London WC2A 3LJ, ☎020 7993 7600 ✉info@gclaw.co.uk
Call Date: Nov 1996, Inner Temple
Qualifications: [LLB]
shereenerb@gclaw.co.uk

BROWNE MR SIMON PETER BUCHANAN QC (2011)

Temple Garden Chambers
1 Harcourt Buildings, Temple, London EC4Y 9DA, ☎020 7583 1315
✉clerks@tgchambers.com
Call Date: Nov 1982, Middle Temple
Pupil Supervisor
Qualifications: [LLB (Hons)]
simonbrowne@tgchambers.com

BROWNE MR TREVOR PAUL

Nexus Chambers
7 New Square, Lincolns Inn, London WC2A 3QS,
☎020 7404 1147 / 020 7831 8309
✉info@nexuschambers.com
Call Date: Mar 2003, Lincoln's Inn
Qualifications: [AB (Hons) (L'pool) LLM (Keele) PgDL (Wolves)]

BROWNE-WILKINSON MR SIMON QC (1998)

Fountain Court Chambers
Fountain Court, Temple, London EC4Y 9DH, ☎020 7583 3335
✉chambers@fountaincourt.co.uk
Call Date: Nov 1981, Lincoln's Inn
Recorder
Qualifications: [BA (Oxon)]
sbw@fountaincourt.co.uk

BROWNHILL MR IAN PETER

Doughty Street Chambers
53-54 Doughty Street, London WC1N 2LS, ☎020 7404 1313
✉enquiries@doughtystreet.co.uk
Call Date: Mar 2009, Lincoln's Inn
Qualifications: [BA (Oxon)]

BROWNHILL MISS JOANNA FRANCESA

Five Paper
Ground Floor, 5 Paper Buildings, Temple, London EC4Y 7HB, ☎020 7815 3200
Call Date: Oct 1997, Gray's Inn
Qualifications: [MA (Oxon)]

BRUCE MR ANDREW JONATHAN

Serle Court
6 New Square, Lincoln's Inn, London WC2A 3QS, ☎020 7242 6105
✉clerks@serlecourt.co.uk
Call Date: Oct 1992, Middle Temple
Pupil Supervisor, Recorder
Qualifications: [MA (Oxon)]
abruce@serlecourt.co.uk

BRUCE MR DAVID LIVINGSTONE

St Johns Buildings
24a - 28 St John Street, Manchester M3 4DJ, ☎0161 214 1500
✉clerk@stjohnsbuildings.co.uk
St Johns Buildings
21 White Friars, Chester CH1 1NZ, ☎01244 323070
✉clerk@stjohnsbuildings.co.uk
16 Winckley Square
Preston PR1 3JJ, ☎01772 256100
Call Date: July 1982, Middle Temple
Qualifications: [LLB (Lond)]
clerk@stjohnsbuildings.co.uk

BRUCE MISS ELEANOR

Pump Court Chambers
Upper Ground Floor, 3 Pump Court, Temple, London EC4Y 7AJ, ☎020 7353 0711
✉clerks@3pumpcourt.com
Pump Court Chambers
5 Temple Chambers, Temple Street, Swindon SN1 1SQ, ☎01793 539899
✉clerks@3pumpcourt.com
Riverview Chambers
Hamilton House, 1 Temple Avenue, London EC4Y 0HA, ☎0844 225 3999
✉chrisbaylis@riverviewchambers.com
Call Date: July 2008, Middle Temple
Qualifications: [BA (Hons) (Lond) PgDl (Lond)]

E

BRUCE MR LAWRENCE ALLAN

Fenners Chambers
3 Madingley Road, Cambridge CB3 0EE,
☎01223 368761
✉clerks@fennerschambers.com
Call Date: Nov 2000, Lincoln's Inn
Qualifications: [LLB (Hons) (L'Pool) LLM (LSE)]
lawrence.bruce@fennerschambers.com

BRUCE MR RICHARD HENDERSON

Chambers of Mr R H Bruce
P.O. Box 748, Richmond TW9 2WU,
☎020 8940 5895 ✉richardhbruce@aol.com
Call Date: July 1974, Gray's Inn
Recorder
Qualifications: [LLB FCIArb LLM (Bris)]

BRUCE MISS ZOE

37 Park Square Chambers
37 Park Square, Leeds LS1 2NY,
☎0113 243 9422 ✉chambers@no37.co.uk
Call Date: July 2009, Inner Temple
Qualifications: [LLB (Newc)]
chambers@no37.co.uk

BRUDENELL MR THOMAS MERVYN

Queen Elizabeth Building
3rd Floor, Queen Elizabeth Building, Temple, London EC4Y 9BS, ☎020 7797 7837
✉clerks@qeb.co.uk
Call Date: Nov 1977, Inner Temple
Pupil Supervisor

BRUNNER MS CATHERINE JANE

Albion Chambers
Broad Street, Bristol BS1 1DR,
☎0117 927 2144
✉clerks@albionchambers.co.uk
36 Bedford Row
London WC1R 4JH, ☎020 7421 8000
✉chambers@36bedfordrow.co.uk
Call Date: Oct 1997, Inner Temple
Qualifications: [MA (Edin) CPE (Lond)]
kate.brunner@albionchambers.co.uk

BRUNNER MR PETER ROLAND

Brick Court Chambers
7-8 Essex Street, London WC2R 3LD,
☎020 7379 3550 ✉clerks@brickcourt.co.uk
Call Date: July 1971, Middle Temple
Pupil Supervisor
Qualifications: [BA LLB (Cantab)]
brunner@Brickcourt.co.uk

BRUNNING MR MATTHEW DAVID GEORGE

No5 Chambers
Fountain Court, Steelhouse Lane, Birmingham B4 6DR, ☎0845 210 5555 ✉info@no5.com
No5 Chambers
Greenwood House, 4-7 Salisbury Court, London EC4Y 8AA, ☎0845 210 5555
No5 Chambers
38 Queen Square, Bristol BS1 4QS,
☎0845 210 5555
Call Date: Nov 1997, Middle Temple
Qualifications: [BA (Hons)]
mdb@no5.com

BRUNSDON-TULLY MR MATTHEW PAUL

1 Hare Court
1 Hare Court, Temple, London EC4Y 7BE,
☎020 7797 7070 ✉clerks@1hc.com
Call Date: Oct 2007, Lincoln's Inn
Qualifications: [LLB (Lond)]
mbt@1hc.com

BRUNT MR PHILIP EDWIN

No 8 Chambers
8 Fountain Court, Steelhouse Lane, Birmingham B4 6DR, ☎0121 236 5514
✉clerks@no8chambers.co.uk
Call Date: Nov 1991, Lincoln's Inn
Qualifications: [BSc (Econ) (Hons) Dip Law]
philipbrunt@no8chambers.co.uk

BRUNTON MR SEAN ALEXANDER MCKAY

Colleton Chambers
Colleton Crescent, Exeter, Devon EX2 4DG,
☎01392 274898
✉clerks@colletonchambers.co.uk
3 PB Barristers
Royal Talbot House, 2 Victoria Street, Bristol, Avon BS1 6BB, ☎0117 928 1520
Call Date: Oct 1990, Middle Temple
Qualifications: [BA (Cantab)]

BRYAN MISS CARMEL MARY

Rougemont Chambers
Victory House, Dean Clarke Gardens, Southernhay East, Exeter EX2 4AA,
☎01392 208484
✉clerks@rougemontchambers.co.uk
Call Date: Nov 1993, Middle Temple
Qualifications: [LLB (Hons)(Lond)]
cbryan@rougemontchambers.co.uk

BRYAN MR REX VICTOR

East Anglian Chambers
140 New London Road, Chelmsford, Essex CM2 0AW, ☎01473 214481
✉chelmsford@ealaw.co.uk
East Anglian Chambers
Gresham House, 5 Museum Street, Ipswich, Suffolk IP1 1HQ, ☎01473 214481
✉ipswich@ealaw.co.uk
East Anglian Chambers
15 The Close, Norwich, Norfolk NR1 4DZ, ☎01473 214481 ✉norwich@ealaw.co.uk
Call Date: Nov 1971, Lincoln's Inn
Pupil Supervisor, Recorder
Qualifications: [MA (Oxon)]
rexbryan@ealaw.co.uk

BRYAN MR ROBERT JOHN

1 Paper Buildings
1st Floor, 1 Paper Buildings, Temple, London EC4Y 7EP, ☎020 7353 3728
✉clerks@onepaper.co.uk
Call Date: Oct 1992, Middle Temple
Pupil Supervisor
Qualifications: [LLB (Hons)]
robertbryan@onepaper.co.uk

BRYAN MR SIMON JAMES QC (2006)

Essex Court Chambers
24 Lincoln's Inn Fields, London WC2A 3EG, ☎020 7813 8000
✉clerksroom@essexcourt.net
Call Date: July 1988, Lincoln's Inn
Qualifications: [MA (Hons) (Cantab)]
sbryan@essexcourt.net

BRYANT MISS CAROLINE

East Anglian Chambers
Gresham House, 5 Museum Street, Ipswich, Suffolk IP1 1HQ, ☎01473 214481
✉ipswich@ealaw.co.uk
East Anglian Chambers
140 New London Road, Chelmsford, Essex CM2 0AW, ☎01473 214481
✉chelmsford@ealaw.co.uk
East Anglian Chambers
15 The Close, Norwich, Norfolk NR1 4DZ, ☎01473 214481 ✉norwich@ealaw.co.uk
Call Date: July 1976, Middle Temple
Pupil Supervisor
Qualifications: [LLB]
carolinebryant@ealaw.co.uk

BRYANT MISS CERI JANE QC (2012)

Erskine Chambers
33 Chancery Lane, London WC2A 1EN, ☎020 7242 5532
✉clerks@erskinechambers.com
Call Date: July 1984, Lincoln's Inn
Pupil Supervisor
Qualifications: [MA LLM (Cantab)]
cbryant@erskine-chambers.co.uk

BRYANT MR JOHN MALCOLM CORNELIUS

1 Chancery Lane
London WC2A 1LF, ☎0845 634 6666
✉clerks@1chancerylane.com
Call Date: Nov 1976, Inner Temple
Pupil Supervisor
Qualifications: [MA (Cantab)]
jbryant@1chancerylane.com

BRYANT MISS JUDITH ANNE

Wilberforce Chambers
8 New Square, Lincoln's Inn, London WC2A 3QP, ☎020 7306 0102
✉chambers@wilberforce.co.uk
Call Date: July 1987, Lincoln's Inn
Pupil Supervisor
Qualifications: [BA LLM (Cantab)]
jbryant@wilberforce.co.uk

Types of work: Capital tax, Chancery (general), Charities, Conflict of laws, Equity, Family provision, Inheritance and cohabitees, Offshore trust litigation, Professional negligence, Trust litigation, Trusts, Wills

BRYANT MR KEITH

Outer Temple Chambers
The Outer Temple, 222 Strand, London WC2R 1BA, ☎020 7353 6381
✉clerks@outertemple.com
Call Date: Oct 1991, Middle Temple
Pupil Supervisor
Qualifications: [BA (Hons) (Cantab) CPE Dip Com Sci (Cantab) MA (Cantab)]
keith.bryant@outertemple.com

BRYANT-HERON MR MARK NICHOLAS

9-12 Bell Yard
London WC2A 2JR, ☎020 7400 1800
✉clerks@9-12bellyard.com
Call Date: Nov 1986, Middle Temple
Pupil Supervisor, Recorder
Qualifications: [MA(Cantab)]
m.bryantheron@9-12bellyard.com

E

BRYDEN MR CHRISTOPHER JAMES YUEN KANG

4 King's Bench Walk
2nd Floor, 4 King's Bench Walk, Temple, London EC4Y 7DL, ☎ 020 7822 7000
✉ clerks@4kbw.co.uk
Call Date: July 2003, Gray's Inn
Qualifications: [BA (Oxon) LLM]
✉ cxb@4kbw.co.uk

BRYSON MR ALAN DAVID

Chambers of Mr Alan Bryson
Hatherley House, Grundisburgh Road, Burgh, Woodbridge, Suffolk IP13 6QA,
☎ 01473 735266
✉ alan.bryson@btinternet.com
Call Date: July 2004, Inner Temple
✉ alan.bryson@btinternet.com

BUBB MR TIMOTHY MICHAEL ANTHONY

39 Park Square
Leeds LS1 2NU, ☎ 0113 245 6633
✉ seniorclerk@39parksquarechambers.co.uk
Call Date: July 1970, Gray's Inn
Pupil Supervisor
Qualifications: [LLB]

BUCHAN MR ANDREW

Cloisters
1 Pump Court, Temple, London EC4Y 7AA,
☎ 020 7827 4000 ✉ clerks@cloisters.com
Call Date: July 1981, Gray's Inn
Pupil Supervisor
Qualifications: [LLB (Leeds)]
✉ abu@cloisters.com

BUCHAN MISS CAROLINE VENETIA

Chambers of Miss C Buchan
9 Savill Road, Haywards Heath, East Sussex RH16 2NY, ☎ 01444 482222
✉ carolinebuchan@yahoo.com
Call Date: Oct 2000, Middle Temple
Qualifications: [MA (Hons) (St. Andrew's) CPE]
✉ carolinebuchan@yahoo.com

BUCHAN MR JONATHAN MAXFIELD

15 Winckley Square
Preston PR1 3JJ, ☎ 01772 252828
✉ clerks@15winckleysq.co.uk
Call Date: Oct 1994, Middle Temple
Pupil Supervisor
Qualifications: [MA (Cantab) CPE]

BUCHANAN MR JAMES IAN CHARLES

2 Hare Court
Lower Ground, Ground, 1st & 2nd Floor, 2 Hare Court, Temple, London EC4Y 7BH,
☎ 020 7353 3982 ✉ clerks@2harecourt.com
Call Date: Nov 1993, Gray's Inn
Qualifications: [BA (Nott'm)]

BUCHANAN MISS VIVIEN JEAN

St Mary's Family Law Chambers
26-28 High Pavement, The Lace Market, Nottingham NG1 1HN, ☎ 0115 950 3503
✉ clerks@stmarysflc.co.uk
Call Date: July 1981, Inner Temple
Qualifications: [LLB (Hons) (So'ton)]
✉ vivien.buchanan@stmarysflc.co.uk

BUCK MR JOHN

Tanfield Chambers
2-5 Warwick Court, London WC1R 5DJ,
☎ 020 7421 5300
✉ clerks@tanfieldchambers.co.uk
Call Date: Nov 1987, Gray's Inn
Pupil Supervisor
Qualifications: [MA (Oxon)]
✉ jbuck@tanfieldchambers.co.uk

BUCK MR WILLIAM EDWARD

Chancery House Chambers
7 Lisbon Square, Leeds, West Yorkshire LS1 4LY, ☎ 0113 244 6691
✉ clerks@chanceryhouse.co.uk
Call Date: July 2001, Lincoln's Inn
Pupil Supervisor
Qualifications: [BA (Hons) LLM]
✉ william.buck@chanceryhouse.co.uk

BUCKETT MR EDWIN GORDON

The Chambers of Grahame Aldous QC
9 Gough Square, London EC4A 3DG,
☎ 020 7832 0500
✉ clerks@9goughsquare.co.uk
Call Date: July 1988, Inner Temple
Pupil Supervisor
Qualifications: [LLB (Hull)]
✉ ebuckett@9goughsquare.co.uk

BUCKHAVEN MRS CHARLOTTE VANDERLIP

2 Dr Johnson's Buildings
2 Dr Johnson's Buildings, Temple, London EC4Y 7AY, ☎ 020 7936 2613
✉ clerks@2drj.com
Call Date: July 1969, Middle Temple
Qualifications: [MA (St Andrews)]

BUCKHAVEN MR SIMON

Hardwicke
New Square, Lincoln's Inn, London WC2A 3SB, ☎ 020 7242 2523
✉ enquiries@hardwicke.co.uk
Call Date: July 1970, Gray's Inn
Pupil Supervisor

BUCKINGHAM MR CHRISTOPHER JOHN

42 Bedford Row
London WC1R 4LL, ☎ 020 7831 0222
✉ clerks@42br.com
Call Date: July 2009, Lincoln's Inn
Qualifications: [BA (Oxon) CPE UZOBU]
✉ chris_j_36@hotmail.com, christopherb@42br.com

BUCKINGHAM MR PAUL RICHARD

Keating Chambers
15 Essex Street, London WC2R 3AA, ☎ 020 7544 2600
✉ clerks@keatingchambers.com
Call Date: Nov 1995, Middle Temple
Pupil Supervisor
Qualifications: [BSc (Hons) CEng FIChemE Dip in Law]

BUCKINGHAM MISS SARAH-JAYNE

No5 Chambers
Fountain Court, Steelhouse Lane, Birmingham B4 6DR, ☎ 0845 210 5555 ✉ info@no5.com
No5 Chambers
Greenwood House, 4-7 Salisbury Court, London EC4Y 8AA, ☎ 0845 210 5555
No5 Chambers
38 Queen Square, Bristol BS1 4QS, ☎ 0845 210 5555
Call Date: Oct 1991, Inner Temple
Pupil Supervisor
Qualifications: [LLB (Hons)]
✉ sbu@no5.com

BUCKINGHAM MR STEWART JOHN

Quadrant Chambers
Quadrant House, 10 Fleet Street, London EC4Y 1AU, ☎ 020 7583 4444
✉ info@quadrantchambers.com
Call Date: Nov 1996, Middle Temple
Pupil Supervisor
Qualifications: [BA (Hons) BCL]
✉ stewart.buckingham@quadrantchambers.com

BUCKLAND MR MATTHEW STEPHEN

Carmelite Chambers
9 Carmelite Street, London EC4Y 0DR, ☎ 020 7936 6300
✉ clerks@carmelitechambers.co.uk
Call Date: Mar 1998, Lincoln's Inn
Qualifications: [BA (Hons)]
✉ mbuckland@carmelitechambers.co.uk

BUCKLAND MR ROBERT JAMES

Apex
Harlech House, 20 Cathedral Road, Cardiff CF11 9LJ, ☎ 02920 232 032
✉ clerks@apexchambers.net
Call Date: Oct 1991, Inner Temple
Pupil Supervisor
Qualifications: [BA (Dunelm)]
✉ robert.buckland@apexchambers.net

BUCKLE MR COLIN DEREK

Kenworthy's Chambers
Arlington House, Bloom Street, Salford, Manchester M3 6AJ, ☎ 0161 832 4036
Call Date: Mar 2002, Middle Temple
Qualifications: [LLB (Hons)]

BUCKLE MR JONATHAN

Regency Chambers
45 Priestgate, Peterborough PE1 1LB, ☎ 01733 315215
✉ clerks@regencychambers.law.co.uk
Regency Chambers
Sheraton House, Castle Park, Cambridge CB3 0AX, ☎ 01223 301517
Call Date: Nov 1990, Lincoln's Inn
Pupil Supervisor
Qualifications: [BA (Hons) Dip Law]
✉ clerks@regencychambers.law.co.uk

BUCKLEY MR CHRISTOPHER DAVID

Radcliffe Chambers
Ground Floor, 11 New Square, Lincoln's Inn, London WC2A 3QB, ☎ 020 7831 0081
✉ clerks@radcliffechambers.com
Call Date: July 2004, Lincoln's Inn
Qualifications: [MA (Hons) (Cantab)]
✉ cbuckley@radcliffechambers.com

BUCKLEY MISS GEORGINA LOUISE

Iscoed Chambers
86 St Helen's Road, Swansea SA1 4BQ, ☎ 01792 652988
✉ clerks@iscoedchambers.co.uk
Call Date: July 2007, Lincoln's Inn
Qualifications: [LLB (Cardiff)]
✉ gb@iscoedchambers.co.uk

BUCKLEY MISS GERARDINE MARIA

Stour Chambers
Mill Studio, 17a Stour Street, Canterbury, Kent CT1 2NR, ☎01227 764899
✉clerks@stourchambers.co.uk
Call Date: Nov 1991, Gray's Inn
Qualifications: [BA (Kent)]
✉clerks@stourchambers.co.uk

BUCKLEY MR PATRICK JAMES

St Johns Buildings
24a - 28 St John Street, Manchester M3 4DJ, ☎0161 214 1500
✉clerk@stjohnsbuildings.co.uk
St Johns Buildings
21 White Friars, Chester CH1 1NZ, ☎01244 323070
✉clerk@stjohnsbuildings.co.uk
16 Winckley Square
Preston PR1 3JJ, ☎01772 256100
Call Date: July 1998, Gray's Inn
Qualifications: [BA (Hons)(Keele) Dip Law]
✉clerk@stjohnsbuildings.co.uk

BUCKLEY MR PETER EVERED

Cobden House Chambers
19 Quay Street, Manchester M3 3HN, ☎0161 833 6000 ✉Clerks@Cobden.co.uk
Call Date: July 1972, Gray's Inn
Pupil Supervisor
Qualifications: [BA (Oxon)]
✉clerks@cobden.co.uk, peter.buckley@cobden.co.uk

BUCKLEY MR WILLIAM JAMES STERLING

1 Paper Buildings
1st Floor, 1 Paper Buildings, Temple, London EC4Y 7EP, ☎020 7353 3728
✉clerks@onepaper.co.uk
Call Date: Nov 1987, Middle Temple
Qualifications: [BA (Cantab)]
✉willbuckley@onepaper.co.uk

BUCKLEY-CLARKE MRS AMANDA VICTORIA

3 PB Barristers
23 Beaumont Street, Oxford OX1 2NP, ☎01865 793 736
3 PB Barristers
30 Christchurch Road, Bournemouth, Dorset BH1 3PD, ☎01202 292102
✉clerks.bournemouth@3paper.co.uk
3 PB Barristers
3 Paper Buildings, Temple, London EC4Y 7EU, ☎020 7583 8055
3 PB Barristers
Royal Talbot House, 2 Victoria Street, Bristol, Avon BS1 6BB, ☎0117 928 1520
3 PB Barristers
4 St Peter Street, Winchester SO23 8BW, ☎01962 868884
✉clerks.winchester@3paper.co.uk
Call Date: Oct 1991, Lincoln's Inn
Qualifications: [BA (Oxon)]

BUCKNALL MISS BELINDA QC (1988)

Quadrant Chambers
Quadrant House, 10 Fleet Street, London EC4Y 1AU, ☎020 7583 4444
✉info@quadrantchambers.com
Call Date: Nov 1974, Middle Temple
Recorder
Qualifications: [MA (Oxon)]
✉belinda.bucknall@quadrantchambers.com

BUCKPITT MR MICHAEL DAVID

Tanfield Chambers
2-5 Warwick Court, London WC1R 5DJ, ☎020 7421 5300
✉clerks@tanfieldchambers.co.uk
Call Date: Feb 1988, Gray's Inn
Pupil Supervisor
Qualifications: [LLB]
✉michaelbuckpitt@tanfieldchambers.co.uk
URL: www.tanfieldchambers.co.uk

Types of work: Chancery (land law), Landlord and tenant, Leasehold enfranchisement

BUDé MISS YVETTE ANOUK

Cloisters
1 Pump Court, Temple, London EC4Y 7AA, ☎020 7827 4000 ✉clerks@cloisters.com
Call Date: Nov 2003, Middle Temple
Qualifications: [LLB LLM]

BUDDEN MISS CAROLINE RACHEL

1 KBW Chambers
1 King's Bench Walk, Temple, London EC4Y 7DB, ☎020 7936 1500
✉clerks@1kbw.co.uk
King's Bench Chambers
174 High Street, Lewes BN7 1YE, ☎01273 402600
Call Date: Nov 1977, Inner Temple
Pupil Supervisor, Recorder
Qualifications: [LLB (Bris)]
✉cbudden@1kbw.co.uk

BUDDEN MISS ROSEMARY CHRISTINE

Queen Elizabeth Building
3rd Floor, Queen Elizabeth Building, Temple, London EC4Y 9BS, ☎ 020 7797 7837
✉ clerks@qeb.co.uk
Call Date: Mar 2003, Lincoln's Inn
Qualifications: [MA (Hons) (Oxon)]
✉ r.budden@qeb.co.uk

BUDWORTH MR ADAM JOHN DUTTON

2 Bedford Row
London WC1R 4BU, ☎ 020 7440 8888
✉ clerks@2bedfordrow.co.uk
Call Date: Nov 1992, Inner Temple
Pupil Supervisor
Qualifications: [BA (Lond) Dip Law]
✉ abudworth@2bedfordrow.co.uk

BUDWORTH MR MARTIN JAMES

Kings Chambers
36 Young Street, Manchester M3 3FT, ☎ 0845 034 3444
✉ clerks@kingschambers.com
Kings Chambers
5 Park Square East, Leeds LS1 2NE, ☎ 0845 034 3444
✉ clerks@kingschambers.com
Kings Chambers
Embassy House, 60 Church Street, Birmingham B3 2DJ, ☎ 0845 034 3444
✉ clerks@kingschambers.com
Call Date: Nov 1999, Inner Temple
Qualifications: [LLB (Dunelm)]
✉ mbudworth@kingschambers.com

BUDWORTH MR RICHARD DUTTON

2-3 Hind Court Chambers
2-3 Hind Court, Fleet Street, London EC4A 3DL, ☎ 020 7822 2150
✉ david@2-3hindcourt.com
Call Date: July 1982, Inner Temple
Qualifications: [BA (Hons) (Notts), Dip Law (Notts) Cert Ed LLB]

BUEHRLEN MISS VERONIQUE EIRA QC (2010)

Keating Chambers
15 Essex Street, London WC2R 3AA, ☎ 020 7544 2600
✉ clerks@keatingchambers.com
Call Date: Oct 1991, Middle Temple
Qualifications: [MA Hons Dip Law]

BUENO MR ANTONIO DE PADUA JOSE MARIA QC (1989)

Clerksroom (Taunton)
Equity House, Administration Centre, Blackbrook Park Avenue, Taunton, Somerset TA1 2PX, ☎ 0845 083 3000
✉ mail@clerksroom.com
Call Date: June 1964, Middle Temple
Recorder
✉ bueno@clerksroom.com

BUGEJA MISS EVELYN

Cornwall Street Chambers
85-87 Cornwall Street, Birmingham B3 3BY, ☎ 0121 233 7500
✉ clerks@cornwallstreet.co.uk
Call Date: Oct 1997, Middle Temple
Qualifications: [LLB (Hons)(L'pool)]
✉ eve.bugeja@cornwallstreet.co.uk

BUGG MR IAN STEPHEN

1 Garden Court Family Law Chambers
Ground Floor, One Garden Court, Temple, London EC4Y 9BJ, ☎ 020 7797 7900
✉ clerks@1gc.com
Call Date: Oct 1992, Middle Temple
Pupil Supervisor
Qualifications: [LLB (Hons)]
✉ bugg@1gc.com

BULEY MR TIMOTHY LAWRENCE HOWARD

Landmark Chambers
180 Fleet Street, London EC4A 2HG, ☎ 020 7430 1221
✉ clerks@landmarkchambers.co.uk
Call Date: Oct 2000, Inner Temple
Pupil Supervisor
Qualifications: [BA (Oxon) CPE (City)]
✉ tbuley@landmarkchambers.co.uk

BULL MR GREGORY QC (2003)

Lombard Chambers
1 Sekforde Street, Clerkenwell, London EC1R 0BE, ☎ 020 7107 2100
Aspect Chambers
Aspect Court, 4 Temple Row, Birmingham B2 5HG, ☎ 0121 222 2447
✉ clerks@aspectchambers.com
Call Date: July 1976, Inner Temple
Qualifications: [LLB (B'ham)]

BULL MRS NATHALIE CLAIRE

New Walk Chambers
27 New Walk, Leicester, Leicestershire LE1 6TE, ☎ 0871 200 1298 / 0116 255 9144
✉ clerks@newwalkchambers.co.uk
Call Date: July 2004, Inner Temple
Qualifications: [LLB (Hons) BVC]

E

BULL MR NICHOLAS DAVID

Old Bailey Chambers
15 Old Bailey, London EC4M 7EF,
☎ 020 3008 6404
✉ clerks@15oldbaileychambers.com
Call Date: Oct 2004, Inner Temple
Qualifications: [LLB (L'pool) LLM (Lond)]
n.bull@15oldbaileychambers.com

BULL MR ROGER

Five Paper
Ground Floor, 5 Paper Buildings, Temple, London EC4Y 7HB, ☎ 020 7815 3200
Call Date: July 1974, Middle Temple
Pupil Supervisor
Qualifications: [LLB (Lond)]
rogerbull@fivepaper.com

BULLEN MRS MARY

The Chambers Of Mary Bullen
7 Grovely Mews, Shaftsbury Road, Wilton SP2 0JW, ☎ 01722 742204
✉ marybullen123@btinternet.com
Call Date: Mar 2005, Inner Temple
Qualifications: [BA (Hons) Southampton Dip. Law Kingston CPE]

BULLOCK MR DAVID NEIL

Coram Chambers
9-11 Fulwood Place, London WC1V 6HG,
☎ 020 7092 3700
✉ mail@coramchambers.co.uk
Call Date: Nov 1989, Middle Temple
Qualifications: [BA]
neil.bullock@coramchambers.co.uk

BULLOCK MR IAN DAVID

St John's Chambers
101 Victoria Street, Bristol BS1 6PU,
☎ 0117 923 4700
✉ clerks@stjohnschambers.co.uk
Call Date: Nov 1975, Inner Temple
Pupil Supervisor
Qualifications: [LLB]
ianbullock@stjohnschambers.co.uk

BULLOCK MR ROBERT GUSTAF

The Chambers of Mr Bullock
Arden Lodge, 11 Montpelier Villas, Brighton BN1 3DG, ☎ 01273 321050
Call Date: Nov 2000, Middle Temple
Qualifications: [BA (Cantab)]

BULLOCK MRS SALLY

New Court
Ground Floor, New Court, Temple, London EC4Y 9BE, ☎ 020 7583 5123
✉ clerks@newcourtchambers.com
Call Date: Oct 1995, Middle Temple
Qualifications: [CPE BA (OU) SFLA CLS]

BULMAN MR WILLIAM GREGORY

New Court
Ground Floor, New Court, Temple, London EC4Y 9BE, ☎ 020 7583 5123
✉ clerks@newcourtchambers.com
Call Date: Oct 2008, Inner Temple
Qualifications: [BA (Oxon)]
wbulman@newcourtchambers.com

BUMPUS MISS LAURA RACHEL

The Chambers of Grahame Aldous QC
9 Gough Square, London EC4A 3DG,
☎ 020 7832 0500
✉ clerks@9goughsquare.co.uk
Call Date: July 2008, Middle Temple
Qualifications: [BSc (Hons) (UEA) PgDl (Lond)]
lbumpus@9goughsquare.co.uk

BUNBURY MISS CLAIRE LOUISE

St James's Chambers
68 Quay Street, Manchester M3 3EJ,
☎ 0161 834 7000
✉ clerks@stjameschambers.com
Call Date: Oct 2006, Middle Temple
Qualifications: [BA (Hons) (Oxon) BCL (Oxon)]
clairebunbury@stjameschambers.com

BUNDELL MISS KATHARINE MICHELLE

Octagon House
19 Colegate, Norwich NR3 1AT,
☎ 01603 623186
✉ clerks@octagonhouse.co.uk
Call Date: Oct 1991, Middle Temple
Pupil Supervisor
Qualifications: [MA (Hons)(Cantab)]

BUNDRED MISS GILLIAN SARAH

Oriel Chambers
14 Water Street, Liverpool, Merseyside L2 8TD, ☎ 0151 236 7191
✉ clerks@orielchambers.co.uk
Oriel Chambers
18 Ribblesdale Place, Preston PR1 3NA,
☎ 01772 254 764
✉ clerks@oriel-chambers.co.uk
Call Date: July 1982, Gray's Inn
Qualifications: [LLB (Lond)]
gillian.bundred@orielchambers.co.uk

E

BUNTING MR DANIEL ALEXANDER JAMES

2 Dr Johnson's Buildings
2 Dr Johnson's Buildings, Temple, London EC4Y 7AY, ☎020 7936 2613
✉clerks@2drj.com
Call Date: Nov 2001, Middle Temple
Qualifications: [BSc (Hons) Dip Law]
✉d.bunting@2drj.com

BUNTING MR JUDE JAMES

Tooks Chambers
81 Farringdon Street, London EC4A 4BL, ☎020 7842 7575 ✉clerks@tooks.co.uk
Call Date: July 2006, Gray's Inn
Qualifications: [BA (Oxon)]
✉jude.bunting@tooks.co.uk

BUNYAN MR ANGUS GUY

2 Hare Court
Lower Ground, Ground, 1st & 2nd Floor, 2 Hare Court, Temple, London EC4Y 7BH, ☎020 7353 3982 ✉clerks@2harecourt.com
Call Date: Oct 1999, Lincoln's Inn
Qualifications: [BA (Hons) MA (Lond) Dip in Law (Lond)]
✉angusbunyan@2harecourt.com

BURCH MR SIMON DAVID

7 Bell Yard
London WC2A 2JR, ☎020 7831 0636
✉kevintarrant@btconnect.com
Call Date: July 2007, Lincoln's Inn
Qualifications: [LLB (Cardiff)]
✉simon.burch@burchandmay.com

BURDEN MR EDWARD ANGUS

St Philips Chambers
55 Temple Row, Birmingham B2 5LS, ☎0121 246 7000 ✉clerks@st-philips.com
Call Date: Nov 1994, Lincoln's Inn
Qualifications: [BA (Hons)(Exon) CPE]
✉aburden@st-philips.com

BURDEN MISS EMMA LOUISE VERENA

New Street Chambers
2 New Street, Leicester LE1 5NA, ☎0116 262 5906 ✉clerks@2newstreet.co.uk
Call Date: Oct 1994, Lincoln's Inn
Qualifications: [LLB (Hons)(Newc)]

BURDIN MR CHRISTOPHER JAMES

3 Verulam Buildings
London WC1R 5NT, ☎020 7831 8441
✉chambers@3vb.com
Call Date: July 2010, Middle Temple
Qualifications: [BA (Hons) (Oxon) BCL]

BURDIS-SMITH MR ALAN

Chambers of Mr A Burdis-Smith
43 Mill Lane, Clophill, Bedford MK45 4BX, ☎07766 014583
✉burdissmith.alan@gmail.com
Call Date: Oct 1998, Inner Temple
Qualifications: [BSc (Open) CPE (Lancs)]

BURDON MR MICHAEL STEWART

37 Park Square Chambers
37 Park Square, Leeds LS1 2NY, ☎0113 243 9422 ✉chambers@no37.co.uk
Call Date: Nov 1993, Lincoln's Inn
Pupil Supervisor
Qualifications: [LLB (Hons)(Leeds)]
✉chambers@no37.co.uk, msb@no37.co.uk

BUREAU MR TOM PETER HAMILTON

Linenhall Chambers
1 Stanley Place, Chester CH1 2LU, ☎01244 348282
✉clerks@linenhallchambers.co.uk
Call Date: Nov 2007, Lincoln's Inn
Qualifications: [MA (Edin)]

BURGE MISS ALISON JAYNE

Pump Court Chambers
31 Southgate Street, Winchester, Hampshire SO23 9EB, ☎01962 868 161
✉clerks@3pumpcourt.com
Pump Court Chambers
Upper Ground Floor, 3 Pump Court, Temple, London EC4Y 7AJ, ☎020 7353 0711
✉clerks@3pumpcourt.com
Pump Court Chambers
5 Temple Chambers, Temple Street, Swindon SN1 1SQ, ☎01793 539899
✉clerks@3pumpcourt.com
Call Date: July 2002, Gray's Inn
Qualifications: [LLB (B'ham) (Hons) LLM (B'ham)]
✉ajb@3pumpcourt.com

BURGE MR EDMUND JOHN

Five St Andrew's Hill
5 St Andrew's Hill, London EC4V 5BZ, ☎020 7332 5400 ✉Clerks@5sah.co.uk
Call Date: Oct 1997, Lincoln's Inn
Qualifications: [BA (Hons)(York) Dip in Law]
✉edmundburge@5sah.co.uk

E

BURGESS MR DAVID CLIFFORD

Nine Bedford Row
9 Bedford Row, London WC1R 4AZ,
☎ 020 7489 2727
✉ clerks@9bedfordrow.co.uk
Call Date: July 1975, Lincoln's Inn
Pupil Supervisor
Qualifications: [LLB (Hons)]
david.burgess@9bedfordrow.co.uk

BURGESS MR EDWARD NORMAN

Albion Chambers
Broad Street, Bristol BS1 1DR,
☎ 0117 927 2144
✉ clerks@albionchambers.co.uk
Call Date: Nov 1993, Inner Temple
Recorder
Qualifications: [BA (Hons)(Oxon) MA (Bris) CPE (Bris)]
edward.burgess@albionchambers.co.uk

BURGESS MISS EMMA LOUISE

2 Hare Court
Lower Ground, Ground, 1st & 2nd Floor, 2 Hare Court, Temple, London EC4Y 7BH,
☎ 020 7353 3982 ✉ clerks@2harecourt.com
Call Date: Oct 2009, Lincoln's Inn
Qualifications: [LLB (Sussex)]

E

BURGESS DR JENNY CLAIRE

Atkinson Bevan Chambers
1st Floor, 2 Harcourt Buildings, Temple, London EC4Y 9DB, ☎ 020 7353 2112
✉ clerks@2hb.co.uk
Call Date: July 2008, Middle Temple
Qualifications: [MPhil (B'ham) MA (Oxon) PhD (B'ham) PgDl (Lond)]

BURGESS MISS VICTORIA CLAIRE

7 Bell Yard
London WC2A 2JR, ☎ 020 7831 0636
✉ kevintarrant@btconnect.com
Call Date: Oct 2006, Gray's Inn
Qualifications: [BA]

BURGHER MR BENJIMIN GEORGE

Outer Temple Chambers
The Outer Temple, 222 Strand, London WC2R 1BA, ☎ 020 7353 6381
✉ clerks@outertemple.com
Call Date: Nov 1995, Gray's Inn
Qualifications: [LLB PG Dip]
benjimin.burgher@outertemple.com

BURKE MR BRENDAN EDWARD

Number 7 Harrington Street Chambers
7 Harrington Street, Liverpool L2 9YH,
☎ 0151 242 0707 ✉ clerks@7hs.co.uk
Call Date: Oct 1995, Inner Temple
Qualifications: [BA (Cantab) CPE (Northumbria)]
brendan.burke@7hs.co.uk

BURKE MISS PATRICIA ANN

Fountain Chambers
Cleveland Business Centre, 1 Watson Street, Middlesbrough TS1 2RQ, ☎ 01642 804040
✉ clerks@fountainchambers.co.uk
Call Date: Oct 1990, Gray's Inn
Pupil Supervisor
Qualifications: [LLB (Newc)]

BURKE MR SAMUEL JAMES

Deans Court Chambers
24 St John Street, Manchester M3 4DF,
☎ 0161 214 6000 ✉ clerks@deanscourt.co.uk
Call Date: Nov 2009, Lincoln's Inn
Qualifications: [LLB (Lond)]
burke@deanscourt.co.uk

BURKE MR TREVOR MICHAEL QC (2001)

3 Raymond Buildings
3 Raymond Buildings, Gray's Inn, London WC1R 5BH, ☎ 020 7400 6400
✉ clerks@3rblaw.com
Call Date: July 1981, Middle Temple
Qualifications: [BA]
trevor.burke@3raymondbuildings.com

BURKILL MR GUY ALEXANDER QC (2002)

Three New Square IP
3 New Square, Lincoln's Inn, London WC2A 3RS, ☎ 020 7405 1111
✉ clerks@3newsquare.co.uk
Call Date: Feb 1981, Middle Temple
Qualifications: [MA (Cantab)]
gb@3newsquare.co.uk

BURKITT MR DANIEL JAMES

13 Old Square Chambers
Ground Floor, 14 Old Square, Lincoln's Inn, London WC2A 3UE, ☎ 020 7831 4445
✉ clerks@13oldsquare.com
Call Date: Oct 2008, Gray's Inn
Qualifications: [LLB LLM MSt DPhil]
danielburkitt@13oldsquare.com

BURLES MR DAVID JOHN

1 Garden Court Family Law Chambers
Ground Floor, One Garden Court, Temple, London EC4Y 9BJ, ☎020 7797 7900
✉clerks@1gc.com
Call Date: Nov 1984, Middle Temple
Pupil Supervisor
Qualifications: [LLB (Bris) Postgraduate Cert in Sports Law]
✉burles@1gc.com, burles@1gc.com

BURLING MR JULIAN MICHAEL

Serle Court
6 New Square, Lincoln's Inn, London WC2A 3QS, ☎020 7242 6105
✉clerks@serlecourt.co.uk
Call Date: July 1976, Middle Temple
Pupil Supervisor
Qualifications: [MA LLB (Cantab)]

Types of work: Financial services, Insurance

BURMAN MR MATTHEW JONATHAN LEE

St Albans Chambers
2 - 4 St Peter's Street, St Albans, Hertfordshire AL1 3LF, ☎01727 843383
✉clerks@stalbanschambers.com
Call Date: Oct 2007, Middle Temple
Qualifications: [LLB (Hons) (Lond)]
✉clerks@stalbanschambers.com

BURNELL MISS KATE

St Johns Buildings Liverpool
8th Floor India Buildings, Water Street, Liverpool L2 0XG, ☎0151 243 6000
✉clerk@stjohnsbuildings.co.uk
16 Winckley Square
Preston PR1 3JJ, ☎01772 256100
St Johns Buildings
24a - 28 St John Street, Manchester M3 4DJ, ☎0161 214 1500
✉clerk@stjohnsbuildings.co.uk
Call Date: Oct 1998, Middle Temple
Qualifications: [LLB (Hons)(L'pool)]

BURNETT MR IAIN

4 King's Bench Walk
2nd Floor, 4 King's Bench Walk, Temple, London EC4Y 7DL, ☎020 7822 7000
✉clerks@4kbw.co.uk
Call Date: Oct 1993, Lincoln's Inn
Qualifications: [LLB (Hons)(Wales)]
✉ib@4kbw.co.uk

BURNHAM MISS ULELE IMOINDA

Doughty Street Chambers
53-54 Doughty Street, London WC1N 2LS, ☎020 7404 1313
✉enquiries@doughtystreet.co.uk
Doughty Street Chambers
Pall Mall Court, 61-67 King Street, Manchester M2 4PD, ☎0161 618 1066
Doughty Street Chambers
5th Floor, Broad Quay House, Prince Street, Bristol BS1 4DJ, ☎01179 058 717
Call Date: Mar 1997, Inner Temple
Qualifications: [BA (Sussex) MPhil (Cantab) CPE (Sussex)]
✉u.burnham@doughtystreet.co.uk

BURNS MR ALEXANDER LAURENCE

New Court Chambers
3 Broad Chare, Newcastle Upon Tyne NE1 3DQ, ☎0191 232 1980
✉clerks@newcourt-chambers.co.uk
Call Date: July 1988, Inner Temple
Pupil Supervisor
Qualifications: [LLB (Sheff)]
✉alexander.burns@newcourt-chambers.co.uk

BURNS MR ANDREW PHILIP

Devereux Chambers
Queen Elizabeth Building, Temple, London EC4Y 9BS, ☎020 7353 7534
✉clerks@devchambers.co.uk
Call Date: Oct 1993, Middle Temple
Pupil Supervisor, Recorder
Qualifications: [BA (Hons)(Cantab)]
✉burns@devchambers.co.uk

BURNS MR FRANCIS JOSEPH

Kenworthy's Chambers
Arlington House, Bloom Street, Salford, Manchester M3 6AJ, ☎0161 832 4036
Call Date: May 1971, Gray's Inn
Pupil Supervisor
Qualifications: [LLB]
✉f.burns@kenworthysbarristers.co.uk

BURNS MR JEREMY STUART

12 College Place
Fauvelle Buildings, 12 College Place, Southampton SO15 2FE, ☎023 8032 0320
✉clerks@12cp.co.uk
Call Date: Nov 1996, Lincoln's Inn
Qualifications: [BA (Cape Town) LLB (Natal) LLM (Cantab)]
✉JBurns@12cp.co.uk

BURNS MISS JUDITH LINDA

Oriel Chambers
14 Water Street, Liverpool, Merseyside L2 8TD, ☎0151 236 7191
✉clerks@orielchambers.co.uk
Oriel Chambers
18 Ribblesdale Place, Preston PR1 3NA, ☎01772 254 764
✉clerks@oriel-chambers.co.uk
Call Date: Mar 2001, Middle Temple
Qualifications: [LLB (Hons) (Sheff)]
judith.burns@orielchambers.co.uk

BURNS MR PAUL ANDREW

Exchange Chambers
One Derby Square, Derby Square, Liverpool L2 9XX, ☎0151 236 7747
✉info@exchangechambers.co.uk
Exchange Chambers
7 Ralli Courts, West Riverside, Manchester M3 5FT, ☎0161 833 2722
Exchange Chambers
Oxford House, Oxford Row, Leeds LS1 3BE, ☎0113 203 1970
✉spencer@exchangechambers.co.uk
Call Date: Oct 1998, Lincoln's Inn
Pupil Supervisor
Qualifications: [LLB (Hons)(L'pool)]
burns@exchangechambers.co.uk

BURNS MR PETER RICHARD

Byrom Street Chambers
12 Byrom Street, Manchester M3 4PP, ☎0161 829 2100 ✉clerks@byromstreet.com
Crown Office Chambers
2 Crown Office Row, Temple, London EC4Y 7HJ, ☎020 7797 8100
✉mail@crownofficechambers.com
42 Bedford Row
London WC1R 4LL, ☎020 7831 0222
✉clerks@42br.com
Call Date: Oct 1993, Gray's Inn
Pupil Supervisor
Qualifications: [BA]

BURNS MR RICHARD HARCOURT

Ropewalk Chambers
24 The Ropewalk, Nottingham NG1 5EF, ☎0115 947 2581 ✉clerks@ropewalk.co.uk
Call Date: Nov 1967, Middle Temple
Recorder
Qualifications: [LLB]
richardburns@ropewalk.co.uk

BURNS MRS ROSEMARY ANNE MACMAHON

4 Breams Buildings
Chancery Lane, London EC4A 1HP, ☎020 7092 1900 ✉clerks@4bb.co.uk
Call Date: Nov 1978, Inner Temple
Pupil Supervisor

BURNS MR SIMON HAMER

Albion Chambers
Broad Street, Bristol BS1 1DR, ☎0117 927 2144
✉clerks@albionchambers.co.uk
Call Date: Oct 1992, Middle Temple
Qualifications: [LLB (Hons)]
simon.burns@albionchambers.co.uk

BURNS MR TERENCE

Chartlands Chambers
3 St Giles Terrace, Northampton NN1 2BN, ☎01604 603322
✉enquiries@chartlands-chambers.co.uk
Call Date: Oct 1990, Middle Temple
Qualifications: [BA (Hons)]

BURR MR ANDREW CHARLES

Atkin Chambers
1 Atkin Building, Gray's Inn, London WC1R 5AT, ☎020 7404 0102
✉clerks@atkinchambers.com
Call Date: Nov 1981, Inner Temple
Pupil Supervisor
Qualifications: [MA (Cantab) ACIArb]
aburr@atkinchambers.com

BURRETT MR ALEX

1 Gray's Inn Square
Ground Floor, 1 Gray's Inn Square, London WC1R 5AA, ☎020 7405 0001
Call Date: July 1999, Inner Temple
Qualifications: [LLB (Lancs)]
aburrett@1gis.co.uk

BURRETT MRS CATHERINE

12 College Place
Fauvelle Buildings, 12 College Place, Southampton SO15 2FE, ☎023 8032 0320
✉clerks@12cp.co.uk
Call Date: Oct 1992, Middle Temple
Pupil Supervisor
Qualifications: [LLB (Hons) (Lond)]
CBurrett@12cp.co.uk

E

BURRINGTON MR RICHARD JAMES HENRY

2 Pump Court
1st Floor, 2 Pump Court, Temple, London EC4Y 7AH, ☎ 020 7353 5597
✉ clerks@2pumpcourt.co.uk
Call Date: Nov 1993, Inner Temple
Qualifications: [BA (Hons)(So'ton)]
✉ rburrington@2pumpcourt.co.uk

BURROUGHS MR NIGEL ALFRED

Four New Square
Four New Square, Lincoln's Inn, London WC2A 3RJ, ☎ 020 7822 2000
✉ barristers@4newsquare.com
Call Date: Apr 1991, Middle Temple
Qualifications: [BA (Hons) (Lond) Dip Law]
✉ n.burroughs@4newsquare.com

BURROWS MR ANDREW STEPHEN

Fountain Court Chambers
Fountain Court, Temple, London EC4Y 9DH, ☎ 020 7583 3335
✉ chambers@fountaincourt.co.uk
Call Date: Feb 1985, Middle Temple
Qualifications: [MA LLM (USA) BCL (Oxon)]

BURROWS MR GARETH JAMES

Westgate Chambers
64 High Street, Lewes, East Sussex BN7 1XG, ☎ 01273 480510
✉ clerks@westgate-chambers.co.uk
Call Date: Nov 2006, Gray's Inn
Qualifications: [LLB]
✉ gbu@westgate-chambers.co.uk

BURROWS MR MICHAEL PETER QC (2008)

No5 Chambers
Fountain Court, Steelhouse Lane, Birmingham B4 6DR, ☎ 0845 210 5555 ✉ info@no5.com
No5 Chambers
Greenwood House, 4-7 Salisbury Court, London EC4Y 8AA, ☎ 0845 210 5555
No5 Chambers
38 Queen Square, Bristol BS1 4QS, ☎ 0845 210 5555
Call Date: Nov 1979, Inner Temple
Pupil Supervisor, Recorder
Qualifications: [BA (Cantab)]
✉ mpb@no5.com

BURROWS MR SIMON PAUL

Kings Chambers
36 Young Street, Manchester M3 3FT, ☎ 0845 034 3444
✉ clerks@kingschambers.com
Kings Chambers
5 Park Square East, Leeds LS1 2NE, ☎ 0845 034 3444
✉ clerks@kingschambers.com
Kings Chambers
Embassy House, 60 Church Street, Birmingham B3 2DJ, ☎ 0845 034 3444
✉ clerks@kingschambers.com
Call Date: Nov 1990, Inner Temple
Qualifications: [BA (Dunelm) Dip Law (City)]
✉ sburrows@kingschambers.com

BURT MISS JOANNA MARIE

Maidstone Chambers
33 Earl Street, Maidstone, Kent ME14 1PF, ☎ 01622 688592
✉ clerks@maidstonechambers.co.uk
Call Date: Oct 1998, Gray's Inn
Qualifications: [LLB (Leic)]
✉ j.burt@maidstonechambers.co.uk

BURTON MR CHARLES DOMINIC PAUL

9-12 Bell Yard
London WC2A 2JR, ☎ 020 7400 1800
✉ clerks@9-12bellyard.com
Call Date: Nov 1983, Inner Temple
Pupil Supervisor
Qualifications: [BA (Lond)]
✉ c.burton@9-12bellyard.com

BURTON MR DANIEL JOSEPH OLDCORN

Radcliffe Chambers
Ground Floor, 11 New Square, Lincoln's Inn, London WC2A 3QB, ☎ 020 7831 0081
✉ clerks@radcliffechambers.com
Call Date: July 2009, Inner Temple
Qualifications: [BA MSt (Oxon)]
✉ dburton@radcliffechambers.com

BURTON MR FRANK QC (1998)

12 King's Bench Walk
12 King's Bench Walk, Temple, London EC4Y 7EL, ☎ 020 7583 0811
Call Date: July 1982, Gray's Inn
Pupil Supervisor, Recorder
Qualifications: [BA (Kent) PhD (Lond)]
✉ burton@12kbw.co.uk

E

BURTON MR JAMES WILLIAM

39 Essex Street
London WC2R 3AT, ☎ 020 7832 1111
✉ clerks@39essex.com
82 King Street
Manchester M2 4WQ, ☎ 0161 870 9969
Call Date: Oct 2001, Lincoln's Inn
Qualifications: [BA (Hons) (Oxon) Dip in Law]
james.burton@39essex.com

BURTON MR JAMIE

Doughty Street Chambers
53-54 Doughty Street, London WC1N 2LS,
☎ 020 7404 1313
✉ enquiries@doughtystreet.co.uk
Doughty Street Chambers
Pall Mall Court, 61-67 King Street, Manchester M2 4PD, ☎ 0161 618 1066
Doughty Street Chambers
5th Floor, Broad Quay House, Prince Street, Bristol BS1 4DJ, ☎ 01179 058 717
Call Date: Oct 1999, Inner Temple
Qualifications: [LLB (Bris)]
j.burton@doughtystreet.co.uk

BURTON MR JOHN MALCOLM QC (2010)

3 Temple Gardens
Lower Ground Floor, 3 Temple Gardens, Temple, London EC4Y 9AU, ☎ 020 7353 3102
✉ clerks@3tg.co.uk
Call Date: July 1979, Inner Temple
Pupil Supervisor
Qualifications: [LLB (Lond) (Hons)]

BURTON MRS KATHERINE

Tooks Chambers
81 Farringdon Street, London EC4A 4BL,
☎ 020 7842 7575 ✉ clerks@tooks.co.uk
Call Date: Mar 2007, Inner Temple
Qualifications: [LLB (Lond)]

BURTON MR PAUL

3 Stone Buildings
Ground Floor, 3 Stone Buildings, Lincoln's Inn, London WC2A 3XL, ☎ 020 7242 4937
✉ clerks@3sb.law.co.uk
Call Date: Oct 1998, Lincoln's Inn
Qualifications: [LLB (Hons) LLM (Lond)]
pburton@3sb.law.co.uk

BURTWISTLE MS CLAIRE LOUISE

Old Bailey Chambers
15 Old Bailey, London EC4M 7EF,
☎ 020 3008 6404
✉ clerks@15oldbaileychambers.com
Call Date: July 2008, Middle Temple
Qualifications: [LLB (Hons) (Lond) LLM (Lond)]

BURY MR PAUL

Keating Chambers
15 Essex Street, London WC2R 3AA,
☎ 020 7544 2600
✉ clerks@keatingchambers.com
Call Date: Nov 2008, Inner Temple
Qualifications: [BA (Hons) (Oxon)]
pbury@keatingchambers.com

BUSBY MR THOMAS ANDREW

Call Date: July 1975, Lincoln's Inn
Qualifications: [LLB (Lond)]

BUSCH MS LISA VIRGINIA

4-5 Gray's Inn Square
Gray's Inn, London WC1R 5AH,
☎ 020 7404 5252 ✉ clerks@4-5.co.uk
Call Date: Nov 2000, Inner Temple
Qualifications: [BA LLB (Australia) BPhil MStud (Oxon)]
lbusch@4-5.co.uk

BUSH MR DOMINIC LUKE

Castle Chambers
The Old Fire Station, 90 High Street, Harrow-on-the-Hill, Middlesex HA1 3LP,
☎ 020 8423 6579 ✉ info@castlechambers.net
Call Date: July 1999, Middle Temple
Qualifications: [LLB (Hons)]
mail@castlechambers.net

BUSH MISS HANNAH KATHERINE

St Philips Chambers
55 Temple Row, Birmingham B2 5LS,
☎ 0121 246 7000 ✉ clerks@st-philips.com
Call Date: Oct 2007, Middle Temple
Qualifications: [LLB (Hons) (B'ham)]
hbush@st-philips.com

BUSH MR PETER TREVOR

King's Bench Chambers
Wellington House, 175 Holdenhurst Road, Bournemouth, Dorset BH8 8DQ,
☎ 01202 250025
Call Date: Oct 2008, Inner Temple
Qualifications: [LLB LLM (South Africa)]

BUSS MR SIMON

Ropewalk Chambers
24 The Ropewalk, Nottingham NG1 5EF,
☎ 0115 947 2581 ✉ clerks@ropewalk.co.uk
Call Date: July 2007, Lincoln's Inn
Qualifications: [BA (Leic)]
simonbuss@ropewalk.co.uk

BUSSEY-JONES MRS ELISABETH BARBARA

2 King's Bench Walk
2 King's Bench Walk, Temple, London
EC4Y 7DE, ☎ 020 7353 1746
✉ clerks@2kbw.com
Call Date: Nov 1997, Inner Temple
Pupil Supervisor
Qualifications: [LLB (Australia)]
✉ ebusseyjones@2kbw.com

BUSTANI MS NAVAZ

The Chambers Of Navaz Bustani
5 St John's Lane, London EC1M 4BH,
☎ 07957 394258/020 7060 9760
✉ navaz13@yahoo.co.uk
Call Date: Nov 1995, Lincoln's Inn
Qualifications: [BA (Hons) LLB (Hons)]

BUSUTTIL MR GODWIN JOHN ANTOINE

5RB
1st Floor, 5 Raymond Buildings, Gray's Inn,
London WC1R 5BP, ☎ 020 7242 2902
✉ clerks@5rb.com
Call Date: Oct 1994, Lincoln's Inn
Pupil Supervisor
Qualifications: [MA Dip Law (Lond) MPhil (Cantab)]

BUSWELL MR RICHARD THOMAS

Hardwicke
New Square, Lincoln's Inn, London
WC2A 3SB, ☎ 020 7242 2523
✉ enquiries@hardwicke.co.uk
Call Date: July 1985, Middle Temple
Pupil Supervisor
Qualifications: [LLB (Lond)]

BUTCHER MR CHRISTOPHER JOHN QC (2001)

7 King's Bench Walk
Ground Floor, 7 King's Bench Walk, Temple,
London EC4Y 7DS, ☎ 020 7910 8300
✉ clerks@7kbw.co.uk
Call Date: July 1986, Gray's Inn
Qualifications: [MA(Oxon) Dip Eur Law Dip Law]
✉ cbutcher@7kbw.co.uk

BUTCHER MISS HELEN

1 Pump Court
Elm Court, Temple, London EC4Y 7AB,
☎ 020 7842 7070
✉ (name)@pumpcourt.co.uk
Call Date: Nov 1999, Middle Temple
Qualifications: [BA (Hons)(Oxon)]
✉ helenbutcher@1pumpcourt.co.uk

BUTCHER MR RICHARD

Lombard Chambers
1 Sekforde Street, Clerkenwell, London
EC1R 0BE, ☎ 020 7107 2100
Aspect Chambers
Aspect Court, 4 Temple Row, Birmingham
B2 5HG, ☎ 0121 222 2447
✉ clerks@aspectchambers.com
187 Fleet Street
London EC4A 2AT, ☎ 020 7430 7430
✉ chambers@187fleetstreet.com
Lincoln House Chambers
Tower 12, The Avenue North, Spinningfields,
18-22 Bridge Street, Manchester M3 3BZ,
☎ 0161 832 5701
✉ info@lincolnhousechambers.com
Call Date: Nov 1985, Gray's Inn
Pupil Supervisor
Qualifications: [LLB (Wales)]

BUTCHER MR RUSSELL HENRY

East Anglian Chambers
Gresham House, 5 Museum Street, Ipswich,
Suffolk IP1 1HQ, ☎ 01473 214481
✉ ipswich@ealaw.co.uk
East Anglian Chambers
53 North Hill, Colchester, Essex CO1 1QA,
☎ 01473 214481 ✉ colchester@ealaw.co.uk
East Anglian Chambers
140 New London Road, Chelmsford, Essex
CM2 0AW, ☎ 01473 214481
✉ chelmsford@ealaw.co.uk
Call Date: Oct 1992, Middle Temple
Qualifications: [BA (Hons) Dip Law(Lond)]
✉ russellbutcher@ealaw.co.uk

BUTLER MR ADAM MICHAEL

187 Fleet Street
London EC4A 2AT, ☎ 020 7430 7430
✉ chambers@187fleetstreet.com
Call Date: Oct 1997, Lincoln's Inn
Qualifications: [LLB (Hons)(Manc)]

BUTLER MR ANDREW

Tanfield Chambers
2-5 Warwick Court, London WC1R 5DJ,
☎ 020 7421 5300
✉ clerks@tanfieldchambers.co.uk
Call Date: Nov 1993, Middle Temple
Pupil Supervisor
Qualifications: [BA MA]
✉ andrewbutler@tanfieldchambers.co.uk

Fax: 020 7421 5333;
DX: 46 London, Chancery Lane;
URL: www.tanfieldchambers.co.uk

Other professional qualifications: Accredited Mediator

E

Types of work: Boundaries, Chancery (commercial), Chancery (general), Chancery (land law), Civil fraud, Civil law, Commercial litigation, Commercial property, Disasters, Fire and other property damage claims, Insolvency, Insurance, Landlord and tenant, Litigation, Mediation, Professional negligence, Real property, Rights of way

Awards and memberships: Property Bar Association; Professional Negligence Bar Association

Publications: 'Transmission Failure' *Solicitors' Journal,* May 11, 2010; 'Dubious Privilege' *Solicitors' Journal,* March 16, 2010; 'If the Cap Fits' *Solicitors' Journal,* October 27, 2009; 'Lean on Me' *Solicitors' Journal,* January 11, 2011; 'World Service' Solicitors Journal February 28, 2012

Reported Cases: *Collier v Williams,* [2006] 1 WLR 1945 Service of process; application of CPR 6.5; meaning of 'last known residence'.
Hart Investments Ltd v Fidler & Another, [2007] BLR 30 Enforceability of adjudication award; time limits; written contracts; insolvent liquidation; default judgment; set aside.
Kyle Bay Ltd v Various Underwriters, [2007] 1 CLC 264; (2006)The Times, 29 May Mistake and misrepresentation in compromise of insurance claim.
Griffin v UHY Hacker Young, [2010] PNLR 20 Professional negligence: ex turpi causa.
Eco Power UK Ltd v Transport for London, [2010] ACD 69 Judicial review: private law claims: issue estoppel.

E

BUTLER MISS AZEB MAGUEDA

Clabenz Chambers
Palladia, Central Court, 25 Southampton Buildings, London WC2A 1AL,
☎ 020 7129 1428
Call Date: July 1966, Lincoln's Inn
Qualifications: [MA LLB (Hons)]

BUTLER MR GEORGE VICTOR

4 Brick Court
4 Brick Court, Temple, London EC4Y 9AD,
☎ 020 7832 3200 ✉ clerks@4bc.co.uk
Call Date: July 2004, Inner Temple
✉ george.butler@4bc.co.uk

BUTLER MR JONATHAN CHARLES

Deans Court Chambers
24 St John Street, Manchester M3 4DF,
☎ 0161 214 6000 ✉ clerks@deanscourt.co.uk
Call Date: Oct 1992, Gray's Inn
Pupil Supervisor
Qualifications: [BA (Hons)(Lond) MA MED]

BUTLER MISS JUDITH JANE SCOTT

29 Bedford Row Chambers
London WC1R 4HE, ☎ 020 7404 1044
✉ clerks@29br.co.uk
Call Date: Oct 1993, Middle Temple
Qualifications: [BA (Hons)(Lond)]

BUTLER MRS MARIANNE JANE

Fountain Court Chambers
Fountain Court, Temple, London EC4Y 9DH,
☎ 020 7583 3335
✉ chambers@fountaincourt.co.uk
Call Date: July 2003, Lincoln's Inn
Qualifications: [BA (Hons) BVC CPE]
✉ mpb@fountaincourt.co.uk

BUTLER MS MICHELLE

Matrix Chambers
Griffin Building, Gray's Inn, London WC1R 5LN, ☎ 020 7404 3447
✉ matrix@matrixlaw.co.uk / Iscott@matrixlaw.co.uk
Call Date: July 2007, Inner Temple
Qualifications: [BA LLB (Queensland) LLM (Cantab)]
✉ michellebutler@matrixlaw.co.uk

BUTLER MR OLIVER

One Essex Court
Ground Floor, One Essex Court, Temple, London EC4Y 9AR, ☎ 020 7583 2000
✉ clerks@oeclaw.co.uk
Call Date: Oct 2010, Inner Temple
Qualifications: [BA (Oxon)]
✉ obutler@oeclaw.co.uk

BUTLER MS REBECCA SOPHIE

Willingdon Chambers
Chapel Wood House, Knapp Lane, Ampfield, Romsey SO51 9BT
✉ rebecca@willingdonmediation.co.uk
Call Date: July 2001, Inner Temple
Qualifications: [LLB (So'ton) SRN]

BUTLER MR RUPERT JAMES

3 Hare Court
3 Hare Court, Temple, London EC4Y 7BJ,
☎ 020 7415 7800 ✉ clerks@3harecourt.com
Call Date: July 1988, Middle Temple
Qualifications: [LLB (Hons) (Manch)]

BUTLER MR SIMON DAVID

The Chambers of Grahame Aldous QC
9 Gough Square, London EC4A 3DG,
☎ 020 7832 0500
✉ clerks@9goughsquare.co.uk
Call Date: Oct 1996, Inner Temple
Qualifications: [LLB (Hons)]
✉ sbutler@9goughsquare.co.uk

BUTLER-COLE MS VICTORIA

39 Essex Street
London WC2R 3AT, ☎ 020 7832 1111
✉ clerks@39essex.com
82 King Street
Manchester M2 4WQ, ☎ 0161 870 9969
Call Date: July 2005, Middle Temple
Qualifications: [BA (Hons) MA (Cantab) MA (Lond)]
✉ vb@39essex.com

BUTT MR MATTHEW PAUL

3 Raymond Buildings
3 Raymond Buildings, Gray's Inn, London WC1R 5BH, ☎ 020 7400 6400
✉ clerks@3rblaw.com
Call Date: July 2002, Gray's Inn
Qualifications: [LLB (Lond)]
✉ matthew.butt@3raymondbuildings.com

BUTT MR MICHAEL ROBERT

Pump Court Chambers
31 Southgate Street, Winchester, Hampshire SO23 9EB, ☎ 01962 868 161
✉ clerks@3pumpcourt.com
Pump Court Chambers
Upper Ground Floor, 3 Pump Court, Temple, London EC4Y 7AJ, ☎ 020 7353 0711
✉ clerks@3pumpcourt.com
Pump Court Chambers
5 Temple Chambers, Temple Street, Swindon SN1 1SQ, ☎ 01793 539899
✉ clerks@3pumpcourt.com
Call Date: Nov 1974, Middle Temple
Pupil Supervisor
Qualifications: [LLB (Lond)]

BUTT MISS NASRA TALAT

Five St Andrew's Hill
5 St Andrew's Hill, London EC4V 5BZ,
☎ 020 7332 5400 ✉ Clerks@5sah.co.uk
St Paul's Chambers
5th Floor, St Paul's House, 23 Park Square South, Leeds LS1 2ND, ☎ 0113 245 5866
Call Date: Oct 2002, Gray's Inn
Qualifications: [LLB (Leeds)]

BUTT MISS NASSERA

No5 Chambers
Greenwood House, 4-7 Salisbury Court, London EC4Y 8AA, ☎ 0845 210 5555
No5 Chambers
38 Queen Square, Bristol BS1 4QS,
☎ 0845 210 5555
No5 Chambers
Fountain Court, Steelhouse Lane, Birmingham B4 6DR, ☎ 0845 210 5555 ✉ info@no5.com
Call Date: July 1999, Middle Temple
Qualifications: [LLB (Hons)]
✉ ndb@no5.com

BUTTERFIELD MR CHRISTOPHER JOHN

29 Bedford Row Chambers
London WC1R 4HE, ☎ 020 7404 1044
✉ clerks@29br.co.uk
Call Date: Oct 2004, Middle Temple
Qualifications: [MA (Hons) Cantab]
✉ cbutterfield@29br.co.uk

BUTTERFIELD MR JOHN ARTHUR

No5 Chambers
Fountain Court, Steelhouse Lane, Birmingham B4 6DR, ☎ 0845 210 5555 ✉ info@no5.com
No5 Chambers
Greenwood House, 4-7 Salisbury Court, London EC4Y 8AA, ☎ 0845 210 5555
No5 Chambers
38 Queen Square, Bristol BS1 4QS,
☎ 0845 210 5555
Call Date: Oct 1995, Lincoln's Inn
Pupil Supervisor, Recorder
Qualifications: [LLB (Hons)(L'pool)]
✉ jab@no5.com

BUTTERS MR JONATHAN BRYN

Devereux Chambers
Queen Elizabeth Building, Temple, London EC4Y 9BS, ☎ 020 7353 7534
✉ clerks@devchambers.co.uk
Call Date: Nov 2003, Middle Temple
Qualifications: [BA (Hons) (Oxon)]

BUTTERS MR RICHARD JOHN

37 Park Square Chambers
37 Park Square, Leeds LS1 2NY,
☎ 0113 243 9422 ✉ chambers@no37.co.uk
Call Date: Oct 2001, Middle Temple
Qualifications: [LLB (Hons) (Leeds)]
✉ chambers@no37.co.uk

E

BUTTERWORTH MR MARTIN FRANK

Citadel Chambers
The Citadel, 190 Corporation Street, Birmingham B4 6QD, ☎0121 233 8500
✉clerks@citadelchambers.com
Call Date: July 1985, Lincoln's Inn
Pupil Supervisor, Recorder
Qualifications: [BA]
clerks@citadelchambers.com

BUTTERWORTH MR PAUL ANTHONY

Octagon House
19 Colegate, Norwich NR3 1AT,
☎01603 623186
✉clerks@octagonhouse.co.uk
Call Date: July 1982, Middle Temple
Pupil Supervisor
Qualifications: [BA (Lond)]
clerks@octagonhouse.co.uk

BUTTIMORE MR GABRIEL

13 King's Bench Walk
13 King's Bench Walk, Temple, London EC4Y 7EN, ☎020 7353 7204
✉clerks@13kbw.co.uk
13 KBW
32 Beaumont Street, Oxford OX1 2NP, ☎01865 311066 ✉clerks@13kbw.co.uk
Call Date: Feb 1993, Gray's Inn
Qualifications: [LLB (UEA)]
gbuttimore@13kbw.co.uk

BUTTLER MR CHRISTOPHER STEPHEN

4-5 Gray's Inn Square
Gray's Inn, London WC1R 5AH,
☎020 7404 5252 ✉clerks@4-5.co.uk
Call Date: Oct 2004, Inner Temple
Qualifications: [BA (Cantab) MPhil (Sussex) CPE]
cb@4-5.co.uk

BUTTON MR RICHARD JAMES

Carmelite Chambers
9 Carmelite Street, London EC4Y 0DR,
☎020 7936 6300
✉clerks@carmelitechambers.co.uk
Call Date: Oct 1993, Gray's Inn
Qualifications: [LLB]
rbutton@carmelitechambers.co.uk

BUXTON MISS SARAH RUTH

St Philips Chambers
55 Temple Row, Birmingham B2 5LS,
☎0121 246 7000 ✉clerks@st-philips.com
Call Date: July 1988, Inner Temple
Qualifications: [LLB (Sheff)]
sbuxton@st-philips.com

BUXTON MR THOMAS JUSTIN

Charter Chambers
33 John Street, London WC1N 2AT,
☎020 7618 4400
✉clerks@charterchambers.com
Call Date: July 1983, Gray's Inn
Qualifications: [LLB (Nottm)]

BYAM-COOK MR HENRY JAMES

20 Essex Street
London WC2R 3AL, ☎020 7842 1200
✉clerks@20essexst.com
Call Date: Oct 2000, Inner Temple
Pupil Supervisor
Qualifications: [BA (Oxon) CPE (City)]
clerks@20essexst.com

BYASS MR ANDREW BARTON

Landmark Chambers
180 Fleet Street, London EC4A 2HG,
☎020 7430 1221
✉clerks@landmarkchambers.co.uk
Call Date: July 2010, Lincoln's Inn
Qualifications: [LLB (Australia) LLM (Melbourne)]
abyass@landmarkchambers.co.uk

BYLES MR ANDREW PETER

Chambers of Ian Macdonald QC
Garden Court North, 22 Oxford Court, Manchester M2 3WQ, ☎0161 236 1840
✉clerks@gcnchambers.co.uk
Call Date: July 2003, Lincoln's Inn
Qualifications: [BA (Hons) CPE (City)]

BYRD MISS NOEMI CSILLA MARIA

6 Pump Court Chambers
6-8 Mill Street, Maidstone, Kent ME15 6XH,
☎01622 688094
✉annexe@6pumpcourt.co.uk
6 Pump Court
1st Floor, 6 Pump Court, Temple, London EC4Y 7AR, ☎020 7797 8400
✉richardconstable@6pumpcourt.co.uk
Call Date: Oct 2004, Gray's Inn
Qualifications: [BA]
noemibyrd@6PumpCourt.co.uk

BYRNE MR GARRETT THOMAS

4-5 Gray's Inn Square
Gray's Inn, London WC1R 5AH,
☎020 7404 5252 ✉clerks@4-5.co.uk
Call Date: Nov 1986, Gray's Inn
Pupil Supervisor
Qualifications: [LLB (Bris) LLM (Lond)]
gbyrne@4-5.co.uk

BYRNE MR JAMES PATRICK

Number 7 Harrington Street Chambers
7 Harrington Street, Liverpool L2 9YH,
☎0151 242 0707 ✉clerks@7hs.co.uk
Call Date: July 1983, Gray's Inn
Pupil Supervisor
Qualifications: [LLB (Hons L'Pool)]
✉james.byrne@7hs.co.uk

BYRNE MR JAMES PAUL

The Chambers of Grahame Aldous QC
9 Gough Square, London EC4A 3DG,
☎020 7832 0500
✉clerks@9goughsquare.co.uk
Call Date: July 2006, Lincoln's Inn
Qualifications: [BA (Lond)]

BYRNE MR WILLIAM HENRY RICHARD

Trinity Chambers
The Custom House, 39 Quayside, Newcastle Upon Tyne NE1 3DE, ☎0191 232 1927
✉info@trinitychambers.co.uk
Trinity Chambers
Multi Media Exchange, 72-80 Corporation Road, Middlesbrough TS1 2RF,
☎01642 247569
✉info@trinitychambers.co.uk
Call Date: July 2006, Gray's Inn
Qualifications: [BA (Hons) LLM]
✉w.byrne@trinitychambers.co.uk

BYRNES MISS AISLING ALICE ELIZABETH

25 Bedford Row
London WC1R 4HD, ☎020 7067 1500
✉clerks@25bedfordrow.com
Call Date: Oct 1994, Gray's Inn
Pupil Supervisor
Qualifications: [LLB]
✉abyrnes@25bedfordrow.com

CABEZA MISS RUTH ROBERTA ELIZABETH

Field Court Chambers
5 Field Court, Gray's Inn, London WC1R 5EF,
☎020 7405 6114 ✉clerks@fieldcourt.co.uk
Call Date: Mar 1998, Middle Temple
Pupil Supervisor
Qualifications: [LLB (Hons)(Kent)]
✉ruth.cabeza@fieldcourt.co.uk

CADDICK MR NICHOLAS DAVID QC (2011)

Hogarth Chambers
5 New Square, Lincoln's Inn, London WC2A 3RJ, ☎020 7404 0404
✉barristers@hogarthchambers.com
Octagon House
19 Colegate, Norwich NR3 1AT,
☎01603 623186
✉clerks@octagonhouse.co.uk
Call Date: Nov 1986, Middle Temple
Pupil Supervisor
Qualifications: [MA BCL (Oxon)]
✉ncaddick@hogarthchambers.com

CADDLE MISS SHERRIE LORETTA

Charter Chambers
33 John Street, London WC1N 2AT,
☎020 7618 4400
✉clerks@charterchambers.com
Call Date: Nov 1983, Lincoln's Inn
Pupil Supervisor
Qualifications: [BSc (Hons) Soc & Law (Brunel)]
✉sherrie.caddle@charterchambers.com

CADE MRS DIANA

Trinity Chambers
Highfield House, Moulsham Street, Chelmsford, Essex CM2 9AH,
☎01245 605040
✉clerks@trinitychambers.com
Call Date: Nov 1994, Inner Temple
Qualifications: [LLB (UEA) LLM (Essex)]

CADE-DAVIES MISS LYNSEY NICOLA

29 Bedford Row Chambers
London WC1R 4HE, ☎020 7404 1044
✉clerks@29br.co.uk
Call Date: Oct 2005, Inner Temple
Qualifications: [LLB University of Bristol]
✉lcadedavies@29br.co.uk

CADMAN MR TOBY MACE

Nine Bedford Row
9 Bedford Row, London WC1R 4AZ,
☎020 7489 2727
✉clerks@9bedfordrow.co.uk
Call Date: Oct 2001, Middle Temple
Qualifications: [LLB (Hons)]
✉toby.cadman@9bedfordrow.co.uk

CADWALADR MR STEPHEN KENNETH

Cornwall Street Chambers
85-87 Cornwall Street, Birmingham B3 3BY,
☎0121 233 7500
✉clerks@cornwallstreet.co.uk
Call Date: July 1992, Middle Temple
Pupil Supervisor
stephen.cadwaladr@cornwallstreet.co.uk

CADWALLADER MR NEIL ANTHONY

Exchange Chambers
One Derby Square, Derby Square, Liverpool L2 9XX, ☎0151 236 7747
✉info@exchangechambers.co.uk
5 Stone Buildings
5 Stone Buildings, Lincoln's Inn, London WC2A 3XT, ☎020 7242 6201
✉clerks@5sblaw.com
Exchange Chambers
Oxford House, Oxford Row, Leeds LS1 3BE,
☎0113 203 1970
✉spencer@exchangechambers.co.uk
Call Date: July 1984, Inner Temple
Pupil Supervisor
Qualifications: [MA (Cantab) Dip Law FSALS FCIArb]

CADWALLADER MR PETER

9 St John Street
Manchester M3 4DN, ☎0161 955 9000
✉civilclerks@9sjs.com / criminalclerks@9sjs.com
Call Date: July 1973, Gray's Inn
Pupil Supervisor
Qualifications: [LLB (Lond)]

CAFFERKEY MISS ANNETTE MARIE

Arden Chambers
20 Bloomsbury Square, London WC1A 2NS,
☎020 7242 4244
✉clerks@ardenchambers.com
Call Date: Nov 1994, Inner Temple
Qualifications: [LLB (Hons)]
annette.cafferkey@ardenchambers.com

CAFFERKEY MISS NICHOLA JANE

Old Bailey Chambers
15 Old Bailey, London EC4M 7EF,
☎020 3008 6404
✉clerks@15oldbaileychambers.com
Call Date: Oct 1998, Middle Temple
Qualifications: [LLB (Hons)(Warwick)]

CAHILL MR PAUL JEREMY QC (2002)

No5 Chambers
Fountain Court, Steelhouse Lane, Birmingham B4 6DR, ☎0845 210 5555 ✉info@no5.com
No5 Chambers
Greenwood House, 4-7 Salisbury Court, London EC4Y 8AA, ☎0845 210 5555
No5 Chambers
38 Queen Square, Bristol BS1 4QS,
☎0845 210 5555
Call Date: July 1975, Middle Temple
Qualifications: [LLB (L'pool)]
jc@no5.com

CAHILL MISS ROWENA COLETTE

Chambers of Marion Smullen and Kerim Fuad QC
1 Inner Temple Lane, London EC4Y 1AF,
☎020 7427 4400 ✉clerks@1itl.com
Call Date: July 2008, Gray's Inn
Qualifications: [BMus (Hons) PgDI (Lond)]

CAIDEN MR NATHANIEL JOSEPH

Cloisters
1 Pump Court, Temple, London EC4Y 7AA,
☎020 7827 4000 ✉clerks@cloisters.com
Call Date: Nov 2009, Gray's Inn
Qualifications: [LLB]
nc@cloisters.com

CAINS MS LINDA HILARY

37 Park Square Chambers
37 Park Square, Leeds LS1 2NY,
☎0113 243 9422 ✉chambers@no37.co.uk
Call Date: Oct 1990, Middle Temple
Pupil Supervisor
Qualifications: [BA (Leeds)]
chambers@no37.co.uk

CAIRNES MR SIMON PAUL STEVEN

No5 Chambers
38 Queen Square, Bristol BS1 4QS,
☎0845 210 5555
No5 Chambers
Greenwood House, 4-7 Salisbury Court, London EC4Y 8AA, ☎0845 210 5555
No5 Chambers
Fountain Court, Steelhouse Lane, Birmingham B4 6DR, ☎0845 210 5555 ✉info@no5.com
3 PB Barristers
4 St Peter Street, Winchester SO23 8BW,
☎01962 868884
✉clerks.winchester@3paper.co.uk
Call Date: Nov 1980, Gray's Inn
Pupil Supervisor
Qualifications: [LLB (Wales)]
psc@no5.com

E

CAIRNS MS SALLY

No 8 Chambers
8 Fountain Court, Steelhouse Lane, Birmingham B4 6DR, ☎ 0121 236 5514
✉ clerks@no8chambers.co.uk
Call Date: July 2006, Gray's Inn
Qualifications: [BA (Bristol) MA (OU) LLB (OU)]
✉ clerks@no8chambers.co.uk

CAKEBREAD MR STUART ALAN CHARLES

Selborne Chambers
10 Essex Street, London WC2R 3AA, ☎ 020 7420 9500
✉ clerks@selbornechambers.co.uk
Call Date: Nov 1978, Middle Temple
Pupil Supervisor
Qualifications: [BA (Exon)]

CALA DR GUISEPPE

New Court
Ground Floor, New Court, Temple, London EC4Y 9BE, ☎ 020 7583 5123
✉ clerks@newcourtchambers.com
Call Date: 1971, Inner Temple
Qualifications: [LLD]
✉ gcala@newcourtchambers.net

CALAS-PROLINGHEUER MISS SOPHIE LOUISE

5 Pump Court
Ground Floor, 5 Pump Court, Temple, London EC4Y 7AP, ☎ 020 7353 2532
✉ clerks@5pumpcourt.com
Call Date: July 2006, Middle Temple
Qualifications: [BA (Hons) (Kent)]
✉ sophieprolingheuer@5pumpcourt.com

CALDECOTT MR ANDREW HILARY QC (1994)

One Brick Court
1st Floor, One Brick Court, Temple, London EC4Y 9BY, ☎ 020 7353 8845
✉ clerks@onebrickcourt.com
Call Date: July 1975, Inner Temple
Qualifications: [BA (Oxon)]
✉ ac@onebrickcourt.com, acaldecott@onebrickcourt.com

CALDER MR DANIEL

18 St John Street
Manchester M3 4EA, ☎ 0161 278 1800
✉ clerks@18sjs.com
Call Date: July 2008, Lincoln's Inn
Qualifications: [LLB (Manch)]

CALDER MRS LYNETTE MARIE

Maidstone Chambers
33 Earl Street, Maidstone, Kent ME14 1PF, ☎ 01622 688592
✉ clerks@maidstonechambers.co.uk
Call Date: July 2003, Lincoln's Inn
Qualifications: [BA (Hons) (Oxon)]

CALDWELL MR ANDREW FREW

Chambers of Mr Ami Feder
Ground Floor, Lamb Building, Temple, London EC4Y 7AS, ☎ 020 7797 7788
✉ clerks@lambbuilding.co.uk
Chambers of Mr Ami Feder
Ground Floor, Lamb Building, Temple, London EC4Y 7AS, ☎ 020 7797 7788
✉ clerks@lambbuilding.co.uk
Call Date: July 1984, Middle Temple
Qualifications: [MA (Edin)]

CALDWELL MR PETER HUGH COYLES

Dyers Chambers
35 Bedford Row, London WC1R 4JH, ☎ 020 7404 1881
✉ admin@dyerschambers.com
Call Date: Oct 1995, Gray's Inn
Pupil Supervisor
Qualifications: [BA (York) MA]
✉ peter.caldwell@2dyersbuildings.com

CALHAEM MR SIMON MALCOLM

29 Bedford Row Chambers
London WC1R 4HE, ☎ 020 7404 1044
✉ clerks@29br.co.uk
Call Date: Oct 1999, Lincoln's Inn
Qualifications: [MA (Hons)(Oxon)]
✉ scalhaem@29br.co.uk

CALLAGHAN MS CATHERINE EILEEN

Blackstone Chambers
Blackstone House, Temple, London EC4Y 9BW, ☎ 020 7583 1770
✉ clerks@blackstonechambers.com
Call Date: Nov 1999, Inner Temple
Pupil Supervisor
Qualifications: [BA, LLB(New Zealand) LLM (Cantab)]
✉ catherinecallaghan@blackstonechambers.com

E

CALLAGHAN MRS ELIZABETH MARY

Dere Street Barristers
14 Toft Green, York YO1 6JT, ☎0844 3351551
✉clerks@derestreet.co.uk
York Chambers
Rotterdam House, 116 The Quayside, Newcastle Upon Tyne NE1 3DY,
☎0191 206 4677
Call Date: July 1998, Lincoln's Inn
Qualifications: [LLB (Hons)(Teesside)]
clerks@yorkchambers.co.uk

CALLAGHAN DR NIGEL JOHN

7 Bell Yard
London WC2A 2JR, ☎020 7831 0636
✉kevintarrant@btconnect.com
Call Date: Oct 2002, Inner Temple
Qualifications: [LMSSA (Lond) LLB (Northumbria) Dip of Prison Medicine (RCPP&GP)]
papadoc@nigel85.freeserve.co.uk

CALLAN MR DAVID ST CLAIR

Trinity Chambers
The Custom House, 39 Quayside, Newcastle Upon Tyne NE1 3DE, ☎0191 232 1927
✉info@trinitychambers.co.uk
Trinity Chambers
Multi Media Exchange, 72-80 Corporation Road, Middlesbrough TS1 2RF,
☎01642 247569
✉info@trinitychambers.co.uk
Call Date: July 1979, Middle Temple
Pupil Supervisor
Qualifications: [MA]
d.callan@trinitychambers.co.uk

CALLAN MS JANE ELIZABETH

Trinity Chambers
The Custom House, 39 Quayside, Newcastle Upon Tyne NE1 3DE, ☎0191 232 1927
✉info@trinitychambers.co.uk
Trinity Chambers
Multi Media Exchange, 72-80 Corporation Road, Middlesbrough TS1 2RF,
☎01642 247569
✉info@trinitychambers.co.uk
Call Date: Nov 1995, Middle Temple
Pupil Supervisor
Qualifications: [BA (Hons) MSc]

CALLAND MR TIMOTHY PATRICK

Enterprise Chambers
9 Old Square, Lincoln's Inn, London WC2A 3SR, ☎020 7405 9471
✉london@enterprisechambers.com
Enterprise Chambers
65 Quayside, Newcastle Upon Tyne NE1 3DE,
☎0191 222 3344
✉newcastle@enterprisechambers.com
Enterprise Chambers
43 Park Square, Leeds LS1 2NP,
☎0113 246 0391
✉leeds@enterprisechambers.com
Call Date: Oct 1999, Lincoln's Inn
Qualifications: [BA (Hons)]
timcalland@enterprisechambers.com

CALLERY MR MARTIN

Cobden House Chambers
19 Quay Street, Manchester M3 3HN,
☎0161 833 6000 ✉Clerks@Cobden.co.uk
Call Date: Mar 1997, Middle Temple
Qualifications: [LLB (Hons)(Wales)]
clerks@cobden.co.uk

CALLINAN MISS CLODAGHMUIRE

15 New Bridge Street
London EC4V 6AU, ☎020 7842 1900
✉clerks@15nbs.com
Call Date: Mar 2007, Middle Temple
Qualifications: [LLB (Hons) LLM (Dub)]

CALLMAN MR JEREMY DAVID

Ten Old Square
Ground Floor, Ten Old Square, Lincoln's Inn, London WC2A 3SU, ☎020 7405 0758
✉clerks@tenoldsquare.com
Call Date: Oct 1991, Middle Temple
Pupil Supervisor
Qualifications: [MA (Hons) (Cantab)]
jeremycallman@tenoldsquare.com

CALLMAN MISS TANYA SARA

Edulaw Chambers
127 Abbots Gardens, London N2 0JJ
Call Date: Oct 1993, Middle Temple
Qualifications: [MA (Hons)(Cantab)]

CALLOW MR DAVID RICHARD

12 King's Bench Walk
12 King's Bench Walk, Temple, London EC4Y 7EL, ☎020 7583 0811
Call Date: Nov 1998, Middle Temple
Pupil Supervisor
Qualifications: [LLB (Hons)(Wales)]
callow@12kbw.co.uk

CALNAN MISS ELEANOR KATHARINE GRACE

14 Gray's Inn Square
14 Gray's Inn Square, Gray's Inn, London WC1R 5JP, ☎020 7242 0858
✉clerks@14gis.co.uk
Call Date: Nov 2007, Inner Temple
Qualifications: [BA (Cantab)]

E

CALVER MR NEIL RICHARD QC (2006)

Brick Court Chambers
7-8 Essex Street, London WC2R 3LD,
☎ 020 7379 3550 ✉ clerks@brickcourt.co.uk
Call Date: Nov 1987, Gray's Inn
Recorder
Qualifications: [MA (Cantab)]
✉ Neil.Calver@Brickcourt.co.uk

CALVERT MR DAVID EDWARD

St James's Chambers
68 Quay Street, Manchester M3 3EJ,
☎ 0161 834 7000
✉ clerks@stjameschambers.com
12 King's Bench Walk
12 King's Bench Walk, Temple, London
EC4Y 7EL, ☎ 020 7583 0811
Call Date: Nov 1995, Inner Temple
Qualifications: [BA (Oxon)]
✉ david.calvert@stjameschambers.com

CALVERT MR PETER CHARLES

Hardwicke
New Square, Lincoln's Inn, London
WC2A 3SB, ☎ 020 7242 2523
✉ enquiries@hardwicke.co.uk
Call Date: July 1975, Middle Temple
Qualifications: [BA]
✉ charles.calvert@hardwicke.co.uk

CALWAY MR MARK EDWARD

Renaissance Chambers
5th Floor, Gray's Inn Chambers, Gray's Inn,
London WC1R 5JA, ☎ 020 7404 1111
✉ clerks@renaissancechambers.co.uk
Call Date: Feb 1989, Inner Temple
Qualifications: [BA (Kent)]

CAMERON MR ALLAN ALEXANDER QC (2003)

3 Raymond Buildings
3 Raymond Buildings, Gray's Inn, London
WC1R 5BH, ☎ 020 7400 6400
✉ clerks@3rblaw.com
Call Date: Nov 1986, Inner Temple
Qualifications: [LLB (Bris)]

CAMERON MR GILLON

14 Gray's Inn Square
14 Gray's Inn Square, Gray's Inn, London
WC1R 5JP, ☎ 020 7242 0858
✉ clerks@14gis.co.uk
Call Date: Nov 2002, Lincoln's Inn
Qualifications: [BA (Hons)(Bris)]
✉ clerks@14graysinnsquare.co.uk

CAMERON MR NEIL ALEXANDER

Wilberforce Chambers
7 Bishop Lane, Hull HU1 1PA,
☎ 01482 323264
Call Date: July 1984, Gray's Inn
Pupil Supervisor
Qualifications: [LLB (Leics)]

CAMERON MR NEIL ST CLAIR QC (2009)

Landmark Chambers
180 Fleet Street, London EC4A 2HG,
☎ 020 7430 1221
✉ clerks@landmarkchambers.co.uk
Call Date: July 1982, Gray's Inn
Qualifications: [BA (Dunelm)]
✉ neilcameron@landmarkchambers.co.uk

CAMERON MR ROBERT

42 Bedford Row
London WC1R 4LL, ☎ 020 7831 0222
✉ clerks@42br.com
Call Date: Mar 2003, Lincoln's Inn
Qualifications: [LLB (Hons) (Dunelm) MA (Hons) (Cantab)]
✉ robert.cameron@42br.com

CAMMEGH MR JOHN STEPHEN

Nine Bedford Row
9 Bedford Row, London WC1R 4AZ,
☎ 020 7489 2727
✉ clerks@9bedfordrow.co.uk
Call Date: Nov 1987, Inner Temple
Qualifications: [LLB (Lond)]
✉ john.cammegh@9bedfordrow.co.uk

CAMMERMAN MR GIDEON SAUL

187 Fleet Street
London EC4A 2AT, ☎ 020 7430 7430
✉ chambers@187fleetstreet.com
Call Date: Nov 1996, Middle Temple
Qualifications: [BA (Hons) (Cantab) Dip Law]
✉ gideoncammerman@187fleetstreet.com

CAMP MR CHRISTOPHER JOHN DAVID

Hardwicke
New Square, Lincoln's Inn, London
WC2A 3SB, ☎ 020 7242 2523
✉ enquiries@hardwicke.co.uk
Call Date: Oct 1996, Inner Temple
Qualifications: [MA (Cantab)]

E

CAMPBELL MR ALASDAIR JAMES

St Paul's Chambers
5th Floor, St Paul's House, 23 Park Square South, Leeds LS1 2ND, ☎0113 245 5866
Call Date: Oct 1999, Lincoln's Inn
Qualifications: [LLB (Hons)(Northumb)]

CAMPBELL MR ALEXANDER JAMES

Hardwicke
New Square, Lincoln's Inn, London WC2A 3SB, ☎020 7242 2523
✉enquiries@hardwicke.co.uk
Call Date: July 2010, Gray's Inn
Qualifications: [BA LLM (Maitrise en droit)]

CAMPBELL MISS ALEXIS ANNE

29 Bedford Row Chambers
London WC1R 4HE, ☎020 7404 1044
✉clerks@29br.co.uk
Call Date: Nov 1990, Inner Temple
Qualifications: [LLB (Leeds)]
acampbell@29br.co.uk

CAMPBELL MR ANDREW NEVILLE QC (1994)

Zenith Chambers
10 Park Square, Leeds LS1 2LH, ☎0113 245 5438
✉clerks@zenithchambers.co.uk
Call Date: Nov 1972, Middle Temple
Recorder
Qualifications: [BA]
acampbell@zenithchambers.co.uk

CAMPBELL MR BENJAMIN ARCHIBALD

Park Court Chambers
16 Park Place, Leeds LS1 2SJ, ☎0113 243 3277
✉clerks@parkcourtchambers.co.uk
Call Date: July 2008, Middle Temple
Qualifications: [MA (Hons) (St. Andrew's) PgDl (Lond)]
clerks@parkcourtchambers.co.uk

CAMPBELL MRS BERNICE

New Bailey Chambers
4th Floor, Corn Exchange, Fenwick Street, Liverpool, Merseyside L2 7QS, ☎0151 236 9402 ✉clerks@newbailey.com
Call Date: July 2007, Gray's Inn

CAMPBELL MISS BRENDA

Garden Court Chambers
57-60 Lincoln's Inn Fields, London WC2A 3LJ, ☎020 7993 7600 ✉info@gclaw.co.uk
Call Date: July 2002, Middle Temple
Qualifications: [LLB (Hons) (Belfast)]
brendac@gclaw.co.uk

CAMPBELL MISS DIANE EVA

Dere Street Barristers
14 Toft Green, York YO1 6JT, ☎0844 3351551
✉clerks@derestreet.co.uk
Dere Street Barristers
33 Broad Chare, Newcastle Upon Tyne NE1 3DQ, ☎0844 3351551
✉clerks@derestreet.co.uk
Call Date: Oct 1995, Gray's Inn
Qualifications: [LLB]
d.campbell@derestreet.co.uk, clerk@yorkchambers.co.uk

CAMPBELL MR DOUGLAS JAMES

Three New Square IP
3 New Square, Lincoln's Inn, London WC2A 3RS, ☎020 7405 1111
✉clerks@3newsquare.co.uk
Call Date: Oct 1993, Inner Temple
Qualifications: [MA (Oxon) Dip Law (Lond)]
campbell@3newsquare.co.uk

Types of work: Biotechnology, Breach of confidence, Communications, Company, commercial and competition, Computer contracts, Computer litigation, Confidential information, Copyright, Data protection, Design, Entertainment, Franchising, Information technology, Intellectual property, Internet law, Malicious falsehood, Media, Media and entertainment, Passing off, Patents, Pharmaceuticals, Registered designs, Scientific and technical disputes, Technical contracts, Telecommunications, Torts, Trade secrets, Trademarks, Unregistered designs

CAMPBELL MISS ELEANOR CHARLOTTE

One Essex Court
Ground Floor, One Essex Court, Temple, London EC4Y 9AR, ☎020 7583 2000
✉clerks@oeclaw.co.uk
Call Date: July 2005, Lincoln's Inn
Qualifications: [BA (Hons)]
ecampbell@oeclaw.co.uk

CAMPBELL MISS EMILY CHARLOTTE

Wilberforce Chambers
8 New Square, Lincoln's Inn, London
WC2A 3QP, ☎ 020 7306 0102
✉ chambers@wilberforce.co.uk
Call Date: Nov 1995, Lincoln's Inn
Pupil Supervisor
Qualifications: [MA (Oxon) BCL]
✉ ecampbell@wilberforce.co.uk

Types of work: Capital tax, Chancery (general), Chancery (land law), Charities, Conflict of laws, Equity, Income tax, Pensions, Professional negligence, Succession, Trusts, Wills

CAMPBELL MR FRASER

Blackstone Chambers
Blackstone House, Temple, London
EC4Y 9BW, ☎ 020 7583 1770
✉ clerks@blackstonechambers.com
Call Date: Nov 2010, Gray's Inn
✉ frasercampbell@blackstonechambers.com

CAMPBELL MR GLENN

Hailsham Chambers
Ground Floor, 4 Paper Buildings, Temple,
London EC4Y 7EX, ☎ 020 7643 5000
✉ clerks@hailshamchambers.com
Deans Court Chambers
101 Walker Street, Preston PR1 2RR,
☎ 01772 565 600
✉ preston@deanscourt.co.uk
Deans Court Chambers
24 St John Street, Manchester M3 4DF,
☎ 0161 214 6000 ✉ clerks@deanscourt.co.uk
Call Date: July 1985, Lincoln's Inn
Pupil Supervisor
Qualifications: [LLB (Manch) LLM QMWC]
✉ glenn.campbell@hailshamchambers.com

CAMPBELL MRS JANE CHARLOTTE

6 Pump Court
1st Floor, 6 Pump Court, Temple, London
EC4Y 7AR, ☎ 020 7797 8400
✉ richardconstable@6pumpcourt.co.uk
6 Pump Court Chambers
6-8 Mill Street, Maidstone, Kent ME15 6XH,
☎ 01622 688094
✉ annexe@6pumpcourt.co.uk
Call Date: Oct 1990, Inner Temple
Qualifications: [BA (Newc) Dip Law]

CAMPBELL MISS JOAN CAROLYN

Trent Chambers
9 Regent Street, Nottingham NG1 5BS,
☎ 0115 941 9596
✉ clerks@trentchambers.co.uk
Call Date: Nov 1996, Lincoln's Inn
Qualifications: [LLB(Jnt Hons)(Wales)]
✉ clerks@trentchambers.co.uk

CAMPBELL MR JOHN WALTER GANT

4-5 Gray's Inn Square
Gray's Inn, London WC1R 5AH,
☎ 020 7404 5252 ✉ clerks@4-5.co.uk
Call Date: Mar 2009, Gray's Inn
✉ jcampbell@4-5.co.uk

CAMPBELL MR MONTCLARE ORLANDO

Clerksroom (London)
3rd Floor, 218 Strand, London WC2R 1AT,
☎ 0845 083 3000 ✉ mail@clerksroom.com
Clerksroom (Taunton)
Equity House, Administration Centre,
Blackbrook Park Avenue, Taunton, Somerset
TA1 2PX, ☎ 0845 083 3000
✉ mail@clerksroom.com
Call Date: Nov 2011, Inner Temple
Qualifications: [LLB (Lond)]

CAMPBELL MR NICHOLAS CHARLES WILSON QC (2000)

KBW
The Engine House, No 1 Foundry Square,
Leeds LS11 5DL, ☎ 0113 297 1200
✉ clerks@kbwchambers.com
Call Date: July 1978, Inner Temple
Recorder
Qualifications: [BA (Cantab)]
✉ nicholascampbell@kbwchambers.com

CAMPBELL MR OLIVER EDWARD WILHELM

Henderson Chambers
2 Harcourt Buildings, Temple, London
EC4Y 9DB, ☎ 020 7583 9020
✉ clerks@hendersonchambers.co.uk
Call Date: Oct 1992, Middle Temple
Pupil Supervisor
Qualifications: [MA (Hons)]
✉ ocampbell@hendersonchambers.co.uk

E

CAMPBELL MISS RHONA LYNN

No5 Chambers
Fountain Court, Steelhouse Lane, Birmingham B4 6DR, ☎0845 210 5555 ✉info@no5.com
No5 Chambers
Greenwood House, 4-7 Salisbury Court, London EC4Y 8AA, ☎0845 210 5555
No5 Chambers
38 Queen Square, Bristol BS1 4QS, ☎0845 210 5555
Call Date: Oct 1993, Inner Temple
Qualifications: [BA (Dunelm)]

CAMPBELL MS SARAH JANE

23 Essex Street
London WC2R 3AA, ☎020 7413 0353
✉clerks@23es.com
Call Date: Oct 1997, Inner Temple
Qualifications: [BA (Cantab)]
sarahcampbell@23es.com

CAMPBELL MR STAFFORD GRAHAM

Westgate Chambers
64 High Street, Lewes, East Sussex BN7 1XG, ☎01273 480510
✉clerks@westgate-chambers.co.uk
Call Date: July 1979, Gray's Inn
Pupil Supervisor
Qualifications: [LLB (Lond)]
sgc@westgate-chambers.co.uk

CAMPBELL MR STEPHEN GORDON

No5 Chambers
Fountain Court, Steelhouse Lane, Birmingham B4 6DR, ☎0845 210 5555 ✉info@no5.com
No5 Chambers
Greenwood House, 4-7 Salisbury Court, London EC4Y 8AA, ☎0845 210 5555
No5 Chambers
38 Queen Square, Bristol BS1 4QS, ☎0845 210 5555
Call Date: July 1982, Middle Temple
Recorder
Qualifications: [LLB (L'pool)]
sgc@no5.com

CAMPBELL MISS SUSAN CLAIRE QC (2009)

Pump Court Chambers
Upper Ground Floor, 3 Pump Court, Temple, London EC4Y 7AJ, ☎020 7353 0711
✉clerks@3pumpcourt.com
Pump Court Chambers
31 Southgate Street, Winchester, Hampshire SO23 9EB, ☎01962 868 161
✉clerks@3pumpcourt.com
Southernhay Chambers
33 Southernhay East, Exeter EX1 1NX, ☎01392 255777
✉clerks@southernhaychambers.co.uk
Call Date: Nov 1986, Middle Temple
Qualifications: [MA (Cantab)]

CAMPBELL-BROWN MISS ANNE LOUISE

One Essex Court
1st Floor, Temple, London EC4Y 9AR, ☎020 7936 3030 ✉clerks@1ec.co.uk
Call Date: Nov 1993, Middle Temple
Pupil Supervisor
Qualifications: [BA (Hons)(York) MA (Lond) Dip Law (Lond) LLM (Lond)]
lcampbellbrown@1ec.co.uk

CAMPBELL-TIECH MR ANDREW QC (2003)

Dyers Chambers
35 Bedford Row, London WC1R 4JH, ☎020 7404 1881
✉admin@dyerschambers.com
Call Date: July 1978, Inner Temple
Recorder

CAMPION MR DAVID RICHARD

Chambers of Ian Macdonald QC
Garden Court North, 22 Oxford Court, Manchester M2 3WQ, ☎0161 236 1840
✉clerks@gcnchambers.co.uk
Call Date: Nov 2004, Inner Temple
Qualifications: [LLB Sheffield Hallam University]
dcampion@gcnchambers.co.uk

CANAVAN MISS SHEELAGH MARY

5 King's Bench Walk
5 King's Bench Walk, Temple, London EC4Y 7DN, ☎020 7353 5638
✉clerks@5kbw.co.uk
Call Date: July 1987, Lincoln's Inn
Pupil Supervisor, Recorder
Qualifications: [LLB (Hons) (Lond)]
sheelagh.canavan@5kbw.co.uk

CANBY MISS FIONA JANE

Temple Garden Chambers
1 Harcourt Buildings, Temple, London EC4Y 9DA, ☎020 7583 1315
✉clerks@tgchambers.com
Call Date: July 2001, Middle Temple
Qualifications: [LLB (Hons)]
fc@tgchambers.com

E

CANDILIO MISS MARIA ELENA

Agnus Chambers
PO Box 64196, London WC1A 9FE,
☎ 020 7637 9670
Call Date: Mar 1998, Middle Temple
Qualifications: [BSc MPhil LLB LLM]

CANDLIN MR JAMES RICHARD

12 King's Bench Walk
12 King's Bench Walk, Temple, London
EC4Y 7EL, ☎ 020 7583 0811
Call Date: Oct 1991, Lincoln's Inn
Pupil Supervisor
Qualifications: [BSc (Hons) Dip Law]
candlin@12kbw.co.uk

CANDLIN MISS NAOMI HELEN

St Philips Chambers
55 Temple Row, Birmingham B2 5LS,
☎ 0121 246 7000 ✉ clerks@st-philips.com
Call Date: Oct 2003, Lincoln's Inn
Qualifications: [MA (Cantab)]
ncandlin@st-philips.co.uk

CANE-SOOTHILL MR MICHAEL STEPHEN

Bank House Chambers
Old Bank House, Hartshead, Sheffield S1 2EL,
☎ 0114 275 1223
✉ w.digby@bankhousechambers.co.uk
Call Date: Oct 1997, Lincoln's Inn
Qualifications: [LLB (Hons)(Sheff)]
m.canesoothill@bankhousechambers.co.uk

CANEY MISS MICHELLE ANN

St Ive's Chambers
Whittall Street, Birmingham B4 6DH,
☎ 0121 236 0863
✉ clerks@stiveschambers.co.uk
Call Date: Oct 2004, Middle Temple
Qualifications: [LLB (Hons) BVC]
michelle.caney@stiveschambers.co.uk

CANNING MR RICHARD

39 Park Square
Leeds LS1 2NU, ☎ 0113 245 6633
✉ seniorclerk@39parksquarechambers.co.uk
Call Date: Nov 2004, Lincoln's Inn
Qualifications: [LLB (Hons)]
canning@39parksquare.com

CANNINGS MR MATTHEW JAMES

3 PB Barristers
Royal Talbot House, 2 Victoria Street, Bristol,
Avon BS1 6BB, ☎ 0117 928 1520
3 PB Barristers
23 Beaumont Street, Oxford OX1 2NP,
☎ 01865 793 736
3 PB Barristers
30 Christchurch Road, Bournemouth, Dorset
BH1 3PD, ☎ 01202 292102
✉ clerks.bournemouth@3paper.co.uk
3 PB Barristers
4 St Peter Street, Winchester SO23 8BW,
☎ 01962 868884
✉ clerks.winchester@3paper.co.uk
3 PB Barristers
3 Paper Buildings, Temple, London EC4Y 7EU,
☎ 020 7583 8055
Call Date: July 2006, Middle Temple
Qualifications: [LLB (Lond) AKC (Lond) PG Dip LLM (Dunelm)]
matthew.cannings@3pb.co.uk

CANNOCK MR GILES MICHAEL MORGAN

Kings Chambers
36 Young Street, Manchester M3 3FT,
☎ 0845 034 3444
✉ clerks@kingschambers.com
Kings Chambers
5 Park Square East, Leeds LS1 2NE,
☎ 0845 034 3444
✉ clerks@kingschambers.com
Kings Chambers
Embassy House, 60 Church Street,
Birmingham B3 2DJ, ☎ 0845 034 3444
✉ clerks@kingschambers.com
Call Date: Oct 1998, Gray's Inn
Qualifications: [BA, LLM (Cantab)]
gcannock@kingschambers.com

CANNON MR JOSEF DAVID

Cornerstone Barristers
2-3 Gray's Inn Square, Gray's Inn, London
WC1R 5JH, ☎ 020 7242 4986
✉ chambers@2-3gis.co.uk
Call Date: July 2002, Lincoln's Inn
Qualifications: [LLB (Hons)(Lond)]
josefc@cornerstonebarristers.com

CANNON MISS LAUREN BEVERLEY

Guildford Chambers
Stoke House, Leapale Lane, Guildford, Surrey
GU1 4LY, ☎ 01483 539131
✉ clerks@guildfordchambers.co.uk
Call Date: Oct 2004, Middle Temple
Qualifications: [MA (Cantab) CPE]

E

CANNON MR MARK RENNISON NORRIS QC (2008)

Four New Square
Four New Square, Lincoln's Inn, London WC2A 3RJ, ☎ 020 7822 2000
✉ barristers@4newsquare.com
Call Date: July 1985, Middle Temple
Pupil Supervisor
Qualifications: [BA(Oxon)]
✉ m.cannon@4newsquare.com

CANNON MR PATRICK SEAN

Taxchambers
15 Old Square, Lincoln's Inn, London WC2A 3UE, ☎ 020 7242 2744
✉ taxchambers@15oldsquare.co.uk
Call Date: July 2003, Lincoln's Inn
Qualifications: [LLB (Hons) (Lond) BCL (Oxon) CTA]
✉ taxchambers@15oldsquare.co.uk

CANT MR CHRISTOPHER IAN

9 Stone Buildings
Lincoln's Inn, London WC2A 3NN, ☎ 020 7404 5055
✉ clerks@9stonebuildings.com
Call Date: July 1973, Lincoln's Inn
Pupil Supervisor
Qualifications: [MA (Cantab)]
✉ clerks@9stonebuildings.com, CCant@9StoneBuildings.com

CANTER MR SIMON ALEXANDER

Richmond Canter Immigration Barristers
1 Fetter Lane, London EC4A 1BR, ☎ 020 3440 5820
✉ info@immigrationbarrister.co.uk
Call Date: Oct 2000, Inner Temple
Pupil Supervisor
Qualifications: [BA (Sussex) CPE]

CANTOR MS ESTHER

12 Old Square Chambers
1st Floor, 12 Old Square, Lincoln's Inn, London WC2A 3TX, ☎ 020 7404 0875
✉ clerks@12oldsquare.com
Call Date: July 2004, Lincoln's Inn
Qualifications: [LLB Hons (Lond)]

CAPEWELL MR EDWARD JACK

11 King's Bench Walk
11 King's Bench Walk, Temple, London EC4Y 7EQ, ☎ 020 7632 8500
✉ clerksroom@11kbw.com
Call Date: Nov 2009, Lincoln's Inn
Qualifications: [BA (Cantab) CPE UCU]
✉ edward.capewell@11kbw.com

CAPLAN MR DAVID ASHER

One Essex Court
Ground Floor, One Essex Court, Temple, London EC4Y 9AR, ☎ 020 7583 2000
✉ clerks@oeclaw.co.uk
Call Date: Nov 2006, Inner Temple
Qualifications: [BA (Cantab)]
✉ dcaplan@oeclaw.co.uk

CAPLAN MR JONATHAN MICHAEL QC (1991)

Five Paper Buildings
1st Floor, Five Paper Buildings, Temple, London EC4Y 7HB, ☎ 020 7583 6117
✉ clerks@5pb.co.uk
Riverview Chambers
Hamilton House, 1 Temple Avenue, London EC4Y 0HA, ☎ 0844 225 3999
✉ chrisbaylis@riverviewchambers.com
Call Date: July 1973, Gray's Inn
Recorder
Qualifications: [MA (Cantab)]
✉ JC@5pb.co.uk

CAPLAN MRS LEONIE SUSAN

18 St John Street
Manchester M3 4EA, ☎ 0161 278 1800
✉ clerks@18sjs.com
Call Date: Mar 2001, Inner Temple
Qualifications: [BA (Keele)]

CAPLAN MR OLIVER LEIGH

18 St John Street
Manchester M3 4EA, ☎ 0161 278 1800
✉ clerks@18sjs.com
Call Date: Oct 2007, Lincoln's Inn
Qualifications: [LLB (Leeds)]

CAPON MR PHILIP CHRISTOPHER WILLIAM

East Anglian Chambers
Gresham House, 5 Museum Street, Ipswich, Suffolk IP1 1HQ, ☎ 01473 214481
✉ ipswich@ealaw.co.uk
East Anglian Chambers
140 New London Road, Chelmsford, Essex CM2 0AW, ☎ 01473 214481
✉ chelmsford@ealaw.co.uk
East Anglian Chambers
15 The Close, Norwich, Norfolk NR1 4DZ, ☎ 01473 214481 ✉ norwich@ealaw.co.uk
St Philips Chambers
55 Temple Row, Birmingham B2 5LS, ☎ 0121 246 7000 ✉ clerks@st-philips.com
Call Date: Oct 1990, Inner Temple
Pupil Supervisor
Qualifications: [LLB (B'ham)]

CAPPS MR DEVERAL CARMICHAEL

Trinity Chambers
The Custom House, 39 Quayside, Newcastle Upon Tyne NE1 3DE, ☎0191 232 1927
✉info@trinitychambers.co.uk
Trinity Chambers
Multi Media Exchange, 72-80 Corporation Road, Middlesbrough TS1 2RF,
☎01642 247569
✉info@trinitychambers.co.uk
Call Date: Oct 1995, Inner Temple
Qualifications: [LLB (Sheff) LLM (Ireland) Cert Ed]
✉d.capps@trinitychambers.co.uk

CAPSTICK MR TIMOTHY

No.6 Park Square
Leeds LS1 2LW, ☎0113 245 9763
✉Tim@no6.co.uk
Call Date: July 1986, Gray's Inn
Pupil Supervisor
Qualifications: [BA]
✉capstick@no6.co.uk

CARDEN MR NICHOLAS

1 Hare Court
1 Hare Court, Temple, London EC4Y 7BE,
☎020 7797 7070 ✉clerks@1hc.com
Call Date: July 1981, Gray's Inn
Pupil Supervisor
Qualifications: [LLB (Lond)]
✉carden@1hc.com

CAREW POLE MRS REBECCA JANE

1 Hare Court
1 Hare Court, Temple, London EC4Y 7BE,
☎020 7797 7070 ✉clerks@1hc.com
Call Date: Oct 1999, Inner Temple
Qualifications: [LLB (Bris)]
✉carewpole@1hc.com

CAREY MR CHRISTOPHER JOHN

Castle Chambers
The Old Fire Station, 90 High Street, Harrow-on-the-Hill, Middlesex HA1 3LP,
☎020 8423 6579 ✉info@castlechambers.net
Call Date: Oct 2001, Middle Temple
Qualifications: [BA (Hons) CPE]

CAREY MISS JACQUELINE ANNE

2 Bedford Row
London WC1R 4BU, ☎020 7440 8888
✉clerks@2bedfordrow.co.uk
Call Date: Oct 1999, Lincoln's Inn
Pupil Supervisor
Qualifications: [LLB (Hons)(Bris)]
✉jcarey@2bedfordrow.co.uk

CAREY-HUGHES MR RICHARD JOHN QC (2000)

Nine Bedford Row
9 Bedford Row, London WC1R 4AZ,
☎020 7489 2727
✉clerks@9bedfordrow.co.uk
Call Date: July 1977, Gray's Inn
Recorder
✉richard.carey-hughesqc@9bedfordrow.co.uk

CARINGTON MR ALEXANDER MICHAEL

12 King's Bench Walk
12 King's Bench Walk, Temple, London EC4Y 7EL, ☎020 7583 0811
Call Date: Oct 2006, Lincoln's Inn
Qualifications: [LLB (Exon)]
✉carington@12kbw.co.uk

CARLETON MISS ERICA JANE

15 Winckley Square
Preston PR1 3JJ, ☎01772 252828
✉clerks@15winckleysq.co.uk
Call Date: Mar 2000, Middle Temple
Qualifications: [LLB]

CARLILE OF BERRIEW LORD ALEXANDER CHARLES QC (1984)

9-12 Bell Yard
London WC2A 2JR, ☎020 7400 1800
✉clerks@9-12bellyard.com
Linenhall Chambers
1 Stanley Place, Chester CH1 2LU,
☎01244 348282
✉clerks@linenhallchambers.co.uk
St Johns Buildings Liverpool
8th Floor India Buildings, Water Street, Liverpool L2 0XG, ☎0151 243 6000
✉clerk@stjohnsbuildings.co.uk
Call Date: July 1970, Gray's Inn
Recorder
Qualifications: [LLB (AKC) FKC]
✉a.carlile@9-12bellyard.com

CARLIN MR NIALL

Broadway House Chambers
Broadway House, 9 Bank Street, Bradford, West Yorkshire BD1 1TW, ☎01274 722560
✉clerks@broadwayhouse.co.uk
Call Date: Oct 2009, Inner Temple
Qualifications: [LLB (L'pool)]

E

CARLISLE MR TIMOTHY ST JOHN OGILVIE

Field Court Chambers
5 Field Court, Gray's Inn, London WC1R 5EF, ☎020 7405 6114 ✉clerks@fieldcourt.co.uk
Call Date: Nov 1984, Gray's Inn
Pupil Supervisor
Qualifications: [Dip Law]
timothy.carlisle@fieldcourt.co.uk

CARMICHAEL MR JOHN

4 Breams Buildings
Chancery Lane, London EC4A 1HP, ☎020 7092 1900 ✉clerks@4bb.co.uk
Call Date: July 1984, Inner Temple
Pupil Supervisor
Qualifications: [BA (Leeds) Dip Law (City)]

CARNE MR ROGER ENYS

Nine Bedford Row
9 Bedford Row, London WC1R 4AZ, ☎020 7489 2727
✉clerks@9bedfordrow.co.uk
Call Date: Nov 1969, Inner Temple
Pupil Supervisor
Qualifications: [LLB (Lond)]
roger.carne@9bedfordrow.co.uk

E

CARNES MR ANDREW JAMES

4-5 Gray's Inn Square
Gray's Inn, London WC1R 5AH, ☎020 7404 5252 ✉clerks@4-5.co.uk
Call Date: July 1984, Lincoln's Inn
Pupil Supervisor
Qualifications: [LLB (Leics)]
acarnes@4-5.co.uk

CARNEY MR ANDREW PATRICK

Number 7 Harrington Street Chambers
7 Harrington Street, Liverpool L2 9YH, ☎0151 242 0707 ✉clerks@7hs.co.uk
Call Date: Oct 1995, Inner Temple
Qualifications: [BA (Dunelm) MSc (Lond)]
andrew.carney@7hs.co.uk

CARNEY MISS CAROLINE MARY

QEB Hollis Whiteman
1-2 Laurence Pountney Hill, London EC4R 0EU, ☎020 7933 8855
✉barristers@qebhw.co.uk
Call Date: Nov 1980, Middle Temple
Qualifications: [BA (Belfast)]

CARNEY MR JOSEPH PATRICK

3 Stone Buildings
Ground Floor, 3 Stone Buildings, Lincoln's Inn, London WC2A 3XL, ☎020 7242 4937
✉clerks@3sb.law.co.uk
Call Date: Nov 2004, Lincoln's Inn
Qualifications: [BEc LLB (Hons)]
jcarney@3sb.law.co.uk

CARNIE MR ALAN

Wilberforce Chambers
7 Bishop Lane, Hull HU1 1PA, ☎01482 323264
Call Date: July 2006, Lincoln's Inn
Qualifications: [LLB (Hull)]

CARON PROF DAVID DENNIS

20 Essex Street
London WC2R 3AL, ☎020 7842 1200
✉clerks@20essexst.com
Call Date: Oct 2009, Inner Temple
Qualifications: [BSc (USA) MSc (Wales) LLB(USA) DipLP PhD]
dcaron@20essexst.com

CARPENTER MISS CHLOE

Fountain Court Chambers
Fountain Court, Temple, London EC4Y 9DH, ☎020 7583 3335
✉chambers@fountaincourt.co.uk
Call Date: Oct 2001, Lincoln's Inn
Pupil Supervisor
Qualifications: [LLB (Hons) (Lond) BCL (Oxon)]
ccarpenter@fountaincourt.co.uk

CARPENTER MR JAMES FREDERICK HORATIO

Hailsham Chambers
Ground Floor, 4 Paper Buildings, Temple, London EC4Y 7EX, ☎020 7643 5000
✉clerks@hailshamchambers.com
Call Date: July 2000, Inner Temple
Pupil Supervisor
Qualifications: [MA (Hons) (Cantab) CPE]
jamie.carpenter@hailshamchambers.com

CARPENTER MISS JANE PATRICIA ANNE

Atkinson Bevan Chambers
1st Floor, 2 Harcourt Buildings, Temple, London EC4Y 9DB, ☎020 7353 2112
✉clerks@2hb.co.uk
Call Date: Nov 1984, Inner Temple
Pupil Supervisor
Qualifications: [BSc (Hons)]

CARPENTER MISS NAOMI FLEUR

4 King's Bench Walk
2nd Floor, 4 King's Bench Walk, Temple, London EC4Y 7DL, ☎020 7822 7000
✉clerks@4kbw.co.uk
Call Date: Oct 2004, Inner Temple
Qualifications: [BSc (Lond) CPE (Lond)]

CARPENTER-LEITCH MR TOM GORDON

Tanfield Chambers
2-5 Warwick Court, London WC1R 5DJ, ☎020 7421 5300
✉clerks@tanfieldchambers.co.uk
Call Date: Mar 2002, Lincoln's Inn
Qualifications: [BA (Hons) MA (Cantab)]
✉carpenter-leitch@tanfieldchambers.co.uk

CARR MR ADRIAN JAMES SELDEN

Tanfield Chambers
2-5 Warwick Court, London WC1R 5DJ, ☎020 7421 5300
✉clerks@tanfieldchambers.co.uk
Call Date: Nov 1999, Inner Temple
Qualifications: [BA (Dunelm) Dip Law]
✉adriancarr@tanfieldchambers.co.uk

Fax: 020 7421 5333;
DX: 46 London, Chancery Lane;
URL: www.tanfieldchambers.co.uk

Types of work: Chancery, Landlord and tenant, Real property, Succession, Trusts

CARR MR BRUCE CONRAD QC (2009)

Devereux Chambers
Queen Elizabeth Building, Temple, London EC4Y 9BS, ☎020 7353 7534
✉clerks@devchambers.co.uk
Call Date: Nov 1986, Inner Temple
Recorder
Qualifications: [BSc(Econ)(Lond)]
✉carr@devchambers.co.uk

CARR MR CHRISTOPHER DAVID

Maitland Chambers
7 Stone Buildings, Lincoln's Inn, London WC2A 3SZ, ☎020 7406 1200
✉clerks@maitlandchambers.com
Call Date: July 2010, Lincoln's Inn
Qualifications: [BA LLM (Cantab)]
✉ccarr@maitlandchambers.com

CARR MR CHRISTOPHER SEAN

36 Bedford Row
London WC1R 4JH, ☎020 7421 8000
✉chambers@36bedfordrow.co.uk
Call Date: Oct 2002, Inner Temple
Qualifications: [BA (Nott'm) CPE]
✉ccarr@36bedfordrow.co.uk

CARR MR CRAIG FREDERICK

Seven Bedford Row
7 Bedford Row, London WC1R 4BS, ☎020 7242 3555 ✉clerks@7br.co.uk
Call Date: Nov 2005, Middle Temple
Qualifications: [BA (Hons) Oxford]
✉ccarr@7br.co.uk

CARR MR HENRY JAMES QC (1998)

11 South Square
1st Floor, 11 South Square, Gray's Inn, London WC1R 5EY, ☎020 7405 1222
✉clerks@11southsquare.com
Call Date: May 1982, Gray's Inn
Qualifications: [BA (Oxon) LLM (Canada)]
✉hcarr@11southsquare.com

CARR MR JAMES CHRISTOPHER DANIEL

4 Breams Buildings
Chancery Lane, London EC4A 1HP, ☎020 7092 1900 ✉clerks@4bb.co.uk
Call Date: Nov 2001, Middle Temple
Qualifications: [BA (Hons)]

CARR MR JONATHAN OLSON

Dere Street Barristers
33 Broad Chare, Newcastle Upon Tyne NE1 3DQ, ☎0844 3351551
✉clerks@derestreet.co.uk
Call Date: Nov 1990, Middle Temple
Pupil Supervisor
Qualifications: [LLB (Newc)]
✉clerks@broadcharechambers.co.uk

CARR MISS SUE LASCELLES QC (2003)

Four New Square
Four New Square, Lincoln's Inn, London WC2A 3RJ, ☎020 7822 2000
✉barristers@4newsquare.com
Call Date: July 1987, Inner Temple
Qualifications: [MA (Cantab)]

Fax: 020 7822 2001;
DX: 1041 London, Chancery Lane

Other professional qualifications: Accredited mediator; Recorder (2009)

E

Types of work: Commercial litigation, Insurance, Professional negligence

Membership of foreign bars: New South Wales

Awards and memberships: Former Chairman of Complaints Committee; Former Chairman of Professional Negligence Bar Association; Chancery Bar Association; COMBAR; LCLBA; Governing Bencher of the Inner Temple; Former Member of Bar Standards Board; Complaint Commissioner of ICC.

Publications: *Jackson & Powell: Professional Liability Precedents* (General Editor), 2000

Reported Cases: *Football League Ltd v Edge Ellison & Active Rights Management*, [2007] PNLR 2 (Chancery), 2006. Solicitors' duties/commercial advisors' duties.
Cheshire Building Society v Dunlop Haywards Ltd, [2008] 4 EG 169 (Commercial), 2008. Insurance business/limitation.
Axa Insurance Ltd v Various Solicitors, [2009] EWHC 635 (Comm); [2010] PNLR 10 (CA) (Commercial and Court of Appeal), 2009. Insurance business/limitation.
Persimmon Homes Ltd v Great Lakes Reinsurance Plc, [2010] EWHC 1705 (Comm) (Commercial), 2010. ATE insurance/non disclosure
Astrazeneca UK Limited v Albermarie International Corpn and another, [2011] EWHC 1574 (Comm) (Commercial), 2011. Breach of commercial contract; right of first refusal clause; construction of limitation clause.

E

CARRASCO MR GLENN LAWRENCE

9-12 Bell Yard
London WC2A 2JR, ☎ 020 7400 1800
✉ clerks@9-12bellyard.com
Call Date: Oct 1997, Inner Temple
Pupil Supervisor
Qualifications: [BA (London) MSc (LSE) CPE]
✉ glenncar01@hotmail.com

CARRINGTON MR DOMINIC

Chambers of Martin Burr
15 Old Bailey, London EC4M 7EF,
☎ 0845 123 1234 ✉ clerks@barristerweb.com
Call Date: Nov 1996, Middle Temple
Qualifications: [LLB (Hons)]

CARRINGTON MR MARK ANTHONY

Hillwood Chambers
Hillwood, Stockers Hill Road, Rodmersham Green, Sittingbourne, Kent ME9 0PJ,
☎ 01795 472741
Call Date: Oct 1991, Inner Temple
Qualifications: [BA (Kent) Dip Soc (Kent)]
✉ mark.carrington@me.com

CARRION BENITEZ MS MIRIAM

36 Bedford Row
London WC1R 4JH, ☎ 020 7421 8000
✉ chambers@36bedfordrow.co.uk
Call Date: July 2001, Gray's Inn
Qualifications: [MA Diploma in Human Rights BA (Hons)]
✉ mbenitez@36bedfordrow.co.uk

CARRODUS MISS GAIL CAROLINE

Huntercombe Chambers
Timbers Farmhouse, Henley-On-Thames RG9 5SY, ☎ 01491 641934
Call Date: Nov 1978, Gray's Inn
Qualifications: [BSc (Hons) (L'pool)]
✉ gail@carrodus.co.uk
DX: 80516 Henley-on-Thames;
URL: www.carrodus.co.uk

Types of work: Care proceedings, Civil partnerships, Cohabitation, Divorce, Family provision, Financial provision, Matrimonial finance, Mediation, Personal insolvency, Private children law

CARROLL MR GRANT SPENCER

College Chambers
19 Carlton Crescent, Southampton, Hampshire SO15 2ET, ☎ 023 8023 0338
✉ clerks@college-chambers.co.uk
Call Date: July 2005, Middle Temple
Qualifications: [BSc (Hons) Loughborough PgDip Law]
✉ gcarroll@college-chambers.co.uk

CARRON MR RICHARD BYRON

Queen Square Chambers
56 Queen Square, Bristol BS1 4PR,
☎ 0117 921 1966 ✉ crime@qs-c.co.uk
Call Date: Oct 1992, Middle Temple
Qualifications: [BA (Hons) (Cantab)]
✉ rbc@qs-c.co.uk

CARROTT MR SYLVESTER EMANUEL

1 Pump Court
Elm Court, Temple, London EC4Y 7AB,
☎ 020 7842 7070
✉ (name)@pumpcourt.co.uk
Call Date: July 1980, Gray's Inn
Pupil Supervisor
Qualifications: [LLB (Lond)]
✉ sylvestercarrott@mac.com

CARSE MS ALICE LOUISE

Devereux Chambers
Queen Elizabeth Building, Temple, London EC4Y 9BS, ☎ 020 7353 7534
✉ clerks@devchambers.co.uk
Call Date: July 2008, Gray's Inn
Qualifications: [BA (Oxon) LLM]
✉ carse@devchambers.co.uk

CARSE MR GORDON WILLIAM LESLIE

5 King's Bench Walk
5 King's Bench Walk, Temple, London EC4Y 7DN, ☎ 020 7353 5638
✉ clerks@5kbw.co.uk
Call Date: Oct 2002, Inner Temple
Qualifications: [LLB (Derby) LLM]

CARSS-FRISK MISS MONICA GUNNEL CONSTANCE QC (2001)

Blackstone Chambers
Blackstone House, Temple, London EC4Y 9BW, ☎ 020 7583 1770
✉ clerks@blackstonechambers.com
Call Date: July 1985, Gray's Inn
Qualifications: [LLB (Lond) BCL (Oxon)]
✉ monicacarss-frisk@blackstonechambers.com

CARTER MR DAVID JOHN

Doughty Street Chambers
53-54 Doughty Street, London WC1N 2LS, ☎ 020 7404 1313
✉ enquiries@doughtystreet.co.uk
Call Date: Nov 1971, Gray's Inn
Pupil Supervisor
Qualifications: [LLB]

CARTER MISS HOLLY EUGENIE SOPHIA

3 Dr Johnson's Buildings
Ground Floor, 3 Dr Johnson's Buildings, Temple, London EC4Y 7BA, ☎ 020 7353 4854
✉ clerks@3djb.co.uk
Call Date: Oct 1993, Inner Temple
Pupil Supervisor
Qualifications: [BA (Manch) CPE]
✉ hcarter@3djb.co.uk

CARTER MR JAMES MATTHEW OLIVER

KCH Garden Square
1 Oxford Street, Nottingham NG1 5BH, ☎ 0115 941 8851
✉ clerks@kchgardensquare.co.uk
Call Date: July 2010, Lincoln's Inn
Qualifications: [LLB (Leic) BCL (Oxon)]
✉ JCarter@kchgardensquare.co.uk

CARTER MISS LESLEY ANNE

Crystal Chambers
Chambers of Miss L A Carter, PO Box 7502, Chelmsford CM2 0WR, ☎ 01245 496515
✉ lesley@crystalchambers.co.uk
Call Date: Nov 1986, Inner Temple
Qualifications: [BA]
✉ lesley@crystalchambers.co.uk

CARTER MR MARTIN RICHARD

Kings Chambers
36 Young Street, Manchester M3 3FT, ☎ 0845 034 3444
✉ clerks@kingschambers.com
Kings Chambers
5 Park Square East, Leeds LS1 2NE, ☎ 0845 034 3444
✉ clerks@kingschambers.com
Kings Chambers
Embassy House, 60 Church Street, Birmingham B3 2DJ, ☎ 0845 034 3444
✉ clerks@kingschambers.com
Call Date: Nov 1992, Middle Temple
Pupil Supervisor
Qualifications: [MA(Oxon)]
✉ mcarter@kingschambers.com

CARTER MISS NATHALIE VERONIQUE

1 Gray's Inn Square
Ground Floor, 1 Gray's Inn Square, London WC1R 5AA, ☎ 020 7405 0001
Call Date: July 2004, Inner Temple

CARTER MR PETER QC (1995)

18 Red Lion Court
London EC4A 3EB, ☎ 020 7520 6000
✉ chambers@18rlc.co.uk
Park Court Chambers
16 Park Place, Leeds LS1 2SJ, ☎ 0113 243 3277
✉ clerks@parkcourtchambers.co.uk
18 Red Lion Court (Annexe)
Thornwood House, 102 New London Road, Chelmsford, Essex CM2 0RG, ☎ 01245 280880
Call Date: July 1974, Gray's Inn
Pupil Supervisor
Qualifications: [LLB (Lond)]
✉ peter.carter@18rlc.co.uk

CARTER MR RICHARD CHARLES

St Johns Buildings
24a - 28 St John Street, Manchester M3 4DJ, ☎ 0161 214 1500
✉ clerk@stjohnsbuildings.co.uk
St Johns Buildings
21 White Friars, Chester CH1 1NZ, ☎ 01244 323070
✉ clerk@stjohnsbuildings.co.uk

E

16 Winckley Square
Preston PR1 3JJ, ☎01772 256100
Call Date: Nov 1990, Inner Temple
Pupil Supervisor
Qualifications: [LLB (Hons)(Manch)]
clerk@stjohnsbuildings.co.uk, rcarter@stjohnsbuildings.co.uk

CARTER MISS ROSALYN FRANCES

St Philips Chambers
55 Temple Row, Birmingham B2 5LS,
☎0121 246 7000 ✉clerks@st-philips.com
Call Date: Nov 1994, Lincoln's Inn
Pupil Supervisor
Qualifications: [LLB (Hons)(Leeds)]
rcarter@st-philips.co.uk

CARTER MR THOMAS EDWARD

1 Hare Court
1 Hare Court, Temple, London EC4Y 7BE,
☎020 7797 7070 ✉clerks@1hc.com
Call Date: Oct 2001, Gray's Inn
Pupil Supervisor
Qualifications: [BA (Manch)]
carter@1hc.com

CARTER MR WILLIAM ANDREW

1 Paper Buildings
1st Floor, 1 Paper Buildings, Temple, London EC4Y 7EP, ☎020 7353 3728
✉clerks@onepaper.co.uk
Call Date: July 1989, Gray's Inn
Pupil Supervisor
Qualifications: [MA (Oxon)]
williamcarter@onepaper.co.uk

CARTER-MANNING MISS JENNIFER ANNE

Seven Bedford Row
7 Bedford Row, London WC1R 4BS,
☎020 7242 3555 ✉clerks@7br.co.uk
Call Date: Oct 1999, Middle Temple
Pupil Supervisor
Qualifications: [BA (Hons)(Oxon)]

CARTER-MANNING MR JEREMY JAMES QC (1993)

Furnival Chambers
32 Furnival Street, London EC4A 1JQ,
☎020 7405 3232
Call Date: Apr 1975, Middle Temple
clerks@furnivallaw.co.uk

CARTER-STEPHENSON MR GEORGE ANTHONY QC (1998)

25 Bedford Row
London WC1R 4HD, ☎020 7067 1500
✉clerks@25bedfordrow.com
Call Date: July 1975, Inner Temple
Qualifications: [LLB (Leeds)]
gcarter-stephenson@25bedfordrow.com

CARTMELL MR NICHOLAS JAMES

New Court Chambers
3 Broad Chare, Newcastle Upon Tyne NE1 3DQ, ☎0191 232 1980
✉clerks@newcourt-chambers.co.uk
Call Date: Oct 1990, Inner Temple
Qualifications: [LLB (Hons)]
nicholas.cartmell@newcourt-chambers.co.uk

CARTWRIGHT MR DAVID CRISPIAN HIMLEY

5 Pump Court
Ground Floor, 5 Pump Court, Temple, London EC4Y 7AP, ☎020 7353 2532
✉clerks@5pumpcourt.com
Call Date: Nov 1976, Middle Temple
Pupil Supervisor, Recorder
Qualifications: [MA (Oxon)]
crispiancartwright@5pumpcourt.com

CARTWRIGHT MR IVAN MATTHEW

KCH Garden Square
1 Oxford Street, Nottingham NG1 5BH,
☎0115 941 8851
✉clerks@kchgardensquare.co.uk
Call Date: Nov 1993, Gray's Inn
Qualifications: [LLB (Hons)]

CARTWRIGHT MR JAMES D'ARCY CAYLEY

10 King's Bench Walk
Ground Floor, 10 King's Bench Walk, Temple, London EC4Y 7EB, ☎020 7353 7742
✉Chambers@10kingsbenchwalk.co.uk
Call Date: Feb 1968, Gray's Inn
Pupil Supervisor
james.cartwright@10kingsbenchwalk.co.uk

CARTWRIGHT MR NICOLAS FREDERICK

St Philips Chambers
55 Temple Row, Birmingham B2 5LS,
☎0121 246 7000 ✉clerks@st-philips.com
Call Date: July 1986, Middle Temple
Recorder
Qualifications: [LLB (L'Pool)]
ncartwright@st-philips.co.uk

E

CARTWRIGHT MR RICHARD JOHN

Devereux Chambers
Queen Elizabeth Building, Temple, London
EC4Y 9BS, ☎ 020 7353 7534
✉ clerks@devchambers.co.uk
Call Date: Nov 1994, Inner Temple
Qualifications: [BA (Hons)(Manch) FCA]
✉ cartwright@devchambers.co.uk

CARTWRIGHT MISS SOPHIE PAMELA

Deans Court Chambers
24 St John Street, Manchester M3 4DF,
☎ 0161 214 6000 ✉ clerks@deanscourt.co.uk
Deans Court Chambers
101 Walker Street, Preston PR1 2RR,
☎ 01772 565 600
✉ preston@deanscourt.co.uk
Call Date: Oct 1998, Inner Temple
Qualifications: [LLB (Warw) MA]
✉ cartwright@deanscourt.co.uk

CARUS MR RODERICK QC (1990)

9 St John Street
Manchester M3 4DN, ☎ 0161 955 9000
✉ civilclerks@9sjs.com /
criminalclerks@9sjs.com
Bank House Chambers
Old Bank House, Hartshead, Sheffield S1 2EL,
☎ 0114 275 1223
✉ w.digby@bankhousechambers.co.uk
Call Date: Nov 1971, Gray's Inn
Recorder
Qualifications: [BA (Oxon)]

CARVALHO GOMES MISS ANA ALEXANDRA

St Albans Chambers
2 - 4 St Peter's Street, St Albans, Hertfordshire
AL1 3LF, ☎ 01727 843383
✉ clerks@stalbanschambers.com
Call Date: Oct 1996, Middle Temple
Qualifications: [LLB (Hons)(Wales) MA]
✉ acg@stalbanschambers.com

CARVILLE MR OWEN BRENDAN NEVILLE

Number 7 Harrington Street Chambers
7 Harrington Street, Liverpool L2 9YH,
☎ 0151 242 0707 ✉ clerks@7hs.co.uk
Call Date: July 1980, Inner Temple
Qualifications: [BA]
✉ brendan.carville@7hs.co.uk

CASE MISS JULIE

Exchange Chambers
One Derby Square, Derby Square, Liverpool
L2 9XX, ☎ 0151 236 7747
✉ info@exchangechambers.co.uk
Exchange Chambers
7 Ralli Courts, West Riverside, Manchester
M3 5FT, ☎ 0161 833 2722
Exchange Chambers
Oxford House, Oxford Row, Leeds LS1 3BE,
☎ 0113 203 1970
✉ spencer@exchangechambers.co.uk
Call Date: Oct 1990, Middle Temple
Pupil Supervisor
Qualifications: [LLB (Leics)]
✉ case@exchangechambers.co.uk

CASE MISS MAGDALEN MARY CLAIRE

St Johns Buildings
24a - 28 St John Street, Manchester M3 4DJ,
☎ 0161 214 1500
✉ clerk@stjohnsbuildings.co.uk
16 Winckley Square
Preston PR1 3JJ, ☎ 01772 256100
St Johns Buildings Liverpool
8th Floor India Buildings, Water Street,
Liverpool L2 0XG, ☎ 0151 243 6000
✉ clerk@stjohnsbuildings.co.uk
Call Date: Oct 1992, Middle Temple
Qualifications: [MA (Oxon) Dip Law]
✉ clerk@stjohnsbuildings.co.uk

CASE MR RICHARD JOHN

No5 Chambers
Greenwood House, 4-7 Salisbury Court,
London EC4Y 8AA, ☎ 0845 210 5555
No5 Chambers
38 Queen Square, Bristol BS1 4QS,
☎ 0845 210 5555
No5 Chambers
Fountain Court, Steelhouse Lane, Birmingham
B4 6DR, ☎ 0845 210 5555 ✉ info@no5.com
Call Date: Oct 1996, Middle Temple
Qualifications: [BA (Hons)(Cantab)]
✉ rjc@no5.com

CASELLA MR BARTHOLOMEW ROMOLO SOINI

23 Essex Street
London WC2R 3AA, ☎ 020 7413 0353
✉ clerks@23es.com
Call Date: Oct 1995, Lincoln's Inn
Qualifications: [LLB (Hons)(Midd)]
✉ BartCasella@23es.com

E

CASEMENT MR DAVID JOHN QC (2008)

Kings Chambers
36 Young Street, Manchester M3 3FT,
☎0845 034 3444
✉clerks@kingschambers.com
Kings Chambers
5 Park Square East, Leeds LS1 2NE,
☎0845 034 3444
✉clerks@kingschambers.com
Serle Court
6 New Square, Lincoln's Inn, London
WC2A 3QS, ☎020 7242 6105
✉clerks@serlecourt.co.uk
Call Date: Oct 1992, Middle Temple
Qualifications: [BA (Hons) (Oxon)]
dcasementqc@kingschambers.com

CASEY MR AIDAN PATRICK

3 Hare Court
3 Hare Court, Temple, London EC4Y 7BJ,
☎020 7415 7800 ✉clerks@3harecourt.com
Call Date: Nov 1992, Gray's Inn
Pupil Supervisor
Qualifications: [LLB]
aidancasey@3harecourt.com

CASEY MR BENJAMIN FRANCIS

Temple Garden Chambers
1 Harcourt Buildings, Temple, London
EC4Y 9DA, ☎020 7583 1315
✉clerks@tgchambers.com
Call Date: Oct 2000, Inner Temple
Qualifications: [BA (York) CPE (City)]
benjamincasey@tgchambers.com

CASEY MR DERMOT FINTAN

Coram Chambers
9-11 Fulwood Place, London WC1V 6HG,
☎020 7092 3700
✉mail@coramchambers.co.uk
Call Date: Nov 1994, Middle Temple
Pupil Supervisor
Qualifications: [BA (Hons) M Sc (Lond) CQSW Dip Law (Lond)]
dermot.casey@coramchambers.co.uk

CASEY MISS MELANIE ANNE

33 Bedford Row
London WC1R 4JH, ☎020 7242 6476
✉clerks@33bedfordrow.co.uk
Call Date: July 2008, Inner Temple
Qualifications: [MA (Oxon)]
clerks@33bedfordrow.co.uk

CASEY MR NOEL

18 Red Lion Court
London EC4A 3EB, ☎020 7520 6000
✉chambers@18rlc.co.uk
Call Date: Nov 1995, Lincoln's Inn
Pupil Supervisor
Qualifications: [BA (Hons)]

CASEY MR NOEL GAVIN

7 King's Bench Walk
Ground Floor, 7 King's Bench Walk, Temple,
London EC4Y 7DS, ☎020 7910 8300
✉clerks@7kbw.co.uk
Call Date: Oct 2005, Lincoln's Inn
Pupil Supervisor
Qualifications: [BA (Hons) (Oxon) ACA]
ncasey@7kbw.co.uk

CASEY MR PAUL JOSEPH

Chambers of Marion Smullen and Kerim Fuad QC
1 Inner Temple Lane, London EC4Y 1AE,
☎020 7427 4400 ✉clerks@1itl.com
Call Date: July 1999, Middle Temple
Qualifications: [BA (Hons)(Exon) Dip in Law]
clerks@1itl.com, paul.casey@1itl.com

CASEY MR PAUL THOMAS JOSEPH

Fountain Court Chambers
Fountain Court, Temple, London EC4Y 9DH,
☎020 7583 3335
✉chambers@fountaincourt.co.uk
Call Date: Oct 2002, Inner Temple
Qualifications: [BA (Cantab) MPhil (Cantab) CPE]
PC@fountaincourt.co.uk

CASHMAN MISS VANESSA JANE

12 King's Bench Walk
12 King's Bench Walk, Temple, London
EC4Y 7EL, ☎020 7583 0811
Call Date: July 2009, Lincoln's Inn
Qualifications: [BA (Oxon) CPE UCU]
cashman@12kbw.co.uk

CASON MR DAVID LEE

2 KBW Ipswich
1st Floor, Fisons House, 159 Princes Street,
Ipswich, Suffolk IP1 1QH, ☎01473 287518
✉kbwipswich@btconnect.com
Call Date: July 2003, Inner Temple
Qualifications: [BA MSc CPE PgDl]

E

CASPI MISS JACQUELINE ELISA

Principal Chambers
15 Lime Tree Walk, Sevenoaks, Kent
TN13 1YH, ☎0845 209 8080
Call Date: Oct 2010, Lincoln's Inn
Qualifications: [LLB (Lond) LLM]

CASSEL MISS BATHSHEBA ANNA

Walnut House
63 St. David's Hill, Exeter, Devon EX4 4DW,
☎01392 279751
✉clerks@walnuthouse.co.uk
Call Date: July 2005, Inner Temple
Qualifications: [BA (Manch) CPE (City)]

CASSERLEY MISS CATHERINE

Cloisters
1 Pump Court, Temple, London EC4Y 7AA,
☎020 7827 4000 ✉clerks@cloisters.com
Call Date: Feb 1991, Gray's Inn
Qualifications: [LLB (Leics) LLM]
✉cc@cloisters.com

CASSIDY MR FRANCIS JOHN JAMES

42 Bedford Row
London WC1R 4LL, ☎020 7831 0222
✉clerks@42br.com
Call Date: Nov 2000, Middle Temple
Qualifications: [LLB (Hons) Dip Law]
✉francis.cassidy@42br.com

CASSIDY MR PATRICK STEPHEN

Kenworthy's Chambers
Arlington House, Bloom Street, Salford,
Manchester M3 6AJ, ☎0161 832 4036
Call Date: July 1982, Lincoln's Inn
Pupil Supervisor
Qualifications: [BA (Hons)]
✉p.cassidy@kenworthysbarristers.co.uk

CASSIDY MISS SHEENA ANNE

3 PB Barristers
3 Paper Buildings, Temple, London EC4Y 7EU,
☎020 7583 8055
3 PB Barristers
Royal Talbot House, 2 Victoria Street, Bristol,
Avon BS1 6BB, ☎0117 928 1520
3 PB Barristers
4 St Peter Street, Winchester SO23 8BW,
☎01962 868884
✉clerks.winchester@3paper.co.uk
3 PB Barristers
23 Beaumont Street, Oxford OX1 2NP,
☎01865 793 736
3 PB Barristers
30 Christchurch Road, Bournemouth, Dorset
BH1 3PD, ☎01202 292102
✉clerks.bournemouth@3paper.co.uk
Call Date: Oct 2001, Inner Temple
Qualifications: [MA (Cantab)]

CASSIE MR IAIN CHARLES

Chambers of Mr I C Cassie
Brackens, Captains Row, Lymington,
Hampshire SO41 9RP,
☎020 7243 0316/07785 394253
Call Date: July 2003, Inner Temple
Qualifications: [BA (Lond) CPE (College of Law)]
✉iain.cassie@btopenworld.com, iain.cassie@btopenworld.com

CASTLE MR PETER BOLTON

13 Old Square Chambers
Ground Floor, 14 Old Square, Lincoln's Inn,
London WC2A 3UE, ☎020 7831 4445
✉clerks@13oldsquare.com
Call Date: July 1970, Middle Temple
Pupil Supervisor
Qualifications: [LCIA LMAA LLB (Lond) ADR]
✉petercastle@13oldsquare.com

CASTLE MR RICHARD DAVID NICHOLAS

1 KBW Chambers
1 King's Bench Walk, Temple, London
EC4Y 7DB, ☎020 7936 1500
✉clerks@1kbw.co.uk
King's Bench Chambers
174 High Street, Lewes BN7 1YE,
☎01273 402600
Call Date: Oct 1998, Gray's Inn
Pupil Supervisor
Qualifications: [LLB (Bris)]
✉rcastle@1kbw.co.uk

CASWELL MR BENJAMIN CECIL

No.6 Park Square
Leeds LS1 2LW, ☎0113 245 9763
✉Tim@no6.co.uk
Call Date: Oct 1993, Middle Temple
Qualifications: [BA (Hons)(Oxon) MA (Lond)]
✉caswell@no6.co.uk

E

CATCHPOLE MR STUART PAUL QC (2002)

39 Essex Street
London WC2R 3AT, ☎020 7832 1111
✉clerks@39essex.com
82 King Street
Manchester M2 4WQ, ☎0161 870 9969
Call Date: July 1987, Inner Temple
Recorder
Qualifications: [BA (Dunelm)]
stuart.catchpole@39essex.com

CATFORD MR GORDON BAXTER

Crown Office Chambers
2 Crown Office Row, Temple, London
EC4Y 7HJ, ☎020 7797 8100
✉mail@crownofficechambers.com
Call Date: July 1980, Lincoln's Inn
Pupil Supervisor
Qualifications: [LLB (Lond)]
catford@crownofficechambers.com

CATHERWOOD MR SHAEN MATTHEW STUART

Devereux Chambers
Queen Elizabeth Building, Temple, London
EC4Y 9BS, ☎020 7353 7534
✉clerks@devchambers.co.uk
Call Date: July 2000, Gray's Inn
Pupil Supervisor
Qualifications: [BA (Oxon)]
catherwood@devchambers.co.uk

CATTERMOLE MISS REBECCA ELKE

Tanfield Chambers
2-5 Warwick Court, London WC1R 5DJ,
☎020 7421 5300
✉clerks@tanfieldchambers.co.uk
Call Date: Oct 1999, Middle Temple
Qualifications: [BA (Hons)(Bris)]

CATTERMULL MISS EMMA JAYNE

East Anglian Chambers
Gresham House, 5 Museum Street, Ipswich,
Suffolk IP1 1HQ, ☎01473 214481
✉ipswich@ealaw.co.uk
East Anglian Chambers
140 New London Road, Chelmsford, Essex
CM2 0AW, ☎01473 214481
✉chelmsford@ealaw.co.uk
East Anglian Chambers
15 The Close, Norwich, Norfolk NR1 4DZ,
☎01473 214481 ✉norwich@ealaw.co.uk
Call Date: Oct 2004, Inner Temple
Qualifications: [LLB (Hons)]
emmacattermull@ealaw.co.uk

E

CATTON-NEWELL MS SALLY ELIZABETH

Trinity Chambers
Highfield House, Moulsham Street,
Chelmsford, Essex CM2 9AH,
☎01245 605040
✉clerks@trinitychambers.com
Call Date: July 2009, Gray's Inn
Qualifications: [BSc PgDL]

CAUDLE MR JOHN ARTHUR

2 Bedford Row
London WC1R 4BU, ☎020 7440 8888
✉clerks@2bedfordrow.co.uk
Call Date: Nov 1976, Middle Temple
Pupil Supervisor
Qualifications: [LLB (Lond)]
jcaudle@2bedfordrow.co.uk

CAULFIELD MS BARBARA MARY ELIZABETH

St Philips Chambers
55 Temple Row, Birmingham B2 5LS,
☎0121 246 7000 ✉clerks@st-philips.com
Call Date: Oct 1999, Inner Temple
Qualifications: [BSc (Hons)(Bris) CPE]
bcaulfield@st-philips.com

CAUN MR LAWRENCE

Lamb Chambers
Lamb Building, Elm Court, Temple, London
EC4Y 7AS, ☎020 7797 8300
✉info@lambchambers.co.uk
Call Date: Nov 1977, Lincoln's Inn
Pupil Supervisor
Qualifications: [MA (Oxon)]
lawrencecaun@lambchambers.co.uk

CAUSER MR JOHN CHARLES

23 Essex Street
London WC2R 3AA, ☎020 7413 0353
✉clerks@23es.com
Call Date: July 1979, Inner Temple
Qualifications: [BA (Lond)]
johncauser@23es.com

CAVANAGH MR JOHN PATRICK QC (2001)

11 King's Bench Walk
11 King's Bench Walk, Temple, London
EC4Y 7EQ, ☎020 7632 8500
✉clerksroom@11kbw.com
Call Date: Nov 1985, Middle Temple
Recorder
Qualifications: [MA (Oxon) LLM (Cantab)]
john.cavanagh@11kbw.com

CAVANAGH MISS LORRAINE

St Johns Buildings
24a - 28 St John Street, Manchester M3 4DJ,
☎ 0161 214 1500
✉ clerk@stjohnsbuildings.co.uk
St Johns Buildings
21 White Friars, Chester CH1 1NZ,
☎ 01244 323070
✉ clerk@stjohnsbuildings.co.uk
16 Winckley Square
Preston PR1 3JJ, ☎ 01772 256100
Call Date: July 2000, Gray's Inn
Qualifications: [LLB (Hons)(Manch)]

CAVE MR JEREMY STEPHEN

Crown Office Row Chambers
119 Church Street, Brighton, Sussex
BN1 1UD, ☎ 01273 625625
✉ clerks@1cor.com
1 Crown Office Row
1 Crown Office Row, Temple, London
EC4Y 7HH, ☎ 020 7797 7500
✉ mail@1cor.com
Call Date: Nov 1992, Middle Temple
Pupil Supervisor
Qualifications: [LLB (Hons) (Manch)]
🖃 jeremy.cave@1cor.com

CAVE MISS PATRICIA ANN

36 Bedford Row
London WC1R 4JH, ☎ 020 7421 8000
✉ chambers@36bedfordrow.co.uk
Call Date: Nov 1989, Middle Temple
Qualifications: [BA Hons (Manch) Dip Law]

CAVENDER MR DAVID JOHN QC (2010)

One Essex Court
Ground Floor, One Essex Court, Temple,
London EC4Y 9AR, ☎ 020 7583 2000
✉ clerks@oeclaw.co.uk
Call Date: July 1993, Middle Temple
Qualifications: [LLB (Lond)]
🖃 dcavender@oeclaw.co.uk

CAVENDER MS SUSAN PENELOPE

Guildhall Chambers
23 Broad Street, Bristol BS1 2HG,
☎ 0117 930 9000
✉ hoc@guildhallchambers.co.uk
Call Date: Oct 2004, Gray's Inn
Qualifications: [BA]
🖃 susan.cavender@guildhallchambers.co.uk

CAVIN MR PAUL RENE

Atkinson Bevan Chambers
1st Floor, 2 Harcourt Buildings, Temple,
London EC4Y 9DB, ☎ 020 7353 2112
✉ clerks@2hb.co.uk
Call Date: Nov 1995, Gray's Inn
Pupil Supervisor
Qualifications: [BA (E.Anglia)]
🖃 paul.cavin@2hb.co.uk

CAWS MR EIAN RICHARD EDWIN

Landmark Chambers
180 Fleet Street, London EC4A 2HG,
☎ 020 7430 1221
✉ clerks@landmarkchambers.co.uk
Call Date: Nov 1974, Inner Temple
Pupil Supervisor
Qualifications: [BA (Oxon)]
🖃 ecaws@landmarkchambers.co.uk

CAWSEY MR BARRY DONALD

Clerksroom (Taunton)
Equity House, Administration Centre,
Blackbrook Park Avenue, Taunton, Somerset
TA1 2PX, ☎ 0845 083 3000
✉ mail@clerksroom.com
Clerksroom (London)
3rd Floor, 218 Strand, London WC2R 1AT,
☎ 0845 083 3000 ✉ mail@clerksroom.com
Call Date: July 2001, Inner Temple
Qualifications: [BSc (Manch) CPE (Lond)]
🖃 Cawsey@clerksroom.com

CAWSEY MS LAURA

Chambers of Ian Macdonald QC
Garden Court North, 22 Oxford Court,
Manchester M2 3WQ, ☎ 0161 236 1840
✉ clerks@gcnchambers.co.uk
Call Date: Nov 2004, Lincoln's Inn
Qualifications: [BSc (Hons) PGDL]
🖃 clerks@gcnchambers.co.uk

CAWSON MR PETER MARK QC (2001)

Exchange Chambers
7 Ralli Courts, West Riverside, Manchester
M3 5FT, ☎ 0161 833 2722
Exchange Chambers
One Derby Square, Derby Square, Liverpool
L2 9XX, ☎ 0151 236 7747
✉ info@exchangechambers.co.uk
Exchange Chambers
Oxford House, Oxford Row, Leeds LS1 3BE,
☎ 0113 203 1970
✉ spencer@exchangechambers.co.uk
Call Date: July 1982, Lincoln's Inn
Recorder
Qualifications: [LLB]
🖃 cawsonqc@exchangechambers.co.uk

E

CAYFORD MR PHILIP JOHN BERKELEY QC (2002)

29 Bedford Row Chambers
London WC1R 4HE, ☎ 020 7404 1044
✉ clerks@29br.co.uk
Call Date: July 1975, Middle Temple
Qualifications: [LLB (Hons)]
✉ pcayford@29br.co.uk

CECIL MISS JOANNE MICHELLE

1 Pump Court
Elm Court, Temple, London EC4Y 7AB,
☎ 020 7842 7070
✉ (name)@pumpcourt.co.uk
Call Date: Nov 2005, Inner Temple
Qualifications: [LLB University of Wales Cardiff]
✉ jce@1pumpcourt.co.uk

CELIKOZ MISS TARA JADE

Eastbourne Chambers
5 Chiswick Place, Eastbourne, East Sussex
BN21 4NH, ☎ 01323 642102
✉ clerks@eastbournechambers.co.uk
Call Date: Oct 2007, Middle Temple
Qualifications: [LLB (Hons) (Sussex)]

CELLAN-JONES MR DEINIOL JAMES

1 KBW Chambers
1 King's Bench Walk, Temple, London
EC4Y 7DB, ☎ 020 7936 1500
✉ clerks@1kbw.co.uk
King's Bench Chambers
174 High Street, Lewes BN7 1YE,
☎ 01273 402600
Call Date: Nov 1988, Middle Temple
Pupil Supervisor
Qualifications: [BA (Oxon)]
✉ dcellan-jones@1kbw.co.uk

CHACKO MR THOMAS JOSEPH

Pump Court Tax Chambers
16 Bedford Row, London WC1R 4EF,
☎ 020 7414 8080 ✉ clerks@pumptax.com
Call Date: Nov 2007, Inner Temple
Qualifications: [BA (Cantab)]
✉ tchacko@pumptax.com

Types of work: Capital tax, Corporation tax, Customs, Excise, Income tax, National Insurance, Private client, Stamp duty, Tax investigations, Tax tribunal, Trusts, VAT

CHACKSFIELD MR MARK ANDREW

8 New Square
8 New Square, Lincoln's Inn, London
WC2A 3QP, ☎ 020 7405 4321
✉ clerks@8newsquare.co.uk
Call Date: Oct 1999, Middle Temple
Pupil Supervisor
Qualifications: [BA (Hons)(Cantab)]
✉ mark.chacksfield@8newsquare.co.uk

Types of work: Breach of confidence, Competition law, Copyright, Data protection, EC competition law, Entertainment, Franchising, Information technology, Intellectual property, Malicious falsehood, Media and entertainment, Patents, Trade secrets, Trademarks

CHADWICK MR DANIEL JAMES

25 Bedford Row
London WC1R 4HD, ☎ 020 7067 1500
✉ clerks@25bedfordrow.com
Call Date: Oct 2006, Middle Temple
Qualifications: [LLB (Hons)]
✉ dchadwick@25bedfordrow.com

CHADWICK MISS JOANNA CERIDWEN

No5 Chambers
Fountain Court, Steelhouse Lane, Birmingham
B4 6DR, ☎ 0845 210 5555 ✉ info@no5.com
No5 Chambers
Greenwood House, 4-7 Salisbury Court,
London EC4Y 8AA, ☎ 0845 210 5555
No5 Chambers
38 Queen Square, Bristol BS1 4QS,
☎ 0845 210 5555
Call Date: Nov 1988, Middle Temple
Qualifications: [LLB (Leeds)]
✉ jcc@no5.com

CHAFFIN-LAIRD MISS OLIVIA CAROLYN

No5 Chambers
Fountain Court, Steelhouse Lane, Birmingham
B4 6DR, ☎ 0845 210 5555 ✉ info@no5.com
No5 Chambers
Greenwood House, 4-7 Salisbury Court,
London EC4Y 8AA, ☎ 0845 210 5555
No5 Chambers
38 Queen Square, Bristol BS1 4QS,
☎ 0845 210 5555
Call Date: July 2001, Gray's Inn
Qualifications: [LLB (Nott'm)]

E

CHAGGAR MRS MANINDER

No 8 Chambers
8 Fountain Court, Steelhouse Lane, Birmingham B4 6DR, ☎ 0121 236 5514
✉ clerks@no8chambers.co.uk
Call Date: Nov 1992, Inner Temple
Qualifications: [LLB]

CHAISTY MR PAUL QC (2001)

Kings Chambers
36 Young Street, Manchester M3 3FT, ☎ 0845 034 3444
✉ clerks@kingschambers.com
Kings Chambers
5 Park Square East, Leeds LS1 2NE, ☎ 0845 034 3444
✉ clerks@kingschambers.com
Kings Chambers
Embassy House, 60 Church Street, Birmingham B3 2DJ, ☎ 0845 034 3444
✉ clerks@kingschambers.com
Serle Court
6 New Square, Lincoln's Inn, London WC2A 3QS, ☎ 020 7242 6105
✉ clerks@serlecourt.co.uk
Call Date: July 1982, Lincoln's Inn
Recorder
Qualifications: [LLB (Notts) BCL (Oxon)]
pchaisty@kingschambers.com

CHAIZE MR TRISTAN PAUL

5 Pump Court
Ground Floor, 5 Pump Court, Temple, London EC4Y 7AP, ☎ 020 7353 2532
✉ clerks@5pumpcourt.com
Call Date: Nov 1977, Inner Temple
Pupil Supervisor
tristanchaize@5pumpcourt.com

CHAKMAKJIAN MR ALEX

1 Mitre Court Buildings
1 Mitre Court Buildings, Temple, London EC4Y 7BS, ☎ 020 7452 8900
✉ clerks@1mcb.com
Call Date: Oct 2009, Middle Temple
Qualifications: [LLB (Hons) (So'ton) LLM (Lond)]
clerks@1mcb.com

CHAKRAVARTY MISS ANUSHKA

42 Bedford Row
London WC1R 4LL, ☎ 020 7831 0222
✉ clerks@42br.com
Call Date: Oct 2010, Lincoln's Inn
Qualifications: [BA (Cantab)]

CHALK MR ALEXANDER JOHN GERVASE

6 King's Bench Walk
Ground Floor, 6 King's Bench Walk, Temple, London EC4Y 7DR, ☎ 020 7583 0410
✉ clerks@6kbw.com
Call Date: Oct 2001, Middle Temple
Qualifications: [BA (Hons) (Oxon) Dip Law]

CHALKLEY MISS REBECCA ELIZABETH

18 Red Lion Court
London EC4A 3EB, ☎ 020 7520 6000
✉ chambers@18rlc.co.uk
18 Red Lion Court (Annexe)
Thornwood House, 102 New London Road, Chelmsford, Essex CM2 0RG, ☎ 01245 280880
Call Date: Oct 1999, Middle Temple
Qualifications: [BA (Hons)]
rebecca.chalkley@18rlc.co.uk

CHALLACOMBE MR THOMAS HENRY

King's Bench and Godolphin (KBG)Chambers
115 North Hill, Plymouth, Devon PL4 8JY, ☎ 01752 221551
✉ clerks@kbgchambers.co.uk
Call Date: July 2006, Gray's Inn
Qualifications: [LLB (Derby)]
thomas.challacombe@kingsbenchchambers.co.uk

CHALLENGER MR COLIN WESTCOTT

Lamb Chambers
Lamb Building, Elm Court, Temple, London EC4Y 7AS, ☎ 020 7797 8300
✉ info@lambchambers.co.uk
Call Date: Nov 1970, Inner Temple
Pupil Supervisor
Qualifications: [LLB (Lond) MBA (Berkeley)]
colinchallenger@lambchambers.co.uk

CHALLINOR MR JONATHAN GERALD

Cornwall Street Chambers
85-87 Cornwall Street, Birmingham B3 3BY, ☎ 0121 233 7500
✉ clerks@cornwallstreet.co.uk
Call Date: Nov 1998, Inner Temple
Qualifications: [BA (Oxon)]
jonathan.challinor@cornwallstreet.co.uk

E

CHALLINOR MR THOMAS MICHAEL

Citadel Chambers
The Citadel, 190 Corporation Street, Birmingham B4 6QD, ☎0121 233 8500
✉clerks@citadelchambers.com
Call Date: July 2004, Gray's Inn
Qualifications: [LLB (Sheff)]
clerks@citadelchambers.com

CHALMERS MISS SUZANNE FRANCES

Crown Office Chambers
2 Crown Office Row, Temple, London EC4Y 7HJ, ☎020 7797 8100
✉mail@crownofficechambers.com
Call Date: Oct 1995, Gray's Inn
Pupil Supervisor
Qualifications: [MA]
chalmers@crownofficechambers.com

CHALONER MR MARK

42 Bedford Row
London WC1R 4LL, ☎020 7831 0222
✉clerks@42br.com
Call Date: July 2002, Middle Temple
Qualifications: [BA (Hons) (Cantab)]

CHAMBERLAIN MS EMMA JANE MARY

Pump Court Tax Chambers
16 Bedford Row, London WC1R 4EF, ☎020 7414 8080 ✉clerks@pumptax.com
Call Date: Nov 1998, Lincoln's Inn
Qualifications: [BA (Hons)(Oxon)]
echamberlain@pumptax.com

Types of work: Offshore trust litigation, Private client, Succession, Tax, Trust litigation, Trusts

CHAMBERLAIN MR KEVIN JOHN

York Chambers
Rotterdam House, 116 The Quayside, Newcastle Upon Tyne NE1 3DY, ☎0191 206 4677
Dere Street Barristers
14 Toft Green, York YO1 6JT, ☎0844 3351551
✉clerks@derestreet.co.uk
Call Date: July 1965, Inner Temple
Qualifications: [LLB (Lond)]

CHAMBERLAIN MR MARTIN DANIEL

Brick Court Chambers
7-8 Essex Street, London WC2R 3LD, ☎020 7379 3550 ✉clerks@brickcourt.co.uk
Call Date: Oct 1997, Middle Temple
Pupil Supervisor
Qualifications: [BA (Hons)(Oxon) CPE (Lond) BCL (Oxon)]
Martin.Chamberlain@Brickcourt.co.uk

CHAMBERLAYNE MR PATRICK ALLIN GERRARD TANKERVI QC (2010)

29 Bedford Row Chambers
London WC1R 4HE, ☎020 7404 1044
✉clerks@29br.co.uk
Call Date: Nov 1992, Inner Temple
Qualifications: [BA (Hons)(Cantab) MA (Cantab)]
pchamberlayne@29br.co.uk

CHAMBERS MR ADAM RUSHBY

12 King's Bench Walk
12 King's Bench Walk, Temple, London EC4Y 7EL, ☎020 7583 0811
Call Date: July 1989, Middle Temple
Pupil Supervisor
Qualifications: [BA (Leeds) Dip Law]
achambers@12kbw.co.uk

CHAMBERS MR DOMINIC KERN QC (2008)

Maitland Chambers
7 Stone Buildings, Lincoln's Inn, London WC2A 3SZ, ☎020 7406 1200
✉clerks@maitlandchambers.com
Call Date: Nov 1987, Gray's Inn
Qualifications: [LLB (Lond)]
dchambers@maitlandchambers.com

CHAMBERS MISS GAYNOR MARIE

Keating Chambers
15 Essex Street, London WC2R 3AA, ☎020 7544 2600
✉clerks@keatingchambers.com
Call Date: Nov 1998, Middle Temple
Pupil Supervisor
Qualifications: [BSc (Hons)]
gchambers@keatingchambers.com

CHAMBERS MR JONATHAN

Quadrant Chambers
Quadrant House, 10 Fleet Street, London EC4Y 1AU, ☎020 7583 4444
✉info@quadrantchambers.com
Call Date: Oct 1996, Inner Temple
Qualifications: [BA(Oxon) CPLS BCL (Oxon)]

CHAMBERS MS RACHEL ELIZABETH

Cloisters
1 Pump Court, Temple, London EC4Y 7AA, ☎020 7827 4000 ✉clerks@cloisters.com
Call Date: Oct 2002, Inner Temple
Qualifications: [MA (Oxon)]

CHAMPION MISS DEBORAH CURTIS

2 Bedford Row
London WC1R 4BU, ☎020 7440 8888
✉clerks@2bedfordrow.co.uk
Call Date: July 1970, Gray's Inn
✉dchampion@2bedfordrow.co.uk

CHAMPION MISS KARINA ELIZABETH

Oriel Chambers
14 Water Street, Liverpool, Merseyside L2 8TD, ☎0151 236 7191
✉clerks@orielchambers.co.uk
Oriel Chambers
18 Ribblesdale Place, Preston PR1 3NA, ☎01772 254 764
✉clerks@oriel-chambers.co.uk
Call Date: Oct 2005, Inner Temple
Qualifications: [BA Exeter College University of Oxford CPE Col]
✉karina.champion@orielchambers.co.uk

CHAMPION MISS ROWENA ELIZABETH

Field Court Chambers
5 Field Court, Gray's Inn, London WC1R 5EF, ☎020 7405 6114 ✉clerks@fieldcourt.co.uk
Call Date: Feb 1990, Middle Temple
Qualifications: [BSc]
✉rowena.champion@fieldcourt.co.uk

CHAN MISS ABBERLAINE DIANNE PAO CHE

9-12 Bell Yard
London WC2A 2JR, ☎020 7400 1800
✉clerks@9-12bellyard.com
Call Date: July 1979, Gray's Inn
Qualifications: [LLB (Bris)]
✉d.chan@9-12bellyard.com

CHAN MISS EVONNIE HEUNG YEN

18 St John Street
Manchester M3 4EA, ☎0161 278 1800
✉clerks@18sjs.com
Call Date: Nov 2006, Middle Temple
Qualifications: [BA (Hons) (Oxon)]

CHAN MISS RACHEL SIU YEE

Stour Chambers
Mill Studio, 17a Stour Street, Canterbury, Kent CT1 2NR, ☎01227 764899
✉clerks@stourchambers.co.uk
Call Date: July 2004, Lincoln's Inn
Qualifications: [LLB]

CHAN MISS REBECCA CHUI YEE

Arden Chambers
20 Bloomsbury Square, London WC1A 2NS, ☎020 7242 4244
✉clerks@ardenchambers.com
Call Date: Nov 2006, Middle Temple
Qualifications: [LLB (Hons) (Sussex)]

CHAN MISS SUSAN

13 King's Bench Walk
13 King's Bench Walk, Temple, London EC4Y 7EN, ☎020 7353 7204
✉clerks@13kbw.co.uk
13 KBW
32 Beaumont Street, Oxford OX1 2NP, ☎01865 311066 ✉clerks@13kbw.co.uk
Call Date: Oct 1994, Gray's Inn
Qualifications: [BA (Hons)(Oxon)]
✉schan@13kbw.co.uk

CHAN MISS WING YAN

New Court
Ground Floor, New Court, Temple, London EC4Y 9BE, ☎020 7583 5123
✉clerks@newcourtchambers.com
Call Date: Mar 2002, Lincoln's Inn
Qualifications: [LLB (Hons) LLM]

CHAND MR RAGVEER

Charter Chambers
33 John Street, London WC1N 2AT, ☎020 7618 4400
✉clerks@charterchambers.com
Call Date: Nov 1994, Lincoln's Inn
Pupil Supervisor
Qualifications: [LLB (Hons)(Wolves)]
✉rag.chand@charterchambers.com

CHANDARANA MR YOGAIN JITENDRA

Nine Bedford Row
9 Bedford Row, London WC1R 4AZ, ☎020 7489 2727
✉clerks@9bedfordrow.co.uk
Call Date: Oct 1997, Lincoln's Inn
Qualifications: [LLB (Hons)(Lond)]
✉yogainchandarana@9bedfordrow.co.uk

CHANDLER MR ALEXANDER CHARLES ROSS

1 Garden Court Family Law Chambers
Ground Floor, One Garden Court, Temple, London EC4Y 9BJ, ☎020 7797 7900
✉clerks@1gc.com
Call Date: Oct 1995, Middle Temple
Pupil Supervisor
Qualifications: [MA (Oxon) Dip Law (Lond)]
✉chandler@1gc.com

E

CHANDLER MISS KATE

12 King's Bench Walk
12 King's Bench Walk, Temple, London EC4Y 7EL, ☎ 020 7583 0811
Call Date: Oct 1990, Inner Temple
Qualifications: [LLB (Lond)]

CHANDRAN MISS PAROSHA

1 Pump Court
Elm Court, Temple, London EC4Y 7AB, ☎ 020 7842 7070
✉ (name)@pumpcourt.co.uk
Call Date: Oct 1997, Lincoln's Inn
Qualifications: [LLB (Hons) LLM (Lond) Dip Human Rights (Germany)]
pch@1pumpcourt.co.uk

CHANNER MR BENJAMIN CHARLES

5 Pump Court
Ground Floor, 5 Pump Court, Temple, London EC4Y 7AP, ☎ 020 7353 2532
✉ clerks@5pumpcourt.com
Call Date: July 2008, Middle Temple
Qualifications: [BA (Hons) (B'ham) PgDl (B'ham) LLB (B'ham)]
clerks@5pumpcourt.com

CHANNON MISS REBECCA ANNE

Dyers Chambers
35 Bedford Row, London WC1R 4JH, ☎ 020 7404 1881
✉ admin@dyerschambers.com
Call Date: July 2007, Middle Temple
Qualifications: [LLB (Bris) LLM (Bris)]
rebecca.channion@dyerschambers.com

CHANTEAU MS DIANE HELENE GENEVIEVE MARJORI

Staple Inn Chambers
1st Floor, 9 Staple Inn, Holborn Bars, London WC1V 7QH, ☎ 020 7242 5240
✉ clerks@stapleinn.co.uk
Call Date: Oct 1997, Middle Temple
Qualifications: [LLB (Hons)]

CHAPLIN MR ADRIAN ROLAND

9-12 Bell Yard
London WC2A 2JR, ☎ 020 7400 1800
✉ clerks@9-12bellyard.com
Call Date: Oct 1990, Gray's Inn
Pupil Supervisor
Qualifications: [BA (Cantab) MA (London)]
a.chaplin@9-12bellyard.com

CHAPLIN MISS SOPHIE ESTHER

4 King's Bench Walk
2nd Floor, 4 King's Bench Walk, Temple, London EC4Y 7DL, ☎ 020 7822 7000
✉ clerks@4kbw.co.uk
Call Date: Oct 2007, Middle Temple
Qualifications: [LLB (Hons) (Nott'm)]

CHAPMAN MISS CLAIRE LOUISE

St Ive's Chambers
Whittall Street, Birmingham B4 6DH, ☎ 0121 236 0863
✉ clerks@stiveschambers.co.uk
Call Date: Nov 2001, Middle Temple
Qualifications: [BA (Hons)(Leeds)]
claire.chapman@stiveschambers.co.uk

CHAPMAN MRS DAWN LILLIAN

Chambers of Mr Ami Feder
Ground Floor, Lamb Building, Temple, London EC4Y 7AS, ☎ 020 7797 7788
✉ clerks@lambbuilding.co.uk
Chambers of Mr Ami Feder
Ground Floor, Lamb Building, Temple, London EC4Y 7AS, ☎ 020 7797 7788
✉ clerks@lambbuilding.co.uk
Call Date: Oct 2001, Middle Temple
Qualifications: [LLB (Hons)]

CHAPMAN MISS GEMMA RENNAI ALICE

Regency Chambers
45 Priestgate, Peterborough PE1 1LB, ☎ 01733 315215
✉ clerks@regencychambers.law.co.uk
Regency Chambers
Sheraton House, Castle Park, Cambridge CB3 0AX, ☎ 01223 301517
Call Date: Mar 2002, Lincoln's Inn
Qualifications: [LLB (Hons)]
clerks@regencychambers.law.co.uk

CHAPMAN MR GRAHAM ANDREW

Four New Square
Four New Square, Lincoln's Inn, London WC2A 3RJ, ☎ 020 7822 2000
✉ barristers@4newsquare.com
Call Date: Oct 1998, Inner Temple
Pupil Supervisor
Qualifications: [BA (Oxon)]
g.chapman@4newsquare.com

CHAPMAN MISS HELEN CLARE

37 Park Square Chambers
37 Park Square, Leeds LS1 2NY, ☎ 0113 243 9422 ✉ chambers@no37.co.uk
Call Date: July 2006, Middle Temple
Qualifications: [BA (Hons) (Cantab)]

CHAPMAN MR JEFFREY PAUL QC (2010)

Fountain Court Chambers
Fountain Court, Temple, London EC4Y 9DH,
☎ 020 7583 3335
✉ chambers@fountaincourt.co.uk
Call Date: Nov 1989, Middle Temple
Pupil Supervisor
Qualifications: [BA (Hons) (Sussex) LLM (Cantab)]
✉ jpc@fountaincourt.co.uk

CHAPMAN MR JOHN FARRAR

Pump Court Chambers
Upper Ground Floor, 3 Pump Court, Temple, London EC4Y 7AJ, ☎ 020 7353 0711
✉ clerks@3pumpcourt.com
Pump Court Chambers
5 Temple Chambers, Temple Street, Swindon SN1 1SQ, ☎ 01793 539899
✉ clerks@3pumpcourt.com
Pump Court Chambers
31 Southgate Street, Winchester, Hampshire SO23 9EB, ☎ 01962 868 161
✉ clerks@3pumpcourt.com
Call Date: July 2003, Lincoln's Inn
Pupil Supervisor
Qualifications: [Dip Law BA (Hons) (Lond)]
✉ jc@3pumpcourt.com

CHAPMAN MISS JULIET PHOEBE

Chambers of Mr Ami Feder
Ground Floor, Lamb Building, Temple, London EC4Y 7AS, ☎ 020 7797 7788
✉ clerks@lambbuilding.co.uk
Chambers of Mr Ami Feder
Ground Floor, Lamb Building, Temple, London EC4Y 7AS, ☎ 020 7797 7788
✉ clerks@lambbuilding.co.uk
Call Date: Oct 2009, Lincoln's Inn
Qualifications: [LLB (Bris)]

CHAPMAN MR MATTHEW JAMES

1 Chancery Lane
London WC2A 1LF, ☎ 0845 634 6666
✉ clerks@1chancerylane.com
Call Date: Oct 1994, Gray's Inn
Pupil Supervisor
Qualifications: [LLB LLM]
✉ mchapman@1chancerylane.com

CHAPMAN MR NICHOLAS

9-12 Bell Yard
London WC2A 2JR, ☎ 020 7400 1800
✉ clerks@9-12bellyard.com
Call Date: Nov 2001, Middle Temple
Qualifications: [LLB (Hons)]
✉ n.chapman@9-12bellyard.com

CHAPMAN MR NICHOLAS JOHN

29 Bedford Row Chambers
London WC1R 4HE, ☎ 020 7404 1044
✉ clerks@29br.co.uk
Call Date: Oct 1990, Inner Temple
Pupil Supervisor
Qualifications: [BSc (Lond) Dip Law (Lond)]
✉ nchapman@29br.co.uk

CHAPMAN MS REBECCA KATE

Tooks Chambers
81 Farringdon Street, London EC4A 4BL,
☎ 020 7842 7575 ✉ clerks@tooks.co.uk
Call Date: Nov 1990, Inner Temple
Pupil Supervisor
Qualifications: [BA (York) Dip Law]
✉ rebecca.chapman@tooks.co.uk

CHAPMAN MR RICHARD HAROLD

18 St John Street
Manchester M3 4EA, ☎ 0161 278 1800
✉ clerks@18sjs.com
Call Date: Oct 1998, Gray's Inn
Pupil Supervisor
Qualifications: [BA (Oxon)]
✉ rchapman@18sjs.com

CHAPMAN MR RUPERT LEANDER

Southernhay Chambers
33 Southernhay East, Exeter EX1 1NX,
☎ 01392 255777
✉ clerks@southernhaychambers.co.uk
Call Date: Oct 2000, Inner Temple
Qualifications: [LLB (Exon)]

CHAPMAN MS TRACY

Coram Chambers
9-11 Fulwood Place, London WC1V 6HG,
☎ 020 7092 3700
✉ mail@coramchambers.co.uk
Call Date: July 2009, Middle Temple
Qualifications: [BA (Hons) (B'ham) MSc (Oxon) Grad Dip Law (Lond)]
✉ tracy.chapman@coramchambers.co.uk

E

CHAPMAN MR VIVIAN ROBERT QC (2006)

9 Stone Buildings
Lincoln's Inn, London WC2A 3NN,
☎020 7404 5055
✉clerks@9stonebuildings.com
New Street Chambers
2 New Street, Leicester LE1 5NA,
☎0116 262 5906 ✉clerks@2newstreet.co.uk
Call Date: July 1970, Middle Temple
Qualifications: [MA LLM (Cantab)]
✉clerks@9stonebuildings.com

Fax: 020 7405 1551
Other comms: clerks@9stonebuildings.com

Types of work: Boundaries, Chancery (general), Chancery (land law), Charities, Commercial property, Common land, Compulsory Purchase, Conveyancing, Damages, Equity, Family provision, Highways, Land compensation, Landlord and tenant, Lands Tribunal, Markets and fairs, Mineral rights, Mining, Mortgages, Partnerships, Professional negligence, Public inquiries, Real property, Restitution, Rights of light, Rights of way, School sites, Succession, Title to land, Trust litigation, Trusts, Water, Wills

E

CHAPMAN MR WILLIAM WAKEFIELD

Seven Bedford Row
7 Bedford Row, London WC1R 4BS,
☎020 7242 3555 ✉clerks@7br.co.uk
Call Date: July 2003, Gray's Inn
Pupil Supervisor
Qualifications: [MA (Cantab)]
✉wchapman@7br.co.uk

CHAPPLE MR JAMES MALCOLM DUNDAS

New Square Chambers
12 New Square, Lincoln's Inn, London WC2A 3SW, ☎020 7419 8000
✉robin.hollington@newsquarechambers.co.uk
Call Date: Nov 1975, Gray's Inn
Pupil Supervisor
Qualifications: [BSc (Hons) FCIArb]
✉malcolm.chapple@newsquarechambers.co.uk

CHARALAMBIDES MR LEONIDAS

Francis Taylor Building
Inner Temple, London EC4Y 7BY,
☎020 7353 8415 ✉clerks@ftb.eu.com
Call Date: July 1998, Inner Temple
Qualifications: [BA (Lond) MA (Lond)]

CHARBIT MISS VALERIE JUDITH

2 Bedford Row
London WC1R 4BU, ☎020 7440 8888
✉clerks@2bedfordrow.co.uk
Call Date: Oct 1992, Middle Temple
Pupil Supervisor
Qualifications: [LLB (Hons) (Sheff)]

CHARKHAM MR GRAHAM HAROLD

20 Essex Street
London WC2R 3AL, ☎020 7842 1200
✉clerks@20essexst.com
Call Date: May 1993, Inner Temple
Qualifications: [BSc (Bris)]
✉clerks@20essexst.com

CHARLES MR HENRY FREDERICK

12 King's Bench Walk
12 King's Bench Walk, Temple, London EC4Y 7EL, ☎020 7583 0811
Call Date: Nov 1987, Inner Temple
Pupil Supervisor
Qualifications: [LLB LLM (Lond)]
✉Charles@12kbw.co.uk

CHARLES MS KATRINA SKEVI

Farringdon Chambers
180 Bermondsey Street, London SE1 3TQ,
☎020 7089 5700
Call Date: Oct 1999, Inner Temple
Qualifications: [LLB (Lond)]
✉katrinacharles@farringdon-law.co.uk

CHARLES MR SIMON WILLIAM EDWARD

18 St John Street
Manchester M3 4EA, ☎0161 278 1800
✉clerks@18sjs.com
Call Date: July 2004, Lincoln's Inn
Qualifications: [LLB Hons (Nott'm)]

CHARLESWORTH-JONES DR STEPHEN GRANT

Cornwall Street Chambers
85-87 Cornwall Street, Birmingham B3 3BY,
☎0121 233 7500
✉clerks@cornwallstreet.co.uk
Call Date: July 2009, Middle Temple
Qualifications: [BMed (Manch) LLDip (Wolves)]

CHARLTON MR ALEXANDER MURRAY QC (2008)

4 Pump Court
4 Pump Court, Temple, London EC4Y 7AN,
☎020 7842 5555
✉chambers@4pumpcourt.com
Call Date: July 1983, Middle Temple
Qualifications: [MA (Hons) (St Andrews) Dip Law (City)]
✉acharlton@4pumpcourt.com

CHARLTON MISS JUDITH ANNE DOROTHY

New Court
Ground Floor, New Court, Temple, London EC4Y 9BE, ☎020 7583 5123
✉clerks@newcourtchambers.com
Call Date: Nov 1991, Inner Temple
Pupil Supervisor
Qualifications: [LLB (Lond)]
✉jcharlton@newcourtchambers.net

CHARLTON MR TIMOTHY ROGER QC (1993)

Brick Court Chambers
7-8 Essex Street, London WC2R 3LD,
☎020 7379 3550 ✉clerks@brickcourt.co.uk
Call Date: Nov 1974, Inner Temple
Qualifications: [BA (Oxon)]
✉Timothy.Charlton@Brickcourt.co.uk

CHARLWOOD MR SPIKE LLEWELLYN

Hailsham Chambers
Ground Floor, 4 Paper Buildings, Temple, London EC4Y 7EX, ☎020 7643 5000
✉clerks@hailshamchambers.com
Call Date: Nov 1994, Inner Temple
Pupil Supervisor
Qualifications: [BA (Law) MA (Cantab)]
✉spike.charlwood@hailshamchambers.com

CHARMAN MR ANDREW JULIAN

St Philips Chambers
55 Temple Row, Birmingham B2 5LS,
☎0121 246 7000 ✉clerks@st-philips.com
Selborne Chambers
10 Essex Street, London WC2R 3AA,
☎020 7420 9500
✉clerks@selbornechambers.co.uk
Call Date: Nov 1994, Lincoln's Inn
Qualifications: [MA (Cantab) MCIArb]
✉ac@st-philips.co.uk

CHARNLEY MISS BETHAN REBECCA

Nine Bedford Row
9 Bedford Row, London WC1R 4AZ,
☎020 7489 2727
✉clerks@9bedfordrow.co.uk
Call Date: Oct 2007, Lincoln's Inn
Qualifications: [BA (Oxon)]
✉bethan.charnley@9bedfordrow.co.uk

CHASEMORE MISS CATHERINE MARGARET

1 High Pavement
Nottingham NG1 1HF, ☎0115 941 8218
✉clerks@1highpavement.co.uk
Call Date: Oct 2004, Lincoln's Inn
Qualifications: [LLB (Hons) Exeter]

CHATAWAY MR BENJAMIN THOMAS MARY

Doughty Street Chambers
53-54 Doughty Street, London WC1N 2LS,
☎020 7404 1313
✉enquiries@doughtystreet.co.uk
Call Date: Nov 1995, Lincoln's Inn
Qualifications: [BA (Hons)]

CHATTERJEE MISS ADREEJA JULIA

No5 Chambers
Fountain Court, Steelhouse Lane, Birmingham B4 6DR, ☎0845 210 5555 ✉info@no5.com
No5 Chambers
Greenwood House, 4-7 Salisbury Court, London EC4Y 8AA, ☎0845 210 5555
No5 Chambers
38 Queen Square, Bristol BS1 4QS,
☎0845 210 5555
Call Date: Nov 1997, Gray's Inn
Qualifications: [BA (Cantab)]
✉ach@no5.com

CHATTERJEE DR CHARLES

Temple Court Chambers
2nd Floor, 2 Dr Johnson's Building, Temple, London EC4Y 7AY, ☎020 7353 7888
✉clerks@templecourt.co.uk
Call Date: Nov 1992, Inner Temple
Qualifications: [LLB PhD LLM LLM]
✉clerks@templecourt.co.uk

CHATTERJEE MISS MIRA

4 Brick Court
4 Brick Court, Temple, London EC4Y 9AD,
☎020 7832 3200 ✉clerks@4bc.co.uk
Call Date: Nov 1973, Middle Temple
Pupil Supervisor
✉mira.chatterjee@4bc.co.uk

E

CHATTERJEE MR RANGAN NARAYAN

4 Pump Court
4 Pump Court, Temple, London EC4Y 7AN,
☎020 7842 5555
✉chambers@4pumpcourt.com
Call Date: July 2004, Lincoln's Inn
Qualifications: [MA (Cantab) MPhil (Cantab) PGDL]
✉rchatterjee@4pumpcourt.com

CHATTERTON MR MARK

Number 7 Harrington Street Chambers
7 Harrington Street, Liverpool L2 9YH,
☎0151 242 0707 ✉clerks@7hs.co.uk
Call Date: July 1983, Gray's Inn
Qualifications: [LLB (L'Pool)]
✉mark.chatterton@7hs.co.uk

CHAUDHRY DR FAROOQ AHMAD

25 Springwater Avenue
25 Springwater Avenue, Holcombe Brook, Bury, Lancashire BL0 9RH, ☎01204 883 630
✉dr.f.chaudhry@hotmail.co.uk
Call Date: July 1970, Lincoln's Inn
Qualifications: [Ph D LLM]

E

CHAUDHRY MISS MEHVISH

Renaissance Chambers
5th Floor, Gray's Inn Chambers, Gray's Inn, London WC1R 5JA, ☎020 7404 1111
✉clerks@renaissancechambers.co.uk
Call Date: Oct 2008, Lincoln's Inn
Qualifications: [LLB (Lond) LLM (Lond)]
✉mc2@renaissancechambers.co.uk

CHAUDHRY MISS SABUHI ASHFAQ

Coram Chambers
9-11 Fulwood Place, London WC1V 6HG,
☎020 7092 3700
✉mail@coramchambers.co.uk
Call Date: Oct 1993, Lincoln's Inn
Qualifications: [LLB (Hons)(Lond)]
✉sc@coramchambers.co.uk, sabuhi.chaudhry@coramchambers.co.uk

CHAUDHRY MISS SAIQA BANO

18 St John Street
Manchester M3 4EA, ☎0161 278 1800
✉clerks@18sjs.com
Call Date: July 2005, Inner Temple
Qualifications: [BA Kings College University of Cambridge]

CHAUDHRY MISS SHABNAM

Liverpool Civil Law
3rd Floor, 1 Old Hall Street, Liverpool L3 9HF,
☎0151 242 0500
✉clerks@liverpoolcivillaw.com
Call Date: July 2005, Lincoln's Inn
Qualifications: [LLB (Hons)]
✉clerks@liverpoolcivillaw.com

CHAUDHRY MR ZIA UDDIN

Call Date: Nov 1991, Inner Temple
Qualifications: [LLB (Hons)(Manch)]

CHAUDHURI MR AVIRUP

187 Fleet Street
London EC4A 2AT, ☎020 7430 7430
✉chambers@187fleetstreet.com
Call Date: Feb 1990, Middle Temple
Pupil Supervisor
Qualifications: [LLB (Hons) (Lond)]
✉avichaudhuri@187fleetstreet.com

CHAVASSE MISS HILARY ANN

St Ive's Chambers
Whittall Street, Birmingham B4 6DH,
☎0121 236 0863
✉clerks@stiveschambers.co.uk
Call Date: May 1971, Gray's Inn
Pupil Supervisor
Qualifications: [LLB (Bris)]
✉ann.chavasse@stiveschambers.co.uk

CHAWATAMA MR SYDNEY

1 Crown Office Row
1 Crown Office Row, Temple, London EC4Y 7HH, ☎020 7797 7500
✉mail@1cor.com
Call Date: Oct 1994, Middle Temple
Pupil Supervisor
Qualifications: [LLB (Hons)(Essex)]
✉sydney.chawatama@1cor.com

CHAWLA MR MUKUL QC (2001)

9-12 Bell Yard
London WC2A 2JR, ☎020 7400 1800
✉clerks@9-12bellyard.com
Call Date: July 1983, Gray's Inn
Qualifications: [LLB (Lond)]
✉m.chawla@9-12bellyard.com

CHAWLA MR NEIL

No5 Chambers
Fountain Court, Steelhouse Lane, Birmingham B4 6DR, ☎0845 210 5555 ✉info@no5.com
No5 Chambers
Greenwood House, 4-7 Salisbury Court, London EC4Y 8AA, ☎0845 210 5555
No5 Chambers
38 Queen Square, Bristol BS1 4QS, ☎0845 210 5555
Call Date: July 2000, Lincoln's Inn
Qualifications: [LLB(Hons) (Nott'm)]
✉nc@no5.com

CHBAT MISS NADIA MARIA

4 King's Bench Walk
2nd Floor, 4 King's Bench Walk, Temple, London EC4Y 7DL, ☎020 7822 7000
✉clerks@4kbw.co.uk
Call Date: Nov 1996, Middle Temple
Qualifications: [LLB (Hons)(Sheff)]
✉clerks@4kbw.co.uk

CHECA-DOVER MISS OLIVIA

KBW
The Engine House, No 1 Foundry Square, Leeds LS11 5DL, ☎0113 297 1200
✉clerks@kbwchambers.com
Call Date: July 2007, Lincoln's Inn
Qualifications: [LLB (Dunelm)]
✉ocd@kbwchambers.com

CHEEMA MISS PARMJIT KAUR

2 Hare Court
Lower Ground, Ground, 1st & 2nd Floor, 2 Hare Court, Temple, London EC4Y 7BH, ☎020 7353 3982 ✉clerks@2harecourt.com
Call Date: July 1989, Gray's Inn
Pupil Supervisor, Recorder
Qualifications: [LLB (Lond)]
✉bobbiecheema@2harecourt.com

CHEETHAM DR GARETH JOHN

St Ive's Chambers
Whittall Street, Birmingham B4 6DH, ☎0121 236 0863
✉clerks@stiveschambers.co.uk
Call Date: Oct 2005, Lincoln's Inn
Qualifications: [MA MSc DPhil GDL]
✉gareth.cheetham@stiveschambers.co.uk

CHEETHAM MR JAMES SIMON

Old Square Chambers
10-11 Bedford Row, London WC1R 4BU, ☎020 7269 0300 ✉clerks@oldsquare.co.uk
Call Date: Oct 1991, Middle Temple
Pupil Supervisor
Qualifications: [MA]
✉Cheetham@oldsquare.co.uk

CHEETHAM MISS JULIA ANN

Deans Court Chambers
24 St John Street, Manchester M3 4DF, ☎0161 214 6000 ✉clerks@deanscourt.co.uk
Deans Court Chambers
101 Walker Street, Preston PR1 2RR, ☎01772 565 600
✉preston@deanscourt.co.uk
Call Date: Oct 1990, Lincoln's Inn
Pupil Supervisor
Qualifications: [LLB (Nott'm)]
✉cheetham@deanscourt.co.uk

CHEETHAM MISS LUCY HELEN

4 Paper Buildings
1st Floor, 4 Paper Buildings, Temple, London EC4Y 7EX, ☎020 7427 5200
✉clerks@4pb.com
Call Date: Oct 1999, Gray's Inn
Qualifications: [MA (Cantab)]
✉lc@4pb.com

CHEGWIDDEN MR JAMES PETER

6 King's Bench Walk
Ground Floor, 6 King's Bench Walk, Temple, London EC4Y 7DR, ☎020 7583 0410
✉clerks@6kbw.com
3 PB Barristers
Royal Talbot House, 2 Victoria Street, Bristol, Avon BS1 6BB, ☎0117 928 1520
3 PB Barristers
4 St Peter Street, Winchester SO23 8BW, ☎01962 868884
✉clerks.winchester@3paper.co.uk
3 PB Barristers
30 Christchurch Road, Bournemouth, Dorset BH1 3PD, ☎01202 292102
✉clerks.bournemouth@3paper.co.uk
Call Date: Oct 2008, Lincoln's Inn
Qualifications: [BCL (Oxon) BA LLB (Australia)]

CHELVAN MR S

No5 Chambers
Greenwood House, 4-7 Salisbury Court, London EC4Y 8AA, ☎0845 210 5555
No5 Chambers
Fountain Court, Steelhouse Lane, Birmingham B4 6DR, ☎0845 210 5555 ✉info@no5.com
Trent Chambers
9 Regent Street, Nottingham NG1 5BS, ☎0115 941 9596
✉clerks@trentchambers.co.uk
No5 Chambers
38 Queen Square, Bristol BS1 4QS, ☎0845 210 5555
Call Date: Oct 1999, Inner Temple
Pupil Supervisor
Qualifications: [BSc (So'ton) LLM (Harvard)]
✉chelvs@yahoo.co.uk

E

CHENG MISS SERENA HUEY-NING

Atkin Chambers
1 Atkin Building, Gray's Inn, London
WC1R 5AT, ☎ 020 7404 0102
✉ clerks@atkinchambers.com
Call Date: Oct 2000, Lincoln's Inn
Pupil Supervisor
Qualifications: [LLB (Hons) (Lond)]
✉ clerks@atkinchambers.com

CHENNELLS MR MARK PAUL

Atkin Chambers
1 Atkin Building, Gray's Inn, London
WC1R 5AT, ☎ 020 7404 0102
✉ clerks@atkinchambers.com
Call Date: Oct 2002, Gray's Inn
Qualifications: [BA (Cantab)]
✉ clerks@atkinchambers.com

CHERN MR CYRIL

Crown Office Chambers
2 Crown Office Row, Temple, London
EC4Y 7HJ, ☎ 020 7797 8100
✉ mail@crownofficechambers.com
Call Date: Nov 2001, Gray's Inn
Qualifications: [BArch]

CHERRETT MR DARRYL JOSEPH

Carmelite Chambers
9 Carmelite Street, London EC4Y 0DR,
☎ 020 7936 6300
✉ clerks@carmelitechambers.co.uk
Call Date: July 2004, Middle Temple
Qualifications: [LLB PGDLS]

CHERRILL MRS BEVERLEY SUSAN

Westgate Chambers
64 High Street, Lewes, East Sussex BN7 1XG,
☎ 01273 480510
✉ clerks@westgate-chambers.co.uk
Call Date: Oct 1996, Middle Temple
Qualifications: [BA (Hons)(Sussex)]
✉ bc@westgate-chambers.co.uk

CHERRILL MR RICHARD

Westgate Chambers
64 High Street, Lewes, East Sussex BN7 1XG,
☎ 01273 480510
✉ clerks@westgate-chambers.co.uk
9-12 Bell Yard
London WC2A 2JR, ☎ 020 7400 1800
✉ clerks@9-12bellyard.com
Call Date: July 1965, Middle Temple
Qualifications: [MA (Cantab) LLB]

CHERRY MR JOHN MITCHELL QC (1988)

Lamb Chambers
Lamb Building, Elm Court, Temple, London
EC4Y 7AS, ☎ 020 7797 8300
✉ info@lambchambers.co.uk
Call Date: Nov 1961, Gray's Inn
✉ info@lambchambers.co.uk

Types of work: Clinical negligence, Personal injury, Professional negligence

CHERRY MR PETER JAMES

Chancery House Chambers
7 Lisbon Square, Leeds, West Yorkshire
LS1 4LY, ☎ 0113 244 6691
✉ clerks@chanceryhouse.co.uk
Call Date: Mar 2003, Lincoln's Inn
Qualifications: [BA (Hons) (Dunelm)]

CHERRY MR RICHARD PETER LAURENCE

33 Bedford Row
London WC1R 4JH, ☎ 020 7242 6476
✉ clerks@33bedfordrow.co.uk
Chambers of Mr Ami Feder
Ground Floor, Lamb Building, Temple, London
EC4Y 7AS, ☎ 020 7797 7788
✉ clerks@lambbuilding.co.uk
Call Date: July 2009, Middle Temple
Qualifications: [BA (Hons) (Cantab) MA (Cantab) Grad Dip Law (Lond)]

CHESNER MR HOWARD MICHAEL

One Essex Court
1st Floor, Temple, London EC4Y 9AR,
☎ 020 7936 3030 ✉ clerks@1ec.co.uk
Call Date: July 1995, Gray's Inn
Qualifications: [LLB (Hons)(Lond) MBA]
✉ hchesner@1ec.co.uk

CHESTER MR MARK JAMES

Atlantic Chambers
4-6 Cook Street, Liverpool L2 9QU,
☎ 0151 236 4421
✉ info@atlanticchambers.co.uk
Call Date: Nov 2002, Lincoln's Inn
Qualifications: [LLB (Hons)(L'pool)]
✉ markchester@atlanticchambers.co.uk

CHEVES MR SIMON THOMSON

Tanfield Chambers
2-5 Warwick Court, London WC1R 5DJ,
☎ 020 7421 5300
✉ clerks@tanfieldchambers.co.uk
Call Date: July 1980, Inner Temple
Qualifications: [BA(Dunelm)]

CHEW MR JONATHAN MARTIN

Wilberforce Chambers
8 New Square, Lincoln's Inn, London
WC2A 3QP, ☎ 020 7306 0102
✉ chambers@wilberforce.co.uk
Call Date: July 2010, Middle Temple
Qualifications: [Maitrise in Law (Paris) BA (Hons) (Cantab)]
✉ jchew@wilberforce.co.uk

CHHOTU MR JASVANT

Chambers of Mr Julius Seal
189 Randolph Avenue, Maida Vale, London
W9 1DJ, ☎ 020 7328 0158
✉ julius.seal@ntlworld.com
Call Date: July 1979, Gray's Inn
Pupil Supervisor
Qualifications: [BA (Hons)]

CHIBAFA MR JONATHAN

18 Red Lion Court
London EC4A 3EB, ☎ 020 7520 6000
✉ chambers@18rlc.co.uk
Call Date: Nov 2006, Middle Temple
Qualifications: [LLB (Hons)]
✉ jonathan.chibafa@18rlc.co.uk

CHICHESTER-CLARK MR ADAM TAMNIARN

13 Old Square Chambers
Ground Floor, 14 Old Square, Lincoln's Inn, London WC2A 3UE, ☎ 020 7831 4445
✉ clerks@13oldsquare.com
Call Date: Nov 2000, Middle Temple
Qualifications: [BA (Hons) (Oxon) CPE]

CHIDGEY MR DAVID GARETH

Albion Chambers
Broad Street, Bristol BS1 1DR,
☎ 0117 927 2144
✉ clerks@albionchambers.co.uk
Call Date: Oct 2000, Middle Temple
Qualifications: [LLB (Hons) (Nott'm)]
✉ david.chidgey@albionchambers.co.uk

CHIDGEY MISS KATE ANNA POPPY

3 Temple Gardens
Lower Ground Floor, 3 Temple Gardens, Temple, London EC4Y 9AU, ☎ 020 7353 3102
✉ clerks@3tg.co.uk
Call Date: July 2006, Inner Temple
Qualifications: [BA (Oxon)]
✉ kc@3tg.co.uk

CHIDLEY MR MATTHEW ADAM ROCK

Furnival Chambers
32 Furnival Street, London EC4A 1JQ,
☎ 020 7405 3232
Call Date: July 2008, Middle Temple
Qualifications: [LLB (Hons) (UEA)]
✉ mchidley@furnivallaw.co.uk

CHILD MR ANDREW JOHN ALEXANDER

3 Stone Buildings
Ground Floor, 3 Stone Buildings, Lincoln's Inn, London WC2A 3XL, ☎ 020 7242 4937
✉ clerks@3sb.law.co.uk
Call Date: Nov 1997, Lincoln's Inn
Pupil Supervisor
Qualifications: [BA (Hons)(Cantab)]
✉ achild@3sb.law.co.uk

CHILD MR JOHN FREDERICK

Wilberforce Chambers
8 New Square, Lincoln's Inn, London
WC2A 3QP, ☎ 020 7306 0102
✉ chambers@wilberforce.co.uk
Call Date: Nov 1966, Lincoln's Inn
Pupil Supervisor
Qualifications: [BA Dip American Law LLM]
✉ jchild@wilberforce.co.uk

Types of work: Capital tax, Chancery (general), Charities, Commercial law, Conflict of laws, Equity, Income tax, Private client, Professional negligence, Society of Lloyd's, Succession, Trusts, Wills

CHINKIN PROF CHRISTINE MARY

Matrix Chambers
Griffin Building, Gray's Inn, London
WC1R 5LN, ☎ 020 7404 3447
✉ matrix@matrixlaw.co.uk / Iscott@matrixlaw.co.uk
Call Date: Mar 2003, Lincoln's Inn
Qualifications: [LLB (Hons) (Lond)]
✉ christinechinkin@matrixlaw.co.uk

CHINN MR ANTONY NIGEL CATON QC (2003)

Nine Bedford Row
9 Bedford Row, London WC1R 4AZ,
☎ 020 7489 2727
✉ clerks@9bedfordrow.co.uk
Call Date: Nov 1972, Middle Temple
Recorder
✉ antony.chinnqc@9bedfordrow.co.uk

E

CHINNER MISS FER

Furnival Chambers
32 Furnival Street, London EC4A 1JQ,
☎020 7405 3232
Call Date: Oct 1998, Inner Temple
Qualifications: [BA (Hons) CPE]

CHINNOCK MISS CHRISTINA FRANCES

Angel Chambers
Ethos Building, Kings Road, Swansea SA1 8AS,
☎01792 464623
✉clerks@angelchambers.co.uk
Call Date: Nov 1998, Middle Temple
Qualifications: [LLB (Hons)(Wales)]
✉christinachinnock@angelchambers.co.uk

CHIPPECK MR STEPHEN

5 King's Bench Walk
5 King's Bench Walk, Temple, London EC4Y 7DN, ☎020 7353 5638
✉clerks@5kbw.co.uk
Call Date: July 1988, Lincoln's Inn
Qualifications: [LLB (Hons) (Leeds)]
✉stephen.chippeck@5kbw.co.uk

CHIPPENDALE MISS EMMA LORRAINE

37 Park Square Chambers
37 Park Square, Leeds LS1 2NY,
☎0113 243 9422 ✉chambers@no37.co.uk
Call Date: July 2002, Middle Temple
Qualifications: [LLB (Hons) (Leeds)]
✉chambers@no37.co.uk, cp@no37.co.uk

CHIPPERFIELD MR JEREMY STEVEN

Cranford Chambers
8 Warwick Court, London WC1R 5DJ,
☎020 7404 7454
✉jemima.ivens@cranfordchambers.com
Call Date: Oct 1995, Inner Temple
Pupil Supervisor
Qualifications: [BA (Warw) CPE]

CHIPPERFIELD MR WILLIAM JAMES

1 Gray's Inn Square
Ground Floor, 1 Gray's Inn Square, London WC1R 5AA, ☎020 7405 0001
Call Date: Mar 2010, Lincoln's Inn
Qualifications: [BA (Staffs) MSc (Oxon) CPE]

CHIPPINDALL MR ADAM COURTENAY

Guildhall Chambers
23 Broad Street, Bristol BS1 2HG,
☎0117 930 9000
✉hoc@guildhallchambers.co.uk
Call Date: Nov 1975, Gray's Inn
Pupil Supervisor, Recorder
Qualifications: [LLB (So'ton)]
✉ac@guildhallchambers.co.uk

CHIRICO MR DAVID DOMENICO

1 Pump Court
Elm Court, Temple, London EC4Y 7AB,
☎020 7842 7070
✉(name)@pumpcourt.co.uk
Call Date: Nov 2002, Middle Temple
Qualifications: [MA (Hons)(Cantab) PhD (Cantab) CPE]
✉dac@1pumpcourt.co.uk

CHIRNSIDE MR STEWART MURRAY

2 Temple Gardens
2 Temple Gardens, Temple, London EC4Y 9AY, ☎020 7822 1200
✉clerks@2tg.co.uk
Call Date: July 2005, Inner Temple
Qualifications: [BA (Hons) Oxon]
✉schirnside@2tg.co.uk

CHISHOLM MR MALCOLM DAVID

1 Garden Court Family Law Chambers
Ground Floor, One Garden Court, Temple, London EC4Y 9BJ, ☎020 7797 7900
✉clerks@1gc.com
Call Date: Nov 1989, Inner Temple
Pupil Supervisor
Qualifications: [MA(Cantab)]
✉chisholm@1gc.com

CHIVERS MR DAVID QC (2002)

Erskine Chambers
33 Chancery Lane, London WC2A 1EN,
☎020 7242 5532
✉clerks@erskinechambers.com
Call Date: July 1983, Lincoln's Inn
Qualifications: [BA (Cantab)]
✉dchivers@erskine-chambers.co.uk

CHODHA MR TEJPAL SINGH

Chambers of Mr T Chodha
112 Hampton Crescent, Gravesend DA12 4HY, ☎01474 326666
Call Date: July 1984, Inner Temple
✉barristerchodha@yahoo.com

CHOKOWRY MISS KHADIDJAH

Renaissance Chambers
5th Floor, Gray's Inn Chambers, Gray's Inn, London WC1R 5JA, ☎ 020 7404 1111
✉ clerks@renaissancechambers.co.uk
Call Date: Oct 2003, Middle Temple
Qualifications: [LLB (Hons)]
✉ kc@renaissancechambers.co.uk

CHOLERTON MR NIGEL PHILIP

Eighteen Carlton Crescent
Rownhams House, Rownhams, Southampton SO16 8LF, ☎ 023 8063 9001
✉ clerks@18carltoncrescent.co.uk
Midland Chambers
174 Blagreaves Lane, Littleover, Derby DE23 1PU, ☎ 01332 749529
✉ nglchol@aol.com
Call Date: Mar 2007, Lincoln's Inn
Qualifications: [BA (Derby)]

CHOO PROF ANDREW LI-TEIK

Matrix Chambers
Griffin Building, Gray's Inn, London WC1R 5LN, ☎ 020 7404 3447
✉ matrix@matrixlaw.co.uk / lscott@matrixlaw.co.uk
Call Date: July 2002, Inner Temple
Qualifications: [BCom LLB (NSW) DPhil (Oxon)]
✉ andrewchoo@matrixlaw.co.uk

CHOO CHOY MR ALAIN QC (2009)

One Essex Court
Ground Floor, One Essex Court, Temple, London EC4Y 9AR, ☎ 020 7583 2000
✉ clerks@oeclaw.co.uk
Call Date: Nov 1991, Inner Temple
Qualifications: [LLB (London)]
✉ achoochoy@oeclaw.co.uk

CHOONGH MR SATNAM SINGH

No5 Chambers
Fountain Court, Steelhouse Lane, Birmingham B4 6DR, ☎ 0845 210 5555 ✉ info@no5.com
No5 Chambers
Greenwood House, 4-7 Salisbury Court, London EC4Y 8AA, ☎ 0845 210 5555
No5 Chambers
38 Queen Square, Bristol BS1 4QS, ☎ 0845 210 5555
Call Date: Oct 1994, Lincoln's Inn
Qualifications: [LLB (Hons)(Warw) D Phil (Oxon)]
✉ ssc@no5.com

CHOPRA MISS JASBINDER KAUR

Temple Court Chambers
2nd Floor, 2 Dr Johnson's Building, Temple, London EC4Y 7AY, ☎ 020 7353 7888
✉ clerks@templecourt.co.uk
Call Date: Nov 2003, Gray's Inn
Qualifications: [LLB]
✉ clerks@templecourt.co.uk

CHORFI MS CAMILLA

Selborne Chambers
10 Essex Street, London WC2R 3AA, ☎ 020 7420 9500
✉ clerks@selbornechambers.co.uk
Call Date: July 2008, Lincoln's Inn
Qualifications: [BA (Exon) MA (Exon) LLB]
✉ camilla.chorfi@selbornechambers.co.uk

CHOTALIA MR SATYA PRAVIN

187 Fleet Street
London EC4A 2AT, ☎ 020 7430 7430
✉ chambers@187fleetstreet.com
Call Date: July 2008, Inner Temple
Qualifications: [LLB (L'pool)]
✉ satyachotalia@187fleetstreet.com

CHOUDHRY MR KAMRAN SERHAT

Tooks Chambers
81 Farringdon Street, London EC4A 4BL, ☎ 020 7842 7575 ✉ clerks@tooks.co.uk
Call Date: Oct 2001, Lincoln's Inn
Qualifications: [LLN (Hons) MPhil]

CHOUDHURI MISS GULSHANAH

Sen Barristers
30 Sycamore Avenue, Chandlers Ford, Eastleigh, Hampshire SO53 5RH, ☎ 07706 936045 ✉ info@senbarristers.co.uk
Call Date: Nov 1995, Lincoln's Inn
Qualifications: [LLB (Hons)(Aberdeen)]

CHOUDHURY MR AKHLAQ

11 King's Bench Walk
11 King's Bench Walk, Temple, London EC4Y 7EQ, ☎ 020 7632 8500
✉ clerksroom@11kbw.com
Call Date: Oct 1992, Inner Temple
Pupil Supervisor, Recorder
Qualifications: [BSc (Scotland) LLB (Lond)]
✉ akhlaq.choudhury@11kbw.com

CHOUDHURY MRS FAREHA ISLAM

42 Bedford Row
London WC1R 4LL, ☎ 020 7831 0222
✉ clerks@42br.com
Call Date: Nov 1995, Gray's Inn
Qualifications: [LLB (Sussex)]
✉ fareha.choudhury@42br.com

E

CHOUDHURY MR JAMSHED NAWAZISH AHMED

5 Pump Court
Ground Floor, 5 Pump Court, Temple, London EC4Y 7AP, ☎020 7353 2532
✉clerks@5pumpcourt.com
Call Date: July 2003, Lincoln's Inn
Qualifications: [LLB Hons (Lond)]
✉nawazishchoudhury@5pumpcourt.com

CHOUDHURY MISS NAFEESA

Dere Street Barristers
33 Broad Chare, Newcastle Upon Tyne NE1 3DQ, ☎0844 3351551
✉clerks@derestreet.co.uk
Call Date: Nov 1990, Inner Temple
Qualifications: [LLB]
✉n.choudhury@derestreet.co.uk

CHOUDHURY MISS SADIYA ASGHAR

Pump Court Tax Chambers
16 Bedford Row, London WC1R 4EF, ☎020 7414 8080 ✉clerks@pumptax.com
Call Date: Oct 2002, Lincoln's Inn
Qualifications: [BSc (Punjab) BA (Oxon)]
✉schoudhury@pumptax.com

Types of work: Capital tax, Corporation tax, Equity, Income tax, National Insurance, Private client, Stamp duty, Trusts, VAT, Wills

CHOWDHARY MR ISLAMUDDIN

Cassian Chambers
43 Fowey Avenue, Ilford, Essex IG4 5JT, ☎07796 262641
✉islam.chowdhary@ntlworld.com
Call Date: July 1982, Lincoln's Inn
Pupil Supervisor
Qualifications: [BA, LLB (India) LLM (Lond) MCIArb]
✉islam.chowdhary@ntlworld.com

CHOWDHURY MR NAZEER AMIN

Henderson Chambers
2 Harcourt Buildings, Temple, London EC4Y 9DB, ☎020 7583 9020
✉clerks@hendersonchambers.co.uk
Call Date: July 2002, Inner Temple
Qualifications: [BA (Dunelm) M Phil (Cantab) CPE (Nott'm)]
✉nchowdhury@hendersonchambers.co.uk

CHRISTENSEN MR CARLTON

10 King's Bench Walk
Ground Floor, 10 King's Bench Walk, Temple, London EC4Y 7EB, ☎020 7353 7742
✉Chambers@10kingsbenchwalk.co.uk
Call Date: July 1977, Middle Temple
Pupil Supervisor
Qualifications: [BSc PhD (Manch) MSc]
✉chambers@10kingsbenchwalk.co.uk

CHRISTIAN MR NEIL CONNAN

Call Date: Oct 2005, Middle Temple
Qualifications: [MA (Hons) Dip in Law]
✉clerk@stjohnsbuildings.co.uk

CHRISTIE MR AIDAN PATRICK QC (2008)

4 Pump Court
4 Pump Court, Temple, London EC4Y 7AN, ☎020 7842 5555
✉chambers@4pumpcourt.com
Call Date: July 1988, Middle Temple
Qualifications: [BA (Hons) (Oxon) MA (Hons) (Cantab)]
✉achristie@4pumpcourt.com

CHRISTIE MR DAVID HENDERSON

Seven Bedford Row
7 Bedford Row, London WC1R 4BS, ☎020 7242 3555 ✉clerks@7br.co.uk
Call Date: July 1973, Inner Temple
Pupil Supervisor
Qualifications: [BCom]

CHRISTIE MR IAIN ROBERT

5RB
1st Floor, 5 Raymond Buildings, Gray's Inn, London WC1R 5BP, ☎020 7242 2902
✉clerks@5rb.com
Call Date: July 1989, Inner Temple
Qualifications: [BA (Dunelm)]

CHRISTIE MISS MICHELLE ELAINE

Northampton Chambers
10 Spencer Parade, Northampton NN1 5AQ, ☎01604 636271
✉clerks@northampton-chambers.co.uk
Call Date: Oct 1999, Middle Temple
Pupil Supervisor
Qualifications: [LLB (Hons) (Leic)]
✉mchristie@northampton-chambers.co.uk

CHRISTIE MR RICHARD HAMISH QC (2006)

2 Pump Court
1st Floor, 2 Pump Court, Temple, London EC4Y 7AH, ☎ 020 7353 5597
✉ clerks@2pumpcourt.co.uk
Call Date: July 1986, Inner Temple
Qualifications: [LLB (Manch)]
✉ rchristie@2pumpcourt.co.uk

CHRISTIE MR SIMON PAUL WILLIAM

Chavasse Court Chambers
18 Queen Avenue, Liverpool L2 4TX, ☎ 0151 229 2030
✉ clerks@chavassechambers.co.uk
Call Date: Feb 1988, Middle Temple
Pupil Supervisor
Qualifications: [LLB (L'pool)]
✉ simon.christie@chavassechambers.co.uk

CHRISTIE-BROWN MISS SARAH LOUISE

Hailsham Chambers
Ground Floor, 4 Paper Buildings, Temple, London EC4Y 7EX, ☎ 020 7643 5000
✉ clerks@hailshamchambers.com
Call Date: Oct 1994, Middle Temple
Qualifications: [BA (Hons)(Oxon) Dip Law (Lond)]
✉ sarah.christie-brown@hailshamchambers.com

CHRISTOPHER MR JULIAN MARK CARMICHAEL QC (2010)

Five Paper Buildings
1st Floor, Five Paper Buildings, Temple, London EC4Y 7HB, ☎ 020 7583 6117
✉ clerks@5pb.co.uk
Call Date: Nov 1988, Gray's Inn
Pupil Supervisor
Qualifications: [BA (Hons)(Cantab)]
✉ jmc@5pb.co.uk

CHRISTOPHER-CHAMBERS MRS GILLIAN CLARE

Five Paper
Ground Floor, 5 Paper Buildings, Temple, London EC4Y 7HB, ☎ 020 7815 3200
Call Date: July 2003, Middle Temple
Qualifications: [BA (Hons) (Nott'm) PgDL]
✉ gillianchristopher-chambers@fivepaper.com

CHU MISS JOSEPHINE

Bank House Chambers
Old Bank House, Hartshead, Sheffield S1 2EL, ☎ 0114 275 1223
✉ w.digby@bankhousechambers.co.uk
Call Date: Oct 2007, Inner Temple
Qualifications: [LLB (Hull)]
✉ j.chu@bankhousechambers.co.uk

CHUDLEIGH MISS LOUISE KATRINA

Old Square Chambers
10-11 Bedford Row, London WC1R 4BU, ☎ 020 7269 0300 ✉ clerks@oldsquare.co.uk
Old Square Chambers
3 Orchard Court, St Augustine's Yard, Bristol BS1 5DP, ☎ 0117 930 5100
✉ clerks@oldsquare.co.uk
Call Date: July 1987, Lincoln's Inn
Pupil Supervisor
Qualifications: [BA (Law) (Kent)]
✉ chudleigh@oldsquare.co.uk

CHUKWUEMEKA MR JOHN OKECHUKWU

St Johns Buildings Liverpool
8th Floor India Buildings, Water Street, Liverpool L2 0XG, ☎ 0151 243 6000
✉ clerk@stjohnsbuildings.co.uk
16 Winckley Square
Preston PR1 3JJ, ☎ 01772 256100
St Johns Buildings
24a - 28 St John Street, Manchester M3 4DJ, ☎ 0161 214 1500
✉ clerk@stjohnsbuildings.co.uk
Call Date: Nov 1994, Lincoln's Inn
Qualifications: [BSc (Hons)(Lond)]
✉ john.chukwuemeka@stjohnsbuildings.co.uk

CHURCH MISS CAMILLA ROSAMUND HESTER

39 Essex Street
London WC2R 3AT, ☎ 020 7832 1111
✉ clerks@39essex.com
Call Date: Nov 1998, Middle Temple
Qualifications: [MA (Cantab)]
✉ camilla.church@39essex.co.uk

CHURCH MR JOHN STEPHEN

Field Court Chambers
5 Field Court, Gray's Inn, London WC1R 5EF, ☎ 020 7405 6114 ✉ clerks@fieldcourt.co.uk
Call Date: Nov 1984, Lincoln's Inn
Qualifications: [BA]
✉ john.church@fieldcourt.co.uk

E

CHUTE MS ANDREA ALEXANDRA

Tooks Chambers
81 Farringdon Street, London EC4A 4BL, ☎020 7842 7575 ✉clerks@tooks.co.uk
Rougemont Chambers
Victory House, Dean Clarke Gardens, Southernhay East, Exeter EX2 4AA, ☎01392 208484
✉clerks@rougemontchambers.co.uk
Call Date: Oct 1995, Middle Temple
Qualifications: [LLB (Hons) LLM (Hons)]
✉andrea.chute@tooks.co.uk

CIBOROWSKA MS CLARE LOUISE

Crown Office Row Chambers
119 Church Street, Brighton, Sussex BN1 1UD, ☎01273 625625
✉clerks@1cor.com
Call Date: Oct 2009, Inner Temple
Qualifications: [BA (Sussex)]
✉clare.ciborowska@1cor.com

CIFONELLI MR ROSSANO GIUSEPPE

2 Dr Johnson's Buildings
2 Dr Johnson's Buildings, Temple, London EC4Y 7AY, ☎020 7936 2613
✉clerks@2drj.com
Call Date: Oct 1998, Gray's Inn
Qualifications: [BA (Leeds) LLB]
✉clerks@2drj.com, r.cifonelli@2drj.com

CIUMEI MR CHARLES GREGG

Essex Court Chambers
24 Lincoln's Inn Fields, London WC2A 3EG, ☎020 7813 8000
✉clerksroom@essexcourt.net
Call Date: Oct 1991, Middle Temple
Pupil Supervisor
Qualifications: [BA (Hons) (Oxon) Dip Law]
✉cciumei@essexcourt.net

CLAIRE MR RAJINDER

Holborn Chambers
6 Gate Street, Lincoln's Inn Fields, London WC2A 3HP, ☎020 7242 6060
Call Date: Oct 1997, Inner Temple
Qualifications: [LLB (Wolves)]

CLAPHAM MISS PENELOPE FLORA

1 Garden Court Family Law Chambers
Ground Floor, One Garden Court, Temple, London EC4Y 9BJ, ☎020 7797 7900
✉clerks@1gc.com
Call Date: Oct 2007, Inner Temple
Qualifications: [MA (Oxon)]
✉clapham@1gc.com

CLARE MISS ALLISON JEAN

18 Red Lion Court
London EC4A 3EB, ☎020 7520 6000
✉chambers@18rlc.co.uk
Call Date: Oct 1992, Gray's Inn
Pupil Supervisor
Qualifications: [BA BCL (Oxon)]
✉allison.clare@18rlc.co.uk

CLARE MR MICHAEL CHRISTOPHER

Octagon House
19 Colegate, Norwich NR3 1AT, ☎01603 623186
✉clerks@octagonhouse.co.uk
Call Date: Nov 1986, Gray's Inn
Qualifications: [LLB (UEA)]

CLARGO MR JOHN PAUL

3 PB Barristers
3 Paper Buildings, Temple, London EC4Y 7EU, ☎020 7583 8055
3 PB Barristers
Royal Talbot House, 2 Victoria Street, Bristol, Avon BS1 6BB, ☎0117 928 1520
3 PB Barristers
4 St Peter Street, Winchester SO23 8BW, ☎01962 868884
✉clerks.winchester@3paper.co.uk
3 PB Barristers
23 Beaumont Street, Oxford OX1 2NP, ☎01865 793 736
3 PB Barristers
30 Christchurch Road, Bournemouth, Dorset BH1 3PD, ☎01202 292102
✉clerks.bournemouth@3paper.co.uk
Call Date: Oct 1994, Middle Temple
Pupil Supervisor
Qualifications: [BA (Hons)(Oxon) CPE]

CLARIDGE MISS RACHAEL SARAH

Crown Office Row Chambers
119 Church Street, Brighton, Sussex BN1 1UD, ☎01273 625625
✉clerks@1cor.com
Call Date: Oct 1996, Inner Temple
Qualifications: [LLB]
✉rachael.claridge@1cor.com

CLARK MR ANDREW RICHARD

9 St John Street
Manchester M3 4DN, ☎0161 955 9000
✉civilclerks@9sjs.com / criminalclerks@9sjs.com
Call Date: July 1994, Inner Temple
Pupil Supervisor
Qualifications: [MA (Oxon)]

CLARK MR DINGLE

Goldsmith Chambers
Ground Floor, Goldsmith Building, Temple, London EC4Y 7BL, ☎ 020 7353 6802
✉ clerks@goldsmithchambers.com
Call Date: July 1981, Middle Temple
Pupil Supervisor
Qualifications: [BSc (So'ton)]
✉ D.Clark@goldsmithchambers.law.co.uk

CLARK MISS FIONA JANE STEWART

8 New Square
8 New Square, Lincoln's Inn, London WC2A 3QP, ☎ 020 7405 4321
✉ clerks@8newsquare.co.uk
Call Date: July 1982, Middle Temple
Pupil Supervisor
Qualifications: [MA (Cantab)]
✉ fiona.clark@8newsquare.co.uk

Types of work: Breach of confidence, Competition law, Copyright, Copyright Tribunal, Design, EC competition law, Entertainment, Franchising, Information technology, Intellectual property, Malicious falsehood, Media, Media and entertainment, Passing off, Patents, Scientific and technical disputes, Trade Descriptions Act, Trade secrets, Trademarks

CLARK MISS GEORGINA

Field Court Chambers
5 Field Court, Gray's Inn, London WC1R 5EF, ☎ 020 7405 6114 ✉ clerks@fieldcourt.co.uk
Call Date: Oct 2003, Lincoln's Inn

CLARK MISS GERALDINE

Serle Court
6 New Square, Lincoln's Inn, London WC2A 3QS, ☎ 020 7242 6105
✉ clerks@serlecourt.co.uk
Call Date: July 1988, Gray's Inn
Pupil Supervisor, Recorder
Qualifications: [LLB (Hons) Dip Law]
✉ gclark@serlecourt.co.uk

CLARK MS JULIA ELISABETH

Hogarth Chambers
5 New Square, Lincoln's Inn, London WC2A 3RJ, ☎ 020 7404 0404
✉ barristers@hogarthchambers.com
Call Date: July 1984, Gray's Inn
Pupil Supervisor
Qualifications: [MA (Oxon) MA (Lond)]
✉ jclark@hogarthchambers.com

CLARK MR MICHAEL MANNING

One Essex Court
Ground Floor, One Essex Court, Temple, London EC4Y 9AR, ☎ 020 7583 2000
✉ clerks@oeclaw.co.uk
Call Date: July 2005, Lincoln's Inn
Qualifications: [LLB (Hons) City]
✉ mclark@oeclaw.co.uk

CLARK MR NEIL ROXBURGH

42 Bedford Row
London WC1R 4LL, ☎ 020 7831 0222
✉ clerks@42br.com
Call Date: July 2007, Inner Temple
Qualifications: [LLB (Lond)]
✉ neil.clark@42br.com

CLARK MRS PATRICIA JAYNE

15 Winckley Square
Preston PR1 3JJ, ☎ 01772 252828
✉ clerks@15winckleysq.co.uk
Call Date: Nov 2009, Lincoln's Inn
Qualifications: [ORD]

CLARK MR PAUL ROBERT

Exchange Chambers
One Derby Square, Derby Square, Liverpool L2 9XX, ☎ 0151 236 7747
✉ info@exchangechambers.co.uk
Exchange Chambers
7 Ralli Courts, West Riverside, Manchester M3 5FT, ☎ 0161 833 2722
Exchange Chambers
Oxford House, Oxford Row, Leeds LS1 3BE, ☎ 0113 203 1970
✉ spencer@exchangechambers.co.uk
Call Date: May 1994, Middle Temple
Pupil Supervisor
Qualifications: [LLB (Hons)]
✉ clark@exchangechambers.co.uk

CLARK MR PETER GRAHAM

2 Pump Court
1st Floor, 2 Pump Court, Temple, London EC4Y 7AH, ☎ 020 7353 5597
✉ clerks@2pumpcourt.co.uk
Call Date: Oct 2000, Inner Temple
Pupil Supervisor
Qualifications: [Dip in Theatre (Manch)]
✉ pclark@2pumpcourt.co.uk

CLARK MISS REBECCA JANE

Exchange Chambers
One Derby Square, Derby Square, Liverpool L2 9XX, ☎ 0151 236 7747
✉ info@exchangechambers.co.uk
Exchange Chambers
7 Ralli Courts, West Riverside, Manchester M3 5FT, ☎ 0161 833 2722

E

Exchange Chambers
Oxford House, Oxford Row, Leeds LS1 3BE,
☎0113 203 1970
✉spencer@exchangechambers.co.uk
Call Date: July 1989, Inner Temple
Qualifications: [LLB (Sheff)]
✉rclark@exchangechambers.co.uk

CLARK MR ROBERT JAMES

Bank House Chambers
Old Bank House, Hartshead, Sheffield S1 2EL,
☎0114 275 1223
✉w.digby@bankhousechambers.co.uk
Call Date: July 2002, Middle Temple
Qualifications: [LLB (Hons) (Nott'm)]
✉r.clark@bankhousechambers.co.uk

CLARK MR TIMOTHY ELWYN

23 Essex Street
London WC2R 3AA, ☎020 7413 0353
✉clerks@23es.com
Call Date: Feb 1993, Inner Temple
Pupil Supervisor, Recorder
Qualifications: [LLB (Hons) (Bris)]
✉timclark@23es.com

CLARK MR TIMOTHY NOEL

New Street Chambers
2 New Street, Leicester LE1 5NA,
☎0116 262 5906 ✉clerks@2newstreet.co.uk
Call Date: July 1974, Middle Temple
Pupil Supervisor, Recorder
Qualifications: [BA (Hons)]

CLARK MISS TONIA ANNE

3 PB Barristers
3 Paper Buildings, Temple, London EC4Y 7EU,
☎020 7583 8055
3 PB Barristers
Royal Talbot House, 2 Victoria Street, Bristol,
Avon BS1 6BB, ☎0117 928 1520
3 PB Barristers
4 St Peter Street, Winchester SO23 8BW,
☎01962 868884
✉clerks.winchester@3paper.co.uk
3 PB Barristers
23 Beaumont Street, Oxford OX1 2NP,
☎01865 793 736
3 PB Barristers
30 Christchurch Road, Bournemouth, Dorset
BH1 3PD, ☎01202 292102
✉clerks.bournemouth@3paper.co.uk
Call Date: July 1986, Middle Temple
Qualifications: [BSc (Hons)(Aston)]
✉tonia.clark@3pb.co.uk

CLARK MR WAYNE VINCENT

Falcon Chambers
Falcon Court, London EC4Y 1AA,
☎020 7353 2484
✉clerks@falcon-chambers.com
Call Date: July 1982, Middle Temple
Pupil Supervisor
Qualifications: [LLB (Lond) BCL (Oxon)]
✉clark@falcon-chambers.com

Types of work: Chancery (land law), Commercial property, Conveyancing, Landlord and tenant, Mortgages, Professional negligence, Real property

CLARKE MRS AMANDA LESLEY

Westgate Chambers
64 High Street, Lewes, East Sussex BN7 1XG,
☎01273 480510
✉clerks@westgate-chambers.co.uk
Call Date: July 1998, Middle Temple
Pupil Supervisor
Qualifications: [BSc (Hons)(Manch) PGOL (Manch) BVC (BPP Lond)]

CLARKE MR ANDREW BERTRAM QC (1997)

Littleton Chambers
3 King's Bench Walk North, Temple, London
EC4Y 7HR, ☎020 7797 8600
✉fschneider@littletonchambers.co.uk
Call Date: July 1980, Middle Temple
Qualifications: [LLB BCL AKC (Lond)]
✉ac@littletonchambers.com

CLARKE MISS ANNA

Park Lane Plowden
19 Westgate, Leeds LS1 2RD,
☎0113 228 5049
✉clerks@parklaneplowden.co.uk
Call Date: Oct 2009, Inner Temple
Qualifications: [BA (Nott'm)]
✉anna.clakre@parklaneplowden.co.uk

CLARKE MISS ANNA VICTORIA

5 Stone Buildings
5 Stone Buildings, Lincoln's Inn, London
WC2A 3XT, ☎020 7242 6201
✉clerks@5sblaw.com
Call Date: Nov 1994, Inner Temple
Pupil Supervisor
Qualifications: [BA (Lond) CPE (Notts)]
✉aclarke@5sblaw.com

CLARKE MR DAVID ELLIS

Harvest Chambers
83 Cork Street, Eccles, Aylesford, Kent ME20 7HQ, ☎ 01622 790070
✉ harvestchambers@btinternet.com
Call Date: Nov 1995, Inner Temple
Qualifications: [LLB (Kent)]
✉ harvestchambers@btinternet.com

CLARKE MISS ELIZABETH ANNE

Queen Elizabeth Building
3rd Floor, Queen Elizabeth Building, Temple, London EC4Y 9BS, ☎ 020 7797 7837
✉ clerks@qeb.co.uk
Call Date: Nov 1991, Gray's Inn
Pupil Supervisor
Qualifications: [BA (Hons)(Oxon)]
✉ e.clarke@qeb.co.uk

CLARKE MR GEORGE ROBERT IVAN

5 Pump Court
Ground Floor, 5 Pump Court, Temple, London EC4Y 7AP, ☎ 020 7353 2532
✉ clerks@5pumpcourt.com
Call Date: Nov 1973, Gray's Inn
Pupil Supervisor
Qualifications: [LLB (Hons)]

CLARKE MR GERARD JOSEPH PATRICK

Blackstone Chambers
Blackstone House, Temple, London EC4Y 9BW, ☎ 020 7583 1770
✉ clerks@blackstonechambers.com
Call Date: July 1986, Middle Temple
Pupil Supervisor
Qualifications: [MA (Oxon) Dip Law]
✉ gerardclarke@blackstonechambers.com

CLARKE MR IAN GRAEME

1 Chancery Lane
London WC2A 1LF, ☎ 0845 634 6666
✉ clerks@1chancerylane.com
Call Date: Mar 2005, Inner Temple
Qualifications: [BA Exeter College University of Oxford]
✉ iclarke@1chancerylane.com

CLARKE MR IAN JAMES

Selborne Chambers
10 Essex Street, London WC2R 3AA, ☎ 020 7420 9500
✉ clerks@selbornechambers.co.uk
Call Date: Oct 1990, Lincoln's Inn
Pupil Supervisor
Qualifications: [LLB (Hons)(Newc)]
✉ ian.clarke@selbornechambers.co.uk

CLARKE MR JAMIE ROY

Hardwicke
New Square, Lincoln's Inn, London WC2A 3SB, ☎ 020 7242 2523
✉ enquiries@hardwicke.co.uk
Call Date: Nov 1995, Gray's Inn
Qualifications: [MA (Oxon)]
✉ jamie.clarke@hardwicke.co.uk

CLARKE MISS JESSICA ALICE

Westgate Chambers
64 High Street, Lewes, East Sussex BN7 1XG, ☎ 01273 480510
✉ clerks@westgate-chambers.co.uk
Call Date: Oct 2006, Lincoln's Inn
Qualifications: [BA (Leeds)]
✉ jclarke@westgate-chambers.co.uk

CLARKE MR JOHN DANIEL

3 Hare Court
3 Hare Court, Temple, London EC4Y 7BJ, ☎ 020 7415 7800 ✉ clerks@3harecourt.com
Call Date: July 2005, Gray's Inn
Qualifications: [LLB CSDF BCL]
✉ danielclarke@3harecourt.com

CLARKE MR JONATHAN CHRISTOPHER ST JOHN

Old Square Chambers
3 Orchard Court, St Augustine's Yard, Bristol BS1 5DP, ☎ 0117 930 5100
✉ clerks@oldsquare.co.uk
Old Square Chambers
10-11 Bedford Row, London WC1R 4BU, ☎ 020 7269 0300 ✉ clerks@oldsquare.co.uk
Call Date: Oct 1990, Middle Temple
Qualifications: [BA (Hons) Dip Law]
✉ clarke@oldsquare.co.uk

CLARKE MR JONATHAN CLIVE

Exchange Chambers
One Derby Square, Derby Square, Liverpool L2 9XX, ☎ 0151 236 7747
✉ info@exchangechambers.co.uk
Exchange Chambers
7 Ralli Courts, West Riverside, Manchester M3 5FT, ☎ 0161 833 2722
Exchange Chambers
Oxford House, Oxford Row, Leeds LS1 3BE, ☎ 0113 203 1970
✉ spencer@exchangechambers.co.uk
Call Date: Oct 1999, Inner Temple
Qualifications: [BSc (L'borough)]
✉ clarke@exchangechambers.co.uk

E

CLARKE MISS LINDSAY JANE

Oriel Chambers
14 Water Street, Liverpool, Merseyside L2 8TD, ☎0151 236 7191
✉clerks@orielchambers.co.uk
Oriel Chambers
18 Ribblesdale Place, Preston PR1 3NA, ☎01772 254 764
✉clerks@oriel-chambers.co.uk
Call Date: July 1999, Gray's Inn
Qualifications: [BA (N'castle) (Hons)]
lindsay.clarke@orielchambers.co.uk

CLARKE MISS LISA TARIN

Staple Inn Chambers
1st Floor, 9 Staple Inn, Holborn Bars, London WC1V 7QH, ☎020 7242 5240
✉clerks@stapleinn.co.uk
Call Date: Oct 1995, Gray's Inn
Qualifications: [BA (Cantab)]
lc@stapleinn.co.uk

CLARKE MR MALCOLM JOHN

King's Bench and Godolphin (KBG)Chambers
115 North Hill, Plymouth, Devon PL4 8JY, ☎01752 221551
✉clerks@kbgchambers.co.uk
Call Date: Oct 1994, Gray's Inn
Qualifications: [LLB]
malcolm.clarke@kingsbenchchambers.co.uk

CLARKE MR MICHAEL THOMAS

St John's Chambers
101 Victoria Street, Bristol BS1 6PU, ☎0117 923 4700
✉clerks@stjohnschambers.co.uk
Call Date: Nov 2009, Lincoln's Inn
Qualifications: [LLB (Bris)]
michael.clarke@stjohnschambers.co.uk

CLARKE MISS MICHELLE NICOLA

2 King's Bench Walk
2 King's Bench Walk, Temple, London EC4Y 7DE, ☎020 7353 1746
✉clerks@2kbw.com
Call Date: July 1988, Inner Temple
Qualifications: [LLB (So'ton)]

CLARKE MR NICHOLAS PATRICK JAMES

18 St John Street
Manchester M3 4EA, ☎0161 278 1800
✉clerks@18sjs.com
Call Date: Oct 2001, Lincoln's Inn

CLARKE MR NICHOLAS STEPHEN QC (2006)

9 St John Street
Manchester M3 4DN, ☎0161 955 9000
✉civilclerks@9sjs.com / criminalclerks@9sjs.com
Bank House Chambers
Old Bank House, Hartshead, Sheffield S1 2EL, ☎0114 275 1223
✉w.digby@bankhousechambers.co.uk
Call Date: July 1981, Middle Temple
Recorder
Qualifications: [LLB (Hons)]

CLARKE MR NIKOLAS MICHAEL

Field Court Chambers
5 Field Court, Gray's Inn, London WC1R 5EF, ☎020 7405 6114 ✉clerks@fieldcourt.co.uk
Call Date: July 2000, Lincoln's Inn
Qualifications: [BA(Hons) (UEA) PgDL (Nott'm) Dip Law]
Nikolas.clarke@fieldcourt.co.uk

CLARKE MR PATRICK JAMES

Atkin Chambers
1 Atkin Building, Gray's Inn, London WC1R 5AT, ☎020 7404 0102
✉clerks@atkinchambers.com
Call Date: Oct 1997, Gray's Inn
Pupil Supervisor
Qualifications: [BSc]
clerks@atkinchambers.com

CLARKE MR PAUL SEBASTIAN

Maitland Chambers
7 Stone Buildings, Lincoln's Inn, London WC2A 3SZ, ☎020 7406 1200
✉clerks@maitlandchambers.com
Call Date: Nov 1997, Gray's Inn
Qualifications: [MA]
pclarke@maitlandchambers.com

CLARKE MR RICHARD JAMES

Blackstone Chambers
Blackstone House, Temple, London EC4Y 9BW, ☎020 7583 1770
✉clerks@blackstonechambers.com
Call Date: July 2009, Middle Temple
Qualifications: [LLB (Hons) (So'ton) BCL (Oxon)]
richardclarke@blackstonechambers.com

CLARKE MR RORY JAMES

Cornerstone Barristers
2-3 Gray's Inn Square, Gray's Inn, London WC1R 5JH, ☎ 020 7242 4986
✉ chambers@2-3gis.co.uk
Call Date: Nov 1996, Inner Temple
Pupil Supervisor
Qualifications: [BA (Cantab)]
✉ rclarke@2-3gis.co.uk

CLARKE MISS SARAH

3 PB Barristers
3 Paper Buildings, Temple, London EC4Y 7EU, ☎ 020 7583 8055
3 PB Barristers
Royal Talbot House, 2 Victoria Street, Bristol, Avon BS1 6BB, ☎ 0117 928 1520
3 PB Barristers
4 St Peter Street, Winchester SO23 8BW, ☎ 01962 868884
✉ clerks.winchester@3paper.co.uk
3 PB Barristers
23 Beaumont Street, Oxford OX1 2NP, ☎ 01865 793 736
3 PB Barristers
30 Christchurch Road, Bournemouth, Dorset BH1 3PD, ☎ 01202 292102
✉ clerks.bournemouth@3paper.co.uk
Call Date: Oct 2005, Inner Temple
Qualifications: [BA Oriel College University of Oxford]
✉ sarah.clarke@3pb.co.uk

CLARKE MISS SARAH ANNE

3 Serjeants Inn
London EC4Y 1BQ, ☎ 020 7427 5000
✉ clerks@3serjeantsinn.com
Call Date: Oct 1994, Inner Temple
Pupil Supervisor
Qualifications: [BA (Durham)]

CLARKE MISS SARAH LOUISE

11 Stone Buildings
11 Stone Buildings, Lincoln's Inn, London WC2A 3TG, ☎ 020 7831 6381
✉ clerks@11sb.com
Call Date: Oct 2003, Middle Temple
Qualifications: [BA (Hons) (B'ham)]
✉ clarke@11sb.com

CLARKE MISS SUSAN LESLEY

Oriel Chambers
14 Water Street, Liverpool, Merseyside L2 8TD, ☎ 0151 236 7191
✉ clerks@orielchambers.co.uk
Oriel Chambers
18 Ribblesdale Place, Preston PR1 3NA, ☎ 01772 254 764
✉ clerks@oriel-chambers.co.uk
Call Date: Oct 1996, Middle Temple
Pupil Supervisor
Qualifications: [LLB (Hons) LLM (L'pool)]
✉ susan.clarke@orielchambers.co.uk

CLARKE MR TIMOTHY JOHN

Cornwall Street Chambers
85-87 Cornwall Street, Birmingham B3 3BY, ☎ 0121 233 7500
✉ clerks@cornwallstreet.co.uk
Call Date: Oct 1992, Middle Temple
Pupil Supervisor
Qualifications: [MA (Cantab)]
✉ tim.clarke@cornwallstreet.co.uk

CLARKSON MR PATRICK ROBERT JAMES QC (1991)

Landmark Chambers
180 Fleet Street, London EC4A 2HG, ☎ 020 7430 1221
✉ clerks@landmarkchambers.co.uk
Call Date: July 1972, Lincoln's Inn
Recorder
✉ pclarkson@landmarkchambers.co.uk

CLARKSON MR STUART JAMES MACGREGOR

St Ive's Chambers
Whittall Street, Birmingham B4 6DH, ☎ 0121 236 0863
✉ clerks@stiveschambers.co.uk
Call Date: Nov 1987, Gray's Inn
Qualifications: [BA (Hons) (L'pool)]
✉ stuart.clarkson@stiveschambers.co.uk

CLAXTON MR DAVID ROBERT

18 Red Lion Court
London EC4A 3EB, ☎ 020 7520 6000
✉ chambers@18rlc.co.uk
Call Date: Oct 2008, Middle Temple
Qualifications: [LLB (Hons) (Dunelm) LLM (Lond)]

E

CLAXTON MR ELROY GERALDO

Old Bailey Chambers
15 Old Bailey, London EC4M 7EF,
☎ 020 3008 6404
✉ clerks@15oldbaileychambers.com
23 Essex Street
London WC2R 3AA, ☎ 020 7413 0353
✉ clerks@23es.com
Call Date: July 1983, Inner Temple
Pupil Supervisor, Recorder
Qualifications: [LLB (Lond)]
✉ elroyclaxton@23es.com

CLAXTON MISS JUDITH MARY

St Mary's Family Law Chambers
26-28 High Pavement, The Lace Market,
Nottingham NG1 1HN, ☎ 0115 950 3503
✉ clerks@stmarysflc.co.uk
Call Date: Oct 1991, Middle Temple
Qualifications: [LLB (Hons)]

CLAY MR JONATHAN ROGER

Cornerstone Barristers
2-3 Gray's Inn Square, Gray's Inn, London
WC1R 5JH, ☎ 020 7242 4986
✉ chambers@2-3gis.co.uk
Call Date: Oct 1990, Lincoln's Inn
Pupil Supervisor
Qualifications: [BSc LLB]
✉ jclay@2-3gis.co.uk

CLAY MR ROBERT CHARLES

Atkin Chambers
1 Atkin Building, Gray's Inn, London
WC1R 5AT, ☎ 020 7404 0102
✉ clerks@atkinchambers.com
Call Date: July 1989, Inner Temple
Pupil Supervisor
Qualifications: [D Phil (Oxon) MA (Oxon) Dip Law]
✉ clerks@atkinchambers.com

CLAYTON MISS BRYONY LYN

Park Lane Plowden
Lombard House, 4-8 Lombard Street,
Newcastle Upon Tyne NE1 3AE,
☎ 0191 211 4087
✉ clerks@parklaneplowden.co.uk
Call Date: July 2008, Inner Temple
Qualifications: [LLB (Dunelm)]
✉ bryony.clayton@parklaneplowden.co.uk

CLAYTON MR HENRY JAMES DENNETT

4 Paper Buildings
1st Floor, 4 Paper Buildings, Temple, London
EC4Y 7EX, ☎ 020 7427 5200
✉ clerks@4pb.com
Call Date: Oct 2007, Middle Temple
Qualifications: [BA (Hons) (Oxon)]
✉ hc@4pb.com

CLAYTON MISS LUCY ELEANOR

Unity Street Chambers
5 Unity Street, College Green, Bristol
BS1 5HH, ☎ 0117 906 9789
✉ chambers@unitystreetchambers.com
Call Date: July 2009, Gray's Inn
Qualifications: [LLB]
✉ lucy.clayton@unitystreetchambers.com

CLAYTON MR NIGEL GARVIN

Kings Chambers
36 Young Street, Manchester M3 3FT,
☎ 0845 034 3444
✉ clerks@kingschambers.com
Kings Chambers
5 Park Square East, Leeds LS1 2NE,
☎ 0845 034 3444
✉ clerks@kingschambers.com
Kings Chambers
Embassy House, 60 Church Street,
Birmingham B3 2DJ, ☎ 0845 034 3444
✉ clerks@kingschambers.com
Call Date: July 1987, Inner Temple
Pupil Supervisor, Recorder
Qualifications: [LLB]
✉ nclayton@kingschambers.com

CLAYTON MR RICHARD ANTHONY QC (2002)

4-5 Gray's Inn Square
Gray's Inn, London WC1R 5AH,
☎ 020 7404 5252 ✉ clerks@4-5.co.uk
Call Date: Nov 1977, Middle Temple
Qualifications: [MA (Oxon)]
✉ clerks@4-5.co.uk

CLAYTON MR STEPHEN CHARLES RAYNER

Atkinson Bevan Chambers
1st Floor, 2 Harcourt Buildings, Temple,
London EC4Y 9DB, ☎ 020 7353 2112
✉ clerks@2hb.co.uk
Call Date: May 1973, Inner Temple

CLEARY MR JAMES MICHAEL

KCH Garden Square
1 Oxford Street, Nottingham NG1 5BH,
☎0115 941 8851
✉clerks@kchgardensquare.co.uk
Call Date: Nov 2003, Middle Temple
Qualifications: [LLB (Hons) (Hull)]

CLEASBY MR JOHN PAUL

KBW
The Engine House, No 1 Foundry Square, Leeds LS11 5DL, ☎0113 297 1200
✉clerks@kbwchambers.com
Call Date: Oct 1994, Lincoln's Inn
Qualifications: [LLB (Hons)(Leics)]
✉paulcleasby@kbwchambers.com

CLEAVER MR HENRY WILLIAM MANSEL

5 Pump Court
Ground Floor, 5 Pump Court, Temple, London EC4Y 7AP, ☎020 7353 2532
✉clerks@5pumpcourt.com
Call Date: July 1985, Inner Temple
Pupil Supervisor
Qualifications: [BA Dip Law]
✉henrycleaver@5pumpcourt.com

CLEAVER MR THOMAS JAMES

Blackstone Chambers
Blackstone House, Temple, London EC4Y 9BW, ☎020 7583 1770
✉clerks@blackstonechambers.com
Call Date: Oct 2009, Lincoln's Inn
Qualifications: [BA (Cantab) CPE COL]
✉tomcleaver@blackstonechambers.com

CLEAVER MR WAYNE DAVID

Nine Bedford Row
9 Bedford Row, London WC1R 4AZ,
☎020 7489 2727
✉clerks@9bedfordrow.co.uk
Call Date: 1986, Inner Temple
Pupil Supervisor
Qualifications: [LLB (Wales)]

CLEE MR CHRISTOPHER QC (2009)

Angel Chambers
Ethos Building, Kings Road, Swansea SA1 8AS,
☎01792 464623
✉clerks@angelchambers.co.uk
Call Date: July 1983, Gray's Inn
Recorder
Qualifications: [LLB (Hons) (Cardiff)]

CLEEVE MR THOMAS D'AUVERGNE

33 Bedford Row
London WC1R 4JH, ☎020 7242 6476
✉clerks@33bedfordrow.co.uk
Call Date: Feb 1993, Lincoln's Inn
Qualifications: [BSc Dip Law]
✉ThomasCleeve@33bedfordrow.co.uk

CLEGG MR ADAM GORDON

Stour Chambers
Mill Studio, 17a Stour Street, Canterbury, Kent CT1 2NR, ☎01227 764899
✉clerks@stourchambers.co.uk
Call Date: Nov 1994, Gray's Inn
Qualifications: [BA (Kent)]
✉clerks@stourchambers.co.uk

CLEGG MR RICHARD ELLIS

Selborne Chambers
10 Essex Street, London WC2R 3AA,
☎020 7420 9500
✉clerks@selbornechambers.co.uk
Call Date: Oct 1999, Gray's Inn
Qualifications: [MA (Cantab)]
✉richard.clegg@selbornechambers.co.uk

CLEGG MR SEBASTIAN JAMES BARWICK

Deans Court Chambers
24 St John Street, Manchester M3 4DF,
☎0161 214 6000 ✉clerks@deanscourt.co.uk
Deans Court Chambers
101 Walker Street, Preston PR1 2RR,
☎01772 565 600
✉preston@deanscourt.co.uk
Call Date: May 1994, Inner Temple
Pupil Supervisor
Qualifications: [BA (Bris) CPE]
✉clegg@deanscourt.co.uk

CLEGG MR SIMON JOSEPH

Sovereign Chambers
46 Park Place, Leeds LS1 2RY,
☎0113 245 1841
✉clerks@sovereignchambers.co.uk
Call Date: Nov 2005, Inner Temple
Qualifications: [LLB University of Leeds]
✉simon.clegg@sovereignchambers.co.uk

CLEGG MR SIMON ROBERT JONATHAN

St Philips Chambers
55 Temple Row, Birmingham B2 5LS,
☎0121 246 7000 ✉clerks@st-philips.com
Call Date: July 1980, Lincoln's Inn
Pupil Supervisor
Qualifications: [LLB (Hons)(Lond)]
✉sclegg@st-philips.co.uk

E

CLEGG MR WILLIAM QC (1991)

2 Bedford Row
London WC1R 4BU, ☎020 7440 8888
✉clerks@2bedfordrow.co.uk
Call Date: July 1972, Gray's Inn
Qualifications: [LLB]
wclegg@2bedfordrow.co.uk

CLEMENS MR ADAM

Seven Bedford Row
7 Bedford Row, London WC1R 4BS,
☎020 7242 3555 ✉clerks@7br.co.uk
Call Date: July 1985, Lincoln's Inn
Pupil Supervisor
Qualifications: [LLB (Newc)]
aclemens@7br.co.uk

CLEMENT MISS JOANNE MARIE

11 King's Bench Walk
11 King's Bench Walk, Temple, London
EC4Y 7EQ, ☎020 7632 8500
✉clerksroom@11kbw.com
Call Date: Oct 2002, Gray's Inn
Pupil Supervisor
Qualifications: [BA BCL (Oxon)]
joanne.clement@11kbw.com

CLEMENT MR PETER GUY

Atkinson Bevan Chambers
1st Floor, 2 Harcourt Buildings, Temple,
London EC4Y 9DB, ☎020 7353 2112
✉clerks@2hb.co.uk
Call Date: Nov 1988, Inner Temple
Pupil Supervisor
Qualifications: [LLB LLM (Lond)]
pclement@2hb.co.uk

CLEMENT MR RYAN WAYNE

Conference Chambers
P.O. Box 626, Harrow, Middlesex HA2 2DZ,
☎020 8144 0134
✉carole@conferencechambers.com
Call Date: Oct 1996, Middle Temple
Qualifications: [BA (Hons) BSc (Hons) LLM CPE MCIArb]
carole@conferencechambers.com

CLEMENTS MISS PAULA KATE

Alexander Chambers
13 Halstead Road, Wanstead, London E11 2AY,
☎0845 652 0451 / 0854 652 0451
✉clerks@alexanderchambers.co.uk
Guildford Chambers
Stoke House, Leapale Lane, Guildford, Surrey
GU1 4LY, ☎01483 539131
✉clerks@guildfordchambers.co.uk
Call Date: July 1985, Inner Temple
Qualifications: [LLB (So'ton)]

CLEMES MR ANDREW JOHN

Angel Chambers
Ethos Building, Kings Road, Swansea SA1 8AS,
☎01792 464623
✉clerks@angelchambers.co.uk
Call Date: Nov 1984, Gray's Inn
Qualifications: [MA (Oxon)]

CLEMITSON MISS JULIE

Dere Street Barristers
33 Broad Chare, Newcastle Upon Tyne
NE1 3DQ, ☎0844 3351551
✉clerks@derestreet.co.uk
Call Date: Nov 1991, Inner Temple
Pupil Supervisor
Qualifications: [LLB (Newc)]
clerks@broadcharechambers.co.uk

CLEMO MR PHILIP JOHN

Linenhall Chambers
1 Stanley Place, Chester CH1 2LU,
☎01244 348282
✉clerks@linenhallchambers.co.uk
Call Date: July 2007, Inner Temple
Qualifications: [LLB (Dunelm)]

CLEVERLY MR CHRISTOPHER JOHN

11 Gray's Inn Square Chambers
Chambers of Mr Ian Sen, 1st Floor South,
10/11 Gray's Inn Square, London WC1R 5JD,
☎020 7405 6879
✉clerks@11graysinnsquare.com
Call Date: Nov 1990, Middle Temple
Qualifications: [LLB (Lond)]
christopher.cleverly@11graysinnsquare.com

CLEWS MR RICHARD ANTHONY

No.6 Park Square
Leeds LS1 2LW, ☎0113 245 9763
✉Tim@no6.co.uk
Call Date: July 1986, Gray's Inn
Qualifications: [LLB]
rclews@aol.com, clews@no6.co.uk

CLIFF MR BARRY GEORGE

Regent Chambers
Regent House, 3 Pall Mall, Hanley, Stoke On
Trent ST1 1HP, ☎01782 286666
✉clerks@regentchambers.co.uk
Call Date: July 1988, Lincoln's Inn
Pupil Supervisor
Qualifications: [LLB (Hons) LLD]
clerks@regentchambers.co.uk

E

CLIFF MISS ELIZABETH DUNBAR

Chavasse Court Chambers
18 Queen Avenue, Liverpool L2 4TX,
☎0151 229 2030
✉clerks@chavassechambers.co.uk
Call Date: July 1975, Middle Temple

CLIFF MR GRAHAM HILTON

No5 Chambers
Fountain Court, Steelhouse Lane, Birmingham B4 6DR, ☎0845 210 5555 ✉info@no5.com
No5 Chambers
Greenwood House, 4-7 Salisbury Court, London EC4Y 8AA, ☎0845 210 5555
No5 Chambers
38 Queen Square, Bristol BS1 4QS,
☎0845 210 5555
Call Date: July 1973, Middle Temple
Pupil Supervisor, Recorder
Qualifications: [LLB(Hons)(Lond)]
✉gc@no5.com

CLIFF MR PAUL RICHARD

Regent Chambers
Regent House, 3 Pall Mall, Hanley, Stoke On Trent ST1 1HP, ☎01782 286666
✉clerks@regentchambers.co.uk
Call Date: Nov 1992, Gray's Inn
Qualifications: [LLB]
✉paul.cliff@regentchambers.co.uk

CLIFFORD MR JAMES

Maitland Chambers
7 Stone Buildings, Lincoln's Inn, London WC2A 3SZ, ☎020 7406 1200
✉clerks@maitlandchambers.com
Call Date: July 1984, Lincoln's Inn
Pupil Supervisor
Qualifications: [BA (Oxon)]
✉jclifford@maitlandchambers.com

CLIFFORD MR JOHN DAVID

9 King's Bench Walk
Lower Ground Floor South, 9 King's Bench Walk, Temple, London EC4Y 7DX,
☎020 7353 9564 ✉9kbw@btconnect.com
Call Date: July 1998, Inner Temple
Qualifications: [MPhil (Cantab)]
✉9kbw@btconnect.com

CLIFFORD MISS VICTORIA LOUISE

No5 Chambers
Fountain Court, Steelhouse Lane, Birmingham B4 6DR, ☎0845 210 5555 ✉info@no5.com
No5 Chambers
Greenwood House, 4-7 Salisbury Court, London EC4Y 8AA, ☎0845 210 5555
No5 Chambers
38 Queen Square, Bristol BS1 4QS,
☎0845 210 5555
Call Date: July 2002, Gray's Inn
Qualifications: [LLB (B'ham)]
✉vc@no5.com

CLIFT MISS CLAIRE TERESA

Clerksroom (Taunton)
Equity House, Administration Centre, Blackbrook Park Avenue, Taunton, Somerset TA1 2PX, ☎0845 083 3000
✉mail@clerksroom.com
Call Date: Oct 2003, Middle Temple
Qualifications: [BA (Hons) (Oxon)]
✉Clift@clerksroom.com

CLIFTON MISS JANE APRIL

Lamb Chambers
Lamb Building, Elm Court, Temple, London EC4Y 7AS, ☎020 7797 8300
✉info@lambchambers.co.uk
Call Date: Oct 2001, Middle Temple
Qualifications: [BA (Hons)]
✉janeclifton@lambchambers.co.uk

CLIMIE MR ROGER STEPHEN

Outer Temple Chambers
The Outer Temple, 222 Strand, London WC2R 1BA, ☎020 7353 6381
✉clerks@outertemple.com
King's Bench and Godolphin (KBG)Chambers
115 North Hill, Plymouth, Devon PL4 8JY,
☎01752 221551
✉clerks@kbgchambers.co.uk
Call Date: July 1982, Lincoln's Inn
Pupil Supervisor, Recorder
Qualifications: [BA]

CLINE MR ROBERT JAMES

Atlantic Chambers
4-6 Cook Street, Liverpool L2 9QU,
☎0151 236 4421
✉info@atlanticchambers.co.uk
Call Date: Oct 2002, Gray's Inn
Qualifications: [MA (Cantab)]
✉robertcline@atlanticchambers.co.uk

E

CLIVE MR NIGEL PHILIP TREVOR

Wilberforce Chambers
7 Bishop Lane, Hull HU1 1PA,
☎ 01482 323264
Call Date: Nov 1998, Gray's Inn
Qualifications: [LLB (Hons)]

CLOHERTY MR ADAM JOHN

XXIV Old Buildings
Ground Floor, 24 Old Buildings, Lincoln's Inn,
London WC2A 3UP, ☎ 020 7691 2424
✉ clerks@xxiv.co.uk
Call Date: July 2005, Middle Temple
Qualifications: [BA (Hons)]
✉ adam.cloherty@xxiv.co.uk

CLOSE MR BENJAMIN PHILLIP

Citadel Chambers
The Citadel, 190 Corporation Street,
Birmingham B4 6QD, ☎ 0121 233 8500
✉ clerks@citadelchambers.com
Call Date: Nov 2009, Lincoln's Inn
Qualifications: [LLB (Nott'm)]

CLOSE MR JON RICHARD

Exchange Chambers
7 Ralli Courts, West Riverside, Manchester
M3 5FT, ☎ 0161 833 2722
Exchange Chambers
One Derby Square, Derby Square, Liverpool
L2 9XX, ☎ 0151 236 7747
✉ info@exchangechambers.co.uk
Oriel Chambers
18 Ribblesdale Place, Preston PR1 3NA,
☎ 01772 254 764
✉ clerks@oriel-chambers.co.uk
Call Date: Oct 1997, Lincoln's Inn
Qualifications: [LLB (Hons)(Warks)]
✉ close@exchangechambers.co.uk

CLOUGH MR RICHARD WILLIAM BUTLER

Renaissance Chambers
5th Floor, Gray's Inn Chambers, Gray's Inn,
London WC1R 5JA, ☎ 020 7404 1111
✉ clerks@renaissancechambers.co.uk
Call Date: Nov 1971, Inner Temple
Pupil Supervisor
✉ rc@renaissancechambers.co.uk

CLOVER MISS SARAH

Kings Chambers
36 Young Street, Manchester M3 3FT,
☎ 0845 034 3444
✉ clerks@kingschambers.com
Kings Chambers
5 Park Square East, Leeds LS1 2NE,
☎ 0845 034 3444
✉ clerks@kingschambers.com
Call Date: Nov 1993, Lincoln's Inn
Qualifications: [BA (Oxon)(Hons) LLM (USA)]
✉ sc@no5.com

CLUTTEN MISS REBECCA PRIMROSE

Francis Taylor Building
Inner Temple, London EC4Y 7BY,
☎ 020 7353 8415 ✉ clerks@ftb.eu.com
Call Date: Nov 2008, Inner Temple
Qualifications: [BA (Cantab) CPE LLB (Cantab)]
✉ rebecca.clutten@ftb.eu.com

CLUTTERBUCK MR ANDREW MAURICE GRAY

4 Stone Buildings
Ground Floor, 4 Stone Buildings, Lincoln's
Inn, London WC2A 3XT, ☎ 020 7242 5524
✉ clerks@4stonebuildings.com
Call Date: Oct 1992, Middle Temple
Pupil Supervisor
Qualifications: [BA (Hons)]
✉ clerks@4stonebuildings.com

CLYNDES MR SAMUEL THOMAS

Old Bailey Chambers
15 Old Bailey, London EC4M 7EF,
☎ 020 3008 6404
✉ clerks@15oldbaileychambers.com
Call Date: July 2009, Middle Temple
Qualifications: [BA (Hons) (Manch)]
✉ s.clyndes@15oldbaileychambers.com

COADE MISS GEORGINA

No.6 Park Square
Leeds LS1 2LW, ☎ 0113 245 9763
✉ Tim@no6.co.uk
Call Date: July 2005, Gray's Inn
Qualifications: [BA]
✉ coade@no6.co.uk

COATES MR GEORGE ALEXANDER NIGEL

Guildford Chambers
Stoke House, Leapale Lane, Guildford, Surrey GU1 4LY, ☎01483 539131
✉clerks@guildfordchambers.co.uk
Call Date: Nov 1990, Middle Temple
Pupil Supervisor
Qualifications: [MA (Cantab)]
gcoates@guildfordchambers.com

COATES MISS HOLLY GWYNETH

Becket Chambers
17 New Dover Road, Canterbury, Kent CT1 3AS, ☎01227 786331
✉clerks@becket-chambers.co.uk
Call Date: Oct 2008, Lincoln's Inn
Qualifications: [LLB (Cantab)]
hcoates@becket-chambers.co.uk

COATES MR JOHN PAUL

1 Gray's Inn Square
Ground Floor, 1 Gray's Inn Square, London WC1R 5AA, ☎020 7405 0001
Call Date: Nov 1988, Middle Temple
Qualifications: [LLB (Warw)]

COBB MISS JOANNA MARIE

The Chambers of Grahame Aldous QC
9 Gough Square, London EC4A 3DG, ☎020 7832 0500
✉clerks@9goughsquare.co.uk
Call Date: Oct 1999, Middle Temple
Qualifications: [LLB (Hons)(Lond)]
jcobb@9goughsquare.co.uk, JoannaCobb@33bedfordrow.co.uk

COBB MR STEPHEN WILLIAM SCOTT QC (2003)

1 Garden Court Family Law Chambers
Ground Floor, One Garden Court, Temple, London EC4Y 9BJ, ☎020 7797 7900
✉clerks@1gc.com
Atlantic Chambers
4-6 Cook Street, Liverpool L2 9QU, ☎0151 236 4421
✉info@atlanticchambers.co.uk
St Philips Chambers
55 Temple Row, Birmingham B2 5LS, ☎0121 246 7000 ✉clerks@st-philips.com
Trinity Chambers
The Custom House, 39 Quayside, Newcastle Upon Tyne NE1 3DE, ☎0191 232 1927
✉info@trinitychambers.co.uk
Trinity Chambers
Multi Media Exchange, 72-80 Corporation Road, Middlesbrough TS1 2RF, ☎01642 247569
✉info@trinitychambers.co.uk
Call Date: July 1985, Inner Temple
Recorder
Qualifications: [LLB (L'pool)]
cobb@1gc.com

COBBE MR MATTHEW RANDALL

9 Park Place
9 Park Place, Cardiff, South Glamorgan CF10 3DP, ☎029 2038 2731
✉clerks@9parkplace.co.uk
Call Date: Nov 1998, Gray's Inn
Qualifications: [LLB (Exon) MSc (Cardiff)]
clerks@9parkplace.co.uk

COBBS MISS LAURA SUSAN

Studio Legale Cobbs
Via G.B.Morgagni 2, Milan 20129, ☎0039 022 953 2531 ✉lcobbs@alice.it
Call Date: Nov 1989, Middle Temple
Pupil Supervisor
Qualifications: [LLB (Hons)(Bucks)]

COBILL MR NICHOLAS

No5 Chambers
Fountain Court, Steelhouse Lane, Birmingham B4 6DR, ☎0845 210 5555 ✉info@no5.com
No5 Chambers
Greenwood House, 4-7 Salisbury Court, London EC4Y 8AA, ☎0845 210 5555
No5 Chambers
38 Queen Square, Bristol BS1 4QS, ☎0845 210 5555
Call Date: Nov 2003, Middle Temple
Qualifications: [BA (Hons) (Kent) Dip Law]

COBURN MR MICHAEL JEREMY PATRICK QC (2010)

20 Essex Street
London WC2R 3AL, ☎020 7842 1200
✉clerks@20essexst.com
Call Date: Nov 1990, Inner Temple
Pupil Supervisor
Qualifications: [BA (Oxon) Dip Law (Lond)]
clerks@20essexst.com

COCCARO MR CARLO EDUARDO

Fenners Chambers
3 Madingley Road, Cambridge CB3 0EE, ☎01223 368761
✉clerks@fennerschambers.com
Call Date: July 2007, Lincoln's Inn
Qualifications: [LLB (So'ton)]

E

COCHAND MR CHARLES MACLEAN

2 King's Bench Walk
2 King's Bench Walk, Temple, London EC4Y 7DE, ☎ 020 7353 1746
✉ clerks@2kbw.com
Call Date: Feb 1978, Middle Temple
Pupil Supervisor
Qualifications: [BA (Hons)]

COCHRANE MISS STEFANIE LOUISE

Cobden House Chambers
19 Quay Street, Manchester M3 3HN,
☎ 0161 833 6000 ✉ Clerks@Cobden.co.uk
Call Date: July 2008, Middle Temple
Qualifications: [LLB (Hons) (Lancs)]

COCKAYNE MISS KERRY LOUISE

St Mary's Family Law Chambers
26-28 High Pavement, The Lace Market, Nottingham NG1 1HN, ☎ 0115 950 3503
✉ clerks@stmarysflc.co.uk
Call Date: July 2002, Lincoln's Inn
Qualifications: [BA (Hons)(Sheff)]
✉ kerry.cockayne@stmarysflc.co.uk

COCKERILL MISS SARA ELIZABETH QC (2011)

Essex Court Chambers
24 Lincoln's Inn Fields, London WC2A 3EG,
☎ 020 7813 8000
✉ clerksroom@essexcourt.net
Call Date: Oct 1990, Lincoln's Inn
Pupil Supervisor
Qualifications: [MA (Oxon)]
✉ scockerill@essexcourt.net

COCKINGS MR GILES FRANCIS SACHEVERAL

Furnival Chambers
32 Furnival Street, London EC4A 1JQ,
☎ 020 7405 3232
Call Date: Oct 1996, Middle Temple
Pupil Supervisor
Qualifications: [BSc (Hons)(Reading) LLB (Hons)]
✉ gcockings@furnivallaw.co.uk

COCKROFT MR THOMAS PHILIP CARLOS

2 Hare Court
Lower Ground, Ground, 1st & 2nd Floor, 2 Hare Court, Temple, London EC4Y 7BH,
☎ 020 7353 3982 ✉ clerks@2harecourt.com
Call Date: July 2010, Middle Temple
Qualifications: [BA (Hons) (Oxon)]

COCKS MR DAVID JOHN QC (1982)

18 Red Lion Court
London EC4A 3EB, ☎ 020 7520 6000
✉ chambers@18rlc.co.uk
18 Red Lion Court (Annexe)
Thornwood House, 102 New London Road, Chelmsford, Essex CM2 0RG,
☎ 01245 280880
Call Date: June 1961, Lincoln's Inn
Qualifications: [MJuris (Oxon)]

COEN MISS YVONNE ANNE QC (2000)

Seven Bedford Row
7 Bedford Row, London WC1R 4BS,
☎ 020 7242 3555 ✉ clerks@7br.co.uk
Call Date: Nov 1982, Lincoln's Inn
Recorder
Qualifications: [MA (Oxon)]
✉ ycoen@7br.co.uk

COFFER MR BENJAMIN

Quadrant Chambers
Quadrant House, 10 Fleet Street, London EC4Y 1AU, ☎ 020 7583 4444
✉ info@quadrantchambers.com
Call Date: July 2008, Middle Temple
Qualifications: [BA (Hons) (Oxon) PgDl (Lond)]

COFFEY MR JOHN JOSEPH QC (1996)

3 Temple Gardens
Lower Ground Floor, 3 Temple Gardens, Temple, London EC4Y 9AU, ☎ 020 7353 3102
✉ clerks@3tg.co.uk
39 Park Square
Leeds LS1 2NU, ☎ 0113 245 6633
✉ seniorclerk@39parksquarechambers.co.uk
Call Date: Nov 1970, Middle Temple
Recorder
Qualifications: [LLB (Lond)(Hons)]
✉ clerks@3tg.co.uk

COFIE MR EDMUND KPAKPO

Nexus Chambers
7 New Square, Lincolns Inn, London WC2A 3QS,
☎ 020 7404 1147 / 020 7831 8309
✉ info@nexuschambers.com
Call Date: July 1980, Middle Temple
Pupil Supervisor
Qualifications: [LLB Hons (Lond)]
✉ edmund.cofie@nexuschambers.com

COGAN MR MICHAEL JAMES

6 King's Bench Walk
Ground, Third & Fourth Floors, 6 King's Bench Walk, Temple, London EC4Y 7DR, ☎020 7353 4931 ✉clerks@6kbw.co.uk
Call Date: Feb 1986, Middle Temple
Pupil Supervisor
Qualifications: [BA (Hons)]
michael.cogan@6kbw.co.uk

COGHILL-SMITH MRS ABIGAIL CATHERINE

Chambers of Andrew Mitchell QC
33 Chancery Lane, London WC2A 1EN, ☎020 7440 9950 ✉clerks@33cllaw.com
Call Date: Nov 1997, Gray's Inn
Qualifications: [LLB (Bris) LLM (LSE)]
ab@33cllaw.com

COGHLAN MR TERENCE AUGUSTINE QC (1993)

1 Crown Office Row
1 Crown Office Row, Temple, London EC4Y 7HH, ☎020 7797 7500
✉mail@1cor.com
Call Date: Nov 1968, Inner Temple
Recorder
Qualifications: [MA (Oxon) MCIArb]

COGHLIN MR THOMAS ASHLEY

Cloisters
1 Pump Court, Temple, London EC4Y 7AA, ☎020 7827 4000 ✉clerks@cloisters.com
Call Date: Mar 1998, Inner Temple
Pupil Supervisor
Qualifications: [MA BCL (Oxon)]
tac@cloisters.com

COGIN MR LEO ANTHONY

Crown Office Row Chambers
119 Church Street, Brighton, Sussex BN1 1UD, ☎01273 625625
✉clerks@1cor.com
Call Date: Nov 2000, Middle Temple
Qualifications: [BA (Hons) (Lond) LLB (Hons) (Lond) MPhil (Cantab)]
leo.cogin@1cor.com

COGLEY MR STEPHEN WILLIAM QC (2011)

Quadrant Chambers
Quadrant House, 10 Fleet Street, London EC4Y 1AU, ☎020 7583 4444
✉info@quadrantchambers.com
Call Date: Nov 1984, Gray's Inn
Pupil Supervisor
Qualifications: [LLB (Hons) (Newc)]
stephen.cogley@quadrantchambers.com

COHEN MISS ABIGAIL LINDY

Henderson Chambers
2 Harcourt Buildings, Temple, London EC4Y 9DB, ☎020 7583 9020
✉clerks@hendersonchambers.co.uk
Call Date: July 2005, Lincoln's Inn
Qualifications: [LLB (Hons)]
acohen@hendersonchambers.co.uk

COHEN MR ANDREW RONALD

Stanhope Chambers
60 Stanhope Avenue, London N3 3NA, ☎020 8343 1277
✉andrewcohenbarrister@gmail.com
Call Date: Nov 1982, Gray's Inn
Pupil Supervisor
Qualifications: [BA (Hons) (Keele)]

COHEN MR EDWARD MERVYN

11 Stone Buildings
11 Stone Buildings, Lincoln's Inn, London WC2A 3TG, ☎020 7831 6381
✉clerks@11sb.com
Call Date: July 1972, Middle Temple
Recorder
Qualifications: [MA (Cantab)]
cohen@11sb.com

COHEN MR HOWARD JONATHON

Farrar's Building
Farrar's Building, Temple, London EC4Y 7BD, ☎020 7583 9241
✉Chambers@farrarsbuilding.co.uk
Call Date: Oct 1999, Gray's Inn
Pupil Supervisor
Qualifications: [BA (Oxon) MPhil (Cantab)]
hcohen@farrarsbuilding.co.uk

COHEN MR JONATHAN LIONEL QC (1997)

4 Paper Buildings
1st Floor, 4 Paper Buildings, Temple, London EC4Y 7EX, ☎020 7427 5200
✉clerks@4pb.com
Call Date: July 1974, Lincoln's Inn
Recorder
Qualifications: [BA]
jc@4pb.com

COHEN MR JONATHAN MICHAEL

Littleton Chambers
3 King's Bench Walk North, Temple, London EC4Y 7HR, ☎020 7797 8600
✉fschneider@littletonchambers.co.uk
Call Date: Oct 1999, Gray's Inn
Qualifications: [BA (Oxon) Jurisprudence]
jcohen@littletonchambers.co.uk

E

COHEN MR LAWRENCE FRANCIS RICHARD QC (1993)

Wilberforce Chambers
8 New Square, Lincoln's Inn, London WC2A 3QP, ☎ 020 7306 0102
✉ chambers@wilberforce.co.uk
Call Date: July 1974, Gray's Inn
Qualifications: [LLB]
lcohen@wilberforce.co.uk

COHEN MRS MARISA

1 Pump Court
Elm Court, Temple, London EC4Y 7AB, ☎ 020 7842 7070
✉ (name)@pumpcourt.co.uk
Call Date: Mar 2010, Inner Temple
Qualifications: [BA LLM]
mco@1pumpcourt.co.uk

COHEN MR RAPHAEL GIDEON

Broadway House Chambers
Broadway House, 9 Bank Street, Bradford, West Yorkshire BD1 1TW, ☎ 01274 722560
✉ clerks@broadwayhouse.co.uk
Call Date: July 1981, Lincoln's Inn
Pupil Supervisor
Qualifications: [LLB]
rc@cohenr.fsnet.co.uk

COHEN MR ROSS MARCUS

Furnival Chambers
32 Furnival Street, London EC4A 1JQ, ☎ 020 7405 3232
Call Date: Nov 2001, Inner Temple
Qualifications: [BA CPE]

COHEN MISS SAMANTHA LOUISE

Nine Bedford Row
9 Bedford Row, London WC1R 4AZ, ☎ 020 7489 2727
✉ clerks@9bedfordrow.co.uk
Call Date: Nov 1995, Inner Temple
Qualifications: [BA (So'ton) CPE (Lond)]
samantha.cohen@9bedfordrow.co.uk

COHEN MS SUSAN ELIZABETH

Chambers of Ms Susan Cohen
17 John Street, Cronulla 2230, ☎ 00 61 612 9527 9488
✉ suecohen@bigpond.com
Call Date: July 1981, Gray's Inn
Qualifications: [LLB (B'ham) MA]

COKE MR EDWARD PETER

St Ive's Chambers
Whittall Street, Birmingham B4 6DH, ☎ 0121 236 0863
✉ clerks@stiveschambers.co.uk
Call Date: July 1976, Inner Temple
Recorder
Qualifications: [LLB (Hons) (Warwick)]
edward.coke@stiveschambers.co.uk

COKER MR WILLIAM JOHN QC (1994)

Seven Bedford Row
7 Bedford Row, London WC1R 4BS, ☎ 020 7242 3555 ✉ clerks@7br.co.uk
Call Date: Nov 1973, Gray's Inn
Recorder
Qualifications: [LLB]
wcoker@7br.co.uk

COLBEY MR RICHARD

Lamb Chambers
Lamb Building, Elm Court, Temple, London EC4Y 7AS, ☎ 020 7797 8300
✉ info@lambchambers.co.uk
Guildhall Chambers Portsmouth
Prudential Buildings, 16 Guildhall Walk, Portsmouth, Hampshire PO1 2DE, ☎ 023 9275 2400
✉ clerks@gcp-barristers.com
Call Date: July 1984, Inner Temple
Qualifications: [LLB (Exon)]
richardcolbey@lambchambers.co.uk

COLBORNE MISS MICHELLE DIANE QC (2010)

Broadway House Chambers
Broadway House, 9 Bank Street, Bradford, West Yorkshire BD1 1TW, ☎ 01274 722560
✉ clerks@broadwayhouse.co.uk
Broadway House Chambers
25 Park Square West, Leeds, West Yorkshire LS1 2PW, ☎ 0113 246 2600
✉ clerks@broadwayhouse.co.uk
Call Date: May 1993, Gray's Inn
Pupil Supervisor
Qualifications: [LLB (Hons) (Wales)]
mdc@broadwayhouse.co.uk

COLDRICK MR EMMET

Quadrant Chambers
Quadrant House, 10 Fleet Street, London EC4Y 1AU, ☎ 020 7583 4444
✉ info@quadrantchambers.com
Call Date: Oct 2004, Gray's Inn
Qualifications: [LLB BCL]
emmet.coldrick@quadrantchambers.com

COLE MR EDWARD ARTHUR

Falcon Chambers
Falcon Court, London EC4Y 1AA,
☎ 020 7353 2484
✉ clerks@falcon-chambers.com
Call Date: July 1980, Gray's Inn
Pupil Supervisor
Qualifications: [MA (Oxon) Dip Law (Lond)]
✉ cole@falcon-chambers.com

Types of work: Agriculture, Arbitration, Chancery (land law), Commercial property, Dispute resolution and arbitration, Housing, Landlord and tenant, Professional negligence, Property, Real property, Telecommunications

COLE MISS GEORGINA ROSE ELIZABETH

1 Garden Court Family Law Chambers
Ground Floor, One Garden Court, Temple, London EC4Y 9BJ, ☎ 020 7797 7900
✉ clerks@1gc.com
Call Date: July 2007, Lincoln's Inn
Qualifications: [BA (Oxon)]
✉ cole@1gc.com

COLE MR GORDON STEWART QC (2006)

Exchange Chambers
One Derby Square, Derby Square, Liverpool L2 9XX, ☎ 0151 236 7747
✉ info@exchangechambers.co.uk
Exchange Chambers
7 Ralli Courts, West Riverside, Manchester M3 5FT, ☎ 0161 833 2722
Lombard Chambers
1 Sekforde Street, Clerkenwell, London EC1R 0BE, ☎ 020 7107 2100
Call Date: July 1979, Inner Temple
Qualifications: [BA (Hons)(L'pool)]
✉ coleqc@exchangechambers.co.uk

COLE MR JUSTIN MARK

Five Paper Buildings
1st Floor, Five Paper Buildings, Temple, London EC4Y 7HB, ☎ 020 7583 6117
✉ clerks@5pb.co.uk
Call Date: May 1992, Inner Temple
Qualifications: [LLB (Notts)]
✉ jac@5pb.co.uk

COLE MISS JUSTINE AMANDA

Bank House Chambers
Old Bank House, Hartshead, Sheffield S1 2EL,
☎ 0114 275 1223
✉ w.digby@bankhousechambers.co.uk
Call Date: Nov 1994, Inner Temple
Pupil Supervisor
Qualifications: [LLB (Sheff) (Hons)]
✉ j.cole@bankhousechambers.co.uk

COLE MR MAX WILLIAM

Ely Place Chambers
30 Ely Place, London EC1N 6TD,
☎ 020 7400 9600 ✉ admin@elyplace.com
Call Date: Oct 2011, Lincoln's Inn
Qualifications: [BA (Bris)]

COLE MR NICHOLAS ARTHUR

St Ive's Chambers
Whittall Street, Birmingham B4 6DH,
☎ 0121 236 0863
✉ clerks@stiveschambers.co.uk
Call Date: Oct 1993, Lincoln's Inn
Pupil Supervisor
Qualifications: [BSc (Hons)(B'ham) CPE]
✉ nicholas.cole@stiveschambers.co.uk

COLE MR RICHARD ANTHONY

Civitas Chambers
Global Reach, Celtic Gateway, Cardiff Bay, Cardiff CF11 0SN, ☎ 0845 0713 007
✉ clerks@civitaslaw.com
Call Date: Oct 2000, Gray's Inn
Qualifications: [LLB (Warwick)]
✉ richard.cole@civitaslaw.com

COLE MR RICHARD JOHN

Templis Chambers
3rd Floor South, 1A Middle Temple Lane, London EC4Y 9AA, ☎ 020 7649 9808
✉ templis@templis.com
Call Date: July 1988, Gray's Inn
Qualifications: [BSc (Eng) ACGI LLB CEng MIEE MBCS]
✉ Richard.Cole@templis.com

COLE MR ROBERT IAN GAWAIN

Broadway House Chambers
Broadway House, 9 Bank Street, Bradford, West Yorkshire BD1 1TW, ☎ 01274 722560
✉ clerks@broadwayhouse.co.uk
Broadway House Chambers
25 Park Square West, Leeds, West Yorkshire LS1 2PW, ☎ 0113 246 2600
✉ clerks@broadwayhouse.co.uk
Call Date: Oct 1991, Middle Temple
Pupil Supervisor
Qualifications: [LLB]
✉ ric@broadwayhouse.co.uk

COLECLOUGH MRS SUZANNE MARIA

St Philips Chambers
55 Temple Row, Birmingham B2 5LS,
☎ 0121 246 7000 ✉ clerks@st-philips.com
Call Date: Mar 2005, Inner Temple
Qualifications: [BA University of Essex BSc Open University CPE]
✉ scoleclough@st-philips.co.uk

E

COLEMAN MR ANTHONY JOHN SCOTT

3 PB Barristers
3 Paper Buildings, Temple, London EC4Y 7EU, ☎ 020 7583 8055
3 PB Barristers
Royal Talbot House, 2 Victoria Street, Bristol, Avon BS1 6BB, ☎ 0117 928 1520
3 PB Barristers
30 Christchurch Road, Bournemouth, Dorset BH1 3PD, ☎ 01202 292102
✉ clerks.bournemouth@3paper.co.uk
3 PB Barristers
4 St Peter Street, Winchester SO23 8BW, ☎ 01962 868884
✉ clerks.winchester@3paper.co.uk
3 PB Barristers
23 Beaumont Street, Oxford OX1 2NP, ☎ 01865 793 736
Call Date: July 1973, Middle Temple
Pupil Supervisor, Recorder
Qualifications: [MA (Oxon)]
anthony.coleman@3paper.co.uk

COLEMAN MR BRUCE ROBERT

1 Garden Court Family Law Chambers
Ground Floor, One Garden Court, Temple, London EC4Y 9BJ, ☎ 020 7797 7900
✉ clerks@1gc.com
Call Date: July 1972, Inner Temple
Pupil Supervisor, Recorder
Qualifications: [LLB (Hons)]
coleman@1gc.com

COLEMAN MR DANIEL GERALD MAYOW

1 Gray's Inn Square
Ground Floor, 1 Gray's Inn Square, London WC1R 5AA, ☎ 020 7405 0001
Call Date: Nov 1994, Gray's Inn
Qualifications: [BA (Lond)]
dcoleman@1gis.co.uk

COLEMAN MISS ELIZABETH JOANNE

4 Paper Buildings
1st Floor, 4 Paper Buildings, Temple, London EC4Y 7EX, ☎ 020 7427 5200
✉ clerks@4pb.com
Call Date: July 1985, Inner Temple
Qualifications: [MA (Cantab)]
ec@4pb.com

COLEMAN MR GUY ROBERT

Lamb Chambers
Lamb Building, Elm Court, Temple, London EC4Y 7AS, ☎ 020 7797 8300
✉ info@lambchambers.co.uk
Call Date: Oct 1998, Inner Temple
Qualifications: [LLB (Exon)]
guycoleman@lambchambers.co.uk

COLEMAN MR RICHARD JAMES LEE QC (2012)

Fountain Court Chambers
Fountain Court, Temple, London EC4Y 9DH, ☎ 020 7583 3335
✉ chambers@fountaincourt.co.uk
Call Date: Feb 1994, Lincoln's Inn
Pupil Supervisor
Qualifications: [MA (Cantab) LLM (Yale)]
rcoleman@fountaincourt.co.uk

COLEMAN MR RUSSELL ADAM

4 Pump Court
4 Pump Court, Temple, London EC4Y 7AN, ☎ 020 7842 5555
✉ chambers@4pumpcourt.com
Call Date: July 1986, Inner Temple
Qualifications: [LLB (Wales)]
coleslaw@templechmabers.com

COLES MRS CLARE LOUISE

New Street Chambers
2 New Street, Leicester LE1 5NA, ☎ 0116 262 5906 ✉ clerks@2newstreet.co.uk
Call Date: July 2003, Inner Temple
Qualifications: [LLB (Nott'm)]

COLES MR STEVEN FREDERICK

Crown Office Chambers
2 Crown Office Row, Temple, London EC4Y 7HJ, ☎ 020 7797 8100
✉ mail@crownofficechambers.com
Call Date: July 1983, Middle Temple
Pupil Supervisor
Qualifications: [MA (Cantab)]
coles@crownofficechambers.com

COLES-HARRINGTON MS FRANCES JULIA

2 Pump Court
1st Floor, 2 Pump Court, Temple, London EC4Y 7AH, ☎ 020 7353 5597
✉ clerks@2pumpcourt.co.uk
Call Date: Nov 2001, Lincoln's Inn
Qualifications: [BA (Hons) CPE]
fcolesharrington@2pumpcourt.co.uk

COLE-WILSON MS LOIS EKUNDAYO

1 Gray's Inn Square
Ground Floor, 1 Gray's Inn Square, London WC1R 5AA, ☎020 7405 0001
NIPC
Kirklees Media Centre, 7 Northumberland Street, Huddersfield HD1 1RL, ☎0800 862 0055 ✉jill.hayfield@nipclaw.com
Call Date: Nov 1995, Inner Temple
Qualifications: [BA (Warw) MA (Lond) CPE (Lond) LLB (Hons)]

COLEY MISS CLARE LOUISE

Clock Chambers
18 Waterloo Road, Wolverhampton WV1 4BL, ☎01902 313444
✉clockchambers@btconnect.com
Call Date: Nov 1978, Middle Temple
Qualifications: [LLB (Lond) LLM (Lond)]

COLIN MR GILES DAVID

1 Crown Office Row
1 Crown Office Row, Temple, London EC4Y 7HH, ☎020 7797 7500
✉mail@1cor.com
Call Date: Feb 1994, Inner Temple
Pupil Supervisor
Qualifications: [BA (Hons)(Dunelm) Dip Law]
✉giles.colin@1cor.com

COLLACO MORAES MR FRANCIS THOMAS

3 Stone Buildings
Ground Floor, 3 Stone Buildings, Lincoln's Inn, London WC2A 3XL, ☎020 7242 4937
✉clerks@3sb.law.co.uk
Call Date: Nov 1985, Lincoln's Inn
Qualifications: [BA (Hons)]
✉clerks@3sb.law.co.uk

COLLARD MR MICHAEL DAVID

5 Pump Court
Ground Floor, 5 Pump Court, Temple, London EC4Y 7AP, ☎020 7353 2532
✉clerks@5pumpcourt.com
Call Date: July 1986, Middle Temple
Pupil Supervisor
Qualifications: [LLB (Bris)]
✉michaelcollard@5pumpcourt.com

COLLERY MR SHANE EDWARD

18 Red Lion Court
London EC4A 3EB, ☎020 7520 6000
✉chambers@18rlc.co.uk
18 Red Lion Court (Annexe)
Thornwood House, 102 New London Road, Chelmsford, Essex CM2 0RG, ☎01245 280880
Call Date: July 1988, Lincoln's Inn
Pupil Supervisor, Recorder
Qualifications: [LLB (Hons) (Notts)]
✉shane.collery@18rlc.co.uk

COLLETT MR GAVIN CHARLES

Rougemont Chambers
Victory House, Dean Clarke Gardens, Southernhay East, Exeter EX2 4AA, ☎01392 208484
✉clerks@rougemontchambers.co.uk
Call Date: Oct 1993, Inner Temple
Pupil Supervisor
Qualifications: [LLB]
✉gcollett@rougemontchambers.co.uk

COLLETT MR IVOR WILLIAM

1 Chancery Lane
London WC2A 1LF, ☎0845 634 6666
✉clerks@1chancerylane.com
Call Date: Oct 1995, Middle Temple
Pupil Supervisor
Qualifications: [BA (Hons)]
✉icollett@1chancerylane.com

COLLETT MR MICHAEL JOHN

20 Essex Street
London WC2R 3AL, ☎020 7842 1200
✉clerks@20essexst.com
Call Date: Oct 1995, Gray's Inn
Pupil Supervisor
Qualifications: [BA (Oxon) Dip Law]
✉clerks@20essexst.com

Fax: 020 7842 1270
URL: www.20essexst.com

Types of work: Admiralty, Arbitration, Aviation, Banking, Commercial law, Commercial litigation, Commodities, Conflict of laws, Insurance, International trade, Sale and carriage of goods, Shipping

E

COLLEY DR PETER MCLEAN

Hogarth Chambers
5 New Square, Lincoln's Inn, London
WC2A 3RJ, ☎020 7404 0404
✉barristers@hogarthchambers.com
Call Date: July 1989, Gray's Inn
Pupil Supervisor
Qualifications: [BSc (Lond) PhD (Lond) LLB (Lond)]
pcolley@hogarthchambers.com

Fax: 020 7404 0505;
Out of hours telephone: 07885 139106;
DX: 16 LDE;
Other comms: E-mail:
barristers@hogarthchambers.com
URL: www.hogarthchambers.com

Types of work: Copyright, Design, EC competition law, Intellectual property, Patents, Scientific and technical disputes, Trademarks

Awards and memberships: Intellectual Property Bar Association; Member of the Royal Institution; Chancery Bar Association; Associate of the Chartered Institute of Patent Agents

Publications: *Forms and Agreements on Intellectual Property and International Licensing; European Patent Office Reports*

Reported Cases: *R v The Medicines Control Agency, ex parte Smith & Nephew Pharmaceuticals Ltd,* [1999] RPC 705 (High Court, Chancery Division), 1999. The nature of the jurisdiction on a cross-undertaking in damages, and the extent of damages recoverable by a company other than the one in whose favour the undertaking was given.
M W Trading/Theft Prevention Device (T89/00), [2002] EPOR 51 (European Patent Office, Technical Board of Appeal), 2002. Gas burner patent invalid for obviousness as a collocation of two separate inventions. Foreign manufacturer not liable for infringement by importation, either as a joint tortfeasor or as importer on the facts.
Sabaf v MFI & Ors, [2005] RPC 10 (HL) (House of Lords), 2004. Gas burner patent invalid for obviousness as a collocation of two separate inventions. Foreign manufacturer not liable for infringement by importation, either as a joint tortfeasor or as importer on the facts.
Electrocoin v Coinworld & Ors, [2005] FSR 7 (High Court, Chancery Division), 2004. Bar-X & OXO registrations including in Class 9 for amusement machines held not to be infringed by use of 'Bar', 'X', and 'O' symbols on reels and in win tables of amusement machines.
Point Solutions Ltd v Focus Business Solutions Ltd, [2006] FSR 31 (High Court, Chancery Division), 2005. Copyright. Software: Declaration of non-infringement.

COLLIER MISS BEATRICE MARION

5 Essex Court
1st Floor, 5 Essex Court, Temple, London
EC4Y 9AH, ☎020 7410 2000
✉clerks@5essexcourt.co.uk
Call Date: Nov 2004, Middle Temple
Qualifications: [BA (Hons) BA (Hons)]
collier@5essexcourt.co.uk

COLLIER MS JANE SARAH

Blackstone Chambers
Blackstone House, Temple, London
EC4Y 9BW, ☎020 7583 1770
✉clerks@blackstonechambers.com
Call Date: Nov 1994, Middle Temple
Pupil Supervisor
Qualifications: [BA (Hons) MBA (Lond)]
janecollier@blackstonechambers.com

COLLIER MR MARTIN MELTON

Fenners Chambers
3 Madingley Road, Cambridge CB3 0EE,
☎01223 368761
✉clerks@fennerschambers.com
Call Date: July 1982, Gray's Inn
Pupil Supervisor
Qualifications: [MA(Oxon)]
martin.collier@fennerschambers.com

COLLIGNON MISS LAURA JACQUELINE

Thomas More Chambers
7 Lincoln's Inn Fields, London WC2A 3BP,
☎020 7404 7000
✉clerks@thomasmore.co.uk
Call Date: Oct 1998, Lincoln's Inn
Pupil Supervisor
Qualifications: [BA (Hons)]
lcollignon@thomasmore.co.uk

COLLINGS MR ANDREW SIMON JOHN

5 King's Bench Walk
5 King's Bench Walk, Temple, London
EC4Y 7DN, ☎020 7353 5638
✉clerks@5kbw.co.uk
Call Date: Nov 1987, Gray's Inn
Qualifications: [LLB]
andrew.collings@5kbw.co.uk

E

COLLINGS MR MATTHEW GLYNN BURKINSHAW QC (2006)

Maitland Chambers
7 Stone Buildings, Lincoln's Inn, London WC2A 3SZ, ☎ 020 7406 1200
✉ clerks@maitlandchambers.com
Call Date: July 1985, Lincoln's Inn
Qualifications: [LLB (Hons) (Lond)]
✉ mcollings@maitlandchambers.com

COLLINGS MR NICHOLAS STEWART

Atkin Chambers
1 Atkin Building, Gray's Inn, London WC1R 5AT, ☎ 020 7404 0102
✉ clerks@atkinchambers.com
Call Date: Nov 1997, Gray's Inn
Pupil Supervisor
Qualifications: [LLB (Bris)]
✉ clerks@atkinchambers.com

COLLINGWOOD MR TIMOTHY DONALD

Serle Court
6 New Square, Lincoln's Inn, London WC2A 3QS, ☎ 020 7242 6105
✉ clerks@serlecourt.co.uk
Call Date: Oct 1996, Gray's Inn
Pupil Supervisor
Qualifications: [BA BCL (Oxon)]
✉ tcollingwood@serlecourt.co.uk

COLLINS MR BENJAMIN ROGER

Old Square Chambers
10-11 Bedford Row, London WC1R 4BU, ☎ 020 7269 0300 ✉ clerks@oldsquare.co.uk
Call Date: Nov 1996, Middle Temple
Qualifications: [MA (Hons)(Cantab)]

COLLINS MRS CATHERINE MARY

Iscoed Chambers
86 St Helen's Road, Swansea SA1 4BQ, ☎ 01792 652988
✉ clerks@iscoedchambers.co.uk
Call Date: Nov 2000, Middle Temple
Qualifications: [BA (Hons) (Exon)]
✉ cmc@iscoedchambers.co.uk

COLLINS MISS DEBORAH JAYNE

St Philips Chambers
55 Temple Row, Birmingham B2 5LS, ☎ 0121 246 7000 ✉ clerks@st-philips.com
Call Date: Mar 2007, Gray's Inn
✉ dcollins@st-philips.co.uk

COLLINS MS DEIRDRE BERNADETTE

Chambers of Mr Ami Feder
Ground Floor, Lamb Building, Temple, London EC4Y 7AS, ☎ 020 7797 7788
✉ clerks@lambbuilding.co.uk
Chambers of Mr Ami Feder
Ground Floor, Lamb Building, Temple, London EC4Y 7AS, ☎ 020 7797 7788
✉ clerks@lambbuilding.co.uk
Call Date: Nov 1999, Inner Temple
Qualifications: [BA, MA (Galway) LLB]

COLLINS MISS EMMA JANE

3 Raymond Buildings
3 Raymond Buildings, Gray's Inn, London WC1R 5BH, ☎ 020 7400 6400
✉ clerks@3rblaw.com
Call Date: July 2008, Lincoln's Inn
Qualifications: [BA LLB BCL MPHIL]
✉ emma.collins@3raymondbuildings.com

COLLINS MR JAMES

36 Bedford Row
London WC1R 4JH, ☎ 020 7421 8000
✉ chambers@36bedfordrow.co.uk
Central Chambers
89 Princess Street, Manchester M1 4HT, ☎ 0161 236 1133
✉ clerks@centralchambers.co.uk
Call Date: Mar 1997, Gray's Inn
Qualifications: [BA (Lond)]

COLLINS MR JAMES DOUGLAS QC (2012)

Essex Court Chambers
24 Lincoln's Inn Fields, London WC2A 3EG, ☎ 020 7813 8000
✉ clerksroom@essexcourt.net
Call Date: Feb 1995, Gray's Inn
Pupil Supervisor
Qualifications: [BA (Cantab)]
✉ jcollins@essexcourt.net

COLLINS MISS JENNIFER CLAIR

Eastbourne Chambers
5 Chiswick Place, Eastbourne, East Sussex BN21 4NH, ☎ 01323 642102
✉ clerks@eastbournechambers.co.uk
Call Date: Oct 1994, Gray's Inn
Qualifications: [BSc]

E

COLLINS MR JOHN MORRIS

Zenith Chambers
10 Park Square, Leeds LS1 2LH,
☎ 0113 245 5438
✉ clerks@zenithchambers.co.uk
Call Date: Feb 1956, Middle Temple
Pupil Supervisor
Qualifications: [MA (Oxon)]
✉ jcollins@zenithchambers.co.uk

COLLINS MR KENNETH GUY WYNDHAM

29 Bedford Row Chambers
London WC1R 4HE, ☎ 020 7404 1044
✉ clerks@29br.co.uk
Call Date: Oct 1996, Inner Temple
Pupil Supervisor
Qualifications: [LLB LLM (Sussex)]
✉ kcollins@29br.co.uk

COLLINS MISS LOUISA

Argent Chambers
5 Bell Yard, London WC2A 2JR,
☎ 020 7556 5500
✉ briefsin@argentchambers.co.uk
Call Date: Nov 2004, Lincoln's Inn
Qualifications: [LLB (Hons)]
✉ l.collins@argentchambers.co.uk

COLLINS MR MICHAEL

Monckton Chambers
1 & 2 Raymond Buildings, Gray's Inn, London WC1R 5NR, ☎ 020 7405 7211
✉ chambers@monckton.com
Call Date: Feb 1987, Lincoln's Inn
Qualifications: [BA (Hons) MA LLM (UC Dub) LLM (USA)]
✉ mcollins@lawlibrary.ie

COLLINS MR MICHAEL

Temple Tax Chambers
1st Floor, 3 Temple Gardens, Temple, London EC4Y 9AU, ☎ 020 7353 7884
✉ clerks@templetax.com
Call Date: Nov 2003, Lincoln's Inn
Qualifications: [MA (Bris) BCL (Oxon)]
✉ mc@templetax.com

COLLINS MR MICHAEL ANTONY

No.6 Park Square
Leeds LS1 2LW, ☎ 0113 245 9763
✉ Tim@no6.co.uk
Call Date: July 1998, Middle Temple
Qualifications: [LLB (Hons)]
✉ collins@no6.co.uk

COLLINS MR PETER RICHARD

4 King's Bench Walk
2nd Floor, 4 King's Bench Walk, Temple, London EC4Y 7DL, ☎ 020 7822 7000
✉ clerks@4kbw.co.uk
Call Date: Oct 1993, Gray's Inn
Qualifications: [LLB (Hons)]

COLLINS MISS ROSALEEN

Guildhall Chambers
23 Broad Street, Bristol BS1 2HG,
☎ 0117 930 9000
✉ hoc@guildhallchambers.co.uk
Call Date: May 1996, Inner Temple
Recorder
Qualifications: [LLB (Kent) BA]
✉ rosaleen.collins@guildhallchambers.co.uk

COLLINS MRS SALLY

Wilberforce Chambers
7 Bishop Lane, Hull HU1 1PA,
☎ 01482 323264
Call Date: July 2002, Middle Temple
Qualifications: [LLB (Hons)]

COLLINS MISS SIOBHAN ELLEN

Citadel Chambers
The Citadel, 190 Corporation Street, Birmingham B4 6QD, ☎ 0121 233 8500
✉ clerks@citadelchambers.com
Call Date: Oct 2005, Inner Temple
Qualifications: [LLB University of Central England]
✉ se_collins@hotmail.com

COLLINSON MISS ALICIA HESTER

Harcourt Chambers
1st Floor, 2 Harcourt Buildings, Temple, London EC4Y 9DB, ☎ 0844 561 7135
Harcourt Chambers
Churchill House, 3 St Aldate's Courtyard, St Aldate's, Oxford OX1 1BN, ☎ 0844 561 7135
Call Date: July 1982, Middle Temple
Pupil Supervisor
Qualifications: [MA (Oxon) M Phil (Oxon)]
✉ acollinson@harcourtchambers.law.co.uk

COLLIS MR MICHAEL

15 New Bridge Street
London EC4V 6AU, ☎ 020 7842 1900
✉ clerks@15nbs.com
Call Date: Nov 2004, Inner Temple
Qualifications: [BA]
✉ michael.collis@15nbs.com

E

COLMAN MR ANDREW

2 Hare Court
Lower Ground, Ground, 1st & 2nd Floor, 2 Hare Court, Temple, London EC4Y 7BH,
☎ 020 7353 3982 ✉ clerks@2harecourt.com
Call Date: July 1980, Lincoln's Inn
Pupil Supervisor
Qualifications: [LLB (Lond)]
andrewcolman@2harecourt.com

COLOVER MR ROBERT MARK

4 Breams Buildings
Chancery Lane, London EC4A 1HP,
☎ 020 7092 1900 ✉ clerks@4bb.co.uk
Call Date: Nov 1975, Middle Temple
Qualifications: [Cert of Criminology]

COLQUHOUN MISS CELINA DAPHNE MARIAN

No5 Chambers
Greenwood House, 4-7 Salisbury Court, London EC4Y 8AA, ☎ 0845 210 5555
No5 Chambers
38 Queen Square, Bristol BS1 4QS,
☎ 0845 210 5555
No5 Chambers
Fountain Court, Steelhouse Lane, Birmingham B4 6DR, ☎ 0845 210 5555 ✉ info@no5.com
Call Date: Oct 1990, Gray's Inn
Pupil Supervisor
Qualifications: [LLB (Bucks)]

COLTART MR CHRISTOPHER MCCALLUM

2 Hare Court
Lower Ground, Ground, 1st & 2nd Floor, 2 Hare Court, Temple, London EC4Y 7BH,
☎ 020 7353 3982 ✉ clerks@2harecourt.com
Call Date: Nov 1998, Inner Temple
Pupil Supervisor
Qualifications: [MA (Oxon)]

COLTER MISS LUCY CLARE

Four New Square
Four New Square, Lincoln's Inn, London WC2A 3RJ, ☎ 020 7822 2000
✉ barristers@4newsquare.com
Call Date: Oct 2008, Lincoln's Inn
Qualifications: [BA (Oxon)]
l.colter@4newsquare.com

COLTON MR SIMON DAVID

One Essex Court
Ground Floor, One Essex Court, Temple, London EC4Y 9AR, ☎ 020 7583 2000
✉ clerks@oeclaw.co.uk
Call Date: Nov 1999, Inner Temple
Pupil Supervisor
Qualifications: [MA (Cantab)]
scolton@oeclaw.co.uk

COLVILLE MR IAIN DAVID

Arden Chambers
20 Bloomsbury Square, London WC1A 2NS,
☎ 020 7242 4244
✉ clerks@ardenchambers.com
Call Date: July 1989, Inner Temple
Qualifications: [LLB]
iain.colville@ardenchambers.com

COLVIN MR ANDREW DUNCAN ROBSON

Goldsmith Chambers
Ground Floor, Goldsmith Building, Temple, London EC4Y 7BL, ☎ 020 7353 6802
✉ clerks@goldsmithchambers.com
Call Date: July 1972, Middle Temple
Qualifications: [BA (Hons) Dott Giuris (Italy)]

COMAISH MR ANDREW JAMES CHRISTIAN

Wilberforce Chambers
7 Bishop Lane, Hull HU1 1PA,
☎ 01482 323264
Call Date: Nov 1989, Middle Temple
Qualifications: [MA (Hons) (Cantab)]

COMB MR DAVID WILLIAM

Trinity Chambers
The Custom House, 39 Quayside, Newcastle Upon Tyne NE1 3DE, ☎ 0191 232 1927
✉ info@trinitychambers.co.uk
Trinity Chambers
Multi Media Exchange, 72-80 Corporation Road, Middlesbrough TS1 2RF,
☎ 01642 247569
✉ info@trinitychambers.co.uk
Call Date: Oct 2005, Inner Temple
Qualifications: [LLB University of Sheffield]
d.comb@trinitychambers.co.uk

COMERFORD MR HUGH MICHAEL

Nexus Chambers
7 New Square, Lincolns Inn, London WC2A 3QS,
☎ 020 7404 1147 / 020 7831 8309
✉ info@nexuschambers.com
Call Date: Nov 2001, Lincoln's Inn
Qualifications: [BA (Hons) MBA]
hugh.comerford@nexuschambers.com

E

COMERTON MISS JULIE ANNE

4 KBW
Ground Floor, 4 King's Bench Walk, Temple, London EC4Y 7DL, ☎020 7822 8822
✉law@4kbw.net
Call Date: July 2003, Gray's Inn
Qualifications: [LLB (Glas)]
jac@4kbw.net

COMISKEY MR REUBEN

11 Stone Buildings
11 Stone Buildings, Lincoln's Inn, London WC2A 3TG, ☎020 7831 6381
✉clerks@11sb.com
Call Date: Mar 2002, Lincoln's Inn
Qualifications: [BA (Hons)(Oxon)]
comiskey@11sb.com

COMMINS MR ANDREW MARK

St John's Chambers
101 Victoria Street, Bristol BS1 6PU, ☎0117 923 4700
✉clerks@stjohnschambers.co.uk
Call Date: Oct 2004, Middle Temple
Qualifications: [LLB (Hons) LLM]

COMMON MR HAMISH ANDREW

23 Essex Street
London WC2R 3AA, ☎020 7413 0353
✉clerks@23es.com
Call Date: July 2003, Lincoln's Inn
Qualifications: [BEng (Lond) PgDL ACGI Dip Econ]
hamishcommon@23es.com

COMPTON MR ALLAN SPENCER

2 Bedford Row
London WC1R 4BU, ☎020 7440 8888
✉clerks@2bedfordrow.co.uk
Call Date: Nov 1994, Inner Temple
Pupil Supervisor
Qualifications: [LLB (Hons) (So'ton)]
acompton@2bedfordrow.co.uk

COMPTON MR BENJAMIN EDWARD WELSTEAD QC (2011)

Outer Temple Chambers
The Outer Temple, 222 Strand, London WC2R 1BA, ☎020 7353 6381
✉clerks@outertemple.com
Call Date: Nov 1979, Lincoln's Inn
Pupil Supervisor, Recorder

COMPTON MISS CHARLOTTE FRANCESCA ROSAMUND

1 Paper Buildings
1st Floor, 1 Paper Buildings, Temple, London EC4Y 7EP, ☎020 7353 3728
✉clerks@onepaper.co.uk
Call Date: July 2008, Gray's Inn
Qualifications: [BA (Oxon)]

COMPTON MR GARETH FRANCIS THOMAS

No5 Chambers
Fountain Court, Steelhouse Lane, Birmingham B4 6DR, ☎0845 210 5555 ✉info@no5.com
No5 Chambers
Greenwood House, 4-7 Salisbury Court, London EC4Y 8AA, ☎0845 210 5555
No5 Chambers
38 Queen Square, Bristol BS1 4QS, ☎0845 210 5555
Call Date: Mar 1997, Middle Temple
Qualifications: [MA (Cantab)]
gco@no5.com

COMPTON MISS JUSTINE LESLEY

1 Pump Court
Elm Court, Temple, London EC4Y 7AB, ☎020 7842 7070
✉(name)@pumpcourt.co.uk
Call Date: Nov 2005, Middle Temple
Qualifications: [LLM (Leic) BA (Hons) (Lancs)]
jlc@1pumpcourt.co.uk

COMPTON MR TIMOTHY MARK

12 College Place
Fauvelle Buildings, 12 College Place, Southampton SO15 2FE, ☎023 8032 0320
✉clerks@12cp.co.uk
Renaissance Chambers
5th Floor, Gray's Inn Chambers, Gray's Inn, London WC1R 5JA, ☎020 7404 1111
✉clerks@renaissancechambers.co.uk
Call Date: July 1984, Inner Temple
Pupil Supervisor
Qualifications: [BA (Hons) (Bris) Dip Law]
tcompton@12cp.co.uk

COMPTON-RICKETT MISS MARY ANNE

Number 7 Harrington Street Chambers
7 Harrington Street, Liverpool L2 9YH, ☎0151 242 0707 ✉clerks@7hs.co.uk
Call Date: July 1972, Gray's Inn
Qualifications: [LLB]
mary.comptonrickett@7hs.co.uk

COMYN MR TIMOTHY JOHN

Francis Taylor Building
Inner Temple, London EC4Y 7BY,
☎020 7353 8415 ✉clerks@ftb.eu.com
Call Date: July 1980, Inner Temple
Pupil Supervisor
Qualifications: [LLB (Hull)]
timothy.comyn@ftb.eu.com

CONBOY MR ANDREW

Trent Chambers
9 Regent Street, Nottingham NG1 5BS,
☎0115 941 9596
✉clerks@trentchambers.co.uk
Call Date: July 1983, Lincoln's Inn
Qualifications: [LLB (Hons) ADV DIP CRIM]

CONCANNON MR TIMOTHY THOMAS PAUL

Guildhall Chambers Portsmouth
Prudential Buildings, 16 Guildhall Walk,
Portsmouth, Hampshire PO1 2DE,
☎023 9275 2400
✉clerks@gcp-barristers.com
Call Date: May 1993, Inner Temple
Pupil Supervisor
GCPClerks@fsmail.net

CONDRON MR MARTIN

Bedlington Chambers
20 Staffa Road, Maidstone ME15 9ST,
☎01622 744 015
✉clerks@bedlingtonchambers.com
Bedlington Chambers
7 New Square, Lincoln's Inn, London
WC2A 2QS, ☎020 7831 1159
✉clerks@bedlingtonchambers.com
Call Date: July 1987, Middle Temple
Qualifications: [BA (Hons) BSc (Hons) BL (Ireland) LLM LLB]

CONE MR JOHN CRAWFORD

Erskine Chambers
33 Chancery Lane, London WC2A 1EN,
☎020 7242 5532
✉clerks@erskinechambers.com
Call Date: July 1975, Middle Temple
Pupil Supervisor
Qualifications: [LLB (L'pool)]
jcone@erskine-chambers.co.uk

CONEY MR CHRISTOPHER RONALD RAMSDEN

Tanfield Chambers
2-5 Warwick Court, London WC1R 5DJ,
☎020 7421 5300
✉clerks@tanfieldchambers.co.uk
Call Date: July 1979, Inner Temple
Pupil Supervisor
Qualifications: [LLB (Soton)]
coney@tanfieldchambers.co.uk

CONLAN MS TINA ANN

Five Paper
Ground Floor, 5 Paper Buildings, Temple,
London EC4Y 7HB, ☎020 7815 3200
Call Date: July 2002, Gray's Inn
Qualifications: [LLB (Bris) LLM (Prague)]
tinaconlan@fivepaper.com

CONLON MR MICHAEL ANTHONY QC (2002)

Temple Tax Chambers
1st Floor, 3 Temple Gardens, Temple, London
EC4Y 9AU, ☎020 7353 7884
✉clerks@templetax.com
Call Date: July 1974, Inner Temple
Qualifications: [MA (Cantab) FTII FIIT FRSA FICPD FSALS]
Michael.conlon@hoganlovells.com

CONLON MR MICHAEL JOHN PATRICK

Harcourt Chambers
1 Isling Brook, Shenley Brook End, Milton
Keynes MK1 9AP, ☎0845 123 1234
✉clerks@barristerweb.com
Call Date: Nov 1984, Inner Temple
Qualifications: [LLB (Hull)]
clerks@barristerweb.com

CONN MS FRANCESCA GWYN

42 Bedford Row
London WC1R 4LL, ☎020 7831 0222
✉clerks@42br.com
Call Date: July 2010, Lincoln's Inn
Qualifications: [BA (Cantab)]
francesca.conn@42br.com

CONNELL MISS AMY JANE

East Anglian Chambers
140 New London Road, Chelmsford, Essex
CM2 0AW, ☎01473 214481
✉chelmsford@ealaw.co.uk
East Anglian Chambers
53 North Hill, Colchester, Essex CO1 1QA,
☎01473 214481 ✉colchester@ealaw.co.uk

E

East Anglian Chambers
Gresham House, 5 Museum Street, Ipswich, Suffolk IP1 1HQ, ☎01473 214481
✉ipswich@ealaw.co.uk
Call Date: Oct 2006, Middle Temple
Qualifications: [LLB (Hons) (Kent)]
clerks@2drj.com

CONNELL MR EDWARD SAMUEL

Five St Andrew's Hill
5 St Andrew's Hill, London EC4V 5BZ,
☎020 7332 5400 ✉Clerks@5sah.co.uk
Call Date: Oct 1996, Middle Temple
Qualifications: [BA (Hons)(Keele) CPE]
edwardconnell@5sah.co.uk

CONNELL MISS JOAN AGNES

14 Gray's Inn Square
14 Gray's Inn Square, Gray's Inn, London WC1R 5JP, ☎020 7242 0858
✉clerks@14gis.co.uk
Call Date: July 1985, Middle Temple
Qualifications: [BA (Hons) (Notts)]

CONNELL WING COMMANDER PAUL JAMES

Assize Court Chambers
14 Small Street, Bristol BS1 1DE,
☎0117 926 4587 ✉carly@assize.co.uk
Call Date: Apr 1991, Middle Temple
Pupil Supervisor
Qualifications: [MA (Dublin)]
paul.connell@assize.co.uk

CONNERTY MR ANTHONY ROBIN

Lamb Chambers
Lamb Building, Elm Court, Temple, London EC4Y 7AS, ☎020 7797 8300
✉info@lambchambers.co.uk
Zenith Chambers
10 Park Square, Leeds LS1 2LH,
☎0113 245 5438
✉clerks@zenithchambers.co.uk
Arc Chambers
PO Box 256, St Leonards-On-Sea TN38 1GL,
☎01424 204779
Call Date: July 1974, Inner Temple
Pupil Supervisor
Qualifications: [FCIArb]

CONNOLLY MRS BARBARA WINIFRED QC (2011)

Seven Bedford Row
7 Bedford Row, London WC1R 4BS,
☎020 7242 3555 ✉clerks@7br.co.uk
Call Date: July 1986, Inner Temple
Pupil Supervisor
Qualifications: [LLB (Hons)]
bconnolly@7br.co.uk

CONNOLLY MS DEIRDRE JOAN

Old Bailey Chambers
15 Old Bailey, London EC4M 7EF,
☎020 3008 6404
✉clerks@15oldbaileychambers.com
Call Date: Nov 1982, Gray's Inn
Pupil Supervisor
Qualifications: [LLB (L'pool)]

CONNOLLY MR DOMINIC REGAN

Five St Andrew's Hill
5 St Andrew's Hill, London EC4V 5BZ,
☎020 7332 5400 ✉Clerks@5sah.co.uk
Call Date: Feb 1989, Middle Temple
Pupil Supervisor
Qualifications: [LLB (LSE)]
dominicconnolly@5sah.co.uk

CONNOLLY MISS JOANNE MARIE

9 St John Street
Manchester M3 4DN, ☎0161 955 9000
✉civilclerks@9sjs.com /
criminalclerks@9sjs.com
Call Date: Oct 1992, Middle Temple
Pupil Supervisor
Qualifications: [LLB (Hons)(Nott'm)]

CONNOLLY MR SIMON JAMES

3 Temple Gardens
Lower Ground Floor, 3 Temple Gardens, Temple, London EC4Y 9AU, ☎020 7353 3102
✉clerks@3tg.co.uk
Call Date: July 1981, Middle Temple
Pupil Supervisor
Qualifications: [BA]

CONNOLLY MR STEPHEN JAMES

Exchange Chambers
7 Ralli Courts, West Riverside, Manchester M3 5FT, ☎0161 833 2722
Exchange Chambers
One Derby Square, Derby Square, Liverpool L2 9XX, ☎0151 236 7747
✉info@exchangechambers.co.uk
Exchange Chambers
Oxford House, Oxford Row, Leeds LS1 3BE,
☎0113 203 1970
✉spencer@exchangechambers.co.uk
Call Date: Nov 2003, Lincoln's Inn
Pupil Supervisor
Qualifications: [LLB (Hons) (Buck'ham)]
connolly@exchangechambers.co.uk

CONNOLLY MR TIMOTHY RICHARD

St Johns Buildings
24a - 28 St John Street, Manchester M3 4DJ,
☎0161 214 1500
✉clerk@stjohnsbuildings.co.uk
St Johns Buildings
21 White Friars, Chester CH1 1NZ,
☎01244 323070
✉clerk@stjohnsbuildings.co.uk
16 Winckley Square
Preston PR1 3JJ, ☎01772 256100
Call Date: Mar 2004, Inner Temple
Qualifications: [BA (Plymouth)]
✉clerk@stjohnsbuildings.co.uk

CONNOR MR GINO PHILIP

Furnival Chambers
32 Furnival Street, London EC4A 1JQ,
☎020 7405 3232
Call Date: Nov 1974, Gray's Inn
Pupil Supervisor
✉gconnor@furnivallaw.co.uk

CONNOR MR MARK JONATHAN DOMINIC

Call Date: May 1994, Inner Temple
Qualifications: [LLB (Hons)]
✉clerk@stjohnsbuildings.co.uk

CONNORS MISS HANNAH CATHERINE JAMIE

Pump Court Chambers
Upper Ground Floor, 3 Pump Court, Temple, London EC4Y 7AJ, ☎020 7353 0711
✉clerks@3pumpcourt.com
Riverview Chambers
Hamilton House, 1 Temple Avenue, London EC4Y 0HA, ☎0844 225 3999
✉chrisbaylis@riverviewchambers.com
Pump Court Chambers
31 Southgate Street, Winchester, Hampshire SO23 9EB, ☎01962 868 161
✉clerks@3pumpcourt.com
Call Date: Nov 2006, Inner Temple
Qualifications: [BA (Oxon)]
✉hannahc@3pumpcourt.com

CONNORS MISS JESSICA CLARE

39 Essex Street
London WC2R 3AT, ☎020 7832 1111
✉clerks@39essex.com
82 King Street
Manchester M2 4WQ, ☎0161 870 9969
Call Date: July 2000, Lincoln's Inn
Qualifications: [BA (Hons) (Oxon)]
✉jess.connors@39essex.com

CONNORS MRS SOPHIE THEA

4 Paper Buildings
1st Floor, 4 Paper Buildings, Temple, London EC4Y 7EX, ☎020 7427 5200
✉clerks@4pb.com
Call Date: Oct 2009, Middle Temple
Qualifications: [BA (Hons) (Oxon)]
✉stc@4pb.com

CONOLLY DR OLIVER STEPHEN

Pump Court Tax Chambers
16 Bedford Row, London WC1R 4EF,
☎020 7414 8080 ✉clerks@pumptax.com
Call Date: Mar 2003, Lincoln's Inn
Pupil Supervisor
Qualifications: [BA (Hons) PhD]
✉oconolly@pumptax.com

Types of work: Capital tax, Corporation tax, Equity, Income tax, National Insurance, Private client, Stamp duty, Trusts, VAT, Wills

CONRAD MR ALAN DAVID QC (1999)

Lincoln House Chambers
Tower 12, The Avenue North, Spinningfields, 18-22 Bridge Street, Manchester M3 3BZ,
☎0161 832 5701
✉info@lincolnhousechambers.com
St Ive's Chambers
Whittall Street, Birmingham B4 6DH,
☎0121 236 0863
✉clerks@stiveschambers.co.uk
Call Date: July 1976, Middle Temple
Recorder
Qualifications: [BA (Oxon)]
✉alan.conrad@lincolnhousechambers.com

CONRATH MR PHILIP BERNARD

Tanfield Chambers
2-5 Warwick Court, London WC1R 5DJ,
☎020 7421 5300
✉clerks@tanfieldchambers.co.uk
Call Date: July 1972, Gray's Inn
Pupil Supervisor

CONROY MR ALAN PETER

7 Bell Yard
London WC2A 2JR, ☎020 7831 0636
✉kevintarrant@btconnect.com
Call Date: July 2002, Inner Temple
Qualifications: [MBA CPE (Lond)]

E

CONSIDINE MR PAUL RONALD

Bedlington Chambers
7 New Square, Lincoln's Inn, London WC2A 2QS, ☎020 7831 1159
✉clerks@bedlingtonchambers.com
Bedlington Chambers
20 Staffa Road, Maidstone ME15 9ST, ☎01622 744 015
✉clerks@bedlingtonchambers.com
Call Date: July 2005, Inner Temple
Qualifications: [BEng Manchester Metropolitan University CPE Man]

CONSTABLE MR ADAM MICHAEL QC (2011)

Keating Chambers
15 Essex Street, London WC2R 3AA, ☎020 7544 2600
✉clerks@keatingchambers.com
Call Date: Oct 1995, Inner Temple
Pupil Supervisor
Qualifications: [MA (Oxon)]
aconstable@keatingchambers.com

CONSTABLE MR JOHN MARTYN CHESTER

Old Court Chambers
Newham House, 96-98 Borough Road, Middlesbrough TS1 2HJ, ☎01642 232523
✉clerks@oldcourtchambers.com
Call Date: Feb 1972, Gray's Inn
Qualifications: [LLB (Hull) LLM (Leics) MA (York) Dip French (OU)]
clerks@oldcourtchambers.com

CONSTANTINE MR STEPHEN ALLAN

Old Court Chambers
Newham House, 96-98 Borough Road, Middlesbrough TS1 2HJ, ☎01642 232523
✉clerks@oldcourtchambers.com
Call Date: Oct 1992, Middle Temple
Pupil Supervisor
Qualifications: [BSc (Hons)]
clerks@oldcourtchambers.com

CONVEY MR CHRISTOPHER MICHAEL

Chambers of Andrew Mitchell QC
33 Chancery Lane, London WC2A 1EN, ☎020 7440 9950 ✉clerks@33cllaw.com
Call Date: Nov 1994, Lincoln's Inn
Qualifications: [LLB (Hons)(Lond)]
cmc@33cllaw.com

CONWAY MR CHARLES

2 Bedford Row
London WC1R 4BU, ☎020 7440 8888
✉clerks@2bedfordrow.co.uk
Call Date: July 1969, Middle Temple
Qualifications: [MA LLB (Cantab)]
cconway@2bedfordrow.co.uk

CONWAY MR SIMON LEO

5 Pump Court
Ground Floor, 5 Pump Court, Temple, London EC4Y 7AP, ☎020 7353 2532
✉clerks@5pumpcourt.com
Call Date: July 2006, Lincoln's Inn
Qualifications: [BA (Oxon) GDL LLM (Harvard)]
simonconway@5pumpcourt.com

COODE MR JONATHAN GRAHAM

13 King's Bench Walk
13 King's Bench Walk, Temple, London EC4Y 7EN, ☎020 7353 7204
✉clerks@13kbw.co.uk
13 KBW
32 Beaumont Street, Oxford OX1 2NP, ☎01865 311066 ✉clerks@13kbw.co.uk
Call Date: July 1984, Middle Temple
Qualifications: [BA (UEA) Dip Law]
jcoode@13kbw.co.uk

COOK MR ALEXANDER JAMES

4 Stone Buildings
Ground Floor, 4 Stone Buildings, Lincoln's Inn, London WC2A 3XT, ☎020 7242 5524
✉clerks@4stonebuildings.com
Call Date: Oct 2008, Lincoln's Inn
Qualifications: [BA (Oxon) LLM]
a.cook@4stonebuildings.com

COOK MISS ALISON NOELE

St Philips Chambers
55 Temple Row, Birmingham B2 5LS, ☎0121 246 7000 ✉clerks@st-philips.com
Call Date: Feb 1989, Gray's Inn
Qualifications: [LLB (Manch) (Hons)]
acook@st-philips.co.uk

COOK MR CHRISTOPHER GRAHAM

Exchange Chambers
7 Ralli Courts, West Riverside, Manchester M3 5FT, ☎0161 833 2722
Exchange Chambers
One Derby Square, Derby Square, Liverpool L2 9XX, ☎0151 236 7747
✉info@exchangechambers.co.uk

Exchange Chambers
Oxford House, Oxford Row, Leeds LS1 3BE,
☎0113 203 1970
✉spencer@exchangechambers.co.uk
Call Date: Oct 1990, Inner Temple
Qualifications: [BSc Dip Law (Lond) BCom (B'ham)]
✉cook@exchangechambers.co.uk

COOK MISS EMILY JANE

25 Bedford Row
London WC1R 4HD, ☎020 7067 1500
✉clerks@25bedfordrow.com
Call Date: Nov 2002, Lincoln's Inn
Qualifications: [BA (Hons) (Cantab) PgDL]
✉ecook@25bedfordrow.com

COOK MR GARY WILLIAM

No 8 Chambers
8 Fountain Court, Steelhouse Lane, Birmingham B4 6DR, ☎0121 236 5514
✉clerks@no8chambers.co.uk
Call Date: Nov 1989, Middle Temple
Pupil Supervisor
Qualifications: [B Ed Hons]

COOK MR IAN REGINALD BLACKLIN

1 KBW Chambers
1 King's Bench Walk, Temple, London EC4Y 7DB, ☎020 7936 1500
✉clerks@1kbw.co.uk
King's Bench Chambers
174 High Street, Lewes BN7 1YE,
☎01273 402600
Call Date: Nov 1994, Inner Temple
Pupil Supervisor
Qualifications: [BA (Hons)(Lond) CPE (Lond)]
✉icook@1kbw.co.uk

COOK MISS KATHERINE EMMA

1 Hare Court
1 Hare Court, Temple, London EC4Y 7BE,
☎020 7797 7070 ✉clerks@1hc.com
Call Date: July 2007, Lincoln's Inn
Qualifications: [BA (Oxon) LLM (Cantab)]
✉clerks@1hc.com

COOK MS KATHERINE HELEN

Matrix Chambers
Griffin Building, Gray's Inn, London WC1R 5LN, ☎020 7404 3447
✉matrix@matrixlaw.co.uk / Iscott@matrixlaw.co.uk
Call Date: Nov 1990, Middle Temple
Qualifications: [BA (Oxon) LLM (USA)]
✉katecook@matrixlaw.co.uk

COOK MISS MARY JANE

Cornerstone Barristers
2-3 Gray's Inn Square, Gray's Inn, London WC1R 5JH, ☎020 7242 4986
✉chambers@2-3gis.co.uk
Call Date: July 1982, Inner Temple
Pupil Supervisor
Qualifications: [LLB (Cardiff)]
✉mcook@2-3gis.co.uk

COOK MR MATTHEW CHARLES

One Essex Court
Ground Floor, One Essex Court, Temple, London EC4Y 9AR, ☎020 7583 2000
✉clerks@oeclaw.co.uk
Call Date: Nov 1999, Middle Temple
Qualifications: [BA (Hons)(Oxon) BCL]
✉mcook@oeclaw.co.uk

COOK MR OLIVER JAMES ALEXANDER

Chavasse Court Chambers
18 Queen Avenue, Liverpool L2 4TX,
☎0151 229 2030
✉clerks@chavassechambers.co.uk
Call Date: Oct 2004, Gray's Inn
Qualifications: [LLB]
✉olic136@aol.com

COOK MR PAUL GRAHAM WHALLEY

Albion Chambers
Broad Street, Bristol BS1 1DR,
☎0117 927 2144
✉clerks@albionchambers.co.uk
Call Date: Nov 1992, Middle Temple
Pupil Supervisor
Qualifications: [BA (Hons)(Kent) DipLaw]
✉paul.cook@albionchambers.co.uk

COOK MISS TINA GAIL QC (2011)

42 Bedford Row
London WC1R 4LL, ☎020 7831 0222
✉clerks@42br.com
Call Date: July 1988, Middle Temple
Pupil Supervisor
Qualifications: [MA (Hons) (Oxon)]
✉tina.cook@42br.com

COOKE MISS CHARLOTTE JANE

South Square
3-4 South Square, Gray's Inn, London WC1R 5HP, ☎020 7696 9900
✉practicemanagers@southsquare.com
Call Date: July 2008, Middle Temple
Qualifications: [MA (Cantab) BCL (Oxon) MPhil (Cantab)]
✉charlottecooke@southsquare.com

E

COOKE MR DUNCAN MATTHEW

Atkinson Bevan Chambers
1st Floor, 2 Harcourt Buildings, Temple, London EC4Y 9DB, ☎020 7353 2112
✉clerks@2hb.co.uk
Call Date: Mar 2010, Inner Temple
Qualifications: [LLB (Manch) CPE]
✉dcooke@2hb.co.uk

COOKE MR GRAHAM OWEN JOHN

King's Bench Chambers
Wellington House, 175 Holdenhurst Road, Bournemouth, Dorset BH8 8DQ, ☎01202 250025
Call Date: July 1983, Lincoln's Inn
Pupil Supervisor
✉graham.cooke@kingsbench.co.uk

COOKE MR PETER RAYMOND

Cornwall Street Chambers
85-87 Cornwall Street, Birmingham B3 3BY, ☎0121 233 7500
✉clerks@cornwallstreet.co.uk
Call Date: July 1985, Lincoln's Inn
Pupil Supervisor, Recorder
Qualifications: [LLB (Manch)]
✉peter.cooke@cornwallstreet.co.uk

COOKE MR RICHARD ANDREW

No5 Chambers
Fountain Court, Steelhouse Lane, Birmingham B4 6DR, ☎0845 210 5555 ✉info@no5.com
No5 Chambers
Greenwood House, 4-7 Salisbury Court, London EC4Y 8AA, ☎0845 210 5555
No5 Chambers
38 Queen Square, Bristol BS1 4QS, ☎0845 210 5555
Call Date: July 2005, Inner Temple
Qualifications: [BA (Dublin) CPE]
✉rac@no5.com

COOKE MR STEPHEN WADE

3 Temple Gardens
Lower Ground Floor, 3 Temple Gardens, Temple, London EC4Y 9AU, ☎020 7353 3102
✉clerks@3tg.co.uk
Call Date: Oct 2006, Gray's Inn
Qualifications: [BA]

COOKE MR THOMAS WILLIAM ANDREW

Pallant Chambers
12 North Pallant, Chichester, West Sussex PO19 1TQ, ☎01243 784538
✉clerks@pallantchambers.co.uk
Call Date: Mar 2006, Lincoln's Inn
Qualifications: [BA (Hons) (Manch)]
✉tcooke@pallantchambers.co.uk

COOKSEY MR NICHOLAS

River Chambers
81 Underdale Road, Shrewsbury, Shropshire SY2 5EF, ☎01743 350505
✉richard@riverchambers.com
Call Date: Nov 2000, Middle Temple
Qualifications: [BA (Hons) (Wales)]

COOKSLEY MR NIGEL JAMES QC (2002)

Old Square Chambers
10-11 Bedford Row, London WC1R 4BU, ☎020 7269 0300 ✉clerks@oldsquare.co.uk
Old Square Chambers
3 Orchard Court, St Augustine's Yard, Bristol BS1 5DP, ☎0117 930 5100
✉clerks@oldsquare.co.uk
Call Date: July 1975, Inner Temple
Qualifications: [MA (Cantab)]
✉cooksleyqc@oldsquare.co.uk

COOMBE MR PETER MICHAEL AENEAS

13 King's Bench Walk
13 King's Bench Walk, Temple, London EC4Y 7EN, ☎020 7353 7204
✉clerks@13kbw.co.uk
13 KBW
32 Beaumont Street, Oxford OX1 2NP, ☎01865 311066 ✉clerks@13kbw.co.uk
Call Date: Nov 1993, Middle Temple
Pupil Supervisor
Qualifications: [BA (Hons)(Oxon)]
✉pcoombe@13kbw.co.uk

COOMBES MR TIMOTHY JAMES

3 PB Barristers
3 Paper Buildings, Temple, London EC4Y 7EU, ☎020 7583 8055
3 PB Barristers
23 Beaumont Street, Oxford OX1 2NP, ☎01865 793 736
3 PB Barristers
30 Christchurch Road, Bournemouth, Dorset BH1 3PD, ☎01202 292102
✉clerks.bournemouth@3paper.co.uk
3 PB Barristers
Royal Talbot House, 2 Victoria Street, Bristol, Avon BS1 6BB, ☎0117 928 1520
3 PB Barristers
4 St Peter Street, Winchester SO23 8BW, ☎01962 868884
✉clerks.winchester@3paper.co.uk
Call Date: July 1980, Inner Temple
Pupil Supervisor
Qualifications: [BA (Dunelm)]
✉timothy.coombes@3paper.co.uk

COOMBES DAVIES DR MAIR

Lamb Chambers
Lamb Building, Elm Court, Temple, London EC4Y 7AS, ☎ 020 7797 8300
✉ info@lambchambers.co.uk
Civitas Chambers
Global Reach, Celtic Gateway, Cardiff Bay, Cardiff CF11 0SN, ☎ 0845 0713 007
✉ clerks@civitaslaw.com
Call Date: July 1988, Lincoln's Inn
Qualifications: [BSc(Hons) PhD (Wales) CPE BArch]

COONAN MR KIERAN BENET QC (1990)

1 Crown Office Row
1 Crown Office Row, Temple, London EC4Y 7HH, ☎ 020 7797 7500
✉ mail@1cor.com
Call Date: July 1971, Gray's Inn
Recorder
Qualifications: [Dip Eur Law]
✉ kieran.coonan@1cor.com

COOPER MR BEN LION

Doughty Street Chambers
53-54 Doughty Street, London WC1N 2LS, ☎ 020 7404 1313
✉ enquiries@doughtystreet.co.uk
Doughty Street Chambers
Pall Mall Court, 61-67 King Street, Manchester M2 4PD, ☎ 0161 618 1066
Doughty Street Chambers
5th Floor, Broad Quay House, Prince Street, Bristol BS1 4DJ, ☎ 01179 058 717
Call Date: Nov 1999, Middle Temple
Pupil Supervisor
Qualifications: [BA (Hons)(Sussex)]
✉ b.cooper@doughtystreet.co.uk

COOPER MR BEN MICHAEL

Old Square Chambers
10-11 Bedford Row, London WC1R 4BU, ☎ 020 7269 0300 ✉ clerks@oldsquare.co.uk
Old Square Chambers
3 Orchard Court, St Augustine's Yard, Bristol BS1 5DP, ☎ 0117 930 5100
✉ clerks@oldsquare.co.uk
Call Date: Nov 2000, Lincoln's Inn
Pupil Supervisor
Qualifications: [LLB (Hons)]
✉ cooper@oldsquare.co.uk

COOPER MISS CHRISTINE

Field Court Chambers
5 Field Court, Gray's Inn, London WC1R 5EF, ☎ 020 7405 6114 ✉ clerks@fieldcourt.co.uk
Call Date: July 2006, Inner Temple
Qualifications: [MSc (Cardiff) LLB (Lond)]
✉ christine.cooper@fieldcourt.co.uk

COOPER MISS CLAIRE LOUISE

Five St Andrew's Hill
5 St Andrew's Hill, London EC4V 5BZ, ☎ 020 7332 5400 ✉ Clerks@5sah.co.uk
Call Date: Oct 2002, Lincoln's Inn
Qualifications: [LLB]
✉ clairecooper@5sah.co.uk

COOPER MISS DANIELLE SOPHIE

Tooks Chambers
81 Farringdon Street, London EC4A 4BL, ☎ 020 7842 7575 ✉ clerks@tooks.co.uk
Call Date: Oct 1999, Lincoln's Inn
Qualifications: [LLB (Hons)(Notts)]
✉ clerks@tooks.co.uk

COOPER MR DOUGLAS RICHARD

St Johns Buildings Liverpool
8th Floor India Buildings, Water Street, Liverpool L2 0XG, ☎ 0151 243 6000
✉ clerk@stjohnsbuildings.co.uk
16 Winckley Square
Preston PR1 3JJ, ☎ 01772 256100
St Johns Buildings
24a - 28 St John Street, Manchester M3 4DJ, ☎ 0161 214 1500
✉ clerk@stjohnsbuildings.co.uk
Call Date: Oct 2004, Inner Temple
Qualifications: [LLB (Manch)]
✉ dougrcooper@mac.com

COOPER MISS ELISABETH DAWN

St Johns Buildings
24a - 28 St John Street, Manchester M3 4DJ, ☎ 0161 214 1500
✉ clerk@stjohnsbuildings.co.uk
16 Winckley Square
Preston PR1 3JJ, ☎ 01772 256100
St Johns Buildings Liverpool
8th Floor India Buildings, Water Street, Liverpool L2 0XG, ☎ 0151 243 6000
✉ clerk@stjohnsbuildings.co.uk
Call Date: July 2008, Middle Temple
Qualifications: [LLB (Hons) (Manch)]

E

COOPER MR GILEAD PATRICK QC (2006)

3 Stone Buildings
Ground Floor, 3 Stone Buildings, Lincoln's Inn, London WC2A 3XL, ☎020 7242 4937
✉clerks@3sb.law.co.uk
Call Date: Nov 1983, Middle Temple
Qualifications: [MA (Oxon) Dip Law]

COOPER MR IAN MARK

Call Date: Mar 1998, Middle Temple
Qualifications: [BA (Hons)]
mcooper@kingschambers.com

COOPER MR JOHN GORDON QC (2010)

25 Bedford Row
London WC1R 4HD, ☎020 7067 1500
✉clerks@25bedfordrow.com
Call Date: July 1983, Middle Temple
Pupil Supervisor
Qualifications: [LLB (Hons) (Newc)]
jcooper@25bedfordrow.com

COOPER MR JOHN MICHAEL

Crown Office Chambers
2 Crown Office Row, Temple, London EC4Y 7HJ, ☎020 7797 8100
✉mail@crownofficechambers.com
Call Date: July 1985, Inner Temple
Qualifications: [LLB(Reading)]
cooper@crownofficechambers.com

COOPER MR JONATHAN PAUL

Doughty Street Chambers
53-54 Doughty Street, London WC1N 2LS, ☎020 7404 1313
✉enquiries@doughtystreet.co.uk
Doughty Street Chambers
Pall Mall Court, 61-67 King Street, Manchester M2 4PD, ☎0161 618 1066
Doughty Street Chambers
5th Floor, Broad Quay House, Prince Street, Bristol BS1 4DJ, ☎01179 058 717
Call Date: Nov 1992, Gray's Inn
Qualifications: [BA (Kent)]
j.cooper@doughtystreet.co.uk

COOPER MR MARK GRAEME

Oriel Chambers
14 Water Street, Liverpool, Merseyside L2 8TD, ☎0151 236 7191
✉clerks@orielchambers.co.uk
Oriel Chambers
18 Ribblesdale Place, Preston PR1 3NA, ☎01772 254 764
✉clerks@oriel-chambers.co.uk
Call Date: July 2005, Lincoln's Inn
Qualifications: [BA (Hons)]
mark.cooper@orielchambers.co.uk

COOPER MR NICHOLAS JEROME

1 Gray's Inn Square
Ground Floor, 1 Gray's Inn Square, London WC1R 5AA, ☎020 7405 0001
Call Date: July 1997, Middle Temple
Qualifications: [BA (Hons)]

COOPER MR NIGEL STUART QC (2010)

Quadrant Chambers
Quadrant House, 10 Fleet Street, London EC4Y 1AU, ☎020 7583 4444
✉info@quadrantchambers.com
Call Date: July 1987, Lincoln's Inn
Pupil Supervisor
Qualifications: [LLB (Leeds) DIPE 1 (Holland) LLM (Lond)]
Nigel.Cooper@quadrantchambers.com

COOPER MR PAUL ANDREW

Portal Chambers
Blaencwm Mawr, Llandysul SA44 5NS, ☎01559 395 292
Call Date: July 1998, Middle Temple
Qualifications: [LLB (Hons)(Sheff)]
pc@portalchambers.co.uk

COOPER MR PETER JOHN

St Ive's Chambers
Whittall Street, Birmingham B4 6DH, ☎0121 236 0863
✉clerks@stiveschambers.co.uk
Call Date: Nov 1996, Gray's Inn
Pupil Supervisor
Qualifications: [MA (Oxon)]
peter.cooper@stiveschambers.co.uk

COOPER MISS RACHEL MARY

Lincoln House Chambers
Tower 12, The Avenue North, Spinningfields, 18-22 Bridge Street, Manchester M3 3BZ, ☎0161 832 5701
✉info@lincolnhousechambers.com
Call Date: July 2007, Middle Temple
Qualifications: [BA (Dunelm) Dip Law]
rachel.cooper@lincolnhousechambers.com

COOPER MR ROGER BERNARD

Park Lane Plowden
Lombard House, 4-8 Lombard Street, Newcastle Upon Tyne NE1 3AE,
☎ 0191 211 4087
✉ clerks@parklaneplowden.co.uk
Call Date: July 1989, Inner Temple
Pupil Supervisor
Qualifications: [BSc (L'pool) Dip Law]
✉ roger.cooper@parklaneplowden.co.uk

COOPER MISS SAMANTHA ANN

Outer Temple Chambers
The Outer Temple, 222 Strand, London WC2R 1BA, ☎ 020 7353 6381
✉ clerks@outertemple.com
Call Date: Oct 2007, Gray's Inn
Qualifications: [BA (Hons) (Cantab)]
✉ Samantha.cooper@outertemple.com

COOPER MISS SARAH LUCY

Thomas More Chambers
7 Lincoln's Inn Fields, London WC2A 3BP,
☎ 020 7404 7000
✉ clerks@thomasmore.co.uk
Call Date: Nov 1993, Inner Temple
Pupil Supervisor
Qualifications: [BA (Dunelm) Dip Law]
✉ slcooper@thomasmore.co.uk

COPE MRS STEPHANIE LOUISE

St John's Chambers
101 Victoria Street, Bristol BS1 6PU,
☎ 0117 923 4700
✉ clerks@stjohnschambers.co.uk
Call Date: Oct 2008, Lincoln's Inn
Qualifications: [LLB]

COPELAND MR ANDREW JOHN

36 Bedford Row
London WC1R 4JH, ☎ 020 7421 8000
✉ chambers@36bedfordrow.co.uk
Call Date: Nov 1992, Gray's Inn
Qualifications: [LLB]
✉ acopeland@36bedfordrow.co.uk

COPELAND MR MILES JAMES SIMON

Three New Square IP
3 New Square, Lincoln's Inn, London WC2A 3RS, ☎ 020 7405 1111
✉ clerks@3newsquare.co.uk
Call Date: Oct 2004, Lincoln's Inn
Qualifications: [MA (Hons)]
✉ copeland@3newsquare.co.uk

COPLEY MR JAMES EDWARD

4 Paper Buildings
1st Floor, 4 Paper Buildings, Temple, London EC4Y 7EX, ☎ 020 7427 5200
✉ clerks@4pb.com
Call Date: Oct 1997, Inner Temple
Qualifications: [LLB (Manch)]
✉ jec@4pb.com

COPLIN MR RICHARD JAMES

Keating Chambers
15 Essex Street, London WC2R 3AA,
☎ 020 7544 2600
✉ clerks@keatingchambers.com
Call Date: Oct 1997, Middle Temple
Pupil Supervisor
Qualifications: [BA (Hons)(Exon) CPE]
✉ rcoplin@keatingchambers.com

COPNALL MR RICHARD ANTHONY

Park Lane Plowden
19 Westgate, Leeds LS1 2RD,
☎ 0113 228 5049
✉ clerks@parklaneplowden.co.uk
Call Date: Oct 1990, Inner Temple
Pupil Supervisor
Qualifications: [BSc CPE (Nott'm)]
✉ richard.copnall@parklaneplowden.co.uk

COPPEL MR JASON ALASTAIR

11 King's Bench Walk
11 King's Bench Walk, Temple, London EC4Y 7EQ, ☎ 020 7632 8500
✉ clerksroom@11kbw.com
Call Date: Nov 1994, Inner Temple
Qualifications: [BA (Oxon) LLM (Italy)]
✉ jason.coppel@11kbw.com

COPPEL MR PHILIP ANTONY QC (2009)

4-5 Gray's Inn Square
Gray's Inn, London WC1R 5AH,
☎ 020 7404 5252 ✉ clerks@4-5.co.uk
Call Date: Nov 1994, Lincoln's Inn
Pupil Supervisor
Qualifications: [BA LLB (Australia)]
✉ pcoppel@4-5.co.uk

COPPOLA MISS ANNA FRANCESCA

Call Date: Nov 1996, Lincoln's Inn
Qualifications: [BA (Hons)(Lond) Dip Law]

E

CORBEN MR PAUL ANTHONY

5 Pump Court
Ground Floor, 5 Pump Court, Temple, London EC4Y 7AP, ☎ 020 7353 2532
✉ clerks@5pumpcourt.com
Call Date: July 1979, Gray's Inn
Pupil Supervisor
Qualifications: [MA (Cantab) FCIArb]

CORBETT-JONES MR MATTHEW

Linenhall Chambers
1 Stanley Place, Chester CH1 2LU, ☎ 01244 348282
✉ clerks@linenhallchambers.co.uk
Call Date: Oct 1999, Middle Temple
Qualifications: [LLB (Hons)]
🖃 clerks@1stanleyplace.co.uk

CORDARA MR RODERICK CHARLES QC (1994)

Essex Court Chambers
24 Lincoln's Inn Fields, London WC2A 3EG, ☎ 020 7813 8000
✉ clerksroom@essexcourt.net
Call Date: July 1975, Middle Temple
Qualifications: [MA (Cantab)]
🖃 rcordara@essexcourt.net

CORDERY MR PHILIP

New Court Chambers
3 Broad Chare, Newcastle Upon Tyne NE1 3DQ, ☎ 0191 232 1980
✉ clerks@newcourt-chambers.co.uk
Call Date: July 2003, Gray's Inn
Qualifications: [LLB (Hull)]
🖃 philip.cordery@newcourt-chambers.co.uk

CORDEY MR DANIEL ROE

Dere Street Barristers
14 Toft Green, York YO1 6JT, ☎ 0844 3351551
✉ clerks@derestreet.co.uk
Call Date: Nov 1990, Gray's Inn
Pupil Supervisor
Qualifications: [LLB (Lond)]
🖃 d.cordey@derestreet.co.uk

CORDREY MR THOMAS JOHN

Devereux Chambers
Queen Elizabeth Building, Temple, London EC4Y 9BS, ☎ 020 7353 7534
✉ clerks@devchambers.co.uk
Call Date: July 2006, Lincoln's Inn
Qualifications: [BA (Cantab)]
🖃 cordrey@devchambers.co.uk

CORFIELD MISS LOUISE SARAH

No5 Chambers
Fountain Court, Steelhouse Lane, Birmingham B4 6DR, ☎ 0845 210 5555 ✉ info@no5.com
No5 Chambers
Greenwood House, 4-7 Salisbury Court, London EC4Y 8AA, ☎ 0845 210 5555
No5 Chambers
38 Queen Square, Bristol BS1 4QS, ☎ 0845 210 5555
Call Date: Oct 2008, Inner Temple
Qualifications: [BA (Oxon)]
🖃 lc@no5.com

CORFIELD MISS SHEELAGH MARJORIE

St John's Chambers
101 Victoria Street, Bristol BS1 6PU, ☎ 0117 923 4700
✉ clerks@stjohnschambers.co.uk
Call Date: July 1975, Middle Temple
Pupil Supervisor
Qualifications: [LLB (Bristol)]
🖃 clerks@stjohnschambers.co.uk

CORLESS MR JOHN VINCENT

Atlantic Chambers
4-6 Cook Street, Liverpool L2 9QU, ☎ 0151 236 4421
✉ info@atlanticchambers.co.uk
Call Date: Nov 1984, Middle Temple
Pupil Supervisor, Recorder
Qualifications: [MA (St Andrews) M Th]
🖃 johncorless@atlanticchambers.co.uk

CORNBERG MR ANTONY JAMES

Cathedral Chambers
First Floor, 17 Queen Street, Newcastle Upon Tyne NE1 3UG, ☎ 0191 232 1311
✉ mail@cathedralchambers.com
Call Date: July 2003, Lincoln's Inn
Qualifications: [BA (Hons) PgDL LésL ACIL]
🖃 tonycornberg@cathedralchambers.com

CORNELL MISS KATHERINE MARGARET

5 Essex Court
1st Floor, 5 Essex Court, Temple, London EC4Y 9AH, ☎ 020 7410 2000
✉ clerks@5essexcourt.co.uk
Call Date: Oct 2003, Lincoln's Inn
Qualifications: [MA (Hons) (Cantab) CPE]

CORNER MR TIMOTHY FRANK QC (2002)

4-5 Gray's Inn Square
Gray's Inn, London WC1R 5AH,
☎ 020 7404 5252 ✉ clerks@4-5.co.uk
Call Date: Nov 1981, Gray's Inn
Recorder
Qualifications: [MA BCL (Oxon)]
✉ tcorner@4-5.co.uk

CORNWALL MISS NATALIA ELIZABETH

Exchange Chambers
One Derby Square, Derby Square, Liverpool L2 9XX, ☎ 0151 236 7747
✉ info@exchangechambers.co.uk
Exchange Chambers
Oxford House, Oxford Row, Leeds LS1 3BE,
☎ 0113 203 1970
✉ spencer@exchangechambers.co.uk
Call Date: July 2007, Middle Temple
Qualifications: [BA (B'ham)]
✉ cornwall@exchangechambers.co.uk

CORNWALL MISS VIRGINIA MARGARET

Albion Chambers
Broad Street, Bristol BS1 1DR,
☎ 0117 927 2144
✉ clerks@albionchambers.co.uk
Call Date: Oct 1990, Middle Temple
Qualifications: [LLB (Hons)]
✉ virginia.cornwall@albionchambers.co.uk

CORNWELL DR JAMES MATTHEW

11 King's Bench Walk
11 King's Bench Walk, Temple, London EC4Y 7EQ, ☎ 020 7632 8500
✉ clerksroom@11kbw.com
Call Date: July 2002, Middle Temple
Qualifications: [BA (Hons) (Oxon) MPhil (Lond) DPhil (Oxon) Dip Law]
✉ james.cornwell@11kbw.com

Types of work: Administrative law, Commercial law, Data protection, Disciplinary procedures, Discrimination, Education, Employment, Freedom of information, Human rights, Immigration, Judicial review, Local authorities, Public law, Social welfare

CORRE MR NEIL BERNARD

Redbourne Chambers
44 Redbourne Avenue, London N3 2BS,
☎ 020 8346 8524
Call Date: Mar 2005, Lincoln's Inn
Qualifications: [LLB (Hons) Leeds]

CORRIE MR MATTHEW JOHN GALLOWAY

13 King's Bench Walk
13 King's Bench Walk, Temple, London EC4Y 7EN, ☎ 020 7353 7204
✉ clerks@13kbw.co.uk
13 KBW
32 Beaumont Street, Oxford OX1 2NP,
☎ 01865 311066 ✉ clerks@13kbw.co.uk
Call Date: July 2006, Middle Temple
Qualifications: [BA (Hons) (Manch)]
✉ mcorrie@13kbw.co.uk

CORRIGAN MR PETER ANTHONY

Carmelite Chambers
9 Carmelite Street, London EC4Y 0DR,
☎ 020 7936 6300
✉ clerks@carmelitechambers.co.uk
Call Date: July 1972, Middle Temple
Pupil Supervisor
Qualifications: [MA (Oxon)]
✉ pcorrigan@carmelitechambers.co.uk

CORRIN MISS LUCY ELIZABETH

Doughty Street Chambers
53-54 Doughty Street, London WC1N 2LS,
☎ 020 7404 1313
✉ enquiries@doughtystreet.co.uk
Doughty Street Chambers
Pall Mall Court, 61-67 King Street, Manchester M2 4PD, ☎ 0161 618 1066
Doughty Street Chambers
5th Floor, Broad Quay House, Prince Street, Bristol BS1 4DJ, ☎ 01179 058 717
Call Date: Oct 2001, Middle Temple
Qualifications: [LLB (Hons)]
✉ l.corrin@doughtystreet.co.uk

CORSELLIS MR NICHOLAS ROBERT ALEXANDER

3 Temple Gardens
Lower Ground Floor, 3 Temple Gardens, Temple, London EC4Y 9AU, ☎ 020 7353 3102
✉ clerks@3tg.co.uk
Call Date: July 1993, Lincoln's Inn
Qualifications: [LLB (Hons)]
✉ nc@3tg.co.uk

CORY-WRIGHT MR CHARLES ALEXANDER QC (2006)

39 Essex Street
London WC2R 3AT, ☎ 020 7832 1111
✉ clerks@39essex.com
82 King Street
Manchester M2 4WQ, ☎ 0161 870 9969
Call Date: Feb 1984, Middle Temple
Qualifications: [BA (Oxon) Dip Law (Oxon)]
✉ charles.cory-wright@39essex.com

E

COSEDGE MR ANDREW JOHN

3 Stone Buildings
Ground Floor, 3 Stone Buildings, Lincoln's Inn, London WC2A 3XL, ☎ 020 7242 4937
✉ clerks@3sb.law.co.uk
Call Date: July 1972, Inner Temple
Pupil Supervisor
Qualifications: [LLB]
✉ acosedge@3sb.law.co.uk

COSGROVE MR THOMAS JAMES

Cornerstone Barristers
2-3 Gray's Inn Square, Gray's Inn, London WC1R 5JH, ☎ 020 7242 4986
✉ chambers@2-3gis.co.uk
Call Date: Oct 1994, Inner Temple
Pupil Supervisor
Qualifications: [MA (Cantab)]
✉ tcosgrove@2-3gis.co.uk

COSTELLO MR PAUL JAMES

Chambers of Mr Paul J Costello
Apartment 1, Pegasus House, High Street, Biggleswade, Bedfordshire SG18 0FB,
☎ 07846 016 399
✉ costellochambers@gmail.com
Call Date: Nov 1998, Inner Temple
Qualifications: [LLB (Hons)(Leeds)]
✉ costellochambers@gmail.com

COSTER MR RONALD DAVID

42 Bedford Row
London WC1R 4LL, ☎ 020 7831 0222
✉ clerks@42br.com
Call Date: July 1989, Lincoln's Inn
Qualifications: [BSc (Lancs) Dip Law]
✉ ronald.coster@42br.com

COTCHER MISS ANN LOUISE QC (2000)

Farringdon Chambers
180 Bermondsey Street, London SE1 3TQ,
☎ 020 7089 5700
Call Date: July 1979, Middle Temple
Qualifications: [LLB (So'ton)]

COTTAGE MISS ROSINA QC (2011)

The Chambers of Grahame Aldous QC
9 Gough Square, London EC4A 3DG,
☎ 020 7832 0500
✉ clerks@9goughsquare.co.uk
Call Date: Nov 1988, Inner Temple
Pupil Supervisor
Qualifications: [LLB (Bris)]
✉ rcottage@9goughsquare.co.uk

COTTER MR MARK JAMES

Five St Andrew's Hill
5 St Andrew's Hill, London EC4V 5BZ,
☎ 020 7332 5400 ✉ Clerks@5sah.co.uk
Call Date: Nov 1994, Middle Temple
Pupil Supervisor
Qualifications: [LLB (Hons) LLM (Wales)]
✉ markcotter@5sah.co.uk

COTTER MR NICHOLAS ANDREW JAMES HORLOR

1 Paper Buildings
1st Floor, 1 Paper Buildings, Temple, London EC4Y 7EP, ☎ 020 7353 3728
✉ clerks@onepaper.co.uk
Call Date: Oct 1999, Lincoln's Inn
Qualifications: [BA (Hons) CPE (Dip Law)]
✉ nicholascotter@onepaper.co.uk

COTTERELL MR DAVID WILLIAM

Albion Chambers
Broad Street, Bristol BS1 1DR,
☎ 0117 927 2144
✉ clerks@albionchambers.co.uk
Call Date: Nov 2001, Lincoln's Inn
Qualifications: [BSc (Hons)]
✉ david.cotterell@albionchambers.co.uk

COTTERILL MISS SUZANNAH

Field Court Chambers
5 Field Court, Gray's Inn, London WC1R 5EF,
☎ 020 7405 6114 ✉ clerks@fieldcourt.co.uk
Call Date: July 1988, Lincoln's Inn
Pupil Supervisor
Qualifications: [LLB (Hons) (Essex)]
✉ suzannah.cotterill@fieldcourt.co.uk

COTTLE MR MAURICE ANTHONY HAYDEN

Nevern Mansions
Flat 8, 27A Nevern Square, London SW5 9TH,
☎ 07973 320654 ✉ tony@cottle.demon.co.uk
Clerksroom (Taunton)
Equity House, Administration Centre, Blackbrook Park Avenue, Taunton, Somerset TA1 2PX, ☎ 0845 083 3000
✉ mail@clerksroom.com
Call Date: July 1978, Gray's Inn
Qualifications: [LLB (Lond) MPhil (Lond)]

COTTLE MR STEPHEN CHARLES

Garden Court Chambers
57-60 Lincoln's Inn Fields, London WC2A 3LJ,
☎ 020 7993 7600 ✉ info@gclaw.co.uk
Call Date: Nov 1984, Inner Temple
Pupil Supervisor
Qualifications: [BA (Hons) Dip Law]
✉ stephenc@gclaw.co.uk

COTTON MRS HEIDI ELIZABETH

Bank House Chambers
Old Bank House, Hartshead, Sheffield S1 2EL,
☎0114 275 1223
✉w.digby@bankhousechambers.co.uk
Call Date: July 1998, Lincoln's Inn
Qualifications: [LLB (Hons)]
h.cotton@bankhousechambers.co.uk

COTTON MR STEPHEN DAVID

College Chambers
19 Carlton Crescent, Southampton,
Hampshire SO15 2ET, ☎023 8023 0338
✉clerks@college-chambers.co.uk
Call Date: Mar 1998, Lincoln's Inn
Qualifications: [LLB (Hons)(So'ton) LLM]

COTTRELL MRS BEVERLEY DAWN

Clerksroom (Taunton)
Equity House, Administration Centre,
Blackbrook Park Avenue, Taunton, Somerset
TA1 2PX, ☎0845 083 3000
✉mail@clerksroom.com
Call Date: Oct 2009, Middle Temple
Qualifications: [MA (Cantab) Vet MB (Cantab)]

COTTRELL MR MATTHEW ROBERT

Oriel Chambers
18 Ribblesdale Place, Preston PR1 3NA,
☎01772 254 764
✉clerks@oriel-chambers.co.uk
Oriel Chambers
14 Water Street, Liverpool, Merseyside
L2 8TD, ☎0151 236 7191
✉clerks@orielchambers.co.uk
Call Date: Oct 1996, Gray's Inn
Qualifications: [LLB (Sheff)]
matthew.cottrell@orielchambers.co.uk

COTTRELL MR STEPHEN

Devereux Chambers
Queen Elizabeth Building, Temple, London
EC4Y 9BS, ☎020 7353 7534
✉clerks@devchambers.co.uk
Call Date: Oct 1998, Inner Temple
Qualifications: [BA (Oxon)]
scottrell@tgchambers.com

COUGHLAN MR JOHN PHILIP

No5 Chambers
Fountain Court, Steelhouse Lane, Birmingham
B4 6DR, ☎0845 210 5555 ✉info@no5.com
No5 Chambers
Greenwood House, 4-7 Salisbury Court,
London EC4Y 8AA, ☎0845 210 5555
No5 Chambers
38 Queen Square, Bristol BS1 4QS,
☎0845 210 5555
Call Date: Nov 1999, Middle Temple
Pupil Supervisor
Qualifications: [LLB (Bris) BCL (Oxon)]
jco@no5.com

COUGHLIN MR VINCENT WILLIAM QC (2003)

18 Red Lion Court
London EC4A 3EB, ☎020 7520 6000
✉chambers@18rlc.co.uk
Apex
Harlech House, 20 Cathedral Road, Cardiff
CF11 9LJ, ☎02920 232 032
✉clerks@apexchambers.net
Temple Chambers
32 Park Place, Cardiff CF10 3BA,
☎029 2039 7364
✉DBrinning@Temple-Chambers.co.uk
1 High Pavement
Nottingham NG1 1HF, ☎0115 941 8218
✉clerks@1highpavement.co.uk
Call Date: July 1980, Middle Temple
Qualifications: [LLB (Lond)]
vincent.coughlin@18rlc.co.uk

COUGHTRIE MR SCOTT WILSON CURRIE

St Ive's Chambers
Whittall Street, Birmingham B4 6DH,
☎0121 236 0863
✉clerks@stiveschambers.co.uk
Call Date: Nov 2000, Lincoln's Inn
Qualifications: [LLB (Hons)(Wolves)]
scott.coughtrie@stiveschambers.co.uk

COULTER MR BARRY JOHN

Clerksroom (Taunton)
Equity House, Administration Centre,
Blackbrook Park Avenue, Taunton, Somerset
TA1 2PX, ☎0845 083 3000
✉mail@clerksroom.com
Clerksroom (London)
3rd Floor, 218 Strand, London WC2R 1AT,
☎0845 083 3000 ✉mail@clerksroom.com

E

King's Lynn Chambers
26 The Birches, South Wootton, King's Lynn, Norfolk PE30 3JG, ☎01553 672 085
✉timothy.leader@tesco.net
Call Date: Nov 1985, Inner Temple
Qualifications: [LLB]
coulter@clerksroom.com

COUNSELL MR EDWARD FREDERICK

Unity Street Chambers
5 Unity Street, College Green, Bristol BS1 5HH, ☎0117 906 9789
✉chambers@unitystreetchambers.com
Call Date: Nov 1990, Inner Temple
Pupil Supervisor
Qualifications: [BA BCL (Oxon)]
edward_counsell@hotmail.co.uk

COUNSELL MR JAMES HENRY

Outer Temple Chambers
The Outer Temple, 222 Strand, London WC2R 1BA, ☎020 7353 6381
✉clerks@outertemple.com
Call Date: July 1984, Inner Temple
Pupil Supervisor
Qualifications: [MA (Cantab)]
james.counsell@outertemple.com

E

COUNSELL MISS LYNNE MARGARET

9 Stone Buildings
Lincoln's Inn, London WC2A 3NN, ☎020 7404 5055
✉clerks@9stonebuildings.com
Call Date: Nov 1986, Inner Temple
Pupil Supervisor
Qualifications: [BA (Lond) Dip Law (City)]
clerks@9stonebuildings.com

COUPE MR TOBY JOHN ERNEST

Sovereign Chambers
46 Park Place, Leeds LS1 2RY, ☎0113 245 1841
✉clerks@sovereignchambers.co.uk
Call Date: July 2007, Lincoln's Inn
Qualifications: [LLB (Leeds)]
toby.coupe@sovereignchambers.co.uk

COUPLAND MR STEVEN MICHAEL EDWARD

1 High Pavement
Nottingham NG1 1HF, ☎0115 941 8218
✉clerks@1highpavement.co.uk
Call Date: May 1993, Lincoln's Inn
Pupil Supervisor
Qualifications: [LLB (Hons) (Wales)]
stevencoupland@1highpavement.co.uk

COURTNEY MS ANN

New Court
Ground Floor, New Court, Temple, London EC4Y 9BE, ☎020 7583 5123
✉clerks@newcourtchambers.com
Call Date: Nov 1987, Inner Temple
Qualifications: [LLB (Hons)]
acourtney@newcourtchambers.net

COURTNEY MR NICHOLAS PIERS

Deans Court Chambers
24 St John Street, Manchester M3 4DF, ☎0161 214 6000 ✉clerks@deanscourt.co.uk
Deans Court Chambers
101 Walker Street, Preston PR1 2RR, ☎01772 565 600
✉preston@deanscourt.co.uk
Call Date: Nov 1990, Middle Temple
Pupil Supervisor
Qualifications: [LLB (Manch)]
courtney@deanscourt.co.uk

COURTS MR ROBERT ALEXANDER

3 PB Barristers
3 Paper Buildings, Temple, London EC4Y 7EU, ☎020 7583 8055
3 PB Barristers
Royal Talbot House, 2 Victoria Street, Bristol, Avon BS1 6BB, ☎0117 928 1520
3 PB Barristers
23 Beaumont Street, Oxford OX1 2NP, ☎01865 793 736
3 PB Barristers
4 St Peter Street, Winchester SO23 8BW, ☎01962 868884
✉clerks.winchester@3paper.co.uk
3 PB Barristers
30 Christchurch Road, Bournemouth, Dorset BH1 3PD, ☎01202 292102
✉clerks.bournemouth@3paper.co.uk
Call Date: July 2003, Lincoln's Inn
Qualifications: [LLB Hons (Sheff)]

COUSENS MR MICHAEL PATRICK

Carmelite Chambers
9 Carmelite Street, London EC4Y 0DR, ☎020 7936 6300
✉clerks@carmelitechambers.co.uk
Call Date: Feb 1973, Lincoln's Inn
Pupil Supervisor

COUSER MR JAMES ROBERT BURKE

13 Old Square Chambers
Ground Floor, 14 Old Square, Lincoln's Inn, London WC2A 3UE, ☎020 7831 4445
✉clerks@13oldsquare.com
Call Date: July 2000, Lincoln's Inn
Qualifications: [LLB (Herts) LLM (Edin) BCL (Oxon)]

COUSINS MR JEREMY VINCENT QC (1999)

11 Stone Buildings
11 Stone Buildings, Lincoln's Inn, London WC2A 3TG, ☎020 7831 6381
✉clerks@11sb.com
St Philips Chambers
55 Temple Row, Birmingham B2 5LS, ☎0121 246 7000 ✉clerks@st-philips.com
Call Date: July 1977, Middle Temple
Recorder
Qualifications: [LLB (Hons)]
✉cousins@11sb.com

COUTINO MISS MELISSA-LOUISE BARBARA

Chambers of Ms M Coutino
136 De Beauvoir Road, London N1 4DJ, ☎07958 202997
✉mlcoutino@googlemail.com
Call Date: Oct 1997, Middle Temple
Pupil Supervisor
Qualifications: [BA (Hons)(Lond) CPE PGDL]
✉melissa.coutinho@dwp.gsi.gov.uk

COUTTS MR JAMES EDWARD

Linenhall Chambers
1 Stanley Place, Chester CH1 2LU, ☎01244 348282
✉clerks@linenhallchambers.co.uk
Call Date: July 2007, Lincoln's Inn
Qualifications: [LLB (Leeds)]

COVENTRY MR CHARLES CHOPIN

St John's Chambers
101 Victoria Street, Bristol BS1 6PU, ☎0117 923 4700
✉clerks@stjohnschambers.co.uk
Call Date: July 2007, Gray's Inn
Qualifications: [LLB (Bris)]
✉charles.coventry@stjohnschambers.co.uk

COVER MISS MARTHA JUNE

Coram Chambers
9-11 Fulwood Place, London WC1V 6HG, ☎020 7092 3700
✉mail@coramchambers.co.uk
Call Date: Nov 1979, Gray's Inn
Pupil Supervisor
Qualifications: [BA (Canada) LLM (Lond) BA]
✉martha.cover@coramchambers.co.uk, marthacover@hotmail.com

COVINGTON MISS REBECCA LOUISE

St Mary's Family Law Chambers
26-28 High Pavement, The Lace Market, Nottingham NG1 1HN, ☎0115 950 3503
✉clerks@stmarysflc.co.uk
Call Date: Mar 2006, Middle Temple
Qualifications: [BA (Hons) (Oxon)]
✉rebecca.covington@stmarysflc.co.uk

COWAN MR DAVID SIMON

Arden Chambers
20 Bloomsbury Square, London WC1A 2NS, ☎020 7242 4244
✉clerks@ardenchambers.com
Call Date: Nov 2006, Middle Temple
Qualifications: [LLB (Hons) (So'ton)]
✉david.cowan@ardenchambers.com

COWAN MR PETER SHERWOOD MCCREA

Oriel Chambers
14 Water Street, Liverpool, Merseyside L2 8TD, ☎0151 236 7191
✉clerks@orielchambers.co.uk
Oriel Chambers
18 Ribblesdale Place, Preston PR1 3NA, ☎01772 254 764
✉clerks@oriel-chambers.co.uk
Call Date: July 1980, Middle Temple
Pupil Supervisor, Recorder
Qualifications: [MA (Oxon)]
✉peter.cowan@orielchambers.co.uk

COWE MISS MARY ELIZABETH

Guildhall Chambers
23 Broad Street, Bristol BS1 2HG, ☎0117 930 9000
✉hoc@guildhallchambers.co.uk
Call Date: July 2006, Inner Temple
Qualifications: [BA (Oxon)]
✉mary.cowe@guildhallchambers.co.uk

COWEN MISS EMMA LOUISE

Lincoln House Chambers
Tower 12, The Avenue North, Spinningfields, 18-22 Bridge Street, Manchester M3 3BZ, ☎0161 832 5701
✉info@lincolnhousechambers.com
Call Date: Nov 2010, Gray's Inn
Qualifications: [BA MPhil]
✉louise.cowen@lincolnhousechambers.com

E

COWEN MR GARY ADAM

Falcon Chambers
Falcon Court, London EC4Y 1AA,
☎ 020 7353 2484
✉ clerks@falcon-chambers.com
Call Date: Oct 1990, Inner Temple
Pupil Supervisor
Qualifications: [LLB (Bris)]
cowen@falcon-chambers.com

Types of work: Chancery (general), Chancery (land law), Commercial property, Common land, Compulsory Purchase, Conveyancing, Environment, Housing, Land compensation, Landlord and tenant

COWEN MR JONATHAN MICHAEL

Field Court Chambers
5 Field Court, Gray's Inn, London WC1R 5EF,
☎ 020 7405 6114 ✉ clerks@fieldcourt.co.uk
Chartlands Chambers
3 St Giles Terrace, Northampton NN1 2BN,
☎ 01604 603322
✉ enquiries@chartlands-chambers.co.uk
Call Date: Nov 1983, Middle Temple
Pupil Supervisor
Qualifications: [MA (Oxon) Dip Law]
jonathan.cowen@fieldcourt.co.uk

E

COWEN MISS SALLY EMMA

Cloisters
1 Pump Court, Temple, London EC4Y 7AA,
☎ 020 7827 4000 ✉ clerks@cloisters.com
Call Date: Oct 1995, Inner Temple
Pupil Supervisor
Qualifications: [LLB (Leeds)]
sc@Cloisters.com

COWEN MR TIMOTHY ARIEH

11 Stone Buildings
11 Stone Buildings, Lincoln's Inn, London WC2A 3TG, ☎ 020 7831 6381
✉ clerks@11sb.com
Call Date: Oct 1993, Inner Temple
Qualifications: [BA (L'pool)]

COWEY MISS SARAH LOUISE

7 King's Bench Walk
Ground Floor, 7 King's Bench Walk, Temple, London EC4Y 7DS, ☎ 020 7910 8300
✉ clerks@7kbw.co.uk
Call Date: Oct 2006, Middle Temple
Qualifications: [MA (Hons) (Cantab) LLM (Cantab)]
scowey@7kbw.co.uk

COWLEY MR ROBERT

No 8 Chambers
8 Fountain Court, Steelhouse Lane, Birmingham B4 6DR, ☎ 0121 236 5514
✉ clerks@no8chambers.co.uk
Call Date: Oct 1992, Lincoln's Inn
Qualifications: [LLB(Hons)(Leics)]
clerks@no8chambers.co.uk

COWTON MISS CATHERINE JUDITH

Queen Elizabeth Building
3rd Floor, Queen Elizabeth Building, Temple, London EC4Y 9BS, ☎ 020 7797 7837
✉ clerks@qeb.co.uk
Call Date: Nov 1995, Middle Temple
Pupil Supervisor
Qualifications: [MA (Hons)]
c.cowton@qeb.co.uk

COX MR BRYAN RICHARD QC (2006)

Park Court Chambers
16 Park Place, Leeds LS1 2SJ,
☎ 0113 243 3277
✉ clerks@parkcourtchambers.co.uk
Call Date: July 1979, Middle Temple
Recorder
Qualifications: [LLB (Leeds)]
bcox@parkcourtchambers.co.uk

COX MR CARWYN GEORGE

Farrar's Building
Farrar's Building, Temple, London EC4Y 7BD,
☎ 020 7583 9241
✉ Chambers@farrarsbuilding.co.uk
Call Date: Oct 2002, Lincoln's Inn
Qualifications: [LLB Hons (Dunelm) P G Dip Law]
ccox@farrarsbuilding.co.uk

COX MR CHARLES GEOFFREY QC (2003)

Thomas More Chambers
7 Lincoln's Inn Fields, London WC2A 3BP,
☎ 020 7404 7000
✉ clerks@thomasmore.co.uk
Call Date: July 1982, Middle Temple
Qualifications: [BA (Cantab)]
gcox@thomasmore.co.uk

COX MR DOMINIC

Argent Chambers
5 Bell Yard, London WC2A 2JR,
☎ 020 7556 5500
✉ briefsin@argentchambers.co.uk
Call Date: Nov 1994, Lincoln's Inn
Qualifications: [BA (Hons)(Kent)]
d.cox@argentchambers.co.uk

COX MR JASON DAVID

Ropewalk Chambers
24 The Ropewalk, Nottingham NG1 5EF,
☎0115 947 2581 ✉clerks@ropewalk.co.uk
Call Date: Oct 1992, Gray's Inn
Pupil Supervisor
Qualifications: [LLB (Nott'm)]
jasoncox@ropewalk.co.uk

COX MR JONATHAN EDWARD

KCH Garden Square
1 Oxford Street, Nottingham NG1 5BH,
☎0115 941 8851
✉clerks@kchgardensquare.co.uk
Call Date: Oct 2005, Lincoln's Inn
Qualifications: [LLB (Hons) (Lond)]

COX MISS JULIA EMMA GRACE

Devon Chambers
3 St Andrew Street, Plymouth PL1 2AH,
☎01752 661659
✉clerks@devonchambers.co.uk
Call Date: July 2006, Middle Temple
Qualifications: [LLB (Hons)]
jcox@devonchambers.co.uk

COX MR KERRIE IAN ERNEST

Clerksroom (Taunton)
Equity House, Administration Centre, Blackbrook Park Avenue, Taunton, Somerset TA1 2PX, ☎0845 083 3000
✉mail@clerksroom.com
Call Date: Oct 1998, Inner Temple
Qualifications: [LLB (Hons)]

COX MISS KERRY AMANDA

Park Lane Plowden
Lombard House, 4-8 Lombard Street, Newcastle Upon Tyne NE1 3AE,
☎0191 211 4087
✉clerks@parklaneplowden.co.uk
Call Date: Oct 1990, Inner Temple
Pupil Supervisor
Qualifications: [MA (Hons)(St Andrew) Dip Law]
kerry.cox@parklaneplowden.co.uk

COX MR LINDSAY RANDALL

1 Paper Buildings
1st Floor, 1 Paper Buildings, Temple, London EC4Y 7EP, ☎020 7353 3728
✉clerks@onepaper.co.uk
Call Date: July 1984, Middle Temple
Pupil Supervisor
Qualifications: [LLB (UEA)]
lindsaycox@onepaper.co.uk

COX MR NICHOLAS IVAN

4 Stone Buildings
Ground Floor, 4 Stone Buildings, Lincoln's Inn, London WC2A 3XT, ☎020 7242 5524
✉clerks@4stonebuildings.com
Call Date: Oct 1992, Middle Temple
Qualifications: [BA (Hons)(Oxon) MBA (Warw)]
n.cox@4stonebuildings.com

COX MISS OLIVIA RODRIGUES

Atlantic Chambers
4-6 Cook Street, Liverpool L2 9QU,
☎0151 236 4421
✉info@atlanticchambers.co.uk
Call Date: Nov 2007, Middle Temple
Qualifications: [LLB (Hons) (Sheff)]
oliviacox@atlanticchambers.co.uk

COX MR RAYMOND EDWIN QC (2002)

Fountain Court Chambers
Fountain Court, Temple, London EC4Y 9DH,
☎020 7583 3335
✉chambers@fountaincourt.co.uk
Call Date: July 1982, Gray's Inn
Qualifications: [BA (Oxon)]
rcox@fountaincourt.co.uk

COX MISS SIAN

Harcourt Chambers
1st Floor, 2 Harcourt Buildings, Temple, London EC4Y 9DB, ☎0844 561 7135
Call Date: July 2008, Middle Temple
Qualifications: [BA (Hons) (Oxon) LLM (Lond)]
scox@harcourtchambers.law.co.uk

COX MS SITA

Stour Chambers
Mill Studio, 17a Stour Street, Canterbury, Kent CT1 2NR, ☎01227 764899
✉clerks@stourchambers.co.uk
Call Date: Nov 1987, Middle Temple
Pupil Supervisor
Qualifications: [BA (Hons)]
clerks@stourchambers.co.uk

COX MISS TAMSIN VICTORIA ELIZABETH

Falcon Chambers
Falcon Court, London EC4Y 1AA,
☎020 7353 2484
✉clerks@falcon-chambers.com
Call Date: Oct 2005, Lincoln's Inn
Qualifications: [BA (Hons) (Oxon)]
cox@falcon-chambers.com

E

COXHILL MR FRASER

QEB Hollis Whiteman
1-2 Laurence Pountney Hill, London EC4R 0EU, ☎ 020 7933 8855
✉ barristers@qebhw.co.uk
Call Date: July 2004, Lincoln's Inn
Qualifications: [LLB]
barristers@qebhw.co.uk

COYLE MR ANTHONY NOEL

Zenith Chambers
10 Park Square, Leeds LS1 2LH, ☎ 0113 245 5438
✉ clerks@zenithchambers.co.uk
Call Date: Nov 2003, Lincoln's Inn
Qualifications: [LLB (Hons) (Hull)]
tonycoyle27@live.co.uk

COYLE MR STEPHEN DAVID

Renaissance Chambers
5th Floor, Gray's Inn Chambers, Gray's Inn, London WC1R 5JA, ☎ 020 7404 1111
✉ clerks@renaissancechambers.co.uk
Call Date: Oct 1998, Middle Temple
Qualifications: [LLB (Hons)(Manc)]
sc1@renaissancechambers.co.uk

CRABB MR RICHARD BLECHYNDEN

Colleton Chambers
Colleton Crescent, Exeter, Devon EX2 4DG, ☎ 01392 274898
✉ clerks@colletonchambers.co.uk
Call Date: Nov 1975, Middle Temple
richardcrabb@colletonchambers.co.uk

CRABB MISS SAMANTHA JILL

Citadel Chambers
The Citadel, 190 Corporation Street, Birmingham B4 6QD, ☎ 0121 233 8500
✉ clerks@citadelchambers.com
Call Date: Nov 1996, Inner Temple
Qualifications: [LLB (L'pool)]
clerks@citadelchambers.com

CRABTREE MR SIMON JEREMY GERHARD

St Johns Buildings
24a - 28 St John Street, Manchester M3 4DJ, ☎ 0161 214 1500
✉ clerk@stjohnsbuildings.co.uk
16 Winckley Square
Preston PR1 3JJ, ☎ 01772 256100
St Johns Buildings Liverpool
8th Floor India Buildings, Water Street, Liverpool L2 0XG, ☎ 0151 243 6000
✉ clerk@stjohnsbuildings.co.uk
Call Date: Nov 1988, Lincoln's Inn
Qualifications: [LLB (Hons) (Leeds)]
clerk@stjohnsbuildings.co.uk

CRAGG MS JANET ELIZABETH

Kenworthy's Chambers
Arlington House, Bloom Street, Salford, Manchester M3 6AJ, ☎ 0161 832 4036
Call Date: July 2005, Lincoln's Inn
Qualifications: [BA (Hons)]
j.cragg@kenworthysbarristers.co.uk

CRAGG MR STEPHEN JAMES

Doughty Street Chambers
53-54 Doughty Street, London WC1N 2LS, ☎ 020 7404 1313
✉ enquiries@doughtystreet.co.uk
Doughty Street Chambers
Pall Mall Court, 61-67 King Street, Manchester M2 4PD, ☎ 0161 618 1066
Doughty Street Chambers
5th Floor, Broad Quay House, Prince Street, Bristol BS1 4DJ, ☎ 01179 058 717
Call Date: Nov 1996, Middle Temple
Pupil Supervisor
Qualifications: [LLB (Hons)(Lond) MA (Brunel)]
s.cragg@doughtystreet.co.uk

CRAIG MR ALISTAIR TREVOR

Chambers of Mr A Craig
95 Court Lane, Dulwich, London SE21 7EF, ☎ 020 8265 2290
✉ alistaircraig@btinternet.com
Call Date: July 1983, Lincoln's Inn
Qualifications: [MA (TCD)]

CRAIG MR AUBREY JOHN

St Philips Chambers
55 Temple Row, Birmingham B2 5LS, ☎ 0121 246 7000 ✉ clerks@st-philips.com
Chancery House Chambers
7 Lisbon Square, Leeds, West Yorkshire LS1 4LY, ☎ 0113 244 6691
✉ clerks@chanceryhouse.co.uk
Call Date: Nov 1987, Inner Temple
Qualifications: [LLB (Hons)]
acraig@st-philips.co.uk

CRAIG MR DAVID MARK

Essex Court Chambers
24 Lincoln's Inn Fields, London WC2A 3EG, ☎ 020 7813 8000
✉ clerksroom@essexcourt.net
Call Date: Oct 1997, Inner Temple
Qualifications: [BSc (Manch) MPhil (Cantab) CPE]
dcraig@essexcourt.net

E

CRAIG MR NICHOLAS

3 Verulam Buildings
London WC1R 5NT, ☎ 020 7831 8441
✉ chambers@3vb.com
Call Date: Oct 1998, Inner Temple
Pupil Supervisor
Qualifications: [BA (Lond) MPhil (Oxon) CPE]
✉ ncraig@3vb.com

CRAIL MISS ROSS

New Square Chambers
12 New Square, Lincoln's Inn, London WC2A 3SW, ☎ 020 7419 8000
✉ robin.hollington@newsquarechambers.co.uk
Call Date: July 1986, Lincoln's Inn
Qualifications: [MA (Oxon) Dip Law (Lond)]
✉ ross.crail@newsquarechambers.co.uk

CRAMMOND MR ANDREW JAMES

Trinity Chambers
The Custom House, 39 Quayside, Newcastle Upon Tyne NE1 3DE, ☎ 0191 232 1927
✉ info@trinitychambers.co.uk
Trinity Chambers
Multi Media Exchange, 72-80 Corporation Road, Middlesbrough TS1 2RF,
☎ 01642 247569
✉ info@trinitychambers.co.uk
Call Date: Nov 2008, Lincoln's Inn
Qualifications: [LLB (Dunelm)]
✉ a.crammond@trinitychambers.co.uk

CRAMPIN DR CECILY MARY

Tanfield Chambers
2-5 Warwick Court, London WC1R 5DJ,
☎ 020 7421 5300
✉ clerks@tanfieldchambers.co.uk
Call Date: Oct 2008, Middle Temple
Qualifications: [BA (Hons) (Oxon) MA (Oxon) DPhil (Oxon) MSc (Manch)]
✉ cecilycrampin@tanfieldchambers.co.uk

CRAMPIN MR PAUL

Chambers of Mr Ami Feder
Ground Floor, Lamb Building, Temple, London EC4Y 7AS, ☎ 020 7797 7788
✉ clerks@lambbuilding.co.uk
Lamb Building
22 Ship Street, Brighton BN1 1AD,
☎ 01273 820490
✉ admin@lambbuilding.co.uk
Chambers of Mr Ami Feder
Ground Floor, Lamb Building, Temple, London EC4Y 7AS, ☎ 020 7797 7788
✉ clerks@lambbuilding.co.uk
Call Date: Oct 1992, Middle Temple
Pupil Supervisor
Qualifications: [LLB (Hons)]
✉ paulcrampin@lambbuilding.co.uk

CRAMPIN MR PETER QC (1993)

Radcliffe Chambers
Ground Floor, 11 New Square, Lincoln's Inn, London WC2A 3QB, ☎ 020 7831 0081
✉ clerks@radcliffechambers.com
Call Date: Nov 1976, Middle Temple
Recorder
Qualifications: [MA (Oxon)]
✉ pcrampin@radcliffechambers.com

CRAMSIE MR JAMES SINCLAIR BERESFORD

13 King's Bench Walk
13 King's Bench Walk, Temple, London EC4Y 7EN, ☎ 020 7353 7204
✉ clerks@13kbw.co.uk
13 KBW
32 Beaumont Street, Oxford OX1 2NP,
☎ 01865 311066 ✉ clerks@13kbw.co.uk
Call Date: Nov 1988, Inner Temple
Pupil Supervisor
Qualifications: [LLB (Leeds)]
✉ SCramsie@13kbw.co.uk

CRAN MR MARK DYSON GORDON QC (1988)

Brick Court Chambers
7-8 Essex Street, London WC2R 3LD,
☎ 020 7379 3550 ✉ clerks@brickcourt.co.uk
Call Date: July 1973, Gray's Inn
Recorder
Qualifications: [LLB (Bris)]
✉ Mark.Cran@Brickcourt.co.uk

CRANE MR MICHAEL JOHN QC (1994)

Fountain Court Chambers
Fountain Court, Temple, London EC4Y 9DH,
☎ 020 7583 3335
✉ chambers@fountaincourt.co.uk
Call Date: Nov 1975, Middle Temple
Qualifications: [BA (Oxon)]
✉ mc@fountaincourt.co.uk

CRANE MISS SUZANNE DENISE

Middle Temple Lane Chambers
2nd Floor South, 1 Middle Temple Lane, London EC4Y 9AA, ☎ 020 7583 4352
✉ chambers@mtlchambers.com
Call Date: Nov 1995, Lincoln's Inn
Qualifications: [LLB (Hons)]

E

CRANFIELD MR JAMES OLIVER

Albion Chambers
Broad Street, Bristol BS1 1DR,
☎0117 927 2144
✉clerks@albionchambers.co.uk
Call Date: July 2002, Inner Temple
Qualifications: [LLB Hons (Wales)]

CRANFIELD MR PETER ANTHONY

3 Verulam Buildings
London WC1R 5NT, ☎020 7831 8441
✉chambers@3vb.com
Call Date: July 1982, Gray's Inn
Pupil Supervisor
Qualifications: [BA BCL (Oxon)]
✉pcranfield@3vb.com

CRANFIELD MR TONY

Bank House Chambers
Old Bank House, Hartshead, Sheffield S1 2EL,
☎0114 275 1223
✉w.digby@bankhousechambers.co.uk
Call Date: Nov 1975, Middle Temple
Pupil Supervisor
Qualifications: [LLB]
✉t.cranfield@bankhousechambers.co.uk

CRANGLE MR THOMAS PETER

4 Pump Court
4 Pump Court, Temple, London EC4Y 7AN,
☎020 7842 5555
✉chambers@4pumpcourt.com
Call Date: July 2002, Gray's Inn
Qualifications: [BA (Cantab)]
✉tcrangle@4pumpcourt.com

CRANIDGE MISS RUTH SELINA

Park Court Chambers
16 Park Place, Leeds LS1 2SJ,
☎0113 243 3277
✉clerks@parkcourtchambers.co.uk
Call Date: Oct 2001, Lincoln's Inn
Pupil Supervisor
Qualifications: [LLB (Hons) (Warwick)]
✉rcranidge@parkcourtchambers.co.uk

CRANMER-BROWN MR MICHAEL TIMOTHY

KCH Garden Square
1 Oxford Street, Nottingham NG1 5BH,
☎0115 941 8851
✉clerks@kchgardensquare.co.uk
Call Date: Nov 1986, Middle Temple
Qualifications: [BA (Hons)(Oxon) Dip Law (City)]

CRANNY MISS AMANDA LOUISE

KCH Garden Square
1 Oxford Street, Nottingham NG1 5BH,
☎0115 941 8851
✉clerks@kchgardensquare.co.uk
Call Date: Nov 1984, Lincoln's Inn
Qualifications: [LLB (Bris)]

CRANSTON-MORRIS MR WAYNE

23 Essex Street
London WC2R 3AA, ☎020 7413 0353
✉clerks@23es.com
Call Date: July 1986, Lincoln's Inn
Qualifications: [LLB (Brunel)]
✉waynecranstonmorris@23es.com

CRAPPER MS SADIE ELLEN

39 Essex Street
London WC2R 3AT, ☎020 7832 1111
✉clerks@39essex.com
Call Date: Nov 2004, Gray's Inn
Pupil Supervisor
Qualifications: [BA (Oxon)]

CRASNOW MS RACHEL

Cloisters
1 Pump Court, Temple, London EC4Y 7AA,
☎020 7827 4000 ✉clerks@cloisters.com
Call Date: Nov 1994, Middle Temple
Pupil Supervisor
Qualifications: [BA (Hons) (Oxon)]
✉rc@cloisters.com

CRAVEN MR EDWARD

Matrix Chambers
Griffin Building, Gray's Inn, London WC1R 5LN, ☎020 7404 3447
✉matrix@matrixlaw.co.uk / lscott@matrixlaw.co.uk
Call Date: Oct 2007, Lincoln's Inn
Qualifications: [BA Law (Cantab)]

CRAVEN MR ROBERT MICHAEL

Iscoed Chambers
86 St Helen's Road, Swansea SA1 4BQ,
☎01792 652988
✉clerks@iscoedchambers.co.uk
Call Date: Nov 1979, Gray's Inn
Pupil Supervisor, Recorder
Qualifications: [MA BCL (Oxon)]
✉rc@iscoedchambers.co.uk

E

CRAWFORD MR COLIN

Kings Chambers
Embassy House, 60 Church Street, Birmingham B3 2DJ, ☎ 0845 034 3444
✉ clerks@kingschambers.com
Kings Chambers
5 Park Square East, Leeds LS1 2NE, ☎ 0845 034 3444
✉ clerks@kingschambers.com
Kings Chambers
36 Young Street, Manchester M3 3FT, ☎ 0845 034 3444
✉ clerks@kingschambers.com
Call Date: July 1997, Middle Temple
Qualifications: [LLB (Hons) LLM (Edin)]
ccrawford@kingschambers.com

CRAWFORD MISS GEORGINA AYNSLEY

Farrar's Building
Farrar's Building, Temple, London EC4Y 7BD, ☎ 020 7583 9241
✉ Chambers@farrarsbuilding.co.uk
Call Date: Oct 2006, Inner Temple
Qualifications: [LLB (Lond)]
gcrawford@farrarsbuilding.co.uk

CRAWFORD MR GRANT

Radcliffe Chambers
Ground Floor, 11 New Square, Lincoln's Inn, London WC2A 3QB, ☎ 020 7831 0081
✉ clerks@radcliffechambers.com
Call Date: July 1974, Middle Temple
Pupil Supervisor
Qualifications: [MA (Cantab)]
gcrawford@radcliffechambers.com

CRAWFORD PROF JAMES RICHARD

Matrix Chambers
Griffin Building, Gray's Inn, London WC1R 5LN, ☎ 020 7404 3447
✉ matrix@matrixlaw.co.uk / Iscott@matrixlaw.co.uk
Call Date: Mar 1999, Gray's Inn
Qualifications: [LLB DPhil (Oxon) BA]
jamescrawford@matrixlaw.co.uk

CRAWFORD MR LINCOLN SANTO

12 King's Bench Walk
12 King's Bench Walk, Temple, London EC4Y 7EL, ☎ 020 7583 0811
Call Date: Nov 1977, Gray's Inn
Pupil Supervisor
Qualifications: [LLB]
crawford@12kbw.co.uk

CRAWFORD MISS MARIE-BERNADETTE CLAIRE

Eastbourne Chambers
5 Chiswick Place, Eastbourne, East Sussex BN21 4NH, ☎ 01323 642102
✉ clerks@eastbournechambers.co.uk
Call Date: Oct 1992, Lincoln's Inn
Pupil Supervisor
Qualifications: [LLB(Hons)(Leeds)]

CRAWFORD MR ROBERT DAVID

15 Winckley Square
Preston PR1 3JJ, ☎ 01772 252828
✉ clerks@15winckleysq.co.uk
Call Date: July 1976, Lincoln's Inn
Pupil Supervisor, Recorder
Qualifications: [MA (Cantab)]
clerks@15winckleysq.co.uk

CRAWFORD MR SHANE REANEY

St Philips Chambers
55 Temple Row, Birmingham B2 5LS, ☎ 0121 246 7000 ✉ clerks@st-philips.com
Call Date: Oct 1996, Lincoln's Inn
Qualifications: [LLB (Hons) LLM (L'pool)]
scrawford@st-philips.com

CRAWLEY MR GARY THOMAS BERNARD

1 Garden Court Family Law Chambers
Ground Floor, One Garden Court, Temple, London EC4Y 9BJ, ☎ 020 7797 7900
✉ clerks@1gc.com
Call Date: Feb 1988, Middle Temple
Pupil Supervisor
Qualifications: [LLB LLM (Lond)]
crawley@1gc.com

CRAWLEY MR KEVIN JOSEPH

Trinity Chambers
The Custom House, 39 Quayside, Newcastle Upon Tyne NE1 3DE, ☎ 0191 232 1927
✉ info@trinitychambers.co.uk
Trinity Chambers
Multi Media Exchange, 72-80 Corporation Road, Middlesbrough TS1 2RF, ☎ 01642 247569
✉ info@trinitychambers.co.uk
Call Date: July 1998, Gray's Inn
Qualifications: [BSc (Econ) (Wales) DipSW MA (Dunelm)]
k.crawley@trinitychambers.co.uk

E

CRAWLEY MR ROSS ALEXANDER

Middle Temple Lane Chambers
2nd Floor South, 1 Middle Temple Lane, London EC4Y 9AA, ☎020 7583 4352
✉chambers@mtlchambers.com
Call Date: July 2005, Middle Temple
Qualifications: [LLB (Hons) Nottingham]
chambers@mtlchambers.com

CRAWSHAW MR SIMON RICHARD

Atkin Chambers
1 Atkin Building, Gray's Inn, London WC1R 5AT, ☎020 7404 0102
✉clerks@atkinchambers.com
Call Date: July 2005, Lincoln's Inn
Qualifications: [BA (Hons) Oxon]

CRAY MR TIMOTHY JAMES

6 King's Bench Walk
Ground Floor, 6 King's Bench Walk, Temple, London EC4Y 7DR, ☎020 7583 0410
✉clerks@6kbw.com
Call Date: Nov 1989, Inner Temple
Pupil Supervisor
Qualifications: [BA (Hons)(Dunelm)]
timothy.cray@6kbw.com

CREAN MR ANTHONY QC (2006)

Kings Chambers
Embassy House, 60 Church Street, Birmingham B3 2DJ, ☎0845 034 3444
✉clerks@kingschambers.com
Kings Chambers
36 Young Street, Manchester M3 3FT, ☎0845 034 3444
✉clerks@kingschambers.com
Kings Chambers
5 Park Square East, Leeds LS1 2NE, ☎0845 034 3444
✉clerks@kingschambers.com
Call Date: July 1987, Gray's Inn
Qualifications: [MPhil (Manchester)]

CREER MRS ANDY MARY

Hardwicke
New Square, Lincoln's Inn, London WC2A 3SB, ☎020 7242 2523
✉enquiries@hardwicke.co.uk
Call Date: Oct 2005, Lincoln's Inn
Qualifications: [BSc (Hons) (Aston)]
andy.creer@hardwicke.co.uk

CREGAN MR JOHN-PAUL FITZJAMES

Renaissance Chambers
5th Floor, Gray's Inn Chambers, Gray's Inn, London WC1R 5JA, ☎020 7404 1111
✉clerks@renaissancechambers.co.uk
Call Date: Nov 1990, Middle Temple
Qualifications: [BCL (Ireland)]
jpc@renaissancechambers.co.uk

CREW MISS GILLIAN MARY

Ely Place Chambers
30 Ely Place, London EC1N 6TD, ☎020 7400 9600 ✉admin@elyplace.com
Call Date: Oct 1998, Gray's Inn
Pupil Supervisor
Qualifications: [LLB Hons]

CRIDDLE MISS BETSAN HEULYN

Old Square Chambers
10-11 Bedford Row, London WC1R 4BU, ☎020 7269 0300 ✉clerks@oldsquare.co.uk
Old Square Chambers
3 Orchard Court, St Augustine's Yard, Bristol BS1 5DP, ☎0117 930 5100
✉clerks@oldsquare.co.uk
Call Date: July 2002, Middle Temple
Qualifications: [MA (Hons) (Cantab)]
criddle@oldsquare.co.uk

CRIDLAND MR SIMON JAMES

3 Serjeants Inn
London EC4Y 1BQ, ☎020 7427 5000
✉clerks@3serjeantsinn.com
Call Date: Mar 1999, Middle Temple
Pupil Supervisor
Qualifications: [BA (Hons)(Cantab)]
scridland@3serjeantsinn.com

CRIGMAN MR DAVID IAN QC (1989)

St Philips Chambers
55 Temple Row, Birmingham B2 5LS, ☎0121 246 7000 ✉clerks@st-philips.com
Call Date: July 1969, Gray's Inn
Recorder
Qualifications: [LLB]
dcrigman@st-philips.co.uk

CRILLEY DR DARREL

St Johns Buildings
24a - 28 St John Street, Manchester M3 4DJ, ☎0161 214 1500
✉clerk@stjohnsbuildings.co.uk
St Johns Buildings
21 White Friars, Chester CH1 1NZ, ☎01244 323070
✉clerk@stjohnsbuildings.co.uk

16 Winckley Square
Preston PR1 3JJ, ☎01772 256100
Call Date: Mar 1996, Inner Temple
Pupil Supervisor
Qualifications: [BA (Oxon) LLB (London) PhD (London)]
✉clerk@stjohnsbuildings.co.uk

CRINION MR CHARLES EDWARD

1 Mitre Court Buildings
1 Mitre Court Buildings, Temple, London EC4Y 7BS, ☎020 7452 8900
✉clerks@1mcb.com
Call Date: Nov 2002, Middle Temple
Qualifications: [LLB (Hons)(Lond) LLM (Lond)]
✉charles.crinion@1mcb.com

CRINNION MRS NEENA LATIFA

3 Temple Gardens
Lower Ground Floor, 3 Temple Gardens, Temple, London EC4Y 9AU, ☎020 7353 3102
✉clerks@3tg.co.uk
Call Date: Oct 1997, Gray's Inn
Pupil Supervisor
✉nlc@3tg.co.uk

CRISPIN MR STEPHEN BENNETT

Harcourt Chambers
1st Floor, 2 Harcourt Buildings, Temple, London EC4Y 9DB, ☎0844 561 7135
Harcourt Chambers
Churchill House, 3 St Aldate's Courtyard, St Aldate's, Oxford OX1 1BN, ☎0844 561 7135
Call Date: Oct 2008, Lincoln's Inn
Qualifications: [BA (Oxon)]
✉scrispin@harcourtchambers.law.co.uk

CRITCHLEY MISS ANNE-MARIE

4 King's Bench Walk
2nd Floor, 4 King's Bench Walk, Temple, London EC4Y 7DL, ☎020 7822 7000
✉clerks@4kbw.co.uk
Call Date: Oct 1999, Middle Temple
Qualifications: [BA (Hons) MA (Cantab) Dip Law]

CRITCHLEY MR JOHN STEPHEN

Field Court Chambers
5 Field Court, Gray's Inn, London WC1R 5EF, ☎020 7405 6114 ✉clerks@fieldcourt.co.uk
Call Date: July 1985, Gray's Inn
Pupil Supervisor
Qualifications: [LLB (Bris)]
✉john.critchley@fieldcourt.co.uk

CRITELLI MR NICHOLAS

9 Stone Buildings
Lincoln's Inn, London WC2A 3NN, ☎020 7404 5055
✉clerks@9stonebuildings.com
Call Date: July 1991, Middle Temple
Qualifications: [B Juris (USA)]
✉clerks@9stonebuildings.com

CROALL MR SIMON MARTIN QC (2008)

Quadrant Chambers
Quadrant House, 10 Fleet Street, London EC4Y 1AU, ☎020 7583 4444
✉info@quadrantchambers.com
Call Date: Nov 1986, Middle Temple
Qualifications: [MA (Cantab)]
✉simon.croall@quadrantchambers.com

CROALLY MR MILES JAMES

Field Court Chambers
5 Field Court, Gray's Inn, London WC1R 5EF, ☎020 7405 6114 ✉clerks@fieldcourt.co.uk
Call Date: Nov 1987, Middle Temple
Pupil Supervisor
Qualifications: [BA Dip Law]
✉miles.croally@fieldcourt.co.uk

CROCKER MISS ELIZABETH ALEXANDRA

15 New Bridge Street
London EC4V 6AU, ☎020 7842 1900
✉clerks@15nbs.com
Call Date: Nov 2006, Middle Temple
Qualifications: [BA (Hons)]
✉beth.crocker@15nbs.com

CROCKETT MR THOMAS WILLIAM BASIL

1 Chancery Lane
London WC2A 1LF, ☎0845 634 6666
✉clerks@1chancerylane.com
Call Date: July 2009, Gray's Inn
Qualifications: [BA]
✉tcrockett@1hcancerylane.com

CRONIN MISS KATHRYN

Garden Court Chambers
57-60 Lincoln's Inn Fields, London WC2A 3LJ, ☎020 7993 7600 ✉info@gclaw.co.uk
Call Date: July 1980, Middle Temple
Qualifications: [BA PhD]
✉kathrync@gclaw.co.uk

E

CRONSHAW MR MICHAEL JOHN

3 Dr Johnson's Buildings
Ground Floor, 3 Dr Johnson's Buildings, Temple, London EC4Y 7BA, ☎ 020 7353 4854
✉ clerks@3djb.co.uk
Call Date: Oct 1993, Middle Temple
Qualifications: [MA (Hons)(Oxon) MSc Dip Law (Lond)]
✉ mcronshaw@3djb.co.uk

CROOKENDEN MR SIMON ROBERT QC (1996)

Essex Court Chambers
24 Lincoln's Inn Fields, London WC2A 3EG, ☎ 020 7813 8000
✉ clerksroom@essexcourt.net
Call Date: Nov 1975, Gray's Inn
Qualifications: [MA (Cantab) FCIArb]
✉ scrookenden@essexcourt.net

CROOKES MISS ALISON NAOMI

King's Bench and Godolphin (KBG)Chambers
115 North Hill, Plymouth, Devon PL4 8JY, ☎ 01752 221551
✉ clerks@kbgchambers.co.uk
Call Date: Oct 1996, Middle Temple
Qualifications: [LLB (Hons) (Wales)]

E

CROPP MR NICHOLAS

Seven Bedford Row
7 Bedford Row, London WC1R 4BS, ☎ 020 7242 3555 ✉ clerks@7br.co.uk
Call Date: Nov 1999, Gray's Inn
Qualifications: [LLB (Lond) BCL (Oxon)]

CRORIE MR ETHAHAD A ELAHEE

12 College Place
Fauvelle Buildings, 12 College Place, Southampton SO15 2FE, ☎ 023 8032 0320
✉ clerks@12cp.co.uk
Call Date: Nov 2000, Middle Temple
Qualifications: [LLB (Hons) LLM]
✉ ECrorie@12cp.co.uk

CROSFILL MR JOHN

Field Court Chambers
5 Field Court, Gray's Inn, London WC1R 5EF, ☎ 020 7405 6114 ✉ clerks@fieldcourt.co.uk
Call Date: Nov 1995, Middle Temple
Pupil Supervisor
Qualifications: [LLB (Hons) BSc]
✉ john.crosfill@fieldcourt.co.uk

CROSKELL MR MARCUS JAMES

East Anglian Chambers
53 North Hill, Colchester, Essex CO1 1QA, ☎ 01473 214481 ✉ colchester@ealaw.co.uk
East Anglian Chambers
140 New London Road, Chelmsford, Essex CM2 0AW, ☎ 01473 214481
✉ chelmsford@ealaw.co.uk
East Anglian Chambers
15 The Close, Norwich, Norfolk NR1 4DZ, ☎ 01473 214481 ✉ norwich@ealaw.co.uk
East Anglian Chambers
Gresham House, 5 Museum Street, Ipswich, Suffolk IP1 1HQ, ☎ 01473 214481
✉ ipswich@ealaw.co.uk
Call Date: July 2003, Lincoln's Inn
Qualifications: [LLB Hons (So'ton) BSc (Joint Hons)]
✉ marcuscroskell@ealaw.co.uk

CROSLAND MR JAMES BENJAMIN

Broadway House Chambers
Broadway House, 9 Bank Street, Bradford, West Yorkshire BD1 1TW, ☎ 01274 722560
✉ clerks@broadwayhouse.co.uk
Broadway House Chambers
25 Park Square West, Leeds, West Yorkshire LS1 2PW, ☎ 0113 246 2600
✉ clerks@broadwayhouse.co.uk
Call Date: Feb 1993, Gray's Inn
Qualifications: [MA (Cantab)]
✉ jbc@broadwayhouse.co.uk

CROSS MR ANTHONY MAURICE QC (2006)

Lincoln House Chambers
Tower 12, The Avenue North, Spinningfields, 18-22 Bridge Street, Manchester M3 3BZ, ☎ 0161 832 5701
✉ info@lincolnhousechambers.com
Call Date: Nov 1982, Middle Temple
Recorder
Qualifications: [LLB (Manc)]
✉ anthony.cross@lincolnhousechambers.com

CROSS MS CAROLINE ELIZABETH KEATING

1 Crown Office Row
1 Crown Office Row, Temple, London EC4Y 7HH, ☎ 020 7797 7500
✉ mail@1cor.com
Call Date: Oct 2006, Gray's Inn
Qualifications: [LLB (Germany) LLM]
✉ caroline.cross@1cor.com

CROSS MR GEOFFREY PAUL

New Court Chambers
3 Broad Chare, Newcastle Upon Tyne
NE1 3DQ, ☎ 0191 232 1980
✉ clerks@newcourt-chambers.co.uk
Call Date: July 1981, Gray's Inn
Pupil Supervisor
Qualifications: [BA (Cantab)]

CROSS MR JAMES EDWARD MICHAEL QC (2006)

4 Pump Court
4 Pump Court, Temple, London EC4Y 7AN,
☎ 020 7842 5555
✉ chambers@4pumpcourt.com
Call Date: July 1985, Gray's Inn
Qualifications: [MA (Oxon)]
jcross@4pumpcourt.com

CROSS MISS JANE ELIZABETH QC (2010)

Deans Court Chambers
24 St John Street, Manchester M3 4DF,
☎ 0161 214 6000 ✉ clerks@deanscourt.co.uk
Deans Court Chambers
101 Walker Street, Preston PR1 2RR,
☎ 01772 565 600
✉ preston@deanscourt.co.uk
Zenith Chambers
10 Park Square, Leeds LS1 2LH,
☎ 0113 245 5438
✉ clerks@zenithchambers.co.uk
Call Date: July 1982, Middle Temple
Qualifications: [LLB (L'pool)]
cross@deanscourt.co.uk

CROSS MR JASON LEE

Charter Chambers
33 John Street, London WC1N 2AT,
☎ 020 7618 4400
✉ clerks@charterchambers.com
Call Date: Oct 1998, Lincoln's Inn
Qualifications: [LLB (Hons)(Herts)]

CROSS MRS JOANNA

Park Court Chambers
16 Park Place, Leeds LS1 2SJ,
☎ 0113 243 3277
✉ clerks@parkcourtchambers.co.uk
Call Date: Oct 1992, Lincoln's Inn
Pupil Supervisor
Qualifications: [BSc (St Andrew) MB ChB (Manc) Dip Law (Lond)]
clerks@parkcourtchambers.co.uk

CROSS MR RICHARD NOEL

Thomas More Chambers
7 Lincoln's Inn Fields, London WC2A 3BP,
☎ 020 7404 7000
✉ clerks@thomasmore.co.uk
Call Date: Oct 1993, Lincoln's Inn
Qualifications: [BA(Hons)(Bris)]

CROSS MR THOMAS ANDREW

11 King's Bench Walk
11 King's Bench Walk, Temple, London
EC4Y 7EQ, ☎ 020 7632 8500
✉ clerksroom@11kbw.com
Call Date: Oct 2007, Lincoln's Inn
Qualifications: [BA (Oxon)]

CROSSFIELD MISS ANNE

Erimus Chambers
PO Box 1440, Bedford MK43 6AJ,
☎ 01234 720952
✉ clerks@erimuschambers.com
Call Date: July 1993, Lincoln's Inn
Qualifications: [LLB (B'ham) MBA (Nott'm)]

CROSSLEY MR DOMINIC FRANCIS

Chancery House Chambers
7 Lisbon Square, Leeds, West Yorkshire
LS1 4LY, ☎ 0113 244 6691
✉ clerks@chanceryhouse.co.uk
Call Date: Oct 2006, Gray's Inn
Qualifications: [BA MA (Oxon) Dip Law]
dominic.crossley@chanceryhouse.co.uk

CROSSLEY MS JOANNE

St Paul's Chambers
5th Floor, St Paul's House, 23 Park Square
South, Leeds LS1 2ND, ☎ 0113 245 5866
Call Date: Nov 1994, Middle Temple
Qualifications: [BA (Hons) (Oxon)]

CROSSLEY MR SIMON JUSTIN

Zenith Chambers
10 Park Square, Leeds LS1 2LH,
☎ 0113 245 5438
✉ clerks@zenithchambers.co.uk
Call Date: Nov 1993, Inner Temple
Pupil Supervisor
Qualifications: [LLB]
jcrossley@zenithchambers.co.uk

E

CROSSLEY MR STEVEN RICHARD

Exchange Chambers
Oxford House, Oxford Row, Leeds LS1 3BE, ☎0113 203 1970
✉spencer@exchangechambers.co.uk
Exchange Chambers
One Derby Square, Derby Square, Liverpool L2 9XX, ☎0151 236 7747
✉info@exchangechambers.co.uk
Exchange Chambers
7 Ralli Courts, West Riverside, Manchester M3 5FT, ☎0161 833 2722
Call Date: Nov 1992, Inner Temple
Qualifications: [LLB (Exon)]

CROSTHWAITE MR GRAHAM ANDREW

1 KBW Chambers
1 King's Bench Walk, Temple, London EC4Y 7DB, ☎020 7936 1500
✉clerks@1kbw.co.uk
King's Bench Chambers
174 High Street, Lewes BN7 1YE, ☎01273 402600
Call Date: Nov 1995, Inner Temple
Qualifications: [MA (Oxon)]
gcrosthwaite@1kbw.co.uk

E

CROUCH MR ANDREW CHARLES MACKESAY

Park Lane Plowden
Lombard House, 4-8 Lombard Street, Newcastle Upon Tyne NE1 3AE, ☎0191 211 4087
✉clerks@parklaneplowden.co.uk
Call Date: Nov 1990, Inner Temple
Qualifications: [LLB (Lancs)]
andrew.crouch@parklaneplowden.co.uk

CROUCH MR STEPHEN WILLIAM MICHAEL

The Chambers of S W M Crouch
6 The Glebe, Badby, Northamptonshire NN11 3AZ, ☎01327 315 742
Call Date: July 1982, Inner Temple
Qualifications: [BSc (Hons) Dip Law]

CROW MR CHARLES DUNCAN TIMOTHY

No5 Chambers
Fountain Court, Steelhouse Lane, Birmingham B4 6DR, ☎0845 210 5555 ✉info@no5.com
No5 Chambers
Greenwood House, 4-7 Salisbury Court, London EC4Y 8AA, ☎0845 210 5555
No5 Chambers
38 Queen Square, Bristol BS1 4QS, ☎0845 210 5555
Call Date: Oct 1999, Lincoln's Inn
Qualifications: [LLB (Hons)(Exon)]
ctc@no5.com

CROW MR JONATHAN RUPERT QC (2006)

4 Stone Buildings
Ground Floor, 4 Stone Buildings, Lincoln's Inn, London WC2A 3XT, ☎020 7242 5524
✉clerks@4stonebuildings.com
Call Date: July 1981, Lincoln's Inn
Qualifications: [BA (Oxon)]
clerks@4stonebuildings.com

CROWDY MISS ISABELLA ALICE

6 Pump Court
1st Floor, 6 Pump Court, Temple, London EC4Y 7AR, ☎020 7797 8400
✉richardconstable@6pumpcourt.co.uk
6 Pump Court Chambers
6-8 Mill Street, Maidstone, Kent ME15 6XH, ☎01622 688094
✉annexe@6pumpcourt.co.uk
Call Date: Oct 2007, Middle Temple
Qualifications: [BA (Hons) (Nott'm) Dip Law (Nott'm)]

CROWE MR CAMERON

36 Bedford Row
London WC1R 4JH, ☎020 7421 8000
✉chambers@36bedfordrow.co.uk
Call Date: Oct 2002, Inner Temple
Qualifications: [BA (E.Anglia) CPE OgDL]
ccrowe@36bedfordrow.co.uk

CROWLEY MR DANIEL JOHN

2 Temple Gardens
2 Temple Gardens, Temple, London EC4Y 9AY, ☎020 7822 1200
✉clerks@2tg.co.uk
Call Date: Oct 1990, Gray's Inn
Pupil Supervisor
Qualifications: [BA (Australia) BCL (Oxon) FCIArb LLB (Australia)]
dcrowley@2tg.co.uk

CROWLEY MRS JANE ELIZABETH QC (1998)

1 Garden Court Family Law Chambers
Ground Floor, One Garden Court, Temple, London EC4Y 9BJ, ☎020 7797 7900
✉clerks@1gc.com
St Ive's Chambers
Whittall Street, Birmingham B4 6DH, ☎0121 236 0863
✉clerks@stiveschambers.co.uk

St Johns Buildings
24a - 28 St John Street, Manchester M3 4DJ,
☎0161 214 1500
✉clerk@stjohnsbuildings.co.uk
Call Date: July 1976, Gray's Inn
Recorder
Qualifications: [LLB (Lond)]
✉crowley@1gc.com

CROWLEY MISS LAURA LOUISE

4 Pump Court
4 Pump Court, Temple, London EC4Y 7AN,
☎020 7842 5555
✉chambers@4pumpcourt.com
Call Date: July 2005, Inner Temple
Qualifications: [MA (Cantab)]
✉lcrowley@4pumpcourt.com

CROWTHER MR JEREMY GAGE

The Chambers of Grahame Aldous QC
9 Gough Square, London EC4A 3DG,
☎020 7832 0500
✉clerks@9goughsquare.co.uk
Call Date: Oct 1991, Middle Temple
Qualifications: [LLB (Hons) (Reading)]
✉jcrowther@9goughsquare.co.uk

CROWTHER MS LUCY ELLEN

Apex
Harlech House, 20 Cathedral Road, Cardiff
CF11 9LJ, ☎02920 232 032
✉clerks@apexchambers.net
Call Date: Oct 1999, Inner Temple
Qualifications: [BEng (Lond)]
✉lucy.crowther@apexchambers.net

CROWTHER MISS SARAH HELEN

3 Hare Court
3 Hare Court, Temple, London EC4Y 7BJ,
☎020 7415 7800 ✉clerks@3harecourt.com
Call Date: Oct 1999, Middle Temple
Pupil Supervisor
Qualifications: [BA (Hons) MA]
✉sarahcrowther@3harecourt.com

CROWTHER MR THOMAS EDWARD

Apex
Harlech House, 20 Cathedral Road, Cardiff
CF11 9LJ, ☎02920 232 032
✉clerks@apexchambers.net
Call Date: Nov 1993, Inner Temple
Pupil Supervisor
Qualifications: [BSc BA (Exon)]
✉tom.crowther@apexchambers.net

CROXFORD MR IAN LIONEL QC (1993)

Wilberforce Chambers
8 New Square, Lincoln's Inn, London
WC2A 3QP, ☎020 7306 0102
✉chambers@wilberforce.co.uk
Call Date: July 1976, Gray's Inn
Qualifications: [LLB]
✉icroxford@wilberforce.co.uk

CROXFORD MRS KERRIE SUZANNE

5 Pump Court
Ground Floor, 5 Pump Court, Temple, London
EC4Y 7AP, ☎020 7353 2532
✉clerks@5pumpcourt.com
Call Date: Mar 2007, Lincoln's Inn
Qualifications: [LLB (B'ham)]
✉clerks@5pumpcourt.com

CROXFORD MR THOMAS HENRY

Blackstone Chambers
Blackstone House, Temple, London
EC4Y 9BW, ☎020 7583 1770
✉clerks@blackstonechambers.com
Call Date: Oct 1992, Middle Temple
Pupil Supervisor
Qualifications: [MA (Hons)(Cantab)]
✉tomcroxford@blackstonechambers.com

CROZIER MR JESSE EDWARD

Devereux Chambers
Queen Elizabeth Building, Temple, London
EC4Y 9BS, ☎020 7353 7534
✉clerks@devchambers.co.uk
Call Date: July 2009, Inner Temple
Qualifications: [BA (Oxon)]
✉crozier@devchambers.co.uk

CROZIER MR RAWDON ROWLAND CRAIG

King's Bench and Godolphin (KBG)Chambers
115 North Hill, Plymouth, Devon PL4 8JY,
☎01752 221551
✉clerks@kbgchambers.co.uk
Call Date: Nov 1984, Middle Temple
Pupil Supervisor
Qualifications: [LLB (Lond)]
✉rc@kbgchambers.co.uk

CRUICKSHANK MISS CYNTHIA MARILYN BENTON

1 Gray's Inn Square
Ground Floor, 1 Gray's Inn Square, London
WC1R 5AA, ☎020 7405 0001
Call Date: Nov 1968, Lincoln's Inn

E

CRYSTAL MR JONATHAN

Argent Chambers
5 Bell Yard, London WC2A 2JR,
☎ 020 7556 5500
✉ briefsin@argentchambers.co.uk
Call Date: July 1972, Middle Temple
Pupil Supervisor
Qualifications: [LLB (Hons)(Lond)]
jc@argentchambers.co.uk

CRYSTAL MR MICHAEL QC (1984)

South Square
3-4 South Square, Gray's Inn, London
WC1R 5HP, ☎ 020 7696 9900
✉ practicemanagers@southsquare.com
Call Date: Nov 1970, Middle Temple
Qualifications: [LLB (Lond) BCL (Oxon)]
clerks@southsquare.com

CSOKA MR SIMON QC (2011)

Lincoln House Chambers
Tower 12, The Avenue North, Spinningfields,
18-22 Bridge Street, Manchester M3 3BZ,
☎ 0161 832 5701
✉ info@lincolnhousechambers.com
Call Date: Nov 1991, Gray's Inn
Pupil Supervisor
Qualifications: [MA (Cantab)]

E

CUDBY MS MARKANZA NICOLA

1 KBW Chambers
1 King's Bench Walk, Temple, London
EC4Y 7DB, ☎ 020 7936 1500
✉ clerks@1kbw.co.uk
King's Bench Chambers
174 High Street, Lewes BN7 1YE,
☎ 01273 402600
Call Date: July 1983, Middle Temple
Pupil Supervisor, Recorder
Qualifications: [BA]
mcudby@1kbw.co.uk

CUDDIGAN MR HUGO JONATHAN PATRICK

11 South Square
1st Floor, 11 South Square, Gray's Inn,
London WC1R 5EY, ☎ 020 7405 1222
✉ clerks@11southsquare.com
Call Date: Nov 1995, Middle Temple
Pupil Supervisor
Qualifications: [BA (Hons)]
hcuddigan@11southsquare.com

CUDDY MISS NATALIE LOUISE

Atlantic Chambers
4-6 Cook Street, Liverpool L2 9QU,
☎ 0151 236 4421
✉ info@atlanticchambers.co.uk
Call Date: Nov 2005, Inner Temple
Qualifications: [LLB University of Liverpool]
nataliecuddy@atlanticchambers.co.uk

CULLEN MISS CLARE ALICE JANE

Arden Chambers
20 Bloomsbury Square, London WC1A 2NS,
☎ 020 7242 4244
✉ clerks@ardenchambers.com
Call Date: July 2009, Middle Temple
Qualifications: [BA (Hons) (Leeds) Post Grad Dipin Law (Lond)]
clare.cullen@ardentchambers.com

CULLEN MR EDMUND WILLIAM HECTOR QC (2012)

Maitland Chambers
7 Stone Buildings, Lincoln's Inn, London
WC2A 3SZ, ☎ 020 7406 1200
✉ clerks@maitlandchambers.com
Call Date: Oct 1990, Lincoln's Inn
Pupil Supervisor
Qualifications: [BA (Bris)]
ecullen@maitlandchambers.com

CULLEN MRS FELICITY ANN QC (2008)

Gray's Inn Tax Chambers
3rd Floor, Gray's Inn Chambers, Gray's Inn,
London WC1R 5JA, ☎ 020 7242 2642
✉ clerks@taxbar.com
Call Date: July 1985, Lincoln's Inn
Qualifications: [LLB (B'ham) LLM (Cantab)]
fc@taxbar.com

CULLEN MISS GRACE CATHERINE

6 Pump Court
1st Floor, 6 Pump Court, Temple, London
EC4Y 7AR, ☎ 020 7797 8400
✉ richardconstable@6pumpcourt.co.uk
6 Pump Court Chambers
6-8 Mill Street, Maidstone, Kent ME15 6XH,
☎ 01622 688094
✉ annexe@6pumpcourt.co.uk
Call Date: Oct 2005, Lincoln's Inn
Qualifications: [BA (Hons) (Cantab)]
gracecullen@6PumpCourt.co.uk

CULLEN MR JAMES WILLIAM CHRISTOPHER

Linenhall Chambers
1 Stanley Place, Chester CH1 2LU, ☎01244 348282
✉clerks@linenhallchambers.co.uk
Call Date: July 2003, Lincoln's Inn
Qualifications: [LLB Hons (L'pool)]
✉jwc@nicholasstreet.com

CULLEN MR STUART JOHN

33 Bedford Row
London WC1R 4JH, ☎020 7242 6476
✉clerks@33bedfordrow.co.uk
Call Date: Oct 2006, Inner Temple
Qualifications: [BA (NUI) LLM (Lond) MCIArb]
✉stuart.cullen@33bedfordrow.co.uk

CULLETON MISS LOUISE ISABEL HELEN

23 Essex Street
London WC2R 3AA, ☎020 7413 0353
✉clerks@23es.com
Call Date: Oct 2005, Middle Temple
Qualifications: [LLB (Hons)]
✉louiseculleton@23es.com

CULLEY MISS LAURA JOAN

Citadel Chambers
The Citadel, 190 Corporation Street, Birmingham B4 6QD, ☎0121 233 8500
✉clerks@citadelchambers.com
Call Date: Oct 2006, Lincoln's Inn
Qualifications: [LLB (Sheff)]

CULLING MISS MARIA ALEXIA

Middle Temple Lane Chambers
2nd Floor South, 1 Middle Temple Lane, London EC4Y 9AA, ☎020 7583 4352
✉chambers@mtlchambers.com
Call Date: Mar 1997, Gray's Inn
Qualifications: [LLB (Lond)]

CULMER MISS GABRIELLE FIONA

2 King's Bench Walk
2 King's Bench Walk, Temple, London EC4Y 7DE, ☎020 7353 1746
✉clerks@2kbw.com
Call Date: Oct 1999, Gray's Inn
Qualifications: [LLB (Kent) BSc LLM(Lond) LLM]

CULVER MR EDWARD JAMES

4 King's Bench Walk
2nd Floor, 4 King's Bench Walk, Temple, London EC4Y 7DL, ☎020 7822 7000
✉clerks@4kbw.co.uk
Call Date: July 2005, Inner Temple
Qualifications: [LLB]

CULVERHOUSE MISS EMILY ANNA LOUISE

Chambers of Miss E Culverhouse
18 Upper Gladstone Road, Chesham, Buckinghamshire HP5 3AF, ☎07813 007503
✉e.culverhouse@sky.com
Call Date: Nov 1998, Lincoln's Inn
Pupil Supervisor
Qualifications: [LLB (Hons)]

CUMBERLAND MISS MELANIE CLAIRE

6 King's Bench Walk
Ground Floor, 6 King's Bench Walk, Temple, London EC4Y 7DR, ☎020 7583 0410
✉clerks@6kbw.com
Call Date: Oct 2001, Lincoln's Inn
Qualifications: [BA (Hons)(Oxon) Dip law]
✉melanie.cumberland@6kbw.com

CUMMERSON MISS ROMILLY JANE

Hardwicke
New Square, Lincoln's Inn, London WC2A 3SB, ☎020 7242 2523
✉enquiries@hardwicke.co.uk
Call Date: Oct 1998, Middle Temple
Qualifications: [BA (Hons)(Cantab)]
✉romilly.cummerson@hardwicke.co.uk

CUMMING MR EDWARD CHARLES

XXIV Old Buildings
Ground Floor, 24 Old Buildings, Lincoln's Inn, London WC2A 3UP, ☎020 7691 2424
✉clerks@xxiv.co.uk
Call Date: July 2006, Middle Temple
Qualifications: [BA (Hons) (Cantab) LLM (Pennsylvania)]
✉edward.cumming@xxiv.co.uk

CUMMING MR ROBERT JAMES

2 Temple Gardens
2 Temple Gardens, Temple, London EC4Y 9AY, ☎020 7822 1200
✉clerks@2tg.co.uk
Call Date: July 2010, Middle Temple
Qualifications: [BA (Hons) (Cantab)]

E

CUMMING MR SETH NEIL

3 Stone Buildings
Ground Floor, 3 Stone Buildings, Lincoln's Inn, London WC2A 3XL, ☎ 020 7242 4937
✉ clerks@3sb.law.co.uk
Call Date: Oct 2010, Middle Temple
Qualifications: [BSc (Hons) (South Africa) MSc (Lond) LLB BVC]
scumming@3sb.law.co.uk

CUMMINGS MR BRIAN QC (2008)

Exchange Chambers
One Derby Square, Derby Square, Liverpool L2 9XX, ☎ 0151 236 7747
✉ info@exchangechambers.co.uk
Exchange Chambers
7 Ralli Courts, West Riverside, Manchester M3 5FT, ☎ 0161 833 2722
Exchange Chambers
Oxford House, Oxford Row, Leeds LS1 3BE, ☎ 0113 203 1970
✉ spencer@exchangechambers.co.uk
Call Date: Nov 1988, Lincoln's Inn
Recorder
Qualifications: [MA (Cantab)]
cummingsqc@exchangechambers.co.uk

CUMMINGS MISS STEPHANIE ANNE

Oriel Chambers
14 Water Street, Liverpool, Merseyside L2 8TD, ☎ 0151 236 7191
✉ clerks@orielchambers.co.uk
Call Date: Nov 2010, Middle Temple
Qualifications: [BA (Hons) (Oxon)]
stephanie.cummings@orielchambers.co.uk

CUMMINS MR BRIAN DOMINIC

Old Square Chambers
10-11 Bedford Row, London WC1R 4BU, ☎ 020 7269 0300 ✉ clerks@oldsquare.co.uk
Old Square Chambers
3 Orchard Court, St Augustine's Yard, Bristol BS1 5DP, ☎ 0117 930 5100
✉ clerks@oldsquare.co.uk
Call Date: Oct 1992, Middle Temple
Pupil Supervisor
Qualifications: [LLB (Hons) LLM]
cummins@oldsquare.co.uk

CUNDY MS CATHERINE PATRICIA

9 St John Street
Manchester M3 4DN, ☎ 0161 955 9000
✉ civilclerks@9sjs.com /
criminalclerks@9sjs.com
Call Date: July 2011, Middle Temple
Qualifications: [BA (Hons) (Lond) PhD (Kent) PgDL (Manch)]

CUNLIFFE MR ALEXANDER MARTIN

Goldsmith Chambers
Ground Floor, Goldsmith Building, Temple, London EC4Y 7BL, ☎ 020 7353 6802
✉ clerks@goldsmithchambers.com
Call Date: Nov 2001, Inner Temple
Qualifications: [BA CPE]

CUNNINGHAM MISS ELIZABETH ALICE

Albion Chambers
Broad Street, Bristol BS1 1DR, ☎ 0117 927 2144
✉ clerks@albionchambers.co.uk
Call Date: Oct 1995, Middle Temple
Qualifications: [BA (Hons)(Bris)]
liz.cunningham@albionchambers.co.uk

CUNNINGHAM MR GRAHAM TAYLOR

Hardwicke
New Square, Lincoln's Inn, London WC2A 3SB, ☎ 020 7242 2523
✉ enquiries@hardwicke.co.uk
Call Date: July 1976, Gray's Inn
Qualifications: [LLB (Hons)]
graham.cunningham@hardwicke.co.uk

CUNNINGHAM MR MARK JAMES QC (2001)

Maitland Chambers
7 Stone Buildings, Lincoln's Inn, London WC2A 3SZ, ☎ 020 7406 1200
✉ clerks@maitlandchambers.com
Call Date: Nov 1980, Inner Temple
Qualifications: [BA (Oxon)]
MCunningham@MaitlandChambers.com

CUNNINGHAM MS NAOMI BRIGID

Outer Temple Chambers
The Outer Temple, 222 Strand, London WC2R 1BA, ☎ 020 7353 6381
✉ clerks@outertemple.com
Call Date: Feb 1994, Inner Temple
Pupil Supervisor
Qualifications: [LLB (Reading) LLM (Bris)]
naomi.cunningham@outertemple.com

CUNNINGTON MR DAVID JOHN

Old Square Chambers
10-11 Bedford Row, London WC1R 4BU, ☎020 7269 0300 ✉clerks@oldsquare.co.uk
Old Square Chambers
3 Orchard Court, St Augustine's Yard, Bristol BS1 5DP, ☎0117 930 5100
✉clerks@oldsquare.co.uk
Call Date: Oct 2005, Lincoln's Inn
Qualifications: [MA (Oxon) DPhil (Oxon) BA (Oxon)]

CURL MR JOSEPH DAVID

9 Stone Buildings
Lincoln's Inn, London WC2A 3NN,
☎020 7404 5055
✉clerks@9stonebuildings.com
Call Date: July 2007, Lincoln's Inn
Qualifications: [BA LLB (Lond)]
jcurl@9stonebuildings.com

CURRAN MR LEO

3 PB Barristers
3 Paper Buildings, Temple, London EC4Y 7EU, ☎020 7583 8055
3 PB Barristers
Royal Talbot House, 2 Victoria Street, Bristol, Avon BS1 6BB, ☎0117 928 1520
3 PB Barristers
4 St Peter Street, Winchester SO23 8BW, ☎01962 868884
✉clerks.winchester@3paper.co.uk
3 PB Barristers
23 Beaumont Street, Oxford OX1 2NP, ☎01865 793 736
3 PB Barristers
30 Christchurch Road, Bournemouth, Dorset BH1 3PD, ☎01202 292102
✉clerks.bournemouth@3paper.co.uk
Call Date: July 1972, Gray's Inn
Pupil Supervisor
Qualifications: [MA (Oxon) BA (Oxon)]

CURRAN MR PHILIP PETER

Lincoln House Chambers
Tower 12, The Avenue North, Spinningfields, 18-22 Bridge Street, Manchester M3 3BZ, ☎0161 832 5701
✉info@lincolnhousechambers.com
Call Date: May 1979, Lincoln's Inn
Pupil Supervisor, Recorder
Qualifications: [BA (Hons)]
philip.curran@lincolnhousechambers.com

CURRER MR PAUL JOSEPH

Trinity Chambers
The Custom House, 39 Quayside, Newcastle Upon Tyne NE1 3DE, ☎0191 232 1927
✉info@trinitychambers.co.uk
Trinity Chambers
Multi Media Exchange, 72-80 Corporation Road, Middlesbrough TS1 2RF, ☎01642 247569
✉info@trinitychambers.co.uk
Call Date: July 2000, Middle Temple
Qualifications: [LLB(Hons)]
p.currer@trinitychambers.co.uk

CURRIE MR FERGUS HUGH

Unity Street Chambers
5 Unity Street, College Green, Bristol BS1 5HH, ☎0117 906 9789
✉chambers@unitystreetchambers.com
Call Date: Mar 1997, Gray's Inn
Pupil Supervisor
Qualifications: [MA (Oxon)]
fergus.currie@unitystreetchambers.com

CURRIE MR HERIOT WHITSON

Monckton Chambers
1 & 2 Raymond Buildings, Gray's Inn, London WC1R 5NR, ☎020 7405 7211
✉chambers@monckton.com
Call Date: Apr 1991, Gray's Inn
Qualifications: [MA (Oxon) LLb (Edin)]
hcurrie@monckton.com

CURRIE MISS KERRY-ANNE

Thomas More Chambers
7 Lincoln's Inn Fields, London WC2A 3BP, ☎020 7404 7000
✉clerks@thomasmore.co.uk
Call Date: July 2007, Middle Temple
Qualifications: [LLB (Hons) (Belfast) LLM (Belfast)]

CURRIE MR PHILIP STEPHEN

3 PB Barristers
3 Paper Buildings, Temple, London EC4Y 7EU, ☎020 7583 8055
3 PB Barristers
23 Beaumont Street, Oxford OX1 2NP, ☎01865 793 736
3 PB Barristers
30 Christchurch Road, Bournemouth, Dorset BH1 3PD, ☎01202 292102
✉clerks.bournemouth@3paper.co.uk
3 PB Barristers
Royal Talbot House, 2 Victoria Street, Bristol, Avon BS1 6BB, ☎0117 928 1520

3 PB Barristers
4 St Peter Street, Winchester SO23 8BW,
☎01962 868884
✉clerks.winchester@3paper.co.uk
Call Date: July 2009, Middle Temple
Qualifications: [BSc (Lond) Grad Dip Law]

CURRY MS CAROLINE ROSE

9 St John Street
Manchester M3 4DN, ☎0161 955 9000
✉civilclerks@9sjs.com /
criminalclerks@9sjs.com
Call Date: Nov 2003, Middle Temple
Qualifications: [LLB (Hons) (Lond) BVC]

CURRY MR OWEN PETER

XXIV Old Buildings
Ground Floor, 24 Old Buildings, Lincoln's Inn,
London WC2A 3UP, ☎020 7691 2424
✉clerks@xxiv.co.uk
Call Date: Oct 2009, Lincoln's Inn
Qualifications: [MA (Oxon) CPE UCU]
owen.curry@xxiv.co.uk

CURSHAM MRS GEORGINA CLAIRE

Ropewalk Chambers
24 The Ropewalk, Nottingham NG1 5EF,
☎0115 947 2581 ✉clerks@ropewalk.co.uk
Call Date: July 2007, Gray's Inn
Qualifications: [BA (Oxon) LLB]
georginacursham@ropewalk.co.uk

E

CURTAIN MISS HANNAH MARY ROWEN

Henderson Chambers
2 Harcourt Buildings, Temple, London
EC4Y 9DB, ☎020 7583 9020
✉clerks@hendersonchambers.co.uk
Call Date: July 2010, Gray's Inn
Qualifications: [BA]

CURTIS MR CHARLES JOHN

Temple Garden Chambers
1 Harcourt Buildings, Temple, London
EC4Y 9DA, ☎020 7583 1315
✉clerks@tgchambers.com
Call Date: Oct 1992, Lincoln's Inn
Pupil Supervisor
Qualifications: [BA(Hons)(Dunelm)]
charlescurtis@tgchambers.com

CURTIS MS HELEN JANE

Garden Court Chambers
57-60 Lincoln's Inn Fields, London WC2A 3LJ,
☎020 7993 7600 ✉info@gclaw.co.uk
Call Date: Nov 1992, Middle Temple
Pupil Supervisor
Qualifications: [LLB (Hons) (Leics)]
helenc@gclaw.co.uk

CURTIS MR JAMES WILLIAM OCKFORD QC (1993)

6 King's Bench Walk
Ground Floor, 6 King's Bench Walk, Temple,
London EC4Y 7DR, ☎020 7583 0410
✉clerks@6kbw.com
Call Date: July 1970, Inner Temple
Recorder
Qualifications: [MA (Oxon)]
james.curtis@6kbw.com

CURTIS MR MATTHEW

Linenhall Chambers
1 Stanley Place, Chester CH1 2LU,
☎01244 348282
✉clerks@linenhallchambers.co.uk
Call Date: July 2006, Inner Temple
Qualifications: [BA Law (Oxon)]

CURTIS MR MATTHEW PAUL

College Chambers
19 Carlton Crescent, Southampton,
Hampshire SO15 2ET, ☎023 8023 0338
✉clerks@college-chambers.co.uk
Call Date: July 2006, Middle Temple
Qualifications: [LLB (Hons) (Lond)]
mcurtis@college-chambers.co.uk

CURTIS MR MICHAEL ALEXANDER QC (2008)

Crown Office Chambers
2 Crown Office Row, Temple, London
EC4Y 7HJ, ☎020 7797 8100
✉mail@crownofficechambers.com
Call Date: Nov 1982, Middle Temple
Qualifications: [MA (Oxon) MSc ACIArb]
curtis@crownofficechambers.com

CURTIS-RALEIGH MR GILES

23 Essex Street
London WC2R 3AA, ☎020 7413 0353
✉clerks@23es.com
Call Date: Oct 1992, Middle Temple
Pupil Supervisor
Qualifications: [BA (Hons) Dip Law MA]
gilescurtisraleigh@23es.com

CURTIS-ROUSE MISS ALICE JEANETTE

Hailsham Chambers
Ground Floor, 4 Paper Buildings, Temple,
London EC4Y 7EX, ☎020 7643 5000
✉clerks@hailshamchambers.com
Call Date: Oct 2009, Inner Temple
Qualifications: [BA (Cantab)]

CURWEN MR DAVID CHRISTIAN

Unity Street Chambers
5 Unity Street, College Green, Bristol BS1 5HH, ☎0117 906 9789
✉chambers@unitystreetchambers.com
Call Date: July 1982, Gray's Inn
Pupil Supervisor
Qualifications: [BA (Warw) Dip Law]
david.curwen@unitystreetchambers.com

CUSWORTH MR NICHOLAS NEVILLE GRYLLS QC (2009)

1 Hare Court
1 Hare Court, Temple, London EC4Y 7BE, ☎020 7797 7070 ✉clerks@1hc.com
Call Date: Nov 1986, Lincoln's Inn
Qualifications: [MA (Oxon)]
cusworth@1hc.com

CUTLER MR ANTHONY NEIL

Clerksroom (London)
3rd Floor, 218 Strand, London WC2R 1AT, ☎0845 083 3000 ✉mail@clerksroom.com
Call Date: July 2007, Gray's Inn
Qualifications: [BSc (Manch)]

CUTRESS MR JAMES STUART

Fountain Court Chambers
Fountain Court, Temple, London EC4Y 9DH, ☎020 7583 3335
✉chambers@fountaincourt.co.uk
Call Date: Oct 2000, Lincoln's Inn
Pupil Supervisor
Qualifications: [BA (Hons) (Oxon) BCL (Oxon) LLM]
jc@fountaincourt.co.uk

CUTTER MISS SIAN LISA

36 Bedford Row
London WC1R 4JH, ☎020 7421 8000
✉chambers@36bedfordrow.co.uk
Call Date: July 2007, Lincoln's Inn
Qualifications: [BA MPHIL]
scutter@36bedfordrow.co.uk

CUTTING MR CHRISTOPHER HUGH

Chambers of Mr Christopher Cutting
Pansy Cottage, Goram's Mill Lane, Laxfield, Woodbridge, Suffolk IP13 8DW, ☎01986 798499 ✉chcutting@btinternet.com
Call Date: Nov 1973, Middle Temple
Pupil Supervisor
Qualifications: [LLM]

DA COSTA MISS FRANCISCA MARIA

3 PB Barristers
3 Paper Buildings, Temple, London EC4Y 7EU, ☎020 7583 8055
3 PB Barristers
30 Christchurch Road, Bournemouth, Dorset BH1 3PD, ☎01202 292102
✉clerks.bournemouth@3paper.co.uk
3 PB Barristers
Royal Talbot House, 2 Victoria Street, Bristol, Avon BS1 6BB, ☎0117 928 1520
3 PB Barristers
4 St Peter Street, Winchester SO23 8BW, ☎01962 868884
✉clerks.winchester@3paper.co.uk
3 PB Barristers
23 Beaumont Street, Oxford OX1 2NP, ☎01865 793 736
Call Date: Oct 2006, Middle Temple
Qualifications: [LLB (Hons) (Southampton)]

DA COSTA-WALDMAN MRS ELISSA JOSEPHINE

Clerksroom (Taunton)
Equity House, Administration Centre, Blackbrook Park Avenue, Taunton, Somerset TA1 2PX, ☎0845 083 3000
✉mail@clerksroom.com
Clerksroom (London)
3rd Floor, 218 Strand, London WC2R 1AT, ☎0845 083 3000 ✉mail@clerksroom.com
King's Lynn Chambers
26 The Birches, South Wootton, King's Lynn, Norfolk PE30 3JG, ☎01553 672 085
✉timothy.leader@tesco.net
Call Date: Oct 1990, Middle Temple
Qualifications: [BA Dip Law LLM]
Elissa.DaCosta-Waldman@218strand.com

DA SILVA MR DAVID VERE AUSTIN CLEMENT PETE

3 Stone Buildings
Ground Floor, 3 Stone Buildings, Lincoln's Inn, London WC2A 3XL, ☎020 7242 4937
✉clerks@3sb.law.co.uk
Call Date: Nov 1978, Middle Temple
Pupil Supervisor
Qualifications: [MA (Oxon)]
ddasilva@3sb.law.co.uk

DABBS MR DAVID LESLIE

42 Bedford Row
London WC1R 4LL, ☎020 7831 0222
✉clerks@42br.com
Call Date: July 1984, Lincoln's Inn
Pupil Supervisor
Qualifications: [LLB (Manch) MCIArb]
david.dabbs@42br.com

E

DABLE MR JEREMY RICHARD

Clerksroom (Taunton)
Equity House, Administration Centre, Blackbrook Park Avenue, Taunton, Somerset TA1 2PX, ☎ 0845 083 3000
✉ mail@clerksroom.com
64 Bridge Street
3rd Floor, 64 Bridge Street, Manchester M3 3BN, ☎ 0845 083 3000
✉ mail@64bridgestreet.com
Call Date: Nov 1987, Gray's Inn
Pupil Supervisor
Qualifications: [LLB (Leeds)]

DACEY MR MARK

5 King's Bench Walk
5 King's Bench Walk, Temple, London EC4Y 7DN, ☎ 020 7353 5638
✉ clerks@5kbw.co.uk
Call Date: Nov 1985, Middle Temple
Pupil Supervisor
Qualifications: [BA]

DACRE MR IAN THOMAS

New Bailey Chambers
4th Floor, Corn Exchange, Fenwick Street, Liverpool, Merseyside L2 7QS, ☎ 0151 236 9402 ✉ clerks@newbailey.com
Call Date: Nov 1991, Middle Temple
Qualifications: [BA MA (Lond)]

E

DAGG MR JOHN DOUGLAS

Trinity Chambers
Highfield House, Moulsham Street, Chelmsford, Essex CM2 9AH, ☎ 01245 605040
✉ clerks@trinitychambers.com
Call Date: July 1980, Middle Temple
Pupil Supervisor
Qualifications: [BSc (Dunelm) LLB (Lond) MCD (L'pool) MRTPI]
🖃 jdagg@trinitychambers.com

DAGNALL MISS JANE MARY

St Johns Buildings
24a - 28 St John Street, Manchester M3 4DJ, ☎ 0161 214 1500
✉ clerk@stjohnsbuildings.co.uk
St Johns Buildings
21 White Friars, Chester CH1 1NZ, ☎ 01244 323070
✉ clerk@stjohnsbuildings.co.uk
16 Winckley Square
Preston PR1 3JJ, ☎ 01772 256100
Call Date: Nov 1987, Inner Temple
Qualifications: [LLB (Hons)]

DAGNALL MR JOHN MARSHALL ANTHONY

Maitland Chambers
7 Stone Buildings, Lincoln's Inn, London WC2A 3SZ, ☎ 020 7406 1200
✉ clerks@maitlandchambers.com
Call Date: Nov 1983, Lincoln's Inn
Pupil Supervisor
Qualifications: [BA BCL(Oxon)]

D'AGUILAR MR KENNETH HUGH

Staple Inn Chambers
1st Floor, 9 Staple Inn, Holborn Bars, London WC1V 7QH, ☎ 020 7242 5240
✉ clerks@stapleinn.co.uk
Call Date: Nov 1998, Lincoln's Inn
Qualifications: [LLB (Hons)(Lond)]
🖃 khd@stapleinn.co.uk

DAHLSEN MR PETER JOHN MORGAN

2 Dr Johnson's Buildings
2 Dr Johnson's Buildings, Temple, London EC4Y 7AY, ☎ 020 7936 2613
✉ clerks@2drj.com
Call Date: Oct 1996, Gray's Inn
Pupil Supervisor
Qualifications: [LLB (Hons)]
🖃 p.dahlsen@2drj.com

DAICHES MR MICHAEL SALIS

42 Bedford Row
London WC1R 4LL, ☎ 020 7831 0222
✉ clerks@42br.com
Call Date: July 1977, Middle Temple
Pupil Supervisor
🖃 michael.daiches@42br.com

D'AIGREMONT MR GILLES LOUIS

1 Gray's Inn Square
Ground Floor, 1 Gray's Inn Square, London WC1R 5AA, ☎ 020 7405 0001
Call Date: July 1978, Lincoln's Inn
Pupil Supervisor
Qualifications: [Maitrise En Droit Dip de L'Institut d'Etudes Politiques (France) Paris Bar Association]

DAINTY MISS CHERYL JANE

Kings Chambers
36 Young Street, Manchester M3 3FT, ☎ 0845 034 3444
✉ clerks@kingschambers.com
Kings Chambers
5 Park Square East, Leeds LS1 2NE, ☎ 0845 034 3444
✉ clerks@kingschambers.com

Kings Chambers
Embassy House, 60 Church Street, Birmingham B3 2DJ, ☎0845 034 3444
✉clerks@kingschambers.com
Call Date: July 2006, Inner Temple
Qualifications: [BA (Oxon) MA Miur (Comp]
✉cdainty@kingschambers.com

DALAL MR RAJEN CHARLES JAMES

Cobden House Chambers
19 Quay Street, Manchester M3 3HN, ☎0161 833 6000 ✉Clerks@Cobden.co.uk
Derwent Chambers
78 Friar Gate, Derby DE1 1FL, ☎01332 242425
✉admin@derwentchambers.co.uk
Call Date: Oct 1991, Lincoln's Inn
Qualifications: [LLB (Hons) (Manc)]
✉clerks@cobden.co.uk

DALBY MR JOSEPH FRANCIS

4-5 Gray's Inn Square
Gray's Inn, London WC1R 5AH, ☎020 7404 5252 ✉clerks@4-5.co.uk
Call Date: July 1988, Middle Temple
Qualifications: [LLB (Hons) Lic Spec en Droit Eur]
✉jdalby@4-5.co.uk, joseph@dalby.ie

DALE MR DERRICK RALPH QC (2010)

Fountain Court Chambers
Fountain Court, Temple, London EC4Y 9DH, ☎020 7583 3335
✉chambers@fountaincourt.co.uk
Call Date: Oct 1990, Middle Temple
Pupil Supervisor
Qualifications: [BA (Cantab) LLM (USA)]
✉ddale@fountaincourt.co.uk

DALE MR JONATHAN PAUL

18 St John Street
Manchester M3 4EA, ☎0161 278 1800
✉clerks@18sjs.com
Call Date: Oct 1991, Gray's Inn
Pupil Supervisor
Qualifications: [MA (Oxon)]
✉jdale@18sjs.com

DALE MR JULIAN CHARLES RIGBY

Eastbourne Chambers
5 Chiswick Place, Eastbourne, East Sussex BN21 4NH, ☎01323 642102
✉clerks@eastbournechambers.co.uk
Call Date: Nov 1991, Middle Temple
Pupil Supervisor
Qualifications: [LLB (Hons)]

DALE MISS LUCY-ANN GEORGIA

4 Brick Court
4 Brick Court, Temple, London EC4Y 9AD, ☎020 7832 3200 ✉clerks@4bc.co.uk
Call Date: July 2002, Lincoln's Inn
Qualifications: [BSc (Hons)(Bris)]

DALES MR COLIN FRANCIS

Clerksroom (Taunton)
Equity House, Administration Centre, Blackbrook Park Avenue, Taunton, Somerset TA1 2PX, ☎0845 083 3000
✉mail@clerksroom.com
Call Date: Oct 2007, Lincoln's Inn
Qualifications: [LLB (So'ton)]

DALEY MR HOWARD MARTIN

Lamb Chambers
Lamb Building, Elm Court, Temple, London EC4Y 7AS, ☎020 7797 8300
✉info@lambchambers.co.uk
Call Date: Oct 1997, Gray's Inn
Qualifications: [BA (Hons)(Cantab)]
✉howarddaley@lambchambers.co.uk

DALEY MISS NICOLA ELIZABETH

Exchange Chambers
One Derby Square, Derby Square, Liverpool L2 9XX, ☎0151 236 7747
✉info@exchangechambers.co.uk
Exchange Chambers
7 Ralli Courts, West Riverside, Manchester M3 5FT, ☎0161 833 2722
Exchange Chambers
Oxford House, Oxford Row, Leeds LS1 3BE, ☎0113 203 1970
✉spencer@exchangechambers.co.uk
Call Date: July 2000, Gray's Inn
Qualifications: [LLB (Leeds)]
✉daley@exchangechambers.co.uk

DALLAS MR ANDREW THOMAS ALASTAIR

No.6 Park Square
Leeds LS1 2LW, ☎0113 245 9763
✉Tim@no6.co.uk
Call Date: Nov 1978, Gray's Inn
Pupil Supervisor, Recorder
Qualifications: [MA (Cantab)]
✉dallas@no6.co.uk

DALLING MR ROBERT JAMES

Five Paper Buildings
1st Floor, Five Paper Buildings, Temple, London EC4Y 7HB, ☎020 7583 6117
✉clerks@5pb.co.uk
Call Date: Oct 2003, Middle Temple
Qualifications: [BA (Hons)(Oxon)]
✉rd@5pb.co.uk

E

DALTON MR MATTHEW WILLIAM

Blackfriars Chambers
79-83 Temple Chambers, 3-7 Temple Avenue, London EC4Y 0HP, ☎ 020 7353 7400
✉ clerks@blackfriarschambers.com
Call Date: Nov 1999, Middle Temple
Qualifications: [BA (Hons)(Cantab)]
✉ matthewdalton5@yahoo.co.uk

DALY MISS CAOIMHE SARAH

QEB Hollis Whiteman
1-2 Laurence Pountney Hill, London EC4R 0EU, ☎ 020 7933 8855
✉ barristers@qebhw.co.uk
Call Date: July 2005, Inner Temple
Qualifications: [BA (Cantab) LLM]
✉ caoimhe.daly@qebhw.co.uk

DALY MR DAVID

Heathway Chambers
31 Heathway, London SE3 7AN, ☎ 020 8293 0509 ✉ daviddaly@talktalk.net
Call Date: July 1979, Middle Temple
Qualifications: [AKC MSc LLB (Lond) BA]

Types of work: Administrative law, Chancery (general), Chancery (land law), Discrimination, Employment, Equity, Family provision, Housing, Human rights, Landlord and tenant, Local authorities, Mediation, Planning, Professional negligence, Succession, Trusts, Wills

E

DALY MR DENIS MICHAEL PATRICK SHEPSTONE

Chambers of Denis Daly
6 Maresfield Gardens, Hampstead, London NW3 5SU, ☎ 07809 465658
✉ den.daly@gmail.com
11 Stone Buildings
11 Stone Buildings, Lincoln's Inn, London WC2A 3TG, ☎ 020 7831 6381
✉ clerks@11sb.com
Call Date: Feb 1995, Lincoln's Inn
Qualifications: [BA LLB (South Africa) LLM (Cantab)]

DALY MR NIGEL JONATHAN

13 King's Bench Walk
13 King's Bench Walk, Temple, London EC4Y 7EN, ☎ 020 7353 7204
✉ clerks@13kbw.co.uk
13 KBW
32 Beaumont Street, Oxford OX1 2NP, ☎ 01865 311066 ✉ clerks@13kbw.co.uk
Call Date: July 1979, Gray's Inn
Pupil Supervisor, Recorder
Qualifications: [LLB (Lond)]
✉ ndaly@13kbw.co.uk

DALY MISS ORLA MAIRE

5 King's Bench Walk
5 King's Bench Walk, Temple, London EC4Y 7DN, ☎ 020 7353 5638
✉ clerks@5kbw.co.uk
Call Date: Nov 2000, Gray's Inn
Qualifications: [BA (Durham)]
✉ orla.daly@5kbw.co.uk

DANCE MR MATHEW WILLIAM

18 Red Lion Court
London EC4A 3EB, ☎ 020 7520 6000
✉ chambers@18rlc.co.uk
Call Date: July 2001, Lincoln's Inn
Qualifications: [LLB (Hons)]
✉ mathew.dance@18rlc.co.uk

DANCER MS HELEN ELIZABETH

Guildford Chambers
Stoke House, Leapale Lane, Guildford, Surrey GU1 4LY, ☎ 01483 539131
✉ clerks@guildfordchambers.co.uk
Call Date: July 2001, Middle Temple
Qualifications: [LLM (Lond) MA (Oxon) Dip Law (City)]
✉ helen.e.dancer@gmail.com

DANESHYAR MR OSAMA

Equity Chambers
First Floor, McLaren Building, 46 Priory Queensway, Birmingham B4 7LR, ☎ 0121 236 5007
✉ clerks@equitychambers.org.uk
Call Date: Oct 1996, Inner Temple
Qualifications: [BA (Notts)]
✉ clerks@equitychambers.org.uk

DANIEL MISS HAYLEY MICHELLE

Cathedral Chambers
10 Clytha Park Road, Newport NP20 4PB, ☎ 01633 215112
Call Date: Nov 2007, Inner Temple
Qualifications: [LLB (Wales)]

DANIEL MR RICHARD

177 Bittacy Hill
London NW7 1RT, ☎ 07775 535738
✉ rdaniellaw@aol.com
Call Date: Feb 1977, Inner Temple
✉ rdaniellaw@aol.com

DANIEL MR THOMAS MICHAEL

2 Bedford Row
London WC1R 4BU, ☎ 020 7440 8888
✉ clerks@2bedfordrow.co.uk
Call Date: July 2009, Inner Temple
Qualifications: [LLB]

DANIELLS-SMITH MR ROGER CHARLES

1 Mitre Court Buildings
1 Mitre Court Buildings, Temple, London EC4Y 7BS, ☎ 020 7452 8900
✉ clerks@1mcb.com
Call Date: Nov 1974, Middle Temple
Pupil Supervisor
Qualifications: [AKC LLB]
✉ roger.daniells-smith@1mcb.com

DANIELS MR DAVID WILLIAM

Rowchester Chambers
4 Rowchester Court, Whittall Street, Birmingham B4 6DH, ☎ 0121 233 2327
✉ clerks@rowchesterchambers.co.uk
Call Date: Oct 1995, Lincoln's Inn
Qualifications: [LLB (Hons)(Lond) B.Com (B'ham)]

DANIELS MR IAIN JAMES

Ely Place Chambers
30 Ely Place, London EC1N 6TD, ☎ 020 7400 9600 ✉ admin@elyplace.com
Call Date: Oct 1992, Lincoln's Inn
Pupil Supervisor
Qualifications: [LLB(Hons)(Sheff)]
✉ idaniels@elyplace.com

DANIELS MRS LAURA MICHELLE

Kings Chambers
36 Young Street, Manchester M3 3FT, ☎ 0845 034 3444
✉ clerks@kingschambers.com
Kings Chambers
5 Park Square East, Leeds LS1 2NE, ☎ 0845 034 3444
✉ clerks@kingschambers.com
Kings Chambers
Embassy House, 60 Church Street, Birmingham B3 2DJ, ☎ 0845 034 3444
✉ clerks@kingschambers.com
Call Date: July 2009, Lincoln's Inn
Qualifications: [LLB (L'pool)]
✉ clerks@kingschambers.com

DANIELS MR NICHOLAS ANDREW

1 Garden Court Family Law Chambers
Ground Floor, One Garden Court, Temple, London EC4Y 9BJ, ☎ 020 7797 7900
✉ clerks@1gc.com
Call Date: Feb 1988, Inner Temple
Qualifications: [LLB (Bristol)]
✉ daniels@1gc.com

DANIELS MISS PHILIPPA CATHERINE

36 Bedford Row
London WC1R 4JH, ☎ 020 7421 8000
✉ chambers@36bedfordrow.co.uk
Call Date: Oct 1995, Inner Temple
Qualifications: [BA (Hons)(S.Africa)]
✉ pdaniels@36bedfordrow.co.uk

DANN MR GEOFFREY LEONARD KEITH

Clock Chambers
18 Waterloo Road, Wolverhampton WV1 4BL, ☎ 01902 313444
✉ clockchambers@btconnect.com
Call Date: Nov 1978, Gray's Inn
Qualifications: [MA (Cantab)]
✉ geoffrey@pattingham-ringers.org.uk

DANTON MISS KIRSTIE ELIZABETH

New Walk Chambers
27 New Walk, Leicester, Leicestershire LE1 6TE, ☎ 0871 200 1298 / 0116 255 9144
✉ clerks@newwalkchambers.co.uk
Call Date: July 1999, Middle Temple
Pupil Supervisor
Qualifications: [LLB (Hons)(Hull)]
✉ kdanton@newwalkchambers.co.uk

DARBISHIRE MR ADRIAN MUNRO QC (2012)

QEB Hollis Whiteman
1-2 Laurence Pountney Hill, London EC4R 0EU, ☎ 020 7933 8855
✉ barristers@qebhw.co.uk
Call Date: Oct 1993, Lincoln's Inn
Pupil Supervisor
Qualifications: [BA (Hons) Dip Law (Lond) LLM (Lond)]
✉ adrian.darbishire@qebhw.co.uk

DARBY MISS JOHANNA LOUISE

Trinity Chambers
The Custom House, 39 Quayside, Newcastle Upon Tyne NE1 3DE, ☎ 0191 232 1927
✉ info@trinitychambers.co.uk
Trinity Chambers
Multi Media Exchange, 72-80 Corporation Road, Middlesbrough TS1 2RF, ☎ 01642 247569
✉ info@trinitychambers.co.uk
Call Date: Oct 2007, Middle Temple
Qualifications: [BA (Hons) (Newc) MA (Wales)]
✉ j.darby@trinitychambers.co.uk

E

DARBY MR PATRICK MICHAEL

St Philips Chambers
55 Temple Row, Birmingham B2 5LS,
☎0121 246 7000 ✉clerks@st-philips.com
Call Date: July 1978, Middle Temple
Pupil Supervisor
Qualifications: [MA (Cantab)]
pdarby@st-philips.com

DARBY MS RACHEL ZOE

Charter Chambers
33 John Street, London WC1N 2AT,
☎020 7618 4400
✉clerks@charterchambers.com
Call Date: Oct 1997, Inner Temple
Pupil Supervisor
Qualifications: [LLB (Middx)]
clerks@charterchambers.com

DARBYSHIRE MR WILLIAM ROBERT

9 St John Street
Manchester M3 4DN, ☎0161 955 9000
✉civilclerks@9sjs.com /
criminalclerks@9sjs.com
Call Date: Nov 1995, Lincoln's Inn
Pupil Supervisor
Qualifications: [BA (Hons) LLM]

D'ARCY MISS ELEANOR MARY JOANNA

Kings Chambers
36 Young Street, Manchester M3 3FT,
☎0845 034 3444
✉clerks@kingschambers.com
Kings Chambers
5 Park Square East, Leeds LS1 2NE,
☎0845 034 3444
✉clerks@kingschambers.com
Kings Chambers
Embassy House, 60 Church Street,
Birmingham B3 2DJ, ☎0845 034 3444
✉clerks@kingschambers.com
Call Date: Oct 2008, Lincoln's Inn
Qualifications: [BA(Oxon)]
edarcy@kingschambers.com

D'ARCY DR MICHAEL BRENDAN

One Essex Court
Ground Floor, One Essex Court, Temple,
London EC4Y 9AR, ☎020 7583 2000
✉clerks@oeclaw.co.uk
Call Date: July 2008, Inner Temple
Qualifications: [MPhys DPhil (Oxon)]

DARDIS MRS HEATHER JUDITH

Temple Garden Chambers
1 Harcourt Buildings, Temple, London
EC4Y 9DA, ☎020 7583 1315
✉clerks@tgchambers.com
Call Date: Nov 2000, Lincoln's Inn
Qualifications: [LLB (Hons)]
clerks@tgchambers.com

DARIAN MRS ANN

Queen Square Chambers
56 Queen Square, Bristol BS1 4PR,
☎0117 921 1966 ✉crime@qs-c.co.uk
Call Date: July 1974, Middle Temple
Qualifications: [LLB (Hons)(LSE)]
civil@qs-c.co.uk

DARLING MR PAUL ANTONY QC (1999)

Keating Chambers
15 Essex Street, London WC2R 3AA,
☎020 7544 2600
✉clerks@keatingchambers.com
Call Date: July 1983, Middle Temple
Qualifications: [BA BCL (Oxon)]

DARLING MS RACHEL POLLYANNA MARGARET

Nine Bedford Row
9 Bedford Row, London WC1R 4AZ,
☎020 7489 2727
✉clerks@9bedfordrow.co.uk
Call Date: Nov 2000, Inner Temple
Qualifications: [MA (Edin) CPE]
polly.darling@9bedfordrow.co.uk

DARLINGTON MISS ELIZABETH

Zenith Chambers
10 Park Square, Leeds LS1 2LH,
☎0113 245 5438
✉clerks@zenithchambers.co.uk
5 Pump Court
Ground Floor, 5 Pump Court, Temple, London
EC4Y 7AP, ☎020 7353 2532
✉clerks@5pumpcourt.com
Call Date: Oct 1998, Middle Temple
Qualifications: [BA (Hons)(Cantab)]
edarlington@zenithchambers.co.uk

DARLOW MISS ANNABEL CHARLOTTE

6 King's Bench Walk
Ground Floor, 6 King's Bench Walk, Temple, London EC4Y 7DR, ☎020 7583 0410
✉clerks@6kbw.com
Call Date: Oct 1993, Middle Temple
Pupil Supervisor
Qualifications: [BA (Hons)(Cantab) Dip Law (Lond)]
annabel.darlow@6kbw.com

DARNBROUGH MR DANIEL JAMES

Chambers of Mr Ami Feder
Ground Floor, Lamb Building, Temple, London EC4Y 7AS, ☎020 7797 7788
✉clerks@lambbuilding.co.uk
Lamb Building
22 Ship Street, Brighton BN1 1AD, ☎01273 820490
✉admin@lambbuilding.co.uk
Chambers of Mr Ami Feder
Ground Floor, Lamb Building, Temple, London EC4Y 7AS, ☎020 7797 7788
✉clerks@lambbuilding.co.uk
Call Date: Nov 2006, Middle Temple
Qualifications: [BA (Hons) (Manch)]
clerks@lambbuilding.co.uk

DARROCH MISS FIONA CULVERWELL

Clerksroom (Taunton)
Equity House, Administration Centre, Blackbrook Park Avenue, Taunton, Somerset TA1 2PX, ☎0845 083 3000
✉mail@clerksroom.com
Clerksroom (London)
3rd Floor, 218 Strand, London WC2R 1AT, ☎0845 083 3000 ✉mail@clerksroom.com
King's Lynn Chambers
26 The Birches, South Wootton, King's Lynn, Norfolk PE30 3JG, ☎01553 672 085
✉timothy.leader@tesco.net
Call Date: Oct 1994, Inner Temple
Qualifications: [BA (Lond) Dip Music CPE LLM]
darroch@clerksroom.com

DARTON MR CLIFFORD JOHN

Pallant Chambers
12 North Pallant, Chichester, West Sussex PO19 1TQ, ☎01243 784538
✉clerks@pallantchambers.co.uk
Call Date: July 1988, Middle Temple
Pupil Supervisor
Qualifications: [BA (Hons) (Oxon)]
cdarton@pallantchambers.co.uk

DARWIN MISS CLAIRE LOUISE

Matrix Chambers
Griffin Building, Gray's Inn, London WC1R 5LN, ☎020 7404 3447
✉matrix@matrixlaw.co.uk / Iscott@matrixlaw.co.uk
Call Date: Oct 2005, Inner Temple
Qualifications: [MA (Cantab)]
clairedarwin@matrixlaw.co.uk

DAS MISS KAMALA

St John's Chambers
101 Victoria Street, Bristol BS1 6PU, ☎0117 923 4700
✉clerks@stjohnschambers.co.uk
Call Date: Nov 1975, Middle Temple
Qualifications: [BA LLM]
kamala.das@stjohnschambers.co.uk

DASANI MISS KAJAL NARENDRA

New Walk Chambers
27 New Walk, Leicester, Leicestershire LE1 6TE, ☎0871 200 1298 / 0116 255 9144
✉clerks@newwalkchambers.co.uk
Call Date: Oct 2004, Middle Temple
Qualifications: [LLB (Hons) (Sheff)]

DASHANI MISS SONAL

15 New Bridge Street
London EC4V 6AU, ☎020 7842 1900
✉clerks@15nbs.com
Call Date: Nov 2002, Lincoln's Inn
Qualifications: [LLB (Hons) (Brunel)]

DASHWOOD PROF ARTHUR ALAN QC (2010)

Henderson Chambers
2 Harcourt Buildings, Temple, London EC4Y 9DB, ☎020 7583 9020
✉clerks@hendersonchambers.co.uk
Call Date: Nov 1969, Inner Temple
Qualifications: [MA (Oxon)]
adashwood@hendersonchambers.co.uk

DASSA MISS REGINE

9 King's Bench Walk
Lower Ground Floor South, 9 King's Bench Walk, Temple, London EC4Y 7DX, ☎020 7353 9564 ✉9kbw@btconnect.com
Call Date: Oct 1999, Lincoln's Inn
Qualifications: [LLB (Hons)(Manc)]
9kbw@btconnect.com

E

DATE MR JULIAN RICHARD

Field Court Chambers
5 Field Court, Gray's Inn, London WC1R 5EF,
☎ 020 7405 6114 ✉ clerks@fieldcourt.co.uk
Call Date: Nov 1988, Middle Temple
Pupil Supervisor
Qualifications: [BA (Oxon)]
julian.date@fieldcourt.co.uk

DATTA MR SHOMIK

42 Bedford Row
London WC1R 4LL, ☎ 020 7831 0222
✉ clerks@42br.com
Call Date: Nov 2000, Gray's Inn
Qualifications: [BA (Oxon) MA (Oxon)]
shomik.datta@42br.com

DATTA MS WENDY PATRICIA MIZAL

Talloway Chambers
Rivington House, 82 Great Eastern Street,
London EC2A 3JF, ☎ 020 7419 5047
✉ tor@talloway.com
Call Date: Oct 1990, Middle Temple
Qualifications: [Dip Ed (Lond) LLB (Hons)]

DAULTON MRS SALLY JANE

Devon Chambers
3 St Andrew Street, Plymouth PL1 2AH,
☎ 01752 661659
✉ clerks@devonchambers.co.uk
Call Date: July 2009, Gray's Inn
Qualifications: [BA MBA]
sdaulton@devonchambers.co.uk

DAVE MR ISHANRAJ

12 Old Square Chambers
1st Floor, 12 Old Square, Lincoln's Inn,
London WC2A 3TX, ☎ 020 7404 0875
✉ clerks@12oldsquare.com
Call Date: Mar 2006, Middle Temple
Qualifications: [LLB (Hons) (Brunel)]
ishan.dave@12os.com

DAVE MISS PRIYA

3 Temple Gardens
Lower Ground Floor, 3 Temple Gardens,
Temple, London EC4Y 9AU, ☎ 020 7353 3102
✉ clerks@3tg.co.uk
Call Date: Oct 2006, Lincoln's Inn
Qualifications: [LLB (Lond)]
pd@3tg.co.uk

DAVENPORT MISS CLAIRE ALISON

7 Bell Yard
London WC2A 2JR, ☎ 020 7831 0636
✉ kevintarrant@btconnect.com
Call Date: Oct 1996, Inner Temple
Qualifications: [BA (Reading) CPE]
cd@7bellyard.co.uk

DAVENPORT MR RICHARD IAN

Citadel Chambers
The Citadel, 190 Corporation Street,
Birmingham B4 6QD, ☎ 0121 233 8500
✉ clerks@citadelchambers.com
Call Date: Oct 2002, Gray's Inn
Qualifications: [Dip Law]

DAVENPORT MR SIMON NICHOLAS QC (2009)

3 Hare Court
3 Hare Court, Temple, London EC4Y 7BJ,
☎ 020 7415 7800 ✉ clerks@3harecourt.com
Call Date: Nov 1987, Inner Temple
Qualifications: [LLB (Hons)(Leeds) FCIArb]
sdavenport@3harecourt.com

DAVEY MR CHARLES

Clerksroom (Taunton)
Equity House, Administration Centre,
Blackbrook Park Avenue, Taunton, Somerset
TA1 2PX, ☎ 0845 083 3000
✉ mail@clerksroom.com
64 Bridge Street
3rd Floor, 64 Bridge Street, Manchester
M3 3BN, ☎ 0845 083 3000
✉ mail@64bridgestreet.com
Chambers of Mr C Davey
7 Blair Close, Bishop's Stortford CM23 4PR,
☎ 01279 506412 ✉ charlesdavey@gmx.com
Call Date: Feb 1989, Middle Temple
Qualifications: [MA (Oxon)]

DAVEY MR FRANCIS JOHN MALCOLM

Chambers of Francis Davey
Flat 8, Manor Lea, 295 Green Lanes, London
N4 2EU, ☎ 020 8442 8099
✉ fjmdla@gmail.com
Call Date: Oct 2003, Gray's Inn
Qualifications: [MA (Cantab)]
fjmd1a@gmail.com

DAVEY MISS HELEN CLARE

St Mary's Family Law Chambers
26-28 High Pavement, The Lace Market,
Nottingham NG1 1HN, ☎ 0115 950 3503
✉ clerks@stmarysflc.co.uk
Call Date: Mar 2006, Lincoln's Inn
Qualifications: [LLB (Hons) (Manch)]
helen.davey@stmarysflc.co.uk

DAVEY MISS HELEN MARGARET

4 Brick Court
4 Brick Court, Temple, London EC4Y 9AD, ☎020 7832 3200 ✉clerks@4bc.co.uk
Call Date: July 1984, Inner Temple
Pupil Supervisor
Qualifications: [BSc (Cardiff)]

DAVEY MR JONATHAN MICHAEL

Wilberforce Chambers
8 New Square, Lincoln's Inn, London WC2A 3QP, ☎020 7306 0102
✉chambers@wilberforce.co.uk
Call Date: Oct 2003, Lincoln's Inn
Qualifications: [BA (Hons) (Nott'm) MA (Nott'm) CPE (Lond) MPhil (Cantab)]
jdavey@wilberforce.co.uk

DAVEY MS KATHERINE ANNE TERESA

2 Pump Court
1st Floor, 2 Pump Court, Temple, London EC4Y 7AH, ☎020 7353 5597
✉clerks@2pumpcourt.co.uk
Call Date: May 1988, Inner Temple
Qualifications: [MA (Cantab)]

DAVEY MR MICHAEL PHILIP

Quadrant Chambers
Quadrant House, 10 Fleet Street, London EC4Y 1AU, ☎020 7583 4444
✉info@quadrantchambers.com
Call Date: Nov 1990, Gray's Inn
Pupil Supervisor
Qualifications: [LLB (Lond) BCL (Oxon)]
michael.davey@quadrantchambers.com

DAVEY MISS MICHELLE MARIA

Atlantic Chambers
4-6 Cook Street, Liverpool L2 9QU, ☎0151 236 4421
✉info@atlanticchambers.co.uk
Call Date: Nov 1993, Lincoln's Inn
Qualifications: [LLB (Hons) (L'pool)]
michelledavey@atlanticchambers.co.uk

DAVEY MR NEIL MARTIN QC (2001)

39 Park Square
Leeds LS1 2NU, ☎0113 245 6633
✉seniorclerk@39parksquarechambers.co.uk
3 Temple Gardens
Lower Ground Floor, 3 Temple Gardens, Temple, London EC4Y 9AU, ☎020 7353 3102
✉clerks@3tg.co.uk
Old Court Chambers
Newham House, 96-98 Borough Road, Middlesbrough TS1 2HJ, ☎01642 232523
✉clerks@oldcourtchambers.com
Call Date: July 1978, Middle Temple
Qualifications: [MA (Oxon)]

DAVEY MR ROGER LAWRENCE

The Chambers of Mr R L Davey
70 Belgarum Place, Winchester, Hampshire SO23 8SL, ☎01962 865728
✉rldavey@ntlworld.com
5 Pump Court
Ground Floor, 5 Pump Court, Temple, London EC4Y 7AP, ☎020 7353 2532
✉clerks@5pumpcourt.com
Call Date: Feb 1978, Inner Temple

DAVEY MR TOBIAS BENJAMIN

4-5 Gray's Inn Square
Gray's Inn, London WC1R 5AH, ☎020 7404 5252 ✉clerks@4-5.co.uk
Call Date: Feb 1977, Gray's Inn
Pupil Supervisor
Qualifications: [LLB (Hons)]
tdavey@4-5.co.uk

DAVID MR ALASTAIR ROBERT OULPE

New Walk Chambers
27 New Walk, Leicester, Leicestershire LE1 6TE, ☎0871 200 1298 / 0116 255 9144
✉clerks@newwalkchambers.co.uk
Pendragon Chambers
Suite 7, J Shed, Kings Road, SA1 Waterfront, Swansea SA1 8PL, ☎01792 411188
✉clerks@pendragonchambers.com
Call Date: July 2005, Lincoln's Inn
Qualifications: [BA (Hons)]

DAVID MR PAUL WILSON

Chambers of Mr Paul David
P.O. Box 4472, Shortland Street, Auckland 1140, ☎0064 9 379 5589
✉paul@pauldavid.co.nz
Farrar's Building
Farrar's Building, Temple, London EC4Y 7BD, ☎020 7583 9241
✉Chambers@farrarsbuilding.co.uk
Call Date: Nov 1981, Inner Temple
Qualifications: [BA (Hons) LLM (Cantab)]

E

DAVIDGE MISS JUSTINE MARIE

4 King's Bench Walk
2nd Floor, 4 King's Bench Walk, Temple, London EC4Y 7DL, ☎ 020 7822 7000
✉ clerks@4kbw.co.uk
Call Date: July 2001, Gray's Inn
Pupil Supervisor
Qualifications: [LLB (Cardiff)]
✉ jmd@4kbw.co.uk

DAVIDSON MR ANDREW EDWARD

Citadel Chambers
The Citadel, 190 Corporation Street, Birmingham B4 6QD, ☎ 0121 233 8500
✉ clerks@citadelchambers.com
Call Date: Oct 2003, Gray's Inn
Qualifications: [LLB]
✉ clerks@citadelchambers.com

DAVIDSON MISS KATHARINE MARY QC (2011)

1 Hare Court
1 Hare Court, Temple, London EC4Y 7BE, ☎ 020 7797 7070 ✉ clerks@1hc.com
Riverview Chambers
Hamilton House, 1 Temple Avenue, London EC4Y 0HA, ☎ 0844 225 3999
✉ chrisbaylis@riverviewchambers.com
Call Date: Nov 1987, Lincoln's Inn
Qualifications: [MA (Oxon)]
✉ davidson@1hc.com

DAVIDSON MISS LAURA ANNE

No5 Chambers
Greenwood House, 4-7 Salisbury Court, London EC4Y 8AA, ☎ 0845 210 5555
No5 Chambers
38 Queen Square, Bristol BS1 4QS, ☎ 0845 210 5555
No5 Chambers
Fountain Court, Steelhouse Lane, Birmingham B4 6DR, ☎ 0845 210 5555 ✉ info@no5.com
Call Date: Oct 1996, Lincoln's Inn
Qualifications: [MA Dip Law LLM (Cantab) PhD (Cantab)]
✉ lda@no5.com

DAVIDSON MR NICHOLAS RANKING QC (1993)

Four New Square
Four New Square, Lincoln's Inn, London WC2A 3RJ, ☎ 020 7822 2000
✉ barristers@4newsquare.com
Call Date: July 1974, Inner Temple
Qualifications: [MA (Cantab)]
✉ n.davidson@4newsquare.com

DAVIDSON DR RANALD DUNBAR

3 Serjeants Inn
London EC4Y 1BQ, ☎ 020 7427 5000
✉ clerks@3serjeantsinn.com
Call Date: Nov 1996, Inner Temple
Pupil Supervisor
Qualifications: [MB LLB (Lond) ChB (Edin)]
✉ rdavidson@3serjeantsinn.com

DAVIDSON MS ROSEMARY ANNE

6 King's Bench Walk
Ground Floor, 6 King's Bench Walk, Temple, London EC4Y 7DR, ☎ 020 7583 0410
✉ clerks@6kbw.com
Call Date: July 2004, Inner Temple

DAVIDSON MISS SALLY ELIZABETH

College Chambers
19 Carlton Crescent, Southampton, Hampshire SO15 2ET, ☎ 023 8023 0338
✉ clerks@college-chambers.co.uk
Call Date: July 2006, Inner Temple
Qualifications: [LLB (L'pool)]
✉ sdavidson@college-chambers.co.uk

DAVIE MR MICHAEL JAMES QC (2010)

4 Pump Court
4 Pump Court, Temple, London EC4Y 7AN, ☎ 020 7842 5555
✉ chambers@4pumpcourt.com
Call Date: Nov 1993, Middle Temple
Qualifications: [LLB (Hons)(Scotland) D Phil (Oxon)]
✉ mdavie@4pumpcourt.com

DAVIE MISS SARA WOODHOUSE

Chambers of Ian Macdonald QC
Garden Court North, 22 Oxford Court, Manchester M2 3WQ, ☎ 0161 236 1840
✉ clerks@gcnchambers.co.uk
Call Date: July 2007, Middle Temple
Qualifications: [BSc (Hons) (St Andrews) BSc (Hons) (Glasgow) Dip Law LLB]

DAVIES MR ADRIAN MICHAEL

3 Dr Johnson's Buildings
Ground Floor, 3 Dr Johnson's Buildings, Temple, London EC4Y 7BA, ☎ 020 7353 4854
✉ clerks@3djb.co.uk
Call Date: July 1998, Lincoln's Inn
Qualifications: [BA (Hons) (Cantab) MA (Cantab) LLM (Lond)]
✉ adavies@3djb.co.uk

DAVIES MR ALEXANDER JULIAN COLIN

KCH Garden Square
1 Oxford Street, Nottingham NG1 5BH, ☎0115 941 8851
✉clerks@kchgardensquare.co.uk
Call Date: Mar 2008, Lincoln's Inn
Qualifications: [LLB (Leeds)]

DAVIES MR ANDREW

Apex
Harlech House, 20 Cathedral Road, Cardiff CF11 9LJ, ☎02920 232 032
✉clerks@apexchambers.net
Call Date: Oct 1992, Lincoln's Inn
Qualifications: [LLB(Hons)(Lancs) LLM(Hull)]
✉andrew.davies@apexchambers.net

DAVIES MR ANDREW CHRISTOPHER

Henderson Chambers
2 Harcourt Buildings, Temple, London EC4Y 9DB, ☎020 7583 9020
✉clerks@hendersonchambers.co.uk
Call Date: July 1988, Inner Temple
Pupil Supervisor
Qualifications: [BA (Oxon)]
✉adavies@hendersonchambers.co.uk

DAVIES MISS ANGHARAD KATE

Dere Street Barristers
14 Toft Green, York YO1 6JT, ☎0844 3351551
✉clerks@derestreet.co.uk
York Chambers
Rotterdam House, 116 The Quayside, Newcastle Upon Tyne NE1 3DY, ☎0191 206 4677
Dere Street Barristers
33 Broad Chare, Newcastle Upon Tyne NE1 3DQ, ☎0844 3351551
✉clerks@derestreet.co.uk
Call Date: Nov 2006, Middle Temple
Qualifications: [BA (Hons) (Lanc) LLM (Lanc) PgDip Law]
✉clerks@yorkchambers.co.uk

DAVIES MISS ANGHARAD SUSAN

30 Park Place
Cardiff CF10 3BS, ☎029 2039 8421
✉clerks@30parkplace.law.co.uk
Call Date: Oct 2000, Lincoln's Inn
Qualifications: [LLB (Hons) (Wales) Pg Dip Law]
✉angharad@30parkplace.co.uk

DAVIES MR BENJAMIN GUY

30 Park Place
Cardiff CF10 3BS, ☎029 2039 8421
✉clerks@30parkplace.law.co.uk
Call Date: Oct 1999, Lincoln's Inn
Pupil Supervisor
Qualifications: [LLB (Hons)(UEA)]
✉bd@30parkplace.co.uk

DAVIES MISS CAROL ELIZABETH

College Chambers
19 Carlton Crescent, Southampton, Hampshire SO15 2ET, ☎023 8023 0338
✉clerks@college-chambers.co.uk
Call Date: Oct 1995, Middle Temple
Pupil Supervisor
Qualifications: [LLB (Hons)]
✉cdavies@College-Chambers.co.uk

DAVIES MISS CHARLOTTE ELIZABETH

Littleton Chambers
3 King's Bench Walk North, Temple, London EC4Y 7HR, ☎020 7797 8600
✉fschneider@littletonchambers.co.uk
Call Date: Oct 2006, Lincoln's Inn
Qualifications: [BA (Oxon)]
✉cdavies@littletonchambers.co.uk

DAVIES MISS CLAIRE SUZANNE

Farringdon Chambers
180 Bermondsey Street, London SE1 3TQ, ☎020 7089 5700
Call Date: July 1999, Middle Temple
Qualifications: [LLB (Hons)(Leeds)]
✉clairedavies@farringdon-law.co.uk

DAVIES MR DAVID MATTHEW

Essex Court Chambers
24 Lincoln's Inn Fields, London WC2A 3EG, ☎020 7813 8000
✉clerksroom@essexcourt.net
Call Date: Mar 2004, Gray's Inn
Qualifications: [BA (Oxon) BCL (Oxon)]
✉ddavies@essexcourt.net

DAVIES MR DAVID PETER

9 Park Place
9 Park Place, Cardiff, South Glamorgan CF10 3DP, ☎029 2038 2731
✉clerks@9parkplace.co.uk
Call Date: May 1996, Lincoln's Inn
Qualifications: [LLB (Hons) (Hull)]
✉pdavies@9parkplace.co.uk

E

DAVIES MISS DEBORAH SUSAN

Ropewalk Chambers
24 The Ropewalk, Nottingham NG1 5EF, ☎0115 947 2581 ✉clerks@ropewalk.co.uk
Call Date: Oct 1993, Inner Temple
Pupil Supervisor
Qualifications: [LLB (Hons)]
deborahdavies@ropewalk.co.uk

DAVIES MS ELIZABETH MARY

Garden Court Chambers
57-60 Lincoln's Inn Fields, London WC2A 3LJ, ☎020 7993 7600 ✉info@gclaw.co.uk
Call Date: Feb 1994, Inner Temple
Pupil Supervisor
Qualifications: [LLB (Hons)(Lond)]
lizd@gclaw.co.uk

DAVIES MISS EMILY JANE

9 Park Place
9 Park Place, Cardiff, South Glamorgan CF10 3DP, ☎029 2038 2731
✉clerks@9parkplace.co.uk
Call Date: Nov 1989, Gray's Inn
Pupil Supervisor
Qualifications: [LLB (Wales)]
clerks@9parkplace.co.uk

E

DAVIES MISS EMILY SPARHAM

Lamb Chambers
Lamb Building, Elm Court, Temple, London EC4Y 7AS, ☎020 7797 8300
✉info@lambchambers.co.uk
Call Date: Oct 2000, Middle Temple
Qualifications: [LLB (Hons) (Wales)]
emilydavies@lambchambers.co.uk

DAVIES MR EVAN HUW QC (2006)

Essex Court Chambers
24 Lincoln's Inn Fields, London WC2A 3EG, ☎020 7813 8000
✉clerksroom@essexcourt.net
Call Date: Nov 1985, Gray's Inn
Qualifications: [LLB (Wales)]
hdavies@essexcourt.net

DAVIES MISS FELICITY ANNE

Sovereign Chambers
46 Park Place, Leeds LS1 2RY, ☎0113 245 1841
✉clerks@sovereignchambers.co.uk
Call Date: July 1980, Middle Temple
Pupil Supervisor, Recorder
Qualifications: [BA (York)]
felicity.davies@sovereignchambers.co.uk

DAVIES MR GEORGE NICHOLAS ROGER

Temple Garden Chambers
1 Harcourt Buildings, Temple, London EC4Y 9DA, ☎020 7583 1315
✉clerks@tgchambers.com
Call Date: Nov 1998, Gray's Inn
Qualifications: [MA (Oxon)]
georgedavies@tgchambers.com

DAVIES DR GILLIAN

Hogarth Chambers
5 New Square, Lincoln's Inn, London WC2A 3RJ, ☎020 7404 0404
✉barristers@hogarthchambers.com
Call Date: Nov 1961, Lincoln's Inn
Qualifications: [PhD]

DAVIES MR GREGORY HUW

4 Brick Court
4 Brick Court, Temple, London EC4Y 9AD, ☎020 7832 3200 ✉clerks@4bc.co.uk
Call Date: Oct 2005, Middle Temple
Qualifications: [BSc PgDL]
greg.davies@4bc.co.uk

DAVIES MR HAROLD RODNEY OLONINDIEH

Redemption Chambers
121 The Vale, Golders Green, London NW11 8TL, ☎020 8458 5486
✉home@ollennu92.freeserve.co.uk
Call Date: Nov 1978, Lincoln's Inn
Qualifications: [LLB (Hons) MA (Brunel)]

DAVIES MRS HARRIET FEAR

3 PB Barristers
Royal Talbot House, 2 Victoria Street, Bristol, Avon BS1 6BB, ☎0117 928 1520
3 PB Barristers
30 Christchurch Road, Bournemouth, Dorset BH1 3PD, ☎01202 292102
✉clerks.bournemouth@3paper.co.uk
3 PB Barristers
4 St Peter Street, Winchester SO23 8BW, ☎01962 868884
✉clerks.winchester@3paper.co.uk
3 PB Barristers
23 Beaumont Street, Oxford OX1 2NP, ☎01865 793 736
3 PB Barristers
3 Paper Buildings, Temple, London EC4Y 7EU, ☎020 7583 8055
Call Date: Oct 2007, Middle Temple
Qualifications: [Dip Law (Lond) LLB]

DAVIES MISS HELEN LOUISE QC (2008)

Brick Court Chambers
7-8 Essex Street, London WC2R 3LD,
☎ 020 7379 3550 ✉ clerks@brickcourt.co.uk
Call Date: Nov 1991, Inner Temple
Pupil Supervisor
Qualifications: [BA (Cantab)]
✉ Helen.Davies@Brickcourt.co.uk

DAVIES MR HENRY OLUSOLA

Trinity Chambers
Suite 441, 27 Colmore Row, Birmingham B3 2EW, ☎ 0121 346 4672
✉ tchambersb@aol.com
Call Date: Nov 1999, Middle Temple
Pupil Supervisor
Qualifications: [LLB (Hons) Dip Int'l Law Dip Human Rights]

DAVIES MR HUGH CURRY

3 Raymond Buildings
3 Raymond Buildings, Gray's Inn, London WC1R 5BH, ☎ 020 7400 6400
✉ clerks@3rblaw.com
Call Date: Oct 1990, Lincoln's Inn
Pupil Supervisor
Qualifications: [BA (Oxon)]
✉ hugh.davies@3raymondbuildings.com

DAVIES MR HUGH MICHAEL

Deans Court Chambers
24 St John Street, Manchester M3 4DF,
☎ 0161 214 6000 ✉ clerks@deanscourt.co.uk
Deans Court Chambers
101 Walker Street, Preston PR1 2RR,
☎ 01772 565 600
✉ preston@deanscourt.co.uk
Call Date: July 1982, Middle Temple
Pupil Supervisor
Qualifications: [MA (Oxon)]
✉ hdavies@deanscourt.co.uk

DAVIES MR HUW PROTHEROE

Farrar's Building
Farrar's Building, Temple, London EC4Y 7BD,
☎ 020 7583 9241
✉ Chambers@farrarsbuilding.co.uk
Call Date: Oct 1998, Gray's Inn
Pupil Supervisor
Qualifications: [BA (Oxon)]
✉ huwdavies@farrarsbuilding.co.uk

DAVIES MR IWAN RHUN

Iscoed Chambers
86 St Helen's Road, Swansea SA1 4BQ,
☎ 01792 652988
✉ clerks@iscoedchambers.co.uk
Call Date: Feb 1995, Gray's Inn
Qualifications: [LLB (Wales & Cantab) LLM PhD (Wales)]
✉ id@iscoedchambers.co.uk

DAVIES MR JAKE SEBASTIAN HUNTER

Five Paper
Ground Floor, 5 Paper Buildings, Temple, London EC4Y 7HB, ☎ 020 7815 3200
Call Date: Oct 1997, Inner Temple
Qualifications: [BA CPE]
✉ jakedavies@fivepaper.com

DAVIES MR JAMES ALEXANDER

Enterprise Chambers
9 Old Square, Lincoln's Inn, London WC2A 3SR, ☎ 020 7405 9471
✉ london@enterprisechambers.com
Call Date: July 2009, Lincoln's Inn
Qualifications: [LLB (Exon)]
✉ jamesdavies@enterprisechambers.com

DAVIES MR JAMES EDWIN

3 PB Barristers
23 Beaumont Street, Oxford OX1 2NP,
☎ 01865 793 736
3 PB Barristers
30 Christchurch Road, Bournemouth, Dorset BH1 3PD, ☎ 01202 292102
✉ clerks.bournemouth@3paper.co.uk
3 PB Barristers
3 Paper Buildings, Temple, London EC4Y 7EU,
☎ 020 7583 8055
3 PB Barristers
Royal Talbot House, 2 Victoria Street, Bristol, Avon BS1 6BB, ☎ 0117 928 1520
3 PB Barristers
4 St Peter Street, Winchester SO23 8BW,
☎ 01962 868884
✉ clerks.winchester@3paper.co.uk
Call Date: Oct 2004, Lincoln's Inn
Qualifications: [BA (Hons) (Oxon)]

DAVIES MR JOHN MEIRION

30 Park Place
Cardiff CF10 3BS, ☎ 029 2039 8421
✉ clerks@30parkplace.law.co.uk
Call Date: July 1975, Gray's Inn
Pupil Supervisor
Qualifications: [LLB (Wales)]

E

DAVIES MR JONATHAN HUW

Old Square Chambers
10-11 Bedford Row, London WC1R 4BU,
☎ 020 7269 0300 ✉ clerks@oldsquare.co.uk
Old Square Chambers
3 Orchard Court, St Augustine's Yard, Bristol BS1 5DP, ☎ 0117 930 5100
✉ clerks@oldsquare.co.uk
Call Date: July 2003, Lincoln's Inn
Qualifications: [MA (Oxon) CTA PgDL]
davies@oldsquare.co.uk

DAVIES MR JONATHAN NORVAL

9-12 Bell Yard
London WC2A 2JR, ☎ 020 7400 1800
✉ clerks@9-12bellyard.com
Call Date: July 1981, Inner Temple
Pupil Supervisor
Qualifications: [LLB (Lond)]

DAVIES MISS JOSEPHINE CELIA PALFREY

20 Essex Street
London WC2R 3AL, ☎ 020 7842 1200
✉ clerks@20essexst.com
Call Date: Oct 2006, Lincoln's Inn
Qualifications: [BA (Cantab) MSci GDL]
clerks@20essexst.com

DAVIES MR KARL LEONARD

Chambers of Mr Karl Davies
17 Burnhill House, Norman Street, London EC1V 3PQ, ☎ 07932 044635
✉ karlldavies@hotmail.com
Call Date: Nov 1999, Inner Temple
Qualifications: [LLB LLM (Kent)]

DAVIES MR MAX JAMES

30 Park Place
Cardiff CF10 3BS, ☎ 029 2039 8421
✉ clerks@30parkplace.law.co.uk
Call Date: Oct 2005, Middle Temple
Qualifications: [BSc (Hons) (Bournemouth)]

DAVIES MR MICHAEL IWAN

Number 7 Harrington Street Chambers
7 Harrington Street, Liverpool L2 9YH,
☎ 0151 242 0707 ✉ clerks@7hs.co.uk
Call Date: July 1979, Middle Temple
Pupil Supervisor
Qualifications: [LLB (L'pool)]
michael.davies@7hs.co.uk

DAVIES MR NICHOLAS JEREMY

Crown Office Chambers
2 Crown Office Row, Temple, London EC4Y 7HJ, ☎ 020 7797 8100
✉ mail@crownofficechambers.com
Call Date: July 1975, Inner Temple
Qualifications: [BA]
ndavies@crownofficechambers.com

DAVIES MR NICHOLAS MICHAEL

Fenners Chambers
3 Madingley Road, Cambridge CB3 0EE,
☎ 01223 368761
✉ clerks@fennerschambers.com
Call Date: July 2006, Lincoln's Inn
Qualifications: [BA (Oxon)]
nick.davies@fennerschambers.com

DAVIES MR NICHOLAS RICHARD JAMES

3 PB Barristers
23 Beaumont Street, Oxford OX1 2NP,
☎ 01865 793 736
3 PB Barristers
Royal Talbot House, 2 Victoria Street, Bristol, Avon BS1 6BB, ☎ 0117 928 1520
3 PB Barristers
3 Paper Buildings, Temple, London EC4Y 7EU,
☎ 020 7583 8055
3 PB Barristers
4 St Peter Street, Winchester SO23 8BW,
☎ 01962 868884
✉ clerks.winchester@3paper.co.uk
3 PB Barristers
30 Christchurch Road, Bournemouth, Dorset BH1 3PD, ☎ 01202 292102
✉ clerks.bournemouth@3paper.co.uk
Call Date: Nov 2006, Gray's Inn
Qualifications: [BA]

DAVIES MR PHILIP EDWARD HAMILTON

Erskine Chambers
33 Chancery Lane, London WC2A 1EN,
☎ 020 7242 5532
✉ clerks@erskinechambers.com
Call Date: Oct 1998, Inner Temple
Qualifications: [BA (Cantab) BCL (Oxon)]
edavies@erskine-chambers.co.uk

DAVIES MISS REBECCA LUCINDA

Westgate Chambers
64 High Street, Lewes, East Sussex BN7 1XG,
☎ 01273 480510
✉ clerks@westgate-chambers.co.uk
Call Date: Nov 1996, Lincoln's Inn
Qualifications: [LLB (Hons)(Lond)]
rld@westgate-chambers.co.uk

E

DAVIES MISS RHIANNON LAURA

St Ive's Chambers
Whittall Street, Birmingham B4 6DH,
☎ 0121 236 0863
✉ clerks@stiveschambers.co.uk
Call Date: Oct 2001, Gray's Inn
Qualifications: [LLB]

DAVIES MR RHYS POWELL

No5 Chambers
Greenwood House, 4-7 Salisbury Court, London EC4Y 8AA, ☎ 0845 210 5555
No5 Chambers
38 Queen Square, Bristol BS1 4QS,
☎ 0845 210 5555
No5 Chambers
Fountain Court, Steelhouse Lane, Birmingham B4 6DR, ☎ 0845 210 5555 ✉ info@no5.com
Call Date: Oct 2004, Gray's Inn
Qualifications: [MA BA]
🖃 rd@no5.com

DAVIES MR RUPERT AIDAN

18 St John Street
Manchester M3 4EA, ☎ 0161 278 1800
✉ clerks@18sjs.com
Call Date: Mar 2007, Gray's Inn
Qualifications: [BA (Cantab)]

DAVIES MR RUSSELL DEWI THOMAS

Deans Court Chambers
24 St John Street, Manchester M3 4DF,
☎ 0161 214 6000 ✉ clerks@deanscourt.co.uk
Deans Court Chambers
101 Walker Street, Preston PR1 2RR,
☎ 01772 565 600
✉ preston@deanscourt.co.uk
Call Date: Nov 1983, Middle Temple
Pupil Supervisor
Qualifications: [LLB (L'pool)]
🖃 davies@deanscourt.co.uk

DAVIES MS SAMANTHA TERESA

Chambers of Ms Samantha Davies
PO Box 6017, Milton Keynes, Buckinghamshire MK1 9AP, ☎ 0845 123 1234
✉ samanthatdavies@yahoo.co.uk
Warwick House Chambers
8 Warwick Court, Warwick House Chambers, Gray's Inn, London WC1R 5DJ,
☎ 020 7430 2323
✉ clerks@warwickhousechambers.com
Call Date: Oct 2002, Inner Temple
Qualifications: [BSc (Lond) CPE LPC BA (Hons)(Lond)]

DAVIES MISS SARAH JEANNETTE

1 Pump Court
Elm Court, Temple, London EC4Y 7AB,
☎ 020 7842 7070
✉ (name)@pumpcourt.co.uk
Call Date: Feb 1984, Gray's Inn
Pupil Supervisor
Qualifications: [BA (Hons) (Kent)]
🖃 sd@1pumpcourt.co.uk

DAVIES MISS SARAH-JANE

4-5 Gray's Inn Square
Gray's Inn, London WC1R 5AH,
☎ 020 7404 5252 ✉ clerks@4-5.co.uk
Call Date: Oct 1996, Inner Temple
Qualifications: [BA (Cantab)]
🖃 sjdavies@4-5.co.uk

DAVIES MISS SHEILAGH ELIZABETH

4 Breams Buildings
Chancery Lane, London EC4A 1HP,
☎ 020 7092 1900 ✉ clerks@4bb.co.uk
Call Date: Nov 1974, Middle Temple
Pupil Supervisor
Qualifications: [LLB (Lond)]

DAVIES MISS SIAN HELEN

Cornerstone Barristers
2-3 Gray's Inn Square, Gray's Inn, London WC1R 5JH, ☎ 020 7242 4986
✉ chambers@2-3gis.co.uk
Call Date: Oct 1999, Gray's Inn
Qualifications: [BA LLM (LSE)]
🖃 sdavies@2-3gis.co.uk

DAVIES MR STEPHEN REES QC (2000)

Guildhall Chambers
23 Broad Street, Bristol BS1 2HG,
☎ 0117 930 9000
✉ hoc@guildhallchambers.co.uk
Wilberforce Chambers
8 New Square, Lincoln's Inn, London WC2A 3QP, ☎ 020 7306 0102
✉ chambers@wilberforce.co.uk
Call Date: July 1983, Gray's Inn
Qualifications: [LLB (Lond) LLB (Cantab)]
🖃 stephen.davies@guildhallchambers.co.uk

DAVIES MR TREVOR GLYN

The Chambers of Grahame Aldous QC
9 Gough Square, London EC4A 3DG,
☎ 020 7832 0500
✉ clerks@9goughsquare.co.uk
Call Date: July 1978, Gray's Inn
Pupil Supervisor
Qualifications: [BA (Nott'm)]
🖃 daviestg@aol.com

E

DAVIES MISS UNYIME APRIL

1 Paper Buildings
1st Floor, 1 Paper Buildings, Temple, London EC4Y 7EP, ☎ 020 7353 3728
✉ clerks@onepaper.co.uk
Call Date: Nov 2006, Middle Temple
Qualifications: [LLB (Hons) (Lond)]

DAVIES MR WILLIAM RHODRI QC (1999)

One Essex Court
Ground Floor, One Essex Court, Temple, London EC4Y 9AR, ☎ 020 7583 2000
✉ clerks@oeclaw.co.uk
Call Date: July 1979, Middle Temple
Qualifications: [BA (Cantab)]
rdavies@oeclaw.co.uk

DAVIES-JONES MR JONATHAN

3 Verulam Buildings
London WC1R 5NT, ☎ 020 7831 8441
✉ chambers@3vb.com
Call Date: Nov 1994, Middle Temple
Pupil Supervisor
Qualifications: [MA]
jdj@3vb.com

E

DAVIS MR ADAM DAVID QC (2012)

Dyers Chambers
35 Bedford Row, London WC1R 4JH, ☎ 020 7404 1881
✉ admin@dyerschambers.com
Call Date: Nov 1985, Inner Temple
Pupil Supervisor
Qualifications: [LLB (Lond)]

DAVIS MR ADRIAN MARTIN

Field Court Chambers
5 Field Court, Gray's Inn, London WC1R 5EF, ☎ 020 7405 6114 ✉ clerks@fieldcourt.co.uk
Call Date: Oct 1996, Gray's Inn
Pupil Supervisor
Qualifications: [B.Sc (Dunelm) LLB (Notts)]
adrian.davis@fieldcourt.co.uk

DAVIS MR ALAN THOMAS SAMUEL

Goldsmith Chambers
Ground Floor, Goldsmith Building, Temple, London EC4Y 7BL, ☎ 020 7353 6802
✉ clerks@goldsmithchambers.com
Call Date: July 2007, Middle Temple
Qualifications: [BMus (Edin) MA (Bris)]
a.davis@goldsmithchambers.law.co.uk

DAVIS MR ANDREW PAUL

Crown Office Chambers
2 Crown Office Row, Temple, London EC4Y 7HJ, ☎ 020 7797 8100
✉ mail@crownofficechambers.com
Call Date: Oct 1996, Gray's Inn
Pupil Supervisor
Qualifications: [LLB (Hons)]
adavis@crownofficechambers.com

DAVIS MR ANTHONY JOHN

Dere Street Barristers
33 Broad Chare, Newcastle Upon Tyne NE1 3DQ, ☎ 0844 3351551
✉ clerks@derestreet.co.uk
Call Date: Nov 1986, Gray's Inn
Qualifications: [BA (Hons)]
clerks@broadcharechambers.co.uk

DAVIS MISS CAROL JANE

Littleton Chambers
3 King's Bench Walk North, Temple, London EC4Y 7HR, ☎ 020 7797 8600
✉ fschneider@littletonchambers.co.uk
Call Date: Oct 1996, Middle Temple
Qualifications: [BA (Hons)(Sussex)]
cdavis@littletonchambers.co.uk

DAVIS MR GLEN MILTON QC (2011)

South Square
3-4 South Square, Gray's Inn, London WC1R 5HP, ☎ 020 7696 9900
✉ practicemanagers@southsquare.com
Call Date: Oct 1992, Middle Temple
Pupil Supervisor
Qualifications: [MA (Hons)(Oxon) Dip Law (Lond)]
glendavis@southsquare.com

DAVIS MR GREVILLE LEIGH BLAKEMAN

Lombard Chambers
1 Sekforde Street, Clerkenwell, London EC1R 0BE, ☎ 020 7107 2100
Call Date: July 1976, Lincoln's Inn
Pupil Supervisor
Qualifications: [LLB (Lond)]

DAVIS MR JAMES BURNHAM

Angel Chambers
Ethos Building, Kings Road, Swansea SA1 8AS, ☎ 01792 464623
✉ clerks@angelchambers.co.uk
Call Date: July 1997, Gray's Inn

DAVIS MR JONATHAN MURRAY

Cornwall Street Chambers
85-87 Cornwall Street, Birmingham B3 3BY,
☎0121 233 7500
✉clerks@cornwallstreet.co.uk
Call Date: July 1983, Middle Temple
Qualifications: [MA (Oxon)]
✉john.davis@cornwallstreet.co.uk

DAVIS MR JUSTIN ROGER WILLIAM

Crown Office Chambers
2 Crown Office Row, Temple, London
EC4Y 7HJ, ☎020 7797 8100
✉mail@crownofficechambers.com
Call Date: Oct 2003, Lincoln's Inn
Qualifications: [LLB (Hons) (City)]
✉jrd@crownofficechambers.com

DAVIS MISS LUCINDA JANE

Pallant Chambers
12 North Pallant, Chichester, West Sussex
PO19 1TQ, ☎01243 784538
✉clerks@pallantchambers.co.uk
Call Date: Nov 1981, Gray's Inn
Pupil Supervisor, Recorder
Qualifications: [LLB (Hons) (Lond)]
✉ldavissussex@hotmail.com

DAVIS MISS LUCY-VICTORIA

Pump Court Chambers
31 Southgate Street, Winchester, Hampshire
SO23 9EB, ☎01962 868 161
✉clerks@3pumpcourt.com
Pump Court Chambers
Upper Ground Floor, 3 Pump Court, Temple,
London EC4Y 7AJ, ☎020 7353 0711
✉clerks@3pumpcourt.com
Pump Court Chambers
5 Temple Chambers, Temple Street, Swindon
SN1 1SQ, ☎01793 539899
✉clerks@3pumpcourt.com
Call Date: Nov 2003, Gray's Inn
Qualifications: [LLB]
✉ld@3pumpcourt.com

DAVIS MR RICHARD JOLYON HAROLD

Hogarth Chambers
5 New Square, Lincoln's Inn, London
WC2A 3RJ, ☎020 7404 0404
✉barristers@hogarthchambers.com
Call Date: Oct 1992, Gray's Inn
Pupil Supervisor
Qualifications: [MA (Cantab) Dip Law C Eng MIEE]
✉rdavis@hogarthchambers.com

DAVIS MR SIMON JOHN

St Philips Chambers
55 Temple Row, Birmingham B2 5LS,
☎0121 246 7000 ✉clerks@st-philips.com
Call Date: Oct 1990, Middle Temple
Pupil Supervisor
Qualifications: [MA (Cantab) Dip Law]

DAVIS MR WILLIAM NEAL

Charter Chambers
33 John Street, London WC1N 2AT,
☎020 7618 4400
✉clerks@charterchambers.com
Call Date: July 2003, Gray's Inn
Qualifications: [BA (Oxon)]
✉william.davis@charterchambers.com

DAVISON MS ELEANOR LOUISE

Outer Temple Chambers
The Outer Temple, 222 Strand, London
WC2R 1BA, ☎020 7353 6381
✉clerks@outertemple.com
Call Date: Nov 2003, Lincoln's Inn
Qualifications: [MA (Bris)]

DAVISON MR GUY DIXON

1 Gray's Inn Square
Ground Floor, 1 Gray's Inn Square, London
WC1R 5AA, ☎020 7405 0001
Call Date: Oct 1998, Lincoln's Inn
Pupil Supervisor
Qualifications: [LLB (Hons)(Newc)]

DAVISON MR JAMES EDWARD

3 PB Barristers
3 Paper Buildings, Temple, London EC4Y 7EU,
☎020 7583 8055
3 PB Barristers
Royal Talbot House, 2 Victoria Street, Bristol,
Avon BS1 6BB, ☎0117 928 1520
3 PB Barristers
30 Christchurch Road, Bournemouth, Dorset
BH1 3PD, ☎01202 292102
✉clerks.bournemouth@3paper.co.uk
3 PB Barristers
4 St Peter Street, Winchester SO23 8BW,
☎01962 868884
✉clerks.winchester@3paper.co.uk
3 PB Barristers
23 Beaumont Street, Oxford OX1 2NP,
☎01865 793 736
Call Date: Nov 1996, Gray's Inn
Qualifications: [LLB (Wales)]

DAVISON MR RICHARD HAROLD

12 King's Bench Walk
12 King's Bench Walk, Temple, London EC4Y 7EL, ☎020 7583 0811
Call Date: July 1982, Gray's Inn
Pupil Supervisor
Qualifications: [MA (Oxon)]
davison@12kbw.co.uk

DAVIS-WHITE MR MALCOLM QC (2003)

4 Stone Buildings
Ground Floor, 4 Stone Buildings, Lincoln's Inn, London WC2A 3XT, ☎020 7242 5524
✉clerks@4stonebuildings.com
Call Date: July 1984, Middle Temple
Qualifications: [MA, BCL (Oxon)]
m.daviswhite@4stonebuildings.com

DAVITT MISS PAULA AINE

St Johns Buildings
24a - 28 St John Street, Manchester M3 4DJ, ☎0161 214 1500
✉clerk@stjohnsbuildings.co.uk
16 Winckley Square
Preston PR1 3JJ, ☎01772 256100
St Johns Buildings Liverpool
8th Floor India Buildings, Water Street, Liverpool L2 0XG, ☎0151 243 6000
✉clerk@stjohnsbuildings.co.uk
Call Date: Nov 1988, Gray's Inn
Qualifications: [LLB Hons]
clerk@stjohnsbuildings.co.uk, pdavitt@stjohnsbuildings.co.uk

DAVY MISS FELICIA MARIE THERESE

Old Bailey Chambers
15 Old Bailey, London EC4M 7EF, ☎020 3008 6404
✉clerks@15oldbaileychambers.com
Call Date: Oct 2000, Middle Temple
Pupil Supervisor
Qualifications: [LLB (Hons) (Wales)]

DAVY MR NEIL GEOFFREY

3 Serjeants Inn
London EC4Y 1BQ, ☎020 7427 5000
✉clerks@3serjeantsinn.com
Call Date: Oct 2000, Middle Temple
Pupil Supervisor
Qualifications: [BA (Hons) (Oxon)]
ndavy@3serjeantsinn.com

DAVY MR PHILIP HOWARD

Ropewalk Chambers
24 The Ropewalk, Nottingham NG1 5EF, ☎0115 947 2581 ✉clerks@ropewalk.co.uk
Call Date: Nov 2009, Lincoln's Inn
Qualifications: [LLB (Sheff)]
Philipdavy@ropewalk.co.uk

DAWAR MISS ARCHNA

Deans Court Chambers
24 St John Street, Manchester M3 4DF, ☎0161 214 6000 ✉clerks@deanscourt.co.uk
Call Date: Oct 1996, Lincoln's Inn
Qualifications: [LLB (Hons)(L'pool)]

DAWES MISS BEVERLEY RACHEL

KBW
The Engine House, No 1 Foundry Square, Leeds LS11 5DL, ☎0113 297 1200
✉clerks@kbwchambers.com
Call Date: July 2008, Gray's Inn
Qualifications: [LLB (Keele)]

DAWES MR JAMES CHRISTOPHER

Atkinson Bevan Chambers
1st Floor, 2 Harcourt Buildings, Temple, London EC4Y 9DB, ☎020 7353 2112
✉clerks@2hb.co.uk
Call Date: Nov 1993, Inner Temple
Pupil Supervisor
Qualifications: [BA (Dunelm) CPE]

DAWES MR SIMON ROBERT

Atlantic Chambers
4-6 Cook Street, Liverpool L2 9QU, ☎0151 236 4421
✉info@atlanticchambers.co.uk
Call Date: Oct 1990, Inner Temple
Pupil Supervisor
Qualifications: [LLB (Hons) (L'pool)]
simondawes@atlanticchambers.co.uk

DAWID MR DARYUSH JONATHAN

Brick Court Chambers
7-8 Essex Street, London WC2R 3LD, ☎020 7379 3550 ✉clerks@brickcourt.co.uk
Call Date: July 2005, Lincoln's Inn
Qualifications: [BA (Hons) Cantab MA (Harvard) Dip Law]
jonathan.dawid@brickcourt.co.uk

DAWSON MR ADAM DAVID

The Chambers of Grahame Aldous QC
9 Gough Square, London EC4A 3DG,
☎ 020 7832 0500
✉ clerks@9goughsquare.co.uk
Call Date: Oct 2000, Middle Temple
Qualifications: [LLB (Hons) (Leeds)]
✉ adawson@9goughsquare.co.uk

DAWSON MR ALEXANDER WILLIAM

13 King's Bench Walk
13 King's Bench Walk, Temple, London EC4Y 7EN, ☎ 020 7353 7204
✉ clerks@13kbw.co.uk
13 KBW
32 Beaumont Street, Oxford OX1 2NP,
☎ 01865 311066 ✉ clerks@13kbw.co.uk
St John's Chambers
101 Victoria Street, Bristol BS1 6PU,
☎ 0117 923 4700
✉ clerks@stjohnschambers.co.uk
Call Date: July 1969, Middle Temple
Recorder
Qualifications: [MA (Oxon)]
✉ adawson@13kbw.co.uk

DAWSON MISS BEATRICE GRACE

Dere Street Barristers
33 Broad Chare, Newcastle Upon Tyne NE1 3DQ, ☎ 0844 3351551
✉ clerks@derestreet.co.uk
Call Date: July 2006, Lincoln's Inn
Qualifications: [LLB (Leic)]

DAWSON MR JAMES

2 Hare Court
Lower Ground, Ground, 1st & 2nd Floor, 2 Hare Court, Temple, London EC4Y 7BH,
☎ 020 7353 3982 ✉ clerks@2harecourt.com
Call Date: Nov 1984, Middle Temple
Pupil Supervisor, Recorder
Qualifications: [BA (Hons)]
✉ jamesdawson@2harecourt.com

DAWSON MR JAMES ROBERT

3 PB Barristers
3 Paper Buildings, Temple, London EC4Y 7EU,
☎ 020 7583 8055
Oriel Chambers
18 Ribblesdale Place, Preston PR1 3NA,
☎ 01772 254 764
✉ clerks@oriel-chambers.co.uk
Oriel Chambers
14 Water Street, Liverpool, Merseyside L2 8TD, ☎ 0151 236 7191
✉ clerks@orielchambers.co.uk
3 PB Barristers
Royal Talbot House, 2 Victoria Street, Bristol, Avon BS1 6BB, ☎ 0117 928 1520
3 PB Barristers
4 St Peter Street, Winchester SO23 8BW,
☎ 01962 868884
✉ clerks.winchester@3paper.co.uk
3 PB Barristers
23 Beaumont Street, Oxford OX1 2NP,
☎ 01865 793 736
3 PB Barristers
30 Christchurch Road, Bournemouth, Dorset BH1 3PD, ☎ 01202 292102
✉ clerks.bournemouth@3paper.co.uk
Call Date: Nov 1994, Inner Temple
Pupil Supervisor
Qualifications: [LLB (So'ton)]

DAWSON MISS JUDY ELIZABETH

Sovereign Chambers
46 Park Place, Leeds LS1 2RY,
☎ 0113 245 1841
✉ clerks@sovereignchambers.co.uk
Unity Street Chambers
5 Unity Street, College Green, Bristol BS1 5HH, ☎ 0117 906 9789
✉ chambers@unitystreetchambers.com
Call Date: Oct 1993, Gray's Inn
Pupil Supervisor
Qualifications: [MA (Cantab)]
✉ judy.dawson@sovereignchambers.co.uk

DAWSON MISS RACHAEL

Chartlands Chambers
3 St Giles Terrace, Northampton NN1 2BN,
☎ 01604 603322
✉ enquiries@chartlands-chambers.co.uk
Call Date: July 2007, Middle Temple
Qualifications: [LLB (Hons) (Nott'm)]

DAWSON MR RICHARD JON FOSTER

Lincoln House Chambers
Tower 12, The Avenue North, Spinningfields, 18-22 Bridge Street, Manchester M3 3BZ,
☎ 0161 832 5701
✉ info@lincolnhousechambers.com
Call Date: Oct 2001, Middle Temple
Qualifications: [BSc (Hons)(Sheff) CPE]

DAY MR ANDREW JAMES

St Ive's Chambers
Whittall Street, Birmingham B4 6DH,
☎ 0121 236 0863
✉ clerks@stiveschambers.co.uk
Call Date: July 2003, Inner Temple
Qualifications: [LLB (B'ham)]
✉ andrew.day@stiveschambers.co.uk

E

DAY MISS ANNELIESE MARY QC (2012)

Four New Square
Four New Square, Lincoln's Inn, London WC2A 3RJ, ☎020 7822 2000
✉barristers@4newsquare.com
Call Date: Oct 1996, Inner Temple
Pupil Supervisor
Qualifications: [MA (Cantab)]
a.day@4newsquare.com

DAY MR DORIAN STEPHEN

St Philips Chambers
55 Temple Row, Birmingham B2 5LS, ☎0121 246 7000 ✉clerks@st-philips.com
Call Date: July 1987, Middle Temple
Pupil Supervisor
Qualifications: [BA (Hons)]
dday@st-philips.com

DAY MR DOUGLAS HENRY QC (1989)

Farrar's Building
Farrar's Building, Temple, London EC4Y 7BD, ☎020 7583 9241
✉Chambers@farrarsbuilding.co.uk
Call Date: July 1967, Lincoln's Inn
Recorder
Qualifications: [MA (Cantab) MA (Wales)]
dday@farrarsbuilding.co.uk

DAY MR THOMAS CHARLES

2 Hare Court
Lower Ground, Ground, 1st & 2nd Floor, 2 Hare Court, Temple, London EC4Y 7BH, ☎020 7353 3982 ✉clerks@2harecourt.com
Call Date: Nov 2008, Inner Temple
Qualifications: [BA (Dunelm) CPE]

DAYCOCK MR DAVID MARTYN

Iscoed Chambers
86 St Helen's Road, Swansea SA1 4BQ, ☎01792 652988
✉clerks@iscoedchambers.co.uk
Call Date: Nov 1987, Gray's Inn
Qualifications: [LLB PGCE (Wales)]

DAYKIN MISS EMMA

Chambers of Mr Ami Feder
Ground Floor, Lamb Building, Temple, London EC4Y 7AS, ☎020 7797 7788
✉clerks@lambbuilding.co.uk
Chambers of Mr Ami Feder
Ground Floor, Lamb Building, Temple, London EC4Y 7AS, ☎020 7797 7788
✉clerks@lambbuilding.co.uk
Call Date: July 2005, Inner Temple
Qualifications: [LLB (Coventry)]

D'CRUZ MISS LAURA

9 St John Street
Manchester M3 4DN, ☎0161 955 9000
✉civilclerks@9sjs.com / criminalclerks@9sjs.com
Call Date: Nov 2006, Inner Temple
Qualifications: [BA (Oxon) LLM (Bris)]

D'CRUZ MR VINOD RUPERT

Littleton Chambers
3 King's Bench Walk North, Temple, London EC4Y 7HR, ☎020 7797 8600
✉fschneider@littletonchambers.co.uk
Call Date: Nov 1989, Lincoln's Inn
Qualifications: [BA (Nott'm)]
rdc@littletonchambers.co.uk

D'CRUZ MR VIVEK RUFUS

18 Red Lion Court
London EC4A 3EB, ☎020 7520 6000
✉chambers@18rlc.co.uk
18 Red Lion Court (Annexe)
Thornwood House, 102 New London Road, Chelmsford, Essex CM2 0RG, ☎01245 280880
Call Date: Oct 1993, Lincoln's Inn
Pupil Supervisor
Qualifications: [BA (Hons)(B'ham) CPE (Lond)]
rufus.dcruz@18rlc.co.uk

DE BANZIE MR ROBERT LOUIS

Maidstone Chambers
33 Earl Street, Maidstone, Kent ME14 1PF, ☎01622 688592
✉clerks@maidstonechambers.co.uk
Call Date: July 2000, Gray's Inn
Qualifications: [BA (Belfast) (Hons) Dip Law ACIS]
rdebanzie@maidstonechambers.co.uk

DE BERRY MR PHILIP JOHN

18 St John Street
Manchester M3 4EA, ☎0161 278 1800
✉clerks@18sjs.com
Call Date: Oct 2003, Lincoln's Inn
Qualifications: [LLB (Hons) (L'pool)]
pdeberry@18sjs.com

DE BONO MR JOHN HUGH

3 Serjeants Inn
London EC4Y 1BQ, ☎020 7427 5000
✉clerks@3serjeantsinn.com
Call Date: Oct 1995, Gray's Inn
Pupil Supervisor
Qualifications: [BA (Hons) (Oxon) MA (Oxon)]
jdebono@3serjeantsinn.com

DE BURGOS MR JAMIE MICHAEL ABULAFIA

36 Bedford Row
London WC1R 4JH, ☎ 020 7421 8000
✉ chambers@36bedfordrow.co.uk
Call Date: July 1973, Inner Temple
Pupil Supervisor
Qualifications: [MA (Cantab)]
jdeburgos@36bedfordrow.co.uk

DE CORDOVA MISS GEMMA CHARLENE

Tanfield Chambers
2-5 Warwick Court, London WC1R 5DJ,
☎ 020 7421 5300
✉ clerks@tanfieldchambers.co.uk
Call Date: July 2006, Inner Temple
Qualifications: [LLB (Surrey)]

DE FREITAS MR ANTHONY PETER STANLEY

Hailsham Chambers
Ground Floor, 4 Paper Buildings, Temple, London EC4Y 7EX, ☎ 020 7643 5000
✉ clerks@hailshamchambers.com
Call Date: July 1971, Inner Temple
Pupil Supervisor, Recorder
Qualifications: [MA (Oxon)]
anthony.defreitas@hailshamchambers.com

DE FREITAS MISS MELANIE CATHERINE

3 PB Barristers
4 St Peter Street, Winchester SO23 8BW,
☎ 01962 868884
✉ clerks.winchester@3paper.co.uk
3 PB Barristers
Royal Talbot House, 2 Victoria Street, Bristol, Avon BS1 6BB, ☎ 0117 928 1520
3 PB Barristers
30 Christchurch Road, Bournemouth, Dorset BH1 3PD, ☎ 01202 292102
✉ clerks.bournemouth@3paper.co.uk
3 PB Barristers
23 Beaumont Street, Oxford OX1 2NP,
☎ 01865 793 736
3 PB Barristers
3 Paper Buildings, Temple, London EC4Y 7EU,
☎ 020 7583 8055
Call Date: Nov 1995, Middle Temple
Qualifications: [BA (Hons)(W.Indies)]

DE GARR ROBINSON MR ANTHONY JOHN QC (2006)

One Essex Court
Ground Floor, One Essex Court, Temple, London EC4Y 9AR, ☎ 020 7583 2000
✉ clerks@oeclaw.co.uk
Call Date: July 1987, Lincoln's Inn
Qualifications: [BA (Oxon)]
arobinson@oeclaw.co.uk

DE GREGORIO MR MICHELE ERNESTO

Crown Office Chambers
2 Crown Office Row, Temple, London EC4Y 7HJ, ☎ 020 7797 8100
✉ mail@crownofficechambers.com
Call Date: July 2003, Inner Temple
Qualifications: [MA (Oxon) LLM]
degregorio@crownofficechambers.com

DE HAAN MR KEVIN CHARLES QC (2000)

Francis Taylor Building
Inner Temple, London EC4Y 7BY,
☎ 020 7353 8415 ✉ clerks@ftb.eu.com
Call Date: July 1976, Inner Temple
Qualifications: [LLB (Lond) LLM]
kevin.haan@ftb.eu.com

DE JEHAN MR DAVID

Park Lane Plowden
19 Westgate, Leeds LS1 2RD,
☎ 0113 228 5049
✉ clerks@parklaneplowden.co.uk
Call Date: Feb 1988, Inner Temple
Pupil Supervisor
Qualifications: [LLB (Hons) LLM (Bristol)]
david.dejehan@parklaneplowden.co.uk

DE KAUWE MR LALITH CHRISTOPHER

Garden Court Chambers
57-60 Lincoln's Inn Fields, London WC2A 3LJ,
☎ 020 7993 7600 ✉ info@gclaw.co.uk
Call Date: Nov 1978, Gray's Inn
Pupil Supervisor
Qualifications: [BA (Hons)]
lalithdk@gclaw.co.uk

E

DE LA MARE MR THOMAS ORLANDO QC (2012)

Blackstone Chambers
Blackstone House, Temple, London EC4Y 9BW, ☎020 7583 1770
✉clerks@blackstonechambers.com
Call Date: Oct 1995, Middle Temple
Pupil Supervisor
Qualifications: [BA (Hons) (Oxon) LLM]
tomdelamare@blackstonechambers.com

DE LA PIQUERIE MR PAUL EDWARD JEAN MICHEL LE CHEVALIER

Selborne Chambers
10 Essex Street, London WC2R 3AA, ☎020 7420 9500
✉clerks@selbornechambers.co.uk
Call Date: Oct 2006, Gray's Inn
Qualifications: [MA]
pdelap@selbornechambers.co.uk

DE LA POER MR NICHOLAS JOHN

Park Court Chambers
16 Park Place, Leeds LS1 2SJ, ☎0113 243 3277
✉clerks@parkcourtchambers.co.uk
Call Date: July 2003, Gray's Inn
Qualifications: [BA Hons (Dunelm)]
ndelapoer@parkcourtchambers.co.uk

DE LA ROSA MR ANDREW JAMES

5 Stone Buildings
5 Stone Buildings, Lincoln's Inn, London WC2A 3XT, ☎020 7242 6201
✉clerks@5sblaw.com
Call Date: July 1981, Inner Temple
Pupil Supervisor
Qualifications: [BA JD Dip LL]
mrdlondon@aol.com

DE MARCO MR NICHOLAS PETER

Blackstone Chambers
Blackstone House, Temple, London EC4Y 9BW, ☎020 7583 1770
✉clerks@blackstonechambers.com
Call Date: July 2001, Middle Temple
Qualifications: [LLB (Hons)]
nickdemarco@blackstonechambers.com

DE MELLO MR REMBERT JOSEPH JULIUS

No5 Chambers
Fountain Court, Steelhouse Lane, Birmingham B4 6DR, ☎0845 210 5555 ✉info@no5.com
No5 Chambers
Greenwood House, 4-7 Salisbury Court, London EC4Y 8AA, ☎0845 210 5555
No5 Chambers
38 Queen Square, Bristol BS1 4QS, ☎0845 210 5555
Call Date: Feb 1983, Lincoln's Inn
Pupil Supervisor
Qualifications: [BA LLB (Lond) LLM MA (India)]
rdm@no5.com

DE MESTRE MR ANDREW ETIENNE

4 Stone Buildings
Ground Floor, 4 Stone Buildings, Lincoln's Inn, London WC2A 3XT, ☎020 7242 5524
✉clerks@4stonebuildings.com
Call Date: Mar 1998, Middle Temple
Qualifications: [MA (Hons)(Cantab)]
a.demestre@4stonebuildings.com

DE MESTRE MRS LYNDSEY CLAIRE

XXIV Old Buildings
Ground Floor, 24 Old Buildings, Lincoln's Inn, London WC2A 3UP, ☎020 7691 2424
✉clerks@xxiv.co.uk
Call Date: Nov 1999, Middle Temple
Pupil Supervisor
Qualifications: [BA (Hons)(Cantab)]
lyndsey.demestre@xxiv.co.uk

DE MOUNTENEY MR JONATHAN PATRICK

Chambers of Mr J P De Mounteney
1 Whistley Court Farm, Lodge Road, Hurst, Reading, Berkshire RG10 0EJ, ☎0118 934 6822
✉jonathan.demounteney@virgin.net
Call Date: Nov 1994, Gray's Inn
Qualifications: [BA (Bath)]

DE NAVARRO MISS FRANCES ANNE

Call Date: Oct 2005, Inner Temple
Qualifications: [BA University of Nottingham]

DE NAVARRO MR MICHAEL ANTONY QC (1990)

2 Temple Gardens
2 Temple Gardens, Temple, London EC4Y 9AY, ☎020 7822 1200
✉clerks@2tg.co.uk
Call Date: July 1968, Inner Temple
Recorder
Qualifications: [MA (Cantab)]
mdn@2tg.co.uk

DE OLIVEIRA MRS ELIZABETH JANE

No 8 Chambers
8 Fountain Court, Steelhouse Lane, Birmingham B4 6DR, ☎0121 236 5514
✉clerks@no8chambers.co.uk
Call Date: Oct 2000, Lincoln's Inn
Qualifications: [LLB (Hons)(Wolves)]
lizdeoliveira@no8chambers.co.uk

DE POURBAIX MR ROMAN

Warwick House Chambers
8 Warwick Court, Warwick House Chambers, Gray's Inn, London WC1R 5DJ,
☎020 7430 2323
✉clerks@warwickhousechambers.com
Call Date: July 2001, Lincoln's Inn
Pupil Supervisor
Qualifications: [LLB (Hons)]
clerks@warwickhousechambers.com

DE ROHAN MR JONATHAN STEWART

2 Temple Gardens
2 Temple Gardens, Temple, London EC4Y 9AY, ☎020 7822 1200
✉clerks@2tg.co.uk
Call Date: July 1989, Middle Temple
Pupil Supervisor
Qualifications: [BA (Reading) Dip Law]

DE SILVA SIR GEORGE DESMOND LORENZ QC (1984)

Argent Chambers
5 Bell Yard, London WC2A 2JR,
☎020 7556 5500
✉briefsin@argentchambers.co.uk
Call Date: June 1964, Middle Temple
d.desilva@argentchambers.co.uk, dds@argentchambers.co.uk

DE SILVA MR HARENDRA ANEURIN DOMINGO QC (1995)

Argent Chambers
5 Bell Yard, London WC2A 2JR,
☎020 7556 5500
✉briefsin@argentchambers.co.uk
Call Date: July 1970, Middle Temple
Recorder
Qualifications: [MA LLM (Cantab)]
h.desilva@argentchambers.co.uk

DE SILVA MR NIRAN SIMON LIYANAGE

Littleton Chambers
3 King's Bench Walk North, Temple, London EC4Y 7HR, ☎020 7797 8600
✉fschneider@littletonchambers.co.uk
Call Date: Nov 1997, Lincoln's Inn
Pupil Supervisor
Qualifications: [BA (Hons)(Oxon)]
ndesilva@littletonchambers.co.uk

DE VECCHI MR THOMAS ETTORE BERNARD

3 Verulam Buildings
London WC1R 5NT, ☎020 7831 8441
✉chambers@3vb.com
Call Date: July 2009, Inner Temple
Qualifications: [BA (Oxon)]
tdevecchi@3vb.com

DE VERNEUIL SMITH MR PETER ROBERT

3 Verulam Buildings
London WC1R 5NT, ☎020 7831 8441
✉chambers@3vb.com
Call Date: Oct 1998, Lincoln's Inn
Pupil Supervisor
Qualifications: [MA (Cantab)]

Types of work: Arbitration, Banking, Commercial litigation, Fraud, Insurance, Professional negligence

DE WAAL MR JOHN HENRY LOWNDES

Hardwicke
New Square, Lincoln's Inn, London WC2A 3SB, ☎020 7242 2523
✉enquiries@hardwicke.co.uk
Call Date: Oct 1992, Middle Temple
Pupil Supervisor
Qualifications: [MA (Cantab)]

DE WILDE MR ROBIN QC (1993)

Clerksroom (Taunton)
Equity House, Administration Centre, Blackbrook Park Avenue, Taunton, Somerset TA1 2PX, ☎0845 083 3000
✉mail@clerksroom.com
Clerksroom (London)
3rd Floor, 218 Strand, London WC2R 1AT,
☎0845 083 3000 ✉mail@clerksroom.com
Call Date: Nov 1971, Inner Temple
dewilde@clerksroom.com

E

DE ZONIE MISS JANE

14 Gray's Inn Square
14 Gray's Inn Square, Gray's Inn, London WC1R 5JP, ☎ 020 7242 0858
✉ clerks@14gis.co.uk
Call Date: Nov 1993, Middle Temple
Qualifications: [BA (Hons)(Lond) Dip Law (Lond)]
✉ jdz@14graysinnsquare.co.uk

DEACOCK MR ADAM JASON

11 Stone Buildings
11 Stone Buildings, Lincoln's Inn, London WC2A 3TG, ☎ 020 7831 6381
✉ clerks@11sb.com
Call Date: Nov 1991, Middle Temple
Qualifications: [BA (Oxon) Dip Law]

DEACON MS EMMA REBECCA

Five Paper Buildings
1st Floor, Five Paper Buildings, Temple, London EC4Y 7HB, ☎ 020 7583 6117
✉ clerks@5pb.co.uk
Call Date: Nov 1993, Inner Temple
Qualifications: [LLB (Lond)]
✉ ed@5pb.co.uk

DEACON MR ROBERT MURRAY

11 Stone Buildings
11 Stone Buildings, Lincoln's Inn, London WC2A 3TG, ☎ 020 7831 6381
✉ clerks@11sb.com
Call Date: July 1976, Gray's Inn
Pupil Supervisor
Qualifications: [LLB (Manch)]
✉ deacon@11sb.com

DEAKIN MR ANDREW CHARLES

39 Essex Street
London WC2R 3AT, ☎ 020 7832 1111
✉ clerks@39essex.com
82 King Street
Manchester M2 4WQ, ☎ 0161 870 9969
Call Date: Oct 2006, Lincoln's Inn
Qualifications: [BA MPhil PgDipL]

DEAL MISS KATHERINE ALISON FRANCES

3 Hare Court
3 Hare Court, Temple, London EC4Y 7BJ, ☎ 020 7415 7800 ✉ clerks@3harecourt.com
Call Date: Oct 1997, Middle Temple
Pupil Supervisor
Qualifications: [BA (Hons)(Oxon) CPE (Lond)]
✉ katherinedeal@3harecourt.com

DEAL MR TIMOTHY JOHN

Deal Chambers
60 Moordown, Shooters Hill, London SE18 3NG, ☎ 020 8856 8738
✉ clerk@dealchambers.co.uk
Call Date: July 1988, Gray's Inn
Qualifications: [LLB (Warw)]

DEAN MR BRIAN JOHN ANTHONY

No5 Chambers
Fountain Court, Steelhouse Lane, Birmingham B4 6DR, ☎ 0845 210 5555 ✉ info@no5.com
No5 Chambers
Greenwood House, 4-7 Salisbury Court, London EC4Y 8AA, ☎ 0845 210 5555
No5 Chambers
38 Queen Square, Bristol BS1 4QS, ☎ 0845 210 5555
Call Date: Nov 1994, Gray's Inn
Qualifications: [LLB (Hons)(Manch)]
✉ bde@no5.com

DEAN MRS CHRISTINE JACQUELINE

1 Pump Court
Elm Court, Temple, London EC4Y 7AB, ☎ 020 7842 7070
✉ (name)@pumpcourt.co.uk
Call Date: Mar 2007, Lincoln's Inn
Qualifications: [LLB (Lond)]
✉ cd@1pumpcourt.co.uk

DEAN MISS ELIZABETH CATHERINE

3 Temple Gardens
Lower Ground Floor, 3 Temple Gardens, Temple, London EC4Y 9AU, ☎ 020 7353 3102
✉ clerks@3tg.co.uk
Call Date: July 2006, Inner Temple
Qualifications: [LLB (Durham)]
✉ ed@3tg.co.uk

DEAN MR JACOB

5RB
1st Floor, 5 Raymond Buildings, Gray's Inn, London WC1R 5BP, ☎ 020 7242 2902
✉ clerks@5rb.com
Call Date: Oct 1995, Inner Temple
Pupil Supervisor
Qualifications: [BA (Oxon) CPE (Lond)]
✉ jacobdean@5rb.com

DEAN MR JAMES PATRICK

Goldsmith Chambers
Ground Floor, Goldsmith Building, Temple, London EC4Y 7BL, ☎ 020 7353 6802
✉ clerks@goldsmithchambers.com
Call Date: Nov 1977, Lincoln's Inn
Pupil Supervisor
✉ J.Dean@goldsmithchambers.law.co.uk

DEAN MR PAUL BENJAMIN

Crown Office Chambers
2 Crown Office Row, Temple, London
EC4Y 7HJ, ☎020 7797 8100
✉mail@crownofficechambers.com
Call Date: July 1982, Inner Temple
Pupil Supervisor
Qualifications: [BA (Oxon) Dip Law]
dean@crownofficechambers.com

DEAN MR PAUL JASON

St Philips Chambers
55 Temple Row, Birmingham B2 5LS,
☎0121 246 7000 ✉clerks@st-philips.com
Call Date: Nov 2001, Inner Temple
Qualifications: [BSc CPE LPC]
pdean@st-philips.co.uk

DEAN MR PETER THOMAS

36 Bedford Row
London WC1R 4JH, ☎020 7421 8000
✉chambers@36bedfordrow.co.uk
Call Date: Nov 1987, Middle Temple
Pupil Supervisor
Qualifications: [MA (Oxon) Dip Law (Lond)]
pdean@36bedfordrow.co.uk

DEANS MISS JACQUELINE ELAINE

Chavasse Court Chambers
18 Queen Avenue, Liverpool L2 4TX,
☎0151 229 2030
✉clerks@chavassechambers.co.uk
Call Date: July 1997, Lincoln's Inn
Qualifications: [LLB (Hons)(L'pool)]
jacqueline.deans@chavassechambers.co.uk

DEAR MR IAN LESLIE

5 King's Bench Walk
5 King's Bench Walk, Temple, London
EC4Y 7DN, ☎020 7353 5638
✉clerks@5kbw.co.uk
Call Date: July 1999, Lincoln's Inn
Qualifications: [BA (Hons)(Sheff) LLB (Hons)]
ian.dear@5kbw.co.uk

DEARING MR ANTHONY JOHN

4-5 Gray's Inn Square
Gray's Inn, London WC1R 5AH,
☎020 7404 5252 ✉clerks@4-5.co.uk
Call Date: Nov 1998, Middle Temple
Qualifications: [LLB (Hons)(Thames)]
clerks@4-5.co.uk

DEAS MRS SUSAN MAGARET

Call Date: July 1999, Gray's Inn
Qualifications: [BA (B'ham)]
clerk@stjohnsbuildings.co.uk

DEB MISS SHUVRA

9 Stone Buildings
Lincoln's Inn, London WC2A 3NN,
☎020 7404 5055
✉clerks@9stonebuildings.com
Call Date: Nov 2007, Inner Temple
Qualifications: [BA (Lond)]
SDeb@9stonebuildings.com

DEE MR JONATHON ANTHONY

KCH Garden Square
1 Oxford Street, Nottingham NG1 5BH,
☎0115 941 8851
✉clerks@kchgardensquare.co.uk
Call Date: Nov 1989, Inner Temple
Qualifications: [LLB (Bris)]

DEEGAN MR LAWRENCE JEFFREY

Fenners Chambers
3 Madingley Road, Cambridge CB3 0EE,
☎01223 368761
✉clerks@fennerschambers.com
Call Date: July 1989, Inner Temple
Pupil Supervisor
Qualifications: [LLB (Leic)]
jeffrey.deegan@fennerschambers.co.uk

DEGUN MR JASVIR SINGH

One Essex Court
1st Floor, Temple, London EC4Y 9AR,
☎020 7936 3030 ✉clerks@1ec.co.uk
Call Date: Oct 2003, Middle Temple
Qualifications: [BA (Lond)]
jdegun@1ec.co.uk

DEHN MR CONRAD FRANCIS QC (1968)

Fountain Court Chambers
Fountain Court, Temple, London EC4Y 9DH,
☎020 7583 3335
✉chambers@fountaincourt.co.uk
Call Date: July 1952, Gray's Inn
Qualifications: [MA (Oxon)]
cd@fountaincourt.co.uk

DEHON MS ESTELLE ALEXANDRA MICHELLE

4-5 Gray's Inn Square
Gray's Inn, London WC1R 5AH,
☎020 7404 5252 ✉clerks@4-5.co.uk
Call Date: July 2006, Inner Temple
Qualifications: [LLB BCL MPhil (Oxon) BA (Hons)]

E

DEIGNAN DR MARY TERESA

Charter Chambers
33 John Street, London WC1N 2AT,
☎ 020 7618 4400
✉ clerks@charterchambers.com
Call Date: Oct 1991, Middle Temple
Pupil Supervisor
Qualifications: [BSc (Aston) PhD (Ireland)]
✉ mtd@charterchambers.com

DEIN MR JEREMY SYDNEY QC (2003)

25 Bedford Row
London WC1R 4HD, ☎ 020 7067 1500
✉ clerks@25bedfordrow.com
Call Date: Nov 1982, Middle Temple
Recorder
Qualifications: [LLB (Lond)]
✉ jdein@25bedfordrow.com

DEKOVEN MR RONALD

Dekoven Chambers
8 Stone Buildings, Lincoln's Inn, London
WC2A 3TA, ☎ 020 7831 9521
✉ rdk@dekovenchambers.com
South Square
3-4 South Square, Gray's Inn, London
WC1R 5HP, ☎ 020 7696 9900
✉ practicemanagers@southsquare.com
Call Date: Mar 2009, Lincoln's Inn
Qualifications: [BA (USA)]

DEL CANTO GONZALEZ MR LEéN FERNANDO

The Chambers Of Leon Fernando del Canto Gonzalez
29 Carlton Crescent, Southampton SO15 2EW
Call Date: Mar 2006, Lincoln's Inn
Qualifications: [LLB (Madrid)]
✉ fernando@konsilia.es

DEL FABBRO MR OSCAR

23 Essex Street
London WC2R 3AA, ☎ 020 7413 0353
✉ clerks@23es.com
Call Date: July 1982, Gray's Inn
Pupil Supervisor, Recorder
Qualifications: [B Com (South Africa)]
✉ oscardelfabbro@23es.com

DEL PRIORE MISS ASSUNTA MARIA LUISA

9 St John Street
Manchester M3 4DN, ☎ 0161 955 9000
✉ civilclerks@9sjs.com /
criminalclerks@9sjs.com
Call Date: Oct 1998, Middle Temple
Qualifications: [MA (Hons)(Edin) MLitt CPE]
✉ Assunta.delpriore@9sjs.com

DELAHUNTY MS JOHANNE ERICA QC (2006)

4 Paper Buildings
1st Floor, 4 Paper Buildings, Temple, London
EC4Y 7EX, ☎ 020 7427 5200
✉ clerks@4pb.com
Park Lane Plowden
19 Westgate, Leeds LS1 2RD,
☎ 0113 228 5049
✉ clerks@parklaneplowden.co.uk
St Ive's Chambers
Whittall Street, Birmingham B4 6DH,
☎ 0121 236 0863
✉ clerks@stiveschambers.co.uk
Call Date: Oct 1986, Middle Temple
Qualifications: [BA MA (Oxon)]
✉ jd@4pb.com

Fax: 0207 353 4979;
Out of hours telephone: 07810 482 828
URL: www.4pb.com

Other professional qualifications: Recorder (Public Law: Family); Mediator; Bencher of Hon. Society of Middle Temple

Types of work: Adoption, Care proceedings, Children, Court of Protection, Family law

Awards and memberships: Family Law Bar Association (FLBA); Association of Lawyers for Children (ALC); Association of Women Barristers (AWB); Amnesty.

Other professional experience: Qualified Mediator

Reported Cases: *LB Islington v Al Alas,* [2012] EWHC 865 (Fam) FLR Pending (High Court Family Division: Theis J), 2012. Acting for mother accused of inflicting NAI fractures and shaking the child causing its death (TRIAD case). All allegations rejected, injuries attributable to rickets and vitamin D deficiency. Hospital care of baby 'suboptimal'. Major media interest. s12 AJA 1960 disapplied so as to allow parents to talk of their experiences at hands of police, social services and health services without restriction
Re M (a child), [2012] Fam. Law 511; EWCA Civ 165 (Court of Appeal, Thorpe LJJ, Rimer LJJ, Dame Janet Smith), 2012. Acting for local authority. Successfully resisted mother's application to appeal out of time against a finding of

NAI and to adduce fresh expert evidence. Appeal and application dismissed. Guidance given on instruction of non-UK Experts.
Re K (children) 2012, (2012) EWHC 450CO5566 (FLR Pending) (Family Division: Hedley J. High Court), 2012. Acting for Local Authority who had brought care proceedings re 5 children, 2 with severe and global disabilities. War of attrition between LA and parents. Concept of 'good enough parenting' and threshold discussed in context of children with potentially life threatening disabilities. 'Unique solution' found. LA granted permission to withdraw care proceedings and 3 of the minors were made wards of court.
Kent CC v A Mother, [2011] EWHC 402 [Fam] and [2011] 2 FLR 1088 [Fam] (High Court Family Division: Baker J), 2011. Sexual abuse fact finding. Acting for intervenor, wrongly accused of child sex abuse. All allegations withdrawn by LA. Guidence given on lessons to be learnt re: local authority case management duties on disclosure and conduct when dealing with parents who have learning disabilities.
Coventry City Council v X, Y and Z (Care Proceedings: Costs), [2011] 1 FLR 1645 (Coventry County Court, HHJ Bellamy), 2011. Acting for mother, leading case on Factitious Induced Illness. All allegations against mother either withdrawn by LA during the trial or dismissed by the court. Review of FII guidance given, costs of £100,000 awarded against LA.

Additional information

Recommended as a Leading Silk in all successive editions of Legal 500 and Chambers & Partners Directory since taking silk. Described as 'absolutely superb' in Chambers & Partners 2012 Edition whilst the Legal 500 remarked on her 'razor sharp mind with a phenomenal work rate'. Previous editions noted 'her conversational style of advocacy puts witnesses at their ease, yet conceals rapier-like incisiveness, previously describing 'her particular prowess advising on complex care cases'; 'young, dynamic and making waves in every case she gets involved in'; Jo's 'eloquence' was singled out for mention in the leading judgment of Lady Baroness Hale in the House of Lords in Re B (2008) 3 WLR 1 in which Jo appeared on behalf of CAFCASS. Cases in which she is successfully involved are regularly reported for their legal significance (9 in 2011 alone).

Jo has particular expertise in factually complex care proceedings involving

- The death of/catastrophic injuries to a child (TRIAD cases)(see Al Alas and Wray: rickets/vitamin D deficiency)
- Applying to, succeeding in, overturning previous findings of the court of abuse
- Sex abuse/incest/paedophilia (including internet and commercial exploitation)
- Ritualized abuse/cultural practices
- Acting for children who are both the victims of abuse and alleged abusers
- Parents with learning disabilities (see Kent CC v A mother)
- Factitious induced illness (see Coventry CC v A mother)
- Child protection cases with concurrent criminal prosecution/attempted murder/ child cruelty and neglect/sex offences/terrorism
- Article 20 Hague Brussels II Revised issues for children received into care (Re S (2008) 2 FLR 1389).

Complex private law proceedings and adoption matters are a natural corollary to her practice. Instructed by all protagonists in complex family cases at High Court level and above. Jo most recently had notable success acting for the mother in Al Alas and Wray when she successful resisted allegations that her client had battered and ultimately killed her baby. Jo took the lead on all cross-examinations in the course of the 4 week trial and established that the fractures were attributable to rickets – the death to benign causes (vitamin D deficiency and seizures) and that the child had received 'suboptimal' medical care by the treating hospitals. Jo has also had particular success in successfully applying to re-open findings of fact in care proceeding on new evidence in both sex abuse and NAHI cases. She is also highly regarded for her representation of vulnerable adults and acting for children where they are separately represented from their guardians, eg. acting for a child who is both subject victim and respondent abuser in sex cases (including parallel criminal proceedings). Jo has particular expertise in cases involving children giving evidence in court.

Publications and Teaching

Jo regularly delivers seminars to legal and social care professionals in addition to overseas legal delegates upon family law procedure/care proceedings/children giving evidence/the representation of children/management of concurrent care and criminal trials.

Jo is regularly invited to write for specialist family legal journals - eg. 'The Vitamin D and Rickets case: LB Islington v Al Alas', Family Law June 2012. She is a sought after speaker at medico/legal family conference for her insight on how to deal with complex cases

E

involving fresh medical evidence and emerging new science (TRIAD cases) as well as how to manage cross examining of children in court.

DELAMERE MISS ISABEL SARAH

4 Breams Buildings
Chancery Lane, London EC4A 1HP,
☎ 020 7092 1900 ✉ clerks@4bb.co.uk
Call Date: Nov 1985, Middle Temple
Pupil Supervisor
Qualifications: [BA(Hull)]

DELANEY MR JOE

Three New Square IP
3 New Square, Lincoln's Inn, London
WC2A 3RS, ☎ 020 7405 1111
✉ clerks@3newsquare.co.uk
Call Date: Oct 2006, Middle Temple
Qualifications: [MA (Cantab)]
delaney@3newsquare.co.uk

Types of work: Biotechnology, Breach of confidence, Copyright, Intellectual property, Passing off, Patents, Pharmaceuticals, Scientific and technical disputes, Trademarks

DELANEY MR KENNETH JOSEPH

Atlantic Chambers
4-6 Cook Street, Liverpool L2 9QU,
☎ 0151 236 4421
✉ info@atlanticchambers.co.uk
Call Date: Oct 1996, Inner Temple
Pupil Supervisor
Qualifications: [BA MPhil (Cantab) LLB (Hons)]
kennethdelaney@atlanticchambers.co.uk

DELANY MS FRANCESCA

1 Mitre Court Buildings
1 Mitre Court Buildings, Temple, London
EC4Y 7BS, ☎ 020 7452 8900
✉ clerks@1mcb.com
Call Date: Oct 2006, Middle Temple
Qualifications: [BA (Hons) (Cantab) MA]
francesca.delany@1mcb.com

DEMACHKIE MR JAMAL

3 PB Barristers
3 Paper Buildings, Temple, London EC4Y 7EU,
☎ 020 7583 8055
Call Date: Nov 2004, Inner Temple
Qualifications: [BA (Hons) (Lond)]
jamal.demachkie@3pb.co.uk

DEMETRIOU MS MARIE-ELENI QC (2012)

Brick Court Chambers
7-8 Essex Street, London WC2R 3LD,
☎ 020 7379 3550 ✉ clerks@brickcourt.co.uk
Call Date: Nov 1995, Middle Temple
Pupil Supervisor
Qualifications: [BA (Hons) BCL]
Marie.Demetriou@Brickcourt.co.uk

DEMPSEY MISS KAREN MARIE

3 Temple Gardens
Lower Ground Floor, 3 Temple Gardens,
Temple, London EC4Y 9AU, ☎ 020 7353 3102
✉ clerks@3tg.co.uk
Call Date: Mar 1996, Lincoln's Inn
Qualifications: [LLB (Hons) LLM (Lond)]
kd@3tg.co.uk

DEMPSTER MISS JENNIFER MARGARET PERT

18 Red Lion Court
London EC4A 3EB, ☎ 020 7520 6000
✉ chambers@18rlc.co.uk
18 Red Lion Court (Annexe)
Thornwood House, 102 New London Road,
Chelmsford, Essex CM2 0RG,
☎ 01245 280880
Call Date: May 1993, Lincoln's Inn
Pupil Supervisor
Qualifications: [LLB (Hons)]
jenni.dempster@18rlc.co.uk

DEMPSTER DR TINA DOREEN ANNE

KBW
The Engine House, No 1 Foundry Square,
Leeds LS11 5DL, ☎ 0113 297 1200
✉ clerks@kbwchambers.com
Call Date: Nov 1997, Middle Temple
Pupil Supervisor
Qualifications: [LLB (Hons) PhD (B'ham)]
td@kbwchambers.com

DEN BESTEN MRS RUTH MICHELLE

Serle Court
6 New Square, Lincoln's Inn, London
WC2A 3QS, ☎ 020 7242 6105
✉ clerks@serlecourt.co.uk
Call Date: July 2001, Middle Temple
Qualifications: [BA (Hons) CPE]
rdenbesten@serlecourt.co.uk

DENBIN MR JACK ARNOLD

Greenway
Sonning Lane, Sonning-on-Thames, Berkshire RG4 6ST, ☎0118 969 2484
✉jackdenbin@btinternet.com
Call Date: July 1973, Inner Temple
Qualifications: [BSc (Reading) C Biol FCIArb MsB]

DENCER MR MARK RICHARD

Tanfield Chambers
2-5 Warwick Court, London WC1R 5DJ,
☎020 7421 5300
✉clerks@tanfieldchambers.co.uk
Call Date: Apr 1978, Lincoln's Inn
Pupil Supervisor
Qualifications: [LLB (Lond)]
✉clerks@tanfieldchambers.co.uk

DENEHAN MR EDWARD

9 Stone Buildings
Lincoln's Inn, London WC2A 3NN,
☎020 7404 5055
✉clerks@9stonebuildings.com
Call Date: July 1981, Lincoln's Inn
Pupil Supervisor
Qualifications: [LLB (Warw)]
✉clerks@9stonebuildings.com

DENHAM MR IAN JAMES

9 St John Street
Manchester M3 4DN, ☎0161 955 9000
✉civilclerks@9sjs.com /
criminalclerks@9sjs.com
18 St John Street
Manchester M3 4EA, ☎0161 278 1800
✉clerks@18sjs.com
Call Date: July 2003, Middle Temple
Qualifications: [BA Hons (Oxon)]

DENHOLM MR GRAHAM SWANSTON

1 Pump Court
Elm Court, Temple, London EC4Y 7AB,
☎020 7842 7070
✉(name)@pumpcourt.co.uk
Call Date: July 2001, Middle Temple
Pupil Supervisor
Qualifications: [MA (Hons) MPhil]
✉gd@1pumpcourt.co.uk

DENISON MR SIMON NEIL QC (2009)

6 King's Bench Walk
Ground Floor, 6 King's Bench Walk, Temple, London EC4Y 7DR, ☎020 7583 0410
✉clerks@6kbw.com
Call Date: Nov 1984, Lincoln's Inn
Qualifications: [MA (Cantab)]
✉simon.denison@6kbw.com

DENIS-SMITH MR JOHN MICHAEL EDWARD

39 Essex Street
London WC2R 3AT, ☎020 7832 1111
✉clerks@39essex.com
82 King Street
Manchester M2 4WQ, ☎0161 870 9969
Call Date: Mar 1998, Gray's Inn
Qualifications: [BA (Oxon)]
✉john.denis-smith@39essex.com

DENNEY MR STUART HENRY MACDONALD QC (2008)

Deans Court Chambers
24 St John Street, Manchester M3 4DF,
☎0161 214 6000 ✉clerks@deanscourt.co.uk
Deans Court Chambers
101 Walker Street, Preston PR1 2RR,
☎01772 565 600
✉preston@deanscourt.co.uk
Thomas More Chambers
7 Lincoln's Inn Fields, London WC2A 3BP,
☎020 7404 7000
✉clerks@thomasmore.co.uk
Call Date: July 1982, Inner Temple
Qualifications: [MA (Cantab)]
✉denney@deanscourt.co.uk

DENNING MRS LOUISA MICHELLE

No5 Chambers
Fountain Court, Steelhouse Lane, Birmingham B4 6DR, ☎0845 210 5555 ✉info@no5.com
No5 Chambers
Greenwood House, 4-7 Salisbury Court, London EC4Y 8AA, ☎0845 210 5555
No5 Chambers
38 Queen Square, Bristol BS1 4QS,
☎0845 210 5555
Call Date: July 1999, Gray's Inn
Qualifications: [BA]
✉ld@no5.com

E

DENNIS MR MARK JONATHAN QC (2006)

6 King's Bench Walk
Ground Floor, 6 King's Bench Walk, Temple, London EC4Y 7DR, ☎ 020 7583 0410
✉ clerks@6kbw.com
Call Date: July 1977, Middle Temple
Recorder
Qualifications: [MA (Cantab)]
✉ mark.dennis@6kbw.com

DENNIS MR PATRICK STEVEN

2 Dr Johnson's Buildings
2 Dr Johnson's Buildings, Temple, London EC4Y 7AY, ☎ 020 7936 2613
✉ clerks@2drj.com
Call Date: Oct 2006, Lincoln's Inn
Qualifications: [BA (Sheff)]
✉ p.dennis@2drj.com

DENNIS MISS REBECCA LOUISE

Queen Square Chambers
56 Queen Square, Bristol BS1 4PR, ☎ 0117 921 1966 ✉ crime@qs-c.co.uk
Call Date: July 1994, Gray's Inn
Pupil Supervisor
Qualifications: [LLB LLM (Bris)]
✉ red@qs-c.co.uk

DENNISON MR JAMES ANGUS

2 Dr Johnson's Buildings
2 Dr Johnson's Buildings, Temple, London EC4Y 7AY, ☎ 020 7936 2613
✉ clerks@2drj.com
Call Date: July 1986, Inner Temple
Pupil Supervisor
Qualifications: [BA (Dunelm)]
✉ clerks@2drj.com

DENNISON MR STEPHEN RANDELL QC (2001)

Atkin Chambers
1 Atkin Building, Gray's Inn, London WC1R 5AT, ☎ 020 7404 0102
✉ clerks@atkinchambers.com
Call Date: Nov 1985, Middle Temple
Qualifications: [LLB (Manch)]
✉ clerks@atkinchambers.com

DENNY MR ROBIN HENRY ALISDAIR

Dere Street Barristers
14 Toft Green, York YO1 6JT, ☎ 0844 3351551
✉ clerks@derestreet.co.uk
York Chambers
Rotterdam House, 116 The Quayside, Newcastle Upon Tyne NE1 3DY, ☎ 0191 206 4677
Call Date: May 1969, Inner Temple
Pupil Supervisor
Qualifications: [BA (Oxon)]
✉ clerks@yorkchambers.co.uk

DENNYS MR NICHOLAS CHARLES JONATHAN QC (1991)

Atkin Chambers
1 Atkin Building, Gray's Inn, London WC1R 5AT, ☎ 020 7404 0102
✉ clerks@atkinchambers.com
Call Date: Nov 1975, Middle Temple
Qualifications: [BA (Oxon)]
✉ clerks@atkinchambers.com

DENT MR ADRIAN RONALD

Fountain Chambers
Cleveland Business Centre, 1 Watson Street, Middlesbrough TS1 2RQ, ☎ 01642 804040
✉ clerks@fountainchambers.co.uk
Call Date: July 1974, Lincoln's Inn
Pupil Supervisor
Qualifications: [LLB]

DENT MR KEVIN JOSEPH

2 Dr Johnson's Buildings
2 Dr Johnson's Buildings, Temple, London EC4Y 7AY, ☎ 020 7936 2613
✉ clerks@2drj.com
Call Date: Nov 1991, Inner Temple
Pupil Supervisor
Qualifications: [BA (Hons)(Sussex)]

DENT MS SALLY CLAIRE LEIGH

1 Pump Court
Elm Court, Temple, London EC4Y 7AB, ☎ 020 7842 7070
✉ (name)@pumpcourt.co.uk
Call Date: July 1989, Lincoln's Inn
Qualifications: [BA (Reading) Dip Law]

E

DENT MR STEPHEN ROBERT CHARLES

Guildhall Chambers
23 Broad Street, Bristol BS1 2HG,
☎0117 930 9000
✉hoc@guildhallchambers.co.uk
Call Date: Feb 1991, Gray's Inn
Qualifications: [LLB (Manch)]
stephen.dent@guildhallchambers.co.uk

DENTON MISS AMANDA

KBW
The Engine House, No 1 Foundry Square, Leeds LS11 5DL, ☎0113 297 1200
✉clerks@kbwchambers.com
Call Date: Nov 1993, Lincoln's Inn
Pupil Supervisor
Qualifications: [LLB (Hons)]
amandadenton@kbwchambers.com

DENTON MR DOUGLAS

Call Date: Oct 1997, Lincoln's Inn
Qualifications: [LLB (Hons)(L'pool) LLM (Cantab)]
douglas.denton@stjohnsbuildings.co.uk

DENTON-COX MR GREGORY MARK

4 Stone Buildings
Ground Floor, 4 Stone Buildings, Lincoln's Inn, London WC2A 3XT, ☎020 7242 5524
✉clerks@4stonebuildings.com
Call Date: July 2000, Lincoln's Inn
Qualifications: [LLB(Hons) (Nott'm)]
clerks@4stonebuildings.com

DENYER-GREEN MR BARRY PETER DOUGLAS

Falcon Chambers
Falcon Court, London EC4Y 1AA,
☎020 7353 2484
✉clerks@falcon-chambers.com
Call Date: Nov 1972, Middle Temple
Pupil Supervisor
Qualifications: [LLM PhD FRICS]
denyer-green@falcon-chambers.com

Types of work: Agriculture, Chancery (land law), Commercial property, Common land, Compulsory Purchase, Conveyancing, Land compensation, Landlord and tenant, Local authorities, Planning

DERBYSHIRE MR HUGH EDWARD HARTLEY

Atlantic Chambers
4-6 Cook Street, Liverpool L2 9QU,
☎0151 236 4421
✉info@atlanticchambers.co.uk
Call Date: Oct 2004, Gray's Inn
Qualifications: [LLB BCL]
hughderbyshire@atlanticchambers.co.uk

DERRINGTON MR JONATHAN MCCOURT

No5 Chambers
38 Queen Square, Bristol BS1 4QS,
☎0845 210 5555
No5 Chambers
Greenwood House, 4-7 Salisbury Court, London EC4Y 8AA, ☎0845 210 5555
No5 Chambers
Fountain Court, Steelhouse Lane, Birmingham B4 6DR, ☎0845 210 5555 ✉info@no5.com
Call Date: Oct 1998, Inner Temple
Qualifications: [BSC (City) CPE (UWE)]
jde@no5.com

DESAI MR RAJENDRA JOHANNES

Matrix Chambers
Griffin Building, Gray's Inn, London WC1R 5LN, ☎020 7404 3447
✉matrix@matrixlaw.co.uk / lscott@matrixlaw.co.uk
Call Date: Nov 2010, Lincoln's Inn
Qualifications: [BA (Oxon)]
rdesai@matrixlaw.co.uk

DESCHAMPSNEUFS MISS ALICE NORA

4 King's Bench Walk
2nd Floor, 4 King's Bench Walk, Temple, London EC4Y 7DL, ☎020 7822 7000
✉clerks@4kbw.co.uk
Call Date: July 1976, Inner Temple
Pupil Supervisor
Qualifications: [BA (Lond)]

DESMOND MR DENIS JOHN

Cornwall Street Chambers
85-87 Cornwall Street, Birmingham B3 3BY,
☎0121 233 7500
✉clerks@cornwallstreet.co.uk
Call Date: Nov 1974, Middle Temple
Pupil Supervisor, Recorder
Qualifications: [BA]
denis.desmond@cornwallstreet.co.uk

E

DETTER DE LUPIS FRANKOPAN PROFESSOR COUNTESS INGRID HILDEGARD DOIMI

13 Old Square Chambers
Ground Floor, 14 Old Square, Lincoln's Inn, London WC2A 3UE, ☎ 020 7831 4445
✉ clerks@13oldsquare.com
Call Date: July 1977, Middle Temple
Qualifications: [DPhil (Oxon) Lic en droit (France) CESE (Italy) Jur Kand, Jur Lic, Jur Dr (Stockholm)]

DEUCHAR MS JESSICA CHRISTIAN DOROTHY

Castle Chambers
The Old Fire Station, 90 High Street, Harrow-on-the-Hill, Middlesex HA1 3LP, ☎ 020 8423 6579 ✉ info@castlechambers.net
Call Date: Oct 2003, Lincoln's Inn
Qualifications: [LLB (Hons) (Herts)]

DEVAS MS NICOLA JANE

1 Paper Buildings
1st Floor, 1 Paper Buildings, Temple, London EC4Y 7EP, ☎ 020 7353 3728
✉ clerks@onepaper.co.uk
Call Date: July 2003, Inner Temple
Qualifications: [BA (Hons)]
nicoladevas@onepaper.co.uk

DEVEREUX MR EDWARD MARK

Harcourt Chambers
1st Floor, 2 Harcourt Buildings, Temple, London EC4Y 9DB, ☎ 0844 561 7135
Call Date: Oct 2001, Middle Temple
Qualifications: [BA (Hons)(Cantab) Dip Law]
edevereux@harcourtchambers.law.co.uk

DEVEREUX-COOKE MR RICHARD CHARLES

13 Old Square Chambers
Ground Floor, 14 Old Square, Lincoln's Inn, London WC2A 3UE, ☎ 020 7831 4445
✉ clerks@13oldsquare.com
Call Date: Oct 1999, Middle Temple
Pupil Supervisor
Qualifications: [BA (Hons)(Oxon) MA (Oxon)]

DEVINE MR MICHAEL BUXTON

Rougemont Chambers
Victory House, Dean Clarke Gardens, Southernhay East, Exeter EX2 4AA, ☎ 01392 208484
✉ clerks@rougemontchambers.co.uk
Call Date: July 1995, Gray's Inn
Qualifications: [BA LLM FCIArb MPA JD DAILS]

DEVLIN MR BERNARD JOSEPH

Five St Andrew's Hill
5 St Andrew's Hill, London EC4V 5BZ, ☎ 020 7332 5400 ✉ Clerks@5sah.co.uk
Call Date: Nov 1980, Gray's Inn
Pupil Supervisor
Qualifications: [LLB (Reading) LLM (Lond)]
bernarddevlin@5sah.co.uk

DEVLIN MR JONATHAN NICHOLAS PONTON

Dere Street Barristers
33 Broad Chare, Newcastle Upon Tyne NE1 3DQ, ☎ 0844 3351551
✉ clerks@derestreet.co.uk
Dere Street Barristers
14 Toft Green, York YO1 6JT, ☎ 0844 3351551
✉ clerks@derestreet.co.uk
Call Date: Nov 1978, Inner Temple
Pupil Supervisor
Qualifications: [LLB (Leeds)]

DEVLIN MR THOMAS HALCRO

23 Essex Street
London WC2R 3AA, ☎ 020 7413 0353
✉ clerks@23es.com
Call Date: July 2009, Lincoln's Inn
Qualifications: [BA (Oxon) CPE]
clerks@23es.com

DEVLIN MR TIMOTHY ROBERT

Furnival Chambers
32 Furnival Street, London EC4A 1JQ, ☎ 020 7405 3232
Call Date: July 1985, Lincoln's Inn
Pupil Supervisor
Qualifications: [BA, (Lond) Dip Law]
tdevlin@furnivallaw.co.uk

DEVONSHIRE MR SIMON PETER QC (2009)

11 King's Bench Walk
11 King's Bench Walk, Temple, London EC4Y 7EQ, ☎ 020 7632 8500
✉ clerksroom@11kbw.com
Call Date: Feb 1988, Gray's Inn
Qualifications: [BA(Oxon)]
simon.devonshire@11kbw.com

DEW MR RICHARD JOHN

Ten Old Square
Ground Floor, Ten Old Square, Lincoln's Inn, London WC2A 3SU, ☎ 020 7405 0758
✉ clerks@tenoldsquare.com
Call Date: Oct 1999, Inner Temple
Pupil Supervisor
Qualifications: [LLB (Reading)]
richarddew@tenoldsquare.com

DEWAR MISS FIONA MARY

Maitland Chambers
7 Stone Buildings, Lincoln's Inn, London WC2A 3SZ, ☎020 7406 1200
✉clerks@maitlandchambers.com
Call Date: Nov 2005, Lincoln's Inn
Qualifications: [BA (Hons) (Oxon)]
✉fdewar@maitlandchambers.com

DEWHURST MISS ELEANOR FRANCES

Pallant Chambers
12 North Pallant, Chichester, West Sussex PO19 1TQ, ☎01243 784538
✉clerks@pallantchambers.co.uk
Call Date: Nov 2008, Middle Temple
Qualifications: [BA (Hons)(Oxon)]
✉edewhurst@pallantchambers.co.uk

DEWI MISS CADI

Angel Chambers
Ethos Building, Kings Road, Swansea SA1 8AS, ☎01792 464623
✉clerks@angelchambers.co.uk
Call Date: July 2008, Gray's Inn
Qualifications: [LLB (Cardiff)]

DEWJI MR ALI IQBAL

187 Fleet Street
London EC4A 2AT, ☎020 7430 7430
✉chambers@187fleetstreet.com
Call Date: July 2010, Middle Temple
Qualifications: [BSc (Hons) (Lond) LLM (Lond)]
✉alidewji@187fleetstreet.com

DEWSBERY MR RICHARD MARK

St Ive's Chambers
Whittall Street, Birmingham B4 6DH, ☎0121 236 0863
✉clerks@stiveschambers.co.uk
Call Date: Oct 1992, Inner Temple
Qualifications: [LLB (Hons) (Essex)]
✉richard.dewsbery@stiveschambers.co.uk

DHADDA MISS SUKWINDER KAUR

2 King's Bench Walk
2 King's Bench Walk, Temple, London EC4Y 7DE, ☎020 7353 1746
✉clerks@2kbw.com
Call Date: July 2004, Lincoln's Inn
Qualifications: [LLB Hons (B'ham)]
✉sdhadda@2kbw.com

DHADLI MRS PERMINDER

KCH Garden Square
1 Oxford Street, Nottingham NG1 5BH, ☎0115 941 8851
✉clerks@kchgardensquare.co.uk
Call Date: Nov 1984, Middle Temple
Pupil Supervisor
Qualifications: [BA (Hons)]

DHALIWAL MISS DAVINDER KAUR

No 8 Chambers
8 Fountain Court, Steelhouse Lane, Birmingham B4 6DR, ☎0121 236 5514
✉clerks@no8chambers.co.uk
Call Date: Nov 1990, Middle Temple
Qualifications: [LLB (Hons)(B'ham)]
✉clerks@no8chambers.co.uk

DHAR MR SIDDHARTH

Essex Court Chambers
24 Lincoln's Inn Fields, London WC2A 3EG, ☎020 7813 8000
✉clerksroom@essexcourt.net
Call Date: Nov 2005, Middle Temple
Qualifications: [BA (Hons LLM]
✉sdhar@essexcourt.net

DHAR MR ZEESHAN

Hardwicke
New Square, Lincoln's Inn, London WC2A 3SB, ☎020 7242 2523
✉enquiries@hardwicke.co.uk
Call Date: Nov 1999, Gray's Inn
Qualifications: [LLB (Lond)]
✉zeeshan.dhar@hardwicke.co.uk

DHILLON MR AMARDEEP SINGH

3 Serjeants Inn
London EC4Y 1BQ, ☎020 7427 5000
✉clerks@3serjeantsinn.com
Call Date: July 2010, Middle Temple
Qualifications: [BSc (B'ham) BDS (B'ham) MFDS RCS (Eng)]

DHILLON MR JASBIR SINGH

Brick Court Chambers
7-8 Essex Street, London WC2R 3LD, ☎020 7379 3550 ✉clerks@brickcourt.co.uk
Call Date: Oct 1996, Gray's Inn
Pupil Supervisor
Qualifications: [BA (Oxon) LLM]
✉Jasbir.Dhillon@Brickcourt.co.uk

E

DHILLON MISS KIRANDEEP KAUR

Broadway House Chambers
Broadway House, 9 Bank Street, Bradford, West Yorkshire BD1 1TW, ☎01274 722560
✉clerks@broadwayhouse.co.uk
Call Date: July 2005, Inner Temple
Qualifications: [LLB King's College University of London]

DHIR MISS ANUJA RAVINDRA QC (2010)

Five Paper Buildings
1st Floor, Five Paper Buildings, Temple, London EC4Y 7HB, ☎020 7583 6117
✉clerks@5pb.co.uk
Call Date: Nov 1989, Gray's Inn
Pupil Supervisor
Qualifications: [LLB (Scotland)]
ad@5pb.co.uk

DI FRANCESCO MR ALESSANDRO JAMES

Chambers of Mr Ami Feder
Ground Floor, Lamb Building, Temple, London EC4Y 7AS, ☎020 7797 7788
✉clerks@lambbuilding.co.uk
Lamb Building
22 Ship Street, Brighton BN1 1AD, ☎01273 820490
✉admin@lambbuilding.co.uk
Chambers of Mr Ami Feder
Ground Floor, Lamb Building, Temple, London EC4Y 7AS, ☎020 7797 7788
✉clerks@lambbuilding.co.uk
Call Date: July 2008, Middle Temple
Qualifications: [BA (Hons) (B'ham) MSc (LSE) PgDl (Lond)]

DI MAMBRO MR DAVID JESSE ANDREW

Radcliffe Chambers
Ground Floor, 11 New Square, Lincoln's Inn, London WC2A 3QB, ☎020 7831 0081
✉clerks@radcliffechambers.com
Pallant Chambers
12 North Pallant, Chichester, West Sussex PO19 1TQ, ☎01243 784538
✉clerks@pallantchambers.co.uk
Call Date: Nov 1973, Middle Temple
Pupil Supervisor
Qualifications: [LLB (Hons) (Lond) FCIArb]
ddim@radcliffechambers.com

DIAMOND MISS ANNA CATRIONA

No5 Chambers
38 Queen Square, Bristol BS1 4QS, ☎0845 210 5555
No5 Chambers
Greenwood House, 4-7 Salisbury Court, London EC4Y 8AA, ☎0845 210 5555
No5 Chambers
Fountain Court, Steelhouse Lane, Birmingham B4 6DR, ☎0845 210 5555 ✉info@no5.com
Call Date: Oct 1995, Gray's Inn
Qualifications: [BA]
acd@no5.com

DIAMOND MR CHRISTOPHER LESLIE WILLIAM

18 St John Street
Manchester M3 4EA, ☎0161 278 1800
✉clerks@18sjs.com
Call Date: Nov 1975, Gray's Inn
Pupil Supervisor
Qualifications: [LLB]

DIAMOND MR PAUL

Chambers of Mr Paul Diamond
PO Box 1041, Barton, Cambridge CB23 7WY, ☎01223 264544
✉pauldiamond@btconnect.com
Call Date: July 1985, Middle Temple
Qualifications: [BA (Exon) LLM (Cantab)]
pauldiamond@btconnect.com

DIAS MR JUDE DEXTER QC (2009)

Garden Court Chambers
57-60 Lincoln's Inn Fields, London WC2A 3LJ, ☎020 7993 7600 ✉info@gclaw.co.uk
Call Date: Feb 1988, Inner Temple
Qualifications: [BA (Dunelm)]
dexterd@gclaw.co.uk

DIAS MISS JULIA AMANDA QC (2008)

7 King's Bench Walk
Ground Floor, 7 King's Bench Walk, Temple, London EC4Y 7DS, ☎020 7910 8300
✉clerks@7kbw.co.uk
Call Date: July 1982, Inner Temple
Qualifications: [MA (Cantab) MCI Arb]

DIAS MISS SAPPHO

5 King's Bench Walk
5 King's Bench Walk, Temple, London EC4Y 7DN, ☎020 7353 5638
✉clerks@5kbw.co.uk
Call Date: Nov 1982, Gray's Inn
Pupil Supervisor
Qualifications: [BA (Cantab)]
sappho.dias@5kbw.co.uk

DIAZ MISS PAULA ANDREA

Field Court Chambers
5 Field Court, Gray's Inn, London WC1R 5EF, ☎020 7405 6114 ✉clerks@fieldcourt.co.uk
Call Date: Oct 2000, Middle Temple
Qualifications: [BA (Hons) (Kent)]
✉paula.diaz@fieldcourt.co.uk

DICK MR JAMES ANTHONY

Bell Yard Chambers
116/118 Chancery Lane, London WC2A 1PP, ☎020 7306 9292
✉byclerks@bellyardchambers.co.uk
9 King's Bench Walk
Lower Ground Floor South, 9 King's Bench Walk, Temple, London EC4Y 7DX, ☎020 7353 9564 ✉9kbw@btconnect.com
Call Date: July 2003, Middle Temple
Qualifications: [MSci (Bris)]
✉jdick@bellyardchambers.co.uk

DICKASON MR ROBERT JAMES

Outer Temple Chambers
The Outer Temple, 222 Strand, London WC2R 1BA, ☎020 7353 6381
✉clerks@outertemple.com
Call Date: Oct 2007, Lincoln's Inn
Qualifications: [BA (Cantab)]
✉robert.dickason@outertemple.com

DICKENS MR ANDREW WILLIAM

9 King's Bench Walk
Lower Ground Floor South, 9 King's Bench Walk, Temple, London EC4Y 7DX, ☎020 7353 9564 ✉9kbw@btconnect.com
Call Date: Nov 1983, Gray's Inn
Pupil Supervisor
Qualifications: [Dip Law]
✉9kbw@btconnect.com

DICKER MR ROBIN MARK QC (2000)

South Square
3-4 South Square, Gray's Inn, London WC1R 5HP, ☎020 7696 9900
✉practicemanagers@southsquare.com
Call Date: Apr 1986, Middle Temple
Qualifications: [BA BCL (Oxon)]
✉robindicker@southsquare.com

DICKINSON MR GREGORY DAVID MARK QC (2002)

1 High Pavement
Nottingham NG1 1HF, ☎0115 941 8218
✉clerks@1highpavement.co.uk
Call Date: July 1981, Gray's Inn
Recorder
Qualifications: [LLB]
✉gdqc@1highpavement.co.uk

DICKINSON MR JOHN FINCH HENEAGE

St John's Chambers
101 Victoria Street, Bristol BS1 6PU, ☎0117 923 4700
✉clerks@stjohnschambers.co.uk
Call Date: Oct 1995, Middle Temple
Pupil Supervisor
Qualifications: [BA (Hons) ACA Dip Law]
✉john.dickinson@stjohnschambers.co.uk

DICKINSON MR JONATHAN DAVID

Call Date: Nov 1986, Inner Temple
Qualifications: [LLB (Hons) (Bris)]
✉clerk@stjohnsbuildings.co.uk

DICKINSON MISS ROSA GEORGETTE JESSIE

St Philips Chambers
55 Temple Row, Birmingham B2 5LS, ☎0121 246 7000 ✉clerks@st-philips.com
Call Date: July 2006, Inner Temple
Qualifications: [BA (Oxon)]
✉rdickinson@st-philips.co.uk

DICKINSON MR RUSSELL

9 St John Street
Manchester M3 4DN, ☎0161 955 9000
✉civilclerks@9sjs.com / criminalclerks@9sjs.com
Call Date: July 2002, Lincoln's Inn
Qualifications: [BA (Hons) (Durham) PgDL (Nott'M)]

DICKINSON MS ZARAH SHELLEY

5 Pump Court
Ground Floor, 5 Pump Court, Temple, London EC4Y 7AP, ☎020 7353 2532
✉clerks@5pumpcourt.com
No.6 Park Square
Leeds LS1 2LW, ☎0113 245 9763
✉Tim@no6.co.uk
Call Date: July 2002, Inner Temple
Qualifications: [LLB (Dunelm)]
✉zarahdickinson@5pumpcourt.com

DICKS MR ANTHONY RICHARD

Essex Court Chambers
24 Lincoln's Inn Fields, London WC2A 3EG, ☎020 7813 8000
✉clerksroom@essexcourt.net
Call Date: May 1961, Inner Temple
Qualifications: [MA LLB (Cantab)]

E

DIEU MR HOA VINH

30 Park Place
Cardiff CF10 3BS, ☎029 2039 8421
✉clerks@30parkplace.law.co.uk
Call Date: Nov 2006, Gray's Inn
Qualifications: [LLB]

DIGGLE MR MARK JAMES

Ropewalk Chambers
24 The Ropewalk, Nottingham NG1 5EF,
☎0115 947 2581 ✉clerks@ropewalk.co.uk
Call Date: Oct 1996, Inner Temple
Pupil Supervisor
Qualifications: [LLM (Nott'm) LLB]
markdiggle@ropewalk.co.uk

DIGNAN MR FRANCIS PATRICK

Nexus Chambers
7 New Square, Lincolns Inn, London
WC2A 3QS,
☎020 7404 1147 / 020 7831 8309
✉info@nexuschambers.com
Bedlington Chambers
7 New Square, Lincoln's Inn, London
WC2A 2QS, ☎020 7831 1159
✉clerks@bedlingtonchambers.com
Bedlington Chambers
20 Staffa Road, Maidstone ME15 9ST,
☎01622 744 015
✉clerks@bedlingtonchambers.com
Call Date: Nov 2000, Inner Temple
Qualifications: [BA (Leeds) LLB (Leeds)]

DIGNUM MR MARCUS BENEDICT

12 King's Bench Walk
12 King's Bench Walk, Temple, London
EC4Y 7EL, ☎020 7583 0811
Call Date: Oct 1994, Middle Temple
Pupil Supervisor
Qualifications: [BA (Hons)(Lond)]

DILHORNE ???

Chambers of Rt Hon Viscount Dilhorne
The Dower House, Minterne Parva,
Dorchester, Dorset DT2 7AP, ☎01300 341392
✉dilhorne@thelegalguru.co.uk
Call Date: Nov 1979, Inner Temple
Qualifications: [FTII]
dilhorne@thelegalguru.co.uk

DILLIWAY-PARRY MR GUY WILLIAM

5 King's Bench Walk
5 King's Bench Walk, Temple, London
EC4Y 7DN, ☎020 7353 5638
✉clerks@5kbw.co.uk
Call Date: July 2002, Gray's Inn
Qualifications: [BSc (B'ham) LLM (L'pool)]

DILLON MS ANNE VERONICA

13 King's Bench Walk
13 King's Bench Walk, Temple, London
EC4Y 7EN, ☎020 7353 7204
✉clerks@13kbw.co.uk
13 KBW
32 Beaumont Street, Oxford OX1 2NP,
☎01865 311066 ✉clerks@13kbw.co.uk
Call Date: July 2003, Inner Temple
Qualifications: [MA (Hons) CPE (Lond)]
dillon.roberts@virgin.net

DILLON MISS CLARE ANNE CECILIA

St Philips Chambers
55 Temple Row, Birmingham B2 5LS,
☎0121 246 7000 ✉clerks@st-philips.com
Call Date: July 1974, Middle Temple
Qualifications: [LLB]

DILLON MR THOMAS WILLIAM MATTHEW

Chambers of Thomas Dillon
25 Howitt Close, London NW3 4LX,
☎020 7692 2722 ✉post@contentadvice.eu
Call Date: July 1983, Middle Temple
Qualifications: [MA (Cantab) Dip IPL FCIArb]

DILNOT MISS ANNA LOUISE

Essex Court Chambers
24 Lincoln's Inn Fields, London WC2A 3EG,
☎020 7813 8000
✉clerksroom@essexcourt.net
Call Date: Mar 2008, Lincoln's Inn
Qualifications: [LLB (Lond)]

DILWORTH MR NOEL THOMAS

Henderson Chambers
2 Harcourt Buildings, Temple, London
EC4Y 9DB, ☎020 7583 9020
✉clerks@hendersonchambers.co.uk
Call Date: July 2001, Inner Temple
Pupil Supervisor
Qualifications: [BA (Oxon) CPE (South Bank)]
ndilworth@hendersonchambers.co.uk

DIN MR SOOFI PERVAZE IQBAL

Ropewalk Chambers
24 The Ropewalk, Nottingham NG1 5EF,
☎0115 947 2581 ✉clerks@ropewalk.co.uk
Call Date: Nov 1984, Lincoln's Inn
Qualifications: [BA (Manch)]
soofidin@ropewalk.co.uk

DINAN-HAYWARD MISS DEBORAH LOUISE

Albion Chambers
Broad Street, Bristol BS1 1DR,
☎ 0117 927 2144
✉ clerks@albionchambers.co.uk
Call Date: Nov 1988, Inner Temple
Pupil Supervisor
Qualifications: [LLB (Sheff)]
deborah.dinan-hayward@albionchambers.co.uk

DINEEN MS MARIA THERESE

2 Bedford Row
London WC1R 4BU, ☎ 020 7440 8888
✉ clerks@2bedfordrow.co.uk
Call Date: Oct 1997, Inner Temple
Qualifications: [LLB (Nottingham)]
mdineen@2bedfordrow.co.uk

DINES MISS SARAH ELIZABETH

1 Gray's Inn Square
Ground Floor, 1 Gray's Inn Square, London WC1R 5AA, ☎ 020 7405 0001
Call Date: July 1988, Lincoln's Inn
Qualifications: [LLB (Hons) (Brunel)]
sdines@1gis.co.uk

DINGEMANS MR JAMES MICHAEL QC (2002)

3 Hare Court
3 Hare Court, Temple, London EC4Y 7BJ,
☎ 020 7415 7800 ✉ clerks@3harecourt.com
Call Date: July 1987, Inner Temple
Qualifications: [BA (Oxon) FCIArb]
jamesdingemans@3harecourt.com

Types of work: Administrative law, Civil liberties, Commercial litigation, Common law (general), Human rights, Insurance, International arbitration, Personal injury, Public law

DINKIN MR ANTHONY DAVID QC (1991)

Cornerstone Barristers
2-3 Gray's Inn Square, Gray's Inn, London WC1R 5JH, ☎ 020 7242 4986
✉ chambers@2-3gis.co.uk
Call Date: Nov 1968, Lincoln's Inn
Recorder
Qualifications: [BSc (Lond)]
adinkin@2-3gis.co.uk

DIPPENAAR MR DANIEL JACOBUS

Lamb Chambers
Lamb Building, Elm Court, Temple, London EC4Y 7AS, ☎ 020 7797 8300
✉ info@lambchambers.co.uk
Call Date: Mar 2007, Middle Temple
Qualifications: [Baccalaureus Procationis (Johannesburg) Baccalaureus Legum (Johannesburg)]
danieldippenaar@lambchambers.co.uk

DIPRé MR PAUL NICHOLAS AMADEUS

Chambers of Mr P N Dipré
Address withheld ☎ 0845 123 1234
✉ pauldipre@btinternet.com
MK Family Law Chambers
PO Box 6017, Milton Keynes MK1 9AP,
☎ 0845 123 1234
Call Date: Nov 1991, Lincoln's Inn
Qualifications: [MA (Oxon)]

DITCHBURN MR JOHN

4 KBW
Ground Floor, 4 King's Bench Walk, Temple, London EC4Y 7DL, ☎ 020 7822 8822
✉ law@4kbw.net
Call Date: July 2007, Middle Temple
Qualifications: [BA (Oxon)]
jd@4kbw.net

DITCHFIELD MR ANTHONY MICHAEL

Kings Chambers
36 Young Street, Manchester M3 3FT,
☎ 0845 034 3444
✉ clerks@kingschambers.com
Kings Chambers
5 Park Square East, Leeds LS1 2NE,
☎ 0845 034 3444
✉ clerks@kingschambers.com
Kings Chambers
Embassy House, 60 Church Street, Birmingham B3 2DJ, ☎ 0845 034 3444
✉ clerks@kingschambers.com
Call Date: Oct 1993, Middle Temple
Qualifications: [BA (Hons) LLM]

DITE DR ALEXIS

18 Red Lion Court
London EC4A 3EB, ☎ 020 7520 6000
✉ chambers@18rlc.co.uk
Call Date: Nov 2008, Inner Temple
Qualifications: [MMATH (Oxon) PhD(Edin) CPE]

E

DIWAN MR RICKY

Essex Court Chambers
24 Lincoln's Inn Fields, London WC2A 3EG,
☎ 020 7813 8000
✉ clerksroom@essexcourt.net
Call Date: Oct 1998, Lincoln's Inn
Qualifications: [BA (Hons)(Cantab) LLM (Harvard)]
✉ rdiwan@essexcourt.net

DIX MISS REBECCA

2 Bedford Row
London WC1R 4BU, ☎ 020 7440 8888
✉ clerks@2bedfordrow.co.uk
Call Date: July 2004, Inner Temple
Qualifications: [LLB LLM]
✉ rdix@2bedfordrow.co.uk, rebecca.dix@tci-sit.org

DIXEY MR IAN ROGER

Guildhall Chambers
23 Broad Street, Bristol BS1 2HG,
☎ 0117 930 9000
✉ hoc@guildhallchambers.co.uk
Call Date: Nov 1984, Inner Temple
Pupil Supervisor
✉ ian.dixey@guildhallchambers.co.uk

DIXEY MR JONATHAN MARK

5 Essex Court
1st Floor, 5 Essex Court, Temple, London EC4Y 9AH, ☎ 020 7410 2000
✉ clerks@5essexcourt.co.uk
Call Date: July 2007, Lincoln's Inn
Qualifications: [LLB (So'ton) LLM (Bris)]
✉ dixey@5essexcourt.co.uk

DIXON MISS ANNE

1 Pump Court
Elm Court, Temple, London EC4Y 7AB,
☎ 020 7842 7070
✉ (name)@pumpcourt.co.uk
Call Date: Nov 1991, Middle Temple
Qualifications: [LLB (Hons) RGN]
✉ ad@1pumpcourt.co.uk

DIXON MS CLARE ELIZABETH

Four New Square
Four New Square, Lincoln's Inn, London WC2A 3RJ, ☎ 020 7822 2000
✉ barristers@4newsquare.com
Call Date: Nov 2002, Inner Temple
Pupil Supervisor
Qualifications: [BA (Oxon)]
✉ c.dixon@4newsquare.com

DIXON MR DAVID STEVEN

Sovereign Chambers
46 Park Place, Leeds LS1 2RY,
☎ 0113 245 1841
✉ clerks@sovereignchambers.co.uk
Call Date: Oct 1992, Lincoln's Inn
Pupil Supervisor
Qualifications: [LLB(Hons)(Newc)]
✉ david.dixon@sovereignchambers.co.uk

DIXON MS EMMA LOUISE

Blackstone Chambers
Blackstone House, Temple, London EC4Y 9BW, ☎ 020 7583 1770
✉ clerks@blackstonechambers.com
Call Date: Oct 1994, Gray's Inn
Pupil Supervisor
Qualifications: [BA]
✉ emmadixon@blackstonechambers.com

DIXON MR HUW

15 Winckley Square
Preston PR1 3JJ, ☎ 01772 252828
✉ clerks@15winckleysq.co.uk
Call Date: Nov 1999, Lincoln's Inn
Qualifications: [BA (Hons)(Birm'h) LLM (Manch)]
✉ clerks@15winckleysq.co.uk

DIXON MR JAMES MALCOLM

No5 Chambers
Fountain Court, Steelhouse Lane, Birmingham B4 6DR, ☎ 0845 210 5555 ✉ info@no5.com
No5 Chambers
Greenwood House, 4-7 Salisbury Court, London EC4Y 8AA, ☎ 0845 210 5555
No5 Chambers
38 Queen Square, Bristol BS1 4QS,
☎ 0845 210 5555
Call Date: Mar 2001, Lincoln's Inn
Qualifications: [BA (Hons) (Hull) Mphil (Cantab) CPE]
✉ jdi@no5.com

DIXON MR RODNEY THOMAS

Temple Garden Chambers
1 Harcourt Buildings, Temple, London EC4Y 9DA, ☎ 020 7583 1315
✉ clerks@tgchambers.com
Call Date: Mar 2000, Inner Temple
Pupil Supervisor
Qualifications: [BA LLM (USA) LLB]
✉ clerks@tgchambers.com

E

DIXON MISS SORREL HELEN

Garden Court Chambers
57-60 Lincoln's Inn Fields, London WC2A 3LJ, ☎ 020 7993 7600 ✉ info@gclaw.co.uk
Call Date: July 1987, Middle Temple
Qualifications: [LLB (Bris)]
✉ sorreld@gclaw.co.uk

DOBBIE MISS ALICE FELICITY

6 Pump Court
1st Floor, 6 Pump Court, Temple, London EC4Y 7AR, ☎ 020 7797 8400
✉ richardconstable@6pumpcourt.co.uk
6 Pump Court Chambers
6-8 Mill Street, Maidstone, Kent ME15 6XH, ☎ 01622 688094
✉ annexe@6pumpcourt.co.uk
Call Date: Nov 2007, Inner Temple
Qualifications: [BA (Oxon)]
✉ AliceDobbie@6pumpcourt.co.uk

DOBBIE MISS OLIVIA-FAITH

Cloisters
1 Pump Court, Temple, London EC4Y 7AA, ☎ 020 7827 4000 ✉ clerks@cloisters.com
Call Date: Oct 2007, Middle Temple
Qualifications: [LLB (Hons) (Lond)]
✉ ODobbie@Cloisters.com

DOBBIN MISS CLAIR JOSEPHINE CRAWFORD

3 Raymond Buildings
3 Raymond Buildings, Gray's Inn, London WC1R 5BH, ☎ 020 7400 6400
✉ clerks@3rblaw.com
Call Date: Nov 1999, Middle Temple
Pupil Supervisor
Qualifications: [BA (Hons)(Cantab)]
✉ clair.dobbin@3raymondbuildings.com

DOBBY MISS HELEN

4 King's Bench Walk
2nd Floor, 4 King's Bench Walk, Temple, London EC4Y 7DL, ☎ 020 7822 7000
✉ clerks@4kbw.co.uk
Call Date: July 2008, Middle Temple
Qualifications: [LLB (Hons) (Newc) LLM]
✉ hhd@4kbw.co.uk

DOBE MR KULJEET SINGH

Old Bailey Chambers
15 Old Bailey, London EC4M 7EF, ☎ 020 3008 6404
✉ clerks@15oldbaileychambers.com
Call Date: Nov 1993, Lincoln's Inn
Qualifications: [LLB (So'ton)]

DOBIE MISS LISA CARRIE

1 Chancery Lane
London WC2A 1LF, ☎ 0845 634 6666
✉ clerks@1chancerylane.com
Call Date: July 2006, Inner Temple
Qualifications: [LLB (Leeds)]
✉ ldobie@1chancerylane.com

DOBSON MISS CATHERINE ALEXANDRA

39 Essex Street
London WC2R 3AT, ☎ 020 7832 1111
✉ clerks@39essex.com
Call Date: July 2009, Inner Temple
Qualifications: [BA (Cantab) BCL (Oxon) MA (Cantab)]
✉ catherine.dobson@39essex.com

DOBSON MR WILLIAM

Cloisters
1 Pump Court, Temple, London EC4Y 7AA, ☎ 020 7827 4000 ✉ clerks@cloisters.com
Call Date: Oct 2008, Inner Temple
Qualifications: [LLB (B'ham)]

DOCKERY MR PAUL

18 St John Street
Manchester M3 4EA, ☎ 0161 278 1800
✉ clerks@18sjs.com
Call Date: July 1973, Gray's Inn
Pupil Supervisor
Qualifications: [LLB Hons (London)]

DOCTOR MR BRIAN ERNEST QC (1999)

Fountain Court Chambers
Fountain Court, Temple, London EC4Y 9DH, ☎ 020 7583 3335
✉ chambers@fountaincourt.co.uk
Call Date: July 1991, Lincoln's Inn
Qualifications: [BA LLB (South Africa) BCL]
✉ bdoctor@fountaincourt.co.uk

DODD MR DANIEL ANDREW

Linenhall Chambers
1 Stanley Place, Chester CH1 2LU, ☎ 01244 348282
✉ clerks@linenhallchambers.co.uk
Call Date: July 2003, Lincoln's Inn
Qualifications: [LLB (Hons) (Wales)]
✉ daniel@1stanleyplace.co.uk

E

DODD MR JOHN STANISLAUS QC (2006)

2 Bedford Row
London WC1R 4BU, ☎020 7440 8888
✉clerks@2bedfordrow.co.uk
Call Date: Nov 1979, Gray's Inn
Qualifications: [LLB (Leics)]
jdodd@2bedfordrow.co.uk

DODD MRS MARGARET ANN

2 Bedford Row
London WC1R 4BU, ☎020 7440 8888
✉clerks@2bedfordrow.co.uk
Call Date: July 1979, Middle Temple
Qualifications: [LLB (So'ton)]

DODD MISS SARA

Exchange Chambers
7 Ralli Courts, West Riverside, Manchester M3 5FT, ☎0161 833 2722
Exchange Chambers
One Derby Square, Derby Square, Liverpool L2 9XX, ☎0151 236 7747
✉info@exchangechambers.co.uk
Exchange Chambers
Oxford House, Oxford Row, Leeds LS1 3BE, ☎0113 203 1970
✉spencer@exchangechambers.co.uk
Call Date: July 1987, Lincoln's Inn
Pupil Supervisor
Qualifications: [LLB]
dodd@exchangechambers.co.uk

DODD MISS STEPHANIE JANE

9-12 Bell Yard
London WC2A 2JR, ☎020 7400 1800
✉clerks@9-12bellyard.com
Call Date: July 2001, Gray's Inn
Qualifications: [LLB (Hons)]
s.dodd@9-12bellyard.com

DODDS MISS KATHRYN SUZANNE

Fountain Chambers
Cleveland Business Centre, 1 Watson Street, Middlesbrough TS1 2RQ, ☎01642 804040
✉clerks@fountainchambers.co.uk
Call Date: July 2000, Gray's Inn
Pupil Supervisor
Qualifications: [BA (Dunelm)]

DODDS MR SHAUN

KBW
The Engine House, No 1 Foundry Square, Leeds LS11 5DL, ☎0113 297 1200
✉clerks@kbwchambers.com
Call Date: July 1990, Gray's Inn
Qualifications: [LLB (Lond)]

DODGE MR PETER CLIVE

Radcliffe Chambers
Ground Floor, 11 New Square, Lincoln's Inn, London WC2A 3QB, ☎020 7831 0081
✉clerks@radcliffechambers.com
Call Date: Oct 1992, Lincoln's Inn
Pupil Supervisor
Qualifications: [MA (Cantab) Dip Law]
pdodge@radcliffechambers.com

DODGSON MR LANCE MYLES

Bank House Chambers
Old Bank House, Hartshead, Sheffield S1 2EL, ☎0114 275 1223
✉w.digby@bankhousechambers.co.uk
Call Date: Nov 2007, Middle Temple
Qualifications: [LLB (Hons)]
l.dodgson@bankhousechambers.co.uk

DODSON MISS JOANNA QC (1993)

Renaissance Chambers
5th Floor, Gray's Inn Chambers, Gray's Inn, London WC1R 5JA, ☎020 7404 1111
✉clerks@renaissancechambers.co.uk
Park Court Chambers
16 Park Place, Leeds LS1 2SJ, ☎0113 243 3277
✉clerks@parkcourtchambers.co.uk
Call Date: Nov 1971, Middle Temple
Qualifications: [MA (Cantab)]
jd1@renaissancechambers.co.uk

DOERFEL MR JAN HENDRIK JAMISON

Chambers of Mr J H Doerfel
Parkshot House, 5 Kew Road, Richmond, Surrey TW9 2PR, ☎0845 123 1234
✉jandoerfel@yahoo.com
1215 Chambers
1 Fetter Lane, London EC4A 1BR, ☎020 3291 1215
✉admin@1215chambers.com
Call Date: Nov 2000, Inner Temple
Qualifications: [BA (York) CPE LLM (Essex)]

DOERRIES MISS CHANTAL-AIMéE RENEE AEMELIA AN QC (2008)

Atkin Chambers
1 Atkin Building, Gray's Inn, London WC1R 5AT, ☎020 7404 0102
✉clerks@atkinchambers.com
Call Date: Oct 1992, Middle Temple
Qualifications: [MA (Hons) (Cantab)]
cadoerries@atkinchambers.com

DOHERTY MR BERNARD JAMES

39 Essex Street
London WC2R 3AT, ☎ 020 7832 1111
✉ clerks@39essex.com
82 King Street
Manchester M2 4WQ, ☎ 0161 870 9969
Call Date: Nov 1990, Middle Temple
Pupil Supervisor
Qualifications: [MA (Cantab) Dip Law (Lond)]
✉ bernard.doherty@39essex.com

DOHERTY MR NICHOLAS BRUDENELL

4 King's Bench Walk
2nd Floor, 4 King's Bench Walk, Temple, London EC4Y 7DL, ☎ 020 7822 7000
✉ clerks@4kbw.co.uk
Call Date: July 1983, Lincoln's Inn
Qualifications: [LLB]
✉ nb@4kbw.co.uk

DOHERTY MR OLIVER BENEDICT

Old Bailey Chambers
15 Old Bailey, London EC4M 7EF, ☎ 020 3008 6404
✉ clerks@15oldbaileychambers.com
Call Date: Oct 2009, Inner Temple
Qualifications: [LLB (Dunelm)]
✉ o.doherty@15oldbaileychambers.com

DOHERTY MRS PATRIZIA ANNA DORINA

Sovereign Chambers
46 Park Place, Leeds LS1 2RY, ☎ 0113 245 1841
✉ clerks@sovereignchambers.co.uk
Call Date: Nov 2000, Gray's Inn
Qualifications: [BA (Lond)]
✉ patrizia.doherty@sovereignchambers.co.uk

DOHMANN MISS BARBARA QC (1987)

Blackstone Chambers
Blackstone House, Temple, London EC4Y 9BW, ☎ 020 7583 1770
✉ clerks@blackstonechambers.com
Call Date: Nov 1971, Gray's Inn
Recorder
✉ barbaradohmann@blackstonechambers.com

DOIG MR GAVIN ANDREW

New Court Chambers
3 Broad Chare, Newcastle Upon Tyne NE1 3DQ, ☎ 0191 232 1980
✉ clerks@newcourt-chambers.co.uk
Call Date: Oct 1995, Lincoln's Inn
Pupil Supervisor
Qualifications: [LLB (Hons)(Bris)]
✉ gavin.doig@newcourt-chambers.co.uk

DOLAN DR BRIDGET MAURA

3 Serjeants Inn
London EC4Y 1BQ, ☎ 020 7427 5000
✉ clerks@3serjeantsinn.com
Call Date: Oct 1997, Middle Temple
Pupil Supervisor
Qualifications: [BSc (Hons) PhD CPE]
✉ bdolan@3serjeantsinn.com

DOMAN MR RICHARD WILLIAM

2 Dr Johnson's Buildings
2 Dr Johnson's Buildings, Temple, London EC4Y 7AY, ☎ 020 7936 2613
✉ clerks@2drj.com
Call Date: Nov 2003, Lincoln's Inn
Qualifications: [LLB (Hons) (Essex)]
✉ r.doman@2drj.com

DOMENGE MRS VICTORIA JANE

29 Bedford Row Chambers
London WC1R 4HE, ☎ 020 7404 1044
✉ clerks@29br.co.uk
Call Date: Nov 1993, Middle Temple
Qualifications: [BA (Hons)(Exon) DipLaw]
✉ vdomenge@29br.co.uk

DONALDSON MR DAVID TORRANCE QC (1984)

Blackstone Chambers
Blackstone House, Temple, London EC4Y 9BW, ☎ 020 7583 1770
✉ clerks@blackstonechambers.com
Call Date: Nov 1968, Gray's Inn
Recorder
Qualifications: [MA (Cantab) DrJur]
✉ daviddonaldson@blackstonechambers.com

DONALDSON MS SARAH RUTH

18 St John Street
Manchester M3 4EA, ☎ 0161 278 1800
✉ clerks@18sjs.com
Call Date: July 2003, Inner Temple
Qualifications: [BA (Oxon) M Phil (Oxon) CPE (Manch)]

E

DONELON MISS ANNE

Middle Temple Lane Chambers
2nd Floor South, 1 Middle Temple Lane, London EC4Y 9AA, ☎ 020 7583 4352
✉ chambers@mtlchambers.com
Call Date: Oct 1995, Lincoln's Inn
Qualifications: [LLB (Hons)(Hull)]

DONKIN MR ANTHONY MATTHEW

Zenith Chambers
10 Park Square, Leeds LS1 2LH,
☎ 0113 245 5438
✉ clerks@zenithchambers.co.uk
Call Date: July 2004, Inner Temple
Qualifications: [LLB BVC]
mdonkin@zenithchambers.co.uk

DONMALL MR MATTHEW FREDERICK

1 Crown Office Row
1 Crown Office Row, Temple, London EC4Y 7HH, ☎ 020 7797 7500
✉ mail@1cor.com
Call Date: Oct 2006, Lincoln's Inn
Qualifications: [MA (Cantab) MPhil Diplaw]
matthew.donmall@1cor.com

DONNE MR ANTHONY MAURICE QC (1988)

Pump Court Chambers
31 Southgate Street, Winchester, Hampshire SO23 9EB, ☎ 01962 868 161
✉ clerks@3pumpcourt.com
Pump Court Chambers
Upper Ground Floor, 3 Pump Court, Temple, London EC4Y 7AJ, ☎ 020 7353 0711
✉ clerks@3pumpcourt.com
Pump Court Chambers
5 Temple Chambers, Temple Street, Swindon SN1 1SQ, ☎ 01793 539899
✉ clerks@3pumpcourt.com
Queen Square Chambers
56 Queen Square, Bristol BS1 4PR,
☎ 0117 921 1966 ✉ crime@qs-c.co.uk
Call Date: Nov 1973, Middle Temple
Qualifications: [BA (Oxon)]
mirandadonne@btinternet.com, ad@3pumpcourt.com

DONNE MR JEREMY NIGEL QC (2003)

QEB Hollis Whiteman
1-2 Laurence Pountney Hill, London EC4R 0EU, ☎ 020 7933 8855
✉ barristers@qebhw.co.uk
Call Date: Nov 1978, Middle Temple
Recorder

DONNELLAN MR CHRISTOPHER JOHN QC (2008)

36 Bedford Row
London WC1R 4JH, ☎ 020 7421 8000
✉ chambers@36bedfordrow.co.uk
Call Date: July 1981, Inner Temple
Recorder
Qualifications: [BA (Oxon)]
cdonnellan@36bedfordrow.co.uk

DONNELLY MISS CATHERINE MARY

6 Pump Court
1st Floor, 6 Pump Court, Temple, London EC4Y 7AR, ☎ 020 7797 8400
✉ richardconstable@6pumpcourt.co.uk
6 Pump Court Chambers
6-8 Mill Street, Maidstone, Kent ME15 6XH,
☎ 01622 688094
✉ annexe@6pumpcourt.co.uk
Call Date: Mar 1997, Middle Temple
Qualifications: [BA (Hons)(Lond)]
Clerks@6PumpCourt.co.uk

DONNELLY DR CATHERINE MARY

Blackstone Chambers
Blackstone House, Temple, London EC4Y 9BW, ☎ 020 7583 1770
✉ clerks@blackstonechambers.com
Call Date: Nov 2003, Gray's Inn
Qualifications: [LLB (Dub) BCL (Oxon) LLM DPhil (Oxon)]

DONNELLY MR JOHN PATRICK

2 Bedford Row
London WC1R 4BU, ☎ 020 7440 8888
✉ clerks@2bedfordrow.co.uk
Call Date: Nov 1983, Inner Temple
Pupil Supervisor
Qualifications: [LLB (Hull)]
jdonnelly@2bedfordrow.co.uk

DONNELLY MISS KATHLEEN

Henderson Chambers
2 Harcourt Buildings, Temple, London EC4Y 9DB, ☎020 7583 9020
✉clerks@hendersonchambers.co.uk
Call Date: Mar 2005, Lincoln's Inn
Qualifications: [BA (Hons) Oxon LLM (Cantab)]
✉kdonnelly@hendersonchambers.co.uk

DONNELLY MR KEVIN GERARD EASTWOOD

Lincoln House Chambers
Tower 12, The Avenue North, Spinningfields, 18-22 Bridge Street, Manchester M3 3BZ, ☎0161 832 5701
✉info@lincolnhousechambers.com
Call Date: Oct 1991, Lincoln's Inn
Pupil Supervisor
Qualifications: [BA (Hons) (Cantab)]
✉kevin.donnelly@lincolnhousechambers.com

DONNELLY MR LEWIS

Zenith Chambers
10 Park Square, Leeds LS1 2LH, ☎0113 245 5438
✉clerks@zenithchambers.co.uk
Call Date: July 2008, Middle Temple
Qualifications: [LLB (Hons) (Sheff)]

DONNELLY MR STEPHEN JOHN

Dyers Chambers
35 Bedford Row, London WC1R 4JH, ☎020 7404 1881
✉admin@dyerschambers.com
Call Date: Oct 2001, Inner Temple
Qualifications: [CPE (Lond)]
✉stephen.donnelly@dyerschambers.com

DONNELLY MR TIMOTHY GERARD

Dere Street Barristers
33 Broad Chare, Newcastle Upon Tyne NE1 3DQ, ☎0844 3351551
✉clerks@derestreet.co.uk
Call Date: July 2003, Lincoln's Inn
Qualifications: [LLB Hons (Newc)]
✉t.donnelly@broadcharechambers.co.uk

DONNELLY MR WILLIAM HOWARD

Kenworthy's Chambers
Arlington House, Bloom Street, Salford, Manchester M3 6AJ, ☎0161 832 4036
Call Date: Nov 1981, Gray's Inn
Qualifications: [BA]
✉maria@kenworthysbarristers.co.uk

DONOGHUE MR STEVEN MICHAEL

9 Park Place
9 Park Place, Cardiff, South Glamorgan CF10 3DP, ☎029 2038 2731
✉clerks@9parkplace.co.uk
Call Date: Oct 1992, Middle Temple
Pupil Supervisor
Qualifications: [LLB (Hons) (Wales)]
✉clerks@9parkplace.co.uk

DONOVAN MISS ALISON MARY

Angel Chambers
Ethos Building, Kings Road, Swansea SA1 8AS, ☎01792 464623
✉clerks@angelchambers.co.uk
Call Date: Nov 1987, Middle Temple
Pupil Supervisor
Qualifications: [MA (Oxon)]
✉alison.donovan@angelchambers.co.uk

DONOVAN MR ANTHONY FRANCIS SCOTT

Atlantic Chambers
4-6 Cook Street, Liverpool L2 9QU, ☎0151 236 4421
✉info@atlanticchambers.co.uk
Call Date: July 1975, Gray's Inn
Pupil Supervisor, Recorder
Qualifications: [BA (Oxon) MA (USA)]
✉info@atlanticchambers.co.uk

DONOVAN MR JOEL QC (2011)

Cloisters
1 Pump Court, Temple, London EC4Y 7AA, ☎020 7827 4000 ✉clerks@cloisters.com
Call Date: July 1991, Lincoln's Inn
Pupil Supervisor
Qualifications: [BA (Hons) (Dunelm)]
✉jd@cloisters.com

DONOVAN MISS JULIET MARY

East Anglian Chambers
Gresham House, 5 Museum Street, Ipswich, Suffolk IP1 1HQ, ☎01473 214481
✉ipswich@ealaw.co.uk
East Anglian Chambers
53 North Hill, Colchester, Essex CO1 1QA, ☎01473 214481 ✉colchester@ealaw.co.uk
East Anglian Chambers
140 New London Road, Chelmsford, Essex CM2 0AW, ☎01473 214481
✉chelmsford@ealaw.co.uk
Call Date: July 2002, Middle Temple
Pupil Supervisor
Qualifications: [BA (Hons) (Oxon) Polytechnic (Oxon) Dip in Law]

E

DOOLEY MR ALLAN KEITH

No5 Chambers
Fountain Court, Steelhouse Lane, Birmingham B4 6DR, ☎0845 210 5555 ✉info@no5.com
No5 Chambers
Greenwood House, 4-7 Salisbury Court, London EC4Y 8AA, ☎0845 210 5555
No5 Chambers
38 Queen Square, Bristol BS1 4QS, ☎0845 210 5555
Call Date: Apr 1991, Lincoln's Inn
Pupil Supervisor, Recorder
Qualifications: [LLB (Hons) (L'pool)]
ad@no5.com

DOOLEY MS CHRISTINE

2 Pump Court
1st Floor, 2 Pump Court, Temple, London EC4Y 7AH, ☎020 7353 5597
✉clerks@2pumpcourt.co.uk
Call Date: July 1980, Gray's Inn
Pupil Supervisor
Qualifications: [BA (Hons)]
cdooley@2pumpcourt.co.uk

DORAN MISS CATHERINE MARY

Radcliffe Chambers
Ground Floor, 11 New Square, Lincoln's Inn, London WC2A 3QB, ☎020 7831 0081
✉clerks@radcliffechambers.com
Call Date: Oct 2008, Inner Temple
Qualifications: [BA (Cantab)]
cdoran@radcliffechambers.com

DORAN MR GERARD PATRICK

Lincoln House Chambers
Tower 12, The Avenue North, Spinningfields, 18-22 Bridge Street, Manchester M3 3BZ, ☎0161 832 5701
✉info@lincolnhousechambers.com
Call Date: Nov 1993, Gray's Inn
Pupil Supervisor
Qualifications: [LLB (Hons)]
gerard.doran@lincolnhousechambers.com

DORMAN-O'GOWAN MR CHRISTOPHER PATRICK DESMOND

Dere Street Barristers
33 Broad Chare, Newcastle Upon Tyne NE1 3DQ, ☎0844 3351551
✉clerks@derestreet.co.uk
Call Date: Nov 1979, Lincoln's Inn
Qualifications: [BA (Newc) BL (Dublin)]

DORRELL MS ALISON GLENDA

Bank House Chambers
Old Bank House, Hartshead, Sheffield S1 2EL, ☎0114 275 1223
✉w.digby@bankhousechambers.co.uk
Call Date: Feb 1992, Gray's Inn
Pupil Supervisor
Qualifications: [LLB (Sheff)]
a.dorrell@bankhousechambers.co.uk

DORS MR MATTHEW JOHN

Devon Chambers
3 St Andrew Street, Plymouth PL1 2AH, ☎01752 661659
✉clerks@devonchambers.co.uk
Call Date: Oct 2004, Inner Temple
Qualifications: [LLB (Bris)]
matthewdors@devonchambers.co.uk

DOS SANTOS MR ALEXANDER

Charter Chambers
33 John Street, London WC1N 2AT, ☎020 7618 4400
✉clerks@charterchambers.com
Call Date: Oct 1999, Lincoln's Inn
Pupil Supervisor
Qualifications: [LLB (Hons)(Luton)]
alexander.dossantos@charterchambers.com

DOSWELL MR RUPERT JOHN

KBW
The Engine House, No 1 Foundry Square, Leeds LS11 5DL, ☎0113 297 1200
✉clerks@kbwchambers.com
Call Date: Oct 1996, Inner Temple
Pupil Supervisor
Qualifications: [LLB (Hons)]
rjd@kbwchambers.com

DOUGHERTY MR CHARLES EGMONT

2 Temple Gardens
2 Temple Gardens, Temple, London EC4Y 9AY, ☎020 7822 1200
✉clerks@2tg.co.uk
Call Date: Oct 1997, Middle Temple
Pupil Supervisor
Qualifications: [BA (Hons) BCL (Oxon)]
cdougherty@2templegardens.co.uk

DOUGHERTY MR NIGEL PETER

Erskine Chambers
33 Chancery Lane, London WC2A 1EN, ☎020 7242 5532
✉clerks@erskinechambers.com
Call Date: Oct 1993, Gray's Inn
Pupil Supervisor
Qualifications: [BA LLM (Cantab)]
ndougherty@erskine-chambers.co.uk

DOUGHTY MR PETER

12 College Place
Fauvelle Buildings, 12 College Place, Southampton SO15 2FE, ☎023 8032 0320
✉clerks@12cp.co.uk
Call Date: July 1988, Lincoln's Inn
Pupil Supervisor
Qualifications: [LLB (Hons) (Wales)]
pdoughty@12cp.co.uk

DOUGLAS MR COLIN NORMAN

Temple Chambers
32 Park Place, Cardiff CF10 3BA,
☎029 2039 7364
✉DBrinning@Temple-Chambers.co.uk
30 Park Place
Cardiff CF10 3BS, ☎029 2039 8421
✉clerks@30parkplace.law.co.uk
Temple Chambers
12 Clytha Park Road, Newport, Gwent NP20 4PB, ☎01633 267403
✉dbrinning@temple-chambers.co.uk
Call Date: Oct 1998, Lincoln's Inn
Qualifications: [LLB (Hons)(Cardiff) LLM (Cardiff)]

DOUGLAS MR MICHAEL JOHN QC (1997)

4 Pump Court
4 Pump Court, Temple, London EC4Y 7AN,
☎020 7842 5555
✉chambers@4pumpcourt.com
Call Date: Nov 1974, Gray's Inn
Recorder
Qualifications: [BA (Oxon)]
mdouglas@4pumpcourt.com

DOUGLAS MR STEPHEN JOHN

St Johns Buildings
24a - 28 St John Street, Manchester M3 4DJ,
☎0161 214 1500
✉clerk@stjohnsbuildings.co.uk
16 Winckley Square
Preston PR1 3JJ, ☎01772 256100
St Johns Buildings Liverpool
8th Floor India Buildings, Water Street, Liverpool L2 0XG, ☎0151 243 6000
✉clerk@stjohnsbuildings.co.uk
Call Date: Nov 1994, Inner Temple
Qualifications: [LLB (Manc) CPE (Staffs)]
clerk@stjohnsbuildings.co.uk

DOUGLAS MR ZACHARY

Matrix Chambers
Griffin Building, Gray's Inn, London WC1R 5LN, ☎020 7404 3447
✉matrix@matrixlaw.co.uk / lscott@matrixlaw.co.uk
Call Date: Mar 2006, Gray's Inn
Qualifications: [LLB BA BCL (Oxon)]
zacharydouglas@matrixlaw.co.uk

DOUGLAS-JONES MR BENJAMIN TIMOTHY

Five Paper Buildings
1st Floor, Five Paper Buildings, Temple, London EC4Y 7HB, ☎020 7583 6117
✉clerks@5pb.co.uk
Apex
Harlech House, 20 Cathedral Road, Cardiff CF11 9LJ, ☎02920 232 032
✉clerks@apexchambers.net
Call Date: Nov 1998, Gray's Inn
Pupil Supervisor
Qualifications: [LLB (Reading)]
bdj@5pb.co.uk

Types of work: Asset recovery, Copyright, Coroners, Corporate fraud, Crime, Health and safety, Intellectual property, Trademarks

DOUGLASS MISS GERALDINE MAISIE

Portal Chambers
Blaencwm Mawr, Llandysul SA44 5NS,
☎01559 395 292
Call Date: Nov 1976, Middle Temple
td@portalchambers.co.uk

DOUGLASS MR PAUL STEPHEN

9 King's Bench Walk
Lower Ground Floor South, 9 King's Bench Walk, Temple, London EC4Y 7DX,
☎020 7353 9564 ✉9kbw@btconnect.com
Call Date: July 1996, Inner Temple
Qualifications: [BA (Cantab) CPE]
psdouglass1966@yahoo.co.uk

DOUTHWAITE MR CHARLES PHILIP

Four New Square
Four New Square, Lincoln's Inn, London WC2A 3RJ, ☎020 7822 2000
✉barristers@4newsquare.com
Call Date: July 1977, Gray's Inn
Pupil Supervisor
Qualifications: [MA (Cantab)]
c.douthwaite@4newsquare.com

E

DOVAR MR DANIEL

Tanfield Chambers
2-5 Warwick Court, London WC1R 5DJ,
☎ 020 7421 5300
✉ clerks@tanfieldchambers.co.uk
Call Date: Oct 1997, Gray's Inn
Qualifications: [LLB (Bris)]

DOVE MR IAN WILLIAM QC (2003)

No5 Chambers
Fountain Court, Steelhouse Lane, Birmingham B4 6DR, ☎ 0845 210 5555 ✉ info@no5.com
No5 Chambers
Greenwood House, 4-7 Salisbury Court, London EC4Y 8AA, ☎ 0845 210 5555
4-5 Gray's Inn Square
Gray's Inn, London WC1R 5AH,
☎ 020 7404 5252 ✉ clerks@4-5.co.uk
No5 Chambers
38 Queen Square, Bristol BS1 4QS,
☎ 0845 210 5555
Call Date: July 1986, Inner Temple
Recorder
Qualifications: [BA (Oxon)]
id@no5.com

E

DOVE MR JAMES FRANCIS

The Chambers of Grahame Aldous QC
9 Gough Square, London EC4A 3DG,
☎ 020 7832 0500
✉ clerks@9goughsquare.co.uk
Call Date: Nov 2006, Lincoln's Inn
Qualifications: [LLB (Durham) PG Dip]
JDove@9goughsquare.co.uk

DOW MR KENNETH

5 Pump Court
Ground Floor, 5 Pump Court, Temple, London EC4Y 7AP, ☎ 020 7353 2532
✉ clerks@5pumpcourt.com
Call Date: Nov 1970, Lincoln's Inn
Pupil Supervisor
Qualifications: [BA]
kennethdow@5pumpcourt.com

DOWD MR CHRISTOPHER JAMES CHARLES

1 Pump Court
Elm Court, Temple, London EC4Y 7AB,
☎ 020 7842 7070
✉ (name)@pumpcourt.co.uk
Call Date: Mar 2012, Middle Temple
cjd@1pumpcourt.co.uk

DOWDEN MR ANDREW PHILIP

Castle Chambers
The Old Fire Station, 90 High Street, Harrow-on-the-Hill, Middlesex HA1 3LP,
☎ 020 8423 6579 ✉ info@castlechambers.net
Melbury House
55 Manor Road, Oadby, Leicester, Leicestershire LE2 2LL, ☎ 07801 037802
✉ melburyhousechambers@yahoo.co.uk
Call Date: Oct 1991, Lincoln's Inn
Qualifications: [BA (Hons) (Manch) M Phil (Cambs)]
info@andrewdowden.com

DOWDING MR NICHOLAS ALAN TATHAM QC (1997)

Falcon Chambers
Falcon Court, London EC4Y 1AA,
☎ 020 7353 2484
✉ clerks@falcon-chambers.com
Call Date: July 1979, Inner Temple
Qualifications: [MA (Cantab) Hon RICS]
dowding@falcon-chambers.com

Types of work: Arbitration, Chancery (land law), Commercial property, Conveyancing, Landlord and tenant, Professional negligence

DOWELL MR GREGORY HAMILTON

Principal Chambers
15 Lime Tree Walk, Sevenoaks, Kent TN13 1YH, ☎ 0845 209 8080
Call Date: Oct 1990, Middle Temple
Qualifications: [LLB (Hons)]

DOWLEY MR DOMINIC MYLES QC (2002)

Serle Court
6 New Square, Lincoln's Inn, London WC2A 3QS, ☎ 020 7242 6105
✉ clerks@serlecourt.co.uk
Call Date: July 1983, Gray's Inn
Qualifications: [MA (Oxon)]
ddowley@serlecourt.co.uk

Types of work: Administrative law, Arbitration, Banking, Commercial law, Commercial litigation, Commodities, Conflict of laws, Construction law, Corporate finance, Financial services, Fraud, Information technology, Insurance, International trade, Media and entertainment, Partnerships, Professional negligence, Sale and carriage of goods

DOWLING-HUSSEY MR ARRAN PETER

Warrenside Chambers
Blew Garth, The Warren, Caversham, Reading RG4 7TH, ☎00 353 87631 2205
Call Date: Nov 2007, Middle Temple
Qualifications: [BA (Hons) (Dublin) MSc (Dub)]

DOWN MRS BARBARA

Westgate Chambers
64 High Street, Lewes, East Sussex BN7 1XG, ☎01273 480510
✉clerks@westgate-chambers.co.uk
Call Date: Nov 1999, Lincoln's Inn
Qualifications: [LLB (Hons)]
✉BD@westgate-chambers.co.uk

DOWN MRS LISA

Zenith Chambers
10 Park Square, Leeds LS1 2LH, ☎0113 245 5438
✉clerks@zenithchambers.co.uk
Call Date: July 2002, Middle Temple
Qualifications: [LLB (Hons) LLM]

DOWN MISS SUSAN

King's Bench and Godolphin (KBG)Chambers
115 North Hill, Plymouth, Devon PL4 8JY, ☎01752 221551
✉clerks@kbgchambers.co.uk
Call Date: Nov 1984, Middle Temple
Qualifications: [LLB (Hons)(UEA)]
✉susan.down@kingsbenchchambers.co.uk

DOWNES MR PAUL SIMON QC (2010)

2 Temple Gardens
2 Temple Gardens, Temple, London EC4Y 9AY, ☎020 7822 1200
✉clerks@2tg.co.uk
Call Date: Oct 1991, Gray's Inn
Pupil Supervisor
Qualifications: [BA (Oxon) ACIB]
✉pdownes@2tg.co.uk

DOWNEY MISS AILEEN PATRICIA

The Chambers of Grahame Aldous QC
9 Gough Square, London EC4A 3DG, ☎020 7832 0500
✉clerks@9goughsquare.co.uk
Call Date: Nov 1991, Lincoln's Inn
Pupil Supervisor, Recorder
Qualifications: [LLB (Hons) (Lond)]
✉adowney@9goughsquare.co.uk

DOWNEY MR CHARLES BERNARD RAOUL DESCHAMP

Littleton Chambers
3 King's Bench Walk North, Temple, London EC4Y 7HR, ☎020 7797 8600
✉fschneider@littletonchambers.co.uk
Call Date: July 1988, Lincoln's Inn
Qualifications: [BSc (Hons) (LSE) Dip Law]
✉rdowney@littletonchambers.co.uk

DOWNEY MR NEIL JAMES

Atlantic Chambers
4-6 Cook Street, Liverpool L2 9QU, ☎0151 236 4421
✉info@atlanticchambers.co.uk
Call Date: Mar 1997, Middle Temple
Qualifications: [BA (Hons)(Oxon)]
✉neildowney@atlanticchambers.co.uk

DOWNHAM MISS GILLIAN CELIA

1 Garden Court Family Law Chambers
Ground Floor, One Garden Court, Temple, London EC4Y 9BJ, ☎020 7797 7900
✉clerks@1gc.com
Call Date: Nov 1993, Middle Temple
Qualifications: [BSc (Hons) MA (Econ) Dip in Social Work]
✉downham@1gc.com

DOWNIE MR ANDREW JAMES

Number 7 Harrington Street Chambers
7 Harrington Street, Liverpool L2 9YH, ☎0151 242 0707 ✉clerks@7hs.co.uk
Call Date: Nov 1990, Gray's Inn
Qualifications: [BA MA]
✉andrew.downie@7hs.co.uk

DOWNING MISS EMMA

Broadway House Chambers
Broadway House, 9 Bank Street, Bradford, West Yorkshire BD1 1TW, ☎01274 722560
✉clerks@broadwayhouse.co.uk
Broadway House Chambers
25 Park Square West, Leeds, West Yorkshire LS1 2PW, ☎0113 246 2600
✉clerks@broadwayhouse.co.uk
Call Date: Oct 2002, Middle Temple
Qualifications: [MA (Hons) (Cantab)]
✉clerks@broadwayhouse.co.uk

DOWNS MR MARTIN JOHN

1 Crown Office Row
1 Crown Office Row, Temple, London EC4Y 7HH, ☎020 7797 7500
✉mail@1cor.com
Call Date: Nov 1990, Inner Temple
Qualifications: [BA (Oxon) Dip Law (Lond)]
✉martin.downs@1cor.com

E

DOWSE MS CLARE OLIVIA MARY

3 Temple Gardens
Lower Ground Floor, 3 Temple Gardens, Temple, London EC4Y 9AU, ☎ 020 7353 3102
✉ clerks@3tg.co.uk
Call Date: July 2002, Inner Temple
Qualifications: [BA (Lond) LLB (Lond)]

DOYLE MISS HOLLY TERESA

Guildhall Chambers
23 Broad Street, Bristol BS1 2HG,
☎ 0117 930 9000
✉ hoc@guildhallchambers.co.uk
Call Date: Oct 2008, Lincoln's Inn
Qualifications: [BA (Oxon)]
✉ holly.doyle@guildhallchambers.co.uk

DOYLE MR LOUIS GEORGE

Kings Chambers
36 Young Street, Manchester M3 3FT,
☎ 0845 034 3444
✉ clerks@kingschambers.com
Kings Chambers
5 Park Square East, Leeds LS1 2NE,
☎ 0845 034 3444
✉ clerks@kingschambers.com
Kings Chambers
Embassy House, 60 Church Street, Birmingham B3 2DJ, ☎ 0845 034 3444
✉ clerks@kingschambers.com
Call Date: Nov 1996, Lincoln's Inn
Qualifications: [LLB LLM (B'ham)]
✉ ldoyle@kingschambers.com

DOYLE MR PETER JOHN QC (2002)

25 Bedford Row
London WC1R 4HD, ☎ 020 7067 1500
✉ clerks@25bedfordrow.com
Call Date: July 1975, Middle Temple
Qualifications: [LLB]
✉ pdoyle@25bedfordrow.com

DOYLE MR SHANE LAWRENCE

Essex Court Chambers
24 Lincoln's Inn Fields, London WC2A 3EG,
☎ 020 7813 8000
✉ clerksroom@essexcourt.net
Call Date: Nov 2001, Lincoln's Inn
Qualifications: [BEcon LLB (Hons) BCL (Oxon)]
✉ sdoyle@essexcourt.net

DRABBLE MR RICHARD JOHN BLOOR QC (1995)

Landmark Chambers
180 Fleet Street, London EC4A 2HG,
☎ 020 7430 1221
✉ clerks@landmarkchambers.co.uk
Call Date: Nov 1975, Inner Temple
Qualifications: [BA (Cantab)]
✉ RDrabble@landmarkchambers.co.uk

DRACASS MR TIMOTHY WILLIAM

Pump Court Chambers
31 Southgate Street, Winchester, Hampshire SO23 9EB, ☎ 01962 868 161
✉ clerks@3pumpcourt.com
Pump Court Chambers
Upper Ground Floor, 3 Pump Court, Temple, London EC4Y 7AJ, ☎ 020 7353 0711
✉ clerks@3pumpcourt.com
Riverview Chambers
Hamilton House, 1 Temple Avenue, London EC4Y 0HA, ☎ 0844 225 3999
✉ chrisbaylis@riverviewchambers.com
Call Date: Oct 1998, Inner Temple
Pupil Supervisor
Qualifications: [LLB (Wales)]

DRACOS MR MARCOS GREGORIOS

One Essex Court
Ground Floor, One Essex Court, Temple, London EC4Y 9AR, ☎ 020 7583 2000
✉ clerks@oeclaw.co.uk
Call Date: Nov 2005, Middle Temple
Qualifications: [BA (Hons) PHD]
✉ mdracos@oeclaw.co.uk

DRAKE MR DAVID CHRISTOPHER

Serle Court
6 New Square, Lincoln's Inn, London WC2A 3QS, ☎ 020 7242 6105
✉ clerks@serlecourt.co.uk
Call Date: Nov 1994, Inner Temple
Pupil Supervisor
Qualifications: [MA BCL (Oxon)]
✉ ddrake@serlecourt.co.uk

DRAKE MR JAMES FREDERICK QC (2011)

7 King's Bench Walk
Ground Floor, 7 King's Bench Walk, Temple, London EC4Y 7DS, ☎ 020 7910 8300
✉ clerks@7kbw.co.uk
Call Date: July 1998, Lincoln's Inn
Pupil Supervisor
Qualifications: [BA (Australia) LLB (Hons) LLM]
✉ jdrake@7kbw.co.uk

E

DRAKE MISS RACHEL ALEXIA

13 King's Bench Walk
13 King's Bench Walk, Temple, London EC4Y 7EN, ☎ 020 7353 7204
✉ clerks@13kbw.co.uk
Call Date: Nov 1995, Middle Temple
Pupil Supervisor
Qualifications: [LLB (Hons)(Brunel)]
✉ rdrake@13kbw.co.uk

DRAKE MISS REBECCA SUSAN

39 Essex Street
London WC2R 3AT, ☎ 020 7832 1111
✉ clerks@39essex.com
82 King Street
Manchester M2 4WQ, ☎ 0161 870 9969
Call Date: July 2007, Lincoln's Inn
Qualifications: [BA (Cantab)]

DRAKE MISS SOPHIE HELENA

Broadway House Chambers
Broadway House, 9 Bank Street, Bradford, West Yorkshire BD1 1TW, ☎ 01274 722560
✉ clerks@broadwayhouse.co.uk
Broadway House Chambers
25 Park Square West, Leeds, West Yorkshire LS1 2PW, ☎ 0113 246 2600
✉ clerks@broadwayhouse.co.uk
Call Date: Oct 1990, Gray's Inn
Pupil Supervisor, Recorder
Qualifications: [LLB (Hons)(Leics)]
✉ clerks@broadwayhouse.co.uk

DRAPER MR GUY THOMAS EDWARD

Furnival Chambers
32 Furnival Street, London EC4A 1JQ,
☎ 020 7405 3232
Call Date: Mar 2008, Middle Temple
Qualifications: [BA (Hons) (Cantab)]

DRAPER MR OWAIN ROLAND

Monckton Chambers
1 & 2 Raymond Buildings, Gray's Inn, London WC1R 5NR, ☎ 020 7405 7211
✉ chambers@monckton.com
Call Date: Oct 2008, Lincoln's Inn
Qualifications: [MA (Edin)]

DRAY MR MARTIN BENEDICT ANTONY

Falcon Chambers
Falcon Court, London EC4Y 1AA,
☎ 020 7353 2484
✉ clerks@falcon-chambers.com
Call Date: Oct 1992, Gray's Inn
Pupil Supervisor
Qualifications: [LLB (Bris)]
✉ dray@falcon-chambers.com

Types of work: Boundaries, Chancery (land law), Commercial property, Conveyancing, Equity, Landlord and tenant, Leasehold enfranchisement, Mortgages, Professional negligence, Real property, Rights of light, Rights of way, Title to land

DRAYCOTT MR CHRISTOPHER ADAM

4 Breams Buildings
Chancery Lane, London EC4A 1HP,
☎ 020 7092 1900 ✉ clerks@4bb.co.uk
Call Date: July 2005, Inner Temple
Qualifications: [LLB]

DRAYCOTT MISS NATASHA CAROLINE

Five St Andrew's Hill
5 St Andrew's Hill, London EC4V 5BZ,
☎ 020 7332 5400 ✉ Clerks@5sah.co.uk
Call Date: July 2005, Middle Temple
Qualifications: [PgDip Law BA (Hons) Leeds]
✉ natashadraycott@5sah.co.uk

DRAYCOTT MR PAUL RICHARD

Doughty Street Chambers
53-54 Doughty Street, London WC1N 2LS,
☎ 020 7404 1313
✉ enquiries@doughtystreet.co.uk
Doughty Street Chambers
Pall Mall Court, 61-67 King Street, Manchester M2 4PD, ☎ 0161 618 1066
Doughty Street Chambers
5th Floor, Broad Quay House, Prince Street, Bristol BS1 4DJ, ☎ 01179 058 717
Call Date: Nov 1994, Gray's Inn
Qualifications: [LLB (Hull)]

DRAYCOTT MR SIMON DOUGLAS QC (2002)

Five St Andrew's Hill
5 St Andrew's Hill, London EC4V 5BZ,
☎ 020 7332 5400 ✉ Clerks@5sah.co.uk
Citadel Chambers
The Citadel, 190 Corporation Street,
Birmingham B4 6QD, ☎ 0121 233 8500
✉ clerks@citadelchambers.com
Call Date: July 1977, Middle Temple
Recorder
simondraycott@5sah.co.uk

DRAYTON MR HENRY ALEXANDER

Garden Court Chambers
57-60 Lincoln's Inn Fields, London WC2A 3LJ,
☎ 020 7993 7600 ✉ info@gclaw.co.uk
Call Date: Feb 1993, Inner Temple
Qualifications: [BA]
henryd@gclaw.co.uk

DREW MRS CHERYL

Warwick House Chambers
8 Warwick Court, Warwick House Chambers,
Gray's Inn, London WC1R 5DJ,
☎ 020 7430 2323
✉ clerks@warwickhousechambers.com
Call Date: Nov 1972, Gray's Inn
Pupil Supervisor
clerks@warwickhousechambers.co.uk

DREW MR CHRISTOPHER THOMAS

Warwick House Chambers
8 Warwick Court, Warwick House Chambers,
Gray's Inn, London WC1R 5DJ,
☎ 020 7430 2323
✉ clerks@warwickhousechambers.com
Call Date: Nov 1969, Gray's Inn
Pupil Supervisor
Qualifications: [LLB (Lond)]
clerks@warwickhousechambers.co.uk

DREW MISS JANE MARIAN

Coram Chambers
9-11 Fulwood Place, London WC1V 6HG,
☎ 020 7092 3700
✉ mail@coramchambers.co.uk
Call Date: July 1976, Middle Temple
Pupil Supervisor
Qualifications: [BA (Dunelm)]
jane.drew@coramchambers.co.uk

DREW MS SANDHYA

Tooks Chambers
81 Farringdon Street, London EC4A 4BL,
☎ 020 7842 7575 ✉ clerks@tooks.co.uk
Call Date: Oct 1993, Gray's Inn
Pupil Supervisor
Qualifications: [MA (Oxon) Dip Law (Lond)]
sandhya.drew@tooks.co.uk

DREW MR SIMON PATRICK QC (2011)

No5 Chambers
Fountain Court, Steelhouse Lane, Birmingham
B4 6DR, ☎ 0845 210 5555 ✉ info@no5.com
No5 Chambers
Greenwood House, 4-7 Salisbury Court,
London EC4Y 8AA, ☎ 0845 210 5555
No5 Chambers
38 Queen Square, Bristol BS1 4QS,
☎ 0845 210 5555
Call Date: Nov 1987, Lincoln's Inn
Pupil Supervisor
Qualifications: [LLB (Leeds)]
sd@no5.com

DRING MISS EMMA

Cornerstone Barristers
2-3 Gray's Inn Square, Gray's Inn, London
WC1R 5JH, ☎ 020 7242 4986
✉ chambers@2-3gis.co.uk
2-3 Gray's Inn Square
One Caspian Point, Pierhead Street, Cardiff
Bay, Cardiff CF10 4DQ, ☎ 02920 444022
✉ Cardiff@2-3gis.co.uk
Call Date: Oct 2009, Lincoln's Inn
Qualifications: [LLB (Sussex) LLM (Cantab)]
edring@2-3gis.co.uk

DRISCOLL MR MICHAEL JOHN QC (1992)

Maitland Chambers
7 Stone Buildings, Lincoln's Inn, London
WC2A 3SZ, ☎ 020 7406 1200
✉ clerks@maitlandchambers.com
Call Date: July 1970, Middle Temple
Qualifications: [BA LLB (Cantab)]
mdriscoll@maitlandchambers.com

DRIVER MS EMILY ROSE

Boston Manor Chambers
69-75 Boston Manor Road, London TW8 9JJ,
☎ 020 8567 5963
✉ chambers@edriver.plus.com
Call Date: Nov 1988, Inner Temple
Qualifications: [BA (Oxon) Dip Law (Lond)]

DRIVER MR SIMON GREGORY

Number 7 Harrington Street Chambers
7 Harrington Street, Liverpool L2 9YH, ☎0151 242 0707 ✉clerks@7hs.co.uk
Call Date: Nov 1991, Inner Temple
Qualifications: [BA]
✉simon.driver@7hs.co.uk

DRIVER MR STUART FRANK QC (2008)

Atlantic Chambers
4-6 Cook Street, Liverpool L2 9QU, ☎0151 236 4421
✉info@atlanticchambers.co.uk
Call Date: Nov 1988, Gray's Inn
Recorder
Qualifications: [BA (Oxon)]
✉stuartdriver@atlanticchambers.co.uk

DRUCE MR MICHAEL JAMES

Cornerstone Barristers
2-3 Gray's Inn Square, Gray's Inn, London WC1R 5JH, ☎020 7242 4986
✉chambers@2-3gis.co.uk
Call Date: July 1988, Inner Temple
Qualifications: [MA (Hons)]
✉michael@cornerstonebarristers.com

Types of work: Administrative law, Common land, Compulsory Purchase, Energy, Environment, Land compensation, Local authorities, Parliamentary, Planning

DRUDY MISS AOIFE HELEN MARY

6 King's Bench Walk
Ground Floor, 6 King's Bench Walk, Temple, London EC4Y 7DR, ☎020 7583 0410
✉clerks@6kbw.com
Call Date: July 2009, Middle Temple
Qualifications: [LLB (Hons) (Dub) LLM (Cantab)]
✉aoife.drudy@6kbw

DRUMMOND MR BRUCE JONATHON HUTCHEON

Cornwall Street Chambers
85-87 Cornwall Street, Birmingham B3 3BY, ☎0121 233 7500
✉clerks@cornwallstreet.co.uk
Palmyra Chambers
Royal House, 46 Legh Street, Warrington WA1 1UJ, ☎01925 444919
✉clerk@palmyrachambers.com
Call Date: Oct 1992, Gray's Inn
Qualifications: [BSc (Wales)]
✉bruce.drummond@cornwallstreet.co.uk

DRY MR NICHOLAS DAVID

St Paul's Chambers
5th Floor, St Paul's House, 23 Park Square South, Leeds LS1 2ND, ☎0113 245 5866
Call Date: Nov 1996, Lincoln's Inn
Qualifications: [BA (Hons)(Cantab)]

DRYDEN MR SHAUN

Old Court Chambers
Newham House, 96-98 Borough Road, Middlesbrough TS1 2HJ, ☎01642 232523
✉clerks@oldcourtchambers.com
Call Date: Nov 1994, Lincoln's Inn
Qualifications: [LLB (Hons)(Lond)]
✉clerks@oldcourtchambers.com

DSANE MISS VICTORIA TSOTSOO

Chambers of Miss Victoria Dsane
61 Elm Grove, Sutton, Surrey SM1 4EX, ☎020 8722 0990
✉vdsaneidown@hotmail.co.uk
Call Date: Nov 1971, Middle Temple
Pupil Supervisor
Qualifications: [BA MA LLB]

D'SOUZA MISS CAROLYN AMANDA

12 King's Bench Walk
12 King's Bench Walk, Temple, London EC4Y 7EL, ☎020 7583 0811
Call Date: Oct 1994, Middle Temple
Qualifications: [LLB (Hons)(Lond) LLM (Hons)(USA)]
✉cds@12kbw.co.uk

DU CANN MR CHRISTIAN DILLON LOTT

39 Essex Street
London WC2R 3AT, ☎020 7832 1111
✉clerks@39essex.com
82 King Street
Manchester M2 4WQ, ☎0161 870 9969
Call Date: July 1982, Gray's Inn
Pupil Supervisor
Qualifications: [BA Cantab]
✉christian.ducann@39essex.com

DU PREEZ MR HENRY ROBERT

18 Red Lion Court
London EC4A 3EB, ☎020 7520 6000
✉chambers@18rlc.co.uk
18 Red Lion Court (Annexe)
Thornwood House, 102 New London Road, Chelmsford, Essex CM2 0RG, ☎01245 280880
Call Date: Nov 1985, Inner Temple
Pupil Supervisor
Qualifications: [BA (Law)]
✉robin.dupreez@18rlc.co.uk

E

DU TOIT SC MR JOHAN IGNATIUS

Selborne Chambers
10 Essex Street, London WC2R 3AA,
☎ 020 7420 9500
✉ clerks@selbornechambers.co.uk
St Philips Chambers
55 Temple Row, Birmingham B2 5LS,
☎ 0121 246 7000 ✉ clerks@st-philips.com
Call Date: Nov 2008, Middle Temple
Qualifications: [BProc LLB LLM]
✉ johan.dutoit@selbornechambers.co.uk

DUBB MR TARLOWCHAN

Equity Chambers
First Floor, McLaren Building, 46 Priory Queensway, Birmingham B4 7LR,
☎ 0121 236 5007
✉ clerks@equitychambers.org.uk
Call Date: Nov 1997, Lincoln's Inn
Qualifications: [LLB (Hons)]
✉ td@e-c.org.uk

DUBBERY MR MARK EDWARD

Pump Court Chambers
Upper Ground Floor, 3 Pump Court, Temple, London EC4Y 7AJ, ☎ 020 7353 0711
✉ clerks@3pumpcourt.com
Pump Court Chambers
5 Temple Chambers, Temple Street, Swindon SN1 1SQ, ☎ 01793 539899
✉ clerks@3pumpcourt.com
Pump Court Chambers
31 Southgate Street, Winchester, Hampshire SO23 9EB, ☎ 01962 868 161
✉ clerks@3pumpcourt.com
Call Date: Oct 1996, Middle Temple
Pupil Supervisor
Qualifications: [BSc (Hons)(Lond) LLB (Hons)]
✉ med@3pumpcourt.com

DUBIN MR JOSHUA CHARLES

1 Pump Court
Elm Court, Temple, London EC4Y 7AB,
☎ 020 7842 7070
✉ (name)@pumpcourt.co.uk
Call Date: Nov 1997, Middle Temple
Pupil Supervisor
Qualifications: [MA (Cantab)]
✉ jd@1pumpcourt.co.uk

DUBINSKY MS LAURA EMMA NINA

Doughty Street Chambers
53-54 Doughty Street, London WC1N 2LS,
☎ 020 7404 1313
✉ enquiries@doughtystreet.co.uk
Doughty Street Chambers
Pall Mall Court, 61-67 King Street, Manchester M2 4PD, ☎ 0161 618 1066
Doughty Street Chambers
5th Floor, Broad Quay House, Prince Street, Bristol BS1 4DJ, ☎ 01179 058 717
Call Date: Oct 2002, Middle Temple
Qualifications: [BA (Oxon) MA (USA) CPE (Lond)]
✉ l.dubinsky@doughtystreet.co.uk

DUCK MR MICHAEL CHARLES QC (2011)

No5 Chambers
Fountain Court, Steelhouse Lane, Birmingham B4 6DR, ☎ 0845 210 5555 ✉ info@no5.com
No5 Chambers
Greenwood House, 4-7 Salisbury Court, London EC4Y 8AA, ☎ 0845 210 5555
No5 Chambers
38 Queen Square, Bristol BS1 4QS,
☎ 0845 210 5555
Call Date: Nov 1988, Gray's Inn
Pupil Supervisor
Qualifications: [LLB]
✉ mcd@no5.com

DUCKWORTH MS EMILY LOUISE

Kings Chambers
Embassy House, 60 Church Street, Birmingham B3 2DJ, ☎ 0845 034 3444
✉ clerks@kingschambers.com
Kings Chambers
36 Young Street, Manchester M3 3FT,
☎ 0845 034 3444
✉ clerks@kingschambers.com
Kings Chambers
5 Park Square East, Leeds LS1 2NE,
☎ 0845 034 3444
✉ clerks@kingschambers.com
Call Date: July 2003, Inner Temple
Qualifications: [BCL BA (Cantab)]
✉ educkworth@kingschambers.com

DUCKWORTH MR NATHANIEL JAMES DYCE

Falcon Chambers
Falcon Court, London EC4Y 1AA,
☎ 020 7353 2484
✉ clerks@falcon-chambers.com
Call Date: Oct 2002, Lincoln's Inn
Qualifications: [BA (Oxon) PgDL]
✉ duckworth@falcon-chambers.com

DUCKWORTH MR PETER

29 Bedford Row Chambers
London WC1R 4HE, ☎ 020 7404 1044
✉ clerks@29br.co.uk
Call Date: July 1971, Middle Temple
Pupil Supervisor
Qualifications: [LLB]
✉ pduckworth@29br.co.uk

DUDDRIDGE MR ROBERT JAMES

Enterprise Chambers
9 Old Square, Lincoln's Inn, London
WC2A 3SR, ☎020 7405 9471
✉london@enterprisechambers.com
Enterprise Chambers
65 Quayside, Newcastle Upon Tyne NE1 3DE,
☎0191 222 3344
✉newcastle@enterprisechambers.com
Enterprise Chambers
43 Park Square, Leeds LS1 2NP,
☎0113 246 0391
✉leeds@enterprisechambers.com
Call Date: Feb 1992, Lincoln's Inn
Pupil Supervisor
Qualifications: [BA (Hons) (Oxon)]
robertduddridge@enterprisechambers.com

DUDKOWSKI MR DOMINIC CHRISTIAN

Chambers of Dominic Dudkowski
7 White Street, Brighton, East Sussex
BN2 0JH, ☎07905 365189
Call Date: Nov 1986, Inner Temple
Qualifications: [BA(Sussex)]

DUDLEY MR ROBERT MICHAEL

Exchange Chambers
One Derby Square, Derby Square, Liverpool
L2 9XX, ☎0151 236 7747
✉info@exchangechambers.co.uk
Exchange Chambers
7 Ralli Courts, West Riverside, Manchester
M3 5FT, ☎0161 833 2722
Exchange Chambers
Oxford House, Oxford Row, Leeds LS1 3BE,
☎0113 203 1970
✉spencer@exchangechambers.co.uk
Call Date: Oct 1993, Gray's Inn
Qualifications: [MA (Cantab)]
dudley@exchangechambers.co.uk

DUDLEY MR THOMAS GEORGE

1 Garden Court Family Law Chambers
Ground Floor, One Garden Court, Temple,
London EC4Y 9BJ, ☎020 7797 7900
✉clerks@1gc.com
Call Date: Oct 2008, Inner Temple
Qualifications: [BA (Oxon)]
clerks@1gc.com

DUDLEY-JONES MS ELIZABETH SARAH

Deans Court Chambers
24 St John Street, Manchester M3 4DF,
☎0161 214 6000 ✉clerks@deanscourt.co.uk
Deans Court Chambers
101 Walker Street, Preston PR1 2RR,
☎01772 565 600
✉preston@deanscourt.co.uk
Call Date: Oct 1997, Inner Temple
Qualifications: [LLB (Hull)]
dudley-jones@deanscourt.co.uk

Types of work: Asset forfeiture, Asset recovery, Computer crime, Confiscation of the proceeds of crime, Coroner's inquests, Coroners, Corporate fraud, Corporate manslaughter, Crime, Crime and criminal due process, Disability and health, Forfeiture, Fraud, Healthcare law, Inquests, International fraud and asset tracing, Internet crime, Local authority claims, Local authority liability, Medical law, Medicines Act, Mental health, Professional negligence, Regulatory and disciplinary law, Serial crime, Serious fraud, Sexual Offences, Terrorism

DUDNIKOV MR ANTON

Essex Court Chambers
24 Lincoln's Inn Fields, London WC2A 3EG,
☎020 7813 8000
✉clerksroom@essexcourt.net
Call Date: July 2008, Gray's Inn
Qualifications: [LLB (Oxon)]
adudnikov@essexcourt.net

DUFF MR EUAN CAMERON

Dere Street Barristers
33 Broad Chare, Newcastle Upon Tyne
NE1 3DQ, ☎0844 3351551
✉clerks@derestreet.co.uk
Call Date: July 1973, Inner Temple
Pupil Supervisor, Recorder
Qualifications: [MA (Cantab)]

DUFF MISS KATHRYN ANNE

Seven Bedford Row
7 Bedford Row, London WC1R 4BS,
☎020 7242 3555 ✉clerks@7br.co.uk
Call Date: July 2009, Middle Temple
Qualifications: [BA (Hons) (Cantab) LLM (Lond)]
kduff@7br.co.uk

DUFFICY MR CONOR ROBERT

Seven Bedford Row
7 Bedford Row, London WC1R 4BS,
☎020 7242 3555 ✉clerks@7br.co.uk
Call Date: July 2004, Middle Temple
Qualifications: [BA (Dublin) CPE]

E

DUFFIELD MR STEPHEN MICHAEL

Trinity Chambers
The Custom House, 39 Quayside, Newcastle Upon Tyne NE1 3DE, ☎0191 232 1927
✉info@trinitychambers.co.uk
Trinity Chambers
Multi Media Exchange, 72-80 Corporation Road, Middlesbrough TS1 2RF,
☎01642 247569
✉info@trinitychambers.co.uk
Call Date: July 1969, Gray's Inn
Pupil Supervisor
Qualifications: [BA (Oxon)]
s.duffield@trinitychambers.co.uk

DUFFY MS CATHERINE ALISON

Zenith Chambers
10 Park Square, Leeds LS1 2LH,
☎0113 245 5438
✉clerks@zenithchambers.co.uk
Call Date: Oct 2003, Inner Temple
Qualifications: [LLB (B'ham)]
cduffy@zenithchambers.co.uk

DUFFY MR DEREK JAMES

St Paul's Chambers
5th Floor, St Paul's House, 23 Park Square South, Leeds LS1 2ND, ☎0113 245 5866
Call Date: Mar 1997, Gray's Inn
Qualifications: [BA (Hons)(Sheffield)]
djd@stpaulschambers.com

DUFFY MR JAMES MICHAEL

Fountain Court Chambers
Fountain Court, Temple, London EC4Y 9DH,
☎020 7583 3335
✉chambers@fountaincourt.co.uk
Call Date: Oct 2005, Lincoln's Inn
Qualifications: [BA (Hons) (Oxon) BCL (Oxon)]
jd@fountaincourt.co.uk

DUFFY MR JONATHAN

Number 7 Harrington Street Chambers
7 Harrington Street, Liverpool L2 9YH,
☎0151 242 0707 ✉clerks@7hs.co.uk
Call Date: Oct 2002, Gray's Inn
Qualifications: [PGDL CPE]
jonathan.duffy@7hs.co.uk

DUFFY MR MICHAEL

Cathedral Chambers
3 Lion Court, Haddenham, Ely, Cambridgeshire CB6 3XL, ☎07800 851813
✉michaelduffy@orange.net
Call Date: July 1992, Lincoln's Inn

DUFFY MR PATRICK WILLIAM

23 Essex Street
London WC2R 3AA, ☎020 7413 0353
✉clerks@23es.com
Call Date: July 2007, Middle Temple
Qualifications: [MSc (Lond) BCL (Ireland)]
patrickduffy@23es.com

DUGDALE MR JEREMY KEITH

Octagon House
19 Colegate, Norwich NR3 1AT,
☎01603 623186
✉clerks@octagonhouse.co.uk
Call Date: Oct 1992, Inner Temple
Pupil Supervisor
Qualifications: [MA (Oxon)]

DUGDALE MR NICHOLAS

Clerksroom (Taunton)
Equity House, Administration Centre, Blackbrook Park Avenue, Taunton, Somerset TA1 2PX, ☎0845 083 3000
✉mail@clerksroom.com
Clerksroom (London)
3rd Floor, 218 Strand, London WC2R 1AT,
☎0845 083 3000 ✉mail@clerksroom.com
King's Lynn Chambers
26 The Birches, South Wootton, King's Lynn, Norfolk PE30 3JG, ☎01553 672 085
✉timothy.leader@tesco.net
Call Date: Feb 1992, Middle Temple
Qualifications: [BA (Australia) LLB (Australia)]
dugdale@clerksroom.com

DUGGAN MR MICHAEL

Littleton Chambers
3 King's Bench Walk North, Temple, London EC4Y 7HR, ☎020 7797 8600
✉fschneider@littletonchambers.co.uk
Call Date: July 1984, Gray's Inn
Pupil Supervisor
Qualifications: [BA LLM (Cantab) BCL]
mduggan@littletonchambers.co.uk

DULAY MISS RANJEET

1 Mitre Court Buildings
1 Mitre Court Buildings, Temple, London EC4Y 7BS, ☎020 7452 8900
✉clerks@1mcb.com
Call Date: Mar 1999, Inner Temple
Qualifications: [LLB]

DUMMETT MISS EMILY

2 Hare Court
Lower Ground, Ground, 1st & 2nd Floor, 2 Hare Court, Temple, London EC4Y 7BH, ☎ 020 7353 3982 ✉ clerks@2harecourt.com
Call Date: Nov 2006, Middle Temple
Qualifications: [BA (Hons) (Oxon)]
✉ emilydummett@2harecourt.com

DUMONT MR THOMAS JULIAN BRADLEY

Radcliffe Chambers
Ground Floor, 11 New Square, Lincoln's Inn, London WC2A 3QB, ☎ 020 7831 0081
✉ clerks@radcliffechambers.com
Call Date: Nov 1979, Gray's Inn
Pupil Supervisor
Qualifications: [MA (Cantab)]
✉ tdumont@radcliffechambers.com

DUNCAN MR GARETH JOHN

30 Park Place
Cardiff CF10 3BS, ☎ 029 2039 8421
✉ clerks@30parkplace.law.co.uk
Call Date: Oct 2010, Lincoln's Inn
Qualifications: [LLB (Cardiff)]

DUNCAN MS HANNAH GILLIAN ISOBELLA

Atkinson Bevan Chambers
1st Floor, 2 Harcourt Buildings, Temple, London EC4Y 9DB, ☎ 020 7353 2112
✉ clerks@2hb.co.uk
Call Date: Oct 2002, Inner Temple
Qualifications: [LLB (So'ton) BVC ICSL]
✉ HDuncan@2hb.co.uk

DUNCAN MISS KATHERINE MARY

9-12 Bell Yard
London WC2A 2JR, ☎ 020 7400 1800
✉ clerks@9-12bellyard.com
Call Date: Nov 2008, Gray's Inn
Qualifications: [BA]

DUNFORD MR MATTHEW SIMON

Linenhall Chambers
1 Stanley Place, Chester CH1 2LU, ☎ 01244 348282
✉ clerks@linenhallchambers.co.uk
Call Date: Oct 1992, Lincoln's Inn
Pupil Supervisor
Qualifications: [LLB(Hons)(Newc)]
✉ md@nicholasstreet.com

DUNHAM MR NICHOLAS DANIEL

9-12 Bell Yard
London WC2A 2JR, ☎ 020 7400 1800
✉ clerks@9-12bellyard.com
Call Date: Oct 1999, Middle Temple
Qualifications: [BA (Hons)(Dunelm)]
✉ n.dunham@9-12bellyard.com

DUNKELS MR ANTONY LAWRENCE RENTON

Garden Court Chambers
57-60 Lincoln's Inn Fields, London WC2A 3LJ, ☎ 020 7993 7600 ✉ info@gclaw.co.uk
Call Date: Oct 2002, Inner Temple
Qualifications: [BSc (Bris) CPE]
✉ antonyd@gclaw.co.uk

DUNKELS MR PAUL RENTON QC (1993)

Walnut House
63 St. David's Hill, Exeter, Devon EX4 4DW, ☎ 01392 279751
✉ clerks@walnuthouse.co.uk
Albion Chambers
Broad Street, Bristol BS1 1DR, ☎ 0117 927 2144
✉ clerks@albionchambers.co.uk
Call Date: May 1972, Inner Temple
Recorder

DUNKIN MR OLIVER WULFSTAN

23 Essex Street
London WC2R 3AA, ☎ 020 7413 0353
✉ clerks@23es.com
Call Date: Oct 1999, Gray's Inn
Pupil Supervisor
Qualifications: [MA(Hons)(Edin) Dip Law (Lond)]
✉ oliverdunkin@23es.com

DUNLOP MR HAMISH MICHAEL

3 PB Barristers
3 Paper Buildings, Temple, London EC4Y 7EU, ☎ 020 7583 8055
3 PB Barristers
Royal Talbot House, 2 Victoria Street, Bristol, Avon BS1 6BB, ☎ 0117 928 1520
3 PB Barristers
30 Christchurch Road, Bournemouth, Dorset BH1 3PD, ☎ 01202 292102
✉ clerks.bournemouth@3paper.co.uk

E

3 PB Barristers
4 St Peter Street, Winchester SO23 8BW,
☎01962 868884
✉clerks.winchester@3paper.co.uk
3 PB Barristers
23 Beaumont Street, Oxford OX1 2NP,
☎01865 793 736
Call Date: Nov 1991, Middle Temple
Pupil Supervisor
Qualifications: [LLB (Hons) (Warw)]
hamish.dunlop@3paper.co.uk

DUNLOP MRS PATRICIA

Regency Chambers
45 Priestgate, Peterborough PE1 1LB,
☎01733 315215
✉clerks@regencychambers.law.co.uk
Call Date: July 2009, Middle Temple
Qualifications: [BA (Hons) (Dub) Dip Law (Dub)]
clerks@regencychambers.law.co.uk

DUNLOP MR RORY JAMES

39 Essex Street
London WC2R 3AT, ☎020 7832 1111
✉clerks@39essex.com
82 King Street
Manchester M2 4WQ, ☎0161 870 9969
Call Date: Nov 2002, Lincoln's Inn
Pupil Supervisor
Qualifications: [BA (Hons) (Oxon) PgDL]
rory.dunlop@39essex.com

DUNN MR ALEXANDER

Farringdon Chambers
180 Bermondsey Street, London SE1 3TQ,
☎020 7089 5700
Call Date: Feb 1985, Middle Temple
Pupil Supervisor
Qualifications: [BA]

DUNN MR CHRISTOPHER

Sovereign Chambers
46 Park Place, Leeds LS1 2RY,
☎0113 245 1841
✉clerks@sovereignchambers.co.uk
Call Date: Oct 1996, Gray's Inn
Qualifications: [BSc MA LLM (Newc)]
christopher.dunn@sovereignchambers.co.uk

DUNN MISS KATHERINE LOUISE

Trinity Chambers
The Custom House, 39 Quayside, Newcastle Upon Tyne NE1 3DE, ☎0191 232 1927
✉info@trinitychambers.co.uk
Trinity Chambers
Multi Media Exchange, 72-80 Corporation Road, Middlesbrough TS1 2RF,
☎01642 247569
✉info@trinitychambers.co.uk
Call Date: Oct 1993, Lincoln's Inn
Qualifications: [LLB (Hons)(Lond)]
k.dunn@trinitychambers.co.uk

DUNN MR PAUL GRAHAM

No.6 Park Square
Leeds LS1 2LW, ☎0113 245 9763
✉Tim@no6.co.uk
Call Date: Oct 2011, Middle Temple
Qualifications: [LLB (Hons) (EAnglia)]

DUNN MISS SAMANTHA

Regency Chambers
45 Priestgate, Peterborough PE1 1LB,
☎01733 315215
✉clerks@regencychambers.law.co.uk
Regency Chambers
Sheraton House, Castle Park, Cambridge CB3 0AX, ☎01223 301517
Call Date: July 2008, Middle Temple
Qualifications: [LLB (Hons) (Derby)]
sdunn@regencychambers.law.co.uk

DUNN MS SARAH PATRICIA QUINCEY

Pump Court Tax Chambers
16 Bedford Row, London WC1R 4EF,
☎020 7414 8080 ✉clerks@pumptax.com
Call Date: Nov 1998, Lincoln's Inn
Qualifications: [BA (Hons)(Oxon)]
sdunn@pumptax.com

Types of work: Capital tax, Employee benefit trusts, Equity, Income tax, National Insurance, Private client, Trusts, VAT, Wills

DUNN MR THOMAS HENRY

Maidstone Chambers
33 Earl Street, Maidstone, Kent ME14 1PF,
☎01622 688592
✉clerks@maidstonechambers.co.uk
Call Date: Nov 1998, Lincoln's Inn
Qualifications: [LLB (Hons)(N'castle)]
tdunn@maidstonechambers.co.uk

E

DUNNE MR ANTHONY JAMES

KBW
The Engine House, No 1 Foundry Square, Leeds LS11 5DL, ☎ 0113 297 1200
✉ clerks@kbwchambers.com
Call Date: Nov 1999, Lincoln's Inn
Qualifications: [LLB (Hons)(Hull)]
ajd@kbwchambers.com

DUNNE MR DAVID JAMES

Number 7 Harrington Street Chambers
7 Harrington Street, Liverpool L2 9YH, ☎ 0151 242 0707 ✉ clerks@7hs.co.uk
Call Date: July 2005, Middle Temple
Qualifications: [LLB (Hons)]
david.dunne@7hs.co.uk

DUNNE MR JONATHAN ANTHONY

4 Breams Buildings
Chancery Lane, London EC4A 1HP, ☎ 020 7092 1900 ✉ clerks@4bb.co.uk
Call Date: July 1986, Inner Temple
Pupil Supervisor
Qualifications: [LLB (Leics)]

DUNNING MR FRANCIS JOHN GROVE

37 Park Square Chambers
37 Park Square, Leeds LS1 2NY, ☎ 0113 243 9422 ✉ chambers@no37.co.uk
Call Date: July 1973, Inner Temple
Pupil Supervisor
Qualifications: [BSc]
chambers@no37.co.uk

DUNNING MR GRAHAM QC (2001)

Essex Court Chambers
24 Lincoln's Inn Fields, London WC2A 3EG, ☎ 020 7813 8000
✉ clerksroom@essexcourt.net
Call Date: July 1982, Lincoln's Inn
Qualifications: [MA (Cantab) LLM (USA)]
gdunning@essexcourt.net

DUNN-SHAW MR JASON DAVID

6 King's Bench Walk
Ground Floor, 6 King's Bench Walk, Temple, London EC4Y 7DR, ☎ 020 7583 0410
✉ clerks@6kbw.com
Call Date: Oct 1992, Lincoln's Inn
Pupil Supervisor
Qualifications: [BA(Hons)(Manch)]
jason.dunn-shaw@6kbw.com

DUNSEATH MISS KATHERINE SUZANNE MAY

3 PB Barristers
3 Paper Buildings, Temple, London EC4Y 7EU, ☎ 020 7583 8055
3 PB Barristers
23 Beaumont Street, Oxford OX1 2NP, ☎ 01865 793 736
3 PB Barristers
4 St Peter Street, Winchester SO23 8BW, ☎ 01962 868884
✉ clerks.winchester@3paper.co.uk
3 PB Barristers
Royal Talbot House, 2 Victoria Street, Bristol, Avon BS1 6BB, ☎ 0117 928 1520
3 PB Barristers
30 Christchurch Road, Bournemouth, Dorset BH1 3PD, ☎ 01202 292102
✉ clerks.bournemouth@3paper.co.uk
Call Date: Oct 2008, Gray's Inn
Qualifications: [BSc LLM]

DUNSTAN MR JAMES PETER

St Philips Chambers
55 Temple Row, Birmingham B2 5LS, ☎ 0121 246 7000 ✉ clerks@st-philips.com
Call Date: Feb 1995, Gray's Inn
Qualifications: [BA (Oxon)]
jdunstan@st-philips.com

DURANCE MR ALEXANDER CHRISTIAN JOHN

Doughty Street Chambers
53-54 Doughty Street, London WC1N 2LS, ☎ 020 7404 1313
✉ enquiries@doughtystreet.co.uk
Doughty Street Chambers
Pall Mall Court, 61-67 King Street, Manchester M2 4PD, ☎ 0161 618 1066
Doughty Street Chambers
5th Floor, Broad Quay House, Prince Street, Bristol BS1 4DJ, ☎ 01179 058 717
Call Date: Nov 1997, Middle Temple
Qualifications: [BA (Hons)]

DURANT MS REBECCA ELIZABETH ANNE

Bedlington Chambers
20 Staffa Road, Maidstone ME15 9ST, ☎ 01622 744 015
✉ clerks@bedlingtonchambers.com
Bedlington Chambers
7 New Square, Lincoln's Inn, London WC2A 2QS, ☎ 020 7831 1159
✉ clerks@bedlingtonchambers.com
Call Date: July 2005, Inner Temple
Qualifications: [BEd LLM CPE Dip OT BSc (York)]

E

DURBER MRS JOANNA LORRAINE

4 King's Bench Walk
2nd Floor, 4 King's Bench Walk, Temple, London EC4Y 7DL, ☎020 7822 7000
✉clerks@4kbw.co.uk
Call Date: Oct 2005, Lincoln's Inn
Qualifications: [BA (Hons) (Oxon)]
jld@4kbw.co.uk

DURHAM HALL MR CHRISTIAN TOBIAS

Broadway House Chambers
Broadway House, 9 Bank Street, Bradford, West Yorkshire BD1 1TW, ☎01274 722560
✉clerks@broadwayhouse.co.uk
Call Date: July 2009, Gray's Inn
Qualifications: [BA LLM PDip Law]
cdh@broadwayhouse.co.uk

DUROSE MR DAVID WILLIAM

Furnival Chambers
32 Furnival Street, London EC4A 1JQ, ☎020 7405 3232
Call Date: Oct 1996, Lincoln's Inn
Qualifications: [MA (Hons)(Oxon)]
ddurose@furnivallaw.co.uk

DURR MR JUDE PATRICK

Octagon House
19 Colegate, Norwich NR3 1AT, ☎01603 623186
✉clerks@octagonhouse.co.uk
Call Date: Oct 1995, Inner Temple
Pupil Supervisor
Qualifications: [MA CPE Dip Law]
clerks@octagonhouse.co.uk

DURRAN MISS ALEXIA GRAINNE

23 Essex Street
London WC2R 3AA, ☎020 7413 0353
✉clerks@23es.com
Call Date: Oct 1995, Middle Temple
Pupil Supervisor, Recorder
Qualifications: [MA (Hons)]
alexiadurran@23es.com

DURRANT MR CHARLES HENRY

3 Temple Gardens
Lower Ground Floor, 3 Temple Gardens, Temple, London EC4Y 9AU, ☎020 7353 3102
✉clerks@3tg.co.uk
Call Date: July 2006, Inner Temple
Qualifications: [LLB (Lond)]

DURSTON MR IAN JEREMY

Exchange Chambers
One Derby Square, Derby Square, Liverpool L2 9XX, ☎0151 236 7747
✉info@exchangechambers.co.uk
Exchange Chambers
Oxford House, Oxford Row, Leeds LS1 3BE, ☎0113 203 1970
✉spencer@exchangechambers.co.uk
Call Date: July 2008, Inner Temple
Qualifications: [BComm LLB (L'pool)]
durston@exchangechambers.co.uk

DUTHIE MISS CATRIONA ANN MACPHERSON

St John's Chambers
101 Victoria Street, Bristol BS1 6PU, ☎0117 923 4700
✉clerks@stjohnschambers.co.uk
Call Date: July 1981, Inner Temple
Qualifications: [LLB (Nott'm) MSc (Edin)]
catriona.duthie@stjohnschambers.co.uk

DUTHIE MR MALCOLM JAMES

No5 Chambers
Fountain Court, Steelhouse Lane, Birmingham B4 6DR, ☎0845 210 5555 ✉info@no5.com
No5 Chambers
Greenwood House, 4-7 Salisbury Court, London EC4Y 8AA, ☎0845 210 5555
No5 Chambers
38 Queen Square, Bristol BS1 4QS, ☎0845 210 5555
Call Date: July 1989, Inner Temple
Pupil Supervisor
Qualifications: [LLB (Buck) LLM (Lond)]
md@no5.com

DUTT MISS NISHA

Middle Temple Lane Chambers
2nd Floor South, 1 Middle Temple Lane, London EC4Y 9AA, ☎020 7583 4352
✉chambers@mtlchambers.com
Call Date: July 2007, Lincoln's Inn
Qualifications: [LLB (Cardiff)]

DUTTA MISS NANDINI

No5 Chambers
Fountain Court, Steelhouse Lane, Birmingham B4 6DR, ☎0845 210 5555 ✉info@no5.com
No5 Chambers
Greenwood House, 4-7 Salisbury Court, London EC4Y 8AA, ☎0845 210 5555
No5 Chambers
38 Queen Square, Bristol BS1 4QS, ☎0845 210 5555
Call Date: Feb 1993, Middle Temple
Qualifications: [LLB (Hons)]
family@no5.com, nd@no5.com

DUTTON MR TIMOTHY CHRISTOPHER

Maitland Chambers
7 Stone Buildings, Lincoln's Inn, London WC2A 3SZ, ☎ 020 7406 1200
✉ clerks@maitlandchambers.com
Call Date: July 1985, Inner Temple
Pupil Supervisor
Qualifications: [BA (Dunelm)]
✉ tdutton@maitlandchambers.com

DUTTON MR TIMOTHY JAMES QC (1998)

Fountain Court Chambers
Fountain Court, Temple, London EC4Y 9DH, ☎ 020 7583 3335
✉ chambers@fountaincourt.co.uk
Call Date: Nov 1979, Middle Temple
Qualifications: [BA (Oxon)]
✉ tdutton@fountaincourt.co.uk

Types of work: Administrative law, Arbitration, Chancery (general), Commercial law, Commercial litigation, Insurance, Partnerships, Professional negligence, Public law, Regulatory and disciplinary law

DUVAL MR ROBERT MICHAEL LOUIS

Albion Chambers
Broad Street, Bristol BS1 1DR, ☎ 0117 927 2144
✉ clerks@albionchambers.co.uk
Call Date: Nov 1979, Gray's Inn
Pupil Supervisor
Qualifications: [LLB (Wales)]
✉ robert.duval@albionchambers.co.uk

DUXBURY MS SARAH LISA

East Anglian Chambers
140 New London Road, Chelmsford, Essex CM2 0AW, ☎ 01473 214481
✉ chelmsford@ealaw.co.uk
East Anglian Chambers
53 North Hill, Colchester, Essex CO1 1QA, ☎ 01473 214481 ✉ colchester@ealaw.co.uk
East Anglian Chambers
15 The Close, Norwich, Norfolk NR1 4DZ, ☎ 01473 214481 ✉ norwich@ealaw.co.uk
East Anglian Chambers
Gresham House, 5 Museum Street, Ipswich, Suffolk IP1 1HQ, ☎ 01473 214481
✉ ipswich@ealaw.co.uk
Call Date: Mar 2010, Middle Temple
Qualifications: [LLB (Leeds)]
✉ chelmsford@ealaw.co.uk

DWOMOH MS ELIZABETH

Lamb Chambers
Lamb Building, Elm Court, Temple, London EC4Y 7AS, ☎ 020 7797 8300
✉ info@lambchambers.co.uk
Call Date: Oct 2005, Middle Temple
Qualifications: [LLB (Hons) (Dub)]
✉ elizabethdwomoh@lambchambers.co.uk

DYAL MR DANIEL ANTONIO GONCALVES

Cloisters
1 Pump Court, Temple, London EC4Y 7AA, ☎ 020 7827 4000 ✉ clerks@cloisters.com
Call Date: Oct 2006, Inner Temple
Qualifications: [BA (Nottingham) MA (Lond) City (CPE)]
✉ ddyal@cloisters.com

DYAL MISS MANDEEP

Cornwall Street Chambers
85-87 Cornwall Street, Birmingham B3 3BY, ☎ 0121 233 7500
✉ clerks@cornwallstreet.co.uk
Call Date: July 2008, Inner Temple
Qualifications: [LLB (B'ham)]
✉ mandeep.dyal@cornwallstreet.co.uk

DYBLE MR STEVEN JOHN

18 Red Lion Court
London EC4A 3EB, ☎ 020 7520 6000
✉ chambers@18rlc.co.uk
18 Red Lion Court (Annexe)
Thornwood House, 102 New London Road, Chelmsford, Essex CM2 0RG, ☎ 01245 280880
Call Date: Nov 1986, Lincoln's Inn
Qualifications: [LLB (UWE)]
✉ steven.dyble@18rlc.co.uk

DYE MR BRIAN WILLIAM

Essex Court Chambers
24 Lincoln's Inn Fields, London WC2A 3EG, ☎ 020 7813 8000
✉ clerksroom@essexcourt.net
Call Date: Oct 1991, Middle Temple
Qualifications: [MA (Hons) (Oxon)]
✉ bdye@essexcourt.net

DYE MR JOHN GEOFFREY

Goldsmith Chambers
Ground Floor, Goldsmith Building, Temple, London EC4Y 7BL, ☎ 020 7353 6802
✉ clerks@goldsmithchambers.com
Call Date: Nov 2002, Inner Temple
Qualifications: [BA (Newc) CPE]
✉ J.Dye@goldsmithchambers.law.co.uk

E

DYER MR ALLEN GORDON

4 Pump Court
4 Pump Court, Temple, London EC4Y 7AN, ☎ 020 7842 5555
✉ chambers@4pumpcourt.com
Call Date: July 1976, Inner Temple
Pupil Supervisor
Qualifications: [BA (Bris)]
adyer@4pumpcourt.com

DYER MR DAVID ROGER

St Philips Chambers
55 Temple Row, Birmingham B2 5LS, ☎ 0121 246 7000 ✉ clerks@st-philips.com
Call Date: Nov 1980, Middle Temple
Qualifications: [BA RIBA FASI FCIArb Dip Arch]
rdyer@st-philips.co.uk

DYER MR JACOB JACKSON

15 Winckley Square
Preston PR1 3JJ, ☎ 01772 252828
✉ clerks@15winckleysq.co.uk
Call Date: Nov 1995, Lincoln's Inn
Pupil Supervisor
Qualifications: [MA (Cantab)]

DYER MR JOHN ROBERT

King's Bench Chambers
Wellington House, 175 Holdenhurst Road, Bournemouth, Dorset BH8 8DQ, ☎ 01202 250025
Assize Court Chambers
14 Small Street, Bristol BS1 1DE, ☎ 0117 926 4587 ✉ carly@assize.co.uk
Call Date: July 2002, Middle Temple
Qualifications: [BA (Hons) (Cantab) MA (Cantab) Dip in Law]
john.dyer@kingsbench.co.uk

DYER MR NIGEL INGRAM JOHN QC (2006)

1 Hare Court
1 Hare Court, Temple, London EC4Y 7BE, ☎ 020 7797 7070 ✉ clerks@1hc.com
Call Date: Feb 1982, Inner Temple
Pupil Supervisor
Qualifications: [BA Hons (Dunelm)]
dyer@1hc.com

DYER MISS POLLY EMMA

QEB Hollis Whiteman
1-2 Laurence Pountney Hill, London EC4R 0EU, ☎ 020 7933 8855
✉ barristers@qebhw.co.uk
Call Date: July 2010, Middle Temple
Qualifications: [BA (Hons) (Warw)]

DYER MR SIMON CHRISTOPHER

Cloisters
1 Pump Court, Temple, London EC4Y 7AA, ☎ 020 7827 4000 ✉ clerks@cloisters.com
Call Date: July 1987, Middle Temple
Pupil Supervisor
Qualifications: [BA (Kent)]
sd@cloisters.com

DYKE MR THOMAS EDWARD

Great James Street Chambers
37 Great James Street, London WC1N 3HB, ☎ 020 7440 4949
✉ chambers@greatjames.co.uk
Call Date: July 2007, Inner Temple
Qualifications: [BA (Sheff) MSc (Lond) Pg Dip Law (B'ham)]
thom.dyke@greatjames.co.uk

DYKERS MISS CORNELIA JOY

Chambers of Mr Ami Feder
Ground Floor, Lamb Building, Temple, London EC4Y 7AS, ☎ 020 7797 7788
✉ clerks@lambbuilding.co.uk
Lamb Building
22 Ship Street, Brighton BN1 1AD, ☎ 01273 820490
✉ admin@lambbuilding.co.uk
Chambers of Mr Ami Feder
Ground Floor, Lamb Building, Temple, London EC4Y 7AS, ☎ 020 7797 7788
✉ clerks@lambbuilding.co.uk
Call Date: Oct 1995, Gray's Inn
Qualifications: [BA]

DYMOND MR ANDREW MARK

Arden Chambers
20 Bloomsbury Square, London WC1A 2NS, ☎ 020 7242 4244
✉ clerks@ardenchambers.com
Call Date: Nov 1991, Middle Temple
Qualifications: [MA (Oxon)]
andrew.dymond@ardenchambers.com

DYSON MR DANIEL BRYN WILLIAM

Southernhay Chambers
33 Southernhay East, Exeter EX1 1NX, ☎ 01392 255777
✉ clerks@southernhaychambers.co.uk
Call Date: Nov 2007, Gray's Inn

EADIE MISS CHARLOTTE LEONIE SHELDON

187 Fleet Street
London EC4A 2AT, ☎ 020 7430 7430
✉ chambers@187fleetstreet.com
Call Date: Oct 2002, Middle Temple
Qualifications: [BA (King's) CPE]

E

EADIE MR JAMES RAYMOND QC (2008)

Blackstone Chambers
Blackstone House, Temple, London EC4Y 9BW, ☎ 020 7583 1770
✉ clerks@blackstonechambers.com
Call Date: July 1984, Middle Temple
Qualifications: [MA (Cantab)]
✉ jameseadie@blackstonechambers.com

EADY MISS JENNIFER JANE QC (2006)

Old Square Chambers
10-11 Bedford Row, London WC1R 4BU, ☎ 020 7269 0300 ✉ clerks@oldsquare.co.uk
Old Square Chambers
3 Orchard Court, St Augustine's Yard, Bristol BS1 5DP, ☎ 0117 930 5100
✉ clerks@oldsquare.co.uk
Call Date: July 1989, Inner Temple
Recorder
Qualifications: [BA (Oxon) Dip Law]
✉ eady@oldsquare.co.uk

EAGLESTONE MR WILLIAM

23 Essex Street
London WC2R 3AA, ☎ 020 7413 0353
✉ clerks@23es.com
Call Date: Nov 2001, Middle Temple
Qualifications: [BA (Hons)(Oxon) LLB (Hons)]
✉ williameaglestone@23es.com

EALES MISS HANNAH JANE

18 Red Lion Court
London EC4A 3EB, ☎ 020 7520 6000
✉ chambers@18rlc.co.uk
Call Date: July 2004, Middle Temple
Qualifications: [LLB Hons (B'ham)]
✉ hannah.eales@18rlc.co.uk

EARDLEY MR AIDAN

One Brick Court
1st Floor, One Brick Court, Temple, London EC4Y 9BY, ☎ 020 7353 8845
✉ clerks@onebrickcourt.com
Call Date: Nov 2002, Lincoln's Inn
Qualifications: [BA (Hons)(Oxon)]
✉ ae@onebrickcourt.com

EARLAM MR SIMON LAWRENCE

Exchange Chambers
One Derby Square, Derby Square, Liverpool L2 9XX, ☎ 0151 236 7747
✉ info@exchangechambers.co.uk
Exchange Chambers
7 Ralli Courts, West Riverside, Manchester M3 5FT, ☎ 0161 833 2722
Exchange Chambers
Oxford House, Oxford Row, Leeds LS1 3BE, ☎ 0113 203 1970
✉ spencer@exchangechambers.co.uk
Call Date: Feb 1975, Gray's Inn
Pupil Supervisor, Recorder
Qualifications: [MA (Oxon) BCL]

EARLE MR JAMES CHRISTOPHER REGINALD ST JOHN

Fenners Chambers
3 Madingley Road, Cambridge CB3 0EE, ☎ 01223 368761
✉ clerks@fennerschambers.com
Call Date: Oct 1996, Gray's Inn
Qualifications: [BA (Kent) MA (Lond)]
✉ james.earle@fennerschambers.com

EARLE MISS JUDY ESTELLE

3 PB Barristers
3 Paper Buildings, Temple, London EC4Y 7EU, ☎ 020 7583 8055
3 PB Barristers
23 Beaumont Street, Oxford OX1 2NP, ☎ 01865 793 736
3 PB Barristers
30 Christchurch Road, Bournemouth, Dorset BH1 3PD, ☎ 01202 292102
✉ clerks.bournemouth@3paper.co.uk
3 PB Barristers
Royal Talbot House, 2 Victoria Street, Bristol, Avon BS1 6BB, ☎ 0117 928 1520
3 PB Barristers
4 St Peter Street, Winchester SO23 8BW, ☎ 01962 868884
✉ clerks.winchester@3paper.co.uk
Call Date: Oct 1994, Middle Temple
Qualifications: [LLB (Hons)(Lond)]
✉ judy.earle@3pb.co.uk

EARLEY MISS SARAH JANE

Pallant Chambers
12 North Pallant, Chichester, West Sussex PO19 1TQ, ☎ 01243 784538
✉ clerks@pallantchambers.co.uk
Call Date: Oct 1998, Inner Temple
Pupil Supervisor
Qualifications: [LLB (Reading)]
✉ searley@pallantchambers.co.uk

E

EARNSHAW MISS ZOE

Deans Court Chambers
24 St John Street, Manchester M3 4DF, ☎0161 214 6000 ✉clerks@deanscourt.co.uk
Deans Court Chambers
101 Walker Street, Preston PR1 2RR, ☎01772 565 600
✉preston@deanscourt.co.uk
Call Date: Nov 2001, Lincoln's Inn
Qualifications: [LLB (Hons)]
✉earnshaw@deanscourt.co.uk

EAST MR WILLIAM DAVID

5 Stone Buildings
5 Stone Buildings, Lincoln's Inn, London WC2A 3XT, ☎020 7242 6201
✉clerks@5sblaw.com
Call Date: July 2008, Lincoln's Inn
Qualifications: [BA (Oxon)]
✉weast@5sblaw.com

EASTEAL MR ANDREW FRANCIS MARTIN

23 Essex Street
London WC2R 3AA, ☎020 7413 0353
✉clerks@23es.com
Call Date: Feb 1990, Inner Temple
Recorder
Qualifications: [BA (Oxon)]

EASTON MISS ALISON JANE

Coram Chambers
9-11 Fulwood Place, London WC1V 6HG, ☎020 7092 3700
✉mail@coramchambers.co.uk
Call Date: Nov 1994, Inner Temple
Qualifications: [LLB (B'ham)]
✉alison.easton@coramchambers.co.uk

EASTON MR JONATHAN MARK

Kings Chambers
36 Young Street, Manchester M3 3FT, ☎0845 034 3444
✉clerks@kingschambers.com
Kings Chambers
5 Park Square East, Leeds LS1 2NE, ☎0845 034 3444
✉clerks@kingschambers.com
Kings Chambers
Embassy House, 60 Church Street, Birmingham B3 2DJ, ☎0845 034 3444
✉clerks@kingschambers.com
Cornerstone Barristers
2-3 Gray's Inn Square, Gray's Inn, London WC1R 5JH, ☎020 7242 4986
✉chambers@2-3gis.co.uk
Call Date: Nov 1996, Gray's Inn
Qualifications: [LLB (Warw) LLM (Italy)]
✉jeaston@kingschambers.com

EASTWOOD MR CHARLES PETER

Call Date: July 1988, Lincoln's Inn
Pupil Supervisor
Qualifications: [BA (Hons) (Oxon)]
✉clerk@stjohnsbuildings.co.uk

EASTWOOD MISS CHARLOTTE

37 Park Square Chambers
37 Park Square, Leeds LS1 2NY, ☎0113 243 9422 ✉chambers@no37.co.uk
Call Date: Nov 2003, Middle Temple
Qualifications: [LLB (Hons) (Leeds)]
✉chambers@no37.co.uk, ce@no37.co.uk

EASTWOOD MR PETER SHANNON

Atlantic Chambers
4-6 Cook Street, Liverpool L2 9QU, ☎0151 236 4421
✉info@atlanticchambers.co.uk
Call Date: Oct 2007, Inner Temple
Qualifications: [LLB (Manch)]
✉info@atlanticchambers.co.uk, shannoneastwood@atlanticchambers.co.uk

EASTWOOD MISS PHILIPPA CLEMENCY ANNE

Doughty Street Chambers
53-54 Doughty Street, London WC1N 2LS, ☎020 7404 1313
✉enquiries@doughtystreet.co.uk
Call Date: Oct 2003, Lincoln's Inn
Qualifications: [BA (Hons) (Oxon)]
✉p.eastwood@doughtystreet.co.uk

EASTY MISS VALERIE STEPHANIE

Garden Court Chambers
57-60 Lincoln's Inn Fields, London WC2A 3LJ, ☎020 7993 7600 ✉info@gclaw.co.uk
Call Date: Oct 1992, Middle Temple
Qualifications: [BSc (Hons) Dip Law]
✉valeriee@gclaw.co.uk

EATON MR ANDREW ROBERT

Garden Court Chambers
57-60 Lincoln's Inn Fields, London WC2A 3LJ, ☎020 7993 7600 ✉info@gclaw.co.uk
Call Date: Nov 2004, Middle Temple
Qualifications: [BA (Hons)]
✉andrewe@gclaw.co.uk

EATON MISS DEBORAH ANN QC (2008)

1 KBW Chambers
1 King's Bench Walk, Temple, London EC4Y 7DB, ☎ 020 7936 1500
✉ clerks@1kbw.co.uk
King's Bench Chambers
174 High Street, Lewes BN7 1YE,
☎ 01273 402600
Call Date: July 1985, Inner Temple
Recorder
Qualifications: [Dip Law (City) B Soc Sc (Hons)]
✉ deaton@1kbw.co.uk

EATON MR JAMES BERNARD

Thomas More Chambers
7 Lincoln's Inn Fields, London WC2A 3BP,
☎ 020 7404 7000
✉ clerks@thomasmore.co.uk
Call Date: Nov 1978, Middle Temple
Pupil Supervisor
Qualifications: [LLB (Hons) (L'Pool) MA (Lond)]
✉ beaton@thomasmore.co.uk

EATON MR NIGEL TREVOR

Essex Court Chambers
24 Lincoln's Inn Fields, London WC2A 3EG,
☎ 020 7813 8000
✉ clerksroom@essexcourt.net
Call Date: Nov 1991, Gray's Inn
Pupil Supervisor
Qualifications: [BA BCL (Oxon)]
✉ neaton@essexcourt.net

EATON MR TOBIAS BARNABY

Staple Inn Chambers
1st Floor, 9 Staple Inn, Holborn Bars, London WC1V 7QH, ☎ 020 7242 5240
✉ clerks@stapleinn.co.uk
Call Date: Oct 2001, Inner Temple
Pupil Supervisor
Qualifications: [LLB (Hons) (Lond)]
✉ te@stapleinn.co.uk

EATON HART MR ANDREW MICHAEL

Walnut House
63 St. David's Hill, Exeter, Devon EX4 4DW,
☎ 01392 279751
✉ clerks@walnuthouse.co.uk
Call Date: July 1989, Gray's Inn
Pupil Supervisor
Qualifications: [LLB (Exon)]

EATON TURNER MR DAVID MURRAY

New Square Chambers
12 New Square, Lincoln's Inn, London WC2A 3SW, ☎ 020 7419 8000
✉ robin.hollington@newsquarechambers.co.uk
Call Date: July 1984, Lincoln's Inn
Pupil Supervisor
Qualifications: [LLB (Lond)]
✉ david.eatonturner@newsquarechambers.co.uk

EATWELL MISS TATYANA JANE

Tooks Chambers
81 Farringdon Street, London EC4A 4BL,
☎ 020 7842 7575 ✉ clerks@tooks.co.uk
Call Date: July 2007, Inner Temple
Qualifications: [BA MA (Manch)]
✉ tatyana.eatwell@tooks.co.uk

EBORALL MISS CHARLOTTE HELEN

3 Verulam Buildings
London WC1R 5NT, ☎ 020 7831 8441
✉ chambers@3vb.com
Call Date: July 2004, Middle Temple
Qualifications: [BA Hons (Cantab)]
✉ ceborall@3vb.com

ECCLES MR DAVID THOMAS

Deans Court Chambers
24 St John Street, Manchester M3 4DF,
☎ 0161 214 6000 ✉ clerks@deanscourt.co.uk
Deans Court Chambers
101 Walker Street, Preston PR1 2RR,
☎ 01772 565 600
✉ preston@deanscourt.co.uk
Call Date: July 1976, Middle Temple
Pupil Supervisor
Qualifications: [MA (Cantab)]
✉ eccles@deanscourt.co.uk

ECCLES MISS SARAH RHIANNON

Iscoed Chambers
86 St Helen's Road, Swansea SA1 4BQ,
☎ 01792 652988
✉ clerks@iscoedchambers.co.uk
Call Date: July 2008, Middle Temple
Qualifications: [LLB (Hons) (Reading)]
✉ clerks@iscoedchambers.co.uk

ECKERSLEY MR SIMON RICHARD

1 High Pavement
Nottingham NG1 1HF, ☎ 0115 941 8218
✉ clerks@1highpavement.co.uk
Call Date: Mar 1996, Lincoln's Inn
Qualifications: [BA (Hons) (Oxon)]
✉ simoneckersley1@mac.com, simoneckersley@1highpavement.co.uk

E

ECOB MISS JOANNE ANITA

36 Bedford Row
London WC1R 4JH, ☎ 020 7421 8000
✉ chambers@36bedfordrow.co.uk
Call Date: July 1985, Inner Temple
Pupil Supervisor
Qualifications: [LLB (Newc)]

ECONOMOU MR GEORGE COSTAS

Quadrant Chambers
Quadrant House, 10 Fleet Street, London EC4Y 1AU, ☎ 020 7583 4444
✉ info@quadrantchambers.com
Call Date: Nov 1965, Lincoln's Inn
Qualifications: [FCIArb]

EDDY MISS KATHERINE ANNE

11 King's Bench Walk
11 King's Bench Walk, Temple, London EC4Y 7EQ, ☎ 020 7632 8500
✉ clerksroom@11kbw.com
Call Date: Oct 2009, Inner Temple
Qualifications: [BA (Canada) M Phil (Cantab) Dphil (Oxon)]
katherine.eddy@11kbw.com

EDELMAN MR COLIN NEIL QC (1995)

Devereux Chambers
Queen Elizabeth Building, Temple, London EC4Y 9BS, ☎ 020 7353 7534
✉ clerks@devchambers.co.uk
Call Date: July 1977, Middle Temple
Recorder
Qualifications: [MA (Cantab)]
edelman@devchambers.co.uk

EDENBOROUGH MR JAMES ROBERT SCOTT

15 New Bridge Street
London EC4V 6AU, ☎ 020 7842 1900
✉ clerks@15nbs.com
Call Date: Nov 2001, Middle Temple
Qualifications: [BA (Hons) MA]
james.edenborough@15nbs.com

EDENBOROUGH MR MICHAEL SIMON QC (2010)

Serle Court
6 New Square, Lincoln's Inn, London WC2A 3QS, ☎ 020 7242 6105
✉ clerks@serlecourt.co.uk
Call Date: Oct 1992, Middle Temple
Pupil Supervisor
Qualifications: [MA (Cantab) DPhil (Oxon)]
clerks@serlecourt.co.uk

EDEY MR PHILIP DAVID QC (2009)

20 Essex Street
London WC2R 3AL, ☎ 020 7842 1200
✉ clerks@20essexst.com
Call Date: Nov 1994, Gray's Inn
Qualifications: [BA (Oxon)]
clerks@20essexst.com

EDGE MR ALAN JAMES

Argent Chambers
5 Bell Yard, London WC2A 2JR, ☎ 020 7556 5500
✉ briefsin@argentchambers.co.uk
Call Date: July 2006, Lincoln's Inn
Qualifications: [BA (Dub)]
a.edge@argentchambers.co.uk

EDGE MR ANDREW CHARLES

11 King's Bench Walk
11 King's Bench Walk, Temple, London EC4Y 7EQ, ☎ 020 7632 8500
✉ clerksroom@11kbw.com
Call Date: Oct 2003, Inner Temple
Qualifications: [BA (Lond)]

EDGE MISS CHARLOTTE LOUISE

5 Stone Buildings
5 Stone Buildings, Lincoln's Inn, London WC2A 3XT, ☎ 020 7242 6201
✉ clerks@5sblaw.com
Call Date: Oct 2006, Lincoln's Inn
Qualifications: [BA (Oxon)]
cedge@5sblaw.com

EDGE MR IAN DAVID

3 PB Barristers
3 Paper Buildings, Temple, London EC4Y 7EU, ☎ 020 7583 8055
3 PB Barristers
Royal Talbot House, 2 Victoria Street, Bristol, Avon BS1 6BB, ☎ 0117 928 1520
3 PB Barristers
23 Beaumont Street, Oxford OX1 2NP, ☎ 01865 793 736
3 PB Barristers
4 St Peter Street, Winchester SO23 8BW, ☎ 01962 868884
✉ clerks.winchester@3paper.co.uk

3 PB Barristers
30 Christchurch Road, Bournemouth, Dorset BH1 3PD, ☎01202 292102
✉clerks.bournemouth@3paper.co.uk
Call Date: Feb 1981, Middle Temple
Qualifications: [BA LLM (Cantab)]
ian.edge@3paper.co.uk

EDGE MR TIMOTHY RICHARD

Deans Court Chambers
24 St John Street, Manchester M3 4DF, ☎0161 214 6000 ✉clerks@deanscourt.co.uk
Deans Court Chambers
101 Walker Street, Preston PR1 2RR, ☎01772 565 600
✉preston@deanscourt.co.uk
Call Date: Oct 1992, Gray's Inn
Pupil Supervisor
Qualifications: [MA (Oxon)]
edge@deanscourt.co.uk

EDGINTON MR HORACE RONALD

Becket Chambers
17 New Dover Road, Canterbury, Kent CT1 3AS, ☎01227 786331
✉clerks@becket-chambers.co.uk
Call Date: Nov 1984, Gray's Inn
Qualifications: [RGN BA(Hons)(Law) LLM (Exon)]
redginton@becket-chambers.co.uk

EDHEM MISS EMMA

No5 Chambers
Greenwood House, 4-7 Salisbury Court, London EC4Y 8AA, ☎0845 210 5555
No5 Chambers
38 Queen Square, Bristol BS1 4QS, ☎0845 210 5555
No5 Chambers
Fountain Court, Steelhouse Lane, Birmingham B4 6DR, ☎0845 210 5555 ✉info@no5.com
Call Date: Oct 1993, Gray's Inn
Pupil Supervisor
Qualifications: [BSc (Hons)]
emma_edhem@yahoo.co.uk

EDIE MR ALASTAIR SCOTT KER

Garden Court Chambers
57-60 Lincoln's Inn Fields, London WC2A 3LJ, ☎020 7993 7600 ✉info@gclaw.co.uk
Call Date: Oct 1992, Middle Temple
Qualifications: [BA(Hons)(Kent)]
alastair@gclaw.co.uk

EDINGTON MRS FIONA ANNE RIDER

Thomas More Chambers
7 Lincoln's Inn Fields, London WC2A 3BP, ☎020 7404 7000
✉clerks@thomasmore.co.uk
Call Date: Oct 1998, Middle Temple
Qualifications: [MA (Hons)(Cantab) MSSc]
fedington@thomasmore.co.uk

Types of work: Administrative law, Constitutional and administrative law, Courts martial, Crime, European law, Family law, Foreign law, Human rights, International law, Military law, Public inquiries, War crimes tribunals

EDIS MR ANDREW JEREMY COULTER QC (1997)

2 Hare Court
Lower Ground, Ground, 1st & 2nd Floor, 2 Hare Court, Temple, London EC4Y 7BH, ☎020 7353 3982 ✉clerks@2harecourt.com
Atlantic Chambers
4-6 Cook Street, Liverpool L2 9QU, ☎0151 236 4421
✉info@atlanticchambers.co.uk
Call Date: July 1980, Middle Temple
Recorder
Qualifications: [MA (Oxon)]
clerks@2harecourt.com

EDIS MR ANGUS WILLIAM BUTLER QC (2008)

1 Crown Office Row
1 Crown Office Row, Temple, London EC4Y 7HH, ☎020 7797 7500
✉mail@1cor.com
Call Date: July 1985, Lincoln's Inn
Recorder
Qualifications: [BA(Oxon) DipLaw (Lond)]
william.edis@1cor.com

EDMONDS MR DANIEL

Fountain Court Chambers
Fountain Court, Temple, London EC4Y 9DH, ☎020 7583 3335
✉chambers@fountaincourt.co.uk
Call Date: Oct 2010, Inner Temple
Qualifications: [BA (Oxon) BA (Cantab) LLM (USA)]

EDMONDS MR MICHAEL JONATHAN

4 Breams Buildings
Chancery Lane, London EC4A 1HP, ☎020 7092 1900 ✉clerks@4bb.co.uk
Call Date: Nov 2000, Inner Temple
Qualifications: [BA (Lond) CPE]

E

EDMONDS MISS VICTORIA JANE

St Philips Chambers
55 Temple Row, Birmingham B2 5LS,
☎0121 246 7000 ✉clerks@st-philips.com
Call Date: July 2004, Gray's Inn
Qualifications: [LLB (B'ham)]
ves@st-philips.com

EDMONDSON MISS HARRIET JANE

30 Park Place
Cardiff CF10 3BS, ☎029 2039 8421
✉clerks@30parkplace.law.co.uk
Call Date: Nov 1997, Gray's Inn
Pupil Supervisor
Qualifications: [LLB (Wales)]
hje@30parkplace.co.uk

EDMUNDS MS LISA ELLEN

Number 7 Harrington Street Chambers
7 Harrington Street, Liverpool L2 9YH,
☎0151 242 0707 ✉clerks@7hs.co.uk
Call Date: Oct 2002, Inner Temple
Qualifications: [LLB]
lisa.edmunds@7hs.co.uk

EDUSEI MR FRANCIS VICTOR BURG

Kenworthy's Chambers
Arlington House, Bloom Street, Salford,
Manchester M3 6AJ, ☎0161 832 4036
Call Date: July 1989, Inner Temple
Qualifications: [LLB]
f.edusei@kenworthysbarristers.co.uk

EDWARDS MS ANN MERERID

Call Date: Oct 1991, Gray's Inn
Pupil Supervisor, Recorder
Qualifications: [LLB (Wales)]
edwards@paradise-sq.co.uk

EDWARDS MR ANTHONY

Chancery House Chambers
7 Lisbon Square, Leeds, West Yorkshire
LS1 4LY, ☎0113 244 6691
✉clerks@chanceryhouse.co.uk
Call Date: July 1999, Middle Temple
Qualifications: [BSc (Hons)]

EDWARDS MR CHARLES EDWIN

Clapham Law Chambers
85 Landor Road, Clapham North, London
SW9 9RT, ☎020 7978 8482
✉DANNY@claphamlawchambers.co.uk
Call Date: Nov 2002, Middle Temple
Qualifications: [BSc (Hons) (Lond)]

EDWARDS MR CHRISTOPHER HOWELL ASHOK

3 PB Barristers
3 Paper Buildings, Temple, London EC4Y 7EU,
☎020 7583 8055
3 PB Barristers
Royal Talbot House, 2 Victoria Street, Bristol,
Avon BS1 6BB, ☎0117 928 1520
3 PB Barristers
30 Christchurch Road, Bournemouth, Dorset
BH1 3PD, ☎01202 292102
✉clerks.bournemouth@3paper.co.uk
3 PB Barristers
4 St Peter Street, Winchester SO23 8BW,
☎01962 868884
✉clerks.winchester@3paper.co.uk
3 PB Barristers
23 Beaumont Street, Oxford OX1 2NP,
☎01865 793 736
Call Date: July 2008, Lincoln's Inn
Qualifications: [BA (Oxon) LLB MPhil (Oxon)]
christopher.edwards@3pb.co.uk

EDWARDS MR CHRISTOPHER JAMES

Old Square Chambers
10-11 Bedford Row, London WC1R 4BU,
☎020 7269 0300 ✉clerks@oldsquare.co.uk
Old Square Chambers
3 Orchard Court, St Augustine's Yard, Bristol
BS1 5DP, ☎0117 930 5100
✉clerks@oldsquare.co.uk
Call Date: Nov 2006, Gray's Inn
Qualifications: [BA]
edwards@oldsquare.co.uk

EDWARDS MR DANIEL HUGH

Dere Street Barristers
14 Toft Green, York YO1 6JT, ☎0844 3351551
✉clerks@derestreet.co.uk
York Chambers
Rotterdam House, 116 The Quayside,
Newcastle Upon Tyne NE1 3DY,
☎0191 206 4677
Call Date: Oct 1993, Lincoln's Inn
Pupil Supervisor
Qualifications: [BA (Hons)(York) Dip Law (Lond)]

EDWARDS MR DAVID LESLIE QC (2006)

7 King's Bench Walk
Ground Floor, 7 King's Bench Walk, Temple,
London EC4Y 7DS, ☎020 7910 8300
✉clerks@7kbw.co.uk
Call Date: July 1989, Lincoln's Inn
Qualifications: [MA (Cantab)]
dedwards@7kbw.co.uk

E

EDWARDS MR DENIS

Francis Taylor Building
Inner Temple, London EC4Y 7BY,
☎ 020 7353 8415 ✉ clerks@ftb.eu.com
Call Date: Oct 2002, Middle Temple
Qualifications: [LLB (Glas)]
✉ denis.edwards@ftb.eu.com

EDWARDS MR DICKON HARRISON

5 Pump Court
Ground Floor, 5 Pump Court, Temple, London EC4Y 7AP, ☎ 020 7353 2532
✉ clerks@5pumpcourt.com
Call Date: Nov 2004, Inner Temple
Qualifications: [BA Pembroke College University of Cambridge CPE]
✉ dickonedwards@5pumpcourt.com

EDWARDS MR GLYN TUDOR

St John's Chambers
101 Victoria Street, Bristol BS1 6PU,
☎ 0117 923 4700
✉ clerks@stjohnschambers.co.uk
Call Date: July 1987, Lincoln's Inn
Pupil Supervisor
Qualifications: [MA (Cantab) LLM (Cantab)]
✉ glyn.edwards@stjohnschambers.co.uk

EDWARDS MR HEATH IAN

9 Park Place
9 Park Place, Cardiff, South Glamorgan CF10 3DP, ☎ 029 2038 2731
✉ clerks@9parkplace.co.uk
Call Date: Oct 1996, Gray's Inn
Qualifications: [LLB (Warks)]
✉ hedwards@9parkplace.co.uk

EDWARDS MRS HELEN LOUISE

Five Paper
Ground Floor, 5 Paper Buildings, Temple, London EC4Y 7HB, ☎ 020 7815 3200
Call Date: July 2005, Lincoln's Inn
Qualifications: [LLB (Hons)]

EDWARDS MR IAIN FREDERICK

1 Mitre Court Buildings
1 Mitre Court Buildings, Temple, London EC4Y 7BS, ☎ 020 7452 8900
✉ clerks@1mcb.com
Call Date: Oct 2000, Middle Temple
Qualifications: [LLB (Hons) LLM]
✉ iain.edwards@1mcb.com

EDWARDS MR JACOB STEWART

1 Paper Buildings
1st Floor, 1 Paper Buildings, Temple, London EC4Y 7EP, ☎ 020 7353 3728
✉ clerks@onepaper.co.uk
Call Date: July 2007, Lincoln's Inn
Qualifications: [LLB (Notts)]
✉ jacobedwards@onepaper.co.uk

EDWARDS MISS JENNIFER MARY

13 King's Bench Walk
13 King's Bench Walk, Temple, London EC4Y 7EN, ☎ 020 7353 7204
✉ clerks@13kbw.co.uk
13 KBW
32 Beaumont Street, Oxford OX1 2NP,
☎ 01865 311066 ✉ clerks@13kbw.co.uk
Call Date: Oct 1992, Gray's Inn
Pupil Supervisor
Qualifications: [BA (Nott'm)]
✉ jedwards@13kbw.co.uk

EDWARDS MR JOHN DAVID

St Philips Chambers
55 Temple Row, Birmingham B2 5LS,
☎ 0121 246 7000 ✉ clerks@st-philips.com
Call Date: July 1983, Inner Temple
Pupil Supervisor, Recorder
Qualifications: [BA]
✉ jedwards@st-philips.co.uk

EDWARDS MR JONATHAN GWYN MENDUS

Cambria Chambers
The Coal Exchange, Mount Stuart Square, Cardiff Bay, Cardiff CF10 5EB,
☎ 0845 123 1234
✉ Info@cambriachambers.co.uk
Call Date: July 1981, Lincoln's Inn
Pupil Supervisor

EDWARDS MR JONATHAN WILLIAM

Westgate Chambers
64 High Street, Lewes, East Sussex BN7 1XG,
☎ 01273 480510
✉ clerks@westgate-chambers.co.uk
Call Date: Nov 1994, Lincoln's Inn
Qualifications: [LLB (Hons)]
✉ je@westgate-chambers.co.uk

EDWARDS MS KATHERINE LAURA

Outer Temple Chambers
The Outer Temple, 222 Strand, London WC2R 1BA, ☎ 020 7353 6381
✉ clerks@outertemple.com
Call Date: July 2006, Middle Temple
Qualifications: [BA (Hons) (Cantab)]
✉ katherine.edwards@outertemple.com

E

EDWARDS MR MARTIN RICHARD

39 Essex Street
London WC2R 3AT, ☎ 020 7832 1111
✉ clerks@39essex.com
82 King Street
Manchester M2 4WQ, ☎ 0161 870 9969
Call Date: Nov 1995, Inner Temple
Qualifications: [BA (Hons) MA]
✉ martin.edwards@39essex.com

EDWARDS MR MATTHEW STUART

East Anglian Chambers
Gresham House, 5 Museum Street, Ipswich, Suffolk IP1 1HQ, ☎ 01473 214481
✉ ipswich@ealaw.co.uk
East Anglian Chambers
53 North Hill, Colchester, Essex CO1 1QA, ☎ 01473 214481 ✉ colchester@ealaw.co.uk
East Anglian Chambers
140 New London Road, Chelmsford, Essex CM2 0AW, ☎ 01473 214481
✉ chelmsford@ealaw.co.uk
Call Date: July 2006, Gray's Inn
Qualifications: [BSc (Lond) MA (Lond)]
✉ matthewedwards@ealaw.co.uk

EDWARDS MR MICHAEL ALEXANDER

4 Paper Buildings
1st Floor, 4 Paper Buildings, Temple, London EC4Y 7EX, ☎ 020 7427 5200
✉ clerks@4pb.com
Call Date: July 2010, Inner Temple
Qualifications: [BA (Bris) CPE (Lond)]
✉ me@4pb.com

EDWARDS MR NIGEL DAVID HARRINGTON

Exchange Chambers
7 Ralli Courts, West Riverside, Manchester M3 5FT, ☎ 0161 833 2722
Exchange Chambers
One Derby Square, Derby Square, Liverpool L2 9XX, ☎ 0151 236 7747
✉ info@exchangechambers.co.uk
Exchange Chambers
Oxford House, Oxford Row, Leeds LS1 3BE, ☎ 0113 203 1970
✉ spencer@exchangechambers.co.uk
Call Date: Mar 1999, Lincoln's Inn
Qualifications: [MA (Hons)(Cantab)]
✉ edwards@exchangechambers.co.uk

EDWARDS MR NIGEL ROYSTON

St Paul's Chambers
5th Floor, St Paul's House, 23 Park Square South, Leeds LS1 2ND, ☎ 0113 245 5866
Call Date: Nov 1995, Lincoln's Inn
Qualifications: [LLB (Hons)(Sheff)]
✉ nedbar1@aol.com

EDWARDS MR OWEN MEIRION

Linenhall Chambers
1 Stanley Place, Chester CH1 2LU, ☎ 01244 348282
✉ clerks@linenhallchambers.co.uk
Call Date: Oct 1992, Lincoln's Inn
Pupil Supervisor
Qualifications: [LLB(Hons)(Wales)]
✉ clerks@1stanleyplace.co.uk

EDWARDS MISS PATRICIA ELIZABETH JEAN

20 Essex Street
London WC2R 3AL, ☎ 020 7842 1200
✉ clerks@20essexst.com
Call Date: Oct 2006, Inner Temple
Qualifications: [LLB (Lond) BCL (Oxon)]
✉ clerks@20essexst.com

EDWARDS MR PAUL

37 Park Square Chambers
37 Park Square, Leeds LS1 2NY, ☎ 0113 243 9422 ✉ chambers@no37.co.uk
Call Date: Mar 2002, Lincoln's Inn
Qualifications: [LLB (Hons)]
✉ chambers@no37.co.uk

EDWARDS MR PETER ALAN

Devereux Chambers
Queen Elizabeth Building, Temple, London EC4Y 9BS, ☎ 020 7353 7534
✉ clerks@devchambers.co.uk
Call Date: Oct 1992, Inner Temple
Qualifications: [BA (Kent)]
✉ edwards@devchambers.co.uk

EDWARDS MR PHILIP DOUGLAS QC (2010)

Francis Taylor Building
Inner Temple, London EC4Y 7BY, ☎ 020 7353 8415 ✉ clerks@ftb.eu.com
Call Date: Nov 1992, Lincoln's Inn
Pupil Supervisor
Qualifications: [LLB (Hons)(B'ham) Dip EC Law (Lond)]
✉ douglas.edwardsqc@ftb.eu.com

EDWARDS MR RICHARD JULIAN HENSHAW

3 Verulam Buildings
London WC1R 5NT, ☎020 7831 8441
✉chambers@3vb.com
Call Date: Oct 1993, Middle Temple
Pupil Supervisor
Qualifications: [MA (Cantab) M Phil (Cantab)]
✉redwards@3vb.com

EDWARDS MISS SARAH LOUISE ELIZABETH

Queen Elizabeth Building
3rd Floor, Queen Elizabeth Building, Temple, London EC4Y 9BS, ☎020 7797 7837
✉clerks@qeb.co.uk
Call Date: Nov 1990, Inner Temple
Qualifications: [MA (Cantab)]
✉s.edwards@qeb.co.uk

EDWARDS MR SIMON JOHN MAY

39 Essex Street
London WC2R 3AT, ☎020 7832 1111
✉clerks@39essex.com
82 King Street
Manchester M2 4WQ, ☎0161 870 9969
Call Date: Nov 1978, Middle Temple
Qualifications: [MA (Cantab)]
✉simon.edwards@39essex.com

EDWARDS MISS SUSAN ANN

Call Date: Nov 1998, Lincoln's Inn
Qualifications: [LLB (Hons) (Jmu)]
✉susan.edwards2@btinternet.com

EDWARDS PROF SUSAN SHEILA MARIA

1 Gray's Inn Square
Ground Floor, 1 Gray's Inn Square, London WC1R 5AA, ☎020 7405 0001
Call Date: July 2004, Inner Temple

EDWARDS MR THOMAS CHARLES

Old Bailey Chambers
15 Old Bailey, London EC4M 7EF,
☎020 3008 6404
✉clerks@15oldbaileychambers.com
9-12 Bell Yard
London WC2A 2JR, ☎020 7400 1800
✉clerks@9-12bellyard.com
Call Date: Mar 2008, Lincoln's Inn
Qualifications: [LLB (Lond)]

EDWARDS MR THOMAS HUW ELGAN

St Johns Buildings
24a - 28 St John Street, Manchester M3 4DJ,
☎0161 214 1500
✉clerk@stjohnsbuildings.co.uk
Call Date: July 2009, Gray's Inn
Qualifications: [BA]

EDWARDS MR WILLIAM JOHN

3 Verulam Buildings
London WC1R 5NT, ☎020 7831 8441
✉chambers@3vb.com
Call Date: Oct 2002, Middle Temple
Pupil Supervisor
Qualifications: [BA (Cantab)]
✉wedwards@3vb.com

EDWARDS-STUART DR ANNA COLETTE

11 South Square
1st Floor, 11 South Square, Gray's Inn, London WC1R 5EY, ☎020 7405 1222
✉clerks@11southsquare.com
Call Date: Oct 2002, Lincoln's Inn
Pupil Supervisor
Qualifications: [MA (Cantab) DPhil (Oxon) PgDL]
✉aedwards-stuart@11southsquare.com

EELEY MISS REBECCA ELIZABETH ANTONIA

9 St John Street
Manchester M3 4DN, ☎0161 955 9000
✉civilclerks@9sjs.com / criminalclerks@9sjs.com
Call Date: Oct 2001, Middle Temple
Qualifications: [BA (Hons) (Oxon) BCL (Oxon)]

EGAN MR EUGENE CHRISTOPHER

30 Park Place
Cardiff CF10 3BS, ☎029 2039 8421
✉clerks@30parkplace.law.co.uk
Call Date: Oct 1993, Lincoln's Inn
Qualifications: [MA (Oxon)]
✉ece@30parkplace.co.uk

EGAN MR PATRICK MANUS DERMOT

Thomas More Chambers
7 Lincoln's Inn Fields, London WC2A 3BP,
☎020 7404 7000
✉clerks@thomasmore.co.uk
Call Date: Nov 1991, Middle Temple
Qualifications: [LLB (Hons)]
✉megan@thomasmore.co.uk

E

EGBUNA MR ROBERT OBIORA

1 High Pavement
Nottingham NG1 1HF, ☎0115 941 8218
✉clerks@1highpavement.co.uk
Call Date: Nov 1988, Gray's Inn
Pupil Supervisor
Qualifications: [LLB]
robertegbuna@1highpavement.co.uk

EGERTON MISS CHRISTINE ANNE

KBW
The Engine House, No 1 Foundry Square, Leeds LS11 5DL, ☎0113 297 1200
✉clerks@kbwchambers.com
Call Date: Oct 1992, Inner Temple
Pupil Supervisor
Qualifications: [LLB (Lond) LLM (Lond)]
cae@kbwchambers.com

EGLETON MR RICHARD WILDMAN

Pallant Chambers
12 North Pallant, Chichester, West Sussex PO19 1TQ, ☎01243 784538
✉clerks@pallantchambers.co.uk
Call Date: July 1981, Gray's Inn
Pupil Supervisor
Qualifications: [MA (Oxon)]
regleton@pallantchambers.co.uk, richardengleton@gmail.com

EICKE MR TIM QC (2011)

Essex Court Chambers
24 Lincoln's Inn Fields, London WC2A 3EG, ☎020 7813 8000
✉clerksroom@essexcourt.net
Call Date: Oct 1993, Middle Temple
Pupil Supervisor
Qualifications: [LLB (Hons)(Dundee)]
teicke@essexcourt.net

EIDINOW MR JOHN SAMUEL CHRISTOPHER

New Square Chambers
12 New Square, Lincoln's Inn, London WC2A 3SW, ☎020 7419 8000
✉robin.hollington@newsquarechambers.co.uk
Call Date: Nov 1992, Middle Temple
Qualifications: [BA (Hons) Dip Law]
john.eidinow@newsquarechambers.co.uk

EILLEDGE MISS AMANDA GAIL CAROLINE

11 Stone Buildings
11 Stone Buildings, Lincoln's Inn, London WC2A 3TG, ☎020 7831 6381
✉clerks@11sb.com
Call Date: Oct 1991, Lincoln's Inn
Pupil Supervisor
Qualifications: [BA (Hons) BCL (Oxon)]
eilledge@11sb.com

EISSA MR ADRIAN NADIR

25 Bedford Row
London WC1R 4HD, ☎020 7067 1500
✉clerks@25bedfordrow.com
Call Date: Nov 1988, Inner Temple
Qualifications: [LLB (Warw)]

EKANEY MR NKUMBE QC (2011)

Albion Chambers
Broad Street, Bristol BS1 1DR, ☎0117 927 2144
✉clerks@albionchambers.co.uk
Walnut House
63 St. David's Hill, Exeter, Devon EX4 4DW, ☎01392 279751
✉clerks@walnuthouse.co.uk
Call Date: Oct 1990, Gray's Inn
Pupil Supervisor
Qualifications: [LLB (Hons)(Bris)]
nkumbe.ekaney@albionchambers.co.uk

EKELEDO MS PEGGY NWAKAEGO

Tooks Chambers
81 Farringdon Street, London EC4A 4BL, ☎020 7842 7575 ✉clerks@tooks.co.uk
Call Date: Nov 2007, Lincoln's Inn
Qualifications: [BSc (Hons)]

EKLUND MR GRAHAM NICHOLAS QC (2002)

Four New Square
Four New Square, Lincoln's Inn, London WC2A 3RJ, ☎020 7822 2000
✉barristers@4newsquare.com
Call Date: May 1984, Inner Temple
Qualifications: [BA LLB (Hons)(Auckland) FCIArb]
g.eklund@4newsquare.com

EL GADHY MR AMEAN

1 Pump Court
Elm Court, Temple, London EC4Y 7AB, ☎020 7842 7070
✉(name)@pumpcourt.co.uk
Call Date: Mar 2008, Lincoln's Inn
Qualifications: [LLB (L'pool)]
ame@1pumpcourt.co.uk

ELAGAB MR YOUSIF OMER

23 Essex Street
London WC2R 3AA, ☎020 7413 0353
✉clerks@23es.com
Call Date: July 2010, Gray's Inn
Qualifications: [BA LLM]
✉clerks@23es.com

ELCOMBE MR NICHOLAS JOHN

East Anglian Chambers
53 North Hill, Colchester, Essex CO1 1QA,
☎01473 214481 ✉colchester@ealaw.co.uk
East Anglian Chambers
140 New London Road, Chelmsford, Essex
CM2 0AW, ☎01473 214481
✉chelmsford@ealaw.co.uk
East Anglian Chambers
15 The Close, Norwich, Norfolk NR1 4DZ,
☎01473 214481 ✉norwich@ealaw.co.uk
East Anglian Chambers
Gresham House, 5 Museum Street, Ipswich,
Suffolk IP1 1HQ, ☎01473 214481
✉ipswich@ealaw.co.uk
Call Date: July 1987, Inner Temple
Pupil Supervisor
Qualifications: [LLB]
✉nickelcombe@ealaw.co.uk

ELDER MISS FIONA ANN MORAG

Albion Chambers
Broad Street, Bristol BS1 1DR,
☎0117 927 2144
✉clerks@albionchambers.co.uk
Call Date: July 1988, Gray's Inn
Pupil Supervisor
Qualifications: [LLB (Hons)(Sheff)]
✉fiona.elder@albionchambers.co.uk

ELDERGILL MR EDMUND MALCOLM

1 Pump Court
Elm Court, Temple, London EC4Y 7AB,
☎020 7842 7070
✉(name)@pumpcourt.co.uk
Call Date: Nov 1991, Inner Temple
Qualifications: [BA (UEA) Dip Law PCGE]
✉ee@1pumpcourt.co.uk

ELDRIDGE MR MARK

5 Pump Court
Ground Floor, 5 Pump Court, Temple, London
EC4Y 7AP, ☎020 7353 2532
✉clerks@5pumpcourt.com
Call Date: July 1982, Gray's Inn
Pupil Supervisor
Qualifications: [BA (Hons)(Lancs) Dip Law]

ELEFTHERIADIS DR PAVLOS

Francis Taylor Building
Inner Temple, London EC4Y 7BY,
☎020 7353 8415 ✉clerks@ftb.eu.com
Call Date: July 2006, Lincoln's Inn
Qualifications: [BA (Athens) LLM PhD (Cantab) MA (Oxon)]
✉Pavlos.eleftheriadis@ftb.eu.com

ELESINNLA MR AYOADE

Igbobi Chambers
c/o Lawyers' Club, 3rd Floor, 218 Strand,
London WC2R 1AT, ☎0203 2867626
✉aelesinnla@igbobichambers.com
Call Date: Nov 2000, Inner Temple
Qualifications: [LLB (Hons)]

ELEY MISS JOANNE MARY

1 Paper Buildings
1st Floor, 1 Paper Buildings, Temple, London
EC4Y 7EP, ☎020 7353 3728
✉clerks@onepaper.co.uk
Call Date: Oct 1997, Middle Temple
Qualifications: [BA (Hull) CPE]

ELEY MR JOHNATHAN DESMOND HUGH

KCH Garden Square
1 Oxford Street, Nottingham NG1 5BH,
☎0115 941 8851
✉clerks@kchgardensquare.co.uk
Call Date: July 1987, Middle Temple
Qualifications: [BA]
✉JEley@kchgardensquare.co.uk

ELFIELD MISS LAURA ELAINE

The Chambers of Grahame Aldous QC
9 Gough Square, London EC4A 3DG,
☎020 7832 0500
✉clerks@9goughsquare.co.uk
Call Date: Mar 1996, Gray's Inn
Qualifications: [BA]
✉lelfield@9goughsquare.co.uk

ELFORD MS CAROLINE JAYNE

Queen Square Chambers
56 Queen Square, Bristol BS1 4PR,
☎0117 921 1966 ✉crime@qs-c.co.uk
Call Date: Oct 2002, Inner Temple
Qualifications: [BMus (B'ham) MA (Bris)]
✉cje@qs-c.co.uk

E

ELGOT MR HOWARD CHARLES

Park Lane Plowden
19 Westgate, Leeds LS1 2RD,
☎0113 228 5049
✉clerks@parklaneplowden.co.uk
Call Date: July 1974, Gray's Inn
Pupil Supervisor
Qualifications: [BA BCL (Oxon)]
howard.elgot@parklaneplowden.co.uk

ELIA MISS ELENA

23 Essex Street
London WC2R 3AA, ☎020 7413 0353
✉clerks@23es.com
Call Date: Oct 2009, Middle Temple
Qualifications: [LLB (Hons) (Lond)]
elenaelia@23es.com

ELIAS MR DAVID

9 Park Place
9 Park Place, Cardiff, South Glamorgan
CF10 3DP, ☎029 2038 2731
✉clerks@9parkplace.co.uk
Call Date: May 1994, Inner Temple
Pupil Supervisor
Qualifications: [MA (Cantab)]
delias@9parkplace.co.uk,
davidelias9parkplace@hotmail.com

ELIAS MR GERARD QC (1984)

Farrar's Building
Farrar's Building, Temple, London EC4Y 7BD,
☎020 7583 9241
✉Chambers@farrarsbuilding.co.uk
9 Park Place
9 Park Place, Cardiff, South Glamorgan
CF10 3DP, ☎029 2038 2731
✉clerks@9parkplace.co.uk
Call Date: July 1968, Inner Temple
Recorder
Qualifications: [LLB]
gelias@farrarsbuilding.co.uk

ELIAS MR ROBERT WILLOUGHBY

Lincoln House Chambers
Tower 12, The Avenue North, Spinningfields,
18-22 Bridge Street, Manchester M3 3BZ,
☎0161 832 5701
✉info@lincolnhousechambers.com
Call Date: July 1979, Middle Temple
Pupil Supervisor
Qualifications: [LLB (Hons) (Sheff)]
robert.elias@lincolnhousechambers.com

ELIAS MR THOMAS PATRICK

Serle Court
6 New Square, Lincoln's Inn, London
WC2A 3QS, ☎020 7242 6105
✉clerks@serlecourt.co.uk
Call Date: Oct 2008, Inner Temple
Qualifications: [BA MPhil MA PhD (Cantab)]
telias@serlecourt.co.uk

ELJADI MR OMAR MUKHTAR

Atkin Chambers
1 Atkin Building, Gray's Inn, London
WC1R 5AT, ☎020 7404 0102
✉clerks@atkinchambers.com
Call Date: July 2009, Middle Temple
Qualifications: [BA (Hons) (Oxon) BCL (Oxon)]

ELKINGTON MR BENJAMIN MICHAEL GORDON QC (2012)

Four New Square
Four New Square, Lincoln's Inn, London
WC2A 3RJ, ☎020 7822 2000
✉barristers@4newsquare.com
Call Date: Oct 1996, Gray's Inn
Pupil Supervisor
Qualifications: [MA (Cantab) LLM (Virginia)]
b.elkington@4newsquare.com

ELLENBOGEN MISS NAOMI LISA QC (2010)

Littleton Chambers
3 King's Bench Walk North, Temple, London
EC4Y 7HR, ☎020 7797 8600
✉fschneider@littletonchambers.co.uk
Call Date: Oct 1992, Gray's Inn
Pupil Supervisor
Qualifications: [MA (Oxon)]
nellenbogen@littletonchambers.co.uk

ELLERAY MR ANTHONY JOHN QC (1993)

Exchange Chambers
7 Ralli Courts, West Riverside, Manchester
M3 5FT, ☎0161 833 2722
Exchange Chambers
One Derby Square, Derby Square, Liverpool
L2 9XX, ☎0151 236 7747
✉info@exchangechambers.co.uk
Call Date: July 1977, Inner Temple
Recorder
Qualifications: [MA (Cantab)]
ellerayqc@exchangechambers.co.uk

E

ELLIN MISS NINA CAROLINE

6 Pump Court
1st Floor, 6 Pump Court, Temple, London EC4Y 7AR, ☎020 7797 8400
✉richardconstable@6pumpcourt.co.uk
6 Pump Court Chambers
6-8 Mill Street, Maidstone, Kent ME15 6XH, ☎01622 688094
✉annexe@6pumpcourt.co.uk
Call Date: Nov 1994, Inner Temple
Qualifications: [LLB (Lond) Maitrise en Droit Francais (France)]
✉ninaellin@6pumpcourt.co.uk

ELLIOTT MR COLIN DOUGLAS

King's Bench and Godolphin (KBG)Chambers
115 North Hill, Plymouth, Devon PL4 8JY, ☎01752 221551
✉clerks@kbgchambers.co.uk
Call Date: July 1987, Gray's Inn
Qualifications: [BSc (Lond) Dip Law]
✉theclerks@godolphinchambers.co.uk

ELLIOTT MR EDWARD ANTHONY JOHN

Garden Court Chambers
57-60 Lincoln's Inn Fields, London WC2A 3LJ, ☎020 7993 7600 ✉info@gclaw.co.uk
Call Date: Oct 2000, Gray's Inn
Qualifications: [LLB (Lond)]

ELLIOTT MISS ELIZABETH JULIE-ANN

Queen Square Chambers
56 Queen Square, Bristol BS1 4PR, ☎0117 921 1966 ✉crime@qs-c.co.uk
Sovereign Chambers
46 Park Place, Leeds LS1 2RY, ☎0113 245 1841
✉clerks@sovereignchambers.co.uk
Call Date: July 2001, Gray's Inn
Qualifications: [LLB]

ELLIOTT MR ERIC ALAN QC (2006)

Trinity Chambers
The Custom House, 39 Quayside, Newcastle Upon Tyne NE1 3DE, ☎0191 232 1927
✉info@trinitychambers.co.uk
Trinity Chambers
Multi Media Exchange, 72-80 Corporation Road, Middlesbrough TS1 2RF, ☎01642 247569
✉info@trinitychambers.co.uk
York Chambers
Rotterdam House, 116 The Quayside, Newcastle Upon Tyne NE1 3DY, ☎0191 206 4677
Sovereign Chambers
46 Park Place, Leeds LS1 2RY, ☎0113 245 1841
✉clerks@sovereignchambers.co.uk
Call Date: July 1974, Gray's Inn
Recorder
Qualifications: [LLB]
✉e.elliottqc@trinitychambers.co.uk

ELLIOTT MR JASON

Dere Street Barristers
33 Broad Chare, Newcastle Upon Tyne NE1 3DQ, ☎0844 3351551
✉clerks@derestreet.co.uk
Call Date: Oct 1993, Inner Temple
Qualifications: [BA]
✉clerks@broadcharechambers.co.uk

ELLIOTT MISS MARGOT MARY

Regency Chambers
45 Priestgate, Peterborough PE1 1LB, ☎01733 315215
✉clerks@regencychambers.law.co.uk
Regency Chambers
Sheraton House, Castle Park, Cambridge CB3 0AX, ☎01223 301517
Call Date: Nov 1989, Gray's Inn
Pupil Supervisor
Qualifications: [LLB (Newc)]
✉clerks@regencychambers.law.co.uk

ELLIOTT MR MARK DANIEL

3 PB Barristers
3 Paper Buildings, Temple, London EC4Y 7EU, ☎020 7583 8055
3 PB Barristers
30 Christchurch Road, Bournemouth, Dorset BH1 3PD, ☎01202 292102
✉clerks.bournemouth@3paper.co.uk
3 PB Barristers
4 St Peter Street, Winchester SO23 8BW, ☎01962 868884
✉clerks.winchester@3paper.co.uk
3 PB Barristers
Royal Talbot House, 2 Victoria Street, Bristol, Avon BS1 6BB, ☎0117 928 1520
3 PB Barristers
23 Beaumont Street, Oxford OX1 2NP, ☎01865 793 736
Call Date: July 2007, Lincoln's Inn
Qualifications: [BA (Hons) LLB]
✉mark.elliott@3pb.co.uk

E

ELLIOTT MR NICHOLAS BLETHYN QC (1995)

3 Verulam Buildings
London WC1R 5NT, ☎020 7831 8441
✉chambers@3vb.com
Call Date: July 1972, Gray's Inn
Qualifications: [LLB]
nelliott@3vb.com

ELLIOTT MR RICHARD ANDREW

3 Temple Gardens
Lower Ground Floor, 3 Temple Gardens, Temple, London EC4Y 9AU, ☎020 7353 3102
✉clerks@3tg.co.uk
Call Date: Oct 2001, Middle Temple
Pupil Supervisor
Qualifications: [BA (Hons)(Lond) CPE]

ELLIOTT MS SARAH JULIA

Doughty Street Chambers
5th Floor, Broad Quay House, Prince Street, Bristol BS1 4DJ, ☎01179 058 717
Doughty Street Chambers
Pall Mall Court, 61-67 King Street, Manchester M2 4PD, ☎0161 618 1066
Doughty Street Chambers
53-54 Doughty Street, London WC1N 2LS, ☎020 7404 1313
✉enquiries@doughtystreet.co.uk
Call Date: Oct 1996, Gray's Inn
Qualifications: [BA (Sussex)]
s.elliott@doughtystreet.co.uk

ELLIOTT MR SIMON PETER

Chambers of Marion Smullen and Kerim Fuad QC
1 Inner Temple Lane, London EC4Y 1AF, ☎020 7427 4400 ✉clerks@1itl.com
Call Date: July 2007, Inner Temple
Qualifications: [LLB (Nott'm)]

ELLIOTT MR STEVEN BALLANTYNE

One Essex Court
Ground Floor, One Essex Court, Temple, London EC4Y 9AR, ☎020 7583 2000
✉clerks@oeclaw.co.uk
Call Date: July 2001, Lincoln's Inn
Pupil Supervisor
Qualifications: [BA (Hons) JD (Hons) DPhil]
selliott@oeclaw.co.uk

ELLIOTT MR TIMOTHY STANLEY QC (1992)

Keating Chambers
15 Essex Street, London WC2R 3AA, ☎020 7544 2600
✉clerks@keatingchambers.com
Call Date: July 1975, Middle Temple
Qualifications: [MA (Oxon)]

ELLIS MR AIDAN BRIND

Temple Garden Chambers
1 Harcourt Buildings, Temple, London EC4Y 9DA, ☎020 7583 1315
✉clerks@tgchambers.com
Call Date: July 2005, Middle Temple
Qualifications: [LLM Cantab BA (Hons) Cantab]
aidan.ellis@tgchambers.com

ELLIS MISS CATHERINE ANNE

Oriel Chambers
14 Water Street, Liverpool, Merseyside L2 8TD, ☎0151 236 7191
✉clerks@orielchambers.co.uk
Oriel Chambers
18 Ribblesdale Place, Preston PR1 3NA, ☎01772 254 764
✉clerks@oriel-chambers.co.uk
Call Date: July 1987, Lincoln's Inn
Qualifications: [LLB (Lanc)]
catherine.ellis@orielchambers.co.uk

ELLIS MISS DIANA QC (2001)

25 Bedford Row
London WC1R 4HD, ☎020 7067 1500
✉clerks@25bedfordrow.com
Call Date: July 1978, Inner Temple
Recorder
Qualifications: [LLB Hons (Lond)]
dellis@25bedfordrow.com

ELLIS MR HENRY JAMES

Stone Chambers
4 Field Court, Gray's Inn, London WC1R 5EF, ☎020 7440 6900
✉clerks@stonechambers.com
Call Date: Nov 2008, Lincoln's Inn
Qualifications: [BA (Cantab) CPE UCU]
henry.ellis@stonechambers.com

ELLIS DR PETER SIMON

Seven Bedford Row
7 Bedford Row, London WC1R 4BS, ☎020 7242 3555 ✉clerks@7br.co.uk
Call Date: Nov 1997, Middle Temple
Pupil Supervisor
Qualifications: [MB MRCP Dip Law DHMSA CEDR BS (Lond)]

ELLIS MISS RACHEL

187 Fleet Street
London EC4A 2AT, ☎020 7430 7430
✉chambers@187fleetstreet.com
Call Date: Oct 2004, Lincoln's Inn
Qualifications: [LLB (Hons) Nott'm]
rachelellis@187fleetstreet.com

E

ELLIS MISS ROSALIND MORAG QC (2006)

Cornerstone Barristers
2-3 Gray's Inn Square, Gray's Inn, London WC1R 5JH, ☎ 020 7242 4986
✉ chambers@2-3gis.co.uk
Call Date: July 1984, Gray's Inn
Qualifications: [MA (Cantab)]
✉ mellis@2-3gis.co.uk, morage@cornerstonebarristers.com

Types of work: Common land, Highways, Local authorities, Local government and public services, Planning

ELLIS MISS SARAH LOUISE

9-12 Bell Yard
London WC2A 2JR, ☎ 020 7400 1800
✉ clerks@9-12bellyard.com
Call Date: Nov 1989, Gray's Inn
Qualifications: [LLB (Wales)]
✉ s.ellis@9-12bellyard.com

ELLISON MR MARK CHRISTOPHER QC (2008)

QEB Hollis Whiteman
1-2 Laurence Pountney Hill, London EC4R 0EU, ☎ 020 7933 8855
✉ barristers@qebhw.co.uk
Call Date: Nov 1979, Gray's Inn
Recorder
Qualifications: [LLB (Wales)]
✉ barristers@qebhw.co.uk

ELLISON MR ROBERT LEONARD

5 King's Bench Walk
5 King's Bench Walk, Temple, London EC4Y 7DN, ☎ 020 7353 5638
✉ clerks@5kbw.co.uk
Call Date: Oct 1996, Middle Temple
Qualifications: [LLB (Hons)(Lond)]
✉ robert.ellison@5kbw.co.uk

ELMER MR THOMAS WILLIAM

Seven Bedford Row
7 Bedford Row, London WC1R 4BS, ☎ 020 7242 3555 ✉ clerks@7br.co.uk
Call Date: Oct 2001, Middle Temple
Qualifications: [BA (Hons) CPE]
✉ telmer@7br.co.uk

ELTON MR EDWARD SCOTT OLIVER

12 College Place
Fauvelle Buildings, 12 College Place, Southampton SO15 2FE, ☎ 023 8032 0320
✉ clerks@12cp.co.uk
Call Date: Nov 2000, Gray's Inn
Pupil Supervisor
Qualifications: [LLB (Lond)]
✉ eelton@12cp.co.uk

ELVIDGE MR JOHN COWIE QC (2010)

Dere Street Barristers
14 Toft Green, York YO1 6JT, ☎ 0844 3351551
✉ clerks@derestreet.co.uk
York Chambers
Rotterdam House, 116 The Quayside, Newcastle Upon Tyne NE1 3DY, ☎ 0191 206 4677
Dere Street Barristers
33 Broad Chare, Newcastle Upon Tyne NE1 3DQ, ☎ 0844 3351551
✉ clerks@derestreet.co.uk
Call Date: Nov 1988, Gray's Inn
Pupil Supervisor
Qualifications: [LLB (Newc)]
✉ clerks@yorkchambers.co.uk

ELVIN MR DAVID JOHN QC (2000)

Landmark Chambers
180 Fleet Street, London EC4A 2HG, ☎ 020 7430 1221
✉ clerks@landmarkchambers.co.uk
Call Date: Nov 1983, Middle Temple
Qualifications: [BA (Oxon) BCL (Oxon)]
✉ delvin@landmarkchambers.co.uk

ELWICK MR BRYAN MARTIN

1 High Pavement
Nottingham NG1 1HF, ☎ 0115 941 8218
✉ clerks@1highpavement.co.uk
Call Date: July 1981, Middle Temple
Qualifications: [LLB (Nott'm)]
✉ martinelwick@1highpavement.co.uk

EMANUEL MR DAVID HENRY

Garden Court Chambers
57-60 Lincoln's Inn Fields, London WC2A 3LJ, ☎ 020 7993 7600 ✉ info@gclaw.co.uk
Call Date: Nov 1996, Gray's Inn
Qualifications: [LLB (Hons) MPhil (Cantab)]
✉ davide@gclaw.co.uk

E

EMANUEL MR MARK PERING WOLFF

29 Bedford Row Chambers
London WC1R 4HE, ☎ 020 7404 1044
✉ clerks@29br.co.uk
Call Date: Nov 1985, Inner Temple
Pupil Supervisor
Qualifications: [BA (Hons)]
✉ memanuel@29br.co.uk

EMERSON MR PAUL MICHAEL

Lamb Chambers
Lamb Building, Elm Court, Temple, London EC4Y 7AS, ☎ 020 7797 8300
✉ info@lambchambers.co.uk
Call Date: July 1984, Middle Temple
Pupil Supervisor
Qualifications: [LLB]
✉ paulemerson@lambchambers.co.uk

EMERSON MR WILLIAM BRADLEY

Pallant Chambers
12 North Pallant, Chichester, West Sussex PO19 1TQ, ☎ 01243 784538
✉ clerks@pallantchambers.co.uk
Call Date: Nov 1992, Middle Temple
Pupil Supervisor
Qualifications: [LLB (Hons)]
✉ clerks@pallantchambers.co.uk

EMERY MR ANDREW JAMES

Malins Chambers
115 Temple Chambers, Temple Avenue, London EC4Y 0DA, ☎ 020 7353 8868
✉ malins@btinternet.com
Call Date: Mar 2004, Lincoln's Inn
Qualifications: [MA (Oxon) LLM (Lond)]
✉ andrew.emery@malinschambers.com

EMERY MR PHILIP ANTHONY GILES

Oriel Chambers
14 Water Street, Liverpool, Merseyside L2 8TD, ☎ 0151 236 7191
✉ clerks@orielchambers.co.uk
Call Date: Mar 2008, Middle Temple
Qualifications: [LLB (Hons) (L'pool)]

EMLYN JONES MR WILLIAM NICHOLAS

3 Raymond Buildings
3 Raymond Buildings, Gray's Inn, London WC1R 5BH, ☎ 020 7400 6400
✉ clerks@3rblaw.com
Call Date: Oct 1996, Inner Temple
Pupil Supervisor
Qualifications: [LLB (So'ton)]
✉ william.emlynjones@3raymondbuildings.com

EMMANUEL MISS JOYCE CLARE

Kenworthy's Chambers
Arlington House, Bloom Street, Salford, Manchester M3 6AJ, ☎ 0161 832 4036
Call Date: Oct 2001, Middle Temple
Qualifications: [LLB (Hons)(L'pool)]
✉ j.emmanuel@kenworthysbarristers.co.uk

EMMERSON MR BENEDICT QC (2000)

Matrix Chambers
Griffin Building, Gray's Inn, London WC1R 5LN, ☎ 020 7404 3447
✉ matrix@matrixlaw.co.uk / Iscott@matrixlaw.co.uk
Call Date: Nov 1986, Middle Temple
Qualifications: [LLB (Bristol)]
✉ benemmerson@matrixlaw.co.uk

EMMERSON MISS HEATHER LOUISE

4-5 Gray's Inn Square
Gray's Inn, London WC1R 5AH,
☎ 020 7404 5252 ✉ clerks@4-5.co.uk
Call Date: Oct 2009, Lincoln's Inn
Qualifications: [BA (Cantab)]
✉ clerks@4-5.co.uk

EMMETT DR LAURENCE ARTHUR HENNESSEY

One Essex Court
Ground Floor, One Essex Court, Temple, London EC4Y 9AR, ☎ 020 7583 2000
✉ clerks@oeclaw.co.uk
Call Date: Nov 2004, Lincoln's Inn
Qualifications: [PgDl BA DPhil]
✉ lemmett@oeclaw.co.uk

EMSLEY-SMITH MRS ROSALIND LUCY

Deans Court Chambers
24 St John Street, Manchester M3 4DF,
☎ 0161 214 6000 ✉ clerks@deanscourt.co.uk
Deans Court Chambers
101 Walker Street, Preston PR1 2RR,
☎ 01772 565 600
✉ preston@deanscourt.co.uk
Call Date: Oct 2001, Gray's Inn
Qualifications: [LLB (Manch)]
✉ emsley-smith@deanscourt.co.uk

EMSLIE MR SIMON GEORGE ANDREW

Albion Chambers
Broad Street, Bristol BS1 1DR,
☎0117 927 2144
✉clerks@albionchambers.co.uk
Call Date: July 2007, Inner Temple
Qualifications: [MA LLB (Lond)]
simon.emslie@albionchambers.co.uk

ENGELMAN MR MARK TREVOR

Hardwicke
New Square, Lincoln's Inn, London
WC2A 3SB, ☎020 7242 2523
✉enquiries@hardwicke.co.uk
Call Date: Nov 1987, Gray's Inn
Pupil Supervisor
Qualifications: [BSc Dip Law]
mark.engelman@hardwicke.co.uk

ENGELMAN MR PHILIP

Cloisters
1 Pump Court, Temple, London EC4Y 7AA,
☎020 7827 4000 ✉clerks@cloisters.com
Trinity Chambers
Multi Media Exchange, 72-80 Corporation Road, Middlesbrough TS1 2RF,
☎01642 247569
✉info@trinitychambers.co.uk
Trinity Chambers
The Custom House, 39 Quayside, Newcastle Upon Tyne NE1 3DE, ☎0191 232 1927
✉info@trinitychambers.co.uk
Call Date: July 1979, Gray's Inn
Pupil Supervisor
Qualifications: [LLB (Lond)]
p.engelman@trinitychambers.co.uk

ENGLAND MISS LAURA PATRICIA

St Johns Buildings
24a - 28 St John Street, Manchester M3 4DJ,
☎0161 214 1500
✉clerk@stjohnsbuildings.co.uk
16 Winckley Square
Preston PR1 3JJ, ☎01772 256100
St Johns Buildings Liverpool
8th Floor India Buildings, Water Street, Liverpool L2 0XG, ☎0151 243 6000
✉clerk@stjohnsbuildings.co.uk
Call Date: Oct 2008, Middle Temple
Qualifications: [LLB (Hons) (Manch)]
laura.england@stjohnsbuildings.co.uk

ENGLAND MRS LISA JOHANNA LOUISE

Guildhall Chambers Portsmouth
Prudential Buildings, 16 Guildhall Walk, Portsmouth, Hampshire PO1 2DE,
☎023 9275 2400
✉clerks@gcp-barristers.com
Call Date: Nov 1992, Gray's Inn
Pupil Supervisor
Qualifications: [LLB (Hons)(Lond)]
GCPClerks@fsmail.net

ENGLAND MR WILLIAM EDWARD CHARLES

Carmelite Chambers
9 Carmelite Street, London EC4Y 0DR,
☎020 7936 6300
✉clerks@carmelitechambers.co.uk
Call Date: Nov 1991, Inner Temple
Qualifications: [LLB LLM (Lond)]
wengland@carmelitechambers.co.uk

ENGLEHART MR ROBERT MICHAEL QC (1986)

Blackstone Chambers
Blackstone House, Temple, London
EC4Y 9BW, ☎020 7583 1770
✉clerks@blackstonechambers.com
Call Date: Nov 1969, Middle Temple
Recorder
Qualifications: [MA (Oxon) LLM (USA)]
robertenglehart@blackstonechambers.com

ENGLISH MISS CAROLINE FRANCES

Furnival Chambers
32 Furnival Street, London EC4A 1JQ,
☎020 7405 3232
Call Date: Nov 1989, Inner Temple
Qualifications: [LLB]

ENGLISH MR RICHARD HENRY

Lincoln House Chambers
Tower 12, The Avenue North, Spinningfields, 18-22 Bridge Street, Manchester M3 3BZ,
☎0161 832 5701
✉info@lincolnhousechambers.com
Call Date: July 2003, Lincoln's Inn
Qualifications: [ACL PGDip Law BA (Dublin)]
richard.english@lincolnhousechambers.com

E

ENGLISH MR ROBERT ANTHONY

1 Pump Court
Elm Court, Temple, London EC4Y 7AB,
☎ 020 7842 7070
✉ (name)@pumpcourt.co.uk
Call Date: Oct 1996, Inner Temple
Pupil Supervisor
Qualifications: [BA (Sussex) LLM (Lond)]
re@1pumpcourt.co.uk

ENOCH MR DAFYDD HUW QC (2008)

23 Essex Street
London WC2R 3AA, ☎ 020 7413 0353
✉ clerks@23es.com
Apex
Harlech House, 20 Cathedral Road, Cardiff CF11 9LJ, ☎ 02920 232 032
✉ clerks@apexchambers.net
Call Date: Nov 1985, Gray's Inn
Recorder
Qualifications: [LLB (Bucks)]
dafyddenoch@23es.com

ENONCHONG PROF NELSON EGBE

No5 Chambers
Fountain Court, Steelhouse Lane, Birmingham B4 6DR, ☎ 0845 210 5555 ✉ info@no5.com
No5 Chambers
Greenwood House, 4-7 Salisbury Court, London EC4Y 8AA, ☎ 0845 210 5555
No5 Chambers
38 Queen Square, Bristol BS1 4QS,
☎ 0845 210 5555
Call Date: Oct 2006, Inner Temple
Qualifications: [LLB MA LLM (Cantab) PhD (Cantab)]
ne@no5.com

ENRIGHT MS JOHANNE

Chambers of Ms Johanne Enright
19 William Blake House, 1 - 6 Dufour's Place, London W1F 7SQ, ☎ 020 7287 7557
Call Date: Nov 1996, Lincoln's Inn
Qualifications: [LLB (Hons) CAAW]
Johanne.Enright@btinternet.com, johanne.enright@btinternet.com

ENSAFF MR OMAR SHERIF

No5 Chambers
Fountain Court, Steelhouse Lane, Birmingham B4 6DR, ☎ 0845 210 5555 ✉ info@no5.com
No5 Chambers
Greenwood House, 4-7 Salisbury Court, London EC4Y 8AA, ☎ 0845 210 5555
No5 Chambers
38 Queen Square, Bristol BS1 4QS,
☎ 0845 210 5555
Call Date: Oct 2000, Gray's Inn
Qualifications: [LLB (LSE)]
oe@no5.com

ENTWISTLE MR JOHN REID

Liverpool Civil Law
3rd Floor, 1 Old Hall Street, Liverpool L3 9HF,
☎ 0151 242 0500
✉ clerks@liverpoolcivillaw.com
Call Date: Nov 1995, Gray's Inn
Qualifications: [LLB]
clerks@liverpoolcivillaw.com

ENTWISTLE MR MATTHEW JAMES

15 Winckley Square
Preston PR1 3JJ, ☎ 01772 252828
✉ clerks@15winckleysq.co.uk
Call Date: July 2011, Lincoln's Inn
Qualifications: [BA (Lincs)]
matthewentwistle@15ws.co.uk

ENTWISTLE MR THOMAS FRANCIS

5 Stone Buildings
5 Stone Buildings, Lincoln's Inn, London WC2A 3XT, ☎ 020 7242 6201
✉ clerks@5sblaw.com
Call Date: Nov 2001, Gray's Inn
Qualifications: [BA (Oxon) CPE (City)]
tentwistle@5sblaw.com

EPHGRAVE MISS AMY JOANNA

Pump Court Chambers
5 Temple Chambers, Temple Street, Swindon SN1 1SQ, ☎ 01793 539899
✉ clerks@3pumpcourt.com
Pump Court Chambers
Upper Ground Floor, 3 Pump Court, Temple, London EC4Y 7AJ, ☎ 020 7353 0711
✉ clerks@3pumpcourt.com
Pump Court Chambers
31 Southgate Street, Winchester, Hampshire SO23 9EB, ☎ 01962 868 161
✉ clerks@3pumpcourt.com
Call Date: Nov 1997, Gray's Inn
Qualifications: [BA (Hons)(Exon) BA (Hons)(Exon)]

EPHRAIM-ADEJUMO MRS HILDA EKPO

12 Old Square Chambers
1st Floor, 12 Old Square, Lincoln's Inn, London WC2A 3TX, ☎ 020 7404 0875
✉ clerks@12oldsquare.com
Call Date: Nov 1989, Lincoln's Inn
Qualifications: [BSc (Nigeria) LLB (Hons) (Lond) LLM (Lond) QDR BL (Lond)]

E

EPSTEIN MR MICHAEL PAUL

2 Bedford Row
London WC1R 4BU, ☎ 020 7440 8888
✉ clerks@2bedfordrow.co.uk
Call Date: Nov 1992, Middle Temple
Qualifications: [LLB (Hons) (Manch)]
✉ mepstein@2bedfordrow.co.uk

EPSTEIN MR PAUL JEREMY QC (2006)

Cloisters
1 Pump Court, Temple, London EC4Y 7AA,
☎ 020 7827 4000 ✉ clerks@cloisters.com
Call Date: Nov 1988, Middle Temple
Qualifications: [BA (Oxon)]
✉ pje@cloisters.com

ERIERA MR ANTON JUSTIN

29 Bedford Row Chambers
London WC1R 4HE, ☎ 020 7404 1044
✉ clerks@29br.co.uk
Call Date: July 2010, Lincoln's Inn
Qualifications: [BA (Cantab) LLM (USA)]
✉ aeriera@29br.co.uk

ERINLE MISS OMOBONIKE OMOLABAKE

Farrar's Building
Farrar's Building, Temple, London EC4Y 7BD,
☎ 020 7583 9241
✉ Chambers@farrarsbuilding.co.uk
Call Date: Oct 2008, Lincoln's Inn
Qualifications: [BA (Hons)]
✉ berinle@farrarsbuilding.co.uk

ERLEN MISS NICOLE

Call Date: Mar 2007, Inner Temple
Qualifications: [BA (Bristol) MA (Sheff)]

ERNSTZEN MR OLAV GUSTAV

Eurolawyer Chambers
PO Box 3621, London N7 0BQ,
☎ 020 7607 0075
✉ OLav@eurolawyer.plus.com
1 Mitre Court Buildings
1 Mitre Court Buildings, Temple, London
EC4Y 7BS, ☎ 020 7452 8900
✉ clerks@1mcb.com
Call Date: July 1981, Middle Temple
Pupil Supervisor

ERWOOD MISS HEATHER MARY ELLISTON

Linenhall Chambers
1 Stanley Place, Chester CH1 2LU,
☎ 01244 348282
✉ clerks@linenhallchambers.co.uk
3 Dr Johnson's Buildings
Ground Floor, 3 Dr Johnson's Buildings,
Temple, London EC4Y 7BA, ☎ 020 7353 4854
✉ clerks@3djb.co.uk
Call Date: Oct 1993, Middle Temple
Qualifications: [LLB (Hons) LLM (Lond)]
✉ heather.erwood@linenhallchambers.co.uk

ESCHWEGE MR RICHARD JOHN

Brick Court Chambers
7-8 Essex Street, London WC2R 3LD,
☎ 020 7379 3550 ✉ clerks@brickcourt.co.uk
Call Date: July 2008, Gray's Inn
Qualifications: [BA (Oxon)]
✉ richard.eschwege@brickcourt.co.uk

ESCORIZA MISS NATALIA

Park Court Chambers
16 Park Place, Leeds LS1 2SJ,
☎ 0113 243 3277
✉ clerks@parkcourtchambers.co.uk
Call Date: Nov 2002, Middle Temple
Qualifications: [BSc (Hons) (Aston) MSc (Edin) Dip Law]

ESHAGHIAN MISS YASMINE

Call Date: Feb 1995, Lincoln's Inn
Qualifications: [BA (Hons)(Lond)]

ESKERIE MR KARWAN ALI

1 Crown Office Row
1 Crown Office Row, Temple, London
EC4Y 7HH, ☎ 020 7797 7500
✉ mail@1cor.com
Call Date: Oct 2010, Inner Temple
Qualifications: [BA LLB (Auckland)]

ESPLEY MR ANDREW ROBERT

6 Pump Court
1st Floor, 6 Pump Court, Temple, London
EC4Y 7AR, ☎ 020 7797 8400
✉ richardconstable@6pumpcourt.co.uk
6 Pump Court Chambers
6-8 Mill Street, Maidstone, Kent ME15 6XH,
☎ 01622 688094
✉ annexe@6pumpcourt.co.uk
Call Date: Nov 1993, Gray's Inn
Pupil Supervisor
Qualifications: [LLB]
✉ andrewespley@6pumpcourt.co.uk

E

ESPLEY MISS SUSAN

Fenners Chambers
3 Madingley Road, Cambridge CB3 0EE,
☎01223 368761
✉clerks@fennerschambers.com
Call Date: July 1976, Gray's Inn
Qualifications: [LLB (Leeds)]
susan.espley@fennerschambers.com

ESPOSITO MR VINCENZO NUNZIO

Charter Chambers
33 John Street, London WC1N 2AT,
☎020 7618 4400
✉clerks@charterchambers.com
Call Date: Oct 2005, Middle Temple

ESPRIT MR BENOIT

Barristers Chambers
89A High Road, Wood Green, London
N22 6BB, ☎020 3417 6461
✉clerk@barristerschambers.org
Legis Chambers
Cherat House, 32 Havelock Street, Aylesbury, Buckinghamshire HP20 2NX,
☎01296 431125 ✉espritbenoit@yahoo.co.uk
Call Date: Nov 1982, Inner Temple
Qualifications: [BA MA (Lond) ADV Dip EDU (Lond) LLM (London) BSc (Brunel)]
espritbenoit@yahoo.co.uk

ESPRIT MR SHAUN ANDREW

33 Bedford Row
London WC1R 4JH, ☎020 7242 6476
✉clerks@33bedfordrow.co.uk
Call Date: Nov 1996, Lincoln's Inn
Qualifications: [BA (Hons) CPE]
ShaunEsprit@33bedfordrow.co.uk

ETHERINGTON MR DAVID CHARLES LYNCH QC (1998)

18 Red Lion Court
London EC4A 3EB, ☎020 7520 6000
✉chambers@18rlc.co.uk
18 Red Lion Court (Annexe)
Thornwood House, 102 New London Road, Chelmsford, Essex CM2 0RG,
☎01245 280880
Call Date: Nov 1979, Middle Temple
Recorder
Qualifications: [MA (Oxon) Dip Soc Pub Admin (Oxon)]
david.etherington@18rlc.co.uk

ETHERTON MISS GILLIAN FELICITY AMANADA QC (2011)

Atkinson Bevan Chambers
1st Floor, 2 Harcourt Buildings, Temple, London EC4Y 9DB, ☎020 7353 2112
✉clerks@2hb.co.uk
Call Date: July 1988, Middle Temple
Pupil Supervisor
Qualifications: [LLB (Hons)]
getherton@2hb.co.uk

ETIEBET MISS PEGGY EKAETE

Cornerstone Barristers
2-3 Gray's Inn Square, Gray's Inn, London
WC1R 5JH, ☎020 7242 4986
✉chambers@2-3gis.co.uk
Call Date: Oct 2001, Gray's Inn
Qualifications: [BA Hons (Cantab)]
petiebet@2-3gis.co.uk

EVANS MR ALAN

Kings Chambers
36 Young Street, Manchester M3 3FT,
☎0845 034 3444
✉clerks@kingschambers.com
Kings Chambers
5 Park Square East, Leeds LS1 2NE,
☎0845 034 3444
✉clerks@kingschambers.com
Kings Chambers
Embassy House, 60 Church Street, Birmingham B3 2DJ, ☎0845 034 3444
✉clerks@kingschambers.com
Call Date: July 1978, Lincoln's Inn
Pupil Supervisor
Qualifications: [MA LLB (Cantab)]
aevans@kingschambers.com

EVANS MR ALUN HOWARD

7 Bell Yard
London WC2A 2JR, ☎020 7831 0636
✉kevintarrant@btconnect.com
Call Date: Nov 1971, Gray's Inn
Pupil Supervisor
Qualifications: [BSc (Lond)]

EVANS MR ANDREW DAVID

St Philips Chambers
55 Temple Row, Birmingham B2 5LS,
☎0121 246 7000 ✉clerks@st-philips.com
Call Date: Nov 2000, Lincoln's Inn
Qualifications: [LLB (Hons) (B'ham)]
aevans@st-philips.com

EVANS MR ANDREW SUTHERLAND

2 Dr Johnson's Buildings
2 Dr Johnson's Buildings, Temple, London EC4Y 7AY, ☎ 020 7936 2613
✉ clerks@2drj.com
Call Date: July 1984, Gray's Inn
Qualifications: [LLB (Manch)]

EVANS MS CATRIN MIRANDA

One Brick Court
1st Floor, One Brick Court, Temple, London EC4Y 9BY, ☎ 020 7353 8845
✉ clerks@onebrickcourt.com
Call Date: Nov 1994, Inner Temple
Pupil Supervisor
Qualifications: [BA (Essex) CPE]
✉ ce@onebrickcourt.com

EVANS MR CHARLES HENRY FREDERICK

Furnival Chambers
32 Furnival Street, London EC4A 1JQ, ☎ 020 7405 3232
Call Date: Nov 1988, Middle Temple
Pupil Supervisor
Qualifications: [LLB]
✉ cevans@furnivallaw.co.uk

EVANS MISS CLARE MARSHALL

7 Bell Yard
London WC2A 2JR, ☎ 020 7831 0636
✉ kevintarrant@btconnect.com
Call Date: Oct 1995, Inner Temple
Qualifications: [BA (Lond) CPE]

EVANS MR DAVID ALEXANDER

Walnut House
63 St. David's Hill, Exeter, Devon EX4 4DW, ☎ 01392 279751
✉ clerks@walnuthouse.co.uk
Call Date: Mar 1996, Gray's Inn
Pupil Supervisor
Qualifications: [BA]

EVANS MR DAVID ANTHONY QC (1983)

Furnival Chambers
32 Furnival Street, London EC4A 1JQ, ☎ 020 7405 3232
Call Date: July 1965, Gray's Inn
Qualifications: [BA (Cantab)]

EVANS MR DAVID GARETH EVAN

9 Park Place
9 Park Place, Cardiff, South Glamorgan CF10 3DP, ☎ 029 2038 2731
✉ clerks@9parkplace.co.uk
Call Date: July 2008, Gray's Inn
Qualifications: [LLB (Cardiff)]

EVANS MR DAVID HOWARD QC (1991)

Chambers of Andrew Mitchell QC
33 Chancery Lane, London WC2A 1EN, ☎ 020 7440 9950 ✉ clerks@33cllaw.com
Aspect Chambers
Aspect Court, 4 Temple Row, Birmingham B2 5HG, ☎ 0121 222 2447
✉ clerks@aspectchambers.com
Call Date: Nov 1972, Middle Temple
Qualifications: [MSc (Lond) BA (Oxon)]
✉ de@33cllaw.com

EVANS MR DAVID HUW

30 Park Place
Cardiff CF10 3BS, ☎ 029 2039 8421
✉ clerks@30parkplace.law.co.uk
Call Date: July 1985, Lincoln's Inn
Pupil Supervisor
Qualifications: [BA (Hons)]
✉ dhe@30parkplace.co.uk

EVANS MR DAVID LEWIS QC (2012)

1 Crown Office Row
1 Crown Office Row, Temple, London EC4Y 7HH, ☎ 020 7797 7500
✉ mail@1cor.com
Call Date: July 1988, Middle Temple
Pupil Supervisor
Qualifications: [MA (Hons)(Cantab) FCIArb]
✉ david.evans@1cor.com

EVANS MR DYLAN

14 Gray's Inn Square
14 Gray's Inn Square, Gray's Inn, London WC1R 5JP, ☎ 020 7242 0858
✉ clerks@14gis.co.uk
Call Date: Apr 1989, Gray's Inn
Qualifications: [LLB (UEA) BA (Hons)(Lond)]
✉ clerks@14graysinnsquare.co.uk

EVANS MISS ELWEN MAIR QC (2002)

Iscoed Chambers
86 St Helen's Road, Swansea SA1 4BQ,
☎ 01792 652988
✉ clerks@iscoedchambers.co.uk
Farrar's Building
Farrar's Building, Temple, London EC4Y 7BD,
☎ 020 7583 9241
✉ Chambers@farrarsbuilding.co.uk
Call Date: July 1980, Gray's Inn
Recorder
Qualifications: [MA (Cantab)]
eme@iscoedchambers.co.uk

EVANS MR FRANCIS WALTON HERMIT QC (1994)

1 Gray's Inn Square
Ground Floor, 1 Gray's Inn Square, London
WC1R 5AA, ☎ 020 7405 0001
Call Date: July 1977, Middle Temple
Qualifications: [BA]

EVANS MR FRANKLIN ST CLAIR MELVILLE

Field Court Chambers
5 Field Court, Gray's Inn, London WC1R 5EF,
☎ 020 7405 6114 ✉ clerks@fieldcourt.co.uk
Call Date: Nov 1981, Gray's Inn
Pupil Supervisor
Qualifications: [BA Hons (Lancs)]
franklin.evans@fieldcourt.co.uk

EVANS MR GARETH ROBERT WILLIAM QC (1994)

No5 Chambers
Fountain Court, Steelhouse Lane, Birmingham
B4 6DR, ☎ 0845 210 5555 ✉ info@no5.com
No5 Chambers
Greenwood House, 4-7 Salisbury Court,
London EC4Y 8AA, ☎ 0845 210 5555
No5 Chambers
38 Queen Square, Bristol BS1 4QS,
☎ 0845 210 5555
Call Date: Nov 1973, Gray's Inn
Recorder
Qualifications: [LLB (Lond)]

EVANS MR GWYNFOR OWEN

Tanfield Chambers
2-5 Warwick Court, London WC1R 5DJ,
☎ 020 7421 5300
✉ clerks@tanfieldchambers.co.uk
Call Date: July 2007, Gray's Inn
Qualifications: [MA (Cantab) Dip Law (Lond)]

EVANS MISS HELEN MARY

Four New Square
Four New Square, Lincoln's Inn, London
WC2A 3RJ, ☎ 020 7822 2000
✉ barristers@4newsquare.com
Call Date: Oct 2001, Middle Temple
Qualifications: [BA (Hons)(Oxon) CPE]
hm.evans@4newsquare.com

EVANS MR HUGH LEWIS

Four New Square
Four New Square, Lincoln's Inn, London
WC2A 3RJ, ☎ 020 7822 2000
✉ barristers@4newsquare.com
Call Date: Nov 1987, Middle Temple
Pupil Supervisor
Qualifications: [MA (Cantab) BCL (Oxon)]
h.evans@4newsquare.com

EVANS MR JAMES ANDREW

18 St John Street
Manchester M3 4EA, ☎ 0161 278 1800
✉ clerks@18sjs.com
Call Date: Mar 2007, Middle Temple
Qualifications: [MA (Cantab) LLM]

EVANS MR JAMES FREDERICK MEURIG

3 Verulam Buildings
London WC1R 5NT, ☎ 020 7831 8441
✉ chambers@3vb.com
Call Date: Nov 1991, Gray's Inn
Pupil Supervisor
Qualifications: [BA (Cantab) LLM (Lond)]
jevans@3vb.com

EVANS MISS JANE LOIS

Temple Chambers
32 Park Place, Cardiff CF10 3BA,
☎ 029 2039 7364
✉ DBrinning@Temple-Chambers.co.uk
Temple Chambers
12 Clytha Park Road, Newport, Gwent
NP20 4PB, ☎ 01633 267403
✉ dbrinning@temple-chambers.co.uk
Call Date: July 1971, Gray's Inn

EVANS MS JILL ANNALIESE

Doughty Street Chambers
53-54 Doughty Street, London WC1N 2LS,
☎ 020 7404 1313
✉ enquiries@doughtystreet.co.uk
Doughty Street Chambers
Pall Mall Court, 61-67 King Street, Manchester
M2 4PD, ☎ 0161 618 1066

Doughty Street Chambers
5th Floor, Broad Quay House, Prince Street, Bristol BS1 4DJ, ☎01179 058 717
Call Date: July 1986, Gray's Inn
Pupil Supervisor
Qualifications: [BA (Hons) (Kent)]
j.evans@doughtystreet.co.uk

EVANS MR JOHN JAMES

Temple Chambers
32 Park Place, Cardiff CF10 3BA,
☎029 2039 7364
✉DBrinning@Temple-Chambers.co.uk
Temple Chambers
12 Clytha Park Road, Newport, Gwent NP20 4PB, ☎01633 267403
✉dbrinning@temple-chambers.co.uk
Call Date: July 2002, Lincoln's Inn
Qualifications: [LLB (Hons)]

EVANS MR JOHN WAINWRIGHT

St Philips Chambers
55 Temple Row, Birmingham B2 5LS,
☎0121 246 7000 ✉clerks@st-philips.com
Call Date: July 1983, Inner Temple
Qualifications: [LLB (Leic)]
jevans@st-philips.com

EVANS MR JONATHAN EDWARD

Wilberforce Chambers
8 New Square, Lincoln's Inn, London WC2A 3QP, ☎020 7306 0102
✉chambers@wilberforce.co.uk
Call Date: Nov 1994, Middle Temple
Pupil Supervisor
Qualifications: [BA (Hons)]
jevans@wilberforce.co.uk

EVANS MISS JUDI

St John's Chambers
101 Victoria Street, Bristol BS1 6PU,
☎0117 923 4700
✉clerks@stjohnschambers.co.uk
Call Date: Nov 1996, Middle Temple
Qualifications: [LLB (Hons)(Bucks) MPhil (Cantab)]
judi.evans@stjohnschambers.co.uk

EVANS MR JULIAN JACOB

QEB Hollis Whiteman
1-2 Laurence Pountney Hill, London EC4R 0EU, ☎020 7933 8855
✉barristers@qebhw.co.uk
Call Date: Oct 1997, Middle Temple
Pupil Supervisor
Qualifications: [BA (Hons)(Cantab)]
julian.evans@qebhw.co.uk

EVANS MR LEE JOHN

Farrar's Building
Farrar's Building, Temple, London EC4Y 7BD,
☎020 7583 9241
✉Chambers@farrarsbuilding.co.uk
Call Date: Nov 1996, Gray's Inn
Pupil Supervisor
Qualifications: [MA (Cantab)]
levans@farrarsbuilding.co.uk

EVANS MR MARK QC (1995)

Chambers of Mr Mark Evans
Grove Farm, Wapley, Bristol BS37 8RW,
☎01454 312150 ✉evansmlaw@fsmail.net
Call Date: Nov 1971, Gray's Inn
Qualifications: [LLB]

EVANS MR MARTIN ALAN LANGHAM

Chambers of Andrew Mitchell QC
33 Chancery Lane, London WC2A 1EN,
☎020 7440 9950 ✉clerks@33cllaw.com
Call Date: Nov 1989, Middle Temple
Pupil Supervisor
Qualifications: [BA (Hons) (Sussex) Dip Law]
me@33cllaw.com

Fax: 020 7430 2818

Types of work: Asset forfeiture, Civil recovery, Confiscation, Fraud, Money laundering

EVANS MR MICHAEL RITHO

1 High Pavement
Nottingham NG1 1HF, ☎0115 941 8218
✉clerks@1highpavement.co.uk
Call Date: Nov 1988, Middle Temple
Qualifications: [LLB]
michaelevans@1highpavement.co.uk

EVANS MR PAUL HUGH

No5 Chambers
Fountain Court, Steelhouse Lane, Birmingham B4 6DR, ☎0845 210 5555 ✉info@no5.com
No5 Chambers
Greenwood House, 4-7 Salisbury Court, London EC4Y 8AA, ☎0845 210 5555
No5 Chambers
38 Queen Square, Bristol BS1 4QS,
☎0845 210 5555
Call Date: July 2001, Inner Temple
Qualifications: [BSc (Lond) CPE (Nott'm)]
pe@no5.com

E

EVANS MR PAUL JAMES

2 Pump Court
1st Floor, 2 Pump Court, Temple, London EC4Y 7AH, ☎ 020 7353 5597
✉ clerks@2pumpcourt.co.uk
Call Date: Oct 2001, Gray's Inn
Qualifications: [LLB]
pevans@2pumpcourt.co.uk

EVANS MR PAUL TIMOTHY

Exchange Chambers
One Derby Square, Derby Square, Liverpool L2 9XX, ☎ 0151 236 7747
✉ info@exchangechambers.co.uk
Exchange Chambers
7 Ralli Courts, West Riverside, Manchester M3 5FT, ☎ 0161 833 2722
Call Date: Nov 1992, Gray's Inn
Qualifications: [MA (Oxon) LLM (Lond) LLM (UEA)]
evans@exchangechambers.co.uk

EVANS MR PHILIP

QEB Hollis Whiteman
1-2 Laurence Pountney Hill, London EC4R 0EU, ☎ 020 7933 8855
✉ barristers@qebhw.co.uk
Call Date: Oct 1995, Lincoln's Inn
Pupil Supervisor
Qualifications: [LLB (Hons)(Wales) MA (So'ton)]
philip.evans@qebhw.co.uk

E

EVANS MR RHYS JOHN

30 Park Place
Cardiff CF10 3BS, ☎ 029 2039 8421
✉ clerks@30parkplace.law.co.uk
Call Date: July 2008, Gray's Inn
Qualifications: [LLB (Cardiff)]

EVANS MR RICHARD

6 King's Bench Walk
Ground Floor, 6 King's Bench Walk, Temple, London EC4Y 7DR, ☎ 020 7583 0410
✉ clerks@6kbw.com
Call Date: July 2008, Gray's Inn
Qualifications: [Double Maitrise (Cantab)]
richard.evans@6kbw.com

EVANS MR ROBERT JONATHAN

Keating Chambers
15 Essex Street, London WC2R 3AA, ☎ 020 7544 2600
✉ clerks@keatingchambers.com
Call Date: July 1989, Gray's Inn
Pupil Supervisor
Qualifications: [MA (Cantab) LLB (Lond) C Eng FCIArb MHKIE FICE]

EVANS MR ROBERT WILLIAM JOSEPH

9 King's Bench Walk
Lower Ground Floor South, 9 King's Bench Walk, Temple, London EC4Y 7DX, ☎ 020 7353 9564 ✉ 9kbw@btconnect.com
Call Date: Nov 1996, Gray's Inn
Qualifications: [LLB (Brunel)]
9kbw@btconnect.com

EVANS MR ROGER KENNETH

Harcourt Chambers
1st Floor, 2 Harcourt Buildings, Temple, London EC4Y 9DB, ☎ 0844 561 7135
Harcourt Chambers
Churchill House, 3 St Aldate's Courtyard, St Aldate's, Oxford OX1 1BN, ☎ 0844 561 7135
Call Date: Nov 1970, Middle Temple
Pupil Supervisor, Recorder
Qualifications: [MA (Cantab)]
revans@harcourtchambers.law.co.uk

EVANS MISS SARAH REBECCA

1 Garden Court Family Law Chambers
Ground Floor, One Garden Court, Temple, London EC4Y 9BJ, ☎ 020 7797 7900
✉ clerks@1gc.com
Call Date: Nov 2004, Inner Temple
Qualifications: [LLB University of Manchester]

EVANS MR SIMEON VAUGHAN

St Johns Buildings
24a - 28 St John Street, Manchester M3 4DJ, ☎ 0161 214 1500
✉ clerk@stjohnsbuildings.co.uk
16 Winckley Square
Preston PR1 3JJ, ☎ 01772 256100
St Johns Buildings Liverpool
8th Floor India Buildings, Water Street, Liverpool L2 0XG, ☎ 0151 243 6000
✉ clerk@stjohnsbuildings.co.uk
Call Date: Nov 1997, Lincoln's Inn
Qualifications: [BA (Hons)(Manch)]

EVANS MR STEPHEN JAMES

Five Paper
Ground Floor, 5 Paper Buildings, Temple, London EC4Y 7HB, ☎ 020 7815 3200
Call Date: Oct 1992, Middle Temple
Qualifications: [BA (Hons)]
stephenevans@fivepaper.com

EVANS MR STEVEN DAVID

36 Bedford Row
London WC1R 4JH, ☎ 020 7421 8000
✉ chambers@36bedfordrow.co.uk
Call Date: Oct 1997, Middle Temple
Recorder
Qualifications: [LLB (Hons) CQSW]
✉ clerks@36bedfordrow.co.uk, sevans@36bedfordrow.co.uk

EVANS MISS SUZANNE MARIE

Oriel Chambers
14 Water Street, Liverpool, Merseyside L2 8TD, ☎ 0151 236 7191
✉ clerks@orielchambers.co.uk
Oriel Chambers
18 Ribblesdale Place, Preston PR1 3NA, ☎ 01772 254 764
✉ clerks@oriel-chambers.co.uk
Call Date: Nov 1985, Middle Temple
Pupil Supervisor
Qualifications: [MA (Oxon)]
✉ suzanne.evans@orielchambers.co.uk

EVANS MR THOMAS GARETH

Colleton Chambers
Colleton Crescent, Exeter, Devon EX2 4DG, ☎ 01392 274898
✉ clerks@colletonchambers.co.uk
Call Date: Oct 1996, Middle Temple
Qualifications: [LLB (Hons)(Exon)]
✉ garethevans@colletonchambers.co.uk

EVANS MR THOMAS JONATHAN CHARLES

Henderson Chambers
2 Harcourt Buildings, Temple, London EC4Y 9DB, ☎ 020 7583 9020
✉ clerks@hendersonchambers.co.uk
Call Date: Oct 2008, Lincoln's Inn
Qualifications: [BA (Oxon)]
✉ tevans@hendersonchambers.co.uk

EVANS MR TIMOTHY AYLMER

Assize Court Chambers
14 Small Street, Bristol BS1 1DE, ☎ 0117 926 4587 ✉ carly@assize.co.uk
Call Date: July 1982, Gray's Inn
Pupil Supervisor
Qualifications: [LLB (Lond)]
✉ taylmer.evans@hotmail.com, timothy.evans@assize.co.uk

EVANS MR TIMOTHY JOHN

Apex
Harlech House, 20 Cathedral Road, Cardiff CF11 9LJ, ☎ 02920 232 032
✉ clerks@apexchambers.net
Call Date: July 1984, Gray's Inn
Pupil Supervisor
Qualifications: [LLB (Nottm)]
✉ tim.evans@apexchambers.net

EVANS MR TIMOTHY WENTWORTH EYRE

Maitland Chambers
7 Stone Buildings, Lincoln's Inn, London WC2A 3SZ, ☎ 020 7406 1200
✉ clerks@maitlandchambers.com
Call Date: July 1979, Lincoln's Inn
Pupil Supervisor
Qualifications: [MA (Oxon)]
✉ tevans@maitlandchambers.com

EVANS MR WILLIAM ANTHONY

Ely Place Chambers
30 Ely Place, London EC1N 6TD, ☎ 020 7400 9600 ✉ admin@elyplace.com
Call Date: July 1977, Gray's Inn
Recorder
Qualifications: [BA (Hons)]

EVANS-GORDON MRS JANE-ANNE MARY

New Square Chambers
12 New Square, Lincoln's Inn, London WC2A 3SW, ☎ 020 7419 8000
✉ robin.hollington@newsquarechambers.co.uk
Call Date: Nov 1992, Inner Temple
Pupil Supervisor
Qualifications: [LLB (Reading)]
✉ jane.evansgordon@newsquarechambers.co.uk

EVANS-TOVEY MR JASON ROBERT

Crown Office Chambers
2 Crown Office Row, Temple, London EC4Y 7HJ, ☎ 020 7797 8100
✉ mail@crownofficechambers.com
Call Date: Oct 1990, Gray's Inn
Pupil Supervisor
Qualifications: [MA (Cantab) LLM]
✉ evans-tovey@crownofficechambers.com

EVELEIGH-WINSTONE MISS ADELLE

New Walk Chambers
27 New Walk, Leicester, Leicestershire LE1 6TE, ☎ 0871 200 1298 / 0116 255 9144
✉ clerks@newwalkchambers.co.uk
Call Date: Oct 2003, Gray's Inn
Qualifications: [LLB]

E

EVISON MR JOHN

5 Pump Court
Ground Floor, 5 Pump Court, Temple, London EC4Y 7AP, ☎ 020 7353 2532
✉ clerks@5pumpcourt.com
Call Date: July 1974, Lincoln's Inn
Pupil Supervisor
Qualifications: [LLB (Lond)]
✉ johnevison@5pumpcourt.com

EWART MR DAVID SCOTT QC (2006)

Pump Court Tax Chambers
16 Bedford Row, London WC1R 4EF,
☎ 020 7414 8080 ✉ clerks@pumptax.com
Call Date: Nov 1987, Gray's Inn
Qualifications: [BA (Oxon)]
✉ dewart@pumptax.com

Types of work: Capital tax, Corporation tax, Equity, Income tax, National Insurance, Private client, Professional negligence, Stamp duty, Trusts, VAT, Wills

EWING MR HARALD RICHARD WOLF

KCH Garden Square
1 Oxford Street, Nottingham NG1 5BH,
☎ 0115 941 8851
✉ clerks@kchgardensquare.co.uk
Call Date: Nov 1997, Gray's Inn
Qualifications: [BA (Cantab)]

EWINGS MR DAVID JOHN

Charter Chambers
33 John Street, London WC1N 2AT,
☎ 020 7618 4400
✉ clerks@charterchambers.com
Call Date: Nov 2009, Gray's Inn
Qualifications: [BA LLB]

EWINS MISS CATHERINE JANE

Hailsham Chambers
Ground Floor, 4 Paper Buildings, Temple, London EC4Y 7EX, ☎ 020 7643 5000
✉ clerks@hailshamchambers.com
Call Date: Nov 1995, Gray's Inn
Qualifications: [BA MA (Cantab)]
✉ catherine.ewins@hailshamchambers.com

EWINS MR DAVID JAMES

Queen Elizabeth Building
3rd Floor, Queen Elizabeth Building, Temple, London EC4Y 9BS, ☎ 020 7797 7837
✉ clerks@qeb.co.uk
Call Date: Nov 1996, Middle Temple
Pupil Supervisor
Qualifications: [BA (Hons)]
✉ j.ewins@qeb.co.uk

EXALL MR GORDON DAVID

Zenith Chambers
10 Park Square, Leeds LS1 2LH,
☎ 0113 245 5438
✉ clerks@zenithchambers.co.uk
Call Date: Apr 1991, Lincoln's Inn
Qualifications: [BA (Warw)]
✉ gexall@zenithchambers.co.uk

EYRE MR GILES STEPHEN

The Chambers of Grahame Aldous QC
9 Gough Square, London EC4A 3DG,
☎ 020 7832 0500
✉ clerks@9goughsquare.co.uk
Call Date: July 1974, Gray's Inn
Pupil Supervisor, Recorder
Qualifications: [LLB]

EYRE MISS JUDITH MARY

2-3 Hind Court Chambers
2-3 Hind Court, Fleet Street, London EC4A 3DL, ☎ 020 7822 2150
✉ david@2-3hindcourt.com
Call Date: Oct 2008, Middle Temple
Qualifications: [BA (Hons) (Cantab)]

EYRE MR STEPHEN JOHN ARTHUR

St Philips Chambers
55 Temple Row, Birmingham B2 5LS,
☎ 0121 246 7000 ✉ clerks@st-philips.com
Call Date: July 1981, Inner Temple
Pupil Supervisor, Recorder
Qualifications: [MA BCL (Oxon)]

EZE MISS SANDRA OGECHI

9 King's Bench Walk
Lower Ground Floor South, 9 King's Bench Walk, Temple, London EC4Y 7DX,
☎ 020 7353 9564 ✉ 9kbw@btconnect.com
Call Date: July 2004, Lincoln's Inn
Qualifications: [LLB Hons (Lancashire)]

EZEKIEL MS ADINA SEJI

6 King's Bench Walk
Ground Floor, 6 King's Bench Walk, Temple, London EC4Y 7DR, ☎ 020 7583 0410
✉ clerks@6kbw.com
Call Date: Oct 1997, Inner Temple
Qualifications: [LLB (Lond)]
✉ adina.ezekiel@6kbw.com

E

FACENNA MR GERALD CARLO

Monckton Chambers
1 & 2 Raymond Buildings, Gray's Inn, London WC1R 5NR, ☎020 7405 7211
✉chambers@monckton.com
Call Date: Oct 2001, Lincoln's Inn
Pupil Supervisor
Qualifications: [BA (Hons)(Cantab) LLB (Hons)]
✉gfacenna@monckton.com

FADIPE MR GABRIEL CHARLES

Wilberforce Chambers
8 New Square, Lincoln's Inn, London WC2A 3QP, ☎020 7306 0102
✉chambers@wilberforce.co.uk
Call Date: Nov 1991, Inner Temple
Pupil Supervisor
Qualifications: [BA (Kent) M en D (France)]
✉gfadipe@wilberforce.co.uk

FAGAN MISS CATHERINE JOSEPHINE

Old Court Chambers
Newham House, 96-98 Borough Road, Middlesbrough TS1 2HJ, ☎01642 232523
✉clerks@oldcourtchambers.com
Call Date: Oct 1993, Gray's Inn
Pupil Supervisor
Qualifications: [BA (Hons)]
✉clerks@oldcourtchambers.com

FAGBORUN BENNETT MS MORAYO ABOSEDE

Hardwicke
New Square, Lincoln's Inn, London WC2A 3SB, ☎020 7242 2523
✉enquiries@hardwicke.co.uk
Call Date: July 2004, Lincoln's Inn
Qualifications: [BA Hons (Oxon)]
✉morayo.bennett@hardwicke.co.uk

FAGGIONATO MISS MARINA CAROLINE HELENE

Queen Elizabeth Building
3rd Floor, Queen Elizabeth Building, Temple, London EC4Y 9BS, ☎020 7797 7837
✉clerks@qeb.co.uk
Call Date: July 2006, Lincoln's Inn
Qualifications: [LLM (Lond) BA (Oxon)]
✉m.faggionato@QEB.co.uk

FAHY MISS SARAH ELIZABETH

St Ive's Chambers
Whittall Street, Birmingham B4 6DH, ☎0121 236 0863
✉clerks@stiveschambers.co.uk
Call Date: July 2009, Middle Temple
Qualifications: [LLB (Hons) (Exon) LLM]
✉sarah.fahy@stiveschambers.co.uk

FAIN MR CARL IAN

Tanfield Chambers
2-5 Warwick Court, London WC1R 5DJ, ☎020 7421 5300
✉clerks@tanfieldchambers.co.uk
Call Date: Oct 2001, Lincoln's Inn
Qualifications: [MA (Hons)(Oxon)]
✉carlfain@tanfieldchambers.co.uk
URL: http://www.tanfieldchambers.co.uk

Types of work: Chancery (land law), Commercial litigation, Common law (general), Insolvency, Landlord and tenant, Real property

FAIRBAIRN MISS REBECCA LOUISE

1 Paper Buildings
1st Floor, 1 Paper Buildings, Temple, London EC4Y 7EP, ☎020 7353 3728
✉clerks@onepaper.co.uk
Call Date: Nov 2000, Middle Temple
Qualifications: [LLB (Hons)]

FAIRBANK MR NICHOLAS JAMES

4 Paper Buildings
1st Floor, 4 Paper Buildings, Temple, London EC4Y 7EX, ☎020 7427 5200
✉clerks@4pb.com
Call Date: Nov 1996, Lincoln's Inn
Pupil Supervisor
Qualifications: [MA (Hons)(Cantab) CPE]
✉nf@4pb.com

FAIRBURN MR GEORGE EDWARD HENRY

Cornwall Street Chambers
85-87 Cornwall Street, Birmingham B3 3BY, ☎0121 233 7500
✉clerks@cornwallstreet.co.uk
Cornwall Street Chambers
Shrewsbury Annex, Rural Enterprise Centre, Stafford Drive, Battlefield Enterprise Park, Shrewsbury SY1 3FE, ☎01743 363 611 / 0121 233 7500
Call Date: Oct 1995, Lincoln's Inn
Pupil Supervisor
Qualifications: [BSc (Hons)]
✉george.fairburn@cornwallstreet.co.uk

E

FAIRCLOUGH MISS LUCY HELEN

Northampton Chambers
10 Spencer Parade, Northampton NN1 5AQ,
☎01604 636271
✉clerks@northampton-chambers.co.uk
Call Date: Oct 2005, Gray's Inn
Qualifications: [LLB (Newcastle upon Tyne)]
LFairclough@northampton-chambers.co.uk

FAIRGRIEVE DR DUNCAN NEILL

1 Crown Office Row
1 Crown Office Row, Temple, London
EC4Y 7HH, ☎020 7797 7500
✉mail@1cor.com
Call Date: Nov 2008, Inner Temple
Qualifications: [LLB (Lond) MGJR (Oxon)
DPhil (Oxon)]

FAIRHEAD MR ALLEN JOHN HUBERT

5 King's Bench Walk
5 King's Bench Walk, Temple, London
EC4Y 7DN, ☎020 7353 5638
✉clerks@5kbw.co.uk
Call Date: Nov 1978, Middle Temple
Pupil Supervisor
Qualifications: [BA (Dunelm)]
allen.fairhead@5kbw.co.uk

FAIRLEY MISS CHLOE ALICE

Park Court Chambers
16 Park Place, Leeds LS1 2SJ,
☎0113 243 3277
✉clerks@parkcourtchambers.co.uk
Call Date: Oct 2004, Gray's Inn
Qualifications: [BA]
cfairley@parkcourtchambers.co.uk

FAIRLEY MR IAN PAUL

2 King's Bench Walk
2 King's Bench Walk, Temple, London
EC4Y 7DE, ☎020 7353 1746
✉clerks@2kbw.com
Call Date: Oct 2007, Middle Temple
Qualifications: [LLB (Hons) (So'ton)]
pfairley@2kbw.com

FAIRPO MS CATHERINE ANNE

Atlas Chambers
3 Field Court, Gray's Inn, London WC1R 5EP,
☎020 7269 7980
✉clerks@atlaschambers.com
Call Date: Nov 2009, Gray's Inn
fairpo@atlaschambers.com

FALK MR CHARLES MORTON JAMES

3 PB Barristers
3 Paper Buildings, Temple, London EC4Y 7EU,
☎020 7583 8055
Call Date: Oct 1994, Middle Temple
Qualifications: [BA (Hons)(Keele) CPE
(Middx)]

FALKOWSKI MR DAMIAN

4-5 Gray's Inn Square
Gray's Inn, London WC1R 5AH,
☎020 7404 5252 ✉clerks@4-5.co.uk
Call Date: Oct 1994, Gray's Inn
Pupil Supervisor
Qualifications: [ARCM LLDip MMus BMus]
dfalkowski@4-5.co.uk

FALLOWS MISS MARY PAULA

Cobden House Chambers
19 Quay Street, Manchester M3 3HN,
☎0161 833 6000 ✉Clerks@Cobden.co.uk
Call Date: July 1981, Lincoln's Inn
Pupil Supervisor
Qualifications: [BA (Hons)]
clerks@cobden.co.uk

FAMA MRS GUDRUN HILDEGARD

Middle Temple Lane Chambers
2nd Floor South, 1 Middle Temple Lane,
London EC4Y 9AA, ☎020 7583 4352
✉chambers@mtlchambers.com
Call Date: Oct 1991, Gray's Inn
Pupil Supervisor
Qualifications: [BA LLB MA]

FANCOURT MR TIMOTHY MILES QC (2003)

Falcon Chambers
Falcon Court, London EC4Y 1AA,
☎020 7353 2484
✉clerks@falcon-chambers.com
Call Date: Nov 1987, Lincoln's Inn
Recorder
Qualifications: [MA (Cantab)]
fancourt@falcon-chambers.com

Fax: 020 7353 1261
URL: www.falconchambers.com

Types of work: Chancery (general), Chancery (land law), Commercial litigation, Commercial property, Landlord and tenant, Professional negligence, Real property

FANE MISS ANGELA ELIZABETH

Goldsmith Chambers
Ground Floor, Goldsmith Building, Temple, London EC4Y 7BL, ☎ 020 7353 6802
✉ clerks@goldsmithchambers.com
Call Date: Nov 1992, Middle Temple
Qualifications: [BA (Lond)]
✉ A.Fane@goldsmithchambers.law.co.uk

FANNERAN MISS MICHELLE

Clerksroom (Taunton)
Equity House, Administration Centre, Blackbrook Park Avenue, Taunton, Somerset TA1 2PX, ☎ 0845 083 3000
✉ mail@clerksroom.com
Call Date: July 2003, Gray's Inn
Qualifications: [LLB (Lond)]

FANSHAWE MISS LYNN HELEN CALISTA

Castle Chambers
The Old Fire Station, 90 High Street, Harrow-on-the-Hill, Middlesex HA1 3LP, ☎ 020 8423 6579 ✉ info@castlechambers.net
Call Date: Oct 1999, Middle Temple
Qualifications: [BA (Hons)(Sheff)]

FAPOHUNDA MRS OLUKEMI

Furnival Chambers
32 Furnival Street, London EC4A 1JQ, ☎ 020 7405 3232
Call Date: July 2002, Gray's Inn
Qualifications: [LLB]
✉ kfapohunda@furnivallaw.co.uk

FARBER MR JAMES HENRY MARTIN

5 Stone Buildings
5 Stone Buildings, Lincoln's Inn, London WC2A 3XT, ☎ 020 7242 6201
✉ clerks@5sblaw.com
Call Date: July 1976, Gray's Inn
Pupil Supervisor
✉ mfarber@5sblaw.com

FARBEY MISS JUDITH SARAH QC (2011)

Doughty Street Chambers
53-54 Doughty Street, London WC1N 2LS, ☎ 020 7404 1313
✉ enquiries@doughtystreet.co.uk
Doughty Street Chambers
Pall Mall Court, 61-67 King Street, Manchester M2 4PD, ☎ 0161 618 1066
Doughty Street Chambers
5th Floor, Broad Quay House, Prince Street, Bristol BS1 4DJ, ☎ 01179 058 717
Call Date: Oct 1992, Middle Temple
Pupil Supervisor
Qualifications: [BA (Hons)(Oxon) Dip Law (City)]
✉ j.farbey@doughtystreet.co.uk

FARLEY MR DAVID DUNBAR

St Johns Buildings
24a - 28 St John Street, Manchester M3 4DJ, ☎ 0161 214 1500
✉ clerk@stjohnsbuildings.co.uk
16 Winckley Square
Preston PR1 3JJ, ☎ 01772 256100
St Johns Buildings Liverpool
8th Floor India Buildings, Water Street, Liverpool L2 0XG, ☎ 0151 243 6000
✉ clerk@stjohnsbuildings.co.uk
Call Date: Oct 2001, Middle Temple
Qualifications: [BA (Hons) (Lanc) Dip Law]

FARLEY MR ROGER BOYD QC (1993)

Cobden House Chambers
19 Quay Street, Manchester M3 3HN, ☎ 0161 833 6000 ✉ Clerks@Cobden.co.uk
3 PB Barristers
23 Beaumont Street, Oxford OX1 2NP, ☎ 01865 793 736
3 PB Barristers
4 St Peter Street, Winchester SO23 8BW, ☎ 01962 868884
✉ clerks.winchester@3paper.co.uk
3 PB Barristers
Royal Talbot House, 2 Victoria Street, Bristol, Avon BS1 6BB, ☎ 0117 928 1520
3 PB Barristers
3 Paper Buildings, Temple, London EC4Y 7EU, ☎ 020 7583 8055
3 PB Barristers
30 Christchurch Road, Bournemouth, Dorset BH1 3PD, ☎ 01202 292102
✉ clerks.bournemouth@3paper.co.uk
Call Date: May 1974, Middle Temple
Recorder
Qualifications: [LLB (L'pool)]

FARMER MR GABRIEL JOHN-HENRY

Guildhall Chambers
23 Broad Street, Bristol BS1 2HG, ☎ 0117 930 9000
✉ hoc@guildhallchambers.co.uk
Call Date: Nov 1994, Gray's Inn
Pupil Supervisor
Qualifications: [BSc (Reading)]
✉ gabriel.farmer@guildhallchambers.co.uk

E

FARMER MR JOHN MICHAEL HEREWARD

1 Paper Buildings
1st Floor, 1 Paper Buildings, Temple, London EC4Y 7EP, ☎ 020 7353 3728
✉ clerks@onepaper.co.uk
Octagon House
19 Colegate, Norwich NR3 1AT,
☎ 01603 623186
✉ clerks@octagonhouse.co.uk
Call Date: Nov 1970, Gray's Inn
Pupil Supervisor
Qualifications: [MA (Cantab)]
johnfarmer@onepaper.co.uk

FARMER MR MATTHEW JONATHAN

Atkinson Bevan Chambers
1st Floor, 2 Harcourt Buildings, Temple, London EC4Y 9DB, ☎ 020 7353 2112
✉ clerks@2hb.co.uk
Call Date: July 1987, Inner Temple
Pupil Supervisor
Qualifications: [BA (Lond) Dip Law]
mfarmer@2hb.co.uk

FARMER MS SARAH LOUISE

Thomas More Chambers
7 Lincoln's Inn Fields, London WC2A 3BP,
☎ 020 7404 7000
✉ clerks@thomasmore.co.uk
Call Date: Nov 1991, Lincoln's Inn
Pupil Supervisor
Qualifications: [BA (Hons) (Oxon)]
sfarmer@thomasmore.co.uk

FARNON MS PATRICIA RONA GABRIELLE

Tooks Chambers
81 Farringdon Street, London EC4A 4BL,
☎ 020 7842 7575 ✉ clerks@tooks.co.uk
Call Date: Nov 1986, Inner Temple
Qualifications: [LLB (Lond)]
patricia.farnon@tooks.co.uk

FAROOQI MRS NIGHAT SHAHEEN

Brompton Chambers
1st Floor, 353A Station Road, Harrow, Middlesex HA1 1LN, ☎ 0560 3685647
✉ bromptonchamber@aol.com
Call Date: July 2005, Lincoln's Inn
Qualifications: [LLB (Hons)]

FARQUHAR MS FIONA MACDONALD

Queen Square Chambers
56 Queen Square, Bristol BS1 4PR,
☎ 0117 921 1966 ✉ crime@qs-c.co.uk
Call Date: Oct 2002, Inner Temple
Qualifications: [BSc (So'ton) CPE]
ff@qs-c.co.uk

FARQUHARSON MR JONATHAN

Colleton Chambers
Colleton Crescent, Exeter, Devon EX2 4DG,
☎ 01392 274898
✉ clerks@colletonchambers.co.uk
Call Date: July 1988, Inner Temple
Pupil Supervisor
Qualifications: [BA (Hons) (Dunelm)]
jonathanfarquharson@colletonchambers.co.uk

FARR MR PHILIP EDWARD

1 Paper Buildings
1st Floor, 1 Paper Buildings, Temple, London EC4Y 7EP, ☎ 020 7353 3728
✉ clerks@onepaper.co.uk
Call Date: Nov 2001, Middle Temple
Qualifications: [LLB (Hons)]

FARRANT MISS JULIA ANNE

Furnival Chambers
32 Furnival Street, London EC4A 1JQ,
☎ 020 7405 3232
Call Date: Nov 2010, Gray's Inn
Qualifications: [BA]
clerks@furnivallaw.co.uk

FARRELL MR SIMON HENRY QC (2003)

3 Raymond Buildings
3 Raymond Buildings, Gray's Inn, London WC1R 5BH, ☎ 020 7400 6400
✉ clerks@3rblaw.com
Call Date: Nov 1983, Lincoln's Inn
Qualifications: [MA (Cantab) Dip Law]

FARRELLY MISS CATHERINE LOUISE

5 King's Bench Walk
5 King's Bench Walk, Temple, London EC4Y 7DN, ☎ 020 7353 5638
✉ clerks@5kbw.co.uk
Call Date: Nov 1999, Middle Temple
Qualifications: [LLB (Hons)]

FARRELLY MR KEVIN JAMES

Ten Old Square
Ground Floor, Ten Old Square, Lincoln's Inn, London WC2A 3SU, ☎ 020 7405 0758
✉ clerks@tenoldsquare.com
Call Date: May 1993, Middle Temple
Qualifications: [BA (Hons)]
kevinfarrelly@tenoldsquare.com

FARRER MR ADAM MICHAEL

No5 Chambers
Fountain Court, Steelhouse Lane, Birmingham B4 6DR, ☎0845 210 5555 ✉info@no5.com
No5 Chambers
Greenwood House, 4-7 Salisbury Court, London EC4Y 8AA, ☎0845 210 5555
No5 Chambers
38 Queen Square, Bristol BS1 4QS, ☎0845 210 5555
Call Date: Oct 1992, Gray's Inn
Pupil Supervisor
Qualifications: [LLB (Nott'n)]
✉af@no5.com

FARRINGTON MRS GAIL LISA

St Mary's Family Law Chambers
26-28 High Pavement, The Lace Market, Nottingham NG1 1HN, ☎0115 950 3503
✉clerks@stmarysflc.co.uk
Call Date: July 2011, Gray's Inn
✉gail.farrington@stmarysflc.co.uk

FARRINGTON MS GEMMA

Stour Chambers
Mill Studio, 17a Stour Street, Canterbury, Kent CT1 2NR, ☎01227 764899
✉clerks@stourchambers.co.uk
Call Date: Oct 1994, Gray's Inn
Pupil Supervisor
Qualifications: [BA (Hons) CPE]
✉clerks@stourchambers.co.uk

FARROW MR ADRIAN JOHN

Exchange Chambers
7 Ralli Courts, West Riverside, Manchester M3 5FT, ☎0161 833 2722
Exchange Chambers
One Derby Square, Derby Square, Liverpool L2 9XX, ☎0151 236 7747
✉info@exchangechambers.co.uk
Exchange Chambers
Oxford House, Oxford Row, Leeds LS1 3BE, ☎0113 203 1970
✉spencer@exchangechambers.co.uk
Call Date: July 1997, Middle Temple
Pupil Supervisor
Qualifications: [LLB (Hons)(Leics)]
✉farrow@exchangechambers.co.uk

FARYL MISS ALAHA BEGUM

Central Chambers
89 Princess Street, Manchester M1 4HT, ☎0161 236 1133
✉clerks@centralchambers.co.uk
Call Date: Nov 2003, Lincoln's Inn
Qualifications: [LLB (Hons) (Manch)]

FATIMA MISS SHAHEED

Blackstone Chambers
Blackstone House, Temple, London EC4Y 9BW, ☎020 7583 1770
✉clerks@blackstonechambers.com
Call Date: Oct 2001, Gray's Inn
Qualifications: [LLB (Hons) (Glas) BCL (Oxon) LLM]
✉shaheedfatima@blackstonechambers.com

FAUL MISS ANNE FRANCES LOUISE

Nine Bedford Row
9 Bedford Row, London WC1R 4AZ, ☎020 7489 2727
✉clerks@9bedfordrow.co.uk
Call Date: Oct 1996, Middle Temple
Pupil Supervisor
Qualifications: [LLB (Hons)]
✉anne.faul@9bedfordrow.co.uk

FAULKNER MR BENJAMIN CHARLES GATEHOUSE

Wilberforce Chambers
8 New Square, Lincoln's Inn, London WC2A 3QP, ☎020 7306 0102
✉chambers@wilberforce.co.uk
Call Date: Oct 2008, Lincoln's Inn
Qualifications: [BA (Cantab)]
✉bfaulkner@wilberforce.co.uk

FAULKS LORD EDWARD PETER LAWLESS QC (1996)

1 Chancery Lane
London WC2A 1LF, ☎0845 634 6666
✉clerks@1chancerylane.com
Call Date: Nov 1973, Middle Temple
Qualifications: [MA (Oxon)]
✉efaulks@1chancerylane.com

FAULKS MR SAMUEL JAMES

Fountain Chambers
Cleveland Business Centre, 1 Watson Street, Middlesbrough TS1 2RQ, ☎01642 804040
✉clerks@fountainchambers.co.uk
Call Date: Oct 1997, Inner Temple
Pupil Supervisor
Qualifications: [LLB (Hons)(Northumbria)]

FAURE WALKER MISS JULIA FRANCES

2 Hare Court
Lower Ground, Ground, 1st & 2nd Floor, 2 Hare Court, Temple, London EC4Y 7BH, ☎020 7353 3982 ✉clerks@2harecourt.com
Call Date: July 2004, Lincoln's Inn
Qualifications: [PgDL BA BVC]
✉juliafaurewalker@2harecourt.com

E

FAUX MR ANDREW JOHN

Cornwall Street Chambers
85-87 Cornwall Street, Birmingham B3 3BY,
☎0121 233 7500
✉clerks@cornwallstreet.co.uk
Call Date: Nov 1995, Inner Temple
Qualifications: [BA (Sheff) CPE (Manc)]
andrew.faux@cornwallstreet.co.uk

FAUX MISS RACHEL ELIZABETH

18 St John Street
Manchester M3 4EA, ☎0161 278 1800
✉clerks@18sjs.com
Call Date: Oct 1997, Lincoln's Inn
Qualifications: [LLB (Hons)(Notts)]

FAVATA MISS EMMA JEAN

Garden Court Chambers
57-60 Lincoln's Inn Fields, London WC2A 3LJ,
☎020 7993 7600 ✉info@gclaw.co.uk
Call Date: Oct 1999, Lincoln's Inn
Qualifications: [MA (Hons)(Dundee) LLM (Lond) DEA (France)]
emmaf@gclaw.co.uk

E

FAWCETT MISS MICHELLE EVELYN

Furnival Chambers
32 Furnival Street, London EC4A 1JQ,
☎020 7405 3232
Call Date: Nov 1993, Inner Temple
Qualifications: [LLB (Kent)]
mfawcett@furnivallaw.co.uk

FAWCETT MR NEIL

St Ive's Chambers
Whittall Street, Birmingham B4 6DH,
☎0121 236 0863
✉clerks@stiveschambers.co.uk
Call Date: Oct 2006, Lincoln's Inn
Qualifications: [BSc (B'ham)]
neil.fawcett@stiveschambers.co.uk

FAZACKERLEY MR THOMAS BRIAN JOSEPH

Atlantic Chambers
4-6 Cook Street, Liverpool L2 9QU,
☎0151 236 4421
✉info@atlanticchambers.co.uk
Call Date: Oct 2010, Gray's Inn

FEALY MR MICHAEL

One Essex Court
Ground Floor, One Essex Court, Temple, London EC4Y 9AR, ☎020 7583 2000
✉clerks@oeclaw.co.uk
Call Date: May 1997, Middle Temple
Pupil Supervisor
Qualifications: [BCL (NUI) LLM (Cantab)]
mfealy@oeclaw.co.uk

FEARNLEY MR BENJAMIN MARK

29 Bedford Row Chambers
London WC1R 4HE, ☎020 7404 1044
✉clerks@29br.co.uk
Call Date: Nov 2001, Middle Temple
Qualifications: [BA (Hons) (Oxon)]
bfearnley@29br.co.uk

FEARON MISS SARAH LOUISE

Wilberforce Chambers
7 Bishop Lane, Hull HU1 1PA,
☎01482 323264
Call Date: Oct 2000, Middle Temple
Qualifications: [BA (Hons) (Sheff)]

FEATHERBY MR WILLIAM ALAN QC (2008)

12 King's Bench Walk
12 King's Bench Walk, Temple, London EC4Y 7EL, ☎020 7583 0811
Call Date: Nov 1978, Middle Temple
Recorder
Qualifications: [MA (Oxon)]
featherby@12kbw.co.uk

FEDER MR AMI

Chambers of Mr Ami Feder
Ground Floor, Lamb Building, Temple, London EC4Y 7AS, ☎020 7797 7788
✉clerks@lambbuilding.co.uk
Lamb Building
22 Ship Street, Brighton BN1 1AD,
☎01273 820490
✉admin@lambbuilding.co.uk
Chambers of Mr Ami Feder
Ground Floor, Lamb Building, Temple, London EC4Y 7AS, ☎020 7797 7788
✉clerks@lambbuilding.co.uk
Call Date: July 1965, Inner Temple
Qualifications: [LLB]
afeder@lambbuilding.co.uk

FEE MR CHARLES JONATHAN CONOR

29 Bedford Row Chambers
London WC1R 4HE, ☎020 7404 1044
✉clerks@29br.co.uk
Call Date: July 2006, Gray's Inn
Qualifications: [BA (Oxon)]

FEEHAN MR FRANCIS THOMAS QC (2010)

42 Bedford Row
London WC1R 4LL, ☎ 020 7831 0222
✉ clerks@42br.com
Call Date: July 1988, Lincoln's Inn
Pupil Supervisor
Qualifications: [BA (Hons) (Cantab)]
frank.feehan@42br.com

FEELY MISS JULIA FRANCES

1 Gray's Inn Square
Ground Floor, 1 Gray's Inn Square, London WC1R 5AA, ☎ 020 7405 0001
Call Date: July 2009, Lincoln's Inn
Qualifications: [LLB (Hons) (Leeds)]
jfeely@1gis.co.uk

FEENEY MISS KATIE MARIA

No5 Chambers
Fountain Court, Steelhouse Lane, Birmingham B4 6DR, ☎ 0845 210 5555 ✉ info@no5.com
No5 Chambers
Greenwood House, 4-7 Salisbury Court, London EC4Y 8AA, ☎ 0845 210 5555
No5 Chambers
38 Queen Square, Bristol BS1 4QS, ☎ 0845 210 5555
Call Date: July 2005, Inner Temple
Qualifications: [LLB(Leeds)]
kf@no5.com, katiefeeney@hotmail.com

FEENY MR CHARLES SHERIDAN

Call Date: Nov 1977, Inner Temple
Pupil Supervisor
Qualifications: [BA (Cantab)]

FEENY MR JACK

No5 Chambers
Greenwood House, 4-7 Salisbury Court, London EC4Y 8AA, ☎ 0845 210 5555
No5 Chambers
38 Queen Square, Bristol BS1 4QS, ☎ 0845 210 5555
No5 Chambers
Fountain Court, Steelhouse Lane, Birmingham B4 6DR, ☎ 0845 210 5555 ✉ info@no5.com
Call Date: Nov 2005, Inner Temple
Qualifications: [BA University of York MA University of Liverpoo]

FEEST MR ADAM SEBASTIAN

3 PB Barristers
3 Paper Buildings, Temple, London EC4Y 7EU, ☎ 020 7583 8055
3 PB Barristers
Royal Talbot House, 2 Victoria Street, Bristol, Avon BS1 6BB, ☎ 0117 928 1520
3 PB Barristers
30 Christchurch Road, Bournemouth, Dorset BH1 3PD, ☎ 01202 292102
✉ clerks.bournemouth@3paper.co.uk
3 PB Barristers
4 St Peter Street, Winchester SO23 8BW, ☎ 01962 868884
✉ clerks.winchester@3paper.co.uk
3 PB Barristers
23 Beaumont Street, Oxford OX1 2NP, ☎ 01865 793 736
Call Date: Feb 1994, Inner Temple
Pupil Supervisor
Qualifications: [BA (Oxon)]
adam.feest@3pb.co.uk

FELDBERG MR PAUL GABRIEL

Chambers of Andrew Mitchell QC
33 Chancery Lane, London WC2A 1EN, ☎ 020 7440 9950 ✉ clerks@33cllaw.com
Call Date: Oct 1997, Inner Temple
Qualifications: [BA (Bris) CPE]
paulfeldberg@fulcrumchambers.com

FELDMAN MR MATTHEW RICHARD BANKES

42 Bedford Row
London WC1R 4LL, ☎ 020 7831 0222
✉ clerks@42br.com
Call Date: Oct 1995, Inner Temple
Pupil Supervisor
Qualifications: [BA (Joint Hons)(Manc) CPE]
matthew.feldman@42br.com

FELDSCHREIBER DR PETER

Four New Square
Four New Square, Lincoln's Inn, London WC2A 3RJ, ☎ 020 7822 2000
✉ barristers@4newsquare.com
Call Date: Nov 2000, Middle Temple
Qualifications: [MBBS(Lond) LLB (Hons) FFPM (RCP)]
p.feldschreiber@4newsquare.com

E

FELIX MISS ALEXANDRA MIRNALINI

QEB Hollis Whiteman
1-2 Laurence Pountney Hill, London
EC4R 0EU, ☎020 7933 8855
✉barristers@qebhw.co.uk
Call Date: Oct 1999, Middle Temple
Pupil Supervisor
Qualifications: [LLB (Hons) LLM (Lond)]
✉alexandra.felix@qebhw.co.uk

FELL MR ALISTAIR ALEXANDER

18 Red Lion Court
London EC4A 3EB, ☎020 7520 6000
✉chambers@18rlc.co.uk
Call Date: Nov 1994, Middle Temple
Qualifications: [LLB (Hons) LLM]
✉Alistair.fell@18RLC.co.uk

FELL MR MARK ANTHONY

Radcliffe Chambers
Ground Floor, 11 New Square, Lincoln's Inn,
London WC2A 3QB, ☎020 7831 0081
✉clerks@radcliffechambers.com
Call Date: July 2004, Lincoln's Inn
Qualifications: [MA MSc CPE]
✉mfell@radcliffechambers.com

FELLOWS MR PHILIP DAVID ANDREW

Hardwicke
New Square, Lincoln's Inn, London
WC2A 3SB, ☎020 7242 2523
✉enquiries@hardwicke.co.uk
Call Date: July 2007, Lincoln's Inn
Qualifications: [MA (Cantab)]
✉philip.fellows@hardwicke.co.uk

FELSTEAD MR CHRISTOPHER JAMES

9 Park Place
9 Park Place, Cardiff, South Glamorgan
CF10 3DP, ☎029 2038 2731
✉clerks@9parkplace.co.uk
Call Date: Oct 1998, Lincoln's Inn
Pupil Supervisor
Qualifications: [LLB (Hons)(Wales)]
✉cfelstead@9parkplace.co.uk

FELTHAM MR PIERS JONATHAN

Radcliffe Chambers
Ground Floor, 11 New Square, Lincoln's Inn,
London WC2A 3QB, ☎020 7831 0081
✉clerks@radcliffechambers.com
Call Date: July 1985, Gray's Inn
Pupil Supervisor
Qualifications: [BA (Cantab)]
✉pfeltham@radcliffechambers.com

FELTON MR TIMOTHY JOHN FOWLER

Rougemont Chambers
Victory House, Dean Clarke Gardens,
Southernhay East, Exeter EX2 4AA,
☎01392 208484
✉clerks@rougemontchambers.co.uk
Call Date: July 1977, Middle Temple
Qualifications: [LLB (Hons)]
✉tfelton@rougemontchambers.co.uk

FEMI-OLA MR ABIODUN JOHN

3 Temple Gardens
Lower Ground Floor, 3 Temple Gardens,
Temple, London EC4Y 9AU, ☎020 7353 3102
✉clerks@3tg.co.uk
Call Date: Nov 1985, Gray's Inn
Pupil Supervisor
Qualifications: [BA]
✉jfo@3tg.co.uk

FENDER MR CARL DAVID

Regency Chambers
45 Priestgate, Peterborough PE1 1LB,
☎01733 315215
✉clerks@regencychambers.law.co.uk
Regency Chambers
Sheraton House, Castle Park, Cambridge
CB3 0AX, ☎01223 301517
Call Date: Feb 1994, Middle Temple
Pupil Supervisor
Qualifications: [BA (Hons)(Kent)]
✉clerks@regencychambers.law.co.uk

FENHALLS MR MARK ROYDON ALLEN

23 Essex Street
London WC2R 3AA, ☎020 7413 0353
✉clerks@23es.com
Call Date: Oct 1992, Gray's Inn
Pupil Supervisor
Qualifications: [MA MSc]

FENN MR ANDREW JAMES

Atkin Chambers
1 Atkin Building, Gray's Inn, London
WC1R 5AT, ☎020 7404 0102
✉clerks@atkinchambers.com
Call Date: Mar 2007, Gray's Inn
Qualifications: [BA (Cantab)]
✉clerks@atkinchambers.com, fender1983@hotmail.com

E

FENNY MR IAN CHARLES

Guildhall Chambers
23 Broad Street, Bristol BS1 2HG,
☎0117 930 9000
✉hoc@guildhallchambers.co.uk
Call Date: July 1978, Gray's Inn
Pupil Supervisor
Qualifications: [LLB]
ian.fenny@guildhallchambers.co.uk

FENTEM MR ROSS DAVID

Guildhall Chambers
23 Broad Street, Bristol BS1 2HG,
☎0117 930 9000
✉hoc@guildhallchambers.co.uk
Call Date: July 2003, Lincoln's Inn
Qualifications: [MA (Lond) BA Hons (Cantab) PgDL (Lond)]
ross.fentem@guildhallchambers.co.uk

FENTON MR ADAM TIMOTHY DOWNS QC (2003)

7 King's Bench Walk
Ground Floor, 7 King's Bench Walk, Temple, London EC4Y 7DS, ☎020 7910 8300
✉clerks@7kbw.co.uk
Call Date: Nov 1984, Inner Temple
Qualifications: [BA (Oxon)]
afenton@7kbw.co.uk

FENWICK MR JUSTIN FRANCIS QUINTUS QC (1993)

Four New Square
Four New Square, Lincoln's Inn, London WC2A 3RJ, ☎020 7822 2000
✉barristers@4newsquare.com
Call Date: Nov 1980, Inner Temple
Recorder
Qualifications: [MA (Cantab)]
j.fenwick@4newsquare.com

FERBER MS IRIS

42 Bedford Row
London WC1R 4LL, ☎020 7831 0222
✉clerks@42br.com
Call Date: July 2005, Inner Temple
Qualifications: [BA M Phil Selwyn College University of Cambridg]
Iris.Ferber@42br.com

Fax: 020 7831 2239
URL: www.42bedfordrow.com

Types of work: Chancery, Commercial law, Employment, Housing, Landlord and tenant, Property, Public law

FERGUSON MR CHRISTOPHER MARK

Sovereign Chambers
46 Park Place, Leeds LS1 2RY,
☎0113 245 1841
✉clerks@sovereignchambers.co.uk
Court Yard Chambers
Eltham Palace, P.O.370, London SE9 2RP,
☎020 7936 2710
Unity Street Chambers
5 Unity Street, College Green, Bristol BS1 5HH, ☎0117 906 9789
✉chambers@unitystreetchambers.com
Call Date: May 1979, Middle Temple
Pupil Supervisor
christopher.ferguson@sovereignchambers.co.uk

FERGUSON MR CRAIG CHARLES

2 Hare Court
Lower Ground, Ground, 1st & 2nd Floor, 2 Hare Court, Temple, London EC4Y 7BH,
☎020 7353 3982 ✉clerks@2harecourt.com
Call Date: Feb 1992, Middle Temple
Pupil Supervisor
Qualifications: [LLB (Hons)]
craigferguson@2harecourt.com

FERGUSON MISS EVA ENID

Hailsham Chambers
Ground Floor, 4 Paper Buildings, Temple, London EC4Y 7EX, ☎020 7643 5000
✉clerks@hailshamchambers.com
Call Date: Nov 1999, Middle Temple
Qualifications: [BA (Hons)(Dunelm)]
eva.ferguson@hailshamchambers.com

FERGUSON MS JASMINE

Argent Chambers
5 Bell Yard, London WC2A 2JR,
☎020 7556 5500
✉briefsin@argentchambers.co.uk
Call Date: Nov 2011, Middle Temple
Qualifications: [BA (Australia) LLB (Hons) (Australia)]

FERGUSON MRS KATHARINE ANN

Fenners Chambers
3 Madingley Road, Cambridge CB3 0EE,
☎01223 368761
✉clerks@fennerschambers.com
Call Date: Feb 1995, Inner Temple
Qualifications: [BA (Oxon)]
katharine.ferguson@fennerschambers.com

E

FERGUSON MR STEPHEN MICHAEL

2 Bedford Row
London WC1R 4BU, ☎ 020 7440 8888
✉ clerks@2bedfordrow.co.uk
Call Date: Nov 1991, Inner Temple
Qualifications: [MA (Oxon)]
sferguson@2bedfordrow.co.uk

FERM MR RODNEY ERIC

Broadway House Chambers
Broadway House, 9 Bank Street, Bradford, West Yorkshire BD1 1TW, ☎ 01274 722560
✉ clerks@broadwayhouse.co.uk
Broadway House Chambers
25 Park Square West, Leeds, West Yorkshire LS1 2PW, ☎ 0113 246 2600
✉ clerks@broadwayhouse.co.uk
Call Date: July 1972, Middle Temple
Pupil Supervisor
Qualifications: [BA (Oxon)]
Rosieferm@yahoo.co.uk

FERN MR GARY

7 Stones IP
88 Kingsway, Holborn, London WC2B 6AA, ☎ 020 7193 4033
Call Date: Oct 1992, Lincoln's Inn
Pupil Supervisor
Qualifications: [B Eng (Hons) LLM CPE]
g.fern@hotmail.co.uk

E

FERNANDES MISS SUE-ELLEN CASSIANA

No5 Chambers
Greenwood House, 4-7 Salisbury Court, London EC4Y 8AA, ☎ 0845 210 5555
No5 Chambers
38 Queen Square, Bristol BS1 4QS, ☎ 0845 210 5555
No5 Chambers
Fountain Court, Steelhouse Lane, Birmingham B4 6DR, ☎ 0845 210 5555 ✉ info@no5.com
Call Date: Oct 2005, Middle Temple
Qualifications: [LLM MA (Hons) Cantab]
sfe@no5.com

FERNANDO MR GILES RUDYARD

11 South Square
1st Floor, 11 South Square, Gray's Inn, London WC1R 5EY, ☎ 020 7405 1222
✉ clerks@11southsquare.com
Call Date: Mar 1998, Gray's Inn
Pupil Supervisor
Qualifications: [BA (Oxon)]
gfernando@11southsquare.com

FERNANDO MR PRAVIN NATH

3 Serjeants Inn
London EC4Y 1BQ, ☎ 020 7427 5000
✉ clerks@3serjeantsinn.com
Call Date: Oct 2009, Inner Temple
Qualifications: [LLB (Lond) LLM (Lond)]
pfernando@3serjeantsinn.com

FERRARI MR NICHOLAS JAMES DINO

1 Gray's Inn Square
Ground Floor, 1 Gray's Inn Square, London WC1R 5AA, ☎ 020 7405 0001
Rougemont Chambers
Victory House, Dean Clarke Gardens, Southernhay East, Exeter EX2 4AA, ☎ 01392 208484
✉ clerks@rougemontchambers.co.uk
Call Date: Nov 2005, Gray's Inn
Qualifications: [BA (Bris)]
nferrari@1gis.co.uk

FERRER MR PETER ANDREW

Quadrant Chambers
Quadrant House, 10 Fleet Street, London EC4Y 1AU, ☎ 020 7583 4444
✉ info@quadrantchambers.com
Call Date: Oct 1998, Inner Temple
Pupil Supervisor
Qualifications: [BA (Wales) CPE]
peter.ferrer@quadrantchambers.com

FERRIER MRS SUSAN

Apex
Harlech House, 20 Cathedral Road, Cardiff CF11 9LJ, ☎ 02920 232 032
✉ clerks@apexchambers.net
Call Date: Nov 1985, Gray's Inn
Pupil Supervisor
Qualifications: [BSc (Hons)(Wales)]
susan.ferrier@apexchambers.net

FERRIS MS CAITLIN TARA

Coram Chambers
9-11 Fulwood Place, London WC1V 6HG, ☎ 020 7092 3700
✉ mail@coramchambers.co.uk
Call Date: Mar 1996, Inner Temple
Qualifications: [BA (Leeds)]
caitlin.ferris@coramchambers.co.uk

FERRIS MR SHAUN

Crown Office Chambers
2 Crown Office Row, Temple, London
EC4Y 7HJ, ☎020 7797 8100
✉mail@crownofficechambers.com
Call Date: Nov 1985, Gray's Inn
Pupil Supervisor
Qualifications: [MA (Oxon)]
✉ferris@crownofficechambers.com

FERRO MR JACK

Crown Office Chambers
2 Crown Office Row, Temple, London
EC4Y 7HJ, ☎020 7797 8100
✉mail@crownofficechambers.com
Call Date: Oct 1998, Inner Temple
Qualifications: [BA (Oxon)]
✉ferro@crownofficechambers.com

FERRY-SWAINSON MR RICHARD JOSEPH

2 Bedford Row
London WC1R 4BU, ☎020 7440 8888
✉clerks@2bedfordrow.co.uk
Call Date: Oct 1994, Lincoln's Inn
Qualifications: [LLB (Hons)(Lond)]
✉rferry-swainson@2bedfordrow.co.uk

FESSAL MR IGNATIUS

1 Mitre Court Buildings
1 Mitre Court Buildings, Temple, London
EC4Y 7BS, ☎020 7452 8900
✉clerks@1mcb.com
Call Date: Nov 1981, Inner Temple
Qualifications: [LLB]
✉ignatius.fessal@1mcb.com

FETHERSTONHAUGH MR GUY CUTHBERT CHARLES QC (2003)

Falcon Chambers
Falcon Court, London EC4Y 1AA,
☎020 7353 2484
✉clerks@falcon-chambers.com
Call Date: July 1983, Inner Temple
Qualifications: [BSc (Bris)]
✉fetherstonhaugh@falcon-chambers.com

Types of work: Chancery, Landlord and tenant, Litigation, Mining, Property, Real property, Water

FETTO MR NIAZI PETER

2 Temple Gardens
2 Temple Gardens, Temple, London
EC4Y 9AY, ☎020 7822 1200
✉clerks@2tg.co.uk
Call Date: Oct 1999, Inner Temple
Pupil Supervisor
Qualifications: [MA (Cantab)]
✉nfetto@2tg.co.uk

FEWTRELL MR NICHOLAS AUSTIN

18 St John Street
Manchester M3 4EA, ☎0161 278 1800
✉clerks@18sjs.com
Call Date: Nov 1977, Inner Temple
Pupil Supervisor, Recorder
Qualifications: [LLB (Lond)]

FFITCH MR NIGEL ANTHONY

Clerksroom (Taunton)
Equity House, Administration Centre,
Blackbrook Park Avenue, Taunton, Somerset
TA1 2PX, ☎0845 083 3000
✉mail@clerksroom.com
64 Bridge Street
3rd Floor, 64 Bridge Street, Manchester
M3 3BN, ☎0845 083 3000
✉mail@64bridgestreet.com
Clerksroom (London)
3rd Floor, 218 Strand, London WC2R 1AT,
☎0845 083 3000 ✉mail@clerksroom.com
Call Date: Oct 1996, Gray's Inn
Qualifications: [LLB (Hons) (Lond)]

FICKLIN MR JARED DUANE

Chambers of Ian Macdonald QC
Garden Court North, 22 Oxford Court,
Manchester M2 3WQ, ☎0161 236 1840
✉clerks@gcnchambers.co.uk
Call Date: July 2007, Middle Temple
Qualifications: [BA (Nebraska) MSc (Bath)]
✉clerks@gcnchambers.co.uk

FIELD MR JULIAN NIGEL

Crown Office Chambers
2 Crown Office Row, Temple, London
EC4Y 7HJ, ☎020 7797 8100
✉mail@crownofficechambers.com
Call Date: Nov 1980, Gray's Inn
Pupil Supervisor
Qualifications: [LLB (Lond)]
✉field@crownofficechambers.com

FIELD MISS LAURA

2 Pump Court
1st Floor, 2 Pump Court, Temple, London EC4Y 7AH, ☎020 7353 5597
✉clerks@2pumpcourt.co.uk
Call Date: July 2009, Middle Temple
Qualifications: [LLB (Hons) (Leeds)]

FIELD MR RORY DOMINIC

15 New Bridge Street
London EC4V 6AU, ☎020 7842 1900
✉clerks@15nbs.com
Call Date: July 1980, Middle Temple
Qualifications: [BA (Hons) (Cantab)]

FIELD MR STEPHEN ANTHONY

1 Pump Court
Elm Court, Temple, London EC4Y 7AB, ☎020 7842 7070
✉(name)@pumpcourt.co.uk
Call Date: Nov 1993, Gray's Inn
Pupil Supervisor
Qualifications: [LLB (Lond)]

FIELDEN DR CHRISTA MARIA

1 Mitre Court Buildings
1 Mitre Court Buildings, Temple, London EC4Y 7BS, ☎020 7452 8900
✉clerks@1mcb.com
Call Date: Nov 1982, Lincoln's Inn
Pupil Supervisor
Qualifications: [BSc (Hons) MSc PhD BSC(Hons)]

FIELDING MR JANICK RAPHAEL ALEXANDER

4 King's Bench Walk
2nd Floor, 4 King's Bench Walk, Temple, London EC4Y 7DL, ☎020 7822 7000
✉clerks@4kbw.co.uk
Call Date: Oct 1997, Inner Temple
Qualifications: [BA (LSE)]
jrf@4kbw.co.uk

FIELDSEND MR JAMES WILLIAM

Tanfield Chambers
2-5 Warwick Court, London WC1R 5DJ, ☎020 7421 5300
✉clerks@tanfieldchambers.co.uk
Call Date: Oct 1997, Lincoln's Inn
Qualifications: [LLB (Hons)(Newc)]
jamesfieldsend@tanfieldchambers.co.uk

FINCH MR ANTHONY WILLIAM

Derwent Chambers
78 Friar Gate, Derby DE1 1FL, ☎01332 242425
✉admin@derwentchambers.co.uk
Call Date: Oct 2006, Lincoln's Inn
Qualifications: [LLB (Hons) (Manch)]
ants21uk@yahoo.com

FINCH MR LEE WILLIAM

Gough Square Chambers
6-7 Gough Square, London EC4A 3DE, ☎020 7353 0924 ✉gsc@goughsq.co.uk
Call Date: July 2010, Inner Temple
Qualifications: [LLB LLM (Dunelm)]
lee.finch@goughsq.co.uk

FINCH MS NADINE ELIZABETH

Garden Court Chambers
57-60 Lincoln's Inn Fields, London WC2A 3LJ, ☎020 7993 7600 ✉info@gclaw.co.uk
Call Date: Oct 1991, Middle Temple
Pupil Supervisor
Qualifications: [BA (Hons) (UEA) DipLaw]
nadinef@gclaw.co.uk

Fax: 020 7993 7700;
DX: 34 London, Chancery Lane

Types of work: Civil liberties, Community care, Family law, Human rights, Immigration

Other professional experience: Nine years as local government officer specialising in work with local communities and equalities

Publications: *Putting Children First: A Guide for Immigration Practitioners* (LAG; Contributor), 2010; *Levelling the Playing Field* (UNICEF UK)(co-author 2010), 2008; *Seeking Asylum Alone: Unaccompanied and Separated Children and Refugee Protection in the UK* (Harvard University Committee on Human Rights Studies), 2006; *Integrating Diversity; The Collected Papers of the 2007 Interdisciplinary Conference, Darlington Hall* (Contributor), 2007; *Levelling the Playing Field* (UNICEF UK)(co-author 2010), 2010

Reported Cases: *R (Clue) v Birmingham City Council & Another (Shelter intervening)*, [2010] EWCA Civ 460 A local authority is under a duty to support a family under Section 17 of the Children Act 1989 when they have an outstanding application for leave to remain based on human rights grounds.
ID & others v The Home Office, [2005] EWCA Civ 38 Immigration officers enjoy no immunity from suit in respect of a damages claim for false imprisonment arising out of a discharge of functions under the Immigration Act 1971
AA (Afghanistan) v Secretary of State for the Home Department, Medical Foundation for the

Care of Victims of Torture intervening, [2007] EWCA Civ 12 The test to be applied as to whether a child was unaccompanied or could be returned to their country of origin.
Sepet v Secretary of State for the Home Department, [2003] UKHL 15 Whether a conscientious objector to military service is entitled to the protection of the Refugee Convention.
Berhe v London Borough of Hillingdon, [2003] EWHC 2075 Admin Immigration officers enjoy no immunity from suit in respect of a damages claim for false imprisonment arising out of a discharge of functions under the Immigration Act 1971.

FINCH MR THOMAS MICHAEL

Dere Street Barristers
33 Broad Chare, Newcastle Upon Tyne
NE1 3DQ, ☎0844 3351551
✉clerks@derestreet.co.uk
Call Date: Nov 1981, Lincoln's Inn
Pupil Supervisor
Qualifications: [BA Hons]
✉t.finch@derestreet.co.uk, clerks@broadcharechambers.co.uk

FINDLAY MR JAMES DE CARDONNEL QC (2008)

Cornerstone Barristers
2-3 Gray's Inn Square, Gray's Inn, London
WC1R 5JH, ☎020 7242 4986
✉chambers@2-3gis.co.uk
Call Date: Nov 1984, Middle Temple
Qualifications: [MA (Cantab)]
✉jfindlay@2-3gis.co.uk

FINLAY MR DARREN

Sovereign Chambers
46 Park Place, Leeds LS1 2RY,
☎0113 245 1841
✉clerks@sovereignchambers.co.uk
Call Date: Oct 1994, Gray's Inn
Qualifications: [BA (Keele)]
✉darren.finlay@sovereignchambers.co.uk

FINN MR TERENCE

Forest Chambers
Chambers of Terence Finn, 13 Rutland Gardens, Gosberton, Boston, Lincolnshire
PE11 4HR, ☎01775 840827
✉forestchambers@btinternet.com
Erimus Chambers
PO Box 1440, Bedford MK43 6AJ,
☎01234 720952
✉clerks@erimuschambers.com
Call Date: Oct 1995, Lincoln's Inn
Qualifications: [LLB (Hons)(Bournem)]
✉forestchambers@btinternet.com

FINNIGAN MR PETER ANTHONY QC (2009)

QEB Hollis Whiteman
1-2 Laurence Pountney Hill, London
EC4R 0EU, ☎020 7933 8855
✉barristers@qebhw.co.uk
Call Date: July 1978, Lincoln's Inn
Qualifications: [LLB (Newc)]
✉barristers@qebhw.co.uk, peter.finnigan@qebhw.co.uk

FINUCANE MR BRENDAN GODFREY EAMONN QC (2003)

Outer Temple Chambers
The Outer Temple, 222 Strand, London
WC2R 1BA, ☎020 7353 6381
✉clerks@outertemple.com
Call Date: July 1976, Middle Temple
Qualifications: [BSc (Lond)]
✉brendan.finucaneqc@outertemple.com

FIRBANK MR KIT JAMES

18 St John Street
Manchester M3 4EA, ☎0161 278 1800
✉clerks@18sjs.com
Call Date: Oct 2005, Middle Temple
Qualifications: [BSc (Hons) (Lond) Dip in Law]

FIRTH MS ALISON MARY LESTER

Ingenuity IP Chambers
Chambers Legal Service, 71b Queensway, Petts Wood, Kent BR5 1DQ
✉lp@chamberslegalservice.com
Call Date: Nov 1980, Middle Temple
Qualifications: [MA (Oxon) MSc]

FIRTH MR MATTHEW ALEXANDER

Queen Elizabeth Building
3rd Floor, Queen Elizabeth Building, Temple, London EC4Y 9BS, ☎020 7797 7837
✉clerks@qeb.co.uk
Call Date: Oct 1991, Gray's Inn
Pupil Supervisor
Qualifications: [MA (Oxon)]
✉m.firth@qeb.co.uk

FISCHEL MR ROBERT GUSTAV QC (1998)

Chambers of Robert Fischel QC
2é Molino, Camino La Lobilla, Estepona
29680, ☎0034 95280 4346
✉rgfischel@gmail.com
Call Date: July 1975, Middle Temple
Qualifications: [LLB (Lond)]

E

FISH MR DAVID THOMAS QC (1997)

Deans Court Chambers
24 St John Street, Manchester M3 4DF,
☎0161 214 6000 ✉clerks@deanscourt.co.uk
Deans Court Chambers
101 Walker Street, Preston PR1 2RR,
☎01772 565 600
✉preston@deanscourt.co.uk
Goldsmith Chambers
Ground Floor, Goldsmith Building, Temple,
London EC4Y 7BL, ☎020 7353 6802
✉clerks@goldsmithchambers.com
Call Date: July 1973, Inner Temple
Recorder
Qualifications: [LLB]
✉fish@deanscourt.co.uk

FISH MR LEE STEPHEN

New Court Chambers
3 Broad Chare, Newcastle Upon Tyne
NE1 3DQ, ☎0191 232 1980
✉clerks@newcourt-chambers.co.uk
Call Date: July 2003, Lincoln's Inn
Qualifications: [LLB (Hons)(Newc)]
✉lee.fish@newcourt-chambers.co.uk

E

FISHER MR CRAIG SIMON

Number 7 Harrington Street Chambers
7 Harrington Street, Liverpool L2 9YH,
☎0151 242 0707 ✉clerks@7hs.co.uk
Call Date: July 2004, Middle Temple
Qualifications: [LLB Hons (Newc)]
✉craig.fisher@7hs.co.uk.

FISHER MR DAVID

New Square Chambers
12 New Square, Lincoln's Inn, London
WC2A 3SW, ☎020 7419 8000
✉robin.hollington@newsquarechambers.co.uk
Call Date: Nov 1985, Lincoln's Inn
Pupil Supervisor
Qualifications: [BA (Cantab)]
✉david.fisher@newsquarechambers.co.uk

FISHER MR DAVID PAUL QC (1996)

6 King's Bench Walk
Ground Floor, 6 King's Bench Walk, Temple,
London EC4Y 7DR, ☎020 7583 0410
✉clerks@6kbw.com
Call Date: July 1973, Gray's Inn
Recorder
✉david.fisher@6kbw.com

FISHER MR JERVIS ANDREW QC (2009)

Citadel Chambers
The Citadel, 190 Corporation Street,
Birmingham B4 6QD, ☎0121 233 8500
✉clerks@citadelchambers.com
Call Date: July 1980, Gray's Inn
Qualifications: [LLB (Lond)]
✉clerks@citadelchambers.com

FISHER MR JONATHAN SIMON QC (2003)

Devereux Chambers
Queen Elizabeth Building, Temple, London
EC4Y 9BS, ☎020 7353 7534
✉clerks@devchambers.co.uk
Call Date: July 1980, Gray's Inn
Qualifications: [BA LLB (Cantab)]
✉fisher@devchambers.co.uk

Types of work: Asset forfeiture, Asset recovery, Banking and Finance, Civil fraud, Computer crime, Confiscation, Corporate fraud, Corporate manslaughter, Crime, Criminal judicial review, Forfeiture, Fraud, International fraud and asset tracing, Litigation, Money laundering, Securities law and regulation, Serious fraud, Tax, Tax investigations, Taxation and duties

FISHER MISS JUSTINE STACEY

Chambers of Mr Ami Feder
Ground Floor, Lamb Building, Temple, London
EC4Y 7AS, ☎020 7797 7788
✉clerks@lambbuilding.co.uk
Chambers of Mr Ami Feder
Ground Floor, Lamb Building, Temple, London
EC4Y 7AS, ☎020 7797 7788
✉clerks@lambbuilding.co.uk
Call Date: Nov 1994, Inner Temple
Qualifications: [LLB LLM (Notts)]

FISHER MR RICHARD ALAN

Doughty Street Chambers
53-54 Doughty Street, London WC1N 2LS,
☎020 7404 1313
✉enquiries@doughtystreet.co.uk
Doughty Street Chambers
Pall Mall Court, 61-67 King Street, Manchester
M2 4PD, ☎0161 618 1066
Doughty Street Chambers
5th Floor, Broad Quay House, Prince Street,
Bristol BS1 4DJ, ☎01179 058 717
Call Date: Nov 1994, Lincoln's Inn
Pupil Supervisor
Qualifications: [LLB (Bris)]
✉r.fisher@doughtystreet.co.uk

FISHER MR RICHARD MARK

South Square
3-4 South Square, Gray's Inn, London WC1R 5HP, ☎ 020 7696 9900
✉ practicemanagers@southsquare.com
Call Date: Oct 2000, Lincoln's Inn
Qualifications: [LLB (Hons) (Lond) BCL (Oxon)]
richardfisher@southsquare.com

FISHER MS SANDRA

Renaissance Chambers
5th Floor, Gray's Inn Chambers, Gray's Inn, London WC1R 5JA, ☎ 020 7404 1111
✉ clerks@renaissancechambers.co.uk
Call Date: Nov 1993, Inner Temple
Qualifications: [LLB]
sf@renaissancechambers.co.uk

FISHER MR STEVEN DAVID

Kew Chambers
354 Kew Road, Kew, Surrey TW9 3DU, ☎ 0844 8099991
✉ admin@kewchambers.co.uk
Call Date: July 2000, Gray's Inn
Qualifications: [LLB (Hons)]
sfisher.barrister@tiscali.co.uk

FISHER MR TOBY RICHARD

Landmark Chambers
180 Fleet Street, London EC4A 2HG, ☎ 020 7430 1221
✉ clerks@landmarkchambers.co.uk
Call Date: Oct 2008, Lincoln's Inn
Qualifications: [BA (Cantab) LLM (Lse)]
TFisher@landmarkchambers.co.uk

FISHWICK MR GREGORY DAVID PHILIP KYLE

187 Fleet Street
London EC4A 2AT, ☎ 020 7430 7430
✉ chambers@187fleetstreet.com
Call Date: Oct 1996, Gray's Inn
Qualifications: [LLB LLM (Exon)]
gregoryfishwick@187fleetstreet.com

FITCH-HOLLAND MR ANDREW ROBERT

Argent Chambers
5 Bell Yard, London WC2A 2JR, ☎ 020 7556 5500
✉ briefsin@argentchambers.co.uk
Call Date: Nov 1990, Inner Temple
Qualifications: [LLB (Bucks)]

FITT MR ROBERT WILLIAM

Old Bailey Chambers
15 Old Bailey, London EC4M 7EF, ☎ 020 3008 6404
✉ clerks@15oldbaileychambers.com
Call Date: July 2008, Middle Temple
Qualifications: [BA (Hons) (York) PgDl (Lond)]

FITTON MR MICHAEL DAVID GUY QC (2006)

Albion Chambers
Broad Street, Bristol BS1 1DR, ☎ 0117 927 2144
✉ clerks@albionchambers.co.uk
Call Date: Nov 1991, Gray's Inn
Recorder
Qualifications: [MA (Oxon)]
michael.fittonqc@albionchambers.co.uk

FITTON-BROWN MISS REBECCA MARY

New Walk Chambers
27 New Walk, Leicester, Leicestershire LE1 6TE, ☎ 0871 200 1298 / 0116 255 9144
✉ clerks@newwalkchambers.co.uk
Call Date: July 1981, Inner Temple
Pupil Supervisor
Qualifications: [LLB]

FITZGERALD MR BENEDICT ANDREW

QEB Hollis Whiteman
1-2 Laurence Pountney Hill, London EC4R 0EU, ☎ 020 7933 8855
✉ barristers@qebhw.co.uk
Call Date: Oct 2000, Lincoln's Inn
Pupil Supervisor
Qualifications: [BA (Hons) (Cantab)]
ben.fitzgerald@qebhw.co.uk

FITZGERALD MR EDWARD HAMILTON QC (1995)

Doughty Street Chambers
53-54 Doughty Street, London WC1N 2LS, ☎ 020 7404 1313
✉ enquiries@doughtystreet.co.uk
Doughty Street Chambers
Pall Mall Court, 61-67 King Street, Manchester M2 4PD, ☎ 0161 618 1066
Doughty Street Chambers
5th Floor, Broad Quay House, Prince Street, Bristol BS1 4DJ, ☎ 01179 058 717
Call Date: Nov 1978, Inner Temple
Qualifications: [BA (Oxon) MPhil]
e.fitzgerald@doughtystreet.co.uk

E

FITZGERALD MISS ELIZABETH HELEN

Falcon Chambers
Falcon Court, London EC4Y 1AA,
☎ 020 7353 2484
✉ clerks@falcon-chambers.com
Call Date: Oct 2001, Inner Temple
Pupil Supervisor
Qualifications: [LLB (Lond)]
fitzgerald@falcon-chambers.com

Types of work: Chancery (land law), Commercial property, Landlord and tenant, Real property

FITZGERALD MR JOHN VINCENT

Ingenuity IP Chambers
Chambers Legal Service, 71b Queensway, Petts Wood, Kent BR5 1DQ
✉ lp@chamberslegalservice.com
Call Date: July 1971, Middle Temple
Pupil Supervisor
Qualifications: [BSc (Hons)]

FITZGERALD MR JOHN WILLIAM

Maidstone Chambers
33 Earl Street, Maidstone, Kent ME14 1PF,
☎ 01622 688592
✉ clerks@maidstonechambers.co.uk
Call Date: Oct 1998, Inner Temple
Pupil Supervisor
Qualifications: [BA (Hons)(Lond) CPE]
jfitzgerald@maidstonechambers.co.uk

FITZGERALD MR MICHAEL EDWARD

Monckton Chambers
1 & 2 Raymond Buildings, Gray's Inn, London WC1R 5NR, ☎ 020 7405 7211
✉ chambers@monckton.com
Call Date: May 1979, Lincoln's Inn
mfitzgerald@monckton.com

FITZGERALD MR PETER MICHAEL PATRICK

6 King's Bench Walk
Ground Floor, 6 King's Bench Walk, Temple, London EC4Y 7DR, ☎ 020 7583 0410
✉ clerks@6kbw.com
Call Date: July 2007, Middle Temple
Qualifications: [BA (Hons) (Cantab) LLB (Hons)]

FITZGERALD MISS SUSANNA QC (1999)

One Essex Court
Ground Floor, One Essex Court, Temple, London EC4Y 9AR, ☎ 020 7583 2000
✉ clerks@oeclaw.co.uk
Call Date: July 1973, Inner Temple
Qualifications: [LLB (Hons)]
sfitzgerald@oeclaw.co.uk

FITZGERALD MR TOBY JONATHAN

Atkinson Bevan Chambers
1st Floor, 2 Harcourt Buildings, Temple, London EC4Y 9DB, ☎ 020 7353 2112
✉ clerks@2hb.co.uk
Call Date: Oct 1993, Lincoln's Inn
Pupil Supervisor
Qualifications: [BSc (Hons)(Bris)]
tfitzgerald@2hb.co.uk

FITZGIBBON MR FRANCIS GEORGE HERBERT DILLON QC (2010)

Doughty Street Chambers
53-54 Doughty Street, London WC1N 2LS,
☎ 020 7404 1313
✉ enquiries@doughtystreet.co.uk
Doughty Street Chambers
Pall Mall Court, 61-67 King Street, Manchester M2 4PD, ☎ 0161 618 1066
Doughty Street Chambers
5th Floor, Broad Quay House, Prince Street, Bristol BS1 4DJ, ☎ 01179 058 717
Call Date: Feb 1986, Middle Temple
Pupil Supervisor
Qualifications: [BA (Oxon)]
f.fitzgibbon@doughtystreet.co.uk

FITZGIBBON MR NEIL KEVIN

Carmelite Chambers
9 Carmelite Street, London EC4Y 0DR,
☎ 020 7936 6300
✉ clerks@carmelitechambers.co.uk
Call Date: Nov 1989, Lincoln's Inn
Qualifications: [LLB (Hons) (Lond)]
nfitzgibbon@carmelitechambers.co.uk

FITZHARRIS MISS GINNETTE

Call Date: Nov 1993, Lincoln's Inn
Qualifications: [LLB (Hons) (Leeds)]
gf.robb@sky.com, clerk@stjohnsbuildings.co.uk

FITZHERBERT MR FRANCIS BRIAN ROYDS

Walnut House
63 St. David's Hill, Exeter, Devon EX4 4DW,
☎ 01392 279751
✉ clerks@walnuthouse.co.uk
Call Date: Oct 2008, Lincoln's Inn
Qualifications: [BA (Cantab)]

FITZMAURICE MR GUY EDWARD CHRISTIAN

Staple Inn Chambers
1st Floor, 9 Staple Inn, Holborn Bars, London WC1V 7QH, ☎ 020 7242 5240
✉ clerks@stapleinn.co.uk
Call Date: July 1999, Lincoln's Inn
Qualifications: [LLB (Hons)]

FITZPATRICK MR ANDREW JOSEPH

Chambers of Ian Macdonald QC
Garden Court North, 22 Oxford Court, Manchester M2 3WQ, ☎ 0161 236 1840
✉ clerks@gcnchambers.co.uk
Call Date: Nov 2003, Gray's Inn
Qualifications: [LLB (L'pool)]

FITZPATRICK MISS DENISE

Kenworthy's Chambers
Arlington House, Bloom Street, Salford, Manchester M3 6AJ, ☎ 0161 832 4036
Call Date: July 2000, Middle Temple
Pupil Supervisor
Qualifications: [LLB(Hons) (Lanc)]
✉ d.fitzpatrick@kenworthysbarristers.co.uk

FITZPATRICK MR EDWARD JAMES

Garden Court Chambers
57-60 Lincoln's Inn Fields, London WC2A 3LJ,
☎ 020 7993 7600 ✉ info@gclaw.co.uk
Call Date: Nov 1990, Gray's Inn
Pupil Supervisor
Qualifications: [LLB (L'pool)]
✉ edwardf@gclaw.co.uk

FITZPATRICK MR FRANCIS PAUL

11 New Square
1st Floor, 11 New Square, Lincoln's Inn, London WC2A 3QB, ☎ 020 7242 4017
✉ john.moore@11newsquare.com
Call Date: Nov 1990, Inner Temple
Pupil Supervisor
Qualifications: [BA (Hons)(Oxon) BCL (Oxon)]
✉ john.moore@11newsquare.com

FITZPATRICK MR JEREMY PAUL

Coram Chambers
9-11 Fulwood Place, London WC1V 6HG,
☎ 020 7092 3700
✉ mail@coramchambers.co.uk
Call Date: Mar 1996, Middle Temple
Qualifications: [BA (Hons) PGCE]
✉ jerryfitz02@aol.com

FITZPATRICK MR STEVEN MARK

2 Pump Court
1st Floor, 2 Pump Court, Temple, London EC4Y 7AH, ☎ 020 7353 5597
✉ clerks@2pumpcourt.co.uk
Call Date: Oct 2004, Lincoln's Inn
Qualifications: [LLB (Hons)]

FITZPATRICK MR THOMAS ANDREW MICHAEL

9 St John Street
Manchester M3 4DN, ☎ 0161 955 9000
✉ civilclerks@9sjs.com / criminalclerks@9sjs.com
Call Date: Nov 1988, Lincoln's Inn
Qualifications: [LLB]

FLANAGAN MR HUGH JAMES

Cornerstone Barristers
2-3 Gray's Inn Square, Gray's Inn, London WC1R 5JH, ☎ 020 7242 4986
✉ chambers@2-3gis.co.uk
Call Date: July 2008, Lincoln's Inn
Qualifications: [BA (Oxon)]
✉ hflanagan@2-3gis.co.uk

FLANAGAN MISS JULIA MARY ALICE

Charter Chambers
33 John Street, London WC1N 2AT,
☎ 020 7618 4400
✉ clerks@charterchambers.com
Call Date: Oct 1993, Lincoln's Inn
Qualifications: [BA (Hons) Dip Law (Lond) CPE]
✉ julia.flanagan@charterchambers.com

FLANAGAN MR NICHOLAS MARK

Cobden House Chambers
19 Quay Street, Manchester M3 3HN,
☎ 0161 833 6000 ✉ Clerks@Cobden.co.uk
Call Date: July 2004, Lincoln's Inn
Qualifications: [LLB Hons (Bris)]
✉ clerks@cobden.co.uk

E

FLATT MS CATHERINE

Victor House Chambers
Victor House, Westfied Road, Pitstone, Bedfordshire LU7 9GW, ☎01296 664043
✉clerks@victorhouse.co.uk
Call Date: July 2002, Inner Temple
Qualifications: [BSc (Bris) CPE (Middx)]
✉clerks@victorhouse.co.uk

FLATTERY MS AMANDA NICHOLE

Kenworthy's Chambers
Arlington House, Bloom Street, Salford, Manchester M3 6AJ, ☎0161 832 4036
Call Date: Oct 1993, Lincoln's Inn
Pupil Supervisor
Qualifications: [BA (Hons)(Lancs) MA (York) CPE]
✉maria@kenworthysbarristers.co.uk

FLAVIN MR MARCUS BENEDICT SEAN

Radcliffe Chambers
Ground Floor, 11 New Square, Lincoln's Inn, London WC2A 3QB, ☎020 7831 0081
✉clerks@radcliffechambers.com
Call Date: Nov 2001, Lincoln's Inn
Pupil Supervisor
Qualifications: [BA (Hons) MSt]
✉mflavin@radcliffechambers.com

FLECK MISS NICOLA LOUISE

Atkinson Bevan Chambers
1st Floor, 2 Harcourt Buildings, Temple, London EC4Y 9DB, ☎020 7353 2112
✉clerks@2hb.co.uk
Call Date: Nov 2006, Middle Temple
Qualifications: [BSc (Lond) PgDip Law]
✉nflick@2hb.co.uk

FLEMING MR ADRIAN

2 King's Bench Walk
2 King's Bench Walk, Temple, London EC4Y 7DE, ☎020 7353 1746
✉clerks@2kbw.com
Call Date: Nov 1991, Middle Temple
Pupil Supervisor
Qualifications: [BA (Hons)(Cantab) Dip Law]
✉afleming@2kbw.com

FLEMING MR PAUL STEPHEN

37 Park Square Chambers
37 Park Square, Leeds LS1 2NY, ☎0113 243 9422 ✉chambers@no37.co.uk
Call Date: Nov 1983, Gray's Inn
Pupil Supervisor
✉chambers@no37.co.uk

FLENLEY MR WILLIAM DAVID WINGATE QC (2010)

Hailsham Chambers
Ground Floor, 4 Paper Buildings, Temple, London EC4Y 7EX, ☎020 7643 5000
✉clerks@hailshamchambers.com
Call Date: Nov 1988, Middle Temple
Pupil Supervisor
Qualifications: [MA LLM (USA) BCL (Oxon)]
✉william.flenley@hailshamchambers.com

FLESCH MR MICHAEL CHARLES QC (1983)

Gray's Inn Tax Chambers
3rd Floor, Gray's Inn Chambers, Gray's Inn, London WC1R 5JA, ☎020 7242 2642
✉clerks@taxbar.com
Call Date: May 1963, Gray's Inn
Qualifications: [LLB]
✉mf@taxbar.com

FLETCHER MR ANDREW FITZROY STEPHEN QC (2006)

3 Verulam Buildings
London WC1R 5NT, ☎020 7831 8441
✉chambers@3vb.com
Call Date: Nov 1980, Inner Temple
Qualifications: [MA (Hons)(Cantab)]
✉afletcher@3vb.com

FLETCHER MR CHRISTOPHER MICHAEL

Octagon House
19 Colegate, Norwich NR3 1AT, ☎01603 623186
✉clerks@octagonhouse.co.uk
Call Date: Nov 1984, Inner Temple
Pupil Supervisor
Qualifications: [LLB (Exeter)]

FLETCHER MR DAVID HAMILTON

St John's Chambers
101 Victoria Street, Bristol BS1 6PU, ☎0117 923 4700
✉clerks@stjohnschambers.co.uk
Call Date: July 1971, Gray's Inn
Pupil Supervisor
Qualifications: [MA (Cantab)]
✉david.fletcher@stjohnschambers.co.uk

FLETCHER MISS ELEANOR KATHLEEN

Chambers of Mr Ami Feder
Ground Floor, Lamb Building, Temple, London EC4Y 7AS, ☎ 020 7797 7788
✉ clerks@lambbuilding.co.uk
Chambers of Mr Ami Feder
Ground Floor, Lamb Building, Temple, London EC4Y 7AS, ☎ 020 7797 7788
✉ clerks@lambbuilding.co.uk
Call Date: Oct 2010, Middle Temple
Qualifications: [BA (Hons) (Oxon)]
clerks@lambbuildings.co.uk

FLETCHER PROF IAN FRANK

South Square
3-4 South Square, Gray's Inn, London WC1R 5HP, ☎ 020 7696 9900
✉ practicemanagers@southsquare.com
Call Date: May 1971, Lincoln's Inn
Qualifications: [MA MCL LLD PhD LLM]
ianfletcher@southsquare.com

FLETCHER MR JAMES WATFORD

Five St Andrew's Hill
5 St Andrew's Hill, London EC4V 5BZ, ☎ 020 7332 5400 ✉ Clerks@5sah.co.uk
Call Date: Oct 2000, Middle Temple
Qualifications: [BA (Hons) (Warw) CPE]
jamesfletcher@5sah.co.uk

FLETCHER MR MARCUS ALEXANDER

1 KBW Chambers
1 King's Bench Walk, Temple, London EC4Y 7DB, ☎ 020 7936 1500
✉ clerks@1kbw.co.uk
King's Bench Chambers
174 High Street, Lewes BN7 1YE, ☎ 01273 402600
Call Date: Oct 1990, Lincoln's Inn
Pupil Supervisor
Qualifications: [BA (Hons)]
mfletcher@1kbw.co.uk

FLETCHER MR MATTHEW

Renaissance Chambers
5th Floor, Gray's Inn Chambers, Gray's Inn, London WC1R 5JA, ☎ 020 7404 1111
✉ clerks@renaissancechambers.co.uk
Call Date: July 2003, Lincoln's Inn
Qualifications: [LLB Hons (LSE)]
mf@renaissancechambers.co.uk

FLETCHER MR STEPHEN JEFFREY

Dere Street Barristers
33 Broad Chare, Newcastle Upon Tyne NE1 3DQ, ☎ 0844 3351551
✉ clerks@derestreet.co.uk
Call Date: Nov 1987, Middle Temple
Qualifications: [LLB (Hons) (Lond)]
clerks@broadcharechambers.co.uk

FLETCHER MR THOMAS ALLAN

New Square Chambers
12 New Square, Lincoln's Inn, London WC2A 3SW, ☎ 020 7419 8000
✉ robin.hollington@newsquarechambers.co.uk
Call Date: Nov 2009, Inner Temple
Qualifications: [BA (Cantab) CPE (Lond)]
thomas.flecther@newsquarechambers.co.uk

FLEWITT MR NEIL QC (2003)

Number 7 Harrington Street Chambers
7 Harrington Street, Liverpool L2 9YH, ☎ 0151 242 0707 ✉ clerks@7hs.co.uk
Call Date: July 1981, Middle Temple
Recorder
Qualifications: [LLB (Hons) (L'pool)]
neil.flewitt@7hs.co.uk

FLEXMAN MRS CARLA ANN

Albion Chambers
Broad Street, Bristol BS1 1DR, ☎ 0117 927 2144
✉ clerks@albionchambers.co.uk
Call Date: Oct 2002, Inner Temple
Qualifications: [LLB (Exon) LLM (Exon)]
CarlaFlexman@albionchambers.co.uk

FLINN MR MATTHEW EDWARD

1 Crown Office Row
1 Crown Office Row, Temple, London EC4Y 7HH, ☎ 020 7797 7500
✉ mail@1cor.com
Call Date: Mar 2010, Lincoln's Inn
Qualifications: [BA (Cantab)]
matthew.flinn@1cor.com

FLINT MR CHARLES JOHN RAFFLES QC (1995)

Blackstone Chambers
Blackstone House, Temple, London EC4Y 9BW, ☎ 020 7583 1770
✉ clerks@blackstonechambers.com
Call Date: July 1975, Middle Temple
Qualifications: [MA (Cantab) CEDR CIArb]

E

FLOOD MR DAVID EDWARD

St Johns Buildings Liverpool
8th Floor India Buildings, Water Street, Liverpool L2 0XG, ☎0151 243 6000
✉clerk@stjohnsbuildings.co.uk
16 Winckley Square
Preston PR1 3JJ, ☎01772 256100
St Johns Buildings
24a - 28 St John Street, Manchester M3 4DJ, ☎0161 214 1500
✉clerk@stjohnsbuildings.co.uk
Call Date: Feb 1993, Middle Temple
Pupil Supervisor
Qualifications: [LLB (Hons)]
chateauflood@aol.com

FLOOD MR DIARMUID BRENDAN MARTIN

Number 7 Harrington Street Chambers
7 Harrington Street, Liverpool L2 9YH, ☎0151 242 0707 ✉clerks@7hs.co.uk
Call Date: Apr 1989, Lincoln's Inn
Pupil Supervisor
Qualifications: [LLB (Lond) Maitrise (France)]
diarmuid.flood@7hs.co.uk

E

FLOOD MR EDWARD ALBERT

1 Garden Court Family Law Chambers
Ground Floor, One Garden Court, Temple, London EC4Y 9BJ, ☎020 7797 7900
✉clerks@1gc.com
Call Date: Oct 2002, Middle Temple
Qualifications: [BA (Oxon) MA]
flood@1gc.com

FLOWER MR PHILIP RONALD

9 Stone Buildings
Lincoln's Inn, London WC2A 3NN, ☎020 7404 5055
✉clerks@9stonebuildings.com
Call Date: Nov 1979, Inner Temple
Qualifications: [MA]
clerks@9stonebuildings.com, pflower@9stonebuildings.com

FLOWERS MISS VICTORIA

Field Court Chambers
5 Field Court, Gray's Inn, London WC1R 5EF, ☎020 7405 6114 ✉clerks@fieldcourt.co.uk
Call Date: July 2009, Lincoln's Inn
Qualifications: [BA (Oxon)]
victoria.flowers@fieldcourt.co.uk

FLYNN MR JAMES EDWARD QC (2003)

Brick Court Chambers
7-8 Essex Street, London WC2R 3LD, ☎020 7379 3550 ✉clerks@brickcourt.co.uk
Call Date: July 1978, Middle Temple
Qualifications: [BA (Oxon)]
James.Flynn@Brickcourt.co.uk

FLYNN MR STEVEN EDMOND

Call Date: Nov 2006, Gray's Inn
Qualifications: [LLB]
steven.flynn@stjohnsbuildings.co.uk

FLYNN MR VERNON JAMES HENNESSY QC (2008)

Essex Court Chambers
24 Lincoln's Inn Fields, London WC2A 3EG, ☎020 7813 8000
✉clerksroom@essexcourt.net
Call Date: Oct 1991, Lincoln's Inn
Qualifications: [BA (Cantab)]
vflynn@essexcourt.net

FODDER MR MARTIN JOHN

Littleton Chambers
3 King's Bench Walk North, Temple, London EC4Y 7HR, ☎020 7797 8600
✉fschneider@littletonchambers.co.uk
Call Date: July 1983, Inner Temple
Pupil Supervisor
Qualifications: [BA (Lond) LLM (Cantab) Dip Law (Lond)]
mfodder@littletonchambers.co.uk

FOINETTE MR IAN

Five St Andrew's Hill
5 St Andrew's Hill, London EC4V 5BZ, ☎020 7332 5400 ✉Clerks@5sah.co.uk
Call Date: Nov 1986, Middle Temple
Pupil Supervisor
Qualifications: [BA (Kent)]
ianfoinette@5sah.co.uk

FOLEY MISS JANE

Trinity Chambers
The Custom House, 39 Quayside, Newcastle Upon Tyne NE1 3DE, ☎0191 232 1927
✉info@trinitychambers.co.uk
Trinity Chambers
Multi Media Exchange, 72-80 Corporation Road, Middlesbrough TS1 2RF, ☎01642 247569
✉info@trinitychambers.co.uk
Call Date: July 2003, Gray's Inn
Qualifications: [LLB (Sheff)]
j.foley@trinitychambers.co.uk

FOLKES MISS SANDRA GILLIAN

2 Dr Johnson's Buildings
2 Dr Johnson's Buildings, Temple, London EC4Y 7AY, ☎ 020 7936 2613
✉ clerks@2drj.com
Call Date: Nov 1989, Lincoln's Inn
Qualifications: [LLB]
✉ s.folkes@2drj.com

FOLLAND MR DAVID JAMES

Victory Chambers
Dan-Y-Coed, New Mill, St Clears, Carmarthen SA33 4HS, ☎ 01994 231704
✉ legaleyes@btinternet.com
Call Date: Oct 1976, Lincoln's Inn
Qualifications: [BSc]

FOLLON MR DANIEL RICHARD THOMAS

1 Gray's Inn Square
Ground Floor, 1 Gray's Inn Square, London WC1R 5AA, ☎ 020 7405 0001
Call Date: July 2003, Middle Temple
Qualifications: [LLB Hons (Leeds)]
✉ dfollon@1gis.com

FONYONGA MS KRYSTLE

Dyers Chambers
35 Bedford Row, London WC1R 4JH, ☎ 020 7404 1881
✉ admin@dyerschambers.com
Call Date: July 2008, Middle Temple
Qualifications: [BSc (Hons) (Bris) PgDl (Lond) LLM (Bris)]

FOOKES MR ROBERT LAWRENCE

Francis Taylor Building
Inner Temple, London EC4Y 7BY, ☎ 020 7353 8415 ✉ clerks@ftb.eu.com
Call Date: July 1975, Lincoln's Inn
Pupil Supervisor
Qualifications: [MA (Oxon)]
✉ robert.fookes@ftb.eu.com

FOOKS MR NICHOLAS DAVID

Five Paper Buildings
1st Floor, Five Paper Buildings, Temple, London EC4Y 7HB, ☎ 020 7583 6117
✉ clerks@5pb.co.uk
Call Date: Nov 1978, Inner Temple
Pupil Supervisor
Qualifications: [MA (L'pool)]
✉ nf@5pb.co.uk

FOOT MS HELEN RACHAEL

Garden Court Chambers
57-60 Lincoln's Inn Fields, London WC2A 3LJ, ☎ 020 7993 7600 ✉ info@gclaw.co.uk
Call Date: July 2008, Gray's Inn
Qualifications: [MA BA (Oxon)]
✉ helenf@gclaw.co.uk

FORBES MR ALEXANDER DAVID

Harcourt Chambers
1st Floor, 2 Harcourt Buildings, Temple, London EC4Y 9DB, ☎ 0844 561 7135
Call Date: Oct 2003, Lincoln's Inn
Qualifications: [BA (Hons) (Lond)]
✉ aforbes@harcourtchambers.law.co.uk

FORBES MR PETER GEORGE

6 Pump Court
1st Floor, 6 Pump Court, Temple, London EC4Y 7AR, ☎ 020 7797 8400
✉ richardconstable@6pumpcourt.co.uk
6 Pump Court Chambers
6-8 Mill Street, Maidstone, Kent ME15 6XH, ☎ 01622 688094
✉ annexe@6pumpcourt.co.uk
Call Date: Oct 1990, Inner Temple
Qualifications: [LLB (Lond)]
✉ peterforbes@6pumpcourt.co.uk

FORBES MISS VICTORIA EVA COLREIN

Argent Chambers
5 Bell Yard, London WC2A 2JR, ☎ 020 7556 5500
✉ briefsin@argentchambers.co.uk
Call Date: July 2007, Inner Temple
Qualifications: [BA CPE]
✉ briefsin@argentchambers.co.uk

FORD MR ANDREW JAMES

Number 7 Harrington Street Chambers
7 Harrington Street, Liverpool L2 9YH, ☎ 0151 242 0707 ✉ clerks@7hs.co.uk
Call Date: Oct 1997, Middle Temple
Qualifications: [BA (Hons)(Sheff) CPE]
✉ andrew.ford@7hs.co.uk

FORD MISS CAROLINE EMMA

Call Date: Oct 1993, Gray's Inn
Qualifications: [LLM (Bucks)]

E

FORD MISS CHARLOTTE JENNIFER

New Square Chambers
12 New Square, Lincoln's Inn, London WC2A 3SW, ☎ 020 7419 8000
✉ robin.hollington@newsquarechambers.co.uk
Call Date: Nov 2007, Lincoln's Inn
Qualifications: [BA (Cantab)]
✉ charlotte.ford@newsquarechambers.co.uk

FORD MR GERARD JAMES

Old Court Chambers
Newham House, 96-98 Borough Road, Middlesbrough TS1 2HJ, ☎ 01642 232523
✉ clerks@oldcourtchambers.com
Call Date: July 1986, Inner Temple
Pupil Supervisor
Qualifications: [BSc CQSW MA (Wark)]
✉ clerks@oldcourtchambers.com

Fax: 01642 232896;
DX: 60591 Middlesbrough

Types of work: Ancillary relief, Care proceedings, Common law (general), Consumer law, Costs, Family law, Family provision, Housing, Landlord and tenant, Personal injury, Sale and carriage of goods

FORD MR JEREMY MICHAEL

The Chambers of Grahame Aldous QC
9 Gough Square, London EC4A 3DG,
☎ 020 7832 0500
✉ clerks@9goughsquare.co.uk
Call Date: Oct 1996, Lincoln's Inn
Qualifications: [LLB (Hons)(Leeds)]
✉ jford@9goughsquare.co.uk

FORD MR MARK STEVEN

Lincoln House Chambers
Tower 12, The Avenue North, Spinningfields, 18-22 Bridge Street, Manchester M3 3BZ,
☎ 0161 832 5701
✉ info@lincolnhousechambers.com
Call Date: Nov 1991, Gray's Inn
Qualifications: [LLB (Hons) (B'ham)]

FORD MR MICHAEL DAVID

Old Square Chambers
3 Orchard Court, St Augustine's Yard, Bristol BS1 5DP, ☎ 0117 930 5100
✉ clerks@oldsquare.co.uk
Call Date: July 1992, Middle Temple
Pupil Supervisor
Qualifications: [LLB (Hons) (Brist) MA (Sheff)]
✉ ford@oldsquare.co.uk

FORD MISS MONICA DOROTHY PATIENCE

14 Gray's Inn Square
14 Gray's Inn Square, Gray's Inn, London WC1R 5JP, ☎ 020 7242 0858
✉ clerks@14gis.co.uk
Call Date: July 1984, Middle Temple
Pupil Supervisor
Qualifications: [LLB (Hons)(L'pool)]
✉ clerks@14graysinnsquare.co.uk

FORD MRS SARAH LOUISE

Brick Court Chambers
7-8 Essex Street, London WC2R 3LD,
☎ 020 7379 3550 ✉ clerks@brickcourt.co.uk
Call Date: Nov 2002, Lincoln's Inn
Pupil Supervisor
Qualifications: [LLB (Hons)(Warw) LLM]
✉ Sarah.Ford@Brickcourt.co.uk

FORD MR STEVEN CHARLES QC (2010)

Seven Bedford Row
7 Bedford Row, London WC1R 4BS,
☎ 020 7242 3555 ✉ clerks@7br.co.uk
Call Date: Oct 1992, Middle Temple
Pupil Supervisor
Qualifications: [LLB (Hons) LRAM]
✉ sford@7br.co.uk

FORD MR THOMAS GRAYSON

Essex Court Chambers
24 Lincoln's Inn Fields, London WC2A 3EG,
☎ 020 7813 8000
✉ clerksroom@essexcourt.net
Call Date: Oct 2008, Gray's Inn
Qualifications: [BA LLM (Hons)]
✉ tford@essexcourt.net

FORDE MR MARTIN ANDREW QC (2006)

1 Crown Office Row
1 Crown Office Row, Temple, London EC4Y 7HH, ☎ 020 7797 7500
✉ mail@1cor.com
Call Date: Feb 1984, Middle Temple
Qualifications: [BA (Oxon)]
✉ martin.forde@1cor.com

FORDHAM MISS CHLOE AUGUSTA

Furnival Chambers
32 Furnival Street, London EC4A 1JQ,
☎ 020 7405 3232
Call Date: July 2005, Inner Temple
Qualifications: [MA CPE]
✉ cfordham@furnivallaw.co.uk

FORDHAM MRS JUDITH

Exchange Chambers
One Derby Square, Derby Square, Liverpool L2 9XX, ☎ 0151 236 7747
✉ info@exchangechambers.co.uk
Exchange Chambers
7 Ralli Courts, West Riverside, Manchester M3 5FT, ☎ 0161 833 2722
Exchange Chambers
Oxford House, Oxford Row, Leeds LS1 3BE, ☎ 0113 203 1970
✉ spencer@exchangechambers.co.uk
Call Date: July 1991, Inner Temple
fordham@exchangechambers.co.uk

FORDHAM MRS MARGARET ALLISON

Principal Chambers
15 Lime Tree Walk, Sevenoaks, Kent TN13 1YH, ☎ 0845 209 8080
Call Date: Oct 1990, Gray's Inn
Qualifications: [BA (West Indies) LLB (Hons)(Bucks)]

FORDHAM MR MICHAEL JOHN QC (2006)

Blackstone Chambers
Blackstone House, Temple, London EC4Y 9BW, ☎ 020 7583 1770
✉ clerks@blackstonechambers.com
Call Date: Feb 1990, Gray's Inn
Qualifications: [BA (Oxon) BCL (Oxon) LLM (USA)]
michaelfordham@blackstonechambers.com

FORGAN MR HUGH MALCOLM

23 Essex Street
London WC2R 3AA, ☎ 020 7413 0353
✉ clerks@23es.com
Call Date: Nov 1989, Lincoln's Inn
Pupil Supervisor
Qualifications: [BA (Cantab)]
hughforgan@23es.com

FORLIN MR GERARD EMLYN QC (2010)

Cornerstone Barristers
2-3 Gray's Inn Square, Gray's Inn, London WC1R 5JH, ☎ 020 7242 4986
✉ chambers@2-3gis.co.uk
Call Date: Feb 1984, Lincoln's Inn
Pupil Supervisor
Qualifications: [LLB (Hons) (Lond) LLM (Lond) M Phil (Cantab) Dip Air & Space law]
gforlin@2-3gis.co.uk

FORMBY MS EMILY JANE

39 Essex Street
London WC2R 3AT, ☎ 020 7832 1111
✉ clerks@39essex.com
Call Date: Oct 1993, Middle Temple
Pupil Supervisor
Qualifications: [BA (Hons)(Oxon) CPE (Lond)]
emily.formby@39essex.com

FORREST MR ALASTAIR JOHN

18 St John Street
Manchester M3 4EA, ☎ 0161 278 1800
✉ clerks@18sjs.com
Call Date: July 1972, Gray's Inn
Pupil Supervisor
Qualifications: [MA (Oxon)]

FORREST MR ROBERT

2 King's Bench Walk
2 King's Bench Walk, Temple, London EC4Y 7DE, ☎ 020 7353 1746
✉ clerks@2kbw.com
Call Date: Oct 2007, Lincoln's Inn
Qualifications: [BA (Cantab)]
rforrest@2kbw.com

FORSDICK MR DAVID JOHN

Landmark Chambers
180 Fleet Street, London EC4A 2HG, ☎ 020 7430 1221
✉ clerks@landmarkchambers.co.uk
Call Date: Oct 1993, Gray's Inn
Pupil Supervisor
Qualifications: [BA (Warw)]
dforsdick@landmarkchambers.co.uk

FORSHALL MS ISABELLA LOUISE QC (2010)

Doughty Street Chambers
53-54 Doughty Street, London WC1N 2LS, ☎ 020 7404 1313
✉ enquiries@doughtystreet.co.uk
Doughty Street Chambers
Pall Mall Court, 61-67 King Street, Manchester M2 4PD, ☎ 0161 618 1066
Doughty Street Chambers
5th Floor, Broad Quay House, Prince Street, Bristol BS1 4DJ, ☎ 01179 058 717
Call Date: Feb 1982, Gray's Inn
Pupil Supervisor
Qualifications: [BA (Cantab)]
i.forshall@doughtystreet.co.uk

E

FORSHAW MISS SARAH ANNE QC (2008)

5 King's Bench Walk
5 King's Bench Walk, Temple, London EC4Y 7DN, ☎020 7353 5638
✉clerks@5kbw.co.uk
Call Date: Nov 1987, Middle Temple
Qualifications: [LLB (Lond)]

FORSHAW MR SIMON CHARLES

11 King's Bench Walk
11 King's Bench Walk, Temple, London EC4Y 7EQ, ☎020 7632 8500
✉clerksroom@11kbw.com
Call Date: Mar 2004, Gray's Inn
Qualifications: [MA (Oxon)]

FORSTER MS BRIDGET ANNE

No5 Chambers
38 Queen Square, Bristol BS1 4QS, ☎0845 210 5555
No5 Chambers
Greenwood House, 4-7 Salisbury Court, London EC4Y 8AA, ☎0845 210 5555
No5 Chambers
Fountain Court, Steelhouse Lane, Birmingham B4 6DR, ☎0845 210 5555 ✉info@no5.com
Call Date: July 2001, Inner Temple
Qualifications: [BA (Oxon) CPE BPP]
bf@no5.com

FORSTER MR MICHAEL WILLIAMS

12 College Place
Fauvelle Buildings, 12 College Place, Southampton SO15 2FE, ☎023 8032 0320
✉clerks@12cp.co.uk
Call Date: Feb 1984, Gray's Inn
Qualifications: [LLB (Lond)]
mforster@12cp.co.uk

FORSTER MS SARAH JUDITH

14 Gray's Inn Square
14 Gray's Inn Square, Gray's Inn, London WC1R 5JP, ☎020 7242 0858
✉clerks@14gis.co.uk
Westgate Chambers
64 High Street, Lewes, East Sussex BN7 1XG, ☎01273 480510
✉clerks@westgate-chambers.co.uk
Call Date: Nov 1976, Middle Temple
Pupil Supervisor
Qualifications: [LLB Dip Law]
sf@14graysinnsquare.co.uk

FORSTER MR THOMAS BERNARD

18 Red Lion Court
London EC4A 3EB, ☎020 7520 6000
✉chambers@18rlc.co.uk
18 Red Lion Court (Annexe)
Thornwood House, 102 New London Road, Chelmsford, Essex CM2 0RG, ☎01245 280880
Call Date: Nov 1993, Inner Temple
Pupil Supervisor
Qualifications: [LLB (Lond)]
tom.forster@18rlc.co.uk

FORSTER MR TIMOTHY SHANE CAVANAGH

Furnival Chambers
32 Furnival Street, London EC4A 1JQ, ☎020 7405 3232
Call Date: Oct 1990, Middle Temple
Pupil Supervisor
Qualifications: [LLB (Hons) (Cardiff)]
tforster@furnivallaw.co.uk

FORSTER-JONES MR WILFRED JENNER EMANUEL

Chambers of Wilfred Forster-Jones
79 Grays Inn Road, London WC1X 8TT, ☎020 7831 0037
✉chambers_79graysinnroad@yahoo.co.uk
Call Date: Nov 1976, Middle Temple
Pupil Supervisor
Qualifications: [BA (Lond)]

FORSYTH MR ANDREW ALLAN

15 New Bridge Street
London EC4V 6AU, ☎020 7842 1900
✉clerks@15nbs.com
Call Date: Nov 1989, Inner Temple
Qualifications: [LLB (Hons) (Wales)]
andrew.forsyth@15nbs.com

FORSYTH PROF CHRISTOPHER FORBES

Atlas Chambers
3 Field Court, Gray's Inn, London WC1R 5EP, ☎020 7269 7980
✉clerks@atlaschambers.com
Call Date: May 1987, Inner Temple
Qualifications: [BSc PhD LLB LLB]
forsyth@atlaschambers.com

E

FORSYTH MISS JULIE PATRICIA

Chavasse Court Chambers
18 Queen Avenue, Liverpool L2 4TX,
☎0151 229 2030
✉clerks@chavassechambers.co.uk
Call Date: July 1983, Gray's Inn
Pupil Supervisor
Qualifications: [LLB (L'pool)]
✉julie.forsyth@chavassechambers.co.uk

FORSYTH MISS SAMANTHA

No5 Chambers
Fountain Court, Steelhouse Lane, Birmingham B4 6DR, ☎0845 210 5555 ✉info@no5.com
No5 Chambers
Greenwood House, 4-7 Salisbury Court, London EC4Y 8AA, ☎0845 210 5555
No5 Chambers
38 Queen Square, Bristol BS1 4QS,
☎0845 210 5555
Call Date: July 1988, Inner Temple
Pupil Supervisor
Qualifications: [LLB (Wales)]

FORTE MR TIMOTHY AXEL

Dyers Chambers
35 Bedford Row, London WC1R 4JH,
☎020 7404 1881
✉admin@dyerschambers.com
Call Date: Oct 1994, Gray's Inn
Pupil Supervisor
Qualifications: [BA]
✉tim.forte@dyerschambers.com

FORTSON MR RUDI FLETCHER QC (2010)

25 Bedford Row
London WC1R 4HD, ☎020 7067 1500
✉clerks@25bedfordrow.com
Call Date: Nov 1976, Middle Temple
Pupil Supervisor
Qualifications: [LLB (Lond)]
✉rfortson@25bedfordrow.com

FORTT MR RUSSELL MARK

5 Essex Court
1st Floor, 5 Essex Court, Temple, London EC4Y 9AH, ☎020 7410 2000
✉clerks@5essexcourt.co.uk
Call Date: Nov 1999, Inner Temple
Qualifications: [LLB]
✉fortt@5essexcourt.co.uk, fortte@5essexcourt.co.uk

FORTUNE MR MALCOLM DONALD PORTER

3 Serjeants Inn
London EC4Y 1BQ, ☎020 7427 5000
✉clerks@3serjeantsinn.com
Call Date: July 1972, Middle Temple
Pupil Supervisor, Recorder
✉mfortune@3serjeantsinn.com

FORTUNE MR PETER CARL MICHAEL

4 King's Bench Walk
2nd Floor, 4 King's Bench Walk, Temple, London EC4Y 7DL, ☎020 7822 7000
✉clerks@4kbw.co.uk
Guildhall Chambers Portsmouth
Prudential Buildings, 16 Guildhall Walk, Portsmouth, Hampshire PO1 2DE,
☎023 9275 2400
✉clerks@gcp-barristers.com
Call Date: July 1978, Inner Temple
Pupil Supervisor
Qualifications: [BA (Leeds)]
✉pkf@4kbw.co.uk

FORTUNE MR ROBERT ANDREW QC (2003)

Nine Bedford Row
9 Bedford Row, London WC1R 4AZ,
☎020 7489 2727
✉clerks@9bedfordrow.co.uk
Call Date: Feb 1976, Middle Temple
Qualifications: [LLB (Lond)]
✉robert.fortune@9bedfordrow.co.uk

FORWARD MR BARRY MILES

10 King's Bench Walk
Ground Floor, 10 King's Bench Walk, Temple, London EC4Y 7EB, ☎020 7353 7742
✉Chambers@10kingsbenchwalk.co.uk
Call Date: July 1981, Gray's Inn
Pupil Supervisor
Qualifications: [BSc (Econ) Dip Law]
✉chambers@10kingsbenchwalk.co.uk

FOSKETT MISS ROSANNA MARIE

Maitland Chambers
7 Stone Buildings, Lincoln's Inn, London WC2A 3SZ, ☎020 7406 1200
✉clerks@maitlandchambers.com
Call Date: July 2008, Lincoln's Inn
Qualifications: [BA MPHIL (Cantab)]
✉rfoskett@maitlandchambers.com

E

FOSTER MISS ALISON LEE CAROLINE QC (2002)

39 Essex Street
London WC2R 3AT, ☎020 7832 1111
✉clerks@39essex.com
82 King Street
Manchester M2 4WQ, ☎0161 870 9969
Call Date: July 1984, Inner Temple
Qualifications: [BA (Oxon) DipLaw MPhil]
alison.foster@39essex.com

FOSTER MR BRIAN IAN

Exchange Chambers
7 Ralli Courts, West Riverside, Manchester M3 5FT, ☎0161 833 2722
Exchange Chambers
One Derby Square, Derby Square, Liverpool L2 9XX, ☎0151 236 7747
✉info@exchangechambers.co.uk
Exchange Chambers
Oxford House, Oxford Row, Leeds LS1 3BE, ☎0113 203 1970
✉spencer@exchangechambers.co.uk
Call Date: July 1988, Lincoln's Inn
Qualifications: [LLB (Hons) (Newc)]
foster@exchangechambers.co.uk

FOSTER MISS CATHERINE MARY

Crown Office Chambers
2 Crown Office Row, Temple, London EC4Y 7HJ, ☎020 7797 8100
✉mail@crownofficechambers.com
Call Date: July 1986, Inner Temple
Pupil Supervisor
Qualifications: [LLB (Nott'm)]
foster@crownofficechambers.com

FOSTER MR CHARLES ANDREW

Outer Temple Chambers
The Outer Temple, 222 Strand, London WC2R 1BA, ☎020 7353 6381
✉clerks@outertemple.com
Call Date: July 1988, Inner Temple
Pupil Supervisor, Recorder
Qualifications: [MA MRCVS Vet MB (Cantab)]
charles.foster@outertemple.com

FOSTER MS ERICA

2 King's Bench Walk
2 King's Bench Walk, Temple, London EC4Y 7DE, ☎020 7353 1746
✉clerks@2kbw.com
Call Date: July 2007, Lincoln's Inn
Qualifications: [LLB (So'ton)]
efoster@2kbw.com

FOSTER MR FRANCIS ALEXANDER

Park Lane Plowden
19 Westgate, Leeds LS1 2RD,
☎0113 228 5049
✉clerks@parklaneplowden.co.uk
Call Date: Oct 1990, Inner Temple
Pupil Supervisor
Qualifications: [LLB (Huddersfield)]
alex.foster@parklaneplowden.co.uk

FOSTER MR JULIEN ANDREW STEWART

1 Garden Court Family Law Chambers
Ground Floor, One Garden Court, Temple, London EC4Y 9BJ, ☎020 7797 7900
✉clerks@1gc.com
Call Date: Oct 1995, Middle Temple
Pupil Supervisor
Qualifications: [BA (Hons) (York)]

FOSTER MR PETER

Oriel Chambers
14 Water Street, Liverpool, Merseyside L2 8TD, ☎0151 236 7191
✉clerks@orielchambers.co.uk
Oriel Chambers
18 Ribblesdale Place, Preston PR1 3NA,
☎01772 254 764
✉clerks@oriel-chambers.co.uk
Call Date: Nov 1992, Middle Temple
Pupil Supervisor
Qualifications: [LLB (Hons) (Manch)]
peter.foster@orielchambers.co.uk

FOSTER MR SIMON HARVEY STENNETT

2 King's Bench Walk
2 King's Bench Walk, Temple, London EC4Y 7DE, ☎020 7353 1746
✉clerks@2kbw.com
Call Date: July 1982, Middle Temple
Pupil Supervisor
Qualifications: [LLB (Exon)]

FOSTER MISS WENDY

Wilberforce Chambers
7 Bishop Lane, Hull HU1 1PA,
☎01482 323264
Call Date: Oct 2005, Inner Temple
Qualifications: [BA Newnham College University of Cambridge]
wfoster@hullbar.co.uk

FOSUHENE MISS AMELIA TRACY

Carmelite Chambers
9 Carmelite Street, London EC4Y 0DR,
☎ 020 7936 6300
✉ clerks@carmelitechambers.co.uk
Call Date: Nov 1996, Middle Temple
Qualifications: [LLB (Hons)(Lond)]
afosuhene@carmelitechambers.co.uk

FOTHERGILL MRS FRANCESCA ELIZABETH

Deans Court Chambers
24 St John Street, Manchester M3 4DF,
☎ 0161 214 6000 ✉ clerks@deanscourt.co.uk
St Johns Buildings
21 White Friars, Chester CH1 1NZ,
☎ 01244 323070
✉ clerk@stjohnsbuildings.co.uk
16 Winckley Square
Preston PR1 3JJ, ☎ 01772 256100
Call Date: Oct 1994, Middle Temple
Qualifications: [BA (Hons)(Oxon)]

FOTTRELL MISS DEIRDRE MAY

Coram Chambers
9-11 Fulwood Place, London WC1V 6HG,
☎ 020 7092 3700
✉ mail@coramchambers.co.uk
Call Date: Oct 2001, Middle Temple
Qualifications: [BA LLB LLM MA]
deirdre.fottrell@coramchambers.co.uk

FOULKES MR CHRISTOPHER DAVID

2 Hare Court
Lower Ground, Ground, 1st & 2nd Floor, 2 Hare Court, Temple, London EC4Y 7BH,
☎ 020 7353 3982 ✉ clerks@2harecourt.com
Call Date: Oct 1994, Lincoln's Inn
Pupil Supervisor
Qualifications: [MA (Cantab) LLB (Hons)(Leeds)]
christfoulkes@2harecourt.com

FOULKES MISS REBECCA

4 Paper Buildings
1st Floor, 4 Paper Buildings, Temple, London EC4Y 7EX, ☎ 020 7427 5200
✉ clerks@4pb.com
Call Date: July 2001, Lincoln's Inn
Qualifications: [BA (Hons) (Oxon)]
rf@4pb.com

FOULKES MISS REBECCA

5 Pump Court
Ground Floor, 5 Pump Court, Temple, London EC4Y 7AP, ☎ 020 7353 2532
✉ clerks@5pumpcourt.com
Call Date: Mar 2003, Lincoln's Inn
Qualifications: [LLB (Hons) (So'ton)]
rebeccafoulkes@5pumpcourt.com

FOULSER MCFARLANE MRS JANE HELENA SUSAN

30 Park Place
Cardiff CF10 3BS, ☎ 029 2039 8421
✉ clerks@30parkplace.law.co.uk
Call Date: Feb 1994, Gray's Inn
Qualifications: [LLB (Wales) LLM (Wales)]

FOUND MR TIMOTHY PAUL

Farrar's Building
Farrar's Building, Temple, London EC4Y 7BD,
☎ 020 7583 9241
✉ Chambers@farrarsbuilding.co.uk
Call Date: July 2006, Lincoln's Inn
Qualifications: [LLB (Exon)]
tfound@farrarsbuilding.co.uk

FOUNDLING-MIAH MR MATHIAS MUHON

No. 3 Fleet Street Chambers
3 Fleet Street, London EC4Y 1DP,
☎ 020 7936 4474 ✉ clerks@3fleetstreet.com
Call Date: Nov 2002, Inner Temple
Qualifications: [BSc (L'pool) LLB (Nott'm)]

FOWLER MR DAVID SIMPSON

Field Court Chambers
5 Field Court, Gray's Inn, London WC1R 5EF,
☎ 020 7405 6114 ✉ clerks@fieldcourt.co.uk
Call Date: Oct 2004, Lincoln's Inn
Qualifications: [BA (Hons) Dunelm]
david.fowler@fieldcourt.co.uk

FOWLER MR EDMUND IAN CARLOSS

5 King's Bench Walk
5 King's Bench Walk, Temple, London EC4Y 7DN, ☎ 020 7353 5638
✉ clerks@5kbw.co.uk
Call Date: Oct 1992, Gray's Inn
Qualifications: [LLB]

E

FOWLER MR RICHARD

Maitland Chambers
7 Stone Buildings, Lincoln's Inn, London WC2A 3SZ, ☎020 7406 1200
✉clerks@maitlandchambers.com
Call Date: Nov 2003, Inner Temple
Qualifications: [MA BA (Hons) (Oxon) DPhil (Oxon)]
rfowler@maitlandchambers.com

FOWLES MR JONATHAN JAMES

Serle Court
6 New Square, Lincoln's Inn, London WC2A 3QS, ☎020 7242 6105
✉clerks@serlecourt.co.uk
Call Date: July 2004, Gray's Inn
Qualifications: [BA (Oxon) PgDL]

FOX MISS ANNA KATHERINE HELEN

Oriel Chambers
14 Water Street, Liverpool, Merseyside L2 8TD, ☎0151 236 7191
✉clerks@orielchambers.co.uk
Oriel Chambers
18 Ribblesdale Place, Preston PR1 3NA, ☎01772 254 764
✉clerks@oriel-chambers.co.uk
Call Date: July 1986, Middle Temple
Qualifications: [LLB (L'pool)]
anna.fox@orielchambers.co.uk

E

FOX MISS CLAIRE

Renaissance Chambers
5th Floor, Gray's Inn Chambers, Gray's Inn, London WC1R 5JA, ☎020 7404 1111
✉clerks@renaissancechambers.co.uk
Call Date: Oct 2003, Middle Temple
Qualifications: [LLB (Hons) (Manc)]
cf@renaissancechambers.co.uk

FOX DR DAVID MURRAY

Maitland Chambers
7 Stone Buildings, Lincoln's Inn, London WC2A 3SZ, ☎020 7406 1200
✉clerks@maitlandchambers.com
Call Date: July 2005, Lincoln's Inn
Qualifications: [BA LLB PhD]

FOX MR IAN ANTONY

Field Court Chambers
5 Field Court, Gray's Inn, London WC1R 5EF, ☎020 7405 6114 ✉clerks@fieldcourt.co.uk
Call Date: Oct 1990, Middle Temple
Qualifications: [LLB]

FOX MR JOHN HARVEY

Chambers of Mr Ami Feder
Ground Floor, Lamb Building, Temple, London EC4Y 7AS, ☎020 7797 7788
✉clerks@lambbuilding.co.uk
Lamb Building
22 Ship Street, Brighton BN1 1AD, ☎01273 820490
✉admin@lambbuilding.co.uk
Chambers of Mr Ami Feder
Ground Floor, Lamb Building, Temple, London EC4Y 7AS, ☎020 7797 7788
✉clerks@lambbuilding.co.uk
Call Date: July 1973, Inner Temple
Qualifications: [LLB (Lond) LDS BDS]
clerks@lambbuilding.co.uk

FOX MR MARTIN GEORGE

Warwick House Chambers
8 Warwick Court, Warwick House Chambers, Gray's Inn, London WC1R 5DJ, ☎020 7430 2323
✉clerks@warwickhousechambers.com
Call Date: July 1981, Middle Temple
Pupil Supervisor
Qualifications: [LLB]
clerks@warwickhousechambers.com

FOX MISS NICOLA SUSAN

1 Garden Court Family Law Chambers
Ground Floor, One Garden Court, Temple, London EC4Y 9BJ, ☎020 7797 7900
✉clerks@1gc.com
Call Date: Oct 1996, Middle Temple
Pupil Supervisor
Qualifications: [BSc (Hons)(Lond) MSc CPE (Lond)]
fox@1gc.com

FOX MR PETER

Hind Court Chambers
London East, 100 Burford Wharf, 3 Cam Road, London E15 2SL, ☎020 8534 2495
✉peter_fox@btinternet.com
Call Date: July 2004, Gray's Inn
Qualifications: [LLB (Hons) LLM (Hons) (Lond)]
info@hindcourtchambers.co.uk

FOX DR SIMON JAMES

No5 Chambers
Fountain Court, Steelhouse Lane, Birmingham B4 6DR, ☎0845 210 5555 ✉info@no5.com
No5 Chambers
Greenwood House, 4-7 Salisbury Court, London EC4Y 8AA, ☎0845 210 5555
No5 Chambers
38 Queen Square, Bristol BS1 4QS, ☎0845 210 5555

Exchange Chambers
One Derby Square, Derby Square, Liverpool L2 9XX, ☎0151 236 7747
✉info@exchangechambers.co.uk
Exchange Chambers
7 Ralli Courts, West Riverside, Manchester M3 5FT, ☎0161 833 2722
Call Date: Nov 1994, Inner Temple
Qualifications: [MB CPE (Lond) BS]
✉sf@no5.com

FOXTON MR DAVID ANDREW QC (2006)

Essex Court Chambers
24 Lincoln's Inn Fields, London WC2A 3EG, ☎020 7813 8000
✉clerksroom@essexcourt.net
Call Date: Feb 1989, Gray's Inn
Qualifications: [BA BCL (Oxon)]
✉dfoxton@essexcourt.net

FOY MR JOHN LEONARD QC (1998)

The Chambers of Grahame Aldous QC
9 Gough Square, London EC4A 3DG, ☎020 7832 0500
✉clerks@9goughsquare.co.uk
Call Date: July 1969, Gray's Inn
Recorder
Qualifications: [LLB]
✉jfoy@9goughsquare.co.uk

FOYLE MR ANDREW WILLIAM

One Essex Court
Ground Floor, One Essex Court, Temple, London EC4Y 9AR, ☎020 7583 2000
✉clerks@oeclaw.co.uk
Call Date: July 2006, Lincoln's Inn
Qualifications: [BA (Cantab)]
✉afoyle@oeclaw.co.uk

FRAIN-BELL MR WILLIAM JOHN

Hardwicke
New Square, Lincoln's Inn, London WC2A 3SB, ☎020 7242 2523
✉enquiries@hardwicke.co.uk
Call Date: July 2000, Middle Temple
Qualifications: [LLB MA]

FRAME MR STUART JAMES

Staple Inn Chambers
1st Floor, 9 Staple Inn, Holborn Bars, London WC1V 7QH, ☎020 7242 5240
✉clerks@stapleinn.co.uk
Call Date: May 1997, Gray's Inn
Qualifications: [LLB (Kingston) MA (Brunel)]
✉sf@stapleinn.co.uk

FRAMPTON MR STUART

Devon Chambers
3 St Andrew Street, Plymouth PL1 2AH, ☎01752 661659
✉clerks@devonchambers.co.uk
Call Date: Oct 1998, Inner Temple
Qualifications: [BSc (Hons_, CPE]
✉stuartframpton@devonchambers.co.uk

FRANCE-HAYHURST MRS JEAN GAYNOR

Linenhall Chambers
1 Stanley Place, Chester CH1 2LU, ☎01244 348282
✉clerks@linenhallchambers.co.uk
Call Date: Nov 1972, Gray's Inn
Qualifications: [LLB (Hons) (Wales)]

FRANCE-HAYHURST MS LUCINDA KATHERINE ROSE

Atlantic Chambers
4-6 Cook Street, Liverpool L2 9QU, ☎0151 236 4421
✉info@atlanticchambers.co.uk
Call Date: July 2009, Gray's Inn
Qualifications: [BA]
✉lucinda@atlanticchambers.co.uk

FRANCIS MR ADRIAN

Selborne Chambers
10 Essex Street, London WC2R 3AA, ☎020 7420 9500
✉clerks@selbornechambers.co.uk
Call Date: Nov 1988, Lincoln's Inn
Pupil Supervisor
Qualifications: [LLB (Hons) (Wales) BCL (Oxon)]

FRANCIS MR ANDREW JAMES

Serle Court
6 New Square, Lincoln's Inn, London WC2A 3QS, ☎020 7242 6105
✉clerks@serlecourt.co.uk
Zenith Chambers
10 Park Square, Leeds LS1 2LH, ☎0113 245 5438
✉clerks@zenithchambers.co.uk
Call Date: Nov 1977, Lincoln's Inn
Qualifications: [MA (Oxon)]
✉afrancis@serlecourt.co.uk

Types of work: Chancery (general), Chancery (land law), Commercial property, Conveyancing, Equity, Family provision, Landlord and tenant, Partnerships, Professional negligence, Rights of light, Succession, Trusts, Wills

E

FRANCIS MR EDWARD GERALD FRANCIS

Enterprise Chambers
9 Old Square, Lincoln's Inn, London
WC2A 3SR, ☎ 020 7405 9471
✉ london@enterprisechambers.com
Enterprise Chambers
65 Quayside, Newcastle Upon Tyne NE1 3DE,
☎ 0191 222 3344
✉ newcastle@enterprisechambers.com
Enterprise Chambers
43 Park Square, Leeds LS1 2NP,
☎ 0113 246 0391
✉ leeds@enterprisechambers.com
Call Date: Nov 1995, Inner Temple
Pupil Supervisor
Qualifications: [BA (Oxon) CPE (Lond)]
edwardfrancis@enterprisechambers.com

FRANCIS MR NICHOLAS QC (2002)

29 Bedford Row Chambers
London WC1R 4HE, ☎ 020 7404 1044
✉ clerks@29br.co.uk
Call Date: July 1981, Middle Temple
Qualifications: [MA (Cantab)]
nfrancis@29br.co.uk

E

Fax: 020 7831 0626;
Out of hours telephone: 020 7404 1044;
DX: 1044 1044

Other professional qualifications: Recorder since 1999; Deputy High Court Judge 2011, Family Law Arbitrator

Types of work: Family law

Membership of foreign bars: International Academy of Matrimonial Lawyers

Awards and memberships: FLBA; Panel Member of COIC Complaints Tribunal

Other professional experience: Regular lecturer and Chair of Jordans and Butterworths Family Law Conferences; frequently chairs private FDRs and Early Neutral Evaluation Hearings.

Publications: *Ancillary Relief after Miller and McFarlane*, Lime Legal Ltd, August 2006; Numerous articles in *Family Law*; Editor and Co-Author of IAML publication: 'International Pre-Nuptial Agreements', 2011

Reported Cases: *Martin Dye v Martin Dye*, [2006] 2 FLR 901 Leading case on treatment of pensions: family law.
A v B, [2005] 2 FLR 730 Leading case on agreements and inherited wealth.
Re C, [2007] 2 FLR 13 Leading case under Schedule 1 CA 1989.
MT v MT, [2008] 2 FLR 1311
Walkden v Walkden, [2010] 1 FLR 1311

FRANCIS MR RICHARD MAURICE

9 Park Place
9 Park Place, Cardiff, South Glamorgan
CF10 3DP, ☎ 029 2038 2731
✉ clerks@9parkplace.co.uk
Call Date: Nov 1974, Gray's Inn
Pupil Supervisor
Qualifications: [BA (Dunelm)]
richardfrancis@9parkplace.co.uk

FRANCIS MR ROBERT ANTHONY QC (1992)

3 Serjeants Inn
London EC4Y 1BQ, ☎ 020 7427 5000
✉ clerks@3serjeantsinn.com
Call Date: July 1973, Inner Temple
Qualifications: [LLB (Exon)]
rfrancis@3serjeantsinn.com

Types of work: Administrative law, Common law (general), Medical negligence, Mental health, Personal injury, Public inquiries

FRANCIS MISS VICTORIA MARIA

29 Bedford Row Chambers
London WC1R 4HE, ☎ 020 7404 1044
✉ clerks@29br.co.uk
Call Date: Oct 2001, Middle Temple
Qualifications: [BA (Hons) (Cantab) CPE]
vfrancis@29br.co.uk

FRANCO MR GIANPIERO

Holborn Chambers
6 Gate Street, Lincoln's Inn Fields, London
WC2A 3HP, ☎ 020 7242 6060
Call Date: Nov 1988, Inner Temple
Qualifications: [MA (Cantab) LLB (Lond)]

FRANK MR IVOR RICHARD BAINTON

7 Bell Yard
London WC2A 2JR, ☎ 020 7831 0636
✉ kevintarrant@btconnect.com
Call Date: July 1979, Gray's Inn
Pupil Supervisor
Qualifications: [LLB (Lond) LLM (USA)]

FRANKLIN MR EDWARD THOMAS ROBERT

Atkinson Bevan Chambers
1st Floor, 2 Harcourt Buildings, Temple,
London EC4Y 9DB, ☎ 020 7353 2112
✉ clerks@2hb.co.uk
Call Date: July 2006, Gray's Inn
Qualifications: [MA (Oxon) Dip Law]
EFranklin@2hb.co.uk

FRANKLIN MISS KIM

Crown Office Chambers
2 Crown Office Row, Temple, London EC4Y 7HJ, ☎020 7797 8100
✉mail@crownofficechambers.com
Call Date: Nov 1984, Middle Temple
Pupil Supervisor
Qualifications: [LLB (Warwick) FCIArb]
franklin@crownofficechambers.com

FRANKLIN MISS REBECCA JANE

St Philips Chambers
55 Temple Row, Birmingham B2 5LS, ☎0121 246 7000 ✉clerks@st-philips.com
Call Date: July 2001, Lincoln's Inn
Qualifications: [BA (Hons), BVC, PgDL]
rfranklin@st-philips.co.uk

FRANSES MISS JESSICA LOUISE

36 Bedford Row
London WC1R 4JH, ☎020 7421 8000
✉chambers@36bedfordrow.co.uk
Call Date: Nov 2000, Gray's Inn
Qualifications: [BA (Newc)]

FRANSMAN MR LAURENS FRANCOIS QC (2000)

Garden Court Chambers
57-60 Lincoln's Inn Fields, London WC2A 3LJ, ☎020 7993 7600 ✉info@gclaw.co.uk
Call Date: July 1979, Middle Temple
Qualifications: [LLB]
laurief@gclaw.co.uk

FRANTZIS MISS ROXANNE

KBW
The Engine House, No 1 Foundry Square, Leeds LS11 5DL, ☎0113 297 1200
✉clerks@kbwchambers.com
Call Date: Nov 2003, Middle Temple
Qualifications: [LLB (Hons) LLM (Lond)]
roxannefrantzis@kbwchambers.com

FRASER MISS CLAIRE

7 Bell Yard
London WC2A 2JR, ☎020 7831 0636
✉kevintarrant@btconnect.com
Call Date: Oct 2000, Lincoln's Inn
Qualifications: [LLB (Hons)(Staffs)]
cf@7bellyard.co.uk

FRASER MR DONALD

Atlantic Chambers
4-6 Cook Street, Liverpool L2 9QU, ☎0151 236 4421
✉info@atlanticchambers.co.uk
Call Date: July 2003, Inner Temple
Qualifications: [LLB (Bris)]
donaldfraser@atlanticchambers.co.uk

FRASER MR MARK-ANTHONY

Dyers Chambers
35 Bedford Row, London WC1R 4JH, ☎020 7404 1881
✉admin@dyerschambers.com
Call Date: Nov 2000, Middle Temple
Qualifications: [LLB (Hons)]
mark.fraser@dyerschambers.com

FRASER MR ORLANDO GREGORY

4 Stone Buildings
Ground Floor, 4 Stone Buildings, Lincoln's Inn, London WC2A 3XT, ☎020 7242 5524
✉clerks@4stonebuildings.com
Call Date: Nov 1994, Inner Temple
Qualifications: [BA (Cantab) CPE (Lond)]
clerks@4stonebuildings.com

FRASER MR PETER DONALD QC (2009)

Atkin Chambers
1 Atkin Building, Gray's Inn, London WC1R 5AT, ☎020 7404 0102
✉clerks@atkinchambers.com
Call Date: Nov 1989, Middle Temple
Recorder
Qualifications: [MA (Hons) LLM (Cantab)]
clerks@atkinchambers.com

FRASER MR QUINTIN ROBSON

39 Essex Street
London WC2R 3AT, ☎020 7832 1111
✉clerks@39essex.com
Call Date: Oct 2006, Middle Temple
Qualifications: [BA (Hons) (Oxon)]

FRASER MR VINCENT QC (2001)

Kings Chambers
36 Young Street, Manchester M3 3FT, ☎0845 034 3444
✉clerks@kingschambers.com
Kings Chambers
5 Park Square East, Leeds LS1 2NE, ☎0845 034 3444
✉clerks@kingschambers.com
Kings Chambers
Embassy House, 60 Church Street, Birmingham B3 2DJ, ☎0845 034 3444
✉clerks@kingschambers.com

E

Cornerstone Barristers
2-3 Gray's Inn Square, Gray's Inn, London WC1R 5JH, ☎ 020 7242 4986
✉ chambers@2-3gis.co.uk
Call Date: July 1981, Gray's Inn
Recorder
Qualifications: [MA (Oxon)]
vfraser@kingschambers.com

FRASER BUTLIN MRS SARAH KATE

Cloisters
1 Pump Court, Temple, London EC4Y 7AA, ☎ 020 7827 4000 ✉ clerks@cloisters.com
Call Date: July 2005, Middle Temple
Qualifications: [MA (cantab)]
sfb@cloisters.com

FRASER-URQUHART MR ANDREW

4-5 Gray's Inn Square
Gray's Inn, London WC1R 5AH,
☎ 020 7404 5252 ✉ clerks@4-5.co.uk
Call Date: Oct 1993, Middle Temple
Qualifications: [MA (Hons) (Cantab)]

FRAWLEY MS LYNDSEY ANNE

Quorum Chambers
2 Victoria Square, Victoria Street, St Albans AL1 3TF, ☎ 01727 884516
✉ clerks@quorumchambers.co.uk
Quorum Tax Chambers
25 Southampton Buildings, London WC2A 1AL, ☎ 020 7043 5189
✉ clerks@quorumchambers.co.uk
Call Date: Oct 1995, Middle Temple
Qualifications: [B.Sc Dip Law (CPE)]
lyndsey.frawley@quorumchambers.co.uk
URL: www.quorumchambers.co.uk

Types of work: Capital tax, Chancery (general), Chancery (land law), Commercial litigation, Contracts, Corporation tax, Employment, Income tax, Taxation and duties, VAT

FRAZER MS ALISON

Queen Square Chambers
56 Queen Square, Bristol BS1 4PR,
☎ 0117 921 1966 ✉ crime@qs-c.co.uk
Call Date: Nov 1999, Gray's Inn
Qualifications: [LLB LLM (Bris)]
civil@qs-c.co.uk, alison_frazer@hotmail.com

FRAZER MISS LUCY CLAIRE

South Square
3-4 South Square, Gray's Inn, London WC1R 5HP, ☎ 020 7696 9900
✉ practicemanagers@southsquare.com
Call Date: Oct 1996, Middle Temple
Pupil Supervisor
Qualifications: [MA (Hons)(Cantab)]
lucyfrazer@southsquare.com

FREDMAN MS SANDRA DEBBE

Old Square Chambers
10-11 Bedford Row, London WC1R 4BU,
☎ 020 7269 0300 ✉ clerks@oldsquare.co.uk
Old Square Chambers
3 Orchard Court, St Augustine's Yard, Bristol BS1 5DP, ☎ 0117 930 5100
✉ clerks@oldsquare.co.uk
Call Date: Mar 2002, Gray's Inn
Qualifications: [BA MA (Oxon) BCL (Oxon)]

FREEDMAN MR BENJAMIN CLIVE QC (1997)

Littleton Chambers
3 King's Bench Walk North, Temple, London EC4Y 7HR, ☎ 020 7797 8600
✉ fschneider@littletonchambers.co.uk
Kings Chambers
Embassy House, 60 Church Street, Birmingham B3 2DJ, ☎ 0845 034 3444
✉ clerks@kingschambers.com
Kings Chambers
36 Young Street, Manchester M3 3FT,
☎ 0845 034 3444
✉ clerks@kingschambers.com
Kings Chambers
5 Park Square East, Leeds LS1 2NE,
☎ 0845 034 3444
✉ clerks@kingschambers.com
Call Date: July 1978, Middle Temple
Recorder
Qualifications: [MA (Cantab)]
cf@littletonchambers.co.uk

FREEDMAN MR JEREMY STUART

Park Lane Plowden
Lombard House, 4-8 Lombard Street, Newcastle Upon Tyne NE1 3AE,
☎ 0191 211 4087
✉ clerks@parklaneplowden.co.uk
Call Date: July 1982, Middle Temple
Pupil Supervisor, Recorder
Qualifications: [BA (Hons) Dip Law (Lond)]
jeremy.freedman@parklaneplowden.co.uk

FREEDMAN MS MICHELLE

Clerksroom (Taunton)
Equity House, Administration Centre, Blackbrook Park Avenue, Taunton, Somerset TA1 2PX, ☎0845 083 3000
✉mail@clerksroom.com
Call Date: Nov 2002, Lincoln's Inn
Qualifications: [BSc (Hons) (Lond)]

FREEDMAN MR SAMPSON CLIVE

3 Verulam Buildings
London WC1R 5NT, ☎020 7831 8441
✉chambers@3vb.com
Call Date: July 1975, Gray's Inn
Pupil Supervisor
Qualifications: [MA (Cantab) FBCS FCI Arb]

FREEMAN MS EMMA JANE

Number 7 Harrington Street Chambers
7 Harrington Street, Liverpool L2 9YH, ☎0151 242 0707 ✉clerks@7hs.co.uk
Call Date: Oct 2002, Inner Temple
Qualifications: [BA (Hons)(L'pool) CPE PgDL]
✉emma.freeman@7hs.co.uk

FREEMAN MRS HANNAH ABIGAIL

Old Square Chambers
10-11 Bedford Row, London WC1R 4BU, ☎020 7269 0300 ✉clerks@oldsquare.co.uk
Old Square Chambers
3 Orchard Court, St Augustine's Yard, Bristol BS1 5DP, ☎0117 930 5100
✉clerks@oldsquare.co.uk
Call Date: July 2004, Lincoln's Inn
Qualifications: [BA Hons (Oxon) PGDipLaw]
✉freeman@oldsquare.co.uk

FREEMAN MR KEITH NICHOLAS

Harrogate Chambers
5 The Grove, Harrogate HG1 5NN, ☎01423 520771
Call Date: July 1985, Lincoln's Inn
Qualifications: [MA (Lond) BA (Reading) Dip Law]

FREEMAN MISS LISA CLAIRE

Furnival Chambers
32 Furnival Street, London EC4A 1JQ, ☎020 7405 3232
Call Date: Oct 2005, Lincoln's Inn
Qualifications: [LLB (Hons) LLM]
✉lfreeman@furnivallaw.co.uk

FREEMAN MR PETER MARK

Farrar's Building
Farrar's Building, Temple, London EC4Y 7BD, ☎020 7583 9241
✉Chambers@farrarsbuilding.co.uk
Call Date: Oct 1992, Middle Temple
Pupil Supervisor
Qualifications: [LLB (Hons)]
✉pfreeman@farrarsbuilding.co.uk

FREEMAN MRS SALLY JANE

East Anglian Chambers
15 The Close, Norwich, Norfolk NR1 4DZ, ☎01473 214481 ✉norwich@ealaw.co.uk
East Anglian Chambers
53 North Hill, Colchester, Essex CO1 1QA, ☎01473 214481 ✉colchester@ealaw.co.uk
East Anglian Chambers
140 New London Road, Chelmsford, Essex CM2 0AW, ☎01473 214481
✉chelmsford@ealaw.co.uk
East Anglian Chambers
Gresham House, 5 Museum Street, Ipswich, Suffolk IP1 1HQ, ☎01473 214481
✉ipswich@ealaw.co.uk
Call Date: Nov 1995, Lincoln's Inn
Pupil Supervisor
Qualifications: [LLB (Hons)]
✉sallyfreeman@ealaw.co.uk

FREEMANTLE MISS KATE PATRICIA

2 King's Bench Walk
2 King's Bench Walk, Temple, London EC4Y 7DE, ☎020 7353 1746
✉clerks@2kbw.com
Call Date: July 2003, Lincoln's Inn
Qualifications: [BA PgDL]
✉kfreemantle@2kbw.com

FREESTON MISS LYNN ROBERTA

Coram Chambers
9-11 Fulwood Place, London WC1V 6HG, ☎020 7092 3700
✉mail@coramchambers.co.uk
Call Date: Oct 1996, Gray's Inn
Qualifications: [BA (Canada) LLB (Hons) DipM DipCam]
✉lynn.freeston@coramchambers.co.uk

FRENCH MISS CHARLOTTE LUCIE ELIZABETH

St Philips Chambers
55 Temple Row, Birmingham B2 5LS, ☎0121 246 7000 ✉clerks@st-philips.com
Call Date: July 2008, Inner Temple
Qualifications: [BA (Cantab)]

E

FRENCH MR GERALD HUGH

Atkinson Bevan Chambers
1st Floor, 2 Harcourt Buildings, Temple, London EC4Y 9DB, ☎020 7353 2112
✉clerks@2hb.co.uk
Call Date: Oct 2004, Inner Temple
Qualifications: [BA (Newc) CPE]
✉hfrench@2hb.co.uk

FRENCH MR JONATHAN GABRIEL

Exchange Chambers
Oxford House, Oxford Row, Leeds LS1 3BE, ☎0113 203 1970
✉spencer@exchangechambers.co.uk
Exchange Chambers
One Derby Square, Derby Square, Liverpool L2 9XX, ☎0151 236 7747
✉info@exchangechambers.co.uk
Exchange Chambers
7 Ralli Courts, West Riverside, Manchester M3 5FT, ☎0161 833 2722
Call Date: Nov 1997, Lincoln's Inn
Pupil Supervisor
Qualifications: [LLB (Hons)(Manch)]
✉french@exchangechambers.co.uk

FRENCH MR LOUIS CHARLES

Nine Bedford Row
9 Bedford Row, London WC1R 4AZ, ☎020 7489 2727
✉clerks@9bedfordrow.co.uk
Call Date: Nov 1979, Inner Temple
Pupil Supervisor
Qualifications: [MA (Oxon)]

FRENCH MR PAUL BECKINTON

Guildhall Chambers
23 Broad Street, Bristol BS1 2HG, ☎0117 930 9000
✉hoc@guildhallchambers.co.uk
Call Date: July 1989, Inner Temple
Qualifications: [LLB (Hons)]

FREW MR BRUCE LIMA

Dere Street Barristers
14 Toft Green, York YO1 6JT, ☎0844 3351551
✉clerks@derestreet.co.uk
York Chambers
Rotterdam House, 116 The Quayside, Newcastle Upon Tyne NE1 3DY, ☎0191 206 4677
Call Date: Nov 2005, Lincoln's Inn
Qualifications: [LLB (Hons) (Dundee) LLM (Leeds)]
✉clerks@yorkchambers.co.uk

FRICKER MISS SUSAN KATHERINE

Sovereign Chambers
46 Park Place, Leeds LS1 2RY, ☎0113 245 1841
✉clerks@sovereignchambers.co.uk
Call Date: July 1988, Gray's Inn
Qualifications: [BA (Keele)]
✉susan.fricker@sovereignchambers.co.uk

FRIDAY MR STEPHEN JOHN

Park Lane Plowden
19 Westgate, Leeds LS1 2RD, ☎0113 228 5049
✉clerks@parklaneplowden.co.uk
Call Date: Oct 1996, Lincoln's Inn
Qualifications: [LLB (Hons)(UEA)]
✉stephen.friday@parklaneplowden.co.uk

FRIDD MR NICHOLAS TIMOTHY

Albion Chambers
Broad Street, Bristol BS1 1DR, ☎0117 927 2144
✉clerks@albionchambers.co.uk
Bell Yard Chambers
116/118 Chancery Lane, London WC2A 1PP, ☎020 7306 9292
✉byclerks@bellyardchambers.co.uk
Call Date: Nov 1975, Inner Temple
Pupil Supervisor
Qualifications: [MA (Oxon)]
✉nicholas.fridd@albionchambers.co.uk

FRIEDMAN MR DANIEL SIMON

Matrix Chambers
Griffin Building, Gray's Inn, London WC1R 5LN, ☎020 7404 3447
✉matrix@matrixlaw.co.uk / lscott@matrixlaw.co.uk
Call Date: Oct 1996, Middle Temple
Pupil Supervisor
Qualifications: [BA (Hons) (Oxon) LLM (Lond)]
✉dannyfriedman@matrixlaw.co.uk

FRIEDMAN MR DAVID PETER QC (1990)

4 Pump Court
4 Pump Court, Temple, London EC4Y 7AN, ☎020 7842 5555
✉chambers@4pumpcourt.com
Call Date: July 1968, Inner Temple
Recorder
Qualifications: [MA (Oxon) CEDR BCL]
✉dfriedman@4pumpcourt.com

E

FRIEL MR JOHN ANTHONY

Hardwicke
New Square, Lincoln's Inn, London
WC2A 3SB, ☎020 7242 2523
✉enquiries@hardwicke.co.uk
Call Date: July 1974, Gray's Inn
Qualifications: [LLB (Lond)]

FRIEL MISS MICHELE

No5 Chambers
Fountain Court, Steelhouse Lane, Birmingham
B4 6DR, ☎0845 210 5555 ✉info@no5.com
No5 Chambers
Greenwood House, 4-7 Salisbury Court,
London EC4Y 8AA, ☎0845 210 5555
No5 Chambers
38 Queen Square, Bristol BS1 4QS,
☎0845 210 5555
Call Date: Oct 1991, Lincoln's Inn
Qualifications: [LLB (Hons)]
✉mfr@no5.com

FRIEND MR MARK OWEN

Lincoln House Chambers
Tower 12, The Avenue North, Spinningfields,
18-22 Bridge Street, Manchester M3 3BZ,
☎0161 832 5701
✉info@lincolnhousechambers.com
Call Date: Mar 2002, Lincoln's Inn
Qualifications: [LLB (Hons)(Leeds)]

FRIER MR DANIEL ROBERT

Eastbourne Chambers
5 Chiswick Place, Eastbourne, East Sussex
BN21 4NH, ☎01323 642102
✉clerks@eastbournechambers.co.uk
Call Date: Oct 2005, Gray's Inn
Qualifications: [LLB (Nott'm)]

FRIEZE MR DANIEL ISAAC

St Johns Buildings
24a - 28 St John Street, Manchester M3 4DJ,
☎0161 214 1500
✉clerk@stjohnsbuildings.co.uk
16 Winckley Square
Preston PR1 3JJ, ☎01772 256100
St Johns Buildings Liverpool
8th Floor India Buildings, Water Street,
Liverpool L2 0XG, ☎0151 243 6000
✉clerk@stjohnsbuildings.co.uk
Call Date: Oct 1994, Gray's Inn
Pupil Supervisor
Qualifications: [BA (Hons) (Manch)]
✉clerk@stjohnsbuildings.co.uk,
daniel.frieze@stjohnsbuildings.co.uk

FRIEZE MR ROBIN BENNETT

No.6 Park Square
Leeds LS1 2LW, ☎0113 245 9763
✉Tim@no6.co.uk
Call Date: July 1985, Lincoln's Inn
Pupil Supervisor
Qualifications: [LLB (Leeds)]
✉frieze@no6.co.uk

FRIPP MR ERIC WILLIAM BURTIN

Chambers of Mr Ami Feder
Ground Floor, Lamb Building, Temple, London
EC4Y 7AS, ☎020 7797 7788
✉clerks@lambbuilding.co.uk
Chambers of Mr Ami Feder
Ground Floor, Lamb Building, Temple, London
EC4Y 7AS, ☎020 7797 7788
✉clerks@lambbuilding.co.uk
Call Date: Oct 1994, Gray's Inn
Pupil Supervisor
Qualifications: [MA LLM MA]

FRISTON DR MARK HARPHAM

Kings Chambers
36 Young Street, Manchester M3 3FT,
☎0845 034 3444
✉clerks@kingschambers.com
Kings Chambers
5 Park Square East, Leeds LS1 2NE,
☎0845 034 3444
✉clerks@kingschambers.com
Kings Chambers
Embassy House, 60 Church Street,
Birmingham B3 2DJ, ☎0845 034 3444
✉clerks@kingschambers.com
Ely Place Chambers
30 Ely Place, London EC1N 6TD,
☎020 7400 9600 ✉admin@elyplace.com
Call Date: Nov 1997, Middle Temple
Qualifications: [MA, BS BChirMRCP (UK) Dip Law BM (Cantab)]
✉mfriston@kingschambers.com

FRITH MS ALEXANDRA HELEN

Westgate Chambers
64 High Street, Lewes, East Sussex BN7 1XG,
☎01273 480510
✉clerks@westgate-chambers.co.uk
Call Date: Feb 1993, Lincoln's Inn
Pupil Supervisor
Qualifications: [LLB (Hons)]
✉af@westgate-chambers.co.uk

E

FRITH MISS HEATHER VIVIEN

Pendragon Chambers
Suite 7, J Shed, Kings Road, SA1 Waterfront, Swansea SA1 8PL, ☎01792 411188
✉clerks@pendragonchambers.com
Call Date: July 1989, Middle Temple
Qualifications: [LLB (Hons) (Bristol)]
heatherfrith@pendragonchambers.com

FRITH MR NICHOLAS JOHN

37 Park Square Chambers
37 Park Square, Leeds LS1 2NY,
☎0113 243 9422 ✉chambers@no37.co.uk
Call Date: Oct 1992, Gray's Inn
Qualifications: [LLB LLM (Bucks)]
chambers@no37.co.uk

FRITH MR TIMOTHY GEORGE

Devereux Chambers
Queen Elizabeth Building, Temple, London EC4Y 9BS, ☎020 7353 7534
✉clerks@devchambers.co.uk
Call Date: Nov 1996, Middle Temple
Qualifications: [MA (Hons) Dip Law LLM (Commercial Law)]

E

FRODSHAM MR ALEXANDER MILES

Oriel Chambers
14 Water Street, Liverpool, Merseyside L2 8TD, ☎0151 236 7191
✉clerks@orielchambers.co.uk
Oriel Chambers
18 Ribblesdale Place, Preston PR1 3NA,
☎01772 254 764
✉clerks@oriel-chambers.co.uk
Call Date: Oct 1996, Lincoln's Inn
Qualifications: [LLB (Hons)(L'pool)]
alexander.frodsham@orielchambers.co.uk

FROST MISS ANGELA MARIE

12 King's Bench Walk
12 King's Bench Walk, Temple, London EC4Y 7EL, ☎020 7583 0811
Call Date: Oct 2001, Inner Temple
Qualifications: [BA (Sheff)]
frost@12kbw.co.uk

FROST MISS NICOLA MARTINE

3 PB Barristers
Royal Talbot House, 2 Victoria Street, Bristol, Avon BS1 6BB, ☎0117 928 1520
Call Date: July 2009, Inner Temple
Qualifications: [LLB (Bris)]
nicola.frost@3pb.co.uk

FRY MISS ELEANOR KATE

Park Court Chambers
16 Park Place, Leeds LS1 2SJ,
☎0113 243 3277
✉clerks@parkcourtchambers.co.uk
Call Date: Nov 2007, Middle Temple
Qualifications: [LLB (Hons) MA (Leeds)]
efry@parkcourtchambers.co.uk

FRY MR NEIL JOHN

Coram Chambers
9-11 Fulwood Place, London WC1V 6HG,
☎020 7092 3700
✉mail@coramchambers.co.uk
Call Date: Feb 1992, Inner Temple
Qualifications: [LLB (Hons) (Exon)]
nf@coramchambers.co.uk, neil.fry@coramchambers.co.uk

FRYER MR NIGEL MCCRAE

Queen Square Chambers
56 Queen Square, Bristol BS1 4PR,
☎0117 921 1966 ✉crime@qs-c.co.uk
Call Date: Nov 1999, Middle Temple
Qualifications: [LLB (Hons)]

FRYER-SPEDDING MR JAMES WALTER

9 St John Street
Manchester M3 4DN, ☎0161 955 9000
✉civilclerks@9sjs.com /
criminalclerks@9sjs.com
Call Date: Feb 1994, Gray's Inn
Pupil Supervisor
Qualifications: [LLB (Lond) BCL (Oxon)]
james.fryer-spedding@9sjs.com

FRYMAN MR NEIL

Lincoln House Chambers
Tower 12, The Avenue North, Spinningfields, 18-22 Bridge Street, Manchester M3 3BZ,
☎0161 832 5701
✉info@lincolnhousechambers.com
Call Date: July 1989, Middle Temple
Qualifications: [LLB (Leics)]
neil.fryman@lincolnhousechambers.com

FRYMANN MR ANDREW PHILIP

187 Fleet Street
London EC4A 2AT, ☎020 7430 7430
✉chambers@187fleetstreet.com
Call Date: Nov 1995, Inner Temple
Pupil Supervisor
Qualifications: [LLB (Dunelm)]

FUAD MR KERIM QC (2010)

Chambers of Marion Smullen and Kerim Fuad QC
1 Inner Temple Lane, London EC4Y 1AF, ☎ 020 7427 4400 ✉ clerks@1itl.com
Call Date: Nov 1992, Inner Temple
Pupil Supervisor
Qualifications: [LLB (Hons)(Lond)]
✉ kerim.fuad@1itl.com

FUDAKOWSKI MRS KATHERINE ELIZABETH

Old Square Chambers
10-11 Bedford Row, London WC1R 4BU, ☎ 020 7269 0300 ✉ clerks@oldsquare.co.uk
Old Square Chambers
3 Orchard Court, St Augustine's Yard, Bristol BS1 5DP, ☎ 0117 930 5100
✉ clerks@oldsquare.co.uk
Call Date: Oct 2008, Lincoln's Inn
Qualifications: [BA (Cantab)]

FUDGE MRS SALLY RUTH

Furnival Chambers
32 Furnival Street, London EC4A 1JQ, ☎ 020 7405 3232
Call Date: Nov 1998, Lincoln's Inn
Qualifications: [LLB (Hons)(Middx)]
✉ sfudge@furnivallaw.co.uk

FUGALLO MR DANIEL JOSEPH MARK

23 Essex Street
London WC2R 3AA, ☎ 020 7413 0353
✉ clerks@23es.com
Call Date: Oct 1999, Middle Temple
Pupil Supervisor
Qualifications: [MA (Hons)(Cantab)]
✉ danielfugallo@23es.com

FULLER MR ALAN PETER

Albion Chambers
Broad Street, Bristol BS1 1DR, ☎ 0117 927 2144
✉ clerks@albionchambers.co.uk
Call Date: Oct 1993, Gray's Inn
Qualifications: [LLB (Warw)]
✉ alan.fuller@albionchambers.co.uk

FULLER MR JONATHAN PAUL QC (2002)

187 Fleet Street
London EC4A 2AT, ☎ 020 7430 7430
✉ chambers@187fleetstreet.com
Call Date: July 1977, Lincoln's Inn
Recorder
Qualifications: [LLB (Lond)]

FULLER MR STEVEN DAVID

Field Court Chambers
5 Field Court, Gray's Inn, London WC1R 5EF, ☎ 020 7405 6114 ✉ clerks@fieldcourt.co.uk
Call Date: July 2008, Middle Temple
Qualifications: [BA (Hons) (Oxon) MSc (LSE) PgDl (Lond)]

FULLER MR STUART KENNETH

Albion Chambers
Broad Street, Bristol BS1 1DR, ☎ 0117 927 2144
✉ clerks@albionchambers.co.uk
Call Date: Mar 2007, Inner Temple
Qualifications: [BA MA (Cantab)]

FULLERTON MR MICHAEL ANDREW

Chambers of Mr Michael Fullerton
5 Pembroke Avenue, Hove, East Sussex BN3 5DA, ☎ 01273 772050
7 Bell Yard
London WC2A 2JR, ☎ 020 7831 0636
✉ kevintarrant@btconnect.com
Call Date: Feb 1990, Inner Temple
Pupil Supervisor
Qualifications: [BA LLB (Australia)]

FULLWOOD MR ADAM GARRETT

Kings Chambers
36 Young Street, Manchester M3 3FT, ☎ 0845 034 3444
✉ clerks@kingschambers.com
Kings Chambers
5 Park Square East, Leeds LS1 2NE, ☎ 0845 034 3444
✉ clerks@kingschambers.com
Kings Chambers
Embassy House, 60 Church Street, Birmingham B3 2DJ, ☎ 0845 034 3444
✉ clerks@kingschambers.com
Call Date: Mar 1996, Gray's Inn
Pupil Supervisor
Qualifications: [BA MA (Bris)]
✉ afullwood@kingschambers.com

FULTON MR ANDREW JOHN

20 Essex Street
London WC2R 3AL, ☎ 020 7842 1200
✉ clerks@20essexst.com
Call Date: Nov 1999, Middle Temple
Qualifications: [BA (Hons)(Oxon) Dip Law]
✉ AFulton@20essexst.com

E

FURBER MR JOHN QC (1995)

Wilberforce Chambers
8 New Square, Lincoln's Inn, London
WC2A 3QP, ☎020 7306 0102
✉chambers@wilberforce.co.uk
Call Date: July 1973, Inner Temple
Qualifications: [MA (Cantab)]
jfurber@wilberforce.co.uk

FURLONG MR LEONARD WILLIAM

Holborn Chambers
6 Gate Street, Lincoln's Inn Fields, London
WC2A 3HP, ☎020 7242 6060
Call Date: July 2009, Inner Temple
Qualifications: [CPE (So'ton)]
len.furlong@holbornchambers.co.uk

FURLONG MR RICHARD CRAVEN

25 Bedford Row
London WC1R 4HD, ☎020 7067 1500
✉clerks@25bedfordrow.com
Call Date: Oct 1994, Lincoln's Inn
Pupil Supervisor
Qualifications: [MA CPE (Lond)]
rfurlong@25bedfordrow.com

FURMINGER MR MICHAEL ASHLEY

Chambers of Michael Furminger
4 Marcent Row, St Mary's Hill, Brixham,
Devon TQ5 9GQ, ☎01803 414 545
✉michaelfurminger@live.com
Call Date: Oct 1991, Gray's Inn
Qualifications: [LLB (Lond)]

FURNESS MR CORIN JOHN

Park Lane Plowden
19 Westgate, Leeds LS1 2RD,
☎0113 228 5049
✉clerks@parklaneplowden.co.uk
Call Date: Oct 1994, Lincoln's Inn
Pupil Supervisor
Qualifications: [LLB (Hons)(Hull)]
corin.furness@parklaneplowden.co.uk

FURNESS MR JONATHAN QC (2003)

30 Park Place
Cardiff CF10 3BS, ☎029 2039 8421
✉clerks@30parkplace.law.co.uk
Call Date: July 1979, Gray's Inn
Recorder
Qualifications: [MA (Cantab)]
hjf@30parkplace.co.uk

FURNESS MR MICHAEL JAMES QC (2000)

Wilberforce Chambers
8 New Square, Lincoln's Inn, London
WC2A 3QP, ☎020 7306 0102
✉chambers@wilberforce.co.uk
Call Date: July 1982, Lincoln's Inn
Qualifications: [MA (Cantab) BCL (Oxon)]
mfurness@wilberforce.co.uk

Types of work: Capital tax, Chancery (general), Charities, Equity, Income tax, Pensions, Professional negligence, Trusts, Wills

FURNISS MR RICHARD ALEXANDER

42 Bedford Row
London WC1R 4LL, ☎020 7831 0222
✉clerks@42br.com
Call Date: Oct 1991, Middle Temple
Pupil Supervisor
Qualifications: [MA (Cantab)]
rf@42br.com

Types of work: Clinical negligence, Personal injury, Professional negligence

FURST MR STEPHEN ANDREW QC (1991)

Keating Chambers
15 Essex Street, London WC2R 3AA,
☎020 7544 2600
✉clerks@keatingchambers.com
Call Date: July 1975, Middle Temple
Recorder
Qualifications: [BA (Oxon) LLB (Hons)(Leeds)]

GABB MR CHARLES HENRY ESCOTT

Pump Court Chambers
31 Southgate Street, Winchester, Hampshire
SO23 9EB, ☎01962 868 161
✉clerks@3pumpcourt.com
Pump Court Chambers
Upper Ground Floor, 3 Pump Court, Temple,
London EC4Y 7AJ, ☎020 7353 0711
✉clerks@3pumpcourt.com
Pump Court Chambers
5 Temple Chambers, Temple Street, Swindon
SN1 1SQ, ☎01793 539899
✉clerks@3pumpcourt.com
Call Date: Feb 1975, Middle Temple
Qualifications: [LLB]

GABBITAS MR CHRISTOPHER PETER DAVID

1 High Pavement
Nottingham NG1 1HF, ☎0115 941 8218
✉clerks@1highpavement.co.uk
Call Date: Nov 2009, Lincoln's Inn
Qualifications: [LLB (Lincoln)]
✉christophergabbitas@1highpavement.co.uk

GADD MR ADAM BRIAN

Pump Court Chambers
Upper Ground Floor, 3 Pump Court, Temple, London EC4Y 7AJ, ☎020 7353 0711
✉clerks@3pumpcourt.com
Pump Court Chambers
31 Southgate Street, Winchester, Hampshire SO23 9EB, ☎01962 868 161
✉clerks@3pumpcourt.com
Riverview Chambers
Hamilton House, 1 Temple Avenue, London EC4Y 0HA, ☎0844 225 3999
✉chrisbaylis@riverviewchambers.com
Call Date: July 2004, Gray's Inn
Qualifications: [MA (Glas)]
✉abg@3pumpcourt.com

GADD MR MICHAEL JOHN

XXIV Old Buildings
Ground Floor, 24 Old Buildings, Lincoln's Inn, London WC2A 3UP, ☎020 7691 2424
✉clerks@xxiv.co.uk
Call Date: July 1981, Lincoln's Inn
Pupil Supervisor
Qualifications: [BA (Dunelm)]

GADSDEN MR MARK JEREMY

Atkinson Bevan Chambers
1st Floor, 2 Harcourt Buildings, Temple, London EC4Y 9DB, ☎020 7353 2112
✉clerks@2hb.co.uk
Call Date: July 1980, Middle Temple
Pupil Supervisor
Qualifications: [MA (Oxon)]

GADZAMA CHIEF JOE-KYARI

Middle Temple Lane Chambers
2nd Floor South, 1 Middle Temple Lane, London EC4Y 9AA, ☎020 7583 4352
✉chambers@mtlchambers.com
Great James Street Chambers
37 Great James Street, London WC1N 3HB, ☎020 7440 4949
✉chambers@greatjames.co.uk
Call Date: Oct 2008, Lincoln's Inn
Qualifications: [LLB (Nigeria)]
✉chambers@mtlchambers.com

GAINER MR RICHARD ST CLAIR

St Margaret's Chambers
44 Sidney Road, St Margaret's, Twickenham, Middlesex TW1 1JR, ☎020 8241 3516
Call Date: Nov 1983, Middle Temple
Qualifications: [BA (Kent)]

GAIR MR CHRISTOPHER

King's Bench Chambers
Wellington House, 175 Holdenhurst Road, Bournemouth, Dorset BH8 8DQ, ☎01202 250025
Call Date: July 2000, Middle Temple
Qualifications: [LLB(Hons) (Northbr)]
✉cgair@bar-law.co.uk

GAISFORD MR PHILIP DAVID

3 Serjeants Inn
London EC4Y 1BQ, ☎020 7427 5000
✉clerks@3serjeantsinn.com
Call Date: Nov 1969, Gray's Inn
Qualifications: [LLB (Soton)]
✉pgaisford@3serjeantsinn.com

GAISMAN MR JONATHAN NICHOLAS CRISPIN QC (1995)

7 King's Bench Walk
Ground Floor, 7 King's Bench Walk, Temple, London EC4Y 7DS, ☎020 7910 8300
✉clerks@7kbw.co.uk
Call Date: Nov 1979, Inner Temple
Recorder
Qualifications: [MA Assocrina BCL (Oxon)]
✉jgaisman@7kbw.co.uk

GAITSKELL MR ROBERT QC (1994)

Keating Chambers
15 Essex Street, London WC2R 3AA, ☎020 7544 2600
✉clerks@keatingchambers.com
Call Date: July 1978, Gray's Inn
Recorder
Qualifications: [BSc (Eng) FCIArb PhD AKC FIMechE CEng FIET]

GAL MS SONIA

St Johns Buildings
24a - 28 St John Street, Manchester M3 4DJ, ☎0161 214 1500
✉clerk@stjohnsbuildings.co.uk
St Johns Buildings
21 White Friars, Chester CH1 1NZ, ☎01244 323070
✉clerk@stjohnsbuildings.co.uk

E

16 Winckley Square
Preston PR1 3JJ, ☎01772 256100
Call Date: Nov 1982, Inner Temple
Recorder
Qualifications: [BA]
clerk@stjohnsbuildings.co.uk

GALBRAITH-MARTEN MR JASON NICHOLAS

Cloisters
1 Pump Court, Temple, London EC4Y 7AA,
☎020 7827 4000 ✉clerks@cloisters.com
Call Date: Oct 1991, Middle Temple
Pupil Supervisor
Qualifications: [MA (Hons) (Cantab)]
jngm@cloisters.com

GALE MR JOCELIN LANSELL HUDD

7 King's Bench Walk
Ground Floor, 7 King's Bench Walk, Temple,
London EC4Y 7DS, ☎020 7910 8300
✉clerks@7kbw.co.uk
Call Date: July 2009, Inner Temple
Qualifications: [BA (Lond) M Phil (Cantab) M Phil]
clerks@7kbw.co.uk

GALE MR JONATHAN RAPHAEL

Chancery House Chambers
7 Lisbon Square, Leeds, West Yorkshire
LS1 4LY, ☎0113 244 6691
✉clerks@chanceryhouse.co.uk
Call Date: Oct 2009, Gray's Inn
Qualifications: [BA MA]
jonathan.gale@chanceryhouse.co.uk

GALE MR PHILLIP STEPHEN JOHN

Enterprise Chambers
9 Old Square, Lincoln's Inn, London
WC2A 3SR, ☎020 7405 9471
✉london@enterprisechambers.com
Enterprise Chambers
65 Quayside, Newcastle Upon Tyne NE1 3DE,
☎0191 222 3344
✉newcastle@enterprisechambers.com
Enterprise Chambers
43 Park Square, Leeds LS1 2NP,
☎0113 246 0391
✉leeds@enterprisechambers.com
Call Date: Oct 2008, Lincoln's Inn
Qualifications: [BA BCL (Oxon)]
phillipgale@enterprisechambers.com

GALLACHER MISS KIRSTY MARIE

No5 Chambers
Fountain Court, Steelhouse Lane, Birmingham
B4 6DR, ☎0845 210 5555 ✉info@no5.com
No5 Chambers
Greenwood House, 4-7 Salisbury Court,
London EC4Y 8AA, ☎0845 210 5555
No5 Chambers
38 Queen Square, Bristol BS1 4QS,
☎0845 210 5555
Call Date: Nov 2006, Gray's Inn
Qualifications: [LLB]

GALLAFENT MS KATE SELINA

Blackstone Chambers
Blackstone House, Temple, London
EC4Y 9BW, ☎020 7583 1770
✉clerks@blackstonechambers.com
Call Date: Oct 1997, Gray's Inn
Pupil Supervisor
Qualifications: [BA (Hons) (Cantab)]
kategallafent@blackstonechambers.com

GALLAGHER MR BRIAN JOSEPH

12 King's Bench Walk
12 King's Bench Walk, Temple, London
EC4Y 7EL, ☎020 7583 0811
Call Date: July 1975, Inner Temple
Pupil Supervisor
Qualifications: [LLB]
gallagher@12kbw.co.uk

GALLAGHER MS CAOILFHIONN ANNA

Doughty Street Chambers
53-54 Doughty Street, London WC1N 2LS,
☎020 7404 1313
✉enquiries@doughtystreet.co.uk
Doughty Street Chambers
Pall Mall Court, 61-67 King Street, Manchester
M2 4PD, ☎0161 618 1066
Doughty Street Chambers
5th Floor, Broad Quay House, Prince Street,
Bristol BS1 4DJ, ☎01179 058 717
Call Date: Oct 2006, Lincoln's Inn
Qualifications: [BCL (Dub) LLM (Cantab) PHD (Dub) BL]
c.gallagher@doughtystreet.co.uk

GALLAGHER MR JOHN DAVID EDMUND

Hardwicke
New Square, Lincoln's Inn, London
WC2A 3SB, ☎020 7242 2523
✉enquiries@hardwicke.co.uk
Call Date: Nov 1974, Gray's Inn
Pupil Supervisor, Recorder
Qualifications: [BA AKC (Lond)]
john.gallagher@hardwicke.co.uk

GALLAGHER MS MARIA THERESA

Pump Court Chambers
5 Temple Chambers, Temple Street, Swindon SN1 1SQ, ☎01793 539899
✉clerks@3pumpcourt.com
Pump Court Chambers
Upper Ground Floor, 3 Pump Court, Temple, London EC4Y 7AJ, ☎020 7353 0711
✉clerks@3pumpcourt.com
Pump Court Chambers
31 Southgate Street, Winchester, Hampshire SO23 9EB, ☎01962 868 161
✉clerks@3pumpcourt.com
Call Date: Nov 1997, Inner Temple
Qualifications: [LLB (L'pool)]

GALLAGHER MR PATRICK

KCH Garden Square
1 Oxford Street, Nottingham NG1 5BH, ☎0115 941 8851
✉clerks@kchgardensquare.co.uk
Call Date: July 1984, Gray's Inn
Qualifications: [BSc (Econ) LLB (Lond)]
pgallagher@kchgardensquare.co.uk

GALLAGHER MR STANLEY HAROLD

Tanfield Chambers
2-5 Warwick Court, London WC1R 5DJ, ☎020 7421 5300
✉clerks@tanfieldchambers.co.uk
Call Date: Feb 1994, Lincoln's Inn
Qualifications: [BEc LLB (Australia)]
stangallagher@tanfieldchambers.co.uk

Types of work: Chancery (land law), Commercial property, Conveyancing, Landlord and tenant, Lands Tribunal, Leasehold enfranchisement

Awards and memberships: Chancery Bar Association; Property Bar Association

Reported Cases: *Cawthorne v Hamdan (CA)*, [2007] EWCA Civ 6; [2007] Ch 187 (Court of Appeal), 2007.
Grosvenor Estates Ltd v Prospect Estates Ltd (CA), [2009] WLR 1313 (Court of Appeal), 2009.

GALLEY MRS HELEN MARGARET

XXIV Old Buildings
Ground Floor, 24 Old Buildings, Lincoln's Inn, London WC2A 3UP, ☎020 7691 2424
✉clerks@xxiv.co.uk
Call Date: July 1987, Gray's Inn
Pupil Supervisor
Qualifications: [LLB (Lond)]

GALLIVAN MR TERENCE JOHN

Five Paper
Ground Floor, 5 Paper Buildings, Temple, London EC4Y 7HB, ☎020 7815 3200
Call Date: July 1981, Inner Temple
Qualifications: [BA (Dunelm) LLB (Cantab)]

GALLOWAY MR MALCOLM KENNITH WILLIAM

Colleton Chambers
Colleton Crescent, Exeter, Devon EX2 4DG, ☎01392 274898
✉clerks@colletonchambers.co.uk
Call Date: Oct 1992, Inner Temple
Pupil Supervisor
Qualifications: [BA (Hons)]
malcolmgalloway@colletonchambers.co.uk

GALLOWAY MISS RACHEL JOSEPHINE

Kings Chambers
36 Young Street, Manchester M3 3FT, ☎0845 034 3444
✉clerks@kingschambers.com
Kings Chambers
5 Park Square East, Leeds LS1 2NE, ☎0845 034 3444
✉clerks@kingschambers.com
Kings Chambers
Embassy House, 60 Church Street, Birmingham B3 2DJ, ☎0845 034 3444
✉clerks@kingschambers.com
Call Date: Oct 2004, Gray's Inn
Qualifications: [BA]
rgalloway@kingschambers.com

GALVIN MR KIERAN JOHN MICHAEL CHRISTOPHE

2 Bedford Row
London WC1R 4BU, ☎020 7440 8888
✉clerks@2bedfordrow.co.uk
Call Date: Nov 1996, Middle Temple
Qualifications: [LLB (Hons)(Lond) BA (Hons)(Newc)]
kgalvin@2bedfordrow.co.uk

GALWAY-COOPER DR PHILIP ANTHONY

Five St Andrew's Hill
5 St Andrew's Hill, London EC4V 5BZ, ☎020 7332 5400 ✉Clerks@5sah.co.uk
Call Date: Oct 1993, Inner Temple
Qualifications: [MRCS LRCP (Lond) MA]
philipgalway-cooper@5sah.co.uk

E

GAMBLE MRS ESTHER RUTH

No5 Chambers
Fountain Court, Steelhouse Lane, Birmingham B4 6DR, ☎0845 210 5555 ✉info@no5.com
No5 Chambers
Greenwood House, 4-7 Salisbury Court, London EC4Y 8AA, ☎0845 210 5555
No5 Chambers
38 Queen Square, Bristol BS1 4QS, ☎0845 210 5555
St Philips Chambers
55 Temple Row, Birmingham B2 5LS, ☎0121 246 7000 ✉clerks@st-philips.com
Call Date: July 2001, Middle Temple
Qualifications: [BSc (Hons) CPE]

GAMBLE MISS HELEN LOUISE

Fountain Chambers
Cleveland Business Centre, 1 Watson Street, Middlesbrough TS1 2RQ, ☎01642 804040 ✉clerks@fountainchambers.co.uk
Call Date: Nov 1998, Inner Temple
Qualifications: [LLB (Hull)]

GAMBLE MR JAMES RICHARD

No5 Chambers
Fountain Court, Steelhouse Lane, Birmingham B4 6DR, ☎0845 210 5555 ✉info@no5.com
No5 Chambers
Greenwood House, 4-7 Salisbury Court, London EC4Y 8AA, ☎0845 210 5555
No5 Chambers
38 Queen Square, Bristol BS1 4QS, ☎0845 210 5555
Call Date: Oct 1999, Middle Temple
Qualifications: [BA (Hons)(Cantab)]
🖃jg@no5.com

GAMMIE MR MALCOLM JAMES QC (2002)

One Essex Court
Ground Floor, One Essex Court, Temple, London EC4Y 9AR, ☎020 7583 2000 ✉clerks@oeclaw.co.uk
Call Date: Oct 1997, Middle Temple
Qualifications: [MA (Hons)(Cantab)]
🖃mgammie@oeclaw.co.uk

GAMMON MISS CHARMIAN RUTH

St Ive's Chambers
Whittall Street, Birmingham B4 6DH, ☎0121 236 0863 ✉clerks@stiveschambers.co.uk
Call Date: Oct 2007, Lincoln's Inn
Qualifications: [LLB (Nott'm)]
🖃charmian.gammon@stiveschambers.co.uk

GANDHI MS PAULENE

Renaissance Chambers
5th Floor, Gray's Inn Chambers, Gray's Inn, London WC1R 5JA, ☎020 7404 1111 ✉clerks@renaissancechambers.co.uk
Call Date: Oct 1995, Inner Temple
Qualifications: [BSc (Aberdeen) BA]

GANDOLFI MRS JOAN

Chambers of Joan Gandolfi
47 Shackleton Place, Oldbrook, Milton Keynes MK6 2PT, ☎0845 123 1234 ✉joangandolfi@sky.com
Call Date: May 1997, Lincoln's Inn
Qualifications: [LLB (Hons)]

GANESAN MR MUTHUPANDI PETER

Furnival Chambers
32 Furnival Street, London EC4A 1JQ, ☎020 7405 3232
Call Date: Oct 2003, Lincoln's Inn
Qualifications: [LLB (Hons) (Wales) LL (Lond)]
🖃mganesan@furnivallaw.co.uk

GANNER MR JOSEPH MICHAEL

Furnival Chambers
32 Furnival Street, London EC4A 1JQ, ☎020 7405 3232
Linenhall Chambers
1 Stanley Place, Chester CH1 2LU, ☎01244 348282 ✉clerks@linenhallchambers.co.uk
Call Date: July 1983, Inner Temple
Pupil Supervisor
Qualifications: [LLB]

GANNON MR KEVIN FRANCIS

1 Pump Court
Elm Court, Temple, London EC4Y 7AB, ☎020 7842 7070 ✉(name)@pumpcourt.co.uk
Call Date: Nov 1993, Inner Temple
Qualifications: [BSc (Loughborough) CPE]
🖃kg@1pumpcourt.co.uk

GANTEAUME MISS NATALIE ANNE

42 Bedford Row
London WC1R 4LL, ☎020 7831 0222 ✉clerks@42br.com
Call Date: Nov 2001, Middle Temple
Qualifications: [LLB (Hons)]
🖃natalie.ganteaume@42br.com

GAPE MR CHRISTIAN DAVID

Southernhay Chambers
33 Southernhay East, Exeter EX1 1NX,
☎01392 255777
✉clerks@southernhaychambers.co.uk
Call Date: July 2005, Middle Temple
Qualifications: [BSc Econ (Wales) MSc Econ (Wales)]
✉c.gape@southernhaychambers.co.uk

GARCHA MR GURDEEP SINGH

Citadel Chambers
The Citadel, 190 Corporation Street, Birmingham B4 6QD, ☎0121 233 8500
✉clerks@citadelchambers.com
Call Date: Nov 1997, Lincoln's Inn
Qualifications: [LLB (Hons)(Warw)]
✉clerks@citadelchambers.com

GARCHA MR SUKHDEV SINGH

Call Date: July 2008, Middle Temple
Qualifications: [LLB (Hons) (Manch)]

GARDINER MR BRUCE DOUGLAS

2 Temple Gardens
2 Temple Gardens, Temple, London EC4Y 9AY, ☎020 7822 1200
✉clerks@2tg.co.uk
Call Date: Oct 1994, Middle Temple
Pupil Supervisor
Qualifications: [MA (Oxon)]
✉bgardiner@2tg.co.uk

GARDINER MISS HELEN MARGERY RUTH

Chancery House Chambers
7 Lisbon Square, Leeds, West Yorkshire LS1 4LY, ☎0113 244 6691
✉clerks@chanceryhouse.co.uk
Call Date: Oct 2007, Gray's Inn
Qualifications: [BA (Oxon)]
✉helen.gardiner@chanceryhouse.co.uk

GARDINER MR JOHN RALPH QC (1982)

11 New Square
1st Floor, 11 New Square, Lincoln's Inn, London WC2A 3QB, ☎020 7242 4017
✉john.moore@11newsquare.com
Call Date: Nov 1968, Middle Temple
Qualifications: [MA LLM (Cantab)]
✉john.moore@11newsquare.com

GARDINER MISS KERRY ANN

Queen Square Chambers
56 Queen Square, Bristol BS1 4PR,
☎0117 921 1966 ✉crime@qs-c.co.uk
Call Date: Oct 2006, Middle Temple
Qualifications: [LLB (Hons) (Bris)]
✉civil@qs-c.co.uk, kg@qs-c.co.uk

GARDINER MR SEBASTIAN

25 Bedford Row
London WC1R 4HD, ☎020 7067 1500
✉clerks@25bedfordrow.com
Call Date: Oct 1997, Inner Temple
Pupil Supervisor
Qualifications: [BA (Manchester) CPE]
✉sgardiner@25bedfordrow.com

GARDINER MR WILLIAM DAVID HUGH

Holborn Chambers
6 Gate Street, Lincoln's Inn Fields, London WC2A 3HP, ☎020 7242 6060
Call Date: Nov 1976, Middle Temple
Qualifications: [BSc (Chemistry)]

GARDNER MR ALAN JAMES

1 KBW Chambers
1 King's Bench Walk, Temple, London EC4Y 7DB, ☎020 7936 1500
✉clerks@1kbw.co.uk
King's Bench Chambers
174 High Street, Lewes BN7 1YE,
☎01273 402600
Call Date: Oct 1997, Middle Temple
Pupil Supervisor
Qualifications: [BA (Hons)(Leeds) CPE (Leeds)]
✉agardner@1kbw.co.uk

GARDNER MR BEN JOHN

Quadrant Chambers
Quadrant House, 10 Fleet Street, London EC4Y 1AU, ☎020 7583 4444
✉info@quadrantchambers.com
Call Date: July 2010, Middle Temple
Qualifications: [BA (Hons) (Cantab) LLM (Cantab) LLM (USA)]
✉ben.gardner@quadrantchambers.com

GARDNER MISS CHLOE

Nexus Chambers
7 New Square, Lincolns Inn, London WC2A 3QS,
☎020 7404 1147 / 020 7831 8309
✉info@nexuschambers.com
Call Date: Oct 2005, Gray's Inn
Qualifications: [BA (Hull) MS (USA)]

GARDNER MISS EILIDH ANNE MAIRI

42 Bedford Row
London WC1R 4LL, ☎ 020 7831 0222
✉ clerks@42br.com
Call Date: Oct 1997, Middle Temple
Qualifications: [LLB (Hons)(Newc)]
✉ eilidh.gardner@42br.com

GARDNER MISS FRANCESCA MARIA ASSUNTA

Kings Chambers
36 Young Street, Manchester M3 3FT,
☎ 0845 034 3444
✉ clerks@kingschambers.com
Kings Chambers
5 Park Square East, Leeds LS1 2NE,
☎ 0845 034 3444
✉ clerks@kingschambers.com
Kings Chambers
Embassy House, 60 Church Street,
Birmingham B3 2DJ, ☎ 0845 034 3444
✉ clerks@kingschambers.com
Call Date: July 2004, Lincoln's Inn
Qualifications: [LLB Hons (Sheff)]
✉ fgardner@kingschambers.com

E

GARDNER MR JAMES PIERS

Monckton Chambers
1 & 2 Raymond Buildings, Gray's Inn, London
WC1R 5NR, ☎ 020 7405 7211
✉ chambers@monckton.com
Call Date: Mar 2000, Gray's Inn
Qualifications: [MA (Oxon)]
✉ pgardner@monckton.com

GARGAN MISS CATHERINE JANE

36 Bedford Row
London WC1R 4JH, ☎ 020 7421 8000
✉ chambers@36bedfordrow.co.uk
Call Date: July 1978, Middle Temple
Pupil Supervisor
Qualifications: [LLB (L'pool)]

GARGAN MR MARK PATRICK

No.6 Park Square
Leeds LS1 2LW, ☎ 0113 245 9763
✉ Tim@no6.co.uk
Call Date: July 1983, Middle Temple
Pupil Supervisor, Recorder
Qualifications: [MA (Oxon)]

GARGITTER MISS EMMA CAROLINE

18 Red Lion Court
London EC4A 3EB, ☎ 020 7520 6000
✉ chambers@18rlc.co.uk
Call Date: Nov 2003, Lincoln's Inn
Qualifications: [BA (Hons) (Cantab)]
✉ emma.gargitter@18rlc.co.uk

GARLICK MRS HELEN MARY

18 Red Lion Court
London EC4A 3EB, ☎ 020 7520 6000
✉ chambers@18rlc.co.uk
Call Date: Nov 1974, Middle Temple
Qualifications: [LLB]
✉ helengarlick@fulcrumchambers.com

GARLICK MR PAUL RICHARD QC (1996)

Furnival Chambers
32 Furnival Street, London EC4A 1JQ,
☎ 020 7405 3232
Call Date: July 1974, Middle Temple
✉ pgarlick@furnivallaw.co.uk

GARNER MISS SOPHIE JANE

St Philips Chambers
55 Temple Row, Birmingham B2 5LS,
☎ 0121 246 7000 ✉ clerks@st-philips.com
Call Date: Nov 1990, Middle Temple
Pupil Supervisor
Qualifications: [LLB (Hons)]
✉ sgarner@st-philips.com

GARNER MR STEPHEN JOHN PETER

Guildhall Chambers
23 Broad Street, Bristol BS1 2HG,
☎ 0117 930 9000
✉ hoc@guildhallchambers.co.uk
Call Date: Oct 1994, Gray's Inn
Qualifications: [LLB (Hons)]
✉ stephen.garner@guildhallchambers.co.uk

GARNETT MRS SUSAN JANE LOUISE

Chambers of Mrs Susan J L Garnett
Widenmayerstrasse 44, Lehel,
Munich☎ 0892 4218798
✉ susanjlgarnett@aol.com
Call Date: July 1973, Lincoln's Inn
Pupil Supervisor
Qualifications: [BA]

GARNHAM MS CLARE LOUISE

Zenith Chambers
10 Park Square, Leeds LS1 2LH,
☎ 0113 245 5438
✉ clerks@zenithchambers.co.uk
Call Date: Oct 2005, Gray's Inn
Qualifications: [BA (Hudds) LLB (Hons) (Hudds)]
✉ cgarnham@zenithchambers.co.uk

GARNHAM MR NEIL STEPHEN QC (2001)

1 Crown Office Row
1 Crown Office Row, Temple, London EC4Y 7HH, ☎020 7797 7500
✉mail@1cor.com
Call Date: July 1982, Middle Temple
Recorder
Qualifications: [MA (Cantab)]
✉neil.garnham@1cor.com

GARRETT MISS LUCY MARGARET

Keating Chambers
15 Essex Street, London WC2R 3AA, ☎020 7544 2600
✉clerks@keatingchambers.com
Call Date: Oct 2001, Gray's Inn
Pupil Supervisor
Qualifications: [BA Hons (Manch) PgDL BVC]
✉lgarrett@keatingchambers.com

GARRETT MR LUKE JOHN

30 Park Place
Cardiff CF10 3BS, ☎029 2039 8421
✉clerks@30parkplace.law.co.uk
Call Date: July 2005, Gray's Inn
Qualifications: [BSc MA]
✉lgarrett@30parkplace.co.uk

GARRETT MR MICHAEL OWEN

St Philips Chambers
55 Temple Row, Birmingham B2 5LS, ☎0121 246 7000 ✉clerks@st-philips.com
Call Date: July 1967, Gray's Inn
Pupil Supervisor
✉mgarrett@st-philips.co.uk

GARRIDO MR DAMIAN ROBIN LEON

Harcourt Chambers
1st Floor, 2 Harcourt Buildings, Temple, London EC4Y 9DB, ☎0844 561 7135
Call Date: Nov 1993, Middle Temple
Pupil Supervisor
Qualifications: [BA (Hons)(Kent) Dip Law (Lond)]
✉dgarrido@harcourtchambers.law.co.uk

GARROD MR NEIL

Warwick House Chambers
8 Warwick Court, Warwick House Chambers, Gray's Inn, London WC1R 5DJ, ☎020 7430 2323
✉clerks@warwickhousechambers.com
Call Date: Nov 2000, Inner Temple
Qualifications: [LLB (Lond)]
✉clerks@warwickhousechambers.com

GARSIDE MR CHARLES ROGER QC (1993)

9 St John Street
Manchester M3 4DN, ☎0161 955 9000
✉civilclerks@9sjs.com / criminalclerks@9sjs.com
Nine Bedford Row
9 Bedford Row, London WC1R 4AZ, ☎020 7489 2727
✉clerks@9bedfordrow.co.uk
Bank House Chambers
Old Bank House, Hartshead, Sheffield S1 2EL, ☎0114 275 1223
✉w.digby@bankhousechambers.co.uk
Call Date: Nov 1971, Gray's Inn
Recorder

GARSIDE MR DAVID VERNON

St Johns Buildings
24a - 28 St John Street, Manchester M3 4DJ, ☎0161 214 1500
✉clerk@stjohnsbuildings.co.uk
16 Winckley Square
Preston PR1 3JJ, ☎01772 256100
St Johns Buildings Liverpool
8th Floor India Buildings, Water Street, Liverpool L2 0XG, ☎0151 243 6000
✉clerk@stjohnsbuildings.co.uk
Call Date: Nov 1982, Gray's Inn
Pupil Supervisor
Qualifications: [LLB (Hons)]
✉david.garside@stjohnsbuildings.co.uk

GARSIDE MR MARK KIRKLAND

Exchange Chambers
7 Ralli Courts, West Riverside, Manchester M3 5FT, ☎0161 833 2722
Exchange Chambers
One Derby Square, Derby Square, Liverpool L2 9XX, ☎0151 236 7747
✉info@exchangechambers.co.uk
Exchange Chambers
Oxford House, Oxford Row, Leeds LS1 3BE, ☎0113 203 1970
✉spencer@exchangechambers.co.uk
St Philips Chambers
55 Temple Row, Birmingham B2 5LS, ☎0121 246 7000 ✉clerks@st-philips.com
Call Date: Feb 1993, Inner Temple
Pupil Supervisor
Qualifications: [BA]

E

GARSON MR ROBERT DAVID MOSHE

2 Bedford Row
London WC1R 4BU, ☎ 020 7440 8888
✉ clerks@2bedfordrow.co.uk
Furnival Chambers
32 Furnival Street, London EC4A 1JQ,
☎ 020 7405 3232
Call Date: Nov 1999, Inner Temple
Qualifications: [BA (Manch)]

GARTH MR STEVEN DAVID

Wilberforce Chambers
7 Bishop Lane, Hull HU1 1PA,
☎ 01482 323264
Call Date: Nov 1983, Gray's Inn
Pupil Supervisor
Qualifications: [LLB (Hons) (Leeds)]

GARTLAND MS DOROTHEA SUSAN

4 Paper Buildings
1st Floor, 4 Paper Buildings, Temple, London
EC4Y 7EX, ☎ 020 7427 5200
✉ clerks@4pb.com
Call Date: Oct 2004, Inner Temple
Qualifications: [BA (Cantab) CPE]
🖃 dsg@4pb.com

GARVIE MR CARL PETER

St Philips Chambers
55 Temple Row, Birmingham B2 5LS,
☎ 0121 246 7000 ✉ clerks@st-philips.com
Call Date: Mar 2008, Lincoln's Inn
Qualifications: [BA (Cantab)]
🖃 cgarvie@st-philips.com

GASH MR WILLIAM SIMON WALKER

Ropewalk Chambers
24 The Ropewalk, Nottingham NG1 5EF,
☎ 0115 947 2581 ✉ clerks@ropewalk.co.uk
Call Date: July 1977, Gray's Inn
Pupil Supervisor
🖃 simongash@ropewalk.co.uk

GASK MR ALEXANDER WILLIAM

Doughty Street Chambers
53-54 Doughty Street, London WC1N 2LS,
☎ 020 7404 1313
✉ enquiries@doughtystreet.co.uk
Call Date: Oct 2008, Middle Temple
Qualifications: [BA (Hons) (Oxon)]
🖃 a.gask@doughtystreet.co.uk

GASKELL MR NICHOLAS JOSEPH JAMES

Quadrant Chambers
Quadrant House, 10 Fleet Street, London
EC4Y 1AU, ☎ 020 7583 4444
✉ info@quadrantchambers.com
Call Date: July 1976, Inner Temple

GASKIN MR FRANCIS JOHN GERALD

4 Breams Buildings
Chancery Lane, London EC4A 1HP,
☎ 020 7092 1900 ✉ clerks@4bb.co.uk
Call Date: July 2000, Middle Temple
Qualifications: [MSc (Dunelm)]

GASKIN MISS LEILA

Charter Chambers
33 John Street, London WC1N 2AT,
☎ 020 7618 4400
✉ clerks@charterchambers.com
Call Date: Oct 2000, Middle Temple
Qualifications: [LLB (Hons) (Dunelm)]
🖃 leila.gaskin@charterchambers.com

GASPARRO MISS JULIA MARIE

Renaissance Chambers
5th Floor, Gray's Inn Chambers, Gray's Inn,
London WC1R 5JA, ☎ 020 7404 1111
✉ clerks@renaissancechambers.co.uk
Call Date: July 1999, Lincoln's Inn
Pupil Supervisor
Qualifications: [BA (Hons)]
🖃 jg2@renaissancechambers.co.uk

GASSMAN MISS CAROLINE DORA

1 Mitre Court Buildings
1 Mitre Court Buildings, Temple, London
EC4Y 7BS, ☎ 020 7452 8900
✉ clerks@1mcb.com
Call Date: July 1974, Inner Temple
Qualifications: [LLB (Leeds)(Hons)]
🖃 caroline.gassman@1mcb.com

GASTON MR GRAEME

Fountain Chambers
Cleveland Business Centre, 1 Watson Street,
Middlesbrough TS1 2RQ, ☎ 01642 804040
✉ clerks@fountainchambers.co.uk
Call Date: Oct 1991, Lincoln's Inn
Qualifications: [LLB (Hons) (Leeds)]

GASZTOWICZ MR STEVEN QC (2009)

Cornerstone Barristers
2-3 Gray's Inn Square, Gray's Inn, London WC1R 5JH, ☎ 020 7242 4986
✉ chambers@2-3gis.co.uk
New Street Chambers
2 New Street, Leicester LE1 5NA,
☎ 0116 262 5906 ✉ clerks@2newstreet.co.uk
Call Date: July 1981, Gray's Inn
Qualifications: [LLB]
✉ sgasztowicz@2-3gis.co.uk

GATENBY MR JAMES MICHAEL

Chavasse Court Chambers
18 Queen Avenue, Liverpool L2 4TX,
☎ 0151 229 2030
✉ clerks@chavassechambers.co.uk
Call Date: Oct 1994, Middle Temple
Pupil Supervisor
Qualifications: [LLB (Hons)(L'pool)]
✉ james.gatenby@chavassechambers.co.uk

GATES MR HARRY

4 Paper Buildings
1st Floor, 4 Paper Buildings, Temple, London EC4Y 7EX, ☎ 020 7427 5200
✉ clerks@4pb.com
Call Date: Nov 2001, Lincoln's Inn
Pupil Supervisor
Qualifications: [BA (Hons) LLB (Hons)]
✉ hg@4pb.com

GATES MISS SERENA JANE

Five St Andrew's Hill
5 St Andrew's Hill, London EC4V 5BZ,
☎ 020 7332 5400 ✉ Clerks@5sah.co.uk
Call Date: Nov 2001, Middle Temple
Qualifications: [BA (Hons) LLM]
✉ serenagates@5sah.co.uk

GATESHILL MR JOSEPH BERNARD

Wilberforce Chambers
7 Bishop Lane, Hull HU1 1PA,
☎ 01482 323264
Call Date: July 1972, Lincoln's Inn
Pupil Supervisor, Recorder
Qualifications: [MA (Cantab)]

GATLAND MR GLENN DALE

New Court Chambers
3 Broad Chare, Newcastle Upon Tyne NE1 3DQ, ☎ 0191 232 1980
✉ clerks@newcourt-chambers.co.uk
Call Date: Nov 1972, Gray's Inn
Pupil Supervisor
Qualifications: [LLB (Hons) Fellow of Caribbean Law Institute]

GATLEY MR MARK DOUGLAS

Argent Chambers
5 Bell Yard, London WC2A 2JR,
☎ 020 7556 5500
✉ briefsin@argentchambers.co.uk
Call Date: Oct 1993, Gray's Inn
Qualifications: [BA]
✉ m.gatley@argentchambers.co.uk

GATTO MISS NICOLA ESTERINA

9 St John Street
Manchester M3 4DN, ☎ 0161 955 9000
✉ civilclerks@9sjs.com /
criminalclerks@9sjs.com
Call Date: Nov 1987, Middle Temple
Qualifications: [LLB (B'ham)]

GATTY MR DANIEL SIMON

Hardwicke
New Square, Lincoln's Inn, London WC2A 3SB, ☎ 020 7242 2523
✉ enquiries@hardwicke.co.uk
Call Date: Oct 1990, Middle Temple
Pupil Supervisor
Qualifications: [BA (Manch) Dip Law]
✉ daniel.gatty@hardwicke.co.uk

GATWARD MR WILLIAM EUGENE

9 King's Bench Walk
Lower Ground Floor South, 9 King's Bench Walk, Temple, London EC4Y 7DX,
☎ 020 7353 9564 ✉ 9kbw@btconnect.com
Call Date: Oct 2009, Middle Temple
Qualifications: [BA (USA) LLB (Canada) BCL (Canada)]
✉ gatward9kbw@gmail.com

GAU MR JUSTIN CHARLES

Pump Court Chambers
Upper Ground Floor, 3 Pump Court, Temple, London EC4Y 7AJ, ☎ 020 7353 0711
✉ clerks@3pumpcourt.com
Pump Court Chambers
5 Temple Chambers, Temple Street, Swindon SN1 1SQ, ☎ 01793 539899
✉ clerks@3pumpcourt.com
Pump Court Chambers
31 Southgate Street, Winchester, Hampshire SO23 9EB, ☎ 01962 868 161
✉ clerks@3pumpcourt.com
Call Date: July 1989, Middle Temple
Pupil Supervisor
Qualifications: [LLB (Lond)]
✉ jg@3pumpcourt.com

E

GAUNT MR JONATHAN ROBERT QC (1991)

Falcon Chambers
Falcon Court, London EC4Y 1AA,
☎ 020 7353 2484
✉ clerks@falcon-chambers.com
Call Date: July 1972, Lincoln's Inn
Qualifications: [BA (Oxon)]
gaunt@falcon-chambers.com

GAUNT MISS SARAH LEVINA

36 Bedford Row
London WC1R 4JH, ☎ 020 7421 8000
✉ chambers@36bedfordrow.co.uk
Call Date: Oct 1992, Lincoln's Inn
Qualifications: [LLB(Hons)(Wales) MPhil (Cantab)]
clerks@36bedfordrow.co.uk

GAVAGHAN MR JONATHAN DAVID

Ten Old Square
Ground Floor, Ten Old Square, Lincoln's Inn, London WC2A 3SU, ☎ 020 7405 0758
✉ clerks@tenoldsquare.com
Call Date: Oct 1992, Lincoln's Inn
Pupil Supervisor
Qualifications: [MA(Hons) BCL (Oxon)]
clerks@tenoldsquare.com

E

GAYAN MR ANIL KUMARSINGH

Clapham Law Chambers
85 Landor Road, Clapham North, London SW9 9RT, ☎ 020 7978 8482
✉ DANNY@claphamlawchambers.co.uk
Call Date: Nov 1972, Inner Temple
Qualifications: [LLB (Lond)]

GAYFORD MISS JUSTINE BEVERLEY

College Chambers
19 Carlton Crescent, Southampton, Hampshire SO15 2ET, ☎ 023 8023 0338
✉ clerks@college-chambers.co.uk
Call Date: Oct 2005, Middle Temple
Qualifications: [LLB (Hons)]
jgayford@College-Chambers.co.uk

GEADAH MR ANTHONY EDWARD

29 Bedford Row Chambers
London WC1R 4HE, ☎ 020 7404 1044
✉ clerks@29br.co.uk
Call Date: July 2000, Gray's Inn
Qualifications: [LLB (Hons)(KCL)]
ageadah@29br.co.uk

GEARTY PROF CONOR ANTHONY

Matrix Chambers
Griffin Building, Gray's Inn, London WC1R 5LN, ☎ 020 7404 3447
✉ matrix@matrixlaw.co.uk / Iscott@matrixlaw.co.uk
Call Date: Nov 1995, Middle Temple
Qualifications: [BCL LLB (Hons) PhD (Cantab)]
conorgearty@matrixlaw.co.uk

GEARY MR GAVIN JOHN

7 King's Bench Walk
Ground Floor, 7 King's Bench Walk, Temple, London EC4Y 7DS, ☎ 020 7910 8300
✉ clerks@7kbw.co.uk
Call Date: Feb 1989, Gray's Inn
Pupil Supervisor
Qualifications: [BA (Oxon)]
ggeary@7kbw.co.uk

GEDDES MISS GILLIAN MARY

2-3 Hind Court Chambers
2-3 Hind Court, Fleet Street, London EC4A 3DL, ☎ 020 7822 2150
✉ david@2-3hindcourt.com
Call Date: Oct 1997, Gray's Inn
Qualifications: [LLB]

GEDDES MS JOANNA FAY

Sovereign Chambers
46 Park Place, Leeds LS1 2RY,
☎ 0113 245 1841
✉ clerks@sovereignchambers.co.uk
Call Date: Nov 1992, Gray's Inn
Pupil Supervisor
Qualifications: [BA (Lond) Dip Law]
joanna.geddes@sovereignchambers.co.uk

GEDGE MR NICHOLAS PAUL JOHNSON

Apex
Harlech House, 20 Cathedral Road, Cardiff CF11 9LJ, ☎ 02920 232 032
✉ clerks@apexchambers.net
Call Date: Oct 2000, Middle Temple
Qualifications: [MA (Hons) CPE]
nick.gedge@apexchambers.net

GEDRYCH MISS JANET ANNE

Angel Chambers
Ethos Building, Kings Road, Swansea SA1 8AS,
☎ 01792 464623
✉ clerks@angelchambers.co.uk
Call Date: Oct 2000, Gray's Inn
Qualifications: [LLB (Warwick)]
janetgedrych@angelchambers.co.uk

GEE MISS CAROLINE

Exchange Chambers
7 Ralli Courts, West Riverside, Manchester M3 5FT, ☎0161 833 2722
Exchange Chambers
One Derby Square, Derby Square, Liverpool L2 9XX, ☎0151 236 7747
✉info@exchangechambers.co.uk
Exchange Chambers
Oxford House, Oxford Row, Leeds LS1 3BE, ☎0113 203 1970
✉spencer@exchangechambers.co.uk
Call Date: July 2003, Gray's Inn
Qualifications: [LLB (Leeds)]
✉gee@exchangechambers.co.uk

GEE MR STEVEN MARK QC (1993)

Stone Chambers
4 Field Court, Gray's Inn, London WC1R 5EF, ☎020 7440 6900
✉clerks@stonechambers.com
Call Date: July 1975, Middle Temple
Recorder
Qualifications: [MA (Oxon)]
✉steven.gee@stonechambers.com

GEE MR TOBY DAVID

Crown Office Chambers
2 Crown Office Row, Temple, London EC4Y 7HJ, ☎020 7797 8100
✉mail@crownofficechambers.com
Call Date: Oct 1992, Inner Temple
Qualifications: [MA (Cantab) CPE]
✉gee@crownofficechambers.com

GEEKIE MR CHARLES NAIRN QC (2006)

1 Garden Court Family Law Chambers
Ground Floor, One Garden Court, Temple, London EC4Y 9BJ, ☎020 7797 7900
✉clerks@1gc.com
St Ive's Chambers
Whittall Street, Birmingham B4 6DH, ☎0121 236 0863
✉clerks@stiveschambers.co.uk
St Mary's Family Law Chambers
26-28 High Pavement, The Lace Market, Nottingham NG1 1HN, ☎0115 950 3503
✉clerks@stmarysflc.co.uk
Call Date: July 1985, Inner Temple
Qualifications: [LLB (Bris)]
✉geekie@1gc.com

GEERING MR CHRISTOPHER ROBERT

2 Hare Court
Lower Ground, Ground, 1st & 2nd Floor, 2 Hare Court, Temple, London EC4Y 7BH, ☎020 7353 3982 ✉clerks@2harecourt.com
Call Date: July 2009, Lincoln's Inn
Qualifications: [BA (Oxon) CPE UCU]

GEESON MR CHRISTOPHER PAUL

1 High Pavement
Nottingham NG1 1HF, ☎0115 941 8218
✉clerks@1highpavement.co.uk
Call Date: Nov 1989, Gray's Inn
Qualifications: [BA]
✉chrisgeeson@1highpavement.co.uk

GEEY MR DAVID SIMON

Number 7 Harrington Street Chambers
7 Harrington Street, Liverpool L2 9YH, ☎0151 242 0707 ✉clerks@7hs.co.uk
Call Date: July 1970, Inner Temple
Pupil Supervisor, Recorder
Qualifications: [LLB]
✉david.geey@7hs.co.uk

GELBART MR GEOFF ALAN

1 Gray's Inn Square
Ground Floor, 1 Gray's Inn Square, London WC1R 5AA, ☎020 7405 0001
Call Date: Nov 1982, Lincoln's Inn
Pupil Supervisor
Qualifications: [BA (Hons) LLM (Lond)]

GENN MS YVETTE NAOMI

Cloisters
1 Pump Court, Temple, London EC4Y 7AA, ☎020 7827 4000 ✉clerks@cloisters.com
Call Date: Oct 1991, Inner Temple
Pupil Supervisor
Qualifications: [BA (Hons) (Warw) Dip Law]
✉yg@cloisters.com

GENNEY MR PAUL WALTON

Wilberforce Chambers
7 Bishop Lane, Hull HU1 1PA, ☎01482 323264
Call Date: May 1976, Middle Temple
Qualifications: [BDS]

GENT MR MATTHEW THOMAS

Sovereign Chambers
46 Park Place, Leeds LS1 2RY, ☎0113 245 1841
✉clerks@sovereignchambers.co.uk
Call Date: Nov 1998, Gray's Inn
Qualifications: [BA (Cantab)]
✉tom.gent@sovereignchambers.co.uk

E

GENTLEMAN MR TOM

4 Stone Buildings
Ground Floor, 4 Stone Buildings, Lincoln's Inn, London WC2A 3XT, ☎ 020 7242 5524
✉ clerks@4stonebuildings.com
Call Date: Oct 2005, Lincoln's Inn
Qualifications: [MA (Hons) (Oxon)]
t.gentleman@4stonebuildings.com

GEORGE MR ANDREW JAMES

Blackstone Chambers
Blackstone House, Temple, London EC4Y 9BW, ☎ 020 7583 1770
✉ clerks@blackstonechambers.com
Call Date: Oct 1997, Gray's Inn
Pupil Supervisor
Qualifications: [BA (Hons) (Oxon)]
andrewgeorge@blackstonechambers.com

GEORGE MR CHARLES RICHARD QC (1992)

Francis Taylor Building
Inner Temple, London EC4Y 7BY, ☎ 020 7353 8415 ✉ clerks@ftb.eu.com
Call Date: July 1974, Inner Temple
Recorder
Qualifications: [MA (Oxon)]
charles.george@ftb.eu.com

GEORGE MR DEAN ROBERT

2 Bedford Row
London WC1R 4BU, ☎ 020 7440 8888
✉ clerks@2bedfordrow.co.uk
Call Date: July 2002, Gray's Inn
Qualifications: [BA (Sussex)]
dgeorge@2bedfordrow.co.uk

GEORGE MR DOMINICK GILES

Quarry Chambers
64 Quarry Road, Winchester, Hants S023 0JS, ☎ 01962 622202
Call Date: July 1998, Gray's Inn
Qualifications: [BA LLM]

GEORGE MISS JUDITH SARAH

St Philips Chambers
55 Temple Row, Birmingham B2 5LS, ☎ 0121 246 7000 ✉ clerks@st-philips.com
Call Date: Oct 1991, Middle Temple
Qualifications: [MA (Hons) (Cantab)]
sgeorge@st-Philips.com

GEORGE MR MARK MCHALLAM QC (2009)

Chambers of Ian Macdonald QC
Garden Court North, 22 Oxford Court, Manchester M2 3WQ, ☎ 0161 236 1840
✉ clerks@gcnchambers.co.uk
Garden Court Chambers
57-60 Lincoln's Inn Fields, London WC2A 3LJ, ☎ 020 7993 7600 ✉ info@gclaw.co.uk
Call Date: Nov 1976, Inner Temple
Qualifications: [BA (Cantab)]
mgeorge@gcnchambers.co.uk

GEORGE MR MICHAEL DAVID ROBERTS

St Philips Chambers
55 Temple Row, Birmingham B2 5LS, ☎ 0121 246 7000 ✉ clerks@st-philips.com
Call Date: Nov 1990, Gray's Inn
Pupil Supervisor
Qualifications: [LLB]
mgeorge@st-philips.com

GEORGE MR NICHOLAS FRANK RAYMOND

New Walk Chambers
27 New Walk, Leicester, Leicestershire LE1 6TE, ☎ 0871 200 1298 / 0116 255 9144
✉ clerks@newwalkchambers.co.uk
Call Date: July 1983, Inner Temple
Qualifications: [LLB (Manch)]
ngeorge@newwalkchambers.co.uk

GEORGE MISS SUSAN DEBORAH

Coram Chambers
9-11 Fulwood Place, London WC1V 6HG, ☎ 020 7092 3700
✉ mail@coramchambers.co.uk
Call Date: Nov 1990, Gray's Inn
Qualifications: [LLB Hons (Lond)]
susan.george@coramchambers.co.uk

GEORGE MR TIMOTHY DAVID

KCH Garden Square
1 Oxford Street, Nottingham NG1 5BH, ☎ 0115 941 8851
✉ clerks@kchgardensquare.co.uk
Call Date: Nov 2000, Inner Temple
Qualifications: [LLB]

GEORGIOU MS ANGELA KYRIACOS

Cobden House Chambers
19 Quay Street, Manchester M3 3HN, ☎ 0161 833 6000 ✉ Clerks@Cobden.co.uk
Call Date: Oct 1997, Inner Temple
Qualifications: [LLB (Hons)(Sheff)]
clerks@cobden.co.uk

GERASIMIDIS MR NICOLAS

Guildhall Chambers
23 Broad Street, Bristol BS1 2HG,
☎ 0117 930 9000
✉ hoc@guildhallchambers.co.uk
Call Date: Nov 1988, Inner Temple
Pupil Supervisor, Recorder
Qualifications: [LLB (So'ton)]
✉ nicolas.gerasimidis@guildhallchambers.co.uk

GERMAIN MR RICHARD

Nine Bedford Row
9 Bedford Row, London WC1R 4AZ,
☎ 020 7489 2727
✉ clerks@9bedfordrow.co.uk
Call Date: July 1968, Inner Temple
Pupil Supervisor
✉ richard.germain@9bedfordrow.co.uk

GERMAN MISS KELLY ANNE

Eastbourne Chambers
5 Chiswick Place, Eastbourne, East Sussex BN21 4NH, ☎ 01323 642102
✉ clerks@eastbournechambers.co.uk
Call Date: July 2000, Lincoln's Inn
Qualifications: [LLB(Hons) (So'ton)]

GERRY MS ALISON PATRICIA

Doughty Street Chambers
53-54 Doughty Street, London WC1N 2LS,
☎ 020 7404 1313
✉ enquiries@doughtystreet.co.uk
Doughty Street Chambers
Pall Mall Court, 61-67 King Street, Manchester M2 4PD, ☎ 0161 618 1066
Doughty Street Chambers
5th Floor, Broad Quay House, Prince Street, Bristol BS1 4DJ, ☎ 01179 058 717
Call Date: Oct 2003, Inner Temple
Qualifications: [LLB LLM (Essex)]
✉ a.gerry@doughtystreet.co.uk

GERRY MISS FELICITY RUTH

36 Bedford Row
London WC1R 4JH, ☎ 020 7421 8000
✉ chambers@36bedfordrow.co.uk
Call Date: Oct 1994, Middle Temple
Pupil Supervisor
Qualifications: [LLB (Hons)]
✉ fgerry@36bedfordrow.co.uk

GERSCH MR ADAM NISSEN

Argent Chambers
5 Bell Yard, London WC2A 2JR,
☎ 020 7556 5500
✉ briefsin@argentchambers.co.uk
Call Date: Oct 1993, Lincoln's Inn
Pupil Supervisor
Qualifications: [LLB (Hons)]
✉ a.gersch@argentchambers.co.uk

GESER MS ANITA

Pallant Chambers
12 North Pallant, Chichester, West Sussex PO19 1TQ, ☎ 01243 784538
✉ clerks@pallantchambers.co.uk
Call Date: Feb 1992, Middle Temple
Qualifications: [BA (Econ) (Lond)]

GHAFFAR MR ARSHAD

XXIV Old Buildings
Ground Floor, 24 Old Buildings, Lincoln's Inn, London WC2A 3UP, ☎ 020 7691 2424
✉ clerks@xxiv.co.uk
Call Date: Oct 1991, Middle Temple
Pupil Supervisor
Qualifications: [LLB (Hons) (Exon) LLM (Cantab)]
✉ arshad.ghaffar@xxiv.co.uk

GHALY MR KARIM RAOUF GEORGE

39 Essex Street
London WC2R 3AT, ☎ 020 7832 1111
✉ clerks@39essex.com
82 King Street
Manchester M2 4WQ, ☎ 0161 870 9969
Call Date: July 2001, Inner Temple
Qualifications: [BA (Oxon)]
✉ karim.ghaly@39essex.com

GHATTAORA MR KULDIP SINGH

Derwent Chambers
78 Friar Gate, Derby DE1 1FL,
☎ 01332 242425
✉ admin@derwentchambers.co.uk
Call Date: July 2005, Middle Temple
Qualifications: [LLB (Hons) BSc (Hons)]

GHOSH MR INDRANIL JULIAN QC (2006)

Pump Court Tax Chambers
16 Bedford Row, London WC1R 4EF,
☎ 020 7414 8080 ✉ clerks@pumptax.com
Call Date: July 1993, Lincoln's Inn
Qualifications: [LLB (Edin) LLM (Lond)]
✉ jghosh@pumptax.com

Types of work: Capital tax, Corporation tax, European Union, Income tax, National Insurance, Stamp duty, VAT

GIACHARDI MISS LAURA ANNE

1 Gray's Inn Square
Ground Floor, 1 Gray's Inn Square, London WC1R 5AA, ☎ 020 7405 0001
Call Date: Oct 2009, Lincoln's Inn
Qualifications: [LLB MA (Lond)]
lgiachardi@1gis.co.uk

GIANI MR HARPREET SINGH

Chambers of Andrew Mitchell QC
33 Chancery Lane, London WC2A 1EN, ☎ 020 7440 9950 clerks@33cllaw.com
Call Date: Oct 2006, Gray's Inn
Qualifications: [BA LLB]

GIANOTA MISS CATERINA

Chambers of Miss C Gianota
10 Lake Road, Hoylake, Wirral CH47 2BX, ☎ 0151 632 5805 gianota@gmail.co.uk
Call Date: Oct 2002, Lincoln's Inn
Qualifications: [BSc (Hons) PgDL]

GIBAUD MISS CATHERINE ALISON ANNETTA

3 Verulam Buildings
London WC1R 5NT, ☎ 020 7831 8441
chambers@3vb.com
Call Date: Oct 1996, Gray's Inn
Pupil Supervisor
Qualifications: [BSc (Hons) CPE (City)]
cgibaud@3vb.com

GIBB MISS FIONA MARGARET

Coram Chambers
9-11 Fulwood Place, London WC1V 6HG, ☎ 020 7092 3700
mail@coramchambers.co.uk
Call Date: July 1983, Middle Temple
Qualifications: [LLB (B'ham)]
fiona.gibb@coramchambers.co.uk

GIBB MS KATHERINE ANNE

Guildhall Chambers
23 Broad Street, Bristol BS1 2HG, ☎ 0117 930 9000
hoc@guildhallchambers.co.uk
Call Date: Oct 1999, Gray's Inn
Qualifications: [BA (Oxon)]
katie.gibb@guildhallchambers.co.uk

GIBBON MISS JULIET REBECCA

30 Park Place
Cardiff CF10 3BS, ☎ 029 2039 8421
clerks@30parkplace.law.co.uk
Call Date: Oct 1994, Lincoln's Inn
Qualifications: [LLB (Hons)(Wales)]
juliet.gibbon@30parkplace.co.uk

GIBBON MR MICHAEL NEIL QC (2011)

Maitland Chambers
7 Stone Buildings, Lincoln's Inn, London WC2A 3SZ, ☎ 020 7406 1200
clerks@maitlandchambers.com
Call Date: Nov 1993, Gray's Inn
Pupil Supervisor
Qualifications: [BA M Phil]
clerks@maitlandchambers.com, mgibbon@maitlandchambers.com

GIBBON MISS ZOE LOUISE CHRISTINE

Fenners Chambers
3 Madingley Road, Cambridge CB3 0EE, ☎ 01223 368761
clerks@fennerschambers.com
Call Date: Nov 2009, Inner Temple
Qualifications: [BSc (So'ton) CPE (College of Law)]
zoe.gibbon@fennerchambers.com

GIBBONS MR CHRISTOPHER CHARLES

Rowchester Chambers
4 Rowchester Court, Whittall Street, Birmingham B4 6DH, ☎ 0121 233 2327
clerks@rowchesterchambers.co.uk
Call Date: July 1977, Gray's Inn
Pupil Supervisor
Qualifications: [BSc (B'ham)]

GIBBONS MS ELLODIE

Tanfield Chambers
2-5 Warwick Court, London WC1R 5DJ, ☎ 020 7421 5300
clerks@tanfieldchambers.co.uk
Call Date: Oct 1999, Inner Temple
Qualifications: [MA (Cantab)]
egibbons@tanfieldchambers.co.uk

GIBBONS MR JAMES FRANCIS

3 Stone Buildings
Ground Floor, 3 Stone Buildings, Lincoln's Inn, London WC2A 3XL, ☎ 020 7242 4937
clerks@3sb.law.co.uk
Call Date: July 1974, Gray's Inn
Pupil Supervisor
jgibbons@3sb.law.co.uk

GIBBONS MISS MARY REGINA

Stone Chambers
4 Field Court, Gray's Inn, London WC1R 5EF, ☎020 7440 6900
✉clerks@stonechambers.com
Call Date: Mar 1999, Lincoln's Inn
Qualifications: [Dip Law]
✉mary.gibbons@stonechambers.com

GIBBONS MR ORLANDO ADZIMA

10 King's Bench Walk
Ground Floor, 10 King's Bench Walk, Temple, London EC4Y 7EB, ☎020 7353 7742
✉Chambers@10kingsbenchwalk.co.uk
Pallant Chambers
12 North Pallant, Chichester, West Sussex PO19 1TQ, ☎01243 784538
✉clerks@pallantchambers.co.uk
Call Date: Nov 1982, Gray's Inn
Pupil Supervisor
Qualifications: [LLB (Lond)]
✉orlando.gibbons@10kingsbenchwalk.co.uk

GIBBONS MISS PERRIN

The Chambers of Grahame Aldous QC
9 Gough Square, London EC4A 3DG, ☎020 7832 0500
✉clerks@9goughsquare.co.uk
Call Date: Oct 1998, Middle Temple
Qualifications: [BA (Hons)(Cantab)]

GIBBONS MRS SARAH ISOBEL

Harcourt Chambers
1st Floor, 2 Harcourt Buildings, Temple, London EC4Y 9DB, ☎0844 561 7135
Call Date: Nov 1987, Middle Temple
Qualifications: [BA (Hons) (B'ham) Dip Law (City)]
✉sgibbons@harcourtchambers.law.co.uk

GIBBONS MISS SHARON LOUISE

Phoenix Chambers
106 Normanton Lane, Littleover, Derby DE23 6GR, ☎07939 545788
✉sharongibbons@email.com
Call Date: Nov 1999, Lincoln's Inn
Qualifications: [LLB (Hons)(Derby)]

GIBBS MRS JOCELYN IDA

1 Mitre Court Buildings
1 Mitre Court Buildings, Temple, London EC4Y 7BS, ☎020 7452 8900
✉clerks@1mcb.com
Call Date: Nov 1972, Lincoln's Inn
Pupil Supervisor
Qualifications: [LLB (Hons) (Lond)]
✉jocelyn.gibbs@1mcb.com

GIBBS MR PATRICK MICHAEL EVAN QC (2006)

3 Raymond Buildings
3 Raymond Buildings, Gray's Inn, London WC1R 5BH, ☎020 7400 6400
✉clerks@3rblaw.com
Call Date: Nov 1986, Middle Temple
Qualifications: [BA(Oxon) Dip Law (Lond)]

GIBBS MR PHILIP MARK

KCH Garden Square
1 Oxford Street, Nottingham NG1 5BH, ☎0115 941 8851
✉clerks@kchgardensquare.co.uk
Call Date: Oct 1991, Inner Temple
Pupil Supervisor
Qualifications: [BA (UEA) Dip Law]

GIBNEY MR MALCOLM THOMAS PATRICK

12 College Place
Fauvelle Buildings, 12 College Place, Southampton SO15 2FE, ☎023 8032 0320
✉clerks@12cp.co.uk
Call Date: July 1981, Inner Temple
Pupil Supervisor, Recorder
Qualifications: [LLB (Cardiff)]
✉mgibney@12cp.co.uk

E

GIBSON MR ARTHUR GEORGE ADRIAN

Number 7 Harrington Street Chambers
7 Harrington Street, Liverpool L2 9YH, ☎0151 242 0707 ✉clerks@7hs.co.uk
Call Date: July 1980, Lincoln's Inn
Qualifications: [LLB Hons (Lond)]
✉arthur.gibson@7hs.co.uk

GIBSON MR CHARLES ANTHONY WARNEFORD QC (2001)

Henderson Chambers
2 Harcourt Buildings, Temple, London EC4Y 9DB, ☎020 7583 9020
✉clerks@hendersonchambers.co.uk
Call Date: July 1984, Inner Temple
Recorder
Qualifications: [BA (Dunelm) Dip Law]

GIBSON MR CHRISTOPHER ALLEN WOOD QC (1995)

Outer Temple Chambers
The Outer Temple, 222 Strand, London WC2R 1BA, ☎020 7353 6381
✉clerks@outertemple.com
Doughty Street Chambers
Pall Mall Court, 61-67 King Street, Manchester M2 4PD, ☎0161 618 1066

Doughty Street Chambers
53-54 Doughty Street, London WC1N 2LS,
☎020 7404 1313
✉enquiries@doughtystreet.co.uk
Call Date: July 1976, Middle Temple
Recorder
Qualifications: [BA (Oxon)]
christopher.gibsonqc@outertemple.com

GIBSON MISS CLAIRE MICHELLE

Dere Street Barristers
33 Broad Chare, Newcastle Upon Tyne
NE1 3DQ, ☎0844 3351551
✉clerks@derestreet.co.uk
Call Date: Oct 2004, Lincoln's Inn
Qualifications: [LLB (Hons)]
c.Gibson@broadcharechambers.co.uk

GIBSON MR JOHN ARTHUR

Call Date: Nov 1993, Lincoln's Inn
Pupil Supervisor, Recorder
Qualifications: [LLB (Hons) (B'ham)]
johngibson@indiabuildings.co.uk

GIBSON MR JOHN WILLIAM

36 Bedford Row
London WC1R 4JH, ☎020 7421 8000
✉chambers@36bedfordrow.co.uk
Call Date: Nov 1991, Inner Temple
Qualifications: [BA (Dunelm)]
jwgibson@btinternet.com

GIBSON MR NICHOLAS TOBY JEFFREY

Matrix Chambers
Griffin Building, Gray's Inn, London
WC1R 5LN, ☎020 7404 3447
✉matrix@matrixlaw.co.uk / Iscott@
matrixlaw.co.uk
Call Date: Oct 2009, Lincoln's Inn
Qualifications: [LLM (Lond) PgDL MA
(Cantab)]
nicholasgibson@matrixlaw.co.uk

GIBSON-LEE MR DAVID MICHAEL

Bell Yard Chambers
116/118 Chancery Lane, London WC2A 1PP,
☎020 7306 9292
✉byclerks@bellyardchambers.co.uk
Call Date: July 1970, Lincoln's Inn
Pupil Supervisor
Qualifications: [LLB]
dgibsonlee@bellyardchambers.co.uk

GIDDENS MISS SARAH ELIZABETH ANNE

Atkinson Bevan Chambers
1st Floor, 2 Harcourt Buildings, Temple,
London EC4Y 9DB, ☎020 7353 2112
✉clerks@2hb.co.uk
Call Date: Oct 1999, Lincoln's Inn
Qualifications: [BA (Hons)(Soton) Dip in Law]

GIDNEY MR JONATHAN ALFRED

St Philips Chambers
55 Temple Row, Birmingham B2 5LS,
☎0121 246 7000 ✉clerks@st-philips.com
Call Date: Oct 1991, Inner Temple
Pupil Supervisor
Qualifications: [BA (Hons)]
jgidney@st-philips.com

GIFFIN MR NIGEL DYSON QC (2003)

11 King's Bench Walk
11 King's Bench Walk, Temple, London
EC4Y 7EQ, ☎020 7632 8500
✉clerksroom@11kbw.com
Call Date: Nov 1986, Inner Temple
Qualifications: [MA (Oxon)]

Types of work: Administrative law, Civil liberties, Commercial litigation, Discrimination, Education, Employment, Environment, Human rights, Local authorities, Procurement

GIFFORD LORD ANTHONY MAURICE QC (1982)

1 Mitre Court Buildings
1 Mitre Court Buildings, Temple, London
EC4Y 7BS, ☎020 7452 8900
✉clerks@1mcb.com
Call Date: July 1962, Middle Temple
Qualifications: [MA (Cantab)]
anthony.gifford@1mcb.com

GILBART MR THOMAS CHRISTIE

9 St John Street
Manchester M3 4DN, ☎0161 955 9000
✉civilclerks@9sjs.com /
criminalclerks@9sjs.com
Call Date: Nov 2003, Middle Temple
Qualifications: [LLB (Hons) (Lond)]

GILBERT MR ANDREW WILLIAM

1 Pump Court
Elm Court, Temple, London EC4Y 7AB,
☎020 7842 7070
✉(name)@pumpcourt.co.uk
Call Date: July 2009, Middle Temple
Qualifications: [BA (Hons) (Oxon) Post Grad
Dip Law (Lond)]
agi@1pumpcourt.co.uk

E

GILBERT MR BARRY DAVID

2 Bedford Row
London WC1R 4BU, ☎ 020 7440 8888
✉ clerks@2bedfordrow.co.uk
Call Date: July 1978, Gray's Inn
Pupil Supervisor
Qualifications: [LLB (So'ton) Dip Ara (Lond)]
✉ bgilbert@2bedfordrow.co.uk

GILBERT MISS DANIELLA LOUISE

Pump Court Chambers
Upper Ground Floor, 3 Pump Court, Temple, London EC4Y 7AJ, ☎ 020 7353 0711
✉ clerks@3pumpcourt.com
Pump Court Chambers
31 Southgate Street, Winchester, Hampshire SO23 9EB, ☎ 01962 868 161
✉ clerks@3pumpcourt.com
Riverview Chambers
Hamilton House, 1 Temple Avenue, London EC4Y 0HA, ☎ 0844 225 3999
✉ chrisbaylis@riverviewchambers.com
Call Date: Oct 2007, Inner Temple
Qualifications: [BSc (Manch)]

GILBERT MR FRANCIS PETER

Chambers of Mr Ami Feder
Ground Floor, Lamb Building, Temple, London EC4Y 7AS, ☎ 020 7797 7788
✉ clerks@lambbuilding.co.uk
Chambers of Mr Ami Feder
Ground Floor, Lamb Building, Temple, London EC4Y 7AS, ☎ 020 7797 7788
✉ clerks@lambbuilding.co.uk
Call Date: July 1980, Lincoln's Inn
Pupil Supervisor
Qualifications: [BD MA AKC]

GILBERT MR ROBERT JOHN

Fountain Chambers
Cleveland Business Centre, 1 Watson Street, Middlesbrough TS1 2RQ, ☎ 01642 804040
✉ clerks@fountainchambers.co.uk
Call Date: Apr 1986, Middle Temple
Qualifications: [LLB (L'pool) PGCE]

GILBERTHORPE MR JAMES CHRISTOPHER

Hailsham Chambers
Ground Floor, 4 Paper Buildings, Temple, London EC4Y 7EX, ☎ 020 7643 5000
✉ clerks@hailshamchambers.com
Call Date: Nov 2002, Middle Temple
Qualifications: [BA (Hons) (Cantab) MA (Cantab)]
✉ james.gilberthorpe@hailshamchambers.com

GILBERTSON MRS HELEN ALISON

Octagon House
19 Colegate, Norwich NR3 1AT,
☎ 01603 623186
✉ clerks@octagonhouse.co.uk
Call Date: Nov 1993, Middle Temple
Qualifications: [LLB (Hons)(UEA)]

GILCHRIST MR DAVID SOMERLED

9 St John Street
Manchester M3 4DN, ☎ 0161 955 9000
✉ civilclerks@9sjs.com / criminalclerks@9sjs.com
Call Date: Nov 1987, Inner Temple
Pupil Supervisor
Qualifications: [BA (Dunelm)]

GILCHRIST MISS NAOMI ROBERTA

St Philips Chambers
55 Temple Row, Birmingham B2 5LS,
☎ 0121 246 7000 ✉ clerks@st-philips.com
Call Date: July 1996, Inner Temple
Qualifications: [LLB (Reading)]
✉ ngilchrist@st-philips.com

GILEAD MISS BERYL LOUISE

St Mary's Family Law Chambers
26-28 High Pavement, The Lace Market, Nottingham NG1 1HN, ☎ 0115 950 3503
✉ clerks@stmarysflc.co.uk
Call Date: Feb 1989, Inner Temple
Pupil Supervisor
Qualifications: [BA (Keele)]
✉ beryl.gilead@stmarysflc.co.uk

GILES MR DAVID WILLIAM

1 Gray's Inn Square
Ground Floor, 1 Gray's Inn Square, London WC1R 5AA, ☎ 020 7405 0001
Call Date: Nov 1988, Lincoln's Inn
Pupil Supervisor
Qualifications: [LLB (Hons)]

GILES MISS MOLLY

Cornwall Street Chambers
85-87 Cornwall Street, Birmingham B3 3BY,
☎ 0121 233 7500
✉ clerks@cornwallstreet.co.uk
Call Date: July 2005, Gray's Inn
Qualifications: [LLB]
✉ molly.giles@cornwallstreet.co.uk

GILES MR ROGER STEPHEN

No5 Chambers
Fountain Court, Steelhouse Lane, Birmingham B4 6DR, ☎0845 210 5555 ✉info@no5.com
No5 Chambers
Greenwood House, 4-7 Salisbury Court, London EC4Y 8AA, ☎0845 210 5555
No5 Chambers
38 Queen Square, Bristol BS1 4QS, ☎0845 210 5555
Call Date: July 1976, Gray's Inn
Qualifications: [BA]
rgiles@no5.com

GILL MR ANTHONY THOMAS

Kings Chambers
36 Young Street, Manchester M3 3FT, ☎0845 034 3444
✉clerks@kingschambers.com
Kings Chambers
5 Park Square East, Leeds LS1 2NE, ☎0845 034 3444
✉clerks@kingschambers.com
Kings Chambers
Embassy House, 60 Church Street, Birmingham B3 2DJ, ☎0845 034 3444
✉clerks@kingschambers.com
Call Date: Nov 2008, Lincoln's Inn
Qualifications: [BA (Oxon) CPE COL]
agill@kingschambers.com

E

GILL MISS BALJINDER

10 King's Bench Walk
Ground Floor, 10 King's Bench Walk, Temple, London EC4Y 7EB, ☎020 7353 7742
✉Chambers@10kingsbenchwalk.co.uk
Call Date: Oct 1996, Inner Temple
Qualifications: [BA (Wolves)]

GILL MR GURNAM SINGH

Rowchester Chambers
4 Rowchester Court, Whittall Street, Birmingham B4 6DH, ☎0121 233 2327
✉clerks@rowchesterchambers.co.uk
Call Date: Nov 1978, Middle Temple
Qualifications: [BSc (Lond)]

GILL MR JULIAN CLIVE

Chambers of Mr J C Gill
Baytree House, 2 Lampeter Close, Oakwood, Derby DE21 2RB, ☎01332 666 135
✉julian.gill1@googlemail.com
Call Date: July 1987, Gray's Inn
Qualifications: [LLB]

GILL MR MANJIT SINGH QC (2000)

No5 Chambers
Greenwood House, 4-7 Salisbury Court, London EC4Y 8AA, ☎0845 210 5555
No5 Chambers
38 Queen Square, Bristol BS1 4QS, ☎0845 210 5555
No5 Chambers
Fountain Court, Steelhouse Lane, Birmingham B4 6DR, ☎0845 210 5555 ✉info@no5.com
Call Date: July 1982, Gray's Inn
Qualifications: [LLB (Lond)]
mgq@no5.com, manjit.gill@virgin.net

GILL MISS MEENA

Coram Chambers
9-11 Fulwood Place, London WC1V 6HG, ☎020 7092 3700
✉mail@coramchambers.co.uk
Call Date: July 1982, Middle Temple
meena.gill@coramchambers.co.uk

GILL MR NED IRVINE OWEN

Iscoed Chambers
86 St Helen's Road, Swansea SA1 4BQ, ☎01792 652988
✉clerks@iscoedchambers.co.uk
Call Date: July 2004, Middle Temple
Qualifications: [LLB Hons]
ng@iscoedchambers.co.uk

GILL MISS PAMILLA

Goldsmith Chambers
Ground Floor, Goldsmith Building, Temple, London EC4Y 7BL, ☎020 7353 6802
✉clerks@goldsmithchambers.com
Call Date: Apr 1989, Lincoln's Inn
Qualifications: [LLB(Hons)]
P.Gill@goldsmithchambers.law.co.uk

GILL MR RAJINDER SINGH

Charter Chambers
33 John Street, London WC1N 2AT, ☎020 7618 4400
✉clerks@charterchambers.com
Call Date: Nov 2001, Inner Temple
Qualifications: [LLB (Lond)]

GILL MR SATINDERJIT SINGH

Five Paper
Ground Floor, 5 Paper Buildings, Temple, London EC4Y 7HB, ☎020 7815 3200
Call Date: Feb 1991, Middle Temple
Qualifications: [LLB (Manch)]
SatinderGill@fivepaper.com

GILLAN MRS DOMINIQUE LYE-PING

Guildford Chambers
Stoke House, Leapale Lane, Guildford, Surrey GU1 4LY, ☎01483 539131
✉clerks@guildfordchambers.co.uk
Call Date: Oct 1998, Gray's Inn
Qualifications: [LLB (Belfast)]

GILLARD MISS ISABELLE

Carmelite Chambers
9 Carmelite Street, London EC4Y 0DR, ☎020 7936 6300
✉clerks@carmelitechambers.co.uk
Call Date: July 1980, Middle Temple
Pupil Supervisor
Qualifications: [LLB (B'Ham)]
✉igillard@carmelitechambers.co.uk

GILLESPIE MR CHRISTOPHER MICHAEL

2 Hare Court
Lower Ground, Ground, 1st & 2nd Floor, 2 Hare Court, Temple, London EC4Y 7BH, ☎020 7353 3982 ✉clerks@2harecourt.com
Call Date: Nov 1991, Gray's Inn
Qualifications: [BA (Cantab)]

GILLESPIE MISS JANE FRANCES

St Mary's Family Law Chambers
26-28 High Pavement, The Lace Market, Nottingham NG1 1HN, ☎0115 950 3503
✉clerks@stmarysflc.co.uk
Call Date: Oct 2001, Middle Temple
Pupil Supervisor
Qualifications: [LLB (Hons)]
✉jane.gillespie@stmarysflc.co.uk

GILLET MS GEMMA LOUISE

Dyers Chambers
35 Bedford Row, London WC1R 4JH, ☎020 7404 1881
✉admin@dyerschambers.com
Call Date: July 2003, Inner Temple
Qualifications: [BA (Sheff) CPE (College of Law) PgDL]
✉gemma.gillet@dyerschambers.com

GILLETT MISS AMANDA JOSEPHINE

College Chambers
19 Carlton Crescent, Southampton, Hampshire SO15 2ET, ☎023 8023 0338
✉clerks@college-chambers.co.uk
Call Date: Oct 1998, Gray's Inn
Qualifications: [LLB (S'ton)]
✉agillett@College-Chambers.co.uk

GILLETT MISS EMILY ADELE

New Square Chambers
12 New Square, Lincoln's Inn, London WC2A 3SW, ☎020 7419 8000
✉robin.hollington@newsquarechambers.co.uk
Call Date: Oct 2005, Lincoln's Inn
Qualifications: [LLB (Hons) (Lond)]
✉emily.gillett@newsquarechambers.co.uk

GILLETT MS TONIA JANE

15 New Bridge Street
London EC4V 6AU, ☎020 7842 1900
✉clerks@15nbs.com
Call Date: Oct 1997, Inner Temple
Qualifications: [LLB]

GILLETTE MR JOHN CHARLES

Old Court Chambers
Newham House, 96-98 Borough Road, Middlesbrough TS1 2HJ, ☎01642 232523
✉clerks@oldcourtchambers.com
Call Date: Oct 1990, Middle Temple
Pupil Supervisor
Qualifications: [LLB (Manc)]
✉clerks@oldcourtchambers.com

GILLIATT MS JACQUELINE

4 Brick Court
4 Brick Court, Temple, London EC4Y 9AD, ☎020 7832 3200 ✉clerks@4bc.co.uk
Call Date: Feb 1992, Middle Temple
Pupil Supervisor
Qualifications: [BA (Hon) (Oxon) Dip Law]
✉jacqui.gilliatt@4bc.co.uk

GILLIES MISS JENNIE

4 Pump Court
4 Pump Court, Temple, London EC4Y 7AN, ☎020 7842 5555
✉chambers@4pumpcourt.com
Call Date: July 2000, Middle Temple
Qualifications: [MA(Hons) (Canatab)]
✉jgillies@4pumpcourt.com

GILLING MISS DENISE ANN

Renaissance Chambers
5th Floor, Gray's Inn Chambers, Gray's Inn, London WC1R 5JA, ☎020 7404 1111
✉clerks@renaissancechambers.co.uk
Call Date: Oct 1992, Lincoln's Inn
Qualifications: [LLB(Hons)]
✉dg@renaissancechambers.co.uk

E

GILLIS MR RICHARD LESLIE IRVINE QC (2006)

One Essex Court
Ground Floor, One Essex Court, Temple, London EC4Y 9AR, ☎ 020 7583 2000
✉ clerks@oeclaw.co.uk
Call Date: Nov 1982, Lincoln's Inn
Qualifications: [BA BCL (Oxon)]
✉ rgillis@oeclaw.co.uk

GILLMAN MISS RACHEL MARY

1 Garden Court Family Law Chambers
Ground Floor, One Garden Court, Temple, London EC4Y 9BJ, ☎ 020 7797 7900
✉ clerks@1gc.com
Call Date: July 1988, Gray's Inn
Pupil Supervisor
Qualifications: [LLB (Lond)]

GILLOTT MR PAUL ALAN ASHLEY

15 Winckley Square
Preston PR1 3JJ, ☎ 01772 252828
✉ clerks@15winckleysq.co.uk
Call Date: Oct 1996, Middle Temple
Qualifications: [BA (Hons)(Oxon) CPE (Lond)]
✉ paulgillott@15ws.co.uk

E

GILLYON MR PHILIP JEFFREY

Erskine Chambers
33 Chancery Lane, London WC2A 1EN, ☎ 020 7242 5532
✉ clerks@erskinechambers.com
Call Date: July 1988, Middle Temple
Pupil Supervisor
Qualifications: [MA (Hons) (Cantab)]
✉ pgillyon@erskine-chambers.co.uk

GILMAN MR JONATHAN CHARLES BAGOT QC (1990)

Essex Court Chambers
24 Lincoln's Inn Fields, London WC2A 3EG, ☎ 020 7813 8000
✉ clerksroom@essexcourt.net
Call Date: Feb 1965, Middle Temple
Qualifications: [MA (Oxon)]

GILMORE MS ALEXANDRA HANNAH HELEN

Goldsmith Chambers
Ground Floor, Goldsmith Building, Temple, London EC4Y 7BL, ☎ 020 7353 6802
✉ clerks@goldsmithchambers.com
Call Date: July 2005, Lincoln's Inn
Qualifications: [BSc (Hons) PgDl]
✉ A.Gilmore@goldsmithchambers.law.co.uk

GILMORE MISS MARY SEANIN

Four New Square
Four New Square, Lincoln's Inn, London WC2A 3RJ, ☎ 020 7822 2000
✉ barristers@4newsquare.com
Call Date: Nov 1996, Gray's Inn
Qualifications: [MA (Cantab)]
✉ s.gilmore@4newsquare.com

GILROY MR PAUL QC (2006)

9 St John Street
Manchester M3 4DN, ☎ 0161 955 9000
✉ civilclerks@9sjs.com / criminalclerks@9sjs.com
Old Square Chambers
10-11 Bedford Row, London WC1R 4BU, ☎ 020 7269 0300 ✉ clerks@oldsquare.co.uk
Call Date: Nov 1985, Gray's Inn
Qualifications: [LLB (Scotland)]

GIMLETTE MR JOHN ELIOT

1 Crown Office Row
1 Crown Office Row, Temple, London EC4Y 7HH, ☎ 020 7797 7500
✉ mail@1cor.com
Call Date: July 1986, Inner Temple
Pupil Supervisor
Qualifications: [BA (Cantab)]
✉ john.gimlette@1cor.com

GINN MISS ALISON IRENE

4 Breams Buildings
Chancery Lane, London EC4A 1HP, ☎ 020 7092 1900 ✉ clerks@4bb.co.uk
Call Date: July 1980, Gray's Inn
Pupil Supervisor
Qualifications: [BA LLM (Lond)]

GINNIFF MR NIGEL THOMAS

Atlantic Chambers
4-6 Cook Street, Liverpool L2 9QU, ☎ 0151 236 4421
✉ info@atlanticchambers.co.uk
Call Date: July 1978, Inner Temple
Qualifications: [LLB]
✉ nigelginniff@atlanticchambers.co.uk

GINSBURG MRS AMANDA

37 Park Square Chambers
37 Park Square, Leeds LS1 2NY, ☎ 0113 243 9422 ✉ chambers@no37.co.uk
Call Date: July 1986, Lincoln's Inn
Qualifications: [LLB (Hons)(Lond)]
✉ chambers@no37.co.uk

GIOSERANO MR RICHARD STEPHEN

No.6 Park Square
Leeds LS1 2LW, ☎0113 245 9763
✉Tim@no6.co.uk
Call Date: Nov 1992, Gray's Inn
Pupil Supervisor
Qualifications: [LLB (Newc)]
✉gioserano@no6.co.uk

GIOVANNETTI MISS LISA CATERINA QC (2011)

39 Essex Street
London WC2R 3AT, ☎020 7832 1111
✉clerks@39essex.com
82 King Street
Manchester M2 4WQ, ☎0161 870 9969
Call Date: Nov 1990, Gray's Inn
Qualifications: [LLB]
✉lg@39essex.com

GIOVANNINI MRS ANGELA MICHELLE

Trinity Chambers
The Custom House, 39 Quayside, Newcastle Upon Tyne NE1 3DE, ☎0191 232 1927
✉info@trinitychambers.co.uk
Trinity Chambers
Multi Media Exchange, 72-80 Corporation Road, Middlesbrough TS1 2RF,
☎01642 247569
✉info@trinitychambers.co.uk
Call Date: Nov 2000, Gray's Inn
Qualifications: [LLB (Newc)]

GIROLAMI MR PAUL JULIAN QC (2002)

Maitland Chambers
7 Stone Buildings, Lincoln's Inn, London WC2A 3SZ, ☎020 7406 1200
✉clerks@maitlandchambers.com
Call Date: Nov 1983, Middle Temple
Qualifications: [BA (Cantab)]
✉pgirolami@maitlandchambers.com

GITTINS MR TIMOTHY JAMES

Trinity Chambers
The Custom House, 39 Quayside, Newcastle Upon Tyne NE1 3DE, ☎0191 232 1927
✉info@trinitychambers.co.uk
Trinity Chambers
Multi Media Exchange, 72-80 Corporation Road, Middlesbrough TS1 2RF,
☎01642 247569
✉info@trinitychambers.co.uk
Call Date: Oct 1990, Middle Temple
Pupil Supervisor, Recorder
Qualifications: [LLB (Manch)]

GIZ MISS ALEV AYSE

1 Garden Court Family Law Chambers
Ground Floor, One Garden Court, Temple, London EC4Y 9BJ, ☎020 7797 7900
✉clerks@1gc.com
Call Date: Nov 1988, Gray's Inn
Qualifications: [LLB (Hons) (Lond)]
✉giz@1gc.com

GLADWELL MR SIMON MARK

East Anglian Chambers
Gresham House, 5 Museum Street, Ipswich, Suffolk IP1 1HQ, ☎01473 214481
✉ipswich@ealaw.co.uk
Call Date: Oct 1996, Inner Temple
Qualifications: [BA (Lond)]

GLAISTER-YOUNG MISS SHELLY JANE

Staple Inn Chambers
1st Floor, 9 Staple Inn, Holborn Bars, London WC1V 7QH, ☎020 7242 5240
✉clerks@stapleinn.co.uk
Call Date: July 2004, Inner Temple
Qualifications: [BA PgDL]
✉sgy@stapleinn.co.uk

GLANCY MR ROBERT PETER QC (1997)

Devereux Chambers
Queen Elizabeth Building, Temple, London EC4Y 9BS, ☎020 7353 7534
✉clerks@devchambers.co.uk
Call Date: July 1972, Middle Temple
Recorder
Qualifications: [MA (Cantab)]
✉glancy@devchambers.co.uk

GLANVILLE MISS SUSAN ELIZABETH

3 Dr Johnson's Buildings
Ground Floor, 3 Dr Johnson's Buildings, Temple, London EC4Y 7BA, ☎020 7353 4854
✉clerks@3djb.co.uk
Call Date: Oct 1991, Inner Temple
Qualifications: [BA (Lond) CPE]
✉sglanville@3djb.co.uk

GLASER MR MICHAEL SAMSON

14 Gray's Inn Square
14 Gray's Inn Square, Gray's Inn, London WC1R 5JP, ☎020 7242 0858
✉clerks@14gis.co.uk
Call Date: Nov 1998, Middle Temple
Pupil Supervisor
Qualifications: [LLB (Hons)(Middx)]
✉mg2@14gis.co.uk

E

GLASGOW MR EDWIN JOHN QC (1987)

39 Essex Street
London WC2R 3AT, ☎ 020 7832 1111
✉ clerks@39essex.com
82 King Street
Manchester M2 4WQ, ☎ 0161 870 9969
Call Date: Nov 1969, Gray's Inn
Qualifications: [LLB (Lond)]

GLASGOW MR OLIVER EDWIN JAMES

2 Hare Court
Lower Ground, Ground, 1st & 2nd Floor, 2 Hare Court, Temple, London EC4Y 7BH,
☎ 020 7353 3982 ✉ clerks@2harecourt.com
Call Date: Nov 1995, Middle Temple
Pupil Supervisor
Qualifications: [BA (Oxon) MA (Oxon)]
oliverglasgow@2harecourt.com

GLASS MR ANTHONY TREVOR QC (1986)

QEB Hollis Whiteman
1-2 Laurence Pountney Hill, London EC4R 0EU, ☎ 020 7933 8855
✉ barristers@qebhw.co.uk
Call Date: July 1965, Inner Temple
Recorder
Qualifications: [BA (Oxon)]
barristers@qebhw.co.uk

E

GLASS MISS MARY CATHERINE

Five Paper
Ground Floor, 5 Paper Buildings, Temple, London EC4Y 7HB, ☎ 020 7815 3200
Call Date: Oct 2001, Middle Temple
Qualifications: [LLB (Hons)]
maryglass@fivepaper.com

GLASS MRS MARY PATRICIA

12 Old Square Chambers
1st Floor, 12 Old Square, Lincoln's Inn, London WC2A 3TX, ☎ 020 7404 0875
✉ clerks@12oldsquare.com
Redemption Chambers
121 The Vale, Golders Green, London NW11 8TL, ☎ 020 8458 5486
✉ home@ollennu92.freeserve.co.uk
Call Date: Nov 2000, Gray's Inn
Qualifications: [BA LLB LLM MA]

GLASSBROOK MR ALEXANDER JAMES

Temple Garden Chambers
1 Harcourt Buildings, Temple, London EC4Y 9DA, ☎ 020 7583 1315
✉ clerks@tgchambers.com
Call Date: Oct 1995, Middle Temple
Qualifications: [BA (Bris) Dip Law (Lond) Dip European community (Lond)]
aglassbrook@tgchambers.com

GLASSON MR JONATHAN JOSEPH

Matrix Chambers
Griffin Building, Gray's Inn, London WC1R 5LN, ☎ 020 7404 3447
✉ matrix@matrixlaw.co.uk / Iscott@matrixlaw.co.uk
Call Date: Mar 1996, Middle Temple
Qualifications: [MA (Oxon)]

GLEDHILL MR ANDREAS NIKOLAUS

Blackstone Chambers
Blackstone House, Temple, London EC4Y 9BW, ☎ 020 7583 1770
✉ clerks@blackstonechambers.com
Call Date: Nov 1992, Middle Temple
Pupil Supervisor
Qualifications: [MA (Hons) (Cantab) CPE]
andreasgledhill@blackstonechambers.com

GLEDHILL MR LEE ANDRE

Trident Barristers Chambers
Peter House, Oxford Street, Manchester M1 5AN, ☎ 0161 663 3123
✉ clerks@tridentchambers.com
Alexander Chambers
13 Halstead Road, Wanstead, London E11 2AY, ☎ 0845 652 0451 / 0854 652 0451
✉ clerks@alexanderchambers.co.uk
Call Date: Mar 1998, Lincoln's Inn
Qualifications: [BA (Hons)(Leeds) Registered Nurse]

GLEDHILL MR ORLANDO JOHN

One Essex Court
Ground Floor, One Essex Court, Temple, London EC4Y 9AR, ☎ 020 7583 2000
✉ clerks@oeclaw.co.uk
Call Date: Oct 1998, Inner Temple
Pupil Supervisor
Qualifications: [BA (Hons) MPhil (Oxon) Dip Law]
ogledhill@oeclaw.co.uk

GLEDHILL MR SIMON CHRISTOPHER

Thomas More Chambers
7 Lincoln's Inn Fields, London WC2A 3BP,
☎ 020 7404 7000
✉ clerks@thomasmore.co.uk
Call Date: July 2005, Middle Temple
Qualifications: [LLB (Hons)]
✉ sgledhill@thomasmore.co.uk

GLEESON MR MICHAEL GERARD

Field Court Chambers
5 Field Court, Gray's Inn, London WC1R 5EF,
☎ 020 7405 6114 ✉ clerks@fieldcourt.co.uk
Call Date: July 2004, Middle Temple
Qualifications: [BA Hons (Cantab) PGDip Law MA (Cantab)]
✉ michael.gleeson@fieldcourt.co.uk

GLEN MR ALASTAIR DAVID ROBERT

One Brick Court
1st Floor, One Brick Court, Temple, London EC4Y 9BY, ☎ 020 7353 8845
✉ clerks@onebrickcourt.com
Call Date: Mar 2002, Middle Temple
Qualifications: [MA (Edin)]
✉ dg@onebrickcourt.com

GLEN MR IAN DOUGLAS QC (1996)

5 King's Bench Walk
5 King's Bench Walk, Temple, London EC4Y 7DN, ☎ 020 7353 5638
✉ clerks@5kbw.co.uk
Call Date: Nov 1973, Gray's Inn
Recorder
Qualifications: [LLB (Lond)]
✉ ian.glen@5kbw.co.uk

GLEN MR PHILIP ALEXANDER

12 College Place
Fauvelle Buildings, 12 College Place, Southampton SO15 2FE, ☎ 023 8032 0320
✉ clerks@12cp.co.uk
Call Date: July 1983, Middle Temple
Qualifications: [LLB(Lond)]
✉ PGlen@12cp.co.uk

Types of work: Housing, Landlord and tenant, Real property

GLENSER MR PETER HEATH

Nine Bedford Row
9 Bedford Row, London WC1R 4AZ,
☎ 020 7489 2727
✉ clerks@9bedfordrow.co.uk
Call Date: Oct 1993, Inner Temple
Pupil Supervisor
Qualifications: [LLB (So'ton)]
✉ peter.glenser@9bedfordrow.co.uk

GLICK MR IAN BERNARD QC (1987)

One Essex Court
Ground Floor, One Essex Court, Temple, London EC4Y 9AR, ☎ 020 7583 2000
✉ clerks@oeclaw.co.uk
Call Date: Nov 1970, Inner Temple
Recorder
Qualifications: [MA BCL (Oxon)]
✉ iglick@oeclaw.co.uk

GLOAG MR ANGUS ROBIN

1 Gray's Inn Square
Ground Floor, 1 Gray's Inn Square, London WC1R 5AA, ☎ 020 7405 0001
Rougemont Chambers
Victory House, Dean Clarke Gardens, Southernhay East, Exeter EX2 4AA,
☎ 01392 208484
✉ clerks@rougemontchambers.co.uk
Call Date: Oct 1992, Inner Temple
Pupil Supervisor
Qualifications: [LLB (Hons)]

GLOVER MISS ANNE-MARIE

Coram Chambers
9-11 Fulwood Place, London WC1V 6HG,
☎ 020 7092 3700
✉ mail@coramchambers.co.uk
Call Date: Oct 2000, Middle Temple
Qualifications: [BA (Hons) (Manch) CPE (Manch)]
✉ annemarie.glover@coramchambers.co.uk

GLOVER MR MARC PHILIP

Tanfield Chambers
2-5 Warwick Court, London WC1R 5DJ,
☎ 020 7421 5300
✉ clerks@tanfieldchambers.co.uk
Call Date: Oct 1999, Lincoln's Inn
Qualifications: [LLB (Hons) LLM (Lancs)]
✉ mglover@tanfieldchambers.co.uk

GLOVER MR RICHARD MICHAEL QC (2009)

Francis Taylor Building
Inner Temple, London EC4Y 7BY,
☎ 020 7353 8415 ✉ clerks@ftb.eu.com
Call Date: July 1984, Inner Temple
Qualifications: [BA (Cantab)]
✉ richard.glover@ftb.eu.com

E

GLOVER MR STEPHEN JULIAN

37 Park Square Chambers
37 Park Square, Leeds LS1 2NY,
☎0113 243 9422 ✉chambers@no37.co.uk
Call Date: July 1978, Middle Temple
Pupil Supervisor
Qualifications: [LLB]
sjg@no37.co.uk

GLYN MR CASPAR HILARY GORDON QC (2012)

Cloisters
1 Pump Court, Temple, London EC4Y 7AA,
☎020 7827 4000 ✉clerks@cloisters.com
Call Date: Nov 1992, Inner Temple
Pupil Supervisor
Qualifications: [LLB (Manch)]
cg@cloisters.com

GLYNN MISS JOANNA ELIZABETH QC (2002)

1 Crown Office Row
1 Crown Office Row, Temple, London
EC4Y 7HH, ☎020 7797 7500
✉mail@1cor.com
Call Date: Nov 1983, Middle Temple
Qualifications: [BA (Lond)]
joanna.glynn@1cor.com

GLYNN MR STEPHEN PETER

The Chambers of Grahame Aldous QC
9 Gough Square, London EC4A 3DG,
☎020 7832 0500
✉clerks@9goughsquare.co.uk
Call Date: Oct 1990, Middle Temple
Pupil Supervisor
Qualifications: [LLB (Bris)]
sglynn@9goughsquare.co.uk

GOATLEY MR PETER SEAMUS PATRICK

No5 Chambers
38 Queen Square, Bristol BS1 4QS,
☎0845 210 5555
No5 Chambers
Greenwood House, 4-7 Salisbury Court,
London EC4Y 8AA, ☎0845 210 5555
No5 Chambers
Fountain Court, Steelhouse Lane, Birmingham
B4 6DR, ☎0845 210 5555 ✉info@no5.com
Call Date: May 1992, Inner Temple
Qualifications: [MA (Oxon)]
pg@no5.com

GOBIR MR NUHU GARBA

9 Park Place
9 Park Place, Cardiff, South Glamorgan
CF10 3DP, ☎029 2038 2731
✉clerks@9parkplace.co.uk
Call Date: Oct 1998, Middle Temple
Qualifications: [LLB (Hons)(Wales) LLM (Warw)]
Nuhugobir@9parkplace.co.uk

GODDARD MR ANDREW STEPHEN QC (2003)

Atkin Chambers
1 Atkin Building, Gray's Inn, London
WC1R 5AT, ☎020 7404 0102
✉clerks@atkinchambers.com
Call Date: Nov 1985, Inner Temple
Qualifications: [BA Law]
agoddard@atkinchambers.com

GODDARD MR CHRISTOPHER JOHN FRANCIS

The Chambers of Grahame Aldous QC
9 Gough Square, London EC4A 3DG,
☎020 7832 0500
✉clerks@9goughsquare.co.uk
Call Date: July 1973, Middle Temple
Pupil Supervisor
Qualifications: [LLB]
cgoddard@9goughsquare.co.uk

GODDARD MISS KATHERINE LESLEY

Bank House Chambers
Old Bank House, Hartshead, Sheffield S1 2EL,
☎0114 275 1223
✉w.digby@bankhousechambers.co.uk
Call Date: Nov 1987, Inner Temple
Qualifications: [BA (Keele)]
k.goddard@bankhousechambers.co.uk

GODDARD MR PHILIP DAMIAN

Chambers of Mr P Goddard
Couching House, Oxford, Oxford OX49 5PX,
☎01608 811550 ✉pdgevil@tiscali.co.uk
Call Date: Nov 1985, Inner Temple
Qualifications: [BA (Kent)]

GODDARD MR RICHARD ANDREW KEITH

Cobden House Chambers
19 Quay Street, Manchester M3 3HN,
☎0161 833 6000 ✉Clerks@Cobden.co.uk
Call Date: Mar 1999, Gray's Inn
Qualifications: [BA]
clerks@cobden.co.uk

GODDARD MR RODERICK IAN

1 Gray's Inn Square
Ground Floor, 1 Gray's Inn Square, London WC1R 5AA, ☎ 020 7405 0001
Call Date: July 2007, Middle Temple
Qualifications: [LLB (Hons) LLM (Lond)]
rgoddard@1gis.co.uk

GODDARD MISS SUZANNE HAZEL QC (2008)

Lincoln House Chambers
Tower 12, The Avenue North, Spinningfields, 18-22 Bridge Street, Manchester M3 3BZ, ☎ 0161 832 5701
info@lincolnhousechambers.com
Call Date: Nov 1986, Gray's Inn
Recorder
Qualifications: [LLB (Hons) (Manch)]
suzanne.goddard@lincolnhousechambers.com

GODFREY MR CHRISTOPHER NICHOLAS

Colleton Chambers
Colleton Crescent, Exeter, Devon EX2 4DG, ☎ 01392 274898
clerks@colletonchambers.co.uk
Call Date: Feb 1993, Lincoln's Inn
Qualifications: [BA (Hons)]
christophergodfrey@colletonchambers.co.uk

GODFREY MISS EMMA CHARLOTTE

Field Court Chambers
5 Field Court, Gray's Inn, London WC1R 5EF, ☎ 020 7405 6114 clerks@fieldcourt.co.uk
Call Date: Nov 1995, Lincoln's Inn
Qualifications: [BA (Hons)]
emma.godfrey@fieldcourt.co.uk

GODFREY MS HANNAH KATE

Cloisters
1 Pump Court, Temple, London EC4Y 7AA, ☎ 020 7827 4000 clerks@cloisters.com
Call Date: Nov 2002, Lincoln's Inn
Pupil Supervisor
Qualifications: [BA (Hons) (Cantab)]
hg@cloisters.com

GODFREY MR HOWARD ANTHONY QC (1991)

2 Bedford Row
London WC1R 4BU, ☎ 020 7440 8888
clerks@2bedfordrow.co.uk
Call Date: Nov 1970, Middle Temple
Qualifications: [LLB (Lond)]
hgodfrey@2bedfordrow.co.uk

GODFREY MR JOHN PAUL

Wilberforce Chambers
7 Bishop Lane, Hull HU1 1PA, ☎ 01482 323264
Call Date: May 1985, Gray's Inn
Qualifications: [BSc(Econ) (Lond)]

GODFREY MR JONATHAN SAUL

Park Lane Plowden
19 Westgate, Leeds LS1 2RD, ☎ 0113 228 5049
clerks@parklaneplowden.co.uk
Call Date: Nov 1990, Inner Temple
Qualifications: [LLB (Essex)]
jonathan.godfrey@parklaneplowden.co.uk

GODFREY MR LAUREN JOHN

Crown Office Row Chambers
119 Church Street, Brighton, Sussex BN1 1UD, ☎ 01273 625625
clerks@1cor.com
Call Date: Oct 2007, Inner Temple
Qualifications: [BA (Australia) LLB (Lond)]
lauren.godfrey@1cor.com

GODFREY MR THOMAS WILLIAM NETHERTON

23 Essex Street
London WC2R 3AA, ☎ 020 7413 0353
clerks@23es.com
Call Date: July 2003, Inner Temple
Qualifications: [BA (Exon) CPE (Nott'm)]
TomGodfrey@23es.com

GODFREY MR TIMOTHY ANDREW ELLINGER

The Chambers of Grahame Aldous QC
9 Gough Square, London EC4A 3DG, ☎ 020 7832 0500
clerks@9goughsquare.co.uk
Call Date: Oct 1997, Middle Temple
Pupil Supervisor
Qualifications: [LLB (Hons)(Sheff)]
tgodfrey@9goughsquare.co.uk

GODWIN MR WILLIAM GEORGE HENRY

3 Hare Court
3 Hare Court, Temple, London EC4Y 7BJ, ☎ 020 7415 7800 clerks@3harecourt.com
St John's Chambers
101 Victoria Street, Bristol BS1 6PU, ☎ 0117 923 4700
clerks@stjohnschambers.co.uk
Call Date: Nov 1986, Middle Temple
Qualifications: [BA (Lond) B Phil (Oxon) D Phil (Oxon)]
williamgodwin@3harecourt.com

E

GOFF MR ANTHONY THOMAS

Exchange Chambers
One Derby Square, Derby Square, Liverpool L2 9XX, ☎ 0151 236 7747
✉ info@exchangechambers.co.uk
Exchange Chambers
7 Ralli Courts, West Riverside, Manchester M3 5FT, ☎ 0161 833 2722
Exchange Chambers
Oxford House, Oxford Row, Leeds LS1 3BE, ☎ 0113 203 1970
✉ spencer@exchangechambers.co.uk
Call Date: July 1978, Middle Temple
Qualifications: [BA (Oxon)]
goff@exchangechambers.co.uk

GOFUR MR ABDUL

Thomas More Chambers
7 Lincoln's Inn Fields, London WC2A 3BP, ☎ 020 7404 7000
✉ clerks@thomasmore.co.uk
Call Date: Oct 1999, Inner Temple
Qualifications: [LLM (UCL) PhD (UCL) LLB (Hons)]
agofur@thomasmore.co.uk

GOH MR ALLAN LEE GUAN

4 Breams Buildings
Chancery Lane, London EC4A 1HP, ☎ 020 7092 1900 ✉ clerks@4bb.co.uk
Call Date: July 1984, Gray's Inn
Pupil Supervisor
Qualifications: [LLB]

GOH MISS SUSAN GUAT ENG

Redemption Chambers
121 The Vale, Golders Green, London NW11 8TL, ☎ 020 8458 5486
✉ home@ollennu92.freeserve.co.uk
Call Date: Mar 1997, Gray's Inn
Qualifications: [LLB (Hons)(L'pool)]

GOHIL MISS PUSHPANJALI

Queen Square Chambers
56 Queen Square, Bristol BS1 4PR, ☎ 0117 921 1966 ✉ crime@qs-c.co.uk
Call Date: Nov 2000, Middle Temple
Qualifications: [LLB (Hons) (Lond)]
ag@qs-c.co.uk

GOKANI MISS RACHNA

QEB Hollis Whiteman
1-2 Laurence Pountney Hill, London EC4R 0EU, ☎ 020 7933 8855
✉ barristers@qebhw.co.uk
Call Date: July 2006, Lincoln's Inn
Qualifications: [LLB (Leic)]
barristers@qebhw.co.uk

GOLD MISS DEBRA ANNE

Fenners Chambers
3 Madingley Road, Cambridge CB3 0EE, ☎ 01223 368761
✉ clerks@fennerschambers.com
Call Date: July 1985, Middle Temple
Qualifications: [BA (Oxon) Dip Law]
debra.gold@fennerschambers.com

GOLD MR ELLIOT

5 Essex Court
1st Floor, 5 Essex Court, Temple, London EC4Y 9AH, ☎ 020 7410 2000
✉ clerks@5essexcourt.co.uk
Call Date: Nov 2001, Inner Temple
Qualifications: [LLB (Manch)]
gold@5essexcourt.co.uk

GOLD MR JONATHAN

Blackfriars Chambers
79-83 Temple Chambers, 3-7 Temple Avenue, London EC4Y 0HP, ☎ 020 7353 7400
✉ clerks@blackfriarschambers.com
Call Date: Oct 2005, Middle Temple
Qualifications: [BA (Hons) Bristol]
jonathan.gold@blackfriarschambers.com

GOLD MR RICHARD DAVID

St John's Chambers
101 Victoria Street, Bristol BS1 6PU, ☎ 0117 923 4700
✉ clerks@stjohnschambers.co.uk
Call Date: Nov 2006, Inner Temple
Qualifications: [BA (Oxon)]
richard.gold@stjohnschambers.co.uk

GOLDBERG MR DAVID GERARD QC (1987)

Gray's Inn Tax Chambers
3rd Floor, Gray's Inn Chambers, Gray's Inn, London WC1R 5JA, ☎ 020 7242 2642
✉ clerks@taxbar.com
Call Date: July 1971, Lincoln's Inn
Qualifications: [LLM]
dg@taxbar.com

GOLDBERG MR JONATHAN JACOB QC (1989)

North Square Chambers
15 North Square, London NW11 7AD, ☎ 020 8455 3735 ✉ jongold@talk21.com
Cobden House Chambers
19 Quay Street, Manchester M3 3HN, ☎ 0161 833 6000 ✉ Clerks@Cobden.co.uk
Call Date: Feb 1971, Middle Temple
Recorder
Qualifications: [MA LLB (Cantab)]
Jg@goldbergqc.com

GOLDBERG MR SIMON IAN

Trinity Chambers
The Custom House, 39 Quayside, Newcastle Upon Tyne NE1 3DE, ☎ 0191 232 1927
✉ info@trinitychambers.co.uk
Trinity Chambers
Multi Media Exchange, 72-80 Corporation Road, Middlesbrough TS1 2RF,
☎ 01642 247569
✉ info@trinitychambers.co.uk
Call Date: July 1999, Middle Temple
Pupil Supervisor
Qualifications: [BA (Hons)(Oxon)]
✉ s.goldberg@trinitychambers.co.uk

GOLDBLATT MR SIMON QC (1972)

39 Essex Street
London WC2R 3AT, ☎ 020 7832 1111
✉ clerks@39essex.com
82 King Street
Manchester M2 4WQ, ☎ 0161 870 9969
Call Date: June 1953, Gray's Inn
Qualifications: [MA (Cantab)]
✉ clerks@39essex.com

GOLDIE MISS KATIE JANE

Albion Chambers
Broad Street, Bristol BS1 1DR,
☎ 0117 927 2144
✉ clerks@albionchambers.co.uk
Call Date: Oct 2004, Inner Temple
Qualifications: [LLB (Staffs)]
✉ kate.goldie@albionchambers.co.uk

GOLDMAN MRS LINDA

Henderson Chambers
2 Harcourt Buildings, Temple, London EC4Y 9DB, ☎ 020 7583 9020
✉ clerks@hendersonchambers.co.uk
Call Date: Oct 1990, Middle Temple
Pupil Supervisor
Qualifications: [BDS (Lond) LLB (Lond) Dip Crim (Lond) Dip Psych (Lond) Dip Forensic Odontology]

GOLDREIN MR IAIN SAVILLE QC (1997)

Number 7 Harrington Street Chambers
7 Harrington Street, Liverpool L2 9YH,
☎ 0151 242 0707 ✉ clerks@7hs.co.uk
7 Bell Yard
London WC2A 2JR, ☎ 020 7831 0636
✉ kevintarrant@btconnect.com
Call Date: July 1975, Inner Temple
Recorder
Qualifications: [MA (Cantab)]
✉ iain.goldrein@7hs.co.uk

GOLDRING MISS JENNIFER LEONIE

Five St Andrew's Hill
5 St Andrew's Hill, London EC4V 5BZ,
☎ 020 7332 5400 ✉ Clerks@5sah.co.uk
Call Date: Nov 1993, Middle Temple
Qualifications: [MA (Hons)(Oxon)]
✉ jennygoldring@5sah.co.uk

GOLDRING MR JEREMY EDWARD

South Square
3-4 South Square, Gray's Inn, London WC1R 5HP, ☎ 020 7696 9900
✉ practicemanagers@southsquare.com
Call Date: Oct 1996, Lincoln's Inn
Pupil Supervisor
Qualifications: [BA (Hons)(Oxon) MA (USA) Dip in Law (Lond)]
✉ jeremygoldring@southsquare.com

GOLDSACK MR IAN

Call Date: May 1997, Gray's Inn
Pupil Supervisor
Qualifications: [BA (Oxon)]

GOLDSMITH MR JAMES DANIEL

One Essex Court
Ground Floor, One Essex Court, Temple, London EC4Y 9AR, ☎ 020 7583 2000
✉ clerks@oeclaw.co.uk
Call Date: Oct 2002, Gray's Inn
Qualifications: [BA (Cantab)]
✉ jgoldsmith@oeclaw.co.uk

GOLDSMITH MR JOSEPH ADAM

5 Stone Buildings
5 Stone Buildings, Lincoln's Inn, London WC2A 3XT, ☎ 020 7242 6201
✉ clerks@5sblaw.com
Call Date: Oct 2003, Lincoln's Inn
Qualifications: [BA (Hons) (Oxon)]
✉ jgoldsmith@5sblaw.com

GOLDSTEIN MR WAYNE NATHAN

18 St John Street
Manchester M3 4EA, ☎ 0161 278 1800
✉ clerks@18sjs.com
Call Date: Nov 1999, Lincoln's Inn
Qualifications: [BLS]

GOLDSTONE MR DAVID JULIAN QC (2006)

Quadrant Chambers
Quadrant House, 10 Fleet Street, London EC4Y 1AU, ☎ 020 7583 4444
✉ info@quadrantchambers.com
Call Date: Apr 1986, Middle Temple
Qualifications: [MA (Cantab) BCL (Oxon)]
✉ david.goldstone@quadrantchambers.com

GOLDSTONE MR SIMON LEWIS

4 Pump Court
4 Pump Court, Temple, London EC4Y 7AN,
☎020 7842 5555
✉chambers@4pumpcourt.com
Call Date: July 2004, Middle Temple
Qualifications: [BA (Oxon) PGDip Law (BPP)]

GOLDWATER MR MICHAEL PHILIP

Cobden House Chambers
19 Quay Street, Manchester M3 3HN,
☎0161 833 6000 ✉Clerks@Cobden.co.uk
Call Date: July 1977, Middle Temple
Pupil Supervisor
Qualifications: [MA (Oxon)]
clerks@cobden.co.uk

GOLINSKI MR ROBERT FELIX

Exchange Chambers
7 Ralli Courts, West Riverside, Manchester M3 5FT, ☎0161 833 2722
Exchange Chambers
One Derby Square, Derby Square, Liverpool L2 9XX, ☎0151 236 7747
✉info@exchangechambers.co.uk
Exchange Chambers
Oxford House, Oxford Row, Leeds LS1 3BE,
☎0113 203 1970
✉spencer@exchangechambers.co.uk
Call Date: Oct 1990, Middle Temple
Qualifications: [BA]
golinski@exchangechambers.co.uk

GOLLANCZ MR DAVID

Keating Chambers
15 Essex Street, London WC2R 3AA,
☎020 7544 2600
✉clerks@keatingchambers.com
Call Date: Nov 2010, Inner Temple
Qualifications: [BA (Sussex)]

GOLLOP MS KATHARINE SUSANNAH

3 Serjeants Inn
London EC4Y 1BQ, ☎020 7427 5000
✉clerks@3serjeantsinn.com
Call Date: Nov 1993, Gray's Inn
Qualifications: [BA (Hons) CPE ICSL]
kgollop@3serjeantsinn.com

GOMER MR ELIS MEREDYDD

Call Date: July 2008, Gray's Inn
Qualifications: [LLB (Cardiff)]
elis.gomer@stjohnsbuildings.co.uk

GOMULKA MR MICHAEL SVEND

25 Bedford Row
London WC1R 4HD, ☎020 7067 1500
✉clerks@25bedfordrow.com
Call Date: Nov 2002, Inner Temple
Pupil Supervisor
Qualifications: [BSc (Bris) CPE]
mgomulka@25bedfordrow.com

GONZALEZ MERELLO MRS MARIA DOLORES

Holborn Chambers
6 Gate Street, Lincoln's Inn Fields, London WC2A 3HP, ☎020 7242 6060
Call Date: Oct 2006, Lincoln's Inn
Qualifications: [LLB (Lond)]

GOODALL MR CHARLES VERNON MACHIN-

Queen Square Chambers
56 Queen Square, Bristol BS1 4PR,
☎0117 921 1966 ✉crime@qs-c.co.uk
Call Date: July 1986, Inner Temple
Qualifications: [BA Dip Law]
cvmg@qs-c.co.uk

GOODALL MISS EMMA

Dyers Chambers
35 Bedford Row, London WC1R 4JH,
☎020 7404 1881
✉admin@dyerschambers.com
Call Date: Nov 1996, Gray's Inn
Qualifications: [LLB]
emma.goodall@dyerschambers.com

GOODALL MR PATRICK JOHN

Fountain Court Chambers
Fountain Court, Temple, London EC4Y 9DH,
☎020 7583 3335
✉chambers@fountaincourt.co.uk
Call Date: Mar 1998, Inner Temple
Pupil Supervisor
Qualifications: [LLB (So'ton) BCL (Oxon)]
pgoodall@fountaincourt.co.uk

GOODALL MISS RACHAEL JANE

3 PB Barristers
3 Paper Buildings, Temple, London EC4Y 7EU,
☎020 7583 8055
3 PB Barristers
23 Beaumont Street, Oxford OX1 2NP,
☎01865 793 736
3 PB Barristers
30 Christchurch Road, Bournemouth, Dorset BH1 3PD, ☎01202 292102
✉clerks.bournemouth@3paper.co.uk
3 PB Barristers
Royal Talbot House, 2 Victoria Street, Bristol, Avon BS1 6BB, ☎0117 928 1520

3 PB Barristers
4 St Peter Street, Winchester SO23 8BW, ☎01962 868884
✉clerks.winchester@3paper.co.uk
Call Date: July 2000, Gray's Inn
Pupil Supervisor
Qualifications: [BA]

GOODBODY MR PETER JAMES

Oriel Chambers
14 Water Street, Liverpool, Merseyside L2 8TD, ☎0151 236 7191
✉clerks@orielchambers.co.uk
Oriel Chambers
18 Ribblesdale Place, Preston PR1 3NA, ☎01772 254 764
✉clerks@oriel-chambers.co.uk
Call Date: July 1986, Lincoln's Inn
Pupil Supervisor
Qualifications: [LLB (Manch)]
🖃peter.goodbody@orielchambers.co.uk

GOODE MR JULIAN LEIGH ALEXANDER

St Johns Buildings
24a - 28 St John Street, Manchester M3 4DJ, ☎0161 214 1500
✉clerk@stjohnsbuildings.co.uk
16 Winckley Square
Preston PR1 3JJ, ☎01772 256100
St Johns Buildings Liverpool
8th Floor India Buildings, Water Street, Liverpool L2 0XG, ☎0151 243 6000
✉clerk@stjohnsbuildings.co.uk
Call Date: Nov 2006, Lincoln's Inn
Qualifications: [LLB (Manch)]

GOODE MISS ROWENA MARGARET

Exchange Chambers
One Derby Square, Derby Square, Liverpool L2 9XX, ☎0151 236 7747
✉info@exchangechambers.co.uk
Exchange Chambers
7 Ralli Courts, West Riverside, Manchester M3 5FT, ☎0161 833 2722
Exchange Chambers
Oxford House, Oxford Row, Leeds LS1 3BE, ☎0113 203 1970
✉spencer@exchangechambers.co.uk
Call Date: July 1974, Gray's Inn
Pupil Supervisor, Recorder
Qualifications: [LLB]
🖃goode@exchangechambers.co.uk

GOODERHAM MISS ELIZABETH ANN

Northampton Chambers
10 Spencer Parade, Northampton NN1 5AQ, ☎01604 636271
✉clerks@northampton-chambers.co.uk
Call Date: July 2001, Inner Temple
Qualifications: [LLB (Derby)]

GOODFELLOW MR GILES WILLIAM JEREMY QC (2003)

Pump Court Tax Chambers
16 Bedford Row, London WC1R 4EF, ☎020 7414 8080 ✉clerks@pumptax.com
Call Date: July 1983, Middle Temple
Qualifications: [MA (Cantab) LLM (USA)]
🖃ggoodfellow@pumptax.com

Types of work: Asset finance, Capital tax, Corporation tax, Employee benefit trusts, Equity, Income tax, National Insurance, Private client, Professional negligence, Stamp duty, Trusts, VAT, Wills

GOODFELLOW MR NICHOLAS WILLIAM SIMON

Littleton Chambers
3 King's Bench Walk North, Temple, London EC4Y 7HR, ☎020 7797 8600
✉fschneider@littletonchambers.co.uk
Call Date: Oct 2009, Lincoln's Inn
Qualifications: [BSc (B'ham) CPE OBPP]
🖃ngoodfellow@littletonchambers.co.uk

GOODFELLOW MR STEPHEN JOHN

East Anglian Chambers
140 New London Road, Chelmsford, Essex CM2 0AW, ☎01473 214481
✉chelmsford@ealaw.co.uk
East Anglian Chambers
Gresham House, 5 Museum Street, Ipswich, Suffolk IP1 1HQ, ☎01473 214481
✉ipswich@ealaw.co.uk
East Anglian Chambers
15 The Close, Norwich, Norfolk NR1 4DZ, ☎01473 214481 ✉norwich@ealaw.co.uk
Call Date: Nov 1997, Middle Temple
Qualifications: [BSc (Hons)(Bris)]

GOODFIELD MISS ELEANOR FRANCES

2 Hare Court
Lower Ground, Ground, 1st & 2nd Floor, 2 Hare Court, Temple, London EC4Y 7BH, ☎020 7353 3982 ✉clerks@2harecourt.com
Call Date: Oct 2009, Lincoln's Inn
Qualifications: [BA (Hons)(Cantab)]

E

GOODHEAD MR THOMAS ARTHUR MORGAN

Clerksroom (London)
3rd Floor, 218 Strand, London WC2R 1AT, ☎0845 083 3000 ✉mail@clerksroom.com
Call Date: July 2010, Lincoln's Inn
Qualifications: [BA (Oxon)]
goodhead@clerksroom.com

GOODING MISS LAURA-JANE

Exchange Chambers
One Derby Square, Derby Square, Liverpool L2 9XX, ☎0151 236 7747
✉info@exchangechambers.co.uk
Exchange Chambers
7 Ralli Courts, West Riverside, Manchester M3 5FT, ☎0161 833 2722
Exchange Chambers
Oxford House, Oxford Row, Leeds LS1 3BE, ☎0113 203 1970
✉spencer@exchangechambers.co.uk
Call Date: Oct 2001, Lincoln's Inn
Qualifications: [BA (Hons) (Oxon) CPE]
gooding@exchangechambers.co.uk

GOODISON MR ADAM HENRY

South Square
3-4 South Square, Gray's Inn, London WC1R 5HP, ☎020 7696 9900
✉practicemanagers@southsquare.com
Call Date: Oct 1990, Middle Temple
Qualifications: [BA (Dunelm)]
adamgoodison@southsquare.com

GOODKIN MR DANIEL LAURENCE

4 Pump Court
4 Pump Court, Temple, London EC4Y 7AN, ☎020 7842 5555
✉chambers@4pumpcourt.com
Call Date: Oct 2008, Lincoln's Inn
Qualifications: [BA (Lond)]
dgoodkin@4pumpcourt.com

GOODLAD MR GRANT DAVID

Farrar's Building
Farrar's Building, Temple, London EC4Y 7BD, ☎020 7583 9241
✉Chambers@farrarsbuilding.co.uk
Call Date: Nov 2006, Lincoln's Inn
Qualifications: [LLB (B'ham)]

GOODMAN MR ALEXANDER DAVID EDMUND

4-5 Gray's Inn Square
Gray's Inn, London WC1R 5AH, ☎020 7404 5252 ✉clerks@4-5.co.uk
Atlas Chambers
3 Field Court, Gray's Inn, London WC1R 5EP, ☎020 7269 7980
✉clerks@atlaschambers.com
Call Date: Nov 2003, Lincoln's Inn
Qualifications: [MA (Hons) (Oxon)]

GOODMAN MR ANDREW DAVID

1 Chancery Lane
London WC2A 1LF, ☎0845 634 6666
✉clerks@1chancerylane.com
Call Date: July 1978, Inner Temple
Pupil Supervisor
Qualifications: [LLB (So'ton) FCIArb]
agoodman@1chancerylane.com

GOODMAN MISS BERNADETTE TRACY

15 Winckley Square
Preston PR1 3JJ, ☎01772 252828
✉clerks@15winckleysq.co.uk
Call Date: Nov 1983, Inner Temple
Pupil Supervisor
Qualifications: [BA (Keele)]

GOODMAN MR JONATHAN ANDREW

Octagon House
19 Colegate, Norwich NR3 1AT, ☎01603 623186
✉clerks@octagonhouse.co.uk
Call Date: Nov 1999, Inner Temple
Pupil Supervisor
Qualifications: [LLB (Luton)]

GOODMAN MR SIMON CHARLES

Queen Square Chambers
56 Queen Square, Bristol BS1 4PR, ☎0117 921 1966 ✉crime@qs-c.co.uk
Call Date: Nov 1996, Gray's Inn
Pupil Supervisor
Qualifications: [BA (Bris)]
sg@qs-c.co.uk

GOODRICH MISS SIOBHAN CATHERINE

3 Serjeants Inn
London EC4Y 1BQ, ☎020 7427 5000
✉clerks@3serjeantsinn.com
Call Date: Nov 1980, Gray's Inn
Pupil Supervisor
Qualifications: [LLB (Lond)]

E

GOODWILL MR GRAHAM

Chambers of Mr G Goodwill
Three Trees Farm, 20 Prickwillow Road, Isleham, Ely, Cambridgeshire CB7 5RG, ☎07801729877
Call Date: July 1983, Inner Temple
Qualifications: [MA LLB(Cantab)]
grahamgoodwill@hotmail.co.uk

GOODWIN MISS CAROLINE TRACY

Trinity Chambers
The Custom House, 39 Quayside, Newcastle Upon Tyne NE1 3DE, ☎0191 232 1927
✉info@trinitychambers.co.uk
Trinity Chambers
Multi Media Exchange, 72-80 Corporation Road, Middlesbrough TS1 2RF, ☎01642 247569
✉info@trinitychambers.co.uk
Call Date: Nov 1988, Inner Temple
Pupil Supervisor, Recorder
Qualifications: [Dip Law]
c.goodwin@trinitychambers.co.uk

GOODWIN MISS DEIRDRE EVELYN

13 King's Bench Walk
13 King's Bench Walk, Temple, London EC4Y 7EN, ☎020 7353 7204
✉clerks@13kbw.co.uk
13 KBW
32 Beaumont Street, Oxford OX1 2NP, ☎01865 311066 ✉clerks@13kbw.co.uk
Call Date: July 1974, Gray's Inn
Pupil Supervisor
Qualifications: [LLB]
dgoodwin@13kbw.co.uk

GOODWIN MR JAMES ANDREW

37 Park Square Chambers
37 Park Square, Leeds LS1 2NY, ☎0113 243 9422 ✉chambers@no37.co.uk
Call Date: Oct 2008, Inner Temple
Qualifications: [LLB (Leeds)]
chambers@no37.co.uk

GOODWIN MR MICHAEL

Old Bailey Chambers
15 Old Bailey, London EC4M 7EF, ☎020 3008 6404
✉clerks@15oldbaileychambers.com
Call Date: Oct 1996, Inner Temple
Pupil Supervisor
Qualifications: [BSc Hons (Leeds) CPE (Lond)]
m.goodwin@15oldbaileychambers.com

GOODWIN MR NICHOLAS ALEXANDER JOHN

Harcourt Chambers
1st Floor, 2 Harcourt Buildings, Temple, London EC4Y 9DB, ☎0844 561 7135
Call Date: Oct 1995, Inner Temple
Recorder
Qualifications: [MA (Oxon)]
ngoodwin@harcourtchambers.law.co.uk

GOODWIN-GILL PROF GUY SERLE

Blackstone Chambers
Blackstone House, Temple, London EC4Y 9BW, ☎020 7583 1770
✉clerks@blackstonechambers.com
Call Date: July 1971, Inner Temple
Qualifications: [MA (Oxon) D Phil (Oxon)]
guygoodwin-gill@blackstonechambers.com

GOOLAMALI MISS NINA SORAYA

2 Temple Gardens
2 Temple Gardens, Temple, London EC4Y 9AY, ☎020 7822 1200
✉clerks@2tg.co.uk
Call Date: Oct 1995, Middle Temple
Pupil Supervisor
Qualifications: [BA (Hons) MA]
ngoolamali@2tg.co.uk

GOOLD MR ALEXANDER MICHAEL

Selborne Chambers
10 Essex Street, London WC2R 3AA, ☎020 7420 9500
✉clerks@selbornechambers.co.uk
Call Date: Nov 1994, Lincoln's Inn
Pupil Supervisor
Qualifications: [MA (Cantab) ACIArb, FCIArb]

GOOSE MR JULIAN NICHOLAS QC (2002)

Zenith Chambers
10 Park Square, Leeds LS1 2LH, ☎0113 245 5438
✉clerks@zenithchambers.co.uk
2 Hare Court
Lower Ground, Ground, 1st & 2nd Floor, 2 Hare Court, Temple, London EC4Y 7BH, ☎020 7353 3982 ✉clerks@2harecourt.com
Call Date: July 1984, Lincoln's Inn
Qualifications: [LLB (Leeds)]

E

GORASIA MR PARAS RAVJI

Kings Chambers
36 Young Street, Manchester M3 3FT,
☎0845 034 3444
✉clerks@kingschambers.com
Kings Chambers
5 Park Square East, Leeds LS1 2NE,
☎0845 034 3444
✉clerks@kingschambers.com
Kings Chambers
Embassy House, 60 Church Street, Birmingham B3 2DJ, ☎0845 034 3444
✉clerks@kingschambers.com
Call Date: July 2005, Inner Temple
Qualifications: [LLB University of Kent at Canterbury BCL M Phil LLM]
pgorasia@kingschambers.com

GORDON MR BENJAMIN JAMES GREGORY

Furnival Chambers
32 Furnival Street, London EC4A 1JQ,
☎020 7405 3232
Call Date: Nov 2005, Inner Temple
Qualifications: [MA University of Edinburgh CPE BPP Law School]
bgordon@furnivallaw.co.uk

E

GORDON MISS CATHERINE ANNE

3 Wayside Green
3 Wayside Green, Woodcote, Reading, South Oxfordshire RG8 0PR, ☎01491 680722
✉cathy@cathygordon.co.uk
Call Date: July 1989, Middle Temple
Qualifications: [LLB]
cathy@cathygordon.co.uk

GORDON MS CLARE

Farringdon Chambers
180 Bermondsey Street, London SE1 3TQ,
☎020 7089 5700
1 Pump Court
Elm Court, Temple, London EC4Y 7AB,
☎020 7842 7070
✉(name)@pumpcourt.co.uk
Call Date: Oct 1995, Middle Temple
Qualifications: [LLB (Hons)]

GORDON MR DAVID MYER

Sovereign Chambers
46 Park Place, Leeds LS1 2RY,
☎0113 245 1841
✉clerks@sovereignchambers.co.uk
Call Date: July 1984, Inner Temple
Pupil Supervisor, Recorder
Qualifications: [MA (Oxon) Dip Law (Lond)]
david.gordon@sovereignchambers.co.uk

GORDON MR HENRY GEORGE

5 Pump Court
Ground Floor, 5 Pump Court, Temple, London EC4Y 7AP, ☎020 7353 2532
✉clerks@5pumpcourt.com
Call Date: July 2007, Inner Temple
Qualifications: [LLB (Warw) LLM (Brussels)]
henrygordon@5pumpcourt.com

GORDON MR JAMES COSMO ALEXANDER

Atkinson Bevan Chambers
1st Floor, 2 Harcourt Buildings, Temple, London EC4Y 9DB, ☎020 7353 2112
✉clerks@2hb.co.uk
Call Date: Oct 2004, Middle Temple
Qualifications: [BA PGDip Law]
JGordon@2hb.co.uk

GORDON MR JEREMY

Chambers of Mr Ami Feder
Ground Floor, Lamb Building, Temple, London EC4Y 7AS, ☎020 7797 7788
✉clerks@lambbuilding.co.uk
Lamb Building
22 Ship Street, Brighton BN1 1AD,
☎01273 820490
✉admin@lambbuilding.co.uk
Chambers of Mr Ami Feder
Ground Floor, Lamb Building, Temple, London EC4Y 7AS, ☎020 7797 7788
✉clerks@lambbuilding.co.uk
Call Date: July 1974, Inner Temple
Pupil Supervisor
Qualifications: [LLB]
clerks@lambbuilding.co.uk

GORDON MR KEITH MICHAEL

Atlas Chambers
3 Field Court, Gray's Inn, London WC1R 5EP,
☎020 7269 7980
✉clerks@atlaschambers.com
Call Date: July 2003, Lincoln's Inn
Qualifications: [BA Hons (Oxon) MA (Oxon) CTA (Fellow) FCA]

GORDON MR RICHARD JOHN FRANCIS QC (1994)

Brick Court Chambers
7-8 Essex Street, London WC2R 3LD,
☎020 7379 3550 ✉clerks@brickcourt.co.uk
Call Date: July 1972, Middle Temple
Recorder
Qualifications: [MA (Oxon) LLM (Lond)]
Richard.Gordon@Brickcourt.co.uk

GORDON WALKER MISS EMILY CLARE

12 King's Bench Walk
12 King's Bench Walk, Temple, London EC4Y 7EL, ☎ 020 7583 0811
Call Date: July 2007, Middle Temple
Qualifications: [MA (Edin) Dip Law]
gordonwalker@12kbw.co.uk

GORE MR ANDREW JULIAN MARK

37 Park Square Chambers
37 Park Square, Leeds LS1 2NY, ☎ 0113 243 9422 ✉ chambers@no37.co.uk
Call Date: Nov 1994, Middle Temple
Pupil Supervisor
Qualifications: [LLB (Hons)]
chambers@no37.co.uk

GORE MR ANDREW ROGER

Fenners Chambers
3 Madingley Road, Cambridge CB3 0EE, ☎ 01223 368761
✉ clerks@fennerschambers.com
Call Date: Nov 1973, Middle Temple
Pupil Supervisor
Qualifications: [MA (Cantab) FCIArb]
andrew.gore@fennerschambers.com

GORE MRS HARRIET NKECHI ADIMORA

Kensington Chambers
5A Philbeach Gardens, London SW5 9DY, ☎ 020 7373 2217
✉ harrietgore.kensingtonchambers@btinternet.com
Call Date: Mar 1997, Middle Temple
Qualifications: [BA (Hons) CPE]

GORE MISS KEIRA JOANNE

Outer Temple Chambers
The Outer Temple, 222 Strand, London WC2R 1BA, ☎ 020 7353 6381
✉ clerks@outertemple.com
Call Date: July 2008, Middle Temple
Qualifications: [BA (Hons) (York) PgDl (Lond)]
keira.gore@outertemple.com

GORE MS SALLY ELIZABETH

14 Gray's Inn Square
14 Gray's Inn Square, Gray's Inn, London WC1R 5JP, ☎ 020 7242 0858
✉ clerks@14gis.co.uk
Call Date: July 2006, Inner Temple
Qualifications: [MA M Phil (Cantab) LLM PHD]
clerks@14graysinnsquare.co.uk

GORE MRS SUSAN DIANA

Coram Chambers
9-11 Fulwood Place, London WC1V 6HG, ☎ 020 7092 3700
✉ mail@coramchambers.co.uk
Call Date: Nov 1993, Middle Temple
Qualifications: [LLB (Hons)(UEA) BA (Hons)(Manch)]

GORTON MR CARL ROBERT

Atlantic Chambers
4-6 Cook Street, Liverpool L2 9QU, ☎ 0151 236 4421
✉ info@atlanticchambers.co.uk
Call Date: Nov 1999, Inner Temple
Qualifications: [BA (Lond) CPE]
carlgorton@atlanticchambers.co.uk

GORTON MR SIMON ANTHONY QC (2011)

Atlantic Chambers
4-6 Cook Street, Liverpool L2 9QU, ☎ 0151 236 4421
✉ info@atlanticchambers.co.uk
Old Square Chambers
10-11 Bedford Row, London WC1R 4BU, ☎ 020 7269 0300 ✉ clerks@oldsquare.co.uk
Call Date: July 1988, Inner Temple
Pupil Supervisor
Qualifications: [LLB (Lond)]
simongorton@atlanticchambers.co.uk

GOSLING MRS DEBORAH

Chavasse Court Chambers
18 Queen Avenue, Liverpool L2 4TX, ☎ 0151 229 2030
✉ clerks@chavassechambers.co.uk
Call Date: Mar 2004, Lincoln's Inn
Qualifications: [BA (Hons) (L'pool)]
deborah.gosling@chavassechambers.co.uk

GOSLING MR TOM ADAM

Oriel Chambers
14 Water Street, Liverpool, Merseyside L2 8TD, ☎ 0151 236 7191
✉ clerks@orielchambers.co.uk
Oriel Chambers
18 Ribblesdale Place, Preston PR1 3NA, ☎ 01772 254 764
✉ clerks@oriel-chambers.co.uk
Call Date: Nov 2004, Lincoln's Inn
Qualifications: [LLB (Hons) (Sheff)]
tom.gosling@orielchambers.co.uk

E

GOSNELL MR STEVEN JAMES

1 High Pavement
Nottingham NG1 1HF, ☎0115 941 8218
✉clerks@1highpavement.co.uk
Call Date: Nov 1995, Gray's Inn
Qualifications: [BSc (Wales)]
✉stevengosnell@1highpavement.co.uk

GOSS MISS KATHERINE

Park Lane Plowden
19 Westgate, Leeds LS1 2RD,
☎0113 228 5049
✉clerks@parklaneplowden.co.uk
Call Date: July 2002, Gray's Inn
Qualifications: [BA (York)]
✉katherine.goss@parklaneplowden.co.uk

GOTT MR PAUL ANDREW QC (2012)

Fountain Court Chambers
Fountain Court, Temple, London EC4Y 9DH,
☎020 7583 3335
✉chambers@fountaincourt.co.uk
Call Date: Oct 1991, Lincoln's Inn
Pupil Supervisor
Qualifications: [MA (Hons) (Cantab) BCL]
✉pgott@fountaincourt.co.uk

GOTTLIEB MR DAVID ANTHONY

Thomas More Chambers
7 Lincoln's Inn Fields, London WC2A 3BP,
☎020 7404 7000
✉clerks@thomasmore.co.uk
Call Date: Nov 1988, Inner Temple
Pupil Supervisor
Qualifications: [LLB (Bris)]
✉DGottlieb@thomasmore.co.uk, clerks@thomasmore.co.uk

GOTTS MISS ANNA CATHERINE

7 King's Bench Walk
Ground Floor, 7 King's Bench Walk, Temple, London EC4Y 7DS, ☎020 7910 8300
✉clerks@7kbw.co.uk
Call Date: Oct 2001, Lincoln's Inn
Qualifications: [BA (Hons)(Oxon)]
✉agotts@7kbw.co.uk

GOUDARZI MISS SARAH LOUISE

Chambers of Mr Ami Feder
Ground Floor, Lamb Building, Temple, London EC4Y 7AS, ☎020 7797 7788
✉clerks@lambbuilding.co.uk
Chambers of Mr Ami Feder
Ground Floor, Lamb Building, Temple, London EC4Y 7AS, ☎020 7797 7788
✉clerks@lambbuilding.co.uk
Call Date: July 2007, Lincoln's Inn
Qualifications: [LLB (Kingston)]
✉clerks@lambbuilding.co.uk

GOUDIE MR ALEXANDER JULIAN COOPER

Argent Chambers
5 Bell Yard, London WC2A 2JR,
☎020 7556 5500
✉briefsin@argentchambers.co.uk
Call Date: Nov 2000, Inner Temple
Qualifications: [LLB (Dundee)]
✉a.goudie@argentchambers.co.uk

GOUDIE MR JAMES QC (1984)

11 King's Bench Walk
11 King's Bench Walk, Temple, London EC4Y 7EQ, ☎020 7632 8500
✉clerksroom@11kbw.com
Call Date: July 1970, Inner Temple
Qualifications: [LLB (Lond)]
✉james.goudie@11kbw.com

Fax: 020 7583 3690/9123;
Out of hours telephone: 07831 304714;
DX: 368 LDE;
Other comms: E-mail: clerksroom@11kbw.com
URL: www.11kbw.com

Other professional qualifications: Fellow of the Chartered Institute of Arbitrators; Fellow of the Society of Advanced Legal Studies

Types of work: Administrative law, Commercial litigation, Discrimination, Education, Employment, Entertainment, Environment, Local authorities, Sport

Membership of foreign bars: Antigua and Barbuda, Virgin Islands

Awards and memberships: Past Chairman, Administrative Law Bar Association; Past Chairman, Bar European Group

Other professional experience: Deputy High Court Judge, Queen's Bench and Chancery Divisions; President, Data Protection Tribunal (National Security Appeals)

Publications: *Judicial Review* (Co-editor) 2010 (4th edn), 1999; *Butterworths (now Bloomsbury) Local Government Law* (Co-editor),

1998; *Butterworths Local Government Reports* (Consultant Editor); 'Audit Commission Act 1998', *Current Law Statutes*; *Local Authorities and the Human Rights Act 1998* (Co-editor), 1999

Reported Cases: *R (Midlands Co-op) v Birmingham City Council*, [2012] EWHC 620 (Admin) Sale and development of Local authority land
Pannu v Geo W King Ltd, [2012] IRLR 193 Service provision changes.
R (JM & NT) v Isle of Wight Council, [2012] EqLR 34 Social care and public sector equality duty
KV, [2012] EuLR 302 Export of hazardous waste
Charles Terence Estates Ltd v Cornwall Council, (2011) LGR 813 Ultra vires contract and its consequences

GOUDIE MR WILLIAM MARTIN PHILLIP

Charter Chambers
33 John Street, London WC1N 2AT, ☎ 020 7618 4400
✉ clerks@charterchambers.com
Call Date: Oct 1996, Inner Temple
Pupil Supervisor
Qualifications: [LLB (Exon)]
✉ m.goudie@charterchambers.com

GOUGH MISS KAREN LOUISE

39 Essex Street
London WC2R 3AT, ☎ 020 7832 1111
✉ clerks@39essex.com
82 King Street
Manchester M2 4WQ, ☎ 0161 870 9969
Arbitration Chambers
22 Willes Road, London NW5 3DS, ☎ 020 7267 2137
✉ john.tackaberry@39essex.com
Call Date: July 1983, Inner Temple
Pupil Supervisor
Qualifications: [LLB (So'ton) FCIArb Dip IC Arb]
✉ karen.gough@39essex.com

GOUGH MRS SIAN LOUISE MORLEY

College Chambers
19 Carlton Crescent, Southampton, Hampshire SO15 2ET, ☎ 023 8023 0338
✉ clerks@college-chambers.co.uk
Call Date: Nov 2003, Gray's Inn
Qualifications: [LLB (Leic)]

GOULD MR JAMES ANDREW

Bank House Chambers
Old Bank House, Hartshead, Sheffield S1 2EL, ☎ 0114 275 1223
✉ w.digby@bankhousechambers.co.uk
Call Date: Nov 1997, Gray's Inn
Pupil Supervisor
Qualifications: [LLB (Leeds)]
✉ j.gould@bankhousechambers.co.uk

GOULDING MR JONATHAN STEVEN

Gough Square Chambers
6-7 Gough Square, London EC4A 3DE, ☎ 020 7353 0924 ✉ gsc@goughsq.co.uk
Call Date: July 1984, Inner Temple
Pupil Supervisor
Qualifications: [LLB (Manch)]
✉ jonathan.goulding@goughsq.co.uk

GOULDING MR PAUL ANTHONY QC (2000)

Blackstone Chambers
Blackstone House, Temple, London EC4Y 9BW, ☎ 020 7583 1770
✉ clerks@blackstonechambers.com
Call Date: Nov 1984, Middle Temple
Qualifications: [MA, BCL (Oxon)]
✉ paulgoulding@blackstonechambers.com

GOURGEY MR ALAN QC (2003)

11 Stone Buildings
11 Stone Buildings, Lincoln's Inn, London WC2A 3TG, ☎ 020 7831 6381
✉ clerks@11sb.com
Call Date: July 1984, Lincoln's Inn
Qualifications: [LL.B (Bris)]
✉ gourgey@11sb.com

GOURIET MR GERALD WILLIAM QC (2006)

Francis Taylor Building
Inner Temple, London EC4Y 7BY, ☎ 020 7353 8415 ✉ clerks@ftb.eu.com
Call Date: July 1974, Inner Temple
Qualifications: [BMus (Lond)]
✉ Gerald.gouriet@ftb.eu.com

GOURLAY MISS AMANDA KIRSTEN

Tanfield Chambers
2-5 Warwick Court, London WC1R 5DJ, ☎ 020 7421 5300
✉ clerks@tanfieldchambers.co.uk
Call Date: July 2004, Gray's Inn
Qualifications: [MA (Cantab)]
✉ agourlay@tanfieldchambers.co.uk

E

GOURLEY MISS CLAIRE ROBERTA JEAN

Exchange Chambers
One Derby Square, Derby Square, Liverpool L2 9XX, ☎0151 236 7747
✉info@exchangechambers.co.uk
Exchange Chambers
7 Ralli Courts, West Riverside, Manchester M3 5FT, ☎0161 833 2722
Exchange Chambers
Oxford House, Oxford Row, Leeds LS1 3BE, ☎0113 203 1970
✉spencer@exchangechambers.co.uk
Call Date: Oct 1996, Middle Temple
Qualifications: [MA (Cantab)]

GOW MR FERGUS BENJAMIN HARPER

KCH Garden Square
1 Oxford Street, Nottingham NG1 5BH, ☎0115 941 8851
✉clerks@kchgardensquare.co.uk
Call Date: Nov 1994, Inner Temple
Qualifications: [BA (Newc) CPE (Lond)]

GOW MR HENRY

New Bailey Chambers
4th Floor, Corn Exchange, Fenwick Street, Liverpool, Merseyside L2 7QS, ☎0151 236 9402 ✉clerks@newbailey.com
Call Date: Oct 1995, Gray's Inn
Pupil Supervisor
Qualifications: [LLB]

GOWEN MR MATTHEW ROBERT

18 Red Lion Court
London EC4A 3EB, ☎020 7520 6000
✉chambers@18rlc.co.uk
18 Red Lion Court (Annexe)
Thornwood House, 102 New London Road, Chelmsford, Essex CM2 0RG, ☎01245 280880
Call Date: Oct 1992, Lincoln's Inn
Pupil Supervisor
Qualifications: [LLB(Hons)]
matthew.gowen@18rlc.co.uk

GOWER MISS HELEN CLARE

Old Square Chambers
3 Orchard Court, St Augustine's Yard, Bristol BS1 5DP, ☎0117 930 5100
✉clerks@oldsquare.co.uk
Old Square Chambers
10-11 Bedford Row, London WC1R 4BU, ☎020 7269 0300 ✉clerks@oldsquare.co.uk
Call Date: Oct 1992, Middle Temple
Pupil Supervisor
Qualifications: [BA (Hons) LLM]
gower@oldsquare.co.uk

GOWER MR PETER JOHN DE PEAULY QC (2006)

6 Pump Court
1st Floor, 6 Pump Court, Temple, London EC4Y 7AR, ☎020 7797 8400
✉richardconstable@6pumpcourt.co.uk
6 Pump Court Chambers
6-8 Mill Street, Maidstone, Kent ME15 6XH, ☎01622 688094
✉annexe@6pumpcourt.co.uk
Call Date: July 1985, Lincoln's Inn
Recorder
Qualifications: [MA (Oxon)]
petergower@6pumpcourt.co.uk

GOWLING MR CHRISTOPHER NIGEL

Agri-Law Chambers
Penterry Farm, St Arvans NP16 6HG, ☎01989 720675
Call Date: Oct 2000, Gray's Inn
Qualifications: [LLB (Wolves)]

GOWLING MRS SERENA MARY

Agri-Law Chambers
Penterry Farm, St Arvans NP16 6HG, ☎01989 720675
Agri-Law Chambers
Briery Lodge, Briery Hill Lane, Gloucester, Gloucestershire GL18 1NH, ☎07989 720675
✉serena@agri-law.co.uk
Call Date: July 2005, Middle Temple
Qualifications: [LL Dip (Wolves) BSc (Hons) Kent]

GOY MR DAVID JOHN LISTER QC (1991)

Gray's Inn Tax Chambers
3rd Floor, Gray's Inn Chambers, Gray's Inn, London WC1R 5JA, ☎020 7242 2642
✉clerks@taxbar.com
Call Date: May 1973, Middle Temple
Qualifications: [LLM]
dgy@taxbar.com

GOZEM MR GAIAS QC (1997)

Lincoln House Chambers
Tower 12, The Avenue North, Spinningfields, 18-22 Bridge Street, Manchester M3 3BZ, ☎0161 832 5701
✉info@lincolnhousechambers.com
Call Date: Nov 1972, Middle Temple
Qualifications: [LLB (Lond)]
gaias.gozem@lincolnhousechambers.com

GRABINER LORD ANTHONY STEPHEN QC (1981)

One Essex Court
Ground Floor, One Essex Court, Temple, London EC4Y 9AR, ☎ 020 7583 2000
✉ clerks@oeclaw.co.uk
Call Date: Nov 1968, Lincoln's Inn
Recorder
Qualifications: [LLB LLM (Lond)]
✉ agrabiner@oeclaw.co.uk

GRACE MR JONATHAN ROBERT

Deans Court Chambers
24 St John Street, Manchester M3 4DF, ☎ 0161 214 6000 ✉ clerks@deanscourt.co.uk
Deans Court Chambers
101 Walker Street, Preston PR1 2RR, ☎ 01772 565 600
✉ preston@deanscourt.co.uk
Call Date: Feb 1989, Middle Temple
Pupil Supervisor
Qualifications: [BA (Oxon) Dip Law]
✉ jonathangrace@deanscourt.co.uk

GRACE MR TIMOTHY MICHAEL

Atlantic Chambers
4-6 Cook Street, Liverpool L2 9QU, ☎ 0151 236 4421
✉ info@atlanticchambers.co.uk
Call Date: Nov 1993, Middle Temple
Qualifications: [BA (Hons)(Oxon)]
✉ timgrace@atlanticchambers.co.uk

GRADY DR KATE

Doughty Street Chambers
53-54 Doughty Street, London WC1N 2LS, ☎ 020 7404 1313
✉ enquiries@doughtystreet.co.uk
Call Date: Oct 2007, Gray's Inn
Qualifications: [LLB (Leeds) LLM (Bris) PGDip]
✉ k.grady@doughtystreet.co.uk

GRAFFIUS MR MARK NARAYAN

187 Fleet Street
London EC4A 2AT, ☎ 020 7430 7430
✉ chambers@187fleetstreet.com
Call Date: Oct 1990, Middle Temple
Qualifications: [LLB (Leics)]
✉ markgraffius@187fleetstreet.com

GRAHAM MRS ALANA NICOLE

9 Stone Buildings
Lincoln's Inn, London WC2A 3NN, ☎ 020 7404 5055
✉ clerks@9stonebuildings.com
Chambers of Alana Graham
Chemix Buildings, Maypole Fields, Cradley, Halesowen, West Midlands B63 2QB, ☎ 01384 894560
Call Date: Nov 1993, Lincoln's Inn
Qualifications: [BA (Hons) LLB (Hons) (Brunel)]

GRAHAM MR CHARLES ROBERT STEPHEN QC (2003)

One Essex Court
Ground Floor, One Essex Court, Temple, London EC4Y 9AR, ☎ 020 7583 2000
✉ clerks@oeclaw.co.uk
Call Date: Nov 1986, Middle Temple
Qualifications: [MA (Oxon) Dip Law (Lond)]
✉ cgraham@oeclaw.co.uk

GRAHAM MR DAVID JAMES

Francis Taylor Building
Inner Temple, London EC4Y 7BY, ☎ 020 7353 8415 ✉ clerks@ftb.eu.com
Call Date: Oct 2010, Lincoln's Inn
Qualifications: [BA (Cantab)]
✉ david.graham@ftb.eu.com

GRAHAM MR GARETH DAVID

Queen Square Chambers
56 Queen Square, Bristol BS1 4PR, ☎ 0117 921 1966 ✉ crime@qs-c.co.uk
Call Date: Nov 2006, Middle Temple
Qualifications: [LLB (Hons) (Bris)]

GRAHAM MR IRVING BENJAMIN

Clifford Chambers
26 Clifford Road, Chafford Hundred, Essex RM16 6NY, ☎ 07961 556294
✉ igraham745@btinternet.com
Call Date: Nov 2003, Middle Temple
Qualifications: [BSc (Hons) (Lond) LLM Dip.Law]
✉ igraham745@btinternet.com

E

GRAHAM MR MICHAEL JOHN GEOFFREY

Trinity Chambers
The Custom House, 39 Quayside, Newcastle Upon Tyne NE1 3DE, ☎0191 232 1927
✉info@trinitychambers.co.uk
Trinity Chambers
Multi Media Exchange, 72-80 Corporation Road, Middlesbrough TS1 2RF,
☎01642 247569
✉info@trinitychambers.co.uk
Call Date: Mar 1999, Lincoln's Inn
Pupil Supervisor
Qualifications: [BA (Hons)]
m.graham@trinitychambers.co.uk

GRAHAM MR ROGER

Kew Chambers
354 Kew Road, Kew, Surrey TW9 3DU,
☎0844 8099991
✉admin@kewchambers.co.uk
Call Date: July 1973, Middle Temple

GRAHAM MR STUART CHARLES

New Court Chambers
3 Broad Chare, Newcastle Upon Tyne NE1 3DQ, ☎0191 232 1980
✉clerks@newcourt-chambers.co.uk
Call Date: July 1996, Lincoln's Inn
Qualifications: [LLB (Hons)]
clerks@newcourt-chambers.co.uk, stuart.graham@newcourt-chambers.co.uk

GRAHAM MR THOMAS PATRICK HENRY

New Square Chambers
12 New Square, Lincoln's Inn, London WC2A 3SW, ☎020 7419 8000
✉robin.hollington@newsquarechambers.co.uk
Call Date: Nov 1985, Middle Temple
Pupil Supervisor
Qualifications: [MA (Cantab)]
thomas.graham@newsquarechambers.co.uk

GRAHAM PAUL MRS ANNABEL

Francis Taylor Building
Inner Temple, London EC4Y 7BY,
☎020 7353 8415 ✉clerks@ftb.eu.com
Call Date: July 2008, Middle Temple
Qualifications: [BA (Hons) (Oxon)]
annabel.grahampaul@ftb.eu.com

GRAHAME MISS NINA STEPHANIE

Chambers of Ian Macdonald QC
Garden Court North, 22 Oxford Court, Manchester M2 3WQ, ☎0161 236 1840
✉clerks@gcnchambers.co.uk
Call Date: Nov 1993, Middle Temple
Pupil Supervisor
Qualifications: [BA (Hons)(Warw) CPE (Lond)]

GRAHAM-WELLS MISS ALISON CHRISTINE

Exchange Chambers
7 Ralli Courts, West Riverside, Manchester M3 5FT, ☎0161 833 2722
Exchange Chambers
One Derby Square, Derby Square, Liverpool L2 9XX, ☎0151 236 7747
✉info@exchangechambers.co.uk
Exchange Chambers
Oxford House, Oxford Row, Leeds LS1 3BE,
☎0113 203 1970
✉spencer@exchangechambers.co.uk
Call Date: July 1992, Inner Temple
Qualifications: [BA (Hons)]

GRAINGER MR ALISTAIR JAMES GEORGE

13 King's Bench Walk
13 King's Bench Walk, Temple, London EC4Y 7EN, ☎020 7353 7204
✉clerks@13kbw.co.uk
13 KBW
32 Beaumont Street, Oxford OX1 2NP,
☎01865 311066 ✉clerks@13kbw.co.uk
Call Date: Nov 1998, Inner Temple
Qualifications: [LLB (L'pool) LLM (Lond)]
agrainger@13kbw.co.uk

GRANDISON MR MYLES CLAYTON

Dyers Chambers
35 Bedford Row, London WC1R 4JH,
☎020 7404 1881
✉admin@dyerschambers.com
Call Date: Oct 2002, Lincoln's Inn
Qualifications: [BSc (Surrey) PgDL]

GRANGE MISS KATHERINE ELIZABETH

39 Essex Street
London WC2R 3AT, ☎020 7832 1111
✉clerks@39essex.com
Call Date: Nov 1998, Middle Temple
Pupil Supervisor
Qualifications: [BA (Hons)(Cantab)]
kate.grange@39essex.com

GRANSHAW MR JAMES DENNIS

Staple Inn Chambers
1st Floor, 9 Staple Inn, Holborn Bars, London WC1V 7QH, ☎ 020 7242 5240
✉ clerks@stapleinn.co.uk
Call Date: Mar 2010, Middle Temple
Qualifications: [BA (Loughborough) LLB (Lond)]
✉ jg@stapleinn.co.uk

GRANSHAW MISS SARA ELIZABETH

Harcourt Chambers
1st Floor, 2 Harcourt Buildings, Temple, London EC4Y 9DB, ☎ 0844 561 7135
New Street Chambers
2 New Street, Leicester LE1 5NA, ☎ 0116 262 5906 ✉ clerks@2newstreet.co.uk
Call Date: Oct 1991, Lincoln's Inn
Qualifications: [MA (Hons) (Oxon)]
✉ Sgranshaw@harcourtchambers.law.co.uk

GRANT MR CHUDI PAUL

Kenworthy's Chambers
Arlington House, Bloom Street, Salford, Manchester M3 6AJ, ☎ 0161 832 4036
Call Date: Nov 2002, Lincoln's Inn
Qualifications: [LLB (Hons) (Manch)]
✉ c.grant@kenworthysbarristers.co.uk

GRANT MR DAVID ERICSON

Outer Temple Chambers
The Outer Temple, 222 Strand, London WC2R 1BA, ☎ 020 7353 6381
✉ clerks@outertemple.com
Call Date: Mar 1999, Inner Temple
Pupil Supervisor
Qualifications: [BA BCL (Oxon)]
✉ david.grant@outertemple.com

GRANT MR EDWARD ALEXANDER GORDON

No5 Chambers
Fountain Court, Steelhouse Lane, Birmingham B4 6DR, ☎ 0845 210 5555 ✉ info@no5.com
No5 Chambers
38 Queen Square, Bristol BS1 4QS, ☎ 0845 210 5555
No5 Chambers
Greenwood House, 4-7 Salisbury Court, London EC4Y 8AA, ☎ 0845 210 5555
Call Date: Nov 1991, Inner Temple
Qualifications: [LLB (So'ton)]
✉ eg@no5.com

GRANT MR EDWARD WILLIAM

6 Pump Court
1st Floor, 6 Pump Court, Temple, London EC4Y 7AR, ☎ 020 7797 8400
✉ richardconstable@6pumpcourt.co.uk
6 Pump Court Chambers
6-8 Mill Street, Maidstone, Kent ME15 6XH, ☎ 01622 688094
✉ annexe@6pumpcourt.co.uk
Call Date: Nov 1994, Inner Temple
Qualifications: [BA (Oxon) CPE]
✉ edwardgrant@6pumpcourt.co.uk

GRANT MR GARY ANDREW

12 College Place
Fauvelle Buildings, 12 College Place, Southampton SO15 2FE, ☎ 023 8032 0320
✉ clerks@12cp.co.uk
Call Date: Nov 1985, Middle Temple
Qualifications: [MA (Oxon)]
✉ GGrant@12cp.co.uk

GRANT MR GARY STEVEN

Francis Taylor Building
Inner Temple, London EC4Y 7BY, ☎ 020 7353 8415 ✉ clerks@ftb.eu.com
Call Date: Oct 1994, Gray's Inn
Qualifications: [BA (Hons)]

GRANT MS KAREN DENISE

Invictus Chambers London
First Floor, 1 Mitre Court Buildings, Temple, London EC4Y 7BS
✉ admin@invictuschamberslondon.co.uk
Call Date: Nov 2004, Inner Temple
Qualifications: [BSc MSc]

GRANT MR KENNETH JOHN

Number 7 Harrington Street Chambers
7 Harrington Street, Liverpool L2 9YH, ☎ 0151 242 0707 ✉ clerks@7hs.co.uk
Call Date: Mar 1998, Inner Temple
Qualifications: [BA (Hons)]
✉ kenneth.grant@7hs.co.uk

GRANT MR MARCUS H JAMES

Temple Garden Chambers
1 Harcourt Buildings, Temple, London EC4Y 9DA, ☎ 020 7583 1315
✉ clerks@tgchambers.com
Call Date: Oct 1993, Lincoln's Inn
Pupil Supervisor
Qualifications: [BA (Hons)(Reading)]
✉ mg@tgchambers.com

E

GRANT MR MURRAY ROSS

13 King's Bench Walk
13 King's Bench Walk, Temple, London EC4Y 7EN, ☎ 020 7353 7204
✉ clerks@13kbw.co.uk
13 KBW
32 Beaumont Street, Oxford OX1 2NP, ☎ 01865 311066 ✉ clerks@13kbw.co.uk
Call Date: Oct 2003, Inner Temple
Qualifications: [BA (Oxon)]

GRANT MISS ORLA CATHERINE SIUBHAN

No5 Chambers
Fountain Court, Steelhouse Lane, Birmingham B4 6DR, ☎ 0845 210 5555 ✉ info@no5.com
No5 Chambers
Greenwood House, 4-7 Salisbury Court, London EC4Y 8AA, ☎ 0845 210 5555
No5 Chambers
38 Queen Square, Bristol BS1 4QS, ☎ 0845 210 5555
Call Date: July 2005, Lincoln's Inn
Qualifications: [BA (Hons)]
og@no5.com

GRANT MISS REBECCA

1 Chancery Lane
London WC2A 1LF, ☎ 0845 634 6666
✉ clerks@1chancerylane.com
Call Date: Nov 2008, Inner Temple
Qualifications: [BA (Dunelm) CPE]
rgrant@1chancerylane.com

GRANT MR THOMAS PAUL WENTWORTH

Maitland Chambers
7 Stone Buildings, Lincoln's Inn, London WC2A 3SZ, ☎ 020 7406 1200
✉ clerks@maitlandchambers.com
Call Date: Oct 1993, Middle Temple
Pupil Supervisor
Qualifications: [BA (Hons)(Bris) Dip Law (Lond)]
tgrant@maitlandchambers.com

GRANT-GARWOOD MR JOSHUA DAHREN

1 Pump Court
Elm Court, Temple, London EC4Y 7AB, ☎ 020 7842 7070
✉ (name)@pumpcourt.co.uk
Call Date: Nov 1992, Middle Temple
Qualifications: [BA (Hons)(Lancs)]
jg@1pumpcourt.co.uk

GRANTHAM MR ANDREW TIMOTHY

Kings Chambers
36 Young Street, Manchester M3 3FT, ☎ 0845 034 3444
✉ clerks@kingschambers.com
Kings Chambers
5 Park Square East, Leeds LS1 2NE, ☎ 0845 034 3444
✉ clerks@kingschambers.com
Kings Chambers
Embassy House, 60 Church Street, Birmingham B3 2DJ, ☎ 0845 034 3444
✉ clerks@kingschambers.com
Serle Court
6 New Square, Lincoln's Inn, London WC2A 3QS, ☎ 020 7242 6105
✉ clerks@serlecourt.co.uk
Call Date: Oct 1991, Middle Temple
Pupil Supervisor
Qualifications: [MA BCL (Oxon)]
agrantham@kingschambers.com

GRANVILLE STAFFORD MR ANDREW

4 King's Bench Walk
2nd Floor, 4 King's Bench Walk, Temple, London EC4Y 7DL, ☎ 020 7822 7000
✉ clerks@4kbw.co.uk
Call Date: July 1987, Gray's Inn
Pupil Supervisor
Qualifications: [MA (Cantab)]

GRASSO MISS ANTONIETTA

College Chambers
19 Carlton Crescent, Southampton, Hampshire SO15 2ET, ☎ 023 8023 0338
✉ clerks@college-chambers.co.uk
Call Date: Nov 2004, Middle Temple
Qualifications: [LLB (Hons)]
agrasso@college-chambers.co.uk

GRATION MR MICHAEL ALLAN

4 Paper Buildings
1st Floor, 4 Paper Buildings, Temple, London EC4Y 7EX, ☎ 020 7427 5200
✉ clerks@4pb.com
Call Date: Nov 2007, Inner Temple
Qualifications: [LLB (Brunel)]
mg@4pb.com

GRATTAGE MR STEPHEN TREVOR

Exchange Chambers
Oxford House, Oxford Row, Leeds LS1 3BE, ☎ 0113 203 1970
✉ spencer@exchangechambers.co.uk
Exchange Chambers
One Derby Square, Derby Square, Liverpool L2 9XX, ☎ 0151 236 7747
✉ info@exchangechambers.co.uk

E

Exchange Chambers
7 Ralli Courts, West Riverside, Manchester M3 5FT, ☎ 0161 833 2722
Furnival Chambers
32 Furnival Street, London EC4A 1JQ, ☎ 020 7405 3232
Call Date: Nov 2000, Lincoln's Inn
Qualifications: [BA (Hons) (Warw)]

GRATWICKE MISS SUSAN AILEEN

Lavenham Chambers
Rookery Farm, Lavenham (near Sudbury), Suffolk CO10 0BJ, ☎ 01787 248247
✉ susangratwicke@yahoo.co.uk
Call Date: Nov 1976, Gray's Inn
Qualifications: [LLB]
✉ susangratwicke@yahoo.co.uk

GRAVES MISS CELIA TERESE ROSANNA

Garden Court Chambers
57-60 Lincoln's Inn Fields, London WC2A 3LJ, ☎ 020 7993 7600 ✉ info@gclaw.co.uk
Call Date: July 1981, Gray's Inn
Qualifications: [BA]
✉ celiag@gclaw.co.uk

GRAY MRS ANNE FIONA MARIA

2 KBW Ipswich
1st Floor, Fisons House, 159 Princes Street, Ipswich, Suffolk IP1 1QH, ☎ 01473 287518
✉ kbwipswich@btconnect.com
Call Date: July 2005, Gray's Inn
Qualifications: [LLB (Hons) (Essex)]

GRAY MISS JENNIFER

Chambers of Mr Ami Feder
Ground Floor, Lamb Building, Temple, London EC4Y 7AS, ☎ 020 7797 7788
✉ clerks@lambbuilding.co.uk
Lamb Building
22 Ship Street, Brighton BN1 1AD, ☎ 01273 820490
✉ admin@lambbuilding.co.uk
Chambers of Mr Ami Feder
Ground Floor, Lamb Building, Temple, London EC4Y 7AS, ☎ 020 7797 7788
✉ clerks@lambbuilding.co.uk
Call Date: Oct 1992, Middle Temple
Pupil Supervisor
Qualifications: [LLB (Hons)]
✉ clerks@lambbuilding.co.uk, jennifergray@lambbuilding.co.uk

GRAY MR JOHN KEVIN

Oriel Chambers
14 Water Street, Liverpool, Merseyside L2 8TD, ☎ 0151 236 7191
✉ clerks@orielchambers.co.uk
Oriel Chambers
18 Ribblesdale Place, Preston PR1 3NA, ☎ 01772 254 764
✉ clerks@oriel-chambers.co.uk
Call Date: Oct 2001, Lincoln's Inn
Qualifications: [LLB (Hons)(L'pool) MA]
✉ john.gray@orielchambers.co.uk

GRAY MR JUSTIN HENRY WALFORD

Trinity Chambers
The Custom House, 39 Quayside, Newcastle Upon Tyne NE1 3DE, ☎ 0191 232 1927
✉ info@trinitychambers.co.uk
Trinity Chambers
Multi Media Exchange, 72-80 Corporation Road, Middlesbrough TS1 2RF, ☎ 01642 247569
✉ info@trinitychambers.co.uk
Call Date: Nov 1993, Inner Temple
Pupil Supervisor
Qualifications: [BA CPE]
✉ j.gray@trinitychambers.co.uk

GRAY MISS MARGARET OLIVIA

Brick Court Chambers
7-8 Essex Street, London WC2R 3LD, ☎ 020 7379 3550 ✉ clerks@brickcourt.co.uk
Call Date: Oct 1998, Gray's Inn
Qualifications: [BA LLM (Bruges) BCL (Oxon)]

GRAY MISS NICHOLA JAYNE

1 Hare Court
1 Hare Court, Temple, London EC4Y 7BE, ☎ 020 7797 7070 ✉ clerks@1hc.com
Call Date: Oct 1991, Lincoln's Inn
Qualifications: [BA (Hons) (Oxon)]
✉ gray@1hc.com

GRAY MR PETER HENRY ST JOHN

5 Pump Court
Ground Floor, 5 Pump Court, Temple, London EC4Y 7AP, ☎ 020 7353 2532
✉ clerks@5pumpcourt.com
Call Date: Nov 1984, Inner Temple
Pupil Supervisor
Qualifications: [BA PCL Dip Law]
✉ petergray@5pumpcourt.com

E

GRAY MR RICHARD

St Johns Buildings
24a - 28 St John Street, Manchester M3 4DJ, ☎0161 214 1500
✉clerk@stjohnsbuildings.co.uk
16 Winckley Square
Preston PR1 3JJ, ☎01772 256100
St Johns Buildings Liverpool
8th Floor India Buildings, Water Street, Liverpool L2 0XG, ☎0151 243 6000
✉clerk@stjohnsbuildings.co.uk
Call Date: Nov 1986, Middle Temple
Qualifications: [LLB (L'pool)]
✉clerk@stjohnsbuildings.co.uk, rgray@stjohnsbuildings.co.uk

GRAY MR ROGER ANDERSON

5 Pump Court
Ground Floor, 5 Pump Court, Temple, London EC4Y 7AP, ☎020 7353 2532
✉clerks@5pumpcourt.com
Call Date: July 1984, Lincoln's Inn
Pupil Supervisor
Qualifications: [MA Dip Law]
✉rogergray@5pumpcourt.com

GRAY MISS RUTH ELIZABETH

Dere Street Barristers
33 Broad Chare, Newcastle Upon Tyne NE1 3DQ, ☎0844 3351551
✉clerks@derestreet.co.uk
Call Date: July 2000, Lincoln's Inn
Qualifications: [LLB(Hons) CPE]
✉clerks@broadcharechambers.co.uk

GRAY MR STEVEN

Seven Bedford Row
7 Bedford Row, London WC1R 4BS, ☎020 7242 3555 ✉clerks@7br.co.uk
Call Date: Oct 2000, Gray's Inn
Qualifications: [BA (Oxon)]
✉sgray@7br.co.uk

GREANEY MS NICOLA CLARE

39 Essex Street
London WC2R 3AT, ☎020 7832 1111
✉clerks@39essex.com
82 King Street
Manchester M2 4WQ, ☎0161 870 9969
Call Date: Nov 1999, Inner Temple
Qualifications: [BA (Cantab)]
✉nicola.greaney@39essex.com

GREANEY MR PAUL RICHARD QC (2010)

Park Court Chambers
16 Park Place, Leeds LS1 2SJ, ☎0113 243 3277
✉clerks@parkcourtchambers.co.uk
6 King's Bench Walk
Ground Floor, 6 King's Bench Walk, Temple, London EC4Y 7DR, ☎020 7583 0410
✉clerks@6kbw.com
Call Date: Oct 1993, Inner Temple
Pupil Supervisor
Qualifications: [BA (Hons) (Dunelm)]
✉pgreaney@parkcourtchambers.co.uk

GREATOREX MS HELEN LOUISE

Zenith Chambers
10 Park Square, Leeds LS1 2LH, ☎0113 245 5438
✉clerks@zenithchambers.co.uk
Call Date: Nov 1997, Inner Temple
Qualifications: [BSc (Edin)]
✉hgreatorex@zenithchambers.co.uk

GREATOREX MR PAUL

4-5 Gray's Inn Square
Gray's Inn, London WC1R 5AH, ☎020 7404 5252 ✉clerks@4-5.co.uk
Call Date: Oct 1999, Lincoln's Inn
Pupil Supervisor
Qualifications: [MA (Hons)]
✉pgreatorex@4-5.co.uk

GREEN MR ALAN DONALD

Chambers of Mr A. Don Green
32 Durham Avenue, Cleveleys, Lancashire FY5 2DP, ☎01253 866307
✉dongreenccbb@hotmail.com
Call Date: July 2004, Inner Temple
✉dongreenccbb@hotmail.com

GREEN MISS ALISON ANNE

2 Temple Gardens
2 Temple Gardens, Temple, London EC4Y 9AY, ☎020 7822 1200
✉clerks@2tg.co.uk
Call Date: July 1974, Middle Temple
Pupil Supervisor
Qualifications: [LLM (Lond) LLB]

GREEN SIR ALLAN DAVID QC (1987)

2 Hare Court
Lower Ground, Ground, 1st & 2nd Floor, 2 Hare Court, Temple, London EC4Y 7BH, ☎020 7353 3982 ✉clerks@2harecourt.com
Call Date: June 1959, Inner Temple
Qualifications: [MA (Cantab)]
✉allangreen@2harecourt.com

GREEN MR ANDREW

30 Park Place
Cardiff CF10 3BS, ☎029 2039 8421
✉clerks@30parkplace.law.co.uk
Call Date: July 1974, Gray's Inn
Pupil Supervisor
Qualifications: [BA (Oxon) (Hons) MA (Oxon) LLB (Dublin)]
ag@30parkplace.co.uk

GREEN MR ANDREW JAMES

St Johns Buildings
24a - 28 St John Street, Manchester M3 4DJ, ☎0161 214 1500
✉clerk@stjohnsbuildings.co.uk
16 Winckley Square
Preston PR1 3JJ, ☎01772 256100
St Johns Buildings Liverpool
8th Floor India Buildings, Water Street, Liverpool L2 0XG, ☎0151 243 6000
✉clerk@stjohnsbuildings.co.uk
Call Date: Oct 1992, Gray's Inn
Qualifications: [LLB (Sheff)]
clerk@stjohnsbuildings.co.uk

GREEN MR ANDREW JAMES DOMINIC QC (2010)

Blackstone Chambers
Blackstone House, Temple, London EC4Y 9BW, ☎020 7583 1770
✉clerks@blackstonechambers.com
Call Date: Nov 1988, Inner Temple
Pupil Supervisor
Qualifications: [LLB (LSE) (Lond)]
andrewgreen@blackstonechambers.com

GREEN MR BRIAN RUSSELL QC (1997)

Wilberforce Chambers
8 New Square, Lincoln's Inn, London WC2A 3QP, ☎020 7306 0102
✉chambers@wilberforce.co.uk
Call Date: Nov 1980, Middle Temple
Qualifications: [BA BCL (Oxon)]
bgreen@wilberforce.co.uk

Types of work: Capital tax, Chancery (general), Charities, Equity, Income tax, Pensions, Professional negligence, Succession, Trusts, Wills

GREEN MR COLIN RICHARD

Cobden House Chambers
19 Quay Street, Manchester M3 3HN, ☎0161 833 6000 ✉Clerks@Cobden.co.uk
Call Date: July 1982, Lincoln's Inn
Qualifications: [BA (Leeds) DipLaw]

GREEN MR DAVID CAMERON

Atlantic Chambers
4-6 Cook Street, Liverpool L2 9QU, ☎0151 236 4421
✉info@atlanticchambers.co.uk
Call Date: Oct 1993, Lincoln's Inn
Pupil Supervisor
Qualifications: [LLB (Hons)(Lancs)]
davidgreen@atlanticchambers.co.uk

GREEN MR DORE JOHN

2 Temple Gardens
2 Temple Gardens, Temple, London EC4Y 9AY, ☎020 7822 1200
✉clerks@2tg.co.uk
Call Date: Feb 1994, Lincoln's Inn
Pupil Supervisor
Qualifications: [BA (Hons)]
dgreen@2templegardens.co.uk

GREEN MR GARRY ANTHONY

Tooks Chambers
81 Farringdon Street, London EC4A 4BL, ☎020 7842 7575 ✉clerks@tooks.co.uk
Call Date: Oct 1999, Inner Temple
Pupil Supervisor
Qualifications: [LLB]
garry.green@tooks.co.uk

GREEN MR JASON

Harcourt Chambers
1st Floor, 2 Harcourt Buildings, Temple, London EC4Y 9DB, ☎0844 561 7135
Call Date: Nov 2001, Gray's Inn
Qualifications: [BA Dip Law MA]

GREEN MR JONATHAN PAUL

Dyers Chambers
35 Bedford Row, London WC1R 4JH, ☎020 7404 1881
✉admin@dyerschambers.com
Call Date: Oct 1993, Gray's Inn
Qualifications: [B Sc (L'pool)]

E

GREEN MR KENNETH CHARLES

Broadway House Chambers
Broadway House, 9 Bank Street, Bradford, West Yorkshire BD1 1TW, ☎01274 722560
✉clerks@broadwayhouse.co.uk
Broadway House Chambers
25 Park Square West, Leeds, West Yorkshire LS1 2PW, ☎0113 246 2600
✉clerks@broadwayhouse.co.uk
Call Date: July 2001, Lincoln's Inn
Qualifications: [BA (Hons)]
clerks@broadwayhouse.co.uk

GREEN MISS LOUISE ELIZABETH

St James's Chambers
68 Quay Street, Manchester M3 3EJ,
☎0161 834 7000
✉clerks@stjameschambers.com
Call Date: July 2009, Gray's Inn
Qualifications: [LLB]

GREEN MR MARK MORRIS BERNARD

3 PB Barristers
3 Paper Buildings, Temple, London EC4Y 7EU,
☎020 7583 8055
3 PB Barristers
Royal Talbot House, 2 Victoria Street, Bristol, Avon BS1 6BB, ☎0117 928 1520
3 PB Barristers
4 St Peter Street, Winchester SO23 8BW,
☎01962 868884
✉clerks.winchester@3paper.co.uk
3 PB Barristers
23 Beaumont Street, Oxford OX1 2NP,
☎01865 793 736
3 PB Barristers
30 Christchurch Road, Bournemouth, Dorset BH1 3PD, ☎01202 292102
✉clerks.bournemouth@3paper.co.uk
Call Date: Oct 2006, Lincoln's Inn
Qualifications: [BA (Cantab)]
mark.green@3paper.co.uk

GREEN MR MICHAEL ANTHONY QC (2009)

Fountain Court Chambers
Fountain Court, Temple, London EC4Y 9DH,
☎020 7583 3335
✉chambers@fountaincourt.co.uk
Call Date: July 1987, Lincoln's Inn
Qualifications: [MA (Cantab)]
mgreen@fountaincourt.co.uk

GREEN MR NICHOLAS NIGEL QC (1998)

Brick Court Chambers
7-8 Essex Street, London WC2R 3LD,
☎020 7379 3550 ✉clerks@brickcourt.co.uk
Call Date: July 1986, Inner Temple
Recorder
Qualifications: [LLB Ph D LLM]
Nicholas.Green@brickcourt.co.uk

GREEN MR PATRICK CURTIS QC (2012)

Henderson Chambers
2 Harcourt Buildings, Temple, London EC4Y 9DB, ☎020 7583 9020
✉clerks@hendersonchambers.co.uk
Call Date: Oct 1990, Middle Temple
Pupil Supervisor
Qualifications: [BA (Cantab) MCI Arb]

GREEN MR ROBIN CHARLES DAVID MAGNUS

Cornerstone Barristers
2-3 Gray's Inn Square, Gray's Inn, London WC1R 5JH, ☎020 7242 4986
✉chambers@2-3gis.co.uk
Call Date: Oct 1992, Inner Temple
Pupil Supervisor
Qualifications: [LLB (Lond)]
rgreen@2-3gis.co.uk

GREEN MR ROGER JOHN BAILEY

Call Date: July 1972, Lincoln's Inn
Pupil Supervisor
Qualifications: [LLB (Lond)]
clerk@stjohnsbuildings.co.uk

GREEN MR SAMUEL

Park Court Chambers
16 Park Place, Leeds LS1 2SJ,
☎0113 243 3277
✉clerks@parkcourtchambers.co.uk
3 Serjeants Inn
London EC4Y 1BQ, ☎020 7427 5000
✉clerks@3serjeantsinn.com
Call Date: Oct 1998, Lincoln's Inn
Qualifications: [BA (Hons)]
clerks@parkcourtchambers.co.uk

GREEN MR TIMOTHY SINCLAIR

St Philips Chambers
55 Temple Row, Birmingham B2 5LS,
☎0121 246 7000 ✉clerks@st-philips.com
Call Date: Oct 1996, Gray's Inn
Qualifications: [BA (Oxon)]
tgreen@st-philips.com

GREEN MISS VICTORIA LOUISE

1 KBW Chambers
1 King's Bench Walk, Temple, London
EC4Y 7DB, ☎020 7936 1500
✉clerks@1kbw.co.uk
King's Bench Chambers
174 High Street, Lewes BN7 1YE,
☎01273 402600
Call Date: Oct 1994, Gray's Inn
Pupil Supervisor
Qualifications: [LLB (Hons)]
vgreen@1kbw.co.uk

GREEN MR WILLIAM HENRY DUNCAN

Trinity Chambers
Highfield House, Moulsham Street,
Chelmsford, Essex CM2 9AH,
☎01245 605040
✉clerks@trinitychambers.com
Call Date: July 1998, Middle Temple
Qualifications: [LLB (Hons)(Wolves)]

GREENAN MR JOHN JOSEPH GILCHRIST

15 New Bridge Street
London EC4V 6AU, ☎020 7842 1900
✉clerks@15nbs.com
Call Date: July 1984, Gray's Inn
Pupil Supervisor
Qualifications: [LLB (B'ham)]
john.greenan@15nbs.com

GREENAN MISS SARAH OCTAVIA

Zenith Chambers
10 Park Square, Leeds LS1 2LH,
☎0113 245 5438
✉clerks@zenithchambers.co.uk
Call Date: July 1987, Gray's Inn
Pupil Supervisor
Qualifications: [BA (Oxon)]

GREENBERG MISS JOANNA ELISHEVER GABRIELLE QC (1994)

Charter Chambers
33 John Street, London WC1N 2AT,
☎020 7618 4400
✉clerks@charterchambers.com
Call Date: July 1972, Gray's Inn
Qualifications: [LLB (Hons) (Lond)]

GREENBOURNE MR JOHN HUGO

Crown Office Chambers
2 Crown Office Row, Temple, London
EC4Y 7HJ, ☎020 7797 8100
✉mail@crownofficechambers.com
Call Date: July 1978, Gray's Inn
Pupil Supervisor
Qualifications: [MA (Cantab)]
greenbourne@crownofficechambers.com

GREENE MR PAUL MARTIN

Maidstone Chambers
33 Earl Street, Maidstone, Kent ME14 1PF,
☎01622 688592
✉clerks@maidstonechambers.co.uk
Call Date: Oct 1994, Middle Temple
Qualifications: [LLB (Hons)(Bris)]

GREENFIELD MR ALEX JEREMY

Number 7 Harrington Street Chambers
7 Harrington Street, Liverpool L2 9YH,
☎0151 242 0707 ✉clerks@7hs.co.uk
Call Date: Oct 1995, Inner Temple
Qualifications: [B.Com (L'pool) CPE (Wolves)]
jeremy.greenfield@7hs.co.uk

GREENFIELD MR PETER CHARLES

King's Bench Chambers
Wellington House, 175 Holdenhurst Road,
Bournemouth, Dorset BH8 8DQ,
☎01202 250025
Call Date: Nov 1989, Middle Temple
Pupil Supervisor
Qualifications: [BA (Lond)]
peter.greenfield@kingsbench.co.uk

GREENHALGH MISS EMMA CLARE

9 St John Street
Manchester M3 4DN, ☎0161 955 9000
✉civilclerks@9sjs.com /
criminalclerks@9sjs.com
Call Date: Nov 2010, Middle Temple
Qualifications: [LLB (Hons) (Nott'm)]
emma.greenhalgh@9sjs.com

GREENHALGH MISS JANE LOUISE

St Johns Buildings
24a - 28 St John Street, Manchester M3 4DJ,
☎0161 214 1500
✉clerk@stjohnsbuildings.co.uk
16 Winckley Square
Preston PR1 3JJ, ☎01772 256100
St Johns Buildings Liverpool
8th Floor India Buildings, Water Street,
Liverpool L2 0XG, ☎0151 243 6000
✉clerk@stjohnsbuildings.co.uk
Call Date: Mar 2004, Lincoln's Inn
Qualifications: [BA (Hons) (Manch)]
clerk@stjohnsbuildings.co.uk

E

GREENHALGH MR MICHAEL

No.6 Park Square
Leeds LS1 2LW, ☎0113 245 9763
✉Tim@no6.co.uk
Call Date: Oct 2004, Middle Temple
Qualifications: [LLB (Hons)]
✉greenhalgh@no6.co.uk

GREENHILL MR JULIAN RUTHERFORD

Wilberforce Chambers
8 New Square, Lincoln's Inn, London WC2A 3QP, ☎020 7306 0102
✉chambers@wilberforce.co.uk
Call Date: Oct 1997, Inner Temple
Pupil Supervisor
Qualifications: [MA (Cantab)]
✉jgreenhill@wilberforce.co.uk

GREENWOOD MR ALEXANDER BARTON

Apex
Harlech House, 20 Cathedral Road, Cardiff CF11 9LJ, ☎02920 232 032
✉clerks@apexchambers.net
Call Date: Mar 2002, Gray's Inn
Qualifications: [LLB (Leeds)]
✉alex.greenwood@apexchambers.net

E

GREENWOOD MISS CELESTINE LESLEY

Chavasse Court Chambers
18 Queen Avenue, Liverpool L2 4TX, ☎0151 229 2030
✉clerks@chavassechambers.co.uk
Call Date: Oct 1991, Lincoln's Inn
Qualifications: [LLB (Hons)(L'pool)]
✉celestine.greenwood@chavassechambers.co.uk

GREENWOOD MR CHRISTOPHER DAVID

Four New Square
Four New Square, Lincoln's Inn, London WC2A 3RJ, ☎020 7822 2000
✉barristers@4newsquare.com
Call Date: Nov 2009, Inner Temple
Qualifications: [LLB (Warw)]

GREENWOOD MR PAUL JEROME

4 Stone Buildings
Ground Floor, 4 Stone Buildings, Lincoln's Inn, London WC2A 3XT, ☎020 7242 5524
✉clerks@4stonebuildings.com
Call Date: Nov 1991, Lincoln's Inn
Pupil Supervisor
Qualifications: [BA (Hons) BCL (Oxon)]
✉clerks@4stonebuildings.com

GREENWOOD MISS RACHEL CLAIRE

Deans Court Chambers
24 St John Street, Manchester M3 4DF, ☎0161 214 6000 ✉clerks@deanscourt.co.uk
Deans Court Chambers
101 Walker Street, Preston PR1 2RR, ☎01772 565 600
✉preston@deanscourt.co.uk
Call Date: July 2008, Middle Temple
Qualifications: [BA (Hons) (Cantab)]

GREGG MISS REBECCA MARY

Cobden House Chambers
19 Quay Street, Manchester M3 3HN, ☎0161 833 6000 ✉Clerks@Cobden.co.uk
Call Date: Mar 2003, Lincoln's Inn
Qualifications: [LLB (Hons) (Nott'm)]
✉clerks@cobden.co.uk

GREGG MR WILLIAM JONATHAN

St Paul's Chambers
5th Floor, St Paul's House, 23 Park Square South, Leeds LS1 2ND, ☎0113 245 5866
Call Date: Oct 1990, Gray's Inn
Pupil Supervisor
Qualifications: [LLB (Hons)(Newc)]
✉jg@stpaulschambers.com

GREGO MR KEVIN CHRISTOPHER

Citadel Chambers
The Citadel, 190 Corporation Street, Birmingham B4 6QD, ☎0121 233 8500
✉clerks@citadelchambers.com
Call Date: Nov 2001, Gray's Inn
Qualifications: [BA]
✉clerks@citadelchambers.com

GREGORY MS ANN MARIE

St Paul's Chambers
5th Floor, St Paul's House, 23 Park Square South, Leeds LS1 2ND, ☎0113 245 5866
Call Date: Nov 1994, Middle Temple
Qualifications: [LLB (Hons)]

GREGORY MR BARRY GEORGE

Furnival Chambers
32 Furnival Street, London EC4A 1JQ, ☎020 7405 3232
Call Date: Nov 1987, Gray's Inn
Pupil Supervisor
✉bgregory@furnivallaw.co.uk

GREGORY MR JAMES HANS

Lincoln House Chambers
Tower 12, The Avenue North, Spinningfields, 18-22 Bridge Street, Manchester M3 3BZ, ☎0161 832 5701
✉info@lincolnhousechambers.com
Call Date: Feb 1970, Gray's Inn
Pupil Supervisor
Qualifications: [BA (Lond)]
✉james.gregory@lincolnhousechambers.com

GREGORY MR JULIAN THOMAS

Monckton Chambers
1 & 2 Raymond Buildings, Gray's Inn, London WC1R 5NR, ☎020 7405 7211
✉chambers@monckton.com
Call Date: Nov 2000, Inner Temple
Qualifications: [MA (Cantab) BCL (Oxon)]
✉jgregory@monckton.com

GREGORY MISS KAREN ANN

Exchange Chambers
One Derby Square, Derby Square, Liverpool L2 9XX, ☎0151 236 7747
✉info@exchangechambers.co.uk
Exchange Chambers
7 Ralli Courts, West Riverside, Manchester M3 5FT, ☎0161 833 2722
Exchange Chambers
Oxford House, Oxford Row, Leeds LS1 3BE, ☎0113 203 1970
✉spencer@exchangechambers.co.uk
Call Date: July 1985, Middle Temple
Pupil Supervisor
Qualifications: [BA (L'pool) Dip Law]
✉gregory@exchangechambers.co.uk

GREGORY MR PETER JOSEPH

Number 7 Harrington Street Chambers
7 Harrington Street, Liverpool L2 9YH, ☎0151 242 0707 ✉clerks@7hs.co.uk
Call Date: July 1982, Gray's Inn
Pupil Supervisor, Recorder
Qualifications: [LLB(Manch)]
✉peter.gregory@7hs.co.uk

GREGORY MR RICHARD EDWARD

42 Bedford Row
London WC1R 4LL, ☎020 7831 0222
✉clerks@42br.com
Call Date: Oct 2000, Middle Temple
Qualifications: [BA (Hons) (Oxon)]
✉richard.gregory@42br.com

GREGORY MR RICHARD HAMILTON

Ropewalk Chambers
24 The Ropewalk, Nottingham NG1 5EF, ☎0115 947 2581 ✉clerks@ropewalk.co.uk
Call Date: Oct 1993, Middle Temple
Pupil Supervisor
Qualifications: [BA (Hons)(Cantab) CPE (Notts)]
✉richardgregory@ropewalk.co.uk

GREGORY MR RUPERT GILES CONAL

Argent Chambers
5 Bell Yard, London WC2A 2JR, ☎020 7556 5500
✉briefsin@argentchambers.co.uk
Call Date: July 1998, Lincoln's Inn
Qualifications: [LLB (Hons)]
✉r.gregory@argentchambers.co.uk

GRENFELL MR GIBSON QC (1994)

6 King's Bench Walk
Ground Floor, 6 King's Bench Walk, Temple, London EC4Y 7DR, ☎020 7583 0410
✉clerks@6kbw.com
Call Date: Nov 1969, Middle Temple
Qualifications: [MA (Cantab)]
✉gibson.grenfell@6kbw.com

GRENNAN MR BARRY EDWARD

Kenworthy's Chambers
Arlington House, Bloom Street, Salford, Manchester M3 6AJ, ☎0161 832 4036
Call Date: July 1977, Lincoln's Inn
Pupil Supervisor
Qualifications: [BA (Hons)]
✉b.grennan@kenworthysbarristers.co.uk

GRENNAN MISS DEBBIE MARIA

Guildhall Chambers
23 Broad Street, Bristol BS1 2HG, ☎0117 930 9000
✉hoc@guildhallchambers.co.uk
Call Date: Oct 1997, Gray's Inn
Qualifications: [LLB (Wolves) LLM (Wolves)]
✉debbie.grennan@guildhallchambers.co.uk

GREY MISS ELEANOR MARY GRACE QC (2011)

39 Essex Street
London WC2R 3AT, ☎020 7832 1111
✉clerks@39essex.com
82 King Street
Manchester M2 4WQ, ☎0161 870 9969
Call Date: Oct 1990, Gray's Inn
Pupil Supervisor
Qualifications: [BA (Oxon) Dip Law LLM]
✉eleanor.grey@39essex.com

E

GREY MR MICHAEL HENRY JOHN

Citadel Chambers
The Citadel, 190 Corporation Street, Birmingham B4 6QD, ☎ 0121 233 8500
✉ clerks@citadelchambers.com
Call Date: Nov 1975, Middle Temple
Pupil Supervisor
Qualifications: [LLB]
mhj.grey@gmail.com

GREY MR ROBERT WILLIAM

3 PB Barristers
3 Paper Buildings, Temple, London EC4Y 7EU, ☎ 020 7583 8055
3 PB Barristers
Royal Talbot House, 2 Victoria Street, Bristol, Avon BS1 6BB, ☎ 0117 928 1520
3 PB Barristers
30 Christchurch Road, Bournemouth, Dorset BH1 3PD, ☎ 01202 292102
✉ clerks.bournemouth@3paper.co.uk
3 PB Barristers
4 St Peter Street, Winchester SO23 8BW, ☎ 01962 868884
✉ clerks.winchester@3paper.co.uk
3 PB Barristers
23 Beaumont Street, Oxford OX1 2NP, ☎ 01865 793 736
Call Date: July 1979, Gray's Inn
Pupil Supervisor
Qualifications: [BA (Lancs)]

E

GREY MR ROBIN DOUGLAS QC (1979)

QEB Hollis Whiteman
1-2 Laurence Pountney Hill, London EC4R 0EU, ☎ 020 7933 8855
✉ barristers@qebhw.co.uk
Call Date: Feb 1957, Gray's Inn
Qualifications: [LLB (Lond)]
robin.grey@qebhw.co.uk

GREY MS SHARON MONICA

Octagon House
19 Colegate, Norwich NR3 1AT, ☎ 01603 623186
✉ clerks@octagonhouse.co.uk
Call Date: Oct 2003, Inner Temple
Qualifications: [LLB (Nott'm)]
clerks@octagonhouse.co.uk

GREY MISS SIOBHAN

Doughty Street Chambers
53-54 Doughty Street, London WC1N 2LS, ☎ 020 7404 1313
✉ enquiries@doughtystreet.co.uk
Call Date: Oct 1994, Gray's Inn
Qualifications: [BA]

GRIBBIN MR LIAM DOMINIC

Fenners Chambers
3 Madingley Road, Cambridge CB3 0EE, ☎ 01223 368761
✉ clerks@fennerschambers.com
Call Date: July 2001, Inner Temple
Qualifications: [LLB (Lond) LLM (Lond)]
liam.gribbin@fennerschambers.com

GRIBBLE MR PETER JOHN

Chambers of Mr Peter Gribble
Flat D, 2 Surrendale Place, London W9 2QW, ☎ 020 7289 2744
✉ petergribble@compuserve.com
Call Date: July 1972, Gray's Inn
Pupil Supervisor

GRICE MR ALAN KEVIN

Number 7 Harrington Street Chambers
7 Harrington Street, Liverpool L2 9YH, ☎ 0151 242 0707 ✉ clerks@7hs.co.uk
Call Date: July 1977, Gray's Inn
Pupil Supervisor, Recorder
Qualifications: [LLB]
kevin.grice@7hs.co.uk

GRICE MR TIMOTHY JAMES

St John's Chambers
101 Victoria Street, Bristol BS1 6PU, ☎ 0117 923 4700
✉ clerks@stjohnschambers.co.uk
Call Date: July 1975, Middle Temple
Pupil Supervisor, Recorder
Qualifications: [MA (Oxon)]
timothy.grice@stjohnschambers.co.uk

GRIEF MISS ALISON SARAH

4 Paper Buildings
1st Floor, 4 Paper Buildings, Temple, London EC4Y 7EX, ☎ 020 7427 5200
✉ clerks@4pb.com
Call Date: Oct 1990, Inner Temple
Recorder
Qualifications: [LLB (Hons)]
ag@4pb.com

GRIEF PROF NICHOLAS JOHN

Doughty Street Chambers
Pall Mall Court, 61-67 King Street, Manchester M2 4PD, ☎ 0161 618 1066
Doughty Street Chambers
5th Floor, Broad Quay House, Prince Street, Bristol BS1 4DJ, ☎ 01179 058 717
Doughty Street Chambers
53-54 Doughty Street, London WC1N 2LS, ☎ 020 7404 1313
✉ enquiries@doughtystreet.co.uk
Call Date: Mar 1996, Gray's Inn
Qualifications: [BA PhD (Kent)]
✉ ngrief@bournemouth.ac.uk

GRIERSON MR NIGEL JONATHAN

18 St John Street
Manchester M3 4EA, ☎ 0161 278 1800
✉ clerks@18sjs.com
Call Date: Nov 1999, Middle Temple
Qualifications: [LLB (Hons)(Hull)]

GRIERSON MR ROBERT JAMES

Chambers of Mr R J Grierson
2 Kenilworth Close, Four Oaks, Sutton Coldfield, West Midlands B74 2SE, ☎ 0121 343 1460
✉ linkrgstps@btinternet.com
Call Date: Oct 1991, Middle Temple
Pupil Supervisor
Qualifications: [MA LLM (Cantab)]

GRIEVE MISS KATE MAKEPEACE

36 Bedford Row
London WC1R 4JH, ☎ 020 7421 8000
✉ chambers@36bedfordrow.co.uk
Call Date: July 2006, Lincoln's Inn
Qualifications: [BFA]
✉ kgrieve@36bedfordrow.co.uk

GRIEVES MR EDWARD JAMES

Garden Court Chambers
57-60 Lincoln's Inn Fields, London WC2A 3LJ, ☎ 020 7993 7600 ✉ info@gclaw.co.uk
Call Date: Oct 1996, Middle Temple
Qualifications: [BSc (Hons) CPE (Notts)]
✉ edwardg@gclaw.co.uk

GRIFFIN MISS FIONA ELIZABETH

Guildford Chambers
Stoke House, Leapale Lane, Guildford, Surrey GU1 4LY, ☎ 01483 539131
✉ clerks@guildfordchambers.co.uk
Call Date: July 2003, Gray's Inn
Qualifications: [LLB (Wales) LLM]

GRIFFIN MR IAN ROSS

4 Brick Court
4 Brick Court, Temple, London EC4Y 9AD, ☎ 020 7832 3200 ✉ clerks@4bc.co.uk
Call Date: Nov 1997, Middle Temple
Qualifications: [LLB (Hons) MA (Lond)]
✉ ian.griffin@4bc.co.uk

GRIFFIN MISS LYNN MYFANWY

23 Essex Street
London WC2R 3AA, ☎ 020 7413 0353
✉ clerks@23es.com
Call Date: Oct 1991, Gray's Inn
Pupil Supervisor
Qualifications: [LLB (Brunel)]
✉ lynngriffin@23es.com

GRIFFIN MISS MARGARET DELIA

Enterprise Chambers
43 Park Square, Leeds LS1 2NP, ☎ 0113 246 0391
✉ leeds@enterprisechambers.com
Enterprise Chambers
65 Quayside, Newcastle Upon Tyne NE1 3DE, ☎ 0191 222 3344
✉ newcastle@enterprisechambers.com
Call Date: July 2004, Gray's Inn
Qualifications: [BA (Cantab)]
✉ margaretgriffin@enterprisechambers.com

E

GRIFFIN MR NEIL PATRICK LUKE

9-12 Bell Yard
London WC2A 2JR, ☎ 020 7400 1800
✉ clerks@9-12bellyard.com
Call Date: Oct 1996, Gray's Inn
Qualifications: [LLB (Hons) (Lond)]
✉ n.griffin@9-12bellyard.com

GRIFFIN MR NICHOLAS JOHN QC (2012)

Five Paper Buildings
1st Floor, Five Paper Buildings, Temple, London EC4Y 7HB, ☎ 020 7583 6117
✉ clerks@5pb.co.uk
Call Date: Oct 1992, Inner Temple
Pupil Supervisor
Qualifications: [LLB (Hons) (Bris)]

GRIFFITH DR GAVAN

Essex Court Chambers
24 Lincoln's Inn Fields, London WC2A 3EG, ☎ 020 7813 8000
✉ clerksroom@essexcourt.net
Call Date: Nov 1969, Lincoln's Inn
Qualifications: [LLB (Australia) DPhil (Oxon)]
✉ ggriffith@essexcourt.net

GRIFFITH MR SHELLEY RAPHAEL WALSH

Farringdon Chambers
180 Bermondsey Street, London SE1 3TQ,
☎ 020 7089 5700
Call Date: Nov 1998, Middle Temple
Qualifications: [BSc (Hons)(Kingston)]
shelleygriffith@farringdon-law.co.uk

GRIFFITHS MR ALAN PAUL

One Essex Court
Ground Floor, One Essex Court, Temple,
London EC4Y 9AR, ☎ 020 7583 2000
clerks@oeclaw.co.uk
Call Date: Feb 1981, Gray's Inn
Pupil Supervisor
Qualifications: [MA BCL (Oxon)]
agriffiths@oeclaw.co.uk

GRIFFITHS MISS ALISON CLARE

4 King's Bench Walk
2nd Floor, 4 King's Bench Walk, Temple,
London EC4Y 7DL, ☎ 020 7822 7000
clerks@4kbw.co.uk
Call Date: Oct 2001, Inner Temple
Qualifications: [LLB (Leics)]
acg@4kbw.co.uk

GRIFFITHS MR BEN TYSSUL

Erskine Chambers
33 Chancery Lane, London WC2A 1EN,
☎ 020 7242 5532
clerks@erskinechambers.com
Call Date: Oct 2004, Middle Temple
Qualifications: [BA (Hons) Cantab]
bgriffiths@erskine-chambers.co.uk

GRIFFITHS MR BRIAN JOHN

Kings Chambers
36 Young Street, Manchester M3 3FT,
☎ 0845 034 3444
clerks@kingschambers.com
Kings Chambers
5 Park Square East, Leeds LS1 2NE,
☎ 0845 034 3444
clerks@kingschambers.com
Kings Chambers
Embassy House, 60 Church Street,
Birmingham B3 2DJ, ☎ 0845 034 3444
clerks@kingschambers.com
Call Date: Nov 1999, Gray's Inn
Qualifications: [BA (Lincoln)]

GRIFFITHS MR COURTENAY QC (1998)

Garden Court Chambers
57-60 Lincoln's Inn Fields, London WC2A 3LJ,
☎ 020 7993 7600 info@gclaw.co.uk
Call Date: July 1980, Gray's Inn
Recorder
Qualifications: [LLB (Hons)(Lond) Honorary Doctorate of Law (Leeds) Honorary Doctorate of Law (Coventry)]
courtenayg@gclaw.co.uk

GRIFFITHS MR DAFYDD

29 Bedford Row Chambers
London WC1R 4HE, ☎ 020 7404 1044
clerks@29br.co.uk
Call Date: Mar 1997, Gray's Inn
Qualifications: [LLB (Lond)]
dgriffiths@29br.co.uk

GRIFFITHS MR DAVID

St Philips Chambers
55 Temple Row, Birmingham B2 5LS,
☎ 0121 246 7000 clerks@st-philips.com
Call Date: Oct 2001, Inner Temple
Qualifications: [LLB (Notts) MBA (Sheff)]

GRIFFITHS MISS EMMA JANE

3 PB Barristers
3 Paper Buildings, Temple, London EC4Y 7EU,
☎ 020 7583 8055
3 PB Barristers
Royal Talbot House, 2 Victoria Street, Bristol,
Avon BS1 6BB, ☎ 0117 928 1520
3 PB Barristers
4 St Peter Street, Winchester SO23 8BW,
☎ 01962 868884
clerks.winchester@3paper.co.uk
3 PB Barristers
23 Beaumont Street, Oxford OX1 2NP,
☎ 01865 793 736
3 PB Barristers
30 Christchurch Road, Bournemouth, Dorset
BH1 3PD, ☎ 01202 292102
clerks.bournemouth@3paper.co.uk
Call Date: Oct 1998, Gray's Inn
Qualifications: [BA (Bristol)]

GRIFFITHS MR HUGH ROBERT JAMES

Furnival Chambers
32 Furnival Street, London EC4A 1JQ,
☎ 020 7405 3232
Call Date: Nov 1972, Inner Temple
Qualifications: [LLB (Edin)]
hgriffiths@furnivallaw.co.uk

E

GRIFFITHS MR MARTIN ALEXANDER QC (2006)

Essex Court Chambers
24 Lincoln's Inn Fields, London WC2A 3EG,
☎ 020 7813 8000
✉ clerksroom@essexcourt.net
Call Date: Nov 1986, Inner Temple
Qualifications: [MA (Oxon) Dip Law (City)]
✉ mgriffiths@essexcourt.net

GRIFFITHS MR MICHAEL DAVID

Cornwall Street Chambers
85-87 Cornwall Street, Birmingham B3 3BY,
☎ 0121 233 7500
✉ clerks@cornwallstreet.co.uk
Call Date: May 1993, Middle Temple
Qualifications: [LLB (Hons)(Wales)]

GRIFFITHS MR PATRICK THOMAS JOHN

Iscoed Chambers
86 St Helen's Road, Swansea SA1 4BQ,
☎ 01792 652988
✉ clerks@iscoedchambers.co.uk
Call Date: Nov 1972, Gray's Inn
Qualifications: [MA (Oxon)]
✉ pg@iscoedchambers.co.uk

GRIFFITHS MR PETER QC (1995)

2 Bedford Row
London WC1R 4BU, ☎ 020 7440 8888
✉ clerks@2bedfordrow.co.uk
30 Park Place
Cardiff CF10 3BS, ☎ 029 2039 8421
✉ clerks@30parkplace.law.co.uk
Call Date: Nov 1970, Gray's Inn
Qualifications: [LLB (Lond)]
✉ pgriffiths@2bedfordrow.co.uk

GRIFFITHS MR PETER ROBERT

4 Stone Buildings
Ground Floor, 4 Stone Buildings, Lincoln's Inn, London WC2A 3XT, ☎ 020 7242 5524
✉ clerks@4stonebuildings.com
Call Date: July 1977, Inner Temple
Pupil Supervisor
Qualifications: [MA (Cantab)]
✉ p.griffiths@4stonebuildings.com

GRIFFITHS MRS REBECCA ANN

Apex
Harlech House, 20 Cathedral Road, Cardiff CF11 9LJ, ☎ 02920 232 032
✉ clerks@apexchambers.net
Call Date: Oct 2005, Gray's Inn
Qualifications: [LLB (Wales)]
✉ rebecca.oakley@apexchambers.net

GRIFFITHS MR RICHARD LLOYD

King's Bench Chambers
Wellington House, 175 Holdenhurst Road, Bournemouth, Dorset BH8 8DQ,
☎ 01202 250025
Call Date: July 2000, Middle Temple
Qualifications: [LLB(Hons) (Kent) LLM (Helsinski)]
✉ richardgriffiths@yahoo.com

GRIFFITHS MR RICHARD STEPHEN

Carmarthen Chambers
30 Spilman Street, Carmarthen, Dyfed SA31 1LQ, ☎ 01267 234410
✉ richard@griffiths2833.freeserve.co.uk
Pendragon Chambers
Suite 7, J Shed, Kings Road, SA1 Waterfront, Swansea SA1 8PL, ☎ 01792 411188
✉ clerks@pendragonchambers.com
Call Date: Nov 1983, Gray's Inn
Pupil Supervisor
Qualifications: [BA]
✉ richard@griffiths2833.freeserve.co.uk

GRIFFITHS MR ROBERT QC (1993)

4-5 Gray's Inn Square
Gray's Inn, London WC1R 5AH,
☎ 020 7404 5252 ✉ clerks@4-5.co.uk
Call Date: Nov 1974, Middle Temple
Qualifications: [MA BCL (Oxon)]
✉ rgriffiths@4-5.co.uk

GRIFFITHS MR ROBERT NORTON

12 College Place
Fauvelle Buildings, 12 College Place, Southampton SO15 2FE, ☎ 023 8032 0320
✉ clerks@12cp.co.uk
Call Date: July 1988, Middle Temple
Pupil Supervisor
Qualifications: [LLB (Hons) (Reading)]
✉ RGriffiths@12cp.co.uk

GRIFFITHS MR ROBIN CLIVE

2 Dr Johnson's Buildings
2 Dr Johnson's Buildings, Temple, London EC4Y 7AY, ☎ 020 7936 2613
✉ clerks@2drj.com
Call Date: Nov 1970, Middle Temple
Pupil Supervisor
Qualifications: [BA (Hons)(Oxon) Dip Crim (Cantab)]

E

GRIFFITHS MR ROGER VAUGHAN

9 Park Place
9 Park Place, Cardiff, South Glamorgan CF10 3DP, ☎ 029 2038 2731
✉ clerks@9parkplace.co.uk
Call Date: July 1983, Gray's Inn
Pupil Supervisor
Qualifications: [LLB (Wales)]

GRIFFITHS MISS SIAN HAYLEY

3 PB Barristers
3 Paper Buildings, Temple, London EC4Y 7EU, ☎ 020 7583 8055
3 PB Barristers
Royal Talbot House, 2 Victoria Street, Bristol, Avon BS1 6BB, ☎ 0117 928 1520
3 PB Barristers
4 St Peter Street, Winchester SO23 8BW, ☎ 01962 868884
✉ clerks.winchester@3paper.co.uk
3 PB Barristers
23 Beaumont Street, Oxford OX1 2NP, ☎ 01865 793 736
3 PB Barristers
30 Christchurch Road, Bournemouth, Dorset BH1 3PD, ☎ 01202 292102
✉ clerks.bournemouth@3paper.co.uk
Call Date: Oct 1990, Inner Temple
Qualifications: [LLB (Cardiff)]
hayley.griffiths@3paper.co.uk

GRIFFITHS MISS TANIA VERONICA QC (2006)

Exchange Chambers
One Derby Square, Derby Square, Liverpool L2 9XX, ☎ 0151 236 7747
✉ info@exchangechambers.co.uk
Exchange Chambers
7 Ralli Courts, West Riverside, Manchester M3 5FT, ☎ 0161 833 2722
Exchange Chambers
Oxford House, Oxford Row, Leeds LS1 3BE, ☎ 0113 203 1970
✉ spencer@exchangechambers.co.uk
Call Date: July 1982, Gray's Inn
Recorder
Qualifications: [BA]
griffithsqc@exchangechambers.co.uk

GRIGG MR ALEXANDER HENRY CAMPBELL

Garden Court Chambers
57-60 Lincoln's Inn Fields, London WC2A 3LJ, ☎ 020 7993 7600 ✉ info@gclaw.co.uk
Call Date: July 2007, Inner Temple
Qualifications: [MA LLB BVC]
alexg@gclaw.co.uk

GRIME MR JOHN ANDREW

Pump Court Chambers
5 Temple Chambers, Temple Street, Swindon SN1 1SQ, ☎ 01793 539899
✉ clerks@3pumpcourt.com
Pump Court Chambers
Upper Ground Floor, 3 Pump Court, Temple, London EC4Y 7AJ, ☎ 020 7353 0711
✉ clerks@3pumpcourt.com
Pump Court Chambers
31 Southgate Street, Winchester, Hampshire SO23 9EB, ☎ 01962 868 161
✉ clerks@3pumpcourt.com
Call Date: Oct 1997, Lincoln's Inn
Pupil Supervisor
Qualifications: [LLB (Hons)(B'ham)]

GRIME MR MARK STEPHEN EASTBURN QC (1987)

Deans Court Chambers
24 St John Street, Manchester M3 4DF, ☎ 0161 214 6000 ✉ clerks@deanscourt.co.uk
Deans Court Chambers
101 Walker Street, Preston PR1 2RR, ☎ 01772 565 600
✉ preston@deanscourt.co.uk
2 Pump Court
1st Floor, 2 Pump Court, Temple, London EC4Y 7AH, ☎ 020 7353 5597
✉ clerks@2pumpcourt.co.uk
Call Date: Feb 1970, Middle Temple
Qualifications: [MA (Oxon) FCIArb]
grime@deanscourt.co.uk

GRIMSHAW MR NICHOLAS EDWARD

Deans Court Chambers
24 St John Street, Manchester M3 4DF, ☎ 0161 214 6000 ✉ clerks@deanscourt.co.uk
Deans Court Chambers
101 Walker Street, Preston PR1 2RR, ☎ 01772 565 600
✉ preston@deanscourt.co.uk
Call Date: Nov 1988, Inner Temple
Pupil Supervisor
Qualifications: [BA (Oxon)]
grimshaw@deanscourt.co.uk

GRIMSHAW MR RICHARD PAUL

No5 Chambers
Fountain Court, Steelhouse Lane, Birmingham B4 6DR, ☎ 0845 210 5555 ✉ info@no5.com
No5 Chambers
Greenwood House, 4-7 Salisbury Court, London EC4Y 8AA, ☎ 0845 210 5555
No5 Chambers
38 Queen Square, Bristol BS1 4QS, ☎ 0845 210 5555
Call Date: July 2010, Inner Temple
Qualifications: [BA (Warw)]

E

GRIMWOOD MR OLIVER JAMES

7 Bell Yard
London WC2A 2JR, ☎ 020 7831 0636
✉ kevintarrant@btconnect.com
Call Date: Nov 2003, Lincoln's Inn
Qualifications: [LLB (Hons) (Lond)]
✉ og@7bellyard.co.uk

GRITT MR EDMUND MATTHEW WILLIAM

3 Raymond Buildings
3 Raymond Buildings, Gray's Inn, London WC1R 5BH, ☎ 020 7400 6400
✉ clerks@3rblaw.com
Call Date: Nov 1997, Gray's Inn
Pupil Supervisor
Qualifications: [BA]
✉ edmund.gritt@3raymondbuildings.com

GROCOTT MISS SUSAN QC (2008)

Deans Court Chambers
24 St John Street, Manchester M3 4DF, ☎ 0161 214 6000 ✉ clerks@deanscourt.co.uk
Deans Court Chambers
101 Walker Street, Preston PR1 2RR, ☎ 01772 565 600
✉ preston@deanscourt.co.uk
Call Date: Nov 1986, Middle Temple
Recorder
Qualifications: [BA (Oxon)]
✉ grocott@deanscourt.co.uk

GRODZINSKI MR SAMUEL MARC QC (2011)

Matrix Chambers
Griffin Building, Gray's Inn, London WC1R 5LN, ☎ 020 7404 3447
✉ matrix@matrixlaw.co.uk / lscott@matrixlaw.co.uk
Call Date: Mar 1996, Middle Temple
Pupil Supervisor
Qualifications: [BA (Hons)]
✉ samgrodzinski@matrixlaw.co.uk

GROGAN MISS HELEN ROSE

39 Essex Street
London WC2R 3AT, ☎ 020 7832 1111
✉ clerks@39essex.com
Call Date: July 2010, Lincoln's Inn
Qualifications: [BA (Oxon) LLM (Canada)]
✉ rose.grogan@39essext.com

GROOM MR IAN JOHN

Call Date: Nov 1990, Middle Temple
Pupil Supervisor
Qualifications: [LLB (Wales)]
✉ groom@paradise-sq.co.uk

GROOME MR DAVID

QEB Hollis Whiteman
1-2 Laurence Pountney Hill, London EC4R 0EU, ☎ 020 7933 8855
✉ barristers@qebhw.co.uk
Call Date: Nov 1987, Middle Temple
Pupil Supervisor
Qualifications: [LLB (Hons) (Lond)]
✉ barristers@qebhw.co.uk

GROUND MR PATRICK QC (1981)

Chambers of Mr Patrick Ground QC
13 Ranelagh Avenue, London SW6 3PJ, ☎ 020 7736 0131 ✉ post@patrickground.com
Call Date: Feb 1960, Inner Temple
Qualifications: [MA (Cantab) MLitt (Oxon)]

GROUND MR RICHARD WILLIAM SCOTT

Cornerstone Barristers
2-3 Gray's Inn Square, Gray's Inn, London WC1R 5JH, ☎ 020 7242 4986
✉ chambers@2-3gis.co.uk
Call Date: Oct 1994, Inner Temple
Pupil Supervisor
Qualifications: [MA (Cantab) CPE]
✉ rground@2-3gis.co.uk

GROUT MR CHRISTOPHER KENNETH

15 New Bridge Street
London EC4V 6AU, ☎ 020 7842 1900
✉ clerks@15nbs.com
Call Date: July 2007, Inner Temple
Qualifications: [LLB (Newc)]
✉ Christopher.Grout@15nbs.com

GROVER MR TIM RUSSELL

Number 7 Harrington Street Chambers
7 Harrington Street, Liverpool L2 9YH, ☎ 0151 242 0707 ✉ clerks@7hs.co.uk
Call Date: Nov 1991, Inner Temple
Qualifications: [LLB (Essex)]
✉ tim.grover@7hs.co.uk

GROVES MR HUGO GERARD

Enterprise Chambers
43 Park Square, Leeds LS1 2NP,
☎0113 246 0391
✉leeds@enterprisechambers.com
Enterprise Chambers
65 Quayside, Newcastle Upon Tyne NE1 3DE,
☎0191 222 3344
✉newcastle@enterprisechambers.com
Call Date: July 1980, Gray's Inn
Pupil Supervisor
Qualifications: [LLB (Leic) LLM (Lond)]
hugogroves@enterprisechambers.com

GROVES MR MATTHEW AUSTIN

1 Mitre Court Buildings
1 Mitre Court Buildings, Temple, London EC4Y 7BS, ☎020 7452 8900
✉clerks@1mcb.com
Call Date: July 1998, Middle Temple
Pupil Supervisor
Qualifications: [LLB (Hons)(Nott'm)]
matthew.groves@1mcb.com

GRUBB MISS CATHRINE SARAH

Civitas Chambers
Global Reach, Celtic Gateway, Cardiff Bay, Cardiff CF11 0SN, ☎0845 0713 007
✉clerks@civitaslaw.com
Call Date: Oct 2007, Middle Temple
Qualifications: [LLB (Hons) (Lond)]
catherine.grubb@civitaslaw.com

GRUBECK MR NIKOLAUS

Doughty Street Chambers
53-54 Doughty Street, London WC1N 2LS,
☎020 7404 1313
✉enquiries@doughtystreet.co.uk
Call Date: Oct 2010, Inner Temple
Qualifications: [BA (Oxon) LLM (USA)]
n.grubeck@doughtystreet.co.uk

GRUCHY MR SIMON GEOFFREY

Carmelite Chambers
9 Carmelite Street, London EC4Y 0DR,
☎020 7936 6300
✉clerks@carmelitechambers.co.uk
Call Date: May 1993, Middle Temple
Qualifications: [BSc DipLaw]
sgruchy@carmelitechambers.co.uk

GRUDER MR JEFFREY NIGEL QC (1997)

Essex Court Chambers
24 Lincoln's Inn Fields, London WC2A 3EG,
☎020 7813 8000
✉clerksroom@essexcourt.net
Call Date: July 1977, Middle Temple
Qualifications: [MA (Cantab)]
jgruder@essexcourt.net

GRUFFYDD MR JOHN

Oriel Chambers
14 Water Street, Liverpool, Merseyside L2 8TD, ☎0151 236 7191
✉clerks@orielchambers.co.uk
Oriel Chambers
18 Ribblesdale Place, Preston PR1 3NA,
☎01772 254 764
✉clerks@oriel-chambers.co.uk
Call Date: Feb 1992, Gray's Inn
Pupil Supervisor
Qualifications: [LLB (Lond)]
john.gruffydd@glentonhouse.demon.co.uk

GRUMBAR MR PAUL HARRY JULIAN

Albion Chambers
Broad Street, Bristol BS1 1DR,
☎0117 927 2144
✉clerks@albionchambers.co.uk
Call Date: Nov 1974, Middle Temple
Pupil Supervisor, Recorder
Qualifications: [BA]
paul.grumbar@albionchambers.co.uk

GRUNDY MS CLARE

St Johns Buildings
24a - 28 St John Street, Manchester M3 4DJ,
☎0161 214 1500
✉clerk@stjohnsbuildings.co.uk
16 Winckley Square
Preston PR1 3JJ, ☎01772 256100
St Johns Buildings Liverpool
8th Floor India Buildings, Water Street, Liverpool L2 0XG, ☎0151 243 6000
✉clerk@stjohnsbuildings.co.uk
Call Date: July 1989, Gray's Inn
Pupil Supervisor
Qualifications: [LLB (B'ham)]
clare.grundy@stjohnsbuildings.co.uk, clerk@stjohnsbuildings.co.uk

GRUNDY MR JAMES MILTON

Gray's Inn Tax Chambers
3rd Floor, Gray's Inn Chambers, Gray's Inn, London WC1R 5JA, ☎ 020 7242 2642
✉ clerks@taxbar.com
Call Date: Nov 1954, Inner Temple
Qualifications: [MA (Cantab) FTII TEP]
✉ mg@taxbar.com

GRUNDY MR LIAM

Atlantic Chambers
4-6 Cook Street, Liverpool L2 9QU,
☎ 0151 236 4421
✉ info@atlanticchambers.co.uk
Call Date: July 1995, Inner Temple
Qualifications: [LLB (Hull) LLM (Cantab)]
✉ liamgrundy@atlanticchambers.co.uk

GRUNDY MR NICHOLAS JOHN

Five Paper
Ground Floor, 5 Paper Buildings, Temple, London EC4Y 7HB, ☎ 020 7815 3200
Call Date: Oct 1993, Gray's Inn
Pupil Supervisor
Qualifications: [MA (Cantab) MSc Dip Law]
✉ nicholasgrundy@fivepaper.com

GRUNDY MR NIGEL LAWRENCE JOHN

9 St John Street
Manchester M3 4DN, ☎ 0161 955 9000
✉ civilclerks@9sjs.com / criminalclerks@9sjs.com
Call Date: July 1983, Middle Temple
Pupil Supervisor, Recorder
Qualifications: [MA (Oxon)]
✉ nigel.grundy@9sjs.com

GRUNDY MR PHILIP MICHAEL DAVID

Call Date: July 1980, Middle Temple
Pupil Supervisor, Recorder
Qualifications: [LLB (Wales)]

GRUNDY MISS SHONA JANE

3 Temple Gardens
Lower Ground Floor, 3 Temple Gardens, Temple, London EC4Y 9AU, ☎ 020 7353 3102
✉ clerks@3tg.co.uk
Call Date: Oct 2008, Inner Temple
Qualifications: [LLB (Dunelm)]
✉ sg@3tg.co.uk

GRUNWALD MR HENRY CYRIL QC (1999)

Charter Chambers
33 John Street, London WC1N 2AT,
☎ 020 7618 4400
✉ clerks@charterchambers.com
Call Date: July 1972, Gray's Inn
Qualifications: [LLB (Lond)]
✉ henry.grunwald@charterchambers.com

GUBBAY MR JEFFREY

1 Gray's Inn Square
Ground Floor, 1 Gray's Inn Square, London WC1R 5AA, ☎ 020 7405 0001
Call Date: Oct 1992, Inner Temple
Pupil Supervisor
Qualifications: [LLB (Hons) (Bucks)]

GUEST MS HELEN

4 Breams Buildings
Chancery Lane, London EC4A 1HP,
☎ 020 7092 1900 ✉ clerks@4bb.co.uk
Call Date: Oct 1996, Lincoln's Inn
Qualifications: [BA (Hons)(Lond)]

GUEST MR NEIL

4 Breams Buildings
Chancery Lane, London EC4A 1HP,
☎ 020 7092 1900 ✉ clerks@4bb.co.uk
Call Date: July 1989, Lincoln's Inn
Pupil Supervisor
Qualifications: [LLB (Hons)]

GUEST MR PETER LIAM

187 Fleet Street
London EC4A 2AT, ☎ 020 7430 7430
✉ chambers@187fleetstreet.com
Call Date: July 1975, Inner Temple
Pupil Supervisor, Recorder
Qualifications: [BA (Hons) (Dunelm)]

GUHA MISS ANITA SANGHMITA

Seven Bedford Row
7 Bedford Row, London WC1R 4BS,
☎ 020 7242 3555 ✉ clerks@7br.co.uk
Call Date: Oct 1997, Middle Temple
Qualifications: [LLB (Hons)(Manc)]

GUILOFF MISS CAROLINA ADELA

25 Bedford Row
London WC1R 4HD, ☎ 020 7067 1500
✉ clerks@25bedfordrow.com
Call Date: Oct 1996, Middle Temple
Qualifications: [LLB (Hons)(Kent)]
✉ cguiloff@25bedfordrow.com

E

GUIRGUIS MISS SHEREN

Exchange Chambers
One Derby Square, Derby Square, Liverpool L2 9XX, ☎0151 236 7747
✉info@exchangechambers.co.uk
Exchange Chambers
7 Ralli Courts, West Riverside, Manchester M3 5FT, ☎0161 833 2722
Exchange Chambers
Oxford House, Oxford Row, Leeds LS1 3BE, ☎0113 203 1970
✉spencer@exchangechambers.co.uk
Call Date: Oct 1996, Inner Temple
Qualifications: [LLB (B'ham)]
guirguis@exchangechambers.co.uk

GULLICK MR MATHEW JAMES

3 PB Barristers
3 Paper Buildings, Temple, London EC4Y 7EU, ☎020 7583 8055
3 PB Barristers
Royal Talbot House, 2 Victoria Street, Bristol, Avon BS1 6BB, ☎0117 928 1520
3 PB Barristers
23 Beaumont Street, Oxford OX1 2NP, ☎01865 793 736
3 PB Barristers
4 St Peter Street, Winchester SO23 8BW, ☎01962 868884
✉clerks.winchester@3paper.co.uk
3 PB Barristers
30 Christchurch Road, Bournemouth, Dorset BH1 3PD, ☎01202 292102
✉clerks.bournemouth@3paper.co.uk
Call Date: July 2003, Gray's Inn
Qualifications: [MA (Oxon)]
mathew.gullick@3paper.co.uk

GULRAIZ MR YASSER

Equity Chambers
First Floor, McLaren Building, 46 Priory Queensway, Birmingham B4 7LR, ☎0121 236 5007
✉clerks@equitychambers.org.uk
Call Date: Mar 2003, Lincoln's Inn
Qualifications: [LLB (Hons)(B'ham)]
yg@e-c.org.uk

GUMBEL MISS ELIZABETH ANNE QC (1999)

1 Crown Office Row
1 Crown Office Row, Temple, London EC4Y 7HH, ☎020 7797 7500
✉mail@1cor.com
Call Date: Nov 1974, Inner Temple
Qualifications: [MA (Oxon)]
lizanne.gumbel@1cor.com

GUMBS MISS ANNETTE PATRICIA

Call Date: Oct 1994, Gray's Inn
Pupil Supervisor
Qualifications: [LLB]

GUN CUNINGHAME MR JULIAN ARTHUR

Gough Square Chambers
6-7 Gough Square, London EC4A 3DE, ☎020 7353 0924 ✉gsc@goughsq.co.uk
Call Date: Nov 1989, Lincoln's Inn
Qualifications: [MA (Edin)]
jgc@goughsq.co.uk

GUNARATNA MR KAVAN GEHAN

Enterprise Chambers
9 Old Square, Lincoln's Inn, London WC2A 3SR, ☎020 7405 9471
✉london@enterprisechambers.com
Enterprise Chambers
65 Quayside, Newcastle Upon Tyne NE1 3DE, ☎0191 222 3344
✉newcastle@enterprisechambers.com
Enterprise Chambers
43 Park Square, Leeds LS1 2NP, ☎0113 246 0391
✉leeds@enterprisechambers.com
Call Date: Nov 2004, Lincoln's Inn
Qualifications: [BA (Hons) MA (Cantab)]
kavangunaratna@enterprisechambers.com

GUNASEKARA MR PRINS

Stone Chambers
Ground Floor, 67 Queens Road, Leytonstone, London E11 1BA, ☎020 8518 7416
✉prinsgunaskara@yahoo.com
Call Date: Nov 1993, Middle Temple
Qualifications: [BA (Hons) (Lond)]

GUNNING MR ALEXANDER RUPERT QC (2012)

4 Pump Court
4 Pump Court, Temple, London EC4Y 7AN, ☎020 7842 5555
✉chambers@4pumpcourt.com
Call Date: Nov 1994, Inner Temple
Pupil Supervisor
Qualifications: [LLB LLM (Lond)]
agunning@4pumpcourt.com

GUNSTONE MR ROBERT GILES

KCH Garden Square
1 Oxford Street, Nottingham NG1 5BH, ☎0115 941 8851
✉clerks@kchgardensquare.co.uk
Call Date: July 2007, Middle Temple
Qualifications: [BA (Hons) (Newc)]

GUPTA MR AMIT

St Philips Chambers
55 Temple Row, Birmingham B2 5LS,
☎0121 246 7000 ✉clerks@st-philips.com
Call Date: July 2006, Gray's Inn
Qualifications: [LLB (Lond)]
✉agupta@st-philips.com

GUPTA MISS MAMTA

No5 Chambers
Greenwood House, 4-7 Salisbury Court, London EC4Y 8AA, ☎0845 210 5555
No5 Chambers
38 Queen Square, Bristol BS1 4QS,
☎0845 210 5555
No5 Chambers
Fountain Court, Steelhouse Lane, Birmingham B4 6DR, ☎0845 210 5555 ✉info@no5.com
Call Date: Oct 2004, Lincoln's Inn
Qualifications: [BSc (Hons) PgDI]
✉mgu@no5.com

GUPTA MR TEERTHA QC (2012)

4 Paper Buildings
1st Floor, 4 Paper Buildings, Temple, London EC4Y 7EX, ☎020 7427 5200
✉clerks@4pb.com
Call Date: Nov 1990, Inner Temple
Pupil Supervisor, Recorder
Qualifications: [LLB (Leeds)]
✉tg@4pb.com

GURDEN MISS ALISON LOUISE

1 Gray's Inn Square
Ground Floor, 1 Gray's Inn Square, London WC1R 5AA, ☎020 7405 0001
Call Date: Mar 2001, Lincoln's Inn
Qualifications: [LLB (Hons) (London) LLM]

GURNEY MR SIMON JAMES

Lincoln House Chambers
Tower 12, The Avenue North, Spinningfields, 18-22 Bridge Street, Manchester M3 3BZ,
☎0161 832 5701
✉info@lincolnhousechambers.com
Call Date: July 2006, Inner Temple
Qualifications: [BA (Hons)(Manch)]
✉simon.gurney@lincolnhousechambers.com

GURNHAM MR PAUL ANTHONY

13 King's Bench Walk
13 King's Bench Walk, Temple, London EC4Y 7EN, ☎020 7353 7204
✉clerks@13kbw.co.uk
13 KBW
32 Beaumont Street, Oxford OX1 2NP,
☎01865 311066 ✉clerks@13kbw.co.uk
Call Date: July 2004, Lincoln's Inn
Qualifications: [BA Hons (Cantab)]
✉pgurnham@13kbw.co.uk

GURSOY MR RAMIZ ALI

18 Red Lion Court
London EC4A 3EB, ☎020 7520 6000
✉chambers@18rlc.co.uk
18 Red Lion Court (Annexe)
Thornwood House, 102 New London Road, Chelmsford, Essex CM2 0RG,
☎01245 280880
Call Date: Nov 1991, Middle Temple
Pupil Supervisor
Qualifications: [BA (Hons) (Essex) Dip Law (Lond)]
✉ramiz.gursoy@18rlc.co.uk

GUTHRIE MS CARA MELISSA

Outer Temple Chambers
The Outer Temple, 222 Strand, London WC2R 1BA, ☎020 7353 6381
✉clerks@outertemple.com
Call Date: Oct 2000, Inner Temple
Pupil Supervisor
Qualifications: [MA (Cantab)]
✉cara.guthrie@outertemple.com

GUTHRIE MR JAMES DALGLISH QC (1993)

3 Hare Court
3 Hare Court, Temple, London EC4Y 7BJ,
☎020 7415 7800 ✉clerks@3harecourt.com
Call Date: July 1975, Inner Temple
Recorder
Qualifications: [BA (Oxon)]
✉james@guthrieqc.com

GUTTERIDGE MISS BEVERLEY JANE

Call Date: July 1987, Middle Temple
Qualifications: [BA (Keele)]

E

GUTTERIDGE MR CHRISTOPHER NEIL

Exchange Chambers
7 Ralli Courts, West Riverside, Manchester M3 5FT, ☎0161 833 2722
Exchange Chambers
One Derby Square, Derby Square, Liverpool L2 9XX, ☎0151 236 7747
✉info@exchangechambers.co.uk
Exchange Chambers
Oxford House, Oxford Row, Leeds LS1 3BE, ☎0113 203 1970
✉spencer@exchangechambers.co.uk
Call Date: July 2006, Inner Temple
Qualifications: [LLB (Durham)]
✉gutteridge@exchangechambers.co.uk

GUY MR JOHN DAVID COLIN

Tanfield Chambers
2-5 Warwick Court, London WC1R 5DJ, ☎020 7421 5300
✉clerks@tanfieldchambers.co.uk
Call Date: July 1972, Gray's Inn
Pupil Supervisor
Qualifications: [BA FCIArb]
✉david_guy@elawuk.com

GUY MR RICHARD PERRAN

Southernhay Chambers
33 Southernhay East, Exeter EX1 1NX, ☎01392 255777
✉clerks@southernhaychambers.co.uk
King's Bench and Godolphin (KBG)Chambers
115 North Hill, Plymouth, Devon PL4 8JY, ☎01752 221551
✉clerks@kbgchambers.co.uk
Chambers of Mr Ami Feder
Ground Floor, Lamb Building, Temple, London EC4Y 7AS, ☎020 7797 7788
✉clerks@lambbuilding.co.uk
Call Date: Nov 1970, Inner Temple
Pupil Supervisor
Qualifications: [MA (Oxon)]
✉rpguy43@hotmail.com

HABBOO MISS CAMILLE FRANCES

14 Gray's Inn Square
14 Gray's Inn Square, Gray's Inn, London WC1R 5JP, ☎020 7242 0858
✉clerks@14gis.co.uk
Call Date: July 1987, Gray's Inn
Pupil Supervisor
Qualifications: [LLB (L'pool)]
✉clerks@14graysinnsquare.co.uk

HABEL MRS JESSICA JENNET

12 College Place
Fauvelle Buildings, 12 College Place, Southampton SO15 2FE, ☎023 8032 0320
✉clerks@12cp.co.uk
Call Date: July 1991, Middle Temple
Pupil Supervisor
Qualifications: [MA (Oxon)]
✉JHabel@12cp.co.uk

HABIB MISS SHYSTA

Kenworthy's Chambers
Arlington House, Bloom Street, Salford, Manchester M3 6AJ, ☎0161 832 4036
Call Date: July 2002, Lincoln's Inn
Qualifications: [LLB (Hons)]
✉s.habib@kenworthysbarristers.co.uk

HACKER MR RICHARD DANIEL QC (1998)

South Square
3-4 South Square, Gray's Inn, London WC1R 5HP, ☎020 7696 9900
✉practicemanagers@southsquare.com
Call Date: July 1977, Lincoln's Inn
Qualifications: [MA (Cantab) LicSpec en Driot Euro (Brussels)]
✉richardhacker@southsquare.com

HACKETT MR MARTIN JOHN

Lincoln House Chambers
Tower 12, The Avenue North, Spinningfields, 18-22 Bridge Street, Manchester M3 3BZ, ☎0161 832 5701
✉info@lincolnhousechambers.com
Call Date: Feb 1995, Middle Temple
Qualifications: [LLB (Hons)(Wales)]
✉martin.hackett@lincolnhousechambers.com

HACKETT MR PHILIP GEORGE QC (1999)

Argent Chambers
5 Bell Yard, London WC2A 2JR, ☎020 7556 5500
✉briefsin@argentchambers.co.uk
Call Date: Nov 1978, Middle Temple
Pupil Supervisor
Qualifications: [BA]

HACON MR RICHARD DAVID

11 South Square
1st Floor, 11 South Square, Gray's Inn, London WC1R 5EY, ☎020 7405 1222
✉clerks@11southsquare.com
Call Date: Nov 1979, Gray's Inn
Pupil Supervisor
Qualifications: [BSc (Leeds)]

HADDEN MR JASON MARK

St Ive's Chambers
Whittall Street, Birmingham B4 6DH,
☎ 0121 236 0863
✉ clerks@stiveschambers.co.uk
Call Date: Mar 2011, Inner Temple
Qualifications: [BA (So'ton)]
✉ jason.hadden@stiveschambers.co.uk

HADDEN MR RHYS THOMAS

Field Court Chambers
5 Field Court, Gray's Inn, London WC1R 5EF,
☎ 020 7405 6114 ✉ clerks@fieldcourt.co.uk
Call Date: Nov 2006, Middle Temple
Qualifications: [BA (Hons) Manch MA (Hons) (Manch)]
✉ rhys.hadden@fieldcourt.co.uk

HADDON MISS CLARE

Ropewalk Chambers
24 The Ropewalk, Nottingham NG1 5EF,
☎ 0115 947 2581 ✉ clerks@ropewalk.co.uk
Call Date: July 1999, Gray's Inn
Qualifications: [BA (B'ham)]
✉ clarehaddon@ropewalk.co.uk

HADFIELD MS CHARLOTTE SINCLAIR

3 PB Barristers
3 Paper Buildings, Temple, London EC4Y 7EU,
☎ 020 7583 8055
Call Date: Nov 1999, Inner Temple
Qualifications: [LLB LLM (LSE)]
✉ charlotte.hadfield@3paper.co.uk

HADGILL MR CLINTON ALEXANDER

St Albans Chambers
2 - 4 St Peter's Street, St Albans, Hertfordshire AL1 3LF, ☎ 01727 843383
✉ clerks@stalbanschambers.com
Call Date: Oct 1998, Middle Temple
Qualifications: [LLB (Hons)(Herts)]
✉ ch@stalbanschambers.com

HADLEY MR RICHARD MARK ANDREW

No5 Chambers
Fountain Court, Steelhouse Lane, Birmingham B4 6DR, ☎ 0845 210 5555 ✉ info@no5.com
No5 Chambers
Greenwood House, 4-7 Salisbury Court, London EC4Y 8AA, ☎ 0845 210 5555
No5 Chambers
38 Queen Square, Bristol BS1 4QS,
☎ 0845 210 5555
Call Date: Oct 1997, Gray's Inn
Qualifications: [BA (Wolves)]
✉ rmh@no5.com

HADLEY MR STEVEN FRANK

9-12 Bell Yard
London WC2A 2JR, ☎ 020 7400 1800
✉ clerks@9-12bellyard.com
Call Date: July 1987, Inner Temple
Pupil Supervisor
Qualifications: [BA (Hons)(Wales) Phil BIB Studies BD (Hons)(Wales) Dip Law]
✉ s.hadley@9-12bellyard.com

HADRILL MR KEITH PAUL

Furnival Chambers
32 Furnival Street, London EC4A 1JQ,
☎ 020 7405 3232
Call Date: July 1977, Lincoln's Inn
Pupil Supervisor
✉ khadrill@furnivallaw.co.uk

HAEEMS MR DAVID RALPH

Carmelite Chambers
9 Carmelite Street, London EC4Y 0DR,
☎ 020 7936 6300
✉ clerks@carmelitechambers.co.uk
Call Date: Oct 1996, Inner Temple
Qualifications: [LLB]

HAFIZ MR MOHAMMED GHULAM

Chambers of Mr M G Hafiz
8 Clairview Road, London SW16 6TU,
☎ 020 8677 5778 ✉ mghafiz@hotmail.co.uk
Call Date: Nov 1970, Inner Temple
Qualifications: [BA LLB]

HAGEN MR DAKIS STEVEN

Serle Court
6 New Square, Lincoln's Inn, London WC2A 3QS, ☎ 020 7242 6105
✉ clerks@serlecourt.co.uk
Call Date: Oct 2002, Lincoln's Inn
Qualifications: [BA (Cantab)]
✉ dhagen@serlecourt.co.uk

HAGGAN MR NICHOLAS SOMERSET QC (2003)

12 College Place
Fauvelle Buildings, 12 College Place, Southampton SO15 2FE, ☎ 023 8032 0320
✉ clerks@12cp.co.uk
Outer Temple Chambers
The Outer Temple, 222 Strand, London WC2R 1BA, ☎ 020 7353 6381
✉ clerks@outertemple.com
Call Date: July 1977, Middle Temple
Recorder
✉ NHaggan@12cp.co.uk

HAGGERTY MISS ELIZABETH FRANCES

Lamb Chambers
Lamb Building, Elm Court, Temple, London EC4Y 7AS, ☎ 020 7797 8300
✉ info@lambchambers.co.uk
Call Date: Feb 1994, Lincoln's Inn
Qualifications: [LLB (Hons)]
elizabethhaggerty@lambchambers.co.uk

HAGGIS MR ANDREW PETER

Call Date: Mar 2007, Middle Temple
Qualifications: [LLB (Hons) (Sheff)]

HAGUE MR PAUL FRANCIS

15 Winckley Square
Preston PR1 3JJ, ☎ 01772 252828
✉ clerks@15winckleysq.co.uk
Call Date: July 1983, Lincoln's Inn
Qualifications: [BA]
clerks@15winckleysq.co.uk

HAIGH MR MARTIN JAMES

Sovereign Chambers
46 Park Place, Leeds LS1 2RY, ☎ 0113 245 1841
✉ clerks@sovereignchambers.co.uk
Call Date: Nov 1970, Gray's Inn
Qualifications: [LLB]
martin.haigh@sovereignchambers.co.uk

HAINES MR ALEXANDRE PHILIPPE

4 Breams Buildings
Chancery Lane, London EC4A 1HP, ☎ 020 7092 1900 ✉ clerks@4bb.co.uk
Call Date: July 2007, Lincoln's Inn
Qualifications: [LLB LLM]

HAINES DR DAVID JOHN

Doughty Street Chambers
5th Floor, Broad Quay House, Prince Street, Bristol BS1 4DJ, ☎ 01179 058 717
Doughty Street Chambers
Pall Mall Court, 61-67 King Street, Manchester M2 4PD, ☎ 0161 618 1066
Doughty Street Chambers
53-54 Doughty Street, London WC1N 2LS, ☎ 020 7404 1313
✉ enquiries@doughtystreet.co.uk
Call Date: Nov 2005, Inner Temple
Qualifications: [BmedSci BMBS University of Nottingham CPE Univ]
d.haines@doughtystreet.co.uk

HAINES MISS HANNAH

9 St John Street
Manchester M3 4DN, ☎ 0161 955 9000
✉ civilclerks@9sjs.com / criminalclerks@9sjs.com
Call Date: Nov 2005, Inner Temple
Qualifications: [BA Keble College University of Oxford CPE Coll]

HAINES MR JOHN WILLIAM

Cornerstone Barristers
2-3 Gray's Inn Square, Gray's Inn, London WC1R 5JH, ☎ 020 7242 4986
✉ chambers@2-3gis.co.uk
Call Date: Nov 1967, Middle Temple
Pupil Supervisor
Qualifications: [BA (Oxon)]

HAISLEY MR MATTHEW JOHN

9 St John Street
Manchester M3 4DN, ☎ 0161 955 9000
✉ civilclerks@9sjs.com / criminalclerks@9sjs.com
Call Date: Oct 1999, Lincoln's Inn
Qualifications: [LLB (Hons)(B'ham)]
matthew.haisley@9sjs.com

HAJI MISS SHAHEEN

The Chambers of Shaheen Haji
89F Philbeach Gardens, London SW5 9EU, ☎ 07553 867153 ✉ sheni1@hotmail.com
Call Date: Mar 1997, Middle Temple
Qualifications: [BA LLB (Hons)]

HAJIMITSIS MR ANTHONY PAUL

Zenith Chambers
10 Park Square, Leeds LS1 2LH, ☎ 0113 245 5438
✉ clerks@zenithchambers.co.uk
Call Date: Nov 1984, Inner Temple
Pupil Supervisor
Qualifications: [BA (Oxon)]
ahajimitsis@zenithchambers.co.uk

HAKME MR MUSTAPHA ADIB

Nine Bedford Row
9 Bedford Row, London WC1R 4AZ, ☎ 020 7489 2727
✉ clerks@9bedfordrow.co.uk
Call Date: Oct 2000, Middle Temple
Qualifications: [LLB (Hons) (Thames Valley) DipLaw (Lond) LLM (Lond)]
mustapha.hakme@9bedfordrow.co.uk

HALBAN MR ALEXANDER JONATHAN

3 Hare Court
3 Hare Court, Temple, London EC4Y 7BJ,
☎020 7415 7800 ✉clerks@3harecourt.com
Call Date: July 2009, Middle Temple
Qualifications: [BA (Hons) (Oxon)]
✉alexanderhalban@3harecourt.com

HALDEN MR ANGUS ROBERT

Queen Square Chambers
56 Queen Square, Bristol BS1 4PR,
☎0117 921 1966 ✉crime@qs-c.co.uk
Call Date: July 1999, Middle Temple
✉arh@qs-c.co.uk

HALE MR CHARLES STANLEY

4 Paper Buildings
1st Floor, 4 Paper Buildings, Temple, London EC4Y 7EX, ☎020 7427 5200
✉clerks@4pb.com
Call Date: Oct 1992, Middle Temple
Pupil Supervisor
Qualifications: [LLB (Hons)]
✉csh@4pb.com

HALE MRS GRACE WAI YI

KCH Garden Square
1 Oxford Street, Nottingham NG1 5BH,
☎0115 941 8851
✉clerks@kchgardensquare.co.uk
Call Date: Mar 1998, Gray's Inn
Qualifications: [LLB LLM (Lond)]

HALE MR SIMON MARK

Hardwicke
New Square, Lincoln's Inn, London WC2A 3SB, ☎020 7242 2523
✉enquiries@hardwicke.co.uk
Call Date: Oct 2006, Gray's Inn
Qualifications: [BA]
✉Simon.Hale@hardwicke.co.uk

HALE MISS VICTORIA LOUISE

Argent Chambers
5 Bell Yard, London WC2A 2JR,
☎020 7556 5500
✉briefsin@argentchambers.co.uk
Call Date: July 2006, Middle Temple
Qualifications: [LLB (Hons) (Exon)]
✉v.hale@argentchambers.co.uk

HALES MISS SALLY ANN QC (2012)

18 Red Lion Court
London EC4A 3EB, ☎020 7520 6000
✉chambers@18rlc.co.uk
18 Red Lion Court (Annexe)
Thornwood House, 102 New London Road, Chelmsford, Essex CM2 0RG,
☎01245 280880
Call Date: July 1988, Gray's Inn
Pupil Supervisor, Recorder
Qualifications: [LLB (Hons)]
✉sally-ann.hales@18rlc.co.uk

HALIM MR RAZA

Garden Court Chambers
57-60 Lincoln's Inn Fields, London WC2A 3LJ,
☎020 7993 7600 ✉info@gclaw.co.uk
Call Date: Oct 2009, Inner Temple
Qualifications: [BA (Oxon) MSc (Lond)]

HALKERSTON MR GRAEME ALEXANDER

Wilberforce Chambers
8 New Square, Lincoln's Inn, London WC2A 3QP, ☎020 7306 0102
✉chambers@wilberforce.co.uk
Call Date: Nov 1994, Middle Temple
Qualifications: [BA (Hons) LLM (USA)]

HALKERSTON MISS SALLY

Atkinson Bevan Chambers
1st Floor, 2 Harcourt Buildings, Temple, London EC4Y 9DB, ☎020 7353 2112
✉clerks@2hb.co.uk
Call Date: Oct 1994, Middle Temple
Pupil Supervisor
Qualifications: [BA (Hons)]
✉shalkerston@2hb.co.uk

HALKYARD MISS KAY

1 Garden Court Family Law Chambers
Ground Floor, One Garden Court, Temple, London EC4Y 9BJ, ☎020 7797 7900
✉clerks@1gc.com
Call Date: July 1980, Gray's Inn
Pupil Supervisor
Qualifications: [LLB (Lond)]
✉halkyard@1gc.com

HALL MR ADRIAN

5 Pump Court
Ground Floor, 5 Pump Court, Temple, London EC4Y 7AP, ☎020 7353 2532
✉clerks@5pumpcourt.com
Call Date: July 1989, Inner Temple
Qualifications: [LLB (Hull) B Ed (Hull)]
✉adrianhall@5pumpcourt.com

E

HALL MISS AJA CHANTELLE

18 Red Lion Court
London EC4A 3EB, ☎020 7520 6000
✉chambers@18rlc.co.uk
Call Date: July 2009, Middle Temple
Qualifications: [LLB (Hons) (Wales)]

HALL MR ANDREW JOSEPH QC (2002)

Doughty Street Chambers
53-54 Doughty Street, London WC1N 2LS, ☎020 7404 1313
✉enquiries@doughtystreet.co.uk
Doughty Street Chambers
Pall Mall Court, 61-67 King Street, Manchester M2 4PD, ☎0161 618 1066
Doughty Street Chambers
5th Floor, Broad Quay House, Prince Street, Bristol BS1 4DJ, ☎01179 058 717
Call Date: Feb 1991, Gray's Inn
Qualifications: [LLB (B'ham) MA (Sheff)]
a.hall@doughtystreet.co.uk

HALL MISS ANGELA RACHEL

Five Paper
Ground Floor, 5 Paper Buildings, Temple, London EC4Y 7HB, ☎020 7815 3200
Call Date: July 2000, Gray's Inn
Pupil Supervisor
Qualifications: [BA (Oxon)]
angelahall@fivepaper.com

HALL MR CHRISTOPHER MICHAEL

11 South Square
1st Floor, 11 South Square, Gray's Inn, London WC1R 5EY, ☎020 7405 1222
✉clerks@11southsquare.com
Call Date: Oct 2010, Middle Temple
Qualifications: [MSci (Hons) (Lond)]
chall@11southsquare.com

HALL MR DAVID PERCY

Zenith Chambers
10 Park Square, Leeds LS1 2LH, ☎0113 245 5438
✉clerks@zenithchambers.co.uk
Call Date: July 1980, Gray's Inn
Pupil Supervisor
Qualifications: [BA]
dhall@zenithchambers.co.uk

HALL MR DEREK

Amicus Chambers
Queens Court, Newport Road, Middlesbrough TS1 5EH, ☎01642 876334
✉amicus.clerk@amicuschambers.co.uk
Call Date: Nov 1994, Middle Temple
Pupil Supervisor
Qualifications: [LLB (Hons)]

HALL MR JAMES EDWARD

Cornwall Street Chambers
85-87 Cornwall Street, Birmingham B3 3BY, ☎0121 233 7500
✉clerks@cornwallstreet.co.uk
Call Date: Oct 2000, Lincoln's Inn
Qualifications: [LLB (Hons) (Cardiff)]

HALL MR JEREMY JOHN

Becket Chambers
17 New Dover Road, Canterbury, Kent CT1 3AS, ☎01227 786331
✉clerks@becket-chambers.co.uk
Call Date: Feb 1988, Gray's Inn
Qualifications: [LLB (Hons) (UEA)]
jhall@becket-chambers.co.uk

HALL MISS JOANNA MARY

14 Gray's Inn Square
14 Gray's Inn Square, Gray's Inn, London WC1R 5JP, ☎020 7242 0858
✉clerks@14gis.co.uk
Call Date: Nov 1973, Inner Temple
Pupil Supervisor
Qualifications: [LLB (Lond)]
jh@14graysinnsquare.co.uk

HALL MR JONATHAN RUPERT

6 King's Bench Walk
Ground Floor, 6 King's Bench Walk, Temple, London EC4Y 7DR, ☎020 7583 0410
✉clerks@6kbw.com
9-12 Bell Yard
London WC2A 2JR, ☎020 7400 1800
✉clerks@9-12bellyard.com
Call Date: Nov 1994, Inner Temple
Pupil Supervisor
Qualifications: [BA (Oxon) CPE (Lond)]

HALL MR MATTHEW

Kings Chambers
36 Young Street, Manchester M3 3FT, ☎0845 034 3444
✉clerks@kingschambers.com
Kings Chambers
5 Park Square East, Leeds LS1 2NE, ☎0845 034 3444
✉clerks@kingschambers.com
Kings Chambers
Embassy House, 60 Church Street, Birmingham B3 2DJ, ☎0845 034 3444
✉clerks@kingschambers.com
Call Date: Mar 1999, Middle Temple
Qualifications: [BA (Hons)(Oxon)]
mhall@kingschambers.com

HALL MRS MELANIE RUTH QC (2002)

Monckton Chambers
1 & 2 Raymond Buildings, Gray's Inn, London WC1R 5NR, ☎020 7405 7211
✉chambers@monckton.com
Call Date: Nov 1982, Inner Temple
Qualifications: [BA Law (Dunelm)]
✉mhall@monckton.com

HALL MR MICHAEL LEBERT

Garden Court Chambers
57-60 Lincoln's Inn Fields, London WC2A 3LJ, ☎020 7993 7600 ✉info@gclaw.co.uk
Call Date: July 1983, Middle Temple
Qualifications: [BA]
✉michaelha@gclaw.co.uk

HALL MR MICHAEL RICHARD

Pump Court Chambers
5 Temple Chambers, Temple Street, Swindon SN1 1SQ, ☎01793 539899
✉clerks@3pumpcourt.com
Pump Court Chambers
Upper Ground Floor, 3 Pump Court, Temple, London EC4Y 7AJ, ☎020 7353 0711
✉clerks@3pumpcourt.com
Pump Court Chambers
31 Southgate Street, Winchester, Hampshire SO23 9EB, ☎01962 868 161
✉clerks@3pumpcourt.com
Call Date: Oct 1996, Inner Temple
Pupil Supervisor
Qualifications: [LLB (Hons)(Reading)]
✉mrh@3pumpcourt.com

HALL MR NICHOLAS

Westgate Chambers
64 High Street, Lewes, East Sussex BN7 1XG, ☎01273 480510
✉clerks@westgate-chambers.co.uk
Call Date: July 1973, Gray's Inn
Pupil Supervisor
Qualifications: [MA (Oxon)]
✉nhall@westgate-chambers.co.uk

HALL MISS NICOLA JAYNE

Goldsmith Chambers
Ground Floor, Goldsmith Building, Temple, London EC4Y 7BL, ☎020 7353 6802
✉clerks@goldsmithchambers.com
Call Date: July 2006, Gray's Inn
Qualifications: [BSc (Leeds)]
✉n.hall@goldsmithchambers.law.co.uk

HALL MR NIGEL DOMINIC

King's Bench and Godolphin (KBG)Chambers
115 North Hill, Plymouth, Devon PL4 8JY, ☎01752 221551
✉clerks@kbgchambers.co.uk
Cornwall Street Chambers
85-87 Cornwall Street, Birmingham B3 3BY, ☎0121 233 7500
✉clerks@cornwallstreet.co.uk
Call Date: July 2001, Inner Temple
Qualifications: [RMN (Bath) LLB (So'ton)]
✉nigel.hall@kingsbenchchambers.co.uk

HALL MR RICHARD ANDREW

Pump Court Chambers
31 Southgate Street, Winchester, Hampshire SO23 9EB, ☎01962 868 161
✉clerks@3pumpcourt.com
Pump Court Chambers
Upper Ground Floor, 3 Pump Court, Temple, London EC4Y 7AJ, ☎020 7353 0711
✉clerks@3pumpcourt.com
Pump Court Chambers
5 Temple Chambers, Temple Street, Swindon SN1 1SQ, ☎01793 539899
✉clerks@3pumpcourt.com
Call Date: Nov 1995, Inner Temple
Qualifications: [LLB (Soton)]
✉rh@3pumpcourt.com

HALL MR TOBY RALPH

1 Pump Court
Elm Court, Temple, London EC4Y 7AB, ☎020 7842 7070
✉(name)@pumpcourt.co.uk
Call Date: July 2008, Inner Temple
Qualifications: [BA MA (York)]

HALL MRS YASMIN MUNIR

Guildhall Chambers Portsmouth
Prudential Buildings, 16 Guildhall Walk, Portsmouth, Hampshire PO1 2DE, ☎023 9275 2400
✉clerks@gcp-barristers.com
Call Date: Nov 1993, Lincoln's Inn
Qualifications: [LLB (Hons)]
✉GCPClerks@fsmail.net

HALL TAYLOR MR ALEXANDER EDWARD

Four New Square
Four New Square, Lincoln's Inn, London WC2A 3RJ, ☎020 7822 2000
✉barristers@4newsquare.com
Call Date: Oct 1996, Inner Temple
Pupil Supervisor
Qualifications: [BA (Hons)(Bris) CPE (Lond)]
✉a.halltaylor@4newsquare.com

E

HALLAM MR JACOB WILLIAM

6 King's Bench Walk
Ground Floor, 6 King's Bench Walk, Temple, London EC4Y 7DR, ☎ 020 7583 0410
✉ clerks@6kbw.com
Call Date: Oct 1996, Gray's Inn
Pupil Supervisor
Qualifications: [MA (Cantab) Dip Law]
jacob.hallam@6kbw.com

HALLETT MISS KATHERINE ELIZABETH

13 Old Square Chambers
Ground Floor, 14 Old Square, Lincoln's Inn, London WC2A 3UE, ☎ 020 7831 4445
✉ clerks@13oldsquare.com
Call Date: Oct 2006, Lincoln's Inn
Qualifications: [BA (Oxon)]

HALLIDAY MR IAN NICOLAS

Queen Square Chambers
56 Queen Square, Bristol BS1 4PR, ☎ 0117 921 1966 ✉ crime@qs-c.co.uk
Call Date: Nov 1989, Lincoln's Inn
Pupil Supervisor
Qualifications: [LLB (Leeds)]

E

HALLIDAY MR PATRICK JAMES TOLLEMACHE

11 King's Bench Walk
11 King's Bench Walk, Temple, London EC4Y 7EQ, ☎ 020 7632 8500
✉ clerksroom@11kbw.com
Call Date: July 2005, Gray's Inn
Qualifications: [BA]
patrick.halliday@11kbw.com

HALLIDAY-DAVIS MS DEBORAH LEE

Carmelite Chambers
9 Carmelite Street, London EC4Y 0DR, ☎ 020 7936 6300
✉ clerks@carmelitechambers.co.uk
Call Date: Nov 1999, Inner Temple
Pupil Supervisor
Qualifications: [LLB]
lhalliday-davis@carmelitechambers.co.uk

HALLIGAN MR RODNEY LEWTON

Number 7 Harrington Street Chambers
7 Harrington Street, Liverpool L2 9YH, ☎ 0151 242 0707 ✉ clerks@7hs.co.uk
Call Date: July 1972, Gray's Inn
Qualifications: [LLB]
rodney.halligan@7hs.co.uk

HALLIN MR CONRAD LAURENCE

3 Serjeants Inn
London EC4Y 1BQ, ☎ 020 7427 5000
✉ clerks@3serjeantsinn.com
Call Date: July 2004, Inner Temple
challin@3serjeantsinn.com

HALLISSEY MS CAROLINE MARIA

Outer Temple Chambers
The Outer Temple, 222 Strand, London WC2R 1BA, ☎ 020 7353 6381
✉ clerks@outertemple.com
Call Date: Feb 1990, Inner Temple
Qualifications: [BA (UEA) Dip Law MA]
caroline.hallissey@outertemple.com

HALLISSEY MR JOHN JAMES ANTHONY

KCH Garden Square
1 Oxford Street, Nottingham NG1 5BH, ☎ 0115 941 8851
✉ clerks@kchgardensquare.co.uk
Call Date: July 2003, Middle Temple
Qualifications: [LLB Hons (De Mont) LLM (Lond)]
jhallissey@kchgardensquare.co.uk

HALLIWELL MR MARK GARETH

Kings Chambers
36 Young Street, Manchester M3 3FT, ☎ 0845 034 3444
✉ clerks@kingschambers.com
Kings Chambers
5 Park Square East, Leeds LS1 2NE, ☎ 0845 034 3444
✉ clerks@kingschambers.com
Kings Chambers
Embassy House, 60 Church Street, Birmingham B3 2DJ, ☎ 0845 034 3444
✉ clerks@kingschambers.com
Call Date: July 1985, Lincoln's Inn
Pupil Supervisor, Recorder
Qualifications: [BSc (Econ) Diploma]
mhalliwell@kingschambers.com

HALLIWELL MR TOBY GEORGE

Unity Street Chambers
5 Unity Street, College Green, Bristol BS1 5HH, ☎ 0117 906 9789
✉ chambers@unitystreetchambers.com
Call Date: Nov 1992, Middle Temple
Qualifications: [LLB (Hons) (Manch)]
toby.halliwell@unitystreetchambers.com

HALLOWES MR RUPERT JOHN MICHAEL

3 Temple Gardens
Lower Ground Floor, 3 Temple Gardens, Temple, London EC4Y 9AU, ☎020 7353 3102
✉clerks@3tg.co.uk
Call Date: Oct 1995, Inner Temple
Qualifications: [BA (Bris) CPE]
rjh@3tg.co.uk

HALLWORTH MR ANDREW MARC

Carmelite Chambers
9 Carmelite Street, London EC4Y 0DR,
☎020 7936 6300
✉clerks@carmelitechambers.co.uk
Call Date: Mar 2002, Gray's Inn
Qualifications: [BA (Leeds)]
ahallworth@carmelitechambers.co.uk

HALPERN MR DAVID ANTHONY QC (2006)

Four New Square
Four New Square, Lincoln's Inn, London WC2A 3RJ, ☎020 7822 2000
✉barristers@4newsquare.com
Call Date: July 1978, Gray's Inn
Qualifications: [MA (Oxon)]
d.halpern@4newsquare.com

HALSALL MISS LOUISE KIM

Linenhall Chambers
1 Stanley Place, Chester CH1 2LU,
☎01244 348282
✉clerks@linenhallchambers.co.uk
Call Date: July 1982, Middle Temple
Pupil Supervisor
kimhalsall2004@yahoo.co.uk

HALSALL MR STEPHEN JAMES

Warwick House Chambers
8 Warwick Court, Warwick House Chambers, Gray's Inn, London WC1R 5DJ,
☎020 7430 2323
✉clerks@warwickhousechambers.com
Call Date: Oct 1997, Inner Temple
Qualifications: [BA (Cantab) Dip Law CPE]

HALSEY MR MARK STEPHEN

2 Bedford Row
London WC1R 4BU, ☎020 7440 8888
✉clerks@2bedfordrow.co.uk
Call Date: Feb 1974, Inner Temple
Qualifications: [LLB (Bris)]
mhalsey@2bedfordrow.co.uk

HALSTEAD MR ROBIN BERNARD

One Essex Court
1st Floor, Temple, London EC4Y 9AR,
☎020 7936 3030 ✉clerks@1ec.co.uk
Call Date: Oct 1996, Inner Temple
Qualifications: [BA (Oxon)]
rhalstead@1ec.co.uk

HAM MR NICHOLAS TREHARNE

Dyers Chambers
35 Bedford Row, London WC1R 4JH,
☎020 7404 1881
✉admin@dyerschambers.com
Call Date: Oct 1997, Middle Temple
Qualifications: [BA (Hons)(Bris) CPE]
nick.ham@dyerschambers.com

HAM MR ROBERT WALLACE QC (1994)

Wilberforce Chambers
8 New Square, Lincoln's Inn, London WC2A 3QP, ☎020 7306 0102
✉chambers@wilberforce.co.uk
Call Date: Nov 1973, Middle Temple
Qualifications: [BCL BA (Oxon)]
rham@wilberforce.co.uk

Types of work: Chancery (general), Charities, Equity, Pensions, Succession, Trusts, Wills

HAMBLIN MR NICHOLAS HOWARD

Westgate Chambers
64 High Street, Lewes, East Sussex BN7 1XG,
☎01273 480510
✉clerks@westgate-chambers.co.uk
Call Date: Nov 1981, Lincoln's Inn
Pupil Supervisor
Qualifications: [LLB (Hons)]
nh@westgate-chambers.co.uk

HAMER MR CHARLES HENRY

Citadel Chambers
The Citadel, 190 Corporation Street, Birmingham B4 6QD, ☎0121 233 8500
✉clerks@citadelchambers.com
Call Date: Mar 2007, Middle Temple
Qualifications: [LLB (Hons) (Lond) LLM (Bris)]
chh_bar@yahoo.co.uk

HAMER MR GEORGE CLEMENS

8 New Square
8 New Square, Lincoln's Inn, London WC2A 3QP, ☎020 7405 4321
✉clerks@8newsquare.co.uk
Call Date: Nov 1974, Gray's Inn
Pupil Supervisor
Qualifications: [BSc ARCS (Lond)]

E

Types of work: Competition law, Confidential information, Copyright, Defamation, Design, EC competition law, Entertainment, Franchising, Information technology, Intellectual property, Malicious falsehood, Media and entertainment, Patents, Professional negligence, Sport, Telecommunications, Trade secrets, Trademarks

HAMER MR MICHAEL HOWARD KENNETH

Henderson Chambers
2 Harcourt Buildings, Temple, London EC4Y 9DB, ☎ 020 7583 9020
✉ clerks@hendersonchambers.co.uk
Call Date: Apr 1975, Inner Temple
Pupil Supervisor, Recorder

HAMES MR CHRISTOPHER WILLIAM

4 Paper Buildings
1st Floor, 4 Paper Buildings, Temple, London EC4Y 7EX, ☎ 020 7427 5200
✉ clerks@4pb.com
Call Date: July 1987, Inner Temple
Pupil Supervisor
Qualifications: [LLB (Sheff)]
✉ ch@4pb.com

HAMEY MR JOHN ANTHONY

East Anglian Chambers
15 The Close, Norwich, Norfolk NR1 4DZ, ☎ 01473 214481 ✉ norwich@ealaw.co.uk
East Anglian Chambers
Gresham House, 5 Museum Street, Ipswich, Suffolk IP1 1HQ, ☎ 01473 214481
✉ ipswich@ealaw.co.uk
East Anglian Chambers
140 New London Road, Chelmsford, Essex CM2 0AW, ☎ 01473 214481
✉ chelmsford@ealaw.co.uk
Call Date: July 1979, Inner Temple
Pupil Supervisor
Qualifications: [MA (Cantab)]
✉ johnhamey@ealaw.co.uk

HAMID MRS BEEBEE NAZMOON

Clapham Law Chambers
85 Landor Road, Clapham North, London SW9 9RT, ☎ 020 7978 8482
✉ DANNY@claphamlawchambers.co.uk
Call Date: July 1980, Lincoln's Inn
Pupil Supervisor
Qualifications: [BA (Hons) (Lond)]

HAMID MS RUBY

18 Red Lion Court
London EC4A 3EB, ☎ 020 7520 6000
✉ chambers@18rlc.co.uk
18 Red Lion Court (Annexe)
Thornwood House, 102 New London Road, Chelmsford, Essex CM2 0RG,
☎ 01245 280880
Call Date: Oct 2002, Lincoln's Inn
Qualifications: [MA Hons (Cantab) Pg Dip Law BVC]
✉ ruby.hamid@18rlc.co.uk

HAMILL MR HUGH ANTHONY

12 King's Bench Walk
12 King's Bench Walk, Temple, London EC4Y 7EL, ☎ 020 7583 0811
Call Date: July 1988, Inner Temple
Qualifications: [BA (Dublin) Dip Law (Lond)]
✉ hamill@12kbw.co.uk

HAMILTON MISS AMANDA JEAN

Furnival Chambers
32 Furnival Street, London EC4A 1JQ,
☎ 020 7405 3232
Call Date: Oct 1995, Lincoln's Inn
Pupil Supervisor
Qualifications: [BA (Hons)(Lond)]

HAMILTON MISS ANNABEL CLAIRE LOUISE

St Ive's Chambers
Whittall Street, Birmingham B4 6DH,
☎ 0121 236 0863
✉ clerks@stiveschambers.co.uk
Call Date: July 2009, Gray's Inn
Qualifications: [LLB]
✉ annabel.hamilton@stiveschambers.co.uk

HAMILTON MS CAROLYN PAULA

1 KBW Chambers
1 King's Bench Walk, Temple, London EC4Y 7DB, ☎ 020 7936 1500
✉ clerks@1kbw.co.uk
Call Date: July 1996, Gray's Inn
Qualifications: [LLB (Bris)]
✉ chamilton@1kbw.co.uk

HAMILTON MR GAVIN

3 PB Barristers
3 Paper Buildings, Temple, London EC4Y 7EU, ☎ 020 7583 8055
3 PB Barristers
Royal Talbot House, 2 Victoria Street, Bristol, Avon BS1 6BB, ☎ 0117 928 1520
3 PB Barristers
23 Beaumont Street, Oxford OX1 2NP, ☎ 01865 793 736

3 PB Barristers
4 St Peter Street, Winchester SO23 8BW,
☎01962 868884
✉clerks.winchester@3paper.co.uk
3 PB Barristers
30 Christchurch Road, Bournemouth, Dorset BH1 3PD, ☎01202 292102
✉clerks.bournemouth@3paper.co.uk
Call Date: July 1979, Gray's Inn
Pupil Supervisor
Qualifications: [BA (Oxon)]
gavin.hamilton@3pb.co.uk

HAMILTON MR JAIME RICHARD

9 St John Street
Manchester M3 4DN, ☎0161 955 9000
✉civilclerks@9sjs.com / criminalclerks@9sjs.com
Call Date: Oct 1993, Gray's Inn
Pupil Supervisor
Qualifications: [LLB (Wales)]

HAMILTON MR JOHN CONRAD

Field Court Chambers
5 Field Court, Gray's Inn, London WC1R 5EF,
☎020 7405 6114 ✉clerks@fieldcourt.co.uk
Call Date: Nov 1988, Gray's Inn
Pupil Supervisor
Qualifications: [BSc (Lond) Dip Law]
john.hamilton@fieldcourt.co.uk

HAMILTON MR NIGEL

Broadway House Chambers
Broadway House, 9 Bank Street, Bradford, West Yorkshire BD1 1TW, ☎01274 722560
✉clerks@broadwayhouse.co.uk
Broadway House Chambers
25 Park Square West, Leeds, West Yorkshire LS1 2PW, ☎0113 246 2600
✉clerks@broadwayhouse.co.uk
Call Date: Oct 2004, Inner Temple
Qualifications: [BSc CPE]
clerks@broadwayhouse.co.uk

HAMILTON MR NIGEL JOHN MAWDESLEY QC (1981)

New Bailey Chambers
4th Floor, Corn Exchange, Fenwick Street, Liverpool, Merseyside L2 7QS,
☎0151 236 9402 ✉clerks@newbailey.com
Call Date: Nov 1965, Inner Temple
Qualifications: [MA (Cantab)]

HAMILTON MRS PENELOPE ANN

Pump Court Tax Chambers
16 Bedford Row, London WC1R 4EF,
☎020 7414 8080 ✉clerks@pumptax.com
Call Date: July 1972, Gray's Inn
Qualifications: [LLB (Hons) (Bris) FTII]
phamilton@pumptax.com

Types of work: Corporation tax, Customs, VAT

HAMILTON MR PETER BERNARD

4 Pump Court
4 Pump Court, Temple, London EC4Y 7AN,
☎020 7842 5555
✉chambers@4pumpcourt.com
Call Date: Feb 1968, Inner Temple
Pupil Supervisor
Qualifications: [BA (Rhodes) MA (Cantab)]
phamilton@4pumpcourt.com

HAMILTON MISS PHILIPPA ANNE

Fountain Court Chambers
Fountain Court, Temple, London EC4Y 9DH,
☎020 7583 3335
✉chambers@fountaincourt.co.uk
Call Date: Oct 1996, Lincoln's Inn
Qualifications: [MA (Hons)(Oxon) Dip in Law (Lond)]
ph@fountaincourt.co.uk

HAMILTON MR RUPERT ARTHUR ROBERT

20 Essex Street
London WC2R 3AL, ☎020 7842 1200
✉clerks@20essexst.com
Call Date: July 2010, Middle Temple
Qualifications: [BA (Hons) (Oxon)]
rhamilton@20essexst.com

HAMILTON MR WILLIAM JAMES

9 St John Street
Manchester M3 4DN, ☎0161 955 9000
✉civilclerks@9sjs.com / criminalclerks@9sjs.com
Call Date: Nov 2008, Lincoln's Inn
Qualifications: [LLB (Manch)]

HAMILTON-SHIELD MISS ANNA-MARIA

Charter Chambers
33 John Street, London WC1N 2AT,
☎020 7618 4400
✉clerks@charterchambers.com
Call Date: Nov 1989, Middle Temple
Qualifications: [LLB (Hons)]
anna.hamilton-shield@charterchambers.com

E

HAMLIN MR PATRICK LINDOP

42 Bedford Row
London WC1R 4LL, ☎ 020 7831 0222
✉ clerks@42br.com
Call Date: Nov 1970, Gray's Inn
Pupil Supervisor
✉ patrick.hamlin@42br.com

HAMMERTON MR ALASTAIR ROLF

1 Chancery Lane
London WC2A 1LF, ☎ 0845 634 6666
✉ clerks@1chancerylane.com
Call Date: July 1983, Inner Temple
Pupil Supervisor, Recorder
Qualifications: [MA (Cantab) LLM (USA)]

HAMMETT MR MICHAEL GREVILLE

9 Park Place
9 Park Place, Cardiff, South Glamorgan
CF10 3DP, ☎ 029 2038 2731
✉ clerks@9parkplace.co.uk
Call Date: July 2001, Gray's Inn
Qualifications: [LLB (Southampton)]
✉ clerks@9parkplace.co.uk

E

HAMMOND MRS CLAIRE LOUISE

St James's Chambers
68 Quay Street, Manchester M3 3EJ,
☎ 0161 834 7000
✉ clerks@stjameschambers.com
Call Date: July 2003, Lincoln's Inn
Qualifications: [LLB Hons (Manch)]
✉ claire.hammond@stjameschambers.com

HAMMOND MR DAVID EUAN

Quadrant Chambers
Quadrant House, 10 Fleet Street, London
EC4Y 1AU, ☎ 020 7583 4444
✉ info@quadrantchambers.com
Call Date: Oct 2006, Middle Temple
Qualifications: [BSc (Hons) (L'pool) Dip Law GDL (Lond)]
✉ david.hammond@quadrantchambers.com

HAMMOND MR FAYAZ BENJAMIN

St James's Chambers
68 Quay Street, Manchester M3 3EJ,
☎ 0161 834 7000
✉ clerks@stjameschambers.com
Call Date: Oct 1999, Gray's Inn
Pupil Supervisor
Qualifications: [LLB (Sheff)]
✉ fayaz.hammond@stjameschambers.com

HAMMOND MISS SARA LOUISE

14 Gray's Inn Square
14 Gray's Inn Square, Gray's Inn, London
WC1R 5JP, ☎ 020 7242 0858
✉ clerks@14gis.co.uk
Call Date: Mar 2009, Middle Temple
Qualifications: [BA (Hons) (Keele)]
✉ slh@14graysinnsquare.co.uk

HAMMOND MR SEAN FRANCIS

2 Bedford Row
London WC1R 4BU, ☎ 020 7440 8888
✉ clerks@2bedfordrow.co.uk
Call Date: Oct 1991, Lincoln's Inn
Pupil Supervisor
Qualifications: [LLB (Hons)]
✉ shammond@2bedfordrow.co.uk

HAMMOND MR TIM MARK

Tanfield Chambers
2-5 Warwick Court, London WC1R 5DJ,
☎ 020 7421 5300
✉ clerks@tanfieldchambers.co.uk
Call Date: Mar 2003, Lincoln's Inn
Qualifications: [MA (Hons) (Oxon) LLM]
✉ thammond@tanfieldchambers.co.uk

HAMMOND MR TIMOTHY DARREN

Rougemont Chambers
Victory House, Dean Clarke Gardens,
Southernhay East, Exeter EX2 4AA,
☎ 01392 208484
✉ clerks@rougemontchambers.co.uk
Call Date: July 2007, Inner Temple
Qualifications: [BA (Hons) (Bris) PG Dip]
✉ thammond@rougemontchambers.co.uk

HAMPTON MR PETER JOSEPH GEORGE

Broadway House Chambers
Broadway House, 9 Bank Street, Bradford,
West Yorkshire BD1 1TW, ☎ 01274 722560
✉ clerks@broadwayhouse.co.uk
Broadway House Chambers
25 Park Square West, Leeds, West Yorkshire
LS1 2PW, ☎ 0113 246 2600
✉ clerks@broadwayhouse.co.uk
Call Date: July 2003, Gray's Inn
Qualifications: [LLB (Kent)]
✉ clerks@broadwayhouse.co.uk

HANBURY MR WILLIAM EDMUND

Exchange Chambers
7 Ralli Courts, West Riverside, Manchester
M3 5FT, ☎ 0161 833 2722
Exchange Chambers
One Derby Square, Derby Square, Liverpool
L2 9XX, ☎ 0151 236 7747
✉ info@exchangechambers.co.uk

Exchange Chambers
Oxford House, Oxford Row, Leeds LS1 3BE,
☎0113 203 1970
✉spencer@exchangechambers.co.uk
Call Date: Nov 1985, Inner Temple
Pupil Supervisor
Qualifications: [LLB (Manch)]
hanbury@exchangechambers.co.uk

HANCOCK MR CHRISTOPHER PATRICK QC (2000)

20 Essex Street
London WC2R 3AL, ☎020 7842 1200
✉clerks@20essexst.com
Call Date: July 1983, Middle Temple
Recorder
Qualifications: [MA (Cantab) LLM (USA)]
clerks@20essexst.com

HANCOCK MS MARIA

Westgate Chambers
64 High Street, Lewes, East Sussex BN7 1XG,
☎01273 480510
✉clerks@westgate-chambers.co.uk
Call Date: Oct 1995, Gray's Inn
Pupil Supervisor
Qualifications: [BA (Hons)]
mh@westgate-chambers.co.uk

HANCOX MISS LISA MARIE

Cornwall Street Chambers
85-87 Cornwall Street, Birmingham B3 3BY,
☎0121 233 7500
✉clerks@cornwallstreet.co.uk
Call Date: Oct 2006, Inner Temple
Qualifications: [LLB (Sheff)]
lisa.hancox@cornwallstreet.co.uk

HANCOX MISS SALLY ELIZABETH

No5 Chambers
Fountain Court, Steelhouse Lane, Birmingham B4 6DR, ☎0845 210 5555 ✉info@no5.com
No5 Chambers
Greenwood House, 4-7 Salisbury Court, London EC4Y 8AA, ☎0845 210 5555
No5 Chambers
38 Queen Square, Bristol BS1 4QS,
☎0845 210 5555
Call Date: Oct 1996, Lincoln's Inn
Recorder
Qualifications: [BSc (Hons)(Bath)]
seh@no5.com

HAND MR ANTHONY RICHARD

College Chambers
19 Carlton Crescent, Southampton, Hampshire SO15 2ET, ☎023 8023 0338
✉clerks@college-chambers.co.uk
Call Date: July 1989, Lincoln's Inn
Pupil Supervisor
Qualifications: [LLB (Lond)]
ahand@College-Chambers.co.uk

HAND MR JONATHAN ELLIOTT SHEERMAN

Outer Temple Chambers
The Outer Temple, 222 Strand, London WC2R 1BA, ☎020 7353 6381
✉clerks@outertemple.com
Call Date: Nov 1990, Inner Temple
Pupil Supervisor
Qualifications: [BA (Oxon)]
jonathan.hand@outertemple.com

HANDA MS RADHIKA

Coram Chambers
9-11 Fulwood Place, London WC1V 6HG,
☎020 7092 3700
✉mail@coramchambers.co.uk
Call Date: July 2008, Inner Temple
Qualifications: [LLB (Lond) LLM (Lond)]

HANDY MR BENJAMIN GORDON

Number 7 Harrington Street Chambers
7 Harrington Street, Liverpool L2 9YH,
☎0151 242 0707 ✉clerks@7hs.co.uk
Call Date: Oct 2008, Lincoln's Inn
Qualifications: [LLB (Manch)]
ben.handy@7hs.co.uk

HANDYSIDE MR RICHARD NEIL QC (2009)

Fountain Court Chambers
Fountain Court, Temple, London EC4Y 9DH,
☎020 7583 3335
✉chambers@fountaincourt.co.uk
Call Date: Oct 1993, Lincoln's Inn
Qualifications: [LLB (Hons)(Bris) BCL (Oxon)]
richardhandyside@fountaincourt.co.uk

HANHAM THE HON JAMES CHARLES FERGUSON

Maitland Chambers
7 Stone Buildings, Lincoln's Inn, London WC2A 3SZ, ☎020 7406 1200
✉clerks@maitlandchambers.com
Call Date: Oct 1996, Middle Temple
Qualifications: [MA (Oxon) LLB (Hons)(Lond)]
jhanham@maitlandchambers.com

E

HANIF MISS SAIMA NAZ

4-5 Gray's Inn Square
Gray's Inn, London WC1R 5AH,
☎ 020 7404 5252 ✉ clerks@4-5.co.uk
Call Date: July 2002, Lincoln's Inn
Pupil Supervisor
Qualifications: [BA (Hons) (Oxon)]
shanif@4-5.co.uk, shanif@4-5graysinnsquare.co.uk

HANKE MR RICHARD PAUL

3 Verulam Buildings
London WC1R 5NT, ☎ 020 7831 8441
✉ chambers@3vb.com
Call Date: Oct 2006, Lincoln's Inn
Qualifications: [BA (Cantab) BCL (Oxon)]
rhanke@3vb.com

HANKIN MR JONAS KEITH

St Philips Chambers
55 Temple Row, Birmingham B2 5LS,
☎ 0121 246 7000 ✉ clerks@st-philips.com
Call Date: Nov 1994, Middle Temple
Qualifications: [BA (Hons)]
jhankin@st-philips.com

HANLON MR JAMES TOBIAS

Old Bailey Chambers
15 Old Bailey, London EC4M 7EF,
☎ 020 3008 6404
✉ clerks@15oldbaileychambers.com
Call Date: Nov 2006, Middle Temple
Qualifications: [LLB]

HANNA MR RONAN GEAROID

Atkin Chambers
1 Atkin Building, Gray's Inn, London
WC1R 5AT, ☎ 020 7404 0102
✉ clerks@atkinchambers.com
Call Date: Oct 2006, Inner Temple
Qualifications: [BA (Oxon) BCL (Oxon)]
clerks@atkinchambers.com

HANNAFORD MISS SARAH JANE QC (2008)

Keating Chambers
15 Essex Street, London WC2R 3AA,
☎ 020 7544 2600
✉ clerks@keatingchambers.com
Call Date: July 1989, Middle Temple
Pupil Supervisor
Qualifications: [BA (Oxon)]
shannaford@keatingchambers.com

HANNAH MISS SARAH ELEANOR

7 Bell Yard
London WC2A 2JR, ☎ 020 7831 0636
✉ kevintarrant@btconnect.com
Call Date: July 2005, Gray's Inn
Qualifications: [LLB]

HANNAM MR TIMOTHY JAMES

Citadel Chambers
The Citadel, 190 Corporation Street,
Birmingham B4 6QD, ☎ 0121 233 8500
✉ clerks@citadelchambers.com
Call Date: Oct 1995, Gray's Inn
Qualifications: [BA (Hons)]
clerks@citadelchambers.com

HANNANT MISS LISA DIANE

5 Pump Court
Ground Floor, 5 Pump Court, Temple, London
EC4Y 7AP, ☎ 020 7353 2532
✉ clerks@5pumpcourt.com
Call Date: Oct 2005, Lincoln's Inn
Qualifications: [BA (Hons) (Cantab) Dip Law]
lisahannant@5pumpcourt.com

HANNETT MS SARAH RUTH

4-5 Gray's Inn Square
Gray's Inn, London WC1R 5AH,
☎ 020 7404 5252 ✉ clerks@4-5.co.uk
Call Date: July 2003, Lincoln's Inn
Qualifications: [LLB Hons (Nott'm) LLM (McGill)]
srh@4-5.co.uk

HANSEN MR WILLIAM JOSEPH

No5 Chambers
Greenwood House, 4-7 Salisbury Court,
London EC4Y 8AA, ☎ 0845 210 5555
No5 Chambers
38 Queen Square, Bristol BS1 4QS,
☎ 0845 210 5555
No5 Chambers
Fountain Court, Steelhouse Lane, Birmingham
B4 6DR, ☎ 0845 210 5555 ✉ info@no5.com
Call Date: Nov 1992, Lincoln's Inn
Qualifications: [BSc (Econ)(Hons) M Phil (Cantab)]
wh@no5.com

HANSON MR TIMOTHY VINCENT RICHARD

Hanson Renouf
Regency House, Regent Road, Hill Street, St
Helier, Jersey JE2 4UZ, ☎ 01534 767764
✉ enquiries@hansonrenouf.com
No5 Chambers
38 Queen Square, Bristol BS1 4QS,
☎ 0845 210 5555

No5 Chambers
Greenwood House, 4-7 Salisbury Court, London EC4Y 8AA, ☎0845 210 5555
No5 Chambers
Fountain Court, Steelhouse Lane, Birmingham B4 6DR, ☎0845 210 5555 ✉info@no5.com
Call Date: July 1989, Inner Temple
Pupil Supervisor
Qualifications: [LLB (Hons)]
✉timothy.hanson@hansonrenouf.com

HANTUSCH MR ROBERT ANTHONY

3 Stone Buildings
Ground Floor, 3 Stone Buildings, Lincoln's Inn, London WC2A 3XL, ☎020 7242 4937
✉clerks@3sb.law.co.uk
Call Date: July 1982, Inner Temple
Pupil Supervisor
Qualifications: [MA (Cantab)]

HAPGOOD MR MARK BERNARD QC (1994)

Brick Court Chambers
7-8 Essex Street, London WC2R 3LD, ☎020 7379 3550 ✉clerks@brickcourt.co.uk
Call Date: Feb 1979, Gray's Inn
Qualifications: [LLB (Nott'm)]
✉Mark.Hapgood@Brickcourt.co.uk

HAPPE MR DOMINIC PETER ALEXANDER

Stone Chambers
4 Field Court, Gray's Inn, London WC1R 5EF, ☎020 7440 6900
✉clerks@stonechambers.com
Call Date: Nov 1993, Gray's Inn
Pupil Supervisor
Qualifications: [BA (Hons) Oxon]
✉dominic.happe@stonechambers.com

HAPPOLD DR MATTHEW CHARLES EDMUND

3 Hare Court
3 Hare Court, Temple, London EC4Y 7BJ, ☎020 7415 7800 ✉clerks@3harecourt.com
Call Date: Nov 1995, Middle Temple
Qualifications: [BA (Hons) MA (Oxon) LLM MSc]

HAQ MR MAHMOODUL

Trinity House
11 Spratt Hall Road, Wanstead, London E11 2RQ, ☎020 8989 1331
✉trinity_house@yahoo.com
Call Date: Feb 1981, Middle Temple
Qualifications: [BA LLB]

HAQ MISS YASMEEN UL

Chambers of Mr Ami Feder
Ground Floor, Lamb Building, Temple, London EC4Y 7AS, ☎020 7797 7788
✉clerks@lambbuilding.co.uk
Lamb Building
22 Ship Street, Brighton BN1 1AD, ☎01273 820490
✉admin@lambbuilding.co.uk
Chambers of Mr Ami Feder
Ground Floor, Lamb Building, Temple, London EC4Y 7AS, ☎020 7797 7788
✉clerks@lambbuilding.co.uk
Call Date: July 2008, Inner Temple
Qualifications: [LLB (Reading)]
✉clerks@lambbuilding.co.uk

HAQUE MR GAZI MOSTA GAWSAL

Dollis Hill Chambers
197 Ellesmere Road, London NW10 1LG, ☎020 8208 1663
Call Date: July 1970, Inner Temple
Qualifications: [MA]

HAQUE MR MUHAMMED LUTHFUL

Crown Office Chambers
2 Crown Office Row, Temple, London EC4Y 7HJ, ☎020 7797 8100
✉mail@crownofficechambers.com
Call Date: Oct 1997, Lincoln's Inn
Pupil Supervisor
Qualifications: [BA (Hons) MA]
✉haque@crownofficechambers.com

HAQUE MISS SARA CAROLINE

Kenworthy's Chambers
Arlington House, Bloom Street, Salford, Manchester M3 6AJ, ☎0161 832 4036
Call Date: Nov 2000, Middle Temple
Qualifications: [LLB (Hons) (Manch)]
✉s.haque@kenworthysbarristers.co.uk

HARBAGE MR WILLIAM JOHN HIRONS QC (2003)

36 Bedford Row
London WC1R 4JH, ☎020 7421 8000
✉chambers@36bedfordrow.co.uk
37 Park Square Chambers
37 Park Square, Leeds LS1 2NY, ☎0113 243 9422 ✉chambers@no37.co.uk
Call Date: July 1983, Middle Temple
Recorder
Qualifications: [MA (Cantab)]
✉wharbage@36bedfordrow.co.uk

E

HARBINSON MR ADAM JAMES

Dyers Chambers
35 Bedford Row, London WC1R 4JH,
☎020 7404 1881
✉admin@dyerschambers.com
Call Date: Nov 2006, Middle Temple
Qualifications: [BA (Hons) (Oxon)]
✉adam.harbinson@dyerschambers.cjsm.net

HARBOTTLE MR GWILYM THOMAS

Hogarth Chambers
5 New Square, Lincoln's Inn, London WC2A 3RJ, ☎020 7404 0404
✉barristers@hogarthchambers.com
Call Date: Nov 1987, Lincoln's Inn
Pupil Supervisor
Qualifications: [BA (Oxon) Dip Law (City)]
✉GwilymHarbottle@hogarthchambers.com

HARBY MR DAVID MICHAEL

College Chambers
19 Carlton Crescent, Southampton, Hampshire SO15 2ET, ☎023 8023 0338
✉clerks@college-chambers.co.uk
Call Date: July 2006, Middle Temple
Qualifications: [LLB (Hons) (B'ham) LLM (Lond)]
✉dharby@College-Chambers.co.uk

HARDCASTLE MISS KATHERINE LOUISE

6 King's Bench Walk
Ground Floor, 6 King's Bench Walk, Temple, London EC4Y 7DR, ☎020 7583 0410
✉clerks@6kbw.com
Call Date: Nov 2011, Inner Temple
Qualifications: [MA (Cantab)]
✉katherine.hardcastle@6kbw.com

HARDEN MISS CLAIRE MARY

The Chambers of Grahame Aldous QC
9 Gough Square, London EC4A 3DG,
☎020 7832 0500
✉clerks@9goughsquare.co.uk
Call Date: Nov 2000, Middle Temple
Pupil Supervisor
Qualifications: [BA (Hons) CPE]
✉charden@9goughsquare.co.uk

HARDING MR BENJAMIN CHRISTOPHER

Kings Chambers
36 Young Street, Manchester M3 3FT,
☎0845 034 3444
✉clerks@kingschambers.com
Kings Chambers
5 Park Square East, Leeds LS1 2NE,
☎0845 034 3444
✉clerks@kingschambers.com
Kings Chambers
Embassy House, 60 Church Street, Birmingham B3 2DJ, ☎0845 034 3444
✉clerks@kingschambers.com
Call Date: Oct 2005, Inner Temple
Qualifications: [BA Balliol College University of Oxford CPE Ci]
✉bharding@kingschambers.com

HARDING MISS CHERRY JACINTA

1 KBW Chambers
1 King's Bench Walk, Temple, London EC4Y 7DB, ☎020 7936 1500
✉clerks@1kbw.co.uk
King's Bench Chambers
174 High Street, Lewes BN7 1YE,
☎01273 402600
Call Date: Nov 1978, Gray's Inn
Pupil Supervisor
Qualifications: [LLB (Lond)]
✉charding@1kbw.co.uk

HARDING MR CHRISTOPHER JAMES

Thomas More Chambers
7 Lincoln's Inn Fields, London WC2A 3BP,
☎020 7404 7000
✉clerks@thomasmore.co.uk
Call Date: Nov 1992, Inner Temple
Pupil Supervisor
Qualifications: [LLB (Lond)]
✉charding@thomasmore.co.uk

HARDING MR JACK

1 Chancery Lane
London WC2A 1LF, ☎0845 634 6666
✉clerks@1chancerylane.com
Call Date: July 2004, Middle Temple
Qualifications: [BA Hons (Cantab)]
✉jharding@1chancerylane.com

HARDING MR MATTHEW AUSTIN

39 Park Square
Leeds LS1 2NU, ☎0113 245 6633
✉seniorclerk@39parksquarechambers.co.uk
Call Date: Nov 2002, Lincoln's Inn
Qualifications: [LLB (Hons)(Leeds)]
✉harding@39parksquare.com

HARDING MR RICHARD ANTHONY QC (2009)

Keating Chambers
15 Essex Street, London WC2R 3AA,
☎020 7544 2600
✉clerks@keatingchambers.com
Call Date: Oct 1992, Middle Temple
Qualifications: [MA (Hons) CPE]
✉rharding@keatingchambers.com

HARDING MR SIMON JOHN

36 Bedford Row
London WC1R 4JH, ☎020 7421 8000
✉chambers@36bedfordrow.co.uk
Call Date: Oct 1998, Middle Temple
Qualifications: [BA (Hons)(York) CPE (Sussex)]
✉sharding@thomasmore.co.uk

HARDWICK MR MATTHEW RICHARD

3 Verulam Buildings
London WC1R 5NT, ☎020 7831 8441
✉chambers@3vb.com
Call Date: Oct 1994, Gray's Inn
Pupil Supervisor
Qualifications: [MA (Cantab) Lic Spec En Droit Euro]
✉mhardwick@3vb.com

HARDY MRS AMANDA JANE

Taxchambers
15 Old Square, Lincoln's Inn, London WC2A 3UE, ☎020 7242 2744
✉taxchambers@15oldsquare.co.uk
Call Date: Nov 1993, Middle Temple
Pupil Supervisor
Qualifications: [LLB (Hons) LLM (Lond) AKC]
✉taxchambers@15oldsquare.co.uk

HARDY MISS JOANNA EMILY

Chambers of Marion Smullen and Kerim Fuad QC
1 Inner Temple Lane, London EC4Y 1AF, ☎020 7427 4400 ✉clerks@1itl.com
Call Date: July 2010, Middle Temple
Qualifications: [LLB (Hons) (Lond) LLM (Lond)]
✉clerks@1itl.com

HARDY MR JOHN SYDNEY QC (2008)

3 Raymond Buildings
3 Raymond Buildings, Gray's Inn, London WC1R 5BH, ☎020 7400 6400
✉clerks@3rblaw.com
Call Date: Nov 1988, Gray's Inn
Recorder
Qualifications: [BA (Hons) (Oxon) Dip Law]
✉john.hardy@3raymondbuildings.com

HARDY MRS LISA MARIE

1 High Pavement
Nottingham NG1 1HF, ☎0115 941 8218
✉clerks@1highpavement.co.uk
Call Date: July 2011, Lincoln's Inn
Qualifications: [LLB (Hull)]

HARDY MR MAXIMILIAN JOHN LEE

Nine Bedford Row
9 Bedford Row, London WC1R 4AZ, ☎020 7489 2727
✉clerks@9bedfordrow.co.uk
Call Date: Oct 2004, Gray's Inn
Qualifications: [BA Oxon]

HARDY DR STEPHEN THOMAS

9 St John Street
Manchester M3 4DN, ☎0161 955 9000
✉civilclerks@9sjs.com / criminalclerks@9sjs.com
Call Date: Oct 2005, Lincoln's Inn
Qualifications: [LLB (Hons) (Lond) PhD MCIArb]

HARDYMAN MR MATTHEW JAMES

15 New Bridge Street
London EC4V 6AU, ☎020 7842 1900
✉clerks@15nbs.com
Call Date: Oct 1997, Lincoln's Inn
Qualifications: [BA (Hons)(Brunel)]
✉matthew.hardyman@15nbs.com

HARE MR IVAN CHARLES

Blackstone Chambers
Blackstone House, Temple, London EC4Y 9BW, ☎020 7583 1770
✉clerks@blackstonechambers.com
Call Date: Oct 1991, Gray's Inn
Qualifications: [LLB (Lond) BCL (Oxon) LLM (USA) MA (Cantab)]
✉ivanhare@blackstonechambers.com

HAREN MISS SARAH JANET ELSPETH

5 Stone Buildings
5 Stone Buildings, Lincoln's Inn, London WC2A 3XT, ☎020 7242 6201
✉clerks@5sblaw.com
Call Date: Nov 1999, Middle Temple
Pupil Supervisor
Qualifications: [BA (Oxon) BCL (Oxon)]
✉sharen@5sblaw.com

HARFORD-BELL MISS NERIDA

Garden Court Chambers
57-60 Lincoln's Inn Fields, London WC2A 3LJ, ☎020 7993 7600 ✉info@gclaw.co.uk
Call Date: Nov 1984, Middle Temple
Pupil Supervisor
Qualifications: [MA (Sussex) BA (Hons)]
✉neridahb@gclaw.co.uk

E

HARGAN MR JAMES JOHN

Sovereign Chambers
46 Park Place, Leeds LS1 2RY,
☎0113 245 1841
✉clerks@sovereignchambers.co.uk
Call Date: Feb 1990, Middle Temple
Qualifications: [LLB (Hons)]
james.hargan@sovereignchambers.co.uk

HARGAN MR JOHN CARL

St Johns Buildings
24a - 28 St John Street, Manchester M3 4DJ,
☎0161 214 1500
✉clerk@stjohnsbuildings.co.uk
16 Winckley Square
Preston PR1 3JJ, ☎01772 256100
St Johns Buildings Liverpool
8th Floor India Buildings, Water Street, Liverpool L2 0XG, ☎0151 243 6000
✉clerk@stjohnsbuildings.co.uk
Call Date: Nov 1995, Lincoln's Inn
Qualifications: [LLB (Hons)]
clerk@stjohnsbuildings.co.uk

HARGREAVES MR BENJAMIN THOMAS

Carmelite Chambers
9 Carmelite Street, London EC4Y 0DR,
☎020 7936 6300
✉clerks@carmelitechambers.co.uk
Call Date: Nov 1989, Lincoln's Inn
Pupil Supervisor
Qualifications: [LLB (Hons) (Wales)]
bhargreaves@carmelitechambers.co.uk

HARGREAVES MR SIMON JOHN ROBERT QC (2009)

Keating Chambers
15 Essex Street, London WC2R 3AA,
☎020 7544 2600
✉clerks@keatingchambers.com
Call Date: Oct 1991, Inner Temple
Qualifications: [BA (Oxon)]
shargreaves@keatingchambers.com

HARGREAVES MISS TERESA MARIE

No5 Chambers
Fountain Court, Steelhouse Lane, Birmingham B4 6DR, ☎0845 210 5555 ✉info@no5.com
No5 Chambers
Greenwood House, 4-7 Salisbury Court, London EC4Y 8AA, ☎0845 210 5555
No5 Chambers
38 Queen Square, Bristol BS1 4QS,
☎0845 210 5555
Call Date: Oct 1999, Lincoln's Inn
Qualifications: [LLB (Hons)(B'ham)]
th@no5.com

HARING MR SIMON NICHOLAS

Sovereign Chambers
46 Park Place, Leeds LS1 2RY,
☎0113 245 1841
✉clerks@sovereignchambers.co.uk
Call Date: July 1982, Lincoln's Inn
Qualifications: [LLB (Leeds)]
simon.haring@sovereignchambers.co.uk

HARINGTON MISS AMANDA

XXIV Old Buildings
Ground Floor, 24 Old Buildings, Lincoln's Inn, London WC2A 3UP, ☎020 7691 2424
✉clerks@xxiv.co.uk
Call Date: July 1989, Inner Temple
Qualifications: [BA (Cantab)]

HARKUS MR GEORGE EVERARD

Goldsmith Chambers
Ground Floor, Goldsmith Building, Temple, London EC4Y 7BL, ☎020 7353 6802
✉clerks@goldsmithchambers.com
Call Date: Nov 1975, Inner Temple
Pupil Supervisor
Qualifications: [LLB (Leeds) MA (Lond) DPA (Bris)]
G.Harkus@goldsmithchambers.law.co.uk

HARLAND MR ROBERT ANDREW

Seven Bedford Row
7 Bedford Row, London WC1R 4BS,
☎020 7242 3555 ✉clerks@7br.co.uk
Call Date: Oct 2006, Middle Temple
Qualifications: [BA (Hons) (Oxon)]
rharland@7br.co.uk, clerks@7br.co.uk

HARLING-PHILLIPS MISS EMMA ABIGAIL

Landmark Chambers
180 Fleet Street, London EC4A 2HG,
☎020 7430 1221
✉clerks@landmarkchambers.co.uk
Call Date: July 2009, Gray's Inn
Qualifications: [LLB LLM]
eharlingphillips@landmarkchambers.co.uk

HARMAN MISS SARAH JANE

4 Stone Buildings
Ground Floor, 4 Stone Buildings, Lincoln's Inn, London WC2A 3XT, ☎020 7242 5524
✉clerks@4stonebuildings.com
Call Date: Nov 1987, Lincoln's Inn
Pupil Supervisor
Qualifications: [BA (Oxon)]
clerks@4stonebuildings.com

HARMER MISS CHRISTINE

Dere Street Barristers
33 Broad Chare, Newcastle Upon Tyne
NE1 3DQ, ☎ 0844 3351551
✉ clerks@derestreet.co.uk
Call Date: July 1973, Middle Temple
Pupil Supervisor
Qualifications: [BA (Hons)]

HAROUNOFF MR DAVID

9-12 Bell Yard
London WC2A 2JR, ☎ 020 7400 1800
✉ clerks@9-12bellyard.com
Call Date: Nov 1984, Middle Temple
Pupil Supervisor
Qualifications: [BA (Sussex)]
✉ d.harounoff@9-12bellyard.com

HARPER MR ANDREW GRAHAM

New Street Chambers
2 New Street, Leicester LE1 5NA,
☎ 0116 262 5906 ✉ clerks@2newstreet.co.uk
Call Date: Feb 1989, Middle Temple
Qualifications: [LLB (Leics)]
✉ andrew.harper@2newstreet.co.uk

HARPER MISS HELEN CATHERINE

Renaissance Chambers
5th Floor, Gray's Inn Chambers, Gray's Inn,
London WC1R 5JA, ☎ 020 7404 1111
✉ clerks@renaissancechambers.co.uk
Call Date: Nov 2002, Middle Temple
Qualifications: [LLB (Hons) (Reading)]
✉ h.harper@2drj.com

HARPER MR JOSEPH CHARLES QC (1992)

Landmark Chambers
180 Fleet Street, London EC4A 2HG,
☎ 020 7430 1221
✉ clerks@landmarkchambers.co.uk
Trinity Chambers
Highfield House, Moulsham Street,
Chelmsford, Essex CM2 9AH,
☎ 01245 605040
✉ clerks@trinitychambers.com
Call Date: July 1970, Gray's Inn
Qualifications: [BA LLM (Lond)]
✉ jharper@landmarkchambers.co.uk

HARPER MR MARK ELIOT GEORGE

Kings Chambers
36 Young Street, Manchester M3 3FT,
☎ 0845 034 3444
✉ clerks@kingschambers.com
Kings Chambers
5 Park Square East, Leeds LS1 2NE,
☎ 0845 034 3444
✉ clerks@kingschambers.com
Kings Chambers
Embassy House, 60 Church Street,
Birmingham B3 2DJ, ☎ 0845 034 3444
✉ clerks@kingschambers.com
Call Date: Oct 1993, Lincoln's Inn
Pupil Supervisor
Qualifications: [BA (Hons)]
✉ mharper@kingschambers.com

HARPER MRS VIVIAN

Chambers of Mrs V Harper
Address withheld
✉ railtonharper@btopenworld.com
Call Date: Oct 1990, Gray's Inn
Qualifications: [BA]

HARPUM MR CHARLES

Falcon Chambers
Falcon Court, London EC4Y 1AA,
☎ 020 7353 2484
✉ clerks@falcon-chambers.com
Call Date: July 1976, Lincoln's Inn
Qualifications: [MA LLB (Cantab) LLD (Cantab)]
✉ harpum@falcon-chambers.com

Types of work: Boundaries, Chancery (general), Chancery (land law), Commercial property, Common land, Conveyancing, Landlord and tenant, Mineral rights, Mortgages, Real property, Rights of way, Title to land, Water

HARRAP MR GILES THRESHER

Pump Court Chambers
31 Southgate Street, Winchester, Hampshire
SO23 9EB, ☎ 01962 868 161
✉ clerks@3pumpcourt.com
Pump Court Chambers
Upper Ground Floor, 3 Pump Court, Temple,
London EC4Y 7AJ, ☎ 020 7353 0711
✉ clerks@3pumpcourt.com
Pump Court Chambers
5 Temple Chambers, Temple Street, Swindon
SN1 1SQ, ☎ 01793 539899
✉ clerks@3pumpcourt.com
Call Date: Nov 1971, Inner Temple
Pupil Supervisor, Recorder
Qualifications: [LLB (Lond)]

HARRAP MR ROBERT PHILIP

Five Paper
Ground Floor, 5 Paper Buildings, Temple,
London EC4Y 7HB, ☎ 020 7815 3200
Call Date: Oct 1997, Inner Temple
Qualifications: [BA (Lond) CPE]
✉ robertharrap@fivepaper.com

E

HARRIES MR MARK ROBERT

Carmelite Chambers
9 Carmelite Street, London EC4Y 0DR,
☎ 020 7936 6300
✉ clerks@carmelitechambers.co.uk
Call Date: Oct 1995, Lincoln's Inn
Qualifications: [LLB (Hons)(Lond)]
✉ mharries@carmelitechambers.co.uk

HARRILL MISS JAYNE ANNE

4 Brick Court
4 Brick Court, Temple, London EC4Y 9AD,
☎ 020 7832 3200 ✉ clerks@4bc.co.uk
Call Date: Oct 1990, Middle Temple
Pupil Supervisor
Qualifications: [BA]
✉ jayne.harrill@4bc.co.uk

HARRINGTON MISS CLARE STEPHANIE

13 King's Bench Walk
13 King's Bench Walk, Temple, London
EC4Y 7EN, ☎ 020 7353 7204
✉ clerks@13kbw.co.uk
13 KBW
32 Beaumont Street, Oxford OX1 2NP,
☎ 01865 311066 ✉ clerks@13kbw.co.uk
Call Date: Oct 1998, Lincoln's Inn
Qualifications: [LLB (Hons)(Lond) LLM]
✉ charrington@13kbw.co.uk

E

HARRINGTON MR PATRICK JOHN QC (1993)

Farrar's Building
Farrar's Building, Temple, London EC4Y 7BD,
☎ 020 7583 9241
✉ Chambers@farrarsbuilding.co.uk
30 Park Place
Cardiff CF10 3BS, ☎ 029 2039 8421
✉ clerks@30parkplace.law.co.uk
Call Date: July 1973, Gray's Inn
Recorder
Qualifications: [LLB (Lond)]
✉ p.j.harrington@btinternet.com

HARRINGTON MISS REBECCA FRANCES

30 Park Place
Cardiff CF10 3BS, ☎ 029 2039 8421
✉ clerks@30parkplace.law.co.uk
Call Date: July 2004, Gray's Inn
Pupil Supervisor
Qualifications: [BSc (Warw) PGDip Law BVC (Cardiff)]
✉ rfh@30parkplace.co.uk

HARRINGTON MR TIMOTHY MARK

Citadel Chambers
The Citadel, 190 Corporation Street,
Birmingham B4 6QD, ☎ 0121 233 8500
✉ clerks@citadelchambers.com
Call Date: Mar 1997, Gray's Inn
Qualifications: [LLB]
✉ clerks@citadelchambers.com

HARRINGTON MISS TINA AMANDA

Trinity Chambers
Highfield House, Moulsham Street,
Chelmsford, Essex CM2 9AH,
☎ 01245 605040
✉ clerks@trinitychambers.com
Call Date: Nov 1985, Middle Temple
Pupil Supervisor
Qualifications: [BA]

HARRIS MR ADRIAN DAVID

23 Essex Street
London WC2R 3AA, ☎ 020 7413 0353
✉ clerks@23es.com
Call Date: Oct 2001, Inner Temple
Pupil Supervisor
Qualifications: [LLB (Hons) (Leics)]
✉ adrhar@23es.com

HARRIS MISS ANNMARIE

3 Dr Johnson's Buildings
Ground Floor, 3 Dr Johnson's Buildings,
Temple, London EC4Y 7BA, ☎ 020 7353 4854
✉ clerks@3djb.co.uk
Call Date: July 1975, Middle Temple
Qualifications: [BA]
✉ aharris@3djb.co.uk

HARRIS MS BETHAN ELEANOR

Garden Court Chambers
57-60 Lincoln's Inn Fields, London WC2A 3LJ,
☎ 020 7993 7600 ✉ info@gclaw.co.uk
Call Date: May 1990, Middle Temple
Pupil Supervisor
Qualifications: [BA (Oxon)]
✉ bethanh@gclaw.co.uk

HARRIS MISS CAROLINE

Linenhall Chambers
1 Stanley Place, Chester CH1 2LU,
☎ 01244 348282
✉ clerks@linenhallchambers.co.uk
Call Date: Oct 2001, Gray's Inn
Qualifications: [LLB (Hons)]
✉ clerks@1stanleyplace.co.uk

HARRIS MISS CAROLINE ELIZABETH

1 KBW Chambers
1 King's Bench Walk, Temple, London EC4Y 7DB, ☎ 020 7936 1500
✉ clerks@1kbw.co.uk
King's Bench Chambers
174 High Street, Lewes BN7 1YE,
☎ 01273 402600
Call Date: Nov 2004, Inner Temple
Qualifications: [BA University of Bristol CPE Nottingham Law Sch]
✉ charris@1kbw.co.uk

HARRIS MR CHRISTOPHER ANDREW

3 Verulam Buildings
London WC1R 5NT, ☎ 020 7831 8441
✉ chambers@3vb.com
Call Date: Oct 2002, Lincoln's Inn
Qualifications: [LLB (Bris) LLM Ph.D]
✉ charris@3vb.com

HARRIS MR CRAIG LEE

Furnival Chambers
32 Furnival Street, London EC4A 1JQ,
☎ 020 7405 3232
Call Date: July 2006, Middle Temple
Qualifications: [LLB (Hons) (Lond)]
✉ charris@furnivallaw.co.uk

HARRIS MR DAVID ANDREW WALLACE

Iscoed Chambers
86 St Helen's Road, Swansea SA1 4BQ,
☎ 01792 652988
✉ clerks@iscoedchambers.co.uk
Call Date: Oct 1990, Gray's Inn
Pupil Supervisor
Qualifications: [BA (Sussex)]
✉ dh@iscoedchambers.co.uk

HARRIS MR DAVID RAYMOND

Prince Henry's Chambers
2 Tamar House, 12 Tavistock Place, London WC1H 9RD, ☎ 020 7837 1645
✉ d.harris4@btconnect.com
Call Date: Nov 1973, Lincoln's Inn
Qualifications: [LLM (Lond)]
✉ d.harris4@btconnect.com

HARRIS MR DAVID ROBERT

St Albans Chambers
2 - 4 St Peter's Street, St Albans, Hertfordshire AL1 3LF, ☎ 01727 843383
✉ clerks@stalbanschambers.com
Call Date: Oct 1997, Lincoln's Inn
Qualifications: [LLB (Hons)(Luton)]
✉ drh@stalbanschambers.com

HARRIS MISS ELEANOR ELIZABETH

1 Hare Court
1 Hare Court, Temple, London EC4Y 7BE,
☎ 020 7797 7070 ✉ clerks@1hc.com
Call Date: July 2000, Middle Temple
Pupil Supervisor
Qualifications: [BA(Hons) (Cantab)]
✉ harris@1hc.com

HARRIS MISS ELIZABETH MARY

St John's Chambers
101 Victoria Street, Bristol BS1 6PU,
☎ 0117 923 4700
✉ clerks@stjohnschambers.co.uk
Call Date: Nov 1992, Inner Temple
Pupil Supervisor
Qualifications: [LLB (Hull)]
✉ elizabeth.harris@stjohnschambers.co.uk

HARRIS MR FRANCIS RICHARD

Field Court Chambers
5 Field Court, Gray's Inn, London WC1R 5EF,
☎ 020 7405 6114 ✉ clerks@fieldcourt.co.uk
Call Date: July 1997, Inner Temple
Qualifications: [BA (Australia) LLB (Australia)]
✉ richard.harris@fieldcourt.co.uk

HARRIS MR GLENN PETER

33 Bedford Row
London WC1R 4JH, ☎ 020 7242 6476
✉ clerks@33bedfordrow.co.uk
Call Date: Oct 1994, Lincoln's Inn
Pupil Supervisor
Qualifications: [LLB (Hons)(Hull)]
✉ glennpeterharris@yahoo.co.uk, glennharris@33bedfordrow.co.uk

HARRIS MR IAN ROBERT

Exchange Chambers
One Derby Square, Derby Square, Liverpool L2 9XX, ☎ 0151 236 7747
✉ info@exchangechambers.co.uk
Exchange Chambers
7 Ralli Courts, West Riverside, Manchester M3 5FT, ☎ 0161 833 2722

E

Exchange Chambers
Oxford House, Oxford Row, Leeds LS1 3BE,
☎0113 203 1970
✉spencer@exchangechambers.co.uk
Call Date: Nov 1990, Inner Temple
Pupil Supervisor
✉harris@exchangechambers.co.uk

HARRIS MR JACK HENRY RALPH

2 Temple Gardens
2 Temple Gardens, Temple, London
EC4Y 9AY, ☎020 7822 1200
✉clerks@2tg.co.uk
Call Date: Oct 2006, Lincoln's Inn
Qualifications: [MA (Cantab)]
✉jharris@2tg.co.uk

HARRIS MR JAMES

Five St Andrew's Hill
5 St Andrew's Hill, London EC4V 5BZ,
☎020 7332 5400 ✉Clerks@5sah.co.uk
Call Date: Nov 1975, Gray's Inn
Pupil Supervisor
Qualifications: [MA (Oxon)]
✉jamesharris@5sah.co.uk

HARRIS PROF JONATHAN MALCOLM

Serle Court
6 New Square, Lincoln's Inn, London
WC2A 3QS, ☎020 7242 6105
✉clerks@serlecourt.co.uk
St Philips Chambers
55 Temple Row, Birmingham B2 5LS,
☎0121 246 7000 ✉clerks@st-philips.com
Call Date: Mar 2006, Lincoln's Inn
Qualifications: [BA (Hons) MA (Oxon) BCL (Oxon) PhD (B'ham)]
✉jharris@serlecourt.co.uk

HARRIS MR JULIAN GILBERT VAUGHAN

Citadel Chambers
The Citadel, 190 Corporation Street,
Birmingham B4 6QD, ☎0121 233 8500
✉clerks@citadelchambers.com
Call Date: Nov 1982, Middle Temple
Qualifications: [BA]

HARRIS MISS KATIE ANNE

Octagon House
19 Colegate, Norwich NR3 1AT,
☎01603 623186
✉clerks@octagonhouse.co.uk
Call Date: Nov 2005, Inner Temple
Qualifications: [LLB University of East Anglia]
✉katieharris@octagonhouse.co.uk

HARRIS MR KEVIN LYN

Chambers of Mr K Harris
229 Tolcarne Drive, Pinner, Middlesex
HA5 2DW, ☎0845 123 1234
✉kevinlynharris@gmail.com
Call Date: Oct 1999, Inner Temple
Qualifications: [LLB (L'pool)]

HARRIS MR LANCE

Old Square Chambers
10-11 Bedford Row, London WC1R 4BU,
☎020 7269 0300 ✉clerks@oldsquare.co.uk
Call Date: Oct 2009, Lincoln's Inn
Qualifications: [BSc (Sussex) CPE UCU]
✉clerksroom@oldsquare.co.uk

HARRIS MR LEE JAMES

4 King's Bench Walk
2nd Floor, 4 King's Bench Walk, Temple,
London EC4Y 7DL, ☎020 7822 7000
✉clerks@4kbw.co.uk
Call Date: Nov 1999, Middle Temple
Qualifications: [LLB (Hons)(Lond)]
✉lh@4kbw.co.uk

HARRIS MISS LUCINDA CLAIRE

Devereux Chambers
Queen Elizabeth Building, Temple, London
EC4Y 9BS, ☎020 7353 7534
✉clerks@devchambers.co.uk
Call Date: July 2004, Middle Temple
Qualifications: [BA Hons (Cantab)]
✉harris@devchambers.co.uk

HARRIS MR LUKE RICHARD

3 Stone Buildings
Ground Floor, 3 Stone Buildings, Lincoln's
Inn, London WC2A 3XL, ☎020 7242 4937
✉clerks@3sb.law.co.uk
Call Date: July 2001, Inner Temple
Qualifications: [LLB Hons (Lond)]
✉lharris@3sb.law.co.uk

HARRIS MR MARK GEOFFREY CHARLES

6 Pump Court
1st Floor, 6 Pump Court, Temple, London
EC4Y 7AR, ☎020 7797 8400
✉richardconstable@6pumpcourt.co.uk
6 Pump Court Chambers
6-8 Mill Street, Maidstone, Kent ME15 6XH,
☎01622 688094
✉annexe@6pumpcourt.co.uk
Call Date: July 1980, Gray's Inn
Qualifications: [BA (Oxon)]

HARRIS MR MELVYN

5 Essex Court
1st Floor, 5 Essex Court, Temple, London EC4Y 9AH, ☎020 7410 2000
✉clerks@5essexcourt.co.uk
Call Date: Oct 1997, Lincoln's Inn
Qualifications: [LLB (Hons)(Middx)]

HARRIS MR MICHAEL PETER

10 King's Bench Walk
Ground Floor, 10 King's Bench Walk, Temple, London EC4Y 7EB, ☎020 7353 7742
✉Chambers@10kingsbenchwalk.co.uk
Call Date: Oct 1993, Gray's Inn
Qualifications: [BA (Hons)(Cantab)]
michael.harris@10kingsbenchwalk.co.uk

HARRIS MISS MICHELLE FAYE

1 Pump Court
Elm Court, Temple, London EC4Y 7AB, ☎020 7842 7070
✉(name)@pumpcourt.co.uk
Call Date: July 2000, Middle Temple
Qualifications: [LLB(Hons) (Lond)]

HARRIS MR MILES RICHARD BOOTH

Four New Square
Four New Square, Lincoln's Inn, London WC2A 3RJ, ☎020 7822 2000
✉barristers@4newsquare.com
Call Date: Oct 2003, Gray's Inn
Pupil Supervisor
Qualifications: [MA (Cantab)]
m.harris@4newsquare.com

HARRIS MISS NICOLA JANE

Apex
Harlech House, 20 Cathedral Road, Cardiff CF11 9LJ, ☎02920 232 032
✉clerks@apexchambers.net
Call Date: Oct 1992, Middle Temple
Qualifications: [MA (Hons) (Cantab) MA (Canada)]

HARRIS MISS OLIVIA JANE

2-3 Hind Court Chambers
2-3 Hind Court, Fleet Street, London EC4A 3DL, ☎020 7822 2150
✉david@2-3hindcourt.com
Call Date: July 2009, Middle Temple
Qualifications: [BA (Hons) (Oxon) Grad Dip Law (Lond)]

HARRIS MR PAUL

Doughty Street Chambers
Pall Mall Court, 61-67 King Street, Manchester M2 4PD, ☎0161 618 1066
Doughty Street Chambers
5th Floor, Broad Quay House, Prince Street, Bristol BS1 4DJ, ☎01179 058 717
Doughty Street Chambers
53-54 Doughty Street, London WC1N 2LS, ☎020 7404 1313
✉enquiries@doughtystreet.co.uk
Call Date: Feb 1976, Lincoln's Inn
Qualifications: [MA Hons (Oxon)]

HARRIS MR PAUL BEST QC (2011)

Monckton Chambers
1 & 2 Raymond Buildings, Gray's Inn, London WC1R 5NR, ☎020 7405 7211
✉chambers@monckton.com
Call Date: Oct 1994, Gray's Inn
Pupil Supervisor
Qualifications: [LLB LLM]
pharris@monckton.com

HARRIS MS REBECCA ELIZABETH

QEB Hollis Whiteman
1-2 Laurence Pountney Hill, London EC4R 0EU, ☎020 7933 8855
✉barristers@qebhw.co.uk
Call Date: Oct 1997, Inner Temple
Pupil Supervisor
Qualifications: [LLB (Lond)]
rebecca.harris@qebhw.co.uk

HARRIS MR RODGER PETER

Overseas Chambers
Chestnut Farm, Le Mont du Ouaisne, Saint Brelade, Jersey JE3 8AW, ☎01534 625879
✉peter.harris@overseaschambers.com
Call Date: July 1980, Middle Temple
Qualifications: [LLB (Hons)(Manc) Dip ICEI (Amsterdam)]
peter.harris@overseaschambers.com

HARRIS MR ROGER CHARLES JAMES

2 Temple Gardens
2 Temple Gardens, Temple, London EC4Y 9AY, ☎020 7822 1200
✉clerks@2tg.co.uk
Call Date: Oct 1996, Inner Temple
Pupil Supervisor
Qualifications: [BA (Exon)]
rharris@2tg.co.uk

E

HARRIS MR RUSSELL JAMES QC (2003)

Landmark Chambers
180 Fleet Street, London EC4A 2HG,
☎020 7430 1221
✉clerks@landmarkchambers.co.uk
Call Date: Nov 1986, Gray's Inn
Qualifications: [MA (Cantab)]
✉rharris@landmarkchambers.co.uk

HARRIS MISS STELLA CASSANDRA METHVEN

Tooks Chambers
81 Farringdon Street, London EC4A 4BL,
☎020 7842 7575 ✉clerks@tooks.co.uk
Call Date: Nov 2002, Gray's Inn
Qualifications: [LLB (L'pool)]
✉stella.harris@tooks.co.uk

HARRIS MR WILBERT ARTHURLYN

Rowchester Chambers
4 Rowchester Court, Whittall Street,
Birmingham B4 6DH, ☎0121 233 2327
✉clerks@rowchesterchambers.co.uk
Call Date: Nov 1973, Inner Temple
Pupil Supervisor
Qualifications: [BA FCIArb]
✉WHarris@rowchesterchambers.co.uk,
safeene@rowchesterchambers.co.uk

E

HARRIS-JENKINS MR PHILIP LEIGH

Angel Chambers
Ethos Building, Kings Road, Swansea SA1 8AS,
☎01792 464623
✉clerks@angelchambers.co.uk
Call Date: Nov 1990, Gray's Inn
Pupil Supervisor, Recorder
Qualifications: [LLB (Hons)(Wales)]
✉philipharrisjenkins@angelchambers.co.uk

HARRISON MR ANTHONY MATTHEW

Tooks Chambers
81 Farringdon Street, London EC4A 4BL,
☎020 7842 7575 ✉clerks@tooks.co.uk
Call Date: July 2004, Lincoln's Inn
Qualifications: [BA Hons (Cantab)]
✉anthony.harrison@tooks.co.uk

HARRISON MR CARL MATTHEW

30 Park Place
Cardiff CF10 3BS, ☎029 2039 8421
✉clerks@30parkplace.law.co.uk
Call Date: Nov 1997, Gray's Inn
Qualifications: [LLB (Wales)]
✉cmh@30parkplace.co.uk

HARRISON MS CAROLINE MARY ALICE

2 Temple Gardens
2 Temple Gardens, Temple, London
EC4Y 9AY, ☎020 7822 1200
✉clerks@2tg.co.uk
Call Date: July 1986, Lincoln's Inn
Pupil Supervisor
Qualifications: [MA (Oxon) Dip Law (Lond) MA (Lond)]
✉charrison@2tg.co.uk

HARRISON MISS CERI DAWN

12 College Place
Fauvelle Buildings, 12 College Place,
Southampton SO15 2FE, ☎023 8032 0320
✉clerks@12cp.co.uk
Call Date: Mar 2008, Gray's Inn
✉charrison@12cp.co.uk

HARRISON MR CHRISTOPHER JOHN

4 Stone Buildings
Ground Floor, 4 Stone Buildings, Lincoln's
Inn, London WC2A 3XT, ☎020 7242 5524
✉clerks@4stonebuildings.com
Call Date: Nov 1988, Gray's Inn
Pupil Supervisor
Qualifications: [MA (Cantab)]
✉clerks@4stonebuildings.com

HARRISON MR EDWARD ALFRED WILLIAM

Brick Court Chambers
7-8 Essex Street, London WC2R 3LD,
☎020 7379 3550 ✉clerks@brickcourt.co.uk
Call Date: Nov 2008, Lincoln's Inn
Qualifications: [BA (Oxon) BCL (Oxon)]
✉edward.harrison@brickcourt.co.uk

HARRISON MS ESTHER

KCH Garden Square
1 Oxford Street, Nottingham NG1 5BH,
☎0115 941 8851
✉clerks@kchgardensquare.co.uk
1 High Pavement
Nottingham NG1 1HF, ☎0115 941 8218
✉clerks@1highpavement.co.uk
Call Date: Oct 2002, Inner Temple
Qualifications: [LLB (Leic)]

HARRISON MR GORDON WILLIAM

Chambers of Mr Gordon Harrison
Manor Farm, Witton, Norfolk NR28 9TU,
☎020 7556 5500
Call Date: Oct 1996, Inner Temple
Qualifications: [LLB (Reading)]
✉gwharrison@hotmail.co.uk

HARRISON DR GRAEME

12 College Place
Fauvelle Buildings, 12 College Place, Southampton SO15 2FE, ☎ 023 8032 0320
✉ clerks@12cp.co.uk
Call Date: Mar 1997, Inner Temple
Qualifications: [MA (Oxon) DPhil (Oxon)]
✉ gharrison@12cp.co.uk

HARRISON MR JAMES MICHAEL

2 Bedford Row
London WC1R 4BU, ☎ 020 7440 8888
✉ clerks@2bedfordrow.co.uk
Call Date: Nov 2002, Lincoln's Inn
Qualifications: [BA(Hons) (Leeds)]
✉ jharrison@2bedfordrow.co.uk

HARRISON MR JOHN FOSTER

St Paul's Chambers
5th Floor, St Paul's House, 23 Park Square South, Leeds LS1 2ND, ☎ 0113 245 5866
Call Date: Oct 1994, Lincoln's Inn
Pupil Supervisor
Qualifications: [BA (Hons)(Notts) LLB (Hons)(Leeds) M Soc Sc (B'ham)]
✉ jh@stpaulschambers.com

HARRISON MR JON

Chambers of Mr Ami Feder
Ground Floor, Lamb Building, Temple, London EC4Y 7AS, ☎ 020 7797 7788
✉ clerks@lambbuilding.co.uk
Lamb Building
22 Ship Street, Brighton BN1 1AD, ☎ 01273 820490
✉ admin@lambbuilding.co.uk
Chambers of Mr Ami Feder
Ground Floor, Lamb Building, Temple, London EC4Y 7AS, ☎ 020 7797 7788
✉ clerks@lambbuilding.co.uk
Call Date: Mar 2003, Lincoln's Inn
Qualifications: [BA (Hons) (Sheff)]
✉ clerks@lambbuilding.co.uk

HARRISON MR KEITH

St Johns Buildings
24a - 28 St John Street, Manchester M3 4DJ, ☎ 0161 214 1500
✉ clerk@stjohnsbuildings.co.uk
St Johns Buildings
21 White Friars, Chester CH1 1NZ, ☎ 01244 323070
✉ clerk@stjohnsbuildings.co.uk
St Johns Buildings Liverpool
8th Floor India Buildings, Water Street, Liverpool L2 0XG, ☎ 0151 243 6000
✉ clerk@stjohnsbuildings.co.uk
Call Date: Nov 1983, Lincoln's Inn
Pupil Supervisor
Qualifications: [LLB (Hons) (Newc)]
✉ clerk@stjohnsbuildings.co.uk

HARRISON MISS LEONA MELANIE

St Johns Buildings Liverpool
8th Floor India Buildings, Water Street, Liverpool L2 0XG, ☎ 0151 243 6000
✉ clerk@stjohnsbuildings.co.uk
16 Winckley Square
Preston PR1 3JJ, ☎ 01772 256100
St Johns Buildings
24a - 28 St John Street, Manchester M3 4DJ, ☎ 0161 214 1500
✉ clerk@stjohnsbuildings.co.uk
Call Date: Oct 1993, Middle Temple
Pupil Supervisor, Recorder
Qualifications: [LLB (Hons)(Manch)]
✉ gailc@indiabuildings.co.uk

HARRISON MR MICHAEL LEE

23 Essex Street
London WC2R 3AA, ☎ 020 7413 0353
✉ clerks@23es.com
Call Date: Nov 1979, Inner Temple
Pupil Supervisor
Qualifications: [LLB (Hons) (Sheff)]

HARRISON MR NICHOLAS FRANCIS

Serle Court
6 New Square, Lincoln's Inn, London WC2A 3QS, ☎ 020 7242 6105
✉ clerks@serlecourt.co.uk
Call Date: July 1988, Lincoln's Inn
Qualifications: [BA (Oxon)]
✉ nharrison@serlecourt.co.uk

HARRISON MR PAUL JOHN

13 King's Bench Walk
13 King's Bench Walk, Temple, London EC4Y 7EN, ☎ 020 7353 7204
✉ clerks@13kbw.co.uk
13 KBW
32 Beaumont Street, Oxford OX1 2NP, ☎ 01865 311066 ✉ clerks@13kbw.co.uk
Call Date: July 2006, Lincoln's Inn
✉ pharrison@13kbw.co.uk

HARRISON MS PETA

St Johns Buildings Liverpool
8th Floor India Buildings, Water Street, Liverpool L2 0XG, ☎ 0151 243 6000
✉ clerk@stjohnsbuildings.co.uk
16 Winckley Square
Preston PR1 3JJ, ☎ 01772 256100
St Johns Buildings
24a - 28 St John Street, Manchester M3 4DJ, ☎ 0161 214 1500
✉ clerk@stjohnsbuildings.co.uk
Call Date: July 2004, Inner Temple
Qualifications: [BA (Hons) CPE]
harrison_peta@yahoo.co.uk

HARRISON MR PETER JOHN QC (2006)

6 Pump Court
1st Floor, 6 Pump Court, Temple, London EC4Y 7AR, ☎ 020 7797 8400
✉ richardconstable@6pumpcourt.co.uk
6 Pump Court Chambers
6-8 Mill Street, Maidstone, Kent ME15 6XH, ☎ 01622 688094
✉ annexe@6pumpcourt.co.uk
Call Date: July 1987, Inner Temple
Qualifications: [BA (Hons) (Dunelm)]
peterharrison@6pumpcourt.co.uk

HARRISON MR PETER JOHN

St Johns Buildings
24a - 28 St John Street, Manchester M3 4DJ, ☎ 0161 214 1500
✉ clerk@stjohnsbuildings.co.uk
16 Winckley Square
Preston PR1 3JJ, ☎ 01772 256100
St Johns Buildings Liverpool
8th Floor India Buildings, Water Street, Liverpool L2 0XG, ☎ 0151 243 6000
✉ clerk@stjohnsbuildings.co.uk
Call Date: July 1983, Middle Temple
Pupil Supervisor
Qualifications: [LLB Hons (L'pool)]
clerk@stjohnsbuildings.co.uk

HARRISON MISS PHILOMENA MARY

Maitland Chambers
7 Stone Buildings, Lincoln's Inn, London WC2A 3SZ, ☎ 020 7406 1200
✉ clerks@maitlandchambers.com
Call Date: Nov 1985, Middle Temple
Pupil Supervisor
Qualifications: [BA (Lond) Dip Law (Lond)]
pharrison@maitlandchambers.com

HARRISON MR PIERS WILLIAM BENEDICT

Tanfield Chambers
2-5 Warwick Court, London WC1R 5DJ, ☎ 020 7421 5300
✉ clerks@tanfieldchambers.co.uk
Call Date: Mar 1997, Lincoln's Inn
Qualifications: [BA (Hons) (Manch)]

HARRISON MISS RACHAEL

Call Date: Nov 1993, Inner Temple
Qualifications: [LLB (Hons)]
harrison@paradise-sq.co.uk

HARRISON MR RICHARD ANDREW

Devereux Chambers
Queen Elizabeth Building, Temple, London EC4Y 9BS, ☎ 020 7353 7534
✉ clerks@devchambers.co.uk
Call Date: Nov 1991, Lincoln's Inn
Pupil Supervisor
Qualifications: [MA (Hons)(Cantab)]
harrison@devchambers.co.uk

HARRISON MR RICHARD TRISTAN QC (2012)

1 KBW Chambers
1 King's Bench Walk, Temple, London EC4Y 7DB, ☎ 020 7936 1500
✉ clerks@1kbw.co.uk
King's Bench Chambers
174 High Street, Lewes BN7 1YE, ☎ 01273 402600
Call Date: Nov 1993, Inner Temple
Pupil Supervisor
Qualifications: [MA (Hons)(Cantab) Dip law (Lond)]
rharrison@1kbw.co.uk

HARRISON MR ROBERT JOHN MACKINTOSH

30 Park Place
Cardiff CF10 3BS, ☎ 029 2039 8421
✉ clerks@30parkplace.law.co.uk
Call Date: Feb 1988, Lincoln's Inn
Pupil Supervisor
Qualifications: [LLB (Cardiff)]
rjmh@30parkplace.co.uk

E

HARRISON MR ROBIN JAMES

Nexus Chambers
7 New Square, Lincolns Inn, London WC2A 3QS,
☎ 020 7404 1147 / 020 7831 8309
✉ info@nexuschambers.com
Call Date: Oct 1995, Gray's Inn
Pupil Supervisor
Qualifications: [B.Sc]
robin.harrison@nexuschambers.com

HARRISON MR ROGER DONALD

1 Paper Buildings
1st Floor, 1 Paper Buildings, Temple, London EC4Y 7EP, ☎ 020 7353 3728
✉ clerks@onepaper.co.uk
Octagon House
19 Colegate, Norwich NR3 1AT,
☎ 01603 623186
✉ clerks@octagonhouse.co.uk
Call Date: Feb 1970, Gray's Inn
Pupil Supervisor, Recorder
Qualifications: [LLB]
rogerharrison@onepaper.co.uk

HARRISON MISS SALLY QC (2010)

Call Date: Oct 1992, Gray's Inn
Qualifications: [B Sc (Reading) Dip Law (Lond)]

HARRISON MS SARAH LOUISE

Chancery House Chambers
7 Lisbon Square, Leeds, West Yorkshire LS1 4LY, ☎ 0113 244 6691
✉ clerks@chanceryhouse.co.uk
Call Date: Nov 1989, Lincoln's Inn
Qualifications: [LLB (Hons) (Leics)]

HARRISON MS STEPHANIE JAYNE

Garden Court Chambers
57-60 Lincoln's Inn Fields, London WC2A 3LJ,
☎ 020 7993 7600 ✉ info@gclaw.co.uk
Call Date: Nov 1991, Middle Temple
Pupil Supervisor
Qualifications: [BSc (Hons) (Bris) MSc (Lond) Dip Law]
stephanieh@gclaw.co.uk

HARRISON MISS SUSAN KATHRYN

18 St John Street
Manchester M3 4EA, ☎ 0161 278 1800
✉ clerks@18sjs.com
Call Date: Oct 1993, Middle Temple
Qualifications: [BA (Hons)(Bris)]

HARRISON MISS VICTORIA ANN

Deans Court Chambers
24 St John Street, Manchester M3 4DF,
☎ 0161 214 6000 ✉ clerks@deanscourt.co.uk
Deans Court Chambers
101 Walker Street, Preston PR1 2RR,
☎ 01772 565 600
✉ preston@deanscourt.co.uk
Call Date: Nov 2006, Lincoln's Inn
Qualifications: [LLB (L'pool)]

HARRISON-HALL MR GILES ARTHUR

St Philips Chambers
55 Temple Row, Birmingham B2 5LS,
☎ 0121 246 7000 ✉ clerks@st-philips.com
Call Date: July 1977, Gray's Inn
Pupil Supervisor
Qualifications: [MA (Oxon)]
gharrisonhall@st-philips.com

HARROD MR HENRY MARK

5 Stone Buildings
5 Stone Buildings, Lincoln's Inn, London WC2A 3XT, ☎ 020 7242 6201
✉ clerks@5sblaw.com
Call Date: July 1963, Lincoln's Inn
Pupil Supervisor
Qualifications: [MA (Oxon)]
hharrod@5sblaw.com

HARROP-GRIFFITHS MR HILTON

Field Court Chambers
5 Field Court, Gray's Inn, London WC1R 5EF,
☎ 020 7405 6114 ✉ clerks@fieldcourt.co.uk
Call Date: July 1978, Inner Temple
Pupil Supervisor
Qualifications: [BA (Hons) (Manch)]
tony.harrop-griffith@fieldcourt.co.uk

HARROW MISS JULIA MARIA

Sovereign Chambers
46 Park Place, Leeds LS1 2RY,
☎ 0113 245 1841
✉ clerks@sovereignchambers.co.uk
Call Date: July 2009, Gray's Inn
Qualifications: [LLB (Hons) (Newc)]
julia.harrow@sovereignchambers.co.uk

HARROWING DR PETER DIX

St John's Chambers
101 Victoria Street, Bristol BS1 6PU,
☎ 0117 923 4700
✉ clerks@stjohnschambers.co.uk
Call Date: Oct 2011, Middle Temple
Qualifications: [BPharm (Hons) (Bath) PhD (Bath) LLB (Hons) (Lond) LLM (Wales) BA (Hons) (Open University)]

E

HARRY MR MARCUS JONATHAN

KCH Garden Square
1 Oxford Street, Nottingham NG1 5BH,
☎0115 941 8851
✉clerks@kchgardensquare.co.uk
Call Date: July 2008, Lincoln's Inn
Qualifications: [LLB (Hull)]
marcusharry14@googlemail.com

HARRY MR TIMOTHY HAWKINS

Maitland Chambers
7 Stone Buildings, Lincoln's Inn, London WC2A 3SZ, ☎020 7406 1200
✉clerks@maitlandchambers.com
Call Date: July 1983, Lincoln's Inn
Pupil Supervisor
Qualifications: [MA BCL (Oxon)]

HART MISS AMANDA MARIJHE

Doughty Street Chambers
53-54 Doughty Street, London WC1N 2LS,
☎020 7404 1313
✉enquiries@doughtystreet.co.uk
Doughty Street Chambers
Pall Mall Court, 61-67 King Street, Manchester M2 4PD, ☎0161 618 1066
Doughty Street Chambers
5th Floor, Broad Quay House, Prince Street, Bristol BS1 4DJ, ☎01179 058 717
Call Date: July 2001, Middle Temple
Qualifications: [BSc (Hons) CPE]
a.hart@doughtystreet.co.uk

E

HART MR COLIN JOHN JEFFREY DINE

10 King's Bench Walk
Ground Floor, 10 King's Bench Walk, Temple, London EC4Y 7EB, ☎020 7353 7742
✉Chambers@10kingsbenchwalk.co.uk
Call Date: Nov 1966, Middle Temple
Pupil Supervisor
Qualifications: [MA (Oxon) Dip Ecom]
chambers@10kingsbenchwalk.co.uk

HART MR DAVID TIMOTHY NELSON QC (2003)

1 Crown Office Row
1 Crown Office Row, Temple, London EC4Y 7HH, ☎020 7797 7500
✉mail@1cor.com
Call Date: July 1982, Middle Temple
Qualifications: [BA (Cantab)]
david.hart@1cor.com

HART MS JENNY

Chambers of Ms Hart
The Old Rectory, North Tawton, Devon EX20 2EX
Call Date: Oct 1993, Middle Temple
Qualifications: [BA (Hons)(Lond) LLB (Reading)]

HART MR JOSEPH WILLIAM

Deans Court Chambers
24 St John Street, Manchester M3 4DF,
☎0161 214 6000 ✉clerks@deanscourt.co.uk
Deans Court Chambers
101 Walker Street, Preston PR1 2RR,
☎01772 565 600
✉preston@deanscourt.co.uk
Call Date: Oct 2000, Inner Temple
Qualifications: [MA (Oxon)]
hart@deanscourt.co.uk

HART MR NEIL HUGH THOMAS

Essex Court Chambers
24 Lincoln's Inn Fields, London WC2A 3EG,
☎020 7813 8000
✉clerksroom@essexcourt.net
Call Date: Oct 1998, Gray's Inn
Qualifications: [BA (Oxon)]
nhart@essexcourt.net

HART MR PAUL

15 Winckley Square
Preston PR1 3JJ, ☎01772 252828
✉clerks@15winckleysq.co.uk
Call Date: July 1982, Gray's Inn
Pupil Supervisor
Qualifications: [LLB (Newc)]

HARTE MR PATRICK DUDDY

3 Temple Gardens
Lower Ground Floor, 3 Temple Gardens, Temple, London EC4Y 9AU, ☎020 7353 3102
✉clerks@3tg.co.uk
Call Date: Nov 2006, Lincoln's Inn
Qualifications: [LLB (Ireland)]
ph@3tg.co.uk

HARTLEY MR ANTONY ARNOLD

No 8 Chambers
8 Fountain Court, Steelhouse Lane, Birmingham B4 6DR, ☎0121 236 5514
✉clerks@no8chambers.co.uk
Call Date: Feb 1991, Gray's Inn
Qualifications: [LLB (Bris)]
antonyhartley@no8chambers.co.uk

HARTLEY MISS BRONIA ELISABETH

Zenith Chambers
10 Park Square, Leeds LS1 2LH,
☎0113 245 5438
✉clerks@zenithchambers.co.uk
Call Date: July 2006, Gray's Inn
Qualifications: [MA (Edin) Pg DL (Nothumbria)]
✉bhartley@zenithchambers.co.uk

HARTLEY MRS CAROLINE ANNE

Pump Court Chambers
31 Southgate Street, Winchester, Hampshire SO23 9EB, ☎01962 868 161
✉clerks@3pumpcourt.com
Pump Court Chambers
Upper Ground Floor, 3 Pump Court, Temple, London EC4Y 7AJ, ☎020 7353 0711
✉clerks@3pumpcourt.com
Pump Court Chambers
5 Temple Chambers, Temple Street, Swindon SN1 1SQ, ☎01793 539899
✉clerks@3pumpcourt.com
Call Date: July 2002, Middle Temple
Pupil Supervisor
Qualifications: [BA (Hons) CPE]
✉ch@3pumpcourt.com

HARTLEY MISS CHARLOTTE LAURA

1 KBW Chambers
1 King's Bench Walk, Temple, London EC4Y 7DB, ☎020 7936 1500
✉clerks@1kbw.co.uk
Call Date: July 2009, Gray's Inn
Qualifications: [BA]
✉chartley@1kbw.co.uk

HARTLEY MISS LOUISE MICHELLE

15 New Bridge Street
London EC4V 6AU, ☎020 7842 1900
✉clerks@15nbs.com
Call Date: July 2008, Middle Temple
Qualifications: [LLB (Hons) (Lond)]
✉louise.hartley@15nbs.com

HARTLEY MR RICHARD ANTHONY QC (2008)

Cobden House Chambers
19 Quay Street, Manchester M3 3HN,
☎0161 833 6000 ✉Clerks@Cobden.co.uk
Call Date: July 1985, Middle Temple
Recorder
Qualifications: [LLB (Hons)]
✉clerks@cobden.co.uk, rahartley123@hotmail.com

HARTLEY MR RICHARD JAMES

Central Chambers
89 Princess Street, Manchester M1 4HT,
☎0161 236 1133
✉clerks@centralchambers.co.uk
Call Date: Oct 2001, Lincoln's Inn
Qualifications: [LLB (Hons)]

HARTLEY MR TIMOTHY GUY

Park Court Chambers
16 Park Place, Leeds LS1 2SJ,
☎0113 243 3277
✉clerks@parkcourtchambers.co.uk
Call Date: July 1970, Gray's Inn
Qualifications: [LLB]
✉thartley@parkcourtchambers.co.uk

HARTLEY-DAVIES MR PAUL KEVIL

30 Park Place
Cardiff CF10 3BS, ☎029 2039 8421
✉clerks@30parkplace.law.co.uk
Call Date: July 1977, Gray's Inn
Pupil Supervisor, Recorder
Qualifications: [LLB (Hons) (Wales)]
✉pkhd@30parkplace.co.uk

HARTMAN MR MICHAEL

One Essex Court
1st Floor, Temple, London EC4Y 9AR,
☎020 7936 3030 ✉clerks@1ec.co.uk
Call Date: Nov 1975, Lincoln's Inn
Pupil Supervisor
✉mhartman@1ec.co.uk

HARTNETT MISS ELIZABETH ANN MARIE

5 Pump Court
Ground Floor, 5 Pump Court, Temple, London EC4Y 7AP, ☎020 7353 2532
✉clerks@5pumpcourt.com
Call Date: July 2005, Middle Temple
Qualifications: [BA (Hons) Cantab]
✉elizabethhartnett@5pumpcourt.com

HARTSHORN MISS SABRINA

Zenith Chambers
10 Park Square, Leeds LS1 2LH,
☎0113 245 5438
✉clerks@zenithchambers.co.uk
Call Date: Nov 2001, Middle Temple
Qualifications: [MA]
✉shartshorn@zenithchambers.co.uk

E

HARTSON MR JAMES LEE

Angel Chambers
Ethos Building, Kings Road, Swansea SA1 8AS, ☎01792 464623
✉clerks@angelchambers.co.uk
Call Date: July 2010, Inner Temple
Qualifications: [LLB (Open University)]
james.hartson@angelchambers.co.uk

HARTY MR PATRICK WILLIAM MARTIN

Erskine Chambers
33 Chancery Lane, London WC2A 1EN, ☎020 7242 5532
✉clerks@erskinechambers.com
Call Date: Oct 2008, Lincoln's Inn
Qualifications: [BA (Cantab)]

HARVEY MR COLIN TREVOR

Dere Street Barristers
14 Toft Green, York YO1 6JT, ☎0844 3351551
✉clerks@derestreet.co.uk
Call Date: July 1975, Middle Temple
Qualifications: [LLB (Lond)]
clerks@yorkchambers.co.uk, charvey@yorkchambers.co.uk

HARVEY MR JOHN GILBERT

No5 Chambers
Fountain Court, Steelhouse Lane, Birmingham B4 6DR, ☎0845 210 5555 ✉info@no5.com
No5 Chambers
Greenwood House, 4-7 Salisbury Court, London EC4Y 8AA, ☎0845 210 5555
No5 Chambers
38 Queen Square, Bristol BS1 4QS, ☎0845 210 5555
Call Date: July 1973, Gray's Inn
Recorder
Qualifications: [LLB (Hons) FCIArb]

HARVEY MR JONATHAN ROBERT WILLIAM

Henderson Chambers
2 Harcourt Buildings, Temple, London EC4Y 9DB, ☎020 7583 9020
✉clerks@hendersonchambers.co.uk
Call Date: July 1974, Inner Temple
Pupil Supervisor
Qualifications: [BA (Cantab)]
jharvey@hendersonchambers.co.uk

HARVEY MISS LOUISE

College Chambers
19 Carlton Crescent, Southampton, Hampshire SO15 2ET, ☎023 8023 0338
✉clerks@college-chambers.co.uk
Call Date: July 2000, Middle Temple
Pupil Supervisor
Qualifications: [LLB(Hons)]
lharvey@College-Chambers.co.uk

Types of work: Adoption, Assessment of costs, Care proceedings, Children, Common law (general), Domestic violence injunctions, Family law, Licensing, Private children law

HARVEY MISS LOUISE BARBARA

15 Winckley Square
Preston PR1 3JJ, ☎01772 252828
✉clerks@15winckleysq.co.uk
Call Date: Oct 1991, Lincoln's Inn
Qualifications: [LLB (Hons)]

HARVEY MR MICHAEL LLEWELLYN TUCKER QC (1982)

Crown Office Chambers
2 Crown Office Row, Temple, London EC4Y 7HJ, ☎020 7797 8100
✉mail@crownofficechambers.com
Call Date: July 1966, Gray's Inn
Recorder
Qualifications: [MA LLB (Cantab)]
harvey@crownofficechambers.com

HARVEY MR RICHARD JOHN

Garden Court Chambers
57-60 Lincoln's Inn Fields, London WC2A 3LJ, ☎020 7993 7600 ✉info@gclaw.co.uk
Call Date: Nov 1971, Lincoln's Inn
Qualifications: [BA (Cantab)]
richardh@gclaw.co.uk

HARVEY MISS SHONA JULIE

East Anglian Chambers
15 The Close, Norwich, Norfolk NR1 4DZ, ☎01473 214481 ✉norwich@ealaw.co.uk
East Anglian Chambers
Gresham House, 5 Museum Street, Ipswich, Suffolk IP1 1HQ, ☎01473 214481
✉ipswich@ealaw.co.uk
East Anglian Chambers
140 New London Road, Chelmsford, Essex CM2 0AW, ☎01473 214481
✉chelmsford@ealaw.co.uk
Call Date: Nov 1999, Middle Temple
Qualifications: [LLB (Hons)(Sheff)]
shonaharvey@ealaw.co.uk

E

HARVEY MR STEPHEN FRANK QC (2006)

18 Red Lion Court
London EC4A 3EB, ☎ 020 7520 6000
✉ chambers@18rlc.co.uk
18 Red Lion Court (Annexe)
Thornwood House, 102 New London Road, Chelmsford, Essex CM2 0RG,
☎ 01245 280880
Call Date: July 1979, Gray's Inn
Qualifications: [LLB (Lond) AICArb]
✉ stephen.harvey@18rlc.co.uk

HARVEY MR TRISTAN RICHARD GEORGE

Queen Elizabeth Building
3rd Floor, Queen Elizabeth Building, Temple, London EC4Y 9BS, ☎ 020 7797 7837
✉ clerks@qeb.co.uk
Call Date: Nov 2002, Middle Temple
Qualifications: [BA (Hons) (Cantab)]
✉ t.harvey@qeb.co.uk

HARVIE MR JONATHAN ALEXANDER QC (1992)

Blackstone Chambers
Blackstone House, Temple, London EC4Y 9BW, ☎ 020 7583 1770
✉ clerks@blackstonechambers.com
Call Date: July 1973, Middle Temple
Recorder
Qualifications: [MA (Oxon)]
✉ jonathanharvie@blackstonechambers.com

HARWOOD MR RICHARD JOHN

39 Essex Street
London WC2R 3AT, ☎ 020 7832 1111
✉ clerks@39essex.com
82 King Street
Manchester M2 4WQ, ☎ 0161 870 9969
Call Date: Nov 1993, Middle Temple
Pupil Supervisor
Qualifications: [MA LLM (Cantab)]
✉ clerks@39essex.com

HARWOOD-GRAY MR BARRY JOHN

Kenworthy's Chambers
Arlington House, Bloom Street, Salford, Manchester M3 6AJ, ☎ 0161 832 4036
Call Date: Nov 1998, Lincoln's Inn
Pupil Supervisor
Qualifications: [BA (Hons)(So'ton) Dip Law LCGI]

HASAN MISS AYESHA

3 Dr Johnson's Buildings
Ground Floor, 3 Dr Johnson's Buildings, Temple, London EC4Y 7BA, ☎ 020 7353 4854
✉ clerks@3djb.co.uk
Call Date: July 1987, Gray's Inn
Pupil Supervisor
Qualifications: [LLB (Nigeria) LLM (Cantab)]
✉ ahasan@3djb.co.uk

HASELHURST MR IAN SHAND

Atlantic Chambers
4-6 Cook Street, Liverpool L2 9QU,
☎ 0151 236 4421
✉ info@atlanticchambers.co.uk
Call Date: July 1976, Gray's Inn
Pupil Supervisor
Qualifications: [LLB (L'pool)]
✉ ianhaselhurst@atlanticchambers.co.uk

HASHIM MR MU'MIN IRAN MUHAMMAD

Chambers of Marion Smullen and Kerim Fuad QC
1 Inner Temple Lane, London EC4Y 1AF,
☎ 020 7427 4400 ✉ clerks@1itl.com
Paragon Chambers
8 Creed Lane, St. Paul, London EC4V 5BR,
☎ 020 3318 9988
✉ contact@paragonchambers.com
Call Date: Nov 2000, Middle Temple
Qualifications: [BA (Hons) (Lond) PgDL]

HASHMI MS AFSHAN

Park Court Chambers
16 Park Place, Leeds LS1 2SJ,
☎ 0113 243 3277
✉ clerks@parkcourtchambers.co.uk
Call Date: Oct 2005, Lincoln's Inn
Qualifications: [LLB (Hons) (Essex)]
✉ ahashmi@parkcourtchambers.co.uk

HASHMI MISS NAYYERA MAHMOOD

The Chambers Of Miss Nayyera Mahmood Hashmi
Suite 162, 4 Montpelier Street, Knightsbridge, London SW7 1EE
Temple Court Chambers
2nd Floor, 2 Dr Johnson's Building, Temple, London EC4Y 7AY, ☎ 020 7353 7888
✉ clerks@templecourt.co.uk
Call Date: Nov 1998, Middle Temple
Qualifications: [LLB (Hons) (Leic)]
✉ nayyerarahashmi@gmail.com

E

HASKELL MR JAMES MATTHEW

Guildhall Chambers
23 Broad Street, Bristol BS1 2HG,
☎0117 930 9000
✉hoc@guildhallchambers.co.uk
Call Date: July 2004, Inner Temple
Qualifications: [LLB]
james.haskell@guildhallchambers.co.uk

HASLAM MR ANDREW PETER

St Paul's Chambers
5th Floor, St Paul's House, 23 Park Square South, Leeds LS1 2ND, ☎0113 245 5866
Call Date: Oct 1991, Gray's Inn
Pupil Supervisor
Qualifications: [LLB (Hons((Leics)]
aph@stpaulschambers.com

HASSALL MR CRAIG JONATHAN

Sovereign Chambers
46 Park Place, Leeds LS1 2RY,
☎0113 245 1841
✉clerks@sovereignchambers.co.uk
Call Date: Nov 1999, Inner Temple
Pupil Supervisor
Qualifications: [BA (Hons)(Oxon)]
craig.hassall@sovereignchambers.co.uk

E

HASSON MR JAMES DAVID

New Walk Chambers
27 New Walk, Leicester, Leicestershire LE1 6TE, ☎0871 200 1298 / 0116 255 9144
✉clerks@newwalkchambers.co.uk
Call Date: Nov 2006, Inner Temple
Qualifications: [LLB (Sheff) LLM (Sheff)]

HATCH MISS LISA SHARMILA

One Essex Court
1st Floor, Temple, London EC4Y 9AR,
☎020 7936 3030 ✉clerks@1ec.co.uk
Call Date: May 1995, Middle Temple
Qualifications: [LLB (Hons) LLM]
lhatch@1ec.co.uk

HATFIELD MS SALLY ANNE

Byrom Street Chambers
12 Byrom Street, Manchester M3 4PP,
☎0161 829 2100 ✉clerks@byromstreet.com
Doughty Street Chambers
53-54 Doughty Street, London WC1N 2LS,
☎020 7404 1313
✉enquiries@doughtystreet.co.uk
Crown Office Chambers
2 Crown Office Row, Temple, London EC4Y 7HJ, ☎020 7797 8100
✉mail@crownofficechambers.com
42 Bedford Row
London WC1R 4LL, ☎020 7831 0222
✉clerks@42br.com
Call Date: Nov 1988, Inner Temple
Pupil Supervisor, Recorder
Qualifications: [BA (Oxon)]
sally.hatfield@byromstreet.com

HATFIELD-HADJIIOANNOU MRS RUTH ELIZABETH

Chambers of Mrs Hatfield-Hadjiioannou
Office 105, 1st Floor, Nicolaou Court, Corner of Eleftheriou, Venizelou & Kaningos, Paphos 8021 ✉harisruth@cytanet.com.cy
Call Date: Nov 1986, Gray's Inn
Qualifications: [LLB (Nott'm)]

HATT MR JAMES WILLIAM REGINALD

4 Pump Court
4 Pump Court, Temple, London EC4Y 7AN,
☎020 7842 5555
✉chambers@4pumpcourt.com
Call Date: July 2003, Lincoln's Inn
Qualifications: [BA Hons (Oxon)]
jhatt@4pumpcourt.com

HATTAN MR SIMON JUSTIN

Serle Court
6 New Square, Lincoln's Inn, London WC2A 3QS, ☎020 7242 6105
✉clerks@serlecourt.co.uk
Call Date: Oct 1999, Middle Temple
Pupil Supervisor
Qualifications: [BSc (Hons)]
shattan@serlecourt.co.uk

Types of work: Chancery (commercial), Commercial fraud, Commercial litigation, Financial services, Professional negligence, Trust litigation

HAUGHEY MISS CAROLINE PHILIPPA

Furnival Chambers
32 Furnival Street, London EC4A 1JQ,
☎020 7405 3232
Aspect Chambers
Aspect Court, 4 Temple Row, Birmingham B2 5HG, ☎0121 222 2447
✉clerks@aspectchambers.com
Call Date: Nov 1999, Middle Temple
Qualifications: [LLB (Hons)]
chaughey@furnivallaw.co.uk

HAUGHTY MR JEREMY NICHOLAS

Rougemont Chambers
Victory House, Dean Clarke Gardens, Southernhay East, Exeter EX2 4AA, ☎01392 208484
✉clerks@rougemontchambers.co.uk
Chambers of Mr Ami Feder
Ground Floor, Lamb Building, Temple, London EC4Y 7AS, ☎020 7797 7788
✉clerks@lambbuilding.co.uk
Chambers of Mr Ami Feder
Ground Floor, Lamb Building, Temple, London EC4Y 7AS, ☎020 7797 7788
✉clerks@lambbuilding.co.uk
Call Date: Nov 1989, Lincoln's Inn
Qualifications: [LLB LLM (Exon)]
jhaughty@rougemontchambers.co.uk

HAUGSTAD MISS ANNELISE CHARLOTTE

Fountain Chambers
Cleveland Business Centre, 1 Watson Street, Middlesbrough TS1 2RQ, ☎01642 804040
✉clerks@fountainchambers.co.uk
Call Date: Nov 1996, Lincoln's Inn
Qualifications: [BA (Hons)(Keele)]

HAUKELAND MR MARTIN JONATHAN

42 Bedford Row
London WC1R 4LL, ☎020 7831 0222
✉clerks@42br.com
Call Date: Feb 1989, Middle Temple
Qualifications: [Dip Law BA]
martin.haukeland@42br.com

HAVEN MR KEVIN

Pallant Chambers
12 North Pallant, Chichester, West Sussex PO19 1TQ, ☎01243 784538
✉clerks@pallantchambers.co.uk
Call Date: July 1982, Gray's Inn
Qualifications: [LLM (Lond) DipIPL (Lond) BA (Hons)(Kent)]

HAVENHAND MR JOHN BARRY

Clerksroom (Taunton)
Equity House, Administration Centre, Blackbrook Park Avenue, Taunton, Somerset TA1 2PX, ☎0845 083 3000
✉mail@clerksroom.com
Clerksroom (London)
3rd Floor, 218 Strand, London WC2R 1AT, ☎0845 083 3000 ✉mail@clerksroom.com
King's Lynn Chambers
26 The Birches, South Wootton, King's Lynn, Norfolk PE30 3JG, ☎01553 672 085
✉timothy.leader@tesco.net
Call Date: July 1976, Middle Temple
Qualifications: [MA (Oxon)]

HAVERS THE HON PHILIP NIGEL QC (1995)

1 Crown Office Row
1 Crown Office Row, Temple, London EC4Y 7HH, ☎020 7797 7500
✉mail@1cor.com
Crown Office Row Chambers
119 Church Street, Brighton, Sussex BN1 1UD, ☎01273 625625
✉clerks@1cor.com
Call Date: July 1974, Inner Temple
Qualifications: [BA (Cantab)]
philip.havers@1cor.com

HAWES MR NEIL ASHLEY QC (2010)

Charter Chambers
33 John Street, London WC1N 2AT, ☎020 7618 4400
✉clerks@charterchambers.com
Call Date: Nov 1989, Inner Temple
Qualifications: [LLB]
neil.hawes@charterchambers.com

HAWKER MR GEOFFREY FORT

Chambers of Mr G F Hawker
3rd Floor, Flat North, 2 Raymond Buildings, Gray's Inn, London WC1R 5BH, ☎020 7405 1953
✉geoffreyhawker@cuthbertlake.co.uk
Call Date: Apr 1970, Gray's Inn
Pupil Supervisor
Qualifications: [BSc(Eng) C Eng FIEI FIStructE MSocIS(France) MConsE FCIArb FCIArb FCensE FREnff FICE]

HAWKES MR MALCOLM ALEXANDER

Dyers Chambers
35 Bedford Row, London WC1R 4JH, ☎020 7404 1881
✉admin@dyerschambers.com
Call Date: Oct 2006, Middle Temple
Qualifications: [BA (Hons) (Lond) LLM (Essex)]
malcolm.hawkes@dyerschambers.com

E

HAWKES MISS NAOMI NANTEZA ASTRID WALLUSIMB

42 Bedford Row
London WC1R 4LL, ☎ 020 7831 0222
✉ clerks@42br.com
Call Date: Oct 1994, Middle Temple
Pupil Supervisor
Qualifications: [MA (Hons)(Cantab)]
✉ naomi.hawkes@42br.com

HAWKIN MR BENJAMIN

1 Mitre Court Buildings
1 Mitre Court Buildings, Temple, London EC4Y 7BS, ☎ 020 7452 8900
✉ clerks@1mcb.com
Call Date: Nov 1998, Middle Temple
Qualifications: [LLB (Hons)(LSE)]
✉ benh@1mcb.com

HAWKINS MISS CHARLENE VERONICA

Littleton Chambers
3 King's Bench Walk North, Temple, London EC4Y 7HR, ☎ 020 7797 8600
✉ fschneider@littletonchambers.co.uk
Call Date: July 2008, Middle Temple
Qualifications: [BA (Hons) (Oxon)]
✉ chawkins@littletonchambers.co.uk

HAWKINS MR DAVID JAMES

Bank House Chambers
Old Bank House, Hartshead, Sheffield S1 2EL, ☎ 0114 275 1223
✉ w.digby@bankhousechambers.co.uk
Call Date: Oct 1991, Gray's Inn
Pupil Supervisor
Qualifications: [B Ed (Exeter) LLB (Sheff)]
✉ d.hawkins@bankhousechambers.co.uk

HAWKINS MR JAMES PETER

3 Hare Court
3 Hare Court, Temple, London EC4Y 7BJ, ☎ 020 7415 7800 ✉ clerks@3harecourt.com
Call Date: Nov 2003, Middle Temple
Qualifications: [BA (Hons) (Cantab) LLM]
✉ jameshawkins@3harecourt.com

HAWKINS MISS LUCY ELIZABETH

St Ive's Chambers
Whittall Street, Birmingham B4 6DH, ☎ 0121 236 0863
✉ clerks@stiveschambers.co.uk
Call Date: Nov 1994, Lincoln's Inn
Qualifications: [BA (Hons)(Dunelm) CPE]
✉ lucy.hawkins@stiveschambers.co.uk

HAWKINS MR QUINN ALEXANDER

2 Hare Court
Lower Ground, Ground, 1st & 2nd Floor, 2 Hare Court, Temple, London EC4Y 7BH, ☎ 020 7353 3982 ✉ clerks@2harecourt.com
Call Date: Mar 1999, Lincoln's Inn
Qualifications: [LLB (Hons) (Lond)]
✉ quinnhawkins@2harecourt.com

HAWKINS MR ROBERT EDWARD

Temple Chambers
32 Park Place, Cardiff CF10 3BA, ☎ 029 2039 7364
✉ DBrinning@Temple-Chambers.co.uk
Temple Chambers
12 Clytha Park Road, Newport, Gwent NP20 4PB, ☎ 01633 267403
✉ dbrinning@temple-chambers.co.uk
Call Date: Nov 1998, Lincoln's Inn
Qualifications: [BSc (UWIST) MSc (Swansea) Dip Law]

HAWKS MR ANTHONY JOSEPH VINCENT

Trinity Chambers
The Custom House, 39 Quayside, Newcastle Upon Tyne NE1 3DE, ☎ 0191 232 1927
✉ info@trinitychambers.co.uk
Trinity Chambers
Multi Media Exchange, 72-80 Corporation Road, Middlesbrough TS1 2RF, ☎ 01642 247569
✉ info@trinitychambers.co.uk
Call Date: Nov 1975, Middle Temple
Pupil Supervisor, Recorder
Qualifications: [LLB]
✉ a.hawks@trinitychambers.co.uk

HAWKS MR JAMES PHILIP

Chavasse Court Chambers
18 Queen Avenue, Liverpool L2 4TX, ☎ 0151 229 2030
✉ clerks@chavassechambers.co.uk
Call Date: Nov 2003, Gray's Inn
Qualifications: [BA (Oxon) MA Mth (Lond)]
✉ james.hawks@chavassechambers.co.uk

HAWLEY MS CAROL ANNE

Tooks Chambers
81 Farringdon Street, London EC4A 4BL, ☎ 020 7842 7575 ✉ clerks@tooks.co.uk
Call Date: Oct 1990, Gray's Inn
Qualifications: [LLB (Hons) (Lond)]

E

HAWORTH MR PHILIP MARTIN

33 Bedford Row
London WC1R 4JH, ☎ 020 7242 6476
✉ clerks@33bedfordrow.co.uk
Call Date: Mar 2006, Lincoln's Inn
Qualifications: [LLB (Hons) (Lond)]

HAWORTH MR RICHARD ANTHONY

15 Winckley Square
Preston PR1 3JJ, ☎ 01772 252828
✉ clerks@15winckleysq.co.uk
Call Date: Nov 1978, Inner Temple
Pupil Supervisor
Qualifications: [LLB (Leeds)]

HAWORTH MISS SARAH CAROLYN

4 Brick Court
4 Brick Court, Temple, London EC4Y 9AD,
☎ 020 7832 3200 ✉ clerks@4bc.co.uk
Call Date: Oct 2006, Middle Temple
Qualifications: [BA (Hons) (Manch) Dip Law]
✉ sarah.haworth@4bc.co.uk

HAY MR BENJAMIN JAMES

Temple Garden Chambers
1 Harcourt Buildings, Temple, London EC4Y 9DA, ☎ 020 7583 1315
✉ clerks@tgchambers.com
Call Date: July 2004, Middle Temple
Qualifications: [BA Hons (Cantab) PGDip Law (BPP) MA (Hons)(Cantab) PGDip Law]
✉ benjaminhay@tgchambers.com

HAY MS DEBORAH JANE

Hardwicke
New Square, Lincoln's Inn, London WC2A 3SB, ☎ 020 7242 2523
✉ enquiries@hardwicke.co.uk
Call Date: Apr 1991, Middle Temple
Qualifications: [BA]
✉ deborah.hay@hardwicke.co.uk

HAY MISS FIONA RUTH

Harcourt Chambers
1st Floor, 2 Harcourt Buildings, Temple, London EC4Y 9DB, ☎ 0844 561 7135
Call Date: Nov 1989, Inner Temple
Pupil Supervisor, Recorder
Qualifications: [BSc BA (Exon)]
✉ fhay@harcourtchambers.law.co.uk

HAY MS GEORGIA SUE

Penlan Chambers
The Coach House, Penlan, Croeslan, Llandysul, Ceredigion SA44 4SL,
☎ 01559 363333
✉ georgiahay@btconnect.com
Call Date: Oct 1999, Inner Temple
Qualifications: [LLB Hons (Lond)]

HAY MR MALCOLM JOHN MARSHALL

3 Dr Johnson's Buildings
Ground Floor, 3 Dr Johnson's Buildings, Temple, London EC4Y 7BA, ☎ 020 7353 4854
✉ clerks@3djb.co.uk
Call Date: Nov 1972, Gray's Inn
Pupil Supervisor
Qualifications: [BA (Oxon)]
✉ mhay@3djb.co.uk

HAY MR MOHAMMED ABDUL

Equity Court Chambers
3 Rectory Close, London SW20 9DQ,
☎ 07890 994550 ✉ m_a_hay@yahoo.co.uk
Call Date: July 2001, Inner Temple
Qualifications: [LLB (Bris)]
✉ mhay@equitycourt.co.uk

HAY MR ROBIN WILLIAM PATRICK HAMILTON

Lamb Chambers
Lamb Building, Elm Court, Temple, London EC4Y 7AS, ☎ 020 7797 8300
✉ info@lambchambers.co.uk
Call Date: Nov 1964, Inner Temple
Pupil Supervisor
Qualifications: [MA LLB (Cantab)]
✉ robinhay@lambchambers.co.uk

HAY MISS TERESA MARY

Five Paper Buildings
1st Floor, Five Paper Buildings, Temple, London EC4Y 7HB, ☎ 020 7583 6117
✉ clerks@5pb.co.uk
Call Date: July 2001, Middle Temple
Qualifications: [BA (Hons) CPE]
✉ tmh@5pb.co.uk

HAYCROFT MR ANTHONY MARK

Outer Temple Chambers
The Outer Temple, 222 Strand, London WC2R 1BA, ☎ 020 7353 6381
✉ clerks@outertemple.com
Call Date: Nov 1982, Middle Temple
Pupil Supervisor
Qualifications: [LLB (Reading) BCL (Oxon)]

E

HAYDEN MR ANTHONY PAUL QC (2002)

St Johns Buildings
24a - 28 St John Street, Manchester M3 4DJ,
☎0161 214 1500
✉clerk@stjohnsbuildings.co.uk
16 Winckley Square
Preston PR1 3JJ, ☎01772 256100
1 Pump Court
Elm Court, Temple, London EC4Y 7AB,
☎020 7842 7070
✉(name)@pumpcourt.co.uk
Call Date: Nov 1987, Middle Temple
Recorder
Qualifications: [BA (Manch) Dip Law (Lond)]
✉clerk@stjohnsbuildings.co.uk

HAYDEN MISS STELLA CONSTANCE

Furnival Chambers
32 Furnival Street, London EC4A 1JQ,
☎020 7405 3232
Call Date: Nov 2009, Middle Temple
Qualifications: [BA (Hons) (Cantab)]

HAYDEN MR STEVEN JOHN

Nexus Chambers
7 New Square, Lincolns Inn, London
WC2A 3QS,
☎020 7404 1147 / 020 7831 8309
✉info@nexuschambers.com
Call Date: Nov 2009, Middle Temple
Qualifications: [LLB (Hons) (Kent)]

HAYDON MR ALEC GUY

Brick Court Chambers
7-8 Essex Street, London WC2R 3LD,
☎020 7379 3550 ✉clerks@brickcourt.co.uk
Call Date: Oct 1993, Gray's Inn
Pupil Supervisor
Qualifications: [BA (Cantab) LLM (USA)]
✉Alec.Haydon@Brickcourt.co.uk

HAYES MRS CHRISTINE ELIZABETH

East Anglian Chambers
Gresham House, 5 Museum Street, Ipswich,
Suffolk IP1 1HQ, ☎01473 214481
✉ipswich@ealaw.co.uk
Call Date: Nov 1999, Middle Temple
Qualifications: [LLB (Hons)(L'pool)]
✉christinehayes@ealaw.co.uk

HAYES MR JEREMY JOSEPH JAMES

Argent Chambers
5 Bell Yard, London WC2A 2JR,
☎020 7556 5500
✉briefsin@argentchambers.co.uk
Call Date: Nov 1977, Middle Temple
Pupil Supervisor
Qualifications: [LLB]

HAYES MR JOHN ALLAN

Zenith Chambers
10 Park Square, Leeds LS1 2LH,
☎0113 245 5438
✉clerks@zenithchambers.co.uk
Call Date: Nov 1992, Lincoln's Inn
Pupil Supervisor
Qualifications: [BA (Hons)]
✉jhayes@zenithchambers.co.uk

HAYES MISS JOSEPHINE MARY

Gough Square Chambers
6-7 Gough Square, London EC4A 3DE,
☎020 7353 0924 ✉gsc@goughsq.co.uk
Call Date: July 1980, Lincoln's Inn
Pupil Supervisor
Qualifications: [MA (Oxon) LLM (USA)]
✉josephine.hayes@goughsq.co.uk

HAYES MRS KATHRYN ELIZABETH

Call Date: Oct 2000, Middle Temple
Qualifications: [BA (Hons) (Sheff)]

HAYES MR RICHARD JAMES

Lamb Chambers
Lamb Building, Elm Court, Temple, London
EC4Y 7AS, ☎020 7797 8300
✉info@lambchambers.co.uk
Call Date: Oct 1995, Lincoln's Inn
Qualifications: [LLB (Hons)(Durham)]
✉richardhayes@lambchambers.co.uk

HAYFORD MISS JANE HELENE

New Court
Ground Floor, New Court, Temple, London
EC4Y 9BE, ☎020 7583 5123
✉clerks@newcourtchambers.com
Call Date: Oct 1997, Gray's Inn
Qualifications: [LLB (Bucks)]
✉jhayford@newcourtchambers.net

HAYGARTH MR EDMUND BRUCE

Chavasse Court Chambers
18 Queen Avenue, Liverpool L2 4TX,
☎0151 229 2030
✉clerks@chavassechambers.co.uk
Call Date: Nov 1988, Gray's Inn
Qualifications: [LLB (Lond)]
✉edmundbhaygarth@aol.com

HAYHOE THE HON CRISPIN BERNARD GASCOIGNE

33 Bedford Row
London WC1R 4JH, ☎020 7242 6476
✉clerks@33bedfordrow.co.uk
Call Date: Nov 2004, Lincoln's Inn
Qualifications: [MA]
✉crispinhayhoe@33bedfordrow.co.uk

HAYHURST MR BENJAMIN DAVID

2 Pump Court
1st Floor, 2 Pump Court, Temple, London EC4Y 7AH, ☎020 7353 5597
✉clerks@2pumpcourt.co.uk
Call Date: July 2004, Gray's Inn
Qualifications: [LLB (Dunelm)]
✉bhayhurst@2pumpcourt.co.uk

HAYMAN MR GEORGE EDWARD

Maitland Chambers
7 Stone Buildings, Lincoln's Inn, London WC2A 3SZ, ☎020 7406 1200
✉clerks@maitlandchambers.com
Call Date: Oct 1998, Middle Temple
Pupil Supervisor
Qualifications: [MA (Hons)(Cantab)]
✉ghayman@maitlandchambers.com

HAYMERLE MR FRIEDRICH CHRISTIAN

Tooks Chambers
81 Farringdon Street, London EC4A 4BL,
☎020 7842 7575 ✉clerks@tooks.co.uk
Call Date: Oct 2000, Inner Temple
Qualifications: [MA CPE]
✉friedrich.haymerle@tooks.co.uk

HAYNE MISS JANETTE ELIZABETH

4 Breams Buildings
Chancery Lane, London EC4A 1HP,
☎020 7092 1900 ✉clerks@4bb.co.uk
Call Date: Nov 1991, Inner Temple
Qualifications: [BA (Lond)]

HAYNES MR MATTHEW THOMAS BONIFACE

St Ive's Chambers
Whittall Street, Birmingham B4 6DH,
☎0121 236 0863
✉clerks@stiveschambers.co.uk
Call Date: Nov 1991, Lincoln's Inn
Qualifications: [MA (Hons) (Oxon)]
✉matthew.haynes@stiveschambers.co.uk

HAYNES MR MICHAEL JOHN

2 Bedford Row
London WC1R 4BU, ☎020 7440 8888
✉clerks@2bedfordrow.co.uk
Call Date: July 1979, Gray's Inn
Qualifications: [LLB (Leic)]
✉mhaynes@2bedfordrow.co.uk

HAYNES MR PETER QC (2008)

St Philips Chambers
55 Temple Row, Birmingham B2 5LS,
☎0121 246 7000 ✉clerks@st-philips.com
Call Date: July 1983, Gray's Inn
Qualifications: [LLB (B'ham)]
✉phaynes@st-philips.co.uk

HAYNES MISS REBECCA

Monckton Chambers
1 & 2 Raymond Buildings, Gray's Inn, London WC1R 5NR, ☎020 7405 7211
✉chambers@monckton.com
Call Date: Nov 1994, Inner Temple
Qualifications: [LLB (Lond) LLM (Lond)]
✉rhaynes@monckton.com

HAYS MR WILLIAM STORMONT

6 King's Bench Walk
Ground Floor, 6 King's Bench Walk, Temple, London EC4Y 7DR, ☎020 7583 0410
✉clerks@6kbw.com
Call Date: Nov 2006, Middle Temple
Qualifications: [BA (Hons) (Oxon) LLM (Lond) PgDip Law]
✉william.hays@6kbw.com

HAYTER MRS KATHLEEN

New Street Chambers
2 New Street, Leicester LE1 5NA,
☎0116 262 5906 ✉clerks@2newstreet.co.uk
Call Date: July 1982, Middle Temple
Pupil Supervisor
Qualifications: [LLB (Leics)]

E

HAYTON MR MICHAEL PEARSON

Deans Court Chambers
24 St John Street, Manchester M3 4DF,
☎ 0161 214 6000 ✉ clerks@deanscourt.co.uk
Deans Court Chambers
101 Walker Street, Preston PR1 2RR,
☎ 01772 565 600
✉ preston@deanscourt.co.uk
Call Date: Oct 1993, Lincoln's Inn
Pupil Supervisor
Qualifications: [MA (Hons) (Oxon)]
hayton@deanscourt.co.uk

HAYTON MISS VIRGINA SUFEIYA

Deans Court Chambers
24 St John Street, Manchester M3 4DF,
☎ 0161 214 6000 ✉ clerks@deanscourt.co.uk
Call Date: Oct 1999, Lincoln's Inn
Pupil Supervisor
Qualifications: [BSc (Hons)(Dunelm)]
vhayton@deanscourt.co.uk

HAYWARD MISS CICELY ALBINIA

5 Essex Court
1st Floor, 5 Essex Court, Temple, London
EC4Y 9AH, ☎ 020 7410 2000
✉ clerks@5essexcourt.co.uk
Call Date: Oct 2009, Lincoln's Inn
Qualifications: [BA (Oxon) CPE UZOBU]
hayward@5essexcourt.co.uk

E

HAYWARD MR JAMES GERALD STEPHEN

Colleton Chambers
Colleton Crescent, Exeter, Devon EX2 4DG,
☎ 01392 274898
✉ clerks@colletonchambers.co.uk
Call Date: July 1985, Middle Temple
Pupil Supervisor
Qualifications: [MA (Cantab)]
jameshayward@colletonchambers.co.uk

HAYWARD MR PETER MICHAEL

30 Brooksby Street
London N1 1HA, ☎ 020 7607 3854
✉ peter.hayward@orange.net
Call Date: July 1974, Gray's Inn
Qualifications: [BA BCL (Oxon)]
peter.hayward@orange.net

HAYWOOD MISS JANET

Guildford Chambers
Stoke House, Leapale Lane, Guildford, Surrey
GU1 4LY, ☎ 01483 539131
✉ clerks@guildfordchambers.co.uk
Call Date: July 1985, Inner Temple
Qualifications: [BA Dip Law (Lond)]
jhaywood@guildfordchambers.com

HAYWOOD MISS JANETTE

Renaissance Chambers
5th Floor, Gray's Inn Chambers, Gray's Inn,
London WC1R 5JA, ☎ 020 7404 1111
✉ clerks@renaissancechambers.co.uk
Call Date: Nov 1977, Middle Temple
Qualifications: [LLM (Lond) LLB (Wales)]
jh@renaissancechambers.co.uk

HAYWOOD DR JENNIFER MARGARET

Serle Court
6 New Square, Lincoln's Inn, London
WC2A 3QS, ☎ 020 7242 6105
✉ clerks@serlecourt.co.uk
Call Date: July 2001, Lincoln's Inn
Pupil Supervisor
Qualifications: [MA (Hons) MBBCh Dip Law]
jhaywood@serlecourt.co.uk

HAYWOOD MR MARCUS EDWARD

South Square
3-4 South Square, Gray's Inn, London
WC1R 5HP, ☎ 020 7696 9900
✉ practicemanagers@southsquare.com
Call Date: Nov 2002, Lincoln's Inn
Qualifications: [BA (Hons) CPE]
marcushaywood@southsquare.com

HAYWOOD MR PHIL

Doughty Street Chambers
53-54 Doughty Street, London WC1N 2LS,
☎ 020 7404 1313
✉ enquiries@doughtystreet.co.uk
Doughty Street Chambers
Pall Mall Court, 61-67 King Street, Manchester
M2 4PD, ☎ 0161 618 1066
Doughty Street Chambers
5th Floor, Broad Quay House, Prince Street,
Bristol BS1 4DJ, ☎ 01179 058 717
Call Date: Mar 2001, Middle Temple
Qualifications: [BA (Hons) (London) CPE]
p.haywood@doughtystreet.co.uk

HEAD MR DAVID IAN

3 Verulam Buildings
London WC1R 5NT, ☎ 020 7831 8441
✉ chambers@3vb.com
Call Date: Nov 1997, Middle Temple
Pupil Supervisor
Qualifications: [BA (Hons)(Oxon)]
dhead@3vb.com

HEAD MR PETER JAMES

11 Stone Buildings
11 Stone Buildings, Lincoln's Inn, London WC2A 3TG, ☎020 7831 6381
✉clerks@11sb.com
Call Date: Oct 2008, Lincoln's Inn
Qualifications: [BA MA (Cantab) LLB]
✉head@11sb.com

HEADLAM MR ROY WASHINGTON

Furnival Chambers
32 Furnival Street, London EC4A 1JQ, ☎020 7405 3232
Call Date: Nov 1983, Gray's Inn
Qualifications: [BA]
✉rheadlam@furnivallaw.co.uk

HEAL MRS MADELEINE

New Square Chambers
12 New Square, Lincoln's Inn, London WC2A 3SW, ☎020 7419 8000
✉robin.hollington@newsquarechambers.co.uk
Call Date: May 1996, Lincoln's Inn
Qualifications: [BA (New Zealand) LLB (New Zealand) LLM (Lond)]
✉madeleine.heal@newsquarechambers.co.uk

HEALD MR JEREMY RICHARD LANE

Three New Square IP
3 New Square, Lincoln's Inn, London WC2A 3RS, ☎020 7405 1111
✉clerks@3newsquare.co.uk
Call Date: Oct 2010, Middle Temple
Qualifications: [BSc (Hons) (Durham)]
✉heald@3newsquare.co.uk

HEALEY MR GREVILLE CHARLES

Falcon Chambers
Falcon Court, London EC4Y 1AA, ☎020 7353 2484
✉clerks@falcon-chambers.com
Call Date: Oct 2002, Inner Temple
Qualifications: [MA (Cantab) B.Phil (Oxon) DPhil (Oxon)]
✉healey@falcon-chambers.com

HEALEY MS SUSAN HILARY

Crown Office Row Chambers
119 Church Street, Brighton, Sussex BN1 1UD, ☎01273 625625
✉clerks@1cor.com
Call Date: Nov 1995, Middle Temple
Qualifications: [BA (Hons)]
✉susan.healey@1cor.com

HEALING MISS YVONNE MARY

18 St John Street
Manchester M3 4EA, ☎0161 278 1800
✉clerks@18sjs.com
Call Date: May 1987, Inner Temple
Pupil Supervisor
Qualifications: [LLB (L'pool)]

HEALY MISS ALEXANDRA QC (2011)

9-12 Bell Yard
London WC2A 2JR, ☎020 7400 1800
✉clerks@9-12bellyard.com
Call Date: Oct 1992, Gray's Inn
Pupil Supervisor
Qualifications: [MA (Cantab)]
✉a.healy@9-12bellyard.com

HEALY MR SAMUEL ANDREW

Dere Street Barristers
14 Toft Green, York YO1 6JT, ☎0844 3351551
✉clerks@derestreet.co.uk
Call Date: Nov 1999, Lincoln's Inn
Pupil Supervisor
Qualifications: [BA (Hons)(Cantab)]
✉clerks@yorkchambers.co.uk, shealy@yorkchambers.co.uk

HEALY MISS SANDRA ITA

Stone Chambers
4 Field Court, Gray's Inn, London WC1R 5EF, ☎020 7440 6900
✉clerks@stonechambers.com
Call Date: July 2007, Middle Temple
Qualifications: [BA (Hons) (Cantab)]
✉sandra.healy@stonechambers.com

HEALY MISS SIOBAN QC (2010)

7 King's Bench Walk
Ground Floor, 7 King's Bench Walk, Temple, London EC4Y 7DS, ☎020 7910 8300
✉clerks@7kbw.co.uk
Call Date: July 1993, Inner Temple
Qualifications: [BA LLM]
✉shealy@7kbw.co.uk

HEAP MR GERARD MILES

Clerksroom (Taunton)
Equity House, Administration Centre, Blackbrook Park Avenue, Taunton, Somerset TA1 2PX, ☎0845 083 3000
✉mail@clerksroom.com
Call Date: July 1985, Gray's Inn
Pupil Supervisor
Qualifications: [MA (Cantab)]
✉heap@clerksroom.com

E

HEARD MR JONATHAN COLIN

Queen Square Chambers
56 Queen Square, Bristol BS1 4PR,
☎0117 921 1966 ✉crime@qs-c.co.uk
Call Date: July 2004, Middle Temple
Qualifications: [LLB Hons (Lond) LLM (Lond)]
jch@qs-c.co.uk

HEARN MR NICHOLAS MILES

Furnival Chambers
32 Furnival Street, London EC4A 1JQ,
☎020 7405 3232
Call Date: Mar 2007, Middle Temple
Qualifications: [LLB (Hons) (Lond)]

HEARNDEN MISS ALEXIS KATRINA

39 Essex Street
London WC2R 3AT, ☎020 7832 1111
✉clerks@39essex.com
82 King Street
Manchester M2 4WQ, ☎0161 870 9969
Call Date: Oct 2005, Inner Temple
Qualifications: [BA (Hons) (Oxon) CPE]
alexis.hearnden@39essex.com

E

HEARNDEN MR RICHARD CHRISTOPHER

Furnival Chambers
32 Furnival Street, London EC4A 1JQ,
☎020 7405 3232
Call Date: Nov 1998, Gray's Inn
Pupil Supervisor
Qualifications: [LLB Hons LSE]

HEARNE MISS JULIET AUDREY

Cornwall Street Chambers
Shrewsbury Annex, Rural Enterprise Centre, Stafford Drive, Battlefield Enterprise Park, Shrewsbury SY1 3FE,
☎01743 363 611 / 0121 233 7500
Cornwall Street Chambers
85-87 Cornwall Street, Birmingham B3 3BY,
☎0121 233 7500
✉clerks@cornwallstreet.co.uk
Call Date: Nov 1989, Gray's Inn
Qualifications: [BA (Bris)]

HEATH MR DUNCAN ROBERT

Enterprise Chambers
9 Old Square, Lincoln's Inn, London WC2A 3SR, ☎020 7405 9471
✉london@enterprisechambers.com
Call Date: Nov 2007, Lincoln's Inn
Qualifications: [BA (Cantab)]

HEATH MR STEPHEN DAVID

Tanfield Chambers
2-5 Warwick Court, London WC1R 5DJ,
☎020 7421 5300
✉clerks@tanfieldchambers.co.uk
Call Date: Feb 1992, Lincoln's Inn
Qualifications: [BA (Hons) (Cantab) Dip Law]

HEATHER MR CHRISTOPHER MARK

Tanfield Chambers
2-5 Warwick Court, London WC1R 5DJ,
☎020 7421 5300
✉clerks@tanfieldchambers.co.uk
Call Date: Oct 1995, Middle Temple
Pupil Supervisor
Qualifications: [MA (Cantab)]
cheather@tanfieldchambers.co.uk

Fax: 020 7421 5333;
DX: 46 London;
URL: www.tanfieldchambers.co.uk

Types of work: Chancery (general), Chancery (land law), Commercial property, Landlord and tenant, Leasehold enfranchisement, Mortgages, Real property

HEATON MS BETH SUSANNAH

Colleton Chambers
Colleton Crescent, Exeter, Devon EX2 4DG,
☎01392 274898
✉clerks@colletonchambers.co.uk
Call Date: Mar 2010, Gray's Inn
Qualifications: [BA]
betheaton@colletonchambers.co.uk

HEATON MR DAVID MICHAEL QC (2008)

Byrom Street Chambers
12 Byrom Street, Manchester M3 4PP,
☎0161 829 2100 ✉clerks@byromstreet.com
Crown Office Chambers
2 Crown Office Row, Temple, London EC4Y 7HJ, ☎020 7797 8100
✉mail@crownofficechambers.com
42 Bedford Row
London WC1R 4LL, ☎020 7831 0222
✉clerks@42br.com
Call Date: July 1983, Middle Temple
Recorder
Qualifications: [MA (Cantab)]
david.heaton@byromstreet.com

HEATON MISS FRANCES MARGARET QC (2012)

Deans Court Chambers
24 St John Street, Manchester M3 4DF, ☎0161 214 6000 ✉clerks@deanscourt.co.uk
Deans Court Chambers
101 Walker Street, Preston PR1 2RR, ☎01772 565 600
✉preston@deanscourt.co.uk
Call Date: Nov 1985, Gray's Inn
Pupil Supervisor, Recorder
Qualifications: [LLB (Hons)]
heaton@deanscourt.co.uk

HEATON MISS LAURA JANE

29 Bedford Row Chambers
London WC1R 4HE, ☎020 7404 1044
✉clerks@29br.co.uk
Call Date: Oct 1998, Middle Temple
Pupil Supervisor
Qualifications: [MA (Hons)(Cantab)]
lheaton@29br.co.uk

HEATON-ARMSTRONG MR ANTHONY EUSTACE JOHN

9-12 Bell Yard
London WC2A 2JR, ☎020 7400 1800
✉clerks@9-12bellyard.com
Call Date: July 1973, Gray's Inn
Pupil Supervisor
Qualifications: [LLB]
a.heatonarmstrong@9-12bellyard.com

HEAVEN MRS KIRSTEN LUCY

Garden Court Chambers
57-60 Lincoln's Inn Fields, London WC2A 3LJ, ☎020 7993 7600 ✉info@gclaw.co.uk
Call Date: July 2007, Lincoln's Inn
Qualifications: [MA (Oxon) LLM (Essex)]
kirstenh@gclaw.co.uk

HECKSCHER MR WILLIAM MARTIN

Albion Chambers
Broad Street, Bristol BS1 1DR,
☎0117 927 2144
✉clerks@albionchambers.co.uk
Call Date: Oct 2006, Inner Temple
Qualifications: [LLB (Lond)]

HEDGECOE MR JOHN PHILIP

St Johns Buildings
24a - 28 St John Street, Manchester M3 4DJ,
☎0161 214 1500
✉clerk@stjohnsbuildings.co.uk
St Johns Buildings
21 White Friars, Chester CH1 1NZ,
☎01244 323070
✉clerk@stjohnsbuildings.co.uk
16 Winckley Square
Preston PR1 3JJ, ☎01772 256100
Call Date: Nov 1972, Inner Temple
Pupil Supervisor
Qualifications: [LLB (Hull)]

HEDWORTH MR ALAN TOBY QC (1996)

Trinity Chambers
The Custom House, 39 Quayside, Newcastle Upon Tyne NE1 3DE, ☎0191 232 1927
✉info@trinitychambers.co.uk
Trinity Chambers
Multi Media Exchange, 72-80 Corporation Road, Middlesbrough TS1 2RF,
☎01642 247569
✉info@trinitychambers.co.uk
Call Date: July 1975, Inner Temple
Recorder
Qualifications: [MA (Cantab)]
t.hedworthqc@trinitychambers.co.uk

HEDWORTH MR JOSEPH PIERS

Cathedral Chambers
First Floor, 17 Queen Street, Newcastle Upon Tyne NE1 3UG, ☎0191 232 1311
✉mail@cathedralchambers.com
Call Date: July 2002, Inner Temple
Qualifications: [LLB (Northumbria)]

HEDWORTH MR LEONARD

10 King's Bench Walk
Ground Floor, 10 King's Bench Walk, Temple, London EC4Y 7EB, ☎020 7353 7742
✉Chambers@10kingsbenchwalk.co.uk
Call Date: July 1979, Lincoln's Inn
Qualifications: [BSc (Lond)]
chambers@10kingsbenchwalk.co.uk

HEDWORTH MS RACHEL CLAIRE

Trinity Chambers
The Custom House, 39 Quayside, Newcastle Upon Tyne NE1 3DE, ☎0191 232 1927
✉info@trinitychambers.co.uk
Trinity Chambers
Multi Media Exchange, 72-80 Corporation Road, Middlesbrough TS1 2RF,
☎01642 247569
✉info@trinitychambers.co.uk
Call Date: July 1999, Inner Temple
Qualifications: [LLB]

E

HEELEY MISS MICHELLE LOUISE

No5 Chambers
Fountain Court, Steelhouse Lane, Birmingham B4 6DR, ☎0845 210 5555 ✉info@no5.com
No5 Chambers
Greenwood House, 4-7 Salisbury Court, London EC4Y 8AA, ☎0845 210 5555
No5 Chambers
38 Queen Square, Bristol BS1 4QS, ☎0845 210 5555
Call Date: July 2001, Gray's Inn
Qualifications: [LLB]
mlh@no5.com

HEER MISS DEANNA MARY

Five Paper Buildings
1st Floor, Five Paper Buildings, Temple, London EC4Y 7HB, ☎020 7583 6117
✉clerks@5pb.co.uk
Call Date: Oct 1994, Gray's Inn
Pupil Supervisor
Qualifications: [LLB]
dh@5pb.co.uk

HEFFORD MISS ANNA NOBLE

New Court
Ground Floor, New Court, Temple, London EC4Y 9BE, ☎020 7583 5123
✉clerks@newcourtchambers.com
Call Date: Mar 2004, Middle Temple
Qualifications: [LLB (Hons) (Leic) MSc]
ahefford@newcourtchambers.net

HEGARTY MR KEVIN JOHN QC (2010)

St Philips Chambers
55 Temple Row, Birmingham B2 5LS, ☎0121 246 7000 ✉clerks@st-philips.com
Call Date: Nov 1982, Middle Temple
Pupil Supervisor, Recorder
Qualifications: [LLB (Hons) (Newc) MA (Salford)]
khegarty@st-philips.co.uk

HEHIR MR CHRISTOPHER JOSEPH

6 King's Bench Walk
Ground Floor, 6 King's Bench Walk, Temple, London EC4Y 7DR, ☎020 7583 0410
✉clerks@6kbw.com
Call Date: Oct 1990, Inner Temple
Pupil Supervisor
Qualifications: [BA (Oxon)]
chris.hehir@6kbw.com

HEILBRON MISS HILARY NORA QC (1987)

Brick Court Chambers
7-8 Essex Street, London WC2R 3LD, ☎020 7379 3550 ✉clerks@brickcourt.co.uk
Call Date: July 1971, Gray's Inn
Qualifications: [MA (Oxon) BA (Oxon)]
Hilary.Heilbron@Brickcourt.co.uk

HEIMLER MR GEORGE ERNEST

4 Breams Buildings
Chancery Lane, London EC4A 1HP, ☎020 7092 1900 ✉clerks@4bb.co.uk
Call Date: July 1978, Inner Temple
Pupil Supervisor
Qualifications: [LLB]
georgeeheimler@yahoo.co.uk

HELLEBRONTH MISS ROSANNA RUTH

Crown Office Chambers
2 Crown Office Row, Temple, London EC4Y 7HJ, ☎020 7797 8100
✉mail@crownofficechambers.com
Call Date: Oct 2004, Middle Temple
Qualifications: [BA (Hons) (Cantab)]
hellebronth@crownofficechambers.com

HELLENS MR MATTHEW JAMES

3 Dr Johnson's Buildings
Ground Floor, 3 Dr Johnson's Buildings, Temple, London EC4Y 7BA, ☎020 7353 4854
✉clerks@3djb.co.uk
Call Date: Oct 1992, Lincoln's Inn
Qualifications: [MA (Cantab)]
mhellens@3djb.co.uk

HELLER MRS ANNE

10 King's Bench Walk
Ground Floor, 10 King's Bench Walk, Temple, London EC4Y 7EB, ☎020 7353 7742
✉Chambers@10kingsbenchwalk.co.uk
Call Date: Nov 1995, Gray's Inn
Qualifications: [BA (Kent) LLB]
anne.heller@10kingsbenchwalk.co.uk

HELLER MR RICHARD MARC

Dyers Chambers
35 Bedford Row, London WC1R 4JH, ☎020 7404 1881
✉admin@dyerschambers.com
Call Date: Oct 1998, Lincoln's Inn
Qualifications: [BA (Hons) CPE]

E

HELLMAN MR STEPHEN GEOFFREY

Chambers of Andrew Mitchell QC
33 Chancery Lane, London WC2A 1EN,
☎ 020 7440 9950 ✉ clerks@33cllaw.com
Call Date: July 1988, Inner Temple
Pupil Supervisor
Qualifications: [BA (Oxon) Dip Law]
✉ sh@33cllaw.com

HELME MR EDWARD MICHAEL

4-5 Gray's Inn Square
Gray's Inn, London WC1R 5AH,
☎ 020 7404 5252 ✉ clerks@4-5.co.uk
Call Date: Oct 2006, Lincoln's Inn
Qualifications: [BA (Oxon)]

HELME MR IAN KEIR STACEY

One Brick Court
1st Floor, One Brick Court, Temple, London EC4Y 9BY, ☎ 020 7353 8845
✉ clerks@onebrickcourt.com
Call Date: July 2005, Middle Temple
Qualifications: [BA (Hons) Cantab]
✉ ih@onebrickcourt.com

HELMI MISS HALA

3 PB Barristers
3 Paper Buildings, Temple, London EC4Y 7EU,
☎ 020 7583 8055
Call Date: July 2000, Middle Temple
Qualifications: [BA(Hons) (Lond) MA (Bris)]

HELMORE MISS KATHERINE LUCY ANNE

Landmark Chambers
180 Fleet Street, London EC4A 2HG,
☎ 020 7430 1221
✉ clerks@landmarkchambers.co.uk
Call Date: Oct 2009, Lincoln's Inn
Qualifications: [LLB (Exon)]
✉ khelmore@landmarkchambers.co.uk

HEMERY MISS PHILIPPA ANNABEL

1 Pump Court
Elm Court, Temple, London EC4Y 7AB,
☎ 020 7842 7070
✉ (name)@pumpcourt.co.uk
Call Date: Mar 2009, Inner Temple
Qualifications: [BA (Oxon) CPE (Oxon)]

HEMINGWAY MISS SARAH MARIE

Garden Court Chambers
57-60 Lincoln's Inn Fields, London WC2A 3LJ,
☎ 020 7993 7600 ✉ info@gclaw.co.uk
Call Date: July 2006, Middle Temple
Qualifications: [BA (Hons) LLM PgDL]
✉ sarahh@gclaw.co.uk

HENDERSON MR ALASDAIR IAIN

1 Crown Office Row
1 Crown Office Row, Temple, London EC4Y 7HH, ☎ 020 7797 7500
✉ mail@1cor.com
Call Date: July 2009, Inner Temple
Qualifications: [BA (Oxon) LLM (Pennsylvania)]
✉ alasdair.henderson@1cor.com

HENDERSON MISS CHARLENE

Northampton Chambers
10 Spencer Parade, Northampton NN1 5AQ,
☎ 01604 636271
✉ clerks@northampton-chambers.co.uk
Call Date: July 2009, Lincoln's Inn
Qualifications: [LLB (Sussex)]

HENDERSON MR IAN FRANCIS

Farringdon Chambers
180 Bermondsey Street, London SE1 3TQ,
☎ 020 7089 5700
Call Date: Nov 1990, Inner Temple
Pupil Supervisor
Qualifications: [LLB]
✉ ianhenderson@farringdon-law.co.uk

HENDERSON MR JAMES THOMAS

Pump Court Tax Chambers
16 Bedford Row, London WC1R 4EF,
☎ 020 7414 8080 ✉ clerks@pumptax.com
Kings Chambers
36 Young Street, Manchester M3 3FT,
☎ 0845 034 3444
✉ clerks@kingschambers.com
Kings Chambers
5 Park Square East, Leeds LS1 2NE,
☎ 0845 034 3444
✉ clerks@kingschambers.com
Call Date: Nov 1997, Gray's Inn
Pupil Supervisor
Qualifications: [BA]
✉ jhenderson@pumptax.com

Types of work: Capital tax, Corporation tax, Employee benefit trusts, Equity, Income tax, National Insurance, Private client, Stamp duty, Trusts, VAT, Wills

HENDERSON MISS JOSEPHINE

Five Paper
Ground Floor, 5 Paper Buildings, Temple, London EC4Y 7HB, ☎ 020 7815 3200
Call Date: Nov 1990, Inner Temple
Qualifications: [BSc (Bris) Dip Law]
✉ josephinehenderson@fivepaper.com

E

HENDERSON MR LAWRENCE MARK

9-12 Bell Yard
London WC2A 2JR, ☎ 020 7400 1800
✉ clerks@9-12bellyard.com
Call Date: Nov 1990, Middle Temple
Pupil Supervisor
Qualifications: [LLB]
l.henderson@9-12bellyard.com

HENDERSON MR MARK

Doughty Street Chambers
53-54 Doughty Street, London WC1N 2LS,
☎ 020 7404 1313
✉ enquiries@doughtystreet.co.uk
Doughty Street Chambers
Pall Mall Court, 61-67 King Street, Manchester M2 4PD, ☎ 0161 618 1066
Doughty Street Chambers
5th Floor, Broad Quay House, Prince Street, Bristol BS1 4DJ, ☎ 01179 058 717
Call Date: Oct 1994, Gray's Inn
Qualifications: [BA (Oxon)]
m.henderson@doughtystreet.co.uk

HENDERSON MR NEIL JOHN

Stone Chambers
4 Field Court, Gray's Inn, London WC1R 5EF,
☎ 020 7440 6900
✉ clerks@stonechambers.com
Call Date: Oct 2004, Inner Temple
Qualifications: [BA (Hons) (B'ham) CPE PGDL]
neil.henderson@stonechambers.com

HENDERSON MR SIMON ALEXANDER

4 Pump Court
4 Pump Court, Temple, London EC4Y 7AN,
☎ 020 7842 5555
✉ chambers@4pumpcourt.com
Call Date: Oct 1993, Inner Temple
Pupil Supervisor
Qualifications: [BA (Dunelm) Dip Law (Lond)]
shenderson@4pumpcourt.com

HENDERSON MR WILLIAM HUGO

Serle Court
6 New Square, Lincoln's Inn, London WC2A 3QS, ☎ 020 7242 6105
✉ clerks@serlecourt.co.uk
Call Date: July 1978, Inner Temple
Pupil Supervisor
Qualifications: [BA (Cantab)]
whenderson@serlecourt.co.uk

HENDRON MR ASHLEY PATRICK

Carmelite Chambers
9 Carmelite Street, London EC4Y 0DR,
☎ 020 7936 6300
✉ clerks@carmelitechambers.co.uk
Call Date: July 2005, Lincoln's Inn
Qualifications: [LLB (Hons)]
clerks@2drj.com

HENDRON MR GERALD JAMES

Broadway House Chambers
Broadway House, 9 Bank Street, Bradford, West Yorkshire BD1 1TW, ☎ 01274 722560
✉ clerks@broadwayhouse.co.uk
Broadway House Chambers
25 Park Square West, Leeds, West Yorkshire LS1 2PW, ☎ 0113 246 2600
✉ clerks@broadwayhouse.co.uk
Call Date: Oct 1992, Lincoln's Inn
Pupil Supervisor
Qualifications: [LLB(Hons)(Leeds)]
gjh@broadwayhouse.co.uk

HENDRON MR HENRY JOSEPH CHRISTOPHER

Strand Chambers
226 The Strand, London WC2R 1BA,
☎ 020 7117 6920 ✉ Henry@lawsurgery.com
Call Date: Nov 2006, Middle Temple
Qualifications: [BA (Hons) (Lond)]

HENDRY MRS LUCY HENRIETTA WESLEY

3 PB Barristers
3 Paper Buildings, Temple, London EC4Y 7EU,
☎ 020 7583 8055
3 PB Barristers
Royal Talbot House, 2 Victoria Street, Bristol, Avon BS1 6BB, ☎ 0117 928 1520
3 PB Barristers
23 Beaumont Street, Oxford OX1 2NP,
☎ 01865 793 736
3 PB Barristers
4 St Peter Street, Winchester SO23 8BW,
☎ 01962 868884
✉ clerks.winchester@3paper.co.uk
3 PB Barristers
30 Christchurch Road, Bournemouth, Dorset BH1 3PD, ☎ 01202 292102
✉ clerks.bournemouth@3paper.co.uk
Call Date: Nov 1988, Inner Temple
Qualifications: [LLB]
lucy.hendry@3paper.co.uk

HENDY MR JOHN GILES QC (1987)

Old Square Chambers
10-11 Bedford Row, London WC1R 4BU,
☎020 7269 0300 ✉clerks@oldsquare.co.uk
Old Square Chambers
3 Orchard Court, St Augustine's Yard, Bristol BS1 5DP, ☎0117 930 5100
✉clerks@oldsquare.co.uk
Call Date: July 1972, Gray's Inn
Qualifications: [LLB LLM]
hendyqc@oldsquare.co.uk

HENKE MISS RUTH SARA MARGARET QC (2006)

30 Park Place
Cardiff CF10 3BS, ☎029 2039 8421
✉clerks@30parkplace.law.co.uk
Linenhall Chambers
1 Stanley Place, Chester CH1 2LU,
☎01244 348282
✉clerks@linenhallchambers.co.uk
Call Date: Nov 1987, Inner Temple
Pupil Supervisor
Qualifications: [MA (Oxon)]
rmh@30parkplace.co.uk

HENLEY MR ANDREW MICHAEL

Furnival Chambers
32 Furnival Street, London EC4A 1JQ,
☎020 7405 3232
Call Date: Oct 1992, Middle Temple
Pupil Supervisor
Qualifications: [LLB(Hons)(Lond)]
ahenley@furnivallaw.co.uk

HENLEY MISS CARLY ELIZABETH

Dere Street Barristers
33 Broad Chare, Newcastle Upon Tyne NE1 3DQ, ☎0844 3351551
✉clerks@derestreet.co.uk
Call Date: July 2003, Lincoln's Inn
Qualifications: [LLB Hons (L'pool)]
clerks@broadcharechambers.co.uk

HENLEY MR CHRISTOPHER MICHAEL

Carmelite Chambers
9 Carmelite Street, London EC4Y 0DR,
☎020 7936 6300
✉clerks@carmelitechambers.co.uk
Call Date: July 1989, Gray's Inn
Pupil Supervisor
Qualifications: [LLB (Bris)]
chenley@carmelitechambers.co.uk

HENLEY MR MARK ROBERT DANIEL

Zenith Chambers
10 Park Square, Leeds LS1 2LH,
☎0113 245 5438
✉clerks@zenithchambers.co.uk
Call Date: Oct 1994, Lincoln's Inn
Qualifications: [MA (Cantab)]
mhenley@zenithchambers.co.uk

HENLEY MR MARTIN BRETT

Great James Street Chambers
37 Great James Street, London WC1N 3HB,
☎020 7440 4949
✉chambers@greatjames.co.uk
Call Date: Oct 2004, Inner Temple
Qualifications: [BA (Essex) LLB]

HENNELL MR PETER GORDON

Linenhall Chambers
1 Stanley Place, Chester CH1 2LU,
☎01244 348282
✉clerks@linenhallchambers.co.uk
Call Date: July 1982, Middle Temple
Pupil Supervisor
Qualifications: [MA (Cantab)]

HENNESSEY CAPTAIN PATRICK RUPERT

39 Essex Street
London WC2R 3AT, ☎020 7832 1111
✉clerks@39essex.com
Call Date: July 2010, Middle Temple
Qualifications: [BA (Hons) (Oxon)]
patrick.hennessey@39essexstreet.com

HENNESSEY MRS TRACEY

12 College Place
Fauvelle Buildings, 12 College Place, Southampton SO15 2FE, ☎023 8032 0320
✉clerks@12cp.co.uk
Call Date: Oct 2001, Lincoln's Inn
Qualifications: [LLB (Hons)]
thennessey@12cp.co.uk

HENNESSY MISS CLARE DANIELLE

18 Red Lion Court
London EC4A 3EB, ☎020 7520 6000
✉chambers@18rlc.co.uk
Call Date: July 2009, Gray's Inn
Qualifications: [BA]

E

HENNESSY MISS SHIRLEY JANE

Oriel Chambers
14 Water Street, Liverpool, Merseyside L2 8TD, ☎0151 236 7191
✉clerks@orielchambers.co.uk
Oriel Chambers
18 Ribblesdale Place, Preston PR1 3NA, ☎01772 254 764
✉clerks@oriel-chambers.co.uk
Call Date: Oct 1997, Lincoln's Inn
Qualifications: [BA (Hons)(Oxon)]
shirley.hennessy@orielchambers.co.uk

HENRY MISS ANNETTE PHYLLIS

25 Bedford Row
London WC1R 4HD, ☎020 7067 1500
✉clerks@25bedfordrow.com
Call Date: July 1984, Gray's Inn
Qualifications: [LLB (Hons) (Manch)]
ahenry@25bedfordrow.com

HENRY MRS CAROLE ANNE

Chambers of Mrs Carole Anne Henry
78 Moorhen Way, Buckingham, Buckinghamshire MK18 1GU,
☎01280 824520 ✉caroleahenry@aol.com
Call Date: Oct 1993, Inner Temple
Qualifications: [LLB (Hons)(Leics)]
caroleahenry@aol.com

HENRY MR DELROY

Citadel Chambers
The Citadel, 190 Corporation Street, Birmingham B4 6QD, ☎0121 233 8500
✉clerks@citadelchambers.com
Call Date: Oct 1999, Inner Temple
Qualifications: [LLB]
clerks@citadelchambers.com

HENRY MR EDWARD JOSEPH ALOYSIUS

QEB Hollis Whiteman
1-2 Laurence Pountney Hill, London EC4R 0EU, ☎020 7933 8855
✉barristers@qebhw.co.uk
Call Date: Nov 1988, Lincoln's Inn
Pupil Supervisor
Qualifications: [BA (Hons) (Cantab) Dip Law (Lond)]
edward.henry@qebhw.co.uk

HENSHAW MR ANDREW RAYWOOD

Brick Court Chambers
7-8 Essex Street, London WC2R 3LD,
☎020 7379 3550 ✉clerks@brickcourt.co.uk
Call Date: Oct 2000, Inner Temple
Pupil Supervisor
Qualifications: [MA (Cantab) BA]
Andrew.Henshaw@Brickcourt.co.uk

HENSHAW MISS GWEN LADI

Central Chambers
89 Princess Street, Manchester M1 4HT,
☎0161 236 1133
✉clerks@centralchambers.co.uk
Call Date: Nov 2000, Middle Temple
Qualifications: [BA (Hons) (Manch)]

HENSON MISS CHRISTINE RUTH

Crown Office Row Chambers
119 Church Street, Brighton, Sussex BN1 1UD, ☎01273 625625
✉clerks@1cor.com
Call Date: Oct 1994, Middle Temple
Pupil Supervisor
Qualifications: [BA (Warw)]
christine.henson@1cor.com

HENSON MR GRAHAM STANLEY

No5 Chambers
Fountain Court, Steelhouse Lane, Birmingham B4 6DR, ☎0845 210 5555 ✉info@no5.com
No5 Chambers
Greenwood House, 4-7 Salisbury Court, London EC4Y 8AA, ☎0845 210 5555
No5 Chambers
38 Queen Square, Bristol BS1 4QS,
☎0845 210 5555
Call Date: July 1976, Gray's Inn
Pupil Supervisor
Qualifications: [BA (Cantab)]
gh@no5.com

HENSTOCK-TURNER MRS SARAH ELIZABETH

College Chambers
19 Carlton Crescent, Southampton, Hampshire SO15 2ET, ☎023 8023 0338
✉clerks@college-chambers.co.uk
Call Date: Oct 2004, Middle Temple
Qualifications: [LLB (Hons) LLM]

HENTHORN MISS KATE MARIE

18 St John Street
Manchester M3 4EA, ☎0161 278 1800
✉clerks@18sjs.com
7 Bell Yard
London WC2A 2JR, ☎020 7831 0636
✉kevintarrant@btconnect.com
Call Date: Mar 2005, Middle Temple
Qualifications: [LLB (Hons)]

HENTON MR PAUL MICHAEL PETER

Quadrant Chambers
Quadrant House, 10 Fleet Street, London EC4Y 1AU, ☎ 020 7583 4444
✉ info@quadrantchambers.com
Call Date: July 2004, Inner Temple
Qualifications: [LLM (Cantab) LLB (UCL)]
✉ paul.henton@quadrantchambers.com

HEPHER MR PAUL ARTHUR RICHARD

4 Paper Buildings
1st Floor, 4 Paper Buildings, Temple, London EC4Y 7EX, ☎ 020 7427 5200
✉ clerks@4pb.com
Call Date: Oct 1994, Gray's Inn
Qualifications: [MA (Oxon)]
✉ pah@4pb.com

HEPPENSTALL MISS CLAIRE NORAH

1 Garden Court Family Law Chambers
Ground Floor, One Garden Court, Temple, London EC4Y 9BJ, ☎ 020 7797 7900
✉ clerks@1gc.com
Call Date: Nov 1990, Inner Temple
Pupil Supervisor
Qualifications: [LLB (Hons)(Lond) LLM (Lond)]
✉ heppenstall@1gc.com

HEPPINSTALL MR ADAM JOHN

Henderson Chambers
2 Harcourt Buildings, Temple, London EC4Y 9DB, ☎ 020 7583 9020
✉ clerks@hendersonchambers.co.uk
Call Date: Oct 1999, Middle Temple
Pupil Supervisor
Qualifications: [MA (Oxon)]
✉ aheppinstall@hendersonchambers.co.uk

HEPWORTH MRS ELIZABETH MARY

3 PB Barristers
3 Paper Buildings, Temple, London EC4Y 7EU, ☎ 020 7583 8055
3 PB Barristers
30 Christchurch Road, Bournemouth, Dorset BH1 3PD, ☎ 01202 292102
✉ clerks.bournemouth@3paper.co.uk
3 PB Barristers
Royal Talbot House, 2 Victoria Street, Bristol, Avon BS1 6BB, ☎ 0117 928 1520
3 PB Barristers
4 St Peter Street, Winchester SO23 8BW, ☎ 01962 868884
✉ clerks.winchester@3paper.co.uk
3 PB Barristers
23 Beaumont Street, Oxford OX1 2NP, ☎ 01865 793 736
Call Date: Mar 2004, Middle Temple
Qualifications: [LLB (Hons) (So'ton)]

HERBERG MR JAVAN WILLIAM QC (2011)

Blackstone Chambers
Blackstone House, Temple, London EC4Y 9BW, ☎ 020 7583 1770
✉ clerks@blackstonechambers.com
Call Date: Oct 1992, Lincoln's Inn
Pupil Supervisor
Qualifications: [LLB(Hons)(Lond) BCL]
✉ javanherberg@blackstonechambers.com

HERBERT MR DAVID RICHARD

36 Bedford Row
London WC1R 4JH, ☎ 020 7421 8000
✉ chambers@36bedfordrow.co.uk
Call Date: Nov 1992, Gray's Inn
Pupil Supervisor
Qualifications: [BA (So'ton)]
✉ dherbert@36bedford.co.uk

HERBERT MR DOUGLAS CHURCHILL

Ropewalk Chambers
24 The Ropewalk, Nottingham NG1 5EF, ☎ 0115 947 2581 ✉ clerks@ropewalk.co.uk
Call Date: July 1973, Middle Temple
Pupil Supervisor, Recorder
Qualifications: [LLB]
✉ douglasherbert@ropewalk.co.uk

HERBERT MISS JANE ELIZABETH

Rougemont Chambers
Victory House, Dean Clarke Gardens, Southernhay East, Exeter EX2 4AA, ☎ 01392 208484
✉ clerks@rougemontchambers.co.uk
Call Date: July 2008, Gray's Inn
Qualifications: [BA (Exon)]

HERBERT MISS KATE

Ropewalk Chambers
24 The Ropewalk, Nottingham NG1 5EF, ☎ 0115 947 2581 ✉ clerks@ropewalk.co.uk
Call Date: July 2004, Gray's Inn
Qualifications: [LLB Hons (Nott'm) BVC (Nott'm)]
✉ kateherbert@ropewalk.co.uk

E

HERBERT MR MARK JEREMY QC (1995)

5 Stone Buildings
5 Stone Buildings, Lincoln's Inn, London WC2A 3XT, ☎ 020 7242 6201
✉ clerks@5sblaw.com
Call Date: July 1974, Lincoln's Inn
Qualifications: [BA (Lond)]
mherbert@5sblaw.com

Fax: 020 7831 8102;
DX: 304 London;
URL: www.5sblaw.com

Other professional qualifications: Accredited mediator

Types of work: Capital tax, Chancery (general), Equity, Income tax, Professional negligence, Succession, Trusts, Wills

Awards and memberships: Chancery Bar Association; Revenue Bar Association; Society of Trust and Estate Practitioners; Charity Law Association; Association of Contentious Trust and Probate Specialists

Publications: *Whiteman on Capital Gains Tax* (Co-editor), 1989; *Drafting and Variation of Wills*, 1989

Reported Cases: *Sieff v Fox*, [2005] 1 WLR 3811 Re-examination of the rule in Hastings-Bass.
Edge v Pensions Ombudsman, [2000] Ch 602 Leading case on the Ombudsman's jurisdiction, and on challenges to the exercise of trustees' powers.
R v OPRA, ex parte Littlewoods, [1998] PLR 63 Application of the *Ramsay* principle to capital transfer tax.
IRC v Fitzwilliam, [1993] 1 WLR 1189 Application of the *Ramsay* principle to capital transfer tax.
Mettoy Pension Trustees v Evans, [1990] 1 WLR 1587 Exercise of fiduciary powers conferred by pension scheme.

HERBERT MR PETER

Justice House
67 Wentworth Avenue, Finchley, London N3 1YN, ☎ 07973 794 946
✉ pherb5law@aol.com
Call Date: Nov 1982, Gray's Inn
Pupil Supervisor
Qualifications: [LLB (Lond)]

HERBERT MRS REBECCA MARY

36 Bedford Row
London WC1R 4JH, ☎ 020 7421 8000
✉ chambers@36bedfordrow.co.uk
Call Date: Oct 1993, Gray's Inn
Qualifications: [LLB (Manch)]

HERCOCK MR DAVID LEONARD

Sovereign Chambers
46 Park Place, Leeds LS1 2RY,
☎ 0113 245 1841
✉ clerks@sovereignchambers.co.uk
Call Date: July 2001, Inner Temple
Qualifications: [LLB (Hons)(Nott'm)]
david.hercock@soveringchambrs.co.uk

HERMAN MR RAYMOND CHARLES

Call Date: Feb 1972, Inner Temple
Pupil Supervisor, Recorder
Qualifications: [LLB]

HERMAN MR SAUL MEYER

3 Temple Gardens
Lower Ground Floor, 3 Temple Gardens, Temple, London EC4Y 9AU, ☎ 020 7353 3102
✉ clerks@3tg.co.uk
Call Date: July 2007, Inner Temple
Qualifications: [BA (Oxon)]

HERMER MR RICHARD SIMON QC (2009)

Matrix Chambers
Griffin Building, Gray's Inn, London WC1R 5LN, ☎ 020 7404 3447
✉ matrix@matrixlaw.co.uk / lscott@matrixlaw.co.uk
Doughty Street Chambers
Pall Mall Court, 61-67 King Street, Manchester M2 4PD, ☎ 0161 618 1066
Doughty Street Chambers
53-54 Doughty Street, London WC1N 2LS,
☎ 020 7404 1313
✉ enquiries@doughtystreet.co.uk
Call Date: Oct 1993, Middle Temple
Qualifications: [BA (Hons)(Manch)]

HERRITY MR PETER

Chambers of Mr P Herrity
75 Provene Gardens, Waltham Chase, Winchester, Hampshire SO32 2RW,
☎ 01489 894408 ✉ peter.herrity@talktalk.net
Call Date: July 1982, Lincoln's Inn
Qualifications: [BSc (Lond)]

HERRMANN MR RICHARD MICHAEL

Dere Street Barristers
14 Toft Green, York YO1 6JT, ☎0844 3351551
✉clerks@derestreet.co.uk
York Chambers
Rotterdam House, 116 The Quayside, Newcastle Upon Tyne NE1 3DY, ☎0191 206 4677
Call Date: Oct 2004, Inner Temple
Qualifications: [BA CPE]
clerks@yorkchambers.co.uk, rherrmann@yorkchambers.co.uk

HERTZOG MISS FRANCES DAWN

Number 7 Harrington Street Chambers
7 Harrington Street, Liverpool L2 9YH, ☎0151 242 0707 ✉clerks@7hs.co.uk
Call Date: Nov 2001, Gray's Inn
Qualifications: [LLB (L'Pool)]
frances.hertzog@7hs.co.uk

HESLOP MR MARTIN SYDNEY QC (1995)

2 Hare Court
Lower Ground, Ground, 1st & 2nd Floor, 2 Hare Court, Temple, London EC4Y 7BH, ☎020 7353 3982 ✉clerks@2harecourt.com
Call Date: July 1972, Lincoln's Inn
Recorder
Qualifications: [LLB (Hons)]

HESTER MR JAMES FRANCIS WILLIAM

Park Lane Plowden
Lombard House, 4-8 Lombard Street, Newcastle Upon Tyne NE1 3AE, ☎0191 211 4087
✉clerks@parklaneplowden.co.uk
Call Date: July 2010, Middle Temple
Qualifications: [BA (Hons) (Bris)]
jim.hester@parklaneplowden.co.uk

HESTER MR PAUL STEPHEN

3 PB Barristers
3 Paper Buildings, Temple, London EC4Y 7EU, ☎020 7583 8055
3 PB Barristers
Royal Talbot House, 2 Victoria Street, Bristol, Avon BS1 6BB, ☎0117 928 1520
3 PB Barristers
30 Christchurch Road, Bournemouth, Dorset BH1 3PD, ☎01202 292102
✉clerks.bournemouth@3paper.co.uk
3 PB Barristers
4 St Peter Street, Winchester SO23 8BW, ☎01962 868884
✉clerks.winchester@3paper.co.uk
3 PB Barristers
23 Beaumont Street, Oxford OX1 2NP, ☎01865 793 736
Call Date: July 1989, Middle Temple
Pupil Supervisor
Qualifications: [BA (Warw) Dip Law]
paul.hester@3paper.co.uk

HETHERINGTON MR EDWARD RONALD

Assize Court Chambers
14 Small Street, Bristol BS1 1DE, ☎0117 926 4587 ✉carly@assize.co.uk
Call Date: Nov 2006, Middle Temple
Qualifications: [LLB (Hons) (Durham)]
carly@assize.co.uk

HETT MR JAMES

The Chambers Of Mr Hett
53 Foxhill Road, Burton Joyce, Nottingham NG14 5DB, ☎0115 9313958/07727 688337
Call Date: Nov 1991, Middle Temple
Pupil Supervisor
Qualifications: [LLB (Hons) (B'ham)]
jameshett@hotmail.com

HEVINGHAM MR PAUL WILLIAM

Heavenwood Chambers
Heavenwood Chambers, Heavenwood House, 71 Bownham Park, Rodborough Common, Stroud, Gloucestershire GL5 5BZ, ☎01453 873444 ✉kms@heavenwood.co.uk
No 8 Chambers
8 Fountain Court, Steelhouse Lane, Birmingham B4 6DR, ☎0121 236 5514
✉clerks@no8chambers.co.uk
Call Date: Nov 2006, Gray's Inn
Qualifications: [LLB]
pwh@heavenwood.co.uk

HEWERTSON MR CHRISTOPHER NEIL

2 King's Bench Walk
2 King's Bench Walk, Temple, London EC4Y 7DE, ☎020 7353 1746
✉clerks@2kbw.com
Call Date: July 2007, Lincoln's Inn
Qualifications: [LLB (Notts)]

HEWITT MISS ALEXANDRA HELEN

Linenhall Chambers
1 Stanley Place, Chester CH1 2LU, ☎01244 348282
✉clerks@linenhallchambers.co.uk
Call Date: Oct 1995, Middle Temple
Qualifications: [MA (Oxon)]
ah@nicholasstreet.com

E

HEWITT MISS ALISON BRYDIE

Temple Garden Chambers
1 Harcourt Buildings, Temple, London EC4Y 9DA, ☎020 7583 1315
✉clerks@tgchambers.com
Call Date: July 1984, Middle Temple
Pupil Supervisor
Qualifications: [LLB (Lond)]
✉a.hewitt@tgchambers.com

HEWITT MISS CATHERINE EILEEN

Cathedral Chambers
First Floor, 17 Queen Street, Newcastle Upon Tyne NE1 3UG, ☎0191 232 1311
✉mail@cathedralchambers.com
Call Date: July 2001, Lincoln's Inn
Qualifications: [LLB (Hons) LLM (Dunelm)]

HEWITT MR DAVID EDWARD MILES

Five St Andrew's Hill
5 St Andrew's Hill, London EC4V 5BZ, ☎020 7332 5400 ✉Clerks@5sah.co.uk
Call Date: Feb 1991, Middle Temple
Pupil Supervisor
Qualifications: [BSc (Wales)]
✉harryhewitt@5sah.co.uk

HEWITT MR EDWARD WILLIAM JAMES

9 Stone Buildings
Lincoln's Inn, London WC2A 3NN, ☎020 7404 5055
✉clerks@9stonebuildings.com
Call Date: Oct 2007, Lincoln's Inn
Qualifications: [LLB (Lond) BCL (Lond)]
✉EHewitt@9stonebuildings.com

HEWITT MISS WENDY ELIZABETH

Five St Andrew's Hill
5 St Andrew's Hill, London EC4V 5BZ, ☎020 7332 5400 ✉Clerks@5sah.co.uk
Call Date: Nov 1999, Middle Temple
Qualifications: [LLB (Hons)]
✉wendyhewitt@5sah.co.uk

HEWSON MS BARBARA MARY

Hardwicke
New Square, Lincoln's Inn, London WC2A 3SB, ☎020 7242 2523
✉enquiries@hardwicke.co.uk
Call Date: Nov 1985, Middle Temple
Pupil Supervisor
Qualifications: [MA (Cantab)]

HEXT MR NEIL FRASER

Four New Square
Four New Square, Lincoln's Inn, London WC2A 3RJ, ☎020 7822 2000
✉barristers@4newsquare.com
Call Date: Oct 1995, Gray's Inn
Pupil Supervisor
Qualifications: [LLB (Bris)]
✉n.hext@4newsquare.com

HEY MR TERENCE MICHAEL

Chambers of Mr T M Hey
Folly Hall Farm, Tranmire, Whitby, North Yorkshire YO21 2BW, ☎07771 665397
✉terencehey@hotmail.co.uk
Call Date: Oct 1997, Lincoln's Inn
Qualifications: [LLB (Hons)(Teesside)]

HEYBROEK MS MYRNA-JANE

Bell Yard Chambers
116/118 Chancery Lane, London WC2A 1PP, ☎020 7306 9292
✉byclerks@bellyardchambers.co.uk
Call Date: Oct 2003, Inner Temple
Qualifications: [LLB (Open Uni)]
✉jheybroek@bellyardchambers.co.uk

HEYWOOD MR MARK ADRIAN QC (2010)

5 King's Bench Walk
5 King's Bench Walk, Temple, London EC4Y 7DN, ☎020 7353 5638
✉clerks@5kbw.co.uk
Call Date: July 1985, Gray's Inn
Pupil Supervisor, Recorder
Qualifications: [BA(Cantab)]

HEYWOOD MR MARK STEPHEN QC (2012)

No5 Chambers
Fountain Court, Steelhouse Lane, Birmingham B4 6DR, ☎0845 210 5555 ✉info@no5.com
No5 Chambers
Greenwood House, 4-7 Salisbury Court, London EC4Y 8AA, ☎0845 210 5555
No5 Chambers
38 Queen Square, Bristol BS1 4QS, ☎0845 210 5555
Call Date: July 1986, Gray's Inn
Qualifications: [LLB (Newc)]
✉mh@no5.com

HEYWOOD MR MATTHEW ALEXANDER

Eastbourne Chambers
5 Chiswick Place, Eastbourne, East Sussex BN21 4NH, ☎ 01323 642102
✉ clerks@eastbournechambers.co.uk
Call Date: July 2006, Middle Temple
Qualifications: [LLB (Hons) (Sussex)]

HEYWOOD MR MICHAEL EDMUNDSON

Radcliffe Chambers
Ground Floor, 11 New Square, Lincoln's Inn, London WC2A 3QB, ☎ 020 7831 0081
✉ clerks@radcliffechambers.com
Call Date: July 1975, Inner Temple
Pupil Supervisor
Qualifications: [BSc Soc(Lond) FCIArb]

HEYWORTH MS ALISON

9 St John Street
Manchester M3 4DN, ☎ 0161 955 9000
✉ civilclerks@9sjs.com / criminalclerks@9sjs.com
Call Date: Oct 2001, Inner Temple
Qualifications: [BA (Warw) CPE (Manch)]

HEYWORTH MISS CATHERINE LOUISE

30 Park Place
Cardiff CF10 3BS, ☎ 029 2039 8421
✉ clerks@30parkplace.law.co.uk
Call Date: Nov 1991, Inner Temple
Pupil Supervisor
Qualifications: [LLB (Hons)]
🖃 ch@30parkplace.co.uk

HEYWORTH MR JAMES EDWARD WATSON

Lincoln House Chambers
Tower 12, The Avenue North, Spinningfields, 18-22 Bridge Street, Manchester M3 3BZ, ☎ 0161 832 5701
✉ info@lincolnhousechambers.com
Call Date: Nov 2006, Gray's Inn
Qualifications: [BSc GDip Law]
🖃 james.heyworth@lincolnhousechambers.com

HEYWORTH MISS VICTORIA SOPHIE DOROTHEA

Deans Court Chambers
24 St John Street, Manchester M3 4DF, ☎ 0161 214 6000 ✉ clerks@deanscourt.co.uk
Deans Court Chambers
101 Walker Street, Preston PR1 2RR, ☎ 01772 565 600
✉ preston@deanscourt.co.uk
Call Date: July 2003, Gray's Inn
Qualifications: [LLB (Leeds)]
🖃 heyworth@deanscourt.co.uk

HIBBERT MR WILLIAM JOHN

Henderson Chambers
2 Harcourt Buildings, Temple, London EC4Y 9DB, ☎ 020 7583 9020
✉ clerks@hendersonchambers.co.uk
Call Date: July 1979, Inner Temple
Pupil Supervisor
Qualifications: [MA (Oxon)]

HICK MR MICHAEL ANDREW

Five Paper Buildings
1st Floor, Five Paper Buildings, Temple, London EC4Y 7HB, ☎ 020 7583 6117
✉ clerks@5pb.co.uk
Call Date: Oct 1995, Gray's Inn
Pupil Supervisor
Qualifications: [BA ACA]
🖃 mh@5pb.co.uk

HICKEY MR ALEXANDER FREDERICK

4 Pump Court
4 Pump Court, Temple, London EC4Y 7AN, ☎ 020 7842 5555
✉ chambers@4pumpcourt.com
Call Date: Nov 1995, Lincoln's Inn
Pupil Supervisor
Qualifications: [BA (Oxon)]
🖃 ahickey@4pumpcourt.com

HICKIE DR THOMAS VINCENT

Seven Bedford Row
7 Bedford Row, London WC1R 4BS, ☎ 020 7242 3555 ✉ clerks@7br.co.uk
Call Date: Oct 2009, Gray's Inn
Qualifications: [BA (Hons) LLB PhD]
🖃 tvhickie@7br.co.uk

HICKINBOTTOM MISS ABIGAIL JEAN

Call Date: Nov 2004, Inner Temple
Qualifications: [BA CPE]
🖃 hickinbottom@paradisechambers.co.uk

E

HICKMAN DR THOMAS RICHARD

Blackstone Chambers
Blackstone House, Temple, London EC4Y 9BW, ☎ 020 7583 1770
✉ clerks@blackstonechambers.com
Call Date: Oct 2003, Lincoln's Inn
Qualifications: [MA (Cantab) PhD (Cantab) LLM (Toronto)]
✉ Tomhickman@blackstonechambers.com

HICKMET MR RICHARD SALADIN

The Chambers of Richard Hickmet
The Chantry, Rhode, North Petherton, Somerset TA5 2AD, ☎ 01278 663388
✉ law@richardhickmet.co.uk
Call Date: July 1974, Inner Temple
Pupil Supervisor
Qualifications: [BA]

HICKS MR BENJAMIN DAVID

1 Chancery Lane
London WC2A 1LF, ☎ 0845 634 6666
✉ clerks@1chancerylane.com
Call Date: July 2001, Inner Temple
Qualifications: [LLB (So'ton)]
✉ bhicks@1chancerylane.com

HICKS MR EDWARD GORDON DAVID

Radcliffe Chambers
Ground Floor, 11 New Square, Lincoln's Inn, London WC2A 3QB, ☎ 020 7831 0081
✉ clerks@radcliffechambers.com
Call Date: Nov 2004, Middle Temple
Qualifications: [MA (Hons) (Cantab) BCL (Oxon)]
✉ ehicks@radcliffechambers.com

HICKS MR MARTIN LESLIE ARTHUR QC (2003)

2 Hare Court
Lower Ground, Ground, 1st & 2nd Floor, 2 Hare Court, Temple, London EC4Y 7BH, ☎ 020 7353 3982 ✉ clerks@2harecourt.com
Call Date: May 1977, Inner Temple
Qualifications: [LLB (Lond)]
✉ martinhicks@2harecourt.com

HICKS MR MICHAEL CHARLES

Hogarth Chambers
5 New Square, Lincoln's Inn, London WC2A 3RJ, ☎ 020 7404 0404
✉ barristers@hogarthchambers.com
Call Date: Nov 1976, Inner Temple
Pupil Supervisor
Qualifications: [BA (Cantab)]
✉ mhicks@hogarthchambers.com

HICKS MISS PASCALE ANNE

Deans Court Chambers
24 St John Street, Manchester M3 4DF, ☎ 0161 214 6000 ✉ clerks@deanscourt.co.uk
Deans Court Chambers
101 Walker Street, Preston PR1 2RR, ☎ 01772 565 600
✉ preston@deanscourt.co.uk
Call Date: Oct 1999, Lincoln's Inn
Qualifications: [LLB (Hons) (L'pool) Licence en Droit]

HICKS MR WILLIAM DAVID ANTHONY QC (1995)

Landmark Chambers
180 Fleet Street, London EC4A 2HG, ☎ 020 7430 1221
✉ clerks@landmarkchambers.co.uk
Call Date: July 1975, Inner Temple
Qualifications: [MA (Cantab)]
✉ whicks@landmarkchambers.co.uk

HIDDLESTON MR ADAM WALLACE

3 PB Barristers
3 Paper Buildings, Temple, London EC4Y 7EU, ☎ 020 7583 8055
3 PB Barristers
Royal Talbot House, 2 Victoria Street, Bristol, Avon BS1 6BB, ☎ 0117 928 1520
3 PB Barristers
4 St Peter Street, Winchester SO23 8BW, ☎ 01962 868884
✉ clerks.winchester@3paper.co.uk
3 PB Barristers
23 Beaumont Street, Oxford OX1 2NP, ☎ 01865 793 736
3 PB Barristers
30 Christchurch Road, Bournemouth, Dorset BH1 3PD, ☎ 01202 292102
✉ clerks.bournemouth@3paper.co.uk
Call Date: Oct 1990, Inner Temple
Pupil Supervisor
Qualifications: [LLB (Newc)]
✉ adam.hiddleston@3paper.co.uk

HIGGINS MR ADRIAN JOHN

13 King's Bench Walk
13 King's Bench Walk, Temple, London EC4Y 7EN, ☎ 020 7353 7204
✉ clerks@13kbw.co.uk
13 KBW
32 Beaumont Street, Oxford OX1 2NP, ☎ 01865 311066 ✉ clerks@13kbw.co.uk
Call Date: Oct 1990, Lincoln's Inn
Qualifications: [MA (Hons)(Oxon)]
✉ ahiggins@13kbw.co.uk

E

HIGGINS MR ANTHONY PAUL

13 King's Bench Walk
13 King's Bench Walk, Temple, London EC4Y 7EN, ☎ 020 7353 7204
✉ clerks@13kbw.co.uk
Call Date: Nov 1978, Gray's Inn
Qualifications: [BA (Oxon) LLM]
ahiggins@13kbw.co.uk

HIGGINS MR DANIEL MALCOLM BUHLEA

Nine Bedford Row
9 Bedford Row, London WC1R 4AZ,
☎ 020 7489 2727
✉ clerks@9bedfordrow.co.uk
Call Date: July 2003, Inner Temple
Qualifications: [BA (Hons)(Cantab)]
daniel.higgins@9bedfordrow.co.uk

HIGGINS MISS GABRIELLE MARGARET

Maitland Chambers
7 Stone Buildings, Lincoln's Inn, London WC2A 3SZ, ☎ 020 7406 1200
✉ clerks@maitlandchambers.com
Call Date: July 2002, Lincoln's Inn
Qualifications: [BA (Hons)(Oxon) Dip Law]
ghiggins@maitlandchambers.com

HIGGINS MISS GILLIAN KAY

Nine Bedford Row
9 Bedford Row, London WC1R 4AZ,
☎ 020 7489 2727
✉ clerks@9bedfordrow.co.uk
Call Date: Nov 1997, Gray's Inn
Pupil Supervisor
Qualifications: [LLB LLM (Cantab)]

HIGGINS MISS LOUISE

Clock Chambers
18 Waterloo Road, Wolverhampton WV1 4BL,
☎ 01902 313444
✉ clockchambers@btconnect.com
Call Date: July 2003, Gray's Inn
Qualifications: [LLB (Warw)]

HIGGINS MR MARK EDWARD

Harcourt Chambers
1st Floor, 2 Harcourt Buildings, Temple, London EC4Y 9DB, ☎ 0844 561 7135
Call Date: July 2005, Inner Temple
Qualifications: [MA St. John's College University of Oxford]
mhiggins@harcourtchambers.law.co.uk

HIGGINS MISS NICHOLA CLAIRE LESLEY

Doughty Street Chambers
53-54 Doughty Street, London WC1N 2LS,
☎ 020 7404 1313
✉ enquiries@doughtystreet.co.uk
Call Date: July 2005, Lincoln's Inn
Qualifications: [BA (Hons)]
n.higgins@doughtystreet.co.uk

HIGGINS MR PAUL ANDREW

Deans Court Chambers
24 St John Street, Manchester M3 4DF,
☎ 0161 214 6000 ✉ clerks@deanscourt.co.uk
Deans Court Chambers
101 Walker Street, Preston PR1 2RR,
☎ 01772 565 600
✉ preston@deanscourt.co.uk
Call Date: Mar 1996, Lincoln's Inn
Qualifications: [BA (Hons)(Oxon)]

HIGGINS MR RUPERT JAMES HALE

Hardwicke
New Square, Lincoln's Inn, London WC2A 3SB, ☎ 020 7242 2523
✉ enquiries@hardwicke.co.uk
Call Date: Oct 1991, Inner Temple
Pupil Supervisor
Qualifications: [BA (Cantab)]
rupert.higgins@hardwicke.co.uk

HIGGINSON MR PETER ST GEORGE

Charter Chambers
33 John Street, London WC1N 2AT,
☎ 020 7618 4400
✉ clerks@charterchambers.com
Call Date: July 1975, Lincoln's Inn
Pupil Supervisor
Qualifications: [BA (Canada)]

HIGGINSON MR TIMOTHY NICHOLAS BENNETT

Littleton Chambers
3 King's Bench Walk North, Temple, London EC4Y 7HR, ☎ 020 7797 8600
✉ fschneider@littletonchambers.co.uk
St John's Chambers
101 Victoria Street, Bristol BS1 6PU,
☎ 0117 923 4700
✉ clerks@stjohnschambers.co.uk
Call Date: Nov 1977, Inner Temple
Qualifications: [LLB]

E

HIGGINSON MR WILLIAM EDWARD

King's Bench and Godolphin (KBG)Chambers
115 North Hill, Plymouth, Devon PL4 8JY, ☎01752 221551
✉clerks@kbgchambers.co.uk
Call Date: Oct 2001, Lincoln's Inn
Qualifications: [LLB (Hons)(Wolves)]
✉william.higginson@kingsbenchchambers.co.uk

HIGGO MR JUSTIN BERESFORD

Serle Court
6 New Square, Lincoln's Inn, London WC2A 3QS, ☎020 7242 6105
✉clerks@serlecourt.co.uk
Call Date: Feb 1995, Gray's Inn
Pupil Supervisor
Qualifications: [BA (Oxon)]
✉jhiggo@serlecourt.co.uk

HIGGS MR JONATHAN ALEXANDER CAMERON QC (2011)

5 King's Bench Walk
5 King's Bench Walk, Temple, London EC4Y 7DN, ☎020 7353 5638
✉clerks@5kbw.co.uk
Call Date: Nov 1987, Middle Temple
Pupil Supervisor
Qualifications: [BA]
✉jonathan.higgs@5kbw.co.uk

HIGGS MISS JOSEPHINE AMY

7 King's Bench Walk
Ground Floor, 7 King's Bench Walk, Temple, London EC4Y 7DS, ☎020 7910 8300
✉clerks@7kbw.co.uk
Call Date: Nov 2000, Middle Temple
Pupil Supervisor
Qualifications: [BA (Hons) (Oxon) CPE]

HIGNETT MR RICHARD JAMES

No5 Chambers
Greenwood House, 4-7 Salisbury Court, London EC4Y 8AA, ☎0845 210 5555
No5 Chambers
38 Queen Square, Bristol BS1 4QS, ☎0845 210 5555
No5 Chambers
Fountain Court, Steelhouse Lane, Birmingham B4 6DR, ☎0845 210 5555 ✉info@no5.com
Call Date: Nov 1995, Inner Temple
Pupil Supervisor
Qualifications: [BA (Keele)]
✉rjh@no5.com

HIKMET MISS BERIN SIMGE

Argent Chambers
5 Bell Yard, London WC2A 2JR, ☎020 7556 5500
✉briefsin@argentchambers.co.uk
Call Date: Oct 2000, Middle Temple
Qualifications: [BSc (Hons) (Bris) Dip in Law]

HILDYARD MISS MARIANNA CATHERINE THOROTON QC (2002)

4 Brick Court
4 Brick Court, Temple, London EC4Y 9AD, ☎020 7832 3200 ✉clerks@4bc.co.uk
Call Date: Nov 1977, Inner Temple
Recorder
✉marianna.hildyard@4bc.co.uk

HILKEN MS ALICE MARY

1 Pump Court
Elm Court, Temple, London EC4Y 7AB, ☎020 7842 7070
✉(name)@pumpcourt.co.uk
Call Date: Nov 1994, Middle Temple
Qualifications: [BA (Hons)]

HILL MR ANDREW CHARLES ROWLAND

Great James Street Chambers
37 Great James Street, London WC1N 3HB, ☎020 7440 4949
✉chambers@greatjames.co.uk
Chambers of Mr A C Hill
16 Hart Grove, London W5 3NB, ☎07792 682928 ✉acrhill@yahoo.co.uk
Call Date: Nov 1982, Gray's Inn
Qualifications: [LLB]

HILL MISS CATHERINE LOUISE

Sovereign Chambers
46 Park Place, Leeds LS1 2RY, ☎0113 245 1841
✉clerks@sovereignchambers.co.uk
Call Date: July 1988, Gray's Inn
Qualifications: [BA (Hons)(Dunelm)]
✉louise.hill@sovereignchambers.co.uk

HILL MS ELEANOR MARY HENRIETTA

Doughty Street Chambers
53-54 Doughty Street, London WC1N 2LS, ☎020 7404 1313
✉enquiries@doughtystreet.co.uk
Doughty Street Chambers
Pall Mall Court, 61-67 King Street, Manchester M2 4PD, ☎0161 618 1066

Doughty Street Chambers
5th Floor, Broad Quay House, Prince Street, Bristol BS1 4DJ, ☎01179 058 717
Call Date: Oct 1997, Inner Temple
Qualifications: [MA (Cantab)]
h.hill@doughtystreet.co.uk

HILL MR GREGORY JOHN SUMMERS

Ten Old Square
Ground Floor, Ten Old Square, Lincoln's Inn, London WC2A 3SU, ☎020 7405 0758
clerks@tenoldsquare.com
Call Date: July 1972, Lincoln's Inn
Pupil Supervisor
Qualifications: [MA BCL (Oxon)]
gregoryhill@tenoldsquare.com

HILL MR JAMES MICHAEL QC (2006)

Fountain Chambers
Cleveland Business Centre, 1 Watson Street, Middlesbrough TS1 2RQ, ☎01642 804040
clerks@fountainchambers.co.uk
Broadway House Chambers
Broadway House, 9 Bank Street, Bradford, West Yorkshire BD1 1TW, ☎01274 722560
clerks@broadwayhouse.co.uk
Broadway House Chambers
25 Park Square West, Leeds, West Yorkshire LS1 2PW, ☎0113 246 2600
clerks@broadwayhouse.co.uk
Call Date: July 1984, Inner Temple
Recorder
Qualifications: [LLB (Manch)]

HILL MR JONATHAN

8 New Square
8 New Square, Lincoln's Inn, London WC2A 3QP, ☎020 7405 4321
clerks@8newsquare.co.uk
Call Date: Oct 2000, Lincoln's Inn
Qualifications: [BA (Hons) (Oxon)]
jonathan.hill@8newsquare.co.uk

Types of work: Breach of confidence, Competition law, Confidential information, Copyright, Data protection, Entertainment, Information technology, Intellectual property, Media, Media and entertainment, Patents, Pharmaceuticals, Privacy, Scientific cases, Telecommunications, Trademarks

HILL MR JONATHAN MARCUS

Pendragon Chambers
Suite 7, J Shed, Kings Road, SA1 Waterfront, Swansea SA1 8PL, ☎01792 411188
clerks@pendragonchambers.com
Call Date: Oct 1997, Middle Temple
Qualifications: [LLB (Hons)(Lond)]

HILL MR MATTHEW STEPHEN

1 Crown Office Row
1 Crown Office Row, Temple, London EC4Y 7HH, ☎020 7797 7500
mail@1cor.com
Call Date: Oct 2009, Inner Temple
Qualifications: [BA MSt (Oxon)]
matthew.hill@1cor.com

HILL MR MAX BENJAMIN ROWLAND QC (2008)

18 Red Lion Court
London EC4A 3EB, ☎020 7520 6000
chambers@18rlc.co.uk
18 Red Lion Court (Annexe)
Thornwood House, 102 New London Road, Chelmsford, Essex CM2 0RG, ☎01245 280880
Call Date: Nov 1987, Middle Temple
Recorder
Qualifications: [BA (Oxon)]
max.hill@18rlc.co.uk

HILL MR MICHAEL GORDON

Trinity Chambers
The Custom House, 39 Quayside, Newcastle Upon Tyne NE1 3DE, ☎0191 232 1927
info@trinitychambers.co.uk
Trinity Chambers
Multi Media Exchange, 72-80 Corporation Road, Middlesbrough TS1 2RF, ☎01642 247569
info@trinitychambers.co.uk
Call Date: July 2004, Gray's Inn
Pupil Supervisor
Qualifications: [BDS (Newc)]
m.hill@trinitychambers.co.uk

HILL MISS MIRANDA JANE

6 King's Bench Walk
Ground Floor, 6 King's Bench Walk, Temple, London EC4Y 7DR, ☎020 7583 0410
clerks@6kbw.com
Call Date: Oct 1999, Middle Temple
Pupil Supervisor
Qualifications: [BA (Hons)(Manch) Dip law]
miranda.hill@6kbw.com

HILL MR NICHOLAS DANIEL GEORGE

Outer Temple Chambers
The Outer Temple, 222 Strand, London WC2R 1BA, ☎020 7353 6381
clerks@outertemple.com
Call Date: July 2008, Inner Temple
Qualifications: [BA (Hons) LLB (Hons)]
nicholas.hill@outertemple.com

E

HILL MR NICHOLAS IAN

No.6 Park Square
Leeds LS1 2LW, ☎0113 245 9763
✉Tim@no6.co.uk
Call Date: Oct 1993, Lincoln's Inn
Qualifications: [BA (Hons)]
hill@no6.co.uk

HILL MR NICHOLAS MARK QC (2009)

Pump Court Chambers
Upper Ground Floor, 3 Pump Court, Temple, London EC4Y 7AJ, ☎020 7353 0711
✉clerks@3pumpcourt.com
Pump Court Chambers
5 Temple Chambers, Temple Street, Swindon SN1 1SQ, ☎01793 539899
✉clerks@3pumpcourt.com
St Philips Chambers
55 Temple Row, Birmingham B2 5LS, ☎0121 246 7000 ✉clerks@st-philips.com
Call Date: July 1987, Middle Temple
Recorder
Qualifications: [LLB (Lond) AKC LLM]
mh@3pumpcourt.com

E

HILL MR PATRICK CHRISTOPHER

3 Raymond Buildings
3 Raymond Buildings, Gray's Inn, London WC1R 5BH, ☎020 7400 6400
✉clerks@3rblaw.com
Call Date: Oct 2010, Lincoln's Inn
Qualifications: [BA (Cantab)]
patrick.hill@3raymondbuildings.com

HILL MR PIERS NICHOLAS

37 Park Square Chambers
37 Park Square, Leeds LS1 2NY, ☎0113 243 9422 ✉chambers@no37.co.uk
Call Date: July 1987, Inner Temple
Pupil Supervisor
Qualifications: [LLB (Hull)]
ph@no37.co.uk

HILL MR RAYMOND

Monckton Chambers
1 & 2 Raymond Buildings, Gray's Inn, London WC1R 5NR, ☎020 7405 7211
✉chambers@monckton.com
Call Date: Oct 1992, Lincoln's Inn
Qualifications: [BA (Hons) LLM]
rhill@monckton.com

HILL MISS REBECCA CLAIRE

Garden Court Chambers
57-60 Lincoln's Inn Fields, London WC2A 3LJ, ☎020 7993 7600 ✉info@gclaw.co.uk
Call Date: July 2004, Middle Temple
Qualifications: [LLB Hons (Nottingham)]

HILL MR RICHARD GEOFFREY QC (2012)

4 Stone Buildings
Ground Floor, 4 Stone Buildings, Lincoln's Inn, London WC2A 3XT, ☎020 7242 5524
✉clerks@4stonebuildings.com
Call Date: Oct 1993, Gray's Inn
Pupil Supervisor
Qualifications: [BA (Cantab)]
clerks@4stonebuildings.com

HILL MISS RINA-MARIE

Goldsmith Chambers
Ground Floor, Goldsmith Building, Temple, London EC4Y 7BL, ☎020 7353 6802
✉clerks@goldsmithchambers.com
Call Date: July 2002, Lincoln's Inn
Pupil Supervisor
Qualifications: [LLB (Hons)]
r.hill@goldsmithchambers.law.co.uk

HILL MR SIMON MICHAEL

33 Bedford Row
London WC1R 4JH, ☎020 7242 6476
✉clerks@33bedfordrow.co.uk
Call Date: Nov 2001, Middle Temple
Qualifications: [BA (Hons) (Cantab)]
SimonHill@33bedfordrow.co.uk

HILL MISS SOPHIE THERESA AMELIA

5 Pump Court
Ground Floor, 5 Pump Court, Temple, London EC4Y 7AP, ☎020 7353 2532
✉clerks@5pumpcourt.com
Call Date: Oct 2003, Middle Temple
Qualifications: [BA (Hons) (Cantab)]
sophiehill@5pumpcourt.com

HILL MR THOMAS PATRICK JAMES QC (2009)

4-5 Gray's Inn Square
Gray's Inn, London WC1R 5AH, ☎020 7404 5252 ✉clerks@4-5.co.uk
Call Date: July 1988, Lincoln's Inn
Qualifications: [MA (Hons) (Cantab)]
thill@4-5.co.uk

HILL MR TIMOTHY JOHN QC (2009)

Stone Chambers
4 Field Court, Gray's Inn, London WC1R 5EF, ☎020 7440 6900
✉clerks@stonechambers.com
Call Date: Oct 1990, Middle Temple
Pupil Supervisor
Qualifications: [LLB (Lond) DLS (Cantab) BCL (Oxon)]
timothy.hill@stonechambers.com

HILLAS MISS SAMANTHA

Atlantic Chambers
4-6 Cook Street, Liverpool L2 9QU, ☎0151 236 4421
✉info@atlanticchambers.co.uk
Call Date: Oct 1996, Inner Temple
Qualifications: [LLB (Hull) Pg DipLaw]
samanthahillas@atlanticchambers.co.uk

HILL-BAKER MR JEREMY ROBERT

No.6 Park Square
Leeds LS1 2LW, ☎0113 245 9763
✉Tim@no6.co.uk
Call Date: July 1983, Inner Temple
Pupil Supervisor, Recorder
Qualifications: [LLB (Leeds)]
hill-baker@no6.co.uk

HILLIARD MISS ALEXANDRA QC (2009)

11 Stone Buildings
11 Stone Buildings, Lincoln's Inn, London WC2A 3TG, ☎020 7831 6381
✉clerks@11sb.com
Call Date: Nov 1987, Middle Temple
Qualifications: [LLB (Lond)]
Hilliard@11SB.com

HILLIARD MISS EMMA MARGARET

7 King's Bench Walk
Ground Floor, 7 King's Bench Walk, Temple, London EC4Y 7DS, ☎020 7910 8300
✉clerks@7kbw.co.uk
Call Date: July 2006, Lincoln's Inn
Qualifications: [MA (Hons) (Cantab) LLM (Cantab)]
ehilliard@7kbw.co.uk

HILLIARD MR JONATHAN ADAM

Wilberforce Chambers
8 New Square, Lincoln's Inn, London WC2A 3QP, ☎020 7306 0102
✉chambers@wilberforce.co.uk
Call Date: Oct 2003, Lincoln's Inn
Qualifications: [BA (Hons) (Cantab) LLM (Cantab)]
jhilliard@wilberforce.co.uk

Types of work: Capital tax, Chancery (general), Chancery (land law), Commercial litigation, Commercial property, Equity, Income tax, Landlord and tenant, Pensions, Professional negligence, Trusts, Wills

HILLIARD MR SPENSER RODNEY

Field Court Chambers
5 Field Court, Gray's Inn, London WC1R 5EF, ☎020 7405 6114 ✉clerks@fieldcourt.co.uk
Call Date: Nov 1975, Middle Temple
Pupil Supervisor
Qualifications: [LLB]

HILLIER MR NICOLAS PETER

The Chambers of Grahame Aldous QC
9 Gough Square, London EC4A 3DG, ☎020 7832 0500
✉clerks@9goughsquare.co.uk
Call Date: July 1982, Inner Temple
Pupil Supervisor
Qualifications: [LLB (So'ton)]
nhillier@9goughsquare.co.uk

HILLIER MISS VICTORIA JANE

Civitas Chambers
Global Reach, Celtic Gateway, Cardiff Bay, Cardiff CF11 0SN, ☎0845 0713 007
✉clerks@civitaslaw.com
Call Date: July 2005, Gray's Inn
Qualifications: [LLB]
victoria.hillier@civitaslaw.com

HILLIER MR WILLIAM

New Street Chambers
2 New Street, Leicester LE1 5NA, ☎0116 262 5906 ✉clerks@2newstreet.co.uk
Call Date: July 2001, Inner Temple
Qualifications: [LLB (Nott'm)]

HILLIS MR JOHN

Bank House Chambers
Old Bank House, Hartshead, Sheffield S1 2EL, ☎0114 275 1223
✉w.digby@bankhousechambers.co.uk
Call Date: July 1982, Gray's Inn
Pupil Supervisor
Qualifications: [LLB (Sheff)]
j.hillis@bankhousechambers.co.uk

E

HILLMAN MR BASIL

4 King's Bench Walk
2nd Floor, 4 King's Bench Walk, Temple, London EC4Y 7DL, ☎ 020 7822 7000
✉ clerks@4kbw.co.uk
Call Date: Nov 1968, Gray's Inn
Qualifications: [MA (MOD)]

HILLMAN MR GERARD PAUL

Carmelite Chambers
9 Carmelite Street, London EC4Y 0DR, ☎ 020 7936 6300
✉ clerks@carmelitechambers.co.uk
Call Date: Oct 1999, Gray's Inn
Qualifications: [LLB (Wales)]
ghillman@carmelitechambers.co.uk

HILLMAN MR ROGER JOHN

Exchange Chambers
One Derby Square, Derby Square, Liverpool L2 9XX, ☎ 0151 236 7747
✉ info@exchangechambers.co.uk
Exchange Chambers
7 Ralli Courts, West Riverside, Manchester M3 5FT, ☎ 0161 833 2722
Exchange Chambers
Oxford House, Oxford Row, Leeds LS1 3BE, ☎ 0113 203 1970
✉ spencer@exchangechambers.co.uk
Call Date: July 1983, Gray's Inn
Pupil Supervisor
Qualifications: [LLB (L'Pool)]
hillman@exchangechambers.co.uk

HILLS MR TIMOTHY JAMES

Albion Chambers
Broad Street, Bristol BS1 1DR, ☎ 0117 927 2144
✉ clerks@albionchambers.co.uk
Call Date: July 1968, Lincoln's Inn
Pupil Supervisor
timothy.hills@albionchambers.co.uk

HILL-SMITH MR ALEXANDER GEORGE LAVANDER

New Square Chambers
12 New Square, Lincoln's Inn, London WC2A 3SW, ☎ 020 7419 8000
✉ robin.hollington@newsquarechambers.co.uk
Call Date: July 1978, Gray's Inn
Pupil Supervisor, Recorder
Qualifications: [LLB MA (Cantab)]

HILTON MR ALAN JOHN HOWARD QC (1990)

QEB Hollis Whiteman
1-2 Laurence Pountney Hill, London EC4R 0EU, ☎ 020 7933 8855
✉ barristers@qebhw.co.uk
Call Date: Nov 1964, Middle Temple
Recorder
Qualifications: [LLB (Manch)]
barristers@qebhw.co.uk

HILTON MR OLIVER JAMES

3 Stone Buildings
Ground Floor, 3 Stone Buildings, Lincoln's Inn, London WC2A 3XL, ☎ 020 7242 4937
✉ clerks@3sb.law.co.uk
Call Date: July 2002, Lincoln's Inn
Pupil Supervisor
Qualifications: [LLB (Hons) (London)]
ohilton@3sb.law.co.uk

HILTON MS SAISAMPAN

Holborn Chambers
6 Gate Street, Lincoln's Inn Fields, London WC2A 3HP, ☎ 020 7242 6060
Call Date: Oct 1994, Gray's Inn
Qualifications: [BA MA]

HILTON MR SIMON JONATHAN

Kings Chambers
36 Young Street, Manchester M3 3FT, ☎ 0845 034 3444
✉ clerks@kingschambers.com
Kings Chambers
5 Park Square East, Leeds LS1 2NE, ☎ 0845 034 3444
✉ clerks@kingschambers.com
Kings Chambers
Embassy House, 60 Church Street, Birmingham B3 2DJ, ☎ 0845 034 3444
✉ clerks@kingschambers.com
Call Date: Nov 1987, Gray's Inn
Pupil Supervisor, Recorder
Qualifications: [BA (Oxon)]
shilton@kingschambers.com

HIMSWORTH MISS EMMA KATHERINE QC (2012)

One Essex Court
Ground Floor, One Essex Court, Temple, London EC4Y 9AR, ☎ 020 7583 2000
✉ clerks@oeclaw.co.uk
Call Date: Oct 1993, Gray's Inn
Pupil Supervisor
Qualifications: [BSc (Edin) Dip Law (Lond) Dip EC Law (Lond)]
ehimsworth@oeclaw.co.uk

HIMSWORTH MR MARK STEPHEN

Dyers Chambers
35 Bedford Row, London WC1R 4JH,
☎ 020 7404 1881
✉ admin@dyerschambers.com
Call Date: Oct 1999, Middle Temple
Qualifications: [LLB (Hons)(Kent) LLM (Bris)]
✉ mark.himsworth@dyerschambers.com

HINCHLIFFE MR PHILIP NICHOLAS QC (1999)

9 St John Street
Manchester M3 4DN, ☎ 0161 955 9000
✉ civilclerks@9sjs.com / criminalclerks@9sjs.com
1 Gray's Inn Square
Ground Floor, 1 Gray's Inn Square, London WC1R 5AA, ☎ 020 7405 0001
Call Date: Nov 1980, Middle Temple
Recorder
Qualifications: [LLB (Manch)]

HINCHLIFFE MR THOMAS RICHARD

Three New Square IP
3 New Square, Lincoln's Inn, London WC2A 3RS, ☎ 020 7405 1111
✉ clerks@3newsquare.co.uk
Call Date: Oct 1997, Middle Temple
Pupil Supervisor
Qualifications: [BA (Hons)(Oxon) CPE (Lond)]
✉ hinchliffe@3newsquare.co.uk

HIND MR KENNETH HARVARD

Oriel Chambers
14 Water Street, Liverpool, Merseyside L2 8TD, ☎ 0151 236 7191
✉ clerks@orielchambers.co.uk
Oriel Chambers
18 Ribblesdale Place, Preston PR1 3NA,
☎ 01772 254 764
✉ clerks@oriel-chambers.co.uk
Call Date: July 1973, Gray's Inn
Pupil Supervisor
Qualifications: [LLB (Hons)]

HINDMARSH MISS ELIZABETH

Chambers of Miss Elizabeth Hindmarsh
Over Court, Bisley, Stroud, Gloucestershire GL6 7BE, ☎ 01452 770170
✉ john.cowen@virgin.net
Call Date: July 1974, Inner Temple
Qualifications: [BA (Dunelm)]

HINDMARSH MR LUKE EDWARD THOMAS

9-12 Bell Yard
London WC2A 2JR, ☎ 020 7400 1800
✉ clerks@9-12bellyard.com
Call Date: Mar 2007, Middle Temple
Qualifications: [LLB (Hons) (Kent) LLM (Kent)]
✉ l.hindmarsh@9-12bellyard.com

HINDS MR ORIEL GLENVERE

Clerksroom (Taunton)
Equity House, Administration Centre, Blackbrook Park Avenue, Taunton, Somerset TA1 2PX, ☎ 0845 083 3000
✉ mail@clerksroom.com
Clerksroom (London)
3rd Floor, 218 Strand, London WC2R 1AT,
☎ 0845 083 3000 ✉ mail@clerksroom.com
66 Worthington Road
66 Worthington Road, Surbiton, Kingston Upon Thames, Surrey KT6 7RX,
☎ 020 8390 6359 ✉ OrielG@aol.com
Call Date: July 1988, Inner Temple
Qualifications: [LLB (Hons)]
✉ hinds@clerksroom.com

HINE MR CHARLES RODERICK JOHN

King's Bench Chambers
Wellington House, 175 Holdenhurst Road, Bournemouth, Dorset BH8 8DQ,
☎ 01202 250025
Call Date: Nov 1985, Gray's Inn
Pupil Supervisor
Qualifications: [B Com (B'ham) DipLaw Cert Ed]

HINE MISS STEPHANIE ALISON

New Court
Ground Floor, New Court, Temple, London EC4Y 9BE, ☎ 020 7583 5123
✉ clerks@newcourtchambers.com
Call Date: Oct 2003, Gray's Inn
Qualifications: [LLB (Teeside) LLM (Lond)]
✉ shine@newcourtchambers.net

HINES MR JAMES PHILIP

3 Raymond Buildings
3 Raymond Buildings, Gray's Inn, London WC1R 5BH, ☎ 020 7400 6400
✉ clerks@3rblaw.com
Call Date: July 1982, Gray's Inn
Pupil Supervisor
Qualifications: [BA]

E

HINGSTON MR JOE

Carmelite Chambers
9 Carmelite Street, London EC4Y 0DR,
☎ 020 7936 6300
✉ clerks@carmelitechambers.co.uk
Call Date: Oct 2007, Lincoln's Inn
Qualifications: [LLB (Manch)]
jhingston@carmelitechambers.co.uk

HINKS MR FRANK PETER QC (2000)

Serle Court
6 New Square, Lincoln's Inn, London WC2A 3QS, ☎ 020 7242 6105
✉ clerks@serlecourt.co.uk
Call Date: July 1973, Lincoln's Inn
Qualifications: [MA BCL (Oxon)]
fhinks@serlecourt.co.uk

Types of work: Chancery (general), Chancery (land law), Common land, Equity, Litigation, Offshore trust litigation, Partnerships, Private client, Property, Real property, Succession, Trust litigation, Trusts, Wills

HINKS MR PHILIP MARTYN JOHN

11 Stone Buildings
11 Stone Buildings, Lincoln's Inn, London WC2A 3TG, ☎ 020 7831 6381
✉ clerks@11sb.com
Call Date: Oct 2008, Lincoln's Inn
Qualifications: [LLB (Bris) BCL (Oxon)]
hinks@11sb.com

HINTON MS HANNAH FRANCESCA

Dyers Chambers
35 Bedford Row, London WC1R 4JH,
☎ 020 7404 1881
✉ admin@dyerschambers.com
Call Date: Mar 2008, Gray's Inn
Qualifications: [BA (Newc)]

HINTON MR NEIL PEARSE

King's Bench Chambers
Wellington House, 175 Holdenhurst Road, Bournemouth, Dorset BH8 8DQ,
☎ 01202 250025
Call Date: Nov 1997, Lincoln's Inn
Qualifications: [BA (Hons)(Nott'm)]
neil.hinton@kingsbench.co.uk

HIORNS MR ROGER MARTIN FAIRCHILD

The Chambers of Grahame Aldous QC
9 Gough Square, London EC4A 3DG,
☎ 020 7832 0500
✉ clerks@9goughsquare.co.uk
Call Date: July 1983, Middle Temple
Pupil Supervisor
Qualifications: [LLB (B'ham)]
rhiorns@9goughsquare.co.uk

HIPKIN MR JOHN LESLIE

Iscoed Chambers
86 St Helen's Road, Swansea SA1 4BQ,
☎ 01792 652988
✉ clerks@iscoedchambers.co.uk
Call Date: Nov 1989, Gray's Inn
Pupil Supervisor
Qualifications: [LLB (Manch)]
jh@iscoedchambers.co.uk

HIRSCH MS GEORGINA ELIZABETH RUTH

Devereux Chambers
Queen Elizabeth Building, Temple, London EC4Y 9BS, ☎ 020 7353 7534
✉ clerks@devchambers.co.uk
Call Date: Nov 2009, Gray's Inn
hirsch@devchambers.co.uk

HIRST MR DAVID WATSON

5RB
1st Floor, 5 Raymond Buildings, Gray's Inn, London WC1R 5BP, ☎ 020 7242 2902
✉ clerks@5rb.com
Call Date: Oct 2003, Gray's Inn
Qualifications: [BA (Cantab) MA (Cantab) MPhil (Cantab)]
davidhirst@5rb.com

HIRST MR JONATHAN WILLIAM QC (1990)

Brick Court Chambers
7-8 Essex Street, London WC2R 3LD,
☎ 020 7379 3550 ✉ clerks@brickcourt.co.uk
Call Date: July 1975, Inner Temple
Recorder
Qualifications: [MA (Cantab)]
jonathan.hirst@brickcourt.co.uk

HIRST MR KARL DOUGLAS

No5 Chambers
Fountain Court, Steelhouse Lane, Birmingham B4 6DR, ☎0845 210 5555 ✉info@no5.com
No5 Chambers
Greenwood House, 4-7 Salisbury Court, London EC4Y 8AA, ☎0845 210 5555
No5 Chambers
38 Queen Square, Bristol BS1 4QS, ☎0845 210 5555
Call Date: Oct 1997, Inner Temple
Pupil Supervisor
Qualifications: [LLB (Lancs)]
kh@no5.com

HIRST MISS KATHRYN ANNE

Furnival Chambers
32 Furnival Street, London EC4A 1JQ, ☎020 7405 3232
Call Date: Nov 1986, Inner Temple
Qualifications: [BA]
khirst@furnivallaw.co.uk

HIRST MS LEONIE CLAIRE

Tooks Chambers
81 Farringdon Street, London EC4A 4BL, ☎020 7842 7575 ✉clerks@tooks.co.uk
Call Date: Oct 2006, Inner Temple
Qualifications: [BA (Oxon) MSc (Lond)]
leonie.hirst@tooks.co.uk

HIRST MR MARTIN LEWIS

13 King's Bench Walk
13 King's Bench Walk, Temple, London EC4Y 7EN, ☎020 7353 7204
✉clerks@13kbw.co.uk
13 KBW
32 Beaumont Street, Oxford OX1 2NP, ☎01865 311066 ✉clerks@13kbw.co.uk
Call Date: Nov 1998, Lincoln's Inn
Qualifications: [BSc (Hons) PG Dip Law LLM Dip Land Admin]
mhirst@13kbw.co.uk

HIRST MISS REBECCA ELISABETH

Cobden House Chambers
19 Quay Street, Manchester M3 3HN, ☎0161 833 6000 ✉Clerks@Cobden.co.uk
Call Date: Nov 1999, Gray's Inn
Qualifications: [LLB (Lancs)]
clerks@cobden.co.uk

HIRST MR SIMON DAVID

Wilberforce Chambers
7 Bishop Lane, Hull HU1 1PA, ☎01482 323264
Call Date: Oct 1993, Lincoln's Inn
Pupil Supervisor
Qualifications: [LLB (Hons)(Hull)]

HIRST MISS SUSAN CAROLINE

New Court Chambers
3 Broad Chare, Newcastle Upon Tyne NE1 3DQ, ☎0191 232 1980
✉clerks@newcourt-chambers.co.uk
Call Date: July 2001, Middle Temple
Qualifications: [LLB (Hons)]
susan.hirst@newcourt-chambers.co.uk

HIRST MR WILLIAM TIMOTHY JOHN

Park Lane Plowden
19 Westgate, Leeds LS1 2RD, ☎0113 228 5049
✉clerks@parklaneplowden.co.uk
Call Date: Nov 1970, Inner Temple
Recorder
Qualifications: [BA (Oxon) IDIL (German)]
tim.hirst@parklaneplowden.co.uk

HISLOP MR DAVID SEYMOUR QC (2010)

Doughty Street Chambers
53-54 Doughty Street, London WC1N 2LS, ☎020 7404 1313
✉enquiries@doughtystreet.co.uk
Doughty Street Chambers
Pall Mall Court, 61-67 King Street, Manchester M2 4PD, ☎0161 618 1066
Doughty Street Chambers
5th Floor, Broad Quay House, Prince Street, Bristol BS1 4DJ, ☎01179 058 717
Call Date: Feb 1989, Gray's Inn
Pupil Supervisor
Qualifications: [LLB (Australia)]
d.hislop@doughtystreet.co.uk

HITCHCOCK MISS JODIE JANE

3 Temple Gardens
Lower Ground Floor, 3 Temple Gardens, Temple, London EC4Y 9AU, ☎020 7353 3102
✉clerks@3tg.co.uk
Call Date: July 2006, Middle Temple
Qualifications: [LLB (Hons) (Exon)]

HITCHCOCK MS PATRICIA ANN QC (2011)

Cloisters
1 Pump Court, Temple, London EC4Y 7AA, ☎020 7827 4000 ✉clerks@cloisters.com
Call Date: Nov 1988, Inner Temple
Pupil Supervisor
Qualifications: [BA (Oxon) Dip Law]

E

HITCHCOCK MR RICHARD GUY

Outer Temple Chambers
The Outer Temple, 222 Strand, London WC2R 1BA, ☎ 020 7353 6381
✉ clerks@outertemple.com
Call Date: Nov 1989, Gray's Inn
Pupil Supervisor
Qualifications: [BA (Oxon)]
richard.hitchcock@outertemple.com

HITCHENS MISS ERIN CLAIRE

XXIV Old Buildings
Ground Floor, 24 Old Buildings, Lincoln's Inn, London WC2A 3UP, ☎ 020 7691 2424
✉ clerks@xxiv.co.uk
Call Date: Oct 2006, Lincoln's Inn
Qualifications: [BA (Cantab)]
erin.hitchens@xxiv.co.uk

HITCHING MISS ISABEL JOY

Crown Office Chambers
2 Crown Office Row, Temple, London EC4Y 7HJ, ☎ 020 7797 8100
✉ mail@crownofficechambers.com
Call Date: Oct 1992, Middle Temple
Qualifications: [MA(Hons)(Oxon) BCL(Oxon)]

HITCHMOUGH MR ANDREW JOHN

Pump Court Tax Chambers
16 Bedford Row, London WC1R 4EF, ☎ 020 7414 8080 ✉ clerks@pumptax.com
Call Date: Oct 1991, Inner Temple
Pupil Supervisor
Qualifications: [LLB (So'ton)]
ahitchmough@pumptax.com

Types of work: Corporation tax, Customs, VAT

HO MR EDWARD ALEXANDER

20 Essex Street
London WC2R 3AL, ☎ 020 7842 1200
✉ clerks@20essexst.com
Call Date: July 2009, Middle Temple
Qualifications: [BA (Hons) (Cantab)]
eho@20essexst.com

HOAR MR FRANCIS JOHN PATRICK

Field Court Chambers
5 Field Court, Gray's Inn, London WC1R 5EF, ☎ 020 7405 6114 ✉ clerks@fieldcourt.co.uk
Call Date: Nov 2001, Lincoln's Inn
Qualifications: [LLB (Hons) (Bris)]

HOARE MR GREGORY BLAKE

Exchange Chambers
One Derby Square, Derby Square, Liverpool L2 9XX, ☎ 0151 236 7747
✉ info@exchangechambers.co.uk
Exchange Chambers
7 Ralli Courts, West Riverside, Manchester M3 5FT, ☎ 0161 833 2722
Exchange Chambers
Oxford House, Oxford Row, Leeds LS1 3BE, ☎ 0113 203 1970
✉ spencer@exchangechambers.co.uk
Call Date: Nov 1992, Gray's Inn
Qualifications: [LLB]

HOBBS MR DANIEL STUART

13 King's Bench Walk
13 King's Bench Walk, Temple, London EC4Y 7EN, ☎ 020 7353 7204
✉ clerks@13kbw.co.uk
13 KBW
32 Beaumont Street, Oxford OX1 2NP, ☎ 01865 311066 ✉ clerks@13kbw.co.uk
Call Date: Oct 1998, Lincoln's Inn

HOBBS MISS EMMA-JANE

Temple Garden Chambers
1 Harcourt Buildings, Temple, London EC4Y 9DA, ☎ 020 7583 1315
✉ clerks@tgchambers.com
Call Date: Oct 1996, Gray's Inn
Qualifications: [BA (Bris)]
ejh@tgchambers.com

HOBBS MR GEOFFREY WILLIAM QC (1991)

One Essex Court
Ground Floor, One Essex Court, Temple, London EC4Y 9AR, ☎ 020 7583 2000
✉ clerks@oeclaw.co.uk
Call Date: July 1977, Inner Temple
Qualifications: [LLB (So'ton)]
teamb@oeclaw.co.uk, clerks@oeclaw.co.uk

HOBBS MS NAOMI JOSEPHINE

No 8 Chambers
8 Fountain Court, Steelhouse Lane, Birmingham B4 6DR, ☎ 0121 236 5514
✉ clerks@no8chambers.co.uk
Call Date: Oct 1993, Gray's Inn
Qualifications: [LLB]
naomihobbs@no8chambers.co.uk

HOBCRAFT MISS GEMMA KIERNAN

Doughty Street Chambers
53-54 Doughty Street, London WC1N 2LS,
☎ 020 7404 1313
✉ enquiries@doughtystreet.co.uk
Call Date: July 2006, Lincoln's Inn
Qualifications: [BA (Sussex)]
✉ g.hobcraft@doughtystreet.co.uk

HOBHOUSE MS HELEN ROSAMUND

Farrar's Building
Farrar's Building, Temple, London EC4Y 7BD,
☎ 020 7583 9241
✉ Chambers@farrarsbuilding.co.uk
Call Date: Oct 1990, Inner Temple
Pupil Supervisor
Qualifications: [B Soc Sci Dip Law]
✉ hhobhouse@farrarsbuilding.co.uk

HOBSON MR FREDERICK PAUL PHILIP

Brick Court Chambers
7-8 Essex Street, London WC2R 3LD,
☎ 020 7379 3550 ✉ clerks@brickcourt.co.uk
Call Date: Oct 2005, Lincoln's Inn
Qualifications: [MA (Cantab) MA]

HOBSON MISS HEATHER FIONA

Deans Court Chambers
24 St John Street, Manchester M3 4DF,
☎ 0161 214 6000 ✉ clerks@deanscourt.co.uk
Deans Court Chambers
101 Walker Street, Preston PR1 2RR,
☎ 01772 565 600
✉ preston@deanscourt.co.uk
Call Date: Nov 1987, Lincoln's Inn
Pupil Supervisor
Qualifications: [LLB (Hons) (Lond)]
✉ hobson@deanscourt.co.uk

HOBSON MR JOHN GRAHAM QC (2000)

4-5 Gray's Inn Square
Gray's Inn, London WC1R 5AH,
☎ 020 7404 5252 ✉ clerks@4-5.co.uk
Call Date: July 1980, Inner Temple
Recorder
Qualifications: [LLM (Cantab)]
✉ jhobson@4-5.co.uk

HOBSON MR JOHN SIMON

Doughty Street Chambers
Pall Mall Court, 61-67 King Street, Manchester M2 4PD, ☎ 0161 618 1066
Doughty Street Chambers
5th Floor, Broad Quay House, Prince Street, Bristol BS1 4DJ, ☎ 01179 058 717
Doughty Street Chambers
53-54 Doughty Street, London WC1N 2LS,
☎ 020 7404 1313
✉ enquiries@doughtystreet.co.uk
Call Date: Oct 1999, Lincoln's Inn
Qualifications: [BA (Hons)(Sheff) MSc (Lond) Dip Law]

HOBSON MISS LAURA ELISE

Citadel Chambers
The Citadel, 190 Corporation Street, Birmingham B4 6QD, ☎ 0121 233 8500
✉ clerks@citadelchambers.com
Call Date: July 2003, Gray's Inn
Qualifications: [BA (Hons)(Lond)]
✉ clerks@citadelchambers.com

HOBSON MR PAUL

Iscoed Chambers
86 St Helen's Road, Swansea SA1 4BQ,
☎ 01792 652988
✉ clerks@iscoedchambers.co.uk
Call Date: July 2000, Gray's Inn
Pupil Supervisor
Qualifications: [BA (Oxon)]
✉ ph@iscoedchambers.co.uk

HOBSON MISS SALLY ANNE

1 Paper Buildings
1st Floor, 1 Paper Buildings, Temple, London EC4Y 7EP, ☎ 020 7353 3728
✉ clerks@onepaper.co.uk
Call Date: Apr 1991, Inner Temple
Qualifications: [LLB (Nott'm) LLM (Nott'm)]
✉ sallyhobson@onepaper.co.uk

HOCHBERG MR DANIEL ALAN

Wilberforce Chambers
8 New Square, Lincoln's Inn, London WC2A 3QP, ☎ 020 7306 0102
✉ chambers@wilberforce.co.uk
Call Date: July 1982, Lincoln's Inn
Pupil Supervisor
Qualifications: [MA (Oxon) BA (Hons) (Oxon)]
✉ dhochberg@wilberforce.co.uk

Types of work: Chancery (general), Chancery (land law), Charities, Commercial litigation, Commercial property, Equity, Landlord and tenant, Partnerships, Professional negligence, Succession, Trusts, Wills

E

HOCHHAUSER MR ANDREW ROMAIN QC (1997)

Essex Court Chambers
24 Lincoln's Inn Fields, London WC2A 3EG, ☎020 7813 8000
✉clerksroom@essexcourt.net
Call Date: July 1977, Middle Temple
Qualifications: [FCIArb LLB (Bris) LLM (Lond)]
ahochhauser@essexcourt.net

HOCKMAN MR STEPHEN ALEXANDER QC (1990)

6 Pump Court
1st Floor, 6 Pump Court, Temple, London EC4Y 7AR, ☎020 7797 8400
✉richardconstable@6pumpcourt.co.uk
Regency Chambers
45 Priestgate, Peterborough PE1 1LB, ☎01733 315215
✉clerks@regencychambers.law.co.uk
6 Pump Court Chambers
6-8 Mill Street, Maidstone, Kent ME15 6XH, ☎01622 688094
✉annexe@6pumpcourt.co.uk
Call Date: July 1970, Middle Temple
Pupil Supervisor
Qualifications: [MA (Cantab)]
qc@shed31.demon.co.uk

Fax: 020 7797 8401;
Out of hours telephone: 07775 894862;
DX: 293 LDE;
Other comms: E-mail: stephenhockmanqc@6pumpcourt.co.uk or qc@shed31.demon.co.uk
URL: www.6pumpcourt.co.uk

Types of work: Administrative law, Common law (general), Crime, Energy, Environment, Health and safety, Local authorities, Personal injury, Planning, Water

HOCKNELL MISS LAURA ANNE

Carmelite Chambers
9 Carmelite Street, London EC4Y 0DR, ☎020 7936 6300
✉clerks@carmelitechambers.co.uk
Call Date: July 2005, Inner Temple
Qualifications: [BA (Cantab) MSc (Leics)]
lhocknell@carmelitechambers.co.uk

HOCKTON MR ANDREW IAN CALLINAN

3 Serjeants Inn
London EC4Y 1BQ, ☎020 7427 5000
✉clerks@3serjeantsinn.com
Call Date: Nov 1984, Middle Temple
Pupil Supervisor
Qualifications: [BA (Oxon) Dip Law]
ahockton@3serjeantsinn.com

HODDER MR PHILIP JAMES

Clerksroom (Taunton)
Equity House, Administration Centre, Blackbrook Park Avenue, Taunton, Somerset TA1 2PX, ☎0845 083 3000
✉mail@clerksroom.com
King's Lynn Chambers
26 The Birches, South Wootton, King's Lynn, Norfolk PE30 3JG, ☎01553 672 085
✉timothy.leader@tesco.net
Call Date: Mar 2005, Lincoln's Inn
Qualifications: [LLB (Hons) Wales]
hodder@clerksroom.com

HODES MISS ANGELA EVE

Field Court Chambers
5 Field Court, Gray's Inn, London WC1R 5EF, ☎020 7405 6114 ✉clerks@fieldcourt.co.uk
Call Date: Nov 1979, Middle Temple
Pupil Supervisor
Qualifications: [BA]
angela.hodes@fieldcourt.co.uk

HODGE MR ALASTAIR BLACKWOOD

5 Essex Court
1st Floor, 5 Essex Court, Temple, London EC4Y 9AH, ☎020 7410 2000
✉clerks@5essexcourt.co.uk
Call Date: Nov 1997, Inner Temple
Pupil Supervisor
Qualifications: [LLB (Bris)]
hodge@5essexcourt.co.uk

HODGES MISS VICTORIA LESLEY

St Mary's Family Law Chambers
26-28 High Pavement, The Lace Market, Nottingham NG1 1HN, ☎0115 950 3503
✉clerks@stmarysflc.co.uk
Call Date: July 1980, Gray's Inn
Qualifications: [LLB (B'ham)]
vickie.hodges@stmarysflc.co.uk

HODGETTS MISS ELIZABETH MARY

St Philips Chambers
55 Temple Row, Birmingham B2 5LS, ☎0121 246 7000 ✉clerks@st-philips.com
Call Date: Nov 1998, Middle Temple
Pupil Supervisor
Qualifications: [BA (Hons)(Oxon)]
ehodgetts@st-philips.co.uk

HODGETTS MR GLEN

Tooks Chambers
81 Farringdon Street, London EC4A 4BL, ☎020 7842 7575 ✉clerks@tooks.co.uk
Call Date: Nov 1995, Inner Temple
Qualifications: [LLB (Hons)]
glen.hodgetts@tooks.co.uk

HODGKIN MR HARRY JOHN

The Chambers of J Dingle & H Hodgkin
3rd Floor, 218 Strand, London WC2R 1DR,
☎0845 083 3000 ✉mail@clerksroom.com
Clerksroom (London)
3rd Floor, 218 Strand, London WC2R 1AT,
☎0845 083 3000 ✉mail@clerksroom.com
Call Date: July 1983, Middle Temple
Pupil Supervisor
Qualifications: [LLB]

HODGKINSON MR JOHN ROBERT

St Philips Chambers
55 Temple Row, Birmingham B2 5LS,
☎0121 246 7000 ✉clerks@st-philips.com
Call Date: Nov 1968, Inner Temple
Pupil Supervisor
Qualifications: [MA (Cantab)]
✉rhodgkinson@st-philips.com

HODGKINSON MR PAUL GEORGE

Call Date: July 2002, Lincoln's Inn
Qualifications: [LLB (Hons)]
✉clerk@stjohnsbuildings.co.uk

HODGKISS MS SUZANNE JANE

43 Temple Row Chambers
6th Floor, 43 Temple Row, Birmingham
B2 5LS, ☎0121 237 6035
✉clerks@43templerow.co.uk
Call Date: Nov 2000, Inner Temple
Qualifications: [LLB (Staffs) MPhil (Keele)]
✉clerks@43templerow.co.uk

HODGSON MISS ELIZABETH JANE

Park Lane Plowden
Lombard House, 4-8 Lombard Street,
Newcastle Upon Tyne NE1 3AE,
☎0191 211 4087
✉clerks@parklaneplowden.co.uk
Call Date: Oct 1993, Gray's Inn
Qualifications: [LLB (Hons) (L'pool)]
✉elizabeth.hodgson@parklaneplowden.co.uk

HODGSON MRS JANE LEE

Five Paper
Ground Floor, 5 Paper Buildings, Temple,
London EC4Y 7HB, ☎020 7815 3200
Call Date: Oct 2000, Lincoln's Inn
Qualifications: [BSc (Hons) Nottingham Trent PgDL (UWE)]

HODGSON MRS MARGARET ANN

The Chambers of Mrs Magaret Hodgson
1 Court Crescent, Slough, Berkshire SL1 3JP,
☎01753 539260
✉r.andm.hodgson@talk21.com
Call Date: Oct 1996, Lincoln's Inn
Qualifications: [BA (Hons)]

HODGSON MR MARTIN DERRICK

1 Pump Court
Elm Court, Temple, London EC4Y 7AB,
☎020 7842 7070
✉(name)@pumpcourt.co.uk
Call Date: July 1980, Middle Temple
Pupil Supervisor
Qualifications: [BA]
✉mho@1pumpcourt.co.uk

HODGSON MR RICHARD ANDREW

Design Chambers
24 Arterberry Road, Wimbledon, London
SW20 8AH, ☎020 7353 0747
✉manager@designchambers.com
Call Date: Nov 1980, Inner Temple
Qualifications: [BSc (Eng) (Lond)]
✉rh@designchambers.com

HODGSON MISS ROSIE OLIVIA

Blackfriars Chambers
79-83 Temple Chambers, 3-7 Temple Avenue,
London EC4Y 0HP, ☎020 7353 7400
✉clerks@blackfriarschambers.com
Call Date: Oct 2008, Inner Temple
Qualifications: [BA (Cantab)]

HODGSON DR TIMOTHY PAUL

Cobden House Chambers
19 Quay Street, Manchester M3 3HN,
☎0161 833 6000 ✉Clerks@Cobden.co.uk
Call Date: Nov 1991, Inner Temple
Pupil Supervisor
Qualifications: [BA (New Zealand) BA (Hons) D Phil (Oxon) Dip Law (Lond)]
✉clerks@cobden.co.uk

HODIVALA MR JAMAS RUSI

2 Bedford Row
London WC1R 4BU, ☎020 7440 8888
✉clerks@2bedfordrow.co.uk
Call Date: Oct 1998, Lincoln's Inn
Pupil Supervisor
Qualifications: [LLB (Hons)(Leic)]
✉jhodivala@2bedfordrow.co.uk

E

HODKINSON MR GARY STEPHEN

Chambers of Mr Ami Feder
Ground Floor, Lamb Building, Temple, London EC4Y 7AS, ☎ 020 7797 7788
✉ clerks@lambbuilding.co.uk
Chambers of Mr Ami Feder
Ground Floor, Lamb Building, Temple, London EC4Y 7AS, ☎ 020 7797 7788
✉ clerks@lambbuilding.co.uk
Call Date: July 2010, Middle Temple
Qualifications: [LLB (Coventry)]
garyhodkinson@lambbuilding.co.uk

HODSON MS KATHERINE

Goldsmith Chambers
Ground Floor, Goldsmith Building, Temple, London EC4Y 7BL, ☎ 020 7353 6802
✉ clerks@goldsmithchambers.com
Call Date: Nov 2000, Inner Temple
Qualifications: [LLB (Hons)(Leeds)]
k.hodson@goldsmithchambers.law.co.uk

HODSON MR MATTHEW PAUL

Farrar's Building
Farrar's Building, Temple, London EC4Y 7BD, ☎ 020 7583 9241
✉ Chambers@farrarsbuilding.co.uk
Call Date: Nov 2004, Lincoln's Inn
Qualifications: [LLB (Hons) (Lond)]
mhodson@farrarsbuilding.co.uk

E

HODSON MR MICHAEL JOHN

New Court Chambers
3 Broad Chare, Newcastle Upon Tyne NE1 3DQ, ☎ 0191 232 1980
✉ clerks@newcourt-chambers.co.uk
Call Date: Feb 1977, Middle Temple
Pupil Supervisor
michael.hodson@newcourt-chambers.co.uk

HODSON MR PETER DAVID

Chambers of Ian Macdonald QC
Garden Court North, 22 Oxford Court, Manchester M2 3WQ, ☎ 0161 236 1840
✉ clerks@gcnchambers.co.uk
Call Date: Nov 1994, Inner Temple
Pupil Supervisor
Qualifications: [LLB (Hons) Dip CE]
peterhodson@gardencourtnorth.co.uk

Types of work: Asbestos-related diseases, Health and safety, Industrial diseases, Personal injury

HOFFMAN MR DAVID ALEXANDER

18 St John Street
Manchester M3 4EA, ☎ 0161 278 1800
✉ clerks@18sjs.com
Atlas Chambers
3 Field Court, Gray's Inn, London WC1R 5EP, ☎ 020 7269 7980
✉ clerks@atlaschambers.com
Call Date: Oct 1997, Lincoln's Inn
Qualifications: [MA (Oxon) BCL]
dhoffman@18sjs.com

HOFFMAN MR NICKY ELVIS

Seven Bedford Row
7 Bedford Row, London WC1R 4BS, ☎ 020 7242 3555 ✉ clerks@7br.co.uk
Call Date: July 2001, Middle Temple
Qualifications: [BA (Hons) CPE MA]
nhoffman@7br.co.uk

HOFMEYR MR STEPHEN MURRAY QC (2000)

7 King's Bench Walk
Ground Floor, 7 King's Bench Walk, Temple, London EC4Y 7DS, ☎ 020 7910 8300
✉ clerks@7kbw.co.uk
Call Date: July 1982, Gray's Inn
Recorder
Qualifications: [MA (Oxon) LLB (South Africa) BCom]
shofmeyr@7kbw.co.uk

HOGAN MR ANDREW PETER JOSEPH EDWARD

Ropewalk Chambers
24 The Ropewalk, Nottingham NG1 5EF, ☎ 0115 947 2581 ✉ clerks@ropewalk.co.uk
Call Date: Oct 1996, Inner Temple
Pupil Supervisor
Qualifications: [LLB (Bris) LLM (Sussex)]
andrewhogan@ropewalk.co.uk

HOGARTH MR ALASTAIR MARK CRAWFORD

The Chambers of Grahame Aldous QC
9 Gough Square, London EC4A 3DG, ☎ 020 7832 0500
✉ clerks@9goughsquare.co.uk
Call Date: Oct 2005, Lincoln's Inn
Qualifications: [MA (Edin)]
ahogarth@9goughsquare.co.uk

HOGARTH MR ANDREW ALLAN QC (2003)

12 King's Bench Walk
12 King's Bench Walk, Temple, London EC4Y 7EL, ☎ 020 7583 0811
Call Date: July 1974, Lincoln's Inn
Qualifications: [MA (Cantab)]
hogarth@12kbw.co.uk

HOGBEN MRS HELEN JANE

Fountain Chambers
Cleveland Business Centre, 1 Watson Street, Middlesbrough TS1 2RQ, ☎ 01642 804040
✉ clerks@fountainchambers.co.uk
Call Date: July 2006, Gray's Inn
Qualifications: [MA]

HOGBEN MR PAUL RAYMOND

5 Pump Court
Ground Floor, 5 Pump Court, Temple, London EC4Y 7AP, ☎ 020 7353 2532
✉ clerks@5pumpcourt.com
Call Date: Feb 1993, Gray's Inn
Pupil Supervisor
Qualifications: [LLB]

HOGG THE RIGHT HON DOUGLAS MARTIN QC (1990)

37 Park Square Chambers
37 Park Square, Leeds LS1 2NY, ☎ 0113 243 9422 ✉ chambers@no37.co.uk
Carmelite Chambers
9 Carmelite Street, London EC4Y 0DR, ☎ 020 7936 6300
✉ clerks@carmelitechambers.co.uk
Hailsham Chambers
Ground Floor, 4 Paper Buildings, Temple, London EC4Y 7EX, ☎ 020 7643 5000
✉ clerks@hailshamchambers.com
Call Date: July 1968, Lincoln's Inn
Qualifications: [MA (Oxon)]

HOGG MR JAMES ALEXANDER

St James's Chambers
68 Quay Street, Manchester M3 3EJ, ☎ 0161 834 7000
✉ clerks@stjameschambers.com
Call Date: Oct 2006, Inner Temple
Qualifications: [BA (Cantab)]
james.hogg@stjameschambers.com

HOGGETT-JONES MRS CAROLINE LOUISE

4 Breams Buildings
Chancery Lane, London EC4A 1HP, ☎ 020 7092 1900 ✉ clerks@4bb.co.uk
Call Date: July 2006, Gray's Inn
Qualifications: [BSc (Teeside) BSc (Northumbria)]

HOGMAN MR TIMOTHY JOHN

2 Bedford Row
London WC1R 4BU, ☎ 020 7440 8888
✉ clerks@2bedfordrow.co.uk
Call Date: July 2008, Middle Temple
Qualifications: [BA (Hons) (Lond) PgDl (Lond)]
thogman@2bedfordrow.co.uk

HOILE MRS ELINOR JANE

Pallant Chambers
12 North Pallant, Chichester, West Sussex PO19 1TQ, ☎ 01243 784538
✉ clerks@pallantchambers.co.uk
Call Date: Mar 2008, Lincoln's Inn
Qualifications: [LLB (Wales)]
ehoile@pallantchambers.co.uk

HOLBECH MR CHARLES EDWARD

New Square Chambers
12 New Square, Lincoln's Inn, London WC2A 3SW, ☎ 020 7419 8000
✉ robin.hollington@newsquarechambers.co.uk
Call Date: July 1988, Lincoln's Inn
Qualifications: [BA (Hons) (Oxon)]

HOLBORN MR DAVID REGINALD

18 Red Lion Court (Annexe)
Thornwood House, 102 New London Road, Chelmsford, Essex CM2 0RG, ☎ 01245 280880
18 Red Lion Court
London EC4A 3EB, ☎ 020 7520 6000
✉ chambers@18rlc.co.uk
Call Date: Oct 1991, Inner Temple
Pupil Supervisor, Recorder
Qualifications: [LLB (Essex)]

HOLBORN MR JACK NATHANIEL NEWTON

39 Essex Street
London WC2R 3AT, ☎ 020 7832 1111
✉ clerks@39essex.com
82 King Street
Manchester M2 4WQ, ☎ 0161 870 9969
Call Date: July 2008, Lincoln's Inn
Qualifications: [BA (Dunelm)]

E

HOLBROOK MR JON

Cornerstone Barristers
2-3 Gray's Inn Square, Gray's Inn, London WC1R 5JH, ☎020 7242 4986
✉chambers@2-3gis.co.uk
Call Date: Nov 1991, Inner Temple
Pupil Supervisor
Qualifications: [BA (Sheff)]
jholbrook@2-3gis.co.uk

HOLCOMBE MISS SOPHIE MARIE

Serle Court
6 New Square, Lincoln's Inn, London WC2A 3QS, ☎020 7242 6105
✉clerks@serlecourt.co.uk
Quadrant Chambers
Quadrant House, 10 Fleet Street, London EC4Y 1AU, ☎020 7583 4444
✉info@quadrantchambers.com
Call Date: July 2009, Inner Temple
Qualifications: [LLB (Cardiff)]
sholcombe@serlecourt.co.uk

HOLDCROFT MR MATTHEW JAMES

5 Essex Court
1st Floor, 5 Essex Court, Temple, London EC4Y 9AH, ☎020 7410 2000
✉clerks@5essexcourt.co.uk
Call Date: Oct 1998, Lincoln's Inn
Qualifications: [BA (Hons)]
holdcroft@5essexcourt.co.uk

HOLDEN MR ANDREW PAUL

XXIV Old Buildings
Ground Floor, 24 Old Buildings, Lincoln's Inn, London WC2A 3UP, ☎020 7691 2424
✉clerks@xxiv.co.uk
Call Date: Nov 2007, Inner Temple
Qualifications: [BA MSt (Oxon)]
andrew.holden@xxiv.co.uk

HOLDEN MR PHILIP ANTHONY

Lincoln House Chambers
Tower 12, The Avenue North, Spinningfields, 18-22 Bridge Street, Manchester M3 3BZ, ☎0161 832 5701
✉info@lincolnhousechambers.com
Call Date: Oct 1994, Lincoln's Inn
Qualifications: [LLB (Hons)(Northumbria)]
phil.holden@lincolnhousechambers.com

HOLDER MR SIMON MICHAEL

Call Date: July 1989, Inner Temple
Pupil Supervisor
Qualifications: [LLB (Lond)]
simonholder@indiabuildings.co.uk

HOLDER MR TERENCE

Colleton Chambers
Colleton Crescent, Exeter, Devon EX2 4DG, ☎01392 274898
✉clerks@colletonchambers.co.uk
Call Date: Nov 1984, Gray's Inn
terenceholder@colletonchambers.co.uk

HOLDERNESS MS KATE JULIA

3 Verulam Buildings
London WC1R 5NT, ☎020 7831 8441
✉chambers@3vb.com
Call Date: Nov 2008, Gray's Inn
Qualifications: [LLB LLM]
kholderness@3vb.com

HOLDSWORTH MR JAMES ARTHUR

Temple Garden Chambers
1 Harcourt Buildings, Temple, London EC4Y 9DA, ☎020 7583 1315
✉clerks@tgchambers.com
Call Date: Feb 1977, Middle Temple
Pupil Supervisor
Qualifications: [MA (Oxon)]
jamesholdsworth@tgchambers.com

HOLE MISS CHARLOTTE ELIZABETH

5 King's Bench Walk
5 King's Bench Walk, Temple, London EC4Y 7DN, ☎020 7353 5638
✉clerks@5kbw.co.uk
Call Date: July 2009, Middle Temple
Qualifications: [BA (Hons) (Oxon) Grad Dip Law (Staffs)]

HOLGATE MR DAVID JOHN QC (1997)

Landmark Chambers
180 Fleet Street, London EC4A 2HG, ☎020 7430 1221
✉clerks@landmarkchambers.co.uk
Call Date: July 1978, Middle Temple
Qualifications: [BA (Oxon)]
dholgate@landmarkchambers.co.uk

HOLINER MR DREW PATRICK

Monckton Chambers
1 & 2 Raymond Buildings, Gray's Inn, London WC1R 5NR, ☎020 7405 7211
✉chambers@monckton.com
Call Date: July 2005, Lincoln's Inn
Qualifications: [Dip Law]
dholiner@monckton.com

E

HOLL-ALLEN MR JONATHAN GUY

3 Serjeants Inn
London EC4Y 1BQ, ☎020 7427 5000
✉clerks@3serjeantsinn.com
Call Date: Nov 1990, Inner Temple
Pupil Supervisor
Qualifications: [MA LLM (Cantab)]
✉jholl-allen@3serjeantsinn.com

HOLLAND MRS ANNE ROSEMARY

King's Bench and Godolphin (KBG)Chambers
115 North Hill, Plymouth, Devon PL4 8JY, ☎01752 221551
✉clerks@kbgchambers.co.uk
Call Date: Nov 1994, Middle Temple
Qualifications: [LLB (Hons) RGN]
✉theclerks@godolphinchambers.co.uk

HOLLAND MR CHARLES CHRISTOPHER

Trinity Chambers
The Custom House, 39 Quayside, Newcastle Upon Tyne NE1 3DE, ☎0191 232 1927
✉info@trinitychambers.co.uk
Trinity Chambers
Multi Media Exchange, 72-80 Corporation Road, Middlesbrough TS1 2RF, ☎01642 247569
✉info@trinitychambers.co.uk
Francis Taylor Building
Inner Temple, London EC4Y 7BY, ☎020 7353 8415 ✉clerks@ftb.eu.com
Call Date: Nov 1994, Inner Temple
Pupil Supervisor
Qualifications: [LLB (Notts)]

HOLLAND MISS CHARLOTTE KATE

Lincoln House Chambers
Tower 12, The Avenue North, Spinningfields, 18-22 Bridge Street, Manchester M3 3BZ, ☎0161 832 5701
✉info@lincolnhousechambers.com
Call Date: Oct 1996, Lincoln's Inn
Pupil Supervisor
Qualifications: [BA (Hons)(B'ham) CPE (Manc)]
✉charlotte.holland@lincolnhousechambers.com

HOLLAND MR DAVID MOORE QC (2011)

Landmark Chambers
180 Fleet Street, London EC4A 2HG, ☎020 7430 1221
✉clerks@landmarkchambers.co.uk
Call Date: July 1986, Inner Temple
Pupil Supervisor
Qualifications: [MA (Cantab) LLM (Canada)]
✉dholland@landmarkchambers.co.uk

HOLLAND MRS ELEANOR JOY

4 Stone Buildings
Ground Floor, 4 Stone Buildings, Lincoln's Inn, London WC2A 3XT, ☎020 7242 5524
✉clerks@4stonebuildings.com
Call Date: July 2010, Lincoln's Inn
Qualifications: [BA (Oxon)]
✉eleanor.holland@4stonebuildings.com

HOLLAND MR JAMES PETER

4 Breams Buildings
Chancery Lane, London EC4A 1HP, ☎020 7092 1900 ✉clerks@4bb.co.uk
Call Date: July 2004, Inner Temple

HOLLAND MR JORDAN DEAN

5 Stone Buildings
5 Stone Buildings, Lincoln's Inn, London WC2A 3XT, ☎020 7242 6201
✉clerks@5sblaw.com
Call Date: Oct 2009, Inner Temple
Qualifications: [BA (Cantab) LLB (Nott'm)]
✉jholland@5sblaw.com

HOLLAND MISS KATHARINE JANE QC (2010)

Landmark Chambers
180 Fleet Street, London EC4A 2HG, ☎020 7430 1221
✉clerks@landmarkchambers.co.uk
Call Date: July 1989, Middle Temple
Qualifications: [BA (Oxon) BCL (Oxon)]

HOLLAND MR MICHAEL FREDERICK RICHARD QC (2006)

9-12 Bell Yard
London WC2A 2JR, ☎020 7400 1800
✉clerks@9-12bellyard.com
Call Date: Nov 1984, Inner Temple
Qualifications: [BA (Dunelm)]
✉m.holland@9-12bellyard.com

E

HOLLAND MR NADEEM JOHN

Castle Chambers
The Old Fire Station, 90 High Street, Harrow-on-the-Hill, Middlesex HA1 3LP, ☎ 020 8423 6579 ✉ info@castlechambers.net
Call Date: Oct 2006, Lincoln's Inn
Qualifications: [BA (Sussex)]

HOLLAND MR RICKY JOHN

Lincoln House Chambers
Tower 12, The Avenue North, Spinningfields, 18-22 Bridge Street, Manchester M3 3BZ, ☎ 0161 832 5701
✉ info@lincolnhousechambers.com
Call Date: Nov 1994, Gray's Inn
Qualifications: [LLB LLM (Cantab)]
✉ rick.holland@lincolnhousechambers.com

HOLLAND MRS ROBERTA

12 College Place
Fauvelle Buildings, 12 College Place, Southampton SO15 2FE, ☎ 023 8032 0320
✉ clerks@12cp.co.uk
Call Date: Nov 1989, Lincoln's Inn
Pupil Supervisor
Qualifications: [BSc (Bath) LLB]
✉ RHolland@12cp.co.uk

HOLLAND MR ROWAN GUY

Five Paper
Ground Floor, 5 Paper Buildings, Temple, London EC4Y 7HB, ☎ 020 7815 3200
Call Date: Mar 2001, Middle Temple
Qualifications: [LLB (Hons) (Newc)]
✉ guyholland@fivepaper.com

HOLLAND MR RUSSELL STEPHEN

12 King's Bench Walk
12 King's Bench Walk, Temple, London EC4Y 7EL, ☎ 020 7583 0811
Call Date: Nov 2008, Lincoln's Inn
Qualifications: [MA (Oxon)]
✉ holland@12kbw.co.uk

HOLLAND MR WILLIAM

1 Gray's Inn Square
Ground Floor, 1 Gray's Inn Square, London WC1R 5AA, ☎ 020 7405 0001
Call Date: July 1982, Gray's Inn
Pupil Supervisor
Qualifications: [LLB (Lond)]

HOLLANDER MR CHARLES SIMON QC (1999)

Brick Court Chambers
7-8 Essex Street, London WC2R 3LD, ☎ 020 7379 3550 ✉ clerks@brickcourt.co.uk
Call Date: July 1978, Gray's Inn
Recorder
Qualifications: [MA (Cantab)]
✉ Charles.hollander@brickcourt.co.uk

HOLLIMAN MR ADAM GRAHAM

4 Stone Buildings
Ground Floor, 4 Stone Buildings, Lincoln's Inn, London WC2A 3XT, ☎ 020 7242 5524
✉ clerks@4stonebuildings.com
Call Date: Oct 2005, Lincoln's Inn
Qualifications: [LLB (Hons) (Lond) BCL (Oxon)]
✉ a.holliman@4stonebuildings.com

HOLLINGSWORTH MR EDWARD MICHAEL ALASTAIR

2 King's Bench Walk
2 King's Bench Walk, Temple, London EC4Y 7DE, ☎ 020 7353 1746
✉ clerks@2kbw.com
Call Date: Nov 2007, Middle Temple
Qualifications: [MA (Edin) PgDL (Lond) MA (Sussex)]
✉ clerks@2kbw.com

HOLLINGTON MR ROBIN FRANK QC (1999)

New Square Chambers
12 New Square, Lincoln's Inn, London WC2A 3SW, ☎ 020 7419 8000
✉ robin.hollington@newsquarechambers.co.uk
Call Date: July 1979, Lincoln's Inn
Recorder
Qualifications: [MA (Oxon) LLM]
✉ robin.hollington@newsquarechambers.co.uk

HOLLINGWORTH MR GUY WILMER RISELEY

One Essex Court
Ground Floor, One Essex Court, Temple, London EC4Y 9AR, ☎ 020 7583 2000
✉ clerks@oeclaw.co.uk
Call Date: Oct 2001, Lincoln's Inn
Qualifications: [BSc (Hons)]
✉ ghollingworth@oeclaw.co.uk

E

HOLLIS MRS KIM QC (2002)

25 Bedford Row
London WC1R 4HD, ☎020 7067 1500
✉clerks@25bedfordrow.com
Call Date: July 1979, Gray's Inn
Qualifications: [LLB (Lond)]
✉kholis@25bedfordrow.com

HOLLORAN MS FIONA ANNE

18 St John Street
Manchester M3 4EA, ☎0161 278 1800
✉clerks@18sjs.com
Call Date: Nov 1989, Gray's Inn
Qualifications: [LLB (Hons) (Warw)]
✉family@18sjs.com

HOLLOW MR PAUL JOHN

Fenners Chambers
3 Madingley Road, Cambridge CB3 0EE,
☎01223 368761
✉clerks@fennerschambers.com
Call Date: Nov 1981, Gray's Inn
Pupil Supervisor
Qualifications: [LLB (UEA)]
✉paul.hollow@fennerschambers.com

HOLLOWAY MR DAVID JOHN

No5 Chambers
Greenwood House, 4-7 Salisbury Court,
London EC4Y 8AA, ☎0845 210 5555
No5 Chambers
38 Queen Square, Bristol BS1 4QS,
☎0845 210 5555
No5 Chambers
Fountain Court, Steelhouse Lane, Birmingham
B4 6DR, ☎0845 210 5555 ✉info@no5.com
Call Date: July 1996, Gray's Inn
Pupil Supervisor
Qualifications: [MA (Cantab) MCIArb]
✉dh@no5.com

HOLLOWAY MR ORLANDO AIDAN

42 Bedford Row
London WC1R 4LL, ☎020 7831 0222
✉clerks@42br.com
Call Date: Oct 2004, Lincoln's Inn
Qualifications: [LLB (Hons) Exon]
✉orlando.holloway@42br.com

HOLLOWAY MR RICHARD MARK

KCH Garden Square
1 Oxford Street, Nottingham NG1 5BH,
☎0115 941 8851
✉clerks@kchgardensquare.co.uk
Call Date: Nov 1993, Gray's Inn
Qualifications: [B Phil Dip Law]
✉rholloway@kchgardensquare.co.uk

HOLLOWAY MR TIMOTHY RICHARD

Oriel Chambers
14 Water Street, Liverpool, Merseyside
L2 8TD, ☎0151 236 7191
✉clerks@orielchambers.co.uk
Oriel Chambers
18 Ribblesdale Place, Preston PR1 3NA,
☎01772 254 764
✉clerks@oriel-chambers.co.uk
Call Date: Nov 1991, Inner Temple
Pupil Supervisor
Qualifications: [MA (Cantab)]
✉timothy.holloway@orielchambers.co.uk

HOLME MR GAVIN JAMES

4 King's Bench Walk
2nd Floor, 4 King's Bench Walk, Temple,
London EC4Y 7DL, ☎020 7822 7000
✉clerks@4kbw.co.uk
Call Date: Oct 1999, Inner Temple
Qualifications: [BA (Leeds)]
✉gh@4kbw.co.uk

HOLME MRS SOPHIE LAURA

Guildhall Chambers
23 Broad Street, Bristol BS1 2HG,
☎0117 930 9000
✉hoc@guildhallchambers.co.uk
Call Date: Oct 2009, Gray's Inn
Qualifications: [BA MSt]
✉sophie.holme@guildhallchambers.co.uk

HOLMES MR ANDREW CHRISTOPHER

42 Bedford Row
London WC1R 4LL, ☎020 7831 0222
✉clerks@42br.com
Dere Street Barristers
33 Broad Chare, Newcastle Upon Tyne
NE1 3DQ, ☎0844 3351551
✉clerks@derestreet.co.uk
Call Date: July 2000, Lincoln's Inn
Qualifications: [LLB(Hons) (Leeds)]

HOLMES MISS CLAIRE AMANDA

Wilberforce Chambers
7 Bishop Lane, Hull HU1 1PA,
☎01482 323264
Call Date: Oct 2009, Gray's Inn

E

HOLMES MS ELISA

Monckton Chambers
1 & 2 Raymond Buildings, Gray's Inn, London WC1R 5NR, ☎020 7405 7211
✉chambers@monckton.com
Call Date: Nov 2003, Inner Temple
Pupil Supervisor
Qualifications: [BCL (Oxon) BA (Austalia) LLB (Australia)]
eholmes@monckton.com

HOLMES MISS HELEN

No.6 Park Square
Leeds LS1 2LW, ☎0113 245 9763
✉Tim@no6.co.uk
Call Date: Oct 2000, Inner Temple
Qualifications: [BA (Dunelm) CPE (Nott'm)]
holmes@no6.co.uk

HOLMES MS JESSICA HELEN

Argent Chambers
5 Bell Yard, London WC2A 2JR, ☎020 7556 5500
✉briefsin@argentchambers.co.uk
Call Date: Oct 2003, Inner Temple
Qualifications: [BA (Lond)]
j.holmes@argentchambers.co.uk

E

HOLMES MR JOSEPH HENRY

Chambers of Mr Ami Feder
Ground Floor, Lamb Building, Temple, London EC4Y 7AS, ☎020 7797 7788
✉clerks@lambbuilding.co.uk
Chambers of Mr Ami Feder
Ground Floor, Lamb Building, Temple, London EC4Y 7AS, ☎020 7797 7788
✉clerks@lambbuilding.co.uk
Call Date: Oct 2009, Middle Temple
Qualifications: [BA (Hons) (Nott'm)]

HOLMES MR JOSHUA PETER FREDERICK

Monckton Chambers
1 & 2 Raymond Buildings, Gray's Inn, London WC1R 5NR, ☎020 7405 7211
✉chambers@monckton.com
Call Date: Oct 1997, Inner Temple
Pupil Supervisor
Qualifications: [MA (Oxon) BCL (Oxon) LLM (USA)]
jholmes@monckton.com

HOLMES MR JUSTIN FRANCIS

Radcliffe Chambers
Ground Floor, 11 New Square, Lincoln's Inn, London WC2A 3QB, ☎020 7831 0081
✉clerks@radcliffechambers.com
Pallant Chambers
12 North Pallant, Chichester, West Sussex PO19 1TQ, ☎01243 784538
✉clerks@pallantchambers.co.uk
Call Date: Feb 1994, Inner Temple
Qualifications: [MA (Cantab)]
jholmes@radcliffechambers.com

HOLMES MS MARTHA FELICITY

1 KBW Chambers
1 King's Bench Walk, Temple, London EC4Y 7DB, ☎020 7936 1500
✉clerks@1kbw.co.uk
King's Bench Chambers
174 High Street, Lewes BN7 1YE, ☎01273 402600
Call Date: July 2003, Inner Temple
Qualifications: [MA (Cantab)]

HOLMES MR MICHAEL DENZIL

7 King's Bench Walk
Ground Floor, 7 King's Bench Walk, Temple, London EC4Y 7DS, ☎020 7910 8300
✉clerks@7kbw.co.uk
Call Date: Oct 1999, Middle Temple
Qualifications: [MPhil (Cantab) MA (Cantab)]
mholmes@7kbw.co.uk

HOLMES MR RORY THOMAS LITTLEWOOD

Crown Office Chambers
2 Crown Office Row, Temple, London EC4Y 7HJ, ☎020 7797 8100
✉mail@crownofficechambers.com
Call Date: Nov 2009, Middle Temple
Qualifications: [BA (Hons) (Cantab)]
holmes@crownofficechambers.com

HOLMES-MILNER MR JAMES NEIL

The Chambers of Grahame Aldous QC
9 Gough Square, London EC4A 3DG, ☎020 7832 0500
✉clerks@9goughsquare.co.uk
Call Date: July 1989, Middle Temple
Pupil Supervisor
Qualifications: [MA (Cantab) Dip Law]
JHolmes-Milner@9goughsquare.co.uk

HOLROYD MR CHARLES WILFRID

7 King's Bench Walk
Ground Floor, 7 King's Bench Walk, Temple, London EC4Y 7DS, ☎ 020 7910 8300
✉ clerks@7kbw.co.uk
Call Date: Oct 1997, Gray's Inn
Pupil Supervisor
Qualifications: [BA (Oxon)]
✉ cholroyd@7kbw.co.uk

HOLROYD MR JOHN JAMES

Zenith Chambers
10 Park Square, Leeds LS1 2LH,
☎ 0113 245 5438
✉ clerks@zenithchambers.co.uk
Call Date: Nov 1989, Gray's Inn
Pupil Supervisor
Qualifications: [BSc (Nott'm) LLB MICE C Eng FCI Arb]
✉ jholroyd@zenithchambers.co.uk

HOLSGROVE MR JONATHAN PETER

Bank House Chambers
Old Bank House, Hartshead, Sheffield S1 2EL,
☎ 0114 275 1223
✉ w.digby@bankhousechambers.co.uk
Call Date: Mar 2011, Gray's Inn
✉ j.holsgrove@bankhousechambers.co.uk

HOLSGROVE MISS LARA LOUISA JANE

Call Date: Oct 1999, Middle Temple
Qualifications: [LLB (Hons)(L'pool)]

HOLT MISS ABIGAIL CLAIRE

Lincoln House Chambers
Tower 12, The Avenue North, Spinningfields, 18-22 Bridge Street, Manchester M3 3BZ,
☎ 0161 832 5701
✉ info@lincolnhousechambers.com
Call Date: Oct 1993, Lincoln's Inn
Qualifications: [MA (Hons)(Oxon)]
✉ abi.holt@lincolnhousechambers.com

HOLT MR BENJAMIN RICHARD

5 King's Bench Walk
5 King's Bench Walk, Temple, London EC4Y 7DN, ☎ 020 7353 5638
✉ clerks@5kbw.co.uk
Call Date: Oct 2006, Inner Temple
Qualifications: [BA (Dunelm)]
✉ benjamin.holt@5kbw.co.uk

HOLT MR CRAIG JOHN

Huntwyck Chambers
The Huntwyck, Hamilton Place, Melton Mowbray LE13 0LX, ☎ 07843 620473
✉ craig@qualitysolicitors.com
Call Date: Nov 2002, Gray's Inn
Qualifications: [BA (Oxon)]

HOLT MRS JANE ROSEMARY

KCH Garden Square
1 Oxford Street, Nottingham NG1 5BH,
☎ 0115 941 8851
✉ clerks@kchgardensquare.co.uk
Call Date: Oct 2006, Middle Temple
Qualifications: [BA (Hons)]
✉ jholt@kchgardensquare.co.uk

HOLT MR JONATHAN DAVID JAMES

Central Chambers
89 Princess Street, Manchester M1 4HT,
☎ 0161 236 1133
✉ clerks@centralchambers.co.uk
Lamb Building
22 Ship Street, Brighton BN1 1AD,
☎ 01273 820490
✉ admin@lambbuilding.co.uk
Call Date: July 2009, Middle Temple
Qualifications: [MPhys (Hons) (Manch) Grad Dip Law (Lond)]

HOLT MISS KAREN JANE

23 Essex Street
London WC2R 3AA, ☎ 020 7413 0353
✉ clerks@23es.com
Call Date: Nov 1987, Lincoln's Inn
Pupil Supervisor, Recorder
Qualifications: [LLB (Leeds)]
✉ karenholt@23es.com

HOLT MISS KERRY

Dere Street Barristers
33 Broad Chare, Newcastle Upon Tyne NE1 3DQ, ☎ 0844 3351551
✉ clerks@derestreet.co.uk
Call Date: July 2009, Inner Temple
Qualifications: [LLB (Keele)]

HOLT MR MICHAEL JULIAN

St Johns Buildings
24a - 28 St John Street, Manchester M3 4DJ,
☎ 0161 214 1500
✉ clerk@stjohnsbuildings.co.uk
St Johns Buildings
21 White Friars, Chester CH1 1NZ,
☎ 01244 323070
✉ clerk@stjohnsbuildings.co.uk

E

16 Winckley Square
Preston PR1 3JJ, ☎01772 256100
Call Date: Feb 1982, Middle Temple
Pupil Supervisor
Qualifications: [BA]
✉clerk@stjohnsbuildings.co.uk

HOLT MISS SARAH LOUISE

Number 7 Harrington Street Chambers
7 Harrington Street, Liverpool L2 9YH,
☎0151 242 0707 ✉clerks@7hs.co.uk
Call Date: Oct 1999, Middle Temple
Qualifications: [LLB (Hons)]
✉sarah.holt@7hs.co.uk

HOLWILL MR DEREK PAUL WINSOR

Hailsham Chambers
Ground Floor, 4 Paper Buildings, Temple,
London EC4Y 7EX, ☎020 7643 5000
✉clerks@hailshamchambers.com
Call Date: July 1982, Gray's Inn
Pupil Supervisor
Qualifications: [MA (Cantab)]
✉derek.holwill@hailshamchambers.com

HONE MR BARNABY MICHAEL LOCHIE

1 Paper Buildings
1st Floor, 1 Paper Buildings, Temple, London
EC4Y 7EP, ☎020 7353 3728
✉clerks@onepaper.co.uk
Call Date: Oct 2006, Middle Temple
Qualifications: [LLB (Hons) (UEA)]

HONEY MR RICHARD ARTHUR

Francis Taylor Building
Inner Temple, London EC4Y 7BY,
☎020 7353 8415 ✉clerks@ftb.eu.com
Call Date: July 2003, Inner Temple
Qualifications: [BSc MSc (Lond) CPE (Nott'm) MRICS MCIARb]
✉Richard.honey@ftb.eu.com

HONEYMAN MS GILLIAN

Coram Chambers
9-11 Fulwood Place, London WC1V 6HG,
☎020 7092 3700
✉mail@coramchambers.co.uk
Call Date: July 2011, Gray's Inn

HOOD MR DAVID

Prince of Wales Chambers
90 Overstrand Mansions, Prince of Wales
Drive, London SW11 4EU, ☎020 7622 7415
✉DavidHoodEsq@aol.com
Call Date: Nov 1980, Inner Temple
Qualifications: [LLB (Lond)]
✉DavidHoodEsq@aol.com

HOOD MR NIGEL ANTHONY

New Square Chambers
12 New Square, Lincoln's Inn, London
WC2A 3SW, ☎020 7419 8000
✉robin.hollington@newsquarechambers.co.uk
Call Date: Oct 1993, Inner Temple
Pupil Supervisor
Qualifications: [BA (Bournemouth) MBA (USA) CPE]
✉nigel.hood@newsquarechambers.co.uk

HOOKWAY MR RICHARD AELRED

Zenith Chambers
10 Park Square, Leeds LS1 2LH,
☎0113 245 5438
✉clerks@zenithchambers.co.uk
Call Date: Nov 1990, Gray's Inn
Pupil Supervisor
Qualifications: [LLB (B'ham)]

HOON MR PRITHVIJIT NOTU SINGH

Argent Chambers
5 Bell Yard, London WC2A 2JR,
☎020 7556 5500
✉briefsin@argentchambers.co.uk
Call Date: Nov 1975, Inner Temple
Pupil Supervisor
✉n.hoon@argentchambers.co.uk

HOOPER MR BENJAMIN RICHARD

11 King's Bench Walk
11 King's Bench Walk, Temple, London
EC4Y 7EQ, ☎020 7632 8500
✉clerksroom@11kbw.com
Call Date: Oct 2000, Inner Temple
Pupil Supervisor
Qualifications: [MA (Oxon) CPE (City)]
✉ben.hooper@11kbw.com

HOOPER MR DAVID JOHN QC (2010)

25 Bedford Row
London WC1R 4HD, ☎020 7067 1500
✉clerks@25bedfordrow.com
Call Date: Feb 1971, Middle Temple
Pupil Supervisor
✉dhooper@25bedfordrow.com

HOOPER MR GOPAL ARTHUR JOHN

Thomas More Chambers
7 Lincoln's Inn Fields, London WC2A 3BP,
☎020 7404 7000
✉clerks@thomasmore.co.uk
Call Date: July 1973, Middle Temple
Pupil Supervisor
Qualifications: [LLB]
✉ghooper@thomasmore.co.uk

HOOPER MS LOUISE

Garden Court Chambers
57-60 Lincoln's Inn Fields, London WC2A 3LJ,
☎ 020 7993 7600 ✉ info@gclaw.co.uk
Call Date: Nov 1997, Gray's Inn
Qualifications: [BA (Lond)]
louiseh@gclaw.co.uk

HOOPER MR MARTIN CHARLES

5 King's Bench Walk
5 King's Bench Walk, Temple, London
EC4Y 7DN, ☎ 020 7353 5638
✉ clerks@5kbw.co.uk
Call Date: July 1988, Middle Temple
Pupil Supervisor
Qualifications: [LLB (Hons)]
martin.hooper@5kbw.co.uk

HOPE MR ANDREW JOHN

Chambers of Marion Smullen and Kerim Fuad QC
1 Inner Temple Lane, London EC4Y 1AF,
☎ 020 7427 4400 ✉ clerks@1itl.com
Call Date: Oct 2003, Gray's Inn
Qualifications: [LLB (Sheff) LLM (Lond)]

HOPE MISS HEATHER ROSALIND

Goldsmith Chambers
Ground Floor, Goldsmith Building, Temple,
London EC4Y 7BL, ☎ 020 7353 6802
✉ clerks@goldsmithchambers.com
Call Date: Oct 1993, Gray's Inn
Qualifications: [LLB (Hons)]
H.Hope@goldsmithchambers.law.co.uk

HOPE MR IAN STUART

23 Essex Street
London WC2R 3AA, ☎ 020 7413 0353
✉ clerks@23es.com
Call Date: Nov 1996, Inner Temple
Qualifications: [BA (Wales) CPE]
ianhope@23es.com

HOPEWELL MR GREGORY TURTLE

2 Dr Johnson's Buildings
2 Dr Johnson's Buildings, Temple, London
EC4Y 7AY, ☎ 020 7936 2613
✉ clerks@2drj.com
Call Date: Feb 1992, Inner Temple
Qualifications: [BA LLB (Hons)]
g.hopewell@2drj.com

HOPKIN MR WILLIAM WALTER

Rougemont Chambers
Victory House, Dean Clarke Gardens,
Southernhay East, Exeter EX2 4AA,
☎ 01392 208484
✉ clerks@rougemontchambers.co.uk
St Leonards Chambers
Address withheld ☎ 07734 706185
✉ william.hopkin@btinternet.com
Call Date: Oct 2000, Inner Temple
Qualifications: [BA (Hons) (Exon) CPE]
whopkin@rougemontchambers.co.uk

HOPKINS MR ADRIAN MARK QC (2003)

3 Serjeants Inn
London EC4Y 1BQ, ☎ 020 7427 5000
✉ clerks@3serjeantsinn.com
Call Date: Nov 1984, Lincoln's Inn
Qualifications: [BA (Oxon)]
ahopkins@3serjeantsinn.com

HOPKINS MR PAUL ANDREW QC (2009)

9 Park Place
9 Park Place, Cardiff, South Glamorgan
CF10 3DP, ☎ 029 2038 2731
✉ clerks@9parkplace.co.uk
Call Date: July 1989, Gray's Inn
Recorder
Qualifications: [LLB (B'ham)]
paulgroeswen2@aol.com

HOPKINS MISS PHILIPPA MARY

Essex Court Chambers
24 Lincoln's Inn Fields, London WC2A 3EG,
☎ 020 7813 8000
✉ clerksroom@essexcourt.net
Call Date: Oct 1994, Middle Temple
Pupil Supervisor
Qualifications: [BA (Hons) BCL (Oxon)]
phopkins@essexcourt.net

HOPKINS MR ROBIN

11 King's Bench Walk
11 King's Bench Walk, Temple, London
EC4Y 7EQ, ☎ 020 7632 8500
✉ clerksroom@11kbw.com
Call Date: July 2008, Lincoln's Inn
Qualifications: [BA (Oxon) BSc MSt (Oxon) CPE BVC (ICSL)]

E

HOPPER MR STEPHEN JOHN

Five Paper Buildings
1st Floor, Five Paper Buildings, Temple, London EC4Y 7HB, ☎ 020 7583 6117
✉ clerks@5pb.co.uk
Call Date: Nov 2001, Middle Temple
Qualifications: [BA (Hons)(Oxon) CPE]
sjh@5pb.co.uk

HORAN MR JOHN PATRICK

Cloisters
1 Pump Court, Temple, London EC4Y 7AA, ☎ 020 7827 4000 ✉ clerks@cloisters.com
Call Date: Feb 1993, Inner Temple
Qualifications: [BA DipLaw]
jh@cloisters.com

HORAN MR STEPHEN JOHN

Erskine Chambers
33 Chancery Lane, London WC2A 1EN, ☎ 020 7242 5532
✉ clerks@erskinechambers.com
Call Date: Nov 2002, Lincoln's Inn
Qualifications: [LLB BA]
shoran@erskine-chambers.co.uk

HORDER MR THOMAS EDWARD

3 PB Barristers
3 Paper Buildings, Temple, London EC4Y 7EU, ☎ 020 7583 8055
3 PB Barristers
Royal Talbot House, 2 Victoria Street, Bristol, Avon BS1 6BB, ☎ 0117 928 1520
3 PB Barristers
30 Christchurch Road, Bournemouth, Dorset BH1 3PD, ☎ 01202 292102
✉ clerks.bournemouth@3paper.co.uk
3 PB Barristers
4 St Peter Street, Winchester SO23 8BW, ☎ 01962 868884
✉ clerks.winchester@3paper.co.uk
3 PB Barristers
23 Beaumont Street, Oxford OX1 2NP, ☎ 01865 793 736
Call Date: July 2004, Middle Temple
Qualifications: [BA Hons (Newc) PGDip Law (BPP)]
tom.horder@3paper.co.uk

HORGAN MR PETER THOMAS

Deans Court Chambers
24 St John Street, Manchester M3 4DF, ☎ 0161 214 6000 ✉ clerks@deanscourt.co.uk
Deans Court Chambers
101 Walker Street, Preston PR1 2RR, ☎ 01772 565 600
✉ preston@deanscourt.co.uk
Call Date: Oct 1993, Middle Temple
Qualifications: [BA (Hons)(Manch) Dip Law (Lond)]
horgan@deanscourt.co.uk

HORGAN MR TIMOTHY GEORGE

Argent Chambers
5 Bell Yard, London WC2A 2JR, ☎ 020 7556 5500
✉ briefsin@argentchambers.co.uk
Call Date: July 1982, Inner Temple
Pupil Supervisor
Qualifications: [LLB (Leeds)]
t.horgan@argentchambers.co.uk

HORLICK MISS FIONA

Outer Temple Chambers
The Outer Temple, 222 Strand, London WC2R 1BA, ☎ 020 7353 6381
✉ clerks@outertemple.com
Call Date: May 1992, Middle Temple
Pupil Supervisor
Qualifications: [LLB (Hons) (Lond)]

HORLOCK MR TIMOTHY JOHN QC (1997)

Deans Court Chambers
24 St John Street, Manchester M3 4DF, ☎ 0161 214 6000 ✉ clerks@deanscourt.co.uk
Call Date: July 1981, Middle Temple
Qualifications: [BA (Cantab) MA]

HORMAECHE MISS ALEJANDRA

Tanfield Chambers
2-5 Warwick Court, London WC1R 5DJ, ☎ 020 7421 5300
✉ clerks@tanfieldchambers.co.uk
Call Date: Oct 1998, Middle Temple
Qualifications: [LLB (Hons)(Manc)]
ahormaeche@tanfieldchambers.co.uk

HORNBLOWER MRS SARAH PATIENCE

Rougemont Chambers
Victory House, Dean Clarke Gardens, Southernhay East, Exeter EX2 4AA, ☎ 01392 208484
✉ clerks@rougemontchambers.co.uk
Call Date: July 2005, Gray's Inn
Qualifications: [LLB (Cardiff)]

HORNBY MR ROBERT CHRISTOPHER

Linenhall Chambers
1 Stanley Place, Chester CH1 2LU,
☎ 01244 348282
✉ clerks@linenhallchambers.co.uk
Call Date: Oct 1990, Lincoln's Inn
Pupil Supervisor, Recorder
Qualifications: [LLB]
✉ clerks@1stanleyplace.co.uk

HORNE MR CHARLES HUGH WILSON

Kings Chambers
36 Young Street, Manchester M3 3FT,
☎ 0845 034 3444
✉ clerks@kingschambers.com
Kings Chambers
5 Park Square East, Leeds LS1 2NE,
☎ 0845 034 3444
✉ clerks@kingschambers.com
Kings Chambers
Embassy House, 60 Church Street,
Birmingham B3 2DJ, ☎ 0845 034 3444
✉ clerks@kingschambers.com
Call Date: Oct 1992, Lincoln's Inn
Pupil Supervisor
Qualifications: [LLB(Hons)(Leeds)]
✉ whorne@kingschambers.com

HORNE MR DAVID MICHAEL

Bank House Chambers
Old Bank House, Hartshead, Sheffield S1 2EL,
☎ 0114 275 1223
✉ w.digby@bankhousechambers.co.uk
Call Date: July 2009, Gray's Inn
Qualifications: [LLB]

HORNE MR JAMES MICHAEL

Bank House Chambers
Old Bank House, Hartshead, Sheffield S1 2EL,
☎ 0114 275 1223
✉ w.digby@bankhousechambers.co.uk
Call Date: July 2004, Middle Temple
Qualifications: [LLB (Hons)]
✉ j.horne@bankhousechambers.co.uk

HORNE MR JOSEPH MERIVS BRERETON

11 Gray's Inn Square Chambers
Chambers of Mr Ian Sen, 1st Floor South,
10/11 Gray's Inn Square, London WC1R 5JD,
☎ 020 7405 6879
✉ clerks@11graysinnsquare.com
Call Date: Oct 1999, Lincoln's Inn
Qualifications: [LLB (Hons)(Lond) LLM (Lond)]

HORNE MR JULIAN

St John's Chambers
101 Victoria Street, Bristol BS1 6PU,
☎ 0117 923 4700
✉ clerks@stjohnschambers.co.uk
Call Date: Nov 1998, Middle Temple
Qualifications: [BA (Hons)(Oxon) BCL (Oxon)]
✉ julian.horne@stjohnschambers.co.uk

HORNE MR KENDERIK THOMAS CLARKE

Atlantic Chambers
4-6 Cook Street, Liverpool L2 9QU,
☎ 0151 236 4421
✉ info@atlanticchambers.co.uk
Call Date: Mar 1996, Lincoln's Inn
Qualifications: [BA (Hons)]
✉ kenderikhorne@atlanticchambers.co.uk

HORNE MR MICHAEL ANDREW

3 Serjeants Inn
London EC4Y 1BQ, ☎ 020 7427 5000
✉ clerks@3serjeantsinn.com
Call Date: Oct 1992, Gray's Inn
Pupil Supervisor
Qualifications: [MA]
✉ mhorne@3serjeantsinn.com

HORNER MR ROBERT DAVID

3 PB Barristers
3 Paper Buildings, Temple, London EC4Y 7EU,
☎ 020 7583 8055
3 PB Barristers
23 Beaumont Street, Oxford OX1 2NP,
☎ 01865 793 736
3 PB Barristers
4 St Peter Street, Winchester SO23 8BW,
☎ 01962 868884
✉ clerks.winchester@3paper.co.uk
3 PB Barristers
Royal Talbot House, 2 Victoria Street, Bristol,
Avon BS1 6BB, ☎ 0117 928 1520
3 PB Barristers
30 Christchurch Road, Bournemouth, Dorset
BH1 3PD, ☎ 01202 292102
✉ clerks.bournemouth@3paper.co.uk
Call Date: Oct 1999, Lincoln's Inn
Pupil Supervisor
Qualifications: [LLB (Hons)(Dunelm)]
✉ robert.horner@3pb.co.uk

HORNER MR ROBIN MICHAEL

Dere Street Barristers
33 Broad Chare, Newcastle Upon Tyne
NE1 3DQ, ☎ 0844 3351551
✉ clerks@derestreet.co.uk
Call Date: July 1975, Lincoln's Inn
Pupil Supervisor
Qualifications: [LLB]

E

HORNE-ROBERTS MRS JENNIFER

Goldsmith Chambers
Ground Floor, Goldsmith Building, Temple, London EC4Y 7BL, ☎ 020 7353 6802
✉ clerks@goldsmithchambers.com
Call Date: Nov 1976, Middle Temple
Qualifications: [BA (Hons)(Lond)]

HORNETT MR STUART IAN

Selborne Chambers
10 Essex Street, London WC2R 3AA,
☎ 020 7420 9500
✉ clerks@selbornechambers.co.uk
Call Date: Oct 1992, Middle Temple
Pupil Supervisor
Qualifications: [LLB (Hons) MPhil (Leic)]
✉ stuart.hornett@selbornechambers.co.uk

HORNSBY MR WALTON FRANCIS PETRE

1 KBW Chambers
1 King's Bench Walk, Temple, London EC4Y 7DB, ☎ 020 7936 1500
✉ clerks@1kbw.co.uk
King's Bench Chambers
174 High Street, Lewes BN7 1YE,
☎ 01273 402600
Call Date: July 1980, Lincoln's Inn
Pupil Supervisor
Qualifications: [BA (Oxon)]
✉ whornsby@1kbw.co.uk

HOROWITZ DR DEBORAH MARGUERITE

Fountain Court Chambers
Fountain Court, Temple, London EC4Y 9DH,
☎ 020 7583 3335
✉ chambers@fountaincourt.co.uk
Call Date: Nov 2010, Inner Temple
Qualifications: [LLB BA (Australia) BCL MPhil Dphil (Oxon)]

HORROCKS MR PETER LESLIE

1 Garden Court Family Law Chambers
Ground Floor, One Garden Court, Temple, London EC4Y 9BJ, ☎ 020 7797 7900
✉ clerks@1gc.com
Call Date: Nov 1977, Middle Temple
Pupil Supervisor
Qualifications: [MA (Cantab)]
✉ horrocks@1gc.com

HORSELL MR ANDREW MARTIN

3 Temple Gardens
Lower Ground Floor, 3 Temple Gardens, Temple, London EC4Y 9AU, ☎ 020 7353 3102
✉ clerks@3tg.co.uk
Call Date: Oct 2009, Lincoln's Inn
Qualifications: [BBusSc (Hons) LLB (South Africa) CPE OBPP]
✉ clerks@3tg.co.uk

HORSLEY MR NICHOLAS PETER

Coram Chambers
9-11 Fulwood Place, London WC1V 6HG,
☎ 020 7092 3700
✉ mail@coramchambers.co.uk
Call Date: Oct 1998, Middle Temple
Qualifications: [BA (Hons)(Cantab) LLB (Hons)(Lond)]

HORSTEAD MR SEAN KEVAN

Garden Court Chambers
57-60 Lincoln's Inn Fields, London WC2A 3LJ,
☎ 020 7993 7600 ✉ info@gclaw.co.uk
Call Date: Oct 1996, Middle Temple
Pupil Supervisor
Qualifications: [BA (Hons)(Sussex) MA CPE]
✉ seanh@gclaw.co.uk

HORTON MISS CAROLINE ANN

Fenners Chambers
3 Madingley Road, Cambridge CB3 0EE,
☎ 01223 368761
✉ clerks@fennerschambers.com
Call Date: Oct 1993, Middle Temple
Qualifications: [LLB (Nott'm)]
✉ caroline.horton@fennerschambers.com

HORTON MR MATTHEW BETHELL QC (1989)

39 Essex Street
London WC2R 3AT, ☎ 020 7832 1111
✉ clerks@39essex.com
82 King Street
Manchester M2 4WQ, ☎ 0161 870 9969
Call Date: July 1969, Middle Temple
Qualifications: [MA LLM (Cantab)]

HORTON MR MICHAEL JOHN EDWARD

Coram Chambers
9-11 Fulwood Place, London WC1V 6HG,
☎ 020 7092 3700
✉ mail@coramchambers.co.uk
Call Date: Nov 1993, Gray's Inn
Pupil Supervisor
Qualifications: [MA (Hons) (Cantab)]
✉ michael.horton@coramchambers.co.uk

HORWELL MR RICHARD ERIC QC (2006)

3 Raymond Buildings
3 Raymond Buildings, Gray's Inn, London WC1R 5BH, ☎ 020 7400 6400
✉ clerks@3rblaw.com
Call Date: Nov 1976, Gray's Inn

HOSFORD-TANNER MR MICHAEL

Queen Elizabeth Building
3rd Floor, Queen Elizabeth Building, Temple, London EC4Y 9BS, ☎ 020 7797 7837
✉ clerks@qeb.co.uk
Call Date: Nov 1974, Inner Temple
Pupil Supervisor
Qualifications: [BA LLB]

HOSKING MISS RUTH JESSICA

Quadrant Chambers
Quadrant House, 10 Fleet Street, London EC4Y 1AU, ☎ 020 7583 4444
✉ info@quadrantchambers.com
Call Date: Nov 2002, Lincoln's Inn
Pupil Supervisor
Qualifications: [BA (Hons) (Oxon) LLM (Lond)]
✉ ruth.hosking@quadrantchambers.com

HOSKING MR STEVE

7 Bell Yard
London WC2A 2JR, ☎ 020 7831 0636
✉ kevintarrant@btconnect.com
Call Date: Nov 1988, Inner Temple
Pupil Supervisor
Qualifications: [BA (Nott'm)]

HOSKINS MR MARK GEORGE QC (2009)

Brick Court Chambers
7-8 Essex Street, London WC2R 3LD,
☎ 020 7379 3550 ✉ clerks@brickcourt.co.uk
Call Date: Nov 1991, Gray's Inn
Pupil Supervisor
Qualifications: [MA (Oxon) Lic Spec Dr Eur (Brussels) BCL (Oxon)]
✉ Mark.Hoskins@Brickcourt.co.uk

HOSKINS MR THOMAS FREDERICK

9-12 Bell Yard
London WC2A 2JR, ☎ 020 7400 1800
✉ clerks@9-12bellyard.com
Call Date: July 2007, Lincoln's Inn
Qualifications: [BA (Oxon) CPE BVC]
✉ t.hoskins@9-12bellyard.com

HOSKINS MR WILLIAM GUERIN

Temple Garden Chambers
1 Harcourt Buildings, Temple, London EC4Y 9DA, ☎ 020 7583 1315
✉ clerks@tgchambers.com
Call Date: Nov 1980, Middle Temple
Pupil Supervisor
Qualifications: [MA (Oxon)]
✉ whoskins@tgchambers.com

HOSSAIN MR AJMALUL QC (1998)

Selborne Chambers
10 Essex Street, London WC2R 3AA,
☎ 020 7420 9500
✉ clerks@selbornechambers.co.uk
St Philips Chambers
55 Temple Row, Birmingham B2 5LS,
☎ 0121 246 7000 ✉ clerks@st-philips.com
Call Date: Nov 1976, Lincoln's Inn
Qualifications: [LLB (Hons)LLM (Lond) FCIArb]
✉ ajmalul.hossain@selbornechambers.co.uk

HOSSAIN MR MOHAMMAD MOZAMMEL

187 Fleet Street
London EC4A 2AT, ☎ 020 7430 7430
✉ chambers@187fleetstreet.com
Call Date: July 2001, Inner Temple
Qualifications: [LLB (L'Pool)]

HOSSAIN MR MOHAMMED MONWAR

No. 3 Fleet Street Chambers
3 Fleet Street, London EC4Y 1DP,
☎ 020 7936 4474 ✉ clerks@3fleetstreet.com
Call Date: July 1998, Lincoln's Inn
Qualifications: [LLB (Hons)(Lond) MCom]

HOSSAIN MR SYED AHMED IZHARUL

23 Essex Street
London WC2R 3AA, ☎ 020 7413 0353
✉ clerks@23es.com
Call Date: Nov 1996, Gray's Inn
Qualifications: [LLB (Newc)]
✉ ahmedhossain@23es.com

HOSSAIN MR SYED AHRARUL

Temple Court Chambers
2nd Floor, 2 Dr Johnson's Building, Temple, London EC4Y 7AY, ☎ 020 7353 7888
✉ clerks@templecourt.co.uk
Call Date: Oct 2005, Lincoln's Inn
Qualifications: [LLB (Hons) (Kingston)]
✉ syed.hossain@templecourt.co.uk

E

HOSSAIN MR SYED MOHAMMAD SA'AD ANSARUL

One Essex Court
Ground Floor, One Essex Court, Temple, London EC4Y 9AR, ☎ 020 7583 2000
✉ clerks@oeclaw.co.uk
Call Date: Nov 1995, Gray's Inn
Pupil Supervisor
Qualifications: [BA]
✉ shossain@oeclaw.co.uk

HOTTEN MR CHRISTOPHER PETER QC (1994)

No5 Chambers
Fountain Court, Steelhouse Lane, Birmingham B4 6DR, ☎ 0845 210 5555 ✉ info@no5.com
No5 Chambers
38 Queen Square, Bristol BS1 4QS, ☎ 0845 210 5555
Seven Bedford Row
7 Bedford Row, London WC1R 4BS, ☎ 020 7242 3555 ✉ clerks@7br.co.uk
No5 Chambers
Greenwood House, 4-7 Salisbury Court, London EC4Y 8AA, ☎ 0845 210 5555
Call Date: Nov 1972, Inner Temple
Recorder
Qualifications: [LLB (Leics)]
✉ ch@no5.com

E

HOUGH MR CHRISTOPHER SIMON

Doughty Street Chambers
53-54 Doughty Street, London WC1N 2LS, ☎ 020 7404 1313
✉ enquiries@doughtystreet.co.uk
Doughty Street Chambers
Pall Mall Court, 61-67 King Street, Manchester M2 4PD, ☎ 0161 618 1066
Doughty Street Chambers
5th Floor, Broad Quay House, Prince Street, Bristol BS1 4DJ, ☎ 01179 058 717
Call Date: July 1981, Middle Temple
Pupil Supervisor
Qualifications: [LLB (Hons)]
✉ c.hough@doughtystreet.co.uk

HOUGH MISS JACQUELINE ANN

4 Breams Buildings
Chancery Lane, London EC4A 1HP, ☎ 020 7092 1900 ✉ clerks@4bb.co.uk
Call Date: Nov 2001, Lincoln's Inn
Qualifications: [LLB (Hons) (Leic)]

HOUGH MR JONATHAN ANTHONY

Four New Square
Four New Square, Lincoln's Inn, London WC2A 3RJ, ☎ 020 7822 2000
✉ barristers@4newsquare.com
Call Date: Oct 1997, Middle Temple
Pupil Supervisor
Qualifications: [MA (Hons)(Oxon) CPE (Lond)]
✉ j.hough@4newsquare.com

HOUGHTON MISS LISA JAYNE

Call Date: Oct 1994, Gray's Inn
Qualifications: [BA (Lancs)]
✉ clerk@stjohnsbuildings.co.uk

HOUGHTON MR PETER

Crown Office Chambers
2 Crown Office Row, Temple, London EC4Y 7HJ, ☎ 020 7797 8100
✉ mail@crownofficechambers.com
Call Date: Oct 2005, Lincoln's Inn
Qualifications: [BA (Hons) (Cantab) PgDl (Lond) MPhil (Cantab)]
✉ houghton@crownofficechambers.com

HOUSE MR JAMES MICHAEL

Seven Bedford Row
7 Bedford Row, London WC1R 4BS, ☎ 020 7242 3555 ✉ clerks@7br.co.uk
Call Date: Oct 1995, Inner Temple
Qualifications: [BA (Lanc) CPE]

HOUSE MR MICHAEL JOHN

Garden Court Chambers
57-60 Lincoln's Inn Fields, London WC2A 3LJ, ☎ 020 7993 7600 ✉ info@gclaw.co.uk
Call Date: July 1972, Inner Temple
Qualifications: [MA (Oxon)]
✉ michaelh@gclaw.co.uk

HOUSEMAN MR STEPHEN TERENCE

Essex Court Chambers
24 Lincoln's Inn Fields, London WC2A 3EG, ☎ 020 7813 8000
✉ clerksroom@essexcourt.net
Call Date: Nov 1995, Inner Temple
Qualifications: [BA BCL (Oxon)]
✉ shouseman@essexcourt.net

HOUSHYARI-DARIAN MISS ALICE

Queen Square Chambers
56 Queen Square, Bristol BS1 4PR, ☎ 0117 921 1966 ✉ crime@qs-c.co.uk
Call Date: Nov 2006, Middle Temple
Qualifications: [LLB (Hons) (Cardiff)]
✉ asd@qs-c.co.uk

HOUSTON MR ANDREW

Pump Court Chambers
31 Southgate Street, Winchester, Hampshire SO23 9EB, ☎01962 868 161
✉clerks@3pumpcourt.com
Pump Court Chambers
Upper Ground Floor, 3 Pump Court, Temple, London EC4Y 7AJ, ☎020 7353 0711
✉clerks@3pumpcourt.com
Pump Court Chambers
5 Temple Chambers, Temple Street, Swindon SN1 1SQ, ☎01793 539899
✉clerks@3pumpcourt.com
Call Date: July 1989, Inner Temple
Qualifications: [LLB (So'ton)]

HOWARD MISS AMANDA JAYNE

Atlantic Chambers
4-6 Cook Street, Liverpool L2 9QU, ☎0151 236 4421
✉info@atlanticchambers.co.uk
37 Park Square Chambers
37 Park Square, Leeds LS1 2NY, ☎0113 243 9422 ✉chambers@no37.co.uk
Call Date: Nov 1994, Inner Temple
Qualifications: [LLB (Hons)]
✉amandahoward@atlanticchambers.co.uk

HOWARD MISS ANNELI CLAIRE

Monckton Chambers
1 & 2 Raymond Buildings, Gray's Inn, London WC1R 5NR, ☎020 7405 7211
✉chambers@monckton.com
Call Date: July 2002, Gray's Inn
Qualifications: [BA (Oxon) BCL (Oxon)]
✉ahoward@monckton.com

HOWARD MR ANTHONY JOHN

9 St John Street
Manchester M3 4DN, ☎0161 955 9000
✉civilclerks@9sjs.com / criminalclerks@9sjs.com
Call Date: Oct 1992, Inner Temple
Qualifications: [LLB (Lancs)]
✉Anthony.howard@9sjs.com

HOWARD MR CHARLES ANTHONY FREDERICK QC (1999)

1 KBW Chambers
1 King's Bench Walk, Temple, London EC4Y 7DB, ☎020 7936 1500
✉clerks@1kbw.co.uk
King's Bench Chambers
174 High Street, Lewes BN7 1YE, ☎01273 402600
Call Date: July 1975, Inner Temple
Qualifications: [MA (Cantab)]
✉chowardqc@1kbw.co.uk

HOWARD MR GRAHAM JOHN

Devon Chambers
3 St Andrew Street, Plymouth PL1 2AH, ☎01752 661659
✉clerks@devonchambers.co.uk
King's Lynn Chambers
26 The Birches, South Wootton, King's Lynn, Norfolk PE30 3JG, ☎01553 672 085
✉timothy.leader@tesco.net
Call Date: Nov 1987, Lincoln's Inn
Qualifications: [LLB (Hons)]

HOWARD MR IAN

Broadway House Chambers
25 Park Square West, Leeds, West Yorkshire LS1 2PW, ☎0113 246 2600
✉clerks@broadwayhouse.co.uk
Broadway House Chambers
Broadway House, 9 Bank Street, Bradford, West Yorkshire BD1 1TW, ☎01274 722560
✉clerks@broadwayhouse.co.uk
Call Date: Nov 1987, Lincoln's Inn
Qualifications: [LLB(Hons) (Newc)]
✉ih@broadwayhouse.co.uk

HOWARD MR JOSEPH HENRY

Atlas Chambers
3 Field Court, Gray's Inn, London WC1R 5EP, ☎020 7269 7980
✉clerks@atlaschambers.com
Call Date: July 2006, Gray's Inn
Qualifications: [BA (Cantab) LLM (Lond)]
✉howard@atlaschambers.com

HOWARD MISS LOUISE

1 Paper Buildings
1st Floor, 1 Paper Buildings, Temple, London EC4Y 7EP, ☎020 7353 3728
✉clerks@onepaper.co.uk
Call Date: July 2004, Middle Temple
Qualifications: [LLB (Hons)]

HOWARD MR MARK STEVEN QC (1996)

Brick Court Chambers
7-8 Essex Street, London WC2R 3LD, ☎020 7379 3550 ✉clerks@brickcourt.co.uk
Call Date: July 1980, Gray's Inn
Qualifications: [LLB LLM (Lond)]
✉Mark.Howard@Brickcourt.co.uk

E

HOWARD MR MICHAEL NEWMAN QC (1986)

Quadrant Chambers
Quadrant House, 10 Fleet Street, London EC4Y 1AU, ☎ 020 7583 4444
✉ info@quadrantchambers.com
Call Date: May 1971, Gray's Inn
Recorder
Qualifications: [MA BCL]

HOWARD MISS NICOLA

25 Bedford Row
London WC1R 4HD, ☎ 020 7067 1500
✉ clerks@25bedfordrow.com
Call Date: Oct 1995, Middle Temple
Pupil Supervisor
Qualifications: [B.Sc (Hons)]
✉ nhoward@25bedfordrow.com

HOWARD MR ROBIN WILLIAM JOHN

Fenners Chambers
3 Madingley Road, Cambridge CB3 0EE, ☎ 01223 368761
✉ clerks@fennerschambers.com
Call Date: Feb 1986, Middle Temple
Pupil Supervisor
Qualifications: [MA (Oxon)]
✉ robin.howard@fennerschambers.com

E

HOWARD MR STEVEN JAMES

3 PB Barristers
30 Christchurch Road, Bournemouth, Dorset BH1 3PD, ☎ 01202 292102
✉ clerks.bournemouth@3paper.co.uk
3 PB Barristers
3 Paper Buildings, Temple, London EC4Y 7EU, ☎ 020 7583 8055
Call Date: Nov 2009, Inner Temple
Qualifications: [BSc (Dunelm) CPE]

HOWARTH MR ANDREW

36 Bedford Row
London WC1R 4JH, ☎ 020 7421 8000
✉ chambers@36bedfordrow.co.uk
Call Date: Nov 1988, Lincoln's Inn
Qualifications: [BA (Oxon)]
✉ clerks@36bedfordrow.co.uk

HOWARTH MISS KATHRYN ANNE

36 Bedford Row
London WC1R 4JH, ☎ 020 7421 8000
✉ chambers@36bedfordrow.co.uk
Call Date: Nov 2005, Lincoln's Inn
Qualifications: [BA (Hons) (Cantab) LLM (Toronto) MA (Cantab)]
✉ khowarth@36bedfordrow.co.uk

HOWARTH MR SIMON STUART

Hailsham Chambers
Ground Floor, 4 Paper Buildings, Temple, London EC4Y 7EX, ☎ 020 7643 5000
✉ clerks@hailshamchambers.com
Call Date: Oct 1991, Gray's Inn
Qualifications: [BA (Oxon)]
✉ howarth@crownofficechambers.com

HOWAT MR ROBIN DAVID CHALMERS

1 Gray's Inn Square
Ground Floor, 1 Gray's Inn Square, London WC1R 5AA, ☎ 020 7405 0001
Call Date: Nov 1986, Inner Temple
Pupil Supervisor
Qualifications: [BA(Dunelm)]

HOWD MR STEPHEN EDMUND JEFFERSON

Zenith Chambers
10 Park Square, Leeds LS1 2LH, ☎ 0113 245 5438
✉ clerks@zenithchambers.co.uk
Call Date: July 1989, Middle Temple
Qualifications: [BA (Oxon) Dip Law]
✉ showd@zenithchambers.co.uk

HOWE MR ANDREW PETER

Oriel Chambers
14 Water Street, Liverpool, Merseyside L2 8TD, ☎ 0151 236 7191
✉ clerks@orielchambers.co.uk
Oriel Chambers
18 Ribblesdale Place, Preston PR1 3NA, ☎ 01772 254 764
✉ clerks@oriel-chambers.co.uk
Call Date: Nov 2002, Lincoln's Inn
Qualifications: [LLB(Hons)(Lanc)]
✉ andrew.howe@orielchambers.co.uk

HOWE MR DARREN FRANCIS

1 Garden Court Family Law Chambers
Ground Floor, One Garden Court, Temple, London EC4Y 9BJ, ☎ 020 7797 7900
✉ clerks@1gc.com
Call Date: Oct 1992, Gray's Inn
Pupil Supervisor
Qualifications: [LLB (Hull)]
✉ howe@1gc.com

HOWE MR GAVIN PAUL

Crown Office Row Chambers
119 Church Street, Brighton, Sussex BN1 1UD, ☎ 01273 625625
✉ clerks@1cor.com
Call Date: Nov 2003, Gray's Inn
Qualifications: [BA]
✉ gavin.howe@1cor.com

HOWE MR MARTIN RUSSELL THOMSON QC (1996)

8 New Square
8 New Square, Lincoln's Inn, London WC2A 3QP, ☎ 020 7405 4321
✉ clerks@8newsquare.co.uk
Call Date: July 1978, Middle Temple
Qualifications: [BA (Cantab)]
martin.howe@8newsquare.co.uk

Types of work: Breach of confidence, Competition law, Computer litigation, Copyright, Copyright theft, Copyright Tribunal, Data protection, Design, E-commerce, EC competition law, Entertainment, Franchising, Information technology, Intellectual property, Media, Media and entertainment, Passing off, Patents, Pharmaceuticals, Scientific and technical disputes, Telecommunications, Trade Descriptions Act, Trade secrets, Trademarks

HOWE MISS PENELOPE ANNE MACGREGOR

Pump Court Chambers
Upper Ground Floor, 3 Pump Court, Temple, London EC4Y 7AJ, ☎ 020 7353 0711
✉ clerks@3pumpcourt.com
Pump Court Chambers
5 Temple Chambers, Temple Street, Swindon SN1 1SQ, ☎ 01793 539899
✉ clerks@3pumpcourt.com
Pump Court Chambers
31 Southgate Street, Winchester, Hampshire SO23 9EB, ☎ 01962 868 161
✉ clerks@3pumpcourt.com
Call Date: Nov 1991, Inner Temple
Qualifications: [BA (Cambs)]
tonya@3pumpcourt.com

HOWE MR ROBERT PAUL THOMPSON QC (2008)

Blackstone Chambers
Blackstone House, Temple, London EC4Y 9BW, ☎ 020 7583 1770
✉ clerks@blackstonechambers.com
Call Date: Nov 1988, Middle Temple
Qualifications: [MA (Cantab) BCL (Oxon)]
roberthowe@blackstonechambers.com

HOWE MISS RUTH ALYSON

Atlantic Chambers
4-6 Cook Street, Liverpool L2 9QU, ☎ 0151 236 4421
✉ info@atlanticchambers.co.uk
Call Date: July 1983, Lincoln's Inn
Pupil Supervisor
Qualifications: [BA (Hons)]
ruthhowe@atlanticchambers.co.uk

HOWE MISS SARA-LISE ANGELIQUE

Westgate Chambers
64 High Street, Lewes, East Sussex BN7 1XG, ☎ 01273 480510
✉ clerks@westgate-chambers.co.uk
Call Date: Oct 1993, Lincoln's Inn
Qualifications: [BA (Hons)(Leics)]
SLH@westgate-chambers.co.uk

HOWE MR TIMOTHY JEAN-PAUL QC (2008)

Fountain Court Chambers
Fountain Court, Temple, London EC4Y 9DH, ☎ 020 7583 3335
✉ chambers@fountaincourt.co.uk
Call Date: Nov 1987, Middle Temple
Qualifications: [MA (Oxon)]
th@fountaincourt.co.uk

HOWELL MS CLAIRE ELIZABETH SIOBHAN

36 Bedford Row
London WC1R 4JH, ☎ 020 7421 8000
✉ chambers@36bedfordrow.co.uk
Call Date: Nov 2003, Inner Temple
Qualifications: [BA (Oxon)]
chowell@36bedfordrow.co.uk

HOWELL MISS CLAIRE LOUISE

New Street Chambers
2 New Street, Leicester LE1 5NA, ☎ 0116 262 5906 ✉ clerks@2newstreet.co.uk
Call Date: Oct 2006, Lincoln's Inn
Qualifications: [LLB]

HOWELL MR JACQUES KEVIN

1 Mitre Court Buildings
1 Mitre Court Buildings, Temple, London EC4Y 7BS, ☎ 020 7452 8900
✉ clerks@1mcb.com
Call Date: Oct 2000, Lincoln's Inn
Qualifications: [LLB (Hons) (Essex) LLM]
jacques.howell@1mcb.com

HOWELL MR JOHN QC (1993)

Blackstone Chambers
Blackstone House, Temple, London EC4Y 9BW, ☎ 020 7583 1770
✉ clerks@blackstonechambers.com
Call Date: Feb 1979, Middle Temple
Recorder
Qualifications: [BA (Oxon)]
johnhowell@blackstonechambers.com

E

HOWELL WILLIAMS MR CRAIG QC (2009)

Francis Taylor Building
Inner Temple, London EC4Y 7BY,
☎020 7353 8415 ✉clerks@ftb.eu.com
Call Date: July 1983, Gray's Inn
Qualifications: [BA (Leeds) Dip Law]
✉chw@ftb.eu.com
URL: www.ftb.ev.com

Types of work: Environment, Planning

HOWELL-JONES MR NICHOLAS

St Philips Chambers
55 Temple Row, Birmingham B2 5LS,
☎0121 246 7000 ✉clerks@st-philips.com
Call Date: July 2000, Gray's Inn
Qualifications: [LLB (Staffs)]

HOWELLS MISS CATHERINE JANE

Exchange Chambers
One Derby Square, Derby Square, Liverpool L2 9XX, ☎0151 236 7747
✉info@exchangechambers.co.uk
Exchange Chambers
7 Ralli Courts, West Riverside, Manchester M3 5FT, ☎0161 833 2722
Exchange Chambers
Oxford House, Oxford Row, Leeds LS1 3BE,
☎0113 203 1970
✉spencer@exchangechambers.co.uk
Call Date: July 1989, Gray's Inn
Pupil Supervisor
Qualifications: [LLB (L'pool)]

HOWELLS MR CHRISTIAN JAMES

30 Park Place
Cardiff CF10 3BS, ☎029 2039 8421
✉clerks@30parkplace.law.co.uk
Call Date: July 2007, Inner Temple
Qualifications: [LLB (Bris)]
✉cjh@30parkplace.co.uk

HOWELLS MR CHRISTOPHER

Civitas Chambers
Global Reach, Celtic Gateway, Cardiff Bay, Cardiff CF11 0SN, ☎0845 0713 007
✉clerks@civitaslaw.com
Call Date: Nov 1999, Lincoln's Inn
Qualifications: [LLB (Hons)(Lond) MPhil BA (Cantab)]
✉christopher.howells@civitaslaw.com

HOWELLS MR GERAINT GORDON

Gough Square Chambers
6-7 Gough Square, London EC4A 3DE,
☎020 7353 0924 ✉gsc@goughsq.co.uk
Call Date: Nov 2002, Inner Temple
Qualifications: [LLB (Brunel)]
✉gsc@goughsq.co.uk

HOWELLS MR JAMES RICHARD

Atkin Chambers
1 Atkin Building, Gray's Inn, London WC1R 5AT, ☎020 7404 0102
✉clerks@atkinchambers.com
Call Date: Nov 1995, Middle Temple
Pupil Supervisor
Qualifications: [BA (Hons) BCL MA]
✉clerks@atkinchambers.com

HOWELLS MR JORDAN RHYS

Bretton Woods Law
New Broad Street House, 35 New Broad Street, London EC2M 1NH
Dyers Chambers
35 Bedford Row, London WC1R 4JH,
☎020 7404 1881
✉admin@dyerschambers.com
Call Date: Mar 2008, Lincoln's Inn
Qualifications: [BA (LSE)]

HOWELLS MISS KATHERINE JANE

Old Square Chambers
10-11 Bedford Row, London WC1R 4BU,
☎020 7269 0300 ✉clerks@oldsquare.co.uk
Old Square Chambers
3 Orchard Court, St Augustine's Yard, Bristol BS1 5DP, ☎0117 930 5100
✉clerks@oldsquare.co.uk
Call Date: Oct 1994, Gray's Inn
Qualifications: [BA (Oxon)]
✉khowells@oldsquare.co.uk

Fax: 020 7405 1387;
DX: 1046 London, Chancery Lane;
URL: www.oldsquare.co.uk

Types of work: Aviation, Clinical negligence, Common law (general), Health and safety, Highways, Holiday injury and damages, Holiday law, Industrial deafness, Industrial diseases, Local authority claims, Local authority liability, Medical negligence, Occupational diseases, Overseas accidents, Personal injury, Travel law

HOWELLS MRS MARION DYMPNA ANN

St Ive's Chambers
Whittall Street, Birmingham B4 6DH, ☎0121 236 0863
✉clerks@stiveschambers.co.uk
Call Date: July 2009, Lincoln's Inn
Qualifications: [BA (Coventry)]
dympna.howells@stiveschambers.co.uk

HOWELLS MR STEPHEN JOHN

Stone Chambers
4 Field Court, Gray's Inn, London WC1R 5EF, ☎020 7440 6900
✉clerks@stonechambers.com
Call Date: July 2006, Middle Temple
Qualifications: [LLB (Melbourne) BA (Melbourne)]
stephen.howells@stonechambers.com

HOWES MISS PAMELA ANN

Holborn Chambers
6 Gate Street, Lincoln's Inn Fields, London WC2A 3HP, ☎020 7242 6060
Call Date: Mar 1999, Lincoln's Inn
Qualifications: [LLB (Hons)(Sussex)]
pamelahowes@holbornchambers.co.uk

HOWES MISS SALLY MARGARET QC (2003)

Atkinson Bevan Chambers
1st Floor, 2 Harcourt Buildings, Temple, London EC4Y 9DB, ☎020 7353 2112
✉clerks@2hb.co.uk
Call Date: Nov 1983, Middle Temple
Qualifications: [BA (Hons)(Newc) Dip Law]
smhowes@2hb.co.uk

HOWEY MS ALISON

Call Date: July 1999, Inner Temple
Pupil Supervisor
Qualifications: [LLB (Hons)(Northumb)]
Alisonhowey@aol.com

HOWIE MR KEIR SIMON

7 King's Bench Walk
Ground Floor, 7 King's Bench Walk, Temple, London EC4Y 7DS, ☎020 7910 8300
✉clerks@7kbw.co.uk
Call Date: July 2010, Middle Temple
Qualifications: [BA (Hons) (Leeds) MA BA (Hons) (Oxon)]
khowie@7kbw.co.uk

HOWKER MR DAVID THOMAS QC (2002)

No5 Chambers
Fountain Court, Steelhouse Lane, Birmingham B4 6DR, ☎0845 210 5555 ✉info@no5.com
No5 Chambers
Greenwood House, 4-7 Salisbury Court, London EC4Y 8AA, ☎0845 210 5555
No5 Chambers
38 Queen Square, Bristol BS1 4QS, ☎0845 210 5555
Call Date: July 1982, Inner Temple
Qualifications: [LLB (B'ham)]

HOWLETT MR JAMES ANTHONY

KCH Garden Square
1 Oxford Street, Nottingham NG1 5BH, ☎0115 941 8851
✉clerks@kchgardensquare.co.uk
Call Date: July 1980, Middle Temple
Pupil Supervisor, Recorder
Qualifications: [LLB (Bris) FCIArb]
jhowlett@kch.co.uk

HOWLING MR REX ANDREW QC (2011)

4 Paper Buildings
1st Floor, 4 Paper Buildings, Temple, London EC4Y 7EX, ☎020 7427 5200
✉clerks@4pb.com
Call Date: Oct 1991, Middle Temple
Pupil Supervisor
Qualifications: [BSc (Hons) (Sussex) Dip Law]
rh@4pb.com

HOYAL MS JANE

1 Pump Court
Elm Court, Temple, London EC4Y 7AB, ☎020 7842 7070
✉(name)@pumpcourt.co.uk
Call Date: Nov 1976, Middle Temple
Pupil Supervisor
Qualifications: [LLB MA]

HUBBARD MR DANIEL ZACHARY

One Essex Court
Ground Floor, One Essex Court, Temple, London EC4Y 9AR, ☎020 7583 2000
✉clerks@oeclaw.co.uk
Call Date: July 2003, Lincoln's Inn
Qualifications: [LLB Hons (Lond) BCL (Oxon)]
dhubbard@oeclaw.co.uk

E

HUBBARD MR MARK IAIN

New Square Chambers
12 New Square, Lincoln's Inn, London WC2A 3SW, ☎ 020 7419 8000
✉ robin.hollington@newsquarechambers.co.uk
Call Date: Nov 1991, Middle Temple
Pupil Supervisor
Qualifications: [BA (Hons) (Oxon) Dip Law (Lond)]
✉ mark.hubbard@newsquarechambers.co.uk

HUBBARD MR MICHAEL JOSEPH QC (1985)

1 Paper Buildings
1st Floor, 1 Paper Buildings, Temple, London EC4Y 7EP, ☎ 020 7353 3728
✉ clerks@onepaper.co.uk
Call Date: May 1972, Gray's Inn
Recorder
✉ michaelhubbard@onepaper.co.uk

HUBBLE MR BENEDICT JOHN WAKELIN QC (2009)

Four New Square
Four New Square, Lincoln's Inn, London WC2A 3RJ, ☎ 020 7822 2000
✉ barristers@4newsquare.com
Call Date: Nov 1992, Middle Temple
Qualifications: [BA (Hons) Dip Law]
✉ b.hubble@4newsquare.com

HUCKLE MR THEODORE DAVID QC (2011)

Civitas Chambers
Global Reach, Celtic Gateway, Cardiff Bay, Cardiff CF11 0SN, ☎ 0845 0713 007
✉ clerks@civitaslaw.com
Call Date: July 1985, Lincoln's Inn
Pupil Supervisor
Qualifications: [BA (Cantab) LLM (Cantab)]
✉ theodore.huckle@civitaslaw.com

HUCKLESBY MR ANTHONY JOHN

Five Paper Buildings
1st Floor, Five Paper Buildings, Temple, London EC4Y 7HB, ☎ 020 7583 6117
✉ clerks@5pb.co.uk
Call Date: Nov 2008, Lincoln's Inn
Qualifications: [BA (Oxon) CPE COL]

HUDA MISS ABIDA ALIA JEHAN

1 Pump Court
Elm Court, Temple, London EC4Y 7AB, ☎ 020 7842 7070
✉ (name)@pumpcourt.co.uk
Call Date: Nov 1989, Middle Temple
Qualifications: [LLB (Hons)]

HUDD MISS ANNE MARGUERITA JANE

29 Bedford Row Chambers
London WC1R 4HE, ☎ 020 7404 1044
✉ clerks@29br.co.uk
Call Date: Oct 2000, Gray's Inn
Qualifications: [MA (Cantab)]
✉ ahudd@29br.co.uk

HUDSON MISS ABIGAIL RACHEL

Call Date: Oct 2003, Gray's Inn
Qualifications: [MA (Aberdeen)]
✉ clerk@stjohnsbuildings.co.uk, abigail.hudson@stjohnsbuildings.co.uk

HUDSON MR ANTHONY SEAN

Doughty Street Chambers
53-54 Doughty Street, London WC1N 2LS, ☎ 020 7404 1313
✉ enquiries@doughtystreet.co.uk
Doughty Street Chambers
Pall Mall Court, 61-67 King Street, Manchester M2 4PD, ☎ 0161 618 1066
Doughty Street Chambers
5th Floor, Broad Quay House, Prince Street, Bristol BS1 4DJ, ☎ 01179 058 717
Call Date: Nov 1996, Middle Temple
Pupil Supervisor
Qualifications: [LLB (Hons)(Exon)]
✉ a.hudson@doughtystreet.co.uk

HUDSON MISS CHLOE JENNIFER

Park Court Chambers
16 Park Place, Leeds LS1 2SJ, ☎ 0113 243 3277
✉ clerks@parkcourtchambers.co.uk
Call Date: July 2003, Lincoln's Inn
Qualifications: [BA Hons (Oxon)]
✉ chudson@parkcourtchambers.co.uk

HUDSON MR CHRISTOPHER JOHN

Deans Court Chambers
24 St John Street, Manchester M3 4DF, ☎ 0161 214 6000 ✉ clerks@deanscourt.co.uk
Deans Court Chambers
101 Walker Street, Preston PR1 2RR, ☎ 01772 565 600
✉ preston@deanscourt.co.uk
Call Date: May 1987, Lincoln's Inn
Pupil Supervisor, Recorder
Qualifications: [MA (Oxon)]
✉ hudson@deanscourt.co.uk

HUDSON MISS ELISABETH HELEN

3 PB Barristers
3 Paper Buildings, Temple, London EC4Y 7EU, ☎020 7583 8055
3 PB Barristers
Royal Talbot House, 2 Victoria Street, Bristol, Avon BS1 6BB, ☎0117 928 1520
3 PB Barristers
23 Beaumont Street, Oxford OX1 2NP, ☎01865 793 736
3 PB Barristers
4 St Peter Street, Winchester SO23 8BW, ☎01962 868884
✉clerks.winchester@3paper.co.uk
3 PB Barristers
30 Christchurch Road, Bournemouth, Dorset BH1 3PD, ☎01202 292102
✉clerks.bournemouth@3paper.co.uk
Call Date: Nov 1987, Gray's Inn
Pupil Supervisor
Qualifications: [LLB (Bucks)]
✉elisabeth.hudson@3paper.co.uk

HUDSON MS EMMA CAROLYN VAUGHAN

1 Garden Court Family Law Chambers
Ground Floor, One Garden Court, Temple, London EC4Y 9BJ, ☎020 7797 7900
✉clerks@1gc.com
Call Date: Feb 1995, Inner Temple
Qualifications: [MA (Edin) CPE (Lond)]
✉hudson@1gc.com

HUDSON MR JOHN EDWARD GERARD

Zenith Chambers
10 Park Square, Leeds LS1 2LH, ☎0113 245 5438
✉clerks@zenithchambers.co.uk
Call Date: Nov 2006, Middle Temple
Qualifications: [LLB (Hudds)]

HUDSON MISS KATHRYN JANE

Coram Chambers
9-11 Fulwood Place, London WC1V 6HG, ☎020 7092 3700
✉mail@coramchambers.co.uk
Call Date: July 1981, Middle Temple
Pupil Supervisor
Qualifications: [LLB (Bris)]
✉kate.hudson@coramchambers.co.uk

HUFFER MR THOMAS IAN

18 St John Street
Manchester M3 4EA, ☎0161 278 1800
✉clerks@18sjs.com
Call Date: Nov 1979, Gray's Inn
Qualifications: [MA (Oxon)]

HUGGINS MRS BIANCA

Bank House Chambers
Old Bank House, Hartshead, Sheffield S1 2EL, ☎0114 275 1223
✉w.digby@bankhousechambers.co.uk
Call Date: July 2004, Gray's Inn
Qualifications: [LLB]

HUGGINS MR TOBY JAMES

Unity Street Chambers
5 Unity Street, College Green, Bristol BS1 5HH, ☎0117 906 9789
✉chambers@unitystreetchambers.com
Call Date: Nov 1998, Middle Temple
Qualifications: [BSc (Hons)(Bris)]
✉toby.huggins@unitystreetchambers.com

HUGHES MR ADRIAN WARWICK QC (2006)

39 Essex Street
London WC2R 3AT, ☎020 7832 1111
✉clerks@39essex.com
82 King Street
Manchester M2 4WQ, ☎0161 870 9969
Call Date: July 1984, Middle Temple
Qualifications: [MA (Oxon)]
✉adrian.hughes@39essex.com

HUGHES MISS ANNA

2 Temple Gardens
2 Temple Gardens, Temple, London EC4Y 9AY, ☎020 7822 1200
✉clerks@2tg.co.uk
Call Date: July 2008, Middle Temple
Qualifications: [BA (Hons) (Cantab)]
✉ahughes@2tg.co.uk

HUGHES MISS ANNA CARINA

Angel Chambers
Ethos Building, Kings Road, Swansea SA1 8AS, ☎01792 464623
✉clerks@angelchambers.co.uk
Call Date: Oct 2003, Middle Temple
Qualifications: [LLB (Hons) (Brunel) LLM (Wales)]
✉carinahughes@angelchambers.co.uk

HUGHES MISS ANNA GABRIEL

Wilberforce Chambers
8 New Square, Lincoln's Inn, London WC2A 3QP, ☎020 7306 0102
✉chambers@wilberforce.co.uk
Call Date: Apr 1978, Lincoln's Inn
Qualifications: [BA (Cantab)]
✉ghughes@wilberforce.co.uk

E

HUGHES MS ANNA LISA

4 Breams Buildings
Chancery Lane, London EC4A 1HP,
☎ 020 7092 1900 ✉ clerks@4bb.co.uk
Call Date: July 2007, Gray's Inn
Qualifications: [BA (Warw)]

HUGHES DR CONSTANCE MARY

1 Pump Court
Elm Court, Temple, London EC4Y 7AB,
☎ 020 7842 7070
✉ (name)@pumpcourt.co.uk
Call Date: Oct 1994, Inner Temple
Pupil Supervisor
Qualifications: [BA (Hull) MPhil (Notts) PhD CPE (Middx)]
✉ mhu@1pumpcourt.co.uk

HUGHES MR DAVID GORDON

30 Park Place
Cardiff CF10 3BS, ☎ 029 2039 8421
✉ clerks@30parkplace.law.co.uk
Farrar's Building
Farrar's Building, Temple, London EC4Y 7BD,
☎ 020 7583 9241
✉ Chambers@farrarsbuilding.co.uk
Call Date: Oct 1997, Middle Temple
Qualifications: [BA (Hons)(Wolves) CPE (Glamorgan)]
✉ dgh@30parkplace.co.uk

HUGHES MR DAVID LLOYD

Nine Bedford Row
9 Bedford Row, London WC1R 4AZ,
☎ 020 7489 2727
✉ clerks@9bedfordrow.co.uk
Call Date: July 1980, Inner Temple
Pupil Supervisor
Qualifications: [LLB (Hons)(Hull)]
✉ david.hughes@9bedfordrow.co.uk

HUGHES MR DERMOT FRANCIS

Call Date: Nov 1993, Gray's Inn
Pupil Supervisor
Qualifications: [LLB LLM]
✉ hughes@paradise-sq.co.uk

HUGHES MR DOMINIC WYNDHAM

Three New Square IP
3 New Square, Lincoln's Inn, London WC2A 3RS, ☎ 020 7405 1111
✉ clerks@3newsquare.co.uk
Call Date: July 2001, Gray's Inn
Qualifications: [BSc (Lond) DPhil (Oxon)]
✉ hughes@3newsquare.co.uk

HUGHES MR GARETH DUNCAN

2 Pump Court
1st Floor, 2 Pump Court, Temple, London EC4Y 7AH, ☎ 020 7353 5597
✉ clerks@2pumpcourt.co.uk
Call Date: Dec 1985, Gray's Inn
Pupil Supervisor
Qualifications: [LLB (Lond)]
✉ ghughes@2pumpcourt.co.uk

HUGHES MISS HANNAH DAISY

Coram Chambers
9-11 Fulwood Place, London WC1V 6HG,
☎ 020 7092 3700
✉ mail@coramchambers.co.uk
Call Date: Oct 1999, Middle Temple
Qualifications: [BA (Hons)(Oxon)]
✉ daisy.hughes@coramchambers.co.uk

HUGHES MR HENRY WINSTONE

187 Fleet Street
London EC4A 2AT, ☎ 020 7430 7430
✉ chambers@187fleetstreet.com
Call Date: Oct 2003, Inner Temple
Qualifications: [MA (Edin)]
✉ henryhughes@187fleetstreet.com

HUGHES MR HYWEL TUDOR

30 Park Place
Cardiff CF10 3BS, ☎ 029 2039 8421
✉ clerks@30parkplace.law.co.uk
Call Date: Oct 1995, Gray's Inn
Qualifications: [LLB (Wales)]
✉ hth@30parkplace.co.uk

HUGHES MR IGNATIUS LOYOLA QC (2009)

Albion Chambers
Broad Street, Bristol BS1 1DR,
☎ 0117 927 2144
✉ clerks@albionchambers.co.uk
Nine Bedford Row
9 Bedford Row, London WC1R 4AZ,
☎ 020 7489 2727
✉ clerks@9bedfordrow.co.uk
Call Date: Apr 1986, Middle Temple
Recorder
Qualifications: [LLB (Newc)]
✉ ignatius.hughesqc@albionchambers.co.uk

HUGHES MR JASON PHILLIP

College Chambers
19 Carlton Crescent, Southampton, Hampshire SO15 2ET, ☎ 023 8023 0338
✉ clerks@college-chambers.co.uk
Call Date: July 2009, Inner Temple
Qualifications: [MSc LLB]
✉ jhughes@college-chambers.co.uk

HUGHES MRS JESSICA KATHARINE

XXIV Old Buildings
Ground Floor, 24 Old Buildings, Lincoln's Inn, London WC2A 3UP, ☎ 020 7691 2424
✉ clerks@xxiv.co.uk
Call Date: Nov 1997, Lincoln's Inn
Pupil Supervisor
Qualifications: [BA (Hons)]
✉ jessica.hughes@xxiv.co.uk

HUGHES MISS JOANNA ELIZABETH

Temple Garden Chambers
1 Harcourt Buildings, Temple, London EC4Y 9DA, ☎ 020 7583 1315
✉ clerks@tgchambers.com
Call Date: July 2007, Middle Temple
Qualifications: [BA (Cantab) LLB (Lond)]
✉ clerks@tgchambers.com

HUGHES MISS KATHRYN ANN

30 Park Place
Cardiff CF10 3BS, ☎ 029 2039 8421
✉ clerks@30parkplace.law.co.uk
Call Date: Nov 1992, Inner Temple
Pupil Supervisor
Qualifications: [LLB (Bris)]
✉ kh@30parkplace.co.uk

HUGHES MRS KATHRYN SALLY

Chavasse Court Chambers
18 Queen Avenue, Liverpool L2 4TX, ☎ 0151 229 2030
✉ clerks@chavassechambers.co.uk
Call Date: Mar 2003, Inner Temple
Qualifications: [BA (Sheff)]
✉ kathryn.hughes@chavassechambers.co.uk

HUGHES MR LEIGHTON ALEXANDER

9 Park Place
9 Park Place, Cardiff, South Glamorgan CF10 3DP, ☎ 029 2038 2731
✉ clerks@9parkplace.co.uk
Call Date: July 1989, Inner Temple
Pupil Supervisor
Qualifications: [LLB (Hons)]

HUGHES MISS MERYL ELIZABETH

Fenners Chambers
3 Madingley Road, Cambridge CB3 0EE, ☎ 01223 368761
✉ clerks@fennerschambers.com
Call Date: Nov 1987, Gray's Inn
Qualifications: [LLB (Leeds)]
✉ meryl.hughes@fennerschambers.com

HUGHES MISS OLAJUMOKE

Middle Temple Lane Chambers
2nd Floor South, 1 Middle Temple Lane, London EC4Y 9AA, ☎ 020 7583 4352
✉ chambers@mtlchambers.com
Call Date: July 1999, Inner Temple
Qualifications: [LLB]

HUGHES MR PAUL STUART

Kings Chambers
36 Young Street, Manchester M3 3FT, ☎ 0845 034 3444
✉ clerks@kingschambers.com
Kings Chambers
5 Park Square East, Leeds LS1 2NE, ☎ 0845 034 3444
✉ clerks@kingschambers.com
Kings Chambers
Embassy House, 60 Church Street, Birmingham B3 2DJ, ☎ 0845 034 3444
✉ clerks@kingschambers.com
Call Date: Oct 2001, Middle Temple
Qualifications: [BA (Hons)(Oxon)]
✉ phughes@kingschambers.com

HUGHES MISS RACHEL

Oriel Chambers
14 Water Street, Liverpool, Merseyside L2 8TD, ☎ 0151 236 7191
✉ clerks@orielchambers.co.uk
Oriel Chambers
18 Ribblesdale Place, Preston PR1 3NA, ☎ 01772 254 764
✉ clerks@oriel-chambers.co.uk
Call Date: Nov 1995, Gray's Inn
Qualifications: [BA (Oxon)]
✉ rachel.hughes@orielchambers.co.uk

HUGHES MISS RUTH MICHELE

5 Stone Buildings
5 Stone Buildings, Lincoln's Inn, London WC2A 3XT, ☎ 020 7242 6201
✉ clerks@5sblaw.com
Call Date: July 2007, Lincoln's Inn
Qualifications: [BA (Cantab)]
✉ rhughes@5sblaw.com

HUGHES MR SIMON DAVID QC (2011)

Keating Chambers
15 Essex Street, London WC2R 3AA, ☎ 020 7544 2600
✉ clerks@keatingchambers.com
Call Date: Nov 1995, Gray's Inn
Pupil Supervisor
Qualifications: [MA]
✉ shughes@keatingchambers.com

E

HUGHES MR SIMON IEUAN

Civitas Chambers
Global Reach, Celtic Gateway, Cardiff Bay, Cardiff CF11 0SN, ☎ 0845 0713 007
✉ clerks@civitaslaw.com
Call Date: Oct 2003, Gray's Inn
Qualifications: [LLB (L'pool)]
✉ simon.hughes@civitaslaw.com

HUGHES MR WILLIAM LLOYD

9-12 Bell Yard
London WC2A 2JR, ☎ 020 7400 1800
✉ clerks@9-12bellyard.com
Call Date: Nov 1989, Gray's Inn
Pupil Supervisor, Recorder
Qualifications: [BSc (Leics)]
✉ w.hughes@9-12bellyard.com

HUGHES MR YWAIN GWYDION

9 Park Place
9 Park Place, Cardiff, South Glamorgan CF10 3DP, ☎ 029 2038 2731
✉ clerks@9parkplace.co.uk
Call Date: Nov 1994, Gray's Inn
Pupil Supervisor
Qualifications: [LLB (Wales)]
✉ ygwydionhughes@mac.com

E

HUGHES-DEANE MS CHARLOTTE BARBARA

Atlantic Chambers
4-6 Cook Street, Liverpool L2 9QU, ☎ 0151 236 4421
✉ info@atlanticchambers.co.uk
Call Date: Nov 2002, Lincoln's Inn
Qualifications: [LLB (Hons)(L'pool)]
✉ charlotte@atlanticchambers.co.uk

HUGHESTON-ROBERTS MR CHARLES JUSTIN

4 Breams Buildings
Chancery Lane, London EC4A 1HP, ☎ 020 7092 1900 ✉ clerks@4bb.co.uk
Call Date: Mar 2009, Gray's Inn
Qualifications: [Transferring Solicitor]
✉ jhr@4bb.co.uk

HUGH-JONES MR GEORGE QC (2010)

3 Serjeants Inn
London EC4Y 1BQ, ☎ 020 7427 5000
✉ clerks@3serjeantsinn.com
Call Date: Nov 1983, Middle Temple
Pupil Supervisor
Qualifications: [MA (Cantab) Dip Law]
✉ ghugh-jones@3serjeantsinn.com

HULME MR JOHN TRELAWNEY STEWART

Castle Chambers
The Old Fire Station, 90 High Street, Harrow-on-the-Hill, Middlesex HA1 3LP, ☎ 020 8423 6579 ✉ info@castlechambers.net
Call Date: Nov 1983, Middle Temple
Pupil Supervisor
Qualifications: [BSC Dip Law]

HULSE MRS CECILIA HELEN

Chambers of Mr Ami Feder
Ground Floor, Lamb Building, Temple, London EC4Y 7AS, ☎ 020 7797 7788
✉ clerks@lambbuilding.co.uk
Chambers of Mr Ami Feder
Ground Floor, Lamb Building, Temple, London EC4Y 7AS, ☎ 020 7797 7788
✉ clerks@lambbuilding.co.uk
Call Date: Nov 1998, Middle Temple
Qualifications: [BA (Hons)]

HUMMERSTONE MS REBEKAH MARY WICLIF

2 Hare Court
Lower Ground, Ground, 1st & 2nd Floor, 2 Hare Court, Temple, London EC4Y 7BH, ☎ 020 7353 3982 ✉ clerks@2harecourt.com
Call Date: July 2002, Gray's Inn
Qualifications: [BA (Oxon) Dip Law]
✉ rebekahhummerstone@2harecourt.com

HUMPHERSON MR PAUL GARETH

6 King's Bench Walk
Ground Floor, 6 King's Bench Walk, Temple, London EC4Y 7DR, ☎ 020 7583 0410
✉ clerks@6kbw.com
Call Date: July 2010, Gray's Inn
Qualifications: [BA MSc]
✉ paul.humpherson@6kbw.com

HUMPHREYS MS ELIZABETH HARRIET

Henderson Chambers
2 Harcourt Buildings, Temple, London EC4Y 9DB, ☎ 020 7583 9020
✉ clerks@hendersonchambers.co.uk
Call Date: July 2009, Middle Temple
Qualifications: [BSc (Hons) (Lond) MA (Oxon) Post Grad Dip Law]
✉ ehumphreys@hendersonchambers.co.uk

HUMPHREYS MRS JACQUELINE LOUISE

St John's Chambers
101 Victoria Street, Bristol BS1 6PU,
☎0117 923 4700
✉clerks@stjohnschambers.co.uk
Call Date: Oct 1994, Lincoln's Inn
Qualifications: [MA (Hons) LLM]

HUMPHREYS MR RICHARD WILLIAM QC (2006)

Francis Taylor Building
Inner Temple, London EC4Y 7BY,
☎020 7353 8415 ✉clerks@ftb.eu.com
No5 Chambers
Fountain Court, Steelhouse Lane, Birmingham B4 6DR, ☎0845 210 5555 ✉info@no5.com
No5 Chambers
38 Queen Square, Bristol BS1 4QS,
☎0845 210 5555
No5 Chambers
Greenwood House, 4-7 Salisbury Court, London EC4Y 8AA, ☎0845 210 5555
Call Date: July 1986, Inner Temple
Qualifications: [LLB (Notts) LLM (Cantab)]
🖃Richard.humphreys@ftb.eu.com

HUMPHRIES MR MICHAEL JOHN QC (2003)

Francis Taylor Building
Inner Temple, London EC4Y 7BY,
☎020 7353 8415 ✉clerks@ftb.eu.com
Call Date: July 1982, Inner Temple
Qualifications: [LLB (Leic)]
🖃michael.humphries@ftb.eu.com

HUMPHRIES MR PAUL BENEDICT

Deans Court Chambers
24 St John Street, Manchester M3 4DF,
☎0161 214 6000 ✉clerks@deanscourt.co.uk
Deans Court Chambers
101 Walker Street, Preston PR1 2RR,
☎01772 565 600
✉preston@deanscourt.co.uk
Call Date: Nov 1986, Middle Temple
Pupil Supervisor
Qualifications: [MA (Oxon)]
🖃humphries@deanscourt.co.uk

HUMPHRYES MISS JANE CAROLE QC (2003)

3 Raymond Buildings
3 Raymond Buildings, Gray's Inn, London WC1R 5BH, ☎020 7400 6400
✉clerks@3rblaw.com
Call Date: July 1983, Middle Temple
Recorder
Qualifications: [BA (Kent)]

HUNJAN MR SATINDER PAL SINGH QC (2002)

No5 Chambers
Fountain Court, Steelhouse Lane, Birmingham B4 6DR, ☎0845 210 5555 ✉info@no5.com
No5 Chambers
Greenwood House, 4-7 Salisbury Court, London EC4Y 8AA, ☎0845 210 5555
No5 Chambers
38 Queen Square, Bristol BS1 4QS,
☎0845 210 5555
Call Date: July 1984, Gray's Inn
Recorder
Qualifications: [LLB (B'ham)]
🖃sh@no5.com

HUNKA MR SIMON PETER

No5 Chambers
Fountain Court, Steelhouse Lane, Birmingham B4 6DR, ☎0845 210 5555 ✉info@no5.com
No5 Chambers
Greenwood House, 4-7 Salisbury Court, London EC4Y 8AA, ☎0845 210 5555
No5 Chambers
38 Queen Square, Bristol BS1 4QS,
☎0845 210 5555
Call Date: July 2007, Middle Temple
Qualifications: [PHSCSc (Dunelm)]
🖃shu@no5.com

HUNT MISS ALISON JANET

No.6 Park Square
Leeds LS1 2LW, ☎0113 245 9763
✉Tim@no6.co.uk
Call Date: July 1986, Gray's Inn
Pupil Supervisor
Qualifications: [BA (Cantab)]
🖃hunt@no6.co.uk

HUNT MISS ALISON LORNA

Regency Chambers
45 Priestgate, Peterborough PE1 1LB,
☎01733 315215
✉clerks@regencychambers.law.co.uk
Regency Chambers
Sheraton House, Castle Park, Cambridge CB3 0AX, ☎01223 301517
Call Date: Nov 2001, Middle Temple
Pupil Supervisor
Qualifications: [BA (Hons)]
🖃clerks@regencychambers.law.co.uk

E

HUNT MR DAVID RODERIC NOTLEY QC (1987)

Blackstone Chambers
Blackstone House, Temple, London
EC4Y 9BW, ☎ 020 7583 1770
✉ clerks@blackstonechambers.com
Call Date: July 1969, Gray's Inn
Recorder
Qualifications: [MA (Hons) (Cantab)]
✉ davidhunt@blackstonechambers.com

HUNT MS NICOLA ANN

Atlantic Chambers
4-6 Cook Street, Liverpool L2 9QU,
☎ 0151 236 4421
✉ info@atlanticchambers.co.uk
Call Date: Nov 1989, Gray's Inn
Qualifications: [LLB]
✉ info@atlanticchambers.co.uk

HUNT MR QUENTIN JOHN

2 Bedford Row
London WC1R 4BU, ☎ 020 7440 8888
✉ clerks@2bedfordrow.co.uk
Call Date: Oct 2000, Gray's Inn
Pupil Supervisor
Qualifications: [BA (Warw)]
✉ qhunt@2bedfordrow.co.uk

HUNT MR RICHARD MARK

15 Winckley Square
Preston PR1 3JJ, ☎ 01772 252828
✉ clerks@15winckleysq.co.uk
Call Date: July 1985, Lincoln's Inn
Qualifications: [LLB]

HUNT MR RODERICK IRVIN

Dere Street Barristers
14 Toft Green, York YO1 6JT, ☎ 0844 3351551
✉ clerks@derestreet.co.uk
Call Date: July 1981, Middle Temple
Qualifications: [MA (Cantab)]

HUNT MR STEPHEN

4 Stone Buildings
Ground Floor, 4 Stone Buildings, Lincoln's Inn, London WC2A 3XT, ☎ 020 7242 5524
✉ clerks@4stonebuildings.com
Call Date: July 1968, Lincoln's Inn
Pupil Supervisor
Qualifications: [MA (Oxon)]
✉ clerks@4stonebuildings.com

HUNT MISS THERESA ELEANORE

43 Temple Row Chambers
6th Floor, 43 Temple Row, Birmingham
B2 5LS, ☎ 0121 237 6035
✉ clerks@43templerow.co.uk
Call Date: July 2007, Gray's Inn
Qualifications: [LLB (Cardiff)]
✉ clerks@43templerow.co.uk

HUNTER MR ANDREW MICHAEL QC (2012)

Blackstone Chambers
Blackstone House, Temple, London
EC4Y 9BW, ☎ 020 7583 1770
✉ clerks@blackstonechambers.com
Call Date: Oct 1993, Middle Temple
Pupil Supervisor
Qualifications: [BA (Hons)(Oxon) BCL (Oxon)]
✉ andrewhunter@blackstonechambers.com

HUNTER MR DAVID ALEXANDER

Assize Court Chambers
14 Small Street, Bristol BS1 1DE,
☎ 0117 926 4587 ✉ carly@assize.co.uk
Call Date: Nov 2002, Lincoln's Inn
Qualifications: [BA (Hons)(Wales)]

HUNTER MR IAN GERALD ADAMSON QC (1980)

Essex Court Chambers
24 Lincoln's Inn Fields, London WC2A 3EG,
☎ 020 7813 8000
✉ clerksroom@essexcourt.net
Call Date: Nov 1967, Inner Temple
Recorder
Qualifications: [MA LLM (USA) LLB (Cantab)]
✉ ihunter@essexcourt.net

HUNTER MR JAMES MARTIN HUGH

Essex Court Chambers
24 Lincoln's Inn Fields, London WC2A 3EG,
☎ 020 7813 8000
✉ clerksroom@essexcourt.net
Call Date: May 1994, Lincoln's Inn
Qualifications: [BA (Cantab)]
✉ mhunter@essexcourt.net

HUNTER MISS JANE ALLISON

Furnival Chambers
32 Furnival Street, London EC4A 1JQ,
☎ 020 7405 3232
Call Date: July 1986, Lincoln's Inn
Pupil Supervisor
Qualifications: [BA (Lond)]
✉ ahunter@furnivallaw.co.uk

HUNTER MR JOHN ZUCCOLOTTO

Kings Chambers
36 Young Street, Manchester M3 3FT,
☎ 0845 034 3444
✉ clerks@kingschambers.com
Kings Chambers
5 Park Square East, Leeds LS1 2NE,
☎ 0845 034 3444
✉ clerks@kingschambers.com
Kings Chambers
Embassy House, 60 Church Street,
Birmingham B3 2DJ, ☎ 0845 034 3444
✉ clerks@kingschambers.com
Call Date: Nov 2002, Lincoln's Inn
Qualifications: [BA (Hons)(Oxon) MSt CPE]
✉ jhunter@kingschambers.com

HUNTER MR ROBERT JAMES

12 Gray's Inn Square
Gray's Inn, London WC1R 5JP,
☎ 020 7067 1960 ✉ almqc@12graysinn.com
Call Date: Mar 2012, Gray's Inn
✉ rh@12graysinn.com

HUNTER MR ROBERT NEIL

Devereux Chambers
Queen Elizabeth Building, Temple, London
EC4Y 9BS, ☎ 020 7353 7534
✉ clerks@devchambers.co.uk
Call Date: Oct 2000, Gray's Inn
Pupil Supervisor
Qualifications: [BA (Hons) (Manch)]
✉ hunter@devchambers.co.uk

HUNTER MR SIMON CHRISTOPHER

13 Old Square Chambers
Ground Floor, 14 Old Square, Lincoln's Inn,
London WC2A 3UE, ☎ 020 7831 4445
✉ clerks@13oldsquare.com
Call Date: Nov 2009, Gray's Inn
Qualifications: [MA MPhil]
✉ simonhunter@13oldsquare.com

HUNTER MISS SUSAN CLARE

St John's Chambers
101 Victoria Street, Bristol BS1 6PU,
☎ 0117 923 4700
✉ clerks@stjohnschambers.co.uk
Call Date: July 1985, Inner Temple
Pupil Supervisor
Qualifications: [MA (Cantab) DipLaw]
✉ susan.hunter@stjohnschambers.co.uk

HUNTER MR TIMOTHY CHARLES

Atkinson Bevan Chambers
1st Floor, 2 Harcourt Buildings, Temple,
London EC4Y 9DB, ☎ 020 7353 2112
✉ clerks@2hb.co.uk
Call Date: Oct 1998, Inner Temple
Qualifications: [BA (Bris) CPE Dip in Law]
✉ timothyhunter@2hb.co.uk

HUNTER MR WILLIAM QUIGLEY

1 Chancery Lane
London WC2A 1LF, ☎ 0845 634 6666
✉ clerks@1chancerylane.com
Call Date: July 1972, Inner Temple
Pupil Supervisor
Qualifications: [MA (Cantab)]
✉ whunter@1chancerylane.com

HUNTER MR WINSTON RONALD QC (2000)

Byrom Street Chambers
12 Byrom Street, Manchester M3 4PP,
☎ 0161 829 2100 ✉ clerks@byromstreet.com
Crown Office Chambers
2 Crown Office Row, Temple, London
EC4Y 7HJ, ☎ 020 7797 8100
✉ mail@crownofficechambers.com
42 Bedford Row
London WC1R 4LL, ☎ 020 7831 0222
✉ clerks@42br.com
Call Date: July 1985, Lincoln's Inn
Recorder
Qualifications: [LLB (Leeds)]
✉ winston.hunter@byromstreet.com

HUNTLEY MISS CLARE HELEN PATRICIA

9-12 Bell Yard
London WC2A 2JR, ☎ 020 7400 1800
✉ clerks@9-12bellyard.com
Call Date: July 2000, Gray's Inn
Qualifications: [LLB (Warw)]

HURD MR JAMES ROBERT

St James's Chambers
68 Quay Street, Manchester M3 3EJ,
☎ 0161 834 7000
✉ clerks@stjameschambers.com
Call Date: Oct 1994, Gray's Inn
Pupil Supervisor
Qualifications: [LLB]
✉ james.hurd@stjameschambers.com

E

HURLOCK MR LUGARD JOHN

2 Bedford Row
London WC1R 4BU, ☎ 020 7440 8888
✉ clerks@2bedfordrow.co.uk
Call Date: Oct 1993, Gray's Inn
Qualifications: [LLB (Coventry)]
✉ jhurlock@2bedfordrow.co.uk

HURST MR ANDREW ROBERT

23 Essex Street
London WC2R 3AA, ☎ 020 7413 0353
✉ clerks@23es.com
Call Date: Nov 1992, Inner Temple
Pupil Supervisor, Recorder
Qualifications: [BA (Oxon)]
✉ andrewhurst@23es.com

HURST MR BRIAN

39 Park Square
Leeds LS1 2NU, ☎ 0113 245 6633
✉ seniorclerk@39parksquarechambers.co.uk
Call Date: July 1983, Middle Temple
Pupil Supervisor
Qualifications: [MA (Hons)(Oxon)]

E

HURST MR MARTIN RICHARD JOHN

1 High Pavement
Nottingham NG1 1HF, ☎ 0115 941 8218
✉ clerks@1highpavement.co.uk
Call Date: July 1985, Middle Temple
Pupil Supervisor
Qualifications: [LLB (L'pool)]
✉ martinhurst@1highpavement.co.uk

HURWORTH MISS JILLIAN MARY

1 Garden Court Family Law Chambers
Ground Floor, One Garden Court, Temple, London EC4Y 9BJ, ☎ 020 7797 7900
✉ clerks@1gc.com
Call Date: Oct 1993, Inner Temple
Qualifications: [BA (Cantab)]
✉ Hurworth@1gc.com

HUSAIN MISS LAUREEN ANWAR

2 Pump Court
1st Floor, 2 Pump Court, Temple, London EC4Y 7AH, ☎ 020 7353 5597
✉ clerks@2pumpcourt.co.uk
Call Date: Mar 1997, Lincoln's Inn
Qualifications: [LLB (Warw)]
✉ lhusain@2pumpcourt.co.uk

HUSAIN MR SYED RAZA QC (2010)

Matrix Chambers
Griffin Building, Gray's Inn, London WC1R 5LN, ☎ 020 7404 3447
✉ matrix@matrixlaw.co.uk / lscott@matrixlaw.co.uk
Call Date: Nov 1993, Middle Temple
Pupil Supervisor
Qualifications: [BA (Hons)(Oxon) CPE (Lond)]
✉ razahusain@matrixlaw.co.uk

HUSBANDS MISS ABIGAIL

23 Essex Street
London WC2R 3AA, ☎ 020 7413 0353
✉ clerks@23es.com
Call Date: Nov 2000, Middle Temple
Qualifications: [Dip in Law BA (Hons) (Lond)]
✉ abigailhusbands@23es.com

HUSEYIN MR MARTIN TREVOR

Tooks Chambers
81 Farringdon Street, London EC4A 4BL, ☎ 020 7842 7575 ✉ clerks@tooks.co.uk
Call Date: Nov 1988, Inner Temple
Pupil Supervisor
Qualifications: [BA (Sussex) DipLaw]
✉ martin.huseyin@tooks.co.uk

HUSSAIN MR AMJAD

Trent Chambers
9 Regent Street, Nottingham NG1 5BS, ☎ 0115 941 9596
✉ clerks@trentchambers.co.uk
Call Date: Nov 1999, Lincoln's Inn
Qualifications: [LLB (Hons) PG Dip]

HUSSAIN MR BASHARAT

Cornwall Street Chambers
85-87 Cornwall Street, Birmingham B3 3BY, ☎ 0121 233 7500
✉ clerks@cornwallstreet.co.uk
Call Date: Nov 1997, Gray's Inn
Qualifications: [LLB (Manch)]
✉ basharat.hussain@cornwallstreet.co.uk

HUSSAIN MISS FRIDA KHANAM

Furnival Chambers
32 Furnival Street, London EC4A 1JQ, ☎ 020 7405 3232
Call Date: Oct 1995, Inner Temple
Qualifications: [LLB (Hons) (Huddersfield)]
✉ fhussain@furnivallaw.co.uk

HUSSAIN MR GHULAM

Crown Office Row Chambers
119 Church Street, Brighton, Sussex BN1 1UD, ☎ 01273 625625
✉ clerks@1cor.com
Call Date: Oct 1998, Inner Temple
Qualifications: [LLB (Leeds)]
✉ ghulam.hussain@1cor.com

HUSSAIN MR GUL NAWAZ MAHBOOB

Bank House Chambers
Old Bank House, Hartshead, Sheffield S1 2EL, ☎ 0114 275 1223
✉ w.digby@bankhousechambers.co.uk
Tooks Chambers
81 Farringdon Street, London EC4A 4BL, ☎ 020 7842 7575 ✉ clerks@tooks.co.uk
Park Court Chambers
16 Park Place, Leeds LS1 2SJ, ☎ 0113 243 3277
✉ clerks@parkcourtchambers.co.uk
Call Date: Oct 2000, Gray's Inn
Qualifications: [LLB]

HUSSAIN MR MUHAMMAD ALTAF

Chambers of Mr M A Hussain
29 Strathbrook Road, London SW16 3AT, ☎ 020 8679 2398
✉ altafhussain06@yahoo.co.uk
Call Date: July 1970, Middle Temple
Qualifications: [MA LLB]

HUSSAIN MR MUKHTAR QC (1992)

Lincoln House Chambers
Tower 12, The Avenue North, Spinningfields, 18-22 Bridge Street, Manchester M3 3BZ, ☎ 0161 832 5701
✉ info@lincolnhousechambers.com
Call Date: July 1971, Middle Temple
Recorder
✉ mukhtar.hussain@lincolnhousechambers.com

HUSSAIN MR RAFAQUAT MAHMOOD

Bell Yard Chambers
116/118 Chancery Lane, London WC2A 1PP, ☎ 020 7306 9292
✉ byclerks@bellyardchambers.co.uk
Call Date: Oct 1996, Middle Temple
Qualifications: [BA (Hons) Dip Law]
✉ rhussain@bellyardchambers.co.uk, rafaquathussain@gmail.com

HUSSAIN MR RIAZ

Atkin Chambers
1 Atkin Building, Gray's Inn, London WC1R 5AT, ☎ 020 7404 0102
✉ clerks@atkinchambers.com
Call Date: July 2001, Gray's Inn
Pupil Supervisor
Qualifications: [LLB (Lond)]
✉ clerks@atkinchambers.com

HUSSAIN MISS RUKHSHANDA JABEEN

St Paul's Chambers
5th Floor, St Paul's House, 23 Park Square South, Leeds LS1 2ND, ☎ 0113 245 5866
Call Date: Nov 1998, Gray's Inn
Qualifications: [LLB (L'pool)]

HUSSAIN MR TASADDAT

Broadway House Chambers
Broadway House, 9 Bank Street, Bradford, West Yorkshire BD1 1TW, ☎ 01274 722560
✉ clerks@broadwayhouse.co.uk
Broadway House Chambers
25 Park Square West, Leeds, West Yorkshire LS1 2PW, ☎ 0113 246 2600
✉ clerks@broadwayhouse.co.uk
Call Date: Oct 1998, Lincoln's Inn
Qualifications: [LLB (Hons) (Notts)]
✉ clerks@broadwayhouse.co.uk

HUSSAIN MR ZAHID

St John's Chambers
101 Victoria Street, Bristol BS1 6PU, ☎ 0117 923 4700
✉ clerks@stjohnschambers.co.uk
Call Date: July 2001, Lincoln's Inn
Qualifications: [LLB (Hons)]
✉ zahid.hussain@stjohnschambers.co.uk

HUSSAIN MISS ZIRA

St Philips Chambers
55 Temple Row, Birmingham B2 5LS, ☎ 0121 246 7000 ✉ clerks@st-philips.com
Call Date: Oct 1998, Lincoln's Inn
Qualifications: [LLB (Hons)(Huddes)]
✉ zhussain@st-philips.com

HUSSEIN MR TIMUR

1 Pump Court
Elm Court, Temple, London EC4Y 7AB, ☎ 020 7842 7070
✉ (name)@pumpcourt.co.uk
Call Date: Oct 1993, Inner Temple
Pupil Supervisor
Qualifications: [LLB]
✉ th@1pumpcourt.co.uk

E

HUSSEY MISS ANN ELIZABETH QC (2009)

1 Hare Court
1 Hare Court, Temple, London EC4Y 7BE,
☎020 7797 7070 ✉clerks@1hc.com
Call Date: July 1981, Middle Temple
Qualifications: [BA (Hons)]
✉hussey@1hc.com

HUSTON MR GRAHAM MARTIN

Seven Bedford Row
7 Bedford Row, London WC1R 4BS,
☎020 7242 3555 ✉clerks@7br.co.uk
Call Date: Feb 1991, Inner Temple
Pupil Supervisor
Qualifications: [LLB (Lond)]
✉ghuston@7br.co.uk

HUTCHIN MR EDWARD ALISTER DAVID

Temple Garden Chambers
1 Harcourt Buildings, Temple, London EC4Y 9DA, ☎020 7583 1315
✉clerks@tgchambers.com
Call Date: Oct 1996, Middle Temple
Qualifications: [LLB (Hons)(Notts)]

E

HUTCHINGS MR MARK JOHANNES

Stour Chambers
Mill Studio, 17a Stour Street, Canterbury, Kent CT1 2NR, ☎01227 764899
✉clerks@stourchambers.co.uk
Call Date: Nov 2005, Gray's Inn
Qualifications: [BSc]
✉clerks@stourchambers.co.uk

HUTCHINGS MR MARTIN ANTHONY QC (2011)

Wilberforce Chambers
8 New Square, Lincoln's Inn, London WC2A 3QP, ☎020 7306 0102
✉chambers@wilberforce.co.uk
Call Date: Feb 1986, Middle Temple
Pupil Supervisor
Qualifications: [MA (Oxon)]
✉mhutchings@wilberforce.co.uk

Types of work: Chancery (land law), Commercial litigation, Commercial property, Landlord and tenant, Professional negligence

HUTCHINGS MR MATTHEW HOWARD OLSEN

Cornerstone Barristers
2-3 Gray's Inn Square, Gray's Inn, London WC1R 5JH, ☎020 7242 4986
✉chambers@2-3gis.co.uk
Call Date: Nov 1993, Inner Temple
Qualifications: [BA (Oxon) DipLaw (Lond)]

HUTCHINGS MR RICHARD PETER MARK

Chambers of Marion Smullen and Kerim Fuad QC
1 Inner Temple Lane, London EC4Y 1AF,
☎020 7427 4400 ✉clerks@1itl.com
Call Date: Nov 2001, Lincoln's Inn
Qualifications: [BA (Hons)(Dunelm) Dip Law]
✉richard.hutchings@1itl.com

HUTCHINSON MR COLIN THOMAS

Garden Court Chambers
57-60 Lincoln's Inn Fields, London WC2A 3LJ,
☎020 7993 7600 ✉info@gclaw.co.uk
Call Date: Oct 1990, Middle Temple
Pupil Supervisor
Qualifications: [LLB (Hons)]
✉colinh@gclaw.co.uk

HUTCHISON MISS ELEANOR CLAIRE

1 Pump Court
Elm Court, Temple, London EC4Y 7AB,
☎020 7842 7070
✉(name)@pumpcourt.co.uk
Call Date: July 2007, Middle Temple
Qualifications: [BA (Lond)]
✉eh@1pumpcourt.co.uk

HUTTON MR ALEXANDER FORBES QC (2012)

Hailsham Chambers
Ground Floor, 4 Paper Buildings, Temple, London EC4Y 7EX, ☎020 7643 5000
✉clerks@hailshamchambers.com
Call Date: Oct 1992, Gray's Inn
Pupil Supervisor
Qualifications: [BSc (Bris)]
✉alexander.hutton@hailshamchambers.com

HUTTON MISS CAROLINE

Enterprise Chambers
9 Old Square, Lincoln's Inn, London WC2A 3SR, ☎020 7405 9471
✉london@enterprisechambers.com
Enterprise Chambers
65 Quayside, Newcastle Upon Tyne NE1 3DE,
☎0191 222 3344
✉newcastle@enterprisechambers.com
Enterprise Chambers
43 Park Square, Leeds LS1 2NP,
☎0113 246 0391
✉leeds@enterprisechambers.com
Call Date: Nov 1979, Middle Temple
Pupil Supervisor
Qualifications: [MA (Cantab) FCIArb]

Fax: 020 7242 1447
URL: www.enterprisechambers.com

Types of work: Agriculture, Arbitration, Chancery (land law), Commercial property, Common land, Conveyancing, Landlord and tenant

HUTTON MISS LOUISE MARY

Maitland Chambers
7 Stone Buildings, Lincoln's Inn, London WC2A 3SZ, ☎ 020 7406 1200
✉ clerks@maitlandchambers.com
Call Date: Oct 1998, Inner Temple
Pupil Supervisor
Qualifications: [BA (Oxon)]
lhutton@maitlandchambers.com

HYAM MR JEREMY RUPERT DANIEL

1 Crown Office Row
1 Crown Office Row, Temple, London EC4Y 7HH, ☎ 020 7797 7500
✉ mail@1cor.com
Call Date: Nov 1995, Gray's Inn
Pupil Supervisor
Qualifications: [BA (Hons)]
jeremy.hyam@1cor.com

HYAMS MISS NATALIE ANNE

Goresbrook Chambers
PO Box 6017, Milton Keynes MK1 9AP, ☎ 0845 123 1234
✉ thomas.john6@btinternet.com
Call Date: Oct 1998, Lincoln's Inn
Qualifications: [BA (Hons)(Westmin) CPE]

HYAMS MR OLIVER MARK

Devereux Chambers
Queen Elizabeth Building, Temple, London EC4Y 9BS, ☎ 020 7353 7534
✉ clerks@devchambers.co.uk
Call Date: July 1989, Middle Temple
Qualifications: [LLB]
hyams@devchambers.co.uk

HYDE MR CHARLES GORDON QC (2006)

Queen Elizabeth Building
3rd Floor, Queen Elizabeth Building, Temple, London EC4Y 9BS, ☎ 020 7797 7837
✉ clerks@qeb.co.uk
Call Date: July 1988, Middle Temple
Recorder
Qualifications: [LLB (Hons) (Manch)]
c.hyde@qeb.co.uk

HYDE MS MARCIA

Coram Chambers
9-11 Fulwood Place, London WC1V 6HG, ☎ 020 7092 3700
✉ mail@coramchambers.co.uk
Call Date: Oct 1992, Inner Temple
Qualifications: [BA (Leeds) MA Dip Law]
marcia.hyde@coramchambers.co.uk

HYDE MR MICHAEL THOMAS

Chambers of Mr Ami Feder
Ground Floor, Lamb Building, Temple, London EC4Y 7AS, ☎ 020 7797 7788
✉ clerks@lambbuilding.co.uk
Chambers of Mr Ami Feder
Ground Floor, Lamb Building, Temple, London EC4Y 7AS, ☎ 020 7797 7788
✉ clerks@lambbuilding.co.uk
Call Date: Nov 2006, Inner Temple
Qualifications: [LLB (Hons) (Nott'm)]
m.hyde@lambbuilding.co.uk

HYDE MS SARAH-JANE

One Essex Court
1st Floor, Temple, London EC4Y 9AR, ☎ 020 7936 3030 ✉ clerks@1ec.co.uk
Call Date: July 2001, Inner Temple
Qualifications: [BA (Swansea) CPE]

HYLAND MR JAMES GRAHAM KEITH QC (1998)

Broadway House Chambers
Broadway House, 9 Bank Street, Bradford, West Yorkshire BD1 1TW, ☎ 01274 722560
✉ clerks@broadwayhouse.co.uk
Dere Street Barristers
33 Broad Chare, Newcastle Upon Tyne NE1 3DQ, ☎ 0844 3351551
✉ clerks@derestreet.co.uk
Broadway House Chambers
25 Park Square West, Leeds, West Yorkshire LS1 2PW, ☎ 0113 246 2600
✉ clerks@broadwayhouse.co.uk
Call Date: July 1978, Inner Temple
Recorder
Qualifications: [BA (Newc)]

HYLTON MISS NASSTASSIA DIONNE

Harcourt Chambers
1st Floor, 2 Harcourt Buildings, Temple, London EC4Y 9DB, ☎ 0844 561 7135
Call Date: July 2007, Inner Temple
Qualifications: [BA (Manch)]
nhylton@harcourtchambers.law.co.uk

E

HYMANSON MISS DEANNA SUSAN

Cobden House Chambers
19 Quay Street, Manchester M3 3HN,
☎0161 833 6000 ✉Clerks@Cobden.co.uk
Call Date: Feb 1988, Middle Temple
Qualifications: [LLB (Hons) (Lond)]
✉clerks@cobden.co.uk, dhilton@hotmail.com

HYNES MR PAUL RICHARD QC (2010)

25 Bedford Row
London WC1R 4HD, ☎020 7067 1500
✉clerks@25bedfordrow.com
Call Date: Nov 1987, Lincoln's Inn
Pupil Supervisor
Qualifications: [BA (Hons)]
✉phynes@25bedfordrow.com

HYPOLITE-DE-SOUZA MRS JOSEPHINE CLAUDIA

12 Old Square Chambers
1st Floor, 12 Old Square, Lincoln's Inn,
London WC2A 3TX, ☎020 7404 0875
✉clerks@12oldsquare.com
Call Date: Nov 1992, Lincoln's Inn
Qualifications: [LLB (Hons) RHV SCM SRN Cert Ed]
✉clerks@12oldsquare.com

E

IBEKWE MISS FRANCES UCHENNA

Furnival Chambers
32 Furnival Street, London EC4A 1JQ,
☎020 7405 3232
Call Date: Mar 2008, Middle Temple
Qualifications: [LLB (Hons) (Lond) LLM (Lond)]
✉clerks@furnivallaw.co.uk

IBRAHIM MR IAN

Angel Chambers
Ethos Building, Kings Road, Swansea SA1 8AS,
☎01792 464623
✉clerks@angelchambers.co.uk
Temple Chambers
12 Clytha Park Road, Newport, Gwent
NP20 4PB, ☎01633 267403
✉dbrinning@temple-chambers.co.uk
Call Date: Oct 1997, Middle Temple
Qualifications: [BSc (Hons) MSc Dip in Law (Plymou)]
✉ian.ibrahim@angelchambers.co.uk

IBRAHIM MISS SARA ELISE LEWIS

3 Hare Court
3 Hare Court, Temple, London EC4Y 7BJ,
☎020 7415 7800 ✉clerks@3harecourt.com
Call Date: Oct 2006, Lincoln's Inn
Qualifications: [BA (Cantab)]
✉saraibrahim@3harecourt.com

IDEH MR DONALD

Chambers of Mr Donald Ideh
12 Ashburnham Tower, Edith Grove, Chelsea,
London SW10 0EE
Call Date: Nov 1999, Middle Temple
Qualifications: [LLB (Hons)(Essex) LLM (LSE)]

IFE MISS LINDEN ELIZABETH

Enterprise Chambers
9 Old Square, Lincoln's Inn, London
WC2A 3SR, ☎020 7405 9471
✉london@enterprisechambers.com
Enterprise Chambers
65 Quayside, Newcastle Upon Tyne NE1 3DE,
☎0191 222 3344
✉newcastle@enterprisechambers.com
Enterprise Chambers
43 Park Square, Leeds LS1 2NP,
☎0113 246 0391
✉leeds@enterprisechambers.com
Call Date: Nov 1982, Middle Temple
Pupil Supervisor
Qualifications: [MA (Oxon)]
✉lindenife@enterprisechambers.com

ILES MR DAVID

No5 Chambers
Fountain Court, Steelhouse Lane, Birmingham
B4 6DR, ☎0845 210 5555 ✉info@no5.com
No5 Chambers
Greenwood House, 4-7 Salisbury Court,
London EC4Y 8AA, ☎0845 210 5555
No5 Chambers
38 Queen Square, Bristol BS1 4QS,
☎0845 210 5555
Call Date: July 1977, Inner Temple
Qualifications: [LLB (Lond)]
✉di@no5.com

ILYAS MR DAUD

Temple Court Chambers
2nd Floor, 2 Dr Johnson's Building, Temple,
London EC4Y 7AY, ☎020 7353 7888
✉clerks@templecourt.co.uk
Call Date: Nov 1959, Gray's Inn
Pupil Supervisor
Qualifications: [BCL MA (Oxon)]
✉daudilyas@templecourt.co.uk, daudilyas@hotmail.com

ILYAS MR SHAIBA

Enterprise Chambers
9 Old Square, Lincoln's Inn, London
WC2A 3SR, ☎020 7405 9471
✉london@enterprisechambers.com
Enterprise Chambers
65 Quayside, Newcastle Upon Tyne NE1 3DE,
☎0191 222 3344
✉newcastle@enterprisechambers.com

Enterprise Chambers
43 Park Square, Leeds LS1 2NP,
☎0113 246 0391
✉leeds@enterprisechambers.com
Call Date: Mar 1998, Lincoln's Inn
Pupil Supervisor
Qualifications: [LLB (Hons)(Herts) LLM]
✉shaibailyas@enterprisechambers.com

INDULSKA MRS NAOMI LYDIA

Pendragon Chambers
Suite 7, J Shed, Kings Road, SA1 Waterfront, Swansea SA1 8PL, ☎01792 411188
✉clerks@pendragonchambers.com
Call Date: July 2006, Gray's Inn
Qualifications: [LLB (Sheff)]
✉Naomi.indulska@pendragonchamber.com

INFIELD MR PAUL LOUIS

Clerksroom (Taunton)
Equity House, Administration Centre, Blackbrook Park Avenue, Taunton, Somerset TA1 2PX, ☎0845 083 3000
✉mail@clerksroom.com
Clerksroom (London)
3rd Floor, 218 Strand, London WC2R 1AT, ☎0845 083 3000 ✉mail@clerksroom.com
King's Lynn Chambers
26 The Birches, South Wootton, King's Lynn, Norfolk PE30 3JG, ☎01553 672 085
✉timothy.leader@tesco.net
Call Date: July 1980, Inner Temple
Pupil Supervisor
Qualifications: [LLB (Sheff)]
✉infield@clerksroom.com

INGHAM MISS ELIZABETH CLAIRE

Colleton Chambers
Colleton Crescent, Exeter, Devon EX2 4DG, ☎01392 274898
✉clerks@colletonchambers.co.uk
36 Bedford Row
London WC1R 4JH, ☎020 7421 8000
✉chambers@36bedfordrow.co.uk
Call Date: Nov 1989, Middle Temple
Qualifications: [BA (Hons) (Oxon)]
✉lizingham@colletonchambers.co.uk

INGLIS MR ALAN

Coram Chambers
9-11 Fulwood Place, London WC1V 6HG, ☎020 7092 3700
✉mail@coramchambers.co.uk
Call Date: July 1989, Middle Temple
Pupil Supervisor
Qualifications: [BA (Essex) MA (Warw) Dip Law CQSW]
✉alan.inglis@coramchambers.co.uk

INGRAM MR JONATHAN ANTONY

Five St Andrew's Hill
5 St Andrew's Hill, London EC4V 5BZ, ☎020 7332 5400 ✉Clerks@5sah.co.uk
Call Date: July 1984, Inner Temple
Pupil Supervisor
Qualifications: [BA (Lond)]
✉jonathaningram@5sah.co.uk

INGRAM MR NIGEL COLQUHOUN

2 Bedford Row
London WC1R 4BU, ☎020 7440 8888
✉clerks@2bedfordrow.co.uk
Call Date: July 1972, Inner Temple
Pupil Supervisor
✉ningram@2bedfordrow.co.uk

INNES MR STEPHEN JAMES

Four New Square
Four New Square, Lincoln's Inn, London WC2A 3RJ, ☎020 7822 2000
✉barristers@4newsquare.com
Call Date: Oct 2000, Gray's Inn
Pupil Supervisor
Qualifications: [BA (Oxon)]
✉s.innes@4newsquare.com

INYUNDO MR RICHARD KWAME SWAKA

6 King's Bench Walk
Ground Floor, 6 King's Bench Walk, Temple, London EC4Y 7DR, ☎020 7583 0410
✉clerks@6kbw.com
Call Date: Mar 1997, Gray's Inn
Pupil Supervisor
Qualifications: [BA (L'pool)]
✉kwame.Inyundo@6kbw.com

IQBAL MR ABDUL SHAFFAQ

No.6 Park Square
Leeds LS1 2LW, ☎0113 245 9763
✉Tim@no6.co.uk
Call Date: Oct 1994, Gray's Inn
Qualifications: [B Pharm (Bradford) Dip Law]
✉iqbal@no6.co.uk

IQBAL MR MASHOOD

London View Chambers
24 Highgate Grove, Sawbridgeworth CM21 0DD, ☎07788 912493
Call Date: Oct 2011, Lincoln's Inn
Qualifications: [LLM (Lond)]

IQBAL MR MAZHAR ADAM

The Chambers of Mr M A Iqbal
111 West Street, Sheffield S1 4EQ,
☎0114 201 4321 ✉maziqbal@hotmail.com
Call Date: Oct 1999, Inner Temple
Qualifications: [LLB (Hons) CeMAP PG Dip MCIArb]

IQBAL MISS SAMINA

Renaissance Chambers
5th Floor, Gray's Inn Chambers, Gray's Inn, London WC1R 5JA, ☎020 7404 1111
✉clerks@renaissancechambers.co.uk
Call Date: Oct 1999, Lincoln's Inn
Pupil Supervisor
Qualifications: [LLB (Hons)(Leic) Dip Law (ICSL)]

IRELAND MISS PENELOPE JANE

Southernhay Chambers
33 Southernhay East, Exeter EX1 1NX,
☎01392 255777
✉clerks@southernhaychambers.co.uk
Call Date: Oct 1996, Gray's Inn
Qualifications: [LLB (Bris)]

IRONFIELD MISS JANET RUTH

Deans Court Chambers
24 St John Street, Manchester M3 4DF,
☎0161 214 6000 ✉clerks@deanscourt.co.uk
Deans Court Chambers
101 Walker Street, Preston PR1 2RR,
☎01772 565 600
✉preston@deanscourt.co.uk
Call Date: Oct 1992, Gray's Inn
Qualifications: [BA]
🖃ironfield@deanscourt.co.uk

IRVIN MR PETER

Brick Court Chambers
7-8 Essex Street, London WC2R 3LD,
☎020 7379 3550 ✉clerks@brickcourt.co.uk
Call Date: July 1972, Gray's Inn
Pupil Supervisor
Qualifications: [BA (Oxon)]
🖃Peter.Irvin@Brickcourt.co.uk

IRVINE MISS CELESTE

Goldsmith Chambers
Ground Floor, Goldsmith Building, Temple, London EC4Y 7BL, ☎020 7353 6802
✉clerks@goldsmithchambers.com
Call Date: Oct 2007, Inner Temple
Qualifications: [LLB (Lond)]
🖃c.irvine@goldsmithchambers.com

IRVING MR DANIEL JAMES

Blackfriars Chambers
79-83 Temple Chambers, 3-7 Temple Avenue, London EC4Y 0HP, ☎020 7353 7400
✉clerks@blackfriarschambers.com
Call Date: July 2007, Middle Temple
Qualifications: [LLB (Hons)]

IRVING MISS GILLIAN QC (2006)

9 St John Street
Manchester M3 4DN, ☎0161 955 9000
✉civilclerks@9sjs.com / criminalclerks@9sjs.com
Linenhall Chambers
1 Stanley Place, Chester CH1 2LU,
☎01244 348282
✉clerks@linenhallchambers.co.uk
15 Winckley Square
Preston PR1 3JJ, ☎01772 252828
✉clerks@15winckleysq.co.uk
Call Date: July 1984, Inner Temple
Qualifications: [BA (Hons)]

IRWIN MR BENEDICT TOWNS

4 Breams Buildings
Chancery Lane, London EC4A 1HP,
☎020 7092 1900 ✉clerks@4bb.co.uk
Call Date: Mar 2006, Lincoln's Inn
Qualifications: [BA (Hons) (Leeds) PgDl]

IRWIN MR GAVIN DAVID

Dyers Chambers
35 Bedford Row, London WC1R 4JH,
☎020 7404 1881
✉admin@dyerschambers.com
Call Date: Nov 1996, Gray's Inn
Qualifications: [LLB (Newc)]
🖃gavin.irwin@dyerschambers.com

IRWIN MR WILLIAM JOHN LAWRENCE

Temple Garden Chambers
1 Harcourt Buildings, Temple, London EC4Y 9DA, ☎020 7583 1315
✉clerks@tgchambers.com
Call Date: Nov 2010, Gray's Inn
Qualifications: [BA]
🖃clerks@tgchambers.com

ISAAC MR NICHOLAS DUDLEY

Tanfield Chambers
2-5 Warwick Court, London WC1R 5DJ,
☎020 7421 5300
✉clerks@tanfieldchambers.co.uk
Call Date: Oct 1993, Gray's Inn
Pupil Supervisor
Qualifications: [BA (Leeds)]
🖃nisaac@tanfieldchambers.co.uk

ISAAC MR SEBASTIAN MARK

One Essex Court
Ground Floor, One Essex Court, Temple, London EC4Y 9AR, ☎ 020 7583 2000
✉ clerks@oeclaw.co.uk
Call Date: Oct 2005, Lincoln's Inn
Qualifications: [BA (Hons) PgDip Law]
✉ sisaac@oeclaw.co.uk

ISAACS MR BARRY RUSSELL QC (2011)

South Square
3-4 South Square, Gray's Inn, London WC1R 5HP, ☎ 020 7696 9900
✉ practicemanagers@southsquare.com
Call Date: Nov 1994, Inner Temple
Pupil Supervisor
Qualifications: [MA (Oxon) MA (USA)]
✉ barryisaacs@southsquare.com

ISAACS MR BENJAMIN

Seven Bedford Row
7 Bedford Row, London WC1R 4BS, ☎ 020 7242 3555 ✉ clerks@7br.co.uk
Call Date: Mar 2009, Middle Temple
Qualifications: [BA (Hons)(Oxon) Dip in Law]
✉ bisaacs@7br.co.uk

ISAACS MISS ELIZABETH

St Ive's Chambers
Whittall Street, Birmingham B4 6DH, ☎ 0121 236 0863
✉ clerks@stiveschambers.co.uk
Call Date: Oct 1998, Lincoln's Inn
Pupil Supervisor
Qualifications: [BA (Hons)(Dunelm) MA (Leic) LLB (Hons)(Coventry)]
✉ elizabeth.isaacs@stiveschambers.co.uk

ISAACS DR NICOLA JANE

Colleton Chambers
Colleton Crescent, Exeter, Devon EX2 4DG, ☎ 01392 274898
✉ clerks@colletonchambers.co.uk
Call Date: July 2007, Gray's Inn
Qualifications: [LLB PhD (Exon)]

ISAACS MR OLIVER DUNCAN JOHN

3 PB Barristers
3 Paper Buildings, Temple, London EC4Y 7EU, ☎ 020 7583 8055
3 PB Barristers
23 Beaumont Street, Oxford OX1 2NP, ☎ 01865 793 736
3 PB Barristers
4 St Peter Street, Winchester SO23 8BW, ☎ 01962 868884
✉ clerks.winchester@3paper.co.uk
3 PB Barristers
Royal Talbot House, 2 Victoria Street, Bristol, Avon BS1 6BB, ☎ 0117 928 1520
3 PB Barristers
30 Christchurch Road, Bournemouth, Dorset BH1 3PD, ☎ 01202 292102
✉ clerks.bournemouth@3paper.co.uk
Call Date: Oct 2000, Middle Temple
Qualifications: [BA (Hons) (Newc) Dip in Law (Oxon)]
✉ oliver.isaacs@3paper.co.uk

ISAACS MR PAUL RICHARD

Broadway House Chambers
Broadway House, 9 Bank Street, Bradford, West Yorkshire BD1 1TW, ☎ 01274 722560
✉ clerks@broadwayhouse.co.uk
Broadway House Chambers
25 Park Square West, Leeds, West Yorkshire LS1 2PW, ☎ 0113 246 2600
✉ clerks@broadwayhouse.co.uk
Call Date: Feb 1974, Middle Temple
Pupil Supervisor, Recorder
Qualifications: [MA (Cantab)]
✉ pi@broadwayhouse.co.uk

ISHERWOOD MR JOHN STANLEY

Unity Street Chambers
5 Unity Street, College Green, Bristol BS1 5HH, ☎ 0117 906 9789
✉ chambers@unitystreetchambers.com
Call Date: July 1978, Gray's Inn
Pupil Supervisor
Qualifications: [MA (Cantab)]
✉ john.isherwood@unitystreetchambers.com

ISHMAEL MR KHALID

Ashtead Park Chambers
15 Gaywood Road, Ashtead, Surrey KT21 1BL, ☎ 01372 813053
✉ khalid@ashteadparkchambers.com / admin@ashteadparkchambers.com
Call Date: Feb 1989, Lincoln's Inn
Qualifications: [BA]
✉ khalid@ashteadparkchambers.com

ISLAM MR AMINUL RUHUL

Chambers of Mr Aminul R. Islam
14 Fakruddin Street, London E1 5BU, ☎ 020 7247 1977 ✉ aminul2@hotmail.co.uk
Call Date: Oct 1997, Lincoln's Inn
Qualifications: [LLB (Hons)]

E

ISLAM MR MOHAMMAD FAKRUL

18 Red Lion Court
London EC4A 3EB, ☎ 020 7520 6000
✉ chambers@18rlc.co.uk
Call Date: Oct 2002, Middle Temple
Qualifications: [LLB (South Bank)]
dara.islam@hotmail.co.uk

ISLAM MISS NAZNIN

Pump Court Chambers
Upper Ground Floor, 3 Pump Court, Temple, London EC4Y 7AJ, ☎ 020 7353 0711
✉ clerks@3pumpcourt.com
Pump Court Chambers
5 Temple Chambers, Temple Street, Swindon SN1 1SQ, ☎ 01793 539899
✉ clerks@3pumpcourt.com
Pump Court Chambers
31 Southgate Street, Winchester, Hampshire SO23 9EB, ☎ 01962 868 161
✉ clerks@3pumpcourt.com
Call Date: Oct 2000, Lincoln's Inn
Qualifications: [LLB (Hons) (Lond)]
ni@3pumpcourt.com

ISLAM MR SAIFUL

3 Dr Johnson's Buildings
Ground Floor, 3 Dr Johnson's Buildings, Temple, London EC4Y 7BA, ☎ 020 7353 4854
✉ clerks@3djb.co.uk
Call Date: Oct 2005, Lincoln's Inn
Qualifications: [LLB (Hons)]

ISLAM-CHOUDHURY MR MUGNI

No5 Chambers
Fountain Court, Steelhouse Lane, Birmingham B4 6DR, ☎ 0845 210 5555 ✉ info@no5.com
No5 Chambers
Greenwood House, 4-7 Salisbury Court, London EC4Y 8AA, ☎ 0845 210 5555
No5 Chambers
38 Queen Square, Bristol BS1 4QS, ☎ 0845 210 5555
Call Date: Oct 1996, Lincoln's Inn
Qualifications: [LLB (Hons)(Lond)]
info@no5.com, mic@no5.com

ISMAIL MR MOHAMMED

1 Mitre Court Buildings
1 Mitre Court Buildings, Temple, London EC4Y 7BS, ☎ 020 7452 8900
✉ clerks@1mcb.com
Call Date: Nov 2007, Middle Temple
Qualifications: [LLB (Hons)]
mohammed.ismail@1mcb.com

ISMAIL MISS NAZMUN NISHA

Central Chambers
89 Princess Street, Manchester M1 4HT, ☎ 0161 236 1133
✉ clerks@centralchambers.co.uk
No5 Chambers
Greenwood House, 4-7 Salisbury Court, London EC4Y 8AA, ☎ 0845 210 5555
No5 Chambers
Fountain Court, Steelhouse Lane, Birmingham B4 6DR, ☎ 0845 210 5555 ✉ info@no5.com
No5 Chambers
38 Queen Square, Bristol BS1 4QS, ☎ 0845 210 5555
Call Date: Oct 1992, Lincoln's Inn
Qualifications: [BA(Hons)]
nazmun@btinternet.com, nazmun@btinternet.com

ISMAIL MISS SHAHIN

Fenners Chambers
3 Madingley Road, Cambridge CB3 0EE, ☎ 01223 368761
✉ clerks@fennerschambers.com
Call Date: Nov 1993, Lincoln's Inn
Qualifications: [LLB (Hons)]

ISRAEL MR JEFFREY ANTHONY

5 King's Bench Walk
5 King's Bench Walk, Temple, London EC4Y 7DN, ☎ 020 7353 5638
✉ clerks@5kbw.co.uk
Call Date: Oct 2000, Middle Temple
Qualifications: [BA (Hons) (Leeds) CPE]

ITEN MISS CORINNE BEATRICE

Pump Court Chambers
Upper Ground Floor, 3 Pump Court, Temple, London EC4Y 7AJ, ☎ 020 7353 0711
✉ clerks@3pumpcourt.com
Call Date: Oct 2006, Inner Temple
Qualifications: [BA PhD (Lond)]
ci@3pumpcourt.com

IVENS MS JEMIMA

Cranford Chambers
8 Warwick Court, London WC1R 5DJ, ☎ 020 7404 7454
✉ jemima.ivens@cranfordchambers.com
1 Mitre Court Buildings
1 Mitre Court Buildings, Temple, London EC4Y 7BS, ☎ 020 7452 8900
✉ clerks@1mcb.com
Call Date: Feb 1994, Lincoln's Inn
Qualifications: [LLB (Hons)]

E

IVERS MR MICHAEL JOSEPH

Garden Court Chambers
57-60 Lincoln's Inn Fields, London WC2A 3LJ, ☎ 020 7993 7600 ✉ info@gclaw.co.uk
Call Date: Nov 1994, Middle Temple
Pupil Supervisor
Qualifications: [LLB (Hons) (Lond)]
✉ michaeli@gclaw.co.uk

IVILL MR SCOTT ASHLEY

2 Hare Court
Lower Ground, Ground, 1st & 2nd Floor, 2 Hare Court, Temple, London EC4Y 7BH, ☎ 020 7353 3982 ✉ clerks@2harecourt.com
Call Date: Nov 1997, Gray's Inn
Pupil Supervisor
Qualifications: [LLB (Leic)]

IYENGAR MS HARINI

11 King's Bench Walk
11 King's Bench Walk, Temple, London EC4Y 7EQ, ☎ 020 7632 8500
✉ clerksroom@11kbw.com
Call Date: Oct 1999, Inner Temple
Qualifications: [MA BCL (Oxon)]

IYER MISS SHOBANA

Swan Chambers
Parkshot House, 5 Kew Road, Richmond, Surrey TW9 2PR, ☎ 0845 123 1234
✉ shobana@mycommercialbarrister.com
Call Date: July 1998, Gray's Inn
Qualifications: [BSc (Lond) LLB (Brunel) LLM (Lond)]

JABATI MISS MARIA HANNAH

Holborn Chambers
6 Gate Street, Lincoln's Inn Fields, London WC2A 3HP, ☎ 020 7242 6060
Call Date: Nov 1986, Lincoln's Inn
Qualifications: [BA LLM (Lond)]
✉ mariajabati@holbornchambers.co.uk

JACK MR ADRIAN LAURENCE ROBERT

Enterprise Chambers
9 Old Square, Lincoln's Inn, London WC2A 3SR, ☎ 020 7405 9471
✉ london@enterprisechambers.com
Enterprise Chambers
65 Quayside, Newcastle Upon Tyne NE1 3DE, ☎ 0191 222 3344
✉ newcastle@enterprisechambers.com
Enterprise Chambers
43 Park Square, Leeds LS1 2NP, ☎ 0113 246 0391
✉ leeds@enterprisechambers.com
Call Date: Nov 1986, Middle Temple
Pupil Supervisor, Recorder
Qualifications: [MA(Oxon)]
✉ adrianjack@enterprisechambers.com

JACK MR NICHOLAS ROBERT

Octagon House
19 Colegate, Norwich NR3 1AT, ☎ 01603 623186
✉ clerks@octagonhouse.co.uk
Call Date: Oct 2002, Lincoln's Inn
Qualifications: [BSc (Manch) CPE]

JACKLIN MISS SUSAN ELIZABETH QC (2006)

St John's Chambers
101 Victoria Street, Bristol BS1 6PU, ☎ 0117 923 4700
✉ clerks@stjohnschambers.co.uk
Harcourt Chambers
1st Floor, 2 Harcourt Buildings, Temple, London EC4Y 9DB, ☎ 0844 561 7135
Harcourt Chambers
Churchill House, 3 St Aldate's Courtyard, St Aldate's, Oxford OX1 1BN, ☎ 0844 561 7135
Call Date: Nov 1980, Inner Temple
Recorder
Qualifications: [BA (Dunelm)]
✉ susan.jacklin@stjohnschambers.co.uk

JACKSON MR ADRIAN PHILIP

Call Date: Oct 1990, Lincoln's Inn
Pupil Supervisor
Qualifications: [MA (Hons)(Cantab) MCI ARB]

JACKSON MISS AMY

St Ive's Chambers
Whittall Street, Birmingham B4 6DH, ☎ 0121 236 0863
✉ clerks@stiveschambers.co.uk
Call Date: July 2009, Middle Temple
Qualifications: [LLB (Hons) (Nott'm)]
✉ clerks@stiveschambers.co.uk

JACKSON MR ANDREW FRASER

5 Pump Court
Ground Floor, 5 Pump Court, Temple, London EC4Y 7AP, ☎ 020 7353 2532
✉ clerks@5pumpcourt.com
Call Date: Oct 1990, Inner Temple
Qualifications: [BA (Hons)]

E

JACKSON MR ANDREW JOHN

St Philips Chambers
55 Temple Row, Birmingham B2 5LS,
☎0121 246 7000 ✉clerks@st-philips.com
Call Date: July 1986, Lincoln's Inn
Pupil Supervisor
Qualifications: [BA (Manch) DipLaw]
✉ajackson@st-philips.com

JACKSON MR CALVIN LEIGH RAPHAEL

Charter Chambers
33 John Street, London WC1N 2AT,
☎020 7618 4400
✉clerks@charterchambers.com
Call Date: July 1975, Lincoln's Inn
Qualifications: [LLB MPhil (Cantab) LLM (Lond)]

JACKSON MR CHRISTOPHER MARSHALL

Liverpool Civil Law
3rd Floor, 1 Old Hall Street, Liverpool L3 9HF,
☎0151 242 0500
✉clerks@liverpoolcivillaw.com
Call Date: Nov 2002, Middle Temple
Pupil Supervisor
Qualifications: [LLB (Hons)]

E

JACKSON MISS CLAIRE

Enterprise Chambers
43 Park Square, Leeds LS1 2NP,
☎0113 246 0391
✉leeds@enterprisechambers.com
Enterprise Chambers
65 Quayside, Newcastle Upon Tyne NE1 3DE,
☎0191 222 3344
✉newcastle@enterprisechambers.com
Call Date: Mar 2002, Lincoln's Inn
Qualifications: [LLB (Hons)]
✉clairejackson@enterprisechambers.com

JACKSON MR DAVID

St Ive's Chambers
Whittall Street, Birmingham B4 6DH,
☎0121 236 0863
✉clerks@stiveschambers.co.uk
Call Date: July 1986, Gray's Inn
Pupil Supervisor
Qualifications: [Dip Mag Law]
✉david.jackson@stiveschambers.co.uk

JACKSON MISS FIONA ROSALIND

Chambers of Andrew Mitchell QC
33 Chancery Lane, London WC2A 1EN,
☎020 7440 9950 ✉clerks@33cllaw.com
Call Date: Nov 1998, Inner Temple
Qualifications: [LLB (Brunel)]
✉fj@33cllaw.com

JACKSON MR HUGH WOODWARD

Selborne Chambers
10 Essex Street, London WC2R 3AA,
☎020 7420 9500
✉clerks@selbornechambers.co.uk
Call Date: July 1981, Middle Temple
Pupil Supervisor
Qualifications: [LLB (Sheff) (Hons)]
✉hugh.jackson@selbornechambers.co.uk

JACKSON MR JOHN GREGORY

Park Lane Plowden
19 Westgate, Leeds LS1 2RD,
☎0113 228 5049
✉clerks@parklaneplowden.co.uk
Call Date: Oct 2006, Inner Temple
Qualifications: [LLB (Leeds)]
✉john.jackson@parklaneplowden.co.uk

JACKSON MISS JUDITH QC (1994)

Maitland Chambers
7 Stone Buildings, Lincoln's Inn, London WC2A 3SZ, ☎020 7406 1200
✉clerks@maitlandchambers.com
Call Date: Nov 1975, Inner Temple
Qualifications: [LLB (Hons) LLM (Lond)]
✉jjackson@maitlandchambers.com

JACKSON MR KEVIN ROY

Becket Chambers
17 New Dover Road, Canterbury, Kent CT1 3AS, ☎01227 786331
✉clerks@becket-chambers.co.uk
Call Date: Nov 1984, Middle Temple
Qualifications: [BA (Hons)(Law)]
✉kjackson@becket-chambers.co.uk

JACKSON MR MARK JOSEPH

No 8 Chambers
8 Fountain Court, Steelhouse Lane, Birmingham B4 6DR, ☎0121 236 5514
✉clerks@no8chambers.co.uk
Call Date: Oct 1997, Lincoln's Inn
Qualifications: [MA (Keele) LLB (Hons)(B'ham)]
✉markjackson@no8chambers.co.uk

JACKSON MR MATTHEW DAVID EVERARD

Hailsham Chambers
Ground Floor, 4 Paper Buildings, Temple, London EC4Y 7EX, ☎020 7643 5000
✉clerks@hailshamchambers.com
Call Date: July 1986, Middle Temple
Qualifications: [MA(Cantab)]
✉matthew.jackson@hailshamchambers.com

JACKSON MR MYLES GERALD

Chambers of Mr M G Jackson
37 Old Deer Park Gardens, Richmond, Surrey TW9 2TN, ☎ 020 8251 7661
✉ mylesgjackson@hotmail.com
Call Date: Oct 1995, Lincoln's Inn
Qualifications: [LLB (Hons)(Lond) MA (York)]

JACKSON MR NICHOLAS DAVID KINGSLEY

Atlantic Chambers
4-6 Cook Street, Liverpool L2 9QU,
☎ 0151 236 4421
✉ info@atlanticchambers.co.uk
Call Date: Nov 1992, Lincoln's Inn
Pupil Supervisor
Qualifications: [LLB (Hons)(Newc)]
✉ nicholasjackson@atlanticchambers.co.uk

Types of work: Chancery (general), Commercial litigation, Commercial property, Copyright, Equity, Family provision, Insolvency, Landlord and tenant, Partnerships, Passing off, Planning, Professional negligence, Real property, Succession, Trademarks, Trusts, Wills

JACKSON MR PAUL

5 King's Bench Walk
5 King's Bench Walk, Temple, London EC4Y 7DN, ☎ 020 7353 5638
✉ clerks@5kbw.co.uk
Call Date: July 2002, Inner Temple
Qualifications: [LLB (So'ton)]
✉ paul.jackson@5kbw.co.uk

JACKSON MISS PHILIPPA CHARLOTTE

4-5 Gray's Inn Square
Gray's Inn, London WC1R 5AH,
☎ 020 7404 5252 ✉ clerks@4-5.co.uk
Call Date: Oct 2008, Lincoln's Inn
Qualifications: [BA (Oxon)]

JACKSON MISS ROSEMARY ELIZABETH QC (2006)

Keating Chambers
15 Essex Street, London WC2R 3AA,
☎ 020 7544 2600
✉ clerks@keatingchambers.com
Call Date: July 1981, Middle Temple
Recorder
Qualifications: [LLB (Lond) CEDR AKC]

JACKSON MS RUTH ELISABETH

Teucro Chambers
Global House, 1 Ashley Avenue, Epsom, Surrey KT18 5AD
Call Date: July 2002, Inner Temple
Qualifications: [BMus (Lond) CPE]

JACKSON MISS SALLY

New Court
Ground Floor, New Court, Temple, London EC4Y 9BE, ☎ 020 7583 5123
✉ clerks@newcourtchambers.com
Call Date: Oct 2006, Lincoln's Inn
Qualifications: [BA (Cantab)]
✉ sjackson@newcourtchambers.com

JACKSON MISS SAMANTHA JANE

1 Chancery Lane
London WC2A 1LF, ☎ 0845 634 6666
✉ clerks@1chancerylane.com
Call Date: Nov 1996, Middle Temple
Qualifications: [LLB (Hons) LLM]
✉ SJackson@1chancerylane.com

JACKSON MR SIMON MALCOLM DERMOT QC (2003)

Park Court Chambers
16 Park Place, Leeds LS1 2SJ,
☎ 0113 243 3277
✉ clerks@parkcourtchambers.co.uk
9 St John Street
Manchester M3 4DN, ☎ 0161 955 9000
✉ civilclerks@9sjs.com / criminalclerks@9sjs.com
Temple Garden Chambers
1 Harcourt Buildings, Temple, London EC4Y 9DA, ☎ 020 7583 1315
✉ clerks@tgchambers.com
Call Date: Nov 1982, Gray's Inn
Recorder
Qualifications: [LLB (Leeds)]
✉ sjackson@parkcourtchambers.co.uk

JACKSON MISS STEPHANIE

12 King's Bench Walk
12 King's Bench Walk, Temple, London EC4Y 7EL, ☎ 020 7583 0811
Call Date: Oct 1992, Inner Temple
Qualifications: [LLB (Reading)]
✉ jackson@12kbw.co.uk

JACKSON MR WAYNE THOMAS

Deans Court Chambers
24 St John Street, Manchester M3 4DF,
☎ 0161 214 6000 ✉ clerks@deanscourt.co.uk
Deans Court Chambers
101 Walker Street, Preston PR1 2RR,
☎ 01772 565 600
✉ preston@deanscourt.co.uk
Call Date: Nov 1984, Middle Temple
Qualifications: [LLB (Sheff)]
✉ jackson@deanscourt.co.uk

E

JACOB MR ISAAC ELLIS

9 Stone Buildings
Lincoln's Inn, London WC2A 3NN,
☎020 7404 5055
✉clerks@9stonebuildings.com
Call Date: July 1963, Lincoln's Inn
Pupil Supervisor
Qualifications: [LLB (Manchester) FCIArb]
clerks@9stonebuildings.com

JACOB MR VAUGHAN

Lamb Chambers
Lamb Building, Elm Court, Temple, London EC4Y 7AS, ☎020 7797 8300
✉info@lambchambers.co.uk
Call Date: Oct 2009, Middle Temple
Qualifications: [BA (Hons) (Warw)]
clerksroom@lambchambers.co.uk

JACOB MR WINSTON EDWARD HILDEBRAND

Lamb Chambers
Lamb Building, Elm Court, Temple, London EC4Y 7AS, ☎020 7797 8300
✉info@lambchambers.co.uk
Call Date: July 2005, Middle Temple
Qualifications: [BA (Hons) Oxon]

E

JACOBS MR ALEXANDER MARC

St Ive's Chambers
Whittall Street, Birmingham B4 6DH,
☎0121 236 0863
✉clerks@stiveschambers.co.uk
Call Date: Oct 1997, Gray's Inn
Pupil Supervisor
Qualifications: [LLB (Hons)(Manch)]
alexander.jacobs@stiveschambers.co.uk

JACOBS MISS AMY CAROLINE

St Ive's Chambers
Whittall Street, Birmingham B4 6DH,
☎0121 236 0863
✉clerks@stiveschambers.co.uk
Call Date: July 2005, Middle Temple
Qualifications: [BA (Hons)]
amy.jacobs@stiveschambers.co.uk

JACOBS MR CHRISTOPHER PETER

Landmark Chambers
180 Fleet Street, London EC4A 2HG,
☎020 7430 1221
✉clerks@landmarkchambers.co.uk
Call Date: Oct 1994, Lincoln's Inn
Qualifications: [LLB (Hons)(Hull)]
cjacobs@landmarkchambers.co.uk

JACOBS SIR FRANCIS GEOFFREY QC (1984)

Fountain Court Chambers
Fountain Court, Temple, London EC4Y 9DH,
☎020 7583 3335
✉chambers@fountaincourt.co.uk
Call Date: June 1964, Middle Temple
Qualifications: [MA DPhil (Oxon)]

JACOBS MISS LINDA DIANE

Cloisters
1 Pump Court, Temple, London EC4Y 7AA,
☎020 7827 4000 ✉clerks@cloisters.com
Call Date: Oct 2000, Middle Temple
Qualifications: [BSc (Hons) (Surrey) Dip Law RN LLM (Lond)]
lj@cloisters.com

JACOBS MS MICHAELLA PAULA

4 King's Bench Walk
2nd Floor, 4 King's Bench Walk, Temple, London EC4Y 7DL, ☎020 7822 7000
✉clerks@4kbw.co.uk
Call Date: July 2003, Middle Temple
Qualifications: [BA Hons (Manch) PG Dip Law]

JACOBS MR NIGEL ROBERT QC (2006)

Quadrant Chambers
Quadrant House, 10 Fleet Street, London EC4Y 1AU, ☎020 7583 4444
✉info@quadrantchambers.com
Call Date: Nov 1983, Middle Temple
Qualifications: [BA LLM (Cantab)]
nigel.jacobs@quadrantchambers.com

JACOBS MR RICHARD DAVID QC (1998)

Essex Court Chambers
24 Lincoln's Inn Fields, London WC2A 3EG,
☎020 7813 8000
✉clerksroom@essexcourt.net
Call Date: Nov 1979, Middle Temple
Qualifications: [BA (Cantab)]
rjacobs@essexcourt.net

JACOBS MR ROBIN EDWARD

Hardwicke
New Square, Lincoln's Inn, London WC2A 3SB, ☎020 7242 2523
✉enquiries@hardwicke.co.uk
Call Date: July 2006, Middle Temple
Qualifications: [BA (Hons) (Cantab)]
robin.jacobs@hardwicke.co.uk

JACOBSON MR LAWRENCE

Five Paper
Ground Floor, 5 Paper Buildings, Temple, London EC4Y 7HB, ☎ 020 7815 3200
Call Date: Nov 1985, Gray's Inn
Qualifications: [BA Dip Law LLB (South Africa)]
lawrencejacobson@fivepaper.com

JACOBSON MS MARY INGE

Maidstone Chambers
33 Earl Street, Maidstone, Kent ME14 1PF, ☎ 01622 688592
clerks@maidstonechambers.co.uk
Call Date: Oct 1992, Middle Temple
Qualifications: [MA (Cantab) LLB (Hons)(Lond)]

JACQUES MR GARETH EDWARD

Regency Chambers
45 Priestgate, Peterborough PE1 1LB, ☎ 01733 315215
clerks@regencychambers.law.co.uk
Call Date: Oct 2007, Inner Temple
Qualifications: [BA (Oxon)]
gjacques@regencychambers.law.co.uk

JACQUES MR TIMOTHY OLIVER

Cornwall Street Chambers
85-87 Cornwall Street, Birmingham B3 3BY, ☎ 0121 233 7500
clerks@cornwallstreet.co.uk
Call Date: Oct 2008, Middle Temple
Qualifications: [BA (Hons) (Oxon) Dip in Law]
tim.jacques@cornwallstreet.co.uk

JAFAR MR ABDURAHMAN AKHTAR

Chambers of Mr Abdurahman Jafar
16 Madras Road, Ilford, Essex IG1 2EY, ☎ 07828 937338
abdurahmanjafar@yahoo.co.uk
Call Date: Nov 1997, Lincoln's Inn
Qualifications: [LLB (Hons)]
abdurahmanjafar@yahoo.co.uk

JAFFA MR RONALD MERVYN

25 Bedford Row
London WC1R 4HD, ☎ 020 7067 1500
clerks@25bedfordrow.com
Call Date: July 1974, Gray's Inn
Pupil Supervisor
Qualifications: [LLB]
rjaffa@25bedfordrow.com

JAFFERJEE MR AFTAB ASGER QC (2008)

Atkinson Bevan Chambers
1st Floor, 2 Harcourt Buildings, Temple, London EC4Y 9DB, ☎ 020 7353 2112
clerks@2hb.co.uk
Call Date: Nov 1980, Inner Temple
Qualifications: [BA (Dunelm)]

JAFFERJI MR ZAINULABEDIN HATIM

Chambers of Mr Jafferji
89 Lamborne Road, Leicester LE2 6HQ, ☎ 07957 198777 zjafferji@gmail.com
Call Date: Mar 1999, Lincoln's Inn
Qualifications: [BSc (Hons) (Lond)]

JAFFEY MR BEN WILLIAM

Blackstone Chambers
Blackstone House, Temple, London EC4Y 9BW, ☎ 020 7583 1770
clerks@blackstonechambers.com
Call Date: Oct 1999, Middle Temple
Pupil Supervisor
Qualifications: [BA (Hons)(Cantab)]
benjaffey@blackstonechambers.com

JAGADESHAM MR VIJAY PULLOORI

Chambers of Ian Macdonald QC
Garden Court North, 22 Oxford Court, Manchester M2 3WQ, ☎ 0161 236 1840
clerks@gcnchambers.co.uk
Call Date: July 2004, Inner Temple
Qualifications: [LLB Hons (Dunelm)]

JAGUTPAL MR PREVIN SING

4 Brick Court
4 Brick Court, Temple, London EC4Y 9AD, ☎ 020 7832 3200 clerks@4bc.co.uk
Call Date: Oct 2005, Middle Temple
Qualifications: [BA (Hons) (Warw)]
previn.jagutpal@4bc.co.uk

JAISRI MR SHASHI SATYENDRA

1 Mitre Court Buildings
1 Mitre Court Buildings, Temple, London EC4Y 7BS, ☎ 020 7452 8900
clerks@1mcb.com
Call Date: Nov 1995, Lincoln's Inn
Qualifications: [LLB (Hons)]

E

JAJA MS AFOLAKE SASEGBON

Blackfriars Chambers
79-83 Temple Chambers, 3-7 Temple Avenue, London EC4Y 0HP, ☎020 7353 7400
✉clerks@blackfriarschambers.com
Call Date: Nov 1989, Gray's Inn
Pupil Supervisor
Qualifications: [LLB LLM (Lond)]
✉afolake.jaja@blackfriarschambers.com

JAMAL MISS ISABEL LEILA

8 New Square
8 New Square, Lincoln's Inn, London WC2A 3QP, ☎020 7405 4321
✉clerks@8newsquare.co.uk
Call Date: Nov 2008, Lincoln's Inn
Qualifications: [MPHIL (Oxon) CPE OBPP]

Types of work: Biotechnology, Breach of confidence, Commercial contracts, Competition law, Confidential information, Copyright, Copyright theft, Copyright Tribunal, Cultural property law, Design, Passing off, Patents, Pharmaceuticals, Registered designs, Scientific and technical disputes, Technical contracts, Trade secrets, Trademarks, Unregistered designs

E

JAMES MR ALUN EDWARD

Temple Tax Chambers
1st Floor, 3 Temple Gardens, Temple, London EC4Y 9AU, ☎020 7353 7884
✉clerks@templetax.com
Exchange Chambers
One Derby Square, Derby Square, Liverpool L2 9XX, ☎0151 236 7747
✉info@exchangechambers.co.uk
Exchange Chambers
7 Ralli Courts, West Riverside, Manchester M3 5FT, ☎0161 833 2722
Call Date: Nov 1986, Middle Temple
Pupil Supervisor
Qualifications: [MA (Oxon) BCL]
✉clerks@templetax.com

JAMES MR BYRON DENNIS

14 Gray's Inn Square
14 Gray's Inn Square, Gray's Inn, London WC1R 5JP, ☎020 7242 0858
✉clerks@14gis.co.uk
Call Date: Oct 2006, Gray's Inn
Qualifications: [LLB]

JAMES MR CHRISTOPHER GLYNNE LAWRENCE

Angel Chambers
Ethos Building, Kings Road, Swansea SA1 8AS, ☎01792 464623
✉clerks@angelchambers.co.uk
Call Date: Nov 1997, Gray's Inn
Qualifications: [LLB (B'ham)]
✉chrisjames@angelchambers.co.uk

JAMES MR DAVID JOHN

Call Date: Oct 1998, Inner Temple
Pupil Supervisor
Qualifications: [BSc LLB]

JAMES MR EDWARD PETER

Ropewalk Chambers
24 The Ropewalk, Nottingham NG1 5EF, ☎0115 947 2581 ✉clerks@ropewalk.co.uk
Call Date: July 2002, Inner Temple
Pupil Supervisor
Qualifications: [MA (Hon) (Edin) CPE]
✉edwardjames@ropewalk.co.uk

JAMES MISS EMILY

5 Pump Court
Ground Floor, 5 Pump Court, Temple, London EC4Y 7AP, ☎020 7353 2532
✉clerks@5pumpcourt.com
Call Date: Nov 1999, Middle Temple
Pupil Supervisor
Qualifications: [BA (Hons)(Kent)]
✉emilyjames@5pumpcourt.com

JAMES MR GEORGE CHRISTOPHER MOHUN

No5 Chambers
Fountain Court, Steelhouse Lane, Birmingham B4 6DR, ☎0845 210 5555 ✉info@no5.com
No5 Chambers
Greenwood House, 4-7 Salisbury Court, London EC4Y 8AA, ☎0845 210 5555
No5 Chambers
38 Queen Square, Bristol BS1 4QS, ☎0845 210 5555
Call Date: July 1977, Middle Temple
Qualifications: [LLB]
✉cj@no5.com

JAMES MR GRAHAME HOWARD

Carmelite Chambers
9 Carmelite Street, London EC4Y 0DR, ☎020 7936 6300
✉clerks@carmelitechambers.co.uk
Call Date: Apr 1989, Gray's Inn
Qualifications: [LLB]
✉gjames@carmelitechambers.co.uk

JAMES MR HENRY TRISTRAM

13 King's Bench Walk
13 King's Bench Walk, Temple, London EC4Y 7EN, ☎ 020 7353 7204
✉ clerks@13kbw.co.uk
13 KBW
32 Beaumont Street, Oxford OX1 2NP, ☎ 01865 311066 ✉ clerks@13kbw.co.uk
Call Date: Nov 1999, Gray's Inn
Pupil Supervisor
Qualifications: [MA]
hjames@13kbw.co.uk

JAMES MR IAN FREDERICK

Octagon House
19 Colegate, Norwich NR3 1AT, ☎ 01603 623186
✉ clerks@octagonhouse.co.uk
Call Date: July 1981, Gray's Inn
Pupil Supervisor
Qualifications: [LLB (Lond)]

JAMES MISS JOANNA MARGARET

Apex
Harlech House, 20 Cathedral Road, Cardiff CF11 9LJ, ☎ 02920 232 032
✉ clerks@apexchambers.net
Call Date: July 2008, Middle Temple
Qualifications: [BA (Econ) (Hons) (Wales) BSc Dip in Law BScEcon PGDipLaw]
joanna.jones@apexchambers.net

JAMES MR MARK DAVID BARTON

Temple Garden Chambers
1 Harcourt Buildings, Temple, London EC4Y 9DA, ☎ 020 7583 1315
✉ clerks@tgchambers.com
Call Date: Nov 1987, Middle Temple
Pupil Supervisor
Qualifications: [MA (Oxon)]
mark.james@tgchambers.com

JAMES MR MICHAEL FRANK

Enterprise Chambers
43 Park Square, Leeds LS1 2NP, ☎ 0113 246 0391
✉ leeds@enterprisechambers.com
Enterprise Chambers
65 Quayside, Newcastle Upon Tyne NE1 3DE, ☎ 0191 222 3344
✉ newcastle@enterprisechambers.com
Call Date: Feb 1976, Lincoln's Inn
michaeljames@enterprisechambers.com

JAMES MR MICHAEL PETER

Park Lane Plowden
Lombard House, 4-8 Lombard Street, Newcastle Upon Tyne NE1 3AE, ☎ 0191 211 4087
✉ clerks@parklaneplowden.co.uk
Call Date: Nov 1989, Gray's Inn
Qualifications: [LLB]
michael.james@parklaneplowden.co.uk

JAMES MR NICHOLAS CHRISTOPHER

Argent Chambers
5 Bell Yard, London WC2A 2JR, ☎ 020 7556 5500
✉ briefsin@argentchambers.co.uk
Call Date: July 2001, Middle Temple
Qualifications: [BA (Hons) CPE]
n.james@argentchambers.co.uk

JAMES MR NIGEL

Clock Chambers
18 Waterloo Road, Wolverhampton WV1 4BL, ☎ 01902 313444
✉ clockchambers@btconnect.com
Call Date: Mar 2008, Inner Temple
Qualifications: [BSc (Open University)]
mail@clockchambers.com

JAMES MISS RACHAEL ELIZABETH

14 Gray's Inn Square
14 Gray's Inn Square, Gray's Inn, London WC1R 5JP, ☎ 020 7242 0858
✉ clerks@14gis.co.uk
Call Date: Oct 1992, Middle Temple
Qualifications: [BA (Hons) (Leics) Dip Law(Lond)]
RachaelJames@33bedfordrow.co.uk

JAMES MR RHODRI WILLIAM MARTIN

Chambers of Mr Ami Feder
Ground Floor, Lamb Building, Temple, London EC4Y 7AS, ☎ 020 7797 7788
✉ clerks@lambbuilding.co.uk
Lamb Building
22 Ship Street, Brighton BN1 1AD, ☎ 01273 820490
✉ admin@lambbuilding.co.uk
Chambers of Mr Ami Feder
Ground Floor, Lamb Building, Temple, London EC4Y 7AS, ☎ 020 7797 7788
✉ clerks@lambbuilding.co.uk
Call Date: July 2002, Inner Temple
Qualifications: [LLB (Cardiff)]

E

JAMES MR RODERICK IAN

Charter Chambers
33 John Street, London WC1N 2AT,
☎ 020 7618 4400
✉ clerks@charterchambers.com
Call Date: Mar 1999, Lincoln's Inn
Pupil Supervisor
Qualifications: [BA (Hons)]
roddy.james@charterchambers.com

JAMES MR RUSSELL JOHN

Devon Chambers
3 St Andrew Street, Plymouth PL1 2AH,
☎ 01752 661659
✉ clerks@devonchambers.co.uk
Call Date: July 2001, Lincoln's Inn
Qualifications: [LLB (Hons)]
russelljames@devonchambers.co.uk

JAMES MISS SHARON ANN SARAH

Angel Chambers
Ethos Building, Kings Road, Swansea SA1 8AS,
☎ 01792 464623
✉ clerks@angelchambers.co.uk
Call Date: Oct 1995, Gray's Inn
Qualifications: [LLB (Wales) LLM (Bris)]
sharonjames@angelchambers.co.uk

JAMES MRS VENICE IMOGEN

No 8 Chambers
8 Fountain Court, Steelhouse Lane,
Birmingham B4 6DR, ☎ 0121 236 5514
✉ clerks@no8chambers.co.uk
Call Date: July 1983, Lincoln's Inn
Qualifications: [BA (Warw) Dip Law (Lond)]
venicejames@no8chambers.co.uk

JAMES MISS VICTORIA JANE

No.6 Park Square
Leeds LS1 2LW, ☎ 0113 245 9763
✉ Tim@no6.co.uk
Call Date: Mar 2012, Inner Temple
james@no6.co.uk

JAMES MR WINSTON

64 Bridge Street
3rd Floor, 64 Bridge Street, Manchester
M3 3BN, ☎ 0845 083 3000
✉ mail@64bridgestreet.com
Clerksroom (Taunton)
Equity House, Administration Centre,
Blackbrook Park Avenue, Taunton, Somerset
TA1 2PX, ☎ 0845 083 3000
✉ mail@clerksroom.com
Clerksroom (London)
3rd Floor, 218 Strand, London WC2R 1AT,
☎ 0845 083 3000 ✉ mail@clerksroom.com
Call Date: Oct 1999, Middle Temple
Qualifications: [LLB (Hons)(Sussex)]
james@clerksroom.com

JAMES-MOORE MR SIWARD PATRICK JOSEPH

KCH Garden Square
1 Oxford Street, Nottingham NG1 5BH,
☎ 0115 941 8851
✉ clerks@kchgardensquare.co.uk
Call Date: July 2000, Lincoln's Inn
Qualifications: [LLB(Hons) (Derby)]

JAMESON MR BARNABY LUKE CONRAD

18 Red Lion Court
London EC4A 3EB, ☎ 020 7520 6000
✉ chambers@18rlc.co.uk
18 Red Lion Court (Annexe)
Thornwood House, 102 New London Road,
Chelmsford, Essex CM2 0RG,
☎ 01245 280880
Call Date: Nov 1993, Middle Temple
Qualifications: [BA (Hons)(Lond) CPE (Lond)]

JAMESON MR DANIEL ROBERT

Furnival Chambers
32 Furnival Street, London EC4A 1JQ,
☎ 020 7405 3232
Call Date: Nov 2004, Middle Temple
Qualifications: [LLB (Hons) (Sussex)]
djameson@furnivallaw.co.uk

JAMESON MR RODNEY MELLOR MAPLES QC (2003)

No.6 Park Square
Leeds LS1 2LW, ☎ 0113 245 9763
✉ Tim@no6.co.uk
New Court Chambers
3 Broad Chare, Newcastle Upon Tyne
NE1 3DQ, ☎ 0191 232 1980
✉ clerks@newcourt-chambers.co.uk
Call Date: July 1976, Middle Temple
Recorder
Qualifications: [BA (Hons) (York)]
jamesonqc@no6.co.uk

JAMIESON MR ALEXANDER WILLIAM

Charter Chambers
33 John Street, London WC1N 2AT,
☎ 020 7618 4400
✉ clerks@charterchambers.com
Call Date: Mar 2007, Gray's Inn
Qualifications: [MA (Cantab)]
alex.jamieson@charterchambers.com

JAMIESON MR ANTHONY GEORGE

Linenhall Chambers
1 Stanley Place, Chester CH1 2LU,
☎01244 348282
✉clerks@linenhallchambers.co.uk
Call Date: July 1974, Gray's Inn
Pupil Supervisor
Qualifications: [BA LLB (Wales)]

JAMIESON MRS FIONA MARY

Linenhall Chambers
1 Stanley Place, Chester CH1 2LU,
☎01244 348282
✉clerks@linenhallchambers.co.uk
Call Date: Nov 2002, Gray's Inn
Qualifications: [LLB]

JAMIESON MISS KATRINA ANN

2 Bedford Row
London WC1R 4BU, ☎020 7440 8888
✉clerks@2bedfordrow.co.uk
Call Date: July 2007, Gray's Inn
Qualifications: [LL.B (Manch)]
🖃kjamieson@2bedfordrow.co.uk

JAMIESON MR STUART OWEN

Park Lane Plowden
19 Westgate, Leeds LS1 2RD,
☎0113 228 5049
✉clerks@parklaneplowden.co.uk
Park Lane Plowden
Lombard House, 4-8 Lombard Street, Newcastle Upon Tyne NE1 3AE,
☎0191 211 4087
✉clerks@parklaneplowden.co.uk
Call Date: Oct 2003, Gray's Inn
Qualifications: [BA (Cantab)]
🖃Stuart.Jamieson@parklaneplowden.co.uk

JAMIL MISS YASMEEN

4 Brick Court
4 Brick Court, Temple, London EC4Y 9AD,
☎020 7832 3200 ✉clerks@4bc.co.uk
Call Date: Oct 1998, Lincoln's Inn
Qualifications: [LLB (Hons)(Notts)]
🖃yasmeen.jamil@4bc.co.uk

JANES MR JEREMY NICHOLAS

KCH Garden Square
1 Oxford Street, Nottingham NG1 5BH,
☎0115 941 8851
✉clerks@kchgardensquare.co.uk
Call Date: Oct 1992, Lincoln's Inn
Qualifications: [BA(Hons)(Bris) Dip Law]

JANNER THE HON DANIEL JOSEPH MITCHELL QC (2002)

23 Essex Street
London WC2R 3AA, ☎020 7413 0353
✉clerks@23es.com
Exchange Chambers
7 Ralli Courts, West Riverside, Manchester M3 5FT, ☎0161 833 2722
St Philips Chambers
55 Temple Row, Birmingham B2 5LS,
☎0121 246 7000 ✉clerks@st-philips.com
Call Date: July 1980, Middle Temple
Qualifications: [MA (Cantab)]

JANUSZ MR PIERRE PHILIP

3 Hare Court
3 Hare Court, Temple, London EC4Y 7BJ,
☎020 7415 7800 ✉clerks@3harecourt.com
Call Date: July 1979, Middle Temple
Pupil Supervisor
Qualifications: [BA (Lond)]
🖃pierrejanusz@3harecourt.com

JAPHETH MISS BETHAN

Linenhall Chambers
1 Stanley Place, Chester CH1 2LU,
☎01244 348282
✉clerks@linenhallchambers.co.uk
Call Date: Oct 1997, Gray's Inn
Qualifications: [LLB (Wales)]
🖃bethan@1stanleyplace.co.uk

JARMAIN MR STEPHEN ROBERT

1 Garden Court Family Law Chambers
Ground Floor, One Garden Court, Temple, London EC4Y 9BJ, ☎020 7797 7900
✉clerks@1gc.com
Call Date: July 2005, Middle Temple
Qualifications: [BSc PGDL]
🖃jarmain@1gc.com

JARMAN MR MARK CHRISTOPHER

4 Paper Buildings
1st Floor, 4 Paper Buildings, Temple, London EC4Y 7EX, ☎020 7427 5200
✉clerks@4pb.com
Call Date: Nov 1989, Inner Temple
Pupil Supervisor
Qualifications: [LLB (Hons)]
🖃mcj@4pb.com

E

JARMAN MR SAMUEL JAMES GUTHRIE

4 KBW
Ground Floor, 4 King's Bench Walk, Temple, London EC4Y 7DL, ☎020 7822 8822
✉law@4kbw.net
Lombard Chambers
1 Sekforde Street, Clerkenwell, London EC1R 0BE, ☎020 7107 2100
Call Date: July 1989, Inner Temple
Pupil Supervisor
Qualifications: [LLB (Lond)]
sja@4kbw.net

JARMOLA MR JUSTIN ANDREW MARK

St Ive's Chambers
Whittall Street, Birmingham B4 6DH, ☎0121 236 0863
✉clerks@stiveschambers.co.uk
Call Date: Oct 2009, Inner Temple
Qualifications: [BA (Manch)]
justin.jarmola@stiveschambers.co.uk

JARRATT MISS ALICE CORDELIA BETCHWORTH

Carmelite Chambers
9 Carmelite Street, London EC4Y 0DR, ☎020 7936 6300
✉clerks@carmelitechambers.co.uk
Call Date: Oct 2007, Inner Temple
Qualifications: [MA (Edin)]

JARRON MISS STEPHANIE ALLAN

Enterprise Chambers
65 Quayside, Newcastle Upon Tyne NE1 3DE, ☎0191 222 3344
✉newcastle@enterprisechambers.com
Enterprise Chambers
43 Park Square, Leeds LS1 2NP, ☎0113 246 0391
✉leeds@enterprisechambers.com
Enterprise Chambers
9 Old Square, Lincoln's Inn, London WC2A 3SR, ☎020 7405 9471
✉london@enterprisechambers.com
Call Date: Oct 1990, Lincoln's Inn
Pupil Supervisor
Qualifications: [BA MCIArb]

JARVIS MR JOHN MANNERS QC (1989)

3 Verulam Buildings
London WC1R 5NT, ☎020 7831 8441
✉chambers@3vb.com
Call Date: July 1970, Lincoln's Inn
Recorder
Qualifications: [MA (Cantab)]
jjarvis@3vb.com

JARVIS DR MALCOLM ANDREW

20 Essex Street
London WC2R 3AL, ☎020 7842 1200
✉clerks@20essexst.com
Call Date: Oct 1998, Middle Temple
Pupil Supervisor
Qualifications: [MA LLM (Cantab) LLD]
clerks@20essexst.com

JARVIS MR OLIVER MARTIN

Exchange Chambers
7 Ralli Courts, West Riverside, Manchester M3 5FT, ☎0161 833 2722
Exchange Chambers
One Derby Square, Derby Square, Liverpool L2 9XX, ☎0151 236 7747
✉info@exchangechambers.co.uk
Exchange Chambers
Oxford House, Oxford Row, Leeds LS1 3BE, ☎0113 203 1970
✉spencer@exchangechambers.co.uk
Call Date: Nov 1992, Inner Temple
Pupil Supervisor
Qualifications: [LLB]

JARVIS MR PAUL

6 King's Bench Walk
Ground Floor, 6 King's Bench Walk, Temple, London EC4Y 7DR, ☎020 7583 0410
✉clerks@6kbw.com
Call Date: Nov 2001, Lincoln's Inn
Pupil Supervisor
Qualifications: [MA (Hons) (Cantab)]

JASPAL MR KAMALJIT SINGH

Ropewalk Chambers
24 The Ropewalk, Nottingham NG1 5EF, ☎0115 947 2581 ✉clerks@ropewalk.co.uk
Call Date: Nov 2005, Lincoln's Inn
Qualifications: [LLB (Hons) (L'pool)]
kamjaspal@ropewalk.co.uk

E

JAWAD-SALLAR MS TARA

Clerksroom (London)
3rd Floor, 218 Strand, London WC2R 1AT, ☎0845 083 3000 ✉mail@clerksroom.com
Clerksroom (Taunton)
Equity House, Administration Centre, Blackbrook Park Avenue, Taunton, Somerset TA1 2PX, ☎0845 083 3000
✉mail@clerksroom.com
Call Date: Mar 2007, Middle Temple
Qualifications: [LLB (Hons) Dip Law CIA FCIArb]
✉tarasallar@tinet.ie

JAY MR CHRISTOPHER JOHN

Quadrant Chambers
Quadrant House, 10 Fleet Street, London EC4Y 1AU, ☎020 7583 4444
✉info@quadrantchambers.com
Call Date: Nov 2009, Inner Temple
Qualifications: [BA (Oxon) CPE (College of Law)]

JAY MR GRENVILLE RICHARD

Regent Chambers
Regent House, 3 Pall Mall, Hanley, Stoke On Trent ST1 1HP, ☎01782 286666
✉clerks@regentchambers.co.uk
Call Date: Nov 1975, Inner Temple
Qualifications: [MA (Cantab)]
✉grenville.jay@regentchambers.co.uk

JAY MR ROBERT MAURICE QC (1998)

39 Essex Street
London WC2R 3AT, ☎020 7832 1111
✉clerks@39essex.com
82 King Street
Manchester M2 4WQ, ☎0161 870 9969
Call Date: July 1981, Middle Temple
Recorder
Qualifications: [BA (Oxon)]
✉robert.jay@39essex.com

JAYAKRISHNAN MR HARRY SISUBALAN

Trent Chambers
9 Regent Street, Nottingham NG1 5BS, ☎0115 941 9596
✉clerks@trentchambers.co.uk
Call Date: Nov 2000, Middle Temple
Qualifications: [LLB (Hons) LLM (L'Pool)]

JEAKINGS MR CRAIG DEAN

Harcourt Chambers
1st Floor, 2 Harcourt Buildings, Temple, London EC4Y 9DB, ☎0844 561 7135
Call Date: Nov 2000, Inner Temple
Qualifications: [BSc (Portsmouth) CPE (Bris)]

JEANS MR CHRISTOPHER JAMES MARWOOD QC (1997)

11 King's Bench Walk
11 King's Bench Walk, Temple, London EC4Y 7EQ, ☎020 7632 8500
✉clerksroom@11kbw.com
Call Date: July 1980, Gray's Inn
Qualifications: [LLB (Lond) BCL (Oxon)]
✉christopher.jeans@11kbw.com

Fax: 020 7583 9123/3690;
Out of hours telephone: 07831 304714;
DX: 368 LDE;
URL: www.kbw.com

Types of work: Discrimination, Employment

Awards and memberships: Fellow of the Institute of Professional Development; Member of Employment Law Bar Association; Member of Employment Lawyers Association; Bencher of Gray's Inn; Advisory Board Equality Law Reports.

Other professional experience: Two years as lecturer in law (Employment law and European Community law); City of London Polytechnic (1981-3); Employment Judge (Part-Time) 1998-2008; Recorder 2009- ; PresidentCommonwealth Secretariat Arbitral Tribunal 2010-

Languages spoken: French, German

Reported Cases: *Andrew Coulson v News Group Newspapers*, [2012] ICR 385 (High Court, proceeding to Court of Appeal), 2011. Claim by editor for indemnity under compromise agreement
Haq v Audit Commission, To be reported (EAT and Court of Appeal), 2011. Genuine material factor defence in equal pay
Proactive Sports Management v Wayne Rooney and others, [2012] IRLR 241 (Court of Appeal), 2011. Restraint of trade concerning footballer's commercial rights
Wardle v Calyon, [2011] ICR 1290 (Court of Appeal), 2011. Career loss in discrimination
Williams v British Airways, [2010] IRLR 541 (Supreme Court) [2011] IRLR 948 (ET, EAT, Court of Appeal, Supreme Court (two hearings), CJEU), 2011. Computation of leave pay under Working Time Directives

JEARY MR STEPHEN JOHN

30 Park Place
Cardiff CF10 3BS, ☎029 2039 8421
✉clerks@30parkplace.law.co.uk
Call Date: July 1987, Inner Temple
Qualifications: [LLB APMI]

E

JEAVONS MS ANNE ELIZABETH

3 Verulam Buildings
London WC1R 5NT, ☎ 020 7831 8441
✉ chambers@3vb.com
Call Date: Nov 2008, Middle Temple
Qualifications: [BA (Hons)(Oxon) BCL (Oxon)]
✉ ajeavons@3vb.com

JEBB MR ANDREW JOHN

Exchange Chambers
One Derby Square, Derby Square, Liverpool L2 9XX, ☎ 0151 236 7747
✉ info@exchangechambers.co.uk
Exchange Chambers
Oxford House, Oxford Row, Leeds LS1 3BE, ☎ 0113 203 1970
✉ spencer@exchangechambers.co.uk
Call Date: Oct 1993, Gray's Inn
Pupil Supervisor
Qualifications: [LLB (Hons) (Exon)]
✉ jebb@exchangechambers.co.uk

JEFFERIES MR ANDREW QC (2009)

Dyers Chambers
35 Bedford Row, London WC1R 4JH, ☎ 020 7404 1881
✉ admin@dyerschambers.com
Westgate Chambers
64 High Street, Lewes, East Sussex BN7 1XG, ☎ 01273 480510
✉ clerks@westgate-chambers.co.uk
Call Date: Oct 1990, Middle Temple
Qualifications: [LLB (UEA)]

JEFFERIES MR THOMAS ROBERT

Landmark Chambers
180 Fleet Street, London EC4A 2HG, ☎ 020 7430 1221
✉ clerks@landmarkchambers.co.uk
Call Date: Nov 1981, Middle Temple
Pupil Supervisor
Qualifications: [BA Dip Law]

JEFFERIS MR ARTHUR MICHAEL QUENTIN

13 Old Square Chambers
Ground Floor, 14 Old Square, Lincoln's Inn, London WC2A 3UE, ☎ 020 7831 4445
✉ clerks@13oldsquare.com
Atlas Chambers
3 Field Court, Gray's Inn, London WC1R 5EP, ☎ 020 7269 7980
✉ clerks@atlaschambers.com
Call Date: July 1976, Middle Temple
Pupil Supervisor
Qualifications: [LLB (Hons) (Lond) AKC]
✉ michaeljefferis@13oldsquare.com

JEFFERSON MISS HELEN SUSAN

2-3 Hind Court Chambers
2-3 Hind Court, Fleet Street, London EC4A 3DL, ☎ 020 7822 2150
✉ david@2-3hindcourt.com
Call Date: Oct 2000, Lincoln's Inn
Qualifications: [LLB (Hons) (B'Ham)]

JEFFORD MISS NERYS ANGHARAD QC (2008)

Keating Chambers
15 Essex Street, London WC2R 3AA, ☎ 020 7544 2600
✉ clerks@keatingchambers.com
Call Date: Nov 1986, Gray's Inn
Recorder
Qualifications: [MA (Oxon) LLM (USA)]
✉ njefford@keatingchambers.com

JEFFREYS MR ALAN HOWARD QC (1996)

Farrar's Building
Farrar's Building, Temple, London EC4Y 7BD, ☎ 020 7583 9241
✉ Chambers@farrarsbuilding.co.uk
Call Date: July 1970, Gray's Inn
Qualifications: [LLB]
✉ ajeffreys@farrarsbuilding.co.uk

JEGARAJAH MISS SHIVANI

Renaissance Chambers
5th Floor, Gray's Inn Chambers, Gray's Inn, London WC1R 5JA, ☎ 020 7404 1111
✉ clerks@renaissancechambers.co.uk
Call Date: July 1993, Middle Temple
Qualifications: [BA (Hons)(Lond)]
✉ sj@renaissancechambers.co.uk

JELF MR SIMON EDWARD

48 Bedford Row
London WC1R 4LR, ☎ 020 7430 2005
✉ tyroon@partnershipcounsel.co.uk
Call Date: Oct 1996, Gray's Inn
Qualifications: [LLB]
✉ sjelf@partnershipcounsel.co.uk

JENKING-REES MISS LAURA

Guildhall Chambers Portsmouth
Prudential Buildings, 16 Guildhall Walk, Portsmouth, Hampshire PO1 2DE, ☎ 023 9275 2400
✉ clerks@gcp-barristers.com
Call Date: Mar 2002, Lincoln's Inn
Pupil Supervisor
Qualifications: [LLB (Hons)]
✉ GCPClerks@fsmail.net

JENKINS MR ALAN MICHAEL

Outer Temple Chambers
The Outer Temple, 222 Strand, London WC2R 1BA, ☎020 7353 6381
✉clerks@outertemple.com
Call Date: Feb 1984, Middle Temple
Pupil Supervisor
Qualifications: [BA (Warw) DipLaw (Lond)]
alan.jenkins@outertemple.com

JENKINS MR ALUN AUSTEN

Goldsmith Chambers
Ground Floor, Goldsmith Building, Temple, London EC4Y 7BL, ☎020 7353 6802
✉clerks@goldsmithchambers.com
Call Date: May 1981, Gray's Inn
Pupil Supervisor
Qualifications: [LLB (Warw)]
A.Jenkins@goldsmithchambers.law.co.uk

JENKINS MR BENJAMIN EDWARD

Albion Chambers
Broad Street, Bristol BS1 1DR,
☎0117 927 2144
✉clerks@albionchambers.co.uk
Call Date: July 2004, Gray's Inn
Qualifications: [LLB (Cardiff)]
benjamin.jenkins@albionchambers.co.uk

JENKINS MISS CATHERINE PHILLIDA

1 Garden Court Family Law Chambers
Ground Floor, One Garden Court, Temple, London EC4Y 9BJ, ☎020 7797 7900
✉clerks@1gc.com
Call Date: Nov 1990, Middle Temple
Qualifications: [BA (Keele)]
jenkins@1gc.com

JENKINS MISS CATRIN ANGHARAD

Angel Chambers
Ethos Building, Kings Road, Swansea SA1 8AS,
☎01792 464623
✉clerks@angelchambers.co.uk
Call Date: July 2010, Gray's Inn
Qualifications: [LLB]
catrin.jenkins@angelchambers.co.uk

JENKINS MR DAVID CROFTON

2 King's Bench Walk
2 King's Bench Walk, Temple, London EC4Y 7DE, ☎020 7353 1746
✉clerks@2kbw.com
Call Date: Nov 1967, Inner Temple
Pupil Supervisor
Qualifications: [LLB]
djenkins@2kbw.com

JENKINS MR EDWARD NICHOLAS QC (2000)

Five Paper Buildings
1st Floor, Five Paper Buildings, Temple, London EC4Y 7HB, ☎020 7583 6117
✉clerks@5pb.co.uk
Call Date: July 1977, Middle Temple
Recorder
Qualifications: [BA (Cantab)]
ej@5pb.co.uk

JENKINS MR HYWEL IESTYN

Outer Temple Chambers
The Outer Temple, 222 Strand, London WC2R 1BA, ☎020 7353 6381
✉clerks@outertemple.com
Call Date: July 1974, Inner Temple
Pupil Supervisor
Qualifications: [LLB]
hywel.jenkins@outertemple.com

JENKINS MR JAMES DOUGLAS

Linenhall Chambers
1 Stanley Place, Chester CH1 2LU,
☎01244 348282
✉clerks@linenhallchambers.co.uk
Call Date: July 2008, Middle Temple
Qualifications: [LLB (Hons) (Sheff)]
jamie.jenkins@linenhallchambers.co.uk

JENKINS MR JAMES JOHN

Iscoed Chambers
86 St Helen's Road, Swansea SA1 4BQ,
☎01792 652988
✉clerks@iscoedchambers.co.uk
Call Date: Nov 1974, Gray's Inn
Pupil Supervisor
Qualifications: [LLB]
jj@iscoedchambers.co.uk

JENKINS MR JEREMY DAVID

Apex
Harlech House, 20 Cathedral Road, Cardiff CF11 9LJ, ☎02920 232 032
✉clerks@apexchambers.net
Call Date: July 1984, Inner Temple
Pupil Supervisor
Qualifications: [BA]
jeremy.jenkins@apexchambers.net

JENKINS MISS JOANNE FRANCES

Wilberforce Chambers
7 Bishop Lane, Hull HU1 1PA,
☎01482 323264
Call Date: July 2009, Middle Temple
Qualifications: [LLB (Hons) (UEA)]

E

JENKINS MR PHILIP

St John's Chambers
101 Victoria Street, Bristol BS1 6PU,
☎0117 923 4700
✉clerks@stjohnschambers.co.uk
Call Date: Oct 2003, Middle Temple
Qualifications: [BA PhD]
philip.jenkins@stjohnschambers.co.uk

JENKINS MISS PHILIPPA EMILY

New Court
Ground Floor, New Court, Temple, London EC4Y 9BE, ☎020 7583 5123
✉clerks@newcourtchambers.com
Call Date: Nov 2008, Middle Temple
Qualifications: [LLB (Hons) (Lond)]
pjenkins@newcourtchambers.net

JENKINS MR ROWAN MATTHEW

Crown Office Row Chambers
119 Church Street, Brighton, Sussex BN1 1UD, ☎01273 625625
✉clerks@1cor.com
Call Date: Nov 1994, Lincoln's Inn
Pupil Supervisor
Qualifications: [MA D Phil CPE]
rowan.jenkins@1cor.com

JENKINS MISS SUSAN HELEN

Angel Chambers
Ethos Building, Kings Road, Swansea SA1 8AS,
☎01792 464623
✉clerks@angelchambers.co.uk
Call Date: Nov 1998, Gray's Inn
Qualifications: [BSc PgDip Law]
susanjenkins@angelchambers.co.uk

JENKINS MR THOMAS ALUN QC (1996)

Queen Square Chambers
56 Queen Square, Bristol BS1 4PR,
☎0117 921 1966 ✉crime@qs-c.co.uk
2 Bedford Row
London WC1R 4BU, ☎020 7440 8888
✉clerks@2bedfordrow.co.uk
Call Date: July 1972, Lincoln's Inn
Recorder
Qualifications: [LLB (Hons)(Brist)]

JENKINSON MR LEE DAVID

Number 7 Harrington Street Chambers
7 Harrington Street, Liverpool L2 9YH,
☎0151 242 0707 ✉clerks@7hs.co.uk
Call Date: Mar 2001, Gray's Inn
Qualifications: [LLB]
lee.jenkinson@7hs.co.uk

JENNINGS MISS CAROLINE MARY

No5 Chambers
Greenwood House, 4-7 Salisbury Court, London EC4Y 8AA, ☎0845 210 5555
No5 Chambers
38 Queen Square, Bristol BS1 4QS,
☎0845 210 5555
No5 Chambers
Fountain Court, Steelhouse Lane, Birmingham B4 6DR, ☎0845 210 5555 ✉info@no5.com
Call Date: Oct 2010, Lincoln's Inn
Qualifications: [BA (Leeds)]

JENNINGS MR PETER NIGEL

3 PB Barristers
3 Paper Buildings, Temple, London EC4Y 7EU,
☎020 7583 8055
3 PB Barristers
Royal Talbot House, 2 Victoria Street, Bristol, Avon BS1 6BB, ☎0117 928 1520
3 PB Barristers
4 St Peter Street, Winchester SO23 8BW,
☎01962 868884
✉clerks.winchester@3paper.co.uk
3 PB Barristers
23 Beaumont Street, Oxford OX1 2NP,
☎01865 793 736
3 PB Barristers
30 Christchurch Road, Bournemouth, Dorset BH1 3PD, ☎01202 292102
✉clerks.bournemouth@3paper.co.uk
Portal Chambers
Blaencwm Mawr, Llandysul SA44 5NS,
☎01559 395 292
Call Date: July 1972, Middle Temple
Pupil Supervisor
Qualifications: [MA (Cantab) LLM (Lond)]

JENNINGS MISS SARAH ANNE

Queen Square Chambers
56 Queen Square, Bristol BS1 4PR,
☎0117 921 1966 ✉crime@qs-c.co.uk
Call Date: Oct 2009, Inner Temple
Qualifications: [LL (Bris) LLM (Leeds)]
saj@qs-c.co.uk

JENNS MR TIMOTHY RODERICK

7 King's Bench Walk
Ground Floor, 7 King's Bench Walk, Temple, London EC4Y 7DS, ☎020 7910 8300
✉clerks@7kbw.co.uk
Call Date: Nov 2009, Lincoln's Inn
Qualifications: [LLB BA (Hons) (New Zealand) BCL (Oxon)]

E

JEPSON MRS AMANDA JANE

1 Gray's Inn Square
Ground Floor, 1 Gray's Inn Square, London WC1R 5AA, ☎ 020 7405 0001
Call Date: Oct 2005, Gray's Inn
Qualifications: [LLB (Hons) (Lond) LLM (Lond)]
ajepson@1gis.co.uk

JERAM MISS KIRTI

Park Lane Plowden
Lombard House, 4-8 Lombard Street, Newcastle Upon Tyne NE1 3AE, ☎ 0191 211 4087
✉ clerks@parklaneplowden.co.uk
Call Date: Nov 1996, Gray's Inn
Qualifications: [LLB (Hons) (Newc)]
kirti.jeram@parklaneplowden.co.uk

JEREMY MR DAVID HUGH THOMAS QC (2006)

QEB Hollis Whiteman
1-2 Laurence Pountney Hill, London EC4R 0EU, ☎ 020 7933 8855
✉ barristers@qebhw.co.uk
Call Date: July 1977, Middle Temple
Recorder
Qualifications: [LLB]

JERMAN MR ANTHONY IVAN

42 Bedford Row
London WC1R 4LL, ☎ 020 7831 0222
✉ clerks@42br.com
Call Date: Nov 1989, Middle Temple
Pupil Supervisor
Qualifications: [BA (Hons) (Lond) DipLaw]
anthony.jerman@42br.com

JERRAM MS HARRIET ANNE

Outer Temple Chambers
The Outer Temple, 222 Strand, London WC2R 1BA, ☎ 020 7353 6381
✉ clerks@outertemple.com
Call Date: Oct 1998, Gray's Inn
Qualifications: [MA (Cantab)]
harriet.jerram@outertemple.com

Types of work: Clinical negligence, Healthcare law, Medical negligence, Personal injury, Professional negligence, Public inquiries, Regulatory and disciplinary law

JERVIS MR CHRISTOPHER ROBERT

Albion Chambers
Broad Street, Bristol BS1 1DR, ☎ 0117 927 2144
✉ clerks@albionchambers.co.uk
Call Date: July 1966, Inner Temple
Pupil Supervisor
Qualifications: [MA (Oxon)]
christopher.jervis@albionchambers.co.uk

JESHANI MR SURESH

Temple Court Chambers
2nd Floor, 2 Dr Johnson's Building, Temple, London EC4Y 7AY, ☎ 020 7353 7888
✉ clerks@templecourt.co.uk
Call Date: Oct 2002, Lincoln's Inn
Qualifications: [LLB (Hons) (Lancaster) LLM (UCL)]
clerks@templecourt.co.uk

JESS DR DIGBY CHARLES

Exchange Chambers
7 Ralli Courts, West Riverside, Manchester M3 5FT, ☎ 0161 833 2722
Exchange Chambers
One Derby Square, Derby Square, Liverpool L2 9XX, ☎ 0151 236 7747
✉ info@exchangechambers.co.uk
Exchange Chambers
Oxford House, Oxford Row, Leeds LS1 3BE, ☎ 0113 203 1970
✉ spencer@exchangechambers.co.uk
Call Date: July 1978, Gray's Inn
Pupil Supervisor
Qualifications: [BSc (Hons) (Aston) LLM (Manch) PhD (Manch) FCIArb CArb TECBAR Arbitrator (2011)]
jess@exchangechambers.co.uk

Fax: 0161 833 2789;
DX: 14330 Manchester 1

Other professional qualifications: TECBAR Arbitrator (2011); Chartered Arbitrator (1999); FCIArb (1992)

Types of work: Arbitration, Commercial litigation, Common law (general), Construction law, Insurance, Professional negligence, Regulatory and disciplinary law

Circuit: Northern

Awards and memberships: Treasury Counsel (Northern Region Panel A) 1990-2003

Other professional experience: Arbitrator; Legal Assessor to General Medical Council Fitness to Practise Panels; Panel Member of ACCA Disciplinary and Licensing Committees; Legal Advisor to General Dental Council Fitness to Practise Committees.

E

Publications: The Insurance of Professional Negligence Risks: Law & Practice (Butterworths), 2011 (4th edn); Professional Indemnity Insurance Law (Sweet & Maxwell), 1989 (2nd edn); Butterworths Insurance Law Handbook (editor), 1992 (3rd edn); The Encyclopaedia of Forms & Precedents Vol 20 (Butterworths), 1988 (5th edn); The Insurance of Professional Negligence Risks: Law & Practice (Butterworths), 1989 (2nd edn)

Reported Cases: *EL Trigger Litigation*, [2012] 1 WLR 867 (Supeme Court), 2011. Construction of wilful default exclusion in household liability insurance.
Rolls Royce v Tyco Fire & Integrated Systems, [2008] BLR 285 (Court of Appeal), 2008. Joint contractors' insurance - coverage of package contractor - whether package contractor liable in negligence.
Patrick v Royal London Insurance, [2007] Lloyd's Rep IR 85 (Court of Appeal), 2007. Construction of wilful default exclusion in household liability insurance.
Bolton MBC v MMU & CU Insurance, [2006] 1 WLR 1492 (Court of Appeal), 2006. Test case to determine which public liability policy covers mesothelioma claims.
Doheny & Doheny v New India Assurance, [2005] Lloyd's Rep IR 251 (Court of Appeal), 2005. Proposal form question regarding previous bankruptcies - extent of duty of disclosure owed.

E

JESSOP MR STUART ANDREW

Nine Bedford Row
9 Bedford Row, London WC1R 4AZ,
☎ 020 7489 2727
✉ clerks@9bedfordrow.co.uk
Call Date: July 2002, Gray's Inn
Qualifications: [BSc (Lond)]
✉ stuart.jessop@9bedfordrow.co.uk

JESURUM MR RAPHAEL RENZO

Chambers of Mr Ami Feder
Ground Floor, Lamb Building, Temple, London EC4Y 7AS, ☎ 020 7797 7788
✉ clerks@lambbuilding.co.uk
Chambers of Mr Ami Feder
Ground Floor, Lamb Building, Temple, London EC4Y 7AS, ☎ 020 7797 7788
✉ clerks@lambbuilding.co.uk
Call Date: Nov 2006, Gray's Inn
Qualifications: [BSc MSc]
✉ r.jesurum@mitrehouse.co.uk

JEWELL MR MATTHEW

1 Paper Buildings
1st Floor, 1 Paper Buildings, Temple, London EC4Y 7EP, ☎ 020 7353 3728
✉ clerks@onepaper.co.uk
Call Date: Nov 1989, Lincoln's Inn
Pupil Supervisor
Qualifications: [BA (Oxon) Dip Law (Lond)]
✉ matthewjewell@onepaper.co.uk

JHITTAY MISS NARINDER KAUR

Maitland Chambers
7 Stone Buildings, Lincoln's Inn, London WC2A 3SZ, ☎ 020 7406 1200
✉ clerks@maitlandchambers.com
Call Date: July 2010, Lincoln's Inn
Qualifications: [BA (Cantab) BCL (Oxon)]
✉ njhittay@maitlandchambers.com

JIBOWU MR OLUMUYIWA OLUBUKUNOLA A.O.

Mount Pleasant Chambers
2 Mount Pleasant Lane, Bricket Wood, St Albans AL2 3UZ, ☎ 01923 678938
Call Date: Oct 1993, Middle Temple
Qualifications: [LLB (Hons)(Lond)]

JIMENEZ MATTSSON MISS LINA MARGARETA

Hardwicke
New Square, Lincoln's Inn, London WC2A 3SB, ☎ 020 7242 2523
✉ enquiries@hardwicke.co.uk
Call Date: July 2010, Lincoln's Inn
Qualifications: [LLB (Lanc)]

JINADU MR ABDUL-LATEEF ABODURIN OLAYINKA

Keating Chambers
15 Essex Street, London WC2R 3AA,
☎ 020 7544 2600
✉ clerks@keatingchambers.com
Call Date: Nov 1995, Middle Temple
Pupil Supervisor
Qualifications: [BA (Hons) LLM (Hons) (Cantab)]
✉ ajinadu@keatingchambers.com

JOB MR RICHARD LESLIE

Chambers of Mr Richard Job
16 Aberdeen Court, Aberdeen Park, London N5 2BH, ☎ 020 7226 3811
✉ richardjob11@gmail.com
Call Date: July 1998, Lincoln's Inn
Qualifications: [LLB (Hons)(Lond)]

JOBLING MR IAN MICHAEL THOMAS

2 Hare Court
Lower Ground, Ground, 1st & 2nd Floor, 2 Hare Court, Temple, London EC4Y 7BH, ☎ 020 7353 3982 ✉ clerks@2harecourt.com
Call Date: Nov 1982, Gray's Inn
Pupil Supervisor
Qualifications: [LLB (Lond)]
ianjobling@2harecourt.com

JOFFE MS NATASHA JULIET LOUISE

Outer Temple Chambers
The Outer Temple, 222 Strand, London WC2R 1BA, ☎ 020 7353 6381
✉ clerks@outertemple.com
Call Date: Oct 1992, Gray's Inn
Qualifications: [BA (Hons)]
natasha.joffe@outertemple.com

JOHAL MISS DEVINDER KAUR

5 Pump Court
Ground Floor, 5 Pump Court, Temple, London EC4Y 7AP, ☎ 020 7353 2532
✉ clerks@5pumpcourt.com
Call Date: Oct 1995, Gray's Inn
Qualifications: [LLB]

JOHAL MISS SUKI KAUR

3 Dr Johnson's Buildings
Ground Floor, 3 Dr Johnson's Buildings, Temple, London EC4Y 7BA, ☎ 020 7353 4854
✉ clerks@3djb.co.uk
Call Date: Nov 1991, Middle Temple
Pupil Supervisor
Qualifications: [LLB (Hons) (Wales)]
sukijohal@rocketmail.com

JOHN MR BENJAMIN DAVID

Maitland Chambers
7 Stone Buildings, Lincoln's Inn, London WC2A 3SZ, ☎ 020 7406 1200
✉ clerks@maitlandchambers.com
Call Date: Oct 2002, Inner Temple
Pupil Supervisor
Qualifications: [MChem CPE (Oxon) Dip Law]
bjohn@maitlandchambers.com

JOHN MISS CATRIN

30 Park Place
Cardiff CF10 3BS, ☎ 029 2039 8421
✉ clerks@30parkplace.law.co.uk
Call Date: Oct 1992, Gray's Inn
Qualifications: [LLB (Wales)]
ecj@30parkplace.co.uk

JOHN MS CHARLOTTE EMMA

Crown Office Row Chambers
119 Church Street, Brighton, Sussex BN1 1UD, ☎ 01273 625625
✉ clerks@1cor.com
Call Date: July 2008, Middle Temple
Qualifications: [BA (Hons) (So'ton) MA (Sussex) PgDl (Lond)]
charlotte.john@1cor.com

JOHN MISS KATHERINE VICTORIA

4 King's Bench Walk
2nd Floor, 4 King's Bench Walk, Temple, London EC4Y 7DL, ☎ 020 7822 7000
✉ clerks@4kbw.co.uk
Call Date: July 2010, Middle Temple
Qualifications: [BA (Hons) (Oxon)]

JOHN MISS LAURA ELIZABETH

Monckton Chambers
1 & 2 Raymond Buildings, Gray's Inn, London WC1R 5NR, ☎ 020 7405 7211
✉ chambers@monckton.com
Call Date: Oct 2007, Inner Temple
Qualifications: [BA BCL]
ljohn@monckton.com

JOHN MISS LAURA KATHERINE

3 Verulam Buildings
London WC1R 5NT, ☎ 020 7831 8441
✉ chambers@3vb.com
Call Date: Oct 2001, Gray's Inn
Pupil Supervisor
Qualifications: [BA (Oxon)]
laurajohn@3vb.com

JOHN MR MORGAN

Lamb Chambers
Lamb Building, Elm Court, Temple, London EC4Y 7AS, ☎ 020 7797 8300
✉ info@lambchambers.co.uk
Call Date: July 2004, Gray's Inn
Qualifications: [BA (Oxon)]
morganjohn@lambchambers.co.uk

JOHN MR PETER CHARLES

Five Paper
Ground Floor, 5 Paper Buildings, Temple, London EC4Y 7HB, ☎ 020 7815 3200
Call Date: Nov 1989, Inner Temple
Pupil Supervisor
Qualifications: [LLB (Lond)]
peterjohn@fivepaper.com

E

JOHN MR SIMON PAUL

12 King's Bench Walk
12 King's Bench Walk, Temple, London EC4Y 7EL, ☎ 020 7583 0811
Call Date: July 1996, Lincoln's Inn
Qualifications: [BA (Hons)(Wales)]
sjohn@12kbw.co.uk

JOHN MR THOMAS HUW

Goresbrook Chambers
PO Box 6017, Milton Keynes MK1 9AP, ☎ 0845 123 1234
thomas.john6@btinternet.com
Call Date: Oct 1997, Middle Temple
Qualifications: [LLB (Hons)(Lond) BPharm (Lond) MSc MRPharms]
thomas.john6@btinternet.com

JOHN-JULES MR CHARLES

Farringdon Chambers
180 Bermondsey Street, London SE1 3TQ, ☎ 020 7089 5700
Call Date: July 1983, Gray's Inn
Qualifications: [LLB (Hons) (So'ton)]
cjohn-jules@farringdon-law.co.uk

E

JOHNS MR ALAN GRANT

Maitland Chambers
7 Stone Buildings, Lincoln's Inn, London WC2A 3SZ, ☎ 020 7406 1200
clerks@maitlandchambers.com
Call Date: Oct 1994, Gray's Inn
Pupil Supervisor
Qualifications: [BA]
ajohns@maitlandchambers.com

JOHNS MR DAVID THOMAS

Pendragon Chambers
Suite 7, J Shed, Kings Road, SA1 Waterfront, Swansea SA1 8PL, ☎ 01792 411188
clerks@pendragonchambers.com
Call Date: Mar 2012, Gray's Inn

JOHNS MR RHYS ALLAN

Pendragon Chambers
Suite 7, J Shed, Kings Road, SA1 Waterfront, Swansea SA1 8PL, ☎ 01792 411188
clerks@pendragonchambers.com
Call Date: Nov 2005, Gray's Inn
Qualifications: [BA (Cantab)]

JOHNSON MISS AMANDA

Exchange Chambers
7 Ralli Courts, West Riverside, Manchester M3 5FT, ☎ 0161 833 2722
Exchange Chambers
One Derby Square, Derby Square, Liverpool L2 9XX, ☎ 0151 236 7747
info@exchangechambers.co.uk
Exchange Chambers
Oxford House, Oxford Row, Leeds LS1 3BE, ☎ 0113 203 1970
spencer@exchangechambers.co.uk
Call Date: Oct 1992, Gray's Inn
Qualifications: [LLB (Wales)]

JOHNSON MISS AMANDA JANE

36 Bedford Row
London WC1R 4JH, ☎ 020 7421 8000
chambers@36bedfordrow.co.uk
Call Date: Nov 1990, Middle Temple
Qualifications: [LLB (Lond)]
clerks@36bedfordrow.co.uk

JOHNSON MR ANDREW DAVID

Five Paper Buildings
1st Floor, Five Paper Buildings, Temple, London EC4Y 7HB, ☎ 020 7583 6117
clerks@5pb.co.uk
Call Date: Oct 2008, Lincoln's Inn
Qualifications: [BA (Cantab)]
aaj@5pb.co.uk

JOHNSON MR ANTHONY ROBERT

Temple Garden Chambers
1 Harcourt Buildings, Temple, London EC4Y 9DA, ☎ 020 7583 1315
clerks@tgchambers.com
Call Date: Nov 2006, Middle Temple
Qualifications: [MA (Hons) (Oxon)]

JOHNSON MRS CAROLYN ANN

Cobden House Chambers
19 Quay Street, Manchester M3 3HN, ☎ 0161 833 6000 Clerks@Cobden.co.uk
Call Date: Nov 1974, Gray's Inn
Pupil Supervisor
clerks@cobden.co.uk

JOHNSON MISS CHRISTINE MARGARET

Atlantic Chambers
4-6 Cook Street, Liverpool L2 9QU, ☎ 0151 236 4421
info@atlanticchambers.co.uk
Call Date: Nov 1991, Middle Temple
Qualifications: [LLB (Hons)]
christinejohnson@atlanticchambers.co.uk

JOHNSON MISS CLARA

3 Hare Court
3 Hare Court, Temple, London EC4Y 7BJ,
☎ 020 7415 7800 ✉ clerks@3harecourt.com
Call Date: Nov 2005, Inner Temple
Qualifications: [BA University College University of Oxford MA (Lond)]
✉ cjohnson@3harecourt.com

JOHNSON MR DAVID RICHARD

Atkin Chambers
1 Atkin Building, Gray's Inn, London WC1R 5AT, ☎ 020 7404 0102
✉ clerks@atkinchambers.com
Call Date: July 2010, Middle Temple
Qualifications: [BA (Hons) (Oxon)]

JOHNSON MR EDWIN GEOFFREY QC (2006)

Maitland Chambers
7 Stone Buildings, Lincoln's Inn, London WC2A 3SZ, ☎ 020 7406 1200
✉ clerks@maitlandchambers.com
Call Date: Nov 1987, Lincoln's Inn
Qualifications: [BA (Oxon)]
✉ ejohnson@maitlandchambers.com

JOHNSON MR GREGORY THOMAS

Carmelite Chambers
9 Carmelite Street, London EC4Y 0DR,
☎ 020 7936 6300
✉ clerks@carmelitechambers.co.uk
Call Date: Oct 1998, Inner Temple
Qualifications: [LLB (Sussex)]
✉ gjohnson@carmelitechambers.co.uk

JOHNSON MR JEREMY CHARLES QC (2011)

5 Essex Court
1st Floor, 5 Essex Court, Temple, London EC4Y 9AH, ☎ 020 7410 2000
✉ clerks@5essexcourt.co.uk
Call Date: Oct 1994, Middle Temple
Pupil Supervisor, Recorder
Qualifications: [MA (Hons)(Oxon)]
✉ johnson@5essexcourt.co.uk

JOHNSON MR JOHN RICHARD HENESEY

Regent Chambers
Regent House, 3 Pall Mall, Hanley, Stoke On Trent ST1 1HP, ☎ 01782 286666
✉ clerks@regentchambers.co.uk
Call Date: Oct 1993, Middle Temple
Qualifications: [MA (Hons)(Oxon) Dip B Admin CPE]

JOHNSON MS KATHRYN MARGARET

Lincoln House Chambers
Tower 12, The Avenue North, Spinningfields, 18-22 Bridge Street, Manchester M3 3BZ,
☎ 0161 832 5701
✉ info@lincolnhousechambers.com
Call Date: July 1989, Gray's Inn
Pupil Supervisor
Qualifications: [LLB (Sheff)]
✉ katherine.johnson@lincolnhousechambers.com

JOHNSON MISS LAURA WENDY

1 Chancery Lane
London WC2A 1LF, ☎ 0845 634 6666
✉ clerks@1chancerylane.com
Call Date: Oct 2001, Gray's Inn
Pupil Supervisor
Qualifications: [BA (Hons)(Oxon)]
✉ ljohnson@1chancerylane.com

JOHNSON MR LINDSAY CHARLES WHITLEY

Doughty Street Chambers
53-54 Doughty Street, London WC1N 2LS,
☎ 020 7404 1313
✉ enquiries@doughtystreet.co.uk
Call Date: Oct 1997, Inner Temple
Qualifications: [BSc (Brunel) MA (London)]

JOHNSON MISS MELANIE JANE

1 Pump Court
Elm Court, Temple, London EC4Y 7AB,
☎ 020 7842 7070
✉ (name)@pumpcourt.co.uk
Call Date: Oct 1996, Middle Temple
Pupil Supervisor
Qualifications: [BSc (Hons) (Bucks)]
✉ mj@1pumpcourt.co.uk

JOHNSON MR NICHOLAS JAMES

Exchange Chambers
Oxford House, Oxford Row, Leeds LS1 3BE,
☎ 0113 203 1970
✉ spencer@exchangechambers.co.uk
Exchange Chambers
One Derby Square, Derby Square, Liverpool L2 9XX, ☎ 0151 236 7747
✉ info@exchangechambers.co.uk
Call Date: Nov 1994, Inner Temple
Pupil Supervisor
Qualifications: [BA (York) CPE]
✉ johnson@exchangechambers.co.uk

E

JOHNSON MR NICHOLAS ROBERT QC (2006)

Number 7 Harrington Street Chambers
7 Harrington Street, Liverpool L2 9YH,
☎0151 242 0707 ✉clerks@7hs.co.uk
Call Date: July 1987, Inner Temple
Qualifications: [BA (Leeds)]
nicholas.johnson@7hs.co.uk

JOHNSON MR PAUL

Kings Chambers
36 Young Street, Manchester M3 3FT,
☎0845 034 3444
✉clerks@kingschambers.com
Kings Chambers
5 Park Square East, Leeds LS1 2NE,
☎0845 034 3444
✉clerks@kingschambers.com
Kings Chambers
Embassy House, 60 Church Street,
Birmingham B3 2DJ, ☎0845 034 3444
✉clerks@kingschambers.com
Call Date: Nov 2006, Gray's Inn
Qualifications: [LLB]

JOHNSON MR PHILLIP MICHAEL

Chambers of Mr P Johnson
8 Packington Street, London N1 8QB,
☎020 7288 2256
✉phill_m_johnson@hotmail.com
Call Date: Oct 1998, Inner Temple
Qualifications: [LLB (Dunelm) PG Dip (Lond) LLM (Lond) PhD (Lond)]
phill_m_johnson@hotmail.com

JOHNSON MR RODERICK STOWERS QC (2006)

Argent Chambers
5 Bell Yard, London WC2A 2JR,
☎020 7556 5500
✉briefsin@argentchambers.co.uk
Call Date: Nov 1975, Lincoln's Inn
Qualifications: [MA (Oxon)]
r.johnson@argentchambers.co.uk

JOHNSON MISS SARAH SUSAN

Kenworthy's Chambers
Arlington House, Bloom Street, Salford,
Manchester M3 6AJ, ☎0161 832 4036
Call Date: Oct 2001, Lincoln's Inn
Qualifications: [LLB (Hons) (Manch)]

JOHNSON MR SIMON MARMONT

Enterprise Chambers
9 Old Square, Lincoln's Inn, London
WC2A 3SR, ☎020 7405 9471
✉london@enterprisechambers.com
Enterprise Chambers
65 Quayside, Newcastle Upon Tyne NE1 3DE,
☎0191 222 3344
✉newcastle@enterprisechambers.com
Enterprise Chambers
43 Park Square, Leeds LS1 2NP,
☎0113 246 0391
✉leeds@enterprisechambers.com
Call Date: Oct 2000, Middle Temple
Qualifications: [MA (Oxon) CPE]
simonjohnson@enterprisechambers.com

JOHNSON MR SIMON NICHOLAS

Stour Chambers
Mill Studio, 17a Stour Street, Canterbury, Kent
CT1 2NR, ☎01227 764899
✉clerks@stourchambers.co.uk
Call Date: July 1987, Gray's Inn
Pupil Supervisor
Qualifications: [LLB (Hons) (Wales)]

JOHNSON MISS SUSANNAH MALEHLOHONOLO

Seven Bedford Row
7 Bedford Row, London WC1R 4BS,
☎020 7242 3555 ✉clerks@7br.co.uk
Call Date: Nov 1996, Middle Temple
Qualifications: [LLB (Hons)(Kent)]
sjohnson@7br.co.uk

JOHNSON MRS SYLVIA ELIZABETH

2-3 Hind Court Chambers
2-3 Hind Court, Fleet Street, London
EC4A 3DL, ☎020 7822 2150
✉david@2-3hindcourt.com
Call Date: Oct 1999, Middle Temple
Qualifications: [BSc (Georgia) LLB (Hons)(Herts)]

JOHNSON MISS ZOE ELISABETH QC (2012)

QEB Hollis Whiteman
1-2 Laurence Pountney Hill, London
EC4R 0EU, ☎020 7933 8855
✉barristers@qebhw.co.uk
Call Date: Nov 1990, Inner Temple
Pupil Supervisor
Qualifications: [BA (Oxon) Dip Law]
zoe.johnson@qebhw.co.uk

JOHNSTON MISS ANNE-MARIE

Carmelite Chambers
9 Carmelite Street, London EC4Y 0DR,
☎ 020 7936 6300
✉ clerks@carmelitechambers.co.uk
Call Date: Oct 1990, Inner Temple
Qualifications: [LLB]

JOHNSTON MR ANTHONY PAUL

St Philips Chambers
55 Temple Row, Birmingham B2 5LS,
☎ 0121 246 7000 ✉ clerks@st-philips.com
Call Date: Nov 1993, Middle Temple
Qualifications: [BA (Hons)(Cantab)]
✉ ajohnston@st-philips.com

JOHNSTON MISS CAREY ANN QC (2003)

18 Red Lion Court
London EC4A 3EB, ☎ 020 7520 6000
✉ chambers@18rlc.co.uk
18 Red Lion Court (Annexe)
Thornwood House, 102 New London Road, Chelmsford, Essex CM2 0RG,
☎ 01245 280880
Queen Square Chambers
56 Queen Square, Bristol BS1 4PR,
☎ 0117 921 1966 ✉ crime@qs-c.co.uk
Call Date: July 1977, Middle Temple
Qualifications: [LLM (Warwick)]
✉ carey.johnston@18rlc.co.uk

JOHNSTON MR CHRISTOPHER GEORGE QC (2011)

3 Serjeants Inn
London EC4Y 1BQ, ☎ 020 7427 5000
✉ clerks@3serjeantsinn.com
Call Date: Nov 1990, Gray's Inn
Pupil Supervisor
Qualifications: [MA (Cantab) (Hons)]
✉ cjohnston@3serjeantsinn.com

JOHNSTON MR CHRISTOPHER MARK

Chambers of Marion Smullen and Kerim Fuad QC
1 Inner Temple Lane, London EC4Y 1AF,
☎ 020 7427 4400 ✉ clerks@1itl.com
Call Date: Nov 1983, Gray's Inn
Pupil Supervisor
Qualifications: [BA LLB]

JOHNSTON MISS JUSTINE JANE

4 Paper Buildings
1st Floor, 4 Paper Buildings, Temple, London EC4Y 7EX, ☎ 020 7427 5200
✉ clerks@4pb.com
Call Date: Oct 1997, Middle Temple
Qualifications: [BA (Sydney) LLB (Hons)(Lond)]
✉ jj@4pb.com

JOHNSTON MISS SARAH LOUISE

Exchange Chambers
7 Ralli Courts, West Riverside, Manchester M3 5FT, ☎ 0161 833 2722
Exchange Chambers
One Derby Square, Derby Square, Liverpool L2 9XX, ☎ 0151 236 7747
✉ info@exchangechambers.co.uk
Exchange Chambers
Oxford House, Oxford Row, Leeds LS1 3BE,
☎ 0113 203 1970
✉ spencer@exchangechambers.co.uk
Call Date: July 2004, Gray's Inn
Qualifications: [LLB (Nott'm)]
✉ johnston@exchangechambers.co.uk

JOHNSTONE MR MARK ANTHONY

4 Paper Buildings
1st Floor, 4 Paper Buildings, Temple, London EC4Y 7EX, ☎ 020 7427 5200
✉ clerks@4pb.com
Call Date: July 1984, Inner Temple
Pupil Supervisor
Qualifications: [MSc (Lond) LLB (Lond)]
✉ mj@4pb.com

JOLLIE MRS MIRANDA MARY ELIZABETH

Blackfriars Chambers
79-83 Temple Chambers, 3-7 Temple Avenue, London EC4Y 0HP, ☎ 020 7353 7400
✉ clerks@blackfriarschambers.com
Call Date: Oct 2007, Middle Temple
Qualifications: [BA (Hons) (Oxon) LLB (Hons) (Lond)]

JOLLIFFE MR JOHN RAYMOND EDWARD ARTHUR

1 Crown Office Row
1 Crown Office Row, Temple, London EC4Y 7HH, ☎ 020 7797 7500
✉ mail@1cor.com
Call Date: Oct 2005, Inner Temple
Qualifications: [BA Trinity College Dublin CPE City University]
✉ john.jolliffe@1cor.com

E

JOLLIFFE MRS VICTORIA ESTHER JEAN

5RB
1st Floor, 5 Raymond Buildings, Gray's Inn, London WC1R 5BP, ☎ 020 7242 2902
✉ clerks@5rb.com
Call Date: Nov 2005, Lincoln's Inn
Qualifications: [BA (Hons) (Leeds) GDL]
✉ victoriajolliffe@5rb.com

JOLLY MS SCHONA KAUR

Cloisters
1 Pump Court, Temple, London EC4Y 7AA, ☎ 020 7827 4000 ✉ clerks@cloisters.com
Call Date: Oct 1999, Gray's Inn
Qualifications: [BA (Oxon)]
✉ sj@cloisters.com

JONATHAN-JONES MR GARETH

30 Park Place
Cardiff CF10 3BS, ☎ 029 2039 8421
✉ clerks@30parkplace.law.co.uk
Call Date: Oct 1991, Inner Temple
Qualifications: [LLB (Wales)]

JONES MR ALUN

St Paul's Chambers
5th Floor, St Paul's House, 23 Park Square South, Leeds LS1 2ND, ☎ 0113 245 5866
Call Date: July 2003, Lincoln's Inn
Qualifications: [BSc Hons (L'pool) MSc (Manch) PgDL SRO]

JONES MISS AMANDA VIOLET

Great James Street Chambers
37 Great James Street, London WC1N 3HB, ☎ 020 7440 4949
✉ chambers@greatjames.co.uk
Call Date: Nov 2001, Middle Temple
Qualifications: [LLB (Hons)]
✉ amanda.jones@greatjames.co.uk

JONES MISS AMY RUTH ELIZABETH

Assize Court Chambers
14 Small Street, Bristol BS1 1DE, ☎ 0117 926 4587 ✉ carly@assize.co.uk
Call Date: Oct 2010, Inner Temple
Qualifications: [BA (Oxon)]

JONES MR ANDREW CRAIG

30 Park Place
Cardiff CF10 3BS, ☎ 029 2039 8421
✉ clerks@30parkplace.law.co.uk
Call Date: Oct 1996, Inner Temple
Pupil Supervisor
Qualifications: [LLB (Bris)]
✉ andrew.jones@30parkplace.co.uk

JONES MS ANIKA MARSHA

1 Mitre Court Buildings
1 Mitre Court Buildings, Temple, London EC4Y 7BS, ☎ 020 7452 8900
✉ clerks@1mcb.com
Call Date: Mar 2002, Gray's Inn
Qualifications: [BSc]

JONES MR BENJAMIN WILLIAM

St Johns Buildings Liverpool
8th Floor India Buildings, Water Street, Liverpool L2 0XG, ☎ 0151 243 6000
✉ clerk@stjohnsbuildings.co.uk
16 Winckley Square
Preston PR1 3JJ, ☎ 01772 256100
St Johns Buildings
24a - 28 St John Street, Manchester M3 4DJ, ☎ 0161 214 1500
✉ clerk@stjohnsbuildings.co.uk
Call Date: Feb 1993, Middle Temple
Qualifications: [LLB (Hons)(L'pool)]

JONES MS BRONWEN ELSPETH

Tooks Chambers
81 Farringdon Street, London EC4A 4BL, ☎ 020 7842 7575 ✉ clerks@tooks.co.uk
Call Date: July 2009, Middle Temple
Qualifications: [BA (Canada) MA Post Grad Dip Law (Lond)]

JONES MISS CAROLYN NERYS

St Philips Chambers
55 Temple Row, Birmingham B2 5LS, ☎ 0121 246 7000 ✉ clerks@st-philips.com
Call Date: Oct 1995, Lincoln's Inn
Qualifications: [LLB (Hons)(Lond)]
✉ cjones@st-philips.com

JONES MISS CHARLOTTE

Crown Office Chambers
2 Crown Office Row, Temple, London EC4Y 7HJ, ☎ 020 7797 8100
✉ mail@crownofficechambers.com
Call Date: July 1982, Middle Temple
Pupil Supervisor, Recorder
Qualifications: [MA (Cantab)]
✉ jones@crownofficechambers.com

JONES MISS CHARLOTTE HEATHER

Old Square Chambers
3 Orchard Court, St Augustine's Yard, Bristol BS1 5DP, ☎ 0117 930 5100
✉ clerks@oldsquare.co.uk
Call Date: Oct 2008, Lincoln's Inn
Qualifications: [BA (Oxon)]
✉ cjones@oldsquare.co.uk

JONES MS CHERYL STEPHANIE

No5 Chambers
Greenwood House, 4-7 Salisbury Court, London EC4Y 8AA, ☎0845 210 5555
No5 Chambers
38 Queen Square, Bristol BS1 4QS, ☎0845 210 5555
No5 Chambers
Fountain Court, Steelhouse Lane, Birmingham B4 6DR, ☎0845 210 5555 ✉info@no5.com
Call Date: Oct 1996, Gray's Inn
Qualifications: [LLB (Lancs)]

JONES MR CHRISTOPHER DAVID HARRIES

St John's Chambers
101 Victoria Street, Bristol BS1 6PU, ☎0117 923 4700
✉clerks@stjohnschambers.co.uk
Call Date: July 2004, Gray's Inn
Qualifications: [LLB (Bristol)]
✉christopher.jones@stjohnschambers.co.uk

JONES MISS CLAIRE-LOUISE

Chavasse Court Chambers
18 Queen Avenue, Liverpool L2 4TX, ☎0151 229 2030
✉clerks@chavassechambers.co.uk
Call Date: Oct 1999, Lincoln's Inn
Qualifications: [LLB (Hons)(L'pool)]
✉claire.jones@chavassechambers.co.uk

JONES MISS CLARE LOUISE

Linenhall Chambers
1 Stanley Place, Chester CH1 2LU, ☎01244 348282
✉clerks@linenhallchambers.co.uk
Call Date: Oct 2006, Gray's Inn
Qualifications: [BA]
✉clerks@1stanleyplace.co.uk, clare.jones@linenhallchambers.co.uk

JONES MR CRAIG LYN

Iscoed Chambers
86 St Helen's Road, Swansea SA1 4BQ, ☎01792 652988
✉clerks@iscoedchambers.co.uk
Call Date: Nov 2003, Inner Temple
Qualifications: [BA (Cantab)]
✉cj@iscoedchambers.co.uk

JONES MR DANIEL

Argent Chambers
5 Bell Yard, London WC2A 2JR, ☎020 7556 5500
✉briefsin@argentchambers.co.uk
Call Date: Mar 2002, Gray's Inn
Qualifications: [LLB (Lond)]
✉djones@argent.co.uk

JONES MR DAVID ELWYN

2 Dr Johnson's Buildings
2 Dr Johnson's Buildings, Temple, London EC4Y 7AY, ☎020 7936 2613
✉clerks@2drj.com
Call Date: Oct 1996, Inner Temple
Qualifications: [BA (E.Ang) CPE]
✉d.jones@2drj.com

JONES MR DAVID JAMES

Garden Court Chambers
57-60 Lincoln's Inn Fields, London WC2A 3LJ, ☎020 7993 7600 ✉info@gclaw.co.uk
Call Date: Nov 1994, Lincoln's Inn
Qualifications: [LLB (Hons) LLM (Lond)]
✉davidj@gclaw.co.uk

JONES MR DAVID NICHOLAS

Broadway House Chambers
Broadway House, 9 Bank Street, Bradford, West Yorkshire BD1 1TW, ☎01274 722560
✉clerks@broadwayhouse.co.uk
Broadway House Chambers
25 Park Square West, Leeds, West Yorkshire LS1 2PW, ☎0113 246 2600
✉clerks@broadwayhouse.co.uk
Cloisters
1 Pump Court, Temple, London EC4Y 7AA, ☎020 7827 4000 ✉clerks@cloisters.com
Call Date: July 1985, Gray's Inn
Pupil Supervisor
Qualifications: [LLB (Hons) (Lond)]
✉dnj@broadwayhouse.co.uk

JONES MR EDWARD BARTLEY QC (1997)

Exchange Chambers
One Derby Square, Derby Square, Liverpool L2 9XX, ☎0151 236 7747
✉info@exchangechambers.co.uk
Exchange Chambers
7 Ralli Courts, West Riverside, Manchester M3 5FT, ☎0161 833 2722
13 Old Square Chambers
Ground Floor, 14 Old Square, Lincoln's Inn, London WC2A 3UE, ☎020 7831 4445
✉clerks@13oldsquare.com
Call Date: July 1975, Lincoln's Inn
Recorder
Qualifications: [BA (Hons)(Oxon)]
✉jonesqc@exchangechambers.co.uk

E

JONES MISS ELERI ANGHARAD

1 Garden Court Family Law Chambers
Ground Floor, One Garden Court, Temple, London EC4Y 9BJ, ☎ 020 7797 7900
✉ clerks@1gc.com
Call Date: July 2009, Middle Temple
Qualifications: [BA (Hons) (Cantab)]
✉ ejones@1gc.com

JONES MISS ELIZABETH SIAN QC (2000)

Serle Court
6 New Square, Lincoln's Inn, London WC2A 3QS, ☎ 020 7242 6105
✉ clerks@serlecourt.co.uk
Call Date: Nov 1984, Middle Temple
Qualifications: [BA (Cantab)]

JONES MISS EMILIE KATHERINE

Four New Square
Four New Square, Lincoln's Inn, London WC2A 3RJ, ☎ 020 7822 2000
✉ barristers@4newsquare.com
Call Date: July 2005, Middle Temple
Qualifications: [BA (Hons) BCL (Oxon)]
✉ e.jones@4newsquare.com

JONES MISS EMILY LOUISE

Temple Garden Chambers
1 Harcourt Buildings, Temple, London EC4Y 9DA, ☎ 020 7583 1315
✉ clerks@tgchambers.com
Call Date: July 2004, Middle Temple
Qualifications: [BA Hons (Oxon) MSt (Oxon) CPE]
✉ louisejones@tgchambers.com

JONES MISS EMMA LOUISE

One Essex Court
Ground Floor, One Essex Court, Temple, London EC4Y 9AR, ☎ 020 7583 2000
✉ clerks@oeclaw.co.uk
Call Date: July 2010, Inner Temple
Qualifications: [BA (Oxon) CPE]
✉ ejones@oeclaw.co.uk

JONES MR EMYR GWEIRYDD

9 Park Place
9 Park Place, Cardiff, South Glamorgan CF10 3DP, ☎ 029 2038 2731
✉ clerks@9parkplace.co.uk
Call Date: Oct 1999, Gray's Inn
Pupil Supervisor
Qualifications: [BA (Oxon) MPhil (Oxon)]
✉ emyrjones@9parkplace.co.uk

JONES MR FRANCIS HUMPHREY

Iscoed Chambers
86 St Helen's Road, Swansea SA1 4BQ, ☎ 01792 652988
✉ clerks@iscoedchambers.co.uk
Call Date: July 1980, Inner Temple
Pupil Supervisor
Qualifications: [MA (Oxon)]
✉ fj@iscoedchambers.co.uk

JONES MR GARETH EDWARD

Lincoln House Chambers
Tower 12, The Avenue North, Spinningfields, 18-22 Bridge Street, Manchester M3 3BZ, ☎ 0161 832 5701
✉ info@lincolnhousechambers.com
Call Date: Oct 2002, Middle Temple
Qualifications: [LLB (Wales)]
✉ gareth.jones@lincolnhousechambers.com

JONES MR GARETH JOHN

Civitas Chambers
Global Reach, Celtic Gateway, Cardiff Bay, Cardiff CF11 0SN, ☎ 0845 0713 007
✉ clerks@civitaslaw.com
Call Date: Feb 1992, Inner Temple
Pupil Supervisor
Qualifications: [MA (Cantab)]
✉ gareth.jones@civitaslaw.com

JONES MR GERAINT ANTHONY QC (2001)

Tanfield Chambers
2-5 Warwick Court, London WC1R 5DJ, ☎ 020 7421 5300
✉ clerks@tanfieldchambers.co.uk
9 St John Street
Manchester M3 4DN, ☎ 0161 955 9000
✉ civilclerks@9sjs.com / criminalclerks@9sjs.com
New Walk Chambers
27 New Walk, Leicester, Leicestershire LE1 6TE, ☎ 0871 200 1298 / 0116 255 9144
✉ clerks@newwalkchambers.co.uk
Call Date: July 1976, Middle Temple
Qualifications: [MA (Cantab) MCI Arb]
✉ geraintjones@tanfieldchambers.co.uk

JONES MR GERAINT MARTYN

Fenners Chambers
3 Madingley Road, Cambridge CB3 0EE, ☎ 01223 368761
✉ clerks@fennerschambers.com
Call Date: Nov 1972, Gray's Inn
Pupil Supervisor
Qualifications: [MA LLM (Cantab)]
✉ geraint.jones@fennerschambers.com

JONES MR GERALD WILLIAM

Number 7 Harrington Street Chambers
7 Harrington Street, Liverpool L2 9YH,
☎ 0151 242 0707 ✉ clerks@7hs.co.uk
Call Date: July 1995, Gray's Inn
Qualifications: [LLB (Sheff)]
✉ gerald.jones@7hs.co.uk

JONES MISS GILLIAN HUNTER

18 Red Lion Court
London EC4A 3EB, ☎ 020 7520 6000
✉ chambers@18rlc.co.uk
18 Red Lion Court (Annexe)
Thornwood House, 102 New London Road, Chelmsford, Essex CM2 0RG,
☎ 01245 280880
Call Date: Oct 1996, Lincoln's Inn
Pupil Supervisor
Qualifications: [LLB (Hons)(Leic)]
✉ gillian.jones@18rlc.co.uk

JONES MR GREGORY PERCY QC (2011)

Francis Taylor Building
Inner Temple, London EC4Y 7BY,
☎ 020 7353 8415 ✉ clerks@ftb.eu.com
Call Date: Nov 1991, Lincoln's Inn
Pupil Supervisor
Qualifications: [MA (Oxon) LLM (Lond)]
✉ gregory.jones@ftb.eu.com

JONES MRS HETTIE GEORGIA

Liberty Chambers
Crackwell Farm, Penally, Tenby, Pembrokeshire SA70 7RY, ☎ 01834 844458
✉ hj@libertylaw.co.uk
Call Date: Oct 2002, Lincoln's Inn
Qualifications: [LLB]

JONES MR HOWARD PETER

Carmelite Chambers
9 Carmelite Street, London EC4Y 0DR,
☎ 020 7936 6300
✉ clerks@carmelitechambers.co.uk
Call Date: Oct 1992, Gray's Inn
Qualifications: [MA (Hons)(Cantab)]
✉ hjones@carmelitechambers.co.uk

JONES MR HUW MICHAEL REES

St Philips Chambers
55 Temple Row, Birmingham B2 5LS,
☎ 0121 246 7000 ✉ clerks@st-philips.com
Call Date: Oct 1997, Lincoln's Inn
Qualifications: [LLB (Hons)(Essex)]
✉ hjones@st-philips.co.uk

JONES MR IAN HARVEY

Holbrook Chambers
PO Box 9327, Leicester LE21 3EL,
☎ 07771 961962 ✉ legal@direct-barrister.com
Call Date: Oct 1993, Inner Temple
Pupil Supervisor
Qualifications: [MA (Oxon)]
✉ ihjones@tiscali.co.uk

JONES MR IFAN WYN LLOYD

Linenhall Chambers
1 Stanley Place, Chester CH1 2LU,
☎ 01244 348282
✉ clerks@linenhallchambers.co.uk
Call Date: Nov 1979, Lincoln's Inn
Pupil Supervisor, Recorder
Qualifications: [LLB (Wales) BCL (Oxon)]
✉ clerks@1stanleyplace.co.uk

JONES MISS JACINTA ELIZABETH BARRETT

1 Mitre Court Buildings
1 Mitre Court Buildings, Temple, London EC4Y 7BS, ☎ 020 7452 8900
✉ clerks@1mcb.com
Call Date: July 2002, Gray's Inn
Qualifications: [MA (Edin)]
✉ jacinta.jones@1mcb.com

JONES MR JEFFREY RODERICK EMLYN

30 Park Place
Cardiff CF10 3BS, ☎ 029 2039 8421
✉ clerks@30parkplace.law.co.uk
Call Date: July 2003, Gray's Inn
Qualifications: [LLB (Wales)]
✉ jeff.jones@30parkplace.co.uk

JONES MISS JENNIFER RACHAEL

Atkin Chambers
1 Atkin Building, Gray's Inn, London WC1R 5AT, ☎ 020 7404 0102
✉ clerks@atkinchambers.com
Call Date: Oct 2003, Lincoln's Inn
Qualifications: [BA (Hons) (Oxon) BVC CSDF]
✉ clerks@atkinchambers.com

E

JONES MR JOHN RICHARD QC (2002)

Exchange Chambers
One Derby Square, Derby Square, Liverpool L2 9XX, ☎0151 236 7747
✉info@exchangechambers.co.uk
Carmelite Chambers
9 Carmelite Street, London EC4Y 0DR, ☎020 7936 6300
✉clerks@carmelitechambers.co.uk
Call Date: July 1981, Middle Temple
Recorder
Qualifications: [LLB]
johnrjonesqc@exchangechambers.co.uk

JONES MR JOHN RICHARD WILLIAM

Doughty Street Chambers
53-54 Doughty Street, London WC1N 2LS, ☎020 7404 1313
✉enquiries@doughtystreet.co.uk
Doughty Street Chambers
Pall Mall Court, 61-67 King Street, Manchester M2 4PD, ☎0161 618 1066
Doughty Street Chambers
5th Floor, Broad Quay House, Prince Street, Bristol BS1 4DJ, ☎01179 058 717
Call Date: Oct 1992, Lincoln's Inn
Pupil Supervisor
Qualifications: [MA(Hons)(Oxon) MA (Lond) LLM (USA)]

JONES MR JONATHAN ARTHUR DAVID

No5 Chambers
Fountain Court, Steelhouse Lane, Birmingham B4 6DR, ☎0845 210 5555 ✉info@no5.com
No5 Chambers
Greenwood House, 4-7 Salisbury Court, London EC4Y 8AA, ☎0845 210 5555
No5 Chambers
38 Queen Square, Bristol BS1 4QS, ☎0845 210 5555
Call Date: Oct 1994, Gray's Inn
Pupil Supervisor
Qualifications: [MA]
jjo@no5.com

JONES MR JULIAN EDWARD

9 King's Bench Walk
Lower Ground Floor South, 9 King's Bench Walk, Temple, London EC4Y 7DX, ☎020 7353 9564 ✉9kbw@btconnect.com
Call Date: Nov 1999, Gray's Inn
Qualifications: [LLB (B'ham)(Hons)]
9kbw@btconnect.com

JONES DR KAREN PATRICIA NIEVERGELT

Tanfield Chambers
2-5 Warwick Court, London WC1R 5DJ, ☎020 7421 5300
✉clerks@tanfieldchambers.co.uk
Call Date: Nov 1995, Middle Temple
Qualifications: [BSc (Hons)(Wales) PhD (Cantab)]

JONES MS KATIE LAURA

Lincoln House Chambers
Tower 12, The Avenue North, Spinningfields, 18-22 Bridge Street, Manchester M3 3BZ, ☎0161 832 5701
✉info@lincolnhousechambers.com
Call Date: Oct 2003, Gray's Inn
Qualifications: [LLB (B'ham)]
katie.jones@lincolnhousechambers.com

JONES MISS KAY MARY

Field Court Chambers
5 Field Court, Gray's Inn, London WC1R 5EF, ☎020 7405 6114 ✉clerks@fieldcourt.co.uk
Call Date: July 1974, Gray's Inn
Pupil Supervisor
Qualifications: [BA (Hons) (Sussex) Cert Universit (France)]
kay.jones@fieldcourt.co.uk

JONES MR KEITH RICHARD

Central Chambers
89 Princess Street, Manchester M1 4HT, ☎0161 236 1133
✉clerks@centralchambers.co.uk
Call Date: July 2009, Middle Temple
Qualifications: [LLB (Hons) (L'pool)]

JONES MR KELVIN MCALLISTER

Templis Chambers
3rd Floor South, 1A Middle Temple Lane, London EC4Y 9AA, ☎020 7649 9808
✉templis@templis.com
Call Date: Oct 1995, Inner Temple
Qualifications: [LLB (Hons) London LLM]
kelvin.jones@templis.com

Types of work: Administrative law, Breach of confidence, Chancery (commercial), Commercial litigation, Competition law, Computer contracts, Computer litigation, Confidential information, Constitutional and administrative law, Contracts, Copyright, Copyright theft, Copyright Tribunal, Data protection, Design, E-commerce, EC competition law, Employment, Entertainment, Factoring, Freedom of information, Freezing orders, Information technology, Intellectual property, Internet law, Media and entertainment, Passing off, Patents, Publishing, Registered designs, Restraint of trade, Sale of business, Scientific and technical disputes, Scientific cases, Sport, Technical contracts, Trademarks, Unregistered designs

JONES MR KEVIN OWEN

Bank House Chambers
Old Bank House, Hartshead, Sheffield S1 2EL,
☎0114 275 1223
✉w.digby@bankhousechambers.co.uk
Call Date: Oct 2003, Middle Temple
Qualifications: [BA (Hons) (Midd'x)]
✉k.jones@bankhousechambers.co.uk

JONES MR LAURENCE ANDREW

Temple Chambers
32 Park Place, Cardiff CF10 3BA,
☎029 2039 7364
✉DBrinning@Temple-Chambers.co.uk
9 Park Place
9 Park Place, Cardiff, South Glamorgan
CF10 3DP, ☎029 2038 2731
✉clerks@9parkplace.co.uk
Temple Chambers
12 Clytha Park Road, Newport, Gwent
NP20 4PB, ☎01633 267403
✉dbrinning@temple-chambers.co.uk
Call Date: Oct 1997, Gray's Inn
Qualifications: [BA (Wales) MSc]

JONES MR LAWRENCE VICTOR

Chambers of Lawrence Jones
8 Stone Buildings, Lincoln's Inn, London
WC2A 3TA, ☎020 7831 1444
✉clerks@8stonebuildings.com
Call Date: July 1988, Lincoln's Inn
Pupil Supervisor
Qualifications: [LLB (Hons)]
✉lawrencejones@8stonebuildings.com

JONES MISS LEANNE HOLLY

New Walk Chambers
27 New Walk, Leicester, Leicestershire
LE1 6TE, ☎0871 200 1298 / 0116 255 9144
✉clerks@newwalkchambers.co.uk
Call Date: July 2008, Middle Temple
Qualifications: [LLB (Hons) (Notts)]

JONES MISS MARGARET EMMA

Garden Court Chambers
57-60 Lincoln's Inn Fields, London WC2A 3LJ,
☎020 7993 7600 ✉info@gclaw.co.uk
Call Date: Nov 1990, Middle Temple
Qualifications: [BA (Dunelm) Dip Law]
✉maggiej@gclaw.co.uk

JONES MR MARK ANDREW

St Ive's Chambers
Whittall Street, Birmingham B4 6DH,
☎0121 236 0863
✉clerks@stiveschambers.co.uk
Call Date: Oct 2000, Middle Temple
Qualifications: [LLB (Hons) (Wales)]
✉mark.jones@stiveschambers.co.uk

JONES MR MARK SIMEON

3 Dr Johnson's Buildings
Ground Floor, 3 Dr Johnson's Buildings,
Temple, London EC4Y 7BA, ☎020 7353 4854
✉clerks@3djb.co.uk
Call Date: July 1997, Middle Temple
Qualifications: [MA (Hons)(Cantab)]
✉mjones@3djb.co.uk

JONES MR MARK WINGATE

Stone Chambers
4 Field Court, Gray's Inn, London WC1R 5EF,
☎020 7440 6900
✉clerks@stonechambers.com
Call Date: Nov 2000, Lincoln's Inn
Pupil Supervisor
Qualifications: [BA (Hons) (Oxon)]
✉mark.jones@stonechambers.com

JONES MR MARTIN WYNNE

Cranford Chambers
8 Warwick Court, London WC1R 5DJ,
☎020 7404 7454
✉jemima.ivens@cranfordchambers.com
1 Mitre Court Buildings
1 Mitre Court Buildings, Temple, London
EC4Y 7BS, ☎020 7452 8900
✉clerks@1mcb.com
Call Date: Nov 1977, Inner Temple
Pupil Supervisor
Qualifications: [MA (Warwick) LLB (Lond)]
✉martin.wynne-jones@1mcb.com

JONES MR MICHAEL

Cobden House Chambers
19 Quay Street, Manchester M3 3HN,
☎0161 833 6000 ✉Clerks@Cobden.co.uk
Call Date: Oct 1998, Lincoln's Inn
Pupil Supervisor
Qualifications: [LLB (Hons)(B'ham)]
✉clerks@cobden.co.uk

E

JONES MR MICHAEL ADRIAN LYSTER

Guildford Chambers
Stoke House, Leapale Lane, Guildford, Surrey GU1 4LY, ☎01483 539131
✉clerks@guildfordchambers.co.uk
Call Date: July 1972, Inner Temple
Pupil Supervisor
Qualifications: [BA]
mjones@guildfordchambers.co.uk

JONES MR MICHAEL DAVID

15 Winckley Square
Preston PR1 3JJ, ☎01772 252828
✉clerks@15winckleysq.co.uk
Call Date: July 2008, Gray's Inn
Qualifications: [BA (Leeds)]
clerks@15winckleysq.co.uk

JONES MR MICHAEL THOMAS

Gray's Inn Tax Chambers
3rd Floor, Gray's Inn Chambers, Gray's Inn, London WC1R 5JA, ☎020 7242 2642
✉clerks@taxbar.com
Call Date: July 2006, Lincoln's Inn
Qualifications: [LLB BCL (Oxon)]
mj@taxbar.com

JONES MR MICHAEL WYN

Number 7 Harrington Street Chambers
7 Harrington Street, Liverpool L2 9YH, ☎0151 242 0707 ✉clerks@7hs.co.uk
Call Date: Mar 1999, Gray's Inn
michael.jones@7hs.co.uk

JONES MR NATHAN RICHARD

30 Park Place
Cardiff CF10 3BS, ☎029 2039 8421
✉clerks@30parkplace.law.co.uk
Call Date: July 2008, Lincoln's Inn
Qualifications: [LLB (Bris)]

JONES MR NICHOLAS DAVID JULIAN

Civitas Chambers
Global Reach, Celtic Gateway, Cardiff Bay, Cardiff CF11 0SN, ☎0845 0713 007
✉clerks@civitaslaw.com
Call Date: Nov 1987, Gray's Inn
Pupil Supervisor
Qualifications: [BSc Econ (Wales) LLM (Cantab)]
ndj@civitaslaw.com

JONES MR NICHOLAS GARETH

Apex
Harlech House, 20 Cathedral Road, Cardiff CF11 9LJ, ☎02920 232 032
✉clerks@apexchambers.net
Call Date: Nov 1970, Gray's Inn
Pupil Supervisor
nicholas.jones@apexchambers.net

JONES MR NIGEL DOUGLAS QC (1999)

Hardwicke
New Square, Lincoln's Inn, London WC2A 3SB, ☎020 7242 2523
✉enquiries@hardwicke.co.uk
Call Date: July 1976, Gray's Inn
Recorder
Qualifications: [LLB (Lond)]

JONES MR OLIVER

Brick Court Chambers
7-8 Essex Street, London WC2R 3LD, ☎020 7379 3550 ✉clerks@brickcourt.co.uk
Call Date: July 2009, Lincoln's Inn
Qualifications: [BA LLB (Sydney) BCL (Oxon)]
oliver.jones@brickcourt.co.uk

JONES MR OLIVER EGERTON

4 Paper Buildings
1st Floor, 4 Paper Buildings, Temple, London EC4Y 7EX, ☎020 7427 5200
✉clerks@4pb.com
Call Date: Nov 1998, Inner Temple
Pupil Supervisor
Qualifications: [LLB (Lond) LLM (London)]
oj@4pb.com

JONES MR PAUL ALAN

Staple Inn Chambers
1st Floor, 9 Staple Inn, Holborn Bars, London WC1V 7QH, ☎020 7242 5240
✉clerks@stapleinn.co.uk
Call Date: July 1981, Inner Temple
Qualifications: [BA (Hons)]
pj@stapleinn.co.uk

JONES MR PHILIP ALUN

The Chambers of Grahame Aldous QC
9 Gough Square, London EC4A 3DG, ☎020 7832 0500
✉clerks@9goughsquare.co.uk
Call Date: Nov 1990, Middle Temple
Pupil Supervisor
Qualifications: [BA (Cantab) LLM (Lond)]
pjones@9goughsquare.co.uk

E

JONES MR PHILIP JOHN QC (2006)

Serle Court
6 New Square, Lincoln's Inn, London
WC2A 3QS, ☎ 020 7242 6105
✉ clerks@serlecourt.co.uk
Call Date: July 1985, Lincoln's Inn
Qualifications: [MA (Oxon) LLM (Canada) BCL (Oxon)]
✉ pjones@serlecourt.co.uk

JONES MR PHILIP WALTER

64 Bridge Street
3rd Floor, 64 Bridge Street, Manchester
M3 3BN, ☎ 0845 083 3000
✉ mail@64bridgestreet.com
Clerksroom (Taunton)
Equity House, Administration Centre,
Blackbrook Park Avenue, Taunton, Somerset
TA1 2PX, ☎ 0845 083 3000
✉ mail@clerksroom.com
Clerksroom (London)
3rd Floor, 218 Strand, London WC2R 1AT,
☎ 0845 083 3000 ✉ mail@clerksroom.com
Call Date: July 2007, Gray's Inn

JONES MISS RHIAN

30 Park Place
Cardiff CF10 3BS, ☎ 029 2039 8421
✉ clerks@30parkplace.law.co.uk
Call Date: July 2008, Gray's Inn
Qualifications: [LLB (Cardiff)]

JONES MISS RHIANNON

Farrar's Building
Farrar's Building, Temple, London EC4Y 7BD,
☎ 020 7583 9241
✉ Chambers@farrarsbuilding.co.uk
Call Date: Nov 1993, Inner Temple
Qualifications: [B Mus MA Dip Law AKC]
✉ rjones@farrarsbuilding.co.uk

JONES MR RHYS CHARLES MANSEL

14 Gray's Inn Square
14 Gray's Inn Square, Gray's Inn, London
WC1R 5JP, ☎ 020 7242 0858
✉ clerks@14gis.co.uk
Call Date: May 1990, Middle Temple
Qualifications: [MA (Cantab)]

JONES MR RHYS MATTHEW

Angel Chambers
Ethos Building, Kings Road, Swansea SA1 8AS,
☎ 01792 464623
✉ clerks@angelchambers.co.uk
Call Date: Nov 1998, Gray's Inn
Qualifications: [LLB (Hons)(Wales)]
✉ rhysjones@angelchambers.co.uk

JONES MR RICHARD FREDERICK THOMAS

Heavenwood Chambers
Heavenwood Chambers, Heavenwood House,
71 Bownham Park, Rodborough Common,
Stroud, Gloucestershire GL5 5BZ,
☎ 01453 873444 ✉ kms@heavenwood.co.uk
Call Date: July 1979, Gray's Inn
Pupil Supervisor
Qualifications: [LLB (Bris) FCIArb MICE]

JONES MR RICHARD GWYN

1 Garden Court Family Law Chambers
Ground Floor, One Garden Court, Temple,
London EC4Y 9BJ, ☎ 020 7797 7900
✉ clerks@1gc.com
Call Date: Oct 2003, Inner Temple
Qualifications: [BA (Cantab)]
✉ jones@1gc.com

JONES MR RICHARD HENRY QC (1996)

No5 Chambers
Greenwood House, 4-7 Salisbury Court,
London EC4Y 8AA, ☎ 0845 210 5555
No5 Chambers
38 Queen Square, Bristol BS1 4QS,
☎ 0845 210 5555
No5 Chambers
Fountain Court, Steelhouse Lane, Birmingham
B4 6DR, ☎ 0845 210 5555 ✉ info@no5.com
Call Date: Nov 1972, Inner Temple
Recorder
Qualifications: [MA (Oxon)]

JONES MR RICHARD HUW FRANKLYN

4 Breams Buildings
Chancery Lane, London EC4A 1HP,
☎ 020 7092 1900 ✉ clerks@4bb.co.uk
Call Date: July 1984, Gray's Inn
Qualifications: [LLB (Wales)]

JONES MR ROBERT ALUN QC (1989)

Great James Street Chambers
37 Great James Street, London WC1N 3HB,
☎ 020 7440 4949
✉ chambers@greatjames.co.uk
Call Date: Nov 1972, Gray's Inn
Recorder
Qualifications: [BSc]
✉ alun.jones@greatjames.co.uk

E

JONES MR ROBERT FFRANCON WYN

Exchange Chambers
One Derby Square, Derby Square, Liverpool L2 9XX, ☎ 0151 236 7747
✉ info@exchangechambers.co.uk
Exchange Chambers
7 Ralli Courts, West Riverside, Manchester M3 5FT, ☎ 0161 833 2722
Exchange Chambers
Oxford House, Oxford Row, Leeds LS1 3BE, ☎ 0113 203 1970
✉ spencer@exchangechambers.co.uk
187 Fleet Street
London EC4A 2AT, ☎ 020 7430 7430
✉ chambers@187fleetstreet.com
Call Date: Nov 1993, Lincoln's Inn
Qualifications: [BA (Hons)]
wynjones@exchangechambers.co.uk

JONES MR ROBERT SAMUEL

Guildhall Chambers
23 Broad Street, Bristol BS1 2HG, ☎ 0117 930 9000
✉ hoc@guildhallchambers.co.uk
Call Date: Oct 2008, Gray's Inn
Pupil Supervisor
Qualifications: [LLB]
sam.jones@guildhallchambers.co.uk

JONES MR RUPERT TREVELYAN

6 King's Bench Walk
Ground Floor, 6 King's Bench Walk, Temple, London EC4Y 7DR, ☎ 020 7583 0410
✉ clerks@6kbw.com
3 PB Barristers
23 Beaumont Street, Oxford OX1 2NP, ☎ 01865 793 736
Call Date: Oct 2000, Middle Temple
Pupil Supervisor
Qualifications: [BA (Hons) (Oxon)]
rupert.jones@6kbw.com, rupert.jones@6kbw.com.cjsm.net

JONES MISS RUTH

Nine Bedford Row
9 Bedford Row, London WC1R 4AZ, ☎ 020 7489 2727
✉ clerks@9bedfordrow.co.uk
Call Date: July 2004, Inner Temple
Qualifications: [LLB (Hons)]
ruth.jones@9bedfordrow.co.uk

JONES MISS SARAH FRANCES

Pump Court Chambers
Upper Ground Floor, 3 Pump Court, Temple, London EC4Y 7AJ, ☎ 020 7353 0711
✉ clerks@3pumpcourt.com
Pump Court Chambers
5 Temple Chambers, Temple Street, Swindon SN1 1SQ, ☎ 01793 539899
✉ clerks@3pumpcourt.com
Pump Court Chambers
31 Southgate Street, Winchester, Hampshire SO23 9EB, ☎ 01962 868 161
✉ clerks@3pumpcourt.com
Call Date: Nov 1996, Lincoln's Inn
Pupil Supervisor
Qualifications: [BA (Hons)]
clerks@3pumpcourt.com

JONES MR SEAN WILLIAM PAUL QC (2012)

11 King's Bench Walk
11 King's Bench Walk, Temple, London EC4Y 7EQ, ☎ 020 7632 8500
✉ clerksroom@11kbw.com
Call Date: Oct 1991, Inner Temple
Pupil Supervisor
Qualifications: [BA BCL (Oxon)]
sean.jones@11kbw.com

JONES MISS SIAN SCOTT

Exchange Chambers
7 Ralli Courts, West Riverside, Manchester M3 5FT, ☎ 0161 833 2722
Exchange Chambers
One Derby Square, Derby Square, Liverpool L2 9XX, ☎ 0151 236 7747
✉ info@exchangechambers.co.uk
Exchange Chambers
Oxford House, Oxford Row, Leeds LS1 3BE, ☎ 0113 203 1970
✉ spencer@exchangechambers.co.uk
Call Date: Oct 1998, Lincoln's Inn
Qualifications: [MA (Hons) (Cantab)]
jones@exchangechambers.co.uk

JONES MR STEFFAN ROBERT

Cathedral Chambers
10 Clytha Park Road, Newport NP20 4PB, ☎ 01633 215112
Call Date: Nov 1997, Gray's Inn
Qualifications: [LLB (Thames Valley)]

E

JONES MR STEPHEN HUGH

Pump Court Chambers
31 Southgate Street, Winchester, Hampshire SO23 9EB, ☎01962 868 161
✉clerks@3pumpcourt.com
Pump Court Chambers
5 Temple Chambers, Temple Street, Swindon SN1 1SQ, ☎01793 539899
✉clerks@3pumpcourt.com
Call Date: Nov 1978, Inner Temple
Pupil Supervisor
Qualifications: [MA (Oxon)]

JONES MR STEWART ELGAN QC (1994)

3 PB Barristers
3 Paper Buildings, Temple, London EC4Y 7EU, ☎020 7583 8055
3 PB Barristers
23 Beaumont Street, Oxford OX1 2NP, ☎01865 793 736
3 PB Barristers
4 St Peter Street, Winchester SO23 8BW, ☎01962 868884
✉clerks.winchester@3paper.co.uk
3 PB Barristers
Royal Talbot House, 2 Victoria Street, Bristol, Avon BS1 6BB, ☎0117 928 1520
3 PB Barristers
30 Christchurch Road, Bournemouth, Dorset BH1 3PD, ☎01202 292102
✉clerks.bournemouth@3paper.co.uk
Call Date: Nov 1972, Gray's Inn
Recorder
Qualifications: [MA (Oxon)]
🖃stewart.jones@3paper.co.uk

JONES MS SUSANNAH ALICE

20 Essex Street
London WC2R 3AL, ☎020 7842 1200
✉clerks@20essexst.com
Call Date: Nov 1999, Gray's Inn
Pupil Supervisor
Qualifications: [LLB (Lond)]
🖃clerks@20essexst.com

JONES MISS SUSANNAH LUCY

Octagon House
19 Colegate, Norwich NR3 1AT, ☎01603 623186
✉clerks@octagonhouse.co.uk
Call Date: Oct 1997, Middle Temple
Qualifications: [B.Ed (Hons)(Cantab) CPE (Lond)]
🖃clerks@octagonhouse.co.uk, Susannahjones@octagonhouse.co.uk

JONES MR TIMOTHY ARTHUR

No5 Chambers
Fountain Court, Steelhouse Lane, Birmingham B4 6DR, ☎0845 210 5555 ✉info@no5.com
No5 Chambers
Greenwood House, 4-7 Salisbury Court, London EC4Y 8AA, ☎0845 210 5555
No5 Chambers
38 Queen Square, Bristol BS1 4QS, ☎0845 210 5555
Call Date: July 1975, Inner Temple
Pupil Supervisor
Qualifications: [LLB (Lond) FRGS FRSA FCIArb]

JONES MR TRISTAN

Blackstone Chambers
Blackstone House, Temple, London EC4Y 9BW, ☎020 7583 1770
✉clerks@blackstonechambers.com
Call Date: Nov 2006, Gray's Inn
Qualifications: [BA MA]
🖃tristanjones@blackstonechambers.com

JONES MISS VICTORIA

3 PB Barristers
Royal Talbot House, 2 Victoria Street, Bristol, Avon BS1 6BB, ☎0117 928 1520
3 PB Barristers
30 Christchurch Road, Bournemouth, Dorset BH1 3PD, ☎01202 292102
✉clerks.bournemouth@3paper.co.uk
3 PB Barristers
4 St Peter Street, Winchester SO23 8BW, ☎01962 868884
✉clerks.winchester@3paper.co.uk
3 PB Barristers
23 Beaumont Street, Oxford OX1 2NP, ☎01865 793 736
3 PB Barristers
3 Paper Buildings, Temple, London EC4Y 7EU, ☎020 7583 8055
Call Date: Oct 2003, Lincoln's Inn
Qualifications: [LLB (Hons) (B'ham)]
🖃victoria.jones@3pb.co.uk

JONES MR WILLIAM JOHN

2 Hare Court
Lower Ground, Ground, 1st & 2nd Floor, 2 Hare Court, Temple, London EC4Y 7BH, ☎020 7353 3982 ✉clerks@2harecourt.com
Call Date: Nov 1972, Inner Temple
Pupil Supervisor, Recorder
🖃johnjones@2harecourt.com

E

JONES MISS XIMENA CANDELARIA

3 PB Barristers
4 St Peter Street, Winchester SO23 8BW, ☎01962 868884
✉clerks.winchester@3paper.co.uk
3 PB Barristers
Royal Talbot House, 2 Victoria Street, Bristol, Avon BS1 6BB, ☎0117 928 1520
3 PB Barristers
23 Beaumont Street, Oxford OX1 2NP, ☎01865 793 736
3 PB Barristers
3 Paper Buildings, Temple, London EC4Y 7EU, ☎020 7583 8055
3 PB Barristers
30 Christchurch Road, Bournemouth, Dorset BH1 3PD, ☎01202 292102
✉clerks.bournemouth@3paper.co.uk
Call Date: Nov 2007, Middle Temple
Qualifications: [BA (Hons) (Leeds)]

JONES-FENLEIGH MISS HARRIET CHRISTABEL CLARE

Fountain Court Chambers
Fountain Court, Temple, London EC4Y 9DH, ☎020 7583 3335
✉chambers@fountaincourt.co.uk
Call Date: July 2007, Lincoln's Inn
Qualifications: [BA (Cantab)]
hjf@fountaincourt.co.uk

E

JONSON MISS LYDIA ESME

18 Red Lion Court (Annexe)
Thornwood House, 102 New London Road, Chelmsford, Essex CM2 0RG, ☎01245 280880
18 Red Lion Court
London EC4A 3EB, ☎020 7520 6000
✉chambers@18rlc.co.uk
Call Date: Oct 2000, Middle Temple
Qualifications: [MA (Hons) (Cantab) CPE]
lydia.jonson@18rlc.co.uk

JOPLING MR ADRIAN ROLAND

Phydeaux Chambers
Maison Phydeaux, 44a The Grove, Biggin Hill, Westerham, Kent TN16 3TB, ☎01209 821442
✉arjo_1@tiscali.co.uk
Call Date: Nov 1985, Middle Temple
Qualifications: [BA]

JORDAN MR ANDREW

Furnival Chambers
32 Furnival Street, London EC4A 1JQ, ☎020 7405 3232
Call Date: July 2006, Inner Temple
Qualifications: [BSc (Belfast) MBA]
andrew@ajordan.net

JORDAN DR RUTH ANNE

Serle Court
6 New Square, Lincoln's Inn, London WC2A 3QS, ☎020 7242 6105
✉clerks@serlecourt.co.uk
Call Date: Oct 2001, Inner Temple
Qualifications: [BA (Dub) MPhil (Cantab) PHd (Cantab) CPE]
rjordan@serlecourt.co.uk

JORDASH MR WAYNE DARREN

Doughty Street Chambers
53-54 Doughty Street, London WC1N 2LS, ☎020 7404 1313
✉enquiries@doughtystreet.co.uk
Doughty Street Chambers
Pall Mall Court, 61-67 King Street, Manchester M2 4PD, ☎0161 618 1066
Doughty Street Chambers
5th Floor, Broad Quay House, Prince Street, Bristol BS1 4DJ, ☎01179 058 717
Call Date: Nov 1995, Middle Temple
Qualifications: [BSc (Hons)]
w.jordash@doughtystreet.co.uk

JORRO MR PETER ANTONIO RAIMO

Garden Court Chambers
57-60 Lincoln's Inn Fields, London WC2A 3LJ, ☎020 7993 7600 ✉info@gclaw.co.uk
Call Date: Nov 1986, Lincoln's Inn
Qualifications: [LLB (Hons) (LSE)]
peterj@gclaw.co.uk

JORY MR RICHARD NORMAN

9-12 Bell Yard
London WC2A 2JR, ☎020 7400 1800
✉clerks@9-12bellyard.com
Call Date: Oct 1993, Middle Temple
Pupil Supervisor
Qualifications: [BA (Hons)(Reading) CPE (Middx)]

JORY MR ROBERT JOHN HUGH

Enterprise Chambers
43 Park Square, Leeds LS1 2NP,
☎ 0113 246 0391
✉ leeds@enterprisechambers.com
Enterprise Chambers
65 Quayside, Newcastle Upon Tyne NE1 3DE,
☎ 0191 222 3344
✉ newcastle@enterprisechambers.com
Call Date: Oct 1992, Lincoln's Inn
Qualifications: [MA Dip Law]
✉ hughjory@enterprisechambers.com

JOSEPH MR ANDREW ROBIN

30 Park Place
Cardiff CF10 3BS, ☎ 029 2039 8421
✉ clerks@30parkplace.law.co.uk
Call Date: July 2004, Gray's Inn
Qualifications: [BA (Hons) Notts]
✉ arj@30parkplace.co.uk

JOSEPH MR CHARLES HENRY

Tanfield Chambers
2-5 Warwick Court, London WC1R 5DJ,
☎ 020 7421 5300
✉ clerks@tanfieldchambers.co.uk
Call Date: July 1980, Lincoln's Inn
Pupil Supervisor
Qualifications: [BA (Hons) FCIArb]
✉ cjoseph@tanfieldchambers.co.uk

JOSEPH MR CLIFFORD DEREK

Chambers of Mr Clifford Joseph
Tiggers, Hall Place Lane, Burchetts Green,
Maidenhead, Berkshire SL6 6QY,
☎ 01628 822267
✉ planning.cliffordjoseph@tinyworld.co.uk
Call Date: Apr 1975, Gray's Inn
Pupil Supervisor
Qualifications: [MA (Oxon) LMRTPI]
✉ planning.cliffordjoseph@tinyworld.co.uk

JOSEPH MR DAVID PHILIP QC (2003)

Essex Court Chambers
24 Lincoln's Inn Fields, London WC2A 3EG,
☎ 020 7813 8000
✉ clerksroom@essexcourt.net
Call Date: Nov 1984, Middle Temple
Qualifications: [MA (Cantab)]
✉ djoseph@essexcourt.net

JOSEPH MRS ELIZABETH ANNE AYODELE

Emmanuel Chambers
66 Daubeney Road, London E5 0EF,
☎ 020 8985 3030 ✉ AYOJOSEPH@aol.com
Call Date: July 1983, Gray's Inn
Qualifications: [BA (Hons) LLM (Lond)]

JOSEPH MR PAUL WOLFE

No5 Chambers
Fountain Court, Steelhouse Lane, Birmingham
B4 6DR, ☎ 0845 210 5555 ✉ info@no5.com
No5 Chambers
Greenwood House, 4-7 Salisbury Court,
London EC4Y 8AA, ☎ 0845 210 5555
No5 Chambers
38 Queen Square, Bristol BS1 4QS,
☎ 0845 210 5555
Call Date: Oct 2005, Inner Temple
Qualifications: [MA Robinson College
University of Cambridge]
✉ pj@no5.com

JOSEPH DR SANDRADEE THERESA

13 Old Square Chambers
Ground Floor, 14 Old Square, Lincoln's Inn,
London WC2A 3UE, ☎ 020 7831 4445
✉ clerks@13oldsquare.com
Call Date: July 1998, Inner Temple
Qualifications: [LLB MPhil (Cantab)]

JOSEPH MR SELLAPPAH JOB

Chambers of Mr S J Joseph
39 Hermitage Road, Haringey, London
N4 1LU, ☎ 020 8809 3083 / 020 8802 9889
✉ sjoe333@yahoo.co.uk
Call Date: Nov 1983, Middle Temple
Pupil Supervisor
Qualifications: [LLB (Lond) LLB (Sri Lanka)]
✉ sjoe333@yahoo.co.uk

JOSEPHS MISS JENNIFER LOUISE

St Philips Chambers
55 Temple Row, Birmingham B2 5LS,
☎ 0121 246 7000 ✉ clerks@st-philips.com
Call Date: July 2000, Middle Temple
Qualifications: [LLB(Hons)(Newc)]
✉ jjosephs@st-philips.co.uk

E

JOSHI MR PRAMOD KUMAR

One Essex Court
1st Floor, Temple, London EC4Y 9AR,
☎020 7936 3030 ✉clerks@1ec.co.uk
Call Date: Nov 1992, Inner Temple
Qualifications: [LLB (Hons) MBA (Sheff)]
pjoshi@1ec.co.uk

JOSHI MR RAJENDRA JUGATRAY

18 Red Lion Court
London EC4A 3EB, ☎020 7520 6000
✉chambers@18rlc.co.uk
18 Red Lion Court (Annexe)
Thornwood House, 102 New London Road, Chelmsford, Essex CM2 0RG,
☎01245 280880
Call Date: Nov 1983, Inner Temple
Pupil Supervisor
Qualifications: [BA (Hons)]

JOSLING MR WILLIAM HENRY CHARLES

37 Park Square Chambers
37 Park Square, Leeds LS1 2NY,
☎0113 243 9422 ✉chambers@no37.co.uk
Call Date: Nov 1995, Lincoln's Inn
Qualifications: [MA (Cantab) Dip.Law]
chambers@no37.co.uk

E

JOSS MR NORMAN JAMES

Chambers of Mr N J Joss
8 Albert Road, Epsom, Surrey KT17 4EH,
☎07734 104551 ✉normjoss@btinternet.com
Call Date: July 1982, Lincoln's Inn
Pupil Supervisor
Qualifications: [BA (Hons)]

JOSSE MR DAVID BENJAMIN QC (2009)

Five St Andrew's Hill
5 St Andrew's Hill, London EC4V 5BZ,
☎020 7332 5400 ✉Clerks@5sah.co.uk
Call Date: July 1985, Middle Temple
Qualifications: [BA (Lond)]

JOSTY MR DAVID STEPHEN

College Chambers
19 Carlton Crescent, Southampton, Hampshire SO15 2ET, ☎023 8023 0338
✉clerks@college-chambers.co.uk
Call Date: July 2002, Gray's Inn
Qualifications: [BSc (Kingston) MSc (Lond)]
djosty@College-Chambers.co.uk

JOURDAN MR STEPHEN ERIC QC (2009)

Falcon Chambers
Falcon Court, London EC4Y 1AA,
☎020 7353 2484
✉clerks@falcon-chambers.com
Call Date: Nov 1989, Gray's Inn
Qualifications: [MA (Cantab)]
jourdan@falcon-chambers.com

Types of work: Agriculture, Chancery (land law), Commercial property, Common land, Conveyancing, Insolvency, Landlord and tenant, Professional negligence

JOWELL MR DANIEL SIMON SUZMAN QC (2011)

Brick Court Chambers
7-8 Essex Street, London WC2R 3LD,
☎020 7379 3550 ✉clerks@brickcourt.co.uk
Call Date: Nov 1995, Middle Temple
Pupil Supervisor
Qualifications: [BA (Hons) LLM]
daniel.jowell@brickcourt.co.uk

JOWELL PROF JEFFREY LIONEL QC (1993)

Blackstone Chambers
Blackstone House, Temple, London EC4Y 9BW, ☎020 7583 1770
✉clerks@blackstonechambers.com
Call Date: Feb 1965, Middle Temple
Qualifications: [BA MA (Oxon) LLM LLD CEDR Accredited Mediator LLB (South Africa) SJD (USA)]

JOWETT MR JOHN MICHAEL

No.6 Park Square
Leeds LS1 2LW, ☎0113 245 9763
✉Tim@no6.co.uk
Call Date: July 2009, Middle Temple
Qualifications: [LLB (Hons) (Leeds)]

JOWETT MR TIMOTHY DAVID CHRISTIAN

9 Park Place
9 Park Place, Cardiff, South Glamorgan CF10 3DP, ☎029 2038 2731
✉clerks@9parkplace.co.uk
Call Date: Oct 1999, Gray's Inn
Qualifications: [LLB (Lond) LLM (Lond)]
cjowett@9parkplace.co.uk

JOYCE MISS ABIGAIL HELEN

1 High Pavement
Nottingham NG1 1HF, ☎0115 941 8218
✉clerks@1highpavement.co.uk
Call Date: Oct 1998, Inner Temple
Qualifications: [LLB (Nott'm)]
✉Abigailjoyce@1highpavement.co.uk

JOYCE MR PETER STUART LANGFORD QC (1991)

1 High Pavement
Nottingham NG1 1HF, ☎0115 941 8218
✉clerks@1highpavement.co.uk
36 Bedford Row
London WC1R 4JH, ☎020 7421 8000
✉chambers@36bedfordrow.co.uk
Call Date: July 1968, Inner Temple
Recorder
✉peterjoyceqc@1highpavement.co.uk

JUBB MR BRIAN PATRICK

Renaissance Chambers
5th Floor, Gray's Inn Chambers, Gray's Inn, London WC1R 5JA, ☎020 7404 1111
✉clerks@renaissancechambers.co.uk
Call Date: Nov 1971, Gray's Inn
Pupil Supervisor
✉bj@renaissancechambers.co.uk

JUBB MR DAVID ANTHONY

Goldsmith Chambers
Ground Floor, Goldsmith Building, Temple, London EC4Y 7BL, ☎020 7353 6802
✉clerks@goldsmithchambers.com
Call Date: Oct 2002, Inner Temple
Qualifications: [BA (Lond)]
✉D.Jubb@goldsmithchambers.law.co.uk

JUCKES MR DAVID

Hailsham Chambers
Ground Floor, 4 Paper Buildings, Temple, London EC4Y 7EX, ☎020 7643 5000
✉clerks@hailshamchambers.com
Call Date: Oct 2008, Inner Temple
Qualifications: [BA (Lond)]

JUDD MISS FRANCES JEAN QC (2006)

Harcourt Chambers
1st Floor, 2 Harcourt Buildings, Temple, London EC4Y 9DB, ☎0844 561 7135
St John's Chambers
101 Victoria Street, Bristol BS1 6PU, ☎0117 923 4700
✉clerks@stjohnschambers.co.uk
Harcourt Chambers
Churchill House, 3 St Aldate's Courtyard, St Aldate's, Oxford OX1 1BN, ☎0844 561 7135
Call Date: Nov 1984, Middle Temple
Qualifications: [BA(Cantab)]
✉fjudd@harcourtchambers.law.co.uk

JUDGE MR ANDREW JOHN

Westgate Chambers
64 High Street, Lewes, East Sussex BN7 1XG, ☎01273 480510
✉clerks@westgate-chambers.co.uk
Call Date: July 1986, Middle Temple
Pupil Supervisor
Qualifications: [BA (Hons) MSc]

JUDGE MR CHARLES JOSEPH

Five Paper Buildings
1st Floor, Five Paper Buildings, Temple, London EC4Y 7HB, ☎020 7583 6117
✉clerks@5pb.co.uk
Call Date: July 1981, Inner Temple
Pupil Supervisor
Qualifications: [BA (Hons)]
✉cj@5pb.co.uk

JUDGE MISS LISA JANE

Deans Court Chambers
24 St John Street, Manchester M3 4DF, ☎0161 214 6000 ✉clerks@deanscourt.co.uk
Deans Court Chambers
101 Walker Street, Preston PR1 2RR, ☎01772 565 600
✉preston@deanscourt.co.uk
Call Date: Oct 1993, Gray's Inn
Pupil Supervisor
Qualifications: [LLB (Hons)]
✉judge@deanscourt.co.uk

JUDGE MISS PARVEEN

1 Mitre Court Buildings
1 Mitre Court Buildings, Temple, London EC4Y 7BS, ☎020 7452 8900
✉clerks@1mcb.com
Call Date: Mar 2001, Lincoln's Inn
Qualifications: [LLB (Hons) (Brunel)]

JUGNARAIN MR DAVID

2 Dr Johnson's Buildings
2 Dr Johnson's Buildings, Temple, London EC4Y 7AY, ☎020 7936 2613
✉clerks@2drj.com
Call Date: Oct 2002, Inner Temple
Qualifications: [LLB (Kent)]
✉clerks@2drj.com

E

JULIEN MISS CHRISTINE HELEN

Guildford Chambers
Stoke House, Leapale Lane, Guildford, Surrey GU1 4LY, ☎01483 539131
✉clerks@guildfordchambers.co.uk
Call Date: Nov 1991, Inner Temple
Qualifications: [LLB (Hons)(L'pool)]

JULYAN MS JAQUELINE ANNE

Seven Bedford Row
7 Bedford Row, London WC1R 4BS, ☎020 7242 3555 ✉clerks@7br.co.uk
Call Date: July 2009, Gray's Inn
Qualifications: [BA LLB LLM]
✉jjulyan@7br.co.uk

JUNG MISS BO-EUN

3 Raymond Buildings
3 Raymond Buildings, Gray's Inn, London WC1R 5BH, ☎020 7400 6400
✉clerks@3rblaw.com
Call Date: July 2005, Lincoln's Inn
Qualifications: [BSc (Hons) PgDI]
✉bo-eun.jung@3raymondbuildings.com

E

JUNG MISS CATHERINE FELICITY

Essex Court Chambers
24 Lincoln's Inn Fields, London WC2A 3EG, ☎020 7813 8000
✉clerksroom@essexcourt.net
Call Date: July 2010, Gray's Inn
Qualifications: [BA BCL]

JURENKO MISS RENATA ANNA

33 Bedford Row
London WC1R 4JH, ☎020 7242 6476
✉clerks@33bedfordrow.co.uk
Call Date: Oct 1993, Middle Temple
Qualifications: [B Ed (Hons)]
✉renatajurenko@33bedfordrow.co.uk

JUSS PROF SATVINDER SINGH

3 Hare Court
3 Hare Court, Temple, London EC4Y 7BJ, ☎020 7415 7800 ✉clerks@3harecourt.com
Call Date: Nov 1989, Gray's Inn
Qualifications: [BA Ph D (Cantab)]

JUTLA MR CHARANJIT SINGH

Equity Chambers
First Floor, McLaren Building, 46 Priory Queensway, Birmingham B4 7LR, ☎0121 236 5007
✉clerks@equitychambers.org.uk
Call Date: Oct 2003, Lincoln's Inn
Qualifications: [LLB (Hons) LLM (Wolves)]
✉csj@e-c.org.uk

KABRA MISS MADHAVI

1 Hare Court
1 Hare Court, Temple, London EC4Y 7BE, ☎020 7797 7070 ✉clerks@1hc.com
Call Date: July 2008, Middle Temple
Qualifications: [LLB (Hons) (LSE)]
✉mr@ihc.com

KABWERU-NAMULEMU MISS KAREN HASASHA

KCH Garden Square
1 Oxford Street, Nottingham NG1 5BH, ☎0115 941 8851
✉clerks@kchgardensquare.co.uk
Call Date: July 2001, Lincoln's Inn
Qualifications: [LLB (Hons)]
✉kknamulemu@kch.co.uk

KADRI MR SADAKAT

Doughty Street Chambers
Pall Mall Court, 61-67 King Street, Manchester M2 4PD, ☎0161 618 1066
Doughty Street Chambers
5th Floor, Broad Quay House, Prince Street, Bristol BS1 4DJ, ☎01179 058 717
Doughty Street Chambers
53-54 Doughty Street, London WC1N 2LS, ☎020 7404 1313
✉enquiries@doughtystreet.co.uk
Call Date: Nov 1989, Inner Temple
Qualifications: [BA (Cantab) LLM (USA)]
✉s.kadri@doughtystreet.co.uk

KADRI MR SIBGHATULLAH QC (1989)

6 King's Bench Walk
Ground, Third & Fourth Floors, 6 King's Bench Walk, Temple, London EC4Y 7DR, ☎020 7353 4931 ✉clerks@6kbw.co.uk
Call Date: Nov 1969, Inner Temple
Qualifications: [FRSA]
✉sibghat.kadri@6kbw.co.uk

KAGABA-MENDOZA MS ELIZABETH

Trinity Chambers
The Custom House, 39 Quayside, Newcastle Upon Tyne NE1 3DE, ☎0191 232 1927
✉info@trinitychambers.co.uk
Trinity Chambers
Multi Media Exchange, 72-80 Corporation Road, Middlesbrough TS1 2RF, ☎01642 247569
✉info@trinitychambers.co.uk
Call Date: July 1999, Inner Temple
Qualifications: [BA LLB]
✉e.mendoza@trinitychambers.co.uk

KAJUE MISS SORIA KEZIAH

18 St John Street
Manchester M3 4EA, ☎0161 278 1800
✉clerks@18sjs.com
Call Date: Oct 2001, Middle Temple
Qualifications: [LLB (Hons) LLM]

KAKONGE MS ARTIS OBONYO

Garden Court Chambers
57-60 Lincoln's Inn Fields, London WC2A 3LJ,
☎020 7993 7600 ✉info@gclaw.co.uk
Call Date: July 2006, Lincoln's Inn
Qualifications: [LLB (Oxon)]
✉artisk@gclaw.co.uk

KALER MISS MANJEET KAUR

1 Pump Court
Elm Court, Temple, London EC4Y 7AB,
☎020 7842 7070
✉(name)@pumpcourt.co.uk
Call Date: Feb 1993, Middle Temple
Qualifications: [LLB (Hons)(Middx)]

KALFON MR OLIVIER

Enterprise Chambers
9 Old Square, Lincoln's Inn, London
WC2A 3SR, ☎020 7405 9471
✉london@enterprisechambers.com
Enterprise Chambers
65 Quayside, Newcastle Upon Tyne NE1 3DE,
☎0191 222 3344
✉newcastle@enterprisechambers.com
Enterprise Chambers
43 Park Square, Leeds LS1 2NP,
☎0113 246 0391
✉leeds@enterprisechambers.com
Call Date: Oct 2003, Inner Temple
Qualifications: [BSc (LSE)]
✉olivierkalfon@enterprisechambers.com

KALLIPETIS MR MICHEL LOUIS QC (1989)

Quadrant Chambers
Quadrant House, 10 Fleet Street, London
EC4Y 1AU, ☎020 7583 4444
✉info@quadrantchambers.com
Call Date: July 1968, Gray's Inn
Qualifications: [LLB (Lond) LCIArb]
✉michel.kallipetis@quadrantchambers.com

KAMAL MR SETU

Taxchambers
15 Old Square, Lincoln's Inn, London
WC2A 3UE, ☎020 7242 2744
✉taxchambers@15oldsquare.co.uk
St James's Chambers
68 Quay Street, Manchester M3 3EJ,
☎0161 834 7000
✉clerks@stjameschambers.com
Call Date: Mar 2004, Lincoln's Inn
Qualifications: [BA (Hons) (LOnd) PgDI]
✉taxchambers@15oldsquare.co.uk

KAMLISH MR STEPHEN MICHAEL ADRIAN QC (2003)

Tooks Chambers
81 Farringdon Street, London EC4A 4BL,
☎020 7842 7575 ✉clerks@tooks.co.uk
Call Date: July 1979, Gray's Inn
Qualifications: [BA (Hons)]
✉stephen.kamlish@tooks.co.uk

KAMM MISS RACHEL MAJ

11 King's Bench Walk
11 King's Bench Walk, Temple, London
EC4Y 7EQ, ☎020 7632 8500
✉clerksroom@11kbw.com
Call Date: Oct 2006, Lincoln's Inn
Qualifications: [BA (Oxon)]
✉rachel.kamm@11kbw.com

KANE MR ADAM VINCENT SIMON

Carmelite Chambers
9 Carmelite Street, London EC4Y 0DR,
☎020 7936 6300
✉clerks@carmelitechambers.co.uk
Call Date: Nov 1993, Gray's Inn
Qualifications: [BA (Oxon) CPE]
✉akane@carmelitechambers.co.uk

KANE DR GILLIAN MARGARET

Fountain Chambers
Cleveland Business Centre, 1 Watson Street,
Middlesbrough TS1 2RQ, ☎01642 804040
✉clerks@fountainchambers.co.uk
Call Date: July 2002, Gray's Inn
Qualifications: [BSc PhD (Manch) MSc (Leeds)]

KANNANGARA MR HARSHAKA HEMANTHA

Temple Court Chambers
2nd Floor, 2 Dr Johnson's Building, Temple,
London EC4Y 7AY, ☎020 7353 7888
✉clerks@templecourt.co.uk
Call Date: Nov 2000, Lincoln's Inn
Pupil Supervisor
Qualifications: [LLB (Hons) LLM]
✉hk@templecourt.co.uk

E

KANSAL MISS SEEMA

12 Old Square Chambers
1st Floor, 12 Old Square, Lincoln's Inn, London WC2A 3TX, ☎020 7404 0875
✉clerks@12oldsquare.com
Call Date: Mar 2007, Middle Temple
Qualifications: [BA (Hons) (York) PGDL (Lond)]
✉clerks@12oldsquare.com, seema.kansal@1208.com

KAPILA MISS RACHEL PRAKASH

3 Raymond Buildings
3 Raymond Buildings, Gray's Inn, London WC1R 5BH, ☎020 7400 6400
✉clerks@3rblaw.com
Call Date: Oct 2006, Middle Temple
Qualifications: [BA (Hons) (Oxon)]

KAPOOR MR SHAMAN

Temple Garden Chambers
1 Harcourt Buildings, Temple, London EC4Y 9DA, ☎020 7583 1315
✉clerks@tgchambers.com
Call Date: Oct 1999, Lincoln's Inn
Qualifications: [LLM Pgdl LLB (Hons) CEP]
✉sk@tgchambers.com

E

KARAISKOS MISS MARIA

Old Bailey Chambers
15 Old Bailey, London EC4M 7EF, ☎020 3008 6404
✉clerks@15oldbaileychambers.com
Call Date: Nov 2000, Middle Temple
Qualifications: [LLB (Hons) (London)]

KARAS MR JONATHAN MARCUS QC (2006)

Wilberforce Chambers
8 New Square, Lincoln's Inn, London WC2A 3QP, ☎020 7306 0102
✉chambers@wilberforce.co.uk
Call Date: July 1986, Middle Temple
Qualifications: [MA (Oxon) Dip Law]
✉jkaras@wilberforce.co.uk

Types of work: Boundaries, Chancery (land law), Commercial property, Common land, Compulsory Purchase, Conveyancing, Highways, Land compensation, Landlord and tenant, Lands Tribunal, Leasehold enfranchisement, Local authorities, Planning, Real property, Rights of light, Rights of way, Title to land, Water

KARBHARI MR NAEEM

1 Gray's Inn Square
Ground Floor, 1 Gray's Inn Square, London WC1R 5AA, ☎020 7405 0001
Call Date: Nov 2003, Middle Temple
Qualifications: [LLB (Hons) LLM]

KARIA MR CHIRAG QC (2012)

Quadrant Chambers
Quadrant House, 10 Fleet Street, London EC4Y 1AU, ☎020 7583 4444
✉info@quadrantchambers.com
Call Date: Nov 1988, Lincoln's Inn
Pupil Supervisor
Qualifications: [BA (Hons)(Cantab) MA (Hons)(Cantab) LLM (USA)]
✉chirag.karia@quadrantchambers.com

KARIM MR MOHAMMED SHAHADOTH

12 Old Square Chambers
1st Floor, 12 Old Square, Lincoln's Inn, London WC2A 3TX, ☎020 7404 0875
✉clerks@12oldsquare.com
Call Date: July 2008, Lincoln's Inn
Qualifications: [LLB (Lond)]

KARIM MR SHEIKH MOHAMMED SAMIUL

Kings Chambers
36 Young Street, Manchester M3 3FT, ☎0845 034 3444
✉clerks@kingschambers.com
Kings Chambers
5 Park Square East, Leeds LS1 2NE, ☎0845 034 3444
✉clerks@kingschambers.com
Kings Chambers
Embassy House, 60 Church Street, Birmingham B3 2DJ, ☎0845 034 3444
✉clerks@kingschambers.com
Call Date: Nov 2002, Gray's Inn
Qualifications: [LLB (B'ham) LLM (Lond)]
✉skarim@kingschambers.com

KARK MR THOMAS VICTOR WILLIAM QC (2010)

QEB Hollis Whiteman
1-2 Laurence Pountney Hill, London EC4R 0EU, ☎020 7933 8855
✉barristers@qebhw.co.uk
Call Date: July 1982, Inner Temple
Pupil Supervisor, Recorder
✉barristers@qebholliswhiteman.co.uk

KARMY-JONES MISS RIEL MEREDITH

18 Red Lion Court
London EC4A 3EB, ☎ 020 7520 6000
✉ chambers@18rlc.co.uk
Call Date: Nov 1995, Lincoln's Inn
Pupil Supervisor
Qualifications: [BA (Alberta) LLB (Hons)]
✉ riel.karmy-jones@18rlc.co.uk

KARNIK MR MIKHIL

Central Chambers
89 Princess Street, Manchester M1 4HT,
☎ 0161 236 1133
✉ clerks@centralchambers.co.uk
Call Date: July 2005, Gray's Inn
Qualifications: [BSc (Leic) MSc (Manch)]

KARSERAS MISS ANASTASIA ANDREA

2 Temple Gardens
2 Temple Gardens, Temple, London
EC4Y 9AY, ☎ 020 7822 1200
✉ clerks@2tg.co.uk
Call Date: Oct 2000, Gray's Inn
Pupil Supervisor
Qualifications: [LLB (Lond)]
✉ ak@2tg.co.uk

KARU MR LEE QC (2010)

Nine Bedford Row
9 Bedford Row, London WC1R 4AZ,
☎ 020 7489 2727
✉ clerks@9bedfordrow.co.uk
Call Date: July 1985, Lincoln's Inn
Pupil Supervisor
Qualifications: [BA (Hons) Dip. Law]
✉ leekaru@9bedfordrow.co.uk

KASASIAN MS LAURA ANN

Cornwall Street Chambers
85-87 Cornwall Street, Birmingham B3 3BY,
☎ 0121 233 7500
✉ clerks@cornwallstreet.co.uk
Call Date: July 2002, Middle Temple
Qualifications: [BA (Hons) (Sussex) CPE]
✉ laura.kasasian@cornwallstreet.co.uk

KASRIEL MR ANDREW THOMAS

5 Pump Court
Ground Floor, 5 Pump Court, Temple, London
EC4Y 7AP, ☎ 020 7353 2532
✉ clerks@5pumpcourt.com
Call Date: Oct 2001, Gray's Inn
Qualifications: [MA(Oxon), DIC, MICE, MIStructE, FCIArb, DipLaw (City)]

KATKOWSKI MR CHRISTOPHER ANDREW MARK QC (1999)

Landmark Chambers
180 Fleet Street, London EC4A 2HG,
☎ 020 7430 1221
✉ clerks@landmarkchambers.co.uk
Call Date: Feb 1982, Gray's Inn
Qualifications: [MA, LLB (Cantab)]
✉ ckatkowski@landmarkchambers.co.uk

KATRAK MR CYRUS PESI

3 PB Barristers
3 Paper Buildings, Temple, London EC4Y 7EU,
☎ 020 7583 8055
3 PB Barristers
Royal Talbot House, 2 Victoria Street, Bristol,
Avon BS1 6BB, ☎ 0117 928 1520
3 PB Barristers
23 Beaumont Street, Oxford OX1 2NP,
☎ 01865 793 736
3 PB Barristers
4 St Peter Street, Winchester SO23 8BW,
☎ 01962 868884
✉ clerks.winchester@3paper.co.uk
3 PB Barristers
30 Christchurch Road, Bournemouth, Dorset
BH1 3PD, ☎ 01202 292102
✉ clerks.bournemouth@3paper.co.uk
Call Date: Oct 1991, Gray's Inn
Pupil Supervisor
Qualifications: [LLB]
✉ cyrus.katrak@3paper.co.uk

KATYAR MR ARUN KUMAR

12 King's Bench Walk
12 King's Bench Walk, Temple, London
EC4Y 7EL, ☎ 020 7583 0811
Call Date: Nov 1993, Lincoln's Inn
Qualifications: [LLB (Hons)]
✉ katyar@12kbw.co.uk

KATZ MR ANTHONY STEPHEN

1 Mitre Court Buildings
1 Mitre Court Buildings, Temple, London
EC4Y 7BS, ☎ 020 7452 8900
✉ clerks@1mcb.com
Call Date: Nov 2007, Middle Temple
Qualifications: [BSc (Hons) (Lond) PgDL (Lond)]
✉ Anthony.Katz@1mcb.com

E

KATZ MR PHILIP ALEC JACKSON QC (2000)

9-12 Bell Yard
London WC2A 2JR, ☎020 7400 1800
✉clerks@9-12bellyard.com
Call Date: Nov 1976, Middle Temple
Qualifications: [MA (Oxon)]
✉p.katz@9-12bellyard.com

Types of work: Corporate fraud, Corporate manslaughter, Crime, Crime and criminal due process, Serious fraud

KAUFMANN MS PHILLIPPA JANE QC (2011)

Doughty Street Chambers
53-54 Doughty Street, London WC1N 2LS, ☎020 7404 1313
✉enquiries@doughtystreet.co.uk
Doughty Street Chambers
Pall Mall Court, 61-67 King Street, Manchester M2 4PD, ☎0161 618 1066
Doughty Street Chambers
5th Floor, Broad Quay House, Prince Street, Bristol BS1 4DJ, ☎01179 058 717
Call Date: Oct 1991, Gray's Inn
Pupil Supervisor
Qualifications: [MA (Sheff) LLB (Bris)]
✉p.kaufmann@doughtystreet.co.uk

KAUL MISS KALYANI QC (2011)

9-12 Bell Yard
London WC2A 2JR, ☎020 7400 1800
✉clerks@9-12bellyard.com
Call Date: July 1983, Middle Temple
Pupil Supervisor
Qualifications: [LLB]
✉k.kaul@9-12bellyard.com

KAUR MISS HARINDER

Seven Bedford Row
7 Bedford Row, London WC1R 4BS, ☎020 7242 3555 ✉clerks@7br.co.uk
Call Date: May 1995, Inner Temple
Pupil Supervisor
Qualifications: [LLB (Hons) LLM]

KAUR MISS LUKHVINDER

18 St John Street
Manchester M3 4EA, ☎0161 278 1800
✉clerks@18sjs.com
Call Date: Nov 2000, Inner Temple
Qualifications: [LLB (Hons)]
✉lkaur@18sjs.com

KAVANAGH MR DENNIS NOEL

Westgate Chambers
64 High Street, Lewes, East Sussex BN7 1XG, ☎01273 480510
✉clerks@westgate-chambers.co.uk
Call Date: Mar 2003, Lincoln's Inn
Qualifications: [BA (Hons) PgDl LCC BVC]
✉dk@westgate-chambers.co.uk

KAVANAGH MRS JENNIFER

Goldsmith Chambers
Ground Floor, Goldsmith Building, Temple, London EC4Y 7BL, ☎020 7353 6802
✉clerks@goldsmithchambers.com
Call Date: Nov 1993, Lincoln's Inn
Pupil Supervisor
Qualifications: [LLB (Hons) (L'pool)]
✉J.Kavanagh@goldsmithchambers.com

KAY MR DOMINIC MATTHEW

Crown Office Chambers
2 Crown Office Row, Temple, London EC4Y 7HJ, ☎020 7797 8100
✉mail@crownofficechambers.com
Call Date: Oct 1997, Gray's Inn
Qualifications: [BSc (Hons) (Sussex)]
✉kay@crownofficechambers.com

KAY MR STEVEN WALTON QC (1997)

Nine Bedford Row
9 Bedford Row, London WC1R 4AZ, ☎020 7489 2727
✉clerks@9bedfordrow.co.uk
Call Date: Nov 1977, Inner Temple
Pupil Supervisor, Recorder
Qualifications: [LLB (Leeds)]
✉steven.kayqc@9bedfordrow.co.uk

KAYNE MR CHARLES ADRIAN

Carmelite Chambers
9 Carmelite Street, London EC4Y 0DR, ☎020 7936 6300
✉clerks@carmelitechambers.co.uk
Call Date: Nov 1989, Inner Temple
Qualifications: [LLB (Hons)]
✉akayne@carmelitechambers.co.uk

KAZA MISS AJANTA

1 Pump Court
Elm Court, Temple, London EC4Y 7AB, ☎020 7842 7070
✉(name)@pumpcourt.co.uk
Call Date: Nov 1998, Lincoln's Inn
Qualifications: [LLB (Hons)]
✉aka@1pumpcourt.co.uk

KAZAKOS MR LEON SAMUEL

187 Fleet Street
London EC4A 2AT, ☎ 020 7430 7430
✉ chambers@187fleetstreet.com
Call Date: Oct 1999, Lincoln's Inn
Pupil Supervisor
Qualifications: [BA (Hons)(Manc)]
leonkazakos@187fleetstreet.com

KE MISS LISI

18 St John Street
Manchester M3 4EA, ☎ 0161 278 1800
✉ clerks@18sjs.com
Call Date: Mar 2009, Middle Temple
Qualifications: [LLB (Hons) (Leeds)]
lke@18sjs.com

KEAL MR JOHN CHARLES

Five St Andrew's Hill
5 St Andrew's Hill, London EC4V 5BZ,
☎ 020 7332 5400 ✉ Clerks@5sah.co.uk
Call Date: July 2004, Lincoln's Inn
Qualifications: [BA Hons (Warw)]
johnkeal@5sah.co.uk

KEALEY MR GAVIN SEAN JAMES QC (1994)

7 King's Bench Walk
Ground Floor, 7 King's Bench Walk, Temple,
London EC4Y 7DS, ☎ 020 7910 8300
✉ clerks@7kbw.co.uk
Call Date: Feb 1977, Inner Temple
Recorder
Qualifications: [BA (Oxon)]
gkealey@7kbw.co.uk

KEALEY MR SIMON THOMAS

Zenith Chambers
10 Park Square, Leeds LS1 2LH,
☎ 0113 245 5438
✉ clerks@zenithchambers.co.uk
Call Date: Apr 1991, Inner Temple
Pupil Supervisor
Qualifications: [LLB (L'pool)]
skealey@zenithchambers.co.uk

KEAN MR GRAHAM EDWARD

3 PB Barristers
Royal Talbot House, 2 Victoria Street, Bristol,
Avon BS1 6BB, ☎ 0117 928 1520
Call Date: Mar 2012, Inner Temple
gkean@btinternet.com

KEANE MR OWEN ASHLEY

Design Chambers
24 Arterberry Road, Wimbledon, London
SW20 8AH, ☎ 020 7353 0747
✉ manager@designchambers.com
Call Date: Nov 1988, Inner Temple
Qualifications: [LLB]

KEARNEY MR ANDREW

St John's Chambers
101 Victoria Street, Bristol BS1 6PU,
☎ 0117 923 4700
✉ clerks@stjohnschambers.co.uk
Call Date: Mar 2007, Inner Temple
Qualifications: [BA (Oxon)]
andrew.kearney@stjohnschambers.co.uk

KEARNEY MR JAMES MARTIN

Chambers of Mr Ami Feder
Ground Floor, Lamb Building, Temple, London
EC4Y 7AS, ☎ 020 7797 7788
✉ clerks@lambbuilding.co.uk
Lamb Building
22 Ship Street, Brighton BN1 1AD,
☎ 01273 820490
✉ admin@lambbuilding.co.uk
Chambers of Mr Ami Feder
Ground Floor, Lamb Building, Temple, London
EC4Y 7AS, ☎ 020 7797 7788
✉ clerks@lambbuilding.co.uk
Call Date: Feb 1992, Gray's Inn
Pupil Supervisor
Qualifications: [LLB (Ireland)]
clerks@lambbuilding.co.uk

KEARNEY MR JOHN

Furnival Chambers
32 Furnival Street, London EC4A 1JQ,
☎ 020 7405 3232
Call Date: Nov 1994, Middle Temple
Qualifications: [LLB (Hons)]
jkearney@furnivallaw.co.uk

KEARNEY MR ROBERT MICHAEL

Lincoln House Chambers
Tower 12, The Avenue North, Spinningfields,
18-22 Bridge Street, Manchester M3 3BZ,
☎ 0161 832 5701
✉ info@lincolnhousechambers.com
16 Winckley Square
Preston PR1 3JJ, ☎ 01772 256100
Call Date: Nov 1996, Inner Temple
Qualifications: [LLB]
rob.kearney@lincolnhousechambers.com

E

KEATING MR DERMOT JOHN

25 Bedford Row
London WC1R 4HD, ☎ 020 7067 1500
✉ clerks@25bedfordrow.com
Call Date: Nov 1997, Inner Temple
Pupil Supervisor
Qualifications: [LLB (Brunel)]
✉ dkeating@25bedfordrow.com

KEATING MR JOSEPH PAUL

43 Temple Row Chambers
6th Floor, 43 Temple Row, Birmingham B2 5LS, ☎ 0121 237 6035
✉ clerks@43templerow.co.uk
Call Date: July 2001, Inner Temple
Qualifications: [LLB Dip Law]
✉ clerks@43templerow.co.uk

KEAY PROF ANDREW RICHARD

Kings Chambers
36 Young Street, Manchester M3 3FT,
☎ 0845 034 3444
✉ clerks@kingschambers.com
Kings Chambers
Embassy House, 60 Church Street, Birmingham B3 2DJ, ☎ 0845 034 3444
✉ clerks@kingschambers.com
Kings Chambers
5 Park Square East, Leeds LS1 2NE,
☎ 0845 034 3444
✉ clerks@kingschambers.com
Call Date: Mar 2010, Lincoln's Inn
Qualifications: [LLB LLM PhD]
✉ akeay@kingschambers.com

KEE MR PETER WILLIAM

Becket Chambers
17 New Dover Road, Canterbury, Kent CT1 3AS, ☎ 01227 786331
✉ clerks@becket-chambers.co.uk
Call Date: July 1983, Middle Temple
Qualifications: [BA (Oxon) LLM (Leic)]

KEEGAN MR LESLIE FRANCIS

Seven Bedford Row
7 Bedford Row, London WC1R 4BS,
☎ 020 7242 3555 ✉ clerks@7br.co.uk
Call Date: Nov 1989, Middle Temple
Qualifications: [BA (Dub) BSc DipLaw]
✉ lkeegan@7br.co.uk

KEEHAN MR MICHAEL JOSEPH QC (2001)

St Ive's Chambers
Whittall Street, Birmingham B4 6DH,
☎ 0121 236 0863
✉ clerks@stiveschambers.co.uk
Queen Square Chambers
56 Queen Square, Bristol BS1 4PR,
☎ 0117 921 1966 ✉ crime@qs-c.co.uk
Call Date: July 1982, Middle Temple
Recorder
Qualifications: [LLB (Hons) (B'ham)]
✉ michael.keehan@stiveschambers.co.uk

KEEL MR DOUGLAS VINCENT

11 Stone Buildings
11 Stone Buildings, Lincoln's Inn, London WC2A 3TG, ☎ 020 7831 6381
✉ clerks@11sb.com
Call Date: Oct 1997, Lincoln's Inn
Qualifications: [MA (Oxon) DIP in Law (Westmin)]
✉ keel@11sb.com

KEELEY MR JAMES FRANCIS

Sovereign Chambers
46 Park Place, Leeds LS1 2RY,
☎ 0113 245 1841
✉ clerks@sovereignchambers.co.uk
Call Date: Oct 1993, Middle Temple
Qualifications: [LLB (Hons)(Kingston) LLM]
✉ james.keeley@sovereignchambers.co.uk

KEELING MR ADRIAN FRANCIS QC (2011)

No5 Chambers
Fountain Court, Steelhouse Lane, Birmingham B4 6DR, ☎ 0845 210 5555 ✉ info@no5.com
No5 Chambers
Greenwood House, 4-7 Salisbury Court, London EC4Y 8AA, ☎ 0845 210 5555
No5 Chambers
38 Queen Square, Bristol BS1 4QS,
☎ 0845 210 5555
Call Date: Oct 1990, Inner Temple
Pupil Supervisor
Qualifications: [BA (Cantab)]
✉ afk@no5.com

KEELING-ROBERTS MR SAM

Cobden House Chambers
19 Quay Street, Manchester M3 3HN,
☎ 0161 833 6000 ✉ Clerks@Cobden.co.uk
Call Date: July 2005, Inner Temple
Qualifications: [BA LLM University of Sheffield]
✉ clerks@cobden.co.uk

KEEN MR GRAEME

Landmark Chambers
180 Fleet Street, London EC4A 2HG,
☎ 020 7430 1221
✉ clerks@landmarkchambers.co.uk
Call Date: Oct 1995, Middle Temple
Pupil Supervisor
Qualifications: [LLB (Hons)]
✉ gkeen@landmarkchambers.co.uk

KEEN MR RICHARD SANDERSON

Blackstone Chambers
Blackstone House, Temple, London
EC4Y 9BW, ☎ 020 7583 1770
✉ clerks@blackstonechambers.com
Call Date: Nov 2009, Middle Temple
Qualifications: [LLB (Hons) (Edin)]

KEEN MR SPENCER JOHN

Pump Court Chambers
31 Southgate Street, Winchester, Hampshire
SO23 9EB, ☎ 01962 868 161
✉ clerks@3pumpcourt.com
Pump Court Chambers
5 Temple Chambers, Temple Street, Swindon
SN1 1SQ, ☎ 01793 539899
✉ clerks@3pumpcourt.com
Riverview Chambers
Hamilton House, 1 Temple Avenue, London
EC4Y 0HA, ☎ 0844 225 3999
✉ chrisbaylis@riverviewchambers.com
Call Date: Nov 1998, Middle Temple
Qualifications: [LLB (Hons)(Essex)]
✉ sk@3pumpcourt.com

KEENE MRS GILLIAN MARGARET

Farrar's Building
Farrar's Building, Temple, London EC4Y 7BD,
☎ 020 7583 9241
✉ Chambers@farrarsbuilding.co.uk
Call Date: Nov 1980, Gray's Inn
Pupil Supervisor
Qualifications: [MA (Oxon)]
✉ gkeene@farrarsbuilding.co.uk, chambers@farrarsbuilding.co.uk

KEENE MR RUAIRI FELIX

Five Paper Buildings
1st Floor, Five Paper Buildings, Temple,
London EC4Y 7HB, ☎ 020 7583 6117
✉ clerks@5pb.co.uk
Call Date: Oct 2001, Middle Temple
Qualifications: [BSc (Hons) CPE]
✉ rk@5pb.co.uk

KEFFORD MR ANTHONY JOHN ROLAND

Octagon House
19 Colegate, Norwich NR3 1AT,
☎ 01603 623186
✉ clerks@octagonhouse.co.uk
Call Date: Nov 1980, Middle Temple
Qualifications: [BSc]
✉ clerks@octagon.co.uk

KEIGHLEY MISS MARY ANNA

187 Fleet Street
London EC4A 2AT, ☎ 020 7430 7430
✉ chambers@187fleetstreet.com
Call Date: Oct 2006, Middle Temple
Qualifications: [BA (Hons) (Leeds) PgDL]
✉ annakeighley@187fleetstreet.com

KEITH MR ALISTAIR JOHN

5 Pump Court
Ground Floor, 5 Pump Court, Temple, London
EC4Y 7AP, ☎ 020 7353 2532
✉ clerks@5pumpcourt.com
Call Date: Nov 1974, Middle Temple
Qualifications: [BD (Lond)]
✉ alistairkeith@5pumpcourt.com

KEITH MR BENJAMIN CHARLES ANDREW

Five St Andrew's Hill
5 St Andrew's Hill, London EC4V 5BZ,
☎ 020 7332 5400 ✉ Clerks@5sah.co.uk
Call Date: Oct 2004, Lincoln's Inn
Qualifications: [BA (Hons) PgDL]

KEITH MR HUGO GEORGE QC (2009)

3 Raymond Buildings
3 Raymond Buildings, Gray's Inn, London
WC1R 5BH, ☎ 020 7400 6400
✉ clerks@3rblaw.com
Call Date: Nov 1989, Gray's Inn
Qualifications: [MA (Oxon)]
✉ hugo.keith@3raymondbuildings.com

KEITH MR PATRICK JAMES BUCHANAN

Cornwall Street Chambers
85-87 Cornwall Street, Birmingham B3 3BY,
☎ 0121 233 7500
✉ clerks@cornwallstreet.co.uk
Call Date: Oct 2006, Inner Temple
Qualifications: [BA (Newc)]

E

KELBRICK MR ANTHONY MICHAEL

No.6 Park Square
Leeds LS1 2LW, ☎0113 245 9763
✉Tim@no6.co.uk
Call Date: Feb 1992, Gray's Inn
Pupil Supervisor, Recorder
Qualifications: [BA]
kelbrick@no6.co.uk

KELEHER MR PAUL ROBERT QC (2009)

25 Bedford Row
London WC1R 4HD, ☎020 7067 1500
✉clerks@25bedfordrow.com
Call Date: July 1980, Gray's Inn
Qualifications: [BA (Cantab)]
paul.keleher@25bedfordrow.com

KELLAR MR ROBERT ALEXANDER

1 Crown Office Row
1 Crown Office Row, Temple, London EC4Y 7HH, ☎020 7797 7500
✉mail@1cor.com
Call Date: Oct 1999, Gray's Inn
Pupil Supervisor
Qualifications: [BA (Oxon) LLM (Cantab)]
robert.kellar@1cor.com

KELLEHER MR BENEDICT PETER JOHN

Atkinson Bevan Chambers
1st Floor, 2 Harcourt Buildings, Temple, London EC4Y 9DB, ☎020 7353 2112
✉clerks@2hb.co.uk
Call Date: Nov 1994, Inner Temple
Qualifications: [LLB MSc (Bris)]
bkelleher@2hb.co.uk

KELLER MR CIARAN JOSEPH

Maitland Chambers
7 Stone Buildings, Lincoln's Inn, London WC2A 3SZ, ☎020 7406 1200
✉clerks@maitlandchambers.com
Call Date: July 2004, Lincoln's Inn
Qualifications: [BA Hons (Oxon) MA (Oxon) PGDip Law]
ckeller@maitlandchambers.com

KELLETT MR JOHN CHARLES

1 Paper Buildings
1st Floor, 1 Paper Buildings, Temple, London EC4Y 7EP, ☎020 7353 3728
✉clerks@onepaper.co.uk
Octagon House
19 Colegate, Norwich NR3 1AT, ☎01603 623186
✉clerks@octagonhouse.co.uk
Call Date: Nov 1971, Middle Temple
Pupil Supervisor
Qualifications: [BA (Cantab)]
charleskellett@onepaper.co.uk

KELLY MRS AMY LOUISE

12 College Place
Fauvelle Buildings, 12 College Place, Southampton SO15 2FE, ☎023 8032 0320
✉clerks@12cp.co.uk
Call Date: Nov 2000, Middle Temple
Qualifications: [BA (Hons) (Oxon)]
AKelly@12cp.co.uk

KELLY MR BENJAMIN KEITH

St Johns Buildings
24a - 28 St John Street, Manchester M3 4DJ, ☎0161 214 1500
✉clerk@stjohnsbuildings.co.uk
St Johns Buildings
21 White Friars, Chester CH1 1NZ, ☎01244 323070
✉clerk@stjohnsbuildings.co.uk
16 Winckley Square
Preston PR1 3JJ, ☎01772 256100
Call Date: Oct 2006, Lincoln's Inn
Qualifications: [BA]

KELLY MR BRENDAN DAMIEN QC (2008)

2 Hare Court
Lower Ground, Ground, 1st & 2nd Floor, 2 Hare Court, Temple, London EC4Y 7BH, ☎020 7353 3982 ✉clerks@2harecourt.com
Call Date: July 1988, Gray's Inn
Recorder
Qualifications: [LLB (Hons)]
brendankelly@2harecourt.com

KELLY MR DAVID THOMAS

Rowchester Chambers
4 Rowchester Court, Whittall Street, Birmingham B4 6DH, ☎0121 233 2327
✉clerks@rowchesterchambers.co.uk
Call Date: Oct 2003, Gray's Inn
Qualifications: [LLB (Derby)]

KELLY MR EAMONN

No. 3 Fleet Street Chambers
3 Fleet Street, London EC4Y 1DP,
☎ 020 7936 4474 ✉ clerks@3fleetstreet.com
Call Date: Oct 1997, Inner Temple
Qualifications: [BA (Cork) LLB (South Bank)]

KELLY MISS EMMA LOUISE

St Philips Chambers
55 Temple Row, Birmingham B2 5LS,
☎ 0121 246 7000 ✉ clerks@st-philips.com
Call Date: Oct 1997, Lincoln's Inn
Qualifications: [LLB (Hons)(Sheff)]
✉ ekelly@st-philips.com

KELLY MISS GEMMA JANE

Harcourt Chambers
1st Floor, 2 Harcourt Buildings, Temple,
London EC4Y 9DB, ☎ 0844 561 7135
Call Date: Nov 2007, Inner Temple
Qualifications: [BA (Oxon)]
✉ gkelly@harcourtchambers.law.co.uk

KELLY MR GEOFFREY ROBERT

Pump Court Chambers
Upper Ground Floor, 3 Pump Court, Temple,
London EC4Y 7AJ, ☎ 020 7353 0711
✉ clerks@3pumpcourt.com
Pump Court Chambers
5 Temple Chambers, Temple Street, Swindon
SN1 1SQ, ☎ 01793 539899
✉ clerks@3pumpcourt.com
Pump Court Chambers
31 Southgate Street, Winchester, Hampshire
SO23 9EB, ☎ 01962 868 161
✉ clerks@3pumpcourt.com
Call Date: Feb 1992, Middle Temple
Pupil Supervisor
Qualifications: [LLB (Hons) (Lond) LLM (Lond)]
✉ gk@3pumpcourt.com

KELLY MISS GERALDINE THERESE

Zenith Chambers
10 Park Square, Leeds LS1 2LH,
☎ 0113 245 5438
✉ clerks@zenithchambers.co.uk
Call Date: Oct 1996, Gray's Inn
Pupil Supervisor
Qualifications: [LLB]
✉ gkelly@zenithchambers.co.uk

KELLY MR MARK

No5 Chambers
Fountain Court, Steelhouse Lane, Birmingham
B4 6DR, ☎ 0845 210 5555 ✉ info@no5.com
No5 Chambers
Greenwood House, 4-7 Salisbury Court,
London EC4Y 8AA, ☎ 0845 210 5555
No5 Chambers
38 Queen Square, Bristol BS1 4QS,
☎ 0845 210 5555
Call Date: Nov 1985, Gray's Inn
Pupil Supervisor
Qualifications: [LLB (Bris) DipLaw (Belgium)]
✉ mrk@no5.com

KELLY MR MARTYN ALEXANDER

Apex
Harlech House, 20 Cathedral Road, Cardiff
CF11 9LJ, ☎ 02920 232 032
✉ clerks@apexchambers.net
Call Date: Nov 1972, Inner Temple
Pupil Supervisor
Qualifications: [MA (Oxon)]
✉ martyn.kelly@apexchambers.net

KELLY MR MATTHIAS JOHN QC (1999)

39 Essex Street
London WC2R 3AT, ☎ 020 7832 1111
✉ clerks@39essex.com
Call Date: Feb 1979, Gray's Inn
Qualifications: [BA (Hons) LLB (Dub)]

KELLY MR RICHARD BERNARD

East Anglian Chambers
140 New London Road, Chelmsford, Essex
CM2 0AW, ☎ 01473 214481
✉ chelmsford@ealaw.co.uk
East Anglian Chambers
53 North Hill, Colchester, Essex CO1 1QA,
☎ 01473 214481 ✉ colchester@ealaw.co.uk
East Anglian Chambers
15 The Close, Norwich, Norfolk NR1 4DZ,
☎ 01473 214481 ✉ norwich@ealaw.co.uk
East Anglian Chambers
Gresham House, 5 Museum Street, Ipswich,
Suffolk IP1 1HQ, ☎ 01473 214481
✉ ipswich@ealaw.co.uk
Call Date: Oct 1994, Gray's Inn
Qualifications: [BA]
✉ richardkelly@ealaw.co.uk

KELLY MR SEAN

Chancery House Chambers
7 Lisbon Square, Leeds, West Yorkshire
LS1 4LY, ☎ 0113 244 6691
✉ clerks@chanceryhouse.co.uk
Call Date: Oct 1990, Gray's Inn
Qualifications: [MA (Cantab)]

E

KELLY MR SHAW MARTIN

Staple Inn Chambers
1st Floor, 9 Staple Inn, Holborn Bars, London WC1V 7QH, ☎020 7242 5240
✉clerks@stapleinn.co.uk
Call Date: Oct 1997, Middle Temple
Qualifications: [BA (Hons)(Lond)]
smk@stapleinn.co.uk

KELLY MS SIOBHAN FRANCES

Coram Chambers
9-11 Fulwood Place, London WC1V 6HG, ☎020 7092 3700
✉mail@coramchambers.co.uk
Call Date: Oct 1995, Middle Temple
Qualifications: [BA (Hons)]
siobhan.kelly@coramchambers.co.uk

KELLY MISS SIOBHAN MARIE

Call Date: Oct 1995, Gray's Inn
Pupil Supervisor
Qualifications: [BA]
kelly@paradise-sq.co.uk

KELSEY MISS KATHERINE LAUREN

1 KBW Chambers
1 King's Bench Walk, Temple, London EC4Y 7DB, ☎020 7936 1500
✉clerks@1kbw.co.uk
King's Bench Chambers
174 High Street, Lewes BN7 1YE, ☎01273 402600
Call Date: July 2003, Lincoln's Inn
Qualifications: [BA Hons (Oxon)]

KELSEY-FRY MR JOHN QC (2000)

Cloth Fair Chambers
39-40 Cloth Fair, London EC1A 7NT, ☎020 7710 6444
✉email@clothfairchambers.com
Call Date: Nov 1978, Gray's Inn
johnkelsey-fry@clothfairchambers.com

KEMBER MR RICHARD

9 Park Place
9 Park Place, Cardiff, South Glamorgan CF10 3DP, ☎029 2038 2731
✉clerks@9parkplace.co.uk
Call Date: Oct 1993, Middle Temple
Pupil Supervisor
Qualifications: [MA (Oxon)]
rkember@9parkplace.co.uk

KEMP MR CHRISTOPHER MARK

Outer Temple Chambers
The Outer Temple, 222 Strand, London WC2R 1BA, ☎020 7353 6381
✉clerks@outertemple.com
Call Date: Nov 1984, Middle Temple
Pupil Supervisor, Recorder
Qualifications: [BA (Oxon) Dip Law]
christopher.kemp@outertemple.com

KEMP MR DAVID MICHAEL

Chambers of Martin Burr
15 Old Bailey, London EC4M 7EF, ☎0845 123 1234 ✉clerks@barristerweb.com
Call Date: Nov 2000, Inner Temple
Qualifications: [LLB (Lond)]

KEMP MR EDWARD WILLIAM

12 King's Bench Walk
12 King's Bench Walk, Temple, London EC4Y 7EL, ☎020 7583 0811
Call Date: Oct 2005, Inner Temple
Qualifications: [LLB (Lond) LLM (Lond)]
kemp@12kbw.co.uk

KEMP MR JAMES RUPERT

Trinity Chambers
The Custom House, 39 Quayside, Newcastle Upon Tyne NE1 3DE, ☎0191 232 1927
✉info@trinitychambers.co.uk
Trinity Chambers
Multi Media Exchange, 72-80 Corporation Road, Middlesbrough TS1 2RF, ☎01642 247569
✉info@trinitychambers.co.uk
Call Date: Oct 1999, Inner Temple
Qualifications: [LLB (Brunel) LLM]
j.kemp@trinitychambers.co.uk

KEMP MR STEPHEN RICHARD

1 High Pavement
Nottingham NG1 1HF, ☎0115 941 8218
✉clerks@1highpavement.co.uk
Call Date: Oct 1995, Lincoln's Inn
Qualifications: [BA (Hons)(York) Dip in Law]
Stephenkemp@1highpavement.co.uk.cjsm.net

KEMPSTER MR IVOR TOBY CHALMERS

Old Square Chambers
3 Orchard Court, St Augustine's Yard, Bristol BS1 5DP, ☎ 0117 930 5100
✉ clerks@oldsquare.co.uk
Old Square Chambers
10-11 Bedford Row, London WC1R 4BU, ☎ 020 7269 0300 ✉ clerks@oldsquare.co.uk
Call Date: July 1980, Inner Temple
Pupil Supervisor
Qualifications: [LLB (Leic)]
✉ kempster@oldsquare.co.uk

Types of work: Discrimination, Employment, Personal injury

KENDAL MR TIMOTHY JAMES

2 Bedford Row
London WC1R 4BU, ☎ 020 7440 8888
✉ clerks@2bedfordrow.co.uk
Call Date: Nov 1985, Gray's Inn
Pupil Supervisor
Qualifications: [LLB]
✉ tkendal@2bedfordrow.co.uk

KENDALL MR JOEL CAMILO TEPLITZ

12 King's Bench Walk
12 King's Bench Walk, Temple, London EC4Y 7EL, ☎ 020 7583 0811
Call Date: Oct 1993, Middle Temple
Qualifications: [MA (Oxon)]
✉ kendall@12kbw.co.uk

KENDRICK MR DOMINIC JOHN QC (1997)

7 King's Bench Walk
Ground Floor, 7 King's Bench Walk, Temple, London EC4Y 7DS, ☎ 020 7910 8300
✉ clerks@7kbw.co.uk
Call Date: July 1981, Middle Temple
Qualifications: [MA (Cantab)]
✉ dkendrick@7kbw.law.co.uk

KENDRICK MISS JULIA ELIZABETH

Crown Office Chambers
2 Crown Office Row, Temple, London EC4Y 7HJ, ☎ 020 7797 8100
✉ mail@crownofficechambers.com
Call Date: Oct 2005, Middle Temple
Qualifications: [BA (Hons) Oxford Dip Law]
✉ kendrick@crownofficechambers.com

KENEFICK MR TIMOTHY

7 King's Bench Walk
Ground Floor, 7 King's Bench Walk, Temple, London EC4Y 7DS, ☎ 020 7910 8300
✉ clerks@7kbw.co.uk
Call Date: Oct 1996, Gray's Inn
Pupil Supervisor
Qualifications: [BA (Cantab)]
✉ tkenefick@7kbw.co.uk

KENNEDY MR ANDREW IAN

1 Crown Office Row
1 Crown Office Row, Temple, London EC4Y 7HH, ☎ 020 7797 7500
✉ mail@1cor.com
Call Date: Nov 1989, Middle Temple
Pupil Supervisor
Qualifications: [BA (Hons) (Newc) Dip Law]
✉ andrew.kennedy@1cor.com

KENNEDY MR BERESFORD ROLAND GEORGE

Eighteen Carlton Crescent
Rownhams House, Rownhams, Southampton SO16 8LF, ☎ 023 8063 9001
✉ clerks@18carltoncrescent.co.uk
Call Date: Oct 1995, Middle Temple
Pupil Supervisor
Qualifications: [LLB (Hons) LLM]
✉ clerks@18carltoncrescent.co.uk

KENNEDY MR BRIAN JAMES

Chambers of Mr Brian James Kennedy
72 Linzee Road, London N8 7RE, ☎ 07891 747 342
Call Date: Mar 1996, Inner Temple
Qualifications: [BA]

KENNEDY MR CHRISTOPHER LAURENCE PAUL QC (2010)

9 St John Street
Manchester M3 4DN, ☎ 0161 955 9000
✉ civilclerks@9sjs.com / criminalclerks@9sjs.com
Call Date: July 1989, Gray's Inn
Pupil Supervisor
Qualifications: [BA (Cantab)]

KENNEDY MISS LUCY JULIA

QEB Hollis Whiteman
1-2 Laurence Pountney Hill, London EC4R 0EU, ☎ 020 7933 8855
✉ barristers@qebhw.co.uk
Call Date: Nov 2000, Middle Temple
Qualifications: [BA (Hons) (York) LPC CPE (Notts)]
✉ lucy.kennedy@qebhw.co.uk

E

KENNEDY MR MICHAEL JOHN

Call Date: May 1985, Middle Temple
Pupil Supervisor
Qualifications: [LLB (Bris)]
michael.kennedy@stjohnsbuildings.co.uk

KENNEDY MR PETER NICHOLAS DODGSON

15 Winckley Square
Preston PR1 3JJ, ☎01772 252828
clerks@15winckleysq.co.uk
Call Date: July 1977, Lincoln's Inn
Pupil Supervisor
Qualifications: [LLB (Lond)]

KENNEDY MISS ROISIN

12 King's Bench Walk
12 King's Bench Walk, Temple, London EC4Y 7EL, ☎020 7583 0811
Call Date: Nov 2006, Inner Temple
Qualifications: [BA (Oxon)]

KENNEDY MR STUART VICTOR

3 PB Barristers
3 Paper Buildings, Temple, London EC4Y 7EU, ☎020 7583 8055
3 PB Barristers
23 Beaumont Street, Oxford OX1 2NP, ☎01865 793 736
3 PB Barristers
30 Christchurch Road, Bournemouth, Dorset BH1 3PD, ☎01202 292102
clerks.bournemouth@3paper.co.uk
3 PB Barristers
Royal Talbot House, 2 Victoria Street, Bristol, Avon BS1 6BB, ☎0117 928 1520
3 PB Barristers
4 St Peter Street, Winchester SO23 8BW, ☎01962 868884
clerks.winchester@3paper.co.uk
Call Date: Oct 1999, Lincoln's Inn
Pupil Supervisor
Qualifications: [LLB (Hons)]
stuart.kennedy@3paper.co.uk

KENNEDY OF THE SHAWS BARONESS HELENA ANN QC (1991)

Doughty Street Chambers
53-54 Doughty Street, London WC1N 2LS, ☎020 7404 1313
enquiries@doughtystreet.co.uk
Doughty Street Chambers
Pall Mall Court, 61-67 King Street, Manchester M2 4PD, ☎0161 618 1066
Doughty Street Chambers
5th Floor, Broad Quay House, Prince Street, Bristol BS1 4DJ, ☎01179 058 717
Call Date: July 1972, Gray's Inn
h.kennedy@doughtystreet.co.uk

KENNEDY-MCGREGOR MS MARILYN

11 Stone Buildings
11 Stone Buildings, Lincoln's Inn, London WC2A 3TG, ☎020 7831 6381
clerks@11sb.com
Call Date: July 1989, Gray's Inn
Pupil Supervisor
Qualifications: [BA (Dunelm) DipLaw]
kennedy-mcgregor@11sb.com

KENNELLY MR BRIAN ANTHONY MARC

Blackstone Chambers
Blackstone House, Temple, London EC4Y 9BW, ☎020 7583 1770
clerks@blackstonechambers.com
Call Date: Oct 1999, Middle Temple
Pupil Supervisor
Qualifications: [BA (Hons) (Cantab)]
briankennelly@blackstonechambers.com

KENNING MR THOMAS PATRICK

Citadel Chambers
The Citadel, 190 Corporation Street, Birmingham B4 6QD, ☎0121 233 8500
clerks@citadelchambers.com
Call Date: Feb 1989, Lincoln's Inn
Pupil Supervisor
Qualifications: [BSc (Wales)]
clerks@citadelchambers.com, kevincgrego@aol.com

KENNY MISS CHARLOTTE

Exchange Chambers
One Derby Square, Derby Square, Liverpool L2 9XX, ☎0151 236 7747
info@exchangechambers.co.uk
Exchange Chambers
7 Ralli Courts, West Riverside, Manchester M3 5FT, ☎0161 833 2722
Exchange Chambers
Oxford House, Oxford Row, Leeds LS1 3BE, ☎0113 203 1970
spencer@exchangechambers.co.uk
Call Date: Nov 1993, Gray's Inn
Qualifications: [BA (Hull) Dip Law (Lond)]
kenny@exchangechambers.co.uk

E

KENNY MR CHRISTIAN EDWARD MACKENZIE

1 Hare Court
1 Hare Court, Temple, London EC4Y 7BE,
☎ 020 7797 7070 ✉ clerks@1hc.com
Call Date: Oct 2003, Inner Temple
Pupil Supervisor
Qualifications: [BA (Hons)(Bris)]
kenny@1hc.com

KENNY MR DAVID JOSEPH

Cobden House Chambers
19 Quay Street, Manchester M3 3HN,
☎ 0161 833 6000 ✉ Clerks@Cobden.co.uk
Call Date: Nov 1982, Middle Temple
Pupil Supervisor
Qualifications: [BA MPhil (Nott'm)]
clerks@cobden.co.uk

KENNY MR EDWARD ALEXANDER

Becket Chambers
17 New Dover Road, Canterbury, Kent
CT1 3AS, ☎ 01227 786331
✉ clerks@becket-chambers.co.uk
Call Date: July 2009, Middle Temple
Qualifications: [BA (Hons) (Oxon) MSt (Oxon) Grad Dip Law (Lond)]
ekenny@becket-chambers.co.uk

KENNY MR JULIAN HECTOR MARRIOTT

20 Essex Street
London WC2R 3AL, ☎ 020 7842 1200
✉ clerks@20essexst.com
Call Date: Nov 1997, Gray's Inn
Pupil Supervisor
Qualifications: [BA (Oxon)]
clerks@20essexst.com

KENNY MR MARTIN WILLIAM

Walnut House
63 St. David's Hill, Exeter, Devon EX4 4DW,
☎ 01392 279751
✉ clerks@walnuthouse.co.uk
Call Date: July 1998, Inner Temple
Pupil Supervisor
Qualifications: [BA (Sheff)]

KENNY MR STEPHEN CHARLES WILFRID QC (2006)

7 King's Bench Walk
Ground Floor, 7 King's Bench Walk, Temple,
London EC4Y 7DS, ☎ 020 7910 8300
✉ clerks@7kbw.co.uk
Call Date: July 1987, Inner Temple
Qualifications: [MA BCL (Oxon)]
skenny@7kbw.co.uk

KENT MR ALAN PETER QC (2009)

23 Essex Street
London WC2R 3AA, ☎ 020 7413 0353
✉ clerks@23es.com
Maidstone Chambers
33 Earl Street, Maidstone, Kent ME14 1PF,
☎ 01622 688592
✉ clerks@maidstonechambers.co.uk
Call Date: Nov 1986, Inner Temple
Qualifications: [LLB]
alankent@23es.com

KENT MR MICHAEL HARCOURT QC (1996)

Crown Office Chambers
2 Crown Office Row, Temple, London
EC4Y 7HJ, ☎ 020 7797 8100
✉ mail@crownofficechambers.com
Call Date: July 1975, Middle Temple
Recorder
Qualifications: [BA (Sussex)]
kent@crownofficechambers.com

KENT MR PETER BRYAN CARLYLE

3 PB Barristers
3 Paper Buildings, Temple, London EC4Y 7EU,
☎ 020 7583 8055
3 PB Barristers
Royal Talbot House, 2 Victoria Street, Bristol,
Avon BS1 6BB, ☎ 0117 928 1520
3 PB Barristers
23 Beaumont Street, Oxford OX1 2NP,
☎ 01865 793 736
3 PB Barristers
4 St Peter Street, Winchester SO23 8BW,
☎ 01962 868884
✉ clerks.winchester@3paper.co.uk
3 PB Barristers
30 Christchurch Road, Bournemouth, Dorset
BH1 3PD, ☎ 01202 292102
✉ clerks.bournemouth@3paper.co.uk
Call Date: Nov 1978, Gray's Inn
Pupil Supervisor
Qualifications: [LLB FCI (Arb)]

KENT MR RUPERT HAWORTH HARCOURT

Atkinson Bevan Chambers
1st Floor, 2 Harcourt Buildings, Temple,
London EC4Y 9DB, ☎ 020 7353 2112
✉ clerks@2hb.co.uk
Call Date: Nov 2006, Middle Temple
Qualifications: [BA (Hons) (Bris)]

E

KENTRIDGE MRS JANET ROCHELLE

Matrix Chambers
Griffin Building, Gray's Inn, London WC1R 5LN, ☎ 020 7404 3447
✉ matrix@matrixlaw.co.uk / Iscott@matrixlaw.co.uk
Call Date: July 1999, Lincoln's Inn
Qualifications: [BA (Hons) LLM (Africa) MA (Oxon) LLM (Lond) LLB]
janetkentridge@matrixlaw.co.uk

KENTRIDGE SIR SYDNEY QC (1984)

Brick Court Chambers
7-8 Essex Street, London WC2R 3LD, ☎ 020 7379 3550 ✉ clerks@brickcourt.co.uk
Call Date: July 1977, Lincoln's Inn
Qualifications: [BA (South Africa) MA (Oxon)]

KENWARD MR TIMOTHY DAVID NELSON

Number 7 Harrington Street Chambers
7 Harrington Street, Liverpool L2 9YH, ☎ 0151 242 0707 ✉ clerks@7hs.co.uk
Call Date: Nov 1987, Gray's Inn
Pupil Supervisor
Qualifications: [MA (Oxon)]
tim.kenward@7hs.co.uk

KENYON MRS FLAVIA ALEXANDRA

3 Temple Gardens
Lower Ground Floor, 3 Temple Gardens, Temple, London EC4Y 9AU, ☎ 020 7353 3102
✉ clerks@3tg.co.uk
Call Date: Oct 2005, Lincoln's Inn
Qualifications: [BA (Hons) (Oxon)]

KENYON MISS LAURA JANE

18 Red Lion Court
London EC4A 3EB, ☎ 020 7520 6000
✉ chambers@18rlc.co.uk
18 Red Lion Court (Annexe)
Thornwood House, 102 New London Road, Chelmsford, Essex CM2 0RG,
☎ 01245 280880
Call Date: Nov 2009, Inner Temple
Qualifications: [BA (Oxon)]

KEOGH MR ANDREW JOHN

No5 Chambers
Fountain Court, Steelhouse Lane, Birmingham B4 6DR, ☎ 0845 210 5555 ✉ info@no5.com
No5 Chambers
Greenwood House, 4-7 Salisbury Court, London EC4Y 8AA, ☎ 0845 210 5555
No5 Chambers
38 Queen Square, Bristol BS1 4QS,
☎ 0845 210 5555
Call Date: Nov 1978, Inner Temple
Pupil Supervisor
Qualifications: [BSc (Econ)]
ajk@no5.com

KEOGH MR RICHARD THOMAS

Farringdon Chambers
180 Bermondsey Street, London SE1 3TQ,
☎ 020 7089 5700
Call Date: Nov 1991, Middle Temple
Pupil Supervisor
Qualifications: [LLB (Hons) (Essex)]
richardkeogh@farringdon-law.co.uk

KERLY MISS VICTORIA LOUISE

Garden Court Chambers
57-60 Lincoln's Inn Fields, London WC2A 3LJ, ☎ 020 7993 7600 ✉ info@gclaw.co.uk
Call Date: July 2005, Inner Temple
Qualifications: [LLB (Hons) (L'pool) LLM]
vikkik@gclaw.co.uk

KERNER MRS ANGELA

Bell Yard Chambers
116/118 Chancery Lane, London WC2A 1PP,
☎ 020 7306 9292
✉ byclerks@bellyardchambers.co.uk
Call Date: July 1965, Inner Temple
Qualifications: [LLB (Lond)]
akerner@bellyardchambers.co.uk, akerner@btinternet.com.

KERR MR CHRISTOPHER RICHARD

2 Pump Court
1st Floor, 2 Pump Court, Temple, London EC4Y 7AH, ☎ 020 7353 5597
✉ clerks@2pumpcourt.co.uk
Call Date: Nov 1988, Middle Temple
Pupil Supervisor
Qualifications: [MA (Oxon)]
christopher.kerr@2pumpcourt.cjsm.net

E

KERR MR DEREK WILLIAM

Lamb Chambers
Lamb Building, Elm Court, Temple, London EC4Y 7AS, ☎020 7797 8300
✉info@lambchambers.co.uk
Call Date: Oct 1994, Middle Temple
Pupil Supervisor
Qualifications: [LLB (Hons)(Reading)]
✉derekkerr@lambchambers.co.uk

KERR DR JOANNA

Lamb Chambers
Lamb Building, Elm Court, Temple, London EC4Y 7AS, ☎020 7797 8300
✉info@lambchambers.co.uk
Call Date: Oct 2001, Gray's Inn
Qualifications: [MA PhD]
✉joannakerr@lambchambers.com

KERR MR NEIL FORSYTH

3 Dr Johnson's Buildings
Ground Floor, 3 Dr Johnson's Buildings, Temple, London EC4Y 7BA, ☎020 7353 4854
✉clerks@3djb.co.uk
Call Date: Nov 2001, Inner Temple
Qualifications: [LLB (Hons) CPE]
✉nkerr@3djb.co.uk

KERR MR PATRICK BRIAN

12 King's Bench Walk
12 King's Bench Walk, Temple, London EC4Y 7EL, ☎020 7583 0811
Call Date: Oct 2006, Gray's Inn
Qualifications: [MA (Oxon)]
✉kerr@12kbw.co.uk

KERR MR SIMON ALEXANDER

7 King's Bench Walk
Ground Floor, 7 King's Bench Walk, Temple, London EC4Y 7DS, ☎020 7910 8300
✉clerks@7kbw.co.uk
Call Date: Oct 1997, Lincoln's Inn
Pupil Supervisor
Qualifications: [BA (Hons) (Oxon) Dip Law (Lond) MA (Oxon)]
✉skerr@7kbw.co.uk

KERR MR TIM JULIAN QC (2001)

11 King's Bench Walk
11 King's Bench Walk, Temple, London EC4Y 7EQ, ☎020 7632 8500
✉clerksroom@11kbw.com
Call Date: Nov 1983, Gray's Inn
Recorder
Qualifications: [BA (Oxon)]
✉tim.kerr@11kbw.com

KER-REID MR JOHN

Pump Court Chambers
Upper Ground Floor, 3 Pump Court, Temple, London EC4Y 7AJ, ☎020 7353 0711
✉clerks@3pumpcourt.com
Pump Court Chambers
5 Temple Chambers, Temple Street, Swindon SN1 1SQ, ☎01793 539899
✉clerks@3pumpcourt.com
Pump Court Chambers
31 Southgate Street, Winchester, Hampshire SO23 9EB, ☎01962 868 161
✉clerks@3pumpcourt.com
Call Date: Nov 1974, Inner Temple
Qualifications: [MA (Cantab)]
✉jkr@3pumpcourt.com

KERRIGAN MR HERBERT AIRD

9-12 Bell Yard
London WC2A 2JR, ☎020 7400 1800
✉clerks@9-12bellyard.com
Call Date: July 1990, Middle Temple
Qualifications: [LLB (Hons) MA (Keele) PGDip TH (Oxon)]
✉herbert.kerrigan@blackchambers.co.uk

KERRUISH-JONES MR MATTHEW JOHN

Farrar's Building
Farrar's Building, Temple, London EC4Y 7BD, ☎020 7583 9241
✉Chambers@farrarsbuilding.co.uk
Linenhall Chambers
1 Stanley Place, Chester CH1 2LU, ☎01244 348282
✉clerks@linenhallchambers.co.uk
Call Date: Nov 2003, Lincoln's Inn
Qualifications: [BA (Hons) (Manch) PgDl]
✉mkerruishjones@farrarsbuilding.co.uk

KERSHAW MR ANDREW

Broadway House Chambers
Broadway House, 9 Bank Street, Bradford, West Yorkshire BD1 1TW, ☎01274 722560
✉clerks@broadwayhouse.co.uk
Broadway House Chambers
25 Park Square West, Leeds, West Yorkshire LS1 2PW, ☎0113 246 2600
✉clerks@broadwayhouse.co.uk
Call Date: July 1975, Middle Temple
Pupil Supervisor, Recorder
Qualifications: [LLB (Lond)]
✉clerks@broadwayhouse.co.uk

KERSHAW MR DEAN EARL

No5 Chambers
Fountain Court, Steelhouse Lane, Birmingham B4 6DR, ☎0845 210 5555 ✉info@no5.com
No5 Chambers
Greenwood House, 4-7 Salisbury Court, London EC4Y 8AA, ☎0845 210 5555
No5 Chambers
38 Queen Square, Bristol BS1 4QS, ☎0845 210 5555
Call Date: Nov 1995, Lincoln's Inn
Recorder
Qualifications: [LLB (Hons)]
dk@no5.com

KESSLER MR JAMES RICHARD QC (2003)

Taxchambers
15 Old Square, Lincoln's Inn, London WC2A 3UE, ☎020 7242 2744
✉taxchambers@15oldsquare.co.uk
Call Date: July 1984, Gray's Inn
Qualifications: [MA (Oxon)]
taxchambers@15oldsquare.co.uk

KESSLING MR CHRISTOPHER DAVID

Chambers of Mr Christopher Kessling
14 Belvoir Street, Leicester LE1 6QH, ☎01509 890690 ✉ck@cklaw.co.uk
Call Date: Oct 1992, Middle Temple
Pupil Supervisor
Qualifications: [LLB (Hons)]

E

KETTLE-WILLIAMS MISS ALEXANDRA MARGARET

Chambers of Marion Smullen and Kerim Fuad QC
1 Inner Temple Lane, London EC4Y 1AF, ☎020 7427 4400 ✉clerks@1itl.com
Call Date: Oct 2004, Inner Temple
Qualifications: [BA (Hons) Exeter CPE]
clerks@1itl.com

KEY DR PAUL ANTHONY

Essex Court Chambers
24 Lincoln's Inn Fields, London WC2A 3EG, ☎020 7813 8000
✉clerksroom@essexcourt.net
Call Date: July 1997, Inner Temple
Pupil Supervisor
Qualifications: [PhD (Cantab) LLB (Auckland)]
pkey@essexcourt.net

KEYES MR GRANT ANDREW

Northampton Chambers
10 Spencer Parade, Northampton NN1 5AQ, ☎01604 636271
✉clerks@northampton-chambers.co.uk
Call Date: July 2007, Gray's Inn
Qualifications: [BA (Leic) MBA (Warwick)]

KHALID MR JAMES

Goulds Green Chambers
Room D, 2 Bakers Yard, High Street, Uxbridge UB8 1JZ, ☎01895 422574
Goulds Green Chambers
48 Goulds Green, Uxbridge UB8 3DG, ☎01895 422574 ✉jamkha@tiscali.co.uk
Call Date: Nov 1999, Lincoln's Inn
Qualifications: [LLB (Hons)(Lond)]
jamkha@tiscali.co.uk

KHALID MR SALEEM

1 Chancery Lane
London WC2A 1LF, ☎0845 634 6666
✉clerks@1chancerylane.com
Call Date: Mar 2001, Lincoln's Inn
Qualifications: [LLB (Hons) (London) LLM]
skhalid@1chancerylane.com

KHALIL MR KARIM SHAKIR QC (2003)

1 Paper Buildings
1st Floor, 1 Paper Buildings, Temple, London EC4Y 7EP, ☎020 7353 3728
✉clerks@onepaper.co.uk
Octagon House
19 Colegate, Norwich NR3 1AT, ☎01603 623186
✉clerks@octagonhouse.co.uk
Call Date: July 1984, Lincoln's Inn
Recorder
Qualifications: [MA (Cantab)]
karimkhalil@onepaper.co.uk

KHALIQUE MISS NAGEENA

No5 Chambers
Fountain Court, Steelhouse Lane, Birmingham B4 6DR, ☎0845 210 5555 ✉info@no5.com
No5 Chambers
Greenwood House, 4-7 Salisbury Court, London EC4Y 8AA, ☎0845 210 5555
No5 Chambers
38 Queen Square, Bristol BS1 4QS, ☎0845 210 5555
Call Date: Oct 1994, Gray's Inn
Qualifications: [BDS LDSRCS]
nk@no5.com

KHAMISA MR MOHAMMED JAFFER QC (2006)

Old Bailey Chambers
15 Old Bailey, London EC4M 7EF,
☎020 3008 6404
✉clerks@15oldbaileychambers.com
Call Date: Nov 1985, Middle Temple
Qualifications: [BA (Hons) (Lond)]

KHAN MISS ABDAH

Dyers Chambers
35 Bedford Row, London WC1R 4JH,
☎020 7404 1881
✉admin@dyerschambers.com
Call Date: Oct 2000, Lincoln's Inn
Qualifications: [LLB (Hons) (Middlesex)]

KHAN MR ABDUL ALEEM

Gray's Chambers
10 Heathside Close, Newbury, Essex IG2 7PD,
☎020 8518 2525
✉aleem.khan@btinternet.com
Call Date: July 2003, Inner Temple
Qualifications: [BA (Osmania) LLB (Osmania)]

KHAN MISS AISHA

Nine Bedford Row
9 Bedford Row, London WC1R 4AZ,
☎020 7489 2727
✉clerks@9bedfordrow.co.uk
Call Date: Oct 2002, Lincoln's Inn
Qualifications: [LLB]
✉aisha.khan@9bedfordrow.co.uk

KHAN DR ALEXANDER

Coral House
42 Charles Street, Manchester, Lancashire M1 7DB
Call Date: Nov 2000, Lincoln's Inn
Qualifications: [BSc (Hons) (Leic) MSc UMIST PhD (B'Ham) CPE (B'Ham)]

KHAN MR ARFAN

Field Court Chambers
5 Field Court, Gray's Inn, London WC1R 5EF,
☎020 7405 6114 ✉clerks@fieldcourt.co.uk
Call Date: Nov 2001, Lincoln's Inn
Qualifications: [LLB (Hons) LLM (Lond)]
✉arfan.khan@fieldcourt.co.uk

KHAN MR AYOUB

Chambers of Mr Ayoub Khan
127 Albert Road, Aston, Birmingham B6 5ND,
☎07930 987202
✉ayoub_khan64@hotmail.com
Call Date: July 2005, Lincoln's Inn
Qualifications: [CPE]

KHAN MR BASHARAT JAMIL

Number 7 Harrington Street Chambers
7 Harrington Street, Liverpool L2 9YH,
☎0151 242 0707 ✉clerks@7hs.co.uk
Call Date: July 1986, Lincoln's Inn
Qualifications: [LLB (Hons)]
✉jamil.khan@7hs.co.uk

KHAN MR CHANGEZ ALI

Farrar's Building
Farrar's Building, Temple, London EC4Y 7BD,
☎020 7583 9241
✉Chambers@farrarsbuilding.co.uk
Call Date: July 2008, Lincoln's Inn
Qualifications: [LLB (Lond)]
✉ckhan@farrarsbuilding.co.uk

KHAN MR FORZ

Chambers of Mr F Khan
19 Glenwood Road, Hounslow, London TW3 1SW, ☎07854 109584
✉forzkhan@live.co.uk
6 King's Bench Walk
Ground, Third & Fourth Floors, 6 King's Bench Walk, Temple, London EC4Y 7DR,
☎020 7353 4931 ✉clerks@6kbw.co.uk
Call Date: July 1988, Middle Temple
Qualifications: [LLB (Hons)(Lond)]

KHAN MR HASSAN AHMED

4 Paper Buildings
1st Floor, 4 Paper Buildings, Temple, London EC4Y 7EX, ☎020 7427 5200
✉clerks@4pb.com
Call Date: Nov 1999, Lincoln's Inn
Pupil Supervisor
Qualifications: [LLB (Hons)(L'pool)]
✉hk@4pb.com

KHAN MISS HELEN MARY GRACE

Pump Court Chambers
Upper Ground Floor, 3 Pump Court, Temple, London EC4Y 7AJ, ☎020 7353 0711
✉clerks@3pumpcourt.com
Pump Court Chambers
5 Temple Chambers, Temple Street, Swindon SN1 1SQ, ☎01793 539899
✉clerks@3pumpcourt.com
Pump Court Chambers
31 Southgate Street, Winchester, Hampshire SO23 9EB, ☎01962 868 161
✉clerks@3pumpcourt.com
Call Date: Nov 1990, Middle Temple
Pupil Supervisor
Qualifications: [LLB (Hons)(Leics)]
✉hk@3pumpcourt.com

E

KHAN MR IMRAN

St Albans Chambers
2 - 4 St Peter's Street, St Albans, Hertfordshire AL1 3LF, ☎01727 843383
✉clerks@stalbanschambers.com
Call Date: Nov 2001, Lincoln's Inn
Qualifications: [LLB (Hons)]
✉ik@stalbanschambers.com

KHAN MS JUDITH QC (2010)

Garden Court Chambers
57-60 Lincoln's Inn Fields, London WC2A 3LJ, ☎020 7993 7600 ✉info@gclaw.co.uk
Call Date: Nov 1989, Middle Temple
Pupil Supervisor
Qualifications: [LLB (Hons)]
✉judyk@gclaw.co.uk

KHAN MR JULFIKHAR FARHAZ

Outer Temple Chambers
The Outer Temple, 222 Strand, London WC2R 1BA, ☎020 7353 6381
✉clerks@outertemple.com
Call Date: Oct 2005, Middle Temple
Qualifications: [BA (Hons) (Bris) MSt (Oxon)]
✉julfikhar.khan@outertemple.com

KHAN MR KARIM ASAD AHMAD QC (2011)

Temple Garden Chambers
1 Harcourt Buildings, Temple, London EC4Y 9DA, ☎020 7583 1315
✉clerks@tgchambers.com
Call Date: Oct 1992, Lincoln's Inn
Qualifications: [LLB(Hons)(Lond) AKC (Lond) Dip Int Rel (Italy)]
✉kk@tgchambers.com

KHAN MR MAHMOOD SHAFI

Willesden Chambers
5 Mora Road, London NW2 6SD, ☎020 3273 1042 ✉syril@btinternet.com
Luton Chambers
103 Wexham Close, Luton LU3 3TX, ☎01582 598394 ✉mshafikhan@hotmail.com
Call Date: Feb 1994, Lincoln's Inn
Qualifications: [BA MA (Brunel) LLB]

KHAN MR MOHAMMAD TAYYAB

Melbury House
55 Manor Road, Oadby, Leicester, Leicestershire LE2 2LL, ☎07801 037802
✉melburyhousechambers@yahoo.co.uk
Call Date: Feb 1972, Lincoln's Inn
Qualifications: [LLM (Lond) MLitt (Cantab)]
✉melburyhousechambers@yahoo.co.uk

KHAN MR MOHAMMED ASIF

Citadel Chambers
The Citadel, 190 Corporation Street, Birmingham B4 6QD, ☎0121 233 8500
✉clerks@citadelchambers.com
Call Date: Nov 1983, Lincoln's Inn
Qualifications: [LLB DPL]
✉clerks@citadelchambers.com

KHAN MR NAWAB MUHAMMAD BABAR

Chambers of Mr N M B Khan
452 Dunstable Road, Luton, Bedfordshire LU4 8DJ, ☎07508 876022
✉chambers.nbk@gmx.com
Call Date: Nov 1999, Inner Temple
Qualifications: [LLB (Thames)]

KHAN MISS RUWENA AFROZE

Zenith Chambers
10 Park Square, Leeds LS1 2LH, ☎0113 245 5438
✉clerks@zenithchambers.co.uk
Call Date: July 2005, Inner Temple
Qualifications: [LLB University of Manchester]
✉rkhan@zenithchambers.co.uk

KHAN MR SAADALLAH FRANS HASSAN

Blackfriars Chambers
79-83 Temple Chambers, 3-7 Temple Avenue, London EC4Y 0HP, ☎020 7353 7400
✉clerks@blackfriarschambers.com
Call Date: Nov 1991, Lincoln's Inn
Pupil Supervisor
Qualifications: [BSc LLB (Hons)]
✉frans.khan@blackfriarschambers.com

KHAN MR SHAHNAWAZ ZULFIQUAR

1 Gray's Inn Square
Ground Floor, 1 Gray's Inn Square, London WC1R 5AA, ☎020 7405 0001
Call Date: July 2001, Lincoln's Inn
Qualifications: [LLB (Hons) LLM]
✉skhan@1gis.co.uk

KHAN MR SHAUKAT ALI

Chambers of Mr S A Khan
1 Wolverton Avenue, Kingston Upon Thames, Surrey KT2 7QF, ☎020 8541 3875
✉shaukou.ali.khan73@hotmail.com
Call Date: July 1971, Lincoln's Inn
Pupil Supervisor
Qualifications: [BA LLB]

KHAN MISS SHAZIA

Kenworthy's Chambers
Arlington House, Bloom Street, Salford, Manchester M3 6AJ, ☎0161 832 4036
Call Date: July 2000, Lincoln's Inn
Qualifications: [LLB(Hons) (Sheff) LLM]
s.khan@kenworthysbarristers.co.uk

KHAN MR SHOKAT

Kings Chambers
36 Young Street, Manchester M3 3FT, ☎0845 034 3444
clerks@kingschambers.com
Kings Chambers
5 Park Square East, Leeds LS1 2NE, ☎0845 034 3444
clerks@kingschambers.com
Kings Chambers
Embassy House, 60 Church Street, Birmingham B3 2DJ, ☎0845 034 3444
clerks@kingschambers.com
Call Date: Nov 1979, Middle Temple
Qualifications: [LLB (Warw) LLM (Lond)]
skhan@kingschambers.com

KHAN MR SHUFQAT MAHMOOD

No.6 Park Square
Leeds LS1 2LW, ☎0113 245 9763
Tim@no6.co.uk
Call Date: Nov 1996, Lincoln's Inn
Qualifications: [LLB (Hons)(Notts)]

KHAN MR SOHEIL JAVED

No.6 Park Square
Leeds LS1 2LW, ☎0113 245 9763
Tim@no6.co.uk
Call Date: Mar 2007, Lincoln's Inn
Qualifications: [LLB]

KHAN MR TAHIR QC (2011)

Broadway House Chambers
Broadway House, 9 Bank Street, Bradford, West Yorkshire BD1 1TW, ☎01274 722560
clerks@broadwayhouse.co.uk
Broadway House Chambers
25 Park Square West, Leeds, West Yorkshire LS1 2PW, ☎0113 246 2600
clerks@broadwayhouse.co.uk
Call Date: July 1986, Lincoln's Inn
Pupil Supervisor, Recorder
Qualifications: [LLB (Hons)]
tzk@broadwayhouse.co.uk

KHAN MR TARIQ ALI

Chambers of Mr T A Khan
St. Paulés Chambers, First Floor, 459 Foleshill Road, Coventry CV6 5AQ, ☎02476 666 400
tkhan@stpaulslaw.co.uk
Call Date: Nov 1996, Lincoln's Inn
Qualifications: [LLB (Hons)]

KHAN MR ZARIF

Dyers Chambers
35 Bedford Row, London WC1R 4JH, ☎020 7404 1881
admin@dyerschambers.com
Call Date: Oct 1996, Lincoln's Inn
Pupil Supervisor
Qualifications: [LLB (Hons)(Manc)]

KHANDKER MISS MONISHA ELEONORA

Albion Chambers
Broad Street, Bristol BS1 1DR, ☎0117 927 2144
clerks@albionchambers.co.uk
Call Date: July 2005, Middle Temple
Qualifications: [BA (Hons) PGDip Law]
monisha.khandker@albionchambers.co.uk

KHANGURE MR AVTAR AMARJIT SINGH QC (2003)

St Philips Chambers
55 Temple Row, Birmingham B2 5LS, ☎0121 246 7000 clerks@st-philips.com
Call Date: Nov 1985, Gray's Inn
Recorder
Qualifications: [BA LLM (Cantab)]
akhangure@st-philips.co.uk

KHANNA MS PRIYADARSHANI

18 Red Lion Court
London EC4A 3EB, ☎020 7520 6000
chambers@18rlc.co.uk
18 Red Lion Court (Annexe)
Thornwood House, 102 New London Road, Chelmsford, Essex CM2 0RG, ☎01245 280880
Call Date: July 2001, Middle Temple
Qualifications: [LLB (Hons) MA]
priya.khanna@18rlc.co.uk

KHAWAR MR AFTAB

Call Date: July 1983, Gray's Inn
Qualifications: [LLB (Hons)(Lancs)]

E

KHAYUM MR ZULFIKAR

Atkin Chambers
1 Atkin Building, Gray's Inn, London WC1R 5AT, ☎020 7404 0102
✉clerks@atkinchambers.com
Call Date: Oct 2006, Gray's Inn
Qualifications: [LLB (Hons)]
zkhayum@atkinchambers.com

KHOKHANI MISS ERIKA

Goldsmith Chambers
Ground Floor, Goldsmith Building, Temple, London EC4Y 7BL, ☎020 7353 6802
✉clerks@goldsmithchambers.com
Call Date: Oct 2007, Inner Temple
Qualifications: [LLB (Lond)]

KHUBBER MR RANJIV

1 Pump Court
Elm Court, Temple, London EC4Y 7AB, ☎020 7842 7070
✉(name)@pumpcourt.co.uk
Call Date: Nov 1994, Middle Temple
Pupil Supervisor
Qualifications: [BA (Hons) (Kent) MA (Sussex)]
rkh@1pumpcourt.co.uk

KHURSHID MR JAWDAT

7 King's Bench Walk
Ground Floor, 7 King's Bench Walk, Temple, London EC4Y 7DS, ☎020 7910 8300
✉clerks@7kbw.co.uk
Call Date: Oct 1994, Lincoln's Inn
Pupil Supervisor
Qualifications: [BA (Hons)(Oxon)]
jkhurshid@7kbw.co.uk

KIAI MISS GILDA

1 Pump Court
Elm Court, Temple, London EC4Y 7AB, ☎020 7842 7070
✉(name)@pumpcourt.co.uk
Call Date: July 2004, Gray's Inn
Qualifications: [LLB (Sussex)]
gki@1pumpcourt.co.uk

KIBLING MR THOMAS

Matrix Chambers
Griffin Building, Gray's Inn, London WC1R 5LN, ☎020 7404 3447
✉matrix@matrixlaw.co.uk / Iscott@matrixlaw.co.uk
Call Date: Nov 1990, Middle Temple
Pupil Supervisor
Qualifications: [LLB]
ThomasKibling@matrixlaw.co.uk

KIDD MISS JOANNE TERESA

Fountain Chambers
Cleveland Business Centre, 1 Watson Street, Middlesbrough TS1 2RQ, ☎01642 804040
✉clerks@fountainchambers.co.uk
Call Date: Oct 1995, Lincoln's Inn
Qualifications: [BA (Hons)(Cantab) MA (Cantab)]

KIDD MR PETER WILLIAM

Number 7 Harrington Street Chambers
7 Harrington Street, Liverpool L2 9YH, ☎0151 242 0707 ✉clerks@7hs.co.uk
Call Date: July 1987, Lincoln's Inn
Qualifications: [LLB (L'pool)]
peter.kidd@7hs.co.uk

KILCOYNE MR PATRICK DESMOND OLIVER

42 Bedford Row
London WC1R 4LL, ☎020 7831 0222
✉clerks@42br.com
Call Date: May 1990, Inner Temple
Qualifications: [LLB (So'ton) LLM (Lond)]
desmond.kilcoyne@42br.com

KILCOYNE MR PAUL ANTHONY JAMES

Temple Garden Chambers
1 Harcourt Buildings, Temple, London EC4Y 9DA, ☎020 7583 1315
✉clerks@tgchambers.com
Call Date: Nov 1985, Lincoln's Inn
Pupil Supervisor
Qualifications: [LLB (B'ham)]
pkilcoyne@tgchambers.com

KILLALEA MR STEPHEN JOSEPH QC (2006)

Devereux Chambers
Queen Elizabeth Building, Temple, London EC4Y 9BS, ☎020 7353 7534
✉clerks@devchambers.co.uk
Call Date: July 1981, Middle Temple
Qualifications: [LLB]
killalea@devchambers.co.uk

KILLEEN MR ROBERT WILLIAM

Capital Fortune Chambers
Third Floor, 14 Nicholas Lane, London EC4N 7BN, ☎0845 3630 430
✉rk@cfchambers.com
Call Date: Oct 1995, Middle Temple
Qualifications: [LLB (Hons) CeMAP Dip Law CeFA]

KILLEEN MR SIMON JOHN

Number 7 Harrington Street Chambers
7 Harrington Street, Liverpool L2 9YH,
☎0151 242 0707 ✉clerks@7hs.co.uk
Call Date: July 1984, Inner Temple
Recorder
Qualifications: [BA]
✉simon.killeen@7hs.co.uk

KILLEN MR GEOFFREY JAMES

Clerksroom (Taunton)
Equity House, Administration Centre, Blackbrook Park Avenue, Taunton, Somerset TA1 2PX, ☎0845 083 3000
✉mail@clerksroom.com
King's Lynn Chambers
26 The Birches, South Wootton, King's Lynn, Norfolk PE30 3JG, ☎01553 672 085
✉timothy.leader@tesco.net
Call Date: Oct 1990, Inner Temple
Qualifications: [LLB]
✉killen@clerksroom.com

KILLEN MR TIMOTHY JAMES

2 Temple Gardens
2 Temple Gardens, Temple, London EC4Y 9AY, ☎020 7822 1200
✉clerks@2tg.co.uk
Call Date: Oct 2010, Gray's Inn
Qualifications: [BA]
✉tkillen@2tg.co.uk

KILROY MS CHARLOTTE LOUISE

Doughty Street Chambers
53-54 Doughty Street, London WC1N 2LS, ☎020 7404 1313
✉enquiries@doughtystreet.co.uk
Doughty Street Chambers
Pall Mall Court, 61-67 King Street, Manchester M2 4PD, ☎0161 618 1066
Doughty Street Chambers
5th Floor, Broad Quay House, Prince Street, Bristol BS1 4DJ, ☎01179 058 717
Call Date: Oct 1999, Inner Temple
Qualifications: [BA (Oxon)]
✉c.kilroy@doughtystreet.co.uk

KILVINGTON MISS SARAH ELIZABETH

18 St John Street
Manchester M3 4EA, ☎0161 278 1800
✉clerks@18sjs.com
Call Date: Oct 1999, Middle Temple
Pupil Supervisor
Qualifications: [BA (Oxon)]

KILVINGTON MR SIMON CHARLES

18 St John Street
Manchester M3 4EA, ☎0161 278 1800
✉clerks@18sjs.com
Call Date: Nov 1995, Lincoln's Inn
Pupil Supervisor
Qualifications: [BA (Hons) (Oxon)]
✉skilvington@18sjs.com

KIMBELL MR JOHN ASHLEY

Quadrant Chambers
Quadrant House, 10 Fleet Street, London EC4Y 1AU, ☎020 7583 4444
✉info@quadrantchambers.com
Call Date: Nov 1995, Inner Temple
Pupil Supervisor
Qualifications: [BA MPhil (Cantab)]

KIMBLIN DR RICHARD THOMAS

No5 Chambers
Fountain Court, Steelhouse Lane, Birmingham B4 6DR, ☎0845 210 5555 ✉info@no5.com
No5 Chambers
Greenwood House, 4-7 Salisbury Court, London EC4Y 8AA, ☎0845 210 5555
No5 Chambers
38 Queen Square, Bristol BS1 4QS, ☎0845 210 5555
Call Date: July 1998, Middle Temple
Pupil Supervisor
Qualifications: [BSc (Hons)(Dunelm) PhD]
✉rk@no5.com, kimblin@cwcom.net

KIME MR MATTHEW JONATHAN

Ingenuity IP Chambers
Chambers Legal Service, 71b Queensway, Petts Wood, Kent BR5 1DQ
✉lp@chamberslegalservice.com
No. 3 Fleet Street Chambers
3 Fleet Street, London EC4Y 1DP, ☎020 7936 4474 ✉clerks@3fleetstreet.com
Cobden House Chambers
19 Quay Street, Manchester M3 3HN, ☎0161 833 6000 ✉Clerks@Cobden.co.uk
Call Date: July 1988, Middle Temple
Pupil Supervisor
Qualifications: [MA, DPhil (Oxon) LLB (Lond) Dip Law (Lond)]

KIMMINS MR CHARLES DOMINIC QC (2010)

20 Essex Street
London WC2R 3AL, ☎020 7842 1200
✉clerks@20essexst.com
Call Date: Nov 1994, Inner Temple
Pupil Supervisor
Qualifications: [BA (Cantab)]
✉clerks@20essexst.com

E

KIMSEY MR MARK FENTON

Castle Chambers
The Old Fire Station, 90 High Street, Harrow-on-the-Hill, Middlesex HA1 3LP,
☎ 020 8423 6579 ✉ info@castlechambers.net
Call Date: Oct 1990, Inner Temple
Qualifications: [LLB (Hons)]

KINCH MISS HANNAH MAITZE JANE

23 Essex Street
London WC2R 3AA, ☎ 020 7413 0353
✉ clerks@23es.com
Call Date: July 2006, Middle Temple
Qualifications: [LLB (Hons) (Lond) LLM (Lond)]

KING MR ADAM HENRY PETER

QEB Hollis Whiteman
1-2 Laurence Pountney Hill, London EC4R 0EU, ☎ 020 7933 8855
✉ barristers@qebhw.co.uk
Call Date: Nov 2005, Inner Temple
Qualifications: [BA University of Bristol CPE BPP Law School]
adam.king@qebhw.co.uk

E

KING MISS ALISON EMMA

1 Pump Court
Elm Court, Temple, London EC4Y 7AB,
☎ 020 7842 7070
✉ (name)@pumpcourt.co.uk
Call Date: Oct 2005, Gray's Inn
Qualifications: [KLLB (Kent)]
eki@1pumpcourt.co.uk

KING MISS ANNE FAWZIA

42 Bedford Row
London WC1R 4LL, ☎ 020 7831 0222
✉ clerks@42br.com
Call Date: Nov 1985, Middle Temple
Pupil Supervisor
Qualifications: [BA (Law)]
fawzia.king@42br.com

KING MR CHARLES GRANVILLE

Chambers of Mr C G King
6 All Saints Field, Stroud GL5 1NE,
☎ 07949 461717 ✉ ckingesq@yahoo.co.uk
Call Date: Nov 1995, Middle Temple
Qualifications: [LLB (Hons)]

KING MR EDMUND GRAHAM RALPH

Essex Court Chambers
24 Lincoln's Inn Fields, London WC2A 3EG,
☎ 020 7813 8000
✉ clerksroom@essexcourt.net
Call Date: Nov 1999, Inner Temple
Pupil Supervisor
Qualifications: [BA (Oxon) LLM (Harvard)]
eking@essexcourt.net

KING MS EMMA

2 Bedford Row
London WC1R 4BU, ☎ 020 7440 8888
✉ clerks@2bedfordrow.co.uk
Call Date: Nov 1999, Inner Temple
Qualifications: [BA (Oxon)]
eking@2bedfordrow.co.uk

KING MR GELAGA PERRY

2 Bedford Row
London WC1R 4BU, ☎ 020 7440 8888
✉ clerks@2bedfordrow.co.uk
Call Date: July 1985, Gray's Inn
Pupil Supervisor
Qualifications: [LLB (Hull)]
gpking@2bedfordrow.co.uk

KING MR GRAHAM ANTHONY

1 Gray's Inn Square
Ground Floor, 1 Gray's Inn Square, London WC1R 5AA, ☎ 020 7405 0001
Call Date: July 2007, Gray's Inn
Qualifications: [MA (Oxon)]
gking@1gis.co.uk

KING MR HENRY GEORGE JOHN

Fountain Court Chambers
Fountain Court, Temple, London EC4Y 9DH,
☎ 020 7583 3335
✉ chambers@fountaincourt.co.uk
Call Date: Nov 1998, Inner Temple
Pupil Supervisor
Qualifications: [MA (Oxon)]
hking@fountaincourt.co.uk

KING MR JOHN PATRICK

Nine Bedford Row
9 Bedford Row, London WC1R 4AZ,
☎ 020 7489 2727
✉ clerks@9bedfordrow.co.uk
Call Date: July 1983, Gray's Inn
Pupil Supervisor
john.king@9bedfordrow.co.uk

KING MR JOHN SAWREY

12 King's Bench Walk
12 King's Bench Walk, Temple, London EC4Y 7EL, ☎ 020 7583 0811
Call Date: Nov 1973, Inner Temple
Pupil Supervisor
Qualifications: [LLB (Lond)]
king@12kbw.co.uk

KING MR JONATHAN DAVID

Deans Court Chambers
24 St John Street, Manchester M3 4DF, ☎ 0161 214 6000 ✉ clerks@deanscourt.co.uk
Call Date: Mar 2009, Inner Temple
Qualifications: [BA (Cantab) MA (Cantab)]
king@deanscourt.co.uk

KING MRS JUDITH ANN

Maidstone Chambers
33 Earl Street, Maidstone, Kent ME14 1PF, ☎ 01622 688592
✉ clerks@maidstonechambers.co.uk
Call Date: July 2002, Middle Temple
Qualifications: [LLB (Hons) MA (Lond) CPE (Lond)]

KING MISS JULIA LOUISE

1 High Pavement
Nottingham NG1 1HF, ☎ 0115 941 8218
✉ clerks@1highpavement.co.uk
Call Date: July 1998, Inner Temple
Qualifications: [LLB]
juliaking@1highpavement.co.uk

KING MR KARL ERROL

Hardwicke
New Square, Lincoln's Inn, London WC2A 3SB, ☎ 020 7242 2523
✉ enquiries@hardwicke.co.uk
Call Date: Nov 1985, Gray's Inn
Pupil Supervisor, Recorder
Qualifications: [BA (Lond)]
karl.king@hardwicke.co.uk

KING MR MARK COURTNEY DILKE

Lamb Chambers
Lamb Building, Elm Court, Temple, London EC4Y 7AS, ☎ 020 7797 8300
✉ info@lambchambers.co.uk
Call Date: Oct 1997, Inner Temple
Qualifications: [BSc (London)]
markking@lambchambers.co.uk

KING MR MICHAEL RICHARD

XXIV Old Buildings
Ground Floor, 24 Old Buildings, Lincoln's Inn, London WC2A 3UP, ☎ 020 7691 2424
✉ clerks@xxiv.co.uk
Call Date: July 1971, Gray's Inn
Pupil Supervisor
Qualifications: [BA (Cantab)]

KING MR NEIL ANTHONY

4 Breams Buildings
Chancery Lane, London EC4A 1HP, ☎ 020 7092 1900 ✉ clerks@4bb.co.uk
Call Date: Oct 2003, Lincoln's Inn
Qualifications: [BA (Hons) (Oxon)]

KING MR NEIL GERALD ALEXANDER QC (2000)

Landmark Chambers
180 Fleet Street, London EC4A 2HG, ☎ 020 7430 1221
✉ clerks@landmarkchambers.co.uk
Call Date: July 1980, Inner Temple
Qualifications: [MA (Oxon)]
nking@landmarkchambers.co.uk

KING MR OLIVER

St Johns Buildings
24a - 28 St John Street, Manchester M3 4DJ, ☎ 0161 214 1500
✉ clerk@stjohnsbuildings.co.uk
St Johns Buildings
21 White Friars, Chester CH1 1NZ, ☎ 01244 323070
✉ clerk@stjohnsbuildings.co.uk
16 Winckley Square
Preston PR1 3JJ, ☎ 01772 256100
Call Date: July 2001, Gray's Inn
Qualifications: [LLB (Hons)]
clerk@stjohnsbuildings.co.uk

KING MR PHILIP HENRY RUSSELL QC (2002)

187 Fleet Street
London EC4A 2AT, ☎ 020 7430 7430
✉ chambers@187fleetstreet.com
Call Date: Nov 1974, Inner Temple
Qualifications: [BA]
chambers@187fleetstreet.com

KING MISS SAMANTHA LEONIE

4 Paper Buildings
1st Floor, 4 Paper Buildings, Temple, London EC4Y 7EX, ☎ 020 7427 5200
✉ clerks@4pb.com
Call Date: Nov 1990, Middle Temple
Qualifications: [BA (Cantab)]
sk@4pb.com

E

KING MR SIMON PAUL

Seven Bedford Row
7 Bedford Row, London WC1R 4BS,
☎ 020 7242 3555 ✉ clerks@7br.co.uk
Call Date: Nov 1987, Gray's Inn
Pupil Supervisor, Recorder
Qualifications: [MA (Oxon)]
✉ sking@7br.co.uk

KING MS SINEAD AOIFE

Principal Chambers
15 Lime Tree Walk, Sevenoaks, Kent
TN13 1YH, ☎ 0845 209 8080
Cornerstone Barristers
2-3 Gray's Inn Square, Gray's Inn, London
WC1R 5JH, ☎ 020 7242 4986
✉ chambers@2-3gis.co.uk
Call Date: Mar 2006, Lincoln's Inn
Qualifications: [BA (Hons) (Oxon)]

KINGERLEY MR MARTIN GODDARD

36 Bedford Row
London WC1R 4JH, ☎ 020 7421 8000
✉ chambers@36bedfordrow.co.uk
Call Date: July 1999, Lincoln's Inn
Qualifications: [LLB (Newc)]
✉ clerks@36bedfordrow.co.uk, mkingerley@36bedfordrow.co.uk

KINGSCOTE MR GEOFFREY LLEWELYN WOODWARD

1 Hare Court
1 Hare Court, Temple, London EC4Y 7BE,
☎ 020 7797 7070 ✉ clerks@1hc.com
Call Date: Nov 1993, Inner Temple
Pupil Supervisor
Qualifications: [BA (Hons) (Oxon) M Phil (Cantab)]
✉ kingscote@1hc.com

KINGSLEY MR RICHARD CHARLES

14 Gray's Inn Square
14 Gray's Inn Square, Gray's Inn, London
WC1R 5JP, ☎ 020 7242 0858
✉ clerks@14gis.co.uk
Call Date: July 1977, Inner Temple
Pupil Supervisor
Qualifications: [LLB (Hons)]
✉ clerks@14graysinnsquare.co.uk

KING-SMITH MR JAMES

Crown Office Row Chambers
119 Church Street, Brighton, Sussex
BN1 1UD, ☎ 01273 625625
✉ clerks@1cor.com
1 Crown Office Row
1 Crown Office Row, Temple, London
EC4Y 7HH, ☎ 020 7797 7500
✉ mail@1cor.com
Call Date: Nov 1980, Middle Temple
Pupil Supervisor
Qualifications: [MA (Oxon)]

KINGSTON MR WILLIAM MARTIN QC (1992)

No5 Chambers
Fountain Court, Steelhouse Lane, Birmingham
B4 6DR, ☎ 0845 210 5555 ✉ info@no5.com
No5 Chambers
Greenwood House, 4-7 Salisbury Court,
London EC4Y 8AA, ☎ 0845 210 5555
No5 Chambers
38 Queen Square, Bristol BS1 4QS,
☎ 0845 210 5555
Call Date: July 1972, Middle Temple
Qualifications: [LLB]
✉ martink@no5.com

KINGSWELL MISS GEMMA LOUISE

18 Red Lion Court
London EC4A 3EB, ☎ 020 7520 6000
✉ chambers@18rlc.co.uk
Call Date: July 2008, Inner Temple
Qualifications: [LLB (Manch)]

KING-UNDERWOOD MR GREGORY

Carmelite Chambers
9 Carmelite Street, London EC4Y 0DR,
☎ 020 7936 6300
✉ clerks@carmelitechambers.co.uk
Call Date: Oct 2002, Middle Temple
Qualifications: [BA (Leeds) Dip Law (BPP)]
✉ gkingunderwood@carmelitechambers.co.uk

KINLOCH-JONES MS CAROLINE PARKER

12 College Place
Fauvelle Buildings, 12 College Place,
Southampton SO15 2FE, ☎ 023 8032 0320
✉ clerks@12cp.co.uk
Call Date: Nov 2002, Inner Temple
Qualifications: [CPE (Bris)]

KINNEAR MISS ELISE

Field Court Chambers
5 Field Court, Gray's Inn, London WC1R 5EF, ☎ 020 7405 6114 ✉ clerks@fieldcourt.co.uk
Call Date: Oct 2003, Gray's Inn
Qualifications: [BA (Oxon)]
elise.kinnear@fieldcourt.co.uk

KINNEAR MR JONATHAN SHEA QC (2012)

9-12 Bell Yard
London WC2A 2JR, ☎ 020 7400 1800
✉ clerks@9-12bellyard.com
Call Date: Oct 1994, Gray's Inn
Pupil Supervisor
Qualifications: [LLB]
j.kinnear@9-12bellyard.com

KINNIER MR ANDREW JOHN

Henderson Chambers
2 Harcourt Buildings, Temple, London EC4Y 9DB, ☎ 020 7583 9020
✉ clerks@hendersonchambers.co.uk
30 Park Place
Cardiff CF10 3BS, ☎ 029 2039 8421
✉ clerks@30parkplace.law.co.uk
Call Date: Oct 1996, Middle Temple
Pupil Supervisor
Qualifications: [MA (Cantab)]
akinnier@hendersonchambers.co.uk

KINSKY MR CYRIL NORMAN FRANCIS QC (2010)

3 Verulam Buildings
London WC1R 5NT, ☎ 020 7831 8441
✉ chambers@3vb.com
Call Date: Nov 1988, Middle Temple
Pupil Supervisor
Qualifications: [BA (Cantab) Dip Law (Lond)]

KINSLER MISS MARIE LOUISE

2 Temple Gardens
2 Temple Gardens, Temple, London EC4Y 9AY, ☎ 020 7822 1200
✉ clerks@2tg.co.uk
Call Date: July 1992, Inner Temple
Qualifications: [BA (Cantab) Dip Ad Eur Studies]
mlkinsler@2tg.co.uk

KIRBY MR PETER JOHN

Hardwicke
New Square, Lincoln's Inn, London WC2A 3SB, ☎ 020 7242 2523
✉ enquiries@hardwicke.co.uk
Call Date: July 1989, Inner Temple
Pupil Supervisor
Qualifications: [LLB (Hull)]
peter.kirby@hardwicke.co.uk

KIRBY MISS RHIAN FAITH

30 Park Place
Cardiff CF10 3BS, ☎ 029 2039 8421
✉ clerks@30parkplace.law.co.uk
Call Date: Oct 2000, Lincoln's Inn
Qualifications: [LLB (Hons) (Cardiff)]
rfk@30parkplace.co.uk

KIRBY MISS RUTH MARY ANTHONY

4 Paper Buildings
1st Floor, 4 Paper Buildings, Temple, London EC4Y 7EX, ☎ 020 7427 5200
✉ clerks@4pb.com
Call Date: Oct 1994, Middle Temple
Pupil Supervisor
Qualifications: [BCL LLM (Lond) CEDR]
rk@4pb.com

KIRK MR ANTHONY JAMES NIGEL QC (2001)

1 KBW Chambers
1 King's Bench Walk, Temple, London EC4Y 7DB, ☎ 020 7936 1500
✉ clerks@1kbw.co.uk
King's Bench Chambers
174 High Street, Lewes BN7 1YE, ☎ 01273 402600
Call Date: July 1981, Gray's Inn
Qualifications: [LLB (Lond) AKC]

KIRK MR GRAEME CHARLES

One Essex Court
1st Floor, Temple, London EC4Y 9AR, ☎ 020 7936 3030 ✉ clerks@1ec.co.uk
Call Date: Nov 2001, Middle Temple
Qualifications: [BA (Hons)(Oxon) CPE]
gkirk@1ec.co.uk

KIRK MR JONATHAN QC (2010)

36 Bedford Row
London WC1R 4JH, ☎ 020 7421 8000
✉ chambers@36bedfordrow.co.uk
Gough Square Chambers
6-7 Gough Square, London EC4A 3DE, ☎ 020 7353 0924 ✉ gsc@goughsq.co.uk
Call Date: Nov 1995, Lincoln's Inn
Pupil Supervisor
Qualifications: [LLB (Hons)]
jkirk@36bedfordrow.co.uk

KIRK MR ROBERT WILSON

Chambers of Mr R W Kirk
20 Redcliffe Square, London SW10 9JZ, ☎ 020 7373 7364
✉ robert.kirk@btinternet.com
Call Date: Nov 1972, Lincoln's Inn
Pupil Supervisor
Qualifications: [MA (Cantab) FCIArb]
robert.kirk@btinternet.com

E

KIRK MR THOMAS SEAN ROBINSON

12 College Place
Fauvelle Buildings, 12 College Place, Southampton SO15 2FE, ☎ 023 8032 0320
✉ clerks@12cp.co.uk
Call Date: July 2007, Lincoln's Inn
Qualifications: [BCL (Oxon) LLB (Lond)]
tkirk@12cp.co.uk

KIRKWOOD MR EDWARD TOBY

Harcourt Chambers
1st Floor, 2 Harcourt Buildings, Temple, London EC4Y 9DB, ☎ 0844 561 7135
Call Date: Nov 1999, Inner Temple
Qualifications: [LLB (Exon)]
ekirkwood@harcourtchambers.law.co.uk

KIRTLEY MR PAUL GEORGE

Exchange Chambers
Oxford House, Oxford Row, Leeds LS1 3BE, ☎ 0113 203 1970
✉ spencer@exchangechambers.co.uk
Exchange Chambers
One Derby Square, Derby Square, Liverpool L2 9XX, ☎ 0151 236 7747
✉ info@exchangechambers.co.uk
Littleton Chambers
3 King's Bench Walk North, Temple, London EC4Y 7HR, ☎ 020 7797 8600
✉ fschneider@littletonchambers.co.uk
Call Date: July 1982, Middle Temple
Pupil Supervisor, Recorder
Qualifications: [MA (Cantab)]

KISSER MISS AMY HANNAH

Queen Elizabeth Building
3rd Floor, Queen Elizabeth Building, Temple, London EC4Y 9BS, ☎ 020 7797 7837
✉ clerks@qeb.co.uk
Call Date: July 2009, Inner Temple
Qualifications: [BA (Oxon) BCL (Oxon)]
a.kisser@qeb.co.uk

KISSIN MISS CLARE NICOLA

One Brick Court
1st Floor, One Brick Court, Temple, London EC4Y 9BY, ☎ 020 7353 8845
✉ clerks@onebrickcourt.com
Call Date: Oct 2009, Middle Temple
Qualifications: [BA (Hons) (Cantab)]
ck@onebrickcourt.com

KITCHEN MR SIMON DUGALD OWEN RALPH

Dyers Chambers
35 Bedford Row, London WC1R 4JH, ☎ 020 7404 1881
✉ admin@dyerschambers.com
Call Date: Nov 1988, Lincoln's Inn
Qualifications: [LLB (Hons)]

KITCHENER MR NEIL DAVID QC (2008)

One Essex Court
Ground Floor, One Essex Court, Temple, London EC4Y 9AR, ☎ 020 7583 2000
✉ clerks@oeclaw.co.uk
Call Date: Oct 1991, Middle Temple
Qualifications: [BA (Oxon)]
nkitchener@oeclaw.co.uk

KITCHIN MISS LOUISE JANE

Lincoln House Chambers
Tower 12, The Avenue North, Spinningfields, 18-22 Bridge Street, Manchester M3 3BZ, ☎ 0161 832 5701
✉ info@lincolnhousechambers.com
Call Date: Oct 1998, Middle Temple
Qualifications: [BA (Hons)(Leeds) CPE (Manc)]
louise.kitchin@lincolnhousechambers.com

KITCHING MRS KOSSAR

Trinity Chambers
The Custom House, 39 Quayside, Newcastle Upon Tyne NE1 3DE, ☎ 0191 232 1927
✉ info@trinitychambers.co.uk
Trinity Chambers
Multi Media Exchange, 72-80 Corporation Road, Middlesbrough TS1 2RF, ☎ 01642 247569
✉ info@trinitychambers.co.uk
Call Date: July 1999, Inner Temple
Qualifications: [LLB (Teeside)]
k.kitching@trinitychambers.co.uk

KITCHING MR ROBIN MILES

Deans Court Chambers
24 St John Street, Manchester M3 4DF, ☎ 0161 214 6000 ✉ clerks@deanscourt.co.uk
Deans Court Chambers
101 Walker Street, Preston PR1 2RR, ☎ 01772 565 600
✉ preston@deanscourt.co.uk
Call Date: Nov 1989, Middle Temple
Qualifications: [BA (Hons) (Manch) CPE]
kitching@deanscourt.co.uk

KITSON MR JUSTIN JAMES PETER

Selborne Chambers
10 Essex Street, London WC2R 3AA,
☎020 7420 9500
✉clerks@selbornechambers.co.uk
Call Date: July 2000, Gray's Inn
Pupil Supervisor
Qualifications: [MA (Hons) PgDL]
✉justin.kitson@selbornechambers.co.uk

KITZING MISS SUSANNA LORAINE

Park Court Chambers
16 Park Place, Leeds LS1 2SJ,
☎0113 243 3277
✉clerks@parkcourtchambers.co.uk
Call Date: Nov 2005, Middle Temple
Qualifications: [BA (Hons) Bristol]
✉skitzing@parkcourtchambers.co.uk

KIVDEH MR SHAHROKH-SEAN

1 Mitre Court Buildings
1 Mitre Court Buildings, Temple, London EC4Y 7BS, ☎020 7452 8900
✉clerks@1mcb.com
Call Date: Nov 1992, Middle Temple
Pupil Supervisor
Qualifications: [LLB (Hons) (Lond) LLM (Lond)]
✉sean.kivdeh@1mcb.com

KLAEDES MISS ANDRIANNA PANTELLI

Temple Court Chambers
2nd Floor, 2 Dr Johnson's Building, Temple, London EC4Y 7AY, ☎020 7353 7888
✉clerks@templecourt.co.uk
Call Date: Oct 2006, Middle Temple
Qualifications: [LLB]
✉clerks@templecourt.co.uk

KLEAR MR NAJINDER SINGH

12 Old Square Chambers
1st Floor, 12 Old Square, Lincoln's Inn, London WC2A 3TX, ☎020 7404 0875
✉clerks@12oldsquare.com
Call Date: Nov 2004, Middle Temple
Qualifications: [LLB (Hons)]

KLEIN MR JONATHAN SIMON

Enterprise Chambers
43 Park Square, Leeds LS1 2NP,
☎0113 246 0391
✉leeds@enterprisechambers.com
Enterprise Chambers
65 Quayside, Newcastle Upon Tyne NE1 3DE,
☎0191 222 3344
✉newcastle@enterprisechambers.com
Call Date: Oct 1992, Lincoln's Inn
Qualifications: [LLB(Hons)(Essex) BCL]
✉jonathanklein@enterprisechambers.com

KLEIN MS LEONORA JANE

Chambers of Ms Leonora Klein
Address withheld☎020 7419 7841
✉leoklein7@hotmail.com
Call Date: Nov 1989, Gray's Inn
Qualifications: [BA (Lond)]

KLOSS MR ALEXANDER WOLFGANG

St Johns Buildings
24a - 28 St John Street, Manchester M3 4DJ,
☎0161 214 1500
✉clerk@stjohnsbuildings.co.uk
16 Winckley Square
Preston PR1 3JJ, ☎01772 256100
St Johns Buildings Liverpool
8th Floor India Buildings, Water Street, Liverpool L2 0XG, ☎0151 243 6000
✉clerk@stjohnsbuildings.co.uk
Call Date: Oct 1993, Gray's Inn
Pupil Supervisor
Qualifications: [BA (Bris)]
✉clerk@stjohnsbuildings.co.uk

KNAFLER MR STEPHEN QC (2010)

Garden Court Chambers
57-60 Lincoln's Inn Fields, London WC2A 3LJ,
☎020 7993 7600 ✉info@gclaw.co.uk
Call Date: May 1993, Lincoln's Inn
Pupil Supervisor
Qualifications: [MA (Cantab)]
✉stephenk@gclaw.co.uk

KNAGG MR CHRISTOPHER DAVID

Number 7 Harrington Street Chambers
7 Harrington Street, Liverpool L2 9YH,
☎0151 242 0707 ✉clerks@7hs.co.uk
Call Date: Nov 2005, Gray's Inn
Qualifications: [LLB]
✉christopher.knagg@7hs.co.uk

E

KNAPP MISS SOPHIE JACQUELINE

3 PB Barristers
3 Paper Buildings, Temple, London EC4Y 7EU, ☎020 7583 8055
3 PB Barristers
Royal Talbot House, 2 Victoria Street, Bristol, Avon BS1 6BB, ☎0117 928 1520
3 PB Barristers
23 Beaumont Street, Oxford OX1 2NP, ☎01865 793 736
3 PB Barristers
4 St Peter Street, Winchester SO23 8BW, ☎01962 868884
✉clerks.winchester@3paper.co.uk
3 PB Barristers
30 Christchurch Road, Bournemouth, Dorset BH1 3PD, ☎01202 292102
✉clerks.bournemouth@3paper.co.uk
Call Date: Feb 1990, Gray's Inn
Qualifications: [BA (Lond)]
sophie.knapp@3paper.co.uk

KNAPP MR STEPHEN JOHN

Number 7 Harrington Street Chambers
7 Harrington Street, Liverpool L2 9YH, ☎0151 242 0707 ✉clerks@7hs.co.uk
Call Date: July 1986, Gray's Inn
Pupil Supervisor
Qualifications: [LLB (Lond)]
stephen.knapp@7hs.co.uk

KNIFTON MR DAVID ALAN

Exchange Chambers
One Derby Square, Derby Square, Liverpool L2 9XX, ☎0151 236 7747
✉info@exchangechambers.co.uk
Exchange Chambers
7 Ralli Courts, West Riverside, Manchester M3 5FT, ☎0161 833 2722
Exchange Chambers
Oxford House, Oxford Row, Leeds LS1 3BE, ☎0113 203 1970
✉spencer@exchangechambers.co.uk
Call Date: July 1986, Inner Temple
Pupil Supervisor
Qualifications: [LLB (Nott'm)]
knifton@exchangechambers.co.uk

KNIGHT MISS ADRIENNE

3 Temple Gardens
Lower Ground Floor, 3 Temple Gardens, Temple, London EC4Y 9AU, ☎020 7353 3102
✉clerks@3tg.co.uk
Call Date: July 1981, Gray's Inn
Pupil Supervisor
Qualifications: [LLB]
akn@3tg.co.uk

KNIGHT MISS ALEXIA EMMA CHARLOTTE

3 Verulam Buildings
London WC1R 5NT, ☎020 7831 8441
✉chambers@3vb.com
Call Date: Oct 2007, Middle Temple
Qualifications: [BA (Hons) (Cantab) LLM (Cantab)]
aknight@3vb.com

KNIGHT MR BENJAMIN JAMES

Central Chambers
89 Princess Street, Manchester M1 4HT, ☎0161 236 1133
✉clerks@centralchambers.co.uk
Call Date: July 2004, Middle Temple
Qualifications: [LLB Hons BVC]

KNIGHT MR CHRISTOPHER JAMES SEXTON

11 King's Bench Walk
11 King's Bench Walk, Temple, London EC4Y 7EQ, ☎020 7632 8500
✉clerksroom@11kbw.com
Call Date: July 2008, Inner Temple
Qualifications: [MA (Cantab) BCL (Oxon)]

KNIGHT MR EDWARD MALYN

XXIV Old Buildings
Ground Floor, 24 Old Buildings, Lincoln's Inn, London WC2A 3UP, ☎020 7691 2424
✉clerks@xxiv.co.uk
Call Date: Nov 1999, Middle Temple
Pupil Supervisor
Qualifications: [MA (Cantab)]
edward.knight@xxiv.co.uk

KNIGHT MRS EMMA LOUISE

13 Old Square Chambers
Ground Floor, 14 Old Square, Lincoln's Inn, London WC2A 3UE, ☎020 7831 4445
✉clerks@13oldsquare.com
Call Date: July 2008, Lincoln's Inn
Qualifications: [LLB (Sheff)]

KNIGHT MR GRAEME EDWARD VERDON

7 Bell Yard
London WC2A 2JR, ☎020 7831 0636
✉kevintarrant@btconnect.com
The Barristers Chambers
Address withheld☎07966 056368
✉gevknight@hotmail.com

Carmelite Chambers
9 Carmelite Street, London EC4Y 0DR,
☎ 020 7936 6300
✉ clerks@carmelitechambers.co.uk
Call Date: Oct 1999, Middle Temple
Pupil Supervisor
Qualifications: [BA (Hons)(Dunelm)]

KNIGHT MISS HEIDI CARINA HEMMINGS

3 Serjeants Inn
London EC4Y 1BQ, ☎ 020 7427 5000
✉ clerks@3serjeantsinn.com
Call Date: Oct 2001, Lincoln's Inn
Qualifications: [MA (Hons) (Cantab)]

KNIGHT MISS JENNIFER CLAUDIA

Atkinson Bevan Chambers
1st Floor, 2 Harcourt Buildings, Temple, London EC4Y 9DB, ☎ 020 7353 2112
✉ clerks@2hb.co.uk
Call Date: Oct 1996, Gray's Inn
Pupil Supervisor
Qualifications: [LLB (Exon)]
✉ JenniferKnight@2hb.co.uk

KNIGHT MR KEITH LESLIE FRANCIS

4 King's Bench Walk
2nd Floor, 4 King's Bench Walk, Temple, London EC4Y 7DL, ☎ 020 7822 7000
✉ clerks@4kbw.co.uk
Call Date: Nov 1969, Gray's Inn
Pupil Supervisor
Qualifications: [BCL]
✉ kk@4kbw.co.uk

KNIGHT MISS SARAH LOUISE

1 High Pavement
Nottingham NG1 1HF, ☎ 0115 941 8218
✉ clerks@1highpavement.co.uk
Call Date: July 1996, Middle Temple
Qualifications: [BA (Hons)(Notts) Dip Law (Lond)]
✉ sarahknight@1highpavement.co.uk

KNIGHTS MISS SAMANTHA JANE

Matrix Chambers
Griffin Building, Gray's Inn, London WC1R 5LN, ☎ 020 7404 3447
✉ matrix@matrixlaw.co.uk / Iscott@matrixlaw.co.uk
Call Date: Nov 1996, Lincoln's Inn
Pupil Supervisor
Qualifications: [BA (Hons)(Oxon) CPE LLM (Lond)]
✉ samanthaknights@matrixlaw.co.uk

KNORR MISS MICHELLE FRANCES

Doughty Street Chambers
53-54 Doughty Street, London WC1N 2LS,
☎ 020 7404 1313
✉ enquiries@doughtystreet.co.uk
Call Date: July 2008, Lincoln's Inn
Qualifications: [BA (USA) LLM (Essex)]

KNOTT MS BARBARA HELEN

4 Brick Court
4 Brick Court, Temple, London EC4Y 9AD,
☎ 020 7832 3200 ✉ clerks@4bc.co.uk
Call Date: July 2002, Middle Temple
Qualifications: [BA (Hons) (Kent) Dip in Law]
✉ helen.knott@4bc.co.uk

KNOTT MR JAMES ALAN STANIFORTH

4 Stone Buildings
Ground Floor, 4 Stone Buildings, Lincoln's Inn, London WC2A 3XT, ☎ 020 7242 5524
✉ clerks@4stonebuildings.com
Call Date: Oct 2008, Inner Temple
Qualifications: [BA (Warwick)]
✉ j.knott@4stonebuildings.com

KNOTT MISS SAMANTHA LOUISE

Crown Office Row Chambers
119 Church Street, Brighton, Sussex BN1 1UD, ☎ 01273 625625
✉ clerks@1cor.com
Call Date: July 2005, Lincoln's Inn
Qualifications: [LLB (Hons)]
✉ samantha.knott@1cor.com

KNOTTS MISS CAROL ELAINE

No5 Chambers
38 Queen Square, Bristol BS1 4QS,
☎ 0845 210 5555
No5 Chambers
Greenwood House, 4-7 Salisbury Court, London EC4Y 8AA, ☎ 0845 210 5555
No5 Chambers
Fountain Court, Steelhouse Lane, Birmingham B4 6DR, ☎ 0845 210 5555 ✉ info@no5.com
Call Date: Nov 1996, Inner Temple
Qualifications: [LLB (B'ham)]

KNOWLES MISS CATHERINE JULIA

Park Court Chambers
16 Park Place, Leeds LS1 2SJ,
☎ 0113 243 3277
✉ clerks@parkcourtchambers.co.uk
Call Date: July 2004, Middle Temple
Qualifications: [BA Hons (Oxon)]
✉ cknowles@parkcourtchambers.co.uk

E

KNOWLES MR CHARLES GEOFFREY

Cathedral Chambers
First Floor, 17 Queen Street, Newcastle Upon Tyne NE1 3UG, ☎0191 232 1311
✉mail@cathedralchambers.com
Call Date: July 1998, Middle Temple
Pupil Supervisor
Qualifications: [LLB (Hons)]

KNOWLES MS GWYNNETH FRANCES QC (2011)

Atlantic Chambers
4-6 Cook Street, Liverpool L2 9QU,
☎0151 236 4421
✉info@atlanticchambers.co.uk
4 Brick Court
4 Brick Court, Temple, London EC4Y 9AD,
☎020 7832 3200 ✉clerks@4bc.co.uk
Call Date: Oct 1993, Gray's Inn
Qualifications: [BA M Sc]
gwynnethknowles@atlanticchambers.co.uk

KNOWLES MR JULIAN BERNARD QC (2011)

Matrix Chambers
Griffin Building, Gray's Inn, London WC1R 5LN, ☎020 7404 3447
✉matrix@matrixlaw.co.uk / lscott@matrixlaw.co.uk
Call Date: Nov 1994, Inner Temple
Pupil Supervisor
Qualifications: [BA (Oxon) CPE]
julianknowles@matrixlaw.co.uk

KNOWLES MISS LINSEY

Albion Chambers
Broad Street, Bristol BS1 1DR,
☎0117 927 2144
✉clerks@albionchambers.co.uk
6 Pump Court
1st Floor, 6 Pump Court, Temple, London EC4Y 7AR, ☎020 7797 8400
✉richardconstable@6pumpcourt.co.uk
6 Pump Court Chambers
6-8 Mill Street, Maidstone, Kent ME15 6XH,
☎01622 688094
✉annexe@6pumpcourt.co.uk
Call Date: July 2000, Lincoln's Inn
Qualifications: [MA (Hons) Dip Law]
linsey.knowles@albionchambers.co.uk

KNOWLES MR MARK DAVID

KCH Garden Square
1 Oxford Street, Nottingham NG1 5BH,
☎0115 941 8851
✉clerks@kchgardensquare.co.uk
Call Date: Nov 1989, Middle Temple
Pupil Supervisor
Qualifications: [LLB (Hons) (Leics)]

KNOWLES MR MICHAEL JOHN

Cobden House Chambers
19 Quay Street, Manchester M3 3HN,
☎0161 833 6000 ✉Clerks@Cobden.co.uk
Call Date: Oct 2000, Middle Temple
Qualifications: [LLB (Hons) (Manch)]
clerks@cobden.co.uk

KNOWLES MR ROBIN ST JOHN QC (1999)

South Square
3-4 South Square, Gray's Inn, London WC1R 5HP, ☎020 7696 9900
✉practicemanagers@southsquare.com
Call Date: July 1982, Middle Temple
Recorder
Qualifications: [MA (Cantab)]
robinknowles@southsquare.com

KNOX MR CHRISTOPHER JOHN

Trinity Chambers
The Custom House, 39 Quayside, Newcastle Upon Tyne NE1 3DE, ☎0191 232 1927
✉info@trinitychambers.co.uk
Trinity Chambers
Multi Media Exchange, 72-80 Corporation Road, Middlesbrough TS1 2RF,
☎01642 247569
✉info@trinitychambers.co.uk
Call Date: July 1974, Inner Temple
Pupil Supervisor, Recorder
Qualifications: [BA (Hons)(Dunelm)]
c.knox@trinitychambers.co.uk

KNOX MR SIMON CHRISTOPHER PETER QC (2006)

3 Hare Court
3 Hare Court, Temple, London EC4Y 7BJ,
☎020 7415 7800 ✉clerks@3harecourt.com
Call Date: Nov 1983, Middle Temple
Qualifications: [BA (Oxon)]
peterknox@3harecourt.com

KOCHNARI MISS KATE

Stour Chambers
Mill Studio, 17a Stour Street, Canterbury, Kent CT1 2NR, ☎01227 764899
✉clerks@stourchambers.co.uk
Call Date: July 2008, Inner Temple
Qualifications: [LLB (Canterbury)]
kate.kochnari@stourchambers.co.uk

KODAGODA MR FRITZ ST CLAIR

12 Old Square Chambers
1st Floor, 12 Old Square, Lincoln's Inn, London WC2A 3TX, ☎ 020 7404 0875
✉ clerks@12oldsquare.com
Call Date: Nov 1993, Lincoln's Inn
Pupil Supervisor
✉ clerks@12oldsquare.com

KOGAN MR BARRY IAN

Carmelite Chambers
9 Carmelite Street, London EC4Y 0DR, ☎ 020 7936 6300
✉ clerks@carmelitechambers.co.uk
Call Date: July 1973, Inner Temple
Pupil Supervisor
Qualifications: [LLB (Hull)]
✉ bkogan@carmelitechambers.co.uk

KOHANZAD MR RAD

Atlantic Chambers
4-6 Cook Street, Liverpool L2 9QU, ☎ 0151 236 4421
✉ info@atlanticchambers.co.uk
Call Date: Nov 2007, Middle Temple
Qualifications: [BSc (Hons) (Lond) LLM (Lond)]

KOHLI MR RYAN SINGH

Cornerstone Barristers
2-3 Gray's Inn Square, Gray's Inn, London WC1R 5JH, ☎ 020 7242 4986
✉ chambers@2-3gis.co.uk
Call Date: July 2006, Inner Temple
Qualifications: [BA (Oxon)]
✉ rkohli@2-3gis.co.uk

KOKELAAR MR SEBASTIAN

13 Old Square Chambers
Ground Floor, 14 Old Square, Lincoln's Inn, London WC2A 3UE, ☎ 020 7831 4445
✉ clerks@13oldsquare.com
Call Date: Nov 2004, Lincoln's Inn
Qualifications: [BA (Hons) MA MPhil]

KOLA MISS FATIMA

Garden Court Chambers
57-60 Lincoln's Inn Fields, London WC2A 3LJ, ☎ 020 7993 7600 ✉ info@gclaw.co.uk
Call Date: Nov 2007, Middle Temple
Qualifications: [LLB (Hons) (Lond) LLM (Lond)]
✉ fatimak@gclaw.co.uk

KOLHATKAR MR ISHAN KAUNTEYA

Chambers of Ishan Kolhatkar
76 Cedar Lawn Avenue, Barnet, Hertfordshire EN5 2LN, ☎ 07703 441010
✉ ishan@kolhatkar.co.uk
Call Date: Oct 2002, Middle Temple
Qualifications: [BSc (Lond) PgDL]

KOLINSKY MR DANIEL JOSEPH

Landmark Chambers
180 Fleet Street, London EC4A 2HG, ☎ 020 7430 1221
✉ clerks@landmarkchambers.co.uk
Call Date: Oct 1998, Inner Temple
Pupil Supervisor
Qualifications: [BA (Oxon)]
✉ dkolinsky@landmarkchambers.co.uk

KOLODYNSKI MR STEFAN RICHARD

St Philips Chambers
55 Temple Row, Birmingham B2 5LS, ☎ 0121 246 7000 ✉ clerks@st-philips.com
Call Date: Oct 1993, Lincoln's Inn
Qualifications: [BSc (Hons)(Lond) CPE (Huddesfield) Dip Law]
✉ skolodynski@st-philips.com

KOLVIN MR PHILIP ALAN QC (2009)

Cornerstone Barristers
2-3 Gray's Inn Square, Gray's Inn, London WC1R 5JH, ☎ 020 7242 4986
✉ chambers@2-3gis.co.uk
Kings Chambers
36 Young Street, Manchester M3 3FT, ☎ 0845 034 3444
✉ clerks@kingschambers.com
Kings Chambers
5 Park Square East, Leeds LS1 2NE, ☎ 0845 034 3444
✉ clerks@kingschambers.com
Call Date: July 1985, Inner Temple
Qualifications: [BA (Oxon)]
✉ pkolvin@2-3gis.co.uk

KONG MR SENGHIN

5 King's Bench Walk
5 King's Bench Walk, Temple, London EC4Y 7DN, ☎ 020 7353 5638
✉ clerks@5kbw.co.uk
Call Date: July 2008, Middle Temple
Qualifications: [BA (Hons) (Oxon)]

E

KOPEL MISS BEATA BARBARA

Nexus Chambers
7 New Square, Lincolns Inn, London
WC2A 3QS,
☎ 020 7404 1147 / 020 7831 8309
✉ info@nexuschambers.com
Call Date: Oct 2000, Lincoln's Inn
Qualifications: [BA (Hons) (Lond) PGDipLaw]

KORDA MR ANTHONY

187 Fleet Street
London EC4A 2AT, ☎ 020 7430 7430
✉ chambers@187fleetstreet.com
Call Date: July 1988, Inner Temple
Pupil Supervisor
Qualifications: [LLB (Lond)]

KORN MR ADAM RICHARD

Seven Bedford Row
7 Bedford Row, London WC1R 4BS,
☎ 020 7242 3555 ✉ clerks@7br.co.uk
Call Date: Oct 1992, Middle Temple
Pupil Supervisor
Qualifications: [BA (Hons) DipLaw AKC MA]
✉ akorn@7br.co.uk

E

KORN MR ANTHONY HENRY

No5 Chambers
Greenwood House, 4-7 Salisbury Court,
London EC4Y 8AA, ☎ 0845 210 5555
No5 Chambers
38 Queen Square, Bristol BS1 4QS,
☎ 0845 210 5555
No5 Chambers
Fountain Court, Steelhouse Lane, Birmingham
B4 6DR, ☎ 0845 210 5555 ✉ info@no5.com
Call Date: Nov 1978, Gray's Inn
Qualifications: [BA (Oxon)]

KORNER MISS JOANNA CHRISTIAN MARY QC (1993)

6 King's Bench Walk
Ground Floor, 6 King's Bench Walk, Temple,
London EC4Y 7DR, ☎ 020 7583 0410
✉ clerks@6kbw.com
Call Date: Nov 1974, Inner Temple

KORNIEJ MRS REBEKAH RACHEL

East Anglian Chambers
140 New London Road, Chelmsford, Essex
CM2 0AW, ☎ 01473 214481
✉ chelmsford@ealaw.co.uk
East Anglian Chambers
53 North Hill, Colchester, Essex CO1 1QA,
☎ 01473 214481 ✉ colchester@ealaw.co.uk
East Anglian Chambers
Gresham House, 5 Museum Street, Ipswich,
Suffolk IP1 1HQ, ☎ 01473 214481
✉ ipswich@ealaw.co.uk
Call Date: Oct 1999, Middle Temple
Qualifications: [LLB (Hons)(Anglia)]
✉ rebekahkorniej@ealaw.co.uk

KOROBOWICZ MISS NATALIA WANDA

No.6 Park Square
Leeds LS1 2LW, ☎ 0113 245 9763
✉ Tim@no6.co.uk
Call Date: Oct 2004, Inner Temple
Qualifications: [LLB (B'ham)]
✉ korobowicz@no6.co.uk

KOROL MS KATHRYN MARGARET

15 Winckley Square
Preston PR1 3JJ, ☎ 01772 252828
✉ clerks@15winckleysq.co.uk
Call Date: Mar 1996, Middle Temple
Pupil Supervisor
Qualifications: [LLB (Hons)]

KOTAK MISS PRAGATI

1 Pump Court
Elm Court, Temple, London EC4Y 7AB,
☎ 020 7842 7070
✉ (name)@pumpcourt.co.uk
Call Date: Mar 2000, Inner Temple
Qualifications: [BA]

KOTHARI MISS SIMA

Coram Chambers
9-11 Fulwood Place, London WC1V 6HG,
☎ 020 7092 3700
✉ mail@coramchambers.co.uk
Call Date: Oct 1992, Gray's Inn
Pupil Supervisor
Qualifications: [LLB (Lond)]
✉ clerks@coramchambers.co.uk

KOVALEVSKY MR RICHARD TARAS QC (2003)

2 Bedford Row
London WC1R 4BU, ☎ 020 7440 8888
✉ clerks@2bedfordrow.co.uk
Call Date: July 1983, Gray's Inn
Qualifications: [LLB (Manch)]
✉ rkovalevsky@2bedfordrow.co.uk

KOVATS MR STEVEN LASZLO QC (2010)

39 Essex Street
London WC2R 3AT, ☎ 020 7832 1111
✉ clerks@39essex.com
82 King Street
Manchester M2 4WQ, ☎ 0161 870 9969
Call Date: July 1989, Middle Temple
Pupil Supervisor
Qualifications: [BA (Cantab)]
✉ steven.kovats@39essex.com

KRAEHLING-SMITH MR MARCUS ANDREW CHARLES

Rowchester Chambers
4 Rowchester Court, Whittall Street, Birmingham B4 6DH, ☎ 0121 233 2327
✉ clerks@rowchesterchambers.co.uk
Call Date: July 1998, Lincoln's Inn
Qualifications: [LLB (Hons)]

KRAMER MR ADAM MARTIN

3 Verulam Buildings
London WC1R 5NT, ☎ 020 7831 8441
✉ chambers@3vb.com
Call Date: July 2004, Gray's Inn
Pupil Supervisor
Qualifications: [BA (Oxon) LLM]
✉ akramer@3vb.com

KRAMER MR PHILIP ANTHONY

Park Lane Plowden
Lombard House, 4-8 Lombard Street, Newcastle Upon Tyne NE1 3AE,
☎ 0191 211 4087
✉ clerks@parklaneplowden.co.uk
Call Date: July 1982, Inner Temple
Pupil Supervisor, Recorder
Qualifications: [LLB (Newc) FCIArb]
✉ philip.kramer@parklaneplowden.co.uk

KRAUSE MS FLORENCE

Meritz Chambers
PO Box 110, Hebben Bridge HX7 9AQ,
☎ 0845 094 0856
✉ clerk@meritzchambers.co.uk
Call Date: July 1998, Lincoln's Inn
Pupil Supervisor
Qualifications: [LLB (Hons)(Sheff)]
✉ flokrause@meritzchambers.co.uk

KREBS MR MICHAEL GORDON

Liverpool Civil Law
3rd Floor, 1 Old Hall Street, Liverpool L3 9HF,
☎ 0151 242 0500
✉ clerks@liverpoolcivillaw.com
Call Date: Nov 1999, Gray's Inn
Qualifications: [LLB (B'ham)]

KREISBERGER MISS RONIT CHARLOTTE

Monckton Chambers
1 & 2 Raymond Buildings, Gray's Inn, London WC1R 5NR, ☎ 020 7405 7211
✉ chambers@monckton.com
Call Date: Mar 1999, Middle Temple
Pupil Supervisor
Qualifications: [BA (Hons), BCL(Oxon)]
✉ rkreisberger@monckton.com

KREMEN MR PHILIP MICHAEL

Selborne Chambers
10 Essex Street, London WC2R 3AA,
☎ 020 7420 9500
✉ clerks@selbornechambers.co.uk
Call Date: Nov 1975, Gray's Inn
Pupil Supervisor
Qualifications: [BSc (Hons)]
✉ philip.kremen@selbornechambers.co.uk

KRIEGER MR GREGORY DANIEL

Farringdon Chambers
180 Bermondsey Street, London SE1 3TQ,
☎ 020 7089 5700
Call Date: Nov 2005, Inner Temple
Qualifications: [LLB University of Birmingham]

KRIKLER MR ALEXANDER RICHARD

4 Breams Buildings
Chancery Lane, London EC4A 1HP,
☎ 020 7092 1900 ✉ clerks@4bb.co.uk
Call Date: Nov 1995, Middle Temple
Qualifications: [BA (Hons)(Manch)]

KRISH MISS JULIA ROSALIE

Garden Court Chambers
57-60 Lincoln's Inn Fields, London WC2A 3LJ,
☎ 020 7993 7600 ✉ info@gclaw.co.uk
Call Date: Feb 1992, Middle Temple
Pupil Supervisor
Qualifications: [MA (Oxon)]
✉ juliak@gclaw.co.uk

KRISHNADASAN MISS DOUSHKA

1 Garden Court Family Law Chambers
Ground Floor, One Garden Court, Temple, London EC4Y 9BJ, ☎ 020 7797 7900
✉ clerks@1gc.com
Call Date: July 1991, Middle Temple
Qualifications: [LLB (Hons) (Lond)]
✉ krish@1gc.com

E

KRISHNAN MISS DAVINA

St Albans Chambers
2 - 4 St Peter's Street, St Albans, Hertfordshire AL1 3LF, ☎01727 843383
✉clerks@stalbanschambers.com
Call Date: July 2004, Lincoln's Inn
Qualifications: [LLB (Hons) (Leic)]
dk@stalbanschambers.com

KROLICK MR IVAN

Chambers of Mr Ami Feder
Ground Floor, Lamb Building, Temple, London EC4Y 7AS, ☎020 7797 7788
✉clerks@lambbuilding.co.uk
Lamb Building
22 Ship Street, Brighton BN1 1AD,
☎01273 820490
✉admin@lambbuilding.co.uk
Chambers of Mr Ami Feder
Ground Floor, Lamb Building, Temple, London EC4Y 7AS, ☎020 7797 7788
✉clerks@lambbuilding.co.uk
Call Date: Nov 1966, Gray's Inn
Pupil Supervisor
Qualifications: [LLB (Dunelm) FCIArb]
clerks@lambbuilding.co.uk, injkrolick@ntlworld.com

KRUSHNER MR DAMIAN MARK

Oakwood Chambers
46a Oakwood Court, London W14 8JY,
☎07789 435485
Call Date: Nov 2001, Middle Temple
Qualifications: [BA (Hons) (Lond) MPhil (Cantab) CPE]

KUBIK MISS HEIDI MARIE

St Philips Chambers
55 Temple Row, Birmingham B2 5LS,
☎0121 246 7000 ✉clerks@st-philips.com
Call Date: Oct 1993, Lincoln's Inn
Qualifications: [BA (Hons)(Notts)]
hkubik@st-philips.com

KULKARNI MR YASH

Quadrant Chambers
Quadrant House, 10 Fleet Street, London EC4Y 1AU, ☎020 7583 4444
✉info@quadrantchambers.com
Call Date: Oct 1998, Lincoln's Inn
Pupil Supervisor
Qualifications: [BA (Hons)(Cantab)]
yash.kulkarni@quadrantchambers.com

KUMAR MISS CAMINI ANOOP

2-3 Hind Court Chambers
2-3 Hind Court, Fleet Street, London EC4A 3DL, ☎020 7822 2150
✉david@2-3hindcourt.com
Call Date: July 2008, Middle Temple
Qualifications: [LLB (Hons) (Wales) MA (Oxon) LLM (Dunelm)]

KUMAR MISS JASMINE

Sapphire Chambers
The Gatehouse, 43B Churchgate, Loughborough, Leicestershire LE11 1UE,
☎07805 852724
Call Date: Oct 2009, Gray's Inn

KUMETA MISS JENNIFER MARY

King's Bench and Godolphin (KBG)Chambers
115 North Hill, Plymouth, Devon PL4 8JY,
☎01752 221551
✉clerks@kbgchambers.co.uk
Call Date: Oct 2005, Middle Temple
Qualifications: [BA (Hons)]

KUMI MR ISHMAEL JOB

Cromwell-Ayeh-Kumi Chambers
25 Taylors Green, London W3 7PF,
☎020 8740 6982 ✉ishmaelkumi@gmail.com
Call Date: Nov 1977, Gray's Inn
Qualifications: [MA (Oxon) Maitrise (Paris)]

KURJI MS FATIM RAZAHUSEIN

No5 Chambers
Fountain Court, Steelhouse Lane, Birmingham B4 6DR, ☎0845 210 5555 ✉info@no5.com
No5 Chambers
38 Queen Square, Bristol BS1 4QS,
☎0845 210 5555
No5 Chambers
Greenwood House, 4-7 Salisbury Court, London EC4Y 8AA, ☎0845 210 5555
Call Date: July 2003, Inner Temple
Qualifications: [LLB (B'ham)]
fk@no5.com

KURZNER MS EMMA LOUISE

187 Fleet Street
London EC4A 2AT, ☎020 7430 7430
✉chambers@187fleetstreet.com
Call Date: Mar 1999, Middle Temple
Qualifications: [BSc (Hons)(Lond)]
emma.kurzner@187fleetstreet.com

E

KUSHNER MISS MARTINE

St Philips Chambers
55 Temple Row, Birmingham B2 5LS,
☎ 0121 246 7000 ✉ clerks@st-philips.com
Call Date: July 1980, Middle Temple
Pupil Supervisor, Recorder
Qualifications: [LLB (Hons)(B'ham) MA]
✉ mkushner@st-philips.co.uk

KVERNDAL MR SIMON RICHARD QC (2002)

Quadrant Chambers
Quadrant House, 10 Fleet Street, London EC4Y 1AU, ☎ 020 7583 4444
✉ info@quadrantchambers.com
Call Date: Nov 1982, Middle Temple
Qualifications: [MA (Cantab)]
✉ simon.kverndal@quadrantchambers.com

KWIATKOWSKI MR FELIKS JERZY

Kew Chambers
354 Kew Road, Kew, Surrey TW9 3DU,
☎ 0844 8099991
✉ admin@kewchambers.co.uk
Call Date: July 1977, Middle Temple
Qualifications: [LLB (Hons)(Bris)]

KYNOCH MR DUNCAN STUART SANDERSON

Selborne Chambers
10 Essex Street, London WC2R 3AA,
☎ 020 7420 9500
✉ clerks@selbornechambers.co.uk
Call Date: Nov 1994, Gray's Inn
Qualifications: [LLB (Bris)]
✉ duncan.kynoch@selbornechambers.co.uk

KYRIAKIDES MISS TINA

11 Stone Buildings
11 Stone Buildings, Lincoln's Inn, London WC2A 3TG, ☎ 020 7831 6381
✉ clerks@11sb.com
Call Date: July 1984, Lincoln's Inn
Pupil Supervisor
Qualifications: [MA(Cantab)]

KYTE MR PETER ERIC QC (1996)

QEB Hollis Whiteman
1-2 Laurence Pountney Hill, London EC4R 0EU, ☎ 020 7933 8855
✉ barristers@qebhw.co.uk
Call Date: July 1970, Gray's Inn
Recorder
Qualifications: [MA (Cantab)]
✉ peter.kyte@qebhw.co.uk

LA GRUA MRS JAYNE

Linenhall Chambers
1 Stanley Place, Chester CH1 2LU,
☎ 01244 348282
✉ clerks@linenhallchambers.co.uk
Call Date: July 2004, Gray's Inn
Qualifications: [LLB (L'pool)]

LACHKOVIC MR JAMES ADRIAN GEORGE

187 Fleet Street
London EC4A 2AT, ☎ 020 7430 7430
✉ chambers@187fleetstreet.com
Call Date: Nov 1987, Gray's Inn
Pupil Supervisor
Qualifications: [LLB (Hull)]

LACK MR JEREMY

Quadrant Chambers
Quadrant House, 10 Fleet Street, London EC4Y 1AU, ☎ 020 7583 4444
✉ info@quadrantchambers.com
Call Date: Nov 1989, Middle Temple
Qualifications: [MA (Oxon)]
✉ jeremy.lack@quadrantchambers.com

LACOB MS LISA MARA

3 Verulam Buildings
London WC1R 5NT, ☎ 020 7831 8441
✉ chambers@3vb.com
Call Date: Mar 2004, Gray's Inn
Qualifications: [LLB (UCT) LLM (Cantab)]
✉ llacob@3vb.com

LACY MR BRIAN STEPHEN ANDREW

Littleton Chambers
3 King's Bench Walk North, Temple, London EC4Y 7HR, ☎ 020 7797 8600
✉ fschneider@littletonchambers.co.uk
Call Date: Nov 2006, Lincoln's Inn
Qualifications: [MA (Edin)]
✉ blacy@littletonchambers.co.uk

LADAK MISS TAHERA

1 Pump Court
Elm Court, Temple, London EC4Y 7AB,
☎ 020 7842 7070
✉ (name)@pumpcourt.co.uk
Call Date: Nov 1986, Gray's Inn
Pupil Supervisor
Qualifications: [LLB (Essex)]
✉ tl@1pumpcourt.co.uk

E

LADDIE MR JAMES MATTHEW LANG QC (2012)

Matrix Chambers
Griffin Building, Gray's Inn, London WC1R 5LN, ☎ 020 7404 3447
✉ matrix@matrixlaw.co.uk / lscott@matrixlaw.co.uk
Call Date: Nov 1995, Middle Temple
Pupil Supervisor
Qualifications: [BA (Hons) (Cantab)]
✉ jamesladdie@matrixlaw.co.uk

LADENBURG MR GUY ALEXANDER

3 Raymond Buildings
3 Raymond Buildings, Gray's Inn, London WC1R 5BH, ☎ 020 7400 6400
✉ clerks@3rblaw.com
Call Date: Nov 2000, Middle Temple
Qualifications: [BA (Hons) (Oxon) CPE (Oxon)]

LAHHAM DR KARIM

Chambers of Dr K Lahham
6 Leckford Place, Oxford OX2 6JB, ☎ 07876 441513 ✉ kl@littmanchambers.com
Call Date: Nov 1999, Inner Temple
Qualifications: [BA MA (RCA) PhD MA DIPLAW]

LAHIFFE MR MARTIN PATRICK JOSEPH

3 Temple Gardens
Lower Ground Floor, 3 Temple Gardens, Temple, London EC4Y 9AU, ☎ 020 7353 3102
✉ clerks@3tg.co.uk
Call Date: Nov 1984, Middle Temple
Pupil Supervisor
Qualifications: [BA (Hons)]
✉ mla@3tg.co.uk

LAHTI MISS LIISA MAARIA

Stone Chambers
4 Field Court, Gray's Inn, London WC1R 5EF, ☎ 020 7440 6900
✉ clerks@stonechambers.com
Call Date: Oct 2009, Lincoln's Inn
Qualifications: [BA (Cantab) BCL (Oxon)]
✉ liisa.lahti@stonechambers.com

LAIDLAW MR JONATHAN JAMES QC (2008)

2 Hare Court
Lower Ground, Ground, 1st & 2nd Floor, 2 Hare Court, Temple, London EC4Y 7BH, ☎ 020 7353 3982 ✉ clerks@2harecourt.com
Call Date: July 1982, Inner Temple
Recorder
Qualifications: [LLB (Hull)]
✉ jonathanlaidlaw@2harecourt.com

LAING MISS CHRISTINE KATHERINE QC (2006)

3 Temple Gardens
Lower Ground Floor, 3 Temple Gardens, Temple, London EC4Y 9AU, ☎ 020 7353 3102
✉ clerks@3tg.co.uk
Call Date: July 1984, Lincoln's Inn
Recorder
Qualifications: [LLB]
✉ cl@3tg.co.uk

LAING MISS ELISABETH MARY CAROLINE QC (2008)

11 King's Bench Walk
11 King's Bench Walk, Temple, London EC4Y 7EQ, ☎ 020 7632 8500
✉ clerksroom@11kbw.com
Call Date: July 1980, Middle Temple
Recorder
Qualifications: [BA (Cantab)]
✉ elisabeth.laing@11kbw.com

LAIRD MR FRANCIS JOSEPH QC (2011)

St Philips Chambers
55 Temple Row, Birmingham B2 5LS, ☎ 0121 246 7000 ✉ clerks@st-philips.com
Call Date: Nov 1986, Gray's Inn
Recorder
Qualifications: [LLB (Newc)]
✉ flaird@st-philips.com

LAKE MR JAMES EDWARD

St Paul's Chambers
5th Floor, St Paul's House, 23 Park Square South, Leeds LS1 2ND, ☎ 0113 245 5866
Call Date: Oct 2005, Inner Temple
Qualifications: [LLB University of Lancaster]

LAKHA MR ABBAS QC (2003)

Nine Bedford Row
9 Bedford Row, London WC1R 4AZ, ☎ 020 7489 2727
✉ clerks@9bedfordrow.co.uk
Call Date: Nov 1984, Inner Temple
Qualifications: [BA (Hons)]
✉ abbaslakha@9bedfordrow.co.uk

LAKHA MR SHABBIR

Farrar's Building
Farrar's Building, Temple, London EC4Y 7BD,
☎ 020 7583 9241
✉ Chambers@farrarsbuilding.co.uk
Call Date: July 1989, Lincoln's Inn
Qualifications: [LLB (Hons) M Phil (Cantab)]
✉ slakha@farrarsbuilding.co.uk

LAKIN MR ADRIAN PAUL

Kings Chambers
36 Young Street, Manchester M3 3FT,
☎ 0845 034 3444
✉ clerks@kingschambers.com
Kings Chambers
5 Park Square East, Leeds LS1 2NE,
☎ 0845 034 3444
✉ clerks@kingschambers.com
Kings Chambers
Embassy House, 60 Church Street,
Birmingham B3 2DJ, ☎ 0845 034 3444
✉ clerks@kingschambers.com
Call Date: July 2000, Middle Temple
Qualifications: [LLB(Hons) (Leeds)]

LAKIN MISS TRACY

St Ive's Chambers
Whittall Street, Birmingham B4 6DH,
☎ 0121 236 0863
✉ clerks@stiveschambers.co.uk
Call Date: Oct 1993, Inner Temple
Qualifications: [LLB]
✉ tracy.lakin@stiveschambers.co.uk

LAL MR SANJAY

4 King's Bench Walk
2nd Floor, 4 King's Bench Walk, Temple,
London EC4Y 7DL, ☎ 020 7822 7000
✉ clerks@4kbw.co.uk
Call Date: Oct 1993, Lincoln's Inn
Qualifications: [LLB (Hons) LLM (Lond)]

LALANI MRS SALMA HAMEEDA

12 Old Square Chambers
1st Floor, 12 Old Square, Lincoln's Inn,
London WC2A 3TX, ☎ 020 7404 0875
✉ clerks@12oldsquare.com
Call Date: Oct 1998, Middle Temple
Qualifications: [BA (Hons) LLB]
✉ clerks@12oldsquare.com

LALL MR TARLOCHAN

Monckton Chambers
1 & 2 Raymond Buildings, Gray's Inn, London
WC1R 5NR, ☎ 020 7405 7211
✉ chambers@monckton.com
Call Date: Nov 2010, Middle Temple
Qualifications: [LLB (Hons) (Warw) LLM (Lond)]
✉ tlall@monckton.com

LALLIE MR RANJIT SINGH

Equity Chambers
First Floor, McLaren Building, 46 Priory
Queensway, Birmingham B4 7LR,
☎ 0121 236 5007
✉ clerks@equitychambers.org.uk
Call Date: Oct 1997, Lincoln's Inn
Pupil Supervisor
Qualifications: [LLB (Hons)]
✉ ranjit.lallie@equitychambers.org.uk

LALLY MR HARBINDER SINGH

No5 Chambers
Fountain Court, Steelhouse Lane, Birmingham
B4 6DR, ☎ 0845 210 5555 ✉ info@no5.com
No5 Chambers
Greenwood House, 4-7 Salisbury Court,
London EC4Y 8AA, ☎ 0845 210 5555
No5 Chambers
38 Queen Square, Bristol BS1 4QS,
☎ 0845 210 5555
Call Date: Oct 1997, Lincoln's Inn
Qualifications: [BSc (Hons) LLB (Hons)(Staffs)]
✉ hl@no5.com

LALLY MR JONATHAN MARTIN

Deans Court Chambers
24 St John Street, Manchester M3 4DF,
☎ 0161 214 6000 ✉ clerks@deanscourt.co.uk
Deans Court Chambers
101 Walker Street, Preston PR1 2RR,
☎ 01772 565 600
✉ preston@deanscourt.co.uk
Call Date: Oct 2005, Inner Temple
Qualifications: [BA Magdalene College University of Cambridge CP]
✉ lally@deanscourt.co.uk

LAM MR CHUEN FAT

Chambers of Martin Burr
15 Old Bailey, London EC4M 7EF,
☎ 0845 123 1234 ✉ clerks@barristerweb.com
Call Date: Nov 1994, Lincoln's Inn
Qualifications: [BA (Hons)(Wolves) Dip Law]

E

LAMACRAFT MR IAN RICHARD

Chambers of Mr Lamacraft
93 Pine Walk, Charlshalton Beeches, Sutton, Surrey SM5 4HL, ☎020 8643 1593
✉ianlamacraft@gicham.co.uk
Call Date: July 1989, Lincoln's Inn
Qualifications: [LLB]

LAMB MR DAVID STEPHEN

Dere Street Barristers
14 Toft Green, York YO1 6JT, ☎0844 3351551
✉clerks@derestreet.co.uk
York Chambers
Rotterdam House, 116 The Quayside, Newcastle Upon Tyne NE1 3DY, ☎0191 206 4677
Call Date: Nov 1987, Middle Temple
Qualifications: [LLB (Hons) (Wales)]
clerks@yorkchambers.co.uk

LAMB MR EDWARD CHARLES

The Chambers of Grahame Aldous QC
9 Gough Square, London EC4A 3DG, ☎020 7832 0500
✉clerks@9goughsquare.co.uk
Call Date: Oct 2006, Lincoln's Inn
Qualifications: [LLB (Lond) MSc (Lond) BVC (BPP)]
elamb@9goughsquare.co.uk

LAMB MR ERIC ALAN

Exchange Chambers
One Derby Square, Derby Square, Liverpool L2 9XX, ☎0151 236 7747
✉info@exchangechambers.co.uk
Exchange Chambers
7 Ralli Courts, West Riverside, Manchester M3 5FT, ☎0161 833 2722
Exchange Chambers
Oxford House, Oxford Row, Leeds LS1 3BE, ☎0113 203 1970
✉spencer@exchangechambers.co.uk
Call Date: July 1975, Lincoln's Inn
Pupil Supervisor
Qualifications: [LLB]
lamb@exchangechambers.co.uk

LAMB MR HENRY DAVID

14 Gray's Inn Square
14 Gray's Inn Square, Gray's Inn, London WC1R 5JP, ☎020 7242 0858
✉clerks@14gis.co.uk
Call Date: July 2004, Lincoln's Inn
Qualifications: [LLB Hons (Lond)]
clerks@14graysinnsquare.co.uk

LAMB MR JEFFREY THOMAS

Westgate Chambers
64 High Street, Lewes, East Sussex BN7 1XG, ☎01273 480510
✉clerks@westgate-chambers.co.uk
Call Date: Oct 1992, Middle Temple
Pupil Supervisor
Qualifications: [BA(Hons)(Sussex) MA(Sussex) Dip Law]

LAMB MR JOHN RICHARD

1 Pump Court
Elm Court, Temple, London EC4Y 7AB, ☎020 7842 7070
✉(name)@pumpcourt.co.uk
Call Date: May 1990, Middle Temple
Pupil Supervisor
Qualifications: [BA (Hons)]
jl@1pumpcourt.co.uk

LAMB MISS MARIA-JANE CARMEL

1 Paper Buildings
1st Floor, 1 Paper Buildings, Temple, London EC4Y 7EP, ☎020 7353 3728
✉clerks@onepaper.co.uk
Call Date: Nov 1984, Gray's Inn
Recorder
Qualifications: [MA (Cantab)]
mariajanelamb@onepaper.co.uk

LAMB MR ROBERT GLASSON

13 King's Bench Walk
13 King's Bench Walk, Temple, London EC4Y 7EN, ☎020 7353 7204
✉clerks@13kbw.co.uk
13 KBW
32 Beaumont Street, Oxford OX1 2NP, ☎01865 311066 ✉clerks@13kbw.co.uk
Call Date: July 1973, Middle Temple
Qualifications: [MA (Cantab)]
rlamb@13kbw.co.uk

LAMBALLE MISS VICTORIA JANE

Old Court Chambers
Newham House, 96-98 Borough Road, Middlesbrough TS1 2HJ, ☎01642 232523
✉clerks@oldcourtchambers.com
Call Date: Nov 2002, Middle Temple
Qualifications: [LLB (Hons)(Sheff)]
clerks@oldcourtchambers.com

E

LAMBERT MRS ALISON JANET

Trinity Chambers
Highfield House, Moulsham Street, Chelmsford, Essex CM2 9AH,
☎ 01245 605040
✉ clerks@trinitychambers.com
Call Date: July 2005, Middle Temple
Qualifications: [LLB (Hons)]
alambert@trinitychambers.com

LAMBERT MISS CHRISTINA CAROLINE QC (2009)

1 Crown Office Row
1 Crown Office Row, Temple, London EC4Y 7HH, ☎ 020 7797 7500
✉ mail@1cor.com
Call Date: Nov 1988, Inner Temple
Qualifications: [MA (Cantab) Dip Law (Lond)]
christina.lambert@1cor.com

LAMBERT MISS ELIZABETH CHARLOTTE

7 Bell Yard
London WC2A 2JR, ☎ 020 7831 0636
✉ kevintarrant@btconnect.com
Call Date: Nov 2001, Lincoln's Inn
Qualifications: [LLB (Hons)]
el@7bellyard.co.uk

LAMBERT MRS EMMALINE

6 Pump Court
1st Floor, 6 Pump Court, Temple, London EC4Y 7AR, ☎ 020 7797 8400
✉ richardconstable@6pumpcourt.co.uk
6 Pump Court Chambers
6-8 Mill Street, Maidstone, Kent ME15 6XH,
☎ 01622 688094
✉ annexe@6pumpcourt.co.uk
Call Date: Oct 2003, Middle Temple
Qualifications: [LLB (Hons) (Lond)]
Clerks@6PumpCourt.co.uk

LAMBERT MR HARRY NATHANIEL

Doughty Street Chambers
53-54 Doughty Street, London WC1N 2LS,
☎ 020 7404 1313
✉ enquiries@doughtystreet.co.uk
Call Date: July 2008, Gray's Inn
Qualifications: [BA (Cantab) LLB]

LAMBERT MISS JANE ELIZABETH

NIPC
Kirklees Media Centre, 7 Northumberland Street, Huddersfield HD1 1RL,
☎ 0800 862 0055 ✉ jill.hayfield@nipclaw.com
Call Date: July 1977, Lincoln's Inn
Pupil Supervisor
Qualifications: [MA FCIArb]
jane.lambert@nipclaw.com

LAMBERT MR NIGEL ROBERT WOOLF QC (1999)

Carmelite Chambers
9 Carmelite Street, London EC4Y 0DR,
☎ 020 7936 6300
✉ clerks@carmelitechambers.co.uk
Call Date: Nov 1974, Gray's Inn
Recorder

LAMBERT MISS SARAH KATRINA

1 Crown Office Row
1 Crown Office Row, Temple, London EC4Y 7HH, ☎ 020 7797 7500
✉ mail@1cor.com
Call Date: Oct 1994, Gray's Inn
Pupil Supervisor
Qualifications: [BA]
sarah.lambert@1cor.com

LAMBERT MS SUZANNE JULIA

1 Crown Office Row
1 Crown Office Row, Temple, London EC4Y 7HH, ☎ 020 7797 7500
✉ mail@1cor.com
Call Date: Oct 2002, Lincoln's Inn
Qualifications: [BA (Oxon)]
suzanne.lambert@1cor.com

LAMBERTSEN MISS SIOBHAN

Crown Office Chambers
2 Crown Office Row, Temple, London EC4Y 7HJ, ☎ 020 7797 8100
✉ mail@crownofficechambers.com
Call Date: Nov 2007, Middle Temple
Qualifications: [BA (Hons) (Oxon)]
lambertsen@crownofficechambers.com

LAMBERTY MR MARK JULIAN HARKER

St Johns Buildings
24a - 28 St John Street, Manchester M3 4DJ,
☎ 0161 214 1500
✉ clerk@stjohnsbuildings.co.uk
St Johns Buildings
21 White Friars, Chester CH1 1NZ,
☎ 01244 323070
✉ clerk@stjohnsbuildings.co.uk
16 Winckley Square
Preston PR1 3JJ, ☎ 01772 256100
Call Date: Nov 1970, Gray's Inn
Qualifications: [BCL MA (Oxon)]
clerk@stjohnsbuildings.co.uk, mark.lamberty@stjohnsbuildings.co.uk

E

LAMBIS MR MARIOS PAMBOS

2 Hare Court
Lower Ground, Ground, 1st & 2nd Floor, 2 Hare Court, Temple, London EC4Y 7BH, ☎020 7353 3982 ✉clerks@2harecourt.com
Call Date: Nov 1989, Middle Temple
Recorder
Qualifications: [BA Hons (Sussex) Dip Law]
marioslambis@2harecourt.com

LAMMING MR DAVID JOHN

Cornerstone Barristers
2-3 Gray's Inn Square, Gray's Inn, London WC1R 5JH, ☎020 7242 4986
✉chambers@2-3gis.co.uk
Call Date: Nov 1972, Gray's Inn
Pupil Supervisor
Qualifications: [LLB (Lond) LLM (Lond)]
dlamming@2-3gis.co.uk

LAMONT MR CALUM

Keating Chambers
15 Essex Street, London WC2R 3AA,
☎020 7544 2600
✉clerks@keatingchambers.com
Call Date: Oct 2004, Inner Temple
Pupil Supervisor
Qualifications: [MA (Cantab) MPhil (Cantab) CPE]

LAMONT MISS CAMILLA ROSE

Landmark Chambers
180 Fleet Street, London EC4A 2HG,
☎020 7430 1221
✉clerks@landmarkchambers.co.uk
Call Date: Nov 1995, Middle Temple
Pupil Supervisor
Qualifications: [MA BCL (Oxon)]
clamont@landmarkchambers.co.uk

LAMONT MISS KATE ANGHARAD

The Chambers of Grahame Aldous QC
9 Gough Square, London EC4A 3DG,
☎020 7832 0500
✉clerks@9goughsquare.co.uk
Call Date: July 2007, Inner Temple
Qualifications: [LLB (Bris)]
klamont@9goughsquare.co.uk

LAMS MR BARNABAS JEFFREY

4 Brick Court
4 Brick Court, Temple, London EC4Y 9AD,
☎020 7832 3200 ✉clerks@4bc.co.uk
Call Date: Oct 1995, Gray's Inn
Qualifications: [BA (Hons) (Bris) MA (UEA)]
barnabas.lams@4bc.co.uk

LANCASTER MR ROGER

Kings Chambers
36 Young Street, Manchester M3 3FT,
☎0845 034 3444
✉clerks@kingschambers.com
Kings Chambers
5 Park Square East, Leeds LS1 2NE,
☎0845 034 3444
✉clerks@kingschambers.com
Kings Chambers
Embassy House, 60 Church Street, Birmingham B3 2DJ, ☎0845 034 3444
✉clerks@kingschambers.com
Call Date: Nov 2002, Middle Temple
Qualifications: [LLB (Hons)(Leic)]
rlancaster@kingschambers.com

LANCHESTER MR MARTIN JOHN

Guildhall Chambers
23 Broad Street, Bristol BS1 2HG,
☎0117 930 9000
✉hoc@guildhallchambers.co.uk
Call Date: Nov 2001, Middle Temple
Qualifications: [BSc (Hons)(Cantab) Dip Law]
martin.lanchester@guildhallchambers.co.uk

LAND MR PETER JAMES

Atkin Chambers
1 Atkin Building, Gray's Inn, London WC1R 5AT, ☎020 7404 0102
✉clerks@atkinchambers.com
Call Date: Oct 2007, Middle Temple
Qualifications: [MA (Hons) (Cantab) Dip Law]
pland@atkinchambers.com

LANDALE MISS TINA JEANETTE

Exchange Chambers
7 Ralli Courts, West Riverside, Manchester M3 5FT, ☎0161 833 2722
Exchange Chambers
One Derby Square, Derby Square, Liverpool L2 9XX, ☎0151 236 7747
✉info@exchangechambers.co.uk
Exchange Chambers
Oxford House, Oxford Row, Leeds LS1 3BE,
☎0113 203 1970
✉spencer@exchangechambers.co.uk
Call Date: July 1988, Middle Temple
Pupil Supervisor
Qualifications: [LLB (Hons)]
landale@exchangechambers.co.uk

LANDAU MR TOBY THOMAS QC (2008)

Essex Court Chambers
24 Lincoln's Inn Fields, London WC2A 3EG,
☎020 7813 8000
✉clerksroom@essexcourt.net
Call Date: Nov 1993, Middle Temple
Qualifications: [MA (Hons) BCL (Oxon) LLM (USA)]
✉tlandau@essexcourt.net

LANDER MR CHARLES GIDEON

Chavasse Court Chambers
18 Queen Avenue, Liverpool L2 4TX,
☎0151 229 2030
✉clerks@chavassechambers.co.uk
Call Date: Nov 1993, Lincoln's Inn
Qualifications: [LLB (Leeds)]
✉charles@charleslander.orangehome.co.uk

LANDER MR RICHARD MARK

Kings Chambers
36 Young Street, Manchester M3 3FT,
☎0845 034 3444
✉clerks@kingschambers.com
Kings Chambers
5 Park Square East, Leeds LS1 2NE,
☎0845 034 3444
✉clerks@kingschambers.com
Kings Chambers
Embassy House, 60 Church Street,
Birmingham B3 2DJ, ☎0845 034 3444
✉clerks@kingschambers.com
Call Date: Oct 1993, Lincoln's Inn
Qualifications: [MA (Hons)]
✉rlander@kingschambers.com

LANDIN MISS RACHAEL CAROLINE

Old Court Chambers
Newham House, 96-98 Borough Road,
Middlesbrough TS1 2HJ, ☎01642 232523
✉clerks@oldcourtchambers.com
Call Date: Oct 2008, Lincoln's Inn
Qualifications: [BA (Leic)]

LANE MR ANDREW JOHN

Hardwicke
New Square, Lincoln's Inn, London
WC2A 3SB, ☎020 7242 2523
✉enquiries@hardwicke.co.uk
Call Date: Oct 1999, Lincoln's Inn
Qualifications: [LLB (Hons)(Leic)]
✉andrew.lane@hardwicke.co.uk

LANE MR CHRISTOPHER PAUL

No 8 Chambers
8 Fountain Court, Steelhouse Lane,
Birmingham B4 6DR, ☎0121 236 5514
✉clerks@no8chambers.co.uk
Call Date: Oct 2002, Lincoln's Inn
Qualifications: [BA (Oxon)]
✉christopherlane@no8chambers.co.uk

LANE MS LINDSAY RUTH BUSFIELD

8 New Square
8 New Square, Lincoln's Inn, London
WC2A 3QP, ☎020 7405 4321
✉clerks@8newsquare.co.uk
Call Date: Oct 1996, Middle Temple
Qualifications: [BA (Hons) (Camb) MA]
✉lindsay.lane@8newsquare.co.uk

Types of work: Breach of confidence, Copyright, Copyright theft, Copyright Tribunal, Data protection, Design, E-commerce, Entertainment, Information technology, Intellectual property, Malicious falsehood, Media, Media and entertainment, Passing off, Patents, Scientific and technical disputes, Trade Descriptions Act, Trade secrets, Trademarks

LANE MR MICHAEL JOHN

East Anglian Chambers
53 North Hill, Colchester, Essex CO1 1QA,
☎01473 214481 ✉colchester@ealaw.co.uk
East Anglian Chambers
Gresham House, 5 Museum Street, Ipswich,
Suffolk IP1 1HQ, ☎01473 214481
✉ipswich@ealaw.co.uk
East Anglian Chambers
15 The Close, Norwich, Norfolk NR1 4DZ,
☎01473 214481 ✉norwich@ealaw.co.uk
Call Date: July 1983, Middle Temple
Pupil Supervisor
Qualifications: [BA (Cantab) Dip Soc (Kent)]
✉mlane@ealaw.co.uk

LANE MR NICHOLAS

New Court Chambers
3 Broad Chare, Newcastle Upon Tyne
NE1 3DQ, ☎0191 232 1980
✉clerks@newcourt-chambers.co.uk
Call Date: July 2008, Inner Temple
Qualifications: [BSc]
✉nicholas.lane@newcourt-chambers.co.uk

E

LANE MR PATRICK MICHAEL MACE

82 King Street
Manchester M2 4WQ, ☎0161 870 9969
39 Essex Street
London WC2R 3AT, ☎020 7832 1111
✉clerks@39essex.com
Call Date: July 1997, Gray's Inn
Qualifications: [BA LLB]
patrick.lane@39essex.com

LANE MISS RACHAEL CAROLINE

2 King's Bench Walk
2 King's Bench Walk, Temple, London
EC4Y 7DE, ☎020 7353 1746
✉clerks@2kbw.com
Call Date: Nov 2002, Lincoln's Inn
Qualifications: [LLB (Hons) (Lond)]
rlane@2kbw.com

LANE MR SIMON CHARLES

Rougemont Chambers
Victory House, Dean Clarke Gardens,
Southernhay East, Exeter EX2 4AA,
☎01392 208484
✉clerks@rougemontchambers.co.uk
Call Date: July 2002, Inner Temple
Qualifications: [LLB (Bris) LLM (Bris)]
slane@rougemontchambers.co.uk

E

LANE-SMITH MISS ZOE VICTORIA

Chambers of Miss Z Lane-Smith
PO Box 6017, Milton Keynes
Call Date: Mar 1997, Middle Temple
Qualifications: [BA (Hons)(Dunelm)]
clerks@barristerweb.com

LANEY MISS ANNA MARIE

Crown Office Chambers
2 Crown Office Row, Temple, London
EC4Y 7HJ, ☎020 7797 8100
✉mail@crownofficechambers.com
Call Date: Oct 1998, Lincoln's Inn
Pupil Supervisor
Qualifications: [LLB (Hons)(Manc)]
laney@crownofficechambers.com

Types of work: Adjudication, Alternative dispute resolution, Arbitration, Commercial litigation, Construction law, Engineering disputes, Fire and other property damage claims, Professional negligence

LANGDALE MR ADRIAN MARK

Seven Bedford Row
7 Bedford Row, London WC1R 4BS,
☎020 7242 3555 ✉clerks@7br.co.uk
Call Date: Mar 1996, Gray's Inn
Pupil Supervisor
Qualifications: [LLB (L'pool)]
alangdale@7br.co.uk, clerks@7br.co.uk

LANGDALE MR TIMOTHY JAMES QC (1992)

Cloth Fair Chambers
39-40 Cloth Fair, London EC1A 7NT,
☎020 7710 6444
✉email@clothfairchambers.com
Call Date: July 1966, Lincoln's Inn
Qualifications: [MA (St Andrews)]

LANGDON MR ANDREW DOMINIC QC (2006)

Guildhall Chambers
23 Broad Street, Bristol BS1 2HG,
☎0117 930 9000
✉hoc@guildhallchambers.co.uk
Call Date: July 1986, Middle Temple
Qualifications: [LLB (Bris)]
andrew.langdon@guildhallchambers.co.uk

LANGDON MS KATIE JANE

Cornwall Street Chambers
85-87 Cornwall Street, Birmingham B3 3BY,
☎0121 233 7500
✉clerks@cornwallstreet.co.uk
Call Date: Oct 2007, Middle Temple
Qualifications: [LLB (Hons) (Bris)]
katie.langdon@cornwallstreet.co.uk

LANGE MR PETER DAVID

Great James Street Chambers
37 Great James Street, London WC1N 3HB,
☎020 7440 4949
✉chambers@greatjames.co.uk
Call Date: July 2001, Inner Temple
Qualifications: [BSc (Hons) JD(Hons) LLB(Hons) BCL(Hons) LLM(Hons)]
PDL@LangeLaw.com

LANGEVAD MISS CLAIRE THERESA MANUELA

Chambers of Marion Smullen and Kerim Fuad QC
1 Inner Temple Lane, London EC4Y 1AF,
☎020 7427 4400 ✉clerks@1itl.com
Call Date: Oct 2005, Lincoln's Inn
Qualifications: [BA (Hons) (Lond) PgDl (Lond)]
clerks@1itl.com

LANGFORD MISS ABIGAIL LOUISE

Broadway House Chambers
Broadway House, 9 Bank Street, Bradford, West Yorkshire BD1 1TW, ☎01274 722560
✉clerks@broadwayhouse.co.uk
Broadway House Chambers
25 Park Square West, Leeds, West Yorkshire LS1 2PW, ☎0113 246 2600
✉clerks@broadwayhouse.co.uk
Call Date: Nov 2005, Lincoln's Inn
Qualifications: [LLM (Northumbria) LLB (Hons)]
✉al@broadwayhouse.co.uk

LANGFORD MISS SARAH MARGARET

3 PB Barristers
3 Paper Buildings, Temple, London EC4Y 7EU, ☎020 7583 8055
3 PB Barristers
30 Christchurch Road, Bournemouth, Dorset BH1 3PD, ☎01202 292102
✉clerks.bournemouth@3paper.co.uk
3 PB Barristers
4 St Peter Street, Winchester SO23 8BW, ☎01962 868884
✉clerks.winchester@3paper.co.uk
3 PB Barristers
Royal Talbot House, 2 Victoria Street, Bristol, Avon BS1 6BB, ☎0117 928 1520
3 PB Barristers
23 Beaumont Street, Oxford OX1 2NP, ☎01865 793 736
Call Date: July 2005, Gray's Inn
Qualifications: [BA]
✉sarah.langford@3paper.co.uk

LANGHAM MR RICHARD GEOFFREY

Landmark Chambers
180 Fleet Street, London EC4A 2HG, ☎020 7430 1221
✉clerks@landmarkchambers.co.uk
Call Date: Nov 1986, Lincoln's Inn
Pupil Supervisor
Qualifications: [BA (Oxon)]
✉rlangham@landmarkchambers.co.uk

LANGHORN MR ALEXANDER JAMES

9 St John Street
Manchester M3 4DN, ☎0161 955 9000
✉civilclerks@9sjs.com / criminalclerks@9sjs.com
Call Date: July 2010, Middle Temple
Qualifications: [LLB (Hons) (Nott'm)]
✉alex.langhorn@9sjs.com

LANGLEY MR CHARLES HOWARD

2 Bedford Row
London WC1R 4BU, ☎020 7440 8888
✉clerks@2bedfordrow.co.uk
Call Date: Nov 1999, Middle Temple
Pupil Supervisor
Qualifications: [BA (Hons)(Hull)]
✉clangley@2bedfordrow.co.uk

LANGLEY MISS SARAH ELIZABETH

Number 7 Harrington Street Chambers
7 Harrington Street, Liverpool L2 9YH, ☎0151 242 0707 ✉clerks@7hs.co.uk
Call Date: Nov 2001, Lincoln's Inn
Qualifications: [LLB (Hons) (Wales)]
✉sarah.langley@7hs.co.uk

LANGLOIS MS NICOLE-LOUISE MAEVE

XXIV Old Buildings
Ground Floor, 24 Old Buildings, Lincoln's Inn, London WC2A 3UP, ☎020 7691 2424
✉clerks@xxiv.co.uk
Call Date: Mar 2008, Lincoln's Inn
Qualifications: [LLB (Exon)]

LANGRIDGE MS NICOLA DAWN

Coram Chambers
9-11 Fulwood Place, London WC1V 6HG, ☎020 7092 3700
✉mail@coramchambers.co.uk
Call Date: Nov 1993, Lincoln's Inn
Pupil Supervisor
Qualifications: [LLB (Hons) (Sheff)]
✉niki.langridge@coramchambers.co.uk

LANGRISH MR ADAM STUART

College Chambers
19 Carlton Crescent, Southampton, Hampshire SO15 2ET, ☎023 8023 0338
✉clerks@college-chambers.co.uk
Call Date: July 2006, Inner Temple
Qualifications: [LLB (L'pool)]
✉alangrish@college-chambers.co.uk

LANLEHIN MR OLAJIDE ADEBOLA

Great James Street Chambers
37 Great James Street, London WC1N 3HB, ☎020 7440 4949
✉chambers@greatjames.co.uk
Inner Temple Chambers
P.O.Box 1677 Aba, 58 Pound Road, Abia State☎70 3189 9078
✉chimaumez@msn.com
Call Date: Nov 1994, Inner Temple
Pupil Supervisor
Qualifications: [LLB (Lond)]
✉jlanlehin@yahoo.co.uk

E

LANSON MISS LAUREN ELIZABETH

1 Gray's Inn Square
Ground Floor, 1 Gray's Inn Square, London WC1R 5AA, ☎020 7405 0001
Call Date: Nov 2006, Middle Temple
Qualifications: [LLB (Hons) (Sheff)]
llanson@1gis.co.uk

LAPRELL MR MARK DIETER

18 St John Street
Manchester M3 4EA, ☎0161 278 1800
clerks@18sjs.com
Call Date: Nov 1979, Gray's Inn
Pupil Supervisor, Recorder
Qualifications: [BA (Oxon)]

LARGE MR BARNABY

Eighteen Carlton Crescent
Rownhams House, Rownhams, Southampton SO16 8LF, ☎023 8063 9001
clerks@18carltoncrescent.co.uk
Call Date: July 2007, Inner Temple
Qualifications: [LLB (Canterbury)]
clerks@18carltoncrescent.co.uk

LARIZADEH MR CYRUS RAIS

4 Paper Buildings
1st Floor, 4 Paper Buildings, Temple, London EC4Y 7EX, ☎020 7427 5200
clerks@4pb.com
Call Date: Nov 1992, Inner Temple
Pupil Supervisor
Qualifications: [BA (Kent) Cert De Droit Francais (France)]
cl@4pb.com

LARKIN MR SEAN QC (2010)

QEB Hollis Whiteman
1-2 Laurence Pountney Hill, London EC4R 0EU, ☎020 7933 8855
barristers@qebhw.co.uk
Call Date: July 1987, Inner Temple
Pupil Supervisor
Qualifications: [LLB (Lond)]

LARTON MISS CLAIRE

Broadway House Chambers
Broadway House, 9 Bank Street, Bradford, West Yorkshire BD1 1TW, ☎01274 722560
clerks@broadwayhouse.co.uk
Broadway House Chambers
25 Park Square West, Leeds, West Yorkshire LS1 2PW, ☎0113 246 2600
clerks@broadwayhouse.co.uk
Call Date: Nov 2005, Lincoln's Inn
Qualifications: [LLB (Hons) (Leeds)]
clerks@broadwayhouse.co.uk

LASCELLES MR RICHARD JAMES DAVID

Littleton Chambers
3 King's Bench Walk North, Temple, London EC4Y 7HR, ☎020 7797 8600
fschneider@littletonchambers.co.uk
Call Date: Nov 2003, Lincoln's Inn
Qualifications: [BCL (Oxon) MA (Hons) (Cantab)]
dlascelles@littletonchambers.co.uk

LASHBROOK MS KELLIE

3 Dr Johnson's Buildings
Ground Floor, 3 Dr Johnson's Buildings, Temple, London EC4Y 7BA, ☎020 7353 4854
clerks@3djb.co.uk
Call Date: July 2001, Inner Temple
Qualifications: [LLB (Hons)]
klashbrook@3djb.co.uk

LASK MR BENJAMIN BELA DAVID

Monckton Chambers
1 & 2 Raymond Buildings, Gray's Inn, London WC1R 5NR, ☎020 7405 7211
chambers@monckton.com
Call Date: Nov 2003, Middle Temple
Qualifications: [BA (Hons) (Sussex) Dip Law]
blask@monckton.com

LASKER MR JEREMY STEWART

Lincoln House Chambers
Tower 12, The Avenue North, Spinningfields, 18-22 Bridge Street, Manchester M3 3BZ, ☎0161 832 5701
info@lincolnhousechambers.com
Call Date: July 1976, Inner Temple
Pupil Supervisor, Recorder
Qualifications: [LLB (B'ham)]
jeremy.lasker@lincolnhousechambers.com

LASOK MR KAROL PAUL EDWARD QC (1994)

Monckton Chambers
1 & 2 Raymond Buildings, Gray's Inn, London WC1R 5NR, ☎020 7405 7211
chambers@monckton.com
Call Date: July 1977, Middle Temple
Recorder
Qualifications: [MA (Cantab) LLM,PhD (Exon)]
plasok@monckton.com

E

LAST MR PETER RAYMOND

Clerksroom (Taunton)
Equity House, Administration Centre, Blackbrook Park Avenue, Taunton, Somerset TA1 2PX, ☎0845 083 3000
✉mail@clerksroom.com
Clerksroom (London)
3rd Floor, 218 Strand, London WC2R 1AT, ☎0845 083 3000 ✉mail@clerksroom.com
King's Lynn Chambers
26 The Birches, South Wootton, King's Lynn, Norfolk PE30 3JG, ☎01553 672 085
✉timothy.leader@tesco.net
Call Date: Oct 1995, Lincoln's Inn
Qualifications: [LLB (Hons)(Lond) LLM (Lond)]
last@clerksroom.com

LATHAM MR KEVIN DAVID

Kings Chambers
36 Young Street, Manchester M3 3FT, ☎0845 034 3444
✉clerks@kingschambers.com
Kings Chambers
5 Park Square East, Leeds LS1 2NE, ☎0845 034 3444
✉clerks@kingschambers.com
Kings Chambers
Embassy House, 60 Church Street, Birmingham B3 2DJ, ☎0845 034 3444
✉clerks@kingschambers.com
Call Date: Oct 2007, Middle Temple
Qualifications: [LLB (Hons) (Hull)]

LATHAM MR MICHAEL RAYMOND HENRI

Furnival Chambers
32 Furnival Street, London EC4A 1JQ, ☎020 7405 3232
Melbury House
55 Manor Road, Oadby, Leicester, Leicestershire LE2 2LL, ☎07801 037802
✉melburyhousechambers@yahoo.co.uk
Call Date: Nov 1975, Gray's Inn
Pupil Supervisor
Qualifications: [LLB]
mlatham@furnivallaw.co.uk

LATHAM MR RICHARD BRUNTON QC (1991)

Seven Bedford Row
7 Bedford Row, London WC1R 4BS, ☎020 7242 3555 ✉clerks@7br.co.uk
Call Date: July 1971, Gray's Inn
Recorder
Qualifications: [LLB (B'ham)]
rlatham@7br.co.uk

LATHAM MR ROBERT JAMES

Doughty Street Chambers
53-54 Doughty Street, London WC1N 2LS, ☎020 7404 1313
✉enquiries@doughtystreet.co.uk
Doughty Street Chambers
Pall Mall Court, 61-67 King Street, Manchester M2 4PD, ☎0161 618 1066
Doughty Street Chambers
5th Floor, Broad Quay House, Prince Street, Bristol BS1 4DJ, ☎01179 058 717
Call Date: July 1976, Middle Temple
Pupil Supervisor
Qualifications: [MA (Cantab) CEDR]
r.latham@doughtystreet.co.uk

LATIMER MR ANDREW GERARD

Kings Chambers
36 Young Street, Manchester M3 3FT, ☎0845 034 3444
✉clerks@kingschambers.com
Kings Chambers
5 Park Square East, Leeds LS1 2NE, ☎0845 034 3444
✉clerks@kingschambers.com
Kings Chambers
Embassy House, 60 Church Street, Birmingham B3 2DJ, ☎0845 034 3444
✉clerks@kingschambers.com
Call Date: Nov 1995, Gray's Inn
Pupil Supervisor
Qualifications: [BA (Oxon) BCL]
alatimer@kingschambers.com

LATIMER-SAYER MR WILLIAM LAURENCE

Cloisters
1 Pump Court, Temple, London EC4Y 7AA, ☎020 7827 4000 ✉clerks@cloisters.com
Call Date: Oct 1995, Gray's Inn
Qualifications: [LLB (Leic) MA (Lond)]
wls@cloisters.com

Fax: 020 7827 4100
URL: www.cloisters.com

Types of work: Clinical negligence, Personal injury

LATTIMER MISS JUSTINE ADELE

St Ive's Chambers
Whittall Street, Birmingham B4 6DH, ☎0121 236 0863
✉clerks@stiveschambers.co.uk
Call Date: May 1992, Inner Temple
Pupil Supervisor
Qualifications: [BA (Oxon)]
justine.lattimer@stiveschambers.co.uk

E

LATYMER MR TAM

Chambers of Tam Latymer
144/145 Temple Chambers, Temple Avenue, London EC4Y 0DA, ☎020 7353 2795
✉tlatymer@hotmail.com
Call Date: Nov 1998, Lincoln's Inn
Qualifications: [LLB (Hons)]

LAU DR MARTIN WILHELM

Essex Court Chambers
24 Lincoln's Inn Fields, London WC2A 3EG, ☎020 7813 8000
✉clerksroom@essexcourt.net
Call Date: Oct 1996, Middle Temple
Qualifications: [MA (Lond) CPE (Lond)]
mlau@essexcourt.net

LAU MISS VANESSA HOI CHUN

18 St John Street
Manchester M3 4EA, ☎0161 278 1800
✉clerks@18sjs.com
Call Date: Mar 2005, Middle Temple
Qualifications: [LLB (Hons)]

LAUGHLAND MR JAMES RUSSELL

Temple Garden Chambers
1 Harcourt Buildings, Temple, London EC4Y 9DA, ☎020 7583 1315
✉clerks@tgchambers.com
Call Date: Nov 1991, Inner Temple
Pupil Supervisor
Qualifications: [BA (Kent)]
jlaughland@tgchambers.com

LAUGHTON MR SAMUEL DENNIS

Ten Old Square
Ground Floor, Ten Old Square, Lincoln's Inn, London WC2A 3SU, ☎020 7405 0758
✉clerks@tenoldsquare.com
Call Date: Feb 1993, Middle Temple
Qualifications: [MA (Cantab) DipLaw]
clerks@tenoldsquare.com

LAUGHTON MISS VICTORIA JANE

Chambers of Mr Ami Feder
Ground Floor, Lamb Building, Temple, London EC4Y 7AS, ☎020 7797 7788
✉clerks@lambbuilding.co.uk
Chambers of Mr Ami Feder
Ground Floor, Lamb Building, Temple, London EC4Y 7AS, ☎020 7797 7788
✉clerks@lambbuilding.co.uk
Call Date: Oct 1998, Lincoln's Inn
Qualifications: [LLB (Hons)(Leic)]

LAURENCE MR GEORGE FREDERICK QC (1991)

New Square Chambers
12 New Square, Lincoln's Inn, London WC2A 3SW, ☎020 7419 8000
✉robin.hollington@newsquarechambers.co.uk
Call Date: Nov 1972, Middle Temple
Qualifications: [MA (Oxon) BA (South Africa)]
george.laurence@newsquarechambers.co.uk

LAUTERPACHT SIR ELIHU QC (1970)

20 Essex Street
London WC2R 3AL, ☎020 7842 1200
✉clerks@20essexst.com
Call Date: Nov 1950, Gray's Inn
Qualifications: [MA LLB (Cantab)]
clerks@20essexst.com

LAVENDER MR NICHOLAS QC (2008)

Serle Court
6 New Square, Lincoln's Inn, London WC2A 3QS, ☎020 7242 6105
✉clerks@serlecourt.co.uk
Call Date: July 1989, Inner Temple
Qualifications: [MA (Cantab) BCL (Oxon)]
nlavender@serlecourt.co.uk

Types of work: Arbitration, Banking, Civil litigation, Financial services, Insurance

LAVERS MR MICHAEL

Charter Chambers
33 John Street, London WC1N 2AT, ☎020 7618 4400
✉clerks@charterchambers.com
Call Date: Oct 1990, Middle Temple
Qualifications: [BA (Sussex) Dip Law (Lond)]
michael.lavers@charterchambers.com

LAVERY MR MICHAEL JAMES

Exchange Chambers
7 Ralli Courts, West Riverside, Manchester M3 5FT, ☎0161 833 2722
Exchange Chambers
One Derby Square, Derby Square, Liverpool L2 9XX, ☎0151 236 7747
✉info@exchangechambers.co.uk
Exchange Chambers
Oxford House, Oxford Row, Leeds LS1 3BE, ☎0113 203 1970
✉spencer@exchangechambers.co.uk
Call Date: Feb 1990, Gray's Inn
Qualifications: [LLB (Hons)]
lavery@exchangechambers.co.uk

LAVIN MISS MARY MANDIE JANE

196 Temple Chamber
3-7 Temple Avenue, London EC4Y 0HP,
☎ 020 7099 9257
✉ davidsimpson@lawandregulation.com
Call Date: Oct 1993, Middle Temple
Qualifications: [LLB (Hons)(Lond) RN MA]

LAVY DR MATTHEW MONTAGUE

4 Pump Court
4 Pump Court, Temple, London EC4Y 7AN,
☎ 020 7842 5555
✉ chambers@4pumpcourt.com
Call Date: July 2004, Lincoln's Inn
Qualifications: [BA Hons (Cantab) MPhil (Cantab) PhD (Cantab)]

LAW MISS CHARLOTTE HOLLY

Kings Chambers
36 Young Street, Manchester M3 3FT,
☎ 0845 034 3444
✉ clerks@kingschambers.com
Kings Chambers
5 Park Square East, Leeds LS1 2NE,
☎ 0845 034 3444
✉ clcrks@kingschambers.com
Kings Chambers
Embassy House, 60 Church Street, Birmingham B3 2DJ, ☎ 0845 034 3444
✉ clerks@kingschambers.com
Call Date: Oct 2005, Middle Temple
Qualifications: [BA (Hons) (Cantab) Dip in Law]
✉ claw@kingschambers.com

LAW MISS HELEN ELIZABETH

Matrix Chambers
Griffin Building, Gray's Inn, London WC1R 5LN, ☎ 020 7404 3447
✉ matrix@matrixlaw.co.uk / Iscott@matrixlaw.co.uk
Call Date: Oct 2005, Gray's Inn
Qualifications: [LLB (B'ham) LLM]
✉ helenlaw@matrixlaw.co.uk

LAW MR JOHN EDWARD

The Chambers of Grahame Aldous QC
9 Gough Square, London EC4A 3DG,
☎ 020 7832 0500
✉ clerks@9goughsquare.co.uk
Call Date: Oct 1996, Lincoln's Inn
Qualifications: [BA (Hons)(Oxon) Dip Law (Lomd)]
✉ JohnLaw@33bedfordrow.co.uk

LAWLER MR DONAL JOHN

187 Fleet Street
London EC4A 2AT, ☎ 020 7430 7430
✉ chambers@187fleetstreet.com
Call Date: July 2008, Middle Temple
Qualifications: [BA (Hons) (York) PgDl (Lond)]
✉ donallawler@187fleetstreet.com

LAWLEY MISS FRANCES ELIZABETH

Zenith Chambers
10 Park Square, Leeds LS1 2LH,
☎ 0113 245 5438
✉ clerks@zenithchambers.co.uk
Call Date: July 2007, Lincoln's Inn
Qualifications: [LLB (Oxon)]
✉ flawley@zenithchambers.co.uk

LAWRENCE MISS ANNE MARY

Atlas Chambers
3 Field Court, Gray's Inn, London WC1R 5EP,
☎ 020 7269 7980
✉ clerks@atlaschambers.com
Call Date: July 2003, Lincoln's Inn
Qualifications: [BSc Hons MSc Diploma in Law LLM]
✉ lawrence@atlaschambers.com

LAWRENCE MR BENJAMIN RICHARD

St Johns Buildings
24a - 28 St John Street, Manchester M3 4DJ,
☎ 0161 214 1500
✉ clerk@stjohnsbuildings.co.uk
16 Winckley Square
Preston PR1 3JJ, ☎ 01772 256100
St Johns Buildings Liverpool
8th Floor India Buildings, Water Street, Liverpool L2 0XG, ☎ 0151 243 6000
✉ clerk@stjohnsbuildings.co.uk
Call Date: Mar 2003, Lincoln's Inn
Qualifications: [LLB (Hons) (Manch)]
✉ clerk@stjohnsbuildings.co.uk

LAWRENCE DR HEATHER BUNTING ELIZABETH

11 South Square
1st Floor, 11 South Square, Gray's Inn, London WC1R 5EY, ☎ 020 7405 1222
✉ clerks@11southsquare.com
Call Date: Oct 1990, Middle Temple
Pupil Supervisor
Qualifications: [BA (Hons) MA DPhil (Oxon)]

Types of work: Breach of confidence, Computer litigation, Copyright, Copyright Tribunal, Data protection, Design, Information technology, Intellectual property, Passing off, Patents, Scientific and technical disputes, Trademarks

E

LAWRENCE SIR IVAN JOHN QC (1981)

5 Pump Court
Ground Floor, 5 Pump Court, Temple, London EC4Y 7AP, ☎ 020 7353 2532
✉ clerks@5pumpcourt.com
Call Date: Feb 1962, Inner Temple
Qualifications: [MA (Oxon)]

Fax: 0207 3535 321;
Out of hours telephone: 0193 2224 692 and 0779 8626 188;
DX: 497 LDE;
URL: www.5pumpcourt.com

Other professional qualifications: Inner Temple Approved Advocacy Trainer; Bar Council Approved Human Rights Trainer

Types of work: Corporate fraud, Crime, Defamation, War crimes tribunals

Awards and memberships: Criminal Bar Association; Recorder (1985-2002); Bencher (Inner Temple (1990-); Knighted (1992); Head of Chambers at One Essex Court (1998-2001); Visiting Professor of Law at University of Buckingham (2004-); elected Member of the Bar Council (2004-10); Fellow of Soc of Advanced Legal Studies

Other professional experience: MP (1974-97); Chairman Home Affairs Select Committee (1992-7); Chairman Conservative Legal and Home Affairs Committees (1987-97); Chairman All Party Barristers Group (1987-94); Chairman Commonwealth Parliamentary Association (UK Branch) (1995-7)

Publications: *My Life of Crime*, (Memoir: Book Guild Ltd), 2010; Numerous articles in various periodicals and national newspapers on legal topics., 2010

Reported Cases: *R v Kray and others*, (1969) 53 Cr App R (Court of Appeal), 2005. Joinder of counts in an indictment: what is a sufficient nexus and part of a series.
R v Emmett and Another, [1998] AC 773 (House of Lords), 2005. Crimes against humanity, murder, persecutions and war crimes.
Sikirica, Dosen, Kolundzija, IT-95-8 (ICTY) (ICTY (Hague)), 2001. Crimes against humanity, murder, persecutions and war crimes.
R v Ely, (2005) EWCA Crim 3248 (Court of Appeal), 2005. Historic child abuse: abuse of process; fresh evidence: appropriate sentence for multi-counts.
R v Faulds, (2010) All ER (D) 91 (Apr) (Court of Appeal), 2010. Joint Enterprise: sentence for manslaughter excessive.

LAWRENCE MR NIGEL STUART

Number 7 Harrington Street Chambers
7 Harrington Street, Liverpool L2 9YH, ☎ 0151 242 0707 ✉ clerks@7hs.co.uk
Call Date: July 1988, Lincoln's Inn
Pupil Supervisor
Qualifications: [LLB (Hons) (Leics)]
✉ nigel.lawrence@7hs.co.uk

LAWRENCE MISS PAMELA AVRIL

Nexus Chambers
7 New Square, Lincolns Inn, London WC2A 3QS,
☎ 020 7404 1147 / 020 7831 8309
✉ info@nexuschambers.com
Call Date: Nov 1975, Inner Temple
Pupil Supervisor
Qualifications: [LLB (Lond)]
✉ pamela.lawrence@nexuschambers.com

LAWRENCE THE HON PATRICK JOHN TRISTRAM QC (2002)

Four New Square
Four New Square, Lincoln's Inn, London WC2A 3RJ, ☎ 020 7822 2000
✉ barristers@4newsquare.com
Call Date: Feb 1985, Inner Temple
Qualifications: [BA (Oxon)]
✉ p.lawrence@4newsquare.com

LAWRENCE MISS RACHEL CAMILLA

Argent Chambers
5 Bell Yard, London WC2A 2JR,
☎ 020 7556 5500
✉ briefsin@argentchambers.co.uk
Call Date: Oct 1992, Inner Temple
Qualifications: [LLB (Lond)]
✉ r.lawrence@argentchambers.co.uk

LAWRENCE MISS SAMANTHA DIONNE

3 Dr Johnson's Buildings
Ground Floor, 3 Dr Johnson's Buildings, Temple, London EC4Y 7BA, ☎ 020 7353 4854
✉ clerks@3djb.co.uk
Call Date: July 2005, Inner Temple
Qualifications: [LLB University of Sheffield]

E

LAWRENCE MS SORAYA DAWN

Carmelite Chambers
9 Carmelite Street, London EC4Y 0DR,
☎ 020 7936 6300
✉ clerks@carmelitechambers.co.uk
Call Date: Oct 1999, Inner Temple
Pupil Supervisor
Qualifications: [BA (B'ham)]
✉ slawrence@carmelitechambers.co.uk

LAWRENSON MRS MARY CHRISTINE

Farringdon Chambers
180 Bermondsey Street, London SE1 3TQ,
☎ 020 7089 5700
Call Date: Nov 1994, Lincoln's Inn
Qualifications: [B Ed (Hons)(Lancs) LLB (Hons)(Northumbria)]
✉ marylawrenson@farringdon-law.co.uk

LAWRENSON MISS SARAH

St James's Chambers
68 Quay Street, Manchester M3 3EJ,
☎ 0161 834 7000
✉ clerks@stjameschambers.com
Zenith Chambers
10 Park Square, Leeds LS1 2LH,
☎ 0113 245 5438
✉ clerks@zenithchambers.co.uk
Call Date: Oct 2003, Middle Temple
Qualifications: [BA (Hons) (Nott'm)]
✉ sarah.lawrenson@stjameschambers.com

LAWRIE MR IAN DOUGLAS QC (2011)

3 PB Barristers
3 Paper Buildings, Temple, London EC4Y 7EU,
☎ 020 7583 8055
3 PB Barristers
Royal Talbot House, 2 Victoria Street, Bristol, Avon BS1 6BB, ☎ 0117 928 1520
3 PB Barristers
23 Beaumont Street, Oxford OX1 2NP,
☎ 01865 793 736
3 PB Barristers
4 St Peter Street, Winchester SO23 8BW,
☎ 01962 868884
✉ clerks.winchester@3paper.co.uk
3 PB Barristers
30 Christchurch Road, Bournemouth, Dorset BH1 3PD, ☎ 01202 292102
✉ clerks.bournemouth@3paper.co.uk
Call Date: Nov 1985, Gray's Inn
Pupil Supervisor, Recorder
Qualifications: [LLB (Wark)]
✉ ian.lawrie@3paper.co.uk

LAWS MISS ELEANOR JANE QC (2011)

6 Pump Court
1st Floor, 6 Pump Court, Temple, London EC4Y 7AR, ☎ 020 7797 8400
✉ richardconstable@6pumpcourt.co.uk
6 Pump Court Chambers
6-8 Mill Street, Maidstone, Kent ME15 6XH,
☎ 01622 688094
✉ annexe@6pumpcourt.co.uk
Call Date: Oct 1990, Inner Temple
Pupil Supervisor
Qualifications: [BA (B'ham) Dip Law]
✉ eleanorlaws@6pumpcourt.co.uk

LAWS MR SIMON REGINALD QC (2011)

Walnut House
63 St. David's Hill, Exeter, Devon EX4 4DW,
☎ 01392 279751
✉ clerks@walnuthouse.co.uk
6 King's Bench Walk
Ground Floor, 6 King's Bench Walk, Temple, London EC4Y 7DR, ☎ 020 7583 0410
✉ clerks@6kbw.com
Call Date: Oct 1991, Inner Temple
Pupil Supervisor
Qualifications: [BA (York) Dip Law]

LAWSON MR ANDREW CHARLES

St Johns Buildings
24a - 28 St John Street, Manchester M3 4DJ,
☎ 0161 214 1500
✉ clerk@stjohnsbuildings.co.uk
16 Winckley Square
Preston PR1 3JJ, ☎ 01772 256100
St Johns Buildings Liverpool
8th Floor India Buildings, Water Street, Liverpool L2 0XG, ☎ 0151 243 6000
✉ clerk@stjohnsbuildings.co.uk
Call Date: Oct 1995, Inner Temple
Pupil Supervisor
Qualifications: [BA (Hons) (Leeds) Dip Law (Lancs)]
✉ andrew.lawson@stjohnsbuildings.co.uk

LAWSON MR DANIEL GEORGE

The Chambers of Grahame Aldous QC
9 Gough Square, London EC4A 3DG,
☎ 020 7832 0500
✉ clerks@9goughsquare.co.uk
Call Date: Nov 1994, Inner Temple
Pupil Supervisor
Qualifications: [BA (Oxon) MA (Lond) CPE]
✉ dlawson@9goughsquare.co.uk

E

LAWSON MR DAVID ALISTAIR

Hardwicke
New Square, Lincoln's Inn, London WC2A 3SB, ☎ 020 7242 2523
✉ enquiries@hardwicke.co.uk
Call Date: July 2000, Middle Temple
Qualifications: [BA(Hons) (Oxon) LLM (Lond) CPE]
✉ david.lawson@hardwicke.co.uk

LAWSON MR MATTHEW CHRISTOPHER

Carmelite Chambers
9 Carmelite Street, London EC4Y 0DR, ☎ 020 7936 6300
✉ clerks@carmelitechambers.co.uk
Call Date: Nov 1995, Gray's Inn
Qualifications: [LLB]
✉ mlawson@carmelitechambers.co.uk

LAWSON MR ROBERT JOHN QC (2009)

Quadrant Chambers
Quadrant House, 10 Fleet Street, London EC4Y 1AU, ☎ 020 7583 4444
✉ info@quadrantchambers.com
Call Date: Nov 1989, Inner Temple
Qualifications: [BA (Oxon) Dip Law (Lond)]

LAWSON MISS SARA

18 Red Lion Court
London EC4A 3EB, ☎ 020 7520 6000
✉ chambers@18rlc.co.uk
18 Red Lion Court (Annexe)
Thornwood House, 102 New London Road, Chelmsford, Essex CM2 0RG, ☎ 01245 280880
Call Date: Oct 1990, Inner Temple
Pupil Supervisor
Qualifications: [LLB (Hons)]
✉ sara.lawson@18rlc.co.uk

LAWSON ROGERS MR GEORGE STUART QC (1994)

Number 7 Harrington Street Chambers
7 Harrington Street, Liverpool L2 9YH, ☎ 0151 242 0707 ✉ clerks@7hs.co.uk
9-12 Bell Yard
London WC2A 2JR, ☎ 020 7400 1800
✉ clerks@9-12bellyard.com
Call Date: July 1969, Gray's Inn
Recorder
Qualifications: [LLB Hons]
✉ stuart.lawsonrogers@7hs.co.uk

LAWTON MR PAUL ANTHONY

Lincoln House Chambers
Tower 12, The Avenue North, Spinningfields, 18-22 Bridge Street, Manchester M3 3BZ, ☎ 0161 832 5701
✉ info@lincolnhousechambers.com
18 Red Lion Court
London EC4A 3EB, ☎ 020 7520 6000
✉ chambers@18rlc.co.uk
Call Date: Nov 1987, Lincoln's Inn
Pupil Supervisor, Recorder
Qualifications: [LLB(Hons) (Manch)]
✉ paul.lawton@lincolnhousechambers.com

LAYNE MR RONALD BALFOUR ROBERT

12 Old Square Chambers
1st Floor, 12 Old Square, Lincoln's Inn, London WC2A 3TX, ☎ 020 7404 0875
✉ clerks@12oldsquare.com
Call Date: Oct 1992, Lincoln's Inn
Qualifications: [LLB (Hons)(Lond) LLM]
✉ clerks@12oldsquare.com

LAYTON MR ALEXANDER WILLIAM QC (1995)

20 Essex Street
London WC2R 3AL, ☎ 020 7842 1200
✉ clerks@20essexst.com
Call Date: July 1976, Middle Temple
Recorder
Qualifications: [MA (Oxon)]

LAZARIDES MR MARCUS

Queen Elizabeth Building
3rd Floor, Queen Elizabeth Building, Temple, London EC4Y 9BS, ☎ 020 7797 7837
✉ clerks@qeb.co.uk
Call Date: Nov 1999, Middle Temple
Qualifications: [MA (Oxon) DPhil (Oxon) Dip Law]
✉ m.lazarides@qeb.co.uk

LAZARUS MR GRANT PHILIP

Number 7 Harrington Street Chambers
7 Harrington Street, Liverpool L2 9YH, ☎ 0151 242 0707 ✉ clerks@7hs.co.uk
Call Date: Nov 1981, Gray's Inn
Pupil Supervisor
Qualifications: [LLB (Hons)]
✉ grant.lazarus@7hs.co.uk

E

LAZARUS MISS MARY HELEN

42 Bedford Row
London WC1R 4LL, ☎ 020 7831 0222
✉ clerks@42br.com
Call Date: Oct 1991, Middle Temple
Pupil Supervisor
Qualifications: [MA (Cantab) CPE]
✉ mary.lazarus@42br.com

LAZARUS MR MICHAEL STEVEN

3 Verulam Buildings
London WC1R 5NT, ☎ 020 7831 8441
✉ chambers@3vb.com
Call Date: Nov 1987, Middle Temple
Pupil Supervisor
Qualifications: [MA (Cantab)]
✉ mlazarus@3vb.com

LAZARUS MR ROBERT JUSTIN

39 Essex Street
London WC2R 3AT, ☎ 020 7832 1111
✉ clerks@39essex.com
82 King Street
Manchester M2 4WQ, ☎ 0161 870 9969
Call Date: Oct 2004, Inner Temple
Qualifications: [MB LLB (Lond) ChB (Manch)]
✉ robert.lazarus@39essex.com

LAZUR MR THOMAS JAMES

Keating Chambers
15 Essex Street, London WC2R 3AA,
☎ 020 7544 2600
✉ clerks@keatingchambers.com
Call Date: Nov 2005, Inner Temple
Qualifications: [BA University of Bristol CPE BPP Law School]
✉ tlazur@keatingchambers.com

LE BROCQ MR MARK WILLIAM

Linenhall Chambers
1 Stanley Place, Chester CH1 2LU,
☎ 01244 348282
✉ clerks@linenhallchambers.co.uk
Call Date: Nov 1982, Middle Temple
Pupil Supervisor
Qualifications: [MA (Cantab)]
✉ mlb@nicholasstreet.com

LE FEVRE MISS SARAH MARGARET

3 Raymond Buildings
3 Raymond Buildings, Gray's Inn, London WC1R 5BH, ☎ 020 7400 6400
✉ clerks@3rblaw.com
Call Date: July 2001, Lincoln's Inn
Qualifications: [MA (Hons) (Cantab) PgDL LLM]
✉ sarah.lefevre@3raymondbuildings.com

LE FORT MR MICHAEL CAMERON RAOUL

King's Bench Chambers
Wellington House, 175 Holdenhurst Road, Bournemouth, Dorset BH8 8DQ,
☎ 01202 250025
Call Date: Oct 2000, Middle Temple
Qualifications: [BSc Econ (Wales) CPE]

LE GRICE MR VALENTINE QC (2002)

1 Hare Court
1 Hare Court, Temple, London EC4Y 7BE,
☎ 020 7797 7070 ✉ clerks@1hc.com
Riverview Chambers
Hamilton House, 1 Temple Avenue, London EC4Y 0HA, ☎ 0844 225 3999
✉ chrisbaylis@riverviewchambers.com
Call Date: July 1977, Middle Temple
Qualifications: [BA (Hons) (Dunelm)]
✉ legrice@1hc.com

LE POIDEVIN MR NICHOLAS PETER QC (2010)

New Square Chambers
12 New Square, Lincoln's Inn, London WC2A 3SW, ☎ 020 7419 8000
✉ robin.hollington@newsquarechambers.co.uk
Call Date: Nov 1975, Middle Temple
Pupil Supervisor
Qualifications: [MA LLB (Cantab)]
✉ nicholas.lepoidevin@newsquarechambers.co.uk

LE PREVOST MRS AVIVA

Crown Office Row Chambers
119 Church Street, Brighton, Sussex BN1 1UD, ☎ 01273 625625
✉ clerks@1cor.com
Call Date: Nov 1990, Inner Temple
Qualifications: [BA (Manch) Dip Law]

LE QUESNE MS CATHERINE MARY

3 Dr Johnson's Buildings
Ground Floor, 3 Dr Johnson's Buildings, Temple, London EC4Y 7BA, ☎ 020 7353 4854
✉ clerks@3djb.co.uk
Call Date: Nov 1993, Inner Temple
Qualifications: [BA (Manch)]
✉ clequesne@3drjb.co.uk

E

LE SUEUR PROF ANDREW PHILIP

Brick Court Chambers
7-8 Essex Street, London WC2R 3LD,
☎020 7379 3550 ✉clerks@brickcourt.co.uk
Call Date: July 1987, Middle Temple
Qualifications: [LLB (Lond)]
✉a.lesueur@qmul.ac.uk

LEABEATER MR JAMES FERGUSON

4 Pump Court
4 Pump Court, Temple, London EC4Y 7AN,
☎020 7842 5555
✉chambers@4pumpcourt.com
Call Date: Oct 1999, Lincoln's Inn
Pupil Supervisor
Qualifications: [BA (Oxon) PG Dip (Leeds)]
✉jleabeater@4pumpcourt.com

LEACH MR ALEXANDER JAMES

Lincoln House Chambers
Tower 12, The Avenue North, Spinningfields, 18-22 Bridge Street, Manchester M3 3BZ,
☎0161 832 5701
✉info@lincolnhousechambers.com
Call Date: Oct 2001, Inner Temple
Qualifications: [LLB (Hons)(Manch)]
✉alexander.leach@lincolnhousechambers.com

E

LEACH MR DOUGLAS COLIN

Guildhall Chambers
23 Broad Street, Bristol BS1 2HG,
☎0117 930 9000
✉hoc@guildhallchambers.co.uk
Call Date: Oct 2003, Inner Temple
Qualifications: [LLB (So'ton) LLM (Lond)]

LEACH MISS NATASHA JANE

Call Date: Nov 2000, Lincoln's Inn
Qualifications: [LLB (Hons) (Bris)]
✉clerk@stjohnsbuildings.co.uk

LEACH MR ROBIN ANTHONY LANGLEY

3 PB Barristers
3 Paper Buildings, Temple, London EC4Y 7EU,
☎020 7583 8055
3 PB Barristers
30 Christchurch Road, Bournemouth, Dorset BH1 3PD, ☎01202 292102
✉clerks.bournemouth@3paper.co.uk
3 PB Barristers
Royal Talbot House, 2 Victoria Street, Bristol, Avon BS1 6BB, ☎0117 928 1520
3 PB Barristers
4 St Peter Street, Winchester SO23 8BW,
☎01962 868884
✉clerks.winchester@3paper.co.uk
3 PB Barristers
23 Beaumont Street, Oxford OX1 2NP,
☎01865 793 736
Call Date: July 1979, Lincoln's Inn
Pupil Supervisor
Qualifications: [MA (St Andrews)]

LEACH MR STUART ANDREW WARWICK

Pump Court Chambers
5 Temple Chambers, Temple Street, Swindon SN1 1SQ, ☎01793 539899
✉clerks@3pumpcourt.com
Pump Court Chambers
Upper Ground Floor, 3 Pump Court, Temple, London EC4Y 7AJ, ☎020 7353 0711
✉clerks@3pumpcourt.com
Pump Court Chambers
31 Southgate Street, Winchester, Hampshire SO23 9EB, ☎01962 868 161
✉clerks@3pumpcourt.com
Call Date: July 2004, Gray's Inn
Qualifications: [MA (Oxon)]
✉sl@3pumpcourt.com

LEADER MISS LUCY ELAINE

Angel Chambers
Ethos Building, Kings Road, Swansea SA1 8AS,
☎01792 464623
✉clerks@angelchambers.co.uk
Call Date: Oct 2002, Lincoln's Inn
Qualifications: [LLB (L'Pool)]
✉lucyleader@angelchambers.co.uk

LEADER MR TIMOTHY JAMES

Clerksroom (Taunton)
Equity House, Administration Centre, Blackbrook Park Avenue, Taunton, Somerset TA1 2PX, ☎0845 083 3000
✉mail@clerksroom.com
64 Bridge Street
3rd Floor, 64 Bridge Street, Manchester M3 3BN, ☎0845 083 3000
✉mail@64bridgestreet.com
Clerksroom (London)
3rd Floor, 218 Strand, London WC2R 1AT,
☎0845 083 3000 ✉mail@clerksroom.com
Call Date: Oct 1994, Middle Temple
Pupil Supervisor
Qualifications: [BSc (Hons)(B'ham) MA (Sheff) CPE (B'ham)]

LEAFE MR DANIEL JOHN

Albion Chambers
Broad Street, Bristol BS1 1DR,
☎0117 927 2144
✉clerks@albionchambers.co.uk
Call Date: Nov 1996, Gray's Inn
Pupil Supervisor
Qualifications: [LLB (Bris)]
✉daniel.leafe@albionchambers.co.uk

LEAHY MS BLAIR PATRICIA

20 Essex Street
London WC2R 3AL, ☎020 7842 1200
✉clerks@20essexst.com
Call Date: July 2001, Inner Temple
Qualifications: [BA (York) MA (Essex) Dip in Law]
✉BLeahy@20essexst.com

LEAKE MR LABAN PHILIP

Furnival Chambers
32 Furnival Street, London EC4A 1JQ,
☎020 7405 3232
Call Date: Oct 1996, Middle Temple
Qualifications: [MA (Hons) (Oxon)]

LEAKE MR STEPHEN

Carmelite Chambers
9 Carmelite Street, London EC4Y 0DR,
☎020 7936 6300
✉clerks@carmelitechambers.co.uk
Call Date: Mar 2002, Middle Temple
Qualifications: [BSc (Hons)]
✉sleake@carmelitechambers.co.uk

LEAN MISS JACQUELINE ANNE

Landmark Chambers
180 Fleet Street, London EC4A 2HG,
☎020 7430 1221
✉clerks@landmarkchambers.co.uk
Call Date: July 2007, Gray's Inn
Qualifications: [BA (Cantab) LL.M (USA) MA (Cantab) (Hons)]
✉jlean@landmarkchambers.co.uk

LEAR MISS ESTELLE CHRISTINE

Tanfield Chambers
2-5 Warwick Court, London WC1R 5DJ,
☎020 7421 5300
✉clerks@tanfieldchambers.co.uk
Call Date: July 2006, Lincoln's Inn
Qualifications: [LLB (Lanc)]
✉estellelear@tanfieldchambers.co.uk

LEARMONTH MR ALEXANDER ROBERT MAGNUS

New Square Chambers
12 New Square, Lincoln's Inn, London WC2A 3SW, ☎020 7419 8000
✉robin.hollington@newsquarechambers.co.uk
Call Date: Oct 2000, Lincoln's Inn
Pupil Supervisor
Qualifications: [BA (Hons) (Oxon)]
✉Alexander.Learmonth@NewSquareChambers.co.uk

LEATHLEY MR DAVID JONATHAN

Cambria Chambers
The Coal Exchange, Mount Stuart Square, Cardiff Bay, Cardiff CF10 5EB,
☎0845 123 1234
✉Info@cambriachambers.co.uk
Call Date: July 1980, Lincoln's Inn
Pupil Supervisor
Qualifications: [LLB (Hons)(B'ham)]
✉d.leathley@mandmsolicitors.co.uk

LEAVER MR PETER LAWRENCE OPPENHEIM QC (1987)

One Essex Court
Ground Floor, One Essex Court, Temple, London EC4Y 9AR, ☎020 7583 2000
✉clerks@oeclaw.co.uk
Call Date: July 1967, Lincoln's Inn
Recorder
✉pleaver@oeclaw.co.uk

LEAVESLEY MISS LAURA MARIEL

Angel Chambers
Ethos Building, Kings Road, Swansea SA1 8AS,
☎01792 464623
✉clerks@angelchambers.co.uk
Call Date: July 2005, Inner Temple
Qualifications: [LLB]
✉lauraleavesley@angelchambers.co.uk

LECOINTE MS ELPHA MARY

Coram Chambers
9-11 Fulwood Place, London WC1V 6HG,
☎020 7092 3700
✉mail@coramchambers.co.uk
Call Date: Nov 1988, Lincoln's Inn
Pupil Supervisor
Qualifications: [LLB (Hons)]
✉elpha.lecointe@coramchambers.co.uk

LEDDEN MR THOMAS MATTHEW

Wilberforce Chambers
7 Bishop Lane, Hull HU1 1PA,
☎01482 323264
Call Date: Nov 2009, Gray's Inn
Qualifications: [LLB]

E

LEDERMAN MR DAVID QC (1990)

Carmelite Chambers
9 Carmelite Street, London EC4Y 0DR,
☎ 020 7936 6300
✉ clerks@carmelitechambers.co.uk
Call Date: July 1966, Inner Temple
Recorder
Qualifications: [BA (Cantab)]

LEDERMAN MR HOWARD DAVID

42 Bedford Row
London WC1R 4LL, ☎ 020 7831 0222
✉ clerks@42br.com
Call Date: July 1982, Gray's Inn
Pupil Supervisor
Qualifications: [BA (Hons) (Oxon)]
howard.lederman@42br.com

LEDGISTER MR ROY ANDREW

25 Bedford Row
London WC1R 4HD, ☎ 020 7067 1500
✉ clerks@25bedfordrow.com
Call Date: Nov 2005, Inner Temple
Qualifications: [LLB University of Coventry]

E

LEDWARD MISS JOCELYN VICTORIA

QEB Hollis Whiteman
1-2 Laurence Pountney Hill, London
EC4R 0EU, ☎ 020 7933 8855
✉ barristers@qebhw.co.uk
Call Date: Nov 1999, Middle Temple
Pupil Supervisor
Qualifications: [BA (Hons)(Oxon)]
jocelyn.ledward@qebhw.co.uk

LEE MISS ANNABEL LAI TING

4-5 Gray's Inn Square
Gray's Inn, London WC1R 5AH,
☎ 020 7404 5252 ✉ clerks@4-5.co.uk
Call Date: July 2010, Middle Temple
Qualifications: [BA (Hons) (Oxon) LLM (Lond)]

LEE MR DAVID CHARLES

36 Bedford Row
London WC1R 4JH, ☎ 020 7421 8000
✉ chambers@36bedfordrow.co.uk
Call Date: July 1973, Gray's Inn
Pupil Supervisor
Qualifications: [BA (Cantab) BA (USA)]
dlee@36bedfordrow.co.uk

LEE MR GORDON

Chambers of Mr Ami Feder
Ground Floor, Lamb Building, Temple, London
EC4Y 7AS, ☎ 020 7797 7788
✉ clerks@lambbuilding.co.uk
Chambers of Mr Ami Feder
Ground Floor, Lamb Building, Temple, London
EC4Y 7AS, ☎ 020 7797 7788
✉ clerks@lambbuilding.co.uk
Call Date: Nov 1998, Middle Temple
Pupil Supervisor
Qualifications: [LLB (Hons)(Kingston)]

LEE MS JENNIFER EN ZE

Pump Court Chambers
Upper Ground Floor, 3 Pump Court, Temple,
London EC4Y 7AJ, ☎ 020 7353 0711
✉ clerks@3pumpcourt.com
Pump Court Chambers
31 Southgate Street, Winchester, Hampshire
SO23 9EB, ☎ 01962 868 161
✉ clerks@3pumpcourt.com
Riverview Chambers
Hamilton House, 1 Temple Avenue, London
EC4Y 0HA, ☎ 0844 225 3999
✉ chrisbaylis@riverviewchambers.com
Call Date: July 2007, Lincoln's Inn
Qualifications: [LLB (Lond)]
jl@3pumpcourt.com

LEE MR JONATHAN JAMES WILTON

Keating Chambers
15 Essex Street, London WC2R 3AA,
☎ 020 7544 2600
✉ clerks@keatingchambers.com
Call Date: Oct 1993, Gray's Inn
Pupil Supervisor
Qualifications: [B Eng (Sheff)]
jlee@keatingchambers.com

LEE MISS KRISTA CHUI LAN

Keating Chambers
15 Essex Street, London WC2R 3AA,
☎ 020 7544 2600
✉ clerks@keatingchambers.com
Call Date: Nov 1996, Lincoln's Inn
Pupil Supervisor
Qualifications: [MA BCL (Oxon) BSc (Open) FCIArb]
klee@keatingchambers.com

LEE MR MICHAEL JAMES ARTHUR

20 Essex Street
London WC2R 3AL, ☎ 020 7842 1200
✉ clerks@20essexst.com
Call Date: July 2001, Middle Temple
Qualifications: [LLB (Hons)]
clerks@20essexst.com

LEE MR MICHAEL JOSEPH

11 King's Bench Walk
11 King's Bench Walk, Temple, London EC4Y 7EQ, ☎ 020 7632 8500
✉ clerksroom@11kbw.com
Call Date: July 2009, Lincoln's Inn
Qualifications: [BA (Cantab)]
✉ michael.lee@11kbw.com

LEE MS REBECCA JANE

187 Fleet Street
London EC4A 2AT, ☎ 020 7430 7430
✉ chambers@187fleetstreet.com
Call Date: Nov 2004, Lincoln's Inn
Qualifications: [BA (Hons) MA]
✉ rebeccalee@187fleetstreet.com

LEE MR ROSSLYN ALEXANDER

Dere Street Barristers
14 Toft Green, York YO1 6JT, ☎ 0844 3351551
✉ clerks@derestreet.co.uk
York Chambers
Rotterdam House, 116 The Quayside, Newcastle Upon Tyne NE1 3DY, ☎ 0191 206 4677
Call Date: Nov 1987, Gray's Inn
Qualifications: [BA MA (Oxon)]
✉ clerks@yorkchambers.co.uk

LEE MISS SARAH JOANNE

Brick Court Chambers
7-8 Essex Street, London WC2R 3LD, ☎ 020 7379 3550 ✉ clerks@brickcourt.co.uk
Call Date: Nov 1990, Middle Temple
Qualifications: [BA BCL (Oxon)]
✉ Sarah.Lee@Brickcourt.co.uk

LEE MISS SARAH-JANE

15 Winckley Square
Preston PR1 3JJ, ☎ 01772 252828
✉ clerks@15winckleysq.co.uk
Call Date: Nov 2002, Lincoln's Inn
Qualifications: [LLB (Hons)]

LEE MISS TARYN JANE QC (2012)

37 Park Square Chambers
37 Park Square, Leeds LS1 2NY, ☎ 0113 243 9422 ✉ chambers@no37.co.uk
Call Date: July 1992, Inner Temple
Pupil Supervisor, Recorder
Qualifications: [LLB (Hons)]
✉ chambers@no37.co.uk

LEECH MR BENEDICT

12 King's Bench Walk
12 King's Bench Walk, Temple, London EC4Y 7EL, ☎ 020 7583 0811
Call Date: Oct 1997, Inner Temple
Qualifications: [MA (Cantab) CPE]
✉ leech@12kbw.co.uk

LEECH MR STEWART QC (2011)

Queen Elizabeth Building
3rd Floor, Queen Elizabeth Building, Temple, London EC4Y 9BS, ☎ 020 7797 7837
✉ clerks@qeb.co.uk
Call Date: Oct 1992, Lincoln's Inn
Pupil Supervisor
Qualifications: [MA(Oxon)]
✉ s.leech@qeb.co.uk

LEECH MR THOMAS ALEXANDER CRISPIN QC (2010)

Maitland Chambers
7 Stone Buildings, Lincoln's Inn, London WC2A 3SZ, ☎ 020 7406 1200
✉ clerks@maitlandchambers.com
Call Date: Nov 1988, Middle Temple
Pupil Supervisor
Qualifications: [MA BCL (Oxon)]
✉ tleech@maitlandchambers.com

LEEK MISS SAMANTHA LOUISE QC (2012)

5 Essex Court
1st Floor, 5 Essex Court, Temple, London EC4Y 9AH, ☎ 020 7410 2000
✉ clerks@5essexcourt.co.uk
Call Date: Oct 1993, Gray's Inn
Pupil Supervisor
Qualifications: [BA (Oxon) CPE]
✉ leek@5essexcourt.co.uk

LEEMING MISS LUCINDA CLARE

9 St John Street
Manchester M3 4DN, ☎ 0161 955 9000
✉ civilclerks@9sjs.com / criminalclerks@9sjs.com
Call Date: Oct 1999, Middle Temple
Qualifications: [LLB (Hons)]

E

LEEPER MR THOMAS RICHARD GEOFFREY

St John's Chambers
101 Victoria Street, Bristol BS1 6PU,
☎0117 923 4700
✉clerks@stjohnschambers.co.uk
Outer Temple Chambers
The Outer Temple, 222 Strand, London WC2R 1BA, ☎020 7353 6381
✉clerks@outertemple.com
Call Date: Nov 1991, Middle Temple
Qualifications: [BA (Hons) (Dunelm)]

LEES MISS CHARLOTTE ELIZABETH

12 College Place
Fauvelle Buildings, 12 College Place, Southampton SO15 2FE, ☎023 8032 0320
✉clerks@12cp.co.uk
Call Date: Nov 2001, Lincoln's Inn
Qualifications: [LLB (Hons)(Lanc) LLM]
✉clees@12cp.co.uk

LEES MR KESTER GERRARD WILLIAM

Falcon Chambers
Falcon Court, London EC4Y 1AA,
☎020 7353 2484
✉clerks@falcon-chambers.com
Call Date: Oct 2010, Inner Temple
Qualifications: [BA (B'ham) LLB (Lond)]
✉lees@falcon-chambers.com

LEFTERI MR KYRIACOS

New Court
Ground Floor, New Court, Temple, London EC4Y 9BE, ☎020 7583 5123
✉clerks@newcourtchambers.com
Call Date: Nov 2006, Inner Temple
Qualifications: [LLB (Lond)]
✉klefteri@newcourtchambers.net

LEGARD MR EDWARD THOMAS

Dere Street Barristers
14 Toft Green, York YO1 6JT, ☎0844 3351551
✉clerks@derestreet.co.uk
York Chambers
Rotterdam House, 116 The Quayside, Newcastle Upon Tyne NE1 3DY,
☎0191 206 4677
Call Date: Oct 1996, Gray's Inn
Qualifications: [MA]
✉clerks@yorkchambers.co.uk, e.legard@derestreet.co.uk

LEGG MR ANDREW JOHN

Essex Court Chambers
24 Lincoln's Inn Fields, London WC2A 3EG,
☎020 7813 8000
✉clerksroom@essexcourt.net
Call Date: Oct 2010, Lincoln's Inn
Qualifications: [BA BCL MPHIL DPHIL (Oxon)]
✉alegg@essexcourt.net

LEGGATT MR GEORGE ANDREW MIDSOMER QC (1997)

Brick Court Chambers
7-8 Essex Street, London WC2R 3LD,
☎020 7379 3550 ✉clerks@brickcourt.co.uk
Call Date: July 1983, Middle Temple
Recorder
Qualifications: [MA (Cantab)]
✉George.Leggatt@Brickcourt.co.uk

LEGGE MR HENRY QC (2012)

5 Stone Buildings
5 Stone Buildings, Lincoln's Inn, London WC2A 3XT, ☎020 7242 6201
✉clerks@5sblaw.com
Call Date: Nov 1993, Middle Temple
Pupil Supervisor
Qualifications: [BA (Hons)(Oxon) CPE (Lond)]
✉hlegge@5sblaw.com

LEIGH MR KEVIN

No5 Chambers
Greenwood House, 4-7 Salisbury Court, London EC4Y 8AA, ☎0845 210 5555
No5 Chambers
38 Queen Square, Bristol BS1 4QS,
☎0845 210 5555
No5 Chambers
Fountain Court, Steelhouse Lane, Birmingham B4 6DR, ☎0845 210 5555 ✉info@no5.com
Call Date: July 1986, Lincoln's Inn
Pupil Supervisor
Qualifications: [LLB (Leics)]
✉kl@no5.com

LEIGH MISS SAMANTHA CERI

18 Red Lion Court
London EC4A 3EB, ☎020 7520 6000
✉chambers@18rlc.co.uk
18 Red Lion Court (Annexe)
Thornwood House, 102 New London Road, Chelmsford, Essex CM2 0RG,
☎01245 280880
Call Date: Nov 1995, Inner Temple
Pupil Supervisor, Recorder
Qualifications: [BA (Essex) CPE]
✉samantha.leigh@18RLC.co.uk

LEIGHTON MR PETER LEONARD

4 King's Bench Walk
2nd Floor, 4 King's Bench Walk, Temple, London EC4Y 7DL, ☎ 020 7822 7000
✉ clerks@4kbw.co.uk
Call Date: July 1966, Inner Temple
Pupil Supervisor
Qualifications: [LLB (Lond)]

LEIPER MR RICHARD THOMAS

11 King's Bench Walk
11 King's Bench Walk, Temple, London EC4Y 7EQ, ☎ 020 7632 8500
✉ clerksroom@11kbw.com
Call Date: Oct 1996, Gray's Inn
Pupil Supervisor
Qualifications: [LLB (B'ham) M.Jur (Oxon)]
✉ richard.leiper@11kbw.com

LEIVESLEY MISS JULIE ANNE

Five Paper
Ground Floor, 5 Paper Buildings, Temple, London EC4Y 7HB, ☎ 020 7815 3200
Call Date: Nov 2000, Lincoln's Inn
Qualifications: [LLB (Hons) (London)]
✉ julieleivesley@fivepaper.com

LEMER MR DAVID JAMES

Doughty Street Chambers
53-54 Doughty Street, London WC1N 2LS, ☎ 020 7404 1313
✉ enquiries@doughtystreet.co.uk
Call Date: Oct 2000, Middle Temple
Qualifications: [LLB (Hons) (Leeds)]

LEMER MR SAUL

One Essex Court
Ground Floor, One Essex Court, Temple, London EC4Y 9AR, ☎ 020 7583 2000
✉ clerks@oeclaw.co.uk
Call Date: Oct 2007, Gray's Inn
Qualifications: [BA (Cantab) BCL (Oxon) LLM]
✉ slemer@oeclaw.co.uk

LEMMY MR MICHAEL DAVID

9 St John Street
Manchester M3 4DN, ☎ 0161 955 9000
✉ civilclerks@9sjs.com / criminalclerks@9sjs.com
Call Date: Nov 1994, Middle Temple
Pupil Supervisor
Qualifications: [LLB (Hons)]
✉ michael.lemmy@9sjs.com

LEMON MISS JANE KATHERINE

Keating Chambers
15 Essex Street, London WC2R 3AA, ☎ 020 7544 2600
✉ clerks@keatingchambers.com
Call Date: Nov 1993, Inner Temple
Pupil Supervisor
Qualifications: [BA (Hons) CPE]
✉ jlemon@keatingchambers.com

LEMOS MISS MARIKA CHRISTOS

Gray's Inn Tax Chambers
3rd Floor, Gray's Inn Chambers, Gray's Inn, London WC1R 5JA, ☎ 020 7242 2642
✉ clerks@taxbar.com
Call Date: Oct 2002, Middle Temple
Qualifications: [MA (Cantab) Dip Law LLM]
✉ mcl@taxbar.com

LENAGHAN MR ANTHONY

Dyers Chambers
35 Bedford Row, London WC1R 4JH, ☎ 020 7404 1881
✉ admin@dyerschambers.com
Call Date: Nov 1996, Middle Temple
Qualifications: [LLB (Hons)(Lond)]
✉ anthony@lenaghan.demon.co.uk

LENNARD MR STEPHEN CHARLES

Hardwicke
New Square, Lincoln's Inn, London WC2A 3SB, ☎ 020 7242 2523
✉ enquiries@hardwicke.co.uk
Call Date: July 1976, Gray's Inn
Pupil Supervisor
Qualifications: [LLB (Manch) Dip Crim (Cantab)]
✉ stephen.lennard@hardwicke.co.uk

LENNON MR DESMOND JOSEPH

Number 7 Harrington Street Chambers
7 Harrington Street, Liverpool L2 9YH, ☎ 0151 242 0707 ✉ clerks@7hs.co.uk
Call Date: Nov 1986, Gray's Inn
Qualifications: [BA]
✉ desmond.lennon@7hs.co.uk

LENNON MR JOHN FRANCIS

23 Essex Street
London WC2R 3AA, ☎ 020 7413 0353
✉ clerks@23es.com
Call Date: Mar 1997, Lincoln's Inn
Pupil Supervisor
Qualifications: [BA (Hons)]
✉ jonathanlennon@23es.com

E

LENNON MISS KAREN JANE

Dere Street Barristers
14 Toft Green, York YO1 6JT, ☎0844 3351551
✉clerks@derestreet.co.uk
York Chambers
Rotterdam House, 116 The Quayside, Newcastle Upon Tyne NE1 3DY, ☎0191 206 4677
Call Date: July 2003, Inner Temple
Qualifications: [LLB (Northumbria) LLB (Hons)]
✉clerks@yorkchambers.co.uk, klennon@yorkchambers.co.uk, k.lennon@derestreet.co.uk

LENON MR ANDREW RALPH FITZMAURICE QC (2006)

One Essex Court
Ground Floor, One Essex Court, Temple, London EC4Y 9AR, ☎020 7583 2000
✉clerks@oeclaw.co.uk
Call Date: Nov 1982, Lincoln's Inn
Qualifications: [BA (Oxon) Dip Law (Lond)]
✉alenon@oeclaw.co.uk

LEON MR MARC EDWARD

Chambers of Marc E. Leon Esq.
Suite 526, 275 Deansgate, Manchester M3 4EL, ☎07875 340598
✉marc@eleon.fsnet.co.uk
Call Date: May 1988, Middle Temple
Qualifications: [LLB (Hons)]
✉marc@eleon.fsnet.co.uk

LEONARD MR CHARLES ROBERT WESTON

Hardwicke
New Square, Lincoln's Inn, London WC2A 3SB, ☎020 7242 2523
✉enquiries@hardwicke.co.uk
Call Date: July 1976, Inner Temple
Pupil Supervisor
Qualifications: [BA (Dublin)]
✉robert.leonard@hardwicke.co.uk

LEONARD MISS CLAIRE HELEN

St John's Chambers
101 Victoria Street, Bristol BS1 6PU, ☎0117 923 4700
✉clerks@stjohnschambers.co.uk
Call Date: Oct 2009, Inner Temple
Qualifications: [BA (Cantab) LLM (Bris)]
✉claire.leonard@stjohnschambers.co.uk

LEONARD MS EDNA JEAN

KCH Garden Square
1 Oxford Street, Nottingham NG1 5BH, ☎0115 941 8851
✉clerks@kchgardensquare.co.uk
Call Date: Oct 1992, Gray's Inn
Qualifications: [BSc (Hons) (Oxon)]

LEONARD MR JAMES ALEXANDER

Outer Temple Chambers
The Outer Temple, 222 Strand, London WC2R 1BA, ☎020 7353 6381
✉clerks@outertemple.com
Call Date: Nov 1989, Inner Temple
Pupil Supervisor
Qualifications: [BA]

LEONARD MS PATRICIA

Seven Bedford Row
7 Bedford Row, London WC1R 4BS, ☎020 7242 3555 ✉clerks@7br.co.uk
Call Date: July 2007, Lincoln's Inn
Qualifications: [BCL(Dub) BCL (Oxon)]
✉pleonard@7br.co.uk

LEONG MR ANDREW SENG POH

Harcourt Chambers
1st Floor, 2 Harcourt Buildings, Temple, London EC4Y 9DB, ☎0844 561 7135
Call Date: Oct 1998, Middle Temple
Pupil Supervisor
Qualifications: [LLB (Hons)(Bris)]
✉aleong@harcourtchambers.law.co.uk

LEONG MR SIMON GEORGE

New Bailey Chambers
4th Floor, Corn Exchange, Fenwick Street, Liverpool, Merseyside L2 7QS, ☎0151 236 9402 ✉clerks@newbailey.com
Call Date: Oct 2001, Middle Temple
Qualifications: [LLB (Hons)]
✉silong1978@hotmail.co.uk

LESLIE MISS CLARE

Chambers of Mr Ami Feder
Ground Floor, Lamb Building, Temple, London EC4Y 7AS, ☎020 7797 7788
✉clerks@lambbuilding.co.uk
Lamb Building
22 Ship Street, Brighton BN1 1AD, ☎01273 820490
✉admin@lambbuilding.co.uk
Chambers of Mr Ami Feder
Ground Floor, Lamb Building, Temple, London EC4Y 7AS, ☎020 7797 7788
✉clerks@lambbuilding.co.uk
Call Date: Nov 2002, Middle Temple
Qualifications: [BA (Hons) (Oxon) CPE]
✉clerks@lambbuilding.co.uk

LESLIE MR JAMES JOSEPH

No5 Chambers
Fountain Court, Steelhouse Lane, Birmingham B4 6DR, ☎0845 210 5555 ✉info@no5.com
No5 Chambers
Greenwood House, 4-7 Salisbury Court, London EC4Y 8AA, ☎0845 210 5555
No5 Chambers
38 Queen Square, Bristol BS1 4QS, ☎0845 210 5555
Call Date: July 2004, Middle Temple
Qualifications: [LLB Hons]
jl@no5.com

LESLIE MISS MARIE RITA

Albion Chambers
Broad Street, Bristol BS1 1DR, ☎0117 927 2144
✉clerks@albionchambers.co.uk
Call Date: Mar 2000, Inner Temple
Qualifications: [LLB]
marie.leslie@albionchambers.co.uk

LESLIE MR NICHOLAS EMMET GRAHAM

Fountain Court Chambers
Fountain Court, Temple, London EC4Y 9DH, ☎020 7583 3335
✉chambers@fountaincourt.co.uk
Call Date: Oct 2010, Lincoln's Inn
Qualifications: [BA (Cantab)]

LESLIE MR STEPHEN WINDSOR QC (1993)

Furnival Chambers
32 Furnival Street, London EC4A 1JQ, ☎020 7405 3232
Cobden House Chambers
19 Quay Street, Manchester M3 3HN, ☎0161 833 6000 ✉Clerks@Cobden.co.uk
Call Date: Feb 1971, Lincoln's Inn
Qualifications: [LLB (Lond)]

LESSING MISS DIANA RUTH

No.6 Park Square
Leeds LS1 2LW, ☎0113 245 9763
✉Tim@no6.co.uk
Call Date: Nov 2010, Inner Temple
Qualifications: [BSc (Bris)]

LESTER MISS MAYA

Brick Court Chambers
7-8 Essex Street, London WC2R 3LD, ☎020 7379 3550 ✉clerks@brickcourt.co.uk
Call Date: Oct 2000, Lincoln's Inn
Pupil Supervisor
Qualifications: [BA (Hons) (Cantab) MSL CPE]
Maya.Lester@Brickcourt.co.uk

LESTER OF HERNE HILL LORD QC (1975)

Blackstone Chambers
Blackstone House, Temple, London EC4Y 9BW, ☎020 7583 1770
✉clerks@blackstonechambers.com
Call Date: Feb 1963, Lincoln's Inn
Qualifications: [BA (Cantab) LLM (USA)]
anthonylester@blackstonechambers.com

LETMAN MR PAUL ST JOHN

3 Hare Court
3 Hare Court, Temple, London EC4Y 7BJ, ☎020 7415 7800 ✉clerks@3harecourt.com
Call Date: Nov 1987, Middle Temple
Pupil Supervisor
Qualifications: [BSc Dip Law]
paulletman@3harecourt.com

LETT MR HUGH BRIAN GORDON QC (2008)

Argent Chambers
5 Bell Yard, London WC2A 2JR, ☎020 7556 5500
✉briefsin@argentchambers.co.uk
Call Date: Nov 1971, Inner Temple
Recorder
b.lett@argentchambers.co.uk

LEUNG MR ANDREW SING YAN

Stone Chambers
4 Field Court, Gray's Inn, London WC1R 5EF, ☎020 7440 6900
✉clerks@stonechambers.com
Call Date: Oct 2010, Lincoln's Inn
Qualifications: [BA MPHIL (Cantab)]

LEVENE MISS RACHAEL DOROTHY

9 St John Street
Manchester M3 4DN, ☎0161 955 9000
✉civilclerks@9sjs.com / criminalclerks@9sjs.com
Call Date: Oct 2006, Gray's Inn
Qualifications: [BA]

LEVENE MR SIMON

12 King's Bench Walk
12 King's Bench Walk, Temple, London EC4Y 7EL, ☎020 7583 0811
Call Date: July 1977, Middle Temple
Pupil Supervisor, Recorder
Qualifications: [MA (Cantab)]
levene@12kbw.co.uk

E

LEVETT MISS FRANCESCA ANNA

Five St Andrew's Hill
5 St Andrew's Hill, London EC4V 5BZ,
☎ 020 7332 5400 ✉ Clerks@5sah.co.uk
Call Date: Oct 1997, Lincoln's Inn
Qualifications: [LLB (Hons)]
francescalevett@5sah.co.uk

LEVETT MR MARTYN NEALE

18 Red Lion Court
London EC4A 3EB, ☎ 020 7520 6000
✉ chambers@18rlc.co.uk
18 Red Lion Court (Annexe)
Thornwood House, 102 New London Road, Chelmsford, Essex CM2 0RG,
☎ 01245 280880
Call Date: Nov 1978, Middle Temple
Pupil Supervisor, Recorder
Qualifications: [BSc (Leeds)]
mnlevett@eachambers17.freeserve.co.uk

LEVEY MR EDWARD MICHAEL

Fountain Court Chambers
Fountain Court, Temple, London EC4Y 9DH,
☎ 020 7583 3335
✉ chambers@fountaincourt.co.uk
Call Date: Nov 1999, Inner Temple
Pupil Supervisor
Qualifications: [BA (Cantab) BCL (Oxon)]
elevey@fountaincourt.co.uk

LEVINE MISS NATALIA MARIA

Park Lane Plowden
19 Westgate, Leeds LS1 2RD,
☎ 0113 228 5049
✉ clerks@parklaneplowden.co.uk
Call Date: July 2007, Lincoln's Inn
Qualifications: [BA (L'pool)]
Natalia.levine@parklaneplowden.co.uk

LEVINE MR STEVEN ADRIAN

Palmyra Chambers
Royal House, 46 Legh Street, Warrington WA1 1UJ, ☎ 01925 444919
✉ clerk@palmyrachambers.com
Call Date: Nov 1989, Lincoln's Inn
Qualifications: [LLB (Hons) LLM (Lond)]

LEVINSON MISS JEMMA

1 Mitre Court Buildings
1 Mitre Court Buildings, Temple, London EC4Y 7BS, ☎ 020 7452 8900
✉ clerks@1mcb.com
Call Date: Nov 2001, Gray's Inn
Qualifications: [LLB (Leeds)]
jemma.levinson@1mcb.com

LEVINSON MR JUSTIN MAURICE

1 Crown Office Row
1 Crown Office Row, Temple, London EC4Y 7HH, ☎ 020 7797 7500
✉ mail@1cor.com
Call Date: Oct 1994, Middle Temple
Pupil Supervisor
Qualifications: [LLB (Hons)]
justin.levinson@1cor.com

LEVISEUR MR NICHOLAS TEMPLAR

3 PB Barristers
3 Paper Buildings, Temple, London EC4Y 7EU,
☎ 020 7583 8055
3 PB Barristers
Royal Talbot House, 2 Victoria Street, Bristol, Avon BS1 6BB, ☎ 0117 928 1520
3 PB Barristers
23 Beaumont Street, Oxford OX1 2NP,
☎ 01865 793 736
3 PB Barristers
4 St Peter Street, Winchester SO23 8BW,
☎ 01962 868884
✉ clerks.winchester@3paper.co.uk
3 PB Barristers
30 Christchurch Road, Bournemouth, Dorset BH1 3PD, ☎ 01202 292102
✉ clerks.bournemouth@3paper.co.uk
Call Date: Nov 1979, Gray's Inn
Pupil Supervisor
Qualifications: [MA(Oxon)]

LEVY MR JACOB

The Chambers of Grahame Aldous QC
9 Gough Square, London EC4A 3DG,
☎ 020 7832 0500
✉ clerks@9goughsquare.co.uk
Call Date: July 1986, Inner Temple
Pupil Supervisor
Qualifications: [LLB (Lond)]
jlevy@9goughsquare.co.uk

LEVY MISS JULIETTE

Selborne Chambers
10 Essex Street, London WC2R 3AA,
☎ 020 7420 9500
✉ clerks@selbornechambers.co.uk
Call Date: Nov 1992, Middle Temple
Pupil Supervisor
Qualifications: [BA (Hons) MA (Lond)]
juliette.levy@selbornechambers.co.uk

LEVY MR MICHAEL PETER

2 Bedford Row
London WC1R 4BU, ☎ 020 7440 8888
✉ clerks@2bedfordrow.co.uk
Call Date: Nov 1979, Gray's Inn
Pupil Supervisor
Qualifications: [LLB Hons]
mlevy@2bedfordrow.co.uk

LEVY MR NEIL HOWARD

Guildhall Chambers
23 Broad Street, Bristol BS1 2HG,
☎ 0117 930 9000
✉ hoc@guildhallchambers.co.uk
Guildhall Chambers
5-8 Broad Street, Bristol BS1 2HW,
☎ 0117 930 9000
Call Date: July 1986, Lincoln's Inn
Pupil Supervisor
Qualifications: [LLB (Exeter)]
neil.levy@guildhallchambers.co.uk

LEVY MR PHILIP GRENVILLE

4 Breams Buildings
Chancery Lane, London EC4A 1HP,
☎ 020 7092 1900 ✉ clerks@4bb.co.uk
Call Date: Nov 1968, Inner Temple
Pupil Supervisor
Qualifications: [LLB (Manch)]

LEVY MR ROBERT STUART QC (2010)

XXIV Old Buildings
Ground Floor, 24 Old Buildings, Lincoln's Inn,
London WC2A 3UP, ☎ 020 7691 2424
✉ clerks@xxiv.co.uk
Queen Square Chambers
56 Queen Square, Bristol BS1 4PR,
☎ 0117 921 1966 ✉ crime@qs-c.co.uk
Call Date: Nov 1988, Middle Temple
Pupil Supervisor
Qualifications: [LLB LLM (Cantab)]
robert.levy@xxiv.co.uk

LEW DR JULIAN DAVID MATHEW

20 Essex Street
London WC2R 3AL, ☎ 020 7842 1200
✉ clerks@20essexst.com
Call Date: Nov 1970, Middle Temple
Qualifications: [LLB (Hons) (Lond)]
clerks@20essexst.com

LEWERS MR NIGEL CHRISTOPHER

12 King's Bench Walk
12 King's Bench Walk, Temple, London
EC4Y 7EL, ☎ 020 7583 0811
Call Date: Nov 1986, Gray's Inn
Pupil Supervisor
Qualifications: [MA (Oxon)]
lewers@12kbw.co.uk

LEWIECKI MISS MARIE

Old Bailey Chambers
15 Old Bailey, London EC4M 7EF,
☎ 020 3008 6404
✉ clerks@15oldbaileychambers.com
Call Date: Nov 2006, Middle Temple
Qualifications: [BA (Hons) (Durham) PgDip Law]
m.lewiecki@15oldbaileychambers.com

LEWIN MR NICHOLAS ANTON

King's Bench and Godolphin (KBG)Chambers
115 North Hill, Plymouth, Devon PL4 8JY,
☎ 01752 221551
✉ clerks@kbgchambers.co.uk
Call Date: July 1989, Gray's Inn
Qualifications: [BA]
nicholas.lewin@kingsbenchchambers.co.uk

LEWINGTON MISS FRANCESCA ANNA

Crown Office Row Chambers
119 Church Street, Brighton, Sussex
BN1 1UD, ☎ 01273 625625
✉ clerks@1cor.com
Call Date: Nov 2001, Inner Temple
Qualifications: [MA (Oxon)]
francesca.lewington@1cor.com

LEWIS MR ADAM VALENTINE SHERVEY QC (2009)

Blackstone Chambers
Blackstone House, Temple, London
EC4Y 9BW, ☎ 020 7583 1770
✉ clerks@blackstonechambers.com
Call Date: July 1985, Gray's Inn
Qualifications: [MA (Cantab)]
adamlewis@blackstonechambers.com

LEWIS MR ANDREW SIMON

4 Breams Buildings
Chancery Lane, London EC4A 1HP,
☎ 020 7092 1900 ✉ clerks@4bb.co.uk
Call Date: Nov 1986, Middle Temple
Pupil Supervisor
Qualifications: [BA(Oxon)]
clerks@4bb.co.uk

E

LEWIS MR ANDREW WILLIAM QC (2009)

Sovereign Chambers
46 Park Place, Leeds LS1 2RY,
☎0113 245 1841
✉clerks@sovereignchambers.co.uk
Byrom Street Chambers
12 Byrom Street, Manchester M3 4PP,
☎0161 829 2100 ✉clerks@byromstreet.com
Call Date: July 1985, Lincoln's Inn
Pupil Supervisor, Recorder
Qualifications: [BA]
andrew.lewis@sovereignchambers.co.uk

LEWIS MS ANYA LOUISE

Garden Court Chambers
57-60 Lincoln's Inn Fields, London WC2A 3LJ,
☎020 7993 7600 ✉info@gclaw.co.uk
Call Date: Nov 1997, Inner Temple
Qualifications: [LLB (So'ton)]
anyal@gclaw.co.uk

LEWIS MS CATRIN ELUNED

Garden Court Chambers
57-60 Lincoln's Inn Fields, London WC2A 3LJ,
☎020 7993 7600 ✉info@gclaw.co.uk
Call Date: Nov 1991, Middle Temple
Pupil Supervisor
Qualifications: [BA (Hons)(Lond) Dip Law]

LEWIS MR CHRISTOPHER DAVID

Atkin Chambers
1 Atkin Building, Gray's Inn, London
WC1R 5AT, ☎020 7404 0102
✉clerks@atkinchambers.com
Call Date: Nov 1998, Middle Temple
Pupil Supervisor
Qualifications: [BA (Hons)(Oxon) BCL]
clerks@atkinchambers.com

LEWIS MR CLIVE BUCKLAND QC (2006)

11 King's Bench Walk
11 King's Bench Walk, Temple, London
EC4Y 7EQ, ☎020 7632 8500
✉clerksroom@11kbw.com
Call Date: Nov 1987, Middle Temple
Recorder
Qualifications: [MA (Cantab) LLM (Canada)]
clive.lewis@11kbw.com

LEWIS MR DANIEL CERI

3 Hare Court
3 Hare Court, Temple, London EC4Y 7BJ,
☎020 7415 7800 ✉clerks@3harecourt.com
Call Date: Oct 2003, Lincoln's Inn
Qualifications: [BA (Hons) (Oxon) BA (Hons) (Cantab)]
daniellewis@3harecourt.com

LEWIS MISS DANIELLE SORAYA

Coram Chambers
9-11 Fulwood Place, London WC1V 6HG,
☎020 7092 3700
✉mail@coramchambers.co.uk
Call Date: Nov 1995, Lincoln's Inn
Qualifications: [LLB (Hons)]
danielle.lewis@coramchambers.co.uk

LEWIS MR DARREN EURWYN

St John's Chambers
101 Victoria Street, Bristol BS1 6PU,
☎0117 923 4700
✉clerks@stjohnschambers.co.uk
Call Date: Oct 2004, Inner Temple
Qualifications: [LLB (Warw)]
darren.lewis@stjohnschambers.co.uk

LEWIS MR DAVID ALEXANDER GOWER

Institute for Human Rights
Abo Akademi University, Biskopsgaton 19,
Turku 20500 ✉dlewis@abo.fi
Call Date: Mar 2006, Lincoln's Inn
Qualifications: [LLB (Hons) (Durham) Dip (IHL) Dip (Int'l Law) PLL BA Double Major and Minor (Magna Cum Laude) LLM (Int'l Human Rights) LLM (European Law) AILS]
dlewis@abo.fi

LEWIS MR DAVID NICHOLAS

Hardwicke
New Square, Lincoln's Inn, London
WC2A 3SB, ☎020 7242 2523
✉enquiries@hardwicke.co.uk
Call Date: Nov 1997, Lincoln's Inn
Pupil Supervisor
Qualifications: [LLB (Hons)(Sheff)]
david.lewis@hardwicke.co.uk

LEWIS MR DAVID PATRICK

20 Essex Street
London WC2R 3AL, ☎020 7842 1200
✉clerks@20essexst.com
Call Date: Nov 1999, Middle Temple
Qualifications: [BA (Hons)(Oxon)]
clerks@20essexst.com

LEWIS MR DOMINIC

Five Paper Buildings
1st Floor, Five Paper Buildings, Temple,
London EC4Y 7HB, ☎020 7583 6117
✉clerks@5pb.co.uk
Call Date: July 2000, Inner Temple
Pupil Supervisor
Qualifications: [BA (Oxon)]
djl@5pb.co.uk

LEWIS MR EDWARD TREVOR GWYN

4 Breams Buildings
Chancery Lane, London EC4A 1HP, ☎020 7092 1900 ✉clerks@4bb.co.uk
Call Date: July 1972, Gray's Inn

LEWIS MR GARY JAMES

Cobden House Chambers
19 Quay Street, Manchester M3 3HN, ☎0161 833 6000 ✉Clerks@Cobden.co.uk
Call Date: July 2010, Lincoln's Inn
Qualifications: [LLB (L'pool)]

LEWIS MR GWION RHISIART

Landmark Chambers
180 Fleet Street, London EC4A 2HG, ☎020 7430 1221 ✉clerks@landmarkchambers.co.uk
Call Date: July 2005, Gray's Inn
Qualifications: [BA BCL (Oxon) LLM (USA)]
glewis@landmarkchambers.co.uk

LEWIS MR JAMES THOMAS QC (2002)

3 Raymond Buildings
3 Raymond Buildings, Gray's Inn, London WC1R 5BH, ☎020 7400 6400 ✉clerks@3rblaw.com
Call Date: July 1987, Gray's Inn
Pupil Supervisor, Recorder
Qualifications: [BSc (Hons) DipLaw]
james.lewis@3raymondbuildings.com

LEWIS MISS JANE ALEXIS

2 Hare Court
Lower Ground, Ground, 1st & 2nd Floor, 2 Hare Court, Temple, London EC4Y 7BH, ☎020 7353 3982 ✉clerks@2harecourt.com
Call Date: Nov 1990, Middle Temple
Pupil Supervisor
Qualifications: [BA (Canada) Dip Law]
alexlewis@2harecourt.com

LEWIS MR JEREMY STEPHEN

Littleton Chambers
3 King's Bench Walk North, Temple, London EC4Y 7HR, ☎020 7797 8600 ✉fschneider@littletonchambers.co.uk
Call Date: May 1992, Lincoln's Inn
Pupil Supervisor
Qualifications: [BA BCL]
jlewis@littletonchambers.co.uk

LEWIS MISS JOANNA RUTH

Queen Square Chambers
56 Queen Square, Bristol BS1 4PR, ☎0117 921 1966 ✉crime@qs-c.co.uk
Call Date: July 2004, Middle Temple
Qualifications: [MA PGDip Law]
jrl@qs-c.co.uk

LEWIS MR JOHN HAROLD FRANK

Chambers of Mr T Ballantine Dykes
Ewe Close, Arkleby, Wigton, Cumbria CA7 2DS, ☎01697 321917 ✉t.ballantinedykes@btinternet.com
Call Date: Nov 2003, Middle Temple
Qualifications: [BA (Hons) (Wales) MA (Wales) CPE]

LEWIS MR JONATHAN MARK

4 Pump Court
4 Pump Court, Temple, London EC4Y 7AN, ☎020 7842 5555 ✉chambers@4pumpcourt.com
Call Date: Mar 1996, Inner Temple
Qualifications: [LLB (Manch)]

LEWIS MR JONATHAN SIMON

Henderson Chambers
2 Harcourt Buildings, Temple, London EC4Y 9DB, ☎020 7583 9020 ✉clerks@hendersonchambers.co.uk
Call Date: Nov 2007, Middle Temple
Qualifications: [BA (Hons) (Oxon)]
jlewis@hendersonchambers.co.uk

LEWIS MISS KATHERINE CHARLOTTE

Maidstone Chambers
33 Earl Street, Maidstone, Kent ME14 1PF, ☎01622 688592 ✉clerks@maidstonechambers.co.uk
Call Date: July 2009, Inner Temple
Qualifications: [LLB]

LEWIS MISS MARIAN ELENA

30 Park Place
Cardiff CF10 3BS, ☎029 2039 8421 ✉clerks@30parkplace.law.co.uk
Farrar's Building
Farrar's Building, Temple, London EC4Y 7BD, ☎020 7583 9241 ✉Chambers@farrarsbuilding.co.uk
Call Date: Nov 1977, Middle Temple
Pupil Supervisor
Qualifications: [LLB (Lond) (Hons)]
mel@30parkplace.co.uk

E

LEWIS MR MARTIN RICHARD

Castle Chambers
The Old Fire Station, 90 High Street, Harrow-on-the-Hill, Middlesex HA1 3LP,
☎ 020 8423 6579 ✉ info@castlechambers.net
Call Date: July 1998, Gray's Inn
Qualifications: [BA]
m.lewis@castlechambers.net

LEWIS MR MAX MYER

29 Bedford Row Chambers
London WC1R 4HE, ☎ 020 7404 1044
✉ clerks@29br.co.uk
Call Date: Mar 2002, Gray's Inn
Qualifications: [BA (Bris)]
mlewis@29br.co.uk

LEWIS MR MEYRIC

Francis Taylor Building
Inner Temple, London EC4Y 7BY,
☎ 020 7353 8415 ✉ clerks@ftb.eu.com
Call Date: Nov 1986, Gray's Inn
Pupil Supervisor
Qualifications: [BA (Bris)]
meyric.lewis@ftb.eu.com

E

LEWIS MR OWEN PRYS

9 Park Place
9 Park Place, Cardiff, South Glamorgan CF10 3DP, ☎ 029 2038 2731
✉ clerks@9parkplace.co.uk
Call Date: July 1985, Middle Temple
Pupil Supervisor
Qualifications: [LLM (Cantab) LLB (Wales)]

LEWIS MR PATRICK JOHN

Garden Court Chambers
57-60 Lincoln's Inn Fields, London WC2A 3LJ,
☎ 020 7993 7600 ✉ info@gclaw.co.uk
Call Date: Nov 1997, Middle Temple
Qualifications: [BSc LLM]
patrickl@gclaw.co.uk

LEWIS MR PAUL KEITH QC (2001)

Farrar's Building
Farrar's Building, Temple, London EC4Y 7BD,
☎ 020 7583 9241
✉ Chambers@farrarsbuilding.co.uk
30 Park Place
Cardiff CF10 3BS, ☎ 029 2039 8421
✉ clerks@30parkplace.law.co.uk
Equity Chambers
First Floor, McLaren Building, 46 Priory Queensway, Birmingham B4 7LR,
☎ 0121 236 5007
✉ clerks@equitychambers.org.uk
Call Date: Feb 1981, Gray's Inn
Recorder
Qualifications: [LLB (Leic) (Hons)]
plewis@farrarsbuilding.co.uk

LEWIS MRS PAULINE GRACE

Holborn Chambers
6 Gate Street, Lincoln's Inn Fields, London WC2A 3HP, ☎ 020 7242 6060
Call Date: Nov 1984, Lincoln's Inn
Qualifications: [LLB (Hons)]

LEWIS MISS RACHAEL JEAN

9 St John Street
Manchester M3 4DN, ☎ 0161 955 9000
✉ civilclerks@9sjs.com / criminalclerks@9sjs.com
Call Date: Nov 2006, Middle Temple
Qualifications: [LLB (Hons)]
rachael.lewis@9sjs.com

LEWIS MR RAYMOND JOSEPH

Furnival Chambers
32 Furnival Street, London EC4A 1JQ,
☎ 020 7405 3232
Call Date: July 1971, Middle Temple
Pupil Supervisor

LEWIS PROF ROY MALCOLM

Old Square Chambers
10-11 Bedford Row, London WC1R 4BU,
☎ 020 7269 0300 ✉ clerks@oldsquare.co.uk
Old Square Chambers
3 Orchard Court, St Augustine's Yard, Bristol BS1 5DP, ☎ 0117 930 5100
✉ clerks@oldsquare.co.uk
Call Date: May 1992, Lincoln's Inn
Qualifications: [LLB MSc (Econ)]
prof.lewis@oldsquare.co.uk

LEWIS MISS SARA JABBARI

Tanfield Chambers
2-5 Warwick Court, London WC1R 5DJ,
☎ 020 7421 5300
✉ clerks@tanfieldchambers.co.uk
Call Date: Oct 2007, Inner Temple
Qualifications: [LLB (Manch)]

LEWIS MISS SARA MICHELLE

9 St John Street
Manchester M3 4DN, ☎ 0161 955 9000
✉ civilclerks@9sjs.com / criminalclerks@9sjs.com
Call Date: Oct 1996, Inner Temple
Pupil Supervisor
Qualifications: [MA (Aberdeen) CPE (York)]
✉ sara.lewis@9sjs.com

LEWIS MRS SARAH LOUISE

4 Paper Buildings
1st Floor, 4 Paper Buildings, Temple, London EC4Y 7EX, ☎ 020 7427 5200
✉ clerks@4pb.com
Call Date: Nov 1995, Middle Temple
Qualifications: [MA (Hons)]
✉ sl@4pb.com

LEWIS MISS SARAH NATALIE

18 Red Lion Court
London EC4A 3EB, ☎ 020 7520 6000
✉ chambers@18rlc.co.uk
Call Date: July 2006, Middle Temple
Qualifications: [BA (Hons) (Dublin) MA (Hons) (Dublin)]
✉ sarah.lewis@18rlc.co.uk

LEWIS MR STUART JOHN

New Walk Chambers
27 New Walk, Leicester, Leicestershire LE1 6TE, ☎ 0871 200 1298 / 0116 255 9144
✉ clerks@newwalkchambers.co.uk
Call Date: July 2002, Lincoln's Inn
Qualifications: [LLB (Hons)(Leic)]

LEWIS MR THOMAS ROBIN ARWEL

St Philips Chambers
55 Temple Row, Birmingham B2 5LS,
☎ 0121 246 7000 ✉ clerks@st-philips.com
Call Date: Nov 1991, Inner Temple
Qualifications: [MA (Cantab)]
✉ rlewis@st-philips.co.uk

LEWIS MR WAYNE ANTHONY

Access Lawyers
800 High Road, Tottenham, London N17 0DH,
☎ 020 8801 2345
Call Date: Nov 1982, Lincoln's Inn
Qualifications: [LLB]
✉ Wayne.Lewis@accesslawyers.co.uk

LEWIS-JONES MR MEIRION

Linenhall Chambers
1 Stanley Place, Chester CH1 2LU,
☎ 01244 348282
✉ clerks@linenhallchambers.co.uk
Call Date: Nov 1971, Gray's Inn
Pupil Supervisor
Qualifications: [LLB (Lond)]
✉ clerks@1stanleyplace.co.uk

LEWIS-MURRAY MRS REBECCA-JANE

Hampshire
Call Date: Nov 1990, Inner Temple
Qualifications: [LLB, LLM (UCL), PGCE MA (Oxon)]

LEWISON MR JOSH

Radcliffe Chambers
Ground Floor, 11 New Square, Lincoln's Inn, London WC2A 3QB, ☎ 020 7831 0081
✉ clerks@radcliffechambers.com
Call Date: July 2005, Lincoln's Inn
Qualifications: [MA (Cantab)]
✉ jlewison@radcliffechambers.com

LEWSLEY MR CHRISTOPHER STANTON

Landmark Chambers
180 Fleet Street, London EC4A 2HG,
☎ 020 7430 1221
✉ clerks@landmarkchambers.co.uk
Call Date: July 1976, Lincoln's Inn
Qualifications: [BSc MiStructE CEng PhD]
✉ clewsley@landmarkchambers.co.uk

LEWTHWAITE MISS JOANNE ELIZABETH

Oriel Chambers
14 Water Street, Liverpool, Merseyside L2 8TD, ☎ 0151 236 7191
✉ clerks@orielchambers.co.uk
Oriel Chambers
18 Ribblesdale Place, Preston PR1 3NA,
☎ 01772 254 764
✉ clerks@oriel-chambers.co.uk
Call Date: Oct 1990, Inner Temple
Qualifications: [LLB (L'pool)]

E

LEY MR NIGEL JOSEPH

Chambers of Nigel Ley
23 Vale Farm Road, Woking, Surrey GU21 6DE, ☎07947 221077
Hind Court Chambers
London East, 100 Burford Wharf, 3 Cam Road, London E15 2SL, ☎020 8534 2495
✉peter_fox@btinternet.com
Call Date: Nov 1969, Gray's Inn
Qualifications: [LLM (Manch)]

LEY MR SPENCER

Farrar's Building
Farrar's Building, Temple, London EC4Y 7BD, ☎020 7583 9241
✉Chambers@farrarsbuilding.co.uk
Call Date: July 1985, Middle Temple
Qualifications: [MA (Cantab)]

LEY-MORGAN MR MARK JOHN

3 Serjeants Inn
London EC4Y 1BQ, ☎020 7427 5000
✉clerks@3serjeantsinn.com
Call Date: Oct 1994, Gray's Inn
Qualifications: [BSc LLB]
✉mley-morgan@3serjeantsinn.com

LééF DR ROBIN

QEB Hollis Whiteman
1-2 Laurence Pountney Hill, London EC4R 0EU, ☎020 7933 8855
✉barristers@qebhw.co.uk
Call Date: July 2009, Lincoln's Inn
Qualifications: [MAT (France) BA MA (Cantab) PHD (EUI)]
✉robin.loof@qebhw.co.uk

LICKLEY MR NIGEL JAMES DOMINIC QC (2006)

3 PB Barristers
3 Paper Buildings, Temple, London EC4Y 7EU, ☎020 7583 8055
3 PB Barristers
Royal Talbot House, 2 Victoria Street, Bristol, Avon BS1 6BB, ☎0117 928 1520
3 PB Barristers
4 St Peter Street, Winchester SO23 8BW, ☎01962 868884
✉clerks.winchester@3paper.co.uk
3 PB Barristers
23 Beaumont Street, Oxford OX1 2NP, ☎01865 793 736
3 PB Barristers
30 Christchurch Road, Bournemouth, Dorset BH1 3PD, ☎01202 292102
✉clerks.bournemouth@3paper.co.uk
Devon Chambers
3 St Andrew Street, Plymouth PL1 2AH, ☎01752 661659
✉clerks@devonchambers.co.uk
Call Date: July 1983, Gray's Inn
Recorder
Qualifications: [LLB (Lond)]
✉nigel.lickley@3paper.co.uk

LIDBURY MR DAVID JAMES AUSTIN

Southernhay Chambers
33 Southernhay East, Exeter EX1 1NX, ☎01392 255777
✉clerks@southernhaychambers.co.uk
Call Date: Oct 2006, Inner Temple
Qualifications: [BA (Newc)]
✉d.lidbury@southernhaychambers.co.uk

LIDDELL MR RICHARD IAN

Four New Square
Four New Square, Lincoln's Inn, London WC2A 3RJ, ☎020 7822 2000
✉barristers@4newsquare.com
Call Date: Oct 1999, Middle Temple
Pupil Supervisor
Qualifications: [BA (Hons) LLM (Cantab)]
✉r.liddell@4newsquare.com

LIDDIARD MR MARTIN THOMAS

No5 Chambers
Fountain Court, Steelhouse Lane, Birmingham B4 6DR, ☎0845 210 5555 ✉info@no5.com
No5 Chambers
Greenwood House, 4-7 Salisbury Court, London EC4Y 8AA, ☎0845 210 5555
No5 Chambers
38 Queen Square, Bristol BS1 4QS, ☎0845 210 5555
Call Date: Nov 1989, Inner Temple
Qualifications: [LLB (B'ham)]
✉ml@no5.com

LIDINGTON MR GARY MARK

11 Stone Buildings
11 Stone Buildings, Lincoln's Inn, London WC2A 3TG, ☎020 7831 6381
✉clerks@11sb.com
Call Date: Oct 2000, Middle Temple
Qualifications: [BSc (Econ) (LSE) Diploma in Law]
✉lidington@11sb.com

LIEBERMAN MS GEMMA FREDA

Kings Chambers
36 Young Street, Manchester M3 3FT,
☎ 0845 034 3444
✉ clerks@kingschambers.com
Kings Chambers
5 Park Square East, Leeds LS1 2NE,
☎ 0845 034 3444
✉ clerks@kingschambers.com
Kings Chambers
Embassy House, 60 Church Street, Birmingham B3 2DJ, ☎ 0845 034 3444
✉ clerks@kingschambers.com
Call Date: Oct 2006, Middle Temple
Qualifications: [BA (Manch) MA (Manch)]
✉ glieberman@kingschambers.com

LIEBRECHT MR JOHN MICHAEL

1 Garden Court Family Law Chambers
Ground Floor, One Garden Court, Temple, London EC4Y 9BJ, ☎ 020 7797 7900
✉ clerks@1gc.com
Call Date: Nov 1989, Inner Temple
Qualifications: [BA (Oxon) LLM (Cantab)]
✉ liebrecht@1gc.com

LIEVEN MS NATHALIE MARIE DANIELLA QC (2006)

Landmark Chambers
180 Fleet Street, London EC4A 2HG,
☎ 020 7430 1221
✉ clerks@landmarkchambers.co.uk
Call Date: July 1989, Gray's Inn
Qualifications: [BA (Cantab)]
✉ nlieven@landmarkchambers.co.uk

LIGHT PROF ROY ALAN

St John's Chambers
101 Victoria Street, Bristol BS1 6PU,
☎ 0117 923 4700
✉ clerks@stjohnschambers.co.uk
Call Date: Feb 1992, Gray's Inn
Qualifications: [LLM (Lond) MPhil PhD (Cantab)]

LIGHTFOOT MR JEREMY ALEXANDER

Stone Chambers
4 Field Court, Gray's Inn, London WC1R 5EF,
☎ 020 7440 6900
✉ clerks@stonechambers.com
Call Date: July 2006, Lincoln's Inn
Qualifications: [BA (Oxon)]
✉ jeremy.lightfoot@stonechambers.com

LIGHTMAN MR DANIEL

Serle Court
6 New Square, Lincoln's Inn, London WC2A 3QS, ☎ 020 7242 6105
✉ clerks@serlecourt.co.uk
Call Date: Oct 1995, Lincoln's Inn
Pupil Supervisor
Qualifications: [BA (Oxon) CPE]
✉ dlightman@serlecourt.co.uk

Types of work: Chancery (commercial), Chancery (general), Civil fraud, Commercial litigation, Company law, Corporate insolvency, Equity, Insolvency, Personal insolvency, Professional negligence, Wills

LIGHTWING MR STUART WILLIAM

Chambers of Stuart Lightwing
8 Thirsk Road, Yarm, Stockton-on-Tees TS15 9HE, ☎ 01642 650550
✉ stuartlightwing@yahoo.co.uk
Call Date: July 1972, Middle Temple
Pupil Supervisor
Qualifications: [LLB MCMI MBA FCIArb FRSA FCIS]

LILL MR STUART MARK

Argent Chambers
5 Bell Yard, London WC2A 2JR,
☎ 020 7556 5500
✉ briefsin@argentchambers.co.uk
Call Date: July 2004, Inner Temple
Qualifications: [BA (Hons) PgDL BVC]
✉ briefsin@argentchambers.co.uk

LILLINGTON MR SIMON DOUGLAS

College Chambers
19 Carlton Crescent, Southampton, Hampshire SO15 2ET, ☎ 023 8023 0338
✉ clerks@college-chambers.co.uk
Renaissance Chambers
5th Floor, Gray's Inn Chambers, Gray's Inn, London WC1R 5JA, ☎ 020 7404 1111
✉ clerks@renaissancechambers.co.uk
Call Date: Nov 1980, Middle Temple
Pupil Supervisor
Qualifications: [BA LLM]
✉ slillington@college-chambers.co.uk

LILLY MR WILLIAM DONALD

4 Stone Buildings
Ground Floor, 4 Stone Buildings, Lincoln's Inn, London WC2A 3XT, ☎ 020 7242 5524
✉ clerks@4stonebuildings.com
Call Date: Nov 2006, Middle Temple
Qualifications: [BA (Hons) (Oxon) BCL (Oxon)]

E

LIM MR MALCOLM KIAN-LENG

3 Serjeants Inn
London EC4Y 1BQ, ☎020 7427 5000
✉clerks@3serjeantsinn.com
Call Date: July 1989, Inner Temple
Qualifications: [BA (Keele) LLM (Lond)]

LIMB MR CHRISTOPHER

18 St John Street
Manchester M3 4EA, ☎0161 278 1800
✉clerks@18sjs.com
Call Date: July 1975, Gray's Inn
Pupil Supervisor
Qualifications: [LLB]

LIMB MR PATRICK FRANCIS QC (2006)

Ropewalk Chambers
24 The Ropewalk, Nottingham NG1 5EF,
☎0115 947 2581 ✉clerks@ropewalk.co.uk
Call Date: July 1987, Middle Temple
Qualifications: [MA (Cantab)]
✉patricklimbqc@ropewalk.co.uk

LIMBREY MR BERNARD MARTIN

3 Dr Johnson's Buildings
Ground Floor, 3 Dr Johnson's Buildings,
Temple, London EC4Y 7BA, ☎020 7353 4854
✉clerks@3djb.co.uk
Call Date: Nov 1980, Middle Temple
Pupil Supervisor
Qualifications: [MSc (Lond)]

LINCE MISS ELIZABETH LOUISE

Chartlands Chambers
3 St Giles Terrace, Northampton NN1 2BN,
☎01604 603322
✉enquiries@chartlands-chambers.co.uk
Call Date: July 2007, Middle Temple
Qualifications: [BA (Wales)]

LINDEN MR THOMAS DOMINIC QC (2006)

Matrix Chambers
Griffin Building, Gray's Inn, London
WC1R 5LN, ☎020 7404 3447
✉matrix@matrixlaw.co.uk / Iscott@
matrixlaw.co.uk
Call Date: Nov 1989, Gray's Inn
Pupil Supervisor, Recorder
Qualifications: [BA,(Oxon) BCL]
✉tomlinden@matrixlaw.co.uk

LINDESAY MS ELIZABETH LORNA

7 King's Bench Walk
Ground Floor, 7 King's Bench Walk, Temple,
London EC4Y 7DS, ☎020 7910 8300
✉clerks@7kbw.co.uk
Call Date: July 2009, Gray's Inn
Qualifications: [BA (Oxon) LLM (USA)]
✉elindesay@7kbw.co.uk

LINDFIELD MS GEMMA ANGELA

Seven Bedford Row
7 Bedford Row, London WC1R 4BS,
☎020 7242 3555 ✉clerks@7br.co.uk
Call Date: Oct 2002, Inner Temple
Qualifications: [LLB (Exon)]
✉glindfield@7br.co.uk

LINDHORST MR GORDON JOHN

Dere Street Barristers
14 Toft Green, York YO1 6JT, ☎0844 3351551
✉clerks@derestreet.co.uk
Call Date: July 2008, Middle Temple
Qualifications: [LLB (Hons) (Edin) DipLP (Glas) LLM]
✉clerks@yorkchambers.co.uk

LINDOP MISS SARAH LOUISE

Westgate Chambers
64 High Street, Lewes, East Sussex BN7 1XG,
☎01273 480510
✉clerks@westgate-chambers.co.uk
Call Date: Nov 1989, Gray's Inn
Pupil Supervisor
Qualifications: [LLB (Hons)]

LINDQVIST MR ANDREW NILS GUNNAR

Octagon House
19 Colegate, Norwich NR3 1AT,
☎01603 623186
✉clerks@octagonhouse.co.uk
Call Date: Nov 1968, Middle Temple
Pupil Supervisor
Qualifications: [MA (Cantab)]

LINDSAY MR ALISTAIR DAVID

Monckton Chambers
1 & 2 Raymond Buildings, Gray's Inn, London
WC1R 5NR, ☎020 7405 7211
✉chambers@monckton.com
Call Date: Oct 1993, Inner Temple
Qualifications: [BA]

LINDSAY MISS CLAIRE LOUISE

Park Lane Plowden
Lombard House, 4-8 Lombard Street, Newcastle Upon Tyne NE1 3AE,
☎0191 211 4087
✉clerks@parklaneplowden.co.uk
Call Date: Oct 1991, Middle Temple
Qualifications: [LLB (Leics)]
claire.lindsay@parklaneplowden.co.uk

LINDSAY MR FRASER THOMAS

Number 7 Harrington Street Chambers
7 Harrington Street, Liverpool L2 9YH,
☎0151 242 0707 ✉clerks@7hs.co.uk
Call Date: July 2006, Middle Temple
Qualifications: [LLB (Hons) (L'pool)]
fraser.lindsay@7hs.co.uk

LINDSAY MR JEREMY MARK HENRY

37 Park Square Chambers
37 Park Square, Leeds LS1 2NY,
☎0113 243 9422 ✉chambers@no37.co.uk
Call Date: July 1986, Gray's Inn
Pupil Supervisor
Qualifications: [LLB (Hons)(Nott'm) Postgraduate Diploma in Radio Journalism]
chambers@no37.co.uk

LINDSAY MR WILLIAM GRAEME

No.6 Park Square
Leeds LS1 2LW, ☎0113 245 9763
✉Tim@no6.co.uk
Call Date: July 2009, Inner Temple
Qualifications: [BA (Manch)]
lindsay@no6.co.uk

LINDSEY MISS AMY CLAIRE

Regency Chambers
45 Priestgate, Peterborough PE1 1LB,
☎01733 315215
✉clerks@regencychambers.law.co.uk
Regency Chambers
Sheraton House, Castle Park, Cambridge CB3 0AX, ☎01223 301517
Call Date: Nov 2001, Middle Temple
Qualifications: [LLB (Hons)]
clerks@regencychambers.law.co.uk

LINDSEY MS SUSAN

Crown Office Chambers
2 Crown Office Row, Temple, London EC4Y 7HJ, ☎020 7797 8100
✉mail@crownofficechambers.com
Call Date: Nov 1997, Inner Temple
Qualifications: [BSc (Lond) MSc (Lond) RIBA]
lindsey@crownofficechambers.com

LINE MR ALEXANDER ANTHONY

3 PB Barristers
3 Paper Buildings, Temple, London EC4Y 7EU,
☎020 7583 8055
Call Date: July 2009, Gray's Inn
Qualifications: [LLB LLM]
alex.line@3pb.co.uk

LINEHAN MR STEPHEN JOHN QC (1993)

St Philips Chambers
55 Temple Row, Birmingham B2 5LS,
☎0121 246 7000 ✉clerks@st-philips.com
Call Date: Feb 1970, Lincoln's Inn
Recorder
Qualifications: [LLB (Lond)]
slinehan@st-philips.co.uk

LINFORD MR ROBERT FRANK

Devon Chambers
3 St Andrew Street, Plymouth PL1 2AH,
☎01752 661659
✉clerks@devonchambers.co.uk
Call Date: Nov 1987, Gray's Inn
Pupil Supervisor, Recorder
Qualifications: [LLB (Hons) (Wales)]
rlinford@devonchambers.co.uk

LING MS NAOMI

Outer Temple Chambers
The Outer Temple, 222 Strand, London WC2R 1BA, ☎020 7353 6381
✉clerks@outertemple.com
Call Date: Nov 2001, Middle Temple
Qualifications: [BA (Hons) Dip Law]
naomi.ling@outertemple.com

LINKLATER MISS LISA MARGARET

Exchange Chambers
Oxford House, Oxford Row, Leeds LS1 3BE,
☎0113 203 1970
✉spencer@exchangechambers.co.uk
Exchange Chambers
One Derby Square, Derby Square, Liverpool L2 9XX, ☎0151 236 7747
✉info@exchangechambers.co.uk
Exchange Chambers
7 Ralli Courts, West Riverside, Manchester M3 5FT, ☎0161 833 2722
Call Date: Oct 1995, Inner Temple
Qualifications: [BA (Cantab)]

LINNEMANN MR BERNARD MARIA

St Philips Chambers
55 Temple Row, Birmingham B2 5LS,
☎0121 246 7000 ✉clerks@st-philips.com
Call Date: Nov 1980, Gray's Inn
Qualifications: [BA (Tcd)]
blinnemann@st-philips.com

E

LINSTEAD MR PETER JAMES

Tanfield Chambers
2-5 Warwick Court, London WC1R 5DJ,
☎ 020 7421 5300
✉ clerks@tanfieldchambers.co.uk
Call Date: Oct 1994, Gray's Inn
Pupil Supervisor
Qualifications: [BA MA]
plinstead@tanfieldchambers.co.uk

Fax: 020 7421 5333;
Out of hours telephone: 020 7421 5341;
DX: 46 London, Chancery Lane;
URL: www.tanfieldchambers.co.uk

Other professional qualifications: MA (Oxon)

Types of work: Discrimination, Employment, Industrial diseases

Awards and memberships: Wilfred Watson scholar and holder of William McNair award (Gray's Inn); Employment Lawyers Association; Employment Law Bar Association; Employment Law Appeal Advice Scheme; PIBA

Other professional experience: Advocacy trainer; lecturer for CLT (and other legal training organisations); leadership coach; treasurer of Hertford College Lawyers Association

Publications: 'Psychiatric Injury in the Workplace Under Review', *ELA Briefing*, 2009; 'In Brief' Editorial, *ELA Briefing*, 2012; 'Taking Time off for Gender Reassignment', *HR Magazine*, 2008; 'Staff Suing Customers', *Personnel Today*, 2008; 'Permanent Shift' on the use of permanent staff in the financial services industry, *The Lawyer*, 2009

Reported Cases: *St Christopher's Fellowship v Walters-Ennis*, [2010] EqLR; EWCA Civ 252 (Court of Appeal), 2010. Whether the burden of proof in race discrimination under s.54A RRA 1976 had been correctly applied.
Keane v Investigo & Ors, [2009] UKEAT 0389/09/1112 (Lawtel) (EAT), 2009. Whether claimant's rejection for a job which she did not intend to do amounted to a detriment or disadvantage under the Employment Equality (Age) Regulations 2006. Whether Respondent's costs award in employment tribunal properly made.
Ebbs v Oxford Brookes University, EWCA [2009] (Court of Appeal), 2009. Successfully resisted application for permission to appeal in Public Sector Equal Pay Claim.
Millbrook Proving Ground Ltd v Jefferson, UKEAT/0014/08 (Employment Appeal Tribunal), 2008. Unfair dismissal and procedural fairness; interviewing witnesses in internal disciplinary hearings.
Lewisham LBC v Colbourne, [2006] All ER (D) 200 (Nov) (Employment Appeal Tribunal), 2007. Whether claimant's rejection for a job which she did not intend to do amounted to a detriment or disadvantage under the Employment Equality (Age) Regulations 2006. Whether Respondent's costs award in employment tribunal properly made.

LINTOTT MR DAVID JAMES

Cornerstone Barristers
2-3 Gray's Inn Square, Gray's Inn, London WC1R 5JH, ☎ 020 7242 4986
✉ chambers@2-3gis.co.uk
Call Date: Oct 1996, Gray's Inn
Qualifications: [BA (Cantab)]
dlintott@2-3gis.co.uk

LIPPIATT MR HUW JOHN

Sovereign Chambers
46 Park Place, Leeds LS1 2RY,
☎ 0113 245 1841
✉ clerks@sovereignchambers.co.uk
Call Date: Mar 2010, Gray's Inn

LIPPOLD MS SARAH IDA LOUISE

13 King's Bench Walk
13 King's Bench Walk, Temple, London EC4Y 7EN, ☎ 020 7353 7204
✉ clerks@13kbw.co.uk
13 KBW
32 Beaumont Street, Oxford OX1 2NP,
☎ 01865 311066 ✉ clerks@13kbw.co.uk
Call Date: Nov 1999, Inner Temple
Pupil Supervisor
Qualifications: [BA (Oxon)]
slippold@13kbw.co.uk

LISSACK MR RICHARD ANTHONY QC (1994)

Outer Temple Chambers
The Outer Temple, 222 Strand, London WC2R 1BA, ☎ 020 7353 6381
✉ clerks@outertemple.com
Riverview Chambers
Hamilton House, 1 Temple Avenue, London EC4Y 0HA, ☎ 0844 225 3999
✉ chrisbaylis@riverviewchambers.com
Call Date: Nov 1978, Inner Temple
Recorder
richard.lissackqc@outertemple.com

LISTER MISS CAROLINE JANE

1 KBW Chambers
1 King's Bench Walk, Temple, London EC4Y 7DB, ☎ 020 7936 1500
✉ clerks@1kbw.co.uk
King's Bench Chambers
174 High Street, Lewes BN7 1YE,
☎ 01273 402600
Call Date: Nov 1980, Middle Temple
Pupil Supervisor, Recorder
Qualifications: [BSc (Lond)]
✉ clister@1kbw.co.uk

LISTER MR DANIEL JAMES

23 Essex Street
London WC2R 3AA, ☎ 020 7413 0353
✉ clerks@23es.com
Call Date: July 2009, Inner Temple
Qualifications: [BA (Sheff)]

LISTER MR KEVIN JAMES

Kenworthy's Chambers
Arlington House, Bloom Street, Salford, Manchester M3 6AJ, ☎ 0161 832 4036
Call Date: July 2012, Middle Temple
✉ k.lister@kenworthysbarristers.co.uk

LITHMAN MR NIGEL LLOYD QC (1997)

2 Bedford Row
London WC1R 4BU, ☎ 020 7440 8888
✉ clerks@2bedfordrow.co.uk
Call Date: Nov 1976, Inner Temple
Qualifications: [LLB (Hons)]
✉ nlithman@2bedfordrow.co.uk

LITTLE MISS HELEN AMANDA

Harcourt Chambers
1st Floor, 2 Harcourt Buildings, Temple, London EC4Y 9DB, ☎ 0844 561 7135
Call Date: Oct 1999, Lincoln's Inn
Pupil Supervisor
Qualifications: [LLB (Hons)(Lancs)]
✉ hlittle@harcourtchambers.law.co.uk

LITTLE MR IAN

9 St John Street
Manchester M3 4DN, ☎ 0161 955 9000
✉ civilclerks@9sjs.com / criminalclerks@9sjs.com
Call Date: Feb 1989, Middle Temple
Qualifications: [BA (Oxon) Dip Law (Lond)]
✉ ian.little.1@9sjs.com

LITTLE MR MICHAEL JOHN

King's Bench Chambers
Wellington House, 175 Holdenhurst Road, Bournemouth, Dorset BH8 8DQ,
☎ 01202 250025
Call Date: Mar 2010, Lincoln's Inn
Qualifications: [LLB (So'ton)]

LITTLE MR RICHARD JOHN

42 Bedford Row
London WC1R 4LL, ☎ 020 7831 0222
✉ clerks@42br.com
Call Date: July 2000, Inner Temple
Qualifications: [MA (Oxon)]
✉ richard.little@42br.com

LITTLE MR TOM CHARLES

The Chambers of Grahame Aldous QC
9 Gough Square, London EC4A 3DG,
☎ 020 7832 0500
✉ clerks@9goughsquare.co.uk
Call Date: Oct 1997, Middle Temple
Pupil Supervisor
Qualifications: [BA (Hons)(Notts) CPE]
✉ tlittle@9goughsquare.co.uk

LITTLE MRS TRINA ANNE-MARIE

Westgate Chambers
64 High Street, Lewes, East Sussex BN7 1XG,
☎ 01273 480510
✉ clerks@westgate-chambers.co.uk
Call Date: Oct 2010, Lincoln's Inn
Qualifications: [BA (L'pool)]
✉ clerks@westgate-chambers.co.uk

LITTLER MISS ANNA MARY HALLOWAY

New Square Chambers
12 New Square, Lincoln's Inn, London WC2A 3SW, ☎ 020 7419 8000
✉ robin.hollington@newsquarechambers.co.uk
Call Date: July 2008, Lincoln's Inn
Qualifications: [BA (Oxon)]
✉ anna.littler@newsquarechambers.co.uk

LITTLER MR MARTIN GORDON

Cobden House Chambers
19 Quay Street, Manchester M3 3HN,
☎ 0161 833 6000 ✉ Clerks@Cobden.co.uk
Call Date: Nov 1989, Gray's Inn
Qualifications: [LLB]
✉ clerks@cobden.co.uk

E

LITTLER MR RICHARD MARK

Exchange Chambers
7 Ralli Courts, West Riverside, Manchester M3 5FT, ☎0161 833 2722
Exchange Chambers
One Derby Square, Derby Square, Liverpool L2 9XX, ☎0151 236 7747
✉info@exchangechambers.co.uk
Exchange Chambers
Oxford House, Oxford Row, Leeds LS1 3BE, ☎0113 203 1970
✉spencer@exchangechambers.co.uk
Call Date: Oct 1994, Gray's Inn
Qualifications: [LLB (Hons)]
littler@exchangechambers.co.uk

LITTLEWOOD MISS REBECCA MAE

1 Pump Court
Elm Court, Temple, London EC4Y 7AB, ☎020 7842 7070
✉(name)@pumpcourt.co.uk
Call Date: Nov 1988, Inner Temple
Pupil Supervisor
Qualifications: [LLB (So'ton)]
bl@1pumpcourt.co.uk

LITTLEWOOD MR ROBERT

4 Paper Buildings
1st Floor, 4 Paper Buildings, Temple, London EC4Y 7EX, ☎020 7427 5200
✉clerks@4pb.com
Call Date: Oct 1993, Inner Temple
Qualifications: [BA CPE]
rl2@4pb.com

LITTMAN MR JEFFREY JAMES

9 Park Place
9 Park Place, Cardiff, South Glamorgan CF10 3DP, ☎029 2038 2731
✉clerks@9parkplace.co.uk
Chambers of Mr Jeffrey Littman
25 Heriot Road, Hendon, London NW4 2EG, ☎020 8922 6844 ✉jeffreylittman@aol.com
Call Date: July 1974, Middle Temple
Pupil Supervisor
Qualifications: [MA (Cantab)]
jlittman@9parkplace.co.uk

LITTON MR JOHN LETABLERE QC (2010)

Landmark Chambers
180 Fleet Street, London EC4A 2HG, ☎020 7430 1221
✉clerks@landmarkchambers.co.uk
Call Date: July 1989, Middle Temple
Pupil Supervisor
Qualifications: [LLB (So'ton)]
jlitton@landmarkchambers.co.uk

LIVESEY MR BERNARD JOSEPH EDWARD QC (1990)

Hailsham Chambers
Ground Floor, 4 Paper Buildings, Temple, London EC4Y 7EX, ☎020 7643 5000
✉clerks@hailshamchambers.com
Call Date: July 1969, Lincoln's Inn
Qualifications: [MA LLB (Cantab)]

LIVESEY MR FRASER MICHAEL STANIER

Deans Court Chambers
24 St John Street, Manchester M3 4DF, ☎0161 214 6000 ✉clerks@deanscourt.co.uk
Deans Court Chambers
101 Walker Street, Preston PR1 2RR, ☎01772 565 600
✉preston@deanscourt.co.uk
Call Date: Oct 1992, Lincoln's Inn
Qualifications: [LLB(Hons)(Newc)]

LIVESEY MR JOHN WILLIAM ALLAN

Albion Chambers
Broad Street, Bristol BS1 1DR, ☎0117 927 2144
✉clerks@albionchambers.co.uk
Call Date: Nov 1990, Lincoln's Inn
Pupil Supervisor
Qualifications: [LLB (Bris)]
john.livesey@albionchambers.co.uk

LIVESEY MISS KATE LOUISE

4 Pump Court
4 Pump Court, Temple, London EC4Y 7AN, ☎020 7842 5555
✉chambers@4pumpcourt.com
Call Date: Nov 2001, Middle Temple
Qualifications: [MA (Cantab) Dip Law]
klivesey@4pumpcourt.com

LIVESLEY MISS RHIAN DANIELLE

Atlantic Chambers
4-6 Cook Street, Liverpool L2 9QU, ☎0151 236 4421
✉info@atlanticchambers.co.uk
Call Date: July 2000, Gray's Inn
Qualifications: [LLB (Warw)]
rhianlivesley@atlanticchambers.co.uk

LIVING MR MARC STEPHEN

Pallant Chambers
12 North Pallant, Chichester, West Sussex PO19 1TQ, ☎01243 784538
✉clerks@pallantchambers.co.uk
Call Date: July 1983, Middle Temple
Pupil Supervisor
Qualifications: [BA (Hons) (Kent)]
mliving@pallantchambers.co.uk

E

LIVINGSTON MR RICHARD JACK

Kings Chambers
36 Young Street, Manchester M3 3FT,
☎ 0845 034 3444
✉ clerks@kingschambers.com
Kings Chambers
5 Park Square East, Leeds LS1 2NE,
☎ 0845 034 3444
✉ clerks@kingschambers.com
Kings Chambers
Embassy House, 60 Church Street, Birmingham B3 2DJ, ☎ 0845 034 3444
✉ clerks@kingschambers.com
Call Date: Oct 2006, Middle Temple
Qualifications: [BA (Hons) (Manch) PGDL (Manch) PGDL]
✉ rlivingston@kingschambers.com

LIVINGSTON MR RICHARD JOHN

2 Bedford Row
London WC1R 4BU, ☎ 020 7440 8888
✉ clerks@2bedfordrow.co.uk
Call Date: July 1980, Gray's Inn
Pupil Supervisor
Qualifications: [BA (Oxon) LLM (Lond)]
✉ rjlivingston@2bedfordrow.co.uk

LIVINGSTONE MR SIMON JOHN

Thomas More Chambers
7 Lincoln's Inn Fields, London WC2A 3BP,
☎ 020 7404 7000
✉ clerks@thomasmore.co.uk
Call Date: Oct 1990, Inner Temple
Qualifications: [LLB (Bris)]
✉ slivingstone@thomasmore.co.uk

LIVINGSTONE MR THOMAS DOUGLAS

Crescent Chambers
14 The Crescent, Belmont, Surrey SM2 6BJ,
☎ 020 8643 4286
✉ douglivingstone@btinternet.com
Call Date: Nov 1989, Inner Temple
Qualifications: [LLB (Lond)]
✉ douglivingstone@btinternet.com

LIXENBERG MR MARC RAPHAEL

Atkin Chambers
1 Atkin Building, Gray's Inn, London WC1R 5AT, ☎ 020 7404 0102
✉ clerks@atkinchambers.com
Call Date: July 2005, Gray's Inn
Qualifications: [BA]
✉ clerks@atkinchambers.com

LLEWELLYN MR CHARLES IVOR

Staple Inn Chambers
1st Floor, 9 Staple Inn, Holborn Bars, London WC1V 7QH, ☎ 020 7242 5240
✉ clerks@stapleinn.co.uk
Call Date: July 1978, Gray's Inn
Qualifications: [LLB (Hons) (Lond)]
✉ cl@stapleinn.co.uk

LLEWELLYN-WATERS MISS HANNA CLAIRE

2 Bedford Row
London WC1R 4BU, ☎ 020 7440 8888
✉ clerks@2bedfordrow.co.uk
Call Date: Nov 2000, Middle Temple
Pupil Supervisor
Qualifications: [BA (Hons) (Oxon) CPE]

LLEWELYN MR PATRICK JAMES

Angel Chambers
Ethos Building, Kings Road, Swansea SA1 8AS,
☎ 01792 464623
✉ clerks@angelchambers.co.uk
Call Date: July 2009, Inner Temple
Qualifications: [BSc (Cardiff)]
✉ patrick.llewelyn@angelchambers.co.uk

LLOYD MR BENJAMIN JOHN

6 King's Bench Walk
Ground Floor, 6 King's Bench Walk, Temple, London EC4Y 7DR, ☎ 020 7583 0410
✉ clerks@6kbw.com
Call Date: July 2004, Lincoln's Inn
Qualifications: [LLB Hons (Warwick) LLM (Warw)]
✉ ben.lloyd@6kbw.com

LLOYD MR DAVID GARETH BEECHEY

Tyddewi Chambers
Felin Isaf, St David's, Pembrokeshire SA62 6QB, ☎ 01437 720 853
✉ dgill@btinternet.com
Call Date: Mar 1996, Gray's Inn
Qualifications: [BA (Hons)(Durham)]

LLOYD MR DOUGLAS JOHN

15 New Bridge Street
London EC4V 6AU, ☎ 020 7842 1900
✉ clerks@15nbs.com
Call Date: July 2008, Inner Temple
Qualifications: [LLB (Leic) LLM (Bris)]
✉ tim.banks@15nbs.com

LLOYD MR FRANCIS ZACHARY

15 New Bridge Street
London EC4V 6AU, ☎020 7842 1900
✉clerks@15nbs.com
Call Date: July 1987, Inner Temple
Qualifications: [BA (Exon) Dip Law]
francis.lloyd@15nbs.com

LLOYD MISS GAYNOR ELIZABETH

Call Date: Oct 1992, Lincoln's Inn
Pupil Supervisor
Qualifications: [LLB(Hons)(Nott'm)]
gaynor.lloyd@stjohnsbuildings.co.uk, gaynor.moore@virgin.net

LLOYD MR HUW

3 Serjeants Inn
London EC4Y 1BQ, ☎020 7427 5000
✉clerks@3serjeantsinn.com
Call Date: July 1975, Middle Temple
Qualifications: [LLB (Leics),Merge Data:,Contact Number: 19763,Quantity: ,Activity Date: ,Notes : LLB (Hons) (Leics),]
hlloyd@3serjeantsinn.com

LLOYD MR JOHN NESBITT

Rougemont Chambers
Victory House, Dean Clarke Gardens, Southernhay East, Exeter EX2 4AA,
☎01392 208484
✉clerks@rougemontchambers.co.uk
Call Date: Nov 1988, Inner Temple
Pupil Supervisor
Qualifications: [BA (Brazil) MA LLB (Exon)]
jlloyd@rougemontchambers.co.uk

LLOYD MR JULIAN ALASTAIR

St Johns Buildings
24a - 28 St John Street, Manchester M3 4DJ,
☎0161 214 1500
✉clerk@stjohnsbuildings.co.uk
St Johns Buildings
21 White Friars, Chester CH1 1NZ,
☎01244 323070
✉clerk@stjohnsbuildings.co.uk
16 Winckley Square
Preston PR1 3JJ, ☎01772 256100
Call Date: July 1985, Gray's Inn
Pupil Supervisor
Qualifications: [MA LLM (Cantab)]

LLOYD MR LLOYD

Chambers of L Lloyd
3 Archery Fields House, Wharton Street, London WC1X 9PN, ☎020 7837 4727
✉lloyd.lloyd@cantab.net
Call Date: July 1973, Gray's Inn
Qualifications: [MA (Cantab) LLM (Lond) MA (Lond)]

LLOYD MISS MARISA RACHEL

Chancery House Chambers
7 Lisbon Square, Leeds, West Yorkshire LS1 4LY, ☎0113 244 6691
✉clerks@chanceryhouse.co.uk
Call Date: Nov 1994, Inner Temple
Qualifications: [BA (Essex) CPE (Wales)]
Marisa.Lloyd@chanceryhouse.co.uk

LLOYD MISS PATRICIA

Chambers of Miss P Lloyd
53 St John's Road, Grove, Wantage, Oxford, Oxford OX12 7NP, ☎01235 762 312
Call Date: July 1979, Gray's Inn
Qualifications: [LLB(Hons)]

LLOYD MS RHIANNON

4 Paper Buildings
1st Floor, 4 Paper Buildings, Temple, London EC4Y 7EX, ☎020 7427 5200
✉clerks@4pb.com
Call Date: Oct 2002, Inner Temple
Qualifications: [LLB (Wales)]
rl@4pb.com

LLOYD MISS SARAH DIANA

1 High Pavement
Nottingham NG1 1HF, ☎0115 941 8218
✉clerks@1highpavement.co.uk
Call Date: July 2005, Middle Temple
Qualifications: [LLB (Hons)]
sarahlloyd@1highpavement.co.uk

LLOYD MS SIOBHAN KATHERINE

Tooks Chambers
81 Farringdon Street, London EC4A 4BL,
☎020 7842 7575 ✉clerks@tooks.co.uk
Call Date: Mar 2010, Gray's Inn
Qualifications: [BA]

LLOYD MR STEPHEN JAMES GEORGE

13 Old Square Chambers
Ground Floor, 14 Old Square, Lincoln's Inn, London WC2A 3UE, ☎020 7831 4445
✉clerks@13oldsquare.com
Call Date: July 1971, Middle Temple
Stephenlloyd@13oldsquare.com

Fax: 020 7841 5825;
DX: DX 52 London, Chancery Lane;
URL: http://www.13oldsquare.com/stephen_lloyd.htm

Types of work: Chancery (general), Chancery (land law), Charities, Company, commercial and competition, Conveyancing, Equity, Family provision, Insolvency, Landlord and tenant,

Partnerships, Personal insolvency, Professional negligence, Succession, Trusts, Wills

LLOYD MR TREFOR

Linenhall Chambers
1 Stanley Place, Chester CH1 2LU,
☎01244 348282
✉clerks@linenhallchambers.co.uk
Portal Chambers
Blaencwm Mawr, Llandysul SA44 5NS,
☎01559 395 292
Call Date: July 2001, Gray's Inn
Qualifications: [BSc (Hons)(Wales) MRICS FAAV]

LLOYD-ELEY MR ANDREW JAMES QC (2010)

Old Bailey Chambers
15 Old Bailey, London EC4M 7EF,
☎020 3008 6404
✉clerks@15oldbaileychambers.com
Call Date: Nov 1979, Middle Temple
Pupil Supervisor
Qualifications: [LLB]
✉clerks@15oldbaileychambers.com

LLOYD-JONES MR JOHN BENEDICT

36 Bedford Row
London WC1R 4JH, ☎020 7421 8000
✉chambers@36bedfordrow.co.uk
Call Date: Nov 1993, Inner Temple
Pupil Supervisor
Qualifications: [BA (Hons) (Dunelm) CPE]
✉jlloyd-jones@36bedfordrow.co.uk

LLOYD-NESLING MISS TRACEY NORMA BEATRICE

30 Park Place
Cardiff CF10 3BS, ☎029 2039 8421
✉clerks@30parkplace.law.co.uk
Call Date: July 1988, Middle Temple
Pupil Supervisor
Qualifications: [LLB (Hons) (Bucks)]
✉tln@30parkplace.co.uk

LO MR BERNARD NORMAN

Field Court Chambers
5 Field Court, Gray's Inn, London WC1R 5EF,
☎020 7405 6114 ✉clerks@fieldcourt.co.uk
Call Date: Nov 1991, Inner Temple
Pupil Supervisor
Qualifications: [BA (Bris) Dip Law]
✉bernard.lo@fieldcourt.co.uk

LOADES MR JONATHAN CHARLES

The Chambers of Grahame Aldous QC
9 Gough Square, London EC4A 3DG,
☎020 7832 0500
✉clerks@9goughsquare.co.uk
Call Date: Nov 1986, Middle Temple
Pupil Supervisor
Qualifications: [BSc (Bradford) DipLaw]
✉jloades@9goughsquare.co.uk

LOBBENBERG MR NICHOLAS

4 Breams Buildings
Chancery Lane, London EC4A 1HP,
☎020 7092 1900 ✉clerks@4bb.co.uk
Call Date: Nov 1987, Gray's Inn
Pupil Supervisor
Qualifications: [BA (Oxon)]

LOCK MR DAVID ANTHONY QC (2011)

No5 Chambers
Fountain Court, Steelhouse Lane, Birmingham B4 6DR, ☎0845 210 5555 ✉info@no5.com
No5 Chambers
Greenwood House, 4-7 Salisbury Court, London EC4Y 8AA, ☎0845 210 5555
No5 Chambers
38 Queen Square, Bristol BS1 4QS,
☎0845 210 5555
Call Date: Nov 1985, Gray's Inn
Qualifications: [MA (Cantab) DipLaw]
✉dl@no5.com

LOCKE MR ANDREW PETER

Nexus Chambers
7 New Square, Lincolns Inn, London WC2A 3QS,
☎020 7404 1147 / 020 7831 8309
✉info@nexuschambers.com
Call Date: Oct 2008, Inner Temple
Qualifications: [LLB (Lond)]
✉andrew.locke@nexuschambers.com

LOCKEY MR JOHN CHARLTON GERARD QC (2006)

Essex Court Chambers
24 Lincoln's Inn Fields, London WC2A 3EG,
☎020 7813 8000
✉clerksroom@essexcourt.net
Call Date: July 1987, Middle Temple
Qualifications: [MA (Cantab) LLM (Lond)]
✉jlockey@essexcourt.net

E

LOCKHART MR ANDREW WILLIAM JARDINE QC (2010)

St Philips Chambers
55 Temple Row, Birmingham B2 5LS,
☎0121 246 7000 ✉clerks@st-philips.com
Call Date: Oct 1991, Lincoln's Inn
Pupil Supervisor, Recorder
Qualifications: [LLB (Hons) (Lond)]
alockhart@st-philips.co.uk

LOCKHART-MUMMERY MR CHRISTOPHER JOHN QC (1986)

Landmark Chambers
180 Fleet Street, London EC4A 2HG,
☎020 7430 1221
✉clerks@landmarkchambers.co.uk
Call Date: July 1971, Inner Temple
Recorder
Qualifications: [BA (Cantab)]

LODDER DR ANDREW VERE METCALFE

One Essex Court
Ground Floor, One Essex Court, Temple,
London EC4Y 9AR, ☎020 7583 2000
✉clerks@oeclaw.co.uk
Call Date: Mar 2012, Inner Temple
alodder@oeclaw.co.uk

E

LODDER MR PETER NORMAN QC (2001)

2 Bedford Row
London WC1R 4BU, ☎020 7440 8888
✉clerks@2bedfordrow.co.uk
Call Date: July 1981, Middle Temple
Qualifications: [LLB (B'ham)]
pnlodder@2bedfordrow.co.uk

LODGE MR ADAM ROBERT

18 St John Street
Manchester M3 4EA, ☎0161 278 1800
✉clerks@18sjs.com
Call Date: Oct 1996, Gray's Inn
Qualifications: [LLB]

LODGE MR ANTON JAMES CORDUFF QC (1989)

Park Court Chambers
16 Park Place, Leeds LS1 2SJ,
☎0113 243 3277
✉clerks@parkcourtchambers.co.uk
Furnival Chambers
32 Furnival Street, London EC4A 1JQ,
☎020 7405 3232
Call Date: Nov 1966, Gray's Inn
Recorder
Qualifications: [MA (Cantab)]
alodge@parkcourtchambers.co.uk

LODGE MR HUGO DANIEL PAUL

Atkinson Bevan Chambers
1st Floor, 2 Harcourt Buildings, Temple,
London EC4Y 9DB, ☎020 7353 2112
✉clerks@2hb.co.uk
Call Date: Oct 1998, Gray's Inn
Pupil Supervisor
Qualifications: [MA (Cantab)]

LODY MISS CAROLINE ANN

Seven Bedford Row
7 Bedford Row, London WC1R 4BS,
☎020 7242 3555 ✉clerks@7br.co.uk
Call Date: July 2009, Middle Temple
Qualifications: [BA (Hons) (Oxon)]
clody@7br.co.uk

LODY MR TUSTIAN STUART

KCH Garden Square
1 Oxford Street, Nottingham NG1 5BH,
☎0115 941 8851
✉clerks@kchgardensquare.co.uk
Call Date: Nov 1991, Gray's Inn
Pupil Supervisor
Qualifications: [BA]

LOEB MISS DINAH YOLANDE

Westgate Chambers
64 High Street, Lewes, East Sussex BN7 1XG,
☎01273 480510
✉clerks@westgate-chambers.co.uk
Call Date: Nov 2004, Middle Temple
Qualifications: [LLB (Hons)]
dl@westgate-chambers.co.uk

LOFTHOUSE MR JAMES

1 Gray's Inn Square
Ground Floor, 1 Gray's Inn Square, London
WC1R 5AA, ☎020 7405 0001
Call Date: Oct 1996, Inner Temple
Pupil Supervisor
Qualifications: [BA (Dunelm)]
jlofthouse@1gis.co.uk

LOFTHOUSE MR JOHN CHARLES

2 King's Bench Walk
2 King's Bench Walk, Temple, London
EC4Y 7DE, ☎020 7353 1746
✉clerks@2kbw.com
Call Date: May 1979, Middle Temple
Pupil Supervisor
Qualifications: [MA (Oxon)]

LOFTHOUSE MR SIMON TIMOTHY QC (2006)

Atkin Chambers
1 Atkin Building, Gray's Inn, London WC1R 5AT, ☎ 020 7404 0102
✉ clerks@atkinchambers.com
Call Date: Nov 1988, Gray's Inn
Recorder
Qualifications: [LLB (Hons)(Lond)]
✉ slofthouse@atkinchambers.com

LOFTUS MISS TERESA ANNE MARTINE

Number 7 Harrington Street Chambers
7 Harrington Street, Liverpool L2 9YH, ☎ 0151 242 0707 ✉ clerks@7hs.co.uk
Call Date: Feb 1995, Lincoln's Inn
Qualifications: [LLB (Hull)]
✉ teresa.loftus@7hs.co.uk

LOGAN MR GRAEME ALEXANDER

15 New Bridge Street
London EC4V 6AU, ☎ 020 7842 1900
✉ clerks@15nbs.com
4 Breams Buildings
Chancery Lane, London EC4A 1HP, ☎ 020 7092 1900 ✉ clerks@4bb.co.uk
Call Date: Oct 1998, Middle Temple
Qualifications: [LLB (Hons)]

LOGAN MISS MAURA

St John's House Chambers
One High Elm Drive, Hale Barns, Altrincham, Cheshire WA15 0JD, ☎ 0161 980 7379
✉ mauraloganllb@aol.com
Call Date: July 1971, Inner Temple

LOGAN MS RACHEL ROSE IDA

Matrix Chambers
Griffin Building, Gray's Inn, London WC1R 5LN, ☎ 020 7404 3447
✉ matrix@matrixlaw.co.uk / lscott@matrixlaw.co.uk
Call Date: Nov 2008, Inner Temple
Qualifications: [BA(Oxon) MA CPE]

LOGSDON MR MICHAEL ANTHONY

2 Hare Court
Lower Ground, Ground, 1st & 2nd Floor, 2 Hare Court, Temple, London EC4Y 7BH, ☎ 020 7353 3982 ✉ clerks@2harecourt.com
Call Date: Feb 1988, Inner Temple
Qualifications: [LLB (So'ton)]
✉ michaellogsdon@2harecourt.com

LOGUE MISS VICTORIA SUZANNE

Park Lane Plowden
19 Westgate, Leeds LS1 2RD, ☎ 0113 228 5049
✉ clerks@parklaneplowden.co.uk
Call Date: July 2005, Middle Temple
Qualifications: [LLB (Hons) Newcastle Upon Tyne]
✉ victoria.logue@parklaneplowden.co.uk

LOHMUS MR MICHAEL KENNETH HEINDRIK

St Ive's Chambers
Whittall Street, Birmingham B4 6DH, ☎ 0121 236 0863
✉ clerks@stiveschambers.co.uk
Call Date: Mar 2005, Gray's Inn
Qualifications: [LLB (Sheffield)]
✉ michael.lohmus@stiveschambers.co.uk

LOKE MISS SIEW YING

Chambers of Mr Ami Feder
Ground Floor, Lamb Building, Temple, London EC4Y 7AS, ☎ 020 7797 7788
✉ clerks@lambbuilding.co.uk
Lamb Building
22 Ship Street, Brighton BN1 1AD, ☎ 01273 820490
✉ admin@lambbuilding.co.uk
Chambers of Mr Ami Feder
Ground Floor, Lamb Building, Temple, London EC4Y 7AS, ☎ 020 7797 7788
✉ clerks@lambbuilding.co.uk
Call Date: July 2003, Gray's Inn
Qualifications: [BA (Exon)]
✉ clerks@lambbuilding.co.uk, siewloke@lambbuilding.co.uk

LOMAS MR MARK HENRY QC (2003)

Littleton Chambers
3 King's Bench Walk North, Temple, London EC4Y 7HR, ☎ 020 7797 8600
✉ fschneider@littletonchambers.co.uk
Call Date: Nov 1977, Middle Temple
Qualifications: [MA (Cantab)]
✉ ml@littletonchambers.co.uk

LOMAS MR MARK STEPHEN

3 PB Barristers
3 Paper Buildings, Temple, London EC4Y 7EU, ☎ 020 7583 8055
3 PB Barristers
Royal Talbot House, 2 Victoria Street, Bristol, Avon BS1 6BB, ☎ 0117 928 1520
3 PB Barristers
30 Christchurch Road, Bournemouth, Dorset BH1 3PD, ☎ 01202 292102
✉ clerks.bournemouth@3paper.co.uk

E

3 PB Barristers
4 St Peter Street, Winchester SO23 8BW, ☎01962 868884
✉clerks.winchester@3paper.co.uk
3 PB Barristers
23 Beaumont Street, Oxford OX1 2NP, ☎01865 793 736
Call Date: July 1983, Middle Temple
Pupil Supervisor
Qualifications: [BA (Keele)]
mark.lomas@3paper.co.uk

LOMAS MISS SOPHIE

Citadel Chambers
The Citadel, 190 Corporation Street, Birmingham B4 6QD, ☎0121 233 8500
✉clerks@citadelchambers.com
Call Date: Oct 2006, Inner Temple
Qualifications: [LLB]

LOMAX MS EMILY ELIZABETH JOY

Central Chambers
89 Princess Street, Manchester M1 4HT, ☎0161 236 1133
✉clerks@centralchambers.co.uk
Call Date: Oct 2004, Gray's Inn
Qualifications: [BA MA]

LOMNICKA PROF EVA ZOFIA

Four New Square
Four New Square, Lincoln's Inn, London WC2A 3RJ, ☎020 7822 2000
✉barristers@4newsquare.com
Call Date: July 1974, Middle Temple
Qualifications: [MA LLB (Cantab)]

LONG MR ANDREW PETER

St Johns Buildings
24a - 28 St John Street, Manchester M3 4DJ, ☎0161 214 1500
✉clerk@stjohnsbuildings.co.uk
St Johns Buildings
21 White Friars, Chester CH1 1NZ, ☎01244 323070
✉clerk@stjohnsbuildings.co.uk
16 Winckley Square
Preston PR1 3JJ, ☎01772 256100
Call Date: July 1981, Inner Temple
Pupil Supervisor
Qualifications: [LLB (Sheff)]
clerk@stjohnsbuildings.co.uk

LONG MR BENJAMIN NICHOLAS JAMES

5 Pump Court
Ground Floor, 5 Pump Court, Temple, London EC4Y 7AP, ☎020 7353 2532
✉clerks@5pumpcourt.com
Call Date: Nov 2000, Inner Temple
Qualifications: [BA (Lond) CPE (Kingston)]

LONG MR BENJAMIN PHILIP JACKSON

Pump Court Chambers
Upper Ground Floor, 3 Pump Court, Temple, London EC4Y 7AJ, ☎020 7353 0711
✉clerks@3pumpcourt.com
Pump Court Chambers
5 Temple Chambers, Temple Street, Swindon SN1 1SQ, ☎01793 539899
✉clerks@3pumpcourt.com
Pump Court Chambers
31 Southgate Street, Winchester, Hampshire SO23 9EB, ☎01962 868 161
✉clerks@3pumpcourt.com
Call Date: July 2006, Middle Temple
Qualifications: [BSc (Lond) PGDL]
bl@3pumpcourt.com

LONG MISS KAYLEIGH

Dere Street Barristers
14 Toft Green, York YO1 6JT, ☎0844 3351551
✉clerks@derestreet.co.uk
Call Date: Oct 2009, Middle Temple
Qualifications: [LLB (Hons) (Leeds)]

LONG MISS MADELIENE MARIE

Kenworthy's Chambers
Arlington House, Bloom Street, Salford, Manchester M3 6AJ, ☎0161 832 4036
Call Date: Nov 1999, Gray's Inn
Qualifications: [BA (Kent) LLM (Leics) MBA (Birm'h)]

LONGHURST-WOODS MS LESLEY

2 Louisa Close
2 Louisa Close, Wetherell Road, London E9 7BZ, ☎020 8985 8716
✉lezwoo@btopenworld.com
Call Date: Nov 1992, Gray's Inn
Qualifications: [BA LLB]

LONGSTAFF MR BENJAMIN MATTHEW KENNETH

Hogarth Chambers
5 New Square, Lincoln's Inn, London
WC2A 3RJ, ☎020 7404 0404
✉barristers@hogarthchambers.com
Call Date: Oct 2009, Gray's Inn
Qualifications: [BSc]
✉blongstaff@hogarthchambers.com

LONGSTAFF MR OLIVER ROBERT

Park Lane Plowden
19 Westgate, Leeds LS1 2RD,
☎0113 228 5049
✉clerks@parklaneplowden.co.uk
Call Date: Oct 1999, Middle Temple
Qualifications: [BA (Hons)(Dunelm)]
✉oliver.longstaff@parklaneplowden.co.uk

LONGWORTH MR ANTONY STEPHEN

St Johns Buildings
24a - 28 St John Street, Manchester M3 4DJ,
☎0161 214 1500
✉clerk@stjohnsbuildings.co.uk
16 Winckley Square
Preston PR1 3JJ, ☎01772 256100
St Johns Buildings Liverpool
8th Floor India Buildings, Water Street,
Liverpool L2 0XG, ☎0151 243 6000
✉clerk@stjohnsbuildings.co.uk
Call Date: July 1978, Middle Temple
Pupil Supervisor
Qualifications: [BA (Oxon)]
✉clerk@stjohnsbuildings.co.uk

LONSDALE MR DAVID JAMES

33 Bedford Row
London WC1R 4JH, ☎020 7242 6476
✉clerks@33bedfordrow.co.uk
Call Date: Nov 1988, Inner Temple
Qualifications: [BA (Oxon)(Hons)]
✉DavidLonsdale@33bedfordrow.co.uk

LONSDALE MISS MARION MARY

Academy Chambers
63 Brim Hill, London N2 0HA,
☎020 8455 2503
✉marionlonsdale@gmail.com
Call Date: July 1984, Gray's Inn
Qualifications: [BSC (Hons) (Nott'm) LLB (Hons) (Lond) ATII (CTA)]

LOOSEMORE MRS MARY

Pallant Chambers
12 North Pallant, Chichester, West Sussex
PO19 1TQ, ☎01243 784538
✉clerks@pallantchambers.co.uk
Call Date: May 1992, Inner Temple
Qualifications: [BSc (Lond)]
✉clerks@pallantchambers.co.uk

LOPEZ MR JUAN NEMESIO

Francis Taylor Building
Inner Temple, London EC4Y 7BY,
☎020 7353 8415 ✉clerks@ftb.eu.com
Call Date: Oct 2002, Lincoln's Inn
Qualifications: [LLB (Hons)]
✉juan.lopez@ftb.eu.com

LOPEZ MR PAUL ANTHONY

St Ive's Chambers
Whittall Street, Birmingham B4 6DH,
☎0121 236 0863
✉clerks@stiveschambers.co.uk
Call Date: July 1982, Middle Temple
Pupil Supervisor, Recorder
Qualifications: [LLB (Hons) (B'ham)]
✉paul.lopez@stiveschambers.co.uk

LOPIAN DR JONATHAN BERNARD

11 Stone Buildings
11 Stone Buildings, Lincoln's Inn, London
WC2A 3TG, ☎020 7831 6381
✉clerks@11sb.com
Call Date: Nov 1994, Middle Temple
Pupil Supervisor
Qualifications: [MA Dip Law (Lond) Ph D (Cantab)]
✉lopian@11sb.com

LORAINE MISS KARA KINMOND

Old Square Chambers
3 Orchard Court, St Augustine's Yard, Bristol
BS1 5DP, ☎0117 930 5100
✉clerks@oldsquare.co.uk
Old Square Chambers
10-11 Bedford Row, London WC1R 4BU,
☎020 7269 0300 ✉clerks@oldsquare.co.uk
Call Date: Nov 2006, Middle Temple
Qualifications: [LLB (Hons) (Durham)]
✉loraine@oldsquare.co.uk

LORAM MISS MARY CAROLINE

36 Bedford Row
London WC1R 4JH, ☎020 7421 8000
✉chambers@36bedfordrow.co.uk
Call Date: Nov 1995, Inner Temple
Qualifications: [BA (Oxon) MPhil (Cantab)]
✉mloram@36bedfordrow.co.uk

E

LORD MR ANDREW JAMES

Call Date: Oct 1999, Gray's Inn
Qualifications: [LLB (Dunelm)]
lord@paradise-sq.co.uk

LORD MR DAVID WILLIAM QC (2009)

3 Stone Buildings
Ground Floor, 3 Stone Buildings, Lincoln's Inn, London WC2A 3XL, ☎ 020 7242 4937
clerks@3sb.law.co.uk
Call Date: July 1987, Middle Temple
Qualifications: [LLB (Bris)]
dlord@3sb.law.co.uk

LORD MR RICHARD DENYER QC (2002)

Brick Court Chambers
7-8 Essex Street, London WC2R 3LD,
☎ 020 7379 3550 clerks@brickcourt.co.uk
Call Date: Nov 1981, Inner Temple
Qualifications: [MA (Cantab)]
Richard.Lord@Brickcourt.co.uk

LORD MR THOMAS BAXTER

15 Winckley Square
Preston PR1 3JJ, ☎ 01772 252828
clerks@15winckleysq.co.uk
Call Date: Nov 2009, Gray's Inn
Qualifications: [BSc MA]
tomlord@15ws.co.uk

LORD MR TIMOTHY MICHAEL QC (2008)

Brick Court Chambers
7-8 Essex Street, London WC2R 3LD,
☎ 020 7379 3550 clerks@brickcourt.co.uk
Call Date: Nov 1992, Inner Temple
Pupil Supervisor
Qualifications: [MA (Cantab)]
Tim.Lord@Brickcourt.co.uk

LORD MR WAYNE EDWARD

Construction Chambers
18 Skiddaw Drive, Mickleover, Derby DE3 9NE, ☎ 01332 617 917
wel@welord.co.uk
Call Date: July 1999, Middle Temple
Qualifications: [BSc (Hons), Dip.Law CEng, MICE,MIStructE]
wel@welord.co.uk

LORENZO MS CLAUDIA

Pump Court Chambers
Upper Ground Floor, 3 Pump Court, Temple, London EC4Y 7AJ, ☎ 020 7353 0711
clerks@3pumpcourt.com
Pump Court Chambers
5 Temple Chambers, Temple Street, Swindon SN1 1SQ, ☎ 01793 539899
clerks@3pumpcourt.com
Pump Court Chambers
31 Southgate Street, Winchester, Hampshire SO23 9EB, ☎ 01962 868 161
clerks@3pumpcourt.com
Call Date: Apr 1991, Inner Temple
Qualifications: [BA (Hons) LLB (Hons) LLM]
cl@3pumpcourt.com

LORIE MR ANDREW GIDEON

3 PB Barristers
4 St Peter Street, Winchester SO23 8BW,
☎ 01962 868884
clerks.winchester@3paper.co.uk
3 PB Barristers
30 Christchurch Road, Bournemouth, Dorset BH1 3PD, ☎ 01202 292102
clerks.bournemouth@3paper.co.uk
3 PB Barristers
3 Paper Buildings, Temple, London EC4Y 7EU,
☎ 020 7583 8055
3 PB Barristers
Royal Talbot House, 2 Victoria Street, Bristol, Avon BS1 6BB, ☎ 0117 928 1520
3 PB Barristers
23 Beaumont Street, Oxford OX1 2NP,
☎ 01865 793 736
Call Date: Oct 1996, Middle Temple
Qualifications: [BA (Hons)(Bris) CPE]

LOUGHRAN MS GEMMA MARY

1 Pump Court
Elm Court, Temple, London EC4Y 7AB,
☎ 020 7842 7070
(name)@pumpcourt.co.uk
Call Date: Nov 2008, Inner Temple
Qualifications: [BA (Sussex) CPE]

LOUIS MS ANGELA

Clapham Law Chambers
85 Landor Road, Clapham North, London SW9 9RT, ☎ 020 7978 8482
DANNY@claphamlawchambers.co.uk
Call Date: Oct 2002, Lincoln's Inn
Qualifications: [LLB]

E

LOURDES MR LOUIS JOSEPH

Chambers of Mr Louis Lourdes
69A, Chertsey Court, Lower Richmond Road, London SW14 7RD, ☎ 020 8288 0133
✉ richmondchambers@googlemail.com
Call Date: Nov 1998, Lincoln's Inn
Qualifications: [LLB (Hons)]

LOVE MR DUDLEY MARK

2 Dr Johnson's Buildings
2 Dr Johnson's Buildings, Temple, London EC4Y 7AY, ☎ 020 7936 2613
✉ clerks@2drj.com
Call Date: Nov 1979, Gray's Inn
Pupil Supervisor
Qualifications: [BSc (Lond)]
✉ clerks@2drj.com

LOVE MISS SARAH ANN

Brick Court Chambers
7-8 Essex Street, London WC2R 3LD,
☎ 020 7379 3550 ✉ clerks@brickcourt.co.uk
Call Date: Oct 2006, Middle Temple
Qualifications: [PPE (Oxon)]
✉ sarah.love@brickcourt.co.uk

LOVE MISS SHARON ANN

Garden Court Chambers
57-60 Lincoln's Inn Fields, London WC2A 3LJ,
☎ 020 7993 7600 ✉ info@gclaw.co.uk
Call Date: Oct 1997, Gray's Inn
Qualifications: [BA]
✉ sharonl@gclaw.co.uk

LOVEDAY MR DAVID ROBERT

4-5 Gray's Inn Square
Gray's Inn, London WC1R 5AH,
☎ 020 7404 5252 ✉ clerks@4-5.co.uk
Call Date: Nov 2007, Inner Temple
Qualifications: [BA (Oxon) LLM (Lond)]

LOVEDAY MR MARK ALAN

Tanfield Chambers
2-5 Warwick Court, London WC1R 5DJ,
☎ 020 7421 5300
✉ clerks@tanfieldchambers.co.uk
Call Date: July 1986, Inner Temple
Pupil Supervisor
Qualifications: [BA (Hons) (Kent) ACI Arb]
✉ markloveday@tanfieldchambers.co.uk

Types of work: Chancery (land law), Commercial property, Landlord and tenant, Leasehold enfranchisement, Professional negligence, Property

LOVELADY MR JOHN GRAHAM

Linenhall Chambers
1 Stanley Place, Chester CH1 2LU,
☎ 01244 348282
✉ clerks@linenhallchambers.co.uk
Call Date: July 1998, Lincoln's Inn
Qualifications: [BSc (Hons)(Leeds)]
✉ jgl@nicholasstreet.com

LOVELAND PROF IAN DAVID

Arden Chambers
20 Bloomsbury Square, London WC1A 2NS,
☎ 020 7242 4244
✉ clerks@ardenchambers.com
Call Date: Mar 2001, Inner Temple
Qualifications: [BA (Warwick) DPhil (Oxon) LLM (Lond)]

LOVELL-PANK MR DORIAN CHRISTOPHER QC (1993)

6 King's Bench Walk
Ground Floor, 6 King's Bench Walk, Temple, London EC4Y 7DR, ☎ 020 7583 0410
✉ clerks@6kbw.com
Call Date: July 1971, Inner Temple
Recorder
✉ dorian.lovell-pank@6kbw.com

LOVERIDGE MR ANDREW ROBERT

Number 7 Harrington Street Chambers
7 Harrington Street, Liverpool L2 9YH,
☎ 0151 242 0707 ✉ clerks@7hs.co.uk
Call Date: July 1983, Lincoln's Inn
Pupil Supervisor, Recorder
Qualifications: [LLB (Newc)]
✉ andrew.loveridge@7hs.co.uk

LOWE MR ALAN VAUGHAN QC (2008)

Essex Court Chambers
24 Lincoln's Inn Fields, London WC2A 3EG,
☎ 020 7813 8000
✉ clerksroom@essexcourt.net
Call Date: Feb 1993, Gray's Inn
Qualifications: [LLB Ph D (Wales) LLM]
✉ vlowe@essexcourt.net

LOWE MR ANTHONY MARSHALL

Cornwall Street Chambers
85-87 Cornwall Street, Birmingham B3 3BY,
☎ 0121 233 7500
✉ clerks@cornwallstreet.co.uk
Call Date: July 1976, Middle Temple
Pupil Supervisor, Recorder
Qualifications: [MA (Oxon)]
✉ anthony.lowe@cornwallstreet.co.uk

E

LOWE MR CHRISTOPHER JOHN

KCH Garden Square
1 Oxford Street, Nottingham NG1 5BH,
☎0115 941 8851
✉clerks@kchgardensquare.co.uk
Call Date: July 2001, Middle Temple
Qualifications: [LLB (Hons)]
✉clowe@kchgardensquare.co.uk

LOWE MR CRAIG DAVID

Call Date: Oct 1994, Lincoln's Inn
Pupil Supervisor
Qualifications: [LLB (Hons)(Lond)]
✉lowe@paradise-sq.co.uk

LOWE MR DAVID ALEXANDER QC (1984)

13 Old Square Chambers
Ground Floor, 14 Old Square, Lincoln's Inn,
London WC2A 3UE, ☎020 7831 4445
✉clerks@13oldsquare.com
Call Date: July 1965, Middle Temple
Qualifications: [MA (Cantab)]

LOWE MR DAVID MARK

Blackstone Chambers
Blackstone House, Temple, London
EC4Y 9BW, ☎020 7583 1770
✉clerks@blackstonechambers.com
Call Date: Nov 2008, Gray's Inn
Qualifications: [BA BCL]
✉davidlowe@blackstonechambers.com

LOWE MISS ELIZABETH HELEN

Argent Chambers
5 Bell Yard, London WC2A 2JR,
☎020 7556 5500
✉briefsin@argentchambers.co.uk
Call Date: Nov 1999, Middle Temple
Qualifications: [BA (Hons)(Oxon) MA (Oxon)]
✉e.lowe@argentchambers.co.uk

LOWE MR GEOFFREY JAMES

St Johns Buildings Liverpool
8th Floor India Buildings, Water Street,
Liverpool L2 0XG, ☎0151 243 6000
✉clerk@stjohnsbuildings.co.uk
16 Winckley Square
Preston PR1 3JJ, ☎01772 256100
St Johns Buildings
24a - 28 St John Street, Manchester M3 4DJ,
☎0161 214 1500
✉clerk@stjohnsbuildings.co.uk
Call Date: July 1975, Gray's Inn
Pupil Supervisor, Recorder
Qualifications: [LLB]
✉geoffrey115@btinternet.com

LOWE MR GEORGE WILLIAM QC (1997)

Call Date: July 1972, Lincoln's Inn
Recorder
Qualifications: [LLB]
✉wlowe@paradise-sq.co.uk, w.loweqc@derestreet.co.uk

LOWE MR JONATHAN RICHARD

Exchange Chambers
7 Ralli Courts, West Riverside, Manchester
M3 5FT, ☎0161 833 2722
Exchange Chambers
One Derby Square, Derby Square, Liverpool
L2 9XX, ☎0151 236 7747
✉info@exchangechambers.co.uk
Exchange Chambers
Oxford House, Oxford Row, Leeds LS1 3BE,
☎0113 203 1970
✉spencer@exchangechambers.co.uk
Call Date: Mar 2008, Lincoln's Inn
Qualifications: [LLB (Newc)]
✉lowe@exchangechambers.co.uk

LOWE MR MATTHEW JUSTIN

36 Bedford Row
London WC1R 4JH, ☎020 7421 8000
✉chambers@36bedfordrow.co.uk
Call Date: Nov 1991, Inner Temple
Pupil Supervisor
Qualifications: [LLB (Exon)]
✉clerks@36bedfordrow.co.uk

LOWE MR MUNGO JAMES

13 Old Square Chambers
Ground Floor, 14 Old Square, Lincoln's Inn,
London WC2A 3UE, ☎020 7831 4445
✉clerks@13oldsquare.com
Call Date: July 2003, Middle Temple
Qualifications: [MA Hons (Edin) CPE]

LOWE MR NICHOLAS MARK QC (1996)

Cornerstone Barristers
2-3 Gray's Inn Square, Gray's Inn, London
WC1R 5JH, ☎020 7242 4986
✉chambers@2-3gis.co.uk
Call Date: July 1972, Gray's Inn
Recorder
Qualifications: [LLB]
✉mlowe@2-3gis.co.uk

LOWE MR RUPERT WILLIAM MANLEY

Guildhall Chambers
23 Broad Street, Bristol BS1 2HG,
☎0117 930 9000
✉hoc@guildhallchambers.co.uk
Call Date: Nov 1998, Inner Temple
Pupil Supervisor
Qualifications: [MA (Cantab) PGDip Law]
✉rupert.lowe@guildhallchambers.co.uk

LOWE MR THOMAS WILLIAM GORDON QC (2008)

Wilberforce Chambers
8 New Square, Lincoln's Inn, London
WC2A 3QP, ☎020 7306 0102
✉chambers@wilberforce.co.uk
Call Date: Nov 1985, Inner Temple
Qualifications: [LLB (Lond) LLM (Cantab)]
✉tlowe@wilberforce.co.uk

Types of work: Chancery (general), Commercial fraud, Commercial litigation, Copyright, Equity, Financial services, Insolvency, Media and entertainment, Offshore trust litigation, Professional negligence, Trusts, Wills

LOWENSTEIN MR PAUL DAVID QC (2009)

3 Verulam Buildings
London WC1R 5NT, ☎020 7831 8441
✉chambers@3vb.com
Call Date: Nov 1988, Middle Temple
Qualifications: [LLB (Manch) LLM (Cantab)]

Types of work: Agency, Alternative dispute resolution, Archaeology, Art, Aviation, Banking, Breach of confidence, Chancery (commercial), Commercial contracts, Commercial fraud, Commercial law, Commercial litigation, Commodities, Computer litigation, Confidential information, Conflict of laws, Cross-border litigation and remedies, Cultural property law, Energy, Entertainment, Freezing orders, Guarantees, Information technology, Insurance, International trade, Internet law, Media and entertainment, Mediation, Multi-party litigation, Professional negligence, Remedies, Sale and carriage of goods, Sale of business, Technical contracts, Telecommunications, Trade secrets, Warranty claims

LOWNDS MR PETER ALEXANDER

Doughty Street Chambers
53-54 Doughty Street, London WC1N 2LS,
☎020 7404 1313
✉enquiries@doughtystreet.co.uk
Doughty Street Chambers
Pall Mall Court, 61-67 King Street, Manchester
M2 4PD, ☎0161 618 1066
Doughty Street Chambers
5th Floor, Broad Quay House, Prince Street,
Bristol BS1 4DJ, ☎01179 058 717
Call Date: Nov 1998, Gray's Inn
Pupil Supervisor
Qualifications: [BSc (Brunel)]
✉p.lownds@doughtystreet.co.uk

LOWNE MR STEPHEN MARK

KCH Garden Square
1 Oxford Street, Nottingham NG1 5BH,
☎0115 941 8851
✉clerks@kchgardensquare.co.uk
Call Date: July 1981, Inner Temple
Pupil Supervisor, Recorder
Qualifications: [BA (Hons)]

LOXTON MR CHRISTOPHER EDWIN

4 KBW
Ground Floor, 4 King's Bench Walk, Temple,
London EC4Y 7DL, ☎020 7822 8822
✉law@4kbw.net
Call Date: Nov 2009, Middle Temple
Qualifications: [BSc (Hons) (Bris)]
✉law@4kbw.net

LUBA MR JAN MICHAEL ANDREW QC (2000)

Garden Court Chambers
57-60 Lincoln's Inn Fields, London WC2A 3LJ,
☎020 7993 7600 ✉info@gclaw.co.uk
Call Date: July 1980, Middle Temple
Recorder
Qualifications: [LLB (Lond) LLM (Leics)]
✉janl@gclaw.co.uk

LUBIMBI MISS THANDEKA BUSISIWE

Chambers of Thandi Lubimbi
46A Cannon Hill, Southgate, London
N14 6LH, ☎07857 034494
✉thandi.lubimbi@gmail.com
Call Date: July 2002, Lincoln's Inn
Qualifications: [LLB (Hons) LLM (Lond)]

LUCAS MISS BRIDGET ANN

Fountain Court Chambers
Fountain Court, Temple, London EC4Y 9DH,
☎020 7583 3335
✉chambers@fountaincourt.co.uk
Call Date: Nov 1989, Inner Temple
Pupil Supervisor
Qualifications: [BA (Oxon)]
✉blucas@fountaincourt.co.uk

E

LUCAS MR EDWARD ALLAN

The Chambers of Grahame Aldous QC
9 Gough Square, London EC4A 3DG,
☎ 020 7832 0500
✉ clerks@9goughsquare.co.uk
Call Date: Oct 1991, Middle Temple
Qualifications: [MA D Phil (Oxon) MLitt]
✉ elucas@9goughsquare.co.uk

LUCAS MISS FELICIE ELISABETH

Cathedral Chambers
10 Clytha Park Road, Newport NP20 4PB,
☎ 01633 215112
Call Date: Oct 1999, Middle Temple
Qualifications: [LLB(Hons)]

LUCAS MISS JOANNA KATE

Queen Square Chambers
56 Queen Square, Bristol BS1 4PR,
☎ 0117 921 1966 ✉ crime@qs-c.co.uk
Call Date: July 2004, Gray's Inn
Qualifications: [LLB]
✉ jkl@qs-c.co.uk

E

LUCAS MR JOHN JOSEPH MAC

7 Bell Yard
London WC2A 2JR, ☎ 020 7831 0636
✉ kevintarrant@btconnect.com
Call Date: July 1998, Middle Temple
Qualifications: [BA (Hons) LLB (Hons)]
✉ jlucas.bar@mail.com, jl@7bellyard.co.uk

LUCAS MR NOEL JOHN MAC QC (2008)

18 Red Lion Court
London EC4A 3EB, ☎ 020 7520 6000
✉ chambers@18rlc.co.uk
Call Date: July 1979, Middle Temple
Recorder
Qualifications: [BSc (Lond)]
✉ noel.lucas@18rlc.co.uk

LUCAS MR PHILLIP JOHN

Goldsmith Chambers
Ground Floor, Goldsmith Building, Temple,
London EC4Y 7BL, ☎ 020 7353 6802
✉ clerks@goldsmithchambers.com
Call Date: Oct 1995, Middle Temple
Qualifications: [LLB (Hons)]
✉ P.Lucas@goldsmithchambers.law.co.uk

LUCEY MISS ANNE MARIE

Trinity Chambers
Highfield House, Moulsham Street,
Chelmsford, Essex CM2 9AH,
☎ 01245 605040
✉ clerks@trinitychambers.com
Call Date: Nov 2005, Middle Temple
Qualifications: [LLB (Hons) (Lond)]

LUCK MS JULIE-ANNE

Kenworthy's Chambers
Arlington House, Bloom Street, Salford,
Manchester M3 6AJ, ☎ 0161 832 4036
Call Date: July 2006, Lincoln's Inn
Qualifications: [LLB (Lond)]
✉ j.luck@kenworthysbarristers.co.uk

LUCKHURST MR JOHN DORMER

Maidstone Chambers
33 Earl Street, Maidstone, Kent ME14 1PF,
☎ 01622 688592
✉ clerks@maidstonechambers.co.uk
Call Date: Oct 2006, Lincoln's Inn
Qualifications: [BSc (Lond)]

LUCKHURST MR PAUL DAVID

Blackstone Chambers
Blackstone House, Temple, London
EC4Y 9BW, ☎ 020 7583 1770
✉ clerks@blackstonechambers.com
Call Date: July 2009, Lincoln's Inn
Qualifications: [BA (Oxon) MPHIL(Cantab) CPE UCU]
✉ paulluckhurst@blackstonechambers.com

LUCKING MRS ADRIENNE SIMONE

36 Bedford Row
London WC1R 4JH, ☎ 020 7421 8000
✉ chambers@36bedfordrow.co.uk
Call Date: Nov 1989, Inner Temple
Pupil Supervisor, Recorder
Qualifications: [LLB (Hons)]
✉ clerks@36bedfordrow.co.uk

LUCRAFT MR MARK QC (2006)

18 Red Lion Court
London EC4A 3EB, ☎ 020 7520 6000
✉ chambers@18rlc.co.uk
18 Red Lion Court (Annexe)
Thornwood House, 102 New London Road,
Chelmsford, Essex CM2 0RG,
☎ 01245 280880
Call Date: July 1984, Inner Temple
Recorder
Qualifications: [BA (Kent)]
✉ mark.lucraft@18rlc.co.uk

LUDBROOK MR TIMOTHY VIVIAN

13 Old Square Chambers
Ground Floor, 14 Old Square, Lincoln's Inn, London WC2A 3UE, ☎ 020 7831 4445
✉ clerks@13oldsquare.com
Call Date: Oct 1996, Inner Temple
Qualifications: [LLB (Hons)]
✉ timludbrook@13oldsquare.com

LUDLOW MR CRAIG DOMINIC

3 PB Barristers
3 Paper Buildings, Temple, London EC4Y 7EU, ☎ 020 7583 8055
3 PB Barristers
Royal Talbot House, 2 Victoria Street, Bristol, Avon BS1 6BB, ☎ 0117 928 1520
3 PB Barristers
30 Christchurch Road, Bournemouth, Dorset BH1 3PD, ☎ 01202 292102
✉ clerks.bournemouth@3paper.co.uk
3 PB Barristers
4 St Peter Street, Winchester SO23 8BW, ☎ 01962 868884
✉ clerks.winchester@3paper.co.uk
3 PB Barristers
23 Beaumont Street, Oxford OX1 2NP, ☎ 01865 793 736
Call Date: Mar 2002, Lincoln's Inn
Qualifications: [LLB (Hons)]
✉ craig.ludlow@3pb.co.uk

LUE MR STEPHEN GEORGE NYUK SHEOUNG

Goldsmith Chambers
Ground Floor, Goldsmith Building, Temple, London EC4Y 7BL, ☎ 020 7353 6802
✉ clerks@goldsmithchambers.com
Call Date: Nov 2006, Middle Temple
Qualifications: [LLB (Hons) (Lond)]

LUGG MISS ELIZABETH CLAIRE

Dere Street Barristers
33 Broad Chare, Newcastle Upon Tyne NE1 3DQ, ☎ 0844 3351551
✉ clerks@derestreet.co.uk
Call Date: Oct 1994, Gray's Inn
Pupil Supervisor
Qualifications: [BA]
✉ e.lugg@derestreet.co.uk

LUGSDIN MR MARTIN

Kenworthy's Chambers
Arlington House, Bloom Street, Salford, Manchester M3 6AJ, ☎ 0161 832 4036
Call Date: Nov 2005, Middle Temple
Qualifications: [LLB (Hons) Lancaster]
✉ m.lugsdin@kenworthysbarristers.co.uk

LUH MISS SHU SHIN

Garden Court Chambers
57-60 Lincoln's Inn Fields, London WC2A 3LJ, ☎ 020 7993 7600 ✉ info@gclaw.co.uk
Call Date: Oct 2006, Middle Temple
Qualifications: [BA (Yale) MSc (Lond)]
✉ shushinl@gclaw.co.uk

LULE MISS JACQUELINE

1 Mitre Court Buildings
1 Mitre Court Buildings, Temple, London EC4Y 7BS, ☎ 020 7452 8900
✉ clerks@1mcb.com
Call Date: Nov 1999, Middle Temple
Qualifications: [LLB (Hons)(Middx)]
✉ jacqueline.lule@1mcb.com

LUMBERS MS KATHERINE ANNE

Seven Bedford Row
7 Bedford Row, London WC1R 4BS, ☎ 020 7242 3555 ✉ clerks@7br.co.uk
Call Date: Oct 1999, Inner Temple
Qualifications: [MA (Edin) MA]
✉ klumbers@7br.co.uk

LUMLEY MR NICHOLAS JAMES HENRY QC (2012)

Park Court Chambers
16 Park Place, Leeds LS1 2SJ, ☎ 0113 243 3277
✉ clerks@parkcourtchambers.co.uk
Melbury House
55 Manor Road, Oadby, Leicester, Leicestershire LE2 2LL, ☎ 07801 037802
✉ melburyhousechambers@yahoo.co.uk
Call Date: Oct 1992, Lincoln's Inn
Pupil Supervisor
Qualifications: [LLB(Hons)(Newc)]
✉ clerks@parkcourtchambers.co.uk

LUMSDAINE MS NAOMI

Tooks Chambers
81 Farringdon Street, London EC4A 4BL, ☎ 020 7842 7575 ✉ clerks@tooks.co.uk
Call Date: July 2008, Middle Temple
Qualifications: [BA (Hons) (Manch)]

LUMSDON MISS KATHERINE JANE

23 Essex Street
London WC2R 3AA, ☎ 020 7413 0353
✉ clerks@23es.com
Call Date: Oct 1993, Middle Temple
Qualifications: [BA (Hons)(Manch) CPE (Lond)]
✉ katelumsdon@23es.com

E

LUND MRS CELIA

Atlantic Chambers
4-6 Cook Street, Liverpool L2 9QU,
☎0151 236 4421
✉info@atlanticchambers.co.uk
5 Stone Buildings
5 Stone Buildings, Lincoln's Inn, London
WC2A 3XT, ☎020 7242 6201
✉clerks@5sblaw.com
Call Date: Nov 1988, Lincoln's Inn
Qualifications: [LLB (Hons)]
✉celialund@atlanticchambers.co.uk

LUNDIE MR CHRISTOPHER CARLTON

2 Temple Gardens
2 Temple Gardens, Temple, London
EC4Y 9AY, ☎020 7822 1200
✉clerks@2tg.co.uk
Call Date: Nov 1991, Inner Temple
Pupil Supervisor
Qualifications: [MA (Cantab)]
✉clundie@2tg.co.uk

LUTTMAN MISS LUCY

6 Pump Court
1st Floor, 6 Pump Court, Temple, London
EC4Y 7AR, ☎020 7797 8400
✉richardconstable@6pumpcourt.co.uk
6 Pump Court Chambers
6-8 Mill Street, Maidstone, Kent ME15 6XH,
☎01622 688094
✉annexe@6pumpcourt.co.uk
Call Date: July 2001, Lincoln's Inn
Qualifications: [LLB (Hons)]

LYCOURGOU MISS OLIVE

4 King's Bench Walk
2nd Floor, 4 King's Bench Walk, Temple,
London EC4Y 7DL, ☎020 7822 7000
✉clerks@4kbw.co.uk
Call Date: July 1997, Gray's Inn
Qualifications: [LLB (Middx)]
✉ol@4kbw.co.uk

LYDIARD MR ANDREW JOHN QC (2003)

Brick Court Chambers
7-8 Essex Street, London WC2R 3LD,
☎020 7379 3550 ✉clerks@brickcourt.co.uk
Call Date: July 1980, Inner Temple
Recorder
Qualifications: [BA (Oxon) LLM]
✉Andrew.Lydiard@Brickcourt.co.uk

LYKIARDOPOULOS MR ANDREW NICOLAS

8 New Square
8 New Square, Lincoln's Inn, London
WC2A 3QP, ☎020 7405 4321
✉clerks@8newsquare.co.uk
Call Date: Oct 2004, Middle Temple
Qualifications: [BA (Hons) Bristol CPE College of Law]
✉andrew.lykiardopoulos@8newsquare.co.uk

Types of work: Breach of confidence, Confidential information, Copyright, Design, Information technology, Intellectual property, Malicious falsehood, Media and entertainment, Patents, Scientific and technical disputes, Trade secrets, Trademarks

LYNAGH MR RICHARD DUDLEY QC (1996)

Crown Office Chambers
2 Crown Office Row, Temple, London
EC4Y 7HJ, ☎020 7797 8100
✉mail@crownofficechambers.com
Call Date: July 1975, Gray's Inn
Recorder
Qualifications: [LLB]
✉lynagh@crownofficechambers.com

LYNCH MR ADRIAN CHARLES EDMUND QC (2000)

11 King's Bench Walk
11 King's Bench Walk, Temple, London
EC4Y 7EQ, ☎020 7632 8500
✉clerksroom@11kbw.com
Call Date: Nov 1983, Gray's Inn
Recorder
Qualifications: [LLB (Lond)]
✉adrian.lynch@11kbw.com

LYNCH MR BENJAMIN JOHN PATRICK

Devereux Chambers
Queen Elizabeth Building, Temple, London
EC4Y 9BS, ☎020 7353 7534
✉clerks@devchambers.co.uk
Call Date: July 2001, Middle Temple
Qualifications: [BA (Hons) LLM]
✉lynch@devchambers.co.uk

LYNCH MR JEROME QC (2000)

Charter Chambers
33 John Street, London WC1N 2AT,
☎020 7618 4400
✉clerks@charterchambers.com
Call Date: July 1983, Lincoln's Inn
Qualifications: [BA (Hons)]
✉jerome.lynch@charterchambers.com

LYNCH MR JOHN PATRICK

QEB Hollis Whiteman
1-2 Laurence Pountney Hill, London EC4R 0EU, ☎ 020 7933 8855
✉ barristers@qebhw.co.uk
Call Date: Mar 2008, Gray's Inn
Qualifications: [BA (Oxon) MA (Bruges)]
john.lynch@qebhw.co.uk

LYNCH MR JOSEPH MICHAEL MARTIN

Central Chambers
89 Princess Street, Manchester M1 4HT, ☎ 0161 236 1133
✉ clerks@centralchambers.co.uk
Call Date: Oct 2007, Middle Temple
Qualifications: [BA (Hons) (Ireland) MA (Ireland)]
mrjosephlynch@gmail.com

LYNCH MR JULIAN

Chambers of Mr Julian Lynch
Mill Barn Cottage, Spring Lane, Old Oxted, Surrey RH8 9PB, ☎ 01883 732 103
✉ bpjlynch@btinternet.com
Call Date: Nov 1976, Inner Temple
Qualifications: [LLB (Lond)]

LYNCH MR JULIAN JAMES

13 King's Bench Walk
13 King's Bench Walk, Temple, London EC4Y 7EN, ☎ 020 7353 7204
✉ clerks@13kbw.co.uk
Call Date: Nov 2009, Gray's Inn
Qualifications: [BA]
jlynch@13kbw.co.uk

LYNCH MISS PATRICIA QC (1998)

18 Red Lion Court
London EC4A 3EB, ☎ 020 7520 6000
✉ chambers@18rlc.co.uk
18 Red Lion Court (Annexe)
Thornwood House, 102 New London Road, Chelmsford, Essex CM2 0RG, ☎ 01245 280880
Call Date: Nov 1979, Inner Temple
Recorder
Qualifications: [LLB (Hull)]
patricia.lynch@18rlc.co.uk

LYNCH MR PETER GARETH

4 Brick Court
4 Brick Court, Temple, London EC4Y 9AD, ☎ 020 7832 3200 ✉ clerks@4bc.co.uk
Call Date: July 1985, Lincoln's Inn
Qualifications: [BSc Dip Law]
peter.lynch@4bc.co.uk

LYNE MR MARK HILARY

Five Paper
Ground Floor, 5 Paper Buildings, Temple, London EC4Y 7HB, ☎ 020 7815 3200
Call Date: Nov 1981, Inner Temple
Pupil Supervisor
Qualifications: [BA (Cantab)]
marklyne@fivepaper.com

LYNESS MR SCOTT EDWARD

Landmark Chambers
180 Fleet Street, London EC4A 2HG, ☎ 020 7430 1221
✉ clerks@landmarkchambers.co.uk
Call Date: Oct 1996, Lincoln's Inn
Pupil Supervisor
Qualifications: [LLB (Hons)(Hull)]
scottlyness@landmarkchambers.co.uk

LYNN MR JEREMY DAVID

Farringdon Chambers
180 Bermondsey Street, London SE1 3TQ, ☎ 020 7089 5700
Call Date: Nov 1983, Inner Temple
Pupil Supervisor
Qualifications: [BSc (Cardiff)]

LYON MR GAVIN

Northampton Chambers
10 Spencer Parade, Northampton NN1 5AQ, ☎ 01604 636271
✉ clerks@northampton-chambers.co.uk
Call Date: Oct 2006, Middle Temple
Qualifications: [BA (Hons) (Southampton)]
glyon@northampton-chambers.co.uk

LYON MRS SHANE VALERIE

King's Bench and Godolphin (KBG)Chambers
115 North Hill, Plymouth, Devon PL4 8JY, ☎ 01752 221551
✉ clerks@kbgchambers.co.uk
Call Date: Nov 1976, Middle Temple
Pupil Supervisor
Qualifications: [LLB (Exon)]

LYON MR STEPHEN JOHN

4 Paper Buildings
1st Floor, 4 Paper Buildings, Temple, London EC4Y 7EX, ☎ 020 7427 5200
✉ clerks@4pb.com
Call Date: July 1987, Inner Temple
Pupil Supervisor
Qualifications: [LLB (Notts)]
sjl@4pb.com

LYONS MR ANDREW SIMON

Ropewalk Chambers
24 The Ropewalk, Nottingham NG1 5EF, ☎0115 947 2581 ✉clerks@ropewalk.co.uk
Call Date: Nov 2002, Inner Temple
Qualifications: [BA (Exon) MA (Dunelm) CPE]
andrewlyons@ropewalk.co.uk

LYONS MS CHRISTINA DIANNE

Seven Bedford Row
7 Bedford Row, London WC1R 4BS, ☎020 7242 3555 ✉clerks@7br.co.uk
Call Date: July 2004, Lincoln's Inn
Qualifications: [MA (Bris) BA (Hons) (UWO)]
clyons@7br.co.uk

LYONS MR DAVID WAKEFIELD

King's Bench Chambers
Wellington House, 175 Holdenhurst Road, Bournemouth, Dorset BH8 8DQ, ☎01202 250025
2 Pump Court
1st Floor, 2 Pump Court, Temple, London EC4Y 7AH, ☎020 7353 5597
✉clerks@2pumpcourt.co.uk
Call Date: July 1987, Middle Temple
Qualifications: [BA (Hons)]

E

LYONS MR JOHN ADAM

18 Red Lion Court
London EC4A 3EB, ☎020 7520 6000
✉chambers@18rlc.co.uk
18 Red Lion Court (Annexe)
Thornwood House, 102 New London Road, Chelmsford, Essex CM2 0RG, ☎01245 280880
Call Date: July 1986, Middle Temple
Pupil Supervisor
Qualifications: [BA (Dunelm) Dip Law]
john.lyons@18rlc.co.uk

LYONS MISS TARA YASMIN

Pump Court Chambers
Upper Ground Floor, 3 Pump Court, Temple, London EC4Y 7AJ, ☎020 7353 0711
✉clerks@3pumpcourt.com
Riverview Chambers
Hamilton House, 1 Temple Avenue, London EC4Y 0HA, ☎0844 225 3999
✉chrisbaylis@riverviewchambers.com
Pump Court Chambers
31 Southgate Street, Winchester, Hampshire SO23 9EB, ☎01962 868 161
✉clerks@3pumpcourt.com
Call Date: Nov 2005, Middle Temple
Qualifications: [BA (Cambs)]
tl@3pumpcourt.com

LYONS MR TIMOTHY JOHN QC (2003)

4-5 Gray's Inn Square
Gray's Inn, London WC1R 5AH, ☎020 7404 5252 ✉clerks@4-5.co.uk
St James's Chambers
68 Quay Street, Manchester M3 3EJ, ☎0161 834 7000
✉clerks@stjameschambers.com
Call Date: July 1980, Inner Temple
Qualifications: [LLB (Bris) LLM (Lond) TEP CTA (Fellow) PhD (Lond)]
clerks@4-5.co.uk

MABB MR DAVID MICHAEL QC (2001)

Erskine Chambers
33 Chancery Lane, London WC2A 1EN, ☎020 7242 5532
✉clerks@erskinechambers.com
Call Date: July 1979, Lincoln's Inn
Qualifications: [MA (Cantab)]
clerks@erskine-chambers.co.uk

MABLY MR LOUIS ASA LUKE ALEXIS DYLAN

6 King's Bench Walk
Ground Floor, 6 King's Bench Walk, Temple, London EC4Y 7DR, ☎020 7583 0410
✉clerks@6kbw.com
Call Date: Oct 1997, Lincoln's Inn
Pupil Supervisor
Qualifications: [BA (Hons)(Leeds) Dip law]
louis.mably@6kbw.com

MABON MRS JANE

9 St John Street
Manchester M3 4DN, ☎0161 955 9000
✉civilclerks@9sjs.com / criminalclerks@9sjs.com
Call Date: July 1998, Gray's Inn
Qualifications: [LLB (B'ham)]

MACADAM MR JASON ANGUS ALAISTER ROBERT

Exchange Chambers
7 Ralli Courts, West Riverside, Manchester M3 5FT, ☎0161 833 2722
Exchange Chambers
One Derby Square, Derby Square, Liverpool L2 9XX, ☎0151 236 7747
✉info@exchangechambers.co.uk
Exchange Chambers
Oxford House, Oxford Row, Leeds LS1 3BE, ☎0113 203 1970
✉spencer@exchangechambers.co.uk

St Paul's Chambers
5th Floor, St Paul's House, 23 Park Square South, Leeds LS1 2ND, ☎0113 245 5866
Call Date: Nov 1990, Lincoln's Inn
Qualifications: [LLB (Wales) B TEC]
jason.macadam@ntlworld.com

MACATONIA MISS EVE CHARLOTTE

2 Dr Johnson's Buildings
2 Dr Johnson's Buildings, Temple, London EC4Y 7AY, ☎020 7936 2613
✉clerks@2drj.com
Call Date: July 2005, Lincoln's Inn
Qualifications: [LLB (Hons)]

MACAULAY MR JACK

Crown Office Chambers
2 Crown Office Row, Temple, London EC4Y 7HJ, ☎020 7797 8100
✉mail@crownofficechambers.com
Call Date: Oct 2009, Lincoln's Inn
Qualifications: [LLB (Lond)]
macaulay@crownofficechambers.com

MACAULAY MR NEIL DAVID

Bretton Woods Law
New Broad Street House, 35 New Broad Street, London EC2M 1NH
Call Date: Nov 1990, Lincoln's Inn
Qualifications: [LLB (Hons)]
macaulaylegal@yahoo.co.uk, neilmacaulay@brettonwoodslaw.com

MACBEAN MR ANDREW HAMISH

Queen Square Chambers
56 Queen Square, Bristol BS1 4PR, ☎0117 921 1966 ✉crime@qs-c.co.uk
Call Date: Nov 2002, Lincoln's Inn
Qualifications: [LLB (Hons) (Leics)]
hm@qs-c.co.uk

MACCABE MR IRVINE JOHN

No5 Chambers
Fountain Court, Steelhouse Lane, Birmingham B4 6DR, ☎0845 210 5555 ✉info@no5.com
No5 Chambers
Greenwood House, 4-7 Salisbury Court, London EC4Y 8AA, ☎0845 210 5555
No5 Chambers
38 Queen Square, Bristol BS1 4QS, ☎0845 210 5555
Call Date: July 1983, Gray's Inn
Qualifications: [MA (Cantab)]
im@no5.com

MACDONALD MR ALEXANDER JAMES

7 King's Bench Walk
Ground Floor, 7 King's Bench Walk, Temple, London EC4Y 7DS, ☎020 7910 8300
✉clerks@7kbw.co.uk
Call Date: Oct 2001, Lincoln's Inn
Qualifications: [BA (Hons) (Cantab) LLM]
amacdonald@7kbw.co.uk

MACDONALD MISS ALISON CATHERINE

Matrix Chambers
Griffin Building, Gray's Inn, London WC1R 5LN, ☎020 7404 3447
✉matrix@matrixlaw.co.uk / Iscott@matrixlaw.co.uk
Call Date: Oct 2000, Gray's Inn
Pupil Supervisor
Qualifications: [MA (Cantab) BCL (Oxon)]
alisonmacdonald@matrixlaw.co.uk

MACDONALD MR ALISTAIR NEIL QC (2000)

Park Court Chambers
16 Park Place, Leeds LS1 2SJ, ☎0113 243 3277
✉clerks@parkcourtchambers.co.uk
Melbury House
55 Manor Road, Oadby, Leicester, Leicestershire LE2 2LL, ☎07801 037802
✉melburyhousechambers@yahoo.co.uk
Call Date: July 1983, Gray's Inn
Recorder
Qualifications: [BSc (Bath) Dip Law (City)]
amacdonald@parkcourtchambers.co.uk

MACDONALD MR ALISTAIR WILLIAM ORCHARD QC (2011)

St Philips Chambers
55 Temple Row, Birmingham B2 5LS, ☎0121 246 7000 ✉clerks@st-philips.com
Call Date: Nov 1995, Inner Temple
Pupil Supervisor, Recorder
Qualifications: [BA (Hons)(Notts) Dip in Law (Lond)]
amacdonald@st-philips.co.uk

MACDONALD MR ANGUS HUGH

St Paul's Chambers
5th Floor, St Paul's House, 23 Park Square South, Leeds LS1 2ND, ☎0113 245 5866
Call Date: July 2009, Gray's Inn
Qualifications: [BA (Hons) (Sheff)]
ama@stpaulschambers.com

MACDONALD MR IAIN

Gough Square Chambers
6-7 Gough Square, London EC4A 3DE,
☎ 020 7353 0924 ✉ gsc@goughsq.co.uk
Call Date: July 1996, Middle Temple
Pupil Supervisor
Qualifications: [BA (Hons)(Oxon)]
✉ iain.macdonald@goughsq.co.uk

MACDONALD MR IAN ALEXANDER QC (1988)

Garden Court Chambers
57-60 Lincoln's Inn Fields, London WC2A 3LJ,
☎ 020 7993 7600 ✉ info@gclaw.co.uk
Kings Court Chambers
3rd Floor, Albert House, 12-26 Albert Street, Birmingham B4 7UD, ☎ 07967 910864
✉ t.rehmanbar@talk21.com
Chambers of Ian Macdonald QC
Garden Court North, 22 Oxford Court, Manchester M2 3WQ, ☎ 0161 236 1840
✉ clerks@gcnchambers.co.uk
Call Date: Feb 1963, Middle Temple
Qualifications: [MA LLB]
✉ ianm@gclaw.co.uk

MACDONALD MR JAMES GEORGE ALEXANDER

3 Verulam Buildings
London WC1R 5NT, ☎ 020 7831 8441
✉ chambers@3vb.com
Call Date: Nov 2005, Inner Temple
Qualifications: [BA Magdalen College University of Oxford MA Ki]
✉ jmacdonald@3vb.com

MACDONALD MR JAMES PHILIP

Seven Bedford Row
7 Bedford Row, London WC1R 4BS,
☎ 020 7242 3555 ✉ clerks@7br.co.uk
Call Date: July 2010, Inner Temple
Qualifications: [MA M Phil (Cantab) CPE]
✉ jmacdonald@7br.co.uki

MACDONALD MR JOHN REGINALD QC (1976)

New Square Chambers
12 New Square, Lincoln's Inn, London WC2A 3SW, ☎ 020 7419 8000
✉ robin.hollington@newsquarechambers.co.uk
Call Date: June 1955, Lincoln's Inn
Qualifications: [MA (Cantab)]
✉ john.macdonald@newsquarechambers.co.uk

MACDONALD LORD KENNETH DONALD JOHN QC (1997)

Matrix Chambers
Griffin Building, Gray's Inn, London WC1R 5LN, ☎ 020 7404 3447
✉ matrix@matrixlaw.co.uk / Iscott@matrixlaw.co.uk
Call Date: July 1978, Inner Temple
Qualifications: [BA (Oxon)]
✉ kenmacdonald@matrixlaw.co.uk

MACDONALD MR MALCOLM

36 Bedford Row
London WC1R 4JH, ☎ 020 7421 8000
✉ chambers@36bedfordrow.co.uk
Call Date: Nov 2010, Inner Temple
Qualifications: [BA (Australia) LLB (Australian)]

MACDONALD MISS SHEILA HAMILTON

Chambers of Sheila Hamilton Macdonald
1 Hanley Street, Nottingham NG1 5BL,
☎ 07986 575399
✉ shm@familyproperty.org.uk
Call Date: Feb 1993, Middle Temple
Pupil Supervisor
Qualifications: [MA (Hons)(Scotland) LLB (Hons)(Lond)]

MACDONALD EGGERS MR PETER JOHN SIBLEY QC (2011)

7 King's Bench Walk
Ground Floor, 7 King's Bench Walk, Temple, London EC4Y 7DS, ☎ 020 7910 8300
✉ clerks@7kbw.co.uk
Call Date: July 1999, Middle Temple
Pupil Supervisor
Qualifications: [LLB (Sydney) LLM (Cantab)]
✉ pme@7kbw.co.uk

MACEVILLY MR CONN JEREMY

9 Stone Buildings
Lincoln's Inn, London WC2A 3NN,
☎ 020 7404 5055
✉ clerks@9stonebuildings.com
Call Date: Oct 1997, Inner Temple
Qualifications: [LLB (Dublin) LLM (LSE)]

E

MACEY-DARE MR THOMAS CHARLES

Quadrant Chambers
Quadrant House, 10 Fleet Street, London EC4Y 1AU, ☎020 7583 4444
✉info@quadrantchambers.com
Call Date: Feb 1994, Middle Temple
Pupil Supervisor
Qualifications: [MA (Cantab) LLM (Cantab) LLM (USA)]
✉thomas.macey-dare@quadrantchambers.com

MACFARLANE MR ANDREW LENNOX

Colleton Chambers
Colleton Crescent, Exeter, Devon EX2 4DG, ☎01392 274898
✉clerks@colletonchambers.co.uk
Call Date: May 1995, Inner Temple
✉andrewmacfarlane@colletonchambers.co.uk

MACFARLANE MISS TABITHA LUCY

Fosters Chambers
17 Small Street, Bristol BS1 1DE, ☎0117927 9604 ✉tabmac@fastmail.fm
Call Date: Nov 1998, Inner Temple
Qualifications: [BA (Hons)]

MACFAUL MR DONALD WILLIAM

Dere Street Barristers
33 Broad Chare, Newcastle Upon Tyne NE1 3DQ, ☎0844 3351551
✉clerks@derestreet.co.uk
Call Date: Mar 1998, Inner Temple
Qualifications: [LLB (Hons(Newc)]
✉d.macfaul@derestreet.co.uk, clerks@broadcharechambers.co.uk

MACGREGOR MR CRAIG

Cobden House Chambers
19 Quay Street, Manchester M3 3HN, ☎0161 833 6000 ✉Clerks@Cobden.co.uk
Call Date: Oct 1999, Lincoln's Inn
Qualifications: [LLB (Hons)(Sheff)]

MACHELL MR JOHN WILLIAM QC (2012)

Serle Court
6 New Square, Lincoln's Inn, London WC2A 3QS, ☎020 7242 6105
✉clerks@serlecourt.co.uk
Call Date: Oct 1993, Inner Temple
Pupil Supervisor
Qualifications: [LLB (So'ton)]
✉jmachell@serlecourt.co.uk

MACHELL MR RAYMOND DONATUS QC (1988)

Byrom Street Chambers
12 Byrom Street, Manchester M3 4PP, ☎0161 829 2100 ✉clerks@byromstreet.com
Crown Office Chambers
2 Crown Office Row, Temple, London EC4Y 7HJ, ☎020 7797 8100
✉mail@crownofficechambers.com
42 Bedford Row
London WC1R 4LL, ☎020 7831 0222
✉clerks@42br.com
Call Date: July 1973, Gray's Inn
Recorder
Qualifications: [MA LLB (Cantab)]
✉raymond.machell@byromstreet.com

MACHIN MR CHARLES KIM

St James's Chambers
68 Quay Street, Manchester M3 3EJ, ☎0161 834 7000
✉clerks@stjameschambers.com
Call Date: Nov 1973, Lincoln's Inn
Pupil Supervisor
Qualifications: [MA (Oxon)]
✉clerks@stjameschambers.com, c.machin@stjameschambers.com

MACHIN MR GRAHAM EDWARD

Ropewalk Chambers
24 The Ropewalk, Nottingham NG1 5EF, ☎0115 947 2581 ✉clerks@ropewalk.co.uk
Call Date: July 1965, Gray's Inn
✉grahammachin@ropewalk.co.uk

MACHIN MS SUSAN

Chavasse Court Chambers
18 Queen Avenue, Liverpool L2 4TX, ☎0151 229 2030
✉clerks@chavassechambers.co.uk
St Johns Buildings
21 White Friars, Chester CH1 1NZ, ☎01244 323070
✉clerk@stjohnsbuildings.co.uk
16 Winckley Square
Preston PR1 3JJ, ☎01772 256100
Call Date: July 1999, Inner Temple
Qualifications: [LLB (Hons)(Lanc)]

MACK MR JONATHAN DAVID

Blackfriars Chambers
79-83 Temple Chambers, 3-7 Temple Avenue, London EC4Y 0HP, ☎020 7353 7400
✉clerks@blackfriarschambers.com
Call Date: July 2009, Lincoln's Inn
Qualifications: [LLB (So'ton) ACIH LLM (Kent)]
✉jon.mack@blackfriarschambers.com

MACKAY MR ARCHIE JOHN CAMERON

Five Paper Buildings
1st Floor, Five Paper Buildings, Temple, London EC4Y 7HB, ☎020 7583 6117
✉clerks@5pb.co.uk
Call Date: July 2003, Middle Temple
Qualifications: [BA Hons (Manch) PG Dip Law]
ama@5pb.co.uk

MACKEAN MS SARAH SUTTON

King's Bench and Godolphin (KBG)Chambers
115 North Hill, Plymouth, Devon PL4 8JY, ☎01752 221551
✉clerks@kbgchambers.co.uk
Call Date: Nov 1992, Inner Temple
Qualifications: [MA (Oxon) Dip Law (Lond)]

MACKENZIE MR ALASDAIR HAMISH

Doughty Street Chambers
53-54 Doughty Street, London WC1N 2LS, ☎020 7404 1313
✉enquiries@doughtystreet.co.uk
Doughty Street Chambers
Pall Mall Court, 61-67 King Street, Manchester M2 4PD, ☎0161 618 1066
Doughty Street Chambers
5th Floor, Broad Quay House, Prince Street, Bristol BS1 4DJ, ☎01179 058 717
Call Date: Oct 2004, Gray's Inn
Qualifications: [BA]
a.mackenzie@doughtystreet.co.uk

MACKENZIE MISS JULIE FIONA

Pump Court Chambers
5 Temple Chambers, Temple Street, Swindon SN1 1SQ, ☎01793 539899
✉clerks@3pumpcourt.com
Pump Court Chambers
Upper Ground Floor, 3 Pump Court, Temple, London EC4Y 7AJ, ☎020 7353 0711
✉clerks@3pumpcourt.com
Pump Court Chambers
31 Southgate Street, Winchester, Hampshire SO23 9EB, ☎01962 868 161
✉clerks@3pumpcourt.com
Call Date: Nov 1978, Lincoln's Inn
Pupil Supervisor

MACKENZIE MR ROBERT SUTHERLAND

Middle Temple Lane Chambers
2nd Floor South, 1 Middle Temple Lane, London EC4Y 9AA, ☎020 7583 4352
✉chambers@mtlchambers.com
Call Date: Mar 1996, Gray's Inn
Qualifications: [BA (Hons)(U.C.L.) FSI]

MACKENZIE SMITH MRS CATHERINE JOANNA

10 King's Bench Walk
Ground Floor, 10 King's Bench Walk, Temple, London EC4Y 7EB, ☎020 7353 7742
✉Chambers@10kingsbenchwalk.co.uk
Call Date: Nov 1960, Inner Temple
chambers@10kingsbenchwalk.co.uk, cmslaw@globalnet.co.uk

MACKIE MS JEANNIE

Doughty Street Chambers
53-54 Doughty Street, London WC1N 2LS, ☎020 7404 1313
✉enquiries@doughtystreet.co.uk
Doughty Street Chambers
Pall Mall Court, 61-67 King Street, Manchester M2 4PD, ☎0161 618 1066
Doughty Street Chambers
5th Floor, Broad Quay House, Prince Street, Bristol BS1 4DJ, ☎01179 058 717
Call Date: July 1995, Inner Temple
Qualifications: [BA (Cantab)]

MACKINNON MISS LAURA CATHERINE

9-12 Bell Yard
London WC2A 2JR, ☎020 7400 1800
✉clerks@9-12bellyard.com
Call Date: Oct 2007, Inner Temple
Qualifications: [BA (Oxon)]

MACKINNON MISS LUCY HANNAH

Hailsham Chambers
Ground Floor, 4 Paper Buildings, Temple, London EC4Y 7EX, ☎020 7643 5000
✉clerks@hailshamchambers.com
Call Date: July 2003, Lincoln's Inn
Qualifications: [LLB Hons (Reading)]
lucy.mackinnon@hailshamchambers.com

MACKINNON MR THOMAS JOSEPH

1 Mitre Court Buildings
1 Mitre Court Buildings, Temple, London EC4Y 7BS, ☎020 7452 8900
✉clerks@1mcb.com
Call Date: July 1982, Middle Temple
Pupil Supervisor
Qualifications: [LLB LLM (Sheff)]
tom.mackinnon@1mcb.com

MACKLEY MR DAVID JOHN

18 St John Street
Manchester M3 4EA, ☎0161 278 1800
✉clerks@18sjs.com
Call Date: Oct 1997, Lincoln's Inn
Qualifications: [BA (Hons)(Wales)]
dmackley@18sjs.com

MACKWORTH MS JULIA KATHLEEN

1 Gray's Inn Square
Ground Floor, 1 Gray's Inn Square, London WC1R 5AA, ☎020 7405 0001
Call Date: July 1999, Inner Temple
Qualifications: [BA (Hons) (Dunelm) LLB (Lond)]

MACLACHLAN MRS ESTHER ANNE

The Chambers of Grahame Aldous QC
9 Gough Square, London EC4A 3DG,
☎020 7832 0500
✉clerks@9goughsquare.co.uk
Call Date: July 2005, Middle Temple
Qualifications: [BA (Hons) Leeds PgDip Law (City)]
✉emaclachlan@9goughsquare.co.uk

MACLAREN MISS CATRIONA LONGUEVILLE

Tanfield Chambers
2-5 Warwick Court, London WC1R 5DJ,
☎020 7421 5300
✉clerks@tanfieldchambers.co.uk
Call Date: Oct 1993, Inner Temple
Pupil Supervisor
Qualifications: [MA (Cantab)]
✉cmaclaren@tanfieldchambers.co.uk

Types of work: Discrimination, Employment, Family provision

MACLEAN MR ALAN JOHN QC (2009)

Brick Court Chambers
7-8 Essex Street, London WC2R 3LD,
☎020 7379 3550 ✉clerks@brickcourt.co.uk
Call Date: Oct 1993, Gray's Inn
Pupil Supervisor
Qualifications: [BA (Oxon)]
✉Alan.Maclean@Brickcourt.co.uk

MACLEAN MR KENNETH WALTER QC (2002)

One Essex Court
Ground Floor, One Essex Court, Temple, London EC4Y 9AR, ☎020 7583 2000
✉clerks@oeclaw.co.uk
Call Date: May 1985, Gray's Inn
Qualifications: [MA (Cantab) LLM (Lond)]
✉kmaclean@oeclaw.co.uk

MACLEAN DR NIALL DONALD

12 King's Bench Walk
12 King's Bench Walk, Temple, London EC4Y 7EL, ☎020 7583 0811
Call Date: July 2008, Lincoln's Inn
Qualifications: [BPHIL (Oxon) MA (Glas) DPHIL (Oxon) GOL (Lond)]
✉maclean@12kbw.co.uk

MACLEAN WATT MR HECTOR WILLIAM GRANTHAM

4 Breams Buildings
Chancery Lane, London EC4A 1HP,
☎020 7092 1900 ✉clerks@4bb.co.uk
Call Date: Nov 2006, Middle Temple
Qualifications: [BSc (Bris) PgDip Law]

MACLENNAN MR EDMUND NICHOLAS

25 Bedford Row
London WC1R 4HD, ☎020 7067 1500
✉clerks@25bedfordrow.com
Call Date: Nov 2010, Middle Temple
Qualifications: [BA (Hons) (Oxon)]

MACLEOD MR DAVID ROSS

Chambers of Andrew Mitchell QC
33 Chancery Lane, London WC2A 1EN,
☎020 7440 9950 ✉clerks@33cllaw.com
Call Date: Mar 2010, Lincoln's Inn
Qualifications: [LLB LLM (Dundee) CPE UGLAS]
✉drm@33cl.com

MACLEOD MR DONALD RODERICK

No. 3 Fleet Street Chambers
3 Fleet Street, London EC4Y 1DP,
☎020 7936 4474 ✉clerks@3fleetstreet.com
Temple Court Chambers
2nd Floor, 2 Dr Johnson's Building, Temple, London EC4Y 7AY, ☎020 7353 7888
✉clerks@templecourt.co.uk
Call Date: Mar 2010, Lincoln's Inn
Qualifications: [LLB (Glas)]

MACLEOD MISS ELENA MARY NADEZHDA

1 Garden Court Family Law Chambers
Ground Floor, One Garden Court, Temple, London EC4Y 9BJ, ☎020 7797 7900
✉clerks@1gc.com
Call Date: July 2007, Lincoln's Inn
Qualifications: [LLB (Exon)]
✉macleod@1gc.com

E

MACLEOD MR MURDO ANGUS

Temple Garden Chambers
1 Harcourt Buildings, Temple, London EC4Y 9DA, ☎ 020 7583 1315
✉ clerks@tgchambers.com
Call Date: July 2011, Middle Temple
Qualifications: [LLB (Hons) (Scotalnd)]
✉ mamacleod@tgchambers.com

MACLEOD-JAMES MR NICHOLAS MARK

Chambers of Mr Macleod-James
105 Chanctonbury Way, Woodside Park, London N12 7AA, ☎ 07789 697477
✉ nmj.clientrecall@gmail.com
Call Date: Nov 1986, Lincoln's Inn
Pupil Supervisor
Qualifications: [BA, BSc (Lond)]

MACLYNN MISS CLAIRE LOUISE

4 Brick Court
4 Brick Court, Temple, London EC4Y 9AD, ☎ 020 7832 3200 ✉ clerks@4bc.co.uk
Call Date: July 2001, Gray's Inn
Qualifications: [BA (Oxon)]
✉ louise.maclynn@4bc.co.uk

MACMANUS MISS SABHA

Carmelite Chambers
9 Carmelite Street, London EC4Y 0DR, ☎ 020 7936 6300
✉ clerks@carmelitechambers.co.uk
Call Date: July 2008, Lincoln's Inn
Qualifications: [BA (Lond)]
✉ smacmanus@carmelitechambers.co.uk

MACNAB MR ALEXANDER ANDREW

Monckton Chambers
1 & 2 Raymond Buildings, Gray's Inn, London WC1R 5NR, ☎ 020 7405 7211
✉ chambers@monckton.com
Call Date: July 1986, Middle Temple
Pupil Supervisor
Qualifications: [MA LLM (Cantab)]

Fax: 020 7405 2084;
DX: 257 (Chancery Lane) LDE;
URL: http://www.monckton.com

Types of work: Commercial litigation, Competition law, Excise, Professional negligence, VAT

MACPHAIL MR ANDREW THOMAS

3 PB Barristers
23 Beaumont Street, Oxford OX1 2NP, ☎ 01865 793 736
3 PB Barristers
Royal Talbot House, 2 Victoria Street, Bristol, Avon BS1 6BB, ☎ 0117 928 1520
3 PB Barristers
4 St Peter Street, Winchester SO23 8BW, ☎ 01962 868884
✉ clerks.winchester@3paper.co.uk
3 PB Barristers
3 Paper Buildings, Temple, London EC4Y 7EU, ☎ 020 7583 8055
3 PB Barristers
30 Christchurch Road, Bournemouth, Dorset BH1 3PD, ☎ 01202 292102
✉ clerks.bournemouth@3paper.co.uk
Call Date: Mar 2007, Middle Temple
Qualifications: [MA (Hons) (Edin) PGDL]

MACPHERSON MR ALEXANDER CHARLES BIRKMYRE

Crown Office Chambers
2 Crown Office Row, Temple, London EC4Y 7HJ, ☎ 020 7797 8100
✉ mail@crownofficechambers.com
Call Date: Nov 2000, Middle Temple
Qualifications: [BA (Hons) (Oxon) CPE]
✉ macpherson@crownofficechambers.com

MACPHERSON MR ANGUS JOHN

Temple Garden Chambers
1 Harcourt Buildings, Temple, London EC4Y 9DA, ☎ 020 7583 1315
✉ clerks@tgchambers.com
Call Date: July 1977, Inner Temple
Pupil Supervisor
Qualifications: [MA (Cantab)]
✉ angusmacpherson@tgchambers.com

MACPHERSON MR DUNCAN CHARLES STEWART

One Essex Court
1st Floor, Temple, London EC4Y 9AR, ☎ 020 7936 3030 ✉ clerks@1ec.co.uk
Call Date: May 1994, Middle Temple
Pupil Supervisor
Qualifications: [BA (Hons)]
✉ dmacpherson@1ec.co.uk

MACRO MISS MORWENNA MARGARET

Five Paper
Ground Floor, 5 Paper Buildings, Temple, London EC4Y 7HB, ☎ 020 7815 3200
Call Date: July 2002, Inner Temple
Qualifications: [LLB (Lond)]

MACRORY MR RICHARD BRABAZON

Brick Court Chambers
7-8 Essex Street, London WC2R 3LD,
☎ 020 7379 3550 ✉ clerks@brickcourt.co.uk
Call Date: Nov 1974, Gray's Inn
Qualifications: [MA (Oxon)]

MACWHANNELL MR IAIN

3 PB Barristers
3 Paper Buildings, Temple, London EC4Y 7EU,
☎ 020 7583 8055
Call Date: Mar 2006, Middle Temple
Qualifications: [LLB (Hons) (Reading)]
✉ imw@3pb.co.uk

MADAN MR PANKAJ

Exchange Chambers
Oxford House, Oxford Row, Leeds LS1 3BE,
☎ 0113 203 1970
✉ spencer@exchangechambers.co.uk
Exchange Chambers
One Derby Square, Derby Square, Liverpool L2 9XX, ☎ 0151 236 7747
✉ info@exchangechambers.co.uk
12 King's Bench Walk
12 King's Bench Walk, Temple, London EC4Y 7EL, ☎ 020 7583 0811
Call Date: Oct 1997, Middle Temple
Qualifications: [BA (Hons)(Cantab)]
✉ madan@exchangechambers.co.uk

MADDAN MR ARCHIE GRACIE

5 Pump Court
Ground Floor, 5 Pump Court, Temple, London EC4Y 7AP, ☎ 020 7353 2532
✉ clerks@5pumpcourt.com
Call Date: Nov 1993, Gray's Inn
Pupil Supervisor
Qualifications: [BA (Dunelm)]

MADDEN MR JOHN ANDREW

187 Fleet Street
London EC4A 2AT, ☎ 020 7430 7430
✉ chambers@187fleetstreet.com
Call Date: Oct 1997, Inner Temple
Qualifications: [BSc (Cardiff) CPE BEng (Hons) Dip Law]

MADDERSON MISS NAOMI MARIA

37 Park Square Chambers
37 Park Square, Leeds LS1 2NY,
☎ 0113 243 9422 ✉ chambers@no37.co.uk
Call Date: Oct 2003, Gray's Inn
Qualifications: [LLB Hons (L'pool)]
✉ chambers@no37.co.uk

MADDISON MR DAVID THOMAS JAMES

Cobden House Chambers
19 Quay Street, Manchester M3 3HN,
☎ 0161 833 6000 ✉ Clerks@Cobden.co.uk
Call Date: Oct 1995, Gray's Inn
Qualifications: [LLB]
✉ clerks@cobden.co.uk

MADDISON MR MATTHEW ROSS

Enterprise Chambers
65 Quayside, Newcastle Upon Tyne NE1 3DE,
☎ 0191 222 3344
✉ newcastle@enterprisechambers.com
Enterprise Chambers
43 Park Square, Leeds LS1 2NP,
☎ 0113 246 0391
✉ leeds@enterprisechambers.com
Enterprise Chambers
9 Old Square, Lincoln's Inn, London WC2A 3SR, ☎ 020 7405 9471
✉ london@enterprisechambers.com
Call Date: July 2010, Middle Temple
Qualifications: [LLB (Hons) (Leeds)]
✉ matthewmaddison@enterprisechambers.com

MADDISON MR SIMON NICHOLAS

Call Date: July 2008, Inner Temple
Qualifications: [LLB (B'ham)]
✉ simonmaddison@indiabuildings.co.uk

MADGE-WYLD MR SAMUEL RICHARD

Arden Chambers
20 Bloomsbury Square, London WC1A 2NS,
☎ 020 7242 4244
✉ clerks@ardenchambers.com
Call Date: July 2008, Middle Temple
Qualifications: [BA (Hons) (Sheff) PgDl (Lond)]
✉ sam.madge-wyld@ardenchambers.com

MAGARIAN MR MICHAEL QC (2011)

Tooks Chambers
81 Farringdon Street, London EC4A 4BL,
☎ 020 7842 7575 ✉ clerks@tooks.co.uk
Call Date: July 1988, Gray's Inn
Pupil Supervisor
Qualifications: [BA (Hons) (Cantab)]

E

MAGEE MR MICHAEL JAMES

Fenners Chambers
3 Madingley Road, Cambridge CB3 0EE,
☎01223 368761
✉clerks@fennerschambers.com
Call Date: Oct 1997, Inner Temple
Pupil Supervisor
Qualifications: [MA (Cantab) CPE Dip Law]
✉mike.magee@fennerschambers.com

MAGEE MISS ROSEIN MOIRA

Pallant Chambers
12 North Pallant, Chichester, West Sussex
PO19 1TQ, ☎01243 784538
✉clerks@pallantchambers.co.uk
Call Date: Oct 1994, Gray's Inn
Qualifications: [BA (Hons)(Keele)]
✉clerks@pallantchambers.co.uk

MAGEE MR SAMUEL CAIRNS

2 Bedford Row
London WC1R 4BU, ☎020 7440 8888
✉clerks@2bedfordrow.co.uk
Call Date: July 2003, Inner Temple
Qualifications: [LLB]
✉smagee@2bedfordrow.co.uk

E

MAGENNIS MISS OLIVIA ANNE

5 Pump Court
Ground Floor, 5 Pump Court, Temple, London
EC4Y 7AP, ☎020 7353 2532
✉clerks@5pumpcourt.com
Call Date: Mar 2005, Lincoln's Inn
Qualifications: [BA (Hons) Cantab]
✉oliviamagennis@5pumpcourt.com

MAGGS MR NICHOLAS PETER

Thomas More Chambers
7 Lincoln's Inn Fields, London WC2A 3BP,
☎020 7404 7000
✉clerks@thomasmore.co.uk
Call Date: July 2006, Middle Temple
Qualifications: [BA (Hons) PGDL]
✉nmaggs@thomasmore.co.uk

MAGGS MR PATRICK TERENCE

15 New Bridge Street
London EC4V 6AU, ☎020 7842 1900
✉clerks@15nbs.com
Call Date: Oct 1996, Inner Temple
Qualifications: [BA (Exon) CPE (Lond)]
✉patrick.maggs@15nbs.com

MAGINN MISS OLIVIA MARIA

New Walk Chambers
27 New Walk, Leicester, Leicestershire
LE1 6TE, ☎0871 200 1298 / 0116 255 9144
✉clerks@newwalkchambers.co.uk
Call Date: July 1998, Lincoln's Inn
Qualifications: [LLB (Hons)]

MAGUIRE MR ANDREW JAMES

St Philips Chambers
55 Temple Row, Birmingham B2 5LS,
☎0121 246 7000 ✉clerks@st-philips.com
Exchange Chambers
One Derby Square, Derby Square, Liverpool
L2 9XX, ☎0151 236 7747
✉info@exchangechambers.co.uk
Exchange Chambers
7 Ralli Courts, West Riverside, Manchester
M3 5FT, ☎0161 833 2722
Call Date: Nov 1988, Inner Temple
Qualifications: [LLB (Hons) (Hull)]
✉amaguire@st-philips.com

MAGUIRE MS CLODAGH MARY

Call Date: Nov 2003, Inner Temple
Qualifications: [BSc (Salford)]

MAGUIRE MR MARTIN BENN

QEB Hollis Whiteman
1-2 Laurence Pountney Hill, London
EC4R 0EU, ☎020 7933 8855
✉barristers@qebhw.co.uk
Call Date: Nov 1994, Inner Temple
Qualifications: [BA (Hons) MA]
✉benn.maguire@qebhw.co.uk

MAGUIRE MR STEPHEN ARTHUR

Kings Chambers
36 Young Street, Manchester M3 3FT,
☎0845 034 3444
✉clerks@kingschambers.com
Kings Chambers
5 Park Square East, Leeds LS1 2NE,
☎0845 034 3444
✉clerks@kingschambers.com
Kings Chambers
Embassy House, 60 Church Street,
Birmingham B3 2DJ, ☎0845 034 3444
✉clerks@kingschambers.com
Call Date: Mar 2007, Inner Temple
Qualifications: [LLB (Lancs)]
✉smaguire@kingschambers.com

MAHER MS MARTHA JOHANNA DOROTHY

St John's Chambers
101 Victoria Street, Bristol BS1 6PU,
☎0117 923 4700
✉clerks@stjohnschambers.co.uk
Call Date: Nov 1987, Inner Temple
Qualifications: [BCL LLM (Cantab) LLB (Cork)]
✉martha.maher@stjohnschambers.co.uk

MAHER MR MICHAEL JAMES

Exchange Chambers
7 Ralli Courts, West Riverside, Manchester M3 5FT, ☎0161 833 2722
Exchange Chambers
One Derby Square, Derby Square, Liverpool L2 9XX, ☎0151 236 7747
✉info@exchangechambers.co.uk
Exchange Chambers
Oxford House, Oxford Row, Leeds LS1 3BE,
☎0113 203 1970
✉spencer@exchangechambers.co.uk
Nine Bedford Row
9 Bedford Row, London WC1R 4AZ,
☎020 7489 2727
✉clerks@9bedfordrow.co.uk
Call Date: Nov 1995, Gray's Inn
Qualifications: [BA (Dunelm) LLM (Edin)]
✉maher@exchangechambers.co.uk

MAHMOOD MR ABID

No5 Chambers
Fountain Court, Steelhouse Lane, Birmingham B4 6DR, ☎0845 210 5555 ✉info@no5.com
No5 Chambers
Greenwood House, 4-7 Salisbury Court, London EC4Y 8AA, ☎0845 210 5555
No5 Chambers
38 Queen Square, Bristol BS1 4QS,
☎0845 210 5555
Central Chambers
89 Princess Street, Manchester M1 4HT,
☎0161 236 1133
✉clerks@centralchambers.co.uk
Call Date: Nov 1992, Inner Temple
Pupil Supervisor
Qualifications: [LLB (Hons)]
✉ama@no5.com

MAHMOOD MR GHAZAN

St Johns Buildings
24a - 28 St John Street, Manchester M3 4DJ,
☎0161 214 1500
✉clerk@stjohnsbuildings.co.uk
16 Winckley Square
Preston PR1 3JJ, ☎01772 256100
St Johns Buildings Liverpool
8th Floor India Buildings, Water Street, Liverpool L2 0XG, ☎0151 243 6000
✉clerk@stjohnsbuildings.co.uk
Call Date: Oct 1997, Inner Temple
Qualifications: [LLB (Brunel)]
✉clerk@stjohnsbuildings.co.uk, ghazan100@hotmail.com

MAHMOOD MR IMRAN WASEEM

5 Pump Court
Ground Floor, 5 Pump Court, Temple, London EC4Y 7AP, ☎020 7353 2532
✉clerks@5pumpcourt.com
Call Date: July 1992, Middle Temple
Pupil Supervisor
Qualifications: [LLB (Hons)]
✉imranmahmood@5pumpcourt.com

MAHMOOD MRS SALEEMA BIBI

Carmelite Chambers
9 Carmelite Street, London EC4Y 0DR,
☎020 7936 6300
✉clerks@carmelitechambers.co.uk
Call Date: Nov 1999, Gray's Inn
Qualifications: [LLB (Sheff)]
✉smahmood@carmelitechambers.co.uk

MAHMUD MR SAAMIR

6 King's Bench Walk
Ground Floor, 6 King's Bench Walk, Temple, London EC4Y 7DR, ☎020 7583 0410
✉clerks@6kbw.com
Principal Chambers
15 Lime Tree Walk, Sevenoaks, Kent TN13 1YH, ☎0845 209 8080
Call Date: July 1996, Lincoln's Inn
Qualifications: [MPhil (Cantab) BA (Oxon) LLM (SOAS)]

MAHMUTAJ MS KLENTIANA

18 Red Lion Court
London EC4A 3EB, ☎020 7520 6000
✉chambers@18rlc.co.uk
Call Date: Nov 2005, Middle Temple
Qualifications: [LLB (Hons) (Leic) LLM (Lond)]

E

MAHTAB MISS SUMITA LAILA-AL

7 Bell Yard
London WC2A 2JR, ☎ 020 7831 0636
✉ kevintarrant@btconnect.com
Call Date: July 2001, Gray's Inn
Pupil Supervisor
Qualifications: [LLB]
sumitamahtab@hotmail.com

MAILER MR CLIFFORD ROWLAND

Goldsmith Chambers
Ground Floor, Goldsmith Building, Temple, London EC4Y 7BL, ☎ 020 7353 6802
✉ clerks@goldsmithchambers.com
Call Date: July 1987, Middle Temple
Pupil Supervisor
Qualifications: [BA LLB (Cantab) LLM (USA) LLB (South Africa)]
C.Mailer@goldsmithchambers.law.co.uk

MAINDS MR ALLAN GILFILLAN

36 Bedford Row
London WC1R 4JH, ☎ 020 7421 8000
✉ chambers@36bedfordrow.co.uk
Call Date: Feb 1977, Inner Temple
Pupil Supervisor, Recorder

MAINWARING MR HENRY

Clerksroom (Taunton)
Equity House, Administration Centre, Blackbrook Park Avenue, Taunton, Somerset TA1 2PX, ☎ 0845 083 3000
✉ mail@clerksroom.com
64 Bridge Street
3rd Floor, 64 Bridge Street, Manchester M3 3BN, ☎ 0845 083 3000
✉ mail@64bridgestreet.com
Clerksroom (London)
3rd Floor, 218 Strand, London WC2R 1AT, ☎ 0845 083 3000 ✉ mail@clerksroom.com
Call Date: Nov 2001, Lincoln's Inn
Qualifications: [BA (Hons) CPE]
Mainwaring@clerksroom.com

MAINWARING MR ROBERT PAUL CLASON

Portal Chambers
Blaencwm Mawr, Llandysul SA44 5NS, ☎ 01559 395 292
Call Date: Nov 1996, Gray's Inn
Qualifications: [LLM (Bris)]
Pm@portalchambers.co.uk

MAIRS MR ROBIN GORDON JAMES

St Paul's Chambers
5th Floor, St Paul's House, 23 Park Square South, Leeds LS1 2ND, ☎ 0113 245 5866
Call Date: Oct 1992, Gray's Inn
Pupil Supervisor
Qualifications: [LLB (Hons) LLM (Cantab)]
rgm@stpaulschambers.com

MAITLAND MR ANDREW HENRY REAVELY

King's Bench and Godolphin (KBG)Chambers
115 North Hill, Plymouth, Devon PL4 8JY, ☎ 01752 221551
✉ clerks@kbgchambers.co.uk
Call Date: July 1970, Lincoln's Inn
Pupil Supervisor, Recorder
Qualifications: [LLB (St Andrews)]
andrew.maitland@kingsbenchchambers.co.uk

MAITLAND MR MARC CLAUDE

King's Bench Chambers
Wellington House, 175 Holdenhurst Road, Bournemouth, Dorset BH8 8DQ, ☎ 01202 250025
Call Date: July 1988, Middle Temple
Qualifications: [LLB (Hons) LLM (Cantab)]

MAITLAND JONES MR MARK GRIFFITH

13 King's Bench Walk
13 King's Bench Walk, Temple, London EC4Y 7EN, ☎ 020 7353 7204
✉ clerks@13kbw.co.uk
13 KBW
32 Beaumont Street, Oxford OX1 2NP, ☎ 01865 311066 ✉ clerks@13kbw.co.uk
Call Date: Nov 1986, Middle Temple
Pupil Supervisor
Qualifications: [MA (Edin) DipLaw (Lond)]

MAITRA MR ADRIAN DILIP

Park Lane Plowden
Lombard House, 4-8 Lombard Street, Newcastle Upon Tyne NE1 3AE, ☎ 0191 211 4087
✉ clerks@parklaneplowden.co.uk
Call Date: May 1997, Gray's Inn
Qualifications: [LLB (Northumbria)]
adrian.maitra@parklaneplowden.co.uk

E

MAJUMDAR MR SHANTANU

Radcliffe Chambers
Ground Floor, 11 New Square, Lincoln's Inn, London WC2A 3QB, ☎020 7831 0081
✉clerks@radcliffechambers.com
Call Date: Nov 1992, Middle Temple
Pupil Supervisor
Qualifications: [BA (Hons)]

MAKA MR ISAAC

4 King's Bench Walk
2nd Floor, 4 King's Bench Walk, Temple, London EC4Y 7DL, ☎020 7822 7000
✉clerks@4kbw.co.uk
Chambers of Mr Isaac Maka
102 Thorold Road, Ilford, Essex IG1 4EX, ☎07973 308 301 ✉isaacmaka@hotmail.com
Call Date: Oct 1998, Lincoln's Inn
Pupil Supervisor
Qualifications: [LLB (Hons)(Manc) Dip Law (ICSL) LLM (Nott)]

MAKEPEACE MR PETER ANTHONY

Dere Street Barristers
14 Toft Green, York YO1 6JT, ☎0844 3351551
✉clerks@derestreet.co.uk
York Chambers
Rotterdam House, 116 The Quayside, Newcastle Upon Tyne NE1 3DY, ☎0191 206 4677
Call Date: July 1988, Lincoln's Inn
Pupil Supervisor
Qualifications: [LLB (Hons) (Wales)]
🖃clerks@yorkchambers.co.uk

MAKEY MR CHRISTOPHER DOUGLAS

Old Square Chambers
10-11 Bedford Row, London WC1R 4BU, ☎020 7269 0300 ✉clerks@oldsquare.co.uk
Old Square Chambers
3 Orchard Court, St Augustine's Yard, Bristol BS1 5DP, ☎0117 930 5100
✉clerks@oldsquare.co.uk
Call Date: July 1975, Middle Temple
Pupil Supervisor, Recorder
Qualifications: [LLB ACIArb]
🖃makey@oldsquare.co.uk

MALAM MR JAMES THOMAS

St Johns Buildings
24a - 28 St John Street, Manchester M3 4DJ, ☎0161 214 1500
✉clerk@stjohnsbuildings.co.uk
St Johns Buildings
21 White Friars, Chester CH1 1NZ, ☎01244 323070
✉clerk@stjohnsbuildings.co.uk
16 Winckley Square
Preston PR1 3JJ, ☎01772 256100
Call Date: July 2002, Gray's Inn
Qualifications: [LLB (Sheff)]

MALCOLM MR ALASTAIR RICHARD QC (1996)

1 Paper Buildings
1st Floor, 1 Paper Buildings, Temple, London EC4Y 7EP, ☎020 7353 3728
✉clerks@onepaper.co.uk
Call Date: Feb 1971, Inner Temple
Recorder
Qualifications: [BA (Oxon)]
🖃alastairmalcolm@onepaper.co.uk

MALCOLM MISS HELEN KATHARINE LUCY QC (2006)

3 Raymond Buildings
3 Raymond Buildings, Gray's Inn, London WC1R 5BH, ☎020 7400 6400
✉clerks@3rblaw.com
Call Date: Nov 1986, Gray's Inn
Recorder
Qualifications: [MA (Oxon)]

MALCOLM MISS ROSALIND NIVEN

Guildford Chambers
Stoke House, Leapale Lane, Guildford, Surrey GU1 4LY, ☎01483 539131
✉clerks@guildfordchambers.co.uk
Call Date: July 1977, Middle Temple
Qualifications: [LLB (Lond)]

MALE MR JOHN MARTIN QC (2000)

Landmark Chambers
180 Fleet Street, London EC4A 2HG, ☎020 7430 1221
✉clerks@landmarkchambers.co.uk
Call Date: July 1976, Lincoln's Inn
Qualifications: [BA (Cantab)]
🖃jmale@landmarkchambers.co.uk

MALECKA DR MARY MARGARET

Chambers of Dr Mary Malecka
Box 365, 43 Bedford Street, Westminster, London WC2E 9HA, ☎07973 425313
✉DRMARYM@TALK21.COM
Call Date: Oct 1994, Inner Temple
Qualifications: [BA (USA) PGCE (Leic) PhD (Notts) CPE (Lond)]
🖃drmarym@talk21.com

E

MALEK MR ALI QC (1996)

3 Verulam Buildings
London WC1R 5NT, ☎ 020 7831 8441
✉ chambers@3vb.com
Call Date: July 1980, Gray's Inn
Recorder
Qualifications: [MA BCL (Oxon)]
✉ am@3vb.com

MALEK MR MEHDI (HODGE) QC (1999)

4-5 Gray's Inn Square
Gray's Inn, London WC1R 5AH,
☎ 020 7404 5252 ✉ clerks@4-5.co.uk
Call Date: July 1983, Gray's Inn
Recorder
Qualifications: [MA BCL (Oxon)]
✉ hmalek@4-5.co.uk

MALES MR STEPHEN MARTIN QC (1998)

20 Essex Street
London WC2R 3AL, ☎ 020 7842 1200
✉ clerks@20essexst.com
Call Date: July 1978, Middle Temple
Recorder
Qualifications: [MA (Cantab) CEDR]
✉ clerks@20essexst.com

MALEY MR WILLIAM RAYMOND

25 Bedford Row
London WC1R 4HD, ☎ 020 7067 1500
✉ clerks@25bedfordrow.com
Call Date: July 1982, Gray's Inn
Qualifications: [LLB (Warw)]
✉ bmaley@25bedfordrow.com

MALHOTRA MISS MEHTAB ROSHAN

12 Old Square Chambers
1st Floor, 12 Old Square, Lincoln's Inn,
London WC2A 3TX, ☎ 020 7404 0875
✉ clerks@12oldsquare.com
Call Date: Oct 1996, Lincoln's Inn
Qualifications: [LLB (Hons)(Lond) LLM (Lond)]

MALHOTRA MISS PRIYA

25 Bedford Row
London WC1R 4HD, ☎ 020 7067 1500
✉ clerks@25bedfordrow.com
Call Date: July 2007, Inner Temple
Qualifications: [BA (Sheff)]
✉ pmalhotra@25bedfordrow.com

MALIK MR AFTAB

Holborn Chambers
6 Gate Street, Lincoln's Inn Fields, London
WC2A 3HP, ☎ 020 7242 6060
Call Date: Oct 2010, Lincoln's Inn
Qualifications: [LLB LLM (B'ham)]

MALIK MR AHMED ABDUL

Clapham Law Chambers
85 Landor Road, Clapham North, London
SW9 9RT, ☎ 020 7978 8482
✉ DANNY@claphamlawchambers.co.uk
Chambers of Ahmed A Malik
243a Whitechapel Road, London E1 1DB,
☎ 020 7978 8482/020 7642 5777
Call Date: Nov 2008, Gray's Inn
✉ malik@claphamlawchambers.co.uk

MALIK MR AMJAD RAZA QC (2010)

36 Bedford Row
London WC1R 4JH, ☎ 020 7421 8000
✉ chambers@36bedfordrow.co.uk
Call Date: Nov 1987, Lincoln's Inn
Pupil Supervisor
Qualifications: [LLM (Lond) BA]
✉ amalik@36bedfordroad.co.uk

MALIK MR OMAR LATIF

12 College Place
Fauvelle Buildings, 12 College Place,
Southampton SO15 2FE, ☎ 023 8032 0320
✉ clerks@12cp.co.uk
Call Date: Nov 1990, Inner Temple
Qualifications: [LLB (So'ton)]

MALIK MISS SARAH

Hardwicke
New Square, Lincoln's Inn, London
WC2A 3SB, ☎ 020 7242 2523
✉ enquiries@hardwicke.co.uk
Call Date: Nov 1999, Lincoln's Inn
Pupil Supervisor
Qualifications: [LLB (Hons)(Manch)]
✉ sarah.malik@hardwicke.co.uk

MALIK MR ZULQARNAIN AKBAR

12 Old Square Chambers
1st Floor, 12 Old Square, Lincoln's Inn,
London WC2A 3TX, ☎ 020 7404 0875
✉ clerks@12oldsquare.com
Call Date: July 2007, Lincoln's Inn
Qualifications: [LLB (Lond)]

MALINS MR JULIAN HENRY QC (1991)

Malins Chambers
115 Temple Chambers, Temple Avenue, London EC4Y 0DA, ☎020 7353 8868
✉malins@btinternet.com
Call Date: July 1972, Middle Temple
Qualifications: [MA (Oxon)]
malins@btinternet.com

MALLALIEU MR ROGER NICHOLAS

Four New Square
Four New Square, Lincoln's Inn, London WC2A 3RJ, ☎020 7822 2000
✉barristers@4newsquare.com
Call Date: Nov 1998, Middle Temple
Qualifications: [LLB (Hons)(N'castle)]

MALLENDER MR PAUL NIGEL

2-3 Hind Court Chambers
2-3 Hind Court, Fleet Street, London EC4A 3DL, ☎020 7822 2150
✉david@2-3hindcourt.com
Call Date: Nov 1974, Lincoln's Inn
Pupil Supervisor
Qualifications: [LLB (Lond)]

MALLETT MISS SARAH JANE VICTORIA

KBW
The Engine House, No 1 Foundry Square, Leeds LS11 5DL, ☎0113 297 1200
✉clerks@kbwchambers.com
Call Date: Nov 1988, Inner Temple
Pupil Supervisor
Qualifications: [BA (Dunelm)]
svm@kbwchambers.com

MALLETT MR SIMON JEREMY

KBW
The Engine House, No 1 Foundry Square, Leeds LS11 5DL, ☎0113 297 1200
✉clerks@kbwchambers.com
Call Date: July 1986, Inner Temple
Pupil Supervisor
Qualifications: [LLB (Sheff)]
sm@kbwchambers.com

MALLICK MISS NABILA HANI

No5 Chambers
Greenwood House, 4-7 Salisbury Court, London EC4Y 8AA, ☎0845 210 5555
No5 Chambers
38 Queen Square, Bristol BS1 4QS, ☎0845 210 5555
No5 Chambers
Fountain Court, Steelhouse Lane, Birmingham B4 6DR, ☎0845 210 5555 ✉info@no5.com
Call Date: Nov 1992, Gray's Inn
Qualifications: [LLB (Lond) LLM]
nma@no5.com

MALLIN MR MAXWELL JAMES

11 Stone Buildings
11 Stone Buildings, Lincoln's Inn, London WC2A 3TG, ☎020 7831 6381
✉clerks@11sb.com
Call Date: Oct 1993, Inner Temple
Pupil Supervisor
Qualifications: [MA (Cantab) CPE (Coventry)]
mallin@11sb.com

MALLINCKRODT MISS SOPHIE

3 Verulam Buildings
London WC1R 5NT, ☎020 7831 8441
✉chambers@3vb.com
Call Date: July 1999, Lincoln's Inn
Pupil Supervisor
Qualifications: [MA]
smallinckrodt@3vb.com

MALLISON MISS CATHERINE MARY HELEN

4 King's Bench Walk
2nd Floor, 4 King's Bench Walk, Temple, London EC4Y 7DL, ☎020 7822 7000
✉clerks@4kbw.co.uk
Call Date: Nov 1974, Middle Temple
Pupil Supervisor
kmm@4kbw.co.uk

MALLON MISS JOANNA

Number 7 Harrington Street Chambers
7 Harrington Street, Liverpool L2 9YH, ☎0151 242 0707 ✉clerks@7hs.co.uk
Call Date: Oct 1996, Lincoln's Inn
Qualifications: [BA (Hons)(Dunelm) Law Dip (Chester)]
joanna.mallon@7hs.co.uk

MALLORY MISS KATHRINE LUCY

9 St John Street
Manchester M3 4DN, ☎0161 955 9000
✉civilclerks@9sjs.com / criminalclerks@9sjs.com
Call Date: Oct 1998, Inner Temple
Qualifications: [BA (Hons) (Leeds) CPE]

E

MALONE MR DAVID JOHN

1 Gray's Inn Square
Ground Floor, 1 Gray's Inn Square, London WC1R 5AA, ☎ 020 7405 0001
Call Date: Oct 1998, Gray's Inn
Pupil Supervisor
Qualifications: [BSc (Hons) (Sheffield) Dip Law (City)]
dmalone@1gis.co.uk

MALONE MISS DEIRDRE EMILIE

Garden Court Chambers
57-60 Lincoln's Inn Fields, London WC2A 3LJ, ☎ 020 7993 7600 ✉ info@gclaw.co.uk
Call Date: Oct 2006, Middle Temple
Qualifications: [LLB (Hons) (Dublin)]
deirdrem@gclaw.co.uk

MALONE MR GERALD FERGUS

Farringdon Chambers
180 Bermondsey Street, London SE1 3TQ, ☎ 020 7089 5700
Call Date: Nov 1998, Inner Temple
Qualifications: [LLB (Hull) LLM]
fergusmalone@farringdon-law.co.uk

MALONE MR MICHAEL JULIAN

One Essex Court
Ground Floor, One Essex Court, Temple, London EC4Y 9AR, ☎ 020 7583 2000
✉ clerks@oeclaw.co.uk
Call Date: Nov 1975, Gray's Inn
Pupil Supervisor
Qualifications: [BA]
mmalone@oeclaw.co.uk

MALTZ MR BEN DANIEL

Five Paper
Ground Floor, 5 Paper Buildings, Temple, London EC4Y 7HB, ☎ 020 7815 3200
Call Date: Oct 1998, Lincoln's Inn
Pupil Supervisor
Qualifications: [LLB (Lond)]
benmaltz@fivepaper.com

MALYNICZ MR SIMON SPIRO

Three New Square IP
3 New Square, Lincoln's Inn, London WC2A 3RS, ☎ 020 7405 1111
✉ clerks@3newsquare.co.uk
Call Date: Oct 1997, Inner Temple
Pupil Supervisor
Qualifications: [BA LLB (Lond) MA]

MANASSE DR PAUL REUBEN

18 St John Street
Manchester M3 4EA, ☎ 0161 278 1800
✉ clerks@18sjs.com
Call Date: Oct 1995, Gray's Inn
Pupil Supervisor
Qualifications: [B.Sc Ph.D (L'pool)]

MANBY MISS PHILIPPA EVE

Four New Square
Four New Square, Lincoln's Inn, London WC2A 3RJ, ☎ 020 7822 2000
✉ barristers@4newsquare.com
Call Date: Oct 2010, Lincoln's Inn
Qualifications: [BA (Oxon)]
p.manby@4newsquare.com

MANDALIA MR VINESH LALJI

St Philips Chambers
55 Temple Row, Birmingham B2 5LS, ☎ 0121 246 7000 ✉ clerks@st-philips.com
Call Date: Oct 1997, Inner Temple
Qualifications: [LLB (Hons)]
vmandalia@st-philips.com

MANDEL MR RICHARD

4 Breams Buildings
Chancery Lane, London EC4A 1HP, ☎ 020 7092 1900 ✉ clerks@4bb.co.uk
Call Date: July 1972, Gray's Inn
Pupil Supervisor
Qualifications: [MA BCL (Oxon)]

MANDER MR CHARLES MARCUS SEPTIMUS GUSTAV

7 King's Bench Walk
Ground Floor, 7 King's Bench Walk, Temple, London EC4Y 7DS, ☎ 020 7910 8300
✉ clerks@7kbw.co.uk
Call Date: Mar 2005, Middle Temple
Qualifications: [MA CPE LPC]
mmander@7kbw.co.uk

MANGAT DR TEJINA KIRAN

Hailsham Chambers
Ground Floor, 4 Paper Buildings, Temple, London EC4Y 7EX, ☎ 020 7643 5000
✉ clerks@hailshamchambers.com
Call Date: Oct 1990, Middle Temple
Qualifications: [BSc MBBS (Lond)]
tejina.mangat@hailshamchambers.com

MANKAU MRS LOUISE

Tanfield Chambers
2-5 Warwick Court, London WC1R 5DJ,
☎ 020 7421 5300
✉ clerks@tanfieldchambers.co.uk
Call Date: Nov 2005, Lincoln's Inn
Qualifications: [LLB Edinburgh]
✉ louisemankau@tanfieldchambers.co.uk

MANKNELL MR DAVID PETER

1 Crown Office Row
1 Crown Office Row, Temple, London
EC4Y 7HH, ☎ 020 7797 7500
✉ mail@1cor.com
Call Date: Oct 2001, Middle Temple
Pupil Supervisor
Qualifications: [BA (Hons) (Oxon) BCL(Oxon)]
✉ david.manknell@1cor.com

MANLEY MR DAVID ERIC QC (2003)

Kings Chambers
36 Young Street, Manchester M3 3FT,
☎ 0845 034 3444
✉ clerks@kingschambers.com
Kings Chambers
5 Park Square East, Leeds LS1 2NE,
☎ 0845 034 3444
✉ clerks@kingschambers.com
Kings Chambers
Embassy House, 60 Church Street,
Birmingham B3 2DJ, ☎ 0845 034 3444
✉ clerks@kingschambers.com
Call Date: July 1981, Inner Temple
Recorder
Qualifications: [BA (Hons) (Leeds)]
✉ dmanley@kingschambers.com

MANLEY MS HILARY

St Paul's Chambers
5th Floor, St Paul's House, 23 Park Square
South, Leeds LS1 2ND, ☎ 0113 245 5866
16 Winckley Square
Preston PR1 3JJ, ☎ 01772 256100
Call Date: Nov 1996, Gray's Inn
Qualifications: [LLB (Lond)]

MANLEY MISS LESLEY PATRICA

Chambers of Marion Smullen and Kerim Fuad QC
1 Inner Temple Lane, London EC4Y 1AF,
☎ 020 7427 4400 ✉ clerks@1itl.com
Call Date: Nov 1983, Middle Temple
Pupil Supervisor
Qualifications: [BA (L'pool)]
✉ Lesley.Manley@1ITL.com

MANLEY MR OLIVER JAMES

30 Park Place
Cardiff CF10 3BS, ☎ 029 2039 8421
✉ clerks@30parkplace.law.co.uk
Call Date: July 2005, Gray's Inn
Qualifications: [BA]
✉ om2005@30parkplace.co.uk

MANN MR CHRISTOPHER

13 King's Bench Walk
13 King's Bench Walk, Temple, London
EC4Y 7EN, ☎ 020 7353 7204
✉ clerks@13kbw.co.uk
13 KBW
32 Beaumont Street, Oxford OX1 2NP,
☎ 01865 311066 ✉ clerks@13kbw.co.uk
Call Date: Oct 1998, Lincoln's Inn
Pupil Supervisor
Qualifications: [BA (Hons)(Oxon)]
✉ cmann@13kbw.co.uk

MANN MISS DAYA LUCIENNE CATHERINE

Southernhay Chambers
33 Southernhay East, Exeter EX1 1NX,
☎ 01392 255777
✉ clerks@southernhaychambers.co.uk
Call Date: Feb 1995, Lincoln's Inn
Qualifications: [BA (Hons)(Lond) Dip Law CPE]
✉ d.mann@southernhaychambers.co.uk

MANN MR JASVIR SINGH

No5 Chambers
Fountain Court, Steelhouse Lane, Birmingham
B4 6DR, ☎ 0845 210 5555 ✉ info@no5.com
No5 Chambers
Greenwood House, 4-7 Salisbury Court,
London EC4Y 8AA, ☎ 0845 210 5555
No5 Chambers
38 Queen Square, Bristol BS1 4QS,
☎ 0845 210 5555
Call Date: Nov 2001, Middle Temple
Qualifications: [LLB (Hons)(Manch)]
✉ jm@no5.com

MANN MR JONATHAN SIMON

25 Bedford Row
London WC1R 4HD, ☎ 020 7067 1500
✉ clerks@25bedfordrow.com
Call Date: Nov 1989, Inner Temple
Qualifications: [LLB (Hons)(Essex)]

E

MANN MR MARTIN EDWARD QC (1983)

XXIV Old Buildings
Ground Floor, 24 Old Buildings, Lincoln's Inn, London WC2A 3UP, ☎ 020 7691 2424
✉ clerks@xxiv.co.uk
Call Date: July 1968, Gray's Inn
✉ martin.mann@xxiv.co.uk

MANN MR PAUL QC (2002)

1 High Pavement
Nottingham NG1 1HF, ☎ 0115 941 8218
✉ clerks@1highpavement.co.uk
Call Date: Nov 1980, Gray's Inn
Recorder
Qualifications: [BA]
✉ paulamannQC@1highpavement.co.uk

MANN MISS REBECCA CLAIRE

Pendragon Chambers
Suite 7, J Shed, Kings Road, SA1 Waterfront, Swansea SA1 8PL, ☎ 01792 411188
✉ clerks@pendragonchambers.com
Call Date: Oct 1995, Lincoln's Inn
Pupil Supervisor
Qualifications: [LLB (Hons)(Leic)]
✉ rebeccamann@pendragonchambers.com

MANN MISS SARA ANGELA

Call Date: Nov 1994, Middle Temple
Qualifications: [LLB (Hons)]
✉ thesaipes@tiscali.co.uk, sara.mann@stjohnsbuildings.co.uk

MANNAN MR CHARLES MADANI FUAD

Temple Court Chambers
2nd Floor, 2 Dr Johnson's Building, Temple, London EC4Y 7AY, ☎ 020 7353 7888
✉ clerks@templecourt.co.uk
Call Date: Nov 1993, Lincoln's Inn
Pupil Supervisor
Qualifications: [BSc (Econ) (Hons)]
✉ charlesmannan@templecourt.co.uk

MANNERING MR STEPHEN JAMES MARION

St Mary's Family Law Chambers
26-28 High Pavement, The Lace Market, Nottingham NG1 1HN, ☎ 0115 950 3503
✉ clerks@stmarysflc.co.uk
Call Date: Nov 2011, Gray's Inn
✉ Stephen.mannering@stmarysflc.co.uk

MANNING MR COLIN

Littleton Chambers
3 King's Bench Walk North, Temple, London EC4Y 7HR, ☎ 020 7797 8600
✉ fschneider@littletonchambers.co.uk
Call Date: July 1970, Gray's Inn
Pupil Supervisor, Recorder
Qualifications: [LLB]

MANNING MR JAMES EDWARD

Nexus Chambers
7 New Square, Lincolns Inn, London WC2A 3QS,
☎ 020 7404 1147 / 020 7831 8309
✉ info@nexuschambers.com
Call Date: Nov 2008, Middle Temple
Qualifications: [MA (Hons) (Cantab) BA (Cantab) MPhil (Cantab)]

MANNING MR JONATHAN DAVID GRANT

Arden Chambers
20 Bloomsbury Square, London WC1A 2NS, ☎ 020 7242 4244
✉ clerks@ardenchambers.com
Call Date: July 1989, Inner Temple
Pupil Supervisor
Qualifications: [MA (Cantab)]
✉ jonathan.manning@ardenchambers.com

MANNING MISS RUTH MARGARET HAYES

No 8 Chambers
8 Fountain Court, Steelhouse Lane, Birmingham B4 6DR, ☎ 0121 236 5514
✉ clerks@no8chambers.co.uk
Call Date: Oct 1993, Gray's Inn
Qualifications: [LLB (Hons)]

MANNION MS AMY ELISABETH

9-12 Bell Yard
London WC2A 2JR, ☎ 020 7400 1800
✉ clerks@9-12bellyard.com
1 Crown Office Row
1 Crown Office Row, Temple, London EC4Y 7HH, ☎ 020 7797 7500
✉ mail@1cor.com
Call Date: Oct 2003, Inner Temple
Qualifications: [BSc (LSE) CPE]
✉ a.mannion@9-12bellyard.com

MANNION MR JOHN DENNIS

Tolzey Chambers
37 Rowlandson Gardens, Lockleaze, Bristol BS7 9UH
Call Date: May 1987, Middle Temple
Pupil Supervisor
Qualifications: [LLM LLB (Hons)]

MANSELL MR JASON FRANCIS GUY

Seven Bedford Row
7 Bedford Row, London WC1R 4BS,
☎ 020 7242 3555 ✉ clerks@7br.co.uk
Call Date: Oct 1991, Lincoln's Inn
Qualifications: [LLB (Hons) (B'ham)]
✉ jmansell@7br.co.uk

MANSELL MR RICHARD AUSTIN QC (2009)

Broadway House Chambers
Broadway House, 9 Bank Street, Bradford, West Yorkshire BD1 1TW, ☎ 01274 722560
✉ clerks@broadwayhouse.co.uk
Broadway House Chambers
25 Park Square West, Leeds, West Yorkshire LS1 2PW, ☎ 0113 246 2600
✉ clerks@broadwayhouse.co.uk
Call Date: Oct 1991, Gray's Inn
Recorder
Qualifications: [LLB (Hons)(Leeds)]

MANSFIELD MR BENJAMIN ELLIOT

KCH Garden Square
1 Oxford Street, Nottingham NG1 5BH,
☎ 0115 941 8851
✉ clerks@kchgardensquare.co.uk
Call Date: Nov 2005, Inner Temple
Qualifications: [BSc London School of Economics & Political Scienc]
✉ bmansfield@kingstreetchambers.com

MANSFIELD MR GAVIN HARRISON

Littleton Chambers
3 King's Bench Walk North, Temple, London EC4Y 7HR, ☎ 020 7797 8600
✉ fschneider@littletonchambers.co.uk
Call Date: Nov 1992, Middle Temple
Pupil Supervisor
Qualifications: [MA (Hons)(Cantab)]
✉ gmansfield@littletonchambers.co.uk

MANSFIELD MR GUY RHYS JOHN QC (1994)

1 Crown Office Row
1 Crown Office Row, Temple, London EC4Y 7HH, ☎ 020 7797 7500
✉ mail@1cor.com
Call Date: Nov 1972, Middle Temple
Recorder
Qualifications: [MA (Oxon)]
✉ guy.mansfield@1cor.com

MANSFIELD MISS KATHRINE JANE

Charter Chambers
33 John Street, London WC1N 2AT,
☎ 020 7618 4400
✉ clerks@charterchambers.com
Call Date: July 2001, Lincoln's Inn
Qualifications: [LLB (Hons)]

MANSFIELD MR MICHAEL QC (1989)

Tooks Chambers
81 Farringdon Street, London EC4A 4BL,
☎ 020 7842 7575 ✉ clerks@tooks.co.uk
Call Date: Nov 1967, Gray's Inn
Qualifications: [BA]
✉ michael.mansfield@tooks.co.uk

MANSFIELD MS NADIA

KCH Garden Square
1 Oxford Street, Nottingham NG1 5BH,
☎ 0115 941 8851
✉ clerks@kchgardensquare.co.uk
Call Date: Nov 2006, Inner Temple
Qualifications: [BA (Hons) (Lond)]

MANSFIELD MRS SUZANNE RIVERS

St James's Chambers
68 Quay Street, Manchester M3 3EJ,
☎ 0161 834 7000
✉ clerks@stjameschambers.com
Call Date: July 2010, Middle Temple
Qualifications: [MA (Cantab)]

MANSINGH MS URMILLA ROSHNEE DEVI

Chambers of G. D. Tetteh
Ground Floor, 2 Middle Temple Lane, Temple, London EC4Y 9AA, ☎ 020 7353 7095
18 Red Lion Court
London EC4A 3EB, ☎ 020 7520 6000
✉ chambers@18rlc.co.uk
Call Date: Nov 2009, Lincoln's Inn
Qualifications: [LLB (South Africa) LLM (South Africa)]

MANSON MISS JULIANN

2-3 Hind Court Chambers
2-3 Hind Court, Fleet Street, London EC4A 3DL, ☎ 020 7822 2150
✉ david@2-3hindcourt.com
Call Date: July 1985, Middle Temple
Pupil Supervisor
Qualifications: [BA (Bris) DipLaw]
✉ j.manson@2-3hindcourt.com

E

MANSOOR MISS PARVEEN

Argent Chambers
5 Bell Yard, London WC2A 2JR,
☎ 020 7556 5500
✉ briefsin@argentchambers.co.uk
Call Date: Oct 1996, Inner Temple
Qualifications: [LLB (B'ham)]

MANT MR PETER JOHN

39 Essex Street
London WC2R 3AT, ☎ 020 7832 1111
✉ clerks@39essex.com
82 King Street
Manchester M2 4WQ, ☎ 0161 870 9969
Call Date: Nov 2006, Inner Temple
Qualifications: [BA (Cantab)]
peter.mant@39essex.com

MANTLE MR PETER JOHN

Monckton Chambers
1 & 2 Raymond Buildings, Gray's Inn, London WC1R 5NR, ☎ 020 7405 7211
✉ chambers@monckton.com
Call Date: July 1989, Inner Temple
Pupil Supervisor
Qualifications: [BA (Oxon) LLM (Cantab)]
pmantle@monckton.com

MANTLE MR PHILIP LEONARD

No5 Chambers
Fountain Court, Steelhouse Lane, Birmingham B4 6DR, ☎ 0845 210 5555 ✉ info@no5.com
No5 Chambers
Greenwood House, 4-7 Salisbury Court, London EC4Y 8AA, ☎ 0845 210 5555
No5 Chambers
38 Queen Square, Bristol BS1 4QS,
☎ 0845 210 5555
Call Date: July 2002, Lincoln's Inn
Qualifications: [BA (Hons)(Oxon)]
pm@no5.com

MANYARARA MISS NATSAI

12 Old Square Chambers
1st Floor, 12 Old Square, Lincoln's Inn, London WC2A 3TX, ☎ 020 7404 0875
✉ clerks@12oldsquare.com
Call Date: July 2001, Gray's Inn
Pupil Supervisor
Qualifications: [LLB (Hons)]
clerks@12oldsquare.com

MANZONI MR CHARLES PETER QC (2009)

39 Essex Street
London WC2R 3AT, ☎ 020 7832 1111
✉ clerks@39essex.com
82 King Street
Manchester M2 4WQ, ☎ 0161 870 9969
Call Date: July 1988, Middle Temple
Qualifications: [BSc AMI Mech Eng (Bristol) CEDR HKMC CIARB HKIAC]

MAQSOOD MISS ZABEDA KHATOON

15 Winckley Square
Preston PR1 3JJ, ☎ 01772 252828
✉ clerks@15winckleysq.co.uk
Call Date: Nov 1996, Gray's Inn
Qualifications: [LLB (Derby)]

MARAGH MISS THALIA

Amethyst Chambers
Ground Floor, 9 Kings Bench Walk, Inner Temple, London EC4Y 7DX,
☎ 020 7936 4966
✉ info@amethystchambers.com
Call Date: Mar 2009, Middle Temple
Qualifications: [LLB (Hons) (West Indies) LLM (Lond)]

MARCH MISS NATASHA LAURA

4 Brick Court
4 Brick Court, Temple, London EC4Y 9AD,
☎ 020 7832 3200 ✉ clerks@4bc.co.uk
Call Date: July 2008, Lincoln's Inn
Qualifications: [LLB]

MARCHESI MS CAMILLA-FAY

Guildhall Chambers Portsmouth
Prudential Buildings, 16 Guildhall Walk, Portsmouth, Hampshire PO1 2DE,
☎ 023 9275 2400
✉ clerks@gcp-barristers.com
Call Date: July 2004, Inner Temple
GCPClerks@fsmail.net

MARCUS MR PETER

Zenith Chambers
10 Park Square, Leeds LS1 2LH,
☎ 0113 245 5438
✉ clerks@zenithchambers.co.uk
Call Date: July 2004, Middle Temple
Qualifications: [BA Hons (Manch) PGDip Law]

MARCUS MS RACHEL ROSE

1 Crown Office Row
1 Crown Office Row, Temple, London EC4Y 7HH, ☎ 020 7797 7500
✉ mail@1cor.com
Call Date: Nov 2005, Inner Temple
Qualifications: [BA Magdalen College University of Oxford CPE C]
✉ rachel.marcus@1cor.com

MARDNER MISS SHARN FIONA

Bell Yard Chambers
116/118 Chancery Lane, London WC2A 1PP, ☎ 020 7306 9292
✉ byclerks@bellyardchambers.co.uk
Call Date: Oct 2003, Inner Temple
Qualifications: [BA (Westminster)]

MARGIOTTA MISS NICOLA JANE

Arden Chambers
20 Bloomsbury Square, London WC1A 2NS, ☎ 020 7242 4244
✉ clerks@ardenchambers.com
Call Date: July 2007, Inner Temple
Qualifications: [LLB (Manch)]

MARGO MR SAUL NICHOLAS

Outer Temple Chambers
The Outer Temple, 222 Strand, London WC2R 1BA, ☎ 020 7353 6381
✉ clerks@outertemple.com
Call Date: Oct 2005, Lincoln's Inn
Qualifications: [BA (Hons) (Cantab)]

MARGOLIN MR DANIEL GEORGE

Maitland Chambers
7 Stone Buildings, Lincoln's Inn, London WC2A 3SZ, ☎ 020 7406 1200
✉ clerks@maitlandchambers.com
Call Date: Nov 1995, Gray's Inn
Pupil Supervisor
Qualifications: [BA (Oxon)]
✉ dmargolin@maitlandchambers.com

MARKANDYA MISS SUSANNAH TESSA

Enterprise Chambers
9 Old Square, Lincoln's Inn, London WC2A 3SR, ☎ 020 7405 9471
✉ london@enterprisechambers.com
Enterprise Chambers
65 Quayside, Newcastle Upon Tyne NE1 3DE, ☎ 0191 222 3344
✉ newcastle@enterprisechambers.com
Enterprise Chambers
43 Park Square, Leeds LS1 2NP, ☎ 0113 246 0391
✉ leeds@enterprisechambers.com
Call Date: Oct 2005, Inner Temple
Qualifications: [MA University of Edinburgh LLB City University]
✉ susannahmarkandya@enterprisechambers.com

MARKHAM MISS ANDREA

18 St John Street
Manchester M3 4EA, ☎ 0161 278 1800
✉ clerks@18sjs.com
Call Date: Oct 2000, Gray's Inn
Qualifications: [LLB (Cardiff)]

MARKHAM MISS ANNA VICTORIA

4 Stone Buildings
Ground Floor, 4 Stone Buildings, Lincoln's Inn, London WC2A 3XT, ☎ 020 7242 5524
✉ clerks@4stonebuildings.com
Call Date: Oct 1996, Lincoln's Inn
Qualifications: [BA (Hons) MA (Hons)(Oxon)]
✉ clerks@4stonebuildings.com

MARKHAM MISS HANNAH MEGAN

36 Bedford Row
London WC1R 4JH, ☎ 020 7421 8000
✉ chambers@36bedfordrow.co.uk
Call Date: July 1998, Lincoln's Inn
Qualifications: [BA (Hons)(Middx) MA (Lond)]
✉ clerks@36bedfordrow.co.uk

MARKLEW MR LEE JONATHON

St Philips Chambers
55 Temple Row, Birmingham B2 5LS, ☎ 0121 246 7000 ✉ clerks@st-philips.com
Call Date: May 1993, Gray's Inn
Qualifications: [BA (Sheff)]
✉ lmarklew@st-philips.com

MARKS MR DAVID GEORGES MAINFROY QC (2009)

South Square
3-4 South Square, Gray's Inn, London WC1R 5HP, ☎ 020 7696 9900
✉ practicemanagers@southsquare.com
Call Date: Nov 1974, Gray's Inn
Qualifications: [MA BCL (Oxon)]

E

MARKS MISS GILLIAN

14 Gray's Inn Square
14 Gray's Inn Square, Gray's Inn, London WC1R 5JP, ☎020 7242 0858
✉clerks@14gis.co.uk
Call Date: July 1981, Gray's Inn
Pupil Supervisor, Recorder
Qualifications: [BA (Sussex)]
✉clerks@14graysinnsquare.co.uk, gillianmarks7@googlemail.com

MARKS MISS JACQUELINE STEPHANIE

Coram Chambers
9-11 Fulwood Place, London WC1V 6HG, ☎020 7092 3700
✉mail@coramchambers.co.uk
Call Date: July 1984, Middle Temple
Qualifications: [BA]

MARKS MR JONATHAN CLIVE QC (1995)

4 Pump Court
4 Pump Court, Temple, London EC4Y 7AN, ☎020 7842 5555
✉chambers@4pumpcourt.com
Call Date: July 1975, Inner Temple
Qualifications: [BA (Oxon)]
✉jmarks@4pumpcourt.com

MARKS MR JONATHAN HAROLD

Matrix Chambers
Griffin Building, Gray's Inn, London WC1R 5LN, ☎020 7404 3447
✉matrix@matrixlaw.co.uk / lscott@matrixlaw.co.uk
Call Date: Oct 1992, Inner Temple
Qualifications: [MA (Oxon) BCL]
✉jonathanmarks@matrixlaw.co.uk

MARKS MR LEWIS QC (2002)

Queen Elizabeth Building
3rd Floor, Queen Elizabeth Building, Temple, London EC4Y 9BS, ☎020 7797 7837
✉clerks@qeb.co.uk
Call Date: July 1984, Middle Temple
Qualifications: [BA Hons (Oxon)]

MARKS DR PETER

Chambers of Peter Marks
1 Maxted Road, London SE15 4LL, ☎07885 163086
Call Date: Nov 1987, Middle Temple
Pupil Supervisor
Qualifications: [MB ChB MRCP MSc LLB LLM DCH PhD]

MARKUS MS KATE

Doughty Street Chambers
53-54 Doughty Street, London WC1N 2LS, ☎020 7404 1313
✉enquiries@doughtystreet.co.uk
Doughty Street Chambers
Pall Mall Court, 61-67 King Street, Manchester M2 4PD, ☎0161 618 1066
Doughty Street Chambers
5th Floor, Broad Quay House, Prince Street, Bristol BS1 4DJ, ☎01179 058 717
Call Date: Nov 1981, Gray's Inn
Pupil Supervisor
Qualifications: [LLB (Manch)]
✉k.markus@doughtystreet.co.uk

MARLAND MR TIMOTHY DESMOND HUGH

Quadrant Chambers
Quadrant House, 10 Fleet Street, London EC4Y 1AU, ☎020 7583 4444
✉info@quadrantchambers.com
Call Date: July 2002, Inner Temple
Pupil Supervisor
Qualifications: [BA (Manch) CPE (Manch) Dip Law]
✉timothy.marland@quadrantchambers.com

MARLER LIEUTENANT COLONEL LEE GARY

Bretton Woods Law
New Broad Street House, 35 New Broad Street, London EC2M 1NH
18 Red Lion Court
London EC4A 3EB, ☎020 7520 6000
✉chambers@18rlc.co.uk
Call Date: Nov 1987, Lincoln's Inn
Qualifications: [LLB LLM (Stell) LLM (Lond)]

MARLEY MISS SARAH ANNE

Coram Chambers
9-11 Fulwood Place, London WC1V 6HG, ☎020 7092 3700
✉mail@coramchambers.co.uk
Call Date: Oct 1995, Lincoln's Inn
Qualifications: [LLB (Hons)(Leic)]
✉sarah.marley@coramchambers.co.uk

MARNHAM MRS MICHELLE JOANNE

Tanfield Chambers
2-5 Warwick Court, London WC1R 5DJ, ☎020 7421 5300
✉clerks@tanfieldchambers.co.uk
Call Date: Nov 1994, Inner Temple
Qualifications: [LLB (Hons) (Essex)]
✉mmarnham@tanfieldchambers.co.uk

MAROOF MS LARA ANNE

Charter Chambers
33 John Street, London WC1N 2AT,
☎ 020 7618 4400
✉ clerks@charterchambers.com
Call Date: July 2001, Inner Temple
Qualifications: [LLB (Lond)]
✉ lara.maroof@charterchambers.com

MARQUAND MR CHARLES NICHOLAS HILARY

4 Stone Buildings
Ground Floor, 4 Stone Buildings, Lincoln's Inn, London WC2A 3XT, ☎ 020 7242 5524
✉ clerks@4stonebuildings.com
Call Date: Nov 1987, Inner Temple
Qualifications: [MA (Oxon) MA (Law) (Lond) Dip EC Law (Lond) Dip EC Comp Law (Lond) FCI Arb]
✉ c.marquand@4stonebuildings.com

MARQUIS MR PIERS

Doughty Street Chambers
53-54 Doughty Street, London WC1N 2LS,
☎ 020 7404 1313
✉ enquiries@doughtystreet.co.uk
Call Date: July 2001, Gray's Inn
Qualifications: [BA (Warwick)]
✉ p.marquis@doughtystreet.co.uk

MARRIN MR JOHN WHEELER QC (1990)

Keating Chambers
15 Essex Street, London WC2R 3AA,
☎ 020 7544 2600
✉ clerks@keatingchambers.com
Call Date: Nov 1974, Inner Temple
Recorder
Qualifications: [MA (Cantab)]

MARRIOTT MR ARTHUR LESLIE

12 Gray's Inn Square
Gray's Inn, London WC1R 5JP,
☎ 020 7067 1960 ✉ almqc@12graysinn.com
Call Date: July 2011, Gray's Inn

MARRIOTT MR JAMIE STEPHEN

Cobden House Chambers
19 Quay Street, Manchester M3 3HN,
☎ 0161 833 6000 ✉ Clerks@Cobden.co.uk
Call Date: July 2003, Gray's Inn
Qualifications: [LLB (Derby)]

MARRS MR ANDREW CHARLES

Kenworthy's Chambers
Arlington House, Bloom Street, Salford, Manchester M3 6AJ, ☎ 0161 832 4036
Call Date: Nov 1995, Inner Temple
Qualifications: [BA (Oxon) CPE (Manc)]
✉ maria@kenworthysbarristers.co.uk

MARSDEN MR ANDREW CHARLES

St John's Chambers
101 Victoria Street, Bristol BS1 6PU,
☎ 0117 923 4700
✉ clerks@stjohnschambers.co.uk
Call Date: May 1994, Lincoln's Inn
Qualifications: [BA BCL (Hons)]
✉ andrew.marsden@stjohnschambers.co.uk

MARSDEN MR ANDREW GUY

East Anglian Chambers
53 North Hill, Colchester, Essex CO1 1QA,
☎ 01473 214481 ✉ colchester@ealaw.co.uk
East Anglian Chambers
140 New London Road, Chelmsford, Essex CM2 0AW, ☎ 01473 214481
✉ chelmsford@ealaw.co.uk
East Anglian Chambers
15 The Close, Norwich, Norfolk NR1 4DZ,
☎ 01473 214481 ✉ norwich@ealaw.co.uk
East Anglian Chambers
Gresham House, 5 Museum Street, Ipswich, Suffolk IP1 1HQ, ☎ 01473 214481
✉ ipswich@ealaw.co.uk
Call Date: July 1975, Middle Temple
Pupil Supervisor, Recorder
Qualifications: [MA (Oxon)]
✉ andrewmarsden@ealaw.co.uk

MARSH MISS ELIZABETH ANN QC (1999)

Nine Bedford Row
9 Bedford Row, London WC1R 4AZ,
☎ 020 7489 2727
✉ clerks@9bedfordrow.co.uk
Call Date: Nov 1979, Gray's Inn
Qualifications: [BA (Hons)]
✉ elizabeth.marshqc@9bedfordrow.co.uk

MARSH MR GRAHAM IAN

Clock Chambers
18 Waterloo Road, Wolverhampton WV1 4BL,
☎ 01902 313444
✉ clockchambers@btconnect.com
Call Date: Oct 2004, Lincoln's Inn
Qualifications: [LLB (Hons) Lond]

E

MARSH MR JOHN

Kenworthy's Chambers
Arlington House, Bloom Street, Salford, Manchester M3 6AJ, ☎ 0161 832 4036
Call Date: July 1977, Gray's Inn
Pupil Supervisor
Qualifications: [BA]
j.marsh@kenworthysbarristers.co.uk

MARSH MISS NANCY RUTH

4 King's Bench Walk
2nd Floor, 4 King's Bench Walk, Temple, London EC4Y 7DL, ☎ 020 7822 7000
clerks@4kbw.co.uk
Call Date: July 2008, Inner Temple
Qualifications: [LLB (Leeds)]
nrm@4kbw.co.uk, nrmarsh@ymail.com

MARSH MR STEPHEN BRADLEY

Garden Court Chambers
57-60 Lincoln's Inn Fields, London WC2A 3LJ, ☎ 020 7993 7600 info@gclaw.co.uk
Call Date: July 2005, Middle Temple
Qualifications: [BA (Hons) L'pool MA Leeds PgDip Law]
stephenm@gclaw.co.uk

E

MARSHALL MR ANDREW DAVID MICHAEL CREAGH

3 PB Barristers
3 Paper Buildings, Temple, London EC4Y 7EU, ☎ 020 7583 8055
3 PB Barristers
Royal Talbot House, 2 Victoria Street, Bristol, Avon BS1 6BB, ☎ 0117 928 1520
3 PB Barristers
30 Christchurch Road, Bournemouth, Dorset BH1 3PD, ☎ 01202 292102
clerks.bournemouth@3paper.co.uk
3 PB Barristers
4 St Peter Street, Winchester SO23 8BW, ☎ 01962 868884
clerks.winchester@3paper.co.uk
3 PB Barristers
23 Beaumont Street, Oxford OX1 2NP, ☎ 01865 793 736
Call Date: July 1981, Lincoln's Inn
Pupil Supervisor
Qualifications: [MA (Oxon)]
david.marshall@3paper.co.uk

MARSHALL MR DEREK STANLEY

College Chambers
19 Carlton Crescent, Southampton, Hampshire SO15 2ET, ☎ 023 8023 0338
clerks@college-chambers.co.uk
Call Date: July 1980, Inner Temple
Pupil Supervisor
Qualifications: [LLB (So'ton)]
dmarshall@College-Chambers.co.uk

MARSHALL MRS ELIZABETH SUZANNE

Iscoed Chambers
86 St Helen's Road, Swansea SA1 4BQ, ☎ 01792 652988
clerks@iscoedchambers.co.uk
Call Date: Oct 1995, Inner Temple
Qualifications: [MA (Oxon) LLM (Lond)]
em@iscoedchambers.co.uk

MARSHALL MISS ELOISE MARY KATHERINE SELINA

23 Essex Street
London WC2R 3AA, ☎ 020 7413 0353
clerks@23es.com
Call Date: Oct 1994, Gray's Inn
Pupil Supervisor
Qualifications: [BA]
eloisemarshall@23es.com

MARSHALL MISS ITA DELORIS

12 Old Square Chambers
1st Floor, 12 Old Square, Lincoln's Inn, London WC2A 3TX, ☎ 020 7404 0875
clerks@12oldsquare.com
Call Date: July 1980, Middle Temple
Pupil Supervisor
Qualifications: [LLB (Hons) MA]

MARSHALL MISS LAURA JANE

Call Date: July 2001, Middle Temple
Qualifications: [LLB (Hons)]
marshall@paradisechambers.co.uk

MARSHALL MISS LUCY CHARLOTTE

St Johns Buildings
24a - 28 St John Street, Manchester M3 4DJ, ☎ 0161 214 1500
clerk@stjohnsbuildings.co.uk
16 Winckley Square
Preston PR1 3JJ, ☎ 01772 256100
St Johns Buildings Liverpool
8th Floor India Buildings, Water Street, Liverpool L2 0XG, ☎ 0151 243 6000
clerk@stjohnsbuildings.co.uk
Call Date: Oct 2005, Middle Temple
Qualifications: [LLB (Hons)]
clerk@stjohnsbuildings.co.uk

MARSHALL MR PAUL DAVID JOHN

No5 Chambers
Greenwood House, 4-7 Salisbury Court, London EC4Y 8AA, ☎0845 210 5555
4-5 Gray's Inn Square
Gray's Inn, London WC1R 5AH, ☎020 7404 5252 ✉clerks@4-5.co.uk
No5 Chambers
38 Queen Square, Bristol BS1 4QS, ☎0845 210 5555
No5 Chambers
Fountain Court, Steelhouse Lane, Birmingham B4 6DR, ☎0845 210 5555 ✉info@no5.com
Call Date: Oct 1991, Inner Temple
Pupil Supervisor
Qualifications: [BA (Cantab) BSc (Lond) MCIArb]

MARSHALL MR PETER DAVID

4 Breams Buildings
Chancery Lane, London EC4A 1HP, ☎020 7092 1900 ✉clerks@4bb.co.uk
Call Date: Nov 1991, Lincoln's Inn
Qualifications: [LLB (Hons)(Warw)]

MARSHALL MR PHILIP JOHN QC (2012)

1 KBW Chambers
1 King's Bench Walk, Temple, London EC4Y 7DB, ☎020 7936 1500 ✉clerks@1kbw.co.uk
King's Bench Chambers
174 High Street, Lewes BN7 1YE, ☎01273 402600
Call Date: July 1989, Gray's Inn
Pupil Supervisor
Qualifications: [LLB (L'pool)]
✉pmarshall@1kbw.co.uk

MARSHALL MR PHILIP SCOTT QC (2003)

Serle Court
6 New Square, Lincoln's Inn, London WC2A 3QS, ☎020 7242 6105 ✉clerks@serlecourt.co.uk
Call Date: July 1987, Lincoln's Inn
Recorder
Qualifications: [MA (Cantab) LLM(USA)]
✉p.marshall@serlecourt.co.uk

MARSHALL MISS VANESSA JULIETTE

Seven Bedford Row
7 Bedford Row, London WC1R 4BS, ☎020 7242 3555 ✉clerks@7br.co.uk
Call Date: Oct 1994, Gray's Inn
Pupil Supervisor
Qualifications: [RGN LLB]
✉vmarshall@7br.co.uk

MARSHALL BAIN MISS LYDIA ESTHER

Clapham Law Chambers
85 Landor Road, Clapham North, London SW9 9RT, ☎020 7978 8482 ✉DANNY@claphamlawchambers.co.uk
Call Date: Mar 1998, Lincoln's Inn
Qualifications: [LLB (Hons)]

MARSHALL WILLIAMS MR ADRIAN PAUL

Garden Court Chambers
57-60 Lincoln's Inn Fields, London WC2A 3LJ, ☎020 7993 7600 ✉info@gclaw.co.uk
Call Date: Oct 1998, Inner Temple
Qualifications: [MA (Edin) CPE]
✉adrianmw@gclaw.co.uk

MARSHALL-ANDREWS MR ROBERT GRAHAM QC (1987)

Carmelite Chambers
9 Carmelite Street, London EC4Y 0DR, ☎020 7936 6300 ✉clerks@carmelitechambers.co.uk
Hailsham Chambers
Ground Floor, 4 Paper Buildings, Temple, London EC4Y 7EX, ☎020 7643 5000 ✉clerks@hailshamchambers.com
Call Date: Feb 1967, Gray's Inn
Recorder
Qualifications: [LLB (Bris)]
✉rmarshall-andrewsqc@carmelitechambers.co.uk

MARSLAND MR JAMES JOHN

Five Paper Buildings
1st Floor, Five Paper Buildings, Temple, London EC4Y 7HB, ☎020 7583 6117 ✉clerks@5pb.co.uk
Call Date: Oct 2008, Middle Temple
Qualifications: [LLB (Hons) (Manch)]
✉jjm@5pb.co.uk

MARSON MRS DENISE LYNN

Sovereign Chambers
46 Park Place, Leeds LS1 2RY, ☎0113 245 1841 ✉clerks@sovereignchambers.co.uk
Call Date: Nov 1990, Inner Temple
Pupil Supervisor, Recorder
Qualifications: [LLB (Hons) (Sheff)]
✉denise.marson@sovereignchambers.co.uk

MARTEN MR RICHARD HEDLEY WESTWOOD

Radcliffe Chambers
Ground Floor, 11 New Square, Lincoln's Inn, London WC2A 3QB, ☎020 7831 0081
✉clerks@radcliffechambers.com
Call Date: Nov 1966, Lincoln's Inn
Pupil Supervisor
Qualifications: [MA (Cantab)]
hmarten@radcliffechambers.com, clerks@radcliffechambers.com

MARTIGNETTI MR IAN

Regency Chambers
45 Priestgate, Peterborough PE1 1LB, ☎01733 315215
✉clerks@regencychambers.law.co.uk
Regency Chambers
Sheraton House, Castle Park, Cambridge CB3 0AX, ☎01223 301517
Call Date: Nov 1990, Inner Temple
Pupil Supervisor
Qualifications: [LLB]
clerks@regencychambers.law.co.uk

E

MARTIN MR BRADLEY DAVID

2 Temple Gardens
2 Temple Gardens, Temple, London EC4Y 9AY, ☎020 7822 1200
✉clerks@2tg.co.uk
Call Date: Oct 1990, Lincoln's Inn
Pupil Supervisor
Qualifications: [LLB (Leic)]
bmartin@2tg.co.uk

MARTIN MR CHRISTOPHER BRIAN

2 Bedford Row
London WC1R 4BU, ☎020 7440 8888
✉clerks@2bedfordrow.co.uk
Call Date: July 2008, Middle Temple
Qualifications: [LLB (Hons) (Lond)]
cmartin@2bedfordrow.co.uk

MARTIN MR DALE

Littleton Chambers
3 King's Bench Walk North, Temple, London EC4Y 7HR, ☎020 7797 8600
✉fschneider@littletonchambers.co.uk
Call Date: Oct 1997, Inner Temple
Pupil Supervisor
Qualifications: [LLB (Nottingham)]
dmartin@littletonchambers.co.uk

MARTIN MR DAVID JOHN

9 King's Bench Walk
Lower Ground Floor South, 9 King's Bench Walk, Temple, London EC4Y 7DX, ☎020 7353 9564 ✉9kbw@btconnect.com
Call Date: Oct 1994, Gray's Inn
Qualifications: [MSc]
9kbw@btconnect.com

MARTIN MR DAVID JOHN PATTISON

Queen Square Chambers
56 Queen Square, Bristol BS1 4PR, ☎0117 921 1966 ✉crime@qs-c.co.uk
Call Date: July 1969, Inner Temple
Qualifications: [BA (Cantab)]
crime@qs-c.co.uk

MARTIN MRS DIANNE JOAN ABEGAIL

St John's Chambers
101 Victoria Street, Bristol BS1 6PU, ☎0117 923 4700
✉clerks@stjohnschambers.co.uk
Call Date: Oct 1992, Gray's Inn
Pupil Supervisor
Qualifications: [LLB]
dianne.martin@stjohnschambers.co.uk

MARTIN MR GERARD JAMES QC (2000)

Exchange Chambers
One Derby Square, Derby Square, Liverpool L2 9XX, ☎0151 236 7747
✉info@exchangechambers.co.uk
Exchange Chambers
7 Ralli Courts, West Riverside, Manchester M3 5FT, ☎0161 833 2722
Exchange Chambers
Oxford House, Oxford Row, Leeds LS1 3BE, ☎0113 203 1970
✉spencer@exchangechambers.co.uk
12 King's Bench Walk
12 King's Bench Walk, Temple, London EC4Y 7EL, ☎020 7583 0811
St Philips Chambers
55 Temple Row, Birmingham B2 5LS, ☎0121 246 7000 ✉clerks@st-philips.com
Call Date: July 1978, Middle Temple
Recorder
Qualifications: [MA (Cantab)]
martinqc@exchangechambers.co.uk

MARTIN MISS JADE LINNEA

East Anglian Chambers
Gresham House, 5 Museum Street, Ipswich, Suffolk IP1 1HQ, ☎ 01473 214481
✉ ipswich@ealaw.co.uk
East Anglian Chambers
53 North Hill, Colchester, Essex CO1 1QA, ☎ 01473 214481 ✉ colchester@ealaw.co.uk
East Anglian Chambers
15 The Close, Norwich, Norfolk NR1 4DZ, ☎ 01473 214481 ✉ norwich@ealaw.co.uk
Call Date: Oct 2003, Middle Temple
Qualifications: [BTh (Oxon)]
✉ jademartin@ealaw.co.uk

MARTIN MR JAMES STEPHEN

5 King's Bench Walk
5 King's Bench Walk, Temple, London EC4Y 7DN, ☎ 020 7353 5638
✉ clerks@5kbw.co.uk
Call Date: Mar 2003, Lincoln's Inn
Qualifications: [LLB (Hons)(Bris)]

MARTIN MISS JOANNA MARGARET

Devon Chambers
3 St Andrew Street, Plymouth PL1 2AH, ☎ 01752 661659
✉ clerks@devonchambers.co.uk
Call Date: July 2005, Middle Temple
Qualifications: [BA LLB PgDip Law]
✉ jomartin@devonchambers.co.uk

MARTIN MR JOHN VANDELEUR QC (1991)

Wilberforce Chambers
8 New Square, Lincoln's Inn, London WC2A 3QP, ☎ 020 7306 0102
✉ chambers@wilberforce.co.uk
Call Date: July 1972, Lincoln's Inn
Qualifications: [MA (Cantab)]
✉ jmartin@wilberforce.co.uk

Types of work: Chancery (general), Chancery (land law), Commercial litigation, Commercial property, Company, commercial and competition, Equity, Landlord and tenant, Professional negligence, Trusts, Wills

MARTIN MR JONATHAN DAVID

10 King's Bench Walk
Ground Floor, 10 King's Bench Walk, Temple, London EC4Y 7EB, ☎ 020 7353 7742
✉ Chambers@10kingsbenchwalk.co.uk
Call Date: Nov 1994, Middle Temple
Pupil Supervisor
Qualifications: [BA (Hons) (Oxon)]
✉ jonathan.martin@10kingsbenchwalk.co.uk

MARTIN MISS JOSEPHINE ANNE VANDELEUR

Four New Square
Four New Square, Lincoln's Inn, London WC2A 3RJ, ☎ 020 7822 2000
✉ barristers@4newsquare.com
Call Date: Oct 2008, Lincoln's Inn
Qualifications: [BA (Dunelm)]
✉ j.martin@4newsquare.com

MARTIN MRS NICOLA JANE

3 PB Barristers
3 Paper Buildings, Temple, London EC4Y 7EU, ☎ 020 7583 8055
3 PB Barristers
Royal Talbot House, 2 Victoria Street, Bristol, Avon BS1 6BB, ☎ 0117 928 1520
3 PB Barristers
30 Christchurch Road, Bournemouth, Dorset BH1 3PD, ☎ 01202 292102
✉ clerks.bournemouth@3paper.co.uk
3 PB Barristers
4 St Peter Street, Winchester SO23 8BW, ☎ 01962 868884
✉ clerks.winchester@3paper.co.uk
3 PB Barristers
23 Beaumont Street, Oxford OX1 2NP, ☎ 01865 793 736
Call Date: July 1982, Inner Temple
Qualifications: [LLB (Hons) (B'ham)]
✉ nicola.martin@3paper.co.uk

MARTIN MR PETER JOHN

Chambers of Mr P J Martin
3 Anglesea Terrace, Wellesley Avenue, London W6 0UT, ☎ 020 8746 1207
✉ pmartinbar@btinternet.com
Call Date: July 1969, Gray's Inn
Pupil Supervisor
Qualifications: [BSc MSc]
✉ pmartinbar@btinternet.com

MARTIN MR PHILIP ROGER

Holborn Chambers
6 Gate Street, Lincoln's Inn Fields, London WC2A 3HP, ☎ 020 7242 6060
Call Date: Oct 1995, Inner Temple
Qualifications: [BA (York) CPE (Lond)]

MARTIN MR PIERS JAMES

4 King's Bench Walk
2nd Floor, 4 King's Bench Walk, Temple, London EC4Y 7DL, ☎ 020 7822 7000
✉ clerks@4kbw.co.uk
Call Date: Oct 1997, Inner Temple
Qualifications: [LLB]
✉ pm@4kbw.co.uk

E

MARTIN MISS REBECCA JANE

1 Pump Court
Elm Court, Temple, London EC4Y 7AB,
☎ 020 7842 7070
✉ (name)@pumpcourt.co.uk
Call Date: July 2002, Gray's Inn
Qualifications: [LLB (Warwick)]
✉ rm@1pumpcourt.co.uk

MARTIN MR RICHARD HENRY BOLAM

Rowchester Chambers
4 Rowchester Court, Whittall Street,
Birmingham B4 6DH, ☎ 0121 233 2327
✉ clerks@rowchesterchambers.co.uk
Call Date: Nov 1978, Inner Temple
Qualifications: [BSc (Econ)]

MARTIN MR ROY LOGAN QC (2008)

6 Pump Court
1st Floor, 6 Pump Court, Temple, London
EC4Y 7AR, ☎ 020 7797 8400
✉ richardconstable@6pumpcourt.co.uk
6 Pump Court Chambers
6-8 Mill Street, Maidstone, Kent ME15 6XH,
☎ 01622 688094
✉ annexe@6pumpcourt.co.uk
Landmark Chambers
180 Fleet Street, London EC4A 2HG,
☎ 020 7430 1221
✉ clerks@landmarkchambers.co.uk
Call Date: July 1990, Lincoln's Inn
Qualifications: [LLB (Glas)]
✉ roymartinqc@6pumpcourt.co.uk

MARTIN MISS SARAH GENEVIEVE ANN

7 King's Bench Walk
Ground Floor, 7 King's Bench Walk, Temple,
London EC4Y 7DS, ☎ 020 7910 8300
✉ clerks@7kbw.co.uk
Call Date: Mar 2008, Inner Temple
Qualifications: [BA LLB (Australia) BCL Mphil (Oxon)]
✉ smartin@7kbw.co.uk

MARTIN MR STUART JON

18 St John Street
Manchester M3 4EA, ☎ 0161 278 1800
✉ clerks@18sjs.com
Call Date: Mar 2007, Lincoln's Inn
Qualifications: [LLB (Dundee)]
✉ S.martin@18sjs.com

MARTIN MR WILLIAM JOHN

9-12 Bell Yard
London WC2A 2JR, ☎ 020 7400 1800
✉ clerks@9-12bellyard.com
Call Date: Nov 2010, Gray's Inn
Qualifications: [BA]

MARTIN-CLARK MR DAVID

Stone Chambers
4 Field Court, Gray's Inn, London WC1R 5EF,
☎ 020 7440 6900
✉ clerks@stonechambers.com
Call Date: June 1961, Gray's Inn
✉ david.martin-clark@stonechambers.com

MARTINEAU MR HENRY RALPH ADEANE

Eighteen Carlton Crescent
Rownhams House, Rownhams, Southampton
SO16 8LF, ☎ 023 8063 9001
✉ clerks@18carltoncrescent.co.uk
Call Date: Nov 1966, Inner Temple
Pupil Supervisor, Recorder
Qualifications: [BA (Cantab)]

MARTINO MR ANTHONY R.

9 King's Bench Walk
Lower Ground Floor South, 9 King's Bench
Walk, Temple, London EC4Y 7DX,
☎ 020 7353 9564 ✉ 9kbw@btconnect.com
Call Date: Nov 1982, Inner Temple
Qualifications: [MA BA]

MARTIN-SPERRY MR DAVID ANTHONY

Charter Chambers
33 John Street, London WC1N 2AT,
☎ 020 7618 4400
✉ clerks@charterchambers.com
Call Date: Nov 1971, Inner Temple
Pupil Supervisor
Qualifications: [MA (Cantab)]
✉ dms@charterchambers.com

MARUSZA MR DAVID JOHN

Harcourt Chambers
1st Floor, 2 Harcourt Buildings, Temple,
London EC4Y 9DB, ☎ 0844 561 7135
Call Date: July 2009, Lincoln's Inn
Qualifications: [BA(Cantab) CPE MAC (Cantab) BVC]
✉ dmarusza@harcourtchambers.law.co.uk

MARVEN MR ROBERT

Four New Square
Four New Square, Lincoln's Inn, London WC2A 3RJ, ☎ 020 7822 2000
✉ barristers@4newsquare.com
82 King Street
Manchester M2 4WQ, ☎ 0161 870 9969
39 Essex Street
London WC2R 3AT, ☎ 020 7832 1111
✉ clerks@39essex.com
Unity Street Chambers
5 Unity Street, College Green, Bristol BS1 5HH, ☎ 0117 906 9789
✉ chambers@unitystreetchambers.com
Call Date: Oct 1994, Middle Temple
Qualifications: [MA (Hons)(Cantab)]

MARWICK MR JAMES PETER

Trinity Chambers
The Custom House, 39 Quayside, Newcastle Upon Tyne NE1 3DE, ☎ 0191 232 1927
✉ info@trinitychambers.co.uk
Trinity Chambers
Multi Media Exchange, 72-80 Corporation Road, Middlesbrough TS1 2RF, ☎ 01642 247569
✉ info@trinitychambers.co.uk
Call Date: Nov 2008, Lincoln's Inn
Qualifications: [LLB (Dunelm)]

MARYNIAK MR RUPERT ANDREW WARD

1 Gray's Inn Square
Ground Floor, 1 Gray's Inn Square, London WC1R 5AA, ☎ 020 7405 0001
Call Date: Nov 1991, Inner Temple
Qualifications: [BSc MSc (Lond) Dip Law]

MARZEC MS ALEXANDRA

5RB
1st Floor, 5 Raymond Buildings, Gray's Inn, London WC1R 5BP, ☎ 020 7242 2902
✉ clerks@5rb.com
Call Date: Nov 1990, Middle Temple
Pupil Supervisor
Qualifications: [LLB (Warw)]
🖂 alexmarzec@5rb.com

MASEFIELD MR ROGER FRANCIS

Brick Court Chambers
7-8 Essex Street, London WC2R 3LD, ☎ 020 7379 3550 ✉ clerks@brickcourt.co.uk
Call Date: Nov 1994, Middle Temple
Pupil Supervisor
Qualifications: [MA (Cantab) BCL (Oxon)]
🖂 Roger.Masefield@Brickcourt.co.uk

MASELLI MR MAURO

Chambers of Mr M Maselli
99 St Paul's Road, Peterborough PE1 3DR, ☎ 07786 320064 ✉ maselli@tiscali.co.uk
Priestgate Chambers
26 Priestgate, Peterborough PE1 1WG, ☎ 01733 865 042
✉ clerks@priestgatechambers.co.uk
Call Date: Mar 2007, Middle Temple
Qualifications: [LLB (Hons) (Leic)]

MASHEMBO MRS CAROL

St John's Chambers
101 Victoria Street, Bristol BS1 6PU, ☎ 0117 923 4700
✉ clerks@stjohnschambers.co.uk
Call Date: Oct 1999, Lincoln's Inn
Qualifications: [LLB (Hons)(exon)]
🖂 carol.mashembo@stjohnschambers.co.uk

MASNIUK MR PETER

6 Newman Avenue
6 Newman Avenue, Royston, Hertfordshire SG8 7LE, ☎ 01763 221993
✉ peter.masniuk-bar@ntlworld.com
Call Date: July 1983, Inner Temple
Qualifications: [BA (Hons) BA (Econ)]

MASON MISS CATHERINE JANE

Sovereign Chambers
46 Park Place, Leeds LS1 2RY, ☎ 0113 245 1841
✉ clerks@sovereignchambers.co.uk
Call Date: July 2000, Middle Temple
Qualifications: [BSc(Hons) (Leeds) PGDip]
🖂 catherine.mason@sovereignchambers.co.uk

MASON MR DAVID BUCHANAN QC (2010)

No5 Chambers
Fountain Court, Steelhouse Lane, Birmingham B4 6DR, ☎ 0845 210 5555 ✉ info@no5.com
No5 Chambers
Greenwood House, 4-7 Salisbury Court, London EC4Y 8AA, ☎ 0845 210 5555
No5 Chambers
38 Queen Square, Bristol BS1 4QS, ☎ 0845 210 5555
Call Date: July 1986, Middle Temple
Pupil Supervisor, Recorder
Qualifications: [LLB (Leics)]
🖂 dbm@no5.com

E

MASON MR DAVID HUGH ROTHWELL

Dere Street Barristers
33 Broad Chare, Newcastle Upon Tyne NE1 3DQ, ☎0844 3351551
✉clerks@derestreet.co.uk
Call Date: Feb 1984, Middle Temple
Qualifications: [LLB (Notts)]
clerks@broadcharechambers.co.uk

MASON MR DAVID JOHN

Bank House Chambers
Old Bank House, Hartshead, Sheffield S1 2EL, ☎0114 275 1223
✉w.digby@bankhousechambers.co.uk
Call Date: July 1979, Gray's Inn
Pupil Supervisor
Qualifications: [LLB]
d.mason@bankhousechambers.co.uk

MASON MR IAN DOUGLAS

Amethyst Chambers
Ground Floor, 9 Kings Bench Walk, Inner Temple, London EC4Y 7DX,
☎020 7936 4966
✉info@amethystchambers.com
Call Date: Nov 1978, Lincoln's Inn
Pupil Supervisor
Qualifications: [BA (Hons)]

MASON MR JAMES WILLIAM

Goldsmith Chambers
Ground Floor, Goldsmith Building, Temple, London EC4Y 7BL, ☎020 7353 6802
✉clerks@goldsmithchambers.com
Call Date: July 1969, Gray's Inn
Pupil Supervisor
j.mason@goldsmithchambers.law.co.uk

MASON MR JOHN JOSEPH

Cornwall Street Chambers
85-87 Cornwall Street, Birmingham B3 3BY, ☎0121 233 7500
✉clerks@cornwallstreet.co.uk
Call Date: Nov 1971, Inner Temple
Pupil Supervisor
Qualifications: [LLB]
john.mason@cornwallstreet.co.uk

MASON MR MARC RICHARD

4 Brick Court
4 Brick Court, Temple, London EC4Y 9AD, ☎020 7832 3200 ✉clerks@4bc.co.uk
Call Date: Oct 2006, Middle Temple
Qualifications: [BSc (Hons) (Manch) MSc PgDL]

MASON MR MATTHEW JOHN

No. 3 Fleet Street Chambers
3 Fleet Street, London EC4Y 1DP, ☎020 7936 4474 ✉clerks@3fleetstreet.com
Call Date: Oct 2008, Lincoln's Inn
Qualifications: [LLB (Lond)]
mmason@3fleetstreet.co.uk

MASON MR NICHOLAS ALAN

Park Court Chambers
16 Park Place, Leeds LS1 2SJ, ☎0113 243 3277
✉clerks@parkcourtchambers.co.uk
Linenhall Chambers
1 Stanley Place, Chester CH1 2LU, ☎01244 348282
✉clerks@linenhallchambers.co.uk
Call Date: July 1984, Gray's Inn
Pupil Supervisor
Qualifications: [BA Dip Law]
nmason@parkcourtchambers.co.uk

MASON MR PATRICK DAVID ANTHONY

Octagon Chambers
29 Park Street, Taunton, Somerset TA1 4DG, ☎01823 331919
✉jcload@Octagonchambers.co.uk
Call Date: Oct 1997, Inner Temple
pmason@octagonchambers.co.uk

MASON MR STEPHEN CHARLES WINSTON

Chambers of Mr S C W Mason
19a Church Street, Langford, Biggleswade, Bedfordshire SG18 9QT, ☎01462 701 036
✉stephenmason@stephenmason.co.uk
Call Date: Nov 1988, Middle Temple
Qualifications: [BA (Hons) MA LLM PGCE (FE)]

MASOOD MISS HAFSAH

3 Hare Court
3 Hare Court, Temple, London EC4Y 7BJ, ☎020 7415 7800 ✉clerks@3harecourt.com
Call Date: Oct 2006, Middle Temple
Qualifications: [BA (Hons) (Oxon) LLM (Lond)]
hmasood@3harecourt.com

MASSARELLA MR DAVID PETER

Cloisters
1 Pump Court, Temple, London EC4Y 7AA, ☎020 7827 4000 ✉clerks@cloisters.com
Call Date: Nov 1999, Middle Temple
Pupil Supervisor
Qualifications: [BA (Hons)(Oxon) Dip Law]
dm@cloisters.com

MASSELIS MISS MARIA

Linenhall Chambers
1 Stanley Place, Chester CH1 2LU,
☎01244 348282
✉clerks@linenhallchambers.co.uk
Call Date: Oct 1997, Lincoln's Inn
Qualifications: [LLB (Hons)(Manc)]
✉clerks@1stanleyplace.co.uk

MASSEY MISS STELLA MARIA

Central Chambers
89 Princess Street, Manchester M1 4HT,
☎0161 236 1133
✉clerks@centralchambers.co.uk
Call Date: Feb 1990, Middle Temple
Pupil Supervisor
Qualifications: [BA (Hons) PGCE]

MASSEY MR WAYNE RICHARD

The Chambers of W. Massey
5 Allenby Road, Cadishead, Manchester
M44 5EA, ☎0161 775 6948
Call Date: July 1986, Inner Temple
Qualifications: [BA (Hons)]

MASSEY MR WILLIAM GREVILLE SALE QC (1996)

Pump Court Tax Chambers
16 Bedford Row, London WC1R 4EF,
☎020 7414 8080 ✉clerks@pumptax.com
Call Date: July 1977, Middle Temple
Qualifications: [BA (Oxon)]
✉wmassey@pumptax.com

Types of work: Capital tax, Corporation tax, Equity, Income tax, National Insurance, Private client, Professional negligence, Stamp duty, Trusts, VAT, Wills

MASSIH MR MICHEL GEORGES ABDEL QC (1999)

Tooks Chambers
81 Farringdon Street, London EC4A 4BL,
☎020 7842 7575 ✉clerks@tooks.co.uk
Call Date: Nov 1979, Middle Temple
Qualifications: [LLB (Lond)]
✉michel.massih@tooks.co.uk

MASTERS MR ALAN BRUCE RAYMOND

1 Pump Court
Elm Court, Temple, London EC4Y 7AB,
☎020 7842 7070
✉(name)@pumpcourt.co.uk
Call Date: July 1979, Middle Temple
Pupil Supervisor
Qualifications: [LLB (Wales) BL]
✉am@1pumpcourt.co.uk

MASTERS MISS DEE SUZANNE

Cloisters
1 Pump Court, Temple, London EC4Y 7AA,
☎020 7827 4000 ✉clerks@cloisters.com
Call Date: July 2004, Lincoln's Inn
Qualifications: [LLB Hons (Lond) LLM (Lond)]
✉deemasters@cloisters.com

MASTERS MR JONATHAN

Fenners Chambers
3 Madingley Road, Cambridge CB3 0EE,
☎01223 368761
✉clerks@fennerschambers.com
Call Date: Oct 2009, Middle Temple
Qualifications: [BA (Hons)]
✉jonathan.masters@fennerschambers.com

MASTERS MR LEE AUBREY GEORGE

Citadel Chambers
The Citadel, 190 Corporation Street,
Birmingham B4 6QD, ☎0121 233 8500
✉clerks@citadelchambers.com
Call Date: Nov 1984, Middle Temple
Pupil Supervisor
Qualifications: [BA]
✉clerks@citadelchambers.com

MASTERS MISS SARA ALAYNA QC (2012)

20 Essex Street
London WC2R 3AL, ☎020 7842 1200
✉clerks@20essexst.com
Call Date: Oct 1993, Middle Temple
Pupil Supervisor
Qualifications: [MA (Hons)(Cantab)]
✉clerks@20essexst.com

MATES MR THOMAS RORY

Liverpool Civil Law
3rd Floor, 1 Old Hall Street, Liverpool L3 9HF,
☎0151 242 0500
✉clerks@liverpoolcivillaw.com
Call Date: Oct 1993, Middle Temple
Pupil Supervisor
Qualifications: [BA (Hons)(Kent)]
✉clerks@liverpoolcivillaw.com

MATHER MISS ALISON ELISABETH

Kenworthy's Chambers
Arlington House, Bloom Street, Salford,
Manchester M3 6AJ, ☎0161 832 4036
Call Date: Oct 1997, Lincoln's Inn
Qualifications: [MA Oxon]
✉a.mather@kenworthysbarristers.co.uk

MATHER MR BRIAN HOWARD

Trinity Chambers
The Custom House, 39 Quayside, Newcastle Upon Tyne NE1 3DE, ☎ 0191 232 1927
✉ info@trinitychambers.co.uk
Trinity Chambers
Multi Media Exchange, 72-80 Corporation Road, Middlesbrough TS1 2RF,
☎ 01642 247569
✉ info@trinitychambers.co.uk
Call Date: July 2002, Gray's Inn
✉ b.mather@trinitychambers.co.uk

MATHER MR JAMES DAVID

Serle Court
6 New Square, Lincoln's Inn, London WC2A 3QS, ☎ 020 7242 6105
✉ clerks@serlecourt.co.uk
Call Date: Oct 2006, Lincoln's Inn
Qualifications: [BA (Cantab)]
✉ jmather@serlecourt.co.uk

MATHER MISS KATE

1 Garden Court Family Law Chambers
Ground Floor, One Garden Court, Temple, London EC4Y 9BJ, ☎ 020 7797 7900
✉ clerks@1gc.com
Call Date: Oct 1990, Gray's Inn
Pupil Supervisor
Qualifications: [LLB (Lond)]
✉ mather@1gc.com

E

MATHER MR NICHOLAS IAN STEWART

Furnival Chambers
32 Furnival Street, London EC4A 1JQ,
☎ 020 7405 3232
Call Date: Oct 1998, Middle Temple
Qualifications: [BA (Hons)(Oxon) CPE]
✉ nmather@furnivallaw.co.uk

MATHER MR STEVEN JAMES

4 Breams Buildings
Chancery Lane, London EC4A 1HP,
☎ 020 7092 1900 ✉ clerks@4bb.co.uk
Call Date: Oct 1997, Middle Temple
Pupil Supervisor
Qualifications: [BEd Dip Law]
✉ s.mather@kingston.ac.uk

MATHER-LEES MR MICHAEL ANTHONY QC (2012)

30 Park Place
Cardiff CF10 3BS, ☎ 029 2039 8421
✉ clerks@30parkplace.law.co.uk
Call Date: Feb 1981, Inner Temple
Pupil Supervisor
Qualifications: [LLB (Lond)]
✉ mml@30parkplace.co.uk

MATHERS MISS WENDY ALISON

Radcliffe Chambers
Ground Floor, 11 New Square, Lincoln's Inn, London WC2A 3QB, ☎ 020 7831 0081
✉ clerks@radcliffechambers.com
Call Date: Oct 2005, Inner Temple
Qualifications: [MA St Catherine's College University of Oxford]
✉ wmathers@radcliffechambers.com

MATHEW MISS NERGIS-ANNE

St Philips Chambers
55 Temple Row, Birmingham B2 5LS,
☎ 0121 246 7000 ✉ clerks@st-philips.com
Call Date: Nov 1981, Inner Temple
Pupil Supervisor
Qualifications: [BSc (Hons)]
✉ namathew@st-philips.co.uk

MATHEW MR ROBERT KNOX QC (1992)

New Square Chambers
12 New Square, Lincoln's Inn, London WC2A 3SW, ☎ 020 7419 8000
✉ robin.hollington@newsquarechambers.co.uk
Call Date: Nov 1974, Lincoln's Inn
Qualifications: [BA (Dublin)]
✉ robin.mathew@newsquarechambers.co.uk

MATHEWS MR DENI

King's Bench and Godolphin (KBG)Chambers
115 North Hill, Plymouth, Devon PL4 8JY,
☎ 01752 221551
✉ clerks@kbgchambers.co.uk
Call Date: Oct 1996, Gray's Inn
Qualifications: [BSc (B'ham) LLB (Bucks)]
✉ deni.mathews@kingsbenchchambers.co.uk

MATHIESON MR GUY ALASTAIR DAVID

St Johns Buildings
24a - 28 St John Street, Manchester M3 4DJ,
☎ 0161 214 1500
✉ clerk@stjohnsbuildings.co.uk
St Johns Buildings
21 White Friars, Chester CH1 1NZ,
☎ 01244 323070
✉ clerk@stjohnsbuildings.co.uk
16 Winckley Square
Preston PR1 3JJ, ☎ 01772 256100
Call Date: Oct 1993, Middle Temple
Pupil Supervisor, Recorder
Qualifications: [BA (Hons)]
✉ clerk@stjohnsbuildings.co.uk

MATON MR NEIL FOSTER

Pallant Chambers
12 North Pallant, Chichester, West Sussex
PO19 1TQ, ☎ 01243 784538
✉ clerks@pallantchambers.co.uk
Call Date: July 2001, Middle Temple
Qualifications: [LLB (Hons) BCL]
✉ nmaton@pallantchambers.co.uk

MATOVU MR DANIEL MBUSI SAJABI

2 Temple Gardens
2 Temple Gardens, Temple, London
EC4Y 9AY, ☎ 020 7822 1200
✉ clerks@2tg.co.uk
Call Date: Nov 1985, Inner Temple
Pupil Supervisor
Qualifications: [BA (Hons)(Oxon)]
✉ dmatovu@2tg.co.uk

MATOVU MR HAROLD NSAMBA QC (2010)

Brick Court Chambers
7-8 Essex Street, London WC2R 3LD,
☎ 020 7379 3550 ✉ clerks@brickcourt.co.uk
Call Date: July 1988, Inner Temple
Pupil Supervisor
Qualifications: [BA (Oxon) Dip Law]
✉ Harry.Matovu@Brickcourt.co.uk

MATTHEW MR ALFRED DAVID HUGH

Seven Bedford Row
7 Bedford Row, London WC1R 4BS,
☎ 020 7242 3555 ✉ clerks@7br.co.uk
Call Date: Nov 1987, Inner Temple
Pupil Supervisor
Qualifications: [MA (Edin) Dip Law]
✉ dmatthew@7br.co.uk

MATTHEWS MISS CLAIRE LOUISE

1 Paper Buildings
1st Floor, 1 Paper Buildings, Temple, London
EC4Y 7EP, ☎ 020 7353 3728
✉ clerks@onepaper.co.uk
Call Date: Nov 1998, Inner Temple
Qualifications: [LLB (Hull)]
✉ clairematthews@onepaper.co.uk

MATTHEWS MR DENNIS ROLAND

Crown Office Chambers
2 Crown Office Row, Temple, London
EC4Y 7HJ, ☎ 020 7797 8100
✉ mail@crownofficechambers.com
Call Date: July 1973, Middle Temple
Pupil Supervisor
Qualifications: [LLM]
✉ matthews@crownofficechambers.com

MATTHEWS MR DUNCAN HENRY ROWLAND QC (2002)

20 Essex Street
London WC2R 3AL, ☎ 020 7842 1200
✉ clerks@20essexst.com
Call Date: Nov 1986, Gray's Inn
Qualifications: [MA (Oxon) Dip Law (Lond)]
✉ clerks@20essexst.com

MATTHEWS MR JANEK PAUL

Pump Court Tax Chambers
16 Bedford Row, London WC1R 4EF,
☎ 020 7414 8080 ✉ clerks@pumptax.com
Call Date: July 1972, Gray's Inn
Qualifications: [MA (Cantab) FCA]
✉ jmatthews@pumptax.com

Types of work: Capital tax, Corporation tax, Employee benefit trusts, Equity, Income tax, National Insurance, Private client, Stamp duty, Trusts, VAT, Wills

MATTHEWS MR JULIAN DAVID

Seven Bedford Row
7 Bedford Row, London WC1R 4BS,
☎ 020 7242 3555 ✉ clerks@7br.co.uk
Call Date: July 1979, Middle Temple
Pupil Supervisor, Recorder
Qualifications: [LLB (Lond)]
✉ jmatthews@7br.co.uk

MATTHEWS MISS LISA

Furnival Chambers
32 Furnival Street, London EC4A 1JQ,
☎ 020 7405 3232
Call Date: Nov 1974, Gray's Inn
Pupil Supervisor
✉ lmatthews@furnivallaw.co.uk

MATTHEWS MR MARTIN HUBE

1 Crown Office Row
1 Crown Office Row, Temple, London
EC4Y 7HH, ☎ 020 7797 7500
✉ mail@1cor.com
St Philips Chambers
55 Temple Row, Birmingham B2 5LS,
☎ 0121 246 7000 ✉ clerks@st-philips.com
Call Date: Nov 1970, Gray's Inn
Qualifications: [LLB (Notts) LLB (Cantab)]

MATTHEWS MR RICHARD ANDREW QC (2010)

2 Bedford Row
London WC1R 4BU, ☎ 020 7440 8888
✉ clerks@2bedfordrow.co.uk
Call Date: Feb 1989, Inner Temple
Pupil Supervisor
Qualifications: [MA (Cantab)]
✉ rmatthews@2bedfordrow.co.uk

E

MATTHEWSON MR SCOTT

42 Bedford Row
London WC1R 4LL, ☎020 7831 0222
✉clerks@42br.com
Call Date: Oct 1996, Inner Temple
Qualifications: [BA (Lond) DipLaw QDR]
✉scott.matthewson@42br.com

MATTHEWS-STROUD MISS JACQUELINE

36 Bedford Row
London WC1R 4JH, ☎020 7421 8000
✉chambers@36bedfordrow.co.uk
Call Date: Nov 1984, Gray's Inn
Qualifications: [LLB (Bris)]

MATTHIAS MR DAVID HUW QC (2006)

Francis Taylor Building
Inner Temple, London EC4Y 7BY,
☎020 7353 8415 ✉clerks@ftb.eu.com
Call Date: July 1980, Inner Temple
Pupil Supervisor
Qualifications: [BA]

MATTU MISS GURPRIT KAUR

Dyers Chambers
35 Bedford Row, London WC1R 4JH,
☎020 7404 1881
✉admin@dyerschambers.com
Call Date: Nov 2007, Lincoln's Inn
Qualifications: [LLB (Wales)]

MATUK MS HELEN ANTOINETTE

Southernhay Chambers
33 Southernhay East, Exeter EX1 1NX,
☎01392 255777
✉clerks@southernhaychambers.co.uk
Exchange Chambers
7 Ralli Courts, West Riverside, Manchester
M3 5FT, ☎0161 833 2722
Call Date: July 1990, Gray's Inn
Qualifications: [LLB]

MAUDSLAY MISS DIANA ELIZABETH

Sovereign Chambers
46 Park Place, Leeds LS1 2RY,
☎0113 245 1841
✉clerks@sovereignchambers.co.uk
Call Date: Oct 1997, Gray's Inn
Pupil Supervisor
Qualifications: [LLB (Sheff) LLM (Sheff)]
✉diana.maudslay@sovereignchambers.co.uk

MAUDSLEY MRS PENELOPE KATHLEEN

Central Chambers
89 Princess Street, Manchester M1 4HT,
☎0161 236 1133
✉clerks@centralchambers.co.uk
Trident Barristers Chambers
Peter House, Oxford Street, Manchester
M1 5AN, ☎0161 663 3123
✉clerks@tridentchambers.com
Alexander Chambers
13 Halstead Road, Wanstead, London E11 2AY,
☎0845 652 0451 / 0854 652 0451
✉clerks@alexanderchambers.co.uk
Call Date: Oct 1998, Lincoln's Inn
Qualifications: [LLB (Hons)(Manc)]

MAUGER MISS CLAIRE SHANTI ANDREA

Enterprise Chambers
9 Old Square, Lincoln's Inn, London
WC2A 3SR, ☎020 7405 9471
✉london@enterprisechambers.com
Enterprise Chambers
65 Quayside, Newcastle Upon Tyne NE1 3DE,
☎0191 222 3344
✉newcastle@enterprisechambers.com
Enterprise Chambers
43 Park Square, Leeds LS1 2NP,
☎0113 246 0391
✉leeds@enterprisechambers.com
Call Date: Oct 1996, Inner Temple
Pupil Supervisor
Qualifications: [BA (Oxon)]
✉shantimauger@enterprisechambers.com

MAUGHAM MR JOLYON TOBY DENNIS

11 New Square
1st Floor, 11 New Square, Lincoln's Inn,
London WC2A 3QB, ☎020 7242 4017
✉john.moore@11newsquare.com
Call Date: Mar 1997, Middle Temple
Pupil Supervisor
Qualifications: [LLB (Hons)(Dunelm)]
✉john.moore@11newsquare.com

MAULADAD MISS FARRAH DEEBA

Crown Office Chambers
2 Crown Office Row, Temple, London
EC4Y 7HJ, ☎020 7797 8100
✉mail@crownofficechambers.com
Call Date: Oct 1999, Middle Temple
Qualifications: [LLB (Hons)(Manch)]
✉mauladad@crownofficechambers.com

MAUNDER MR DAVID JAMES

Queen Square Chambers
56 Queen Square, Bristol BS1 4PR,
☎ 0117 921 1966 ✉ crime@qs-c.co.uk
Call Date: Oct 1993, Middle Temple
Qualifications: [BA(Hons)(Oxon) DipLaw (Lond) ISCL]
✉ djm@qs-c.co.uk

MAURICI MR JAMES PATRICK

Landmark Chambers
180 Fleet Street, London EC4A 2HG,
☎ 020 7430 1221
✉ clerks@landmarkchambers.co.uk
Call Date: Oct 1996, Inner Temple
Pupil Supervisor
Qualifications: [BA BCL (Oxon)]
✉ jmaurici@landmarkchambers.co.uk

MAVROGORDATO MR ZANNIS

12 Gray's Inn Square
Gray's Inn, London WC1R 5JP,
☎ 020 7067 1960 ✉ almqc@12graysinn.com
Call Date: Oct 1999, Middle Temple
Qualifications: [MA (Cantab)]

MAWDSLEY MR DAVID JOHN

Chambers of Mr David Mawdsley
17 Clinning Road, Southport, Merseyside PR8 4NU, ☎ 01704 565 387
Call Date: Nov 1995, Gray's Inn
Qualifications: [BA LLB]

MAWDSLEY MR MATTHEW EDWARD

Call Date: Nov 1991, Inner Temple
Pupil Supervisor
Qualifications: [LLB (Hons)]
✉ clerk@stjohnsbuildings.co.uk

MAWHINNEY MR RICHARD MARTIN

Outer Temple Chambers
The Outer Temple, 222 Strand, London WC2R 1BA, ☎ 020 7353 6381
✉ clerks@outertemple.com
St John's Chambers
101 Victoria Street, Bristol BS1 6PU,
☎ 0117 923 4700
✉ clerks@stjohnschambers.co.uk
Call Date: Nov 1977, Middle Temple
Pupil Supervisor
Qualifications: [BA (Oxon)]
✉ richard.mawhinney@outertemple.com

Types of work: Common law (general), Copyright, Costs, Employment, Healthcare law, Intellectual property, Partnerships, Personal injury, Professional negligence

MAWREY MS ELEANOR FRANCES

The Chambers of Grahame Aldous QC
9 Gough Square, London EC4A 3DG,
☎ 020 7832 0500
✉ clerks@9goughsquare.co.uk
Call Date: July 2001, Gray's Inn
Pupil Supervisor
Qualifications: [BA (Leeds)]
✉ emawrey@9goughsquare.co.uk

MAWREY MR RICHARD BROOKS QC (1986)

Henderson Chambers
2 Harcourt Buildings, Temple, London EC4Y 9DB, ☎ 020 7583 9020
✉ clerks@hendersonchambers.co.uk
Call Date: Feb 1964, Gray's Inn
Recorder
Qualifications: [MA (Oxon)]
✉ rmawrey@hendersonchambers.co.uk

MAX MISS SALLY ANN

29 Bedford Row Chambers
London WC1R 4HE, ☎ 020 7404 1044
✉ clerks@29br.co.uk
Call Date: Oct 1991, Lincoln's Inn
Qualifications: [BA (Hons) (Cantab)]

MAXWELL MR ADRIAN ROBERT JOHN

St John's Chambers
101 Victoria Street, Bristol BS1 6PU,
☎ 0117 923 4700
✉ clerks@stjohnschambers.co.uk
Call Date: Nov 1993, Middle Temple
Qualifications: [MA (Hons)(Oxon)]
✉ adrian.maxwell@stjohnschambers.co.uk

MAXWELL MR DAVID

St Philips Chambers
55 Temple Row, Birmingham B2 5LS,
☎ 0121 246 7000 ✉ clerks@st-philips.com
Call Date: Feb 1994, Inner Temple
Qualifications: [LLB (Hons)(Warw)]
✉ dmaxwell@st-philips.co.uk

MAXWELL MISS JUDITH MARY ANGELA

3 Dr Johnson's Buildings
Ground Floor, 3 Dr Johnson's Buildings, Temple, London EC4Y 7BA, ☎ 020 7353 4854
✉ clerks@3djb.co.uk
Call Date: July 1988, Lincoln's Inn
Pupil Supervisor
Qualifications: [LLB (Hons) (B'ham)]
✉ jmaxwell@3djb.co.uk

E

MAXWELL LEWIS MR CAMERON

Lamb Chambers
Lamb Building, Elm Court, Temple, London EC4Y 7AS, ☎020 7797 8300
✉info@lambchambers.co.uk
Call Date: July 1974, Middle Temple

MAXWELL-SCOTT MR JAMES HERBERT

Crown Office Chambers
2 Crown Office Row, Temple, London EC4Y 7HJ, ☎020 7797 8100
✉mail@crownofficechambers.com
Call Date: Nov 1995, Gray's Inn
Pupil Supervisor
Qualifications: [MA (Cantab) BCL (Oxon)]
✉maxwell-scott@crownofficechambers.com

MAXWELL-STEWART MR DUNCAN

Park Lane Plowden
19 Westgate, Leeds LS1 2RD, ☎0113 228 5049
✉clerks@parklaneplowden.co.uk
Call Date: July 2007, Gray's Inn
Qualifications: [BA (Leeds)]
✉duncan.maxwell-stewart@parklaneplowden.co.uk

E

MAY MISS CHARLOTTE LOUISA

8 New Square
8 New Square, Lincoln's Inn, London WC2A 3QP, ☎020 7405 4321
✉clerks@8newsquare.co.uk
Call Date: Nov 1995, Inner Temple
Pupil Supervisor
Qualifications: [BA (Oxon) CPE (Lond)]
✉charlotte.may@8newsquare.co.uk

Types of work: Breach of confidence, Copyright, Copyright theft, Copyright Tribunal, Data protection, Design, E-commerce, EC competition law, Entertainment, Information technology, Intellectual property, Internet law, Malicious falsehood, Media, Media and entertainment, Passing off, Patents, Pharmaceuticals, Scientific and technical disputes, Trade Descriptions Act, Trade secrets, Trademarks

MAY MR CHRISTOPHER JOHN

Five St Andrew's Hill
5 St Andrew's Hill, London EC4V 5BZ, ☎020 7332 5400 ✉Clerks@5sah.co.uk
Call Date: Nov 1983, Middle Temple
Qualifications: [MA (Cantab)]

MAY MISS NICOLA JANE

18 Red Lion Court
London EC4A 3EB, ☎020 7520 6000
✉chambers@18rlc.co.uk
18 Red Lion Court (Annexe)
Thornwood House, 102 New London Road, Chelmsford, Essex CM2 0RG, ☎01245 280880
Call Date: Nov 1993, Gray's Inn
Qualifications: [LLB]
✉nicola.may@18rlc.co.uk

MAY MR NIGEL

Furnival Chambers
32 Furnival Street, London EC4A 1JQ, ☎020 7405 3232
Call Date: July 1974, Inner Temple
Pupil Supervisor, Recorder
Qualifications: [BA (Hons) Dip Crim]
✉nmay@furnivallaw.co.uk

MAY MRS PATRICIA ROSEMARY

Nine Bedford Row
9 Bedford Row, London WC1R 4AZ, ☎020 7489 2727
✉clerks@9bedfordrow.co.uk
Call Date: July 1965, Gray's Inn
Pupil Supervisor, Recorder
Qualifications: [LLB (Lond)]
✉patriciamay@9bedfordrow.co.uk

MAYALL MR DAVID WILLIAM

Lamb Chambers
Lamb Building, Elm Court, Temple, London EC4Y 7AS, ☎020 7797 8300
✉info@lambchambers.co.uk
Call Date: July 1979, Gray's Inn
Pupil Supervisor
Qualifications: [MA (Cantab)]
✉davidmayall@lambchambers.co.uk

MAYES MR IAN QC (1993)

Littleton Chambers
3 King's Bench Walk North, Temple, London EC4Y 7HR, ☎020 7797 8600
✉fschneider@littletonchambers.co.uk
Call Date: July 1974, Middle Temple
Recorder
Qualifications: [BA (Cantab)]

MAYHEW MISS ALICE CANDIDA MARY

Devereux Chambers
Queen Elizabeth Building, Temple, London EC4Y 9BS, ☎020 7353 7534
✉clerks@devchambers.co.uk
Call Date: Nov 2001, Inner Temple
Qualifications: [LLB LLM]
✉mayhew@devchambers.co.uk

MAYHEW MR DAVID WILLIAM

39 Essex Street
London WC2R 3AT, ☎ 020 7832 1111
✉ clerks@39essex.com
Call Date: Nov 2011, Inner Temple
Qualifications: [LLB (N.Zealand)]
David.Mayhew@39essex.com

MAYHEW MISS JUDITH

3 Dr Johnson's Buildings
Ground Floor, 3 Dr Johnson's Buildings, Temple, London EC4Y 7BA, ☎ 020 7353 4854
✉ clerks@3djb.co.uk
Call Date: July 2000, Middle Temple
Qualifications: [LLB(Hons) (Wales)]
jmayhew@3djb.co.uk

MAYNARD MR CHRISTOPHER HOWARD

Tanfield Chambers
2-5 Warwick Court, London WC1R 5DJ,
☎ 020 7421 5300
✉ clerks@tanfieldchambers.co.uk
Call Date: July 1988, Gray's Inn
Pupil Supervisor
Qualifications: [BA (Hons) (York) Dip Law]

MAYNARD MR MATTHEW DAVID

St Ive's Chambers
Whittall Street, Birmingham B4 6DH,
☎ 0121 236 0863
✉ clerks@stiveschambers.co.uk
Call Date: Nov 2003, Inner Temple
Pupil Supervisor
Qualifications: [LLB]

MAYNARD-CONNOR MR GILES

Exchange Chambers
7 Ralli Courts, West Riverside, Manchester M3 5FT, ☎ 0161 833 2722
Exchange Chambers
One Derby Square, Derby Square, Liverpool L2 9XX, ☎ 0151 236 7747
✉ info@exchangechambers.co.uk
13 Old Square Chambers
Ground Floor, 14 Old Square, Lincoln's Inn, London WC2A 3UE, ☎ 020 7831 4445
✉ clerks@13oldsquare.com
Call Date: Nov 1992, Inner Temple
Pupil Supervisor
Qualifications: [LLB (Lancs)]
maynardconnor@exchangechambers.co.uk

MAYO MR SIMON PETER QC (2008)

187 Fleet Street
London EC4A 2AT, ☎ 020 7430 7430
✉ chambers@187fleetstreet.com
Call Date: Nov 1985, Inner Temple
Recorder
Qualifications: [BA (Lond)]

MAYOH MISS MICHELLE

Kings Chambers
36 Young Street, Manchester M3 3FT,
☎ 0845 034 3444
✉ clerks@kingschambers.com
Kings Chambers
5 Park Square East, Leeds LS1 2NE,
☎ 0845 034 3444
✉ clerks@kingschambers.com
Kings Chambers
Embassy House, 60 Church Street, Birmingham B3 2DJ, ☎ 0845 034 3444
✉ clerks@kingschambers.com
Call Date: July 2003, Lincoln's Inn
Qualifications: [LLB (Hons)(L'pool)]

MAZZAG MR ANTHONY JAMES

Cobden House Chambers
19 Quay Street, Manchester M3 3HN,
☎ 0161 833 6000 ✉ Clerks@Cobden.co.uk
Call Date: Nov 1996, Lincoln's Inn
Pupil Supervisor
Qualifications: [MA]
clerks@cobden.co.uk

MCALINDEN MR BARRY O'NEILL

Field Court Chambers
5 Field Court, Gray's Inn, London WC1R 5EF,
☎ 020 7405 6114 ✉ clerks@fieldcourt.co.uk
Call Date: Oct 1993, Inner Temple
Qualifications: [BA (Hons) (Cantab)]

MCALINDEN MR MICHAEL PAUL

2 Dr Johnson's Buildings
2 Dr Johnson's Buildings, Temple, London EC4Y 7AY, ☎ 020 7936 2613
✉ clerks@2drj.com
Call Date: Nov 1997, Middle Temple
Qualifications: [LLB (Hons)(Wales)]
clerks@2drj.com

MCALLISTER MR ROBERT JAMES

The Chambers of Grahame Aldous QC
9 Gough Square, London EC4A 3DG,
☎ 020 7832 0500
✉ clerks@9goughsquare.co.uk
Call Date: Oct 2002, Inner Temple
Qualifications: [MA (Oxon) BCL (Oxon)]
rmcallister@9goughsquare.co.uk

E

MCARDLE MISS ISABEL

1 Crown Office Row
1 Crown Office Row, Temple, London EC4Y 7HH, ☎ 020 7797 7500
✉ mail@1cor.com
Call Date: July 2008, Lincoln's Inn
Qualifications: [BA (Hons) (Oxon)]
✉ isabel.mcardle@1cor.com

MCATASNEY MISS PHILIPPA MARY QC (2006)

Furnival Chambers
32 Furnival Street, London EC4A 1JQ, ☎ 020 7405 3232
Call Date: Nov 1985, Lincoln's Inn
Qualifications: [LLB (Lond)]

MCATEER MISS SHANDA LOUISE

2 Dr Johnson's Buildings
2 Dr Johnson's Buildings, Temple, London EC4Y 7AY, ☎ 020 7936 2613
✉ clerks@2drj.com
Call Date: Oct 1994, Gray's Inn
Qualifications: [BA (Hons)(Oxon)]

E

MCAVOCK MAJOR GABRIELLE

2 King's Bench Walk
2 King's Bench Walk, Temple, London EC4Y 7DE, ☎ 020 7353 1746
✉ clerks@2kbw.com
Call Date: Oct 1994, Lincoln's Inn
Qualifications: [LLB (Hons)(Lond)]

MCBRIDE MR GAVIN JOHN

Kings Chambers
36 Young Street, Manchester M3 3FT, ☎ 0845 034 3444
✉ clerks@kingschambers.com
Kings Chambers
5 Park Square East, Leeds LS1 2NE, ☎ 0845 034 3444
✉ clerks@kingschambers.com
Kings Chambers
Embassy House, 60 Church Street, Birmingham B3 2DJ, ☎ 0845 034 3444
✉ clerks@kingschambers.com
Call Date: Oct 1996, Middle Temple
Qualifications: [MA (Cantab) CPE Dip Law]
✉ gmcbride@kingschambers.com

MCBRIDE MR GEORGE

Hardwicke
New Square, Lincoln's Inn, London WC2A 3SB, ☎ 020 7242 2523
✉ enquiries@hardwicke.co.uk
Call Date: Oct 2010, Inner Temple
Qualifications: [LLB (Lond)]
✉ george.mcbride@hardwicke.co.uk

MCBRIDE MR MARTIN JEREMY

Monckton Chambers
1 & 2 Raymond Buildings, Gray's Inn, London WC1R 5NR, ☎ 020 7405 7211
✉ chambers@monckton.com
Call Date: Nov 2004, Inner Temple
Qualifications: [LLB University of Birmingham LLB Fitzwilliam Co]
✉ jmcbride@monckton.com

MCBRINN MISS DIANE MARGARET

Hardwicke
New Square, Lincoln's Inn, London WC2A 3SB, ☎ 020 7242 2523
✉ enquiries@hardwicke.co.uk
Call Date: July 2002, Gray's Inn
Qualifications: [MA (Glas)]
✉ diane.mcbrinn@hardwicke.co.uk

MCCABE MISS LOUISE ANNE

St Philips Chambers
55 Temple Row, Birmingham B2 5LS, ☎ 0121 246 7000 ✉ clerks@st-philips.com
Call Date: Oct 1996, Inner Temple
Qualifications: [BA (Hons)(Dunelm)]
✉ lmccabe@st-philips.com

MCCABE MS MARGARET ANN

Call Date: July 1981, Middle Temple
Qualifications: [BA LLB (Lond)]

MCCAFFERTY MISS CATHERINE JANE

11 King's Bench Walk
11 King's Bench Walk, Temple, London EC4Y 7EQ, ☎ 020 7632 8500
✉ clerksroom@11kbw.com
Call Date: Nov 1998, Middle Temple
Pupil Supervisor
Qualifications: [BA (Hons)(Cantab) LLM (Cantab)]
✉ jane.mccafferty@11kbw.com

MCCAFFERTY MR JOHN ANTHONY

Arden Chambers
20 Bloomsbury Square, London WC1A 2NS, ☎ 020 7242 4244
✉ clerks@ardenchambers.com
Call Date: July 2000, Gray's Inn
Qualifications: [MA (Glas) CPE]
✉ john.mccafferty@ardenchambers.com

MCCAFFERTY MISS LYNNE

4 Pump Court
4 Pump Court, Temple, London EC4Y 7AN,
☎020 7842 5555
✉chambers@4pumpcourt.com
Call Date: Oct 1997, Middle Temple
Pupil Supervisor
Qualifications: [BA (Hons)(Oxon) CPE (Lond)]
✉lmccafferty@4pumpcourt.com

MCCAFFREY MR STEPHEN PATRICK

Holborn Chambers
6 Gate Street, Lincoln's Inn Fields, London
WC2A 3HP, ☎020 7242 6060
Call Date: Oct 2007, Middle Temple
Qualifications: [LLb (Hons) (Lond)]

MCCAIN MR CHARLES STUART

Dere Street Barristers
33 Broad Chare, Newcastle Upon Tyne
NE1 3DQ, ☎0844 3351551
✉clerks@derestreet.co.uk
Call Date: Oct 2002, Middle Temple
Qualifications: [BA (L'Pool)]
✉clerks@broadcharechambers.co.uk

MCCALL MR CHRISTOPHER HUGH QC (1987)

Maitland Chambers
7 Stone Buildings, Lincoln's Inn, London
WC2A 3SZ, ☎020 7406 1200
✉clerks@maitlandchambers.com
Call Date: Nov 1966, Lincoln's Inn
Qualifications: [BA (Oxon)]
✉cmccall@maitlandchambers.com

MCCALL MR DUNCAN JAMES QC (2008)

4 Pump Court
4 Pump Court, Temple, London EC4Y 7AN,
☎020 7842 5555
✉chambers@4pumpcourt.com
Call Date: Feb 1988, Gray's Inn
Qualifications: [BA (Oxon)]
✉dmccall@4pumpcourt.com

MCCALLUM MS LOUISE MAXINE

Zenith Chambers
10 Park Square, Leeds LS1 2LH,
☎0113 245 5438
✉clerks@zenithchambers.co.uk
Call Date: Nov 1999, Gray's Inn
Qualifications: [BA (Hons)]

MCCAMBLEY MISS DAWN MELLISSA

11 Stone Buildings
11 Stone Buildings, Lincoln's Inn, London
WC2A 3TG, ☎020 7831 6381
✉clerks@11sb.com
Call Date: Oct 2005, Lincoln's Inn
Qualifications: [LLB (Hons) (Bris)]
✉mccambley@11sb.com

MCCANDLESS MR PAUL JAMES

Derwent Chambers
78 Friar Gate, Derby DE1 1FL,
☎01332 242425
✉admin@derwentchambers.co.uk
Call Date: Nov 1991, Lincoln's Inn
Pupil Supervisor
Qualifications: [LLB (Hons) (Manch)]
✉admin@derwentchambers.co.uk

MCCANN MISS CLAIRE

Cloisters
1 Pump Court, Temple, London EC4Y 7AA,
☎020 7827 4000 ✉clerks@cloisters.com
Call Date: Oct 2000, Inner Temple
Qualifications: [BA (Hons)(Oxon) Dip Law (City)]
✉cm@cloisters.com

MCCANN MISS KATIE

Atlantic Chambers
4-6 Cook Street, Liverpool L2 9QU,
☎0151 236 4421
✉info@atlanticchambers.co.uk
Call Date: Oct 2009, Lincoln's Inn
Qualifications: [LLB (L'pool)]
✉info@atlanticchambers.co.uk, katiekm@hotmail.co.uk

MCCANN MISS SARAH JANE

Hardwicke
New Square, Lincoln's Inn, London
WC2A 3SB, ☎020 7242 2523
✉enquiries@hardwicke.co.uk
Call Date: Oct 2001, Lincoln's Inn
Qualifications: [LLB (Hons)]
✉sarah.mccann@hardwicke.co.uk

Types of work: Banking, Chancery (general), Chancery (land law), Commercial law, Commercial litigation, Commercial property, Common law (general), Construction law, Equity, Financial services, Insolvency, Insurance, Landlord and tenant, Partnerships, Personal insolvency, Professional negligence, Sale and carriage of goods, Trusts

E

MCCANN MR SIMON HOWARD

Deans Court Chambers
24 St John Street, Manchester M3 4DF, ☎0161 214 6000 ✉clerks@deanscourt.co.uk
Deans Court Chambers
101 Walker Street, Preston PR1 2RR, ☎01772 565 600
✉preston@deanscourt.co.uk
Call Date: Nov 1996, Gray's Inn
Pupil Supervisor
Qualifications: [BA (Leeds)]
✉mccann@deanscourt.co.uk

MCCARRAHER MR COLIN FRASER

7 Bell Yard
London WC2A 2JR, ☎020 7831 0636
✉kevintarrant@btconnect.com
Call Date: Oct 1990, Lincoln's Inn
Qualifications: [MA (Cantab)]

MCCARROLL MISS ISOBEL SHARON

4 Breams Buildings
Chancery Lane, London EC4A 1HP, ☎020 7092 1900 ✉clerks@4bb.co.uk
Call Date: Nov 2001, Gray's Inn
Qualifications: [BA]

MCCARTHY MISS HUI LING SARITA

Gray's Inn Tax Chambers
3rd Floor, Gray's Inn Chambers, Gray's Inn, London WC1R 5JA, ☎020 7242 2642
✉clerks@taxbar.com
Call Date: July 2005, Inner Temple
Qualifications: [BSc (Dunelm) C Panel MCSI CPE (Lond) LCGI ATT]
✉hlm@taxbar.com

MCCARTHY MS KEELIN NATALIE

Chambers of Mr Ami Feder
Ground Floor, Lamb Building, Temple, London EC4Y 7AS, ☎020 7797 7788
✉clerks@lambbuilding.co.uk
Chambers of Mr Ami Feder
Ground Floor, Lamb Building, Temple, London EC4Y 7AS, ☎020 7797 7788
✉clerks@lambbuilding.co.uk
Call Date: July 2007, Gray's Inn
Qualifications: [BA (Cantab) MA (Essex) MSc (Lond) GDL]
✉k.mccarthy@mitrehouse.co.uk

MCCARTHY MR MARTIN RAYMOND

Farringdon Chambers
180 Bermondsey Street, London SE1 3TQ, ☎020 7089 5700
Call Date: Nov 1994, Gray's Inn
Pupil Supervisor
Qualifications: [LLB (Hons)]
✉martinmccarthy@farringdon-law.co.uk

MCCARTHY MISS MARY ANN

Walnut House
63 St. David's Hill, Exeter, Devon EX4 4DW, ☎01392 279751
✉clerks@walnuthouse.co.uk
Call Date: Oct 1994, Middle Temple
Pupil Supervisor
Qualifications: [LLB (Hons)(Exon)]
✉mary.mccarthy@walnuthouse.co.uk

MCCARTHY MR ROGER JOHN QC (1996)

Coram Chambers
9-11 Fulwood Place, London WC1V 6HG, ☎020 7092 3700
✉mail@coramchambers.co.uk
Call Date: July 1975, Gray's Inn
Qualifications: [BA (Hons)]
✉roger.mccarthy@coramchambers.co.uk

MCCARTHY MRS SARA REBECCA

KCH Garden Square
1 Oxford Street, Nottingham NG1 5BH, ☎0115 941 8851
✉clerks@kchgardensquare.co.uk
Call Date: July 2009, Gray's Inn
Qualifications: [BA]
✉SMcCarthy@kchgardensquare.co.uk

MCCARTHY MISS TARA MIA INGER

Thomas More Chambers
7 Lincoln's Inn Fields, London WC2A 3BP, ☎020 7404 7000
✉clerks@thomasmore.co.uk
Call Date: Oct 1997, Lincoln's Inn
Qualifications: [LLB (Hons)(Staffs)]
✉tmccarthy@thomasmore.co.uk

MCCARTHY MR WILLIAM

Bridgewater Chambers
5 Bleasefell Chase, Worsley, Manchester M28 1UZ, ☎0161 3877127
✉info@barristers-chambers.com
1 Mitre Court Buildings
1 Mitre Court Buildings, Temple, London EC4Y 7BS, ☎020 7452 8900
✉clerks@1mcb.com
Call Date: Nov 1996, Middle Temple
Qualifications: [LLB (Hons)(Leeds)]

MCCARTNEY MR JOHN KEVIN

Five Paper Buildings
1st Floor, Five Paper Buildings, Temple, London EC4Y 7HB, ☎020 7583 6117
✉clerks@5pb.co.uk
Call Date: Nov 1991, Middle Temple
Pupil Supervisor
Qualifications: [LLB (Hons)(Manch)]
✉jw@5pb.co.uk

MCCAUGHRAN MR JOHN QC (2003)

One Essex Court
Ground Floor, One Essex Court, Temple, London EC4Y 9AR, ☎020 7583 2000
✉clerks@oeclaw.co.uk
Call Date: July 1982, Gray's Inn
Qualifications: [MA (Cantab)]
✉jmccaughran@oeclaw.co.uk

MCCAUL MR COLIN BROWNLIE QC (2003)

39 Essex Street
London WC2R 3AT, ☎020 7832 1111
✉clerks@39essex.com
82 King Street
Manchester M2 4WQ, ☎0161 870 9969
Call Date: July 1978, Gray's Inn
Qualifications: [LLB (Lond)]
✉colin.mccaul@39essex.com

MCCLELLAND MR JAMES ROBERT

Fountain Court Chambers
Fountain Court, Temple, London EC4Y 9DH, ☎020 7583 3335
✉chambers@fountaincourt.co.uk
Call Date: July 2004, Lincoln's Inn
Qualifications: [BA Hons(Cantab) PgDL BCL (Oxon)]
✉jm@fountaincourt.co.uk

MCCLEMENT MS LYNETTE

No5 Chambers
Fountain Court, Steelhouse Lane, Birmingham B4 6DR, ☎0845 210 5555 ✉info@no5.com
No5 Chambers
Greenwood House, 4-7 Salisbury Court, London EC4Y 8AA, ☎0845 210 5555
No5 Chambers
38 Queen Square, Bristol BS1 4QS, ☎0845 210 5555
Citadel Chambers
The Citadel, 190 Corporation Street, Birmingham B4 6QD, ☎0121 233 8500
✉clerks@citadelchambers.com
Call Date: Oct 2002, Inner Temple
Qualifications: [BA (S.Africa) LLM (B'ham) CPE (B'ham)]

MCCLENAGHAN MISS FRANCES SARAH KATHERINE

1 Chancery Lane
London WC2A 1LF, ☎0845 634 6666
✉clerks@1chancerylane.com
Call Date: Mar 2009, Lincoln's Inn
Qualifications: [LLB (Dunelm)]
✉fmcclenaghan@1chancerylane.com

MCCLINTOCK MR JUSTIN JAMES

15 New Bridge Street
London EC4V 6AU, ☎020 7842 1900
✉clerks@15nbs.com
Call Date: Oct 2009, Lincoln's Inn
Qualifications: [LLB (Lond)]
✉justin.mcclintock@15nbs.com

MCCLORY MS ELIZABETH JANE

New Court Chambers
3 Broad Chare, Newcastle Upon Tyne NE1 3DQ, ☎0191 232 1980
✉clerks@newcourt-chambers.co.uk
Call Date: Nov 2003, Inner Temple
Qualifications: [BA (Dunelm) Dip Law]
✉elizabeth.mcclory@newcourt-chambers.co.uk

MCCLOSKEY MISS LOUISE

St Johns Buildings Liverpool
8th Floor India Buildings, Water Street, Liverpool L2 0XG, ☎0151 243 6000
✉clerk@stjohnsbuildings.co.uk
16 Winckley Square
Preston PR1 3JJ, ☎01772 256100
St Johns Buildings
24a - 28 St John Street, Manchester M3 4DJ, ☎0161 214 1500
✉clerk@stjohnsbuildings.co.uk
Call Date: Oct 2002, Gray's Inn
Qualifications: [LLB (L'Pool)]

MCCLUGGAGE MR BRIAN THOMAS

9 St John Street
Manchester M3 4DN, ☎0161 955 9000
✉civilclerks@9sjs.com / criminalclerks@9sjs.com
Call Date: Oct 1995, Middle Temple
Pupil Supervisor
Qualifications: [MA (Cantab) LLM (USA)]
✉brian.mccluggage@9sjs.com

MCCLUSKEY MR ALEC STUART

Maitland Chambers
7 Stone Buildings, Lincoln's Inn, London WC2A 3SZ, ☎020 7406 1200
✉clerks@maitlandchambers.com
Call Date: Oct 2005, Inner Temple
Qualifications: [BA Merton College University of Oxford CPE Cit]
✉amccluskey@maitlandchambers.com

MCCLUSKEY MISS ELLA

Northampton Chambers
10 Spencer Parade, Northampton NN1 5AQ, ☎01604 636271
✉clerks@northampton-chambers.co.uk
Call Date: Oct 2006, Middle Temple
Qualifications: [LLB (Hons)]

MCCLUSKEY MR MARK PATRICK

St Mary's Family Law Chambers
26-28 High Pavement, The Lace Market, Nottingham NG1 1HN, ☎0115 950 3503
✉clerks@stmarysflc.co.uk
Call Date: July 2001, Gray's Inn
Qualifications: [BA (Nott'm) MA]

MCCLYMONT MR GREG

4 KBW
Ground Floor, 4 King's Bench Walk, Temple, London EC4Y 7DL, ☎020 7822 8822
✉law@4kbw.net
Call Date: Mar 2010, Lincoln's Inn
Qualifications: [BA (Oxon)]

MCCOLGAN PROF AILEEN

Matrix Chambers
Griffin Building, Gray's Inn, London WC1R 5LN, ☎020 7404 3447
✉matrix@matrixlaw.co.uk / Iscott@matrixlaw.co.uk
Call Date: Nov 2001, Lincoln's Inn
Qualifications: [BA (Hons) (Cantab) LLM]
aileenmccolgan@matrixlaw.co.uk

MCCOLGAN MISS CAROLINE ANNE

Crown Office Chambers
2 Crown Office Row, Temple, London EC4Y 7HJ, ☎020 7797 8100
✉mail@crownofficechambers.com
Call Date: July 2010, Inner Temple
Qualifications: [BA (Oxon) CPE]
clerks@crownofficechambers.com

MCCOMBIE MR FERGUS ALEXANDER PAUL

1 Gray's Inn Square
Ground Floor, 1 Gray's Inn Square, London WC1R 5AA, ☎020 7405 0001
Call Date: Oct 1999, Gray's Inn
Qualifications: [BA (Oxon)]

MCCONNELL MR CHRISTOPHER RONALD

4 King's Bench Walk
2nd Floor, 4 King's Bench Walk, Temple, London EC4Y 7DL, ☎020 7822 7000
✉clerks@4kbw.co.uk
Call Date: July 1979, Lincoln's Inn
Pupil Supervisor
Qualifications: [MA (Oxon)]
cmc@4kbw.co.uk

MCCORMACK MR ALAN

Staple Inn Chambers
1st Floor, 9 Staple Inn, Holborn Bars, London WC1V 7QH, ☎020 7242 5240
✉clerks@stapleinn.co.uk
Call Date: Oct 1990, Lincoln's Inn
Pupil Supervisor
Qualifications: [LLB (Hons)]
amc@stapleinn.co.uk

MCCORMACK MR BENJAMIN

Chambers of Ian Macdonald QC
Garden Court North, 22 Oxford Court, Manchester M2 3WQ, ☎0161 236 1840
✉clerks@gcnchambers.co.uk
Call Date: Nov 2005, Gray's Inn
Pupil Supervisor
Qualifications: [LLB]
bmccormack@gcnchambers.co.uk

MCCORMACK MISS HELEN

15 New Bridge Street
London EC4V 6AU, ☎020 7842 1900
✉clerks@15nbs.com
Call Date: Feb 1986, Middle Temple
Pupil Supervisor
Qualifications: [LLB(L'pool)]
helen.mccormack@15nbs.com

MCCORMACK MR PHILIP ALEXANDER

42 Bedford Row
London WC1R 4LL, ☎020 7831 0222
✉clerks@42br.com
Call Date: Oct 1994, Gray's Inn
Pupil Supervisor
Qualifications: [LLB (Wales)]
clerks@42br.com

MCCORMACK MISS THERESA MARIE

St Philips Chambers
55 Temple Row, Birmingham B2 5LS, ☎0121 246 7000 ✉clerks@st-philips.com
Call Date: July 2002, Inner Temple
Qualifications: [LLB (Lancaster) LLM (ICSL)]

MCCORMICK MS ALISON CLAIRE

Outer Temple Chambers
The Outer Temple, 222 Strand, London WC2R 1BA, ☎020 7353 6381
✉clerks@outertemple.com
Call Date: Nov 1988, Middle Temple
Pupil Supervisor
Qualifications: [BA (Hons)]
alison.mccormick@outertemple.com

MCCORMICK MISS LUCY

13 King's Bench Walk
13 King's Bench Walk, Temple, London EC4Y 7EN, ☎ 020 7353 7204
✉ clerks@13kbw.co.uk
Call Date: July 2008, Middle Temple
Qualifications: [MA (Hons) (Oxon)]

MCCORMICK DR PAUL MARTIN

Hampshire Chambers
Malton House, 24 Hampshire Terrace, Portsmouth, Hampshire PO1 2QF,
☎ 023 9282 6636
✉ PMC.CLERK@BTCONNECT.COM
Call Date: July 1983, Middle Temple
Qualifications: [Dip Soc Stud B Sc MA MPhil DPhil (Oxon)]

MCCORMICK MR WILLIAM THOMAS QC (2010)

Ely Place Chambers
30 Ely Place, London EC1N 6TD,
☎ 020 7400 9600 ✉ admin@elyplace.com
Call Date: July 1985, Gray's Inn
Pupil Supervisor
Qualifications: [LLB (Hons) (Cardiff)]
✉ wmccormick@elyplace.com

MCCOURT MR CHRISTOPHER

1 KBW Chambers
1 King's Bench Walk, Temple, London EC4Y 7DB, ☎ 020 7936 1500
✉ clerks@1kbw.co.uk
King's Bench Chambers
174 High Street, Lewes BN7 1YE,
☎ 01273 402600
Call Date: Nov 1993, Inner Temple
Pupil Supervisor
Qualifications: [LLB (Nott'm)]
✉ cmccourt@1kbw.co.uk, chrismccourt64@btinternet.com

MCCOURT FRITZ MR DANIEL WILLIAM

Serle Court
6 New Square, Lincoln's Inn, London WC2A 3QS, ☎ 020 7242 6105
✉ clerks@serlecourt.co.uk
Call Date: Nov 2007, Lincoln's Inn
Qualifications: [BA (Cantab)]
✉ dfritz@serlecourt.co.uk

MCCRACKEN MR JAMES

Cornwall Street Chambers
85-87 Cornwall Street, Birmingham B3 3BY,
☎ 0121 233 7500
✉ clerks@cornwallstreet.co.uk
Call Date: Nov 1998, Middle Temple
Qualifications: [LLB (Hons)(Herts)]
✉ jamie.mccracken@cornwallstreet.co.uk

MCCRACKEN MR ROBERT HENRY JOY QC (2003)

Francis Taylor Building
Inner Temple, London EC4Y 7BY,
☎ 020 7353 8415 ✉ clerks@ftb.eu.com
Call Date: July 1973, Inner Temple
Qualifications: [MA (Oxon)]
✉ robert.mccracken@ftb.eu.com

MCCRAE MISS FIONA

Trinity Chambers
The Custom House, 39 Quayside, Newcastle Upon Tyne NE1 3DE, ☎ 0191 232 1927
✉ info@trinitychambers.co.uk
Trinity Chambers
Multi Media Exchange, 72-80 Corporation Road, Middlesbrough TS1 2RF,
☎ 01642 247569
✉ info@trinitychambers.co.uk
Call Date: July 1986, Gray's Inn
Qualifications: [LLB (Newc)]
✉ f.mccrae@trinitychambers.co.uk

MCCREATH MR JAMES WILLIAM

Wilberforce Chambers
8 New Square, Lincoln's Inn, London WC2A 3QP, ☎ 020 7306 0102
✉ chambers@wilberforce.co.uk
Call Date: July 2009, Inner Temple
Qualifications: [BA (Oxon)]
✉ jmccreath@wilberforcechambers.co.uk

MCCREDIE MISS FIONNUALA MARY CONSTANCE

Keating Chambers
15 Essex Street, London WC2R 3AA,
☎ 020 7544 2600
✉ clerks@keatingchambers.com
Call Date: Oct 1992, Middle Temple
Qualifications: [BSc (Hons) (Manch) MA (Brunel) CPE]
✉ fmccredie@keatingchambers.com

Fax: 020 7544 2700;
Out of hours telephone: 020 7544 2600
URL: www.keatingchambers.com

Types of work: Arbitration, Commercial litigation, Construction law, Energy, Environment, European Union, Health and safety, Procurement, Professional negligence

E

MCCRIMMON MISS CATHRYN JANE

4 Breams Buildings
Chancery Lane, London EC4A 1HP,
☎ 020 7092 1900 ✉ clerks@4bb.co.uk
Call Date: Nov 1991, Middle Temple
Qualifications: [LLB (Hons)]

MCCRINDELL MR JAMES DERREY

1 Pump Court
Elm Court, Temple, London EC4Y 7AB,
☎ 020 7842 7070
✉ (name)@pumpcourt.co.uk
Call Date: Oct 1993, Middle Temple
Pupil Supervisor
Qualifications: [BSc (Hons)(Lond) Dip Law (Italy)]
jm@1pumpcourt.co.uk

MCCROSSAN MR SIMON GERARD

New Walk Chambers
27 New Walk, Leicester, Leicestershire
LE1 6TE, ☎ 0871 200 1298 / 0116 255 9144
✉ clerks@newwalkchambers.co.uk
Call Date: July 2010, Gray's Inn
Qualifications: [BA]

E

MCCRUDDEN PROF JOHN CHRISTOPHER

Blackstone Chambers
Blackstone House, Temple, London
EC4Y 9BW, ☎ 020 7583 1770
✉ clerks@blackstonechambers.com
Call Date: May 1996, Gray's Inn
Qualifications: [LLB (Ireland) LLM (USA) MA (Oxon) DPhil (Oxon)]
christophermccrudden@blackstonechambers.com

MCCUBBIN MR IAN WILLIAM

Cobden House Chambers
19 Quay Street, Manchester M3 3HN,
☎ 0161 833 6000 ✉ Clerks@Cobden.co.uk
Call Date: July 2010, Lincoln's Inn
Qualifications: [LLB (Manch)]

MCCUE MR DONALD

11 Stone Buildings
11 Stone Buildings, Lincoln's Inn, London
WC2A 3TG, ☎ 020 7831 6381
✉ clerks@11sb.com
Call Date: July 1974, Lincoln's Inn
Qualifications: [MA (Cantab)]

MCCULLOCH MISS FIONA CATHARINE JANE

Middle Temple Lane Chambers
2nd Floor South, 1 Middle Temple Lane,
London EC4Y 9AA, ☎ 020 7583 4352
✉ chambers@mtlchambers.com
Call Date: July 2002, Middle Temple
Qualifications: [LLB (Hons)]

MCCULLOCH MR NIALL ALAN

Enterprise Chambers
9 Old Square, Lincoln's Inn, London
WC2A 3SR, ☎ 020 7405 9471
✉ london@enterprisechambers.com
Enterprise Chambers
65 Quayside, Newcastle Upon Tyne NE1 3DE,
☎ 0191 222 3344
✉ newcastle@enterprisechambers.com
Enterprise Chambers
43 Park Square, Leeds LS1 2NP,
☎ 0113 246 0391
✉ leeds@enterprisechambers.com
Call Date: Oct 2000, Lincoln's Inn
Qualifications: [BA (Hons) (Oxon) MA]
niallmcculloch@enterprisechambers.com

MCCULLOUGH MR ANGUS MAXWELL THOMAS QC (2010)

1 Crown Office Row
1 Crown Office Row, Temple, London
EC4Y 7HH, ☎ 020 7797 7500
✉ mail@1cor.com
Call Date: Oct 1990, Middle Temple
Pupil Supervisor
Qualifications: [BA (Oxon) Dip Law]
angus.mccullough@1cor.com

MCCULLOUGH MISS LOUISE CLARE

Chambers of Mr Ami Feder
Ground Floor, Lamb Building, Temple, London
EC4Y 7AS, ☎ 020 7797 7788
✉ clerks@lambbuilding.co.uk
Lamb Building
22 Ship Street, Brighton BN1 1AD,
☎ 01273 820490
✉ admin@lambbuilding.co.uk
Chambers of Mr Ami Feder
Ground Floor, Lamb Building, Temple, London
EC4Y 7AS, ☎ 020 7797 7788
✉ clerks@lambbuilding.co.uk
Call Date: Oct 1991, Middle Temple
Pupil Supervisor
Qualifications: [LLB (Hons) (Lond)]
clerks@lambbuilding.co.uk

MCCUNE MR RODNEY JAMES

Goldsmith Chambers
Ground Floor, Goldsmith Building, Temple, London EC4Y 7BL, ☎ 020 7353 6802
✉ clerks@goldsmithchambers.com
Call Date: Nov 2000, Lincoln's Inn
Qualifications: [LLB (Hons) (London)]
✉ R.McCune@goldsmithchambers.law.co.uk

MCDERMOTT MR FRAZER IAN

Dere Street Barristers
33 Broad Chare, Newcastle Upon Tyne NE1 3DQ, ☎ 0844 3351551
✉ clerks@derestreet.co.uk
Call Date: Mar 2004, Inner Temple
Qualifications: [LLB (Northumbria)]

MCDERMOTT MR GERARD FRANCIS QC (1999)

Chambers of Gerard McDermott QC
Weir House, 7 Stamford Street, Stalybridge SK15 1JP, ☎ 0161 304 4301
✉ gerard@mcdermottqc.com
9 St John Street
Manchester M3 4DN, ☎ 0161 955 9000
✉ civilclerks@9sjs.com / criminalclerks@9sjs.com
Outer Temple Chambers
The Outer Temple, 222 Strand, London WC2R 1BA, ☎ 020 7353 6381
✉ clerks@outertemple.com
Call Date: July 1978, Middle Temple
Pupil Supervisor, Recorder
Qualifications: [LLB (Manch)]

MCDERMOTT MR JOHN RAYMUND QC (2003)

Chavasse Court Chambers
18 Queen Avenue, Liverpool L2 4TX, ☎ 0151 229 2030
✉ clerks@chavassechambers.co.uk
Call Date: Nov 1976, Gray's Inn
Qualifications: [LLB]
✉ j.mcdermott@blueyonder.co.uk

MCDERMOTT MR MATHEW DAVID DENIS

5 Pump Court
Ground Floor, 5 Pump Court, Temple, London EC4Y 7AP, ☎ 020 7353 2532
✉ clerks@5pumpcourt.com
Call Date: July 2008, Inner Temple
Qualifications: [LLB (Warw)]
✉ mathewmcdermott@5pumpcourt.com

MCDEVITT MR COLIN JOHN

3 PB Barristers
4 St Peter Street, Winchester SO23 8BW, ☎ 01962 868884
✉ clerks.winchester@3paper.co.uk
3 PB Barristers
23 Beaumont Street, Oxford OX1 2NP, ☎ 01865 793 736
3 PB Barristers
3 Paper Buildings, Temple, London EC4Y 7EU, ☎ 020 7583 8055
3 PB Barristers
Royal Talbot House, 2 Victoria Street, Bristol, Avon BS1 6BB, ☎ 0117 928 1520
3 PB Barristers
30 Christchurch Road, Bournemouth, Dorset BH1 3PD, ☎ 01202 292102
✉ clerks.bournemouth@3paper.co.uk
Call Date: Oct 1995, Inner Temple
Pupil Supervisor
Qualifications: [BSc (Reading)]

MCDONAGH MR MATTHEW BARTLY ANTHONY

23 Essex Street
London WC2R 3AA, ☎ 020 7413 0353
✉ clerks@23es.com
Call Date: Oct 1994, Middle Temple
Pupil Supervisor, Recorder
Qualifications: [LLB (Hons)(B'ham)]
✉ matthewmcdonagh@23es.com

MCDONALD MR ANDREW

Number 7 Harrington Street Chambers
7 Harrington Street, Liverpool L2 9YH, ☎ 0151 242 0707 ✉ clerks@7hs.co.uk
Call Date: July 1971, Gray's Inn
Qualifications: [LLB (L'pool)]
✉ andrew.mcdonald@7hs.co.uk

MCDONALD MR BRENT ANDREW

Old Square Chambers
3 Orchard Court, St Augustine's Yard, Bristol BS1 5DP, ☎ 0117 930 5100
✉ clerks@oldsquare.co.uk
Call Date: Oct 2000, Gray's Inn
Qualifications: [LLB (Hons)(Plymouth)]
✉ mcdonald@oldsquare.co.uk

MCDONALD MR GEORGE ALAN DEWAR

Four New Square
Four New Square, Lincoln's Inn, London WC2A 3RJ, ☎ 020 7822 2000
✉ barristers@4newsquare.com
Call Date: Oct 2007, Lincoln's Inn
Qualifications: [BA (Oxon)]
✉ g.mcdonald@4newsquare.com

E

MCDONALD MISS JANET

9 Park Place
9 Park Place, Cardiff, South Glamorgan CF10 3DP, ☎ 029 2038 2731
✉ clerks@9parkplace.co.uk
Call Date: July 1984, Gray's Inn
Qualifications: [LLB]
✉ jmcdonald@9parkplace.co.uk, clerks@9parkplace.co.uk

MCDONALD MR JOHN WILLIAM

2 Temple Gardens
2 Temple Gardens, Temple, London EC4Y 9AY, ☎ 020 7822 1200
✉ clerks@2tg.co.uk
Call Date: Nov 1981, Middle Temple
Pupil Supervisor
Qualifications: [MA (St Andrews) FRSA FCIArb]
✉ jmcdonald@2tg.co.uk

MCDONALD MR LAWRENCE PATRICK

Atlantic Chambers
4-6 Cook Street, Liverpool L2 9QU, ☎ 0151 236 4421
✉ info@atlanticchambers.co.uk
Call Date: Oct 1996, Inner Temple
Qualifications: [LLB (Lond)]
✉ lawrencemcdonald@atlanticchambers.co.uk

MCDONALD MS MARGARET MARY BERNADETTE

Kenworthy's Chambers
Arlington House, Bloom Street, Salford, Manchester M3 6AJ, ☎ 0161 832 4036
Call Date: Nov 2000, Inner Temple
Pupil Supervisor
Qualifications: [LLB]

MCDONALD MR MARK PAUL

1 Pump Court
Elm Court, Temple, London EC4Y 7AB, ☎ 020 7842 7070
✉ (name)@pumpcourt.co.uk
Call Date: Oct 1997, Lincoln's Inn
Pupil Supervisor
Qualifications: [LLB (Hons)]
✉ mcd@1pumpcourt.co.uk

MCDONALD MS MELANIE SHARON

No5 Chambers
Greenwood House, 4-7 Salisbury Court, London EC4Y 8AA, ☎ 0845 210 5555
No5 Chambers
38 Queen Square, Bristol BS1 4QS, ☎ 0845 210 5555
No5 Chambers
Fountain Court, Steelhouse Lane, Birmingham B4 6DR, ☎ 0845 210 5555 ✉ info@no5.com
Call Date: Nov 1990, Inner Temple
Pupil Supervisor
Qualifications: [MA (Kent) Dip Law (Lond)]
✉ mm@no5.com

MCDONALD MR PAUL

9 St John Street
Manchester M3 4DN, ☎ 0161 955 9000
✉ civilclerks@9sjs.com / criminalclerks@9sjs.com
Call Date: July 1975, Lincoln's Inn
Pupil Supervisor
Qualifications: [LLB (Hons)]

MCDONALD MISS RACHAEL

Alpha Court Chambers
Stuart House, Buckingham Lodge, 23 Kenilworth Road, Leamington Spa CV32 6JD, ☎ 01926 886412 ✉ CP@Payton.uk.net
Call Date: Nov 2000, Lincoln's Inn
Qualifications: [LLB (Hons)]

MCDONNELL MR CONRAD MORTIMER

Gray's Inn Tax Chambers
3rd Floor, Gray's Inn Chambers, Gray's Inn, London WC1R 5JA, ☎ 020 7242 2642
✉ clerks@taxbar.com
Call Date: Oct 1994, Lincoln's Inn
Pupil Supervisor
Qualifications: [MA (Oxon)]
✉ clerks@taxbar.com

MCDONNELL MISS CONSTANCE

3 Stone Buildings
Ground Floor, 3 Stone Buildings, Lincoln's Inn, London WC2A 3XL, ☎ 020 7242 4937
✉ clerks@3sb.law.co.uk
Call Date: July 2000, Lincoln's Inn
Pupil Supervisor
Qualifications: [BA(Hons) MA (Oxon)]
✉ cmcdonnell@3sb.law.co.uk

MCDONNELL MR JOHN BERESFORD WILLIAM QC (1984)

13 Old Square Chambers
Ground Floor, 14 Old Square, Lincoln's Inn, London WC2A 3UE, ☎ 020 7831 4445
✉ clerks@13oldsquare.com
Call Date: July 1968, Inner Temple
Qualifications: [MA (Oxon) LLM (USA)]
✉ clerks@13oldsquare.com

MCDONNELL MR MARTIN JAMES

Warwick House Chambers
8 Warwick Court, Warwick House Chambers, Gray's Inn, London WC1R 5DJ,
☎ 020 7430 2323
✉ clerks@warwickhousechambers.com
Call Date: Oct 1997, Middle Temple
Qualifications: [LLB (Hons)(Lond)]
✉ clerks@warwickhousechambers.com

MCDOWELL MR DANIEL ROBIN

36 Bedford Row
London WC1R 4JH, ☎ 020 7421 8000
✉ chambers@36bedfordrow.co.uk
Call Date: Oct 2001, Gray's Inn
Qualifications: [LLB (Cardiff) MPhil (Cantab) Dip Law]
✉ dmcdowell@36bedfordrow.co.uk

MCELDUFF MR BARRY ANTHONY

2 King's Bench Walk
2 King's Bench Walk, Temple, London EC4Y 7DE, ☎ 020 7353 1746
✉ clerks@2kbw.com
Call Date: July 2002, Lincoln's Inn
Qualifications: [BA (Hons)(Belfast)]
✉ bmcelduff@2kbw.com

MCELEAVY MR PETER EUGENE

1 Garden Court Family Law Chambers
Ground Floor, One Garden Court, Temple, London EC4Y 9BJ, ☎ 020 7797 7900
✉ clerks@1gc.com
Call Date: Oct 1999, Gray's Inn
Qualifications: [BSc (Surrey) PhD]

MCERLEAN MISS AILEEN

Hardwicke
New Square, Lincoln's Inn, London WC2A 3SB, ☎ 020 7242 2523
✉ enquiries@hardwicke.co.uk
Call Date: Mar 2011, Middle Temple
Qualifications: [LLB (Bris)]
✉ aileen.mcerlean@hardwicke.co.uk

MCEWAN MR MALCOLM CHARLES

18 St John Street
Manchester M3 4EA, ☎ 0161 278 1800
✉ clerks@18sjs.com
Call Date: July 1976, Middle Temple
Pupil Supervisor
Qualifications: [MA (Oxon)]

MCEWAN MISS VERA GEORGINA

1 Garden Court Family Law Chambers
Ground Floor, One Garden Court, Temple, London EC4Y 9BJ, ☎ 020 7797 7900
✉ clerks@1gc.com
Call Date: Nov 1979, Inner Temple
Qualifications: [MA Dip Ed MSc LLM]

MCFADYEN MS LYNN JANET

Park Lane Plowden
19 Westgate, Leeds LS1 2RD,
☎ 0113 228 5049
✉ clerks@parklaneplowden.co.uk
Call Date: Oct 2003, Inner Temple
Pupil Supervisor
Qualifications: [LLB (B'ham)]
✉ lynn.mcfadyen@parklaneplowden.co.uk

MCFARLAND MISS DENISE

Three New Square IP
3 New Square, Lincoln's Inn, London WC2A 3RS, ☎ 020 7405 1111
✉ clerks@3newsquare.co.uk
Call Date: July 1987, Inner Temple
Pupil Supervisor
Qualifications: [MA (Cantab)]

MCFARLANE MR ALASTAIR DUNCAN JAMES

Temple Garden Chambers
1 Harcourt Buildings, Temple, London EC4Y 9DA, ☎ 020 7583 1315
✉ clerks@tgchambers.com
Call Date: July 1985, Middle Temple
Qualifications: [LLB]
✉ amcfarlane@tgchambers.com

MCFARLANE MISS CYNTHIA JULLIETT

10 King's Bench Walk
Ground Floor, 10 King's Bench Walk, Temple, London EC4Y 7EB, ☎ 020 7353 7742
✉ Chambers@10kingsbenchwalk.co.uk
Call Date: Nov 2003, Middle Temple
Qualifications: [LLB (Hons) (N'hampton)]
✉ cynthia.mcfarlane@10kingsbenchwalk.co.uk

E

MCGAHEY MISS CATHRYN MARGARET

Temple Garden Chambers
1 Harcourt Buildings, Temple, London EC4Y 9DA, ☎020 7583 1315
✉clerks@tgchambers.com
Call Date: Nov 1990, Inner Temple
Pupil Supervisor
Qualifications: [MA (Cantab)]
CathrynMcGahey@tgchambers.com

MCGAHEY MISS ELIZABETH CLARE

30 Park Place
Cardiff CF10 3BS, ☎029 2039 8421
✉clerks@30parkplace.law.co.uk
Call Date: Nov 1994, Inner Temple
Qualifications: [BA (Wales) CPE (Wales)]
ecm@30parkplace.co.uk

MCGARRY MR STEVEN DAVID

St Johns Buildings
24a - 28 St John Street, Manchester M3 4DJ, ☎0161 214 1500
✉clerk@stjohnsbuildings.co.uk
16 Winckley Square
Preston PR1 3JJ, ☎01772 256100
St Johns Buildings Liverpool
8th Floor India Buildings, Water Street, Liverpool L2 0XG, ☎0151 243 6000
✉clerk@stjohnsbuildings.co.uk
Call Date: Mar 2005, Lincoln's Inn
Qualifications: [BA (Hons) Birmingham]
clerk@stjohnsbuildings.co.uk

MCGARVEY MR TOMAS PATRICK

7 Bell Yard
London WC2A 2JR, ☎020 7831 0636
✉kevintarrant@btconnect.com
Call Date: Mar 2010, Lincoln's Inn
Qualifications: [LLB (Kent)]

MCGEE PROF ANDREW

Kings Chambers
36 Young Street, Manchester M3 3FT, ☎0845 034 3444
✉clerks@kingschambers.com
Kings Chambers
5 Park Square East, Leeds LS1 2NE, ☎0845 034 3444
✉clerks@kingschambers.com
Kings Chambers
Embassy House, 60 Church Street, Birmingham B3 2DJ, ☎0845 034 3444
✉clerks@kingschambers.com
Call Date: Nov 1998, Lincoln's Inn
Qualifications: [BA BCL (Oxon)]
amcgee@kingschambers.com

MCGEE MR ANDREW WILLIAM

2 Bedford Row
London WC1R 4BU, ☎020 7440 8888
✉clerks@2bedfordrow.co.uk
Call Date: July 1999, Middle Temple
Qualifications: [BA (Hons) MA]
amcgee@2bedfordrow.co.uk

MCGEE DR TRISTAN PAUL

Foxhill Chambers
Matterdale, Penrith, Cumbria CA11 0SA, ☎01768 482710
✉clerking@foxhillchambers.com
Call Date: Nov 1997, Middle Temple
Qualifications: [BA MSc PhD]
tpmcgee@tristanmcgee.com, clerking@foxhillchambers.com

MCGEORGE MR ANTHONY WILLIAM

13 King's Bench Walk
13 King's Bench Walk, Temple, London EC4Y 7EN, ☎020 7353 7204
✉clerks@13kbw.co.uk
13 KBW
32 Beaumont Street, Oxford OX1 2NP, ☎01865 311066 ✉clerks@13kbw.co.uk
Call Date: Nov 1969, Inner Temple
Pupil Supervisor
Qualifications: [MA (Cantab)]
amcgeorge@13kbw.co.uk

MCGHEE MR JOHN ALEXANDER QC (2003)

Maitland Chambers
7 Stone Buildings, Lincoln's Inn, London WC2A 3SZ, ☎020 7406 1200
✉clerks@maitlandchambers.com
Call Date: July 1984, Lincoln's Inn
Qualifications: [MA (Oxon)]
jmcghee@maitlandchambers.com

MCGHEE MR PHILIP JAMES

QEB Hollis Whiteman
1-2 Laurence Pountney Hill, London EC4R 0EU, ☎020 7933 8855
✉barristers@qebhw.co.uk
Call Date: Oct 2003, Gray's Inn
Qualifications: [MA (Oxon) BA (Oxon)]
philip.mcghee@qebhw.co.uk

MCGHEE MR STUART EDWARD

College Chambers
19 Carlton Crescent, Southampton, Hampshire SO15 2ET, ☎023 8023 0338
✉clerks@college-chambers.co.uk
Call Date: Mar 2000, Lincoln's Inn
Qualifications: [LLB (Hons) (Sheff) LLM (Dunelm)]
smcghee@College-Chambers.co.uk

MCGINN MR DOMINIC STUART

4 Breams Buildings
Chancery Lane, London EC4A 1HP,
☎020 7092 1900 ✉clerks@4bb.co.uk
Call Date: Nov 1990, Gray's Inn
Qualifications: [LLB (Wales)]

MCGINTY MR ROBERT FRASER

St Johns Buildings
24a - 28 St John Street, Manchester M3 4DJ,
☎0161 214 1500
✉clerk@stjohnsbuildings.co.uk
St Johns Buildings
21 White Friars, Chester CH1 1NZ,
☎01244 323070
✉clerk@stjohnsbuildings.co.uk
St Johns Buildings Liverpool
8th Floor India Buildings, Water Street,
Liverpool L2 0XG, ☎0151 243 6000
✉clerk@stjohnsbuildings.co.uk
Call Date: Nov 1994, Inner Temple
Qualifications: [BA (Oxon)]
🖃clerk@stjohnsbuildings.co.uk

MCGIVERN MR THOMAS AIDAN

Linenhall Chambers
1 Stanley Place, Chester CH1 2LU,
☎01244 348282
✉clerks@linenhallchambers.co.uk
Call Date: Nov 2008, Gray's Inn

MCGONIGAL MR DAVID AMBROSE

Broadway House Chambers
Broadway House, 9 Bank Street, Bradford,
West Yorkshire BD1 1TW, ☎01274 722560
✉clerks@broadwayhouse.co.uk
Broadway House Chambers
25 Park Square West, Leeds, West Yorkshire
LS1 2PW, ☎0113 246 2600
✉clerks@broadwayhouse.co.uk
Call Date: July 1982, Gray's Inn
Pupil Supervisor
Qualifications: [BA (Hons)]
🖃dam@broadwayhouse.co.uk

MCGOWAN MISS MAURA PATRICIA QC (2001)

2 Bedford Row
London WC1R 4BU, ☎020 7440 8888
✉clerks@2bedfordrow.co.uk
Lincoln House Chambers
Tower 12, The Avenue North, Spinningfields,
18-22 Bridge Street, Manchester M3 3BZ,
☎0161 832 5701
✉info@lincolnhousechambers.com
Call Date: Nov 1980, Middle Temple
Qualifications: [LLB (Manch)]
🖃mmcgowan@2bedfordrow.co.uk

MCGRATH MR ANDREW JOHN

No5 Chambers
Fountain Court, Steelhouse Lane, Birmingham
B4 6DR, ☎0845 210 5555 ✉info@no5.com
No5 Chambers
Greenwood House, 4-7 Salisbury Court,
London EC4Y 8AA, ☎0845 210 5555
No5 Chambers
38 Queen Square, Bristol BS1 4QS,
☎0845 210 5555
Call Date: Nov 1983, Gray's Inn
Qualifications: [BA]
🖃am@no5.com

MCGRATH MISS ELIZABETH ANN

St Philips Chambers
55 Temple Row, Birmingham B2 5LS,
☎0121 246 7000 ✉clerks@st-philips.com
Call Date: Nov 1987, Inner Temple
Pupil Supervisor
Qualifications: [LLB (Hull)]
🖃emcgrath@st-philips.co.uk

MCGRATH MR FRANCIS JOSEPH

23 Essex Street
London WC2R 3AA, ☎020 7413 0353
✉clerks@23es.com
Call Date: Oct 1995, Middle Temple
Qualifications: [MA (oxon)]
🖃frankmcgrath@23es.com

MCGRATH MR PAUL ANTHONY QC (2011)

Essex Court Chambers
24 Lincoln's Inn Fields, London WC2A 3EG,
☎020 7813 8000
✉clerksroom@essexcourt.net
Call Date: Nov 1994, Inner Temple
Qualifications: [BA (Hons) BCL (Oxon)]
🖃pmcgrath@essexcourt.net

MCGRATH MR PAUL FRANCIS

Temple Garden Chambers
1 Harcourt Buildings, Temple, London
EC4Y 9DA, ☎020 7583 1315
✉clerks@tgchambers.com
Call Date: Oct 1997, Gray's Inn
Pupil Supervisor
Qualifications: [LLB (Lond)]
🖃paulmcgrath@tgchambers.com

E

MCGREGOR MR ALISTAIR JOHN QC (1997)

11 King's Bench Walk
11 King's Bench Walk, Temple, London EC4Y 7EQ, ☎ 020 7632 8500
✉ clerksroom@11kbw.com
Call Date: July 1974, Middle Temple
Qualifications: [LLB (Lond)]
✉ alistair.mcgregor@11kbw.com

MCGREGOR MS CLAIRE MARY-ASTRID

Garden Court Chambers
57-60 Lincoln's Inn Fields, London WC2A 3LJ, ☎ 020 7993 7600 ✉ info@gclaw.co.uk
Call Date: July 2009, Lincoln's Inn
Qualifications: [BA (Lond) CPE OBPP]

MCGREGOR MR HARVEY QC (1978)

Hailsham Chambers
Ground Floor, 4 Paper Buildings, Temple, London EC4Y 7EX, ☎ 020 7643 5000
✉ clerks@hailshamchambers.com
Call Date: Feb 1955, Inner Temple
Qualifications: [MA SJD (USA) DCL]
✉ harvey.mcgregor@hailshamchambers.com

MCGUINNESS MR JOHN FRANCIS QC (2001)

9-12 Bell Yard
London WC2A 2JR, ☎ 020 7400 1800
✉ clerks@9-12bellyard.com
Call Date: July 1980, Lincoln's Inn
Recorder
Qualifications: [BA (Lond)]
✉ jncqc@hotmail.com

MCGUINNESS MR TERENCE JOSEPH

Garden Court Chambers
57-60 Lincoln's Inn Fields, London WC2A 3LJ, ☎ 020 7993 7600 ✉ info@gclaw.co.uk
Call Date: July 2009, Middle Temple
Qualifications: [LLB (Hons) LLM (Dunelm)]

MCGUINNESS-WAY MR ANDREW JEFFREY SEBASTIAN

Holborn Chambers
6 Gate Street, Lincoln's Inn Fields, London WC2A 3HP, ☎ 020 7242 6060
Call Date: Oct 1992, Middle Temple
Qualifications: [BA (Hons)(Cantab)]

MCGUIRE MR BRYAN NICHOLAS QC (2010)

Cornerstone Barristers
2-3 Gray's Inn Square, Gray's Inn, London WC1R 5JH, ☎ 020 7242 4986
✉ chambers@2-3gis.co.uk
Call Date: July 1983, Middle Temple
Pupil Supervisor
Qualifications: [LLB (Lond) M Phil (Cantab)]
✉ bmcguire@2-3gis.co.uk, bryanm@cornerstonebarristers.com

MCGUIRE MISS DEIRDRE MARIA

Number 7 Harrington Street Chambers
7 Harrington Street, Liverpool L2 9YH, ☎ 0151 242 0707 ✉ clerks@7hs.co.uk
Call Date: Nov 1983, Inner Temple
Qualifications: [LLB (Leeds)]
✉ deirdre.mcguire@7hs.co.uk

MCGUIRE MR DONAL PATRICK

Lombard Chambers
1 Sekforde Street, Clerkenwell, London EC1R 0BE, ☎ 020 7107 2100
Call Date: July 1983, Gray's Inn
Qualifications: [LLB (L'pool) BL (Dub)]

MCGUIRE MR KENNETH

3 PB Barristers
3 Paper Buildings, Temple, London EC4Y 7EU, ☎ 020 7583 8055
Call Date: July 2000, Inner Temple
Qualifications: [LLB (Hons) (Dundee)]

MCGURK MR BRENDAN DAVID STEPHEN

Monckton Chambers
1 & 2 Raymond Buildings, Gray's Inn, London WC1R 5NR, ☎ 020 7405 7211
✉ chambers@monckton.com
Call Date: July 2004, Middle Temple
Qualifications: [BA (Hons) BCL (Oxon) DPhil (Oxon)]

MCHUGH MR DENIS DAVID

Clerksroom (Taunton)
Equity House, Administration Centre, Blackbrook Park Avenue, Taunton, Somerset TA1 2PX, ☎ 0845 083 3000
✉ mail@clerksroom.com
Call Date: Oct 1994, Lincoln's Inn
Qualifications: [LLB (Hons)(Hull) ACIB]
✉ mchugh@clerksroom.com

MCHUGH MR KELAN PATRICK

1 KBW Chambers
1 King's Bench Walk, Temple, London EC4Y 7DB, ☎ 020 7936 1500
✉ clerks@1kbw.co.uk
Call Date: Nov 2007, Inner Temple
Qualifications: [BA (Dub)]
✉ kmchugh@1kbw.co.uk

MCHUGH MISS PAULINE MARY

St Johns Buildings
24a - 28 St John Street, Manchester M3 4DJ, ☎ 0161 214 1500
✉ clerk@stjohnsbuildings.co.uk
16 Winckley Square
Preston PR1 3JJ, ☎ 01772 256100
St Johns Buildings Liverpool
8th Floor India Buildings, Water Street, Liverpool L2 0XG, ☎ 0151 243 6000
✉ clerk@stjohnsbuildings.co.uk
Call Date: Oct 1995, Gray's Inn
Qualifications: [MA (Cantab)]
✉ clerk@stjohnsbuildings.co.uk, mchugh.pauline@btinternet.com

MCHUGH DE CLARE MISS ABIGAIL

North Square Chambers
15 North Square, London NW11 7AD, ☎ 020 8455 3735 ✉ jongold@talk21.com
Call Date: Oct 2006, Middle Temple
Qualifications: [MA (Oxon) PgDL]

MCILROY MR DAVID HALLIDAY

3 PB Barristers
3 Paper Buildings, Temple, London EC4Y 7EU, ☎ 020 7583 8055
3 PB Barristers
Royal Talbot House, 2 Victoria Street, Bristol, Avon BS1 6BB, ☎ 0117 928 1520
3 PB Barristers
4 St Peter Street, Winchester SO23 8BW, ☎ 01962 868884
✉ clerks.winchester@3paper.co.uk
3 PB Barristers
23 Beaumont Street, Oxford OX1 2NP, ☎ 01865 793 736
3 PB Barristers
30 Christchurch Road, Bournemouth, Dorset BH1 3PD, ☎ 01202 292102
✉ clerks.bournemouth@3paper.co.uk
Call Date: Nov 1995, Inner Temple
Pupil Supervisor
Qualifications: [MA (Cantab) PhD (Wales) MtrDt]
✉ david.mcilroy@3paper.co.uk

MCILROY MISS SARA ANNE

2-3 Hind Court Chambers
2-3 Hind Court, Fleet Street, London EC4A 3DL, ☎ 020 7822 2150
✉ david@2-3hindcourt.com
Call Date: Oct 2008, Lincoln's Inn
Qualifications: [BA (Oxon)]

MCILWAIN MISS AMBER STEPHANIE

Cathedral Chambers
First Floor, 17 Queen Street, Newcastle Upon Tyne NE1 3UG, ☎ 0191 232 1311
✉ mail@cathedralchambers.com
Call Date: July 2005, Gray's Inn
Qualifications: [LLB (Leic) LLM]

MCILWAIN MR SYLVESTER DAVID

1 Garden Court Family Law Chambers
Ground Floor, One Garden Court, Temple, London EC4Y 9BJ, ☎ 020 7797 7900
✉ clerks@1gc.com
Call Date: July 1985, Lincoln's Inn
Pupil Supervisor
Qualifications: [LLB (Warw)]

MCINNES MR ANDREW DAVID

Linenhall Chambers
1 Stanley Place, Chester CH1 2LU, ☎ 01244 348282
✉ clerks@linenhallchambers.co.uk
Call Date: Oct 2007, Gray's Inn

MCINTOSH MISS JACQUELINE LORRAINE

1 Mitre Court Buildings
1 Mitre Court Buildings, Temple, London EC4Y 7BS, ☎ 020 7452 8900
✉ clerks@1mcb.com
Call Date: July 1987, Inner Temple
Qualifications: [LLB]
✉ jacqueline.mcintosh@1mcb.com

MCINTOSH MS MELANIE

Becket Chambers
17 New Dover Road, Canterbury, Kent CT1 3AS, ☎ 01227 786331
✉ clerks@becket-chambers.co.uk
Call Date: Mar 2002, Lincoln's Inn
Qualifications: [BA LLB (Hons)]
✉ mmcintosh@Becket-Chambers.co.uk

E

MCINTOSH MISS NICOLA

KCH Garden Square
1 Oxford Street, Nottingham NG1 5BH,
☎0115 941 8851
✉clerks@kchgardensquare.co.uk
Call Date: Nov 2007, Lincoln's Inn
Qualifications: [BA (Wales)]

MCKAY MR CHRISTOPHER ALEXANDER

Cathedral Chambers
10 Clytha Park Road, Newport NP20 4PB,
☎01633 215112
Call Date: Nov 1976, Gray's Inn
Pupil Supervisor
Qualifications: [LLB (Lond)]

MCKECHNIE MISS EMILY JANE

Wilberforce Chambers
8 New Square, Lincoln's Inn, London
WC2A 3QP, ☎020 7306 0102
✉chambers@wilberforce.co.uk
Call Date: Nov 2005, Lincoln's Inn
Qualifications: [MA (Cantab) LLM (Cantab)]
emckechnie@wilberforce.co.uk

MCKECHNIE MRS GAIL LEONORE

Colleton Chambers
Colleton Crescent, Exeter, Devon EX2 4DG,
☎01392 274898
✉clerks@colletonchambers.co.uk
Call Date: July 2007, Gray's Inn
Qualifications: [BVMS LLB CertVOphthal (RVCS)]

MCKECHNIE MR STUART IAIN WILLIAM

The Chambers of Grahame Aldous QC
9 Gough Square, London EC4A 3DG,
☎020 7832 0500
✉clerks@9goughsquare.co.uk
Call Date: Oct 1997, Inner Temple
Qualifications: [LLB (Nottingham)]
smckechnie@9goughsquare.co.uk

MCKEE MR HUGH ANTHONY

16 Winckley Square
Preston PR1 3JJ, ☎01772 256100
St Johns Buildings
21 White Friars, Chester CH1 1NZ,
☎01244 323070
✉clerk@stjohnsbuildings.co.uk
St Johns Buildings Liverpool
8th Floor India Buildings, Water Street,
Liverpool L2 0XG, ☎0151 243 6000
✉clerk@stjohnsbuildings.co.uk
Call Date: Nov 1983, Middle Temple
Pupil Supervisor
Qualifications: [BA]
clerk@stjohnsbuildings.co.uk

MCKENDRICK MR EWAN GORDON

3 Verulam Buildings
London WC1R 5NT, ☎020 7831 8441
✉chambers@3vb.com
Call Date: Mar 1998, Gray's Inn
Qualifications: [LLB (Edin) BCL (Oxon)]

MCKENDRICK MR JOHN DEMPSTER

Outer Temple Chambers
The Outer Temple, 222 Strand, London
WC2R 1BA, ☎020 7353 6381
✉clerks@outertemple.com
Call Date: Nov 1999, Inner Temple
Qualifications: [LLB (LSE) MSc (Oxon)]

MCKENNA MISS ANNA LOUISE

42 Bedford Row
London WC1R 4LL, ☎020 7831 0222
✉clerks@42br.com
Call Date: Nov 1994, Middle Temple
Qualifications: [BA (Hons) (Leeds)]
anna.mckenna@42br.com

MCKENNA MR BRIAN MALACHY

Call Date: July 1983, Middle Temple
Qualifications: [LLB (L'pool)]
clerk@stjohnsbuildings.co.uk

MCKENNA MR JOSEPH THOMAS

Middle Temple Lane Chambers
2nd Floor South, 1 Middle Temple Lane,
London EC4Y 9AA, ☎020 7583 4352
✉chambers@mtlchambers.com
Call Date: July 2005, Lincoln's Inn
Qualifications: [BA (Hons) Lond]

MCKENNA MISS MARY ANN

Holborn Chambers
6 Gate Street, Lincoln's Inn Fields, London
WC2A 3HP, ☎020 7242 6060
Call Date: Nov 2008, Lincoln's Inn
Qualifications: [BSc CPE UZWES]

MCKENZIE MISS LESLEY SHARON

Trinity Chambers
The Custom House, 39 Quayside, Newcastle
Upon Tyne NE1 3DE, ☎0191 232 1927
✉info@trinitychambers.co.uk
Trinity Chambers
Multi Media Exchange, 72-80 Corporation
Road, Middlesbrough TS1 2RF,
☎01642 247569
✉info@trinitychambers.co.uk
Call Date: Feb 1983, Lincoln's Inn
Qualifications: [LLB (Newc)]
l.mckenzie@trinitychambers.co.uk

MCKEON MR JAMES PATRICK

Number 7 Harrington Street Chambers
7 Harrington Street, Liverpool L2 9YH,
☎0151 242 0707 ✉clerks@7hs.co.uk
Call Date: Nov 1982, Lincoln's Inn
Qualifications: [LLB (L'pool)]
james.mckeon@7hs.co.uk

MCKEONE MS MARY BRENDA

Chambers of Ian Macdonald QC
Garden Court North, 22 Oxford Court, Manchester M2 3WQ, ☎0161 236 1840
✉clerks@gcnchambers.co.uk
Call Date: Feb 1986, Gray's Inn
Qualifications: [LLB]
marym@gclaw.co.uk

MCKEOWN MISS SARAH

Arden Chambers
20 Bloomsbury Square, London WC1A 2NS,
☎020 7242 4244
✉clerks@ardenchambers.com
Call Date: Nov 1998, Middle Temple
Qualifications: [MA (Oxon)]
sarah.mckeown@ardenchambers.com

MCKIE MR ANDREW IAN

Clerksroom (Taunton)
Equity House, Administration Centre, Blackbrook Park Avenue, Taunton, Somerset TA1 2PX, ☎0845 083 3000
✉mail@clerksroom.com
Call Date: July 2011, Lincoln's Inn
Qualifications: [LLB (Keele) LLM (Lancs)]

MCKIE MISS JACQUELINE

Amicus Chambers
Queens Court, Newport Road, Middlesbrough TS1 5EH, ☎01642 876334
✉amicus.clerk@amicuschambers.co.uk
Call Date: Oct 1995, Inner Temple
Qualifications: [LLB (Hons)]

MCKIE MISS SUZANNE ELIZABETH QC (2012)

Littleton Chambers
3 King's Bench Walk North, Temple, London EC4Y 7HR, ☎020 7797 8600
✉fschneider@littletonchambers.co.uk
Call Date: Nov 1991, Inner Temple
Pupil Supervisor
Qualifications: [LLB (Notts)]

MCKIERNAN MR EDWARD JOSEPH

Farringdon Chambers
180 Bermondsey Street, London SE1 3TQ,
☎020 7089 5700
Call Date: Nov 1981, Lincoln's Inn
Pupil Supervisor
Qualifications: [LLB(Lond)]
edwardmckiernan@farringdon-law.co.uk

MCKINLAY MRS KATE SUSANNA

Zenith Chambers
10 Park Square, Leeds LS1 2LH,
☎0113 245 5438
✉clerks@zenithchambers.co.uk
Call Date: Oct 2000, Middle Temple
Qualifications: [MA (Hons) (Leeds) Dip in Law]
kmckinlay@zenithchambers.co.uk

MCKINLAY MISS KIRSTY ELIZABETH

9 St John Street
Manchester M3 4DN, ☎0161 955 9000
✉civilclerks@9sjs.com / criminalclerks@9sjs.com
Call Date: Mar 2001, Lincoln's Inn
Qualifications: [LLB (Hons) (Newc)]

MCKINLAY MISS VANESSA JANE

St John's Chambers
101 Victoria Street, Bristol BS1 6PU,
☎0117 923 4700
✉clerks@stjohnschambers.co.uk
Call Date: Oct 2000, Middle Temple
Qualifications: [LLB (Hons) LLM (Cardiff)]
vanessa.mckinlay@stjohnschambers.co.uk

MCKINNEY MISS NICOLA ALEXANDRA

4 KBW
Ground Floor, 4 King's Bench Walk, Temple, London EC4Y 7DL, ☎020 7822 8822
✉law@4kbw.net
Call Date: Oct 2004, Gray's Inn
Qualifications: [BA MSc LLB]

MCKONE MR MARK DESMOND

Sovereign Chambers
46 Park Place, Leeds LS1 2RY,
☎0113 245 1841
✉clerks@sovereignchambers.co.uk
Call Date: Nov 1988, Lincoln's Inn
Pupil Supervisor
Qualifications: [LLB (Hons) (Leeds)]
mark.mckone@sovereignchambers.co.uk

E

MCLACHLAN MR DAVID ROBERT

Number 7 Harrington Street Chambers
7 Harrington Street, Liverpool L2 9YH,
☎0151 242 0707 ✉clerks@7hs.co.uk
Call Date: Oct 1996, Inner Temple
Qualifications: [LLB LLM (Essex)]
✉david.mclachlan@7hs.co.uk

MCLANACHAN MR JOHN

Independent Chambers
Rivendale, 6 Gorse Hill Lane, The Wentworth Estate, Virgina Water, Surrey GU25 4AJ,
☎01344 845315
✉admin@independentchambers.co.uk
Call Date: Feb 1980, Gray's Inn
Qualifications: [LLB (Bris)]

MCLAREN THE HON MICHAEL DUNCAN QC (2002)

Fountain Court Chambers
Fountain Court, Temple, London EC4Y 9DH,
☎020 7583 3335
✉chambers@fountaincourt.co.uk
Call Date: Nov 1981, Middle Temple
Qualifications: [MA (Cantab)]
✉mm@fountaincourt.co.uk

E

MCLARNON MR NEIL SIMON PETER

XXIV Old Buildings
Ground Floor, 24 Old Buildings, Lincoln's Inn, London WC2A 3UP, ☎020 7691 2424
✉clerks@xxiv.co.uk
Call Date: Oct 2004, Lincoln's Inn
Pupil Supervisor
Qualifications: [BA (Hons)]
✉neil.mclarnon@xxiv.co.uk

MCLAUGHLIN MR ANDREW PETER

St John's Chambers
101 Victoria Street, Bristol BS1 6PU,
☎0117 923 4700
✉clerks@stjohnschambers.co.uk
Call Date: Nov 1993, Middle Temple
Qualifications: [BA (Hons)(York) CPE (Lancs)]
✉andrew.mclaughlin@stjohnschambers.co.uk

MCLAUGHLIN MISS KAREN JANET

Crown Office Row Chambers
119 Church Street, Brighton, Sussex BN1 1UD, ☎01273 625625
✉clerks@1cor.com
Call Date: July 1982, Middle Temple
Pupil Supervisor
Qualifications: [BA (Hons)]
✉karen.mclaughlin@1cor.com

MCLAUGHLIN MISS VICTORIA MARY

Guildford Chambers
Stoke House, Leapale Lane, Guildford, Surrey GU1 4LY, ☎01483 539131
✉clerks@guildfordchambers.co.uk
Call Date: Nov 2004, Gray's Inn
Qualifications: [LLB LLM]
✉vmclaughlin@guildfordchambers.com

MCLEESE MR DANIEL STUART

30 Park Place
Cardiff CF10 3BS, ☎029 2039 8421
✉clerks@30parkplace.law.co.uk
Call Date: Oct 2000, Gray's Inn
Qualifications: [LLB (Wales)]

MCLEISH MR MARTYN LEE

Cloisters
1 Pump Court, Temple, London EC4Y 7AA,
☎020 7827 4000 ✉clerks@cloisters.com
Call Date: Oct 1997, Inner Temple
Pupil Supervisor
Qualifications: [BA (Oxon) D.Phil CPE]
✉mm@cloisters.com

MCLEISH MR PHILIP

Chambers of Ian Macdonald QC
Garden Court North, 22 Oxford Court, Manchester M2 3WQ, ☎0161 236 1840
✉clerks@gcnchambers.co.uk
Call Date: Oct 2003, Inner Temple
Qualifications: [BA (York) MA (B'ham)]

MCLEOD MR IAIN

3 Hare Court
3 Hare Court, Temple, London EC4Y 7BJ,
☎020 7415 7800 ✉clerks@3harecourt.com
Call Date: July 1969, Inner Temple
Recorder
Qualifications: [LLB]
✉mcleod@work.gb.com

MCLERNON MR JAMES PATRICK

36 Bedford Row
London WC1R 4JH, ☎020 7421 8000
✉chambers@36bedfordrow.co.uk
Call Date: Oct 2007, Middle Temple
Qualifications: [LLB (Hons) (Belfast)]

MCLINDEN MR JOHN VINCENT BARRY QC (2011)

Field Court Chambers
5 Field Court, Gray's Inn, London WC1R 5EF,
☎ 020 7405 6114 ✉ clerks@fieldcourt.co.uk
Call Date: Apr 1991, Inner Temple
Pupil Supervisor
Qualifications: [LLB (Hons) LLM (New Zealand)]

MCLORINAN MISS HAYLEY

2 Temple Gardens
2 Temple Gardens, Temple, London EC4Y 9AY, ☎ 020 7822 1200
✉ clerks@2tg.co.uk
Call Date: July 2008, Inner Temple
Qualifications: [BA (Cantab) LLM (Pennsylvania)]
hm@2tg.co.uk

MCLOUGHLIN MR IAN

4 Breams Buildings
Chancery Lane, London EC4A 1HP,
☎ 020 7092 1900 ✉ clerks@4bb.co.uk
Call Date: Nov 1993, Lincoln's Inn
Pupil Supervisor
Qualifications: [B Soc Sci (Hons)]
ian.mcloughlin@4bb.cjsm.net

MCLOUGHLIN MR KEVIN

Temple Garden Chambers
1 Harcourt Buildings, Temple, London EC4Y 9DA, ☎ 020 7583 1315
✉ clerks@tgchambers.com
Call Date: May 2007, Middle Temple
Qualifications: [BA (Hons) (Manch) MA (Sheff) MA]
kevin.mcloughlin@tgchambers.com

MCLOUGHLIN MR SIMON PATRICK

Selborne Chambers
10 Essex Street, London WC2R 3AA,
☎ 020 7420 9500
✉ clerks@selbornechambers.co.uk
Call Date: July 2009, Lincoln's Inn
Qualifications: [BA (Cantab) MPHIL (Cantab) CPE UCU]
simon.mcloughlin@selbornechambers.co.uk

MCMAHON MISS HEATHER MARGARET

Hailsham Chambers
Ground Floor, 4 Paper Buildings, Temple, London EC4Y 7EX, ☎ 020 7643 5000
✉ clerks@hailshamchambers.com
Call Date: Nov 1999, Middle Temple
Qualifications: [BA (Hons) (Oxon)]

MCMANUS MR JONATHAN RICHARD QC (1999)

4-5 Gray's Inn Square
Gray's Inn, London WC1R 5AH,
☎ 020 7404 5252 ✉ clerks@4-5.co.uk
Call Date: July 1982, Middle Temple
Qualifications: [MA (Cantab)]
rmcmanus@4-5.co.uk

MCMASTER MR ROBERT JAMES

Deans Court Chambers
24 St John Street, Manchester M3 4DF,
☎ 0161 214 6000 ✉ clerks@deanscourt.co.uk
Deans Court Chambers
101 Walker Street, Preston PR1 2RR,
☎ 01772 565 600
✉ preston@deanscourt.co.uk
Call Date: Nov 2001, Middle Temple
Qualifications: [LLB (Hons)]
mcmaster@deanscourt.co.uk

MCMEECHAN MISS SARAH JANE

New Court
Ground Floor, New Court, Temple, London EC4Y 9BE, ☎ 020 7583 5123
✉ clerks@newcourtchambers.com
Call Date: Oct 2000, Inner Temple
Qualifications: [LLB]

MCMEEKIN MR IAN

2 Bedford Row
London WC1R 4BU, ☎ 020 7440 8888
✉ clerks@2bedfordrow.co.uk
Lincoln House Chambers
Tower 12, The Avenue North, Spinningfields, 18-22 Bridge Street, Manchester M3 3BZ,
☎ 0161 832 5701
✉ info@lincolnhousechambers.com
Call Date: July 1987, Middle Temple
Qualifications: [BA (Hons) (Leeds) Dip Law (City)]
ian.mcmeekin@lincolnhousechambers.com

MCMEEL PROF GERARD PATRICK

Guildhall Chambers
23 Broad Street, Bristol BS1 2HG,
☎ 0117 930 9000
✉ hoc@guildhallchambers.co.uk
Quadrant Chambers
Quadrant House, 10 Fleet Street, London EC4Y 1AU, ☎ 020 7583 4444
✉ info@quadrantchambers.com
Call Date: Nov 1993, Inner Temple
Pupil Supervisor
Qualifications: [BCL MA (Oxon)]
Gerard.McMeel@guildhallchambers.co.uk

E

MCMILLAN MRS CAROL ANN

Westgate Chambers
64 High Street, Lewes, East Sussex BN7 1XG,
☎01273 480510
✉clerks@westgate-chambers.co.uk
Call Date: Nov 1996, Middle Temple
Pupil Supervisor
Qualifications: [BA (Hons)(So'ton) MPhil (Lond)]
cm@westgate-chambers.co.uk

MCMORROW MR PATRICK JOSEPH

4 King's Bench Walk
2nd Floor, 4 King's Bench Walk, Temple, London EC4Y 7DL, ☎020 7822 7000
✉clerks@4kbw.co.uk
Call Date: Oct 1996, Inner Temple
Qualifications: [LLB (LSE)]

MCMULLAN MS LAURA CHRISTINA

Coram Chambers
9-11 Fulwood Place, London WC1V 6HG,
☎020 7092 3700
✉mail@coramchambers.co.uk
Call Date: Nov 2004, Inner Temple
Qualifications: [LLB University of Exeter MA University of Padua]
lauramcmullan1977@hotmail.com

E

MCMULLAN MR MANUS ANTHONY QC (2010)

Atkin Chambers
1 Atkin Building, Gray's Inn, London WC1R 5AT, ☎020 7404 0102
✉clerks@atkinchambers.com
Call Date: Nov 1994, Middle Temple
Pupil Supervisor
Qualifications: [BA (Hons)]
clerks@atkinchambers.com

MCMURTRIE MR CHRISTOPHER JONATHAN

Oriel Chambers
14 Water Street, Liverpool, Merseyside L2 8TD, ☎0151 236 7191
✉clerks@orielchambers.co.uk
Oriel Chambers
18 Ribblesdale Place, Preston PR1 3NA,
☎01772 254 764
✉clerks@oriel-chambers.co.uk
Call Date: July 2003, Gray's Inn
Qualifications: [LLB (Leic) LLM (Keele)]

MCNAB MISS MHAIRI SHUNA ELSPETH

14 Gray's Inn Square
14 Gray's Inn Square, Gray's Inn, London WC1R 5JP, ☎020 7242 0858
✉clerks@14gis.co.uk
Call Date: July 1974, Middle Temple
Pupil Supervisor
clerks@14graysinnsquare.co.uk

MCNAE MR JONATHAN JAMES

Selborne Chambers
10 Essex Street, London WC2R 3AA,
☎020 7420 9500
✉clerks@selbornechambers.co.uk
Call Date: Oct 2001, Gray's Inn
Pupil Supervisor
Qualifications: [MA (Cantab)]
jonathan.mcnae@selbornechambers.co.uk

MCNAIR MR DUNCAN WENDELL HECTOR

Clerksroom (Taunton)
Equity House, Administration Centre, Blackbrook Park Avenue, Taunton, Somerset TA1 2PX, ☎0845 083 3000
✉mail@clerksroom.com
Call Date: July 2003, Middle Temple
Qualifications: [Dip Law MSci (Dunelm) CPE]
mcnair@clerksroom.com

MCNAIR-WILSON MISS LAURA ROSE

Matrix Chambers
Griffin Building, Gray's Inn, London WC1R 5LN, ☎020 7404 3447
✉matrix@matrixlaw.co.uk / Iscott@matrixlaw.co.uk
Call Date: Nov 2007, Gray's Inn
Qualifications: [BA (Oxon)]

MCNALL DR CHRISTOPHER IAN JAMES

18 St John Street
Manchester M3 4EA, ☎0161 278 1800
✉clerks@18sjs.com
Call Date: July 2005, Middle Temple
Qualifications: [MA (Oxon) DPhil (Oxon)]
clerks@18sjs.com

MCNALLY MR JOHN JOSEPH

Dyers Chambers
35 Bedford Row, London WC1R 4JH,
☎020 7404 1881
✉admin@dyerschambers.com
Call Date: Nov 1996, Gray's Inn
Qualifications: [BSc (Surrey) LLM (Lond)]

MCNALLY MR STEPHEN

Exchange Chambers
One Derby Square, Derby Square, Liverpool L2 9XX, ☎0151 236 7747
✉info@exchangechambers.co.uk
Exchange Chambers
7 Ralli Courts, West Riverside, Manchester M3 5FT, ☎0161 833 2722
Exchange Chambers
Oxford House, Oxford Row, Leeds LS1 3BE, ☎0113 203 1970
✉spencer@exchangechambers.co.uk
Call Date: Nov 2003, Gray's Inn
Qualifications: [BA (L'pool)]
McNally@exchangechambers.co.uk

MCNAMARA MR ANDREW DAVID

Ropewalk Chambers
24 The Ropewalk, Nottingham NG1 5EF, ☎0115 947 2581 ✉clerks@ropewalk.co.uk
Call Date: Nov 1992, Inner Temple
Pupil Supervisor
Qualifications: [BA (So'ton) LLB (Leeds)]
andrewmcnamara@ropewalk.co.uk

MCNAMARA MR JAMES

1 High Pavement
Nottingham NG1 1HF, ☎0115 941 8218
✉clerks@1highpavement.co.uk
Call Date: May 1990, Inner Temple
Qualifications: [BA]
jamesmcnamara@1highpavement.co.uk

MCNAMARA MR STEPHEN MICHAEL

Kings Chambers
36 Young Street, Manchester M3 3FT, ☎0845 034 3444
✉clerks@kingschambers.com
Kings Chambers
5 Park Square East, Leeds LS1 2NE, ☎0845 034 3444
✉clerks@kingschambers.com
Kings Chambers
Embassy House, 60 Church Street, Birmingham B3 2DJ, ☎0845 034 3444
✉clerks@kingschambers.com
Call Date: July 2008, Gray's Inn
Qualifications: [BSc (LSE)]
smcnamara@kingschambers.com

MCNEILL MR DAVID MARTIN

Five St Andrew's Hill
5 St Andrew's Hill, London EC4V 5BZ, ☎020 7332 5400 ✉Clerks@5sah.co.uk
Call Date: Nov 2003, Inner Temple
Qualifications: [BA (Oxon)]
davidmcneill@5sah.co.uk

MCNEILL MISS ELIZABETH JANE QC (2002)

Old Square Chambers
10-11 Bedford Row, London WC1R 4BU, ☎020 7269 0300 ✉clerks@oldsquare.co.uk
Old Square Chambers
3 Orchard Court, St Augustine's Yard, Bristol BS1 5DP, ☎0117 930 5100
✉clerks@oldsquare.co.uk
Call Date: Nov 1982, Lincoln's Inn
Recorder
Qualifications: [BA (Oxon) Dip Law (Lond)]

MCNEILL MR JOHN SEDDON

Call Date: July 1974, Gray's Inn
Pupil Supervisor
Qualifications: [BSc (Hons)]

MCNERNEY MR KEVIN JOHN

Call Date: Nov 1992, Inner Temple
Qualifications: [BA LLM Dip Law]
kevin.mcnerney@stjohnsbuildings.co.uk, McNerney64@yahoo.co.uk

MCNICHOLAS MR CHRISTOPHER JOHN

Goresbrook Chambers
PO Box 6017, Milton Keynes MK1 9AP, ☎0845 123 1234
✉thomas.john6@btinternet.com
Call Date: Nov 1995, Lincoln's Inn
Qualifications: [LLB (Hons) ACIB]

MCNICHOLAS MR EAMON JOHN

Temple Tax Chambers
1st Floor, 3 Temple Gardens, Temple, London EC4Y 9AU, ☎020 7353 7884
✉clerks@templetax.com
Call Date: Oct 1994, Lincoln's Inn
Qualifications: [BA (Hons)(Leic) Dip in Law (City) ACMA]
clerks@templetax.com

MCNIFF MR MATTHEW JAMES

EC Chambers
PO Box 825, Bungay, Norfolk NR35 9AR, ☎01508 483931
1 Paper Buildings
1st Floor, 1 Paper Buildings, Temple, London EC4Y 7EP, ☎020 7353 3728
✉clerks@onepaper.co.uk
18 Red Lion Court
London EC4A 3EB, ☎020 7520 6000
✉chambers@18rlc.co.uk
Call Date: Oct 1992, Gray's Inn
Qualifications: [LLB (Hons)]

E

MCNULTY MR LAWRENCE JAMES

Tooks Chambers
81 Farringdon Street, London EC4A 4BL,
☎020 7842 7575 ✉clerks@tooks.co.uk
Lamb Building
22 Ship Street, Brighton BN1 1AD,
☎01273 820490
✉admin@lambbuilding.co.uk
Call Date: Nov 1985, Middle Temple
Qualifications: [BA (Kent) BCL (Oxon)]

MCPARLAND MR MICHAEL JOSEPH

Quadrant Chambers
Quadrant House, 10 Fleet Street, London EC4Y 1AU, ☎020 7583 4444
✉info@quadrantchambers.com
Call Date: July 1983, Inner Temple
Pupil Supervisor
Qualifications: [BA (Oxon)]
michael.mcparland@quadrantchambers.com

MCPHERSON MR GEORGE ROBERT

3 Verulam Buildings
London WC1R 5NT, ☎020 7831 8441
✉chambers@3vb.com
Call Date: Oct 2003, Inner Temple
Qualifications: [BA (Hons) (Oxon) Pg DL]
gmcpherson@3vb.com

MCPHERSON MR GRAEME PAUL QC (2008)

Four New Square
Four New Square, Lincoln's Inn, London WC2A 3RJ, ☎020 7822 2000
✉barristers@4newsquare.com
Call Date: Oct 1993, Gray's Inn
Qualifications: [MA (Hons)]
g.mcpherson@4newsquare.com
URL: www.4newsquare.com/barristers/92/Graeme-b-McPherson-b-QC

Types of work: Commercial law, Commercial litigation, Financial services, Insurance, Professional negligence, Sale and carriage of goods, Sport

MCQUAIL MS KATHERINE EMMA

Radcliffe Chambers
Ground Floor, 11 New Square, Lincoln's Inn, London WC2A 3QB, ☎020 7831 0081
✉clerks@radcliffechambers.com
Call Date: Nov 1989, Middle Temple
Pupil Supervisor
Qualifications: [BA (Hons) (Oxon)]
kmcquail@radcliffechambers.com

MCQUATER MR EWAN ALAN QC (2003)

3 Verulam Buildings
London WC1R 5NT, ☎020 7831 8441
✉chambers@3vb.com
Call Date: July 1985, Middle Temple
Qualifications: [MA (Cantab)]
emcquater@3vb.com

MCREDDIE MS FIONA MARIE

Amicus Chambers
Queens Court, Newport Road, Middlesbrough TS1 5EH, ☎01642 876334
✉amicus.clerk@amicuschambers.co.uk
Call Date: July 2010, Lincoln's Inn
Qualifications: [BA (Newc) LLB (Lond)]

MCSORLEY MISS HANNAH REBECCA

Guildford Chambers
Stoke House, Leapale Lane, Guildford, Surrey GU1 4LY, ☎01483 539131
✉clerks@guildfordchambers.co.uk
Call Date: Mar 2010, Middle Temple
Qualifications: [MA (Oxon) CPE (Oxford Brookes)]
hmcsorley@guildfordchambers.com

MCTAGUE MISS MEGHANN ROSE

2 Temple Gardens
2 Temple Gardens, Temple, London EC4Y 9AY, ☎020 7822 1200
✉clerks@2tg.co.uk
Call Date: Oct 2004, Inner Temple
Qualifications: [BA (Sheff)]
mmctague@2tg.co.uk

MCVAY MS BRIDGET SIOBHAN

Octagon Chambers
29 Park Street, Taunton, Somerset TA1 4DG,
☎01823 331919
✉jcload@Octagonchambers.co.uk
Call Date: Feb 1990, Inner Temple
Qualifications: [LLB (Hons)]
bmcvay@octagonchambers.co.uk

MCWATTERS MR CHRISTOPHER GEORGE

Garden Court Chambers
57-60 Lincoln's Inn Fields, London WC2A 3LJ,
☎020 7993 7600 ✉info@gclaw.co.uk
Call Date: Nov 2004, Lincoln's Inn
Qualifications: [BA (Hons)]
christopherm@gclaw.co.uk

MEACHER MISS ALISON MERYL

Hardwicke
New Square, Lincoln's Inn, London
WC2A 3SB, ☎020 7242 2523
✉enquiries@hardwicke.co.uk
Call Date: Nov 1998, Lincoln's Inn
Pupil Supervisor
Qualifications: [LLB(Jnt Hons)(Wales)]
Alison.Meacher@hardwicke.co.uk

MEACHIN MISS VANESSA VERONICA

St Philips Chambers
55 Temple Row, Birmingham B2 5LS,
☎0121 246 7000 ✉clerks@st-philips.com
Call Date: Oct 1990, Inner Temple
Pupil Supervisor, Recorder
Qualifications: [LLB (B'ham)]
vmeachin@st-philips.co.uk

MEAD MR JOHN PHILIP

Old Square Chambers
10-11 Bedford Row, London WC1R 4BU,
☎020 7269 0300 ✉clerks@oldsquare.co.uk
Old Square Chambers
3 Orchard Court, St Augustine's Yard, Bristol
BS1 5DP, ☎0117 930 5100
✉clerks@oldsquare.co.uk
Call Date: July 1989, Lincoln's Inn
Qualifications: [LLB (B'ham) LLM (Italy)]
mead@oldsquare.co.uk

MEADE MR RICHARD DAVID QC (2008)

8 New Square
8 New Square, Lincoln's Inn, London
WC2A 3QP, ☎020 7405 4321
✉clerks@8newsquare.co.uk
Call Date: Nov 1991, Lincoln's Inn
Qualifications: [BA (Hons) (Oxon)]

Types of work: Breach of confidence, Competition law, Computer litigation, Copyright, Copyright theft, Copyright Tribunal, Design, EC competition law, Entertainment, Information technology, Intellectual property, Malicious falsehood, Media, Media and entertainment, Mediation, Passing off, Patents, Pharmaceuticals, Scientific and technical disputes, Trade Descriptions Act, Trade secrets, Trademarks

MEADOWCROFT MR STEPHEN CHRISTIAN QC (2008)

Exchange Chambers
7 Ralli Courts, West Riverside, Manchester
M3 5FT, ☎0161 833 2722
Exchange Chambers
One Derby Square, Derby Square, Liverpool
L2 9XX, ☎0151 236 7747
✉info@exchangechambers.co.uk
Exchange Chambers
Oxford House, Oxford Row, Leeds LS1 3BE,
☎0113 203 1970
✉spencer@exchangechambers.co.uk
Call Date: Nov 1973, Gray's Inn
meadowcroftqc@exchangechambers.co.uk

MEADS MISS VICTORIA ANNE

Tooks Chambers
81 Farringdon Street, London EC4A 4BL,
☎020 7842 7575 ✉clerks@tooks.co.uk
Call Date: Nov 2002, Gray's Inn
Qualifications: [LLB]

MEADWAY MISS SUSANNAH LAWTON

Ten Old Square
Ground Floor, Ten Old Square, Lincoln's Inn,
London WC2A 3SU, ☎020 7405 0758
✉clerks@tenoldsquare.com
Call Date: July 1988, Middle Temple
Qualifications: [MA (Oxon) Dip Law (Lond)]
susannahmeadway@tenoldsquare.com

MEAGER MRS ROWENA ELISABETH

No5 Chambers
Fountain Court, Steelhouse Lane, Birmingham
B4 6DR, ☎0845 210 5555 ✉info@no5.com
No5 Chambers
Greenwood House, 4-7 Salisbury Court,
London EC4Y 8AA, ☎0845 210 5555
No5 Chambers
38 Queen Square, Bristol BS1 4QS,
☎0845 210 5555
Call Date: July 2007, Lincoln's Inn
Qualifications: [LLB (Oxon) BCL (Oxon)]
rme@no5.com

MEAKIN MR IAN LEONARD

XXIV Old Buildings
Ground Floor, 24 Old Buildings, Lincoln's Inn,
London WC2A 3UP, ☎020 7691 2424
✉clerks@xxiv.co.uk
Call Date: Oct 1991, Gray's Inn
Qualifications: [BD AKC MCIArb Dip Law]
ian.meakin@xxiv.co.uk

MEAKIN MR TIMOTHY WILLIAM

Seven Bedford Row
7 Bedford Row, London WC1R 4BS,
☎020 7242 3555 ✉clerks@7br.co.uk
Call Date: July 1989, Middle Temple
Qualifications: [BA (Leeds) Dip Law LLM (LSE)]

E

MEARES MR NIGEL LESLIE VELLACOTT

11 Stone Buildings
11 Stone Buildings, Lincoln's Inn, London WC2A 3TG, ☎020 7831 6381
✉clerks@11sb.com
Call Date: Nov 1975, Middle Temple
Pupil Supervisor
Qualifications: [BA (Cantab)]
✉meares@11sb.com

MEDCROFT MR NICHOLAS JULIAN

Outer Temple Chambers
The Outer Temple, 222 Strand, London WC2R 1BA, ☎020 7353 6381
✉clerks@outertemple.com
Call Date: Oct 1998, Lincoln's Inn
Qualifications: [LLB (Hons)(Durham)]
✉nick.medcroft@outertemple.com

MEDD MR JAMES POWYS

Crown Office Chambers
2 Crown Office Row, Temple, London EC4Y 7HJ, ☎020 7797 8100
✉mail@crownofficechambers.com
Call Date: July 1985, Middle Temple
Pupil Supervisor
Qualifications: [MA (Cantab)]
✉medd@crownofficechambers.com

MEDHURST MR DAVID CHARLES

4 Brick Court
4 Brick Court, Temple, London EC4Y 9AD, ☎020 7832 3200 ✉clerks@4bc.co.uk
Call Date: Nov 1969, Gray's Inn
Pupil Supervisor
Qualifications: [LLB (Manch)]
✉david.medhurst@4bc.co.uk

MEDLAND MR SIMON EDWARD QC (2011)

Exchange Chambers
One Derby Square, Derby Square, Liverpool L2 9XX, ☎0151 236 7747
✉info@exchangechambers.co.uk
Exchange Chambers
7 Ralli Courts, West Riverside, Manchester M3 5FT, ☎0161 833 2722
Exchange Chambers
Oxford House, Oxford Row, Leeds LS1 3BE, ☎0113 203 1970
✉spencer@exchangechambers.co.uk
Call Date: Oct 1991, Middle Temple
Pupil Supervisor
Qualifications: [BA (Hull) Dip Law]

MEECH MISS JENNIFER CLAIRE

Enterprise Chambers
9 Old Square, Lincoln's Inn, London WC2A 3SR, ☎020 7405 9471
✉london@enterprisechambers.com
Enterprise Chambers
65 Quayside, Newcastle Upon Tyne NE1 3DE, ☎0191 222 3344
✉newcastle@enterprisechambers.com
Enterprise Chambers
43 Park Square, Leeds LS1 2NP, ☎0113 246 0391
✉leeds@enterprisechambers.com
Call Date: Oct 2008, Middle Temple
Qualifications: [MA (Hons) (Cantab)]
✉jennifermeech@enterprisechambers.com

MEEGAN MR TREVOR LEO

Citadel Chambers
The Citadel, 190 Corporation Street, Birmingham B4 6QD, ☎0121 233 8500
✉clerks@citadelchambers.com
Call Date: July 2000, Lincoln's Inn
Qualifications: [LLB(Hons) (Leeds)]
✉clerks@citadelchambers.com

MEEK MISS SUSAN ELIZABETH

Furnival Chambers
32 Furnival Street, London EC4A 1JQ, ☎020 7405 3232
Call Date: Nov 1997, Gray's Inn
Qualifications: [LLB (Lond)]

MEEKE MR ROBERT MARTIN JAMES QC (2000)

Colleton Chambers
Colleton Crescent, Exeter, Devon EX2 4DG, ☎01392 274898
✉clerks@colletonchambers.co.uk
Call Date: July 1973, Gray's Inn
Recorder
Qualifications: [LLB (Bristol)]
✉martinmeeke@colletonchambers.co.uk

MEGGY MR RHYS FRANCIS

QEB Hollis Whiteman
1-2 Laurence Pountney Hill, London EC4R 0EU, ☎020 7933 8855
✉barristers@qebhw.co.uk
Call Date: July 2009, Inner Temple
Qualifications: [LLB (Lond)]
✉rhys.meggy@qebhw.co.uk

E

MEHIGAN MR JAMES GARFIELD

Tooks Chambers
81 Farringdon Street, London EC4A 4BL,
☎020 7842 7575 ✉clerks@tooks.co.uk
Call Date: Nov 2008, Middle Temple
Qualifications: [LLB (Hons) (Dub) MPhil (Cantab) PhD (Open University)]
✉james.mehigan@tooks.co.uk

MEHIGAN MR SIMON PETER QC (1998)

Francis Taylor Building
Inner Temple, London EC4Y 7BY,
☎020 7353 8415 ✉clerks@ftb.eu.com
Albion Chambers
Broad Street, Bristol BS1 1DR,
☎0117 927 2144
✉clerks@albionchambers.co.uk
Call Date: July 1980, Lincoln's Inn
Qualifications: [LLB (Lond)]
✉simon.mehigan@ftb.eu.com

MEHRZAD MR JOHN

Littleton Chambers
3 King's Bench Walk North, Temple, London EC4Y 7HR, ☎020 7797 8600
✉fschneider@littletonchambers.co.uk
Call Date: July 2005, Inner Temple
Qualifications: [MA (Dub) MSt (Oxon)]
✉jm@cloisters.com

MEHTA MISS ANITA ROXANE

Crown Office Row Chambers
119 Church Street, Brighton, Sussex BN1 1UD, ☎01273 625625
✉clerks@1cor.com
Call Date: Oct 2002, Lincoln's Inn
Qualifications: [LLB (Bristol)]
✉anita.mehta@1cor.com

MEHTA MR NIKHIL VASANT

Gray's Inn Tax Chambers
3rd Floor, Gray's Inn Chambers, Gray's Inn, London WC1R 5JA, ☎020 7242 2642
✉clerks@taxbar.com
Call Date: July 1976, Lincoln's Inn
✉nm@taxbar.com

MEHTA MR SAILESH

18 Red Lion Court
London EC4A 3EB, ☎020 7520 6000
✉chambers@18rlc.co.uk
Call Date: July 1986, Lincoln's Inn
Pupil Supervisor
Qualifications: [LLB (Manch)]

MEICHEN MR JONATHAN BRIAN

St Philips Chambers
55 Temple Row, Birmingham B2 5LS,
☎0121 246 7000 ✉clerks@st-philips.com
Call Date: Nov 2006, Inner Temple
Qualifications: [MA (Glasgow)]
✉jmeichen@st-philips.co.uk

MEIKLE MISS KATE ALEXIS

7 Bell Yard
London WC2A 2JR, ☎020 7831 0636
✉kevintarrant@btconnect.com
Call Date: July 2006, Inner Temple
Qualifications: [LLB (Herts) LLM (City)]

MEIKLE MR ROBERT WILLIAM

Goldsmith Chambers
Ground Floor, Goldsmith Building, Temple, London EC4Y 7BL, ☎020 7353 6802
✉clerks@goldsmithchambers.com
Call Date: July 1970, Gray's Inn
Pupil Supervisor
Qualifications: [LLB (B'ham)]
✉R.Meikle@goldsmithchambers.law.co.uk

MEILAND DR JUSTIN OTZEN

Hailsham Chambers
Ground Floor, 4 Paper Buildings, Temple, London EC4Y 7EX, ☎020 7643 5000
✉clerks@hailshamchambers.com
Call Date: July 2010, Lincoln's Inn
Qualifications: [BA (Oxon) MA (Bris) DPHIL (Oxon)]
✉justin.meiland@hailshamchambers.com

MELLENEY MR PETER ROBERT

Charter Chambers
33 John Street, London WC1N 2AT,
☎020 7618 4400
✉clerks@charterchambers.com
Call Date: July 2010, Inner Temple
Qualifications: [LLB (Sheff) MA (Lond)]
✉clerks@charterchambers.com

MELLON MISS GRAINNE BRID

36 Bedford Row
London WC1R 4JH, ☎020 7421 8000
✉chambers@36bedfordrow.co.uk
Call Date: July 2010, Middle Temple
Qualifications: [LLB (Hons) (Dub) LLM (Lond)]
✉gmellon@36befordrow.co.uk

E

MELLOR MR CHRISTOPHER JOHN

1 Crown Office Row
1 Crown Office Row, Temple, London EC4Y 7HH, ☎ 020 7797 7500
✉ mail@1cor.com
Call Date: Nov 1999, Middle Temple
Qualifications: [BA (Hons)(Cantab)]
christopher.mellor@1cor.com

MELLOR MR EDWARD JAMES WILSON QC (2006)

8 New Square
8 New Square, Lincoln's Inn, London WC2A 3QP, ☎ 020 7405 4321
✉ clerks@8newsquare.co.uk
Call Date: July 1986, Middle Temple
Qualifications: [MA (Cantab)]
james.mellor@8newsquare.co.uk

Types of work: Breach of confidence, Competition law, Computer litigation, Copyright, Copyright theft, Copyright Tribunal, Design, E-commerce, EC competition law, Entertainment, Information technology, Intellectual property, Malicious falsehood, Media, Media and entertainment, Passing off, Patents, Pharmaceuticals, Scientific and technical disputes, Telecommunications, Trade secrets, Trademarks

E

MELLOR MISS FAYE ELIZABETH

KCH Garden Square
1 Oxford Street, Nottingham NG1 5BH, ☎ 0115 941 8851
✉ clerks@kchgardensquare.co.uk
Call Date: Oct 2005, Middle Temple
Qualifications: [BSc (Hons) London]

MELLOR MISS RACHEL ELIZABETH

Broadway House Chambers
Broadway House, 9 Bank Street, Bradford, West Yorkshire BD1 1TW, ☎ 01274 722560
✉ clerks@broadwayhouse.co.uk
Broadway House Chambers
25 Park Square West, Leeds, West Yorkshire LS1 2PW, ☎ 0113 246 2600
✉ clerks@broadwayhouse.co.uk
Call Date: July 2004, Lincoln's Inn
Qualifications: [LLB Hons (Nott'm Trent) LLM (Nott'm)]
clerks@broadwayhouse.co.uk

MELLY MISS KAMA LOUISE

No.6 Park Square
Leeds LS1 2LW, ☎ 0113 245 9763
✉ Tim@no6.co.uk
Call Date: Oct 1997, Middle Temple
Pupil Supervisor
Qualifications: [LLB (Hons)(Leeds)]
melly@no6.co.uk

MELTON MR CHRISTOPHER QC (2001)

Byrom Street Chambers
12 Byrom Street, Manchester M3 4PP, ☎ 0161 829 2100 ✉ clerks@byromstreet.com
Crown Office Chambers
2 Crown Office Row, Temple, London EC4Y 7HJ, ☎ 020 7797 8100
✉ mail@crownofficechambers.com
42 Bedford Row
London WC1R 4LL, ☎ 020 7831 0222
✉ clerks@42br.com
Call Date: July 1982, Gray's Inn
Recorder
Qualifications: [LLB (Bris)]
christopher.melton@byromstreet.com

MELVILLE MR RICHARD DAVID QC (2002)

39 Essex Street
London WC2R 3AT, ☎ 020 7832 1111
✉ clerks@39essex.com
82 King Street
Manchester M2 4WQ, ☎ 0161 870 9969
Call Date: July 1975, Inner Temple
Qualifications: [MA (Cantab)]
david.melville@39essex.com

MELVILLE-SHREEVE MR MICHAEL DAVID

Walnut House
63 St. David's Hill, Exeter, Devon EX4 4DW, ☎ 01392 279751
✉ clerks@walnuthouse.co.uk
Call Date: July 1986, Gray's Inn
Pupil Supervisor
Qualifications: [LLB (Exeter)]
michael.melville.sheeve@walnuthouse.co.uk

MELVIN MR JAMES WARREN

Surrey Chambers Richmond
Argyle House, 1 Dee Road, Richmond, Surrey TW9 2JN, ☎ 020 8322 7785
Call Date: Nov 1997, Inner Temple
Qualifications: [LLB (Hons)]

MELWANI MISS POONAM ARJANDAS QC (2011)

Quadrant Chambers
Quadrant House, 10 Fleet Street, London EC4Y 1AU, ☎ 020 7583 4444
✉ info@quadrantchambers.com
Call Date: Nov 1989, Inner Temple
Pupil Supervisor
Qualifications: [MA (Cantab)]
poonam.melwani@quadrantchambers.com

MENARY MR ALEXANDER WILLIAM CHRISTOPHER

KBW
The Engine House, No 1 Foundry Square, Leeds LS11 5DL, ☎0113 297 1200
✉clerks@kbwchambers.com
Call Date: July 2004, Gray's Inn
Qualifications: [LLB (Cardiff)]
alexmenary@kbwchambers.com

MENARY MR ANDREW GWYN QC (2003)

Number 7 Harrington Street Chambers
7 Harrington Street, Liverpool L2 9YH, ☎0151 242 0707 ✉clerks@7hs.co.uk
Furnival Chambers
32 Furnival Street, London EC4A 1JQ, ☎020 7405 3232
Call Date: Nov 1982, Inner Temple
Recorder
Qualifications: [BA (Hons)]
andrew.menary@7hs.co.uk

MENASHY MISS MICHELLE ANN

One Essex Court
Ground Floor, One Essex Court, Temple, London EC4Y 9AR, ☎020 7583 2000
✉clerks@oeclaw.co.uk
Call Date: Oct 2003, Gray's Inn
Qualifications: [BA (Cantab)]
mmenashy@oeclaw.co.uk

MENDELLE MR PAUL MICHAEL QC (2006)

25 Bedford Row
London WC1R 4HD, ☎020 7067 1500
✉clerks@25bedfordrow.com
Call Date: July 1981, Lincoln's Inn
Qualifications: [LLB (Lond)]
paul.mendelle@25bedfordrow.com

MENDELSON MR MAURICE HARVEY QC (1992)

Blackstone Chambers
Blackstone House, Temple, London EC4Y 9BW, ☎020 7583 1770
✉clerks@blackstonechambers.com
Call Date: Nov 1965, Lincoln's Inn
Qualifications: [MA DPhil (Oxon)]
mauricemendelson@blackstonechambers.com

MENDES DA COSTA MR DAVID

Chambers of Mr D Mendes Da Costa
4 Chesterfield Road, Chiswick, London W4 3HG, ☎020 8747 4633
✉mendesdacosta@blueyonder.co.uk
MK Family Law Chambers
PO Box 6017, Milton Keynes MK1 9AP, ☎0845 123 1234
No. 3 Fleet Street Chambers
3 Fleet Street, London EC4Y 1DP, ☎020 7936 4474 ✉clerks@3fleetstreet.com
Call Date: Nov 1976, Inner Temple
Pupil Supervisor

MENDOZA MR COLIN JOHN

Devereux Chambers
Queen Elizabeth Building, Temple, London EC4Y 9BS, ☎020 7353 7534
✉clerks@devchambers.co.uk
Call Date: Nov 1983, Inner Temple
Pupil Supervisor
Qualifications: [BA (Kent) LLM (Cantab)]
mendoza@devchambers.co.uk

MENDOZA MR NEIL DAVID PEREIRA

Selborne Chambers
10 Essex Street, London WC2R 3AA, ☎020 7420 9500
✉clerks@selbornechambers.co.uk
Call Date: July 1982, Inner Temple
Pupil Supervisor
Qualifications: [MA (Cantab)]
neil.mendoza@selbornechambers.co.uk

MENON MR HARIGOVIND

Park Lane Plowden
Lombard House, 4-8 Lombard Street, Newcastle Upon Tyne NE1 3AE, ☎0191 211 4087
✉clerks@parklaneplowden.co.uk
New Court Chambers
3 Broad Chare, Newcastle Upon Tyne NE1 3DQ, ☎0191 232 1980
✉clerks@newcourt-chambers.co.uk
Call Date: July 1989, Gray's Inn
Pupil Supervisor
Qualifications: [BSc (Scotland) LLB (Newc)]
hari.menon@parklaneplowden.co.uk

MENON MR RAJIV QC (2011)

Garden Court Chambers
57-60 Lincoln's Inn Fields, London WC2A 3LJ, ☎020 7993 7600 ✉info@gclaw.co.uk
Call Date: Nov 1993, Middle Temple
Pupil Supervisor
Qualifications: [MSc (Lond) CPE]
rajivm@gclaw.co.uk

E

MENSAH MISS LORRAINE SONIA LOUISE

St Johns Buildings Liverpool
8th Floor India Buildings, Water Street, Liverpool L2 0XG, ☎0151 243 6000
✉clerk@stjohnsbuildings.co.uk
16 Winckley Square
Preston PR1 3JJ, ☎01772 256100
St Johns Buildings
24a - 28 St John Street, Manchester M3 4DJ, ☎0161 214 1500
✉clerk@stjohnsbuildings.co.uk
Call Date: Oct 1997, Gray's Inn
Qualifications: [LLB (L'pool)]
lorraine.mensah@stjohnsbuildings.co.uk

MENSAH MR MARTIN MINTAH

Atlantic Chambers
4-6 Cook Street, Liverpool L2 9QU, ☎0151 236 4421
✉info@atlanticchambers.co.uk
Call Date: Oct 2004, Inner Temple
Qualifications: [LLB (L'pool)]
info@atlanticchambers.co.uk

MENZIES MR GORDON WILLIAM

6 Pump Court
1st Floor, 6 Pump Court, Temple, London EC4Y 7AR, ☎020 7797 8400
✉richardconstable@6pumpcourt.co.uk
6 Pump Court Chambers
6-8 Mill Street, Maidstone, Kent ME15 6XH, ☎01622 688094
✉annexe@6pumpcourt.co.uk
Call Date: Oct 1998, Inner Temple
Pupil Supervisor
Qualifications: [MA (Cantab)]
gordonmenzies@6pumpcourt.co.uk

MENZIES MRS JENNIFER MARY

St Johns Buildings Liverpool
8th Floor India Buildings, Water Street, Liverpool L2 0XG, ☎0151 243 6000
✉clerk@stjohnsbuildings.co.uk
16 Winckley Square
Preston PR1 3JJ, ☎01772 256100
St Johns Buildings
24a - 28 St John Street, Manchester M3 4DJ, ☎0161 214 1500
✉clerk@stjohnsbuildings.co.uk
Call Date: Oct 2002, Middle Temple
Qualifications: [LLB (L'Pool)]

MENZIES MR RICHARD MARK

Lamb Chambers
Lamb Building, Elm Court, Temple, London EC4Y 7AS, ☎020 7797 8300
✉info@lambchambers.co.uk
Call Date: Nov 1993, Middle Temple
Pupil Supervisor
Qualifications: [MA (Cantab)]
richardmenzies@lambchambers.co.uk

Fax: 020 7797 8308;
DX: 418 London, Chancery Lane;
URL: www.lambchambers.co.uk

Types of work: Animals, Clinical negligence, Personal injury, Professional negligence

MERCER MR DAVID PAUL

St Johns Buildings
24a - 28 St John Street, Manchester M3 4DJ, ☎0161 214 1500
✉clerk@stjohnsbuildings.co.uk
St Johns Buildings
21 White Friars, Chester CH1 1NZ, ☎01244 323070
✉clerk@stjohnsbuildings.co.uk
16 Winckley Square
Preston PR1 3JJ, ☎01772 256100
Call Date: July 1980, Lincoln's Inn
Qualifications: [BA (Oxon) Dip Law]
david.mercer@stjohnsbuildings.co.uk, clerk@stjohnsbuildings.co.uk

MERCER MR GEOFFREY MICHAEL QC (2002)

Walnut House
63 St. David's Hill, Exeter, Devon EX4 4DW, ☎01392 279751
✉clerks@walnuthouse.co.uk
Call Date: Nov 1975, Inner Temple
Recorder
Qualifications: [LLB (So'ton)]

MERCER MR HUGH CHARLES QC (2008)

Essex Court Chambers
24 Lincoln's Inn Fields, London WC2A 3EG, ☎020 7813 8000
✉clerksroom@essexcourt.net
Call Date: July 1985, Middle Temple
Pupil Supervisor
Qualifications: [MA (Cantab) Lic Spec En Dr Euro (Brussels)]
hmercer@essexcourt.net

MERCER MISS KIRSTEN REBECCA

Park Court Chambers
16 Park Place, Leeds LS1 2SJ,
☎0113 243 3277
✉clerks@parkcourtchambers.co.uk
Call Date: July 2006, Inner Temple
Qualifications: [LLB (Newc)]
kmercer@parkcourtchambers.co.uk

MERCER MR NEIL STANLEY

Old Bailey Chambers
15 Old Bailey, London EC4M 7EF,
☎020 3008 6404
✉clerks@15oldbaileychambers.com
Call Date: Nov 1988, Lincoln's Inn
Pupil Supervisor
Qualifications: [LLB (Hons) (Wales)]

MEREDITH MISS CATHERINE AMY MORRISROE

Chambers of Mr Ami Feder
Ground Floor, Lamb Building, Temple, London EC4Y 7AS, ☎020 7797 7788
✉clerks@lambbuilding.co.uk
Doughty Street Chambers
53-54 Doughty Street, London WC1N 2LS,
☎020 7404 1313
✉enquiries@doughtystreet.co.uk
Chambers of Mr Ami Feder
Ground Floor, Lamb Building, Temple, London EC4Y 7AS, ☎020 7797 7788
✉clerks@lambbuilding.co.uk
Call Date: July 2008, Gray's Inn
Qualifications: [LLB (Lond)]

MEREDITH MR CHRISTOPHER WILLIAM

Furnival Chambers
32 Furnival Street, London EC4A 1JQ,
☎020 7405 3232
Call Date: Nov 1988, Inner Temple
Pupil Supervisor
Qualifications: [LLB (Hons)]

MEREDITH MR PHILIP GRANVILLE

Westgate Chambers
64 High Street, Lewes, East Sussex BN7 1XG,
☎01273 480510
✉clerks@westgate-chambers.co.uk
Call Date: July 1979, Inner Temple
Pupil Supervisor
Qualifications: [BA (Dunelm)]
pm@westgate-chambers.co.uk

MEREDITH DAVIES MISS GEMMA BETHAN

Park Lane Plowden
19 Westgate, Leeds LS1 2RD,
☎0113 228 5049
✉clerks@parklaneplowden.co.uk
Call Date: July 2007, Lincoln's Inn
Qualifications: [LLB (Dunelm)]
Gemma.Meredith-Davies@parklaneplowden.co.uk

MEREDITH-HARDY MR JOHN OCTAVIAN

Farrar's Building
Farrar's Building, Temple, London EC4Y 7BD,
☎020 7583 9241
✉Chambers@farrarsbuilding.co.uk
Call Date: Nov 1989, Inner Temple
Qualifications: [MA (St Andrews) Dip Law]

MEREDITH-JONES MISS KATE

Linenhall Chambers
1 Stanley Place, Chester CH1 2LU,
☎01244 348282
✉clerks@linenhallchambers.co.uk
Call Date: July 2003, Middle Temple
Qualifications: [BA Hons (B'Ham) LLM (B'ham)]
clerks@1stanleyplace.co.uk

MERRETT MISS LOUISE ANN

Fountain Court Chambers
Fountain Court, Temple, London EC4Y 9DH,
☎020 7583 3335
✉chambers@fountaincourt.co.uk
Call Date: Oct 1995, Gray's Inn
Qualifications: [BA]
lmerrett@fountaincourt.co.uk

MERRICK MISS NICOLA

Furnival Chambers
32 Furnival Street, London EC4A 1JQ,
☎020 7405 3232
Call Date: Nov 1983, Gray's Inn
Qualifications: [BA, LLB]
nmerrick@furnivallaw.co.uk

MERRIGAN MR DAVID

Chambers of Mr Ami Feder
Ground Floor, Lamb Building, Temple, London EC4Y 7AS, ☎020 7797 7788
✉clerks@lambbuilding.co.uk
Lamb Building
22 Ship Street, Brighton BN1 1AD,
☎01273 820490
✉admin@lambbuilding.co.uk

E

Chambers of Mr Ami Feder
Ground Floor, Lamb Building, Temple, London EC4Y 7AS, ☎ 020 7797 7788
✉ clerks@lambbuilding.co.uk
Call Date: July 2004, Lincoln's Inn
Qualifications: [BA Hons (Oxon)]
✉ clerks@lambbuilding.co.uk

MERRY MR HUGH GAIRNS

12 College Place
Fauvelle Buildings, 12 College Place, Southampton SO15 2FE, ☎ 023 8032 0320
✉ clerks@12cp.co.uk
Call Date: July 1979, Inner Temple
Pupil Supervisor
Qualifications: [LLB (Bris)]
✉ hmerry@12cp.co.uk

MERRYLEES MR RICHARD GAVIN

Tanfield Chambers
2-5 Warwick Court, London WC1R 5DJ, ☎ 020 7421 5300
✉ clerks@tanfieldchambers.co.uk
Call Date: Nov 1964, Gray's Inn
Pupil Supervisor
Qualifications: [LLB (Lond)]
✉ gavinmerrylees@tanfieldchambers.co.uk

E

MERTENS MISS SALLY ANN LOUISE

Great James Street Chambers
37 Great James Street, London WC1N 3HB, ☎ 020 7440 4949
✉ chambers@greatjames.co.uk
Call Date: Nov 2002, Middle Temple
Qualifications: [LLB (Hons)(Bournmth)]

MERZ MR RICHARD JAMES

9-12 Bell Yard
London WC2A 2JR, ☎ 020 7400 1800
✉ clerks@9-12bellyard.com
Call Date: July 1972, Inner Temple
Pupil Supervisor, Recorder
Qualifications: [LLB (So'ton)]
✉ r.merz@9-12bellyard.com

MESSENGER MR DANIEL PAUL

Regency Chambers
45 Priestgate, Peterborough PE1 1LB, ☎ 01733 315215
✉ clerks@regencychambers.law.co.uk
Call Date: Nov 2008, Middle Temple
Qualifications: [LLB (Hons) (Essex)]

MESSENGER MISS EMMA JAYNE

Alban Abbey Chambers
16 Albert Street, St Albans, Hertfordshire AL1 1RU, ☎ 01727 830 704
✉ ejmessuk@yahoo.co.uk
Call Date: Mar 1999, Middle Temple
Qualifications: [BA (Hons) LLB (Hons)]

MESSLING MR LAWRENCE DAVID

St Philips Chambers
55 Temple Row, Birmingham B2 5LS, ☎ 0121 246 7000 ✉ clerks@st-philips.com
Call Date: July 1983, Middle Temple
Qualifications: [BA (Keele)]
✉ lmessling@st-philips.co.uk

METAXA MR WILLIAM ALEXANDER

Renaissance Chambers
5th Floor, Gray's Inn Chambers, Gray's Inn, London WC1R 5JA, ☎ 020 7404 1111
✉ clerks@renaissancechambers.co.uk
Call Date: Nov 1995, Middle Temple
Qualifications: [BA (Hons)]
✉ wm@renaissancechambers.co.uk

METCALF MS LOUISE KAREN

Exchange Chambers
One Derby Square, Derby Square, Liverpool L2 9XX, ☎ 0151 236 7747
✉ info@exchangechambers.co.uk
Exchange Chambers
7 Ralli Courts, West Riverside, Manchester M3 5FT, ☎ 0161 833 2722
Exchange Chambers
Oxford House, Oxford Row, Leeds LS1 3BE, ☎ 0113 203 1970
✉ spencer@exchangechambers.co.uk
Call Date: Oct 1997, Inner Temple
Qualifications: [BA (Oxon) CPE]
✉ metcalf@exchangechambers.co.uk

METCALFE MR DANIEL JOSEPH

Call Date: July 2008, Lincoln's Inn
Qualifications: [LLB (Hull)]
✉ daniel.metcalfe@stjohnsbuildings.co.uk

METCALFE DR ERIC WILLIAM

Monckton Chambers
1 & 2 Raymond Buildings, Gray's Inn, London WC1R 5NR, ☎ 020 7405 7211
✉ chambers@monckton.com
Call Date: Nov 1999, Inner Temple
Qualifications: [BA LLM DPhil (Oxon) LLB]

METCALFE MR IAN MICHAEL

Cobden House Chambers
19 Quay Street, Manchester M3 3HN,
☎ 0161 833 6000 ✉ Clerks@Cobden.co.uk
Call Date: Nov 1985, Middle Temple
Qualifications: [LLB (Hons)]

METHUEN MR RICHARD ST BARBE QC (1997)

12 King's Bench Walk
12 King's Bench Walk, Temple, London
EC4Y 7EL, ☎ 020 7583 0811
Call Date: Nov 1972, Lincoln's Inn
Recorder

METTAM MISS HANNAH KATHRYN

Northampton Chambers
10 Spencer Parade, Northampton NN1 5AQ,
☎ 01604 636271
✉ clerks@northampton-chambers.co.uk
Call Date: Nov 2006, Inner Temple
Qualifications: [LLB (Nott'm)]

METZER MR ANTHONY DAVID ERWIN

Argent Chambers
5 Bell Yard, London WC2A 2JR,
☎ 020 7556 5500
✉ briefsin@argentchambers.co.uk
Call Date: Nov 1987, Middle Temple
Pupil Supervisor
Qualifications: [BA (Hons) (Oxon) MA (Oxon)]

METZGER MR KEVIN ALBERT

11 Gray's Inn Square Chambers
Chambers of Mr Ian Sen, 1st Floor South,
10/11 Gray's Inn Square, London WC1R 5JD,
☎ 020 7405 6879
✉ clerks@11graysinnsquare.com
Call Date: Nov 1984, Middle Temple
Pupil Supervisor
Qualifications: [BA (Hons)]
🖃 kevin.metzger@11graysinnsquare.com

MEUSZ MISS AMANDA JANE

Garden Court Chambers
57-60 Lincoln's Inn Fields, London WC2A 3LJ,
☎ 020 7993 7600 ✉ info@gclaw.co.uk
Call Date: July 1986, Gray's Inn
Qualifications: [LLB (UCL)]
🖃 amandam@gclaw.co.uk

MEYER MISS BIRGITTA SARAH GRACE

11 Stone Buildings
11 Stone Buildings, Lincoln's Inn, London
WC2A 3TG, ☎ 020 7831 6381
✉ clerks@11sb.com
Call Date: Nov 1992, Middle Temple
Qualifications: [BA (Hons) (Cantab)]
🖃 meyer@11sb.com

MEYER MISS LORNA GILLIAN QC (2006)

No5 Chambers
Fountain Court, Steelhouse Lane, Birmingham
B4 6DR, ☎ 0845 210 5555 ✉ info@no5.com
No5 Chambers
Greenwood House, 4-7 Salisbury Court,
London EC4Y 8AA, ☎ 0845 210 5555
No5 Chambers
38 Queen Square, Bristol BS1 4QS,
☎ 0845 210 5555
Call Date: July 1986, Inner Temple
Qualifications: [LLB (Sheff)]
🖃 lm@no5.com

MIAH MR AHMED

Temple Court Chambers
2nd Floor, 2 Dr Johnson's Building, Temple,
London EC4Y 7AY, ☎ 020 7353 7888
✉ clerks@templecourt.co.uk
Call Date: Oct 1998, Middle Temple
Pupil Supervisor
Qualifications: [BA (Hons) (Lond) LLM (L'pool)]
🖃 clerks@templecourt.co.uk

MIAH MR ANAWAR BABUL

Great James Street Chambers
37 Great James Street, London WC1N 3HB,
☎ 020 7440 4949
✉ chambers@greatjames.co.uk
Call Date: July 1998, Lincoln's Inn
Qualifications: [LLB (Hons)(Middx)]
🖃 anawar.miah@greatjames.co.uk

MIAH MR ZACHARIAS AZAD AFZAL

Carmelite Chambers
9 Carmelite Street, London EC4Y 0DR,
☎ 020 7936 6300
✉ clerks@carmelitechambers.co.uk
Call Date: Nov 1990, Inner Temple
Pupil Supervisor
Qualifications: [LLB]

E

MIALL MR HUGH THOMAS

13 Old Square Chambers
Ground Floor, 14 Old Square, Lincoln's Inn, London WC2A 3UE, ☎020 7831 4445
✉clerks@13oldsquare.com
Call Date: July 2009, Lincoln's Inn
Qualifications: [BA (Cantab)]
hughmiall@13oldsquare.com

MIAN MR NAEEM MAJID

Tooks Chambers
81 Farringdon Street, London EC4A 4BL,
☎020 7842 7575 ✉clerks@tooks.co.uk
Call Date: Oct 2002, Inner Temple
Qualifications: [BA MPhil (Oxon) CPE]
naeem.mian@tooks.co.uk

MIAN MS NAJMA

St Ive's Chambers
Whittall Street, Birmingham B4 6DH,
☎0121 236 0863
✉clerks@stiveschambers.co.uk
Call Date: Mar 2006, Gray's Inn
Qualifications: [LLB (Lond)]
najma.mian@stiveschambers.co.uk

E

MICAH MS CAROL HELEN

Kenworthy's Chambers
Arlington House, Bloom Street, Salford, Manchester M3 6AJ, ☎0161 832 4036
Call Date: Mar 2009, Lincoln's Inn
Qualifications: [BA (Lond) CPE UZMMU]
c.micah@kenworthysbarristers.co.uk

MICHAEL MR NICHOLAS

East Anglian Chambers
15 The Close, Norwich, Norfolk NR1 4DZ,
☎01473 214481 ✉norwich@ealaw.co.uk
East Anglian Chambers
53 North Hill, Colchester, Essex CO1 1QA,
☎01473 214481 ✉colchester@ealaw.co.uk
East Anglian Chambers
140 New London Road, Chelmsford, Essex CM2 0AW, ☎01473 214481
✉chelmsford@ealaw.co.uk
East Anglian Chambers
Gresham House, 5 Museum Street, Ipswich, Suffolk IP1 1HQ, ☎01473 214481
✉ipswich@ealaw.co.uk
Call Date: July 2003, Middle Temple
Qualifications: [LLB Hons LLM (Lond)]
nicholasmichael@ealaw.co.uk

MICHAEL MR SIMON LAURENCE

No5 Chambers
Fountain Court, Steelhouse Lane, Birmingham B4 6DR, ☎0845 210 5555 ✉info@no5.com
No5 Chambers
Greenwood House, 4-7 Salisbury Court, London EC4Y 8AA, ☎0845 210 5555
No5 Chambers
38 Queen Square, Bristol BS1 4QS,
☎0845 210 5555
Call Date: Nov 1978, Middle Temple
Qualifications: [LLB Hons (Lond)]
slm@no5.com

Types of work: Clinical negligence, Personal injury, Professional negligence

MICHAEL-IHUNDE MR HENRY OSERIEMEN

Middle Temple Lane Chambers
2nd Floor South, 1 Middle Temple Lane, London EC4Y 9AA, ☎020 7583 4352
✉chambers@mtlchambers.com
Great James Street Chambers
37 Great James Street, London WC1N 3HB,
☎020 7440 4949
✉chambers@greatjames.co.uk
Call Date: July 2011, Inner Temple
Qualifications: [LLB (Nigeria)]

MICHAELS MISS AMANDA LOUISE

Hogarth Chambers
5 New Square, Lincoln's Inn, London WC2A 3RJ, ☎020 7404 0404
✉barristers@hogarthchambers.com
Call Date: July 1981, Gray's Inn
Pupil Supervisor
Qualifications: [BA (Dunelm) MA (Belgium)]

MICHAELS MISS SHARON LYNN

Chambers of Miss Sharon Michaels
c/o 5 King Street Cloisters, Clifton Walk, King Street, Hammersmith, London W6 0GY,
☎07877 681003
✉sharonmichaels@btinternet.com
Call Date: Nov 1976, Inner Temple

MICHAELS MISS TALI NATALIE

New Court
Ground Floor, New Court, Temple, London EC4Y 9BE, ☎020 7583 5123
✉clerks@newcourtchambers.com
Call Date: Oct 2001, Lincoln's Inn
Qualifications: [BA (Hons)(Lond) Dip Law]
tmichaels@newcourtchambers.net

MICHALOS MISS CHRISTINA ANTIGONE DIANA

5RB
1st Floor, 5 Raymond Buildings, Gray's Inn, London WC1R 5BP, ☎020 7242 2902
✉clerks@5rb.com
Call Date: Oct 1994, Gray's Inn
Pupil Supervisor
Qualifications: [LLB]
✉christinamichalos@5rb.com

MICHELL MR PAUL JOSEPH

Cloisters
1 Pump Court, Temple, London EC4Y 7AA,
☎020 7827 4000 ✉clerks@cloisters.com
Call Date: Nov 1991, Middle Temple
Pupil Supervisor
Qualifications: [MA (Cantab) Dip Law]
✉pm@cloisters.com

MIDDLETON MS CAROLINE ELIZABETH

1 Garden Court Family Law Chambers
Ground Floor, One Garden Court, Temple, London EC4Y 9BJ, ☎020 7797 7900
✉clerks@1gc.com
Call Date: Oct 2002, Inner Temple
Qualifications: [BA (Nott'm) CPE]
✉middleton@1gc.com

MIDDLETON MR CHRISTOPHER MICHAEL

Oriel Chambers
14 Water Street, Liverpool, Merseyside L2 8TD, ☎0151 236 7191
✉clerks@orielchambers.co.uk
Oriel Chambers
18 Ribblesdale Place, Preston PR1 3NA,
☎01772 254 764
✉clerks@oriel-chambers.co.uk
Call Date: Oct 2002, Inner Temple
Qualifications: [LLB (Nott'm)]
✉christopher.middleton@orielchambers.co.uk

MIDDLETON MISS CLAIRE LOUISE

Dere Street Barristers
33 Broad Chare, Newcastle Upon Tyne NE1 3DQ, ☎0844 3351551
✉clerks@derestreet.co.uk
Chambers of Mr L Rahman
201 Maidstone Road, Rochester, Kent ME1 3ES, ☎07947 588362
✉luthfur99@gmail.com
Call Date: Oct 1991, Lincoln's Inn
Qualifications: [LLB (Hons) (Newc)]
✉clerks@broadcharechambers.co.uk

MIDDLETON MR JOSEPH

Doughty Street Chambers
53-54 Doughty Street, London WC1N 2LS,
☎020 7404 1313
✉enquiries@doughtystreet.co.uk
Doughty Street Chambers
Pall Mall Court, 61-67 King Street, Manchester M2 4PD, ☎0161 618 1066
Doughty Street Chambers
5th Floor, Broad Quay House, Prince Street, Bristol BS1 4DJ, ☎01179 058 717
Call Date: Nov 1997, Inner Temple
Qualifications: [BSc (Surrey) LLM (Lond)]
✉j.middleton@doughtystreet.co.uk

MIDGLEY MR ANDREW LLOYD

Old Square Chambers
3 Orchard Court, St Augustine's Yard, Bristol BS1 5DP, ☎0117 930 5100
✉clerks@oldsquare.co.uk
Old Square Chambers
10-11 Bedford Row, London WC1R 4BU,
☎020 7269 0300 ✉clerks@oldsquare.co.uk
Call Date: Oct 2000, Gray's Inn
Qualifications: [BA (Lond)]
✉midgley@oldsquare.co.uk

MIDGLEY MISS ANNA VICTORIA JANE

Albion Chambers
Broad Street, Bristol BS1 1DR,
☎0117 927 2144
✉clerks@albionchambers.co.uk
Call Date: Oct 2005, Middle Temple
Qualifications: [BA (Hons)]
✉anna.midgley@albionchambers.co.uk

MIDWINTER MR STEPHEN BRIAN

Brick Court Chambers
7-8 Essex Street, London WC2R 3LD,
☎020 7379 3550 ✉clerks@brickcourt.co.uk
Call Date: July 2002, Middle Temple
Pupil Supervisor
Qualifications: [BA (Hons) (Cantab) LLM (Cantab)]
✉Stephen.Midwinter@Brickcourt.co.uk

MIHANGEL MISS OLWEN MAIR

Linenhall Chambers
1 Stanley Place, Chester CH1 2LU,
☎01244 348282
✉clerks@linenhallchambers.co.uk
Call Date: Oct 2002, Gray's Inn
Qualifications: [BA (Cantab)]
✉clerks@1stanleyplace.co.uk

E

MILDON MR DAVID WALLIS QC (2000)

Essex Court Chambers
24 Lincoln's Inn Fields, London WC2A 3EG, ☎ 020 7813 8000
✉ clerksroom@essexcourt.net
Call Date: July 1980, Middle Temple
Qualifications: [MA LLB (Cantab)]
✉ dmildon@essexcourt.net

MILES MR EDWARD NAPIER TREMAYNE

Lamb Chambers
Lamb Building, Elm Court, Temple, London EC4Y 7AS, ☎ 020 7797 8300
✉ info@lambchambers.co.uk
Call Date: Feb 1989, Inner Temple
Qualifications: [BA (Oxon)]
✉ napiermiles@lambchambers.co.uk

MILES MISS NICOLA

Number 7 Harrington Street Chambers
7 Harrington Street, Liverpool L2 9YH, ☎ 0151 242 0707 ✉ clerks@7hs.co.uk
Call Date: Oct 1999, Lincoln's Inn
Qualifications: [LLB (Hons)(Leic)]
✉ nicola.miles@7hs.co.uk

MILES MR RICHARD IAIN

One Essex Court
1st Floor, Temple, London EC4Y 9AR, ☎ 020 7936 3030 ✉ clerks@1ec.co.uk
Call Date: Nov 1997, Gray's Inn
Pupil Supervisor
Qualifications: [BA (Kingston)]
✉ rmiles@1ec.co.uk

MILES MR ROBERT JOHN QC (2002)

4 Stone Buildings
Ground Floor, 4 Stone Buildings, Lincoln's Inn, London WC2A 3XT, ☎ 020 7242 5524
✉ clerks@4stonebuildings.com
Call Date: Nov 1987, Lincoln's Inn
Qualifications: [BA BCL (Oxon)]
✉ clerks@4stonebuildings.com

MILFORD MR JULIAN ROBERT

11 King's Bench Walk
11 King's Bench Walk, Temple, London EC4Y 7EQ, ☎ 020 7632 8500
✉ clerksroom@11kbw.com
Call Date: July 2000, Middle Temple
Qualifications: [BA(Hons) (Oxon)]
✉ julian.milford@11kbw.com

MILL MR IAN ALEXANDER QC (1999)

Blackstone Chambers
Blackstone House, Temple, London EC4Y 9BW, ☎ 020 7583 1770
✉ clerks@blackstonechambers.com
Call Date: July 1981, Middle Temple
Qualifications: [MA (Cantab)]
✉ ianmill@blackstonechambers.com

MILLAR MR GAVIN JAMES QC (2000)

Doughty Street Chambers
53-54 Doughty Street, London WC1N 2LS, ☎ 020 7404 1313
✉ enquiries@doughtystreet.co.uk
Doughty Street Chambers
Pall Mall Court, 61-67 King Street, Manchester M2 4PD, ☎ 0161 618 1066
Doughty Street Chambers
5th Floor, Broad Quay House, Prince Street, Bristol BS1 4DJ, ☎ 01179 058 717
Call Date: July 1981, Lincoln's Inn
Recorder
Qualifications: [BA (Oxon)]
✉ g.millar@doughtystreet.co.uk

MILLER MISS AMANDA CATHERINE ARNOT

Dere Street Barristers
33 Broad Chare, Newcastle Upon Tyne NE1 3DQ, ☎ 0844 3351551
✉ clerks@derestreet.co.uk
Call Date: July 2005, Inner Temple
Qualifications: [LLB (Northumbria)]
✉ clerks@broadcharechambers.co.uk

MILLER MR ANDREW

2 Temple Gardens
2 Temple Gardens, Temple, London EC4Y 9AY, ☎ 020 7822 1200
✉ clerks@2tg.co.uk
Call Date: July 1989, Inner Temple
Pupil Supervisor
Qualifications: [LLB (So'ton) FCIArb]
✉ amiller@2tg.co.uk

MILLER MISS CATHERINE

East Anglian Chambers
Gresham House, 5 Museum Street, Ipswich, Suffolk IP1 1HQ, ☎ 01473 214481
✉ ipswich@ealaw.co.uk
East Anglian Chambers
140 New London Road, Chelmsford, Essex CM2 0AW, ☎ 01473 214481
✉ chelmsford@ealaw.co.uk

East Anglian Chambers
15 The Close, Norwich, Norfolk NR1 4DZ,
☎01473 214481 ✉norwich@ealaw.co.uk
Call Date: July 2003, Gray's Inn
Pupil Supervisor
Qualifications: [BA (Dunelm)]
✉katemiller@ealaw.co.uk

MILLER MR CHRISTOPHER ALBERT

14 Gray's Inn Square
14 Gray's Inn Square, Gray's Inn, London
WC1R 5JP, ☎020 7242 0858
✉clerks@14gis.co.uk
Call Date: Oct 1998, Lincoln's Inn
Qualifications: [LLB (Hons)(Sheff)]
✉cm2@14graysinnsquare.co.uk

MILLER MR DANIEL NORMAN

Crown Office Row Chambers
119 Church Street, Brighton, Sussex
BN1 1UD, ☎01273 625625
✉clerks@1cor.com
Call Date: Oct 2005, Lincoln's Inn
Qualifications: [BA (Hons) Leeds]
✉daniel.miller@1cor.com

MILLER MR DAVID ROBIN

Furnival Chambers
32 Furnival Street, London EC4A 1JQ,
☎020 7405 3232
Call Date: Oct 1998, Inner Temple
Pupil Supervisor
Qualifications: [LLB (Thames)]
✉dmiller@furnivallaw.co.uk

MILLER MR IAN DAUKES DOUGLAS

1 Chancery Lane
London WC2A 1LF, ☎0845 634 6666
✉clerks@1chancerylane.com
Call Date: Oct 1999, Gray's Inn
Pupil Supervisor
Qualifications: [BA (Oxon) MA (Warw)]

MILLER MR IAN ROBERTSON

Broadway House Chambers
Broadway House, 9 Bank Street, Bradford,
West Yorkshire BD1 1TW, ☎01274 722560
✉clerks@broadwayhouse.co.uk
Broadway House Chambers
25 Park Square West, Leeds, West Yorkshire
LS1 2PW, ☎0113 246 2600
✉clerks@broadwayhouse.co.uk
Call Date: Oct 1999, Lincoln's Inn
Pupil Supervisor
Qualifications: [LLB (Hons)(Huddes)]
✉irm@broadwayhouse.co.uk

MILLER MR JOHN NICHOLAS

St John's Chambers
101 Victoria Street, Bristol BS1 6PU,
☎0117 923 4700
✉clerks@stjohnschambers.co.uk
Call Date: July 1994, Inner Temple
Pupil Supervisor
Qualifications: [LLB]
✉jnm@stjohnschambers.co.uk

MILLER MR JONATHAN

One Essex Court
1st Floor, Temple, London EC4Y 9AR,
☎020 7936 3030 ✉clerks@1ec.co.uk
Call Date: Nov 1996, Middle Temple
Qualifications: [BA (Hons)(Oxon)]
✉jmiller@1ec.co.uk

MILLER MR KEITH STEWART HUNTER

Fountain Chambers
Cleveland Business Centre, 1 Watson Street,
Middlesbrough TS1 2RQ, ☎01642 804040
✉clerks@fountainchambers.co.uk
Call Date: July 1973, Middle Temple
Pupil Supervisor, Recorder
Qualifications: [LLB]

MILLER MR PAUL WAIND

Wilberforce Chambers
7 Bishop Lane, Hull HU1 1PA,
☎01482 323264
Call Date: July 1974, Lincoln's Inn
Pupil Supervisor, Recorder
Qualifications: [MA (Oxon)]

MILLER MR PETER OWEN MICHAEL

Cornerstone Barristers
2-3 Gray's Inn Square, Gray's Inn, London
WC1R 5JH, ☎020 7242 4986
✉chambers@2-3gis.co.uk
Call Date: Oct 1993, Lincoln's Inn
Qualifications: [LLB (Hons)(Lond)]
✉pmiller@2-3gis.co.uk

MILLER MR RICHARD HUGH QC (1995)

Three New Square IP
3 New Square, Lincoln's Inn, London
WC2A 3RS, ☎020 7405 1111
✉clerks@3newsquare.co.uk
Call Date: July 1976, Middle Temple
Qualifications: [BSc]
✉rmiller@3newsquare.co.uk

E

MILLER MR RICHARD JAMES

9 Park Place
9 Park Place, Cardiff, South Glamorgan CF10 3DP, ☎029 2038 2731
✉clerks@9parkplace.co.uk
Call Date: Oct 1991, Gray's Inn
Pupil Supervisor
Qualifications: [LLB (Wales)]
clerks@9parkplace.co.uk

MILLER MR SIMON RICHARD ANDREW

Harcourt Chambers
1st Floor, 2 Harcourt Buildings, Temple, London EC4Y 9DB, ☎0844 561 7135
Call Date: Oct 1996, Lincoln's Inn
Pupil Supervisor
Qualifications: [LLB (Hons)(Leic)]
Smiller@harcourtchambers.law.co.uk

MILLER MR STEPHEN MACKENZIE QC (1990)

1 Crown Office Row
1 Crown Office Row, Temple, London EC4Y 7HH, ☎020 7797 7500
✉mail@1cor.com
Call Date: July 1971, Middle Temple
Recorder
Qualifications: [BA Hons (Oxon)]
stephen.miller@1cor.com

MILLER MISS WENDY ANNE MAY

Citadel Chambers
The Citadel, 190 Corporation Street, Birmingham B4 6QD, ☎0121 233 8500
✉clerks@citadelchambers.com
Call Date: July 2001, Middle Temple
Qualifications: [LLB (Hons)]
clerks@citadelchambers.com

MILLETT MR KENNETH JAMES

2 Hare Court
Lower Ground, Ground, 1st & 2nd Floor, 2 Hare Court, Temple, London EC4Y 7BH, ☎020 7353 3982 ✉clerks@2harecourt.com
Call Date: July 1988, Inner Temple
Pupil Supervisor
Qualifications: [LLB]
kenmillett@2harecourt.com

MILLETT MR RICHARD LESTER QC (2003)

Essex Court Chambers
24 Lincoln's Inn Fields, London WC2A 3EG, ☎020 7813 8000
✉clerksroom@essexcourt.net
Call Date: July 1985, Lincoln's Inn
Qualifications: [BA (Cantab)]
rmillett@essexcourt.net

MILLETT MISS TRILBY REBECCA CHARLOTTE

Dyers Chambers
35 Bedford Row, London WC1R 4JH, ☎020 7404 1881
✉admin@dyerschambers.com
Call Date: July 1996, Gray's Inn
Qualifications: [BA (Exon)]

MILLIGAN MR IAIN ANSTRUTHER QC (1991)

20 Essex Street
London WC2R 3AL, ☎020 7842 1200
✉clerks@20essexst.com
Call Date: July 1973, Inner Temple
Qualifications: [MA (Cantab)]
clerks@20essexst.com

MILLIKEN-SMITH MR MARK GORDON QC (2006)

2 Bedford Row
London WC1R 4BU, ☎020 7440 8888
✉clerks@2bedfordrow.co.uk
Call Date: Nov 1986, Gray's Inn
Qualifications: [LLB(Bris)]
mmilliken-smith@2bedfordrow.co.uk

MILLIN MRS LESLIE MARILYN

The Chambers of Mrs Leslie Millin
12 Folly Orchard, Wokingham, Berkshire RG41 2TU, ☎0118 978 8026
✉lmmillin@gmail.com
Call Date: Nov 1988, Gray's Inn
Qualifications: [LLB (Reading)]

MILLIN MRS MELISSA PATRICIA

Goldsmith Chambers
Ground Floor, Goldsmith Building, Temple, London EC4Y 7BL, ☎020 7353 6802
✉clerks@goldsmithchambers.com
Call Date: Nov 1999, Gray's Inn
Qualifications: [LLM (Wales)]

MILLINGTON MR CHRISTOPHER JOHN QC (2001)

St Philips Chambers
55 Temple Row, Birmingham B2 5LS,
☎0121 246 7000 ✉clerks@st-philips.com
Call Date: July 1976, Gray's Inn
Recorder
Qualifications: [LLM(B'ham)]
cmillington@st-philips.com

MILLINGTON MR JOSEPH EDWARD

St Philips Chambers
55 Temple Row, Birmingham B2 5LS,
☎0121 246 7000 ✉clerks@st-philips.com
Call Date: Oct 2009, Inner Temple
Qualifications: [LLB (Nott'm)]
jmillington@st-philips.com

MILLINGTON MR OLIVER JAMES RICHARD

The Chambers of Grahame Aldous QC
9 Gough Square, London EC4A 3DG,
☎020 7832 0500
✉clerks@9goughsquare.co.uk
Call Date: July 2003, Gray's Inn
Qualifications: [BA (Oxon)]
omillington@9goughsquare.co.uk

MILLNS MISS CLAIRE ALICE ELIZABETH

Park Lane Plowden
Lombard House, 4-8 Lombard Street,
Newcastle Upon Tyne NE1 3AE,
☎0191 211 4087
✉clerks@parklaneplowden.co.uk
Call Date: July 2001, Middle Temple
Qualifications: [LLB (Hons)]
claire.millns@parklaneplowden.co.uk

MILLS MR ALEXANDER EDWARD

23 Essex Street
London WC2R 3AA, ☎020 7413 0353
✉clerks@23es.com
Call Date: July 2004, Gray's Inn
Qualifications: [MA (Cantab)]
alexandermills@23es.com

MILLS MISS BARBARA

4 Paper Buildings
1st Floor, 4 Paper Buildings, Temple, London
EC4Y 7EX, ☎020 7427 5200
✉clerks@4pb.com
Call Date: Oct 1990, Inner Temple
Qualifications: [LLB (Hull)]
bm@4pb.com

MILLS MR BENEDICT JOHN

St Philips Chambers
55 Temple Row, Birmingham B2 5LS,
☎0121 246 7000 ✉clerks@st-philips.com
Call Date: Oct 2000, Inner Temple
Qualifications: [BA (Hons)(B'Ham) PGDL BVC]
bmills@st-philips.co.uk

MILLS MR COREY ARTHUR

Becket Chambers
17 New Dover Road, Canterbury, Kent
CT1 3AS, ☎01227 786331
✉clerks@becket-chambers.co.uk
Call Date: Nov 1987, Middle Temple
Qualifications: [LLB (Hons)]
cmills@becket-chambers.co.uk

MILLS MR KRISTIAN ANTHONY

Trinity Chambers
The Custom House, 39 Quayside, Newcastle
Upon Tyne NE1 3DE, ☎0191 232 1927
✉info@trinitychambers.co.uk
Trinity Chambers
Multi Media Exchange, 72-80 Corporation
Road, Middlesbrough TS1 2RF,
☎01642 247569
✉info@trinitychambers.co.uk
Call Date: Nov 1998, Middle Temple
Qualifications: [LLB (Hons)(Wales)]

E

MILLS MR REGINALD STUART

Oriel Chambers
14 Water Street, Liverpool, Merseyside
L2 8TD, ☎0151 236 7191
✉clerks@orielchambers.co.uk
Oriel Chambers
18 Ribblesdale Place, Preston PR1 3NA,
☎01772 254 764
✉clerks@oriel-chambers.co.uk
Call Date: Oct 1992, Middle Temple
Pupil Supervisor
Qualifications: [LLB (Hons)]
stuart.mills@orielchambers.co.uk

MILLS MR SIMON MARK

Linenhall Chambers
1 Stanley Place, Chester CH1 2LU,
☎01244 348282
✉clerks@linenhallchambers.co.uk
Call Date: Nov 1986, Inner Temple
Pupil Supervisor
Qualifications: [LLB (B'ham)]
clerks@1stanleyplace.co.uk

MILLS MR SIMON THOMAS

Five Paper
Ground Floor, 5 Paper Buildings, Temple, London EC4Y 7HB, ☎ 020 7815 3200
Call Date: Nov 1994, Lincoln's Inn
Pupil Supervisor
Qualifications: [MA (Cantab)]
simonmills@fivepaper.com

MILMO MR PATRICK HELENUS QC (1985)

5RB
1st Floor, 5 Raymond Buildings, Gray's Inn, London WC1R 5BP, ☎ 020 7242 2902
clerks@5rb.com
Call Date: July 1962, Middle Temple
Qualifications: [MA (Cantab)]
patrickmilmo@5rb.com

MILNE MR ALEXANDER HUGH QC (2010)

18 Red Lion Court
London EC4A 3EB, ☎ 020 7520 6000
chambers@18rlc.co.uk
18 Red Lion Court (Annexe)
Thornwood House, 102 New London Road, Chelmsford, Essex CM2 0RG,
☎ 01245 280880
Call Date: Nov 1981, Gray's Inn
Pupil Supervisor, Recorder
Qualifications: [BA]
alex.milne@18rlc.co.uk

MILNE MRS ARLENE JOAN

Cobden House Chambers
19 Quay Street, Manchester M3 3HN,
☎ 0161 833 6000 Clerks@Cobden.co.uk
Call Date: Oct 1999, Middle Temple
Qualifications: [LLB (Hons)(Coventry)]
msamilne@hotmail.co.uk

MILNE MR DAVID CALDER QC (1987)

Pump Court Tax Chambers
16 Bedford Row, London WC1R 4EF,
☎ 020 7414 8080 clerks@pumptax.com
Call Date: July 1970, Lincoln's Inn
Qualifications: [MA (Oxon) FCA]
dmilne@pumptax.com

Types of work: Capital tax, Corporation tax, Income tax, National Insurance, Stamp duty, Trusts, VAT

MILNE MR DUNCAN PAUL

12 College Place
Fauvelle Buildings, 12 College Place, Southampton SO15 2FE, ☎ 023 8032 0320
clerks@12cp.co.uk
Call Date: Oct 2007, Lincoln's Inn
Qualifications: [BA (York) MPhil (Cantab)]

MILNE MR MICHAEL

Resolution Chambers
The Old School House, Walwyn Road, Colwall, Malvern, Worcestershire WR13 6PL,
☎ 01684 541008
mmilne@milne-arbitration.co.uk
Call Date: July 1987, Lincoln's Inn
Qualifications: [BA FCIArb FRICS Dip Law]
mmilne5@me.com

MILNE MR RICHARD JAMES

23 Essex Street
London WC2R 3AA, ☎ 020 7413 0353
clerks@23es.com
Call Date: Oct 1992, Middle Temple
Pupil Supervisor
Qualifications: [MA (Hons)(Oxon) Dip Law]
richardmilne@23es.com

MILNER MR ALEXANDER NATHAN

Fountain Court Chambers
Fountain Court, Temple, London EC4Y 9DH,
☎ 020 7583 3335
chambers@fountaincourt.co.uk
Call Date: Oct 2006, Lincoln's Inn
Qualifications: [BA (Cantab)]
anm@fountaincourt.co.uk

MILNER MR JONAS DANIEL

2 Bedford Row
London WC1R 4BU, ☎ 020 7440 8888
clerks@2bedfordrow.co.uk
Call Date: Nov 2008, Middle Temple
Qualifications: [BA (Hons) (Nott'm)]
jmilner@2bedfordrow.co.uk

MILNER MR JONATHAN DAVID BENJAMIN

Francis Taylor Building
Inner Temple, London EC4Y 7BY,
☎ 020 7353 8415 clerks@ftb.eu.com
Call Date: July 1977, Inner Temple
Pupil Supervisor
Qualifications: [LLB (Lond)]
jonathan.milner@ftb.eu.com

MILNES MR PETER HARTLEY

Aegis Chambers
39 Mostyn Avenue, Wembley, Middlesex HA9 8AY
Call Date: Mar 2007, Lincoln's Inn
Qualifications: [LLB (Sheff)]

MILNES MR SIMON CHRISTOPHER

20 Essex Street
London WC2R 3AL, ☎ 020 7842 1200
✉ clerks@20essexst.com
Call Date: Oct 2005, Gray's Inn
Qualifications: [BA (Oxon)]
✉ clerks@20essexst.com

MILROY MISS CAROLINE

Thomas More Chambers
7 Lincoln's Inn Fields, London WC2A 3BP, ☎ 020 7404 7000
✉ clerks@thomasmore.co.uk
Call Date: July 2000, Gray's Inn
Qualifications: [LLB MA]
✉ cmilroy@thomasmore.co.uk

MILSOM MRS CATHERINE MARY

Argent Chambers
5 Bell Yard, London WC2A 2JR, ☎ 020 7556 5500
✉ briefsin@argentchambers.co.uk
Call Date: Nov 1994, Inner Temple
Pupil Supervisor
Qualifications: [BA (Hons) LLM]
✉ c.milsom@argentchambers.co.uk

MILSOM MR CHRISTOPHER ANDREW

Cloisters
1 Pump Court, Temple, London EC4Y 7AA, ☎ 020 7827 4000 ✉ clerks@cloisters.com
Call Date: Oct 2006, Inner Temple
Qualifications: [BA (Oxon)]

MINOPRIO MS DELIA JOY

42 Bedford Row
London WC1R 4LL, ☎ 020 7831 0222
✉ clerks@42br.com
Call Date: July 2007, Middle Temple
Qualifications: [BA (Exon)]
✉ delia.minoprio@42br.com

MINTO MISS AMANDA JAYNE

Guildford Chambers
Stoke House, Leapale Lane, Guildford, Surrey GU1 4LY, ☎ 01483 539131
✉ clerks@guildfordchambers.co.uk
Call Date: Nov 2009, Middle Temple
Qualifications: [LLB (Hons) (Oxon)]
✉ aminto@guildfordchambers.com

MINTZ MR SIMON HAROLD

Call Date: Nov 1996, Inner Temple
Qualifications: [BA (Newcastle)]

MIRCHANDANI MS SIAN

Four New Square
Four New Square, Lincoln's Inn, London WC2A 3RJ, ☎ 020 7822 2000
✉ barristers@4newsquare.com
Call Date: Oct 1997, Inner Temple
Qualifications: [VetMB (Cantab) MA (Cantab) CPE (City)]
✉ s.mirchandani@4newsquare.com

MIRIC MR ROBIN

4 Breams Buildings
Chancery Lane, London EC4A 1HP, ☎ 020 7092 1900 ✉ clerks@4bb.co.uk
Call Date: July 1978, Gray's Inn
Pupil Supervisor
Qualifications: [LLB]

MIRWITCH MISS JANE

Nine Bedford Row
9 Bedford Row, London WC1R 4AZ, ☎ 020 7489 2727
✉ clerks@9bedfordrow.co.uk
Call Date: Nov 1974, Middle Temple
Qualifications: [LLM (Lond)]
✉ jane.mirwitch@9bedfordrow.co.uk

MIRZA MR MUSSADAK

Cobden House Chambers
19 Quay Street, Manchester M3 3HN, ☎ 0161 833 6000 ✉ Clerks@Cobden.co.uk
Call Date: July 2004, Middle Temple
Qualifications: [BA Hons (Manch) MSc (Oxon)]
✉ clerks@cobden.co.uk

MIRZA MR QADEER BUKSH

10 King's Bench Walk
Ground Floor, 10 King's Bench Walk, Temple, London EC4Y 7EB, ☎ 020 7353 7742
✉ Chambers@10kingsbenchwalk.co.uk
Call Date: Nov 2009, Middle Temple
Qualifications: [LLB (Hons) (Lond)]

E

MISHCON MISS JANE MALCA

Hailsham Chambers
Ground Floor, 4 Paper Buildings, Temple, London EC4Y 7EX, ☎ 020 7643 5000
✉ clerks@hailshamchambers.com
Call Date: July 1979, Gray's Inn
Pupil Supervisor
Qualifications: [BA (Oxon) MA (Oxon)]

MISHCON MR OLIVER ZEBEDEE

Chambers of Mr Oliver Mishcon
1 Fetter Lane, London EC4A 1BR,
☎ 020 7993 8890 ✉ info@mishcon.org
Call Date: Nov 1993, Gray's Inn
Qualifications: [LLB]

MISKIN MR CHARLES JAMES MONCKTON QC (1998)

23 Essex Street
London WC2R 3AA, ☎ 020 7413 0353
✉ clerks@23es.com
Call Date: July 1975, Gray's Inn
Recorder
Qualifications: [MA (Oxon)]

E

MISNER MR PHILIP LAWRENCE IAN

4 Breams Buildings
Chancery Lane, London EC4A 1HP,
☎ 020 7092 1900 ✉ clerks@4bb.co.uk
Call Date: July 1984, Middle Temple
Pupil Supervisor
Qualifications: [LLB (B'ham)]

MISRA MISS ELEENA

Littleton Chambers
3 King's Bench Walk North, Temple, London EC4Y 7HR, ☎ 020 7797 8600
✉ fschneider@littletonchambers.co.uk
Call Date: July 2001, Middle Temple
Pupil Supervisor
Qualifications: [MA (Hons) (Oxon)]
✉ emisra@littletonchambers.co.uk

MISZKIEL MS URSULA

12 Old Square Chambers
1st Floor, 12 Old Square, Lincoln's Inn, London WC2A 3TX, ☎ 020 7404 0875
✉ clerks@12oldsquare.com
Call Date: Oct 1994, Gray's Inn
Qualifications: [LLB (Leeds)]

MITCHELL MR ALISTAIR STEPHEN FABIAN

49 Chambers
PO Box 3956, Bridgnorth, Shropshire WV16 4NA, ☎ 01746 761545
✉ 49chambers@googlemail.com
Call Date: Oct 1997, Middle Temple
Qualifications: [LLB (Hons)]
✉ 49chambers@googlemail.com

MITCHELL MR ANDREW EDWARD QC (2011)

Fountain Court Chambers
Fountain Court, Temple, London EC4Y 9DH,
☎ 020 7583 3335
✉ chambers@fountaincourt.co.uk
Call Date: Nov 1992, Middle Temple
Pupil Supervisor
Qualifications: [MA (Hons) (Cantab) BCL (Oxon)]
✉ aem@fountaincourt.co.uk

MITCHELL MR ANDREW JONATHAN MILLS

No.6 Park Square
Leeds LS1 2LW, ☎ 0113 245 9763
✉ Tim@no6.co.uk
Call Date: Nov 1991, Lincoln's Inn
Pupil Supervisor
Qualifications: [LLB (Hons) (Leeds)]
✉ mitchell@no6.co.uk

MITCHELL MR ANDREW ROBERT QC (1998)

Chambers of Andrew Mitchell QC
33 Chancery Lane, London WC2A 1EN,
☎ 020 7440 9950 ✉ clerks@33cllaw.com
Call Date: July 1976, Gray's Inn
✉ arm@33cllaw.com

MITCHELL MS ANNE CUMMING

104 Gypsy Lane
104 Gypsy Lane, Nunthorpe, Middlesbrough, Cleveland TS7 0DR, ☎ 01642 316018
✉ annecmitchell@msn.com
Call Date: Oct 1994, Gray's Inn
Qualifications: [LLB]

MITCHELL MRS CATHERINE LOUISE

Palmyra Chambers
Royal House, 46 Legh Street, Warrington WA1 1UJ, ☎ 01925 444919
✉ clerk@palmyrachambers.com
Call Date: July 2008, Lincoln's Inn
Qualifications: [BSc (Leeds) LLB (Lond)]
✉ cathy.mitchell@palmyrachambers.com

MITCHELL MR CHRISTIAN RICHARD

Guildford Chambers
Stoke House, Leapale Lane, Guildford, Surrey GU1 4LY, ☎01483 539131
✉clerks@guildfordchambers.co.uk
Alexander Chambers
13 Halstead Road, Wanstead, London E11 2AY, ☎0845 652 0451 / 0854 652 0451
✉clerks@alexanderchambers.co.uk
Call Date: July 2001, Middle Temple
Qualifications: [BSc (Hons) DipLaw]
cmitchell@guildfordchambers.com

MITCHELL MR DAVID GORDON

Ely Place Chambers
30 Ely Place, London EC1N 6TD, ☎020 7400 9600 ✉admin@elyplace.com
Call Date: Nov 2004, Inner Temple
Qualifications: [BA University of Manchester CPE College of Law]
dmitchell@elyplace.com

MITCHELL MR DAVID JOHN

No5 Chambers
Fountain Court, Steelhouse Lane, Birmingham B4 6DR, ☎0845 210 5555 ✉info@no5.com
No5 Chambers
Greenwood House, 4-7 Salisbury Court, London EC4Y 8AA, ☎0845 210 5555
No5 Chambers
38 Queen Square, Bristol BS1 4QS, ☎0845 210 5555
Call Date: Oct 1995, Lincoln's Inn
Pupil Supervisor
Qualifications: [BSc (Hons)(Lond) LLB (Hons)(Lond)]
dm@no5.com

MITCHELL MR FRANK

Monckton Chambers
1 & 2 Raymond Buildings, Gray's Inn, London WC1R 5NR, ☎020 7405 7211
✉chambers@monckton.com
Call Date: Nov 2010, Gray's Inn
fmitchell@monckton.com

MITCHELL MR GREGORY CHARLES MATHEW QC (1997)

3 Verulam Buildings
London WC1R 5NT, ☎020 7831 8441
✉chambers@3vb.com
Call Date: July 1979, Gray's Inn
Recorder
Qualifications: [BA (Lond) PhD]
gmitchell@3vb.com

MITCHELL MR IAIN QC (2012)

Tanfield Chambers
2-5 Warwick Court, London WC1R 5DJ, ☎020 7421 5300
✉clerks@tanfieldchambers.co.uk
Call Date: May 2012, Middle Temple

MITCHELL MR JACK

3 PB Barristers
3 Paper Buildings, Temple, London EC4Y 7EU, ☎020 7583 8055
3 PB Barristers
Royal Talbot House, 2 Victoria Street, Bristol, Avon BS1 6BB, ☎0117 928 1520
3 PB Barristers
4 St Peter Street, Winchester SO23 8BW, ☎01962 868884
✉clerks.winchester@3paper.co.uk
3 PB Barristers
23 Beaumont Street, Oxford OX1 2NP, ☎01865 793 736
3 PB Barristers
30 Christchurch Road, Bournemouth, Dorset BH1 3PD, ☎01202 292102
✉clerks.bournemouth@3paper.co.uk
Call Date: Oct 1994, Inner Temple
Qualifications: [LLB (Huddersfield)]
jack.mitchell@3paper.co.uk

MITCHELL MR JAMES RONALD

New Court Chambers
3 Broad Chare, Newcastle Upon Tyne NE1 3DQ, ☎0191 232 1980
✉clerks@newcourt-chambers.co.uk
Call Date: July 1973, Inner Temple
james.mitchell@newcourt-chambers.co.uk

MITCHELL MISS JANET VIVIAN

4 Brick Court
4 Brick Court, Temple, London EC4Y 9AD, ☎020 7832 3200 ✉clerks@4bc.co.uk
Call Date: Feb 1978, Middle Temple
Qualifications: [BA (Lond)]
janet.mitchell@4bc.co.uk

MITCHELL MR JONATHAN

1 Gray's Inn Square
Ground Floor, 1 Gray's Inn Square, London WC1R 5AA, ☎020 7405 0001
Holborn Chambers
6 Gate Street, Lincoln's Inn Fields, London WC2A 3HP, ☎020 7242 6060
Call Date: Mar 1998, Inner Temple
Qualifications: [BA]
jmitchell@1gis.co.uk

E

MITCHELL MR JONATHAN HOWARD

Ropewalk Chambers
24 The Ropewalk, Nottingham NG1 5EF, ☎0115 947 2581 ✉clerks@ropewalk.co.uk
Call Date: Oct 1992, Gray's Inn
Pupil Supervisor
Qualifications: [LLB (Wales)]

MITCHELL MR JONATHAN STUART

25 Bedford Row
London WC1R 4HD, ☎020 7067 1500
✉clerks@25bedfordrow.com
Call Date: Nov 1974, Middle Temple
Qualifications: [MA]
✉jmitchell@25bedfordrow.com

MITCHELL MR KEITH ARNO

Chambers of Andrew Mitchell QC
33 Chancery Lane, London WC2A 1EN, ☎020 7440 9950 ✉clerks@33cllaw.com
Call Date: Nov 1981, Inner Temple
Pupil Supervisor
Qualifications: [BA]
✉kam@33cllaw.com

MITCHELL MS LESLEY

Chambers of Lesley Mitchell
Stapleton Lodge, 71 Hamilton Road, Brentford, Middlesex TW8 0QF, ☎020 8568 2164
✉lesley@mitchellsegal.co.uk
Call Date: Nov 1987, Inner Temple
Qualifications: [BSc (Lond) Dip Law]
✉lesley@mitchellsegal.co.uk

MITCHELL MR NIGEL CAMPBELL

3 PB Barristers
3 Paper Buildings, Temple, London EC4Y 7EU, ☎020 7583 8055
3 PB Barristers
Royal Talbot House, 2 Victoria Street, Bristol, Avon BS1 6BB, ☎0117 928 1520
3 PB Barristers
23 Beaumont Street, Oxford OX1 2NP, ☎01865 793 736
3 PB Barristers
4 St Peter Street, Winchester SO23 8BW, ☎01962 868884
✉clerks.winchester@3paper.co.uk
3 PB Barristers
30 Christchurch Road, Bournemouth, Dorset BH1 3PD, ☎01202 292102
✉clerks.bournemouth@3paper.co.uk
Call Date: Feb 1978, Lincoln's Inn
Pupil Supervisor
Qualifications: [LLB (Lond)]

MITCHELL DR PAUL STUART

Hailsham Chambers
Ground Floor, 4 Paper Buildings, Temple, London EC4Y 7EX, ☎020 7643 5000
✉clerks@hailshamchambers.com
Call Date: Oct 1999, Lincoln's Inn
Pupil Supervisor
Qualifications: [MA (Cantab) MA (Lond) PhD (Cantab)]

MITCHELL MR PETER

29 Bedford Row Chambers
London WC1R 4HE, ☎020 7404 1044
✉clerks@29br.co.uk
Call Date: Oct 1996, Inner Temple
Qualifications: [LLB (Lond)]
✉pmitchell@29br.co.uk

MITCHELL MISS REBECCA ELIZABETH

1 Garden Court Family Law Chambers
Ground Floor, One Garden Court, Temple, London EC4Y 9BJ, ☎020 7797 7900
✉clerks@1gc.com
Call Date: Oct 2000, Gray's Inn
Pupil Supervisor
Qualifications: [LLB]

MITCHELL MISS SOPHIE JANE

St Paul's Chambers
5th Floor, St Paul's House, 23 Park Square South, Leeds LS1 2ND, ☎0113 245 5866
Call Date: Oct 2010, Gray's Inn
Qualifications: [LLB]
✉sjm@stpaulschambers.com

MITCHELL MR THOMAS JARLETH DAVID

Fountain Chambers
Cleveland Business Centre, 1 Watson Street, Middlesbrough TS1 2RQ, ☎01642 804040
✉clerks@fountainchambers.co.uk
Call Date: Oct 1995, Lincoln's Inn
Pupil Supervisor
Qualifications: [BA (Hons) CPE (Manc) MA (Oxon)]

MITCHESON MR THOMAS GEORGE MOSELEY

Three New Square IP
3 New Square, Lincoln's Inn, London WC2A 3RS, ☎ 020 7405 1111
✉ clerks@3newsquare.co.uk
Call Date: Oct 1996, Inner Temple
Pupil Supervisor
Qualifications: [MA (Cantab) CPE (Lond)]
✉ mitcheson@3newsquare.co.uk

Types of work: Biotechnology, Breach of confidence, Confidential information, Copyright, Design, EC competition law, Entertainment, Information technology, Intellectual property, Passing off, Patents, Pharmaceuticals, Telecommunications, Trademarks

MITFORD MR CHRISTOPHER PETER

Trinity Chambers
The Custom House, 39 Quayside, Newcastle Upon Tyne NE1 3DE, ☎ 0191 232 1927
✉ info@trinitychambers.co.uk
Trinity Chambers
Multi Media Exchange, 72-80 Corporation Road, Middlesbrough TS1 2RF,
☎ 01642 247569
✉ info@trinitychambers.co.uk
Call Date: Nov 2001, Middle Temple

MITROPHANOUS MS ELENI

Matrix Chambers
Griffin Building, Gray's Inn, London WC1R 5LN, ☎ 020 7404 3447
✉ matrix@matrixlaw.co.uk / lscott@matrixlaw.co.uk
Call Date: Oct 1999, Inner Temple
Qualifications: [BA (Cantab) BCL (Oxon) LLM DPhil (Oxon)]
✉ elenimitrophanous@matrixlaw.co.uk

MITROPOULOS MR CHRISTOS

5 Pump Court
Ground Floor, 5 Pump Court, Temple, London EC4Y 7AP, ☎ 020 7353 2532
✉ clerks@5pumpcourt.com
Call Date: Mar 1997, Lincoln's Inn
Qualifications: [BA (Hons) (Cantab)]

MITROPOULOS MS GEORGIA

Coram Chambers
9-11 Fulwood Place, London WC1V 6HG,
☎ 020 7092 3700
✉ mail@coramchambers.co.uk
Call Date: July 1989, Gray's Inn
Pupil Supervisor
Qualifications: [BA (Wales) DipLaw]
✉ georgia.mitropoulos@coramchambers.co.uk

MITTELL MISS JODIE

12 College Place
Fauvelle Buildings, 12 College Place, Southampton SO15 2FE, ☎ 023 8032 0320
✉ clerks@12cp.co.uk
Call Date: July 2004, Inner Temple
Qualifications: [LLB (Southampton)]
✉ jmittell@12cp.co.uk

MLADENOVIC MR DEJAN

Old Bailey Chambers
15 Old Bailey, London EC4M 7EF,
☎ 020 3008 6404
✉ clerks@15oldbaileychambers.com
Tooks Chambers
81 Farringdon Street, London EC4A 4BL,
☎ 020 7842 7575 ✉ clerks@tooks.co.uk
Call Date: Nov 2006, Inner Temple
Qualifications: [LLB (So'ton) MSc (Oxon)]

MOAT MR RICHARD MARK

No5 Chambers
Fountain Court, Steelhouse Lane, Birmingham B4 6DR, ☎ 0845 210 5555 ✉ info@no5.com
No5 Chambers
Greenwood House, 4-7 Salisbury Court, London EC4Y 8AA, ☎ 0845 210 5555
No5 Chambers
38 Queen Square, Bristol BS1 4QS,
☎ 0845 210 5555
Call Date: July 1985, Lincoln's Inn
Pupil Supervisor
Qualifications: [BA (Oxon)]
✉ rm@no5.com

MOATE MS JENNIFER SARAH JANE

Five Paper
Ground Floor, 5 Paper Buildings, Temple, London EC4Y 7HB, ☎ 020 7815 3200
Call Date: July 2006, Middle Temple
Qualifications: [BA (Hons) (Oxon)]
✉ jennifermoate@fivepaper.com

MOBBS MR RICHARD JAMES

Chambers of Mr Ami Feder
Ground Floor, Lamb Building, Temple, London EC4Y 7AS, ☎ 020 7797 7788
✉ clerks@lambbuilding.co.uk
Lamb Building
22 Ship Street, Brighton BN1 1AD,
☎ 01273 820490
✉ admin@lambbuilding.co.uk
Chambers of Mr Ami Feder
Ground Floor, Lamb Building, Temple, London EC4Y 7AS, ☎ 020 7797 7788
✉ clerks@lambbuilding.co.uk
Call Date: July 2007, Lincoln's Inn
Qualifications: [BA (Oxon)]

E

MODGIL MISS SANGITA

Carmelite Chambers
9 Carmelite Street, London EC4Y 0DR, ☎ 020 7936 6300
✉ clerks@carmelitechambers.co.uk
Call Date: Oct 1990, Gray's Inn
Qualifications: [LLB (Leics)]
✉ smodgil@carmelitechambers.co.uk

MODGILL MR ALEXANDER JEFFREY

Broadway House Chambers
Broadway House, 9 Bank Street, Bradford, West Yorkshire BD1 1TW, ☎ 01274 722560
✉ clerks@broadwayhouse.co.uk
Broadway House Chambers
25 Park Square West, Leeds, West Yorkshire LS1 2PW, ☎ 0113 246 2600
✉ clerks@broadwayhouse.co.uk
Call Date: Oct 2002, Lincoln's Inn
Qualifications: [LLB (Lond) LLM (Lond)]
✉ ajm@broadwayhouse.co.uk

MODHA MR NIRAJ

Tanfield Chambers
2-5 Warwick Court, London WC1R 5DJ, ☎ 020 7421 5300
✉ clerks@tanfieldchambers.co.uk
Call Date: Oct 2010, Lincoln's Inn
Qualifications: [MA (Cantab)]

MOERAN MR FENNER ORLANDO

3 Stone Buildings
Ground Floor, 3 Stone Buildings, Lincoln's Inn, London WC2A 3XL, ☎ 020 7242 4937
✉ clerks@3sb.law.co.uk
Call Date: Oct 1996, Lincoln's Inn
Pupil Supervisor
Qualifications: [BSc (Hons)(Bris) Dip in Law]
✉ fmoeran@3sb.law.co.uk

MOFFAT MR RUSSELL DEAN

Linenhall Chambers
1 Stanley Place, Chester CH1 2LU, ☎ 01244 348282
✉ clerks@linenhallchambers.co.uk
Call Date: July 1998, Lincoln's Inn
Pupil Supervisor
Qualifications: [LLB (Hons)(L'pool)]
✉ rdmoffat@aol.com

MOFFATT MR JONATHAN ANDREW

Outer Temple Chambers
The Outer Temple, 222 Strand, London WC2R 1BA, ☎ 020 7353 6381
✉ clerks@outertemple.com
Call Date: July 2009, Middle Temple
Qualifications: [BA (Hons) (Exon) Grad Dip Law (Lond)]
✉ jonathan.moffatt@outertemple.com

MOFFATT MISS ROWENA

Chambers of Mr Ami Feder
Ground Floor, Lamb Building, Temple, London EC4Y 7AS, ☎ 020 7797 7788
✉ clerks@lambbuilding.co.uk
Chambers of Mr Ami Feder
Ground Floor, Lamb Building, Temple, London EC4Y 7AS, ☎ 020 7797 7788
✉ clerks@lambbuilding.co.uk
Call Date: Oct 2009, Inner Temple
Qualifications: [BA (Oxon) LLM CPE (Lond)]
✉ r.moffatt@mitrehouse.co.uk

MOFFETT MR JONATHAN KEITH

4-5 Gray's Inn Square
Gray's Inn, London WC1R 5AH, ☎ 020 7404 5252 ✉ clerks@4-5.co.uk
Call Date: Oct 1996, Inner Temple
Pupil Supervisor
Qualifications: [MA LLM (Cantab)]
✉ jmoffett@4-5.co.uk

MOFFETT MR WILLIAM CHARLES OLIVER

Radcliffe Chambers
Ground Floor, 11 New Square, Lincoln's Inn, London WC2A 3QB, ☎ 020 7831 0081
✉ clerks@radcliffechambers.com
Call Date: Oct 2000, Gray's Inn
Pupil Supervisor
Qualifications: [MA (Cantab)]
✉ wmoffett@radcliffechambers.com

MOGER MR CHRISTOPHER RICHARD DERWENT QC (1992)

4 Pump Court
4 Pump Court, Temple, London EC4Y 7AN, ☎ 020 7842 5555
✉ chambers@4pumpcourt.com
Call Date: July 1972, Inner Temple
Recorder
Qualifications: [LLB (Bris) FCIArb]

MOHABIR MR GERALD YOGIN

Charter Chambers
33 John Street, London WC1N 2AT, ☎ 020 7618 4400
✉ clerks@charterchambers.com
Call Date: Oct 1996, Middle Temple
Pupil Supervisor
Qualifications: [MA LLB]
✉ Gerry.Mohabir@CharterChambers.com

MOHABIR MR RICHARD RAMESH

7 Bell Yard
London WC2A 2JR, ☎ 020 7831 0636
✉ kevintarrant@btconnect.com
Call Date: Nov 2009, Middle Temple
Qualifications: [LLB (Hons) (Nott'm)]

MOHAMED MS LEEANN

Temple Court Chambers
2nd Floor, 2 Dr Johnson's Building, Temple, London EC4Y 7AY, ☎020 7353 7888
✉clerks@templecourt.co.uk
Call Date: July 2011, Middle Temple
Qualifications: [LLB (Hons) (Wolves)]

MOHAMMAD MR NAZAR

No. 3 Fleet Street Chambers
3 Fleet Street, London EC4Y 1DP,
☎020 7936 4474 ✉clerks@3fleetstreet.com
Legis Chambers
Cherat House, 32 Havelock Street, Aylesbury, Buckinghamshire HP20 2NX,
☎01296 431125 ✉espritbenoit@yahoo.co.uk
Call Date: July 2006, Inner Temple
Qualifications: [BSc (Lond) MSc (Lond)]
nkhattak63@hotmail.com

MOHAMMED MR IQBAL

St Philips Chambers
55 Temple Row, Birmingham B2 5LS,
☎0121 246 7000 ✉clerks@st-philips.com
Call Date: Nov 2007, Middle Temple
Qualifications: [LLB (Hons) (Warw)]
imohammed@st-philips.com

MOHAMMED MR RASHAD

23 Essex Street
London WC2R 3AA, ☎020 7413 0353
✉clerks@23es.com
Call Date: July 2004, Lincoln's Inn
Qualifications: [LLB Hons (Birmingham)]

MOHINDRU MR ANURAG

Lombard Chambers
1 Sekforde Street, Clerkenwell, London EC1R 0BE, ☎020 7107 2100
Call Date: July 2004, Middle Temple
Qualifications: [LLB (Hons) LLM]
anumohindru@lombardchambers.com

MOHSIN MISS ANDLIB

6 King's Bench Walk
Ground, Third & Fourth Floors, 6 King's Bench Walk, Temple, London EC4Y 7DR,
☎020 7353 4931 ✉clerks@6kbw.co.uk
Call Date: Mar 2006, Lincoln's Inn
Qualifications: [BSc (Hons) (Lond)]
andlibmohsin@6kbw.co.uk

MOHYUDDIN MR DAVID NIAZ

Exchange Chambers
7 Ralli Courts, West Riverside, Manchester M3 5FT, ☎0161 833 2722
Exchange Chambers
One Derby Square, Derby Square, Liverpool L2 9XX, ☎0151 236 7747
✉info@exchangechambers.co.uk
13 Old Square Chambers
Ground Floor, 14 Old Square, Lincoln's Inn, London WC2A 3UE, ☎020 7831 4445
✉clerks@13oldsquare.com
Call Date: Oct 1999, Lincoln's Inn
Pupil Supervisor
Qualifications: [LLB (Hons)(B'ham)]

MOLD MR ANDREW MATTHEW STEPHEN

Wilberforce Chambers
8 New Square, Lincoln's Inn, London WC2A 3QP, ☎020 7306 0102
✉chambers@wilberforce.co.uk
Call Date: Oct 2003, Lincoln's Inn
Qualifications: [BA (Hons) (Cantab) LLM]
amold@wilberforce.co.uk

Types of work: Arbitration, Banking, Capital tax, Chancery (general), Chancery (land law), Charities, Commercial law, Commercial litigation, Commercial property, Company, commercial and competition, Conflict of laws, Equity, Financial services, Foreign law, Income tax, Insolvency, Landlord and tenant, Partnerships, Pensions, Professional negligence, Succession, Trusts, Wills

MOLD MR DAVID VINCENT

Holborn Chambers
6 Gate Street, Lincoln's Inn Fields, London WC2A 3HP, ☎020 7242 6060
Call Date: Mar 2010, Middle Temple
Qualifications: [LLB (Lond)]
david.mold@holbornchambers.co.uk

MOLE MR JONATHAN JAMES

9 King's Bench Walk
Lower Ground Floor South, 9 King's Bench Walk, Temple, London EC4Y 7DX,
☎020 7353 9564 ✉9kbw@btconnect.com
Call Date: Oct 1999, Inner Temple
Qualifications: [LLB (So'ton)]
jonathanmole@btinternet.com

E

MOLL MR CHRISTIAAN ERIC

Blackfriars Chambers
79-83 Temple Chambers, 3-7 Temple Avenue, London EC4Y 0HP, ☎020 7353 7400
✉clerks@blackfriarschambers.com
Call Date: July 1986, Middle Temple
Pupil Supervisor
Qualifications: [BA (Hons) (Oxon)]
christiaan.moll@blackfriarschambers.com

MOLL MR LOUIS-PETER ALFONSO-MARIA MACK

18 Red Lion Court
London EC4A 3EB, ☎020 7520 6000
✉chambers@18rlc.co.uk
18 Red Lion Court (Annexe)
Thornwood House, 102 New London Road, Chelmsford, Essex CM2 0RG,
☎01245 280880
Call Date: Nov 1998, Middle Temple
Qualifications: [LLB (Hons)(Manch)]
louis.moll@18rlc.co.uk

MOLLER MS ALICE CHRISTINA

Alexander Chambers
13 Halstead Road, Wanstead, London E11 2AY,
☎0845 652 0451 / 0854 652 0451
✉clerks@alexanderchambers.co.uk
Chambers of Ms A C Moller
Address withheld☎07966 448572
✉chris.moller@btinternet.com
Call Date: Nov 2006, Middle Temple
Qualifications: [MA (Hons) (Edin) LLM]

MOLLOY MR ANDREW JOSEPH

St Ive's Chambers
Whittall Street, Birmingham B4 6DH,
☎0121 236 0863
✉clerks@stiveschambers.co.uk
Call Date: July 2004, Gray's Inn
Qualifications: [LLB (Wolves)]
andrew.molloy@stiveschambers.co.uk

MOLLOY MR KEVIN ANTHONY JOSEPH

Chambers of Marion Smullen and Kerim Fuad QC
1 Inner Temple Lane, London EC4Y 1AF,
☎020 7427 4400 ✉clerks@1itl.com
Call Date: Mar 1999, Middle Temple
Qualifications: [BA (Hons) CPE]
clerks@1itl.com

MOLLOY MISS SIOBHAN ANGELA

Chambers of Marion Smullen and Kerim Fuad QC
1 Inner Temple Lane, London EC4Y 1AF,
☎020 7427 4400 ✉clerks@1itl.com
Call Date: Mar 1998, Middle Temple
Qualifications: [BSc (Hons) CPE]

MOLLOY MR STEVEN GERARD

13 King's Bench Walk
13 King's Bench Walk, Temple, London EC4Y 7EN, ☎020 7353 7204
✉clerks@13kbw.co.uk
13 KBW
32 Beaumont Street, Oxford OX1 2NP,
☎01865 311066 ✉clerks@13kbw.co.uk
Call Date: July 2008, Gray's Inn
Qualifications: [LLB (L'pool)]

MOLONEY MR TIMOTHY JOHN QC (2010)

Tooks Chambers
81 Farringdon Street, London EC4A 4BL,
☎020 7842 7575 ✉clerks@tooks.co.uk
Call Date: Nov 1993, Middle Temple
Qualifications: [LLB (Hons)(B'ham) Ph D (B'ham)]
timothy.moloney@tooks.co.uk

MOLYNEUX MR BRENTON JOHN

29 Bedford Row Chambers
London WC1R 4HE, ☎020 7404 1044
✉clerks@29br.co.uk
Call Date: Feb 1994, Lincoln's Inn
Pupil Supervisor
Qualifications: [BA (Hons) (Oxon) Dip Law]
bmolyneux@29br.co.uk

MOLYNEUX MR SIMON ROWLEY

Carmelite Chambers
9 Carmelite Street, London EC4Y 0DR,
☎020 7936 6300
✉clerks@carmelitechambers.co.uk
Call Date: Apr 1986, Inner Temple
Pupil Supervisor
Qualifications: [BSc (Econ) MA (Wales) MPhil]
smolyneux@carmelitechambers.co.uk

MOMTAZ MR SAM

1 Garden Court Family Law Chambers
Ground Floor, One Garden Court, Temple, London EC4Y 9BJ, ☎020 7797 7900
✉clerks@1gc.com
Call Date: Nov 1995, Lincoln's Inn
Qualifications: [LLB (Hons)]
momtaz@1gc.com

MONAGHAN MS KARON QC (2008)

Matrix Chambers
Griffin Building, Gray's Inn, London WC1R 5LN, ☎ 020 7404 3447
✉ matrix@matrixlaw.co.uk / Iscott@matrixlaw.co.uk
Call Date: July 1989, Inner Temple
Qualifications: [LLB]
✉ karonmonaghan@matrixlaw.co.uk

MONAGHAN MR MARK EDWARD

Angel Chambers
Ethos Building, Kings Road, Swansea SA1 8AS, ☎ 01792 464623
✉ clerks@angelchambers.co.uk
Call Date: Oct 2002, Lincoln's Inn
Qualifications: [LLB (Thames Valley) PgDL MCIArb]
✉ markmonaghan@angelchambers.co.uk

MONAGHAN MR MARK TERENCE

9 St John Street
Manchester M3 4DN, ☎ 0161 955 9000
✉ civilclerks@9sjs.com / criminalclerks@9sjs.com
Call Date: July 1987, Lincoln's Inn
Qualifications: [LLB (Hons) (Sheff)]

MONAGHAN MS SUSAN MARY

No5 Chambers
Greenwood House, 4-7 Salisbury Court, London EC4Y 8AA, ☎ 0845 210 5555
No5 Chambers
38 Queen Square, Bristol BS1 4QS, ☎ 0845 210 5555
No5 Chambers
Fountain Court, Steelhouse Lane, Birmingham B4 6DR, ☎ 0845 210 5555 ✉ info@no5.com
Call Date: Oct 1995, Inner Temple
Qualifications: [BA (Galway) LLB (Wales)]
✉ monaghansusan@hotmail.com

MONAH MISS HELEN ANNE

1 Pump Court
Elm Court, Temple, London EC4Y 7AB, ☎ 020 7842 7070
✉ (name)@pumpcourt.co.uk
Call Date: Nov 1996, Lincoln's Inn
Qualifications: [LLB (Hons)(Lond)]

MOND WEDD MS JESSICA JOAN

2 Dr Johnson's Buildings
2 Dr Johnson's Buildings, Temple, London EC4Y 7AY, ☎ 020 7936 2613
✉ clerks@2drj.com
Call Date: Nov 2006, Inner Temple
Qualifications: [BA (Sussex)]
✉ clerks@2drj.com

MONDAY MISS MARTHA ANNE

Stour Chambers
Mill Studio, 17a Stour Street, Canterbury, Kent CT1 2NR, ☎ 01227 764899
✉ clerks@stourchambers.co.uk
Call Date: Oct 1998, Middle Temple
Qualifications: [BA (Hons)(Lond) CPE]
✉ clerks@stourchambers.co.uk

MONK MR DAVID KENNETH

New Walk Chambers
27 New Walk, Leicester, Leicestershire LE1 6TE, ☎ 0871 200 1298 / 0116 255 9144
✉ clerks@newwalkchambers.co.uk
Call Date: July 1991, Middle Temple
Pupil Supervisor
Qualifications: [BA (Hons) LLM]
✉ dmonk@newwalkchambers.co.uk

MONKCOM MR STEPHEN PHILIP

Tanfield Chambers
2-5 Warwick Court, London WC1R 5DJ, ☎ 020 7421 5300
✉ clerks@tanfieldchambers.co.uk
Call Date: Nov 1974, Middle Temple
Pupil Supervisor
Qualifications: [BA (Oxon)]
✉ smonkcom@tanfieldchambers.co.uk

MONKS MR ROBERT FRANCIS

Old Square Chambers
10-11 Bedford Row, London WC1R 4BU, ☎ 020 7269 0300 ✉ clerks@oldsquare.co.uk
Call Date: Oct 1999, Middle Temple
Qualifications: [LLB (Hons) LLM (L'pool)]

MONNINGTON MR BRUCE GILBERT

Fenners Chambers
3 Madingley Road, Cambridge CB3 0EE, ☎ 01223 368761
✉ clerks@fennerschambers.com
Call Date: July 1989, Inner Temple
Qualifications: [MA Dip EU Law LLM]
✉ bruce.monnington@fennerschambers.com

MONSON THE HON ANDREW ANTHONY JOHN

5RB
1st Floor, 5 Raymond Buildings, Gray's Inn, London WC1R 5BP, ☎ 020 7242 2902
✉ clerks@5rb.com
Call Date: Nov 1983, Middle Temple
Pupil Supervisor
Qualifications: [MA (Oxon)]
✉ andrewmonson@5rb.com

E

MONTAGUE MRS SUSAN

Weald Chambers
Address withheld☎01424 882 876
Call Date: Nov 1981, Inner Temple
Qualifications: [BA]
thebarrister@beeb.net

MONTAGU-SMITH MR THOMAS

XXIV Old Buildings
Ground Floor, 24 Old Buildings, Lincoln's Inn, London WC2A 3UP, ☎020 7691 2424
clerks@xxiv.co.uk
Call Date: Oct 2001, Lincoln's Inn
Pupil Supervisor
Qualifications: [MA (Hons) (Oxon)]
tms@xxiv.co.uk

MONTALDO MR NEIL JONATHAN

Call Date: Mar 2002, Lincoln's Inn
Qualifications: [LLB (Hons)]
clerk@stjohnsbuildings.co.uk,
neil.montaldo@stjohnsbuildings.co.uk

MONTEITH MR KEIR BARTLEY

Garden Court Chambers
57-60 Lincoln's Inn Fields, London WC2A 3LJ,
☎020 7993 7600 info@gclaw.co.uk
Call Date: May 1994, Lincoln's Inn
Qualifications: [LLB (Hons) (Essex)]
keirm@gclaw.co.uk

MONTES MANZANO MISS XIMENA

Atlas Chambers
3 Field Court, Gray's Inn, London WC1R 5EP,
☎020 7269 7980
clerks@atlaschambers.com
Call Date: July 2004, Middle Temple
Qualifications: [BSc (Lond) PGDip Law]

MONTGOMERY MISS CLARE PATRICIA QC (1996)

Matrix Chambers
Griffin Building, Gray's Inn, London
WC1R 5LN, ☎020 7404 3447
matrix@matrixlaw.co.uk / lscott@matrixlaw.co.uk
Call Date: Nov 1980, Gray's Inn
Recorder
Qualifications: [LLB (Lond)]
claremontgomery@matrixlaw.co.uk

MONTGOMERY MISS KRISTINA (AILEEN)

St Philips Chambers
55 Temple Row, Birmingham B2 5LS,
☎0121 246 7000 clerks@st-philips.com
Call Date: Oct 1993, Middle Temple
Pupil Supervisor, Recorder
Qualifications: [LLB (Hons)(Lond)]
kmontgomery@st-philips.com

MONTGOMERY MR TONY KEVIN

4 Breams Buildings
Chancery Lane, London EC4A 1HP,
☎020 7092 1900 clerks@4bb.co.uk
Call Date: Nov 1987, Inner Temple
Pupil Supervisor
Qualifications: [LLB (Brunel)]

MONTROSE MR RODNEY STUART

Tooks Chambers
81 Farringdon Street, London EC4A 4BL,
☎020 7842 7575 clerks@tooks.co.uk
Call Date: May 1972, Middle Temple
Pupil Supervisor
Qualifications: [LLB]
stuart.montrose@tooks.co.uk

MONTY MR SIMON TREVOR QC (2003)

Four New Square
Four New Square, Lincoln's Inn, London
WC2A 3RJ, ☎020 7822 2000
barristers@4newsquare.com
Call Date: July 1982, Middle Temple
Qualifications: [LLB]
s.monty@4newsquare.com

MOODY MISS JOANNA ELIZABETH

Deans Court Chambers
24 St John Street, Manchester M3 4DF,
☎0161 214 6000 clerks@deanscourt.co.uk
Call Date: Oct 1998, Lincoln's Inn
Qualifications: [MA (Manch) LLB (Hons)(Leeds)]

MOODY MR NEIL ROBERT QC (2010)

2 Temple Gardens
2 Temple Gardens, Temple, London
EC4Y 9AY, ☎020 7822 1200
clerks@2tg.co.uk
Call Date: Nov 1989, Gray's Inn
Pupil Supervisor
Qualifications: [MA (Oxon)]
nmoody@2tg.co.uk

MOODY-STUART MR THOMAS

8 New Square
8 New Square, Lincoln's Inn, London WC2A 3QP, ☎020 7405 4321
✉clerks@8newsquare.co.uk
Call Date: Nov 1995, Middle Temple
Pupil Supervisor
Qualifications: [BA (Hons) (Cantab)]
✉tom.moodystuart@8newsquare.co.uk

Types of work: Breach of confidence, Competition law, Computer litigation, Copyright, Copyright theft, Copyright Tribunal, Design, E-commerce, EC competition law, Entertainment, Information technology, Intellectual property, Malicious falsehood, Media, Media and entertainment, Passing off, Patents, Pharmaceuticals, Scientific and technical disputes, Telecommunications, Trade Descriptions Act, Trade secrets, Trademarks

MOOLLAN MR IQBAL ABDOOL HAMID

Radcliffe Chambers
Ground Floor, 11 New Square, Lincoln's Inn, London WC2A 3QB, ☎020 7831 0081
✉clerks@radcliffechambers.com
Call Date: Oct 1998, Middle Temple
Qualifications: [LLB (Hons)]
✉imoollan@chambers.sirhamid.intnet.mu

MOOLLAN MR SALIM ABDOOL HAMID

Essex Court Chambers
24 Lincoln's Inn Fields, London WC2A 3EG, ☎020 7813 8000
✉clerksroom@essexcourt.net
Call Date: Oct 1998, Middle Temple
Qualifications: [BA (Hons)(Cantab)]
✉smoollan@essexcourt.net

MOON MR PHILIP CHARLES ANGUS QC (2006)

3 Serjeants Inn
London EC4Y 1BQ, ☎020 7427 5000
✉clerks@3serjeantsinn.com
Call Date: Nov 1986, Middle Temple
Qualifications: [MA (Cantab)]
✉amoon@3serjeantsinn.com

MOONAN MISS CAROLINE MARY SAMANTHA

1 Gray's Inn Square
Ground Floor, 1 Gray's Inn Square, London WC1R 5AA, ☎020 7405 0001
Call Date: Oct 1997, Lincoln's Inn
Qualifications: [LLB (Hons)(Reading)]
✉cmoonan@1gis.co.uk

MOONEY MR GILES JOSEPH

The Chambers of Grahame Aldous QC
9 Gough Square, London EC4A 3DG, ☎020 7832 0500
✉clerks@9goughsquare.co.uk
Call Date: Nov 1998, Gray's Inn
Pupil Supervisor
Qualifications: [BA (Hons)(Lond)]
✉gmooney@9goughsquare.co.uk

MOONEY MR STEPHEN JOHN

Albion Chambers
Broad Street, Bristol BS1 1DR, ☎0117 927 2144
✉clerks@albionchambers.co.uk
Call Date: Nov 1987, Inner Temple
Pupil Supervisor
Qualifications: [LLB (Hull)]
✉stephen.mooney@albionchambers.co.uk

MOORE MISS ALISON DENISE

1 Garden Court Family Law Chambers
Ground Floor, One Garden Court, Temple, London EC4Y 9BJ, ☎020 7797 7900
✉clerks@1gc.com
Call Date: Oct 1994, Middle Temple
Pupil Supervisor
Qualifications: [MA (Hons)(Oxon)]
✉clerks@14graysinnsquare.co.uk

MOORE MR ANDREW DAVID

18 St John Street
Manchester M3 4EA, ☎0161 278 1800
✉clerks@18sjs.com
Call Date: Nov 1996, Inner Temple
Pupil Supervisor
Qualifications: [BA PhD (Manch)]

MOORE MR ARTHUR JAMES

Hardwicke
New Square, Lincoln's Inn, London WC2A 3SB, ☎020 7242 2523
✉enquiries@hardwicke.co.uk
Call Date: Oct 1992, Gray's Inn
Pupil Supervisor
Qualifications: [BA (Oxon) Dip Law (Lond)]
✉arthur.moore@hardwicke.co.uk

MOORE MR CRAIG IAN

Park Lane Plowden
19 Westgate, Leeds LS1 2RD, ☎0113 228 5049
✉clerks@parklaneplowden.co.uk
Call Date: July 1989, Middle Temple
Pupil Supervisor
Qualifications: [LLB (Lond)]
✉craig.moore@parklaneplowden.co.uk

E

MOORE MR DANNY GEORGE

6 Pump Court
1st Floor, 6 Pump Court, Temple, London EC4Y 7AR, ☎020 7797 8400
✉richardconstable@6pumpcourt.co.uk
6 Pump Court Chambers
6-8 Mill Street, Maidstone, Kent ME15 6XH, ☎01622 688094
✉annexe@6pumpcourt.co.uk
Call Date: Nov 1994, Middle Temple
Qualifications: [LLB (Hons)]
clerks@6pumpcourt.co.uk

MOORE MR GEORGE CRAWFORD JACKSON

11 King's Bench Walk
11 King's Bench Walk, Temple, London EC4Y 7EQ, ☎020 7632 8500
✉clerksroom@11kbw.com
Call Date: July 1970, Inner Temple
Qualifications: [BA LLM (Cantab) BPhil MA (Cantab)]

Fax: 020 7583 9123;
Out of hours telephone: 07831 304 714

Types of work: American law, Anguilla law, Antigua and Barbuda law, British Virgin Islands law, British West Indies law, Foreign law, Grenada law, International law, Jamaica law, Montserrat law, St Lucia law, Turks and Caicos Islands law

E

MOORE MR JAMES ANTHONY

39 Park Square
Leeds LS1 2NU, ☎0113 245 6633
✉seniorclerk@39parksquarechambers.co.uk
Goldsmith Chambers
Ground Floor, Goldsmith Building, Temple, London EC4Y 7BL, ☎020 7353 6802
✉clerks@goldsmithchambers.com
Call Date: July 1984, Lincoln's Inn
Qualifications: [BA]
moore@39parksquare.com

MOORE MISS JOAN YVETTE

2 Dr Johnson's Buildings
2 Dr Johnson's Buildings, Temple, London EC4Y 7AY, ☎020 7936 2613
✉clerks@2drj.com
Call Date: Nov 1986, Lincoln's Inn
Qualifications: [LLB]

MOORE MR JONATHAN GUY

Cathedral Chambers
10 Clytha Park Road, Newport NP20 4PB, ☎01633 215112
Cathedral Chambers
28 Cathedral Road, Cardiff CF11 9LJ, ☎02920 660129
Call Date: July 2006, Gray's Inn
Qualifications: [JRC]

MOORE MISS KATHARINE ELIZABETH

Octagon House
19 Colegate, Norwich NR3 1AT, ☎01603 623186
✉clerks@octagonhouse.co.uk
Call Date: Oct 1995, Middle Temple
Qualifications: [BA (Hons)]
clerks@octagonhouse.co.uk

MOORE MISS KIRSTIE ELIZABETH

Regent Chambers
Regent House, 3 Pall Mall, Hanley, Stoke On Trent ST1 1HP, ☎01782 286666
✉clerks@regentchambers.co.uk
Call Date: Oct 1994, Middle Temple
Qualifications: [LLB (Hons)(Lond) LLM (Sheff)]
kirstie.moore@regentchambers.co.uk

MOORE MR MARTIN LUKE QC (2002)

Erskine Chambers
33 Chancery Lane, London WC2A 1EN, ☎020 7242 5532
✉clerks@erskinechambers.com
Call Date: July 1982, Lincoln's Inn
Qualifications: [BA (Oxon)]
mmoore@erskine-chambers.co.uk

MOORE MISS MIRANDA JAYNE QC (2003)

Five Paper Buildings
1st Floor, Five Paper Buildings, Temple, London EC4Y 7HB, ☎020 7583 6117
✉clerks@5pb.co.uk
Call Date: July 1983, Lincoln's Inn
Qualifications: [BSc (Aston)]
mm@5pb.co.uk

MOORE MISS NATALIE

Quadrant Chambers
Quadrant House, 10 Fleet Street, London EC4Y 1AU, ☎020 7583 4444
✉info@quadrantchambers.com
Call Date: Oct 2007, Lincoln's Inn
Qualifications: [BA (Cantab)]

MOORE MR NEIL PATRICK

23 Essex Street
London WC2R 3AA, ☎020 7413 0353
✉clerks@23es.com
Call Date: July 1986, Gray's Inn
Qualifications: [LLB (Hons) (Notts)]

MOORE MR NIGEL RICHARD

Rougemont Chambers
Victory House, Dean Clarke Gardens, Southernhay East, Exeter EX2 4AA,
☎01392 208484
✉clerks@rougemontchambers.co.uk
Call Date: July 1978, Middle Temple
Qualifications: [LLB (So'ton)]

MOORE MR OLIVER RICHARD

Guildhall Chambers
23 Broad Street, Bristol BS1 2HG,
☎0117 930 9000
✉hoc@guildhallchambers.co.uk
Call Date: Mar 2005, Gray's Inn
Qualifications: [BA (Hons) (Nottingham)]
🖃oliver.moore@guildhallchambers.co.uk

MOORE MR RICHARD JOHN

St James's Chambers
68 Quay Street, Manchester M3 3EJ,
☎0161 834 7000
✉clerks@stjameschambers.com
Call Date: Oct 1992, Lincoln's Inn
Pupil Supervisor
Qualifications: [BA(Hons) MA (Oxon)]
🖃richard.moore@stjameschambers.com

MOORE MR RODERICK ANDREW MCGOWAN

Pump Court Chambers
Upper Ground Floor, 3 Pump Court, Temple, London EC4Y 7AJ, ☎020 7353 0711
✉clerks@3pumpcourt.com
Call Date: Nov 1993, Inner Temple
Pupil Supervisor
Qualifications: [LLB (So'ton)]

MOORE MISS SARAH ELIZABETH

11 King's Bench Walk
11 King's Bench Walk, Temple, London EC4Y 7EQ, ☎020 7632 8500
✉clerksroom@11kbw.com
Call Date: Nov 1990, Middle Temple
Qualifications: [BA LLM (Cantab)]
🖃sarah.moore@11kbw.com

MOORE MRS THERESE FINOLA

4 Brick Court
4 Brick Court, Temple, London EC4Y 9AD,
☎020 7832 3200 ✉clerks@4bc.co.uk
Call Date: July 1988, Lincoln's Inn
Pupil Supervisor
Qualifications: [MA BA (Hons) (So'ton)]
🖃finola.moore@4bc.co.uk

MOORES MR TIMOTHY KIERON

12 College Place
Fauvelle Buildings, 12 College Place, Southampton SO15 2FE, ☎023 8032 0320
✉clerks@12cp.co.uk
Call Date: July 1987, Lincoln's Inn
Pupil Supervisor
Qualifications: [LLB (Bris)]
🖃TMoores@12cp.co.uk

MOORHOUSE MR BRENDON SCOTT

Guildhall Chambers
23 Broad Street, Bristol BS1 2HG,
☎0117 930 9000
✉hoc@guildhallchambers.co.uk
Call Date: Nov 1992, Middle Temple
Pupil Supervisor
Qualifications: [LLB (Hons)]

MOOTIEN MISS DAVINA POOLLAY

4 Breams Buildings
Chancery Lane, London EC4A 1HP,
☎020 7092 1900 ✉clerks@4bb.co.uk
Call Date: July 2004, Gray's Inn
Qualifications: [LLB (Herts)]

MORADIFAR MR KAMBIZ

St John's Chambers
101 Victoria Street, Bristol BS1 6PU,
☎0117 923 4700
✉clerks@stjohnschambers.co.uk
Call Date: Nov 1998, Gray's Inn
Pupil Supervisor
Qualifications: [LLB (Lond) Postgraduate Dip]
🖃kambiz.moradifar@stjohnschambers.co.uk

MORAN MR ANDREW GERARD QC (1994)

Number 7 Harrington Street Chambers
7 Harrington Street, Liverpool L2 9YH,
☎0151 242 0707 ✉clerks@7hs.co.uk
Stone Chambers
4 Field Court, Gray's Inn, London WC1R 5EF,
☎020 7440 6900
✉clerks@stonechambers.com
Call Date: Nov 1976, Gray's Inn
Qualifications: [MA (Oxon)]
🖃andrew.moran@7hs.co.uk

E

MORAN MR ANDREW JOHN

Serle Court
6 New Square, Lincoln's Inn, London
WC2A 3QS, ☎ 020 7242 6105
✉ clerks@serlecourt.co.uk
Call Date: Feb 1989, Middle Temple
Pupil Supervisor
Qualifications: [LLB (Lond) BCL (Oxon)]
amoran@serlecourt.co.uk

MORAN MR CHRISTOPHER JOHN

39 Park Square
Leeds LS1 2NU, ☎ 0113 245 6633
✉ seniorclerk@39parksquarechambers.co.uk
Call Date: Oct 2007, Middle Temple
Qualifications: [BA (Hons) (Hull) MJur (Hons) (Hull)]
chris.moran@39parksquare.com

MORAN MISS NATASHA ALEXANDRIA LILLIAN

Iscoed Chambers
86 St Helen's Road, Swansea SA1 4BQ,
☎ 01792 652988
✉ clerks@iscoedchambers.co.uk
Call Date: July 2007, Gray's Inn
Qualifications: [BA (Sheff)]
clerks@iscoedchambers.co.uk

E

MORAN MR PATRICK MICHAEL

15 New Bridge Street
London EC4V 6AU, ☎ 020 7842 1900
✉ clerks@15nbs.com
Call Date: Oct 1997, Inner Temple
Qualifications: [LLB]
patrick.moran@15nbs.com

MORAN MR THOMAS

New Court Chambers
3 Broad Chare, Newcastle Upon Tyne
NE1 3DQ, ☎ 0191 232 1980
✉ clerks@newcourt-chambers.co.uk
Call Date: Nov 1996, Gray's Inn
Pupil Supervisor
Qualifications: [LLB (B'ham)]
thomas.moran@newcourt-chambers.co.uk

MORAN MR VINCENT JOHN QC (2011)

Keating Chambers
15 Essex Street, London WC2R 3AA,
☎ 020 7544 2600
✉ clerks@keatingchambers.com
Call Date: Oct 1991, Gray's Inn
Pupil Supervisor
Qualifications: [MA (Cantab) DipLaw (Lond)]
vmoran@keatingchambers.com

MORCOM MR CHRISTOPHER QC (1991)

Hogarth Chambers
5 New Square, Lincoln's Inn, London
WC2A 3RJ, ☎ 020 7404 0404
✉ barristers@hogarthchambers.com
Call Date: July 1963, Middle Temple
Qualifications: [MA (Cantab)]

MORE O'FERRALL MISS GERALDINE ANN

Renaissance Chambers
5th Floor, Gray's Inn Chambers, Gray's Inn,
London WC1R 5JA, ☎ 020 7404 1111
✉ clerks@renaissancechambers.co.uk
Call Date: July 1983, Middle Temple
Pupil Supervisor
gmo@renaissancechambers.co.uk

MORELLI MISS LUISA TERESA

Crown Office Row Chambers
119 Church Street, Brighton, Sussex
BN1 1UD, ☎ 01273 625625
✉ clerks@1cor.com
Call Date: Nov 1993, Middle Temple
Qualifications: [BA (Hons)(Sussex) CPE (Sussex) Dip Law]
luisa.morelli@1cor.com

MORETTO MR ROBERT SALVATORE

Old Square Chambers
10-11 Bedford Row, London WC1R 4BU,
☎ 020 7269 0300 ✉ clerks@oldsquare.co.uk
Old Square Chambers
3 Orchard Court, St Augustine's Yard, Bristol
BS1 5DP, ☎ 0117 930 5100
✉ clerks@oldsquare.co.uk
Call Date: Oct 2000, Inner Temple
Pupil Supervisor
Qualifications: [MA (Cantab)]
moretto@oldsquare.co.uk

MORGAN MR ADAM GEOFFREY

Argent Chambers
5 Bell Yard, London WC2A 2JR,
☎ 020 7556 5500
✉ briefsin@argentchambers.co.uk
Call Date: Nov 1996, Gray's Inn
Qualifications: [LLB LLM (Lond)]

MORGAN MS ADRIENNE

No5 Chambers
Greenwood House, 4-7 Salisbury Court, London EC4Y 8AA, ☎ 0845 210 5555
No5 Chambers
38 Queen Square, Bristol BS1 4QS, ☎ 0845 210 5555
No5 Chambers
Fountain Court, Steelhouse Lane, Birmingham B4 6DR, ☎ 0845 210 5555 ✉ info@no5.com
Call Date: Nov 1988, Gray's Inn
Pupil Supervisor
Qualifications: [BA (Hons) (Lond)]

MORGAN MISS ALISON ESTHER

6 King's Bench Walk
Ground Floor, 6 King's Bench Walk, Temple, London EC4Y 7DR, ☎ 020 7583 0410
✉ clerks@6kbw.com
Call Date: Nov 2000, Middle Temple
Qualifications: [BA (Hons) (Oxon)]
✉ alison.morgan@6kbw.com

MORGAN MR ANDREW JAMES

St Philips Chambers
55 Temple Row, Birmingham B2 5LS, ☎ 0121 246 7000 ✉ clerks@st-philips.com
Call Date: Oct 1996, Inner Temple
Pupil Supervisor, Recorder
Qualifications: [BA (Cantab) MA (Cantab)]
✉ jmorgan@st-philips.co.uk

MORGAN DR AUSTEN JUDE

33 Bedford Row
London WC1R 4JH, ☎ 020 7242 6476
✉ clerks@33bedfordrow.co.uk
Call Date: Oct 1995, Lincoln's Inn
Qualifications: [BSc (Hons)(Bris) PhD (Belfast) MA (Lond)]
✉ austenmorgan@33bedfordrow.co.uk

MORGAN MR CHARLES JAMES ARTHUR

Enterprise Chambers
65 Quayside, Newcastle Upon Tyne NE1 3DE, ☎ 0191 222 3344
✉ newcastle@enterprisechambers.com
Enterprise Chambers
9 Old Square, Lincoln's Inn, London WC2A 3SR, ☎ 020 7405 9471
✉ london@enterprisechambers.com
Enterprise Chambers
43 Park Square, Leeds LS1 2NP, ☎ 0113 246 0391
✉ leeds@enterprisechambers.com
Call Date: July 1978, Middle Temple
Pupil Supervisor
Qualifications: [MA FCIArb]
✉ charlesmorgan@enterprisechambers.com

MORGAN MR CHRISTOPHER JOHN

1 Paper Buildings
1st Floor, 1 Paper Buildings, Temple, London EC4Y 7EP, ☎ 020 7353 3728
✉ clerks@onepaper.co.uk
Call Date: July 1987, Middle Temple
Qualifications: [LLB (Hons)]
✉ christophermorgan@onepaper.co.uk

MORGAN MR COLIN THOMAS PATRICK

Pallant Chambers
12 North Pallant, Chichester, West Sussex PO19 1TQ, ☎ 01243 784538
✉ clerks@pallantchambers.co.uk
Call Date: Nov 1989, Middle Temple
Qualifications: [BA (Oxon) Dip Law]
✉ cmorgan@pallantchambers.co.uk

MORGAN MR DAVID SIMON SELBY

St John's Chambers
101 Victoria Street, Bristol BS1 6PU, ☎ 0117 923 4700
✉ clerks@stjohnschambers.co.uk
Call Date: Nov 1988, Gray's Inn
Pupil Supervisor
✉ simon.morgan@stjohnschambers.co.uk

MORGAN MR DYLAN ROBERT

12 College Place
Fauvelle Buildings, 12 College Place, Southampton SO15 2FE, ☎ 023 8032 0320
✉ clerks@12cp.co.uk
Call Date: July 1986, Gray's Inn
Pupil Supervisor
Qualifications: [LLB (CNAA)]
✉ DMorgan@12cp.co.uk

MORGAN MR EDWARD PATRICK

9 St John Street
Manchester M3 4DN, ☎ 0161 955 9000
✉ civilclerks@9sjs.com / criminalclerks@9sjs.com
Call Date: July 1989, Lincoln's Inn
Pupil Supervisor
Qualifications: [LLB (Hons) FCIArb LLM]

MORGAN MISS GEMMA ELIZABETH

Quadrant Chambers
Quadrant House, 10 Fleet Street, London EC4Y 1AU, ☎ 020 7583 4444
✉ info@quadrantchambers.com
Call Date: Oct 2006, Middle Temple
Qualifications: [BA (Hons) (Cantab)]
✉ gemma.morgan@quadrantchambers.com

E

MORGAN MR JAMIE PETER

Trinity Chambers
The Custom House, 39 Quayside, Newcastle Upon Tyne NE1 3DE, ☎0191 232 1927
✉info@trinitychambers.co.uk
Trinity Chambers
Multi Media Exchange, 72-80 Corporation Road, Middlesbrough TS1 2RF, ☎01642 247569
✉info@trinitychambers.co.uk
Call Date: July 2006, Inner Temple
Qualifications: [LLB (Durham)]

MORGAN MR JEREMY QC (2003)

39 Essex Street
London WC2R 3AT, ☎020 7832 1111
✉clerks@39essex.com
82 King Street
Manchester M2 4WQ, ☎0161 870 9969
Call Date: Apr 1989, Middle Temple
Qualifications: [BA (Oxon) BA (Kent) FCIArb]
jeremy.morgan@39essex.com

MORGAN MR JOHN

Bedlington Chambers
7 New Square, Lincoln's Inn, London WC2A 2QS, ☎020 7831 1159
✉clerks@bedlingtonchambers.com
Call Date: July 1999, Gray's Inn
Qualifications: [BSc (Lond) PGCE CPE MIM PgDip (Law)]

MORGAN MS KATY REBECCA

30 Park Place
Cardiff CF10 3BS, ☎029 2039 8421
✉clerks@30parkplace.law.co.uk
Call Date: July 2002, Inner Temple
Qualifications: [LLB (Cardiff)]
km@30parkplace.co.uk

MORGAN MR LLOYD JOHN

Chavasse Court Chambers
18 Queen Avenue, Liverpool L2 4TX, ☎0151 229 2030
✉clerks@chavassechambers.co.uk
Call Date: Mar 1999, Middle Temple
Qualifications: [BAppSC MBA LLB]
clerks@chavassechambers.co.uk

MORGAN MR MATTHEW DAVID

2 Pump Court
1st Floor, 2 Pump Court, Temple, London EC4Y 7AH, ☎020 7353 5597
✉clerks@2pumpcourt.co.uk
Call Date: Oct 2004, Lincoln's Inn
Qualifications: [BA (Hons) (Lond)]
mmorgan@2pumpcourt.co.uk

MORGAN MR PHILIP DAVID

Dere Street Barristers
14 Toft Green, York YO1 6JT, ☎0844 3351551
✉clerks@derestreet.co.uk
Call Date: July 2010, Middle Temple
Qualifications: [BA (Hons) (Cantab)]
P.Morgan@derestreet.co.uk

MORGAN MR RICHARD HUGO LYNDON QC (2011)

Maitland Chambers
7 Stone Buildings, Lincoln's Inn, London WC2A 3SZ, ☎020 7406 1200
✉clerks@maitlandchambers.com
Call Date: Nov 1988, Gray's Inn
Pupil Supervisor
Qualifications: [LLB (Bucks) LLM (Cantab)]
rmorgan@maitlandchambers.com

MORGAN MISS SARAH MARY QC (2011)

1 Garden Court Family Law Chambers
Ground Floor, One Garden Court, Temple, London EC4Y 9BJ, ☎020 7797 7900
✉clerks@1gc.com
Call Date: Nov 1988, Gray's Inn
Pupil Supervisor
Qualifications: [LLB (Brunel)]
morgan@1gc.com

MORGAN MISS SARAH-JAYNE

Linenhall Chambers
1 Stanley Place, Chester CH1 2LU, ☎01244 348282
✉clerks@linenhallchambers.co.uk
Call Date: Mar 2009, Middle Temple
Qualifications: [LLB (Hons) (Manch)]

MORGAN MR STEPHEN FRANCIS

Landmark Chambers
180 Fleet Street, London EC4A 2HG, ☎020 7430 1221
✉clerks@landmarkchambers.co.uk
Call Date: Nov 1983, Gray's Inn
Pupil Supervisor
Qualifications: [LLB (Warw) MA (Nottm)]
smorgan@landmarkchambers.co.uk

MORGAN DR VICTORIA CLARE ESTELLE

Thomas More Chambers
7 Lincoln's Inn Fields, London WC2A 3BP, ☎020 7404 7000
✉clerks@thomasmore.co.uk
Call Date: Oct 2005, Inner Temple
Qualifications: [BA St. John's College University of Oxford PhD]
vmorgan@thomasmore.co.uk

MORGANS MR JOHN MORGAN

Octagon House
19 Colegate, Norwich NR3 1AT,
☎01603 623186
✉clerks@octagonhouse.co.uk
Call Date: Nov 1996, Middle Temple
Qualifications: [LLB (Hons)(Lancs) LLM]
✉clerks@octagonhouse.co.uk

MORIARTY MR STEPHEN QC (1999)

Fountain Court Chambers
Fountain Court, Temple, London EC4Y 9DH,
☎020 7583 3335
✉chambers@fountaincourt.co.uk
Call Date: Nov 1986, Middle Temple
Qualifications: [BCL MA (Oxon)]
✉smoriarty@fountaincourt.co.uk

MORLAND MS CAMILLE

Broadway House Chambers
Broadway House, 9 Bank Street, Bradford, West Yorkshire BD1 1TW, ☎01274 722560
✉clerks@broadwayhouse.co.uk
Broadway House Chambers
25 Park Square West, Leeds, West Yorkshire LS1 2PW, ☎0113 246 2600
✉clerks@broadwayhouse.co.uk
Call Date: Nov 1996, Gray's Inn
Qualifications: [BA (Hons) (Bradford)]
✉cm@broadwayhouse.co.uk

MORLEY MR GARETH EDWARD

Farringdon Chambers
180 Bermondsey Street, London SE1 3TQ,
☎020 7089 5700
Call Date: July 1982, Middle Temple
Pupil Supervisor
Qualifications: [LLB (Hons)]
✉garethmorley@farringdon-law.co.uk

MORLEY MR IAIN CHARLES QC (2009)

23 Essex Street
London WC2R 3AA, ☎020 7413 0353
✉clerks@23es.com
Call Date: July 1988, Inner Temple
Qualifications: [MA (Oxon)]
✉iainmorley@23es.com

MORLEY MISS KATE

Chavasse Court Chambers
18 Queen Avenue, Liverpool L2 4TX,
☎0151 229 2030
✉clerks@chavassechambers.co.uk
Call Date: Oct 2004, Inner Temple
Qualifications: [LLB]
✉kate.morley@chavassechambers.co.uk

MORLEY MISS KATHERINE JANE

Bank House Chambers
Old Bank House, Hartshead, Sheffield S1 2EL,
☎0114 275 1223
✉w.digby@bankhousechambers.co.uk
Call Date: Oct 2006, Lincoln's Inn
Qualifications: [LLB (Sheff)]
✉k.morley@bankhousechambers.co.uk

MORLEY MISS LAURA

4 Paper Buildings
1st Floor, 4 Paper Buildings, Temple, London EC4Y 7EX, ☎020 7427 5200
✉clerks@4pb.com
Call Date: July 2006, Middle Temple
Qualifications: [BSc PgDL]
✉lm@4pb.com

MORLEY MR STEPHEN DOUGLAS

3 Serjeants Inn
London EC4Y 1BQ, ☎020 7427 5000
✉clerks@3serjeantsinn.com
Call Date: Oct 1996, Inner Temple
Qualifications: [LLB (Westminster)]
✉smorley@3serjeantsinn.com

MORPUSS MR GUY QC (2008)

20 Essex Street
London WC2R 3AL, ☎020 7842 1200
✉clerks@20essexst.com
Call Date: Oct 1991, Lincoln's Inn
Qualifications: [LLB (Hons) (B'ham)]
✉clerks@20essexst.com

MORRELL MISS ROXANNE TRACIE

Carmelite Chambers
9 Carmelite Street, London EC4Y 0DR,
☎020 7936 6300
✉clerks@carmelitechambers.co.uk
Call Date: July 1996, Middle Temple
Qualifications: [LLB (Hons)]
✉rmorrell@carmelitechambers.co.uk

MORRIS MISS ANNA CLAIRE

Garden Court Chambers
57-60 Lincoln's Inn Fields, London WC2A 3LJ,
☎020 7993 7600 ✉info@gclaw.co.uk
Call Date: Mar 2006, Middle Temple
Qualifications: [LLB (Hons) (Nott'm) LLM]
✉annam@gclaw.co.uk

MORRIS MR ANTHONY JOSEPH

Kenworthy's Chambers
Arlington House, Bloom Street, Salford, Manchester M3 6AJ, ☎0161 832 4036
Call Date: Nov 1986, Gray's Inn
✉a.morris@kenworthysbarristers.co.uk

E

MORRIS MR ARTHUR ROWLAND

Eastbourne Chambers
5 Chiswick Place, Eastbourne, East Sussex BN21 4NH, ☎01323 642102
✉clerks@eastbournechambers.co.uk
Call Date: Nov 1997, Gray's Inn
Qualifications: [BSc (Econ) (LSE) MA]

MORRIS MISS BELLA LOUISE

Old Square Chambers
10-11 Bedford Row, London WC1R 4BU, ☎020 7269 0300 ✉clerks@oldsquare.co.uk
Old Square Chambers
3 Orchard Court, St Augustine's Yard, Bristol BS1 5DP, ☎0117 930 5100
✉clerks@oldsquare.co.uk
Call Date: Oct 2000, Middle Temple
Qualifications: [BA (Hons) (Oxon)]
morris@oldsquare.co.uk

MORRIS MR BEN

Chavasse Court Chambers
18 Queen Avenue, Liverpool L2 4TX, ☎0151 229 2030
✉clerks@chavassechambers.co.uk
Call Date: Oct 1996, Middle Temple
Qualifications: [LLB (Hons)(L'pool)]
bennmorris@btinternet.com

MORRIS MR BENJAMIN

9 St John Street
Manchester M3 4DN, ☎0161 955 9000
✉civilclerks@9sjs.com / criminalclerks@9sjs.com
Call Date: Oct 2004, Lincoln's Inn
Qualifications: [BA (Hons) Cantab]
benjamin.morris@9sjs.com

MORRIS MISS BRENDA ALISON

14 Gray's Inn Square
14 Gray's Inn Square, Gray's Inn, London WC1R 5JP, ☎020 7242 0858
✉clerks@14gis.co.uk
Call Date: July 1978, Middle Temple
Qualifications: [BSc (Lond) PGCE]
clerks@14graysinnsquare.co.uk

MORRIS MR BRENDAN ANTHONY

18 Red Lion Court
London EC4A 3EB, ☎020 7520 6000
✉chambers@18rlc.co.uk
18 Red Lion Court (Annexe)
Thornwood House, 102 New London Road, Chelmsford, Essex CM2 0RG, ☎01245 280880
Call Date: July 1985, Middle Temple
Pupil Supervisor
Qualifications: [BA Dip Law (Lond)]
brendan.morris@18rlc.co.uk

MORRIS MS CHRISTINA GAYE

Coram Chambers
9-11 Fulwood Place, London WC1V 6HG, ☎020 7092 3700
✉mail@coramchambers.co.uk
Call Date: Nov 1983, Gray's Inn
Pupil Supervisor
Qualifications: [BA (Warw)]
christina.morris@coramchambers.co.uk

MORRIS MR DAVID PAUL

Outer Temple Chambers
The Outer Temple, 222 Strand, London WC2R 1BA, ☎020 7353 6381
✉clerks@outertemple.com
Call Date: July 1976, Inner Temple
Pupil Supervisor
Qualifications: [LLB (Bris)]

MORRIS MISS DEBORAH ANNE

Westbourne Chambers
62 Westbourne Park Villas, London W2 5EB, ☎07956 950350
✉DeborahBarrister@aol.com
Call Date: July 1989, Gray's Inn
Pupil Supervisor
Qualifications: [BEd (Hons) Dip Law]
DeborahBarrister@aol.com

MORRIS MISS FENELLA QC (2012)

39 Essex Street
London WC2R 3AT, ☎020 7832 1111
✉clerks@39essex.com
82 King Street
Manchester M2 4WQ, ☎0161 870 9969
Call Date: Oct 1990, Middle Temple
Qualifications: [BA (Hons) (Oxon) Dip Law (Lond)]

MORRIS MS GILLIAN SUSAN

Matrix Chambers
Griffin Building, Gray's Inn, London WC1R 5LN, ☎020 7404 3447
✉matrix@matrixlaw.co.uk / lscott@matrixlaw.co.uk
Call Date: Nov 1997, Inner Temple
Qualifications: [LLB (Bris) PhD (Cantab)]
gillianmorris@matrixlaw.co.uk

MORRIS MR IEUAN JOHN

9 Park Place
9 Park Place, Cardiff, South Glamorgan CF10 3DP, ☎029 2038 2731
✉clerks@9parkplace.co.uk
Call Date: July 1979, Gray's Inn
Pupil Supervisor
Qualifications: [LLB (Lond)]
ijmorrisbar@aol.com, imorris@9parkplace.co.uk

MORRIS MS JOHANNA

Chambers of Marion Smullen and Kerim Fuad QC
1 Inner Temple Lane, London EC4Y 1AF,
☎ 020 7427 4400 ✉ clerks@1itl.com
Call Date: Nov 2003, Middle Temple
Qualifications: [BA (Hons) (Kent) CPE]

MORRIS MISS MARY-FRANCES

Malins Chambers
115 Temple Chambers, Temple Avenue, London EC4Y 0DA, ☎ 020 7353 8868
✉ malins@btinternet.com
Call Date: Nov 2004, Middle Temple
Qualifications: [MA (Hons) BA (Oxon)]

MORRIS MR MICHAEL HARVEY

Goldsmith Chambers
Ground Floor, Goldsmith Building, Temple, London EC4Y 7BL, ☎ 020 7353 6802
✉ clerks@goldsmithchambers.com
Call Date: July 1984, Gray's Inn
Qualifications: [BSc (Eng) (Lond)]
✉ M.Morris@goldsmithchambers.law.co.uk

MORRIS MR PHILIP JAMES

39 Park Square
Leeds LS1 2NU, ☎ 0113 245 6633
✉ seniorclerk@39parksquarechambers.co.uk
Call Date: July 2011, Middle Temple
Qualifications: [LLB (Hons) (Huddersfield)]

MORRIS MR PHILLIP JOHN

9 Park Place
9 Park Place, Cardiff, South Glamorgan CF10 3DP, ☎ 029 2038 2731
✉ clerks@9parkplace.co.uk
Call Date: July 2003, Gray's Inn
Qualifications: [BA (Oxon)]
✉ pmorris@9parkplace.co.uk

MORRIS MR ROBERT EDWARD

3 Raymond Buildings
3 Raymond Buildings, Gray's Inn, London WC1R 5BH, ☎ 020 7400 6400
✉ clerks@3rblaw.com
Call Date: Nov 2008, Inner Temple
Qualifications: [BA (Oxon) M Phil (Lond) CPE]
✉ robert.morris@3raymondbuildings.com

MORRIS MISS SARAH

Chambers of Marion Smullen and Kerim Fuad QC
1 Inner Temple Lane, London EC4Y 1AF,
☎ 020 7427 4400 ✉ clerks@1itl.com
Call Date: Mar 1996, Lincoln's Inn
Qualifications: [LLB (Hons)(L'pool)]
✉ sarahmorris2k@hotmail.com

MORRIS MISS SHAN ELIZABETH

Linenhall Chambers
1 Stanley Place, Chester CH1 2LU,
☎ 01244 348282
✉ clerks@linenhallchambers.co.uk
Call Date: Oct 1991, Middle Temple
Pupil Supervisor
Qualifications: [LLB (Hons) (Hull)]
✉ clerks@1stanleyplace.co.uk

MORRIS MR STEPHEN NATHAN QC (2002)

20 Essex Street
London WC2R 3AL, ☎ 020 7842 1200
✉ clerks@20essexst.com
Call Date: July 1981, Lincoln's Inn
Recorder
Qualifications: [MA (Cantab)]
✉ clerks@20essexst.com, smorris@20essexst.com

MORRIS-COOLE MR CHRISTOPHER

Crown Office Row Chambers
119 Church Street, Brighton, Sussex BN1 1UD, ☎ 01273 625625
✉ clerks@1cor.com
Call Date: July 1974, Inner Temple
Pupil Supervisor, Recorder
Qualifications: [LLB BSC MSB FRSA FRSM]
✉ christopher.morris-coole@1cor.com

MORRISON MR CHRISTOPHER QUINTIN

Old Court Chambers
Newham House, 96-98 Borough Road, Middlesbrough TS1 2HJ, ☎ 01642 232523
✉ clerks@oldcourtchambers.com
Call Date: Nov 1986, Inner Temple
Pupil Supervisor
Qualifications: [LLB (Leics) BA (Dunelm)]
✉ clerks@oldcourtchambers.com

MORRISON MR CRAIG DAVID

Brick Court Chambers
7-8 Essex Street, London WC2R 3LD,
☎ 020 7379 3550 ✉ clerks@brickcourt.co.uk
Call Date: July 2008, Middle Temple
Qualifications: [BA (Hons) (Cantab)]
✉ craig.morrison@brickcourt.co.uk

MORRISON MR GILES BENEDICT

15 New Bridge Street
London EC4V 6AU, ☎ 020 7842 1900
✉ clerks@15nbs.com
Call Date: Nov 2002, Middle Temple
Qualifications: [LLB (Hons) (Wales)]
✉ giles.morrison@15nbs.com

E

MORRISON MR MATTHEW JOHN

Serle Court
6 New Square, Lincoln's Inn, London WC2A 3QS, ☎020 7242 6105
✉clerks@serlecourt.co.uk
Call Date: Nov 2004, Lincoln's Inn
Qualifications: [MA BCL]
✉mmorrison@serlecourt.co.uk

MORRISSEY MS JOANNA MICHELLE AUGUSTINA

12 College Place
Fauvelle Buildings, 12 College Place, Southampton SO15 2FE, ☎023 8032 0320
✉clerks@12cp.co.uk
Call Date: July 1999, Inner Temple
Qualifications: [LLB (Hons)]

MORSE MR ANDREW PHILIP RICHARD

30 Park Place
Cardiff CF10 3BS, ☎029 2039 8421
✉clerks@30parkplace.law.co.uk
Call Date: July 2000, Gray's Inn
Qualifications: [B.Soc.Sci(Manch)]
✉aprm@30parkplace.co.uk

MORSE MR MALCOLM GEORGE MCEWAN

St Philips Chambers
55 Temple Row, Birmingham B2 5LS, ☎0121 246 7000 ✉clerks@st-philips.com
Call Date: July 1967, Inner Temple
Pupil Supervisor, Recorder
Qualifications: [MA (Cantab)]
✉mmorse@st-philips.com

MORSHEAD MR TIMOTHY FRANCIS QC (2011)

Landmark Chambers
180 Fleet Street, London EC4A 2HG, ☎020 7430 1221
✉clerks@landmarkchambers.co.uk
Call Date: Feb 1995, Lincoln's Inn
Qualifications: [MA (Hons) Dip Law (Lond)]
✉tmorshead@landmarkchambers.co.uk

MORT MR JUSTIN JOHN GLASBROOK

Keating Chambers
15 Essex Street, London WC2R 3AA, ☎020 7544 2600
✉clerks@keatingchambers.com
Call Date: Oct 1994, Middle Temple
Pupil Supervisor
Qualifications: [BA (Hons)(Dunelm) MSc (Lond)]
✉jmort@keatingchambers.com

MORTIMER MISS SOPHIE KATE

1 Chancery Lane
London WC2A 1LF, ☎0845 634 6666
✉clerks@1chancerylane.com
Call Date: Oct 1996, Lincoln's Inn
Pupil Supervisor
Qualifications: [BA (Hons)(Sussex)]
✉smortimer@1chancerylane.com

MORTIMORE MR SIMON ANTHONY QC (1991)

South Square
3-4 South Square, Gray's Inn, London WC1R 5HP, ☎020 7696 9900
✉practicemanagers@southsquare.com
Call Date: July 1972, Inner Temple
Qualifications: [LLB (Exon)]

MORTON MR DAVID MICHAEL

Kenworthy's Chambers
Arlington House, Bloom Street, Salford, Manchester M3 6AJ, ☎0161 832 4036
Call Date: Nov 1999, Inner Temple
Qualifications: [LLB]
✉d.morton@kenworthysbarristers.co.uk

MORTON MS ELIZABETH ROSE

Deans Court Chambers
24 St John Street, Manchester M3 4DF, ☎0161 214 6000 ✉clerks@deanscourt.co.uk
4 King's Bench Walk
2nd Floor, 4 King's Bench Walk, Temple, London EC4Y 7DL, ☎020 7822 7000
✉clerks@4kbw.co.uk
Call Date: Oct 1999, Gray's Inn
Qualifications: [LLB (Manch)]
✉morton@deanscourt.co.uk

MORTON MR GARY DAVID

Pump Court Chambers
Upper Ground Floor, 3 Pump Court, Temple, London EC4Y 7AJ, ☎020 7353 0711
✉clerks@3pumpcourt.com
Pump Court Chambers
5 Temple Chambers, Temple Street, Swindon SN1 1SQ, ☎01793 539899
✉clerks@3pumpcourt.com

E

Pump Court Chambers
31 Southgate Street, Winchester, Hampshire SO23 9EB, ☎ 01962 868 161
✉ clerks@3pumpcourt.com
Call Date: Nov 1993, Gray's Inn
Qualifications: [B Sc (Econ) MA (Warw) Dip Law (Middx)]

MORTON MR KEITH FARRANCE QC (2011)

Temple Garden Chambers
1 Harcourt Buildings, Temple, London EC4Y 9DA, ☎ 020 7583 1315
✉ clerks@tgchambers.com
Riverview Chambers
Hamilton House, 1 Temple Avenue, London EC4Y 0HA, ☎ 0844 225 3999
✉ chrisbaylis@riverviewchambers.com
Call Date: Oct 1990, Lincoln's Inn
Pupil Supervisor
Qualifications: [BSc (Hull) Dip Law (Lond)]
kmorton@tgchambers.com

MORTON MR PETER JOHN

Crown Office Chambers
2 Crown Office Row, Temple, London EC4Y 7HJ, ☎ 020 7797 8100
✉ mail@crownofficechambers.com
Call Date: Nov 1988, Middle Temple
Qualifications: [LLB (Lanc) LLM (Cantab)]
morton@crownofficechambers.com

MORTON MISS RACHAEL JOANNA EADEN

4 Brick Court
4 Brick Court, Temple, London EC4Y 9AD, ☎ 020 7832 3200 ✉ clerks@4bc.co.uk
Call Date: Feb 1995, Lincoln's Inn
Qualifications: [LLB (Hons)(Warw) LLM (Lond)]

MORTON MISS ROWAN FRANCES

Guildford Chambers
Stoke House, Leapale Lane, Guildford, Surrey GU1 4LY, ☎ 01483 539131
✉ clerks@guildfordchambers.co.uk
Alexander Chambers
13 Halstead Road, Wanstead, London E11 2AY, ☎ 0845 652 0451 / 0854 652 0451
✉ clerks@alexanderchambers.co.uk
Call Date: Nov 2004, Lincoln's Inn
Qualifications: [BSc (Hons)]

MORTON JACK MR HENRY

2 Temple Gardens
2 Temple Gardens, Temple, London EC4Y 9AY, ☎ 020 7822 1200
✉ clerks@2tg.co.uk
Call Date: July 2009, Lincoln's Inn
Qualifications: [MA (Oxon)]
hmj@2tg.co.uk

MORWOOD MR JONATHAN THOMAS BOYD

Hardwicke
New Square, Lincoln's Inn, London WC2A 3SB, ☎ 020 7242 2523
✉ enquiries@hardwicke.co.uk
Call Date: Nov 1996, Middle Temple
Pupil Supervisor
Qualifications: [BA (Hons)(Keele) LLB]
boyd.morwood@hardwicke.co.uk

MOSELEY MISS JULIE RUTH

St Philips Chambers
55 Temple Row, Birmingham B2 5LS, ☎ 0121 246 7000 ✉ clerks@st-philips.com
Call Date: Oct 1992, Inner Temple
Qualifications: [LLB (Leics)]
jmoseley@st-philips.com

MOSER MR PHILIP CURT HAROLD QC (2012)

Monckton Chambers
1 & 2 Raymond Buildings, Gray's Inn, London WC1R 5NR, ☎ 020 7405 7211
✉ chambers@monckton.com
Call Date: Oct 1992, Inner Temple
Qualifications: [MA (Cantab)]

Types of work: Commercial law, Conflict of laws, EC competition law, European Union

MOSES MR DYLAN

4 Breams Buildings
Chancery Lane, London EC4A 1HP, ☎ 020 7092 1900 ✉ clerks@4bb.co.uk
Call Date: Oct 2003, Gray's Inn
Qualifications: [BA (York)]

MOSES MR STEPHEN COLIN

Furnival Chambers
32 Furnival Street, London EC4A 1JQ, ☎ 020 7405 3232
Call Date: Nov 1997, Gray's Inn
Pupil Supervisor
Qualifications: [LLB (Hons) (London)]
smoses@furnivallaw.co.uk

E

MOSS MR CHRISTOPHER STEPHEN

St Johns Buildings
24a - 28 St John Street, Manchester M3 4DJ,
☎0161 214 1500
✉clerk@stjohnsbuildings.co.uk
16 Winckley Square
Preston PR1 3JJ, ☎01772 256100
St Johns Buildings Liverpool
8th Floor India Buildings, Water Street,
Liverpool L2 0XG, ☎0151 243 6000
✉clerk@stjohnsbuildings.co.uk
Call Date: Oct 2002, Lincoln's Inn
Qualifications: [LLB (Hons)]
christopher.moss@stjohnsbuildings.co.uk

MOSS MR EDWARD JOHN

Exchange Chambers
7 Ralli Courts, West Riverside, Manchester
M3 5FT, ☎0161 833 2722
Exchange Chambers
One Derby Square, Derby Square, Liverpool
L2 9XX, ☎0151 236 7747
✉info@exchangechambers.co.uk
Exchange Chambers
Oxford House, Oxford Row, Leeds LS1 3BE,
☎0113 203 1970
✉spencer@exchangechambers.co.uk
Call Date: July 2005, Inner Temple
Qualifications: [LLB Liverpool John Moores University]

MOSS MR GABRIEL STEPHEN QC (1989)

South Square
3-4 South Square, Gray's Inn, London
WC1R 5HP, ☎020 7696 9900
✉practicemanagers@southsquare.com
Call Date: July 1974, Lincoln's Inn
Qualifications: [MA BCL (Oxon)]
gabrielmoss@southsquare.com

MOSS MS JOANNE ROSEMARY

Falcon Chambers
Falcon Court, London EC4Y 1AA,
☎020 7353 2484
✉clerks@falcon-chambers.com
Call Date: July 1976, Inner Temple
Qualifications: [MA (Cantab) LLM (Lond)]

MOSS MR JONATHAN HENRY METSON

Hogarth Chambers
5 New Square, Lincoln's Inn, London
WC2A 3RJ, ☎020 7404 0404
✉barristers@hogarthchambers.com
Call Date: Mar 2009, Inner Temple
Qualifications: [BSc (Bris) LLM (USA)]
jmoss@hogarthchambers.com

MOSS MR NICHOLAS SIMON

Temple Garden Chambers
1 Harcourt Buildings, Temple, London
EC4Y 9DA, ☎020 7583 1315
✉clerks@tgchambers.com
Call Date: Nov 1995, Middle Temple
Qualifications: [MA (Hons)(Cantab)]
n.moss@tgchambers.com

MOSS MR NORMAN WILLIAM

3 Dr Johnson's Buildings
Ground Floor, 3 Dr Johnson's Buildings,
Temple, London EC4Y 7BA, ☎020 7353 4854
✉clerks@3djb.co.uk
Call Date: Oct 1990, Inner Temple
Qualifications: [LLB (Hons)(Wales) DipLaw]
Nmoss@3djb.co.uk

MOSS MR PETER

Linenhall Chambers
1 Stanley Place, Chester CH1 2LU,
☎01244 348282
✉clerks@linenhallchambers.co.uk
Call Date: Nov 1980, Middle Temple
Pupil Supervisor
clerks@1stanleyplace.co.uk

MOSS MR RICHARD JOHN

4 King's Bench Walk
2nd Floor, 4 King's Bench Walk, Temple,
London EC4Y 7DL, ☎020 7822 7000
✉clerks@4kbw.co.uk
Call Date: Oct 2005, Lincoln's Inn
Qualifications: [LLB (Hons) (Leeds)]
rm@4kbw.co.uk

MOSTAFA MISS MARGIA

2 Pump Court
1st Floor, 2 Pump Court, Temple, London
EC4Y 7AH, ☎020 7353 5597
✉clerks@2pumpcourt.co.uk
Call Date: Oct 1999, Lincoln's Inn
Qualifications: [LLB (Hons)(Derby)]
mmostafa@2pumpcourt.co.uk

MOSTESHAR PROF SA'ID

Hardwicke
New Square, Lincoln's Inn, London
WC2A 3SB, ☎020 7242 2523
✉enquiries@hardwicke.co.uk
Call Date: July 1975, Lincoln's Inn
Qualifications: [DPhil BSC MSc (Econ) FCA]
sa'id.mosteshar@hardwicke.co.uk

MOSTYN MR PIERS NICHOLAS

Tooks Chambers
81 Farringdon Street, London EC4A 4BL,
☎020 7842 7575 ✉clerks@tooks.co.uk
Call Date: Nov 1989, Middle Temple
Qualifications: [BSc (Hons) (Bris) DipLaw]
✉piers.mostyn@tooks.co.uk

MOTRAGHI MISS NADIA ARTEMIS

Old Square Chambers
10-11 Bedford Row, London WC1R 4BU,
☎020 7269 0300 ✉clerks@oldsquare.co.uk
Old Square Chambers
3 Orchard Court, St Augustine's Yard, Bristol BS1 5DP, ☎0117 930 5100
✉clerks@oldsquare.co.uk
Call Date: July 2004, Gray's Inn
Qualifications: [BA (Oxon) LLM]
✉motraghi@oldsquare.co.uk

MOTT MR GEOFFREY EDWARD

Clerksroom (Taunton)
Equity House, Administration Centre, Blackbrook Park Avenue, Taunton, Somerset TA1 2PX, ☎0845 083 3000
✉mail@clerksroom.com
Clerksroom (London)
3rd Floor, 218 Strand, London WC2R 1AT,
☎0845 083 3000 ✉mail@clerksroom.com
King's Lynn Chambers
26 The Birches, South Wootton, King's Lynn, Norfolk PE30 3JG, ☎01553 672 085
✉timothy.leader@tesco.net
Call Date: July 1982, Gray's Inn
Pupil Supervisor
Qualifications: [BA Dip Law]
✉mott@clerksroom.com

MOTT MR PHILIP CHARLES QC (1991)

Outer Temple Chambers
The Outer Temple, 222 Strand, London WC2R 1BA, ☎020 7353 6381
✉clerks@outertemple.com
Call Date: July 1970, Inner Temple
Recorder
Qualifications: [BA (Oxon) MA]
✉pm@pmqc.co.uk

MOTT MR RICHARD STEPHEN PAUL

One Essex Court
Ground Floor, One Essex Court, Temple, London EC4Y 9AR, ☎020 7583 2000
✉clerks@oeclaw.co.uk
Call Date: Oct 2006, Middle Temple
Qualifications: [BA (Hons) (Cantab)]
✉rmott@oeclaw.co.uk

MOTTRAM MISS CHERYL LEE

St Johns Buildings Liverpool
8th Floor India Buildings, Water Street, Liverpool L2 0XG, ☎0151 243 6000
✉clerk@stjohnsbuildings.co.uk
16 Winckley Square
Preston PR1 3JJ, ☎01772 256100
St Johns Buildings
24a - 28 St John Street, Manchester M3 4DJ,
☎0161 214 1500
✉clerk@stjohnsbuildings.co.uk
Call Date: Oct 2002, Lincoln's Inn
Qualifications: [LLB (L'Pool)]
✉cherylmottram@yahoo.com

MOULD MR TIMOTHY JAMES QC (2006)

Landmark Chambers
180 Fleet Street, London EC4A 2HG,
☎020 7430 1221
✉clerks@landmarkchambers.co.uk
Call Date: Nov 1987, Gray's Inn
Qualifications: [BA (Oxon) Dip Law]
✉tmould@landmarkchambers.co.uk

MOULDER MR PAUL JOHN

Guildford Chambers
Stoke House, Leapale Lane, Guildford, Surrey GU1 4LY, ☎01483 539131
✉clerks@guildfordchambers.co.uk
Alexander Chambers
13 Halstead Road, Wanstead, London E11 2AY,
☎0845 652 0451 / 0854 652 0451
✉clerks@alexanderchambers.co.uk
Call Date: Oct 1997, Lincoln's Inn
Qualifications: [LLB (Hons)(Lond)]
✉pmoulder@guildfordchambers.com

MOULDER MISS PAULINE MARY

Dere Street Barristers
33 Broad Chare, Newcastle Upon Tyne NE1 3DQ, ☎0844 3351551
✉clerks@derestreet.co.uk
Call Date: July 1983, Lincoln's Inn
Qualifications: [LLB (Hons) (Newc)]
✉clerks@broadcharechambers.co.uk

MOULES MR RICHARD JAMES

Landmark Chambers
180 Fleet Street, London EC4A 2HG,
☎020 7430 1221
✉clerks@landmarkchambers.co.uk
Call Date: Mar 2005, Middle Temple
Qualifications: [BA (Hons) LLM]

E

MOULSON MR PETER CHARLES EDWARD QC (2011)

No.6 Park Square
Leeds LS1 2LW, ☎0113 245 9763
✉Tim@no6.co.uk
Call Date: Oct 1991, Gray's Inn
Qualifications: [LLB MBA]
moulson@no6.co.uk

MOUNTFIELD MS HELEN QC (2010)

Matrix Chambers
Griffin Building, Gray's Inn, London WC1R 5LN, ☎020 7404 3447
✉matrix@matrixlaw.co.uk / Iscott@matrixlaw.co.uk
Call Date: Oct 1991, Gray's Inn
Pupil Supervisor
Qualifications: [BA (Oxon) Dip Law (Lond) Dip Euro Law]

MOUNTFORD MR THOMAS DAVID HENRY

Blackstone Chambers
Blackstone House, Temple, London EC4Y 9BW, ☎020 7583 1770
✉clerks@blackstonechambers.com
Call Date: Oct 2009, Inner Temple
Qualifications: [BA (Oxon) CPE (Lond)]
tommountford@blackstonechambers.com

MOUSLEY MR TIMOTHY JOHN QC (2003)

2 King's Bench Walk
2 King's Bench Walk, Temple, London EC4Y 7DE, ☎020 7353 1746
✉clerks@2kbw.com
King's Bench and Godolphin (KBG)Chambers
115 North Hill, Plymouth, Devon PL4 8JY, ☎01752 221551
✉clerks@kbgchambers.co.uk
St Philips Chambers
55 Temple Row, Birmingham B2 5LS, ☎0121 246 7000 ✉clerks@st-philips.com
Call Date: July 1979, Middle Temple
Recorder
Qualifications: [BA (Keele)]

MOUSLEY MR WILLIAM HOWARD QC (2011)

2 King's Bench Walk
2 King's Bench Walk, Temple, London EC4Y 7DE, ☎020 7353 1746
✉clerks@2kbw.com
Call Date: July 1986, Middle Temple
Pupil Supervisor, Recorder
Qualifications: [LLB (Warks)]
wmousley@2kbw.com

MOVERLEY SMITH MR STEPHEN PHILIP QC (2002)

XXIV Old Buildings
Ground Floor, 24 Old Buildings, Lincoln's Inn, London WC2A 3UP, ☎020 7691 2424
✉clerks@xxiv.co.uk
Call Date: Feb 1985, Middle Temple
Qualifications: [MA (Oxon)]
Stephen.moverley.smith@xxiv.co.uk

MOWSCHENSON MR TERENCE RENNIE QC (1995)

Wilberforce Chambers
8 New Square, Lincoln's Inn, London WC2A 3QP, ☎020 7306 0102
✉chambers@wilberforce.co.uk
Call Date: July 1977, Middle Temple
Recorder
Qualifications: [LLB (Lond) BCL (Oxon) FCIArb]
tmowschenson@wilberforce.co.uk

MOXON MR NATHAN ANDREW

KBW
The Engine House, No 1 Foundry Square, Leeds LS11 5DL, ☎0113 297 1200
✉clerks@kbwchambers.com
Call Date: July 2006, Inner Temple
Qualifications: [BA]
nathanmoxon@kbwchambers.com

MOXON BROWNE MR ROBERT WILLIAM QC (1990)

2 Temple Gardens
2 Temple Gardens, Temple, London EC4Y 9AY, ☎020 7822 1200
✉clerks@2tg.co.uk
Call Date: July 1969, Gray's Inn
Recorder
Qualifications: [BA (Oxon)]
rmoxonbrowne@2tg.co.uk

MOYS MR CLIVE JOHN

Radcliffe Chambers
Ground Floor, 11 New Square, Lincoln's Inn, London WC2A 3QB, ☎020 7831 0081
✉clerks@radcliffechambers.com
Pallant Chambers
12 North Pallant, Chichester, West Sussex PO19 1TQ, ☎01243 784538
✉clerks@pallantchambers.co.uk
Call Date: July 1998, Lincoln's Inn
Qualifications: [LLB (Hons)]
cmoys@radcliffechambers.com

E

MOYS MISS LAURA ANN

1 KBW Chambers
1 King's Bench Walk, Temple, London EC4Y 7DB, ☎020 7936 1500
✉clerks@1kbw.co.uk
Call Date: July 2008, Gray's Inn
Qualifications: [BA (Oxon)]
✉lmoys@1kbw.co.uk

MUCHLINSKI MR PETER THOMAS

Brick Court Chambers
7-8 Essex Street, London WC2R 3LD, ☎020 7379 3550 ✉clerks@brickcourt.co.uk
Call Date: July 1981, Lincoln's Inn
Qualifications: [LLB (Cantab) LLB (Lond)]

MUGLISTON MR ADAM JAMES

Dere Street Barristers
14 Toft Green, York YO1 6JT, ☎0844 3351551
✉clerks@derestreet.co.uk
Call Date: Oct 2008, Lincoln's Inn
Qualifications: [BA LLB]
✉clerks@yorkchambers.co.uk

MUHAREMI-MLINAKU MRS BRIKENA

Chambers of Brikena Muharemi-Mlinaku
9a Bulwer Road, London E11 1DE, ☎020 8279 2247
Call Date: Nov 2003, Lincoln's Inn
Qualifications: [LLB (Hons) (Westminster)]
✉bmuharemi@yahoo.co.uk

MUIR MISS NICOLA JANE

Hardwicke
New Square, Lincoln's Inn, London WC2A 3SB, ☎020 7242 2523
✉enquiries@hardwicke.co.uk
Call Date: Nov 1998, Inner Temple
Qualifications: [LLB (Edinburgh)]
✉nicola.muir@hardwicke.co.uk

MUIR-WILSON MISS LOUISE SARAH

Carmelite Chambers
9 Carmelite Street, London EC4Y 0DR, ☎020 7936 6300
✉clerks@carmelitechambers.co.uk
Call Date: Nov 1999, Middle Temple
Qualifications: [BA (Hons) (E.Anglia)]

MUKHERJEE MR AVIK

1 High Pavement
Nottingham NG1 1HF, ☎0115 941 8218
✉clerks@1highpavement.co.uk
Call Date: Oct 1990, Gray's Inn
Pupil Supervisor
Qualifications: [LLB]
✉avikmukherjee@1highpavement.co.uk

MUKHERJEE MR TUBLU KRISHNENDU

Doughty Street Chambers
53-54 Doughty Street, London WC1N 2LS, ☎020 7404 1313
✉enquiries@doughtystreet.co.uk
Doughty Street Chambers
Pall Mall Court, 61-67 King Street, Manchester M2 4PD, ☎0161 618 1066
Doughty Street Chambers
5th Floor, Broad Quay House, Prince Street, Bristol BS1 4DJ, ☎01179 058 717
Call Date: May 1996, Inner Temple
Qualifications: [BA (Hons) MA (Newc)]
✉t.mukherjee@doughtystreet.co.uk

MUKULU MR MATONDO KAMAU

Amethyst Chambers
Ground Floor, 9 Kings Bench Walk, Inner Temple, London EC4Y 7DX, ☎020 7936 4966
✉info@amethystchambers.com
Call Date: Mar 2002, Lincoln's Inn
Qualifications: [LLB (Hons)]
✉m.kmukulu@yahoo.co.uk

MULCAHY MS JANE SUZANNE

Blackstone Chambers
Blackstone House, Temple, London EC4Y 9BW, ☎020 7583 1770
✉clerks@blackstonechambers.com
Call Date: Oct 1995, Middle Temple
Pupil Supervisor
Qualifications: [BA (Hons) (Lond)]
✉janemulcahy@blackstonechambers.com

MULCAHY MISS LEIGH-ANN MARIA QC (2009)

Four New Square
Four New Square, Lincoln's Inn, London WC2A 3RJ, ☎020 7822 2000
✉barristers@4newsquare.com
Call Date: Oct 1993, Inner Temple
Qualifications: [MA Dip EC Law LLM]
✉l.mulcahy@4newsquare.com

MULCHRONE MR RORY THOMAS

Middle Temple Lane Chambers
2nd Floor South, 1 Middle Temple Lane, London EC4Y 9AA, ☎020 7583 4352
✉chambers@mtlchambers.com
Call Date: Oct 2009, Middle Temple
Qualifications: [BA (Hons) (Lond) LLB (Hons) (Lond)]

MULDERIG MR JOSEPH PAUL

St James's Chambers
68 Quay Street, Manchester M3 3EJ,
☎0161 834 7000
✉clerks@stjameschambers.com
Call Date: Nov 2002, Lincoln's Inn
Qualifications: [LLB (Hons) (Lanc)]
joseph.mulderig@stjameschambers.com

MULHOLLAND MISS HELEN MAUREEN

Kings Chambers
36 Young Street, Manchester M3 3FT,
☎0845 034 3444
✉clerks@kingschambers.com
Kings Chambers
5 Park Square East, Leeds LS1 2NE,
☎0845 034 3444
✉clerks@kingschambers.com
Kings Chambers
Embassy House, 60 Church Street,
Birmingham B3 2DJ, ☎0845 034 3444
✉clerks@kingschambers.com
Call Date: Oct 1999, Middle Temple
Pupil Supervisor
Qualifications: [BA (Hons)(B'ham)]
hmullholland@kingschambers.com

E

MULHOLLAND MR JAMES MALACHI QC (2011)

15 New Bridge Street
London EC4V 6AU, ☎020 7842 1900
✉clerks@15nbs.com
Call Date: July 1986, Inner Temple
Pupil Supervisor, Recorder
Qualifications: [LLB (Leeds)]
james.mulholland@15nbs.com

MULHOLLAND MR JAMES PETER

2-3 Hind Court Chambers
2-3 Hind Court, Fleet Street, London
EC4A 3DL, ☎020 7822 2150
✉david@2-3hindcourt.com
Call Date: Nov 2008, Gray's Inn
Qualifications: [MA]
j.manson@2-3hindcourt.com

MULHOLLAND MR MICHAEL

St James's Chambers
68 Quay Street, Manchester M3 3EJ,
☎0161 834 7000
✉clerks@stjameschambers.com
Call Date: Nov 1976, Gray's Inn
Pupil Supervisor
Qualifications: [MA (Oxon) Dip Crim (Cantab)]
michael.mulholland@stjameschambers.com

MULLA MISS MARIA JULIETTE

Palmyra Chambers
Royal House, 46 Legh Street, Warrington
WA1 1UJ, ☎01925 444919
✉clerk@palmyrachambers.com
Call Date: Mar 2005, Lincoln's Inn
Qualifications: [LLB (Hons) LLM]

MULLAN MR RICHARD FRANCIS

Linenhall Chambers
1 Stanley Place, Chester CH1 2LU,
☎01244 348282
✉clerks@linenhallchambers.co.uk
Call Date: Oct 1994, Gray's Inn
Qualifications: [BA (Wales)]
clerks@1stanleyplace.co.uk

MULLAN MR RORY EDWARD

Taxchambers
15 Old Square, Lincoln's Inn, London
WC2A 3UE, ☎020 7242 2744
✉taxchambers@15oldsquare.co.uk
Call Date: July 2000, Gray's Inn
Pupil Supervisor
Qualifications: [MA (Cantab)]
rorymullan@15oldsquare.co.uk

MULLANY MR NICHOLAS JAY

3 Serjeants Inn
London EC4Y 1BQ, ☎020 7427 5000
✉clerks@3serjeantsinn.com
Call Date: Oct 2007, Inner Temple
Qualifications: [LLB (Australia) BCL (Oxon)]
nmullany@3serjeantsinn.com

MULLARKEY MR IAN

KBW
The Engine House, No 1 Foundry Square,
Leeds LS11 5DL, ☎0113 297 1200
✉clerks@kbwchambers.com
Call Date: July 2003, Inner Temple
Qualifications: [LLB (Lond)]
ianmullarkey@kbwchambers.com

MULLEE MR BRENDAN PAUL

Hardwicke
New Square, Lincoln's Inn, London
WC2A 3SB, ☎020 7242 2523
✉enquiries@hardwicke.co.uk
Call Date: Oct 1996, Middle Temple
Qualifications: [LLB (Hons)]
brendan.mullee@hardwicke.co.uk

MULLEN MISS JAYNE ALISON

St Ive's Chambers
Whittall Street, Birmingham B4 6DH,
☎0121 236 0863
✉clerks@stiveschambers.co.uk
Call Date: July 1989, Gray's Inn
Pupil Supervisor
Qualifications: [LLB (Hons) (Wales)]
jayne.mullen@stiveschambers.co.uk

MULLEN MR MARK ROBERT

Radcliffe Chambers
Ground Floor, 11 New Square, Lincoln's Inn, London WC2A 3QB, ☎020 7831 0081
✉clerks@radcliffechambers.com
Call Date: July 2001, Lincoln's Inn
Pupil Supervisor
Qualifications: [BA (Hons) PgDL]
mmullen@radcliffechambers.com

MULLEN MR PATRICK ANTHONY

Argent Chambers
5 Bell Yard, London WC2A 2JR,
☎020 7556 5500
✉briefsin@argentchambers.co.uk
Call Date: July 1967, Gray's Inn
Pupil Supervisor
Qualifications: [MA (Cantab)]
p.mullen@argentchambers.co.uk

MULLEN MR PETER

1 Mitre Court Buildings
1 Mitre Court Buildings, Temple, London EC4Y 7BS, ☎020 7452 8900
✉clerks@1mcb.com
Call Date: July 1977, Lincoln's Inn
Pupil Supervisor
Qualifications: [BA (Lond)]
peter.mullen@1mcb.com

MULLER MR ANTONIE SEAN

Citadel Chambers
The Citadel, 190 Corporation Street, Birmingham B4 6QD, ☎0121 233 8500
✉clerks@citadelchambers.com
Call Date: July 1990, Middle Temple
Pupil Supervisor
Qualifications: [MA (Cantab)]
clerks@citadelchambers.com

MULLER MR MARK OLIVER BENJAMIN QC (2006)

Garden Court Chambers
57-60 Lincoln's Inn Fields, London WC2A 3LJ,
☎020 7993 7600 ✉info@gclaw.co.uk
Call Date: Apr 1991, Lincoln's Inn
Qualifications: [BSC(Econ) LLB]
markm@gclaw.co.uk

MULLIGAN MS ANN COLLETTE

15 New Bridge Street
London EC4V 6AU, ☎020 7842 1900
✉clerks@15nbs.com
Call Date: July 1989, Gray's Inn
Pupil Supervisor, Recorder
Qualifications: [BA (Oxon)]
ann.mulligan@15nbs.com

MULLIN MR MICHAEL GEORGE

Staple Inn Chambers
1st Floor, 9 Staple Inn, Holborn Bars, London WC1V 7QH, ☎020 7242 5240
✉clerks@stapleinn.co.uk
Call Date: Mar 2010, Middle Temple
Qualifications: [BA(Dunelm) LLB (Lond)]

MULLINS MR MARK

Outer Temple Chambers
The Outer Temple, 222 Strand, London WC2R 1BA, ☎020 7353 6381
✉clerks@outertemple.com
Call Date: Nov 1988, Lincoln's Inn
Pupil Supervisor
Qualifications: [BA Hons (Oxon) DipLaw (City) Dip Forensic Mental Health (Lond)]
mark.mullins@outertemple.com

MULLINS MR MARK LOVEL RUPERT

Five St Andrew's Hill
5 St Andrew's Hill, London EC4V 5BZ,
☎020 7332 5400 ✉Clerks@5sah.co.uk
Call Date: Nov 1995, Inner Temple
Pupil Supervisor
Qualifications: [BA (Dunelm) CPE (Lond)]
markmullins@5sah.co.uk

MULLIS MR ANTHONY ROGER

Radcliffe Chambers
Ground Floor, 11 New Square, Lincoln's Inn, London WC2A 3QB, ☎020 7831 0081
✉clerks@radcliffechambers.com
Pallant Chambers
12 North Pallant, Chichester, West Sussex PO19 1TQ, ☎01243 784538
✉clerks@pallantchambers.co.uk
Call Date: Nov 1987, Lincoln's Inn
Pupil Supervisor
Qualifications: [BA (Oxon) BCL]
rmullis@radcliffechambers.com

E

MULRENNAN MISS MARIA HELEN ANNE

St Mary's Family Law Chambers
26-28 High Pavement, The Lace Market, Nottingham NG1 1HN, ☎0115 950 3503
✉clerks@stmarysflc.co.uk
Call Date: Nov 1990, Inner Temple
Pupil Supervisor
Qualifications: [BA (Sussex) LLM (Nott'm)]
maria.mulrennan@stmarysflc.co.uk

MULROONEY MR MARK TERENCE DANIEL

Exchange Chambers
One Derby Square, Derby Square, Liverpool L2 9XX, ☎0151 236 7747
✉info@exchangechambers.co.uk
Exchange Chambers
7 Ralli Courts, West Riverside, Manchester M3 5FT, ☎0161 833 2722
Exchange Chambers
Oxford House, Oxford Row, Leeds LS1 3BE, ☎0113 203 1970
✉spencer@exchangechambers.co.uk
Call Date: July 1988, Middle Temple
Qualifications: [BA (Hons) Kent MPhil (Cantab)]
mulrooney@exchangechambers.co.uk

E

MULVANNY MISS BERENICE HELEN LOUISE

2 King's Bench Walk
2 King's Bench Walk, Temple, London EC4Y 7DE, ☎020 7353 1746
✉clerks@2kbw.com
Call Date: July 2009, Middle Temple
Qualifications: [LLB (Hons) (Kent)]
clerks@2kbw.com

MUMAN MR VIJAY KUMAR

43 Temple Row Chambers
6th Floor, 43 Temple Row, Birmingham B2 5LS, ☎0121 237 6035
✉clerks@43templerow.co.uk
Call Date: Nov 2001, Gray's Inn
Qualifications: [LLB]
clerks@43templerow.co.uk

MUMFORD MR DAVID STEWART

Maitland Chambers
7 Stone Buildings, Lincoln's Inn, London WC2A 3SZ, ☎020 7406 1200
✉clerks@maitlandchambers.com
Call Date: Oct 2000, Lincoln's Inn
Pupil Supervisor
Qualifications: [MA (Hons (Oxon) Dip in Law (City)]
dmumford@maitlandchambers.com

MUMFORD MR RICHARD STEPHEN JAMES

1 Crown Office Row
1 Crown Office Row, Temple, London EC4Y 7HH, ☎020 7797 7500
✉mail@1cor.com
Call Date: Nov 2004, Lincoln's Inn
Qualifications: [MA (Cantab) LLM]
richard.mumford@1cor.com

MUNBY MR THOMAS EDWARD

Maitland Chambers
7 Stone Buildings, Lincoln's Inn, London WC2A 3SZ, ☎020 7406 1200
✉clerks@maitlandchambers.com
Call Date: Oct 2006, Inner Temple
Qualifications: [BA (Oxon)]
tmunby@maitlandchambers.com

MUNDAY MR ANDREW HUGH QC (1996)

2 Bedford Row
London WC1R 4BU, ☎020 7440 8888
✉clerks@2bedfordrow.co.uk
Call Date: Nov 1973, Middle Temple
Qualifications: [LLB (Hons)]
amunday@2bedfordrow.co.uk

MUNDAY MR GARETH

The Chambers of Grahame Aldous QC
9 Gough Square, London EC4A 3DG, ☎020 7832 0500
✉clerks@9goughsquare.co.uk
Call Date: Nov 2000, Middle Temple
Qualifications: [LLB (Hons)]
gmunday@9goughsquare.co.uk

MUNDEN MR RICHARD ALEXANDER JOHN

5RB
1st Floor, 5 Raymond Buildings, Gray's Inn, London WC1R 5BP, ☎020 7242 2902
✉clerks@5rb.com
Call Date: July 2003, Lincoln's Inn
Qualifications: [LLB Hons (Warw) BCL (Oxon)]
richardmunden@5rb.com

MUNDY MR ROBERT

St Philips Chambers
55 Temple Row, Birmingham B2 5LS, ☎0121 246 7000 ✉clerks@st-philips.com
Call Date: July 2008, Middle Temple
Qualifications: [BA (Hons) (Cantab)]

MUNIR DR ASHLEY EDWARD

Five St Andrew's Hill
5 St Andrew's Hill, London EC4V 5BZ, ☎020 7332 5400 ✉Clerks@5sah.co.uk
Call Date: June 1956, Gray's Inn
Pupil Supervisor
Qualifications: [MA (Cantab) PhD (Lond) MPhil]
✉edwardmunir@5sah.co.uk

MUNRO MR ALEXANDER IAN

2 Dr Johnson's Buildings
2 Dr Johnson's Buildings, Temple, London EC4Y 7AY, ☎020 7936 2613
✉clerks@2drj.com
Call Date: July 2001, Lincoln's Inn
Qualifications: [LLB (Hons)]
✉a.munro@2drj.com, alex_munro78@hotmail.com

MUNRO MR DAVID PHILIP

St Philips Chambers
55 Temple Row, Birmingham B2 5LS, ☎0121 246 7000 ✉clerks@st-philips.com
Call Date: Nov 2001, Gray's Inn
Qualifications: [LLB (B'Ham)]
✉dmunro@st-philips.com

MUNRO MR IAIN

4 Pump Court
4 Pump Court, Temple, London EC4Y 7AN, ☎020 7842 5555
✉chambers@4pumpcourt.com
Call Date: Oct 2009, Lincoln's Inn
Qualifications: [BA (Oxon)]
✉imunro@4pumpcourt.com

MUNRO MR JOSHUA NEIL

Hailsham Chambers
Ground Floor, 4 Paper Buildings, Temple, London EC4Y 7EX, ☎020 7643 5000
✉clerks@hailshamchambers.com
Call Date: Oct 2001, Gray's Inn
Pupil Supervisor
Qualifications: [BA (Oxon)]
✉joshua.munro@hailshamchambers.com

MUNRO MR KENNETH STUART

New Square Chambers
12 New Square, Lincoln's Inn, London WC2A 3SW, ☎020 7419 8000
✉robin.hollington@newsquarechambers.co.uk
Call Date: Nov 1973, Inner Temple
Pupil Supervisor
Qualifications: [MA (Cantab)]
✉kenneth.munro@newsquarechambers.co.uk

MUNRO MISS SARAH TIFFANY

1 High Pavement
Nottingham NG1 1HF, ☎0115 941 8218
✉clerks@1highpavement.co.uk
Call Date: Oct 1990, Middle Temple
Qualifications: [LLB]

MUNROE MISS VERONICA ALLISON

Tooks Chambers
81 Farringdon Street, London EC4A 4BL, ☎020 7842 7575 ✉clerks@tooks.co.uk
Call Date: Oct 1992, Middle Temple
Qualifications: [BA (Hons)(Cantab) Diploma in Law]
✉allison.munroe@tooks.co.uk

MUNT MR ALASTAIR HENRY MCLAREN

KCH Garden Square
1 Oxford Street, Nottingham NG1 5BH, ☎0115 941 8851
✉clerks@kchgardensquare.co.uk
Call Date: July 1989, Gray's Inn
Qualifications: [LLB (Reading) LLM (Cantab) MPhil (Cantab)]

MUNYARD MR TERRY

Garden Court Chambers
57-60 Lincoln's Inn Fields, London WC2A 3LJ, ☎020 7993 7600 ✉info@gclaw.co.uk
Call Date: July 1972, Gray's Inn
Pupil Supervisor
Qualifications: [LLB (Hons) (Lond)]
✉terrym@gclaw.co.uk

MUQIT MISS PIYA DILRUBA

Chambers of Miss P Muqit
149 Riverside Mansions, Milk Yard, Wapping, London E1W 3SU, ☎07888 606866
✉piyamuqit@gmail.com
Call Date: Oct 2001, Inner Temple
Qualifications: [LLB CPE LLM (Lond)]
✉pmuqit@freedomfromtorture.org

MUQUIT MR MOHAMMED SHUYEB

1 Mitre Court Buildings
1 Mitre Court Buildings, Temple, London EC4Y 7BS, ☎020 7452 8900
✉clerks@1mcb.com
Call Date: July 1998, Inner Temple
Qualifications: [BSc (LSE) LI Dip (B'ham)]

E

MURCH MR STEPHEN JAMES

42 Bedford Row
London WC1R 4LL, ☎020 7831 0222
✉clerks@42br.com
Advolex Chambers
70 Coulsdon Road, Coulsdon, Croydon, Surrey CR5 2LB, ☎0871 951 9000
Call Date: Oct 1991, Lincoln's Inn
Pupil Supervisor
Qualifications: [LLB (Hons) (Bucks)]
Stephen.Murch@42br.com

MURDEN MISS CLAIRE ELIZABETH

Sovereign Chambers
46 Park Place, Leeds LS1 2RY,
☎0113 245 1841
✉clerks@sovereignchambers.co.uk
Call Date: Nov 1999, Gray's Inn
Qualifications: [BA (Hons)(Oxon) Dip Law]
Claire.murden@sovereignchambers.co.uk

MURDIN MR LIAM

St Johns Buildings
24a - 28 St John Street, Manchester M3 4DJ,
☎0161 214 1500
✉clerk@stjohnsbuildings.co.uk
St Johns Buildings
21 White Friars, Chester CH1 1NZ,
☎01244 323070
✉clerk@stjohnsbuildings.co.uk
16 Winckley Square
Preston PR1 3JJ, ☎01772 256100
Call Date: July 1998, Lincoln's Inn
Pupil Supervisor
Qualifications: [BA (Hons)(Salford)]

MURDOCH MISS CATRIONA JANE

Crown Office Row Chambers
119 Church Street, Brighton, Sussex BN1 1UD, ☎01273 625625
✉clerks@1cor.com
Call Date: Oct 2009, Gray's Inn
Qualifications: [LLB]
catriona.murdoch@1cor.com

MURKIN MRS SANDRIA

Becket Chambers
17 New Dover Road, Canterbury, Kent CT1 3AS, ☎01227 786331
✉clerks@becket-chambers.co.uk
Call Date: Oct 2004, Inner Temple
Qualifications: [LLB (Hons) Bristol]
smurkin@becket-chambers.co.uk

MURPHY MRS CATRIONA ANNE

10 King's Bench Walk
Ground Floor, 10 King's Bench Walk, Temple, London EC4Y 7EB, ☎020 7353 7742
✉Chambers@10kingsbenchwalk.co.uk
Call Date: Nov 1995, Lincoln's Inn
Qualifications: [BA (Hons) LLM]

MURPHY MR DAMIAN

Enterprise Chambers
65 Quayside, Newcastle Upon Tyne NE1 3DE,
☎0191 222 3344
✉newcastle@enterprisechambers.com
Enterprise Chambers
43 Park Square, Leeds LS1 2NP,
☎0113 246 0391
✉leeds@enterprisechambers.com
Enterprise Chambers
9 Old Square, Lincoln's Inn, London WC2A 3SR, ☎020 7405 9471
✉london@enterprisechambers.com
Call Date: July 2001, Middle Temple
Pupil Supervisor
Qualifications: [BA (Hons) (Cantab) CPE]
damianmurphy@enterprisechambers.com

MURPHY MS DIANA LOUISE

Goldsmith Chambers
Ground Floor, Goldsmith Building, Temple, London EC4Y 7BL, ☎020 7353 6802
✉clerks@goldsmithchambers.com
Call Date: May 2010, Middle Temple
Qualifications: [BA (Hons) Wales]
d.murphy@goldsmithchambers.com

MURPHY MISS EMER MéIRE

Wilberforce Chambers
8 New Square, Lincoln's Inn, London WC2A 3QP, ☎020 7306 0102
✉chambers@wilberforce.co.uk
Call Date: Oct 2009, Inner Temple
Qualifications: [BA (Oxon)]
EMurphy@wilberforce.co.uk

MURPHY MISS HEATHER

XXIV Old Buildings
Ground Floor, 24 Old Buildings, Lincoln's Inn, London WC2A 3UP, ☎020 7691 2424
✉clerks@xxiv.co.uk
Call Date: July 2009, Lincoln's Inn
Qualifications: [BA (Cantab)]
heather.murphy@xxiv.co.uk

E

MURPHY MR IAN PATRICK QC (1992)

Farrar's Building
Farrar's Building, Temple, London EC4Y 7BD, ☎ 020 7583 9241
✉ Chambers@farrarsbuilding.co.uk
9 Park Place
9 Park Place, Cardiff, South Glamorgan CF10 3DP, ☎ 029 2038 2731
✉ clerks@9parkplace.co.uk
Call Date: July 1972, Middle Temple
Recorder
Qualifications: [LLB (Lond)]
imurphy@farrarsbuilding.co.uk

MURPHY MR JAMES ST JOHN

Park Lane Plowden
19 Westgate, Leeds LS1 2RD, ☎ 0113 228 5049
✉ clerks@parklaneplowden.co.uk
Call Date: Nov 1993, Inner Temple
Pupil Supervisor
Qualifications: [BA (L'pool) CPE]
james.murphy@parklaneplowden.co.uk

MURPHY MRS JASMINE ANNE

Hardwicke
New Square, Lincoln's Inn, London WC2A 3SB, ☎ 020 7242 2523
✉ enquiries@hardwicke.co.uk
Call Date: July 2002, Gray's Inn
Qualifications: [LLB (Hons) (Exon)]
jasmine.murphy@hardwicke.co.uk

MURPHY MISS LIANNE CLARE

Northampton Chambers
10 Spencer Parade, Northampton NN1 5AQ, ☎ 01604 636271
✉ clerks@northampton-chambers.co.uk
Call Date: Nov 2001, Lincoln's Inn
Pupil Supervisor
Qualifications: [LLB (Hons)]
liannecmurphy@aol.co.uk

MURPHY MISS MELISSA ROSALIND GILLIAN

Cornerstone Barristers
2-3 Gray's Inn Square, Gray's Inn, London WC1R 5JH, ☎ 020 7242 4986
✉ chambers@2-3gis.co.uk
Call Date: Nov 2001, Middle Temple
Pupil Supervisor
Qualifications: [BA (Hons)]
mmurphy@2-3gis.co.uk

MURPHY MR MICHAEL PATRICK

10 King's Bench Walk
Ground Floor, 10 King's Bench Walk, Temple, London EC4Y 7EB, ☎ 020 7353 7742
✉ Chambers@10kingsbenchwalk.co.uk
Central Chambers
89 Princess Street, Manchester M1 4HT, ☎ 0161 236 1133
✉ clerks@centralchambers.co.uk
Call Date: Nov 1992, Inner Temple
Pupil Supervisor
Qualifications: [LLB (Essex)]

MURPHY MISS OLIVIA BRIDGET

Tanfield Chambers
2-5 Warwick Court, London WC1R 5DJ, ☎ 020 7421 5300
✉ clerks@tanfieldchambers.co.uk
Call Date: Nov 2001, Middle Temple
Qualifications: [BA (Hons)(Manch)]

MURPHY MR PAUL RICHARD

Call Date: July 2004, Gray's Inn
Qualifications: [BA Hons (Dunelm)]
clerk@stjohnsbuildings.co.uk

MURPHY MR PETER JOHN QC (2002)

30 Park Place
Cardiff CF10 3BS, ☎ 029 2039 8421
✉ clerks@30parkplace.law.co.uk
Call Date: Nov 1980, Gray's Inn
Qualifications: [LLB (Leics)]

MURRAY MR ANIL PETER

Wilberforce Chambers
7 Bishop Lane, Hull HU1 1PA, ☎ 01482 323264
Call Date: July 1989, Middle Temple
Pupil Supervisor
Qualifications: [LLB (Hull)]

MURRAY MR ASHLEY CHARLES

Oriel Chambers
14 Water Street, Liverpool, Merseyside L2 8TD, ☎ 0151 236 7191
✉ clerks@orielchambers.co.uk
Oriel Chambers
18 Ribblesdale Place, Preston PR1 3NA, ☎ 01772 254 764
✉ clerks@oriel-chambers.co.uk
Call Date: July 1974, Middle Temple
Pupil Supervisor, Recorder
Qualifications: [LLB (B'ham)]
ashley.murray@orielchambers.co.uk

E

MURRAY MS CAROLE JEANNE

No5 Chambers
Greenwood House, 4-7 Salisbury Court, London EC4Y 8AA, ☎0845 210 5555
No5 Chambers
38 Queen Square, Bristol BS1 4QS, ☎0845 210 5555
No5 Chambers
Fountain Court, Steelhouse Lane, Birmingham B4 6DR, ☎0845 210 5555 ✉info@no5.com
Call Date: Nov 1989, Middle Temple
Qualifications: [MA (Hons) (Cantab) DipLaw]
cm@no5.com

MURRAY MR CHARLES HUMPHREY STEWART

Rougemont Chambers
Victory House, Dean Clarke Gardens, Southernhay East, Exeter EX2 4AA, ☎01392 208484
✉clerks@rougemontchambers.co.uk
Call Date: Mar 2005, Inner Temple
Qualifications: [LLB University of Southampton]
cmurray@rougemontchambers.co.uk

MURRAY MR DANIEL EVAN DUNCAN

Old Bailey Chambers
15 Old Bailey, London EC4M 7EF, ☎020 3008 6404
✉clerks@15oldbaileychambers.com
Call Date: Nov 1996, Lincoln's Inn
Qualifications: [LLB (Hons)(Lond)]
d.murray@15oldbaileychambers.com

MURRAY MR DAVID JOHN

Fountain Court Chambers
Fountain Court, Temple, London EC4Y 9DH, ☎020 7583 3335
✉chambers@fountaincourt.co.uk
Call Date: July 2004, Lincoln's Inn
Qualifications: [BA (Hons)]

MURRAY MISS ELIZABETH EMILY

18 St John Street
Manchester M3 4EA, ☎0161 278 1800
✉clerks@18sjs.com
Call Date: Oct 2005, Inner Temple
Qualifications: [LLB University of Liverpool]

MURRAY MR EWAN DOUGLAS

14 Gray's Inn Square
14 Gray's Inn Square, Gray's Inn, London WC1R 5JP, ☎020 7242 0858
✉clerks@14gis.co.uk
Call Date: Oct 2008, Lincoln's Inn
Qualifications: [BA (York)]

MURRAY MR HARVEY

Fountain Chambers
Cleveland Business Centre, 1 Watson Street, Middlesbrough TS1 2RQ, ☎01642 804040
✉clerks@fountainchambers.co.uk
Call Date: Mar 2004, Middle Temple
Qualifications: [LLB (Hons) (Newc)]

MURRAY MISS JOANNE

St Paul's Chambers
5th Floor, St Paul's House, 23 Park Square South, Leeds LS1 2ND, ☎0113 245 5866
Call Date: Mar 2006, Middle Temple
Qualifications: [BA (Hons) (Newc)]

MURRAY MR JOHN MICHAEL ANDREW

18 St John Street
Manchester M3 4EA, ☎0161 278 1800
✉clerks@18sjs.com
Call Date: Nov 1979, Middle Temple
Pupil Supervisor
Qualifications: [BA]

MURRAY MISS JUDITH ROWENA

4 Paper Buildings
1st Floor, 4 Paper Buildings, Temple, London EC4Y 7EX, ☎020 7427 5200
✉clerks@4pb.com
Call Date: Oct 1994, Middle Temple
Qualifications: [BA (Hons)(Oxon)]
jm@4pb.com

MURRAY MR LANCE JOHN MOLE

Nexus Chambers
7 New Square, Lincolns Inn, London WC2A 3QS,
☎020 7404 1147 / 020 7831 8309
✉info@nexuschambers.com
Call Date: Oct 2007, Middle Temple
Qualifications: [BA (Hons) PgDL (Lond) PgD]
lance.murray@nexuschambers.com

MURRAY MISS LUCY JANE

Call Date: May 1997, Lincoln's Inn
Qualifications: [BA (Hons)(Exon) MA (Exon) CPE]

MURRAY MR PAUL MARTIN

Garden Court Chambers
57-60 Lincoln's Inn Fields, London WC2A 3LJ, ☎020 7993 7600 ✉info@gclaw.co.uk
Call Date: Mar 2009, Lincoln's Inn
Qualifications: [BSc (Buckinghamshire) CPE PWOLV]
paulm@gclaw.co.uk

E

MURRAY MISS REBECCA LOUISE ELIZABETH

Temple Tax Chambers
1st Floor, 3 Temple Gardens, Temple, London EC4Y 9AU, ☎ 020 7353 7884
✉ clerks@templetax.com
Call Date: Nov 2001, Lincoln's Inn
Qualifications: [LLB (Hons)]
rebecca.murray@templetax.com

MURRAY MR SIMON PEREGRINE GAUVAIN

1 Chancery Lane
London WC2A 1LF, ☎ 0845 634 6666
✉ clerks@1chancerylane.com
Call Date: Oct 2000, Inner Temple
Pupil Supervisor
Qualifications: [MA CPE (Lond)]
smurray@1chancerylane.com

MURRAY MR SIMON STEWART

St Johns Buildings
24a - 28 St John Street, Manchester M3 4DJ, ☎ 0161 214 1500
✉ clerk@stjohnsbuildings.co.uk
St Johns Buildings
21 White Friars, Chester CH1 1NZ, ☎ 01244 323070
✉ clerk@stjohnsbuildings.co.uk
16 Winckley Square
Preston PR1 3JJ, ☎ 01772 256100
Call Date: Oct 2008, Inner Temple
Qualifications: [PGDip BA (Cantab)]
simon.murray@stjohnsbuildings.co.uk

MURRAY MR STEPHEN JOHN

18 St John Street
Manchester M3 4EA, ☎ 0161 278 1800
✉ clerks@18sjs.com
Call Date: July 1986, Inner Temple
Pupil Supervisor
Qualifications: [LLB (Leic)]

MURRAY-SMITH MR JAMES MICHAEL

1 Mitre Court Buildings
1 Mitre Court Buildings, Temple, London EC4Y 7BS, ☎ 020 7452 8900
✉ clerks@1mcb.com
Call Date: May 1990, Middle Temple
Pupil Supervisor
Qualifications: [BA]
james.murraysmith@1mcb.com

MURSHED MISS TANYA HASAN

1 Mitre Court Buildings
1 Mitre Court Buildings, Temple, London EC4Y 7BS, ☎ 020 7452 8900
✉ clerks@1mcb.com
Call Date: Oct 2006, Middle Temple
Qualifications: [BA (Hons) (Lond)]
tanya.murshed@gmail.com

MUSAALA MUKASA MISS CHRISTINE ROSE MIRANDA

Musaala & Co
Address withheld ☎ 07762 627336
✉ mulugero-blog@yahoo.co.uk
Call Date: Nov 1985, Gray's Inn
Qualifications: [LLB LLM]

MUSAHEB MR IKBAL KEVIN

Cobden House Chambers
19 Quay Street, Manchester M3 3HN, ☎ 0161 833 6000 ✉ Clerks@Cobden.co.uk
Call Date: Oct 1990, Middle Temple
Qualifications: [LLB]
clerks@cobden.co.uk

MUSGRAVE MISS ANARKALI AVRIL

3 PB Barristers
3 Paper Buildings, Temple, London EC4Y 7EU, ☎ 020 7583 8055
3 PB Barristers
Royal Talbot House, 2 Victoria Street, Bristol, Avon BS1 6BB, ☎ 0117 928 1520
3 PB Barristers
4 St Peter Street, Winchester SO23 8BW, ☎ 01962 868884
✉ clerks.winchester@3paper.co.uk
3 PB Barristers
23 Beaumont Street, Oxford OX1 2NP, ☎ 01865 793 736
3 PB Barristers
30 Christchurch Road, Bournemouth, Dorset BH1 3PD, ☎ 01202 292102
✉ clerks.bournemouth@3paper.co.uk
Call Date: Nov 2005, Inner Temple
Qualifications: [BA Worcester College University of Oxford]
anarkali.musgrave@3paper.co.uk

MUSGRAVE MS CAROLINE ELIZABETH

Cloisters
1 Pump Court, Temple, London EC4Y 7AA, ☎ 020 7827 4000 ✉ clerks@cloisters.com
Call Date: Nov 2008, Inner Temple
Qualifications: [MA (Cantab) CPE]
cem@cloisters.com

E

MUSHTAQ MS ERIMNAZ

Doughty Street Chambers
Pall Mall Court, 61-67 King Street, Manchester M2 4PD, ☎0161 618 1066
Doughty Street Chambers
5th Floor, Broad Quay House, Prince Street, Bristol BS1 4DJ, ☎01179 058 717
Doughty Street Chambers
53-54 Doughty Street, London WC1N 2LS, ☎020 7404 1313
✉enquiries@doughtystreet.co.uk
Call Date: Nov 2000, Inner Temple
Qualifications: [LLB (Manc)]
e.mushtaq@doughtystreet.co.uk

MUSSA MISS AZREEN

Fenners Chambers
3 Madingley Road, Cambridge CB3 0EE, ☎01223 368761
✉clerks@fennerschambers.com
Call Date: Oct 2003, Middle Temple
Qualifications: [LLB (Hons) (Leic)]
azreen.mussa@fennerschambers.com

MUSSA MR HANIF MOHAMED IQBAL

Blackstone Chambers
Blackstone House, Temple, London EC4Y 9BW, ☎020 7583 1770
✉clerks@blackstonechambers.com
Call Date: July 2007, Inner Temple
Qualifications: [BA (Cantab) Dip Law]
hanifmussa@blackstonechambers.com

MUSTAFA MS HALA MOHAMED KAMEL

1 Crown Office Row
1 Crown Office Row, Temple, London EC4Y 7HH, ☎020 7797 7500
✉mail@1cor.com
Crown Office Row Chambers
119 Church Street, Brighton, Sussex BN1 1UD, ☎01273 625625
✉clerks@1cor.com
Call Date: July 2004, Middle Temple
Qualifications: [LLB Hons (Middlesex)]
hala.mustafa@1cor.com

MUSTAKIM MR ABDUL YUNUS AL

Chambers of Mr Mustakim
6 Shandy Street, London E1 4LX
Call Date: May 1997, Lincoln's Inn
Pupil Supervisor
Qualifications: [BCL (Oxon) LLB (Hons)]

MUSTARD MISS LORRAINE

Dere Street Barristers
33 Broad Chare, Newcastle Upon Tyne NE1 3DQ, ☎0844 3351551
✉clerks@derestreet.co.uk
Call Date: July 1999, Lincoln's Inn
Qualifications: [LLB (Hons)]
clerks@broadcharechambers.co.uk

MUTCH MR IAIN RICHARD ALISTAIR

Palmyra Chambers
Royal House, 46 Legh Street, Warrington WA1 1UJ, ☎01925 444919
✉clerk@palmyrachambers.com
Call Date: Mar 2002, Lincoln's Inn
Qualifications: [LLB (Hons) MA (Liverpool)]
wecarter@care2.com

MUTH MISS SUSANNE

St Johns Buildings
24a - 28 St John Street, Manchester M3 4DJ, ☎0161 214 1500
✉clerk@stjohnsbuildings.co.uk
St Johns Buildings
21 White Friars, Chester CH1 1NZ, ☎01244 323070
✉clerk@stjohnsbuildings.co.uk
16 Winckley Square
Preston PR1 3JJ, ☎01772 256100
Call Date: July 1998, Inner Temple
Qualifications: [LLB (Lancs) LLM (Sheff)]
clerk@stjohnsbuildings.co.uk

MUZAFFER MR ADEM BEHCET

St Ive's Chambers
Whittall Street, Birmingham B4 6DH, ☎0121 236 0863
✉clerks@stiveschambers.co.uk
Call Date: July 2007, Lincoln's Inn
Qualifications: [BA (Cardiff)]

MYATT MR CHARLES EDWARD

1 Paper Buildings
1st Floor, 1 Paper Buildings, Temple, London EC4Y 7EP, ☎020 7353 3728
✉clerks@onepaper.co.uk
Call Date: Nov 1993, Gray's Inn
Qualifications: [BA (Dunelm)]
charlesmyatt@onepaper.co.uk

MYDEEN MR KALANDAR

Chambers of Mr K Mydeen
3 Kempston House, The Downsway, Sutton SM2 5RE, ☎020 8643 3633
✉kenmydeen@blueyonder.co.uk
Call Date: Nov 1973, Lincoln's Inn
Qualifications: [LLB]

MYERS MR BARRY

4 Breams Buildings
Chancery Lane, London EC4A 1HP,
☎ 020 7092 1900 ✉ clerks@4bb.co.uk
Call Date: Nov 1988, Inner Temple
Pupil Supervisor
Qualifications: [BA (Hull) DipLaw]

MYERS MR BENJAMIN JOHN

Exchange Chambers
7 Ralli Courts, West Riverside, Manchester M3 5FT, ☎ 0161 833 2722
Exchange Chambers
One Derby Square, Derby Square, Liverpool L2 9XX, ☎ 0151 236 7747
✉ info@exchangechambers.co.uk
Call Date: Oct 1994, Inner Temple
Pupil Supervisor
Qualifications: [BA (Hons)(Leeds) CPE (Lond) LLM (Leeds)]

MYERS MR JOHN ERNEST

Zenith Chambers
10 Park Square, Leeds LS1 2LH,
☎ 0113 245 5438
✉ clerks@zenithchambers.co.uk
Call Date: Mar 2007, Inner Temple
Qualifications: [LLB (Exon)]
✉ jmyers@zenithchambers.co.uk

MYERS MR RUPERT EDMUND FRANCIS

East Anglian Chambers
Gresham House, 5 Museum Street, Ipswich, Suffolk IP1 1HQ, ☎ 01473 214481
✉ ipswich@ealaw.co.uk
East Anglian Chambers
53 North Hill, Colchester, Essex CO1 1QA,
☎ 01473 214481 ✉ colchester@ealaw.co.uk
East Anglian Chambers
15 The Close, Norwich, Norfolk NR1 4DZ,
☎ 01473 214481 ✉ norwich@ealaw.co.uk
Call Date: Nov 2008, Inner Temple
Qualifications: [BA (Cantab) CPE]

MYERS MR SIMON MARTIN

Broadway House Chambers
Broadway House, 9 Bank Street, Bradford, West Yorkshire BD1 1TW, ☎ 01274 722560
✉ clerks@broadwayhouse.co.uk
Broadway House Chambers
25 Park Square West, Leeds, West Yorkshire LS1 2PW, ☎ 0113 246 2600
✉ clerks@broadwayhouse.co.uk
Call Date: Nov 1987, Middle Temple
Pupil Supervisor
Qualifications: [BA (Bris) DipLaw (Lond)]
✉ clerks@broadwayhouse.co.uk

MYERSON MR DAVID SIMON QC (2003)

St Paul's Chambers
5th Floor, St Paul's House, 23 Park Square South, Leeds LS1 2ND, ☎ 0113 245 5866
Byrom Street Chambers
12 Byrom Street, Manchester M3 4PP,
☎ 0161 829 2100 ✉ clerks@byromstreet.com
42 Bedford Row
London WC1R 4LL, ☎ 020 7831 0222
✉ clerks@42br.com
Call Date: July 1986, Middle Temple
Recorder
Qualifications: [MA (Cantab)]
✉ sm@stpaulschambers.com

MYHILL MR DAVID WILLIAM

Crown Office Chambers
2 Crown Office Row, Temple, London EC4Y 7HJ, ☎ 020 7797 8100
✉ mail@crownofficechambers.com
Call Date: Nov 2006, Lincoln's Inn
Qualifications: [BA (Cantab)]
✉ myhill@crownofficechambers.com

MYLONAS MR MICHAEL JOHN QC (2012)

3 Serjeants Inn
London EC4Y 1BQ, ☎ 020 7427 5000
✉ clerks@3serjeantsinn.com
Call Date: July 1988, Gray's Inn
Pupil Supervisor
Qualifications: [LLB (Bucks)]
✉ mmylonas@3serjeantsinn.com

MYLVAGANAM MR PAUL JOSEPH PARAM SOTHY

Argent Chambers
5 Bell Yard, London WC2A 2JR,
☎ 020 7556 5500
✉ briefsin@argentchambers.co.uk
Call Date: Nov 1993, Middle Temple
Pupil Supervisor
Qualifications: [BA (Hons)(Oxon) CPE (Lond)]
✉ p.mylvaganam@argentchambers.co.uk

MYLVAGANAM MS TANOO

1 Gray's Inn Square
Ground Floor, 1 Gray's Inn Square, London WC1R 5AA, ☎ 020 7405 0001
Call Date: July 1983, Gray's Inn
Qualifications: [BA (Kent)]

MYNORS DR CHARLES BASKERVILLE

Francis Taylor Building
Inner Temple, London EC4Y 7BY,
☎ 020 7353 8415 ✉ clerks@ftb.eu.com
Call Date: Nov 1988, Middle Temple
Pupil Supervisor
Qualifications: [MA (Cantab) MA (Sheff) Dip Law FRTPI IHBC MRICS]
charles.mynors@ftb.eu.com

MYTTON MR PAUL VINCENT

St Philips Chambers
55 Temple Row, Birmingham B2 5LS,
☎ 0121 246 7000 ✉ clerks@st-philips.com
Call Date: July 1982, Lincoln's Inn
Pupil Supervisor
Qualifications: [LLB]
pmytton@st-philips.com

NABI MR SAJJAD

5 Pump Court
Ground Floor, 5 Pump Court, Temple, London EC4Y 7AP, ☎ 020 7353 2532
✉ clerks@5pumpcourt.com
Call Date: Oct 2003, Middle Temple
Qualifications: [LLB (Hons) (Nott'm)]
sajjadnabi@5pumpcourt.com

NABI MR ZIA UL-HAQ

1 Pump Court
Elm Court, Temple, London EC4Y 7AB,
☎ 020 7842 7070
✉ (name)@pumpcourt.co.uk
Call Date: Nov 1991, Middle Temple
Pupil Supervisor
Qualifications: [LLB (Hons)(Essex)]

NABIJOU DR SHERRY

10 King's Bench Walk
Ground Floor, 10 King's Bench Walk, Temple, London EC4Y 7EB, ☎ 020 7353 7742
✉ Chambers@10kingsbenchwalk.co.uk
Call Date: Oct 1996, Inner Temple
Qualifications: [BSc (Leeds) MScDIC PhD (Lond) CPE]
chambers@10kingsbenchwalk.co.uk

NADIM MR AHMED

Lincoln House Chambers
Tower 12, The Avenue North, Spinningfields, 18-22 Bridge Street, Manchester M3 3BZ,
☎ 0161 832 5701
✉ info@lincolnhousechambers.com
Call Date: July 1982, Lincoln's Inn
Pupil Supervisor
Qualifications: [BA]

NADIN MR JAMES

One Essex Court
Ground Floor, One Essex Court, Temple, London EC4Y 9AR, ☎ 020 7583 2000
✉ clerks@oeclaw.co.uk
Call Date: Nov 2002, Lincoln's Inn
Qualifications: [MA (Cantab) BCL (Oxon)]
jnadin@oeclaw.co.uk

NAGPAL MR DEEPAK

1 KBW Chambers
1 King's Bench Walk, Temple, London EC4Y 7DB, ☎ 020 7936 1500
✉ clerks@1kbw.co.uk
King's Bench Chambers
174 High Street, Lewes BN7 1YE,
☎ 01273 402600
Call Date: Oct 2002, Lincoln's Inn
Qualifications: [MA (Oxon) BCL (Oxon)]
dnagpal@1kbw.co.uk

NAIDOO MISS MAYA LAKSHMI

Garden Court Chambers
57-60 Lincoln's Inn Fields, London WC2A 3LJ,
☎ 020 7993 7600 ✉ info@gclaw.co.uk
Call Date: Nov 2002, Middle Temple
Qualifications: [LLM BA (Hons) (Oxon) CPE]
mayan@gclaw.co.uk

NAIK MR GAURANG RAMANLAL

The Chambers of Grahame Aldous QC
9 Gough Square, London EC4A 3DG,
☎ 020 7832 0500
✉ clerks@9goughsquare.co.uk
Call Date: July 1985, Gray's Inn
Pupil Supervisor
Qualifications: [BSc Dip Law]
gnaik@9goughsquare.co.uk

NAIK MISS SONALI

Garden Court Chambers
57-60 Lincoln's Inn Fields, London WC2A 3LJ,
☎ 020 7993 7600 ✉ info@gclaw.co.uk
Call Date: Nov 1991, Middle Temple
Pupil Supervisor
Qualifications: [BA (Hons)(Oxon)]
sonalin@gclaw.co.uk

NAIK MR TIMOTHY ANIL

4 Breams Buildings
Chancery Lane, London EC4A 1HP,
☎ 020 7092 1900 ✉ clerks@4bb.co.uk
Call Date: Nov 1994, Gray's Inn
Pupil Supervisor
Qualifications: [LLB (Hons)]

NAISH MR CHRISTOPHER JOHN

Southernhay Chambers
33 Southernhay East, Exeter EX1 1NX, ☎01392 255777
✉clerks@southernhaychambers.co.uk
Call Date: July 1980, Inner Temple
Pupil Supervisor
Qualifications: [LLB]
✉c.naish@southernhaychambers.co.uk

NAJIB MR MOHAMMED SHAKIL

St Philips Chambers
55 Temple Row, Birmingham B2 5LS, ☎0121 246 7000 ✉clerks@st-philips.com
Call Date: Oct 1999, Lincoln's Inn
Qualifications: [LLB (Hons)(B'ham) LLM (Lond)]
✉snajib@st-philips.co.uk

NALL-CAIN THE HON RICHARD CHRISTOPHER PHILIP

St Albans Chambers
2 - 4 St Peter's Street, St Albans, Hertfordshire AL1 3LF, ☎01727 843383
✉clerks@stalbanschambers.com
Call Date: Oct 1997, Inner Temple
Pupil Supervisor
Qualifications: [LLB (Hons)(Herts) LLM Dip Law]
✉rnc@stalbanschambers.com

NAMBISAN MR DEEPAK DAMODARAN

Fountain Court Chambers
Fountain Court, Temple, London EC4Y 9DH, ☎020 7583 3335
✉chambers@fountaincourt.co.uk
Call Date: Oct 1998, Gray's Inn
Qualifications: [BA (Hons) (Cantab) BCL (Oxon) LLM (Lond)]
✉dnambisan@fountaincourt.co.uk

NANAYAKKARA MS DINALI SAMANTHIKA

New Court
Ground Floor, New Court, Temple, London EC4Y 9BE, ☎020 7583 5123
✉clerks@newcourtchambers.com
Call Date: July 2000, Inner Temple
Qualifications: [BSc (Herts) CPE]
✉dnanayakkara@newcourtchambers.com

NANCE MR FRANCIS PETER

Exchange Chambers
One Derby Square, Derby Square, Liverpool L2 9XX, ☎0151 236 7747
✉info@exchangechambers.co.uk
Exchange Chambers
7 Ralli Courts, West Riverside, Manchester M3 5FT, ☎0161 833 2722
Exchange Chambers
Oxford House, Oxford Row, Leeds LS1 3BE, ☎0113 203 1970
✉spencer@exchangechambers.co.uk
Call Date: Nov 1970, Gray's Inn
Pupil Supervisor
✉nance@exchangechambers.co.uk

NANHOO-ROBINSON MISS AMANDA MARQUARITE

Great Russell Street Chambers
265, 10 Great Russell Street, London WC1B 3BQ, ☎020 3239 0650/07581 248366
Call Date: July 2000, Gray's Inn
Qualifications: [LL.B (Leeds) MA]
✉anmrobinson@hotmail.com

NAPIER PROF BRIAN WILLIAM

Cloisters
1 Pump Court, Temple, London EC4Y 7AA, ☎020 7827 4000 ✉clerks@cloisters.com
Call Date: July 1990, Middle Temple
Qualifications: [MA LLB (Edin) PhD (Cantab)]
✉bn@cloisters.com

NAPTHINE MR DAVID ROBERT GUY

1 High Pavement
Nottingham NG1 1HF, ☎0115 941 8218
✉clerks@1highpavement.co.uk
Call Date: Nov 1979, Inner Temple
Pupil Supervisor
Qualifications: [BA]
✉guynapthine@1highpavement.co.uk

NAQSHBANDI MISS SABA SHAFIQUE

3 Raymond Buildings
3 Raymond Buildings, Gray's Inn, London WC1R 5BH, ☎020 7400 6400
✉clerks@3rblaw.com
Call Date: Oct 1996, Middle Temple
Pupil Supervisor
Qualifications: [LLB (Hons) LLM (Lond)]
✉saba.naqshbandi@3raymondbuildings.com

E

NARAIN MR BENJAMIN ROBERT

Doughty Street Chambers
53-54 Doughty Street, London WC1N 2LS,
☎020 7404 1313
✉enquiries@doughtystreet.co.uk
Doughty Street Chambers
Pall Mall Court, 61-67 King Street, Manchester M2 4PD, ☎0161 618 1066
Doughty Street Chambers
5th Floor, Broad Quay House, Prince Street, Bristol BS1 4DJ, ☎01179 058 717
Call Date: Nov 1999, Middle Temple
Qualifications: [LLB (Hons)(LSE)]
b.narain@doughtystreet.co.uk

NARAYAN MR HIRANYA GARBHA

Cobden House Chambers
19 Quay Street, Manchester M3 3HN,
☎0161 833 6000 ✉Clerks@Cobden.co.uk
Call Date: Nov 1970, Lincoln's Inn
Pupil Supervisor
clerks@cobden.co.uk

NARDELL MR GORDON LAWRENCE QC (2010)

39 Essex Street
London WC2R 3AT, ☎020 7832 1111
✉clerks@39essex.com
82 King Street
Manchester M2 4WQ, ☎0161 870 9969
Call Date: Nov 1995, Inner Temple
Qualifications: [LLB (Hons)(Leeds)]
gordon.nardell@39essex.com

Fax: 020 7353 3978;
Out of hours telephone: 07711 351093;
DX: 298 London, Chancery Lane;
Other comms: E-mail:
gordon.nardell@39essex.com
URL: www.39essex.com

Types of work: Administrative law, Civil liberties, Commercial litigation, EC competition law, Environment, Financial services, Parliamentary, Planning, Telecommunications

NARTEY MISS ELIZABETH

Argent Chambers
5 Bell Yard, London WC2A 2JR,
☎020 7556 5500
✉briefsin@argentchambers.co.uk
Call Date: Mar 2003, Middle Temple
Qualifications: [BA (Hons) (Sheff)]
e.nartey@argentchambers.co.uk

NASH MS ALICE

Hailsham Chambers
Ground Floor, 4 Paper Buildings, Temple, London EC4Y 7EX, ☎020 7643 5000
✉clerks@hailshamchambers.com
Call Date: July 2006, Inner Temple
Qualifications: [BA (Oxon) CPe]
Alice.Nash@hailshamchambers.com

NASH MS EMMA JANE

2 Pump Court
1st Floor, 2 Pump Court, Temple, London EC4Y 7AH, ☎020 7353 5597
✉clerks@2pumpcourt.co.uk
Call Date: July 2001, Inner Temple
Qualifications: [LLB (Plymouth)]
enash@2pumpcourt.co.uk

NASH MR JONATHAN SCOTT QC (2006)

3 Verulam Buildings
London WC1R 5NT, ☎020 7831 8441
✉chambers@3vb.com
Call Date: Nov 1986, Gray's Inn
Qualifications: [BA(Oxon)]
jnash@3vb.com

NASH MISS LAURA JANE

St Johns Buildings
24a - 28 St John Street, Manchester M3 4DJ,
☎0161 214 1500
✉clerk@stjohnsbuildings.co.uk
St Johns Buildings
21 White Friars, Chester CH1 1NZ,
☎01244 323070
✉clerk@stjohnsbuildings.co.uk
St Johns Buildings Liverpool
8th Floor India Buildings, Water Street, Liverpool L2 0XG, ☎0151 243 6000
✉clerk@stjohnsbuildings.co.uk
Call Date: Oct 2009, Lincoln's Inn
Qualifications: [LLB (B'ham)]
laura.nash@stjohnsbuildings.co.uk

NASHASHIBI MR ANWAR DAVID

Seven Bedford Row
7 Bedford Row, London WC1R 4BS,
☎020 7242 3555 ✉clerks@7br.co.uk
Call Date: Nov 1995, Middle Temple
Qualifications: [BA (Hons)(Manch)]
anashashibi@7br.co.uk

NASIM MR ZIA-UL-MUSTAFA

Milestone Chambers
267 High Road, London NW10 2RX
Call Date: July 2001, Lincoln's Inn
Qualifications: [LLB (Hons) (Lond)]

E

NASSAR MISS VICTORIA KATIE

Fortis Green Chambers
Hillcroft, Wilmslow Park South, Wilmslow SK9 2AY, ☎0161 439 5804
✉victorianassar@yahoo.co.uk
Call Date: Feb 1994, Gray's Inn
Qualifications: [BSc (Hons)]

NATH MR RAKESH

Strand Chambers
226 The Strand, London WC2R 1BA, ☎020 7117 6920 ✉Henry@lawsurgery.com
Call Date: July 1985, Inner Temple
Pupil Supervisor
Qualifications: [LLB (Lond)]

NATHAN MISS APARNA

Gray's Inn Tax Chambers
3rd Floor, Gray's Inn Chambers, Gray's Inn, London WC1R 5JA, ☎020 7242 2642
✉clerks@taxbar.com
Call Date: Nov 1994, Middle Temple
Pupil Supervisor
Qualifications: [LLB (Hons) LLM]
✉an@taxbar.com

NATHAN MR DAVID BRIAN QC (2002)

Zenith Chambers
10 Park Square, Leeds LS1 2LH, ☎0113 245 5438
✉clerks@zenithchambers.co.uk
Argent Chambers
5 Bell Yard, London WC2A 2JR, ☎020 7556 5500
✉briefsin@argentchambers.co.uk
Call Date: Nov 1971, Middle Temple
Qualifications: [LLB]

NATHAN MR PHILIP GABRIEL

Landmark Chambers
180 Fleet Street, London EC4A 2HG, ☎020 7430 1221
✉clerks@landmarkchambers.co.uk
Call Date: Mar 1996, Lincoln's Inn
Qualifications: [LLB (Hons)]
✉pnathan@landmarkchambers.co.uk

NATHAN MR STEPHEN ANDREW QC (1993)

Blackstone Chambers
Blackstone House, Temple, London EC4Y 9BW, ☎020 7583 1770
✉clerks@blackstonechambers.com
Call Date: Nov 1969, Middle Temple
Recorder
Qualifications: [MA (Oxon)]

NATHWANI MR RISHI NAREMDRAKUMAR

5 King's Bench Walk
5 King's Bench Walk, Temple, London EC4Y 7DN, ☎020 7353 5638
✉clerks@5kbw.co.uk
Call Date: July 2006, Middle Temple
Qualifications: [LLB (Hons) (Brunel)]

NAUGHTON MS LIANNE EVE

Number 7 Harrington Street Chambers
7 Harrington Street, Liverpool L2 9YH, ☎0151 242 0707 ✉clerks@7hs.co.uk
Call Date: Oct 1999, Inner Temple
Qualifications: [LLB (Hull)]
✉lianne.naughton@7hs.co.uk

NAUGHTON MR SEBASTIAN HUGH JOSEPH

42 Bedford Row
London WC1R 4LL, ☎020 7831 0222
✉clerks@42br.com
Call Date: Nov 1999, Gray's Inn
Pupil Supervisor
Qualifications: [BA (Bris)]
✉sebastian.naughton@42br.com

NAWAZ MR MOHAMMED

Lincoln House Chambers
Tower 12, The Avenue North, Spinningfields, 18-22 Bridge Street, Manchester M3 3BZ, ☎0161 832 5701
✉info@lincolnhousechambers.com
Call Date: Nov 1995, Lincoln's Inn
Qualifications: [LLB LLM (Cantab)]
✉mohammed.nawaz@lincolnhousechambers.com

NAWBATT MR AKASH VEDANT

Devereux Chambers
Queen Elizabeth Building, Temple, London EC4Y 9BS, ☎020 7353 7534
✉clerks@devchambers.co.uk
Call Date: Oct 1999, Gray's Inn
Pupil Supervisor
Qualifications: [BA (Cantab)]
✉nawbatt@devchambers.co.uk

NAYLOR DR KEVIN MICHAEL THOMAS

Exchange Chambers
7 Ralli Courts, West Riverside, Manchester M3 5FT, ☎0161 833 2722
Exchange Chambers
One Derby Square, Derby Square, Liverpool L2 9XX, ☎0151 236 7747
✉info@exchangechambers.co.uk

E

Exchange Chambers
Oxford House, Oxford Row, Leeds LS1 3BE,
☎0113 203 1970
✉spencer@exchangechambers.co.uk
Call Date: Oct 1992, Lincoln's Inn
Pupil Supervisor
Qualifications: [MB ChB LLB(Hons)(Sheff) LLM MRCGP]

NAYLOR MR MARTYN JAMES

4 Pump Court
4 Pump Court, Temple, London EC4Y 7AN,
☎020 7842 5555
✉chambers@4pumpcourt.com
Call Date: July 2009, Inner Temple
Qualifications: [BA (Cantab) LLM (Berkeley)]

NAYLOR MR TIMOTHY REX

QEB Hollis Whiteman
1-2 Laurence Pountney Hill, London EC4R 0EU, ☎020 7933 8855
✉barristers@qebhw.co.uk
Call Date: July 2010, Middle Temple
Qualifications: [BA (Hons) (USA)]
tim.naylor@qebhw.co.uk

E

NAZARETH MISS MELANIE BERNADETTE

Renaissance Chambers
5th Floor, Gray's Inn Chambers, Gray's Inn, London WC1R 5JA, ☎020 7404 1111
✉clerks@renaissancechambers.co.uk
Call Date: July 1984, Inner Temple
Qualifications: [BSc (Lond) Dip Law]
mn@renaissancechambers.co.uk

NAZIR MR KAISER

Park Lane Plowden
19 Westgate, Leeds LS1 2RD,
☎0113 228 5049
✉clerks@parklaneplowden.co.uk
Call Date: Nov 1991, Lincoln's Inn
Qualifications: [LLB (Hons)]
kaiser.nazir@parklaneplowden.co.uk

NDLOVU MR LAZARUS

12 Old Square Chambers
1st Floor, 12 Old Square, Lincoln's Inn, London WC2A 3TX, ☎020 7404 0875
✉clerks@12oldsquare.com
Call Date: July 1979, Lincoln's Inn
Qualifications: [BA LLM (Lond)]
clerks@12oldsquare.com

NEAL PROF ALAN CHRISTOPHER

New Street Chambers
2 New Street, Leicester LE1 5NA,
☎0116 262 5906 ✉clerks@2newstreet.co.uk
Cloisters
1 Pump Court, Temple, London EC4Y 7AA,
☎020 7827 4000 ✉clerks@cloisters.com
Call Date: July 1975, Gray's Inn
Qualifications: [LLB (Warkw) LLM (Lond) DGLS (Sweden)]

NEALE MISS FIONA ROSALIND

Hailsham Chambers
Ground Floor, 4 Paper Buildings, Temple, London EC4Y 7EX, ☎020 7643 5000
✉clerks@hailshamchambers.com
Call Date: July 1981, Middle Temple
Pupil Supervisor
Qualifications: [LLB (Lond)]

NEALE MR NICHOLAS LAWRENCE

Call Date: July 1972, Gray's Inn
Qualifications: [BA]
neale@paradise-sq.co.uk

NEAMAN MR SAMUEL LISTER

Littleton Chambers
3 King's Bench Walk North, Temple, London EC4Y 7HR, ☎020 7797 8600
✉fschneider@littletonchambers.co.uk
Call Date: July 1988, Inner Temple
Pupil Supervisor
Qualifications: [MA (Oxon) Dip Law (Lond)]
sneaman@littletonchambers.co.uk

NEATHEY MISS RONA VANESSA

6 King's Bench Walk
Ground, Third & Fourth Floors, 6 King's Bench Walk, Temple, London EC4Y 7DR,
☎020 7353 4931 ✉clerks@6kbw.co.uk
Call Date: Nov 1990, Inner Temple
Qualifications: [LLB (Hons)]
rona.neathey@6kbw.co.uk

NEAVES MR ANDREW MICHAEL

St Philips Chambers
55 Temple Row, Birmingham B2 5LS,
☎0121 246 7000 ✉clerks@st-philips.com
Call Date: July 1977, Gray's Inn
Pupil Supervisor
Qualifications: [LLB (Leics)]
aneaves@st-philips.co.uk

NEEDHAM MRS JULIA CHERRY

10 King's Bench Walk
Ground Floor, 10 King's Bench Walk, Temple, London EC4Y 7EB, ☎020 7353 7742
✉Chambers@10kingsbenchwalk.co.uk
Call Date: Nov 2000, Middle Temple
Qualifications: [BA (Hons) (Manch) CPE] •
✉Julia.needham@10kingsbenchwalk.co.uk

NEENAN MISS LESLEY

Brompton Chambers
1st Floor, 353A Station Road, Harrow, Middlesex HA1 1LN, ☎0560 3685647
✉bromptonchamber@aol.com
Call Date: Nov 1990, Inner Temple
Qualifications: [LLB (Hons)]

NEIL MISS JENNIFER ELIZABETH

Five Paper Buildings
1st Floor, Five Paper Buildings, Temple, London EC4Y 7HB, ☎020 7583 6117
✉clerks@5pb.co.uk
Call Date: July 2010, Middle Temple
Qualifications: [BA (Hons) (Cantab)]

NEILL DR DANIEL JAMES

Guildhall Chambers
23 Broad Street, Bristol BS1 2HG,
☎0117 930 9000
✉hoc@guildhallchambers.co.uk
Call Date: Mar 2008, Lincoln's Inn
Qualifications: [BA MA (Cantab) PhD (Cantab)]
✉daniel.neill@guildhallchambers.co.uk

NEILL MISS EMILY CHARLOTTE

Blackstone Chambers
Blackstone House, Temple, London EC4Y 9BW, ☎020 7583 1770
✉clerks@blackstonechambers.com
Call Date: Nov 2008, Inner Temple
Qualifications: [BA (Oxon) CPE]
✉emilyneill@blackstonechambers.com

NEILL MR ROBIN CHARLES RICHARD

St John's Chambers
101 Victoria Street, Bristol BS1 6PU,
☎0117 923 4700
✉clerks@stjohnschambers.co.uk
Call Date: July 1979, Gray's Inn
Qualifications: [LLI, ucb]
✉robin.neill@stjohnschambers.co.uk

NEILL OF BLADEN LORD FRANCIS PATRICK QC (1966)

20 Essex Street
London WC2R 3AL, ☎020 7842 1200
✉clerks@20essexst.com
Call Date: Nov 1951, Gray's Inn
Qualifications: [BCL DCL (Oxon) MA (Hons)]
✉clerks@20essexst.com, pneill@20essexst.com

NEISH MR ANDREW GRAHAM QC (2009)

4 Pump Court
4 Pump Court, Temple, London EC4Y 7AN,
☎020 7842 5555
✉chambers@4pumpcourt.com
Call Date: July 1988, Lincoln's Inn
Qualifications: [MA (Hons) (St Andrews) Dip Law]
✉aneish@4pumpcourt.com

NELSON MR CAIRNS LOUIS DAVID QC (2010)

23 Essex Street
London WC2R 3AA, ☎020 7413 0353
✉clerks@23es.com
Call Date: Nov 1987, Gray's Inn
Pupil Supervisor, Recorder
Qualifications: [LLB (Lond)]
✉cairnsnelson@23es.com

NELSON MR GILES YORICK

Albion Chambers
Broad Street, Bristol BS1 1DR,
☎0117 927 2144
✉clerks@albionchambers.co.uk
Call Date: Feb 1995, Inner Temple
Qualifications: [BSc (Bris) CPE]
✉giles.nelson@albionchambers.co.uk

NELSON MS JULIA MARIA

Park Lane Plowden
19 Westgate, Leeds LS1 2RD,
☎0113 228 5049
✉clerks@parklaneplowden.co.uk
Call Date: Nov 1993, Gray's Inn
Pupil Supervisor
Qualifications: [BA (Manch)]
✉julia.nelson@parklaneplowden.co.uk

NELSON MISS LINDA SINEAD

The Chambers of Grahame Aldous QC
9 Gough Square, London EC4A 3DG,
☎020 7832 0500
✉clerks@9goughsquare.co.uk
Call Date: July 2000, Gray's Inn
Qualifications: [LLB (Exon)]
✉lnelson@9goughsquare.co.uk

E

NELSON MISS MICHELLE

18 Red Lion Court
London EC4A 3EB, ☎020 7520 6000
✉chambers@18rlc.co.uk
18 Red Lion Court (Annexe)
Thornwood House, 102 New London Road, Chelmsford, Essex CM2 0RG,
☎01245 280880
Call Date: Oct 1994, Middle Temple
Qualifications: [BSc (Hons)(Brunel) LLB (Hons)(Lond)]
Michelle.nelson@18rlc.co.uk

NELSON MR VINCENT LEONARD QC (2001)

39 Essex Street
London WC2R 3AT, ☎020 7832 1111
✉clerks@39essex.com
Call Date: Nov 1980, Inner Temple
Qualifications: [LLB]
vincent.nelson@39essex.com

NELSON ROHRER MR KERRON XAVER

E

Exchange Chambers
One Derby Square, Derby Square, Liverpool L2 9XX, ☎0151 236 7747
✉info@exchangechambers.co.uk
Exchange Chambers
7 Ralli Courts, West Riverside, Manchester M3 5FT, ☎0161 833 2722
Exchange Chambers
Oxford House, Oxford Row, Leeds LS1 3BE,
☎0113 203 1970
✉spencer@exchangechambers.co.uk
Call Date: Oct 2005, Inner Temple
Qualifications: [BA London School of Economics & Political Science]
rohrer@exchangechambers.co.uk

NERESHRAAJ MR SRIKANTHARAJAH

Tooks Chambers
81 Farringdon Street, London EC4A 4BL,
☎020 7842 7575 ✉clerks@tooks.co.uk
Call Date: July 2007, Gray's Inn
Qualifications: [MA (Edin) LLB (Lond)]

NERSESSIAN MR TIRAN

4 Stone Buildings
Ground Floor, 4 Stone Buildings, Lincoln's Inn, London WC2A 3XT, ☎020 7242 5524
✉clerks@4stonebuildings.com
Call Date: Nov 2002, Lincoln's Inn
Qualifications: [BA (Hons)(Oxon)]
clerks@4stonebuildings.com

NESBITT MR TIMOTHY JOHN ROBERT

Outer Temple Chambers
The Outer Temple, 222 Strand, London WC2R 1BA, ☎020 7353 6381
✉clerks@outertemple.com
Call Date: Feb 1991, Middle Temple
Qualifications: [BA (Dunelm) Dip Law (Lond) LLM (Lond)]
tim.nesbitt@outertemple.com

NETTLESHIP MISS HELEN

33 Bedford Row
London WC1R 4JH, ☎020 7242 6476
✉clerks@33bedfordrow.co.uk
Call Date: Mar 2009, Inner Temple
Qualifications: [LLB]

NEUBERGER MR EDMUND PHILIP JAMES

Atkin Chambers
1 Atkin Building, Gray's Inn, London WC1R 5AT, ☎020 7404 0102
✉clerks@atkinchambers.com
Call Date: July 2008, Lincoln's Inn
Qualifications: [MENG]

NEUBERT MR JOLYON NICHOLAS

1 Gray's Inn Square
Ground Floor, 1 Gray's Inn Square, London WC1R 5AA, ☎020 7405 0001
Call Date: July 1989, Middle Temple
Qualifications: [LLB (Hons)]

NEUFELD MISS MICHAELA

Chambers of Ms M Neufeld
PO Box 6017, Milton Keynes MK1 9AP,
☎01908 330 134 ✉clerks@barristerweb.com
Call Date: July 1990, Middle Temple
Qualifications: [LLB (Lond)]

NEVILL MS PENELOPE JUNE

20 Essex Street
London WC2R 3AL, ☎020 7842 1200
✉clerks@20essexst.com
Call Date: July 2010, Middle Temple
Qualifications: [LLB (Hons) (Auckland) LLM (Auckland)]

NEVILLE MR JOSEPH RICHARD

43 Temple Row Chambers
6th Floor, 43 Temple Row, Birmingham B2 5LS, ☎0121 237 6035
✉clerks@43templerow.co.uk
Call Date: Nov 2007, Lincoln's Inn
Qualifications: [LLB (Hull)]

NEVILLE MR STEPHEN JOHN

Gough Square Chambers
6-7 Gough Square, London EC4A 3DE,
☎020 7353 0924 ✉gsc@goughsq.co.uk
Call Date: Nov 1986, Middle Temple
Pupil Supervisor
Qualifications: [MA(Cantab)]
✉stephen.neville@goughsq.co.uk

NEVILLE-CLARKE MR SEBASTIAN ADRIAN BENNETT

3 Hare Court
3 Hare Court, Temple, London EC4Y 7BJ,
☎020 7415 7800 ✉clerks@3harecourt.com
Call Date: Nov 1973, Inner Temple
Pupil Supervisor
Qualifications: [BA (Oxon)]
✉snevilleclarke@3harecourt.com

NEWBEGIN MS NICOLA LOUISE

Old Square Chambers
10-11 Bedford Row, London WC1R 4BU,
☎020 7269 0300 ✉clerks@oldsquare.co.uk
Old Square Chambers
3 Orchard Court, St Augustine's Yard, Bristol BS1 5DP, ☎0117 930 5100
✉clerks@oldsquare.co.uk
Call Date: July 2008, Middle Temple
Qualifications: [BA (Hons) (Oxon)]
✉newbegin@oldsquare.co.uk

NEWBERRY MR CLIVE DOUGLAS QC (1993)

Francis Taylor Building
Inner Temple, London EC4Y 7BY,
☎020 7353 8415 ✉clerks@ftb.eu.com
Call Date: July 1978, Inner Temple
Qualifications: [FRSA]
✉clive.newberry@ftb.eu.com

NEWBERY MISS FREYA PATRICIA

12 King's Bench Walk
12 King's Bench Walk, Temple, London EC4Y 7EL, ☎020 7583 0811
Call Date: Nov 1986, Middle Temple
Pupil Supervisor, Recorder
Qualifications: [MA (Cantab)]
✉newbery@12kbw.co.uk

NEWBOLD DR ANNE LORRAINE ELSIE

Minerva Chambers
704 Grand Ocean Plaza, Ocean Village☎00 350 20042779
✉l.newbold@minervachambers.com
Call Date: Nov 1990, Lincoln's Inn
Pupil Supervisor
Qualifications: [LLB PhD (Lond)]

NEWBOLD MR MICHAEL PAUL

9-12 Bell Yard
London WC2A 2JR, ☎020 7400 1800
✉clerks@9-12bellyard.com
Call Date: July 2004, Inner Temple
Qualifications: [BA (Oxon)]
✉m.newbold@9-12bellyard.com

NEWCOMB MRS JENNIFER ELIZABETH

The Chambers of Grahame Aldous QC
9 Gough Square, London EC4A 3DG,
☎020 7832 0500
✉clerks@9goughsquare.co.uk
Call Date: July 2006, Inner Temple
Qualifications: [LLB (Nottingham)]
✉jnewcomb@9goughsquare.co.uk

NEWCOMB MR QUINTON JOHN

1 Paper Buildings
1st Floor, 1 Paper Buildings, Temple, London EC4Y 7EP, ☎020 7353 3728
✉clerks@onepaper.co.uk
Call Date: July 2005, Middle Temple
Qualifications: [LLB (Hons)]

NEWCOMBE MR ANDREW BENNETT QC (2010)

Francis Taylor Building
Inner Temple, London EC4Y 7BY,
☎020 7353 8415 ✉clerks@ftb.eu.com
Call Date: July 1987, Middle Temple
Pupil Supervisor
Qualifications: [BA (Dunelm)]
✉andrew.newcombe@ftb.eu.com

NEWCOMBE MR PAUL ANTHONY

Old Court Chambers
Newham House, 96-98 Borough Road, Middlesbrough TS1 2HJ, ☎01642 232523
✉clerks@oldcourtchambers.com
Call Date: Feb 1991, Inner Temple
Qualifications: [LLB (Hons)(Law)]
✉clerks@oldcourtchambers.com

NEWCOMBE MR ROBERT WILLIAM

7 Bell Yard
London WC2A 2JR, ☎020 7831 0636
✉kevintarrant@btconnect.com
Call Date: May 1996, Lincoln's Inn
Qualifications: [LLB (Hons)]

E

NEWDICK PROF CHRISTOPHER

No5 Chambers
Fountain Court, Steelhouse Lane, Birmingham B4 6DR, ☎0845 210 5555 ✉info@no5.com
No5 Chambers
Greenwood House, 4-7 Salisbury Court, London EC4Y 8AA, ☎0845 210 5555
No5 Chambers
38 Queen Square, Bristol BS1 4QS, ☎0845 210 5555
Call Date: Feb 1983, Gray's Inn
Qualifications: [BA LLM (Lond)]

NEWELL MISS CHARLOTTE ANNE

5 King's Bench Walk
5 King's Bench Walk, Temple, London EC4Y 7DN, ☎020 7353 5638
✉clerks@5kbw.co.uk
Call Date: Oct 1994, Gray's Inn
Pupil Supervisor
Qualifications: [LLB (Hons)]
charlotte.newell@5kbw.co.uk

NEWELL MR GILES JAMES BANKS

Tooks Chambers
81 Farringdon Street, London EC4A 4BL, ☎020 7842 7575 ✉clerks@tooks.co.uk
Call Date: Mar 2007, Middle Temple
Qualifications: [BA (Hons) (Cantab) MA (Cantab)]
giles.newell@tooks.co.uk

NEWMAN MR ALAN RONALD HARVEY QC (1989)

Argent Chambers
5 Bell Yard, London WC2A 2JR, ☎020 7556 5500
✉briefsin@argentchambers.co.uk
Call Date: Nov 1968, Middle Temple
Qualifications: [MA LLB (Cantab)]

NEWMAN MS ANYA HELEN

St Ive's Chambers
Whittall Street, Birmingham B4 6DH, ☎0121 236 0863
✉clerks@stiveschambers.co.uk
Call Date: July 2007, Inner Temple
Qualifications: [LLB (B'ham)]

NEWMAN MR AUSTIN ERIC

Zenith Chambers
10 Park Square, Leeds LS1 2LH, ☎0113 245 5438
✉clerks@zenithchambers.co.uk
Call Date: Nov 1987, Inner Temple
Qualifications: [LLB LLM]
anewman@zenithchambers.co.uk

NEWMAN MISS CATHERINE MARY QC (1995)

Maitland Chambers
7 Stone Buildings, Lincoln's Inn, London WC2A 3SZ, ☎020 7406 1200
✉clerks@maitlandchambers.com
Call Date: July 1979, Middle Temple
Recorder
Qualifications: [LLB (Hons) (Lond)]
cnewman@maitlandchambers.com

NEWMAN MR CHRISTOPHER ROGER

Littleton Chambers
3 King's Bench Walk North, Temple, London EC4Y 7HR, ☎020 7797 8600
✉fschneider@littletonchambers.co.uk
Call Date: Nov 2003, Inner Temple
Qualifications: [BA, MEng (Cantab)]
cnewman@littletonchambers.co.uk

NEWMAN MR JAMES ANDREW

Ely Place Chambers
30 Ely Place, London EC1N 6TD, ☎020 7400 9600 ✉admin@elyplace.com
Call Date: July 2000, Gray's Inn
Qualifications: [LLB (Hons)(Leic)]
jnewman@elyplace.com

NEWMAN MR JONATHAN PHILIP SIMEON

42 Bedford Row
London WC1R 4LL, ☎020 7831 0222
✉clerks@42br.com
Call Date: July 2009, Middle Temple
Qualifications: [BA (Hons) (Cantab)]
Jonathan.Newman@42br.com

NEWMAN MR PAUL

3 PB Barristers
3 Paper Buildings, Temple, London EC4Y 7EU, ☎020 7583 8055
3 PB Barristers
30 Christchurch Road, Bournemouth, Dorset BH1 3PD, ☎01202 292102
✉clerks.bournemouth@3paper.co.uk
3 PB Barristers
4 St Peter Street, Winchester SO23 8BW, ☎01962 868884
✉clerks.winchester@3paper.co.uk
3 PB Barristers
Royal Talbot House, 2 Victoria Street, Bristol, Avon BS1 6BB, ☎0117 928 1520

3 PB Barristers
23 Beaumont Street, Oxford OX1 2NP,
☎01865 793 736
Call Date: Nov 1982, Gray's Inn
Qualifications: [MA (Cantab) Dip Law (Lond) FCIArb]
paul.newman@3paper.co.uk

NEWMAN MR PAUL LANCE QC (2009)

Wilberforce Chambers
8 New Square, Lincoln's Inn, London WC2A 3QP, ☎020 7306 0102
✉chambers@wilberforce.co.uk
Call Date: Oct 1991, Lincoln's Inn
Qualifications: [MA (Hons) (Cantab) LLM (USA)]
pnewman@wilberforce.co.uk

NEWMAN MR PETER ROBERT

1 KBW Chambers
1 King's Bench Walk, Temple, London EC4Y 7DB, ☎020 7936 1500
✉clerks@1kbw.co.uk
King's Bench Chambers
174 High Street, Lewes BN7 1YE,
☎01273 402600
Call Date: July 2005, Inner Temple
Qualifications: [BA University of Liverpool LLB City University]
pnewman@1kbw.co.uk

NEWMAN MR PHILIP ADRIAN

42 Bedford Row
London WC1R 4LL, ☎020 7831 0222
✉clerks@42br.com
Call Date: Nov 1977, Gray's Inn
Pupil Supervisor
Qualifications: [QDR LLM (Lond) FCIArb DiplCArb]
philip.newman@42br.com

NEWMAN MISS REBECCA JANE

Clerksroom (Taunton)
Equity House, Administration Centre, Blackbrook Park Avenue, Taunton, Somerset TA1 2PX, ☎0845 083 3000
✉mail@clerksroom.com
King's Lynn Chambers
26 The Birches, South Wootton, King's Lynn, Norfolk PE30 3JG, ☎01553 672 085
✉timothy.leader@tesco.net
Call Date: Nov 1991, Lincoln's Inn
Qualifications: [LLB (Hons) (Wales) LLM (Edin)]
newman@clerksroom.com

NEWMAN MR TIMOTHY JOHN

No5 Chambers
Fountain Court, Steelhouse Lane, Birmingham B4 6DR, ☎0845 210 5555 ✉info@no5.com
No5 Chambers
Greenwood House, 4-7 Salisbury Court, London EC4Y 8AA, ☎0845 210 5555
No5 Chambers
38 Queen Square, Bristol BS1 4QS,
☎0845 210 5555
Call Date: July 1981, Gray's Inn
Qualifications: [BA]
tn@no5.com

NEWMAN MRS VERONICA

Chambers of Mrs V Newman
77 Roath Court Road, Roath, Cardiff CF24 3SF, ☎029 2048 8797
✉newmanv@tiscali.co.uk
Call Date: Nov 1984, Gray's Inn
Qualifications: [BA DipLaw]

NEWNHAM MISS MARY JANE

12 King's Bench Walk
12 King's Bench Walk, Temple, London EC4Y 7EL, ☎020 7583 0811
Call Date: Nov 2003, Lincoln's Inn
Qualifications: [MA (Oxon) CPE]
newnham@12kbw.co.uk

NEWPORT MR IAN ALUN

College Chambers
19 Carlton Crescent, Southampton, Hampshire SO15 2ET, ☎023 8023 0338
✉clerks@college-chambers.co.uk
Call Date: Oct 2000, Gray's Inn
Pupil Supervisor
Qualifications: [LLB (Wales) LLM (Wales)]
inewport@college-chambers.co.uk

NEWPORT MR MICHAEL ANDREW

Chambers of Mr Ami Feder
Ground Floor, Lamb Building, Temple, London EC4Y 7AS, ☎020 7797 7788
✉clerks@lambbuilding.co.uk
Lamb Building
22 Ship Street, Brighton BN1 1AD,
☎01273 820490
✉admin@lambbuilding.co.uk
Chambers of Mr Ami Feder
Ground Floor, Lamb Building, Temple, London EC4Y 7AS, ☎020 7797 7788
✉clerks@lambbuilding.co.uk
Call Date: July 1999, Middle Temple
Qualifications: [BSc (Hons)]
clerks@lambbuilding.co.uk

E

NEWSOM MR GEORGE LUCIEN

Guildhall Chambers
23 Broad Street, Bristol BS1 2HG,
☎ 0117 930 9000
✉ hoc@guildhallchambers.co.uk
Call Date: Nov 1973, Lincoln's Inn
Qualifications: [MA (Oxon) ADR FCIArb]
george.newsom@guildhallchambers.co.uk

Types of work: Agriculture, Arbitration, Chancery (general), Charities, Common land, Compulsory Purchase, Dispute resolution, Ecclesiastical law, Equity, Highways, Inheritance and cohabitees, Land compensation, Landlord and tenant, Lands Tribunal, Partnerships, Planning, Real property, Trusts, Wills

NEWSTEAD MS JENNIFER ELIZABETH

Call Date: Nov 2003, Gray's Inn
Qualifications: [BA (Nott'm) MA (Nott'm) PGDip BVC]
clerk@stjohnsbuildings.co.uk

NEWTON MRS ALEXANDRA

15 Winckley Square
Preston PR1 3JJ, ☎ 01772 252828
✉ clerks@15winckleysq.co.uk
Call Date: Mar 2007, Lincoln's Inn

NEWTON MISS ALICE HENRIETTA

East Anglian Chambers
53 North Hill, Colchester, Essex CO1 1QA,
☎ 01473 214481 ✉ colchester@ealaw.co.uk
East Anglian Chambers
Gresham House, 5 Museum Street, Ipswich, Suffolk IP1 1HQ, ☎ 01473 214481
✉ ipswich@ealaw.co.uk
East Anglian Chambers
15 The Close, Norwich, Norfolk NR1 4DZ,
☎ 01473 214481 ✉ norwich@ealaw.co.uk
Call Date: July 2009, Inner Temple
Qualifications: [BA (Oxon)]
colchester@ealaw.co.uk

NEWTON MR ANDREW DAVID

187 Fleet Street
London EC4A 2AT, ☎ 020 7430 7430
✉ chambers@187fleetstreet.com
Call Date: Nov 1989, Inner Temple
Qualifications: [MA (Oxon) Dip Law (Lond) LLM]
andrewnewton@187fleetstreet.com

NEWTON MR BENJAMIN ANTHONY

Doughty Street Chambers
53-54 Doughty Street, London WC1N 2LS,
☎ 020 7404 1313
✉ enquiries@doughtystreet.co.uk
Doughty Street Chambers
Pall Mall Court, 61-67 King Street, Manchester M2 4PD, ☎ 0161 618 1066
Doughty Street Chambers
5th Floor, Broad Quay House, Prince Street, Bristol BS1 4DJ, ☎ 01179 058 717
Call Date: Oct 2004, Lincoln's Inn
Qualifications: [BA (Hons) Oxon]
b.newton@doughtystreet.co.uk

NEWTON MISS CLAIRE ELAINE MARIA BAILEY

Middle Temple Lane Chambers
2nd Floor South, 1 Middle Temple Lane, London EC4Y 9AA, ☎ 020 7583 4352
✉ chambers@mtlchambers.com
Call Date: Oct 1992, Gray's Inn
Qualifications: [LLB (Lond)]

NEWTON MR CLIVE RICHARD QC (2002)

1 KBW Chambers
1 King's Bench Walk, Temple, London EC4Y 7DB, ☎ 020 7936 1500
✉ clerks@1kbw.co.uk
King's Bench Chambers
174 High Street, Lewes BN7 1YE,
☎ 01273 402600
Call Date: Nov 1968, Middle Temple
Qualifications: [MA BCL (Oxon)]
cnewton@1kbw.co.uk

NEWTON MISS KATHARINE JULIA

Old Square Chambers
10-11 Bedford Row, London WC1R 4BU,
☎ 020 7269 0300 ✉ clerks@oldsquare.co.uk
Old Square Chambers
3 Orchard Court, St Augustine's Yard, Bristol BS1 5DP, ☎ 0117 930 5100
✉ clerks@oldsquare.co.uk
Call Date: Oct 1999, Middle Temple
Qualifications: [LLB (Hons)(Manch) LLM (Lond)]
newton@oldsquare.co.uk

NEWTON MISS LAURA AMY

11 Stone Buildings
11 Stone Buildings, Lincoln's Inn, London WC2A 3TG, ☎ 020 7831 6381
✉ clerks@11sb.com
Call Date: Oct 2009, Middle Temple
Qualifications: [LLB (Hons) (Dunelm) BCL (Hons) (Oxon)]
newton@11sb.com

NEWTON MR PHILIP

Becket Chambers
17 New Dover Road, Canterbury, Kent CT1 3AS, ☎ 01227 786331
✉ clerks@becket-chambers.co.uk
Call Date: July 1984, Middle Temple
Pupil Supervisor
Qualifications: [BA (Hons) Dip Int Human Rights (Germany) LLM]
pnewton@becket-chambers.co.uk

NEWTON MR STUART RICHARD JAMES

Call Date: Nov 1993, Middle Temple
Qualifications: [BA (Hons)(Lond) CPE]
newton@paradise-sq.co.uk

NEWTON-PRICE MR JAMES EDWARD

Pump Court Chambers
31 Southgate Street, Winchester, Hampshire SO23 9EB, ☎ 01962 868 161
✉ clerks@3pumpcourt.com
Pump Court Chambers
Upper Ground Floor, 3 Pump Court, Temple, London EC4Y 7AJ, ☎ 020 7353 0711
✉ clerks@3pumpcourt.com
Pump Court Chambers
5 Temple Chambers, Temple Street, Swindon SN1 1SQ, ☎ 01793 539899
✉ clerks@3pumpcourt.com
Call Date: Oct 1992, Middle Temple
Pupil Supervisor
Qualifications: [BA (Hons)]

NG MR ALEX CHING-WONG

Blackfriars Chambers
79-83 Temple Chambers, 3-7 Temple Avenue, London EC4Y 0HP, ☎ 020 7353 7400
✉ clerks@blackfriarschambers.com
Call Date: Feb 1991, Gray's Inn
Qualifications: [BA LLB (Lond) MA (Hong Kong)]

NG MR JERN-FEI

Essex Court Chambers
24 Lincoln's Inn Fields, London WC2A 3EG, ☎ 020 7813 8000
✉ clerksroom@essexcourt.net
Call Date: July 2002, Lincoln's Inn
Qualifications: [BA (Hons)(Cantab)]
jfng@essexcourt.net

NI GHRALAIGH MISS BLINNE

Matrix Chambers
Griffin Building, Gray's Inn, London WC1R 5LN, ☎ 020 7404 3447
✉ matrix@matrixlaw.co.uk / Iscott@matrixlaw.co.uk
Call Date: Nov 2005, Lincoln's Inn
Qualifications: [BA (Hons) (Cantab)]
blinnenighralaigh@matrixlaw.co.uk

NIAZ MISS ANISA

Kenworthy's Chambers
Arlington House, Bloom Street, Salford, Manchester M3 6AJ, ☎ 0161 832 4036
Call Date: Oct 2004, Middle Temple
Qualifications: [LLB (Hons) LLM]
a.niaz@kenworthysbarristers.co.uk

NICE SIR GEOFFREY QC (1990)

Temple Garden Chambers
1 Harcourt Buildings, Temple, London EC4Y 9DA, ☎ 020 7583 1315
✉ clerks@tgchambers.com
Call Date: July 1971, Inner Temple
Recorder
Qualifications: [MA (Oxon)]
geoffreynice@hotmail.com

NICHOL MR SIMON BEDE

Cobden House Chambers
19 Quay Street, Manchester M3 3HN, ☎ 0161 833 6000 ✉ Clerks@Cobden.co.uk
Call Date: May 1994, Lincoln's Inn
Qualifications: [BSc (Hons) (Manch)]
simon.nichol@cobden.co.uk

NICHOLAS MS CHRISTINA MICHALINA DE WELD

Chambers of Martin Burr
15 Old Bailey, London EC4M 7EF, ☎ 0845 123 1234 ✉ clerks@barristerweb.com
Call Date: Nov 1997, Inner Temple
Qualifications: [MA CPE]

NICHOLES MS CATHERINE MARGARET ELIZABETH

Coram Chambers
9-11 Fulwood Place, London WC1V 6HG, ☎ 020 7092 3700
✉ mail@coramchambers.co.uk
Call Date: May 1977, Inner Temple
Pupil Supervisor
Qualifications: [LLB (Lond)]
catherine.nicholes@coramchambers.co.uk

E

NICHOLLS MR CHRISTOPHER BENJAMIN

Citadel Chambers
The Citadel, 190 Corporation Street, Birmingham B4 6QD, ☎0121 233 8500
✉clerks@citadelchambers.com
Call Date: July 1978, Gray's Inn
Recorder
Qualifications: [BA (Cantab) Dip ECL (Lond) LLM (Wales)]
✉clerks@citadelchambers.com

NICHOLLS MR CLIVE VICTOR QC (1982)

3 Raymond Buildings
3 Raymond Buildings, Gray's Inn, London WC1R 5BH, ☎020 7400 6400
✉clerks@3rblaw.com
Call Date: May 1957, Gray's Inn
Qualifications: [MA LLM]
✉clive.nicholls@3raymondbuildings.com

NICHOLLS MR COLIN ALFRED ARTHUR QC (1981)

3 Raymond Buildings
3 Raymond Buildings, Gray's Inn, London WC1R 5BH, ☎020 7400 6400
✉clerks@3rblaw.com
Call Date: July 1957, Gray's Inn
Qualifications: [MA LLB]

NICHOLLS MR DAVID JAMES

11 Stone Buildings
11 Stone Buildings, Lincoln's Inn, London WC2A 3TG, ☎020 7831 6381
✉clerks@11sb.com
Call Date: Nov 2002, Lincoln's Inn
Qualifications: [BA(Hons) (Oxon)]
✉nicholls@11sb.com

NICHOLLS MISS ELIZABETH JANE

Lincoln House Chambers
Tower 12, The Avenue North, Spinningfields, 18-22 Bridge Street, Manchester M3 3BZ, ☎0161 832 5701
✉info@lincolnhousechambers.com
Call Date: July 1984, Inner Temple
Pupil Supervisor, Recorder
Qualifications: [BA (Manch) Dip Law]
✉elizabeth.nicholls@lincolnhousechambers.com

NICHOLLS MR JESSE CHRISTOPHER

Tooks Chambers
81 Farringdon Street, London EC4A 4BL, ☎020 7842 7575 ✉clerks@tooks.co.uk
Call Date: Nov 2010, Inner Temple
Qualifications: [BA (Cantab)]
✉jesse.nicholls@tooks.co.uk

NICHOLLS MR JOHN PETER QC (2006)

Maitland Chambers
7 Stone Buildings, Lincoln's Inn, London WC2A 3SZ, ☎020 7406 1200
✉clerks@maitlandchambers.com
Call Date: July 1986, Middle Temple
Qualifications: [MA (Cantab)]
✉jnicholls@maitlandchambers.com

NICHOLLS MR MICHAEL JOHN GADSBY QC (2006)

1 Hare Court
1 Hare Court, Temple, London EC4Y 7BE, ☎020 7797 7070 ✉clerks@1hc.com
Dere Street Barristers
33 Broad Chare, Newcastle Upon Tyne NE1 3DQ, ☎0844 3351551
✉clerks@derestreet.co.uk
Call Date: July 1975, Middle Temple
✉nicholls@1hc.com

NICHOLLS MR PAUL RICHARD QC (2012)

11 King's Bench Walk
11 King's Bench Walk, Temple, London EC4Y 7EQ, ☎020 7632 8500
✉clerksroom@11kbw.com
Call Date: Oct 1992, Inner Temple
Pupil Supervisor
Qualifications: [LLB (Sheff) BCL (Oxon)]
✉paul.nicholls@11kbw.com

NICHOLLS MR PETER JOHN

5 Pump Court
Ground Floor, 5 Pump Court, Temple, London EC4Y 7AP, ☎020 7353 2532
✉clerks@5pumpcourt.com
Call Date: Nov 1991, Inner Temple
Pupil Supervisor
Qualifications: [BA(Hons)(Dunelm)]
✉john@fivepumpcourt.demon.co.uk

Types of work: Corporate liability, Health and safety, Personal injury, Professional negligence

NICHOLLS MR RICHARD JOHN

Brunel Chambers
24 Magdalen Ave, Bath BA2 4QB,
☎ 01225 447730
✉ richardjnicholls@btinternet.com
Call Date: Oct 1994, Gray's Inn
Qualifications: [LLB (Manch)]

NICHOLLS MR SAMUEL DAVID

Devereux Chambers
Queen Elizabeth Building, Temple, London
EC4Y 9BS, ☎ 020 7353 7534
✉ clerks@devchambers.co.uk
Call Date: Nov 2006, Inner Temple
Qualifications: [LLM (Cantab) LLB (Leic)]

NICHOLS MR STUART RICHARD

1 Garden Court Family Law Chambers
Ground Floor, One Garden Court, Temple,
London EC4Y 9BJ, ☎ 020 7797 7900
✉ clerks@1gc.com
Call Date: Nov 1989, Lincoln's Inn
Pupil Supervisor
Qualifications: [LLB (Leics)]

NICHOLSON EUR ING DR BRIAN ANDREW

11 South Square
1st Floor, 11 South Square, Gray's Inn,
London WC1R 5EY, ☎ 020 7405 1222
✉ clerks@11southsquare.com
Call Date: July 2000, Lincoln's Inn
Pupil Supervisor
Qualifications: [B.Eng Ph.D (Bath) PgDipLaw PgDipPLS CEngIntPE (UK)]
🖃 bnicholson@11southsquare.com

NICHOLSON MR EDWARD GRAVES

No5 Chambers
Greenwood House, 4-7 Salisbury Court,
London EC4Y 8AA, ☎ 0845 210 5555
No5 Chambers
38 Queen Square, Bristol BS1 4QS,
☎ 0845 210 5555
No5 Chambers
Fountain Court, Steelhouse Lane, Birmingham
B4 6DR, ☎ 0845 210 5555 ✉ info@no5.com
Call Date: Nov 1993, Middle Temple
Qualifications: [BA (Hons)(Lanc) CPE]

NICHOLSON MR JEREMY MARK QC (2000)

4 Pump Court
4 Pump Court, Temple, London EC4Y 7AN,
☎ 020 7842 5555
✉ chambers@4pumpcourt.com
Call Date: July 1977, Middle Temple
Qualifications: [MA (Cantab)]

NICHOLSON DR JOHN ROBERT

Kenworthy's Chambers
Arlington House, Bloom Street, Salford,
Manchester M3 6AJ, ☎ 0161 832 4036
Call Date: July 2004, Gray's Inn
Qualifications: [LLB BA PhD MA]
🖃 j.nicholson@kenworthysbarristers.co.uk

NICHOLSON MR MICHAEL HUGH

Old Square Chambers
10-11 Bedford Row, London WC1R 4BU,
☎ 020 7269 0300 ✉ clerks@oldsquare.co.uk
Old Square Chambers
3 Orchard Court, St Augustine's Yard, Bristol
BS1 5DP, ☎ 0117 930 5100
✉ clerks@oldsquare.co.uk
Call Date: Oct 1993, Middle Temple
Qualifications: [LLB (Hons)(Lond)]
🖃 nicholson@oldsquare.co.uk

NICHOLSON MR THOMAS EDWARD CYRIL

Atkinson Bevan Chambers
1st Floor, 2 Harcourt Buildings, Temple,
London EC4Y 9DB, ☎ 020 7353 2112
✉ clerks@2hb.co.uk
Call Date: July 2001, Gray's Inn
Qualifications: [BA (Durham)]
🖃 tnicholson@2hb.co.uk

NICHOLSON PRATT MR THOMAS HYCY

15 New Bridge Street
London EC4V 6AU, ☎ 020 7842 1900
✉ clerks@15nbs.com
Call Date: July 1986, Lincoln's Inn
Recorder
Qualifications: [LLB (Lond)]
🖃 tom.nicholson-pratt@15nbs.com

NICKLESS MR JASON ALAN

College Chambers
19 Carlton Crescent, Southampton,
Hampshire SO15 2ET, ☎ 023 8023 0338
✉ clerks@college-chambers.co.uk
Call Date: Oct 2001, Gray's Inn
Qualifications: [LLB (Hons) LLM]
🖃 jnickless@College-Chambers.co.uk

NICKLIN MR ANDREW RUSSELL

East Anglian Chambers
140 New London Road, Chelmsford, Essex
CM2 0AW, ☎ 01473 214481
✉ chelmsford@ealaw.co.uk
East Anglian Chambers
53 North Hill, Colchester, Essex CO1 1QA,
☎ 01473 214481 ✉ colchester@ealaw.co.uk

E

East Anglian Chambers
Gresham House, 5 Museum Street, Ipswich, Suffolk IP1 1HQ, ☎01473 214481
✉ipswich@ealaw.co.uk
Call Date: July 2010, Middle Temple
Qualifications: [BA (Hons) (Bris)]

NICKLIN MR MATTHEW JAMES

5RB
1st Floor, 5 Raymond Buildings, Gray's Inn, London WC1R 5BP, ☎020 7242 2902
✉clerks@5rb.com
Call Date: Oct 1993, Lincoln's Inn
Pupil Supervisor
Qualifications: [LLB (Hons)(Newc)]
matthewnicklin@5rb.com

NICOL MR ANDREW ROBERT

Four New Square
Four New Square, Lincoln's Inn, London WC2A 3RJ, ☎020 7822 2000
✉barristers@4newsquare.com
Call Date: Nov 1991, Inner Temple
Pupil Supervisor
Qualifications: [MA (Cantab)]
a.nicol@4newsquare.com

E

NICOL MR NICHOLAS KEITH

1 Pump Court
Elm Court, Temple, London EC4Y 7AB, ☎020 7842 7070
✉(name)@pumpcourt.co.uk
Call Date: Nov 1986, Inner Temple
Pupil Supervisor
Qualifications: [LLB (Lond)]
nn@1pumpcourt.co.uk

NICOL MR STUART HENRY DAVID

13 King's Bench Walk
13 King's Bench Walk, Temple, London EC4Y 7EN, ☎020 7353 7204
✉clerks@13kbw.co.uk
Call Date: Nov 1994, Lincoln's Inn
Qualifications: [LLB (Hons)(Lond)]

NIELD MS ZOE JUSTINE KATHRYN

Lincoln House Chambers
Tower 12, The Avenue North, Spinningfields, 18-22 Bridge Street, Manchester M3 3BZ, ☎0161 832 5701
✉info@lincolnhousechambers.com
Call Date: Oct 1998, Gray's Inn
Qualifications: [LLB (Nottingham)]
zoe.nield@lincolnhousechambers.com

NIETO MS REBECCA

7 Bell Yard
London WC2A 2JR, ☎020 7831 0636
✉kevintarrant@btconnect.com
Call Date: Nov 2006, Lincoln's Inn
Qualifications: [BA (Durham)]

NIJABAT MISS SHAMA BATOOL

Call Date: Nov 1993, Middle Temple
Qualifications: [LLB (Hons) LLM (Lond)]

NISSEN MR ALEXANDER DAVID QC (2006)

Keating Chambers
15 Essex Street, London WC2R 3AA, ☎020 7544 2600
✉clerks@keatingchambers.com
Call Date: July 1985, Middle Temple
Recorder
Qualifications: [LLB (Manch) FCIArb]

NIXON MISS ABIGAIL LISA BARBARA

Citadel Chambers
The Citadel, 190 Corporation Street, Birmingham B4 6QD, ☎0121 233 8500
✉clerks@citadelchambers.com
Call Date: Oct 1991, Inner Temple
Qualifications: [BA (Dunelm)]

NIXON MR ANDREW IAN

St Paul's Chambers
5th Floor, St Paul's House, 23 Park Square South, Leeds LS1 2ND, ☎0113 245 5866
Call Date: July 2006, Gray's Inn
Qualifications: [BA (Hudds) LLB (Hudds)]
an@stpaulschambers.com

NIXON MR COLIN ROSSINGTON

Crown Office Chambers
2 Crown Office Row, Temple, London EC4Y 7HJ, ☎020 7797 8100
✉mail@crownofficechambers.com
Call Date: July 1973, Lincoln's Inn
Qualifications: [BA (Natal)]
nixon@crownofficechambers.com

NIXON MRS ELAINE VIOLET

Cathedral Chambers
10 Clytha Park Road, Newport NP20 4PB, ☎01633 215112
Call Date: July 2003, Lincoln's Inn
Qualifications: [LLB (Hons)]
enixon@cathedralchambers.co.uk

NNAMANI MISS NWAMAKA YVONNE LOUISE

Staple Inn Chambers
1st Floor, 9 Staple Inn, Holborn Bars, London WC1V 7QH, ☎020 7242 5240
✉clerks@stapleinn.co.uk
Call Date: Nov 2000, Lincoln's Inn
Qualifications: [LLB (Hons) (Bristol)]

NOBLE MR ANDREW

Enterprise Chambers
43 Park Square, Leeds LS1 2NP, ☎0113 246 0391
✉leeds@enterprisechambers.com
Call Date: Nov 1992, Lincoln's Inn
Qualifications: [LLB (Hons)(Manch) FRICS FCIArb]

NOBLE MR PHILIP ROBERT

Thomas More Chambers
7 Lincoln's Inn Fields, London WC2A 3BP, ☎020 7404 7000
✉clerks@thomasmore.co.uk
Call Date: July 1978, Inner Temple
Pupil Supervisor
✉pnoble@thomasmore.co.uk

NOBLE MR RODERICK GRANT

39 Essex Street
London WC2R 3AT, ☎020 7832 1111
✉clerks@39essex.com
82 King Street
Manchester M2 4WQ, ☎0161 870 9969
Call Date: Nov 1977, Gray's Inn
Pupil Supervisor
Qualifications: [BSc]
✉roderick.noble@39essex.com

NOBLE MR WILLIAM THOMAS

Nine Bedford Row
9 Bedford Row, London WC1R 4AZ, ☎020 7489 2727
✉clerks@9bedfordrow.co.uk
Call Date: July 2000, Gray's Inn
Qualifications: [BA (Wales)]
✉will.noble@9bedfordrow.co.uk

NOLAN MR BENJAMIN QC (1992)

Dere Street Barristers
33 Broad Chare, Newcastle Upon Tyne NE1 3DQ, ☎0844 3351551
✉clerks@derestreet.co.uk
Kenworthy's Chambers
Arlington House, Bloom Street, Salford, Manchester M3 6AJ, ☎0161 832 4036
St Paul's Chambers
5th Floor, St Paul's House, 23 Park Square South, Leeds LS1 2ND, ☎0113 245 5866
Call Date: July 1971, Middle Temple
Recorder
Qualifications: [LLB (Lond)]
✉b.nolan@broadcharechambers.co.uk

NOLAN MR DAMIAN FRANCIS

Exchange Chambers
One Derby Square, Derby Square, Liverpool L2 9XX, ☎0151 236 7747
✉info@exchangechambers.co.uk
Exchange Chambers
7 Ralli Courts, West Riverside, Manchester M3 5FT, ☎0161 833 2722
Exchange Chambers
Oxford House, Oxford Row, Leeds LS1 3BE, ☎0113 203 1970
✉spencer@exchangechambers.co.uk
Call Date: Oct 1994, Lincoln's Inn
Qualifications: [BSc (Hons)(Wales)]
✉nolan@exchangechambers.co.uk

NOLAN MR DOMINIC THOMAS QC (2006)

Ropewalk Chambers
24 The Ropewalk, Nottingham NG1 5EF, ☎0115 947 2581 ✉clerks@ropewalk.co.uk
Call Date: July 1985, Lincoln's Inn
Recorder
Qualifications: [LLB (Nott'm)]
✉dominicnolanqc@ropewalk.co.uk

NOLAN MISS GEORGINA

Park Lane Plowden
Lombard House, 4-8 Lombard Street, Newcastle Upon Tyne NE1 3AE, ☎0191 211 4087
✉clerks@parklaneplowden.co.uk
Call Date: July 2006, Middle Temple
Qualifications: [MA (Hons) (Edin) PGDL]
✉clerks@broadcharechambers.co.uk

NOLAN MR MICHAEL ALFRED ANTHONY

Quadrant Chambers
Quadrant House, 10 Fleet Street, London EC4Y 1AU, ☎020 7583 4444
✉info@quadrantchambers.com
Call Date: July 1981, Middle Temple
Pupil Supervisor
Qualifications: [MA (Oxon)]
✉michael.nolan@quadrantchambers.com

E

E

NOLAN MR RICHARD CHARLES

Erskine Chambers
33 Chancery Lane, London WC2A 1EN, ☎020 7242 5532
✉clerks@erskinechambers.com
Call Date: July 1999, Middle Temple
Qualifications: [MA]

NOLTEN MISS SONIA JAYNE

2 Temple Gardens
2 Temple Gardens, Temple, London EC4Y 9AY, ☎020 7822 1200
✉clerks@2tg.co.uk
Call Date: Nov 2002, Inner Temple
Qualifications: [MA (Oxon) MSt (Oxon) CPE (City)]
sjn@2tg.co.uk

NOOR MR OUSMAN BABIR

Centurion Chambers
Chambers of Mer Nazir Ahmed, 1st Floor Paragon House, 79 Birmingham Road, West Bromwich B70 6PX, ☎0121 553 4613
✉clerks@centurionchambers.com
Call Date: July 2010, Lincoln's Inn
Qualifications: [LLB (Lond)]

NORBURY MR HUGH ROBERT QC (2012)

Serle Court
6 New Square, Lincoln's Inn, London WC2A 3QS, ☎020 7242 6105
✉clerks@serlecourt.co.uk
Call Date: Nov 1995, Lincoln's Inn
Pupil Supervisor
Qualifications: [BA (Oxon) LLM Dip Law]
hnorbury@serlecourt.co.uk

NORIE-MILLER MR JEFFREY REGINALD

12 College Place
Fauvelle Buildings, 12 College Place, Southampton SO15 2FE, ☎023 8032 0320
✉clerks@12cp.co.uk
Call Date: July 1996, Inner Temple
Qualifications: [LLB (So'ton)]
jnorie-miller@12cp.co.uk

NORMAN MR BENJAMIN EDWARD

18 St John Street
Manchester M3 4EA, ☎0161 278 1800
✉clerks@18sjs.com
Call Date: Mar 2000, Gray's Inn
Pupil Supervisor
Qualifications: [LLB (Manch)]
bnormal@18sjs.com

NORMAN MR CHRISTOPHER JOHN GEORGE

1 Chancery Lane
London WC2A 1LF, ☎0845 634 6666
✉clerks@1chancerylane.com
Call Date: Nov 1979, Lincoln's Inn
Pupil Supervisor
Qualifications: [LLB (Hons) (Lond)]
jnorman@1chancerylane.com

NORMAN MISS ELIZABETH ANNE

Rowchester Chambers
4 Rowchester Court, Whittall Street, Birmingham B4 6DH, ☎0121 233 2327
✉clerks@rowchesterchambers.co.uk
Call Date: Nov 1977, Middle Temple
Qualifications: [MA (Cantab)]

NORMAN MRS HELEN ELIZABETH

Heavenwood Chambers
Heavenwood Chambers, Heavenwood House, 71 Bownham Park, Rodborough Common, Stroud, Gloucestershire GL5 5BZ, ☎01453 873444 ✉kms@heavenwood.co.uk
Call Date: Nov 1973, Gray's Inn
Qualifications: [LLB LLM]
H.E.Norman@bris.ac.uk

NORMAN MR JAMES ANDREW

Five Paper Buildings
1st Floor, Five Paper Buildings, Temple, London EC4Y 7HB, ☎020 7583 6117
✉clerks@5pb.co.uk
Call Date: Nov 2000, Middle Temple
Pupil Supervisor
Qualifications: [BA (Hons) (Oxon) Dip in Law (Oxon)]

NORMAN MR JAMES STEVEN EDWARD

4 Brick Court
4 Brick Court, Temple, London EC4Y 9AD, ☎020 7832 3200 ✉clerks@4bc.co.uk
Call Date: Nov 2008, Middle Temple
Qualifications: [BA (Hons) (Cantab)]
james.norman@4bc.co.uk

NORMAN MR JARED SIMON GREGORY

Field Court Chambers
5 Field Court, Gray's Inn, London WC1R 5EF, ☎020 7405 6114 ✉clerks@fieldcourt.co.uk
Call Date: Nov 2001, Middle Temple
Qualifications: [BA (Hons)(Lond) CPE LLM (Lond)]
jared.norman@fieldcourt.co.uk

NORMAN MS JULIAN ELIZABETH

11 Gray's Inn Square Chambers
Chambers of Mr Ian Sen, 1st Floor South, 10/11 Gray's Inn Square, London WC1R 5JD, ☎020 7405 6879
✉clerks@11graysinnsquare.com
Call Date: Mar 2012, Middle Temple

NORMAN MR MICHAEL CHARLES

3 PB Barristers
3 Paper Buildings, Temple, London EC4Y 7EU, ☎020 7583 8055
3 PB Barristers
Royal Talbot House, 2 Victoria Street, Bristol, Avon BS1 6BB, ☎0117 928 1520
3 PB Barristers
4 St Peter Street, Winchester SO23 8BW, ☎01962 868884
✉clerks.winchester@3paper.co.uk
3 PB Barristers
23 Beaumont Street, Oxford OX1 2NP, ☎01865 793 736
3 PB Barristers
30 Christchurch Road, Bournemouth, Dorset BH1 3PD, ☎01202 292102
✉clerks.bournemouth@3paper.co.uk
Call Date: Feb 1971, Gray's Inn
Pupil Supervisor, Recorder
Qualifications: [MA (Hons) LLB (Cantab)]
michael.norman@3pb.co.uk

NORMAN MR RICHARD HENRY

St John's Chambers
101 Victoria Street, Bristol BS1 6PU, ☎0117 923 4700
✉clerks@stjohnschambers.co.uk
Call Date: July 2009, Gray's Inn
Qualifications: [BA]
richard.norman@stjohnschambers.co.uk

NORMINGTON MR JAMES ADAM

Park Court Chambers
16 Park Place, Leeds LS1 2SJ, ☎0113 243 3277
✉clerks@parkcourtchambers.co.uk
Call Date: Nov 2005, Inner Temple
Qualifications: [MA University of St. Andrews CPE Leeds Metropol]
jnormington@parkcourtchambers.co.uk

NORRIS MR ANDREW JAMES STEEDSMAN

Hogarth Chambers
5 New Square, Lincoln's Inn, London WC2A 3RJ, ☎020 7404 0404
✉barristers@hogarthchambers.com
Call Date: Nov 1995, Middle Temple
Qualifications: [BSc (Hons)]
anorris@hogarthchambers.com

NORRIS MR JOHN GERAINT

Albion Chambers
Broad Street, Bristol BS1 1DR, ☎0117 927 2144
✉clerks@albionchambers.co.uk
Call Date: July 1980, Lincoln's Inn
Pupil Supervisor
Qualifications: [MA (Oxon)]
geraint.norris@albionchambers.co.uk

NORRIS MS JOSEPHINE CHARLOTTE

39 Essex Street
London WC2R 3AT, ☎020 7832 1111
✉clerks@39essex.com
Call Date: July 2008, Gray's Inn
Qualifications: [BA (Cantab)]
josephine.norris@39essex.com

NORRIS MR PAUL HOWARD

Five Paper
Ground Floor, 5 Paper Buildings, Temple, London EC4Y 7HB, ☎020 7815 3200
Call Date: May 1963, Middle Temple
Pupil Supervisor
Qualifications: [BA (Oxon)]
paulnorris@fivepaper.com

NORRIS MR WILLIAM JOHN QC (1997)

39 Essex Street
London WC2R 3AT, ☎020 7832 1111
✉clerks@39essex.com
82 King Street
Manchester M2 4WQ, ☎0161 870 9969
Call Date: July 1974, Middle Temple
Qualifications: [MA (Oxon)]
william.norris@39essex.com

NORRMAN MS EDITH MARY

Furnival Chambers
32 Furnival Street, London EC4A 1JQ, ☎020 7405 3232
Call Date: Nov 2000, Inner Temple
Qualifications: [LLB (Bris)]
enorrman@furnivallaw.co.uk

NORSWORTHY MR PIERS GERARD REEVE

Devon Chambers
3 St Andrew Street, Plymouth PL1 2AH, ☎01752 661659
✉clerks@devonchambers.co.uk
Call Date: Mar 2001, Lincoln's Inn
Pupil Supervisor
Qualifications: [LLB (Hons)]
piersnorsworthy@devonchambers.co.uk

E

NORTH MS CLAIRE VICTORIA

Cathedral Chambers
10 Clytha Park Road, Newport NP20 4PB, ☎01633 215112
Cathedral Chambers
28 Cathedral Road, Cardiff CF11 9LJ, ☎02920 660129
Call Date: Oct 2003, Inner Temple
Qualifications: [LLB (Bournemouth)]

NORTHALL MR DANIEL

9 St John Street
Manchester M3 4DN, ☎0161 955 9000
✉civilclerks@9sjs.com / criminalclerks@9sjs.com
Call Date: July 2004, Lincoln's Inn
Qualifications: [BA Hons (Cantab)]

NORTHEY MRS EMMA JANE

Temple Garden Chambers
1 Harcourt Buildings, Temple, London EC4Y 9DA, ☎020 7583 1315
✉clerks@tgchambers.com
Call Date: Oct 2009, Lincoln's Inn
Qualifications: [BSc (University of Stirling) CPE OBPP]
en@tgchambers.com

NORTON MR ANDREW DAVID

1 Garden Court Family Law Chambers
Ground Floor, One Garden Court, Temple, London EC4Y 9BJ, ☎020 7797 7900
✉clerks@1gc.com
Call Date: Oct 1992, Inner Temple
Pupil Supervisor
Qualifications: [BSc (So'ton) CPE]
norton@1gc.com

NORTON MR GILES

Enigma Chambers
Troway Hall, Troway Marsh Lane, Sheffield S21 5RU, ☎07779 576499
✉law@enigmachambers.co.uk
Holborn Chambers
6 Gate Street, Lincoln's Inn Fields, London WC2A 3HP, ☎020 7242 6060
Call Date: Nov 2004, Inner Temple
Qualifications: [BA LLB LLM Sta MA]

NORTON MR RICHARD DAMIAN

St Johns Buildings
24a - 28 St John Street, Manchester M3 4DJ, ☎0161 214 1500
✉clerk@stjohnsbuildings.co.uk
16 Winckley Square
Preston PR1 3JJ, ☎01772 256100
St Johns Buildings Liverpool
8th Floor India Buildings, Water Street, Liverpool L2 0XG, ☎0151 243 6000
✉clerk@stjohnsbuildings.co.uk
Call Date: Nov 1992, Lincoln's Inn
Pupil Supervisor
Qualifications: [LLB (Hons)(Leeds)]
clerk@stjohnsbuildings.co.uk

NORTON-TAYLOR MR HUGO BENEDICT

36 Bedford Row
London WC1R 4JH, ☎020 7421 8000
✉chambers@36bedfordrow.co.uk
Call Date: Oct 2000, Inner Temple
Qualifications: [LLB (Lond)]

NOSSITER MR THOMAS ALFRED

Park Lane Plowden
19 Westgate, Leeds LS1 2RD, ☎0113 228 5049
✉clerks@parklaneplowden.co.uk
Call Date: Oct 1999, Inner Temple
Qualifications: [BA (B'ham)]
tom.nossiter@parklaneplowden.co.uk

NOSWORTHY MR HARRY EDWARD

4 Paper Buildings
1st Floor, 4 Paper Buildings, Temple, London EC4Y 7EX, ☎020 7427 5200
✉clerks@4pb.com
Call Date: July 2010, Middle Temple
Qualifications: [BA (Hons) (Exon) LLB (Hons)]

NOSWORTHY MR JONATHAN ALEX

St Philips Chambers
55 Temple Row, Birmingham B2 5LS, ☎0121 246 7000 ✉clerks@st-philips.com
Call Date: Nov 2000, Middle Temple
Qualifications: [BSc (Hons) (B'Ham) CPE Dip Law]
jnosworthy@st-philips.co.uk

NOTHER MR DANIEL ROBERT

College Chambers
19 Carlton Crescent, Southampton, Hampshire SO15 2ET, ☎023 8023 0338
✉clerks@college-chambers.co.uk
Call Date: Nov 1994, Inner Temple
Pupil Supervisor
Qualifications: [BA (Oxon)]
dnother@College-Chambers.co.uk

E

NOTT MISS EMMA CATHERINE

Goldsmith Chambers
Ground Floor, Goldsmith Building, Temple, London EC4Y 7BL, ☎020 7353 6802
✉clerks@goldsmithchambers.com
Call Date: Nov 1995, Gray's Inn
Qualifications: [MA (Cantab)]

NOURSE MR EDMUND ALEXANDER MARTIN

One Essex Court
Ground Floor, One Essex Court, Temple, London EC4Y 9AR, ☎020 7583 2000
✉clerks@oeclaw.co.uk
Call Date: Nov 1994, Lincoln's Inn
Pupil Supervisor
Qualifications: [BA (Hons)(Oxon) DipLaw (City)]
✉enourse@oeclaw.co.uk

NOWELL MISS KATIE LOUISE

9 St John Street
Manchester M3 4DN, ☎0161 955 9000
✉civilclerks@9sjs.com / criminalclerks@9sjs.com
Call Date: Oct 1996, Lincoln's Inn
Qualifications: [LLB (Hons)(Cardiff)]

NOWINSKI MR RICHARD

Tanfield Chambers
2-5 Warwick Court, London WC1R 5DJ, ☎020 7421 5300
✉clerks@tanfieldchambers.co.uk
Call Date: July 1977, Middle Temple
Pupil Supervisor
Qualifications: [BA LLM]
✉rnowinski@tanfieldchambers.co.uk

NOWLAND MR LEE PHILIP

Cobden House Chambers
19 Quay Street, Manchester M3 3HN, ☎0161 833 6000 ✉Clerks@Cobden.co.uk
Call Date: May 1997, Lincoln's Inn
Qualifications: [LLB (Hons)(Leics)]
✉lee.nowland@cobden.co.uk

NSUGBE MR OBA ERIC QC (2002)

Pump Court Chambers
Upper Ground Floor, 3 Pump Court, Temple, London EC4Y 7AJ, ☎020 7353 0711
✉clerks@3pumpcourt.com
Pump Court Chambers
5 Temple Chambers, Temple Street, Swindon SN1 1SQ, ☎01793 539899
✉clerks@3pumpcourt.com
Pump Court Chambers
31 Southgate Street, Winchester, Hampshire SO23 9EB, ☎01962 868 161
✉clerks@3pumpcourt.com
Call Date: July 1985, Gray's Inn
Pupil Supervisor, Recorder
Qualifications: [LLB (Hull)]
✉on@3pumpcourt.com

NUGEE MR CHRISTOPHER GEORGE QC (1998)

Wilberforce Chambers
8 New Square, Lincoln's Inn, London WC2A 3QP, ☎020 7306 0102
✉chambers@wilberforce.co.uk
Call Date: July 1983, Inner Temple
Recorder
Qualifications: [BA (Oxon) Dip Law (Lond)]

Types of work: Chancery (general), Chancery (land law), Commercial litigation, Commercial property, Energy, Equity, Landlord and tenant, Pensions, Professional negligence, Trusts, Wills

NUGEE MR EDWARD GEORGE QC (1977)

Wilberforce Chambers
8 New Square, Lincoln's Inn, London WC2A 3QP, ☎020 7306 0102
✉chambers@wilberforce.co.uk
Call Date: June 1955, Inner Temple
Recorder
Qualifications: [MA (Oxon)]
✉enugee@wilberforce.co.uk

Types of work: Capital tax, Chancery (general), Chancery (land law), Charities, Commercial property, Common land, Conveyancing, Ecclesiastical law, Equity, Financial services, Income tax, Landlord and tenant, Partnerships, Pensions, Share options, Succession, Trusts, Unit trusts, Wills

NUGENT MR COLM GERARD

Hardwicke
New Square, Lincoln's Inn, London WC2A 3SB, ☎020 7242 2523
✉enquiries@hardwicke.co.uk
Call Date: Oct 1992, Inner Temple
Pupil Supervisor
Qualifications: [BA (Kent)]
✉colm.nugent@hardwicke.co.uk

E

NURSE MR GORDON BRAMWELL WILLIAM

Radcliffe Chambers
Ground Floor, 11 New Square, Lincoln's Inn, London WC2A 3QB, ☎020 7831 0081
✉clerks@radcliffechambers.com
Call Date: Nov 1973, Middle Temple
Pupil Supervisor
Qualifications: [MA (Cantab)]
✉gnurse@radcliffechambers.com

NUSSEY MR RICHARD JOHN GEORGE

Farrar's Building
Farrar's Building, Temple, London EC4Y 7BD, ☎020 7583 9241
✉Chambers@farrarsbuilding.co.uk
Call Date: Nov 1971, Lincoln's Inn
Pupil Supervisor
Qualifications: [BA]
✉rnussey@farrarsbuilding.co.uk

NUTTALL MR ANDREW PETER

Lincoln House Chambers
Tower 12, The Avenue North, Spinningfields, 18-22 Bridge Street, Manchester M3 3BZ, ☎0161 832 5701
✉info@lincolnhousechambers.com
Call Date: Nov 1978, Lincoln's Inn
Recorder
Qualifications: [LLB]
✉andrew.nuttall@lincolnhousechambers.com

NUTTER MR JULIAN ANDREW

Number 7 Harrington Street Chambers
7 Harrington Street, Liverpool L2 9YH, ☎0151 242 0707 ✉clerks@7hs.co.uk
Call Date: Nov 1979, Gray's Inn
Qualifications: [LLB (Hons) (L'pool)]

NUVOLONI MR STEFANO VINCENZO

No5 Chambers
Fountain Court, Steelhouse Lane, Birmingham B4 6DR, ☎0845 210 5555 ✉info@no5.com
No5 Chambers
Greenwood House, 4-7 Salisbury Court, London EC4Y 8AA, ☎0845 210 5555
No5 Chambers
38 Queen Square, Bristol BS1 4QS, ☎0845 210 5555
Call Date: Nov 1994, Inner Temple
Qualifications: [LLB (Lond) MA (Lond)]

NWOSU MISS SHERYL ADA

4 Breams Buildings
Chancery Lane, London EC4A 1HP, ☎020 7092 1900 ✉clerks@4bb.co.uk
Call Date: Nov 2000, Middle Temple
Qualifications: [LLB (Hons)]

NYE MISS LOUISA

Landmark Chambers
180 Fleet Street, London EC4A 2HG, ☎020 7430 1221
✉clerks@landmarkchambers.co.uk
Call Date: July 2007, Middle Temple
Qualifications: [MA (Cantab) LLM (LSE)]
✉lnye@landmarkchambers.co.uk

OAKES MISS ALISON DENISE

Landmark Chambers
180 Fleet Street, London EC4A 2HG, ☎020 7430 1221
✉clerks@landmarkchambers.co.uk
Call Date: Oct 1996, Inner Temple
Qualifications: [BA (Dunelm) CPE (Lond)]
✉aoakes@landmarkchambers.co.uk

OAKES MR RICHARD MICHAEL

No5 Chambers
Fountain Court, Steelhouse Lane, Birmingham B4 6DR, ☎0845 210 5555 ✉info@no5.com
No5 Chambers
Greenwood House, 4-7 Salisbury Court, London EC4Y 8AA, ☎0845 210 5555
No5 Chambers
38 Queen Square, Bristol BS1 4QS, ☎0845 210 5555
Call Date: Oct 2007, Middle Temple
Qualifications: [LLB (Hons) (B'ham)]
✉ro@no5.com

OAKES MR SIMON JAMES NEVILLE

Outer Temple Chambers
The Outer Temple, 222 Strand, London WC2R 1BA, ☎020 7353 6381
✉clerks@outertemple.com
Call Date: Oct 2010, Lincoln's Inn
Qualifications: [BA (Oxon)]
✉simon.oakes@outertemple.com

OAKES MISS VICTORIA CLARE BAKER

Five Paper Buildings
1st Floor, Five Paper Buildings, Temple, London EC4Y 7HB, ☎020 7583 6117
✉clerks@5pb.co.uk
Call Date: Oct 2005, Inner Temple
Qualifications: [LLB University of Sheffield]
✉vo@5pb.co.uk

OAKESHOTT MISS RACHEL JILL

One Essex Court
Ground Floor, One Essex Court, Temple, London EC4Y 9AR, ☎020 7583 2000
✉clerks@oeclaw.co.uk
Call Date: Nov 2006, Inner Temple
Qualifications: [BA (Oxon)]
✉roakeshott@oeclaw.co.uk

OAKLEY MISS LOUISE MICHELLE

2 Bedford Row
London WC1R 4BU, ☎020 7440 8888
✉clerks@2bedfordrow.co.uk
Call Date: July 2001, Middle Temple
Qualifications: [BA (Hons) PGdip (Law)]
loakley@2bedfordrow.co.uk

OAKLEY MR PAUL JAMES

One Essex Court
1st Floor, Temple, London EC4Y 9AR,
☎020 7936 3030 ✉clerks@1ec.co.uk
Call Date: Nov 1995, Gray's Inn
Qualifications: [LLB MSc (Bris)]
poakley@1ec.co.uk

OATES MR JOHN RICHARD

Call Date: July 1987, Gray's Inn

OBI-EZEKPAZU MS MAUREEN NGOZI

Tooks Chambers
81 Farringdon Street, London EC4A 4BL,
☎020 7842 7575 ✉clerks@tooks.co.uk
Call Date: July 2008, Gray's Inn
maureen.obi@tooks.co.uk

OBORNE MISS JENNIFER ANNE

Carmelite Chambers
9 Carmelite Street, London EC4Y 0DR,
☎020 7936 6300
✉clerks@carmelitechambers.co.uk
Call Date: July 2007, Inner Temple
Qualifications: [LLB (Dunelm)]

O'BRIEN MR BERNARD NICHOLAS

Albion Chambers
Broad Street, Bristol BS1 1DR,
☎0117 927 2144
✉clerks@albionchambers.co.uk
Call Date: July 1968, Middle Temple
Pupil Supervisor
Qualifications: [MA (Dub)]
nicholas.o'brien@albionchambers.co.uk

O'BRIEN MR DAVID

Trinity Chambers
Highfield House, Moulsham Street,
Chelmsford, Essex CM2 9AH,
☎01245 605040
✉clerks@trinitychambers.com
Call Date: Nov 1994, Middle Temple
Qualifications: [LLB (Hons) CQSW ASW Dips W]

O'BRIEN MS HAYLEE FIONA

4 Brick Court
4 Brick Court, Temple, London EC4Y 9AD,
☎020 7832 3200 ✉clerks@4bc.co.uk
Call Date: Nov 1984, Middle Temple
Qualifications: [LLB (Hons)(Lond)]
haylee.obrien@4bc.co.uk

O'BRIEN MR JOSEPH PATRICK ANTONY PETER

Call Date: Nov 1989, Inner Temple
Qualifications: [LLB (Newc) (Hons)]
obrien@paradise-sq.co.uk

O'BRIEN MR LIAM RORY

Old Court Chambers
Newham House, 96-98 Borough Road,
Middlesbrough TS1 2HJ, ☎01642 232523
✉clerks@oldcourtchambers.com
Call Date: Oct 2007, Middle Temple
Qualifications: [LLB (Hons) (L'pool)]

O'BRIEN THE RIGHT HON MICHAEL

No5 Chambers
Greenwood House, 4-7 Salisbury Court,
London EC4Y 8AA, ☎0845 210 5555
No5 Chambers
38 Queen Square, Bristol BS1 4QS,
☎0845 210 5555
No5 Chambers
Fountain Court, Steelhouse Lane, Birmingham
B4 6DR, ☎0845 210 5555 ✉info@no5.com
Call Date: Mar 2011, Middle Temple
Qualifications: [BA (Hons) (Staffs)]

O'BRIEN MISS NIAMH KATRINA

Lamb Chambers
Lamb Building, Elm Court, Temple, London
EC4Y 7AS, ☎020 7797 8300
✉info@lambchambers.co.uk
Call Date: Oct 1998, Middle Temple
Qualifications: [LLB (Hons)(Sussex)]
niamhobrien@lambchambers.co.uk

O'BRIEN MR NICHOLAS JOHN

Coram Chambers
9-11 Fulwood Place, London WC1V 6HG,
☎020 7092 3700
✉mail@coramchambers.co.uk
Call Date: Nov 1985, Middle Temple
Pupil Supervisor
Qualifications: [BA (Oxon)]
nick.obrien@coramchambers.co.uk

E

O'BRIEN MR NICHOLAS WILLIAM WATTEBOT

10 King's Bench Walk
Ground Floor, 10 King's Bench Walk, Temple, London EC4Y 7EB, ☎020 7353 7742
✉Chambers@10kingsbenchwalk.co.uk
Call Date: Nov 1996, Lincoln's Inn
Qualifications: [MA (Oxon) CPE]
nicholas.obrien@10kingsbenchwalk.co.uk

O'BRIEN MR PAUL

18 St John Street
Manchester M3 4EA, ☎0161 278 1800
✉clerks@18sjs.com
Call Date: Nov 1974, Gray's Inn
Recorder
Qualifications: [BA]

O'BRIEN MR RICHARD WILLIAM

Four New Square
Four New Square, Lincoln's Inn, London WC2A 3RJ, ☎020 7822 2000
✉barristers@4newsquare.com
Call Date: Oct 2005, Lincoln's Inn
Qualifications: [BA (Hons) (Oxon) MPhil (Oxon)]
r.obrien@4newsquare.com

O'BRIEN MISS SARAH ANNE LOUISE

Exchange Chambers
One Derby Square, Derby Square, Liverpool L2 9XX, ☎0151 236 7747
✉info@exchangechambers.co.uk
Exchange Chambers
7 Ralli Courts, West Riverside, Manchester M3 5FT, ☎0161 833 2722
Exchange Chambers
Oxford House, Oxford Row, Leeds LS1 3BE, ☎0113 203 1970
✉spencer@exchangechambers.co.uk
Call Date: July 1998, Inner Temple
Qualifications: [LLB MBA]
obrien@exchangechambers.co.uk

O'BRIEN MR SEAN TIMOTHY

St Philips Chambers
55 Temple Row, Birmingham B2 5LS, ☎0121 246 7000 ✉clerks@st-philips.com
Call Date: Oct 2001, Lincoln's Inn
Qualifications: [MA (Oxon) LLB (Hons) MSc]
sobrien@st-philips.co.uk

OBRUSIK MISS KIMBERLEY NICOLE

15 Winckley Square
Preston PR1 3JJ, ☎01772 252828
✉clerks@15winckleysq.co.uk
Call Date: July 2010, Lincoln's Inn
Qualifications: [LLB (Newc)]
kimberleyobrusik@15ws.co.uk

OBUKA MS OBIJUO AGWU

Chambers of Miss O A Obuka
Suite 14502, 2nd Floor, 145-157 St John Street, London EC1V 4PW, ☎020 7936 4474
✉obijuo.obuka@sky.com
Call Date: Oct 1993, Inner Temple
Qualifications: [LLB]

O'BYRNE MR ANDREW JOHN MARTIN QC (2006)

St Johns Buildings
24a - 28 St John Street, Manchester M3 4DJ, ☎0161 214 1500
✉clerk@stjohnsbuildings.co.uk
16 Winckley Square
Preston PR1 3JJ, ☎01772 256100
St Johns Buildings Liverpool
8th Floor India Buildings, Water Street, Liverpool L2 0XG, ☎0151 243 6000
✉clerk@stjohnsbuildings.co.uk
Call Date: July 1978, Gray's Inn
Qualifications: [LLB (L'pool)]
andrew.o'byrne@stjohnsbuildings.co.uk, abqc@hotmail.co.uk

O'CALLAGHAN MR DECLAN MATHEW DENIS MARK

Landmark Chambers
180 Fleet Street, London EC4A 2HG, ☎020 7430 1221
✉clerks@landmarkchambers.co.uk
Colleton Chambers
Colleton Crescent, Exeter, Devon EX2 4DG, ☎01392 274898
✉clerks@colletonchambers.co.uk
Call Date: Oct 1995, Gray's Inn
Pupil Supervisor
Qualifications: [LLB (Exon) LLM (Nottt'm)]
docallaghan@landmarkchambers.co.uk

O'CALLAGHAN MISS LOUISE CHRISTINE SARA

One Essex Court
1st Floor, Temple, London EC4Y 9AR, ☎020 7936 3030 ✉clerks@1ec.co.uk
Call Date: July 2006, Gray's Inn
Qualifications: [LLB (Keele)]
locallaghan@1ec.co.uk

O'CEALLAIGH MR GREAGOIR SEAMUS

1 Pump Court
Elm Court, Temple, London EC4Y 7AB,
☎ 020 7842 7070
✉ (name)@pumpcourt.co.uk
Call Date: Oct 2006, Inner Temple
Qualifications: [BA (Dublin) MA (Lond)]

O'CONNELL MS JOANNA ELIZABETH

36 Bedford Row
London WC1R 4JH, ☎ 020 7421 8000
✉ chambers@36bedfordrow.co.uk
Call Date: Oct 2003, Gray's Inn
Qualifications: [MA BA (Hons) (Belfast) BlegSci (Belfast)]
✉ clerks@36bedfordrow.co.uk

O'CONNOR MR ANDREW MCDOUGAL

Temple Garden Chambers
1 Harcourt Buildings, Temple, London EC4Y 9DA, ☎ 020 7583 1315
✉ clerks@tgchambers.com
Call Date: Oct 1996, Gray's Inn
Pupil Supervisor
Qualifications: [MA (Cantab) Dip in Law]
✉ aoconnor@tgchambers.com

O'CONNOR MS CHARLOTTE JANE ANDREWS

Nine Bedford Row
9 Bedford Row, London WC1R 4AZ,
☎ 020 7489 2727
✉ clerks@9bedfordrow.co.uk
Call Date: Oct 1999, Inner Temple
Pupil Supervisor
Qualifications: [LLB (Lond)]
✉ charlotte.oconnor@9bedfordrow.co.uk

O'CONNOR MR GERARD MICHAEL

23 Essex Street
London WC2R 3AA, ☎ 020 7413 0353
✉ clerks@23es.com
Call Date: Nov 1993, Lincoln's Inn
Qualifications: [MA (Oxon)]
✉ gedoconnor@23es.com

O'CONNOR MISS HILDA ANN

Kidby Chambers
Grundisburgh Road, Woodbridge, Suffolk IP13 6QA
Call Date: Nov 1991, Gray's Inn
Qualifications: [LLB (Essex) LLM (Lond)]

O'CONNOR MR MARK

Landmark Chambers
180 Fleet Street, London EC4A 2HG,
☎ 020 7430 1221
✉ clerks@landmarkchambers.co.uk
Call Date: Oct 1994, Inner Temple
Pupil Supervisor
Qualifications: [LLB (Lond)]
✉ moconnor@landmarkchambers.co.uk

O'CONNOR MR PATRICK MICHAEL JOSEPH QC (1993)

Doughty Street Chambers
53-54 Doughty Street, London WC1N 2LS,
☎ 020 7404 1313
✉ enquiries@doughtystreet.co.uk
Doughty Street Chambers
Pall Mall Court, 61-67 King Street, Manchester M2 4PD, ☎ 0161 618 1066
Doughty Street Chambers
5th Floor, Broad Quay House, Prince Street, Bristol BS1 4DJ, ☎ 01179 058 717
Call Date: Nov 1970, Inner Temple
Qualifications: [LLB (Lond)]
✉ p.oconnor@doughtystreet.co.uk

O'DAIR MR DAVID RICHARD FRAZER

36 Bedford Row
London WC1R 4JH, ☎ 020 7421 8000
✉ chambers@36bedfordrow.co.uk
Call Date: Nov 1987, Gray's Inn
Qualifications: [MA BCL (Oxon)]
✉ rodair@36bedfordrow.co.uk

O'DEMPSEY MR DECLAN JOHN

Cloisters
1 Pump Court, Temple, London EC4Y 7AA,
☎ 020 7827 4000 ✉ clerks@cloisters.com
Call Date: Nov 1987, Middle Temple
Pupil Supervisor
Qualifications: [BA (Hons) (Cantab) Dip Law (Lond)]
✉ dod@cloisters.com

ODGERS MR JOHN ARTHUR QC (2012)

3 Verulam Buildings
London WC1R 5NT, ☎ 020 7831 8441
✉ chambers@3vb.com
Call Date: Oct 1990, Gray's Inn
Pupil Supervisor
Qualifications: [BA (Hons)(Oxon)]
✉ jodgers@3vb.com

E

ODITAH DR FIDELIS HILARY IZUKA QC (2003)

South Square
3-4 South Square, Gray's Inn, London WC1R 5HP, ☎ 020 7696 9900
✉ practicemanagers@southsquare.com
Call Date: July 1992, Lincoln's Inn
Qualifications: [MA D Phil BCL]
✉ fidelisoditah@southsquare.com

O'DOHERTY MR PAUL JOSEPH

3 PB Barristers
3 Paper Buildings, Temple, London EC4Y 7EU, ☎ 020 7583 8055
3 PB Barristers
23 Beaumont Street, Oxford OX1 2NP, ☎ 01865 793 736
3 PB Barristers
30 Christchurch Road, Bournemouth, Dorset BH1 3PD, ☎ 01202 292102
✉ clerks.bournemouth@3paper.co.uk
3 PB Barristers
Royal Talbot House, 2 Victoria Street, Bristol, Avon BS1 6BB, ☎ 0117 928 1520
3 PB Barristers
4 St Peter Street, Winchester SO23 8BW, ☎ 01962 868884
✉ clerks.winchester@3paper.co.uk
Call Date: Nov 2000, Middle Temple
Qualifications: [BA (Hons) (Cantab)]
✉ paul.odoherty@3paper.co.uk

O'DONNELL MISS CATHERINE

Garden Court Chambers
57-60 Lincoln's Inn Fields, London WC2A 3LJ, ☎ 020 7993 7600 ✉ info@gclaw.co.uk
Call Date: Oct 2000, Inner Temple
Qualifications: [BA (B'Ham) MA (Lond) CPE (Lond)]
✉ cathod@gclaw.co.uk

O'DONNELL MR DUNCAN GERARD

1 Paper Buildings
1st Floor, 1 Paper Buildings, Temple, London EC4Y 7EP, ☎ 020 7353 3728
✉ clerks@onepaper.co.uk
Call Date: Oct 1992, Gray's Inn
Qualifications: [MA]
✉ duncanodonnell@onepaper.co.uk

O'DONNELL MR IAIN ROBERT

1 Crown Office Row
1 Crown Office Row, Temple, London EC4Y 7HH, ☎ 020 7797 7500
✉ mail@1cor.com
Call Date: July 2000, Lincoln's Inn
Qualifications: [BA(Hons) (Bristol) CPE]
✉ iain.odonnell@1cor.com

O'DONOGHUE MR HUGH VINCENT

Carmelite Chambers
9 Carmelite Street, London EC4Y 0DR, ☎ 020 7936 6300
✉ clerks@carmelitechambers.co.uk
Call Date: Oct 2004, Inner Temple
Qualifications: [BCL LLB (Cork) LLM]
✉ hodonoghue@carmelitechambers.co.uk

O'DONOGHUE MR ROBERT PETER

Brick Court Chambers
7-8 Essex Street, London WC2R 3LD, ☎ 020 7379 3550 ✉ clerks@brickcourt.co.uk
Call Date: Nov 1996, Lincoln's Inn
Qualifications: [LLB (Hons) LLM (Bris)]
✉ robert.odonoghue@brickcourt.co.uk

O'DONOHOE MR ANTHONY FRANCIS

Chavasse Court Chambers
18 Queen Avenue, Liverpool L2 4TX, ☎ 0151 229 2030
✉ clerks@chavassechambers.co.uk
Call Date: July 1983, Middle Temple
Pupil Supervisor, Recorder
Qualifications: [LLB (L'pool)]
✉ anthony.o'donohoe@chavassechambers.co.uk

O'DONOHOE MR THOMAS CALDER

3 PB Barristers
3 Paper Buildings, Temple, London EC4Y 7EU, ☎ 020 7583 8055
Call Date: July 2007, Lincoln's Inn
Qualifications: [BA (Oxon) PgDL]
✉ thomas.odonohoe@3pb.co.uk

O'DONOHUE MISS KATHERINE ANN

Number 7 Harrington Street Chambers
7 Harrington Street, Liverpool L2 9YH, ☎ 0151 242 0707 ✉ clerks@7hs.co.uk
Call Date: July 2006, Gray's Inn
Qualifications: [LLB (L'pool)]
✉ katherine.odonohue@7hs.co.uk

O'DONOVAN MS DANIELLE MARIE

Chambers of Miss Danielle O'Donovan
Address withheld ☎ 01493 701174
✉ danielodonovan@hotmail.co.uk
Call Date: Oct 2002, Gray's Inn
Qualifications: [LLM (Edin)]

E

O'DONOVAN MR HUGH ROBERT PATRICK

Quadrant Chambers
Quadrant House, 10 Fleet Street, London EC4Y 1AU, ☎ 020 7583 4444
✉ info@quadrantchambers.com
Call Date: Nov 1975, Gray's Inn
Qualifications: [BA (Oxon)]
hugh.odonovan@quadrantchambers.com

O'DONOVAN MR KEVIN JOHN

No5 Chambers
Fountain Court, Steelhouse Lane, Birmingham B4 6DR, ☎ 0845 210 5555 ✉ info@no5.com
No5 Chambers
Greenwood House, 4-7 Salisbury Court, London EC4Y 8AA, ☎ 0845 210 5555
No5 Chambers
38 Queen Square, Bristol BS1 4QS, ☎ 0845 210 5555
Call Date: July 1978, Middle Temple
Pupil Supervisor
Qualifications: [BA]
kjod@no5.com, ko@no5.com

O'DONOVAN MR RONAN DANIEL JAMES

14 Gray's Inn Square
14 Gray's Inn Square, Gray's Inn, London WC1R 5JP, ☎ 020 7242 0858
✉ clerks@14gis.co.uk
Call Date: Nov 1995, Lincoln's Inn
Pupil Supervisor
Qualifications: [BA (Hons)(Nott'm)]
ronano72@hotmail.com, clerks@14graysinnsquare.co.uk

O'DRISCOLL MISS PATRICIA MARY

Pump Court Chambers
Upper Ground Floor, 3 Pump Court, Temple, London EC4Y 7AJ, ☎ 020 7353 0711
✉ clerks@3pumpcourt.com
Pump Court Chambers
5 Temple Chambers, Temple Street, Swindon SN1 1SQ, ☎ 01793 539899
✉ clerks@3pumpcourt.com
Pump Court Chambers
31 Southgate Street, Winchester, Hampshire SO23 9EB, ☎ 01962 868 161
✉ clerks@3pumpcourt.com
Call Date: Oct 2006, Middle Temple
Qualifications: [BA (Hons) (Dublin) MSc (Lond)]
clerks@3pumpcourt.com

O'FARRELL MS FINOLA MARY QC (2002)

Keating Chambers
15 Essex Street, London WC2R 3AA, ☎ 020 7544 2600
✉ clerks@keatingchambers.com
Call Date: July 1983, Inner Temple
Recorder
Qualifications: [BA (Dunelm)]
fofarrell@keatingchambers.com

OFEI-KWATIA MISS DIDO ASANTEWA

12 Old Square Chambers
1st Floor, 12 Old Square, Lincoln's Inn, London WC2A 3TX, ☎ 020 7404 0875
✉ clerks@12oldsquare.com
Call Date: July 2002, Lincoln's Inn
Qualifications: [BA (Hons) MPhil (Cantab) PgDL]
clerks@12oldsquare.com

OFFENBACH MR ROGER LEON

25 Bedford Row
London WC1R 4HD, ☎ 020 7067 1500
✉ clerks@25bedfordrow.com
Call Date: July 1978, Inner Temple
Pupil Supervisor
Qualifications: [ARICS]
roffenbach@25bedfordrow.com

OFFER MR ALEXANDER

Park Court Chambers
16 Park Place, Leeds LS1 2SJ, ☎ 0113 243 3277
✉ clerks@parkcourtchambers.co.uk
Garden Court Chambers
57-60 Lincoln's Inn Fields, London WC2A 3LJ, ☎ 020 7993 7600 ✉ info@gclaw.co.uk
Call Date: Oct 1998, Middle Temple
Pupil Supervisor
Qualifications: [MA (Hons)(Cantab) CPE]
clerks@parkcourtchambers.co.uk

O'FLAHERTY MR JOHN MICHAEL

Matrix Chambers
Griffin Building, Gray's Inn, London WC1R 5LN, ☎ 020 7404 3447
✉ matrix@matrixlaw.co.uk / Iscott@matrixlaw.co.uk
Call Date: Oct 2001, Middle Temple
Qualifications: [BA (Hons) CPE MLitt Dip Law]
johnoflaherty@matrixlaw.co.uk

E

OGANAH MISS JANET MUNANIE

42 Bedford Row
London WC1R 4LL, ☎ 020 7831 0222
✉ clerks@42br.com
Call Date: July 2007, Lincoln's Inn
Qualifications: [LLB (Bris)]

OGDEN MR THOMAS EDWARD DRUMMOND

Four New Square
Four New Square, Lincoln's Inn, London WC2A 3RJ, ☎ 020 7822 2000
✉ barristers@4newsquare.com
Call Date: Oct 2008, Lincoln's Inn
Qualifications: [BA (Cantab)]

OGLE MISS REBECCA THEODOSIA ABIGAIL

Southernhay Chambers
33 Southernhay East, Exeter EX1 1NX, ☎ 01392 255777
✉ clerks@southernhaychambers.co.uk
Call Date: July 1989, Inner Temple
Qualifications: [BA Dip Law]
✉ r.ogle@southernhaychambers.co.uk

O'GORMAN MR CHRISTOPHER FRANCIS

Cornwall Street Chambers
85-87 Cornwall Street, Birmingham B3 3BY, ☎ 0121 233 7500
✉ clerks@cornwallstreet.co.uk
Call Date: Nov 1987, Gray's Inn
Qualifications: [LLB (Sheff)]
✉ chris.ogorman@cornwallstreet.co.uk

O'GRADY MR MATTHEW JAMES STALMEISTERS

St Mary's Family Law Chambers
26-28 High Pavement, The Lace Market, Nottingham NG1 1HN, ☎ 0115 950 3503
✉ clerks@stmarysflc.co.uk
Call Date: Oct 2010, Gray's Inn
Qualifications: [LLB]
✉ clerks@stmarysflc.co.uk

OGUNBIYI MR OLUWOLE AFOLABI

Chambers of Mr O A Ogunbiyi
6 Vicarage Heights, Benfleet, Essex SS7 1QA, ☎ 01268 631 618 ✉ oao@lineone.net
Call Date: July 1995, Lincoln's Inn
Qualifications: [LLB (Hons)]

OGUNBUSOLA MR VICTOR OLANIYI

Chambers of Victor Ogumbusola
23 Cockerell Close, Burnt Mill, Basildon SS13 1QR, ☎ 07413 634231
✉ victorogunbusola@hotmail.com
Call Date: July 2000, Lincoln's Inn
Qualifications: [LLB (Hons) (Middsx) LLM (Lond)]
✉ victorogunbusola@hotmail.com

O'GUNLEYE MISS MARISHA

15 New Bridge Street
London EC4V 6AU, ☎ 020 7842 1900
✉ clerks@15nbs.com
Call Date: Nov 2006, Inner Temple
Qualifications: [LLB (Lond)]
✉ marisha.o'gunleye@15nbs.com

OGUNTAYO MR OLUWATOSIN

Hardwicke
New Square, Lincoln's Inn, London WC2A 3SB, ☎ 020 7242 2523
✉ enquiries@hardwicke.co.uk
Call Date: Nov 2001, Middle Temple
Qualifications: [MA (Cantab) LLB (Hons) LLM (Lond)]
✉ tosin.oguntayo@hardwicke.co.uk

O'HAGAN MS RACHAEL MARY

39 Essex Street
London WC2R 3AT, ☎ 020 7832 1111
✉ clerks@39essex.com
82 King Street
Manchester M2 4WQ, ☎ 0161 870 9969
Call Date: Oct 2006, Inner Temple
Qualifications: [LLB (B'ham)]
✉ rachael.ohagan@39essex.com

O'HAGAN MISS SOPHIA MARIA

Regent Chambers
Regent House, 3 Pall Mall, Hanley, Stoke On Trent ST1 1HP, ☎ 01782 286666
✉ clerks@regentchambers.co.uk
Call Date: Oct 1996, Middle Temple
Qualifications: [LLB (Hons)(Lond) LLM (Lond)]

O'HARA MISS SARAH LOUISE

3 PB Barristers
3 Paper Buildings, Temple, London EC4Y 7EU, ☎ 020 7583 8055
3 PB Barristers
Royal Talbot House, 2 Victoria Street, Bristol, Avon BS1 6BB, ☎ 0117 928 1520
3 PB Barristers
30 Christchurch Road, Bournemouth, Dorset BH1 3PD, ☎ 01202 292102
✉ clerks.bournemouth@3paper.co.uk

3 PB Barristers
4 St Peter Street, Winchester SO23 8BW,
☎ 01962 868884
✉ clerks.winchester@3paper.co.uk
3 PB Barristers
23 Beaumont Street, Oxford OX1 2NP,
☎ 01865 793 736
Call Date: July 1984, Middle Temple
Qualifications: [MA (Cantab)]
✉ Sarah.Ohara@3paper.co.uk

O'HARE MISS ELIZABETH ANNE

Park Lane Plowden
19 Westgate, Leeds LS1 2RD,
☎ 0113 228 5049
✉ clerks@parklaneplowden.co.uk
Call Date: July 1980, Middle Temple
Pupil Supervisor
Qualifications: [LLB]
✉ elizabeth.o'hare@parklaneplowden.co.uk

O'HIGGINS MR JOHN GERARD

6 Pump Court
1st Floor, 6 Pump Court, Temple, London EC4Y 7AR, ☎ 020 7797 8400
✉ richardconstable@6pumpcourt.co.uk
6 Pump Court Chambers
6-8 Mill Street, Maidstone, Kent ME15 6XH,
☎ 01622 688094
✉ annexe@6pumpcourt.co.uk
Call Date: Nov 1990, Middle Temple
Pupil Supervisor
Qualifications: [MA (Cantab)]
✉ Clerks@6PumpCourt.co.uk

OHRENSTEIN MR DOV

Radcliffe Chambers
Ground Floor, 11 New Square, Lincoln's Inn, London WC2A 3QB, ☎ 020 7831 0081
✉ clerks@radcliffechambers.com
Call Date: Oct 1995, Gray's Inn
Qualifications: [MA (Cantab)]

OHRINGER MR ADAM

Cloisters
1 Pump Court, Temple, London EC4Y 7AA,
☎ 020 7827 4000 ✉ clerks@cloisters.com
Call Date: Mar 2001, Middle Temple
Qualifications: [LLB (Hons) (London)]
✉ ao@cloisters.com

OJAKOVOH MR JOHN FRANCIS

9 King's Bench Walk
Lower Ground Floor South, 9 King's Bench Walk, Temple, London EC4Y 7DX,
☎ 020 7353 9564 ✉ 9kbw@btconnect.com
Call Date: Oct 2008, Lincoln's Inn
Qualifications: [BA MA (Oxon)]

OJI MISS ATIM ANENE IFEOMA

Amethyst Chambers
Ground Floor, 9 Kings Bench Walk, Inner Temple, London EC4Y 7DX,
☎ 020 7936 4966
✉ info@amethystchambers.com
Call Date: Nov 1992, Inner Temple
Qualifications: [BA LLB (Hons) (Lond)]
✉ info@amethystchambers.com

OJUTIKU MRS FADEKEMI OMOTAYO

4 King's Bench Walk
2nd Floor, 4 King's Bench Walk, Temple, London EC4Y 7DL, ☎ 020 7822 7000
✉ clerks@4kbw.co.uk
Call Date: Oct 1994, Lincoln's Inn
Qualifications: [BA (Hons)(Nigeria) LLB (Hons)(Lond)]
✉ ko@4kbw.co.uk

OKAI MR ANTHONY SETH

12 Old Square Chambers
1st Floor, 12 Old Square, Lincoln's Inn, London WC2A 3TX, ☎ 020 7404 0875
✉ clerks@12oldsquare.com
Call Date: July 1973, Inner Temple
Pupil Supervisor
Qualifications: [LLB (Lond)]
✉ clerks@12oldsquare.com

E

O'KANE MISS SARAH CAROLINE

Argent Chambers
5 Bell Yard, London WC2A 2JR,
☎ 020 7556 5500
✉ briefsin@argentchambers.co.uk
Call Date: Oct 2001, Middle Temple
Qualifications: [LLB (Hons)]

OKE MR OLANREWAJU OLADIPUPO

Kingsway Chambers
Suite 51, 95 Wilton Road, London SW1V 3BX,
☎ 020 7404 2357
Call Date: July 1979, Lincoln's Inn
Qualifications: [MA(Oxon)]

O'KEEFFE MR DARREN PHILIP DE VOIELS

Oriel Chambers
14 Water Street, Liverpool, Merseyside L2 8TD, ☎ 0151 236 7191
✉ clerks@orielchambers.co.uk
Oriel Chambers
18 Ribblesdale Place, Preston PR1 3NA,
☎ 01772 254 764
✉ clerks@oriel-chambers.co.uk
Call Date: July 1984, Inner Temple
Pupil Supervisor
Qualifications: [MA (Oxon)]

OKEWALE MR TUNDE

Doughty Street Chambers
53-54 Doughty Street, London WC1N 2LS,
☎020 7404 1313
✉enquiries@doughtystreet.co.uk
Call Date: Nov 2007, Inner Temple
Qualifications: [LLB (Lond)]
clerks@4bb.co.uk

OKINE MISS JULIE ANNE

Goldsmith Chambers
Ground Floor, Goldsmith Building, Temple, London EC4Y 7BL, ☎020 7353 6802
✉clerks@goldsmithchambers.com
Call Date: Oct 1996, Lincoln's Inn
Pupil Supervisor
Qualifications: [LLB (Hons)(Lond)]
J.Okine@goldsmithchambers.law.co.uk

OKOYA MR WILLIAM EBIKISE

Arden Chambers
20 Bloomsbury Square, London WC1A 2NS,
☎020 7242 4244
✉clerks@ardenchambers.com
Call Date: Nov 1989, Gray's Inn
Pupil Supervisor
Qualifications: [LLM (Lond) LLB (Wales) FCIArb]
william.okoya@ardenchambers.com

OKOYE MISS JOY NWAMALA

Chambers of Joy Okoye
9 Redbourne Avenue, Finchley Church End, London N3 2BP,
☎07976 426871 / 020 7405 7011
✉okoyejoy@hotmail.com
Call Date: July 1981, Inner Temple
Pupil Supervisor
Qualifications: [BA (Hons)]

OLBOURNE MR BENJAMIN RUPERT

20 Essex Street
London WC2R 3AL, ☎020 7842 1200
✉clerks@20essexst.com
Call Date: Nov 2003, Inner Temple
Qualifications: [BEc (Syndey Australia) BA (Australia) LLB (Sydney Australia) LLM (Cantab)]
clerks@20essexst.com

OLDFIELD MISS JANE LISA CATHERINE

18 Red Lion Court
London EC4A 3EB, ☎020 7520 6000
✉chambers@18rlc.co.uk
18 Red Lion Court (Annexe)
Thornwood House, 102 New London Road, Chelmsford, Essex CM2 0RG,
☎01245 280880
Call Date: Oct 2004, Middle Temple
Qualifications: [BA Oxon CPE City University]

OLDHAM MRS FRANCES MARY THERESA QC (1994)

36 Bedford Row
London WC1R 4JH, ☎020 7421 8000
✉chambers@36bedfordrow.co.uk
37 Park Square Chambers
37 Park Square, Leeds LS1 2NY,
☎0113 243 9422 ✉chambers@no37.co.uk
Call Date: July 1977, Gray's Inn
Recorder
Qualifications: [LLB]

OLDHAM MRS JANE ELIZABETH

11 King's Bench Walk
11 King's Bench Walk, Temple, London EC4Y 7EQ, ☎020 7632 8500
✉clerksroom@11kbw.com
Call Date: July 1985, Middle Temple
Qualifications: [MA (Cantab)]
jane.oldham@11kbw.com

OLDHAM MR PETER ROBERT QC (2010)

11 King's Bench Walk
11 King's Bench Walk, Temple, London EC4Y 7EQ, ☎020 7632 8500
✉clerksroom@11kbw.com
Call Date: Oct 1990, Gray's Inn
Pupil Supervisor
Qualifications: [BA (Cantab) Dip Law (Lond)]
peter.oldham@11kbw.com

O'LEARY MR BRENDAN FINBARR

18 St John Street
Manchester M3 4EA, ☎0161 278 1800
✉clerks@18sjs.com
Call Date: Nov 2007, Middle Temple
Qualifications: [BSc (Econ)(Hons)(Wales) MA (Lond) PgDL (Manch)]

O'LEARY MR JAMES SAMUEL

One Essex Court
Ground Floor, One Essex Court, Temple, London EC4Y 9AR, ☎020 7583 2000
✉clerks@oeclaw.co.uk
Call Date: Nov 2007, Lincoln's Inn
Qualifications: [LLB/BA (First Class Honours) é University of New South Wales, BCL (Distinction) é Oxford University]

O'LEARY MR JOHN JOSEPH IGNATIUS

Number 7 Harrington Street Chambers
7 Harrington Street, Liverpool L2 9YH, ☎0151 242 0707 ✉clerks@7hs.co.uk
Call Date: July 2010, Middle Temple
Qualifications: [BA (Hons)]
john.oleary@7hs.co.uk

O'LEARY MS MICHELE ANN

1 Pump Court
Elm Court, Temple, London EC4Y 7AB, ☎020 7842 7070
✉(name)@pumpcourt.co.uk
Call Date: Nov 1983, Gray's Inn
Pupil Supervisor
Qualifications: [LLB (Hons)(Wales)]
mol@1pumpcourt.co.uk

O'LEARY MR ROBERT MICHAEL

Civitas Chambers
Global Reach, Celtic Gateway, Cardiff Bay, Cardiff CF11 0SN, ☎0845 0713 007
✉clerks@civitaslaw.com
Call Date: Oct 1990, Inner Temple
Pupil Supervisor
Qualifications: [LLB (Cardiff)]
robert.oleary@civitaslaw.com

OLIVARES-CHANDLER MR JOSE ANDRES

7 Bell Yard
London WC2A 2JR, ☎020 7831 0636
✉kevintarrant@btconnect.com
Call Date: Oct 2000, Middle Temple
Qualifications: [LLB (Hons) (Lond)]
jose_olivares_chandler@hotmail.com

OLIVER MR ANDREW JAMES

Octagon House
19 Colegate, Norwich NR3 1AT, ☎01603 623186
✉clerks@octagonhouse.co.uk
Call Date: Nov 1993, Lincoln's Inn
Qualifications: [LLB (Hons)]

OLIVER MR CRISPIN ARTHUR

Dere Street Barristers
14 Toft Green, York YO1 6JT, ☎0844 3351551
✉clerks@derestreet.co.uk
York Chambers
Rotterdam House, 116 The Quayside, Newcastle Upon Tyne NE1 3DY, ☎0191 206 4677
Call Date: Nov 1990, Middle Temple
Pupil Supervisor
Qualifications: [MA (St Andrews) Dip Law]
clerks@yorkchambers.co.uk

OLIVER MR DAVID KEIGHTLEY RIDEAL QC (1986)

13 Old Square Chambers
Ground Floor, 14 Old Square, Lincoln's Inn, London WC2A 3UE, ☎020 7831 4445
✉clerks@13oldsquare.com
Call Date: July 1972, Lincoln's Inn
Qualifications: [BA (Cantab), LicSpec en droit Eur (Belguim)]
davidoliver@13oldsquare.com

OLIVER MR HARRY JOHN WILLIAM

1 KBW Chambers
1 King's Bench Walk, Temple, London EC4Y 7DB, ☎020 7936 1500
✉clerks@1kbw.co.uk
King's Bench Chambers
174 High Street, Lewes BN7 1YE, ☎01273 402600
Call Date: Nov 1999, Gray's Inn
Pupil Supervisor
Qualifications: [BA (Oxon)]
holiver@1kbw.co.uk

OLIVER MISS HEATHER ELIZABETH

3 Raymond Buildings
3 Raymond Buildings, Gray's Inn, London WC1R 5BH, ☎020 7400 6400
✉clerks@3rblaw.com
Call Date: July 2010, Inner Temple
Qualifications: [BA (Oxon) CPE]
heather.oliver@3raymondbuildings.com

OLIVER MISS JULIET DIANNE

5 Pump Court
Ground Floor, 5 Pump Court, Temple, London EC4Y 7AP, ☎020 7353 2532
✉clerks@5pumpcourt.com
Call Date: Nov 1974, Gray's Inn
Qualifications: [LLB]
julietoliver@5pumpcourt.com

E

OLIVER MR MICHAEL RICHARD

15 New Bridge Street
London EC4V 6AU, ☎ 020 7842 1900
✉ clerks@15nbs.com
Call Date: July 1977, Inner Temple
Pupil Supervisor
Qualifications: [MA (Oxon)]
michael.oliver@15nbs.com

OLIVER DR PETER JAMES ROBERT

4 Pump Court
4 Pump Court, Temple, London EC4Y 7AN,
☎ 020 7842 5555
✉ chambers@4pumpcourt.com
Call Date: July 2002, Lincoln's Inn
Qualifications: [MB BS (Lond) CPE Dip Law BVC]
poliver@4pumpcourt.com

OLLECH MR JOSEPH SELWYN

Falcon Chambers
Falcon Court, London EC4Y 1AA,
☎ 020 7353 2484
✉ clerks@falcon-chambers.com
Call Date: July 2006, Lincoln's Inn
Qualifications: [BSc (Lond) PgDL]
ollech@falcon-chambers.com

OLLENNU MR ASHITEY KWAME NII-AMAA

Redemption Chambers
121 The Vale, Golders Green, London NW11 8TL, ☎ 020 8458 5486
✉ home@ollennu92.freeserve.co.uk
Call Date: July 1981, Lincoln's Inn
Pupil Supervisor
Qualifications: [BA (Hons)]

OLLESON MR SIMON PHILIP

13 Old Square Chambers
Ground Floor, 14 Old Square, Lincoln's Inn, London WC2A 3UE, ☎ 020 7831 4445
✉ clerks@13oldsquare.com
Call Date: Oct 2002, Lincoln's Inn
Qualifications: [BA (Cantab) LLM]

OLLEY MISS KATHERINE MARGARET

Landmark Chambers
180 Fleet Street, London EC4A 2HG,
☎ 020 7430 1221
✉ clerks@landmarkchambers.co.uk
Call Date: Oct 1999, Middle Temple
Qualifications: [BA (Hons)]
kolley@landmarkchambers.co.uk

OLSON MR ROSS ALEXANDER

Deans Court Chambers
24 St John Street, Manchester M3 4DF,
☎ 0161 214 6000 ✉ clerks@deanscourt.co.uk
Deans Court Chambers
101 Walker Street, Preston PR1 2RR,
☎ 01772 565 600
✉ preston@deanscourt.co.uk
Call Date: Oct 1999, Gray's Inn
Qualifications: [MA (Cantab)]
olson@deanscourt.co.uk

OLUPITAN-RUBAN MS YETUNDE

Chambers of Yetunde Ruban
9 Grenaby Road, Croydon, London CR0 2EJ,
☎ 020 8665 5834 ✉ yetruban@yahoo.co.uk
Call Date: Nov 1996, Inner Temple
Qualifications: [BA]
yetruban@yahoo.co.uk

O'MAHONY MR DAVID ST JOHN

Seven Bedford Row
7 Bedford Row, London WC1R 4BS,
☎ 020 7242 3555 ✉ clerks@7br.co.uk
Call Date: Oct 2000, Inner Temple
Pupil Supervisor
Qualifications: [LLB (Australia) LLM (Cantab)]
domahony@7br.co.uk

O'MAHONY MR JONATHAN SOLOMON

9 Stone Buildings
Lincoln's Inn, London WC2A 3NN,
☎ 020 7404 5055
✉ clerks@9stonebuildings.com
Call Date: Nov 2000, Inner Temple
Pupil Supervisor
Qualifications: [BA (Dublin) MPhil (Cantab) CPE (City)]
clerks@9stonebuildings.com, jomahony@9stonebuildings.com

Types of work: Chancery (general)

O'MALLEY MR DANIEL WILLIAM

Nexus Chambers
7 New Square, Lincolns Inn, London WC2A 3QS,
☎ 020 7404 1147 / 020 7831 8309
✉ info@nexuschambers.com
Call Date: Nov 2003, Middle Temple
Qualifications: [LLB (Hons) (Lond)]
daniel.omalley@nexuschambers.com

O'MALLEY MS JULIE BERNADETTE

Chambers of Mr Ami Feder
Ground Floor, Lamb Building, Temple, London EC4Y 7AS, ☎ 020 7797 7788
✉ clerks@lambbuilding.co.uk
Lamb Building
22 Ship Street, Brighton BN1 1AD,
☎ 01273 820490
✉ admin@lambbuilding.co.uk
Chambers of Mr Ami Feder
Ground Floor, Lamb Building, Temple, London EC4Y 7AS, ☎ 020 7797 7788
✉ clerks@lambbuilding.co.uk
Call Date: Nov 1983, Gray's Inn
Qualifications: [LLB (Sheff)]
clerks@lambbuilding.co.uk

O'MALLEY MISS LAURA JANE

Northampton Chambers
10 Spencer Parade, Northampton NN1 5AQ,
☎ 01604 636271
✉ clerks@northampton-chambers.co.uk
Call Date: Oct 2007, Lincoln's Inn
Qualifications: [BA (Warwick) LLM (Dub)]

OMAMBALA MISS IJEOMA CHINYELU

Old Square Chambers
10-11 Bedford Row, London WC1R 4BU,
☎ 020 7269 0300 ✉ clerks@oldsquare.co.uk
Old Square Chambers
3 Orchard Court, St Augustine's Yard, Bristol BS1 5DP, ☎ 0117 930 5100
✉ clerks@oldsquare.co.uk
Call Date: Apr 1989, Gray's Inn
Pupil Supervisor
Qualifications: [BA MPhil (Cantab)]
omambala@oldsquare.co.uk

OMAR MISS ROBINA

The Chambers of Robina Omar
Safari, Lake View Road, Furnace Wood, Feldbridge, East Grinstead, West Sussex RH19 2QE, ☎ 01342 712326
✉ robina.omar@hotmail.co.uk
Call Date: Oct 1991, Lincoln's Inn
Qualifications: [LLB (Hons)]

O'MARA MISS AMANDA CHERIS

43 Temple Row Chambers
6th Floor, 43 Temple Row, Birmingham B2 5LS, ☎ 0121 237 6035
✉ clerks@43templerow.co.uk
Call Date: July 1999, Gray's Inn
Qualifications: [BA (Hons) Dip Law]
clerks@43templerow.co.uk

OMARI MS JAZZ

Bretton Woods Law
New Broad Street House, 35 New Broad Street, London EC2M 1NH
Dyers Chambers
35 Bedford Row, London WC1R 4JH,
☎ 020 7404 1881
✉ admin@dyerschambers.com
Call Date: Oct 2006, Middle Temple
Qualifications: [LLB (Hons) (Lond), Maitrise en droit prive (Paris)]
jazz.omari@dyerschambers.com

OMERE MR FRANK FEMI

Garden Court Chambers
57-60 Lincoln's Inn Fields, London WC2A 3LJ,
☎ 020 7993 7600 ✉ info@gclaw.co.uk
Call Date: Nov 1999, Middle Temple
Qualifications: [BA (Hons)(Lond)]

OMERI MS SHERYN

Cloisters
1 Pump Court, Temple, London EC4Y 7AA,
☎ 020 7827 4000 ✉ clerks@cloisters.com
Call Date: July 2010, Middle Temple
Qualifications: [BA (Hons) (Sydney) LLB (Hons) (Sydney)]

OMIDEYI MISS ANUOLUWAPO IYANU

Furnival Chambers
32 Furnival Street, London EC4A 1JQ,
☎ 020 7405 3232
Call Date: July 2001, Lincoln's Inn
Qualifications: [LLB (Hons)]
aomideyi@furnivallaw.co.uk

OMIDEYI MRS CHRISTINA AYINKE

Nexus Chambers
7 New Square, Lincolns Inn, London WC2A 3QS,
☎ 020 7404 1147 / 020 7831 8309
✉ info@nexuschambers.com
Call Date: July 1987, Lincoln's Inn
Pupil Supervisor
Qualifications: [LLB]
christina.omideyi@nexuschambers.com

ONABANJO MISS TENIOLA

3 Verulam Buildings
London WC1R 5NT, ☎ 020 7831 8441
✉ chambers@3vb.com
Call Date: July 2010, Middle Temple
Qualifications: [BA (Hons) (Oxon) BCL]

E

ONALAJA MR JAMES OLUWATOSIN

2 Pump Court
1st Floor, 2 Pump Court, Temple, London EC4Y 7AH, ☎020 7353 5597
✉clerks@2pumpcourt.co.uk
Call Date: Oct 2004, Lincoln's Inn
Qualifications: [LLB (Hons)]
jonalaja@2pumpcourt.co.uk

O'NEILL MR AIDAN MARK

Matrix Chambers
Griffin Building, Gray's Inn, London WC1R 5LN, ☎020 7404 3447
✉matrix@matrixlaw.co.uk / lscott@matrixlaw.co.uk
Call Date: July 1996, Inner Temple
Qualifications: [LLB (Edin) LLM (Australia) LLM (Italy)]

O'NEILL MR BRIAN PATRICK QC (2010)

2 Hare Court
Lower Ground, Ground, 1st & 2nd Floor, 2 Hare Court, Temple, London EC4Y 7BH, ☎020 7353 3982 ✉clerks@2harecourt.com
Call Date: Nov 1987, Gray's Inn
Pupil Supervisor, Recorder
Qualifications: [LLB (Hons) (Brunel)]
brianoneillqc@2harecourt.com

O'NEILL MR JONATHAN NORMAN

Rougemont Chambers
Victory House, Dean Clarke Gardens, Southernhay East, Exeter EX2 4AA, ☎01392 208484
✉clerks@rougemontchambers.co.uk
Call Date: Nov 2007, Inner Temple
Qualifications: [LLB (Bris)]
joneill@rougemontchambers.co.uk

O'NEILL MISS LOUISE CATHERINE

St John's Chambers
101 Victoria Street, Bristol BS1 6PU, ☎0117 923 4700
✉clerks@stjohnschambers.co.uk
Call Date: Feb 1989, Gray's Inn
Qualifications: [BA (Dublin) LLM (Cantab)]
louise.oneill@stjohnschambers.co.uk

O'NEILL MR MICHAEL ALISTAIR HUGH

Clerksroom (Taunton)
Equity House, Administration Centre, Blackbrook Park Avenue, Taunton, Somerset TA1 2PX, ☎0845 083 3000
✉mail@clerksroom.com
Call Date: July 1979, Inner Temple
Pupil Supervisor
Qualifications: [MA (Oxon)]
o'neill@clerksroom.com

O'NEILL MR MICHAEL JOSEPH GERRARD

St James's Chambers
68 Quay Street, Manchester M3 3EJ, ☎0161 834 7000
✉clerks@stjameschambers.com
12 King's Bench Walk
12 King's Bench Walk, Temple, London EC4Y 7EL, ☎020 7583 0811
Call Date: Oct 2007, Lincoln's Inn
Qualifications: [LLB (L'pool)]
michael.oneill@stjameschambers.com

O'NEILL MISS SALLY JANE QC (1997)

Furnival Chambers
32 Furnival Street, London EC4A 1JQ, ☎020 7405 3232
Call Date: Nov 1976, Gray's Inn
Qualifications: [LLB (Lond)]
soneill@furnivallaw.co.uk

ONG DR COLIN YEE CHENG

Essex Court Chambers
24 Lincoln's Inn Fields, London WC2A 3EG, ☎020 7813 8000
✉clerksroom@essexcourt.net
Call Date: Nov 1991, Inner Temple
Qualifications: [LLB (Sheff) LLM PhD (Lond) ACIArb]

ONG MISS GRACE YU MAE

Argent Chambers
5 Bell Yard, London WC2A 2JR, ☎020 7556 5500
✉briefsin@argentchambers.co.uk
Call Date: July 1985, Lincoln's Inn
Pupil Supervisor
Qualifications: [LLB (Lond)]
g.ong@argentchambers.co.uk

E

ONIONS MR JEFFERY PETER QC (1998)

One Essex Court
Ground Floor, One Essex Court, Temple, London EC4Y 9AR, ☎ 020 7583 2000
✉ clerks@oeclaw.co.uk
Call Date: July 1981, Middle Temple
Qualifications: [MA LLM (Cantab)]
🖃 jonions@oeclaw.co.uk

ONIPEDE DR VICTOR OLUSEGUN

Chambers of Dr V O Onipede
34 Meeting House Lane, London SE15 2UN, ☎ 07956 207159
Call Date: Oct 2000, Lincoln's Inn
Pupil Supervisor
Qualifications: [LLB (Hons) (Lond) ACIB PhD MBA]

ONSLOW MR ANDREW GEORGE QC (2002)

3 Verulam Buildings
London WC1R 5NT, ☎ 020 7831 8441
✉ chambers@3vb.com
Call Date: July 1982, Middle Temple
Qualifications: [MA (Oxon)]
🖃 aonslow@3vb.com

ONSLOW MR RICHARD ALAN DOUGLAS

3 PB Barristers
3 Paper Buildings, Temple, London EC4Y 7EU, ☎ 020 7583 8055
3 PB Barristers
Royal Talbot House, 2 Victoria Street, Bristol, Avon BS1 6BB, ☎ 0117 928 1520
3 PB Barristers
30 Christchurch Road, Bournemouth, Dorset BH1 3PD, ☎ 01202 292102
✉ clerks.bournemouth@3paper.co.uk
3 PB Barristers
4 St Peter Street, Winchester SO23 8BW, ☎ 01962 868884
✉ clerks.winchester@3paper.co.uk
3 PB Barristers
23 Beaumont Street, Oxford OX1 2NP, ☎ 01865 793 736
Call Date: July 1982, Inner Temple
Pupil Supervisor
Qualifications: [MA (Oxon)]
🖃 richard.onslow@3paper.co.uk

ONSLOW MR ROBERT DENZIL

8 New Square
8 New Square, Lincoln's Inn, London WC2A 3QP, ☎ 020 7405 4321
✉ clerks@8newsquare.co.uk
Call Date: Oct 1991, Lincoln's Inn
Pupil Supervisor
Qualifications: [BA (Hons) (Oxon) Dip Law]
🖃 robert.onslow@8newsquare.co.uk

Types of work: Breach of confidence, Competition law, Computer litigation, Copyright, Copyright Tribunal, Data protection, Design, E-commerce, EC competition law, Entertainment, Franchising, Information technology, Intellectual property, Malicious falsehood, Media, Media and entertainment, Passing off, Patents, Pharmaceuticals, Scientific and technical disputes, Telecommunications, Trade Descriptions Act, Trade secrets, Trademarks

ONUAGULUCHI MR JONES

10 King's Bench Walk
Ground Floor, 10 King's Bench Walk, Temple, London EC4Y 7EB, ☎ 020 7353 7742
✉ Chambers@10kingsbenchwalk.co.uk
Call Date: Feb 1971, Inner Temple
Qualifications: [LLM (Lond) MA FCIArb]
🖃 chambers@10kingsbenchwalk.co.uk

ONUZO MISS DILICHI

Chambers of Miss Onuzo
38 Gateshead Road, Borehamwood WD6 4NQ
Call Date: July 2002, Gray's Inn
Qualifications: [LLB (Lond)]

OOMMEN MR JACOB

Chambers of Mr Jacob Oommen
1 Stuart Road, East Barnet, Hertfordshire EN4 8XG, ☎ 07958 680272
✉ jacob.oommen@justbarrister.com
Call Date: Mar 2001, Middle Temple
Qualifications: [LLB (Hons) LLM]
🖃 jacob.oommen@justbarrister.com

OON MISS PAMELA BENG SUE

Dyers Chambers
35 Bedford Row, London WC1R 4JH, ☎ 020 7404 1881
✉ admin@dyerschambers.com
Call Date: July 1982, Inner Temple
Pupil Supervisor
Qualifications: [LLB (Bucks)]

E

OPENSHAW MISS SAMANTHA JAYNE

Cobden House Chambers
19 Quay Street, Manchester M3 3HN, ☎0161 833 6000 ✉Clerks@Cobden.co.uk
Call Date: July 2005, Lincoln's Inn
Qualifications: [LLB (Hons)]
clerks@cobden.co.uk

OPPENHEIM MR ROBIN FRANK QC (2006)

Doughty Street Chambers
53-54 Doughty Street, London WC1N 2LS, ☎020 7404 1313
✉enquiries@doughtystreet.co.uk
Doughty Street Chambers
Pall Mall Court, 61-67 King Street, Manchester M2 4PD, ☎0161 618 1066
Doughty Street Chambers
5th Floor, Broad Quay House, Prince Street, Bristol BS1 4DJ, ☎01179 058 717
Call Date: Nov 1988, Middle Temple
Recorder
Qualifications: [BA Hons (Manch) Dip Law]
r.oppenheim@doughtystreet.co.uk

OPPENHEIMER MS TAMARA HELEN PASTERNAK

Fountain Court Chambers
Fountain Court, Temple, London EC4Y 9DH, ☎020 7583 3335
✉chambers@fountaincourt.co.uk
Call Date: Oct 2002, Inner Temple
Pupil Supervisor
Qualifications: [BA (Oxon) BCL (Oxon) CPE LPC DipLaw]
toppenheimer@fountaincourt.co.uk

ORAGWU MISS ADAKU ELIZABETH

6 Pump Court
1st Floor, 6 Pump Court, Temple, London EC4Y 7AR, ☎020 7797 8400
✉richardconstable@6pumpcourt.co.uk
6 Pump Court Chambers
6-8 Mill Street, Maidstone, Kent ME15 6XH, ☎01622 688094
✉annexe@6pumpcourt.co.uk
Call Date: July 2001, Middle Temple
Qualifications: [BA (Hons)]
Clerks@6PumpCourt.co.uk

ORAM MR SEBASTIAN PETER RICHARD

3 PB Barristers
3 Paper Buildings, Temple, London EC4Y 7EU, ☎020 7583 8055
Call Date: Oct 2007, Lincoln's Inn
Qualifications: [BA (Cantab)]
seb.oram@3pb.co.uk

O'RAWE MISS DOLORES

2 Dr Johnson's Buildings
2 Dr Johnson's Buildings, Temple, London EC4Y 7AY, ☎020 7936 2613
✉clerks@2drj.com
Call Date: Nov 1992, Middle Temple
Qualifications: [LLB (Hons) (Lond)]
clerks@2drj.com

ORBAUM MR DAVID MARTIN STEPHEN

Sovereign Chambers
46 Park Place, Leeds LS1 2RY, ☎0113 245 1841
✉clerks@sovereignchambers.co.uk
Call Date: July 1978, Gray's Inn
Qualifications: [BA (Leeds)]
david.orbaum@sovereignchambers.co.uk

ORCHARD MR ANTHONY EDWARD QC (2011)

Carmelite Chambers
9 Carmelite Street, London EC4Y 0DR, ☎020 7936 6300
✉clerks@carmelitechambers.co.uk
Call Date: Oct 1991, Inner Temple
Pupil Supervisor
Qualifications: [LLB (So'ton)]

ORCHARD MISS CATHLYN ESTHER

Citadel Chambers
The Citadel, 190 Corporation Street, Birmingham B4 6QD, ☎0121 233 8500
✉clerks@citadelchambers.com
Call Date: Oct 1999, Lincoln's Inn
Qualifications: [BA (Hons)(B'ham) CPE (Lond)]
clerks@citadelchambers.com

ORCHOVER MS FRANCES RACHEL

Coram Chambers
9-11 Fulwood Place, London WC1V 6HG, ☎020 7092 3700
✉mail@coramchambers.co.uk
Call Date: July 1989, Middle Temple
Pupil Supervisor
Qualifications: [BA (Hons) (Lond) Dip Law]
frances.orchover@coramchambers.co.uk

O'REILLY MISS CATHERINE MARY

Regent Chambers
Regent House, 3 Pall Mall, Hanley, Stoke On Trent ST1 1HP, ☎01782 286666
✉clerks@regentchambers.co.uk
Call Date: Oct 1998, Gray's Inn
Qualifications: [LLB (Staffs)]
catherine.oreilly@regentchambers.co.uk

O'REILLY MISS JANE ANN ELIZABETH

New Street Chambers
2 New Street, Leicester LE1 5NA,
☎ 0116 262 5906 ✉ clerks@2newstreet.co.uk
Call Date: Nov 1991, Lincoln's Inn
Qualifications: [LLB (Hons)]

O'REILLY MS NIAMH ANNE

Hailsham Chambers
Ground Floor, 4 Paper Buildings, Temple, London EC4Y 7EX, ☎ 020 7643 5000
✉ clerks@hailshamchambers.com
Call Date: Oct 2007, Middle Temple
Qualifications: [LLB (Hons) (Dub) BCL (Oxon)]
✉ niamh.oreilly@hailshamchambers.com

ORME MISS EMILY CHARLOTTE

Arden Chambers
20 Bloomsbury Square, London WC1A 2NS,
☎ 020 7242 4244
✉ clerks@ardenchambers.com
Call Date: July 2003, Lincoln's Inn
Qualifications: [BA (Hons) Nottingham Trent Dip Law London]
✉ emily.orme@ardenchambers.com

ORME MR JOHN RICHARD

Chambers of Mr John R Orme
71 Breton House, Barbican, London EC2Y 8DQ, ☎ 020 7628 0755
✉ jrolaw@ronague.plus.com
Call Date: Feb 1995, Lincoln's Inn
Qualifications: [BSc (Hons)(Lond) PhD Dip Law (City)]

ORME MR RICHARD ANDREW

St Johns Buildings
24a - 28 St John Street, Manchester M3 4DJ,
☎ 0161 214 1500
✉ clerk@stjohnsbuildings.co.uk
16 Winckley Square
Preston PR1 3JJ, ☎ 01772 256100
St Johns Buildings Liverpool
8th Floor India Buildings, Water Street, Liverpool L2 0XG, ☎ 0151 243 6000
✉ clerk@stjohnsbuildings.co.uk
Call Date: Oct 1993, Lincoln's Inn
Qualifications: [BA (Hons)(Leeds) CPE (Lond)]
✉ clerk@stjohnsbuildings.co.uk

ORMONDROYD MR MATTHEW CAIN

Francis Taylor Building
Inner Temple, London EC4Y 7BY,
☎ 020 7353 8415 ✉ clerks@ftb.eu.com
Call Date: Oct 2007, Lincoln's Inn
Qualifications: [BA (Oxon)]
✉ cain.ormondroyd@ftb.eu.com

ORNSBY MISS SUZANNE DOREEN QC (2012)

Francis Taylor Building
Inner Temple, London EC4Y 7BY,
☎ 020 7353 8415 ✉ clerks@ftb.eu.com
St John's Chambers
101 Victoria Street, Bristol BS1 6PU,
☎ 0117 923 4700
✉ clerks@stjohnschambers.co.uk
Call Date: Nov 1986, Middle Temple
Pupil Supervisor
Qualifications: [LLB (Lond)]
✉ Suzanne.ornsby@ftb.eu.com

O'ROURKE MISS MARY BERNADETTE QC (2009)

Old Square Chambers
10-11 Bedford Row, London WC1R 4BU,
☎ 020 7269 0300 ✉ clerks@oldsquare.co.uk
Call Date: Nov 1981, Gray's Inn
Qualifications: [Cert des Hautes Etudes Europeenes (Bruges) LLB (Lond) LLB (Hons) Postgraduate Cert in Sports Law]

ORR MR CRAIG WYNDHAM QC (2006)

One Essex Court
Ground Floor, One Essex Court, Temple, London EC4Y 9AR, ☎ 020 7583 2000
✉ clerks@oeclaw.co.uk
Call Date: July 1986, Middle Temple
Qualifications: [MA (Cantab) BCL (Oxon)]

Fax: 0207 583 0118
URL: www.oeclaw.co.uk

Types of work: Arbitration, Aviation, Banking, Commercial law, Commercial litigation, Company, commercial and competition, Corporate finance, Financial services, Insurance, International trade, Professional negligence

ORR MR JULIAN BOYD

Cobden House Chambers
19 Quay Street, Manchester M3 3HN,
☎ 0161 833 6000 ✉ Clerks@Cobden.co.uk
Call Date: Oct 1995, Lincoln's Inn
Pupil Supervisor
Qualifications: [LLB (Hons)(L'pool)]
✉ clerks@cobden.co.uk

ORSULIK MR MICHAEL ANTHONY

9-12 Bell Yard
London WC2A 2JR, ☎ 020 7400 1800
✉ clerks@9-12bellyard.com
Call Date: Nov 1978, Middle Temple
Pupil Supervisor
Qualifications: [BA LLM (Lond)]
✉ m.orsulik@9-12bellyard.com

E

O'RYAN MR RORY CHARLES MARK

Chambers of Ian Macdonald QC
Garden Court North, 22 Oxford Court, Manchester M2 3WQ, ☎ 0161 236 1840
✉ clerks@gcnchambers.co.uk
Call Date: Mar 2000, Middle Temple
Pupil Supervisor
Qualifications: [BSc (Hons) (L'pool) CPE]
rory an@gcnchambers.co.uk

OSBORNE MR DAVID THOMAS

Chambers of Mr D T Osborne
The Granary, Preston Bowyer, Milverton, Taunton, Somerset TA4 1PQ,
☎ 01823 400 705
✉ david@david-osborne.com
Call Date: July 1974, Gray's Inn
Qualifications: [BA (Hons) (Canada) CSS (Spain)]

OSBORNE MR JAMES ROBERT

Clerksroom (London)
3rd Floor, 218 Strand, London WC2R 1AT,
☎ 0845 083 3000 ✉ mail@clerksroom.com
Call Date: July 2006, Lincoln's Inn
Qualifications: [BSc (Manch)]

E

OSBORNE MISS JANE ELIZABETH

Atkinson Bevan Chambers
1st Floor, 2 Harcourt Buildings, Temple, London EC4Y 9DB, ☎ 020 7353 2112
✉ clerks@2hb.co.uk
Call Date: Oct 2000, Lincoln's Inn
Qualifications: [BA (Hons) (Oxon)]
josborne@2hb.co.uk

OSBORNE MR RICHARD

4 Pump Court
4 Pump Court, Temple, London EC4Y 7AN,
☎ 020 7842 5555
✉ chambers@4pumpcourt.com
Call Date: Oct 2005, Inner Temple
Qualifications: [BA Lady Margaret Hall University of Oxford CPE]
rosborne@4pumpcourt.com

OSBORNE-HALSEY MRS THELMA EDWINA

Northeastern Law Chambers
69 Minster Moorgate, Beverley, East Yorkshire HU17 8HP
✉ thelma@northeastern.wanadoo.co.uk
Call Date: July 1982, Gray's Inn
Qualifications: [BA LLB (Hons) MSc MA (West Indies)]
thelmabush53@yahoo.co.uk

OSCROFT MR DANIEL THOMAS WILLIAM

No5 Chambers
Fountain Court, Steelhouse Lane, Birmingham B4 6DR, ☎ 0845 210 5555 ✉ info@no5.com
No5 Chambers
Greenwood House, 4-7 Salisbury Court, London EC4Y 8AA, ☎ 0845 210 5555
No5 Chambers
38 Queen Square, Bristol BS1 4QS,
☎ 0845 210 5555
Call Date: Nov 2003, Middle Temple
Qualifications: [MSci (Lond) Dip in Law]
dto@no5.com

OSCROFT MISS JENNIFER VIVIENNE MARY

Cornerstone Barristers
2-3 Gray's Inn Square, Gray's Inn, London WC1R 5JH, ☎ 020 7242 4986
✉ chambers@2-3gis.co.uk
Call Date: Nov 2006, Middle Temple
Qualifications: [LLM BA (Hons) (Oxon) PgDip Law]
joscroft@2-3gis.co.uk

OSEPCIU MS LIGIA-MARIA

Monckton Chambers
1 & 2 Raymond Buildings, Gray's Inn, London WC1R 5NR, ☎ 020 7405 7211
✉ chambers@monckton.com
Call Date: Oct 2008, Lincoln's Inn
Qualifications: [BA (Cantab) LLM (Cornell)]
losepciu@monckton.com

O'SHEA PROF ANDREAS GORDON

25 Bedford Row
London WC1R 4HD, ☎ 020 7067 1500
✉ clerks@25bedfordrow.com
Call Date: Oct 1992, Lincoln's Inn
Qualifications: [LLB (Hons) Lic Spec en Droit Eur (Leeds)]

O'SHEA MISS JOANNE

No 8 Chambers
8 Fountain Court, Steelhouse Lane, Birmingham B4 6DR, ☎ 0121 236 5514
✉ clerks@no8chambers.co.uk
Call Date: Nov 2000, Middle Temple
Qualifications: [BA (Hons) (L'Pool) CPE]
joanneoshea@no8chambers.co.uk

O'SHEA MR PAUL ANDREW

Bank House Chambers
Old Bank House, Hartshead, Sheffield S1 2EL, ☎0114 275 1223
✉w.digby@bankhousechambers.co.uk
Call Date: July 1989, Inner Temple
Pupil Supervisor
Qualifications: [LLB (Hons)(L'pool)]
✉p.oshea@bankhousechambers.co.uk

OSLER MISS VICTORIA LOUISE

Five Paper
Ground Floor, 5 Paper Buildings, Temple, London EC4Y 7HB, ☎020 7815 3200
Call Date: Nov 2001, Middle Temple
Qualifications: [MA (Hons) CPE]

OSMAN MR FAISAL TARIQ

Chambers of Andrew Mitchell QC
33 Chancery Lane, London WC2A 1EN, ☎020 7440 9950 ✉clerks@33cllaw.com
Call Date: Mar 2002, Lincoln's Inn
Qualifications: [LLB (Hons)]
✉fo@33cllaw.com

OSMAN MR NABEEL TARIQ

187 Fleet Street
London EC4A 2AT, ☎020 7430 7430
✉chambers@187fleetstreet.com
Call Date: Oct 2008, Middle Temple
Qualifications: [LLB (Hons) (Oxon)]

OSMAN MR OSMAN HASAN

25 Bedford Row
London WC1R 4HD, ☎020 7067 1500
✉clerks@25bedfordrow.com
Call Date: Feb 1995, Inner Temple
Qualifications: [LLB (Hons) (Middx)]
✉oosman@25bedfordrow.com

OSMUND-SMITH MISS THEA GRACE

No5 Chambers
Fountain Court, Steelhouse Lane, Birmingham B4 6DR, ☎0845 210 5555 ✉info@no5.com
No5 Chambers
Greenwood House, 4-7 Salisbury Court, London EC4Y 8AA, ☎0845 210 5555
No5 Chambers
38 Queen Square, Bristol BS1 4QS, ☎0845 210 5555
Call Date: July 2010, Inner Temple
Qualifications: [LLB (Warw)]
✉theaos@no5.com

OSSACK MRS TANYA RACHELLE ELISE

3 Temple Gardens
Lower Ground Floor, 3 Temple Gardens, Temple, London EC4Y 9AU, ☎020 7353 3102
✉clerks@3tg.co.uk
Call Date: Oct 1993, Gray's Inn
Qualifications: [MA (Brunel)]
✉to@3tg.co.uk

OSTROWSKI MR NICHOLAS CHARLES

6 Pump Court
1st Floor, 6 Pump Court, Temple, London EC4Y 7AR, ☎020 7797 8400
✉richardconstable@6pumpcourt.co.uk
6 Pump Court Chambers
6-8 Mill Street, Maidstone, Kent ME15 6XH, ☎01622 688094
✉annexe@6pumpcourt.co.uk
Call Date: July 2009, Gray's Inn
Qualifications: [BA MA]

O'SULLIVAN MR BERNARD ANTHONY

Henderson Chambers
2 Harcourt Buildings, Temple, London EC4Y 9DB, ☎020 7583 9020
✉clerks@hendersonchambers.co.uk
Call Date: July 1971, Inner Temple
Pupil Supervisor
Qualifications: [MA (Cantab) MBA (OU)]
✉bosullivan@hendersonchambers.co.uk

O'SULLIVAN MR DEREK ANTHONY

39 Essex Street
London WC2R 3AT, ☎020 7832 1111
✉clerks@39essex.com
82 King Street
Manchester M2 4WQ, ☎0161 870 9969
St John's Chambers
101 Victoria Street, Bristol BS1 6PU, ☎0117 923 4700
✉clerks@stjohnschambers.co.uk
Call Date: Oct 1990, Lincoln's Inn
Pupil Supervisor
Qualifications: [BA (Hons) (Dunelm) Dip Law]
✉derek.osullivan@39essex.com

O'SULLIVAN MR GRAHAM

New Court Chambers
3 Broad Chare, Newcastle Upon Tyne NE1 3DQ, ☎0191 232 1980
✉clerks@newcourt-chambers.co.uk
Call Date: July 2009, Middle Temple
Qualifications: [MA (Cantab)]
✉graham.o'sullivan@newcourt-chambers.co.uk

E

O'SULLIVAN MR JOHN

Trinity Chambers
The Custom House, 39 Quayside, Newcastle Upon Tyne NE1 3DE, ☎0191 232 1927
✉info@trinitychambers.co.uk
Call Date: Nov 1984, Middle Temple
Pupil Supervisor
Qualifications: [LLB (Hons) (Warw) LLM]
✉J.O'Sullivan@trinitychambers.co.uk

O'SULLIVAN MR MICHAEL MORTON

5 Stone Buildings
5 Stone Buildings, Lincoln's Inn, London WC2A 3XT, ☎020 7242 6201
✉clerks@5sblaw.com
Call Date: July 1986, Lincoln's Inn
Qualifications: [MA (Cantab) BCL (Oxon)]
✉mosullivan@5sblaw.com

Fax: 020 7831 82102

Types of work: Chancery (general), Chancery (land law), Conveyancing, Court of Protection, Equity, Family provision, Professional negligence, Succession, Trusts, Wills

O'SULLIVAN MR RICHARD JOHN

1215 Chambers
1 Fetter Lane, London EC4A 1BR, ☎020 3291 1215
✉admin@1215chambers.com
Call Date: Oct 1999, Inner Temple
Qualifications: [LLB (Manch)]
✉richard.osullivan@1215chambers.com

Fax: 020 3291 1216
URL: www.1215chambers.com

Types of work: Administrative law, Chancery (land law), Community care, Constitutional and administrative law, Housing, Human rights, Insolvency, Judicial review, Landlord and tenant, Local government and public services, Mental health, Property, Public law, Social welfare, Trusts

O'SULLIVAN MR RICHARD TERENCE

East Anglian Chambers
140 New London Road, Chelmsford, Essex CM2 0AW, ☎01473 214481
✉chelmsford@ealaw.co.uk
East Anglian Chambers
53 North Hill, Colchester, Essex CO1 1QA, ☎01473 214481 ✉colchester@ealaw.co.uk
East Anglian Chambers
Gresham House, 5 Museum Street, Ipswich, Suffolk IP1 1HQ, ☎01473 214481
✉ipswich@ealaw.co.uk
Call Date: July 2000, Inner Temple
Pupil Supervisor
Qualifications: [BA (York) CPE]
✉richardosullivan@ealaw.co.uk

O'SULLIVAN MR ROBERT MICHAEL QC (2012)

Five Paper Buildings
1st Floor, Five Paper Buildings, Temple, London EC4Y 7HB, ☎020 7583 6117
✉clerks@5pb.co.uk
Call Date: July 1988, Lincoln's Inn
Pupil Supervisor
Qualifications: [LLB (Hons) (Lond)]
✉ro@5pb.co.uk

O'SULLIVAN MR THOMAS SEAN PATRICK

4 Pump Court
4 Pump Court, Temple, London EC4Y 7AN, ☎020 7842 5555
✉chambers@4pumpcourt.com
Call Date: Oct 1997, Middle Temple
Pupil Supervisor
Qualifications: [BA (Hons)(Oxon) CPE (Lond)]
✉sosullivan@4pumpcourt.com

O'SULLIVAN MISS ZOE SIOBHAN

One Essex Court
Ground Floor, One Essex Court, Temple, London EC4Y 9AR, ☎020 7583 2000
✉clerks@oeclaw.co.uk
Call Date: Oct 1993, Middle Temple
Qualifications: [MA (Hons)(Oxon) Dip Law (Lond)]
✉zosullivan@oeclaw.co.uk

OTCHIE MR ANDREW AKUAFO

12 Old Square Chambers
1st Floor, 12 Old Square, Lincoln's Inn, London WC2A 3TX, ☎020 7404 0875
✉clerks@12oldsquare.com
Call Date: Nov 2005, Gray's Inn
Qualifications: [LL.B LLM MCIArb]

O'TOOLE MR ANTHONY JAMES

Linenhall Chambers
1 Stanley Place, Chester CH1 2LU, ☎01244 348282
✉clerks@linenhallchambers.co.uk
Call Date: Feb 1993, Gray's Inn
Pupil Supervisor
Qualifications: [LLB]

O'TOOLE MR BARTHOLOMEW VINCENT

5 King's Bench Walk
5 King's Bench Walk, Temple, London
EC4Y 7DN, ☎020 7353 5638
✉clerks@5kbw.co.uk
Call Date: Nov 1980, Middle Temple
Pupil Supervisor
Qualifications: [BSc (Lond) Dip Law]
✉bartholomew.o'toole@5kbw.co.uk

O'TOOLE MR FRANCIS HENRY

Argent Chambers
5 Bell Yard, London WC2A 2JR,
☎020 7556 5500
✉briefsin@argentchambers.co.uk
Call Date: July 2002, Middle Temple
Qualifications: [BA (Hons)]

O'TOOLE MR SIMON GERARD

5 Pump Court
Ground Floor, 5 Pump Court, Temple, London
EC4Y 7AP, ☎020 7353 2532
✉clerks@5pumpcourt.com
Riverview Chambers
Hamilton House, 1 Temple Avenue, London
EC4Y 0HA, ☎0844 225 3999
✉chrisbaylis@riverviewchambers.com
Call Date: July 1984, Inner Temple
Qualifications: [BA (B'ham) Dip Law (Lond)]
✉simonotoole@5pumpcourt.com

OTTON-GOULDER MISS CATHARINE ANNE QC (2000)

Brick Court Chambers
7-8 Essex Street, London WC2R 3LD,
☎020 7379 3550 ✉clerks@brickcourt.co.uk
Call Date: Nov 1983, Lincoln's Inn
Recorder
Qualifications: [MA (Oxon)]
✉Catharine.Otton-Goulder@Brickcourt.co.uk

OTTY MR TIMOTHY JOHN QC (2006)

Blackstone Chambers
Blackstone House, Temple, London
EC4Y 9BW, ☎020 7583 1770
✉clerks@blackstonechambers.com
Call Date: Oct 1990, Lincoln's Inn
Qualifications: [MA (Cantab)]

OTWAL MR MUKHTIAR SINGH

42 Bedford Row
London WC1R 4LL, ☎020 7831 0222
✉clerks@42br.com
Call Date: Nov 1991, Lincoln's Inn
Qualifications: [LLB (Hons) (Leeds)]

OUDKERK MR DANIEL RICHARD QC (2010)

11 King's Bench Walk
11 King's Bench Walk, Temple, London
EC4Y 7EQ, ☎020 7632 8500
✉clerksroom@11kbw.com
Call Date: Nov 1992, Inner Temple
Pupil Supervisor
Qualifications: [LLB (Bris)]
✉daniel.oudkerk@11kbw.com

OUGHTON MR RICHARD DONALD

Cobden House Chambers
19 Quay Street, Manchester M3 3HN,
☎0161 833 6000 ✉Clerks@Cobden.co.uk
Call Date: July 1978, Lincoln's Inn
Pupil Supervisor
Qualifications: [MA (Cantab) LLM (USA)]
✉clerks@cobden.co.uk

OULTON MR RICHARD ARTHUR COURTENAY

5 Essex Court
1st Floor, 5 Essex Court, Temple, London
EC4Y 9AH, ☎020 7410 2000
✉clerks@5essexcourt.co.uk
Call Date: Nov 1995, Middle Temple
Pupil Supervisor
Qualifications: [MA]
✉oulton@5essexcourt.co.uk

OULTRAM MR JONATHAN RICHARD GERARD

Cobden House Chambers
19 Quay Street, Manchester M3 3HN,
☎0161 833 6000 ✉Clerks@Cobden.co.uk
Call Date: Nov 1988, Middle Temple
Qualifications: [LLB]
✉clerks@cobden.co.uk

OUTTERSIDE MR DAVID MICHAEL

1 High Pavement
Nottingham NG1 1HF, ☎0115 941 8218
✉clerks@1highpavement.co.uk
Call Date: July 2004, Inner Temple
✉davidoutterside@1highpavement.co.uk

E

OVEY MISS ELIZABETH HELEN

Radcliffe Chambers
Ground Floor, 11 New Square, Lincoln's Inn, London WC2A 3QB, ☎020 7831 0081
✉clerks@radcliffechambers.com
Call Date: July 1978, Middle Temple
Pupil Supervisor
Qualifications: [BA (Oxon)]
eovey@radcliffechambers.com

Types of work: Building societies, Chancery (general), Equity, Financial services, Pensions, Professional negligence, Succession, Trusts, Wills

Other professional experience: Sitting as a Deputy Judge of the Upper Tribunal.

Publications: *Wurtzburg and Mills: Building Society Law* (Sweet & Maxwell); *The Law of Investor Protection* (Sweet & Maxwell) 2003 (2nd edn.)

OWEN MISS CARYS

18 Red Lion Court
London EC4A 3EB, ☎020 7520 6000
✉chambers@18rlc.co.uk
18 Red Lion Court (Annexe)
Thornwood House, 102 New London Road, Chelmsford, Essex CM2 0RG,
☎01245 280880
Call Date: Oct 2002, Lincoln's Inn
Qualifications: [BSc (Manch) Dip in Law (B'ham)]

E

OWEN MR DANIEL ROBERT SEISYLLT

Fenners Chambers
3 Madingley Road, Cambridge CB3 0EE,
☎01223 368761
✉clerks@fennerschambers.com
Call Date: Oct 1999, Middle Temple
Qualifications: [BA (Hons) (Oxon) MSc (Newc) Dip Law]
daniel.owen@fennerschambers.com

OWEN MR DAVID CHRISTOPHER QC (2006)

20 Essex Street
London WC2R 3AL, ☎020 7842 1200
✉clerks@20essexst.com
Call Date: Nov 1983, Middle Temple
Qualifications: [BA (Oxon) Dip Law (London)]
clerks@20essexst.com

OWEN MR DAVID MEURIG

Number 7 Harrington Street Chambers
7 Harrington Street, Liverpool L2 9YH,
☎0151 242 0707 ✉clerks@7hs.co.uk
Call Date: July 1981, Gray's Inn
Pupil Supervisor
Qualifications: [BA (Keele)]
david.owen@7hs.co.uk

OWEN MS ELEN MAI

Linenhall Chambers
1 Stanley Place, Chester CH1 2LU,
☎01244 348282
✉clerks@linenhallchambers.co.uk
Call Date: Nov 1985, Gray's Inn
Qualifications: [LLB (Lond)]
clerks@linenhallchambers.co.uk

OWEN REV ERIC CYRIL HAMMERSLEY

Kings Chambers
36 Young Street, Manchester M3 3FT,
☎0845 034 3444
✉clerks@kingschambers.com
Kings Chambers
5 Park Square East, Leeds LS1 2NE,
☎0845 034 3444
✉clerks@kingschambers.com
Kings Chambers
Embassy House, 60 Church Street, Birmingham B3 2DJ, ☎0845 034 3444
✉clerks@kingschambers.com
Call Date: Nov 1969, Gray's Inn
Pupil Supervisor
Qualifications: [LLB (L'pool)]
eowen@kingschambers.com

OWEN MISS GAIL ANN

Call Date: Nov 1980, Gray's Inn
Recorder
Qualifications: [LLB (L'pool)]
dgmaubrey@hotmail.com

OWEN MISS GLENDA CAROLINE

Angel Chambers
Ethos Building, Kings Road, Swansea SA1 8AS,
☎01792 464623
✉clerks@angelchambers.co.uk
Call Date: July 2002, Gray's Inn
Qualifications: [LLB (Wales) LLM (Bris)]
glendaowen@angelchambers.co.uk

OWEN MR HARRY TUDOR EVAN

43 Temple Row Chambers
6th Floor, 43 Temple Row, Birmingham B2 5LS, ☎0121 237 6035
✉ clerks@43templerow.co.uk
Call Date: Nov 2003, Middle Temple
Qualifications: [LLB (Hons) LPC]
✉ clerks@43templerow.co.uk

OWEN MR JONATHAN ROBERT

Ropewalk Chambers
24 The Ropewalk, Nottingham NG1 5EF, ☎0115 947 2581 ✉ clerks@ropewalk.co.uk
Call Date: July 2004, Inner Temple
Pupil Supervisor
✉ jonathanowen@ropewalk.co.uk

OWEN MISS NAOMI JOY EVIE

4 KBW
Ground Floor, 4 King's Bench Walk, Temple, London EC4Y 7DL, ☎020 7822 8822
✉ law@4kbw.net
Call Date: Oct 2008, Lincoln's Inn
Qualifications: [BA (Oxon) MA (Bris)]
✉ njo@4kbw.net

OWEN MS SARA JANE

Cathedral Chambers
10 Clytha Park Road, Newport NP20 4PB, ☎01633 215112
Call Date: Oct 1995, Inner Temple
Pupil Supervisor
Qualifications: [MA (Cantab) BED]
✉ sowen@temple-chambers.co.uk

OWEN MR TIMOTHY WYNN QC (2000)

Matrix Chambers
Griffin Building, Gray's Inn, London WC1R 5LN, ☎020 7404 3447
✉ matrix@matrixlaw.co.uk / Iscott@matrixlaw.co.uk
Call Date: July 1983, Middle Temple
Qualifications: [BA (Lond) Dip Law]
✉ timowen@matrixlaw.co.uk

OWEN MISS WENDY JANE

Call Date: July 2002, Middle Temple
Qualifications: [BA (Hons) (Wales)]
✉ wendy.owen@stjohnsbuildings.co.uk, clerks@liverpoolcivillaw.com

OWEN-CASEY MR NEIL ROBERT

St Johns Buildings
24a - 28 St John Street, Manchester M3 4DJ, ☎0161 214 1500
✉ clerk@stjohnsbuildings.co.uk
St Johns Buildings
21 White Friars, Chester CH1 1NZ, ☎01244 323070
✉ clerk@stjohnsbuildings.co.uk
16 Winckley Square
Preston PR1 3JJ, ☎01772 256100
Call Date: July 2007, Gray's Inn
Qualifications: [BMus LLB MA (B'ham)]
✉ Neil.Owen-Casey@stjohnsbuildings.co.uk

OWENS MISS ELSPETH ELUNED

4 Pump Court
4 Pump Court, Temple, London EC4Y 7AN, ☎020 7842 5555
✉ chambers@4pumpcourt.com
Call Date: Oct 2007, Middle Temple
Qualifications: [BA (Hons) (Oxon) BCL]
✉ eowens@4pumpcourt.com

OWENS MRS LUCY ISABEL

29 Bedford Row Chambers
London WC1R 4HE, ☎020 7404 1044
✉ clerks@29br.co.uk
Call Date: Oct 1997, Middle Temple
Qualifications: [BA (Hons)(Kingston)]
✉ lowens@29br.co.uk

OWEN-THOMAS MR RICHARD MATTHEW

13 King's Bench Walk
13 King's Bench Walk, Temple, London EC4Y 7EN, ☎020 7353 7204
✉ clerks@13kbw.co.uk
13 KBW
32 Beaumont Street, Oxford OX1 2NP, ☎01865 311066 ✉ clerks@13kbw.co.uk
Call Date: Nov 2000, Middle Temple
Pupil Supervisor
Qualifications: [LLB (Hons)]
✉ rowen-thomas@13kbw.co.uk

OWUSU MR KWABENA

11 Gray's Inn Square Chambers
Chambers of Mr Ian Sen, 1st Floor South, 10/11 Gray's Inn Square, London WC1R 5JD, ☎020 7405 6879
✉ clerks@11graysinnsquare.com
Call Date: Nov 1983, Gray's Inn
Qualifications: [LLB (Warks)]
✉ kwabena.owusu@11graysinnsquare.com

E

OWUSU-YIANOMA MR DAVID KWASI DARTEY

1 Mitre Court Buildings
1 Mitre Court Buildings, Temple, London EC4Y 7BS, ☎ 020 7452 8900
✉ clerks@1mcb.com
Call Date: Nov 1992, Inner Temple
Pupil Supervisor
Qualifications: [LLB (Hons)]
✉ david.owusu@1mcb.com

OXTON MR THOMAS JOHN EDWARD

Alexander Chambers
13 Halstead Road, Wanstead, London E11 2AY, ☎ 0845 652 0451 / 0854 652 0451
✉ clerks@alexanderchambers.co.uk
Chambers of Mr T Oxton
Address withheld ☎ 07833 901226
✉ thomasoxton100@yahoo.co.uk
Call Date: July 2002, Gray's Inn
Qualifications: [BA (Bris)]

OZIN MR PAUL DAVID

23 Essex Street
London WC2R 3AA, ☎ 020 7413 0353
✉ clerks@23es.com
Call Date: Nov 1987, Middle Temple
Pupil Supervisor
Qualifications: [BA (Oxon)]
✉ paulozin@23es.com

OZWELL MISS KATHERINE ELIZABETH

1 KBW Chambers
1 King's Bench Walk, Temple, London EC4Y 7DB, ☎ 020 7936 1500
✉ clerks@1kbw.co.uk
Call Date: Nov 2007, Lincoln's Inn
Qualifications: [MA (Oxon)]
✉ kozwell@1kbw.co.uk

PABARY MR RAJESH

7 Bell Yard
London WC2A 2JR, ☎ 020 7831 0636
✉ kevintarrant@btconnect.com
Call Date: Mar 2002, Lincoln's Inn
Qualifications: [LLB (Hons) (Luton)]

PACEY MR THOMAS BENJAMIN

12 King's Bench Walk
12 King's Bench Walk, Temple, London EC4Y 7EL, ☎ 020 7583 0811
Call Date: Nov 2008, Gray's Inn
Qualifications: [BA]
✉ pacey@12kbw.co.uk

PACIFICO MR ADAM LOUIS

18 Red Lion Court
London EC4A 3EB, ☎ 020 7520 6000
✉ chambers@18rlc.co.uk
Call Date: Nov 1991, Inner Temple
Qualifications: [LLB (Hons)]
✉ adampacifico@thepacificopartnership.com

PACK MISS MELISSA ELIZABETH JANE

Temple Garden Chambers
1 Harcourt Buildings, Temple, London EC4Y 9DA, ☎ 020 7583 1315
✉ clerks@tgchambers.com
Call Date: Nov 1995, Middle Temple
Qualifications: [MA (Cantab)]

PACKMAN MISS CLAIRE GERALDINE VANCE

4 Pump Court
4 Pump Court, Temple, London EC4Y 7AN, ☎ 020 7842 5555
✉ chambers@4pumpcourt.com
Call Date: Oct 1996, Inner Temple
Pupil Supervisor
Qualifications: [BA (Oxon) CPE (Lond)]
✉ cpackman@4pumpcourt.com

PADFIELD MS ALISON MARY

Devereux Chambers
Queen Elizabeth Building, Temple, London EC4Y 9BS, ☎ 020 7353 7534
✉ clerks@devchambers.co.uk
Call Date: Oct 1992, Lincoln's Inn
Qualifications: [BA MA BCL (Oxon)]
✉ padfield@devchambers.co.uk

PADFIELD MR NICHOLAS DAVID QC (1991)

Chambers of Nicholas Padfield QC
2 Netherton Grove, Chelsea, London SW10 9TQ, ☎ 020 7351 1961
✉ ndp@nicholaspadfieldqc.com
Call Date: Nov 1972, Inner Temple
Pupil Supervisor
Qualifications: [MA (Oxon) LLM (Cantab) FCIArb]
✉ ndp@nicholaspadfieldqc.com

PAGE MISS ADRIENNE MAY QC (1999)

5RB
1st Floor, 5 Raymond Buildings, Gray's Inn, London WC1R 5BP, ☎ 020 7242 2902
✉ clerks@5rb.com
Call Date: July 1974, Middle Temple
Qualifications: [BA (Kent)]
✉ adriennepage@5rb.com

PAGE MR ARTHUR HUGO MICKLEM QC (2002)

Blackstone Chambers
Blackstone House, Temple, London EC4Y 9BW, ☎020 7583 1770
✉clerks@blackstonechambers.com
Call Date: Nov 1977, Inner Temple
Qualifications: [MA (Cantab)]
hugopage@blackstonechambers.com

PAGE MR DOUGLAS PHILIP

Carmelite Chambers
9 Carmelite Street, London EC4Y 0DR, ☎020 7936 6300
✉clerks@carmelitechambers.co.uk
Call Date: Mar 2003, Lincoln's Inn
Qualifications: [BMus (Hons)]
dpage@carmelitechambers.co.uk

PAGE MRS JANE ELIZABETH

Chartlands Chambers
3 St Giles Terrace, Northampton NN1 2BN, ☎01604 603322
✉enquiries@chartlands-chambers.co.uk
Call Date: July 1982, Inner Temple
Pupil Supervisor
Qualifications: [LLB]
janepage194@btinternet.com

PAGE MR JONATHAN ROWLAND THOMAS

Carmelite Chambers
9 Carmelite Street, London EC4Y 0DR, ☎020 7936 6300
✉clerks@carmelitechambers.co.uk
Call Date: Oct 1996, Middle Temple
Qualifications: [BEng PhD (Lond) CPE]
jpage@carmelitechambers.co.uk

PAGE MR NIGEL BERNARD

St Mary's Family Law Chambers
26-28 High Pavement, The Lace Market, Nottingham NG1 1HN, ☎0115 950 3503
✉clerks@stmarysflc.co.uk
Call Date: July 1976, Gray's Inn
Pupil Supervisor
Qualifications: [LLB (Lond)]
nigel.page@stmarysflc.co.uk

PAGE MISS REBECCA

Enterprise Chambers
9 Old Square, Lincoln's Inn, London WC2A 3SR, ☎020 7405 9471
✉london@enterprisechambers.com
Enterprise Chambers
65 Quayside, Newcastle Upon Tyne NE1 3DE, ☎0191 222 3344
✉newcastle@enterprisechambers.com
Enterprise Chambers
43 Park Square, Leeds LS1 2NP, ☎0113 246 0391
✉leeds@enterprisechambers.com
Call Date: Nov 2001, Gray's Inn
Qualifications: [BA (Cantab)]
rebeccapage@enterprisechambers.com

PAGE MR STEPHEN

Warwick House Chambers
8 Warwick Court, Warwick House Chambers, Gray's Inn, London WC1R 5DJ, ☎020 7430 2323
✉clerks@warwickhousechambers.com
Call Date: Mar 2003, Gray's Inn
Qualifications: [BA (So'ton) MA]

PAGET MS HENRIETTA FRANCES

9-12 Bell Yard
London WC2A 2JR, ☎020 7400 1800
✉clerks@9-12bellyard.com
Call Date: Oct 1999, Inner Temple
Pupil Supervisor
Qualifications: [BA (Worcs)]

PAGET MR MICHAEL RODBOROUGH

Garden Court Chambers
57-60 Lincoln's Inn Fields, London WC2A 3LJ, ☎020 7993 7600 ✉info@gclaw.co.uk
Call Date: Oct 1995, Lincoln's Inn
Qualifications: [BSc (Hons) MA (Bris) CPE]

PAGETT MISS HELEN CATHERINE

Crown Office Chambers
2 Crown Office Row, Temple, London EC4Y 7HJ, ☎020 7797 8100
✉mail@crownofficechambers.com
Call Date: July 2008, Inner Temple
Qualifications: [BSc MA (Dunelm)]
pagett@crownofficechambers.com

PAHLAVANPOUR MR RIO

4 Breams Buildings
Chancery Lane, London EC4A 1HP, ☎020 7092 1900 ✉clerks@4bb.co.uk
Call Date: Mar 2006, Lincoln's Inn
Qualifications: [BSc (Hons) (Surrey) PgDl]

PAIGE MR RICHARD MARK

Sovereign Chambers
46 Park Place, Leeds LS1 2RY, ☎0113 245 1841
✉clerks@sovereignchambers.co.uk
Call Date: Oct 1997, Middle Temple
Pupil Supervisor
Qualifications: [MA (Hons)(Oxon) MA (Lond)]
richard.paige@sovereignchambers.co.uk

E

PAIN MR KEVIN MARK

Pallant Chambers
12 North Pallant, Chichester, West Sussex PO19 1TQ, ☎01243 784538
✉clerks@pallantchambers.co.uk
Call Date: Oct 1995, Gray's Inn
Qualifications: [MA (Oxon)]
clerks@pallantchambers.co.uk

PAINE MR DOUGLAS GEORGE

One Essex Court
Ground Floor, One Essex Court, Temple, London EC4Y 9AR, ☎020 7583 2000
✉clerks@oeclaw.co.uk
Call Date: Oct 2009, Lincoln's Inn
Qualifications: [BA MPHIL PHD (Cantab) CPE UCU]
dpaine@oeclaw.co.uk

PAINES MR NICHOLAS PAUL BILLOT QC (1997)

Monckton Chambers
1 & 2 Raymond Buildings, Gray's Inn, London WC1R 5NR, ☎020 7405 7211
✉chambers@monckton.com
Call Date: Apr 1978, Gray's Inn
Qualifications: [MA Lic Spec en droit Eur]
npaines@monckton.com

PAKROOH MR RAMIN

Guildhall Chambers
23 Broad Street, Bristol BS1 2HG, ☎0117 930 9000
✉hoc@guildhallchambers.co.uk
Call Date: Mar 1996, Lincoln's Inn
Qualifications: [LLB (Hons)]
ramin.pakrooh@guildhallchambers.co.uk

PALEY MS RUTH THERESA ELIZABETH

23 Essex Street
London WC2R 3AA, ☎020 7413 0353
✉clerks@23es.com
Call Date: Oct 2003, Gray's Inn
Qualifications: [LLB (So'ton)]
ruthpaley@23es.com

PALFREY MR MONTAGUE MARK

3 PB Barristers
3 Paper Buildings, Temple, London EC4Y 7EU, ☎020 7583 8055
3 PB Barristers
23 Beaumont Street, Oxford OX1 2NP, ☎01865 793 736
3 PB Barristers
4 St Peter Street, Winchester SO23 8BW, ☎01962 868884
✉clerks.winchester@3paper.co.uk
3 PB Barristers
Royal Talbot House, 2 Victoria Street, Bristol, Avon BS1 6BB, ☎0117 928 1520
3 PB Barristers
30 Christchurch Road, Bournemouth, Dorset BH1 3PD, ☎01202 292102
✉clerks.bournemouth@3paper.co.uk
Call Date: Nov 1985, Middle Temple
Pupil Supervisor
Qualifications: [LLB (Bucks)]
monty.palfrey@3paper.co.uk

PALIN MISS SARAH MCLEAN

One Brick Court
1st Floor, One Brick Court, Temple, London EC4Y 9BY, ☎020 7353 8845
✉clerks@onebrickcourt.com
Call Date: Nov 1999, Middle Temple
Qualifications: [BA (Hons)(Oxon)]
sp@onebrickcourt.com

PALLO MR SIMON RUSSEL

Bank House Chambers
Old Bank House, Hartshead, Sheffield S1 2EL, ☎0114 275 1223
✉w.digby@bankhousechambers.co.uk
Call Date: July 2003, Gray's Inn
Qualifications: [LLB (Leic)]
s.pallo@bankhousechambers.co.uk

PALMER MR ADRIAN OLIVER QC (1992)

Guildhall Chambers
23 Broad Street, Bristol BS1 2HG, ☎0117 930 9000
✉hoc@guildhallchambers.co.uk
Call Date: July 1972, Middle Temple
Recorder
Qualifications: [MA (Cantab) LLM]
adrian.palmer@guildhallchambers.co.uk

PALMER MS ANYA

Old Square Chambers
10-11 Bedford Row, London WC1R 4BU, ☎020 7269 0300 ✉clerks@oldsquare.co.uk
Old Square Chambers
3 Orchard Court, St Augustine's Yard, Bristol BS1 5DP, ☎0117 930 5100
✉clerks@oldsquare.co.uk
Call Date: July 1999, Inner Temple
Qualifications: [BA (Hons)]
palmer@oldsquare.co.uk

PALMER MISS BRIONY MADELAINE

3 Dr Johnson's Buildings
Ground Floor, 3 Dr Johnson's Buildings, Temple, London EC4Y 7BA, ☎ 020 7353 4854
✉ clerks@3djb.co.uk
Call Date: July 2009, Inner Temple
Qualifications: [BA MSt (Oxon)]

PALMER MISS CLAIRE LOUISE

Thomas More Chambers
7 Lincoln's Inn Fields, London WC2A 3BP, ☎ 020 7404 7000
✉ clerks@thomasmore.co.uk
Call Date: Oct 2003, Lincoln's Inn
Pupil Supervisor
Qualifications: [LLB (Hons) (Bris)]
✉ cpalmer@thomasmore.co.uk

PALMER MR EDWARD JAMES

Regent Chambers
Regent House, 3 Pall Mall, Hanley, Stoke On Trent ST1 1HP, ☎ 01782 286666
✉ clerks@regentchambers.co.uk
Call Date: July 2000, Lincoln's Inn
Qualifications: [LLB LLM (Lanc)]
✉ edward.palmer@regentchambers.co.uk

PALMER MR HOWARD WILLIAM ARTHUR QC (1999)

2 Temple Gardens
2 Temple Gardens, Temple, London EC4Y 9AY, ☎ 020 7822 1200
✉ clerks@2tg.co.uk
Call Date: July 1977, Inner Temple
Recorder
Qualifications: [MA (Oxon)]
✉ hpalmer@2tg.co.uk

PALMER MR IAIN FRANKLYN

Renaissance Chambers
5th Floor, Gray's Inn Chambers, Gray's Inn, London WC1R 5JA, ☎ 020 7404 1111
✉ clerks@renaissancechambers.co.uk
Call Date: Nov 1999, Middle Temple
Qualifications: [LLB (Hons)]

PALMER MR JAMES SAVILL

Henderson Chambers
2 Harcourt Buildings, Temple, London EC4Y 9DB, ☎ 020 7583 9020
✉ clerks@hendersonchambers.co.uk
Call Date: Nov 1983, Middle Temple
Qualifications: [MA (Cantab)]

PALMER MR MARTIN ANDREW

Littleton Chambers
3 King's Bench Walk North, Temple, London EC4Y 7HR, ☎ 020 7797 8600
✉ fschneider@littletonchambers.co.uk
Call Date: July 2003, Inner Temple
Qualifications: [MA Hons (Oxon)]
✉ clerks@littletonchambers.co.uk

PALMER MR MICHAEL JOHN ERIC

Serle Court
6 New Square, Lincoln's Inn, London WC2A 3QS, ☎ 020 7242 6105
✉ clerks@serlecourt.co.uk
Call Date: Mar 2004, Lincoln's Inn
Qualifications: [LLB (Hons) (Cantab) BSc (Hons) (Lond) LLD (Lond)]
✉ mpalmer@serlecourt.co.uk

PALMER MR NATHAN EMMANUEL

5 Pump Court
Ground Floor, 5 Pump Court, Temple, London EC4Y 7AP, ☎ 020 7353 2532
✉ clerks@5pumpcourt.com
Call Date: Oct 1994, Middle Temple
Qualifications: [LLB (Hons)(Lond)]
✉ nathanpalmer@5pumpcourt.com

PALMER PROF NORMAN ERNEST

3 Stone Buildings
Ground Floor, 3 Stone Buildings, Lincoln's Inn, London WC2A 3XL, ☎ 020 7242 4937
✉ clerks@3sb.law.co.uk
York Chambers
Rotterdam House, 116 The Quayside, Newcastle Upon Tyne NE1 3DY, ☎ 0191 206 4677
Call Date: July 1973, Gray's Inn
Pupil Supervisor
Qualifications: [MA BCL (Oxon)]
✉ npalmer@3sb.law.co.uk

PALMER MR PATRICK JOHN STEVEN

Sovereign Chambers
46 Park Place, Leeds LS1 2RY, ☎ 0113 245 1841
✉ clerks@sovereignchambers.co.uk
Call Date: July 1978, Inner Temple
Pupil Supervisor, Recorder
Qualifications: [LLB (Lond)]
✉ patrick.palmer@sovereignchambers.co.uk

E

PALMER MR ROBERT HENRY

Monckton Chambers
1 & 2 Raymond Buildings, Gray's Inn, London WC1R 5NR, ☎ 020 7405 7211
✉ chambers@monckton.com
Call Date: Oct 1998, Gray's Inn
Pupil Supervisor
Qualifications: [BA (Oxon) Dip Law]
✉ rpalmer@monckton.com

PALMER DR STEPHANIE MARGARET

Blackstone Chambers
Blackstone House, Temple, London EC4Y 9BW, ☎ 020 7583 1770
✉ clerks@blackstonechambers.com
Call Date: Mar 2000, Middle Temple
Qualifications: [LLB LLM SJD]
✉ stephaniepalmer@blackstonechambers.com

PALMER MISS SUZANNE ELIZABETH JOSEPHINE

4 King's Bench Walk
2nd Floor, 4 King's Bench Walk, Temple, London EC4Y 7DL, ☎ 020 7822 7000
✉ clerks@4kbw.co.uk
Call Date: Nov 1995, Middle Temple
Pupil Supervisor
Qualifications: [BA (Hons) (Oxon)]
✉ sxp@4kbw.co.uk

PALMER MR TIMOTHY NIGEL JOHN

1 High Pavement
Nottingham NG1 1HF, ☎ 0115 941 8218
✉ clerks@1highpavement.co.uk
Call Date: July 1982, Middle Temple
Pupil Supervisor
Qualifications: [LLB]
✉ timothypalmer@1highpavement.co.uk

PALSER MISS ELAINE JAQUELINE

9 Stone Buildings
Lincoln's Inn, London WC2A 3NN, ☎ 020 7404 5055
✉ clerks@9stonebuildings.com
Call Date: Oct 2002, Middle Temple
Qualifications: [MA (Cantab) MA (Oxon)]
✉ epalser@9stonebuildings.com

PALTENGHI MR MARK FRANCIS

Atkinson Bevan Chambers
1st Floor, 2 Harcourt Buildings, Temple, London EC4Y 9DB, ☎ 020 7353 2112
✉ clerks@2hb.co.uk
Call Date: July 1979, Middle Temple
Qualifications: *[LLB]*
✉ MPaltenghi@2hb.co.uk

PANAGIOTOPOULOU MISS SOPHIE THALIA

Staple Inn Chambers
1st Floor, 9 Staple Inn, Holborn Bars, London WC1V 7QH, ☎ 020 7242 5240
✉ clerks@stapleinn.co.uk
Call Date: Oct 1995, Middle Temple
Qualifications: [LLB (Hons) LLM (Hons)]

PANAGIOTOPOULOU MISS TANIA

Staple Inn Chambers
1st Floor, 9 Staple Inn, Holborn Bars, London WC1V 7QH, ☎ 020 7242 5240
✉ clerks@stapleinn.co.uk
Call Date: Oct 1994, Middle Temple
Qualifications: [LLB (Hons) LLM (Bucks)]

PANAYI MR PAVLOS PAUL

Carmelite Chambers
9 Carmelite Street, London EC4Y 0DR, ☎ 020 7936 6300
✉ clerks@carmelitechambers.co.uk
Call Date: Oct 1995, Gray's Inn
Pupil Supervisor
Qualifications: [LLB]
✉ ppanayi@carmelitechambers.co.uk

PANDE MISS KAKOLY

2 Dr Johnson's Buildings
2 Dr Johnson's Buildings, Temple, London EC4Y 7AY, ☎ 020 7936 2613
✉ clerks@2drj.com
Call Date: Oct 2005, Middle Temple
Qualifications: [LLB (Hons)]
✉ clerks@2drj.com

PANDYA MISS ABHA

12 King's Bench Walk
12 King's Bench Walk, Temple, London EC4Y 7EL, ☎ 020 7583 0811
Call Date: Mar 2007, Middle Temple
Qualifications: [LLB (Oxon)]
✉ Pandya@12kbw.co.uk

PANESAR MR DESHPAL SINGH

Old Square Chambers
10-11 Bedford Row, London WC1R 4BU, ☎ 020 7269 0300 ✉ clerks@oldsquare.co.uk
Old Square Chambers
3 Orchard Court, St Augustine's Yard, Bristol BS1 5DP, ☎ 0117 930 5100
✉ clerks@oldsquare.co.uk
Call Date: Feb 1993, Inner Temple
Qualifications: [LLB (Hons)(Lond)]
✉ panesar@oldsquare.co.uk

E

PANESAR MR RASHVINDERJEET SINGH

Lombard Chambers
1 Sekforde Street, Clerkenwell, London EC1R 0BE, ☎020 7107 2100
Call Date: July 2004, Gray's Inn
Qualifications: [LLB (B'ham)]

PANNICK LORD DAVID PHILIP QC (1992)

Blackstone Chambers
Blackstone House, Temple, London EC4Y 9BW, ☎020 7583 1770
✉clerks@blackstonechambers.com
Call Date: July 1979, Gray's Inn
Recorder
Qualifications: [MA BCL (Oxon)]
davidpannick@blackstonechambers.com

PANTON MR ALASTAIR HOWARD

10 King's Bench Walk
Ground Floor, 10 King's Bench Walk, Temple, London EC4Y 7EB, ☎020 7353 7742
✉Chambers@10kingsbenchwalk.co.uk
Call Date: Oct 1996, Inner Temple
Qualifications: [MA (Cantab) CPE]
alastair.panton@10kingsbenchwalk.co.uk

PANTON MR THOMAS PATRICK

Ropewalk Chambers
24 The Ropewalk, Nottingham NG1 5EF, ☎0115 947 2581 ✉clerks@ropewalk.co.uk
Call Date: July 2002, Lincoln's Inn
Pupil Supervisor
Qualifications: [LLB (Hons)]
tompanton@ropewalk.co.uk

PANTON MR WILLIAM DWIGHT

Amethyst Chambers
Ground Floor, 9 Kings Bench Walk, Inner Temple, London EC4Y 7DX, ☎020 7936 4966
✉info@amethystchambers.com
Call Date: Nov 1977, Inner Temple
Pupil Supervisor

PAPADOPOULOS MR SOCRATES PHILIP

20 Essex Street
London WC2R 3AL, ☎020 7842 1200
✉clerks@20essexst.com
Call Date: Oct 2001, Inner Temple
Qualifications: [BA (Oxon) LLM (Lond)]
clerks@20essexst.com

PAPAGEORGIS MR GEORGE MICHAEL

4 Breams Buildings
Chancery Lane, London EC4A 1HP, ☎020 7092 1900 ✉clerks@4bb.co.uk
Call Date: July 1981, Middle Temple
Pupil Supervisor

PAPAZIAN MISS CLIONA CONCEPTA

4 Paper Buildings
1st Floor, 4 Paper Buildings, Temple, London EC4Y 7EX, ☎020 7427 5200
✉clerks@4pb.com
Call Date: Nov 1994, Inner Temple
Pupil Supervisor
Qualifications: [BA (Wales) MA LLB (Ireland)]
cp@4pb.com

PARAMJORTHY MR NISHANTHAN

Renaissance Chambers
5th Floor, Gray's Inn Chambers, Gray's Inn, London WC1R 5JA, ☎020 7404 1111
✉clerks@renaissancechambers.co.uk
Call Date: Nov 1999, Lincoln's Inn
Qualifications: [LLB (Hons)(Wales)]

PARASKOS MR PARASKEVAKIS CHRISTAKIS

11 Gray's Inn Square Chambers
Chambers of Mr Ian Sen, 1st Floor South, 10/11 Gray's Inn Square, London WC1R 5JD, ☎020 7405 6879
✉clerks@11graysinnsquare.com
Call Date: July 2003, Middle Temple
Qualifications: [LLB Hons (WMIN) LLM (WMIN) Pg Dip (ICSL)]

PARATHALINGAM MISS AMRISHA SWAHI AKILA

St Philips Chambers
55 Temple Row, Birmingham B2 5LS, ☎0121 246 7000 ✉clerks@st-philips.com
Call Date: Nov 2004, Lincoln's Inn
Qualifications: [LLB (Hons)]

PARDOE MR MATTHEW JAMES

Dyers Chambers
35 Bedford Row, London WC1R 4JH, ☎020 7404 1881
✉admin@dyerschambers.com
Call Date: Feb 1992, Inner Temple
Qualifications: [BA (Hons) CPE]

E

PARDOE MR RUPERT ADAM CORIN

23 Essex Street
London WC2R 3AA, ☎020 7413 0353
✉clerks@23es.com
Call Date: July 1984, Inner Temple
Pupil Supervisor
Qualifications: [MA (Cantab)]
✉rupertpardoe@23es.com

PARE MR CHRISTOPHER MICHAEL

Call Date: July 2006, Middle Temple
Qualifications: [LLB (Hons) (Sheff)]
✉clerk@stjohnsbuildings.co.uk, chris.pare@stjohnsbuildings.co.uk

PARFITT MR MATTHEW CHARLES

Erskine Chambers
33 Chancery Lane, London WC2A 1EN,
☎020 7242 5532
✉clerks@erskinechambers.com
Call Date: Nov 2005, Lincoln's Inn
Qualifications: [BA (Hons) (Oxon)]
✉mparfitt@erskine-chambers.co.uk

PARHAM MR SAM WILLIAM

1 Pump Court
Elm Court, Temple, London EC4Y 7AB,
☎020 7842 7070
✉(name)@pumpcourt.co.uk
Call Date: Oct 2000, Gray's Inn
Qualifications: [LLB (LSE)]
✉sam@1pumpcourt.co.uk

PARISH MR STEPHEN ADRIAN BURGIS

2 King's Bench Walk
2 King's Bench Walk, Temple, London
EC4Y 7DE, ☎020 7353 1746
✉clerks@2kbw.com
Call Date: July 1966, Inner Temple
Recorder
Qualifications: [LLB]
✉sparish@2kbw.com

PARKE MISS KARA GENEVIEVE JOY

One Essex Court
1st Floor, Temple, London EC4Y 9AR,
☎020 7936 3030 ✉clerks@1ec.co.uk
Call Date: Nov 2006, Middle Temple
Qualifications: [LLB (Hons) (Dub) LLM (Lond)]

PARKER MR BENJAMIN JONATHAN

7 King's Bench Walk
Ground Floor, 7 King's Bench Walk, Temple,
London EC4Y 7DS, ☎020 7910 8300
✉clerks@7kbw.co.uk
Call Date: July 2000, Middle Temple
Qualifications: [MA(Hons) (Oxon) BCL (Oxon) MA (Cantab)]
✉bparker@7kbw.co.uk

PARKER MR CHRISTOPHER JAMES FRANCIS QC (2006)

3 PB Barristers
3 Paper Buildings, Temple, London EC4Y 7EU,
☎020 7583 8055
3 PB Barristers
Royal Talbot House, 2 Victoria Street, Bristol,
Avon BS1 6BB, ☎0117 928 1520
3 PB Barristers
23 Beaumont Street, Oxford OX1 2NP,
☎01865 793 736
3 PB Barristers
4 St Peter Street, Winchester SO23 8BW,
☎01962 868884
✉clerks.winchester@3paper.co.uk
3 PB Barristers
30 Christchurch Road, Bournemouth, Dorset
BH1 3PD, ☎01202 292102
✉clerks.bournemouth@3paper.co.uk
Call Date: July 1986, Gray's Inn
Recorder
Qualifications: [LLB (Hons)(Exon)]
✉cp@3paper.co.uk

PARKER MR CHRISTOPHER ROY QC (2008)

Maitland Chambers
7 Stone Buildings, Lincoln's Inn, London
WC2A 3SZ, ☎020 7406 1200
✉clerks@maitlandchambers.com
Call Date: Nov 1984, Lincoln's Inn
Qualifications: [MA (Oxon) (LLM (Harv) BCL LLM]
✉crparker@maitlandchambers.com

PARKER MRS KAREN LESLEY

Hampshire
Guildhall Chambers Portsmouth
Prudential Buildings, 16 Guildhall Walk,
Portsmouth, Hampshire PO1 2DE,
☎023 9275 2400
✉clerks@gcp-barristers.com
Call Date: July 2001, Inner Temple
Qualifications: [BSc (bedford) CPE (Manch)]

E

PARKER MISS KATE LOUISE

Civitas Chambers
Global Reach, Celtic Gateway, Cardiff Bay, Cardiff CF11 0SN, ☎ 0845 0713 007
✉ clerks@civitaslaw.com
Call Date: July 2010, Inner Temple
Qualifications: [LLB Cardiff University]

PARKER MISS LOUISE NATHALIE MARY

Thomas More Chambers
7 Lincoln's Inn Fields, London WC2A 3BP, ☎ 020 7404 7000
✉ clerks@thomasmore.co.uk
Call Date: Nov 2007, Middle Temple
Qualifications: [BA (Hons) (Cantab) PgDL (Lond) MA (Hons) (Cantab) BVC (Lond)]

PARKER MISS LYCIA LAURE COATS

The Chambers of Grahame Aldous QC
9 Gough Square, London EC4A 3DG, ☎ 020 7832 0500
✉ clerks@9goughsquare.co.uk
Call Date: July 2010, Lincoln's Inn
Qualifications: [BSc (Bris)]
✉ lparker@9goughsquare.co.uk

PARKER MR MATTHEW RICHARD

3 Verulam Buildings
London WC1R 5NT, ☎ 020 7831 8441
✉ chambers@3vb.com
Call Date: Oct 1997, Middle Temple
Pupil Supervisor
Qualifications: [BA (Hons)(Cantab) CPE]
✉ mparker@3vb.com

PARKER MR PAUL ANDREW

Four New Square
Four New Square, Lincoln's Inn, London WC2A 3RJ, ☎ 020 7822 2000
✉ barristers@4newsquare.com
Call Date: July 1986, Middle Temple
Pupil Supervisor
Qualifications: [MA(Cantab)]
✉ p.parker@4newsquare.com

PARKER MR STEVEN NIGEL

Number 7 Harrington Street Chambers
7 Harrington Street, Liverpool L2 9YH, ☎ 0151 242 0707 ✉ clerks@7hs.co.uk
Call Date: Nov 1987, Gray's Inn
Qualifications: [LLB]
✉ steven.parker@7hs.co.uk

PARKER MR TIMOTHY TERENCE

The Chambers of Grahame Aldous QC
9 Gough Square, London EC4A 3DG, ☎ 020 7832 0500
✉ clerks@9goughsquare.co.uk
Call Date: Nov 1995, Gray's Inn
Pupil Supervisor
Qualifications: [BA (Hons) (Lond) Dip Law]

PARKER MISS WENDY

Hardwicke
New Square, Lincoln's Inn, London WC2A 3SB, ☎ 020 7242 2523
✉ enquiries@hardwicke.co.uk
Call Date: July 1978, Middle Temple
Pupil Supervisor
Qualifications: [MA]
✉ wendy.parker@hardwicke.co.uk

PARKIN MISS FIONA JANE QC (2011)

Atkin Chambers
1 Atkin Building, Gray's Inn, London WC1R 5AT, ☎ 020 7404 0102
✉ clerks@atkinchambers.com
Call Date: Oct 1993, Inner Temple
Pupil Supervisor
Qualifications: [LLB (Hons) (Exon) LLB (Hons) (Cantab)]
✉ clerks@atkinchambers.com

PARKINS MR GRAHAM CHARLES QC (1990)

18 Red Lion Court
London EC4A 3EB, ☎ 020 7520 6000
✉ chambers@18rlc.co.uk
18 Red Lion Court (Annexe)
Thornwood House, 102 New London Road, Chelmsford, Essex CM2 0RG, ☎ 01245 280880
Call Date: July 1972, Inner Temple
Qualifications: [LLB (Hons)]
✉ graham.parkins@18rlc.co.uk

PARKINSON MR ANDREW JAMES

Landmark Chambers
180 Fleet Street, London EC4A 2HG, ☎ 020 7430 1221
✉ clerks@landmarkchambers.co.uk
Call Date: Oct 2010, Lincoln's Inn
Qualifications: [BA (Oxon)]
✉ aparkinson@landmarkchambers.co.uk

E

PARKINSON MR WILLIAM HAROLD

64 Bridge Street
3rd Floor, 64 Bridge Street, Manchester M3 3BN, ☎0845 083 3000
✉mail@64bridgestreet.com
Chambers of Mr William Parkinson
St Andrews, 3a Mort Street, Wigan, Lancashire WN6 7AU, ☎0845 083 3000
Call Date: Oct 1997, Lincoln's Inn
Qualifications: [LLB (Hons)]
parkinson@clerksroom.com

PARMAR MISS CHETNA SURESH

Cobden House Chambers
19 Quay Street, Manchester M3 3HN, ☎0161 833 6000 ✉Clerks@Cobden.co.uk
Call Date: July 2003, Gray's Inn
Qualifications: [LLB (Lanc) LLM (Manch)]
clerks@cobden.co.uk

PARNELL MRS CHERIE EILEEN

East Anglian Chambers
Gresham House, 5 Museum Street, Ipswich, Suffolk IP1 1HQ, ☎01473 214481
✉ipswich@ealaw.co.uk
East Anglian Chambers
53 North Hill, Colchester, Essex CO1 1QA, ☎01473 214481 ✉colchester@ealaw.co.uk
East Anglian Chambers
15 The Close, Norwich, Norfolk NR1 4DZ, ☎01473 214481 ✉norwich@ealaw.co.uk
Call Date: Nov 2000, Middle Temple
Qualifications: [LLB (Hons)]
cherieparnell@ealaw.co.uk

PARR MR JOHN EDWARD

Cobden House Chambers
19 Quay Street, Manchester M3 3HN, ☎0161 833 6000 ✉Clerks@Cobden.co.uk
Call Date: July 1989, Middle Temple
Qualifications: [LLB (Reading)]
clerks@cobden.co.uk

PARR MS JUDITH MARGARET

Renaissance Chambers
5th Floor, Gray's Inn Chambers, Gray's Inn, London WC1R 5JA, ☎020 7404 1111
✉clerks@renaissancechambers.co.uk
Call Date: Feb 1994, Inner Temple
Qualifications: [LLB (New Zealand)]
jpa@renaissancechambers.co.uk

PARR MISS MARGARET MARY

Oriel Chambers
14 Water Street, Liverpool, Merseyside L2 8TD, ☎0151 236 7191
✉clerks@orielchambers.co.uk
Call Date: Mar 2008, Lincoln's Inn
Qualifications: [BA (Oxon)]
margaret.parr@orielchambers.co.uk

PARRATT DR DAVID RICHMOND

Crown Office Chambers
2 Crown Office Row, Temple, London EC4Y 7HJ, ☎020 7797 8100
✉mail@crownofficechambers.com
Call Date: Mar 2009, Lincoln's Inn
Qualifications: [LLB (Aberdeen) PHD (Edin)]
david.parratt@advocates.org.uk

PARRISH MR SAMUEL NEVILLE

3 PB Barristers
3 Paper Buildings, Temple, London EC4Y 7EU, ☎020 7583 8055
3 PB Barristers
23 Beaumont Street, Oxford OX1 2NP, ☎01865 793 736
3 PB Barristers
30 Christchurch Road, Bournemouth, Dorset BH1 3PD, ☎01202 292102
✉clerks.bournemouth@3paper.co.uk
3 PB Barristers
Royal Talbot House, 2 Victoria Street, Bristol, Avon BS1 6BB, ☎0117 928 1520
3 PB Barristers
4 St Peter Street, Winchester SO23 8BW, ☎01962 868884
✉clerks.winchester@3paper.co.uk
Call Date: Feb 1962, Inner Temple
Pupil Supervisor
Qualifications: [LLB (Hons)]
samuel.parrish@3paper.co.uk

PARROY MR MICHAEL PICTON QC (1991)

3 PB Barristers
3 Paper Buildings, Temple, London EC4Y 7EU, ☎020 7583 8055
3 PB Barristers
23 Beaumont Street, Oxford OX1 2NP, ☎01865 793 736
3 PB Barristers
4 St Peter Street, Winchester SO23 8BW, ☎01962 868884
✉clerks.winchester@3paper.co.uk
3 PB Barristers
Royal Talbot House, 2 Victoria Street, Bristol, Avon BS1 6BB, ☎0117 928 1520

3 PB Barristers
30 Christchurch Road, Bournemouth, Dorset BH1 3PD, ☎01202 292102
✉clerks.bournemouth@3paper.co.uk
Call Date: Nov 1969, Middle Temple
Recorder
Qualifications: [BA (Oxon) MA (Oxon)]

PARRY MISS ANGHARAD MYRA

20 Essex Street
London WC2R 3AL, ☎020 7842 1200
✉clerks@20essexst.com
Call Date: Oct 2002, Gray's Inn
Qualifications: [BA (Hons) (Oxon) LLM (Cantab)]
✉clerks@20essexst.com

PARRY MR CHARLES ROBERT

Pump Court Chambers
31 Southgate Street, Winchester, Hampshire SO23 9EB, ☎01962 868 161
✉clerks@3pumpcourt.com
Pump Court Chambers
Upper Ground Floor, 3 Pump Court, Temple, London EC4Y 7AJ, ☎020 7353 0711
✉clerks@3pumpcourt.com
Pump Court Chambers
5 Temple Chambers, Temple Street, Swindon SN1 1SQ, ☎01793 539899
✉clerks@3pumpcourt.com
Call Date: Nov 1973, Middle Temple
Pupil Supervisor
Qualifications: [LLB (Lond)]

PARRY MS CLARE ELEANOR

Cornerstone Barristers
2-3 Gray's Inn Square, Gray's Inn, London WC1R 5JH, ☎020 7242 4986
✉chambers@2-3gis.co.uk
Call Date: Nov 2005, Middle Temple
Qualifications: [BA (Hons) Oxford]
✉cparry@2-3gis.co.uk

PARRY MR PHILIP CHRISTOPHER

Call Date: Oct 1995, Lincoln's Inn
Pupil Supervisor
Qualifications: [LLB (Hons)(Sheff)]

PARRY MISS SIAN RACHEL

9 Park Place
9 Park Place, Cardiff, South Glamorgan CF10 3DP, ☎029 2038 2731
✉clerks@9parkplace.co.uk
Call Date: Oct 1994, Gray's Inn
Qualifications: [LLB (Hons)(Wales)]
✉sparry@9parkplace.co.uk

PARRY MR SIMON EDWARD

Call Date: Nov 1997, Inner Temple
Qualifications: [LLB (Wales)]
✉clerk@stjohnsbuildings.co.uk

PARRY EVANS MS MARY ALETHEA

30 Park Place
Cardiff CF10 3BS, ☎029 2039 8421
✉clerks@30parkplace.law.co.uk
Call Date: June 1953, Inner Temple
Pupil Supervisor
Qualifications: [BCL MA]

PARRY-JONES MRS CAROLE ANN

East Anglian Chambers
15 The Close, Norwich, Norfolk NR1 4DZ, ☎01473 214481 ✉norwich@ealaw.co.uk
East Anglian Chambers
140 New London Road, Chelmsford, Essex CM2 0AW, ☎01473 214481
✉chelmsford@ealaw.co.uk
East Anglian Chambers
Gresham House, 5 Museum Street, Ipswich, Suffolk IP1 1HQ, ☎01473 214481
✉ipswich@ealaw.co.uk
Call Date: Nov 1992, Middle Temple
Qualifications: [LLB (Hons) (Lond)]
✉caroleparry-jones@ealaw.co.uk

PARRY-JONES MR JOHN TREVOR

Number 7 Harrington Street Chambers
7 Harrington Street, Liverpool L2 9YH, ☎0151 242 0707 ✉clerks@7hs.co.uk
Call Date: Feb 1992, Gray's Inn
Pupil Supervisor
Qualifications: [LLB (Hons) (Wales)]
✉trevor.parryjones@7hs.co.uk

PARSLEY MR CHARLES RONALD

30 Park Place
Cardiff CF10 3BS, ☎029 2039 8421
✉clerks@30parkplace.law.co.uk
Call Date: July 1973, Inner Temple
Qualifications: [LLB (Exon)]
✉crp@30parkplace.co.uk

PARSONS MR ANDREW JAMES

Portsmouth Barristers'Chambers
Victory House, 7 Bellevue Terrace, Portsmouth, Hampshire PO5 3AT, ☎023 9283 1292
✉clerks@portsmouthbar.com
Call Date: July 1985, Inner Temple
Pupil Supervisor
Qualifications: [LLB (Hons)(Lond) FCI Arb]

E

PARSONS MR GLEN ANDREW

Park Court Chambers
16 Park Place, Leeds LS1 2SJ,
☎0113 243 3277
✉clerks@parkcourtchambers.co.uk
Call Date: Oct 1999, Lincoln's Inn
Pupil Supervisor
Qualifications: [LLB (Hons)(Hudders)]
clerks@parkcourtchambers.co.uk

PARSONS MR LUKE ARTHUR QC (2003)

Quadrant Chambers
Quadrant House, 10 Fleet Street, London EC4Y 1AU, ☎020 7583 4444
✉info@quadrantchambers.com
Call Date: July 1985, Inner Temple
Qualifications: [LLB (Bris)]
luke.parsons@quadrantchambers.com

PARSONS MS NAOMI PHILIPPA

18 Red Lion Court
London EC4A 3EB, ☎020 7520 6000
✉chambers@18rlc.co.uk
Call Date: Oct 2008, Inner Temple
Qualifications: [BA (Nott'm)]

E

PARTINGTON MR DAVID JOHN

Sovereign Chambers
46 Park Place, Leeds LS1 2RY,
☎0113 245 1841
✉clerks@sovereignchambers.co.uk
Call Date: July 1987, Middle Temple
Pupil Supervisor
Qualifications: [MA (Cantab)]
david.partington@sovereignchambers.co.uk

PARTINGTON MISS LISA SHIRLEY

Call Date: July 1989, Inner Temple
Qualifications: [LLB (Hons)]
clerk@stjohnsbuildings.co.uk

PARTRIDGE MR IAN SIMON

3 PB Barristers
3 Paper Buildings, Temple, London EC4Y 7EU, ☎020 7583 8055
3 PB Barristers
30 Christchurch Road, Bournemouth, Dorset BH1 3PD, ☎01202 292102
✉clerks.bournemouth@3paper.co.uk
3 PB Barristers
4 St Peter Street, Winchester SO23 8BW, ☎01962 868884
✉clerks.winchester@3paper.co.uk
3 PB Barristers
Royal Talbot House, 2 Victoria Street, Bristol, Avon BS1 6BB, ☎0117 928 1520
3 PB Barristers
23 Beaumont Street, Oxford OX1 2NP, ☎01865 793 736
Call Date: July 1979, Inner Temple
Pupil Supervisor
Qualifications: [MA (Oxon)]
ian.partridge@3paper.co.uk

PARTRIDGE MR JAMES CHRISTOPHER LEWIS

Eastbourne Chambers
5 Chiswick Place, Eastbourne, East Sussex BN21 4NH, ☎01323 642102
✉clerks@eastbournechambers.co.uk
Call Date: Nov 2009, Lincoln's Inn
Qualifications: [LLB (UEA)]
clerks@eastbournechambers.co.uk

PARTRIDGE DR RICHARD CHARLES

3 Serjeants Inn
London EC4Y 1BQ, ☎020 7427 5000
✉clerks@3serjeantsinn.com
Call Date: July 1994, Lincoln's Inn
Pupil Supervisor
Qualifications: [MBBch LLB (Hons) (Wales)]
rpartridge@3serjeantsinn.com

PARTRIDGE MR RICHARD JACK

7 Bell Yard
London WC2A 2JR, ☎020 7831 0636
✉kevintarrant@btconnect.com
Call Date: Oct 1997, Inner Temple
Qualifications: [LLB (Manch)]
rp@7bellyard.co.uk

PARUK MISS SAIRA

Quadrant Chambers
Quadrant House, 10 Fleet Street, London EC4Y 1AU, ☎020 7583 4444
✉info@quadrantchambers.com
Call Date: July 2004, Lincoln's Inn
Qualifications: [BA Hons (Oxon)]
saira.paruk@quadrantchambers.com

PASCALL MR MATTHEW STEPHEN

Guildford Chambers
Stoke House, Leapale Lane, Guildford, Surrey GU1 4LY, ☎01483 539131
✉clerks@guildfordchambers.co.uk
Alexander Chambers
13 Halstead Road, Wanstead, London E11 2AY, ☎0845 652 0451 / 0854 652 0451
✉clerks@alexanderchambers.co.uk
Call Date: July 1984, Middle Temple
Pupil Supervisor
Qualifications: [BA]
mpascall@guildfordchambers.com

PASCOE MR MARTIN MICHAEL QC (2002)

South Square
3-4 South Square, Gray's Inn, London
WC1R 5HP, ☎ 020 7696 9900
✉ practicemanagers@southsquare.com
Call Date: July 1977, Lincoln's Inn
Qualifications: [BA BCL (Oxon)]
✉ martinpascoe@southsquare.com

PASCOE MR NIGEL SPENCER KNIGHT QC (1988)

Pump Court Chambers
31 Southgate Street, Winchester, Hampshire
SO23 9EB, ☎ 01962 868 161
✉ clerks@3pumpcourt.com
Pump Court Chambers
Upper Ground Floor, 3 Pump Court, Temple,
London EC4Y 7AJ, ☎ 020 7353 0711
✉ clerks@3pumpcourt.com
Pump Court Chambers
5 Temple Chambers, Temple Street, Swindon
SN1 1SQ, ☎ 01793 539899
✉ clerks@3pumpcourt.com
Queen Square Chambers
56 Queen Square, Bristol BS1 4PR,
☎ 0117 921 1966 ✉ crime@qs-c.co.uk
Call Date: July 1966, Inner Temple
Recorder
✉ np@3pumpcourt.com

PASCOE MS SORAYA

1 Gray's Inn Square
Ground Floor, 1 Gray's Inn Square, London
WC1R 5AA, ☎ 020 7405 0001
Call Date: July 1999, Gray's Inn
Qualifications: [LLB (Essex)]

PASIUK MS JANINA STEFANIA

Chambers of Janina Pasiuk
7 Marlborough Drive, Heaton Chapel,
Stockport, Cheshire SK4 2QZ,
☎ 0161 442 5576
✉ janinapasiuk@hotmail.co.uk
Call Date: July 1983, Middle Temple
Qualifications: [LLB (B'ham)]

PASSFIELD MR SIMON ALAN

Guildhall Chambers
23 Broad Street, Bristol BS1 2HG,
☎ 0117 930 9000
✉ hoc@guildhallchambers.co.uk
Call Date: July 2009, Gray's Inn
Qualifications: [LLB]
✉ simon.passfield@guildhallchambers.co.uk

PASSMORE MR JOHN WILLIAM

Quadrant Chambers
Quadrant House, 10 Fleet Street, London
EC4Y 1AU, ☎ 020 7583 4444
✉ info@quadrantchambers.com
Call Date: Oct 1992, Lincoln's Inn
Pupil Supervisor
Qualifications: [LLB(Hons)(Bris)]

PATCHETT-JOYCE MR MICHAEL THURSTON

Outer Temple Chambers
The Outer Temple, 222 Strand, London
WC2R 1BA, ☎ 020 7353 6381
✉ clerks@outertemple.com
Call Date: July 1981, Middle Temple
Pupil Supervisor
Qualifications: [MA (Hons) (Cantab)]

PATEL MR BHAVIN VINUBHAI

Middle Temple Lane Chambers
2nd Floor South, 1 Middle Temple Lane,
London EC4Y 9AA, ☎ 020 7583 4352
✉ chambers@mtlchambers.com
Call Date: Nov 1991, Lincoln's Inn
Qualifications: [BA (Oxon)]

PATEL MISS CHETNA

4 Breams Buildings
Chancery Lane, London EC4A 1HP,
☎ 020 7092 1900 ✉ clerks@4bb.co.uk
Call Date: Nov 1995, Lincoln's Inn
Qualifications: [LLB (Hons)]

PATEL MR ELYAS MOHAMMED

Park Court Chambers
16 Park Place, Leeds LS1 2SJ,
☎ 0113 243 3277
✉ clerks@parkcourtchambers.co.uk
Call Date: Nov 1991, Gray's Inn
Qualifications: [LLB (Hons) LLM (Cantab)]
✉ epatel@parkcourtchambers.co.uk

PATEL MISS GITA

Kenworthy's Chambers
Arlington House, Bloom Street, Salford,
Manchester M3 6AJ, ☎ 0161 832 4036
Call Date: July 1988, Inner Temple
Pupil Supervisor
Qualifications: [LLB (B'ham)]
✉ g.patel@kenworthysbarristers.co.uk

E

PATEL MISS HANISHA

Seven Bedford Row
7 Bedford Row, London WC1R 4BS,
☎020 7242 3555 ✉clerks@7br.co.uk
Call Date: Oct 2002, Lincoln's Inn
Qualifications: [LLB (City) BVC]
clerks@7br.co.uk

PATEL MR JAI JAGDISH

4 Breams Buildings
Chancery Lane, London EC4A 1HP,
☎020 7092 1900 ✉clerks@4bb.co.uk
Call Date: Oct 1999, Lincoln's Inn
Qualifications: [LLB (Hons)(Lond) LLM (Lond)]
clerks@4bb.co.uk

PATEL MISS JAYABEN

Chambers of Miss J Patel
77 Chesterfield Road, London E10 6EN,
☎020 8539 7147
✉jaya.patel1@btinternet.com
Call Date: Oct 1990, Inner Temple
Qualifications: [BA (Sussex) LLM (Lond)]
jaya.patel1@btinternet.com

PATEL MR JAYANTILAL LALJI

Chambers of Mr Julius Seal
189 Randolph Avenue, Maida Vale, London
W9 1DJ, ☎020 7328 0158
✉julius.seal@ntlworld.com
Call Date: Nov 1999, Inner Temple
Qualifications: [BSc (City)]

PATEL MS NAINA NIKITA

Blackstone Chambers
Blackstone House, Temple, London
EC4Y 9BW, ☎020 7583 1770
✉clerks@blackstonechambers.com
Call Date: Oct 2005, Inner Temple
Qualifications: [MA (Cantab) BCL (Oxon)]
nainapatel@blackstonechambers.com

PATEL MR PARISHIL JAYANTILAL

39 Essex Street
London WC2R 3AT, ☎020 7832 1111
✉clerks@39essex.com
82 King Street
Manchester M2 4WQ, ☎0161 870 9969
Call Date: Nov 1996, Middle Temple
Pupil Supervisor
Qualifications: [BA (Hons) LLM (Cantab)]
parishil.patel@39essex.com

PATEL MR SANDIP

Furnival Chambers
32 Furnival Street, London EC4A 1JQ,
☎020 7405 3232
Call Date: July 1991, Middle Temple
Pupil Supervisor
Qualifications: [LLB (Hons) (Essex)]

PATEL MR SHAIL

Four New Square
Four New Square, Lincoln's Inn, London
WC2A 3RJ, ☎020 7822 2000
✉barristers@4newsquare.com
Call Date: Nov 2006, Inner Temple
Qualifications: [BA (Oxon) LLM]
s.patel@4newsquare.com

PATEL MR SHERIYAR

The Chambers Of Mr S Patel
35 Ravenscroft Avenue, London NW11 8BH,
☎020 8458 7501
Call Date: Oct 1996, Gray's Inn
Qualifications: [BSc LLB]

PATEL MR YASIN AHMED

25 Bedford Row
London WC1R 4HD, ☎020 7067 1500
✉clerks@25bedfordrow.com
Call Date: July 2002, Gray's Inn
Qualifications: [BA (Kent)]
ypatel@25bedfordrow.com

PATERSON MISS FIONA MARGARET FLEUR

3 Serjeants Inn
London EC4Y 1BQ, ☎020 7427 5000
✉clerks@3serjeantsinn.com
Call Date: Mar 2003, Middle Temple
Qualifications: [LLB (Edin)]
fpaterson@3serjeantsinn.com

PATERSON MR JAMES STUART IAN

Deans Court Chambers
24 St John Street, Manchester M3 4DF,
☎0161 214 6000 ✉clerks@deanscourt.co.uk
Call Date: July 2010, Middle Temple
Qualifications: [BA (Hons) (Dunelm) DipLaw]
paterson@deanscourt.co.uk

PATHAK MR PANKAJ KUMAR

2 Dr Johnson's Buildings
2 Dr Johnson's Buildings, Temple, London
EC4Y 7AY, ☎020 7936 2613
✉clerks@2drj.com
Call Date: Oct 1992, Lincoln's Inn
Pupil Supervisor
Qualifications: [MA (Cantab) LLM (Lond)]
clerks@2drj.com

PATIENCE MR DAVID WILLIAM ANDREW

2 Bedford Row
London WC1R 4BU, ☎ 020 7440 8888
✉ clerks@2bedfordrow.co.uk
Call Date: July 2009, Gray's Inn
Qualifications: [BA]
✉ dpatience@2bedfordrow.co.uk

PATIENCE MR JAMES

Atlantic Chambers
4-6 Cook Street, Liverpool L2 9QU,
☎ 0151 236 4421
✉ info@atlanticchambers.co.uk
Call Date: Oct 2007, Middle Temple
Qualifications: [BA (Hons) (L'pool) Dip Law (Nott'm)]
✉ jamespatience@atlanticchambers.co.uk

PATON MISS DANIELLE

Number 7 Harrington Street Chambers
7 Harrington Street, Liverpool L2 9YH,
☎ 0151 242 0707 ✉ clerks@7hs.co.uk
Call Date: July 2007, Inner Temple
Qualifications: [LLB (Sheff)]

PATON MR EWAN WILLIAM

Guildhall Chambers
23 Broad Street, Bristol BS1 2HG,
☎ 0117 930 9000
✉ hoc@guildhallchambers.co.uk
Call Date: Oct 1996, Inner Temple
Pupil Supervisor
Qualifications: [MA (Oxon) BCL]
✉ ewan.paton@guildhallchambers.co.uk

PATON MR IAN FRANCIS

QEB Hollis Whiteman
1-2 Laurence Pountney Hill, London EC4R 0EU, ☎ 020 7933 8855
✉ barristers@qebhw.co.uk
Call Date: Apr 1975, Middle Temple
Pupil Supervisor, Recorder
✉ barristers@qebholliswhiteman.co.uk

PATON-PHILIP MR RICHARD HENRY

Nine Bedford Row
9 Bedford Row, London WC1R 4AZ,
☎ 020 7489 2727
✉ clerks@9bedfordrow.co.uk
Call Date: Nov 2004, Inner Temple
Qualifications: [LLB London School of Economics & Political Scienc]
✉ clerks@9bedfordrow.co.uk

PATRICK MRS CAROLINE

Central Chambers
89 Princess Street, Manchester M1 4HT,
☎ 0161 236 1133
✉ clerks@centralchambers.co.uk
Call Date: Nov 1999, Lincoln's Inn
Qualifications: [LLB (Hons)(Manch)]

PATRY MS CARINE ANNE ISABELLE

Landmark Chambers
180 Fleet Street, London EC4A 2HG,
☎ 020 7430 1221
✉ clerks@landmarkchambers.co.uk
Call Date: Nov 1999, Inner Temple
Pupil Supervisor
Qualifications: [LLB LLM (Cantab)]
✉ cpatryhoskins@landmarkchambers.co.uk

PATTEN MR BENEDICT JOSEPH QC (2010)

Four New Square
Four New Square, Lincoln's Inn, London WC2A 3RJ, ☎ 020 7822 2000
✉ barristers@4newsquare.com
Call Date: July 1986, Middle Temple
Pupil Supervisor
Qualifications: [BA (Oxon)]
✉ b.patten@4newsquare.com

PATTERSON MR GARETH THOMAS

6 King's Bench Walk
Ground Floor, 6 King's Bench Walk, Temple, London EC4Y 7DR, ☎ 020 7583 0410
✉ clerks@6kbw.com
Call Date: July 1995, Gray's Inn
Pupil Supervisor
Qualifications: [BA (Hons) (Cantab)]
✉ gareth.patterson@6kbw.com

PATTERSON MISS HOLLIE LOUISE VIOLET

18 St John Street
Manchester M3 4EA, ☎ 0161 278 1800
✉ clerks@18sjs.com
Call Date: Oct 2008, Lincoln's Inn
Qualifications: [LLB (Manch)]

PATTERSON MR PHILLIP JOHN DEMIAN

4 Stone Buildings
Ground Floor, 4 Stone Buildings, Lincoln's Inn, London WC2A 3XT, ☎ 020 7242 5524
✉ clerks@4stonebuildings.com
Call Date: Nov 2008, Gray's Inn
Qualifications: [BA]

E

PATTERSON MR STEWART

Pump Court Chambers
31 Southgate Street, Winchester, Hampshire SO23 9EB, ☎ 01962 868 161
✉ clerks@3pumpcourt.com
Pump Court Chambers
Upper Ground Floor, 3 Pump Court, Temple, London EC4Y 7AJ, ☎ 020 7353 0711
✉ clerks@3pumpcourt.com
Pump Court Chambers
5 Temple Chambers, Temple Street, Swindon SN1 1SQ, ☎ 01793 539899
✉ clerks@3pumpcourt.com
Call Date: Nov 1967, Middle Temple
Pupil Supervisor, Recorder
Qualifications: [BA (Oxon)]
stp@3pumpcourt.com

PATTISON MISS CATHERINE ELIZABETH

2 King's Bench Walk
2 King's Bench Walk, Temple, London EC4Y 7DE, ☎ 020 7353 1746
✉ clerks@2kbw.com
Call Date: July 2000, Gray's Inn
Qualifications: [LLB (Lancsh)]
cpattison@2kbw.com

PATTON MR CONALL

One Essex Court
Ground Floor, One Essex Court, Temple, London EC4Y 9AR, ☎ 020 7583 2000
✉ clerks@oeclaw.co.uk
Call Date: Oct 2004, Gray's Inn
Pupil Supervisor
Qualifications: [BA (Cantab)]
cpatton@oeclaw.co.uk

PATTON MR ROBIN MICHAEL

New Court Chambers
3 Broad Chare, Newcastle Upon Tyne NE1 3DQ, ☎ 0191 232 1980
✉ clerks@newcourt-chambers.co.uk
Chambers of Mr Ami Feder
Ground Floor, Lamb Building, Temple, London EC4Y 7AS, ☎ 020 7797 7788
✉ clerks@lambbuilding.co.uk
Chambers of Mr Ami Feder
Ground Floor, Lamb Building, Temple, London EC4Y 7AS, ☎ 020 7797 7788
✉ clerks@lambbuilding.co.uk
Call Date: July 1983, Inner Temple
Pupil Supervisor
Qualifications: [BA]
robin.patton@newcourt-chambers.co.uk

PAUL MR DANIEL JOHN

Deans Court Chambers
24 St John Street, Manchester M3 4DF, ☎ 0161 214 6000 ✉ clerks@deanscourt.co.uk
Deans Court Chambers
101 Walker Street, Preston PR1 2RR, ☎ 01772 565 600
✉ preston@deanscourt.co.uk
Call Date: Oct 1998, Middle Temple
Pupil Supervisor
Qualifications: [BA (Hons) CPE]
paul@deanscourt.co.uk

PAUL MR MATTHEW GRAHAM

Argent Chambers
5 Bell Yard, London WC2A 2JR, ☎ 020 7556 5500
✉ briefsin@argentchambers.co.uk
Call Date: Oct 2000, Inner Temple
Qualifications: [BA (Oxon) CPE]
m.paul@argentchambers.co.uk

PAUL MR NICHOLAS MARTIN

Doughty Street Chambers
53-54 Doughty Street, London WC1N 2LS, ☎ 020 7404 1313
✉ enquiries@doughtystreet.co.uk
Call Date: July 1980, Gray's Inn
Pupil Supervisor
Qualifications: [BA (York)]

PAULIN MR MICHAEL AMRIT SINGH

3 PB Barristers
3 Paper Buildings, Temple, London EC4Y 7EU, ☎ 020 7583 8055
3 PB Barristers
Royal Talbot House, 2 Victoria Street, Bristol, Avon BS1 6BB, ☎ 0117 928 1520
3 PB Barristers
4 St Peter Street, Winchester SO23 8BW, ☎ 01962 868884
✉ clerks.winchester@3paper.co.uk
3 PB Barristers
23 Beaumont Street, Oxford OX1 2NP, ☎ 01865 793 736
3 PB Barristers
30 Christchurch Road, Bournemouth, Dorset BH1 3PD, ☎ 01202 292102
✉ clerks.bournemouth@3paper.co.uk
Call Date: July 2007, Inner Temple
Qualifications: [BA (Leeds) M Phil (Lond)]

PAVLOU MR PAVLOS KYRIACOU

4 Brick Court
4 Brick Court, Temple, London EC4Y 9AD, ☎ 020 7832 3200 ✉ clerks@4bc.co.uk
Call Date: Nov 1993, Lincoln's Inn
Pupil Supervisor
Qualifications: [LLB (Hons)]
paul.pavlou@4bc.co.uk

PAWAR-PRICE MRS SUKHVINDER KUMARI

Citadel Chambers
The Citadel, 190 Corporation Street, Birmingham B4 6QD, ☎0121 233 8500
✉clerks@citadelchambers.com
Call Date: July 2010, Lincoln's Inn
Qualifications: [LLB (Wolves)]

PAWSON MR ROBERT EDWARD CRUICKSHANK

Pump Court Chambers
31 Southgate Street, Winchester, Hampshire SO23 9EB, ☎01962 868 161
✉clerks@3pumpcourt.com
Pump Court Chambers
Upper Ground Floor, 3 Pump Court, Temple, London EC4Y 7AJ, ☎020 7353 0711
✉clerks@3pumpcourt.com
Pump Court Chambers
5 Temple Chambers, Temple Street, Swindon SN1 1SQ, ☎01793 539899
✉clerks@3pumpcourt.com
Call Date: Nov 1994, Inner Temple
Pupil Supervisor
Qualifications: [BA MA (Lond) CPE]
rep@3pumpcourt.com

PAWSON MISS TAMARA SHAHAN

KBW
The Engine House, No 1 Foundry Square, Leeds LS11 5DL, ☎0113 297 1200
✉clerks@kbwchambers.com
Call Date: Oct 2003, Lincoln's Inn
Qualifications: [LLB (Hons) (Hull)]
tamarapawson@kbwchambers.com

PAWSON-POUNDS MR DANIEL JAMES

6 King's Bench Walk
Ground Floor, 6 King's Bench Walk, Temple, London EC4Y 7DR, ☎020 7583 0410
✉clerks@6kbw.com
Call Date: July 2007, Middle Temple
Qualifications: [MA (Hons) (Oxon)]
daniel.pawson@6kbw.com

PAXI-CATO MR SIMAO

Invictus Chambers London
First Floor, 1 Mitre Court Buildings, Temple, London EC4Y 7BS
✉admin@invictuschamberslondon.co.uk
Call Date: Oct 2010, Gray's Inn
Qualifications: [BA]

PAXTON MR CHRISTOPHER

18 Red Lion Court
London EC4A 3EB, ☎020 7520 6000
✉chambers@18rlc.co.uk
18 Red Lion Court (Annexe)
Thornwood House, 102 New London Road, Chelmsford, Essex CM2 0RG, ☎01245 280880
Call Date: Nov 1991, Gray's Inn
Qualifications: [LLB]
christopher.paxton@18rlc.co.uk

PAY MR ADRIAN JAMES

New Square Chambers
12 New Square, Lincoln's Inn, London WC2A 3SW, ☎020 7419 8000
✉robin.hollington@newsquarechambers.co.uk
Call Date: Mar 1999, Middle Temple
Pupil Supervisor
Qualifications: [BA (Hons)(Oxon)]
adrian.pay@newsquarechambers.co.uk

PAYNE MR ALAN PATRICK

5 Essex Court
1st Floor, 5 Essex Court, Temple, London EC4Y 9AH, ☎020 7410 2000
✉clerks@5essexcourt.co.uk
Call Date: Nov 1996, Middle Temple
Qualifications: [LLB (Hons)(LSE)]
payne@5essexcourt.co.uk

PAYNE MR DAVID JAMES

No 8 Chambers
8 Fountain Court, Steelhouse Lane, Birmingham B4 6DR, ☎0121 236 5514
✉clerks@no8chambers.co.uk
Call Date: July 2003, Gray's Inn
Qualifications: [LLB (Cardiff)]
davidpayne@no8chambers.co.uk

PAYNE MISS FELICITY PRIMOSE

Walnut House
63 St. David's Hill, Exeter, Devon EX4 4DW, ☎01392 279751
✉clerks@walnuthouse.co.uk
Call Date: July 2010, Middle Temple
Qualifications: [LLB (Hons) (So'ton)]

PAYNE MR GEOFFREY DONALD STEPHEN

25 Bedford Row
London WC1R 4HD, ☎020 7067 1500
✉clerks@25bedfordrow.com
Call Date: Oct 2000, Inner Temple
Qualifications: [BA (Oxon) CPE]
gpayne@25bedfordrow.com

E

PAYNE MR JOHNATHAN EDWARD

The Chambers of Grahame Aldous QC
9 Gough Square, London EC4A 3DG,
☎ 020 7832 0500
✉ clerks@9goughsquare.co.uk
Call Date: Oct 1997, Gray's Inn
Qualifications: [BSc Hons (Wales)]

PAYNE MR THOMAS HENRY

18 Red Lion Court
London EC4A 3EB, ☎ 020 7520 6000
✉ chambers@18rlc.co.uk
Call Date: Oct 1998, Middle Temple
Pupil Supervisor
Qualifications: [MA (Hons) (Oxon) LLM]
✉ thomas.payne@18rlc.co.uk

PAYTER MR ADAM WAYNE

6 King's Bench Walk
Ground Floor, 6 King's Bench Walk, Temple, London EC4Y 7DR, ☎ 020 7583 0410
✉ clerks@6kbw.com
Call Date: July 2008, Lincoln's Inn
Qualifications: [LLB (Nott'm)]
✉ adam.payter@6kbw.com

E

PAYTON MR ALEXANDER CLIFFORD BASIL LEE

Alpha Court Chambers
Stuart House, Buckingham Lodge, 23 Kenilworth Road, Leamington Spa CV32 6JD,
☎ 01926 886412 ✉ CP@Payton.uk.net
12 King's Bench Walk
12 King's Bench Walk, Temple, London EC4Y 7EL, ☎ 020 7583 0811
Call Date: Nov 1998, Lincoln's Inn
Qualifications: [BA (Hons)(Oxon)]
✉ apayton@alphacourtchambers.co.uk

PAYTON MR CLIFFORD CONINGSBY

Alpha Court Chambers
Stuart House, Buckingham Lodge, 23 Kenilworth Road, Leamington Spa CV32 6JD,
☎ 01926 886412 ✉ CP@Payton.uk.net
Call Date: July 1972, Inner Temple
Qualifications: [BCL MA (Oxon)]
✉ cp@payton.uk.net

PEACHEY MR DAVID JAMES

1 Gray's Inn Square
Ground Floor, 1 Gray's Inn Square, London WC1R 5AA, ☎ 020 7405 0001
Call Date: July 2007, Middle Temple
Qualifications: [BSc (Warw) GDL]

PEACOCK MR IAN CHRISTOPHER

New Square Chambers
12 New Square, Lincoln's Inn, London WC2A 3SW, ☎ 020 7419 8000
✉ robin.hollington@newsquarechambers.co.uk
Call Date: Oct 1990, Gray's Inn
Pupil Supervisor
Qualifications: [BA (Cantab)]
✉ ian.peacock@newsquarechambers.co.uk

PEACOCK MR JONATHAN DAVID QC (2001)

11 New Square
1st Floor, 11 New Square, Lincoln's Inn, London WC2A 3QB, ☎ 020 7242 4017
✉ john.moore@11newsquare.com
Call Date: July 1987, Middle Temple
Qualifications: [MA (Oxon)]
✉ john.moore@11newsquare.com

PEACOCK MISS LISA JAYNE

3 Dr Johnson's Buildings
Ground Floor, 3 Dr Johnson's Buildings, Temple, London EC4Y 7BA, ☎ 020 7353 4854
✉ clerks@3djb.co.uk
Call Date: Oct 1992, Lincoln's Inn
Qualifications: [MA (Hons)(Cantab)]
✉ lpeacock@3djb.co.uk

PEACOCK MR NICHOLAS ALLEN

Hailsham Chambers
Ground Floor, 4 Paper Buildings, Temple, London EC4Y 7EX, ☎ 020 7643 5000
✉ clerks@hailshamchambers.com
Call Date: Oct 1992, Gray's Inn
Pupil Supervisor
Qualifications: [MA (Cantab)]
✉ nicholas.peacock@hailshamchambers.com

PEACOCK MR NICHOLAS CHRISTOPHER QC (2009)

Maitland Chambers
7 Stone Buildings, Lincoln's Inn, London WC2A 3SZ, ☎ 020 7406 1200
✉ clerks@maitlandchambers.com
Call Date: Nov 1989, Middle Temple
Qualifications: [BA (Oxon)]
✉ npeacock@maitlandchambers.com

PEACOCKE MRS TERESA ANNE ROSEN

3 Stone Buildings
Ground Floor, 3 Stone Buildings, Lincoln's Inn, London WC2A 3XL, ☎ 020 7242 4937
✉ clerks@3sb.law.co.uk
Call Date: Nov 1982, Lincoln's Inn
Pupil Supervisor
Qualifications: [BA MA (USA) LLM (USA)]

PEARCE MISS EMMA PATRICIA

King's Bench and Godolphin (KBG)Chambers
115 North Hill, Plymouth, Devon PL4 8JY,
☎ 01752 221551
✉ clerks@kbgchambers.co.uk
Call Date: July 2006, Lincoln's Inn
Qualifications: [BA]
✉ emma.pearce@kingsbenchchambers.co.uk

PEARCE MR IVAN JAMES

Chambers of Andrew Mitchell QC
33 Chancery Lane, London WC2A 1EN,
☎ 020 7440 9950 ✉ clerks@33cllaw.com
Call Date: Oct 1994, Gray's Inn
Qualifications: [LLB]
✉ ivanpearce@fulcrumchambers.com

PEARCE MR LUKE RICARDO

20 Essex Street
London WC2R 3AL, ☎ 020 7842 1200
✉ clerks@20essexst.com
Call Date: Nov 2007, Lincoln's Inn
Qualifications: [BA (Oxon)]
✉ clerks@20essexst.com

PEARCE MR RICHARD WILLIAM

Byrom Street Chambers
12 Byrom Street, Manchester M3 4PP,
☎ 0161 829 2100 ✉ clerks@byromstreet.com
Crown Office Chambers
2 Crown Office Row, Temple, London EC4Y 7HJ, ☎ 020 7797 8100
✉ mail@crownofficechambers.com
42 Bedford Row
London WC1R 4LL, ☎ 020 7831 0222
✉ clerks@42br.com
Call Date: July 1985, Middle Temple
Pupil Supervisor, Recorder
Qualifications: [BA (Cantab)]
✉ richard.pearce@byromstreet.com

PEARCE MR ROBERT EDGAR QC (2006)

Radcliffe Chambers
Ground Floor, 11 New Square, Lincoln's Inn, London WC2A 3QB, ☎ 020 7831 0081
✉ clerks@radcliffechambers.com
Call Date: July 1977, Middle Temple
Qualifications: [MA BCL (Oxon)]

PEARCE-SMITH MR JAMES GEORGE KENNETH

St John's Chambers
101 Victoria Street, Bristol BS1 6PU,
☎ 0117 923 4700
✉ clerks@stjohnschambers.co.uk
Call Date: Mar 2002, Inner Temple
Qualifications: [MA (Cantab)]
✉ james.pearce-smith@stjohnschambers.co.uk

PEARMAN MR LEE CHARLES

4 Brick Court
4 Brick Court, Temple, London EC4Y 9AD,
☎ 020 7832 3200 ✉ clerks@4bc.co.uk
Call Date: July 2003, Middle Temple
Qualifications: [LLM (Lond)]
✉ lee.pearman@4bc.co.uk

PEARMAN MR RICHARD SCOTT

Ely Place Chambers
30 Ely Place, London EC1N 6TD,
☎ 020 7400 9600 ✉ admin@elyplace.com
Call Date: Oct 1999, Middle Temple
Pupil Supervisor
Qualifications: [BA (Georgetown, USA) BA (Hons) (Oxon)]
✉ spearman@elyplace.com

PEARS MR DERRICK ALLAN

Tanfield Chambers
2-5 Warwick Court, London WC1R 5DJ,
☎ 020 7421 5300
✉ clerks@tanfieldchambers.co.uk
Call Date: July 1975, Inner Temple
Pupil Supervisor
Qualifications: [MA (Oxon)]
✉ dapears@tanfieldchambers.co.uk

PEARSON MR ADAM WILLIAM

36 Bedford Row
London WC1R 4JH, ☎ 020 7421 8000
✉ chambers@36bedfordrow.co.uk
Call Date: Oct 2000, Middle Temple
Qualifications: [LLB (Hons) (Nott'm)]
✉ apearson@36bedfordrow.co.uk

E

PEARSON MS CAROLYN

14 Gray's Inn Square
14 Gray's Inn Square, Gray's Inn, London WC1R 5JP, ☎ 020 7242 0858
✉ clerks@14gis.co.uk
Call Date: Nov 1990, Gray's Inn
Pupil Supervisor
Qualifications: [LLB (Warw) MA (Lond)]
✉ clerks@14graysinnsquare.co.uk

PEARSON MR CHRISTOPHER

Lamb Chambers
Lamb Building, Elm Court, Temple, London EC4Y 7AS, ☎ 020 7797 8300
✉ info@lambchambers.co.uk
Call Date: Oct 1995, Inner Temple
Qualifications: [BSc (Dunelm) CPE]

PEART MR ICAH DELANO EVERARD QC (2002)

Garden Court Chambers
57-60 Lincoln's Inn Fields, London WC2A 3LJ, ☎ 020 7993 7600 ✉ info@gclaw.co.uk
Call Date: Nov 1978, Middle Temple
Recorder
Qualifications: [LLB (LSE)]
✉ icahp@gclaw.co.uk

PEASE MISS ALEXANDRA JANE

Chambers of Mr Ami Feder
Ground Floor, Lamb Building, Temple, London EC4Y 7AS, ☎ 020 7797 7788
✉ clerks@lambbuilding.co.uk
Lamb Building
22 Ship Street, Brighton BN1 1AD, ☎ 01273 820490
✉ admin@lambbuilding.co.uk
Chambers of Mr Ami Feder
Ground Floor, Lamb Building, Temple, London EC4Y 7AS, ☎ 020 7797 7788
✉ clerks@lambbuilding.co.uk
Call Date: Nov 1999, Middle Temple
Qualifications: [LLB (Hons)(Lond) LLM]
✉ clerks@lambbuilding.co.uk, alexpease@lambbuilding.co.uk

PEAT MR CHARLIE ANDREW

1 Pump Court
Elm Court, Temple, London EC4Y 7AB, ☎ 020 7842 7070
✉ (name)@pumpcourt.co.uk
Call Date: July 2003, Middle Temple
Qualifications: [BSc (LSE) CPE (LGU)]
✉ cpe@1pumpcourt.co.uk

PEAT MR RICHARD COLIN

13 Old Square Chambers
Ground Floor, 14 Old Square, Lincoln's Inn, London WC2A 3UE, ☎ 020 7831 4445
✉ clerks@13oldsquare.com
Call Date: Oct 1993, Gray's Inn
Qualifications: [BA LLM]
✉ richardpeat@13oldsquare.com

PECK MISS CATHERINE MARY ELIZABETH

12 King's Bench Walk
12 King's Bench Walk, Temple, London EC4Y 7EL, ☎ 020 7583 0811
Call Date: Oct 1995, Gray's Inn
Qualifications: [LLB]
✉ peck@12kbw.co.uk

PECKHAM MS JANE LOUISE

1 Crown Office Row
1 Crown Office Row, Temple, London EC4Y 7HH, ☎ 020 7797 7500
✉ mail@1cor.com
Crown Office Row Chambers
119 Church Street, Brighton, Sussex BN1 1UD, ☎ 01273 625625
✉ clerks@1cor.com
Call Date: Oct 1999, Inner Temple
Pupil Supervisor
Qualifications: [LLB (So'ton)]

PEDDER MR PETER THOMAS PAUL

2 Dr Johnson's Buildings
2 Dr Johnson's Buildings, Temple, London EC4Y 7AY, ☎ 020 7936 2613
✉ clerks@2drj.com
Call Date: July 1999, Middle Temple
Qualifications: [BSc (Hons)(Herts)]

PEDDIE MR IAN JAMES CROFTON QC (1992)

Garden Court Chambers
57-60 Lincoln's Inn Fields, London WC2A 3LJ, ☎ 020 7993 7600 ✉ info@gclaw.co.uk
St Johns Buildings Liverpool
8th Floor India Buildings, Water Street, Liverpool L2 0XG, ☎ 0151 243 6000
✉ clerk@stjohnsbuildings.co.uk
Westgate Chambers
64 High Street, Lewes, East Sussex BN7 1XG, ☎ 01273 480510
✉ clerks@westgate-chambers.co.uk
Call Date: July 1971, Inner Temple
Qualifications: [LLB (Hons) (Lond)]
✉ ianp@gclaw.co.uk

PEDRO MR TERRY ADEBISI

1 Pump Court
Elm Court, Temple, London EC4Y 7AB,
☎ 020 7842 7070
✉ (name)@pumpcourt.co.uk
Call Date: Oct 1996, Middle Temple
Qualifications: [LLB (Hons)(Lond)]
✉ tpe@1pumpcourt.co.uk

PEEBLES MR ANDREW JAMES

Farrar's Building
Farrar's Building, Temple, London EC4Y 7BD,
☎ 020 7583 9241
✉ Chambers@farrarsbuilding.co.uk
Call Date: Nov 1987, Inner Temple
Pupil Supervisor
Qualifications: [MA (Cantab) Dip Law (Lond)]
✉ apeebles@farrarsbuilding.co.uk

PEEL MR ROBERT ROGER QC (2010)

29 Bedford Row Chambers
London WC1R 4HE, ☎ 020 7404 1044
✉ clerks@29br.co.uk
Call Date: Oct 1990, Middle Temple
Qualifications: [BA (Oxon) Dip Law (City)]
✉ rpeel@29br.co.uk

PEERS MR BENEDICT GILES FREDERICK

Fenners Chambers
3 Madingley Road, Cambridge CB3 0EE,
☎ 01223 368761
✉ clerks@fennerschambers.com
Call Date: Mar 1998, Middle Temple
Qualifications: [BA (Oxon) Dip Law]
✉ benedict.peers@fennerschambers.com

PEERS MS HEATHER LOUISE

King's Bench and Godolphin (KBG)Chambers
115 North Hill, Plymouth, Devon PL4 8JY,
☎ 01752 221551
✉ clerks@kbgchambers.co.uk
Call Date: Oct 1991, Gray's Inn
Qualifications: [BA (Dunelm) M Phil (Camb)]
✉ theclerks@godolphinchambers.co.uk

PEERS MISS NICOLA JANE

Broadway House Chambers
Broadway House, 9 Bank Street, Bradford, West Yorkshire BD1 1TW, ☎ 01274 722560
✉ clerks@broadwayhouse.co.uk
Broadway House Chambers
25 Park Square West, Leeds, West Yorkshire LS1 2PW, ☎ 0113 246 2600
✉ clerks@broadwayhouse.co.uk
Call Date: Oct 1996, Inner Temple
Qualifications: [MA (Hons) (Oxon)]
✉ clerks@broadwayhouse.co.uk

PEET MR ANDREW GERAINT

Chambers of Mr Andrew Peet
2 Sycamore Close, Stretton Hall, Leicester LE2 4QU, ☎ 07966 238437
✉ andrew@peet593.orangehome.co.uk
Call Date: Oct 1991, Inner Temple
Pupil Supervisor
Qualifications: [LLB (Manch)(Hons)]
✉ andy.peet@apeet.cjsm.net

PEEVERS MISS CHARLOTTE EMMA

Doughty Street Chambers
53-54 Doughty Street, London WC1N 2LS,
☎ 020 7404 1313
✉ enquiries@doughtystreet.co.uk
Doughty Street Chambers
Pall Mall Court, 61-67 King Street, Manchester M2 4PD, ☎ 0161 618 1066
Doughty Street Chambers
5th Floor, Broad Quay House, Prince Street, Bristol BS1 4DJ, ☎ 01179 058 717
Call Date: Nov 2009, Middle Temple
Qualifications: [MA (Hons) (Edin) MSc (Glas)]

PEHAR MISS VEDRANA

2 Bedford Row
London WC1R 4BU, ☎ 020 7440 8888
✉ clerks@2bedfordrow.co.uk
Call Date: July 2008, Middle Temple
Qualifications: [BA (Hons) (Cantab) PgDl (Lond)]

PEIRSON MR OLIVER JAMES

Pump Court Chambers
31 Southgate Street, Winchester, Hampshire SO23 9EB, ☎ 01962 868 161
✉ clerks@3pumpcourt.com
Pump Court Chambers
Upper Ground Floor, 3 Pump Court, Temple, London EC4Y 7AJ, ☎ 020 7353 0711
✉ clerks@3pumpcourt.com

E

Pump Court Chambers
5 Temple Chambers, Temple Street, Swindon SN1 1SQ, ☎ 01793 539899
✉ clerks@3pumpcourt.com
Call Date: Oct 1993, Lincoln's Inn
Qualifications: [LLB (Hons)(Lond)]
op@3pumpcourt.com

PELLING MR RICHARD ALEXANDER

XXIV Old Buildings
Ground Floor, 24 Old Buildings, Lincoln's Inn, London WC2A 3UP, ☎ 020 7691 2424
✉ clerks@xxiv.co.uk
Call Date: Oct 1995, Middle Temple
Pupil Supervisor
Qualifications: [MA (Hons) DPhil]
alexander.pelling@xxiv.co.uk

PEMA MR ANES BHUMIN LALOO

Zenith Chambers
10 Park Square, Leeds LS1 2LH,
☎ 0113 245 5438
✉ clerks@zenithchambers.co.uk
Call Date: Nov 1994, Middle Temple
Pupil Supervisor
Qualifications: [BA (Hons)]
aneshpema@zenithchambers.co.uk

PEMBERTON MS JESSICA LOUISE

Call Date: Mar 2007, Inner Temple
Qualifications: [BA (Keele)]

PEMBERTON MISS LYDIA JOY

St Philips Chambers
55 Temple Row, Birmingham B2 5LS,
☎ 0121 246 7000 ✉ clerks@st-philips.com
Call Date: July 2006, Lincoln's Inn
Qualifications: [LLB (Dunelm)]

PEMBERTON MISS YOLANDA ERICA

St Philips Chambers
55 Temple Row, Birmingham B2 5LS,
☎ 0121 246 7000 ✉ clerks@st-philips.com
Call Date: Mar 2002, Lincoln's Inn
Qualifications: [LLB (Hons)]
ypemberton@st-philips.com

PENDLEBURY MR JEREMY JOHN STRINGFELLOW

Seven Bedford Row
7 Bedford Row, London WC1R 4BS,
☎ 020 7242 3555 ✉ clerks@7br.co.uk
Call Date: July 1980, Inner Temple
Pupil Supervisor
Qualifications: [BA (Kent)]
jpendlebury@7br.co.uk

PENNI MISS SALLY SELORM-JULIET

Kenworthy's Chambers
Arlington House, Bloom Street, Salford, Manchester M3 6AJ, ☎ 0161 832 4036
Call Date: Oct 2000, Gray's Inn
Pupil Supervisor
Qualifications: [LLB]

PENNICOTT MR IAN QC (2003)

Keating Chambers
15 Essex Street, London WC2R 3AA,
☎ 020 7544 2600
✉ clerks@keatingchambers.com
Call Date: July 1982, Middle Temple
Qualifications: [BA, LLM (Cantab)]
ipennicott@keatingchambers.com

PENNIFER MISS KELLY

Kings Chambers
36 Young Street, Manchester M3 3FT,
☎ 0845 034 3444
✉ clerks@kingschambers.com
Kings Chambers
5 Park Square East, Leeds LS1 2NE,
☎ 0845 034 3444
✉ clerks@kingschambers.com
Kings Chambers
Embassy House, 60 Church Street, Birmingham B3 2DJ, ☎ 0845 034 3444
✉ clerks@kingschambers.com
Call Date: Nov 1994, Middle Temple
Qualifications: [LLB (Hons) Maitrise en Droit]

PENNINGTON-BENTON MR ROWAN

3 Hare Court
3 Hare Court, Temple, London EC4Y 7BJ,
☎ 020 7415 7800 ✉ clerks@3harecourt.com
Call Date: July 2008, Middle Temple
Qualifications: [LLB (Hons) (Essex)]
rowanbenton@3harecourt.com

PENNINGTON-LEGH MR JONATHAN PIERS

Field Court Chambers
5 Field Court, Gray's Inn, London WC1R 5EF,
☎ 020 7405 6114 ✉ clerks@fieldcourt.co.uk
Call Date: Oct 2000, Inner Temple
Qualifications: [BA (Oxon) LLB (Lond)]
penningtonlegh@fieldcourt.co.uk

PENNOCK MR IAN

Park Lane Plowden
19 Westgate, Leeds LS1 2RD,
☎ 0113 228 5049
✉ clerks@parklaneplowden.co.uk
Call Date: July 2001, Lincoln's Inn
Qualifications: [LLB (Hons)]
ian.pennock@parklaneplowden.co.uk

PENNY MISS ABIGAIL SARAH PRUDENCE

4 Breams Buildings
Chancery Lane, London EC4A 1HP,
☎ 020 7092 1900 ✉ clerks@4bb.co.uk
Call Date: Oct 1999, Middle Temple
Qualifications: [BA (Hons)]

PENNY MR DUNCAN JOHN WILLIAM

6 King's Bench Walk
Ground Floor, 6 King's Bench Walk, Temple, London EC4Y 7DR, ☎ 020 7583 0410
✉ clerks@6kbw.com
Call Date: Oct 1992, Middle Temple
Pupil Supervisor
Qualifications: [BA (Hons)(Oxon)]
🖃 duncan.penny@6kbw.com

PENNY MR TIMOTHY CHARLES

11 Stone Buildings
11 Stone Buildings, Lincoln's Inn, London WC2A 3TG, ☎ 020 7831 6381
✉ clerks@11sb.com
Call Date: July 1988, Inner Temple
Pupil Supervisor
Qualifications: [LLB (Hons)]
🖃 penny@11sb.com

PENTOL MR SIMON ALEX

25 Bedford Row
London WC1R 4HD, ☎ 020 7067 1500
✉ clerks@25bedfordrow.com
Call Date: Nov 1982, Middle Temple
Pupil Supervisor
Qualifications: [LLB (Lond)]
🖃 spentol@25bedfordrow.com

PEPPER MISS JUDITH LEAH

4 Brick Court
4 Brick Court, Temple, London EC4Y 9AD,
☎ 020 7832 3200 ✉ clerks@4bc.co.uk
Call Date: Oct 1999, Middle Temple
Qualifications: [LLB (Hons)(Lond)]
🖃 judith.pepper@4bc.co.uk

PEPPER MR LIAM GEORGE

Chambers of Mr Liam Pepper
65L Warwick Square, London SW1V 2AL,
☎ 07889 172288
✉ liamgeorgepepper@gmail.com
Call Date: July 2003, Lincoln's Inn
Qualifications: [BA]
🖃 liamgeorgepepper@gMail.com

PEPPER MISS THERESA

Chavasse Court Chambers
18 Queen Avenue, Liverpool L2 4TX,
☎ 0151 229 2030
✉ clerks@chavassechambers.co.uk
Call Date: Nov 1973, Gray's Inn
Pupil Supervisor, Recorder
🖃 theresa.pepper@chavassechambers.co.uk

PEPPERALL MR EDWARD BRIAN

St Philips Chambers
55 Temple Row, Birmingham B2 5LS,
☎ 0121 246 7000 ✉ clerks@st-philips.com
Call Date: July 1989, Lincoln's Inn
Pupil Supervisor, Recorder
Qualifications: [LLB (B'ham)]
🖃 epepperall@st-philips.co.uk

PERCIVAL MR ROBERT ELDON

Five Paper
Ground Floor, 5 Paper Buildings, Temple, London EC4Y 7HB, ☎ 020 7815 3200
Call Date: Nov 1971, Inner Temple
Pupil Supervisor
Qualifications: [MA (Cantab)]
🖃 robertpercival@fivepaper.com

PEREIRA MR JAMES ALEXANDER

Francis Taylor Building
Inner Temple, London EC4Y 7BY,
☎ 020 7353 8415 ✉ clerks@ftb.eu.com
Call Date: Oct 1996, Middle Temple
Pupil Supervisor
Qualifications: [MA (Hons)(Cantab) LLM (Lond)]
🖃 james.pereira@ftb.eu.com

PERETZ MR GEORGE MICHAEL JOHN

Monckton Chambers
1 & 2 Raymond Buildings, Gray's Inn, London WC1R 5NR, ☎ 020 7405 7211
✉ chambers@monckton.com
Call Date: Nov 1990, Middle Temple
Pupil Supervisor
Qualifications: [BA (Oxon) Dip Law (Lond)]
🖃 gperetz@monckton.com

PERFECT MR ANDREW CHRISTOPHER

3 PB Barristers
3 Paper Buildings, Temple, London EC4Y 7EU,
☎ 020 7583 8055
3 PB Barristers
23 Beaumont Street, Oxford OX1 2NP,
☎ 01865 793 736

E

3 PB Barristers
4 St Peter Street, Winchester SO23 8BW, ☎01962 868884
✉clerks.winchester@3paper.co.uk
3 PB Barristers
Royal Talbot House, 2 Victoria Street, Bristol, Avon BS1 6BB, ☎0117 928 1520
3 PB Barristers
30 Christchurch Road, Bournemouth, Dorset BH1 3PD, ☎01202 292102
✉clerks.bournemouth@3paper.co.uk
Call Date: Mar 2007, Inner Temple
Qualifications: [BA (Manch)]

PERIAN MR STEVEN

3 Temple Gardens
Lower Ground Floor, 3 Temple Gardens, Temple, London EC4Y 9AU, ☎020 7353 3102
✉clerks@3tg.co.uk
Call Date: Nov 1987, Lincoln's Inn
Pupil Supervisor
Qualifications: [LLB (Lond)]
spe@3tg.co.uk

PERKINS MR ALISTAIR GEOFFREY

4 Paper Buildings
1st Floor, 4 Paper Buildings, Temple, London EC4Y 7EX, ☎020 7427 5200
✉clerks@4pb.com
Call Date: July 1986, Middle Temple
Pupil Supervisor
Qualifications: [BA (Keele)]
AGP@4pb.com

PERKINS MISS AMY LAURA

1 Hare Court
1 Hare Court, Temple, London EC4Y 7BE, ☎020 7797 7070 ✉clerks@1hc.com
Call Date: July 2010, Lincoln's Inn
Qualifications: [BA (Cantab)]
perkins@1hc.com

PERKINS DR JOANNA RUTH

South Square
3-4 South Square, Gray's Inn, London WC1R 5HP, ☎020 7696 9900
✉practicemanagers@southsquare.com
Call Date: July 2001, Middle Temple
Qualifications: [BA (Hons) (Cantab) LLM (Cantab) D.Phil (Oxon)]

PERKINS MR SIMON JOHN BENJAMIN

Zenith Chambers
10 Park Square, Leeds LS1 2LH, ☎0113 245 5438
✉clerks@zenithchambers.co.uk
Call Date: Oct 1999, Gray's Inn
Qualifications: [BA (Buckingham)]
sperkins@zenithchambers.co.uk

PERKOFF MR RICHARD MICHAEL

Littleton Chambers
3 King's Bench Walk North, Temple, London EC4Y 7HR, ☎020 7797 8600
✉fschneider@littletonchambers.co.uk
Call Date: July 1971, Middle Temple
Pupil Supervisor
Qualifications: [MA (Oxon)]

PERPLUS MISS STEPHANIE ALISON

15 Winckley Square
Preston PR1 3JJ, ☎01772 252828
✉clerks@15winckleysq.co.uk
Call Date: Oct 2008, Lincoln's Inn
Qualifications: [BA (Leeds)]

PERRINS MR GREGORY LLOYD

1 Paper Buildings
1st Floor, 1 Paper Buildings, Temple, London EC4Y 7EP, ☎020 7353 3728
✉clerks@onepaper.co.uk
Call Date: Oct 1997, Inner Temple
Pupil Supervisor
Qualifications: [LLB LLM]

PERRINS MISS JENNIFER JOAN

1 KBW Chambers
1 King's Bench Walk, Temple, London EC4Y 7DB, ☎020 7936 1500
✉clerks@1kbw.co.uk
King's Bench Chambers
174 High Street, Lewes BN7 1YE, ☎01273 402600
Call Date: July 2004, Lincoln's Inn
Qualifications: [LLB Hons (Manch)]
jperrins@1kbw.co.uk

PERRINS MR PHILIP MICHAEL JAMES

1 Garden Court Family Law Chambers
Ground Floor, One Garden Court, Temple, London EC4Y 9BJ, ☎020 7797 7900
✉clerks@1gc.com
Call Date: July 2002, Middle Temple
Qualifications: [LLB (Hons) (Luton) LLM (Cantab)]
perrins@1gc.com

PERRY MR ALEXANDER WILLIAM MARK

Harcourt Chambers
1st Floor, 2 Harcourt Buildings, Temple, London EC4Y 9DB, ☎ 0844 561 7135
Call Date: Nov 2007, Middle Temple
Qualifications: [BA (Hons) (York) PgDL (Lond) LLB (Lond) LLM (Lond)]
✉ aperry@harcourtchambers.law.co.uk

PERRY MR CHRISTOPHER EDWARD

Palmyra Chambers
Royal House, 46 Legh Street, Warrington WA1 1UJ, ☎ 01925 444919
✉ clerk@palmyrachambers.com
Call Date: Nov 2002, Lincoln's Inn
Qualifications: [LLB (Hons) (Hull)]

PERRY MISS CLEO

4 Paper Buildings
1st Floor, 4 Paper Buildings, Temple, London EC4Y 7EX, ☎ 020 7427 5200
✉ clerks@4pb.com
Call Date: Oct 2000, Gray's Inn
Pupil Supervisor
Qualifications: [BA (Cantab)]
✉ cpp@4pb.com

PERRY MR DAVID QC (2006)

6 King's Bench Walk
Ground Floor, 6 King's Bench Walk, Temple, London EC4Y 7DR, ☎ 020 7583 0410
✉ clerks@6kbw.com
Call Date: July 1980, Lincoln's Inn
Pupil Supervisor
Qualifications: [LLB, MA]
✉ david.perry@6kbw.com

PERRY MR DEREK ANEURIN

Albion Chambers
Broad Street, Bristol BS1 1DR, ☎ 0117 927 2144
✉ clerks@albionchambers.co.uk
Call Date: Nov 2006, Gray's Inn
Qualifications: [BA]

PERRY MISS JACQUELINE ANNE QC (2006)

2 Temple Gardens
2 Temple Gardens, Temple, London EC4Y 9AY, ☎ 020 7822 1200
✉ clerks@2tg.co.uk
Call Date: Feb 1975, Gray's Inn
Qualifications: [MA (Oxon)]
✉ jperry@2tg.co.uk

PERRY MR LEWIS KENNETH

Rowchester Chambers
4 Rowchester Court, Whittall Street, Birmingham B4 6DH, ☎ 0121 233 2327
✉ clerks@rowchesterchambers.co.uk
Call Date: Mar 2002, Gray's Inn
Qualifications: [LLB]

PERRY MRS NAOMI MELANIE

4 King's Bench Walk
2nd Floor, 4 King's Bench Walk, Temple, London EC4Y 7DL, ☎ 020 7822 7000
✉ clerks@4kbw.co.uk
Call Date: July 1974, Middle Temple
Pupil Supervisor
Qualifications: [BA (B'ham)]

PERSAUD DR MARCIA CHITROUTIE

1 Gray's Inn Square
Ground Floor, 1 Gray's Inn Square, London WC1R 5AA, ☎ 020 7405 0001
Call Date: Oct 2000, Middle Temple
Pupil Supervisor
Qualifications: [BA (Hons) (Lond) MSc CPE PhD]
✉ mpersaud@1gis.law.co.uk

PERSEY MR LIONEL EDWARD QC (1997)

Quadrant Chambers
Quadrant House, 10 Fleet Street, London EC4Y 1AU, ☎ 020 7583 4444
✉ info@quadrantchambers.com
Call Date: July 1981, Gray's Inn
Qualifications: [LLB DEJF (France)]
✉ lionel.persey@quadrantchambers.com

PERSSON MR MATTHEW STEPHEN

4 Paper Buildings
1st Floor, 4 Paper Buildings, Temple, London EC4Y 7EX, ☎ 020 7427 5200
✉ clerks@4pb.com
Call Date: Nov 2003, Inner Temple
Qualifications: [MA (Bris)]
✉ mp@4pb.com

PESTER MR IAIN BRUCE

11 Stone Buildings
11 Stone Buildings, Lincoln's Inn, London WC2A 3TG, ☎ 020 7831 6381
✉ clerks@11sb.com
Call Date: Oct 1999, Lincoln's Inn
Pupil Supervisor
Qualifications: [BA (Oxon) BCL]
✉ pester@11sb.com

E

PETCHEY MR PHILIP NEIL

Francis Taylor Building
Inner Temple, London EC4Y 7BY,
☎ 020 7353 8415 ✉ clerks@ftb.eu.com
Call Date: July 1976, Middle Temple
Pupil Supervisor
Qualifications: [MA (Oxon)]
philip.petchey@ftb.eu.com

PETER MS NATASHA

4-5 Gray's Inn Square
Gray's Inn, London WC1R 5AH,
☎ 020 7404 5252 ✉ clerks@4-5.co.uk
Call Date: Oct 2001, Lincoln's Inn
Qualifications: [BA (Hons)(Cantab)]
npeter@4-5.co.uk

PETERS MR DAVID DANIEL

Essex Court Chambers
24 Lincoln's Inn Fields, London WC2A 3EG,
☎ 020 7813 8000
✉ clerksroom@essexcourt.net
11 Stone Buildings
11 Stone Buildings, Lincoln's Inn, London
WC2A 3TG, ☎ 020 7831 6381
✉ clerks@11sb.com
Call Date: July 2005, Middle Temple
Qualifications: [BA (Hons) Cantab]

PETERS MR EDWARD JAMES HEDLEY

Falcon Chambers
Falcon Court, London EC4Y 1AA,
☎ 020 7353 2484
✉ clerks@falcon-chambers.com
Call Date: Nov 1998, Middle Temple
Pupil Supervisor
Qualifications: [MA (Hons)(Cantab)]
peters@falcon-chambers.com

Types of work: Agriculture, Chancery (land law), Landlord and tenant, Mineral rights, Real property

PETERS MISS GEORGINA SARAH

South Square
3-4 South Square, Gray's Inn, London
WC1R 5HP, ☎ 020 7696 9900
✉ practicemanagers@southsquare.com
Call Date: July 2005, Lincoln's Inn
Qualifications: [MA (Hons) Cantab]
georginapeters@southsquare.com

PETERSEN MR NEIL

2 Dr Johnson's Buildings
2 Dr Johnson's Buildings, Temple, London
EC4Y 7AY, ☎ 020 7936 2613
✉ clerks@2drj.com
Call Date: July 1983, Middle Temple
Qualifications: [BA Dip Crim (Cantab) LLB (South Africa)]

PETERSEN MR THOMAS JAMES

Goldsmith Chambers
Ground Floor, Goldsmith Building, Temple,
London EC4Y 7BL, ☎ 020 7353 6802
✉ clerks@goldsmithchambers.com
Call Date: July 2004, Lincoln's Inn
Qualifications: [BSc Hons (Wales) MSc (Lond) Pg Dip Law (Lond) MRICS]
T.Petersen@goldsmithchambers.law.co.uk

PETERSON MISS GERALDINE SHELDA

Chambers of Mr Ami Feder
Ground Floor, Lamb Building, Temple, London
EC4Y 7AS, ☎ 020 7797 7788
✉ clerks@lambbuilding.co.uk
Lamb Building
22 Ship Street, Brighton BN1 1AD,
☎ 01273 820490
✉ admin@lambbuilding.co.uk
Chambers of Mr Ami Feder
Ground Floor, Lamb Building, Temple, London
EC4Y 7AS, ☎ 020 7797 7788
✉ clerks@lambbuilding.co.uk
Call Date: Oct 1997, Middle Temple
Pupil Supervisor
Qualifications: [MA (Hons)(Cantab)]
clerks@lambbuilding.co.uk

PETKOVIC MR JAMES ALEXANDER

One Essex Court
Ground Floor, One Essex Court, Temple,
London EC4Y 9AR, ☎ 020 7583 2000
✉ clerks@oeclaw.co.uk
Call Date: July 2009, Lincoln's Inn
Qualifications: [BA(Cantab)]

PETO MR ANTHONY NICHOLAS GEORGE QC (2009)

Blackstone Chambers
Blackstone House, Temple, London
EC4Y 9BW, ☎ 020 7583 1770
✉ clerks@blackstonechambers.com
Call Date: Feb 1985, Middle Temple
Qualifications: [MA BCL (Oxon)]
tonypeto@blackstonechambers.com

PETTERSON MR ANDREW CUTHBERT

Exchange Chambers
Oxford House, Oxford Row, Leeds LS1 3BE, ☎ 0113 203 1970
✉ spencer@exchangechambers.co.uk
Exchange Chambers
One Derby Square, Derby Square, Liverpool L2 9XX, ☎ 0151 236 7747
✉ info@exchangechambers.co.uk
Exchange Chambers
7 Ralli Courts, West Riverside, Manchester M3 5FT, ☎ 0161 833 2722
Call Date: Oct 2004, Middle Temple
Qualifications: [BA (Hons)]

PETTICAN MR KEVIN

11 Stone Buildings
11 Stone Buildings, Lincoln's Inn, London WC2A 3TG, ☎ 020 7831 6381
✉ clerks@11sb.com
Call Date: Nov 1994, Inner Temple
Qualifications: [BA BCL (Oxon)]
pettican@11sb.com

PETTIT MR SEAN

1 Pump Court
Elm Court, Temple, London EC4Y 7AB, ☎ 020 7842 7070
✉ (name)@pumpcourt.co.uk
Call Date: Oct 1997, Inner Temple
Qualifications: [BA]

PETTITT MR ROBERT

Northampton Chambers
10 Spencer Parade, Northampton NN1 5AQ, ☎ 01604 636271
✉ clerks@northampton-chambers.co.uk
Call Date: July 2002, Middle Temple
Qualifications: [LLB (Hons) (Nott'm Trent)]
rpettitt@northampton-chambers.co.uk

PETTS MR JAMES EDWIN

1 Gray's Inn Square
Ground Floor, 1 Gray's Inn Square, London WC1R 5AA, ☎ 020 7405 0001
Call Date: July 2002, Middle Temple
Pupil Supervisor
Qualifications: [LLB (Hons) BCC]
jpetts@1gis.co.uk

PETTS MR PETER SIMON TINSLEY

Hardwicke
New Square, Lincoln's Inn, London WC2A 3SB, ☎ 020 7242 2523
✉ enquiries@hardwicke.co.uk
Call Date: Oct 1998, Inner Temple
Pupil Supervisor
Qualifications: [LLB (Lond)]
pp@hardwicke.co.uk

PETTS MR TIMOTHY DAVID

12 King's Bench Walk
12 King's Bench Walk, Temple, London EC4Y 7EL, ☎ 020 7583 0811
Call Date: Oct 1996, Inner Temple
Pupil Supervisor, Recorder
Qualifications: [MA (Oxon) MJur (Oxon)]
petts@12kbw.co.uk

PEZZANI MR ROGER ROBERT NICHOLAS

Garden Court Chambers
57-60 Lincoln's Inn Fields, London WC2A 3LJ, ☎ 020 7993 7600 ✉ info@gclaw.co.uk
Call Date: Nov 1997, Middle Temple
Qualifications: [BA (Hons)(Sussex)]

PHELAN MS SARAH JANE DOROTHY

Chavasse Court Chambers
18 Queen Avenue, Liverpool L2 4TX, ☎ 0151 229 2030
✉ clerks@chavassechambers.co.uk
Call Date: Nov 1999, Inner Temple
Qualifications: [BA (Leeds)]

PHELPS MISS ROSALIND JAYNE

Fountain Court Chambers
Fountain Court, Temple, London EC4Y 9DH, ☎ 020 7583 3335
✉ chambers@fountaincourt.co.uk
Call Date: Nov 1998, Lincoln's Inn
Pupil Supervisor
Qualifications: [BA (Hons)(Oxon) BCL (Oxon)]
rphelps@fountaincourt.co.uk

PHIL-EBOSIE MISS EUNICE SHEILA NNEKA

42 Bedford Row
London WC1R 4LL, ☎ 020 7831 0222
✉ clerks@42br.com
Call Date: Nov 1988, Gray's Inn
Qualifications: [LLB (Nigeria) LLM (Lond) BL (Nigeria)]
sheila.phil-ebosie@42br.com

E

PHILIPPOU MISS MARIE-ANN

Garden Court Chambers
57-60 Lincoln's Inn Fields, London WC2A 3LJ,
☎ 020 7993 7600 ✉ info@gclaw.co.uk
Call Date: Nov 2007, Inner Temple
Qualifications: [LLB LLM (Lond)]
✉ mariep@gclaw.co.uk

PHILIPPS MR GUY WOGAN QC (2002)

Fountain Court Chambers
Fountain Court, Temple, London EC4Y 9DH,
☎ 020 7583 3335
✉ chambers@fountaincourt.co.uk
Call Date: July 1986, Inner Temple
Qualifications: [MA (Oxon) Dip Law]
✉ gphilipps@fountaincourt.co.uk

PHILIPSON MISS AMY VICTORIA

Sovereign Chambers
46 Park Place, Leeds LS1 2RY,
☎ 0113 245 1841
✉ clerks@sovereignchambers.co.uk
Call Date: Nov 2006, Inner Temple
Qualifications: [LLB]
✉ amy.philipson@sovereignchambers.co.uk

PHILLIMORE MISS SARAH VICTORIA

St John's Chambers
101 Victoria Street, Bristol BS1 6PU,
☎ 0117 923 4700
✉ clerks@stjohnschambers.co.uk
Call Date: Oct 1994, Lincoln's Inn
Pupil Supervisor
Qualifications: [LLB (Hons)(Lond)]

PHILLIPS MR ANDREW CHARLES

Crown Office Chambers
2 Crown Office Row, Temple, London
EC4Y 7HJ, ☎ 020 7797 8100
✉ mail@crownofficechambers.com
Call Date: July 1978, Middle Temple
Pupil Supervisor
Qualifications: [BA (Oxon) MA (Cantab)]
✉ phillips@crownofficechambers.com

PHILLIPS MR DAVID JOHN

37 Park Square Chambers
37 Park Square, Leeds LS1 2NY,
☎ 0113 243 9422 ✉ chambers@no37.co.uk
Call Date: Nov 2010, Inner Temple
✉ dp@no37.co.uk

PHILLIPS MR DAVID JOHN QC (1997)

Wilberforce Chambers
8 New Square, Lincoln's Inn, London
WC2A 3QP, ☎ 020 7306 0102
✉ chambers@wilberforce.co.uk
30 Park Place
Cardiff CF10 3BS, ☎ 029 2039 8421
✉ clerks@30parkplace.law.co.uk
Call Date: Nov 1976, Gray's Inn
Recorder
Qualifications: [MA (Oxon)]
✉ dphillips@wilberforce.co.uk

PHILLIPS MISS EMMA LOUISE

1 Pump Court
Elm Court, Temple, London EC4Y 7AB,
☎ 020 7842 7070
✉ (name)@pumpcourt.co.uk
Call Date: Nov 2001, Middle Temple
Qualifications: [LLB (Hons)]
✉ ep@1pumpcourt.co.uk

PHILLIPS MR FRANK

Iscoed Chambers
86 St Helen's Road, Swansea SA1 4BQ,
☎ 01792 652988
✉ clerks@iscoedchambers.co.uk
Call Date: Nov 1972, Lincoln's Inn
Pupil Supervisor
Qualifications: [LLB (Bris) ATCL LRSM]
✉ fp@iscoedchambers.co.uk

PHILLIPS MR HENRY ELLIOT GORDON

South Square
3-4 South Square, Gray's Inn, London
WC1R 5HP, ☎ 020 7696 9900
✉ practicemanagers@southsquare.com
Call Date: July 2008, Lincoln's Inn
Qualifications: [BA (Oxon) BCL (Oxon)]
✉ henryphillips@southsquare.com

PHILLIPS MR IAN ROBERT REES

6 Pump Court
1st Floor, 6 Pump Court, Temple, London
EC4Y 7AR, ☎ 020 7797 8400
✉ richardconstable@6pumpcourt.co.uk
6 Pump Court Chambers
6-8 Mill Street, Maidstone, Kent ME15 6XH,
☎ 01622 688094
✉ annexe@6pumpcourt.co.uk
Call Date: Mar 2009, Middle Temple
Qualifications: [BA (Hons) (Oxon)]

PHILLIPS MISS JANE ROSE

One Brick Court
1st Floor, One Brick Court, Temple, London EC4Y 9BY, ☎ 020 7353 8845
✉ clerks@onebrickcourt.com
Call Date: July 1989, Inner Temple
Pupil Supervisor
Qualifications: [BA (Oxon)(Hons)]
jrp@onebrickcourt.com

PHILLIPS MR JEREMY GAVIN

Francis Taylor Building
Inner Temple, London EC4Y 7BY,
☎ 020 7353 8415 ✉ clerks@ftb.eu.com
Call Date: Mar 2004, Inner Temple
Qualifications: [BA (Southampton)]
jeremy.phillips@ftb.eu.com

PHILLIPS MR JONATHAN MARK

3 Verulam Buildings
London WC1R 5NT, ☎ 020 7831 8441
✉ chambers@3vb.com
Call Date: Nov 1991, Inner Temple
Pupil Supervisor
Qualifications: [BA (Hons)(Cantab)]

PHILLIPS MISS KATIE

42 Bedford Row
London WC1R 4LL, ☎ 020 7831 0222
✉ clerks@42br.com
Call Date: July 2002, Lincoln's Inn
Qualifications: [BA (Oxon)]
katie.phillips@42br.com

PHILLIPS MISS LAURA MAYA CLAIRE

6 Pump Court
1st Floor, 6 Pump Court, Temple, London EC4Y 7AR, ☎ 020 7797 8400
✉ richardconstable@6pumpcourt.co.uk
6 Pump Court Chambers
6-8 Mill Street, Maidstone, Kent ME15 6XH,
☎ 01622 688094
✉ annexe@6pumpcourt.co.uk
Call Date: July 2009, Middle Temple
Qualifications: [MA (Hons) (Edin) MSc Post Grad Dip Law (Lond)]

PHILLIPS MR MARK PAUL QC (1999)

South Square
3-4 South Square, Gray's Inn, London WC1R 5HP, ☎ 020 7696 9900
✉ practicemanagers@southsquare.com
Call Date: July 1984, Inner Temple
Recorder
Qualifications: [LLB LLM (Bris)]
markphillips@southsquare.com

PHILLIPS MR MATTHEW JAMES

Outer Temple Chambers
The Outer Temple, 222 Strand, London WC2R 1BA, ☎ 020 7353 6381
✉ clerks@outertemple.com
Call Date: Nov 1993, Lincoln's Inn
Qualifications: [BA (Hons)]
matthew.phillips@outertemple.com

Types of work: Asbestos-related diseases, Clinical negligence, Personal injury

PHILLIPS MR MICHAEL CHARLES JOSEPH

Chambers of Mr Ami Feder
Ground Floor, Lamb Building, Temple, London EC4Y 7AS, ☎ 020 7797 7788
✉ clerks@lambbuilding.co.uk
Lamb Building
22 Ship Street, Brighton BN1 1AD,
☎ 01273 820490
✉ admin@lambbuilding.co.uk
Chambers of Mr Ami Feder
Ground Floor, Lamb Building, Temple, London EC4Y 7AS, ☎ 020 7797 7788
✉ clerks@lambbuilding.co.uk
Call Date: Feb 1980, Middle Temple
Pupil Supervisor
Qualifications: [LLB (Lond)]
clerks@lambbuilding.co.uk

PHILLIPS MRS MOIRA ELYNWY

No5 Chambers
Fountain Court, Steelhouse Lane, Birmingham B4 6DR, ☎ 0845 210 5555 ✉ info@no5.com
No5 Chambers
38 Queen Square, Bristol BS1 4QS,
☎ 0845 210 5555
No5 Chambers
Greenwood House, 4-7 Salisbury Court, London EC4Y 8AA, ☎ 0845 210 5555
Call Date: July 1989, Gray's Inn
Qualifications: [LLB (Wales) BCL (Oxon)]
mp@no5.com

PHILLIPS MR NEVIL DAVID

Quadrant Chambers
Quadrant House, 10 Fleet Street, London EC4Y 1AU, ☎ 020 7583 4444
✉ info@quadrantchambers.com
Call Date: Oct 1992, Gray's Inn
Qualifications: [BA (So'ton) Dip Law (Lond) LLM (Lond)]
nevil.phillips@quadrantchambers.com

E

PHILLIPS MR OLIVER FREDERICK GEORGE

Maitland Chambers
7 Stone Buildings, Lincoln's Inn, London WC2A 3SZ, ☎ 020 7406 1200
✉ clerks@maitlandchambers.com
Call Date: July 2009, Middle Temple
Qualifications: [MA (Cantab) MPhil (Cantab) Grad Dip Law (Lond)]
✉ ophillips@maitlandchambers.com

PHILLIPS MR PAUL STUART

Charter Chambers
33 John Street, London WC1N 2AT,
☎ 020 7618 4400
✉ clerks@charterchambers.com
Call Date: Feb 1991, Gray's Inn
Qualifications: [LLB (Wales)]
✉ clerks@charterchambers.com

PHILLIPS MR RICHARD CHARLES JONATHAN QC (1990)

Francis Taylor Building
Inner Temple, London EC4Y 7BY,
☎ 020 7353 8415 ✉ clerks@ftb.eu.com
Call Date: Nov 1970, Inner Temple
Qualifications: [MA (Cantab)]
✉ Richard.phillips@ftb.eu.com

E

PHILLIPS MR RORY ANDREW LIVINGSTONE QC (2002)

3 Verulam Buildings
London WC1R 5NT, ☎ 020 7831 8441
✉ chambers@3vb.com
Call Date: July 1984, Inner Temple
Qualifications: [MA (Cantab)]

PHILLIPS MISS RUTH

Trinity Chambers
The Custom House, 39 Quayside, Newcastle Upon Tyne NE1 3DE, ☎ 0191 232 1927
✉ info@trinitychambers.co.uk
Trinity Chambers
Multi Media Exchange, 72-80 Corporation Road, Middlesbrough TS1 2RF,
☎ 01642 247569
✉ info@trinitychambers.co.uk
Call Date: July 2001, Middle Temple
Qualifications: [LLB (Hons)]
✉ r.phillips@trinitychambers.co.uk

PHILLIPS MR S J QC (2009)

7 King's Bench Walk
Ground Floor, 7 King's Bench Walk, Temple, London EC4Y 7DS, ☎ 020 7910 8300
✉ clerks@7kbw.co.uk
Call Date: Oct 1993, Lincoln's Inn
Qualifications: [MA (Oxon) BCL]
✉ sphillips@7kbw.co.uk

PHILLIPS MR SIMON BENJAMIN QC (2010)

Park Court Chambers
16 Park Place, Leeds LS1 2SJ,
☎ 0113 243 3277
✉ clerks@parkcourtchambers.co.uk
Francis Taylor Building
Inner Temple, London EC4Y 7BY,
☎ 020 7353 8415 ✉ clerks@ftb.eu.com
Call Date: July 1985, Inner Temple
Pupil Supervisor, Recorder
Qualifications: [BA (Sussex) LLM (Cantab)]
✉ sphillips@parkcourtchambers.co.uk

PHILLIPS MR SIMON DAVID

St Philips Chambers
55 Temple Row, Birmingham B2 5LS,
☎ 0121 246 7000 ✉ clerks@st-philips.com
Call Date: Oct 1996, Inner Temple
Qualifications: [MA (Cantab)]
✉ sphillips@st-philips.co.uk

PHILLIPS MR STEPHEN EDMUND QC (2002)

3 Verulam Buildings
London WC1R 5NT, ☎ 020 7831 8441
✉ chambers@3vb.com
Call Date: July 1984, Gray's Inn
Recorder
Qualifications: [MA (Oxon)]
✉ sphillips@3vb.com

PHILLIPS MR WILLIAM BERNARD

Call Date: July 1970, Inner Temple
Pupil Supervisor, Recorder
Qualifications: [MA (Oxon)]
✉ phillips@paradise-sq.co.uk

PHILLIPSON MISS NICOLA JANE

Zenith Chambers
10 Park Square, Leeds LS1 2LH,
☎ 0113 245 5438
✉ clerks@zenithchambers.co.uk
Call Date: Nov 1999, Lincoln's Inn
Qualifications: [BA (Hons)]
✉ nphillipson@zenithchambers.co.uk

PHILLPOT MR HEREWARD LINDON

Francis Taylor Building
Inner Temple, London EC4Y 7BY,
☎ 020 7353 8415 ✉ clerks@ftb.eu.com
Call Date: Oct 1997, Gray's Inn
Pupil Supervisor
Qualifications: [BA (York)]
hereward.phillpot@ftb.eu.com

PHILO MR NOEL PHILIP

KCH Garden Square
1 Oxford Street, Nottingham NG1 5BH,
☎ 0115 941 8851
✉ clerks@kchgardensquare.co.uk
Call Date: Feb 1975, Gray's Inn
Pupil Supervisor
Qualifications: [MA (Oxon)]

PHILPOTT MR ANTHONY LUKE

12 Old Square Chambers
1st Floor, 12 Old Square, Lincoln's Inn,
London WC2A 3TX, ☎ 020 7404 0875
✉ clerks@12oldsquare.com
Call Date: Nov 1987, Gray's Inn
Qualifications: [BA MSc Construction Law & Arbitration MCIArb]

PHILPOTT MR FREDERICK ALAN

Gough Square Chambers
6-7 Gough Square, London EC4A 3DE,
☎ 020 7353 0924 ✉ gsc@goughsq.co.uk
Call Date: July 1974, Gray's Inn
Pupil Supervisor
Qualifications: [LLB (Lond)]
fred.philpott@goughsq.co.uk

PHILPOTTS MR ROBERT JOHN

Linenhall Chambers
1 Stanley Place, Chester CH1 2LU,
☎ 01244 348282
✉ clerks@linenhallchambers.co.uk
Call Date: Oct 1990, Gray's Inn
Pupil Supervisor
Qualifications: [BA MPhil (L'pool)]
jp@nicholasstreet.com

PHIPPS MR ALEXANDER JAMES

3 Verulam Buildings
London WC1R 5NT, ☎ 020 7831 8441
✉ chambers@3vb.com
Call Date: Nov 2008, Lincoln's Inn
Qualifications: [BA LLB (Australia) BSc (Oxon)]
sphipps@3vb.com

PHIPPS MR CHARLES MACKENZIE

Four New Square
Four New Square, Lincoln's Inn, London
WC2A 3RJ, ☎ 020 7822 2000
✉ barristers@4newsquare.com
Call Date: Nov 1992, Middle Temple
Pupil Supervisor
Qualifications: [BA (Oxon) DipLaw (Lond)]
c.phipps@4newsquare.com

PHIPPS MISS SARAH ELIZABETH

Queen Elizabeth Building
3rd Floor, Queen Elizabeth Building, Temple,
London EC4Y 9BS, ☎ 020 7797 7837
✉ clerks@qeb.co.uk
Call Date: Nov 1997, Lincoln's Inn
Pupil Supervisor
Qualifications: [BA (Hons)]
s.phipps@qeb.co.uk

PHYSSAS MISS CLAIRE

Renaissance Chambers
5th Floor, Gray's Inn Chambers, Gray's Inn,
London WC1R 5JA, ☎ 020 7404 1111
✉ clerks@renaissancechambers.co.uk
Call Date: Oct 2004, Lincoln's Inn
Qualifications: [LLB (Hons) (Lond) LLM]
cp@renaissancechambers.co.uk

PICARDA MR HUBERT ALISTAIR PAUL QC (1992)

Chambers of Mr Hubert Picarda QC
Third Floor North, 9 Old Square, Lincoln's
Inn, London WC2A 3SR, ☎ 020 7242 3566
✉ hpicarda@aol.com
Call Date: Feb 1962, Inner Temple
Qualifications: [MA BCL (Oxon)]
hpicarda@aol.com

PICCININ MR DANIEL PETER CLEMENT

Brick Court Chambers
7-8 Essex Street, London WC2R 3LD,
☎ 020 7379 3550 ✉ clerks@brickcourt.co.uk
Call Date: July 2010, Lincoln's Inn
Qualifications: [LLB BCo (Australia)]
daniel.piccinin@brickcourt.co.uk

PICKARD MISS KATHRYN MARY

11 South Square
1st Floor, 11 South Square, Gray's Inn,
London WC1R 5EY, ☎ 020 7405 1222
✉ clerks@11southsquare.com
Call Date: Oct 2001, Inner Temple
Qualifications: [MA (Cantab) BCL (Oxon)]
kpickard@11southsquare.com

E

PICKAVANCE MR GRAHAM MICHAEL

Chavasse Court Chambers
18 Queen Avenue, Liverpool L2 4TX,
☎0151 229 2030
✉clerks@chavassechambers.co.uk
Call Date: Nov 1973, Gray's Inn
Pupil Supervisor
Qualifications: [LLB]
graham.pickavance@chavassechambers.co.uk

PICKAVANCE MR MICHAEL JOHN

Number 7 Harrington Street Chambers
7 Harrington Street, Liverpool L2 9YH,
☎0151 242 0707 ✉clerks@7hs.co.uk
Call Date: July 1974, Middle Temple
Qualifications: [LLB (Hons)]
michael.pickavance@7hs.co.uk

PICKEN MR JAMES EDWARD

St Ive's Chambers
Whittall Street, Birmingham B4 6DH,
☎0121 236 0863
✉clerks@stiveschambers.co.uk
Call Date: Oct 2004, Gray's Inn
Qualifications: [LLB]
james.picken@stiveschambers.co.uk

PICKEN MR SIMON DEREK QC (2006)

7 King's Bench Walk
Ground Floor, 7 King's Bench Walk, Temple, London EC4Y 7DS, ☎020 7910 8300
✉clerks@7kbw.co.uk
30 Park Place
Cardiff CF10 3BS, ☎029 2039 8421
✉clerks@30parkplace.law.co.uk
Call Date: July 1989, Middle Temple
Recorder
Qualifications: [LLB (Wales) LLM (Cantab)]
spicken@7kbw.co.uk

PICKERING MRS CHARLOTTE LOUISE

King's Bench and Godolphin (KBG)Chambers
115 North Hill, Plymouth, Devon PL4 8JY,
☎01752 221551
✉clerks@kbgchambers.co.uk
Call Date: July 2007, Middle Temple
Qualifications: [LLB (Hons) (Bris)]

PICKERING MR JAMES PATRICK

Enterprise Chambers
9 Old Square, Lincoln's Inn, London WC2A 3SR, ☎020 7405 9471
✉london@enterprisechambers.com
Enterprise Chambers
65 Quayside, Newcastle Upon Tyne NE1 3DE,
☎0191 222 3344
✉newcastle@enterprisechambers.com
Enterprise Chambers
43 Park Square, Leeds LS1 2NP,
☎0113 246 0391
✉leeds@enterprisechambers.com
Call Date: Oct 1991, Middle Temple
Pupil Supervisor
Qualifications: [BSc (Hons) (So'ton)]
jamespickering@enterprisechambers.com

PICKERING MR LEON EDWARD

Ten Old Square
Ground Floor, Ten Old Square, Lincoln's Inn, London WC2A 3SU, ☎020 7405 0758
✉clerks@tenoldsquare.com
Call Date: July 2010, Lincoln's Inn
Qualifications: [BA (Oxon) MA (Oxon) M Phil (Oxon)]
leonpickering@tenoldsquare.com

PICKERING MISS REBECCA ANNE

Kenworthy's Chambers
Arlington House, Bloom Street, Salford, Manchester M3 6AJ, ☎0161 832 4036
Call Date: July 2007, Inner Temple
Qualifications: [BA (York)]
r.pickering@kenworthysbarristers.co.uk

PICKERING MR RICHARD ANDREW

Atlantic Chambers
4-6 Cook Street, Liverpool L2 9QU,
☎0151 236 4421
✉info@atlanticchambers.co.uk
12 King's Bench Walk
12 King's Bench Walk, Temple, London EC4Y 7EL, ☎020 7583 0811
Call Date: Nov 1987, Lincoln's Inn
Pupil Supervisor
Qualifications: [MA (Hons) (Cantab) Dip Law (Lond)]
andrewpickering@atlanticchambers.co.uk

PICKERING MR SIMON TOBY

Wilberforce Chambers
7 Bishop Lane, Hull HU1 1PA,
☎01482 323264
Call Date: Oct 1996, Inner Temple
Qualifications: [LLB (Hull) MA (York)]

E

PICKFORD MR MEREDITH WILLIAM

Monckton Chambers
1 & 2 Raymond Buildings, Gray's Inn, London WC1R 5NR, ☎ 020 7405 7211
✉ chambers@monckton.com
Call Date: Oct 1999, Middle Temple
Pupil Supervisor
Qualifications: [MA (Cantab)]
✉ mpickford@monckton.com

PICKLES MR SIMON ROBERT

Landmark Chambers
180 Fleet Street, London EC4A 2HG,
☎ 020 7430 1221
✉ clerks@landmarkchambers.co.uk
Call Date: July 1978, Inner Temple
Pupil Supervisor
Qualifications: [MA (Cantab)]
✉ spickles@landmarkchambers.co.uk

PICKTHALL MS CLAIRE LOUISE

Temple Chambers
32 Park Place, Cardiff CF10 3BA,
☎ 029 2039 7364
✉ DBrinning@Temple-Chambers.co.uk
Temple Chambers
12 Clytha Park Road, Newport, Gwent NP20 4PB, ☎ 01633 267403
✉ dbrinning@temple-chambers.co.uk
Call Date: Nov 1999, Gray's Inn
Qualifications: [LLB (Wales)]
✉ cpickthall@temple-chambers.co.uk

PICKUP MISS ALISON MARGARET

Doughty Street Chambers
53-54 Doughty Street, London WC1N 2LS,
☎ 020 7404 1313
✉ enquiries@doughtystreet.co.uk
Doughty Street Chambers
Pall Mall Court, 61-67 King Street, Manchester M2 4PD, ☎ 0161 618 1066
Doughty Street Chambers
5th Floor, Broad Quay House, Prince Street, Bristol BS1 4DJ, ☎ 01179 058 717
Call Date: Oct 2007, Middle Temple
Qualifications: [BA (Hons) (Cantab) PgDL (Lond) MA (Lond)]
✉ a.pickup@doughtystreet.co.uk

PICKUP MR DAVID MICHAEL WALKER

St Johns Buildings
24a - 28 St John Street, Manchester M3 4DJ,
☎ 0161 214 1500
✉ clerk@stjohnsbuildings.co.uk
16 Winckley Square
Preston PR1 3JJ, ☎ 01772 256100
St Johns Buildings Liverpool
8th Floor India Buildings, Water Street, Liverpool L2 0XG, ☎ 0151 243 6000
✉ clerk@stjohnsbuildings.co.uk
Call Date: July 1984, Inner Temple
Pupil Supervisor
Qualifications: [LLB (Leeds)]
✉ clerk@stjohnsbuildings.co.uk

PICKUP MR JAMES KENNETH QC (2000)

Lincoln House Chambers
Tower 12, The Avenue North, Spinningfields, 18-22 Bridge Street, Manchester M3 3BZ,
☎ 0161 832 5701
✉ info@lincolnhousechambers.com
2 Hare Court
Lower Ground, Ground, 1st & 2nd Floor, 2 Hare Court, Temple, London EC4Y 7BH,
☎ 020 7353 3982 ✉ clerks@2harecourt.com
Call Date: July 1976, Gray's Inn
Recorder
Qualifications: [MA (Oxon) BCL]
✉ james.pickup@lincolnhousechambers.com

PICTON MR JULIAN MARK QC (2010)

Hailsham Chambers
Ground Floor, 4 Paper Buildings, Temple, London EC4Y 7EX, ☎ 020 7643 5000
✉ clerks@hailshamchambers.com
Call Date: Feb 1988, Middle Temple
Pupil Supervisor
Qualifications: [BA (Oxon)]
✉ julian.picton@hailshamchambers.com

PIDDINGTON MR DANIEL EDWARD

College Chambers
19 Carlton Crescent, Southampton, Hampshire SO15 2ET, ☎ 023 8023 0338
✉ clerks@college-chambers.co.uk
Call Date: Nov 2008, Inner Temple
Qualifications: [LLB (Bris) CPE]

PIEARS MISS ANGELA KATHRYN AMY

Cobden House Chambers
19 Quay Street, Manchester M3 3HN,
☎ 0161 833 6000 ✉ Clerks@Cobden.co.uk
Call Date: Oct 2001, Middle Temple
Qualifications: [BA (Hons) CPE]
✉ clerks@cobden.co.uk

E

PIERCY MISS ARLETTE MARY

25 Bedford Row
London WC1R 4HD, ☎ 020 7067 1500
✉ clerks@25bedfordrow.com
Call Date: Nov 1990, Lincoln's Inn
Pupil Supervisor
Qualifications: [LLB (Leeds)]
✉ apiercy@25bedfordrow.com

PIERCY MISS CATHERINE

Hardwicke
New Square, Lincoln's Inn, London
WC2A 3SB, ☎ 020 7242 2523
✉ enquiries@hardwicke.co.uk
Call Date: July 2007, Middle Temple
Qualifications: [BA (Hons) (Oxon)]

PIERPOINT MISS KATHERINE ANNE

Lincoln House Chambers
Tower 12, The Avenue North, Spinningfields,
18-22 Bridge Street, Manchester M3 3BZ,
☎ 0161 832 5701
✉ info@lincolnhousechambers.com
Call Date: Oct 1998, Lincoln's Inn
Pupil Supervisor
Qualifications: [LLB (Hons) (Nott'm)]
✉ katherine.pierpoint@
lincolnhousechambers.com

E

PIEVSKY MR DAVID RICHARD

Blackstone Chambers
Blackstone House, Temple, London
EC4Y 9BW, ☎ 020 7583 1770
✉ clerks@blackstonechambers.com
Call Date: July 2001, Inner Temple
Qualifications: [BA (Cantab) M Phil (Cantab)
CPE]
✉ davidpievsky@blackstonechambers.com

PIGOT MISS DIANA MARGUERITE

2 Pump Court
1st Floor, 2 Pump Court, Temple, London
EC4Y 7AH, ☎ 020 7353 5597
✉ clerks@2pumpcourt.co.uk
Call Date: Nov 1978, Inner Temple
Qualifications: [BA (Lond)]
✉ dpigot@2pumpcourt.co.uk

PIGOTT MRS FRANCES WINIFRED

Atkin Chambers
1 Atkin Building, Gray's Inn, London
WC1R 5AT, ☎ 020 7404 0102
✉ clerks@atkinchambers.com
St Philips Chambers
55 Temple Row, Birmingham B2 5LS,
☎ 0121 246 7000 ✉ clerks@st-philips.com
Call Date: Oct 1994, Gray's Inn
Qualifications: [LLB]
✉ fpigott@atkinchambers.com

PIGRAM MR CHRISTOPHER STUART

East Anglian Chambers
53 North Hill, Colchester, Essex CO1 1QA,
☎ 01473 214481 ✉ colchester@ealaw.co.uk
East Anglian Chambers
140 New London Road, Chelmsford, Essex
CM2 0AW, ☎ 01473 214481
✉ chelmsford@ealaw.co.uk
East Anglian Chambers
Gresham House, 5 Museum Street, Ipswich,
Suffolk IP1 1HQ, ☎ 01473 214481
✉ ipswich@ealaw.co.uk
Call Date: July 2000, Gray's Inn
Pupil Supervisor
Qualifications: [BMus (Manch)]
✉ christopherpigram@ealaw.co.uk

PIKE MR JEREMY JOHN

Francis Taylor Building
Inner Temple, London EC4Y 7BY,
☎ 020 7353 8415 ✉ clerks@ftb.eu.com
Call Date: July 2001, Middle Temple
Qualifications: [LLB (Hons) LLM]
✉ jeremy.pike@ftb.eu.com

PIKE MISS OLIVIA TERESA

30 Park Place
Cardiff CF10 3BS, ☎ 029 2039 8421
✉ clerks@30parkplace.law.co.uk
Call Date: July 2008, Middle Temple
Qualifications: [LLB (Hons) (Wales)]
✉ op@30parkplace.co.uk

PILBROW MR FIONN PETER ALEXANDER

Brick Court Chambers
7-8 Essex Street, London WC2R 3LD,
☎ 020 7379 3550 ✉ clerks@brickcourt.co.uk
Call Date: Oct 2001, Inner Temple
Pupil Supervisor
Qualifications: [BA (Oxon) M Phil (Cantab)
CPE]
✉ Fionn.Pilbrow@Brickcourt.co.uk

PILGERSTORFER MR MARCUS JAMES

11 King's Bench Walk
11 King's Bench Walk, Temple, London
EC4Y 7EQ, ☎ 020 7632 8500
✉ clerksroom@11kbw.com
Call Date: July 2002, Gray's Inn
Pupil Supervisor
Qualifications: [MA (Oxon)]
✉ Marcus.Pilgerstorfer@11kbw.com

PILKINGTON MISS ABIGAIL JANE

Fenners Chambers
3 Madingley Road, Cambridge CB3 0EE,
☎01223 368761
✉clerks@fennerschambers.com
Call Date: July 2008, Inner Temple
Qualifications: [BA (Dunelm)]
abigail.pilkington@fennerschambers.com

PILKINGTON MR ANDREW JAMES

Doughty Street Chambers
Pall Mall Court, 61-67 King Street, Manchester M2 4PD, ☎0161 618 1066
Doughty Street Chambers
5th Floor, Broad Quay House, Prince Street, Bristol BS1 4DJ, ☎01179 058 717
Doughty Street Chambers
53-54 Doughty Street, London WC1N 2LS,
☎020 7404 1313
✉enquiries@doughtystreet.co.uk
Call Date: July 2010, Inner Temple
Qualifications: [MA (Cantab) LLM (Warw)]

PILLAI MR RAJESH

3 Verulam Buildings
London WC1R 5NT, ☎020 7831 8441
✉chambers@3vb.com
Call Date: Nov 2002, Middle Temple
Qualifications: [BA (Hons) (Oxon) BA (Hons) (Cantab) LLM (NYU)]
rpillai@3vb.com

PILLING MR BENJAMIN

4 Pump Court
4 Pump Court, Temple, London EC4Y 7AN,
☎020 7842 5555
✉chambers@4pumpcourt.com
Call Date: Oct 1997, Inner Temple
Pupil Supervisor
Qualifications: [BA (Oxon) CPE MA]
bpilling@4pumpcourt.com

PILLING MR DAVID JONATHAN

Liverpool Civil Law
3rd Floor, 1 Old Hall Street, Liverpool L3 9HF,
☎0151 242 0500
✉clerks@liverpoolcivillaw.com
Call Date: Oct 1999, Middle Temple
Qualifications: [BA (Hons)(Sheff)]
clerks@liverpoolcivillaw.com

PILLOW MR NATHAN CHARLES

Essex Court Chambers
24 Lincoln's Inn Fields, London WC2A 3EG,
☎020 7813 8000
✉clerksroom@essexcourt.net
Call Date: Nov 1997, Gray's Inn
Pupil Supervisor
Qualifications: [BA (Oxon)]
npillow@essexcourt.net

PILSBURY MR NICHOLAS

Hailsham Chambers
Ground Floor, 4 Paper Buildings, Temple, London EC4Y 7EX, ☎020 7643 5000
✉clerks@hailshamchambers.com
Call Date: Nov 2008, Inner Temple
Qualifications: [BA (Oxon) CPE]
Nicholas.pilsbury@hailshamchambers.com

PIMLOTT MR CHARLES ROBERT

Crown Office Chambers
2 Crown Office Row, Temple, London EC4Y 7HJ, ☎020 7797 8100
✉mail@crownofficechambers.com
Call Date: Nov 2001, Middle Temple
Qualifications: [MA (Cantab)]
pimlott@crownofficechambers.com

PIMM MR PETER JULIAN

Bank House Chambers
Old Bank House, Hartshead, Sheffield S1 2EL,
☎0114 275 1223
✉w.digby@bankhousechambers.co.uk
Call Date: Apr 1991, Gray's Inn
Pupil Supervisor, Recorder
Qualifications: [BSC (Bristol)]
p.pimm@bankhousechambers.co.uk

PINDER MISS SARAH

Renaissance Chambers
5th Floor, Gray's Inn Chambers, Gray's Inn, London WC1R 5JA, ☎020 7404 1111
✉clerks@renaissancechambers.co.uk
Call Date: Oct 2006, Middle Temple
Qualifications: [BA (Hons) (Warw)]
sp2@renaissancechambers.co.uk

PINE MISS MIKA KATE

East Anglian Chambers
140 New London Road, Chelmsford, Essex CM2 0AW, ☎01473 214481
✉chelmsford@ealaw.co.uk
East Anglian Chambers
53 North Hill, Colchester, Essex CO1 1QA,
☎01473 214481 ✉colchester@ealaw.co.uk

E

East Anglian Chambers
Gresham House, 5 Museum Street, Ipswich, Suffolk IP1 1HQ, ☎01473 214481
✉ipswich@ealaw.co.uk
Call Date: Nov 2007, Middle Temple
Qualifications: [BA PgDL]
mikapine@ealaw.co.uk

PINE-COFFIN MISS MARGARET ANN

12 College Place
Fauvelle Buildings, 12 College Place, Southampton SO15 2FE, ☎023 8032 0320
✉clerks@12cp.co.uk
Call Date: July 1981, Inner Temple
Qualifications: [BA (Leeds)]

PINFOLD MR MARTIN FRANKS

The Chambers of Grahame Aldous QC
9 Gough Square, London EC4A 3DG, ☎020 7832 0500
✉clerks@9goughsquare.co.uk
Call Date: July 1981, Middle Temple
Pupil Supervisor
Qualifications: [LLB (London)]
mpinfold@9goughsquare.co.uk

PINHORN MR RICHARD JOHN

Derwent Chambers
78 Friar Gate, Derby DE1 1FL, ☎01332 242425
✉admin@derwentchambers.co.uk
Call Date: July 1998, Middle Temple
Qualifications: [LLB (Hons)(Nott'm)]
admin@derwentchambers.co.uk

PINI MR JOHN PETER JULIAN QC (2006)

Seven Bedford Row
7 Bedford Row, London WC1R 4BS, ☎020 7242 3555 ✉clerks@7br.co.uk
Call Date: July 1981, Gray's Inn
Recorder
Qualifications: [BA]
jpini@7br.co.uk

PINKHAM MRS JOY EMMA

Chartlands Chambers
3 St Giles Terrace, Northampton NN1 2BN, ☎01604 603322
✉enquiries@chartlands-chambers.co.uk
Call Date: Feb 1993, Gray's Inn
Pupil Supervisor
Qualifications: [LLB (Bucks)]
joyemmapinkham@aol.com

PINKNEY MR ANDREW GILES FREDERICK

Fountain Chambers
Cleveland Business Centre, 1 Watson Street, Middlesbrough TS1 2RQ, ☎01642 804040
✉clerks@fountainchambers.co.uk
Call Date: Nov 1978, Gray's Inn
Pupil Supervisor
Qualifications: [BA (Hons)]

PINKUS MISS MOLLY CARLA

Farringdon Chambers
180 Bermondsey Street, London SE1 3TQ, ☎020 7089 5700
Call Date: Oct 1997, Middle Temple
Qualifications: [LLB (Hons) LLM (Lond)]
mollypinkus@farringdon-law.co.uk

PINNELL MR DAVID WILLIAM

9 Park Place
9 Park Place, Cardiff, South Glamorgan CF10 3DP, ☎029 2038 2731
✉clerks@9parkplace.co.uk
Call Date: Mar 2008, Gray's Inn

PINNOCK MR EARL WESTON

No5 Chambers
Fountain Court, Steelhouse Lane, Birmingham B4 6DR, ☎0845 210 5555 ✉info@no5.com
No5 Chambers
Greenwood House, 4-7 Salisbury Court, London EC4Y 8AA, ☎0845 210 5555
No5 Chambers
38 Queen Square, Bristol BS1 4QS, ☎0845 210 5555
Call Date: Nov 2003, Middle Temple
Qualifications: [BA (Hons) (Keele) LLM]
epi@no5.com

PINTO MISS AMANDA EVE QC (2006)

Five Paper Buildings
1st Floor, Five Paper Buildings, Temple, London EC4Y 7HB, ☎020 7583 6117
✉clerks@5pb.co.uk
Call Date: Nov 1983, Middle Temple
Recorder
Qualifications: [MA (Cantab)]

PIPE MR ADAM

No 8 Chambers
8 Fountain Court, Steelhouse Lane, Birmingham B4 6DR, ☎0121 236 5514
✉clerks@no8chambers.co.uk
Call Date: Oct 1999, Middle Temple
Qualifications: [LLB (Hons)(Warw) LLM (Wales)]
adampipe@no8chambers.co.uk

PIPE MR GREGORY SIMON

Chancery House Chambers
7 Lisbon Square, Leeds, West Yorkshire LS1 4LY, ☎ 0113 244 6691
✉ clerks@chanceryhouse.co.uk
Call Date: Oct 1995, Lincoln's Inn
Qualifications: [BA (Hons)(Oxon) LLM (Cantab)]
✉ gregory.pipe@chanceryhouse.co.uk

PIPER MR ANGUS RICHARD

1 Chancery Lane
London WC2A 1LF, ☎ 0845 634 6666
✉ clerks@1chancerylane.com
Call Date: Nov 1991, Lincoln's Inn
Pupil Supervisor
Qualifications: [BA (Hons) (York) Dip Law]
✉ apiper@1chancerylane.com

PIPI MR CHUKWUEMEKA EZEKIEL

Chambers of Martin Burr
15 Old Bailey, London EC4M 7EF, ☎ 0845 123 1234 ✉ clerks@barristerweb.com
Call Date: Apr 1991, Inner Temple
Qualifications: [LLB]

PIRANI MR ROHAN CARL

Old Square Chambers
3 Orchard Court, St Augustine's Yard, Bristol BS1 5DP, ☎ 0117 930 5100
✉ clerks@oldsquare.co.uk
Old Square Chambers
10-11 Bedford Row, London WC1R 4BU, ☎ 020 7269 0300 ✉ clerks@oldsquare.co.uk
Call Date: Oct 1995, Middle Temple
Qualifications: [MA (Oxon) BCL (Oxon) LLM (USA)]
✉ pirani@oldsquare.co.uk

PITCHERS MR HENRY WILLIAM STODART

No5 Chambers
Fountain Court, Steelhouse Lane, Birmingham B4 6DR, ☎ 0845 210 5555 ✉ info@no5.com
No5 Chambers
Greenwood House, 4-7 Salisbury Court, London EC4Y 8AA, ☎ 0845 210 5555
No5 Chambers
38 Queen Square, Bristol BS1 4QS, ☎ 0845 210 5555
Call Date: Nov 1996, Inner Temple
Qualifications: [BA (Oxon)]
✉ hp@no5.com

Types of work: Clinical negligence, Health and safety, Personal injury, Professional negligence

PITCHFORD MISS LAUREN RAE

Southernhay Chambers
33 Southernhay East, Exeter EX1 1NX, ☎ 01392 255777
✉ clerks@southernhaychambers.co.uk
Call Date: July 2001, Gray's Inn
Qualifications: [LLB (Durham) BA]
✉ l.pitchford@southernhaychambers.co.uk

PITHERS MR CLIVE ROBERT

Fenners Chambers
3 Madingley Road, Cambridge CB3 0EE, ☎ 01223 368761
✉ clerks@fennerschambers.com
Call Date: Feb 1989, Gray's Inn
Qualifications: [LLB (Reading)]
✉ clive.pithers@fennerschambers.com

PITMAN MISS LAURA

1 High Pavement
Nottingham NG1 1HF, ☎ 0115 941 8218
✉ clerks@1highpavement.co.uk
Call Date: Oct 2000, Middle Temple
Qualifications: [LLB (Hons) (Nott'm)]
✉ laurapitman@1highpavement.co.uk

PITT MR DANIEL CRAWFORD

Fenners Chambers
3 Madingley Road, Cambridge CB3 0EE, ☎ 01223 368761
✉ clerks@fennerschambers.com
Call Date: Oct 1995, Inner Temple
Qualifications: [BSc (Bath) Dip Law CPE]
✉ daniel.pitt@fennerschambers.com

PITTAWAY MISS AMANDA MICHELLE

Cornwall Street Chambers
85-87 Cornwall Street, Birmingham B3 3BY, ☎ 0121 233 7500
✉ clerks@cornwallstreet.co.uk
Call Date: July 1980, Gray's Inn
Qualifications: [LLB (B'ham)]
✉ amanda.pittaway@cornwallstreet.co.uk

PITTAWAY MR DAVID MICHAEL QC (2000)

Hailsham Chambers
Ground Floor, 4 Paper Buildings, Temple, London EC4Y 7EX, ☎ 020 7643 5000
✉ clerks@hailshamchambers.com
Call Date: July 1977, Inner Temple
Recorder
Qualifications: [MA (Cantab) FCI Arb]
✉ David.PittawayQC@hailshamchambers.com

E

PITTER MR JASON KARL

Park Court Chambers
16 Park Place, Leeds LS1 2SJ,
☎ 0113 243 3277
✉ clerks@parkcourtchambers.co.uk
Call Date: Oct 1994, Gray's Inn
Pupil Supervisor
Qualifications: [LLB (Hons)]
jpitter@parkcourtchambers.co.uk

PITT-LEWIS MRS JANET REBECCA

Cornwall Street Chambers
85-87 Cornwall Street, Birmingham B3 3BY,
☎ 0121 233 7500
✉ clerks@cornwallstreet.co.uk
Cornwall Street Chambers
Shrewsbury Annex, Rural Enterprise Centre, Stafford Drive, Battlefield Enterprise Park, Shrewsbury SY1 3FE,
☎ 01743 363 611 / 0121 233 7500
Call Date: July 1976, Middle Temple
Pupil Supervisor
Qualifications: [MA (Oxon)]
janet.pitt-lewis@cornwallstreet.co.uk

PITT-PAYNE MR TIMOTHY SHERIDAN QC (2010)

11 King's Bench Walk
11 King's Bench Walk, Temple, London EC4Y 7EQ, ☎ 020 7632 8500
✉ clerksroom@11kbw.com
Call Date: Nov 1989, Inner Temple
Pupil Supervisor
Qualifications: [BA BCL (Oxon)]
timothy.pitt-payne@11kbw.com

PITTS MISS CHARLOTTE FRANCES

Albion Chambers
Broad Street, Bristol BS1 1DR,
☎ 0117 927 2144
✉ clerks@albionchambers.co.uk
Call Date: Oct 1999, Inner Temple
Qualifications: [LLB (So'ton)]
charlotte.pitts@albionchambers.co.uk

PITTS MISS EMILY ODETTE

Colleton Chambers
Colleton Crescent, Exeter, Devon EX2 4DG,
☎ 01392 274898
✉ clerks@colletonchambers.co.uk
Call Date: Oct 2000, Inner Temple
Qualifications: [BA (Dunelm) CPE]
emilypitts@colletonchambers.co.uk

PITTS MR KEITH FRANCIS

The Chambers of Mr K F Pitts
'Tussocks', The Causeway, Therfield, Hertfordshire SG8 9PP, ☎ 01763 287 760
✉ keithpitts@keithpitts.f2s.com
Call Date: Oct 1997, Middle Temple
Qualifications: [BSc (Salford) C.Eng, MIMechE Dip Law]

PLANGE MISS JANET NYANCH

Renaissance Chambers
5th Floor, Gray's Inn Chambers, Gray's Inn, London WC1R 5JA, ☎ 020 7404 1111
✉ clerks@renaissancechambers.co.uk
Call Date: July 1981, Gray's Inn
Qualifications: [LLB (B'ham)]
jp1@renaissancechambers.co.uk

PLANT MISS APRIL SUZANNE

East Anglian Chambers
Gresham House, 5 Museum Street, Ipswich, Suffolk IP1 1HQ, ☎ 01473 214481
✉ ipswich@ealaw.co.uk
East Anglian Chambers
53 North Hill, Colchester, Essex CO1 1QA,
☎ 01473 214481 ✉ colchester@ealaw.co.uk
East Anglian Chambers
15 The Close, Norwich, Norfolk NR1 4DZ,
☎ 01473 214481 ✉ norwich@ealaw.co.uk
Call Date: Oct 2002, Lincoln's Inn
Qualifications: [LLB (Leic)]
aprilplant@ealaw.co.uk

PLANT MR JAMES RICHARD

Farrar's Building
Farrar's Building, Temple, London EC4Y 7BD,
☎ 020 7583 9241
✉ Chambers@farrarsbuilding.co.uk
Call Date: Nov 2004, Middle Temple
Qualifications: [BA (Hons) (L'pool) PgDip Law]
jplant@farrarsbuilding.co.uk

PLASCHKES MS SARAH GEORGINA QC (2011)

QEB Hollis Whiteman
1-2 Laurence Pountney Hill, London EC4R 0EU, ☎ 020 7933 8855
✉ barristers@qebhw.co.uk
Call Date: July 1988, Inner Temple
Pupil Supervisor, Recorder
Qualifications: [LLB (So'ton)]
sarah.plaschkes@qebhw.co.uk

E

PLATFORD MR GRAHAM ROY

Five Paper
Ground Floor, 5 Paper Buildings, Temple, London EC4Y 7HB, ☎ 020 7815 3200
Call Date: Nov 1970, Gray's Inn
Pupil Supervisor
Qualifications: [BA]
grahamplatford@fivepaper.com

PLATT MR DAVID WALLACE QC (2011)

Crown Office Chambers
2 Crown Office Row, Temple, London EC4Y 7HJ, ☎ 020 7797 8100
mail@crownofficechambers.com
Call Date: July 1987, Middle Temple
Pupil Supervisor
Qualifications: [MA (Cantab)]
platt@crownofficechambers.com

PLATT MISS ELEANOR FRANCES QC (1982)

1 Garden Court Family Law Chambers
Ground Floor, One Garden Court, Temple, London EC4Y 9BJ, ☎ 020 7797 7900
clerks@1gc.com
Eastbourne Chambers
5 Chiswick Place, Eastbourne, East Sussex BN21 4NH, ☎ 01323 642102
clerks@eastbournechambers.co.uk
Call Date: Feb 1960, Gray's Inn
Recorder
Qualifications: [LLB (Lond)]
platt@1gc.com

PLATT MISS HEATHER LOUISE

Pump Court Chambers
Upper Ground Floor, 3 Pump Court, Temple, London EC4Y 7AJ, ☎ 020 7353 0711
clerks@3pumpcourt.com
Pump Court Chambers
5 Temple Chambers, Temple Street, Swindon SN1 1SQ, ☎ 01793 539899
clerks@3pumpcourt.com
Riverview Chambers
Hamilton House, 1 Temple Avenue, London EC4Y 0HA, ☎ 0844 225 3999
chrisbaylis@riverviewchambers.com
Call Date: Oct 2002, Lincoln's Inn
Pupil Supervisor
Qualifications: [LLB (L'Pool)]
hp@3pumpcourt.com

PLATT MR STEPHEN WILLIAM

23 Essex Street
London WC2R 3AA, ☎ 020 7413 0353
clerks@23es.com
Call Date: Oct 1994, Middle Temple
Qualifications: [LLB (Hons)(Brunel)]
stephenplatt@jerseyibs.com

PLATTS MISS RACHEL ELIZABETH

1 Hare Court
1 Hare Court, Temple, London EC4Y 7BE, ☎ 020 7797 7070 clerks@1hc.com
Riverview Chambers
Hamilton House, 1 Temple Avenue, London EC4Y 0HA, ☎ 0844 225 3999
chrisbaylis@riverviewchambers.com
Call Date: Nov 1989, Inner Temple
Qualifications: [LLB (Hons)(Lond)]
clerks@1hc.com

PLATTS-MILLS MR MARK FORTESCUE QC (1995)

8 New Square
8 New Square, Lincoln's Inn, London WC2A 3QP, ☎ 020 7405 4321
clerks@8newsquare.co.uk
Call Date: July 1974, Inner Temple
Qualifications: [BA (Oxon)]
mark.platts-mills@8newsquare.co.uk

Types of work: Breach of confidence, Competition law, Computer litigation, Copyright, Copyright theft, Copyright Tribunal, Design, EC competition law, Entertainment, Franchising, Information technology, Intellectual property, Malicious falsehood, Media, Media and entertainment, Passing off, Patents, Product liability, Scientific and technical disputes, Trade Descriptions Act, Trade secrets, Trademarks

PLAUT MR SIMON MICHAEL

Kings Chambers
36 Young Street, Manchester M3 3FT, ☎ 0845 034 3444
clerks@kingschambers.com
Kings Chambers
5 Park Square East, Leeds LS1 2NE, ☎ 0845 034 3444
clerks@kingschambers.com

E

Kings Chambers
Embassy House, 60 Church Street, Birmingham B3 2DJ, ☎0845 034 3444
✉clerks@kingschambers.com
Call Date: Oct 1997, Lincoln's Inn
Qualifications: [BA (Hons)]
splaut@kingschambers.com

PLEETH MR EDWARD JAMES

3 Serjeants Inn
London EC4Y 1BQ, ☎020 7427 5000
✉clerks@3serjeantsinn.com
Call Date: July 2005, Inner Temple
Qualifications: [LLB]

PLEMING MR NIGEL PETER QC (1992)

39 Essex Street
London WC2R 3AT, ☎020 7832 1111
✉clerks@39essex.com
82 King Street
Manchester M2 4WQ, ☎0161 870 9969
Call Date: Feb 1971, Inner Temple
Qualifications: [LLM (Lond)]
nigel.pleming@39essex.com

PLEWMAN MR THOMAS

Brick Court Chambers
7-8 Essex Street, London WC2R 3LD, ☎020 7379 3550 ✉clerks@brickcourt.co.uk
Call Date: Oct 2009, Middle Temple
Qualifications: [LLB (South Africa) BCL (Hons) (Oxon)]
thomas.plewman@brickcourt.co.uk

PLIENER MR DAVID JONATHAN

Hardwicke
New Square, Lincoln's Inn, London WC2A 3SB, ☎020 7242 2523
✉enquiries@hardwicke.co.uk
Call Date: Nov 1996, Middle Temple
Pupil Supervisor
Qualifications: [BSc (Hons)(Manch)]
david.pliener@hardwicke.co.uk

PLIMMER MISS MELANIE ANN

Kings Chambers
36 Young Street, Manchester M3 3FT, ☎0845 034 3444
✉clerks@kingschambers.com
Kings Chambers
5 Park Square East, Leeds LS1 2NE, ☎0845 034 3444
✉clerks@kingschambers.com
Kings Chambers
Embassy House, 60 Church Street, Birmingham B3 2DJ, ☎0845 034 3444
✉clerks@kingschambers.com
Call Date: Mar 1996, Gray's Inn
Qualifications: [LLB (Bris) LLM (Lond)]
mplimmer@kingschambers.com, melplimmer@googlemail.com

PLOWDEN MR PHILIP EDWARD HARTLEY STANDISH

Park Lane Plowden
Lombard House, 4-8 Lombard Street, Newcastle Upon Tyne NE1 3AE, ☎0191 211 4087
✉clerks@parklaneplowden.co.uk
Call Date: Mar 2001, Middle Temple
Qualifications: [BA (Hons) (Oxon) CPE LLM (Newc)]

PLOWDEN MRS SARAH SELENA RIXAR

Guildhall Chambers
23 Broad Street, Bristol BS1 2HG, ☎0117 930 9000
✉hoc@guildhallchambers.co.uk
Call Date: Nov 1991, Inner Temple
Qualifications: [BA (Lond) Dip Law]
selena.plowden@guildhallchambers.co.uk

PLOWRIGHT MR JOSEPH EDWARD

1 Gray's Inn Square
Ground Floor, 1 Gray's Inn Square, London WC1R 5AA, ☎020 7405 0001
Call Date: Oct 1999, Inner Temple
Qualifications: [BA (Cantab)]

PLUMMER MISS KATHERINE NORAH

KCH Garden Square
1 Oxford Street, Nottingham NG1 5BH, ☎0115 941 8851
✉clerks@kchgardensquare.co.uk
Call Date: Oct 2010, Inner Temple
Qualifications: [LLB (Sheff)]
kplummer@kchgardensquare.co.uk

PLUNKETT MR RAYMOND JOHN

Cornwall Street Chambers
85-87 Cornwall Street, Birmingham B3 3BY, ☎0121 233 7500
✉clerks@cornwallstreet.co.uk
Call Date: Mar 2004, Gray's Inn
Qualifications: [LLB]
raymond.plunkett@cornwallstreet.co.uk

E

POCOCK MR CHRISTOPHER JAMES QC (2009)

1 KBW Chambers
1 King's Bench Walk, Temple, London
EC4Y 7DB, ☎020 7936 1500
✉clerks@1kbw.co.uk
King's Bench Chambers
174 High Street, Lewes BN7 1YE,
☎01273 402600
Call Date: July 1984, Inner Temple
Qualifications: [BA (Hons)(Oxon)]
✉cpocock@1kbw.co.uk

POINTER MR MARTIN JOHN QC (1996)

1 Hare Court
1 Hare Court, Temple, London EC4Y 7BE,
☎020 7797 7070 ✉clerks@1hc.com
Call Date: July 1976, Gray's Inn
Qualifications: [LLB]
✉mpqc@1hc.com

POINTING MR JOHN ERIC

Chambers of Mr John Pointing
46 Arlington Road, Ealing, London W13 8PE,
☎020 8997 2285
✉johnpointing@hotmail.com
Call Date: Oct 1992, Middle Temple
Qualifications: [BA (Hons) (Keele) M Phil Dip Law]
✉johnpointing@hotmail.com

POINTON MR NICHOLAS LLOYD

St John's Chambers
101 Victoria Street, Bristol BS1 6PU,
☎0117 923 4700
✉clerks@stjohnschambers.co.uk
Call Date: July 2010, Lincoln's Inn
Qualifications: [LLB (Bris)]

POJUR MR DAVID ELLIOT

St Johns Buildings
24a - 28 St John Street, Manchester M3 4DJ,
☎0161 214 1500
✉clerk@stjohnsbuildings.co.uk
16 Winckley Square
Preston PR1 3JJ, ☎01772 256100
St Johns Buildings Liverpool
8th Floor India Buildings, Water Street,
Liverpool L2 0XG, ☎0151 243 6000
✉clerk@stjohnsbuildings.co.uk
Call Date: Nov 2001, Middle Temple
Qualifications: [LLB (Hons)(Manch)]
✉davidpojur@stjohnsbuildings.co.uk

POKU MISS MARY LAUREEN

9-12 Bell Yard
London WC2A 2JR, ☎020 7400 1800
✉clerks@9-12bellyard.com
Call Date: Nov 1993, Lincoln's Inn
Qualifications: [LLB (Hons)]
✉m.poku@9-12bellyard.com

POLE MR TIMOTHY DANIEL

No5 Chambers
Fountain Court, Steelhouse Lane, Birmingham
B4 6DR, ☎0845 210 5555 ✉info@no5.com
No5 Chambers
Greenwood House, 4-7 Salisbury Court,
London EC4Y 8AA, ☎0845 210 5555
No5 Chambers
38 Queen Square, Bristol BS1 4QS,
☎0845 210 5555
Call Date: July 2001, Middle Temple
Qualifications: [BA (Hons) Dip Law]
✉tp@no5.com

POLGLASE MR DAVID SUTHERLAND

St Johns Buildings Liverpool
8th Floor India Buildings, Water Street,
Liverpool L2 0XG, ☎0151 243 6000
✉clerk@stjohnsbuildings.co.uk
16 Winckley Square
Preston PR1 3JJ, ☎01772 256100
St Johns Buildings
24a - 28 St John Street, Manchester M3 4DJ,
☎0161 214 1500
✉clerk@stjohnsbuildings.co.uk
Call Date: Oct 1993, Middle Temple
Qualifications: [BA (Hons)(Oxon) MA (Oxon)]

POLLARD MS ELIZA JOAN

Chambers of Marion Smullen and Kerim Fuad QC
1 Inner Temple Lane, London EC4Y 1AF,
☎020 7427 4400 ✉clerks@1itl.com
Call Date: Nov 2008, Gray's Inn
Qualifications: [BA]

POLLARD MISS JOANNA KATE

Blackstone Chambers
Blackstone House, Temple, London
EC4Y 9BW, ☎020 7583 1770
✉clerks@blackstonechambers.com
Call Date: Oct 1993, Gray's Inn
Pupil Supervisor
Qualifications: [BA (Cantab)]
✉joannapollard@blackstonechambers.com

E

POLLEY MR ALEXANDER RICHARD

One Essex Court
Ground Floor, One Essex Court, Temple, London EC4Y 9AR, ☎ 020 7583 2000
✉ clerks@oeclaw.co.uk
Call Date: July 2005, Inner Temple
Qualifications: [BA (Oxon) M Phil (Oxon) Dip Law]

POLLI MR TIMOTHY JAMES

Tanfield Chambers
2-5 Warwick Court, London WC1R 5DJ, ☎ 020 7421 5300
✉ clerks@tanfieldchambers.co.uk
Call Date: July 1997, Middle Temple
Qualifications: [MA BCL (Oxon)]
timpolli@tanfieldchambers.co.uk, timpolli@tanfieldchambers.co.uk

POLLOCK MR ALAN GORDON SETON QC (1979)

Essex Court Chambers
24 Lincoln's Inn Fields, London WC2A 3EG, ☎ 020 7813 8000
✉ clerksroom@essexcourt.net
Call Date: Nov 1968, Gray's Inn
Qualifications: [MA LLB (Cantab)]
gpollock@essexcourt.net

POLLOCK DR EVELYN MARIAN MARGARET

Hailsham Chambers
Ground Floor, 4 Paper Buildings, Temple, London EC4Y 7EX, ☎ 020 7643 5000
✉ clerks@hailshamchambers.com
Call Date: Oct 1991, Inner Temple
Qualifications: [BSc FRCA MBChB MD (Edin)]
evelyn.pollock@hailshamchambers.com

POLLOCK MISS ROBERTA HILARY

Goldsmith Chambers
Ground Floor, Goldsmith Building, Temple, London EC4Y 7BL, ☎ 020 7353 6802
✉ clerks@goldsmithchambers.com
Call Date: Nov 1993, Inner Temple
Qualifications: [LLB (Brunel)]
H.Pollock@goldsmithchambers.law.co.uk

POLNAY MR JONATHAN SAMUEL

5 King's Bench Walk
5 King's Bench Walk, Temple, London EC4Y 7DN, ☎ 020 7353 5638
✉ clerks@5kbw.co.uk
Call Date: Nov 2000, Middle Temple
Qualifications: [BA (Hons) (Cantab)]

POLSON MR ALISTAIR JAMES

1 Pump Court
Elm Court, Temple, London EC4Y 7AB, ☎ 020 7842 7070
✉ (name)@pumpcourt.co.uk
Call Date: Nov 1989, Middle Temple
Pupil Supervisor
Qualifications: [MA (Hons) (Glas) DipLaw]
ap@1pumpcourt.co.uk

POMFRET MR BRADLEY RUSSELL

St James's Chambers
68 Quay Street, Manchester M3 3EJ, ☎ 0161 834 7000
✉ clerks@stjameschambers.com
Call Date: Oct 2004, Lincoln's Inn
Qualifications: [LLB (Hons)]
brad.pomfret@stjameschambers.com

PONNAMPALAM REILLY MRS LAXMI DEVI

CHL Chambers
50 Colney Hatch Lane, Muswell Hill, London N10 1EA, ☎ 020 8883 7706
✉ acesreill@aol.com
Call Date: Nov 1972, Middle Temple
acesreill@aol.com

PONS MR GARY STEPHEN

Five St Andrew's Hill
5 St Andrew's Hill, London EC4V 5BZ, ☎ 020 7332 5400 ✉ Clerks@5sah.co.uk
Call Date: Oct 1995, Gray's Inn
Qualifications: [BA (Kent) Diploma In Spanish Law]
garypons@5sah.co.uk

PONTE MR LUKE ANTHONY ARCHIBALD

3 Raymond Buildings
3 Raymond Buildings, Gray's Inn, London WC1R 5BH, ☎ 020 7400 6400
✉ clerks@3rblaw.com
Call Date: Nov 2003, Middle Temple
Qualifications: [BA (Hons) (Lond) CPE]

PONTER MR IAN MICHAEL

Kings Chambers
36 Young Street, Manchester M3 3FT, ☎ 0845 034 3444
✉ clerks@kingschambers.com
Kings Chambers
5 Park Square East, Leeds LS1 2NE, ☎ 0845 034 3444
✉ clerks@kingschambers.com
Kings Chambers
Embassy House, 60 Church Street, Birmingham B3 2DJ, ☎ 0845 034 3444
✉ clerks@kingschambers.com

Cornerstone Barristers
2-3 Gray's Inn Square, Gray's Inn, London WC1R 5JH, ☎020 7242 4986
✉chambers@2-3gis.co.uk
Call Date: Oct 1993, Middle Temple
Pupil Supervisor
Qualifications: [BA (Hons) (Keele) LLM (Scotland)]
✉iponter@kingschambers.com

POOLE MR ALEXANDER DAVID

Deans Court Chambers
24 St John Street, Manchester M3 4DF,
☎0161 214 6000 ✉clerks@deanscourt.co.uk
Deans Court Chambers
101 Walker Street, Preston PR1 2RR,
☎01772 565 600
✉preston@deanscourt.co.uk
Call Date: Oct 2002, Inner Temple
Qualifications: [MA (Hons) (Edin) CPE (Manch)]
✉poole@deanscourt.co.uk

POOLE MR CHRISTOPHER ROBERT

New Court
Ground Floor, New Court, Temple, London EC4Y 9BE, ☎020 7583 5123
✉clerks@newcourtchambers.com
Call Date: Nov 1996, Lincoln's Inn
Pupil Supervisor
Qualifications: [LLB (Hons)(Lond)]
✉cpoole@newcourtchambers.net

POOLE MR NIGEL DAVID QC (2012)

Kings Chambers
36 Young Street, Manchester M3 3FT,
☎0845 034 3444
✉clerks@kingschambers.com
Kings Chambers
5 Park Square East, Leeds LS1 2NE,
☎0845 034 3444
✉clerks@kingschambers.com
Kings Chambers
Embassy House, 60 Church Street, Birmingham B3 2DJ, ☎0845 034 3444
✉clerks@kingschambers.com
Call Date: Nov 1989, Middle Temple
Recorder
Qualifications: [BA (Oxon) DipLaw]
✉npoole@kingschambers.com

POOLE MR TOM JOHN DALTON

3 Hare Court
3 Hare Court, Temple, London EC4Y 7BJ,
☎020 7415 7800 ✉clerks@3harecourt.com
Call Date: Oct 2001, Inner Temple
Qualifications: [MA (Cantab)]
✉tompoole@3harecourt.com

POOLE MR WILLIAM

Call Date: July 2004, Middle Temple
Qualifications: [BA Hons (Leeds) CPE]
✉clerk@stjohnsbuildings.co.uk

POOLES MR MICHAEL PHILIP HOLMES QC (1999)

Hailsham Chambers
Ground Floor, 4 Paper Buildings, Temple, London EC4Y 7EX, ☎020 7643 5000
✉clerks@hailshamchambers.com
Call Date: July 1978, Inner Temple
Recorder
Qualifications: [LLB (Lond)]
✉Michael.PoolesQC@hailshamchambers.com

POOTS MISS LAURA JILL

Pump Court Tax Chambers
16 Bedford Row, London WC1R 4EF,
☎020 7414 8080 ✉clerks@pumptax.com
Call Date: Oct 2007, Middle Temple
Qualifications: [BA (Hons) (Oxon)]
✉lpoots@pumptax.com

Types of work: Capital tax, Corporation tax, Equity, Income tax, National Insurance, Private client, Stamp duty, Trusts, VAT, Wills

POPAT MR PRASHANT QC (2008)

Henderson Chambers
2 Harcourt Buildings, Temple, London EC4Y 9DB, ☎020 7583 9020
✉clerks@hendersonchambers.co.uk
Call Date: Feb 1992, Gray's Inn
Qualifications: [MA (Oxon)]
✉ppopat@hendersonchambers.co.uk

POPE MISS ANNA

Linenhall Chambers
1 Stanley Place, Chester CH1 2LU,
☎01244 348282
✉clerks@linenhallchambers.co.uk
Call Date: Oct 2007, Middle Temple
Qualifications: [BA (Hons) (Cantab) PgDL (Nott'm)]

POPE MRS HEATHER

1 Hare Court
1 Hare Court, Temple, London EC4Y 7BE,
☎020 7797 7070 ✉clerks@1hc.com
Call Date: July 1977, Inner Temple
Qualifications: [BA (Hons) (Wales) Dip Ed (Wales)]
✉pope@1hc.com

Fax: 020 7797 7435;
DX: 342 London, Chancery Lane

Types of work: Care proceedings, Children, Family law, Matrimonial, Private children law

E

POPE MISS SANDRA JANE

18 St John Street
Manchester M3 4EA, ☎ 0161 278 1800
✉ clerks@18sjs.com
Call Date: July 2008, Inner Temple
Qualifications: [LLB (Leic)]
✉ spope@18sjs.com

POPE MISS SARAH BLANCHE VICTORIA

14 Gray's Inn Square
14 Gray's Inn Square, Gray's Inn, London WC1R 5JP, ☎ 020 7242 0858
✉ clerks@14gis.co.uk
Call Date: July 2006, Lincoln's Inn
Qualifications: [BA (Hons)]
✉ sp@14graysinnsquare.co.uk

POPLAWSKI MR ROMAN

33 Bedford Row
London WC1R 4JH, ☎ 020 7242 6476
✉ clerks@33bedfordrow.co.uk
Call Date: Nov 1989, Lincoln's Inn
Qualifications: [LLB (B'ham)]

POPLE MISS ALISON RUTH

2 Bedford Row
London WC1R 4BU, ☎ 020 7440 8888
✉ clerks@2bedfordrow.co.uk
Call Date: Nov 1993, Middle Temple
Qualifications: [LLB (Hons)]
✉ apople@2bedfordrow.co.uk

POPLEY MISS HEATHER LOUISE

New Street Chambers
2 New Street, Leicester LE1 5NA, ☎ 0116 262 5906 ✉ clerks@2newstreet.co.uk
Call Date: Nov 2003, Gray's Inn
Qualifications: [LLB (Hull)]

POPPLEWELL MR SIMON JOHN

Gough Square Chambers
6-7 Gough Square, London EC4A 3DE, ☎ 020 7353 0924 ✉ gsc@goughsq.co.uk
Call Date: Oct 2000, Gray's Inn
Qualifications: [BA (Hons)]
✉ simon.popplewell@goughsq.co.uk

PORTEN MR ANTHONY RALPH QC (1988)

Cornerstone Barristers
2-3 Gray's Inn Square, Gray's Inn, London WC1R 5JH, ☎ 020 7242 4986
✉ chambers@2-3gis.co.uk
Call Date: July 1969, Inner Temple
Qualifications: [BA (Cantab)]
✉ aporten@2-3gis.co.uk

PORTER MR DAVID LEONARD

St James's Chambers
68 Quay Street, Manchester M3 3EJ, ☎ 0161 834 7000
✉ clerks@stjameschambers.com
Call Date: July 1980, Lincoln's Inn
Qualifications: [LLB (Manch)]
✉ david.porter@stjameschambers.com

PORTER MR JAMIE ROBERT

King's Bench Chambers
Wellington House, 175 Holdenhurst Road, Bournemouth, Dorset BH8 8DQ,
☎ 01202 250025
Call Date: Oct 1997, Inner Temple
Qualifications: [LLB (Brunel)]
✉ jamie.porter@trialcounsel.co.uk

PORTER MS JOANNE EMILY

Stour Chambers
Mill Studio, 17a Stour Street, Canterbury, Kent CT1 2NR, ☎ 01227 764899
✉ clerks@stourchambers.co.uk
Call Date: Nov 2010, Inner Temple
Qualifications: [LLB (Canterbury)]
✉ joanne.porter@stourchambers.co.uk

PORTER MR MARTIN HUGH QC (2006)

2 Temple Gardens
2 Temple Gardens, Temple, London EC4Y 9AY, ☎ 020 7822 1200
✉ clerks@2tg.co.uk
Call Date: July 1986, Inner Temple
Qualifications: [MA (Cantab) LLM]
✉ mporter@2tg.co.uk

PORTER MR NIGEL JOHN

11 King's Bench Walk
11 King's Bench Walk, Temple, London EC4Y 7EQ, ☎ 020 7632 8500
✉ clerksroom@11kbw.com
Call Date: Nov 1994, Middle Temple
Qualifications: [MA (Cantab) LLM (Hons)(Cantab)]
✉ nigel.porter@11kbw.com

PORTER MR ROBERT GEOFFREY WALDEGRAVE

4 Breams Buildings
Chancery Lane, London EC4A 1HP, ☎ 020 7092 1900 ✉ clerks@4bb.co.uk
Call Date: Nov 1988, Middle Temple
Qualifications: [BA (Dunelm) Dip Law LLM (USA)]

PORTER-BRYANT MR MATTHEW SEYMOUR

Guildhall Chambers
23 Broad Street, Bristol BS1 2HG,
☎ 0117 930 9000
✉ hoc@guildhallchambers.co.uk
Call Date: Nov 1999, Middle Temple
Qualifications: [LLB (Hons)]
✉ matthew.porter-bryant@guildhallchambers.co.uk

PORTER-PHILLIPS MRS CLARE MARY ELIZABETH

Call Date: Mar 2001, Lincoln's Inn
Qualifications: [LLB (Hons)]
✉ clerk@stjohnsbuildings.co.uk, cpp@stjohnsbuildings.co.uk

POSNER MISS GABRIELLE JAN

Renaissance Chambers
5th Floor, Gray's Inn Chambers, Gray's Inn, London WC1R 5JA, ☎ 020 7404 1111
✉ clerks@renaissancechambers.co.uk
Call Date: July 1984, Inner Temple
Pupil Supervisor
Qualifications: [LLB (Soton) LLM (Indiana)]

POST MR ANDREW JOHN QC (2012)

Hailsham Chambers
Ground Floor, 4 Paper Buildings, Temple, London EC4Y 7EX, ☎ 020 7643 5000
✉ clerks@hailshamchambers.com
Call Date: July 1988, Middle Temple
Pupil Supervisor
Qualifications: [BA (Cantab) Dip Law (Lond)]
✉ andrew.post@hailshamchambers.com

POSTA MR ADRIAN MARK

Albion Chambers
Broad Street, Bristol BS1 1DR,
☎ 0117 927 2144
✉ clerks@albionchambers.co.uk
Call Date: Oct 1996, Middle Temple
Qualifications: [LLB (Hons)(Warw)]
✉ adrian.posta@albionchambers.co.uk

POTE MR ANDREW THOMAS

13 King's Bench Walk
13 King's Bench Walk, Temple, London EC4Y 7EN, ☎ 020 7353 7204
✉ clerks@13kbw.co.uk
13 KBW
32 Beaumont Street, Oxford OX1 2NP,
☎ 01865 311066 ✉ clerks@13kbw.co.uk
Call Date: Nov 1983, Gray's Inn
Pupil Supervisor
Qualifications: [LLB (UEA)]
✉ apote@13kbw.co.uk

POTTER MISS ALISON LISA

4 Pump Court
4 Pump Court, Temple, London EC4Y 7AN,
☎ 020 7842 5555
✉ chambers@4pumpcourt.com
Call Date: Feb 1987, Middle Temple
Qualifications: [MA (Oxon)]
✉ apotter@4pumpcourt.com

POTTER MR ANTHONY JOHN

No5 Chambers
Fountain Court, Steelhouse Lane, Birmingham B4 6DR, ☎ 0845 210 5555 ✉ info@no5.com
No5 Chambers
Greenwood House, 4-7 Salisbury Court, London EC4Y 8AA, ☎ 0845 210 5555
No5 Chambers
38 Queen Square, Bristol BS1 4QS,
☎ 0845 210 5555
Call Date: July 1994, Gray's Inn
Qualifications: [BA (Wales)]
✉ ap@no5.com

POTTER MR DAVID ANDREW

Exchange Chambers
One Derby Square, Derby Square, Liverpool L2 9XX, ☎ 0151 236 7747
✉ info@exchangechambers.co.uk
Exchange Chambers
7 Ralli Courts, West Riverside, Manchester M3 5FT, ☎ 0161 833 2722
Farrar's Building
Farrar's Building, Temple, London EC4Y 7BD,
☎ 020 7583 9241
✉ Chambers@farrarsbuilding.co.uk
Call Date: Oct 1990, Lincoln's Inn
Pupil Supervisor
Qualifications: [LLB (UEA)]

POTTER REV HARRY DRUMMOND

25 Bedford Row
London WC1R 4HD, ☎ 020 7067 1500
✉ clerks@25bedfordrow.com
Call Date: Oct 1993, Gray's Inn
Qualifications: [MA M Phil LLB]
✉ hpotter@25bedfordrow.com

POTTER MR IAN EDWARD JAMES

Eastbourne Chambers
5 Chiswick Place, Eastbourne, East Sussex BN21 4NH, ☎ 01323 642102
✉ clerks@eastbournechambers.co.uk
Call Date: Nov 2001, Inner Temple
Pupil Supervisor
Qualifications: [LLB (Kent)]

POTTER MISS LOUISE

Harcourt Chambers
1st Floor, 2 Harcourt Buildings, Temple, London EC4Y 9DB, ☎ 0844 561 7135
Harcourt Chambers
Churchill House, 3 St Aldate's Courtyard, St Aldate's, Oxford OX1 1BN, ☎ 0844 561 7135
Call Date: Nov 1993, Inner Temple
Pupil Supervisor
Qualifications: [MA (Oxon) CPE]
lpotter@harcourtchambers.law.co.uk

POTTER MR TIMOTHY MICHAEL

4 Brick Court
4 Brick Court, Temple, London EC4Y 9AD, ☎ 020 7832 3200 ✉ clerks@4bc.co.uk
Call Date: Oct 2005, Lincoln's Inn
Qualifications: [LLB (Hons) LLM]
tim.potter@4bc.co.uk

POTTINGER MR GAVIN JAMES

4 Breams Buildings
Chancery Lane, London EC4A 1HP, ☎ 020 7092 1900 ✉ clerks@4bb.co.uk
Call Date: Oct 1991, Inner Temple
Qualifications: [BScECON DipLaw]

POTTLE MS EMILIE CATHERINE BEAUDIN

36 Bedford Row
London WC1R 4JH, ☎ 020 7421 8000
✉ chambers@36bedfordrow.co.uk
Call Date: Oct 2008, Lincoln's Inn
Qualifications: [LLB (Dunelm)]
epottle@36bedfordrow.co.uk

POTTS MR JAMES RUPERT

Erskine Chambers
33 Chancery Lane, London WC2A 1EN, ☎ 020 7242 5532
✉ clerks@erskinechambers.com
Call Date: Oct 1994, Gray's Inn
Pupil Supervisor
Qualifications: [BA (Oxon)]
jpotts@erskine-chambers.co.uk

POTTS MR RICHARD ANDREW

2 Pump Court
1st Floor, 2 Pump Court, Temple, London EC4Y 7AH, ☎ 020 7353 5597
✉ clerks@2pumpcourt.co.uk
18 Red Lion Court
London EC4A 3EB, ☎ 020 7520 6000
✉ chambers@18rlc.co.uk
Call Date: Nov 1991, Inner Temple
Qualifications: [LLB (B'ham)]

POTTS MR WARREN NIGEL

St James's Chambers
68 Quay Street, Manchester M3 3EJ, ☎ 0161 834 7000
✉ clerks@stjameschambers.com
Zenith Chambers
10 Park Square, Leeds LS1 2LH, ☎ 0113 245 5438
✉ clerks@zenithchambers.co.uk
Call Date: July 1995, Middle Temple
Pupil Supervisor
Qualifications: [BA (Hons)]
clerks@stjameschambers.com

POULET MRS REBECCA MARIA QC (1995)

QEB Hollis Whiteman
1-2 Laurence Pountney Hill, London EC4R 0EU, ☎ 020 7933 8855
✉ barristers@qebhw.co.uk
Call Date: Nov 1975, Lincoln's Inn
Recorder
barristers@qebholliswhiteman.co.uk

POUNDER MS ESTHER ANTONIA

The Chambers of Grahame Aldous QC
9 Gough Square, London EC4A 3DG, ☎ 020 7832 0500
✉ clerks@9goughsquare.co.uk
Call Date: July 2003, Inner Temple
Qualifications: [BA (Hons) (Lond) CPE(Lond) DipLaw]
epounder@9goughsquare.co.uk

POUNDER MR GERARD

18 Red Lion Court
London EC4A 3EB, ☎ 020 7520 6000
✉ chambers@18rlc.co.uk
Call Date: July 1980, Lincoln's Inn
Pupil Supervisor, Recorder
Qualifications: [LLB (Lond) BA (Lond) MA (Lond)]
gerard.pounder@18rlc.co.uk

E

POUNDS MISS CAROLINE JOANNE

Quadrant Chambers
Quadrant House, 10 Fleet Street, London EC4Y 1AU, ☎020 7583 4444
✉info@quadrantchambers.com
Call Date: Oct 2003, Lincoln's Inn
Qualifications: [BA (Hons) (Oxon)]
✉caroline.pounds@quadrantchambers.com

POVALL MR DAVID JUSTIN

23 Essex Street
London WC2R 3AA, ☎020 7413 0353
✉clerks@23es.com
Call Date: July 2000, Lincoln's Inn
Pupil Supervisor
Qualifications: [LLB(HONS) (Lond)]
✉davidpovall@23es.com

POVOAS MR NIGEL JOHN SPENCER

Seven Bedford Row
7 Bedford Row, London WC1R 4BS, ☎020 7242 3555 ✉clerks@7br.co.uk
Call Date: Oct 1998, Lincoln's Inn
Qualifications: [LLB (Hons)(Notts)]
✉npovoas@7br.co.uk

POVOAS MR SIMON JOHN SPENCER

Chavasse Court Chambers
18 Queen Avenue, Liverpool L2 4TX, ☎0151 229 2030
✉clerks@chavassechambers.co.uk
Call Date: Oct 1996, Lincoln's Inn
Qualifications: [LLB (Hons) MA]
✉simon.povoas@chavassechambers.co.uk

POWELL MR ANDREW CHRISTOPHER

4 Paper Buildings
1st Floor, 4 Paper Buildings, Temple, London EC4Y 7EX, ☎020 7427 5200
✉clerks@4pb.com
Call Date: Nov 2008, Gray's Inn
Qualifications: [BSocSc MA]
✉ap@4pb.com

POWELL MR BERNARD HILSON

Temple Chambers
12 Clytha Park Road, Newport, Gwent NP20 4PB, ☎01633 267403
✉dbrinning@temple-chambers.co.uk
Temple Chambers
32 Park Place, Cardiff CF10 3BA, ☎029 2039 7364
✉DBrinning@Temple-Chambers.co.uk
Call Date: Oct 1991, Gray's Inn
Qualifications: [BSc PhD]

POWELL MISS CATRIN EVA

Four New Square
Four New Square, Lincoln's Inn, London WC2A 3RJ, ☎020 7822 2000
✉barristers@4newsquare.com
Call Date: Oct 2005, Middle Temple
Qualifications: [PPE PgDL]
✉k.powell@4newsquare.com

POWELL MR DAMIAN CENYDD

Field Court Chambers
5 Field Court, Gray's Inn, London WC1R 5EF, ☎020 7405 6114 ✉clerks@fieldcourt.co.uk
Call Date: Oct 2003, Gray's Inn
Qualifications: [LLB LLM]
✉damian.powell@fieldcourt.co.uk

POWELL MISS DEBRA ANN

3 Serjeants Inn
London EC4Y 1BQ, ☎020 7427 5000
✉clerks@3serjeantsinn.com
Call Date: Oct 1995, Middle Temple
Pupil Supervisor
Qualifications: [BA (Hons)]
✉dpowell@3serjeantsinn.com

POWELL MR FREDERICK MANSELL

Regent Chambers
Regent House, 3 Pall Mall, Hanley, Stoke On Trent ST1 1HP, ☎01782 286666
✉clerks@regentchambers.co.uk
Call Date: Nov 1999, Lincoln's Inn
Qualifications: [LLB (Hons)(Staffs)]
✉frederick.powell@regentchambers.co.uk

POWELL MR JOHN LEWIS QC (1990)

Four New Square
Four New Square, Lincoln's Inn, London WC2A 3RJ, ☎020 7822 2000
✉barristers@4newsquare.com
Call Date: July 1974, Middle Temple
Qualifications: [MA LLB (Cantab)]
✉j.powell@4newsquare.com

POWELL MR JONATHAN DAVID

Atlas Chambers
3 Field Court, Gray's Inn, London WC1R 5EP, ☎020 7269 7980
✉clerks@atlaschambers.com
Call Date: Nov 1984, Inner Temple
Qualifications: [LLM Legal Assoc R.T.P.I FRGS]
✉j@plaw.org

E

POWELL MISS LEONA

Blackstone Chambers
Blackstone House, Temple, London EC4Y 9BW, ☎020 7583 1770
✉clerks@blackstonechambers.com
Call Date: Oct 2000, Middle Temple
Pupil Supervisor
Qualifications: [BA (Hons) (Oxon) CPE (Oxon) Dip in Law]
✉leonapowell@blackstonechambers.com

POWELL MS MICHELLE LOUISE

Chambers of Mr Ami Feder
Ground Floor, Lamb Building, Temple, London EC4Y 7AS, ☎020 7797 7788
✉clerks@lambbuilding.co.uk
Lamb Building
22 Ship Street, Brighton BN1 1AD, ☎01273 820490
✉admin@lambbuilding.co.uk
Chambers of Mr Ami Feder
Ground Floor, Lamb Building, Temple, London EC4Y 7AS, ☎020 7797 7788
✉clerks@lambbuilding.co.uk
Call Date: July 2001, Inner Temple
Qualifications: [LLB (Essex)]
✉michellepowell@lambbuilding.co.uk

POWELL MR OLIVER JONATHAN

3 PB Barristers
3 Paper Buildings, Temple, London EC4Y 7EU, ☎020 7583 8055
Call Date: July 2006, Gray's Inn
Qualifications: [LLB (Reading)]
✉oliver.powell@3pb.co.uk

POWELL MR RICHARD ARTHUR GAYLER

Southernhay Chambers
33 Southernhay East, Exeter EX1 1NX, ☎01392 255777
✉clerks@southernhaychambers.co.uk
Call Date: July 1989, Middle Temple
Qualifications: [LLB (Hons) Assoc CIPD LLM]
✉r.powell@southernhaychambers.co.uk

POWELL MR RICHARD FREDERIC

River Chambers
81 Underdale Road, Shrewsbury, Shropshire SY2 5EF, ☎01743 350505
✉richard@riverchambers.com
St Philips Chambers
55 Temple Row, Birmingham B2 5LS, ☎0121 246 7000 ✉clerks@st-philips.com
Call Date: Nov 1991, Inner Temple
Qualifications: [BA (Surrey) QDR]
✉richard@riverchambers.com

POWELL MR ROBIN EDWARD

Tanfield Chambers
2-5 Warwick Court, London WC1R 5DJ, ☎020 7421 5300
✉clerks@tanfieldchambers.co.uk
Call Date: Nov 1993, Inner Temple
Pupil Supervisor
Qualifications: [BA CPE LLM (Lond)]
✉rpowell@tanfieldchambers.co.uk

POWELL MR WILLIAM GILES HUGH

Old Square Chambers
10-11 Bedford Row, London WC1R 4BU, ☎020 7269 0300 ✉clerks@oldsquare.co.uk
Old Square Chambers
3 Orchard Court, St Augustine's Yard, Bristol BS1 5DP, ☎0117 930 5100
✉clerks@oldsquare.co.uk
Call Date: Nov 1990, Gray's Inn
Pupil Supervisor
Qualifications: [LLB (Wales)]
✉powell@oldsquare.co.uk

POWELL MR WILLIAM RHYS

Regency Chambers
45 Priestgate, Peterborough PE1 1LB, ☎01733 315215
✉clerks@regencychambers.law.co.uk
Regency Chambers
Sheraton House, Castle Park, Cambridge CB3 0AX, ☎01223 301517
Call Date: Nov 1971, Lincoln's Inn
Qualifications: [BA (Cantab) DIPArb MCIArb]
✉clerks@regencychambers.law.co.uk

POWER MS ALEXIA CLARE

Furnival Chambers
32 Furnival Street, London EC4A 1JQ, ☎020 7405 3232
Call Date: Oct 1992, Gray's Inn
Pupil Supervisor
Qualifications: [BSc (Hons)(Surrey)]
✉apower@furnivallaw.co.uk

POWER MR ARCHANGELO CARLO

2 Bedford Row
London WC1R 4BU, ☎020 7440 8888
✉clerks@2bedfordrow.co.uk
Call Date: Nov 2001, Middle Temple
Qualifications: [LLB (Hons)]

POWER MISS ELIZABETH JOANNE

No5 Chambers
Fountain Court, Steelhouse Lane, Birmingham B4 6DR, ☎0845 210 5555 ✉info@no5.com
No5 Chambers
Greenwood House, 4-7 Salisbury Court, London EC4Y 8AA, ☎0845 210 5555
No5 Chambers
38 Queen Square, Bristol BS1 4QS, ☎0845 210 5555
Call Date: Oct 1996, Inner Temple
Qualifications: [LLB (Sheff)]
ep@no5.com

POWER MS ELOISE JANE

Doughty Street Chambers
53-54 Doughty Street, London WC1N 2LS, ☎020 7404 1313
✉enquiries@doughtystreet.co.uk
Doughty Street Chambers
Pall Mall Court, 61-67 King Street, Manchester M2 4PD, ☎0161 618 1066
Doughty Street Chambers
5th Floor, Broad Quay House, Prince Street, Bristol BS1 4DJ, ☎01179 058 717
Call Date: Mar 2002, Gray's Inn
Qualifications: [BA (Cantab)]
e.power@doughtystreet.co.uk

POWER MISS ERICA MARGARET

Crown Office Chambers
2 Crown Office Row, Temple, London EC4Y 7HJ, ☎020 7797 8100
✉mail@crownofficechambers.com
Call Date: Oct 1990, Lincoln's Inn
Pupil Supervisor
Qualifications: [MA (Cantab) LLM]
power@crownofficechambers.com

POWER MISS LAURIE-ANNE

Carmelite Chambers
9 Carmelite Street, London EC4Y 0DR, ☎020 7936 6300
✉clerks@carmelitechambers.co.uk
Call Date: July 2000, Middle Temple
Qualifications: [LLB(Hons) (Lond)]
lpower@carmelitechambers.co.uk

POWER MR LAWRENCE IMAM

4 KBW
Ground Floor, 4 King's Bench Walk, Temple, London EC4Y 7DL, ☎020 7822 8822
✉law@4kbw.net
Call Date: Nov 1995, Middle Temple
Pupil Supervisor
Qualifications: [LLB (Hons)(Notts) LLM (Notts)]

POWER MR LEWIS NIALL QC (2011)

Chambers of Mr Ami Feder
Ground Floor, Lamb Building, Temple, London EC4Y 7AS, ☎020 7797 7788
✉clerks@lambbuilding.co.uk
Lamb Building
22 Ship Street, Brighton BN1 1AD, ☎01273 820490
✉admin@lambbuilding.co.uk
Chambers of Mr Ami Feder
Ground Floor, Lamb Building, Temple, London EC4Y 7AS, ☎020 7797 7788
✉clerks@lambbuilding.co.uk
Call Date: Nov 1990, Gray's Inn
Qualifications: [LLB (Hons)]
clerks@lambbuilding.co.uk

POWER MR NICHOLAS JAMES

Broadway House Chambers
Broadway House, 9 Bank Street, Bradford, West Yorkshire BD1 1TW, ☎01274 722560
✉clerks@broadwayhouse.co.uk
Broadway House Chambers
25 Park Square West, Leeds, West Yorkshire LS1 2PW, ☎0113 246 2600
✉clerks@broadwayhouse.co.uk
Call Date: July 2004, Lincoln's Inn
Qualifications: [BA Hons (Humberside)]
np@broadwayhouse.co.uk

POWER MR NIGEL JOHN QC (2010)

Number 7 Harrington Street Chambers
7 Harrington Street, Liverpool L2 9YH, ☎0151 242 0707 ✉clerks@7hs.co.uk
Call Date: Nov 1992, Inner Temple
Pupil Supervisor
Qualifications: [LLB (Reading)]
nigel.power@7hs.co.uk

POWER MR RICHARD JON

Fountain Court Chambers
Fountain Court, Temple, London EC4Y 9DH, ☎020 7583 3335
✉chambers@fountaincourt.co.uk
Call Date: Oct 2007, Lincoln's Inn
Qualifications: [BA (Oxon)]
rjp@fountaincourt.co.uk

POWER MR RICHARD MICHAEL ARTHUR

Lamb Chambers
Lamb Building, Elm Court, Temple, London EC4Y 7AS, ☎020 7797 8300
✉info@lambchambers.co.uk
Call Date: Nov 1983, Middle Temple
Qualifications: [BA (Oxon)]
richardpower@lambchambers.co.uk

E

POWERS DR MICHAEL JOHN QC (1995)

Clerksroom (Taunton)
Equity House, Administration Centre, Blackbrook Park Avenue, Taunton, Somerset TA1 2PX, ☎ 0845 083 3000
✉ mail@clerksroom.com
Clerksroom (London)
3rd Floor, 218 Strand, London WC2R 1AT, ☎ 0845 083 3000 ✉ mail@clerksroom.com
King's Lynn Chambers
26 The Birches, South Wootton, King's Lynn, Norfolk PE30 3JG, ☎ 01553 672 085
✉ timothy.leader@tesco.net
Call Date: July 1979, Lincoln's Inn
Qualifications: [BSc FFFLM DA MB]
✉ powersqc@clerksroom.com

POWIS MISS LUCY ELIZABETH

Kings Chambers
36 Young Street, Manchester M3 3FT, ☎ 0845 034 3444
✉ clerks@kingschambers.com
Kings Chambers
5 Park Square East, Leeds LS1 2NE, ☎ 0845 034 3444
✉ clerks@kingschambers.com
Kings Chambers
Embassy House, 60 Church Street, Birmingham B3 2DJ, ☎ 0845 034 3444
✉ clerks@kingschambers.com
Call Date: Oct 1992, Gray's Inn
Qualifications: [LLB (L'pool)]
✉ lpowis@kingschambers.com

POWIS MISS SAMANTHA INEZ

Citadel Chambers
The Citadel, 190 Corporation Street, Birmingham B4 6QD, ☎ 0121 233 8500
✉ clerks@citadelchambers.com
Call Date: Nov 1985, Lincoln's Inn
Qualifications: [LLB (Wales)]
✉ clerks@citadelchambers.com

POWLES MR STEVEN SACHA

Doughty Street Chambers
53-54 Doughty Street, London WC1N 2LS, ☎ 020 7404 1313
✉ enquiries@doughtystreet.co.uk
Doughty Street Chambers
Pall Mall Court, 61-67 King Street, Manchester M2 4PD, ☎ 0161 618 1066
Doughty Street Chambers
5th Floor, Broad Quay House, Prince Street, Bristol BS1 4DJ, ☎ 01179 058 717
Call Date: Nov 1997, Middle Temple
Qualifications: [LLB (Hons)(LSE) LLM (Cantab)]
✉ s.powles@doughtystreet.co.uk

POWLESLAND MR PAUL DAVID

Ely Place Chambers
30 Ely Place, London EC1N 6TD, ☎ 020 7400 9600 ✉ admin@elyplace.com
Call Date: Oct 2009, Middle Temple
Qualifications: [BA (Hons) (Cantab)]
✉ ppowlesland@elyplace.com

POWNALL MR STEPHEN ORLANDO FLETCHER QC (2002)

2 Hare Court
Lower Ground, Ground, 1st & 2nd Floor, 2 Hare Court, Temple, London EC4Y 7BH, ☎ 020 7353 3982 ✉ clerks@2harecourt.com
Call Date: July 1975, Inner Temple
Recorder
✉ orlandopownall@2harecourt.com

POYNOR MS BRYONY CLARE

Garden Court Chambers
57-60 Lincoln's Inn Fields, London WC2A 3LJ, ☎ 020 7993 7600 ✉ info@gclaw.co.uk
Call Date: Mar 2009, Lincoln's Inn
Qualifications: [BA (Oxon)]

PRAGER MS SARAH JANE

1 Chancery Lane
London WC2A 1LF, ☎ 0845 634 6666
✉ clerks@1chancerylane.com
Call Date: Oct 1997, Inner Temple
Pupil Supervisor
Qualifications: [LLB (Nottingham)]
✉ sprager@1chancerylane.com

PRAKASH MISS AVANTIKA

Blackfriars Chambers
79-83 Temple Chambers, 3-7 Temple Avenue, London EC4Y 0HP, ☎ 020 7353 7400
✉ clerks@blackfriarschambers.com
Call Date: Oct 2000, Lincoln's Inn
Qualifications: [LLB (Hons) (Lond)]
✉ avantika.prakash@blackfriarschambers.com

PRAND MISS ANNETTE BETTINA

Lamb Chambers
Lamb Building, Elm Court, Temple, London EC4Y 7AS, ☎ 020 7797 8300
✉ info@lambchambers.co.uk
Call Date: Nov 1995, Inner Temple
Qualifications: [MA (Cantab)]
✉ drannetteprand@lambchambers.co.uk

E

PRATLEY MS MICHELLE ELIZABETH

4-5 Gray's Inn Square
Gray's Inn, London WC1R 5AH,
☎020 7404 5252 ✉clerks@4-5.co.uk
Call Date: July 2006, Lincoln's Inn
Qualifications: [LLB LLM (Cantab) BA]
✉mpratley@4-5.co.uk

PRATT MR ASHLEY JAMES

Zenith Chambers
10 Park Square, Leeds LS1 2LH,
☎0113 245 5438
✉clerks@zenithchambers.co.uk
Call Date: Oct 2006, Gray's Inn
Qualifications: [LLB]

PRATT MR JAKE STEPHEN

Iscoed Chambers
86 St Helen's Road, Swansea SA1 4BQ,
☎01792 652988
✉clerks@iscoedchambers.co.uk
Call Date: Oct 2004, Lincoln's Inn
Qualifications: [LLB (Hons) (Lond)]

PRATT MR RICHARD CAMDEN QC (1992)

1 KBW Chambers
1 King's Bench Walk, Temple, London
EC4Y 7DB, ☎020 7936 1500
✉clerks@1kbw.co.uk
King's Bench Chambers
174 High Street, Lewes BN7 1YE,
☎01273 402600
Call Date: July 1970, Gray's Inn
Recorder
Qualifications: [MA (Oxon)]
✉cprattqc@1kbw.co.uk

PRATT MR RICHARD JAMES QC (2006)

Number 7 Harrington Street Chambers
7 Harrington Street, Liverpool L2 9YH,
☎0151 242 0707 ✉clerks@7hs.co.uk
Lombard Chambers
1 Sekforde Street, Clerkenwell, London
EC1R 0BE, ☎020 7107 2100
Call Date: July 1980, Gray's Inn
Pupil Supervisor, Recorder
Qualifications: [BA]
✉richard.pratt@7hs.co.uk

PREECE MISS NICOLA JAYNE

Iscoed Chambers
86 St Helen's Road, Swansea SA1 4BQ,
☎01792 652988
✉clerks@iscoedchambers.co.uk
Call Date: Oct 2006, Gray's Inn
Qualifications: [LLB]
✉np@iscoedchambers.co.uk

PREEN MISS CATHERINE LOUISE

St Ive's Chambers
Whittall Street, Birmingham B4 6DH,
☎0121 236 0863
✉clerks@stiveschambers.co.uk
Call Date: Nov 1988, Middle Temple
Qualifications: [LLB (Hons) (Lond)]
✉catherine.preen@stiveschambers.co.uk

PRENTICE PROF DANIEL DAVID

Erskine Chambers
33 Chancery Lane, London WC2A 1EN,
☎020 7242 5532
✉clerks@erskinechambers.com
Call Date: Nov 1982, Lincoln's Inn
Qualifications: [LLB (Hons)(Ireland) JD (USA) MA (Oxon)]
✉dprentice@erskine-chambers.co.uk

PRENTIS MR SEBASTIAN HUGH RUNTON

New Square Chambers
12 New Square, Lincoln's Inn, London
WC2A 3SW, ☎020 7419 8000
✉robin.hollington@newsquarechambers.co.uk
Call Date: Oct 1996, Middle Temple
Qualifications: [BA (Hons) (Cantab)]
✉sebastian.prentis@newsquarechambers.co.uk

PRESLAND MR FREDERICK JAMES ADRIAN

1 Pump Court
Elm Court, Temple, London EC4Y 7AB,
☎020 7842 7070
✉(name)@pumpcourt.co.uk
Call Date: July 1985, Gray's Inn
Pupil Supervisor
Qualifications: [BA (Hons) (UEA)]
✉jp@1pumpcourt.co.uk

PRESLAND MS SAMANTHA LOUISE

Outer Temple Chambers
The Outer Temple, 222 Strand, London
WC2R 1BA, ☎020 7353 6381
✉clerks@outertemple.com
Call Date: Mar 2001, Middle Temple
Qualifications: [BA (Hons) (Oxon) CPE]
✉sam.presland@outertemple.com

E

PRESSDEE MR PIERS CHARLES WILLIAM QC (2010)

29 Bedford Row Chambers
London WC1R 4HE, ☎ 020 7404 1044
✉ clerks@29br.co.uk
St John's Chambers
101 Victoria Street, Bristol BS1 6PU,
☎ 0117 923 4700
✉ clerks@stjohnschambers.co.uk
St Philips Chambers
55 Temple Row, Birmingham B2 5LS,
☎ 0121 246 7000 ✉ clerks@st-philips.com
Call Date: Oct 1991, Middle Temple
Qualifications: [MA (Hons)(Cantab)]
✉ PPressdee@29br.co.uk

PRESSMAN MR BERNARD

Lamb Chambers
Lamb Building, Elm Court, Temple, London EC4Y 7AS, ☎ 020 7797 8300
✉ info@lambchambers.co.uk
Call Date: Nov 2004, Middle Temple
Qualifications: [LLB (Hons) LLM]
✉ bernardpressman@lambchambers.co.uk

PREST MR ADAM CHARLES

No.6 Park Square
Leeds LS1 2LW, ☎ 0113 245 9763
✉ Tim@no6.co.uk
Call Date: Nov 2005, Inner Temple
Qualifications: [MA St John's College University of Cambridge]
✉ prest@no6.co.uk

PRESTON MR DARREN SAMUEL

9 St John Street
Manchester M3 4DN, ☎ 0161 955 9000
✉ civilclerks@9sjs.com / criminalclerks@9sjs.com
Call Date: Oct 1991, Gray's Inn
Qualifications: [LLB (L'pool)]

PRESTON MR DAVID HENRY

Ely Place Chambers
30 Ely Place, London EC1N 6TD,
☎ 020 7400 9600 ✉ admin@elyplace.com
Call Date: Nov 1993, Lincoln's Inn
Pupil Supervisor
Qualifications: [LLB (Australia)]
✉ dpreston@elyplace.com

PRESTON MR DOMINIC

Doughty Street Chambers
53-54 Doughty Street, London WC1N 2LS,
☎ 020 7404 1313
✉ enquiries@doughtystreet.co.uk
Doughty Street Chambers
Pall Mall Court, 61-67 King Street, Manchester M2 4PD, ☎ 0161 618 1066
Doughty Street Chambers
5th Floor, Broad Quay House, Prince Street, Bristol BS1 4DJ, ☎ 01179 058 717
Call Date: Feb 1995, Inner Temple
Qualifications: [BA (Lond) CPE (Lond)]
✉ d.preston@doughtystreet.co.uk

PRESTON MR HUGH GEOFFREY QC (2012)

Seven Bedford Row
7 Bedford Row, London WC1R 4BS,
☎ 020 7242 3555 ✉ clerks@7br.co.uk
Call Date: Oct 1994, Middle Temple
Pupil Supervisor
Qualifications: [BA (Hons)(Durham) CPE]
✉ hpreston@7br.co.uk

PRESTON MISS KIM DEBORAH

4 King's Bench Walk
2nd Floor, 4 King's Bench Walk, Temple, London EC4Y 7DL, ☎ 020 7822 7000
✉ clerks@4kbw.co.uk
Call Date: Nov 1991, Inner Temple
Pupil Supervisor
Qualifications: [BSc (Hons) Dip Law]
✉ kimpreston@4kbw.co.uk

PRESTON MR LEWIS TAYLOR

Five Paper
Ground Floor, 5 Paper Buildings, Temple, London EC4Y 7HB, ☎ 020 7815 3200
Call Date: July 2007, Middle Temple
Qualifications: [BA (Hons) (Cantab)]
✉ lewispreston@fivepaper.com

PRESTON MR NICHOLAS JOHN HOLMAN

Clerksroom (Taunton)
Equity House, Administration Centre, Blackbrook Park Avenue, Taunton, Somerset TA1 2PX, ☎ 0845 083 3000
✉ mail@clerksroom.com
Call Date: July 1986, Gray's Inn
Qualifications: [MA]
✉ preston@clerksroom.com

PRESTON MRS NICOLA

No5 Chambers
Fountain Court, Steelhouse Lane, Birmingham B4 6DR, ☎0845 210 5555 ✉info@no5.com
No5 Chambers
Greenwood House, 4-7 Salisbury Court, London EC4Y 8AA, ☎0845 210 5555
No5 Chambers
38 Queen Square, Bristol BS1 4QS, ☎0845 210 5555
Call Date: Nov 1992, Lincoln's Inn
Qualifications: [LLB (Hons) (Manch) LLM (B'ham)]
✉info@no5.com

PRESTWICH MR ANDREW

Ropewalk Chambers
24 The Ropewalk, Nottingham NG1 5EF, ☎0115 947 2581 ✉clerks@ropewalk.co.uk
Call Date: Nov 1986, Gray's Inn
Pupil Supervisor
Qualifications: [LLB (B'ham)]

PRETSELL MR JAMES DAVIDSON

Farrar's Building
Farrar's Building, Temple, London EC4Y 7BD, ☎020 7583 9241
✉Chambers@farrarsbuilding.co.uk
Call Date: Nov 1998, Gray's Inn
Pupil Supervisor
Qualifications: [BA (Bris) Dip Law (Lond)]
✉jpretsell@farrarsbuilding.co.uk

PRETZELL MR ANDREAS ERICH JOACHIM

Chambers of Mr Ami Feder
Ground Floor, Lamb Building, Temple, London EC4Y 7AS, ☎020 7797 7788
✉clerks@lambbuilding.co.uk
Lamb Building
22 Ship Street, Brighton BN1 1AD, ☎01273 820490
✉admin@lambbuilding.co.uk
Chambers of Mr Ami Feder
Ground Floor, Lamb Building, Temple, London EC4Y 7AS, ☎020 7797 7788
✉clerks@lambbuilding.co.uk
Call Date: Oct 1997, Middle Temple
Pupil Supervisor
Qualifications: [LLB (Hons)(Brunel) LLM (Lond)]
✉clerks@lambbuilding.co.uk

PREVATT MISS BEATRICE HILARY ROSE

Garden Court Chambers
57-60 Lincoln's Inn Fields, London WC2A 3LJ, ☎020 7993 7600 ✉info@gclaw.co.uk
Call Date: Nov 1985, Gray's Inn
Pupil Supervisor
Qualifications: [BA (Oxon)]
✉beatricep@gclaw.co.uk

PRICE MR ALBERT JOHN QC (2009)

23 Essex Street
London WC2R 3AA, ☎020 7413 0353
✉clerks@23es.com
Call Date: July 1982, Inner Temple
Recorder
Qualifications: [BA (Oxon)]
✉johnprice@23es.com

PRICE MR ANDREW ROBERT

Dyers Chambers
35 Bedford Row, London WC1R 4JH, ☎020 7404 1881
✉admin@dyerschambers.com
Call Date: Oct 2003, Middle Temple
Qualifications: [LLB (Hons)]
✉andrew.price@dyerchambers.com, andrew.price@dyerschambers.com

PRICE MR CHARLES JOHN

No5 Chambers
Fountain Court, Steelhouse Lane, Birmingham B4 6DR, ☎0845 210 5555 ✉info@no5.com
No5 Chambers
Greenwood House, 4-7 Salisbury Court, London EC4Y 8AA, ☎0845 210 5555
No5 Chambers
38 Queen Square, Bristol BS1 4QS, ☎0845 210 5555
Call Date: Nov 1999, Middle Temple
Qualifications: [LLB (Hons)(So'ton) LLM (So'ton)]
✉cp@no5.com

PRICE MISS COLLETTE

Fountain Chambers
Cleveland Business Centre, 1 Watson Street, Middlesbrough TS1 2RQ, ☎01642 804040
✉clerks@fountainchambers.co.uk
Call Date: Nov 1997, Gray's Inn
Qualifications: [BA (Hons) (Cantab) MA (Cantab)]

E

PRICE MISS EMMA CHARLOTTE LOUISA

Temple Garden Chambers
1 Harcourt Buildings, Temple, London EC4Y 9DA, ☎020 7583 1315
✉clerks@tgchambers.com
Call Date: Oct 2007, Gray's Inn
Qualifications: [BA (Exon) LLB]

PRICE MR EVAN DAVID LEWIS

Ten Old Square
Ground Floor, Ten Old Square, Lincoln's Inn, London WC2A 3SU, ☎020 7405 0758
✉clerks@tenoldsquare.com
Call Date: Oct 1997, Middle Temple
Qualifications: [LLB (Hons)(Lond)]
evanprice@tenoldsquare.com

PRICE MR GARETH DAVID

Park Lane Plowden
19 Westgate, Leeds LS1 2RD, ☎0113 228 5049
✉clerks@parklaneplowden.co.uk
Call Date: July 2009, Middle Temple
Qualifications: [LLB (Hons)]
gareth.price@parklaneplowden.co.uk

PRICE MRS HUMA SABIH

St Andrews Chambers
St Andrews House, 52 Manor Drive, London N20 0DX, ☎020 8368 3686
✉standrewschambers@live.co.uk
Call Date: Nov 1991, Inner Temple
Qualifications: [LLB]

PRICE MR JAMES RICHARD KENRICK QC (1995)

5RB
1st Floor, 5 Raymond Buildings, Gray's Inn, London WC1R 5BP, ☎020 7242 2902
✉clerks@5rb.com
Call Date: July 1974, Inner Temple
Qualifications: [BA(Oxon)]
jamesprice@5rb.com

PRICE MR JONATHAN RICHARD

Ely Place Chambers
30 Ely Place, London EC1N 6TD, ☎020 7400 9600 ✉admin@elyplace.com
Call Date: Oct 2004, Middle Temple
Qualifications: [MA (Hons) PGDip Law]
jprice@elyplace.com

PRICE MISS KATHARINE CLARE HARDING

Hailsham Chambers
Ground Floor, 4 Paper Buildings, Temple, London EC4Y 7EX, ☎020 7643 5000
✉clerks@hailshamchambers.com
Call Date: July 1988, Middle Temple
Qualifications: [LLB (Hons) (Lond) LLM (Cantab)]
clare.price@hailshamchambers.com

PRICE MISS LOUISE

Doughty Street Chambers
53-54 Doughty Street, London WC1N 2LS, ☎020 7404 1313
✉enquiries@doughtystreet.co.uk
Call Date: July 2006, Inner Temple
Qualifications: [BA MSc (Manch)]
l.price@doughtystreet.co.uk

PRICE MRS LOUISE THERESE

Albion Chambers
Broad Street, Bristol BS1 1DR, ☎0117 927 2144
✉clerks@albionchambers.co.uk
Call Date: Nov 1972, Middle Temple
Qualifications: [MA (Oxon)]
louise.price@albionchambers.co.uk

PRICE MR PETER NICHOLAS

Dere Street Barristers
14 Toft Green, York YO1 6JT, ☎0844 3351551
✉clerks@derestreet.co.uk
York Chambers
Rotterdam House, 116 The Quayside, Newcastle Upon Tyne NE1 3DY, ☎0191 206 4677
Call Date: Nov 1987, Inner Temple
Pupil Supervisor
Qualifications: [LLB (Hull)]
clerks@yorkchambers.co.uk

PRICE MR RICHARD JOHN

9 St John Street
Manchester M3 4DN, ☎0161 955 9000
✉civilclerks@9sjs.com / criminalclerks@9sjs.com
Call Date: July 2010, Lincoln's Inn
Qualifications: [LLB MA (Cantab)]
richard.price@9sjs.com

PRICE MR RICHARD MERVYN QC (1996)

Littleton Chambers
3 King's Bench Walk North, Temple, London EC4Y 7HR, ☎020 7797 8600
✉fschneider@littletonchambers.co.uk
Park Court Chambers
16 Park Place, Leeds LS1 2SJ,
☎0113 243 3277
✉clerks@parkcourtchambers.co.uk
Call Date: Nov 1969, Gray's Inn
Recorder
Qualifications: [LLB (Lond)]

PRICE MR RODERICK MICHAEL THOMAS

187 Fleet Street
London EC4A 2AT, ☎020 7430 7430
✉chambers@187fleetstreet.com
Call Date: Nov 1971, Inner Temple
Pupil Supervisor
Qualifications: [LLB]
🖃chambers@187fleetstreet.com

PRICE MR THOMAS QC (2010)

25 Bedford Row
London WC1R 4HD, ☎020 7067 1500
✉clerks@25bedfordrow.com
Call Date: Nov 1985, Inner Temple
Pupil Supervisor
Qualifications: [LLB (So'ton)]
🖃tprice@25bedfordrow.com

PRICE LEWIS MR RHODRI QC (2001)

Landmark Chambers
180 Fleet Street, London EC4A 2HG,
☎020 7430 1221
✉clerks@landmarkchambers.co.uk
Call Date: July 1975, Middle Temple
Qualifications: [MA (Oxon) DipCrim (Cantab)]
🖃rpricelewis@landmarkchambers.co.uk

PRICE ROWLANDS MR GWYNN

St Ive's Chambers
Whittall Street, Birmingham B4 6DH,
☎0121 236 0863
✉clerks@stiveschambers.co.uk
Call Date: May 1985, Inner Temple
Pupil Supervisor
Qualifications: [MA (Lond) LLB MBA Dip EC Law,Merge Data:,Contact Number: 23730,Quantity: ,Activity Date: ,Notes : LLB (L'pool),]
🖃gwynn.pricerowlands@stiveschambers.co.uk

PRICE-MARMION MISS ALEXANDRA RACHAEL GEORGETTE

2 Pump Court
1st Floor, 2 Pump Court, Temple, London EC4Y 7AH, ☎020 7353 5597
✉clerks@2pumpcourt.co.uk
Call Date: Oct 2002, Middle Temple
Qualifications: [BA (Oxon) Dip Law]
🖃apm@2pumpcourt.co.uk

PRIDAY MR CHARLES NICHOLAS BRUTON

7 King's Bench Walk
Ground Floor, 7 King's Bench Walk, Temple, London EC4Y 7DS, ☎020 7910 8300
✉clerks@7kbw.co.uk
Call Date: Nov 1982, Middle Temple
Pupil Supervisor
Qualifications: [BA (Oxon)]
🖃cpriday@7kbw.co.uk

PRIDE MR PETER ERIC CHARLES

1 Gray's Inn Square
Ground Floor, 1 Gray's Inn Square, London WC1R 5AA, ☎020 7405 0001
Call Date: Oct 1996, Lincoln's Inn
Pupil Supervisor
Qualifications: [LLB (Hons) LLM (Lond)]

PRIESTLEY MR RODERICK CHARLES

Lincoln House Chambers
Tower 12, The Avenue North, Spinningfields, 18-22 Bridge Street, Manchester M3 3BZ,
☎0161 832 5701
✉info@lincolnhousechambers.com
Call Date: Nov 1996, Gray's Inn
Qualifications: [BSc (Bris)]
🖃roderick.priestley@lincolnhousechambers.com

PRINCE MISS LAURA MARGARET

Matrix Chambers
Griffin Building, Gray's Inn, London WC1R 5LN, ☎020 7404 3447
✉matrix@matrixlaw.co.uk / lscott@matrixlaw.co.uk
Call Date: July 2003, Lincoln's Inn
Pupil Supervisor
Qualifications: [LLB (Hons) (Lond)]
🖃lauraprince@matrixlaw.co.uk

E

PRINGLE MR IAN DEREK QC (2003)

Guildhall Chambers
23 Broad Street, Bristol BS1 2HG,
☎ 0117 930 9000
✉ hoc@guildhallchambers.co.uk
Call Date: July 1979, Gray's Inn
Recorder
Qualifications: [MA (Cantab)]
ian.pringle@guildhallchambers.co.uk

PRINGLE MR WATSON MILLER

New Square Chambers
12 New Square, Lincoln's Inn, London WC2A 3SW, ☎ 020 7419 8000
✉ robin.hollington@newsquarechambers.co.uk
Call Date: July 2005, Inner Temple
Qualifications: [BA Brasenose College University of Oxford]
watson.pringle@newsquarechambers.co.uk

PRINN MISS HELEN ELIZABETH

Octagon House
19 Colegate, Norwich NR3 1AT,
☎ 01603 623186
✉ clerks@octagonhouse.co.uk
Call Date: Oct 1993, Middle Temple
Qualifications: [BA (Hons)(Lond) CPE (Lond)]
helenprinn@octagonhouse.co.uk, clerks@octagonhouse.co.uk

PRIOR MR CHARLES ROBERT CHRISTOPHER

Atlantic Chambers
4-6 Cook Street, Liverpool L2 9QU,
☎ 0151 236 4421
✉ info@atlanticchambers.co.uk
Call Date: Oct 1995, Lincoln's Inn
Pupil Supervisor
Qualifications: [BA (Hons)(Oxon) Dip in Law (Lond)]
charlesprior@atlanticchambers.co.uk

PRIOR MR CHRISTOPHER JAMES

Westgate Chambers
64 High Street, Lewes, East Sussex BN7 1XG,
☎ 01273 480510
✉ clerks@westgate-chambers.co.uk
Call Date: July 2007, Lincoln's Inn
Qualifications: [LLB (Notts)]

PRIOR MRS MARY

36 Bedford Row
London WC1R 4JH, ☎ 020 7421 8000
✉ chambers@36bedfordrow.co.uk
Call Date: Oct 1990, Gray's Inn
Pupil Supervisor
Qualifications: [LLB (Hons)]

PRIOR MR PAUL STEPHEN

36 Bedford Row
London WC1R 4JH, ☎ 020 7421 8000
✉ chambers@36bedfordrow.co.uk
Call Date: Nov 2003, Lincoln's Inn
Qualifications: [LLB (Hons) (B' ham)]
pprior@36bedfordrow.co.uk

PRITCHARD MISS CECILIA MARY

Oriel Chambers
18 Ribblesdale Place, Preston PR1 3NA,
☎ 01772 254 764
✉ clerks@oriel-chambers.co.uk
Oriel Chambers
14 Water Street, Liverpool, Merseyside L2 8TD, ☎ 0151 236 7191
✉ clerks@orielchambers.co.uk
Call Date: July 1998, Middle Temple
Qualifications: [LLB (Hons)]

PRITCHARD MR GEOFFREY MICHAEL

Three New Square IP
3 New Square, Lincoln's Inn, London WC2A 3RS, ☎ 020 7405 1111
✉ clerks@3newsquare.co.uk
Call Date: Oct 1998, Middle Temple
Pupil Supervisor
Qualifications: [BSc (Hons)(Bris) PHD (Cantab) CPE (Leic)]
pritchard@3newsquare.co.uk

PRITCHARD MISS SARAH JANE

Kings Chambers
36 Young Street, Manchester M3 3FT,
☎ 0845 034 3444
✉ clerks@kingschambers.com
Kings Chambers
5 Park Square East, Leeds LS1 2NE,
☎ 0845 034 3444
✉ clerks@kingschambers.com
Kings Chambers
Embassy House, 60 Church Street, Birmingham B3 2DJ, ☎ 0845 034 3444
✉ clerks@kingschambers.com
Call Date: Oct 1993, Gray's Inn
Pupil Supervisor
Qualifications: [LLB (Manch)]
spritchard@kingschambers.com

PRITCHARD MISS SARAH LOUISE

St Ive's Chambers
Whittall Street, Birmingham B4 6DH,
☎ 0121 236 0863
✉ clerks@stiveschambers.co.uk
Call Date: Oct 1997, Gray's Inn
Pupil Supervisor
Qualifications: [BA (Hons)(Warwick)]
sarah.pritchard@stiveschambers.co.uk

E

PRITCHARD MR SIMON DAVID

Blackstone Chambers
Blackstone House, Temple, London
EC4Y 9BW, ☎ 020 7583 1770
✉ clerks@blackstonechambers.com
Call Date: July 2007, Lincoln's Inn
Qualifications: [Dip Law MChem (Oxon)]
✉ simonpritchard@blackstonechambers.com

PRITCHARD MRS TERESA JULIA

5 Pump Court
Ground Floor, 5 Pump Court, Temple, London
EC4Y 7AP, ☎ 020 7353 2532
✉ clerks@5pumpcourt.com
Call Date: Oct 1994, Lincoln's Inn
Pupil Supervisor
Qualifications: [MA (Hons)(St Andrew) DipLaw (Lond)]
✉ teresapritchard@5pumpcourt.com

PRITCHETT MR STEPHEN JOHN

Clerksroom (Taunton)
Equity House, Administration Centre,
Blackbrook Park Avenue, Taunton, Somerset
TA1 2PX, ☎ 0845 083 3000
✉ mail@clerksroom.com
5 Stone Buildings
5 Stone Buildings, Lincoln's Inn, London
WC2A 3XT, ☎ 020 7242 6201
✉ clerks@5sblaw.com
Clerksroom (London)
3rd Floor, 218 Strand, London WC2R 1AT,
☎ 0845 083 3000 ✉ mail@clerksroom.com
Call Date: July 1989, Lincoln's Inn
Pupil Supervisor
Qualifications: [LLB (Hons) (L'pool)]
✉ pritchett@clerksroom.com

PROBERT MISS SARAH KATE ELIZABETH

15 Winckley Square
Preston PR1 3JJ, ☎ 01772 252828
✉ clerks@15winckleysq.co.uk
Call Date: Nov 2000, Middle Temple
Qualifications: [LLB (Hons) (Keele)]
✉ sarahprobert@15ws.co.uk

PROBYN MISS CALISTA JANE

4 Paper Buildings
1st Floor, 4 Paper Buildings, Temple, London
EC4Y 7EX, ☎ 020 7427 5200
✉ clerks@4pb.com
Call Date: Feb 1988, Middle Temple
Pupil Supervisor, Recorder
Qualifications: [LLB]
✉ jp@4pb.com

PROCHASKA MS ELIZABETH HARRIET

Matrix Chambers
Griffin Building, Gray's Inn, London
WC1R 5LN, ☎ 020 7404 3447
✉ matrix@matrixlaw.co.uk / Iscott@matrixlaw.co.uk
Call Date: Oct 2007, Inner Temple
Qualifications: [BA (Cantab)]
✉ elizabethprochaska@matrixlaw.co.uk

PROCTER MR ALFRED GEORGE HAYDN

1 Garden Court Family Law Chambers
Ground Floor, One Garden Court, Temple,
London EC4Y 9BJ, ☎ 020 7797 7900
✉ clerks@1gc.com
Call Date: July 2005, Middle Temple
Qualifications: [LLB (Laws) London]
✉ procter@1gc.com

PROCTER MR MICHAEL

Fenners Chambers
3 Madingley Road, Cambridge CB3 0EE,
☎ 01223 368761
✉ clerks@fennerschambers.com
Call Date: Nov 1993, Gray's Inn
Qualifications: [BA (Lond)]
✉ michael.procter@fennerschambers.com

PROGHOULIS MR PHILIP GEORGE

Roehampton Chambers
30 Stoughton Close, Roehampton, London
SW15 4LS, ☎ 020 8788 1238
Call Date: Nov 1963, Inner Temple

PROKOFIEV MR SERGEY

Lincoln House Chambers
Tower 12, The Avenue North, Spinningfields,
18-22 Bridge Street, Manchester M3 3BZ,
☎ 0161 832 5701
✉ info@lincolnhousechambers.com
Call Date: July 2004, Lincoln's Inn
Qualifications: [LLB Hons (Durham)]
✉ sergey.prokofiev@lincolnhousechambers.com

PROOPS MISS ANYA LUCIE VICTORIA

11 King's Bench Walk
11 King's Bench Walk, Temple, London
EC4Y 7EQ, ☎ 020 7632 8500
✉ clerksroom@11kbw.com
Call Date: Oct 1998, Inner Temple
Qualifications: [MA (Cantab) PhD (LSE) CPE]
✉ anya.proops@11kbw.com

PROOPS MISS HELEN JEANETTE

Dere Street Barristers
14 Toft Green, York YO1 6JT, ☎0844 3351551
✉clerks@derestreet.co.uk
York Chambers
Rotterdam House, 116 The Quayside, Newcastle Upon Tyne NE1 3DY, ☎0191 206 4677
Call Date: July 1986, Middle Temple
Recorder
Qualifications: [LLB (Exon)]
✉clerks@yorkchambers.co.uk

PROSSER MR ANTHONY GRIFFITH THOMAS

Five St Andrew's Hill
5 St Andrew's Hill, London EC4V 5BZ,
☎020 7332 5400 ✉Clerks@5sah.co.uk
Call Date: July 1985, Inner Temple
Pupil Supervisor
Qualifications: [LLB (Lond)]
✉anthonyprosser@5sah.co.uk

PROSSER MR KEVIN JOHN QC (1996)

Pump Court Tax Chambers
16 Bedford Row, London WC1R 4EF,
☎020 7414 8080 ✉clerks@pumptax.com
Call Date: July 1982, Lincoln's Inn
Qualifications: [LLB (Lond) BCL (Oxon)]
✉kprosser@pumptax.com

Types of work: Capital tax, Corporation tax, Income tax, National Insurance, Stamp duty, VAT

PRYCE MR GARY DAVID

New Square Chambers
12 New Square, Lincoln's Inn, London WC2A 3SW, ☎020 7419 8000
✉robin.hollington@newsquarechambers.co.uk
Call Date: Oct 1997, Lincoln's Inn
Qualifications: [BA (Hons) LLM (Virginia)]
✉gary.pryce@newsquarechambers.co.uk

PRYCE MR GREGORY HUGH

36 Bedford Row
London WC1R 4JH, ☎020 7421 8000
✉chambers@36bedfordrow.co.uk
Call Date: July 1988, Gray's Inn
Pupil Supervisor, Recorder
Qualifications: [BA (Hons)]
✉clerks@36bedfordrow.co.uk

PRYKE MR STUART

Fiduciary Legal
5 North Court, Clevedon Road, London TW1 2HS, ☎07814 495366
✉stuart.pryke@fiduciarylegal.com
Call Date: Oct 1994, Lincoln's Inn
Qualifications: [BEng (Lond) MSc (Econ) Dip in Law (City)]
✉stuart_pryke@fiduciarylegal.com, stuart_pryke5@hotmail.com

PRYNNE MR ANDREW GEOFFREY LOCKYER QC (1995)

Temple Garden Chambers
1 Harcourt Buildings, Temple, London EC4Y 9DA, ☎020 7583 1315
✉clerks@tgchambers.com
Call Date: July 1975, Middle Temple
Qualifications: [LLB (So'ton)]
✉clerks@tgchambers.com

PRYOR MISS ALISON CLARE

Westgate Chambers
64 High Street, Lewes, East Sussex BN7 1XG, ☎01273 480510
✉clerks@westgate-chambers.co.uk
Call Date: July 2008, Inner Temple
Qualifications: [BA (Leeds)]
✉apr@westgate-chambers.co.uk

PRYOR MR MICHAEL ROBERT

Maitland Chambers
7 Stone Buildings, Lincoln's Inn, London WC2A 3SZ, ☎020 7406 1200
✉clerks@maitlandchambers.com
Call Date: Oct 1992, Inner Temple
Pupil Supervisor
Qualifications: [LLB (Hons)]
✉mpryor@maitlandchambers.com

PRZYBYLSKA MISS SARAH ELLEN

2 Hare Court
Lower Ground, Ground, 1st & 2nd Floor, 2 Hare Court, Temple, London EC4Y 7BH,
☎020 7353 3982 ✉clerks@2harecourt.com
Call Date: Oct 2006, Middle Temple

PUAR MR MIKHAEL

30 Park Place
Cardiff CF10 3BS, ☎029 2039 8421
✉clerks@30parkplace.law.co.uk
Call Date: July 2006, Gray's Inn
Qualifications: [LLB]
✉mp@30parkplace.co.uk

E

PUGH MR DAVID

College Chambers
19 Carlton Crescent, Southampton, Hampshire SO15 2ET, ☎ 023 8023 0338
✉ clerks@college-chambers.co.uk
Call Date: Oct 2008, Middle Temple
Qualifications: [LLB (Hons) (Sheff)]

PUGH MISS HELEN ELIZABETH

3 Hare Court
3 Hare Court, Temple, London EC4Y 7BJ, ☎ 020 7415 7800 ✉ clerks@3harecourt.com
Call Date: Oct 2008, Inner Temple
Qualifications: [BA (Oxon) BCL (Oxon)]
helen.pugh@3harecourt.com

PUGH MR JOHN BISHOP

John Pugh's Chambers
707 - 709, The Corn Exchange, Fenwick Street, Liverpool L2 7RB, ☎ 0151 236 5415
✉ john@johnpughschambers.co.uk
Call Date: July 1972, Lincoln's Inn
Qualifications: [LLB (Hons)]
john@johnpughschambers.co.uk

PUGH MR KIERAN ROY

4 Brick Court
4 Brick Court, Temple, London EC4Y 9AD, ☎ 020 7832 3200 ✉ clerks@4bc.co.uk
Call Date: Nov 2006, Middle Temple
Qualifications: [BA (Hons) (Oxon)]
kieranp@4bc.co.uk

PUGH-SMITH MR JOHN EDGAR

39 Essex Street
London WC2R 3AT, ☎ 020 7832 1111
✉ clerks@39essex.com
East Anglian Chambers
140 New London Road, Chelmsford, Essex CM2 0AW, ☎ 01473 214481
✉ chelmsford@ealaw.co.uk
East Anglian Chambers
15 The Close, Norwich, Norfolk NR1 4DZ, ☎ 01473 214481 ✉ norwich@ealaw.co.uk
Call Date: July 1977, Gray's Inn
Pupil Supervisor
Qualifications: [MA (Oxon)]

PULLE MISS ROSHANI

23 Essex Street
London WC2R 3AA, ☎ 020 7413 0353
✉ clerks@23es.com
Call Date: July 2007, Middle Temple
Qualifications: [BSc (Lond) LLM (Lond)]
roshanipulle@23es.com

PULLEN MR TIMOTHY JOHN

King's Bench and Godolphin (KBG)Chambers
115 North Hill, Plymouth, Devon PL4 8JY, ☎ 01752 221551
✉ clerks@kbgchambers.co.uk
Doughty Street Chambers
53-54 Doughty Street, London WC1N 2LS, ☎ 020 7404 1313
✉ enquiries@doughtystreet.co.uk
Call Date: Nov 1993, Middle Temple
Qualifications: [BSc (Plymouth) CPE (Lond)]
theclerks@godolphinchambers.co.uk

PULLING MR DEAN

Angel Chambers
Ethos Building, Kings Road, Swansea SA1 8AS, ☎ 01792 464623
✉ clerks@angelchambers.co.uk
Call Date: Nov 1993, Middle Temple
Pupil Supervisor
Qualifications: [LLB (Hons)(Wales)]
clerks@angelchambers.co.uk

PULMAN MR GEORGE FREDERICK QC (1989)

Hardwicke
New Square, Lincoln's Inn, London WC2A 3SB, ☎ 020 7242 2523
✉ enquiries@hardwicke.co.uk
Stour Chambers
Mill Studio, 17a Stour Street, Canterbury, Kent CT1 2NR, ☎ 01227 764899
✉ clerks@stourchambers.co.uk
Call Date: July 1971, Middle Temple
Recorder
Qualifications: [MA (Cantab)]
george.pulman@hardwicke.co.uk

PUNIA MISS RAJBIR KAUR

St Philips Chambers
55 Temple Row, Birmingham B2 5LS, ☎ 0121 246 7000 ✉ clerks@st-philips.com
Call Date: Oct 1999, Lincoln's Inn
Qualifications: [BSc (Hons)(Lond) Dip Law]
rpunia@st-philips.com

PUNJANI MISS YASMIN MICHELLE

187 Fleet Street
London EC4A 2AT, ☎ 020 7430 7430
✉ chambers@187fleetstreet.com
Call Date: Nov 2000, Lincoln's Inn
Qualifications: [LLB (Hons) (Lond)]
yasminpunjani@187fleetstreet.com

E

PUNT DR JONATHAN ARTHUR GILBERT

No5 Chambers
Fountain Court, Steelhouse Lane, Birmingham B4 6DR, ☎0845 210 5555 ✉info@no5.com
No5 Chambers
Greenwood House, 4-7 Salisbury Court, London EC4Y 8AA, ☎0845 210 5555
No5 Chambers
38 Queen Square, Bristol BS1 4QS, ☎0845 210 5555
Call Date: July 2005, Inner Temple
Qualifications: [MBBS (Lond)]
jgp@no5.com

PURCELL MISS DEIRDRE MARIE

Oriel Chambers
14 Water Street, Liverpool, Merseyside L2 8TD, ☎0151 236 7191
✉clerks@orielchambers.co.uk
Oriel Chambers
18 Ribblesdale Place, Preston PR1 3NA, ☎01772 254 764
✉clerks@oriel-chambers.co.uk
Call Date: Nov 2000, Lincoln's Inn
Qualifications: [LLB (Hons) (L'Pool)]
deirdre.purcell@orielchambers.co.uk

PURCELL MR GREGOR ALEXANDER MORRISON

1 High Pavement
Nottingham NG1 1HF, ☎0115 941 8218
✉clerks@1highpavement.co.uk
Call Date: Oct 1997, Lincoln's Inn
Qualifications: [LLB (Hons)(Newc)]
georgepurcell@1highpavement.co.uk

PURCHAS MR CHRISTOPHER PATRICK BROOKS QC (1990)

Crown Office Chambers
2 Crown Office Row, Temple, London EC4Y 7HJ, ☎020 7797 8100
✉mail@crownofficechambers.com
Call Date: July 1966, Inner Temple
Recorder
Qualifications: [MA (Cantab)]
purchas@crownofficechambers.com

PURCHAS MR JAMES ALEXANDER FRANCIS

4 Pump Court
4 Pump Court, Temple, London EC4Y 7AN, ☎020 7842 5555
✉chambers@4pumpcourt.com
Call Date: Oct 1997, Inner Temple
Pupil Supervisor
Qualifications: [MA CPE]
jpurchas@4pumpcourt.com

PURCHAS MR ROBIN MICHAEL QC (1987)

Francis Taylor Building
Inner Temple, London EC4Y 7BY, ☎020 7353 8415 ✉clerks@ftb.eu.com
Call Date: Nov 1968, Inner Temple
Recorder
Qualifications: [MA (Cantab)]

PURCHASE MR MATHEW JOHN

Matrix Chambers
Griffin Building, Gray's Inn, London WC1R 5LN, ☎020 7404 3447
✉matrix@matrixlaw.co.uk / Iscott@matrixlaw.co.uk
Call Date: July 2002, Lincoln's Inn
Qualifications: [MA (Oxon) CPE BVC]
mathewpurchase@matrixlaw.co.uk

PURDIE MR ROBERT ANTHONY JAMES

Faringdon Chambers
First Floor, Marlborough House, Bromsgrove, Faringdon, Oxfordshire SN7 7QJ, ☎01367 240598
4 King's Bench Walk
2nd Floor, 4 King's Bench Walk, Temple, London EC4Y 7DL, ☎020 7822 7000
✉clerks@4kbw.co.uk
Call Date: July 1979, Middle Temple
Qualifications: [LLB]

Fax: 01367 240256;
Out of hours telephone: 07770 594456
URL: www.faringdonchambers.co.uk

Types of work: Adoption, Ancillary relief, Care proceedings, Chancery (general), Child abduction, Child abuse, Child care law, Child support, Civil partnerships, Cohabitation, Divorce, Domestic violence injunctions, Ecclesiastical law, Family law, Family provision, Financial provision, Financial provision for children, Forced Marriage, Fostering, Inheritance, Inheritance and cohabitees, Leave to remove, Matrimonial, Matrimonial finance, Private children law, Special Guardianship, Succession, Trusts, Unmarried couples, Wills

Circuit: South Eastern

Awards and memberships: Member: Family Law Bar Association, Ecclesiastical Law Society, Society of Anglo-French Lawyers

E

Languages spoken: French

Publications: Matrimonial and Domestic Injunctions (Co-author), 1st Edition 1982, 2nd Edition 1987; Atkin's Court Forms, Husband and Wife (Contributior), 1985; A Guide to the Family Law Act 1996 (Co-author), 1996; Butterworths Family Law Guide (Contributor), 1997; Rayden and Jackson on Divorce and Family Matters (Contributor), 1997

Reported Cases: *Kennedy v Kennedy*, [2010] 1 FLR 807, CA Whether an unmarried father had 'rights of custody' under Spanish Law for The Hague Convention.
Harries v Bishop of Chester, (2007) 9 Eccl LJ 141 Appeal to Archbishop against the revocation by Bishop of the licence of a priest-in-charge.
J v J (A Minor: Property Transfer), [1993] 2 FLR 56 Meaning of #parent' in Children Act 189, Schedule 1
K v K, [1986] 2 FLR 411 Application for discretionary stay of English divorce proceedings where concurrent foreign proceedings
Re J (A Minor) (Wardship), (1984) 5 FLR 535 Confidential nature of wardship proceedings and the use of wardship documents in criminal proceedings.

PURDY MS CATHERINE LOUISE

3 PB Barristers
3 Paper Buildings, Temple, London EC4Y 7EU, ☎ 020 7583 8055
3 PB Barristers
Royal Talbot House, 2 Victoria Street, Bristol, Avon BS1 6BB, ☎ 0117 928 1520
3 PB Barristers
30 Christchurch Road, Bournemouth, Dorset BH1 3PD, ☎ 01202 292102
✉ clerks.bournemouth@3paper.co.uk
3 PB Barristers
4 St Peter Street, Winchester SO23 8BW, ☎ 01962 868884
✉ clerks.winchester@3paper.co.uk
3 PB Barristers
23 Beaumont Street, Oxford OX1 2NP, ☎ 01865 793 736
Call Date: Oct 1997, Inner Temple
Qualifications: [BA (Oxon)]
✉ Catherine.Purdy@3paper.co.uk

PURKIS MR SIMON FREDERICK GORDON

Pump Court Chambers
Upper Ground Floor, 3 Pump Court, Temple, London EC4Y 7AJ, ☎ 020 7353 0711
✉ clerks@3pumpcourt.com
Pump Court Chambers
5 Temple Chambers, Temple Street, Swindon SN1 1SQ, ☎ 01793 539899
✉ clerks@3pumpcourt.com
Pump Court Chambers
31 Southgate Street, Winchester, Hampshire SO23 9EB, ☎ 01962 868 161
✉ clerks@3pumpcourt.com
Call Date: Oct 2008, Inner Temple
Qualifications: [BA (Cantab) LLB]
✉ clerks@3pumpcourt.com

PURKISS MISS CATHLEEN KAREN

Coram Chambers
9-11 Fulwood Place, London WC1V 6HG, ☎ 020 7092 3700
✉ mail@coramchambers.co.uk
Call Date: July 1988, Lincoln's Inn
Pupil Supervisor
Qualifications: [BA (Hons) (Lond) Dip Law]
✉ kate.purkiss@coramchambers.co.uk

PURNELL MS CATHERINE ANA

Five Paper Buildings
1st Floor, Five Paper Buildings, Temple, London EC4Y 7HB, ☎ 020 7583 6117
✉ clerks@5pb.co.uk
Call Date: Oct 1999, Inner Temple
Qualifications: [BA (Leeds)]
✉ cp@5pb.co.uk

PURNELL MR JAMES DOMINIC

Henderson Chambers
2 Harcourt Buildings, Temple, London EC4Y 9DB, ☎ 020 7583 9020
✉ clerks@hendersonchambers.co.uk
Call Date: Oct 2002, Middle Temple
Pupil Supervisor
Qualifications: [MA (Edin) Dip Law]
✉ jpurnell@hendersonchambers.co.uk

PURNELL MR NICHOLAS ROBERT QC (1985)

Cloth Fair Chambers
39-40 Cloth Fair, London EC1A 7NT, ☎ 020 7710 6444
✉ email@clothfairchambers.com
23 Essex Street
London WC2R 3AA, ☎ 020 7413 0353
✉ clerks@23es.com
Call Date: July 1968, Middle Temple
Qualifications: [MA (Cantab)]
✉ nicholaspurnell@clothfairchambers.com

PURNELL MR PAUL OLIVER QC (1982)

Farringdon Chambers
180 Bermondsey Street, London SE1 3TQ, ☎ 020 7089 5700
Call Date: Nov 1962, Inner Temple
Qualifications: [MA (Oxon)]
✉ paulpurnell@farringdon-law.co.uk

E

PURSS MR CHARLES NAIRN HAY

4 Brick Court
4 Brick Court, Temple, London EC4Y 9AD,
☎ 020 7832 3200 ✉ clerks@4bc.co.uk
Call Date: Oct 1999, Inner Temple
Qualifications: [BA (Lond)]
🖃 nairn.purss@4bc.co.uk

PURVES MR GAVIN BOWMAN

Swan House
P.O.Box 8749, London W13 8ZX,
☎ 020 8998 3035
✉ swanchambers@yahoo.co.uk
Call Date: July 1979, Gray's Inn
Qualifications: [LLB (Hons)(Brunel) DEI (Amsterdam)]

PURVES DR ROBERT LANGLEY

3 Verulam Buildings
London WC1R 5NT, ☎ 020 7831 8441
✉ chambers@3vb.com
Call Date: Nov 2007, Middle Temple
Qualifications: [BA LLB (Cape Town) LLM (Cantab) PhD (Cantab)]
🖃 rpurves@3vb.com

PURVIS MR IAIN YOUNIE QC (2006)

11 South Square
1st Floor, 11 South Square, Gray's Inn, London WC1R 5EY, ☎ 020 7405 1222
✉ clerks@11southsquare.com
Call Date: July 1986, Gray's Inn
Qualifications: [MA (Cantab) BCL (Oxon)]
🖃 ipurvis@11southsquare.com

PUSEY MR WILLIAM JAMES

No5 Chambers
Fountain Court, Steelhouse Lane, Birmingham B4 6DR, ☎ 0845 210 5555 ✉ info@no5.com
No5 Chambers
Greenwood House, 4-7 Salisbury Court, London EC4Y 8AA, ☎ 0845 210 5555
No5 Chambers
38 Queen Square, Bristol BS1 4QS,
☎ 0845 210 5555
Call Date: Nov 1977, Inner Temple
Pupil Supervisor
Qualifications: [LLB (Leeds)]
🖃 wp@no5.com

PUTNAM MRS SHEELAGH

Putnam
14 Keyes Road, London NW2 3XA,
☎ 020 8438 2950 ✉ tom@lending_law.co.uk
Call Date: Nov 1976, Middle Temple
🖃 sheelagh@lending-law.co.uk

PUTNAM MR THOMAS DREW

Putnam
14 Keyes Road, London NW2 3XA,
☎ 020 8438 2950 ✉ tom@lending_law.co.uk
Call Date: July 1976, Gray's Inn
Pupil Supervisor
🖃 tom@lending-law.co.uk

PUZEY MR JAMES RODERICK

St Philips Chambers
55 Temple Row, Birmingham B2 5LS,
☎ 0121 246 7000 ✉ clerks@st-philips.com
Call Date: Oct 1990, Inner Temple
Qualifications: [LLB (L'pool)]
🖃 jpuzey@st-philips.com

PYE MR DEREK

No5 Chambers
Fountain Court, Steelhouse Lane, Birmingham B4 6DR, ☎ 0845 210 5555 ✉ info@no5.com
No5 Chambers
Greenwood House, 4-7 Salisbury Court, London EC4Y 8AA, ☎ 0845 210 5555
No5 Chambers
38 Queen Square, Bristol BS1 4QS,
☎ 0845 210 5555
Zenith Chambers
10 Park Square, Leeds LS1 2LH,
☎ 0113 245 5438
✉ clerks@zenithchambers.co.uk
Call Date: July 2008, Lincoln's Inn
Qualifications: [LLB (Hons) FRICS FCIArb MAE]
🖃 dpye@no5.com

PYE MISS HANNAH RUTH

Five St Andrew's Hill
5 St Andrew's Hill, London EC4V 5BZ,
☎ 020 7332 5400 ✉ Clerks@5sah.co.uk
Call Date: Nov 2007, Gray's Inn
Qualifications: [LLB (Reading)]

PYE MISS MARGARET JAYNE

Zenith Chambers
10 Park Square, Leeds LS1 2LH,
☎ 0113 245 5438
✉ clerks@zenithchambers.co.uk
Call Date: May 1995, Middle Temple
Pupil Supervisor, Recorder
Qualifications: [BA (Hons)]

PYLE MISS SUSAN DEBORAH

1 Garden Court Family Law Chambers
Ground Floor, One Garden Court, Temple, London EC4Y 9BJ, ☎020 7797 7900
✉clerks@1gc.com
Call Date: Nov 1985, Gray's Inn
Pupil Supervisor
Qualifications: [LLB (Newc)]
✉pyle@1gc.com

PYMONT MR CHRISTOPHER HOWARD QC (1996)

Maitland Chambers
7 Stone Buildings, Lincoln's Inn, London WC2A 3SZ, ☎020 7406 1200
✉clerks@maitlandchambers.com
Call Date: July 1979, Gray's Inn
Recorder
Qualifications: [MA (Oxon)]
✉cpymont@maitlandchambers.com

PYNE MR RUSSELL DAVID

2 King's Bench Walk
2 King's Bench Walk, Temple, London EC4Y 7DE, ☎020 7353 1746
✉clerks@2kbw.com
Call Date: Oct 1991, Inner Temple
Pupil Supervisor
Qualifications: [LLB (Bris)]
✉rpyne@2kbw.com

QADRI MR KHALID

Chambers of Mr K Qadri
84 Augustus Road, London SW19 6EL, ☎07956 205798 ✉kkadri1993@yahoo.co.uk
Call Date: Nov 1993, Middle Temple
Qualifications: [BA (Hons) CPE]
✉kkadri1993@yahoo.co.uk

QAZI MR MOHAMMED AYAZ

Carmelite Chambers
9 Carmelite Street, London EC4Y 0DR, ☎020 7936 6300
✉clerks@carmelitechambers.co.uk
Call Date: Feb 1993, Gray's Inn
Qualifications: [LLB]
✉aqazi@carmelitechambers.co.uk

QUAIFE MR RAMSAY JUSTIN MALIN

Devon Chambers
3 St Andrew Street, Plymouth PL1 2AH, ☎01752 661659
✉clerks@devonchambers.co.uk
Call Date: Oct 1995, Middle Temple
Qualifications: [BA (Hons) Dip Law]
✉ramsayquaife@devonchambers.co.uk

QUEGAN MR PETER EDWARD

Kenworthy's Chambers
Arlington House, Bloom Street, Salford, Manchester M3 6AJ, ☎0161 832 4036
Call Date: July 2010, Inner Temple
Qualifications: [LLB (Hull) TACSC]

QUEST MR DAVID CHARLES

3 Verulam Buildings
London WC1R 5NT, ☎020 7831 8441
✉chambers@3vb.com
Call Date: Oct 1993, Gray's Inn
Pupil Supervisor
Qualifications: [MA (Cantab)]
✉dquest@3vb.com

QUICKFALL MR ROGER MARK

Park Lane Plowden
19 Westgate, Leeds LS1 2RD, ☎0113 228 5049
✉clerks@parklaneplowden.co.uk
Call Date: Oct 2003, Middle Temple
Qualifications: [BA (Hons) (Surrey)]
✉roger.quickfall@parklaneplowden.co.uk

Types of work: Employment, Health and safety, Personal injury

QUIGLEY MR CONOR QC (2003)

Serle Court
6 New Square, Lincoln's Inn, London WC2A 3QS, ☎020 7242 6105
✉clerks@serlecourt.co.uk
Call Date: Nov 1985, Gray's Inn
Qualifications: [LLB (Lond) Dip E I (Holland) MA (Oxon)]
✉cquigley@serlecourt.co.uk

QUIGLEY MS LOUISE

St Johns Buildings
24a - 28 St John Street, Manchester M3 4DJ, ☎0161 214 1500
✉clerk@stjohnsbuildings.co.uk
16 Winckley Square
Preston PR1 3JJ, ☎01772 256100
St Johns Buildings Liverpool
8th Floor India Buildings, Water Street, Liverpool L2 0XG, ☎0151 243 6000
✉clerk@stjohnsbuildings.co.uk
Call Date: Nov 2003, Inner Temple
Qualifications: [BA (Manch)]
✉louise.quigley@stjohnsbuildings.co.uk

E

QUINEY MR CHARLES BENEDICTUS ALEXANDER

Crown Office Chambers
2 Crown Office Row, Temple, London EC4Y 7HJ, ☎ 020 7797 8100
✉ mail@crownofficechambers.com
Call Date: Mar 1998, Gray's Inn
Pupil Supervisor
Qualifications: [BA BCL (Oxon)]
quiney@crownofficechambers.com

QUINLAN MR CHRISTOPHER JOHN QC (2011)

Guildhall Chambers
23 Broad Street, Bristol BS1 2HG,
☎ 0117 930 9000
✉ hoc@guildhallchambers.co.uk
Call Date: Nov 1992, Inner Temple
Pupil Supervisor
Qualifications: [LLB (Hons)]
christopher.quinlan@guildhallchambers.co.uk

QUINN MR CHRISTOPHER JOHN

Littleton Chambers
3 King's Bench Walk North, Temple, London EC4Y 7HR, ☎ 020 7797 8600
✉ fschneider@littletonchambers.co.uk
Call Date: Oct 1992, Middle Temple
Pupil Supervisor
Qualifications: [LL.B (Hons) (Cantab) LL.M (Canada)]
cquinn@littletonchambers.co.uk

QUINN MR CONOR HENRY THOMAS

KBW
The Engine House, No 1 Foundry Square, Leeds LS11 5DL, ☎ 0113 297 1200
✉ clerks@kbwchambers.com
Call Date: Oct 2007, Middle Temple
Qualifications: [BA (Hons) (Nott'm)]
conorquinn@kbwchambers.com

QUINN MISS MICHELLE LOUISE

Clerksroom (Taunton)
Equity House, Administration Centre, Blackbrook Park Avenue, Taunton, Somerset TA1 2PX, ☎ 0845 083 3000
✉ mail@clerksroom.com
Call Date: July 2005, Inner Temple
Qualifications: [BA]

QUINN MR STUART JOHN

New Walk Chambers
27 New Walk, Leicester, Leicestershire LE1 6TE, ☎ 0871 200 1298 / 0116 255 9144
✉ clerks@newwalkchambers.co.uk
Call Date: Oct 1990, Gray's Inn
Qualifications: [BSc LLM]

QUINN MS SUSAN ANN

4 Brick Court
4 Brick Court, Temple, London EC4Y 9AD, ☎ 020 7832 3200 ✉ clerks@4bc.co.uk
Call Date: Nov 1983, Gray's Inn
Pupil Supervisor
Qualifications: [LLB (lond)]
susan.quinn@4bc.co.uk

QUINN MR TOMAS ANTHONY

4 King's Bench Walk
2nd Floor, 4 King's Bench Walk, Temple, London EC4Y 7DL, ☎ 020 7822 7000
✉ clerks@4kbw.co.uk
Call Date: July 2006, Lincoln's Inn
Qualifications: [BSc LLB (Wales)]
tq@4kbw.co.uk

QUINN MISS VICTORIA KATHLEEN

Thomas More Chambers
7 Lincoln's Inn Fields, London WC2A 3BP, ☎ 020 7404 7000
✉ clerks@thomasmore.co.uk
Call Date: Oct 1995, Lincoln's Inn
Pupil Supervisor
Qualifications: [BA (Hons)(Lond)]
vquinn@thomasmore.co.uk

QUINNEY MISS NICOLA TAMSIN

Call Date: July 2001, Gray's Inn
Qualifications: [BA (Oxon)]

QUINT MS JOAN FRANCESCA RAE

Radcliffe Chambers
Ground Floor, 11 New Square, Lincoln's Inn, London WC2A 3QB, ☎ 020 7831 0081
✉ clerks@radcliffechambers.com
Call Date: July 1970, Gray's Inn
Pupil Supervisor
Qualifications: [LLB (Lond) AKC]

Fax: 020 7405 2560;
DX: 319 LDE;
URL: http://www.radcliffechambers.com

Types of work: Charities, Equity, Family provision, Succession, Trusts, Wills

QUIRK MR IAIN RICHARD

Essex Court Chambers
24 Lincoln's Inn Fields, London WC2A 3EG, ☎ 020 7813 8000
✉ clerksroom@essexcourt.net
Call Date: Oct 2002, Lincoln's Inn
Qualifications: [LLB (Nott'm)]
iquirk@essexcourt.net

QUIRKE MR GERARD MARTIN

Citadel Chambers
The Citadel, 190 Corporation Street, Birmingham B4 6QD, ☎0121 233 8500
✉clerks@citadelchambers.com
Call Date: Nov 1988, Middle Temple
Qualifications: [BA (Hull) Dip Law (Lond)]

QUIRKE MR JAMES KEIRON

St Philips Chambers
55 Temple Row, Birmingham B2 5LS, ☎0121 246 7000 ✉clerks@st-philips.com
Call Date: Nov 1974, Gray's Inn
Pupil Supervisor
Qualifications: [BA (Oxon)]
jquirke@st-philips.com

QURESHI MR ABDUL SALEEM

Barclay Chambers
Ground Floor, 2a Barclay Road, Leytonstone, London E11 3DG, ☎020 8558 2289
✉barqureshi@hotmail.co.uk
Call Date: July 1972, Middle Temple
Pupil Supervisor
Qualifications: [BA LLB]
barqureshi@hotmail.co.uk

QURESHI MR ASIF HASAN

Quadrant Chambers
Quadrant House, 10 Fleet Street, London EC4Y 1AU, ☎020 7583 4444
✉info@quadrantchambers.com
Call Date: Nov 1978, Lincoln's Inn
Qualifications: [LLB (Lond) LLM (Lond) PhD (Lond)]

QURESHI MISS DILRUBA

Temple Court Chambers
2nd Floor, 2 Dr Johnson's Building, Temple, London EC4Y 7AY, ☎020 7353 7888
✉clerks@templecourt.co.uk
Call Date: Mar 2002, Lincoln's Inn
Qualifications: [LLB (Hons) (Lond)]
clerks@templecourt.co.uk, djqureshi@templecourt.co.uk

QURESHI MR KHAWAR MEHMOOD QC (2006)

Serle Court
6 New Square, Lincoln's Inn, London WC2A 3QS, ☎020 7242 6105
✉clerks@serlecourt.co.uk
Call Date: Oct 1990, Middle Temple
Qualifications: [LLB LLM (Cantab)]
kqureshi@serlecourt.co.uk, kmqureshi@aol.com

QURESHI MR TANVEER AFTAB

25 Bedford Row
London WC1R 4HD, ☎020 7067 1500
✉clerks@25bedfordrow.com
Call Date: Nov 2000, Lincoln's Inn
Qualifications: [LLB (Hons) (Brunel) LLM (Uni Coll Lond)]

RABAIOTTI MISS CATHERINE SEPHORA

Five Paper Buildings
1st Floor, Five Paper Buildings, Temple, London EC4Y 7HB, ☎020 7583 6117
✉clerks@5pb.co.uk
Call Date: Mar 2002, Middle Temple
Qualifications: [BA (Hons)]
cr@5pb.co.uk

RABINOWITZ MR LAURENCE ANTON QC (2002)

One Essex Court
Ground Floor, One Essex Court, Temple, London EC4Y 9AR, ☎020 7583 2000
✉clerks@oeclaw.co.uk
Call Date: Nov 1987, Middle Temple
Qualifications: [BA BCL (Oxon) BA LLB (New Zealand)]
lrabinowitz@oeclaw.co.uk

RADBURN MR MARK CHARLES CRISPIN

No5 Chambers
Fountain Court, Steelhouse Lane, Birmingham B4 6DR, ☎0845 210 5555 ✉info@no5.com
No5 Chambers
Greenwood House, 4-7 Salisbury Court, London EC4Y 8AA, ☎0845 210 5555
No5 Chambers
38 Queen Square, Bristol BS1 4QS, ☎0845 210 5555
Call Date: Oct 1991, Lincoln's Inn
Qualifications: [LLB (Hons)]
mr@no5.com

RADCLIFFE MR ANDREW ALLEN QC (2000)

2 Hare Court
Lower Ground, Ground, 1st & 2nd Floor, 2 Hare Court, Temple, London EC4Y 7BH, ☎020 7353 3982 ✉clerks@2harecourt.com
Call Date: Nov 1975, Middle Temple
Recorder
Qualifications: [BA (Oxon)]
andrewradcliffe@2harecourt.com

E

RADCLIFFE MR FRANCIS CHARLES JOSEPH

KBW
The Engine House, No 1 Foundry Square, Leeds LS11 5DL, ☎ 0113 297 1200
✉ clerks@kbwchambers.com
Call Date: Nov 1962, Gray's Inn
Qualifications: [MA (Cantab)]
fcr@kbwchambers.com

RADCLIFFE MS PAMELA JOAN

20 Course Road
20 Course Road, Ascot, Berks SL5 7HL, ☎ 07932 671509
✉ pamelaradcliffe@estl.demon.co.uk
Call Date: July 1979, Gray's Inn
Qualifications: [LLB (Warw)]
pamelaradcliffe@estl.demon.co.uk

RADCLIFFE MRS SHEILA MARY

Cathedral Chambers
10 Clytha Park Road, Newport NP20 4PB, ☎ 01633 215112
Call Date: July 2003, Middle Temple
Qualifications: [LLB Hons (Bris)]

RADEVSKY MR ANTHONY ERIC

Falcon Chambers
Falcon Court, London EC4Y 1AA, ☎ 020 7353 2484
✉ clerks@falcon-chambers.com
Call Date: July 1978, Inner Temple
Pupil Supervisor
Qualifications: [LLB (So'ton)]
radevsky@falcon-chambers.com

Types of work: Chancery (land law), Commercial property, Conveyancing, Landlord and tenant, Leasehold enfranchisement, Professional negligence, Real property, Rights of way

RADFORD MISS ALTHEA JANE

Chambers of Mr Ami Feder
Ground Floor, Lamb Building, Temple, London EC4Y 7AS, ☎ 020 7797 7788
✉ clerks@lambbuilding.co.uk
Chambers of Mr Ami Feder
Ground Floor, Lamb Building, Temple, London EC4Y 7AS, ☎ 020 7797 7788
✉ clerks@lambbuilding.co.uk
Call Date: July 2009, Lincoln's Inn
Qualifications: [BA (Cantab) CPE UCU MPHIL (Cantab)]

RADFORD MRS NADINE POGGIOLI QC (1995)

187 Fleet Street
London EC4A 2AT, ☎ 020 7430 7430
✉ chambers@187fleetstreet.com
Call Date: Nov 1974, Lincoln's Inn
Qualifications: [BA (Hons)]

RADLEY-GARDNER MR OLIVER

Falcon Chambers
Falcon Court, London EC4Y 1AA, ☎ 020 7353 2484
✉ clerks@falcon-chambers.com
Call Date: Oct 2003, Gray's Inn
Qualifications: [BA (Oxon)]
radley-gardner@falcon-chambers.com

RADSTONE MR MATTHEW ELLIOT

25 Bedford Row
London WC1R 4HD, ☎ 020 7067 1500
✉ clerks@25bedfordrow.com
Call Date: July 2005, Middle Temple
Qualifications: [BA (Hons) Leeds]

RAE MR JAMES ROBERT

Number 7 Harrington Street Chambers
7 Harrington Street, Liverpool L2 9YH, ☎ 0151 242 0707 ✉ clerks@7hs.co.uk
Call Date: July 1976, Inner Temple
Pupil Supervisor
james.rae@7hs.co.uk

RAE MRS LOUISE ELIZABETH

St Johns Buildings
24a - 28 St John Street, Manchester M3 4DJ, ☎ 0161 214 1500
✉ clerk@stjohnsbuildings.co.uk
St Johns Buildings
21 White Friars, Chester CH1 1NZ, ☎ 01244 323070
✉ clerk@stjohnsbuildings.co.uk
16 Winckley Square
Preston PR1 3JJ, ☎ 01772 256100
Call Date: Nov 2006, Middle Temple
Qualifications: [BA (Hons) (Lanc) LLB (Hons)]
louise.scott@stjohnsbuildings.co.uk

RAESIDE MR MARK ANDREW QC (2002)

Atkin Chambers
1 Atkin Building, Gray's Inn, London WC1R 5AT, ☎ 020 7404 0102
✉ clerks@atkinchambers.com
Call Date: Nov 1982, Middle Temple
Qualifications: [MA MPhil (Cantab)]
mraeside@atkinchambers.com

E

RAFATI MR ALI REZA

King's Bench and Godolphin (KBG)Chambers
115 North Hill, Plymouth, Devon PL4 8JY, ☎01752 221551
✉clerks@kbgchambers.co.uk
Call Date: Nov 1993, Gray's Inn
Pupil Supervisor
Qualifications: [LLB]
✉ali.rafati@kingsbenchchambers.co.uk

RAFFERTY MISS ANGELA MARGARET MARY

1 Paper Buildings
1st Floor, 1 Paper Buildings, Temple, London EC4Y 7EP, ☎020 7353 3728
✉clerks@onepaper.co.uk
Call Date: Feb 1995, Lincoln's Inn
Pupil Supervisor
Qualifications: [BA (Cantab)]
✉angelarafferty@onepaper.co.uk

RAFFERTY MR STUART QC (2009)

1 High Pavement
Nottingham NG1 1HF, ☎0115 941 8218
✉clerks@1highpavement.co.uk
Furnival Chambers
32 Furnival Street, London EC4A 1JQ, ☎020 7405 3232
Call Date: July 1975, Gray's Inn
Recorder
Qualifications: [BA]
✉stuartraffertyqc@1highpavement.co.uk

RAFFIN MR CHARLES WILLIAM STEWART

Hardwicke
New Square, Lincoln's Inn, London WC2A 3SB, ☎020 7242 2523
✉enquiries@hardwicke.co.uk
Call Date: Nov 2005, Middle Temple
Qualifications: [BA (Hons) Oxford]

RAFTER MISS KATHRYN MICHELLE

KBW
The Engine House, No 1 Foundry Square, Leeds LS11 5DL, ☎0113 297 1200
✉clerks@kbwchambers.com
Call Date: Oct 2005, Middle Temple
Qualifications: [BA (Hons) (Sheff)]
✉kr@kbwchambers.com

RAFTER MISS LAUREN

Seven Bedford Row
7 Bedford Row, London WC1R 4BS, ☎020 7242 3555 ✉clerks@7br.co.uk
Call Date: Oct 2007, Inner Temple
Qualifications: [BA (Hons) (Nott'm) LLB (Nott'm)]
✉lrafter@7br.co.uk

RAGGATT MR TIMOTHY WALTER HAROLD QC (1993)

4 King's Bench Walk
2nd Floor, 4 King's Bench Walk, Temple, London EC4Y 7DL, ☎020 7822 7000
✉clerks@4kbw.co.uk
St Philips Chambers
55 Temple Row, Birmingham B2 5LS, ☎0121 246 7000 ✉clerks@st-philips.com
Call Date: July 1972, Inner Temple
Recorder
Qualifications: [LLB (Lond)]
✉tr@4kbw.co.uk

RAHAL MISS RAVINDER KAUR

Garden Court Chambers
57-60 Lincoln's Inn Fields, London WC2A 3LJ, ☎020 7993 7600 ✉info@gclaw.co.uk
Call Date: Nov 1983, Middle Temple
Qualifications: [LLB LLM (Cantab)]
✉ravinderr@gclaw.co.uk

RAHMAN MR ANIS

12 Old Square Chambers
1st Floor, 12 Old Square, Lincoln's Inn, London WC2A 3TX, ☎020 7404 0875
✉clerks@12oldsquare.com
Call Date: Nov 1990, Inner Temple
Pupil Supervisor
Qualifications: [MA Dip Law DSL MA]
✉clerks@12oldsquare.com

RAHMAN MR LEO FERHANUR

Chambers of Leo Rahman
30 Balsdean Road, Brighton, Sussex BN2 6PF, ☎07814 004 790 ✉leorahman@aol.com
Call Date: July 1998, Lincoln's Inn
Qualifications: [BA (Hons)(Keele) LLM (Sussex)]

RAHMAN MR LUTHFUR

Chambers of Mr L Rahman
201 Maidstone Road, Rochester, Kent ME1 3ES, ☎07947 588362
✉luthfur99@gmail.com
Call Date: Oct 1996, Middle Temple
Qualifications: [LLB (Hons) Bus Law]
✉luthfur99@gmail.com

E

RAHMAN MR MUSHTAQ ZIA-UR

Clerksroom (Taunton)
Equity House, Administration Centre, Blackbrook Park Avenue, Taunton, Somerset TA1 2PX, ☎0845 083 3000
✉mail@clerksroom.com
Call Date: July 2006, Lincoln's Inn
Qualifications: [LLB (Leic) MA (Manchester)]

RAHMAN MS SADEQA SHAHEEN

1 Crown Office Row
1 Crown Office Row, Temple, London EC4Y 7HH, ☎020 7797 7500
✉mail@1cor.com
Call Date: Nov 1996, Gray's Inn
Pupil Supervisor
Qualifications: [BA (B'ham)]
shaheen.rahman@1cor.com

RAHMAN MR SAMI UR

Field Court Chambers
5 Field Court, Gray's Inn, London WC1R 5EF, ☎020 7405 6114 ✉clerks@fieldcourt.co.uk
Call Date: Oct 1996, Lincoln's Inn
Qualifications: [LLB (Hons)(Middx)]

RAHMAN MISS TAHMINA

4 Brick Court
4 Brick Court, Temple, London EC4Y 9AD, ☎020 7832 3200 ✉clerks@4bc.co.uk
Call Date: July 2001, Lincoln's Inn
Qualifications: [LLB (Hons) (Lond)]
tahmina.rahman@4bc.co.uk

RAHMAN MR YAQUB

Oriel Chambers
14 Water Street, Liverpool, Merseyside L2 8TD, ☎0151 236 7191
✉clerks@orielchambers.co.uk
Oriel Chambers
18 Ribblesdale Place, Preston PR1 3NA, ☎01772 254 764
✉clerks@oriel-chambers.co.uk
Call Date: Oct 1991, Gray's Inn
Pupil Supervisor, Recorder
Qualifications: [BA (Hons) (Oxon) DipLaw]
yaqub.rahman@orielchambers.co.uk

RAI MR AMARJIT SINGH

St Philips Chambers
55 Temple Row, Birmingham B2 5LS, ☎0121 246 7000 ✉clerks@st-philips.com
Call Date: July 1989, Middle Temple
Qualifications: [LLB (Hons)]
arai@st-philips.co.uk

RAI MISS PUNEET KAUR

Thomas More Chambers
7 Lincoln's Inn Fields, London WC2A 3BP, ☎020 7404 7000
✉clerks@thomasmore.co.uk
Call Date: Oct 2004, Lincoln's Inn
Qualifications: [BA (Hons) (Oxon) PgDl]
prai@thomasmore.co.uk

RAI MR RAJESH KUMAR

1 Mitre Court Buildings
1 Mitre Court Buildings, Temple, London EC4Y 7BS, ☎020 7452 8900
✉clerks@1mcb.com
Call Date: Feb 1993, Lincoln's Inn
Qualifications: [LLB (Hons)]

RAI MISS SONIA

Five Paper
Ground Floor, 5 Paper Buildings, Temple, London EC4Y 7HB, ☎020 7815 3200
Call Date: Oct 1998, Gray's Inn
Qualifications: [B.Pharm (Hons)]
soniarai@fivepaper.com

RAILTON MR DAVID QC (1996)

Fountain Court Chambers
Fountain Court, Temple, London EC4Y 9DH, ☎020 7583 3335
✉chambers@fountaincourt.co.uk
Call Date: July 1979, Gray's Inn
Recorder
Qualifications: [BA (Oxon)]
drailton@fountaincourt.co.uk

RAINEY MISS ANGELA LOUISE

39 Essex Street
London WC2R 3AT, ☎020 7832 1111
✉clerks@39essex.com
Call Date: Nov 2010, Inner Temple
Qualifications: [BA BCL (Oxon)]

RAINEY MR KIERAN VINCENT

Fountain Chambers
Cleveland Business Centre, 1 Watson Street, Middlesbrough TS1 2RQ, ☎01642 804040
✉clerks@fountainchambers.co.uk
Call Date: July 2004, Gray's Inn
Qualifications: [LLB (Leic)]

E

RAINEY MR PHILIP CARSLAKE QC (2010)

Tanfield Chambers
2-5 Warwick Court, London WC1R 5DJ,
☎020 7421 5300
✉clerks@tanfieldchambers.co.uk
Call Date: Oct 1990, Middle Temple
Qualifications: [LLB (Leics) MCIArb]
philiprainey@tanfieldchambers.co.uk

RAINEY MR SIMON PIERS NICHOLAS QC (2000)

Quadrant Chambers
Quadrant House, 10 Fleet Street, London EC4Y 1AU, ☎020 7583 4444
✉info@quadrantchambers.com
Call Date: July 1982, Lincoln's Inn
Recorder
Qualifications: [MA (Cantab) LSDE (Belguim)]
simon.rainey@quadrantchambers.com

RAINSFORD MR MARK DAVID QC (2006)

Chambers of Andrew Mitchell QC
33 Chancery Lane, London WC2A 1EN,
☎020 7440 9950 ✉clerks@33cllaw.com
Call Date: Nov 1985, Lincoln's Inn
Qualifications: [LLB (Hons) (LSE)]

RAJAH MR EASON THURAI QC (2011)

Ten Old Square
Ground Floor, Ten Old Square, Lincoln's Inn, London WC2A 3SU, ☎020 7405 0758
✉clerks@tenoldsquare.com
Call Date: July 1989, Gray's Inn
Pupil Supervisor
Qualifications: [LLB]
easonrajah@tenoldsquare.com

RAJGOPAUL-HICKLIN MR CRAIG

Littleton Chambers
3 King's Bench Walk North, Temple, London EC4Y 7HR, ☎020 7797 8600
✉fschneider@littletonchambers.co.uk
Call Date: Nov 2010, Middle Temple
Qualifications: [BA (Hons) (Oxon)]
crh@littletonchambers.co.uk

RAJI-LAWAL MR TOM OMOTOLA

St Ive's Chambers
Whittall Street, Birmingham B4 6DH,
☎0121 236 0863
✉clerks@stiveschambers.co.uk
Call Date: Oct 2008, Middle Temple
Qualifications: [LLB (Hons) (Coventry) LLM of (Nott'm)]
tom.lawal@stiveschambers.co.uk

RALPH MR CRAIG

Kings Chambers
36 Young Street, Manchester M3 3FT,
☎0845 034 3444
✉clerks@kingschambers.com
Kings Chambers
5 Park Square East, Leeds LS1 2NE,
☎0845 034 3444
✉clerks@kingschambers.com
Kings Chambers
Embassy House, 60 Church Street, Birmingham B3 2DJ, ☎0845 034 3444
✉clerks@kingschambers.com
Call Date: Oct 2002, Middle Temple
Qualifications: [LLB (Hons)]
cralph@kingschambers.com

RALSTON ??? SCOTT EDWARD

3 Verulam Buildings
London WC1R 5NT, ☎020 7831 8441
✉chambers@3vb.com
Call Date: Mar 2012, Inner Temple

RALSTON MR WILLIAM ROBB

Number 7 Harrington Street Chambers
7 Harrington Street, Liverpool L2 9YH,
☎0151 242 0707 ✉clerks@7hs.co.uk
Call Date: Oct 2000, Inner Temple
Qualifications: [LLB (Hons) (Northumbria)]
william.ralston@7hs.co.uk

RAMADHAN MISS LUBEYA KAREN

Pump Court Chambers
31 Southgate Street, Winchester, Hampshire SO23 9EB, ☎01962 868 161
✉clerks@3pumpcourt.com
Pump Court Chambers
Upper Ground Floor, 3 Pump Court, Temple, London EC4Y 7AJ, ☎020 7353 0711
✉clerks@3pumpcourt.com
Pump Court Chambers
5 Temple Chambers, Temple Street, Swindon SN1 1SQ, ☎01793 539899
✉clerks@3pumpcourt.com
Call Date: July 2000, Middle Temple
Qualifications: [LLB(Hons) (Sussex)]
clerks@3pumpcourt.com

RAMAMOORTHY MISS DIVYA

1 Gray's Inn Square
Ground Floor, 1 Gray's Inn Square, London WC1R 5AA, ☎020 7405 0001
Call Date: Mar 2006, Middle Temple
Qualifications: [LLB (Hons)]
drobinson@1gis.co.uk

E

RAMASAMY MR SELVARAJU

QEB Hollis Whiteman
1-2 Laurence Pountney Hill, London EC4R 0EU, ☎020 7933 8855
✉barristers@qebhw.co.uk
Call Date: Nov 1992, Inner Temple
Pupil Supervisor
Qualifications: [LLB (Lond) LLM (Lond)]
selva.ramasamy@qebhw.co.uk

RAMBLE MR DONALD ROBERT LOUIS

Five St Andrew's Hill
5 St Andrew's Hill, London EC4V 5BZ,
☎020 7332 5400 ✉Clerks@5sah.co.uk
Call Date: Nov 1998, Middle Temple
Qualifications: [LLB (Hons)(Lond)]
donramble@5sah.co.uk

RAMDAS-HARSIA MR ROHAN MUKESH

1 Pump Court
Elm Court, Temple, London EC4Y 7AB,
☎020 7842 7070
✉(name)@pumpcourt.co.uk
Call Date: Nov 1999, Middle Temple
Pupil Supervisor
Qualifications: [LLB (Hons)]
rrh@1pumpcourt.co.uk

E

RAMEL MR STEFAN PHILIPPE

Guildhall Chambers
23 Broad Street, Bristol BS1 2HG,
☎0117 930 9000
✉hoc@guildhallchambers.co.uk
Call Date: Oct 2002, Inner Temple
Qualifications: [LLB (UWE) LLM (Cantab)]
stefan.ramel@guildhallchambers.co.uk

RAMPTON MR RICHARD QC (1987)

One Brick Court
1st Floor, One Brick Court, Temple, London EC4Y 9BY, ☎020 7353 8845
✉clerks@onebrickcourt.com
Call Date: Nov 1965, Inner Temple
Qualifications: [BA (Oxon)]
rr@onebrickcourt.com

RAMSAHOYE MISS INDIRA KIM

29 Bedford Row Chambers
London WC1R 4HE, ☎020 7404 1044
✉clerks@29br.co.uk
Call Date: Nov 1980, Lincoln's Inn
Pupil Supervisor
Qualifications: [BA]
iramsahoye@29br.co.uk

RAMSDEN MR JAMES MICHAEL SCOTT

4-5 Gray's Inn Square
Gray's Inn, London WC1R 5AH,
☎020 7404 5252 ✉clerks@4-5.co.uk
Call Date: Nov 1987, Middle Temple
Pupil Supervisor
Qualifications: [LLB (Leics)]
jramsden@4-5.co.uk

RAMSDEN MISS JUSTINE LOUISE

Harcourt Chambers
1st Floor, 2 Harcourt Buildings, Temple, London EC4Y 9DB, ☎0844 561 7135
Call Date: July 2010, Lincoln's Inn
Qualifications: [BA (Oxon)]
jramsden@harcourtchambers.law.co.uk

RAMZAN MS FARAH JABEEN

Holborn Chambers
6 Gate Street, Lincoln's Inn Fields, London WC2A 3HP, ☎020 7242 6060
Call Date: July 2003, Lincoln's Inn
Qualifications: [LLB Hons (Manch)]
f.ramzan@6gs.co.uk

RAMZAN MR MOHAMMED ANWAR

Great James Street Chambers
37 Great James Street, London WC1N 3HB,
☎020 7440 4949
✉chambers@greatjames.co.uk
Call Date: Oct 1995, Lincoln's Inn
Qualifications: [LLB (Hons)(Wolves)]

RANA MR MOHAMMED AKRAM

Clapham Law Chambers
85 Landor Road, Clapham North, London SW9 9RT, ☎020 7978 8482
✉DANNY@claphamlawchambers.co.uk
Call Date: Nov 1995, Lincoln's Inn
Qualifications: [BSc (Hons) LLB (Hons)]

RANALES-COTOS MISS TINA LUISA

Kings Chambers
36 Young Street, Manchester M3 3FT,
☎0845 034 3444
✉clerks@kingschambers.com
Kings Chambers
5 Park Square East, Leeds LS1 2NE,
☎0845 034 3444
✉clerks@kingschambers.com
Kings Chambers
Embassy House, 60 Church Street, Birmingham B3 2DJ, ☎0845 034 3444
✉clerks@kingschambers.com
Call Date: Oct 1999, Lincoln's Inn
Qualifications: [LLB (Hons)(Leic) BCL]
tranalescotos@kingschambers.com

RANATUNGA MR ASITHA NANDIKA

Cornerstone Barristers
2-3 Gray's Inn Square, Gray's Inn, London WC1R 5JH, ☎ 020 7242 4986
✉ chambers@2-3gis.co.uk
Call Date: Oct 2001, Inner Temple
Qualifications: [BA (Cantab) MPhil (Cantab) CPE]
✉ aranatunga@2-3gis.co.uk

RANDALL MISS HELEN JULIA

Iscoed Chambers
86 St Helen's Road, Swansea SA1 4BQ,
☎ 01792 652988
✉ clerks@iscoedchambers.co.uk
Call Date: July 2010, Middle Temple
Qualifications: [BA (Hons) (Oxon)]
✉ clerks@iscoedchambers.co.uk

RANDALL MR JOHN YEOMAN QC (1995)

St Philips Chambers
55 Temple Row, Birmingham B2 5LS,
☎ 0121 246 7000 ✉ clerks@st-philips.com
Maitland Chambers
7 Stone Buildings, Lincoln's Inn, London WC2A 3SZ, ☎ 020 7406 1200
✉ clerks@maitlandchambers.com
Call Date: July 1978, Lincoln's Inn
Recorder
Qualifications: [MA (Cantab)]
✉ jrandall@st-philips.co.uk

RANDALL MISS LOUISE ELIZABETH

Keating Chambers
15 Essex Street, London WC2R 3AA,
☎ 020 7544 2600
✉ clerks@keatingchambers.com
Call Date: July 1988, Middle Temple
Pupil Supervisor
Qualifications: [BA (Hons) (Keele)]
✉ lrandall@keatingchambers.com

RANDALL MR NICHOLAS CLIVE

Devereux Chambers
Queen Elizabeth Building, Temple, London EC4Y 9BS, ☎ 020 7353 7534
✉ clerks@devchambers.co.uk
Call Date: Oct 1990, Middle Temple
Qualifications: [LLB (Lond)]
✉ randall@devchambers.co.uk

RANDALL MRS REBECCA

25 Bedford Row
London WC1R 4HD, ☎ 020 7067 1500
✉ clerks@25bedfordrow.com
Call Date: July 2005, Gray's Inn
Qualifications: [BA]
✉ rrandall@25bedfordrow.com

RANDHAWA MISS RAVINDER KAUR

Dere Street Barristers
14 Toft Green, York YO1 6JT, ☎ 0844 3351551
✉ clerks@derestreet.co.uk
York Chambers
Rotterdam House, 116 The Quayside, Newcastle Upon Tyne NE1 3DY,
☎ 0191 206 4677
Call Date: Oct 1995, Lincoln's Inn
Qualifications: [LLB (Hons)(Leeds)]
✉ clerks@yorkchambers.co.uk

RANDLE MR SIMON PATRICK

Atlas Chambers
3 Field Court, Gray's Inn, London WC1R 5EP,
☎ 020 7269 7980
✉ clerks@atlaschambers.com
Call Date: July 1982, Inner Temple
Qualifications: [LLB (Hull)]
✉ randle@atlaschambers.com

RANDOLPH MR FERGUS MARK HARRY QC (2009)

Brick Court Chambers
7-8 Essex Street, London WC2R 3LD,
☎ 020 7379 3550 ✉ clerks@brickcourt.co.uk
Call Date: July 1985, Middle Temple
Qualifications: [LLB Dip French Law]
✉ Fergus.Randolph@Brickcourt.co.uk

RANDOLPH MR PAUL LESLIE

Field Court Chambers
5 Field Court, Gray's Inn, London WC1R 5EF,
☎ 020 7405 6114 ✉ clerks@fieldcourt.co.uk
Call Date: Nov 1971, Inner Temple
Pupil Supervisor
Qualifications: [LLB (Lond)]

RANK MR CHRISTOPHER WILLIAM

Cornwall Street Chambers
85-87 Cornwall Street, Birmingham B3 3BY,
☎ 0121 233 7500
✉ clerks@cornwallstreet.co.uk
Call Date: Oct 2008, Middle Temple
Qualifications: [LLB (Hons) (Staffs)]

RANKIN MR CIARAN EMMANUEL

Deans Court Chambers
24 St John Street, Manchester M3 4DF,
☎ 0161 214 6000 ✉ clerks@deanscourt.co.uk
Deans Court Chambers
101 Walker Street, Preston PR1 2RR,
☎ 01772 565 600
✉ preston@deanscourt.co.uk
Call Date: Nov 1988, Lincoln's Inn
Qualifications: [LLB (Hons)]

E

RANKIN MR JAMES ROWLAND EVELYN

Francis Taylor Building
Inner Temple, London EC4Y 7BY,
☎ 020 7353 8415 ✉ clerks@ftb.eu.com
Call Date: July 1983, Inner Temple
Pupil Supervisor
Qualifications: [LLB (Bucks)]
james.rankin@ftb.eu.com

RANKIN MR WILLIAM KERR

Oriel Chambers
14 Water Street, Liverpool, Merseyside
L2 8TD, ☎ 0151 236 7191
✉ clerks@orielchambers.co.uk
Oriel Chambers
18 Ribblesdale Place, Preston PR1 3NA,
☎ 01772 254 764
✉ clerks@oriel-chambers.co.uk
Call Date: Oct 1994, Gray's Inn
Pupil Supervisor
Qualifications: [LLB]
w.k.rankin@orielchambers.co.uk

RAPHAEL MR THOMAS GEOFFREY

20 Essex Street
London WC2R 3AL, ☎ 020 7842 1200
✉ clerks@20essexst.com
Call Date: Nov 1999, Middle Temple
Qualifications: [BA (Oxon) BA (Hons)(Cantab)]
clerks@20essexst.com

RAPP MR MICHAEL JAMES

Temple Garden Chambers
1 Harcourt Buildings, Temple, London
EC4Y 9DA, ☎ 020 7583 1315
✉ clerks@tgchambers.com
Call Date: July 2002, Inner Temple
Qualifications: [BA (Bris) CPE PGDL]
michaelrapp@tgchambers.com

RASHID MR HAROON

St James's Chambers
68 Quay Street, Manchester M3 3EJ,
☎ 0161 834 7000
✉ clerks@stjameschambers.com
Call Date: Mar 1999, Lincoln's Inn
Qualifications: [LLB (Hons)(Staffs) LLM (Manch)]
haroon.rashid@stjameschambers.com

RASHID MR MIRZA ABDUL

Commonwealth Chambers
354 Moseley Road, Birmingham B12 9AZ,
☎ 0121 446 5732
✉ mirzarashid786@hotmail.com
Call Date: Nov 1981, Lincoln's Inn
Qualifications: [BA LLB (Hons) MA]

RASHID MR SHAHID

Middlesex Chambers
89 Easton Street, High Wycombe HP11 1LT,
☎ 0203 1764186
✉ middlesexchambers@googlemail.com
Call Date: Nov 1982, Middle Temple
Qualifications: [BA (Hons) LLM]

RASHID MR WAQAS

Chartlands Chambers
3 St Giles Terrace, Northampton NN1 2BN,
☎ 01604 603322
✉ enquiries@chartlands-chambers.co.uk
Call Date: July 2006, Lincoln's Inn
Qualifications: [LLB (Wolves) LLM]
waq_rashid@yahoo.co.uk

RASIAH MR NATHAN

23 Essex Street
London WC2R 3AA, ☎ 020 7413 0353
✉ clerks@23es.com
Call Date: Nov 2007, Inner Temple
Qualifications: [BA (Cantab)]
nathanrasiah@23es.com

RASOUL MISS MIRIAM HAMEAN

Trinity Chambers
The Custom House, 39 Quayside, Newcastle
Upon Tyne NE1 3DE, ☎ 0191 232 1927
✉ info@trinitychambers.co.uk
Trinity Chambers
Multi Media Exchange, 72-80 Corporation
Road, Middlesbrough TS1 2RF,
☎ 01642 247569
✉ info@trinitychambers.co.uk
Call Date: July 2001, Lincoln's Inn
Qualifications: [BA (Hons) Law LLM]

RASUL MISS LUBNA

St Albans Chambers
2 - 4 St Peter's Street, St Albans, Hertfordshire
AL1 3LF, ☎ 01727 843383
✉ clerks@stalbanschambers.com
Call Date: Oct 1997, Middle Temple
Qualifications: [LLB (Hons)(Brunel)]
lr@stalbanschambers.com

RATCLIFFE MISS ANNE KIRKPATRICK

5 Pump Court
Ground Floor, 5 Pump Court, Temple, London
EC4Y 7AP, ☎ 020 7353 2532
✉ clerks@5pumpcourt.com
Call Date: Feb 1981, Inner Temple
Pupil Supervisor
Qualifications: [BSc (Soton) Dip Law]
anneratcliffe@5pumpcourt.com

RATCLIFFE MISS FRANCES ANNE

Radcliffe Chambers
Ground Floor, 11 New Square, Lincoln's Inn, London WC2A 3QB, ☎ 020 7831 0081
✉ clerks@radcliffechambers.com
Call Date: Oct 2002, Lincoln's Inn
Qualifications: [LLB (Exon)]
✉ fratcliffe@radcliffechambers.com

RATCLIFFE MR PETER DAVID

3 Verulam Buildings
London WC1R 5NT, ☎ 020 7831 8441
✉ chambers@3vb.com
Call Date: Oct 1998, Middle Temple
Pupil Supervisor
Qualifications: [BA (Hons) MA (Notts) CPE]
✉ pdratcliffe@3vb.com

RATHMELL MR ROBIN WILLIAM ALLEN GEORGE

Serle Court
6 New Square, Lincoln's Inn, London WC2A 3QS, ☎ 020 7242 6105
✉ clerks@serlecourt.co.uk
Call Date: Oct 2006, Inner Temple
Qualifications: [MA Cantab)]
✉ rrathmell@serlecourt.co.uk

RATHOD MR PRITESH

1 Crown Office Row
1 Crown Office Row, Temple, London EC4Y 7HH, ☎ 020 7797 7500
✉ mail@1cor.com
Call Date: July 2006, Middle Temple
Qualifications: [LLB (Hons) (Lond)]
✉ pritesh.rathod@1cor.com

RATLEDGE MR JOHN

Call Date: Nov 1999, Lincoln's Inn
Qualifications: [BA (Hons) MPhil (Cantab)]

RATLIFF MR JOHN HARRISON

Henderson Chambers
2 Harcourt Buildings, Temple, London EC4Y 9DB, ☎ 020 7583 9020
✉ clerks@hendersonchambers.co.uk
Call Date: July 1980, Middle Temple
Pupil Supervisor
Qualifications: [BA (Oxon) Dip European Integration (Holland)]

RATLIFF MR PETER DAVID

6 King's Bench Walk
Ground Floor, 6 King's Bench Walk, Temple, London EC4Y 7DR, ☎ 020 7583 0410
✉ clerks@6kbw.com
Call Date: Oct 2003, Lincoln's Inn
Qualifications: [LLB (Hons) (Sheff)]
✉ peter.ratliff@6kbw.com

RAUDNITZ MR PAUL NIKOLAI

QEB Hollis Whiteman
1-2 Laurence Pountney Hill, London EC4R 0EU, ☎ 020 7933 8855
✉ barristers@qebhw.co.uk
Call Date: Nov 1994, Inner Temple
Pupil Supervisor
Qualifications: [BA (Oxon) CPE]

RAW MR EDWARD

Tanfield Chambers
2-5 Warwick Court, London WC1R 5DJ,
☎ 020 7421 5300
✉ clerks@tanfieldchambers.co.uk
Call Date: July 1963, Inner Temple
Pupil Supervisor
Qualifications: [MA (Oxon)]

RAWAL MISS ANITA

Chambers of Mr Ami Feder
Ground Floor, Lamb Building, Temple, London EC4Y 7AS, ☎ 020 7797 7788
✉ clerks@lambbuilding.co.uk
Lamb Building
22 Ship Street, Brighton BN1 1AD,
☎ 01273 820490
✉ admin@lambbuilding.co.uk
Chambers of Mr Ami Feder
Ground Floor, Lamb Building, Temple, London EC4Y 7AS, ☎ 020 7797 7788
✉ clerks@lambbuilding.co.uk
Call Date: Oct 2004, Middle Temple
Qualifications: [LLB (Hons)]

RAWAT MR BILAL MAHMAD

Seven Bedford Row
7 Bedford Row, London WC1R 4BS,
☎ 020 7242 3555 ✉ clerks@7br.co.uk
Call Date: Oct 1995, Middle Temple
Pupil Supervisor
Qualifications: [B.Sc (Hons) PhD Dip Law]
✉ brawat@7br.co.uk

E

RAWAT MISS HOUZLA BIBI MAHMAD

Carmelite Chambers
9 Carmelite Street, London EC4Y 0DR,
☎ 020 7936 6300
✉ clerks@carmelitechambers.co.uk
Call Date: Oct 2001, Middle Temple
Qualifications: [BSc (Hons) CPE]
✉ hrawat@carmelitechambers.co.uk

RAWAT MRS ISMET PARVEEN

Hermitage Court Chambers
117a-117b Inwood Road, Hounslow, Middlesex TW3 1XJ, ☎ 07852 146056
✉ hermitagecourtchambers@gmx.com
Conference Chambers
P.O. Box 626, Harrow, Middlesex HA2 2DZ,
☎ 020 8144 0134
✉ carole@conferencechambers.com
Call Date: Nov 1992, Inner Temple
Qualifications: [BA (Hons) LLM (Lond)]

RAWCLIFFE MR ANTHONY MARK WILSON

4 Brick Court
4 Brick Court, Temple, London EC4Y 9AD,
☎ 020 7832 3200 ✉ clerks@4bc.co.uk
Call Date: Nov 1996, Middle Temple
Qualifications: [BA (Hons) LLM]
✉ mark.rawcliffe@4bc.co.uk

RAWLEY MR ALAN DAVID QC (1977)

Outer Temple Chambers
The Outer Temple, 222 Strand, London WC2R 1BA, ☎ 020 7353 6381
✉ clerks@outertemple.com
Call Date: June 1958, Middle Temple
Recorder
Qualifications: [MA (Oxon)]

RAWLEY MISS DOMINIQUE JANE QC (2012)

Atkin Chambers
1 Atkin Building, Gray's Inn, London WC1R 5AT, ☎ 020 7404 0102
✉ clerks@atkinchambers.com
Call Date: Nov 1991, Middle Temple
Pupil Supervisor
Qualifications: [BA (Hons) (Cantab)]
✉ clerks@atkinchambers.com

RAWLINGS MISS CARRIE-ANN

King's Bench and Godolphin (KBG)Chambers
115 North Hill, Plymouth, Devon PL4 8JY,
☎ 01752 221551
✉ clerks@kbgchambers.co.uk
Call Date: Oct 2005, Inner Temple
Qualifications: [LLB University of Birmingham]
✉ carrie-anne@kingsbenchchambers.co.uk

RAWLINGS MR CLIVE PATRICK

Hardwicke
New Square, Lincoln's Inn, London WC2A 3SB, ☎ 020 7242 2523
✉ enquiries@hardwicke.co.uk
Call Date: Nov 1994, Inner Temple
Pupil Supervisor
Qualifications: [BA (Hons) (Bradford) CPE (Middx)]
✉ clive.rawlings@hardwicke.co.uk

RAWLINSON MR MICHAEL EDWARD QC (2009)

Kings Chambers
36 Young Street, Manchester M3 3FT,
☎ 0845 034 3444
✉ clerks@kingschambers.com
Kings Chambers
5 Park Square East, Leeds LS1 2NE,
☎ 0845 034 3444
✉ clerks@kingschambers.com
12 King's Bench Walk
12 King's Bench Walk, Temple, London EC4Y 7EL, ☎ 020 7583 0811
Call Date: Nov 1991, Inner Temple
Qualifications: [LLB (Manch)]

RAWLINSON MR MICHAEL JOHN

Call Date: Mar 2002, Lincoln's Inn
Qualifications: [LLB (Hons) (Manch)]
✉ rawlinson@paradise-sq.co.uk

RAY MR JONATHAN RICHARD

Thomas More Chambers
7 Lincoln's Inn Fields, London WC2A 3BP,
☎ 020 7404 7000
✉ clerks@thomasmore.co.uk
Call Date: July 1980, Gray's Inn
Pupil Supervisor
Qualifications: [BA (Hons)]
✉ clerks@thomasmore.co.uk

E

RAY MR SIMON JAMES FRANCIS

6 King's Bench Walk
Ground Floor, 6 King's Bench Walk, Temple, London EC4Y 7DR, ☎ 020 7583 0410
✉ clerks@6kbw.com
Call Date: Nov 2001, Gray's Inn
Qualifications: [BA Hons (Dunelm)]
✉ simon.ray@6kbw.com

RAY-CROSBY MISS IRENA WYVIS

Westgate Chambers
64 High Street, Lewes, East Sussex BN7 1XG, ☎ 01273 480510
✉ clerks@westgate-chambers.co.uk
Call Date: Nov 1990, Middle Temple
Pupil Supervisor
Qualifications: [MA (Oxon)]
✉ irc@westgate-chambers.co.uk

RAYMENT MR BENEDICK MICHAEL

Monckton Chambers
1 & 2 Raymond Buildings, Gray's Inn, London WC1R 5NR, ☎ 020 7405 7211
✉ chambers@monckton.com
Call Date: Oct 1996, Inner Temple
Qualifications: [MA (Hons) BCL (Oxon)]
✉ brayment@monckton.com

RAYNER MS CATHERINE ELIZABETH

Tooks Chambers
81 Farringdon Street, London EC4A 4BL, ☎ 020 7842 7575 ✉ clerks@tooks.co.uk
Call Date: Nov 1988, Gray's Inn
Qualifications: [LLB]
✉ catherine.rayner@tooks.co.uk

RAYNER MISS EMILY ELIZABETH

Harcourt Chambers
1st Floor, 2 Harcourt Buildings, Temple, London EC4Y 9DB, ☎ 0844 561 7135
Harcourt Chambers
Churchill House, 3 St Aldate's Courtyard, St Aldate's, Oxford OX1 1BN, ☎ 0844 561 7135
Call Date: July 2009, Middle Temple
Qualifications: [BA (Hons) (Cantab) LLM]
✉ erayner@harcourtchambers.law.co.uk

RAYNER JAMES MR JONATHAN ELWYN QC (1988)

Hogarth Chambers
5 New Square, Lincoln's Inn, London WC2A 3RJ, ☎ 020 7404 0404
✉ barristers@hogarthchambers.com
Call Date: Nov 1971, Lincoln's Inn
Qualifications: [MA Lic.Sp.en droit Eur LLM (Cantab)]
✉ barristers@hogarthchambers.com

RAYNOR MR KEITH HUGH

23 Essex Street
London WC2R 3AA, ☎ 020 7413 0353
✉ clerks@23es.com
Call Date: Oct 1995, Lincoln's Inn
Qualifications: [LLB (Hons) (Nott'm)]
✉ keithraynor@23es.com

RAYSON MISS JANE VIVIENNE

4 Paper Buildings
1st Floor, 4 Paper Buildings, Temple, London EC4Y 7EX, ☎ 020 7427 5200
✉ clerks@4pb.com
Call Date: July 1982, Gray's Inn
Pupil Supervisor
Qualifications: [LLB (Hons)]
✉ jvr@4pb.com

REA MISS KAREN MARIE-JEANNE

Queen Square Chambers
56 Queen Square, Bristol BS1 4PR, ☎ 0117 921 1966 ✉ crime@qs-c.co.uk
Call Date: July 1980, Gray's Inn
Pupil Supervisor
Qualifications: [BA RGN]

READ MR DANIEL JAMES

Farrar's Building
Farrar's Building, Temple, London EC4Y 7BD, ☎ 020 7583 9241
✉ Chambers@farrarsbuilding.co.uk
Call Date: Oct 2006, Gray's Inn
Qualifications: [BA]
✉ dread@farrarsbuilding.co.uk

READ MISS EMILY MARY

12 King's Bench Walk
12 King's Bench Walk, Temple, London EC4Y 7EL, ☎ 020 7583 0811
Call Date: July 2007, Middle Temple
Qualifications: [BA (Hons) (Cantab) MA (Cantab)]
✉ read@12kbw.co.uk

READ MISS EMMA

One Essex Court
1st Floor, Temple, London EC4Y 9AR, ☎ 020 7936 3030 ✉ clerks@1ec.co.uk
Call Date: Nov 2006, Inner Temple
Qualifications: [BSc (Lond)]

E

READ MR GRAHAM STEPHEN QC (2003)

Devereux Chambers
Queen Elizabeth Building, Temple, London EC4Y 9BS, ☎ 020 7353 7534
✉ clerks@devchambers.co.uk
Call Date: July 1981, Gray's Inn
Qualifications: [MA (Cantab)]
read@devchambers.co.uk

READ MISS SARAH ANN

2 Dr Johnson's Buildings
2 Dr Johnson's Buildings, Temple, London EC4Y 7AY, ☎ 020 7936 2613
✉ clerks@2drj.com
Call Date: Oct 2006, Lincoln's Inn
Qualifications: [LLB (Lond)]
clerks@2drj.com

READ MR SIMON ERIC

Zenith Chambers
10 Park Square, Leeds LS1 2LH,
☎ 0113 245 5438
✉ clerks@zenithchambers.co.uk
Call Date: Nov 1989, Inner Temple
Qualifications: [LLB (Warc)]
sread@zenithchambers.co.uk

READE MR DAVID JARRETT QC (2006)

Littleton Chambers
3 King's Bench Walk North, Temple, London EC4Y 7HR, ☎ 020 7797 8600
✉ fschneider@littletonchambers.co.uk
Park Lane Plowden
19 Westgate, Leeds LS1 2RD,
☎ 0113 228 5049
✉ clerks@parklaneplowden.co.uk
Call Date: July 1983, Middle Temple
Qualifications: [LLB (B'ham)]
dreade@littletonchambers.co.uk

READE MR KEVIN

Number 7 Harrington Street Chambers
7 Harrington Street, Liverpool L2 9YH,
☎ 0151 242 0707 ✉ clerks@7hs.co.uk
Call Date: July 1983, Gray's Inn
Qualifications: [LLB (Hons)(L'pool)]
kevin.reade@7hs.co.uk

READHEAD MR SIMON JOHN HOWARD QC (2006)

1 Chancery Lane
London WC2A 1LF, ☎ 0845 634 6666
✉ clerks@1chancerylane.com
Call Date: July 1979, Middle Temple
Recorder
Qualifications: [BCL MA (Oxon)]
sreadhead@1chancerylane.com

READINGS MR DOUGLAS GEORGE

St Philips Chambers
55 Temple Row, Birmingham B2 5LS,
☎ 0121 246 7000 ✉ clerks@st-philips.com
Call Date: July 1972, Middle Temple
Recorder
Qualifications: [MA (Cantab) FCIArb]
dreadings@st-philips.co.uk

READY MISS HANNAH KATE

One Brick Court
1st Floor, One Brick Court, Temple, London EC4Y 9BY, ☎ 020 7353 8845
✉ clerks@onebrickcourt.com
Call Date: Oct 2010, Lincoln's Inn
Qualifications: [BA (Cantab)]
clerks@onebrickcourt.com

REAL MISS KIRSTY NICHOLA

Albion Chambers
Broad Street, Bristol BS1 1DR,
☎ 0117 927 2144
✉ clerks@albionchambers.co.uk
Call Date: Oct 1996, Inner Temple
Qualifications: [LLB (Notts)]
kirsty.real@albionchambers.co.uk

REANEY MISS JANET ELIZABETH

Number 7 Harrington Street Chambers
7 Harrington Street, Liverpool L2 9YH,
☎ 0151 242 0707 ✉ clerks@7hs.co.uk
Call Date: July 1987, Middle Temple
Qualifications: [MA (Cantab)]
janet.reaney@7hs.co.uk

REARDON MISS MADELEINE JENNY

1 KBW Chambers
1 King's Bench Walk, Temple, London EC4Y 7DB, ☎ 020 7936 1500
✉ clerks@1kbw.co.uk
King's Bench Chambers
174 High Street, Lewes BN7 1YE,
☎ 01273 402600
Call Date: Nov 2001, Middle Temple
Qualifications: [BA (Hons)(Oxon) Dip Law]

RECORD MRS CELIA SAINT CLAIRE

Chambers of Lawrence Jones
8 Stone Buildings, Lincoln's Inn, London WC2A 3TA, ☎ 020 7831 1444
✉ clerks@8stonebuildings.com
Call Date: Mar 1998, Middle Temple
Qualifications: [LLB (Hons)]

REDDIFORD MR ANTHONY JAMES

Guildhall Chambers
23 Broad Street, Bristol BS1 2HG,
☎ 0117 930 9000
✉ hoc@guildhallchambers.co.uk
Call Date: Nov 1991, Inner Temple
Pupil Supervisor
Qualifications: [BA (Warw) Dip Law]
✉ anthony.reddiford@guildhallchambers.co.uk

REDDISH MR JOHN WILSON

1 KBW Chambers
1 King's Bench Walk, Temple, London EC4Y 7DB, ☎ 020 7936 1500
✉ clerks@1kbw.co.uk
King's Bench Chambers
174 High Street, Lewes BN7 1YE,
☎ 01273 402600
Call Date: July 1973, Middle Temple
Pupil Supervisor
Qualifications: [MA (Oxon)]
✉ jreddish@1kbw.co.uk

REDFERN MR DAVID ALAN

One Essex Court
Ground Floor, One Essex Court, Temple, London EC4Y 9AR, ☎ 020 7583 2000
✉ clerks@oeclaw.co.uk
Call Date: May 1995, Middle Temple
Qualifications: [MA (Cantab) FCIArb]
✉ aredfern@oeclaw.co.uk

REDFERN MR MICHAEL HOWARD QC (1993)

St Johns Buildings
24a - 28 St John Street, Manchester M3 4DJ,
☎ 0161 214 1500
✉ clerk@stjohnsbuildings.co.uk
St Johns Buildings
21 White Friars, Chester CH1 1NZ,
☎ 01244 323070
✉ clerk@stjohnsbuildings.co.uk
16 Winckley Square
Preston PR1 3JJ, ☎ 01772 256100
Call Date: July 1970, Inner Temple
Recorder
Qualifications: [LLB (Leeds)]
✉ cronan@stjohnsbuildings.co.uk, michael.redfern@stjohnsbuildings.co.uk

REDGRAVE MR ADRIAN ROBERT FRANK QC (1992)

13 King's Bench Walk
13 King's Bench Walk, Temple, London EC4Y 7EN, ☎ 020 7353 7204
✉ clerks@13kbw.co.uk
13 KBW
32 Beaumont Street, Oxford OX1 2NP,
☎ 01865 311066 ✉ clerks@13kbw.co.uk
Citadel Chambers
The Citadel, 190 Corporation Street, Birmingham B4 6QD, ☎ 0121 233 8500
✉ clerks@citadelchambers.com
Call Date: Nov 1968, Inner Temple
Qualifications: [LLB]

REDHEAD MR LEROY PETER BASIL

25 Bedford Row
London WC1R 4HD, ☎ 020 7067 1500
✉ clerks@25bedfordrow.com
Call Date: Nov 1982, Lincoln's Inn
Qualifications: [LLB (Lond) LLM]
✉ lredhead@25bedfordrow.com

REDLEY MR CLIVE GODFREY

Tooks Chambers
81 Farringdon Street, London EC4A 4BL,
☎ 020 7842 7575 ✉ clerks@tooks.co.uk
Call Date: Nov 2010, Inner Temple
Qualifications: [LLB]
✉ clive.redley@tooks.co.uk

REDMAYNE MR SIMON MARK

East Anglian Chambers
15 The Close, Norwich, Norfolk NR1 4DZ,
☎ 01473 214481 ✉ norwich@ealaw.co.uk
East Anglian Chambers
53 North Hill, Colchester, Essex CO1 1QA,
☎ 01473 214481 ✉ colchester@ealaw.co.uk
East Anglian Chambers
140 New London Road, Chelmsford, Essex CM2 0AW, ☎ 01473 214481
✉ chelmsford@ealaw.co.uk
East Anglian Chambers
Gresham House, 5 Museum Street, Ipswich, Suffolk IP1 1HQ, ☎ 01473 214481
✉ ipswich@ealaw.co.uk
Call Date: July 1982, Inner Temple
Pupil Supervisor
Qualifications: [BA (Oxon)]
✉ sr@ealaw.co.uk

REDMOND MRS CHRISTINE LOUISE

Chavasse Court Chambers
18 Queen Avenue, Liverpool L2 4TX,
☎ 0151 229 2030
✉ clerks@chavassechambers.co.uk
Call Date: Nov 2006, Inner Temple
Qualifications: [BA (Cantab)]

E

REDMOND MR DAVID VICTOR JOHN

St Albans Chambers
2 - 4 St Peter's Street, St Albans, Hertfordshire AL1 3LF, ☎ 01727 843383
✉ clerks@stalbanschambers.com
Call Date: Oct 2006, Middle Temple
Qualifications: [LLB (Hons) (Herts) LLM]
dr@stalbanschambers.com

REDMOND MS HELEN

9 St John Street
Manchester M3 4DN, ☎ 0161 955 9000
✉ civilclerks@9sjs.com / criminalclerks@9sjs.com
Call Date: Oct 1999, Gray's Inn
Qualifications: [LLB LLM (L'pool)]

REDMOND MR JACK WARREN

St Philips Chambers
55 Temple Row, Birmingham B2 5LS, ☎ 0121 246 7000 ✉ clerks@st-philips.com
Call Date: July 2009, Gray's Inn
Qualifications: [BA MA]
jredmond@st-philips.com

REDMOND MR STEVEN

Citadel Chambers
The Citadel, 190 Corporation Street, Birmingham B4 6QD, ☎ 0121 233 8500
✉ clerks@citadelchambers.com
Call Date: July 1975, Gray's Inn
Pupil Supervisor
Qualifications: [BA]
clerks@citadelchambers.com

REDPATH MR JOHN SCOTT

Exchange Chambers
7 Ralli Courts, West Riverside, Manchester M3 5FT, ☎ 0161 833 2722
Exchange Chambers
One Derby Square, Derby Square, Liverpool L2 9XX, ☎ 0151 236 7747
✉ info@exchangechambers.co.uk
Exchange Chambers
Oxford House, Oxford Row, Leeds LS1 3BE, ☎ 0113 203 1970
✉ spencer@exchangechambers.co.uk
Temple Tax Chambers
1st Floor, 3 Temple Gardens, Temple, London EC4Y 9AU, ☎ 020 7353 7884
✉ clerks@templetax.com
Call Date: Oct 1996, Middle Temple
Qualifications: [BA (Hons) MA (Hons) (Lond)]
redpath@exchangechambers.co.uk

REDPATH-STEVENS MR ALASTAIR YATES

Hardwicke
New Square, Lincoln's Inn, London WC2A 3SB, ☎ 020 7242 2523
✉ enquiries@hardwicke.co.uk
Call Date: Oct 1998, Middle Temple
Qualifications: [BSc (Bris) Dip Housing Dip Law MA]
alastair.redpath-stevens@hardwicke.co.uk

REDSTON MS ANNE

Temple Tax Chambers
1st Floor, 3 Temple Gardens, Temple, London EC4Y 9AU, ☎ 020 7353 7884
✉ clerks@templetax.com
Call Date: Nov 2009, Middle Temple
Qualifications: [MA (Oxon) LLB (Hons)]
clerks@templetax.com

REECE MR BRIAN ALFRED WILLIAM

187 Fleet Street
London EC4A 2AT, ☎ 020 7430 7430
✉ chambers@187fleetstreet.com
Call Date: July 1974, Middle Temple
Pupil Supervisor
Qualifications: [LLB (Lond)]

REECE MR JASON

St Mary's Family Law Chambers
26-28 High Pavement, The Lace Market, Nottingham NG1 1HN, ☎ 0115 950 3503
✉ clerks@stmarysflc.co.uk
Call Date: Nov 2000, Inner Temple
Pupil Supervisor
Qualifications: [BA MPhil PGCE (Cantab) PGDL]
reece.jason@stmarysflc.co.uk

REECE MR RUPERT VAUGHAN PAYNTER

2 Temple Gardens
2 Temple Gardens, Temple, London EC4Y 9AY, ☎ 020 7822 1200
✉ clerks@2tg.co.uk
Call Date: Oct 1992, Inner Temple
Qualifications: [BA (Cantab) DESS (France) Examen D'aptitude (France)]
clerks@2tg.co.uk

REED MISS EMMA

Old Bailey Chambers
15 Old Bailey, London EC4M 7EF, ☎ 020 3008 6404
✉ clerks@15oldbaileychambers.com
Call Date: July 2004, Lincoln's Inn
Qualifications: [LLB Hons (Lond)]

E

REED MR JEREMY NIGEL

Hogarth Chambers
5 New Square, Lincoln's Inn, London
WC2A 3RJ, ☎ 020 7404 0404
✉ barristers@hogarthchambers.com
Call Date: Oct 1997, Middle Temple
Pupil Supervisor
Qualifications: [MA (Hons)(Cantab) CPE (Lond)]
jreed@hogarthchambers.com

Types of work: Commercial litigation, Confidential information, Copyright, Copyright Tribunal, Design, EC competition law, Information technology, Intellectual property, Media and entertainment, Passing off, Patents, Privacy, Scientific and technical disputes, Trade secrets, Trademarks

REED MR JOHN WILLIAM RUPERT

Wilberforce Chambers
8 New Square, Lincoln's Inn, London
WC2A 3QP, ☎ 020 7306 0102
✉ chambers@wilberforce.co.uk
Call Date: Oct 1996, Lincoln's Inn
Pupil Supervisor
Qualifications: [BA (Hons)(Oxon) BA (Hons)(Cantab) LLM]
rreed@wilberforce.co.uk

REED MR JULIAN WINN

9 Park Place
9 Park Place, Cardiff, South Glamorgan
CF10 3DP, ☎ 029 2038 2731
✉ clerks@9parkplace.co.uk
Call Date: Nov 1991, Inner Temple
Qualifications: [LLB]
j.reed@9parkplace.co.uk, julian.reed@ymail.com

REED MS LUCY EMMA

St John's Chambers
101 Victoria Street, Bristol BS1 6PU,
☎ 0117 923 4700
✉ clerks@stjohnschambers.co.uk
Call Date: Oct 2002, Lincoln's Inn
Qualifications: [BA (Exon) Mres PgDL]

REED MR MATTHEW ROBERT

Landmark Chambers
180 Fleet Street, London EC4A 2HG,
☎ 020 7430 1221
✉ clerks@landmarkchambers.co.uk
Call Date: Nov 1995, Middle Temple
Pupil Supervisor
Qualifications: [MA (Hons)]
mreed@landmarkchambers.co.uk

REED MR PAUL STUART MALCOLM QC (2010)

Hardwicke
New Square, Lincoln's Inn, London
WC2A 3SB, ☎ 020 7242 2523
✉ enquiries@hardwicke.co.uk
Call Date: July 1988, Inner Temple
Pupil Supervisor
Qualifications: [LLB ACIArb MSc]

REED MISS PENELOPE JANE QC (2009)

5 Stone Buildings
5 Stone Buildings, Lincoln's Inn, London
WC2A 3XT, ☎ 020 7242 6201
✉ clerks@5sblaw.com
Call Date: July 1983, Inner Temple
Qualifications: [LLB (Lond)]
preed@5sblaw.com

REED MR PIERS KNOWLE MOORHOUSE

3 Temple Gardens
Lower Ground Floor, 3 Temple Gardens,
Temple, London EC4Y 9AU, ☎ 020 7353 3102
✉ clerks@3tg.co.uk
Call Date: Nov 1974, Lincoln's Inn
Pupil Supervisor
pr@3tg.co.uk

REED MR SIMON JOHN

New Walk Chambers
27 New Walk, Leicester, Leicestershire
LE1 6TE, ☎ 0871 200 1298 / 0116 255 9144
✉ clerks@newwalkchambers.co.uk
Call Date: Mar 1998, Gray's Inn
Pupil Supervisor
Qualifications: [BA (Lou'brgh)]

REED MR STEVEN WILLIAM

No5 Chambers
Fountain Court, Steelhouse Lane, Birmingham
B4 6DR, ☎ 0845 210 5555 ✉ info@no5.com
No5 Chambers
Greenwood House, 4-7 Salisbury Court,
London EC4Y 8AA, ☎ 0845 210 5555
No5 Chambers
38 Queen Square, Bristol BS1 4QS,
☎ 0845 210 5555
Call Date: July 2005, Inner Temple
Qualifications: [LLB LLM (Lond)]
srt@no5.com

E

REED MISS SUSAN CATHERINE

Seven Bedford Row
7 Bedford Row, London WC1R 4BS,
☎ 020 7242 3555 ✉ clerks@7br.co.uk
Call Date: July 1984, Gray's Inn
Pupil Supervisor
Qualifications: [LLB (Manch)]
sreed@7br.co.uk

REEDER MR JOHN QC (1989)

Stone Chambers
4 Field Court, Gray's Inn, London WC1R 5EF,
☎ 020 7440 6900
✉ clerks@stonechambers.com
Call Date: July 1971, Gray's Inn
Qualifications: [LLM PhD]
john.reeder@stonechambers.com

REEDER MR STEPHEN

Doughty Street Chambers
53-54 Doughty Street, London WC1N 2LS,
☎ 020 7404 1313
✉ enquiries@doughtystreet.co.uk
Doughty Street Chambers
Pall Mall Court, 61-67 King Street, Manchester M2 4PD, ☎ 0161 618 1066
Doughty Street Chambers
5th Floor, Broad Quay House, Prince Street, Bristol BS1 4DJ, ☎ 01179 058 717
Call Date: Nov 1991, Middle Temple
Pupil Supervisor
Qualifications: [LLB (Hons) CEDR]

REEDS MR GARETH DAVID

Canary Wharf Chambers
Level 33, 25 Canada Square, London E14 5LQ,
☎ 020 7183 8011
✉ admin@canarywharfchambers.com
Call Date: Oct 2001, Lincoln's Inn
Qualifications: [LLB European (Hons), LLM European Busin. (Hons), Dip German Law, Attorney of the State of New York, USA]

Fax: 020 7183 8830
Other comms: Tel: 001 (212) 202 0822 (NY)
URL: www.canarywharfchambers.com

Types of work: Arbitration, Chancery (general), Charities, Commercial law, Commercial litigation, Commercial property, Company, commercial and competition, Competition law, Conflict of laws, Consumer law, EC competition law, Employment, Financial services, Foreign law, German law, Insolvency, Landlord and tenant, New York law, Personal insolvency

REES MISS CAROLINE ELIZABETH

30 Park Place
Cardiff CF10 3BS, ☎ 029 2039 8421
✉ clerks@30parkplace.law.co.uk
Call Date: Oct 1994, Gray's Inn
Qualifications: [LLB]
cr@30parkplace.co.uk

REES MR CHRISTOPHER LLOYD

Apex
Harlech House, 20 Cathedral Road, Cardiff CF11 9LJ, ☎ 02920 232 032
✉ clerks@apexchambers.net
Call Date: Nov 1996, Lincoln's Inn
Qualifications: [BA (Cantab)]
christopher.rees@apexchambers.net

REES MR DAVID BENJAMIN

5 Stone Buildings
5 Stone Buildings, Lincoln's Inn, London WC2A 3XT, ☎ 020 7242 6201
✉ clerks@5sblaw.com
Call Date: Oct 1994, Lincoln's Inn
Pupil Supervisor
Qualifications: [BA (Hons) (Oxon)]
drees@5sblaw.com

REES MR EDWARD PARRY QC (1998)

Doughty Street Chambers
53-54 Doughty Street, London WC1N 2LS,
☎ 020 7404 1313
✉ enquiries@doughtystreet.co.uk
Doughty Street Chambers
Pall Mall Court, 61-67 King Street, Manchester M2 4PD, ☎ 0161 618 1066
Doughty Street Chambers
5th Floor, Broad Quay House, Prince Street, Bristol BS1 4DJ, ☎ 01179 058 717
Call Date: Feb 1973, Gray's Inn
Qualifications: [LLB (Wales)]
e.rees@doughtystreet.co.uk

REES MR HEFIN EDNYFED

39 Essex Street
London WC2R 3AT, ☎ 020 7832 1111
✉ clerks@39essex.com
Call Date: Nov 1992, Inner Temple
Pupil Supervisor
Qualifications: [BA (Hons)(Dunelm)]
hefin.rees@39essex.com

REES MR IEUAN

Angel Chambers
Ethos Building, Kings Road, Swansea SA1 8AS, ☎ 01792 464623
✉ clerks@angelchambers.co.uk
Call Date: Nov 1982, Gray's Inn
Pupil Supervisor
Qualifications: [BSc (Cardiff)]
✉ clerks@angelchambers.co.uk

REES MR JAMES WILLIAM STEWART

Southernhay Chambers
33 Southernhay East, Exeter EX1 1NX, ☎ 01392 255777
✉ clerks@southernhaychambers.co.uk
Call Date: Nov 1994, Gray's Inn
Pupil Supervisor
Qualifications: [BA (Hons) (Dunelm)]
✉ j.rees@southernhaychambers.co.uk

REES MR JOHN CHARLES QC (1991)

Chambers of Mr J C Rees QC
Sophia House, 28 Cathedral Road, Cardiff CF11 9LJ, ☎ 02920 233 313
✉ clerks@jcrqc.com
Exchange Chambers
7 Ralli Courts, West Riverside, Manchester M3 5FT, ☎ 0161 833 2722
Furnival Chambers
32 Furnival Street, London EC4A 1JQ, ☎ 020 7405 3232
Call Date: July 1972, Lincoln's Inn
Qualifications: [LLB (Cantab) LLM (Cantab)]

REES MR JONATHAN DAVID QC (2010)

2 Hare Court
Lower Ground, Ground, 1st & 2nd Floor, 2 Hare Court, Temple, London EC4Y 7BH, ☎ 020 7353 3982 ✉ clerks@2harecourt.com
Call Date: Nov 1987, Gray's Inn
Pupil Supervisor, Recorder
Qualifications: [BA (Oxon)]
✉ jonathanrees@2harecourt.com

REES MR JONATHAN ELYSTAN

Apex
Harlech House, 20 Cathedral Road, Cardiff CF11 9LJ, ☎ 02920 232 032
✉ clerks@apexchambers.net
Call Date: Oct 2000, Inner Temple
Qualifications: [BA (Cantab)]
✉ jonathan.rees@apexchambers.net

REES MR MATTHEW

Angel Chambers
Ethos Building, Kings Road, Swansea SA1 8AS, ☎ 01792 464623
✉ clerks@angelchambers.co.uk
Call Date: Oct 1996, Gray's Inn
Pupil Supervisor
Qualifications: [LLB]
✉ matthewrees@angelchambers.co.uk

REES MISS NAOMI ANGELIQUE

3 PB Barristers
3 Paper Buildings, Temple, London EC4Y 7EU, ☎ 020 7583 8055
3 PB Barristers
4 St Peter Street, Winchester SO23 8BW, ☎ 01962 868884
✉ clerks.winchester@3paper.co.uk
Call Date: July 2006, Middle Temple
Qualifications: [LLB (Hons) (Lond)]
✉ naomi.rees@3pb.co.uk

REES MR OWEN HUW

Iscoed Chambers
86 St Helen's Road, Swansea SA1 4BQ, ☎ 01792 652988
✉ clerks@iscoedchambers.co.uk
Call Date: July 1983, Gray's Inn
Pupil Supervisor, Recorder
Qualifications: [LLB (Wales)]
✉ hr@iscoedchambers.co.uk

REES MR PAUL STUART QC (2000)

1 Crown Office Row
1 Crown Office Row, Temple, London EC4Y 7HH, ☎ 020 7797 7500
✉ mail@1cor.com
Call Date: Nov 1980, Gray's Inn
Qualifications: [MA BCL (Oxon) M Phil]
✉ paul.rees@1cor.com

REES MR ROBERT CHARLES DAVID

New Walk Chambers
27 New Walk, Leicester, Leicestershire LE1 6TE, ☎ 0871 200 1298 / 0116 255 9144
✉ clerks@newwalkchambers.co.uk
Call Date: Feb 1978, Middle Temple
Pupil Supervisor
Qualifications: [BA LLB]

E

REES MR STEPHEN ROBERT TRISTRAM

Iscoed Chambers
86 St Helen's Road, Swansea SA1 4BQ,
☎01792 652988
✉clerks@iscoedchambers.co.uk
Call Date: Nov 1979, Gray's Inn
Pupil Supervisor
Qualifications: [LLB (Wales)]
✉sr@iscoedchambers.co.uk

REES PROF WILLIAM MICHAEL

1 Gray's Inn Square
Ground Floor, 1 Gray's Inn Square, London
WC1R 5AA, ☎020 7405 0001
Call Date: July 1973, Inner Temple
Qualifications: [MA (Cantab)]

REESE MR COLIN EDWARD QC (1987)

Atkin Chambers
1 Atkin Building, Gray's Inn, London
WC1R 5AT, ☎020 7404 0102
✉clerks@atkinchambers.com
Call Date: July 1973, Gray's Inn
Qualifications: [MA (Cantab) FCIArb]
✉clerks@atkinchambers.com

REEVE MR MATTHEW FRANCIS

Quadrant Chambers
Quadrant House, 10 Fleet Street, London
EC4Y 1AU, ☎020 7583 4444
✉info@quadrantchambers.com
Call Date: Nov 1987, Inner Temple
Pupil Supervisor
Qualifications: [MA (Cantab)]
✉matthew.reeve@quadrantchambers.com

REEVE MISS VERONICA ELLEN

Chambers of Mr Ami Feder
Ground Floor, Lamb Building, Temple, London
EC4Y 7AS, ☎020 7797 7788
✉clerks@lambbuilding.co.uk
Lamb Building
22 Ship Street, Brighton BN1 1AD,
☎01273 820490
✉admin@lambbuilding.co.uk
Chambers of Mr Ami Feder
Ground Floor, Lamb Building, Temple, London
EC4Y 7AS, ☎020 7797 7788
✉clerks@lambbuilding.co.uk
Call Date: July 2004, Inner Temple
Qualifications: [BA MA (Oxon)]
✉clerks@lambbuilding.co.uk

REEVELL MRS LOUISE MARIE

39 Park Square
Leeds LS1 2NU, ☎0113 245 6633
✉seniorclerk@39parksquarechambers.co.uk
Call Date: Oct 2001, Lincoln's Inn
Qualifications: [LLB (Hons)]

REEVELL MR SIMON JUSTIN

39 Park Square
Leeds LS1 2NU, ☎0113 245 6633
✉seniorclerk@39parksquarechambers.co.uk
Call Date: Oct 1990, Lincoln's Inn
Pupil Supervisor
Qualifications: [BA (Econs) Dip Law]

REEVES MISS SIAN

Temple Garden Chambers
1 Harcourt Buildings, Temple, London
EC4Y 9DA, ☎020 7583 1315
✉clerks@tgchambers.com
Call Date: July 2006, Gray's Inn
Qualifications: [BA (Cantab) BCL (Oxon)]
✉sian.reeves@tgchambers.com

REEVES-CROFT MR CHRISTOPHER DAVID

St Albans Chambers
2 - 4 St Peter's Street, St Albans, Hertfordshire
AL1 3LF, ☎01727 843383
✉clerks@stalbanschambers.com
Call Date: Oct 1992, Lincoln's Inn
Qualifications: [LLB(Hons)(Sheff)]
✉crc@stalbanschambers.com

REFFIN MISS CLARE ALYSON

One Essex Court
Ground Floor, One Essex Court, Temple,
London EC4Y 9AR, ☎020 7583 2000
✉clerks@oeclaw.co.uk
Call Date: July 1981, Middle Temple
Pupil Supervisor
Qualifications: [MA (Cantab)]
✉creffin@oeclaw.co.uk

REGAN MR DAVID ROBERT

St John's Chambers
101 Victoria Street, Bristol BS1 6PU,
☎0117 923 4700
✉clerks@stjohnschambers.co.uk
Call Date: Nov 1994, Inner Temple
Qualifications: [MA (Oxon) CPE (Lond)]
✉david.regan@stjohnschambers.co.uk

REGAN MRS SARAH

Albion Chambers
Broad Street, Bristol BS1 1DR,
☎0117 927 2144
✉clerks@albionchambers.co.uk
Call Date: Oct 2000, Lincoln's Inn
Qualifications: [LLB (Hons) (Bris)]
✉sarah.regan@albionchambers.co.uk

REHMAN MR TARIQ

Kings Court Chambers
3rd Floor, Albert House, 12-26 Albert Street, Birmingham B4 7UD, ☎07967 910864
✉t.rehmanbar@talk21.com
Call Date: Mar 2000, Lincoln's Inn
Qualifications: [BA (Hons) (Luton)]

REICHERT MR KLAUS

Brick Court Chambers
7-8 Essex Street, London WC2R 3LD,
☎020 7379 3550 ✉clerks@brickcourt.co.uk
Call Date: Nov 1996, Middle Temple
Qualifications: [BCL MCIArb PGDipICA]
✉klaus.reichert@brickcourt.co.uk

REID MR ANDREW RICHARD PRICE

Chambers of Andrew Reid
Westport Farm, Ruskway Lane, Westport TA10 0BN, ☎01460 281046
✉andrewreid443@me.com
Call Date: July 1981, Gray's Inn

REID MISS CHERYL LOUISE PEGG

Temple Court Chambers
2nd Floor, 2 Dr Johnson's Building, Temple, London EC4Y 7AY, ☎020 7353 7888
✉clerks@templecourt.co.uk
Call Date: July 2003, Lincoln's Inn
Qualifications: [LLB Hons (B'ham)]
✉cheryl.reid@templecourt.co.uk

REID MISS CLAUDETTE PATRICIA

Chambers of Miss Claudette Reid
C P Reid Direct Access, Barrister, PO Box 583872, London SE27 7BJ
Call Date: Oct 1990, Gray's Inn
Pupil Supervisor
Qualifications: [BA LLM]
✉legalpublicaccess2011@hotmail.co.uk, directaccesspractice@yahoo.com

REID MR DAVID DONALD WILLIAM

3 PB Barristers
3 Paper Buildings, Temple, London EC4Y 7EU,
☎020 7583 8055
3 PB Barristers
23 Beaumont Street, Oxford OX1 2NP,
☎01865 793 736
3 PB Barristers
30 Christchurch Road, Bournemouth, Dorset BH1 3PD, ☎01202 292102
✉clerks.bournemouth@3paper.co.uk
3 PB Barristers
Royal Talbot House, 2 Victoria Street, Bristol, Avon BS1 6BB, ☎0117 928 1520
3 PB Barristers
4 St Peter Street, Winchester SO23 8BW,
☎01962 868884
✉clerks.winchester@3paper.co.uk
Call Date: Nov 1994, Gray's Inn
Pupil Supervisor
Qualifications: [BA (Oxon)]

REID MR DICKON

5 King's Bench Walk
5 King's Bench Walk, Temple, London EC4Y 7DN, ☎020 7353 5638
✉clerks@5kbw.co.uk
Call Date: Nov 2005, Inner Temple
Qualifications: [MA University of Edinburgh MSc London School of]

REID MR ERROL EDISON

Clapham Law Chambers
85 Landor Road, Clapham North, London SW9 9RT, ☎020 7978 8482
✉DANNY@claphamlawchambers.co.uk
Call Date: Feb 1978, Gray's Inn

REID MISS JACQUELINE CLAIRE

11 South Square
1st Floor, 11 South Square, Gray's Inn, London WC1R 5EY, ☎020 7405 1222
✉clerks@11southsquare.com
Call Date: Oct 1992, Middle Temple
Pupil Supervisor
Qualifications: [BSc (Surrey) MPhil (Lond)]
✉jreid@11southsquare.com

REID MR MARTIN JOSEPH

Number 7 Harrington Street Chambers
7 Harrington Street, Liverpool L2 9YH,
☎0151 242 0707 ✉clerks@7hs.co.uk
Call Date: Nov 2003, Inner Temple
Qualifications: [BA (Oxon)]
✉martin.reid@7hs.co.uk

E

REID MR PAUL CAMPBELL QC (2001)

Lincoln House Chambers
Tower 12, The Avenue North, Spinningfields, 18-22 Bridge Street, Manchester M3 3BZ, ☎0161 832 5701
✉info@lincolnhousechambers.com
Call Date: July 1973, Gray's Inn
Recorder
Qualifications: [MA (Cantab)]
paul.reid@lincolnhousechambers.com

REID MR PAUL WILLIAM

Park Court Chambers
16 Park Place, Leeds LS1 2SJ,
☎0113 243 3277
✉clerks@parkcourtchambers.co.uk
13 King's Bench Walk
13 King's Bench Walk, Temple, London EC4Y 7EN, ☎020 7353 7204
✉clerks@13kbw.co.uk
13 KBW
32 Beaumont Street, Oxford OX1 2NP, ☎01865 311066 ✉clerks@13kbw.co.uk
Call Date: July 1975, Inner Temple
Pupil Supervisor, Recorder
Qualifications: [MA (Cantab)]
preid@parkcourtchambers.co.uk

REID MR ROBERT BARCLAY SEYMOUR

Assize Court Chambers
14 Small Street, Bristol BS1 1DE,
☎0117 926 4587 ✉carly@assize.co.uk
Call Date: Oct 1992, Inner Temple
Qualifications: [MA Dip Law]
robert.reid@assize.co.uk

REID MISS SARAH KATRINA

Kings Chambers
36 Young Street, Manchester M3 3FT,
☎0845 034 3444
✉clerks@kingschambers.com
Kings Chambers
Embassy House, 60 Church Street, Birmingham B3 2DJ, ☎0845 034 3444
✉clerks@kingschambers.com
Call Date: July 2004, Lincoln's Inn
Qualifications: [LLB Hons (Lond)]

REID MR SEBASTIAN PETER SCOTT

Tanfield Chambers
2-5 Warwick Court, London WC1R 5DJ,
☎020 7421 5300
✉clerks@tanfieldchambers.co.uk
Call Date: July 1982, Gray's Inn
Qualifications: [BA (Lond) Dip Law AKC]
sreid@tanfieldchambers.co.uk

REID MR SILAS JAMES

2 Dr Johnson's Buildings
2 Dr Johnson's Buildings, Temple, London EC4Y 7AY, ☎020 7936 2613
✉clerks@2drj.com
Call Date: Oct 1995, Lincoln's Inn
Pupil Supervisor
Qualifications: [MA (Hons)(Cantab)]
clerks@2drj.com

REID-CHALMERS MISS EMMA LOUISE

Triangle Chambers
Blair Atholl, 11 The Triangle, North Ferriby, East Yorkshire HU14 3AT, ☎01482 632075
✉emmarc@emmarc.karoo.co.uk
Call Date: July 1996, Lincoln's Inn
Qualifications: [LLB (Hons)]

REIFF-MUSGROVE MISS KAJA

Dyers Chambers
35 Bedford Row, London WC1R 4JH,
☎020 7404 1881
✉admin@dyerschambers.com
Call Date: Nov 1992, Middle Temple
Qualifications: [BA (Hons) (Sussex)]

REILLY MS FFYON EMMA

Castle Chambers
The Old Fire Station, 90 High Street, Harrow-on-the-Hill, Middlesex HA1 3LP, ☎020 8423 6579 ✉info@castlechambers.net
Call Date: Oct 1999, Inner Temple
Qualifications: [BA (Lond) LLB (City)]
clerks@castlechambers.net

REILLY MR JOHN JOSEPH

CHL Chambers
50 Colney Hatch Lane, Muswell Hill, London N10 1EA, ☎020 8883 7706
✉acesreill@aol.com
Call Date: Nov 1972, Inner Temple
Pupil Supervisor
Qualifications: [BL (Dublin)]

REINDORF MISS ANNA KATERINA AWURAKUA

Cloisters
1 Pump Court, Temple, London EC4Y 7AA, ☎020 7827 4000 ✉clerks@cloisters.com
Call Date: Nov 1999, Middle Temple
Qualifications: [BA (Hons)(Sussex) MA (Sussex)]
ar@cloisters.com

REIZ MR STANLEY

Carmelite Chambers
9 Carmelite Street, London EC4Y 0DR,
☎ 020 7936 6300
✉ clerks@carmelitechambers.co.uk
Call Date: Mar 2001, Lincoln's Inn
Pupil Supervisor
Qualifications: [LLB (Hons)]

RENDLE MR JEREMY MARK

9 King's Bench Walk
Lower Ground Floor South, 9 King's Bench Walk, Temple, London EC4Y 7DX,
☎ 020 7353 9564 ✉ 9kbw@btconnect.com
Call Date: July 2000, Inner Temple
Qualifications: [BA (Manc) Dip Law]
9kbw@btconnect.com

RENE MR JACQUES MARIO

Chambers of Mr J M Rene
20 Fairoak Drive, Eltham, London SE9 2QH,
☎ 07768 854321
✉ jacques_rene30@hotmail.com
Call Date: Oct 1998, Lincoln's Inn
Qualifications: [LLB (Hons)]

RENFREE MR PETER GERALD STANLEY

Harbour Court Chambers
140 Warsash Road, Warsash, Hampshire SO31 9JD, ☎ 01489 557999
✉ peter_renfree@harbourcourt.co.uk
Call Date: July 1992, Middle Temple
Qualifications: [LLB (Hons)]
peter_renfree@harbourcourt.co.uk

RENOUF MR GERARD JOHN PETER

2 Pump Court
1st Floor, 2 Pump Court, Temple, London EC4Y 7AH, ☎ 020 7353 5597
✉ clerks@2pumpcourt.co.uk
Call Date: July 1977, Inner Temple
Pupil Supervisor
Qualifications: [MA (Dublin)]
grenouf@2pumpcourt.co.uk

RENOUF MR MARK PHILIP

Hanson Renouf
Regency House, Regent Road, Hill Street, St Helier, Jersey JE2 4UZ, ☎ 01534 767764
✉ enquiries@hansonrenouf.com
No5 Chambers
38 Queen Square, Bristol BS1 4QS,
☎ 0845 210 5555
No5 Chambers
Greenwood House, 4-7 Salisbury Court, London EC4Y 8AA, ☎ 0845 210 5555
No5 Chambers
Fountain Court, Steelhouse Lane, Birmingham B4 6DR, ☎ 0845 210 5555 ✉ info@no5.com
Call Date: Oct 1994, Middle Temple
Qualifications: [LLB (Hons)(Lond)]
mark.renouf@hansonrenouf.com

RENSTEN MS KATHERINE SUSAN

Coram Chambers
9-11 Fulwood Place, London WC1V 6HG,
☎ 020 7092 3700
✉ mail@coramchambers.co.uk
Call Date: July 2010, Inner Temple
Qualifications: [BA (Cantab) CPE]

RENTON THE HON MRS CLARE OLIVIA

29 Bedford Row Chambers
London WC1R 4HE, ☎ 020 7404 1044
✉ clerks@29br.co.uk
Call Date: Nov 1972, Lincoln's Inn
crenton@29br.co.uk

RENTON DR DAVID KURT

Garden Court Chambers
57-60 Lincoln's Inn Fields, London WC2A 3LJ,
☎ 020 7993 7600 ✉ info@gclaw.co.uk
Call Date: Oct 2008, Gray's Inn
Qualifications: [BA PhD MA]
davidr@gclaw.co.uk

RENTON MS JACQUELINE CLAIRE

4 Paper Buildings
1st Floor, 4 Paper Buildings, Temple, London EC4Y 7EX, ☎ 020 7427 5200
✉ clerks@4pb.com
Call Date: July 2007, Middle Temple
Qualifications: [BA (Bris)]
jcr@4pb.com

RENTON MR OLIVER KENNETH MAXWELL

Charter Chambers
33 John Street, London WC1N 2AT,
☎ 020 7618 4400
✉ clerks@charterchambers.com
Call Date: July 2008, Lincoln's Inn
Qualifications: [BA (Leeds) MA (Leeds) GDL]

E

RENVOIZE MR EDWARD PHILIP

1 Paper Buildings
1st Floor, 1 Paper Buildings, Temple, London EC4Y 7EP, ☎ 020 7353 3728
✉ clerks@onepaper.co.uk
No.6 Park Square
Leeds LS1 2LW, ☎ 0113 245 9763
✉ Tim@no6.co.uk
Call Date: Oct 2004, Lincoln's Inn
Qualifications: [BA PgDI]
edwardrenvoize@onepaper.co.uk

REPPER MISS ELIZABETH RUTH GEORGINA

Keating Chambers
15 Essex Street, London WC2R 3AA,
☎ 020 7544 2600
✉ clerks@keatingchambers.com
Call Date: Oct 2002, Inner Temple
Qualifications: [LL.B (UEA) LLM (Lond)]
erepper@keatingchambers.com

REQUENA MR STEPHEN

18 Red Lion Court
London EC4A 3EB, ☎ 020 7520 6000
✉ chambers@18rlc.co.uk
Call Date: Oct 1997, Inner Temple
Qualifications: [LLB (LSE)]
stephen.requena@18rlc.co.uk

E

RESTALL MR THOMAS CHARLES

The Chambers of Grahame Aldous QC
9 Gough Square, London EC4A 3DG,
☎ 020 7832 0500
✉ clerks@9goughsquare.co.uk
Call Date: Oct 2007, Middle Temple
Qualifications: [BA (Hons) (Oxon) PgDL]
TRestall@9goughsquare.co.uk

REVERE MS CARLA

1 Chancery Lane
London WC2A 1LF, ☎ 0845 634 6666
✉ clerks@1chancerylane.com
Call Date: Oct 2001, Inner Temple
Qualifications: [MA CPE]
crevere@1chancerylane.com

REYNOLD MR FREDERIC QC (1982)

Old Square Chambers
10-11 Bedford Row, London WC1R 4BU,
☎ 020 7269 0300 ✉ clerks@oldsquare.co.uk
Old Square Chambers
3 Orchard Court, St Augustine's Yard, Bristol BS1 5DP, ☎ 0117 930 5100
✉ clerks@oldsquare.co.uk
Call Date: July 1960, Gray's Inn
Qualifications: [BA (Oxon)]
reynoldqc@oldsquare.co.uk

REYNOLDS MR ADRIAN LEONARD

1 High Pavement
Nottingham NG1 1HF, ☎ 0115 941 8218
✉ clerks@1highpavement.co.uk
Call Date: Nov 1982, Gray's Inn
Pupil Supervisor, Recorder
Qualifications: [MA (Oxon)]
adrianreynolds@1highpavement.co.uk

REYNOLDS MISS CHARLOTTE NATHALIE

12 King's Bench Walk
12 King's Bench Walk, Temple, London EC4Y 7EL, ☎ 020 7583 0811
Call Date: Nov 2001, Middle Temple
Qualifications: [MA (Cantab)]

REYNOLDS MR CHRISTOPHER MICHAEL

2 Dr Johnson's Buildings
2 Dr Johnson's Buildings, Temple, London EC4Y 7AY, ☎ 020 7936 2613
✉ clerks@2drj.com
Call Date: July 2010, Gray's Inn
Qualifications: [BA]

REYNOLDS PROF FRANCIS MARTIN BAILLIE

7 King's Bench Walk
Ground Floor, 7 King's Bench Walk, Temple, London EC4Y 7DS, ☎ 020 7910 8300
✉ clerks@7kbw.co.uk
Call Date: Feb 1961, Inner Temple
Qualifications: [DCL]

REYNOLDS MR GARY WILLIAM

St Johns Buildings
24a - 28 St John Street, Manchester M3 4DJ,
☎ 0161 214 1500
✉ clerk@stjohnsbuildings.co.uk
St Johns Buildings
21 White Friars, Chester CH1 1NZ,
☎ 01244 323070
✉ clerk@stjohnsbuildings.co.uk
16 Winckley Square
Preston PR1 3JJ, ☎ 01772 256100
Call Date: Nov 1994, Lincoln's Inn
Qualifications: [BSc (Hons)(Portsmith) Dip Law (Staff)]
clerk@stjohnsbuildings.co.uk

REYNOLDS MR JOHN ADAM

King's Bench Chambers
Wellington House, 175 Holdenhurst Road, Bournemouth, Dorset BH8 8DQ,
☎ 01202 250025
Call Date: Oct 1998, Gray's Inn
Qualifications: [BA]

REYNOLDS MR JONATHAN JAMES

Holborn Chambers
6 Gate Street, Lincoln's Inn Fields, London
WC2A 3HP, ☎020 7242 6060
Call Date: Nov 1992, Inner Temple
Qualifications: [LLB (Lond)]
✉jonathanreynolds@holbornchambers.co.uk

REYNOLDS MR KIRK QC (1993)

Falcon Chambers
Falcon Court, London EC4Y 1AA,
☎020 7353 2484
✉clerks@falcon-chambers.com
Call Date: July 1974, Middle Temple
Qualifications: [MA (Cantab) LLD (Hon)]
✉reynolds@falcon-chambers.com

Types of work: Arbitration, Chancery (land law), Commercial property, Landlord and tenant, Professional negligence

REYNOLDS MR LEE JULIAN

Apex
Harlech House, 20 Cathedral Road, Cardiff
CF11 9LJ, ☎02920 232 032
✉clerks@apexchambers.net
Call Date: Oct 2002, Gray's Inn
Qualifications: [LLB (Wales)]
✉lee.reynolds@apexchambers.net

REYNOLDS MR RICHARD

Tooks Chambers
81 Farringdon Street, London EC4A 4BL,
☎020 7842 7575 ✉clerks@tooks.co.uk
Call Date: July 2007, Middle Temple
Qualifications: [BA (Hons) (Oxon) LLM]
✉richard.reynolds@tooks.co.uk

REYNOLDS MISS STELLA LOUISE

187 Fleet Street
London EC4A 2AT, ☎020 7430 7430
✉chambers@187fleetstreet.com
Call Date: July 1983, Gray's Inn
Pupil Supervisor
Qualifications: [LLB (L'pool)]

REYNOLDS MR STEPHEN ALAN

29 Bedford Row Chambers
London WC1R 4HE, ☎020 7404 1044
✉clerks@29br.co.uk
Call Date: Nov 1987, Inner Temple
Pupil Supervisor
Qualifications: [BA]
✉sreynolds@29br.co.uk

REYNOLDS MISS VICTORIA LOIS

Becket Chambers
17 New Dover Road, Canterbury, Kent
CT1 3AS, ☎01227 786331
✉clerks@becket-chambers.co.uk
Call Date: Nov 2008, Middle Temple
Qualifications: [BA (Hons) (Oxon)]

REZA MR HASHIM

Field Court Chambers
5 Field Court, Gray's Inn, London WC1R 5EF,
☎020 7405 6114 ✉clerks@fieldcourt.co.uk
Call Date: July 1981, Middle Temple
Pupil Supervisor
Qualifications: [LLB (Leics)]
✉hashim.reza@fieldcourt.co.uk

RHEE MISS DEOK-JOO

11 King's Bench Walk
11 King's Bench Walk, Temple, London
EC4Y 7EQ, ☎020 7632 8500
✉clerksroom@11kbw.com
Call Date: Oct 1998, Gray's Inn
Pupil Supervisor
Qualifications: [BA BCL (Oxon)]
✉deokjoo.rhee@11kbw.com

RHIND MR MARK ALEXANDER

Exchange Chambers
7 Ralli Courts, West Riverside, Manchester
M3 5FT, ☎0161 833 2722
Exchange Chambers
One Derby Square, Derby Square, Liverpool
L2 9XX, ☎0151 236 7747
✉info@exchangechambers.co.uk
Exchange Chambers
Oxford House, Oxford Row, Leeds LS1 3BE,
☎0113 203 1970
✉spencer@exchangechambers.co.uk
Call Date: Nov 1989, Middle Temple
Qualifications: [LLB (Hons) (Manch)]
✉rhind@exchangechambers.co.uk

RHODES MISS AMANDA LOUISE

Unity Street Chambers
5 Unity Street, College Green, Bristol
BS1 5HH, ☎0117 906 9789
✉chambers@unitystreetchambers.com
Call Date: May 1990, Lincoln's Inn
Qualifications: [LLB (Hons)]
✉amanda.rhodes@unitystreetchambers.com

RHODES MR DAVID LAWRENCE

Doughty Street Chambers
53-54 Doughty Street, London WC1N 2LS,
☎020 7404 1313
✉enquiries@doughtystreet.co.uk
Doughty Street Chambers
Pall Mall Court, 61-67 King Street, Manchester M2 4PD, ☎0161 618 1066
Doughty Street Chambers
5th Floor, Broad Quay House, Prince Street, Bristol BS1 4DJ, ☎01179 058 717
Call Date: July 2002, Middle Temple
Qualifications: [BA (Hons) (York) M.Phil (Oxford) CPE]
d.rhodes@doughtystreet.co.uk

RHODES MR NICHOLAS PIERS QC (2008)

Charter Chambers
33 John Street, London WC1N 2AT,
☎020 7618 4400
✉clerks@charterchambers.com
Call Date: July 1981, Lincoln's Inn
Recorder
Qualifications: [LLB (UEA)]
nick.rhodes@charterchambers.com

RHODES MR ROBERT ELLIOTT QC (1989)

Outer Temple Chambers
The Outer Temple, 222 Strand, London WC2R 1BA, ☎020 7353 6381
✉clerks@outertemple.com
Principal Chambers
15 Lime Tree Walk, Sevenoaks, Kent TN13 1YH, ☎0845 209 8080
St Philips Chambers
55 Temple Row, Birmingham B2 5LS,
☎0121 246 7000 ✉clerks@st-philips.com
Call Date: July 1968, Inner Temple
Qualifications: [MA (Oxon)]
DX: 351 LDE;
URL: http://www.outertemple.com/barristers/robert-rhodes-qc.asp

Types of work: Administrative law, Commercial fraud, Commercial law, Commercial regulation, Confiscation, Crime, Dispute resolution, Extradition, Financial services, Health and safety, Human rights, Money laundering, Professional negligence, Public law, Regulatory and disciplinary law, Tax investigations

RHONE-ADRIEN MISS PAULA CHRISTINA

Chambers of Mr Ami Feder
Ground Floor, Lamb Building, Temple, London EC4Y 7AS, ☎020 7797 7788
✉clerks@lambbuilding.co.uk
Lamb Building
22 Ship Street, Brighton BN1 1AD,
☎01273 820490
✉admin@lambbuilding.co.uk
Chambers of Mr Ami Feder
Ground Floor, Lamb Building, Temple, London EC4Y 7AS, ☎020 7797 7788
✉clerks@lambbuilding.co.uk
Call Date: Oct 1998, Inner Temple
Qualifications: [LLB (Lond)]
clerks@lambbuilding.co.uk

RHYS MISS MEGAN JILL

Call Date: Nov 1994, Inner Temple
Qualifications: [LLB (Sheff)]
megan.rhys@stjohnsbuildings.co.uk

RHYS-DAVIES MR ADAM

Sovereign Chambers
46 Park Place, Leeds LS1 2RY,
☎0113 245 1841
✉clerks@sovereignchambers.co.uk
Call Date: Oct 1998, Middle Temple
Qualifications: [LLB (Hons)(Leeds)]
adam.rhys-davies@sovereignchambers.co.uk

RIAZ MR MOHAMMED AMIR

Rowchester Chambers
4 Rowchester Court, Whittall Street, Birmingham B4 6DH, ☎0121 233 2327
✉clerks@rowchesterchambers.co.uk
Call Date: July 2003, Gray's Inn
Qualifications: [LLB (Wolves)]

RICCIARDI MS ANGELA JANE

Angel Chambers
Ethos Building, Kings Road, Swansea SA1 8AS,
☎01792 464623
✉clerks@angelchambers.co.uk
Call Date: July 2008, Gray's Inn
Qualifications: [BA (Cardiff)]

RICE MR CHRISTOPHER DOUGLAS

Crown Office Row Chambers
119 Church Street, Brighton, Sussex BN1 1UD, ☎01273 625625
✉clerks@1cor.com
Call Date: July 1991, Middle Temple
Qualifications: [BA (Hons)]
christopher.rice@1cor.com

RICH MISS ANN BARBARA

5 Stone Buildings
5 Stone Buildings, Lincoln's Inn, London WC2A 3XT, ☎020 7242 6201
✉clerks@5sblaw.com
Call Date: Oct 1990, Gray's Inn
Pupil Supervisor
Qualifications: [MA (Cantab) Dip Law]

RICH MR BENJAMIN MICHAEL

2 Hare Court
Lower Ground, Ground, 1st & 2nd Floor, 2 Hare Court, Temple, London EC4Y 7BH, ☎020 7353 3982 ✉clerks@2harecourt.com
Call Date: July 2010, Inner Temple
Qualifications: [BA (Hons) (Oxon)]
✉benrich@2harecourt.com

RICH MR CHARLES STEPHEN ANTHONY

Cathedral Chambers
First Floor, 17 Queen Street, Newcastle Upon Tyne NE1 3UG, ☎0191 232 1311
✉mail@cathedralchambers.com
Call Date: July 1972, Gray's Inn
Qualifications: [LLB (Hons) LLM]

RICH MR JONATHAN BERNARD GEORGE

Five Paper
Ground Floor, 5 Paper Buildings, Temple, London EC4Y 7HB, ☎020 7815 3200
Call Date: July 1989, Middle Temple
Qualifications: [MA (Cantab)]
✉jonathanrich@fivepaper.com

RICHARDS MR ALAN JAMES

Five Paper Buildings
1st Floor, Five Paper Buildings, Temple, London EC4Y 7HB, ☎020 7583 6117
✉clerks@5pb.co.uk
Call Date: Oct 2004, Inner Temple
Qualifications: [LLB (Kent)]
✉ar@5pb.co.uk

RICHARDS MS CATHERINE MARY

Iscoed Chambers
86 St Helen's Road, Swansea SA1 4BQ, ☎01792 652988
✉clerks@iscoedchambers.co.uk
Call Date: Nov 2000, Lincoln's Inn
Pupil Supervisor
Qualifications: [LLB (Hons) (London)]
✉cr@iscoedchambers.co.uk

RICHARDS MR DAVID CENNYDD

Angel Chambers
Ethos Building, Kings Road, Swansea SA1 8AS, ☎01792 464623
✉clerks@angelchambers.co.uk
Call Date: Oct 1999, Gray's Inn
Qualifications: [BA (Hons)(Oxon)]
✉cennyddrichards@angelchambers.co.uk

RICHARDS MR DAVID JAMES MARTIN

3 PB Barristers
3 Paper Buildings, Temple, London EC4Y 7EU, ☎020 7583 8055
3 PB Barristers
Royal Talbot House, 2 Victoria Street, Bristol, Avon BS1 6BB, ☎0117 928 1520
3 PB Barristers
30 Christchurch Road, Bournemouth, Dorset BH1 3PD, ☎01202 292102
✉clerks.bournemouth@3paper.co.uk
3 PB Barristers
4 St Peter Street, Winchester SO23 8BW, ☎01962 868884
✉clerks.winchester@3paper.co.uk
3 PB Barristers
23 Beaumont Street, Oxford OX1 2NP, ☎01865 793 736
Call Date: July 1989, Middle Temple
Pupil Supervisor
Qualifications: [LLB (Cantab) MA (Cantab) LLM]

RICHARDS MR DUNCAN JAMES

Chambers of Mr Ami Feder
Ground Floor, Lamb Building, Temple, London EC4Y 7AS, ☎020 7797 7788
✉clerks@lambbuilding.co.uk
Principal Chambers
15 Lime Tree Walk, Sevenoaks, Kent TN13 1YH, ☎0845 209 8080
Chambers of Mr Ami Feder
Ground Floor, Lamb Building, Temple, London EC4Y 7AS, ☎020 7797 7788
✉clerks@lambbuilding.co.uk
Call Date: Oct 2007, Inner Temple
Qualifications: [LLB (Lond) LLM (Lond)]

RICHARDS MISS ELIZABETH

St Philips Chambers
55 Temple Row, Birmingham B2 5LS, ☎0121 246 7000 ✉clerks@st-philips.com
Call Date: Oct 2001, Middle Temple
Qualifications: [LLB (Hons)]
✉erichards@st-philips.co.uk

E

RICHARDS MR HUGH ALAN

No5 Chambers
Fountain Court, Steelhouse Lane, Birmingham B4 6DR, ☎0845 210 5555 ✉info@no5.com
No5 Chambers
Greenwood House, 4-7 Salisbury Court, London EC4Y 8AA, ☎0845 210 5555
No5 Chambers
38 Queen Square, Bristol BS1 4QS, ☎0845 210 5555
Call Date: Nov 1992, Inner Temple
Qualifications: [BSc (Wales) Dip Law]
hr@no5.com

RICHARDS MR IAN

Pump Court Tax Chambers
16 Bedford Row, London WC1R 4EF, ☎020 7414 8080 ✉clerks@pumptax.com
Call Date: Nov 1971, Lincoln's Inn
Qualifications: [BA]
irichards@pumptax.com

Types of work: Capital tax, Equity, Income tax, Trusts, Wills

RICHARDS MISS JENNIFER QC (2011)

39 Essex Street
London WC2R 3AT, ☎020 7832 1111
✉clerks@39essex.com
82 King Street
Manchester M2 4WQ, ☎0161 870 9969
Call Date: Oct 1991, Middle Temple
Pupil Supervisor
Qualifications: [MA (Hons) (Cantab) LLM (Canada)]
jenni.richards@39essex.com

RICHARDS DR JONATHAN NICHOLAS

King's Bench and Godolphin (KBG)Chambers
115 North Hill, Plymouth, Devon PL4 8JY, ☎01752 221551
✉clerks@kbgchambers.co.uk
Lamb Chambers
Lamb Building, Elm Court, Temple, London EC4Y 7AS, ☎020 7797 8300
✉info@lambchambers.co.uk
Call Date: Oct 1995, Middle Temple
Qualifications: [MB CPE ChB (Bris)]
theclerks@godolphinchambers.co.uk

RICHARDS MR THOMAS ALEXANDER

Blackstone Chambers
Blackstone House, Temple, London EC4Y 9BW, ☎020 7583 1770
✉clerks@blackstonechambers.com
Call Date: July 2006, Gray's Inn
Qualifications: [BA (Oxon) Diploma in Law]
tomrichards@blackstonechambers.com

RICHARDSON MR ALISTAIR PAUL GEORGE

6 King's Bench Walk
Ground Floor, 6 King's Bench Walk, Temple, London EC4Y 7DR, ☎020 7583 0410
✉clerks@6kbw.com
Call Date: Oct 2006, Inner Temple
Qualifications: [BA (Oxon)]
alistair.richardson@6kbw.com

RICHARDSON MISS ANNE LYDIA

Dere Street Barristers
33 Broad Chare, Newcastle Upon Tyne NE1 3DQ, ☎0844 3351551
✉clerks@derestreet.co.uk
Call Date: July 1986, Inner Temple
Pupil Supervisor
Qualifications: [LLB (B'ham)]
clerks@broadcharechambers.co.uk

RICHARDSON MR GARTH DOUGLAS ANTHONY

Rougemont Chambers
Victory House, Dean Clarke Gardens, Southernhay East, Exeter EX2 4AA, ☎01392 208484
✉clerks@rougemontchambers.co.uk
Devon Chambers
3 St Andrew Street, Plymouth PL1 2AH, ☎01752 661659
✉clerks@devonchambers.co.uk
Call Date: July 1975, Middle Temple
Pupil Supervisor
Qualifications: [LLB]

RICHARDSON MR GILES JOHN

Serle Court
6 New Square, Lincoln's Inn, London WC2A 3QS, ☎020 7242 6105
✉clerks@serlecourt.co.uk
Call Date: Oct 1997, Inner Temple
Qualifications: [BA BCL (Oxon)]
grichardson@serlecourt.co.uk

RICHARDSON MR GRAHAME CHARLES

Trinity Chambers
Highfield House, Moulsham Street, Chelmsford, Essex CM2 9AH, ☎01245 605040
✉clerks@trinitychambers.com
Call Date: July 2001, Middle Temple
Qualifications: [BA (Hons)]

RICHARDSON MR JAMES DAVID

Trinity Chambers
The Custom House, 39 Quayside, Newcastle Upon Tyne NE1 3DE, ☎0191 232 1927
✉info@trinitychambers.co.uk
Trinity Chambers
Multi Media Exchange, 72-80 Corporation Road, Middlesbrough TS1 2RF, ☎01642 247569
✉info@trinitychambers.co.uk
Call Date: Nov 1982, Gray's Inn
Pupil Supervisor
Qualifications: [LLB (Leic)]
j.richardson@trinitychambers.co.uk

RICHARDSON MR MATTHEW CHARLES FALCO LOMBARDI

Henderson Chambers
2 Harcourt Buildings, Temple, London EC4Y 9DB, ☎020 7583 9020
✉clerks@hendersonchambers.co.uk
Call Date: Nov 2006, Gray's Inn
Qualifications: [BA]
mrichardson@hendersonchambers.co.uk

RICHARDSON MR MATTHEW JAMES

New Court
Ground Floor, New Court, Temple, London EC4Y 9BE, ☎020 7583 5123
✉clerks@newcourtchambers.com
Call Date: Oct 2009, Lincoln's Inn
Qualifications: [BA (Cantab)]

RICHARDSON MR PAUL ANDREW

1 Gray's Inn Square
Ground Floor, 1 Gray's Inn Square, London WC1R 5AA, ☎020 7405 0001
Call Date: Feb 1993, Inner Temple
Qualifications: [LLB (So'ton)]
paulrichardsonbarrister@ntlworld.com, prichardson@1gis.co.uk

RICHARDSON MISS REBECCA EMILY

Hardwicke
New Square, Lincoln's Inn, London WC2A 3SB, ☎020 7242 2523
✉enquiries@hardwicke.co.uk
Call Date: July 2003, Middle Temple
Qualifications: [LLB Hons (Lond) LLM (Lond)]
rebecca.richardson@hardwicke.co.uk

RICHES MR PHILIP GEOFFREY HURRY

Stone Chambers
4 Field Court, Gray's Inn, London WC1R 5EF, ☎020 7440 6900
✉clerks@stonechambers.com
Call Date: Nov 2001, Inner Temple
Pupil Supervisor
Qualifications: [BA (Hons) (Cantab) CPE Dip Law]
philip.riches@stonechambers.com

RICHMAN MRS HELENE PINES

9 Stone Buildings
Lincoln's Inn, London WC2A 3NN, ☎020 7404 5055
✉clerks@9stonebuildings.com
Eighteen Carlton Crescent
Rownhams House, Rownhams, Southampton SO16 8LF, ☎023 8063 9001
✉clerks@18carltoncrescent.co.uk
Stour Chambers
Mill Studio, 17a Stour Street, Canterbury, Kent CT1 2NR, ☎01227 764899
✉clerks@stourchambers.co.uk
Call Date: July 1992, Middle Temple
Pupil Supervisor
Qualifications: [BA (Hons)(USA)]
hprichman@9stonebuildings.com

RICHMOND MR BERNARD GRANT QC (2006)

Chambers of Mr Ami Feder
Ground Floor, Lamb Building, Temple, London EC4Y 7AS, ☎020 7797 7788
✉clerks@lambbuilding.co.uk
Central Chambers
89 Princess Street, Manchester M1 4HT, ☎0161 236 1133
✉clerks@centralchambers.co.uk
Chambers of Mr Ami Feder
Ground Floor, Lamb Building, Temple, London EC4Y 7AS, ☎020 7797 7788
✉clerks@lambbuilding.co.uk
Call Date: July 1988, Middle Temple
Pupil Supervisor
Qualifications: [LLB (Hons)]
bernardrichmond@lambbuilding.co.uk

E

RICHMOND DR CATHERINE ANN

Cloisters
1 Pump Court, Temple, London EC4Y 7AA,
☎020 7827 4000 ✉clerks@cloisters.com
Call Date: July 2011, Inner Temple
Qualifications: [BA (Oxon) DPhil (Italy)]
cr@cloisters.com

RICHMOND MR JEREMY JOHN

Quadrant Chambers
Quadrant House, 10 Fleet Street, London EC4Y 1AU, ☎020 7583 4444
✉info@quadrantchambers.com
St Philips Chambers
55 Temple Row, Birmingham B2 5LS,
☎0121 246 7000 ✉clerks@st-philips.com
Call Date: Oct 2000, Lincoln's Inn
Qualifications: [LLB (Hons) (Edin) BCL (Oxon) LLM (Harvard)]

RICHMOND MR PAUL ANTHONY OLIFFE

Richmond Canter Immigration Barristers
1 Fetter Lane, London EC4A 1BR,
☎020 3440 5820
✉info@immigrationbarrister.co.uk
Call Date: Oct 1998, Inner Temple
Qualifications: [LLB (Soton)]

RICKARBY MR WILLIAM EDMUND

Cornwall Street Chambers
85-87 Cornwall Street, Birmingham B3 3BY,
☎0121 233 7500
✉clerks@cornwallstreet.co.uk
Call Date: July 1975, Gray's Inn
Qualifications: [LLB (Hons)]
william.rickarby@cornwallstreet.co.uk

RICKARD MR MARCUS JOHN REID

18 Red Lion Court
London EC4A 3EB, ☎020 7520 6000
✉chambers@18rlc.co.uk
Call Date: July 2000, Inner Temple
Qualifications: [BA (Newc) CPE Dip T P Dip in Law]

RICKARD MS SUSANNA LOUISA

3 Serjeants Inn
London EC4Y 1BQ, ☎020 7427 5000
✉clerks@3serjeantsinn.com
Call Date: July 2009, Middle Temple
Qualifications: [BA (Hons) (Cantab)]
srickard@3serjeantsinn.com

RICKARDS MR JAMES

Outer Temple Chambers
The Outer Temple, 222 Strand, London WC2R 1BA, ☎020 7353 6381
✉clerks@outertemple.com
Call Date: Mar 2002, Inner Temple
Qualifications: [BA (Newc) CPE LLM (London)]
james.rickards@outertemple.com

RICKETTS MR PAUL CHARLES

Assize Court Chambers
14 Small Street, Bristol BS1 1DE,
☎0117 926 4587 ✉carly@assize.co.uk
Call Date: July 2002, Gray's Inn
Qualifications: [BA(Hons) PGDip]
paul.ricketts@assize.co.uk

RIDD MR DAVID IAN MCGREGOR

Farrar's Building
Farrar's Building, Temple, London EC4Y 7BD,
☎020 7583 9241
✉Chambers@farrarsbuilding.co.uk
Call Date: July 1975, Middle Temple
Pupil Supervisor
Qualifications: [BA (Hons)(Oxon) FCIArb]

RIDGWAY MR PHILIP

Temple Tax Chambers
1st Floor, 3 Temple Gardens, Temple, London EC4Y 9AU, ☎020 7353 7884
✉clerks@templetax.com
Call Date: July 1986, Middle Temple
Qualifications: [BA FTII LLM (Cantab)]

RIDING MR HENRY

Number 7 Harrington Street Chambers
7 Harrington Street, Liverpool L2 9YH,
☎0151 242 0707 ✉clerks@7hs.co.uk
Call Date: July 1981, Middle Temple
Qualifications: [LLB (Hons)]
henry.riding@7hs.co.uk

RIDLEY MISS SAMANTHA JANE

1 KBW Chambers
1 King's Bench Walk, Temple, London EC4Y 7DB, ☎020 7936 1500
✉clerks@1kbw.co.uk
Call Date: July 2009, Inner Temple
Qualifications: [LLB (L'pool)]
sridley@1kbw.co.uk

RIFAT MR MAURICE ALAN

1 Gray's Inn Square
Ground Floor, 1 Gray's Inn Square, London WC1R 5AA, ☎ 020 7405 0001
Call Date: Nov 1990, Inner Temple
Pupil Supervisor
Qualifications: [LLB]
mrifat@1gis.co.uk

RIGBY MR TERENCE

9 St John Street
Manchester M3 4DN, ☎ 0161 955 9000
civilclerks@9sjs.com / criminalclerks@9sjs.com
Call Date: May 1971, Gray's Inn
Pupil Supervisor, Recorder
Qualifications: [LLB (Nottm) BCL (Oxon)]

RIGBY MISS VICTORIA ANNE

9 St John Street
Manchester M3 4DN, ☎ 0161 955 9000
civilclerks@9sjs.com / criminalclerks@9sjs.com
Call Date: Oct 2000, Middle Temple
Qualifications: [BA (Hons) (Cantab) Dip in Law (Nott'm)]

RIGGS MISS SAMANTHA

25 Bedford Row
London WC1R 4HD, ☎ 020 7067 1500
clerks@25bedfordrow.com
Call Date: Oct 1996, Gray's Inn
Qualifications: [BA]
sriggs@25bedfordrow.com

RIGNEY MR ANDREW JAMES QC (2010)

Crown Office Chambers
2 Crown Office Row, Temple, London EC4Y 7HJ, ☎ 020 7797 8100
mail@crownofficechambers.com
Call Date: Oct 1992, Gray's Inn
Pupil Supervisor
Qualifications: [MA (Cantab) Dip Law (Lond)]
rigney@crownofficechambers.com

RILEY MISS CHRISTINE ANNE

9 St John Street
Manchester M3 4DN, ☎ 0161 955 9000
civilclerks@9sjs.com / criminalclerks@9sjs.com
Call Date: July 1974, Gray's Inn
Pupil Supervisor
Qualifications: [LLB]

RILEY MISS DAVINIA

St Philips Chambers
55 Temple Row, Birmingham B2 5LS, ☎ 0121 246 7000 clerks@st-philips.com
Call Date: July 2004, Inner Temple
driley@st-philips.com

RILEY MS GERALDINE MARGARET

Cobden House Chambers
19 Quay Street, Manchester M3 3HN, ☎ 0161 833 6000 Clerks@Cobden.co.uk
Call Date: Oct 2002, Inner Temple
Qualifications: [BA (Manch) B.Phil (Exon) CPE (Manch)]

RILEY MR JAMIE SPENCER

11 Stone Buildings
11 Stone Buildings, Lincoln's Inn, London WC2A 3TG, ☎ 020 7831 6381
clerks@11sb.com
Call Date: Nov 1995, Lincoln's Inn
Qualifications: [MA (Cantab)]
riley@11sb.com

RILEY MR MICHAEL JOHN

23 Essex Street
London WC2R 3AA, ☎ 020 7413 0353
clerks@23es.com
Call Date: Nov 1983, Middle Temple
Pupil Supervisor
Qualifications: [BA (Hons)]
johnriley@23es.com

RILEY-SMITH MR TOBIAS AUGUSTINE WILLIAM

Henderson Chambers
2 Harcourt Buildings, Temple, London EC4Y 9DB, ☎ 020 7583 9020
clerks@hendersonchambers.co.uk
Call Date: Nov 1995, Middle Temple
Pupil Supervisor
Qualifications: [MA (Cantab)]
trileysmith@hendersonchambers.co.uk

RIMMER MR ANTHONY MICHAEL

187 Fleet Street
London EC4A 2AT, ☎ 020 7430 7430
chambers@187fleetstreet.com
Call Date: July 1983, Gray's Inn
Pupil Supervisor
Qualifications: [BA]
tonyrimmer@187fleetstreet.com

RIMMER MISS CATHERINE LOUISE

Call Date: July 2004, Gray's Inn
Qualifications: [LLB (Leeds)]
catrimmer23@hotmail.com

RIMMER MR HUGH

3 PB Barristers
3 Paper Buildings, Temple, London EC4Y 7EU, ☎020 7583 8055
18 St John Street
Manchester M3 4EA, ☎0161 278 1800
✉clerks@18sjs.com
Call Date: Oct 2003, Inner Temple
Qualifications: [BA (Nott'm)]

RIMMER MR NICHOLAS PATRICK EDWARD

23 Essex Street
London WC2R 3AA, ☎020 7413 0353
✉clerks@23es.com
Call Date: July 2004, Lincoln's Inn
Qualifications: [BA Hons (Dub) PGDL]
nicholasrimmer@23es.com

RINDER MR ROBERT MICHAEL

2 Hare Court
Lower Ground, Ground, 1st & 2nd Floor, 2 Hare Court, Temple, London EC4Y 7BH, ☎020 7353 3982 ✉clerks@2harecourt.com
Call Date: Oct 2001, Inner Temple
Qualifications: [BA (Manch) CPE]
clerks@2harecourt.com

RINKER MR ANDREW STUART D'ARTOIS

Chambers of Mr Andrew Rinker
3 Kensington Gate, London W8 5NA, ☎020 7584 1091 ✉a.rinker@btinernet.com
Call Date: July 2011, Middle Temple
Qualifications: [MBA (USA) Jurisdoctorate (USA)]

RIORDAN MR STEPHEN VAUGHAN QC (1992)

Number 7 Harrington Street Chambers
7 Harrington Street, Liverpool L2 9YH, ☎0151 242 0707 ✉clerks@7hs.co.uk
Call Date: July 1972, Inner Temple
Qualifications: [LLB (L'pool)]
stephen.riordan@7hs.co.uk, svr19@btinternet.com

RIPLEY MR MICHAEL EDWARD

11 New Square
1st Floor, 11 New Square, Lincoln's Inn, London WC2A 3QB, ☎020 7242 4017
✉john.moore@11newsquare.com
Call Date: Oct 2008, Lincoln's Inn
Qualifications: [BA (Dunelm)]

RIPPON MRS AMANDA JAYNE

New Court Chambers
3 Broad Chare, Newcastle Upon Tyne NE1 3DQ, ☎0191 232 1980
✉clerks@newcourt-chambers.co.uk
Call Date: Oct 1993, Gray's Inn
Qualifications: [BA Dip Law]
amanda.rippon@newcourt-chambers.co.uk

RIPPON MR SIMON JOHN

Citadel Chambers
The Citadel, 190 Corporation Street, Birmingham B4 6QD, ☎0121 233 8500
✉clerks@citadelchambers.com
Call Date: Nov 1996, Gray's Inn
Qualifications: [BA (Lond)]

RISOLI MR ANDREA ENRICO

Old Square Chambers
3 Orchard Court, St Augustine's Yard, Bristol BS1 5DP, ☎0117 930 5100
✉clerks@oldsquare.co.uk
Call Date: July 2005, Gray's Inn
Qualifications: [LLB]
risoli@oldsquare.co.uk

RISSO-GILL MR EDWARD DAVID CHARLES

Thomas More Chambers
7 Lincoln's Inn Fields, London WC2A 3BP, ☎020 7404 7000
✉clerks@thomasmore.co.uk
Call Date: Nov 1998, Inner Temple
Qualifications: [BA (Oxon)]
edwardrisso-gill@thomasmore.co.uk

RITCHIE MR ANDREW GEORGE QC (2009)

The Chambers of Grahame Aldous QC
9 Gough Square, London EC4A 3DG, ☎020 7832 0500
✉clerks@9goughsquare.co.uk
Call Date: Feb 1985, Inner Temple
Qualifications: [MA (Cantab)]
aritchie@9goughsquare.co.uk

RITCHIE MR RICHARD BULKELEY

XXIV Old Buildings
Ground Floor, 24 Old Buildings, Lincoln's Inn, London WC2A 3UP, ☎020 7691 2424
✉clerks@xxiv.co.uk
Call Date: July 1978, Middle Temple
Pupil Supervisor
Qualifications: [BA (Oxon)]

RITCHIE MISS SHAUNA

2 Bedford Row
London WC1R 4BU, ☎ 020 7440 8888
✉ clerks@2bedfordrow.co.uk
Call Date: Nov 2000, Lincoln's Inn
Pupil Supervisor
Qualifications: [LLB (Hons) (London)]
✉ sritchie@2bedfordrow.co.uk

RITCHIE MR STUART MARTIN QC (2012)

Littleton Chambers
3 King's Bench Walk North, Temple, London EC4Y 7HR, ☎ 020 7797 8600
✉ fschneider@littletonchambers.co.uk
Call Date: Oct 1995, Middle Temple
Pupil Supervisor
Qualifications: [BA (Oxon)]
✉ sritchie@littletonchambers.co.uk

RITSON PROF JOHN

Clock Chambers
18 Waterloo Road, Wolverhampton WV1 4BL, ☎ 01902 313444
✉ clockchambers@btconnect.com
Call Date: July 1967, Lincoln's Inn
Pupil Supervisor
Qualifications: [LLB (Hons)]

RIVALLAND MR MARC-EDOUARD

1 Chancery Lane
London WC2A 1LF, ☎ 0845 634 6666
✉ clerks@1chancerylane.com
Call Date: July 1987, Middle Temple
Pupil Supervisor
Qualifications: [B Com LLB (South Africa) Dip Law LLM]
✉ mrivalland@1chancerylane.com

RIVERS MR DAVID ALEXANDER

Old Square Chambers
10-11 Bedford Row, London WC1R 4BU, ☎ 020 7269 0300 ✉ clerks@oldsquare.co.uk
Old Square Chambers
3 Orchard Court, St Augustine's Yard, Bristol BS1 5DP, ☎ 0117 930 5100
✉ clerks@oldsquare.co.uk
Call Date: Oct 2002, Gray's Inn
Qualifications: [BA (Cantab) PgDip Law LLM]
✉ rivers@oldsquare.co.uk

RIVETT MR JAMES PETER

Pump Court Tax Chambers
16 Bedford Row, London WC1R 4EF, ☎ 020 7414 8080 ✉ clerks@pumptax.com
Call Date: Nov 2004, Lincoln's Inn
Qualifications: [BA (Hons) Pphil]
✉ jrivett@pumptax.com

Types of work: Capital tax, Corporation tax, Equity, Income tax, National Insurance, Private client, Stamp duty, Trusts, VAT, Wills

RIVETT MR TIMOTHY JACK STEWART

Erskine Chambers
33 Chancery Lane, London WC2A 1EN, ☎ 020 7242 5532
✉ clerks@erskinechambers.com
Call Date: July 2010, Lincoln's Inn
Qualifications: [BA (Cantab)]

RIZA MR ALPER ALI QC (1991)

Goldsmith Chambers
Ground Floor, Goldsmith Building, Temple, London EC4Y 7BL, ☎ 020 7353 6802
✉ clerks@goldsmithchambers.com
Call Date: Nov 1973, Gray's Inn
Recorder
✉ A.Riza@goldsmithchambers.law.co.uk

RIZA MISS LILY EUGENIA

Blackfriars Chambers
79-83 Temple Chambers, 3-7 Temple Avenue, London EC4Y 0HP, ☎ 020 7353 7400
✉ clerks@blackfriarschambers.com
Call Date: Nov 2009, Inner Temple
Qualifications: [MA (Oxon) LLB (College of Law) CPE (College of Law)]

ROACH MISS JACQUELINE ALISON

Crown Office Row Chambers
119 Church Street, Brighton, Sussex BN1 1UD, ☎ 01273 625625
✉ clerks@1cor.com
Call Date: Nov 1996, Middle Temple
Qualifications: [LLB (Hons)(Kent)]
✉ jacqueline.roach@1cor.com

ROACH MR OWEN ADRIANI

No. 3 Fleet Street Chambers
3 Fleet Street, London EC4Y 1DP, ☎ 020 7936 4474 ✉ clerks@3fleetstreet.com
Call Date: Mar 2003, Lincoln's Inn
Qualifications: [LLB (Hons)]

E

ROBB MR ADAM DUNCAN

39 Essex Street
London WC2R 3AT, ☎020 7832 1111
✉clerks@39essex.com
82 King Street
Manchester M2 4WQ, ☎0161 870 9969
Call Date: Nov 1995, Inner Temple
Pupil Supervisor
Qualifications: [BA (Oxon) BCL]
adam.robb@39essex.com

ROBBINS MR IAN GEOFFREY

1 Garden Court Family Law Chambers
Ground Floor, One Garden Court, Temple, London EC4Y 9BJ, ☎020 7797 7900
✉clerks@1gc.com
Call Date: Feb 1991, Middle Temple
Qualifications: [LLB]
robbins@1gc.com

ROBERTS MR ALLAN CALVIN

Guildhall Chambers
23 Broad Street, Bristol BS1 2HG,
☎0117 930 9000
✉hoc@guildhallchambers.co.uk
Guildhall Chambers
5-8 Broad Street, Bristol BS1 2HW,
☎0117 930 9000
Call Date: Nov 2004, Middle Temple
Qualifications: [LLB (Hons)]
allan.roberts@guildhallchambers.co.uk

ROBERTS MISS BEVERLEY JAN

4 King's Bench Walk
2nd Floor, 4 King's Bench Walk, Temple, London EC4Y 7DL, ☎020 7822 7000
✉clerks@4kbw.co.uk
Call Date: Mar 1998, Middle Temple
Qualifications: [BArch]
br@4kbw.co.uk

ROBERTS MS CATHERINE

3 Temple Gardens
Lower Ground Floor, 3 Temple Gardens, Temple, London EC4Y 9AU, ☎020 7353 3102
✉clerks@3tg.co.uk
Call Date: Mar 2011, Lincoln's Inn
Qualifications: [BA LLB (Ireland)]

ROBERTS MISS CATHERINE ANN

Erskine Chambers
33 Chancery Lane, London WC2A 1EN,
☎020 7242 5532
✉clerks@erskinechambers.com
Call Date: Nov 1986, Lincoln's Inn
Pupil Supervisor
Qualifications: [MA LLM (Cantab)]
croberts@erskine-chambers.co.uk

ROBERTS MISS CLARE JUSTINE

Arden Chambers
20 Bloomsbury Square, London WC1A 2NS,
☎020 7242 4244
✉clerks@ardenchambers.com
Call Date: Nov 1988, Middle Temple
Pupil Supervisor
Qualifications: [LLB (Hons)(Lond) LLM/DEA (Belgium)]
clare.roberts@ardenchambers.com

ROBERTS MR DAFYDD OWEN

Linenhall Chambers
1 Stanley Place, Chester CH1 2LU,
☎01244 348282
✉clerks@linenhallchambers.co.uk
Call Date: Oct 1998, Gray's Inn
Qualifications: [BA (Wales)]
clerks@1stanleyplace.co.uk

ROBERTS MR DOMINIC PAUL

St Philips Chambers
55 Temple Row, Birmingham B2 5LS,
☎0121 246 7000 ✉clerks@st-philips.com
Call Date: July 2011, Middle Temple
Qualifications: [Lit Hum (Oxon) PgDL (Exon)]

ROBERTS MISS ELLIW FFLUR

St Johns Buildings
24a - 28 St John Street, Manchester M3 4DJ,
☎0161 214 1500
✉clerk@stjohnsbuildings.co.uk
St Johns Buildings
21 White Friars, Chester CH1 1NZ,
☎01244 323070
✉clerk@stjohnsbuildings.co.uk
16 Winckley Square
Preston PR1 3JJ, ☎01772 256100
Call Date: July 2009, Gray's Inn
Qualifications: [LLB]

ROBERTS MR GARETH ROGER

Linenhall Chambers
1 Stanley Place, Chester CH1 2LU,
☎01244 348282
✉clerks@linenhallchambers.co.uk
Riverview Chambers
Hamilton House, 1 Temple Avenue, London EC4Y 0HA, ☎0844 225 3999
✉chrisbaylis@riverviewchambers.com
Call Date: Oct 1999, Gray's Inn
Pupil Supervisor
Qualifications: [BSc (LSE)]

ROBERTS MISS GEMMA VICTORIA

No5 Chambers
Fountain Court, Steelhouse Lane, Birmingham B4 6DR, ☎ 0845 210 5555 ✉ info@no5.com
No5 Chambers
Greenwood House, 4-7 Salisbury Court, London EC4Y 8AA, ☎ 0845 210 5555
No5 Chambers
38 Queen Square, Bristol BS1 4QS, ☎ 0845 210 5555
Call Date: Oct 2006, Gray's Inn
Qualifications: [BA]
✉ gr@no5.com

ROBERTS MR HILARY LLEWELYN ARTHUR

9 Park Place
9 Park Place, Cardiff, South Glamorgan CF10 3DP, ☎ 029 2038 2731
✉ clerks@9parkplace.co.uk
Call Date: Nov 1978, Gray's Inn
Pupil Supervisor
Qualifications: [LLB (Wales)]

ROBERTS MR HUW EIFION

Linenhall Chambers
1 Stanley Place, Chester CH1 2LU, ☎ 01244 348282
✉ clerks@linenhallchambers.co.uk
Call Date: Nov 1993, Gray's Inn
Pupil Supervisor
Qualifications: [LLB LLM]
✉ huwroberts@1stanleyplace.co.uk

ROBERTS MR JACK

Sheldan
Chirk Road, Gobowen, Oswestry, Shropshire SY11 3LB, ☎ 01691 657635
✉ jack@roberts155560.fsnet.co.uk
Call Date: Nov 1998, Middle Temple
Qualifications: [BA (Hons)(Manch) LLB (John Moores)]
✉ jack@roberts155560.fsnet.co.uk

ROBERTS MR JAMES MCCLINTOCK

1 KBW Chambers
1 King's Bench Walk, Temple, London EC4Y 7DB, ☎ 020 7936 1500
✉ clerks@1kbw.co.uk
King's Bench Chambers
174 High Street, Lewes BN7 1YE, ☎ 01273 402600
Call Date: Oct 1993, Gray's Inn
Pupil Supervisor, Recorder
Qualifications: [MA (Hons)(Oxon)]

ROBERTS MRS JENNIFER MARY QC (2009)

Queen Elizabeth Building
3rd Floor, Queen Elizabeth Building, Temple, London EC4Y 9BS, ☎ 020 7797 7837
✉ clerks@qeb.co.uk
Call Date: July 1988, Inner Temple
Recorder
Qualifications: [LLB (Soton)]
✉ j.roberts@qeb.co.uk

ROBERTS DR JULIAN FRANCIS

Ten Old Square
Ground Floor, Ten Old Square, Lincoln's Inn, London WC2A 3SU, ☎ 020 7405 0758
✉ clerks@tenoldsquare.com
Call Date: July 1987, Lincoln's Inn
Qualifications: [BA PhD (Cantab) MA]

ROBERTS MISS LISA

Lincoln House Chambers
Tower 12, The Avenue North, Spinningfields, 18-22 Bridge Street, Manchester M3 3BZ, ☎ 0161 832 5701
✉ info@lincolnhousechambers.com
Call Date: Oct 1993, Lincoln's Inn
Pupil Supervisor
Qualifications: [BA (Hons) (Oxon)]
✉ lisa.roberts@lincolnhousechambers.com

ROBERTS MR MARC ALEXANDER

4 Brick Court
4 Brick Court, Temple, London EC4Y 9AD, ☎ 020 7832 3200 ✉ clerks@4bc.co.uk
Call Date: Nov 1984, Inner Temple
Qualifications: [BA]
✉ marc.roberts@4bc.co.uk

ROBERTS MR MARK

Number 7 Harrington Street Chambers
7 Harrington Street, Liverpool L2 9YH, ☎ 0151 242 0707 ✉ clerks@7hs.co.uk
Call Date: Mar 2001, Gray's Inn
Qualifications: [LLB (Hons)]
✉ mark.roberts@7hs.co.uk

ROBERTS MR MARK VAUGHAN

St Johns Buildings
24a - 28 St John Street, Manchester M3 4DJ, ☎ 0161 214 1500
✉ clerk@stjohnsbuildings.co.uk
St Johns Buildings
21 White Friars, Chester CH1 1NZ, ☎ 01244 323070
✉ clerk@stjohnsbuildings.co.uk
16 Winckley Square
Preston PR1 3JJ, ☎ 01772 256100
Call Date: Nov 1991, Inner Temple
Qualifications: [LLB (Hons)(Sheff)]

E

ROBERTS MR MATTHEW JOHN PIERS

9 Park Place
9 Park Place, Cardiff, South Glamorgan CF10 3DP, ☎029 2038 2731
✉clerks@9parkplace.co.uk
Call Date: Nov 1994, Gray's Inn
Pupil Supervisor
Qualifications: [LLB (Wales) LLM (Bris)]
✉mroberts@9parkplace.co.uk

ROBERTS MR MICHAEL CHARLES

Chambers of Michael Roberts
Fawley House, 100A St Andrews Road, Henley-On-Thames, Oxfordshire RG9 1PL, ☎01844 355 655
✉mcr@michaelrobertsbarrister.co.uk
Call Date: July 1978, Lincoln's Inn
Qualifications: [BA (Cantab)]
✉mcr@michaelrobertsbarrister.co.uk

ROBERTS MISS PATRICIA

14 Gray's Inn Square
14 Gray's Inn Square, Gray's Inn, London WC1R 5JP, ☎020 7242 0858
✉clerks@14gis.co.uk
Call Date: Nov 1987, Gray's Inn
Pupil Supervisor
Qualifications: [LLB (Hons)(L'pool)]
✉clerks@14graysinnsquare.co.uk

ROBERTS MR PHILIP DUNCAN

One Essex Court
Ground Floor, One Essex Court, Temple, London EC4Y 9AR, ☎020 7583 2000
✉clerks@oeclaw.co.uk
Call Date: Oct 1996, Inner Temple
Pupil Supervisor
Qualifications: [BA (Nott'm)]
✉proberts@oeclaw.co.uk

ROBERTS MR RICHARD VAUGHAN

Henderson Chambers
2 Harcourt Buildings, Temple, London EC4Y 9DB, ☎020 7583 9020
✉clerks@hendersonchambers.co.uk
Call Date: Oct 2006, Lincoln's Inn
Qualifications: [BA (Oxon)]
✉rroberts@hendersonchambers.co.uk

ROBERTS MR STEPHEN MICHAEL

Queen Square Chambers
56 Queen Square, Bristol BS1 4PR, ☎0117 921 1966 ✉crime@qs-c.co.uk
Call Date: Nov 2002, Lincoln's Inn
Qualifications: [BA (Hons)(Kent) LLM (Bris)]
✉smr@qs-c.co.uk

ROBERTS MR STUART ROYD

Chancery House Chambers
7 Lisbon Square, Leeds, West Yorkshire LS1 4LY, ☎0113 244 6691
✉clerks@chanceryhouse.co.uk
Call Date: Nov 1994, Middle Temple
Pupil Supervisor
Qualifications: [BA (Hons)]

ROBERTS MR TIMOTHY DAVID QC (2003)

Fountain Chambers
Cleveland Business Centre, 1 Watson Street, Middlesbrough TS1 2RQ, ☎01642 804040
✉clerks@fountainchambers.co.uk
QEB Hollis Whiteman
1-2 Laurence Pountney Hill, London EC4R 0EU, ☎020 7933 8855
✉barristers@qebhw.co.uk
Call Date: July 1978, Gray's Inn
Recorder
Qualifications: [LLB (So'ton)]

ROBERTS MRS VICTORIA

Number 7 Harrington Street Chambers
7 Harrington Street, Liverpool L2 9YH, ☎0151 242 0707 ✉clerks@7hs.co.uk
Call Date: Nov 2005, Lincoln's Inn
Qualifications: [LLB (Hons) (Bris)]
✉victoria.roberts@7hs.co.uk

ROBERTS-HARRY MR TOMOS GWILYM

Angel Chambers
Ethos Building, Kings Road, Swansea SA1 8AS, ☎01792 464623
✉clerks@angelchambers.co.uk
Call Date: July 2008, Gray's Inn
Qualifications: [LLB (Leic)]
✉gwilym.robertsharry@angelchambers.co.uk

ROBERTSHAW MR ALAN STUART

The Chambers of Mr Alan Robertshaw
Ashtree Cottage, Shepards Farm, Fiddlers' Green, St Newlyn East, Cornwall TR8 5NW, ☎01872 245974/07973 825348
Call Date: Oct 1997, Middle Temple
Qualifications: [LLB (Hons)]
✉arobertshaw0901@googlemail.com

ROBERTSHAW MR CHARLES JAMES

12 King's Bench Walk
12 King's Bench Walk, Temple, London EC4Y 7EL, ☎ 020 7583 0811
Call Date: Nov 2007, Middle Temple
Qualifications: [BSc (Hons) (Lond) PgDL (Lond) LLB]
robertshaw@12kbw.co.uk

ROBERTSHAW MR MARTIN ANDREW

39 Park Square
Leeds LS1 2NU, ☎ 0113 245 6633
✉ seniorclerk@39parksquarechambers.co.uk
Call Date: Nov 1977, Middle Temple
Qualifications: [LLB (Sheff)]

ROBERTSON MR AIDAN MALCOLM DAVID QC (2009)

Brick Court Chambers
7-8 Essex Street, London WC2R 3LD, ☎ 020 7379 3550 ✉ clerks@brickcourt.co.uk
Call Date: July 1995, Middle Temple
Qualifications: [MA LLM (Cantab)]
Aidan.Robertson@Brickcourt.co.uk

ROBERTSON MR ANDREW JAMES QC (1996)

KBW
The Engine House, No 1 Foundry Square, Leeds LS11 5DL, ☎ 0113 297 1200
✉ clerks@kbwchambers.com
Call Date: July 1975, Middle Temple
Qualifications: [MA (Cantab)]
ajrqc@kbwchambers.com

ROBERTSON MR ANGUS FREDERICK

2 King's Bench Walk
2 King's Bench Walk, Temple, London EC4Y 7DE, ☎ 020 7353 1746
✉ clerks@2kbw.com
Call Date: July 1978, Middle Temple
Pupil Supervisor
Qualifications: [BA]

ROBERTSON MR GEOFFREY RONALD QC (1988)

Doughty Street Chambers
53-54 Doughty Street, London WC1N 2LS, ☎ 020 7404 1313
✉ enquiries@doughtystreet.co.uk
Doughty Street Chambers
Pall Mall Court, 61-67 King Street, Manchester M2 4PD, ☎ 0161 618 1066
Doughty Street Chambers
5th Floor, Broad Quay House, Prince Street, Bristol BS1 4DJ, ☎ 01179 058 717
Call Date: July 1973, Middle Temple
Recorder
Qualifications: [BA BCL LLB]
g.robertson@doughtystreet.co.uk

ROBERTSON MR JAMES JOLLYON

4 Breams Buildings
Chancery Lane, London EC4A 1HP, ☎ 020 7092 1900 ✉ clerks@4bb.co.uk
Call Date: Feb 1983, Middle Temple
Pupil Supervisor
Qualifications: [BA]

ROBERTSON MISS MARY BLACKADDER

42 Bedford Row
London WC1R 4LL, ☎ 020 7831 0222
✉ clerks@42br.com
Call Date: Nov 2005, Lincoln's Inn
Qualifications: [BD (Hons) (Lond)]
clerks@42br.com

ROBERTSON MISS NICOLE FREYA

Henderson Chambers
2 Harcourt Buildings, Temple, London EC4Y 9DB, ☎ 020 7583 9020
✉ clerks@hendersonchambers.co.uk
Call Date: Oct 2007, Lincoln's Inn
Qualifications: [BA (Oxon)]

ROBERTSON MISS PATRICIA GRACE QC (2006)

Fountain Court Chambers
Fountain Court, Temple, London EC4Y 9DH, ☎ 020 7583 3335
✉ chambers@fountaincourt.co.uk
Call Date: Nov 1988, Inner Temple
Qualifications: [BA (Oxon) Dip Law (Lond)]
probertson@fountaincourt.co.uk

ROBERTSON MS SALLY ELIZABETH

Cloisters
1 Pump Court, Temple, London EC4Y 7AA, ☎ 020 7827 4000 ✉ clerks@cloisters.com
Call Date: Nov 1995, Inner Temple
Qualifications: [BA (Hons) (Reading) MSc (LSE)]
sr@cloisters.com

E

ROBINS MISS IMOGEN

3 PB Barristers
3 Paper Buildings, Temple, London EC4Y 7EU, ☎020 7583 8055
3 PB Barristers
Royal Talbot House, 2 Victoria Street, Bristol, Avon BS1 6BB, ☎0117 928 1520
3 PB Barristers
23 Beaumont Street, Oxford OX1 2NP, ☎01865 793 736
3 PB Barristers
4 St Peter Street, Winchester SO23 8BW, ☎01962 868884
✉clerks.winchester@3paper.co.uk
3 PB Barristers
30 Christchurch Road, Bournemouth, Dorset BH1 3PD, ☎01202 292102
✉clerks.bournemouth@3paper.co.uk
Call Date: Oct 1991, Inner Temple
Qualifications: [LLB]
imogen.robins@3paper.co.uk

ROBINS MR STEPHEN JAMES

South Square
3-4 South Square, Gray's Inn, London WC1R 5HP, ☎020 7696 9900
✉practicemanagers@southsquare.com
Call Date: Nov 2001, Lincoln's Inn
Qualifications: [BA (Hons)]
stephenrobins@southsquare.com

ROBINSON MISS ANNE-LOUISE

Clerksroom (Taunton)
Equity House, Administration Centre, Blackbrook Park Avenue, Taunton, Somerset TA1 2PX, ☎0845 083 3000
✉mail@clerksroom.com
Call Date: July 1978, Lincoln's Inn
Qualifications: [BA (Hons)]
robinson@clerksroom.com

ROBINSON MISS CLAIRE MARIA

Charter Chambers
33 John Street, London WC1N 2AT, ☎020 7618 4400
✉clerks@charterchambers.com
Call Date: Oct 1991, Gray's Inn
Qualifications: [BA (Oxon)]
claire.robinson@charterchambers.com

ROBINSON MR DANIEL JOSEPH

Falcon Chambers
Falcon Court, London EC4Y 1AA, ☎020 7353 2484
✉clerks@falcon-chambers.com
Call Date: Oct 2008, Lincoln's Inn
Qualifications: [BA (Hons)]
robinson@falcon-chambers.com

ROBINSON MR DANIEL MICHAEL

5 King's Bench Walk
5 King's Bench Walk, Temple, London EC4Y 7DN, ☎020 7353 5638
✉clerks@5kbw.co.uk
Call Date: Nov 1993, Lincoln's Inn
Pupil Supervisor
Qualifications: [BSc]
daniel.robinson@5kbw.co.uk

ROBINSON MR DANIEL STEPHEN

18 Red Lion Court
London EC4A 3EB, ☎020 7520 6000
✉chambers@18rlc.co.uk
Call Date: July 2010, Gray's Inn
Qualifications: [BA]
daniel.robinson@18rlc.co.uk

ROBINSON MR GRAHAM ANDREW

9 St John Street
Manchester M3 4DN, ☎0161 955 9000
✉civilclerks@9sjs.com / criminalclerks@9sjs.com
Call Date: July 2009, Middle Temple
Qualifications: [BA (Hons) (Dunelm)]

ROBINSON MRS HELEN LOUISE

Amicus Chambers
Queens Court, Newport Road, Middlesbrough TS1 5EH, ☎01642 876334
✉amicus.clerk@amicuschambers.co.uk
Call Date: July 1998, Gray's Inn
Qualifications: [LLB (Hons)(Notts)]

ROBINSON MR JAMES EDWARD

Dere Street Barristers
14 Toft Green, York YO1 6JT, ☎0844 3351551
✉clerks@derestreet.co.uk
York Chambers
Rotterdam House, 116 The Quayside, Newcastle Upon Tyne NE1 3DY, ☎0191 206 4677
Call Date: Oct 1992, Middle Temple
Pupil Supervisor
Qualifications: [MA (St Andrews) Dip Law]
clerks@yorkchambers.co.uk

ROBINSON MISS KAREN

QEB Hollis Whiteman
1-2 Laurence Pountney Hill, London EC4R 0EU, ☎020 7933 8855
✉barristers@qebhw.co.uk
Call Date: Nov 2000, Lincoln's Inn
Qualifications: [MA (Hons) (Cantab)]
karen.robinson@qebhw.co.uk

ROBINSON MISS KATHERINE ANN

No.6 Park Square
Leeds LS1 2LW, ☎0113 245 9763
✉Tim@no6.co.uk
Call Date: July 2002, Gray's Inn
Qualifications: [BA (Dunelm)]
✉robinson@no6.co.uk

ROBINSON MISS KIRSTY ELIZABETH

Chavasse Court Chambers
18 Queen Avenue, Liverpool L2 4TX,
☎0151 229 2030
✉clerks@chavassechambers.co.uk
Call Date: Oct 2003, Gray's Inn
Qualifications: [MA (Glasgow)]
✉kirsty.robinson@chavassechambers.co.uk

ROBINSON MISS LAURA

Tanfield Chambers
2-5 Warwick Court, London WC1R 5DJ,
☎020 7421 5300
✉clerks@tanfieldchambers.co.uk
Call Date: Oct 2001, Inner Temple
Qualifications: [BSc (Durham) CPE PGDL]

ROBINSON MR MATTHEW JAMIE

Chartlands Chambers
3 St Giles Terrace, Northampton NN1 2BN,
☎01604 603322
✉enquiries@chartlands-chambers.co.uk
Call Date: Nov 1994, Inner Temple
Qualifications: [LLB]
✉mjrobinson.barrister@virgin.net

ROBINSON MR NICHOLAS DAVID JOHN

4 Breams Buildings
Chancery Lane, London EC4A 1HP,
☎020 7092 1900 ✉clerks@4bb.co.uk
Call Date: Oct 2007, Lincoln's Inn
Qualifications: [MA (Cantab)]

ROBINSON MR NICHOLAS GRAHAM

Ropewalk Chambers
24 The Ropewalk, Nottingham NG1 5EF,
☎0115 947 2581 ✉clerks@ropewalk.co.uk
Call Date: July 2007, Lincoln's Inn
Qualifications: [LLB (Dunelm)]
✉nicholasrobinson@ropewalk.co.uk

ROBINSON MR NICHOLAS JAMES LANSDALE

3 PB Barristers
3 Paper Buildings, Temple, London EC4Y 7EU,
☎020 7583 8055
3 PB Barristers
23 Beaumont Street, Oxford OX1 2NP,
☎01865 793 736
3 PB Barristers
4 St Peter Street, Winchester SO23 8BW,
☎01962 868884
✉clerks.winchester@3paper.co.uk
3 PB Barristers
Royal Talbot House, 2 Victoria Street, Bristol, Avon BS1 6BB, ☎0117 928 1520
3 PB Barristers
30 Christchurch Road, Bournemouth, Dorset BH1 3PD, ☎01202 292102
✉clerks.bournemouth@3paper.co.uk
Call Date: July 2006, Inner Temple
Qualifications: [BA (L'pool)]
✉nick.robinson@3paper.co.uk

ROBINSON MR SAM ANDREW

Tooks Chambers
81 Farringdon Street, London EC4A 4BL,
☎020 7842 7575 ✉clerks@tooks.co.uk
Call Date: Oct 2002, Middle Temple
Qualifications: [LLB]
✉sam.robinson@tooks.co.uk

ROBINSON MR STEPHEN MARK

Wilberforce Chambers
7 Bishop Lane, Hull HU1 1PA,
☎01482 323264
Call Date: Nov 1999, Gray's Inn
Qualifications: [BA (Cantab)]

ROBINSON MR THOMAS JAMES DANIELL

11 Stone Buildings
11 Stone Buildings, Lincoln's Inn, London WC2A 3TG, ☎020 7831 6381
✉clerks@11sb.com
Call Date: Oct 2003, Lincoln's Inn
Qualifications: [BA (Hons) (Oxon) Pg DL]
✉robinson@11sb.com

ROBINSON-YOUNG MR DAVID TILLEY

Dere Street Barristers
33 Broad Chare, Newcastle Upon Tyne NE1 3DQ, ☎0844 3351551
✉clerks@derestreet.co.uk
Call Date: July 1999, Lincoln's Inn
Pupil Supervisor
Qualifications: [LLB (Hons)]
✉clerks@broadcharechambers.co.uk, d.robinsonyoung@derestreet.co.uk

E

ROBLIN MISS LARAINE ARIANWEN

Iscoed Chambers
86 St Helen's Road, Swansea SA1 4BQ,
☎01792 652988
✉clerks@iscoedchambers.co.uk
Call Date: July 1981, Lincoln's Inn
Pupil Supervisor
Qualifications: [LLB (Wales)]
lr@iscoedchambers.co.uk

ROBOTTOM MR JAMES MALCOLM

Seven Bedford Row
7 Bedford Row, London WC1R 4BS,
☎020 7242 3555 ✉clerks@7br.co.uk
Call Date: July 2009, Lincoln's Inn
Qualifications: [BA (Sheff) CPE]
jrobottom@7br.co.uk

ROBSON MR ALEXANDER DANIEL NEIL

Littleton Chambers
3 King's Bench Walk North, Temple, London EC4Y 7HR, ☎020 7797 8600
✉fschneider@littletonchambers.co.uk
Call Date: July 2006, Middle Temple
Qualifications: [BA (Hons) (Cantab)]
arobson@littletonchambers.co.uk

ROBSON MR BARRY JAMES

New Court Chambers
3 Broad Chare, Newcastle Upon Tyne NE1 3DQ, ☎0191 232 1980
✉clerks@newcourt-chambers.co.uk
Call Date: July 2004, Gray's Inn
Qualifications: [LLB (Newc)]
barry.robson@newcourt-chambers.co.uk

ROBSON MR DAVID ERNEST HENRY QC (1980)

New Court Chambers
3 Broad Chare, Newcastle Upon Tyne NE1 3DQ, ☎0191 232 1980
✉clerks@newcourt-chambers.co.uk
KBW
The Engine House, No 1 Foundry Square, Leeds LS11 5DL, ☎0113 297 1200
✉clerks@kbwchambers.com
Call Date: Feb 1965, Inner Temple
Recorder
Qualifications: [MA (Oxon)]
drqc@kbwchambers.com

ROBSON MR JEREMY WILLIAM THOMAS

KCH Garden Square
1 Oxford Street, Nottingham NG1 5BH,
☎0115 941 8851
✉clerks@kchgardensquare.co.uk
Call Date: Oct 1999, Middle Temple
Qualifications: [LLB (Hons)]

ROBSON MR JOHN MALCOLM

Arden Chambers
20 Bloomsbury Square, London WC1A 2NS,
☎020 7242 4244
✉clerks@ardenchambers.com
Call Date: July 1974, Inner Temple
Pupil Supervisor
Qualifications: [LLB (Lond) FCIArb]
john.robson@ardenchambers.com

ROBSON MS SARAH JEAN

Alpha Court Chambers
Stuart House, Buckingham Lodge, 23 Kenilworth Road, Leamington Spa CV32 6JD,
☎01926 886412 ✉CP@Payton.uk.net
Call Date: July 2002, Inner Temple
Qualifications: [LLB (Lond)]

ROCHE DR JUANITA LOUISE

Five Paper
Ground Floor, 5 Paper Buildings, Temple, London EC4Y 7HB, ☎020 7815 3200
Call Date: July 2004, Gray's Inn
Qualifications: [MA (Cantab) PhD (Lond)]

ROCHE MISS MARIA

1 Crown Office Row
1 Crown Office Row, Temple, London EC4Y 7HH, ☎020 7797 7500
✉mail@1cor.com
Call Date: Oct 2010, Inner Temple
Qualifications: [BA (Oxon)]
maria.roche@1cor.com

ROCHE MR PATRICK RICHARD REDMOND

Tooks Chambers
81 Farringdon Street, London EC4A 4BL,
☎020 7842 7575 ✉clerks@tooks.co.uk
Call Date: July 1977, Middle Temple
Pupil Supervisor, Recorder
Qualifications: [MA (Oxon)]
patrick.roche@tooks.co.uk

E

ROCHFORD MR THOMAS NICHOLAS BEVERLEY

St Philips Chambers
55 Temple Row, Birmingham B2 5LS,
☎0121 246 7000 ✉clerks@st-philips.com
Call Date: July 1984, Inner Temple
Pupil Supervisor, Recorder
Qualifications: [MA (Cantab)]
✉trochford@st-philips.co.uk

ROCOS MR OLIVER

Chambers of Lawrence Jones
8 Stone Buildings, Lincoln's Inn, London
WC2A 3TA, ☎020 7831 1444
✉clerks@8stonebuildings.com
Call Date: July 2008, Lincoln's Inn
Qualifications: [BA LLB (Cardiff)]
✉oliverrocos@8stonebuildings.com

RODDICK MISS HELEN

9 Park Place
9 Park Place, Cardiff, South Glamorgan
CF10 3DP, ☎029 2038 2731
✉clerks@9parkplace.co.uk
Call Date: July 2004, Gray's Inn
Qualifications: [BA (Exon)]
✉hroddick@9parkplace.co.uk

RODDICK MR WINSTON QC (1986)

9 Park Place
9 Park Place, Cardiff, South Glamorgan
CF10 3DP, ☎029 2038 2731
✉clerks@9parkplace.co.uk
Call Date: Nov 1968, Gray's Inn
Recorder
Qualifications: [LLM]

RODERICK MR DAVID GEORGE

Farrar's Building
Farrar's Building, Temple, London EC4Y 7BD,
☎020 7583 9241
✉Chambers@farrarsbuilding.co.uk
Call Date: Oct 2005, Middle Temple
Qualifications: [LLM BA (Hons) MA (Lond)]
✉droderick@farrarsbuilding.co.uk

RODGER MR JONATHAN JAMES

Enterprise Chambers
65 Quayside, Newcastle Upon Tyne NE1 3DE,
☎0191 222 3344
✉newcastle@enterprisechambers.com
Enterprise Chambers
9 Old Square, Lincoln's Inn, London
WC2A 3SR, ☎020 7405 9471
✉london@enterprisechambers.com
Enterprise Chambers
43 Park Square, Leeds LS1 2NP,
☎0113 246 0391
✉leeds@enterprisechambers.com
Call Date: Nov 1999, Middle Temple
Qualifications: [BA (Hons)(Cantab)]
✉jonathanrodger@enterprisechambers.com

RODGER MR MARTIN OWEN QC (2006)

Falcon Chambers
Falcon Court, London EC4Y 1AA,
☎020 7353 2484
✉clerks@falcon-chambers.com
Call Date: July 1986, Middle Temple
Qualifications: [BA (Oxon)]
✉rodger@falcon-chambers.com

Types of work: Agriculture, Chancery (general), Chancery (land law), Commercial property, Common land, Housing, Landlord and tenant, Mining, Partnerships, Professional negligence

RODGERS MR BENEDICT JAMES

The Chambers of Grahame Aldous QC
9 Gough Square, London EC4A 3DG,
☎020 7832 0500
✉clerks@9goughsquare.co.uk
Call Date: Nov 2007, Inner Temple
Qualifications: [BA (Bris) LLB (Lond)]
✉brodgers@9goughsquare.co.uk

RODGERS MISS DORIS JUNE

Harcourt Chambers
1st Floor, 2 Harcourt Buildings, Temple,
London EC4Y 9DB, ☎0844 561 7135
Harcourt Chambers
Churchill House, 3 St Aldate's Courtyard, St
Aldate's, Oxford OX1 1BN, ☎0844 561 7135
Call Date: Nov 1971, Middle Temple
Pupil Supervisor, Recorder
Qualifications: [MA (Dub) MA (Oxon)]
✉jrodgers@harcourtchambers.law.co.uk

RODHAM MISS SUSAN ANNE

5 King's Bench Walk
5 King's Bench Walk, Temple, London
EC4Y 7DN, ☎020 7353 5638
✉clerks@5kbw.co.uk
Call Date: Nov 1989, Gray's Inn
Pupil Supervisor
Qualifications: [LLB]

E

RODIKIS MISS JOANNA

St Johns Buildings
24a - 28 St John Street, Manchester M3 4DJ, ☎0161 214 1500
✉clerk@stjohnsbuildings.co.uk
St Johns Buildings
21 White Friars, Chester CH1 1NZ, ☎01244 323070
✉clerk@stjohnsbuildings.co.uk
16 Winckley Square
Preston PR1 3JJ, ☎01772 256100
Call Date: Oct 1993, Middle Temple
Qualifications: [LLB (Hons)]
clerk@stjohnsbuildings.co.uk

RODWAY MISS SUSAN CAROLINE QC (2002)

39 Essex Street
London WC2R 3AT, ☎020 7832 1111
✉clerks@39essex.com
82 King Street
Manchester M2 4WQ, ☎0161 870 9969
Call Date: July 1981, Middle Temple
Qualifications: [BA (Hons)(Lond) Dip Law]
susan.rodway@39essex.com

E

RODWELL MR CHRISTOPHER JOHN

7 Bell Yard
London WC2A 2JR, ☎020 7831 0636
✉kevintarrant@btconnect.com
Call Date: Nov 1997, Middle Temple
Qualifications: [BA (Hons)]

ROE MR THOMAS IDRIS

3 Hare Court
3 Hare Court, Temple, London EC4Y 7BJ, ☎020 7415 7800 ✉clerks@3harecourt.com
Call Date: Oct 1995, Middle Temple
Pupil Supervisor
Qualifications: [MA (Cantab)]
thomasroe@3harecourt.com

ROGERS MISS AMY ELIZABETH CLARE

11 King's Bench Walk
11 King's Bench Walk, Temple, London EC4Y 7EQ, ☎020 7632 8500
✉clerksroom@11kbw.com
Call Date: July 2007, Lincoln's Inn
Qualifications: [BA (Cantab)]
amy.rogers@11kbw.com

ROGERS MISS BETHAN GWENLLIAN

Farringdon Chambers
180 Bermondsey Street, London SE1 3TQ, ☎020 7089 5700
Call Date: Oct 2007, Lincoln's Inn
Qualifications: [BA (York)]

ROGERS MISS BEVERLY-ANN

Serle Court
6 New Square, Lincoln's Inn, London WC2A 3QS, ☎020 7242 6105
✉clerks@serlecourt.co.uk
Call Date: July 1978, Middle Temple
Pupil Supervisor
Qualifications: [LLB (Lond)]
brogers@serlecourt.co.uk

ROGERS MR CHRISTOPHER THOMAS

Five Paper
Ground Floor, 5 Paper Buildings, Temple, London EC4Y 7HB, ☎020 7815 3200
Call Date: July 2004, Middle Temple
Qualifications: [MA (Cantab)]
christopherrogers@fivepaper.com

ROGERS MISS CHRISTY ABIGAIL

Ingenuity IP Chambers
Chambers Legal Service, 71b Queensway, Petts Wood, Kent BR5 1DQ
✉lp@chamberslegalservice.com
No. 3 Fleet Street Chambers
3 Fleet Street, London EC4Y 1DP, ☎020 7936 4474 ✉clerks@3fleetstreet.com
Call Date: Oct 1999, Middle Temple
Qualifications: [MA (Cantab) Dip Law]

ROGERS MR DANIEL JAMES

Number 7 Harrington Street Chambers
7 Harrington Street, Liverpool L2 9YH, ☎0151 242 0707 ✉clerks@7hs.co.uk
Call Date: Oct 1997, Inner Temple
Pupil Supervisor
Qualifications: [BA (Nottingham) CPE]
daniel.rogers@7hs.co.uk

ROGERS MR DONALD HALEY

Goldsmith Chambers
Ground Floor, Goldsmith Building, Temple, London EC4Y 7BL, ☎020 7353 6802
✉clerks@goldsmithchambers.com
Call Date: Nov 1991, Middle Temple
Qualifications: [LLB (Hons)]
D.Rogers@goldsmithchambers.law.co.uk

ROGERS MR GREGORY CHARLES

St Ive's Chambers
Whittall Street, Birmingham B4 6DH, ☎0121 236 0863
✉clerks@stiveschambers.co.uk
Call Date: Nov 1992, Gray's Inn
Pupil Supervisor
Qualifications: [BA (Hons)]
gregory.rogers@stiveschambers.co.uk

ROGERS MS HEATHER QC (2006)

Doughty Street Chambers
53-54 Doughty Street, London WC1N 2LS, ☎ 020 7404 1313
✉ enquiries@doughtystreet.co.uk
Doughty Street Chambers
Pall Mall Court, 61-67 King Street, Manchester M2 4PD, ☎ 0161 618 1066
Doughty Street Chambers
5th Floor, Broad Quay House, Prince Street, Bristol BS1 4DJ, ☎ 01179 058 717
Call Date: July 1983, Middle Temple
Recorder
Qualifications: [LLB (LSE)]

ROGERS MR IAN PAUL

Monckton Chambers
1 & 2 Raymond Buildings, Gray's Inn, London WC1R 5NR, ☎ 020 7405 7211
✉ chambers@monckton.com
Call Date: Oct 1995, Gray's Inn
Pupil Supervisor
Qualifications: [MA (Hons) (Oxon) LLM (Italy)]
✉ irogers@monckton.com

ROGERS MR JONATHAN

Exchange Chambers
One Derby Square, Derby Square, Liverpool L2 9XX, ☎ 0151 236 7747
✉ info@exchangechambers.co.uk
Exchange Chambers
7 Ralli Courts, West Riverside, Manchester M3 5FT, ☎ 0161 833 2722
Exchange Chambers
Oxford House, Oxford Row, Leeds LS1 3BE, ☎ 0113 203 1970
✉ spencer@exchangechambers.co.uk
Call Date: Oct 2000, Middle Temple
Qualifications: [LLB (Hons) (Manch)]
✉ rogers@exchangechambers.co.uk

ROGERS MISS KATE LOUISE

St Philips Chambers
55 Temple Row, Birmingham B2 5LS, ☎ 0121 246 7000 ✉ clerks@st-philips.com
Call Date: July 2009, Inner Temple
Qualifications: [LLB (Cardiff)]
✉ krogers@stphilips.com

ROGERS MR KENNETH EDWARD

Assize Court Chambers
14 Small Street, Bristol BS1 1DE, ☎ 0117 926 4587 ✉ carly@assize.co.uk
Invictus Chambers London
First Floor, 1 Mitre Court Buildings, Temple, London EC4Y 7BS
✉ admin@invictuschamberslondon.co.uk
Call Date: Nov 1999, Inner Temple
Qualifications: [LLB Hons (Bristol)]
Types of work: Civil actions against the police, Common law (general), Crime, Customs, Fraud

ROGERS MR MICHAEL PETER

Chambers of Mr Ami Feder
Ground Floor, Lamb Building, Temple, London EC4Y 7AS, ☎ 020 7797 7788
✉ clerks@lambbuilding.co.uk
Chambers of Mr Ami Feder
Ground Floor, Lamb Building, Temple, London EC4Y 7AS, ☎ 020 7797 7788
✉ clerks@lambbuilding.co.uk
Call Date: July 2002, Lincoln's Inn
Qualifications: [LLB (Hons) (London)]

ROGERS MISS SHONA LOUISE

1 KBW Chambers
1 King's Bench Walk, Temple, London EC4Y 7DB, ☎ 020 7936 1500
✉ clerks@1kbw.co.uk
Call Date: Oct 1998, Inner Temple
Qualifications: [LLB (Exon)]
✉ srogers@1kbw.co.uk

ROGERS MR SIMON PETER

Linenhall Chambers
1 Stanley Place, Chester CH1 2LU, ☎ 01244 348282
✉ clerks@linenhallchambers.co.uk
Call Date: Nov 2002, Gray's Inn
Qualifications: [LLB]
✉ spr@nicholasstreet.com

ROGERSON MISS JUDITH MARY

1 Crown Office Row
1 Crown Office Row, Temple, London EC4Y 7HH, ☎ 020 7797 7500
✉ mail@1cor.com
Call Date: July 2003, Lincoln's Inn
Pupil Supervisor
Qualifications: [BA Hons (Oxon)]
✉ judith.rogerson@1cor.com

ROLFE MR PATRICK JOHN BENEDICT

5 Stone Buildings
5 Stone Buildings, Lincoln's Inn, London WC2A 3XT, ☎ 020 7242 6201
✉ clerks@5sblaw.com
Call Date: Nov 1987, Middle Temple
Pupil Supervisor
Qualifications: [LLB (Lond)]
✉ prolfe@5sblaw.com

E

ROLLIN MR ARON DAVID RAPOPORT

Carmelite Chambers
9 Carmelite Street, London EC4Y 0DR,
☎020 7936 6300
✉clerks@carmelitechambers.co.uk
Call Date: Nov 2004, Middle Temple
Qualifications: [MA (Hons) (Edin)]
arollin@carmelitechambers.co.uk

ROLLINSON MR DARRYN ANDREW

15 New Bridge Street
London EC4V 6AU, ☎020 7842 1900
✉clerks@15nbs.com
Call Date: July 2001, Lincoln's Inn
Qualifications: [LLB (Hons)]
darryn.rollinson@15nbs.com

ROMANS MR PHILIP RUTHERS

Furnival Chambers
32 Furnival Street, London EC4A 1JQ,
☎020 7405 3232
Call Date: Nov 1982, Gray's Inn
Qualifications: [MA Oxon]
promans@furnivallaw.co.uk

E

ROMNEY MISS DAPHNE IRENE QC (2009)

Cloisters
1 Pump Court, Temple, London EC4Y 7AA,
☎020 7827 4000 ✉clerks@cloisters.com
Call Date: Nov 1979, Inner Temple
Qualifications: [BA (Cantab)]
dr@cloisters.com

ROOCHOVE MR MARK NATHAN

2 Pump Court
1st Floor, 2 Pump Court, Temple, London
EC4Y 7AH, ☎020 7353 5597
✉clerks@2pumpcourt.co.uk
Call Date: Oct 1994, Gray's Inn
Pupil Supervisor
Qualifications: [BSc (Wales)]
mroochove@2pumpcourt.co.uk

ROOK MISS RACHAEL EMILY

Call Date: Oct 2006, Lincoln's Inn
Qualifications: [BA (Sheff)]

ROOK MR STUART ALAN

Dere Street Barristers
33 Broad Chare, Newcastle Upon Tyne
NE1 3DQ, ☎0844 3351551
✉clerks@derestreet.co.uk
Call Date: Oct 2006, Gray's Inn
Qualifications: [BA]

ROOKE MR ALEXANDER JOHN GILES

Argent Chambers
5 Bell Yard, London WC2A 2JR,
☎020 7556 5500
✉briefsin@argentchambers.co.uk
Call Date: July 2001, Lincoln's Inn
Qualifications: [BA (Hons) MSc]
alexrooke@yahoo.com, A.Rooke@argentchambers.co.uk

ROONEY MR PAUL

QEB Hollis Whiteman
1-2 Laurence Pountney Hill, London
EC4R 0EU, ☎020 7933 8855
✉barristers@qebhw.co.uk
New Court Chambers
3 Broad Chare, Newcastle Upon Tyne
NE1 3DQ, ☎0191 232 1980
✉clerks@newcourt-chambers.co.uk
Call Date: July 2007, Inner Temple
Qualifications: [LLB (Teesside)]
Paul.Rooney@newcourt-chambers.co.uk

ROOTS MR GUY ROBERT GODFREY QC (1989)

Francis Taylor Building
Inner Temple, London EC4Y 7BY,
☎020 7353 8415 ✉clerks@ftb.eu.com
12 College Place
Fauvelle Buildings, 12 College Place,
Southampton SO15 2FE, ☎023 8032 0320
✉clerks@12cp.co.uk
Call Date: July 1969, Middle Temple
Qualifications: [MA (Oxon)]
guy.roots@ftb.eu.com
URL: www.ftb.eu.com

Types of work: Administrative law, Compulsory Purchase, Energy, Environment, Land compensation, Local authorities, Parliamentary, Planning, Rating and CPO

ROQUES MR MICHAEL

4 King's Bench Walk
2nd Floor, 4 King's Bench Walk, Temple,
London EC4Y 7DL, ☎020 7822 7000
✉clerks@4kbw.co.uk
Call Date: Nov 2000, Gray's Inn
Qualifications: [BA (Sussex)]
mar@4kbw.co.uk, clerks@4kbw.co.uk

ROSARIO MR DESMOND DAVID LUKE

Call Date: Nov 1990, Inner Temple
Qualifications: [LLB (Sheff)]
rosario@paradise-sq.co.uk, desrosario@mail.com

ROSCOE MR MARK ST JOHN WILLIAM

1 Mitre Court Buildings
1 Mitre Court Buildings, Temple, London EC4Y 7BS, ☎ 020 7452 8900
✉ clerks@1mcb.com
Call Date: Oct 1999, Lincoln's Inn
Qualifications: [BA (Hons)(Lond) Dip in Law]
mark.roscoe@1mcb.com

ROSCOE MR THOMAS HENRY

Wilberforce Chambers
8 New Square, Lincoln's Inn, London WC2A 3QP, ☎ 020 7306 0102
✉ chambers@wilberforce.co.uk
Call Date: July 2010, Inner Temple
Qualifications: [BA(Oxon)]
troscoe@wilberforce.co.uk

ROSE MR ALEXANDER JAMES

Garden Court Chambers
57-60 Lincoln's Inn Fields, London WC2A 3LJ, ☎ 020 7993 7600 ✉ info@gclaw.co.uk
Call Date: July 2003, Gray's Inn
Qualifications: [LLB (Bris)]
alexr@gclaw.co.uk

ROSE MR ANTHONY KENNETH

Chavasse Court Chambers
18 Queen Avenue, Liverpool L2 4TX, ☎ 0151 229 2030
✉ clerks@chavassechambers.co.uk
Call Date: Nov 1978, Middle Temple
Qualifications: [LLM (Lond)]
anthony.rose@chavassechambers.co.uk

ROSE MR DAVID LESLIE

No.6 Park Square
Leeds LS1 2LW, ☎ 0113 245 9763
✉ Tim@no6.co.uk
Call Date: July 1977, Middle Temple
Pupil Supervisor
Qualifications: [MA LLB (Cantab)]
rose@no6.co.uk

ROSE MISS DINAH GWEN LISON QC (2006)

Blackstone Chambers
Blackstone House, Temple, London EC4Y 9BW, ☎ 020 7583 1770
✉ clerks@blackstonechambers.com
Call Date: July 1989, Gray's Inn
Qualifications: [BA (Oxon)]
dinahrose@blackstonechambers.com

ROSE MR MARTIN CHRISTOPHER

New Court Chambers
3 Broad Chare, Newcastle Upon Tyne NE1 3DQ, ☎ 0191 232 1980
✉ clerks@newcourt-chambers.co.uk
Call Date: July 1999, Lincoln's Inn
Qualifications: [LLB (Hons)]
christopher.rose@newcourt-chambers.co.uk

ROSE MISS PAMELA SUSAN

1 Mitre Court Buildings
1 Mitre Court Buildings, Temple, London EC4Y 7BS, ☎ 020 7452 8900
✉ clerks@1mcb.com
Call Date: July 1980, Inner Temple
Pupil Supervisor
Qualifications: [BA]

ROSE MR PAUL TELFER QC (2002)

Old Square Chambers
10-11 Bedford Row, London WC1R 4BU, ☎ 020 7269 0300 ✉ clerks@oldsquare.co.uk
Old Square Chambers
3 Orchard Court, St Augustine's Yard, Bristol BS1 5DP, ☎ 0117 930 5100
✉ clerks@oldsquare.co.uk
Call Date: Nov 1981, Gray's Inn
Qualifications: [LLB (Reading)]
roseqc@oldsquare.co.uk

ROSE MR STEPHEN PAUL

18 Red Lion Court
London EC4A 3EB, ☎ 020 7520 6000
✉ chambers@18rlc.co.uk
18 Red Lion Court (Annexe)
Thornwood House, 102 New London Road, Chelmsford, Essex CM2 0RG, ☎ 01245 280880
Call Date: Nov 1995, Gray's Inn
Qualifications: [BA (Oxon)]
stephen.rose@18rlc.co.uk

ROSE MR WILLIAM STEVEN

King's Bench and Godolphin (KBG)Chambers
115 North Hill, Plymouth, Devon PL4 8JY, ☎ 01752 221551
✉ clerks@kbgchambers.co.uk
Call Date: July 2007, Inner Temple
Qualifications: [LLB (Derby)]
wr@kbgchambers.co.uk

E

ROSEMAN MR GIDEON TYLER

Ten Old Square
Ground Floor, Ten Old Square, Lincoln's Inn, London WC2A 3SU, ☎ 020 7405 0758
✉ clerks@tenoldsquare.com
Call Date: July 2007, Inner Temple
Qualifications: [LLB (Bris) LLM (Cantab)]
gideonroseman@tenoldsquare.com

ROSEMARINE MR ANDREW MARC

Chambers of Mr A M Rosemarine
International Law Chambers, 78 Cavendish Road, Salford, Manchester M7 4WA, ☎ 0161 740 3861 ✉ help@rosemarine.co.uk
Call Date: Nov 1989, Gray's Inn
Qualifications: [MA (Oxon) Lic Spec en Droit Eur (Belgium) BCL (Oxon)]

ROSEN MR JONATHAN LEON

1 Gray's Inn Square
Ground Floor, 1 Gray's Inn Square, London WC1R 5AA, ☎ 020 7405 0001
Call Date: Nov 1996, Gray's Inn
Qualifications: [BSc (Hons) LLB (Hons)]

ROSENBLATT MR JEREMY GEORGE

42 Bedford Row
London WC1R 4LL, ☎ 020 7831 0222
✉ clerks@42br.com
Call Date: July 1985, Gray's Inn
Qualifications: [LLB (Hons) (LSE)]
jeremy.rosenblatt@42br.com

ROSENTHAL MR ADAM

Falcon Chambers
Falcon Court, London EC4Y 1AA, ☎ 020 7353 2484
✉ clerks@falcon-chambers.com
Call Date: Oct 1999, Gray's Inn
Pupil Supervisor
Qualifications: [MA]
rosenthal@falcon-chambers.com

ROSENTHAL MR DENNIS

Henderson Chambers
2 Harcourt Buildings, Temple, London EC4Y 9DB, ☎ 020 7583 9020
✉ clerks@hendersonchambers.co.uk
Call Date: Nov 2009, Gray's Inn
drosenthal@hendersonchambers.co.uk

ROSS MR ANTHONY JOHN

1 Pump Court
Elm Court, Temple, London EC4Y 7AB, ☎ 020 7842 7070
✉ (name)@pumpcourt.co.uk
Call Date: Oct 1991, Lincoln's Inn
Qualifications: [LLB (Hons) (Leeds)]

ROSS MRS FIONA LOUISE

Sovereign Chambers
46 Park Place, Leeds LS1 2RY, ☎ 0113 245 1841
✉ clerks@sovereignchambers.co.uk
Call Date: Nov 2004, Lincoln's Inn
Qualifications: [MA (Hons) PgDL]
fiona.ross@sovereignchambers.co.uk

ROSS MR GORDON MACRAE

3 Temple Gardens
Lower Ground Floor, 3 Temple Gardens, Temple, London EC4Y 9AU, ☎ 020 7353 3102
✉ clerks@3tg.co.uk
Call Date: July 1986, Inner Temple
Qualifications: [LLB]
gr@3tg.co.uk

ROSS MR IAIN ALASDAIR

3 PB Barristers
3 Paper Buildings, Temple, London EC4Y 7EU, ☎ 020 7583 8055
3 PB Barristers
Royal Talbot House, 2 Victoria Street, Bristol, Avon BS1 6BB, ☎ 0117 928 1520
3 PB Barristers
4 St Peter Street, Winchester SO23 8BW, ☎ 01962 868884
✉ clerks.winchester@3paper.co.uk
3 PB Barristers
23 Beaumont Street, Oxford OX1 2NP, ☎ 01865 793 736
3 PB Barristers
30 Christchurch Road, Bournemouth, Dorset BH1 3PD, ☎ 01202 292102
✉ clerks.bournemouth@3paper.co.uk
Call Date: Nov 1991, Inner Temple
Pupil Supervisor
Qualifications: [LLB (Scotland) Dip Law]
iain.ross@3paper.co.uk

ROSS MR JAMES FRASER

Maidstone Chambers
33 Earl Street, Maidstone, Kent ME14 1PF, ☎ 01622 688592
✉ clerks@maidstonechambers.co.uk
Call Date: Nov 2001, Gray's Inn
Qualifications: [BA (Lond) CPE (City)]

ROSS MR JAMES WILLIAM

Gough Square Chambers
6-7 Gough Square, London EC4A 3DE, ☎ 020 7353 0924 ✉ gsc@goughsq.co.uk
Call Date: Oct 2006, Inner Temple
Qualifications: [LLB (Lond)]
james.ross@goughsq.co.uk

ROSS MS JENNIFER

King's Bench Chambers
Wellington House, 175 Holdenhurst Road, Bournemouth, Dorset BH8 8DQ,
☎01202 250025
Call Date: July 2007, Middle Temple
Qualifications: [BA (Hons) (Nott'm)]

ROSS MR JOHN GRAFFIN QC (2001)

1 Chancery Lane
London WC2A 1LF, ☎0845 634 6666
✉clerks@1chancerylane.com
Call Date: July 1971, Inner Temple
Recorder
Qualifications: [LLB LLM (London)]
jross@1chancerylane.com

ROSS MR SIDNEY DAVID

11 Stone Buildings
11 Stone Buildings, Lincoln's Inn, London WC2A 3TG, ☎020 7831 6381
✉clerks@11sb.com
Call Date: July 1983, Middle Temple
Pupil Supervisor
Qualifications: [LLB (London) MSc PhD FCIArb]

ROSS MR SIMON HADLEIGH

Zenith Chambers
10 Park Square, Leeds LS1 2LH,
☎0113 245 5438
✉clerks@zenithchambers.co.uk
Call Date: Nov 1999, Lincoln's Inn
Pupil Supervisor
Qualifications: [LLB (Hons)(Reading)]
simonross@zenithchambers.co.uk

ROSS MARTYN MR JOHN GREAVES

New Square Chambers
12 New Square, Lincoln's Inn, London WC2A 3SW, ☎020 7419 8000
✉robin.hollington@newsquarechambers.co.uk
Octagon House
19 Colegate, Norwich NR3 1AT,
☎01603 623186
✉clerks@octagonhouse.co.uk
Call Date: July 1969, Middle Temple
Pupil Supervisor
Qualifications: [MA FCIArb LLM]

Fax: 020 7419 8050;
DX: 1056 London

Types of work: Boundaries, Chancery, Chancery (general), Chancery (land law), Charities, Conveyancing, Dispute resolution and arbitration, Equity, Family provision, Inheritance and cohabitees, Landlord and tenant, Mediation, Mortgages, Partnerships, Professional negligence, Real property, Rights of light, Rights of way, Succession, Title to land, Trust litigation, Trusts, Wills

Awards and memberships: Chartered arbitrator; Panel Member, Chartered Institute of Arbitrators; Member, Society of Trust and Estate Practitioners (STEP) and Association of Contentious Trust and Probate Specialists (ACTAPS); qualified mediator

Other professional experience: Lecturer, Birmingham College of Commerce (now the University of Central England at Birmingham) 1966-8

Publications: *Family Provision: Law and Practice*, 2010; *Williams, Mortimer and Sunnucks on Executors, Administrators and Probate* (Joint Editor, 2008), new edition in preparation, 2008; *Family Provision: Law and Practice*, 2010

Reported Cases: *Lankesheer, decd; Rees v Newbery*, [1998] 1 FLR 1041 (High Court), 1998. Inheritance (Provision for Family and Dependants) Act 1975; friend and tenant a person maintained by the deceased.
Taylor v Dickens, [1998] 1 FLR 806 (High Court), 1998. Promise to leave house to gardener gave no rights (an appeal was compromised).
Re B, deceased, [2000] Ch 662 (Court of Appeal), 1999. Mother maintained by daughter; maintenance under the 1975 Act a question of fact.
Re Key deceased, [2010] 1 WLR 2020 (High Court), 2010. Effect of bereavement on testamentary capacity.
Hubbard v Scott, [2012] WTLR 29 (High Court), 2011. Nature of online influence in probate

ROTHERY MR PETER

Deans Court Chambers
24 St John Street, Manchester M3 4DF,
☎0161 214 6000 ✉clerks@deanscourt.co.uk
Deans Court Chambers
101 Walker Street, Preston PR1 2RR,
☎01772 565 600
✉preston@deanscourt.co.uk
Call Date: Oct 1994, Lincoln's Inn
Pupil Supervisor
Qualifications: [BA (Hons)(Oxon)]

E

ROTHSCHILD MR GERARD PHILIP

Brick Court Chambers
7-8 Essex Street, London WC2R 3LD,
☎020 7379 3550 ✉clerks@brickcourt.co.uk
Call Date: July 2005, Lincoln's Inn
Qualifications: [BA (Hons) Oxon BCL Oxon]
gerard.rothschild@brickcourt.co.uk

ROTHWELL MRS JOANNE LESLEY

No5 Chambers
Fountain Court, Steelhouse Lane, Birmingham B4 6DR, ☎0845 210 5555 ✉info@no5.com
No5 Chambers
Greenwood House, 4-7 Salisbury Court, London EC4Y 8AA, ☎0845 210 5555
No5 Chambers
38 Queen Square, Bristol BS1 4QS,
☎0845 210 5555
Call Date: Oct 1993, Inner Temple
Qualifications: [LLB (Hons) RGN Dip Couns]

ROUCH MR PETER CHRISTOPHER QC (1996)

3 Temple Gardens
Lower Ground Floor, 3 Temple Gardens, Temple, London EC4Y 9AU, ☎020 7353 3102
✉clerks@3tg.co.uk
Apex
Harlech House, 20 Cathedral Road, Cardiff CF11 9LJ, ☎02920 232 032
✉clerks@apexchambers.net
Iscoed Chambers
86 St Helen's Road, Swansea SA1 4BQ,
☎01792 652988
✉clerks@iscoedchambers.co.uk
Call Date: July 1972, Gray's Inn
Recorder
Qualifications: [LLB (Wales)]

ROUCH MR ROBIN BENJAMIN FRANCIS

Iscoed Chambers
86 St Helen's Road, Swansea SA1 4BQ,
☎01792 652988
✉clerks@iscoedchambers.co.uk
Call Date: Nov 1999, Gray's Inn
Pupil Supervisor
Qualifications: [BA (Kent)]
rr@iscoedchambers.co.uk

ROUGHT-BROOKS MISS HANNAH MILDRED

Tooks Chambers
81 Farringdon Street, London EC4A 4BL,
☎020 7842 7575 ✉clerks@tooks.co.uk
Call Date: Mar 1999, Middle Temple
Qualifications: [LLB (Hons)(B'ham)]
hannahrought-brooks@tooks.co.uk

ROUGHTON MR ASHLEY WENTWORTH

Hogarth Chambers
5 New Square, Lincoln's Inn, London WC2A 3RJ, ☎020 7404 0404
✉barristers@hogarthchambers.com
Call Date: Oct 1992, Inner Temple
Pupil Supervisor
Qualifications: [BSc (Hons)(Lond) PhD (Cantab) Dip Law MSc (Econ) (City)]
aroughton@hogarthchambers.com

ROUND MS KATHRINE SUSAN

5 Pump Court
Ground Floor, 5 Pump Court, Temple, London EC4Y 7AP, ☎020 7353 2532
✉clerks@5pumpcourt.com
Call Date: Oct 2005, Inner Temple
Qualifications: [BA University of Manchester CPE University of B]
kate.round@btinternet.com, kateround@5pumpcourt.com

ROUSE MR JAMES EDWARD

187 Fleet Street
London EC4A 2AT, ☎020 7430 7430
✉chambers@187fleetstreet.com
Call Date: July 2000, Gray's Inn
Qualifications: [BA (Lond)]
jamesrouse@187fleetstreet.com

ROUSE MR JUSTIN CLIVE DOUGLAS

Nine Bedford Row
9 Bedford Row, London WC1R 4AZ,
☎020 7489 2727
✉clerks@9bedfordrow.co.uk
Call Date: July 1982, Lincoln's Inn
Pupil Supervisor, Recorder
Qualifications: [BA]
justin.rouse@9bedfordrow.co.uk

ROUSSAK MR JEREMY BRIAN

Kings Chambers
36 Young Street, Manchester M3 3FT,
☎0845 034 3444
✉clerks@kingschambers.com
Kings Chambers
5 Park Square East, Leeds LS1 2NE,
☎0845 034 3444
✉clerks@kingschambers.com
Kings Chambers
Embassy House, 60 Church Street, Birmingham B3 2DJ, ☎0845 034 3444
✉clerks@kingschambers.com
Call Date: Oct 1996, Middle Temple
Qualifications: [MA (Cantab) FRCSEd (Lond) BChir (Cantab) MB (Cantab) CPE (Lond)]

E

ROUTLEDGE MR SHAUN WILLIAM

Trinity Chambers
The Custom House, 39 Quayside, Newcastle Upon Tyne NE1 3DE, ☎0191 232 1927
✉info@trinitychambers.co.uk
Trinity Chambers
Multi Media Exchange, 72-80 Corporation Road, Middlesbrough TS1 2RF, ☎01642 247569
✉info@trinitychambers.co.uk
Call Date: Nov 1988, Gray's Inn
Qualifications: [LLB (L'pool)]
✉s.routledge@trinitychambers.co.uk

ROUTLEY MR PATRICK

Goldsmith Chambers
Ground Floor, Goldsmith Building, Temple, London EC4Y 7BL, ☎020 7353 6802
✉clerks@goldsmithchambers.com
Call Date: July 1979, Inner Temple
Pupil Supervisor
Qualifications: [MA (Cantab) DipLaw]
✉P.Routley@goldsmithchambers.law.co.uk

ROW MR CHARLES PHILIP

Queen Square Chambers
56 Queen Square, Bristol BS1 4PR, ☎0117 921 1966 ✉crime@qs-c.co.uk
Call Date: Oct 1993, Lincoln's Inn
Pupil Supervisor
Qualifications: [BA (Hons)(Portsmith)]
✉cpr@qs-c.co.uk

ROWE MISS FREYA EMILY BEATRICE

Thomas More Chambers
7 Lincoln's Inn Fields, London WC2A 3BP, ☎020 7404 7000
✉clerks@thomasmore.co.uk
Call Date: Oct 1996, Inner Temple
Qualifications: [BA (Oxon) CPE (Sussex)]
✉frowe@thomasmore.co.uk

ROWELL MR DAVID STEWART

9 Stone Buildings
Lincoln's Inn, London WC2A 3NN, ☎020 7404 5055
✉clerks@9stonebuildings.com
Call Date: July 1972, Gray's Inn
Pupil Supervisor
Qualifications: [BA (Oxon)]
✉drowell@9stonebuildings.com

ROWELL MR GEORGE EDWARD

St John's Chambers
101 Victoria Street, Bristol BS1 6PU, ☎0117 923 4700
✉clerks@stjohnschambers.co.uk
Call Date: Nov 2004, Lincoln's Inn
Qualifications: [MA (Oxon) MA]
✉george.rowell@stjohnschambers.co.uk

ROWLAND MR NICHOLAS EDWARD

3 PB Barristers
3 Paper Buildings, Temple, London EC4Y 7EU, ☎020 7583 8055
3 PB Barristers
30 Christchurch Road, Bournemouth, Dorset BH1 3PD, ☎01202 292102
✉clerks.bournemouth@3paper.co.uk
3 PB Barristers
4 St Peter Street, Winchester SO23 8BW, ☎01962 868884
✉clerks.winchester@3paper.co.uk
3 PB Barristers
Royal Talbot House, 2 Victoria Street, Bristol, Avon BS1 6BB, ☎0117 928 1520
3 PB Barristers
23 Beaumont Street, Oxford OX1 2NP, ☎01865 793 736
Call Date: July 1988, Inner Temple
Pupil Supervisor, Recorder
Qualifications: [BA (Bristol) Dip Law (Lond)]
✉nicholas.rowland@3paper.co.uk

ROWLAND MR ROBIN FRANK

No5 Chambers
Fountain Court, Steelhouse Lane, Birmingham B4 6DR, ☎0845 210 5555 ✉info@no5.com
No5 Chambers
Greenwood House, 4-7 Salisbury Court, London EC4Y 8AA, ☎0845 210 5555
No5 Chambers
38 Queen Square, Bristol BS1 4QS, ☎0845 210 5555
Call Date: Nov 1977, Middle Temple
Pupil Supervisor, Recorder
Qualifications: [LLB]
✉rr@no5.com

ROWLANDS MS CATHERINE JANET

Cornerstone Barristers
2-3 Gray's Inn Square, Gray's Inn, London WC1R 5JH, ☎020 7242 4986
✉chambers@2-3gis.co.uk
Call Date: Nov 1992, Gray's Inn
Qualifications: [LLB (Hons)(Lond) Maitrise en Droit (Paris)]
✉crowlands@2-3gis.co.uk

E

ROWLANDS MR DAVID PETER ANDREW

Dere Street Barristers
33 Broad Chare, Newcastle Upon Tyne NE1 3DQ, ☎0844 3351551
✉clerks@derestreet.co.uk
Call Date: Nov 1988, Middle Temple
Pupil Supervisor
Qualifications: [LLB (Manch)]
clerks@broadcharechambers.co.uk

ROWLANDS MR MARC HUMPHREYS QC (2012)

Keating Chambers
15 Essex Street, London WC2R 3AA,
☎020 7544 2600
✉clerks@keatingchambers.com
Call Date: Nov 1990, Gray's Inn
Pupil Supervisor
Qualifications: [BA Hons (Oxon)]
mrowlands@keatingchambers.com

ROWLANDS MR MARK ANDREW LEWIS

Thomas More Chambers
7 Lincoln's Inn Fields, London WC2A 3BP,
☎020 7404 7000
✉clerks@thomasmore.co.uk
Call Date: Oct 2009, Lincoln's Inn
Qualifications: [BA (Nott'm) CPE COL]

ROWLANDS MR PETER FRANCIS CLEVELAND

Garden Court Chambers
57-60 Lincoln's Inn Fields, London WC2A 3LJ,
☎020 7993 7600 ✉info@gclaw.co.uk
Call Date: Feb 1990, Middle Temple
Pupil Supervisor
Qualifications: [BA (Hons) (Oxon)]
peterr@gclaw.co.uk

ROWLEY MR JOHN JAMES QC (2006)

Byrom Street Chambers
12 Byrom Street, Manchester M3 4PP,
☎0161 829 2100 ✉clerks@byromstreet.com
Crown Office Chambers
2 Crown Office Row, Temple, London EC4Y 7HJ, ☎020 7797 8100
✉mail@crownofficechambers.com
42 Bedford Row
London WC1R 4LL, ☎020 7831 0222
✉clerks@42br.com
Call Date: July 1987, Lincoln's Inn
Recorder
Qualifications: [MA (Cantab) Dip Law]
james.rowley@byromstreet.com

ROWLEY MR KARL JOHN

St Johns Buildings
24a - 28 St John Street, Manchester M3 4DJ,
☎0161 214 1500
✉clerk@stjohnsbuildings.co.uk
16 Winckley Square
Preston PR1 3JJ, ☎01772 256100
St Johns Buildings Liverpool
8th Floor India Buildings, Water Street, Liverpool L2 0XG, ☎0151 243 6000
✉clerk@stjohnsbuildings.co.uk
Call Date: Nov 1994, Middle Temple
Recorder
Qualifications: [MA (Oxon)]
clerk@stjohnsbuildings.co.uk

ROWLEY MR KEITH NIGEL QC (2001)

Radcliffe Chambers
Ground Floor, 11 New Square, Lincoln's Inn, London WC2A 3QB, ☎020 7831 0081
✉clerks@radcliffechambers.com
Call Date: July 1979, Gray's Inn
Qualifications: [LLB (Lond)]
krowley@radcliffechambers.com

Fax: 020 7405 2560

Types of work: Chancery (general), Commercial property, Company, commercial and competition, Landlord and tenant, Pensions, Professional negligence

ROWLEY MISS LESLEY LENORA JANE

Queen Square Chambers
56 Queen Square, Bristol BS1 4PR,
☎0117 921 1966 ✉crime@qs-c.co.uk
Call Date: July 1988, Gray's Inn
Recorder
Qualifications: [LLB (Wales)]

ROWLEY MRS RACHEL ELISABETH

No5 Chambers
Fountain Court, Steelhouse Lane, Birmingham B4 6DR, ☎0845 210 5555 ✉info@no5.com
No5 Chambers
Greenwood House, 4-7 Salisbury Court, London EC4Y 8AA, ☎0845 210 5555
No5 Chambers
38 Queen Square, Bristol BS1 4QS,
☎0845 210 5555
Call Date: Nov 1997, Middle Temple
Pupil Supervisor
Qualifications: [BA (Hons)(Keele)]
rro@no5.com

E

ROWLEY-FOX MS RACHAEL

Garden Court Chambers
57-60 Lincoln's Inn Fields, London WC2A 3LJ,
☎ 020 7993 7600 ✉ info@gclaw.co.uk
Call Date: July 1998, Gray's Inn
Pupil Supervisor
Qualifications: [BA (Hull) Pg Dip Law]
✉ rachaelrf@gclaw.co.uk

ROWLING MISS FIONA JANE

Westgate Chambers
64 High Street, Lewes, East Sussex BN7 1XG,
☎ 01273 480510
✉ clerks@westgate-chambers.co.uk
Call Date: July 1980, Inner Temple
Qualifications: [LLB (Lond)]
✉ FR@westgate-chambers.co.uk

ROWLINSON MISS WENDY JULIA

Pallant Chambers
12 North Pallant, Chichester, West Sussex
PO19 1TQ, ☎ 01243 784538
✉ clerks@pallantchambers.co.uk
Call Date: July 1981, Gray's Inn
Qualifications: [BA]
✉ wrowlinson@pallantchambers.co.uk

ROWNTREE MR EDWARD JOHN PICKERING

Hardwicke
New Square, Lincoln's Inn, London
WC2A 3SB, ☎ 020 7242 2523
✉ enquiries@hardwicke.co.uk
Call Date: Oct 1996, Lincoln's Inn
Qualifications: [BA (Hons)(Oxon)]
✉ edward.rowntree@hardwicke.co.uk

ROWSELL MISS CLAIRE LOUISE

Albion Chambers
Broad Street, Bristol BS1 1DR,
☎ 0117 927 2144
✉ clerks@albionchambers.co.uk
Call Date: Feb 1991, Middle Temple
Pupil Supervisor
Qualifications: [LLB]
✉ claire.rowsell@albionchambers.co.uk

ROWSELL MR PAUL JOHN

Devon Chambers
3 St Andrew Street, Plymouth PL1 2AH,
☎ 01752 661659
✉ clerks@devonchambers.co.uk
Call Date: July 1971, Inner Temple
Pupil Supervisor
Qualifications: [LLB (Hons)]

ROXBURGH MR ALAN JOHN NORTON

Brick Court Chambers
7-8 Essex Street, London WC2R 3LD,
☎ 020 7379 3550 ✉ clerks@brickcourt.co.uk
Call Date: Oct 1992, Middle Temple
Pupil Supervisor
Qualifications: [MA (Oxon) Dip Law(Lond)]
✉ Alan.Roxburgh@Brickcourt.co.uk

ROY MR ANDREW ROBERT

12 King's Bench Walk
12 King's Bench Walk, Temple, London
EC4Y 7EL, ☎ 020 7583 0811
Call Date: July 2002, Lincoln's Inn
Pupil Supervisor
Qualifications: [LLB (Hons) MA]
✉ roy@12kbw.co.uk

ROY MR STEFAN ALEXANDER HIREN

5 Pump Court
Ground Floor, 5 Pump Court, Temple, London
EC4Y 7AP, ☎ 020 7353 2532
✉ clerks@5pumpcourt.com
Call Date: May 1996, Gray's Inn
Qualifications: [LLB]

ROYCE MR DARRYL FRASER

Atkin Chambers
1 Atkin Building, Gray's Inn, London
WC1R 5AT, ☎ 020 7404 0102
✉ clerks@atkinchambers.com
Call Date: Nov 1976, Gray's Inn
Pupil Supervisor
Qualifications: [BA]
✉ droyce@atkinchambers.com

ROYLE MR CHARLES FANSHAWE

Goldsmith Chambers
Ground Floor, Goldsmith Building, Temple,
London EC4Y 7BL, ☎ 020 7353 6802
✉ clerks@goldsmithchambers.com
Call Date: Oct 1997, Lincoln's Inn
Qualifications: [BSc (Hons) Dip law]
✉ C.Royle@goldsmithchambers.law.co.uk

ROYLE MR CHRISTOPHER ANDREW

Exchange Chambers
Oxford House, Oxford Row, Leeds LS1 3BE,
☎ 0113 203 1970
✉ spencer@exchangechambers.co.uk
Exchange Chambers
One Derby Square, Derby Square, Liverpool
L2 9XX, ☎ 0151 236 7747
✉ info@exchangechambers.co.uk

E

Exchange Chambers
7 Ralli Courts, West Riverside, Manchester M3 5FT, ☎ 0161 833 2722
Call Date: July 2009, Lincoln's Inn
Qualifications: [LLB (Hons) MA (Cantab)]

ROYLE MR RICHARD WILLIAM CARTER

Devereux Chambers
Queen Elizabeth Building, Temple, London EC4Y 9BS, ☎ 020 7353 7534
✉ clerks@devchambers.co.uk
Call Date: Nov 1983, Gray's Inn
Qualifications: [BA (York)]
rroyle@sirowendixon.com.au

ROZIER MR JAMES IAN

1 Gray's Inn Square
Ground Floor, 1 Gray's Inn Square, London WC1R 5AA, ☎ 020 7405 0001
Rougemont Chambers
Victory House, Dean Clarke Gardens, Southernhay East, Exeter EX2 4AA, ☎ 01392 208484
✉ clerks@rougemontchambers.co.uk
Call Date: Nov 2007, Middle Temple
Qualifications: [BSc (Hons) (Wales) CPE (Wales) Dip Law (Wales)]
jrozier@1gis.co.uk

RUBENS MISS JACQUELINE ANN

1 Pump Court
Elm Court, Temple, London EC4Y 7AB, ☎ 020 7842 7070
✉ (name)@pumpcourt.co.uk
Call Date: Nov 1989, Inner Temple
Qualifications: [BA (USA) LLB (Hons) (Lond)]

RUBIN MR STEPHEN CHARLES QC (2000)

Fountain Court Chambers
Fountain Court, Temple, London EC4Y 9DH, ☎ 020 7583 3335
✉ chambers@fountaincourt.co.uk
Call Date: July 1977, Middle Temple
Recorder
Qualifications: [MA (Oxon)]
sr@fountaincourt.co.uk

RUCK MS MARY IDA

Byrom Street Chambers
12 Byrom Street, Manchester M3 4PP, ☎ 0161 829 2100 ✉ clerks@byromstreet.com
Crown Office Chambers
2 Crown Office Row, Temple, London EC4Y 7HJ, ☎ 020 7797 8100
✉ mail@crownofficechambers.com
42 Bedford Row
London WC1R 4LL, ☎ 020 7831 0222
✉ clerks@42br.com
Call Date: Oct 1993, Gray's Inn
Pupil Supervisor
Qualifications: [BA (Hons) MA]
mary.ruck@byromstreet.com

RUCK KEENE MR ALEXANDER CHARLES EDWARD

39 Essex Street
London WC2R 3AT, ☎ 020 7832 1111
✉ clerks@39essex.com
82 King Street
Manchester M2 4WQ, ☎ 0161 870 9969
Call Date: Oct 2002, Lincoln's Inn
Pupil Supervisor
Qualifications: [BA (Hons) (Oxon) MA (USA)]
alex.ruckkeene@39essex.com

RUDD MR MATTHEW ALLAN

Broadway House Chambers
Broadway House, 9 Bank Street, Bradford, West Yorkshire BD1 1TW, ☎ 01274 722560
✉ clerks@broadwayhouse.co.uk
Broadway House Chambers
25 Park Square West, Leeds, West Yorkshire LS1 2PW, ☎ 0113 246 2600
✉ clerks@broadwayhouse.co.uk
Call Date: Nov 1994, Inner Temple
Pupil Supervisor
Qualifications: [LLB (Hons)(Sheff)]
mr@broadwayhouse.co.uk

RUDD MR MICHAEL

36 Bedford Row
London WC1R 4JH, ☎ 020 7421 8000
✉ chambers@36bedfordrow.co.uk
Call Date: Oct 2002, Inner Temple
Qualifications: [BSc (Hons) (Keele) MSc (Dunelm) LLM (Kent) CPE PgDIP]

RUDD MR OLIVER JONATHAN PETER

12 King's Bench Walk
12 King's Bench Walk, Temple, London EC4Y 7EL, ☎ 020 7583 0811
Call Date: Mar 2009, Lincoln's Inn
Qualifications: [BA (Oxon) CPE UCU MSc (Lond)]
rudd@12kbw.co.uk

RUDD MISS ZOE ANN

College Chambers
19 Carlton Crescent, Southampton, Hampshire SO15 2ET, ☎ 023 8023 0338
✉ clerks@college-chambers.co.uk
Call Date: July 2003, Gray's Inn
Qualifications: [LLB (De Mont)]
✉ zrudd@College-Chambers.co.uk

RUDMAN MISS SARA ANN

Pendragon Chambers
Suite 7, J Shed, Kings Road, SA1 Waterfront, Swansea SA1 8PL, ☎ 01792 411188
✉ clerks@pendragonchambers.com
4 King's Bench Walk
2nd Floor, 4 King's Bench Walk, Temple, London EC4Y 7DL, ☎ 020 7822 7000
✉ clerks@4kbw.co.uk
Call Date: Nov 1992, Inner Temple
Pupil Supervisor
Qualifications: [LLB (Hons)]
✉ sararudman@pendragonchambers.com

RUDOLF MR NATHANIEL DAVID

25 Bedford Row
London WC1R 4HD, ☎ 020 7067 1500
✉ clerks@25bedfordrow.com
Call Date: Nov 1996, Middle Temple
Pupil Supervisor
Qualifications: [LLB (Hons)(Warw)]
✉ nrudolf@25bedfordrow.com

RUFFELL MR MARK BERESFORD

Pump Court Chambers
31 Southgate Street, Winchester, Hampshire SO23 9EB, ☎ 01962 868 161
✉ clerks@3pumpcourt.com
Pump Court Chambers
Upper Ground Floor, 3 Pump Court, Temple, London EC4Y 7AJ, ☎ 020 7353 0711
✉ clerks@3pumpcourt.com
Pump Court Chambers
5 Temple Chambers, Temple Street, Swindon SN1 1SQ, ☎ 01793 539899
✉ clerks@3pumpcourt.com
Call Date: Nov 1992, Middle Temple
Qualifications: [BA (Hons) Dip Law]

RULE MR JONATHAN DANIEL

Palmyra Chambers
Royal House, 46 Legh Street, Warrington WA1 1UJ, ☎ 01925 444919
✉ clerk@palmyrachambers.com
Call Date: Nov 1993, Gray's Inn
Qualifications: [BA (Hons) (Oxon)]

RULE MR PHILIP DAVID

Castle Chambers
The Old Fire Station, 90 High Street, Harrow-on-the-Hill, Middlesex HA1 3LP, ☎ 020 8423 6579 ✉ info@castlechambers.net
Call Date: July 2001, Lincoln's Inn
Pupil Supervisor
Qualifications: [LLB (Hons)]

RUMFITT MR NIGEL JOHN QC (1994)

Seven Bedford Row
7 Bedford Row, London WC1R 4BS, ☎ 020 7242 3555 ✉ clerks@7br.co.uk
Call Date: July 1974, Middle Temple
Recorder
Qualifications: [BCL (Oxon) MA (Oxon)]
✉ nrumfitt@7br.co.uk

RUMNEY MR CONRAD WILLIAM ARTHUR

St Philips Chambers
55 Temple Row, Birmingham B2 5LS, ☎ 0121 246 7000 ✉ clerks@st-philips.com
Call Date: Feb 1988, Inner Temple
Qualifications: [MA (Oxon) Dip Law]
✉ crumney@st-philips.co.uk

RUNDLE MR DAVID JOHN HARRIS

Old Bailey Chambers
15 Old Bailey, London EC4M 7EF, ☎ 020 3008 6404
✉ clerks@15oldbaileychambers.com
Call Date: Nov 2007, Middle Temple
Qualifications: [LLB (Hons) (Nott'm)]

RUPASINHA MR SUNIL JAYANTHA

Old Bailey Chambers
15 Old Bailey, London EC4M 7EF, ☎ 020 3008 6404
✉ clerks@15oldbaileychambers.com
Call Date: Nov 1983, Inner Temple
Qualifications: [LLB (Cardiff)]
✉ r.rupasinha@15oldbaileychambers.com

RUSH MR CRAIG PETER

2 Bedford Row
London WC1R 4BU, ☎ 020 7440 8888
✉ clerks@2bedfordrow.co.uk
Call Date: Nov 1989, Inner Temple
Pupil Supervisor
Qualifications: [LLB]

E

RUSHBROOKE MR JUSTIN CHARLES NEIL

5RB
1st Floor, 5 Raymond Buildings, Gray's Inn, London WC1R 5BP, ☎ 020 7242 2902
✉ clerks@5rb.com
Call Date: Oct 1992, Middle Temple
Pupil Supervisor
Qualifications: [MA (Oxon)]
✉ justinrushbrooke@5rb.com

RUSHTON MR JONATHON BARKER

36 Bedford Row
London WC1R 4JH, ☎ 020 7421 8000
✉ chambers@36bedfordrow.co.uk
Call Date: Nov 1997, Inner Temple
Pupil Supervisor
Qualifications: [LLB (Middx)]
✉ jrushton@36bedfordrow.co.uk

RUSHTON MS NICOLA JANE

Five Paper
Ground Floor, 5 Paper Buildings, Temple, London EC4Y 7HB, ☎ 020 7815 3200
Call Date: Oct 1993, Gray's Inn
Pupil Supervisor
Qualifications: [BA (Cantab) LLM (Canada)]
✉ nicolarushton@fivepaper.com

Fax: 020 7815 3201;
DX: 415 LDE;
URL: www.5paper.com

Types of work: Asset finance, Chancery (commercial), Civil fraud, Commercial law, Commercial litigation, Costs, Freezing orders, Insolvency, Legal aid costs

RUSHWORTH MR ADAM DAVID

One Essex Court
Ground Floor, One Essex Court, Temple, London EC4Y 9AR, ☎ 020 7583 2000
✉ clerks@oeclaw.co.uk
Call Date: Nov 2010, Lincoln's Inn
Qualifications: [BA (Oxon)]
✉ arushworth@oeclaw.co.uk

RUSHWORTH MISS GEORGINA ELLEN

Coram Chambers
9-11 Fulwood Place, London WC1V 6HG, ☎ 020 7092 3700
✉ mail@coramchambers.co.uk
Call Date: Oct 2007, Lincoln's Inn
Qualifications: [BA (Hons) Dip Law MA]
✉ nick.obrien@coramchambers.co.uk

RUSSELL MS ALISON ELIZABETH

Pump Court Chambers
Upper Ground Floor, 3 Pump Court, Temple, London EC4Y 7AJ, ☎ 020 7353 0711
✉ clerks@3pumpcourt.com
Pump Court Chambers
5 Temple Chambers, Temple Street, Swindon SN1 1SQ, ☎ 01793 539899
✉ clerks@3pumpcourt.com
Pump Court Chambers
31 Southgate Street, Winchester, Hampshire SO23 9EB, ☎ 01962 868 161
✉ clerks@3pumpcourt.com
Call Date: Oct 1993, Middle Temple
Qualifications: [LLB (Hons) (Essex)]

RUSSELL MS ALISON HUNTER QC (2008)

1 Garden Court Family Law Chambers
Ground Floor, One Garden Court, Temple, London EC4Y 9BJ, ☎ 020 7797 7900
✉ clerks@1gc.com
Call Date: July 1983, Gray's Inn
Recorder
Qualifications: [BA (Hons)]
✉ russell@1gc.com

RUSSELL MR CHRISTOPHER JOHN

2 Temple Gardens
2 Temple Gardens, Temple, London EC4Y 9AY, ☎ 020 7822 1200
✉ clerks@2tg.co.uk
Call Date: Nov 1982, Gray's Inn
Pupil Supervisor
Qualifications: [LLB (Exon)]
✉ cr@2tg.co.uk

RUSSELL MISS FERN

2 King's Bench Walk
2 King's Bench Walk, Temple, London EC4Y 7DE, ☎ 020 7353 1746
✉ clerks@2kbw.com
Call Date: Nov 1994, Middle Temple
Pupil Supervisor
Qualifications: [BA (Hons)]
✉ frussell@2kbw.com

RUSSELL MR GRAHAM ALEXANDER

Citadel Chambers
The Citadel, 190 Corporation Street, Birmingham B4 6QD, ☎ 0121 233 8500
✉ clerks@citadelchambers.com
Call Date: Nov 2004, Inner Temple
Qualifications: [MA Fitzwilliam College University of Cambridge MSc (Lond)]

RUSSELL MR GUY JONOTHON

Westgate Chambers
64 High Street, Lewes, East Sussex BN7 1XG,
☎ 01273 480510
✉ clerks@westgate-chambers.co.uk
Call Date: Nov 1985, Gray's Inn
Qualifications: [BA]
✉ GR@westgate-chambers.co.uk

RUSSELL MRS JANE ELIZABETH

Essex Court Chambers
24 Lincoln's Inn Fields, London WC2A 3EG,
☎ 020 7813 8000
✉ clerksroom@essexcourt.net
Tooks Chambers
81 Farringdon Street, London EC4A 4BL,
☎ 020 7842 7575 ✉ clerks@tooks.co.uk
Call Date: Nov 2004, Middle Temple
Qualifications: [MA (Hons) BA (Hons) MA]

RUSSELL MR JEREMY FRANCIS JOHN

2-3 Hind Court Chambers
2-3 Hind Court, Fleet Street, London
EC4A 3DL, ☎ 020 7822 2150
✉ david@2-3hindcourt.com
Call Date: Nov 1973, Middle Temple
Qualifications: [MA (Cantab) LLB]

RUSSELL MR JEREMY JONATHAN QC (1994)

Quadrant Chambers
Quadrant House, 10 Fleet Street, London
EC4Y 1AU, ☎ 020 7583 4444
✉ info@quadrantchambers.com
Call Date: Nov 1975, Middle Temple
Qualifications: [BA LLM (Lond)]
✉ jeremy.russell@quadrantchambers.com

RUSSELL MISS MARGUERITE

Garden Court Chambers
57-60 Lincoln's Inn Fields, London WC2A 3LJ,
☎ 020 7993 7600 ✉ info@gclaw.co.uk
Call Date: July 1972, Lincoln's Inn
Pupil Supervisor
Qualifications: [LLM]
✉ margueriter@gclaw.co.uk

RUSSELL MR PAUL ANTHONY WELLINGTON QC (2011)

12 King's Bench Walk
12 King's Bench Walk, Temple, London
EC4Y 7EL, ☎ 020 7583 0811
Call Date: July 1984, Middle Temple
Pupil Supervisor
Qualifications: [BA (Dunelm)]
✉ russell@12kbw.co.uk

RUSSELL MISS RACHEL EMMA

St John's Chambers
101 Victoria Street, Bristol BS1 6PU,
☎ 0117 923 4700
✉ clerks@stjohnschambers.co.uk
Call Date: Oct 2001, Gray's Inn
Qualifications: [BA (Oxon)]

RUSSELL MR ROBERT JOHN FINLAY

Quadrant Chambers
Quadrant House, 10 Fleet Street, London
EC4Y 1AU, ☎ 020 7583 4444
✉ info@quadrantchambers.com
Call Date: Oct 1993, Middle Temple
Pupil Supervisor
Qualifications: [BA (Hons)(Oxon)]

RUSSELL MR THOMAS CHARLES WELLDON

KCH Garden Square
1 Oxford Street, Nottingham NG1 5BH,
☎ 0115 941 8851
✉ clerks@kchgardensquare.co.uk
Call Date: Oct 2004, Inner Temple
Qualifications: [LLB (Hull)]

RUSSELL FLINT MR SIMON COLERIDGE QC (2003)

23 Essex Street
London WC2R 3AA, ☎ 020 7413 0353
✉ clerks@23es.com
Eastbourne Chambers
5 Chiswick Place, Eastbourne, East Sussex
BN21 4NH, ☎ 01323 642102
✉ clerks@eastbournechambers.co.uk
Call Date: Nov 1980, Inner Temple
Recorder
Qualifications: [BA]
✉ simonrussellflint@23es.com

RUSSELL-MITRA MISS JESSICA SUPARNA

1 Mitre Court Buildings
1 Mitre Court Buildings, Temple, London
EC4Y 7BS, ☎ 020 7452 8900
✉ clerks@1mcb.com
Call Date: Oct 2003, Middle Temple
Qualifications: [BA (Hons) (Bris)]
✉ jessica.russellmitra@1mcb.com

E

RUSSEN MR JONATHAN HUW SINCLAIR QC (2010)

Maitland Chambers
7 Stone Buildings, Lincoln's Inn, London WC2A 3SZ, ☎ 020 7406 1200
✉ clerks@maitlandchambers.com
Call Date: July 1986, Lincoln's Inn
Pupil Supervisor
Qualifications: [LLB (Wales) LLM (Cantab)]
✉ jrussen@maitlandchambers.com

RUSTOM MR SHIRAZ SAM

1 Mitre Court Buildings
1 Mitre Court Buildings, Temple, London EC4Y 7BS, ☎ 020 7452 8900
✉ clerks@1mcb.com
1215 Chambers
1 Fetter Lane, London EC4A 1BR,
☎ 020 3291 1215
✉ admin@1215chambers.com
Cranford Chambers
8 Warwick Court, London WC1R 5DJ,
☎ 020 7404 7454
✉ jemima.ivens@cranfordchambers.com
Call Date: Oct 1998, Middle Temple
Pupil Supervisor
Qualifications: [BSc (Hons) LLB (Hons)(Lond)]
✉ shiraz.rustom@1mcb.com

E

RUTHERFORD MISS EMMA VICTORIA

No 8 Chambers
8 Fountain Court, Steelhouse Lane, Birmingham B4 6DR, ☎ 0121 236 5514
✉ clerks@no8chambers.co.uk
Call Date: July 2002, Middle Temple
Qualifications: [LLB (Hons)]
✉ emmarutherford@no8chambers.co.uk

RUTHERFORD MISS HELEN KATE

Cobden House Chambers
19 Quay Street, Manchester M3 3HN,
☎ 0161 833 6000 ✉ Clerks@Cobden.co.uk
Call Date: Oct 2010, Middle Temple
Qualifications: [BA (Hons) (Cantab)]

RUTHERFORD MR MARTIN

Furnival Chambers
32 Furnival Street, London EC4A 1JQ,
☎ 020 7405 3232
Call Date: Oct 1990, Lincoln's Inn
Pupil Supervisor
Qualifications: [BA (Cardiff) Dip Law]
✉ mrutherford@furnivallaw.co.uk

RUTKOWSKI MISS CHRISTINE DIANE

43 Temple Row Chambers
6th Floor, 43 Temple Row, Birmingham B2 5LS, ☎ 0121 237 6035
✉ clerks@43templerow.co.uk
Call Date: Oct 1999, Lincoln's Inn
Qualifications: [LLB (Hons) (Kingston)]
✉ clerks@43templerow.co.uk

RUTLEDGE MR DESMOND JOHN

Garden Court Chambers
57-60 Lincoln's Inn Fields, London WC2A 3LJ,
☎ 020 7993 7600 ✉ info@gclaw.co.uk
Call Date: Mar 2001, Middle Temple
Qualifications: [LLB (Hons)]
✉ desmondr@gclaw.co.uk

RUTLEDGE MR KELVIN ALBERT

Cornerstone Barristers
2-3 Gray's Inn Square, Gray's Inn, London WC1R 5JH, ☎ 020 7242 4986
✉ chambers@2-3gis.co.uk
Call Date: July 1989, Middle Temple
Pupil Supervisor
Qualifications: [LLB (Essex) LLB (Lond)]
✉ krutledge@2-3gis.co.uk

RUTTER MR ANDREW MICHAEL

Trinity Chambers
The Custom House, 39 Quayside, Newcastle Upon Tyne NE1 3DE, ☎ 0191 232 1927
✉ info@trinitychambers.co.uk
Trinity Chambers
Multi Media Exchange, 72-80 Corporation Road, Middlesbrough TS1 2RF,
☎ 01642 247569
✉ info@trinitychambers.co.uk
Call Date: July 1990, Middle Temple
Qualifications: [LLB (Lond)]
✉ a.rutter@trinitychambers.co.uk

RUTTER MR GARY MARK

Chambers of Marion Smullen and Kerim Fuad QC
1 Inner Temple Lane, London EC4Y 1AF,
☎ 020 7427 4400 ✉ clerks@1itl.com
Call Date: Nov 1997, Gray's Inn
Qualifications: [LLB (Nott'm)]
✉ clerks@1itl.com

RUTTLE MR STEPHEN QC (1997)

Brick Court Chambers
7-8 Essex Street, London WC2R 3LD,
☎ 020 7379 3550 ✉ clerks@brickcourt.co.uk
Call Date: Nov 1976, Gray's Inn
Qualifications: [BA (Cantab) CEDR]
✉ Stephen.Ruttle@Brickcourt.co.uk

RYAN MR DAVID PATRICK

3 Temple Gardens
Lower Ground Floor, 3 Temple Gardens, Temple, London EC4Y 9AU, ☎ 020 7353 3102
✉ clerks@3tg.co.uk
Call Date: Nov 1985, Inner Temple
Pupil Supervisor
Qualifications: [LLB (Hons)]

RYAN MISS FIONA

5 King's Bench Walk
5 King's Bench Walk, Temple, London EC4Y 7DN, ☎ 020 7353 5638
✉ clerks@5kbw.co.uk
Call Date: Mar 2009, Gray's Inn
Qualifications: [BA (Hons)]
✉ fiona.ryan@5kbw.co.uk

RYAN MR JOHN EMRYS HUGH

Apex
Harlech House, 20 Cathedral Road, Cardiff CF11 9LJ, ☎ 02920 232 032
✉ clerks@apexchambers.net
Call Date: Oct 1997, Gray's Inn
Qualifications: [LLB (Wales)]
✉ john.ryan@apexchambers.net

RYAN MR LIAM MICHAEL

Ely Place Chambers
30 Ely Place, London EC1N 6TD, ☎ 020 7400 9600 ✉ admin@elyplace.com
Call Date: Oct 2007, Inner Temple
Qualifications: [LLM (Nott'm) LLB (Dunelm)]

RYAN MR NICHOLAS JOSEPH

Atlantic Chambers
4-6 Cook Street, Liverpool L2 9QU, ☎ 0151 236 4421
✉ info@atlanticchambers.co.uk
Call Date: July 1984, Gray's Inn
Qualifications: [BA (Lond)]
✉ nicholasryan@atlanticchambers.co.uk

RYAN MR RICHARD COLLUM

Hardwicke
New Square, Lincoln's Inn, London WC2A 3SB, ☎ 020 7242 2523
✉ enquiries@hardwicke.co.uk
Call Date: Oct 2004, Gray's Inn
Qualifications: [LLB LLM]

RYAN MR WILLIAM

Farringdon Chambers
180 Bermondsey Street, London SE1 3TQ, ☎ 020 7089 5700
Corsham Barristers Chambers
New Farm House, Silver Street, Corsham SN13 9PG, ☎ 01225 582582
✉ enquiries@corshamlaw.co.uk
Call Date: Oct 1994, Gray's Inn
Qualifications: [LLB (Hons)]

RYDER MR JOHN QC (2000)

6 King's Bench Walk
Ground Floor, 6 King's Bench Walk, Temple, London EC4Y 7DR, ☎ 020 7583 0410
✉ clerks@6kbw.com
Call Date: Nov 1980, Inner Temple
Recorder
Qualifications: [BA (Hons)]
✉ john.ryder@6kbw.com

RYDER MR MATTHEW CONRAD QC (2010)

Matrix Chambers
Griffin Building, Gray's Inn, London WC1R 5LN, ☎ 020 7404 3447
✉ matrix@matrixlaw.co.uk / lscott@matrixlaw.co.uk
Call Date: Nov 1992, Gray's Inn
Qualifications: [LLB (Hons)(Cantab) LLM (Columbia)]
✉ matthewryder@matrixlaw.co.uk

RYDER MISS TAMSIN ALEXANDRA

2 Dr Johnson's Buildings
2 Dr Johnson's Buildings, Temple, London EC4Y 7AY, ☎ 020 7936 2613
✉ clerks@2drj.com
Call Date: July 2009, Inner Temple
Qualifications: [BA (Cantab)]

RYDER MR TIMOTHY ROBERT

Deans Court Chambers
24 St John Street, Manchester M3 4DF, ☎ 0161 214 6000 ✉ clerks@deanscourt.co.uk
Deans Court Chambers
101 Walker Street, Preston PR1 2RR, ☎ 01772 565 600
✉ preston@deanscourt.co.uk
Call Date: July 1977, Middle Temple
Pupil Supervisor, Recorder
Qualifications: [MA (Cantab)]

E

RYLANDS MISS MARGARET ELIZABETH

18 St John Street
Manchester M3 4EA, ☎ 0161 278 1800
✉ clerks@18sjs.com
Call Date: Nov 1973, Middle Temple
Pupil Supervisor
Qualifications: [LLB (Hons) (Bris)]
✉ erylands@18sjs.com

RYLE MS KATE FRANCES

5 Pump Court
Ground Floor, 5 Pump Court, Temple, London EC4Y 7AP, ☎ 020 7353 2532
✉ clerks@5pumpcourt.com
Call Date: Oct 2002, Inner Temple
Qualifications: [BA (Oxon) CPE]
✉ kateryle@5pumpcourt.com

SABBEN-CLARE MISS REBECCA MARY QC (2012)

7 King's Bench Walk
Ground Floor, 7 King's Bench Walk, Temple, London EC4Y 7DS, ☎ 020 7910 8300
✉ clerks@7kbw.co.uk
Call Date: Oct 1993, Gray's Inn
Pupil Supervisor
Qualifications: [MA (Oxon)]
✉ rsabbenclare@7kbw.co.uk

SABIC MS IRENA

Garden Court Chambers
57-60 Lincoln's Inn Fields, London WC2A 3LJ, ☎ 020 7993 7600 ✉ info@gclaw.co.uk
Call Date: Oct 2002, Inner Temple
Qualifications: [BA Hons (Cantab)]
✉ irenas@gclaw.co.uk

SABIDO MR JOHN HARRIES

3 Dr Johnson's Buildings
Ground Floor, 3 Dr Johnson's Buildings, Temple, London EC4Y 7BA, ☎ 020 7353 4854
✉ clerks@3djb.co.uk
Call Date: July 1976, Lincoln's Inn
Pupil Supervisor
✉ https://www.barristerconnect.org.uk/login/

SABISTON MR PETER JOHN

Old Court Chambers
Newham House, 96-98 Borough Road, Middlesbrough TS1 2HJ, ☎ 01642 232523
✉ clerks@oldcourtchambers.com
Call Date: Feb 1992, Gray's Inn
Qualifications: [LLB (Newc)]
✉ clerks@oldcourtchambers.com

SABRY MR KARIM SAMIR

9 St John Street
Manchester M3 4DN, ☎ 0161 955 9000
✉ civilclerks@9sjs.com / criminalclerks@9sjs.com
Call Date: Nov 1992, Inner Temple
Pupil Supervisor
Qualifications: [BA (Hons)]

SACHDEVA DR VIKRAM

39 Essex Street
London WC2R 3AT, ☎ 020 7832 1111
✉ clerks@39essex.com
82 King Street
Manchester M2 4WQ, ☎ 0161 870 9969
Call Date: Oct 1998, Middle Temple
Qualifications: [MA (Cantab) BCL (Oxon) BM B Ch (Oxon)]
✉ vikram.sachdeva@39essex.com

SACKMAN MISS SARAH REBECCA

Francis Taylor Building
Inner Temple, London EC4Y 7BY, ☎ 020 7353 8415 ✉ clerks@ftb.eu.com
Call Date: Nov 2008, Inner Temple
Qualifications: [BA (Cantab) CPE]
✉ sarah.sackman@ftb.eu.com

SADD MR PATRICK JAMES THOMAS

Outer Temple Chambers
The Outer Temple, 222 Strand, London WC2R 1BA, ☎ 020 7353 6381
✉ clerks@outertemple.com
Call Date: Nov 1984, Middle Temple
Pupil Supervisor
Qualifications: [BA]

SADIQ MR MUHAMMAD FAISEL

Ely Place Chambers
30 Ely Place, London EC1N 6TD, ☎ 020 7400 9600 ✉ admin@elyplace.com
Call Date: Oct 2000, Inner Temple
Pupil Supervisor
Qualifications: [LLB (Lond) LLM (Lond)]

SADIQ MR TARIQ MAHMOOD

St Philips Chambers
55 Temple Row, Birmingham B2 5LS, ☎ 0121 246 7000 ✉ clerks@st-philips.com
Call Date: Nov 1993, Gray's Inn
Qualifications: [BA (Hons) (Kent)]
✉ tsadiq@st-philips.com

SADLER MISS RHIANNON JANE

Westgate Chambers
64 High Street, Lewes, East Sussex BN7 1XG,
☎01273 480510
✉clerks@westgate-chambers.co.uk
Call Date: July 2004, Middle Temple
Qualifications: [LLB Hons (Kingston)]
rhs@westgate-chambers.co.uk

SAGAR MR LEIGH

New Square Chambers
12 New Square, Lincoln's Inn, London
WC2A 3SW, ☎020 7419 8000
✉robin.hollington@newsquarechambers.co.uk
Call Date: July 1983, Lincoln's Inn
Pupil Supervisor
Qualifications: [BA (Lond)]
leigh.sagar@newsquarechambers.co.uk

SAGE MR RICHARD DAVID

Crown Office Chambers
2 Crown Office Row, Temple, London
EC4Y 7HJ, ☎020 7797 8100
✉mail@crownofficechambers.com
Call Date: Nov 2006, Lincoln's Inn
Qualifications: [BA (Oxon)]
sage@crownofficechambers.com

SAGOE MR FREDRICK KOJO

Villa Chambers
33 St Peters Road, Oundle, Peterborough
PE8 4NU, ☎01832 273 097
Call Date: July 1983, Gray's Inn
Qualifications: [LLB]
fredsagoe@yahoo.co.uk

SAHONTE MR RAJINDER KUMAR

Guildhall Chambers
23 Broad Street, Bristol BS1 2HG,
☎0117 930 9000
✉hoc@guildhallchambers.co.uk
Call Date: Nov 1986, Lincoln's Inn
Pupil Supervisor
Qualifications: [LLB (Hons)]
raj@guildhallchambers.co.uk

SAHU MR MARK

Chambers of Mr Ami Feder
Ground Floor, Lamb Building, Temple, London
EC4Y 7AS, ☎020 7797 7788
✉clerks@lambbuilding.co.uk
Chambers of Mr Ami Feder
Ground Floor, Lamb Building, Temple, London
EC4Y 7AS, ☎020 7797 7788
✉clerks@lambbuilding.co.uk
Call Date: Nov 1995, Middle Temple
Qualifications: [LLB (Hons) (Leeds) LLM (Nottingham)]

SAIFEE MR FAISAL AFTAAB

Thomas More Chambers
7 Lincoln's Inn Fields, London WC2A 3BP,
☎020 7404 7000
✉clerks@thomasmore.co.uk
Call Date: July 2003, Middle Temple
Qualifications: [LLB Hons (L'Pool)]
fsaifee@thomasmore.co.uk

SAIFOLAHI MISS SANAZ

Renaissance Chambers
5th Floor, Gray's Inn Chambers, Gray's Inn,
London WC1R 5JA, ☎020 7404 1111
✉clerks@renaissancechambers.co.uk
Call Date: July 2000, Lincoln's Inn
Qualifications: [BA(Hons) (Warw)]

SAILLET MISS REBECCA

Carmelite Chambers
9 Carmelite Street, London EC4Y 0DR,
☎020 7936 6300
✉clerks@carmelitechambers.co.uk
Call Date: July 2009, Middle Temple
Qualifications: [BA (Hons) (UEA) LLB (Hons) (UEA)]

SAINI MR PARMINDER PAUL SINGH

12 Old Square Chambers
1st Floor, 12 Old Square, Lincoln's Inn,
London WC2A 3TX, ☎020 7404 0875
✉clerks@12oldsquare.com
Call Date: Nov 2001, Gray's Inn
Qualifications: [LLB]
clerks@12oldsquare.com

SAINI MR PUSHPINDER QC (2008)

Blackstone Chambers
Blackstone House, Temple, London
EC4Y 9BW, ☎020 7583 1770
✉clerks@blackstonechambers.com
Call Date: Oct 1991, Gray's Inn
Qualifications: [MA (Oxon) BCL (Oxon)]
pushpindersaini@blackstonechambers.com

SAJID MR AHMER

Clerksroom (Taunton)
Equity House, Administration Centre,
Blackbrook Park Avenue, Taunton, Somerset
TA1 2PX, ☎0845 083 3000
✉mail@clerksroom.com
Clerksroom (London)
3rd Floor, 218 Strand, London WC2R 1AT,
☎0845 083 3000 ✉mail@clerksroom.com

E

King's Lynn Chambers
26 The Birches, South Wootton, King's Lynn, Norfolk PE30 3JG, ☎ 01553 672 085
✉ timothy.leader@tesco.net
Call Date: Nov 1998, Lincoln's Inn
Qualifications: [LLB (Hons)(Wolves)]
✉ sajid@clerksroom.com

SALAKO-OLORUNFEMI MISS TOYIN

23 Essex Street
London WC2R 3AA, ☎ 020 7413 0353
✉ clerks@23es.com
Call Date: Nov 1998, Middle Temple
Qualifications: [BA (Hons) LLB (Hons)]
✉ toyinsalako@23es.com

SALIS MR ROBERT GEORGE

4 King's Bench Walk
2nd Floor, 4 King's Bench Walk, Temple, London EC4Y 7DL, ☎ 020 7822 7000
✉ clerks@4kbw.co.uk
Call Date: Nov 1999, Middle Temple
Qualifications: [BA (Hons)(Oxon)]
✉ rs@4kbw.co.uk

E

SALLON MR CHRISTOPHER ROBERT QC (1994)

Doughty Street Chambers
53-54 Doughty Street, London WC1N 2LS, ☎ 020 7404 1313
✉ enquiries@doughtystreet.co.uk
Doughty Street Chambers
Pall Mall Court, 61-67 King Street, Manchester M2 4PD, ☎ 0161 618 1066
Doughty Street Chambers
5th Floor, Broad Quay House, Prince Street, Bristol BS1 4DJ, ☎ 01179 058 717
Call Date: July 1973, Gray's Inn
Recorder
✉ c.sallon@doughtystreet.co.uk

SALMMAN MR HASHIM RIHAB

9 Park Place
9 Park Place, Cardiff, South Glamorgan CF10 3DP, ☎ 029 2038 2731
✉ clerks@9parkplace.co.uk
Call Date: July 2005, Lincoln's Inn
Qualifications: [LLB (Hons)]

SALMON MR CHARLES NATHAN QC (1996)

25 Bedford Row
London WC1R 4HD, ☎ 020 7067 1500
✉ clerks@25bedfordrow.com
Call Date: Nov 1972, Inner Temple
Qualifications: [LLB (Hons)]
✉ csalmon@25bedfordrow.com

SALMON MR JONATHAN CARL

St Philips Chambers
55 Temple Row, Birmingham B2 5LS, ☎ 0121 246 7000 ✉ clerks@st-philips.com
Call Date: Nov 1987, Inner Temple
Pupil Supervisor
Qualifications: [LLB (Nottm)]

SALMON MR KEVIN

St Mary's Family Law Chambers
26-28 High Pavement, The Lace Market, Nottingham NG1 1HN, ☎ 0115 950 3503
✉ clerks@stmarysflc.co.uk
Call Date: Nov 1984, Gray's Inn
Qualifications: [MA (St Andrews)]
✉ kevin.salmon@stmarysflc.co.uk

SALMON MISS SARAH LOUISE

Arden Chambers
20 Bloomsbury Square, London WC1A 2NS, ☎ 020 7242 4244
✉ clerks@ardenchambers.com
Call Date: Oct 2007, Lincoln's Inn
Qualifications: [LLB (Wales)]
✉ sarah.salmon@ardenchambers.com

SALOMAN MR TIMOTHY PETER QC (1993)

7 King's Bench Walk
Ground Floor, 7 King's Bench Walk, Temple, London EC4Y 7DS, ☎ 020 7910 8300
✉ clerks@7kbw.co.uk
Call Date: Nov 1975, Middle Temple
Recorder
Qualifications: [BA (Oxon)]
✉ tsaloman@7kbw.co.uk

SALTER MR ADRIAN NICHOLAS

11 Stone Buildings
11 Stone Buildings, Lincoln's Inn, London WC2A 3TG, ☎ 020 7831 6381
✉ clerks@11sb.com
Call Date: July 1973, Middle Temple
Pupil Supervisor
Qualifications: [MA (Cantab)]
✉ salter@11sb.com

SALTER MR MICHAEL RICHARD

Ely Place Chambers
30 Ely Place, London EC1N 6TD, ☎ 020 7400 9600 ✉ admin@elyplace.com
Call Date: Oct 1999, Inner Temple
Pupil Supervisor
Qualifications: [LLB (Brunel) BCL (Oxon)]
✉ msalter@elyplace.com

SALTER MR RICHARD STANLEY QC (1995)

3 Verulam Buildings
London WC1R 5NT, ☎ 020 7831 8441
✉ chambers@3vb.com
Call Date: July 1975, Inner Temple
Recorder
Qualifications: [MA (Oxon) ACI Arb]
rsalter@3vb.com

SALTER MISS SIBBY ANNE VICTORIA

3 Temple Gardens
Lower Ground Floor, 3 Temple Gardens, Temple, London EC4Y 9AU, ☎ 020 7353 3102
✉ clerks@3tg.co.uk
Call Date: Oct 1991, Middle Temple
Qualifications: [BA (Hons) (Cantab)]
sas@3tg.co.uk

SALZEDO MR SIMON LOPEZ QC (2011)

Brick Court Chambers
7-8 Essex Street, London WC2R 3LD,
☎ 020 7379 3550 ✉ clerks@brickcourt.co.uk
Call Date: Nov 1995, Lincoln's Inn
Pupil Supervisor
Qualifications: [BA (Hons)(Oxon) ACA (City)]
Simon.Salzedo@Brickcourt.co.uk

SAMBROOKS-WRIGHT MISS LYNDSEY KATHERINE

2 Dr Johnson's Buildings
2 Dr Johnson's Buildings, Temple, London EC4Y 7AY, ☎ 020 7936 2613
✉ clerks@2drj.com
Call Date: July 2008, Middle Temple
Qualifications: [BA (Hons) (Oxon) PgDl (Lond)]
clerks@2drj.com, lyndsey.sambrooks-wright@2drj.com

SAMEK MR CHARLES STEPHEN QC (2009)

Littleton Chambers
3 King's Bench Walk North, Temple, London EC4Y 7HR, ☎ 020 7797 8600
✉ fschneider@littletonchambers.co.uk
Call Date: Nov 1989, Middle Temple
Qualifications: [MA (Oxon) Dip Law (Lond)]
clerks@littletonchambers.co.uk, cs@littletonchambers.com

SAMMON MISS SARAH BRIDGET

Linenhall Chambers
1 Stanley Place, Chester CH1 2LU,
☎ 01244 348282
✉ clerks@linenhallchambers.co.uk
Call Date: Oct 1991, Middle Temple
Qualifications: [BA (Hons) Dip Law]

SAMMY MISS NATASHA CLAIRE

1 Pump Court
Elm Court, Temple, London EC4Y 7AB,
☎ 020 7842 7070
✉ (name)@pumpcourt.co.uk
Call Date: Nov 2006, Lincoln's Inn
Qualifications: [LLB (Nott'm)]

SAMPSON MR GRAEME WILLIAM

3 PB Barristers
3 Paper Buildings, Temple, London EC4Y 7EU,
☎ 020 7583 8055
3 PB Barristers
Royal Talbot House, 2 Victoria Street, Bristol, Avon BS1 6BB, ☎ 0117 928 1520
3 PB Barristers
4 St Peter Street, Winchester SO23 8BW,
☎ 01962 868884
✉ clerks.winchester@3paper.co.uk
3 PB Barristers
23 Beaumont Street, Oxford OX1 2NP,
☎ 01865 793 736
3 PB Barristers
30 Christchurch Road, Bournemouth, Dorset BH1 3PD, ☎ 01202 292102
✉ clerks.bournemouth@3paper.co.uk
Call Date: Nov 1981, Gray's Inn
Pupil Supervisor
Qualifications: [BA]
graeme.sampson@3pb.co.uk

SAMPSON MRS HELEN MARY

Sovereign Chambers
46 Park Place, Leeds LS1 2RY,
☎ 0113 245 1841
✉ clerks@sovereignchambers.co.uk
Call Date: Mar 2006, Inner Temple
Qualifications: [BA University of Hull]
helen.sampson@sovereignchambers.co.uk

SAMPSON MR JONATHAN ROBERT

Harcourt Chambers
1st Floor, 2 Harcourt Buildings, Temple, London EC4Y 9DB, ☎ 0844 561 7135
Call Date: Oct 1997, Middle Temple
Qualifications: [MA (Hons)(Cantab)]
jsampson@harcourtchambers.law.co.uk

E

SAMPSON MR RICHARD MICHAEL ANTHONY

Blackfriars Chambers
79-83 Temple Chambers, 3-7 Temple Avenue, London EC4Y 0HP, ☎ 020 7353 7400
✉ clerks@blackfriarschambers.com
Call Date: Nov 2007, Lincoln's Inn
Qualifications: [LLB (Exon)]
✉ clerks@blackfriarschambers.com

SAMPSON DR TIMOTHY MICHAEL GEORGE

One Essex Court
1st Floor, Temple, London EC4Y 9AR,
☎ 020 7936 3030 ✉ clerks@1ec.co.uk
Call Date: Mar 2000, Lincoln's Inn
Qualifications: [BSc (Hons) (Dunelm) PhD (Cantab)]
✉ TSampson@1ec.co.uk

SAMRA MISS SHARN

Broadway House Chambers
Broadway House, 9 Bank Street, Bradford, West Yorkshire BD1 1TW, ☎ 01274 722560
✉ clerks@broadwayhouse.co.uk
Broadway House Chambers
25 Park Square West, Leeds, West Yorkshire LS1 2PW, ☎ 0113 246 2600
✉ clerks@broadwayhouse.co.uk
Call Date: Nov 2002, Lincoln's Inn
Qualifications: [LLB (Hons)(Lond)]
✉ ssamra@broadwayhouse.co.uk

SAMSON MR JOHN

Ely Place Chambers
30 Ely Place, London EC1N 6TD,
☎ 020 7400 9600 ✉ admin@elyplace.com
Call Date: July 2001, Inner Temple
Qualifications: [LLB (Lond)]
✉ jsamson@elyplace.com

SAMUEL MR ADAM GARETH

Old Square Chambers
10-11 Bedford Row, London WC1R 4BU,
☎ 020 7269 0300 ✉ clerks@oldsquare.co.uk
Call Date: July 2003, Inner Temple
Qualifications: [LLB (B'Ham)]
✉ samuel@oldsquare.co.uk

SAMUEL MISS ANA ELIZABETH

Call Date: July 2004, Inner Temple
✉ ana.samuel@stjohnsbuildings.co.uk

SAMUEL MR DAVID GERWYN

Doughty Street Chambers
53-54 Doughty Street, London WC1N 2LS,
☎ 020 7404 1313
✉ enquiries@doughtystreet.co.uk
Doughty Street Chambers
Pall Mall Court, 61-67 King Street, Manchester M2 4PD, ☎ 0161 618 1066
Doughty Street Chambers
5th Floor, Broad Quay House, Prince Street, Bristol BS1 4DJ, ☎ 01179 058 717
Call Date: July 1986, Gray's Inn
Pupil Supervisor
Qualifications: [MA (Oxon)]
✉ g.samuel@doughtystreet.co.uk

SAMUEL MR GLYN ROSS

St Philips Chambers
55 Temple Row, Birmingham B2 5LS,
☎ 0121 246 7000 ✉ clerks@st-philips.com
Call Date: Oct 1991, Lincoln's Inn
Qualifications: [LLB (Hons)]
✉ gsamuel@st-philips.co.uk

SAMUEL MISS JACQUELINE ELEANOR

2 Hare Court
Lower Ground, Ground, 1st & 2nd Floor, 2 Hare Court, Temple, London EC4Y 7BH,
☎ 020 7353 3982 ✉ clerks@2harecourt.com
Call Date: July 1971, Gray's Inn
Pupil Supervisor
Qualifications: [LLB (Hons)(Lond)]
✉ jacquelinesamuel@2harecourt.com

SAMUEL MR RICHARD GEOFFREY GRAHAM

3 Hare Court
3 Hare Court, Temple, London EC4Y 7BJ,
☎ 020 7415 7800 ✉ clerks@3harecourt.com
Call Date: Nov 1996, Middle Temple
Pupil Supervisor
Qualifications: [MA (Hons)(Edin) LLB (Hons) (Lond)]
✉ rsamuel@3harecourt.com

SAMUEL MR TIMOTHY MARK LANSLEY

Invictus Chambers London
First Floor, 1 Mitre Court Buildings, Temple, London EC4Y 7BS
✉ admin@invictuschamberslondon.co.uk
Call Date: Nov 2005, Middle Temple
Qualifications: [BA (Hons) (York) MA (Leic)]

SAMUEL MR ZIMRAN

9 St John Street
Manchester M3 4DN, ☎ 0161 955 9000
✉ civilclerks@9sjs.com / criminalclerks@9sjs.com
Call Date: Nov 2008, Lincoln's Inn
Qualifications: [LLB (Lond)]

SAMUELS MR JEFFREY KEITH QC (2009)

Call Date: July 1988, Middle Temple
Qualifications: [LLB (Hons) (Leeds)]
✉ clerk@stjohnsbuildings.co.uk

SAMUELS MR LESLIE JOHN QC (2011)

Pump Court Chambers
Upper Ground Floor, 3 Pump Court, Temple, London EC4Y 7AJ, ☎ 020 7353 0711
✉ clerks@3pumpcourt.com
Pump Court Chambers
31 Southgate Street, Winchester, Hampshire SO23 9EB, ☎ 01962 868 161
✉ clerks@3pumpcourt.com
Riverview Chambers
Hamilton House, 1 Temple Avenue, London EC4Y 0HA, ☎ 0844 225 3999
✉ chrisbaylis@riverviewchambers.com
Call Date: July 1989, Gray's Inn
Pupil Supervisor
Qualifications: [BA (Cantab) MA (Canada)]
✉ ls@3pumpcourt.com

SAMUELS MR THOMAS DAVID

Gough Square Chambers
6-7 Gough Square, London EC4A 3DE, ☎ 020 7353 0924 ✉ gsc@goughsq.co.uk
Call Date: July 2009, Lincoln's Inn
Qualifications: [BA (Oxon)]
✉ thomas.samuels@goughsq.co.uk

SANDBACH MISS CARLY

Exchange Chambers
7 Ralli Courts, West Riverside, Manchester M3 5FT, ☎ 0161 833 2722
Exchange Chambers
One Derby Square, Derby Square, Liverpool L2 9XX, ☎ 0151 236 7747
✉ info@exchangechambers.co.uk
Exchange Chambers
Oxford House, Oxford Row, Leeds LS1 3BE, ☎ 0113 203 1970
✉ spencer@exchangechambers.co.uk
Call Date: July 2006, Inner Temple
Qualifications: [BA (Cantab)]
✉ sandbach@exchangechambers.co.uk

SANDBROOK-HUGHES MR STEWERT KARL ANTHONY

Iscoed Chambers
86 St Helen's Road, Swansea SA1 4BQ, ☎ 01792 652988
✉ clerks@iscoedchambers.co.uk
Call Date: Nov 1980, Lincoln's Inn
Pupil Supervisor
Qualifications: [BSc Econ (Wales) Dip Law]
✉ sh@iscoedchambers.co.uk

SANDELL MR ADAM

Matrix Chambers
Griffin Building, Gray's Inn, London WC1R 5LN, ☎ 020 7404 3447
✉ matrix@matrixlaw.co.uk / Iscott@matrixlaw.co.uk
Call Date: July 2008, Lincoln's Inn
Qualifications: [BA (Oxon) MSc (Oxon) BM BCh (Oxon) LLB (Lond)]

SANDELLS MS NICOLE

Four New Square
Four New Square, Lincoln's Inn, London WC2A 3RJ, ☎ 020 7822 2000
✉ barristers@4newsquare.com
Call Date: Nov 1994, Inner Temple
Qualifications: [BA (Oxon)]
✉ n.sandells@4newsquare.com

SANDER MISS AMY JEAN CATHERINE

Essex Court Chambers
24 Lincoln's Inn Fields, London WC2A 3EG, ☎ 020 7813 8000
✉ clerksroom@essexcourt.net
Call Date: Oct 2006, Middle Temple
Qualifications: [BA (Hons) (Cantab) MA (Hons) LLM (Cantab)]
✉ asander@essexcourt.net

SANDERCOCK MISS NATALIE JANE

30 Park Place
Cardiff CF10 3BS, ☎ 029 2039 8421
✉ clerks@30parkplace.law.co.uk
Call Date: Oct 2000, Middle Temple
Qualifications: [BA (Hons) (Oxon) CPE]
✉ ns@30parkplace.co.uk

SANDERS MR DAMIAN

Call Date: Nov 1988, Middle Temple
Qualifications: [LLB]
✉ damiansanders@yahoo.co.uk

E

SANDERS MR OLIVER TSCHANZ

1 Crown Office Row
1 Crown Office Row, Temple, London
EC4Y 7HH, ☎ 020 7797 7500
✉ mail@1cor.com
Call Date: July 1995, Inner Temple
Pupil Supervisor
Qualifications: [LLB (Lond) BCL (Oxon)]
oliver.sanders@1cor.com

SANDERSON MR DAVID FRANK

12 King's Bench Walk
12 King's Bench Walk, Temple, London
EC4Y 7EL, ☎ 020 7583 0811
Call Date: Nov 1985, Inner Temple
Pupil Supervisor
Qualifications: [BA (Sussex)]
sanderson@12kbw.co.uk

SANDERSON MS ELEANOR KATHLEEN

2 Bedford Row
London WC1R 4BU, ☎ 020 7440 8888
✉ clerks@2bedfordrow.co.uk
Call Date: July 2005, Inner Temple
Qualifications: [CPE BA]
esanderson@2bedfordrow.co.uk

SANDFORD MR ROBERT STANLEY

Bank House Chambers
Old Bank House, Hartshead, Sheffield S1 2EL,
☎ 0114 275 1223
✉ w.digby@bankhousechambers.co.uk
Call Date: Nov 1999, Middle Temple
Qualifications: [BA (Hons)(Dunelm)]
r.sandford@bankhousechambers.co.uk

SANDFORD MR SIMON JOHN AUSTIN

5 King's Bench Walk
5 King's Bench Walk, Temple, London
EC4Y 7DN, ☎ 020 7353 5638
✉ clerks@5kbw.co.uk
Call Date: Nov 1979, Gray's Inn
Pupil Supervisor
Qualifications: [MA (Cantab)]
simon.sandford@5kbw.co.uk

SANDHAM MR JAMES ANDREW

Arden Chambers
20 Bloomsbury Square, London WC1A 2NS,
☎ 020 7242 4244
✉ clerks@ardenchambers.com
Call Date: Mar 2003, Lincoln's Inn
Qualifications: [LLB (Hons) (Cardiff) LLM (Bris)]
james.sandham@ardenchambers.com

Types of work: Administrative law, Chancery (general), Chancery (land law), Commercial property, Common land, Common law (general), Conveyancing, Equity, Housing, Human rights, Landlord and tenant, Local authorities, Real property, Trusts

SANDHU MR HARPREET SINGH

No5 Chambers
Fountain Court, Steelhouse Lane, Birmingham
B4 6DR, ☎ 0845 210 5555 ✉ info@no5.com
No5 Chambers
Greenwood House, 4-7 Salisbury Court,
London EC4Y 8AA, ☎ 0845 210 5555
No5 Chambers
38 Queen Square, Bristol BS1 4QS,
☎ 0845 210 5555
Call Date: July 2005, Gray's Inn
Qualifications: [BA (Hons) (Dunelm) Dip Law]
hss@no5.com

SANDHU MR SUNIT

Equity Chambers
First Floor, McLaren Building, 46 Priory
Queensway, Birmingham B4 7LR,
☎ 0121 236 5007
✉ clerks@equitychambers.org.uk
Call Date: Feb 1990, Middle Temple
Pupil Supervisor
Qualifications: [LLB(Hons)(B'ham) BA]
sunit.sandhu@equitychambers.org.uk

SANDIFORD MR DAVID CHARLES

Cobden House Chambers
19 Quay Street, Manchester M3 3HN,
☎ 0161 833 6000 ✉ Clerks@Cobden.co.uk
Call Date: Oct 1995, Gray's Inn
Pupil Supervisor
Qualifications: [BA (Hons)(Oxon)]
clerks@cobden.co.uk

SANDIFORD MR JONATHAN

St Paul's Chambers
5th Floor, St Paul's House, 23 Park Square
South, Leeds LS1 2ND, ☎ 0113 245 5866
Call Date: Oct 1992, Gray's Inn
Qualifications: [LLB (Hons) (Newc)]
js@stpaulschambers.com

SANDS PROF PHILIPPE JOSEPH QC (2003)

Matrix Chambers
Griffin Building, Gray's Inn, London WC1R 5LN, ☎ 020 7404 3447
✉ matrix@matrixlaw.co.uk / lscott@matrixlaw.co.uk
Call Date: Nov 1985, Middle Temple
Qualifications: [MA LLM (Cantab)]
✉ philippesands@matrixlaw.co.uk

SANDYS MR NEIL ASHLEY

23 Essex Street
London WC2R 3AA, ☎ 020 7413 0353
✉ clerks@23es.com
Call Date: Oct 1998, Inner Temple
Qualifications: [LLB (Leic)]
✉ neilsandys@23es.com

SANGHERA MISS SHARANDISH KAUR

3 PB Barristers
3 Paper Buildings, Temple, London EC4Y 7EU, ☎ 020 7583 8055
3 PB Barristers
Royal Talbot House, 2 Victoria Street, Bristol, Avon BS1 6BB, ☎ 0117 928 1520
3 PB Barristers
23 Beaumont Street, Oxford OX1 2NP, ☎ 01865 793 736
3 PB Barristers
4 St Peter Street, Winchester SO23 8BW, ☎ 01962 868884
✉ clerks.winchester@3paper.co.uk
3 PB Barristers
30 Christchurch Road, Bournemouth, Dorset BH1 3PD, ☎ 01202 292102
✉ clerks.bournemouth@3paper.co.uk
Call Date: Nov 2009, Inner Temple
Qualifications: [BA (Oxon)]

SANGSTER MR NIGEL QC (1998)

25 Bedford Row
London WC1R 4HD, ☎ 020 7067 1500
✉ clerks@25bedfordrow.com
Call Date: Nov 1976, Middle Temple
Recorder
Qualifications: [LLB (Hons)]
✉ nsangster@25bedfordrow.com

SANTAMERA MISS LOUISE ALEXANDRIA

New Bailey Chambers
4th Floor, Corn Exchange, Fenwick Street, Liverpool, Merseyside L2 7QS, ☎ 0151 236 9402 ✉ clerks@newbailey.com
Call Date: Oct 2002, Gray's Inn
Qualifications: [BA (Manch)]
✉ Clerks@newbailey.com

SAOUL MR DANIEL ABEL ELIE

Four New Square
Four New Square, Lincoln's Inn, London WC2A 3RJ, ☎ 020 7822 2000
✉ barristers@4newsquare.com
Call Date: Nov 2008, Lincoln's Inn
Qualifications: [MA (Edin) BA (Oxon)]
✉ d.saoul@4newsquare.com

SAPIECHA MR DAVID JOHN

Colleton Chambers
Colleton Crescent, Exeter, Devon EX2 4DG, ☎ 01392 274898
✉ clerks@colletonchambers.co.uk
Call Date: Oct 1990, Gray's Inn
Qualifications: [LLB]
✉ davidsapiecha@colletonchambers.co.uk

SAPNARA MISS KHATUN

Coram Chambers
9-11 Fulwood Place, London WC1V 6HG, ☎ 020 7092 3700
✉ mail@coramchambers.co.uk
Call Date: Nov 1990, Middle Temple
Qualifications: [LLB (Lond)]
✉ khatun.sapnara@coramchambers.co.uk

SAPSTEAD MISS LOUISE ANNE

KCH Garden Square
1 Oxford Street, Nottingham NG1 5BH, ☎ 0115 941 8851
✉ clerks@kchgardensquare.co.uk
Call Date: July 2004, Lincoln's Inn
Qualifications: [LLB (Hons)]
✉ lsapstead@kch.co.uk

SAPWELL MR TIMOTHY ROBERT

Cornwall Street Chambers
85-87 Cornwall Street, Birmingham B3 3BY, ☎ 0121 233 7500
✉ clerks@cornwallstreet.co.uk
Call Date: Oct 1997, Lincoln's Inn
Qualifications: [BA (Lond)]
✉ tim.clarke@cornwallstreet.co.uk

SAREEN MR BEN ALAN

Keating Chambers
15 Essex Street, London WC2R 3AA, ☎ 020 7544 2600
✉ clerks@keatingchambers.com
Call Date: Oct 2008, Middle Temple
Qualifications: [MA (Hons) (Oxon) Dip in Law of (Manch)]
✉ bsareen@keatingchambers.com

E

SAREEN MR ELLIS WOLFE

9-12 Bell Yard
London WC2A 2JR, ☎ 020 7400 1800
✉ clerks@9-12bellyard.com
Call Date: Oct 2008, Middle Temple
Qualifications: [Dip in Law BA (Hons) (Cantab)]

SARGINSON MISS JANE ELIZABETH

St Philips Chambers
55 Temple Row, Birmingham B2 5LS,
☎ 0121 246 7000 ✉ clerks@st-philips.com
Call Date: Mar 2000, Middle Temple
Qualifications: [BSc (Manch) CPE]
jsarginson@st-philips.co.uk

SARLL MR RICHARD CHAD GRATWICK

7 King's Bench Walk
Ground Floor, 7 King's Bench Walk, Temple, London EC4Y 7DS, ☎ 020 7910 8300
✉ clerks@7kbw.co.uk
Call Date: Oct 2005, Middle Temple
Qualifications: [BA (Hons) GDL]
richardsarll@7kbw.co.uk

E

SAROOSHI PROF DAN

Essex Court Chambers
24 Lincoln's Inn Fields, London WC2A 3EG,
☎ 020 7813 8000
✉ clerksroom@essexcourt.net
Call Date: July 2005, Middle Temple
Qualifications: [MA PhD LLM LLB]
dsarooshi@essexcourt.net

SARTIN MR LEON JAMES

5 Stone Buildings
5 Stone Buildings, Lincoln's Inn, London WC2A 3XT, ☎ 020 7242 6201
✉ clerks@5sblaw.com
Call Date: Oct 1997, Middle Temple
Pupil Supervisor
Qualifications: [BSc (Hons)(Soton) LLM (Lond)]
lsartin@5sblaw.com

SARWAR MR HASSAN HAMID

Rowchester Chambers
4 Rowchester Court, Whittall Street, Birmingham B4 6DH, ☎ 0121 233 2327
✉ clerks@rowchesterchambers.co.uk
Call Date: Oct 2010, Lincoln's Inn
Qualifications: [LLB (B'ham)]
rsarwar@rowchesterchambers.co.uk

SARWAR MR MOHAMMED

Chambers of Mr Ayoub Khan
127 Albert Road, Aston, Birmingham B6 5ND,
☎ 07930 987202
✉ ayoub_khan64@hotmail.com
Call Date: July 2000, Lincoln's Inn
Qualifications: [LLB(Hons) (Warw)]
shabir6kbw@hotmail.co.uk

SASSE MR TOBY WILLIAM

18 St John Street
Manchester M3 4EA, ☎ 0161 278 1800
✉ clerks@18 s.com
Call Date: July 1988, Middle Temple
Pupil Supervisor
Qualifications: [LLB (Hons) (Exon) Dipo Heath & Safety & Enviro Law]

SASTRY MR BOB AJAY DWARAKANATH

Call Date: Oct 1996, Inner Temple
Qualifications: [LLB (Exon)]

SAUL MISS SONYA DENISE

23 Essex Street
London WC2R 3AA, ☎ 020 7413 0353
✉ clerks@23es.com
Call Date: Oct 2002, Gray's Inn
Qualifications: [BA (Lond) MA (City) Dip Law]
sonyasaul@23es.com

SAUNDERS MISS DENISE AMBER

Crown Office Row Chambers
119 Church Street, Brighton, Sussex BN1 1UD, ☎ 01273 625625
✉ clerks@1cor.com
Call Date: July 2008, Inner Temple
Qualifications: [LLB]
denise.saunders@1cor.com

SAUNDERS MR KEVIN JOHN

St Ive's Chambers
Whittall Street, Birmingham B4 6DH,
☎ 0121 236 0863
✉ clerks@stiveschambers.co.uk
Call Date: Oct 2003, Gray's Inn
Qualifications: [LLB (Wales)]
kevin.saunders@stiveschambers.co.uk

SAUNDERS MR MARK DANIEL

No.6 Park Square
Leeds LS1 2LW, ☎ 0113 245 9763
✉ Tim@no6.co.uk
Call Date: Oct 2002, Inner Temple
Qualifications: [BA (Cantab)]
saunders@no6.co.uk

SAUNDERS MR NEIL

3 Raymond Buildings
3 Raymond Buildings, Gray's Inn, London WC1R 5BH, ☎ 020 7400 6400
✉ clerks@3rblaw.com
Call Date: Nov 1983, Middle Temple
Pupil Supervisor, Recorder
Qualifications: [BA]

SAUNDERS MR NICHOLAS JOSEPH

Fenners Chambers
3 Madingley Road, Cambridge CB3 0EE,
☎ 01223 368761
✉ clerks@fennerschambers.com
Call Date: July 1989, Middle Temple
Qualifications: [LLB (Hull) LLM (Cantab)]

SAUNDERS DR NICHOLAS THOMAS

Brick Court Chambers
7-8 Essex Street, London WC2R 3LD,
☎ 020 7379 3550 ✉ clerks@brickcourt.co.uk
Call Date: Oct 2001, Middle Temple
Pupil Supervisor
Qualifications: [MA (Cantab) PhD (Cantab) Dip Law]
nicholas.saunders@brickcourt.co.uk

SAUNDERS MR WILLIAM ANTHONY

3 Temple Gardens
Lower Ground Floor, 3 Temple Gardens, Temple, London EC4Y 9AU, ☎ 020 7353 3102
✉ clerks@3tg.co.uk
Call Date: Nov 1980, Gray's Inn
Pupil Supervisor
Qualifications: [LLB (B'ham)]
ws@3tg.co.uk

SAUNDERS MISS ZOE ALICE

St John's Chambers
101 Victoria Street, Bristol BS1 6PU,
☎ 0117 923 4700
✉ clerks@stjohnschambers.co.uk
Call Date: Oct 2003, Gray's Inn
Qualifications: [BA (Bris) PgDL]
zoe.saunders@stjohnschambers.co.uk, zoe@straudquise.se

SAUNDERSON MISS EMILY JANE

2 Temple Gardens
2 Temple Gardens, Temple, London EC4Y 9AY, ☎ 020 7822 1200
✉ clerks@2tg.co.uk
Call Date: July 2005, Gray's Inn
Qualifications: [BA (Hons) Southampton]
esaunderson@2tg.co.uk

SAUNT MS LINDA PATRICIA

Chambers of Andrew Mitchell QC
33 Chancery Lane, London WC2A 1EN,
☎ 020 7440 9950 ✉ clerks@33cllaw.com
Call Date: Nov 1986, Inner Temple
Qualifications: [MA (Cantab)]

SAUVAIN MR STEPHEN JOHN QC (1995)

Kings Chambers
36 Young Street, Manchester M3 3FT,
☎ 0845 034 3444
✉ clerks@kingschambers.com
Cornerstone Barristers
2-3 Gray's Inn Square, Gray's Inn, London WC1R 5JH, ☎ 020 7242 4986
✉ chambers@2-3gis.co.uk
Kings Chambers
Embassy House, 60 Church Street, Birmingham B3 2DJ, ☎ 0845 034 3444
✉ clerks@kingschambers.com
Kings Chambers
5 Park Square East, Leeds LS1 2NE,
☎ 0845 034 3444
✉ clerks@kingschambers.com
Call Date: July 1977, Lincoln's Inn
Recorder
Qualifications: [MA LLB (Cantab)]
ssauvain@kingschambers.com

E

SAVAGE MISS AMANDA CLAIRE

Four New Square
Four New Square, Lincoln's Inn, London WC2A 3RJ, ☎ 020 7822 2000
✉ barristers@4newsquare.com
Call Date: Oct 1999, Middle Temple
Pupil Supervisor
Qualifications: [LLB (Lond) BCL (Oxon) BA (Hons)]
a.savage@4newsquare.com

SAVAGE MR JONATHAN HOWARD

9 St John Street
Manchester M3 4DN, ☎ 0161 955 9000
✉ civilclerks@9sjs.com / criminalclerks@9sjs.com
Call Date: Oct 2003, Gray's Inn
Qualifications: [LLB (Manch)]

SAVAGE MISS MAI-LING CARMEN

14 Gray's Inn Square
14 Gray's Inn Square, Gray's Inn, London WC1R 5JP, ☎ 020 7242 0858
✉ clerks@14gis.co.uk
Call Date: Oct 1998, Inner Temple
Qualifications: [BDiv (Lond) CPE]
✉ clerks@14graysinnsquare.co.uk, mls@14gis.co.uk

SAVAGE MR TIMOTHY JOHN

Call Date: Nov 1991, Inner Temple
✉ savage@paradise-sq.co.uk

SAVILL MR MARK ASHLEY

Deans Court Chambers
101 Walker Street, Preston PR1 2RR, ☎ 01772 565 600
✉ preston@deanscourt.co.uk
Deans Court Chambers
24 St John Street, Manchester M3 4DF, ☎ 0161 214 6000 ✉ clerks@deanscourt.co.uk
Call Date: Nov 1993, Inner Temple
Pupil Supervisor
Qualifications: [BA (Dunelm)]

SAVILL MR PETER JOHN

12 College Place
Fauvelle Buildings, 12 College Place, Southampton SO15 2FE, ☎ 023 8032 0320
✉ clerks@12cp.co.uk
Call Date: Nov 1995, Inner Temple
Qualifications: [BA (Warw) CPE]
✉ PSavill@12cp.co.uk

SAVVIDES MISS MARIA

Northampton Chambers
10 Spencer Parade, Northampton NN1 5AQ, ☎ 01604 636271
✉ clerks@northampton-chambers.co.uk
Call Date: July 1986, Middle Temple
Pupil Supervisor
Qualifications: [BA (Hons)]
✉ msavvides@northampton-chambers.co.uk

SAWTELL MR DAVID ROBERT FRASER

4 King's Bench Walk
2nd Floor, 4 King's Bench Walk, Temple, London EC4Y 7DL, ☎ 020 7822 7000
✉ clerks@4kbw.co.uk
Call Date: Nov 2005, Lincoln's Inn
Qualifications: [BA (Hons) (Cantab) PgDl (Lond)]
✉ das@4kbw.co.uk

SAWYER MR EDWARD HUMPHREY

Wilberforce Chambers
8 New Square, Lincoln's Inn, London WC2A 3QP, ☎ 020 7306 0102
✉ chambers@wilberforce.co.uk
Call Date: Oct 2001, Middle Temple
Pupil Supervisor
Qualifications: [BA (Hons) (Oxon) CPE]
✉ esawyer@wilberforce.co.uk

Types of work: Chancery (general), Chancery (land law), Commercial law, Equity, Fraud, Landlord and tenant, Professional negligence, Trusts, Wills

SAWYER MR JAMIE NEIL

18 Red Lion Court
London EC4A 3EB, ☎ 020 7520 6000
✉ chambers@18rlc.co.uk
Call Date: Oct 2003, Inner Temple
Qualifications: [LLB LLM]
✉ jamie.sawyer@18rlc.co.uk

SAWYER MS KATRINE MARY

Hailsham Chambers
Ground Floor, 4 Paper Buildings, Temple, London EC4Y 7EX, ☎ 020 7643 5000
✉ clerks@hailshamchambers.com
Call Date: Nov 1996, Middle Temple
Qualifications: [BA (Hons)(Oxon)]
✉ katrine.sawyer@hailshamchambers.com

SAWYERR MISS SHARON ROSE

Coram Chambers
9-11 Fulwood Place, London WC1V 6HG, ☎ 020 7092 3700
✉ mail@coramchambers.co.uk
Call Date: Nov 1992, Inner Temple
Qualifications: [LLB]
✉ sharon.sawyerr@coramchambers.co.uk

SAXBY MR DANIEL JAMES

3 Hare Court
3 Hare Court, Temple, London EC4Y 7BJ, ☎ 020 7415 7800 ✉ clerks@3harecourt.com
Call Date: Nov 2000, Middle Temple
Qualifications: [BA (Hons) (Cantab)]
✉ danielsaxby@3harecourt.com

SAXBY MR OLIVER CHARLES JOHN

6 Pump Court
1st Floor, 6 Pump Court, Temple, London EC4Y 7AR, ☎020 7797 8400
✉richardconstable@6pumpcourt.co.uk
6 Pump Court Chambers
6-8 Mill Street, Maidstone, Kent ME15 6XH, ☎01622 688094
✉annexe@6pumpcourt.co.uk
Call Date: Nov 1992, Inner Temple
Pupil Supervisor
Qualifications: [LLB (So'ton)]
✉oliversaxby@6pumpcourt.co.uk

SAXENA MISS HANNAH

Farrar's Building
Farrar's Building, Temple, London EC4Y 7BD, ☎020 7583 9241
✉Chambers@farrarsbuilding.co.uk
Call Date: Mar 2010, Middle Temple
Qualifications: [LLB (Exon)]
✉hsaxena@farrarsbuilding.co.uk

SAXTON MISS NICOLA HELEN

St Paul's Chambers
5th Floor, St Paul's House, 23 Park Square South, Leeds LS1 2ND, ☎0113 245 5866
Call Date: Nov 1992, Inner Temple
Pupil Supervisor
Qualifications: [MA (Cantab)]
✉ns@stpaulschambers.com

SAY MR BRADLEY JOHN

Gough Square Chambers
6-7 Gough Square, London EC4A 3DE, ☎020 7353 0924 ✉gsc@goughsq.co.uk
Call Date: Oct 1993, Inner Temple
Pupil Supervisor
Qualifications: [LLB]
✉bradley.say@goughsq.co.uk

SAYED MISS NERMINE ABDEL

Old Bailey Chambers
15 Old Bailey, London EC4M 7EF, ☎020 3008 6404
✉clerks@15oldbaileychambers.com
Call Date: Nov 2001, Middle Temple
Qualifications: [LLB (Hons)]
✉n.abdulsayed@15oldbaileychambers.com

SAYED MISS RUBY

1 Pump Court
Elm Court, Temple, London EC4Y 7AB, ☎020 7842 7070
✉(name)@pumpcourt.co.uk
Call Date: Mar 1999, Inner Temple
Qualifications: [LLB (Sussex)]
✉rs@1pumpcourt.co.uk

SAYEED MR MUHAMMAD ABU

10 Highlever Road
10 Highlever Road, North Kensington, London W10 6PS, ☎020 8969 8514
✉znsayeed@uk2.net
Call Date: July 1973, Inner Temple
Qualifications: [BA]
✉zahirun.sayeed@sky.com

SAYEED MR SADAT

Garden Court Chambers
57-60 Lincoln's Inn Fields, London WC2A 3LJ, ☎020 7993 7600 ✉info@gclaw.co.uk
Call Date: Oct 2001, Inner Temple
Qualifications: [BSc (Manch) CPE]
✉sadats@gclaw.co.uk

SAYER MR PETER EDWIN

Gough Square Chambers
6-7 Gough Square, London EC4A 3DE, ☎020 7353 0924 ✉gsc@goughsq.co.uk
Call Date: July 1975, Middle Temple
Qualifications: [MA (Cantab)]
✉peter.sayer@goughsq.co.uk

SAYER MR SEBASTIAN JAMES

9-12 Bell Yard
London WC2A 2JR, ☎020 7400 1800
✉clerks@9-12bellyard.com
Call Date: July 2007, Lincoln's Inn
Qualifications: [LLB (Warw)]

SAYERS MISS LYNNE

Chambers of Miss L Sayers
45 Orford Green, Warrington WA2 8PQ, ☎07850 366366 ✉lynnesayers@hotmail.com
Call Date: Oct 2002, Lincoln's Inn
Qualifications: [LLB (L'Pool)]
✉lynnesayers@hotmail.com

SAYNOR MR RICHARD WILLIAM

6 King's Bench Walk
Ground Floor, 6 King's Bench Walk, Temple, London EC4Y 7DR, ☎020 7583 0410
✉clerks@6kbw.com
Call Date: Oct 2009, Middle Temple
Qualifications: [BA (Hons) (Oxon) LLB (Hons)]
✉richard.saynor@6kbw.com

SCALLY MISS JOSEPHINE THERESA SARAH

Palmyra Chambers
Royal House, 46 Legh Street, Warrington WA1 1UJ, ☎01925 444919
✉clerk@palmyrachambers.com
Call Date: Feb 1984, Lincoln's Inn
Qualifications: [BA (Manch)]

E

SCAMARDELLA MR ROSSANO

23 Essex Street
London WC2R 3AA, ☎ 020 7413 0353
✉ clerks@23es.com
Call Date: Nov 1998, Gray's Inn
Pupil Supervisor
Qualifications: [BA (Glamorgan) Dip Law (CPE)]
rossanoscamardella@23es.com

SCANNELL MR DAVID LUKE

Brick Court Chambers
7-8 Essex Street, London WC2R 3LD,
☎ 020 7379 3550 ✉ clerks@brickcourt.co.uk
Call Date: Nov 2003, Inner Temple
Qualifications: [LLB (Dub) LLM (Cantab)]
david.scannell@brickcourt.co.uk

SCAPENS MR THOMAS JOSEPH

Iscoed Chambers
86 St Helen's Road, Swansea SA1 4BQ,
☎ 01792 652988
✉ clerks@iscoedchambers.co.uk
Call Date: July 2008, Gray's Inn
Qualifications: [LLB (Wales)]
clerks@iscoedchambers.co.uk

E

SCHAEFER MR MAXIMILIAN MARTIN

Brick Court Chambers
7-8 Essex Street, London WC2R 3LD,
☎ 020 7379 3550 ✉ clerks@brickcourt.co.uk
Call Date: Oct 2010, Inner Temple
Qualifications: [BA (Cantab)]

SCHAFF MR ALISTAIR GRAHAM QC (1999)

7 King's Bench Walk
Ground Floor, 7 King's Bench Walk, Temple, London EC4Y 7DS, ☎ 020 7910 8300
✉ clerks@7kbw.co.uk
Call Date: July 1983, Inner Temple
Qualifications: [MA (Cantab)]
aschaff@7kbw.co.uk

SCHAMA MR STANLEY ANDREW LEE

10 King's Bench Walk
Ground Floor, 10 King's Bench Walk, Temple, London EC4Y 7EB, ☎ 020 7353 7742
✉ Chambers@10kingsbenchwalk.co.uk
Call Date: Nov 2003, Gray's Inn
Qualifications: [MA (Hons) (Edin)]

SCHAW MILLER MR STEPHEN GRANT

New Square Chambers
12 New Square, Lincoln's Inn, London WC2A 3SW, ☎ 020 7419 8000
✉ robin.hollington@newsquarechambers.co.uk
Call Date: Nov 1988, Inner Temple
Pupil Supervisor
Qualifications: [BA (Oxon) Dip Law (Lond)]
stephen.schawmiller@newsquarechambers.co.uk

SCHER MR LAURIE SIMON

Maitland Chambers
7 Stone Buildings, Lincoln's Inn, London WC2A 3SZ, ☎ 020 7406 1200
✉ clerks@maitlandchambers.com
Call Date: July 2008, Middle Temple
Qualifications: [BA (Hons) (Cantab)]
lscher@maitlandchambers.com

SCHERBEL-BALL MR JONATHAN ALEC

One Brick Court
1st Floor, One Brick Court, Temple, London EC4Y 9BY, ☎ 020 7353 8845
✉ clerks@onebrickcourt.com
Call Date: Oct 2010, Middle Temple
Qualifications: [MA (Oxon) MPhil (Cantab)]

SCHMELZER MS MIRIAM KERSTIN

3 Verulam Buildings
London WC1R 5NT, ☎ 020 7831 8441
✉ chambers@3vb.com
Call Date: Nov 2010, Middle Temple
Qualifications: [BA (Hons) (York) MA (Bris)]

SCHMITZ MR DAVID REUBEN

Ten Old Square
Ground Floor, Ten Old Square, Lincoln's Inn, London WC2A 3SU, ☎ 020 7405 0758
✉ clerks@tenoldsquare.com
Call Date: Nov 1976, Lincoln's Inn
Pupil Supervisor
Qualifications: [BA]

SCHOFIELD MISS ELIZABETH ANNE

Middle Temple Lane Chambers
2nd Floor South, 1 Middle Temple Lane, London EC4Y 9AA, ☎ 020 7583 4352
✉ chambers@mtlchambers.com
Call Date: Oct 2000, Middle Temple
Qualifications: [BA (Leeds) MA(Leeds) Dip in Law (Manch)]
chambers@mtlchambers.com

SCHOFIELD MR JAMES JOHN MCMICHAEL

Coram Chambers
9-11 Fulwood Place, London WC1V 6HG, ☎020 7092 3700
✉mail@coramchambers.co.uk
Call Date: July 2004, Gray's Inn
Qualifications: [MA (Oxon)]
✉james.schofield@coramchambers.co.uk

SCHOFIELD MR PETER ANDREW

New Court Chambers
3 Broad Chare, Newcastle Upon Tyne NE1 3DQ, ☎0191 232 1980
✉clerks@newcourt-chambers.co.uk
Call Date: Nov 1982, Gray's Inn
Pupil Supervisor
Qualifications: [BA]
✉peter.schofield@newcourt-chambers.co.uk

SCHOFIELD MR THOMAS LEON

No5 Chambers
Fountain Court, Steelhouse Lane, Birmingham B4 6DR, ☎0845 210 5555 ✉info@no5.com
No5 Chambers
Greenwood House, 4-7 Salisbury Court, London EC4Y 8AA, ☎0845 210 5555
No5 Chambers
38 Queen Square, Bristol BS1 4QS, ☎0845 210 5555
Call Date: Oct 2001, Lincoln's Inn
Qualifications: [LLB (Hons) (L'pool)]
✉tls@no5.com

SCHOLES MR MICHAEL HOWARD

Exchange Chambers
One Derby Square, Derby Square, Liverpool L2 9XX, ☎0151 236 7747
✉info@exchangechambers.co.uk
Exchange Chambers
7 Ralli Courts, West Riverside, Manchester M3 5FT, ☎0161 833 2722
Exchange Chambers
Oxford House, Oxford Row, Leeds LS1 3BE, ☎0113 203 1970
✉spencer@exchangechambers.co.uk
Call Date: July 1996, Inner Temple
Qualifications: [LLB (Hons)(L'pool)]
✉scholes@exchangechambers.co.uk

SCHOLZ MR KARL HUBERTUS

Linenhall Chambers
1 Stanley Place, Chester CH1 2LU, ☎01244 348282
✉clerks@linenhallchambers.co.uk
Call Date: July 1973, Gray's Inn
Pupil Supervisor
Qualifications: [LLB (Lond)]
✉ks@nicholasstreet.com

SCHONEVELD MR FRANK ROBERT

Henderson Chambers
2 Harcourt Buildings, Temple, London EC4Y 9DB, ☎020 7583 9020
✉clerks@hendersonchambers.co.uk
Call Date: May 1992, Inner Temple
Qualifications: [B Juris LLB (Australia) Dip Eur Law (Netherlands)]

SCHUTZER-WEISSMANN MISS ESTHER YOLANDE CECILE

6 King's Bench Walk
Ground Floor, 6 King's Bench Walk, Temple, London EC4Y 7DR, ☎020 7583 0410
✉clerks@6kbw.com
Call Date: Oct 2000, Middle Temple
Pupil Supervisor
Qualifications: [BA (Hons) (Oxon) Dip law]
✉esther.schutzer-weissmann@6kbw.com

SCHWARZ MR JONATHAN SIMON

Temple Tax Chambers
1st Floor, 3 Temple Gardens, Temple, London EC4Y 9AU, ☎020 7353 7884
✉clerks@templetax.com
Call Date: Mar 1998, Middle Temple
Qualifications: [BA (South Africa) LLB (South Africa) LLM (USA)]
✉jonathan.schwarz@taxbarristers.com

SCHWENK MR MARK BERNARD

Kenworthy's Chambers
Arlington House, Bloom Street, Salford, Manchester M3 6AJ, ☎0161 832 4036
Call Date: July 2001, Middle Temple
Qualifications: [LLB (Hons)]
✉m.schwenk@kenworthysbarristers.co.uk

SCOBIE MR JAMES TIMOTHY NORMAN QC (2010)

Garden Court Chambers
57-60 Lincoln's Inn Fields, London WC2A 3LJ, ☎020 7993 7600 ✉info@gclaw.co.uk
Call Date: July 1984, Gray's Inn
Pupil Supervisor
Qualifications: [BA (Hons) (Exon) Dip Law (Lond)]
✉jamess@gclaw.co.uk

SCOLDING MISS FIONA KATE

Hardwicke
New Square, Lincoln's Inn, London WC2A 3SB, ☎020 7242 2523
✉enquiries@hardwicke.co.uk
Call Date: Nov 1996, Gray's Inn
Pupil Supervisor
Qualifications: [BA (Cantab) Dip Law]

E

SCOREY MR DAVID WILLIAM JOHN

Essex Court Chambers
24 Lincoln's Inn Fields, London WC2A 3EG,
☎ 020 7813 8000
✉ clerksroom@essexcourt.net
Call Date: Oct 1997, Lincoln's Inn
Pupil Supervisor
Qualifications: [BA (Hons) LLM]
✉ dscorey@essexcourt.net

SCOTLAND MISS MARIA LYN

Seven Bedford Row
7 Bedford Row, London WC1R 4BS,
☎ 020 7242 3555 ✉ clerks@7br.co.uk
Call Date: Oct 1995, Gray's Inn
Qualifications: [B.Sc (Leeds)]
✉ mscotland@7br.co.uk

SCOTLAND OF ASTHAL ??? PATRICIA JANET QC (1991)

4 Paper Buildings
1st Floor, 4 Paper Buildings, Temple, London EC4Y 7EX, ☎ 020 7427 5200
✉ clerks@4pb.com
Call Date: July 1977, Middle Temple
Qualifications: [LLB (Lond) Honorary PHD (Lond) Honorary PHD (Bucks)]
✉ ps@4pb.com

E

SCOTT MISS ALEXANDRA ELISABETH

New Street Chambers
2 New Street, Leicester LE1 5NA,
☎ 0116 262 5906 ✉ clerks@2newstreet.co.uk
Call Date: July 1983, Gray's Inn
Pupil Supervisor
Qualifications: [LLB (Leic)]

SCOTT MR ANDREW DAVID PETER

Park Lane Plowden
19 Westgate, Leeds LS1 2RD,
☎ 0113 228 5049
✉ clerks@parklaneplowden.co.uk
Call Date: July 2002, Gray's Inn
Qualifications: [LLB (Teeside)]
✉ andrew.scott@parklaneplowden.co.uk

SCOTT MR ANDREW JAMES

Blackstone Chambers
Blackstone House, Temple, London EC4Y 9BW, ☎ 020 7583 1770
✉ clerks@blackstonechambers.com
Call Date: July 2010, Gray's Inn
Qualifications: [BA BCL DPhil]
✉ andrewscott@blackstonechambers.com

SCOTT MR CHARLES EDWIN

13 King's Bench Walk
13 King's Bench Walk, Temple, London EC4Y 7EN, ☎ 020 7353 7204
✉ clerks@13kbw.co.uk
13 KBW
32 Beaumont Street, Oxford OX1 2NP,
☎ 01865 311066 ✉ clerks@13kbw.co.uk
Call Date: July 1980, Middle Temple
Pupil Supervisor
Qualifications: [LLB (Lond) FCIArb]

SCOTT MR CHRISTOPHER GEORGE

Argent Chambers
5 Bell Yard, London WC2A 2JR,
☎ 020 7556 5500
✉ briefsin@argentchambers.co.uk
Call Date: Nov 2005, Gray's Inn
Qualifications: [BA(Law)]
✉ cscott@2hb.co.uk

SCOTT MISS GEMMA DIANNE

12 King's Bench Walk
12 King's Bench Walk, Temple, London EC4Y 7EL, ☎ 020 7583 0811
Call Date: Oct 2005, Inner Temple
Qualifications: [MA (Oxon) CPE]
✉ scott@12kbw.co.uk

SCOTT MR IAN RICHARD

Old Square Chambers
10-11 Bedford Row, London WC1R 4BU,
☎ 020 7269 0300 ✉ clerks@oldsquare.co.uk
Old Square Chambers
3 Orchard Court, St Augustine's Yard, Bristol BS1 5DP, ☎ 0117 930 5100
✉ clerks@oldsquare.co.uk
Call Date: Oct 1991, Lincoln's Inn
Pupil Supervisor
Qualifications: [BA (Hons) (Newc) MSc (Lond) DipLaw (Lond)]
✉ scott@oldsquare.co.uk

Types of work: Employment, Personal injury

SCOTT MR JAMES CAMERON

23 Essex Street
London WC2R 3AA, ☎ 020 7413 0353
✉ clerks@23es.com
Call Date: Mar 2012, Inner Temple

SCOTT MISS JANUARY

Wilberforce Chambers
7 Bishop Lane, Hull HU1 1PA,
☎ 01482 323264
Call Date: July 2000, Gray's Inn
Qualifications: [LLB (Hull)]

SCOTT MR JOHN ANDREW

18 St John Street
Manchester M3 4EA, ☎0161 278 1800
✉clerks@18sjs.com
Call Date: Nov 2000, Middle Temple
Qualifications: [LLB (Hons)]

SCOTT MISS KATHARINE MARY RUSSELL

39 Essex Street
London WC2R 3AT, ☎020 7832 1111
✉clerks@39essex.com
82 King Street
Manchester M2 4WQ, ☎0161 870 9969
Call Date: Mar 2000, Lincoln's Inn
Qualifications: [BA (Hons) (Surrey) MA (Lond) CPE]
✉katharine.scott@39essex.com

SCOTT MS LAURA LOUISE

14 Gray's Inn Square
14 Gray's Inn Square, Gray's Inn, London WC1R 5JP, ☎020 7242 0858
✉clerks@14gis.co.uk
Call Date: July 2001, Inner Temple
Qualifications: [BMus (Hons) CPE LRAM KCL]

SCOTT MR MARTIN JOHN HABERSHON

2 Dr Johnson's Buildings
2 Dr Johnson's Buildings, Temple, London EC4Y 7AY, ☎020 7936 2613
✉clerks@2drj.com
Call Date: Oct 1998, Middle Temple
Qualifications: [BA (Hons)(Cantab) CPE]
✉clerks@2drj.com

SCOTT MR MATTHEW JOHN

Pump Court Chambers
Upper Ground Floor, 3 Pump Court, Temple, London EC4Y 7AJ, ☎020 7353 0711
✉clerks@3pumpcourt.com
Pump Court Chambers
5 Temple Chambers, Temple Street, Swindon SN1 1SQ, ☎01793 539899
✉clerks@3pumpcourt.com
Pump Court Chambers
31 Southgate Street, Winchester, Hampshire SO23 9EB, ☎01962 868 161
✉clerks@3pumpcourt.com
Call Date: Nov 1985, Inner Temple
Pupil Supervisor
Qualifications: [BA (York)]
✉ms@3pumpcourt.com

SCOTT MISS RACHEL

3 Raymond Buildings
3 Raymond Buildings, Gray's Inn, London WC1R 5BH, ☎020 7400 6400
✉clerks@3rblaw.com
Call Date: July 2004, Gray's Inn
Qualifications: [BA PgDL]
✉rachel.scott@3raymondbuildings.com

SCOTT MR STUART

1 Pump Court
Elm Court, Temple, London EC4Y 7AB, ☎020 7842 7070
✉(name)@pumpcourt.co.uk
Call Date: Nov 1998, Inner Temple
Qualifications: [LLB (Lond)]
✉ssc@1pumpcourt.co.uk

SCOTT MISS TIFFANY ANNE

Wilberforce Chambers
8 New Square, Lincoln's Inn, London WC2A 3QP, ☎020 7306 0102
✉chambers@wilberforce.co.uk
Call Date: Nov 1998, Middle Temple
Pupil Supervisor
Qualifications: [BA (Hons)(Oxon)]
✉tscott@wilberforce.co.uk

SCOTT MR TIMOTHY JOHN WHITTAKER QC (1995)

29 Bedford Row Chambers
London WC1R 4HE, ☎020 7404 1044
✉clerks@29br.co.uk
Call Date: Nov 1975, Gray's Inn
Recorder
Qualifications: [BA (Oxon)]
✉tscott@29br.co.uk

SCOTT BELL MRS ROSALIND SARA

Trinity Chambers
The Custom House, 39 Quayside, Newcastle Upon Tyne NE1 3DE, ☎0191 232 1927
✉info@trinitychambers.co.uk
Trinity Chambers
Multi Media Exchange, 72-80 Corporation Road, Middlesbrough TS1 2RF, ☎01642 247569
✉info@trinitychambers.co.uk
Call Date: Oct 1993, Middle Temple
Pupil Supervisor
Qualifications: [LLB (Hons)(Manch)]
✉r.scottbell@trinitychambers.co.uk

E

SCOTT HOLLAND MR GIDEON SILAS

Keating Chambers
15 Essex Street, London WC2R 3AA,
☎ 020 7544 2600
✉ clerks@keatingchambers.com
Call Date: Oct 1999, Lincoln's Inn
Pupil Supervisor
Qualifications: [MA (Oxon) Dip in Law]
gscottholland@keatingchambers.com

SCOTT-BECKETT MISS ALISA-MARIE

Eastbourne Chambers
5 Chiswick Place, Eastbourne, East Sussex
BN21 4NH, ☎ 01323 642102
✉ clerks@eastbournechambers.co.uk
Call Date: July 2000, Inner Temple
Qualifications: [LLB (Hons)(Kent)]

SCOTT-JONES MISS ALISON CLAIRE

No 8 Chambers
8 Fountain Court, Steelhouse Lane,
Birmingham B4 6DR, ☎ 0121 236 5514
✉ clerks@no8chambers.co.uk
Call Date: Feb 1991, Middle Temple
Qualifications: [LLB (Wales)]

SCOTT-MANDERSON MR MARCUS CHARLES WILLIAM QC (2006)

4 Paper Buildings
1st Floor, 4 Paper Buildings, Temple, London
EC4Y 7EX, ☎ 020 7427 5200
✉ clerks@4pb.com
Call Date: July 1980, Lincoln's Inn
Qualifications: [BCL MA (Oxon)]
msm@4pb.com

SCOTT-MASON MISS HOLLY MARIA

Doughty Street Chambers
53-54 Doughty Street, London WC1N 2LS,
☎ 020 7404 1313
✉ enquiries@doughtystreet.co.uk
Call Date: Oct 2010, Middle Temple
Qualifications: [BA (Hons) (Cantab) LLM]

SCOTT-PHILLIPS MR ALEXANDER JAMES

5 Pump Court
Ground Floor, 5 Pump Court, Temple, London
EC4Y 7AP, ☎ 020 7353 2532
✉ clerks@5pumpcourt.com
Call Date: Oct 1995, Inner Temple
Pupil Supervisor
Qualifications: [BA (Hons)(Durham) CPE (Leic)]
clerks@kent-chambers.co.uk, alexanderscott-phillips@5pumpcourt.com

SCREECHE-POWELL MISS GENEVIEVE BERNADETTE FAITH

Field Court Chambers
5 Field Court, Gray's Inn, London WC1R 5EF,
☎ 020 7405 6114 ✉ clerks@fieldcourt.co.uk
Call Date: Oct 1997, Gray's Inn
Qualifications: [BA (Warks)]
genevieve@fieldcourt.co.uk

SCRIVEN MISS PAMELA QC (1992)

1 KBW Chambers
1 King's Bench Walk, Temple, London
EC4Y 7DB, ☎ 020 7936 1500
✉ clerks@1kbw.co.uk
King's Bench Chambers
174 High Street, Lewes BN7 1YE,
☎ 01273 402600
Dere Street Barristers
33 Broad Chare, Newcastle Upon Tyne
NE1 3DQ, ☎ 0844 3351551
✉ clerks@derestreet.co.uk
Call Date: Nov 1970, Inner Temple
Recorder
Qualifications: [LLB (Lond)]
pscrivenqc@1kbw.co.uk

SCRIVENER MISS KELLY LOUISE

Devon Chambers
3 St Andrew Street, Plymouth PL1 2AH,
☎ 01752 661659
✉ clerks@devonchambers.co.uk
Call Date: Oct 2001, Lincoln's Inn
Qualifications: [LLB (Hons)]
kellyscrivener@devonchambers.co.uk

SCUDAMORE MR JEREMY RICHARD

Henderson Chambers
2 Harcourt Buildings, Temple, London
EC4Y 9DB, ☎ 020 7583 9020
✉ clerks@hendersonchambers.co.uk
Call Date: Nov 1982, Middle Temple
Qualifications: [BA (Hons) (Exon)]

SCULLY MRS JENNIFER LESLEY

St Johns Buildings Liverpool
8th Floor India Buildings, Water Street,
Liverpool L2 0XG, ☎ 0151 243 6000
✉ clerk@stjohnsbuildings.co.uk
16 Winckley Square
Preston PR1 3JJ, ☎ 01772 256100
St Johns Buildings
24a - 28 St John Street, Manchester M3 4DJ,
☎ 0161 214 1500
✉ clerk@stjohnsbuildings.co.uk
Call Date: July 2006, Middle Temple
Qualifications: [BA (Hons)]
jenny.scully@stjohnsbuildings.co.uk

E

SCUTT MR DAVID ROBERT

9-12 Bell Yard
London WC2A 2JR, ☎020 7400 1800
✉clerks@9-12bellyard.com
Call Date: Nov 1989, Middle Temple
Pupil Supervisor
Qualifications: [BA (Hons)(Keele)]

SEABROOK MR RICHARD MICHAEL

Ropewalk Chambers
24 The Ropewalk, Nottingham NG1 5EF,
☎0115 947 2581 ✉clerks@ropewalk.co.uk
Call Date: July 1987, Inner Temple
Pupil Supervisor
Qualifications: [LLB]
richardseabrook@ropewalk.co.uk

SEABROOK MR ROBERT JOHN QC (1983)

1 Crown Office Row
1 Crown Office Row, Temple, London
EC4Y 7HH, ☎020 7797 7500
✉mail@1cor.com
Call Date: June 1964, Middle Temple
Recorder
Qualifications: [LLB]

SEAGRIM MR WILLIAM

9 Park Place
9 Park Place, Cardiff, South Glamorgan
CF10 3DP, ☎029 2038 2731
✉clerks@9parkplace.co.uk
Call Date: July 2007, Gray's Inn
Qualifications: [LLB (Hons) (Wales)]
wseagrim@9parkplace.co.uk

SEAL MR JULIUS DAMIEN

Chambers of Mr Julius Seal
189 Randolph Avenue, Maida Vale, London
W9 1DJ, ☎020 7328 0158
✉julius.seal@ntlworld.com
Call Date: Nov 1967, Lincoln's Inn
Pupil Supervisor
julius.seal@ntlworld.com

SEAL MR KEVIN PAUL

9 Park Place
9 Park Place, Cardiff, South Glamorgan
CF10 3DP, ☎029 2038 2731
✉clerks@9parkplace.co.uk
Call Date: July 1998, Gray's Inn
Qualifications: [LLB (Manch)]

SEAL MISS PHILIPPA MARGARET

Lamb Chambers
Lamb Building, Elm Court, Temple, London
EC4Y 7AS, ☎020 7797 8300
✉info@lambchambers.co.uk
Chambers of Mr Julius Seal
189 Randolph Avenue, Maida Vale, London
W9 1DJ, ☎020 7328 0158
✉julius.seal@ntlworld.com
Call Date: Nov 2008, Lincoln's Inn
Qualifications: [BA (Cantab) CPE UCU]
philippaseal@lambchambers.co.uk

SEAMAN MISS JENNIFER ANNE

3 Stone Buildings
Ground Floor, 3 Stone Buildings, Lincoln's
Inn, London WC2A 3XL, ☎020 7242 4937
✉clerks@3sb.law.co.uk
Call Date: Oct 2007, Lincoln's Inn
Qualifications: [BA BCL (Oxon)]
jseaman@3sb.law.co.uk

SEAR MISS JOANNE

13 King's Bench Walk
13 King's Bench Walk, Temple, London
EC4Y 7EN, ☎020 7353 7204
✉clerks@13kbw.co.uk
13 KBW
32 Beaumont Street, Oxford OX1 2NP,
☎01865 311066 ✉clerks@13kbw.co.uk
Call Date: July 2004, Gray's Inn
Qualifications: [LLB (Cardiff)]
jsear@13kbw.co.uk

SEAR MR RICHARD ANTHONY

1 Hare Court
1 Hare Court, Temple, London EC4Y 7BE,
☎020 7797 7070 ✉clerks@1hc.com
Riverview Chambers
Hamilton House, 1 Temple Avenue, London
EC4Y 0HA, ☎0844 225 3999
✉chrisbaylis@riverviewchambers.com
Call Date: July 2005, Middle Temple
Qualifications: [BA MA AKC MSc]
rs@1hc.com

SEARLE MR BARRIE

St James's Chambers
68 Quay Street, Manchester M3 3EJ,
☎0161 834 7000
✉clerks@stjameschambers.com
Call Date: July 1975, Middle Temple
Pupil Supervisor, Recorder
Qualifications: [LLB (Hons)]

E

SEARLE MISS CORINNE LOUISE TEAGUE

Walnut House
63 St. David's Hill, Exeter, Devon EX4 4DW,
☎01392 279751
✉clerks@walnuthouse.co.uk
Call Date: July 1982, Gray's Inn
Pupil Supervisor, Recorder
Qualifications: [LLB (Lond)]

SEARLE MR JASON ARIO XAVIER

Call Date: Oct 1993, Middle Temple
Qualifications: [LLB (Hons)]
jason.searle@stjohnsbuildings.co.uk

SEARS MR ROBERT DAVID MURRAY QC (2003)

Four New Square
Four New Square, Lincoln's Inn, London WC2A 3RJ, ☎020 7822 2000
✉barristers@4newsquare.com
Call Date: Nov 1984, Middle Temple
Qualifications: [MA (Oxon)]
d.sears@4newsquare.com

E

SEAWARD MR MARTIN VINCENT

Cloisters
1 Pump Court, Temple, London EC4Y 7AA,
☎020 7827 4000 ✉clerks@cloisters.com
Call Date: Nov 1978, Gray's Inn
Pupil Supervisor
Qualifications: [BA (Hons) (Dunelm)]
ms@cloisters.com

SEDDON MISS DOROTHY

Cornwall Street Chambers
85-87 Cornwall Street, Birmingham B3 3BY,
☎0121 233 7500
✉clerks@cornwallstreet.co.uk
Call Date: July 1974, Middle Temple
Qualifications: [LLB (B'ham)]
dorothy.seddon@cornwallstreet.co.uk

SEDDON MR JAMES DURAN

Garden Court Chambers
57-60 Lincoln's Inn Fields, London WC2A 3LJ,
☎020 7993 7600 ✉info@gclaw.co.uk
Call Date: Feb 1994, Middle Temple
Qualifications: [BA (Hons)(Oxon) CPE (Manch)]
durans@gclaw.co.uk

SEEBORUTH MR ROYLN JEAN-PAUL

Chambers of Royln Seeboruth
Abbotts Close Chambers, 4 Abbotts Close, Aylesbury, Bucks HP20 1HZ, ☎01296 393329
✉rseeboruth@live.co.uk
Call Date: Nov 1986, Middle Temple
Pupil Supervisor
Qualifications: [LLB (Hons)(Bucks)]
rseeboruth@live.co.uk

SEED MR STEPHEN NICHOLAS

Number 7 Harrington Street Chambers
7 Harrington Street, Liverpool L2 9YH,
☎0151 242 0707 ✉clerks@7hs.co.uk
Call Date: Oct 1991, Gray's Inn
Qualifications: [LLB]
stephen.seed@7hs.co.uk

SEEHRA MISS AMARJIT

10 King's Bench Walk
Ground Floor, 10 King's Bench Walk, Temple, London EC4Y 7EB, ☎020 7353 7742
✉Chambers@10kingsbenchwalk.co.uk
Call Date: Oct 1999, Middle Temple
Qualifications: [LLB (Hons)]
amarjit.seehra@10kingsbenchwalk.co.uk

SEELIG MR LEO WILLIAM

Atkinson Bevan Chambers
1st Floor, 2 Harcourt Buildings, Temple, London EC4Y 9DB, ☎020 7353 2112
✉clerks@2hb.co.uk
Call Date: Nov 2007, Lincoln's Inn
Qualifications: [BSc (Leeds)]
lseelig@2hb.co.uk

SEELY MR JONATHAN SEBASTIAN

1 Paper Buildings
1st Floor, 1 Paper Buildings, Temple, London EC4Y 7EP, ☎020 7353 3728
✉clerks@onepaper.co.uk
Call Date: Nov 1987, Inner Temple
Qualifications: [BA Dip Law]
jonathanseely@onepaper.co.uk

SEFI MR BENEDICT JOHN

Harcourt Chambers
1st Floor, 2 Harcourt Buildings, Temple, London EC4Y 9DB, ☎0844 561 7135
Harcourt Chambers
Churchill House, 3 St Aldate's Courtyard, St Aldate's, Oxford OX1 1BN, ☎0844 561 7135
Call Date: July 1972, Inner Temple
Pupil Supervisor
Qualifications: [BA (Oxon)]
bsefi@harcourtchambers.law.co.uk

SEFTON MRS JOANNE ELIZABETH

Littleton Chambers
3 King's Bench Walk North, Temple, London EC4Y 7HR, ☎ 020 7797 8600
✉ fschneider@littletonchambers.co.uk
Call Date: July 2002, Lincoln's Inn
Pupil Supervisor
Qualifications: [BA (Hons)(Cantab)]
jsefton@littletonchambers.co.uk

SEFTON MR MARK THOMAS DUNBLANE

Falcon Chambers
Falcon Court, London EC4Y 1AA,
☎ 020 7353 2484
✉ clerks@falcon-chambers.com
Call Date: Nov 1996, Middle Temple
Pupil Supervisor
Qualifications: [MA (Hons)(Cantab)]
sefton@falcon-chambers.com

SEFTON MR NICHOLAS EDWARD

Linenhall Chambers
1 Stanley Place, Chester CH1 2LU,
☎ 01244 348282
✉ clerks@linenhallchambers.co.uk
Pendragon Chambers
Suite 7, J Shed, Kings Road, SA1 Waterfront, Swansea SA1 8PL, ☎ 01792 411188
✉ clerks@pendragonchambers.com
Call Date: July 2004, Gray's Inn
Qualifications: [LLB (Hons)]
clerks@1stanleyplace.co.uk

SEFTON-SMITH MR LLOYD

Lamb Chambers
Lamb Building, Elm Court, Temple, London EC4Y 7AS, ☎ 020 7797 8300
✉ info@lambchambers.co.uk
Call Date: Oct 1993, Lincoln's Inn
Pupil Supervisor
Qualifications: [BA (Hons)(Lond)]
lloydseftonsmith@lambchambers.co.uk

SEGAL MR OLIVER LEON QC (2011)

Old Square Chambers
10-11 Bedford Row, London WC1R 4BU,
☎ 020 7269 0300 ✉ clerks@oldsquare.co.uk
Old Square Chambers
3 Orchard Court, St Augustine's Yard, Bristol BS1 5DP, ☎ 0117 930 5100
✉ clerks@oldsquare.co.uk
Call Date: Oct 1992, Middle Temple
Pupil Supervisor
Qualifications: [BA (Hons)]
segal@oldsquare.co.uk

SEGAL MS SHARON MIRIAM

1 Garden Court Family Law Chambers
Ground Floor, One Garden Court, Temple, London EC4Y 9BJ, ☎ 020 7797 7900
✉ clerks@1gc.com
Call Date: July 2000, Inner Temple
Pupil Supervisor
Qualifications: [LLB (Lond)]
segal@1gc.com

SEGAN MR JAMES JEFFREY

Blackstone Chambers
Blackstone House, Temple, London EC4Y 9BW, ☎ 020 7583 1770
✉ clerks@blackstonechambers.com
Call Date: Nov 2004, Inner Temple
Qualifications: [BA (Oxon) Diploma in Law]
jamessegan@blackstonechambers.com

SEGUSS MISS PENELOPE MARIE

The Chambers of Penelope Seguss
28 Burcote Road, London SW18 3LQ,
☎ 020 8877 0707 ✉ pseguss@btinternet.com
Call Date: Oct 1996, Gray's Inn
Qualifications: [LLB (Essex)]

SEHAT MISS AMANDA

Trinity Chambers
The Custom House, 39 Quayside, Newcastle Upon Tyne NE1 3DE, ☎ 0191 232 1927
✉ info@trinitychambers.co.uk
Trinity Chambers
Multi Media Exchange, 72-80 Corporation Road, Middlesbrough TS1 2RF,
☎ 01642 247569
✉ info@trinitychambers.co.uk
Call Date: July 2009, Lincoln's Inn
Qualifications: [LLB (Dunelm)]
a.sehat@trinitychambers.co.uk

SEHMI MR MANDEEP SINGH

9 King's Bench Walk
Lower Ground Floor South, 9 King's Bench Walk, Temple, London EC4Y 7DX,
☎ 020 7353 9564 ✉ 9kbw@btconnect.com
Call Date: Oct 1997, Lincoln's Inn
Qualifications: [LLB (Hons)]

SEIFERT MISS VICTORIA CHARLOTTE

Lamb Chambers
Lamb Building, Elm Court, Temple, London EC4Y 7AS, ☎ 020 7797 8300
✉ info@lambchambers.co.uk
Call Date: Oct 2002, Middle Temple
Qualifications: [MA (Hons) (Edin) CPE]

E

SEITLER MS DEBORAH

Renaissance Chambers
5th Floor, Gray's Inn Chambers, Gray's Inn, London WC1R 5JA, ☎ 020 7404 1111
✉ clerks@renaissancechambers.co.uk
Call Date: Nov 1991, Inner Temple
Qualifications: [BA (Leeds) DipLaw]
✉ ds@renaissancechambers.co.uk

SEITLER MR JONATHAN SIMON QC (2003)

Wilberforce Chambers
8 New Square, Lincoln's Inn, London WC2A 3QP, ☎ 020 7306 0102
✉ chambers@wilberforce.co.uk
Call Date: Nov 1985, Inner Temple
Qualifications: [BA (Oxon)]
✉ jseitler@wilberforce.co.uk

SEKAR MR CHANDRA

Angell Park Chambers
Unit 11, Amberley Court, Angell Road, London SW9 7HL, ☎ 020 7737 5957
✉ info@chandrasekar.co.uk
Call Date: Mar 1996, Gray's Inn
Qualifications: [BA (Bris)]

SEKHON MRS JAGDEEP KAUR

No 8 Chambers
8 Fountain Court, Steelhouse Lane, Birmingham B4 6DR, ☎ 0121 236 5514
✉ clerks@no8chambers.co.uk
Call Date: Nov 1999, Gray's Inn
Qualifications: [LLB]

SEKHON MR NARINDER SINGH

Sovereign Chambers
46 Park Place, Leeds LS1 2RY, ☎ 0113 245 1841
✉ clerks@sovereignchambers.co.uk
Call Date: Nov 2000, Lincoln's Inn
Qualifications: [LLB (Hons)]
✉ narinder.sekhon@sovereignchambers.co.uk

SELBY MR ANDREW ROBERT VINCENT

Chambers of Mr Ami Feder
Ground Floor, Lamb Building, Temple, London EC4Y 7AS, ☎ 020 7797 7788
✉ clerks@lambbuilding.co.uk
Lamb Building
22 Ship Street, Brighton BN1 1AD, ☎ 01273 820490
✉ admin@lambbuilding.co.uk
Chambers of Mr Ami Feder
Ground Floor, Lamb Building, Temple, London EC4Y 7AS, ☎ 020 7797 7788
✉ clerks@lambbuilding.co.uk
Call Date: Nov 1997, Gray's Inn
Pupil Supervisor
Qualifications: [BA (Hons)]
✉ clerks@lambbuilding.co.uk, selby@barristeratlaw.info

SELBY MR JONATHAN LEE

Keating Chambers
15 Essex Street, London WC2R 3AA, ☎ 020 7544 2600
✉ clerks@keatingchambers.com
Call Date: Nov 1999, Gray's Inn
Pupil Supervisor
Qualifications: [MA (Cantab)]
✉ jselby@keatingchambers.com

SELBY MR LAWRENCE JULIAN CATELLO

Nine Bedford Row
9 Bedford Row, London WC1R 4AZ, ☎ 020 7489 2727
✉ clerks@9bedfordrow.co.uk
Call Date: Mar 1997, Gray's Inn
Qualifications: [BA (Hons)(Reading) CPE BVC]
✉ lawrence.selby@9bedfordrow.co.uk

SELBY MISS SARAH ANNE

9-12 Bell Yard
London WC2A 2JR, ☎ 020 7400 1800
✉ clerks@9-12bellyard.com
Call Date: Oct 1998, Gray's Inn
Qualifications: [BA (Cantab)]
✉ s.selby@9-12bellyard.com

SELF MR GARY PETER

College Chambers
19 Carlton Crescent, Southampton, Hampshire SO15 2ET, ☎ 023 8023 0338
✉ clerks@college-chambers.co.uk
St David's Chambers
Myrtle Cottage, Norton Road, Mumbles, Swansea SA3 5TQ, ☎ 01792 559924
✉ j.vallack@ntlworld.com
Call Date: Oct 1991, Lincoln's Inn
Pupil Supervisor
Qualifications: [BA (Hons)(Manc) Dip Law]
✉ gself@College-Chambers.co.uk

SELFE MR MICHAEL ROSS

2 King's Bench Walk
2 King's Bench Walk, Temple, London
EC4Y 7DE, ☎020 7353 1746
✉clerks@2kbw.com
Call Date: Nov 1965, Middle Temple
Pupil Supervisor, Recorder
Qualifications: [LLB (So'ton)]
mselfe@2kbw.com

SELLARS MR MICHAEL JOHN

Atlantic Chambers
4-6 Cook Street, Liverpool L2 9QU,
☎0151 236 4421
✉info@atlanticchambers.co.uk
Call Date: July 1980, Inner Temple
Qualifications: [BA (Dunelm)]
michaelsellars@atlanticchambers.co.uk

SELLERS MR ALAN MITCHELL

Liverpool Civil Law
3rd Floor, 1 Old Hall Street, Liverpool L3 9HF,
☎0151 242 0500
✉clerks@liverpoolcivillaw.com
Call Date: July 1991, Gray's Inn
Qualifications: [LLB (Lancs)]
clerks@liverpoolcivillaw.com

SELLERS MR GRAHAM

Atlantic Chambers
4-6 Cook Street, Liverpool L2 9QU,
☎0151 236 4421
✉info@atlanticchambers.co.uk
Call Date: Oct 1990, Middle Temple
Qualifications: [LLB LLM (Cantab)]
grahamsellers@atlanticchambers.co.uk

SELLERS MR ROBIN ST. JOHN

23 Essex Street
London WC2R 3AA, ☎020 7413 0353
✉clerks@23es.com
Call Date: Nov 1994, Inner Temple
Pupil Supervisor
Qualifications: [LLB (Reading)]
robinsellers@23es.com

SELLICK MR WILLIAM PATRICK LLEWELLYN

King's Bench and Godolphin (KBG)Chambers
115 North Hill, Plymouth, Devon PL4 8JY,
☎01752 221551
✉clerks@kbgchambers.co.uk
Call Date: July 1973, Middle Temple
Pupil Supervisor, Recorder
Qualifications: [LLB]
LlewellynSellick@btinternet.com

SELLS MR OLIVER MATTHEW QC (1995)

Five Paper Buildings
1st Floor, Five Paper Buildings, Temple,
London EC4Y 7HB, ☎020 7583 6117
✉clerks@5pb.co.uk
Call Date: July 1972, Inner Temple
Recorder
os@5pb.co.uk

SELMAN MISS ELIZABETH

1 KBW Chambers
1 King's Bench Walk, Temple, London
EC4Y 7DB, ☎020 7936 1500
✉clerks@1kbw.co.uk
King's Bench Chambers
174 High Street, Lewes BN7 1YE,
☎01273 402600
Call Date: Nov 1989, Inner Temple
Pupil Supervisor
Qualifications: [LLB (Lond)]
eselman@1kbw.co.uk

SELVARATNAM MISS VASANTI EMILY INDRANI QC (2001)

Stone Chambers
4 Field Court, Gray's Inn, London WC1R 5EF,
☎020 7440 6900
✉clerks@stonechambers.com
Call Date: July 1983, Middle Temple
Recorder
Qualifications: [LLM AKC LLB (Lond)]
vasanti.selvaratnam@stonechambers.com

Types of work: Admiralty, Arbitration, Banking, Civil fraud, Commercial law, Commercial litigation, Commodities, Competition law, Conflict of laws, EC competition law, Insurance, International trade, Sale and carriage of goods, Shipping

SELWAY DR KATHERINE EMMA

Radcliffe Chambers
Ground Floor, 11 New Square, Lincoln's Inn,
London WC2A 3QB, ☎020 7831 0081
✉clerks@radcliffechambers.com
Call Date: Nov 1995, Inner Temple
Pupil Supervisor
Qualifications: [BA (Hons)(Bris) D.Phil (Oxon) CPE (Lond)]
kselway@radcliffechambers.com

SELWAY MR MICHAEL DAVID

Guildhall Chambers
23 Broad Street, Bristol BS1 2HG,
☎0117 930 9000
✉hoc@guildhallchambers.co.uk
Call Date: Nov 2007, Middle Temple
Qualifications: [BA (Hons) (Oxon)]
michael.selway@guildhallchambers.co.uk

E

SELWYN SHARPE MR RICHARD CHARLES

St James's Chambers
68 Quay Street, Manchester M3 3EJ,
☎0161 834 7000
✉clerks@stjameschambers.com
Call Date: Nov 1985, Lincoln's Inn
Pupil Supervisor
Qualifications: [LLB(Bris)]
clerks@stjameschambers.com

SEMARK MR DAVID MARTIN

Quadrant Chambers
Quadrant House, 10 Fleet Street, London EC4Y 1AU, ☎020 7583 4444
✉info@quadrantchambers.com
Call Date: Oct 2009, Lincoln's Inn
Qualifications: [LLM LLB BComm]
david.semark@quadrantchambers.com

SEMKEN MR CHRISTOPHER RICHARD

New Square Chambers
12 New Square, Lincoln's Inn, London WC2A 3SW, ☎020 7419 8000
✉robin.hollington@newsquarechambers.co.uk
Call Date: July 1977, Lincoln's Inn
Qualifications: [MA (Oxon)]
christopher.semken@newsquarechambers.co.uk

SEMPLE MR ANDREW BLAIR

Sovereign Chambers
46 Park Place, Leeds LS1 2RY,
☎0113 245 1841
✉clerks@sovereignchambers.co.uk
Call Date: Oct 1993, Inner Temple
Qualifications: [BA (Dunelm)]
andrew.semple@sovereignchambers.co.uk

SEMPLE MR GORDON ROBERT

No.6 Park Square
Leeds LS1 2LW, ☎0113 245 9763
✉Tim@no6.co.uk
Call Date: Oct 2003, Gray's Inn
Qualifications: [BSc (York)]

SEMPLE MISS JANE ELIZABETH

Park Lane Plowden
19 Westgate, Leeds LS1 2RD,
☎0113 228 5049
✉clerks@parklaneplowden.co.uk
Call Date: July 2000, Gray's Inn
Qualifications: [LLB (Dundee)]
jane.semple@parklaneplowden.co.uk

SEN MR ADITYA KUMAR

Coram Chambers
9-11 Fulwood Place, London WC1V 6HG,
☎020 7092 3700
✉mail@coramchambers.co.uk
Call Date: July 1977, Lincoln's Inn
Pupil Supervisor
Qualifications: [MA, LLB (Cantab), FCA, BA (Hons)(India)]

Fax: 020 8922 8435 Chambers Fax: 020 7092 3777;
Out of hours telephone: 020 8458 8697/ 07932 743212;
DX: 404 Chancery Lane or 92008 Temple Fortune;
Other comms: E-mail: seninlondon@hotmail.com

Other professional qualifications: BA (Hons) in Economics, Delhi University; MA, LLB (Cantab); FCA

Types of work: Banking, Chancery (general), Commercial litigation, Company, commercial and competition, Corporate fraud, Foreign law, Indian law, International trade, Partnerships, Professional negligence

Membership of foreign bars: Enrolled in the Supreme Court of India Bar Association and the Bar Library, Calcutta High Court

Circuit: South Eastern

Awards and memberships: Member of the Commonwealth Lawyers Association; Professional Negligence Bar Association; Human Rights Lawyers Association; Justice; Liberty; Society of Asian Lawyers; International Bar Association

Other professional experience: Worked in a firm of chartered accountants; involved in mediation

Languages spoken: Bengali, Hindi

Additional information
I had qualified as an accountant and worked in one of the 'big five' firms of accountants before I was called to the Bar. I have found that my experience in accountancy matters has been of invaluable assistance in my practice particularly in the fields of commercial, company and partnership matters. My practice covers a wide area of both domestic and international law. I have been involved in a considerable number of major commercial disputes which involve different jurisdictions. I have knowledge of Indian law and am presently practising in the Indian High Courts and in the Supreme Court of India. I am in a position to advise on most fields of Indian law

particularly in shipping, commercial and arbitration matters where I have been involved in major cases in the High Courts and in the Supreme Court of India. I advise clients in the UK, India, Far East and the Middle East and I have established and maintained chambers in London and in Calcutta and New Delhi.

Details of cases can be provided on request.

SEN MR DAIPAYAN IAN

11 Gray's Inn Square Chambers
Chambers of Mr Ian Sen, 1st Floor South, 10/11 Gray's Inn Square, London WC1R 5JD, ☎ 020 7405 6879
✉ clerks@11graysinnsquare.com
Call Date: Nov 1998, Middle Temple
Qualifications: [LLB (Hons)(Dublin) LLM (Dublin)]
✉ ian.sen@11graysinnsquare.com

SEN GUPTA MISS DIYA

Blackstone Chambers
Blackstone House, Temple, London EC4Y 9BW, ☎ 020 7583 1770
✉ clerks@blackstonechambers.com
Call Date: Oct 2000, Inner Temple
Pupil Supervisor
Qualifications: [BA (Hons) (Cantab)]
✉ DiyaSenGupta@blackstonechambers.com

SENDALL MR ANTONY JOHN CHRISTMAS

Littleton Chambers
3 King's Bench Walk North, Temple, London EC4Y 7HR, ☎ 020 7797 8600
✉ fschneider@littletonchambers.co.uk
Call Date: July 1984, Lincoln's Inn
Pupil Supervisor
Qualifications: [MA (Cantab)]

SENIOR MR ANTHONY JAMES

Dere Street Barristers
33 Broad Chare, Newcastle Upon Tyne NE1 3DQ, ☎ 0844 3351551
✉ clerks@derestreet.co.uk
Call Date: July 2002, Gray's Inn
Qualifications: [LLB (Hons) (Teesside)]
✉ clerks@broadcharechambers.co.uk

SENIOR MR MARK

St Johns Buildings Liverpool
8th Floor India Buildings, Water Street, Liverpool L2 0XG, ☎ 0151 243 6000
✉ clerk@stjohnsbuildings.co.uk
16 Winckley Square
Preston PR1 3JJ, ☎ 01772 256100
St Johns Buildings
24a - 28 St John Street, Manchester M3 4DJ, ☎ 0161 214 1500
✉ clerk@stjohnsbuildings.co.uk
Call Date: July 2002, Gray's Inn
Qualifications: [LLB (Lancaster) MA (L'pool)]
✉ theseniorfamily@googlemail.com

SEPHTON MR CRAIG GARDNER QC (2001)

Deans Court Chambers
24 St John Street, Manchester M3 4DF, ☎ 0161 214 6000 ✉ clerks@deanscourt.co.uk
Deans Court Chambers
101 Walker Street, Preston PR1 2RR, ☎ 01772 565 600
✉ preston@deanscourt.co.uk
Call Date: July 1981, Middle Temple
Qualifications: [MA BCL (Oxon)]
✉ sephton@deanscourt.co.uk

SERGIDES MS MARINA

Garden Court Chambers
57-60 Lincoln's Inn Fields, London WC2A 3LJ, ☎ 020 7993 7600 ✉ info@gclaw.co.uk
Call Date: Nov 2000, Inner Temple
Qualifications: [LLB (Lond)]
✉ marinas@gclaw.co.uk

SERR MR ASHLEY BARRIE

Park Lane Plowden
19 Westgate, Leeds LS1 2RD, ☎ 0113 228 5049
✉ clerks@parklaneplowden.co.uk
Call Date: Nov 1996, Middle Temple
Pupil Supervisor
Qualifications: [LLB (Hons)(Notts) LLM (Sydney)]
✉ ashley.serr@parklaneplowden.co.uk

SERUGO-LUGO MR YOSEFALY NDAULA KIKWANGWIRA SE

Essex House Chambers
122-126 Kilburn High Road, Kilburn, London NW6 4HY, ☎ 020 7692 0677
✉ essexhousechambers@yahoo.co.uk
Call Date: Nov 1973, Inner Temple
Pupil Supervisor
Qualifications: [BA]
✉ essexhousechambers@yahoo.co.uk

E

SETHI MR MOHINDERPAL SINGH

Devereux Chambers
Queen Elizabeth Building, Temple, London EC4Y 9BS, ☎ 020 7353 7534
✉ clerks@devchambers.co.uk
Call Date: Oct 1996, Middle Temple
Qualifications: [BA (Hons)(Oxon)]
✉ sethi@devchambers.co.uk

SETHI MISS NATASHA

Henderson Chambers
2 Harcourt Buildings, Temple, London EC4Y 9DB, ☎ 020 7583 9020
✉ clerks@hendersonchambers.co.uk
Call Date: Oct 2001, Middle Temple
Qualifications: [LLB (Hons) LLM]
✉ nsethi@hendersonchambers.co.uk

SETHI MS RITA

Tooks Chambers
81 Farringdon Street, London EC4A 4BL, ☎ 020 7842 7575 ✉ clerks@tooks.co.uk
Call Date: Nov 2000, Inner Temple
Qualifications: [BA (Hons) CPE Dip EC Law LSF]
✉ rita.sethi@tooks.co.uk

E

SETRIGHT MR HENRY JOHN QC (2001)

4 Paper Buildings
1st Floor, 4 Paper Buildings, Temple, London EC4Y 7EX, ☎ 020 7427 5200
✉ clerks@4pb.com
Call Date: Nov 1979, Middle Temple
Recorder
Qualifications: [MA (Oxon) DipGerm (German)]
✉ hs@4pb.com

SEYMOUR MS LYDIA RUTH

Outer Temple Chambers
The Outer Temple, 222 Strand, London WC2R 1BA, ☎ 020 7353 6381
✉ clerks@outertemple.com
Call Date: Oct 1997, Inner Temple
Qualifications: [BA (Oxon) CPE]
✉ lydia.seymour@outertemple.com

SEYMOUR MR MARK WILLIAM

9-12 Bell Yard
London WC2A 2JR, ☎ 020 7400 1800
✉ clerks@9-12bellyard.com
Call Date: Oct 1992, Middle Temple
Qualifications: [MA (Hons)]
✉ m.seymour@9-12bellyard.com

SEYMOUR MR THOMAS OLIVER

Wilberforce Chambers
8 New Square, Lincoln's Inn, London WC2A 3QP, ☎ 020 7306 0102
✉ chambers@wilberforce.co.uk
Call Date: July 1975, Inner Temple
Pupil Supervisor
Qualifications: [MA (Cantab)]

SHACKLEFORD MISS SUSAN ANGELA

Octagon House
19 Colegate, Norwich NR3 1AT, ☎ 01603 623186
✉ clerks@octagonhouse.co.uk
Call Date: Nov 1980, Inner Temple
Pupil Supervisor
Qualifications: [BA (Lond)]

SHADAREVIAN MR PAUL

Cornerstone Barristers
2-3 Gray's Inn Square, Gray's Inn, London WC1R 5JH, ☎ 020 7242 4986
✉ chambers@2-3gis.co.uk
Call Date: July 1984, Gray's Inn
Pupil Supervisor
Qualifications: [BA (Hons) Dip Law (Lond)]
✉ pshadarevian@2-3gis.co.uk

SHAFI MR MOHAMMED IMRAN

Exchange Chambers
7 Ralli Courts, West Riverside, Manchester M3 5FT, ☎ 0161 833 2722
Exchange Chambers
One Derby Square, Derby Square, Liverpool L2 9XX, ☎ 0151 236 7747
✉ info@exchangechambers.co.uk
Exchange Chambers
Oxford House, Oxford Row, Leeds LS1 3BE, ☎ 0113 203 1970
✉ spencer@exchangechambers.co.uk
Call Date: Nov 1996, Lincoln's Inn
Qualifications: [LLB (Hons)(Lond) LLM (L'pool)]
✉ imranshafi@btinternet.com

SHAH MR AKHIL QC (2010)

Fountain Court Chambers
Fountain Court, Temple, London EC4Y 9DH, ☎ 020 7583 3335
✉ chambers@fountaincourt.co.uk
Call Date: Nov 1990, Inner Temple
Pupil Supervisor
Qualifications: [BA (Cantab) MA (Cantab)]
✉ ashah@fountaincourt.co.uk

SHAH MR BAJUL AMRATLAL SOMCHAND

XXIV Old Buildings
Ground Floor, 24 Old Buildings, Lincoln's Inn, London WC2A 3UP, ☎020 7691 2424
✉clerks@xxiv.co.uk
Call Date: Oct 1996, Lincoln's Inn
Pupil Supervisor
Qualifications: [BA (Hons) BCL (Oxon)]
✉bajul.shah@xxiv.co.uk

SHAH MISS NEHALI NALIN

One Essex Court
Ground Floor, One Essex Court, Temple, London EC4Y 9AR, ☎020 7583 2000
✉clerks@oeclaw.co.uk
Call Date: Oct 2008, Middle Temple
Qualifications: [BA (Hons) (Cantab) LLM (Lond)]
✉nshah@oeclaw.co.uk

SHAH MR NEIL

Coram Chambers
9-11 Fulwood Place, London WC1V 6HG, ☎020 7092 3700
✉mail@coramchambers.co.uk
Call Date: July 2008, Middle Temple
Qualifications: [LLB (Hons) (LSE)]

SHAH MS SHILPA

Ropewalk Chambers
24 The Ropewalk, Nottingham NG1 5EF, ☎0115 947 2581 ✉clerks@ropewalk.co.uk
Call Date: July 1998, Lincoln's Inn
Qualifications: [LLB LLM]
✉shilpashah@ropewalk.co.uk

SHAH MS SMITA

Garden Court Chambers
57-60 Lincoln's Inn Fields, London WC2A 3LJ, ☎020 7993 7600 ✉info@gclaw.co.uk
Call Date: Oct 2002, Inner Temple
Qualifications: [LLB (Hons) MA (Lond) LLM (Columbia)]
✉smitas@gclaw.co.uk

SHAH MISS WAFA

Garden Court Chambers
57-60 Lincoln's Inn Fields, London WC2A 3LJ, ☎020 7993 7600 ✉info@gclaw.co.uk
Call Date: Oct 2009, Middle Temple
Qualifications: [LLB (Hons) (Bris)]

SHAIKH EUR ING CHRISTOPHER

Avondale Chambers
134 Engel Park, Mill Hill East, London NW7 2HP, ☎020 8346 1126
Call Date: July 1980, Gray's Inn
Qualifications: [BSc Eng (Hons)(Lond) C Eng MRINA FB Eng M I MAR EST]
✉chrisshaikh2002@yahoo.co.uk

SHAIKH MISS SEMAAB

Broadway House Chambers
Broadway House, 9 Bank Street, Bradford, West Yorkshire BD1 1TW, ☎01274 722560
✉clerks@broadwayhouse.co.uk
Broadway House Chambers
25 Park Square West, Leeds, West Yorkshire LS1 2PW, ☎0113 246 2600
✉clerks@broadwayhouse.co.uk
Call Date: Nov 2002, Lincoln's Inn
Qualifications: [LLB (Hons)(B'ham) LLM (B'ham)]
✉clerks@broadwayhouse.co.uk

SHAKESPEARE MISS SUSAN

Park Lane Plowden
Lombard House, 4-8 Lombard Street, Newcastle Upon Tyne NE1 3AE, ☎0191 211 4087
✉clerks@parklaneplowden.co.uk
Call Date: Mar 2007, Inner Temple
Qualifications: [BA (Newc) LLB (Northumbria)]
✉susan.shakespeare@parklaneplowden.co.uk

SHAKOOR MR TARIQ BIN

Cornwall Street Chambers
85-87 Cornwall Street, Birmingham B3 3BY, ☎0121 233 7500
✉clerks@cornwallstreet.co.uk
Call Date: Feb 1992, Inner Temple
Qualifications: [BA (Lancs) CPE]
✉tariq.shakoor@cornwallstreet.co.uk

SHALDON MISS NICOLA

Four New Square
Four New Square, Lincoln's Inn, London WC2A 3RJ, ☎020 7822 2000
✉barristers@4newsquare.com
Call Date: Oct 1994, Middle Temple
Qualifications: [MA (Cantab) LLB (Hons)(Lond)]
✉n.shaldon@4newsquare.com

E

SHALE MR JUSTIN ANTON

King's Bench Chambers
Wellington House, 175 Holdenhurst Road, Bournemouth, Dorset BH8 8DQ, ☎ 01202 250025
Call Date: July 1982, Inner Temple
Pupil Supervisor
Qualifications: [LLB (So'ton)]

SHALOM MISS MIRIAM

Field Court Chambers
5 Field Court, Gray's Inn, London WC1R 5EF, ☎ 020 7405 6114 ✉ clerks@fieldcourt.co.uk
Call Date: July 2003, Middle Temple
Qualifications: [Ba Hons (Oxon) LLM]

SHAMELI MISS SHARDI CLAIRE

Palmyra Chambers
Royal House, 46 Legh Street, Warrington WA1 1UJ, ☎ 01925 444919
✉ clerk@palmyrachambers.com
Call Date: Oct 1998, Lincoln's Inn
Qualifications: [LLB (Hons)(Leic)]

SHAMIM MR MOHAMMED

Clapham Law Chambers
85 Landor Road, Clapham North, London SW9 9RT, ☎ 020 7978 8482
✉ DANNY@claphamlawchambers.co.uk
Call Date: July 1975, Lincoln's Inn
Qualifications: [BA LLB]

SHAMJI MR RAHIM

Chambers of Mr Ami Feder
Ground Floor, Lamb Building, Temple, London EC4Y 7AS, ☎ 020 7797 7788
✉ clerks@lambbuilding.co.uk
Chambers of Mr Ami Feder
Ground Floor, Lamb Building, Temple, London EC4Y 7AS, ☎ 020 7797 7788
✉ clerks@lambbuilding.co.uk
Call Date: Oct 2000, Inner Temple
Qualifications: [LLB (Lond)]

SHANDRO MR PHILIP ALEXANDER

South Square
3-4 South Square, Gray's Inn, London WC1R 5HP, ☎ 020 7696 9900
✉ practicemanagers@southsquare.com
Call Date: Mar 2008, Lincoln's Inn
Qualifications: [BA (Canada) MA (Canada) BA BCL (Oxon)]
🖃 sandyshandro@southsquare.com

SHANKARDASS MR VIJAY SOHAG TRILOKNATH

Maitland Chambers
7 Stone Buildings, Lincoln's Inn, London WC2A 3SZ, ☎ 020 7406 1200
✉ clerks@maitlandchambers.com
Call Date: Nov 1972, Lincoln's Inn
Qualifications: [BSc (India) MA LLM (Cantab)]
🖃 vshankardass@maitlandchambers.com

SHANNON MISS NICOLA ELIZABETH JANE

Chambers of Mr Ami Feder
Ground Floor, Lamb Building, Temple, London EC4Y 7AS, ☎ 020 7797 7788
✉ clerks@lambbuilding.co.uk
Lamb Building
22 Ship Street, Brighton BN1 1AD, ☎ 01273 820490
✉ admin@lambbuilding.co.uk
Chambers of Mr Ami Feder
Ground Floor, Lamb Building, Temple, London EC4Y 7AS, ☎ 020 7797 7788
✉ clerks@lambbuilding.co.uk
Call Date: Oct 1997, Middle Temple
Qualifications: [MA (Hons)(Cantab)]
🖃 nejshannon@hotmail.com

SHANNON MR SIMON JOSEPH

3 Temple Gardens
Lower Ground Floor, 3 Temple Gardens, Temple, London EC4Y 9AU, ☎ 020 7353 3102
✉ clerks@3tg.co.uk
Call Date: Mar 1999, Inner Temple
Qualifications: [BA (Oxon) CPE]
🖃 sts@3tg.co.uk

SHANNON MR THOMAS ERIC

St Johns Buildings
24a - 28 St John Street, Manchester M3 4DJ, ☎ 0161 214 1500
✉ clerk@stjohnsbuildings.co.uk
St Johns Buildings
21 White Friars, Chester CH1 1NZ, ☎ 01244 323070
✉ clerk@stjohnsbuildings.co.uk
16 Winckley Square
Preston PR1 3JJ, ☎ 01772 256100
Call Date: Nov 1974, Middle Temple
Pupil Supervisor
Qualifications: [BA (Oxon)]
🖃 clerk@stjohnsbuildings.co.uk

SHANT MISS NIRMAL KANTA QC (2006)

23 Essex Street
London WC2R 3AA, ☎020 7413 0353
✉clerks@23es.com
36 Bedford Row
London WC1R 4JH, ☎020 7421 8000
✉chambers@36bedfordrow.co.uk
Call Date: July 1984, Gray's Inn
Recorder
Qualifications: [LLB (Leics)]
✉NirmalShantQC@23es.com

SHAPIRO MR DANIEL JONATHAN

Crown Office Chambers
2 Crown Office Row, Temple, London
EC4Y 7HJ, ☎020 7797 8100
✉mail@crownofficechambers.com
Call Date: Oct 1999, Inner Temple
Pupil Supervisor
Qualifications: [BA (Oxon)]
✉shapiro@crownofficechambers.com

SHAPIRO MR SELWYN

2 King's Bench Walk
2 King's Bench Walk, Temple, London
EC4Y 7DE, ☎020 7353 1746
✉clerks@2kbw.com
Call Date: July 1979, Inner Temple
Pupil Supervisor
Qualifications: [LLB (Lond)]

SHARDA MR ASHOK KUMAR

Green Lane Chambers
272 Green Lane, London SW16 3BA,
☎020 8623 1654 ✉a_sharda@hotmail.com
Call Date: Nov 1979, Inner Temple
Qualifications: [BA (Hons)]

SHARGHY MISS PEGAH

Crown Office Row Chambers
119 Church Street, Brighton, Sussex
BN1 1UD, ☎01273 625625
✉clerks@1cor.com
Call Date: Oct 1998, Inner Temple
Qualifications: [BA (E. Lond) CPE (Sussex)]
✉pegah.sharghy@1cor.com

SHARGHY MR SHAHRAM

The Chambers of Grahame Aldous QC
9 Gough Square, London EC4A 3DG,
☎020 7832 0500
✉clerks@9goughsquare.co.uk
Call Date: July 2000, Lincoln's Inn
Pupil Supervisor
Qualifications: [LLB(Hons)(Sussex) LLM (Cantab)]
✉ssharghy@9goughsquare.co.uk

SHARIF MS NADIA

No5 Chambers
Fountain Court, Steelhouse Lane, Birmingham
B4 6DR, ☎0845 210 5555 ✉info@no5.com
No5 Chambers
Greenwood House, 4-7 Salisbury Court,
London EC4Y 8AA, ☎0845 210 5555
No5 Chambers
38 Queen Square, Bristol BS1 4QS,
☎0845 210 5555
Call Date: Nov 1985, Lincoln's Inn
Qualifications: [BA (Hons)]
✉ns@no5.com

SHARKEY MR PAUL JAMES

9-12 Bell Yard
London WC2A 2JR, ☎020 7400 1800
✉clerks@9-12bellyard.com
Call Date: Nov 2000, Middle Temple
Qualifications: [LLB (Hons) MSc]
✉p.sharkey@9-12bellyard.com

SHARLAND MR ANDREW JOHN

4-5 Gray's Inn Square
Gray's Inn, London WC1R 5AH,
☎020 7404 5252 ✉clerks@4-5.co.uk
Call Date: Oct 1996, Gray's Inn
Pupil Supervisor
Qualifications: [LLB (Lond) BCL (Oxon) LLM (USA)]
✉asharland@4-5.co.uk

SHARMA MR JAMIE

187 Fleet Street
London EC4A 2AT, ☎020 7430 7430
✉chambers@187fleetstreet.com
Call Date: Oct 2005, Inner Temple
Qualifications: [LLB University of Bristol]
✉jamiesharma@187fleetstreet.com

SHARMA MISS NAMITA

Osterley Court Chambers
124 Penhill Road, Bexley, Kent DA5 3EL,
☎07956 655265/07825 959604
Call Date: Nov 1999, Gray's Inn
Qualifications: [LLB (Hons) (Nott'm) Dip Law]
✉namita.sharma@live.com

SHARMA MISS NEELAM

187 Fleet Street
London EC4A 2AT, ☎020 7430 7430
✉chambers@187fleetstreet.com
Call Date: July 2000, Lincoln's Inn
Qualifications: [BSc(Hons) (Lond) BA(Hons) (Cantab)]
✉neeliesharma@187fleetstreet.com

E

SHARMA MR PAVAN

Lombard Chambers
1 Sekforde Street, Clerkenwell, London EC1R 0BE, ☎020 7107 2100
Aspect Chambers
Aspect Court, 4 Temple Row, Birmingham B2 5HG, ☎0121 222 2447
✉clerks@aspectchambers.com
Call Date: Oct 1993, Middle Temple
Qualifications: [LLB (Lond) LLM (Lond)]

SHARMA MISS RAKHEE

Kingsway Chambers
Suite 51, 95 Wilton Road, London SW1V 3BX, ☎020 7404 2357
Call Date: Nov 1995, Gray's Inn
Qualifications: [LLB]

SHARMA MR SANJEEV MOHAN

Equity Chambers
First Floor, McLaren Building, 46 Priory Queensway, Birmingham B4 7LR, ☎0121 236 5007
✉clerks@equitychambers.org.uk
Call Date: July 2004, Inner Temple
Qualifications: [LLB (Hons) LLM]
sms@e-c.org.uk

SHARMA MRS SUMAN

Warwick House Chambers
8 Warwick Court, Warwick House Chambers, Gray's Inn, London WC1R 5DJ, ☎020 7430 2323
✉clerks@warwickhousechambers.com
Call Date: May 1994, Middle Temple
Qualifications: [LLB (Hons)]
clerks@warwickhousechambers.com

SHARMA MISS SUNYANA

3 PB Barristers
3 Paper Buildings, Temple, London EC4Y 7EU, ☎020 7583 8055
3 PB Barristers
30 Christchurch Road, Bournemouth, Dorset BH1 3PD, ☎01202 292102
✉clerks.bournemouth@3paper.co.uk
Call Date: July 2006, Inner Temple
Qualifications: [LLB LLM (Lond)]
sunyana.sharma@3pb.co.uk

SHARMAN MR BRIAN FREDERICK

2 King's Bench Walk
2 King's Bench Walk, Temple, London EC4Y 7DE, ☎020 7353 1746
✉clerks@2kbw.com
Call Date: July 2004, Gray's Inn
Qualifications: [LLB (Warwick)]

SHARMAN MR MARK GEOFFREY

Cornwall Street Chambers
85-87 Cornwall Street, Birmingham B3 3BY, ☎0121 233 7500
✉clerks@cornwallstreet.co.uk
Cornwall Street Chambers
Shrewsbury Annex, Rural Enterprise Centre, Stafford Drive, Battlefield Enterprise Park, Shrewsbury SY1 3FE, ☎01743 363 611 / 0121 233 7500
Call Date: July 2004, Lincoln's Inn
Qualifications: [LLB (Hons)]
mark.sharman@cornwallstreet.co.uk

SHARP MR CHRISTOPHER FRANCIS QC (1999)

St John's Chambers
101 Victoria Street, Bristol BS1 6PU, ☎0117 923 4700
✉clerks@stjohnschambers.co.uk
Harcourt Chambers
1st Floor, 2 Harcourt Buildings, Temple, London EC4Y 9DB, ☎0844 561 7135
Harcourt Chambers
Churchill House, 3 St Aldate's Courtyard, St Aldate's, Oxford OX1 1BN, ☎0844 561 7135
Call Date: July 1975, Inner Temple
Recorder
Qualifications: [MA (Oxon)]
christopher.sharpqc@stjohnschambers.co.uk

SHARP MR DAVID IAN

Tanfield Chambers
2-5 Warwick Court, London WC1R 5DJ, ☎020 7421 5300
✉clerks@tanfieldchambers.co.uk
Call Date: Nov 1986, Middle Temple
Pupil Supervisor
Qualifications: [BA (Oxon) MA Dip Law]
dsharp@tanfieldchambers.co.uk

SHARPE MR DAVID ROBERT KITSON

12 King's Bench Walk
12 King's Bench Walk, Temple, London EC4Y 7EL, ☎020 7583 0811
Call Date: Nov 2004, Inner Temple
Qualifications: [MB BCh]

SHARPE MR DENNIS NIGEL

Field Court Chambers
5 Field Court, Gray's Inn, London WC1R 5EF, ☎020 7405 6114 ✉clerks@fieldcourt.co.uk
Call Date: July 1976, Inner Temple
Pupil Supervisor
Qualifications: [LLB (Exon) BCL (Oxon)]
dennis.sharpe@fieldcourt.co.uk

SHARPE MR HARRY EDWARD GRAFTON

XXIV Old Buildings
Ground Floor, 24 Old Buildings, Lincoln's Inn, London WC2A 3UP, ☎ 020 7691 2424
✉ clerks@xxiv.co.uk
Call Date: Oct 2010, Middle Temple
Qualifications: [MMath (Oxon)]
✉ harry.sharpe@xxiv.co.uk

SHARPE MR MALCOLM DAVID

Atlantic Chambers
4-6 Cook Street, Liverpool L2 9QU,
☎ 0151 236 4421
✉ info@atlanticchambers.co.uk
Call Date: July 1989, Lincoln's Inn
Pupil Supervisor, Recorder
Qualifications: [LLB (Sheff) LLM (Belfast)]
✉ malcolmsharpe@atlanticchambers.co.uk

SHARPE MR MARTIN LAURENCE

Park Court Chambers
16 Park Place, Leeds LS1 2SJ,
☎ 0113 243 3277
✉ clerks@parkcourtchambers.co.uk
Call Date: Nov 1989, Middle Temple
Pupil Supervisor
Qualifications: [BA (Hons) (Manch) MA (L'pool)]
✉ msharpe@parkcourtchambers.co.uk

SHARPE MR RICHARD CHARLES CHRISTOPHER

23 Essex Street
London WC2R 3AA, ☎ 020 7413 0353
✉ clerks@23es.com
Call Date: Oct 2002, Middle Temple
Qualifications: [BA (Oxon)]

SHARPE MR THOMAS ANTHONY EDWARD QC (1994)

One Essex Court
Ground Floor, One Essex Court, Temple, London EC4Y 9AR, ☎ 020 7583 2000
✉ clerks@oeclaw.co.uk
Call Date: May 1976, Lincoln's Inn
Qualifications: [MA(Cantab)]
✉ tsharpe@oeclaw.co.uk

SHARPE MR TIMOTHY JAMES

Temple Garden Chambers
1 Harcourt Buildings, Temple, London EC4Y 9DA, ☎ 020 7583 1315
✉ clerks@tgchambers.com
Call Date: Oct 2002, Lincoln's Inn
Qualifications: [MA (Cantab)]
✉ timsharpe@tgchambers.com

SHARPLES MR JOHN EDMUND

St John's Chambers
101 Victoria Street, Bristol BS1 6PU,
☎ 0117 923 4700
✉ clerks@stjohnschambers.co.uk
Call Date: Nov 1992, Middle Temple
Qualifications: [BA (Oxon) LLM (USA) LLM (Cantab)]
✉ john.sharples@stjohnschambers.co.uk

SHARRON MISS ELIZA VOGEL

Deans Court Chambers
24 St John Street, Manchester M3 4DF,
☎ 0161 214 6000 ✉ clerks@deanscourt.co.uk
Call Date: Nov 2009, Inner Temple
Qualifications: [BA (Hons) (Bris) CPE UWE) BVC (UWE)]
✉ sharron@deanscourt.co.uk

SHAW MR ANDREW DAVID

1 Paper Buildings
1st Floor, 1 Paper Buildings, Temple, London EC4Y 7EP, ☎ 020 7353 3728
✉ clerks@onepaper.co.uk
Call Date: Mar 1998, Lincoln's Inn
Pupil Supervisor
Qualifications: [MA (Hons)]
✉ andrewshaw@onepaper.co.uk

SHAW MR ANDREW SCOTT ELLIOT

New Court
Ground Floor, New Court, Temple, London EC4Y 9BE, ☎ 020 7583 5123
✉ clerks@newcourtchambers.com
Call Date: Oct 2001, Inner Temple
Qualifications: [LLB (Bris)]
✉ ashaw@newcourtchambers.net

SHAW MISS ANNABEL VICTORIA

Four New Square
Four New Square, Lincoln's Inn, London WC2A 3RJ, ☎ 020 7822 2000
✉ barristers@4newsquare.com
Call Date: July 2002, Gray's Inn
Qualifications: [BA Hons (Oxon) CPE]
✉ a.shaw@4newsquare.com

SHAW MR ANTONY MICHAEL NINIAN QC (1994)

18 Red Lion Court
London EC4A 3EB, ☎ 020 7520 6000
✉ chambers@18rlc.co.uk
18 Red Lion Court (Annexe)
Thornwood House, 102 New London Road, Chelmsford, Essex CM2 0RG,
☎ 01245 280880
Call Date: July 1975, Middle Temple
Qualifications: [BA (Oxon)]
✉ tony.shaw@18rlc.co.uk

E

SHAW MR BENJAMIN CHRISTOPHER

Erskine Chambers
33 Chancery Lane, London WC2A 1EN,
☎ 020 7242 5532
✉ clerks@erskinechambers.com
Call Date: Nov 2002, Lincoln's Inn
Qualifications: [BA (Hons)]
✉ bshaw@erskine-chambers.co.uk

SHAW MISS ELIZABETH

37 Park Square Chambers
37 Park Square, Leeds LS1 2NY,
☎ 0113 243 9422 ✉ chambers@no37.co.uk
Call Date: Nov 1986, Middle Temple
Qualifications: [BA]
✉ chambers@no37.co.uk

SHAW MISS ELLA MARIE

4 Brick Court
4 Brick Court, Temple, London EC4Y 9AD,
☎ 020 7832 3200 ✉ clerks@4bc.co.uk
Call Date: Oct 2006, Middle Temple
Qualifications: [LLB (Hons) (L'pool)]
✉ ella.shaw@4bc.co.uk

SHAW MISS FRANCES JANE

1 Gray's Inn Square
Ground Floor, 1 Gray's Inn Square, London WC1R 5AA, ☎ 020 7405 0001
Call Date: Nov 2007, Inner Temple
Qualifications: [LLB (Kent)]
✉ fshaw@1gis.co.uk

SHAW MR HOWARD QC (2011)

29 Bedford Row Chambers
London WC1R 4HE, ☎ 020 7404 1044
✉ clerks@29br.co.uk
Call Date: July 1973, Inner Temple
Pupil Supervisor
Qualifications: [LLB (Lond)]
✉ hshaw@29br.co.uk

SHAW MR HOWARD JAMES

Zenith Chambers
10 Park Square, Leeds LS1 2LH,
☎ 0113 245 5438
✉ clerks@zenithchambers.co.uk
Call Date: Oct 1999, Middle Temple
Qualifications: [BSc (Hons)(York)]
✉ hshaw@zenithchambers.co.uk

SHAW MR JAMES NICHOLAS

4 Paper Buildings
1st Floor, 4 Paper Buildings, Temple, London EC4Y 7EX, ☎ 020 7427 5200
✉ clerks@4pb.com
Call Date: Nov 1988, Inner Temple
Qualifications: [LLB (Reading)]
✉ jns@4pb.com

SHAW MISS JENNA LOUISE

14 Gray's Inn Square
14 Gray's Inn Square, Gray's Inn, London WC1R 5JP, ☎ 020 7242 0858
✉ clerks@14gis.co.uk
Call Date: July 2009, Inner Temple
Qualifications: [BA (Bris)]
✉ clerks@14graysinnsquare.co.uk

SHAW MISS JOANNA ELIZABETH

One Essex Court
1st Floor, Temple, London EC4Y 9AR,
☎ 020 7936 3030 ✉ clerks@1ec.co.uk
Call Date: Oct 2000, Middle Temple
Qualifications: [BA (Hons) (Leeds) DipLaw (Lond)]
✉ joannashaw2001@hotmail.com

SHAW MR JONATHAN PAUL

Zenith Chambers
10 Park Square, Leeds LS1 2LH,
☎ 0113 245 5438
✉ clerks@zenithchambers.co.uk
No5 Chambers
Greenwood House, 4-7 Salisbury Court, London EC4Y 8AA, ☎ 0845 210 5555
No5 Chambers
38 Queen Square, Bristol BS1 4QS,
☎ 0845 210 5555
No5 Chambers
Fountain Court, Steelhouse Lane, Birmingham B4 6DR, ☎ 0845 210 5555 ✉ info@no5.com
Call Date: July 2008, Inner Temple
Qualifications: [Bsc LLB FCIArb FInstCES DipArb FRICS]
✉ jshaw@zenithchambers.co.uk

SHAW MR JULIAN

St Johns Buildings
24a - 28 St John Street, Manchester M3 4DJ,
☎ 0161 214 1500
✉ clerk@stjohnsbuildings.co.uk
St Johns Buildings
21 White Friars, Chester CH1 1NZ,
☎ 01244 323070
✉ clerk@stjohnsbuildings.co.uk

St Johns Buildings Liverpool
8th Floor India Buildings, Water Street, Liverpool L2 0XG, ☎0151 243 6000
✉clerk@stjohnsbuildings.co.uk
Call Date: Nov 1984, Gray's Inn
Pupil Supervisor, Recorder
Qualifications: [LLB (Wales)]
js@stjohnsbuildings.co.uk

SHAW PROF MALCOLM NATHAN QC (2002)

Essex Court Chambers
24 Lincoln's Inn Fields, London WC2A 3EG, ☎020 7813 8000
✉clerksroom@essexcourt.net
Call Date: July 1988, Gray's Inn
Qualifications: [LLB (L'pool) LLM (Israel) PhD (Keele)]
mshaw@essexcourt.net

SHAW MR MARK RICHARD QC (2002)

Blackstone Chambers
Blackstone House, Temple, London EC4Y 9BW, ☎020 7583 1770
✉clerks@blackstonechambers.com
Call Date: July 1987, Inner Temple
Qualifications: [BA (Dunelm) LLM (Cantab)]

SHAW MR MICHAEL JOHN

9-12 Bell Yard
London WC2A 2JR, ☎020 7400 1800
✉clerks@9-12bellyard.com
Call Date: Nov 1994, Middle Temple
Qualifications: [LLB (Hons)]
m.shaw@9-12bellyard.com

SHAW MISS NICOLA JANE QC (2012)

Gray's Inn Tax Chambers
3rd Floor, Gray's Inn Chambers, Gray's Inn, London WC1R 5JA, ☎020 7242 2642
✉clerks@taxbar.com
Call Date: Nov 1995, Inner Temple
Pupil Supervisor
Qualifications: [BCL BA (Oxon)]
ns@taxbar.com

SHAW MS NICOLA JANE DUCKWORTH

Trinity Chambers
Multi Media Exchange, 72-80 Corporation Road, Middlesbrough TS1 2RF, ☎01642 247569
✉info@trinitychambers.co.uk
15 Winckley Square
Preston PR1 3JJ, ☎01772 252828
✉clerks@15winckleysq.co.uk
Trinity Chambers
The Custom House, 39 Quayside, Newcastle Upon Tyne NE1 3DE, ☎0191 232 1927
✉info@trinitychambers.co.uk
Call Date: Oct 1992, Lincoln's Inn
Qualifications: [BA(Hons)(Leeds) CPE]

SHAW MR PETER MAURICE

9 Stone Buildings
Lincoln's Inn, London WC2A 3NN, ☎020 7404 5055
✉clerks@9stonebuildings.com
Call Date: Nov 1995, Middle Temple
Pupil Supervisor
Qualifications: [BA (Hons)]
clerks@9stonebuildings.com

SHAW MR ROBERT ANDREW

25 Bedford Row
London WC1R 4HD, ☎020 7067 1500
✉clerks@25bedfordrow.com
Call Date: July 2008, Middle Temple
Qualifications: [BSc (Hons) (B'ham) PgDl (Lond)]
rshaw25br@gmail.com

SHAW MR SAMUEL BENJAMIN BARNABY

1 Paper Buildings
1st Floor, 1 Paper Buildings, Temple, London EC4Y 7EP, ☎020 7353 3728
✉clerks@onepaper.co.uk
Call Date: Nov 1996, Middle Temple
Qualifications: [MA (Hons)]
barnabyshaw@onepaper.co.uk

SHAW MR STEPHEN

Lamb Chambers
Lamb Building, Elm Court, Temple, London EC4Y 7AS, ☎020 7797 8300
✉info@lambchambers.co.uk
Call Date: July 1975, Gray's Inn
Pupil Supervisor
Qualifications: [LLB]

SHAY MR STEPHEN EVERETT

1 KBW Chambers
1 King's Bench Walk, Temple, London EC4Y 7DB, ☎020 7936 1500
✉clerks@1kbw.co.uk
King's Bench Chambers
174 High Street, Lewes BN7 1YE, ☎01273 402600
Call Date: Nov 1984, Middle Temple
Pupil Supervisor
Qualifications: [BA (Hons) (Oxon)]
sshay@1kbw.co.uk

E

SHEA MS CAROLINE MARY

Falcon Chambers
Falcon Court, London EC4Y 1AA,
☎ 020 7353 2484
✉ clerks@falcon-chambers.com
Call Date: Nov 1994, Middle Temple
Pupil Supervisor
Qualifications: [MA (Cantab)]
✉ shea@falcon-chambers.com

SHEARD MR DAVID STEFAN EDWARD

Keating Chambers
15 Essex Street, London WC2R 3AA,
☎ 020 7544 2600
✉ clerks@keatingchambers.com
Call Date: Oct 2010, Lincoln's Inn
Qualifications: [BA (Cantab)]

SHEARS MR PHILIP PETER QC (1996)

Seven Bedford Row
7 Bedford Row, London WC1R 4BS,
☎ 020 7242 3555 ✉ clerks@7br.co.uk
Call Date: July 1972, Middle Temple
Recorder
Qualifications: [LLB (Nott'm) LLB (Cantab)]
✉ pshears@7br.co.uk

E

SHEEHAN MISS ANNE-MARIE

Goldsmith Chambers
Ground Floor, Goldsmith Building, Temple, London EC4Y 7BL, ☎ 020 7353 6802
✉ clerks@goldsmithchambers.com
Call Date: July 1994, Lincoln's Inn
Qualifications: [LLB (Hons) (Ireland)]
✉ A.Sheehan@goldsmithchambers.law.co.uk

SHEEHAN MR JAMES MICHAEL

Maitland Chambers
7 Stone Buildings, Lincoln's Inn, London WC2A 3SZ, ☎ 020 7406 1200
✉ clerks@maitlandchambers.com
Call Date: Oct 2008, Middle Temple
Qualifications: [BA (Hons) (Cantab) Dip in Law]
✉ jsheehan@maitlandchambers.com

SHEEHAN MR MALCOLM PETER

Henderson Chambers
2 Harcourt Buildings, Temple, London EC4Y 9DB, ☎ 020 7583 9020
✉ clerks@hendersonchambers.co.uk
Call Date: Oct 1993, Lincoln's Inn
Pupil Supervisor
Qualifications: [MA (Hons)(Oxon)]
✉ msheehan@hendersonchambers.co.uk

SHEEHAN MR MICHAEL JOHN

East Anglian Chambers
15 The Close, Norwich, Norfolk NR1 4DZ,
☎ 01473 214481 ✉ norwich@ealaw.co.uk
East Anglian Chambers
Gresham House, 5 Museum Street, Ipswich, Suffolk IP1 1HQ, ☎ 01473 214481
✉ ipswich@ealaw.co.uk
East Anglian Chambers
140 New London Road, Chelmsford, Essex CM2 0AW, ☎ 01473 214481
✉ chelmsford@ealaw.co.uk
Call Date: Oct 2010, Middle Temple
Qualifications: [LLB (Hons) (Warw)]

SHEFF MS JANINE RACHEL

18 Red Lion Court
London EC4A 3EB, ☎ 020 7520 6000
✉ chambers@18rlc.co.uk
18 Red Lion Court (Annexe)
Thornwood House, 102 New London Road, Chelmsford, Essex CM2 0RG,
☎ 01245 280880
Call Date: July 1983, Middle Temple
Pupil Supervisor
Qualifications: [LLB (B'ham)]
✉ janine.sheff@18rlc.co.uk

SHEFTEL MR ANDREW LAWSON BAYLIES

Tanfield Chambers
2-5 Warwick Court, London WC1R 5DJ,
☎ 020 7421 5300
✉ clerks@tanfieldchambers.co.uk
Call Date: Nov 2004, Inner Temple
Qualifications: [BA Magdalen College University of Oxford]
✉ asheftel@tanfieldchambers.co.uk

SHEIKH MR IRSHAD AHMED

187 Fleet Street
London EC4A 2AT, ☎ 020 7430 7430
✉ chambers@187fleetstreet.com
Call Date: July 1983, Lincoln's Inn
Pupil Supervisor
Qualifications: [LLB (Hons) (Hull)]
✉ ish@187fleetstreet.com

SHEIKH MS RAANA

12 Old Square Chambers
1st Floor, 12 Old Square, Lincoln's Inn, London WC2A 3TX, ☎ 020 7404 0875
✉ clerks@12oldsquare.com
Call Date: Nov 1977, Middle Temple
Pupil Supervisor
Qualifications: [LLB (Hons) (Lond)]

SHEIKH MS SAIRA KABIR

Francis Taylor Building
Inner Temple, London EC4Y 7BY,
☎ 020 7353 8415 ✉ clerks@ftb.eu.com
Call Date: Nov 2000, Inner Temple
Pupil Supervisor
Qualifications: [LLM (Lond) LLM (USA)]
✉ saira.sheikh@ftb.eu.com

SHEKERDEMIAN MISS MARCIA ANNA-MARIA

11 Stone Buildings
11 Stone Buildings, Lincoln's Inn, London WC2A 3TG, ☎ 020 7831 6381
✉ clerks@11sb.com
Call Date: July 1987, Middle Temple
Pupil Supervisor
Qualifications: [MA (Cantab)]

SHELDON MR CLIVE DAVID QC (2011)

11 King's Bench Walk
11 King's Bench Walk, Temple, London EC4Y 7EQ, ☎ 020 7632 8500
✉ clerksroom@11kbw.com
Call Date: Nov 1991, Inner Temple
Pupil Supervisor
Qualifications: [BA (Cantab) LLM (USA)]
✉ clive.sheldon@11kbw.com

SHELDON MR NEIL JOHN

1 Crown Office Row
1 Crown Office Row, Temple, London EC4Y 7HH, ☎ 020 7797 7500
✉ mail@1cor.com
Call Date: Nov 1998, Gray's Inn
Pupil Supervisor
Qualifications: [MA (Cantab)]
✉ neil.sheldon@1cor.com

SHELDON MR RICHARD MICHAEL QC (1996)

South Square
3-4 South Square, Gray's Inn, London WC1R 5HP, ☎ 020 7696 9900
✉ practicemanagers@southsquare.com
Call Date: July 1979, Gray's Inn
Qualifications: [MA (Cantab)]
✉ richardsheldon@southsquare.com

SHELDON MR RICHARD NEIL

Bank House Chambers
Old Bank House, Hartshead, Sheffield S1 2EL, ☎ 0114 275 1223
✉ w.digby@bankhousechambers.co.uk
Call Date: July 1984, Lincoln's Inn
Pupil Supervisor, Recorder
Qualifications: [LLB (Leeds)]
✉ r.sheldon@bankhousechambers.co.uk

SHELDRAKE MISS CHRISTINE ANNE

Coram Chambers
9-11 Fulwood Place, London WC1V 6HG, ☎ 020 7092 3700
✉ mail@coramchambers.co.uk
Call Date: July 1977, Middle Temple
Pupil Supervisor
Qualifications: [LLB (Lond)]

SHELLARD MR ROBIN JAMES SPENCER

Queen Square Chambers
56 Queen Square, Bristol BS1 4PR, ☎ 0117 921 1966 ✉ crime@qs-c.co.uk
Call Date: Nov 1992, Inner Temple
Pupil Supervisor
Qualifications: [BA (Wales) Dip Law]
✉ rs@qs-c.co.uk

E

SHELLEY MR DOMINIC PAUL

1 High Pavement
Nottingham NG1 1HF, ☎ 0115 941 8218
✉ clerks@1highpavement.co.uk
Call Date: July 2003, Gray's Inn
Qualifications: [LLB (Bris)]
✉ dominicshelly@1highpavement.co.uk

SHELTON MR GORDON EDWARD

Broadway House Chambers
Broadway House, 9 Bank Street, Bradford, West Yorkshire BD1 1TW, ☎ 01274 722560
✉ clerks@broadwayhouse.co.uk
Broadway House Chambers
25 Park Square West, Leeds, West Yorkshire LS1 2PW, ☎ 0113 246 2600
✉ clerks@broadwayhouse.co.uk
Call Date: Nov 1981, Inner Temple
Pupil Supervisor, Recorder
Qualifications: [LLB (Leics)]
✉ ges@broadwayhouse.co.uk

SHENTON MISS RACHEL CLAIRE

18 St John Street
Manchester M3 4EA, ☎ 0161 278 1800
✉ clerks@18sjs.com
Call Date: Nov 1993, Middle Temple
Pupil Supervisor
Qualifications: [LLB (Hons)]

☎ Telephone ✉ E-mail address ✉ Personal e-mail address

SHENTON MISS SUZANNE HELENE

1 Garden Court Family Law Chambers
Ground Floor, One Garden Court, Temple, London EC4Y 9BJ, ☎020 7797 7900
✉clerks@1gc.com
Call Date: July 1973, Middle Temple
Qualifications: [LLB (Manch)]
✉clerks@1gc.com

SHEPHERD MR JAMES EDWARD

Doughty Street Chambers
53-54 Doughty Street, London WC1N 2LS, ☎020 7404 1313
✉enquiries@doughtystreet.co.uk
Doughty Street Chambers
Pall Mall Court, 61-67 King Street, Manchester M2 4PD, ☎0161 618 1066
Doughty Street Chambers
5th Floor, Broad Quay House, Prince Street, Bristol BS1 4DJ, ☎01179 058 717
Call Date: Oct 1998, Middle Temple
Qualifications: [BA (Hons)(Northumbr) CPE (City)]
✉j.shepherd@doughtystreet.co.uk

SHEPHERD MR JAMES MICHAEL

Castle Chambers
The Old Fire Station, 90 High Street, Harrow-on-the-Hill, Middlesex HA1 3LP, ☎020 8423 6579 ✉info@castlechambers.net
Melbury House
55 Manor Road, Oadby, Leicester, Leicestershire LE2 2LL, ☎07801 037802
✉melburyhousechambers@yahoo.co.uk
Call Date: July 2002, Gray's Inn
Qualifications: [BA LLB (Lond)]

SHEPHERD MISS JOANNE ELIZABETH

37 Park Square Chambers
37 Park Square, Leeds LS1 2NY, ☎0113 243 9422 ✉chambers@no37.co.uk
Call Date: Oct 1993, Inner Temple
Qualifications: [BA]
✉jos@no37.co.uk

SHEPHERD MISS JUDITH ELIZABETH

42 Bedford Row
London WC1R 4LL, ☎020 7831 0222
✉clerks@42br.com
Call Date: Oct 1996, Lincoln's Inn
Qualifications: [LLB (Hons)(Derby)]
✉jude.shepherd@42br.com

SHEPHERD MR PHILIP ALEXANDER QC (2003)

XXIV Old Buildings
Ground Floor, 24 Old Buildings, Lincoln's Inn, London WC2A 3UP, ☎020 7691 2424
✉clerks@xxiv.co.uk
Call Date: Nov 1975, Gray's Inn
Qualifications: [BSc (Econ)]

SHEPHERD MR RICHARD ANDREW JOHN

Albion Chambers
Broad Street, Bristol BS1 1DR, ☎0117 927 2144
✉clerks@albionchambers.co.uk
Call Date: July 2001, Middle Temple
Pupil Supervisor
Qualifications: [LLB (Hons)]
✉richard.shepherd@albionchambers.co.uk

SHEPHERD MR THOMAS PAUL

11 Stone Buildings
11 Stone Buildings, Lincoln's Inn, London WC2A 3TG, ☎020 7831 6381
✉clerks@11sb.com
Call Date: Oct 2008, Lincoln's Inn
Qualifications: [LLB (Bris) BCL (Oxon)]
✉shepherd@11sb.com

SHEPPARD MR TIMOTHY DERIE

No5 Chambers
Greenwood House, 4-7 Salisbury Court, London EC4Y 8AA, ☎0845 210 5555
No5 Chambers
38 Queen Square, Bristol BS1 4QS, ☎0845 210 5555
No5 Chambers
Fountain Court, Steelhouse Lane, Birmingham B4 6DR, ☎0845 210 5555 ✉info@no5.com
Call Date: Nov 1995, Inner Temple
Qualifications: [BSc (Edin) LLM (Lond)]

Types of work: Discrimination, Employment, Environment, Planning, Public law

SHEPPARD-JONES MISS VICTORIA LOUISE

Carmelite Chambers
9 Carmelite Street, London EC4Y 0DR, ☎020 7936 6300
✉clerks@carmelitechambers.co.uk
Call Date: Nov 2005, Inner Temple
Qualifications: [LLB King's College University of London]
✉vsheppardjones@carmelitechambers.co.uk

SHER MR ADAM DANIEL

Fountain Court Chambers
Fountain Court, Temple, London EC4Y 9DH,
☎ 020 7583 3335
✉ chambers@fountaincourt.co.uk
Call Date: Oct 2007, Lincoln's Inn
Qualifications: [BA BCL (Oxon) LLM (Harvard)]
✉ ads@fountaincourt.co.uk

SHER MR CHRISTOPHER

Furnival Chambers
32 Furnival Street, London EC4A 1JQ,
☎ 020 7405 3232
Call Date: Nov 1993, Gray's Inn
Qualifications: [BA]

SHER MISS SHAMIM AKHTAR

Chambers of Miss Shamim Sher
3 Coronation Close, Ilford, Essex IG6 1DB,
☎ 07581 201823 ✉ shamim50@live.co.uk
Call Date: May 1995, Lincoln's Inn
Qualifications: [LLB (Hons)]
✉ shamim50@live.co.uk, shamimsher@me.com

SHERAFAT MANSOORI MISS SARA LOUISE

Matrix Chambers
Griffin Building, Gray's Inn, London WC1R 5LN, ☎ 020 7404 3447
✉ matrix@matrixlaw.co.uk / lscott@matrixlaw.co.uk
Call Date: Nov 1997, Lincoln's Inn
Qualifications: [LLB (Hons)(Leeds)]

SHERBORN MISS NATALIE LOUISE

25 Bedford Row
London WC1R 4HD, ☎ 020 7067 1500
✉ clerks@25bedfordrow.com
Call Date: Nov 2000, Gray's Inn
Qualifications: [LLB (Lond)]

SHERBORNE MR DAVID ALEXANDER

5RB
1st Floor, 5 Raymond Buildings, Gray's Inn, London WC1R 5BP, ☎ 020 7242 2902
✉ clerks@5rb.com
Call Date: Oct 1992, Gray's Inn
Pupil Supervisor
Qualifications: [BA (Oxon)]
✉ davidsherborne@5rb.com

SHERIDAN MISS AMBER FAYE

29 Bedford Row Chambers
London WC1R 4HE, ☎ 020 7404 1044
✉ clerks@29br.co.uk
Call Date: July 2008, Middle Temple
Qualifications: [MA (Hons) (Edin)]

SHERIDAN MR IAIN DOUGLAS

London Scottish
183 Loxley Road, Stratford Upon Avon, Warwickshire CV37 7DU, ☎ 07971 681724
✉ isheridan@londonscottishlaw.com
Call Date: Nov 1997, Inner Temple
Qualifications: [MBA (Oxon)]
✉ isheridan@londonscottishlaw.com, iainsheridan@btinternet.com, iainsheridan@lspartnership.com

SHERIDAN MR MATTHEW STEPHEN

Littleton Chambers
3 King's Bench Walk North, Temple, London EC4Y 7HR, ☎ 020 7797 8600
✉ fschneider@littletonchambers.co.uk
Call Date: Oct 2000, Gray's Inn
Qualifications: [MA (Cantab)]
✉ msheridan@littletonchambers.co.uk

SHERIDAN MR MAURICE BERNARD GERARD

Matrix Chambers
Griffin Building, Gray's Inn, London WC1R 5LN, ☎ 020 7404 3447
✉ matrix@matrixlaw.co.uk / lscott@matrixlaw.co.uk
Call Date: July 1984, Middle Temple
Qualifications: [LLM (Cantab)]
✉ mauricesheridan@matrixlaw.co.uk

SHERIDAN MR NORMAN PATRICK

Sheridan Chambers
Knaresbrook, King Edward Road, Shenley, Herts WD7 9BY, ☎ 01923 856 345
✉ norman.sheridan@gmail.com
Call Date: Oct 1990, Middle Temple
Qualifications: [BSc (Lond) MPhil Dip Law (Lond) LLM (Lond)]

SHERIDAN MR PAUL ADRIAN

Cobden House Chambers
19 Quay Street, Manchester M3 3HN,
☎ 0161 833 6000 ✉ Clerks@Cobden.co.uk
Call Date: Nov 1984, Lincoln's Inn
Pupil Supervisor
Qualifications: [LLB (Hons) (Belfast)]
✉ clerks@cobden.co.uk

E

SHERIDAN MR ROBERT JAMES

Southernhay Chambers
33 Southernhay East, Exeter EX1 1NX,
☎ 01392 255777
✉ clerks@southernhaychambers.co.uk
Call Date: Nov 2001, Lincoln's Inn
Qualifications: [BA (Hons)(Oxon) MA (Law)]
r.sheridan@southernhaychambers.co.uk

SHERIFF MR ANDREW MARK

3 PB Barristers
3 Paper Buildings, Temple, London EC4Y 7EU,
☎ 020 7583 8055
3 PB Barristers
23 Beaumont Street, Oxford OX1 2NP,
☎ 01865 793 736
3 PB Barristers
4 St Peter Street, Winchester SO23 8BW,
☎ 01962 868884
✉ clerks.winchester@3paper.co.uk
3 PB Barristers
Royal Talbot House, 2 Victoria Street, Bristol, Avon BS1 6BB, ☎ 0117 928 1520
3 PB Barristers
30 Christchurch Road, Bournemouth, Dorset BH1 3PD, ☎ 01202 292102
✉ clerks.bournemouth@3paper.co.uk
Call Date: Nov 2000, Lincoln's Inn
Qualifications: [BA (Hons) (Oxon) CPE]
andrew.sheriff@3paper.co.uk

E

SHERMAN MR ROBERT LESLIE

Chambers of Mr Ami Feder
Ground Floor, Lamb Building, Temple, London EC4Y 7AS, ☎ 020 7797 7788
✉ clerks@lambbuilding.co.uk
Lamb Building
22 Ship Street, Brighton BN1 1AD,
☎ 01273 820490
✉ admin@lambbuilding.co.uk
Chambers of Mr Ami Feder
Ground Floor, Lamb Building, Temple, London EC4Y 7AS, ☎ 020 7797 7788
✉ clerks@lambbuilding.co.uk
Call Date: July 1977, Gray's Inn
Pupil Supervisor
Qualifications: [LLB (Leeds)]

SHERMAN MISS SUSAN ELIZABETH

Chavasse Court Chambers
18 Queen Avenue, Liverpool L2 4TX,
☎ 0151 229 2030
✉ clerks@chavassechambers.co.uk
Call Date: Nov 1993, Middle Temple
Qualifications: [LLB (Hons)(Lancs)]
susan.sherman@chavassechambers.co.uk

SHERRARD MR CHARLES ISAAC QC (2012)

Furnival Chambers
32 Furnival Street, London EC4A 1JQ,
☎ 020 7405 3232
Call Date: Nov 1986, Middle Temple
Pupil Supervisor
Qualifications: [LLB]
csherrard@furnivallaw.co.uk

SHERRATT MR MATHEW JOHN

Carmelite Chambers
9 Carmelite Street, London EC4Y 0DR,
☎ 020 7936 6300
✉ clerks@carmelitechambers.co.uk
Call Date: July 1994, Inner Temple
Qualifications: [LLB (New Zealand) LLM (USA)]
jsherratt@carmelitechambers.co.uk

SHERRIFF MR SIMON BRUCE

Goldsmith Chambers
Ground Floor, Goldsmith Building, Temple, London EC4Y 7BL, ☎ 020 7353 6802
✉ clerks@goldsmithchambers.com
Call Date: Nov 1999, Inner Temple
Qualifications: [BA(Hons) (Kingston)]
S.Sherriff@goldsmithchambers.law.co.uk

SHERRY MR MICHAEL GABRIEL

Temple Tax Chambers
1st Floor, 3 Temple Gardens, Temple, London EC4Y 9AU, ☎ 020 7353 7884
✉ clerks@templetax.com
Call Date: Nov 1978, Gray's Inn
Pupil Supervisor
Qualifications: [MA (Oxon) ATII FCA]

SHERWIN MISS DEBORAH ANN

Fountain Chambers
Cleveland Business Centre, 1 Watson Street, Middlesbrough TS1 2RQ, ☎ 01642 804040
✉ clerks@fountainchambers.co.uk
Call Date: July 1979, Inner Temple
Pupil Supervisor, Recorder
Qualifications: [LLB (Exon)]

SHETTY MR RAJEEV RAMA

The Chambers of Grahame Aldous QC
9 Gough Square, London EC4A 3DG,
☎ 020 7832 0500
✉ clerks@9goughsquare.co.uk
Call Date: Mar 1996, Inner Temple
Recorder
Qualifications: [LLB (S'ton)]
rshetty@9goughsquare.co.uk

SHIBLI MR FARAZ

10 King's Bench Walk
Ground Floor, 10 King's Bench Walk, Temple, London EC4Y 7EB, ☎020 7353 7742
✉Chambers@10kingsbenchwalk.co.uk
Call Date: Nov 2007, Middle Temple
Qualifications: [LLB (Hons) (Warw)]
✉faraz.shibli@10kingsbenchwalk.co.uk

SHIBLI MR OMAR

Garden Court Chambers
57-60 Lincoln's Inn Fields, London WC2A 3LJ, ☎020 7993 7600 ✉info@gclaw.co.uk
Call Date: Oct 2006, Middle Temple
Qualifications: [MA (Cantab)]
✉omars@gclaw.co.uk

SHIELD MISS DEBORAH

42 Bedford Row
London WC1R 4LL, ☎020 7831 0222
✉clerks@42br.com
Call Date: Nov 1991, Inner Temple
Qualifications: [LLB]
✉deborah.shield@42br.com

SHIELDS MISS CAROLINE ANN

No.6 Park Square
Leeds LS1 2LW, ☎0113 245 9763
✉Tim@no6.co.uk
Call Date: Oct 2006, Middle Temple
Qualifications: [BA (Hons)]
✉shields@no6.co.uk

SHIELDS MR JOSHUA ADAM

Exchange Chambers
7 Ralli Courts, West Riverside, Manchester M3 5FT, ☎0161 833 2722
Exchange Chambers
One Derby Square, Derby Square, Liverpool L2 9XX, ☎0151 236 7747
✉info@exchangechambers.co.uk
Exchange Chambers
Oxford House, Oxford Row, Leeds LS1 3BE, ☎0113 203 1970
✉spencer@exchangechambers.co.uk
Call Date: Mar 2000, Middle Temple
Qualifications: [BA (Hons) (Cantab)]
✉shields@exchangechambers.co.uk

SHIELDS MISS SONJA MARION

Carmelite Chambers
9 Carmelite Street, London EC4Y 0DR, ☎020 7936 6300
✉clerks@carmelitechambers.co.uk
Call Date: July 1977, Inner Temple
Qualifications: [BA (Cantab)]
✉sshields@carmelitechambers.co.uk

SHIELS MR IAN

Sovereign Chambers
46 Park Place, Leeds LS1 2RY, ☎0113 245 1841
✉clerks@sovereignchambers.co.uk
Call Date: Nov 1992, Inner Temple
Pupil Supervisor
Qualifications: [BA (Leeds) DipLaw (Lond)]
✉ian.shiels@sovereignchambers.co.uk

SHIKDER MR KUTUB UDDIN AHMED

T H Barristers Chambers
178 Whitechapel Road, London E1 1BJ, ☎020 7377 8090 ✉thbchambers@aol.com
Call Date: Nov 1990, Lincoln's Inn
Qualifications: [LLB (Hons) MA]
✉shikderka@aol.com

SHILLINGFORD MS JULIA KAY

3 PB Barristers
3 Paper Buildings, Temple, London EC4Y 7EU, ☎020 7583 8055
3 PB Barristers
23 Beaumont Street, Oxford OX1 2NP, ☎01865 793 736
3 PB Barristers
4 St Peter Street, Winchester SO23 8BW, ☎01962 868884
✉clerks.winchester@3paper.co.uk
3 PB Barristers
Royal Talbot House, 2 Victoria Street, Bristol, Avon BS1 6BB, ☎0117 928 1520
3 PB Barristers
30 Christchurch Road, Bournemouth, Dorset BH1 3PD, ☎01202 292102
✉clerks.bournemouth@3paper.co.uk
Call Date: Oct 2002, Middle Temple
Qualifications: [BA (Oxon)]

SHIPMAN MR ANTHONY MICHAEL

Goldsmith Chambers
Ground Floor, Goldsmith Building, Temple, London EC4Y 7BL, ☎020 7353 6802
✉clerks@goldsmithchambers.com
Call Date: July 1992, Middle Temple
Qualifications: [BA (Hons) (Bris) LLB (Hons) (Lond)]

E

SHIRES MR GARETH RICHARD

Exchange Chambers
7 Ralli Courts, West Riverside, Manchester M3 5FT, ☎0161 833 2722
Exchange Chambers
One Derby Square, Derby Square, Liverpool L2 9XX, ☎0151 236 7747
✉info@exchangechambers.co.uk
Exchange Chambers
Oxford House, Oxford Row, Leeds LS1 3BE, ☎0113 203 1970
✉spencer@exchangechambers.co.uk
Call Date: July 2007, Lincoln's Inn
Qualifications: [BA (Oxon) LLB]
shires@exchangechambers.co.uk

SHIRLEY MR JAMES PATRICK

Stone Chambers
4 Field Court, Gray's Inn, London WC1R 5EF, ☎020 7440 6900
✉clerks@stonechambers.com
Call Date: Nov 2002, Middle Temple
Qualifications: [LLB (Hons)(Lond)]
james.shirley@stonechambers.com

SHIRLEY MISS LYNNE

East Anglian Chambers
Gresham House, 5 Museum Street, Ipswich, Suffolk IP1 1HQ, ☎01473 214481
✉ipswich@ealaw.co.uk
East Anglian Chambers
140 New London Road, Chelmsford, Essex CM2 0AW, ☎01473 214481
✉chelmsford@ealaw.co.uk
East Anglian Chambers
15 The Close, Norwich, Norfolk NR1 4DZ, ☎01473 214481 ✉norwich@ealaw.co.uk
Call Date: July 2002, Middle Temple
Qualifications: [LLB (Hons)]
lynneshirley@ealaw.co.uk

SHIU MISS MING YEE

2 Temple Gardens
2 Temple Gardens, Temple, London EC4Y 9AY, ☎020 7822 1200
✉clerks@2tg.co.uk
Call Date: Oct 2000, Middle Temple
Qualifications: [BA (Hons) (Cantab) LLM]
mys@2tg.co.uk

SHIVJI MR SHARIF ASIM

4 Stone Buildings
Ground Floor, 4 Stone Buildings, Lincoln's Inn, London WC2A 3XT, ☎020 7242 5524
✉clerks@4stonebuildings.com
Call Date: July 2001, Lincoln's Inn
Pupil Supervisor
Qualifications: [BSc (Hons) (Lond) MA]
s.shivji@4stonebuildings.com

SHOKER MR CHANVIR SINGH

Cornwall Street Chambers
85-87 Cornwall Street, Birmingham B3 3BY, ☎0121 233 7500
✉clerks@cornwallstreet.co.uk
Call Date: Oct 2006, Middle Temple
Qualifications: [LLB (Hons) (B'ham)]
chanvir.shoker@cornwallstreet.co.uk

SHOKER MR MAKKAN SINGH

St Philips Chambers
55 Temple Row, Birmingham B2 5LS, ☎0121 246 7000 ✉clerks@st-philips.com
Call Date: May 1981, Inner Temple
Pupil Supervisor
Qualifications: [LLB (Lond)]
mshoker@st-philips.co.uk

SHORE MISS VICTORIA LOUISE

5RB
1st Floor, 5 Raymond Buildings, Gray's Inn, London WC1R 5BP, ☎020 7242 2902
✉clerks@5rb.com
Call Date: Nov 2005, Lincoln's Inn
Qualifications: [BA (Hons) (Oxon)]
victoriashore@5rb.com

SHOREY MISS CARRIE LORRAE

Nine Bedford Row
9 Bedford Row, London WC1R 4AZ, ☎020 7489 2727
✉clerks@9bedfordrow.co.uk
Call Date: July 2006, Middle Temple
Qualifications: [LLB (Hons) (Lond)]
carrie.shorey@9bedfordrow.co.uk

SHORROCK MR JOHN MICHAEL QC (1988)

Atkinson Bevan Chambers
1st Floor, 2 Harcourt Buildings, Temple, London EC4Y 9DB, ☎020 7353 2112
✉clerks@2hb.co.uk
Call Date: July 1966, Inner Temple
Recorder
Qualifications: [MA (Cantab)]

SHORT MR ANDREW JOHN QC (2010)

Outer Temple Chambers
The Outer Temple, 222 Strand, London WC2R 1BA, ☎ 020 7353 6381
✉ clerks@outertemple.com
Riverview Chambers
Hamilton House, 1 Temple Avenue, London EC4Y 0HA, ☎ 0844 225 3999
✉ chrisbaylis@riverviewchambers.com
Call Date: Nov 1990, Gray's Inn
Pupil Supervisor
Qualifications: [LLB (Bristol)]
✉ andrew.short@outertemple.com

SHORT MISS ANNA LOUISE

St James's Chambers
68 Quay Street, Manchester M3 3EJ, ☎ 0161 834 7000
✉ clerks@stjameschambers.com
12 King's Bench Walk
12 King's Bench Walk, Temple, London EC4Y 7EL, ☎ 020 7583 0811
Call Date: Nov 1997, Gray's Inn
Qualifications: [MA (Cantab)]
✉ anna.short@stjameschambers.com

SHORT MR GARY PETER

KCH Garden Square
1 Oxford Street, Nottingham NG1 5BH, ☎ 0115 941 8851
✉ clerks@kchgardensquare.co.uk
Call Date: Nov 1996, Gray's Inn
Qualifications: [BA (Lond)]

SHORT MS HARRIET OLIVIA JANE

1 Pump Court
Elm Court, Temple, London EC4Y 7AB, ☎ 020 7842 7070
✉ (name)@pumpcourt.co.uk
Call Date: July 2007, Gray's Inn
Qualifications: [LLB (Lond) LLM (Essex)]

SHORT MS MANDY LISA

14 Gray's Inn Square
14 Gray's Inn Square, Gray's Inn, London WC1R 5JP, ☎ 020 7242 0858
✉ clerks@14gis.co.uk
Call Date: July 2003, Middle Temple
Qualifications: [LLB Hons (Lond) PGCE]

SHOTTON MS SOPHIE DIANA

15 New Bridge Street
London EC4V 6AU, ☎ 020 7842 1900
✉ clerks@15nbs.com
Call Date: Oct 1999, Inner Temple
Qualifications: [MA Hons (Cantab)]
✉ Sophie.Shotton@15nbs.com

SHRAVAT MR NEELOTPAL

Pump Court Chambers
Upper Ground Floor, 3 Pump Court, Temple, London EC4Y 7AJ, ☎ 020 7353 0711
✉ clerks@3pumpcourt.com
Pump Court Chambers
31 Southgate Street, Winchester, Hampshire SO23 9EB, ☎ 01962 868 161
✉ clerks@3pumpcourt.com
Call Date: Nov 2002, Middle Temple
Qualifications: [LLB (Hons) (Edin) Dip in Law]
✉ nes@3pumpcourt.com

SHRIMPTON MS CLAIRE ALISON

Guildford Chambers
Stoke House, Leapale Lane, Guildford, Surrey GU1 4LY, ☎ 01483 539131
✉ clerks@guildfordchambers.co.uk
Call Date: July 1983, Inner Temple
Qualifications: [LLB (Hull)]

SHRIMPTON MR MICHAEL

Chambers of Michael Shrimpton
8 Jusons Glebe, Wendover, Buckinghamshire HP22 6PF, ☎ 01296 291564
✉ michael@mshrimpton.co.uk
Call Date: Nov 1983, Gray's Inn
Qualifications: [LLB (Wales)]

SHROFF MR CYRUS

18 Red Lion Court
London EC4A 3EB, ☎ 020 7520 6000
✉ chambers@18rlc.co.uk
18 Red Lion Court (Annexe)
Thornwood House, 102 New London Road, Chelmsford, Essex CM2 0RG, ☎ 01245 280880
Call Date: July 1983, Gray's Inn
Pupil Supervisor
Qualifications: [BA]
✉ cyrus.shroff@18rlc.co.uk

SHROFF MISS TESSA

Nine Bedford Row
9 Bedford Row, London WC1R 4AZ, ☎ 020 7489 2727
✉ clerks@9bedfordrow.co.uk
Call Date: July 2009, Lincoln's Inn
Qualifications: [LLB (Sussex)]
✉ clerks@9bedfordrow.co.uk

E

SHUMAN MISS KAREN ANN ELIZABETH

1 Chancery Lane
London WC2A 1LF, ☎ 0845 634 6666
✉ clerks@1chancerylane.com
No 8 Chambers
8 Fountain Court, Steelhouse Lane, Birmingham B4 6DR, ☎ 0121 236 5514
✉ clerks@no8chambers.co.uk
Call Date: Oct 1991, Lincoln's Inn
Pupil Supervisor
Qualifications: [LLB (Hons) (B'ham)]
kshuman@1chancerylane.com

SHUTTLEWORTH MR TIMOTHY WILLIAM

Tanfield Chambers
2-5 Warwick Court, London WC1R 5DJ,
☎ 020 7421 5300
✉ clerks@tanfieldchambers.co.uk
Call Date: July 1971, Gray's Inn
Pupil Supervisor
Qualifications: [LLB]
clerks@tanfieldchambers.co.uk

SIBBEL MR SHANE JOSEPH RODERICK

Blackstone Chambers
Blackstone House, Temple, London EC4Y 9BW, ☎ 020 7583 1770
✉ clerks@blackstonechambers.com
Call Date: July 2010, Inner Temple
Qualifications: [BA BCL (Oxon)]
clerks@blackstonechambers.com

SIBERRY MR RICHARD QC (1989)

Essex Court Chambers
24 Lincoln's Inn Fields, London WC2A 3EG,
☎ 020 7813 8000
✉ clerksroom@essexcourt.net
Call Date: July 1974, Middle Temple
Recorder
Qualifications: [MA LLB (Cantab)]
rsiberry@essexcourt.net

SIBSON MRS CLARE ADELE

Cloth Fair Chambers
39-40 Cloth Fair, London EC1A 7NT,
☎ 020 7710 6444
✉ email@clothfairchambers.com
Call Date: Oct 1997, Middle Temple
Qualifications: [BA (Hons)(Cantab)]

SIDDALL MR NICHOLAS MICHAEL

Kings Chambers
36 Young Street, Manchester M3 3FT,
☎ 0845 034 3444
✉ clerks@kingschambers.com
Kings Chambers
5 Park Square East, Leeds LS1 2NE,
☎ 0845 034 3444
✉ clerks@kingschambers.com
Kings Chambers
Embassy House, 60 Church Street, Birmingham B3 2DJ, ☎ 0845 034 3444
✉ clerks@kingschambers.com
Call Date: Oct 1997, Middle Temple
Pupil Supervisor
Qualifications: [BA (Hons)(Cantab)]
nsiddall@kingschambers.com

SIDDIQI MR FAIZUL AQTAB

Justice Court Chambers
23 Wykin Road, Hinckley, Leicestershire LE10 0HU, ☎ 02476 325859
✉ blessedseat@yahoo.co.uk
Call Date: July 1990, Lincoln's Inn
Qualifications: [LLB]
siddiqi@justicecourtchambers.com

SIDDLE MR TREVOR BRYAN

Goldsmith Chambers
Ground Floor, Goldsmith Building, Temple, London EC4Y 7BL, ☎ 020 7353 6802
✉ clerks@goldsmithchambers.com
Call Date: Oct 1991, Gray's Inn
Qualifications: [LLB (Hons)]
T.Siddle@goldsmithchambers.law.co.uk

SIDHU MR AKAAL SINGH

Equity Chambers
First Floor, McLaren Building, 46 Priory Queensway, Birmingham B4 7LR,
☎ 0121 236 5007
✉ clerks@equitychambers.org.uk
Call Date: Nov 2008, Lincoln's Inn
Qualifications: [LLB (Lond)]

SIDHU MR NAVJOT QC (2012)

25 Bedford Row
London WC1R 4HD, ☎ 020 7067 1500
✉ clerks@25bedfordrow.com
Call Date: Nov 1993, Lincoln's Inn
Pupil Supervisor
Qualifications: [MA (Oxon) MSc (Econ) (London)]
nsidhu@25bedfordrow.com

SIDHU-BRAR MR NISHARN SINGH

Citadel Chambers
The Citadel, 190 Corporation Street, Birmingham B4 6QD, ☎0121 233 8500
✉clerks@citadelchambers.com
Call Date: Oct 1991, Gray's Inn
Qualifications: [LLB (Hons) RMN]

SIGEE MR PETER HOWARD

Atlantic Chambers
4-6 Cook Street, Liverpool L2 9QU,
☎0151 236 4421
✉info@atlanticchambers.co.uk
Call Date: Nov 2002, Middle Temple
Qualifications: [LLB (Hons)(B'ham) MA]
petersigee@atlanticchambers.co.uk

SIKAND MISS MAYA

Garden Court Chambers
57-60 Lincoln's Inn Fields, London WC2A 3LJ,
☎020 7993 7600 ✉info@gclaw.co.uk
Call Date: Nov 1997, Middle Temple
Pupil Supervisor
Qualifications: [BA (Hons)(Oxon) MSc (Lond)]
mayas@gclaw.co.uk

SILCOCK MR IAN PETER

Hardwicke
New Square, Lincoln's Inn, London
WC2A 3SB, ☎020 7242 2523
✉enquiries@hardwicke.co.uk
Call Date: Oct 1997, Middle Temple
Qualifications: [LLB (Hons)(Lond) MSc (Lond)]
ian.silcock@hardwicke.co.uk

SILCOTT MR TYRONE JOHN

Charter Chambers
33 John Street, London WC1N 2AT,
☎020 7618 4400
✉clerks@charterchambers.com
Call Date: July 2004, Middle Temple
Pupil Supervisor
Qualifications: [BA Hons (Lond) PGDip Law]
t.silcott@charterchambers.com

SILLS MR DANIEL JAMES

1 Pump Court
Elm Court, Temple, London EC4Y 7AB,
☎020 7842 7070
✉(name)@pumpcourt.co.uk
Call Date: Oct 2011, Gray's Inn
dsi@1pumpcourt.co.uk

SILVA MR DAVID JEROME

4 King's Bench Walk
2nd Floor, 4 King's Bench Walk, Temple,
London EC4Y 7DL, ☎020 7822 7000
✉clerks@4kbw.co.uk
Call Date: Oct 2001, Inner Temple
Qualifications: [LLB (Exeter)]
js@4kbw.co.uk

SILVER MISS NADIA ANGELA MIMI

36 Bedford Row
London WC1R 4JH, ☎020 7421 8000
✉chambers@36bedfordrow.co.uk
Call Date: Oct 2001, Middle Temple
Qualifications: [BA (Hons)(Leeds) Dip Law]

SILVER MISS TAMSIN GABRIELLE

1 Mitre Court Buildings
1 Mitre Court Buildings, Temple, London
EC4Y 7BS, ☎020 7452 8900
✉clerks@1mcb.com
Call Date: Nov 2002, Gray's Inn
Qualifications: [BSc (Hons)]
clerks@1mcb.com

SILVERLEAF MR ALEXANDER MICHAEL QC (1996)

11 South Square
1st Floor, 11 South Square, Gray's Inn,
London WC1R 5EY, ☎020 7405 1222
✉clerks@11southsquare.com
Call Date: May 1980, Gray's Inn
Pupil Supervisor
Qualifications: [BSc (Lond)]

SILVERSTONE MR BENJAMIN MAURICE

Doughty Street Chambers
53-54 Doughty Street, London WC1N 2LS,
☎020 7404 1313
✉enquiries@doughtystreet.co.uk
Call Date: Oct 2009, Lincoln's Inn
Qualifications: [BA (Cantab) CPE LLM]
b.silverstone@doughtystreetchambers.co.uk

SILVERTON MISS CATHERINE ANNE

Sovereign Chambers
46 Park Place, Leeds LS1 2RY,
☎0113 245 1841
✉clerks@sovereignchambers.co.uk
Call Date: Nov 2001, Lincoln's Inn
Qualifications: [BA (Hons) PG Dip Law]

E

SILVESTER MR BRUCE ROSS

Devereux Chambers
Queen Elizabeth Building, Temple, London EC4Y 9BS, ☎ 020 7353 7534
✉ clerks@devchambers.co.uk
Call Date: July 1983, Inner Temple
Pupil Supervisor
Qualifications: [LLB (Lond)]
✉ silvester@devchambers.co.uk

SIMBLET MR STEPHEN JOHN

Garden Court Chambers
57-60 Lincoln's Inn Fields, London WC2A 3LJ, ☎ 020 7993 7600 ✉ info@gclaw.co.uk
Call Date: Oct 1991, Inner Temple
Pupil Supervisor
Qualifications: [MA (Cantab) LLM]
✉ stephens@gclaw.co.uk

SIMCOCK MISS SARAH LOUISE

3 Serjeants Inn
London EC4Y 1BQ, ☎ 020 7427 5000
✉ clerks@3serjeantsinn.com
Call Date: Oct 2001, Inner Temple
Qualifications: [BA (Hons)(Oxon)]
✉ ssimcock@3serjeantsinn.com

E

SIME PROF STUART JOHN

13 King's Bench Walk
13 King's Bench Walk, Temple, London EC4Y 7EN, ☎ 020 7353 7204
✉ clerks@13kbw.co.uk
13 KBW
32 Beaumont Street, Oxford OX1 2NP, ☎ 01865 311066 ✉ clerks@13kbw.co.uk
Call Date: Nov 1983, Gray's Inn
Qualifications: [LLB]

SIMISON MR JEREMY CHARLES

Trinity Chambers
Highfield House, Moulsham Street, Chelmsford, Essex CM2 9AH,
☎ 01245 605040
✉ clerks@trinitychambers.com
Call Date: Oct 1993, Inner Temple
Pupil Supervisor
Qualifications: [BA (B'ham) CPE]

SIMKIN MR IAIN JAMES

Call Date: Feb 1995, Inner Temple
Pupil Supervisor
Qualifications: [BA CPE (Staffs)]

SIMLER MISS INGRID ANN QC (2006)

Devereux Chambers
Queen Elizabeth Building, Temple, London EC4Y 9BS, ☎ 020 7353 7534
✉ clerks@devchambers.co.uk
Call Date: July 1987, Inner Temple
Recorder
Qualifications: [MA (Cantab) Dip EEC Law]
✉ simler@devchambers.co.uk

SIMMONDS MISS ALEXANDRA MARGOT RACHEL

St Johns Buildings
24a - 28 St John Street, Manchester M3 4DJ,
☎ 0161 214 1500
✉ clerk@stjohnsbuildings.co.uk
St Johns Buildings
21 White Friars, Chester CH1 1NZ,
☎ 01244 323070
✉ clerk@stjohnsbuildings.co.uk
16 Winckley Square
Preston PR1 3JJ, ☎ 01772 256100
Call Date: Oct 1998, Gray's Inn
Qualifications: [LLB (Birmingham)]

SIMMONDS MR ANDREW JOHN QC (1999)

5 Stone Buildings
5 Stone Buildings, Lincoln's Inn, London WC2A 3XT, ☎ 020 7242 6201
✉ clerks@5sblaw.com
Call Date: Nov 1980, Middle Temple
Qualifications: [MA (Cantab)]
✉ asimmonds@5sblaw.com

SIMMONS MR JOHN PERRIOR

Chambers of Mr John Simmons
Address withheld ✉ john.simmons@live.co.uk
Call Date: Mar 2000, Middle Temple
Qualifications: [LLB (Oxon)]

SIMMONS MISS KAYLEIGH MARGARET

9 Park Place
9 Park Place, Cardiff, South Glamorgan CF10 3DP, ☎ 029 2038 2731
✉ clerks@9parkplace.co.uk
Call Date: July 2009, Gray's Inn
Qualifications: [LLB]
✉ ksimmons@9parkplace.co.uk

SIMMS MISS SONIA ANGELA

Farringdon Chambers
180 Bermondsey Street, London SE1 3TQ,
☎ 020 7089 5700
Call Date: Nov 1993, Middle Temple
Qualifications: [BSc (Hons) Dip Law (Lond) LLM]

SIMON MR MICHAEL HENRY

4 Paper Buildings
1st Floor, 4 Paper Buildings, Temple, London EC4Y 7EX, ☎ 020 7427 5200
✉ clerks@4pb.com
Call Date: Nov 1992, Inner Temple
Pupil Supervisor
Qualifications: [LLB (L'pool)]
✉ mhs@4pb.com

SIMON MR PAUL HOWARD

9 King's Bench Walk
Lower Ground Floor South, 9 King's Bench Walk, Temple, London EC4Y 7DX,
☎ 020 7353 9564 ✉ 9kbw@btconnect.com
Call Date: Nov 2000, Lincoln's Inn
Qualifications: [LLB (Hons) (Nott'm)]

SIMON MR PHILIPP ARNOLD HEINRICH

4 KBW
Ground Floor, 4 King's Bench Walk, Temple, London EC4Y 7DL, ☎ 020 7822 8822
✉ law@4kbw.net
Call Date: Oct 2004, Inner Temple
Qualifications: [LLB (Kent) Dip iVN]
✉ ps@4kbw.net

SIMONS MR KANE ANTHONY

18 St John Street
Manchester M3 4EA, ☎ 0161 278 1800
✉ clerks@18sjs.com
Call Date: Oct 2007, Lincoln's Inn
Qualifications: [BA LLM (Leeds)]

SIMONS MR RICHARD GRAHAM

Lincoln House Chambers
Tower 12, The Avenue North, Spinningfields, 18-22 Bridge Street, Manchester M3 3BZ,
☎ 0161 832 5701
✉ info@lincolnhousechambers.com
Call Date: Feb 1991, Gray's Inn
Qualifications: [LLB (Hons)]
✉ richard.simons@lincolnhousechambers.com

SIMONS MR ZACK ARTHUR

39 Essex Street
London WC2R 3AT, ☎ 020 7832 1111
✉ clerks@39essex.com
Call Date: July 2009, Inner Temple
Qualifications: [BA (Cantab) MSc (Lond)]
✉ zack.simons@39essex.com

SIMOR MISS JESSICA MARGARET POPPAEA

Matrix Chambers
Griffin Building, Gray's Inn, London WC1R 5LN, ☎ 020 7404 3447
✉ matrix@matrixlaw.co.uk / lscott@matrixlaw.co.uk
Call Date: Nov 1992, Middle Temple
Pupil Supervisor
Qualifications: [MA (Oxon) Dip EU Law]
✉ jessicasimor@matrixlaw.co.uk

SIMPSON MISS CAROL MONICA

Amethyst Chambers
Ground Floor, 9 Kings Bench Walk, Inner Temple, London EC4Y 7DX,
☎ 020 7936 4966
✉ info@amethystchambers.com
Call Date: Mar 1998, Gray's Inn
Qualifications: [LLB Hons (Thames)]

SIMPSON MR DAVID ANDREW

3 Verulam Buildings
London WC1R 5NT, ☎ 020 7831 8441
✉ chambers@3vb.com
Call Date: Oct 2003, Gray's Inn
Qualifications: [BA (Hons) (Oxon) PgDL]
✉ dsimpson@3vb.com

SIMPSON MR DAVID JOSEPH

196 Temple Chamber
3-7 Temple Avenue, London EC4Y 0HP,
☎ 020 7099 9257
✉ davidsimpson@lawandregulation.com
Call Date: Oct 1992, Gray's Inn
Qualifications: [LLB (Hons)]

SIMPSON MR EDWIN JOHN FLETCHER

New Square Chambers
12 New Square, Lincoln's Inn, London WC2A 3SW, ☎ 020 7419 8000
✉ robin.hollington@newsquarechambers.co.uk
Call Date: Nov 1990, Lincoln's Inn
Qualifications: [MA BCL (Oxon)]
✉ edwin.simpson@newsquarechambers.co.uk

E

SIMPSON MR GRAEME MICHAEL

Citadel Chambers
The Citadel, 190 Corporation Street, Birmingham B4 6QD, ☎0121 233 8500
✉clerks@citadelchambers.com
Call Date: Nov 1994, Middle Temple
Qualifications: [LLB (Hons)]

SIMPSON MISS HANNAH JOY

St Mary's Family Law Chambers
26-28 High Pavement, The Lace Market, Nottingham NG1 1HN, ☎0115 950 3503
✉clerks@stmarysflc.co.uk
Call Date: Oct 2000, Middle Temple
Pupil Supervisor
Qualifications: [LLB (Hons) (Nott'm)]
✉hannah.simpson@stmarysflc.co.uk

SIMPSON MR IAN

Clerksroom (Taunton)
Equity House, Administration Centre, Blackbrook Park Avenue, Taunton, Somerset TA1 2PX, ☎0845 083 3000
✉mail@clerksroom.com
Call Date: Oct 1997, Lincoln's Inn
Qualifications: [LLB (Hons)(Lond)]
✉isimpson.barrister@virgin.net

E

SIMPSON MS JACQUELINE LAWRENCE

Hailsham Chambers
Ground Floor, 4 Paper Buildings, Temple, London EC4Y 7EX, ☎020 7643 5000
✉clerks@hailshamchambers.com
Call Date: July 2006, Inner Temple
Qualifications: [BSc (Lond)]
✉jacqueline.simpson@hailshamchambers.com

SIMPSON MR JONATHAN DAVID

Charter Chambers
33 John Street, London WC1N 2AT, ☎020 7618 4400
✉clerks@charterchambers.com
Call Date: Nov 1993, Gray's Inn
Qualifications: [LLB (Hons)]

SIMPSON MR MARK TAYLOR QC (2008)

Fountain Court Chambers
Fountain Court, Temple, London EC4Y 9DH, ☎020 7583 3335
✉chambers@fountaincourt.co.uk
Call Date: Oct 1992, Middle Temple
Qualifications: [MA (Hons) (Oxon) Dip Law (Lond)]
✉ms@fountaincourt.co.uk

SIMPSON MS MELANIE DENISE

25 Bedford Row
London WC1R 4HD, ☎020 7067 1500
✉clerks@25bedfordrow.com
Call Date: Mar 1998, Gray's Inn
Qualifications: [LLB (Lond)]
✉msimpson@25bedfordrow.com,

SIMPSON MR PAUL RICHARD

New Bailey Chambers
4th Floor, Corn Exchange, Fenwick Street, Liverpool, Merseyside L2 7QS, ☎0151 236 9402 ✉clerks@newbailey.com
Call Date: Nov 1980, Lincoln's Inn
Qualifications: [LLB (L'pool)]
✉pr.simpson@blueyonder.co.uk

SIMPSON MS RAQUEL

18 St John Street
Manchester M3 4EA, ☎0161 278 1800
✉clerks@18sjs.com
Call Date: Oct 1990, Inner Temple
Pupil Supervisor
Qualifications: [LLB (LSE)]

SIMS MISS ALICE ANTONIA

Keating Chambers
15 Essex Street, London WC2R 3AA, ☎020 7544 2600
✉clerks@keatingchambers.com
Call Date: July 2004, Inner Temple
Qualifications: [MA Hons (Cantab) PGDip Law BVC]
✉asims@keatingchambers.com

SIMS MR GUY ROHAN

Fenners Chambers
3 Madingley Road, Cambridge CB3 0EE, ☎01223 368761
✉clerks@fennerschambers.com
Call Date: July 2000, Inner Temple
Qualifications: [BSc (Lond) BA (Hons)(Cambridge) ACA]
✉guy.sims@fennerschambers.com

SIMS MR HUGH

Guildhall Chambers
23 Broad Street, Bristol BS1 2HG, ☎0117 930 9000
✉hoc@guildhallchambers.co.uk
Call Date: Oct 1999, Lincoln's Inn
Pupil Supervisor
Qualifications: [BSc (Hons)(Manc)]
✉hugh.sims@guildhallchambers.co.uk

SIMS MR PAUL LLYSTYN

4 Breams Buildings
Chancery Lane, London EC4A 1HP,
☎020 7092 1900 ✉clerks@4bb.co.uk
Call Date: Nov 1990, Gray's Inn
Qualifications: [LLB]

SIN MR JUI FUNG

Kenworthy's Chambers
Arlington House, Bloom Street, Salford, Manchester M3 6AJ, ☎0161 832 4036
Call Date: July 2003, Lincoln's Inn
Qualifications: [LLB (Hons)]

SINAI MR ALI REZA

Ely Place Chambers
30 Ely Place, London EC1N 6TD,
☎020 7400 9600 ✉admin@elyplace.com
Call Date: July 1997, Gray's Inn
Qualifications: [LLB LLM DEA]
🖃asinai@elyplace.com

SINAN MR IZZET MAHMUT

Chambers of Mr Izzet Sinan
Floor 8, 7 Rue Guimard, Brussels B-1040,
☎00 32 2 507 7522
Call Date: July 1981, Inner Temple
Qualifications: [MA Lic Spec En Droit European (Belguim) LLM (Cantab)]

SINCLAIR MISS CAROLINE

1 Pump Court
Elm Court, Temple, London EC4Y 7AB,
☎020 7842 7070
✉(name)@pumpcourt.co.uk
Call Date: July 2005, Middle Temple
Qualifications: [LLB (Hons)]
🖃csi@1pumpcourt.co.uk

SINCLAIR MR DUNCAN EDWARD MACCALLUM

39 Essex Street
London WC2R 3AT, ☎020 7832 1111
✉clerks@39essex.com
Call Date: Oct 1996, Lincoln's Inn
Qualifications: [BA (Hons) LLM (Cantab)]

SINCLAIR MISS FIONA MARY

Four New Square
Four New Square, Lincoln's Inn, London WC2A 3RJ, ☎020 7822 2000
✉barristers@4newsquare.com
Call Date: July 1989, Inner Temple
Pupil Supervisor
Qualifications: [MA (Cantab) LLM (Cantab)]
🖃f.sinclair@4newsquare.com

SINCLAIR MR GRAHAM KELSO

East Anglian Chambers
15 The Close, Norwich, Norfolk NR1 4DZ,
☎01473 214481 ✉norwich@ealaw.co.uk
East Anglian Chambers
53 North Hill, Colchester, Essex CO1 1QA,
☎01473 214481 ✉colchester@ealaw.co.uk
East Anglian Chambers
Gresham House, 5 Museum Street, Ipswich, Suffolk IP1 1HQ, ☎01473 214481
✉ipswich@ealaw.co.uk
Call Date: July 1979, Gray's Inn
Pupil Supervisor
Qualifications: [QDR LLB (Hons) (Lond)]

SINCLAIR MR JEAN-PAUL MEEHAN

14 Gray's Inn Square
14 Gray's Inn Square, Gray's Inn, London WC1R 5JP, ☎020 7242 0858
✉clerks@14gis.co.uk
Call Date: Feb 1989, Middle Temple
Qualifications: [MA (Cantab)]
🖃jps@14gis.co.uk

SINCLAIR MISS LISA ANNE

Chambers of Miss Lisa Sinclair
Glencairn House, 70 Ridgway, London SW19 4RA, ☎020 8946 7201
✉lisaasinclair@yahoo.com
Call Date: July 1993, Gray's Inn
Qualifications: [LLB (Leic) MBA]
🖃lisaasinclair@yahoo.com

SINCLAIR MR MALCOLM DAVID

Chambers of Mr Malcolm Sinclair
First Floor, Holborn Gate, 330, High Holborn, London WC1V 7QT, ☎020 7242 0644
✉malcolmsinclair@gmail.com
Call Date: July 1978, Lincoln's Inn
Pupil Supervisor
Qualifications: [LLB (Lond) BA]

SINCLAIR MR PAUL

Fountain Court Chambers
Fountain Court, Temple, London EC4Y 9DH,
☎020 7583 3335
✉chambers@fountaincourt.co.uk
Call Date: Oct 1997, Middle Temple
Pupil Supervisor
Qualifications: [MA (Hons)(Cantab) LLM (Lond)]
🖃pxs@fountaincourt.co.uk

E

SINCLAIR MR PHILIP JUSTYN

Maidstone Chambers
33 Earl Street, Maidstone, Kent ME14 1PF,
☎01622 688592
✉clerks@maidstonechambers.co.uk
Call Date: Oct 1995, Gray's Inn
Qualifications: [LLB (Hons)]

SINGARAJAH MR FREDERICO

1 Gray's Inn Square
Ground Floor, 1 Gray's Inn Square, London
WC1R 5AA, ☎020 7405 0001
Call Date: July 2009, Gray's Inn
fsingarajah@1gis.co.uk

SINGER MR ANDREW MICHAEL

Kings Chambers
36 Young Street, Manchester M3 3FT,
☎0845 034 3444
✉clerks@kingschambers.com
Kings Chambers
5 Park Square East, Leeds LS1 2NE,
☎0845 034 3444
✉clerks@kingschambers.com
Kings Chambers
Embassy House, 60 Church Street,
Birmingham B3 2DJ, ☎0845 034 3444
✉clerks@kingschambers.com
Call Date: Nov 1990, Gray's Inn
Pupil Supervisor
Qualifications: [MA (Cantab)]
asinger@kingschambers.com

SINGER MR NICHOLAS PAUL

42 Bedford Row
London WC1R 4LL, ☎020 7831 0222
✉clerks@42br.com
Call Date: July 2006, Gray's Inn
Qualifications: [BA (Cantab)]
nick.singer@42br.com

SINGER MR PHILIP FRANCIS QC (1994)

2 Pump Court
1st Floor, 2 Pump Court, Temple, London
EC4Y 7AH, ☎020 7353 5597
✉clerks@2pumpcourt.co.uk
Call Date: Feb 1964, Inner Temple
Recorder
Qualifications: [MA LLM (Cantab)]
psinger@2pumpcourt.co.uk

SINGER MR RICHARD ADAM

1 Gray's Inn Square
Ground Floor, 1 Gray's Inn Square, London
WC1R 5AA, ☎020 7405 0001
Call Date: Oct 2001, Lincoln's Inn
Qualifications: [BA (Hons) (Manch) CPE]
rsinger@1gis.co.uk

SINGER MISS SAMANTHA LAURA CATHERINE

Queen Elizabeth Building
3rd Floor, Queen Elizabeth Building, Temple,
London EC4Y 9BS, ☎020 7797 7837
✉clerks@qeb.co.uk
Call Date: July 2004, Gray's Inn
Qualifications: [LLB (Bris)]
s.singer@qeb.co.uk

SINGH MR ANTHONY BHARAT

Deans Court Chambers
24 St John Street, Manchester M3 4DF,
☎0161 214 6000 ✉clerks@deanscourt.co.uk
Deans Court Chambers
101 Walker Street, Preston PR1 2RR,
☎01772 565 600
✉preston@deanscourt.co.uk
Call Date: Oct 2001, Gray's Inn
Qualifications: [LLB (Sheff)]
singh@deanscourt.co.uk

SINGH MR BALBIR

Equity Chambers
First Floor, McLaren Building, 46 Priory
Queensway, Birmingham B4 7LR,
☎0121 236 5007
✉clerks@equitychambers.org.uk
Call Date: July 1984, Lincoln's Inn
Pupil Supervisor
Qualifications: [BA Dip MRS LLB (Hons)]
balbir.singh@equitychambers.org.uk

SINGH MR DAPINDERPAUL

23 Essex Street
London WC2R 3AA, ☎020 7413 0353
✉clerks@23es.com
Park Court Chambers
16 Park Place, Leeds LS1 2SJ,
☎0113 243 3277
✉clerks@parkcourtchambers.co.uk
Call Date: July 2000, Middle Temple
Qualifications: [LLB(Hons) (Hudd)]

E

SINGH MR GURDIAL

Bank House Chambers
Old Bank House, Hartshead, Sheffield S1 2EL,
☎0114 275 1223
✉w.digby@bankhousechambers.co.uk
Call Date: July 1989, Lincoln's Inn
Pupil Supervisor
Qualifications: [LLB (Leeds)]
g.singh@bankhousechambers.co.uk

SINGH MR KARAMJIT KHAIRA

St Ive's Chambers
Whittall Street, Birmingham B4 6DH,
☎0121 236 0863
✉clerks@stiveschambers.co.uk
Call Date: Mar 2000, Lincoln's Inn
Qualifications: [LLB (Hons)]
karamjit.singh@stiveschambers.co.uk

SINGH MR KULDIP QC (1993)

Serle Court
6 New Square, Lincoln's Inn, London
WC2A 3QS, ☎020 7242 6105
✉clerks@serlecourt.co.uk
Call Date: July 1975, Middle Temple
Recorder
ksingh@serlecourt.co.uk

SINGH MR RANJIT

New Court
Ground Floor, New Court, Temple, London
EC4Y 9BE, ☎020 7583 5123
✉clerks@newcourtchambers.com
Call Date: Oct 2007, Inner Temple
Qualifications: [BA (Lond)]
rsingh@newcourtchambers.net

SINGH MR SANDESH MOHAN

2 Bedford Row
London WC1R 4BU, ☎020 7440 8888
✉clerks@2bedfordrow.co.uk
Call Date: Oct 2004, Inner Temple
Qualifications: [LLB (Bris)]
ssingh@2bedfordrow.co.uk

SINGH MR SARABJIT

1 Crown Office Row
1 Crown Office Row, Temple, London
EC4Y 7HH, ☎020 7797 7500
✉mail@1cor.com
Call Date: Oct 2001, Lincoln's Inn
Pupil Supervisor
Qualifications: [MA (Oxon)]
sarabjit.singh@1cor.com

SINGH MR TALBIR

No5 Chambers
Fountain Court, Steelhouse Lane, Birmingham
B4 6DR, ☎0845 210 5555 ✉info@no5.com
No5 Chambers
Greenwood House, 4-7 Salisbury Court,
London EC4Y 8AA, ☎0845 210 5555
No5 Chambers
38 Queen Square, Bristol BS1 4QS,
☎0845 210 5555
Call Date: July 1997, Gray's Inn
Qualifications: [LLB (Middx) LLM (Warw)]
ts@no5.com

SINGH-HAYER MR BANSA

Deans Court Chambers
24 St John Street, Manchester M3 4DF,
☎0161 214 6000 ✉clerks@deanscourt.co.uk
Deans Court Chambers
101 Walker Street, Preston PR1 2RR,
☎01772 565 600
✉preston@deanscourt.co.uk
Call Date: Nov 1988, Gray's Inn
Pupil Supervisor
Qualifications: [LLB (Hons)]
singhhayer@deanscourt.co.uk

SINGH-TIWANA MR EKWALL

No5 Chambers
Fountain Court, Steelhouse Lane, Birmingham
B4 6DR, ☎0845 210 5555 ✉info@no5.com
No5 Chambers
Greenwood House, 4-7 Salisbury Court,
London EC4Y 8AA, ☎0845 210 5555
No5 Chambers
38 Queen Square, Bristol BS1 4QS,
☎0845 210 5555
Call Date: Nov 1988, Middle Temple
Pupil Supervisor
Qualifications: [LLB(Hons)]
est@no5.com

SINGLA MR NIKKI SHAILINDER

Wilberforce Chambers
8 New Square, Lincoln's Inn, London
WC2A 3QP, ☎020 7306 0102
✉chambers@wilberforce.co.uk
Call Date: July 2000, Middle Temple
Pupil Supervisor
Qualifications: [BA (Hons) (Oxon) BCL (Oxon)]
nsingla@wilberforce.co.uk

E

SINGLA MR SHIVINDER TONY KUMAR

Brick Court Chambers
7-8 Essex Street, London WC2R 3LD,
☎ 020 7379 3550 ✉ clerks@brickcourt.co.uk
Call Date: July 2007, Lincoln's Inn
Qualifications: [BA BCL (Oxon)]
✉ tony.singla@brickcourt.co.uk

SINGLETON MR BARRY NEILL QC (1989)

1 KBW Chambers
1 King's Bench Walk, Temple, London
EC4Y 7DB, ☎ 020 7936 1500
✉ clerks@1kbw.co.uk
King's Bench Chambers
174 High Street, Lewes BN7 1YE,
☎ 01273 402600
Call Date: July 1968, Gray's Inn
Qualifications: [MA (Cantab)]
✉ bsingletonqc@1kbw.co.uk

SINGLETON MR MICHAEL JOHN

St Ive's Chambers
Whittall Street, Birmingham B4 6DH,
☎ 0121 236 0863
✉ clerks@stiveschambers.co.uk
Call Date: July 1987, Middle Temple
Pupil Supervisor
Qualifications: [LLB (Hons) (Leics)]
✉ michael.singleton@stiveschambers.co.uk

SINKER MR ANDREW TENNANT

New Bailey Chambers
4th Floor, Corn Exchange, Fenwick Street,
Liverpool, Merseyside L2 7QS,
☎ 0151 236 9402 ✉ clerks@newbailey.com
Call Date: Oct 1991, Lincoln's Inn
Qualifications: [LLB (Hons) (Leeds)]

SINNATT MR SIMON PETER RANDALL

Crown Office Row Chambers
119 Church Street, Brighton, Sussex
BN1 1UD, ☎ 01273 625625
✉ clerks@1cor.com
Call Date: Oct 1993, Lincoln's Inn
Pupil Supervisor
Qualifications: [BA (Hons)(York) CPE]
✉ simon.sinnatt@1cor.com

SIRIKANDA MR MORGAN

Queen Elizabeth Building
3rd Floor, Queen Elizabeth Building, Temple,
London EC4Y 9BS, ☎ 020 7797 7837
✉ clerks@qeb.co.uk
Call Date: Nov 2002, Middle Temple
Pupil Supervisor
Qualifications: [BA (Hons)(L'pool) CPE]
✉ m.sirikanda@qeb.co.uk

SISLEY MR TIMOTHY JULIAN CRISPIN

9 Stone Buildings
Lincoln's Inn, London WC2A 3NN,
☎ 020 7404 5055
✉ clerks@9stonebuildings.com
Call Date: Feb 1989, Middle Temple
Pupil Supervisor
Qualifications: [BA (Lond) BA (Lond)]
✉ t.sisley@ntlworld.com, clerks@9stonebuildings.com

SISSONS MR PHILIP STEPHEN

Falcon Chambers
Falcon Court, London EC4Y 1AA,
☎ 020 7353 2484
✉ clerks@falcon-chambers.com
Call Date: Nov 2005, Inner Temple
Qualifications: [MA BCL (Oxon)]
✉ sissons@falcon-chambers.com

SIVA MR KANNAN SARAVANAPAVAANANTHAN

Albion Chambers
Broad Street, Bristol BS1 1DR,
☎ 0117 927 2144
✉ clerks@albionchambers.co.uk
Call Date: Nov 1996, Gray's Inn
Pupil Supervisor
Qualifications: [BA (Hons) Dip Law]
✉ kannan.siva@albionchambers.co.uk

SJOLIN MS CATARINA MARIANNE

36 Bedford Row
London WC1R 4JH, ☎ 020 7421 8000
✉ chambers@36bedfordrow.co.uk
Call Date: Nov 1998, Gray's Inn
Qualifications: [MA, LLM (Cantab)]

SJOSTRAND MISS EKATERINA

13 Old Square Chambers
Ground Floor, 14 Old Square, Lincoln's Inn,
London WC2A 3UE, ☎ 020 7831 4445
✉ clerks@13oldsquare.com
Call Date: Oct 2003, Inner Temple
Qualifications: [LLB (Moscow)]
✉ ekaterinasjostrand@13oldsquare.com

SKEATE MR IAN ROBERT

64 Bridge Street
3rd Floor, 64 Bridge Street, Manchester M3 3BN, ☎ 0845 083 3000
✉ mail@64bridgestreet.com
Clerksroom (London)
3rd Floor, 218 Strand, London WC2R 1AT, ☎ 0845 083 3000 ✉ mail@clerksroom.com
Call Date: Nov 2002, Lincoln's Inn
Qualifications: [BA (Hons)(Cantab)]

SKELLEY MR MICHAEL DAVID

18 Red Lion Court
London EC4A 3EB, ☎ 020 7520 6000
✉ chambers@18rlc.co.uk
Call Date: Oct 1991, Inner Temple
Qualifications: [BA (Oxon)]

SKELLORN MISS KATHRYN MAIR

St John's Chambers
101 Victoria Street, Bristol BS1 6PU, ☎ 0117 923 4700
✉ clerks@stjohnschambers.co.uk
Call Date: Nov 1993, Gray's Inn
Qualifications: [MA (Hons)(Oxon)]
🖃 kathryn.skellorn@stjohnschambers.co.uk

SKELLY MR ANDREW JON

Hardwicke
New Square, Lincoln's Inn, London WC2A 3SB, ☎ 020 7242 2523
✉ enquiries@hardwicke.co.uk
Call Date: Oct 1994, Inner Temple
Qualifications: [LLB]
🖃 andrew.skelly@hardwicke.co.uk

SKELT MR IAN STUART

KBW
The Engine House, No 1 Foundry Square, Leeds LS11 5DL, ☎ 0113 297 1200
✉ clerks@kbwchambers.com
Call Date: Oct 1994, Lincoln's Inn
Pupil Supervisor
Qualifications: [LLB (Hons)(Newc)]
🖃 ianskelt@msn.com

SKELTON MR PETER

1 Crown Office Row
1 Crown Office Row, Temple, London EC4Y 7HH, ☎ 020 7797 7500
✉ mail@1cor.com
Call Date: Oct 1997, Middle Temple
Qualifications: [BA (York) MPhil (Cantab)]

SKINNER MR ANDREW MURRAY

College Chambers
19 Carlton Crescent, Southampton, Hampshire SO15 2ET, ☎ 023 8023 0338
✉ clerks@college-chambers.co.uk
Call Date: July 2000, Middle Temple
Qualifications: [BA(Hons) (Loughbr)]
🖃 askinner@College-Chambers.co.uk

SKINNER MISS LORNA JANE

Matrix Chambers
Griffin Building, Gray's Inn, London WC1R 5LN, ☎ 020 7404 3447
✉ matrix@matrixlaw.co.uk / lscott@matrixlaw.co.uk
Call Date: Nov 1997, Middle Temple
Pupil Supervisor
Qualifications: [MA (Cantab)]
🖃 lornaskinner@matrixlaw.co.uk

SKINNER MR PAUL RICHARD

Henderson Chambers
2 Harcourt Buildings, Temple, London EC4Y 9DB, ☎ 020 7583 9020
✉ clerks@hendersonchambers.co.uk
Call Date: Mar 2010, Inner Temple
Qualifications: [Bmus (Lond) BA (Cantab)]

SKINNER MR SAMUEL RICHARD EDWARD

KCH Garden Square
1 Oxford Street, Nottingham NG1 5BH, ☎ 0115 941 8851
✉ clerks@kchgardensquare.co.uk
Call Date: Oct 2007, Gray's Inn
Qualifications: [BA (Oxon)]
🖃 SSkinner@kch.co.uk

SKITTRELL MISS ELAINE ANGELA

Park Court Chambers
16 Park Place, Leeds LS1 2SJ, ☎ 0113 243 3277
✉ clerks@parkcourtchambers.co.uk
Call Date: July 1999, Middle Temple
Qualifications: [BA (Hons)(So'ton)]
🖃 clerks@parkcourtchambers.co.uk

SKYNER MR ROBERT STEPHEN

39 Park Square
Leeds LS1 2NU, ☎ 0113 245 6633
✉ seniorclerk@39parksquarechambers.co.uk
Call Date: Mar 2003, Middle Temple
Qualifications: [LLB (Hons) (Essex)]

E

SLACK MR HENRY ALEXANDER FERGUSSON

Hardwicke
New Square, Lincoln's Inn, London
WC2A 3SB, ☎020 7242 2523
✉enquiries@hardwicke.co.uk
Call Date: Oct 1999, Lincoln's Inn
Qualifications: [BA (Hons)]
henry.slack@hardwicke.co.uk

SLACK MR KEVIN JOHN

Exchange Chambers
One Derby Square, Derby Square, Liverpool
L2 9XX, ☎0151 236 7747
✉info@exchangechambers.co.uk
Exchange Chambers
7 Ralli Courts, West Riverside, Manchester
M3 5FT, ☎0161 833 2722
Exchange Chambers
Oxford House, Oxford Row, Leeds LS1 3BE,
☎0113 203 1970
✉spencer@exchangechambers.co.uk
Call Date: Oct 1997, Gray's Inn
Qualifications: [MA]
slack@exchangechambers.co.uk

E

SLADE MR RICHARD PENKIVIL QC (2010)

Brick Court Chambers
7-8 Essex Street, London WC2R 3LD,
☎020 7379 3550 ✉clerks@brickcourt.co.uk
Call Date: Nov 1987, Lincoln's Inn
Pupil Supervisor
Qualifications: [BA (Hons) (Cantab)]
Richard.Slade@Brickcourt.co.uk

SLADE JONES MR ROBIN

Chartlands Chambers
3 St Giles Terrace, Northampton NN1 2BN,
☎01604 603322
✉enquiries@chartlands-chambers.co.uk
Call Date: Oct 1993, Gray's Inn
Qualifications: [M Eng]

SLATER MISS JULIE ANN

Cornwall Street Chambers
85-87 Cornwall Street, Birmingham B3 3BY,
☎0121 233 7500
✉clerks@cornwallstreet.co.uk
Call Date: July 1988, Lincoln's Inn
Qualifications: [LLB (Hons)]
julie.slater@cornwallstreet.co.uk

SLATER MR JUSTIN WILLIAM

Seven Bedford Row
7 Bedford Row, London WC1R 4BS,
☎020 7242 3555 ✉clerks@7br.co.uk
Call Date: July 1999, Inner Temple
Qualifications: [MA (Cantab)]
clerks@7br.co.uk, jslater@7br.co.uk

SLATER MR MATTHEW JAMES

3 Stone Buildings
Ground Floor, 3 Stone Buildings, Lincoln's
Inn, London WC2A 3XL, ☎020 7242 4937
✉clerks@3sb.law.co.uk
Call Date: Nov 2005, Middle Temple
Qualifications: [BA (Hons) Oxford]

SLATER MR MICHAEL NEAL

Call Date: July 1983, Inner Temple
Pupil Supervisor, Recorder
Qualifications: [LLB (Sheff)]
slater@paradise-sq.co.uk

SLATTER MR ALEXIS ANDREW MALLATRATT

Tooks Chambers
81 Farringdon Street, London EC4A 4BL,
☎020 7842 7575 ✉clerks@tooks.co.uk
Call Date: Nov 1999, Inner Temple
Qualifications: [BSc (Bris) MA (Lond)]

SLAUGHTER MISS JESSICA JANE

East Anglian Chambers
53 North Hill, Colchester, Essex CO1 1QA,
☎01473 214481 ✉colchester@ealaw.co.uk
East Anglian Chambers
140 New London Road, Chelmsford, Essex
CM2 0AW, ☎01473 214481
✉chelmsford@ealaw.co.uk
East Anglian Chambers
Gresham House, 5 Museum Street, Ipswich,
Suffolk IP1 1HQ, ☎01473 214481
✉ipswich@ealaw.co.uk
Call Date: July 2009, Middle Temple
Qualifications: [LLB (Hons) (Dunelm)]

SLEE MISS LYDIA MARJORIE

Stour Chambers
Mill Studio, 17a Stour Street, Canterbury, Kent
CT1 2NR, ☎01227 764899
✉clerks@stourchambers.co.uk
Call Date: Nov 2007, Middle Temple
Qualifications: [LLB (Hons) (Kent) LLM (Kent)]
clerks@stourchambers.co.uk

SLEEMAN MISS RACHEL SARAH ELIZABETH

Five Paper
Ground Floor, 5 Paper Buildings, Temple, London EC4Y 7HB, ☎ 020 7815 3200
Call Date: Nov 1996, Gray's Inn
Pupil Supervisor
Qualifications: [LLB (Lond)]
🖃 rachelsleeman@fivepaper.com

SLEEMAN MS SUSAN JANET

Doughty Street Chambers
53-54 Doughty Street, London WC1N 2LS, ☎ 020 7404 1313
✉ enquiries@doughtystreet.co.uk
Doughty Street Chambers
Pall Mall Court, 61-67 King Street, Manchester M2 4PD, ☎ 0161 618 1066
Doughty Street Chambers
5th Floor, Broad Quay House, Prince Street, Bristol BS1 4DJ, ☎ 01179 058 717
Call Date: Oct 2001, Inner Temple
Qualifications: [BA (Hons) (Lond) MSc CPE]
🖃 s.sleeman@doughtystreet.co.uk

SLEIGHT MR NIGEL

Regency Chambers
45 Priestgate, Peterborough PE1 1LB, ☎ 01733 315215
✉ clerks@regencychambers.law.co.uk
Regency Chambers
Sheraton House, Castle Park, Cambridge CB3 0AX, ☎ 01223 301517
Call Date: Oct 1998, Lincoln's Inn
Pupil Supervisor
Qualifications: [LLB (Hons)(Hull)]
🖃 clerks@regencychambers.law.co.uk

SLEIGHTHOLME MR JOHN TREVOR

37 Park Square Chambers
37 Park Square, Leeds LS1 2NY, ☎ 0113 243 9422 ✉ chambers@no37.co.uk
Call Date: Nov 1982, Gray's Inn
Pupil Supervisor
Qualifications: [LLB (Hons)(Leeds)]
🖃 chambers@no37.co.uk

SLIWINSKI MR ROBERT ANDREW

SWL Chambers
Aston Court, Frederick Place, Loudwater, Buckinghamshire HP11 1LA, ☎ 01494 616007
✉ robert@swl-legal.co.uk
Call Date: Oct 1990, Middle Temple
Qualifications: [BSc LLB (Hons) FRICS FCIArb DipIntArb]

SLOANE MISS VALENTINA

Monckton Chambers
1 & 2 Raymond Buildings, Gray's Inn, London WC1R 5NR, ☎ 020 7405 7211
✉ chambers@monckton.com
Call Date: Oct 2000, Gray's Inn
Qualifications: [BA (Oxon) LLM (Brussels)]
🖃 vsloane@monckton.com

SLOBODA MR NICHOLAS EDMUND ALBERT

One Essex Court
Ground Floor, One Essex Court, Temple, London EC4Y 9AR, ☎ 020 7583 2000
✉ clerks@oeclaw.co.uk
Call Date: Nov 2007, Lincoln's Inn
Qualifications: [BA (Oxon)]
🖃 nsloboda@oeclaw.co.uk

SLOMNICKA MISS BARBARA IRENA

14 Gray's Inn Square
14 Gray's Inn Square, Gray's Inn, London WC1R 5JP, ☎ 020 7242 0858
✉ clerks@14gis.co.uk
Call Date: Nov 1976, Middle Temple
Pupil Supervisor
Qualifications: [LLB MJur]
🖃 clerks@14graysinnsquare.co.uk

SLOW MISS CAMILLE

Atkin Chambers
1 Atkin Building, Gray's Inn, London WC1R 5AT, ☎ 020 7404 0102
✉ clerks@atkinchambers.com
Call Date: July 2002, Middle Temple
Pupil Supervisor
Qualifications: [LLB (Hons) (Bris)]
🖃 clerks@atkinchambers.com

SMALL MRS ARLENE ANNMARIE

Clerksroom (Taunton)
Equity House, Administration Centre, Blackbrook Park Avenue, Taunton, Somerset TA1 2PX, ☎ 0845 083 3000
✉ mail@clerksroom.com
Clerksroom (London)
3rd Floor, 218 Strand, London WC2R 1AT, ☎ 0845 083 3000 ✉ mail@clerksroom.com
King's Lynn Chambers
26 The Birches, South Wootton, King's Lynn, Norfolk PE30 3JG, ☎ 01553 672 085
✉ timothy.leader@tesco.net
Call Date: Oct 1997, Middle Temple
Qualifications: [LLB (Hons)(Brunel)]
🖃 small@clerksroom.com

E

SMALL MR DEVON

Rowchester Chambers
4 Rowchester Court, Whittall Street, Birmingham B4 6DH, ☎0121 233 2327
✉clerks@rowchesterchambers.co.uk
Call Date: Nov 1990, Inner Temple
Qualifications: [LLB]

SMALL MISS GINA LEE

King's Bench and Godolphin (KBG)Chambers
115 North Hill, Plymouth, Devon PL4 8JY, ☎01752 221551
✉clerks@kbgchambers.co.uk
Call Date: Oct 1991, Lincoln's Inn
Pupil Supervisor
Qualifications: [BA (Hons) (Lond) Dip Law]
gina.small@kingsbenchchambers.co.uk

SMALL MR JOHN ROBERT

36 Bedford Row
London WC1R 4JH, ☎020 7421 8000
✉chambers@36bedfordrow.co.uk
Call Date: Oct 2002, Inner Temple
Qualifications: [LLB (Lond) LLM]
jsmall@36bedfordrow.co.uk

SMALL MR JONATHAN EDWIN QC (2006)

Falcon Chambers
Falcon Court, London EC4Y 1AA, ☎020 7353 2484
✉clerks@falcon-chambers.com
Call Date: Oct 1990, Lincoln's Inn
Qualifications: [BA (Nott'm) Dip Law (Lond)]
small@falcon-chambers.com

SMALL MISS PENELOPE SUSAN

Chambers of Andrew Mitchell QC
33 Chancery Lane, London WC2A 1EN, ☎020 7440 9950 ✉clerks@33cllaw.com
Call Date: Oct 1992, Inner Temple
Pupil Supervisor
Qualifications: [BA (Warw) Dip Law(Lond)]
ps@33cllaw.com

SMALLER MISS ELIZABETH ANNE

9-12 Bell Yard
London WC2A 2JR, ☎020 7400 1800
✉clerks@9-12bellyard.com
Call Date: Oct 1995, Gray's Inn
Pupil Supervisor
Qualifications: [BA]
e.smaller@9-12bellyard.com

SMALLWOOD MISS ANNE ELIZABETH

No5 Chambers
Fountain Court, Steelhouse Lane, Birmingham B4 6DR, ☎0845 210 5555 ✉info@no5.com
No5 Chambers
Greenwood House, 4-7 Salisbury Court, London EC4Y 8AA, ☎0845 210 5555
No5 Chambers
38 Queen Square, Bristol BS1 4QS, ☎0845 210 5555
Call Date: Nov 1977, Middle Temple
Pupil Supervisor
Qualifications: [LLB]
as@no5.com, annes@no5.com

SMALLWOOD MR ROBERT ANDREW

No5 Chambers
Fountain Court, Steelhouse Lane, Birmingham B4 6DR, ☎0845 210 5555 ✉info@no5.com
No5 Chambers
Greenwood House, 4-7 Salisbury Court, London EC4Y 8AA, ☎0845 210 5555
No5 Chambers
38 Queen Square, Bristol BS1 4QS, ☎0845 210 5555
Call Date: Oct 1994, Lincoln's Inn
Qualifications: [LLB (Hons)(Sheff)]
ras@no5.com

SMART MISS JACQUELINE ANNE

Trinity Chambers
The Custom House, 39 Quayside, Newcastle Upon Tyne NE1 3DE, ☎0191 232 1927
✉info@trinitychambers.co.uk
Trinity Chambers
Multi Media Exchange, 72-80 Corporation Road, Middlesbrough TS1 2RF, ☎01642 247569
✉info@trinitychambers.co.uk
Call Date: Nov 1981, Middle Temple
Pupil Supervisor
Qualifications: [LLB (Lond)]
j.smart@trinitychambers.co.uk

SMART MISS JULIA ELIZABETH

Goldsmith Chambers
Ground Floor, Goldsmith Building, Temple, London EC4Y 7BL, ☎020 7353 6802
✉clerks@goldsmithchambers.com
Call Date: Oct 1993, Gray's Inn
Qualifications: [LLB (Lond)]
J.Smart@goldsmithchambers.law.co.uk

E

SMART MR ROGER BERNARD

QEB Hollis Whiteman
1-2 Laurence Pountney Hill, London EC4R 0EU, ☎ 020 7933 8855
✉ barristers@qebhw.co.uk
Call Date: July 1989, Inner Temple
Pupil Supervisor
Qualifications: [LLB (Hons)]
roger.smart@qebhw.co.uk

SMEATON MISS JESSICA PRECEY

1 Gray's Inn Square
Ground Floor, 1 Gray's Inn Square, London WC1R 5AA, ☎ 020 7405 0001
Call Date: Oct 2008, Middle Temple
Qualifications: [LLB (Hons) (Leeds)]
jsmeaton@1gis.co.uk

SMILEY MR BEN RICHARD PHILIP DE CRESPIGNY

Four New Square
Four New Square, Lincoln's Inn, London WC2A 3RJ, ☎ 020 7822 2000
✉ barristers@4newsquare.com
Call Date: July 2009, Middle Temple
Qualifications: [BA (Hons) (Oxon) Grad Dip Law (Lond)]

SMITH MS ABIGAIL

Tooks Chambers
81 Farringdon Street, London EC4A 4BL, ☎ 020 7842 7575 ✉ clerks@tooks.co.uk
Call Date: Oct 2003, Lincoln's Inn
Qualifications: [LLB (Hons) LLM (Lond)]
abigail.smith@tooks.co.uk

SMITH MR ADAM HUNTER WEIR

Maitland Chambers
7 Stone Buildings, Lincoln's Inn, London WC2A 3SZ, ☎ 020 7406 1200
✉ clerks@maitlandchambers.com
Call Date: Nov 2001, Gray's Inn
Pupil Supervisor
Qualifications: [BA (Oxon)]
asmith@maitlandchambers.com

SMITH MR ADAM JOHN

Crown Office Row Chambers
119 Church Street, Brighton, Sussex BN1 1UD, ☎ 01273 625625
✉ clerks@1cor.com
Call Date: Nov 1987, Inner Temple
Pupil Supervisor
Qualifications: [LLB (Hull)]
adam.smith@1cor.com

SMITH MR ALAN ARTHUR

Old Square Chambers
10-11 Bedford Row, London WC1R 4BU, ☎ 020 7269 0300 ✉ clerks@oldsquare.co.uk
Old Square Chambers
3 Orchard Court, St Augustine's Yard, Bristol BS1 5DP, ☎ 0117 930 5100
✉ clerks@oldsquare.co.uk
Call Date: July 1981, Middle Temple
Pupil Supervisor
Qualifications: [BA (Hons)]
asmith@oldsquare.co.uk

SMITH MR ALISDAIR ROBERT MACSORLEY

9-12 Bell Yard
London WC2A 2JR, ☎ 020 7400 1800
✉ clerks@9-12bellyard.com
Call Date: July 1981, Gray's Inn
Pupil Supervisor
Qualifications: [LLB (Lond)]

SMITH MR ANDREW

Crown Office Chambers
2 Crown Office Row, Temple, London EC4Y 7HJ, ☎ 020 7797 8100
✉ mail@crownofficechambers.com
Call Date: Nov 2006, Gray's Inn
Qualifications: [LLB]

SMITH MR ANDREW DESMOND

Bank House Chambers
Old Bank House, Hartshead, Sheffield S1 2EL, ☎ 0114 275 1223
✉ w.digby@bankhousechambers.co.uk
Call Date: Oct 1991, Middle Temple
Qualifications: [LLB (Hons) (Sheff)]
a.smith@bankhousechambers.co.uk

SMITH MR ANDREW DUNCAN QC (2012)

St Philips Chambers
55 Temple Row, Birmingham B2 5LS, ☎ 0121 246 7000 ✉ clerks@st-philips.com
Call Date: Oct 1997, Middle Temple
Pupil Supervisor, Recorder
Qualifications: [MA (Hons)(Oxon)]
asmith@st-philips.co.uk

SMITH MR ANDREW PAUL

Matrix Chambers
Griffin Building, Gray's Inn, London WC1R 5LN, ☎ 020 7404 3447
✉ matrix@matrixlaw.co.uk / Iscott@ matrixlaw.co.uk
Call Date: Oct 2008, Lincoln's Inn
Qualifications: [LLB (Sheff)]

E

SMITH MR ANDREW WILLIAM

Exchange Chambers
7 Ralli Courts, West Riverside, Manchester M3 5FT, ☎0161 833 2722
Exchange Chambers
One Derby Square, Derby Square, Liverpool L2 9XX, ☎0151 236 7747
✉info@exchangechambers.co.uk
Exchange Chambers
Oxford House, Oxford Row, Leeds LS1 3BE, ☎0113 203 1970
✉spencer@exchangechambers.co.uk
Call Date: Oct 1996, Lincoln's Inn
Qualifications: [LLB (Hons)(Manc)]
smith@exchangechambers.co.uk

SMITH MR ANTHONY THOMAS QC (1977)

No5 Chambers
Greenwood House, 4-7 Salisbury Court, London EC4Y 8AA, ☎0845 210 5555
No5 Chambers
38 Queen Square, Bristol BS1 4QS, ☎0845 210 5555
No5 Chambers
Fountain Court, Steelhouse Lane, Birmingham B4 6DR, ☎0845 210 5555 ✉info@no5.com
Call Date: Feb 1958, Inner Temple
Recorder
Qualifications: [MA (Cantab)]
tsmqc@no5.com

SMITH MISS CATHERINE EMMA

Furnival Chambers
32 Furnival Street, London EC4A 1JQ, ☎020 7405 3232
Call Date: Nov 1994, Middle Temple
Qualifications: [LLB (Hons) (Essex) Dip French Law (France)]
esmith@furnivallaw.co.uk

SMITH MR CHARLES AUGUSTUS CLIVE

Maitland Chambers
7 Stone Buildings, Lincoln's Inn, London WC2A 3SZ, ☎020 7406 1200
✉clerks@maitlandchambers.com
Call Date: Oct 2002, Lincoln's Inn
Qualifications: [BA (Oxon) Dip Law (City) MSt (Oxon)]
csmith@maitlandchambers.com

SMITH MR CHRISTOPHER FRANK QC (2009)

Essex Court Chambers
24 Lincoln's Inn Fields, London WC2A 3EG, ☎020 7813 8000
✉clerksroom@essexcourt.net
Call Date: July 1989, Inner Temple
Qualifications: [LLB (So'ton)]
csmith@essexcourt.net

SMITH MR CHRISTOPHER JAMES

Zenith Chambers
10 Park Square, Leeds LS1 2LH, ☎0113 245 5438
✉clerks@zenithchambers.co.uk
Call Date: Oct 1997, Lincoln's Inn
Qualifications: [LLB (Hons)(Keele)]
csmith@zenithchambers.co.uk

SMITH MR CHRISTOPHER MICHAEL

Quadrant Chambers
Quadrant House, 10 Fleet Street, London EC4Y 1AU, ☎020 7583 4444
✉info@quadrantchambers.com
Call Date: Nov 1999, Inner Temple
Pupil Supervisor
Qualifications: [BA (Cantab)]
christopher.smith@quadrantchambers.com

SMITH MR CLIVE FRANCIS

Chambers of Marion Smullen and Kerim Fuad QC
1 Inner Temple Lane, London EC4Y 1AF, ☎020 7427 4400 ✉clerks@1itl.com
Call Date: July 2003, Lincoln's Inn
Qualifications: [LLB Hons (E.Anglia)]
Clive.Smith@1itl.com, clerks@1itl.com

SMITH MR DAVID ANDREW

9-12 Bell Yard
London WC2A 2JR, ☎020 7400 1800
✉clerks@9-12bellyard.com
Call Date: July 1988, Middle Temple
Pupil Supervisor
Qualifications: [LLB (Hons)]
d.smith@9-12bellyard.com

SMITH MR DAVID ANTHONY

Landmark Chambers
180 Fleet Street, London EC4A 2HG, ☎020 7430 1221
✉clerks@landmarkchambers.co.uk
Call Date: Nov 1980, Inner Temple
Qualifications: [LLM (Lond) LLB (Brunel)]
dsmith@landmarkchambers.co.uk

E

SMITH MR DUNCAN

York Chambers
Rotterdam House, 116 The Quayside, Newcastle Upon Tyne NE1 3DY, ☎0191 206 4677
Dere Street Barristers
14 Toft Green, York YO1 6JT, ☎0844 3351551
✉clerks@derestreet.co.uk
Melbury House
55 Manor Road, Oadby, Leicester, Leicestershire LE2 2LL, ☎07801 037802
✉melburyhousechambers@yahoo.co.uk
Call Date: July 1979, Inner Temple
Pupil Supervisor, Recorder
Qualifications: [LLB]
clerks@yorkchambers.co.uk

SMITH MISS EILEEN JOAN

Trinity Chambers
The Custom House, 39 Quayside, Newcastle Upon Tyne NE1 3DE, ☎0191 232 1927
✉info@trinitychambers.co.uk
Trinity Chambers
Multi Media Exchange, 72-80 Corporation Road, Middlesbrough TS1 2RF, ☎01642 247569
✉info@trinitychambers.co.uk
Call Date: Oct 2002, Middle Temple
Qualifications: [BA (Hon)(Stafs)]

SMITH MISS ELEANOR RACHEL

Trinity Chambers
The Custom House, 39 Quayside, Newcastle Upon Tyne NE1 3DE, ☎0191 232 1927
✉info@trinitychambers.co.uk
Trinity Chambers
Multi Media Exchange, 72-80 Corporation Road, Middlesbrough TS1 2RF, ☎01642 247569
✉info@trinitychambers.co.uk
Call Date: Feb 1992, Middle Temple
Qualifications: [LLB (Hons) (Sheff)]
r.smith@trinitychambers.co.uk

SMITH MISS EMMA LOUISE

Old Square Chambers
10-11 Bedford Row, London WC1R 4BU, ☎020 7269 0300 ✉clerks@oldsquare.co.uk
Old Square Chambers
3 Orchard Court, St Augustine's Yard, Bristol BS1 5DP, ☎0117 930 5100
✉clerks@oldsquare.co.uk
Call Date: Oct 1995, Lincoln's Inn
Pupil Supervisor
Qualifications: [LLB (Hons)(Leic) MA (Lond)]
smith@oldsquare.co.uk

SMITH MR GRAHAM

23 Essex Street
London WC2R 3AA, ☎020 7413 0353
✉clerks@23es.com
Call Date: Nov 1999, Inner Temple
Pupil Supervisor
Qualifications: [LLB (Thames)]

SMITH MR HENRY FORBES

One Essex Court
Ground Floor, One Essex Court, Temple, London EC4Y 9AR, ☎020 7583 2000
✉clerks@oeclaw.co.uk
Call Date: Nov 2004, Middle Temple
Qualifications: [LLB (Hons) BCL PhD]
hsmith@oeclaw.co.uk

SMITH MR HOWARD JAMES

Radcliffe Chambers
Ground Floor, 11 New Square, Lincoln's Inn, London WC2A 3QB, ☎020 7831 0081
✉clerks@radcliffechambers.com
Call Date: July 1986, Inner Temple
Qualifications: [MA (Oxon) Dip Law]
hsmith@radcliffechambers.com

SMITH MR IAN ALFIO

11 Stone Buildings
11 Stone Buildings, Lincoln's Inn, London WC2A 3TG, ☎020 7831 6381
✉clerks@11sb.com
Call Date: July 2003, Middle Temple
Qualifications: [LLB Hons (B'ham)]
smith@11sb.com

SMITH MR JAMES ALASTAIR

9-12 Bell Yard
London WC2A 2JR, ☎020 7400 1800
✉clerks@9-12bellyard.com
Call Date: Oct 2001, Inner Temple
Qualifications: [BA (Manch) CPE]
a.smith@9-12bellyard.com

SMITH MR JAMIE CHARLES

Four New Square
Four New Square, Lincoln's Inn, London WC2A 3RJ, ☎020 7822 2000
✉barristers@4newsquare.com
Call Date: Oct 1995, Lincoln's Inn
Pupil Supervisor
Qualifications: [BA (Hons)(Cantab)]
j.smith@4newsquare.com

E

SMITH MRS JANE LESLEY

Southernhay Chambers
33 Southernhay East, Exeter EX1 1NX,
☎ 01392 255777
✉ clerks@southernhaychambers.co.uk
Call Date: July 2007, Inner Temple
Qualifications: [LLB (Wolves)]
j.smith@southernhaychambers.co.uk

SMITH MS JENNIFER ANNE

Dere Street Barristers
14 Toft Green, York YO1 6JT, ☎ 0844 3351551
✉ clerks@derestreet.co.uk
York Chambers
Rotterdam House, 116 The Quayside,
Newcastle Upon Tyne NE1 3DY,
☎ 0191 206 4677
Call Date: Oct 2002, Inner Temple
Qualifications: [LLB]

SMITH MISS JOANNA ANGELA QC (2009)

Wilberforce Chambers
8 New Square, Lincoln's Inn, London
WC2A 3QP, ☎ 020 7306 0102
✉ chambers@wilberforce.co.uk
Call Date: Nov 1990, Lincoln's Inn
Pupil Supervisor
Qualifications: [MA (Hons)(Oxon)]

Types of work: Adjudication, Arbitration, Building, Chancery (commercial), Chancery (general), Commercial contracts, Commercial law, Commercial litigation, Construction law, Contracts, Dispute resolution, Economic torts, Engineering disputes, Partnerships, Professional negligence, Solicitor's indemnity, Technical contracts, Technology and Construction Court, Torts

SMITH MR JOEL DAVID GEOFFREY

Furnival Chambers
32 Furnival Street, London EC4A 1JQ,
☎ 020 7405 3232
Call Date: July 2002, Inner Temple
Qualifications: [LLB (Lond)]
jsmith@furnivallaw.co.uk

SMITH MR JOHN STEPHEN QC (2000)

New Square Chambers
12 New Square, Lincoln's Inn, London
WC2A 3SW, ☎ 020 7419 8000
✉ robin.hollington@newsquarechambers.co.uk
Call Date: July 1983, Middle Temple
Recorder
Qualifications: [BA (Oxon)]
stephen.smith@newsquarechambers.co.uk

SMITH MR JONATHAN MICHAEL

St James's Chambers
68 Quay Street, Manchester M3 3EJ,
☎ 0161 834 7000
✉ clerks@stjameschambers.com
Call Date: Oct 1991, Gray's Inn
Pupil Supervisor
Qualifications: [LLB (Hons)]
clerks@stjameschambers.com

SMITH MR JOSEPH PAUL

Broadway House Chambers
Broadway House, 9 Bank Street, Bradford,
West Yorkshire BD1 1TW, ☎ 01274 722560
✉ clerks@broadwayhouse.co.uk
Call Date: Nov 2008, Gray's Inn
Qualifications: [BA LLM]

SMITH MISS JULIA MAIR WHELDON

Henderson Chambers
2 Harcourt Buildings, Temple, London
EC4Y 9DB, ☎ 020 7583 9020
✉ clerks@hendersonchambers.co.uk
Call Date: Nov 1988, Inner Temple
Pupil Supervisor
Qualifications: [LLB (L'pool)]

SMITH MR JULIAN ROBERT

Lincoln's Inn Fields Chambers
88 Kingsway, London WC2B 6AA,
☎ 0845 123 1234
✉ jsmith@lincolnsinnfields.com
Call Date: Mar 1998, Lincoln's Inn
Qualifications: [LLB (Hons)(LSE) DBTS (Oxon)]
jsmith@lincolnsinnfields.com

SMITH MR JULIAN WILLIAM

New Court Chambers
3 Broad Chare, Newcastle Upon Tyne
NE1 3DQ, ☎ 0191 232 1980
✉ clerks@newcourt-chambers.co.uk
Call Date: Nov 1991, Inner Temple
Pupil Supervisor
Qualifications: [LLB (Newc)]
julian.smith@newcourt-chambers.co.uk

SMITH MS KATE

Angel Chambers
Ethos Building, Kings Road, Swansea SA1 8AS,
☎ 01792 464623
✉ clerks@angelchambers.co.uk
Call Date: July 2008, Gray's Inn
Qualifications: [LLB (Swansea)]
kate.smith@angelchambers.co.uk

SMITH MS KATHERINE EMMA

Monckton Chambers
1 & 2 Raymond Buildings, Gray's Inn, London WC1R 5NR, ☎ 020 7405 7211
✉ chambers@monckton.com
Call Date: Nov 1995, Inner Temple
Pupil Supervisor
Qualifications: [BA (Oxon) BCL (Oxon)]
✉ ksmith@monckton.com

SMITH MISS KERRY ANN

Chambers of Ian Macdonald QC
Garden Court North, 22 Oxford Court, Manchester M2 3WQ, ☎ 0161 236 1840
✉ clerks@gcnchambers.co.uk
Call Date: July 2002, Lincoln's Inn
Qualifications: [LLB (Hons)(Sheff)]

SMITH MR LEONARD WAYNE QC (2008)

Carmelite Chambers
9 Carmelite Street, London EC4Y 0DR, ☎ 020 7936 6300
✉ clerks@carmelitechambers.co.uk
Call Date: July 1991, Gray's Inn
Qualifications: [LLB]

SMITH MISS LEONORAH PATRICIA DOLORES

Pump Court Chambers
Upper Ground Floor, 3 Pump Court, Temple, London EC4Y 7AJ, ☎ 020 7353 0711
✉ clerks@3pumpcourt.com
Pump Court Chambers
5 Temple Chambers, Temple Street, Swindon SN1 1SQ, ☎ 01793 539899
✉ clerks@3pumpcourt.com
Pump Court Chambers
31 Southgate Street, Winchester, Hampshire SO23 9EB, ☎ 01962 868 161
✉ clerks@3pumpcourt.com
Call Date: Nov 1993, Inner Temple
Qualifications: [BA (Surrey) CPE (Sussex)]
✉ lps@3pumpcourt.com

SMITH MR LESLIE WILLIAM

King's Bench Chambers
Wellington House, 175 Holdenhurst Road, Bournemouth, Dorset BH8 8DQ, ☎ 01202 250025
Call Date: Mar 1997, Inner Temple
Qualifications: [BA CPE]

SMITH MR MARCUS ALEXANDER QC (2010)

Fountain Court Chambers
Fountain Court, Temple, London EC4Y 9DH, ☎ 020 7583 3335
✉ chambers@fountaincourt.co.uk
Call Date: Oct 1991, Lincoln's Inn
Pupil Supervisor
Qualifications: [MA BCL (Oxon)]
✉ msmith@fountaincourt.co.uk

SMITH MISS MARION HELEN

39 Essex Street
London WC2R 3AT, ☎ 020 7832 1111
✉ clerks@39essex.com
82 King Street
Manchester M2 4WQ, ☎ 0161 870 9969
Call Date: July 1981, Gray's Inn
Pupil Supervisor
Qualifications: [LLB LLM (Lond)]
✉ marion.smith@39essex.com

SMITH MR MARK VALENTINE

Essex Court Chambers
24 Lincoln's Inn Fields, London WC2A 3EG, ☎ 020 7813 8000
✉ clerksroom@essexcourt.net
Call Date: July 1981, Lincoln's Inn
Qualifications: [MA (Cantab)]
✉ msmith@essexcourt.net

SMITH MR MARK WESTMORELAND

Francis Taylor Building
Inner Temple, London EC4Y 7BY, ☎ 020 7353 8415 ✉ clerks@ftb.eu.com
Call Date: Oct 2006, Lincoln's Inn
Qualifications: [BA (Manch)]
✉ mark.westmoreland-smith@ftb.eu.com, mws@ftb.eu.com

SMITH MR MARK WILLIAM

Aegis Chambers
39 Mostyn Avenue, Wembley, Middlesex HA9 8AY
Call Date: Mar 1997, Gray's Inn
Pupil Supervisor
Qualifications: [LLB (Nott'm) Dip Loc. Govt Law]
✉ msmithcounsel@msn.com

SMITH MR MATTHEW JAMES

Maitland Chambers
7 Stone Buildings, Lincoln's Inn, London WC2A 3SZ, ☎ 020 7406 1200
✉ clerks@maitlandchambers.com
Call Date: Oct 2001, Inner Temple
Pupil Supervisor
Qualifications: [BA (Cantab) CPE]
✉ msmith@maitlandchambers.com

E

SMITH MR MATTHEW JAMES

Kings Chambers
36 Young Street, Manchester M3 3FT,
☎ 0845 034 3444
✉ clerks@kingschambers.com
Kings Chambers
5 Park Square East, Leeds LS1 2NE,
☎ 0845 034 3444
✉ clerks@kingschambers.com
Kings Chambers
Embassy House, 60 Church Street,
Birmingham B3 2DJ, ☎ 0845 034 3444
✉ clerks@kingschambers.com
15 Winckley Square
Preston PR1 3JJ, ☎ 01772 252828
✉ clerks@15winckleysq.co.uk
Call Date: Oct 1991, Lincoln's Inn
Pupil Supervisor
Qualifications: [BA (Hons)(Cantab) MA (Cantab)]
msmith@kingschambers.com

SMITH MR MATTHEW ROBERT

Sovereign Chambers
46 Park Place, Leeds LS1 2RY,
☎ 0113 245 1841
✉ clerks@sovereignchambers.co.uk
Call Date: Nov 1996, Inner Temple
Pupil Supervisor
Qualifications: [BA (Dunelm) MPhil (Cantab)]
matthew.smith@sovereignchambers.co.uk

SMITH MR MICHAEL ANTHONY

No.6 Park Square
Leeds LS1 2LW, ☎ 0113 245 9763
✉ Tim@no6.co.uk
Call Date: July 1980, Inner Temple
Pupil Supervisor, Recorder
Qualifications: [LLB (Newc)]
smith@no6.co.uk

SMITH MR MICHAEL CRAIG

Thomas More Chambers
7 Lincoln's Inn Fields, London WC2A 3BP,
☎ 020 7404 7000
✉ clerks@thomasmore.co.uk
Call Date: Oct 2009, Lincoln's Inn
Qualifications: [BA (Lond) CPE OBPP]
clerks@thomasmore.co.uk

SMITH MR MICHAEL DAVID

Kenworthy's Chambers
Arlington House, Bloom Street, Salford,
Manchester M3 6AJ, ☎ 0161 832 4036
Call Date: Oct 2001, Lincoln's Inn
Qualifications: [LLB (Hons)]

SMITH MR MICHAEL EDWARD

13 Old Square Chambers
Ground Floor, 14 Old Square, Lincoln's Inn,
London WC2A 3UE, ☎ 020 7831 4445
✉ clerks@13oldsquare.com
Call Date: Nov 2008, Inner Temple
Qualifications: [MSc (Dunelm) CPE]
michaelsmith@13oldsquare.com

SMITH MR MICHAEL JOSEPH

Deans Court Chambers
24 St John Street, Manchester M3 4DF,
☎ 0161 214 6000 ✉ clerks@deanscourt.co.uk
Deans Court Chambers
101 Walker Street, Preston PR1 2RR,
☎ 01772 565 600
✉ preston@deanscourt.co.uk
Call Date: July 1989, Lincoln's Inn
Pupil Supervisor
Qualifications: [MA BCL (Oxon)]

SMITH DR NATHAN LLEWELLYN

Kings Chambers
36 Young Street, Manchester M3 3FT,
☎ 0845 034 3444
✉ clerks@kingschambers.com
Kings Chambers
5 Park Square East, Leeds LS1 2NE,
☎ 0845 034 3444
✉ clerks@kingschambers.com
Kings Chambers
Embassy House, 60 Church Street,
Birmingham B3 2DJ, ☎ 0845 034 3444
✉ clerks@kingschambers.com
Call Date: Oct 2007, Lincoln's Inn
Qualifications: [MPHYS (Oxon)]
nsmith@kingschambers.com

SMITH MR NICHOLAS GILBERT

Guildhall Chambers
23 Broad Street, Bristol BS1 2HG,
☎ 0117 930 9000
✉ hoc@guildhallchambers.co.uk
Call Date: Nov 1990, Lincoln's Inn
Qualifications: [LLB]
Nicholas.Smith@guildhallchambers.co.uk

SMITH MR NICHOLAS MARTIN

St Philips Chambers
55 Temple Row, Birmingham B2 5LS,
☎ 0121 246 7000 ✉ clerks@st-philips.com
Call Date: Oct 1994, Gray's Inn
Qualifications: [BA (Lond)]
nsmith@st-philips.com

SMITH MISS NICOLA JANE

Northampton Chambers
10 Spencer Parade, Northampton NN1 5AQ,
☎ 01604 636271
✉ clerks@northampton-chambers.co.uk
Call Date: Oct 1994, Gray's Inn
Qualifications: [LLB (Hons)]

SMITH MR PAUL CHARLES

St Johns Buildings
24a - 28 St John Street, Manchester M3 4DJ,
☎ 0161 214 1500
✉ clerk@stjohnsbuildings.co.uk
16 Winckley Square
Preston PR1 3JJ, ☎ 01772 256100
St Johns Buildings Liverpool
8th Floor India Buildings, Water Street,
Liverpool L2 0XG, ☎ 0151 243 6000
✉ clerk@stjohnsbuildings.co.uk
Call Date: Oct 2002, Gray's Inn
Qualifications: [BA (Lond)]
clerk@stjohnsbuildings.co.uk

SMITH DR PETER MICHAEL

Radcliffe Chambers
Ground Floor, 11 New Square, Lincoln's Inn,
London WC2A 3QB, ☎ 020 7831 0081
✉ clerks@radcliffechambers.com
Call Date: Feb 1993, Lincoln's Inn
Qualifications: [LLB F R Hist S Ph D (Sheff)]
psmith@radcliffechambers.com

Types of work: Charities, Ecclesiastical law, Trusts

SMITH MR PETER RICHARD

Deans Court Chambers
24 St John Street, Manchester M3 4DF,
☎ 0161 214 6000 ✉ clerks@deanscourt.co.uk
Call Date: Nov 1988, Inner Temple
Qualifications: [LLB (Hons)(Lancaster)]

SMITH MS RACHEL CATHERINE

Lincoln House Chambers
Tower 12, The Avenue North, Spinningfields,
18-22 Bridge Street, Manchester M3 3BZ,
☎ 0161 832 5701
✉ info@lincolnhousechambers.com
Call Date: Oct 1990, Lincoln's Inn
Pupil Supervisor, Recorder
Qualifications: [BA (Leeds) Dip Law (Lond)]
rachel.smith@lincolnhousechambers.com

SMITH MISS REBECCA ELLEN

St Johns Buildings Liverpool
8th Floor India Buildings, Water Street,
Liverpool L2 0XG, ☎ 0151 243 6000
✉ clerk@stjohnsbuildings.co.uk
16 Winckley Square
Preston PR1 3JJ, ☎ 01772 256100
St Johns Buildings
24a - 28 St John Street, Manchester M3 4DJ,
☎ 0161 214 1500
✉ clerk@stjohnsbuildings.co.uk
Call Date: Nov 2002, Lincoln's Inn
Qualifications: [LLB (Hons) (L'pool)]
clerks@oldcourtchambers.com,
rebecca.smith@stjohnsbuildings.co.uk

SMITH MS REBECCA LOUISE

4 Breams Buildings
Chancery Lane, London EC4A 1HP,
☎ 020 7092 1900 ✉ clerks@4bb.co.uk
Call Date: July 2003, Inner Temple
Qualifications: [LLB (Nott'h)]

SMITH MR RICHARD LLOYD QC (2001)

Guildhall Chambers
23 Broad Street, Bristol BS1 2HG,
☎ 0117 930 9000
✉ hoc@guildhallchambers.co.uk
Call Date: July 1986, Middle Temple
Recorder
Qualifications: [LLB (Lond)]
richard.smith@guildhallchambers.co.uk

SMITH MR RICHARD WILLIAM MEAD

1 Crown Office Row
1 Crown Office Row, Temple, London
EC4Y 7HH, ☎ 020 7797 7500
✉ mail@1cor.com
Call Date: Oct 1999, Inner Temple
Pupil Supervisor
Qualifications: [BA (Hons)(Cantab)]
richard.smith@1cor.com

SMITH MR ROBERT CLIVE

RCS Chambers
Penny Hill, Holme Hall Lane, Stainton
S66 7RD, ☎ 01709 814 147
✉ robert@rcschambers.com
1 Paper Buildings
1st Floor, 1 Paper Buildings, Temple, London
EC4Y 7EP, ☎ 020 7353 3728
✉ clerks@onepaper.co.uk
Call Date: July 1974, Middle Temple
Qualifications: [MA (Cantab)]
robert@rcschambers.com

E

SMITH MR ROBERT IAN

St Paul's Chambers
5th Floor, St Paul's House, 23 Park Square South, Leeds LS1 2ND, ☎ 0113 245 5866
Call Date: Oct 1995, Lincoln's Inn
Pupil Supervisor
Qualifications: [LLB (Hons) (Northumbria)]
rs@stpaulschambers.com

SMITH MR ROBERT NEIL

9 St John Street
Manchester M3 4DN, ☎ 0161 955 9000
✉ civilclerks@9sjs.com / criminalclerks@9sjs.com
Call Date: Oct 2005, Gray's Inn
Qualifications: [LLB (Bris)]

SMITH MR ROBERT STEEN QC (1986)

Park Court Chambers
16 Park Place, Leeds LS1 2SJ,
☎ 0113 243 3277
✉ clerks@parkcourtchambers.co.uk
New Court Chambers
3 Broad Chare, Newcastle Upon Tyne NE1 3DQ, ☎ 0191 232 1980
✉ clerks@newcourt-chambers.co.uk
Call Date: July 1971, Inner Temple
Qualifications: [LLB]
rsmith@parkcourtchambers.co.uk

SMITH MR ROGER DENZIL HOWARD QC (1992)

Cornwall Street Chambers
85-87 Cornwall Street, Birmingham B3 3BY,
☎ 0121 233 7500
✉ clerks@cornwallstreet.co.uk
Call Date: Feb 1972, Gray's Inn
Qualifications: [LLM]
roger.smith@cornwallstreet.co.uk

SMITH MR ROGER GAVIN ABBEY

1 Hare Court
1 Hare Court, Temple, London EC4Y 7BE,
☎ 020 7797 7070 ✉ clerks@1hc.com
Call Date: Nov 1981, Middle Temple
Pupil Supervisor
Qualifications: [MA (Oxon)]

SMITH MR ROGER HUGH TRAYLEN

No5 Chambers
Fountain Court, Steelhouse Lane, Birmingham B4 6DR, ☎ 0845 210 5555 ✉ info@no5.com
No5 Chambers
Greenwood House, 4-7 Salisbury Court, London EC4Y 8AA, ☎ 0845 210 5555
No5 Chambers
38 Queen Square, Bristol BS1 4QS,
☎ 0845 210 5555
Call Date: Nov 1968, Gray's Inn
Pupil Supervisor
Qualifications: [BA (Oxon)]

SMITH MISS RUTH ELIZABETH ANNE

Apex
Harlech House, 20 Cathedral Road, Cardiff CF11 9LJ, ☎ 02920 232 032
✉ clerks@apexchambers.net
Call Date: July 1987, Gray's Inn
Qualifications: [LLB (Wales)]

SMITH MISS SALLY ELIZABETH QC (1997)

1 Crown Office Row
1 Crown Office Row, Temple, London EC4Y 7HH, ☎ 020 7797 7500
✉ mail@1cor.com
Call Date: Nov 1977, Inner Temple
Qualifications: [LLB (Lond)]
sally.smith@1cor.com

SMITH MISS SARAH LORRAINE

7 Bell Yard
London WC2A 2JR, ☎ 020 7831 0636
✉ kevintarrant@btconnect.com
Call Date: Oct 2006, Inner Temple
Qualifications: [LLB (Lond) LLM (Lond)]

SMITH MR SCOTT ALAN NEWEY

Fountain Chambers
Cleveland Business Centre, 1 Watson Street, Middlesbrough TS1 2RQ, ☎ 01642 804040
✉ clerks@fountainchambers.co.uk
Call Date: July 2003, Gray's Inn
Qualifications: [LLB]

SMITH MR SHAUN MALDEN QC (2008)

1 High Pavement
Nottingham NG1 1HF, ☎0115 941 8218
✉clerks@1highpavement.co.uk
Bank House Chambers
Old Bank House, Hartshead, Sheffield S1 2EL, ☎0114 275 1223
✉w.digby@bankhousechambers.co.uk
Call Date: July 1981, Gray's Inn
Qualifications: [LLB (Sheff)]
ShaunSmithQC@1HighPavement.co.uk

SMITH MR SIMON NOEL

3 Temple Gardens
Lower Ground Floor, 3 Temple Gardens, Temple, London EC4Y 9AU, ☎020 7353 3102
✉clerks@3tg.co.uk
Call Date: July 1981, Gray's Inn
Pupil Supervisor
Qualifications: [LLB (Lond)]
ss@3tg.co.uk

SMITH MISS SOPHIE LOUISE ELIZABETH

Atlantic Chambers
4-6 Cook Street, Liverpool L2 9QU, ☎0151 236 4421
✉info@atlanticchambers.co.uk
Call Date: Oct 1999, Lincoln's Inn
Qualifications: [LLB (Hons)(L'pool)]
sophiesmith@atlanticchambers.co.uk

SMITH MISS STEPHANIE ELIZABETH

Arden Chambers
20 Bloomsbury Square, London WC1A 2NS, ☎020 7242 4244
✉clerks@ardenchambers.com
Call Date: Nov 2004, Lincoln's Inn
Qualifications: [BA (Hons) (Oxon)]
stephanie.smith@ardenchambers.com

SMITH MR STEVEN JAMES

Palmyra Chambers
Royal House, 46 Legh Street, Warrington WA1 1UJ, ☎01925 444919
✉clerk@palmyrachambers.com
Call Date: Oct 2011, Gray's Inn
steven.smith@palmyrachambers.com

SMITH MR THOMAS JONATHAN

South Square
3-4 South Square, Gray's Inn, London WC1R 5HP, ☎020 7696 9900
✉practicemanagers@southsquare.com
Call Date: Nov 1999, Middle Temple
Pupil Supervisor
Qualifications: [MA (Hons)(Cantab) LLM (Cantab)]
tomsmith@southsquare.com

SMITH MR TYRONE GREGORY

25 Bedford Row
London WC1R 4HD, ☎020 7067 1500
✉clerks@25bedfordrow.com
Call Date: Oct 1994, Gray's Inn
Pupil Supervisor
Qualifications: [BA (Hons)]
tsmith@25bedfordrow.com

SMITH MR WARWICK TIMOTHY CRESSWELL

Deans Court Chambers
24 St John Street, Manchester M3 4DF, ☎0161 214 6000 ✉clerks@deanscourt.co.uk
Deans Court Chambers
101 Walker Street, Preston PR1 2RR, ☎01772 565 600
✉preston@deanscourt.co.uk
Call Date: July 1982, Middle Temple
Pupil Supervisor, Recorder
Qualifications: [MA (Cantab) FCI Arb]

SMITHERS DR ROGER HOWARD

Guildford Chambers
Stoke House, Leapale Lane, Guildford, Surrey GU1 4LY, ☎01483 539131
✉clerks@guildfordchambers.co.uk
Clerksroom (Taunton)
Equity House, Administration Centre, Blackbrook Park Avenue, Taunton, Somerset TA1 2PX, ☎0845 083 3000
✉mail@clerksroom.com
Alexander Chambers
13 Halstead Road, Wanstead, London E11 2AY, ☎0845 652 0451 / 0854 652 0451
✉clerks@alexanderchambers.co.uk
Call Date: Oct 1990, Inner Temple
Pupil Supervisor
Qualifications: [BSc Dip Law PhD (Lond)]
rsmithers@guildfordchambers.com

E

SMITHIES MISS DEBORAH LUCY

KBW
The Engine House, No 1 Foundry Square, Leeds LS11 5DL, ☎0113 297 1200
✉clerks@kbwchambers.com
Call Date: Nov 2008, Lincoln's Inn
Qualifications: [BA (Oxon) CPE UNOT]
deborahsmithies@kbwchambers.com

SMITTEN MR BEN JAMES

25 Bedford Row
London WC1R 4HD, ☎020 7067 1500
✉clerks@25bedfordrow.com
Call Date: Nov 1999, Middle Temple
Qualifications: [LLB (Hons)(Bris)]
bsmitten@25bedfordrow.com

SMOKER MISS KATHLEEN MARY

Heavenwood Chambers
Heavenwood Chambers, Heavenwood House, 71 Bownham Park, Rodborough Common, Stroud, Gloucestershire GL5 5BZ,
☎01453 873444 ✉kms@heavenwood.co.uk
Call Date: May 1974, Gray's Inn
Pupil Supervisor
Qualifications: [LLB (B'ham)]
kms@heavenwood.co.uk

SMOUHA MR JOSEPH QC (2003)

Essex Court Chambers
24 Lincoln's Inn Fields, London WC2A 3EG,
☎020 7813 8000
✉clerksroom@essexcourt.net
Call Date: July 1986, Middle Temple
Qualifications: [MA (Cantab) LLM (USA)]

SMOULT-HAWTREE MRS KAREN

Dere Street Barristers
14 Toft Green, York YO1 6JT, ☎0844 3351551
✉clerks@derestreet.co.uk
Dere Street Barristers
33 Broad Chare, Newcastle Upon Tyne NE1 3DQ, ☎0844 3351551
✉clerks@derestreet.co.uk
Call Date: July 2000, Gray's Inn
Qualifications: [LLB (Hons) (Hull)]
clerks@yorkchambers.co.uk, ksmoulthawtree@yorkchambers.co.uk

SMOUT MR WILLIAM KINGSLEY

Guildford Chambers
Stoke House, Leapale Lane, Guildford, Surrey GU1 4LY, ☎01483 539131
✉clerks@guildfordchambers.co.uk
Call Date: Oct 2005, Lincoln's Inn
Qualifications: [BSc (Hons) (B'ham) PgDl (Lond)]
wsmout@guildfordchambers.com

SMULLEN MRS MARION

Chambers of Marion Smullen and Kerim Fuad QC
1 Inner Temple Lane, London EC4Y 1AF,
☎020 7427 4400 ✉clerks@1itl.com
Call Date: July 1985, Gray's Inn
Pupil Supervisor
Qualifications: [BA LLB (Lond)]
clerks@1itl.com

SMYTH MR CHRISTOPHER JULIAN WORSLEY

Queen Square Chambers
56 Queen Square, Bristol BS1 4PR,
☎0117 921 1966 ✉crime@qs-c.co.uk
Call Date: Mar 2006, Gray's Inn
Qualifications: [BA (Hons) (Kent)]
cjs@qs-c.co.uk

SMYTH MR JACK ALEXANDER

No5 Chambers
Fountain Court, Steelhouse Lane, Birmingham B4 6DR, ☎0845 210 5555 ✉info@no5.com
No5 Chambers
Greenwood House, 4-7 Salisbury Court, London EC4Y 8AA, ☎0845 210 5555
No5 Chambers
38 Queen Square, Bristol BS1 4QS,
☎0845 210 5555
Call Date: Oct 2007, Middle Temple
Qualifications: [BA (Hons) (Dunelm) PgDL (Lond)]
js@no5.com

SMYTH MISS JULIA MADELEINE

Temple Garden Chambers
1 Harcourt Buildings, Temple, London EC4Y 9DA, ☎020 7583 1315
✉clerks@tgchambers.com
Call Date: Oct 1996, Inner Temple
Qualifications: [LLB (Lond) Dip in German Law]
ksmyth@tgchambers.com

SMYTH MR STEPHEN MARK JAMES ATHELSTAN

Atkinson Bevan Chambers
1st Floor, 2 Harcourt Buildings, Temple, London EC4Y 9DB, ☎020 7353 2112
✉clerks@2hb.co.uk
Call Date: July 1974, Inner Temple
Recorder

SNARR MR MATTHEW JAMES

9 St John Street
Manchester M3 4DN, ☎0161 955 9000
✉civilclerks@9sjs.com / criminalclerks@9sjs.com
Call Date: Nov 2001, Inner Temple
Qualifications: [LLB Hons (Manch)]
✉matthew.snarr@9sjs.com

SNELL MR JOHN

New Walk Chambers
27 New Walk, Leicester, Leicestershire
LE1 6TE, ☎0871 200 1298 / 0116 255 9144
✉clerks@newwalkchambers.co.uk
Call Date: July 1973, Inner Temple
Pupil Supervisor
Qualifications: [LLB]

SNELL MR JOHN MICHAEL

Guildhall Chambers
23 Broad Street, Bristol BS1 2HG,
☎0117 930 9000
✉hoc@guildhallchambers.co.uk
2 Temple Gardens
2 Temple Gardens, Temple, London
EC4Y 9AY, ☎020 7822 1200
✉clerks@2tg.co.uk
Call Date: Oct 1991, Lincoln's Inn
Qualifications: [BA (Hons) (Oxon) Dip Law]
✉john.snell@guildhallchambers.co.uk

SNELLING MR CHARLES WILLIAM

Fenners Chambers
3 Madingley Road, Cambridge CB3 0EE,
☎01223 368761
✉clerks@fennerschambers.com
Call Date: Nov 2005, Middle Temple
Qualifications: [LLB (Hons)]
✉clerks@fennerschambers.com

SNELUS MR JAMES GORDON ERNEST

St Mary's Family Law Chambers
26-28 High Pavement, The Lace Market,
Nottingham NG1 1HN, ☎0115 950 3503
✉clerks@stmarysflc.co.uk
Call Date: Oct 1999, Inner Temple
Qualifications: [MA (Cantab)]
✉james.snelus@stmarysflc.co.uk

SNIDER MR JOHN LEOPOLD

Essex Court Chambers
24 Lincoln's Inn Fields, London WC2A 3EG,
☎020 7813 8000
✉clerksroom@essexcourt.net
Call Date: July 1982, Middle Temple
Pupil Supervisor
Qualifications: [MA (Hons) (Oxon) MBA]
✉jsnider@essexcourt.net

SNODIN MR OLIVER KARL ASTLEY

4 Breams Buildings
Chancery Lane, London EC4A 1HP,
☎020 7092 1900 ✉clerks@4bb.co.uk
Call Date: Nov 2009, Middle Temple
Qualifications: [BA (Hons)(B'ham)]

SNOOK MR HARRY BENEDICK

St Albans Chambers
2 - 4 St Peter's Street, St Albans, Hertfordshire
AL1 3LF, ☎01727 843383
✉clerks@stalbanschambers.com
Call Date: Nov 2006, Inner Temple
Qualifications: [BA (Durham)]
✉hs@stalbanschambers.com

SNOOK MR SEAN EDWARD

20 Essex Street
London WC2R 3AL, ☎020 7842 1200
✉clerks@20essexst.com
Call Date: July 2000, Lincoln's Inn
Pupil Supervisor
Qualifications: [BA(Hons) (Exet)]
✉clerks@20essexst.com

SNOW MR DARREN MARK

Charter Chambers
33 John Street, London WC1N 2AT,
☎020 7618 4400
✉clerks@charterchambers.com
Call Date: Oct 2000, Middle Temple
Qualifications: [LLB (Hons) LLM MCIArb]
✉darren.snow@charterchambers.com

SNOWDEN MR RICHARD ANDREW QC (2003)

Erskine Chambers
33 Chancery Lane, London WC2A 1EN,
☎020 7242 5532
✉clerks@erskinechambers.com
Call Date: July 1986, Lincoln's Inn
Qualifications: [MA (Cantab) LLM (USA)]
✉rsnowden@erskine-chambers.co.uk

SNOWDEN MR STEVEN

Crown Office Chambers
2 Crown Office Row, Temple, London
EC4Y 7HJ, ☎020 7797 8100
✉mail@crownofficechambers.com
Call Date: July 1989, Inner Temple
Pupil Supervisor
Qualifications: [BA (Nott'm)]
✉snowden@crownofficechambers.com

E

SNOWDON MISS MARTINE JAYNE

Exchange Chambers
One Derby Square, Derby Square, Liverpool L2 9XX, ☎ 0151 236 7747
✉ info@exchangechambers.co.uk
Exchange Chambers
7 Ralli Courts, West Riverside, Manchester M3 5FT, ☎ 0161 833 2722
Exchange Chambers
Oxford House, Oxford Row, Leeds LS1 3BE, ☎ 0113 203 1970
✉ spencer@exchangechambers.co.uk
Call Date: Oct 2000, Lincoln's Inn
Qualifications: [LLB (Hons) (L'Pool)]
✉ snowdon@exchangechambers.co.uk

SOARES MR PATRICK CLAUDE

Gray's Inn Tax Chambers
3rd Floor, Gray's Inn Chambers, Gray's Inn, London WC1R 5JA, ☎ 020 7242 2642
✉ clerks@taxbar.com
Call Date: Nov 1983, Lincoln's Inn
Pupil Supervisor
Qualifications: [LLB FTII LLM (Lond)]
✉ ps@taxbar.com

E

SODHA MISS SONAL

Five St Andrew's Hill
5 St Andrew's Hill, London EC4V 5BZ, ☎ 020 7332 5400 ✉ Clerks@5sah.co.uk
Call Date: Nov 2005, Middle Temple
Qualifications: [BA (Hons) (Lond)]
✉ sonalsodha@5sah.co.uk

SOERTSZ MISS LAUREN BRIGITTE

Doughty Street Chambers
53-54 Doughty Street, London WC1N 2LS, ☎ 020 7404 1313
✉ enquiries@doughtystreet.co.uk
Call Date: Feb 1987, Middle Temple
Pupil Supervisor
Qualifications: [LLB]

SOFAER MISS MOIRA

Goldsmith Chambers
Ground Floor, Goldsmith Building, Temple, London EC4Y 7BL, ☎ 020 7353 6802
✉ clerks@goldsmithchambers.com
Call Date: July 1975, Middle Temple
Qualifications: [BSc (Lond)]

SOFFA MISS HELEN ROSEMARY

New Court
Ground Floor, New Court, Temple, London EC4Y 9BE, ☎ 020 7583 5123
✉ clerks@newcourtchambers.com
Call Date: Nov 1990, Inner Temple
✉ hsoffa@newcourtchambers.net

SOKOL MR CHRISTOPHER JOHN FRANCIS QC (2006)

Taxchambers
15 Old Square, Lincoln's Inn, London WC2A 3UE, ☎ 020 7242 2744
✉ taxchambers@15oldsquare.co.uk
Deans Court Chambers
24 St John Street, Manchester M3 4DF, ☎ 0161 214 6000 ✉ clerks@deanscourt.co.uk
Temple Tax Chambers
1st Floor, 3 Temple Gardens, Temple, London EC4Y 9AU, ☎ 020 7353 7884
✉ clerks@templetax.com
Call Date: July 1975, Lincoln's Inn
Qualifications: [MA (Cantab)]
✉ csokol@15oldsquare.co.uk, taxchambers@15oldsquare.co.uk

SOLANKI MISS PRIYA ASHOK

10 King's Bench Walk
Ground Floor, 10 King's Bench Walk, Temple, London EC4Y 7EB, ☎ 020 7353 7742
✉ Chambers@10kingsbenchwalk.co.uk
Call Date: July 2008, Lincoln's Inn
Qualifications: [LLB (L'pool)]
✉ jonathan.martin@10kbw.co.uk

SOLARI MISS YOLANDA ELLEN

5 Pump Court
Ground Floor, 5 Pump Court, Temple, London EC4Y 7AP, ☎ 020 7353 2532
✉ clerks@5pumpcourt.com
Call Date: Nov 1992, Gray's Inn
Qualifications: [LLB (Hons)]
✉ yolandasolari@5pumpcourt.com

SOLE MISS EMMA JAYNE

Farrar's Building
Farrar's Building, Temple, London EC4Y 7BD, ☎ 020 7583 9241
✉ Chambers@farrarsbuilding.co.uk
Call Date: Oct 2005, Inner Temple
Qualifications: [BA Trinity College University of Oxford]
✉ esole@farrarsbuilding.co.uk

SOLLEY MR STEPHEN MALCOLM QC (1989)

Charter Chambers
33 John Street, London WC1N 2AT, ☎ 020 7618 4400
✉ clerks@charterchambers.com
Call Date: Nov 1969, Inner Temple
Recorder
Qualifications: [LLB (Lond)]
✉ stephensolley@charterchambers.com

SOLOMON MR ADAM JONATHAN

Littleton Chambers
3 King's Bench Walk North, Temple, London EC4Y 7HR, ☎020 7797 8600
✉fschneider@littletonchambers.co.uk
Call Date: Oct 1998, Gray's Inn
Pupil Supervisor
Qualifications: [BA (Oxon) MA (Sussex) Dip Law]
✉ASolomon@littletonchambers.co.uk

SOLOMON MR REUBEN

12 Old Square Chambers
1st Floor, 12 Old Square, Lincoln's Inn, London WC2A 3TX, ☎020 7404 0875
✉clerks@12oldsquare.com
Call Date: Oct 1993, Lincoln's Inn
Qualifications: [LLB (Hons)]
✉clerks@12oldsquare.com

SOLOMON MISS SUSAN ISABEL BARBARA

3 PB Barristers
3 Paper Buildings, Temple, London EC4Y 7EU, ☎020 7583 8055
3 PB Barristers
23 Beaumont Street, Oxford OX1 2NP, ☎01865 793 736
3 PB Barristers
30 Christchurch Road, Bournemouth, Dorset BH1 3PD, ☎01202 292102
✉clerks.bournemouth@3paper.co.uk
3 PB Barristers
Royal Talbot House, 2 Victoria Street, Bristol, Avon BS1 6BB, ☎0117 928 1520
3 PB Barristers
4 St Peter Street, Winchester SO23 8BW, ☎01962 868884
✉clerks.winchester@3paper.co.uk
Call Date: July 1967, Middle Temple
Pupil Supervisor
Qualifications: [MA (Oxon)]
✉susan.solomon@3pb.co.uk

SOMERVILLE MR BRYCE EDWARD

Cornwall Street Chambers
85-87 Cornwall Street, Birmingham B3 3BY, ☎0121 233 7500
✉clerks@cornwallstreet.co.uk
Call Date: July 1980, Middle Temple
Pupil Supervisor
Qualifications: [BA (Cantab)]
✉bryce.somerville@cornwallstreet.co.uk

SOMERVILLE MR THOMAS CLINTON

Linenhall Chambers
1 Stanley Place, Chester CH1 2LU, ☎01244 348282
✉clerks@linenhallchambers.co.uk
Call Date: July 1979, Middle Temple
Qualifications: [BA (Bris)]
✉t.somerville@ntlworld.com

SONAIKE MR KOLARELE OLADELE OBAFEMI

One Essex Court
1st Floor, Temple, London EC4Y 9AR, ☎020 7936 3030 ✉clerks@1ec.co.uk
Call Date: Oct 1998, Inner Temple
Qualifications: [BSocSc (B'ham) CPE]
✉ksonaike@1ec.co.uk

SONES MR RICHARD

5 King's Bench Walk
5 King's Bench Walk, Temple, London EC4Y 7DN, ☎020 7353 5638
✉clerks@5kbw.co.uk
Call Date: Nov 1969, Inner Temple
Pupil Supervisor
Qualifications: [LLB (Lond)]
✉richard.sones@5kbw.co.uk

SONI MISS BANSI

Garden Court Chambers
57-60 Lincoln's Inn Fields, London WC2A 3LJ, ☎020 7993 7600 ✉info@gclaw.co.uk
Call Date: Nov 2003, Middle Temple
Qualifications: [Dip. in Law BA (Hons) (Lond)]
✉bansis@gclaw.co.uk

SOOD MRS USHA RANI

Trent Chambers
9 Regent Street, Nottingham NG1 5BS, ☎0115 941 9596
✉clerks@trentchambers.co.uk
Call Date: July 1974, Gray's Inn
Pupil Supervisor
Qualifications: [LLB M Phil]
✉usha.sood@trentchambers.co.uk

SOOLE MR MICHAEL ALEXANDER QC (2002)

Four New Square
Four New Square, Lincoln's Inn, London WC2A 3RJ, ☎020 7822 2000
✉barristers@4newsquare.com
Call Date: July 1977, Inner Temple
Recorder
Qualifications: [MA (Oxon)]
✉m.soole@4newsquare.com

E

SOOR MR SMAIR SINGH

Seven Bedford Row
7 Bedford Row, London WC1R 4BS,
☎ 020 7242 3555 ✉ clerks@7br.co.uk
Call Date: July 1988, Gray's Inn
Qualifications: [LLB]
✉ ssoor@7br.co.uk

SOORA MS BRINDER

5 Pump Court
Ground Floor, 5 Pump Court, Temple, London EC4Y 7AP, ☎ 020 7353 2532
✉ clerks@5pumpcourt.com
Call Date: Nov 2000, Inner Temple
Qualifications: [LLB (Lond) LLM (Lond)]

SOPPITT MR NIGEL

Old Court Chambers
Newham House, 96-98 Borough Road, Middlesbrough TS1 2HJ, ☎ 01642 232523
✉ clerks@oldcourtchambers.com
Call Date: Nov 1996, Gray's Inn
✉ clerks@oldcourtchambers.com

SOREL-CAMERON MR MATTHEW GEORGE

East Anglian Chambers
53 North Hill, Colchester, Essex CO1 1QA,
☎ 01473 214481 ✉ colchester@ealaw.co.uk
East Anglian Chambers
Gresham House, 5 Museum Street, Ipswich, Suffolk IP1 1HQ, ☎ 01473 214481
✉ ipswich@ealaw.co.uk
East Anglian Chambers
15 The Close, Norwich, Norfolk NR1 4DZ,
☎ 01473 214481 ✉ norwich@ealaw.co.uk
Call Date: Oct 2009, Middle Temple
Qualifications: [BA (Hons) (Lond)]
✉ colchester@ealaw.co.uk

SOTO-MIRANDA MR DIEGO FERNANDO

One Essex Court
1st Floor, Temple, London EC4Y 9AR,
☎ 020 7936 3030 ✉ clerks@1ec.co.uk
Call Date: July 2001, Inner Temple
Qualifications: [LLB (LSE)]
✉ dsotomiranda@1ec.co.uk

SOULE MISS NATALIE MERCY NINA

5 King's Bench Walk
5 King's Bench Walk, Temple, London EC4Y 7DN, ☎ 020 7353 5638
✉ clerks@5kbw.co.uk
Call Date: Oct 2008, Lincoln's Inn
Qualifications: [BA (Cantab) MSc (Cantab)]
✉ nataliesoule@5kbw.co.uk

SOULSBY MR EDWARD WILLIAM

Clock Chambers
18 Waterloo Road, Wolverhampton WV1 4BL,
☎ 01902 313444
✉ clockchambers@btconnect.com
Call Date: Oct 1996, Gray's Inn
Qualifications: [LLB (Staffs)]

SOUTER MISS CATHERINE ELISABETH

Park Lane Plowden
19 Westgate, Leeds LS1 2RD,
☎ 0113 228 5049
✉ clerks@parklaneplowden.co.uk
Call Date: July 2002, Gray's Inn
Qualifications: [LLB (Leeds)]
✉ catherine.souter@parklaneplowden.co.uk

SOUTHERN MR DAVID BOARDMAN

Temple Tax Chambers
1st Floor, 3 Temple Gardens, Temple, London EC4Y 9AU, ☎ 020 7353 7884
✉ clerks@templetax.com
Call Date: July 1982, Lincoln's Inn
Qualifications: [MA D Phil (Oxon) FIIT M Phil]
✉ clerks@templetax.com

Fax: 020 7583 2044
URL: www.taxbarrister.co.uk
www.davidsouthern.co.uk

Types of work: Capital tax, Corporation tax, Customs, Income tax, Stamp duty, Tax investigations, VAT

SOUTHERN MISS EMMA CATHERINE

12 College Place
Fauvelle Buildings, 12 College Place, Southampton SO15 2FE, ☎ 023 8032 0320
✉ clerks@12cp.co.uk
Call Date: July 2006, Lincoln's Inn
Qualifications: [LLB (Bris)]
✉ esouthern@12cp.co.uk

SOUTHERN MR RICHARD MICHAEL QC (2006)

7 King's Bench Walk
Ground Floor, 7 King's Bench Walk, Temple, London EC4Y 7DS, ☎ 020 7910 8300
✉ clerks@7kbw.co.uk
Call Date: Nov 1987, Middle Temple
Qualifications: [MA (Cantab)]
✉ rsouthern@7kbw.co.uk

SOUTHEY MR DAVID HUGH QC (2010)

Tooks Chambers
81 Farringdon Street, London EC4A 4BL,
☎020 7842 7575 ✉clerks@tooks.co.uk
Call Date: Nov 1996, Inner Temple
Pupil Supervisor, Recorder
Qualifications: [MEng (Lond)]
hugh.southey@tooks.co.uk

SOUTHGATE MR JONATHAN BLAKE

29 Bedford Row Chambers
London WC1R 4HE, ☎020 7404 1044
✉clerks@29br.co.uk
Call Date: Nov 1992, Middle Temple
Qualifications: [LLB]
jsouthgate@29br.co.uk

SOWDEN MRS LUCY ELIZABETH

Zenith Chambers
10 Park Square, Leeds LS1 2LH,
☎0113 245 5438
✉clerks@zenithchambers.co.uk
Call Date: July 2006, Inner Temple
Qualifications: [LLB (Hull)]

SOWERBY MR MATTHEW GILES

1 Gray's Inn Square
Ground Floor, 1 Gray's Inn Square, London
WC1R 5AA, ☎020 7405 0001
Call Date: July 1987, Middle Temple
Qualifications: [BA (Sussex)]

SOWERSBY MR ROBERT KENNETH

Guildhall Chambers
23 Broad Street, Bristol BS1 2HG,
☎0117 930 9000
✉hoc@guildhallchambers.co.uk
Call Date: July 2000, Gray's Inn
Qualifications: [BA Dip Law MA (Lond)]

SOWLER MR THOMAS RICHARD HOLLAND

The Tax Chambers of Mr Richard Sowler TD
6 Church Road Marina, Douglas IM1 2HQ,
☎07624 235000
Call Date: July 1974, Inner Temple
Qualifications: [MA (Oxon)]
sowler@gmail.com

SPACKMAN MR MARK ANDREW

Iscoed Chambers
86 St Helen's Road, Swansea SA1 4BQ,
☎01792 652988
✉clerks@iscoedchambers.co.uk
Call Date: Nov 1986, Lincoln's Inn
Pupil Supervisor
Qualifications: [LLB (Leic)]
ms@iscoedchambers.co.uk

SPAIN MR TIMOTHY HARRISSON

Trinity Chambers
The Custom House, 39 Quayside, Newcastle
Upon Tyne NE1 3DE, ☎0191 232 1927
✉info@trinitychambers.co.uk
Trinity Chambers
Multi Media Exchange, 72-80 Corporation
Road, Middlesbrough TS1 2RF,
☎01642 247569
✉info@trinitychambers.co.uk
Call Date: July 1983, Gray's Inn
Pupil Supervisor
Qualifications: [LLB (Newc)]
t.spain@trinitychambers.co.uk

SPALTON MR GEORGE DAVID JOHN

Four New Square
Four New Square, Lincoln's Inn, London
WC2A 3RJ, ☎020 7822 2000
✉barristers@4newsquare.com
Call Date: July 2004, Lincoln's Inn
Qualifications: [BA (Oxon) LLM]
g.spalton@4newsquare.com

SPANIER MR SAMSON CURTIS

13 King's Bench Walk
13 King's Bench Walk, Temple, London
EC4Y 7EN, ☎020 7353 7204
✉clerks@13kbw.co.uk
13 KBW
32 Beaumont Street, Oxford OX1 2NP,
☎01865 311066 ✉clerks@13kbw.co.uk
Call Date: Nov 2009, Lincoln's Inn
Qualifications: [MA BA (Cantab) CPE UCU]

SPARKS MISS CATHERINE ALEXANDRA

5 Pump Court
Ground Floor, 5 Pump Court, Temple, London
EC4Y 7AP, ☎020 7353 2532
✉clerks@5pumpcourt.com
Call Date: July 2003, Lincoln's Inn
Qualifications: [LLB Hons (UEA)]
clerks@kent-chambers.co.uk

E

SPARKS MS PAULA DENISE

Doughty Street Chambers
53-54 Doughty Street, London WC1N 2LS,
☎ 020 7404 1313
✉ enquiries@doughtystreet.co.uk
Doughty Street Chambers
Pall Mall Court, 61-67 King Street, Manchester M2 4PD, ☎ 0161 618 1066
Doughty Street Chambers
5th Floor, Broad Quay House, Prince Street, Bristol BS1 4DJ, ☎ 01179 058 717
Call Date: Oct 1994, Gray's Inn
Qualifications: [LLB]
p.sparks@doughtystreet.co.uk

SPARLING MR OLIVER CHARLES

Old Square Chambers
10-11 Bedford Row, London WC1R 4BU,
☎ 020 7269 0300 ✉ clerks@oldsquare.co.uk
Old Square Chambers
3 Orchard Court, St Augustine's Yard, Bristol BS1 5DP, ☎ 0117 930 5100
✉ clerks@oldsquare.co.uk
Call Date: Nov 2006, Inner Temple
Qualifications: [BA MSt (Oxon)]
sparling@oldsquare.co.uk

SPARROW MISS JULIE ELIZABETH

St Philips Chambers
55 Temple Row, Birmingham B2 5LS,
☎ 0121 246 7000 ✉ clerks@st-philips.com
Call Date: Oct 1992, Lincoln's Inn
Qualifications: [LLB(Hons)]
julie@forumlaw.co.uk, contact@forumlaw.co.uk

SPARROW MRS MARIE-CLAIRE

Holborn Chambers
6 Gate Street, Lincoln's Inn Fields, London WC2A 3HP, ☎ 020 7242 6060
Call Date: Nov 1977, Lincoln's Inn
Pupil Supervisor
Qualifications: [Maitrise en droit (France) Chevalier de L'Ordre du Merite DES Driot Public (France) DESS EU LAW (France) Des Political Sciences (France)]

SPEAIGHT MR ANTHONY HUGH QC (1995)

4 Pump Court
4 Pump Court, Temple, London EC4Y 7AN,
☎ 020 7842 5555
✉ chambers@4pumpcourt.com
Call Date: July 1973, Middle Temple
Qualifications: [MA (Oxon)]

SPEAKMAN MR LEE

Exchange Chambers
One Derby Square, Derby Square, Liverpool L2 9XX, ☎ 0151 236 7747
✉ info@exchangechambers.co.uk
Call Date: July 2009, Middle Temple
Qualifications: [BA (Hons) (Dunelm)]
speakman@exchangechambers.co.uk

SPEARING MS RACHEL MICHELLE

Pump Court Chambers
31 Southgate Street, Winchester, Hampshire SO23 9EB, ☎ 01962 868 161
✉ clerks@3pumpcourt.com
Pump Court Chambers
Upper Ground Floor, 3 Pump Court, Temple, London EC4Y 7AJ, ☎ 020 7353 0711
✉ clerks@3pumpcourt.com
Pump Court Chambers
5 Temple Chambers, Temple Street, Swindon SN1 1SQ, ☎ 01793 539899
✉ clerks@3pumpcourt.com
Call Date: Oct 1999, Inner Temple
Pupil Supervisor
Qualifications: [LLB (L'pool)]
rms@3pumpcourt.com

SPEARMAN MR RICHARD QC (1996)

4-5 Gray's Inn Square
Gray's Inn, London WC1R 5AH,
☎ 020 7404 5252 ✉ clerks@4-5.co.uk
Call Date: Nov 1977, Middle Temple
Recorder
Qualifications: [MA (Cantab)]
rspearman@4-5.co.uk

SPEARS MISS FRANCES PORTIA

12 King's Bench Walk
12 King's Bench Walk, Temple, London EC4Y 7EL, ☎ 020 7583 0811
Call Date: Nov 1992, Gray's Inn
Qualifications: [MA (Oxon)]

SPEARS MISS KATHARINE SARAH

Carmelite Chambers
9 Carmelite Street, London EC4Y 0DR,
☎ 020 7936 6300
✉ clerks@carmelitechambers.co.uk
Call Date: Nov 2005, Middle Temple
Qualifications: [BA (Hons)]
kspears@carmelitechambers.co.uk

E

SPECK MR ADRIAN QC (2012)

8 New Square
8 New Square, Lincoln's Inn, London WC2A 3QP, ☎ 020 7405 4321
✉ clerks@8newsquare.co.uk
Call Date: Oct 1993, Gray's Inn
Pupil Supervisor
Qualifications: [BA (Cantab)]
✉ adrian.speck@8newsquare.co.uk

Types of work: Breach of confidence, Competition law, Copyright, Copyright Tribunal, Design, E-commerce, EC competition law, Entertainment, Information technology, Intellectual property, Internet law, Malicious falsehood, Media, Media and entertainment, Passing off, Patents, Pharmaceuticals, Scientific and technical disputes, Trade secrets, Trademarks

SPEED MR GEORGE CLIFFORD

Chambers of Mr George Speed
25 Northfield Way, Hallcroft, Retford, Nottinghamshire DN22 7LJ, ☎ 07968 986926
✉ geo_speed@hotmail.com
Call Date: Oct 1999, Middle Temple
Qualifications: [LLB (Keele)]

SPEED MR IAN JAMES

St Philips Chambers
55 Temple Row, Birmingham B2 5LS, ☎ 0121 246 7000 ✉ clerks@st-philips.com
Call Date: Oct 2000, Gray's Inn
Qualifications: [LLB]
✉ ispeed@st-philips.com

SPEKER MR ADAM SAMUEL EDWARD

5RB
1st Floor, 5 Raymond Buildings, Gray's Inn, London WC1R 5BP, ☎ 020 7242 2902
✉ clerks@5rb.com
Call Date: Oct 1999, Middle Temple
Pupil Supervisor
Qualifications: [BA (Hons)(Bris)]
✉ adamspeker@5rb.com

SPELLER MR BRUCE CHRISTOPHER NORMAN

The White House
Whatlington, Battle, East Sussex TN33 0ND, ☎ 01424 777944
✉ brucespeller@btinternet.com
Call Date: July 1976, Inner Temple
Pupil Supervisor
Qualifications: [MA (Oxon)]

SPENCE MISS ELIZABETH ANNE

Stour Chambers
Mill Studio, 17a Stour Street, Canterbury, Kent CT1 2NR, ☎ 01227 764899
✉ clerks@stourchambers.co.uk
Call Date: July 2006, Gray's Inn
Qualifications: [MA (Edin)]
✉ clerks@stourchambers.co.uk

SPENCE MISS GEMMA LOUISE

East Anglian Chambers
140 New London Road, Chelmsford, Essex CM2 0AW, ☎ 01473 214481
✉ chelmsford@ealaw.co.uk
East Anglian Chambers
53 North Hill, Colchester, Essex CO1 1QA, ☎ 01473 214481 ✉ colchester@ealaw.co.uk
East Anglian Chambers
Gresham House, 5 Museum Street, Ipswich, Suffolk IP1 1HQ, ☎ 01473 214481
✉ ipswich@ealaw.co.uk
Call Date: July 2007, Lincoln's Inn
Qualifications: [LLB (Sheff)]
✉ gemmaspence@ealaw.co.uk

SPENCE MR SIMON PETER QC (2009)

18 Red Lion Court
London EC4A 3EB, ☎ 020 7520 6000
✉ chambers@18rlc.co.uk
18 Red Lion Court (Annexe)
Thornwood House, 102 New London Road, Chelmsford, Essex CM2 0RG, ☎ 01245 280880
Call Date: July 1985, Inner Temple
Recorder
Qualifications: [LLB (Leics)]
✉ simon.spence@18rlc.co.uk

SPENCE MR STEPHEN NICHOLAS

1 Paper Buildings
1st Floor, 1 Paper Buildings, Temple, London EC4Y 7EP, ☎ 020 7353 3728
✉ clerks@onepaper.co.uk
Call Date: July 1983, Gray's Inn
Qualifications: [BSc (Cardiff)]
✉ stephenspence@onepaper.co.uk

SPENCER MR ANDREW NICHOLAS

1 Chancery Lane
London WC2A 1LF, ☎ 0845 634 6666
✉ clerks@1chancerylane.com
Call Date: Oct 2004, Gray's Inn
Qualifications: [BA Hons (Oxon)]
✉ aspencer@1chancerylane.com

E

SPENCER MS ANNA ELIZABETH RUTH

14 Gray's Inn Square
14 Gray's Inn Square, Gray's Inn, London WC1R 5JP, ☎ 020 7242 0858
✉ clerks@14gis.co.uk
Call Date: Oct 2004, Middle Temple
Qualifications: [BA (Hons) Lond PGDip]
✉ clerks@14graysinnsquare.co.uk

SPENCER SIR DEREK HAROLD QC (1980)

18 Red Lion Court
London EC4A 3EB, ☎ 020 7520 6000
✉ chambers@18rlc.co.uk
18 Red Lion Court (Annexe)
Thornwood House, 102 New London Road, Chelmsford, Essex CM2 0RG, ☎ 01245 280880
Call Date: Feb 1961, Gray's Inn
Qualifications: [MA BCL (Oxon)]
✉ derek.spencer@18rlc.co.uk

SPENCER MR JOHN JOSEPH

KBW
The Engine House, No 1 Foundry Square, Leeds LS11 5DL, ☎ 0113 297 1200
✉ clerks@kbwchambers.com
Call Date: July 2001, Gray's Inn
Qualifications: [LLB]
✉ jjspencer@kbwchambers.com

SPENCER MISS LARA SHARON

Walnut House
63 St. David's Hill, Exeter, Devon EX4 4DW, ☎ 01392 279751
✉ clerks@walnuthouse.co.uk
Call Date: July 2000, Lincoln's Inn
Qualifications: [LLB(Hons) (Exon)]

SPENCER MR MARTIN BENEDICT QC (2003)

Hailsham Chambers
Ground Floor, 4 Paper Buildings, Temple, London EC4Y 7EX, ☎ 020 7643 5000
✉ clerks@hailshamchambers.com
Call Date: July 1979, Inner Temple
Recorder
Qualifications: [MA BCL (Oxon)]
✉ martin.spencer@hailshamchambers.com

SPENCER MR MICHAEL GERALD QC (1989)

Crown Office Chambers
2 Crown Office Row, Temple, London EC4Y 7HJ, ☎ 020 7797 8100
✉ mail@crownofficechambers.com
Call Date: July 1970, Inner Temple
Recorder
Qualifications: [MA (Oxon)]
✉ spencer@crownofficechambers.com

SPENCER MR PAUL ANTHONY

3 Serjeants Inn
London EC4Y 1BQ, ☎ 020 7427 5000
✉ clerks@3serjeantsinn.com
Call Date: Nov 1988, Middle Temple
Pupil Supervisor
Qualifications: [LLB]
✉ pspencer@3serjeantsinn.com

SPENCER MR SHAUN ANTHONY

St Johns Buildings
24a - 28 St John Street, Manchester M3 4DJ, ☎ 0161 214 1500
✉ clerk@stjohnsbuildings.co.uk
St Johns Buildings
21 White Friars, Chester CH1 1NZ, ☎ 01244 323070
✉ clerk@stjohnsbuildings.co.uk
16 Winckley Square
Preston PR1 3JJ, ☎ 01772 256100
Call Date: July 2005, Lincoln's Inn
Qualifications: [LLB (Hons)]
✉ Shaun.spencer@stjohnsbuildings.co.uk, shaunspencer_montes@yahoo.co.uk

SPENCER MR TIMOTHY JOHN QC (2001)

Seven Bedford Row
7 Bedford Row, London WC1R 4BS, ☎ 020 7242 3555 ✉ clerks@7br.co.uk
Call Date: July 1982, Middle Temple
Qualifications: [MA (Cantab)]
✉ tspencer@7br.co.uk

SPENCER BERNARD MR ROBERT VERE

4 King's Bench Walk
2nd Floor, 4 King's Bench Walk, Temple, London EC4Y 7DL, ☎ 020 7822 7000
✉ clerks@4kbw.co.uk
Call Date: Nov 1969, Inner Temple
Recorder
Qualifications: [MA (Oxon)]
✉ clerks@4kbw.co.uk

SPENCER-LEWIS MR NEVILLE JULIAN

12 King's Bench Walk
12 King's Bench Walk, Temple, London EC4Y 7EL, ☎ 020 7583 0811
The Chambers of Adrian Turner
4 Charleston Road, Eastbourne BN21 1SF, ☎ 01323 737388
Call Date: July 1970, Inner Temple
Pupil Supervisor
Qualifications: [MA (Oxon)]
spencer-lewis@12kbw.co.uk

SPENS MR DAVID PATRICK QC (1995)

Garden Court Chambers
57-60 Lincoln's Inn Fields, London WC2A 3LJ, ☎ 020 7993 7600 ✉ info@gclaw.co.uk
Call Date: Nov 1973, Inner Temple
Recorder
Qualifications: [BA]
davidsp@gclaw.co.uk

SPENWYN MS MARIE ANN

Carmelite Chambers
9 Carmelite Street, London EC4Y 0DR, ☎ 020 7936 6300
✉ clerks@carmelitechambers.co.uk
Call Date: Oct 1999, Gray's Inn
Pupil Supervisor
Qualifications: [LLB (LSE) LLM (Camtab)]
mspenwyn@carmelitechambers.co.uk

SPICER MR JONATHAN RICHARD

36 Bedford Row
London WC1R 4JH, ☎ 020 7421 8000
✉ chambers@36bedfordrow.co.uk
Call Date: Oct 1995, Lincoln's Inn
Qualifications: [MA (Cantab)]
clerks@36bedfordrow.co.uk, jspicer@36bedfordrow.co.uk

SPICER MISS RACHEL MARTHA

1 Hare Court
1 Hare Court, Temple, London EC4Y 7BE, ☎ 020 7797 7070 ✉ clerks@1hc.com
Riverview Chambers
Hamilton House, 1 Temple Avenue, London EC4Y 0HA, ☎ 0844 225 3999
✉ chrisbaylis@riverviewchambers.com
Call Date: Nov 2002, Middle Temple
Pupil Supervisor
Qualifications: [BA (Hons) (Oxon) Dip in Law]
spicer@1hc.com

SPICER MR ROBERT HADEN

Frederick Place Chambers
9 Frederick Place, Frederick Place Chambers, Clifton, Bristol BS8 1AS, ☎ 0117 946 7059
✉ rsp4593558@aol.com
Call Date: July 1970, Inner Temple
Qualifications: [MA (Cantab) Dip LegStuds (Cantab)]

SPIER MISS SIAN

Chambers of Sian Spier
8 Upper Park Road, Kingston Upon Thames, Surrey KT2 5LD, ☎ 020 8546 7868
✉ sianhines@me.com
Call Date: Nov 1989, Inner Temple
Qualifications: [LLB (Buck)]
sianhines@me.com

SPINK MR ANDREW JOHN MURRAY QC (2003)

Outer Temple Chambers
The Outer Temple, 222 Strand, London WC2R 1BA, ☎ 020 7353 6381
✉ clerks@outertemple.com
Riverview Chambers
Hamilton House, 1 Temple Avenue, London EC4Y 0HA, ☎ 0844 225 3999
✉ chrisbaylis@riverviewchambers.com
Call Date: Nov 1985, Middle Temple
Recorder
Qualifications: [MA (Cantab)]
andrew.spinkqc@outertemple.com

SPINK MR PETER JOHN WILLIAM

12 College Place
Fauvelle Buildings, 12 College Place, Southampton SO15 2FE, ☎ 023 8032 0320
✉ clerks@12cp.co.uk
Call Date: July 1979, Gray's Inn
pspink@12cp.co.uk

SPINKS MR RODERICK CAMERON

Fenners Chambers
3 Madingley Road, Cambridge CB3 0EE, ☎ 01223 368761
✉ clerks@fennerschambers.com
Call Date: Nov 1997, Inner Temple
Qualifications: [LLB (Sheff)]
roderick.spinks@fennerschambers.co.uk

SPIRO MISS DAFNA MIRIAM

Garden Court Chambers
57-60 Lincoln's Inn Fields, London WC2A 3LJ, ☎ 020 7993 7600 ✉ info@gclaw.co.uk
Call Date: Nov 1994, Inner Temple
Pupil Supervisor
Qualifications: [BA (Sussex) CPE]

E

SPITZ MR DEREK BRYAN

One Essex Court
Ground Floor, One Essex Court, Temple, London EC4Y 9AR, ☎ 020 7583 2000
✉ clerks@oeclaw.co.uk
Call Date: Nov 2001, Lincoln's Inn
Qualifications: [LLB MA JD]
dspitz@oeclaw.co.uk

SPOLLON MR GUY MERTON

St Philips Chambers
55 Temple Row, Birmingham B2 5LS, ☎ 0121 246 7000 ✉ clerks@st-philips.com
Call Date: Nov 1976, Gray's Inn
Pupil Supervisor
Qualifications: [BA]
gspollon@st-philips.co.uk

SPOONER MR HENRY NEVILLE

Westgate Chambers
64 High Street, Lewes, East Sussex BN7 1XG, ☎ 01273 480510
✉ clerks@westgate-chambers.co.uk
Tolzey Chambers
37 Rowlandson Gardens, Lockleaze, Bristol BS7 9UH
Call Date: Nov 1971, Lincoln's Inn
Pupil Supervisor

SPOONER MISS JUDITH ANN

14 Gray's Inn Square
14 Gray's Inn Square, Gray's Inn, London WC1R 5JP, ☎ 020 7242 0858
✉ clerks@14gis.co.uk
Call Date: July 1987, Middle Temple
Pupil Supervisor
Qualifications: [LLB (Hons)(Reading)]
js@14graysinnsquare.co.uk

SPRAGG MR ROBERT FORRESTER

Trinity Chambers
The Custom House, 39 Quayside, Newcastle Upon Tyne NE1 3DE, ☎ 0191 232 1927
✉ info@trinitychambers.co.uk
Call Date: July 2003, Middle Temple
Qualifications: [LLB Hons (Newc)]

SPRATLING MRS ANNE VIRGINIA

Coram Chambers
9-11 Fulwood Place, London WC1V 6HG, ☎ 020 7092 3700
✉ mail@coramchambers.co.uk
Call Date: July 1980, Lincoln's Inn
Pupil Supervisor
Qualifications: [BA (Cantab)]
anne.spratling@coramchambers.co.uk

SPRATT MR CHRISTOPHER DAVID RICHARD DEAN

9 Stone Buildings
Lincoln's Inn, London WC2A 3NN, ☎ 020 7404 5055
✉ clerks@9stonebuildings.com
Call Date: Nov 1986, Gray's Inn
Pupil Supervisor
Qualifications: [LLB (Scotland)]

SPRATT-DAWSON MISS JOSEPHINE MARGERY

Trinity Chambers
Highfield House, Moulsham Street, Chelmsford, Essex CM2 9AH, ☎ 01245 605040
✉ clerks@trinitychambers.com
Call Date: Oct 1993, Gray's Inn
Pupil Supervisor
Qualifications: [LLB (UEA)]
jsprattdawson@trinitychambers.com

SPREADBOROUGH MR PAUL RICHARD

Furnival Chambers
32 Furnival Street, London EC4A 1JQ, ☎ 020 7405 3232
Call Date: Oct 2002, Gray's Inn
Qualifications: [LLB (Essex)]
pspreadborough@furnivallaw.co.uk

SPRIGGS MISS KATIE LOUISE

New Walk Chambers
27 New Walk, Leicester, Leicestershire LE1 6TE, ☎ 0871 200 1298 / 0116 255 9144
✉ clerks@newwalkchambers.co.uk
Call Date: July 2010, Gray's Inn
Qualifications: [LLB]

SPRINZ MISS LUCY

1 Garden Court Family Law Chambers
Ground Floor, One Garden Court, Temple, London EC4Y 9BJ, ☎ 020 7797 7900
✉ clerks@1gc.com
Call Date: Oct 2008, Inner Temple
Qualifications: [BA (Nott'm)]
sprinz@1gc.com

SPROSON MISS EILEEN

2 King's Bench Walk
2 King's Bench Walk, Temple, London EC4Y 7DE, ☎ 020 7353 1746
✉ clerks@2kbw.com
Call Date: July 2005, Gray's Inn
Qualifications: [B.Sc Southampton]

SPROULL MR NICHOLAS

Albion Chambers
Broad Street, Bristol BS1 1DR,
☎0117 927 2144
✉clerks@albionchambers.co.uk
Call Date: Nov 1992, Gray's Inn
Pupil Supervisor
Qualifications: [LLB (Bris)]
✉nicholas.sproull@albionchambers.co.uk

SPURLING MR RUDOLPH

10 King's Bench Walk
Ground Floor, 10 King's Bench Walk, Temple, London EC4Y 7EB, ☎020 7353 7742
✉Chambers@10kingsbenchwalk.co.uk
Call Date: Oct 2007, Middle Temple
Qualifications: [MA (Lond) BA (Hons) (Lond)]
✉rudolph.spurling@10kingsbenchwalk.co.uk

SPURRIER MISS MARTHA GABRIELLA

36 Bedford Row
London WC1R 4JH, ☎020 7421 8000
✉chambers@36bedfordrow.co.uk
Call Date: Oct 2010, Middle Temple
Qualifications: [BA (Hons) (Cantab)]
✉clerks@36bedfordrow.co.uk

SQUIRE MR PHILIP DENBY

3 Dr Johnson's Buildings
Ground Floor, 3 Dr Johnson's Buildings, Temple, London EC4Y 7BA, ☎020 7353 4854
✉clerks@3djb.co.uk
Call Date: Nov 1997, Inner Temple
Pupil Supervisor
Qualifications: [BA (Sheff)]

SQUIRES MR DANIEL BENJAMIN

Matrix Chambers
Griffin Building, Gray's Inn, London WC1R 5LN, ☎020 7404 3447
✉matrix@matrixlaw.co.uk / Iscott@matrixlaw.co.uk
Call Date: Nov 1998, Middle Temple
Qualifications: [MA (Cantab) LLM (USA) MSc (Lond)]
✉dansquires@matrixlaw.co.uk

SQUIRRELL MR BENJAMIN

Nine Bedford Row
9 Bedford Row, London WC1R 4AZ,
☎020 7489 2727
✉clerks@9bedfordrow.co.uk
Call Date: Oct 1990, Inner Temple
Pupil Supervisor
Qualifications: [BA (Lond) Dip Law]
✉benjamin.squirrell@9bedfordrow.co.uk

ST LOUIS MR BRIAN LLOYD

15 New Bridge Street
London EC4V 6AU, ☎020 7842 1900
✉clerks@15nbs.com
Call Date: Oct 1994, Middle Temple
Pupil Supervisor
Qualifications: [LLB (Hons) LLM (Lond)]

ST QUINTIN MR THOMAS CHRISTOPHER

Hogarth Chambers
5 New Square, Lincoln's Inn, London WC2A 3RJ, ☎020 7404 0404
✉barristers@hogarthchambers.com
Call Date: Oct 2006, Inner Temple
Qualifications: [MA (Cantab)]
✉tstquintin@hogarthchambers.com

ST VILLE MR LAURENCE JAMES

8 New Square
8 New Square, Lincoln's Inn, London WC2A 3QP, ☎020 7405 4321
✉clerks@8newsquare.co.uk
Call Date: Oct 1995, Gray's Inn
Pupil Supervisor
Qualifications: [MA C.Eng MIEE (Cantab)]
✉st.ville@8newsquare.co.uk

Types of work: Breach of confidence, Competition law, Computer litigation, Copyright, Copyright Tribunal, Data protection, Design, E-commerce, EC competition law, Entertainment, Franchising, Information technology, Intellectual property, Malicious falsehood, Media and entertainment, Passing off, Patents, Pharmaceuticals, Privacy, Scientific and technical disputes, Trade secrets, Trademarks

STABLES MR CHRISTOPHER HILTON

Exchange Chambers
One Derby Square, Derby Square, Liverpool L2 9XX, ☎0151 236 7747
✉info@exchangechambers.co.uk
Exchange Chambers
7 Ralli Courts, West Riverside, Manchester M3 5FT, ☎0161 833 2722
Exchange Chambers
Oxford House, Oxford Row, Leeds LS1 3BE,
☎0113 203 1970
✉spencer@exchangechambers.co.uk
Call Date: Oct 1990, Gray's Inn
Pupil Supervisor
Qualifications: [LLB (L'pool)]
✉stables@exchangechambers.co.uk

STABLES MR GORDON

Call Date: Oct 1995, Lincoln's Inn
Pupil Supervisor
Qualifications: [BA (Hons) MA CPE (Hudds)]

E

STACEY MR DANIEL THOMAS

Hailsham Chambers
Ground Floor, 4 Paper Buildings, Temple, London EC4Y 7EX, ☎020 7643 5000
✉clerks@hailshamchambers.com
Call Date: Nov 1996, Gray's Inn
Pupil Supervisor
Qualifications: [BA (Oxon)]
dan.stacey@hailshamchambers.com

STACEY MISS MYRIAM NICOLE

Landmark Chambers
180 Fleet Street, London EC4A 2HG, ☎020 7430 1221
✉clerks@landmarkchambers.co.uk
Call Date: Oct 1998, Inner Temple
Qualifications: [LLB (Bris)]
mstacey@landmarkchambers.co.uk

STADDON MISS CLAIRE ANN

New Square Chambers
12 New Square, Lincoln's Inn, London WC2A 3SW, ☎020 7419 8000
✉robin.hollington@newsquarechambers.co.uk
Call Date: July 1985, Middle Temple
Qualifications: [LLB (Lond)]
claire.staddon@newsquarechambers.co.uk

STADDON MR PAUL

Tanfield Chambers
2-5 Warwick Court, London WC1R 5DJ, ☎020 7421 5300
✉clerks@tanfieldchambers.co.uk
Call Date: July 1976, Inner Temple
Qualifications: [BSc (Econ) (Lond)]

STAFF MR MARCUS RICHARD

XXIV Old Buildings
Ground Floor, 24 Old Buildings, Lincoln's Inn, London WC2A 3UP, ☎020 7691 2424
✉clerks@xxiv.co.uk
Call Date: Nov 1994, Inner Temple
Pupil Supervisor
Qualifications: [BA (York)]
marcus.staff@xxiv.co.uk

STAFFORD MR ANDREW BRUCE QC (2000)

Littleton Chambers
3 King's Bench Walk North, Temple, London EC4Y 7HR, ☎020 7797 8600
✉fschneider@littletonchambers.co.uk
Trinity Chambers
The Custom House, 39 Quayside, Newcastle Upon Tyne NE1 3DE, ☎0191 232 1927
✉info@trinitychambers.co.uk
Trinity Chambers
Multi Media Exchange, 72-80 Corporation Road, Middlesbrough TS1 2RF, ☎01642 247569
✉info@trinitychambers.co.uk
Call Date: July 1980, Middle Temple
Qualifications: [MA (Cantab)]
astafford@littletonchambers.co.uk

STAFFORD MR PAUL RINALDO

Ten Old Square
Ground Floor, Ten Old Square, Lincoln's Inn, London WC2A 3SU, ☎020 7405 0758
✉clerks@tenoldsquare.com
Call Date: Nov 1987, Gray's Inn
Pupil Supervisor
Qualifications: [MA (Oxon) D Phil (Oxon) Dip Law]
paulstafford@tenoldsquare.com

STAFFORD-MICHAEL MR SIMON ALEXANDER

Lombard Chambers
1 Sekforde Street, Clerkenwell, London EC1R 0BE, ☎020 7107 2100
Call Date: Nov 1982, Gray's Inn
Pupil Supervisor
Qualifications: [LLB(Bristol)]

STAGE MR PETER JAMES

4 Breams Buildings
Chancery Lane, London EC4A 1HP, ☎020 7092 1900 ✉clerks@4bb.co.uk
Call Date: July 1971, Lincoln's Inn
Pupil Supervisor
Qualifications: [LLB]

STAGG MR PAUL ANDREW

1 Chancery Lane
London WC2A 1LF, ☎0845 634 6666
✉clerks@1chancerylane.com
Call Date: Oct 1994, Gray's Inn
Pupil Supervisor
Qualifications: [LLB (Warw)]
pstagg@1chancerylane.com

STAKER MR CHRISTOPHER ROBERT

39 Essex Street
London WC2R 3AT, ☎020 7832 1111
✉clerks@39essex.com
82 King Street
Manchester M2 4WQ, ☎0161 870 9969
Call Date: Oct 2003, Middle Temple
Qualifications: [LLB (Hons) DPhil (Oxon) BA]
christopher.staker@39essex.com

STALLWORTHY MR NICOLAS KYD QC (2011)

Outer Temple Chambers
The Outer Temple, 222 Strand, London WC2R 1BA, ☎020 7353 6381
✉clerks@outertemple.com
Call Date: Oct 1993, Middle Temple
Pupil Supervisor
Qualifications: [MA (Oxon) BLC]
✉nicolas.stallworthy@outertemple.com

Fax: 020 7583 1786;
DX: 351 London

Types of work: Chancery (commercial), Commercial contracts, Commercial litigation, Employee benefit trusts, Financial services, Pensions, Professional negligence, Trust litigation, Trusts

Membership of foreign bars: Northern Ireland

Awards and memberships: Association of Pension Lawyers; Chancery Bar Association; Professional Negligence Bar Association; Commercial Bar Association (COMBAR); Financial Services Lawyers Association

Reported Cases: *Bridge Trustees v Yates, Re the Imperial Home Décor Pension Scheme,* [2011] UKSC 42; [2011] 1 WLR 1912; [2012] 1 All E.R. 659; [2011] I.C.R. 1069; [2011] Pens. L.R. 313; Times, August 9, 2011 (Supreme Court), 2011. Acting for successful representative beneficiaries in case concerning the meaning of the statutory definition of 'money purchase benefit' and the operation of s.73 of the Pensions Act 1995 in relation to hybrid schemes
Bloom & Ors v The Pensions Regulator & Ors, Re: the Nortel and Lehman Brothers administrations, [2011] EWCA Civ 1124; [2012] Bus. L.R. 818; [2012] 1 All E.R. 1455; [2012] B.C.C. 83; [2012] 1 B.C.L.C. 248; [2011] Pens. L.R. 397; and appeal in Supreme Court pending (Court of Appeal), 2011. Acting for the Trustees of the Lehman Brothers Pension Scheme and the Pension Protection Fund, securing declarations that a Financial Support Direction (and any ensuing Contribution Notice) is enforceable within a target's administration or liquidation
Re the Box Clever Pension Scheme, [2012] 014 PBLR (The Determinations Panel of the Pensions Regulator), 2011. Acting for the Pensions Regulator in proceedings determining that a Financial Support Direction should be issued against companies associated with employers in a failed joint venture.
Re the Lehman Brothers Pension Scheme, FS/2010/0031 (Upper Tribunal), 2012. Acting for the Trustees of the Lehman Brothers Pension Scheme defending application to strike out their reference from the Determination that a Financial Support Direction should not be issued against certain companies within the Lehman Brothers group of companies
IBM UK Pensions Trust Ltd v Metcalfe & Others, [2012] EWHC 125 (costs); trial judgment pending (Chancery Division (Warren J)), 2012. Acting for beneficiary in proceedings claiming rectification of early retirement rules in the IBM Pension Plan

STAMFORD MISS SUSAN DEBORAH

Coram Chambers
9-11 Fulwood Place, London WC1V 6HG, ☎020 7092 3700
✉mail@coramchambers.co.uk
Call Date: Oct 1997, Middle Temple
Qualifications: [LLB (Hons)]
✉susan.stamford@coramchambers.co.uk

STAMP MISS ABIGAIL

Guildhall Chambers
23 Broad Street, Bristol BS1 2HG, ☎0117 930 9000
✉hoc@guildhallchambers.co.uk
Call Date: Oct 2004, Gray's Inn
Qualifications: [LLB]
✉abigail.stamp@guildhallchambers.co.uk

STANAGE MR NICK SEAN

Doughty Street Chambers
53-54 Doughty Street, London WC1N 2LS, ☎020 7404 1313
✉enquiries@doughtystreet.co.uk
Doughty Street Chambers
Pall Mall Court, 61-67 King Street, Manchester M2 4PD, ☎0161 618 1066
Doughty Street Chambers
5th Floor, Broad Quay House, Prince Street, Bristol BS1 4DJ, ☎01179 058 717
Call Date: Oct 1997, Inner Temple
Qualifications: [MA CPE (Bris)]
✉n.stanage@doughtystreet.co.uk

STANBROOK MR CLIVE ST GEORGE QC (1989)

Henderson Chambers
2 Harcourt Buildings, Temple, London EC4Y 9DB, ☎020 7583 9020
✉clerks@hendersonchambers.co.uk
Call Date: Nov 1972, Inner Temple
Qualifications: [LLB (Lond)]

E

STANBURY MRS LOUISE EMMA

Bank House Chambers
Old Bank House, Hartshead, Sheffield S1 2EL, ☎0114 275 1223
✉w.digby@bankhousechambers.co.uk
Call Date: Oct 2004, Lincoln's Inn
Qualifications: [LLB (Hons)]
l.rafferty@bankhousechambers.co.uk

STANBURY MR MATTHEW FRANCIS

Chambers of Ian Macdonald QC
Garden Court North, 22 Oxford Court, Manchester M2 3WQ, ☎0161 236 1840
✉clerks@gcnchambers.co.uk
Call Date: Oct 2004, Gray's Inn
Qualifications: [LLB Sheffield]

STANCOMBE MR BARRY TERRENCE

Chambers of Andrew Mitchell QC
33 Chancery Lane, London WC2A 1EN, ☎020 7440 9950 ✉clerks@33cllaw.com
3 PB Barristers
Royal Talbot House, 2 Victoria Street, Bristol, Avon BS1 6BB, ☎0117 928 1520
3 PB Barristers
4 St Peter Street, Winchester SO23 8BW, ☎01962 868884
✉clerks.winchester@3paper.co.uk
3 PB Barristers
23 Beaumont Street, Oxford OX1 2NP, ☎01865 793 736
3 PB Barristers
3 Paper Buildings, Temple, London EC4Y 7EU, ☎020 7583 8055
3 PB Barristers
30 Christchurch Road, Bournemouth, Dorset BH1 3PD, ☎01202 292102
✉clerks.bournemouth@3paper.co.uk
Call Date: July 1983, Gray's Inn
Pupil Supervisor
Qualifications: [LLB (Hons) (Lond)]
bs@33cllaw.com

STANDFAST MR PHILIP ARTHUR

St Paul's Chambers
5th Floor, St Paul's House, 23 Park Square South, Leeds LS1 2ND, ☎0113 245 5866
Call Date: July 1980, Inner Temple
Pupil Supervisor
Qualifications: [BA (Sheff)]

STANFORD MISS KATRIONA ANN ELIZABETH

7 Bell Yard
London WC2A 2JR, ☎020 7831 0636
✉kevintarrant@btconnect.com
Call Date: Nov 2004, Gray's Inn
Qualifications: [BA (Cantab)]

STANFORD MR TONY JAMES

Old Bailey Chambers
15 Old Bailey, London EC4M 7EF, ☎020 3008 6404
✉clerks@15oldbaileychambers.com
Call Date: Nov 1996, Lincoln's Inn
Qualifications: [LLB (Hons)(Lond)]
t.stanford@15oldbaileychambers.com

STANGER MR MARK FULLERTON

Oriel Chambers
14 Water Street, Liverpool, Merseyside L2 8TD, ☎0151 236 7191
✉clerks@orielchambers.co.uk
33 Bedford Row
London WC1R 4JH, ☎020 7242 6476
✉clerks@33bedfordrow.co.uk
Call Date: July 1998, Middle Temple
Qualifications: [LLB (Hons)(B'ham)]
MarkStanger@33bedfordrow.co.uk

STANGOE MISS HEATHER ELIZABETH

Atkinson Bevan Chambers
1st Floor, 2 Harcourt Buildings, Temple, London EC4Y 9DB, ☎020 7353 2112
✉clerks@2hb.co.uk
Call Date: Oct 2001, Inner Temple
Qualifications: [MA (Lond) CPE]
hstangoe@2hb.co.uk

STANISTREET MISS PENELOPE

Call Date: Oct 1993, Lincoln's Inn
Pupil Supervisor
Qualifications: [BA (Hons)(Notts) Dip Law (Lond)]
pennie.stanistreet@stjohnsbuildings.co.uk, stanistreet@paradise-sq.co.uk

STANLEY MISS CLARE FIONA LOUISE

Wilberforce Chambers
8 New Square, Lincoln's Inn, London WC2A 3QP, ☎020 7306 0102
✉chambers@wilberforce.co.uk
Call Date: Nov 1994, Middle Temple
Pupil Supervisor
Qualifications: [BA (Hons) (Cantab)]
cstanley@wilberforce.co.uk

STANLEY MRS GILLIAN FRANCES

1 Garden Court Family Law Chambers
Ground Floor, One Garden Court, Temple, London EC4Y 9BJ, ☎ 020 7797 7900
✉ clerks@1gc.com
Call Date: July 2001, Middle Temple
Pupil Supervisor
Qualifications: [BA CPE]
✉ stanley@1gc.com

STANLEY MR PAUL MALLALIEU QC (2010)

Essex Court Chambers
24 Lincoln's Inn Fields, London WC2A 3EG,
☎ 020 7813 8000
✉ clerksroom@essexcourt.net
Call Date: Nov 1993, Middle Temple
Pupil Supervisor
Qualifications: [BA (Hons)(Cantab) LLM (USA)]
✉ pstanley@essexcourt.net

STANNILAND MR JONATHAN PETER

Albion Chambers
Broad Street, Bristol BS1 1DR,
☎ 0117 927 2144
✉ clerks@albionchambers.co.uk
Call Date: Nov 1993, Inner Temple
Pupil Supervisor
Qualifications: [LLB]
✉ jonathan.stanniland@albionchambers.co.uk

STANSBY MRS HILARY ALEXANDRA

18 St John Street
Manchester M3 4EA, ☎ 0161 278 1800
✉ clerks@18sjs.com
Call Date: Nov 1985, Middle Temple
Pupil Supervisor
Qualifications: [MA (Cantab)]

STANSFELD MR JAMES HUGH

Great James Street Chambers
37 Great James Street, London WC1N 3HB,
☎ 020 7440 4949
✉ chambers@greatjames.co.uk
Call Date: July 2008, Inner Temple
Qualifications: [LLB (Sheff)]
✉ james.stansfeld@greatjames.co.uk

STANSFIELD MR PIERS ALISTAIR QC (2012)

Keating Chambers
15 Essex Street, London WC2R 3AA,
☎ 020 7544 2600
✉ clerks@keatingchambers.com
Call Date: Nov 1993, Inner Temple
Pupil Supervisor
Qualifications: [LLB (Bris)]
✉ pstansfield@keatingchambers.com

STANTON MR DAVID RONALD

4 Breams Buildings
Chancery Lane, London EC4A 1HP,
☎ 020 7092 1900 ✉ clerks@4bb.co.uk
Call Date: July 1979, Gray's Inn
Pupil Supervisor
Qualifications: [BA]

STANZEL MRS SARAH ASTRID

Tanfield Chambers
2-5 Warwick Court, London WC1R 5DJ,
☎ 020 7421 5300
✉ clerks@tanfieldchambers.co.uk
Call Date: July 1999, Inner Temple
Qualifications: [LLB LLM]

STAPLES MISS JOANNA LIDA

Dyers Chambers
35 Bedford Row, London WC1R 4JH,
☎ 020 7404 1881
✉ admin@dyerschambers.com
Call Date: Oct 2003, Lincoln's Inn
Qualifications: [LLB (Hons) (Lond)]

STAPLETON MS ELAINE BRIGID

Carmelite Chambers
9 Carmelite Street, London EC4Y 0DR,
☎ 020 7936 6300
✉ clerks@carmelitechambers.co.uk
Call Date: Nov 1997, Inner Temple
Qualifications: [BCL (Dublin) LLM (Lond)]
✉ estapleton@carmelitechambers.co.uk

STARCEVIC MR PETAR

St Philips Chambers
55 Temple Row, Birmingham B2 5LS,
☎ 0121 246 7000 ✉ clerks@st-philips.com
Call Date: July 1983, Inner Temple
Pupil Supervisor
Qualifications: [LLB (Bris)]
✉ pstarcevic@st-philips.co.uk

STARK MR JAMES HAYDEN ALEXANDER

Chambers of Ian Macdonald QC
Garden Court North, 22 Oxford Court, Manchester M2 3WQ, ☎ 0161 236 1840
✉ clerks@gcnchambers.co.uk
Call Date: Mar 1998, Middle Temple
Qualifications: [LLB (Hons)(Sheff)]

STARK MISS SAMANTHA JANE

15 New Bridge Street
London EC4V 6AU, ☎ 020 7842 1900
✉ clerks@15nbs.com
Call Date: July 2005, Middle Temple
Qualifications: [LLB (Hons)]
✉ samantha.stark@15nbs.com

E

STARKEY MR TIMOTHY LUKE

Castle Chambers
The Old Fire Station, 90 High Street, Harrow-on-the-Hill, Middlesex HA1 3LP, ☎ 020 8423 6579 ✉ info@castlechambers.net
Call Date: Mar 2002, Middle Temple
Qualifications: [BA (Hons)]

STARKS MR NICHOLAS ERNSHAW

St Ive's Chambers
Whittall Street, Birmingham B4 6DH, ☎ 0121 236 0863
✉ clerks@stiveschambers.co.uk
Call Date: July 1989, Middle Temple
Qualifications: [LLB (Hons)(Manch)]
nicholas.starks@stiveschambers.co.uk

STARR MRS TERESA MARGARET

Great James Street Chambers
37 Great James Street, London WC1N 3HB, ☎ 020 7440 4949
✉ chambers@greatjames.co.uk
Call Date: Oct 2000, Middle Temple
Qualifications: [LLB (Hons) (Lond)]

STARTE MR HARVEY NICHOLAS ADRIAN

One Brick Court
1st Floor, One Brick Court, Temple, London EC4Y 9BY, ☎ 020 7353 8845
✉ clerks@onebrickcourt.com
Call Date: Nov 1985, Gray's Inn
Pupil Supervisor
Qualifications: [MA (Cantab)]
hs@onebrickcourt.com

STATHER MISS JULIE

42 Bedford Row
London WC1R 4LL, ☎ 020 7831 0222
✉ clerks@42br.com
Call Date: Oct 2000, Inner Temple
Qualifications: [LLB (Leic)]
Julie.stather@42br.com

STAUNTON MR ULICK

Radcliffe Chambers
Ground Floor, 11 New Square, Lincoln's Inn, London WC2A 3QB, ☎ 020 7831 0081
✉ clerks@radcliffechambers.com
Call Date: July 1984, Middle Temple
Pupil Supervisor
Qualifications: [LLB (Lond)]
ustaunton@radcliffechambers.com

STAUNTON MR WILLIAM JOHN PAUL

Central Chambers
89 Princess Street, Manchester M1 4HT, ☎ 0161 236 1133
✉ clerks@centralchambers.co.uk
Call Date: Feb 1986, Middle Temple
Qualifications: [MA (Cantab)]

STAVROU MISS XENIA

5 King's Bench Walk
5 King's Bench Walk, Temple, London EC4Y 7DN, ☎ 020 7353 5638
✉ clerks@5kbw.co.uk
Call Date: Nov 1998, Middle Temple
Qualifications: [LLB (Hons)(Lond)]

STEAD MR RICHARD JAMES

St John's Chambers
101 Victoria Street, Bristol BS1 6PU, ☎ 0117 923 4700
✉ clerks@stjohnschambers.co.uk
Call Date: July 1979, Middle Temple
Pupil Supervisor, Recorder
Qualifications: [MA (Cantab)]
richard.stead@stjohnschambers.co.uk

STEAD MR TIMOTHY HAROLD

No.6 Park Square
Leeds LS1 2LW, ☎ 0113 245 9763
✉ Tim@no6.co.uk
Call Date: Nov 1979, Gray's Inn
Pupil Supervisor, Recorder
Qualifications: [BA]
stead@no6.co.uk

STEADMAN MR RUSSELL CHARLES

3 Dr Johnson's Buildings
Ground Floor, 3 Dr Johnson's Buildings, Temple, London EC4Y 7BA, ☎ 020 7353 4854
✉ clerks@3djb.co.uk
Call Date: Nov 1995, Inner Temple
Qualifications: [BA (Essex) CPE]
rsteadman@3djb.co.uk

STEBBINGS MR IAN ANTHONY

1 Gray's Inn Square
Ground Floor, 1 Gray's Inn Square, London WC1R 5AA, ☎ 020 7405 0001
Call Date: Oct 2001, Lincoln's Inn
Qualifications: [LLB (Hons) (Lond)]
istebbs@aol.com

E

STEDMAN MR ARYAN JOHN

Chambers of Mr A J Stedman
24a Palm Bay Avenue, Cliftonville, Kent CT9 3DQ, ☎07702 870575
✉aryanstedman@hotmail.com
Call Date: Nov 1997, Middle Temple
Qualifications: [LLB (Hons)(Kent)]

STEEL MR JOHN BRYCHAN QC (1993)

4-5 Gray's Inn Square
Gray's Inn, London WC1R 5AH,
☎020 7404 5252 ✉clerks@4-5.co.uk
Call Date: July 1978, Gray's Inn
Recorder
Qualifications: [BSc (Hons)]

STEEL MISS LOUISE CLARE

Dyers Chambers
35 Bedford Row, London WC1R 4JH,
☎020 7404 1881
✉admin@dyerschambers.com
Call Date: July 2009, Inner Temple
Qualifications: [BA (Lond)]

STEELE MR IAIN THOMAS

Blackstone Chambers
Blackstone House, Temple, London EC4Y 9BW, ☎020 7583 1770
✉clerks@blackstonechambers.com
Call Date: Oct 2005, Inner Temple
Qualifications: [BA Queen's College University of Cambridge BCL Oxon]
✉iainsteele@blackstonechambers.com

STEELE MISS JENNIFER ANNE

New Walk Chambers
27 New Walk, Leicester, Leicestershire LE1 6TE, ☎0871 200 1298 / 0116 255 9144
✉clerks@newwalkchambers.co.uk
Call Date: July 2002, Middle Temple
Pupil Supervisor
Qualifications: [LLB (Hons)]
✉JSteele@newwalkchambers.co.uk

STEEN MR MARTIN GAMPER

Albion Chambers
Broad Street, Bristol BS1 1DR,
☎0117 927 2144
✉clerks@albionchambers.co.uk
Call Date: July 1976, Inner Temple
Pupil Supervisor
Qualifications: [LLB (Hons)]
✉martin.steen@albionchambers.co.uk

STEER MR LEWIS RICHARD

Chambers of Richard Steer
Haywood House North, Dumfries Place, Cardiff CF10 3GA, ☎07950 401818
✉law@richardsteer.com
Call Date: Oct 2001, Gray's Inn
Qualifications: [BA (Hons)]

STEIN MR DANIEL ALEXANDER

No5 Chambers
Fountain Court, Steelhouse Lane, Birmingham B4 6DR, ☎0845 210 5555 ✉info@no5.com
No5 Chambers
Greenwood House, 4-7 Salisbury Court, London EC4Y 8AA, ☎0845 210 5555
No5 Chambers
38 Queen Square, Bristol BS1 4QS,
☎0845 210 5555
Call Date: July 1998, Gray's Inn
Qualifications: [LLB (Guildhall)]
✉ast@no5.com

STEIN MR SAMUEL QC (2009)

Dyers Chambers
35 Bedford Row, London WC1R 4JH,
☎020 7404 1881
✉admin@dyerschambers.com
Westgate Chambers
64 High Street, Lewes, East Sussex BN7 1XG,
☎01273 480510
✉clerks@westgate-chambers.co.uk
Call Date: Nov 1988, Inner Temple
Qualifications: [LLB (Hons)]

STEINBERG MR HARRY DAVID GLYN

12 King's Bench Walk
12 King's Bench Walk, Temple, London EC4Y 7EL, ☎020 7583 0811
Call Date: Nov 1997, Gray's Inn
Pupil Supervisor
Qualifications: [MA (Cantab)]
✉steinberg@12kbw.co.uk

STEINERT MR JONATHAN

Henderson Chambers
2 Harcourt Buildings, Temple, London EC4Y 9DB, ☎020 7583 9020
✉clerks@hendersonchambers.co.uk
Call Date: Feb 1986, Middle Temple
Pupil Supervisor
Qualifications: [BA (Oxon) Dip Law]
✉jsteinert@hendersonchambers.co.uk

E

STEINFELD MR ALAN GEOFFREY QC (1987)

XXIV Old Buildings
Ground Floor, 24 Old Buildings, Lincoln's Inn, London WC2A 3UP, ☎020 7691 2424
✉clerks@xxiv.co.uk
Call Date: Nov 1968, Lincoln's Inn
Qualifications: [BA LLB (Cantab)]
alan.steinfeld@xxiv.co.uk

STEINHARDT MS SARAH DAVIDSON

1 Mitre Court Buildings
1 Mitre Court Buildings, Temple, London EC4Y 7BS, ☎020 7452 8900
✉clerks@1mcb.com
Call Date: Nov 2008, Middle Temple
Qualifications: [BA (Hons) (Lond) LLM (Lond)]
sarah.steinhardt@1mcb.com

STELLING MR NIGEL ROY

Citadel Chambers
The Citadel, 190 Corporation Street, Birmingham B4 6QD, ☎0121 233 8500
✉clerks@citadelchambers.com
Call Date: July 1987, Inner Temple
Qualifications: [BA]
clerks@citadelchambers.com

E

STEMP MR SCOTT

12 College Place
Fauvelle Buildings, 12 College Place, Southampton SO15 2FE, ☎023 8032 0320
✉clerks@12cp.co.uk
Call Date: Oct 2000, Inner Temple
Qualifications: [LLB (Southampton)]
sstemp@12cp.co.uk

STENHOUSE MR JOHN ALEXANDER

Nightingale Chambers
Nightingale Cottage, Drakelow Lane, Wolverley, Worcestershire DY11 5RU, ☎01562 851350
✉john@jasten.free-online.co.uk
Call Date: Nov 1986, Lincoln's Inn
Qualifications: [LLB]
john@stenhouse-law.co.uk

STEPHANOU MISS SARAH

Chambers of Mr Ami Feder
Ground Floor, Lamb Building, Temple, London EC4Y 7AS, ☎020 7797 7788
✉clerks@lambbuilding.co.uk
Chambers of Mr Ami Feder
Ground Floor, Lamb Building, Temple, London EC4Y 7AS, ☎020 7797 7788
✉clerks@lambbuilding.co.uk
Call Date: Oct 2008, Inner Temple
Qualifications: [LLB (Lond) LLM (Lond)]

STEPHENS MR ANDREW XAVIER

Westgate Chambers
64 High Street, Lewes, East Sussex BN7 1XG, ☎01273 480510
✉clerks@westgate-chambers.co.uk
Call Date: July 2004, Lincoln's Inn
Qualifications: [LLB Hons (Sussex)]
astephens@westgate-chambers.co.uk

STEPHENS MISS JESSICA

Keating Chambers
15 Essex Street, London WC2R 3AA, ☎020 7544 2600
✉clerks@keatingchambers.com
Call Date: July 2001, Lincoln's Inn
Pupil Supervisor
Qualifications: [LLB (Hons)]
jstephens@keatingchambers.com

STEPHENS MR JOHN LEWIS

XXIV Old Buildings
Ground Floor, 24 Old Buildings, Lincoln's Inn, London WC2A 3UP, ☎020 7691 2424
✉clerks@xxiv.co.uk
Call Date: July 1975, Middle Temple
Pupil Supervisor
Qualifications: [BA (Oxon)]
john.stephens@xxiv.co.uk

STEPHENS MR MARK TIMOTHY EDWIN

Hardwicke
New Square, Lincoln's Inn, London WC2A 3SB, ☎020 7242 2523
✉enquiries@hardwicke.co.uk
Call Date: Nov 1998, Middle Temple
Qualifications: [BA (Hons) Dip Law]
mark.stephens@hardwicke.co.uk.

STEPHENS MR MICHAEL ALLEN

St Ive's Chambers
Whittall Street, Birmingham B4 6DH, ☎0121 236 0863
✉clerks@stiveschambers.co.uk
Design Chambers
24 Arterberry Road, Wimbledon, London SW20 8AH, ☎020 7353 0747
✉manager@designchambers.com
Call Date: July 1983, Middle Temple
Pupil Supervisor
Qualifications: [BA (Keele) FCIArb QDR FRSA]
michael.stephens@stiveschambers.co.uk

STEPHENSON MR ANTHONY MARK

Exchange Chambers
7 Ralli Courts, West Riverside, Manchester M3 5FT, ☎0161 833 2722
Exchange Chambers
One Derby Square, Derby Square, Liverpool L2 9XX, ☎0151 236 7747
✉info@exchangechambers.co.uk
Exchange Chambers
Oxford House, Oxford Row, Leeds LS1 3BE, ☎0113 203 1970
✉spencer@exchangechambers.co.uk
Call Date: Nov 1997, Gray's Inn
Qualifications: [LLB]
stephenson@exchangechambers.co.uk

STEPHENSON MR CHRISTOPHER JAMES

The Chambers of Grahame Aldous QC
9 Gough Square, London EC4A 3DG, ☎020 7832 0500
✉clerks@9goughsquare.co.uk
Call Date: Nov 1994, Lincoln's Inn
Pupil Supervisor
Qualifications: [MA (Hons)(Edin)]
cstephenson@9goughsquare.co.uk

STEPHENSON MR DAVID MATTHEW

1 Mitre Court Buildings
1 Mitre Court Buildings, Temple, London EC4Y 7BS, ☎020 7452 8900
✉clerks@1mcb.com
Call Date: Oct 2005, Lincoln's Inn
Qualifications: [LLB (Hons) London]
david.stephenson@1mcb.com, clerks@1mcb.com

STEPHENSON MR GEOFFREY CHARLES

Cornerstone Barristers
2-3 Gray's Inn Square, Gray's Inn, London WC1R 5JH, ☎020 7242 4986
✉chambers@2-3gis.co.uk
Call Date: Nov 1971, Gray's Inn
Pupil Supervisor
gstephenson@2-3gis.co.uk

STEPHENSON MR PAUL

St James's Chambers
68 Quay Street, Manchester M3 3EJ, ☎0161 834 7000
✉clerks@stjameschambers.com
Call Date: Oct 1990, Middle Temple
Qualifications: [LLB (Leeds) LLM]
clerks@stjameschambers.com

STEPHENSON MR SIMON HUW PETER

Angel Chambers
Ethos Building, Kings Road, Swansea SA1 8AS, ☎01792 464623
✉clerks@angelchambers.co.uk
Call Date: July 2005, Inner Temple
Qualifications: [LLB (Notts)]
simonstephenson@angelchambers.co.uk

STEPHENSON MR WILLIAM BENEDICT

3 PB Barristers
3 Paper Buildings, Temple, London EC4Y 7EU, ☎020 7583 8055
3 PB Barristers
30 Christchurch Road, Bournemouth, Dorset BH1 3PD, ☎01202 292102
✉clerks.bournemouth@3paper.co.uk
3 PB Barristers
4 St Peter Street, Winchester SO23 8BW, ☎01962 868884
✉clerks.winchester@3paper.co.uk
3 PB Barristers
Royal Talbot House, 2 Victoria Street, Bristol, Avon BS1 6BB, ☎0117 928 1520
3 PB Barristers
23 Beaumont Street, Oxford OX1 2NP, ☎01865 793 736
Call Date: July 1973, Inner Temple
Qualifications: [MA (Oxon)]

STERLING MR ROBERT ALAN

St James's Chambers
68 Quay Street, Manchester M3 3EJ, ☎0161 834 7000
✉clerks@stjameschambers.com
Zenith Chambers
10 Park Square, Leeds LS1 2LH, ☎0113 245 5438
✉clerks@zenithchambers.co.uk
Call Date: July 1970, Gray's Inn
Pupil Supervisor
Qualifications: [MA (Cantab)]
robert.sterling@stjameschambers.com

STERLING MISS VALERIE

Park Court Chambers
16 Park Place, Leeds LS1 2SJ, ☎0113 243 3277
✉clerks@parkcourtchambers.co.uk
Call Date: July 1981, Gray's Inn
Pupil Supervisor
Qualifications: [LLB]
clerks@parkcourtchambers.co.uk

E

STERN MR DAVID PATRICK JULIAN

King's Bench Chambers
Wellington House, 175 Holdenhurst Road, Bournemouth, Dorset BH8 8DQ, ☎ 01202 250025
11 Stone Buildings
11 Stone Buildings, Lincoln's Inn, London WC2A 3TG, ☎ 020 7831 6381
✉ clerks@11sb.com
Call Date: July 1989, Lincoln's Inn
Pupil Supervisor
Qualifications: [LLB (Lond) LLM (Cantab)]

STERN MR IAN MICHAEL QC (2006)

2 Bedford Row
London WC1R 4BU, ☎ 020 7440 8888
✉ clerks@2bedfordrow.co.uk
Call Date: July 1983, Inner Temple
Qualifications: [BA (Warw) Dip Law (Lond)]
istern@2bedfordrow.co.uk

STERN DR KRISTINA ANNE

39 Essex Street
London WC2R 3AT, ☎ 020 7832 1111
✉ clerks@39essex.com
82 King Street
Manchester M2 4WQ, ☎ 0161 870 9969
Call Date: Nov 1996, Inner Temple
Qualifications: [LLB (Melbourne) PhD (Cantab)]
kristina.stern@39essex.com

STERN MR MARK RICHARD ALEXANDER

2 Dr Johnson's Buildings
2 Dr Johnson's Buildings, Temple, London EC4Y 7AY, ☎ 020 7936 2613
✉ clerks@2drj.com
Call Date: Feb 1988, Lincoln's Inn
Qualifications: [MA (Hons) (Cantab)]
m.stern@2drj.com

STERN MR THOMAS WILLIAM PAUL

Maidstone Chambers
33 Earl Street, Maidstone, Kent ME14 1PF, ☎ 01622 688592
✉ clerks@maidstonechambers.co.uk
Call Date: Nov 1995, Gray's Inn
Pupil Supervisor
Qualifications: [LLB (Hons)]
tstern@maidstonechambers.co.uk

STERNBERG MR DANIEL ISAIAH

9-12 Bell Yard
London WC2A 2JR, ☎ 020 7400 1800
✉ clerks@9-12bellyard.com
Call Date: Oct 2006, Gray's Inn
Qualifications: [BA LLB]
d.sternberg@9-12bellyard.com

STERNBERG MR MICHAEL VIVIAN QC (2008)

4 Paper Buildings
1st Floor, 4 Paper Buildings, Temple, London EC4Y 7EX, ☎ 020 7427 5200
✉ clerks@4pb.com
Call Date: July 1975, Gray's Inn
Qualifications: [MA (Cantab) LLM (Cantab)]
mvs@4pb.com

STEVENS MR ANDREW JOHN CHARLES

4 Pump Court
4 Pump Court, Temple, London EC4Y 7AN, ☎ 020 7842 5555
✉ chambers@4pumpcourt.com
Call Date: Oct 2007, Lincoln's Inn
Qualifications: [BA (Cantab)]
astevens@4pumpcourt.com

STEVENS MRS HAZEL ANN

East Anglian Chambers
Gresham House, 5 Museum Street, Ipswich, Suffolk IP1 1HQ, ☎ 01473 214481
✉ ipswich@ealaw.co.uk
East Anglian Chambers
140 New London Road, Chelmsford, Essex CM2 0AW, ☎ 01473 214481
✉ chelmsford@ealaw.co.uk
East Anglian Chambers
15 The Close, Norwich, Norfolk NR1 4DZ, ☎ 01473 214481 ✉ norwich@ealaw.co.uk
Call Date: July 2001, Lincoln's Inn
Qualifications: [BA (Hons) PgDl]
hazelstevens@ealaw.co.uk

STEVENS MISS HEATHER LOUISE

Chambers of Mr Ami Feder
Ground Floor, Lamb Building, Temple, London EC4Y 7AS, ☎ 020 7797 7788
✉ clerks@lambbuilding.co.uk
Chambers of Mr Ami Feder
Ground Floor, Lamb Building, Temple, London EC4Y 7AS, ☎ 020 7797 7788
✉ clerks@lambbuilding.co.uk
Call Date: July 2009, Middle Temple
Qualifications: [BA (Hons) Grad Dip Law]

E

STEVENS MR HENRY ADAM

Guildhall Chambers
23 Broad Street, Bristol BS1 2HG,
☎ 0117 930 9000
✉ hoc@guildhallchambers.co.uk
Call Date: Oct 2002, Inner Temple
Qualifications: [BA (So'ton) LLB (So'ton)]
✉ henry.stevens@guildhallchambers.co.uk

STEVENS MR HOWARD LINTON QC (2012)

3 Hare Court
3 Hare Court, Temple, London EC4Y 7BJ,
☎ 020 7415 7800 ✉ clerks@3harecourt.com
Call Date: Oct 1990, Middle Temple
Pupil Supervisor
Qualifications: [BA (Dunelm) Dip Law (City)]
✉ howardstevens@3harecourt.com

STEVENS MR MARK NICHOLAS

Chambers of Marion Smullen and Kerim Fuad QC
1 Inner Temple Lane, London EC4Y 1AF,
☎ 020 7427 4400 ✉ clerks@1itl.com
Call Date: Nov 1998, Inner Temple
Qualifications: [LLB (Lond) LLM (Lond)]
✉ clerks@1itl.com

STEVENS MISS REBECCA

KBW
The Engine House, No 1 Foundry Square, Leeds LS11 5DL, ☎ 0113 297 1200
✉ clerks@kbwchambers.com
Call Date: Oct 1999, Middle Temple
Qualifications: [LLB (Hons)(Leeds)]
✉ rs@kbwchambers.com

STEVENS MR RICHARD MARK GEORGE

Cobden House Chambers
19 Quay Street, Manchester M3 3HN,
☎ 0161 833 6000 ✉ Clerks@Cobden.co.uk
Call Date: Oct 2008, Lincoln's Inn
Qualifications: [LLB (Leeds)]

STEVENS MR STUART STANDISH

Holborn Chambers
6 Gate Street, Lincoln's Inn Fields, London WC2A 3HP, ☎ 020 7242 6060
Call Date: July 1970, Gray's Inn
Pupil Supervisor
✉ stuartstevens@holbornchambers.co.uk

STEVENS MISS SUSANNAH RACHEL

QEB Hollis Whiteman
1-2 Laurence Pountney Hill, London EC4R 0EU, ☎ 020 7933 8855
✉ barristers@qebhw.co.uk
Call Date: Oct 1997, Middle Temple
Pupil Supervisor
Qualifications: [LLB (Hons)(Manc)]
✉ susannah.stevens@qebhw.co.uk

STEVENS MR THOMAS MICHAEL

Doughty Street Chambers
53-54 Doughty Street, London WC1N 2LS,
☎ 020 7404 1313
✉ enquiries@doughtystreet.co.uk
Call Date: Oct 2008, Middle Temple
Qualifications: [BA (Hons) (Bris) Dip in Law (Nott'm)]

STEVENS-HOARE MISS MICHELLE

Hardwicke
New Square, Lincoln's Inn, London WC2A 3SB, ☎ 020 7242 2523
✉ enquiries@hardwicke.co.uk
Call Date: July 1986, Middle Temple
Pupil Supervisor
Qualifications: [LLB (Lond) LLM (Lond)]
✉ michelle.stevens-hoare@hardwicke.co.uk

STEVENSON MR CHRISTOPHER

14 Gray's Inn Square
14 Gray's Inn Square, Gray's Inn, London WC1R 5JP, ☎ 020 7242 0858
✉ clerks@14gis.co.uk
Call Date: Nov 2009, Gray's Inn
Qualifications: [LLB]
✉ cs@14gis.co.uk

STEVENSON MR DANIEL KEITH

9-12 Bell Yard
London WC2A 2JR, ☎ 020 7400 1800
✉ clerks@9-12bellyard.com
Call Date: Oct 2002, Lincoln's Inn
Qualifications: [LLB (Sheff)]
✉ d.stevenson@9-12bellyard.com

STEVENSON MR JOHN MELFORD

Crown Office Chambers
2 Crown Office Row, Temple, London EC4Y 7HJ, ☎ 020 7797 8100
✉ mail@crownofficechambers.com
Call Date: Nov 1975, Inner Temple
Pupil Supervisor
Qualifications: [MA (Oxon)]
✉ jstevenson@crownofficechambers.com

E

STEVENSON MS MONICA MARGARET

25 Bedford Row
London WC1R 4HD, ☎020 7067 1500
✉clerks@25bedfordrow.com
Call Date: July 2004, Middle Temple
Qualifications: [LLB Hons (Wales) LLM (Nott'm)]
mstevenson@25bedfordrow.com

STEVENSON MR PAUL ANTHONY

Tanfield Chambers
2-5 Warwick Court, London WC1R 5DJ,
☎020 7421 5300
✉clerks@tanfieldchambers.co.uk
Call Date: Oct 2006, Middle Temple
Qualifications: [MA (Hons) (Oxon) Dip Law]
pstevenson@tanfieldchambers.co.uk

STEVENSON MR PETER NICHOLAS

Stone Chambers
4 Field Court, Gray's Inn, London WC1R 5EF,
☎020 7440 6900
✉clerks@stonechambers.com
Call Date: Nov 2008, Inner Temple
Qualifications: [MA (Edin) CPE]
peter.stevenson@stonechambers.com

STEVENSON MR ROBERT LLOYD

Sovereign Chambers
46 Park Place, Leeds LS1 2RY,
☎0113 245 1841
✉clerks@sovereignchambers.co.uk
Call Date: July 2003, Inner Temple
Qualifications: [LLB (Leic)]
robert.stevenson@sovereignchambers.co.uk

STEVENSON DR SIMON JOHN

Park Lane Plowden
19 Westgate, Leeds LS1 2RD,
☎0113 228 5049
✉clerks@parklaneplowden.co.uk
Call Date: Mar 1999, Lincoln's Inn
Qualifications: [BA (Hons) (Cantab) MA(Cantab) DPhil (Oxon) Dip Law]
simon.stevenson@parklaneplowden.co.uk

Fax: 0113 228 1500;
DX: 26404 Leeds, Park Square;
Other comms: E-mail:
clerks@parklaneplowden.co.uk
URL: www.parklaneplowden.co.uk/
member-details.php?practice=
chancery&member=30

Other professional qualifications: Accredited Mediator

Types of work: Agriculture, Boundaries, Chancery (general), Chancery (land law), Charities, Common land, Competition law, Copyright, Court of Protection, Equity, European Union, Family provision, Inheritance, Intellectual property, Landlord and tenant, Partnerships, Pensions, Professional negligence, Real property, Succession, Tax, Trusts, Wills

Awards and memberships: Chancery Bar Association; Charity Law Association; Statute Law Society

Reported Cases: *Adekunle v Richie*, [2007] WTLR 1505
Barron v Woodhead and Waite, [2009] 1 FLR 747
Webster v Webster & Others, [2009] WTLR 339; [2009] 1 FLR 1240

STEVENSON-WATT MR NEVILLE WILLIAM

Crown Office Row Chambers
119 Church Street, Brighton, Sussex
BN1 1UD, ☎01273 625625
✉clerks@1cor.com
Call Date: Nov 1985, Middle Temple
Pupil Supervisor
Qualifications: [MA (Cantab) LLB (Hons)]
neville.stevenson-watt@1cor.com

STEWARD MR MARK

Chavasse Court Chambers
18 Queen Avenue, Liverpool L2 4TX,
☎0151 229 2030
✉clerks@chavassechambers.co.uk
Call Date: Nov 2002, Inner Temple
Qualifications: [BA (Hons)]
mark.steward@chavassechambers.co.uk

STEWART MR ALEXANDER JOSEPH

Hogarth Chambers
5 New Square, Lincoln's Inn, London
WC2A 3RJ, ☎020 7404 0404
✉barristers@hogarthchambers.com
Call Date: July 1975, Gray's Inn
Qualifications: [BA BCL (Oxon)]
astewart@hogarthchambers.com

STEWART MR NICHOLAS JOHN CAMERON QC (1987)

Ely Place Chambers
30 Ely Place, London EC1N 6TD,
☎020 7400 9600 ✉admin@elyplace.com
Call Date: July 1971, Inner Temple
Qualifications: [BA (Oxon) FCIArb CEDR C Dip AF]

E

STEWART MR RICHARD PAUL

Lamb Chambers
Lamb Building, Elm Court, Temple, London EC4Y 7AS, ☎ 020 7797 8300
✉ info@lambchambers.co.uk
Call Date: July 1975, Gray's Inn
Pupil Supervisor
Qualifications: [BA (Belfast)]
✉ paulstewart@lambchambers.co.uk

STEWART MR ROGER PAUL DAVIDSON QC (2001)

Four New Square
Four New Square, Lincoln's Inn, London WC2A 3RJ, ☎ 020 7822 2000
✉ barristers@4newsquare.com
Call Date: July 1986, Inner Temple
Qualifications: [MA (Cantab) LLM]
✉ r.stewart@4newsquare.com

STEWART MR TOBY ALASDAIR CHARLES

Ropewalk Chambers
24 The Ropewalk, Nottingham NG1 5EF, ☎ 0115 947 2581 ✉ clerks@ropewalk.co.uk
Call Date: July 1989, Middle Temple
Pupil Supervisor
Qualifications: [LLB (Sheff)]
✉ tobystewart@ropewalk.co.uk

STEWART SMITH MR WILLIAM RODNEY

New Square Chambers
12 New Square, Lincoln's Inn, London WC2A 3SW, ☎ 020 7419 8000
✉ robin.hollington@newsquarechambers.co.uk
Call Date: June 1964, Middle Temple
Pupil Supervisor
Qualifications: [BA LLB]
✉ rodney.stewartsmith@newsquarechambers.co.uk

STEYN MS KAREN MARGARET

11 King's Bench Walk
11 King's Bench Walk, Temple, London EC4Y 7EQ, ☎ 020 7632 8500
✉ clerksroom@11kbw.com
Call Date: Oct 1995, Middle Temple
Pupil Supervisor
Qualifications: [BA (Hons) (L'pool) Dip Law (Lond) Dip EC Law (KCL)]
✉ karen.steyn@11kbw.com

STEYNOR MR ALAN CHARLES

Keating Chambers
15 Essex Street, London WC2R 3AA, ☎ 020 7544 2600
✉ clerks@keatingchambers.com
Call Date: July 1975, Gray's Inn
Pupil Supervisor, Recorder
Qualifications: [MA (Cantab) FCIArb]

STICKLER MISS REBECCA CINARA

30 Park Place
Cardiff CF10 3BS, ☎ 029 2039 8421
✉ clerks@30parkplace.law.co.uk
Call Date: Oct 2007, Middle Temple
Qualifications: [BA (Hons) (Oxon)]
✉ rs@30parkplace.co.uk

STILITZ MR DANIEL MALACHI QC (2010)

11 King's Bench Walk
11 King's Bench Walk, Temple, London EC4Y 7EQ, ☎ 020 7632 8500
✉ clerksroom@11kbw.com
Call Date: Oct 1992, Lincoln's Inn
Pupil Supervisor
Qualifications: [BA (Hons)(Oxon) MA (Lond)]
✉ daniel.stilitz@11kbw.com

STILL MR JULIAN JAMES

Chancery House Chambers
7 Lisbon Square, Leeds, West Yorkshire LS1 4LY, ☎ 0113 244 6691
✉ clerks@chanceryhouse.co.uk
Call Date: July 1999, Lincoln's Inn
Qualifications: [LLB (Hons)]
✉ julian.still@chanceryhouse.co.uk

STIMMLER MR BENJAMIN JAMES

13 King's Bench Walk
13 King's Bench Walk, Temple, London EC4Y 7EN, ☎ 020 7353 7204
✉ clerks@13kbw.co.uk
13 KBW
32 Beaumont Street, Oxford OX1 2NP, ☎ 01865 311066 ✉ clerks@13kbw.co.uk
Call Date: July 2009, Middle Temple
Qualifications: [BA (Hons) (Cantab) Dip Government and Politics Grad Dip Law (Lond)]

STIMPSON MR CHRISTOPHER HUGH

Atkinson Bevan Chambers
1st Floor, 2 Harcourt Buildings, Temple, London EC4Y 9DB, ☎ 020 7353 2112
✉ clerks@2hb.co.uk
Call Date: Oct 1999, Middle Temple
Qualifications: [MA (Hons)(Edin)]
✉ cstimpson@2hb.co.uk

E

STIMPSON MR MICHAEL EDWARD

Keating Chambers
15 Essex Street, London WC2R 3AA,
☎ 020 7544 2600
✉ clerks@keatingchambers.com
Call Date: Nov 1969, Lincoln's Inn

STINCHCOMBE MR PAUL DAVID QC (2011)

4-5 Gray's Inn Square
Gray's Inn, London WC1R 5AH,
☎ 020 7404 5252 ✉ clerks@4-5.co.uk
Call Date: July 1985, Lincoln's Inn
Pupil Supervisor
Qualifications: [BA (Cantab) LLM (USA)]
pstinchcombe@4-5.co.uk

STIRLING MISS CATRIONA MARIA

Cloisters
1 Pump Court, Temple, London EC4Y 7AA,
☎ 020 7827 4000 ✉ clerks@cloisters.com
Call Date: July 2008, Middle Temple
Qualifications: [MSci (Hons) LLB (Edin) PgDl (Nott'm)]
cs@cloisters.com

STIRLING MR CHRISTOPHER WILLIAM

Field Court Chambers
5 Field Court, Gray's Inn, London WC1R 5EF,
☎ 020 7405 6114 ✉ clerks@fieldcourt.co.uk
Call Date: Oct 1993, Inner Temple
Qualifications: [LLB]
christopher.stirling@fieldcourt.co.uk

STIRLING MR SIMON

Nine Bedford Row
9 Bedford Row, London WC1R 4AZ,
☎ 020 7489 2727
✉ clerks@9bedfordrow.co.uk
Call Date: July 1989, Gray's Inn
Pupil Supervisor
Qualifications: [BA (Hull)]
simon.stirling@9bedfordrow.co.uk

STOBART MRS TRACEY

KCH Garden Square
1 Oxford Street, Nottingham NG1 5BH,
☎ 0115 941 8851
✉ clerks@kchgardensquare.co.uk
Call Date: Oct 1995, Middle Temple
Qualifications: [LLB (Hons)]

STOCK MRS CATHERINE MCKINNON

Alexander Chambers
13 Halstead Road, Wanstead, London E11 2AY,
☎ 0845 652 0451 / 0854 652 0451
✉ clerks@alexanderchambers.co.uk
Trident Barristers Chambers
Peter House, Oxford Street, Manchester M1 5AN, ☎ 0161 663 3123
✉ clerks@tridentchambers.com
Call Date: July 2007, Middle Temple
Qualifications: [BA (Hons) (Glasgow) BSc (Hons) (Glasgow) RGN]

STOCKER MR JOHN CRISPIN

1 Garden Court Family Law Chambers
Ground Floor, One Garden Court, Temple, London EC4Y 9BJ, ☎ 020 7797 7900
✉ clerks@1gc.com
Call Date: Nov 1985, Inner Temple
Pupil Supervisor
Qualifications: [LLB (Exon) LLM (Cantab)]
stocker@1gc.com

STOCKILL MR DAVID ANDREW

St Philips Chambers
55 Temple Row, Birmingham B2 5LS,
☎ 0121 246 7000 ✉ clerks@st-philips.com
Call Date: Nov 1985, Lincoln's Inn
Pupil Supervisor
Qualifications: [MA (Cantab)]

STOCKLEY MISS RUTH ANGELA

Kings Chambers
36 Young Street, Manchester M3 3FT,
☎ 0845 034 3444
✉ clerks@kingschambers.com
Kings Chambers
5 Park Square East, Leeds LS1 2NE,
☎ 0845 034 3444
✉ clerks@kingschambers.com
Kings Chambers
Embassy House, 60 Church Street, Birmingham B3 2DJ, ☎ 0845 034 3444
✉ clerks@kingschambers.com
Call Date: July 1988, Lincoln's Inn
Pupil Supervisor
Qualifications: [LLB (Hons)(Notts)]
rstockley@kingschambers.com

STOCKWELL MR GRAHAM CLIVE

1 High Pavement
Nottingham NG1 1HF, ☎ 0115 941 8218
✉ clerks@1highpavement.co.uk
Call Date: Nov 1988, Inner Temple
Pupil Supervisor
Qualifications: [LLB]
clivestockwell@1highpavement.co.uk

STOCKWELL MR MATTHEW CHARLES

Call Date: Oct 1998, Gray's Inn
Qualifications: [LLB (L'pool)]
matthewstockwell@indiabuildings.co.uk

STOKELL MR ROBERT

Crown Office Chambers
2 Crown Office Row, Temple, London EC4Y 7HJ, ☎020 7797 8100
mail@crownofficechambers.com
Call Date: Oct 1995, Lincoln's Inn
Qualifications: [MA (Hons)(Oxon)]
stokell@crownofficechambers.com

STOKER MR GRAHAM KENNETH ROBERT

Cornerstone Barristers
2-3 Gray's Inn Square, Gray's Inn, London WC1R 5JH, ☎020 7242 4986
chambers@2-3gis.co.uk
Call Date: Nov 1977, Middle Temple
Pupil Supervisor
Qualifications: [LLB LLM]
gstoker@2-3gis.co.uk

STOKES MISS MARY ELIZABETH

Erskine Chambers
33 Chancery Lane, London WC2A 1EN, ☎020 7242 5532
clerks@erskinechambers.com
Call Date: July 1989, Lincoln's Inn
Pupil Supervisor
Qualifications: [MA LLM (USA) BCL (Oxon)]
mstokes@erskine-chambers.co.uk

STOKES-HERBST MISS REBECCA

Amicus Chambers
Queens Court, Newport Road, Middlesbrough TS1 5EH, ☎01642 876334
amicus.clerk@amicuschambers.co.uk
Call Date: July 2006, Lincoln's Inn
Qualifications: [LLB (Warw)]

STOLL MR JAMES ANDREW

No5 Chambers
38 Queen Square, Bristol BS1 4QS, ☎0845 210 5555
No5 Chambers
Greenwood House, 4-7 Salisbury Court, London EC4Y 8AA, ☎0845 210 5555
No5 Chambers
Fountain Court, Steelhouse Lane, Birmingham B4 6DR, ☎0845 210 5555 info@no5.com
Call Date: Nov 1994, Inner Temple
Pupil Supervisor
Qualifications: [LLB (Hons)(So'ton)]
JST@no5.com

STONE MR ANWAR KAREEM

Chambers of Mr A K Stone
97 River Avenue, Palmers Green, London N13 5RP, ☎07956 360101
anwarkstone@yahoo.co.uk
Call Date: Oct 2001, Lincoln's Inn
Qualifications: [BA (Lond)]
anwarkstone@yahoo.co.uk

STONE MR CHRISTOPHER MARK

Devereux Chambers
Queen Elizabeth Building, Temple, London EC4Y 9BS, ☎020 7353 7534
clerks@devchambers.co.uk
Call Date: Oct 2007, Lincoln's Inn
Qualifications: [MA (Oxon) MA]
stone@devchambers.co.uk

STONE MISS JENNY MARIE

Call Date: Nov 2000, Middle Temple
Qualifications: [LLB (Hons) (Exon)]
jstoonline@googlemail.com

STONE MR JOSEPH

Doughty Street Chambers
53-54 Doughty Street, London WC1N 2LS, ☎020 7404 1313
enquiries@doughtystreet.co.uk
Doughty Street Chambers
Pall Mall Court, 61-67 King Street, Manchester M2 4PD, ☎0161 618 1066
Doughty Street Chambers
5th Floor, Broad Quay House, Prince Street, Bristol BS1 4DJ, ☎01179 058 717
Call Date: July 1989, Inner Temple
Pupil Supervisor
Qualifications: [BA (Manch) Dip Law (City)]
j.stone@doughtystreet.co.uk

STONE MS JUDITH RACHAEL

11 King's Bench Walk
11 King's Bench Walk, Temple, London EC4Y 7EQ, ☎020 7632 8500
clerksroom@11kbw.com
Call Date: Oct 2003, Inner Temple
Qualifications: [BA (Oxon) PgDL]
judy.stone@11kbw.com

STONE MISS KATE

Chambers of Ian Macdonald QC
Garden Court North, 22 Oxford Court, Manchester M2 3WQ, ☎0161 236 1840
clerks@gcnchambers.co.uk
Call Date: Oct 2004, Inner Temple
Qualifications: [MA (Edin) CPE]

E

STONE MISS LUCILLE MADELINE QC (2001)

Queen Elizabeth Building
3rd Floor, Queen Elizabeth Building, Temple, London EC4Y 9BS, ☎ 020 7797 7837
✉ clerks@qeb.co.uk
Call Date: July 1983, Middle Temple
Qualifications: [MA (Cantab)]
l.stone@qeb.co.uk

STONE MR RUSSELL CLIVE ANDREW

Ely Place Chambers
30 Ely Place, London EC1N 6TD,
☎ 020 7400 9600 ✉ admin@elyplace.com
Call Date: Oct 1992, Inner Temple
Pupil Supervisor
Qualifications: [BA (Oxon)]
rstone@elyplace.com

STONE MISS SALLY VICTORIA

1 Garden Court Family Law Chambers
Ground Floor, One Garden Court, Temple, London EC4Y 9BJ, ☎ 020 7797 7900
✉ clerks@1gc.com
Call Date: Nov 1994, Inner Temple
Qualifications: [BA (Hons) (Kent)]
stone@1gc.com

STONE MR TURLOUGH FRANCIS

Quadrant Chambers
Quadrant House, 10 Fleet Street, London EC4Y 1AU, ☎ 020 7583 4444
✉ info@quadrantchambers.com
Call Date: Nov 2004, Inner Temple
Qualifications: [BA (Oxon) MSt All]
turlough.stone@quadrantchambers.com

STONEFROST MS HILARY

South Square
3-4 South Square, Gray's Inn, London WC1R 5HP, ☎ 020 7696 9900
✉ practicemanagers@southsquare.com
Call Date: Nov 1991, Middle Temple
Pupil Supervisor
Qualifications: [MSc (Lond)]
hilarystonefrost@southsquare.com

STONER MR CHRISTOPHER PAUL QC (2010)

Serle Court
6 New Square, Lincoln's Inn, London WC2A 3QS, ☎ 020 7242 6105
✉ clerks@serlecourt.co.uk
Call Date: Oct 1991, Lincoln's Inn
Qualifications: [LLB (Hons)(UEA)]
cstoner@serlecourt.co.uk

Types of work: Commercial law, Commercial litigation, Partnerships, Trusts, Wills

STONOR MR NICHOLAS WILLIAM

Trinity Chambers
The Custom House, 39 Quayside, Newcastle Upon Tyne NE1 3DE, ☎ 0191 232 1927
✉ info@trinitychambers.co.uk
Trinity Chambers
Multi Media Exchange, 72-80 Corporation Road, Middlesbrough TS1 2RF,
☎ 01642 247569
✉ info@trinitychambers.co.uk
Call Date: Oct 1993, Middle Temple
Pupil Supervisor
Qualifications: [LLB (Hons)]
n.stonor@trinitychambers.co.uk

STOPA MR CHRISTOPHER PAUL MICHAEL

2 King's Bench Walk
2 King's Bench Walk, Temple, London EC4Y 7DE, ☎ 020 7353 1746
✉ clerks@2kbw.com
Call Date: Nov 1976, Middle Temple
Pupil Supervisor
Qualifications: [LLB (Leeds) FCA]
cstopa@2kbw.com

STOREY MR JEREMY BRIAN QC (1994)

4 Pump Court
4 Pump Court, Temple, London EC4Y 7AN,
☎ 020 7842 5555
✉ chambers@4pumpcourt.com
Call Date: July 1974, Inner Temple
Recorder
Qualifications: [MCIArb MA (Cantab)]

STOREY MR PAUL MARK QC (2001)

29 Bedford Row Chambers
London WC1R 4HE, ☎ 020 7404 1044
✉ clerks@29br.co.uk
Albion Chambers
Broad Street, Bristol BS1 1DR,
☎ 0117 927 2144
✉ clerks@albionchambers.co.uk

Regency Chambers
45 Priestgate, Peterborough PE1 1LB,
☎ 01733 315215
✉ clerks@regencychambers.law.co.uk
Southernhay Chambers
33 Southernhay East, Exeter EX1 1NX,
☎ 01392 255777
✉ clerks@southernhaychambers.co.uk
Call Date: July 1982, Lincoln's Inn
Recorder
Qualifications: [BA]
✉ pstorey@29br.co.uk

STOREY MR RICHARD ALEXANDER

3 Temple Gardens
Lower Ground Floor, 3 Temple Gardens,
Temple, London EC4Y 9AU, ☎ 020 7353 3102
✉ clerks@3tg.co.uk
Call Date: Nov 2005, Lincoln's Inn
Qualifications: [BA (Hons) (Durham) PgDl (Lond)]
✉ rst@3tg.co.uk

STOREY MR THOMAS SEBASTIAN

Zenith Chambers
10 Park Square, Leeds LS1 2LH,
☎ 0113 245 5438
✉ clerks@zenithchambers.co.uk
Call Date: Feb 1993, Gray's Inn
Pupil Supervisor
Qualifications: [BA (Oxon)]
✉ t.storey@zenithchambers.co.uk

STOREY-REA MRS ALEXA ROSEANN

29 Bedford Row Chambers
London WC1R 4HE, ☎ 020 7404 1044
✉ clerks@29br.co.uk
Call Date: Feb 1990, Middle Temple
Qualifications: [LLB]
✉ astorey-rea@29br.co.uk

STORK MR BRIAN RAYMOND

3 Temple Gardens
Lower Ground Floor, 3 Temple Gardens,
Temple, London EC4Y 9AU, ☎ 020 7353 3102
✉ clerks@3tg.co.uk
Call Date: July 1981, Inner Temple
Pupil Supervisor
Qualifications: [LLB (Lond)]
✉ bs@3tg.co.uk

STORRIE MR TIMOTHY JAMES

Lincoln House Chambers
Tower 12, The Avenue North, Spinningfields,
18-22 Bridge Street, Manchester M3 3BZ,
☎ 0161 832 5701
✉ info@lincolnhousechambers.com
Call Date: Oct 1993, Middle Temple
Pupil Supervisor
Qualifications: [LLB BA (Hons)(Oxon) CPE]
✉ tim.storrie@lincolnhousechambers.com

STOTESBURY MR DAVID CHARLES

Chambers of Mr David Stotesbury
21 Redmore Road, London W6 0HZ,
☎ 020 8748 2447
✉ d.c.stotesbury@btinternet.com
Call Date: Feb 1980, Gray's Inn
Qualifications: [LLB (Lond) MA (Cantab)]

STOTON MR JOHN AUSTIN GERALD

2 Bedford Row
London WC1R 4BU, ☎ 020 7440 8888
✉ clerks@2bedfordrow.co.uk
Call Date: Oct 2007, Inner Temple
Qualifications: [BEng PhD (Wales)]
✉ astoton@2bedfordrow.co.uk

STOTT MR MATTHEW GLENN

Field Court Chambers
5 Field Court, Gray's Inn, London WC1R 5EF,
☎ 020 7405 6114 ✉ clerks@fieldcourt.co.uk
Broadway House Chambers
Broadway House, 9 Bank Street, Bradford,
West Yorkshire BD1 1TW, ☎ 01274 722560
✉ clerks@broadwayhouse.co.uk
Broadway House Chambers
25 Park Square West, Leeds, West Yorkshire
LS1 2PW, ☎ 0113 246 2600
✉ clerks@broadwayhouse.co.uk
Call Date: Oct 2005, Middle Temple
✉ matthew.stott@fieldcourt.co.uk

STOTT MR PHILIP GEOFFREY

QEB Hollis Whiteman
1-2 Laurence Pountney Hill, London
EC4R 0EU, ☎ 020 7933 8855
✉ barristers@qebhw.co.uk
Call Date: July 2004, Middle Temple
Qualifications: [BA (Hons) Dip in Law]
✉ philip.stott@qebhw.co.uk

E

STOUT MISS HOLLY EILEEN

11 King's Bench Walk
11 King's Bench Walk, Temple, London EC4Y 7EQ, ☎ 020 7632 8500
✉ clerksroom@11kbw.com
Call Date: July 2003, Lincoln's Inn
Qualifications: [BA Hons (Cantab) PgDL (Lond)]
✉ holly.stout@11kbw.com

STRACHAN MR DOUGLAS MARK ARTHUR QC (1987)

3 Hare Court
3 Hare Court, Temple, London EC4Y 7BJ, ☎ 020 7415 7800 ✉ clerks@3harecourt.com
Call Date: July 1969, Inner Temple
Qualifications: [MA BCL (Oxon)]

STRACHAN MS ELAINE JUNE

3 PB Barristers
3 Paper Buildings, Temple, London EC4Y 7EU, ☎ 020 7583 8055
3 PB Barristers
Royal Talbot House, 2 Victoria Street, Bristol, Avon BS1 6BB, ☎ 0117 928 1520
3 PB Barristers
23 Beaumont Street, Oxford OX1 2NP, ☎ 01865 793 736
3 PB Barristers
4 St Peter Street, Winchester SO23 8BW, ☎ 01962 868884
✉ clerks.winchester@3paper.co.uk
3 PB Barristers
30 Christchurch Road, Bournemouth, Dorset BH1 3PD, ☎ 01202 292102
✉ clerks.bournemouth@3paper.co.uk
Call Date: Nov 1995, Middle Temple
Qualifications: [BA (Hons)]
✉ es@3paper.co.uk

STRACHAN MR JAMES OLIVER JOHN

4-5 Gray's Inn Square
Gray's Inn, London WC1R 5AH, ☎ 020 7404 5252 ✉ clerks@4-5.co.uk
Call Date: Oct 1996, Middle Temple
Pupil Supervisor
Qualifications: [BA (Hons) MA (Oxon) Dip Law]
✉ jstrachan@4-5.co.uk

STRAKER MR TIMOTHY DERRICK QC (1996)

4-5 Gray's Inn Square
Gray's Inn, London WC1R 5AH, ☎ 020 7404 5252 ✉ clerks@4-5.co.uk
Call Date: July 1977, Gray's Inn
Qualifications: [MA (Cantab)]
✉ tstraker@4-5.co.uk

Fax: 020 7242 7803;
Out of hours telephone: 020 7404 5252;
DX: 1029 London;
URL: www.4-5.co.uk

Other professional qualifications: Deputy High Court Judge, Acting Justice Court of Appeal (Falkland Islands), Recorder

Types of work: Administrative law, Civil liberties, Discrimination, Education, Election law, Environment, Housing, Local authorities, Planning

Membership of foreign bars: Trinidad and Tobago; Northern Ireland

Awards and memberships: Administrative Law Bar Association; Local Government and Planning Bar Association; Administrative Court Users' Association; Parliamentary Bar Mess; Downing College Prize for Law; Holt Scholar of Gray's Inn; Lord Justice Holker Senior Award; Bencher of Gray's Inn

Other professional experience: Advocacy Tutor

Publications: 'Public Health and Environmental Protection', Halsbury's Laws of England (4th edn), 2000; 'Local Government', *Halsbury's Laws of England* (4th edn), 2001; 'Markets', *Halsbury's Laws of England* (4th edn), 2002; *Civil Court Practice* (Contributing Editor) (Judicial Review), 2005; Electoral Administration Act 2006 (Commentary: Current Law Status)

Reported Cases: *R v Secretary of State (on application of Devon C.C. and Norfolk C.C.)*, [2011] LGR 64 (High Court), 2010. Procedural fairness.
South Bucks v Porter, [2004] 4 All ER 775 House of Lords determine reasons required in planning decisions.
O'Connor v Wiltshire County Council, [2007] EWCA Civ 426; [2007] RVR 179 (2007), 2007. Case determines the basis of compensation for public works.
R (Breckland Council) v Boundary Committee, [2009] EWCA Civ 239 Court of Appeal determine approach to local authority reorganisation.
M v Lambeth, [2010] 1 ALL ER 469 House of Lords determine reasons required in planning decisions.

E

STRANEX MR ANDREW JOHN

St Paul's Chambers
5th Floor, St Paul's House, 23 Park Square South, Leeds LS1 2ND, ☎0113 245 5866
Call Date: July 2000, Gray's Inn
Qualifications: [BA (Hons)]
asx@stpaulschambers.com

STRANG MR ROBERT STEPHEN

3 Hare Court
3 Hare Court, Temple, London EC4Y 7BJ, ☎020 7415 7800 ✉clerks@3harecourt.com
Call Date: Nov 2003, Middle Temple
Qualifications: [BA (Hons) (Oxon) CPE]
robertstrang@3harecourt.com

STRANGE MS JESSICA

Zenith Chambers
10 Park Square, Leeds LS1 2LH, ☎0113 245 5438
✉clerks@zenithchambers.co.uk
Call Date: July 2003, Inner Temple
Qualifications: [LLB (Sheff)]

STRATFORD MISS JEMIMA LUCY QC (2010)

Brick Court Chambers
7-8 Essex Street, London WC2R 3LD, ☎020 7379 3550 ✉clerks@brickcourt.co.uk
Call Date: Oct 1993, Middle Temple
Pupil Supervisor
Qualifications: [BA (Hons)(Oxon) CPE (Lond)]
Jemima.Stratford@Brickcourt.co.uk

STRAUSS MR NICHOLAS ALBERT QC (1984)

One Essex Court
Ground Floor, One Essex Court, Temple, London EC4Y 9AR, ☎020 7583 2000
✉clerks@oeclaw.co.uk
Call Date: Nov 1965, Middle Temple
Recorder
Qualifications: [MA LLB (Cantab)]
nstrauss@oeclaw.co.uk

STRAW MR ADAM DOUGAL

Tooks Chambers
81 Farringdon Street, London EC4A 4BL, ☎020 7842 7575 ✉clerks@tooks.co.uk
Call Date: Nov 2004, Gray's Inn
Qualifications: [BA]
adam.straw@tooks.co.uk

STRAW MR JONATHAN JAMES

KCH Garden Square
1 Oxford Street, Nottingham NG1 5BH, ☎0115 941 8851
✉clerks@kchgardensquare.co.uk
Call Date: Oct 1992, Lincoln's Inn
Pupil Supervisor
Qualifications: [LLB(Hons)(Newc)]

STREATFEILD-JAMES MR DAVID STEWART QC (2001)

Atkin Chambers
1 Atkin Building, Gray's Inn, London WC1R 5AT, ☎020 7404 0102
✉clerks@atkinchambers.com
Call Date: July 1986, Inner Temple
Qualifications: [BA(Oxon)]
clerks@atkinchambers.com

STREET MS AMY CAROLINE

3 Serjeants Inn
London EC4Y 1BQ, ☎020 7427 5000
✉clerks@3serjeantsinn.com
Call Date: Oct 2002, Inner Temple
Qualifications: [BA (Oxon) MA (Lond)]
as@3serjeantsinn.com

STREET MISS CHARLOTTE ELIZABETH

Pump Court Chambers
31 Southgate Street, Winchester, Hampshire SO23 9EB, ☎01962 868 161
✉clerks@3pumpcourt.com
Pump Court Chambers
5 Temple Chambers, Temple Street, Swindon SN1 1SQ, ☎01793 539899
✉clerks@3pumpcourt.com
Call Date: July 2003, Gray's Inn
Qualifications: [LLB]

STRELITZ MR PAUL STEPHEN

East Anglian Chambers
Gresham House, 5 Museum Street, Ipswich, Suffolk IP1 1HQ, ☎01473 214481
✉ipswich@ealaw.co.uk
East Anglian Chambers
53 North Hill, Colchester, Essex CO1 1QA, ☎01473 214481 ✉colchester@ealaw.co.uk
East Anglian Chambers
140 New London Road, Chelmsford, Essex CM2 0AW, ☎01473 214481
✉chelmsford@ealaw.co.uk
Call Date: Nov 2005, Lincoln's Inn
Qualifications: [LLB (Hons) Southampton]

E

STRIDE MR LIONEL ALEXANDER

Temple Garden Chambers
1 Harcourt Buildings, Temple, London
EC4Y 9DA, ☎020 7583 1315
✉clerks@tgchambers.com
Call Date: Oct 2005, Lincoln's Inn
Qualifications: [BSc (Hons) GDL]
✉las@tgchambers.com

STRINGER MR LEON PETER

15 Winckley Square
Preston PR1 3JJ, ☎01772 252828
✉clerks@15winckleysq.co.uk
Call Date: Oct 1996, Lincoln's Inn
Qualifications: [LLM LLDip BSc (Hons)]
✉leonstringer@15ws.co.uk

STRONG MR ADRIAN PETER CIARAN

KBW
The Engine House, No 1 Foundry Square,
Leeds LS11 5DL, ☎0113 297 1200
✉clerks@kbwchambers.com
Call Date: July 2001, Gray's Inn
Pupil Supervisor
Qualifications: [BA (Lond) LLM (Lond)]
✉adrianstrong@kbwchambers.com

STRONG MR BENJAMIN JAMES QUENTIN

One Essex Court
Ground Floor, One Essex Court, Temple,
London EC4Y 9AR, ☎020 7583 2000
✉clerks@oeclaw.co.uk
Call Date: Nov 2001, Middle Temple
Pupil Supervisor
Qualifications: [MA (Cantab)]
✉bstrong@oeclaw.co.uk

STRONGMAN MRS CAROL ANN

No 8 Chambers
8 Fountain Court, Steelhouse Lane,
Birmingham B4 6DR, ☎0121 236 5514
✉clerks@no8chambers.co.uk
Call Date: Oct 2003, Lincoln's Inn
Qualifications: [LLB (Hons) (Leeds)]
✉carolstrongman@no8chambers.co.uk

STROUD MISS AMY NICOLA

Ely Place Chambers
30 Ely Place, London EC1N 6TD,
☎020 7400 9600 ✉admin@elyplace.com
Call Date: Nov 2004, Inner Temple
Qualifications: [MA CPE]
✉astroud@elyplace.com

STRUDWICK MISS LINDA DIANE

QEB Hollis Whiteman
1-2 Laurence Pountney Hill, London
EC4R 0EU, ☎020 7933 8855
✉barristers@qebhw.co.uk
Call Date: July 1973, Lincoln's Inn
Pupil Supervisor
Qualifications: [BA]
✉barristers@qebholliswhiteman.co.uk

STRUGO MS ANDREA THERESE LINDSAY

Crown Office Row Chambers
119 Church Street, Brighton, Sussex
BN1 1UD, ☎01273 625625
✉clerks@1cor.com
1 Crown Office Row
1 Crown Office Row, Temple, London
EC4Y 7HH, ☎020 7797 7500
✉mail@1cor.com
Call Date: Oct 2003, Inner Temple
Qualifications: [BA (Oxon) Dip Law]
✉andrea.lindsaystrugo@1cor.com

STRUTT MR MARTIN ANDREW

3 PB Barristers
3 Paper Buildings, Temple, London EC4Y 7EU,
☎020 7583 8055
3 PB Barristers
Royal Talbot House, 2 Victoria Street, Bristol,
Avon BS1 6BB, ☎0117 928 1520
3 PB Barristers
30 Christchurch Road, Bournemouth, Dorset
BH1 3PD, ☎01202 292102
✉clerks.bournemouth@3paper.co.uk
3 PB Barristers
4 St Peter Street, Winchester SO23 8BW,
☎01962 868884
✉clerks.winchester@3paper.co.uk
3 PB Barristers
23 Beaumont Street, Oxford OX1 2NP,
☎01865 793 736
Call Date: Nov 1981, Inner Temple
Qualifications: [BA (Cantab)]
✉martin.strutt@3paper.co.uk

STUART MR BRUCE IAN

Lombard Chambers
1 Sekforde Street, Clerkenwell, London
EC1R 0BE, ☎020 7107 2100
Call Date: Nov 1977, Gray's Inn
Pupil Supervisor

STUART MR DAMIAN ANDREW

New Court
Ground Floor, New Court, Temple, London EC4Y 9BE, ☎ 020 7583 5123
✉ clerks@newcourtchambers.com
Call Date: Mar 2009, Inner Temple
Qualifications: [LLB (Lond) LLM]
✉ dstuart@newcourtchambers.net

STUART MR DOUGLAS MARK

Lincoln House Chambers
Tower 12, The Avenue North, Spinningfields, 18-22 Bridge Street, Manchester M3 3BZ, ☎ 0161 832 5701
✉ info@lincolnhousechambers.com
Call Date: Nov 1985, Gray's Inn
Qualifications: [BA (Newc)]

STUART MR JAMES WILLIAM

Lamb Chambers
Lamb Building, Elm Court, Temple, London EC4Y 7AS, ☎ 020 7797 8300
✉ info@lambchambers.co.uk
Call Date: Oct 1990, Gray's Inn
Pupil Supervisor
Qualifications: [MA (Cantab)]
✉ jamesstuart@lambchambers.co.uk

STUART-LOFTHOUSE MISS ELIZABETH MICHELE

Zenith Chambers
10 Park Square, Leeds LS1 2LH, ☎ 0113 245 5438
✉ clerks@zenithchambers.co.uk
Call Date: Nov 2001, Lincoln's Inn
Qualifications: [BA (Hons) (Hull)]
✉ msl@zenithchambers.co.uk

STUART-SMITH MISS EMMA LUCIA

25 Bedford Row
London WC1R 4HD, ☎ 020 7067 1500
✉ clerks@25bedfordrow.com
Call Date: July 2009, Gray's Inn
Qualifications: [BA]

STUART-SMITH MR JEREMY HUGH QC (1997)

Four New Square
Four New Square, Lincoln's Inn, London WC2A 3RJ, ☎ 020 7822 2000
✉ barristers@4newsquare.com
Call Date: July 1978, Gray's Inn
Recorder
Qualifications: [MA (Cantab)]
✉ j.stuartsmith@4newsquare.com

STUBBS MR ANDREW JAMES QC (2008)

St Paul's Chambers
5th Floor, St Paul's House, 23 Park Square South, Leeds LS1 2ND, ☎ 0113 245 5866
Call Date: July 1988, Lincoln's Inn
Recorder
Qualifications: [LLB (Hons) (Notts)]
✉ as@stpaulschambers.com

STUBBS MISS REBECCA QC (2012)

Maitland Chambers
7 Stone Buildings, Lincoln's Inn, London WC2A 3SZ, ☎ 020 7406 1200
✉ clerks@maitlandchambers.com
Call Date: Oct 1994, Middle Temple
Pupil Supervisor
Qualifications: [MA (Hons) (Cantab)]
✉ RStubbs@MaitlandChambers.com

STUBBS MR RICHARD JOHN MORRIS

Trinity Chambers
The Custom House, 39 Quayside, Newcastle Upon Tyne NE1 3DE, ☎ 0191 232 1927
✉ info@trinitychambers.co.uk
Trinity Chambers
Multi Media Exchange, 72-80 Corporation Road, Middlesbrough TS1 2RF, ☎ 01642 247569
✉ info@trinitychambers.co.uk
Call Date: July 2005, Lincoln's Inn
Qualifications: [BA (Hons)]
✉ r.stubbs@trinitychambers.co.uk

STUBLEY MISS ANNA ELIZABETH

Chancery House Chambers
7 Lisbon Square, Leeds, West Yorkshire LS1 4LY, ☎ 0113 244 6691
✉ clerks@chanceryhouse.co.uk
Call Date: July 2010, Gray's Inn
Qualifications: [LLB]

STUCKEY MISS KATHRYN THERESE

39 Park Square
Leeds LS1 2NU, ☎ 0113 245 6633
✉ seniorclerk@39parksquarechambers.co.uk
Call Date: Oct 2004, Inner Temple
Qualifications: [LLB (Leeds)]
✉ k.stuckey@39parksquare.com

STUDD MISS ANNE ELIZABETH QC (2012)

5 Essex Court
1st Floor, 5 Essex Court, Temple, London EC4Y 9AH, ☎ 020 7410 2000
✉ clerks@5essexcourt.co.uk
Call Date: July 1988, Gray's Inn
Pupil Supervisor, Recorder
Qualifications: [BA (Lond)]
✉ studd@5essexcourt.co.uk

STUDER MR MARK EDGAR WALTER

Wilberforce Chambers
8 New Square, Lincoln's Inn, London WC2A 3QP, ☎ 020 7306 0102
✉ chambers@wilberforce.co.uk
Call Date: July 1976, Lincoln's Inn
Pupil Supervisor
Qualifications: [BA (Oxon)]
✉ mstuder@wilberforce.co.uk

Types of work: Chancery (general), Chancery (land law), Charities, Conveyancing, Court of Protection, Equity, Family provision, Inheritance and cohabitees, Professional negligence, Real property, Succession, Trust litigation, Trusts, Wills

STURMAN MR JAMES ANTHONY QC (2002)

2 Bedford Row
London WC1R 4BU, ☎ 020 7440 8888
✉ clerks@2bedfordrow.co.uk
Call Date: July 1982, Gray's Inn
Qualifications: [LLB (Reading)]
✉ jsturman@2bedfordrow.co.uk

STYLES MR CLIVE RICHARD

Becket Chambers
17 New Dover Road, Canterbury, Kent CT1 3AS, ☎ 01227 786331
✉ clerks@becket-chambers.co.uk
Call Date: Oct 1990, Gray's Inn
Qualifications: [LLB (Hons) LLM]
✉ cstyles@becket-chambers.co.uk

STYLES MRS KAY MARGARET

Harcourt Chambers
1st Floor, 2 Harcourt Buildings, Temple, London EC4Y 9DB, ☎ 0844 561 7135
Harcourt Chambers
Churchill House, 3 St Aldate's Courtyard, St Aldate's, Oxford OX1 1BN, ☎ 0844 561 7135
Call Date: Oct 2000, Middle Temple
Qualifications: [MA (Oxon)]
✉ mstyles@harcourtchambers.law.co.uk

STYLES MR MARK PATRICK

Dere Street Barristers
33 Broad Chare, Newcastle Upon Tyne NE1 3DQ, ☎ 0844 3351551
✉ clerks@derestreet.co.uk
Call Date: July 1988, Inner Temple
Pupil Supervisor
Qualifications: [LLB (Lancs)]
✉ clerks@broadcharechambers.co.uk

SUBEDI PROF SURYA PRASAD

Tanfield Chambers
2-5 Warwick Court, London WC1R 5DJ, ☎ 020 7421 5300
✉ clerks@tanfieldchambers.co.uk
Call Date: July 2007, Middle Temple
Qualifications: [LLB LLM DPhil]

SUDDABY MR JOHN ANDREW

Chambers of Mr John Suddaby
29 Rhodes Avenue, London NN22 7UR, ☎ 020 8888 7185 ✉ john@suddaby.com
Call Date: Nov 1990, Inner Temple
Qualifications: [BA (Hons) Dip Law DLGL DGL]

SUGAR MR SIMON GARETH

1 Garden Court Family Law Chambers
Ground Floor, One Garden Court, Temple, London EC4Y 9BJ, ☎ 020 7797 7900
✉ clerks@1gc.com
Call Date: Nov 1990, Middle Temple
Qualifications: [LLB (Hons)]
✉ sugar@1gc.com

SUGARMAN MR ANDREW

Park Lane Plowden
19 Westgate, Leeds LS1 2RD, ☎ 0113 228 5049
✉ clerks@parklaneplowden.co.uk
Call Date: Nov 2001, Lincoln's Inn
Qualifications: [BA (Hons) LLM]
✉ Andrew.Sugarman@parklaneplowden.co.uk

SUGARMAN MR JASON ASHLEY

9-12 Bell Yard
London WC2A 2JR, ☎ 020 7400 1800
✉ clerks@9-12bellyard.com
Call Date: July 1995, Inner Temple
Pupil Supervisor
Qualifications: [BA (Dunelm) CPE (Lond)]
✉ j.sugarman@9-12bellyard.com

SUGDEN MRS AMELIA JANE

1 Hare Court
1 Hare Court, Temple, London EC4Y 7BE,
☎020 7797 7070 ✉clerks@1hc.com
Call Date: July 2006, Middle Temple
Qualifications: [BA (Hons) (Cantab)]
✉amelia.harris@1hc.com

SUGGETT MR IAIN ROBERT OTTAR

Warwick Chambers
959 Chester Road, Birmingham, Birmingham B24 0HQ, ☎0121 382 9122
✉warwickchambers@hotmail.com
Call Date: Nov 1989, Lincoln's Inn
Qualifications: [LLB (Hons)]
✉warwickchambers@hotmail.co.uk

SUKUL MR GANESH SHANKAR

Centurion Chambers
Suite 9, Temple Court, Cathedral Road, Cardiff CF11 9HA, ☎029 2078 6472
Call Date: July 1982, Gray's Inn
Qualifications: [BA]

SUKUL MR RABI SHANKAR

Balham Chambers
Basement, 82 Balham High Road, London SW12 9AG, ☎020 8675 4609
Call Date: July 1988, Lincoln's Inn
Qualifications: [LLB (Hons)]

SULLIVAN MR GEOFFREY CHARLES ALEXANDER

36 Bedford Row
London WC1R 4JH, ☎020 7421 8000
✉chambers@36bedfordrow.co.uk
Call Date: July 2001, Inner Temple
Qualifications: [BA (So'ton) CPE BPP]
✉clerks@36bedfordrow.co.uk

SULLIVAN MR JAMES WILLIAM

12 King's Bench Walk
12 King's Bench Walk, Temple, London EC4Y 7EL, ☎020 7583 0811
Call Date: Oct 2005, Inner Temple
Qualifications: [BSc London School of Economics & Political Scienc MPhil PGDL]
✉sullivan@12kbw.co.uk

SULLIVAN MR JOSEPH PATRICK

2 Temple Gardens
2 Temple Gardens, Temple, London EC4Y 9AY, ☎020 7822 1200
✉clerks@2tg.co.uk
Call Date: July 2006, Middle Temple
Qualifications: [BA (Hons) (Cantab) LLM (Cantab)]
✉jsullivan@2tg.co.uk

SULLIVAN MR LIAM

Trinity Chambers
Highfield House, Moulsham Street, Chelmsford, Essex CM2 9AH,
☎01245 605040
✉clerks@trinitychambers.com
Call Date: July 2009, Lincoln's Inn
Qualifications: [LLB (UEA)]
✉lsullivan@trinitychambers.com

SULLIVAN MS LISA ANN

Cloisters
1 Pump Court, Temple, London EC4Y 7AA,
☎020 7827 4000 ✉clerks@cloisters.com
Call Date: Oct 1997, Inner Temple
Pupil Supervisor
Qualifications: [BA (Oxon)]
✉ls@cloisters.com

SULLIVAN MR MARK ANDREW

3 PB Barristers
3 Paper Buildings, Temple, London EC4Y 7EU,
☎020 7583 8055
3 PB Barristers
Royal Talbot House, 2 Victoria Street, Bristol, Avon BS1 6BB, ☎0117 928 1520
3 PB Barristers
4 St Peter Street, Winchester SO23 8BW,
☎01962 868884
✉clerks.winchester@3paper.co.uk
3 PB Barristers
23 Beaumont Street, Oxford OX1 2NP,
☎01865 793 736
3 PB Barristers
30 Christchurch Road, Bournemouth, Dorset BH1 3PD, ☎01202 292102
✉clerks.bournemouth@3paper.co.uk
Call Date: Oct 1997, Middle Temple
Qualifications: [LLB (Hons)(Bris)]
✉mark.sullivan@3paper.co.uk

SULLIVAN MR MICHAEL JEROME QC (2008)

One Essex Court
Ground Floor, One Essex Court, Temple, London EC4Y 9AR, ☎020 7583 2000
✉clerks@oeclaw.co.uk
Call Date: July 1983, Middle Temple
Qualifications: [LLB (Hons) (Manch)]
✉msullivan@oeclaw.co.uk

SULLIVAN MR SEAN

Nine Bedford Row
9 Bedford Row, London WC1R 4AZ,
☎020 7489 2727
✉clerks@9bedfordrow.co.uk
Call Date: July 2004, Inner Temple
Qualifications: [BA (Oxon)]
✉sean.sullivan@9bedfordrow.co.uk

E

SULTAN MS NEELIM

1 Mitre Court Buildings
1 Mitre Court Buildings, Temple, London EC4Y 7BS, ☎ 020 7452 8900
✉ clerks@1mcb.com
Call Date: Nov 1993, Gray's Inn
Pupil Supervisor
Qualifications: [BA (Hull) LLM (Lond)]
neelim.sultan@1mcb.com

SUMERAY MRS CAROLINE SARAH

No5 Chambers
Greenwood House, 4-7 Salisbury Court, London EC4Y 8AA, ☎ 0845 210 5555
No5 Chambers
38 Queen Square, Bristol BS1 4QS, ☎ 0845 210 5555
No5 Chambers
Fountain Court, Steelhouse Lane, Birmingham B4 6DR, ☎ 0845 210 5555 ✉ info@no5.com
Call Date: July 1993, Middle Temple
Qualifications: [LLB (Hons)(Wolves) DipFMS]
css@no5.com

SUMMERS MISS ALLISON

36 Bedford Row
London WC1R 4JH, ☎ 020 7421 8000
✉ chambers@36bedfordrow.co.uk
Call Date: Nov 2000, Lincoln's Inn
Pupil Supervisor
Qualifications: [MA (Hons) CPE]
asummers@36bedfordrow.co.uk

SUMMERS MR BENJAMIN DYLAN JAMES

3 Raymond Buildings
3 Raymond Buildings, Gray's Inn, London WC1R 5BH, ☎ 020 7400 6400
✉ clerks@3rblaw.com
Call Date: Nov 1994, Inner Temple
Qualifications: [LLB (Sussex)]
ben.summers@3raymondbuildings.com

SUMMERS MR GARY

23 Essex Street
London WC2R 3AA, ☎ 020 7413 0353
✉ clerks@23es.com
Call Date: Nov 1985, Gray's Inn
Pupil Supervisor
Qualifications: [BA (Hons)]
garysummers@23es.com, gary@summersweb.net

SUMMERS MR JOHN EMRYS

Falcon Chambers
Falcon Court, London EC4Y 1AA, ☎ 020 7353 2484
✉ clerks@falcon-chambers.com
Call Date: Oct 2004, Lincoln's Inn
Qualifications: [MA (Oxon) LLM (Cantab)]
summers@falcon-chambers.com

SUMMERS MR MARK JOHN

Matrix Chambers
Griffin Building, Gray's Inn, London WC1R 5LN, ☎ 020 7404 3447
✉ matrix@matrixlaw.co.uk / Iscott@matrixlaw.co.uk
Call Date: Nov 1996, Inner Temple
Pupil Supervisor
Qualifications: [LLB (Exon)]

SUMNALL MISS CHARLENE EMMA LOUISE

Five Paper Buildings
1st Floor, Five Paper Buildings, Temple, London EC4Y 7HB, ☎ 020 7583 6117
✉ clerks@5pb.co.uk
Call Date: July 2003, Lincoln's Inn
Qualifications: [LLB (Hons) LLM (Belfast)]
csu@5pb.co.uk

SUMNER MS DAIAN

Atlantic Chambers
4-6 Cook Street, Liverpool L2 9QU, ☎ 0151 236 4421
✉ info@atlanticchambers.co.uk
Call Date: July 2004, Gray's Inn
Qualifications: [LLB (Hons) PGCE]
daiansumner@atlanticchambers.co.uk

SUMNER MS EMMA

1 Hare Court
1 Hare Court, Temple, London EC4Y 7BE, ☎ 020 7797 7070 ✉ clerks@1hc.com
Call Date: Oct 1999, Inner Temple
Qualifications: [BA (Exon)]
sumner@1hc.com

SUPPLE MR STEPHEN

Holborn Chambers
6 Gate Street, Lincoln's Inn Fields, London WC2A 3HP, ☎ 020 7242 6060
Call Date: Oct 2002, Lincoln's Inn
Qualifications: [LLB (Kent)]

SURTEES-JONES MR CHRISTOPHER GLYN

4 Breams Buildings
Chancery Lane, London EC4A 1HP, ☎020 7092 1900 ✉clerks@4bb.co.uk
Call Date: Oct 1997, Inner Temple
Qualifications: [LLB (Southampton)]

SUSMAN MR PETER JOSEPH QC (1997)

Henderson Chambers
2 Harcourt Buildings, Temple, London EC4Y 9DB, ☎020 7583 9020
✉clerks@hendersonchambers.co.uk
Call Date: Nov 1966, Middle Temple
Recorder
Qualifications: [MA (Oxon) JD (USA)]
psusman@hendersonchambers.co.uk

SUTCLIFFE MR ANDREW HAROLD WENTWORTH QC (2001)

3 Verulam Buildings
London WC1R 5NT, ☎020 7831 8441
✉chambers@3vb.com
Call Date: Nov 1983, Inner Temple
Recorder
Qualifications: [MA (Oxon)]
asutcliffe@3vb.com

SUTER MR ERICH GEORGE BERNARD

Park Chambers
3 Park Drive, Weybridge Park, Surrey KT13 8UU, ☎01932 820082
✉clerks@ParkChambers.co.uk
Call Date: May 1979, Middle Temple
Qualifications: [BA FCIArb FCIPD LLM]

SUTERWALLA MR AZEEM SIRAJ

Doughty Street Chambers
53-54 Doughty Street, London WC1N 2LS, ☎020 7404 1313
✉enquiries@doughtystreet.co.uk
Doughty Street Chambers
Pall Mall Court, 61-67 King Street, Manchester M2 4PD, ☎0161 618 1066
Doughty Street Chambers
5th Floor, Broad Quay House, Prince Street, Bristol BS1 4DJ, ☎01179 058 717
Call Date: Nov 2004, Inner Temple
Qualifications: [BA(Lond) MA (Lond)]
a.suterwalla@doughtystreet.co.uk

SUTHERLAND MR JAMES MORE

Nexus Chambers
7 New Square, Lincolns Inn, London WC2A 3QS,
☎020 7404 1147 / 020 7831 8309
✉info@nexuschambers.com
Call Date: Oct 1999, Middle Temple
Qualifications: [BA (Hons)(Oxon)]
james.sutherland@nexuschambers.com

SUTHERLAND MR JAMIE

Falcon Chambers
Falcon Court, London EC4Y 1AA,
☎020 7353 2484
✉clerks@falcon-chambers.com
Call Date: July 2010, Lincoln's Inn
Qualifications: [BA MPHIL (Cantab)]
sutherland@falcon-chambers.com

SUTHERLAND MISS JESSICA ANN

7 King's Bench Walk
Ground Floor, 7 King's Bench Walk, Temple, London EC4Y 7DS, ☎020 7910 8300
✉clerks@7kbw.co.uk
Call Date: Oct 2003, Middle Temple
Qualifications: [LLM (Cantab) MA (Hons) (Cantab)]
jsutherland@7kbw.co.uk

SUTHERLAND MR PAUL JEFFREY JOHN-PAUL

Four New Square
Four New Square, Lincoln's Inn, London WC2A 3RJ, ☎020 7822 2000
✉barristers@4newsquare.com
Call Date: Nov 1992, Middle Temple
Qualifications: [MA (Oxon) MA (Cantab)]
p.sutherland@4newsquare.com

SUTHERLAND MISS SARA ELIZABETH ALEXANDRA

Exchange Chambers
7 Ralli Courts, West Riverside, Manchester M3 5FT, ☎0161 833 2722
Exchange Chambers
One Derby Square, Derby Square, Liverpool L2 9XX, ☎0151 236 7747
✉info@exchangechambers.co.uk
Exchange Chambers
Oxford House, Oxford Row, Leeds LS1 3BE,
☎0113 203 1970
✉spencer@exchangechambers.co.uk
Call Date: Oct 2004, Lincoln's Inn
Qualifications: [BA (Hons) (Stirling)]

E

SUTHERLAND MISS YVONNE

King's Bench and Godolphin (KBG)Chambers
115 North Hill, Plymouth, Devon PL4 8JY, ☎01752 221551
✉clerks@kbgchambers.co.uk
Call Date: July 2001, Lincoln's Inn
Qualifications: [LLB (Hons)]
✉yvonne.sutherland@kingsbenchchambers.co.uk

SUTHERLAND-MACK MISS JESSICA

Goldsmith Chambers
Ground Floor, Goldsmith Building, Temple, London EC4Y 7BL, ☎020 7353 6802
✉clerks@goldsmithchambers.com
Call Date: Oct 2007, Middle Temple
Qualifications: [LLB (Hons) (Lincoln)]

SUTTON PROF ALASTAIR MORRIS

Brick Court Chambers
7-8 Essex Street, London WC2R 3LD, ☎020 7379 3550 ✉clerks@brickcourt.co.uk
Call Date: May 1972, Middle Temple
Qualifications: [LLB (Scotland) LLM (Lond) Dip Int Air Law]
✉alastair.sutton@brickcourt.co.uk

SUTTON MR CLIVE RAYMOND

Chambers of Mr Clive Sutton
18 Mill Lane, Stoke, Bruerne, Northamptonshire NN12 7SH, ☎07973 386702
✉cs@clivesuttonbarristerdirect.co.uk
Call Date: July 1987, Inner Temple
Pupil Supervisor
Qualifications: [LLB]

SUTTON MR DAVID ST JOHN

20 Essex Street
London WC2R 3AL, ☎020 7842 1200
✉clerks@20essexst.com
Call Date: July 2001, Middle Temple
Qualifications: [BA FCIArb]
✉clerks@20essexst.com

SUTTON MISS EMMA NAOMI

30 Park Place
Cardiff CF10 3BS, ☎029 2039 8421
✉clerks@30parkplace.law.co.uk
Call Date: Oct 2006, Gray's Inn
Qualifications: [LLB LLM]
✉es@30parkplace.co.uk

SUTTON MR KEITH ANDREW

Number 7 Harrington Street Chambers
7 Harrington Street, Liverpool L2 9YH, ☎0151 242 0707 ✉clerks@7hs.co.uk
Call Date: Nov 1988, Gray's Inn
Pupil Supervisor
Qualifications: [LLB (Hons)]
✉keith.sutton@7hs.co.uk

SUTTON MR MARK QC (2011)

Old Square Chambers
10-11 Bedford Row, London WC1R 4BU, ☎020 7269 0300 ✉clerks@oldsquare.co.uk
Old Square Chambers
3 Orchard Court, St Augustine's Yard, Bristol BS1 5DP, ☎0117 930 5100
✉clerks@oldsquare.co.uk
Call Date: July 1982, Middle Temple
Pupil Supervisor
Qualifications: [BA Dip Law]
✉sutton@oldsquare.co.uk

SUTTON MR PHILIP JULIAN

Bell Yard Chambers
116/118 Chancery Lane, London WC2A 1PP, ☎020 7306 9292
✉byclerks@bellyardchambers.co.uk
Call Date: Nov 1971, Inner Temple
Pupil Supervisor
Qualifications: [LLB (Hons)]
✉psutton@bellyardchambers.co.uk

SUTTON MRS REBECCA KATALIN

St Johns Buildings Liverpool
8th Floor India Buildings, Water Street, Liverpool L2 0XG, ☎0151 243 6000
✉clerk@stjohnsbuildings.co.uk
St Johns Buildings
21 White Friars, Chester CH1 1NZ, ☎01244 323070
✉clerk@stjohnsbuildings.co.uk
St Johns Buildings
24a - 28 St John Street, Manchester M3 4DJ, ☎0161 214 1500
✉clerk@stjohnsbuildings.co.uk
Call Date: Nov 2004, Inner Temple
Qualifications: [LLB University of Northumbria]

E

SUTTON MR RICHARD PATRICK QC (1993)

18 Red Lion Court
London EC4A 3EB, ☎ 020 7520 6000
✉ chambers@18rlc.co.uk
18 Red Lion Court (Annexe)
Thornwood House, 102 New London Road, Chelmsford, Essex CM2 0RG,
☎ 01245 280880
Call Date: July 1969, Middle Temple
Recorder
Qualifications: [BA (Oxon)]
✉ richard.sutton@18rlc.co.uk

SUTTON-MATTOCKS MR CHRISTOPHER JOHN

5 King's Bench Walk
5 King's Bench Walk, Temple, London EC4Y 7DN, ☎ 020 7353 5638
✉ clerks@5kbw.co.uk
Call Date: July 1975, Middle Temple
Qualifications: [MA (Oxon)]

SWAIN MISS JACQUELINE SUSAN

Number 7 Harrington Street Chambers
7 Harrington Street, Liverpool L2 9YH,
☎ 0151 242 0707 ✉ clerks@7hs.co.uk
Call Date: Oct 1998, Lincoln's Inn
Qualifications: [LLB (Hons)(Leic) Dip Law]
✉ jacqueline.swain@7hs.co.uk

SWAIN MR JON DAVID

Furnival Chambers
32 Furnival Street, London EC4A 1JQ,
☎ 020 7405 3232
Call Date: Nov 1983, Lincoln's Inn
Pupil Supervisor
Qualifications: [BSc (Hons)]
✉ jswain@furnivallaw.co.uk

SWAINSTON MR MICHAEL GEORGE QC (2002)

Brick Court Chambers
7-8 Essex Street, London WC2R 3LD,
☎ 020 7379 3550 ✉ clerks@brickcourt.co.uk
Call Date: Nov 1985, Lincoln's Inn
Qualifications: [MA (Cantab) BCL (Oxon)]
✉ Michael.Swainston@Brickcourt.co.uk

SWAN MISS JENNIFER JANE

Renaissance Chambers
5th Floor, Gray's Inn Chambers, Gray's Inn, London WC1R 5JA, ☎ 020 7404 1111
✉ clerks@renaissancechambers.co.uk
Call Date: July 2009, Middle Temple
Qualifications: [LLB (Hons) (B'ham)]

SWAROOP MR SUDHANSHU

20 Essex Street
London WC2R 3AL, ☎ 020 7842 1200
✉ clerks@20essexst.com
Call Date: Oct 1997, Inner Temple
Pupil Supervisor
Qualifications: [MA (Cantab) BCL (Oxon)]
✉ clerks@20essexst.com

SWEENEY MR CHRISTIAN NOEL

3 PB Barristers
3 Paper Buildings, Temple, London EC4Y 7EU,
☎ 020 7583 8055
3 PB Barristers
Royal Talbot House, 2 Victoria Street, Bristol, Avon BS1 6BB, ☎ 0117 928 1520
3 PB Barristers
23 Beaumont Street, Oxford OX1 2NP,
☎ 01865 793 736
3 PB Barristers
4 St Peter Street, Winchester SO23 8BW,
☎ 01962 868884
✉ clerks.winchester@3paper.co.uk
3 PB Barristers
30 Christchurch Road, Bournemouth, Dorset BH1 3PD, ☎ 01202 292102
✉ clerks.bournemouth@3paper.co.uk
Call Date: Oct 1992, Gray's Inn
Pupil Supervisor
Qualifications: [LLB (Reading)]

SWEENEY MR JAMES PETER

Park Lane Plowden
Lombard House, 4-8 Lombard Street, Newcastle Upon Tyne NE1 3AE,
☎ 0191 211 4087
✉ clerks@parklaneplowden.co.uk
Call Date: Nov 1989, Inner Temple
Pupil Supervisor
Qualifications: [LLB (Hons)]
✉ seamus.sweeney@parklaneplowden.co.uk

SWEENEY MRS LINDA MARY

Call Date: Nov 1999, Middle Temple
Qualifications: [LLB (Hons)(Manch)]
✉ linda.sweeney@stjohnsbuildings.co.uk, clerk@stjohnsbuildings.co.uk

SWEENEY MS LYDIA

Temple Garden Chambers
1 Harcourt Buildings, Temple, London EC4Y 9DA, ☎ 020 7583 1315
✉ clerks@tgchambers.com
Call Date: Oct 2002, Inner Temple
Qualifications: [BA (Manch) PGDL]
✉ ls@tgchambers.com

E

SWEENEY MR NOEL CHRISTOPHER

Veritas Chambers
186 High Street, Worle, North Somerset
BS22 6JD, ☎01934 853 382
✉nole@nsweeney.plus.com
Call Date: July 1975, Gray's Inn
Pupil Supervisor
Qualifications: [LLB]

SWEENEY MR THOMAS GERARD

Chambers of Mr Thomas Sweeney
4 Parkway, Daisy Hill, Westoughton, Bolton
BL5 2RY, ☎01942 819206
✉Tasjas5@hotmail.co.uk
Call Date: Feb 1988, Gray's Inn
✉tasjas5@hotmail.co.uk

SWEET MISS LOUISE JUNE

Carmelite Chambers
9 Carmelite Street, London EC4Y 0DR,
☎020 7936 6300
✉clerks@carmelitechambers.co.uk
Call Date: Oct 1994, Gray's Inn
Pupil Supervisor
Qualifications: [LLB (Hull)]
✉lsweet@carmelitechambers.co.uk

E

SWEETING MISS MARGARET FRANCIS

Trinity Chambers
The Custom House, 39 Quayside, Newcastle Upon Tyne NE1 3DE, ☎0191 232 1927
✉info@trinitychambers.co.uk
Trinity Chambers
Multi Media Exchange, 72-80 Corporation Road, Middlesbrough TS1 2RF,
☎01642 247569
✉info@trinitychambers.co.uk
Call Date: Oct 1996, Lincoln's Inn
Qualifications: [LLB (Hons)(Notts) MA (Lond)]
✉m.sweeting@trinitychambers.co.uk

SWIFFEN MR GUY CHARLES

Park Lane Plowden
19 Westgate, Leeds LS1 2RD,
☎0113 228 5049
✉clerks@parklaneplowden.co.uk
Call Date: Nov 1991, Lincoln's Inn
Pupil Supervisor
Qualifications: [BA (Hons) Dip Law]
✉guy.swiffen@parklaneplowden.co.uk

SWIFT MR JOHN ANTHONY QC (1981)

Monckton Chambers
1 & 2 Raymond Buildings, Gray's Inn, London
WC1R 5NR, ☎020 7405 7211
✉chambers@monckton.com
Call Date: Nov 1965, Inner Temple
Qualifications: [MA (Oxon)]

SWIFT MR JONATHAN MARK QC (2010)

11 King's Bench Walk
11 King's Bench Walk, Temple, London
EC4Y 7EQ, ☎020 7632 8500
✉clerksroom@11kbw.com
Call Date: July 1989, Inner Temple
Pupil Supervisor, Recorder
Qualifications: [BA (Oxon) LLM (Cantab)]
✉jonathan.swift@11kbw.com

SWIFT MR JONATHAN PETER

29 Bedford Row Chambers
London WC1R 4HE, ☎020 7404 1044
✉clerks@29br.co.uk
Call Date: Nov 1977, Inner Temple
Pupil Supervisor, Recorder
Qualifications: [LLB (Hons)(Lond)]
✉jswift@29br.co.uk

SWIFT MR MALCOLM ROBIN QC (1988)

Wilberforce Chambers
7 Bishop Lane, Hull HU1 1PA,
☎01482 323264
2 Hare Court
Lower Ground, Ground, 1st & 2nd Floor, 2 Hare Court, Temple, London EC4Y 7BH,
☎020 7353 3982 ✉clerks@2harecourt.com
Call Date: July 1970, Gray's Inn
Qualifications: [LLB AKC]
✉malcolm@swiftqc.co.uk

SWINNERTON MR DAVID MICHAEL

Cornwall Street Chambers
85-87 Cornwall Street, Birmingham B3 3BY,
☎0121 233 7500
✉clerks@cornwallstreet.co.uk
Call Date: Nov 1995, Lincoln's Inn
Qualifications: [BA (Hons)]
✉david.swinnerton@cornwallstreet.co.uk

SWINSTEAD MR DAVID LLOYD

3 PB Barristers
3 Paper Buildings, Temple, London EC4Y 7EU, ☎020 7583 8055
3 PB Barristers
Royal Talbot House, 2 Victoria Street, Bristol, Avon BS1 6BB, ☎0117 928 1520
3 PB Barristers
30 Christchurch Road, Bournemouth, Dorset BH1 3PD, ☎01202 292102
✉clerks.bournemouth@3paper.co.uk
3 PB Barristers
4 St Peter Street, Winchester SO23 8BW, ☎01962 868884
✉clerks.winchester@3paper.co.uk
3 PB Barristers
23 Beaumont Street, Oxford OX1 2NP, ☎01865 793 736
Call Date: July 1970, Inner Temple
Pupil Supervisor

SWIRSKY MR ADAM ABRAHAM BURL BRADBURY

Lamb Chambers
Lamb Building, Elm Court, Temple, London EC4Y 7AS, ☎020 7797 8300
✉info@lambchambers.co.uk
Call Date: Nov 1989, Middle Temple
Pupil Supervisor
Qualifications: [BSc (Lond) Dip Law MSc (Lond)]
adamswirsky@lambchambers.co.uk

SWIRSKY MR JOSHUA MAX BRADBURY

Field Court Chambers
5 Field Court, Gray's Inn, London WC1R 5EF, ☎020 7405 6114 ✉clerks@fieldcourt.co.uk
Call Date: Nov 1987, Middle Temple
Pupil Supervisor
Qualifications: [BA (Dunelm)]
joshua.swirsky@fieldcourt.co.uk

SWOBODA MR JOHN-PAUL SELVAN

12 King's Bench Walk
12 King's Bench Walk, Temple, London EC4Y 7EL, ☎020 7583 0811
Call Date: July 2006, Gray's Inn
Qualifications: [LLB (Sheffield)]

SYED MR GULZAR SHAH

Bank House Chambers
Old Bank House, Hartshead, Sheffield S1 2EL, ☎0114 275 1223
✉w.digby@bankhousechambers.co.uk
Call Date: July 1983, Gray's Inn
Qualifications: [LLB (Lanc)]
g.syed@bankhousechambers.co.uk

SYED MISS MARYAM HASSAN

Seven Bedford Row
7 Bedford Row, London WC1R 4BS, ☎020 7242 3555 ✉clerks@7br.co.uk
Call Date: Oct 1993, Lincoln's Inn
Qualifications: [LLB (Hons)(Lond)]
msyed@7br.co.uk

SYED MISS SAFORA

Chambers of Mr Ami Feder
Ground Floor, Lamb Building, Temple, London EC4Y 7AS, ☎020 7797 7788
✉clerks@lambbuilding.co.uk
Chambers of Mr Ami Feder
Ground Floor, Lamb Building, Temple, London EC4Y 7AS, ☎020 7797 7788
✉clerks@lambbuilding.co.uk
Call Date: Nov 2000, Lincoln's Inn
Qualifications: [LLB (Hons)]

SYFRET MR NICHOLAS QC (2008)

13 King's Bench Walk
13 King's Bench Walk, Temple, London EC4Y 7EN, ☎020 7353 7204
✉clerks@13kbw.co.uk
13 KBW
32 Beaumont Street, Oxford OX1 2NP, ☎01865 311066 ✉clerks@13kbw.co.uk
Citadel Chambers
The Citadel, 190 Corporation Street, Birmingham B4 6QD, ☎0121 233 8500
✉clerks@citadelchambers.com
Call Date: July 1979, Middle Temple
Recorder
Qualifications: [MA (Cantab)]
nsyfret@13kbw.co.uk

SYKES MRS CAROLINE

Pendragon Chambers
Suite 7, J Shed, Kings Road, SA1 Waterfront, Swansea SA1 8PL, ☎01792 411188
✉clerks@pendragonchambers.com
Call Date: July 2004, Gray's Inn
Qualifications: [BSc (Hons) (Wales) PGDL]

SYKES MR LAURENT CHARLES

Gray's Inn Tax Chambers
3rd Floor, Gray's Inn Chambers, Gray's Inn, London WC1R 5JA, ☎020 7242 2642
✉clerks@taxbar.com
Call Date: Oct 2007, Gray's Inn
Pupil Supervisor
Qualifications: [BA ACA]

SYME MRS SUZANNE MARIE

2-3 Hind Court Chambers
2-3 Hind Court, Fleet Street, London EC4A 3DL, ☎ 020 7822 2150
✉ david@2-3hindcourt.com
Call Date: July 2004, Inner Temple
Qualifications: [LLB (Hons)]

SYMES MR MARK ADRIAN

Garden Court Chambers
57-60 Lincoln's Inn Fields, London WC2A 3LJ, ☎ 020 7993 7600 ✉ info@gclaw.co.uk
Call Date: Nov 2004, Lincoln's Inn
Qualifications: [BA (Hons) Oxon]
🖃 marks@gclaw.co.uk

SYMINGTON MS ANNA DIMITY ROSE

St John's Chambers
101 Victoria Street, Bristol BS1 6PU, ☎ 0117 923 4700
✉ clerks@stjohnschambers.co.uk
Call Date: Oct 2002, Inner Temple
Qualifications: [LLB (Dunelm)]
🖃 anna.symington@stjohnschambers.co.uk

SYMMS MISS KATHRYN ANN

Number 7 Harrington Street Chambers
7 Harrington Street, Liverpool L2 9YH, ☎ 0151 242 0707 ✉ clerks@7hs.co.uk
Call Date: Oct 1990, Gray's Inn
Qualifications: [BA (Cantab)]
🖃 kate.symms@7hs.co.uk

SYMONS MR CHRISTOPHER JOHN MAURICE QC (1989)

3 Verulam Buildings
London WC1R 5NT, ☎ 020 7831 8441
✉ chambers@3vb.com
Call Date: July 1972, Middle Temple
Recorder
Qualifications: [BA (Kent)]
🖃 csymons@3vb.com

SYRIL MR GEORGE CARMEL

Willesden Chambers
5 Mora Road, London NW2 6SD, ☎ 020 3273 1042 ✉ syril@btinternet.com
Luton Chambers
103 Wexham Close, Luton LU3 3TX, ☎ 01582 598394 ✉ mshafikhan@hotmail.com
Call Date: July 1980, Lincoln's Inn
Pupil Supervisor
Qualifications: [MA LLB]
🖃 syril@btinternet.com

SZERARD MR ANDREI MICHAEL

3 Dr Johnson's Buildings
Ground Floor, 3 Dr Johnson's Buildings, Temple, London EC4Y 7BA, ☎ 020 7353 4854
✉ clerks@3djb.co.uk
Call Date: Apr 1986, Inner Temple
Pupil Supervisor
Qualifications: [LLB (Hull)]
🖃 aszerard@3djb.co.uk

SZWED MISS ELIZABETH MARIA

1 Garden Court Family Law Chambers
Ground Floor, One Garden Court, Temple, London EC4Y 9BJ, ☎ 020 7797 7900
✉ clerks@1gc.com
Call Date: Nov 1974, Middle Temple
Pupil Supervisor
Qualifications: [LLB (Leeds)]
🖃 szwed@1gc.com

SZYSZCZAK PROF ERIKA MARIA

Littleton Chambers
3 King's Bench Walk North, Temple, London EC4Y 7HR, ☎ 020 7797 8600
✉ fschneider@littletonchambers.co.uk
Call Date: July 2004, Middle Temple
Qualifications: [LLB LLM PhD]

TABACHNIK MR ANDREW DANIEL

4-5 Gray's Inn Square
Gray's Inn, London WC1R 5AH, ☎ 020 7404 5252 ✉ clerks@4-5.co.uk
Call Date: Nov 1991, Inner Temple
Qualifications: [MA (Hons) (Cantab) LLM (USA)]
🖃 atabachnik@4-5.co.uk

TABARI MR ALI-REZA

St Philips Chambers
55 Temple Row, Birmingham B2 5LS, ☎ 0121 246 7000 ✉ clerks@st-philips.com
Call Date: Nov 2006, Inner Temple
Qualifications: [LLB (Durham)]
🖃 atabari@st-phillips.com

TACKABERRY MR JOHN ANTONY QC (1982)

39 Essex Street
London WC2R 3AT, ☎ 020 7832 1111
✉ clerks@39essex.com
Assize Court Chambers
14 Small Street, Bristol BS1 1DE, ☎ 0117 926 4587 ✉ carly@assize.co.uk
Arbitration Chambers
22 Willes Road, London NW5 3DS, ☎ 020 7267 2137
✉ john.tackaberry@39essex.com
Call Date: July 1967, Gray's Inn
Qualifications: [MA CEDR FFB FCIARB LLM]

E

TACZALSKI MR CARLO JOHN-PAUL

Crown Office Chambers
2 Crown Office Row, Temple, London EC4Y 7HJ, ☎020 7797 8100
✉mail@crownofficechambers.com
Call Date: July 2010, Middle Temple
Qualifications: [BA (Hons) (Cantab)]
✉taczalski@crownofficechambers.com

TAELOR START MISS ANGHARAD JOCELYN

3 Verulam Buildings
London WC1R 5NT, ☎020 7831 8441
✉chambers@3vb.com
Call Date: Nov 1988, Lincoln's Inn
Qualifications: [BA (Hons) (Dunelm)]
✉astart@3vb.com

TAFADAR MISS SULTANA RAZIA

Tooks Chambers
81 Farringdon Street, London EC4A 4BL, ☎020 7842 7575 ✉clerks@tooks.co.uk
Call Date: Mar 2005, Lincoln's Inn

TAFT MR CHRISTOPHER HEITON

St James's Chambers
68 Quay Street, Manchester M3 3EJ, ☎0161 834 7000
✉clerks@stjameschambers.com
Call Date: Oct 1997, Middle Temple
Qualifications: [LLB (Hons)(Manc)]
✉christopher.taft@stjameschambers.com

TAFUR MRS ISABELLA JOSEPHINE

Francis Taylor Building
Inner Temple, London EC4Y 7BY, ☎020 7353 8415 ✉clerks@ftb.eu.com
Call Date: Oct 2009, Lincoln's Inn
Qualifications: [BA (Oxon) CPE COL]
✉isabella.tafur@ftb.eu.com

TAGER MR ROMIE QC (1995)

Selborne Chambers
10 Essex Street, London WC2R 3AA, ☎020 7420 9500
✉clerks@selbornechambers.co.uk
Call Date: Nov 1970, Middle Temple
Qualifications: [LLM]
✉romie.tager@selbornechambers.co.uk

TAGGART MR NICHOLAS

Landmark Chambers
180 Fleet Street, London EC4A 2HG, ☎020 7430 1221
✉clerks@landmarkchambers.co.uk
Call Date: Oct 1991, Middle Temple
Pupil Supervisor
Qualifications: [LLB (Hons)(Lond) BCL (Oxon)]
✉ntaggart@landmarkchambers.co.uk

TAGHDISSIAN MR JAMES ALI

Colleton Chambers
Colleton Crescent, Exeter, Devon EX2 4DG, ☎01392 274898
✉clerks@colletonchambers.co.uk
Call Date: Oct 2005, Gray's Inn
Qualifications: [LLB (Exeter)]
✉jamestaghdissian@colletonchambers.co.uk

TAGON MISS TAMIA

Call Date: May 1997, Lincoln's Inn
Qualifications: [BA (Hons)(Lond)]

TAHERI MR PETER KIE-ARASH

5 Essex Court
1st Floor, 5 Essex Court, Temple, London EC4Y 9AH, ☎020 7410 2000
✉clerks@5essexcourt.co.uk
Call Date: July 2007, Lincoln's Inn
Qualifications: [BA (Oxon)]
✉taheri@5essexcourt.co.uk

TAHIR MISS PERICAN

6 Pump Court
1st Floor, 6 Pump Court, Temple, London EC4Y 7AR, ☎020 7797 8400
✉richardconstable@6pumpcourt.co.uk
6 Pump Court Chambers
6-8 Mill Street, Maidstone, Kent ME15 6XH, ☎01622 688094
✉annexe@6pumpcourt.co.uk
Call Date: July 2004, Middle Temple
Qualifications: [LLB Hons (Sussex)]
✉Clerks@6PumpCourt.co.uk

TAHTA MISS NATASHA ALEXANDRA

QEB Hollis Whiteman
1-2 Laurence Pountney Hill, London EC4R 0EU, ☎020 7933 8855
✉barristers@qebhw.co.uk
Call Date: Oct 1998, Inner Temple
Qualifications: [BA (Cantab) MA (Cantab) CPE]
✉barristers@qebhw.co.uk

E

TAI MISS FARZANA

Park Lane Plowden
19 Westgate, Leeds LS1 2RD,
☎ 0113 228 5049
✉ clerks@parklaneplowden.co.uk
Pallant Chambers
12 North Pallant, Chichester, West Sussex
PO19 1TQ, ☎ 01243 784538
✉ clerks@pallantchambers.co.uk
Call Date: July 2003, Middle Temple
Qualifications: [LLB Hons (Newcastle)]

TAIT MR ANDREW CHARLES GORDON QC (2003)

Francis Taylor Building
Inner Temple, London EC4Y 7BY,
☎ 020 7353 8415 ✉ clerks@ftb.eu.com
Call Date: July 1981, Inner Temple
Qualifications: [MA (Oxon)]
andrew.tait@ftb.eu.com

TAIT MR DONALD

Albion Chambers
Broad Street, Bristol BS1 1DR,
☎ 0117 927 2144
✉ clerks@albionchambers.co.uk
Call Date: Feb 1987, Inner Temple
Pupil Supervisor, Recorder
Qualifications: [BA (Leic)]

TAITE MS SARAH GEORGINA

Westgate Chambers
64 High Street, Lewes, East Sussex BN7 1XG,
☎ 01273 480510
✉ clerks@westgate-chambers.co.uk
Call Date: July 2008, Inner Temple
Qualifications: [BA]
staite@westgate-chambers.co.uk

TAKATSUKI MISS YUURI

5RB
1st Floor, 5 Raymond Buildings, Gray's Inn,
London WC1R 5BP, ☎ 020 7242 2902
✉ clerks@5rb.com
Call Date: Nov 2007, Lincoln's Inn
Qualifications: [BA (Cantab)]
yulitakatsuki@5rb.com

TALACCHI MR CARLO GIANCARLO

10 King's Bench Walk
Ground Floor, 10 King's Bench Walk, Temple,
London EC4Y 7EB, ☎ 020 7353 7742
✉ Chambers@10kingsbenchwalk.co.uk
Call Date: July 1986, Lincoln's Inn
Qualifications: [BSc (B'ham) LLM (Cantab)]
chambers@10kingsbenchwalk.co.uk

TALALAY MR ROBERT JOSEPH

5 Essex Court
1st Floor, 5 Essex Court, Temple, London
EC4Y 9AH, ☎ 020 7410 2000
✉ clerks@5essexcourt.co.uk
Call Date: Oct 2010, Gray's Inn
Qualifications: [BA]
talalay@5essexcourt.co.uk

TALBOT MR JACK RICHARD

Dyers Chambers
35 Bedford Row, London WC1R 4JH,
☎ 020 7404 1881
✉ admin@dyerschambers.com
Call Date: Oct 2004, Middle Temple
Qualifications: [BA (Hons) (Bris) PgDl]

TALBOT MR KENNEDY VERNON

Chambers of Andrew Mitchell QC
33 Chancery Lane, London WC2A 1EN,
☎ 020 7440 9950 ✉ clerks@33cllaw.com
Call Date: Nov 1984, Gray's Inn
Pupil Supervisor
Qualifications: [BA]
kt@33cllaw.com

TALBOT MISS NICOLA EMMA

1 Paper Buildings
1st Floor, 1 Paper Buildings, Temple, London
EC4Y 7EP, ☎ 020 7353 3728
✉ clerks@onepaper.co.uk
Call Date: Oct 2007, Lincoln's Inn
Qualifications: [BA (Oxon)]
nicola.talbot@environment-agency.gov.uk

TALBOT MR PATRICK JOHN QC (1990)

Serle Court
6 New Square, Lincoln's Inn, London
WC2A 3QS, ☎ 020 7242 6105
✉ clerks@serlecourt.co.uk
Call Date: July 1969, Lincoln's Inn
Recorder
Qualifications: [MA (Oxon)]
ptalbot@serlecourt.co.uk

TALBOT RICE MRS ELSPETH MIDDLETON QC (2008)

XXIV Old Buildings
Ground Floor, 24 Old Buildings, Lincoln's Inn,
London WC2A 3UP, ☎ 020 7691 2424
✉ clerks@xxiv.co.uk
Call Date: Oct 1990, Lincoln's Inn
Pupil Supervisor
Qualifications: [BA (Dunelm)]
etr@xxiv.co.uk

TALBOT-PONSONBY MR THOMAS MARTIN

3 PB Barristers
23 Beaumont Street, Oxford OX1 2NP, ☎ 01865 793 736
3 PB Barristers
3 Paper Buildings, Temple, London EC4Y 7EU, ☎ 020 7583 8055
Call Date: Nov 2011, Middle Temple
Qualifications: [BA (Hons) (Cantab) MA (Cantab)]

TALBOTT MR ROSS DAVID

Lamb Building
22 Ship Street, Brighton BN1 1AD, ☎ 01273 820490
✉ admin@lambbuilding.co.uk
Call Date: July 2008, Middle Temple
Qualifications: [LLB (Hons) (Kent)]

TALLON MR JOHN MARK QC (2000)

Pump Court Tax Chambers
16 Bedford Row, London WC1R 4EF, ☎ 020 7414 8080 ✉ clerks@pumptax.com
Call Date: July 1975, Middle Temple
Qualifications: [FCA]
✉ jtallon@pumptax.com

Types of work: Capital tax, Corporation tax, Employee benefit trusts, Equity, Income tax, National Insurance, Private client, Professional negligence, Stamp duty, Trusts, VAT, Wills

TALMON DR STEFAN ALEXANDER GUSTAV

20 Essex Street
London WC2R 3AL, ☎ 020 7842 1200
✉ clerks@20essexst.com
Call Date: July 2007, Lincoln's Inn
Qualifications: [LLM MA DPHI Habil DPhil]
✉ stalmon@20essexst.com

TAM MR ROBIN BING-KUEN QC (2006)

Temple Garden Chambers
1 Harcourt Buildings, Temple, London EC4Y 9DA, ☎ 020 7583 1315
✉ clerks@tgchambers.com
Call Date: July 1986, Middle Temple
Qualifications: [MA (Cantab)]
✉ robintam@tgchambers.com

TAMBLING MR RICHARD

1 Garden Court Family Law Chambers
Ground Floor, One Garden Court, Temple, London EC4Y 9BJ, ☎ 020 7797 7900
✉ clerks@1gc.com
Call Date: Oct 2005, Middle Temple
Qualifications: [BA (Hons) (GCU) LLB (Hons) Northumbria]
✉ tambling@1gc.com

TAMLYN MR LLOYD JEFFREY

South Square
3-4 South Square, Gray's Inn, London WC1R 5HP, ☎ 020 7696 9900
✉ practicemanagers@southsquare.com
Call Date: Nov 1991, Gray's Inn
Pupil Supervisor
Qualifications: [BA (Hons) (Cantab)]
✉ lloydtamlyn@southsquare.com

TAMPAKOPOULOS MS ALEXANDRA ARGYRO

2 Hare Court
Lower Ground, Ground, 1st & 2nd Floor, 2 Hare Court, Temple, London EC4Y 7BH, ☎ 020 7353 3982 ✉ clerks@2harecourt.com
Call Date: Nov 2007, Lincoln's Inn
Qualifications: [BA (Lond) MSc (Lond) PgDL MSc (Lond)]

TAMPION MS KARIN SALLY

Bedlington Chambers
7 New Square, Lincoln's Inn, London WC2A 2QS, ☎ 020 7831 1159
✉ clerks@bedlingtonchambers.com
Sundridge Chambers
10 Sundridge House, Burnt Ash Lane, Bromley, Kent BR1 5AE, ☎ 020 8464 9772
✉ sundridgechambers@sky.com
Bedlington Chambers
20 Staffa Road, Maidstone ME15 9ST, ☎ 01622 744 015
✉ clerks@bedlingtonchambers.com
Call Date: July 2005, Inner Temple
Qualifications: [BA MSc]

TAN MISS CHARLOTTE LOUISA CHENG-SU

20 Essex Street
London WC2R 3AL, ☎ 020 7842 1200
✉ clerks@20essexst.com
Call Date: July 2008, Middle Temple
Qualifications: [BA (Hons) (Cantab)]
✉ clerks@20essexst.com

E

TANCHEL MISS VIVIENNE JOY

2 Hare Court
Lower Ground, Ground, 1st & 2nd Floor, 2 Hare Court, Temple, London EC4Y 7BH,
☎ 020 7353 3982 ✉ clerks@2harecourt.com
Call Date: Nov 2005, Middle Temple
Qualifications: [LLB (Hons) (Lond) Dip Law (Lond)]
✉ viviennetanchel@2harecourt.com

TANKEL MR BENJAMIN EDWARD DAVID

4-5 Gray's Inn Square
Gray's Inn, London WC1R 5AH,
☎ 020 7404 5252 ✉ clerks@4-5.co.uk
Call Date: Nov 2009, Middle Temple
Qualifications: [BA (Hons) (Cantab)]

TANKEL MRS RUTH SHOSHANA

15 Winckley Square
Preston PR1 3JJ, ☎ 01772 252828
✉ clerks@15winckleysq.co.uk
Call Date: July 1990, Middle Temple
Qualifications: [LLB (Manch)]
✉ ruth@tankel.com

TANNER MISS AMANDA CHARLOTTE

2-3 Hind Court Chambers
2-3 Hind Court, Fleet Street, London EC4A 3DL, ☎ 020 7822 2150
✉ david@2-3hindcourt.com
Call Date: July 2009, Inner Temple
Qualifications: [BA (Oxon)]
✉ m.tanner@2-3hindcourt.com

TANNEY MR ANTHONY

Falcon Chambers
Falcon Court, London EC4Y 1AA,
☎ 020 7353 2484
✉ clerks@falcon-chambers.com
Call Date: Oct 1994, Lincoln's Inn
Pupil Supervisor
Qualifications: [BA (Hons) M Jur (Dunelm)]
✉ tanney@falcon-chambers.com

Types of work: Boundaries, Chancery (land law), Commercial property, Conveyancing, Equity, Landlord and tenant, Lands Tribunal, Leasehold enfranchisement, Professional negligence, Real property, Rights of way, Title to land, Trusts

TANNEY MR MICHAEL

7 Bell Yard
London WC2A 2JR, ☎ 020 7831 0636
✉ kevintarrant@btconnect.com
Call Date: Mar 2004, Lincoln's Inn
Qualifications: [BA (Hons) (Edin)]

TANSEY MISS ANOUSKA

2-3 Hind Court Chambers
2-3 Hind Court, Fleet Street, London EC4A 3DL, ☎ 020 7822 2150
✉ david@2-3hindcourt.com
Call Date: Nov 2004, Gray's Inn
Qualifications: [BA MSsc LLB]

TANSEY MR ROCK BENEDICT QC (1990)

25 Bedford Row
London WC1R 4HD, ☎ 020 7067 1500
✉ clerks@25bedfordrow.com
Call Date: July 1966, Lincoln's Inn
Recorder
Qualifications: [Dip Soc (Bris) LLB (Bris) (Hons)]
✉ rtansey@25bedfordrow.com

TAPPER MR PAUL KENNEDY

Chartlands Chambers
3 St Giles Terrace, Northampton NN1 2BN,
☎ 01604 603322
✉ enquiries@chartlands-chambers.co.uk
Call Date: July 1991, Middle Temple
Qualifications: [LLB (Hons)]
✉ ppk38taps@aol.com

TAPPIN MR MICHAEL JOHN QC (2009)

8 New Square
8 New Square, Lincoln's Inn, London WC2A 3QP, ☎ 020 7405 4321
✉ clerks@8newsquare.co.uk
Call Date: Oct 1991, Middle Temple
Qualifications: [BA (Hons) CPE DPhil (Oxon)]
✉ michael.tappin@8newsquare.co.uk

Types of work: Breach of confidence, Copyright, Copyright theft, Copyright Tribunal, Design, Entertainment, Intellectual property, Malicious falsehood, Media, Media and entertainment, Passing off, Patents, Pharmaceuticals, Scientific and technical disputes, Trade secrets, Trademarks

TAPSELL MR PAUL RICHARD

Becket Chambers
17 New Dover Road, Canterbury, Kent CT1 3AS, ☎ 01227 786331
✉ clerks@becket-chambers.co.uk
Call Date: Oct 1991, Middle Temple
Qualifications: [LLB (Hons) (Lancs)]
✉ ptapsell@becket-chambers.co.uk

TAPSON MISS LESLEY KATHERINE

Field Court Chambers
5 Field Court, Gray's Inn, London WC1R 5EF, ☎ 020 7405 6114 ✉ clerks@fieldcourt.co.uk
Call Date: Nov 1982, Gray's Inn
Pupil Supervisor
Qualifications: [LLB (Newc)]
✉ lesley.tapson@fieldcourt.co.uk

TARBITT MR NICHOLAS EDWARD HENRY

Cornwall Street Chambers
85-87 Cornwall Street, Birmingham B3 3BY, ☎ 0121 233 7500
✉ clerks@cornwallstreet.co.uk
Call Date: July 1988, Inner Temple
Qualifications: [LLB]
✉ nick.tarbitt@cornwallstreet.co.uk

TARGETT-PARKER MISS LEANNE SUSAN

The Chambers of Miss Leanne Targett-Parker
4 Romola Road, London SE24 9AZ, ☎ 020 8674 6694 ✉ parkerls@yahoo.co.uk
No. 3 Fleet Street Chambers
3 Fleet Street, London EC4Y 1DP, ☎ 020 7936 4474 ✉ clerks@3fleetstreet.com
Call Date: Oct 2005, Lincoln's Inn
Qualifications: [BA (Hons) (Lond) PgDl (Lond) LLM (Lond)]

TASKEEN MR WASIM UDDIN

St James's Chambers
68 Quay Street, Manchester M3 3EJ, ☎ 0161 834 7000
✉ clerks@stjameschambers.com
Call Date: Oct 1998, Lincoln's Inn
Qualifications: [LLB (Hons)(Manc)]
✉ wasim.taskeen@stjameschambers.com

TASKIS MS CATHERINE LOUISE

Falcon Chambers
Falcon Court, London EC4Y 1AA, ☎ 020 7353 2484
✉ clerks@falcon-chambers.com
Call Date: Nov 1995, Inner Temple
Qualifications: [MA BCL (Oxon)]
✉ taskis@falcon-chambers.com

Types of work: Agriculture, Chancery (land law), Landlord and tenant, Real property

TATFORD MR WARWICK HENRY PATRICK

9-12 Bell Yard
London WC2A 2JR, ☎ 020 7400 1800
✉ clerks@9-12bellyard.com
Call Date: Oct 1993, Lincoln's Inn
Pupil Supervisor
Qualifications: [BA (Hons)(Oxon)]
✉ w.tatford@9-12bellyard.com

TATLOW MR NICHOLAS MARK

Citadel Chambers
The Citadel, 190 Corporation Street, Birmingham B4 6QD, ☎ 0121 233 8500
✉ clerks@citadelchambers.com
Call Date: May 1996, Gray's Inn
Qualifications: [BA (Wales)]
✉ clerks@citadelchambers.com

TATTERSALL MR GEOFFREY FRANK QC (1992)

Byrom Street Chambers
12 Byrom Street, Manchester M3 4PP, ☎ 0161 829 2100 ✉ clerks@byromstreet.com
Crown Office Chambers
2 Crown Office Row, Temple, London EC4Y 7HJ, ☎ 020 7797 8100
✉ mail@crownofficechambers.com
5 Essex Court
1st Floor, 5 Essex Court, Temple, London EC4Y 9AH, ☎ 020 7410 2000
✉ clerks@5essexcourt.co.uk
42 Bedford Row
London WC1R 4LL, ☎ 020 7831 0222
✉ clerks@42br.com
Call Date: July 1970, Lincoln's Inn
Recorder
Qualifications: [MA (Oxon)]
✉ geoffrey.tattersall@byromstreet.com

TATTERSALL MR SIMON MARK ROGERS

Fenners Chambers
3 Madingley Road, Cambridge CB3 0EE, ☎ 01223 368761
✉ clerks@fennerschambers.com
Call Date: Nov 1977, Middle Temple
Pupil Supervisor
Qualifications: [LLB (Lond)]
✉ simon.tattersall@fennerschambers.com

E

TATTON-BENNETT MR ALEXANDER JAMES

1 KBW Chambers
1 King's Bench Walk, Temple, London EC4Y 7DB, ☎ 020 7936 1500
✉ clerks@1kbw.co.uk
King's Bench Chambers
174 High Street, Lewes BN7 1YE,
☎ 01273 402600
Call Date: Oct 2007, Gray's Inn
Qualifications: [BA (Lond)]
atbennett@1kbw.co.uk

TATTON-BROWN MR DANIEL NICHOLAS

Littleton Chambers
3 King's Bench Walk North, Temple, London EC4Y 7HR, ☎ 020 7797 8600
✉ fschneider@littletonchambers.co.uk
Call Date: Nov 1994, Middle Temple
Pupil Supervisor
Qualifications: [BA (Hons)]
dtb@littletonchambers.co.uk

TAUBE MR SIMON AXEL ROBIN QC (2000)

Ten Old Square
Ground Floor, Ten Old Square, Lincoln's Inn, London WC2A 3SU, ☎ 020 7405 0758
✉ clerks@tenoldsquare.com
Call Date: July 1980, Middle Temple
Qualifications: [MA (Oxon)]
simontaube@tenoldsquare.com

TAURAH MS SHEILA DOOLARY

Clerksroom (Taunton)
Equity House, Administration Centre, Blackbrook Park Avenue, Taunton, Somerset TA1 2PX, ☎ 0845 083 3000
✉ mail@clerksroom.com
Call Date: Oct 1991, Lincoln's Inn
Qualifications: [LLB (Hons)]
taurah@clerksroom.com

TAUSSIG MR GURION

The Chambers of Grahame Aldous QC
9 Gough Square, London EC4A 3DG,
☎ 020 7832 0500
✉ clerks@9goughsquare.co.uk
Call Date: July 2001, Inner Temple
Qualifications: [BA (Cantab) MA (Leeds) PhD (Leeds)]

TAUTZ MR WILLIAM HENRY

Tooks Chambers
81 Farringdon Street, London EC4A 4BL,
☎ 020 7842 7575 ✉ clerks@tooks.co.uk
Call Date: Oct 2004, Gray's Inn
Qualifications: [BA LLB]
william.tautz@tooks.co.uk

TAVARES MR NATHAN WARREN

Outer Temple Chambers
The Outer Temple, 222 Strand, London WC2R 1BA, ☎ 020 7353 6381
✉ clerks@outertemple.com
Call Date: Oct 1992, Middle Temple
Pupil Supervisor
Qualifications: [BSc (Hons) CPE]
nathan.tavares@outertemple.com

Types of work: Clinical negligence, Common law (general), Contracts, Mental health, Personal injury, Professional negligence, Regulatory and disciplinary law

TAVERNER MR MARCUS LOUIS QC (2000)

Keating Chambers
15 Essex Street, London WC2R 3AA,
☎ 020 7544 2600
✉ clerks@keatingchambers.com
Call Date: July 1981, Gray's Inn
Qualifications: [LLB ACI Arb LLM (Lond)]
mtaverner@keatingchambers.com

TAWFIK MISS NADIA

Pallant Chambers
12 North Pallant, Chichester, West Sussex PO19 1TQ, ☎ 01243 784538
✉ clerks@pallantchambers.co.uk
Call Date: July 2010, Middle Temple
Qualifications: [MA (Hons) Dip Law LLB (Hons)]
nadiat@pallantchambers.co.uk

TAYLOR MR ALAN JEREMY

Park Court Chambers
16 Park Place, Leeds LS1 2SJ,
☎ 0113 243 3277
✉ clerks@parkcourtchambers.co.uk
Call Date: July 1986, Lincoln's Inn
Pupil Supervisor
Qualifications: [BA(Bris) MPhil (Oxon) Dip Law]
ajtaylor@parkcourtchambers.co.uk, clerks@parkcourtchambers.co.uk

TAYLOR MR ALEX GEOFFREY

Park Lane Plowden
19 Westgate, Leeds LS1 2RD,
☎0113 228 5049
✉clerks@parklaneplowden.co.uk
Park Court Chambers
16 Park Place, Leeds LS1 2SJ,
☎0113 243 3277
✉clerks@parkcourtchambers.co.uk
Call Date: July 2000, Inner Temple
Qualifications: [BA (Oxon) CPE]

TAYLOR MR ALEXANDER RAYMOND LESLIE

Deans Court Chambers
24 St John Street, Manchester M3 4DF,
☎0161 214 6000 ✉clerks@deanscourt.co.uk
Deans Court Chambers
101 Walker Street, Preston PR1 2RR,
☎01772 565 600
✉preston@deanscourt.co.uk
Call Date: Nov 2003, Lincoln's Inn
Qualifications: [LLB (Hons) (Bris)]
✉taylor@deanscourt.co.uk

TAYLOR MR ANDREW PETER

KCH Garden Square
1 Oxford Street, Nottingham NG1 5BH,
☎0115 941 8851
✉clerks@kchgardensquare.co.uk
Call Date: Nov 1989, Gray's Inn
Qualifications: [BA (Hons)]

TAYLOR MR ANDREW ROBERT

30 Park Place
Cardiff CF10 3BS, ☎029 2039 8421
✉clerks@30parkplace.law.co.uk
Call Date: Nov 1985, Gray's Inn
Pupil Supervisor
Qualifications: [BSc Econ (Wales)]

TAYLOR MISS ARABA ARBA KURANKYIWA

Fenners Chambers
3 Madingley Road, Cambridge CB3 0EE,
☎01223 368761
✉clerks@fennerschambers.com
Call Date: July 1985, Middle Temple
Pupil Supervisor
Qualifications: [MA (Cantab)]
✉araba.taylor@fennerschambers.com

TAYLOR MR CHARLES SPENCER

Pallant Chambers
12 North Pallant, Chichester, West Sussex
PO19 1TQ, ☎01243 784538
✉clerks@pallantchambers.co.uk
Call Date: July 1974, Middle Temple
Pupil Supervisor
Qualifications: [LLB Hons]
✉clerks@pallantchambers.co.uk

TAYLOR MR CHRISTIAN

Exchange Chambers
7 Ralli Courts, West Riverside, Manchester
M3 5FT, ☎0161 833 2722
Exchange Chambers
One Derby Square, Derby Square, Liverpool
L2 9XX, ☎0151 236 7747
✉info@exchangechambers.co.uk
Exchange Chambers
Oxford House, Oxford Row, Leeds LS1 3BE,
☎0113 203 1970
✉spencer@exchangechambers.co.uk
Call Date: July 2003, Lincoln's Inn
Qualifications: [BA Hons (Cantab) PgDL (Manch)]
✉ctaylor@exchangechambers.co.uk

TAYLOR MR CHRISTOPHER JOHN

Queen Square Chambers
56 Queen Square, Bristol BS1 4PR,
☎0117 921 1966 ✉crime@qs-c.co.uk
Call Date: Nov 1982, Gray's Inn
Pupil Supervisor
Qualifications: [BA (Hons)]
✉cht@qs-c.co.uk

TAYLOR MISS CLAIRE ELIZABETH

15 Winckley Square
Preston PR1 3JJ, ☎01772 252828
✉clerks@15winckleysq.co.uk
Call Date: July 2009, Inner Temple
Qualifications: [BSc (Newc) BSc (Hons) GDipL]
✉clairetaylor@15ws.co.uk

TAYLOR MR DAVID BARTHOLOMEW

No5 Chambers
Fountain Court, Steelhouse Lane, Birmingham
B4 6DR, ☎0845 210 5555 ✉info@no5.com
No5 Chambers
Greenwood House, 4-7 Salisbury Court,
London EC4Y 8AA, ☎0845 210 5555
No5 Chambers
38 Queen Square, Bristol BS1 4QS,
☎0845 210 5555
Call Date: Nov 1993, Lincoln's Inn
Qualifications: [BA (Hons)]
✉dt@no5.com

E

TAYLOR MR DAVID CHRISTOPHER

St Johns Buildings Liverpool
8th Floor India Buildings, Water Street, Liverpool L2 0XG, ☎0151 243 6000
✉clerk@stjohnsbuildings.co.uk
16 Winckley Square
Preston PR1 3JJ, ☎01772 256100
St Johns Buildings
24a - 28 St John Street, Manchester M3 4DJ, ☎0161 214 1500
✉clerk@stjohnsbuildings.co.uk
Call Date: Oct 1998, Lincoln's Inn
Qualifications: [LLB (Hons)(L'pool)]
davidtaylor@indiabuildings.co.uk

TAYLOR MR DAVID EDWARD

37 Park Square Chambers
37 Park Square, Leeds LS1 2NY, ☎0113 243 9422 ✉chambers@no37.co.uk
Call Date: May 1995, Inner Temple
Qualifications: [LLB (Lond) LLM (Wolves)]
chambers@no37.co.uk

TAYLOR MR DOUGLAS JAMES

College Chambers
19 Carlton Crescent, Southampton, Hampshire SO15 2ET, ☎023 8023 0338
✉clerks@college-chambers.co.uk
Call Date: July 1981, Middle Temple
Pupil Supervisor
Qualifications: [BA (Hons) (Sheff)]
dtaylor@College-Chambers.co.uk

TAYLOR MISS EVE REBECCA

St John's Chambers
101 Victoria Street, Bristol BS1 6PU, ☎0117 923 4700
✉clerks@stjohnschambers.co.uk
Call Date: Nov 2003, Lincoln's Inn
Qualifications: [LLB (Hons) (Sheff)]
rebecca.taylor@stjohnschambers.co.uk

TAYLOR MISS GEMMA MARY

42 Bedford Row
London WC1R 4LL, ☎020 7831 0222
✉clerks@42br.com
Call Date: Feb 1988, Inner Temple
Qualifications: [LLB (London)]
gemma.taylor@42br.com

TAYLOR MR GREGORY LYNN QC (2001)

9 Park Place
9 Park Place, Cardiff, South Glamorgan CF10 3DP, ☎029 2038 2731
✉clerks@9parkplace.co.uk
Call Date: July 1974, Middle Temple
Qualifications: [BA (Keele)]
gtaylorqc@btinternet.com

TAYLOR MR JASON

Albion Chambers
Broad Street, Bristol BS1 1DR, ☎0117 927 2144
✉clerks@albionchambers.co.uk
Call Date: Nov 1995, Gray's Inn
Qualifications: [LLB (Wales)]
jason.taylor@albionchambers.co.uk

TAYLOR MR JOHN CHARLES

Fountain Court Chambers
Fountain Court, Temple, London EC4Y 9DH, ☎020 7583 3335
✉chambers@fountaincourt.co.uk
Call Date: Oct 1993, Middle Temple
Pupil Supervisor
Qualifications: [MA (Hons)(Cantab)]
jtaylor@fountaincourt.co.uk

TAYLOR MR JOHN DAVID

Charter Chambers
33 John Street, London WC1N 2AT, ☎020 7618 4400
✉clerks@charterchambers.com
Call Date: July 1986, Gray's Inn
Qualifications: [LLB (Cardiff)]
david.taylor@charterchambers.com

TAYLOR MR JONATHAN ANDREW

4 Breams Buildings
Chancery Lane, London EC4A 1HP, ☎020 7092 1900 ✉clerks@4bb.co.uk
Call Date: Nov 1987, Gray's Inn
Qualifications: [BA (Manch)]

TAYLOR MR JONATHAN FORD

St Johns Buildings Liverpool
8th Floor India Buildings, Water Street, Liverpool L2 0XG, ☎0151 243 6000
✉clerk@stjohnsbuildings.co.uk
16 Winckley Square
Preston PR1 3JJ, ☎01772 256100
St Johns Buildings
24a - 28 St John Street, Manchester M3 4DJ, ☎0161 214 1500
✉clerk@stjohnsbuildings.co.uk
Call Date: Nov 1991, Middle Temple
Qualifications: [LLB (Hons) (Reading)]

TAYLOR MR JULIAN RICHARD

St Johns Buildings
24a - 28 St John Street, Manchester M3 4DJ, ☎0161 214 1500
✉clerk@stjohnsbuildings.co.uk
St Johns Buildings
21 White Friars, Chester CH1 1NZ, ☎01244 323070
✉clerk@stjohnsbuildings.co.uk

16 Winckley Square
Preston PR1 3JJ, ☎ 01772 256100
Call Date: July 1986, Middle Temple
Pupil Supervisor, Recorder
Qualifications: [LLB (Bris)]
clerk@stjohnsbuildings.co.uk

TAYLOR MISS JULIE

15 Winckley Square
Preston PR1 3JJ, ☎ 01772 252828
✉ clerks@15winckleysq.co.uk
Call Date: Nov 1992, Inner Temple
Qualifications: [LLB]

TAYLOR MS KAREN ANNE

Themis Chambers
Suite 14067, 145-157 St John's Street, London EC1V 4PY, ☎ 07967 418976
✉ karentaylor@themischambers.co.uk
Call Date: July 2004, Inner Temple
Qualifications: [BA DTS]

TAYLOR MISS KATHRYN ANNE

No5 Chambers
Fountain Court, Steelhouse Lane, Birmingham B4 6DR, ☎ 0845 210 5555 ✉ info@no5.com
No5 Chambers
Greenwood House, 4-7 Salisbury Court, London EC4Y 8AA, ☎ 0845 210 5555
No5 Chambers
38 Queen Square, Bristol BS1 4QS, ☎ 0845 210 5555
Call Date: July 2005, Lincoln's Inn
Qualifications: [BA (Hons)]
kt@no5.com

TAYLOR MRS KITTY ELIZABETH

No.6 Park Square
Leeds LS1 2LW, ☎ 0113 245 9763
✉ Tim@no6.co.uk
Call Date: Oct 1992, Middle Temple
Qualifications: [LLB (Hons)]
taylor@no6.co.uk

TAYLOR MISS LINDA KATHRYN

Westgate Chambers
64 High Street, Lewes, East Sussex BN7 1XG, ☎ 01273 480510
✉ clerks@westgate-chambers.co.uk
Call Date: Oct 1998, Middle Temple
Qualifications: [BA (Hons)(B'ham) MSc (Oxon) CPE]
lt@westgate-chambers.co.uk

TAYLOR MR MARK ANDERSON

Trinity Chambers
Highfield House, Moulsham Street, Chelmsford, Essex CM2 9AH, ☎ 01245 605040
✉ clerks@trinitychambers.com
Call Date: July 2010, Middle Temple
Qualifications: [BSc (Hons) (Lond)]

TAYLOR MR MARTIN JOHN

Carmelite Chambers
9 Carmelite Street, London EC4Y 0DR, ☎ 020 7936 6300
✉ clerks@carmelitechambers.co.uk
Call Date: July 1988, Middle Temple
Pupil Supervisor
Qualifications: [BA (Hons) (Leeds) Dip Law]
mtaylor@carmelitechambers.co.uk

TAYLOR MS MARY-JANE

Coram Chambers
9-11 Fulwood Place, London WC1V 6HG, ☎ 020 7092 3700
✉ mail@coramchambers.co.uk
Call Date: Oct 2003, Inner Temple
Qualifications: [LLM (Sussex) LLM (UEA)]
mary-jane.taylor@coramchambers.co.uk

TAYLOR MR MICHAEL JOHN

Clock Chambers
18 Waterloo Road, Wolverhampton WV1 4BL, ☎ 01902 313444
✉ clockchambers@btconnect.com
Call Date: July 1986, Middle Temple
Qualifications: [LLB (Lond)]

TAYLOR MR MICHAEL JOSEPH FITZ

4 Pump Court
4 Pump Court, Temple, London EC4Y 7AN, ☎ 020 7842 5555
✉ chambers@4pumpcourt.com
Call Date: Nov 1996, Middle Temple
Pupil Supervisor
Qualifications: [BA ((Hons)]
mtaylor@4pumpcourt.com

TAYLOR MR MICHAEL PAUL

6 Pump Court Chambers
6-8 Mill Street, Maidstone, Kent ME15 6XH, ☎ 01622 688094
✉ annexe@6pumpcourt.co.uk
6 Pump Court
1st Floor, 6 Pump Court, Temple, London EC4Y 7AR, ☎ 020 7797 8400
✉ richardconstable@6pumpcourt.co.uk

E

Exchange Chambers
Oxford House, Oxford Row, Leeds LS1 3BE,
☎0113 203 1970
✉spencer@exchangechambers.co.uk
Call Date: Nov 1985, Gray's Inn
Pupil Supervisor
Qualifications: [LL.B (Leeds)]

TAYLOR MR NIGEL STUART

Crown Office Row Chambers
119 Church Street, Brighton, Sussex
BN1 1UD, ☎01273 625625
✉clerks@1cor.com
Call Date: Oct 1993, Inner Temple
Pupil Supervisor
Qualifications: [BA LLB (Lond)]
✉nigel.taylor@1cor.com

TAYLOR MR PAUL RICHARD

Doughty Street Chambers
53-54 Doughty Street, London WC1N 2LS,
☎020 7404 1313
✉enquiries@doughtystreet.co.uk
Doughty Street Chambers
Pall Mall Court, 61-67 King Street, Manchester
M2 4PD, ☎0161 618 1066
Doughty Street Chambers
5th Floor, Broad Quay House, Prince Street,
Bristol BS1 4DJ, ☎01179 058 717
Call Date: Nov 1989, Middle Temple
Pupil Supervisor
Qualifications: [LLB LLM (Cantab) CNAA]
✉p.taylor@doughtystreet.co.uk

TAYLOR MR PHILLIP BRIAN

Richmond Green Chambers
5 Connaught Road, Richmond, Surrey
TW10 6DW, ☎020 8948 4801
✉richmondchambers@btconnect.com
Call Date: Nov 1991, Lincoln's Inn
Qualifications: [LLB (Hons) (Lond) PGCE (Lond)]
✉richmondchambers@btconnect.com

TAYLOR MISS REBECCA

Crown Office Chambers
2 Crown Office Row, Temple, London
EC4Y 7HJ, ☎020 7797 8100
✉mail@crownofficechambers.com
Call Date: Oct 2001, Gray's Inn
Qualifications: [BA (Oxon)]
✉rtaylor@crownofficechambers.com

TAYLOR MR REUBEN MALLINSON

Landmark Chambers
180 Fleet Street, London EC4A 2HG,
☎020 7430 1221
✉clerks@landmarkchambers.co.uk
Call Date: Oct 1990, Gray's Inn
Pupil Supervisor
Qualifications: [LLB (Hons) (Wales)]
✉rtaylor@landmarkchambers.co.uk

TAYLOR MR RHYS STEADMAN

30 Park Place
Cardiff CF10 3BS, ☎029 2039 8421
✉clerks@30parkplace.law.co.uk
Call Date: Nov 1996, Inner Temple
Pupil Supervisor
Qualifications: [LLB (Reading)]

TAYLOR MR RUFUS ALEXANDER OTTLEY

3 PB Barristers
3 Paper Buildings, Temple, London EC4Y 7EU,
☎020 7583 8055
3 PB Barristers
Royal Talbot House, 2 Victoria Street, Bristol,
Avon BS1 6BB, ☎0117 928 1520
3 PB Barristers
23 Beaumont Street, Oxford OX1 2NP,
☎01865 793 736
3 PB Barristers
4 St Peter Street, Winchester SO23 8BW,
☎01962 868884
✉clerks.winchester@3paper.co.uk
3 PB Barristers
30 Christchurch Road, Bournemouth, Dorset
BH1 3PD, ☎01202 292102
✉clerks.bournemouth@3paper.co.uk
Call Date: Oct 1998, Middle Temple
Qualifications: [LLB (Hons)(Edin) Dip in Law]

TAYLOR MR RUPERT LADD

Devon Chambers
3 St Andrew Street, Plymouth PL1 2AH,
☎01752 661659
✉clerks@devonchambers.co.uk
Call Date: July 1990, Gray's Inn
Qualifications: [LLB (Hons) LLM (Lond)]
✉rtaylor@devonchambers.co.uk

TAYLOR MISS RUTH JULIA

Kings Chambers
36 Young Street, Manchester M3 3FT,
☎0845 034 3444
✉clerks@kingschambers.com
Kings Chambers
5 Park Square East, Leeds LS1 2NE,
☎0845 034 3444
✉clerks@kingschambers.com

Kings Chambers
Embassy House, 60 Church Street, Birmingham B3 2DJ, ☎0845 034 3444
✉clerks@kingschambers.com
Call Date: July 2010, Middle Temple
Qualifications: [MA (Cantab) MPhil (Cantab)]
✉rtaylor@kingschambers.com

TAYLOR MR SIMON

Chambers of Andrew Mitchell QC
33 Chancery Lane, London WC2A 1EN, ☎020 7440 9950 ✉clerks@33cllaw.com
Call Date: Oct 1993, Inner Temple
Pupil Supervisor
Qualifications: [BSc (Hons) CPE]
✉st@33cllaw.com

TAYLOR MR SIMON MARK

Keating Chambers
15 Essex Street, London WC2R 3AA, ☎020 7544 2600
✉clerks@keatingchambers.com
Call Date: Nov 1987, Gray's Inn
Qualifications: [BA (Oxon) LicSpec en droit Europeen (Belgium)]
✉staylor@keatingchambers.com

TAYLOR MR SIMON PETER JAMES

6 Pump Court
1st Floor, 6 Pump Court, Temple, London EC4Y 7AR, ☎020 7797 8400
✉richardconstable@6pumpcourt.co.uk
6 Pump Court Chambers
6-8 Mill Street, Maidstone, Kent ME15 6XH, ☎01622 688094
✉annexe@6pumpcourt.co.uk
Call Date: Nov 1997, Inner Temple
Pupil Supervisor
Qualifications: [LLB (Middx)]

TAYLOR DR SIMON WHELDON QC (2003)

Cloisters
1 Pump Court, Temple, London EC4Y 7AA, ☎020 7827 4000 ✉clerks@cloisters.com
Call Date: July 1984, Middle Temple
Qualifications: [BA (Cantab) MA (Cantab) MB BChir]
✉st@cloisters.com

TAYLOR MR STEPHEN NICHOLAS SIMON

KCH Garden Square
1 Oxford Street, Nottingham NG1 5BH, ☎0115 941 8851
✉clerks@kchgardensquare.co.uk
Call Date: July 2002, Inner Temple
Qualifications: [LLB (Hons) (Buckingham)]
✉staylor@kingstreetchambers.com

TAYLOR MR STEVEN JAMES

Unicorn Chambers
P.O.Box 7696, Nottingham NG3 5WZ, ☎0115 985 6602
✉sjt@unicornchambers.co.uk
Call Date: Oct 1992, Lincoln's Inn
Qualifications: [LLB(Hons)]
✉sjt@unicornchambers.co.uk

TAYLOR MS SUE

10 King's Bench Walk
Ground Floor, 10 King's Bench Walk, Temple, London EC4Y 7EB, ☎020 7353 7742
✉Chambers@10kingsbenchwalk.co.uk
Call Date: Oct 1996, Lincoln's Inn
Qualifications: [BEd (Hons)(B'ham) MA (Essex) MEd (Leeds)]
✉chambers@10kingsbenchwalk.co.uk

TAYLOR MRS SUSAN

Trinity Chambers
The Custom House, 39 Quayside, Newcastle Upon Tyne NE1 3DE, ☎0191 232 1927
✉info@trinitychambers.co.uk
Trinity Chambers
Multi Media Exchange, 72-80 Corporation Road, Middlesbrough TS1 2RF, ☎01642 247569
✉info@trinitychambers.co.uk
Call Date: Nov 1987, Middle Temple
Pupil Supervisor, Recorder
Qualifications: [BA]
✉s.taylor@trinitychambers.co.uk

TAYLOR MR WILLIAM JAMES QC (1998)

Carmelite Chambers
9 Carmelite Street, London EC4Y 0DR, ☎020 7936 6300
✉clerks@carmelitechambers.co.uk
Call Date: July 1990, Inner Temple
Qualifications: [MA LLB (Scotland)]
✉wtaylorqc@carmelitechambers.co.uk

TAYLOR MRS YVONNE MARIE

Trinity Chambers
The Custom House, 39 Quayside, Newcastle Upon Tyne NE1 3DE, ☎0191 232 1927
✉info@trinitychambers.co.uk
Trinity Chambers
Multi Media Exchange, 72-80 Corporation Road, Middlesbrough TS1 2RF, ☎01642 247569
✉info@trinitychambers.co.uk
Call Date: July 1998, Inner Temple
Qualifications: [LLB (Newc)]
✉y.taylor@trinitychambers.co.uk

E

TAYLOR-CAMARA MR ALEXANDER ABDU RAHMAN

Garden Court Chambers
57-60 Lincoln's Inn Fields, London WC2A 3LJ,
☎ 020 7993 7600 ✉ info@gclaw.co.uk
Call Date: Nov 1989, Middle Temple
Pupil Supervisor
Qualifications: [LLB (Hons)]
alextc@gclaw.co.uk

TAYO MISS ANN IBILOLA

Cornerstone Chambers
15 Old Bailey, London EC4M 7EF,
☎ 020 3008 8392
✉ anntayo7@gmail.com/anntayo@cornerstonechambrers.co / anntayo@cornerstonechambrers.com
Call Date: Oct 1991, Gray's Inn
Qualifications: [LLB]

TEACHER MISS PETRA ROSE MACNAGHTEN

29 Bedford Row Chambers
London WC1R 4HE, ☎ 020 7404 1044
✉ clerks@29br.co.uk
Call Date: Oct 2006, Inner Temple
Qualifications: [BA (Oxon)]
pteacher@29br.co.uk

TECKS MR JONATHAN HOWARD

Chambers of Jonathan Tecks
Green Gables, Curload, Stoke St Gregory, Taunton, Somerset TA3 6JA, ☎ 01823 491268
✉ jo@jotecks.com
Call Date: July 1978, Gray's Inn
Qualifications: [CEDR MA (Cantab) FCIArb]

TEDD MR REX HILARY QC (1993)

No5 Chambers
Fountain Court, Steelhouse Lane, Birmingham B4 6DR, ☎ 0845 210 5555 ✉ info@no5.com
Atlantic Chambers
4-6 Cook Street, Liverpool L2 9QU,
☎ 0151 236 4421
✉ info@atlanticchambers.co.uk
No5 Chambers
Greenwood House, 4-7 Salisbury Court, London EC4Y 8AA, ☎ 0845 210 5555
No5 Chambers
38 Queen Square, Bristol BS1 4QS,
☎ 0845 210 5555
Call Date: Feb 1970, Inner Temple
Recorder
Qualifications: [MA D Univ BCL (Oxon)]

TEE MR GREGORY JAMES

Guildford Chambers
Stoke House, Leapale Lane, Guildford, Surrey GU1 4LY, ☎ 01483 539131
✉ clerks@guildfordchambers.co.uk
Call Date: July 1999, Inner Temple
Qualifications: [LLB (Hons)]
gtee@guildfordchambers.com

TEGGIN MISS VICTORIA HELEN

3 Dr Johnson's Buildings
Ground Floor, 3 Dr Johnson's Buildings, Temple, London EC4Y 7BA, ☎ 020 7353 4854
✉ clerks@3djb.co.uk
Call Date: Nov 1990, Inner Temple
Qualifications: [BA (Hons) (Lond) Dip Law]
vteggin@3djb.co.uk

TEHRANI MR CHRISTOPHER

Park Court Chambers
16 Park Place, Leeds LS1 2SJ,
☎ 0113 243 3277
✉ clerks@parkcourtchambers.co.uk
Call Date: Nov 1990, Inner Temple
Pupil Supervisor
Qualifications: [LLB]
ctehrani@parkcourtchambers.co.uk

TEJI MISS USHA DEVI

1 Pump Court
Elm Court, Temple, London EC4Y 7AB,
☎ 020 7842 7070
✉ (name)@pumpcourt.co.uk
Call Date: July 1981, Lincoln's Inn
Qualifications: [LLB (Lond)]

TELFORD MR PETER

Yealm House Chambers
88-90 Yealm Road, Plymouth PL8 1BL,
☎ 01752 873227
✉ petertelford@hotmail.co.uk
Southernhay Chambers
33 Southernhay East, Exeter EX1 1NX,
☎ 01392 255777
✉ clerks@southernhaychambers.co.uk
Call Date: July 1985, Lincoln's Inn
Pupil Supervisor
Qualifications: [BA (Hons) (Keele)]
petertelford@hotmail.co.uk

TEMKIN MR DAVID JEREMY

Exchange Chambers
7 Ralli Courts, West Riverside, Manchester M3 5FT, ☎ 0161 833 2722
Exchange Chambers
One Derby Square, Derby Square, Liverpool L2 9XX, ☎ 0151 236 7747
✉ info@exchangechambers.co.uk

Exchange Chambers
Oxford House, Oxford Row, Leeds LS1 3BE, ☎0113 203 1970
✉spencer@exchangechambers.co.uk
Call Date: July 2000, Inner Temple
Qualifications: [BA (Oxon) PGCE]
✉temkin@exchangechambers.co.uk

TEMMINK MR ROBERT-JAN

Quadrant Chambers
Quadrant House, 10 Fleet Street, London EC4Y 1AU, ☎020 7583 4444
✉info@quadrantchambers.com
Call Date: Oct 1996, Middle Temple
Pupil Supervisor
Qualifications: [MA (Hons)(Cantab) FCIArb]

TEMPEST MR ALISTAIR MARK

Field Court Chambers
5 Field Court, Gray's Inn, London WC1R 5EF, ☎020 7405 6114 ✉clerks@fieldcourt.co.uk
Call Date: Oct 1997, Middle Temple
Pupil Supervisor
Qualifications: [LLB (Hons)(Lond)]

TEMPLE MR ADAM JOHN

4 Pump Court
4 Pump Court, Temple, London EC4Y 7AN, ☎020 7842 5555
✉chambers@4pumpcourt.com
Call Date: July 2008, Middle Temple
Qualifications: [BA (Hons) (Oxon) BCL (Oxon)]
✉adamtemple@4pumpcourt.com

TEMPLE MR ANTHONY DOMINIC QC (1986)

4 Pump Court
4 Pump Court, Temple, London EC4Y 7AN, ☎020 7842 5555
✉chambers@4pumpcourt.com
Call Date: July 1968, Inner Temple
Qualifications: [MA (Oxon)]
✉atemple@4pumpcourt.com

TEMPLE MR BENJAMIN TOBY AFAMADO

5 King's Bench Walk
5 King's Bench Walk, Temple, London EC4Y 7DN, ☎020 7353 5638
✉clerks@5kbw.co.uk
Call Date: Oct 1997, Inner Temple
Qualifications: [BA (Manchester) CPE]
✉ben.temple@5kbw.co.uk

TEMPLE MS ELEANOR LOUISE

Kings Chambers
36 Young Street, Manchester M3 3FT, ☎0845 034 3444
✉clerks@kingschambers.com
Kings Chambers
5 Park Square East, Leeds LS1 2NE, ☎0845 034 3444
✉clerks@kingschambers.com
Kings Chambers
Embassy House, 60 Church Street, Birmingham B3 2DJ, ☎0845 034 3444
✉clerks@kingschambers.com
Call Date: July 2000, Inner Temple
Qualifications: [LLB (Dunelm)]
✉etemple@kingschambers.com

TEMPLE MISS MICHELLE JEAN

Trinity Chambers
The Custom House, 39 Quayside, Newcastle Upon Tyne NE1 3DE, ☎0191 232 1927
✉info@trinitychambers.co.uk
Call Date: Oct 1992, Lincoln's Inn
Pupil Supervisor
Qualifications: [MA (Hons) (Oxon)]
✉M.Temple@trinitychambers.co.uk

TEMPLE MISS RACHEL ELISABETH

Chavasse Court Chambers
18 Queen Avenue, Liverpool L2 4TX, ☎0151 229 2030
✉clerks@chavassechambers.co.uk
Call Date: Oct 2004, Gray's Inn
Qualifications: [BA]
✉racheltemple329@hotmail.co.uk

TEMPLE MR VICTOR BEVIS AFOUMADO QC (1993)

6 King's Bench Walk
Ground Floor, 6 King's Bench Walk, Temple, London EC4Y 7DR, ☎020 7583 0410
✉clerks@6kbw.com
Call Date: July 1971, Inner Temple
Recorder
✉victor.temple@6kbw.com

TEMPLE-BONE MISS GILLIAN ELIZABETH

36 Bedford Row
London WC1R 4JH, ☎020 7421 8000
✉chambers@36bedfordrow.co.uk
Call Date: Nov 1978, Gray's Inn
Pupil Supervisor
Qualifications: [BA (Durham) MA (Lond)]

TEMPLEMAN MISS CLARE

Angel Chambers
Ethos Building, Kings Road, Swansea SA1 8AS, ☎01792 464623
✉clerks@angelchambers.co.uk
Call Date: Nov 2004, Inner Temple
Qualifications: [LLB (University of Wales)(Swansea)]
✉claretempleman@angelchambers.co.uk

TEMPLEMAN MR MARK JEREMY QC (2003)

Essex Court Chambers
24 Lincoln's Inn Fields, London WC2A 3EG, ☎020 7813 8000
✉clerksroom@essexcourt.net
Call Date: Nov 1981, Middle Temple
Qualifications: [MA BCL (Oxon)]

TEMPLEMAN MR MICHAEL RICHARD

Guildford Chambers
Stoke House, Leapale Lane, Guildford, Surrey GU1 4LY, ☎01483 539131
✉clerks@guildfordchambers.co.uk
5 Stone Buildings
5 Stone Buildings, Lincoln's Inn, London WC2A 3XT, ☎020 7242 6201
✉clerks@5sblaw.com
Call Date: Nov 1973, Lincoln's Inn
Qualifications: [MA (Oxon)]
✉mtempleman@guildfordchambers.co.uk

E

TEMPLETON MR JOSEPH JAMES

23 Essex Street
London WC2R 3AA, ☎020 7413 0353
✉clerks@23es.com
Call Date: Nov 2006, Middle Temple
Qualifications: [BA (Hons) (Cantab)]
✉josephtempleton@23es.com

TENNET MR MICHAEL JOHN QC (2006)

Wilberforce Chambers
8 New Square, Lincoln's Inn, London WC2A 3QP, ☎020 7306 0102
✉chambers@wilberforce.co.uk
Call Date: July 1985, Inner Temple
Pupil Supervisor
Qualifications: [BA (Oxon)]
✉mtennet@wilberforce.co.uk

TER HAAR MISS CAMILLA CATHERINE

Five Paper
Ground Floor, 5 Paper Buildings, Temple, London EC4Y 7HB, ☎020 7815 3200
Call Date: July 2005, Inner Temple
Qualifications: [MA University of Edinburgh CPE City University]
✉camillaterhaar@fivepaper.com

TERRIS MISS SALLY

Park Court Chambers
16 Park Place, Leeds LS1 2SJ, ☎0113 243 3277
✉clerks@parkcourtchambers.co.uk
Call Date: Nov 1997, Middle Temple
Qualifications: [BA (Hons)(Cantab)]
✉clerks@parkcourtchambers.co.uk

TERRY MR ROBERT JEFFREY

Kings Chambers
36 Young Street, Manchester M3 3FT, ☎0845 034 3444
✉clerks@kingschambers.com
Kings Chambers
5 Park Square East, Leeds LS1 2NE, ☎0845 034 3444
✉clerks@kingschambers.com
Kings Chambers
Embassy House, 60 Church Street, Birmingham B3 2DJ, ☎0845 034 3444
✉clerks@kingschambers.com
Lamb Chambers
Lamb Building, Elm Court, Temple, London EC4Y 7AS, ☎020 7797 8300
✉info@lambchambers.co.uk
Call Date: July 1976, Lincoln's Inn
Pupil Supervisor
Qualifications: [FCIArb LLB MA (Lond) FSALS]
✉jterry@kingschambers.com

TESTAR MISS PHILIPPA KATHERINE

42 Bedford Row
London WC1R 4LL, ☎020 7831 0222
✉clerks@42br.com
Call Date: Nov 2009, Middle Temple
Qualifications: [MA (Hons) (Cantab)]
✉philippat@42br.com

TETHER MS MELANIE GEORGIA KIM

Old Square Chambers
10-11 Bedford Row, London WC1R 4BU,
☎ 020 7269 0300 ✉ clerks@oldsquare.co.uk
Old Square Chambers
3 Orchard Court, St Augustine's Yard, Bristol BS1 5DP, ☎ 0117 930 5100
✉ clerks@oldsquare.co.uk
Call Date: July 1995, Inner Temple
Qualifications: [MA (Oxon)]
✉ mtether@oldsquare.co.uk

TETLOW MR BERNARD GEOFFREY QC (2011)

Charter Chambers
33 John Street, London WC1N 2AT,
☎ 020 7618 4400
✉ clerks@charterchambers.com
Call Date: Nov 1984, Middle Temple
Pupil Supervisor
Qualifications: [BA LLM (Cantab)]
✉ bernard.tetlow@charterchambers.com

TETLOW MR RICHARD HUGH

Exchange Chambers
7 Ralli Courts, West Riverside, Manchester M3 5FT, ☎ 0161 833 2722
Exchange Chambers
One Derby Square, Derby Square, Liverpool L2 9XX, ☎ 0151 236 7747
✉ info@exchangechambers.co.uk
Exchange Chambers
Oxford House, Oxford Row, Leeds LS1 3BE,
☎ 0113 203 1970
✉ spencer@exchangechambers.co.uk
Call Date: July 2006, Middle Temple
Qualifications: [BA (Hons) (Cantab)]
✉ tetlow@exchangechambers.co.uk

TETTEH LADY GIFTY DEDE

Chambers of G. D. Tetteh
Ground Floor, 2 Middle Temple Lane, Temple, London EC4Y 9AA, ☎ 020 7353 7095
Call Date: Nov 2000, Middle Temple
Pupil Supervisor
Qualifications: [LLB (Hons) (London)]
✉ lady@gdtettehchambers.com

TETTEY MR STEPHEN NII OFOSU

Kenworthy's Chambers
Arlington House, Bloom Street, Salford, Manchester M3 6AJ, ☎ 0161 832 4036
Call Date: Mar 2010, Gray's Inn
Qualifications: [LLB LLM]
✉ marla@kenworthysbarristers.co.uk

THACKER MR JAMES CHRISTIAN

The Chambers of Grahame Aldous QC
9 Gough Square, London EC4A 3DG,
☎ 020 7832 0500
✉ clerks@9goughsquare.co.uk
Call Date: Nov 2001, Gray's Inn
Pupil Supervisor
Qualifications: [LLB(Hons)]
✉ jthacker@9goughsquare.co.uk

THACKER MR RAJEEV KUMAR

Garden Court Chambers
57-60 Lincoln's Inn Fields, London WC2A 3LJ,
☎ 020 7993 7600 ✉ info@gclaw.co.uk
Call Date: Oct 1993, Gray's Inn
Pupil Supervisor
Qualifications: [LLB (Wales)]
✉ rajeevt@gclaw.co.uk

THACKRAY MR JOHN RICHARD DOMINIC

Wilberforce Chambers
7 Bishop Lane, Hull HU1 1PA,
☎ 01482 323264
Call Date: Oct 1994, Lincoln's Inn
Pupil Supervisor
Qualifications: [LLB (Hons)(Leeds)]

THAIN MISS ASHLEY

1 KBW Chambers
1 King's Bench Walk, Temple, London EC4Y 7DB, ☎ 020 7936 1500
✉ clerks@1kbw.co.uk
King's Bench Chambers
174 High Street, Lewes BN7 1YE,
☎ 01273 402600
Call Date: Oct 1996, Inner Temple
Pupil Supervisor
Qualifications: [LLB]
✉ athain@1kbw.co.uk

THANKI MR BANKIM QC (2003)

Fountain Court Chambers
Fountain Court, Temple, London EC4Y 9DH,
☎ 020 7583 3335
✉ chambers@fountaincourt.co.uk
Call Date: July 1988, Middle Temple
Qualifications: [MA (Oxon) Dip Law (Lond)]
✉ bthanki@fountaincourt.co.uk

THAROO MRS SAFIA

42 Bedford Row
London WC1R 4LL, ☎ 020 7831 0222
✉ clerks@42br.com
Call Date: July 2004, Inner Temple
Qualifications: [LLB]
✉ st@42br.com, safia.tharoo@42br.com

E

THATCHER MR RICHARD DAVID

1 High Pavement
Nottingham NG1 1HF, ☎ 0115 941 8218
✉ clerks@1highpavement.co.uk
Call Date: July 1989, Inner Temple
Pupil Supervisor
Qualifications: [LLB]
richardthatcher@1highpavement.co.uk

THELEN MISS JENNIFER AILEEN

4-5 Gray's Inn Square
Gray's Inn, London WC1R 5AH,
☎ 020 7404 5252 ✉ clerks@4-5.co.uk
Call Date: Nov 2007, Inner Temple
Qualifications: [PgDL]

THIND MISS ANITA

Regency Chambers
45 Priestgate, Peterborough PE1 1LB,
☎ 01733 315215
✉ clerks@regencychambers.law.co.uk
Regency Chambers
Sheraton House, Castle Park, Cambridge CB3 0AX, ☎ 01223 301517
Call Date: Nov 1988, Inner Temple
Pupil Supervisor
Qualifications: [LLB]
AThind@regencychambers.law.co.uk

THISTLE MR DEAN TERENCE

Becket Chambers
17 New Dover Road, Canterbury, Kent CT1 3AS, ☎ 01227 786331
✉ clerks@becket-chambers.co.uk
Call Date: Nov 2010, Lincoln's Inn
Qualifications: [LLB (Wolves)]

THOM MR JAMES ALEXANDER FRANCIS QC (2003)

New Square Chambers
12 New Square, Lincoln's Inn, London WC2A 3SW, ☎ 020 7419 8000
✉ robin.hollington@newsquarechambers.co.uk
Call Date: Nov 1974, Middle Temple
Recorder
Qualifications: [MA (Oxon) BCL (Oxon)]
james.thom@newsquarechambers.co.uk

THOMANN MR COLIN BENEDIKT

39 Essex Street
London WC2R 3AT, ☎ 020 7832 1111
✉ clerks@39essex.com
82 King Street
Manchester M2 4WQ, ☎ 0161 870 9969
Call Date: Oct 1999, Middle Temple
Qualifications: [LLB (Hons)(Reading)]
colin.thomann@39essex.com

THOMAS MR ADRIAN FRANCIS TREVELYAN

Cornerstone Barristers
2-3 Gray's Inn Square, Gray's Inn, London WC1R 5JH, ☎ 020 7242 4986
✉ chambers@2-3gis.co.uk
Call Date: July 1974, Gray's Inn
Pupil Supervisor
Qualifications: [MA (Cantab)]
atrevelyanthomas@2-3gis.co.uk

THOMAS MR ANDREW MARTIN QC (2008)

Lincoln House Chambers
Tower 12, The Avenue North, Spinningfields, 18-22 Bridge Street, Manchester M3 3BZ,
☎ 0161 832 5701
✉ info@lincolnhousechambers.com
Linenhall Chambers
1 Stanley Place, Chester CH1 2LU,
☎ 01244 348282
✉ clerks@linenhallchambers.co.uk
Call Date: Nov 1989, Gray's Inn
Recorder
Qualifications: [MA (Cantab)]
andrew.thomas@lincolnhousechambers.com

THOMAS MR ANDREW RICHARD

Brick Court Chambers
7-8 Essex Street, London WC2R 3LD,
☎ 020 7379 3550 ✉ clerks@brickcourt.co.uk
Call Date: Oct 1996, Inner Temple
Andrew.Thomas@Brickcourt.co.uk

THOMAS MR ARRON MICHAEL

18 St John Street
Manchester M3 4EA, ☎ 0161 278 1800
✉ clerks@18sjs.com
Call Date: Oct 2005, Lincoln's Inn
Qualifications: [LLB (Hons) (Nott'm)]
athomas@18sjs.com

THOMAS MR BENEDICT TIMOTHY RICHARD

Park Court Chambers
16 Park Place, Leeds LS1 2SJ,
☎ 0113 243 3277
✉ clerks@parkcourtchambers.co.uk
Call Date: July 2010, Middle Temple
Qualifications: [BA (Hons) (York)]
bthomas@parkcourtchambers.co.uk

THOMAS MR BRYAN MICHAEL

Civitas Chambers
Global Reach, Celtic Gateway, Cardiff Bay, Cardiff CF11 0SN, ☎0845 0713 007
✉clerks@civitaslaw.com
Call Date: July 1978, Gray's Inn
Pupil Supervisor
Qualifications: [LLB (Hons)(Wales)]

THOMAS MR CHARLES AUBREY MORGAN

Guildhall Chambers
23 Broad Street, Bristol BS1 2HG, ☎0117 930 9000
✉hoc@guildhallchambers.co.uk
Call Date: Oct 1990, Middle Temple
Qualifications: [BA (Oxon)]

THOMAS MISS CHRISTINA

9 Park Place
9 Park Place, Cardiff, South Glamorgan CF10 3DP, ☎029 2038 2731
✉clerks@9parkplace.co.uk
Call Date: Feb 1994, Inner Temple
Qualifications: [LLB (Wales)]

THOMAS DR CHRISTOPHER SYDNEY QC (1989)

Keating Chambers
15 Essex Street, London WC2R 3AA, ☎020 7544 2600
✉clerks@keatingchambers.com
Call Date: July 1973, Lincoln's Inn
Recorder
Qualifications: [BA Dip de Droit Compare PhD FCIArb]

THOMAS MISS CLARE RACHEL

16 Winckley Square
Preston PR1 3JJ, ☎01772 256100
St Johns Buildings
24a - 28 St John Street, Manchester M3 4DJ, ☎0161 214 1500
✉clerk@stjohnsbuildings.co.uk
St Johns Buildings Liverpool
8th Floor India Buildings, Water Street, Liverpool L2 0XG, ☎0151 243 6000
✉clerk@stjohnsbuildings.co.uk
Call Date: Oct 1998, Inner Temple
Qualifications: [LLB (Hull)]

THOMAS MR CLIVE RICHARD

Farrar's Building
Farrar's Building, Temple, London EC4Y 7BD, ☎020 7583 9241
✉Chambers@farrarsbuilding.co.uk
Call Date: July 2005, Gray's Inn
Qualifications: [BA]
🖃cthomas@farrarsbuilding.co.uk

THOMAS MR DANIEL JAMES

Lincoln House Chambers
Tower 12, The Avenue North, Spinningfields, 18-22 Bridge Street, Manchester M3 3BZ, ☎0161 832 5701
✉info@lincolnhousechambers.com
Call Date: July 2005, Middle Temple
Qualifications: [LLB (Hons)]
🖃daniel.thomas@lincolnhousechambers.com

THOMAS MR DAVID COLIN

2 Temple Gardens
2 Temple Gardens, Temple, London EC4Y 9AY, ☎020 7822 1200
✉clerks@2tg.co.uk
Call Date: Oct 2009, Lincoln's Inn
Qualifications: [BA (Oxon) BCL (Oxon)]
🖃dthomas@2tg.co.uk

THOMAS DR DAVID KEITH

Rougemont Chambers
Victory House, Dean Clarke Gardens, Southernhay East, Exeter EX2 4AA, ☎01392 208484
✉clerks@rougemontchambers.co.uk
1 Gray's Inn Square
Ground Floor, 1 Gray's Inn Square, London WC1R 5AA, ☎020 7405 0001
Call Date: July 2003, Inner Temple
Qualifications: [BMedBiol MBChB CPE]
🖃dthomas@rougemontchambers.co.uk

THOMAS DR DAVID RICHARD BRYNMOR

39 Essex Street
London WC2R 3AT, ☎020 7832 1111
✉clerks@39essex.com
Call Date: Mar 2011, Middle Temple
Qualifications: [MBChB (Edin)]
🖃david.brynmor.thomas@39essex.com

THOMAS MISS DAWN MARIE

9 St John Street
Manchester M3 4DN, ☎0161 955 9000
✉civilclerks@9sjs.com / criminalclerks@9sjs.com
Call Date: Oct 2001, Lincoln's Inn
Qualifications: [LLB (Hons) LLM]

THOMAS MR DYFED LLION

Angel Chambers
Ethos Building, Kings Road, Swansea SA1 8AS, ☎01792 464623
✉clerks@angelchambers.co.uk
Call Date: Oct 1992, Middle Temple
Pupil Supervisor
Qualifications: [BA (Hons)(Oxon)]
🖃dyfedthomas@angelchambers.co.uk

E

THOMAS MRS FELICITY

Westgate Chambers
64 High Street, Lewes, East Sussex BN7 1XG,
☎01273 480510
✉clerks@westgate-chambers.co.uk
Call Date: Nov 2005, Middle Temple
Qualifications: [BA (Hons) Sussex]
ft@westgate-chambers.co.uk

THOMAS MR GARETH

Atlantic Chambers
4-6 Cook Street, Liverpool L2 9QU,
☎0151 236 4421
✉info@atlanticchambers.co.uk
Call Date: July 1977, Gray's Inn
Pupil Supervisor
Qualifications: [LLB (Wales) ACII]
gareththomas@atlanticchambers.co.uk

THOMAS MR GARETH DAVID

9 Park Place
9 Park Place, Cardiff, South Glamorgan
CF10 3DP, ☎029 2038 2731
✉clerks@9parkplace.co.uk
Call Date: Nov 1993, Inner Temple
Pupil Supervisor
Qualifications: [LLB (Wales)]
gthomas@9parkplace.co.uk

THOMAS MISS GEMMA LOUISE

Number 7 Harrington Street Chambers
7 Harrington Street, Liverpool L2 9YH,
☎0151 242 0707 ✉clerks@7hs.co.uk
Call Date: Nov 2010, Middle Temple
Qualifications: [LLB (Hons) (Hull)]
Gemma.thomas@7hs.co.uk

THOMAS MR GEORGE LLEWELLYN

3 Serjeants Inn
London EC4Y 1BQ, ☎020 7427 5000
✉clerks@3serjeantsinn.com
Call Date: Oct 1995, Gray's Inn
Pupil Supervisor
Qualifications: [BA]
gthomas@3serjeantsinn.com

THOMAS MS GWAWR

1 Mitre Court Buildings
1 Mitre Court Buildings, Temple, London
EC4Y 7BS, ☎020 7452 8900
✉clerks@1mcb.com
Call Date: July 2008, Inner Temple
Qualifications: [BA (Cantab) CPE]

THOMAS MISS JACQUELINE LOUISE

37 Park Square Chambers
37 Park Square, Leeds LS1 2NY,
☎0113 243 9422 ✉chambers@no37.co.uk
Call Date: Oct 2000, Lincoln's Inn
Qualifications: [LLB (Hons) (Keele)]
chambers@no37.co.uk, jt@no37.co.uk

THOMAS MR JAMES AUSTIN

KCH Garden Square
1 Oxford Street, Nottingham NG1 5BH,
☎0115 941 8851
✉clerks@kchgardensquare.co.uk
Call Date: July 1999, Middle Temple
Qualifications: [LLB (Hons)]
jim.thomas2@virgin.net

THOMAS MR KEITH SINCLAIR

16 Winckley Square
Preston PR1 3JJ, ☎01772 256100
St Johns Buildings
21 White Friars, Chester CH1 1NZ,
☎01244 323070
✉clerk@stjohnsbuildings.co.uk
St Johns Buildings
24a - 28 St John Street, Manchester M3 4DJ,
☎0161 214 1500
✉clerk@stjohnsbuildings.co.uk
Call Date: July 1969, Gray's Inn
Pupil Supervisor
Qualifications: [BA (Oxon)]

THOMAS MRS LAURA JANE

18 St John Street
Manchester M3 4EA, ☎0161 278 1800
✉clerks@18sjs.com
Call Date: Nov 2003, Lincoln's Inn
Qualifications: [LLB (Hons) (Leic)]

THOMAS MR LESLIE

Garden Court Chambers
57-60 Lincoln's Inn Fields, London WC2A 3LJ,
☎020 7993 7600 ✉info@gclaw.co.uk
Call Date: Nov 1988, Inner Temple
Pupil Supervisor
Qualifications: [LLB]
lesliet@gclaw.co.uk

THOMAS MISS LISA JANE

9 Park Place
9 Park Place, Cardiff, South Glamorgan
CF10 3DP, ☎029 2038 2731
✉clerks@9parkplace.co.uk
Call Date: Oct 1998, Middle Temple
Pupil Supervisor
Qualifications: [LLB (Hons)(Wales)]
clerks@9parkplace.co.uk

THOMAS MR MARK DAVID

5 Essex Court
1st Floor, 5 Essex Court, Temple, London EC4Y 9AH, ☎020 7410 2000
✉clerks@5essexcourt.co.uk
Call Date: Oct 2006, Lincoln's Inn
Qualifications: [MA (Oxon)]
✉thomas@5essexcourt.co.uk

THOMAS MR MARK JOHN

Park Lane Plowden
Lombard House, 4-8 Lombard Street, Newcastle Upon Tyne NE1 3AE,
☎0191 211 4087
✉clerks@parklaneplowden.co.uk
Call Date: July 2003, Middle Temple
Qualifications: [CPE]
✉mark.thomas@parklaneplowden.co.uk

THOMAS MISS MEGAN MOIRA

6 Pump Court
1st Floor, 6 Pump Court, Temple, London EC4Y 7AR, ☎020 7797 8400
✉richardconstable@6pumpcourt.co.uk
6 Pump Court Chambers
6-8 Mill Street, Maidstone, Kent ME15 6XH,
☎01622 688094
✉annexe@6pumpcourt.co.uk
Call Date: July 1987, Gray's Inn
Pupil Supervisor
Qualifications: [BA (Hons)(Sheff)]
✉meganthomas@6pumpcourt.co.uk

THOMAS MR MICHAEL DAVID QC (1973)

Essex Court Chambers
24 Lincoln's Inn Fields, London WC2A 3EG,
☎020 7813 8000
✉clerksroom@essexcourt.net
Call Date: May 1955, Middle Temple
Qualifications: [LLB (Lond) BA]
✉mthomas@essexcourt.net

THOMAS MR MICHAEL JAMES

Gray's Inn Tax Chambers
3rd Floor, Gray's Inn Chambers, Gray's Inn, London WC1R 5JA, ☎020 7242 2642
✉clerks@taxbar.com
Call Date: Mar 2001, Gray's Inn
Qualifications: [BA (Oxon) BCL (Oxon)]
✉mt@taxbar.com

THOMAS MISS NATALIE LOUISE

Erimus Chambers
PO Box 1440, Bedford MK43 6AJ,
☎01234 720952
✉clerks@erimuschambers.com
Warwick Chambers
959 Chester Road, Birmingham, Birmingham B24 0HQ, ☎0121 382 9122
✉warwickchambers@hotmail.com
Call Date: Nov 1999, Middle Temple
Qualifications: [LLB (Hons) LLM]

THOMAS MR NIGEL MATTHEW

Maitland Chambers
7 Stone Buildings, Lincoln's Inn, London WC2A 3SZ, ☎020 7406 1200
✉clerks@maitlandchambers.com
Linenhall Chambers
1 Stanley Place, Chester CH1 2LU,
☎01244 348282
✉clerks@linenhallchambers.co.uk
Call Date: July 1976, Gray's Inn
Pupil Supervisor, Recorder
Qualifications: [LLB (Wales) LLB (Cantab)]
✉nthomas@maitlandchambers.com

THOMAS MR OWEN HUW

9 Park Place
9 Park Place, Cardiff, South Glamorgan CF10 3DP, ☎029 2038 2731
✉clerks@9parkplace.co.uk
Call Date: Oct 1994, Gray's Inn
Qualifications: [BA (Oxon)]
✉owenthomas@9parkplace.co.uk

THOMAS MRS PAULA ANGELIQUE

Regency Chambers
45 Priestgate, Peterborough PE1 1LB,
☎01733 315215
✉clerks@regencychambers.law.co.uk
Call Date: July 2009, Lincoln's Inn
Qualifications: [MA (Bournemouth) CPE OBPP]
✉clerks@regencychambers.co.uk

THOMAS MS REBECCA JANE

42 Bedford Row
London WC1R 4LL, ☎020 7831 0222
✉clerks@42br.com
Call Date: Nov 1999, Inner Temple
Qualifications: [BA (Cantab)]
✉rebecca.thomas@42br.com

E

THOMAS MR RHYS AB OWEN

Iscoed Chambers
86 St Helen's Road, Swansea SA1 4BQ,
☎ 01792 652988
✉ clerks@iscoedchambers.co.uk
Call Date: Nov 2009, Inner Temple
Qualifications: [BA (Oxon)]
rt@iscoedchambers.co.uk

THOMAS MR RICHARD JOHN

Doughty Street Chambers
53-54 Doughty Street, London WC1N 2LS,
☎ 020 7404 1313
✉ enquiries@doughtystreet.co.uk
Doughty Street Chambers
Pall Mall Court, 61-67 King Street, Manchester M2 4PD, ☎ 0161 618 1066
Doughty Street Chambers
5th Floor, Broad Quay House, Prince Street, Bristol BS1 4DJ, ☎ 01179 058 717
Call Date: Oct 2002, Inner Temple
Pupil Supervisor
Qualifications: [MA (Oxon) MA]
r.thomas@doughtystreet.co.uk

THOMAS MR ROBERT OWAIN PHILIP QC (2011)

Quadrant Chambers
Quadrant House, 10 Fleet Street, London EC4Y 1AU, ☎ 020 7583 4444
✉ info@quadrantchambers.com
Call Date: Nov 1992, Lincoln's Inn
Pupil Supervisor
Qualifications: [MA (Cantab) BCL (Oxon) LIC SP Dr Eur (Brussels)]
robert.thomas@quadrantchambers.com

THOMAS MR ROGER CHRISTOPHER

Pump Court Tax Chambers
16 Bedford Row, London WC1R 4EF,
☎ 020 7414 8080 ✉ clerks@pumptax.com
Call Date: July 1979, Lincoln's Inn
Qualifications: [MA BCL (Oxon)]
rthomas@pumptax.com

Types of work: Capital tax, Corporation tax, Equity, Income tax, National Insurance, Private client, Stamp duty, Trusts, VAT, Wills

THOMAS MR ROGER LLOYD QC (1994)

4 King's Bench Walk
2nd Floor, 4 King's Bench Walk, Temple, London EC4Y 7DL, ☎ 020 7822 7000
✉ clerks@4kbw.co.uk
9 Park Place
9 Park Place, Cardiff, South Glamorgan CF10 3DP, ☎ 029 2038 2731
✉ clerks@9parkplace.co.uk
Equity Chambers
First Floor, McLaren Building, 46 Priory Queensway, Birmingham B4 7LR,
☎ 0121 236 5007
✉ clerks@equitychambers.org.uk
Call Date: July 1969, Gray's Inn
Recorder
Qualifications: [LLB (Wales)]
clerks@4kbw.co.uk

THOMAS MR ROGER OWEN

St Ive's Chambers
Whittall Street, Birmingham B4 6DH,
☎ 0121 236 0863
✉ clerks@stiveschambers.co.uk
Call Date: July 2001, Inner Temple
Qualifications: [LLB (Hons)(Lond) ACMA]
roger.thomas@stiveschambers.co.uk

THOMAS MR SIMON CHRISTOPHER

Seven Bedford Row
7 Bedford Row, London WC1R 4BS,
☎ 020 7242 3555 ✉ clerks@7br.co.uk
Call Date: Oct 1995, Inner Temple
Pupil Supervisor
Qualifications: [BA (Oxon)]
sthomas@7br.co.uk

THOMAS MR STEPHEN EDWARD OWEN

St Philips Chambers
55 Temple Row, Birmingham B2 5LS,
☎ 0121 246 7000 ✉ clerks@st-philips.com
Call Date: July 1980, Gray's Inn
Pupil Supervisor, Recorder
Qualifications: [LLB (Exon)]
sthomas@st-philips.com

THOMAS MR STEPHEN JOHN

Temple Chambers
32 Park Place, Cardiff CF10 3BA,
☎ 029 2039 7364
✉ DBrinning@Temple-Chambers.co.uk
Temple Chambers
12 Clytha Park Road, Newport, Gwent NP20 4PB, ☎ 01633 267403
✉ dbrinning@temple-chambers.co.uk
Call Date: Feb 1993, Gray's Inn
Pupil Supervisor
Qualifications: [LLB (Hons)(Wales)]
sthomas@temple-chambers.co.uk

THOMAS MISS SUZANNE ELIZABETH

9 Park Place
9 Park Place, Cardiff, South Glamorgan CF10 3DP, ☎029 2038 2731
✉clerks@9parkplace.co.uk
Call Date: July 2001, Middle Temple
Qualifications: [LLB (Hons)]

THOMAS MR TIMOTHY NICHOLAS

Lombard Chambers
1 Sekforde Street, Clerkenwell, London EC1R 0BE, ☎020 7107 2100
Call Date: Oct 2002, Lincoln's Inn
Qualifications: [BA (Dunelm) PGDL (G'ford)]
✉tthomas@lombardchambers.com

THOMAS MR WILLIAM DAVID QC (2002)

Keating Chambers
15 Essex Street, London WC2R 3AA, ☎020 7544 2600
✉clerks@keatingchambers.com
Call Date: July 1982, Middle Temple
Qualifications: [MA (Oxon)]

THOMAS MR WILLIAM OWAIN

1 Crown Office Row
1 Crown Office Row, Temple, London EC4Y 7HH, ☎020 7797 7500
✉mail@1cor.com
Call Date: Oct 1995, Inner Temple
Pupil Supervisor
Qualifications: [BA (Oxon) BCL]
✉owain.thomas@1cor.com

THOMAS OF GRESFORD LORD DONALD MARTIN QC (1979)

Goldsmith Chambers
Ground Floor, Goldsmith Building, Temple, London EC4Y 7BL, ☎020 7353 6802
✉clerks@goldsmithchambers.com
Linenhall Chambers
1 Stanley Place, Chester CH1 2LU, ☎01244 348282
✉clerks@linenhallchambers.co.uk
No 8 Chambers
8 Fountain Court, Steelhouse Lane, Birmingham B4 6DR, ☎0121 236 5514
✉clerks@no8chambers.co.uk
Call Date: Nov 1967, Gray's Inn
Recorder
Qualifications: [MA LLB]
✉m.thomas@goldsmithchambers.law.co.uk

THOMAS-SYMONDS MR NICKLAUS

Civitas Chambers
Global Reach, Celtic Gateway, Cardiff Bay, Cardiff CF11 0SN, ☎0845 0713 007
✉clerks@civitaslaw.com
Call Date: Oct 2004, Lincoln's Inn
Pupil Supervisor
Qualifications: [MA (Oxon)]
✉nick.thomas-symonds@civitaslaw.com

Types of work: Chancery (general), Civil liberties, Commercial law, Construction law

THOMPSON MR ANDREW EDWARD COURTNEY

Tanfield Chambers
2-5 Warwick Court, London WC1R 5DJ, ☎020 7421 5300
✉clerks@tanfieldchambers.co.uk
Call Date: Nov 1969, Inner Temple
Pupil Supervisor
Qualifications: [BA (Hons) LLB (Dublin)]
✉athompson@tanfieldchambers.co.uk

THOMPSON MR ANDREW IAN

18 Red Lion Court
London EC4A 3EB, ☎020 7520 6000
✉chambers@18rlc.co.uk
Call Date: Oct 1991, Gray's Inn
Pupil Supervisor
Qualifications: [MA (Oxon)]
✉andrew.thompson@18rlc.co.uk

THOMPSON MR ANDREW RICHARD

Erskine Chambers
33 Chancery Lane, London WC2A 1EN, ☎020 7242 5532
✉clerks@erskinechambers.com
Call Date: Nov 1991, Inner Temple
Pupil Supervisor
Qualifications: [MA LLM (Cantab)]
✉athompson@erskine-chambers.co.uk

THOMPSON MR ANTONY CARL

20 Essex Street
London WC2R 3AL, ☎020 7842 1200
✉clerks@20essexst.com
Call Date: Nov 2002, Middle Temple
Qualifications: [BA LLB (Hons) BA (Oxon) MSt (Oxon)]
✉clerks@20essexst.com

E

THOMPSON MISS BLONDEL MARGUERITE

St Philips Chambers
55 Temple Row, Birmingham B2 5LS,
☎0121 246 7000 ✉clerks@st-philips.com
Call Date: July 1987, Middle Temple
Pupil Supervisor
Qualifications: [LLB]
bthompson@st-philips.co.uk

THOMPSON MISS CLAIRE ANITA

Clock Chambers
18 Waterloo Road, Wolverhampton WV1 4BL,
☎01902 313444
✉clockchambers@btconnect.com
Call Date: Oct 2000, Inner Temple
Qualifications: [LLB]
cthompson@clockchambers.com, claire-thompson@btconnect.com

THOMPSON MR COLLINGWOOD FORSTER JAMES QC (1998)

Seven Bedford Row
7 Bedford Row, London WC1R 4BS,
☎020 7242 3555 ✉clerks@7br.co.uk
Call Date: July 1975, Gray's Inn
Recorder
Qualifications: [LLB (Lond)]
cthompson@7br.co.uk

THOMPSON MR DERMOT MICHAEL MAIN

Renaissance Chambers
5th Floor, Gray's Inn Chambers, Gray's Inn, London WC1R 5JA, ☎020 7404 1111
✉clerks@renaissancechambers.co.uk
Call Date: July 1977, Gray's Inn
Pupil Supervisor
Qualifications: [MA LLM (Cantab)]
dmt@renaissancechambers.co.uk

THOMPSON MR GARETH EDWARD GEORGE

Call Date: Nov 2005, Gray's Inn
Qualifications: [LLB]
clerk@stjohnsbuildings.co.uk

THOMPSON MR HOWARD NEIL

No5 Chambers
Fountain Court, Steelhouse Lane, Birmingham B4 6DR, ☎0845 210 5555 ✉info@no5.com
No5 Chambers
Greenwood House, 4-7 Salisbury Court, London EC4Y 8AA, ☎0845 210 5555
No5 Chambers
38 Queen Square, Bristol BS1 4QS,
☎0845 210 5555
Call Date: July 1982, Lincoln's Inn
Pupil Supervisor
Qualifications: [BA]
nt@no5.com

THOMPSON MR IAN CHRISTOPHER

Chambers of Ian C Thompson TD
Spirthill Farm, Spirthill, Calne, Wiltshire SN11 9HP, ☎07714 758579
✉ian.c.thompson@btinternet.com
Call Date: Oct 2000, Inner Temple
Qualifications: [BSc (L'Pool) PGCE PGDipl PG Dip BVC]

THOMPSON MR JONATHAN RICHARD

St Johns Buildings
24a - 28 St John Street, Manchester M3 4DJ,
☎0161 214 1500
✉clerk@stjohnsbuildings.co.uk
St Johns Buildings
21 White Friars, Chester CH1 1NZ,
☎01244 323070
✉clerk@stjohnsbuildings.co.uk
16 Winckley Square
Preston PR1 3JJ, ☎01772 256100
Call Date: Oct 1990, Inner Temple
Qualifications: [MA LLM (Cantab)]
clerk@stjohnsbuildings.co.uk

THOMPSON MR MICHAEL JAMES

Keating Chambers
15 Essex Street, London WC2R 3AA,
☎020 7544 2600
✉clerks@keatingchambers.com
Call Date: July 2005, Middle Temple
Qualifications: [BA (Hons) (Cantab)]
jthompson@keatingchambers.com

THOMPSON MR PATRICK MILES

St Johns Buildings
24a - 28 St John Street, Manchester M3 4DJ,
☎0161 214 1500
✉clerk@stjohnsbuildings.co.uk
16 Winckley Square
Preston PR1 3JJ, ☎01772 256100
St Johns Buildings Liverpool
8th Floor India Buildings, Water Street, Liverpool L2 0XG, ☎0151 243 6000
✉clerk@stjohnsbuildings.co.uk

KBW
The Engine House, No 1 Foundry Square, Leeds LS11 5DL, ☎ 0113 297 1200
✉ clerks@kbwchambers.com
Call Date: Oct 1990, Gray's Inn
Recorder
Qualifications: [LLB (Hons)(Manch)]
✉ clerk@stjohnsbuildings.co.uk

THOMPSON MISS PAULINE SONITA

5 King's Bench Walk
5 King's Bench Walk, Temple, London EC4Y 7DN, ☎ 020 7353 5638
✉ clerks@5kbw.co.uk
Call Date: July 1998, Middle Temple
Pupil Supervisor
Qualifications: [LLB (Hons)]

THOMPSON MISS POLLY

Stour Chambers
Mill Studio, 17a Stour Street, Canterbury, Kent CT1 2NR, ☎ 01227 764899
✉ clerks@stourchambers.co.uk
Renaissance Chambers
5th Floor, Gray's Inn Chambers, Gray's Inn, London WC1R 5JA, ☎ 020 7404 1111
✉ clerks@renaissancechambers.co.uk
Call Date: Nov 1990, Middle Temple
Pupil Supervisor
Qualifications: [BA Dip Law (Lond)]
✉ pt@renaissancechambers.co.uk

THOMPSON MR RHODRI WILLIAM RALPH QC (2002)

Matrix Chambers
Griffin Building, Gray's Inn, London WC1R 5LN, ☎ 020 7404 3447
✉ matrix@matrixlaw.co.uk / Iscott@matrixlaw.co.uk
Call Date: July 1989, Middle Temple
Qualifications: [MA (Oxon) BPhil (Oxon)]

THOMPSON MR RICHARD ANTHONY

Wilberforce Chambers
7 Bishop Lane, Hull HU1 1PA, ☎ 01482 323264
Call Date: July 2007, Middle Temple
Qualifications: [LLB (Hons) (Nott'm)]

THOMPSON MR RYAN JEROME

Dyers Chambers
35 Bedford Row, London WC1R 4JH, ☎ 020 7404 1881
✉ admin@dyerschambers.com
Call Date: Mar 1999, Lincoln's Inn
Qualifications: [LLB (Hons)(Leeds)]
✉ ryan.thompson@dyerschambers.com

THOMPSON MISS SALLY

Atkinson Bevan Chambers
1st Floor, 2 Harcourt Buildings, Temple, London EC4Y 9DB, ☎ 020 7353 2112
✉ clerks@2hb.co.uk
Call Date: Oct 1994, Middle Temple
Qualifications: [Dip Music CPE (Lond)]

THOMPSON MR STEVEN LIM

XXIV Old Buildings
Ground Floor, 24 Old Buildings, Lincoln's Inn, London WC2A 3UP, ☎ 020 7691 2424
✉ clerks@xxiv.co.uk
Call Date: Oct 1996, Inner Temple
Pupil Supervisor
Qualifications: [BA (Cantab)]
✉ steven.thompson@xxiv.co.uk

THOMPSON MRS ZOE CARMELLA

9 St John Street
Manchester M3 4DN, ☎ 0161 955 9000
✉ civilclerks@9sjs.com / criminalclerks@9sjs.com
Call Date: Nov 1999, Middle Temple
Qualifications: [LLB (Hons)(LSE)]
✉ zthompson@9sjs.com

THOMSON DR DAVID JAMES RAMSAY GIBB

1 Chancery Lane
London WC2A 1LF, ☎ 0845 634 6666
✉ clerks@1chancerylane.com
Call Date: Nov 1994, Inner Temple
Pupil Supervisor
Qualifications: [MB Ch B (Sheff) LLB (Lond) LLM (Cantab) FCIArb]
✉ dthomson@1chancerylane.com

THOMSON MRS LOUISE GILLIAN

12 King's Bench Walk
12 King's Bench Walk, Temple, London EC4Y 7EL, ☎ 020 7583 0811
Call Date: Nov 1996, Lincoln's Inn
Qualifications: [BA (Hons)(E.Anglia)]
✉ thomson@12kbw.co.uk

E

THOMSON MR MARTIN HALDANE AHMAD

Wynne Chambers
5 Kimberley Road, London NW6 7SG,
☎ 020 3239 6964
✉ admin@wynnechambers.co.uk
Call Date: July 1979, Gray's Inn
Qualifications: [LLB (Hons) (Exeter) GDL (Lond)]
✉ ahmadthomson@wynnechambers.co.uk

Fax: 020 3014 8839;
Out of hours telephone: 020 3239 6946
URL: www.wynnechambers.co.uk

Types of work: Charities, Discrimination, Employment, Islamic law, Trusts, Wills

THOMSON MISS VANESSA ELIZABETH

9 St John Street
Manchester M3 4DN, ☎ 0161 955 9000
✉ civilclerks@9sjs.com / criminalclerks@9sjs.com
Call Date: Oct 1998, Lincoln's Inn
Qualifications: [LLB (Hons)(L'pool)]

E

THORLEY MR SIMON JOE QC (1989)

Three New Square IP
3 New Square, Lincoln's Inn, London WC2A 3RS, ☎ 020 7405 1111
✉ clerks@3newsquare.co.uk
Call Date: July 1972, Inner Temple
Qualifications: [MA (Oxon)]
✉ thorley@3newsquare.co.uk

Types of work: Arbitration, Biotechnology, Breach of confidence, Confidential information, Copyright, Copyright Tribunal, EC competition law, Entertainment, Intellectual property, Licensing, Media and entertainment, Passing off, Patents, Pharmaceuticals, Telecommunications, Trademarks

THORNDIKE DR TONY EDWARD

Central Chambers
89 Princess Street, Manchester M1 4HT,
☎ 0161 236 1133
✉ clerks@centralchambers.co.uk
Call Date: Oct 1994, Lincoln's Inn
Qualifications: [BSc (Econ) MSc PhD]

THORNE MS KATHERINE HARRIET

Tooks Chambers
81 Farringdon Street, London EC4A 4BL,
☎ 020 7842 7575 ✉ clerks@tooks.co.uk
Call Date: Nov 1994, Inner Temple
Pupil Supervisor
Qualifications: [BA (Leeds) CPE]

THORNE MR OLIVER CHARLES

King's Bench Chambers
Wellington House, 175 Holdenhurst Road, Bournemouth, Dorset BH8 8DQ,
☎ 01202 250025
Call Date: Nov 2005, Gray's Inn
Qualifications: [LLB LLM]

THORNE MR OLIVER WILLIAM

KBW
The Engine House, No 1 Foundry Square, Leeds LS11 5DL, ☎ 0113 297 1200
✉ clerks@kbwchambers.com
Call Date: Oct 2003, Gray's Inn
Qualifications: [BA (Manch)]
✉ oliverthorne@kbwchambers.com

THORNETT MR GARY PAUL

12 King's Bench Walk
12 King's Bench Walk, Temple, London EC4Y 7EL, ☎ 020 7583 0811
Call Date: Nov 1991, Middle Temple
Pupil Supervisor
Qualifications: [B Mus (Lond) ARCO LRAM]
✉ thornett@12kbw.co.uk

THORNHILL MR ANDREW ROBERT QC (1985)

Pump Court Tax Chambers
16 Bedford Row, London WC1R 4EF,
☎ 020 7414 8080 ✉ clerks@pumptax.com
Albion Chambers
Broad Street, Bristol BS1 1DR,
☎ 0117 927 2144
✉ clerks@albionchambers.co.uk
Call Date: July 1969, Middle Temple
Qualifications: [BA (Oxon)]
✉ athornhill@pumptax.com

Types of work: Capital tax, Corporation tax, Employee benefit trusts, Equity, Income tax, National Insurance, Private client, Stamp duty, Trusts, VAT, Wills

THORNHILL MS TERESA

Chambers of Ms T Thornhill
Crowell Brook Mill Cottage, Forthay, North Nibley GL11 6EA, ☎ 07887 490554
✉ tthornhill@childcarelegal.co.uk
Call Date: July 1986, Middle Temple
Qualifications: [BA (Hons) (Oxon) Dip Law (Lond) MA (Lond)]

THORNLEY MISS HANNAH ELISE

South Square
3-4 South Square, Gray's Inn, London WC1R 5HP, ☎ 020 7696 9900
✉ practicemanagers@southsquare.com
Call Date: Oct 2003, Middle Temple
Qualifications: [BA(Hons) (Cantab) BCL (Oxon)]
hannahthornley@southsquare.com

THORNTON MR ANDREW JAMES

Erskine Chambers
33 Chancery Lane, London WC2A 1EN, ☎ 020 7242 5532
✉ clerks@erskinechambers.com
Call Date: Nov 1994, Lincoln's Inn
Qualifications: [LLB (Hons)(Hull)]
athornton@erskine-chambers.co.uk

THORNTON LADY DELIA

St John's Chambers
101 Victoria Street, Bristol BS1 6PU, ☎ 0117 923 4700
✉ clerks@stjohnschambers.co.uk
Call Date: Oct 1999, Lincoln's Inn
Qualifications: [LLB (Hons)(Notts)]
delia.thornton@stjohnschambers.co.uk

THORNTON MR JOHN ROBERT

Stour Chambers
Mill Studio, 17a Stour Street, Canterbury, Kent CT1 2NR, ☎ 01227 764899
✉ clerks@stourchambers.co.uk
Call Date: Nov 2002, Gray's Inn
Qualifications: [BA Hons (Lincoln)]
clerks@stourchambers.co.uk

THORNTON MISS JUSTINE

39 Essex Street
London WC2R 3AT, ☎ 020 7832 1111
✉ clerks@39essex.com
82 King Street
Manchester M2 4WQ, ☎ 0161 870 9969
Call Date: Feb 1994, Lincoln's Inn
Qualifications: [BA (Hons)]
justine.thornton@39essex.com

THORNTON MR STEPHEN JOHN

Dere Street Barristers
14 Toft Green, York YO1 6JT, ☎ 0844 3351551
✉ clerks@derestreet.co.uk
Dere Street Barristers
33 Broad Chare, Newcastle Upon Tyne NE1 3DQ, ☎ 0844 3351551
✉ clerks@derestreet.co.uk
Call Date: Nov 2003, Inner Temple
Qualifications: [MA (Glas)]
clerks@yorkchambers.co.uk, sthornton@yorkchambers.co.uk

THOROGOOD MR BERNARD

No5 Chambers
Fountain Court, Steelhouse Lane, Birmingham B4 6DR, ☎ 0845 210 5555 ✉ info@no5.com
No5 Chambers
Greenwood House, 4-7 Salisbury Court, London EC4Y 8AA, ☎ 0845 210 5555
No5 Chambers
38 Queen Square, Bristol BS1 4QS, ☎ 0845 210 5555
Call Date: July 1986, Gray's Inn
Pupil Supervisor, Recorder
Qualifications: [LLB (Leeds)]
bt@no5.com

THOROWGOOD MR MAX CAMPBELL DE WARRENNE

Field Court Chambers
5 Field Court, Gray's Inn, London WC1R 5EF, ☎ 020 7405 6114 ✉ clerks@fieldcourt.co.uk
Call Date: Nov 1995, Lincoln's Inn
Pupil Supervisor
Qualifications: [MA (Hons)]
max.thorowgood@fieldcourt.co.uk

THORPE MR ALEXANDER LAMBERT

Queen Elizabeth Building
3rd Floor, Queen Elizabeth Building, Temple, London EC4Y 9BS, ☎ 020 7797 7837
✉ clerks@qeb.co.uk
Call Date: Oct 1995, Inner Temple
Pupil Supervisor
Qualifications: [BD (Lond) CPE (Lond)]
a.thorpe@qeb.co.uk

THRELFALL MR RICHARD WILLIAM GEORGE

Queen Square Chambers
56 Queen Square, Bristol BS1 4PR, ☎ 0117 921 1966 ✉ crime@qs-c.co.uk
Call Date: July 1972, Gray's Inn
Pupil Supervisor
crime@qs-c.co.uk

THROWER MR JAMES SIMEON

Chambers of Simeon Thrower
16 Langside Avenue, London SW15 5QT, ☎ 020 8878 7374 ✉ simlawhome@aol.com
Call Date: July 1973, Middle Temple
Pupil Supervisor
Qualifications: [LLB]

THWAITES MR RONALD QC (1987)

Ely Place Chambers
30 Ely Place, London EC1N 6TD, ☎ 020 7400 9600 ✉ admin@elyplace.com
Call Date: Nov 1970, Gray's Inn
Qualifications: [LLB (Lond)]
rthwaites@elyplace.com

E

THYNE MR RICHARD MICHAEL

Call Date: Oct 2002, Lincoln's Inn
Qualifications: [LLB (Sheff)]
thyne@paradise-sq.co.uk

TIBBITTS MISS HOLLY

The Chambers of Grahame Aldous QC
9 Gough Square, London EC4A 3DG,
☎ 020 7832 0500
clerks@9goughsquare.co.uk
Call Date: July 2010, Middle Temple
Qualifications: [BA (Hons) (Cantab)]
htibbitts@9goughsquare.co.uk

TIBBITTS MR SIMON STUART ALAN

Queen Square Chambers
56 Queen Square, Bristol BS1 4PR,
☎ 0117 921 1966 crime@qs-c.co.uk
Call Date: Oct 2006, Inner Temple
Qualifications: [LLB (Hons) (Lond)]
sst@qs-c.co.uk

TICCIATI MR OLIVER

4 Pump Court
4 Pump Court, Temple, London EC4Y 7AN,
☎ 020 7842 5555
chambers@4pumpcourt.com
Call Date: July 1979, Inner Temple
Pupil Supervisor
Qualifications: [MA (Cantab)]

TICEHURST MR JOSS EDWARD

Walnut House
63 St. David's Hill, Exeter, Devon EX4 4DW,
☎ 01392 279751
clerks@walnuthouse.co.uk
Call Date: Nov 2006, Inner Temple
Qualifications: [BA (Lond)]
joss.ticehurst@walnuthouse.co.uk

TIDBURY MR ANDREW HUGH

Queen Elizabeth Building
3rd Floor, Queen Elizabeth Building, Temple, London EC4Y 9BS, ☎ 020 7797 7837
clerks@qeb.co.uk
Call Date: July 1976, Inner Temple
Pupil Supervisor, Recorder
Qualifications: [BA (Cantab)]
a.tidbury@qeb.co.uk

TIDMARSH MR CHRISTOPHER RALPH FRANCIS QC (2002)

5 Stone Buildings
5 Stone Buildings, Lincoln's Inn, London WC2A 3XT, ☎ 020 7242 6201
clerks@5sblaw.com
Call Date: Nov 1985, Lincoln's Inn
Qualifications: [BA (Oxon)]
ctidmarsh@5sblaw.com

TIGHE MISS DAWN

Bank House Chambers
Old Bank House, Hartshead, Sheffield S1 2EL,
☎ 0114 275 1223
w.digby@bankhousechambers.co.uk
Call Date: Nov 1989, Lincoln's Inn
Pupil Supervisor
Qualifications: [LLB (Newc)]
d.tighe@bankhousechambers.co.uk

TILBURY MR JAMES RICHARD

Carmelite Chambers
9 Carmelite Street, London EC4Y 0DR,
☎ 020 7936 6300
clerks@carmelitechambers.co.uk
Call Date: Mar 1996, Gray's Inn
Qualifications: [LLB]
jtilbury@carmelitechambers.co.uk

TILLEY MR GARETH DONALD

Serle Court
6 New Square, Lincoln's Inn, London WC2A 3QS, ☎ 020 7242 6105
clerks@serlecourt.co.uk
Call Date: Nov 2007, Lincoln's Inn
Qualifications: [BA LLB (Australia) BCL (Oxon)]
gtilley@serlecourt.co.uk

TILLYARD MR JAMES HENRY HUGH QC (2002)

30 Park Place
Cardiff CF10 3BS, ☎ 029 2039 8421
clerks@30parkplace.law.co.uk
St Ive's Chambers
Whittall Street, Birmingham B4 6DH,
☎ 0121 236 0863
clerks@stiveschambers.co.uk
Call Date: July 1978, Middle Temple
Recorder
Qualifications: [BSc (Leeds)]
jhht@30parkplace.co.uk

E

TIMAN MISS ANNABEL ESTHER

Doughty Street Chambers
53-54 Doughty Street, London WC1N 2LS,
☎ 020 7404 1313
✉ enquiries@doughtystreet.co.uk
Call Date: Oct 2007, Inner Temple
Qualifications: [BA (Manch)]

TIMMINS MISS NICOLA MICHELLE

4 Stone Buildings
Ground Floor, 4 Stone Buildings, Lincoln's Inn, London WC2A 3XT, ☎ 020 7242 5524
✉ clerks@4stonebuildings.com
Call Date: Oct 2008, Gray's Inn
Qualifications: [BA LLM MA]
✉ n.timmins@4stonebuildings.com

TIMSON MR CORIN JAMES

Kenworthy's Chambers
Arlington House, Bloom Street, Salford, Manchester M3 6AJ, ☎ 0161 832 4036
Call Date: Nov 1994, Inner Temple
Qualifications: [BA (Hons) (B'ham) Dip Law (Lond)]
✉ c.timson@kenworthysbarristers.co.uk

TINDAL MR JAMES STUART

St Philips Chambers
55 Temple Row, Birmingham B2 5LS,
☎ 0121 246 7000 ✉ clerks@st-philips.com
Call Date: Nov 2002, Lincoln's Inn
Qualifications: [LLB (Hons) (B'ham)]

TINDALL MR PAUL ROBERT

St James's Chambers
68 Quay Street, Manchester M3 3EJ,
☎ 0161 834 7000
✉ clerks@stjameschambers.com
Call Date: Oct 1999, Gray's Inn
Qualifications: [BA (Nott'm) LLM (Bris)]
✉ paul.tindall@stjameschambers.com

TINKLER MR DAVID

Atlantic Chambers
4-6 Cook Street, Liverpool L2 9QU,
☎ 0151 236 4421
✉ info@atlanticchambers.co.uk
Call Date: Oct 2004, Lincoln's Inn
Qualifications: [BA (Hons) PgDI]
✉ davidtinkler@atlanticchambers.co.uk

TINNION MR ANTOINE

Trinity Chambers
The Custom House, 39 Quayside, Newcastle Upon Tyne NE1 3DE, ☎ 0191 232 1927
✉ info@trinitychambers.co.uk
Trinity Chambers
Multi Media Exchange, 72-80 Corporation Road, Middlesbrough TS1 2RF,
☎ 01642 247569
✉ info@trinitychambers.co.uk
Call Date: Nov 2004, Lincoln's Inn
Qualifications: [MA (Oxon) BA (Cantab) LLM (Harv)]
✉ a.tinnion@trinitychambers.co.uk

TIPPLES MISS AMANDA JANE QC (2011)

Maitland Chambers
7 Stone Buildings, Lincoln's Inn, London WC2A 3SZ, ☎ 020 7406 1200
✉ clerks@maitlandchambers.com
Call Date: Oct 1991, Gray's Inn
Pupil Supervisor, Recorder
Qualifications: [MA (Cantab)]
✉ atipples@maitlandchambers.com

TITCHMARSH MISS KATHARINE ELIZABETH

Exchange Chambers
One Derby Square, Derby Square, Liverpool L2 9XX, ☎ 0151 236 7747
✉ info@exchangechambers.co.uk
Exchange Chambers
7 Ralli Courts, West Riverside, Manchester M3 5FT, ☎ 0161 833 2722
Exchange Chambers
Oxford House, Oxford Row, Leeds LS1 3BE,
☎ 0113 203 1970
✉ spencer@exchangechambers.co.uk
Call Date: Nov 1998, Lincoln's Inn
Qualifications: [LLB (Hons)(Sheff)]
✉ titchmarsh@exchangechambers.co.uk

TITMUSS MR JONATHAN AUSTIN

Hardwicke
New Square, Lincoln's Inn, London WC2A 3SB, ☎ 020 7242 2523
✉ enquiries@hardwicke.co.uk
Call Date: Nov 2001, Lincoln's Inn
Pupil Supervisor
Qualifications: [BA(Hons)(Lond)]

E

TITUS MISS FRANCESCA ELIZABETH

Carmelite Chambers
9 Carmelite Street, London EC4Y 0DR,
☎ 020 7936 6300
✉ clerks@carmelitechambers.co.uk
Call Date: July 2003, Middle Temple
Qualifications: [LLB Hons (Brunel)]
ftitus@carmelitechambers.co.uk

TIVADAR MR DANIEL

3 Hare Court
3 Hare Court, Temple, London EC4Y 7BJ,
☎ 020 7415 7800 ✉ clerks@3harecourt.com
Call Date: Nov 2005, Middle Temple
Qualifications: [BA (Hons) Cambridge BCL Oxford]
danieltivadar@3harecourt.com

TIZZANO MR FRANCO SALVATORE

Old Bailey Chambers
15 Old Bailey, London EC4M 7EF,
☎ 020 3008 6404
✉ clerks@15oldbaileychambers.com
Call Date: Feb 1989, Middle Temple
Pupil Supervisor
Qualifications: [LLB]
f.tizzano@15oldbaileychambers.com

E

TKACZYNSKA MISS ANNA MARIA

Hardwicke
New Square, Lincoln's Inn, London
WC2A 3SB, ☎ 020 7242 2523
✉ enquiries@hardwicke.co.uk
Call Date: July 2008, Middle Temple
Qualifications: [LLB LLM]
anna.tkaczynska@hardwicke.co.uk

TOAL MR DAVID JOHN

Exchange Chambers
7 Ralli Courts, West Riverside, Manchester
M3 5FT, ☎ 0161 833 2722
Exchange Chambers
One Derby Square, Derby Square, Liverpool
L2 9XX, ☎ 0151 236 7747
✉ info@exchangechambers.co.uk
Exchange Chambers
Oxford House, Oxford Row, Leeds LS1 3BE,
☎ 0113 203 1970
✉ spencer@exchangechambers.co.uk
Call Date: Feb 1990, Gray's Inn
Qualifications: [LLB (Hons)]
toal@exchangechambers.co.uk

TOAL MR RONAN

Garden Court Chambers
57-60 Lincoln's Inn Fields, London WC2A 3LJ,
☎ 020 7993 7600 ✉ info@gclaw.co.uk
Call Date: Nov 1999, Middle Temple
Pupil Supervisor
Qualifications: [BA (Hons)(Cantab) Dip Law]
ronant@gclaw.co.uk

TOBIN MR DANIEL ALPHONSUS JOSEPH

12 King's Bench Walk
12 King's Bench Walk, Temple, London
EC4Y 7EL, ☎ 020 7583 0811
Call Date: Oct 1994, Middle Temple
Qualifications: [LLB (Hons)(Lond)]
tobin@12kbw.co.uk

TOBIN MISS KEZIA ELIZABETH

Renaissance Chambers
5th Floor, Gray's Inn Chambers, Gray's Inn,
London WC1R 5JA, ☎ 020 7404 1111
✉ clerks@renaissancechambers.co.uk
Call Date: Oct 2010, Middle Temple
Qualifications: [BA (Hons) (Sussex)]
kt@renaissancechambers.co.uk

TOCH MISS JOANNA PATRICIA

Chambers of Mr Ami Feder
Ground Floor, Lamb Building, Temple, London
EC4Y 7AS, ☎ 020 7797 7788
✉ clerks@lambbuilding.co.uk
Chambers of Mr Ami Feder
Ground Floor, Lamb Building, Temple, London
EC4Y 7AS, ☎ 020 7797 7788
✉ clerks@lambbuilding.co.uk
Chambers of Miss J P Toch
1 John Brunt VC Court, Church Road,
Paddock Wood, Tonbridge, Kent TH12 6ET,
☎ 01892 833 005 ✉ j.toch@yahoo.co.uk
Call Date: Nov 1988, Middle Temple
Pupil Supervisor
Qualifications: [LLB (Hons)(Lond)]
joanna@joannatoch.com

TOD MR JONATHAN ALAN

29 Bedford Row Chambers
London WC1R 4HE, ☎ 020 7404 1044
✉ clerks@29br.co.uk
Call Date: Nov 1990, Inner Temple
Qualifications: [LLB (Hons)]
jtod@29br.co.uk

TODD MR ALAN JAMES

39 Essex Street
London WC2R 3AT, ☎ 020 7832 1111
✉ clerks@39essex.com
82 King Street
Manchester M2 4WQ, ☎ 0161 870 9969
Call Date: Nov 1990, Gray's Inn
Qualifications: [MA (Cantab)]
james.todd@39essex.com

TODD MISS BRIDGET LOUISE

Five St Andrew's Hill
5 St Andrew's Hill, London EC4V 5BZ,
☎ 020 7332 5400 ✉ Clerks@5sah.co.uk
Call Date: Oct 1996, Gray's Inn
Qualifications: [LLB (Leeds)]
bridgettodd@5sah.co.uk

TODD MRS ELISABETH HELEN MARGARET

1 Hare Court
1 Hare Court, Temple, London EC4Y 7BE,
☎ 020 7797 7070 ✉ clerks@1hc.com
Call Date: Oct 1990, Middle Temple
Qualifications: [LLB (Lond) (Hons)]
todd@1hc.com

TODD MR MARTIN RUSSELL

Dere Street Barristers
14 Toft Green, York YO1 6JT, ☎ 0844 3351551
✉ clerks@derestreet.co.uk
York Chambers
Rotterdam House, 116 The Quayside,
Newcastle Upon Tyne NE1 3DY,
☎ 0191 206 4677
Call Date: Nov 1991, Inner Temple
Pupil Supervisor
Qualifications: [LLB (Hons)]
clerks@yorkchambers.co.uk

TODD MR MICHAEL ALAN QC (1997)

Erskine Chambers
33 Chancery Lane, London WC2A 1EN,
☎ 020 7242 5532
✉ clerks@erskinechambers.com
Call Date: July 1977, Lincoln's Inn
Qualifications: [BA (Keele)]

TODD MR RICHARD FRAZER QC (2009)

1 Hare Court
1 Hare Court, Temple, London EC4Y 7BE,
☎ 020 7797 7070 ✉ clerks@1hc.com
Call Date: July 1988, Middle Temple
Qualifications: [MA (Hons) (Oxon)]
rt@1hc.com

TODMAN MRS DEBORAH

42 Bedford Row
London WC1R 4LL, ☎ 020 7831 0222
✉ clerks@42br.com
Call Date: Oct 1991, Gray's Inn
Qualifications: [LLB (Hons)]

TOLAN MISS JULIANNA

Five Paper Buildings
1st Floor, Five Paper Buildings, Temple,
London EC4Y 7HB, ☎ 020 7583 6117
✉ clerks@5pb.co.uk
Call Date: Mar 2010, Lincoln's Inn
Qualifications: [LLB (Leic)]
jmt@5pb.co.uk

TOLANEY MISS SONIA QC (2011)

3 Verulam Buildings
London WC1R 5NT, ☎ 020 7831 8441
✉ chambers@3vb.com
Call Date: Oct 1995, Middle Temple
Pupil Supervisor
Qualifications: [MA (Hons)]
stolaney@3vb.com

TOLEDANO MR DANIEL ZE'EV QC (2009)

One Essex Court
Ground Floor, One Essex Court, Temple,
London EC4Y 9AR, ☎ 020 7583 2000
✉ clerks@oeclaw.co.uk
Call Date: Oct 1993, Inner Temple
Qualifications: [MA (Hons) (Cantab)]
dtoledano@oeclaw.co.uk

TOLLEY MR ADAM RICHARD

Fountain Court Chambers
Fountain Court, Temple, London EC4Y 9DH,
☎ 020 7583 3335
✉ chambers@fountaincourt.co.uk
Call Date: Oct 1994, Inner Temple
Pupil Supervisor
Qualifications: [BA (Oxon) BCL (Oxon)]
atolley@fountaincourt.co.uk

TOLLEY MR NICHOLAS JAMES

Four New Square
Four New Square, Lincoln's Inn, London
WC2A 3RJ, ☎ 020 7822 2000
✉ barristers@4newsquare.com
Call Date: Nov 2009, Inner Temple
Qualifications: [MA (Cantab) BCL (Oxon)]

E

TOLSON MR ROBIN STEWART QC (2001)

St John's Chambers
101 Victoria Street, Bristol BS1 6PU,
☎0117 923 4700
✉clerks@stjohnschambers.co.uk
12 College Place
Fauvelle Buildings, 12 College Place,
Southampton SO15 2FE, ☎023 8032 0320
✉clerks@12cp.co.uk
Call Date: Nov 1980, Inner Temple
Qualifications: [BA (Cantab)]
robin.tolsonqc@outertemple.com

TOMAN MISS CRISTIN CECILIA

Enterprise Chambers
43 Park Square, Leeds LS1 2NP,
☎0113 246 0391
✉leeds@enterprisechambers.com
Enterprise Chambers
65 Quayside, Newcastle Upon Tyne NE1 3DE,
☎0191 222 3344
✉newcastle@enterprisechambers.com
Call Date: Nov 2004, Lincoln's Inn
Qualifications: [LLB BSc (Hons)]
cristintoman@enterprisechambers.com

E

TOMASSI MR MARK DAVID

Charter Chambers
33 John Street, London WC1N 2AT,
☎020 7618 4400
✉clerks@charterchambers.com
Call Date: Nov 1981, Middle Temple
Pupil Supervisor
Qualifications: [BA (Hons)]
mark.tomassi@charterchambers.com

TOMLINSON MISS ELIZABETH RHODA

Harcourt Chambers
1st Floor, 2 Harcourt Buildings, Temple,
London EC4Y 9DB, ☎0844 561 7135
Harcourt Chambers
Churchill House, 3 St Aldate's Courtyard, St
Aldate's, Oxford OX1 1BN, ☎0844 561 7135
Call Date: July 2004, Inner Temple
Qualifications: [LLB (Hons) LLM (Cantab)]
etomlinson@harcourtchambers.law.co.uk

TOMLINSON MR HUGH RICHARD EDWARD QC (2002)

Matrix Chambers
Griffin Building, Gray's Inn, London
WC1R 5LN, ☎020 7404 3447
✉matrix@matrixlaw.co.uk / lscott@
matrixlaw.co.uk
Call Date: Nov 1983, Gray's Inn
Pupil Supervisor
Qualifications: [BA (Oxon) MA (Sussex)]
hughtomlinson@matrixlaw.co.uk

TOMLINSON MR MICHAEL JAMES

3 PB Barristers
3 Paper Buildings, Temple, London EC4Y 7EU,
☎020 7583 8055
3 PB Barristers
30 Christchurch Road, Bournemouth, Dorset
BH1 3PD, ☎01202 292102
✉clerks.bournemouth@3paper.co.uk
3 PB Barristers
4 St Peter Street, Winchester SO23 8BW,
☎01962 868884
✉clerks.winchester@3paper.co.uk
3 PB Barristers
Royal Talbot House, 2 Victoria Street, Bristol,
Avon BS1 6BB, ☎0117 928 1520
3 PB Barristers
23 Beaumont Street, Oxford OX1 2NP,
☎01865 793 736
Call Date: Nov 2002, Middle Temple
Qualifications: [BA (Hons) (Lond) CPE]
michael.tomlinson@3paper.co.uk

TOMPKINS MISS KATE

36 Bedford Row
London WC1R 4JH, ☎020 7421 8000
✉chambers@36bedfordrow.co.uk
Call Date: July 2003, Lincoln's Inn
Qualifications: [BA Hons (Sheff)]
clerks@36bedfordrow.co.uk

TOMPKINSON MISS DEBORAH ANN

Clerksroom (Taunton)
Equity House, Administration Centre,
Blackbrook Park Avenue, Taunton, Somerset
TA1 2PX, ☎0845 083 3000
✉mail@clerksroom.com
Clerksroom (London)
3rd Floor, 218 Strand, London WC2R 1AT,
☎0845 083 3000 ✉mail@clerksroom.com
Call Date: Nov 1984, Middle Temple
Qualifications: [MA (Oxon) LLM (UCL) ACII]

Types of work: Alternative dispute resolution, Civil actions against the police, Civil law, Commercial litigation, Common law (general), Consumer law, Coroner's inquests, Damages, Employment, Freezing orders, Holiday injury and damages, Insurance, Legal advice, Mediation, Personal injury, Professional negligence,

Restitution, Sale and carriage of goods, Solicitor's indemnity, Torts

TOMS MR NICHOLAS ROBERT

Doughty Street Chambers
53-54 Doughty Street, London WC1N 2LS, ☎ 020 7404 1313
✉ enquiries@doughtystreet.co.uk
Doughty Street Chambers
Pall Mall Court, 61-67 King Street, Manchester M2 4PD, ☎ 0161 618 1066
Doughty Street Chambers
5th Floor, Broad Quay House, Prince Street, Bristol BS1 4DJ, ☎ 01179 058 717
Call Date: Nov 1996, Middle Temple
Qualifications: [LLB (Hons) LLM (Cantab)]
n.toms@doughtystreet.co.uk

TOMS MR PAUL JAMES

Quadrant Chambers
Quadrant House, 10 Fleet Street, London EC4Y 1AU, ☎ 020 7583 4444
✉ info@quadrantchambers.com
Call Date: Oct 2003, Gray's Inn
Qualifications: [BA (Oxon) BCL (Oxon)]
paul.toms@quadrantchambers.com

TOMSON MR ALASTAIR JOHN

4 Stone Buildings
Ground Floor, 4 Stone Buildings, Lincoln's Inn, London WC2A 3XT, ☎ 020 7242 5524
✉ clerks@4stonebuildings.com
Call Date: July 2004, Lincoln's Inn
Qualifications: [MA (Cantab)]
a.tomson@4stonebuildings.com

TONEY MISS RACHEL ELIZABETH

Stone Chambers
4 Field Court, Gray's Inn, London WC1R 5EF, ☎ 020 7440 6900
✉ clerks@stonechambers.com
Call Date: Oct 1998, Lincoln's Inn
Qualifications: [BA (Oxon) MA]
rachel.toney@stonechambers.com

TONGE MR CHRISTOPHER PAUL

Bank House Chambers
Old Bank House, Hartshead, Sheffield S1 2EL, ☎ 0114 275 1223
✉ w.digby@bankhousechambers.co.uk
Call Date: July 1988, Inner Temple
Pupil Supervisor
Qualifications: [LLB (Sheff)]
c.tonge@bankhousechambers.co.uk

TONNA MR JOHN PRINGLE NODWELL

39 Essex Street
London WC2R 3AT, ☎ 020 7832 1111
✉ clerks@39essex.com
82 King Street
Manchester M2 4WQ, ☎ 0161 870 9969
Call Date: July 1974, Gray's Inn
Pupil Supervisor
Qualifications: [BA (Oxon)]
john.tonna@39essex.com

TOOGOOD MISS CLAIRE VICTORIA

Crown Office Chambers
2 Crown Office Row, Temple, London EC4Y 7HJ, ☎ 020 7797 8100
✉ mail@crownofficechambers.com
Call Date: Oct 1995, Middle Temple
Pupil Supervisor
Qualifications: [MA (Hons) (Oxon)]
toogood@crownofficechambers.com

TOOMEY MR KEVIN IAN

2 Bedford Row
London WC1R 4BU, ☎ 020 7440 8888
✉ clerks@2bedfordrow.co.uk
Call Date: July 2004, Gray's Inn
Qualifications: [PGDL]
KToomey@2bedfordrow.co.uk

TOONE MR ROBERT FRANCIS

KBW
The Engine House, No 1 Foundry Square, Leeds LS11 5DL, ☎ 0113 297 1200
✉ clerks@kbwchambers.com
Call Date: Oct 1993, Inner Temple
Qualifications: [BA]
roberttoone@kbwchambers.com

TOPAL MR EROL

Lamb Chambers
Lamb Building, Elm Court, Temple, London EC4Y 7AS, ☎ 020 7797 8300
✉ info@lambchambers.co.uk
Call Date: July 1998, Middle Temple
Qualifications: [LLB (Hons)(Lond)]
eroltopal@lambchambers.co.uk

E

TOPHAM MR JOHN DAVID

Broadway House Chambers
Broadway House, 9 Bank Street, Bradford, West Yorkshire BD1 1TW, ☎01274 722560
✉clerks@broadwayhouse.co.uk
Broadway House Chambers
25 Park Square West, Leeds, West Yorkshire LS1 2PW, ☎0113 246 2600
✉clerks@broadwayhouse.co.uk
Call Date: July 1970, Gray's Inn
Pupil Supervisor
Qualifications: [LLB (Lond)]
jdt@broadwayhouse.co.uk

TOPLISS MISS MEGAN LOUISE

3 PB Barristers
3 Paper Buildings, Temple, London EC4Y 7EU, ☎020 7583 8055
3 PB Barristers
Royal Talbot House, 2 Victoria Street, Bristol, Avon BS1 6BB, ☎0117 928 1520
3 PB Barristers
23 Beaumont Street, Oxford OX1 2NP, ☎01865 793 736
3 PB Barristers
4 St Peter Street, Winchester SO23 8BW, ☎01962 868884
✉clerks.winchester@3paper.co.uk
3 PB Barristers
30 Christchurch Road, Bournemouth, Dorset BH1 3PD, ☎01202 292102
✉clerks.bournemouth@3paper.co.uk
Call Date: Oct 1994, Gray's Inn
Pupil Supervisor
Qualifications: [LLB (Wales)]
megan.topliss@3paper.co.uk

TOPPING MISS CAROLINE WENDY

6 Pump Court
1st Floor, 6 Pump Court, Temple, London EC4Y 7AR, ☎020 7797 8400
✉richardconstable@6pumpcourt.co.uk
6 Pump Court Chambers
6-8 Mill Street, Maidstone, Kent ME15 6XH, ☎01622 688094
✉annexe@6pumpcourt.co.uk
Call Date: Nov 1984, Middle Temple
Qualifications: [MA (Cantab)]
carolinetopping@6pumpcourt.co.uk

TORODE MISS JOANNA DOROTHEA

Chambers of Andrew Mitchell QC
33 Chancery Lane, London WC2A 1EN, ☎020 7440 9950 ✉clerks@33cllaw.com
Call Date: Nov 2006, Middle Temple
Qualifications: [BA (Hons) (Newc) PgDip Law (Newc)]
jt@33cllaw.com

TOUBE MS FELICITY ROSALIND QC (2011)

South Square
3-4 South Square, Gray's Inn, London WC1R 5HP, ☎020 7696 9900
✉practicemanagers@southsquare.com
Call Date: Nov 1995, Inner Temple
Pupil Supervisor
Qualifications: [BA BCL (Oxon)]
felicitytoube@southsquare.com

Types of work: Banking, Chancery (general), Commercial law, Commercial litigation, Company, commercial and competition, Insolvency, Insurance, Personal insolvency, Professional negligence

TOWERS MR MARTIN PETER

Fountain Chambers
Cleveland Business Centre, 1 Watson Street, Middlesbrough TS1 2RQ, ☎01642 804040
✉clerks@fountainchambers.co.uk
Call Date: Nov 1996, Gray's Inn
Qualifications: [LLB (Bris)]

TOWLER MR PETER JEREMY HAMILTON

12 College Place
Fauvelle Buildings, 12 College Place, Southampton SO15 2FE, ☎023 8032 0320
✉clerks@12cp.co.uk
Call Date: July 1974, Middle Temple
Recorder
Qualifications: [MA (Cantab) FCI Arb]
ptowler@12cp.co.uk

TOWNEND MR SAMUEL JOHN

Keating Chambers
15 Essex Street, London WC2R 3AA, ☎020 7544 2600
✉clerks@keatingchambers.com
Call Date: Oct 1999, Lincoln's Inn
Pupil Supervisor
Qualifications: [MA]

TOWNSEND MR EDMUND TIMOTHY

Farrar's Building
Farrar's Building, Temple, London EC4Y 7BD, ☎020 7583 9241
✉Chambers@farrarsbuilding.co.uk
Call Date: Mar 2006, Middle Temple
Qualifications: [LLB (Hons) (Warwick) LLM (Lond)]
etownsend@farrarsbuilding.co.uk

TOWNSEND MRS HARRIET CAROLINE JANE

Cornerstone Barristers
2-3 Gray's Inn Square, Gray's Inn, London WC1R 5JH, ☎ 020 7242 4986
✉ chambers@2-3gis.co.uk
Call Date: Nov 1992, Middle Temple
Qualifications: [B Sc (Hons)]
htownsend@2-3gis.co.uk

TOWNSEND MR JAMES NEVILLE

Guildhall Chambers
23 Broad Street, Bristol BS1 2HG,
☎ 0117 930 9000
✉ hoc@guildhallchambers.co.uk
Call Date: July 1980, Inner Temple
Pupil Supervisor, Recorder
Qualifications: [MA (Oxon)]
james.townsend@guildhallchambers.co.uk

TOWNSHEND MS SAOIRSE ROISIN CURTIN

36 Bedford Row
London WC1R 4JH, ☎ 020 7421 8000
✉ chambers@36bedfordrow.co.uk
Call Date: Oct 2010, Lincoln's Inn
Qualifications: [BA (Leeds)]
stownshend@36bedfordrow.co.uk,
stownshend@36bedfordrow.co.uk

TOZER MISS STEPHANIE

Falcon Chambers
Falcon Court, London EC4Y 1AA,
☎ 020 7353 2484
✉ clerks@falcon-chambers.com
Call Date: Oct 1996, Lincoln's Inn
Pupil Supervisor
Qualifications: [MA (Oxon)]

Types of work: Boundaries, Chancery (general), Chancery (land law), Commercial property, Common land, Landlord and tenant, Mediation, Mortgages, Professional negligence, Rights of light, Rights of way, Title to land

TOZZI MR NIGEL KENNETH QC (2001)

4 Pump Court
4 Pump Court, Temple, London EC4Y 7AN,
☎ 020 7842 5555
✉ chambers@4pumpcourt.com
Call Date: July 1980, Gray's Inn
Qualifications: [LLB (Exon)]

TOZZI MISS SARAH

Farrar's Building
Farrar's Building, Temple, London EC4Y 7BD,
☎ 020 7583 9241
✉ Chambers@farrarsbuilding.co.uk
Call Date: Oct 1998, Inner Temple
Qualifications: [LLB (Hons)]
stozzi@farrarsbuilding.co.uk

TRACE MR ANTHONY JOHN QC (1998)

Maitland Chambers
7 Stone Buildings, Lincoln's Inn, London WC2A 3SZ, ☎ 020 7406 1200
✉ clerks@maitlandchambers.com
Call Date: July 1981, Lincoln's Inn
Qualifications: [MA (Hons) (Cantab)]
atrace@maitlandchambers.com

Fax: 020 7406 1300;
Out of hours telephone: 07767 487537;
DX: 326 LDE

Types of work: Arbitration, Banking, Chancery (general), Chancery (land law), Commercial law, Commercial litigation, Commercial property, Company, commercial and competition, Equity, Fraud, Insolvency, Insurance, Landlord and tenant, Partnerships, Personal insolvency, Professional negligence, Sport, Succession, Trusts, Wills

Membership of foreign bars: British Virgin Islands

Awards and memberships: Bundy Scholarship (Magdalene College, Cambridge University); Hardwicke Scholar, Tancred Studentship and Droop Scholar of Lincoln's Inn; Hon. Secretary, Chancery Bar Association (1997-2001); Vice-Chairman, Chancery Bar Association (2001-4); Member COMBAR, ACTAPS (Association of Contentious Trust and Probate Specialists); CFLA (Commercial Fraud Lawyers Association); R3 (Association of Business Recovery Professionals) and ILA (Insolvency Lawyers Association)

Publications: *Butterworths European Law Service (Company Law)* (Contributor), 2000 to 2002; *Butterworths European Law Service (Company Law)* (Contributor), 1999; *Receivers, Administrators and Liquidators Quarterly* (RALQ) (Deputy Managing Editor), 1993 to 2004; *Briefings in Real Estate Finance* (Member, International Editorial Board), 2000 to 2002

Reported Cases: *Menolly v Cerep Sarl*, LTL 26/3/2009 (Chancery Division), 2009. Estoppel.
Mohammad Zahoor v Sohail Masood, LTL 3/7/2009 (Court of Appeal), 2009. Striking out for abuse of process.

Wirecard Bank AG v Scott, LTL 16/3/2010 (Queen's Bench Division), 2010. Conspiracy; fraudulent misrepresentation
JSC BTA Bank v Ablyazov, [2011] 1 WLR 2996 (Queen's Bench Division), 2011. Act of state/ non-justiciability
Interactive Investor Trading v City Index, LTL 20/7/2011 (Court of Appeal), 2011. Construction of Contracts

Practice
After graduating from Cambridge in 1980 with first-class honours in law, Anthony Trace was a pupil to David Oliver and Colin Rimer (now Lord Justice Rimer). In 1981 he was joint winner of the Observer Mace Debating Competition and won the Crowther Advocacy Shield. He has developed a very substantial practice, both in England and in foreign jurisdictions. He has been involved in a number of cases in the Cayman Islands, the Bahamas, the British Virgin Islands, the Isle of Man and Hong Kong. He has sat as an arbitrator and has considerable experience of mediation.

Reported cases in which he has appeared include:
Plant v Plant [1998] 1 BCLC 38 (individual voluntary arrangements)
Jordan Grand Prix Ltd v Baltic Insurance Group [1999] 2 AC 127 (Brussels Convention)
Goldstein v Conley [2001] L & TR 400 (powers of Lands Tribunal)
Shalson v Russo [2002] LTL (purging contempt)
SMAY Investments Ltd v Sachdev [2003] 1 WLR 1973 (submission to jurisdiction)
Shalson v Russo (No 2) [2003] WTLR 1165 (constructive trusts and tracing)
Zestafoni v Ronley Holdings [2004] (arbitration agreements)
Might SA v Redbus [2004] 2 BCLC 449 (fiduciary duties)
Watford Petroleum Ltd v Interoil Trading SA [2005] (cross-examination in interlocutory proceedings)*Newgate Stud v Penfold* [2005] (account of profits and limitation)
Harley Street Capital v Tchigirinsky [2005] (fortification of a cross-undertaking)
Walker International Holdings Ltd v Congo [2005] (transactions defrauding creditors)
Kyrri-Royle v Burger King [2005] (conspiracy)
Dranez Anstalt v Hayek [2005] (costs against third parties)
Square Mile Partnership Ltd v Fitzmaurice McCall Ltd [2006] (share sale agreements)
Farepak [2006] (constructive trusts)
Donegal v Republic of Lambia [2007] (Illegality)
Prudential Assurance v Ayres [2008] (Enforceability of Contracts by non-parties)

TRACY FORSTER MISS JANE ELIZABETH

Hailsham Chambers
Ground Floor, 4 Paper Buildings, Temple, London EC4Y 7EX, ☎ 020 7643 5000
✉ clerks@hailshamchambers.com
Call Date: July 1975, Inner Temple
Pupil Supervisor
Qualifications: [LLB (Hons) (L'pool)]
jane.tracyforster@hailshamchambers.com

TRAFFORD MR MARK RUSSELL

23 Essex Street
London WC2R 3AA, ☎ 020 7413 0353
✉ clerks@23es.com
Call Date: May 1992, Lincoln's Inn
Pupil Supervisor
Qualifications: [BSc (Hons) (Brunel) Dip Law (Lond)]
marktrafford@23es.com

TRAIN MISS SOPHIE ALEXANDRA

Renaissance Chambers
5th Floor, Gray's Inn Chambers, Gray's Inn, London WC1R 5JA, ☎ 020 7404 1111
✉ clerks@renaissancechambers.co.uk
Call Date: July 2005, Middle Temple
Qualifications: [LLB (Hons)]
st@renaissancechambers.co.uk

TRAUGOTT MS ELISABETH SANTA

3 Stone Buildings
Ground Floor, 3 Stone Buildings, Lincoln's Inn, London WC2A 3XL, ☎ 020 7242 4937
✉ clerks@3sb.law.co.uk
Call Date: July 2011, Lincoln's Inn
Qualifications: [BA (Cantab) MA (Leeds) JD (USA)]

TRAVERS MR DANIEL GRANT

Exchange Chambers
One Derby Square, Derby Square, Liverpool L2 9XX, ☎ 0151 236 7747
✉ info@exchangechambers.co.uk
Exchange Chambers
7 Ralli Courts, West Riverside, Manchester M3 5FT, ☎ 0161 833 2722
Exchange Chambers
Oxford House, Oxford Row, Leeds LS1 3BE, ☎ 0113 203 1970
✉ spencer@exchangechambers.co.uk
Call Date: Oct 1999, Lincoln's Inn
Qualifications: [LLB (Hons)]
travers@exchangechambers.co.uk

E

TRAVERS MR DAVID QC (2010)

6 Pump Court
1st Floor, 6 Pump Court, Temple, London EC4Y 7AR, ☎ 020 7797 8400
✉ richardconstable@6pumpcourt.co.uk
6 Pump Court Chambers
6-8 Mill Street, Maidstone, Kent ME15 6XH, ☎ 01622 688094
✉ annexe@6pumpcourt.co.uk
Call Date: July 1981, Middle Temple
Pupil Supervisor
Qualifications: [LLB AKC LLM]
✉ davidtravers@6pumpcourt.co.uk

TRAVERS MR HUGH

Pump Court Chambers
Upper Ground Floor, 3 Pump Court, Temple, London EC4Y 7AJ, ☎ 020 7353 0711
✉ clerks@3pumpcourt.com
Pump Court Chambers
5 Temple Chambers, Temple Street, Swindon SN1 1SQ, ☎ 01793 539899
✉ clerks@3pumpcourt.com
Pump Court Chambers
31 Southgate Street, Winchester, Hampshire SO23 9EB, ☎ 01962 868 161
✉ clerks@3pumpcourt.com
Call Date: Nov 1988, Middle Temple
Qualifications: [MA (Cantab)]
✉ ht@3pumpcourt.com

TRAVERSI MR JOHN DAVID STEPHEN ANTONA

Nine Bedford Row
9 Bedford Row, London WC1R 4AZ, ☎ 020 7489 2727
✉ clerks@9bedfordrow.co.uk
Call Date: July 1977, Gray's Inn
Pupil Supervisor
Qualifications: [MA (Oxon)]
✉ john.traversi@9bedfordrow.co.uk

TRAYNOR MR DAVID ANDREW

15 Winckley Square
Preston PR1 3JJ, ☎ 01772 252828
✉ clerks@15winckleysq.co.uk
Call Date: Oct 2002, Lincoln's Inn
Qualifications: [BA (Oxon)]

TREADWELL MR BRIAN

Number 7 Harrington Street Chambers
7 Harrington Street, Liverpool L2 9YH, ☎ 0151 242 0707 ✉ clerks@7hs.co.uk
Call Date: Oct 2006, Lincoln's Inn
Qualifications: [LLB (L'pool)]
✉ brian.treadwell@7hs.co.uk

TREASURE MR FRANCIS SETON

42 Bedford Row
London WC1R 4LL, ☎ 020 7831 0222
✉ clerks@42br.com
Call Date: Feb 1980, Gray's Inn
Pupil Supervisor
Qualifications: [MA (Oxon)]
✉ francis.treasure@42br.com

Fax: 020 7831 2239;
DX: 201 London;
URL: www.42br.com/cv.asp?id=16

Types of work: Commercial law, Common law (general), Personal injury, Professional negligence

TREBLE MR PAUL JOSEPH

St Johns Buildings Liverpool
8th Floor India Buildings, Water Street, Liverpool L2 0XG, ☎ 0151 243 6000
✉ clerk@stjohnsbuildings.co.uk
Call Date: Nov 1994, Lincoln's Inn
Pupil Supervisor
Qualifications: [BSc (Hons)(Sheff) CPE (Manch)]
✉ Paul.Treble@stjohnsbuildings.co.uk

TREGEAR MR FRANCIS BENEDICT WILLIAM QC (2003)

XXIV Old Buildings
Ground Floor, 24 Old Buildings, Lincoln's Inn, London WC2A 3UP, ☎ 020 7691 2424
✉ clerks@xxiv.co.uk
Call Date: July 1980, Middle Temple
Qualifications: [BA (Cantab)]

TREGIDGO MR MARC GORDON

4 King's Bench Walk
2nd Floor, 4 King's Bench Walk, Temple, London EC4Y 7DL, ☎ 020 7822 7000
✉ clerks@4kbw.co.uk
Call Date: July 2002, Middle Temple
Qualifications: [LLB (Hons)]
✉ mt@4kbw.co.uk

TREGILGAS-DAVEY MR MARCUS IAN

Pump Court Chambers
31 Southgate Street, Winchester, Hampshire SO23 9EB, ☎ 01962 868 161
✉ clerks@3pumpcourt.com
Pump Court Chambers
Upper Ground Floor, 3 Pump Court, Temple, London EC4Y 7AJ, ☎ 020 7353 0711
✉ clerks@3pumpcourt.com

E

Pump Court Chambers
5 Temple Chambers, Temple Street, Swindon SN1 1SQ, ☎01793 539899
✉clerks@3pumpcourt.com
Call Date: Feb 1993, Gray's Inn
Qualifications: [LLB (So'ton) LLM (Cantab)]

TREGONING MR BRUCE

Crown Office Row Chambers
119 Church Street, Brighton, Sussex BN1 1UD, ☎01273 625625
✉clerks@1cor.com
Call Date: Mar 2009, Middle Temple
Qualifications: [BA (Hons) (Wales) Dip in Law]
bruce.tregoning@1cor.com

TREHARNE MISS JENNET MARY LLOYD

30 Park Place
Cardiff CF10 3BS, ☎029 2039 8421
✉clerks@30parkplace.law.co.uk
Hardwicke
New Square, Lincoln's Inn, London WC2A 3SB, ☎020 7242 2523
✉enquiries@hardwicke.co.uk
Call Date: July 1975, Middle Temple
Pupil Supervisor
Qualifications: [LLB (Lond)]
jmt@30parkplace.co.uk

E

TREHARNE MR NEIL SIMON

Dingle Chambers
1 Chardstock Avenue, Coombe Dingle, Bristol BS9 2RY, ☎07818 827754
✉N.treharne@btinternet.com
Call Date: Nov 2001, Lincoln's Inn
Qualifications: [LLB (Hons)(Bris)]

TREMBATH MR GRAHAM ROBERT QC (2003)

Five Paper Buildings
1st Floor, Five Paper Buildings, Temple, London EC4Y 7HB, ☎020 7583 6117
✉clerks@5pb.co.uk
Westgate Chambers
64 High Street, Lewes, East Sussex BN7 1XG, ☎01273 480510
✉clerks@westgate-chambers.co.uk
Call Date: July 1978, Middle Temple
Qualifications: [LLB (Soton)]
gt@5pb.co.uk

TRENEER MR EDWARD MARK

Walnut House
63 St. David's Hill, Exeter, Devon EX4 4DW, ☎01392 279751
✉clerks@walnuthouse.co.uk
Call Date: July 1987, Inner Temple
Qualifications: [BA (So'ton) Dip Law (Lond) MA (Lond)]

TREPTE MR PETER ARMIN

Littleton Chambers
3 King's Bench Walk North, Temple, London EC4Y 7HR, ☎020 7797 8600
✉fschneider@littletonchambers.co.uk
Call Date: July 1987, Gray's Inn
Qualifications: [BA (Hons) Licence en Droit]

TRESMAN MR LEWIS ROBERT SIMON

Staple Inn Chambers
1st Floor, 9 Staple Inn, Holborn Bars, London WC1V 7QH, ☎020 7242 5240
✉clerks@stapleinn.co.uk
Call Date: Nov 1980, Gray's Inn
Pupil Supervisor
Qualifications: [LLB (Hons) (Reading)]
rt@stapleinn.co.uk

TRESMAN MISS SARAH RACHEL BEATRICE

20 Essex Street
London WC2R 3AL, ☎020 7842 1200
✉clerks@20essexst.com
Call Date: Oct 2008, Middle Temple
Qualifications: [LLB (Hons) (Lond) BCL of (Oxon)]
clerks@20essexst.com

TREVERTON-JONES MR GREGORY DENNIS QC (2002)

39 Essex Street
London WC2R 3AT, ☎020 7832 1111
✉clerks@39essex.com
82 King Street
Manchester M2 4WQ, ☎0161 870 9969
Call Date: Nov 1977, Inner Temple
Qualifications: [MA (Oxon)]
gregtj@39essex.com

TREVIS MR ROBERT JAMES

Clerksroom (Taunton)
Equity House, Administration Centre, Blackbrook Park Avenue, Taunton, Somerset TA1 2PX, ☎0845 083 3000
✉mail@clerksroom.com
King's Lynn Chambers
26 The Birches, South Wootton, King's Lynn, Norfolk PE30 3JG, ☎01553 672 085
✉timothy.leader@tesco.net
Call Date: Feb 1990, Inner Temple
Pupil Supervisor
Qualifications: [LLB]
trevis@clerksroom.com

TRIDIMAS PROF PANAGIOTIS TAKIS

Matrix Chambers
Griffin Building, Gray's Inn, London WC1R 5LN, ☎020 7404 3447
✉matrix@matrixlaw.co.uk / Iscott@matrixlaw.co.uk
Call Date: July 2000, Middle Temple
Qualifications: [LLB (Athens) PhD (Cantab) LLM]
Takistridimas@matrixlaw.co.uk

TRIGG MR MILES HADDON

4 Breams Buildings
Chancery Lane, London EC4A 1HP, ☎020 7092 1900 ✉clerks@4bb.co.uk
Call Date: July 1987, Inner Temple
Qualifications: [LLB (Hons) (Lond)]

TRIGGER MR SIMON

1 Chancery Lane
London WC2A 1LF, ☎0845 634 6666
✉clerks@1chancerylane.com
Call Date: Oct 2000, Middle Temple
Qualifications: [BA (Hons) (Cantab) CPE Dip Law (Guildford)]
strigger@1chancerylane.com

TRIMMER MS CAROL JANE

Wilberforce Chambers
7 Bishop Lane, Hull HU1 1PA, ☎01482 323264
Call Date: Nov 1993, Gray's Inn
Pupil Supervisor
Qualifications: [LLB (Hull)]

TRIMMER MR STUART ALAN QC (2006)

4 Breams Buildings
Chancery Lane, London EC4A 1HP, ☎020 7092 1900 ✉clerks@4bb.co.uk
Call Date: July 1977, Gray's Inn
Qualifications: [LLB (Lond)]

TRIPPIER LADY RUTH

Deans Court Chambers
24 St John Street, Manchester M3 4DF, ☎0161 214 6000 ✉clerks@deanscourt.co.uk
Deans Court Chambers
101 Walker Street, Preston PR1 2RR, ☎01772 565 600
✉preston@deanscourt.co.uk
Call Date: July 1978, Gray's Inn
Qualifications: [LLB (Manch)]
trippier@deanscourt.co.uk

TRITTON MR ROBERT GUY HENTON

Hogarth Chambers
5 New Square, Lincoln's Inn, London WC2A 3RJ, ☎020 7404 0404
✉barristers@hogarthchambers.com
Call Date: July 1987, Inner Temple
Pupil Supervisor
Qualifications: [BSc (Dunelm) Dip Law]
gtritton@hogarthchambers.com

TROLLOPE MR ANDREW DAVID HEDDERWICK QC (1991)

187 Fleet Street
London EC4A 2AT, ☎020 7430 7430
✉chambers@187fleetstreet.com
Call Date: Nov 1971, Inner Temple
Recorder
andrewtrollope@187fleetstreet.com

TROMAN MR CARL RUSSELL

Four New Square
Four New Square, Lincoln's Inn, London WC2A 3RJ, ☎020 7822 2000
✉barristers@4newsquare.com
Call Date: July 2001, Lincoln's Inn
Qualifications: [LLB (Hons) Dip PLS]
c.troman@4newsquare.com

TROMANS MR STEPHEN RICHARD QC (2009)

39 Essex Street
London WC2R 3AT, ☎020 7832 1111
✉clerks@39essex.com
82 King Street
Manchester M2 4WQ, ☎0161 870 9969
Riverview Chambers
Hamilton House, 1 Temple Avenue, London EC4Y 0HA, ☎0844 225 3999
✉chrisbaylis@riverviewchambers.com
Call Date: July 1999, Inner Temple
Qualifications: [MA]

E

TROMPETER MR NICHOLAS SIMEON

Selborne Chambers
10 Essex Street, London WC2R 3AA,
☎020 7420 9500
✉clerks@selbornechambers.co.uk
Call Date: July 2006, Gray's Inn
Qualifications: [MA (Oxon) Dip Law]
nicholas.trompeter@selbornechambers.co.uk

TROOP MR PAUL BENJAMIN

Tooks Chambers
81 Farringdon Street, London EC4A 4BL,
☎020 7842 7575 ✉clerks@tooks.co.uk
Call Date: Oct 1998, Lincoln's Inn
Pupil Supervisor
Qualifications: [LLB (Hons)(B'ham) MA (KCL)]
paul.troop@tooks.co.uk

TRORY MR HENRY NATHANIEL CURTIS

Dere Street Barristers
14 Toft Green, York YO1 6JT, ☎0844 3351551
✉clerks@derestreet.co.uk
York Chambers
Rotterdam House, 116 The Quayside, Newcastle Upon Tyne NE1 3DY,
☎0191 206 4677
Call Date: Nov 2003, Middle Temple
Qualifications: [BA (Hons) (Leeds) CPE]
clerks@yorkchambers.co.uk, htroy@yorkchambers.co.uk

E

TROTMAN MR TIMOTHY OLIVER

Deans Court Chambers
24 St John Street, Manchester M3 4DF,
☎0161 214 6000 ✉clerks@deanscourt.co.uk
Deans Court Chambers
101 Walker Street, Preston PR1 2RR,
☎01772 565 600
✉preston@deanscourt.co.uk
Call Date: July 1983, Middle Temple
Qualifications: [MA (Cantab)]
trotman@deanscourt.co.uk

TROTTER MISS HELEN CLAIRE

Pump Court Chambers
Upper Ground Floor, 3 Pump Court, Temple, London EC4Y 7AJ, ☎020 7353 0711
✉clerks@3pumpcourt.com
Pump Court Chambers
5 Temple Chambers, Temple Street, Swindon SN1 1SQ, ☎01793 539899
✉clerks@3pumpcourt.com
Pump Court Chambers
31 Southgate Street, Winchester, Hampshire SO23 9EB, ☎01962 868 161
✉clerks@3pumpcourt.com
Call Date: Oct 2004, Gray's Inn
Qualifications: [LLB]
hct@3pumpcourt.com

TROUP MR ALEXANDER WILLIAM

St John's Chambers
101 Victoria Street, Bristol BS1 6PU,
☎0117 923 4700
✉clerks@stjohnschambers.co.uk
Call Date: Nov 1998, Gray's Inn
Pupil Supervisor
Qualifications: [MA (Oxon)]
Alex.Troup@stjohnschambers.co.uk

TROUP MISS RACHEL ELIZABETH

Pump Court Chambers
31 Southgate Street, Winchester, Hampshire SO23 9EB, ☎01962 868 161
✉clerks@3pumpcourt.com
Pump Court Chambers
Upper Ground Floor, 3 Pump Court, Temple, London EC4Y 7AJ, ☎020 7353 0711
✉clerks@3pumpcourt.com
Pump Court Chambers
5 Temple Chambers, Temple Street, Swindon SN1 1SQ, ☎01793 539899
✉clerks@3pumpcourt.com
Call Date: Nov 2005, Lincoln's Inn
Qualifications: [LLB (Hons)]
ret@3pumpcourt.com

TROWELL MR STEPHEN MARK

1 Hare Court
1 Hare Court, Temple, London EC4Y 7BE,
☎020 7797 7070 ✉clerks@1hc.com
Call Date: Oct 1995, Middle Temple
Pupil Supervisor
Qualifications: [MA (Oxon) D.Phil (Oxon)]
trowell@1hc.com

TROWER MR WILLIAM SPENCER PHILIP QC (2001)

South Square
3-4 South Square, Gray's Inn, London WC1R 5HP, ☎020 7696 9900
✉practicemanagers@southsquare.com
Call Date: July 1983, Lincoln's Inn
Qualifications: [MA (Oxon)]
williamtrower@southsquare.com

TROWLER MS REBECCA QC (2012)

Doughty Street Chambers
53-54 Doughty Street, London WC1N 2LS, ☎ 020 7404 1313
✉ enquiries@doughtystreet.co.uk
Doughty Street Chambers
Pall Mall Court, 61-67 King Street, Manchester M2 4PD, ☎ 0161 618 1066
Doughty Street Chambers
5th Floor, Broad Quay House, Prince Street, Bristol BS1 4DJ, ☎ 01179 058 717
Call Date: Oct 1995, Gray's Inn
Pupil Supervisor
Qualifications: [B.Sc]
r.trowler@doughtystreet.co.uk

TROY MRS JILL MARY

No.6 Park Square
Leeds LS1 2LW, ☎ 0113 245 9763
✉ Tim@no6.co.uk
Call Date: July 1986, Middle Temple
Pupil Supervisor
Qualifications: [BA (Oxon)]
troy@no6.co.uk

TROY MISS KAREN

Exchange Chambers
One Derby Square, Derby Square, Liverpool L2 9XX, ☎ 0151 236 7747
✉ info@exchangechambers.co.uk
Exchange Chambers
7 Ralli Courts, West Riverside, Manchester M3 5FT, ☎ 0161 833 2722
Exchange Chambers
Oxford House, Oxford Row, Leeds LS1 3BE, ☎ 0113 203 1970
✉ spencer@exchangechambers.co.uk
Call Date: July 1981, Lincoln's Inn
Qualifications: [BA (Oxon) LLM (USA)]
troy@exchangechambers.co.uk

TROY MS PAULINE MARIE

42 Bedford Row
London WC1R 4LL, ☎ 020 7831 0222
✉ clerks@42br.com
Call Date: Oct 2011, Lincoln's Inn
Qualifications: [LLB (Exon)]
clerks@42br.com

TRUMBLE MR JAMES MATTHEW

Field Court Chambers
5 Field Court, Gray's Inn, London WC1R 5EF, ☎ 020 7405 6114 ✉ clerks@fieldcourt.co.uk
Call Date: Mar 2006, Middle Temple
Qualifications: [BA (Hons) (Cardiff) LPC]

TRUMPER MISS SARA KATHERINE

Southernhay Chambers
33 Southernhay East, Exeter EX1 1NX, ☎ 01392 255777
✉ clerks@southernhaychambers.co.uk
Call Date: Nov 1996, Lincoln's Inn
Pupil Supervisor
Qualifications: [BA (Hons)(Lond)]
s.trumper@southernhaychambers.co.uk

TRUMPINGTON MR JOHN HENRY

Staple Inn Chambers
1st Floor, 9 Staple Inn, Holborn Bars, London WC1V 7QH, ☎ 020 7242 5240
✉ clerks@stapleinn.co.uk
Call Date: Feb 1985, Middle Temple
Pupil Supervisor
Qualifications: [BA (Hons)]
jht@stapleinn.co.uk

TRUSCOTT MISS CAROLINE

39 Essex Street
London WC2R 3AT, ☎ 020 7832 1111
✉ clerks@39essex.com
82 King Street
Manchester M2 4WQ, ☎ 0161 870 9969
Call Date: Nov 1998, Lincoln's Inn
Qualifications: [LLB (Hons)(LSE) BCL (Oxon)]
caroline.truscott@39essex.com

TRUSCOTT MR IAN DEREK

Old Square Chambers
10-11 Bedford Row, London WC1R 4BU, ☎ 020 7269 0300 ✉ clerks@oldsquare.co.uk
Old Square Chambers
3 Orchard Court, St Augustine's Yard, Bristol BS1 5DP, ☎ 0117 930 5100
✉ clerks@oldsquare.co.uk
Call Date: Nov 1995, Gray's Inn
Qualifications: [LLB (Edin) LLM (Leeds)]
truscottqc@oldsquare.co.uk

TRUSSLER MR JONATHAN ANDREW

The Chambers Of Mr Jonathan Trussler
3 York Parade, Great West Road, Brentford, Middlesex TW8 9AA
Call Date: Nov 1987, Gray's Inn
Qualifications: [LLB (Hons) (Wales) F Inst BA]

TRUSTED MR JAMES HARRY

Outer Temple Chambers
The Outer Temple, 222 Strand, London WC2R 1BA, ☎ 020 7353 6381
✉ clerks@outertemple.com
Call Date: July 1985, Inner Temple
Pupil Supervisor
Qualifications: [MA (Cantab)]

E

TRUSTMAN MRS JUDITH ANN

Garden Court Chambers
57-60 Lincoln's Inn Fields, London WC2A 3LJ, ☎020 7993 7600 ✉info@gclaw.co.uk
Call Date: Oct 1996, Middle Temple
Qualifications: [LLB (Hons)(Notts)]
✉juditht@gclaw.co.uk

TSELENTIS MR MICHAEL QC (2003)

20 Essex Street
London WC2R 3AL, ☎020 7842 1200
✉clerks@20essexst.com
Call Date: Nov 1995, Gray's Inn
Qualifications: [BA, LLB (Cape Town) BCL (Oxon)]
✉clerks@20essexst.com

TUCK MISS REBECCA LOUISE

Old Square Chambers
10-11 Bedford Row, London WC1R 4BU, ☎020 7269 0300 ✉clerks@oldsquare.co.uk
Old Square Chambers
3 Orchard Court, St Augustine's Yard, Bristol BS1 5DP, ☎0117 930 5100
✉clerks@oldsquare.co.uk
Call Date: Oct 1998, Gray's Inn
Pupil Supervisor
Qualifications: [BA (Oxon)]
✉tuck@oldsquare.co.uk

TUCKER MR ANDREW RICHARD SMETHURST

Cornwall Street Chambers
85-87 Cornwall Street, Birmingham B3 3BY, ☎0121 233 7500
✉clerks@cornwallstreet.co.uk
Call Date: July 1977, Middle Temple
Pupil Supervisor
Qualifications: [LLB (Sheffield)]
✉andrew.tucker@cornwallstreet.co.uk

TUCKER MR ASHLEY RUSSELL

Park Court Chambers
16 Park Place, Leeds LS1 2SJ, ☎0113 243 3277
✉clerks@parkcourtchambers.co.uk
Call Date: Nov 1990, Middle Temple
Pupil Supervisor
Qualifications: [BA (Manch) Dip Law (Lond)]
✉art@parkcourtchambers.co.uk

TUCKER MR IAN JAMES

Exchange Chambers
7 Ralli Courts, West Riverside, Manchester M3 5FT, ☎0161 833 2722
Exchange Chambers
One Derby Square, Derby Square, Liverpool L2 9XX, ☎0151 236 7747
✉info@exchangechambers.co.uk
Exchange Chambers
Oxford House, Oxford Row, Leeds LS1 3BE, ☎0113 203 1970
✉spencer@exchangechambers.co.uk
Call Date: July 2010, Middle Temple
Qualifications: [BSc (Hons)(Lond)]

TUCKER MR JAMES ECKHORD

Queen Square Chambers
56 Queen Square, Bristol BS1 4PR, ☎0117 921 1966 ✉crime@qs-c.co.uk
Call Date: Oct 2004, Gray's Inn
Qualifications: [MA]
✉jet@qs-c.co.uk

TUCKER MR JAMES WILLIAM RICHARD

Teucro Chambers
Global House, 1 Ashley Avenue, Epsom, Surrey KT18 5AD
Call Date: July 2002, Middle Temple
Qualifications: [LLB (Hons)]

TUCKER MRS LORRAINE JEAN

18 Red Lion Court (Annexe)
Thornwood House, 102 New London Road, Chelmsford, Essex CM2 0RG, ☎01245 280880
18 Red Lion Court
London EC4A 3EB, ☎020 7520 6000
✉chambers@18rlc.co.uk
Call Date: Nov 1982, Middle Temple
Pupil Supervisor
Qualifications: [BA]

TUCKER MR LYNTON ANTHONY

New Square Chambers
12 New Square, Lincoln's Inn, London WC2A 3SW, ☎020 7419 8000
✉robin.hollington@newsquarechambers.co.uk
Call Date: Feb 1971, Lincoln's Inn
Pupil Supervisor
Qualifications: [MA BCL (Oxon)]
✉lynton.tucker@newsquarechambers.co.uk

TUCKER MR NICHOLAS JAMES

12 College Place
Fauvelle Buildings, 12 College Place, Southampton SO15 2FE, ☎ 023 8032 0320
✉ clerks@12cp.co.uk
Call Date: Oct 1993, Inner Temple
Pupil Supervisor
Qualifications: [MA]
✉ NTucker@12cp.co.uk

TUCKER MR PAUL GEOFFREY QC (2010)

Kings Chambers
36 Young Street, Manchester M3 3FT, ☎ 0845 034 3444
✉ clerks@kingschambers.com
Kings Chambers
5 Park Square East, Leeds LS1 2NE, ☎ 0845 034 3444
✉ clerks@kingschambers.com
Kings Chambers
Embassy House, 60 Church Street, Birmingham B3 2DJ, ☎ 0845 034 3444
✉ clerks@kingschambers.com
Call Date: Nov 1990, Gray's Inn
Pupil Supervisor
Qualifications: [MA (Cantab)]
✉ ptucker@kingschambers.com

TUDOR-EVANS MR QUINTIN JOHN

12 King's Bench Walk
12 King's Bench Walk, Temple, London EC4Y 7EL, ☎ 020 7583 0811
Call Date: July 1977, Lincoln's Inn
Pupil Supervisor
✉ qte@btinternet.com

TUEJE MISS PATRICIA

1 Pump Court
Elm Court, Temple, London EC4Y 7AB, ☎ 020 7842 7070
✉ (name)@pumpcourt.co.uk
Call Date: Mar 1999, Inner Temple
Qualifications: [BSc (So'ton) CPE]
✉ pt@1pumpcourt.co.uk

TUGHAN MR JOHN CHARLES RONALD

4 Paper Buildings
1st Floor, 4 Paper Buildings, Temple, London EC4Y 7EX, ☎ 020 7427 5200
✉ clerks@4pb.com
Call Date: Nov 1991, Inner Temple
Pupil Supervisor
Qualifications: [LLB (L'pool)]
✉ jt@4pb.com

TULLY MS ANNE MARGARET

Eastbourne Chambers
5 Chiswick Place, Eastbourne, East Sussex BN21 4NH, ☎ 01323 642102
✉ clerks@eastbournechambers.co.uk
Call Date: July 1989, Gray's Inn
Qualifications: [MA (Cantab) LLM (Cantab)]

TULLY MR PHILIP SEAN

Number 7 Harrington Street Chambers
7 Harrington Street, Liverpool L2 9YH, ☎ 0151 242 0707 ✉ clerks@7hs.co.uk
Call Date: Oct 2000, Middle Temple
Pupil Supervisor
Qualifications: [CPE (Manch)]

TULLY MR RAYMOND PETER

Guildhall Chambers
23 Broad Street, Bristol BS1 2HG, ☎ 0117 930 9000
✉ hoc@guildhallchambers.co.uk
Call Date: Nov 1987, Inner Temple
Pupil Supervisor
Qualifications: [BA (Keele) Dip Law (Lond)]
✉ ray.tully@guildhallchambers.co.uk

TUNG MS HELEN

Temple Court Chambers
2nd Floor, 2 Dr Johnson's Building, Temple, London EC4Y 7AY, ☎ 020 7353 7888
✉ clerks@templecourt.co.uk
Call Date: Nov 2009, Gray's Inn
Qualifications: [LLB]
✉ helen.tung@templecourt.co.uk

TUNKEL MR ALAN MICHAEL

3 Stone Buildings
Ground Floor, 3 Stone Buildings, Lincoln's Inn, London WC2A 3XL, ☎ 020 7242 4937
✉ clerks@3sb.law.co.uk
Call Date: July 1976, Middle Temple
Pupil Supervisor
Qualifications: [BA (Oxon)]
✉ atunkel@3sb.law.co.uk

Types of work: Chancery (general), Chancery (land law), Charities, Commercial law, Commercial litigation, Commercial property, Company, commercial and competition, Conveyancing, Equity, Family provision, Insolvency, Landlord and tenant, Partnerships, Personal insolvency, Professional negligence, Succession, Trusts, Wills

E

TUNLEY MR JAMES CHRISTOPHER GORDON

4 KBW
Ground Floor, 4 King's Bench Walk, Temple, London EC4Y 7DL, ☎020 7822 8822
✉law@4kbw.net
Call Date: July 2005, Lincoln's Inn
Qualifications: [LLB (Hons)]
jt@4kbw.net

TURKSON MR NII TETTEH

23 Essex Street
London WC2R 3AA, ☎020 7413 0353
✉clerks@23es.com
Call Date: Oct 1998, Gray's Inn
Qualifications: [LLB (Lond)]
tettehturkson@23es.com

TURNBULL MISS HELEN MARY

Lamb Chambers
Lamb Building, Elm Court, Temple, London EC4Y 7AS, ☎020 7797 8300
✉info@lambchambers.co.uk
Call Date: Nov 2004, Inner Temple
Qualifications: [BA Balliol College University of Oxford]
helenturnbull@lambchambers.co.uk

TURNBULL MRS LINDA ANGELA

1 Gray's Inn Square
Ground Floor, 1 Gray's Inn Square, London WC1R 5AA, ☎020 7405 0001
Call Date: Mar 1998, Lincoln's Inn
Pupil Supervisor
Qualifications: [LLB (Northumbria) LLM (Dunelm)]
clerks@1gis.law.co.uk

TURNER MISS ABIGAIL JAYNE

Northampton Chambers
10 Spencer Parade, Northampton NN1 5AQ, ☎01604 636271
✉clerks@northampton-chambers.co.uk
Call Date: Oct 2006, Middle Temple
Qualifications: [LLB (Hons)]
aturner@northampton-chambers.co.uk

TURNER MR ADAM DAVID CHARLES

7 King's Bench Walk
Ground Floor, 7 King's Bench Walk, Temple, London EC4Y 7DS, ☎020 7910 8300
✉clerks@7kbw.co.uk
Call Date: Oct 2008, Lincoln's Inn
Qualifications: [BA BCL (Oxon)]
aturner@7kbw.co.uk

TURNER MR ADRIAN JOHN

The Chambers of Adrian Turner
4 Charleston Road, Eastbourne BN21 1SF, ☎01323 737388
Call Date: Feb 1978, Gray's Inn
Qualifications: [LLB]
turnerchambers@iorange.net

TURNER MR ALAN JOSEPH

Melbeck Chambers
86 Gospel End Road, Sedgley, Dudley, West Midlands DY3 3YU, ☎020 7404 2166
✉alan.turner@melbeck.com
Call Date: Nov 1984, Gray's Inn
Qualifications: [LLB MSc (Wales) BSc]
alan.turner@melbeck.com

TURNER MR ANDREW THOMAS

Clerksroom (Taunton)
Equity House, Administration Centre, Blackbrook Park Avenue, Taunton, Somerset TA1 2PX, ☎0845 083 3000
✉mail@clerksroom.com
King's Lynn Chambers
26 The Birches, South Wootton, King's Lynn, Norfolk PE30 3JG, ☎01553 672 085
✉timothy.leader@tesco.net
Call Date: Nov 2010, Lincoln's Inn
Qualifications: [LLB (Wolves)]
mail@clerksroom.com

TURNER MR DAVID BENJAMIN QC (2009)

Four New Square
Four New Square, Lincoln's Inn, London WC2A 3RJ, ☎020 7822 2000
✉barristers@4newsquare.com
Call Date: Nov 1992, Gray's Inn
Qualifications: [MA (Cantab)]
d.turner@4newsquare.com

TURNER MR JAMES QC (1998)

1 KBW Chambers
1 King's Bench Walk, Temple, London EC4Y 7DB, ☎020 7936 1500
✉clerks@1kbw.co.uk
King's Bench Chambers
174 High Street, Lewes BN7 1YE, ☎01273 402600
Call Date: July 1976, Inner Temple
Qualifications: [LLB Hons (Hull)]
jturnerqc@1kbw.co.uk

E

TURNER MR JAMES MICHAEL

Quadrant Chambers
Quadrant House, 10 Fleet Street, London EC4Y 1AU, ☎ 020 7583 4444
✉ info@quadrantchambers.com
Call Date: Oct 1990, Inner Temple
Pupil Supervisor
Qualifications: [BA (Dunelm) LLM(Germany) MIL]

TURNER MR JAMES PAUL

Harcourt Chambers
1st Floor, 2 Harcourt Buildings, Temple, London EC4Y 9DB, ☎ 0844 561 7135
Harcourt Chambers
Churchill House, 3 St Aldate's Courtyard, St Aldate's, Oxford OX1 1BN, ☎ 0844 561 7135
Call Date: July 2001, Inner Temple
Qualifications: [BSoc (So'ton)]
clerks@harcourtchambers.law.co.uk, JTurner@harcourtchambers.law.co.uk

TURNER MR JONATHAN CHADWICK QC (2003)

6 King's Bench Walk
Ground Floor, 6 King's Bench Walk, Temple, London EC4Y 7DR, ☎ 020 7583 0410
✉ clerks@6kbw.com
Exchange Chambers
One Derby Square, Derby Square, Liverpool L2 9XX, ☎ 0151 236 7747
✉ info@exchangechambers.co.uk
Exchange Chambers
7 Ralli Courts, West Riverside, Manchester M3 5FT, ☎ 0161 833 2722
Call Date: July 1974, Gray's Inn
Recorder
Qualifications: [LLB (Hons)(Lond)]
jonathan.turner@6kbw.com

TURNER MR JONATHAN DAVID CHATTYN

13 Old Square Chambers
Ground Floor, 14 Old Square, Lincoln's Inn, London WC2A 3UE, ☎ 020 7831 4445
✉ clerks@13oldsquare.com
Call Date: Feb 1982, Gray's Inn
Pupil Supervisor
Qualifications: [MA (Cantab) Lic Sp Dr Eur (Belgium)]
JDCT@13oldsquare.com

TURNER MR JONATHAN JAMES

Argent Chambers
5 Bell Yard, London WC2A 2JR, ☎ 020 7556 5500
✉ briefsin@argentchambers.co.uk
Call Date: Nov 1999, Inner Temple
Qualifications: [LLB (Lond)]

TURNER MR JONATHAN RICHARD QC (2006)

Monckton Chambers
1 & 2 Raymond Buildings, Gray's Inn, London WC1R 5NR, ☎ 020 7405 7211
✉ chambers@monckton.com
Call Date: Nov 1988, Middle Temple
Qualifications: [MA (Cantab) LLM (USA)]
jturner@monckton.com

TURNER MR JUSTIN JOHN QC (2009)

Three New Square IP
3 New Square, Lincoln's Inn, London WC2A 3RS, ☎ 020 7405 1111
✉ clerks@3newsquare.co.uk
Call Date: Nov 1992, Middle Temple
Qualifications: [Vet Med (Lond) Ph D (Cantab) Dip Law AFRC]
clerks@3newsquare.co.uk

TURNER MR JUSTYN ROBERT SURTEES

4 King's Bench Walk
2nd Floor, 4 King's Bench Walk, Temple, London EC4Y 7DL, ☎ 020 7822 7000
✉ clerks@4kbw.co.uk
Call Date: July 2001, Inner Temple
Qualifications: [LLB (Durham)]
jt@4kbw.co.uk

TURNER MR MARK GEORGE QC (1998)

Deans Court Chambers
24 St John Street, Manchester M3 4DF, ☎ 0161 214 6000 ✉ clerks@deanscourt.co.uk
Crown Office Chambers
2 Crown Office Row, Temple, London EC4Y 7HJ, ☎ 020 7797 8100
✉ mail@crownofficechambers.com
Call Date: July 1981, Gray's Inn
Recorder
Qualifications: [BA (Oxon)]
turner@deanscourt.co.uk

TURNER MR MATHEW JAMES LEYSHON

15 New Bridge Street
London EC4V 6AU, ☎ 020 7842 1900
✉ clerks@15nbs.com
Call Date: Oct 2003, Gray's Inn
Qualifications: [BA (Oxon)]
mathew.turner@15nbs.com

E

TURNER MR MICHAEL QC (2002)

Garden Court Chambers
57-60 Lincoln's Inn Fields, London WC2A 3LJ,
☎020 7993 7600 ✉info@gclaw.co.uk
Call Date: July 1981, Gray's Inn
Qualifications: [BA (Hons)]
✉michaelt@gclaw.co.uk

TURNER MS NICOLA GAIL

Number 7 Harrington Street Chambers
7 Harrington Street, Liverpool L2 9YH,
☎0151 242 0707 ✉clerks@7hs.co.uk
Call Date: Nov 1995, Gray's Inn
Qualifications: [LLB (L'pool)]
✉nicola.turner@7hs.co.uk

TURNER MR PAUL ANTONY

10 King's Bench Walk
Ground Floor, 10 King's Bench Walk, Temple, London EC4Y 7EB, ☎020 7353 7742
✉Chambers@10kingsbenchwalk.co.uk
Call Date: Nov 1998, Lincoln's Inn
Qualifications: [LLB (Hons)(Sussex)]
✉chambers@10kingsbenchwalk.co.uk

TURNER MR STEVEN MURRAY

Park Lane Plowden
19 Westgate, Leeds LS1 2RD,
☎0113 228 5049
✉clerks@parklaneplowden.co.uk
Call Date: Nov 1993, Middle Temple
Pupil Supervisor
Qualifications: [BA (Hons) (Kent) CPE (Notts)]
✉steven.turner@parklaneplowden.co.uk

TURNER MRS TARYN JONES

Park Court Chambers
16 Park Place, Leeds LS1 2SJ,
☎0113 243 3277
✉clerks@parkcourtchambers.co.uk
Call Date: Feb 1990, Gray's Inn
Pupil Supervisor, Recorder
Qualifications: [LLB (Hons)]
✉tarynjonesturner@yahoo.co.uk

TURNEY MR RICHARD WILLIAM

Landmark Chambers
180 Fleet Street, London EC4A 2HG,
☎020 7430 1221
✉clerks@landmarkchambers.co.uk
Call Date: Oct 2007, Gray's Inn
Qualifications: [BA (Cantab) LLM (Lond)]
✉rturney@landmarkchambers.co.uk

TURNILL MR EVAN

Pallant Chambers
12 North Pallant, Chichester, West Sussex PO19 1TQ, ☎01243 784538
✉clerks@pallantchambers.co.uk
Call Date: July 2003, Gray's Inn
Qualifications: [LLB (Leic)]
✉eturnill@pallantchambers.co.uk

TURTON MR ANDREW PHILIP

Carmelite Chambers
9 Carmelite Street, London EC4Y 0DR,
☎020 7936 6300
✉clerks@carmelitechambers.co.uk
Call Date: July 1977, Middle Temple
Pupil Supervisor
Qualifications: [LLB (Lond) AKC]
✉aturton@carmelitechambers.co.uk

TURTON MR PHILIP JOHN

Ropewalk Chambers
24 The Ropewalk, Nottingham NG1 5EF,
☎0115 947 2581 ✉clerks@ropewalk.co.uk
Call Date: Nov 1989, Gray's Inn
Pupil Supervisor
Qualifications: [LLB (Wales)]
✉philipturton@ropewalk.co.uk

TURTON MR ROBERT EDMUND

Fountain Chambers
Cleveland Business Centre, 1 Watson Street, Middlesbrough TS1 2RQ, ☎01642 804040
✉clerks@fountainchambers.co.uk
Call Date: July 1996, Inner Temple
Qualifications: [BA (Dunelm) CPE]

TUTT MR RICHARD MICHAEL FRUGARD

Pump Court Chambers
Upper Ground Floor, 3 Pump Court, Temple, London EC4Y 7AJ, ☎020 7353 0711
✉clerks@3pumpcourt.com
Pump Court Chambers
5 Temple Chambers, Temple Street, Swindon SN1 1SQ, ☎01793 539899
✉clerks@3pumpcourt.com
Pump Court Chambers
31 Southgate Street, Winchester, Hampshire SO23 9EB, ☎01962 868 161
✉clerks@3pumpcourt.com
Call Date: July 2000, Middle Temple
Pupil Supervisor
Qualifications: [LLB(Hons) (B'ham)]
✉rt@3pumpcourt.com

E

TWEEDDALE MRS KEREN DANIELLE

Tweeddale Chambers
3 Atwood Avenue, Kew, Richmond, Surrey TW9 4HF, ☎020 8940 9896
✉tweeddale@blueyonder.co.uk
Call Date: Oct 1991, Lincoln's Inn
Qualifications: [BA (Hons) (Lond)]
✉tweeddale@blueyonder.co.uk

TWEEDY MS LAURA ELIZABETH

Hardwicke
New Square, Lincoln's Inn, London WC2A 3SB, ☎020 7242 2523
✉enquiries@hardwicke.co.uk
Call Date: July 2007, Lincoln's Inn
Qualifications: [LLB (Dunelm) MJur (Dunelm)]
✉laura.tweedy@hardwicke.co.uk

TWIGGER MR ANDREW MARK QC (2011)

3 Stone Buildings
Ground Floor, 3 Stone Buildings, Lincoln's Inn, London WC2A 3XL, ☎020 7242 4937
✉clerks@3sb.law.co.uk
Call Date: Nov 1994, Inner Temple
Pupil Supervisor
Qualifications: [BA (Oxon) CPE (City)]
✉atwigger@3sb.law.co.uk

TWINE MISS NICOLA

Park Lane Plowden
19 Westgate, Leeds LS1 2RD, ☎0113 228 5049
✉clerks@parklaneplowden.co.uk
Call Date: July 1999, Middle Temple
Qualifications: [LLB (Hons)]
✉nicola.twine@parklaneplowden.co.uk

TWIST MR STEPHEN JOHN

Dere Street Barristers
33 Broad Chare, Newcastle Upon Tyne NE1 3DQ, ☎0844 3351551
✉clerks@derestreet.co.uk
Call Date: July 1979, Middle Temple
Pupil Supervisor
Qualifications: [LLB (L'pool) CACDPI]
✉s.twist@darestreet.co.uk

TWOMEY MR MARK JAMES JOHN

Coram Chambers
9-11 Fulwood Place, London WC1V 6HG, ☎020 7092 3700
✉mail@coramchambers.co.uk
Call Date: Nov 1990, Inner Temple
Qualifications: [LLB (Bris)]
✉mark.twomey@coramchambers.co.uk

TWYDELL MISS CHERRY LOUISA

Trinity Chambers
Highfield House, Moulsham Street, Chelmsford, Essex CM2 9AH, ☎01245 605040
✉clerks@trinitychambers.com
Call Date: May 1985, Middle Temple
Qualifications: [BA (Hons)]
✉ctwydell@trinitychambers.com

TYACK MR DAVID GUY

No5 Chambers
Fountain Court, Steelhouse Lane, Birmingham B4 6DR, ☎0845 210 5555 ✉info@no5.com
Exchange Chambers
7 Ralli Courts, West Riverside, Manchester M3 5FT, ☎0161 833 2722
Exchange Chambers
Oxford House, Oxford Row, Leeds LS1 3BE, ☎0113 203 1970
✉spencer@exchangechambers.co.uk
No5 Chambers
38 Queen Square, Bristol BS1 4QS, ☎0845 210 5555
No5 Chambers
Greenwood House, 4-7 Salisbury Court, London EC4Y 8AA, ☎0845 210 5555
Exchange Chambers
One Derby Square, Derby Square, Liverpool L2 9XX, ☎0151 236 7747
✉info@exchangechambers.co.uk
Call Date: Nov 1994, Middle Temple
Qualifications: [BA (Hons)]
✉dgt@no5.com

TYERS-SMITH MR PETER JAMES

No5 Chambers
Fountain Court, Steelhouse Lane, Birmingham B4 6DR, ☎0845 210 5555 ✉info@no5.com
No5 Chambers
Greenwood House, 4-7 Salisbury Court, London EC4Y 8AA, ☎0845 210 5555
No5 Chambers
38 Queen Square, Bristol BS1 4QS, ☎0845 210 5555
Call Date: Nov 2005, Lincoln's Inn
Qualifications: [LLB (Hons) Northampton]
✉pts@no5.com

TYLER MISS KATHERINE LOUISE

9-12 Bell Yard
London WC2A 2JR, ☎020 7400 1800
✉clerks@9-12bellyard.com
Call Date: Nov 2007, Inner Temple
Qualifications: [BA (Warwick)]
✉k.tyler@9-12bellyard.com

E

TYLER MISS SARAH ELIZABETH

Coram Chambers
9-11 Fulwood Place, London WC1V 6HG,
☎ 020 7092 3700
✉ mail@coramchambers.co.uk
Call Date: Oct 2009, Inner Temple
Qualifications: [BSc (Bris)]
✉ sarah.tyler@coramchambers.co.uk

TYLER MR THOMAS GEOFFREY

3 PB Barristers
3 Paper Buildings, Temple, London EC4Y 7EU,
☎ 020 7583 8055
3 PB Barristers
Royal Talbot House, 2 Victoria Street, Bristol, Avon BS1 6BB, ☎ 0117 928 1520
3 PB Barristers
4 St Peter Street, Winchester SO23 8BW,
☎ 01962 868884
✉ clerks.winchester@3paper.co.uk
3 PB Barristers
23 Beaumont Street, Oxford OX1 2NP,
☎ 01865 793 736
3 PB Barristers
30 Christchurch Road, Bournemouth, Dorset BH1 3PD, ☎ 01202 292102
✉ clerks.bournemouth@3paper.co.uk
Call Date: Oct 1996, Lincoln's Inn
Qualifications: [LLB (Hons)(Lond)]
✉ tom.tyler@3pb.co.uk

E

TYLER MR WILLIAM JOHN

Deans Court Chambers
24 St John Street, Manchester M3 4DF,
☎ 0161 214 6000 ✉ clerks@deanscourt.co.uk
Deans Court Chambers
101 Walker Street, Preston PR1 2RR,
☎ 01772 565 600
✉ preston@deanscourt.co.uk
Call Date: Oct 2003, Inner Temple
Qualifications: [BA (B'ham)]
✉ tyler@deanscourt.co.uk

TYLER MR WILLIAM JOHN

36 Bedford Row
London WC1R 4JH, ☎ 020 7421 8000
✉ chambers@36bedfordrow.co.uk
Call Date: Oct 1996, Inner Temple
Qualifications: [MA (Hons)(Oxon)]
✉ WTyler@36bedfordrow.co.uk, clerks@36bedfordrow.co.uk

TYRELL MR GLEN

Four New Square
Four New Square, Lincoln's Inn, London WC2A 3RJ, ☎ 020 7822 2000
✉ barristers@4newsquare.com
Call Date: July 1977, Inner Temple
Pupil Supervisor
Qualifications: [LLB]
✉ g.tyrell@4newsquare.com

TYRRELL MR RICHARD MARK LAWRENCE

Crown Office Chambers
2 Crown Office Row, Temple, London EC4Y 7HJ, ☎ 020 7797 8100
✉ mail@crownofficechambers.com
Call Date: Nov 1993, Gray's Inn
Qualifications: [LLB (Sheff)]

TYSON MR RICHARD THEODORE

3 PB Barristers
3 Paper Buildings, Temple, London EC4Y 7EU,
☎ 020 7583 8055
3 PB Barristers
23 Beaumont Street, Oxford OX1 2NP,
☎ 01865 793 736
3 PB Barristers
30 Christchurch Road, Bournemouth, Dorset BH1 3PD, ☎ 01202 292102
✉ clerks.bournemouth@3paper.co.uk
3 PB Barristers
Royal Talbot House, 2 Victoria Street, Bristol, Avon BS1 6BB, ☎ 0117 928 1520
3 PB Barristers
4 St Peter Street, Winchester SO23 8BW,
☎ 01962 868884
✉ clerks.winchester@3paper.co.uk
Call Date: Nov 1975, Inner Temple
Pupil Supervisor, Recorder
Qualifications: [BA (Exon)]

TYSON MR THOMAS DAVID

Zenith Chambers
10 Park Square, Leeds LS1 2LH,
☎ 0113 245 5438
✉ clerks@zenithchambers.co.uk
Call Date: Oct 1995, Gray's Inn
Qualifications: [LLB (Bris)]
✉ tom.tyson@zenithchambers.co.uk

TYTHCOTT MISS ELISABETH CLAIRE

18 St John Street
Manchester M3 4EA, ☎ 0161 278 1800
✉ clerks@18sjs.com
Call Date: Nov 1989, Inner Temple
Pupil Supervisor
Qualifications: [LLB (Hons)]

TYZACK MR WILLIAM DAVID CUBITT

Queen Elizabeth Building
3rd Floor, Queen Elizabeth Building, Temple, London EC4Y 9BS, ☎ 020 7797 7837
✉ clerks@qeb.co.uk
Call Date: Oct 2007, Middle Temple
Qualifications: [BA (Hons) (Oxon)]
✉ w.tyzack@qeb.co.uk

UBEROI MR MICHAEL GERARD

Outer Temple Chambers
The Outer Temple, 222 Strand, London WC2R 1BA, ☎ 020 7353 6381
✉ clerks@outertemple.com
Call Date: July 2004, Middle Temple
Qualifications: [BA Hons (Oxon) CPE (City)]
✉ michael.uberoi@outertemple.com

UDDIN MR TAJ

Guildhall Chambers Portsmouth
Prudential Buildings, 16 Guildhall Walk, Portsmouth, Hampshire PO1 2DE, ☎ 023 9275 2400
✉ clerks@gcp-barristers.com
Call Date: Oct 2010, Gray's Inn

UDOM MISS NANCY INI

Five St Andrew's Hill
5 St Andrew's Hill, London EC4V 5BZ, ☎ 020 7332 5400 ✉ Clerks@5sah.co.uk
Call Date: Nov 2002, Lincoln's Inn
Qualifications: [LLB (Hons)(Lond)]
✉ nancyudom@5sah.co.uk, niudom@5sah.co.uk

UDUJE MR BENJAMIN ELLIOTT

42 Bedford Row
London WC1R 4LL, ☎ 020 7831 0222
✉ clerks@42br.com
Call Date: Nov 1992, Middle Temple
Qualifications: [LLB (Hons)]
✉ benjamin.uduje@42br.com

UFF MR DAVID CHARLES

Call Date: July 1981, Gray's Inn
Pupil Supervisor
Qualifications: [LLB (Hons)]

UFF MR JOHN FRANCIS QC (1983)

Keating Chambers
15 Essex Street, London WC2R 3AA, ☎ 020 7544 2600
✉ clerks@keatingchambers.com
Call Date: July 1970, Gray's Inn
Recorder
Qualifications: [PhD FCIArb FREng BScEng]
✉ juff@keatingchambers.com

UKACHI-LOIS MISS ONYE

12 Old Square Chambers
1st Floor, 12 Old Square, Lincoln's Inn, London WC2A 3TX, ☎ 020 7404 0875
✉ clerks@12oldsquare.com
Call Date: Nov 2003, Lincoln's Inn
Qualifications: [BA (Hons) (Lond)]
✉ clerks@12oldsquare.com

ULLSTEIN MR AUGUSTUS RUPERT PATRICK QC (1992)

39 Essex Street
London WC2R 3AT, ☎ 020 7832 1111
✉ clerks@39essex.com
Call Date: July 1970, Inner Temple
Recorder
Qualifications: [LLB (Lond)]
✉ augustus.ullstein@39essex.com

ULYATT MR CRAIG OWEN

Fountain Court Chambers
Fountain Court, Temple, London EC4Y 9DH, ☎ 020 7583 3335
✉ chambers@fountaincourt.co.uk
Call Date: July 2008, Lincoln's Inn
Qualifications: [BA LLB (New Zealand) BCL MPHIL (Oxon)]
✉ cu@fountaincourt.co.uk

UME MR CYRIL OBIORA

12 Old Square Chambers
1st Floor, 12 Old Square, Lincoln's Inn, London WC2A 3TX, ☎ 020 7404 0875
✉ clerks@12oldsquare.com
Call Date: July 1972, Gray's Inn
Pupil Supervisor
Qualifications: [LLB (Lond) Dip Law MCIArb]

UME-EZEOKE MR MATTHIAS IFEANYI

Amethyst Chambers
Ground Floor, 9 Kings Bench Walk, Inner Temple, London EC4Y 7DX, ☎ 020 7936 4966
✉ info@amethystchambers.com
Call Date: July 2002, Middle Temple
Qualifications: [BSc (Hons) CPE]

UNDERHILL MISS ALISON

East Anglian Chambers
53 North Hill, Colchester, Essex CO1 1QA, ☎ 01473 214481 ✉ colchester@ealaw.co.uk
East Anglian Chambers
140 New London Road, Chelmsford, Essex CM2 0AW, ☎ 01473 214481
✉ chelmsford@ealaw.co.uk
East Anglian Chambers
15 The Close, Norwich, Norfolk NR1 4DZ, ☎ 01473 214481 ✉ norwich@ealaw.co.uk

E

East Anglian Chambers
Gresham House, 5 Museum Street, Ipswich, Suffolk IP1 1HQ, ☎ 01473 214481
✉ ipswich@ealaw.co.uk
Call Date: Oct 1997, Gray's Inn
Qualifications: [LLB (Hons)]
alisonunderhill@ealaw.co.uk

UNDERHILL MR GARETH ADAM

4 Breams Buildings
Chancery Lane, London EC4A 1HP,
☎ 020 7092 1900 ✉ clerks@4bb.co.uk
Call Date: Oct 1995, Lincoln's Inn
Qualifications: [LLB (Hons)(Hudds)]

UNDERHILL MR JONATHAN IAN

Temple Chambers
32 Park Place, Cardiff CF10 3BA,
☎ 029 2039 7364
✉ DBrinning@Temple-Chambers.co.uk
Call Date: Nov 2008, Inner Temple
Qualifications: [LLB (Cardiff) CPE]

UNDERWOOD MR ASHLEY GRENVILLE QC (2001)

Landmark Chambers
180 Fleet Street, London EC4A 2HG,
☎ 020 7430 1221
✉ clerks@landmarkchambers.co.uk
Call Date: July 1976, Gray's Inn
Qualifications: [LLB (Hons) (Lond)]
aunderwood@landmarkchambers.co.uk

UNDERWOOD MR DEAN MICHAEL

Hardwicke
New Square, Lincoln's Inn, London WC2A 3SB, ☎ 020 7242 2523
✉ enquiries@hardwicke.co.uk
Call Date: Nov 2002, Middle Temple
Qualifications: [MA (Oxon) LLB (Hons)]
dean.underwood@hardwicke.co.uk

UNDERWOOD MR ROBERT ANTHONY

36 Bedford Row
London WC1R 4JH, ☎ 020 7421 8000
✉ chambers@36bedfordrow.co.uk
Call Date: July 1986, Lincoln's Inn
Pupil Supervisor
Qualifications: [BA]

UNIGWE MR SYLVESTER EMEFIONA

11 Gray's Inn Square Chambers
Chambers of Mr Ian Sen, 1st Floor South, 10/11 Gray's Inn Square, London WC1R 5JD,
☎ 020 7405 6879
✉ clerks@11graysinnsquare.com
Essex House Chambers
122-126 Kilburn High Road, Kilburn, London NW6 4HY, ☎ 020 7692 0677
✉ essexhousechambers@yahoo.co.uk
Call Date: July 1972, Lincoln's Inn
Qualifications: [ACII LLB (Hons)]

UNSWORTH MR IAN STEPHEN QC (2010)

Number 7 Harrington Street Chambers
7 Harrington Street, Liverpool L2 9YH,
☎ 0151 242 0707 ✉ clerks@7hs.co.uk
Call Date: Oct 1992, Lincoln's Inn
Pupil Supervisor
Qualifications: [LLB(Hons)]

UNTERHALTER MR DAVID NAT

Monckton Chambers
1 & 2 Raymond Buildings, Gray's Inn, London WC1R 5NR, ☎ 020 7405 7211
✉ chambers@monckton.com
Call Date: July 2009, Gray's Inn

UNTHANK MISS NINA CLAIRE

2 Temple Gardens
2 Temple Gardens, Temple, London EC4Y 9AY, ☎ 020 7822 1200
✉ clerks@2tg.co.uk
Call Date: July 2001, Middle Temple
Qualifications: [BA (Hons) MA (Hons)]
nunthank@2tg.co.uk

UNWIN MR GREGORY DAVID

187 Fleet Street
London EC4A 2AT, ☎ 020 7430 7430
✉ chambers@187fleetstreet.com
Call Date: Oct 2008, Middle Temple
Qualifications: [MA (Hons) (Cantab) Dip in Law]
gregunwin@187fleetstreet.com

UPEX PROF ROBERT VAUGHAN

Old Square Chambers
10-11 Bedford Row, London WC1R 4BU,
☎ 020 7269 0300 ✉ clerks@oldsquare.co.uk
Old Square Chambers
3 Orchard Court, St Augustine's Yard, Bristol BS1 5DP, ☎ 0117 930 5100
✉ clerks@oldsquare.co.uk
Call Date: July 1973, Middle Temple
Qualifications: [MA LLM (Cantab) ACI Arb]

UPSON MR MICHAEL JAMES

Bank House Chambers
Old Bank House, Hartshead, Sheffield S1 2EL, ☎0114 275 1223
✉w.digby@bankhousechambers.co.uk
Call Date: Oct 1993, Lincoln's Inn
Pupil Supervisor
Qualifications: [LLB (Hons)]
✉m.upson@bankhousechambers.co.uk

UPTON MR ALEXANDER STUART ALLEN

23 Essex Street
London WC2R 3AA, ☎020 7413 0353
✉clerks@23es.com
Call Date: Oct 2004, Lincoln's Inn
Qualifications: [BA PgDI]
✉alexanderupton@23es.com

UPTON MR JAMES WILLIAM DAVID

6 Pump Court
1st Floor, 6 Pump Court, Temple, London EC4Y 7AR, ☎020 7797 8400
✉richardconstable@6pumpcourt.co.uk
6 Pump Court Chambers
6-8 Mill Street, Maidstone, Kent ME15 6XH, ☎01622 688094
✉annexe@6pumpcourt.co.uk
Call Date: Nov 1990, Inner Temple
Qualifications: [MA (Cantab) LLM (Cantab)]
✉williamupton@6pumpcourt.co.uk

UPTON MR JOHN STEWART

4 King's Bench Walk
2nd Floor, 4 King's Bench Walk, Temple, London EC4Y 7DL, ☎020 7822 7000
✉clerks@4kbw.co.uk
Call Date: Oct 1998, Gray's Inn
Qualifications: [BA]

UPTON MR JONATHAN MICHAEL

Tanfield Chambers
2-5 Warwick Court, London WC1R 5DJ, ☎020 7421 5300
✉clerks@tanfieldchambers.co.uk
Call Date: July 2004, Gray's Inn
Qualifications: [BA (Hons)]
✉JonathanUpton@tanfieldchambers.co.uk

UPTON MISS REBECCA

Eastbourne Chambers
5 Chiswick Place, Eastbourne, East Sussex BN21 4NH, ☎01323 642102
✉clerks@eastbournechambers.co.uk
Call Date: July 1999, Gray's Inn
Qualifications: [BA (Hons)(Middx)]
✉rebecca@eastbournechambers.co.uk

UPTON MISS SHONA MARION

Dere Street Barristers
33 Broad Chare, Newcastle Upon Tyne NE1 3DQ, ☎0844 3351551
✉clerks@derestreet.co.uk
Call Date: July 2007, Inner Temple
Qualifications: [BA (Newc)]

URELL MISS KATHERINE ELLEN

Gough Square Chambers
6-7 Gough Square, London EC4A 3DE, ☎020 7353 0924 ✉gsc@goughsq.co.uk
Call Date: Nov 2002, Middle Temple
Qualifications: [LLB (Hons) (Europe) LLM (Cantab)]
✉kate.urell@goughsq.co.uk

URQUHART MR ANDREW ROBERT HILDYARD

36 Bedford Row
London WC1R 4JH, ☎020 7421 8000
✉chambers@36bedfordrow.co.uk
Call Date: Nov 1963, Middle Temple
Pupil Supervisor
Qualifications: [BA (Oxon)]
✉urqmart@hotmail.com

URQUHART MS CATHERINE MARY

Ely Place Chambers
30 Ely Place, London EC1N 6TD, ☎020 7400 9600 ✉admin@elyplace.com
Call Date: Oct 2010, Middle Temple
Qualifications: [BA (Hons) (Oxon)]
✉curquhart@elyplace.com

URWIN MR THOMAS JAMES

Fenners Chambers
3 Madingley Road, Cambridge CB3 0EE, ☎01223 368761
✉clerks@fennerschambers.com
Call Date: Oct 2007, Middle Temple
Qualifications: [BA (Hons) (Sheff) MSc (Lond) PgDL (Lond)]
✉tom.urwin@fennerschambers.com

USHER MR MAXWELL CHARLES

Paragon Chambers
8 Creed Lane, St. Paul, London EC4V 5BR, ☎020 3318 9988
✉contact@paragonchambers.com
Call Date: Nov 2000, Gray's Inn
Qualifications: [BA (Sussex) Dip in Law]
✉mcusher@paragonchambers.com

E

USHER MR NEIL MORRIS

Lincoln House Chambers
Tower 12, The Avenue North, Spinningfields, 18-22 Bridge Street, Manchester M3 3BZ, ☎0161 832 5701
✉info@lincolnhousechambers.com
Call Date: Oct 1993, Middle Temple
Pupil Supervisor
Qualifications: [BA (Hons)(Hull) CPE (Lond)]
neil.usher@lincolnhousechambers.com

USTYCH MR OLEKSANDR

5 Essex Court
1st Floor, 5 Essex Court, Temple, London EC4Y 9AH, ☎020 7410 2000
✉clerks@5essexcourt.co.uk
Call Date: Nov 2010, Gray's Inn
Qualifications: [LLB]
ustych@5essexcourt.co.uk

UTTLEY MR STEPHEN EDWARD

Park Court Chambers
16 Park Place, Leeds LS1 2SJ, ☎0113 243 3277
✉clerks@parkcourtchambers.co.uk
Call Date: Apr 1986, Inner Temple
Qualifications: [BA (Hons)]

VAHIBOGLU MISS AYSE

Colleton Chambers
Colleton Crescent, Exeter, Devon EX2 4DG, ☎01392 274898
✉clerks@colletonchambers.co.uk
Call Date: July 2003, Middle Temple
Qualifications: [LLB Hons (Warw)]
aysevahib@colletonchambers.co.uk

VAITILINGAM MR ADAM SKANDA QC (2010)

Albion Chambers
Broad Street, Bristol BS1 1DR, ☎0117 927 2144
✉clerks@albionchambers.co.uk
Call Date: Nov 1987, Middle Temple
Pupil Supervisor, Recorder
Qualifications: [MA (Cantab)]
adam.vaitilingam@albionchambers.co.uk

VAJDA MR CHRISTOPHER STEPHEN QC (1997)

Monckton Chambers
1 & 2 Raymond Buildings, Gray's Inn, London WC1R 5NR, ☎020 7405 7211
✉chambers@monckton.com
Call Date: July 1979, Gray's Inn
Qualifications: [MA]
cvajda@monckton.com

VAKIL MR JIMMY

Staple Inn Chambers
1st Floor, 9 Staple Inn, Holborn Bars, London WC1V 7QH, ☎020 7242 5240
✉clerks@stapleinn.co.uk
Call Date: May 1993, Middle Temple
Qualifications: [LLB (Hons)(Lond)]
jv@stapleinn.co.uk

VALDER MR PAUL

Five St Andrew's Hill
5 St Andrew's Hill, London EC4V 5BZ, ☎020 7332 5400 ✉Clerks@5sah.co.uk
Call Date: Nov 1994, Inner Temple
Qualifications: [BA (B'ham) CPE (Lond)]
paulvalder@5sah.co.uk

VALENTIN MR BEN MATTHEW

South Square
3-4 South Square, Gray's Inn, London WC1R 5HP, ☎020 7696 9900
✉practicemanagers@southsquare.com
Call Date: Nov 1995, Inner Temple
Pupil Supervisor
Qualifications: [BA, BCL (Oxon) LLM (Cornell)]
benvalentin@southsquare.com

VALENTINE MR JUSTIN SIMON

Atlantic Chambers
4-6 Cook Street, Liverpool L2 9QU, ☎0151 236 4421
✉info@atlanticchambers.co.uk
Call Date: Oct 1999, Middle Temple
Qualifications: [BSc MSc PGDip Law]
justinvalentine@atlanticchambers.co.uk

VALIOS MR NICHOLAS PAUL QC (1991)

4 Breams Buildings
Chancery Lane, London EC4A 1HP, ☎020 7092 1900 ✉clerks@4bb.co.uk
No 8 Chambers
8 Fountain Court, Steelhouse Lane, Birmingham B4 6DR, ☎0121 236 5514
✉clerks@no8chambers.co.uk
Call Date: June 1964, Inner Temple
Recorder

VALKS MR MICHAEL

Eastbourne Chambers
5 Chiswick Place, Eastbourne, East Sussex BN21 4NH, ☎01323 642102
✉clerks@eastbournechambers.co.uk
Call Date: Oct 1994, Gray's Inn
Qualifications: [LLB (Hons)(Bucks)]

VALLACK MISS JULIE ANN

St David's Chambers
Myrtle Cottage, Norton Road, Mumbles, Swansea SA3 5TQ, ☎01792 559924
✉j.vallack@ntlworld.com
Call Date: Oct 1993, Gray's Inn
Qualifications: [BA (Hons) (Bath) LLB (Hons) (Lond)]
j.vallack@ntlworld.com

VALLANCE MR HENRY

Old Bailey Chambers
15 Old Bailey, London EC4M 7EF, ☎020 3008 6404
✉clerks@15oldbaileychambers.com
Call Date: Nov 2004, Inner Temple
Qualifications: [BA CPE]
h.vallance@15oldbaileychambers.com

VALLAT MR RICHARD JUSTIN

Pump Court Tax Chambers
16 Bedford Row, London WC1R 4EF, ☎020 7414 8080 ✉clerks@pumptax.com
Call Date: Oct 1997, Gray's Inn
Pupil Supervisor
Qualifications: [BA]
rvallat@pumptax.com

Types of work: Capital tax, Corporation tax, Customs, Employee benefit trusts, Equity, Income tax, National Insurance, Private client, Professional negligence, Stamp duty, Trusts, VAT, Wills

VALLEJO MISS JACQUELINE

Tooks Chambers
81 Farringdon Street, London EC4A 4BL, ☎020 7842 7575 ✉clerks@tooks.co.uk
Call Date: Mar 1997, Middle Temple
Qualifications: [BA (Hons)]
jacqueline.vallejo@tooks.co.uk

VALLEY MISS HELEN MARIA

25 Bedford Row
London WC1R 4HD, ☎020 7067 1500
✉clerks@25bedfordrow.com
Call Date: Oct 1990, Middle Temple
Pupil Supervisor
Qualifications: [BA (Hons) (Lond) Dip Law]
hvalley@25bedfordrow.com

VALLI MR YUNUS

No.6 Park Square
Leeds LS1 2LW, ☎0113 245 9763
✉Tim@no6.co.uk
Call Date: Nov 1994, Lincoln's Inn
Qualifications: [LLB (Hons)(Leeds)]
valli@no6.co.uk

VAN BESOUW MR EUFRON

Chartlands Chambers
3 St Giles Terrace, Northampton NN1 2BN, ☎01604 603322
✉enquiries@chartlands-chambers.co.uk
Call Date: Nov 1988, Middle Temple
Qualifications: [LLB]
eufron@live.co.uk

VAN DEN BERG MR BARRIE PATRICK

Devon Chambers
3 St Andrew Street, Plymouth PL1 2AH, ☎01752 661659
✉clerks@devonchambers.co.uk
Call Date: July 1978, Middle Temple
Pupil Supervisor
Qualifications: [BA]

VAN DER CRAATS MS PRUDENCE HELENA GRACE

Queen's Gate Chambers
Flat 2, 27 Stanhope Gardens, London SW7 5QX, ☎07765 404650
Call Date: July 2003, Middle Temple
Qualifications: [LLB Hons (Kingston) PgDL Pharm Sc (Merit)]

VAN DER LEIJ DR MARTINA

Field Court Chambers
5 Field Court, Gray's Inn, London WC1R 5EF, ☎020 7405 6114 ✉clerks@fieldcourt.co.uk
Call Date: July 2001, Inner Temple
Qualifications: [BSc MSc MSc PhD (Lond) CPE UCT BVC]

VAN DER ZWART MR MARK ANDREW

KCH Garden Square
1 Oxford Street, Nottingham NG1 5BH, ☎0115 941 8851
✉clerks@kchgardensquare.co.uk
Call Date: Feb 1988, Middle Temple
Pupil Supervisor
Qualifications: [BA (Hons) (Essex)]

VAN DUYVENBODE MR DAMIAN ANTHONY

Argent Chambers
5 Bell Yard, London WC2A 2JR, ☎020 7556 5500
✉briefsin@argentchambers.co.uk
Call Date: Nov 2001, Middle Temple
Qualifications: [BA (Hons) CPE]
dvd@argentchambers.co.uk

E

VAN HAGEN MR CHRISTOPHER SEYMOUR NIGEL

7 Bell Yard
London WC2A 2JR, ☎ 020 7831 0636
✉ kevintarrant@btconnect.com
Call Date: Nov 1980, Middle Temple
Pupil Supervisor
Qualifications: [BA]

VAN HECK MR DIRK VINCENT

One Essex Court
1st Floor, Temple, London EC4Y 9AR,
☎ 020 7936 3030 ✉ clerks@1ec.co.uk
Call Date: Nov 2001, Middle Temple
Qualifications: [BA (Hons) (Cantab) Dip Law]
dvanheck@1ec.co.uk

VAN OVERDIJK MISS CLAIRE ORIT

No5 Chambers
Greenwood House, 4-7 Salisbury Court,
London EC4Y 8AA, ☎ 0845 210 5555
No5 Chambers
38 Queen Square, Bristol BS1 4QS,
☎ 0845 210 5555
No5 Chambers
Fountain Court, Steelhouse Lane, Birmingham
B4 6DR, ☎ 0845 210 5555 ✉ info@no5.com
Call Date: July 2003, Lincoln's Inn
Qualifications: [LLB (Lond) LLM]
cvo@no5.com

E

VAN ROL MRS KATHERINE ANN

4 Paper Buildings
1st Floor, 4 Paper Buildings, Temple, London
EC4Y 7EX, ☎ 020 7427 5200
✉ clerks@4pb.com
Call Date: July 2002, Lincoln's Inn
Qualifications: [LLB (Hons)]
kvr@4pb.com

VAN SANTE-KENLEY MR THEODOR

3 Verulam Buildings
London WC1R 5NT, ☎ 020 7831 8441
✉ chambers@3vb.com
Call Date: July 2009, Inner Temple
Qualifications: [BSc (Lond) MSc (Stanford)]
tvansante@3ub.com

VAN SPALL MS PENELOPE-JANE

Chartlands Chambers
3 St Giles Terrace, Northampton NN1 2BN,
☎ 01604 603322
✉ enquiries@chartlands-chambers.co.uk
Call Date: July 1998, Gray's Inn
Qualifications: [BA (Sunderland)]

VAN STONE MR GRANT FREDERICK

187 Fleet Street
London EC4A 2AT, ☎ 020 7430 7430
✉ chambers@187fleetstreet.com
Call Date: Nov 1988, Middle Temple
Pupil Supervisor
Qualifications: [LLB (Hons)]
grantvanstone@187fleetstreet.com

VAN TONDER MR GERARD DIRK

New Square Chambers
12 New Square, Lincoln's Inn, London
WC2A 3SW, ☎ 020 7419 8000
✉ robin.hollington@newsquarechambers.co.uk
Call Date: Nov 1990, Middle Temple
Pupil Supervisor
Qualifications: [BA LLB (South Africa)]
gerard.vantonder@newsquarechambers.co.uk

VAN-DER-HAER MS AUDREY

St Johns Buildings
24a - 28 St John Street, Manchester M3 4DJ,
☎ 0161 214 1500
✉ clerk@stjohnsbuildings.co.uk
16 Winckley Square
Preston PR1 3JJ, ☎ 01772 256100
St Johns Buildings Liverpool
8th Floor India Buildings, Water Street,
Liverpool L2 0XG, ☎ 0151 243 6000
✉ clerk@stjohnsbuildings.co.uk
Call Date: Oct 2001, Gray's Inn
Qualifications: [LLB (L'pool)]
clerk@stjohnsbuildings.co.uk

VANDERPUMP MR HENRY JOHN

St Johns Buildings
24a - 28 St John Street, Manchester M3 4DJ,
☎ 0161 214 1500
✉ clerk@stjohnsbuildings.co.uk
St Johns Buildings
21 White Friars, Chester CH1 1NZ,
☎ 01244 323070
✉ clerk@stjohnsbuildings.co.uk
St Johns Buildings Liverpool
8th Floor India Buildings, Water Street,
Liverpool L2 0XG, ☎ 0151 243 6000
✉ clerk@stjohnsbuildings.co.uk
Call Date: July 2007, Inner Temple
Qualifications: [LLB (Bris)]

VANDYCK MR WILLIAM GEORGE

Crown Office Chambers
2 Crown Office Row, Temple, London EC4Y 7HJ, ☎020 7797 8100
✉mail@crownofficechambers.com
Call Date: July 1988, Lincoln's Inn
Pupil Supervisor
Qualifications: [BA (Hons) (Cantab)]
✉vandyck@crownofficechambers.com

VANE THE HON CHRISTOPHER JOHN FLETCHER

Trinity Chambers
The Custom House, 39 Quayside, Newcastle Upon Tyne NE1 3DE, ☎0191 232 1927
✉info@trinitychambers.co.uk
Trinity Chambers
Multi Media Exchange, 72-80 Corporation Road, Middlesbrough TS1 2RF, ☎01642 247569
✉info@trinitychambers.co.uk
Call Date: Nov 1976, Inner Temple
Qualifications: [MA (Cantab)]
✉c.vane@trinitychambers.co.uk

VANHEGAN MR MARK JAMES QC (2009)

11 South Square
1st Floor, 11 South Square, Gray's Inn, London WC1R 5EY, ☎020 7405 1222
✉clerks@11southsquare.com
Call Date: Nov 1990, Lincoln's Inn
Qualifications: [MA (Cantab)]
✉mvanhegan@11southsquare.com

VANHEGAN MR TOBY BARTHOLOMEW

Arden Chambers
20 Bloomsbury Square, London WC1A 2NS, ☎020 7242 4244
✉clerks@ardenchambers.com
Call Date: Oct 1996, Middle Temple
Pupil Supervisor
Qualifications: [BA (Hons) (Oxon) LLM (Lond) MA (Oxon)]
✉toby.vanhegan@ardenchambers.com

VANN MR HARRY MICHAEL

Crown Office Chambers
2 Crown Office Row, Temple, London EC4Y 7HJ, ☎020 7797 8100
✉mail@crownofficechambers.com
Call Date: Oct 2003, Middle Temple
Qualifications: [MA(Hons) (Cantab)]
✉vann@crownofficechambers.com

VANSTONE MISS REBECCA

23 Essex Street
London WC2R 3AA, ☎020 7413 0353
✉clerks@23es.com
Call Date: July 2006, Inner Temple
Qualifications: [LLB (Hon) LLM]

VARDON MR RICHARD STANHOPE

18 St John Street
Manchester M3 4EA, ☎0161 278 1800
✉clerks@18sjs.com
Call Date: Nov 1985, Gray's Inn
Pupil Supervisor
Qualifications: [LLB (B'ham)]

VARLE MISS STEPHANIE MARIE

Kenworthy's Chambers
Arlington House, Bloom Street, Salford, Manchester M3 6AJ, ☎0161 832 4036
Call Date: July 2009, Lincoln's Inn
Qualifications: [LLB (Manch)]

VARLEY MR JAMES ROBERT KENRICK

1 High Pavement
Nottingham NG1 1HF, ☎0115 941 8218
✉clerks@1highpavement.co.uk
Call Date: Nov 1997, Lincoln's Inn
Qualifications: [BA (Hons)(Keele)]

VARMA MR RAHUL

Lamb Chambers
Lamb Building, Elm Court, Temple, London EC4Y 7AS, ☎020 7797 8300
✉info@lambchambers.co.uk
Call Date: Nov 2007, Inner Temple
Qualifications: [LLB (Lond)]

VASILESCU MR ANDREI CONSTANTIN

Chambers of Martin Burr
15 Old Bailey, London EC4M 7EF, ☎0845 123 1234 ✉clerks@barristerweb.com
Call Date: Nov 1993, Lincoln's Inn
Qualifications: [BA (Hons) Dip in Law]

VASS MR HUGH PATRICK

1 Paper Buildings
1st Floor, 1 Paper Buildings, Temple, London EC4Y 7EP, ☎020 7353 3728
✉clerks@onepaper.co.uk
Call Date: Nov 1983, Gray's Inn
Pupil Supervisor
Qualifications: [BA]
✉hughvass@onepaper.co.uk

E

VASSALL-ADAMS MR GUY LUKE

Doughty Street Chambers
53-54 Doughty Street, London WC1N 2LS, ☎ 020 7404 1313
✉ enquiries@doughtystreet.co.uk
Doughty Street Chambers
Pall Mall Court, 61-67 King Street, Manchester M2 4PD, ☎ 0161 618 1066
Doughty Street Chambers
5th Floor, Broad Quay House, Prince Street, Bristol BS1 4DJ, ☎ 01179 058 717
Call Date: Nov 2000, Middle Temple
Pupil Supervisor
Qualifications: [BA (Hons) (Oxon) LLM (Essex) CPE]
g.vassall-adams@doughtystreet.co.uk

VATER MR JOHN ALISTAIR PITT QC (2012)

Harcourt Chambers
1st Floor, 2 Harcourt Buildings, Temple, London EC4Y 9DB, ☎ 0844 561 7135
Call Date: Feb 1995, Gray's Inn
Pupil Supervisor
Qualifications: [MA (Oxon)]
jvater@harcourtchambers.law.co.uk

VAUGHAN MR ANTHONY

Garden Court Chambers
57-60 Lincoln's Inn Fields, London WC2A 3LJ, ☎ 020 7993 7600 ✉ info@gclaw.co.uk
Call Date: Oct 2006, Inner Temple
Qualifications: [MA (Cantab) LLM (Lond)]
antonyv@gclaw.co.uk

VAUGHAN MR DAVID ARTHUR JOHN QC (1981)

Brick Court Chambers
7-8 Essex Street, London WC2R 3LD, ☎ 020 7379 3550 ✉ clerks@brickcourt.co.uk
Call Date: Nov 1963, Inner Temple
Recorder
Qualifications: [MA (Cantab)]
David.Vaughan@Brickcourt.co.uk

VAUGHAN MR KIERAN PATRICK QC (2012)

Garden Court Chambers
57-60 Lincoln's Inn Fields, London WC2A 3LJ, ☎ 020 7993 7600 ✉ info@gclaw.co.uk
Call Date: Nov 1993, Middle Temple
Qualifications: [LLB (Hons)]
kieranv@gclaw.co.uk

VAUGHAN MR SIMON PETER

Exchange Chambers
7 Ralli Courts, West Riverside, Manchester M3 5FT, ☎ 0161 833 2722
Exchange Chambers
One Derby Square, Derby Square, Liverpool L2 9XX, ☎ 0151 236 7747
✉ info@exchangechambers.co.uk
Exchange Chambers
Oxford House, Oxford Row, Leeds LS1 3BE, ☎ 0113 203 1970
✉ spencer@exchangechambers.co.uk
Call Date: Nov 1989, Gray's Inn
Pupil Supervisor
Qualifications: [LLB LLM (Lond)]
vaughan@exchangechambers.co.uk

VAUGHAN MR TERENCE PAUL

Fenners Chambers
3 Madingley Road, Cambridge CB3 0EE, ☎ 01223 368761
✉ clerks@fennerschambers.com
Call Date: Oct 1996, Middle Temple
Qualifications: [BSc (Hons) (Salford) Dip Law (B'ham)]
clerks@fennerschambers.com

VAUGHAN JONES MISS SARAH JANE QC (2008)

2 Temple Gardens
2 Temple Gardens, Temple, London EC4Y 9AY, ☎ 020 7822 1200
✉ clerks@2tg.co.uk
Call Date: Nov 1983, Middle Temple
Recorder
Qualifications: [MA (Cantab)]
svj@2tg.co.uk

VAUGHAN-NEIL MISS CATHERINE MARY BERNARDINE

4 Pump Court
4 Pump Court, Temple, London EC4Y 7AN, ☎ 020 7842 5555
✉ chambers@4pumpcourt.com
Call Date: Oct 1994, Inner Temple
Qualifications: [BA (Oxon) LLM (Cantab)]
kvaughanneil@4pumpcourt.com

VAUGHAN-WILLIAMS MR ARTHUR LAURENCE

13 Old Square Chambers
Ground Floor, 14 Old Square, Lincoln's Inn, London WC2A 3UE, ☎ 020 7831 4445
✉ clerks@13oldsquare.com
Call Date: Nov 1988, Lincoln's Inn
Qualifications: [LLB (Bucks)]

VAVRECKA MR DAVID PAUL FRANK

Coram Chambers
9-11 Fulwood Place, London WC1V 6HG,
☎ 020 7092 3700
✉ mail@coramchambers.co.uk
Call Date: Oct 1992, Middle Temple
Pupil Supervisor
Qualifications: [LLB (Lond) LLM]
✉ dv@coramchambers.co.uk, david.vavrecka@coramchambers.co.uk

VEASEY-PUGH MR JONATHAN CHARLES

Cornwall Street Chambers
85-87 Cornwall Street, Birmingham B3 3BY,
☎ 0121 233 7500
✉ clerks@cornwallstreet.co.uk
Call Date: July 2005, Lincoln's Inn
Qualifications: [BA (Hons) GDL]
✉ johnathan.veasey-pugh@cornwallstreet.co.uk

VEATS MISS ELIZABETH CLEA

Garden Court Chambers
57-60 Lincoln's Inn Fields, London WC2A 3LJ,
☎ 020 7993 7600 ✉ info@gclaw.co.uk
Call Date: July 1986, Middle Temple
Pupil Supervisor
Qualifications: [LLB (B'ham) LLM]
✉ lizv@gclaw.co.uk

VEEDER MR VAN VECHTEN QC (1986)

Essex Court Chambers
24 Lincoln's Inn Fields, London WC2A 3EG,
☎ 020 7813 8000
✉ clerksroom@essexcourt.net
Call Date: Nov 1971, Inner Temple
Recorder
Qualifications: [MA (Cantab)]
✉ vveeder@essexcourt.net

VEITCH MR STEVEN DRUMMOND

KCH Garden Square
1 Oxford Street, Nottingham NG1 5BH,
☎ 0115 941 8851
✉ clerks@kchgardensquare.co.uk
Call Date: Nov 2007, Lincoln's Inn
Qualifications: [BA (York)]

VELOSO MRS LINDA

Call Date: Oct 1996, Lincoln's Inn
Qualifications: [BA (Hons)(Keele)]

VENABLES MR ROBERT QC (1990)

Taxchambers
15 Old Square, Lincoln's Inn, London
WC2A 3UE, ☎ 020 7242 2744
✉ taxchambers@15oldsquare.co.uk
Call Date: July 1973, Middle Temple
Qualifications: [MA (Oxon) TEP FTII LLM]
✉ taxchambers@15oldsquare.co.uk

VENCATACHELLUM MS GLENDA ROXANDE

Rowchester Chambers
4 Rowchester Court, Whittall Street,
Birmingham B4 6DH, ☎ 0121 233 2327
✉ clerks@rowchesterchambers.co.uk
Call Date: Oct 1996, Middle Temple
Qualifications: [BA]

VENN MISS SARAH

Hardwicke
New Square, Lincoln's Inn, London
WC2A 3SB, ☎ 020 7242 2523
✉ enquiries@hardwicke.co.uk
Call Date: July 2002, Gray's Inn
Qualifications: [LLB (B'ham)]

VENTHAM MR ANTHONY MICHAEL

Carmelite Chambers
9 Carmelite Street, London EC4Y 0DR,
☎ 020 7936 6300
✉ clerks@carmelitechambers.co.uk
Call Date: Apr 1991, Middle Temple
Qualifications: [BSc (Hons)]
✉ tventham@carmelitechambers.co.uk

VENTHAM MS CHARLOTTE

5 Essex Court
1st Floor, 5 Essex Court, Temple, London
EC4Y 9AH, ☎ 020 7410 2000
✉ clerks@5essexcourt.co.uk
Call Date: July 2001, Lincoln's Inn
Qualifications: [MA (Hons)]
✉ ventham@5essexcourt.co.uk

VENTURI MR GARY ANTHONY

2 King's Bench Walk
2 King's Bench Walk, Temple, London
EC4Y 7DE, ☎ 020 7353 1746
✉ clerks@2kbw.com
Call Date: Oct 1996, Middle Temple
Qualifications: [LLB (Hons)(Lond)]

VERDAN MR ALEXANDER QC (2006)

4 Paper Buildings
1st Floor, 4 Paper Buildings, Temple, London EC4Y 7EX, ☎020 7427 5200
✉clerks@4pb.com
Call Date: Nov 1987, Inner Temple
Recorder
Qualifications: [BA Dip Law]
av@4pb.com

VERDIRAME DR GUGLIELMO

20 Essex Street
London WC2R 3AL, ☎020 7842 1200
✉clerks@20essexst.com
Call Date: Mar 2006, Inner Temple
Qualifications: [BA University of Bologna LLM SOAS University o]
clerks@20essexst.com, gverdirame@20essexst.com

VERDUYN DR ANTHONY JAMES

St Philips Chambers
55 Temple Row, Birmingham B2 5LS,
☎0121 246 7000 ✉clerks@st-philips.com
Call Date: Oct 1993, Lincoln's Inn
Pupil Supervisor, Recorder
Qualifications: [BA (Hons)(Dunelm) D Phil (Oxon) Dip Law (Lond)]
averduyn@st-philips.co.uk

VERE-HODGE MR MICHAEL JOHN DAVY QC (1993)

3 PB Barristers
3 Paper Buildings, Temple, London EC4Y 7EU,
☎020 7583 8055
3 PB Barristers
23 Beaumont Street, Oxford OX1 2NP,
☎01865 793 736
3 PB Barristers
30 Christchurch Road, Bournemouth, Dorset BH1 3PD, ☎01202 292102
✉clerks.bournemouth@3paper.co.uk
3 PB Barristers
Royal Talbot House, 2 Victoria Street, Bristol, Avon BS1 6BB, ☎0117 928 1520
3 PB Barristers
4 St Peter Street, Winchester SO23 8BW,
☎01962 868884
✉clerks.winchester@3paper.co.uk
Call Date: Nov 1970, Gray's Inn
mverehodge@3paper.co.uk

VERITY MRS EMILY JANE

The Chambers of Grahame Aldous QC
9 Gough Square, London EC4A 3DG,
☎020 7832 0500
✉clerks@9goughsquare.co.uk
Call Date: Oct 2003, Gray's Inn
Pupil Supervisor
Qualifications: [BSc (Edin)]
everity@9goughsquare.co.uk

VERNON MR ELLIOT CURT

No. 3 Fleet Street Chambers
3 Fleet Street, London EC4Y 1DP,
☎020 7936 4474 ✉clerks@3fleetstreet.com
Call Date: Oct 2001, Lincoln's Inn
Qualifications: [BA (Hons)(Lond) MA (Lond) PhD (Cantab) PGDL (BPP)]

VERNON MR ROBERT ANTHONY

9 Park Place
9 Park Place, Cardiff, South Glamorgan CF10 3DP, ☎029 2038 2731
✉clerks@9parkplace.co.uk
Call Date: Nov 2000, Lincoln's Inn
Qualifications: [LLB (Hons) (Cardiff)]
rvernon@9parkplace.co.uk

VERNON-ASIMENG MISS KATHRYN HELENA

St Philips Chambers
55 Temple Row, Birmingham B2 5LS,
☎0121 246 7000 ✉clerks@st-philips.com
Call Date: July 2009, Middle Temple
Qualifications: [BA (Hons) Grad Dip Law of (Manch)]

VIALS DR CORA ANN ELAIN

Chambers of Dr Cora Vials
152 Ulsterville Avenue, Lisburn Road, Belfast BT9 7AR
Call Date: Nov 2000, Gray's Inn
Qualifications: [LLB (Wolves) PhD]

VICARY MISS JOANNA CLAIRE

9 St John Street
Manchester M3 4DN, ☎0161 955 9000
✉civilclerks@9sjs.com / criminalclerks@9sjs.com
Call Date: July 2003, Middle Temple
Qualifications: [BA Hons (Oxon)]
civil.clerks@9sjs.com

VICKERS MR CRAIG JOHN STEVEN

Trinity Chambers
Highfield House, Moulsham Street, Chelmsford, Essex CM2 9AH,
☎01245 605040
✉clerks@trinitychambers.com
Trinity Chambers
36 Museum Street, Ipswich, Suffolk IP1 1JQ,
☎01473 282020
✉clerks@trinity-ipswich.law.co.uk
Call Date: July 2008, Inner Temple
Qualifications: [LLB (Canterbury)]
✉clerks@trinitychambers.law.co.uk

VICKERS MR EDMUND BENEDICT BLYTH

Nine Bedford Row
9 Bedford Row, London WC1R 4AZ,
☎020 7489 2727
✉clerks@9bedfordrow.co.uk
Call Date: Nov 1993, Middle Temple
Pupil Supervisor
Qualifications: [BA (Hons)(Dunelm) Dip Law (City)]
✉edmund.vickers@9bedfordrow.co.uk

VICKERS MR GUY JULIAN COURTNEY

Exchange Chambers
7 Ralli Courts, West Riverside, Manchester M3 5FT, ☎0161 833 2722
Exchange Chambers
One Derby Square, Derby Square, Liverpool L2 9XX, ☎0151 236 7747
✉info@exchangechambers.co.uk
Exchange Chambers
Oxford House, Oxford Row, Leeds LS1 3BE,
☎0113 203 1970
✉spencer@exchangechambers.co.uk
Call Date: Nov 1986, Middle Temple
Qualifications: [BA (Oxon)]
✉vickers@exchangechambers.co.uk

VICKERS MS LAURA ANNALISA DAWN

New Street Chambers
2 New Street, Leicester LE1 5NA,
☎0116 262 5906 ✉clerks@2newstreet.co.uk
Call Date: Oct 2007, Lincoln's Inn
Qualifications: [LLB (Leeds)]

VICKERS MS RACHEL CLARE

Outer Temple Chambers
The Outer Temple, 222 Strand, London WC2R 1BA, ☎020 7353 6381
✉clerks@outertemple.com
Call Date: Oct 1992, Lincoln's Inn
Qualifications: [LLB(Hons)(Bris)]
✉rachel.vickers@outertemple.com

VICKERY MR NEIL MICHAEL

13 King's Bench Walk
13 King's Bench Walk, Temple, London EC4Y 7EN, ☎020 7353 7204
✉clerks@13kbw.co.uk
13 KBW
32 Beaumont Street, Oxford OX1 2NP,
☎01865 311066 ✉clerks@13kbw.co.uk
Call Date: July 1985, Gray's Inn
Pupil Supervisor
Qualifications: [MA (Cantab)]
✉nvickery@13kbw.co.uk

VICTOR-MAZELI MISS JACQUELINE

Bell Yard Chambers
116/118 Chancery Lane, London WC2A 1PP,
☎020 7306 9292
✉byclerks@bellyardchambers.co.uk
Chambers of Martin Burr
15 Old Bailey, London EC4M 7EF,
☎0845 123 1234 ✉clerks@barristerweb.com
Call Date: Nov 1997, Middle Temple
Qualifications: [LLB (Hons)(Leeds) BA (Hons)]

VIGARS MRS ANNA LILIAN

Guildhall Chambers
23 Broad Street, Bristol BS1 2HG,
☎0117 930 9000
✉hoc@guildhallchambers.co.uk
Call Date: Nov 1996, Gray's Inn
Pupil Supervisor
Qualifications: [BA (Oxon)]
✉anna.vigars@guildhallchambers.co.uk

VILLAGE MR PETER MALCOLM QC (2002)

4-5 Gray's Inn Square
Gray's Inn, London WC1R 5AH,
☎020 7404 5252 ✉clerks@4-5.co.uk
Call Date: July 1983, Inner Temple
Qualifications: [LLB (Leeds)]
✉pvillage@4-5.co.uk

VILLAROSA MISS ANNUNZIATA

Clerksroom (London)
3rd Floor, 218 Strand, London WC2R 1AT,
☎0845 083 3000 ✉mail@clerksroom.com
Clerksroom (Taunton)
Equity House, Administration Centre, Blackbrook Park Avenue, Taunton, Somerset TA1 2PX, ☎0845 083 3000
✉mail@clerksroom.com
Call Date: July 1995, Middle Temple
Qualifications: [BA]

E

VINALL MR MARK WYN

Blackstone Chambers
Blackstone House, Temple, London EC4Y 9BW, ☎ 020 7583 1770
✉ clerks@blackstonechambers.com
Call Date: July 2002, Inner Temple
Pupil Supervisor
Qualifications: [BA (Oxon)]
markvinall@blackstonechambers.com

VINCE MISS SARAH LOUISE

Devon Chambers
3 St Andrew Street, Plymouth PL1 2AH, ☎ 01752 661659
✉ clerks@devonchambers.co.uk
Call Date: Oct 2007, Middle Temple
Qualifications: [LLB (Hons)]

VINCENT MR PATRICK BENJAMIN

12 King's Bench Walk
12 King's Bench Walk, Temple, London EC4Y 7EL, ☎ 020 7583 0811
Call Date: Oct 1992, Middle Temple
Pupil Supervisor
Qualifications: [BA (Hons)(Bris) Dip Law]
vincent@12kbw.co.uk

VINDIS MISS TARA

The Chambers of Grahame Aldous QC
9 Gough Square, London EC4A 3DG, ☎ 020 7832 0500
✉ clerks@9goughsquare.co.uk
Call Date: Nov 1996, Inner Temple
Pupil Supervisor
Qualifications: [LLB (Exon)]
tvindis@9goughsquare.co.uk

VINE MR AIDAN JAMES WILSON

Harcourt Chambers
1st Floor, 2 Harcourt Buildings, Temple, London EC4Y 9DB, ☎ 0844 561 7135
Harcourt Chambers
Churchill House, 3 St Aldate's Courtyard, St Aldate's, Oxford OX1 1BN, ☎ 0844 561 7135
Call Date: Oct 1995, Middle Temple
Pupil Supervisor
Qualifications: [BA (Hons) MA]
avine@harcourtchambers.law.co.uk

VINE MS CATRIONA MARY

1 Pump Court
Elm Court, Temple, London EC4Y 7AB, ☎ 020 7842 7070
✉ (name)@pumpcourt.co.uk
Call Date: July 2002, Middle Temple
Qualifications: [BA (Galway) LLB (Hons) (Galway) LLM (Lond)]

VINE MR JAMES PETER STOCKMAN

Five St Andrew's Hill
5 St Andrew's Hill, London EC4V 5BZ, ☎ 020 7332 5400 ✉ Clerks@5sah.co.uk
Call Date: Nov 1977, Middle Temple
Pupil Supervisor
jamesvine@5sah.co.uk

VINE MS SARAH JANE

2 Pump Court
1st Floor, 2 Pump Court, Temple, London EC4Y 7AH, ☎ 020 7353 5597
✉ clerks@2pumpcourt.co.uk
Call Date: Mar 1997, Inner Temple
Qualifications: [BA (B'ham) CPE]
svine@2pumpcourt.co.uk

VINEALL MR NICHOLAS EDWARD JOHN QC (2006)

4 Pump Court
4 Pump Court, Temple, London EC4Y 7AN, ☎ 020 7842 5555
✉ chambers@4pumpcourt.com
Call Date: Nov 1988, Middle Temple
Qualifications: [BA (Cantab) MA (USA) Dip Law (Lond)]

VINES MR ANTHONY ROBERT FRANCIS

Civitas Chambers
Global Reach, Celtic Gateway, Cardiff Bay, Cardiff CF11 0SN, ☎ 0845 0713 007
✉ clerks@civitaslaw.com
Call Date: Nov 1993, Gray's Inn
Pupil Supervisor
Qualifications: [BA (Cantab)]

VINEY MR RICHARD JOHN

12 King's Bench Walk
12 King's Bench Walk, Temple, London EC4Y 7EL, ☎ 020 7583 0811
Call Date: Feb 1994, Middle Temple
Pupil Supervisor
Qualifications: [MA (Cantab) LLM (Cantab)]
viney@12kbw.co.uk

VINEY MISS THEA NEWTON

Blackfriars Chambers
79-83 Temple Chambers, 3-7 Temple Avenue, London EC4Y 0HP, ☎ 020 7353 7400
✉ clerks@blackfriarschambers.com
Call Date: Nov 2006, Middle Temple
Qualifications: [BA (Hons) (Durham) PgDip Law]
thea.viney@blackfriarschambers.com

VINSON MR ANDREW JOHN

Exchange Chambers
7 Ralli Courts, West Riverside, Manchester M3 5FT, ☎0161 833 2722
Exchange Chambers
One Derby Square, Derby Square, Liverpool L2 9XX, ☎0151 236 7747
✉info@exchangechambers.co.uk
Exchange Chambers
Oxford House, Oxford Row, Leeds LS1 3BE, ☎0113 203 1970
✉spencer@exchangechambers.co.uk
Call Date: July 2000, Middle Temple
Pupil Supervisor
Qualifications: [BA(Hons) (Oxon) CPE]
✉vinson@exchangechambers.co.uk

VIR SINGH MS SYLVIA

Call Date: July 2001, Middle Temple
Qualifications: [B.Ed (Hons) LLB (Hons)]
✉clerk@stjohnsbuildings.co.uk

VIRGO MR JOHN ANTHONY

Guildhall Chambers
23 Broad Street, Bristol BS1 2HG, ☎0117 930 9000
✉hoc@guildhallchambers.co.uk
XXIV Old Buildings
Ground Floor, 24 Old Buildings, Lincoln's Inn, London WC2A 3UP, ☎020 7691 2424
✉clerks@xxiv.co.uk
Call Date: Nov 1983, Inner Temple
Pupil Supervisor
Qualifications: [MA (Oxon)]
✉john.virgo@guildhallchambers.co.uk

VIRK MR SUNDEEP SINGH

Cornwall Street Chambers
85-87 Cornwall Street, Birmingham B3 3BY, ☎0121 233 7500
✉clerks@cornwallstreet.co.uk
Call Date: Nov 2004, Gray's Inn
Qualifications: [LLB]

VISSIAN MRS HENA

Chartlands Chambers
3 St Giles Terrace, Northampton NN1 2BN, ☎01604 603322
✉enquiries@chartlands-chambers.co.uk
Call Date: Oct 2002, Lincoln's Inn
Qualifications: [LLB (Leic)]

VITIELLO MR FABIO ANGELO-GIUSEPPE

Staple Inn Chambers
1st Floor, 9 Staple Inn, Holborn Bars, London WC1V 7QH, ☎020 7242 5240
✉clerks@stapleinn.co.uk
Call Date: Oct 1995, Inner Temple
Qualifications: [Dr Jur (Italy) CPE (Lond)]

VODANOVIC MISS VILMA

Zenith Chambers
10 Park Square, Leeds LS1 2LH, ☎0113 245 5438
✉clerks@zenithchambers.co.uk
Call Date: Oct 2002, Gray's Inn
Qualifications: [LLB (Leeds)]
✉vvodanovic@zenithchambers.co.uk

VOKES MR STEPHEN JOHN

No 8 Chambers
8 Fountain Court, Steelhouse Lane, Birmingham B4 6DR, ☎0121 236 5514
✉clerks@no8chambers.co.uk
Call Date: July 1989, Lincoln's Inn
Qualifications: [BA (Wales)]
✉stephenvokes@no8chambers.co.uk

VOLLENWEIDER MR AMIOT MARCUS ELLERTON

Thomas More Chambers
7 Lincoln's Inn Fields, London WC2A 3BP, ☎020 7404 7000
✉clerks@thomasmore.co.uk
Call Date: Oct 2000, Gray's Inn
Pupil Supervisor
Qualifications: [BSc (B'Ham)]
✉avollenweider@thomasmore.co.uk

VOLZ MR KARL ANDREW

2 Pump Court
1st Floor, 2 Pump Court, Temple, London EC4Y 7AH, ☎020 7353 5597
✉clerks@2pumpcourt.co.uk
Call Date: Nov 1993, Middle Temple
Qualifications: [BA (Hons)(Newc) CPE (Lond)]
✉kvolz@2pumpcourt.co.uk

VON BERG MR PIERS

36 Bedford Row
London WC1R 4JH, ☎020 7421 8000
✉chambers@36bedfordrow.co.uk
Call Date: Mar 2009, Gray's Inn
Qualifications: [MA]
✉pvonberg@36bedfordrow.co.uk

E

VON POMMERN-PEGLOW DR MICHAEL ALFRED HERMAN PR.

Brunswick Chambers
2 Middle Temple Lane, Temple, London EC4Y 9AA, ☎ 020 7353 1987
✉ alpha@brunswickchambers.net
Call Date: July 1993, Middle Temple
Qualifications: [D Phil (Oxon) Dr Jur (Saarb) MSc Econ (Saarb) JA (Germany) FAS (Russia)]
✉ pommern@brunswickchambers.net

VON WACHTER LADY VICTORIA NORA CRESSIDA

5 Essex Court
1st Floor, 5 Essex Court, Temple, London EC4Y 9AH, ☎ 020 7410 2000
✉ clerks@5essexcourt.co.uk
Call Date: July 1997, Gray's Inn
Pupil Supervisor
Qualifications: [BSc M Phil (Oxon) LLB]
✉ wachter@5essexcourt.co.uk

VONBERG MR THOMAS CHARLES

Devereux Chambers
Queen Elizabeth Building, Temple, London EC4Y 9BS, ☎ 020 7353 7534
✉ clerks@devchambers.co.uk
Call Date: Nov 2004, Middle Temple
Qualifications: [LLB (Hons) (Dunelm)]

VOOGHT MISS ABIGAIL LOUISE

4 King's Bench Walk
2nd Floor, 4 King's Bench Walk, Temple, London EC4Y 7DL, ☎ 020 7822 7000
✉ clerks@4kbw.co.uk
Call Date: Nov 2006, Inner Temple
Qualifications: [LLB (Lond)]

VOUT MR ANDREW PAUL

1 High Pavement
Nottingham NG1 1HF, ☎ 0115 941 8218
✉ clerks@1highpavement.co.uk
9-12 Bell Yard
London WC2A 2JR, ☎ 020 7400 1800
✉ clerks@9-12bellyard.com
Call Date: Nov 1995, Gray's Inn
Pupil Supervisor
Qualifications: [LLB (Warw)]

VULLO MR STEPHEN

2 Bedford Row
London WC1R 4BU, ☎ 020 7440 8888
✉ clerks@2bedfordrow.co.uk
Call Date: Nov 1996, Middle Temple
Pupil Supervisor
Qualifications: [LLB (Hons)]
✉ svullo@2bedfordrow.co.uk

WACEK MISS KIM MARIE

4 KBW
Ground Floor, 4 King's Bench Walk, Temple, London EC4Y 7DL, ☎ 020 7822 8822
✉ law@4kbw.net
Clerksroom (Taunton)
Equity House, Administration Centre, Blackbrook Park Avenue, Taunton, Somerset TA1 2PX, ☎ 0845 083 3000
✉ mail@clerksroom.com
Call Date: Nov 2003, Middle Temple
Qualifications: [Jurisdoctorate]

WACEY MISS NICOLA JOY

Goldsmith Chambers
Ground Floor, Goldsmith Building, Temple, London EC4Y 7BL, ☎ 020 7353 6802
✉ clerks@goldsmithchambers.com
Call Date: Nov 2004, Middle Temple
Qualifications: [LLB (Hons) (B'ham)]
✉ n.wacey@goldsmithchambers.law.co.uk

WADDELL MISS PHILIPPA

St Johns Buildings
24a - 28 St John Street, Manchester M3 4DJ, ☎ 0161 214 1500
✉ clerk@stjohnsbuildings.co.uk
16 Winckley Square
Preston PR1 3JJ, ☎ 01772 256100
St Johns Buildings Liverpool
8th Floor India Buildings, Water Street, Liverpool L2 0XG, ☎ 0151 243 6000
✉ clerk@stjohnsbuildings.co.uk
Call Date: July 2004, Lincoln's Inn
Qualifications: [LLB Hons (Manch)]
✉ philippa_waddell@yahoo.co.uk

WADDINGTON MR JAMES CHARLES

9-12 Bell Yard
London WC2A 2JR, ☎ 020 7400 1800
✉ clerks@9-12bellyard.com
Call Date: July 1983, Gray's Inn
Pupil Supervisor
Qualifications: [LLB (Exon)]
✉ j.waddington@9-12bellyard.com, jcwaddington@mac.com

WADE MISS CLARE CATHERINE

Tooks Chambers
81 Farringdon Street, London EC4A 4BL, ☎ 020 7842 7575 ✉ clerks@tooks.co.uk
Call Date: Nov 1990, Inner Temple
Qualifications: [BA (Dunelm) Dip Law (Lond)]

WADE MR IAN QC (2010)

Five Paper Buildings
1st Floor, Five Paper Buildings, Temple, London EC4Y 7HB, ☎020 7583 6117
✉clerks@5pb.co.uk
Call Date: Nov 1977, Gray's Inn
Pupil Supervisor
Qualifications: [MA (Cantab)]
✉iw@5pb.co.uk

WADE MR NATHANIEL AERON TREHARNE

Furnival Chambers
32 Furnival Street, London EC4A 1JQ, ☎020 7405 3232
Call Date: Oct 2009, Middle Temple
Qualifications: [MA (Hons) (Edin) MA (Lond) LLB (College of Law)]

WADE MISS REBECCA LUCY

Northampton Chambers
10 Spencer Parade, Northampton NN1 5AQ, ☎01604 636271
✉clerks@northampton-chambers.co.uk
Call Date: July 2003, Gray's Inn
Pupil Supervisor
Qualifications: [LLB (Sussex)]
✉rwade@northampton-chambers.co.uk

WADOODI MISS AISHA

Dere Street Barristers
14 Toft Green, York YO1 6JT, ☎0844 3351551
✉clerks@derestreet.co.uk
Dere Street Barristers
33 Broad Chare, Newcastle Upon Tyne NE1 3DQ, ☎0844 3351551
✉clerks@derestreet.co.uk
Call Date: Oct 1994, Middle Temple
Qualifications: [LLB (Hons)(Newc)]
✉aishawadoodi@gmail.com

WADSLEY MR PETER JOHN CAMPBELL

St John's Chambers
101 Victoria Street, Bristol BS1 6PU, ☎0117 923 4700
✉clerks@stjohnschambers.co.uk
Call Date: July 1984, Middle Temple
Pupil Supervisor
Qualifications: [MA LLM (Cantab)]
✉peter.wadsley@stjohnschambers.co.uk

WADSWORTH MR NICHOLAS STEPHEN

Clock Chambers
18 Waterloo Road, Wolverhampton WV1 4BL, ☎01902 313444
✉clockchambers@btconnect.com
Call Date: Feb 1993, Gray's Inn
Pupil Supervisor
Qualifications: [LLB (Staffs)]

WAGNER MR ADAM MARC

Crown Office Row Chambers
119 Church Street, Brighton, Sussex BN1 1UD, ☎01273 625625
✉clerks@1cor.com
1 Crown Office Row
1 Crown Office Row, Temple, London EC4Y 7HH, ☎020 7797 7500
✉mail@1cor.com
Call Date: Nov 2007, Inner Temple
Qualifications: [BA (Oxon) MA (Columbia)]

WAGSTAFF MR ANDREW MARTIN NICHOLAS

Westgate Chambers
64 High Street, Lewes, East Sussex BN7 1XG, ☎01273 480510
✉clerks@westgate-chambers.co.uk
Call Date: Oct 2006, Gray's Inn
Qualifications: [BA]
✉awagstaff@westgate-chambers.co.uk

WAGSTAFFE MR CHRISTOPHER DAVID QC (2011)

29 Bedford Row Chambers
London WC1R 4HE, ☎020 7404 1044
✉clerks@29br.co.uk
Call Date: Nov 1992, Inner Temple
Qualifications: [LLB (Hons)(Essex)]
✉cwagstaffe@29br.co.uk

WAHEED MR ERUM JUNADE

12 Old Square Chambers
1st Floor, 12 Old Square, Lincoln's Inn, London WC2A 3TX, ☎020 7404 0875
✉clerks@12oldsquare.com
Call Date: Nov 1995, Gray's Inn
Qualifications: [LLB]
✉clerks@12oldsquare.com

WAHIWALA MR AMRIK SINGH

East Anglian Chambers
15 The Close, Norwich, Norfolk NR1 4DZ, ☎ 01473 214481 ✉ norwich@ealaw.co.uk
East Anglian Chambers
53 North Hill, Colchester, Essex CO1 1QA, ☎ 01473 214481 ✉ colchester@ealaw.co.uk
East Anglian Chambers
140 New London Road, Chelmsford, Essex CM2 0AW, ☎ 01473 214481 ✉ chelmsford@ealaw.co.uk
East Anglian Chambers
Gresham House, 5 Museum Street, Ipswich, Suffolk IP1 1HQ, ☎ 01473 214481 ✉ ipswich@ealaw.co.uk
Call Date: July 2003, Middle Temple
Qualifications: [LLB Hons (Essex) LLM (Nott'm)]
🖃 amrikwahiwala@ealaw.co.uk

WAIDHOFER MR BENJAMIN WALTER

2 Bedford Row
London WC1R 4BU, ☎ 020 7440 8888 ✉ clerks@2bedfordrow.co.uk
Call Date: Nov 2008, Inner Temple
Qualifications: [BA (Leeds) CPE]
🖃 bwaidhofer@2bedfordrow.co.uk

WAINWRIGHT MR JEREMY PATRICK

Chambers of Mr Ami Feder
Ground Floor, Lamb Building, Temple, London EC4Y 7AS, ☎ 020 7797 7788 ✉ clerks@lambbuilding.co.uk
Lamb Building
22 Ship Street, Brighton BN1 1AD, ☎ 01273 820490 ✉ admin@lambbuilding.co.uk
Chambers of Mr Ami Feder
Ground Floor, Lamb Building, Temple, London EC4Y 7AS, ☎ 020 7797 7788 ✉ clerks@lambbuilding.co.uk
Call Date: Oct 1990, Gray's Inn
Pupil Supervisor
Qualifications: [BA (Hons) Dip Law]
🖃 clerks@lambbuilding.co.uk

WAINWRIGHT MR JOHN PATRICK HADEN

St Philips Chambers
55 Temple Row, Birmingham B2 5LS, ☎ 0121 246 7000 ✉ clerks@st-philips.com
Call Date: Oct 1994, Lincoln's Inn
Qualifications: [MA (Oxon)]
🖃 pwainwright@st-philips.com

WAINWRIGHT MR MICHAEL WILLIAM

No. 3 Fleet Street Chambers
3 Fleet Street, London EC4Y 1DP, ☎ 020 7936 4474 ✉ clerks@3fleetstreet.com
Call Date: Nov 2008, Lincoln's Inn
Qualifications: [BSc (Hons) (Brunel) GDL]

WAINWRIGHT MR SCOTT ANTHONY

2 Pump Court
1st Floor, 2 Pump Court, Temple, London EC4Y 7AH, ☎ 020 7353 5597 ✉ clerks@2pumpcourt.co.uk
Call Date: Oct 2006, Middle Temple
Qualifications: [LLB (Hons) (Southampton)]

WAINWRIGHT MR THOMAS JAMES

Garden Court Chambers
57-60 Lincoln's Inn Fields, London WC2A 3LJ, ☎ 020 7993 7600 ✉ info@gclaw.co.uk
Call Date: Nov 2003, Gray's Inn
Qualifications: [MA (Oxon)]
🖃 tomw@gclaw.co.uk

WAITE MR JOHN-PAUL TANGYE

5 Essex Court
1st Floor, 5 Essex Court, Temple, London EC4Y 9AH, ☎ 020 7410 2000 ✉ clerks@5essexcourt.co.uk
Call Date: Nov 1995, Middle Temple
Qualifications: [BA (Hons)(Leeds)]
🖃 waite@5essexcourt.co.uk

WAITE MR JONATHAN GILBERT STOKES QC (2002)

Crown Office Chambers
2 Crown Office Row, Temple, London EC4Y 7HJ, ☎ 020 7797 8100 ✉ mail@crownofficechambers.com
Call Date: July 1978, Inner Temple
Qualifications: [MA (Cantab)]
🖃 waite@crownofficechambers.com

WAITE MR KIRIL

1 Chancery Lane
London WC2A 1LF, ☎ 0845 634 6666 ✉ clerks@1chancerylane.com
Call Date: Nov 1997, Gray's Inn
Pupil Supervisor
Qualifications: [LLB (Lond)]
🖃 kwaite@1chancerylane.com

E

WAITHE MR JOHN ALBERT

12 Old Square Chambers
1st Floor, 12 Old Square, Lincoln's Inn, London WC2A 3TX, ☎ 020 7404 0875
✉ clerks@12oldsquare.com
Call Date: Nov 1972, Lincoln's Inn
Pupil Supervisor
Qualifications: [LLB LLM (Lond) MA]
✉ clerks@12oldsquare.com

WAKEFIELD MS VICTORIA ELIZABETH LIVESEY

Brick Court Chambers
7-8 Essex Street, London WC2R 3LD,
☎ 020 7379 3550 ✉ clerks@brickcourt.co.uk
Call Date: July 2003, Gray's Inn
Qualifications: [BA (Cantab)]
✉ victoria.wakefield@brickcourt.co.uk

WAKERLEY MR PAUL CHARLES MACLENNON

QEB Hollis Whiteman
1-2 Laurence Pountney Hill, London EC4R 0EU, ☎ 020 7933 8855
✉ barristers@qebhw.co.uk
Call Date: Nov 1990, Gray's Inn
Pupil Supervisor
Qualifications: [LLB (Hons)]
✉ barristers@qebhw.co.uk

WALBANK MR DAVID NICHOLAS

18 Red Lion Court
London EC4A 3EB, ☎ 020 7520 6000
✉ chambers@18rlc.co.uk
18 Red Lion Court (Annexe)
Thornwood House, 102 New London Road, Chelmsford, Essex CM2 0RG,
☎ 01245 280880
Call Date: Nov 1987, Inner Temple
Qualifications: [MA (Cantab)]
✉ david.walbank@18rlc.co.uk

WALD MR RICHARD DANIEL

39 Essex Street
London WC2R 3AT, ☎ 020 7832 1111
✉ clerks@39essex.com
82 King Street
Manchester M2 4WQ, ☎ 0161 870 9969
Riverview Chambers
Hamilton House, 1 Temple Avenue, London EC4Y 0HA, ☎ 0844 225 3999
✉ chrisbaylis@riverviewchambers.com
Call Date: Nov 1997, Gray's Inn
Pupil Supervisor
Qualifications: [MA (Edin) Dip Law Dip EC Law]
✉ richard.wald@39essex.com

WALDEN-SMITH MR DAVID EDWARD

29 Bedford Row Chambers
London WC1R 4HE, ☎ 020 7404 1044
✉ clerks@29br.co.uk
Call Date: July 1985, Lincoln's Inn
Qualifications: [MA (Cantab)]
✉ dwalden-smith@29br.co.uk

WALDER MR AARON LEE

Landmark Chambers
180 Fleet Street, London EC4A 2HG,
☎ 020 7430 1221
✉ clerks@landmarkchambers.co.uk
Call Date: Nov 2002, Inner Temple
Qualifications: [MPhil (Cantab) LLB (Oxon)]
✉ awalder@landmarkchambers.co.uk

WALDMAN MR AMOS

Doughty Street Chambers
Pall Mall Court, 61-67 King Street, Manchester M2 4PD, ☎ 0161 618 1066
Doughty Street Chambers
5th Floor, Broad Quay House, Prince Street, Bristol BS1 4DJ, ☎ 01179 058 717
Doughty Street Chambers
53-54 Doughty Street, London WC1N 2LS,
☎ 020 7404 1313
✉ enquiries@doughtystreet.co.uk
Call Date: Nov 2001, Middle Temple
Qualifications: [LLB (Hons)]

WALDRON MISS KAY

9 Park Place
9 Park Place, Cardiff, South Glamorgan CF10 3DP, ☎ 029 2038 2731
✉ clerks@9parkplace.co.uk
Call Date: Nov 1989, Inner Temple
Qualifications: [LLB]

WALDRON MISS LORRAINE ANNE

1 Pump Court
Elm Court, Temple, London EC4Y 7AB,
☎ 020 7842 7070
✉ (name)@pumpcourt.co.uk
Call Date: Nov 2004, Gray's Inn
Qualifications: [LLB]

E

WALDRON MR WILLIAM FRANCIS QC (2006)

Exchange Chambers
One Derby Square, Derby Square, Liverpool L2 9XX, ☎0151 236 7747
✉info@exchangechambers.co.uk
Exchange Chambers
7 Ralli Courts, West Riverside, Manchester M3 5FT, ☎0161 833 2722
Call Date: Nov 1986, Gray's Inn
Recorder
Qualifications: [LLB]
waldronqc@exchangechambers.co.uk

WALE MISS ELIZABETH ELLEN

Atlantic Chambers
4-6 Cook Street, Liverpool L2 9QU, ☎0151 236 4421
✉info@atlanticchambers.co.uk
Call Date: July 2004, Inner Temple
Qualifications: [BA (Hons) PG Diplaw]
elizabethwale@atlanticchambers.co.uk

WALES MR ANDREW NIGEL MALCOLM QC (2012)

7 King's Bench Walk
Ground Floor, 7 King's Bench Walk, Temple, London EC4Y 7DS, ☎020 7910 8300
✉clerks@7kbw.co.uk
Call Date: Nov 1992, Gray's Inn
Pupil Supervisor
Qualifications: [MA (Cantab) LLM (USA)]
awales@7kbw.co.uk

WALES MR MATTHEW JAMES

Guildhall Chambers
23 Broad Street, Bristol BS1 2HG, ☎0117 930 9000
✉hoc@guildhallchambers.co.uk
Call Date: Oct 1993, Inner Temple
Pupil Supervisor
Qualifications: [BA (Dunelm)]

WALEY MR ERIC RICHARD THOMAS

Assize Court Chambers
14 Small Street, Bristol BS1 1DE, ☎0117 926 4587 ✉carly@assize.co.uk
Call Date: Nov 1976, Inner Temple
Pupil Supervisor
Qualifications: [MA (Hons) (Cantab)]
eric.waley@assize.co.uk

WALFORD MR PHILIP CHARLES

11 New Square
1st Floor, 11 New Square, Lincoln's Inn, London WC2A 3QB, ☎020 7242 4017
✉john.moore@11newsquare.com
Call Date: Oct 2003, Lincoln's Inn
Qualifications: [MMath (Oxon) Dip Law (City)]
john.moore@11newsquare.com

WALFORD MR RICHARD HENRY HOWARD

Serle Court
6 New Square, Lincoln's Inn, London WC2A 3QS, ☎020 7242 6105
✉clerks@serlecourt.co.uk
Call Date: July 1984, Middle Temple
Pupil Supervisor
Qualifications: [LLB (Exon)]
rwalford@serlecourt.co.uk

Types of work: Civil fraud, Commercial litigation, Equity, International arbitration, Professional negligence, Real property

WALJI MISS SHABNAM

Regency Chambers
45 Priestgate, Peterborough PE1 1LB, ☎01733 315215
✉clerks@regencychambers.law.co.uk
Regency Chambers
Sheraton House, Castle Park, Cambridge CB3 0AX, ☎01223 301517
Call Date: July 2001, Gray's Inn
Qualifications: [LLB (Essex) LLM (Nott'm)]
clerks@regencychambers.law.co.uk

WALKER MR ADAM NIGEL

Seven Bedford Row
7 Bedford Row, London WC1R 4BS, ☎020 7242 3555 ✉clerks@7br.co.uk
Call Date: July 2000, Lincoln's Inn
Qualifications: [LLB(Hons)(L'pool)]
awalker@7br.co.uk

WALKER MR ALLISTER DAVID

Five St Andrew's Hill
5 St Andrew's Hill, London EC4V 5BZ, ☎020 7332 5400 ✉Clerks@5sah.co.uk
Call Date: Nov 1990, Inner Temple
Pupil Supervisor
Qualifications: [LLB (Essex)]

WALKER MISS AMELIA POPPY

Hardwicke
New Square, Lincoln's Inn, London WC2A 3SB, ☎020 7242 2523
✉enquiries@hardwicke.co.uk
Call Date: Oct 2007, Inner Temple
Qualifications: [MA M Phil (Cantab)]
amelia.walker@hardwicke.co.uk

WALKER MR ANDREW JAMES

Dere Street Barristers
33 Broad Chare, Newcastle Upon Tyne NE1 3DQ, ☎0844 3351551
✉clerks@derestreet.co.uk
Call Date: Oct 1998, Inner Temple
Qualifications: [LLB (Leic)]
clerks@broadcharechambers.co.uk

WALKER MR ANDREW PAUL DALTON QC (2011)

Maitland Chambers
7 Stone Buildings, Lincoln's Inn, London WC2A 3SZ, ☎020 7406 1200
✉clerks@maitlandchambers.com
Call Date: Nov 1991, Lincoln's Inn
Pupil Supervisor
Qualifications: [MA (Cantab)]
awalker@maitlandchambers.com

WALKER MISS ANWEN ELIZABETH

Assize Court Chambers
14 Small Street, Bristol BS1 1DE, ☎0117 926 4587 ✉carly@assize.co.uk
Call Date: July 1992, Inner Temple
Qualifications: [LLB]
anwen.walker@assize.co.uk

WALKER MISS CHARLOTTE LUCY

Guildhall Chambers
23 Broad Street, Bristol BS1 2HG, ☎0117 930 9000
✉hoc@guildhallchambers.co.uk
Call Date: Nov 2008, Middle Temple
Qualifications: [BA (Hons) (Dunelm)]
lucy.walker@guildhallchambers.co.uk

WALKER MR CHRISTOPHER DAVID BESTWICK

Old Square Chambers
3 Orchard Court, St Augustine's Yard, Bristol BS1 5DP, ☎0117 930 5100
✉clerks@oldsquare.co.uk
Old Square Chambers
10-11 Bedford Row, London WC1R 4BU, ☎020 7269 0300 ✉clerks@oldsquare.co.uk
Call Date: Oct 1990, Middle Temple
Pupil Supervisor
Qualifications: [MA (Cantab) LicSpec en Driot (Brussels)]
walker@oldsquare.co.uk

WALKER MR DAMIEN ANDREW

Essex Court Chambers
24 Lincoln's Inn Fields, London WC2A 3EG, ☎020 7813 8000
✉clerksroom@essexcourt.net
Call Date: Nov 2006, Lincoln's Inn
Qualifications: [BA (Sydney) LLB (Oxon) BA (Ec Hons) (Sydney) LLB (Sydney) BCL (Oxon)]
dwalker@essexcourt.net

WALKER MR EDWARD JEREMY BRUCE

Exchange Chambers
Oxford House, Oxford Row, Leeds LS1 3BE, ☎0113 203 1970
✉spencer@exchangechambers.co.uk
Exchange Chambers
One Derby Square, Derby Square, Liverpool L2 9XX, ☎0151 236 7747
✉info@exchangechambers.co.uk
Exchange Chambers
7 Ralli Courts, West Riverside, Manchester M3 5FT, ☎0161 833 2722
Call Date: Nov 1994, Gray's Inn
Qualifications: [BSc]

WALKER MRS ELIZABETH MARY

St Philips Chambers
55 Temple Row, Birmingham B2 5LS, ☎0121 246 7000 ✉clerks@st-philips.com
Call Date: Oct 1994, Gray's Inn
Qualifications: [BA (Hons)(Dunelm)]
ewalker@st-philips.co.uk

WALKER MRS FIONA

Trinity Chambers
The Custom House, 39 Quayside, Newcastle Upon Tyne NE1 3DE, ☎0191 232 1927
✉info@trinitychambers.co.uk
Trinity Chambers
Multi Media Exchange, 72-80 Corporation Road, Middlesbrough TS1 2RF, ☎01642 247569
✉info@trinitychambers.co.uk
Call Date: July 1998, Inner Temple
Qualifications: [LLB (Dunelm)]
f.walker@trinitychambers.co.uk

WALKER MRS FIONA

Bank House Chambers
Old Bank House, Hartshead, Sheffield S1 2EL, ☎0114 275 1223
✉w.digby@bankhousechambers.co.uk
Call Date: Feb 1992, Inner Temple
Pupil Supervisor
Qualifications: [LLB (Manc)]
f.walker@bankhousechambers.co.uk

E

WALKER MISS HANNAH

Call Date: Oct 2008, Middle Temple
Qualifications: [LLB (Hons) (Newc)]

WALKER MS HANNAH VICTORIA

Dyers Chambers
35 Bedford Row, London WC1R 4JH,
☎020 7404 1881
✉admin@dyerschambers.com
Call Date: Oct 2010, Inner Temple
Qualifications: [BA (B'ham)]
clerks@dyerschambers.com

WALKER MR JAMES

Carmelite Chambers
9 Carmelite Street, London EC4Y 0DR,
☎020 7936 6300
✉clerks@carmelitechambers.co.uk
Call Date: Oct 1994, Lincoln's Inn
Qualifications: [LLB (Hons)(UEA)]
jwalker@carmelitechambers.co.uk

WALKER MISS JANE

St Johns Buildings
24a - 28 St John Street, Manchester M3 4DJ,
☎0161 214 1500
✉clerk@stjohnsbuildings.co.uk
St Johns Buildings
21 White Friars, Chester CH1 1NZ,
☎01244 323070
✉clerk@stjohnsbuildings.co.uk
16 Winckley Square
Preston PR1 3JJ, ☎01772 256100
Call Date: July 1987, Middle Temple
Qualifications: [MA (Oxon)]
jane.walker@btinternet.com

WALKER MR JONATHAN JOHAR

Fountain Chambers
Cleveland Business Centre, 1 Watson Street, Middlesbrough TS1 2RQ, ☎01642 804040
✉clerks@fountainchambers.co.uk
Call Date: Oct 1997, Lincoln's Inn
Qualifications: [BSc (Hons)(Dundee) Dip in Law (Notts)]

WALKER MR LIAM DAVID

Doughty Street Chambers
53-54 Doughty Street, London WC1N 2LS,
☎020 7404 1313
✉enquiries@doughtystreet.co.uk
Call Date: Nov 2001, Gray's Inn
Pupil Supervisor
Qualifications: [BA (Bris)]

WALKER MS MARIA-AMALIA LUISA

42 Bedford Row
London WC1R 4LL, ☎020 7831 0222
✉clerks@42br.com
Call Date: Oct 2003, Inner Temple
Qualifications: [BA (Hons) (Lond) Dip Law (Lond) MA (Lond)]
amalia.walker@42br.com

WALKER MR MICHAEL PHILLIP

Crown Office Row Chambers
119 Church Street, Brighton, Sussex BN1 1UD, ☎01273 625625
✉clerks@1cor.com
Call Date: July 2008, Middle Temple
Qualifications: [LLB (Hons) (Leic)]
michael.walker@1cor.com

WALKER MR NICHOLAS DAVID FRANCIS

Exchange Chambers
One Derby Square, Derby Square, Liverpool L2 9XX, ☎0151 236 7747
✉info@exchangechambers.co.uk
Exchange Chambers
7 Ralli Courts, West Riverside, Manchester M3 5FT, ☎0161 833 2722
Exchange Chambers
Oxford House, Oxford Row, Leeds LS1 3BE,
☎0113 203 1970
✉spencer@exchangechambers.co.uk
Call Date: Oct 1998, Lincoln's Inn
Qualifications: [LLB (Hons)(Leic)]
walker@exchangechambers.co.uk

WALKER MR PAUL CHRISTOPHER

5 King's Bench Walk
5 King's Bench Walk, Temple, London EC4Y 7DN, ☎020 7353 5638
✉clerks@5kbw.co.uk
Call Date: Oct 1993, Lincoln's Inn
Pupil Supervisor
Qualifications: [LLB (Hons)(Lond)]
paul.walker@5kbw.co.uk

WALKER MR RONALD JACK QC (1983)

12 King's Bench Walk
12 King's Bench Walk, Temple, London EC4Y 7EL, ☎020 7583 0811
Call Date: July 1962, Gray's Inn
Recorder
Qualifications: [LLB]
walker@12kbw.co.uk

WALKER MR STEVEN JOHN QC (2012)

Atkin Chambers
1 Atkin Building, Gray's Inn, London WC1R 5AT, ☎ 020 7404 0102
✉ clerks@atkinchambers.com
Call Date: Nov 1993, Lincoln's Inn
Pupil Supervisor
Qualifications: [LLB (Hons)]
✉ clerks@atkinchambers.com

WALKER MR STEVEN PETER

4-5 Gray's Inn Square
Gray's Inn, London WC1R 5AH,
☎ 020 7404 5252 ✉ clerks@4-5.co.uk
Call Date: Mar 2008, Middle Temple
Qualifications: [LLB (Hons)]

WALKER MR STUART JAMES

Moatlands Chambers
2 Moarlands House, Cromer Street, London WC1H 8DF, ☎ 07813 828697
✉ sjw976@googlemail.com
Call Date: Oct 2005, Middle Temple
Qualifications: [LLB (Hons)]

WALKER-KANE MR JONATHAN CHARLES

Broadway House Chambers
Broadway House, 9 Bank Street, Bradford, West Yorkshire BD1 1TW, ☎ 01274 722560
✉ clerks@broadwayhouse.co.uk
Broadway House Chambers
25 Park Square West, Leeds, West Yorkshire LS1 2PW, ☎ 0113 246 2600
✉ clerks@broadwayhouse.co.uk
Call Date: July 1994, Gray's Inn
Qualifications: [MA (Cantab)]
✉ clerks@broadwayhouse.co.uk

WALKER-MCKEVITT MISS EMMA FINOLA

14 Gray's Inn Square
14 Gray's Inn Square, Gray's Inn, London WC1R 5JP, ☎ 020 7242 0858
✉ clerks@14gis.co.uk
Call Date: July 2006, Inner Temple
Qualifications: [LLB (Sheffield)]

WALKER-NOLAN MR BENJAMIN

Thomas More Chambers
7 Lincoln's Inn Fields, London WC2A 3BP,
☎ 020 7404 7000
✉ clerks@thomasmore.co.uk
Call Date: Mar 2002, Middle Temple
Qualifications: [LLB (Hons)]
✉ bwalkernolan@thomasmore.co.uk

WALKER-SMITH SIR JOHN JONAH

Chambers of Mr Walker-Smith
32 Westbourne Park Villas, London W2 5EA,
☎ 020 7229 6128
Call Date: Nov 1963, Middle Temple
Pupil Supervisor
Qualifications: [MA (Oxon)]

WALKLATE MR ANDREW JAMES

Chambers of Marion Smullen and Kerim Fuad QC
1 Inner Temple Lane, London EC4Y 1AF,
☎ 020 7427 4400 ✉ clerks@1itl.com
Call Date: July 2002, Middle Temple
Qualifications: [BA (Hons) (Cantab)]

WALKLING MR THOMAS

St Philips Chambers
55 Temple Row, Birmingham B2 5LS,
☎ 0121 246 7000 ✉ clerks@st-philips.com
Call Date: July 2001, Lincoln's Inn
Qualifications: [BA (Hons)(Bris) Dip Law]
✉ twalkling@st-philips.com

WALL MR CHRISTOPHER JAMES LYNTON

Becket Chambers
17 New Dover Road, Canterbury, Kent CT1 3AS, ☎ 01227 786331
✉ clerks@becket-chambers.co.uk
Call Date: Nov 1987, Lincoln's Inn
Qualifications: [LLB (Hons)]
✉ cwall@becket-chambers.co.uk

WALL MISS JACQUELINE FRANCOISE

15 Winckley Square
Preston PR1 3JJ, ☎ 01772 252828
✉ clerks@15winckleysq.co.uk
Call Date: July 1986, Gray's Inn
Pupil Supervisor
Qualifications: [LLB (Lanc)]

WALL MR MARK ARTHUR QC (2006)

Citadel Chambers
The Citadel, 190 Corporation Street, Birmingham B4 6QD, ☎ 0121 233 8500
✉ clerks@citadelchambers.com
Call Date: Nov 1985, Lincoln's Inn
Recorder
Qualifications: [MA (Cantab)]
✉ clerks@citadelchambers.com

E

WALLACE MR ANDREW DUNCAN GRAY

No5 Chambers
Fountain Court, Steelhouse Lane, Birmingham B4 6DR, ☎0845 210 5555 ✉info@no5.com
No5 Chambers
Greenwood House, 4-7 Salisbury Court, London EC4Y 8AA, ☎0845 210 5555
No5 Chambers
38 Queen Square, Bristol BS1 4QS, ☎0845 210 5555
Call Date: Nov 1988, Gray's Inn
Qualifications: [LLB]
✉adw@no5.com

WALLACE MS ANN CHRISTINE

King's Bench and Godolphin (KBG)Chambers
115 North Hill, Plymouth, Devon PL4 8JY, ☎01752 221551
✉clerks@kbgchambers.co.uk
Call Date: July 1979, Inner Temple
Qualifications: [LLB (Hons) (Bris)]

WALLACE MR HUGH GEORGE

9 Park Place
9 Park Place, Cardiff, South Glamorgan CF10 3DP, ☎029 2038 2731
✉clerks@9parkplace.co.uk
Call Date: July 1993, Gray's Inn
✉clerks@9parkplace.co.uk

WALLACE MISS NICOLA JANE

4 Paper Buildings
1st Floor, 4 Paper Buildings, Temple, London EC4Y 7EX, ☎020 7427 5200
✉clerks@4pb.com
Call Date: Oct 2006, Inner Temple
Qualifications: [BA (Oxon)]
✉nw@4pb.com

WALLACE MR SAM

New Court
Ground Floor, New Court, Temple, London EC4Y 9BE, ☎020 7583 5123
✉clerks@newcourtchambers.com
Call Date: Nov 2004, Gray's Inn
Qualifications: [LLB]
✉swallace@newcourtchambers.net

WALLACE MR SHAUN ANTHONY

Great James Street Chambers
37 Great James Street, London WC1N 3HB, ☎020 7440 4949
✉chambers@greatjames.co.uk
Call Date: Nov 1984, Inner Temple
Qualifications: [BA]

WALLBANKS MISS JOANNE

Regent Chambers
Regent House, 3 Pall Mall, Hanley, Stoke On Trent ST1 1HP, ☎01782 286666
✉clerks@regentchambers.co.uk
Call Date: Oct 1997, Middle Temple
Qualifications: [LLB (Hons)(Staffs)]

WALLER MR RICHARD BEAUMONT QC (2012)

7 King's Bench Walk
Ground Floor, 7 King's Bench Walk, Temple, London EC4Y 7DS, ☎020 7910 8300
✉clerks@7kbw.co.uk
Call Date: Oct 1994, Gray's Inn
Pupil Supervisor
Qualifications: [MA]
✉rwaller@7kbw.co.uk

WALLING MR PHILIP THOMAS GEORGE

7 Bell Yard
London WC2A 2JR, ☎020 7831 0636
✉kevintarrant@btconnect.com
Call Date: Nov 1986, Lincoln's Inn
Qualifications: [LLB(Lanc) BL (Dublin)]
✉pwa@7bellyard.co.uk

WALLINGTON MR PETER THOMAS QC (2008)

11 King's Bench Walk
11 King's Bench Walk, Temple, London EC4Y 7EQ, ☎020 7632 8500
✉clerksroom@11kbw.com
Call Date: July 1987, Gray's Inn
Qualifications: [MA LLM (Cantab)]
✉peter.wallington@11kbw.com

WALLINGTON MR RICHARD ANTHONY

Ten Old Square
Ground Floor, Ten Old Square, Lincoln's Inn, London WC2A 3SU, ☎020 7405 0758
✉clerks@tenoldsquare.com
Call Date: July 1972, Middle Temple
Qualifications: [MA (Cantab)]
✉richardwallington@tenoldsquare.com

WALLS MR KEVIN ANDREW

4 Breams Buildings
Chancery Lane, London EC4A 1HP, ☎020 7092 1900 ✉clerks@4bb.co.uk
Call Date: July 1999, Gray's Inn
Qualifications: [LLB (L'pool)]

WALMISLEY MRS LISA CATHERINE

Kings Chambers
36 Young Street, Manchester M3 3FT,
☎0845 034 3444
✉clerks@kingschambers.com
Kings Chambers
5 Park Square East, Leeds LS1 2NE,
☎0845 034 3444
✉clerks@kingschambers.com
Kings Chambers
Embassy House, 60 Church Street, Birmingham B3 2DJ, ☎0845 034 3444
✉clerks@kingschambers.com
Call Date: July 2000, Middle Temple
Qualifications: [LLB(Hons) (Newc)]
✉LWalmisley@kingschambers.com

WALMSLEY MR ALAN

5 King's Bench Walk
5 King's Bench Walk, Temple, London EC4Y 7DN, ☎020 7353 5638
✉clerks@5kbw.co.uk
Call Date: Nov 1991, Inner Temple
Qualifications: [BSc]
✉alan.walmsley@5kbw.co.uk

WALMSLEY MR JAMES OLIVER

Wilberforce Chambers
8 New Square, Lincoln's Inn, London WC2A 3QP, ☎020 7306 0102
✉chambers@wilberforce.co.uk
Call Date: Oct 2007, Lincoln's Inn
Qualifications: [MA (Hons) (Oxon)]
✉jwalmsley@wilberforce.co.uk

WALMSLEY MR KEITH BERNARD RUPERT

1 Chancery Lane
London WC2A 1LF, ☎0845 634 6666
✉clerks@1chancerylane.com
York Chambers
Rotterdam House, 116 The Quayside, Newcastle Upon Tyne NE1 3DY,
☎0191 206 4677
Call Date: July 1973, Inner Temple
Pupil Supervisor
Qualifications: [LLB (Bris) DCrim (Cantab)]
✉kwalmsley@1chancerylane.com

WALPOLE MS EILEEN SEAN QUINN

Lamb Chambers
Lamb Building, Elm Court, Temple, London EC4Y 7AS, ☎020 7797 8300
✉info@lambchambers.co.uk
Call Date: July 2008, Middle Temple
Qualifications: [BA (Hons) (Dub)]

WALSH MR DARREN STEPHEN

Queen Square Chambers
56 Queen Square, Bristol BS1 4PR,
☎0117 921 1966 ✉crime@qs-c.co.uk
Call Date: Oct 1997, Inner Temple
Qualifications: [LLB (Staffs)]

WALSH MR DAVID PAUL

Quadrant Chambers
Quadrant House, 10 Fleet Street, London EC4Y 1AU, ☎020 7583 4444
✉info@quadrantchambers.com
Call Date: Oct 2007, Inner Temple
Qualifications: [BA (Oxon) LLM (Lond)]

WALSH MR JACK LAWRENCE

2 Pump Court
1st Floor, 2 Pump Court, Temple, London EC4Y 7AH, ☎020 7353 5597
✉clerks@2pumpcourt.co.uk
Call Date: July 2006, Lincoln's Inn
Qualifications: [BA (Oxon)]
✉jwalsh@2pumpcourt.co.uk

WALSH MR JOHN PATRICK

Doughty Street Chambers
53-54 Doughty Street, London WC1N 2LS,
☎020 7404 1313
✉enquiries@doughtystreet.co.uk
Doughty Street Chambers
Pall Mall Court, 61-67 King Street, Manchester M2 4PD, ☎0161 618 1066
Doughty Street Chambers
5th Floor, Broad Quay House, Prince Street, Bristol BS1 4DJ, ☎01179 058 717
Call Date: Nov 1993, Inner Temple
Pupil Supervisor
Qualifications: [BA LLB (Lond) MA (Ireland)]
✉j.walsh@doughtystreet.co.uk

WALSH MISS KATHRYN MARIE

Broadway House Chambers
Broadway House, 9 Bank Street, Bradford, West Yorkshire BD1 1TW, ☎01274 722560
✉clerks@broadwayhouse.co.uk
Broadway House Chambers
25 Park Square West, Leeds, West Yorkshire LS1 2PW, ☎0113 246 2600
✉clerks@broadwayhouse.co.uk
Call Date: Nov 2008, Middle Temple
Qualifications: [LLB (Hons) (Lond) MSc (Oxon)]
✉clerks@broadwayhouse.co.uk, kmw@broadwayhouse.co.uk

E

WALSH MR KEVIN REDMOND

4 Breams Buildings
Chancery Lane, London EC4A 1HP, ☎020 7092 1900 ✉clerks@4bb.co.uk
Call Date: Mar 2003, Lincoln's Inn
Qualifications: [LLB (Hons) (Cardiff)]

WALSH MISS MARTHA CONDON

Westgate Chambers
64 High Street, Lewes, East Sussex BN7 1XG, ☎01273 480510
✉clerks@westgate-chambers.co.uk
Call Date: Nov 2000, Middle Temple
Qualifications: [BA (Sussex) Post Graduate Dip in Law PGDL MA]
mw@westgate-chambers.co.uk

WALSH MR MICHAEL PATRICK

Tanfield Chambers
2-5 Warwick Court, London WC1R 5DJ, ☎020 7421 5300
✉clerks@tanfieldchambers.co.uk
Call Date: July 2006, Middle Temple
Qualifications: [LLB (Hons) (Lond)]
michaelwalsh@tanfieldchambers.co.uk

E

WALSH MR MICHAEL STEVEN

The Chambers of Grahame Aldous QC
9 Gough Square, London EC4A 3DG, ☎020 7832 0500
✉clerks@9goughsquare.co.uk
Call Date: Oct 1996, Middle Temple
Qualifications: [BA (Hons) (Lond) Dip Law]
mwalsh@9goughsquare.co.uk

WALSH MISS MOIRA

KCH Garden Square
1 Oxford Street, Nottingham NG1 5BH, ☎0115 941 8851
✉clerks@kchgardensquare.co.uk
Call Date: July 2000, Middle Temple
Pupil Supervisor
Qualifications: [Bsc(Hons) (Leic)]

WALSH MISS PATRICIA CLAIRE

East Anglian Chambers
53 North Hill, Colchester, Essex CO1 1QA, ☎01473 214481 ✉colchester@ealaw.co.uk
East Anglian Chambers
140 New London Road, Chelmsford, Essex CM2 0AW, ☎01473 214481
✉chelmsford@ealaw.co.uk
East Anglian Chambers
Gresham House, 5 Museum Street, Ipswich, Suffolk IP1 1HQ, ☎01473 214481
✉ipswich@ealaw.co.uk
Call Date: Nov 1993, Lincoln's Inn
Qualifications: [LLB (Hons)]
patriciawalsh@ealaw.co.uk

WALSH MR PETER ANTHONY JOSEPH

15 New Bridge Street
London EC4V 6AU, ☎020 7842 1900
✉clerks@15nbs.com
Call Date: Nov 1978, Middle Temple
Pupil Supervisor
Qualifications: [LLB (Hons) (Lond)]
peter.walsh@15nbs.com

WALSH MR PETER PAUL

Trinity Chambers
The Custom House, 39 Quayside, Newcastle Upon Tyne NE1 3DE, ☎0191 232 1927
✉info@trinitychambers.co.uk
Trinity Chambers
Multi Media Exchange, 72-80 Corporation Road, Middlesbrough TS1 2RF, ☎01642 247569
✉info@trinitychambers.co.uk
Call Date: May 1982, Gray's Inn
Pupil Supervisor
Qualifications: [BA (Hons)]
p.walsh@trinitychambers.co.uk

WALSH MISS RACHEL ANN

2 Hare Court
Lower Ground, Ground, 1st & 2nd Floor, 2 Hare Court, Temple, London EC4Y 7BH, ☎020 7353 3982 ✉clerks@2harecourt.com
Call Date: July 2010, Gray's Inn
Qualifications: [LLB LLM]

WALSH MISS ROSEMARY

Queen Square Chambers
56 Queen Square, Bristol BS1 4PR, ☎0117 921 1966 ✉crime@qs-c.co.uk
Call Date: July 2006, Middle Temple
Qualifications: [LLB (Hons) (Lond)]
rgw@qs-c.co.uk

WALSH MR STEPHEN PAUL QC (2009)

3 Raymond Buildings
3 Raymond Buildings, Gray's Inn, London WC1R 5BH, ☎020 7400 6400
✉clerks@3rblaw.com
Call Date: Nov 1983, Middle Temple
Qualifications: [LLB]

WALSH MR STEVEN JAMES FRANKLYN

Five Paper
Ground Floor, 5 Paper Buildings, Temple, London EC4Y 7HB, ☎020 7815 3200
Call Date: Feb 1965, Lincoln's Inn
Pupil Supervisor
Qualifications: [BA LLB (Cantab)]
clerks@fivepaper.com

Types of work: Banking, Chancery (general), Commercial litigation, Company, commercial and competition, Conflict of laws, Equity, Personal insolvency, Professional negligence, Trusts, Wills

Circuit: South Eastern

Languages spoken: French, Spanish

Reported Cases: *Noel v Becker*, 1 WLR 355 [1971] (Court of Appeal), 1971. The Trial Court may not interfere and alter the terms of an agreement set out in a Tomlin Order Schedule contrary to the parties' wishes.
Degazon v Barclays Bank International, [1988] 1 FTLR 17 (Court of Appeal), 1988. A foreign administrator incorporated in England appointed by a Court in Dominica could not be sued in England by an English resident with Legal Aid.
Behzadi v Shaftsbury Hotels Ltd, [1992] Ch 1; [1991] 2 All ER 477 (Court of Appeal), 1991. The notice making time of the essence to complete a contract for the sale of land must provide reasonable time for compliance with that notice.
Ashock Patel & Partners v Ibrahim Khan Raja, 13 July, Chancery Division, Robert Walker J (High Court, Chancery Decision), 1995. In a contract to provide both contentious and non-contentious business the Court retained a residual discretion to order the taxation of any Bill of Costs.
Segbedzi v Segbedzi, 1999 Ghanaian Administrators remitting assets to Ghana (for administration) without English Court's permission made English resident Administrator (who took no part) liable under S11(3) Administration of Estates Act 1971.

WALSH MR TIMOTHY EDMUND

Guildhall Chambers
23 Broad Street, Bristol BS1 2HG, ☎0117 930 9000
✉hoc@guildhallchambers.co.uk
Call Date: Oct 2000, Inner Temple
Pupil Supervisor
Qualifications: [BA (Oxon)]
tim.walsh@guildhallchambers.co.uk

WALSH MR WILLIAM JOHN TEASDALE

Old Bailey Chambers
15 Old Bailey, London EC4M 7EF, ☎020 3008 6404
✉clerks@15oldbaileychambers.com
Call Date: Nov 1998, Middle Temple
Qualifications: [LLB (Hons)(Leeds)]
w.walsh@15oldbaileychambers.com

WALTERS MISS CARLY SARAH

Deans Court Chambers
24 St John Street, Manchester M3 4DF, ☎0161 214 6000 ✉clerks@deanscourt.co.uk
Deans Court Chambers
101 Walker Street, Preston PR1 2RR, ☎01772 565 600
✉preston@deanscourt.co.uk
Call Date: Mar 2005, Lincoln's Inn
Qualifications: [LLB (Hons) Lanc]

WALTERS MISS CERYS ANN

9 Park Place
9 Park Place, Cardiff, South Glamorgan CF10 3DP, ☎029 2038 2731
✉clerks@9parkplace.co.uk
Call Date: July 2009, Lincoln's Inn
Qualifications: [LLB (Cardiff)]
cwalters@9parkplace.co.uk

WALTERS MR EDMUND JOHN

13 King's Bench Walk
13 King's Bench Walk, Temple, London EC4Y 7EN, ☎020 7353 7204
✉clerks@13kbw.co.uk
Call Date: Nov 1991, Middle Temple
Qualifications: [BA (Hons) (Bris) Dip Law]

WALTERS MR GERAINT WYN

Angel Chambers
Ethos Building, Kings Road, Swansea SA1 8AS, ☎01792 464623
✉clerks@angelchambers.co.uk
Call Date: Nov 1981, Gray's Inn
Pupil Supervisor, Recorder
Qualifications: [LLB Hons) (Wales)]

WALTERS MR GRAHAM ANTHONY

Civitas Chambers
Global Reach, Celtic Gateway, Cardiff Bay, Cardiff CF11 0SN, ☎0845 0713 007
✉clerks@civitaslaw.com
Call Date: July 1986, Gray's Inn
Pupil Supervisor
Qualifications: [MA (Oxon)]
graham.walters@civitaslaw.com

E

WALTERS MR JOHN LATIMER QC (1997)

Gray's Inn Tax Chambers
3rd Floor, Gray's Inn Chambers, Gray's Inn, London WC1R 5JA, ☎020 7242 2642
✉clerks@taxbar.com
East Anglian Chambers
Gresham House, 5 Museum Street, Ipswich, Suffolk IP1 1HQ, ☎01473 214481
✉ipswich@ealaw.co.uk
East Anglian Chambers
15 The Close, Norwich, Norfolk NR1 4DZ, ☎01473 214481 ✉norwich@ealaw.co.uk
East Anglian Chambers
53 North Hill, Colchester, Essex CO1 1QA, ☎01473 214481 ✉colchester@ealaw.co.uk
East Anglian Chambers
140 New London Road, Chelmsford, Essex CM2 0AW, ☎01473 214481
✉chelmsford@ealaw.co.uk
Call Date: July 1977, Middle Temple
Qualifications: [MA (Oxon) FCA]
✉jw@taxbar.com

WALTERS MR JONATHAN GWYNNE

Civitas Chambers
Global Reach, Celtic Gateway, Cardiff Bay, Cardiff CF11 0SN, ☎0845 0713 007
✉clerks@civitaslaw.com
Call Date: July 1984, Inner Temple
Qualifications: [LLB (Wales)]
✉jonathan.walters@civitaslaw.com

WALTERS MISS VIVIAN IRENE ELIZABETH

Five St Andrew's Hill
5 St Andrew's Hill, London EC4V 5BZ, ☎020 7332 5400 ✉Clerks@5sah.co.uk
Call Date: Nov 1991, Middle Temple
Pupil Supervisor
Qualifications: [BA (Hons) (Leic)]
✉vivianwalters@5sah.co.uk

WALTHALL MR ARRON

Cobden House Chambers
19 Quay Street, Manchester M3 3HN, ☎0161 833 6000 ✉Clerks@Cobden.co.uk
Call Date: July 2005, Inner Temple
Qualifications: [BA (Cantab)]
✉clerks@cobden.co.uk

WALTON MR ALASTAIR HENRY

Maitland Chambers
7 Stone Buildings, Lincoln's Inn, London WC2A 3SZ, ☎020 7406 1200
✉clerks@maitlandchambers.com
Call Date: July 1977, Lincoln's Inn
Pupil Supervisor
Qualifications: [BA (Oxon)]
✉awalton@maitlandchambers.com

WALTON MISS CAROLYN MARGERY

Maitland Chambers
7 Stone Buildings, Lincoln's Inn, London WC2A 3SZ, ☎020 7406 1200
✉clerks@maitlandchambers.com
Call Date: July 1980, Gray's Inn
Pupil Supervisor
Qualifications: [LLB (Lond) LLM (Lond)]
✉cwalton@maitlandchambers.com

WALTON MISS KAREN TANYA

Dyers Chambers
35 Bedford Row, London WC1R 4JH, ☎020 7404 1881
✉admin@dyerschambers.com
Call Date: Mar 1998, Middle Temple
Qualifications: [BA (Hons)(Manch)]

WALTON MR ROBERT JOHN

Landmark Chambers
180 Fleet Street, London EC4A 2HG, ☎020 7430 1221
✉clerks@landmarkchambers.co.uk
Call Date: Mar 1999, Lincoln's Inn
Pupil Supervisor
Qualifications: [BA (Hons) (Edin)]
✉rwalton@landmarkchambers.co.uk

WAN DAUD MR MALEK

Garden Court Chambers
57-60 Lincoln's Inn Fields, London WC2A 3LJ, ☎020 7993 7600 ✉info@gclaw.co.uk
Call Date: Nov 1991, Inner Temple
Pupil Supervisor
Qualifications: [LLB LLM]
✉malekwd@gclaw.co.uk

WANAS MISS SALLY

Clock Chambers
18 Waterloo Road, Wolverhampton WV1 4BL, ☎01902 313444
✉clockchambers@btconnect.com
Call Date: Nov 2005, Inner Temple
Qualifications: [LLB University of Wolverhampton]
✉sallywanas@excite.com

WARBURTON MISS JULIE

KCH Garden Square
1 Oxford Street, Nottingham NG1 5BH,
☎ 0115 941 8851
✉ clerks@kchgardensquare.co.uk
Call Date: Oct 1993, Middle Temple
Qualifications: [LLB (Hons)(Lond)]
✉ JWarburton@kchgardensquare.co.uk, jwarburton@kch.co.uk

WARBY MR MARK DAVID JOHN QC (2002)

5RB
1st Floor, 5 Raymond Buildings, Gray's Inn, London WC1R 5BP, ☎ 020 7242 2902
✉ clerks@5rb.com
Call Date: Nov 1981, Gray's Inn
Qualifications: [MA (Oxon)]

WARD MISS ALEXANDRA

9-12 Bell Yard
London WC2A 2JR, ☎ 020 7400 1800
✉ clerks@9-12bellyard.com
Call Date: July 2000, Lincoln's Inn
Qualifications: [BA(Hons) (Abery)]

WARD MR ANDREW JOHN

Exchange Chambers
7 Ralli Courts, West Riverside, Manchester M3 5FT, ☎ 0161 833 2722
Exchange Chambers
One Derby Square, Derby Square, Liverpool L2 9XX, ☎ 0151 236 7747
✉ info@exchangechambers.co.uk
Exchange Chambers
Oxford House, Oxford Row, Leeds LS1 3BE,
☎ 0113 203 1970
✉ spencer@exchangechambers.co.uk
Call Date: July 2000, Middle Temple
Qualifications: [BA(Hons) (Oxon) BCL (Oxon)]
✉ ward@exchangechambers.co.uk

WARD MRS ANNIE FRANCES

Pump Court Chambers
31 Southgate Street, Winchester, Hampshire SO23 9EB, ☎ 01962 868 161
✉ clerks@3pumpcourt.com
Pump Court Chambers
Upper Ground Floor, 3 Pump Court, Temple, London EC4Y 7AJ, ☎ 020 7353 0711
✉ clerks@3pumpcourt.com
Pump Court Chambers
5 Temple Chambers, Temple Street, Swindon SN1 1SQ, ☎ 01793 539899
✉ clerks@3pumpcourt.com
Call Date: Nov 1997, Gray's Inn
Qualifications: [BA (Oxon) MA (Essex)]
✉ afw@3pumpcourt.com

WARD MR ANTHONY DOUGLAS

3 PB Barristers
Royal Talbot House, 2 Victoria Street, Bristol, Avon BS1 6BB, ☎ 0117 928 1520
Call Date: July 1971, Inner Temple
Pupil Supervisor
Qualifications: [LLB (Lond)]
✉ tony.ward@3pb.co.uk

WARD MISS EMILY VICTORIA

Broadway House Chambers
Broadway House, 9 Bank Street, Bradford, West Yorkshire BD1 1TW, ☎ 01274 722560
✉ clerks@broadwayhouse.co.uk
Call Date: July 2011, Middle Temple
Qualifications: [LLB (Hons) (Manch)]
✉ evw@broadwayhouse.co.uk

WARD MS GALINA

Landmark Chambers
180 Fleet Street, London EC4A 2HG,
☎ 020 7430 1221
✉ clerks@landmarkchambers.co.uk
Call Date: Mar 2000, Gray's Inn
Pupil Supervisor
Qualifications: [BA (Oxon)]
✉ gward@landmarkchambers.co.uk

WARD MR JOHN DAVID

39 Park Square
Leeds LS1 2NU, ☎ 0113 245 6633
✉ seniorclerk@39parksquarechambers.co.uk
Call Date: July 2004, Lincoln's Inn
Qualifications: [LLB Hons (Northumbria)]

WARD MR JOHNNY

Kings Chambers
36 Young Street, Manchester M3 3FT,
☎ 0845 034 3444
✉ clerks@kingschambers.com
Kings Chambers
5 Park Square East, Leeds LS1 2NE,
☎ 0845 034 3444
✉ clerks@kingschambers.com
Kings Chambers
Embassy House, 60 Church Street, Birmingham B3 2DJ, ☎ 0845 034 3444
✉ clerks@kingschambers.com
Call Date: July 2007, Lincoln's Inn
Qualifications: [BA (B'ham)]
✉ jward@kingchambers.com

E

WARD MISS KELLY JANE

Pallant Chambers
12 North Pallant, Chichester, West Sussex PO19 1TQ, ☎01243 784538
✉clerks@pallantchambers.co.uk
Call Date: Oct 2001, Middle Temple
Qualifications: [LLB (Hons)]
✉clerks@pallantchambers.co.uk, kward@pallantchambers.co.uk

WARD MR MARTIN STUART

14 Gray's Inn Square
14 Gray's Inn Square, Gray's Inn, London WC1R 5JP, ☎020 7242 0858
✉clerks@14gis.co.uk
Call Date: Oct 1992, Lincoln's Inn
Pupil Supervisor
Qualifications: [BA(Hons)(Warw)]

WARD MR PETER MARK

The Chambers of Peter Ward
88 Kingsway, London WC2B 6AA, ☎020 3402 2152 ✉whurr@yahoo.com
Call Date: Oct 1996, Inner Temple
Qualifications: [LLB (Lond)]

WARD MISS RACHAEL ANN

New Walk Chambers
27 New Walk, Leicester, Leicestershire LE1 6TE, ☎0871 200 1298 / 0116 255 9144
✉clerks@newwalkchambers.co.uk
Call Date: July 2009, Middle Temple
Qualifications: [LLB (Hons) (Wales)]

WARD MR ROBERT ANDREW

15 New Bridge Street
London EC4V 6AU, ☎020 7842 1900
✉clerks@15nbs.com
Call Date: July 2007, Lincoln's Inn
Qualifications: [LLB (Leeds)]
✉robert.ward@15nbs.com

WARD MR ROBIN HENRY

8 New Square
8 New Square, Lincoln's Inn, London WC2A 3QP, ☎020 7405 4321
✉clerks@8newsquare.co.uk
Call Date: Nov 2000, Middle Temple
Qualifications: [BA (Cantab) B.Eng (Hons)(Cantab) CPE]
✉henry.ward@8newsquare.co.uk

Types of work: Breach of confidence, Competition law, Copyright, EC competition law, Entertainment, Information technology, Intellectual property, Malicious falsehood, Media and entertainment, Patents, Trade secrets, Trademarks

WARD MR SIMON JOHN

St Philips Chambers
55 Temple Row, Birmingham B2 5LS, ☎0121 246 7000 ✉clerks@st-philips.com
Call Date: July 1986, Inner Temple
Pupil Supervisor, Recorder
Qualifications: [LLB (B'ham)]
✉sward@st-philips.com

WARD MR SIMON KENNETH

Argent Chambers
5 Bell Yard, London WC2A 2JR, ☎020 7556 5500
✉briefsin@argentchambers.co.uk
Call Date: Nov 1984, Middle Temple
Qualifications: [BA (Durham) MA (Lond)]
✉s.ward@argentchambers.co.uk

WARD MISS STEPHANIE ELIZABETH MARY

Garden Court Chambers
57-60 Lincoln's Inn Fields, London WC2A 3LJ, ☎020 7993 7600 ✉info@gclaw.co.uk
Call Date: July 2005, Lincoln's Inn
Qualifications: [BA (Hons)]
✉stephaniew@gclaw.co.uk

WARD MR TIMOTHY JUSTIN QC (2011)

Monckton Chambers
1 & 2 Raymond Buildings, Gray's Inn, London WC1R 5NR, ☎020 7405 7211
✉chambers@monckton.com
Call Date: Oct 1994, Gray's Inn
Pupil Supervisor
Qualifications: [BA MA]
✉tward@monckton.com

WARD MR TREVOR ROBERT EDWARD

12 College Place
Fauvelle Buildings, 12 College Place, Southampton SO15 2FE, ☎023 8032 0320
✉clerks@12cp.co.uk
Call Date: Apr 1991, Middle Temple
Qualifications: [LLB (Hons) MSc]
✉TWard@12cp.co.uk

WARD MR VINCENT

New Court Chambers
3 Broad Chare, Newcastle Upon Tyne NE1 3DQ, ☎0191 232 1980
✉clerks@newcourt-chambers.co.uk
Call Date: July 1998, Middle Temple
Qualifications: [LLB (HOns)(N'castle)]
✉clerks@newcourt-chambers.co.uk

WARDELL MR JOHN DAVID MEREDITH QC (2002)

Wilberforce Chambers
8 New Square, Lincoln's Inn, London WC2A 3QP, ☎020 7306 0102
✉chambers@wilberforce.co.uk
Call Date: July 1979, Gray's Inn
Qualifications: [LLB (Exon) MPhil (Cantab)]
jwardell@wilberforce.co.uk

Types of work: Banking, Chancery (general), Commercial litigation, Commercial property, Financial services, Landlord and tenant, Professional negligence

WARDLOW MR JOHN JEFFREY

East Anglian Chambers
15 The Close, Norwich, Norfolk NR1 4DZ, ☎01473 214481 ✉norwich@ealaw.co.uk
East Anglian Chambers
53 North Hill, Colchester, Essex CO1 1QA, ☎01473 214481 ✉colchester@ealaw.co.uk
East Anglian Chambers
Gresham House, 5 Museum Street, Ipswich, Suffolk IP1 1HQ, ☎01473 214481
✉ipswich@ealaw.co.uk
Call Date: July 1971, Gray's Inn
Pupil Supervisor
johnwardlow@ealaw.co.uk

WARD-PROWSE MR JOHN

Chambers of Mr J Ward-Prowse
317 Havant Road, Farlington, Portsmouth, Hampshire PO6 1DD, ☎0239 237 9708
✉j.wp@hotmail.com
Call Date: Nov 1997, Lincoln's Inn

WARE MR CHRISTOPHER EDWARD

2 Hare Court
Lower Ground, Ground, 1st & 2nd Floor, 2 Hare Court, Temple, London EC4Y 7BH, ☎020 7353 3982 ✉clerks@2harecourt.com
Call Date: Nov 2007, Lincoln's Inn
Qualifications: [BA (Oxon)]
chrisware@2harecourt.com

WARENTS MR DANIEL ELIJAH

XXIV Old Buildings
Ground Floor, 24 Old Buildings, Lincoln's Inn, London WC2A 3UP, ☎020 7691 2424
✉clerks@xxiv.co.uk
Call Date: Oct 2009, Middle Temple
Qualifications: [BA (Hons) (Cantab) LLM (Cantab)]
daniel.warents@xxiv.co.uk

WARITAY MR SAMUEL

Chambers of Mr Samuel Waritay
2nd Floor, 145-147 St John Street, London EC1V 4PY, ☎0845 803 7767
✉Waritay@onetel.com
Call Date: Nov 1993, Inner Temple
Qualifications: [BA (Hons)(Sussex)]
waritay@onetel.com

WARNE MR PETER LAWRENCE

Lincoln House Chambers
Tower 12, The Avenue North, Spinningfields, 18-22 Bridge Street, Manchester M3 3BZ,
☎0161 832 5701
✉info@lincolnhousechambers.com
Call Date: Nov 1993, Inner Temple
Qualifications: [BA (Manch) CPE]
peter.warne@lincolnhousechambers.com

WARNER MR ANTHONY CHARLES BROUGHTON

Citadel Chambers
The Citadel, 190 Corporation Street, Birmingham B4 6QD, ☎0121 233 8500
✉clerks@citadelchambers.com
Call Date: July 1979, Gray's Inn
Pupil Supervisor, Recorder
Qualifications: [BA]
clerks@citadelchambers.com

WARNER MR DAVID ALEXANDER

St Philips Chambers
55 Temple Row, Birmingham B2 5LS, ☎0121 246 7000 ✉clerks@st-philips.com
Call Date: Oct 1996, Gray's Inn
Pupil Supervisor
Qualifications: [LLB]
dwarner@st-philips.com

WARNER MR MALCOLM DIGBY

Guildhall Chambers
23 Broad Street, Bristol BS1 2HG,
☎0117 930 9000
✉hoc@guildhallchambers.co.uk
Call Date: July 1979, Lincoln's Inn
Pupil Supervisor
Qualifications: [BScEcon (Hons) (Wales)]
malcolm.warner@guildhallchambers.co.uk

WARNER MISS PAMELA SHARAN

Coram Chambers
9-11 Fulwood Place, London WC1V 6HG,
☎020 7092 3700
✉mail@coramchambers.co.uk
Call Date: Feb 1985, Gray's Inn
Qualifications: [BA (Hons)]
pamela.warner@coramchambers.co.uk

E

WARNOCK MR ANDREW RONALD QC (2012)

1 Chancery Lane
London WC2A 1LF, ☎ 0845 634 6666
✉ clerks@1chancerylane.com
Call Date: Nov 1993, Inner Temple
Pupil Supervisor
Qualifications: [BA Dip French (Cantab)]
awarnock@1chancerylane.com

WARNOCK-SMITH MRS SHAN QC (2002)

5 Stone Buildings
5 Stone Buildings, Lincoln's Inn, London WC2A 3XT, ☎ 020 7242 6201
✉ clerks@5sblaw.com
Call Date: July 1971, Gray's Inn
Qualifications: [LLM]

WARREN MS CAMILLE ELIZABETH

Chambers of Ian Macdonald QC
Garden Court North, 22 Oxford Court, Manchester M2 3WQ, ☎ 0161 236 1840
✉ clerks@gcnchambers.co.uk
Call Date: Nov 2008, Inner Temple
Qualifications: [BA (Manch) MA CPE]
cwarren@gcnchambers.co.uk

WARREN MR MICHAEL JOHN DAVID

1 KBW Chambers
1 King's Bench Walk, Temple, London EC4Y 7DB, ☎ 020 7936 1500
✉ clerks@1kbw.co.uk
King's Bench Chambers
174 High Street, Lewes BN7 1YE, ☎ 01273 402600
Call Date: Nov 1971, Middle Temple
Pupil Supervisor, Recorder
Qualifications: [MA (Oxon)]
mwarren@1kbw.co.uk

WARREN MR PHILIP DAVID CHARLES

Queen Square Chambers
56 Queen Square, Bristol BS1 4PR, ☎ 0117 921 1966 ✉ crime@qs-c.co.uk
Call Date: May 1988, Gray's Inn
Pupil Supervisor
Qualifications: [LLB (Wales)]
pdw@qs-c.co.uk

WARREN MR RUPERT MILES QC (2012)

Landmark Chambers
180 Fleet Street, London EC4A 2HG, ☎ 020 7430 1221
✉ clerks@landmarkchambers.co.uk
Call Date: Oct 1994, Gray's Inn
Pupil Supervisor
Qualifications: [BA (Oxon)]
rwarren@landmarkchambers.co.uk

WARRENDER MISS NICHOLA MARY

Quadrant Chambers
Quadrant House, 10 Fleet Street, London EC4Y 1AU, ☎ 020 7583 4444
✉ info@quadrantchambers.com
Call Date: Nov 1995, Inner Temple
Pupil Supervisor
Qualifications: [LLB (Bris)]
nichola.warrender@quadrantchambers.com

WARRINGTON MR JOHN EDWARD LAWRENCE

Five St Andrew's Hill
5 St Andrew's Hill, London EC4V 5BZ, ☎ 020 7332 5400 ✉ Clerks@5sah.co.uk
Call Date: July 2000, Lincoln's Inn
Qualifications: [LLB(Hons) (Lond)]
johnwarrington@5sah.co.uk

WARSHAW MR JUSTIN ALEXANDER EDWARD

1 Hare Court
1 Hare Court, Temple, London EC4Y 7BE, ☎ 020 7797 7070 ✉ clerks@1hc.com
Call Date: Nov 1995, Gray's Inn
Pupil Supervisor
Qualifications: [MA (Oxon)]
warshaw@1hc.com

WARWICK MR HENRY

Henderson Chambers
2 Harcourt Buildings, Temple, London EC4Y 9DB, ☎ 020 7583 9020
✉ clerks@hendersonchambers.co.uk
Call Date: July 2007, Lincoln's Inn
Qualifications: [BSc (Bris) LLM (Cantab)]
clerks@hendersonchambers.co.uk

WARWICK MISS JOANNA LOUISE

QEB Hollis Whiteman
1-2 Laurence Pountney Hill, London EC4R 0EU, ☎ 020 7933 8855
✉ barristers@qebhw.co.uk
Call Date: July 2004, Lincoln's Inn
Qualifications: [LLB Hons (U.E.A.)]
barristers@qebhw.co.uk

WARWICK MR MARK GRANVILLE

Selborne Chambers
10 Essex Street, London WC2R 3AA,
☎ 020 7420 9500
✉ clerks@selbornechambers.co.uk
Call Date: July 1974, Inner Temple
Qualifications: [LLB (Hons)]
✉ mark.warwick@selbornechambers.co.uk

WASS MISS KRYSTELLE JENNIFER

10 King's Bench Walk
Ground Floor, 10 King's Bench Walk, Temple, London EC4Y 7EB, ☎ 020 7353 7742
✉ Chambers@10kingsbenchwalk.co.uk
Call Date: Mar 2007, Middle Temple
Qualifications: [LLB (Warw)]
✉ chambers@10kingsbenchwalk.co.uk

WASS MISS SASHA QC (2000)

6 King's Bench Walk
Ground Floor, 6 King's Bench Walk, Temple, London EC4Y 7DR, ☎ 020 7583 0410
✉ clerks@6kbw.com
Call Date: Nov 1981, Gray's Inn
Recorder
Qualifications: [LLB (L'pool)]
✉ sasha.wass@6kbw.com

WASTALL MR ANDREW JAMES FREDERICK

Park Court Chambers
16 Park Place, Leeds LS1 2SJ,
☎ 0113 243 3277
✉ clerks@parkcourtchambers.co.uk
Call Date: Oct 2005, Gray's Inn
Qualifications: [BA (Southampton)]
✉ awastall@parkcourtchambers.co.uk

WASTELL MR ROBERT JAMES

1 Crown Office Row
1 Crown Office Row, Temple, London EC4Y 7HH, ☎ 020 7797 7500
✉ mail@1cor.com
Call Date: July 2004, Lincoln's Inn
Qualifications: [BA Hons (Oxon)]
✉ robert.wastell@1cor.com

WASUNNA MR CHRISTIAN CHRISTOPHER PETER

2 Dr Johnson's Buildings
2 Dr Johnson's Buildings, Temple, London EC4Y 7AY, ☎ 020 7936 2613
✉ clerks@2drj.com
Call Date: Nov 2000, Gray's Inn
Qualifications: [BA]
✉ c.wasunna@2drj.com, clerks@2drj.com

WATERMAN MR ADRIAN MARK QC (2006)

KBW
The Engine House, No 1 Foundry Square, Leeds LS11 5DL, ☎ 0113 297 1200
✉ clerks@kbwchambers.com
Tooks Chambers
81 Farringdon Street, London EC4A 4BL,
☎ 020 7842 7575 ✉ clerks@tooks.co.uk
Call Date: July 1988, Inner Temple
Recorder
Qualifications: [LLB (Lond)]
✉ adrianwatermanqc@kbwchambers.com

WATERS MR ANDREW JOHN

5 Essex Court
1st Floor, 5 Essex Court, Temple, London EC4Y 9AH, ☎ 020 7410 2000
✉ clerks@5essexcourt.co.uk
Call Date: Nov 1987, Inner Temple
Pupil Supervisor
Qualifications: [LLB]
✉ waters@5essexcourt.co.uk

WATERS MR DAVID EBSWORTH QC (1999)

2 Hare Court
Lower Ground, Ground, 1st & 2nd Floor, 2 Hare Court, Temple, London EC4Y 7BH,
☎ 020 7353 3982 ✉ clerks@2harecourt.com
Call Date: May 1973, Middle Temple
Recorder
✉ davidwaters@2harecourt.com

WATERS MR JOHN CLOUGH

East Anglian Chambers
Gresham House, 5 Museum Street, Ipswich, Suffolk IP1 1HQ, ☎ 01473 214481
✉ ipswich@ealaw.co.uk
East Anglian Chambers
140 New London Road, Chelmsford, Essex CM2 0AW, ☎ 01473 214481
✉ chelmsford@ealaw.co.uk
East Anglian Chambers
15 The Close, Norwich, Norfolk NR1 4DZ,
☎ 01473 214481 ✉ norwich@ealaw.co.uk
Call Date: May 1974, Lincoln's Inn
Pupil Supervisor
✉ johnwaters@ealaw.co.uk

WATERS MR JULIAN WILLIAM PENROSE

1 Chancery Lane
London WC2A 1LF, ☎ 0845 634 6666
✉ clerks@1chancerylane.com
Call Date: Nov 1986, Middle Temple
Pupil Supervisor
Qualifications: [MA (Cantab)]
✉ jwaters@1chancerylane.com

E

WATERS MR MALCOLM IAN QC (1997)

Radcliffe Chambers
Ground Floor, 11 New Square, Lincoln's Inn, London WC2A 3QB, ☎ 020 7831 0081
✉ clerks@radcliffechambers.com
Call Date: July 1977, Lincoln's Inn
Qualifications: [BA (Oxon) BCL (Oxon)]
✉ mwaters@radcliffechambers.com

Fax: 020 7405 2560;
DX: 319 LDE

Types of work: Banking, Building societies, Chancery (land law), Consumer credit, Conveyancing, Equity, Financial services, Mortgages

Awards and memberships: Member of the Working Party responsible for drafting the Standard Conditions of Sale; Member of the Committee responsible for drafting the Standard Commercial Property Conditions

Publications: *Halsbury's Laws of England*, 'Mutual Societies', 5th edition, 2008; *The Building Societies Act 1986* (Co-author), 1987; *The Law of Investor Protection*, 2nd edition (Joint Author), 2003; *Halsbury's Laws of England*, 'Friendly Societies', 4th edition (Reissue) (Consultant Editor), 2007

Reported Cases: *Halifax v Thomas*, [1996] Ch 217 (Court of Appeal), 1995. Mortgages/restitution.
C & G v Norgan, [1996] 1 WLR 343 (Court of Appeal), 1995. Mortgages.
Director General of Fair Trading v First National Bank, [2002] 1 AC 481 (House of Lords), 2001. Unfair terms in consumer contracts.
OFT v Abbey National and Others, [2008] EWHC (Comm); [2008] WLR(D) 128 (Commercial Court), 2008. Fairness of unarranged overdraft charges.
Southern Pacific Mortgage Ltd v Heath, [2010] Ch 254 (Court of Appeal), 2009. Mortgages.

WATERS MISS SARAH

30 Park Place
Cardiff CF10 3BS, ☎ 029 2039 8421
✉ clerks@30parkplace.law.co.uk
Call Date: Oct 1999, Middle Temple
Pupil Supervisor
Qualifications: [LLB (Hons)(N'castle)]
✉ sjw@30parkplace.co.uk

WATERWORTH MRS CAROLINE LOUISE

Ten Old Square
Ground Floor, Ten Old Square, Lincoln's Inn, London WC2A 3SU, ☎ 020 7405 0758
✉ clerks@tenoldsquare.com
Call Date: July 2008, Lincoln's Inn
Qualifications: [BA (Cantab)]

WATERWORTH MR MICHAEL CHRISTOPHER

Ten Old Square
Ground Floor, Ten Old Square, Lincoln's Inn, London WC2A 3SU, ☎ 020 7405 0758
✉ clerks@tenoldsquare.com
Call Date: Oct 1994, Lincoln's Inn
Qualifications: [MA (Cantab) DipLaw (Lond)]
✉ michaelwaterworth@tenoldsquare.com

WATKIN MR TOBY PAUL

Landmark Chambers
180 Fleet Street, London EC4A 2HG,
☎ 020 7430 1221
✉ clerks@landmarkchambers.co.uk
Call Date: Oct 1996, Inner Temple
Pupil Supervisor
Qualifications: [MA (Cantab)]
✉ twatkin@landmarkchambers.co.uk

WATKIN MR TONY MICHAEL

St Ive's Chambers
Whittall Street, Birmingham B4 6DH,
☎ 0121 236 0863
✉ clerks@stiveschambers.co.uk
Call Date: Oct 1998, Middle Temple
Pupil Supervisor
Qualifications: [LLB (Hons)(De Mont)]
✉ tony.watkin@stiveschambers.co.uk

WATKINS MR AARON JAMES

Matrix Chambers
Griffin Building, Gray's Inn, London WC1R 5LN, ☎ 020 7404 3447
✉ matrix@matrixlaw.co.uk / lscott@matrixlaw.co.uk
Call Date: Oct 2006, Middle Temple
Qualifications: [BA (Hons) (Oxon)]

WATKINS MR ADAM KARL

St Johns Buildings
24a - 28 St John Street, Manchester M3 4DJ,
☎ 0161 214 1500
✉ clerk@stjohnsbuildings.co.uk
16 Winckley Square
Preston PR1 3JJ, ☎ 01772 256100
St Johns Buildings Liverpool
8th Floor India Buildings, Water Street,
Liverpool L2 0XG, ☎ 0151 243 6000
✉ clerk@stjohnsbuildings.co.uk
Call Date: July 2004, Gray's Inn
Qualifications: [LLB Hons (Nott'm)]
✉ clerk@stjohnsbuildings.co.uk

WATKINS MR GUY THOMAS

Farrar's Building
Farrar's Building, Temple, London EC4Y 7BD,
☎ 020 7583 9241
✉ Chambers@farrarsbuilding.co.uk
Call Date: Oct 1999, Lincoln's Inn
Pupil Supervisor
Qualifications: [LLB (Hons)(Bris)]
✉ gwatkins@farrarsbuilding.co.uk

WATKINS MR MICHAEL DAVID VERNON

One Essex Court
Ground Floor, One Essex Court, Temple,
London EC4Y 9AR, ☎ 020 7583 2000
✉ clerks@oeclaw.co.uk
Call Date: Oct 2009, Lincoln's Inn
Qualifications: [BA BCL (Oxon)]
✉ mwatkins@oeclaw.co.uk

WATKINS MISS RACHEL CLAIRE

Chartlands Chambers
3 St Giles Terrace, Northampton NN1 2BN,
☎ 01604 603322
✉ enquiries@chartlands-chambers.co.uk
Call Date: Oct 1998, Middle Temple
Pupil Supervisor
Qualifications: [LLB (Hons)(De Mont)]

WATKINSON MR DAVID ROBERT

Garden Court Chambers
57-60 Lincoln's Inn Fields, London WC2A 3LJ,
☎ 020 7993 7600 ✉ info@gclaw.co.uk
Call Date: July 1972, Middle Temple
Pupil Supervisor
Qualifications: [MA LLB (Cantab)]

WATKINSON MR HOWARD

9-12 Bell Yard
London WC2A 2JR, ☎ 020 7400 1800
✉ clerks@9-12bellyard.com
Call Date: Oct 2006, Lincoln's Inn
Qualifications: [BA (Cantab)]
✉ h.watkinson@9-12bellyard.com

WATKINSON MISS SASHA LOUISE

Deans Court Chambers
24 St John Street, Manchester M3 4DF,
☎ 0161 214 6000 ✉ clerks@deanscourt.co.uk
Deans Court Chambers
101 Walker Street, Preston PR1 2RR,
☎ 01772 565 600
✉ preston@deanscourt.co.uk
Call Date: Oct 1998, Lincoln's Inn
Qualifications: [LLB (Hons)(L'pool)]

WATSON MR ALARIC

11 Stone Buildings
11 Stone Buildings, Lincoln's Inn, London
WC2A 3TG, ☎ 020 7831 6381
✉ clerks@11sb.com
Call Date: Nov 1997, Middle Temple
Qualifications: [BA (Hons)(Bris) PhD (Lond)]
✉ watson@11sb.com

WATSON MR ANTONY EDWARD DOUGLAS QC (1986)

Three New Square IP
3 New Square, Lincoln's Inn, London
WC2A 3RS, ☎ 020 7405 1111
✉ clerks@3newsquare.co.uk
Call Date: Nov 1968, Inner Temple
Qualifications: [MA (Cantab)]
✉ clerks@3newsquare.co.uk

WATSON MR BENJAMIN TURQUAND

3 Raymond Buildings
3 Raymond Buildings, Gray's Inn, London
WC1R 5BH, ☎ 020 7400 6400
✉ clerks@3rblaw.com
Call Date: Oct 2002, Lincoln's Inn
Qualifications: [MA (Cantab) CPE BA (Hons) (Cantab)]
✉ ben.watson@3raymondbuildings.com

WATSON MR CHRISTOPHER JONATHAN

St Philips Chambers
55 Temple Row, Birmingham B2 5LS,
☎ 0121 246 7000 ✉ clerks@st-philips.com
Call Date: July 2003, Inner Temple
Qualifications: [LLB (Hons) (Dundee)]
✉ cwatson@st-philips.co.uk

WATSON MS CLAIRE

East Anglian Chambers
140 New London Road, Chelmsford, Essex
CM2 0AW, ☎ 01473 214481
✉ chelmsford@ealaw.co.uk
East Anglian Chambers
Gresham House, 5 Museum Street, Ipswich,
Suffolk IP1 1HQ, ☎ 01473 214481
✉ ipswich@ealaw.co.uk

East Anglian Chambers
15 The Close, Norwich, Norfolk NR1 4DZ,
☎01473 214481 ✉norwich@ealaw.co.uk
Call Date: Nov 1991, Lincoln's Inn
Pupil Supervisor
Qualifications: [LLB (Hons)]
✉clairewatson@ealaw.co.uk

WATSON MISS CLAIRE ELIZABETH

3 Serjeants Inn
London EC4Y 1BQ, ☎020 7427 5000
✉clerks@3serjeantsinn.com
Call Date: July 2001, Middle Temple
Qualifications: [BA (Hons)]
✉cwatson@3serjeantsinn.com

WATSON MR CRAIG BARRY

9 Stone Buildings
Lincoln's Inn, London WC2A 3NN,
☎020 7404 5055
✉clerks@9stonebuildings.com
Call Date: Oct 2001, Lincoln's Inn
Qualifications: [LLB (Hons)]

WATSON MR DAVID WILLIAM

Call Date: Oct 1990, Middle Temple
Pupil Supervisor
Qualifications: [LLB (Brunel)]

WATSON MR DUNCAN ALLEN

Westgate Chambers
64 High Street, Lewes, East Sussex BN7 1XG,
☎01273 480510
✉clerks@westgate-chambers.co.uk
Call Date: Oct 1997, Inner Temple
Qualifications: [BA (Wales) CPE]
✉dw@westgate-chambers.co.uk

WATSON MR FRANCIS PAUL QC (2002)

Call Date: Nov 1978, Gray's Inn
Recorder
Qualifications: [BA (Leeds)]
✉watson@paradise-sq.co.uk

WATSON MR GRAHAM

Colleton Chambers
Colleton Crescent, Exeter, Devon EX2 4DG,
☎01392 274898
✉clerks@colletonchambers.co.uk
Call Date: Oct 1996, Lincoln's Inn
Pupil Supervisor
Qualifications: [LLB (Hons)(Newc) LLM (Bris)]
✉grahamwatson@colletonchambers.co.uk

WATSON MR HAL CHRISTOPHER JOHN

Dere Street Barristers
33 Broad Chare, Newcastle Upon Tyne
NE1 3DQ, ☎0844 3351551
✉clerks@derestreet.co.uk
9-12 Bell Yard
London WC2A 2JR, ☎020 7400 1800
✉clerks@9-12bellyard.com
Call Date: Nov 2003, Middle Temple
Qualifications: [BA (Hons) (Lond) CPE]

WATSON MR IAN DAVID

3 Stone Buildings
Ground Floor, 3 Stone Buildings, Lincoln's Inn, London WC2A 3XL, ☎020 7242 4937
✉clerks@3sb.law.co.uk
Call Date: July 2005, Lincoln's Inn
Qualifications: [JD BA]
✉iwatson@3sb.law.co.uk

WATSON MISS ISABELLE MARGARET

4 Brick Court
4 Brick Court, Temple, London EC4Y 9AD,
☎020 7832 3200 ✉clerks@4bc.co.uk
Call Date: Oct 1991, Middle Temple
Pupil Supervisor
Qualifications: [BA (Hons) (Cantab) DipLaw]

WATSON MR JAMES VERNON QC (2000)

3 Serjeants Inn
London EC4Y 1BQ, ☎020 7427 5000
✉clerks@3serjeantsinn.com
Call Date: July 1979, Middle Temple
Qualifications: [BA (Cantab)]

WATSON MISS KIRSTIE ANN

St Paul's Chambers
5th Floor, St Paul's House, 23 Park Square South, Leeds LS1 2ND, ☎0113 245 5866
Call Date: Oct 1994, Middle Temple
Qualifications: [LLB (Hons)(Leeds)]

WATSON MR MARK

6 Pump Court
1st Floor, 6 Pump Court, Temple, London EC4Y 7AR, ☎020 7797 8400
✉richardconstable@6pumpcourt.co.uk
6 Pump Court Chambers
6-8 Mill Street, Maidstone, Kent ME15 6XH,
☎01622 688094
✉annexe@6pumpcourt.co.uk
Call Date: Oct 1994, Gray's Inn
Pupil Supervisor
Qualifications: [BA]
✉markwatson@6pumpcourt.co.uk

WATSON MR MARK ANDREW

KCH Garden Square
1 Oxford Street, Nottingham NG1 5BH,
☎0115 941 8851
✉clerks@kchgardensquare.co.uk
Call Date: July 1999, Gray's Inn
Qualifications: [B.Sc (Surrey)]
✉mwatson@kch.co.uk

WATSON PROF PHILIPPA

Essex Court Chambers
24 Lincoln's Inn Fields, London WC2A 3EG,
☎020 7813 8000
✉clerksroom@essexcourt.net
Call Date: July 1988, Middle Temple
Qualifications: [MA (Dublin) LLM BL (Ireland) PhD (Cantab)]
✉pwatson@essexcourt.net

WATSON MISS SARAH FLORENCE

Devereux Chambers
Queen Elizabeth Building, Temple, London EC4Y 9BS, ☎020 7353 7534
✉clerks@devchambers.co.uk
Call Date: Oct 2002, Lincoln's Inn
Qualifications: [BA (Oxon) LLM]
✉watson@devchambers.co.uk

WATSON MS SHARON

15 Winckley Square
Preston PR1 3JJ, ☎01772 252828
✉clerks@15winckleysq.co.uk
Call Date: Nov 1994, Middle Temple
Qualifications: [BA (Hons)]
✉Clerks@newbailey.com

WATSON MR TOM BRADLEY

Chavasse Court Chambers
18 Queen Avenue, Liverpool L2 4TX,
☎0151 229 2030
✉clerks@chavassechambers.co.uk
Call Date: Oct 1990, Inner Temple
Pupil Supervisor
Qualifications: [BA (Hons) (Wales) MA (Keele) Dip Law]
✉tom.watson@chavassechambers.co.uk

WATSON-GANDY PROF MARK

13 Old Square Chambers
Ground Floor, 14 Old Square, Lincoln's Inn, London WC2A 3UE, ☎020 7831 4445
✉clerks@13oldsquare.com
Call Date: Oct 1990, Inner Temple
Pupil Supervisor
Qualifications: [LLB (Hons)]
✉mwg@13oldsquare.com

WATT MISS KATHERINE ANNA MARY

Fountain Court Chambers
Fountain Court, Temple, London EC4Y 9DH,
☎020 7583 3335
✉chambers@fountaincourt.co.uk
Call Date: Oct 2002, Middle Temple
Qualifications: [BA (Cantab) MPhil (Cantab) CPE Dip Law]
✉kw@fountaincourt.co.uk

WATTERS MISS SARAH LOUISE

Number 7 Harrington Street Chambers
7 Harrington Street, Liverpool L2 9YH,
☎0151 242 0707 ✉clerks@7hs.co.uk
Call Date: Oct 2007, Lincoln's Inn
Qualifications: [LLB (Leic)]
✉sarah.watters@7hs.co.uk

WATTERSON MS ANNA ELIZABETH

1 Mitre Court Buildings
1 Mitre Court Buildings, Temple, London EC4Y 7BS, ☎020 7452 8900
✉clerks@1mcb.com
Call Date: Nov 2007, Inner Temple
Qualifications: [BA (Cantab)]
✉anna.watterson@1mcb.com

WATTERSON MR MARK JOSEPH

37 Park Square Chambers
37 Park Square, Leeds LS1 2NY,
☎0113 243 9422 ✉chambers@no37.co.uk
Call Date: Oct 2011, Middle Temple
Qualifications: [LLB (Hons) (Northumbria)]

WATTHEY MR JAMES ROBERTSON

Hardwicke
New Square, Lincoln's Inn, London WC2A 3SB, ☎020 7242 2523
✉enquiries@hardwicke.co.uk
Call Date: Nov 2000, Gray's Inn
Pupil Supervisor
Qualifications: [MA (Cantab) BCL (Oxon)]
✉james.watthey@hardwicke.co.uk

WATT-PRINGLE MR JONATHAN HELIER QC (2008)

Farrar's Building
Farrar's Building, Temple, London EC4Y 7BD,
☎020 7583 9241
✉Chambers@farrarsbuilding.co.uk
Call Date: July 1987, Middle Temple
Qualifications: [MA BA BCL (Oxon) LLB (South Africa)]
✉jwpringle@farrarsbuilding.co.uk

E

WATTS MISS ANDREA LOUISE

1 KBW Chambers
1 King's Bench Walk, Temple, London EC4Y 7DB, ☎ 020 7936 1500
✉ clerks@1kbw.co.uk
King's Bench Chambers
174 High Street, Lewes BN7 1YE, ☎ 01273 402600
Call Date: Oct 2006, Lincoln's Inn
Qualifications: [BA (Oxon)]
awatts@1kbw.co.uk

WATTS MR DARREN CLAUDE

1 Gray's Inn Square
Ground Floor, 1 Gray's Inn Square, London WC1R 5AA, ☎ 020 7405 0001
Call Date: Oct 2005, Middle Temple
Qualifications: [BSc (Hons) (Essex) PgDip Law]

WAUCHOPE MR PIERS ANDREW CHARLES

5 Pump Court
Ground Floor, 5 Pump Court, Temple, London EC4Y 7AP, ☎ 020 7353 2532
✉ clerks@5pumpcourt.com
Call Date: July 1985, Gray's Inn
Pupil Supervisor
Qualifications: [BA (Manch)]
pierswauchope@5pumpcourt.com

WAUGH MR ANDREW PETER QC (1998)

Three New Square IP
3 New Square, Lincoln's Inn, London WC2A 3RS, ☎ 020 7405 1111
✉ clerks@3newsquare.co.uk
Call Date: July 1982, Gray's Inn
Qualifications: [BSc (Lond) Dip Law (Lond)]

WAUGH MS JANE

New Court Chambers
3 Broad Chare, Newcastle Upon Tyne NE1 3DQ, ☎ 0191 232 1980
✉ clerks@newcourt-chambers.co.uk
Call Date: Oct 1992, Inner Temple
Qualifications: [LLB]
jane.waugh@newcourt-chambers.co.uk

WAY MR IAN LEONARD

KCH Garden Square
1 Oxford Street, Nottingham NG1 5BH, ☎ 0115 941 8851
✉ clerks@kchgardensquare.co.uk
Dyers Chambers
35 Bedford Row, London WC1R 4JH, ☎ 020 7404 1881
✉ admin@dyerschambers.com
Call Date: Nov 1988, Inner Temple
Pupil Supervisor
Qualifications: [BA (Lond)]

WAY MR PATRICK EDWARD

Gray's Inn Tax Chambers
3rd Floor, Gray's Inn Chambers, Gray's Inn, London WC1R 5JA, ☎ 020 7242 2642
✉ clerks@taxbar.com
Call Date: May 1994, Lincoln's Inn
Qualifications: [BA (Hons) (Leeds)]
pw@taxbar.com

WAYNE MR NICHOLAS

Argent Chambers
5 Bell Yard, London WC2A 2JR, ☎ 020 7556 5500
✉ briefsin@argentchambers.co.uk
Call Date: July 1994, Middle Temple
Qualifications: [BA (Hons)(Oxon)]
n.wayne@argentchambers.co.uk

WEALE MR JAMES JULIUS

3 Stone Buildings
Ground Floor, 3 Stone Buildings, Lincoln's Inn, London WC2A 3XL, ☎ 020 7242 4937
✉ clerks@3sb.law.co.uk
Call Date: Oct 2007, Inner Temple
Qualifications: [LLB (Hons) (Bris) BCL (Oxon)]
jweale@3sb.law.co.uk

WEATHERALL MISS JULIA

Cathedral Chambers
First Floor, 17 Queen Street, Newcastle Upon Tyne NE1 3UG, ☎ 0191 232 1311
✉ mail@cathedralchambers.com
Call Date: July 1985, Inner Temple
Pupil Supervisor
Qualifications: [LLB (Brunel)]

WEATHERBY MR PETER FRANCIS QC (2012)

Chambers of Ian Macdonald QC
Garden Court North, 22 Oxford Court, Manchester M2 3WQ, ☎ 0161 236 1840
✉ clerks@gcnchambers.co.uk
Garden Court Chambers
57-60 Lincoln's Inn Fields, London WC2A 3LJ, ☎ 020 7993 7600 ✉ info@gclaw.co.uk
Call Date: Nov 1992, Gray's Inn
Pupil Supervisor
Qualifications: [BSc (Hons)]
✉ clerks@gcnchambers.co.uk, pweatherby@talk21.com

WEATHERILL MR BERNARD RICHARD QC (1996)

Enterprise Chambers
9 Old Square, Lincoln's Inn, London WC2A 3SR, ☎ 020 7405 9471
✉ london@enterprisechambers.com
Enterprise Chambers
65 Quayside, Newcastle Upon Tyne NE1 3DE, ☎ 0191 222 3344
✉ newcastle@enterprisechambers.com
Enterprise Chambers
43 Park Square, Leeds LS1 2NP, ☎ 0113 246 0391
✉ leeds@enterprisechambers.com
Pallant Chambers
12 North Pallant, Chichester, West Sussex PO19 1TQ, ☎ 01243 784538
✉ clerks@pallantchambers.co.uk
Call Date: July 1974, Middle Temple
Recorder
Qualifications: [BA FCIArb CIArb]

WEAVER MR BRETT

6 King's Bench Walk
Ground Floor, 6 King's Bench Walk, Temple, London EC4Y 7DR, ☎ 020 7583 0410
✉ clerks@6kbw.com
Call Date: Mar 2003, Lincoln's Inn
Qualifications: [BA (Hons) (Oxon)]
✉ brett.weaver@6kbw.com

WEAVER MISS ELIZABETH ANNE

XXIV Old Buildings
Ground Floor, 24 Old Buildings, Lincoln's Inn, London WC2A 3UP, ☎ 020 7691 2424
✉ clerks@xxiv.co.uk
Call Date: July 1982, Lincoln's Inn
Pupil Supervisor
Qualifications: [LLB (Bris)]
✉ elizabeth.weaver@xxiv.co.uk

WEAVER MR MATTHEW PAUL

St Philips Chambers
55 Temple Row, Birmingham B2 5LS, ☎ 0121 246 7000 ✉ clerks@st-philips.com
Call Date: Nov 2002, Lincoln's Inn
Qualifications: [LLB (Hons)(Kent)]
✉ mweaver@st-philips.com

WEAVER MRS VALERIE JUNE

Sundridge Chambers
10 Sundridge House, Burnt Ash Lane, Bromley, Kent BR1 5AE, ☎ 020 8464 9772
✉ sundridgechambers@sky.com
Call Date: Nov 1979, Middle Temple
Pupil Supervisor
Qualifications: [BA LLM]
✉ valerieweaver@lawyer.com

WEBB MR GERAINT TIMOTHY

Henderson Chambers
2 Harcourt Buildings, Temple, London EC4Y 9DB, ☎ 020 7583 9020
✉ clerks@hendersonchambers.co.uk
Call Date: Oct 1995, Inner Temple
Pupil Supervisor
Qualifications: [BA (Oxon) CPE (Lond)]
✉ gwebb@hendersonchambers.co.uk

WEBB MR HENRY CHARLES DAINES

Selborne Chambers
10 Essex Street, London WC2R 3AA, ☎ 020 7420 9500
✉ clerks@selbornechambers.co.uk
Call Date: Oct 2005, Lincoln's Inn
Qualifications: [BA (Hons) (Oxon) BCL (Oxon)]
✉ henry.webb@selbornechambers.co.uk

WEBB MISS HOLLY ALYSS

23 Essex Street
London WC2R 3AA, ☎ 020 7413 0353
✉ clerks@23es.com
Call Date: Nov 2006, Lincoln's Inn
Qualifications: [MA (Oxon) MSc]
✉ hollywebb@23es.com

WEBB MISS LORRAINE ELIZABETH

Roxwell
Dukes Manor, The Street, Roxwell, Chelmsford, Essex CM1 4PE, ☎ 01245 248341
✉ lorrainewebbbarrister@yahoo.co.uk
Call Date: July 1980, Middle Temple
Qualifications: [BA]

E

WEBB MR PAUL HAYDN COULSON

7 Bell Yard
London WC2A 2JR, ☎020 7831 0636
✉kevintarrant@btconnect.com
Call Date: July 2003, Middle Temple
Qualifications: [LLB Hons (Kingston)]
pw@7bellyard.co.uk

WEBB MR THOMAS ANDREW

3 PB Barristers
4 St Peter Street, Winchester SO23 8BW,
☎01962 868884
✉clerks.winchester@3paper.co.uk
3 PB Barristers
Royal Talbot House, 2 Victoria Street, Bristol, Avon BS1 6BB, ☎0117 928 1520
3 PB Barristers
30 Christchurch Road, Bournemouth, Dorset BH1 3PD, ☎01202 292102
✉clerks.bournemouth@3paper.co.uk
3 PB Barristers
23 Beaumont Street, Oxford OX1 2NP,
☎01865 793 736
3 PB Barristers
3 Paper Buildings, Temple, London EC4Y 7EU,
☎020 7583 8055
Call Date: July 2010, Middle Temple
Qualifications: [LLB (Hons)(Exon)]

E

WEBB MISS VICTORIA ALEXANDRA

Old Square Chambers
10-11 Bedford Row, London WC1R 4BU,
☎020 7269 0300 ✉clerks@oldsquare.co.uk
Old Square Chambers
3 Orchard Court, St Augustine's Yard, Bristol BS1 5DP, ☎0117 930 5100
✉clerks@oldsquare.co.uk
Call Date: July 2009, Middle Temple
Qualifications: [BA (Hons) (Oxon) LLM (Essex)]
webb@oldsquare.co.uk

WEBB MR WILLIAM RUPERT

Keating Chambers
15 Essex Street, London WC2R 3AA,
☎020 7544 2600
✉clerks@keatingchambers.com
Call Date: July 2005, Lincoln's Inn
Qualifications: [BA (Cantab) LLM (Virginia) BCL (Oxon)]
wwebb@keatingchambers.com

WEBBER MR DOMINIC DENZIL FERNANDEZ

5 King's Bench Walk
5 King's Bench Walk, Temple, London EC4Y 7DN, ☎020 7353 5638
✉clerks@5kbw.co.uk
Call Date: Nov 1985, Gray's Inn
Pupil Supervisor
Qualifications: [BA Dip Law]

WEBBER MISS RUTH

42 Bedford Row
London WC1R 4LL, ☎020 7831 0222
✉clerks@42br.com
Call Date: July 2006, Lincoln's Inn
Qualifications: [LLB (Bris)]
ruth.webber@42br.com

WEBSTER MR ALISTAIR STEVENSON QC (1995)

Lincoln House Chambers
Tower 12, The Avenue North, Spinningfields, 18-22 Bridge Street, Manchester M3 3BZ,
☎0161 832 5701
✉info@lincolnhousechambers.com
Chambers of Andrew Mitchell QC
33 Chancery Lane, London WC2A 1EN,
☎020 7440 9950 ✉clerks@33cllaw.com
Call Date: July 1976, Middle Temple
Recorder
Qualifications: [BA (Oxon)]
alistair.webster@lincolnhousechambers.com

WEBSTER MR ANDREW JOHN

Park Lane Plowden
Lombard House, 4-8 Lombard Street, Newcastle Upon Tyne NE1 3AE,
☎0191 211 4087
✉clerks@parklaneplowden.co.uk
Call Date: July 2005, Middle Temple
Qualifications: [LLB (Hons)]
andrew.webster@parklaneplowden.co.uk

WEBSTER MRS BARBARA-LOUISE

Number 7 Harrington Street Chambers
7 Harrington Street, Liverpool L2 9YH,
☎0151 242 0707 ✉clerks@7hs.co.uk
Call Date: Oct 2005, Lincoln's Inn
Qualifications: [LLB (Hons) (Lancs)]
Barbara.webster@7hs.co.uk

WEBSTER MR DAVID

Bank House Chambers
Old Bank House, Hartshead, Sheffield S1 2EL, ☎0114 275 1223
✉w.digby@bankhousechambers.co.uk
Call Date: Mar 1998, Middle Temple
Pupil Supervisor
✉d.webster@bankhousechambers.co.uk

WEBSTER MR DAVID FRANCIS

Temple Chambers
32 Park Place, Cardiff CF10 3BA, ☎029 2039 7364
✉DBrinning@Temple-Chambers.co.uk
Temple Chambers
12 Clytha Park Road, Newport, Gwent NP20 4PB, ☎01633 267403
✉dbrinning@temple-chambers.co.uk
Call Date: Oct 1993, Gray's Inn
Qualifications: [B Sc (Econ) (Wales)]

WEBSTER MR KEITH

4 King's Bench Walk
2nd Floor, 4 King's Bench Walk, Temple, London EC4Y 7DL, ☎020 7822 7000
✉clerks@4kbw.co.uk
Call Date: July 2006, Gray's Inn
Qualifications: [MBA (Warw)]
✉kw@4kbw.co.uk

WEBSTER MISS LINDSAY

Amicus Chambers
Queens Court, Newport Road, Middlesbrough TS1 5EH, ☎01642 876334
✉amicus.clerk@amicuschambers.co.uk
Call Date: July 2005, Middle Temple
Qualifications: [BA (Hons) Manchester Metropolitan CPE Northumbria]

WEBSTER MISS SARAH MARY

Staple Inn Chambers
1st Floor, 9 Staple Inn, Holborn Bars, London WC1V 7QH, ☎020 7242 5240
✉clerks@stapleinn.co.uk
Call Date: July 2006, Middle Temple
Qualifications: [LLB (Hons) (Edin) PgDL]
✉sw@stapleinn.co.uk

WEBSTER MISS SHELLEY ANNE

Carmelite Chambers
9 Carmelite Street, London EC4Y 0DR, ☎020 7936 6300
✉clerks@carmelitechambers.co.uk
Call Date: Oct 2002, Lincoln's Inn
Qualifications: [LLB (LGU) PgDL (LGU) CPE BVC]
✉swebster@carmelitechambers.co.uk

WEBSTER MR SIMON MARK

1 Hare Court
1 Hare Court, Temple, London EC4Y 7BE, ☎020 7797 7070 ✉clerks@1hc.com
Call Date: Oct 1997, Inner Temple
Pupil Supervisor
Qualifications: [LLB (Lond)]
✉webster@1hc.com

WEBSTER MR WILLIAM HOWARD

12 College Place
Fauvelle Buildings, 12 College Place, Southampton SO15 2FE, ☎023 8032 0320
✉clerks@12cp.co.uk
Call Date: July 1975, Middle Temple
Pupil Supervisor
Qualifications: [LLB (Bris)]
✉wwebster@12cp.co.uk

WEDDELL MR GEOFFREY DAVID ANDREW

1 Chancery Lane
London WC2A 1LF, ☎0845 634 6666
✉clerks@1chancerylane.com
Call Date: Nov 1989, Inner Temple
Pupil Supervisor
Qualifications: [LLB]
✉gweddell@1chancerylane.com

WEDDERSPOON MISS RACHEL LEONE

9 St John Street
Manchester M3 4DN, ☎0161 955 9000
✉civilclerks@9sjs.com / criminalclerks@9sjs.com
Call Date: Oct 1993, Middle Temple
Qualifications: [LLB (Hons)(Manch)]

WEDDLE MR STEVEN EDGAR

Hardwicke
New Square, Lincoln's Inn, London WC2A 3SB, ☎020 7242 2523
✉enquiries@hardwicke.co.uk
Call Date: Nov 1977, Gray's Inn
Pupil Supervisor
Qualifications: [BA]

WEE MR PAUL CHOON KIAT

3 Verulam Buildings
London WC1R 5NT, ☎020 7831 8441
✉chambers@3vb.com
Call Date: Oct 2010, Gray's Inn
Qualifications: [BA BCL]
✉pckwee@3vb.com

E

WEEDEN MR ROSS CHARLES

Bell Yard Chambers
116/118 Chancery Lane, London WC2A 1PP, ☎020 7306 9292
✉byclerks@bellyardchambers.co.uk
Call Date: Oct 1996, Middle Temple
Qualifications: [LLB (Hons)]
rweeden@bellyardchambers.co.uk

WEEKES MISS ANESTA GLENDORA QC (1999)

23 Essex Street
London WC2R 3AA, ☎020 7413 0353
✉clerks@23es.com
Call Date: July 1981, Gray's Inn
Recorder
anestaweekes@23es.com

WEEKES MR MARK VINCENT

6 King's Bench Walk
Ground Floor, 6 King's Bench Walk, Temple, London EC4Y 7DR, ☎020 7583 0410
✉clerks@6kbw.com
Call Date: Nov 1999, Lincoln's Inn
Qualifications: [BA (Hons)(Oxon) Dip law]

WEEKES MR ROBERT NICHOLAS

Blackstone Chambers
Blackstone House, Temple, London EC4Y 9BW, ☎020 7583 1770
✉clerks@blackstonechambers.com
Call Date: Oct 2003, Middle Temple
Qualifications: [LLM (New York) MA (Hons)(Cantab)]
robertweekes@blackstonechambers.com

WEEKES MR THOMAS CHARLES

Landmark Chambers
180 Fleet Street, London EC4A 2HG, ☎020 7430 1221
✉clerks@landmarkchambers.co.uk
Call Date: Oct 1995, Inner Temple
Pupil Supervisor
Qualifications: [BA (Oxon) CPE (Lond)]

WEEKS MS JANET KATHLEEN

Five Paper Buildings
1st Floor, Five Paper Buildings, Temple, London EC4Y 7HB, ☎020 7583 6117
✉clerks@5pb.co.uk
Call Date: Oct 1993, Inner Temple
Pupil Supervisor
Qualifications: [LLB (Exon)]
jw@5pb.co.uk

WEERERATNE MS RUFINA ASWINI

Doughty Street Chambers
53-54 Doughty Street, London WC1N 2LS, ☎020 7404 1313
✉enquiries@doughtystreet.co.uk
Doughty Street Chambers
Pall Mall Court, 61-67 King Street, Manchester M2 4PD, ☎0161 618 1066
Doughty Street Chambers
5th Floor, Broad Quay House, Prince Street, Bristol BS1 4DJ, ☎01179 058 717
Call Date: July 1986, Gray's Inn
Pupil Supervisor
Qualifications: [BSc (Sussex) Dip Law]
a.weereratne@doughtystreet.co.uk

WEETCH MR OLIVER PETER MCCALLUM

Chambers of Marion Smullen and Kerim Fuad QC
1 Inner Temple Lane, London EC4Y 1AF, ☎020 7427 4400 ✉clerks@1itl.com
Call Date: Oct 2001, Middle Temple
Qualifications: [BA (Hons) (Bris) CPE]
clerks@1itl.com

WEETMAN MR GARETH JAMES

Seven Bedford Row
7 Bedford Row, London WC1R 4BS, ☎020 7242 3555 ✉clerks@7br.co.uk
Call Date: Oct 1999, Gray's Inn
Pupil Supervisor
Qualifications: [BA (Cantab)]
gweetman@7br.co.uk

WEHRLE MISS JACQUELINE

29 Bedford Row Chambers
London WC1R 4HE, ☎020 7404 1044
✉clerks@29br.co.uk
Call Date: Nov 1984, Lincoln's Inn
Pupil Supervisor
Qualifications: [LLB (Reading)]
jwehrle@29br.co.uk

WEINIGER MR NORMAN NOAH

Renaissance Chambers
5th Floor, Gray's Inn Chambers, Gray's Inn, London WC1R 5JA, ☎020 7404 1111
✉clerks@renaissancechambers.co.uk
Call Date: Nov 1984, Gray's Inn
Pupil Supervisor
Qualifications: [LLB (Manch)]
nw@renaissancechambers.co.uk

WEIR MR ALAN ANTHONY

Park Lane Plowden
19 Westgate, Leeds LS1 2RD,
☎ 0113 228 5049
✉ clerks@parklaneplowden.co.uk
Call Date: Nov 1996, Gray's Inn
Qualifications: [BSc MSc]
✉ alan.weir@parklaneplowden.co.uk

WEIR MISS CLAIRE LOUISE

Blackstone Chambers
Blackstone House, Temple, London
EC4Y 9BW, ☎ 020 7583 1770
✉ clerks@blackstonechambers.com
Call Date: July 1998, Middle Temple
Qualifications: [BA (Hons)(Cantab) LLM]
✉ claireweir@blackstonechambers.com

WEIR MISS OLIVIA

Bank House Chambers
Old Bank House, Hartshead, Sheffield S1 2EL,
☎ 0114 275 1223
✉ w.digby@bankhousechambers.co.uk
Call Date: Nov 1995, Inner Temple
Qualifications: [BA (Hons)]
✉ o.weir@bankhousechambers.co.uk

WEIR MR ROBERT THOMAS MACDONALD QC (2010)

Devereux Chambers
Queen Elizabeth Building, Temple, London
EC4Y 9BS, ☎ 020 7353 7534
✉ clerks@devchambers.co.uk
Call Date: Nov 1992, Middle Temple
Pupil Supervisor
Qualifications: [MA (Hons)]
✉ weir@devchambers.co.uk

WEISS MR ALFRED ANTHONY

Exchange Chambers
One Derby Square, Derby Square, Liverpool
L2 9XX, ☎ 0151 236 7747
✉ info@exchangechambers.co.uk
Call Date: Oct 2006, Lincoln's Inn
Qualifications: [BA (Cantab)]

WEISSELBERG MR TOM

Blackstone Chambers
Blackstone House, Temple, London
EC4Y 9BW, ☎ 020 7583 1770
✉ clerks@blackstonechambers.com
Call Date: Oct 1995, Inner Temple
Pupil Supervisor
Qualifications: [BA (Oxon) CPE (Lond)]
✉ tomweisselberg@blackstonechambers.com

WEITZMAN MR THOMAS EDWARD BENJAMIN QC (2003)

3 Verulam Buildings
London WC1R 5NT, ☎ 020 7831 8441
✉ chambers@3vb.com
Call Date: July 1984, Gray's Inn
Qualifications: [BA (Oxon)]
✉ tweitzman@3vb.com

WELCH MR AUSTIN PETER

Lincoln House Chambers
Tower 12, The Avenue North, Spinningfields,
18-22 Bridge Street, Manchester M3 3BZ,
☎ 0161 832 5701
✉ info@lincolnhousechambers.com
Call Date: Oct 2005, Middle Temple
Qualifications: [LLB (Hons) (Leeds)]
✉ austin.welch@lincolnhousechambers.com

WELCH MR DAVID WILLIAM

Warwick House Chambers
8 Warwick Court, Warwick House Chambers,
Gray's Inn, London WC1R 5DJ,
☎ 020 7430 2323
✉ clerks@warwickhousechambers.com
Alexander Chambers
13 Halstead Road, Wanstead, London E11 2AY,
☎ 0845 652 0451 / 0854 652 0451
✉ clerks@alexanderchambers.co.uk
Call Date: Oct 2005, Inner Temple
Qualifications: [LLB Birkbeck College
University of London]

WELCH MR ROBERT WILLIAM

Unity Street Chambers
5 Unity Street, College Green, Bristol
BS1 5HH, ☎ 0117 906 9789
✉ chambers@unitystreetchambers.com
Call Date: Mar 2007, Middle Temple
Qualifications: [BA (Hons) (Nott'm)]
✉ robert.welch@unitystreetchambers.com

WELCH MR VOLDI BELFIELD

St Paul's Chambers
5th Floor, St Paul's House, 23 Park Square
South, Leeds LS1 2ND, ☎ 0113 245 5866
Call Date: Oct 2008, Middle Temple
Qualifications: [Dip in Law]
✉ vw@stpaulschambers.com

WELFARE MR DAMIEN FRANCIS JOHN

Cornerstone Barristers
2-3 Gray's Inn Square, Gray's Inn, London
WC1R 5JH, ☎ 020 7242 4986
✉ chambers@2-3gis.co.uk
Call Date: July 2001, Inner Temple
Qualifications: [BA (Cantab) MSc (Lond) CPE]
✉ dwelfare@2-3gis.co.uk

E

WELFORD MR DAVID

Selborne Chambers
10 Essex Street, London WC2R 3AA,
☎020 7420 9500
✉clerks@selbornechambers.co.uk
Call Date: Oct 2010, Lincoln's Inn
Qualifications: [BA (Oxon)]

WELLER MS SOPHIE JOANNE

Cornerstone Barristers
2-3 Gray's Inn Square, Gray's Inn, London WC1R 5JH, ☎020 7242 4986
✉chambers@2-3gis.co.uk
Call Date: Oct 2005, Gray's Inn
Qualifications: [BSc (Lond) BA (Oxon) BCL (Oxon)]
sophiew@cornerstonebarristers.com, sweller@2-3gis.co.uk

WELLFARE MISS AIMEE KAY

3 Temple Gardens
Lower Ground Floor, 3 Temple Gardens, Temple, London EC4Y 9AU, ☎020 7353 3102
✉clerks@3tg.co.uk
Call Date: Oct 2004, Lincoln's Inn
Qualifications: [LLB (Hons) (Wales)]

E

WELLINGS MR OLIVER JAMES

2 King's Bench Walk
2 King's Bench Walk, Temple, London EC4Y 7DE, ☎020 7353 1746
✉clerks@2kbw.com
Call Date: Oct 2001, Inner Temple
Qualifications: [BA (Cantab)]

WELLS MISS CAMILLA

Crown Office Row Chambers
119 Church Street, Brighton, Sussex BN1 1UD, ☎01273 625625
✉clerks@1cor.com
Call Date: Oct 1998, Inner Temple
Qualifications: [BA (Manc) CPE (City)]
camilla.wells@1cor.com

WELLS MR CASPAR JOHN MOWLEM

Goldsmith Chambers
Ground Floor, Goldsmith Building, Temple, London EC4Y 7BL, ☎020 7353 6802
✉clerks@goldsmithchambers.com
Call Date: Oct 2000, Middle Temple
Qualifications: [BA (Hons) (Bris) CPE]
C.Wells@goldsmithchambers.com

WELLS MR CHRISTOPHER JAMES

KCH Garden Square
1 Oxford Street, Nottingham NG1 5BH,
☎0115 941 8851
✉clerks@kchgardensquare.co.uk
Call Date: July 2007, Inner Temple
Qualifications: [LLB (Sheff)]

WELLS MR COLIN JOHN

25 Bedford Row
London WC1R 4HD, ☎020 7067 1500
✉clerks@25bedfordrow.com
Call Date: Nov 1987, Inner Temple
Pupil Supervisor
Qualifications: [BSc, MA (Warw) DipLaw]
cwells@25bedfordrow.com

WELLS MR GRAHAM HOLLAND

Oriel Chambers
14 Water Street, Liverpool, Merseyside L2 8TD, ☎0151 236 7191
✉clerks@orielchambers.co.uk
Oriel Chambers
18 Ribblesdale Place, Preston PR1 3NA,
☎01772 254 764
✉clerks@oriel-chambers.co.uk
Call Date: July 1982, Middle Temple
Pupil Supervisor, Recorder
Qualifications: [MA (Oxon)]
graham.wells@orielchambers.co.uk

WELLS DR JASON MARK

18 St John Street
Manchester M3 4EA, ☎0161 278 1800
✉clerks@18sjs.com
Call Date: July 2007, Lincoln's Inn
Qualifications: [LLB FRCS MBChB]

WELLS MRS JESSICA EILUNED

Essex Court Chambers
24 Lincoln's Inn Fields, London WC2A 3EG,
☎020 7813 8000
✉clerksroom@essexcourt.net
Call Date: Nov 2004, Lincoln's Inn
Qualifications: [BA (Hons)]
jwells@essexcourt.net

WELLS MR NATHAN ERNEST JOHN

Radcliffe Chambers
Ground Floor, 11 New Square, Lincoln's Inn, London WC2A 3QB, ☎020 7831 0081
✉clerks@radcliffechambers.com
Call Date: Oct 2000, Lincoln's Inn
Pupil Supervisor
Qualifications: [BA (Hons) (Oxon) LLM (Cantab)]
nwells@radcliffechambers.com

WELLS MR NICHOLAS THOMAS CLINTON

1 Gray's Inn Square
Ground Floor, 1 Gray's Inn Square, London WC1R 5AA, ☎020 7405 0001
Call Date: Nov 1990, Lincoln's Inn
Pupil Supervisor
Qualifications: [BA (Cantab) Dip Law]

WELLS MR STEPHEN DAVID

9 King's Bench Walk
Lower Ground Floor South, 9 King's Bench Walk, Temple, London EC4Y 7DX, ☎020 7353 9564 ✉9kbw@btconnect.com
Call Date: Oct 2000, Lincoln's Inn
Qualifications: [LLB (Hons) (Lond)]

WELSH MRS ABIGAIL

Charter Chambers
33 John Street, London WC1N 2AT, ☎020 7618 4400
✉clerks@charterchambers.com
Call Date: Nov 2001, Inner Temple
Qualifications: [LLB (L'pool)]

WELSH MR JAMES ANTHONY KIRKMAN

Nine Bedford Row
9 Bedford Row, London WC1R 4AZ, ☎020 7489 2727
✉clerks@9bedfordrow.co.uk
Call Date: Nov 1994, Middle Temple
Qualifications: [BA (Hons) (Dunelm) Dip Law]

WELSH MR MICHAEL

Trent Chambers
9 Regent Street, Nottingham NG1 5BS, ☎0115 941 9596
✉clerks@trentchambers.co.uk
Call Date: July 2008, Lincoln's Inn
Qualifications: [BA (Reading)]

WENBAN-SMITH MR MUNGO WILLIAM

4-5 Gray's Inn Square
Gray's Inn, London WC1R 5AH, ☎020 7404 5252 ✉clerks@4-5.co.uk
Call Date: July 2004, Lincoln's Inn
Qualifications: [BA Hons (Cantab)]
✉clerks@4-5.co.uk

WENTWORTH MISS ANNABEL HENRIETTE

29 Bedford Row Chambers
London WC1R 4HE, ☎020 7404 1044
✉clerks@29br.co.uk
Call Date: Oct 1990, Inner Temple
Qualifications: [BA (Nott'm) Dip Law]
✉awentworth@29br.co.uk

WEST MR COLIN

Brick Court Chambers
7-8 Essex Street, London WC2R 3LD, ☎020 7379 3550 ✉clerks@brickcourt.co.uk
Call Date: Nov 1999, Inner Temple
Pupil Supervisor
Qualifications: [BA BCL (Oxon)]
✉Colin.West@Brickcourt.co.uk

WEST DR EWAN DONALD

Monckton Chambers
1 & 2 Raymond Buildings, Gray's Inn, London WC1R 5NR, ☎020 7405 7211
✉chambers@monckton.com
Call Date: July 2006, Lincoln's Inn
Qualifications: [BA (Oxon) LLB (Lond) MA (Oxon) DPhil (Oxon) MBA (Cranfield)]

WEST MR IAN HERBERT

Bank House Chambers
Old Bank House, Hartshead, Sheffield S1 2EL, ☎0114 275 1223
✉w.digby@bankhousechambers.co.uk
Call Date: Nov 1996, Middle Temple
Qualifications: [LLB (Hons)(Auckland)]
✉i.west@bankhousechambers.co.uk

WEST MR IAN STUART

Fountain Chambers
Cleveland Business Centre, 1 Watson Street, Middlesbrough TS1 2RQ, ☎01642 804040
✉clerks@fountainchambers.co.uk
Call Date: Nov 1985, Inner Temple
Pupil Supervisor
Qualifications: [LLB (Hull)]
✉clerks@fountainchambers.co.uk

WEST MR JOHN REDVERS

No5 Chambers
Fountain Court, Steelhouse Lane, Birmingham B4 6DR, ☎0845 210 5555 ✉info@no5.com
No5 Chambers
Greenwood House, 4-7 Salisbury Court, London EC4Y 8AA, ☎0845 210 5555
No5 Chambers
38 Queen Square, Bristol BS1 4QS, ☎0845 210 5555
Call Date: Feb 1965, Middle Temple
Qualifications: [BA (Cantab)]
✉jw@no5.com

E

WEST MS LAURA CLAIRE

Arden Chambers
20 Bloomsbury Square, London WC1A 2NS, ☎ 020 7242 4244
✉ clerks@ardenchambers.com
Call Date: Nov 2006, Gray's Inn
Qualifications: [BA]
laura.west@ardenchambers.com

WEST MR LAWRENCE JOSEPH QC (2003)

Henderson Chambers
2 Harcourt Buildings, Temple, London EC4Y 9DB, ☎ 020 7583 9020
✉ clerks@hendersonchambers.co.uk
Call Date: May 1979, Gray's Inn
Recorder
Qualifications: [LLM (Lond) LLB MCI Arb BA (Canada)]

WEST MR MARK

Radcliffe Chambers
Ground Floor, 11 New Square, Lincoln's Inn, London WC2A 3QB, ☎ 020 7831 0081
✉ clerks@radcliffechambers.com
Call Date: July 1987, Middle Temple
Pupil Supervisor
Qualifications: [MA LLM (Cantab)]
mwest@radcliffechambers.com

Fax: 020 7405 2560;
DX: 319 LDE;
URL: www.radcliffechambers.com

Other professional qualifications: Contributing Editor to Lloyd's Law Reports (professional negligence) 1999-2003

Types of work: Chancery (general), Chancery (land law), Charities, Commercial litigation, Commercial property, Common law (general), Company, commercial and competition, Conveyancing, Equity, Family provision, Insolvency, Landlord and tenant, Partnerships, Personal insolvency, Professional negligence, Real property, Restitution, Succession, Trusts, Wills

Awards and memberships: Chancery Bar Association; Professional Negligence Bar Association; Property Bar Association; Member of Lincoln's Inn

Other professional experience: Deputy Judge of the Upper Tribunal (Administrative Appeals Chamber)

Publications: 'Know Your Limits: Trustees' Mistakes under the Limitation Act 1980, 86 *Trusts & Estate Law Journal* 12, 2007; 'Breach of Warranty of Authority in Solicitors' Liability Claims' (with Professor Francis Reynolds), 25 *Journal of Professional Negligence* 131, 2009; 'The Ownership of Surface Voids Created By Mineral Extraction' in *Conveyancer 30*, 2011; 'Section 5 of the Limitation Act 1980 and Restitutionary Claims for Money Had and Received', *30 Civil Justice Quarterly 366*, 2011

Reported Cases: *Kleinwort Benson v Sandwell BC*, [1994] 4 All ER 890 Restitution of monies paid under *ultra vires* interest rate swap contracts.
Morgan Grenfell v Welwyn Hatfield DC; Islington LBC (third party), [1995] 1 All ER 1 Whether passing on is a defence to restitution of monies paid under a void interest rate swap contract.
Kleinwort Benson v Birmingham CC, [1997] QB 380 Whether passing on is a defence to restitution of monies paid under a void interest rate swap contract.
Chong Kai Tai Ringo v Lee Gee Kee, [1997] HKLRD 491 Provisional agreement for sale of flat; whether obligations of purchaser and vendor concurrent; whether liquidated damage clause a bar to specific performance.
Kleinwort Benson v Lincoln CC, [1999] 2 AC 349 Whether money paid under a void interest rate swap contract is recoverable as being paid under a mistake of law.

WEST MR MARK ROGER

Lamb Chambers
Lamb Building, Elm Court, Temple, London EC4Y 7AS, ☎ 020 7797 8300
✉ info@lambchambers.co.uk
Call Date: May 1973, Inner Temple
Pupil Supervisor, Recorder
Qualifications: [LLB]

WEST MR MATTHEW JAMES ATTOCK

Enterprise Chambers
65 Quayside, Newcastle Upon Tyne NE1 3DE, ☎ 0191 222 3344
✉ newcastle@enterprisechambers.com
Enterprise Chambers
43 Park Square, Leeds LS1 2NP, ☎ 0113 246 0391
✉ leeds@enterprisechambers.com
Enterprise Chambers
9 Old Square, Lincoln's Inn, London WC2A 3SR, ☎ 020 7405 9471
✉ london@enterprisechambers.com
Call Date: Nov 2000, Middle Temple
Qualifications: [MA (Hons) (Oxon) BCL (Oxon)]
matthewwest@enterprisechambers.com

WEST MR PATRICK DAVID

St John's Chambers
101 Victoria Street, Bristol BS1 6PU,
☎ 0117 923 4700
✉ clerks@stjohnschambers.co.uk
Call Date: Oct 2007, Lincoln's Inn
Qualifications: [MA (Oxon)]
✉ patrick.west@stjohnschambers.co.uk

WESTAWAY MR NED JONATHAN

Francis Taylor Building
Inner Temple, London EC4Y 7BY,
☎ 020 7353 8415 ✉ clerks@ftb.eu.com
Call Date: Oct 2009, Lincoln's Inn
Qualifications: [BA LLM (London) CPE USUS]
✉ ned.westaway@ftb.eu.com

WESTCOTT MR DAVID GUY QC (2003)

Outer Temple Chambers
The Outer Temple, 222 Strand, London
WC2R 1BA, ☎ 020 7353 6381
✉ clerks@outertemple.com
Call Date: Nov 1982, Middle Temple
Qualifications: [BA (Oxon) BCL]
✉ david.westcott@outertemple.com

WESTCOTT MISS MARY CATHERINE

Five St Andrew's Hill
5 St Andrew's Hill, London EC4V 5BZ,
☎ 020 7332 5400 ✉ Clerks@5sah.co.uk
Call Date: July 2007, Gray's Inn
Qualifications: [BA (Lond)]

WESTERN MR ADAM JOHN BROOKS

Citadel Chambers
The Citadel, 190 Corporation Street,
Birmingham B4 6QD, ☎ 0121 233 8500
✉ clerks@citadelchambers.com
Call Date: Mar 1997, Gray's Inn
Qualifications: [BA (L'pool)]
✉ clerks@citadelchambers.com

WESTGATE MR MARTIN TREVOR QC (2010)

Doughty Street Chambers
53-54 Doughty Street, London WC1N 2LS,
☎ 020 7404 1313
✉ enquiries@doughtystreet.co.uk
Doughty Street Chambers
Pall Mall Court, 61-67 King Street, Manchester
M2 4PD, ☎ 0161 618 1066
Doughty Street Chambers
5th Floor, Broad Quay House, Prince Street,
Bristol BS1 4DJ, ☎ 01179 058 717
Call Date: Nov 1985, Middle Temple
Pupil Supervisor
Qualifications: [BA (Oxon)]
✉ m.westgate@doughtystreet.co.uk

WEST-KNIGHTS MR LAURENCE JAMES QC (2000)

Hailsham Chambers
Ground Floor, 4 Paper Buildings, Temple,
London EC4Y 7EX, ☎ 020 7643 5000
✉ clerks@hailshamchambers.com
Call Date: Nov 1977, Gray's Inn
Recorder
Qualifications: [MA (Cantab) FCIArb]
✉ laurie.west-knightsqc@hailshamchambers.com

WESTLEY MR NICK DAVID

Queen Elizabeth Building
3rd Floor, Queen Elizabeth Building, Temple,
London EC4Y 9BS, ☎ 020 7797 7837
✉ clerks@qeb.co.uk
Call Date: Oct 2005, Lincoln's Inn
Qualifications: [BA (Hons) (Oxon)]
✉ n.westley@qeb.co.uk

WESTMAAS MR DEREK KEIRON STORM

12 Old Square Chambers
1st Floor, 12 Old Square, Lincoln's Inn,
London WC2A 3TX, ☎ 020 7404 0875
✉ clerks@12oldsquare.com
Call Date: July 1984, Inner Temple
Qualifications: [BA Dip Law (Lond)]
✉ clerks@12oldsquare.com

WESTON MS AMANDA

Tooks Chambers
81 Farringdon Street, London EC4A 4BL,
☎ 020 7842 7575 ✉ clerks@tooks.co.uk
Call Date: Oct 1995, Inner Temple
Pupil Supervisor
Qualifications: [LLB (Hons)]
✉ amanda.weston@tooks.co.uk

WESTON MR CRAIG

Charter Chambers
33 John Street, London WC1N 2AT,
☎ 020 7618 4400
✉ clerks@charterchambers.com
Call Date: July 2007, Lincoln's Inn
Qualifications: [LLB (Cardiff)]
✉ craig.weston@charterchambers.com

E

WESTON MR JAMES PAUL RADOVIC

Seven Bedford Row
7 Bedford Row, London WC1R 4BS,
☎ 020 7242 3555 ✉ clerks@7br.co.uk
Call Date: Oct 2007, Lincoln's Inn
Qualifications: [BSc (Lond) MPhil (Cantab)]

WESTON MR JEREMY PAUL QC (2011)

St Ive's Chambers
Whittall Street, Birmingham B4 6DH,
☎ 0121 236 0863
✉ clerks@stiveschambers.co.uk
Call Date: Oct 1991, Inner Temple
Pupil Supervisor
Qualifications: [LLB (Hons)(Staffs)]
✉ jeremy.weston@stiveschambers.co.uk

WESTON MR LOUIS ROY PAUL

3 PB Barristers
3 Paper Buildings, Temple, London EC4Y 7EU,
☎ 020 7583 8055
3 PB Barristers
30 Christchurch Road, Bournemouth, Dorset BH1 3PD, ☎ 01202 292102
✉ clerks.bournemouth@3paper.co.uk
3 PB Barristers
4 St Peter Street, Winchester SO23 8BW,
☎ 01962 868884
✉ clerks.winchester@3paper.co.uk
3 PB Barristers
Royal Talbot House, 2 Victoria Street, Bristol, Avon BS1 6BB, ☎ 0117 928 1520
3 PB Barristers
23 Beaumont Street, Oxford OX1 2NP,
☎ 01865 793 736
Call Date: Nov 1994, Lincoln's Inn
Pupil Supervisor
Qualifications: [BA (Hons)(Bris) CPE]
✉ louis.weston@3paper.co.uk

WESTWOOD MR ANDREW DAVID

Maitland Chambers
7 Stone Buildings, Lincoln's Inn, London WC2A 3SZ, ☎ 020 7406 1200
✉ clerks@maitlandchambers.com
Call Date: Nov 1994, Inner Temple
Pupil Supervisor
Qualifications: [MA (Oxon) CPE (Huddersfield)]
✉ awestwood@maitlandchambers.com

WHAITES MISS EMMA LOUISE

Exchange Chambers
7 Ralli Courts, West Riverside, Manchester M3 5FT, ☎ 0161 833 2722
Exchange Chambers
One Derby Square, Derby Square, Liverpool L2 9XX, ☎ 0151 236 7747
✉ info@exchangechambers.co.uk
Call Date: Nov 1994, Gray's Inn
Qualifications: [LLB (Hons)]
✉ whaites@exchangechambers.co.uk

WHALAN MR MARK ANDREW

The Chambers of Grahame Aldous QC
9 Gough Square, London EC4A 3DG,
☎ 020 7832 0500
✉ clerks@9goughsquare.co.uk
Call Date: Nov 1988, Middle Temple
Pupil Supervisor
Qualifications: [BA (Leeds) Dip Law (Lond)]
✉ mwhalan@9goughsquare.co.uk

WHALE MR STEPHEN JOHN

4-5 Gray's Inn Square
Gray's Inn, London WC1R 5AH,
☎ 020 7404 5252 ✉ clerks@4-5.co.uk
Call Date: Oct 1999, Gray's Inn
Pupil Supervisor
Qualifications: [B.Soc.Sc (B'ham) Dip Law]
✉ swhale@4-5.co.uk

WHALLEY MISS ALISON CLAIRE

Chambers of Miss A Whalley
18 Mulcaster Crescent, Stanwix, Carlisle, Cumbria CA3 9EA, ☎ 07759 520140
✉ acwabroad@yahoo.com
Call Date: Nov 2000, Lincoln's Inn
Qualifications: [LLB (Hons) (Cardiff)]

WHATLEY MR PAUL DONALD

Cobden House Chambers
19 Quay Street, Manchester M3 3HN,
☎ 0161 833 6000 ✉ Clerks@Cobden.co.uk
Call Date: Oct 2002, Lincoln's Inn
Qualifications: [LLB (Staffordshire)]
✉ clerks@cobden.co.uk

WHAWELL MISS LEESHA CLAIRE

3 Temple Gardens
Lower Ground Floor, 3 Temple Gardens, Temple, London EC4Y 9AU, ☎ 020 7353 3102
✉ clerks@3tg.co.uk
Call Date: July 2005, Lincoln's Inn
Qualifications: [BA (Hons) (Derby) LLDip]
✉ lw@3tg.co.uk

WHEATER MR MICHAEL JOHN

Hardwicke
New Square, Lincoln's Inn, London
WC2A 3SB, ☎ 020 7242 2523
✉ enquiries@hardwicke.co.uk
Call Date: Oct 2003, Lincoln's Inn
Qualifications: [LLB (Hons) LLM (Sheff)]
✉ michael.wheater@hardwicke.co.uk

WHEATLEY MR GERAINT RHYS

Kings Chambers
36 Young Street, Manchester M3 3FT,
☎ 0845 034 3444
✉ clerks@kingschambers.com
Kings Chambers
5 Park Square East, Leeds LS1 2NE,
☎ 0845 034 3444
✉ clerks@kingschambers.com
Kings Chambers
Embassy House, 60 Church Street,
Birmingham B3 2DJ, ☎ 0845 034 3444
✉ clerks@kingschambers.com
Call Date: Oct 2001, Gray's Inn
Qualifications: [BA (Oxon)]
✉ gwheatley@kingschambers.com

WHEATLEY MS JANE

Bank House Chambers
Old Bank House, Hartshead, Sheffield S1 2EL,
☎ 0114 275 1223
✉ w.digby@bankhousechambers.co.uk
Call Date: Nov 2007, Inner Temple
Qualifications: [LLB (Sheff)]
✉ j.wheatley@bankhousechambers.co.uk

WHEATLEY MR SIMON DEREK JOHN

Seven Bedford Row
7 Bedford Row, London WC1R 4BS,
☎ 020 7242 3555 ✉ clerks@7br.co.uk
Call Date: July 1979, Middle Temple
Pupil Supervisor
Qualifications: [LLB]
✉ swheatley@7br.co.uk

WHEATON MR IAN MALCOLM JAMES

Eighteen Carlton Crescent
Rownhams House, Rownhams, Southampton
SO16 8LF, ☎ 023 8063 9001
✉ clerks@18carltoncrescent.co.uk
Call Date: July 2002, Lincoln's Inn
Qualifications: [LLB (Hons)]
✉ clerks@18carltoncrescent.co.uk,
ianwheaton@18carltoncrescent.co.uk

WHEELER MR ANDREW GEORGE

Seven Bedford Row
7 Bedford Row, London WC1R 4BS,
☎ 020 7242 3555 ✉ clerks@7br.co.uk
Call Date: July 1988, Lincoln's Inn
Pupil Supervisor
Qualifications: [LLB (Hons)]
✉ awheeler@7br.co.uk

WHEELER MR GILES NEIL LAURENCE

Fountain Court Chambers
Fountain Court, Temple, London EC4Y 9DH,
☎ 020 7583 3335
✉ chambers@fountaincourt.co.uk
Call Date: Oct 1998, Middle Temple
Qualifications: [BA (Hons) LLM (Cantab)]
✉ gwheeler@fountaincourt.co.uk

WHEELER MISS MARINA CLAIRE

1 Crown Office Row
1 Crown Office Row, Temple, London
EC4Y 7HH, ☎ 020 7797 7500
✉ mail@1cor.com
Call Date: Nov 1987, Gray's Inn
Qualifications: [MA (Cantab)]
✉ marina.wheeler@1cor.com

WHEELER MR RICHARD GEORGE

3 PB Barristers
3 Paper Buildings, Temple, London EC4Y 7EU,
☎ 020 7583 8055
3 PB Barristers
Royal Talbot House, 2 Victoria Street, Bristol,
Avon BS1 6BB, ☎ 0117 928 1520
3 PB Barristers
30 Christchurch Road, Bournemouth, Dorset
BH1 3PD, ☎ 01202 292102
✉ clerks.bournemouth@3paper.co.uk
3 PB Barristers
4 St Peter Street, Winchester SO23 8BW,
☎ 01962 868884
✉ clerks.winchester@3paper.co.uk
3 PB Barristers
23 Beaumont Street, Oxford OX1 2NP,
☎ 01865 793 736
Call Date: July 2004, Inner Temple
Qualifications: [BA Dip Law]
✉ richard.wheeler@3paper.co.uk

WHEELER MR RUPERT ALEC OLIVER

1 Pump Court
Elm Court, Temple, London EC4Y 7AB,
☎ 020 7842 7070
✉ (name)@pumpcourt.co.uk
Call Date: Oct 2010, Inner Temple
Qualifications: [BA LLM (Bris)]

E

WHEETMAN MR ALAN

East Anglian Chambers
15 The Close, Norwich, Norfolk NR1 4DZ, ☎01473 214481 ✉norwich@ealaw.co.uk
East Anglian Chambers
140 New London Road, Chelmsford, Essex CM2 0AW, ☎01473 214481
✉chelmsford@ealaw.co.uk
East Anglian Chambers
Gresham House, 5 Museum Street, Ipswich, Suffolk IP1 1HQ, ☎01473 214481
✉ipswich@ealaw.co.uk
Call Date: Oct 1995, Middle Temple
Qualifications: [LLB (Hons)]
alanwheetman@ealaw.co.uk

WHELAN DR CHRISTOPHER JUDE

3 PB Barristers
23 Beaumont Street, Oxford OX1 2NP, ☎01865 793 736
3 PB Barristers
Royal Talbot House, 2 Victoria Street, Bristol, Avon BS1 6BB, ☎0117 928 1520
3 PB Barristers
4 St Peter Street, Winchester SO23 8BW, ☎01962 868884
✉clerks.winchester@3paper.co.uk
3 PB Barristers
3 Paper Buildings, Temple, London EC4Y 7EU, ☎020 7583 8055
3 PB Barristers
30 Christchurch Road, Bournemouth, Dorset BH1 3PD, ☎01202 292102
✉clerks.bournemouth@3paper.co.uk
Call Date: Nov 2001, Middle Temple
Qualifications: [LLB (Hons) PhD]

WHELAN MR GEOFFREY MICHAEL

Kenworthy's Chambers
Arlington House, Bloom Street, Salford, Manchester M3 6AJ, ☎0161 832 4036
Call Date: Mar 1996, Gray's Inn
Pupil Supervisor
Qualifications: [LLB (Hons)(Sheff)]
g.whelan@kenworthysbarristers.co.uk

WHELAN MISS ROMA FELICITY

4 Brick Court
4 Brick Court, Temple, London EC4Y 9AD, ☎020 7832 3200 ✉clerks@4bc.co.uk
Call Date: May 1984, Gray's Inn
Qualifications: [LLB (Belfast)]
roma.whelan@4bc.co.uk

WHELAN-JOHNSON MS ASHLIE VICTORIA

9 King's Bench Walk
Lower Ground Floor South, 9 King's Bench Walk, Temple, London EC4Y 7DX, ☎020 7353 9564 ✉9kbw@btconnect.com
Call Date: Nov 2000, Inner Temple
Qualifications: [LLB (Lond)]
9kbw@btconnect.com

WHIPPLE MRS PHILIPPA JANE EDWARDS QC (2010)

1 Crown Office Row
1 Crown Office Row, Temple, London EC4Y 7HH, ☎020 7797 7500
✉mail@1cor.com
Call Date: Feb 1994, Middle Temple
Pupil Supervisor
Qualifications: [MA (Oxon)]
philippa.whipple@1cor.com

WHIPPMAN MRS CONSTANCE

33 Bedford Row
London WC1R 4JH, ☎020 7242 6476
✉clerks@33bedfordrow.co.uk
Call Date: Nov 1978, Gray's Inn
Pupil Supervisor
Qualifications: [BA MA]
ConstanceWhippman@33bedfordrow.co.uk, cwhippman@aol.com

WHITAKER MR JOHN STEPHEN

No5 Chambers
Fountain Court, Steelhouse Lane, Birmingham B4 6DR, ☎0845 210 5555 ✉info@no5.com
No5 Chambers
Greenwood House, 4-7 Salisbury Court, London EC4Y 8AA, ☎0845 210 5555
No5 Chambers
38 Queen Square, Bristol BS1 4QS, ☎0845 210 5555
Call Date: Nov 1970, Lincoln's Inn
Pupil Supervisor
Qualifications: [MA BCL (Oxon)]
swhitaker@no5.com

WHITAKER MS QUINCY RACHEL SUZY

Doughty Street Chambers
53-54 Doughty Street, London WC1N 2LS, ☎020 7404 1313
✉enquiries@doughtystreet.co.uk
Doughty Street Chambers
Pall Mall Court, 61-67 King Street, Manchester M2 4PD, ☎0161 618 1066

Doughty Street Chambers
5th Floor, Broad Quay House, Prince Street, Bristol BS1 4DJ, ☎01179 058 717
Call Date: Nov 1991, Middle Temple
Qualifications: [BA (Hons) (Oxon) LLM (Lond)]
q.whitaker@doughtystreet.co.uk

WHITBY MRS JULIE ANNE

Castle Chambers
The Old Fire Station, 90 High Street, Harrow-on-the-Hill, Middlesex HA1 3LP, ☎020 8423 6579 info@castlechambers.net
Call Date: Oct 1997, Lincoln's Inn
Pupil Supervisor
Qualifications: [LLB (Hons)(B'ham)]

WHITCOMBE MR MARK DAVID

Old Square Chambers
3 Orchard Court, St Augustine's Yard, Bristol BS1 5DP, ☎0117 930 5100
clerks@oldsquare.co.uk
Old Square Chambers
10-11 Bedford Row, London WC1R 4BU, ☎020 7269 0300 clerks@oldsquare.co.uk
Call Date: Nov 1994, Middle Temple
Qualifications: [BA (Hons)(Oxon) BCL (Oxon)]
whitcombe@oldsquare.co.uk

WHITE MISS ABIGAIL CLAIRE

Five St Andrew's Hill
5 St Andrew's Hill, London EC4V 5BZ, ☎020 7332 5400 Clerks@5sah.co.uk
Call Date: Nov 2000, Lincoln's Inn
Qualifications: [LLB (Hons) (B'Ham)]
abigailwhite@5sah.co.uk

WHITE MISS AMANDA JANE

No 8 Chambers
8 Fountain Court, Steelhouse Lane, Birmingham B4 6DR, ☎0121 236 5514
clerks@no8chambers.co.uk
Call Date: Nov 1976, Gray's Inn
Qualifications: [BA CNAA]
clerks@no8chambers.co.uk

WHITE MR ANDREW QC (1997)

Atkin Chambers
1 Atkin Building, Gray's Inn, London WC1R 5AT, ☎020 7404 0102
clerks@atkinchambers.com
Call Date: July 1980, Lincoln's Inn
Qualifications: [LLB (Wales)]
clerks@atkinchambers.com

WHITE MR ANTONY DENIS LOWNDES QC (2001)

Matrix Chambers
Griffin Building, Gray's Inn, London WC1R 5LN, ☎020 7404 3447
matrix@matrixlaw.co.uk / lscott@matrixlaw.co.uk
Call Date: Nov 1983, Middle Temple
Qualifications: [MA (Cantab)]
antonywhite@matrixlaw.co.uk

WHITE MR BARRY

Walnut House
63 St. David's Hill, Exeter, Devon EX4 4DW, ☎01392 279751
clerks@walnuthouse.co.uk
Call Date: July 2004, Gray's Inn
Qualifications: [LLB (Bris)]
barry.white@walnuthouse.co.uk

WHITE MS CERI ANN

4 Paper Buildings
1st Floor, 4 Paper Buildings, Temple, London EC4Y 7EX, ☎020 7427 5200
clerks@4pb.com
Call Date: Oct 2002, Gray's Inn
Qualifications: [BA (Oxon)]
caw@4pb.com

WHITE MR DANIEL EDWARD MILLS

Citadel Chambers
The Citadel, 190 Corporation Street, Birmingham B4 6QD, ☎0121 233 8500
clerks@citadelchambers.com
Call Date: Oct 2003, Gray's Inn
Qualifications: [LLB (B'ham)]
clerks@citadelchambers.com

WHITE MR DAVID RICHARD

Temple Garden Chambers
1 Harcourt Buildings, Temple, London EC4Y 9DA, ☎020 7583 1315
clerks@tgchambers.com
Call Date: July 2009, Inner Temple
Qualifications: [BA (Sheff) LLB (Nott'm)]
drwhite@tgchambers.com

WHITE MR DAVID SPENCER

12 King's Bench Walk
12 King's Bench Walk, Temple, London EC4Y 7EL, ☎020 7583 0811
Call Date: Oct 1999, Lincoln's Inn
Qualifications: [MA (Cantab)]
white@12kbw.co.uk

E

WHITE MRS DEBRA ANNE

Call Date: Oct 2005, Gray's Inn
Qualifications: [LLB (Manch)]
clerk@stjohnsbuildings.co.uk

WHITE MISS ELIZABETH ALICIA JANE

East Anglian Chambers
140 New London Road, Chelmsford, Essex CM2 0AW, ☎01473 214481
chelmsford@ealaw.co.uk
East Anglian Chambers
Gresham House, 5 Museum Street, Ipswich, Suffolk IP1 1HQ, ☎01473 214481
ipswich@ealaw.co.uk
East Anglian Chambers
15 The Close, Norwich, Norfolk NR1 4DZ, ☎01473 214481 norwich@ealaw.co.uk
Call Date: July 2006, Inner Temple
Qualifications: [BA (Georgia State)]
elizabethwhite@ealaw.co.uk

WHITE MISS GEMMA SOPHIE GOLDER

Blackstone Chambers
Blackstone House, Temple, London EC4Y 9BW, ☎020 7583 1770
clerks@blackstonechambers.com
Call Date: Nov 1994, Inner Temple
Qualifications: [LLB (Lond) BCL (Oxon)]
gemmawhite@blackstonechambers.com

WHITE MISS HELENA ELIZABETH LOUISE

Hardwicke
New Square, Lincoln's Inn, London WC2A 3SB, ☎020 7242 2523
enquiries@hardwicke.co.uk
Call Date: Oct 2007, Middle Temple
Qualifications: [BA (Hons) (Oxon)]
helena.white@hardwicke.co.uk

WHITE MR JEREMY BARRY

Pump Court Tax Chambers
16 Bedford Row, London WC1R 4EF, ☎020 7414 8080 clerks@pumptax.com
Call Date: July 1976, Gray's Inn
Qualifications: [LLB]
jwhite@pumptax.com

Types of work: Corporation tax, Customs, VAT

WHITE MR MATTHEW JAMES

St John's Chambers
101 Victoria Street, Bristol BS1 6PU, ☎0117 923 4700
clerks@stjohnschambers.co.uk
Call Date: Oct 1997, Gray's Inn
Pupil Supervisor
Qualifications: [MA]
matthew.white@stjohnschambers.co.uk

WHITE MR OLIVER ZACHARY

Littleton Chambers
3 King's Bench Walk North, Temple, London EC4Y 7HR, ☎020 7797 8600
fschneider@littletonchambers.co.uk
Call Date: Nov 2001, Lincoln's Inn
Pupil Supervisor
Qualifications: [BA (Hons)(Leeds)]
ow@littletonchambers.co.uk

WHITE MR PETER-JOHN SPENCER

Great Barford Chambers
Bridge Cottage, 88 Green End Road, Bedford, Bedford MK44 3HD, ☎012134 870004
peter_johnwhite@hotmail.com
Call Date: July 1977, Inner Temple
Pupil Supervisor
Qualifications: [BA (Hons)]
peter_johnwhite@hotmail.com

WHITE MISS RACHEL DOROTHY

Kenworthy's Chambers
Arlington House, Bloom Street, Salford, Manchester M3 6AJ, ☎0161 832 4036
Call Date: Nov 2000, Middle Temple
Qualifications: [BA (Hons) (Manch) Dip in Law (Manch)]
r.white@kenworthysbarristers.co.uk

WHITE MR ROBERT DOUGLAS

4-5 Gray's Inn Square
Gray's Inn, London WC1R 5AH, ☎020 7404 5252 clerks@4-5.co.uk
Call Date: Nov 1993, Inner Temple
Pupil Supervisor
Qualifications: [LLB (Lond)]
rwhite@4-5.co.uk

E

WHITE MS ROBIN MOIRA

Old Square Chambers
10-11 Bedford Row, London WC1R 4BU,
☎ 020 7269 0300 ✉ clerks@oldsquare.co.uk
Old Square Chambers
3 Orchard Court, St Augustine's Yard, Bristol BS1 5DP, ☎ 0117 930 5100
✉ clerks@oldsquare.co.uk
Call Date: Nov 1995, Gray's Inn
Pupil Supervisor
Qualifications: [BSc LLB (Exon) ARCS MCIT]
✉ white@oldsquare.co.uk

WHITE MR SASHA NICHOLAS

Landmark Chambers
180 Fleet Street, London EC4A 2HG,
☎ 020 7430 1221
✉ clerks@landmarkchambers.co.uk
Call Date: Oct 1991, Inner Temple
Qualifications: [BA (Cantab)]
✉ sashawhite@landmarkchambers.co.uk

WHITE MR STEVEN JAMES

Park Court Chambers
16 Park Place, Leeds LS1 2SJ,
☎ 0113 243 3277
✉ clerks@parkcourtchambers.co.uk
Call Date: Nov 1998, Inner Temple
Qualifications: [BA (Manch) Dip Law]
✉ swhite@parkcourtchambers.co.uk

WHITE MRS TANYA

Great Barford Chambers
Bridge Cottage, 88 Green End Road, Bedford, Bedford MK44 3HD, ☎ 012134 870004
✉ peter_johnwhite@hotmail.com
Call Date: Feb 1983, Middle Temple
Qualifications: [BA (Hons)]
✉ peter_johnwhite@hotmail.com

WHITE MR TIMOTHY GORDON

Cobden House Chambers
19 Quay Street, Manchester M3 3HN,
☎ 0161 833 6000 ✉ Clerks@Cobden.co.uk
Call Date: July 1978, Middle Temple
Pupil Supervisor
Qualifications: [BA]
✉ clerks@cobden.co.uk

WHITEHALL MR MARK ANTHONY

Colleton Chambers
Colleton Crescent, Exeter, Devon EX2 4DG,
☎ 01392 274898
✉ clerks@colletonchambers.co.uk
Call Date: July 1983, Inner Temple
Pupil Supervisor
Qualifications: [LLB (Exon)]
✉ markwhitehall@colletonchambers.co.uk

WHITEHALL MR RICHARD LANGDALE

Deans Court Chambers
24 St John Street, Manchester M3 4DF,
☎ 0161 214 6000 ✉ clerks@deanscourt.co.uk
Deans Court Chambers
101 Walker Street, Preston PR1 2RR,
☎ 01772 565 600
✉ preston@deanscourt.co.uk
Call Date: July 1998, Lincoln's Inn
Pupil Supervisor
Qualifications: [LLB (Hons)(Cardiff) LLM (Cardiff)]
✉ whitehall@deanscourt.co.uk

WHITEHEAD MR DARRON MARCUS

St Philips Chambers
55 Temple Row, Birmingham B2 5LS,
☎ 0121 246 7000 ✉ clerks@st-philips.com
Call Date: Nov 1995, Inner Temple
Pupil Supervisor
Qualifications: [LLB (Hons)(Sheff)]
✉ dwhitehead@st-philips.co.uk

WHITEHEAD MR THOMAS PATRICK CROMARTY

Stone Chambers
4 Field Court, Gray's Inn, London WC1R 5EF,
☎ 020 7440 6900
✉ clerks@stonechambers.com
Call Date: Oct 2002, Inner Temple
Pupil Supervisor
Qualifications: [BA (Oxon) BCL (Oxon)]
✉ tom.whitehead@stonechambers.com

WHITEHORN MR NICHOLAS

1 Gray's Inn Square
Ground Floor, 1 Gray's Inn Square, London WC1R 5AA, ☎ 020 7405 0001
Call Date: Mar 2006, Gray's Inn
Qualifications: [BA (Lond)]
✉ nwhitehorn@1gis.co.uk

WHITEHOUSE MISS CAMILLA JANE

10 King's Bench Walk
Ground Floor, 10 King's Bench Walk, Temple, London EC4Y 7EB, ☎ 020 7353 7742
✉ Chambers@10kingsbenchwalk.co.uk
Call Date: July 2010, Middle Temple
Qualifications: [BA (Hons) (Lond)]

WHITEHOUSE MR CHRISTOPHER

Farringdon Chambers
180 Bermondsey Street, London SE1 3TQ,
☎ 020 7089 5700
Call Date: Nov 1997, Gray's Inn
Qualifications: [LLB]
✉ chriswhitehouse@farringdon-law.co.uk

E

WHITEHOUSE MR CHRISTOPHER JOHN

5 Stone Buildings
5 Stone Buildings, Lincoln's Inn, London WC2A 3XT, ☎ 020 7242 6201
✉ clerks@5sblaw.com
Call Date: May 1972, Inner Temple
Qualifications: [BA BCL (Oxon)]
cwhitehouse@5sblaw.com

WHITEHOUSE MRS SARAH ALICE

6 King's Bench Walk
Ground Floor, 6 King's Bench Walk, Temple, London EC4Y 7DR, ☎ 020 7583 0410
✉ clerks@6kbw.com
Call Date: Oct 1993, Lincoln's Inn
Pupil Supervisor
Qualifications: [MA (Hons) Dip law]
sarah.whitehouse@6kbw.com

WHITEHOUSE MR STUART COLIN

Goldsmith Chambers
Ground Floor, Goldsmith Building, Temple, London EC4Y 7BL, ☎ 020 7353 6802
✉ clerks@goldsmithchambers.com
Call Date: July 1987, Middle Temple
Pupil Supervisor
Qualifications: [LLB(Hons) LLM (Exon)]
S.Whitehouse@goldsmithchambers.law.co.uk

WHITEHURST MR IAN JOHN

Number 7 Harrington Street Chambers
7 Harrington Street, Liverpool L2 9YH, ☎ 0151 242 0707 ✉ clerks@7hs.co.uk
Call Date: Nov 1994, Inner Temple
Qualifications: [LLB (Hull)]
ian.whitehurst@7hs.co.uk

WHITELAW MS FRANCESCA LUCY KAYE

5 Essex Court
1st Floor, 5 Essex Court, Temple, London EC4Y 9AH, ☎ 020 7410 2000
✉ clerks@5essexcourt.co.uk
Call Date: July 2003, Inner Temple
Qualifications: [MA (Cantab) CPE MA]
whitelaw@5essexcourt.co.uk

WHITELEY MS GINNY LOUISE

St Johns Buildings Liverpool
8th Floor India Buildings, Water Street, Liverpool L2 0XG, ☎ 0151 243 6000
✉ clerk@stjohnsbuildings.co.uk
Call Date: July 2010, Inner Temple
Qualifications: [BA (Oxon)]
ginny.whiteley@stjohnsbuildings.co.uk

WHITEMAN MR PETER GEORGE QC (1977)

QEB Hollis Whiteman
1-2 Laurence Pountney Hill, London EC4R 0EU, ☎ 020 7933 8855
✉ barristers@qebhw.co.uk
Call Date: July 1967, Lincoln's Inn
Recorder
Qualifications: [LLB LLM]
barristers@qebhw.co.uk

WHITFIELD MR JONATHAN QC (2010)

Doughty Street Chambers
53-54 Doughty Street, London WC1N 2LS, ☎ 020 7404 1313
✉ enquiries@doughtystreet.co.uk
Call Date: July 1985, Middle Temple
Pupil Supervisor
Qualifications: [BA]
j.whitfield@Doughtystreet.co.uk

WHITFIELD MR SIMON WILLIAM

Exchange Chambers
7 Ralli Courts, West Riverside, Manchester M3 5FT, ☎ 0161 833 2722
Exchange Chambers
One Derby Square, Derby Square, Liverpool L2 9XX, ☎ 0151 236 7747
✉ info@exchangechambers.co.uk
Exchange Chambers
Oxford House, Oxford Row, Leeds LS1 3BE, ☎ 0113 203 1970
✉ spencer@exchangechambers.co.uk
Call Date: July 2009, Lincoln's Inn
Qualifications: [BA (Cantab)]
whitfield@exchangechambers.co.uk

WHITLEY MR JONATHAN DENTON

Castle Chambers
The Old Fire Station, 90 High Street, Harrow-on-the-Hill, Middlesex HA1 3LP, ☎ 020 8423 6579 ✉ info@castlechambers.net
Call Date: Nov 1993, Inner Temple
Qualifications: [LLB (Hons) (Exon)]

WHITTAKER MR DAVID JOHN

2 Hare Court
Lower Ground, Ground, 1st & 2nd Floor, 2 Hare Court, Temple, London EC4Y 7BH, ☎ 020 7353 3982 ✉ clerks@2harecourt.com
Nine Bedford Row
9 Bedford Row, London WC1R 4AZ, ☎ 020 7489 2727
✉ clerks@9bedfordrow.co.uk
Call Date: Nov 1986, Middle Temple
Pupil Supervisor, Recorder
Qualifications: [BA (Lond) Dip Law]

WHITTAKER MRS NADEZHDA

Crown Office Chambers
2 Crown Office Row, Temple, London
EC4Y 7HJ, ☎ 020 7797 8100
✉ mail@crownofficechambers.com
Call Date: July 2007, Inner Temple
Qualifications: [BSc (Lond) MA (Lond) LLB (Lond)]
✉ whittaker@crownofficechambers.com

WHITTAKER DR SIMON JOHN

Blackstone Chambers
Blackstone House, Temple, London
EC4Y 9BW, ☎ 020 7583 1770
✉ clerks@blackstonechambers.com
Call Date: Nov 1987, Lincoln's Inn
Qualifications: [BCL DPhil (Oxon) MA]
✉ simon.whittaker@sjc.ox.ac.uk

WHITTAM MS SAMANTHA ABIGAIL

14 Gray's Inn Square
14 Gray's Inn Square, Gray's Inn, London
WC1R 5JP, ☎ 020 7242 0858
✉ clerks@14gis.co.uk
Call Date: Nov 1995, Middle Temple
Qualifications: [BA (Hons)(Bris) MA (Lond)]
✉ clerks@14graysinnsquare.co.uk

WHITTAM MR WILLIAM RICHARD LAMONT QC (2008)

2 Bedford Row
London WC1R 4BU, ☎ 020 7440 8888
✉ clerks@2bedfordrow.co.uk
Call Date: July 1983, Gray's Inn
Qualifications: [LLB (Hons) (Lond)]
✉ rwhittam@2bedfordrow.co.uk

WHITTING MR JOHN JUSTIN QC (2011)

1 Crown Office Row
1 Crown Office Row, Temple, London
EC4Y 7HH, ☎ 020 7797 7500
✉ mail@1cor.com
Call Date: Oct 1991, Middle Temple
Qualifications: [BA (Hons)(Oxon) LLM (Lond)]
✉ john.whitting@1cor.com

WHITTLE-MARTIN MISS LUCIA

3 PB Barristers
3 Paper Buildings, Temple, London EC4Y 7EU,
☎ 020 7583 8055
3 PB Barristers
23 Beaumont Street, Oxford OX1 2NP,
☎ 01865 793 736
3 PB Barristers
30 Christchurch Road, Bournemouth, Dorset
BH1 3PD, ☎ 01202 292102
✉ clerks.bournemouth@3paper.co.uk
3 PB Barristers
Royal Talbot House, 2 Victoria Street, Bristol,
Avon BS1 6BB, ☎ 0117 928 1520
3 PB Barristers
4 St Peter Street, Winchester SO23 8BW,
☎ 01962 868884
✉ clerks.winchester@3paper.co.uk
Call Date: Nov 1985, Middle Temple
Qualifications: [BSc (Lond) DipLaw]
✉ lucia.whittle-martin@3pb.co.uk

WHITTLESTONE MISS KIM

Exchange Chambers
One Derby Square, Derby Square, Liverpool
L2 9XX, ☎ 0151 236 7747
✉ info@exchangechambers.co.uk
Exchange Chambers
7 Ralli Courts, West Riverside, Manchester
M3 5FT, ☎ 0161 833 2722
Exchange Chambers
Oxford House, Oxford Row, Leeds LS1 3BE,
☎ 0113 203 1970
✉ spencer@exchangechambers.co.uk
Call Date: Nov 1994, Middle Temple
Qualifications: [LLB (Hons)]
✉ whittlestone@exchangechambers.co.uk

WHITTOCK DR ROBERT JOHN

Kew Chambers
354 Kew Road, Kew, Surrey TW9 3DU,
☎ 0844 8099991
✉ admin@kewchambers.co.uk
Call Date: July 2006, Lincoln's Inn
Qualifications: [BSc (Cardiff) PhD (Cardiff) PGDipLaw (Nott'm)]

WHITTY MR MICHAEL LEWIS

Linenhall Chambers
1 Stanley Place, Chester CH1 2LU,
☎ 01244 348282
✉ clerks@linenhallchambers.co.uk
Call Date: July 2005, Middle Temple
Qualifications: [LLB (Hons) L'pool]
✉ clerks@1stanleyplace.co.uk

WHYATT MR BERNARD ANTHONY

Chambers of Mr Bernard Whyatt
Stonecroft, Somerton Road, Ardley,
Oxfordshire OX27 7PF, ☎ 01869 346160
✉ bernard.whyatt@bptm.co.uk
Call Date: Oct 1996, Middle Temple
Qualifications: [BA (Hons)(Leeds) LLB (Hons)]

E

WHYATT MR MICHAEL GEORGE

15 Winckley Square
Preston PR1 3JJ, ☎01772 252828
✉clerks@15winckleysq.co.uk
Call Date: Feb 1992, Gray's Inn
Pupil Supervisor
Qualifications: [LLB]

WHYMENT MISS KRYSTAL KELLY

Five St Andrew's Hill
5 St Andrew's Hill, London EC4V 5BZ,
☎020 7332 5400 ✉Clerks@5sah.co.uk
Call Date: July 2008, Middle Temple
Qualifications: [LLB (Hons) (Kent)]

WHYTE MISS ANNE LYNNE QC (2010)

Atlantic Chambers
4-6 Cook Street, Liverpool L2 9QU,
☎0151 236 4421
✉info@atlanticchambers.co.uk
Call Date: Feb 1993, Lincoln's Inn
Pupil Supervisor
Qualifications: [BA Dip Law BA (Hons)(Oxon)]
annewhyte@atlanticchambers.co.uk

WHYTE DR JAMES RICHARD CLELAND

8 New Square
8 New Square, Lincoln's Inn, London
WC2A 3QP, ☎020 7405 4321
✉clerks@8newsquare.co.uk
Call Date: Oct 2005, Lincoln's Inn
Qualifications: [BA (Hons) (Cantab) PhD (Cantab) CPE (Lond)]
james.whyte@8newsquare.co.uk

Types of work: Breach of confidence, Communications, Computer contracts, Computer litigation, Confidential information, Copyright, Copyright Tribunal, Data protection, Design, Entertainment, Information technology, Internet law, Media, Media and entertainment, Passing off, Patents, Pharmaceuticals, Publishing, Registered designs, Scientific and technical disputes, Telecommunications, Trade secrets, Trademarks, Unregistered designs

WHYTE MISS MONICA PATRICIA

42 Bedford Row
London WC1R 4LL, ☎020 7831 0222
✉clerks@42br.com
Call Date: Oct 1996, Inner Temple
Qualifications: [BA (Hons) LLM (L'pool)]
monica.whyte@42br.com

WIBBERLEY MR JAMES MATTHEW

Ropewalk Chambers
24 The Ropewalk, Nottingham NG1 5EF,
☎0115 947 2581 ✉clerks@ropewalk.co.uk
Call Date: July 2009, Lincoln's Inn
Qualifications: [BA (Oxon) LLB]
jameswibberley@ropewalk.co.uk

WIBBERLEY MISS LUCIE ANNE

1 Pump Court
Elm Court, Temple, London EC4Y 7AB,
☎020 7842 7070
✉(name)@pumpcourt.co.uk
Call Date: Nov 2005, Gray's Inn
Qualifications: [BA (Brighton) MA (Lond)]
lwi@1pumpcourt.co.uk

WICKENS MR SIMON

Maidstone Chambers
33 Earl Street, Maidstone, Kent ME14 1PF,
☎01622 688592
✉clerks@maidstonechambers.co.uk
Call Date: Mar 1998, Lincoln's Inn
Qualifications: [BA (Hons)]

WICKINS MISS STEFANIE LORRAINE

Trinity Chambers
Highfield House, Moulsham Street,
Chelmsford, Essex CM2 9AH,
☎01245 605040
✉clerks@trinitychambers.com
Call Date: Nov 1994, Lincoln's Inn
Qualifications: [LLB (Hons)(UEA) LLM (Bris)]

WICKS MR DAVID CHARLES

Pump Court Chambers
Upper Ground Floor, 3 Pump Court, Temple,
London EC4Y 7AJ, ☎020 7353 0711
✉clerks@3pumpcourt.com
Pump Court Chambers
5 Temple Chambers, Temple Street, Swindon
SN1 1SQ, ☎01793 539899
✉clerks@3pumpcourt.com
Pump Court Chambers
31 Southgate Street, Winchester, Hampshire
SO23 9EB, ☎01962 868 161
✉clerks@3pumpcourt.com
Call Date: July 1989, Middle Temple
Qualifications: [BA]
dcw@3pumpcourt.com

E

WICKS MS JOANNE QC (2010)

Wilberforce Chambers
8 New Square, Lincoln's Inn, London
WC2A 3QP, ☎ 020 7306 0102
✉ chambers@wilberforce.co.uk
Call Date: Nov 1990, Lincoln's Inn
Pupil Supervisor
Qualifications: [BA (Hons)(Oxon) BCL]
✉ jwicks@wilberforce.co.uk

Types of work: Chancery (general), Chancery (land law), Commercial litigation, Commercial property, Conveyancing, Equity, Landlord and tenant, Professional negligence, Solicitor's indemnity, Trusts

WICKS MISS LUCINDA JANE MOONEY

Coram Chambers
9-11 Fulwood Place, London WC1V 6HG,
☎ 020 7092 3700
✉ mail@coramchambers.co.uk
Call Date: Nov 2006, Middle Temple
Qualifications: [BSc (Bris)]
✉ Lucinda.Wicks@coramchambers.co.uk

WICKS MR RAYMOND

Prince Henry's Chambers
2 Tamar House, 12 Tavistock Place, London
WC1H 9RD, ☎ 020 7837 1645
✉ d.harris4@btconnect.com
Call Date: Oct 1997, Inner Temple
Qualifications: [BSc (Reading) MBA CPE (Middx) MCIArb]

WIDDETT MS CERI LOUISE

Park Court Chambers
16 Park Place, Leeds LS1 2SJ,
☎ 0113 243 3277
✉ clerks@parkcourtchambers.co.uk
Call Date: Oct 1994, Gray's Inn
Pupil Supervisor
Qualifications: [BA (Keele)]
✉ clerks@parkcourtchambers.co.uk

WIDDISON-THOM MRS STACEY JANE

Kingsley Chambers
104 Tanners Lane, Barkingside, Essex
IG6 1QE, ☎ 07891 441 445
✉ s.widdison@kingsleychambers.com
Call Date: Oct 2000, Inner Temple
Qualifications: [LLB (Lond)]
✉ swiddison@kingsleychambers.com

WIDDUP MR STANLEY JEFFREY PONSONBY

Guildford Chambers
Stoke House, Leapale Lane, Guildford, Surrey
GU1 4LY, ☎ 01483 539131
✉ clerks@guildfordchambers.co.uk
Call Date: Nov 1973, Gray's Inn
Pupil Supervisor, Recorder

WIGGLESWORTH MR RAYMOND QC (1999)

18 St John Street
Manchester M3 4EA, ☎ 0161 278 1800
✉ clerks@18sjs.com
Call Date: July 1974, Gray's Inn
Recorder
Qualifications: [LLB]

WIGGLESWORTH MR TIMOTHY ROBIN

Dere Street Barristers
33 Broad Chare, Newcastle Upon Tyne
NE1 3DQ, ☎ 0844 3351551
✉ clerks@derestreet.co.uk
Call Date: July 2007, Middle Temple
Qualifications: [LLB (Wales)]
✉ clerks@broadcharechambers.co.uk

WIGHTWICK MR IAIN

Unity Street Chambers
5 Unity Street, College Green, Bristol
BS1 5HH, ☎ 0117 906 9789
✉ chambers@unitystreetchambers.com
Riverview Chambers
Hamilton House, 1 Temple Avenue, London
EC4Y 0HA, ☎ 0844 225 3999
✉ chrisbaylis@riverviewchambers.com
Call Date: Nov 1985, Inner Temple
Pupil Supervisor
Qualifications: [BSc (Hons)(Bris) Dip Law]

WIGIN MISS CAROLINE ROSEMARY

Park Court Chambers
16 Park Place, Leeds LS1 2SJ,
☎ 0113 243 3277
✉ clerks@parkcourtchambers.co.uk
Call Date: July 1984, Inner Temple
Pupil Supervisor, Recorder
Qualifications: [BA (Exon)]
✉ cwigin@parkcourtchambers.co.uk

WIGLEY MISS JENNY

No5 Chambers
Greenwood House, 4-7 Salisbury Court, London EC4Y 8AA, ☎0845 210 5555
No5 Chambers
38 Queen Square, Bristol BS1 4QS, ☎0845 210 5555
No5 Chambers
Fountain Court, Steelhouse Lane, Birmingham B4 6DR, ☎0845 210 5555 ✉info@no5.com
Call Date: Nov 2000, Middle Temple
Qualifications: [MA (Hons) Cantab]
jwi@no5.com

WIGLEY MR JOSEPH

4 Stone Buildings
Ground Floor, 4 Stone Buildings, Lincoln's Inn, London WC2A 3XT, ☎020 7242 5524
✉clerks@4stonebuildings.com
Call Date: Oct 2010, Middle Temple
Qualifications: [BA (Hons) (Oxon)]

WIGNALL MR EDWARD GORDON

No5 Chambers
Greenwood House, 4-7 Salisbury Court, London EC4Y 8AA, ☎0845 210 5555
No5 Chambers
38 Queen Square, Bristol BS1 4QS, ☎0845 210 5555
No5 Chambers
Fountain Court, Steelhouse Lane, Birmingham B4 6DR, ☎0845 210 5555 ✉info@no5.com
Call Date: July 1987, Gray's Inn
Qualifications: [MA (Oxon) DipLaw]
gwi@no5.com

WIGODER THE HON LEWIS JUSTIN

1 High Pavement
Nottingham NG1 1HF, ☎0115 941 8218
✉clerks@1highpavement.co.uk
Call Date: July 1977, Gray's Inn
Pupil Supervisor, Recorder
Qualifications: [MA DPhil (Oxon)]
justinwigoder@1highpavement.co.uk

WIJEYARATNE MR ASELA LOCHANA NEVILLE

3 Hare Court
3 Hare Court, Temple, London EC4Y 7BJ, ☎020 7415 7800 ✉clerks@3harecourt.com
Call Date: Nov 2008, Lincoln's Inn
Qualifications: [LLB (Lond) LLM (Cantab)]
asela.wijeyaratne@3harecourt.com

WIKTOROWSKI-SOLECKI MISS TAMARA

Middle Temple Lane Chambers
2nd Floor South, 1 Middle Temple Lane, London EC4Y 9AA, ☎020 7583 4352
✉chambers@mtlchambers.com
Call Date: Oct 1999, Lincoln's Inn
Qualifications: [BA (Hons) (Oxon) Dip in Law (Westmin) MA (Oxon)]

WILBY MR DAVID CHRISTOPHER QC (1998)

Park Lane Plowden
19 Westgate, Leeds LS1 2RD, ☎0113 228 5049
✉clerks@parklaneplowden.co.uk
Park Lane Plowden
Lombard House, 4-8 Lombard Street, Newcastle Upon Tyne NE1 3AE, ☎0191 211 4087
✉clerks@parklaneplowden.co.uk
Old Square Chambers
3 Orchard Court, St Augustine's Yard, Bristol BS1 5DP, ☎0117 930 5100
✉clerks@oldsquare.co.uk
Call Date: July 1974, Inner Temple
Recorder
Qualifications: [MA (Cantab)]
david.wilby@parklaneplowden.co.uk

WILCKEN MR ANTHONY DAVID FELIX

QEB Hollis Whiteman
1-2 Laurence Pountney Hill, London EC4R 0EU, ☎020 7933 8855
✉barristers@qebhw.co.uk
Call Date: Nov 1966, Middle Temple
Pupil Supervisor, Recorder
barristers@qebhw.co.uk

WILCOCK MR PETER LAZENBY QC (2012)

Tooks Chambers
81 Farringdon Street, London EC4A 4BL, ☎020 7842 7575 ✉clerks@tooks.co.uk
Call Date: July 1988, Middle Temple
Pupil Supervisor
Qualifications: [LLB (Hons) (LSE)]
peter.wilcock@tooks.co.uk

WILCOX MR JEROME CARL JEAN

Alexander Chambers
13 Halstead Road, Wanstead, London E11 2AY, ☎0845 652 0451 / 0854 652 0451
✉clerks@alexanderchambers.co.uk
Call Date: Nov 1988, Middle Temple
Qualifications: [LLB(Bucks) Dip Law]

E

WILCOX MR LAWRENCE GAYWOOD

Octagon Chambers
29 Park Street, Taunton, Somerset TA1 4DG, ☎ 01823 331919
✉ jcload@Octagonchambers.co.uk
Call Date: Oct 1996, Lincoln's Inn
Qualifications: [LLB (Hons)(Exon)]
✉ lwilcox@octagonchambers.co.uk

WILCOX MR NICHOLAS HUGH

5 Essex Court
1st Floor, 5 Essex Court, Temple, London EC4Y 9AH, ☎ 020 7410 2000
✉ clerks@5essexcourt.co.uk
Call Date: July 1977, Gray's Inn
Pupil Supervisor
Qualifications: [LLB]
✉ wilcox@5essexcourt.co.uk

WILD MR SIMON PETER

9-12 Bell Yard
London WC2A 2JR, ☎ 020 7400 1800
✉ clerks@9-12bellyard.com
Call Date: July 1977, Inner Temple
Pupil Supervisor
Qualifications: [BA (Lond)]
✉ s.wild@9-12bellyard.com

WILD MR STEVEN

St Johns Buildings
24a - 28 St John Street, Manchester M3 4DJ, ☎ 0161 214 1500
✉ clerk@stjohnsbuildings.co.uk
16 Winckley Square
Preston PR1 3JJ, ☎ 01772 256100
St Johns Buildings Liverpool
8th Floor India Buildings, Water Street, Liverpool L2 0XG, ☎ 0151 243 6000
✉ clerk@stjohnsbuildings.co.uk
Call Date: Oct 1994, Gray's Inn
Pupil Supervisor
Qualifications: [LLB]

WILDE MISS CARMEL JOAN-MARIE

Chavasse Court Chambers
18 Queen Avenue, Liverpool L2 4TX, ☎ 0151 229 2030
✉ clerks@chavassechambers.co.uk
Call Date: Oct 2004, Inner Temple
Qualifications: [LLB (Manch)]
✉ carmelwilde@hotmail.com

WILDING MISS JOANNA MARRIE HARRISON

Garden Court Chambers
57-60 Lincoln's Inn Fields, London WC2A 3LJ, ☎ 020 7993 7600 ✉ info@gclaw.co.uk
Call Date: Mar 2007, Gray's Inn
Qualifications: [BA (Newc) MSc (Bris) PGDip Law (Bris) BVC]

WILDING MR KEITH

Principal Chambers
15 Lime Tree Walk, Sevenoaks, Kent TN13 1YH, ☎ 0845 209 8080
Call Date: Oct 1990, Inner Temple
Pupil Supervisor
Qualifications: [BA B Phil LLM CQSW Dip Law]

WILDING MISS LISA MARIE

Old Bailey Chambers
15 Old Bailey, London EC4M 7EF, ☎ 020 3008 6404
✉ clerks@15oldbaileychambers.com
Call Date: Nov 1993, Inner Temple
Pupil Supervisor
Qualifications: [MA (Hons) (Cantab)]
✉ lwilding@15oldbaileychambers.com

WILES MS ELLEN

39 Essex Street
London WC2R 3AT, ☎ 020 7832 1111
✉ clerks@39essex.com
82 King Street
Manchester M2 4WQ, ☎ 0161 870 9969
Call Date: Oct 2007, Inner Temple
Qualifications: [BA (Oxon) LLM (Lond)]

WILEY MISS FRANCESCA PETRA DENNING

1 Garden Court Family Law Chambers
Ground Floor, One Garden Court, Temple, London EC4Y 9BJ, ☎ 020 7797 7900
✉ clerks@1gc.com
Call Date: May 1996, Gray's Inn
Qualifications: [MA]

WILFORD MR ELLIS DAVID JOHN

Chambers of Mr Ami Feder
Ground Floor, Lamb Building, Temple, London EC4Y 7AS, ☎ 020 7797 7788
✉ clerks@lambbuilding.co.uk
Chambers of Mr Ami Feder
Ground Floor, Lamb Building, Temple, London EC4Y 7AS, ☎ 020 7797 7788
✉ clerks@lambbuilding.co.uk
Call Date: Oct 2006, Gray's Inn
Qualifications: [MA (Cantab)]

E

WILKEN MR SEAN DAVID HENRY QC (2010)

39 Essex Street
London WC2R 3AT, ☎020 7832 1111
✉clerks@39essex.com
82 King Street
Manchester M2 4WQ, ☎0161 870 9969
Call Date: Nov 1991, Middle Temple
Pupil Supervisor
Qualifications: [BA (Hons)(Oxon) Dip Law]

WILKES MISS ALISON VICTORIA

5 King's Bench Walk
5 King's Bench Walk, Temple, London
EC4Y 7DN, ☎020 7353 5638
✉clerks@5kbw.co.uk
Call Date: Oct 2005, Middle Temple
Qualifications: [BA (Hons)]
alison.wilkes@5kbw.co.uk

WILKINS MR ANDREW LEWIS

Cornwall Street Chambers
85-87 Cornwall Street, Birmingham B3 3BY,
☎0121 233 7500
✉clerks@cornwallstreet.co.uk
Call Date: Oct 1995, Lincoln's Inn
Qualifications: [MA (Oxon)]

WILKINS MISS CHLOE ELIZABETH JANE

Harcourt Chambers
1st Floor, 2 Harcourt Buildings, Temple,
London EC4Y 9DB, ☎0844 561 7135
Harcourt Chambers
Churchill House, 3 St Aldate's Courtyard, St
Aldate's, Oxford OX1 1BN, ☎0844 561 7135
Call Date: July 2006, Gray's Inn
Qualifications: [LLB (Cardiff)]
cwilkins@harcourtchambers.law.co.uk

WILKINS MR CHRISTOPHER JOHN

Pallant Chambers
12 North Pallant, Chichester, West Sussex
PO19 1TQ, ☎01243 784538
✉clerks@pallantchambers.co.uk
Call Date: May 1993, Lincoln's Inn
Qualifications: [MA (Oxon)]
cwilkins@pallantchambers.co.uk

WILKINS MR DEAN ROBERT

Chambers of Lawrence Jones
8 Stone Buildings, Lincoln's Inn, London
WC2A 3TA, ☎020 7831 1444
✉clerks@8stonebuildings.com
Call Date: July 2007, Lincoln's Inn
Qualifications: [LLB (Bris)]

WILKINS MISS SUSAN

1 KBW Chambers
1 King's Bench Walk, Temple, London
EC4Y 7DB, ☎020 7936 1500
✉clerks@1kbw.co.uk
King's Bench Chambers
174 High Street, Lewes BN7 1YE,
☎01273 402600
Call Date: July 2004, Lincoln's Inn
Qualifications: [BA Hons (Cantab) BVC GDL]
swilkins@1kbw.co.uk

WILKINS MR THOMAS ALEXANDER

Atkinson Bevan Chambers
1st Floor, 2 Harcourt Buildings, Temple,
London EC4Y 9DB, ☎020 7353 2112
✉clerks@2hb.co.uk
Call Date: Oct 1993, Middle Temple
Pupil Supervisor
Qualifications: [BSc (Hons)(Bris) CPE (Lond)]
twilkins@2hb.co.uk

WILKINSON MISS ANNA LOUISE

Sovereign Chambers
46 Park Place, Leeds LS1 2RY,
☎0113 245 1841
✉clerks@sovereignchambers.co.uk
Call Date: July 2007, Middle Temple
Qualifications: [LLB (Sheff)]
anna.wilkinson@sovereignchambers.co.uk

WILKINSON MR FRANCIS JOHN

Field Court Chambers
5 Field Court, Gray's Inn, London WC1R 5EF,
☎020 7405 6114 ✉clerks@fieldcourt.co.uk
Call Date: Oct 2001, Middle Temple
Pupil Supervisor
Qualifications: [BA (Hons) Dip Law]
francis.wilkinson@fieldcourt.co.uk

WILKINSON MISS HELEN KAY

Harcourt Chambers
1st Floor, 2 Harcourt Buildings, Temple,
London EC4Y 9DB, ☎0844 561 7135
Call Date: July 2007, Middle Temple
Qualifications: [BA (Hons) (Cantab)]
hwilkinson@harcourtchambers.law.co.uk

WILKINSON MR JONATHAN MARK

14 Gray's Inn Square
14 Gray's Inn Square, Gray's Inn, London
WC1R 5JP, ☎020 7242 0858
✉clerks@14gis.co.uk
Call Date: July 2006, Lincoln's Inn
Qualifications: [LLB (Hull)]
jw@14gis.co.uk

E

WILKINSON MISS KATIE

43 Temple Row Chambers
6th Floor, 43 Temple Row, Birmingham
B2 5LS, ☎0121 237 6035
✉clerks@43templerow.co.uk
Call Date: Oct 2003, Lincoln's Inn
Qualifications: [LLB (Hons) (Wolves)]
✉clerks@43templerow.co.uk

WILKINSON MR MARC ASHLEY

No5 Chambers
Fountain Court, Steelhouse Lane, Birmingham
B4 6DR, ☎0845 210 5555 ✉info@no5.com
No5 Chambers
Greenwood House, 4-7 Salisbury Court,
London EC4Y 8AA, ☎0845 210 5555
No5 Chambers
38 Queen Square, Bristol BS1 4QS,
☎0845 210 5555
Call Date: Nov 1992, Lincoln's Inn
Qualifications: [BA (Hons)]
✉mw@no5.com

WILKINSON MR MICHAEL DAVID BARTHOLOMEW

18 St John Street
Manchester M3 4EA, ☎0161 278 1800
✉clerks@18sjs.com
Call Date: Oct 2006, Inner Temple
Qualifications: [LLB (Dunelm) LLM]
✉mwilkinson@18sjs.com

WILKINSON MR MICHAEL JOHN

Trinity Chambers
The Custom House, 39 Quayside, Newcastle
Upon Tyne NE1 3DE, ☎0191 232 1927
✉info@trinitychambers.co.uk
Trinity Chambers
Multi Media Exchange, 72-80 Corporation
Road, Middlesbrough TS1 2RF,
☎01642 247569
✉info@trinitychambers.co.uk
Call Date: July 1979, Gray's Inn
Qualifications: [LLB (Exon)]
✉j.wilkinson@trinitychambers.co.uk

WILKINSON MR NICHOLAS MARSHALL

1 Hare Court
1 Hare Court, Temple, London EC4Y 7BE,
☎020 7797 7070 ✉clerks@1hc.com
Call Date: Oct 2006, Middle Temple
Qualifications: [BA (Hons) (Bris)]
✉wilkinson@1hc.com

WILKINSON MR NIGEL VIVIAN MARSHALL QC (1990)

Temple Garden Chambers
1 Harcourt Buildings, Temple, London
EC4Y 9DA, ☎020 7583 1315
✉clerks@tgchambers.com
Call Date: July 1972, Middle Temple
Recorder
Qualifications: [MA (Hons)(Oxon)]
✉clerks@tgchambers.com

WILKINSON MR PAUL

Dere Street Barristers
33 Broad Chare, Newcastle Upon Tyne
NE1 3DQ, ☎0844 3351551
✉clerks@derestreet.co.uk
Call Date: July 2001, Gray's Inn
Qualifications: [LLB (Hons)]
✉p.wilkinson@broadcharechambers.co.uk

WILKINSON MR PETER MICHAEL

1 Pump Court
Elm Court, Temple, London EC4Y 7AB,
☎020 7842 7070
✉(name)@pumpcourt.co.uk
Call Date: July 2003, Inner Temple
Qualifications: [LLB (Kent)]

WILKINSON MR RICHARD JOHN

Temple Garden Chambers
1 Harcourt Buildings, Temple, London
EC4Y 9DA, ☎020 7583 1315
✉clerks@tgchambers.com
Call Date: Oct 1992, Lincoln's Inn
Pupil Supervisor
Qualifications: [LLB(Hons)(Bris)]
✉rwilkinson@tgchambers.com

WILKINSON DR SARAH CAROLINE ALICE

Blackstone Chambers
Blackstone House, Temple, London
EC4Y 9BW, ☎020 7583 1770
✉clerks@blackstonechambers.com
Call Date: July 2003, Gray's Inn
Qualifications: [DPhil (Oxon) BA (Oxon)]
✉sarahwilkinson@blackstonechambers.com

WILKINSON MS TIFFANY JODIE

Trinity Chambers
Highfield House, Moulsham Street,
Chelmsford, Essex CM2 9AH,
☎01245 605040
✉clerks@trinitychambers.com
Call Date: Nov 2003, Inner Temple
Qualifications: [Dip Law BVC BA (Leics)]
✉twilkinson@trinitychambers.com

E

WILKINSON MR TIMOTHY HENRY PINDER

St Johns Buildings
24a - 28 St John Street, Manchester M3 4DJ,
☎ 0161 214 1500
✉ clerk@stjohnsbuildings.co.uk
16 Winckley Square
Preston PR1 3JJ, ☎ 01772 256100
St Johns Buildings Liverpool
8th Floor India Buildings, Water Street,
Liverpool L2 0XG, ☎ 0151 243 6000
✉ clerk@stjohnsbuildings.co.uk
Call Date: Oct 2006, Middle Temple

WILKINSON MR TIMOTHY JAMES

Park Lane Plowden
Lombard House, 4-8 Lombard Street,
Newcastle Upon Tyne NE1 3AE,
☎ 0191 211 4087
✉ clerks@parklaneplowden.co.uk
Call Date: July 2006, Inner Temple
Qualifications: [LLB]
tim.wilkinson@parklaneplowden.co.uk

WILKS MISS CLARE ANN

Apex
Harlech House, 20 Cathedral Road, Cardiff
CF11 9LJ, ☎ 02920 232 032
✉ clerks@apexchambers.net
Call Date: July 2000, Gray's Inn
Qualifications: [LLB (Cardiff)]
clare.wilks@apexchambers.net

WILLAN MR JAMES CHRISTOPHER

Essex Court Chambers
24 Lincoln's Inn Fields, London WC2A 3EG,
☎ 020 7813 8000
✉ clerksroom@essexcourt.net
Call Date: July 2006, Gray's Inn
Qualifications: [BA (Cantab)]
jwillan@essexcourt.net

WILLANS MR DAVID

Northampton Chambers
10 Spencer Parade, Northampton NN1 5AQ,
☎ 01604 636271
✉ clerks@northampton-chambers.co.uk
Call Date: Oct 1995, Lincoln's Inn
Qualifications: [BSc (Hons)(Lond) LLB (Hons)(City)]
clerks@northampton-chambers.co.uk

WILLBOURNE MISS CAROLINE CATCHPOLE

1 Garden Court Family Law Chambers
Ground Floor, One Garden Court, Temple,
London EC4Y 9BJ, ☎ 020 7797 7900
✉ clerks@1gc.com
Call Date: Nov 1970, Inner Temple
Pupil Supervisor
Qualifications: [BA]

WILLCOCK MISS RACHEL CATHERINE

Crown Office Row Chambers
119 Church Street, Brighton, Sussex
BN1 1UD, ☎ 01273 625625
✉ clerks@1cor.com
Call Date: July 2008, Inner Temple
Qualifications: [MA (Cantab)]

WILLCOCKS MISS HANNAH LEAHCIM

18 Red Lion Court
London EC4A 3EB, ☎ 020 7520 6000
✉ chambers@18rlc.co.uk
Call Date: July 2001, Middle Temple
Qualifications: [BA (Joint Hons) PgDL]
hannah.willcocks@18rlc.co.uk

WILLE MR ANDREW LENTHALL

Farrar's Building
Farrar's Building, Temple, London EC4Y 7BD,
☎ 020 7583 9241
✉ Chambers@farrarsbuilding.co.uk
Call Date: Nov 1998, Lincoln's Inn
Pupil Supervisor
Qualifications: [BA (Hons)(Oxon) Dip Law]
awille@farrarsbuilding.co.uk

WILLEMS MR MARC PAUL BERNARD ALBERT

Cobden House Chambers
19 Quay Street, Manchester M3 3HN,
☎ 0161 833 6000 ✉ Clerks@Cobden.co.uk
Call Date: Nov 1990, Lincoln's Inn
Pupil Supervisor
Qualifications: [BA (Nott'm)]
marc.willems@cobden.co.uk, willems@supanet.com

WILLER MR ROBERT MICHAEL

Ely Place Chambers
30 Ely Place, London EC1N 6TD,
☎ 020 7400 9600 ✉ admin@elyplace.com
Call Date: July 1970, Middle Temple
Pupil Supervisor
Qualifications: [BA (Oxon)]

E

WILLERS MR MARC LAWRENCE GEORGE

Garden Court Chambers
57-60 Lincoln's Inn Fields, London WC2A 3LJ, ☎020 7993 7600 ✉info@gclaw.co.uk
Call Date: Nov 1987, Lincoln's Inn
Pupil Supervisor
Qualifications: [LLB BL]
✉marcw@gclaw.co.uk

WILLETTS MR ANDREW PHILIP

King's Bench and Godolphin (KBG)Chambers
115 North Hill, Plymouth, Devon PL4 8JY, ☎01752 221551
✉clerks@kbgchambers.co.uk
New Walk Chambers
27 New Walk, Leicester, Leicestershire LE1 6TE, ☎0871 200 1298 / 0116 255 9144
✉clerks@newwalkchambers.co.uk
Call Date: Nov 1997, Inner Temple
Pupil Supervisor, Recorder
Qualifications: [BSc (Wales) LLM]

WILLETTS MR GLENN PHILIP

No5 Chambers
Fountain Court, Steelhouse Lane, Birmingham B4 6DR, ☎0845 210 5555 ✉info@no5.com
No5 Chambers
Greenwood House, 4-7 Salisbury Court, London EC4Y 8AA, ☎0845 210 5555
No5 Chambers
38 Queen Square, Bristol BS1 4QS, ☎0845 210 5555
Call Date: July 2000, Middle Temple
Qualifications: [LLB(Hons) (B'ham) BCL (Oxon)]
✉gw@no5.com

WILLIAMS MR A JOHN

Crown Office Chambers
2 Crown Office Row, Temple, London EC4Y 7HJ, ☎020 7797 8100
✉mail@crownofficechambers.com
Call Date: July 1983, Lincoln's Inn
Pupil Supervisor
Qualifications: [MA (Cantab)]
✉williams@crownofficechambers.com

WILLIAMS MR ALAN GREGORY

4 King's Bench Walk
2nd Floor, 4 King's Bench Walk, Temple, London EC4Y 7DL, ☎020 7822 7000
✉clerks@4kbw.co.uk
Call Date: Mar 2006, Lincoln's Inn
Qualifications: [LLB (Hons) (Warwick)]
✉gw@4kbw.co.uk

WILLIAMS MR ALEC BRIAN

1 Gray's Inn Square
Ground Floor, 1 Gray's Inn Square, London WC1R 5AA, ☎020 7405 0001
Call Date: July 1999, Gray's Inn
Qualifications: [BA (N. Wales)]
✉awilliams@1gis.co.uk

WILLIAMS MR ALEXANDER DAVID

Oriel Chambers
14 Water Street, Liverpool, Merseyside L2 8TD, ☎0151 236 7191
✉clerks@orielchambers.co.uk
Oriel Chambers
18 Ribblesdale Place, Preston PR1 3NA, ☎01772 254 764
✉clerks@oriel-chambers.co.uk
Call Date: July 2004, Middle Temple
Qualifications: [BA Hons (Cantab)]
✉alexander.williams@orielchambers.co.uk

WILLIAMS MR ALEXANDER JAMES HYATT

3 Temple Gardens
Lower Ground Floor, 3 Temple Gardens, Temple, London EC4Y 9AU, ☎020 7353 3102
✉clerks@3tg.co.uk
Call Date: Nov 1995, Middle Temple
Pupil Supervisor
Qualifications: [BA (Hons)]
✉aw@3tg.co.uk

WILLIAMS MISS ALISON LOUISE

Harcourt Chambers
1st Floor, 2 Harcourt Buildings, Temple, London EC4Y 9DB, ☎0844 561 7135
Call Date: Oct 2004, Gray's Inn
Qualifications: [BA]
✉awilliams@harcourtchambers.law.co.uk

WILLIAMS MR ANDREW ARTHUR

Atlantic Chambers
4-6 Cook Street, Liverpool L2 9QU, ☎0151 236 4421
✉info@atlanticchambers.co.uk
Call Date: Oct 1994, Gray's Inn
Pupil Supervisor
Qualifications: [LLB]
✉andrewwilliams@atlanticchambers.co.uk

WILLIAMS MISS ANNA

Trinity Chambers
Highfield House, Moulsham Street, Chelmsford, Essex CM2 9AH, ☎01245 605040
✉clerks@trinitychambers.com
Call Date: Nov 1990, Gray's Inn
Qualifications: [LLB]

WILLIAMS MISS ANNE MARGARET

6 Pump Court
1st Floor, 6 Pump Court, Temple, London EC4Y 7AR, ☎020 7797 8400
✉richardconstable@6pumpcourt.co.uk
6 Pump Court Chambers
6-8 Mill Street, Maidstone, Kent ME15 6XH, ☎01622 688094
✉annexe@6pumpcourt.co.uk
Call Date: Nov 1980, Gray's Inn
Pupil Supervisor
Qualifications: [BA (Manch) MPhil (Lond) RTPI]
✉annewilliams@6pumpcourt.co.uk

WILLIAMS MR BEN DYLAN

Kings Chambers
36 Young Street, Manchester M3 3FT, ☎0845 034 3444
✉clerks@kingschambers.com
Kings Chambers
5 Park Square East, Leeds LS1 2NE, ☎0845 034 3444
✉clerks@kingschambers.com
Kings Chambers
Embassy House, 60 Church Street, Birmingham B3 2DJ, ☎0845 034 3444
✉clerks@kingschambers.com
Call Date: July 2001, Middle Temple
Qualifications: [LLB (Hons)]
✉bwilliams@kingschambers.com

WILLIAMS MR BENJAMIN JAMES

39 Essex Street
London WC2R 3AT, ☎020 7832 1111
✉clerks@39essex.com
Call Date: Nov 1994, Lincoln's Inn
Qualifications: [MA (Hons)(Oxon) Dip Law (Lond)]
✉ben.williams@39essex.com

WILLIAMS MR BENJAMIN MATTHEW IAN

St Philips Chambers
55 Temple Row, Birmingham B2 5LS, ☎0121 246 7000 ✉clerks@st-philips.com
Call Date: July 2006, Lincoln's Inn
Qualifications: [BA (B'ham)]
✉bwilliams@st-philips.co.uk

WILLIAMS MR BRIAN DAVID

15 Winckley Square
Preston PR1 3JJ, ☎01772 252828
✉clerks@15winckleysq.co.uk
Call Date: July 1986, Inner Temple
Qualifications: [LLB (Manch)]

WILLIAMS MISS CARYS ELLEN

9 Park Place
9 Park Place, Cardiff, South Glamorgan CF10 3DP, ☎029 2038 2731
✉clerks@9parkplace.co.uk
Call Date: Oct 2007, Lincoln's Inn
Qualifications: [LLB (Cardiff)]
✉cwilliams@9parkplace.co.uk

WILLIAMS MISS CASSANDRA LOUISE

Ropewalk Chambers
24 The Ropewalk, Nottingham NG1 5EF, ☎0115 947 2581 ✉clerks@ropewalk.co.uk
Call Date: July 2010, Inner Temple
Qualifications: [LLB (B'ham)]
✉cassandrawilliams@ropewalk.co.uk

WILLIAMS MISS CASSIE MAXINE

39 Park Square
Leeds LS1 2NU, ☎0113 245 6633
✉seniorclerk@39parksquarechambers.co.uk
Call Date: July 2002, Middle Temple
Qualifications: [LLB (Hons) (Newc)]

WILLIAMS MS CERYS LOUISE

St Johns Buildings Liverpool
8th Floor India Buildings, Water Street, Liverpool L2 0XG, ☎0151 243 6000
✉clerk@stjohnsbuildings.co.uk
16 Winckley Square
Preston PR1 3JJ, ☎01772 256100
St Johns Buildings
24a - 28 St John Street, Manchester M3 4DJ, ☎0161 214 1500
✉clerk@stjohnsbuildings.co.uk
Call Date: July 2008, Gray's Inn
Qualifications: [LLB (L'pool)]
✉cerys.williams@stjohnsbuildings.co.uk

WILLIAMS MISS CHRISTINE MAY

Ridgeway Chambers
3a Ridgeway Avenue, East Barnet, Hertfordshire EN4 8TR, ☎020 8440 0904
✉cmwilliams@ukonline.co.uk
Call Date: Oct 2000, Gray's Inn
Qualifications: [BA (Hons) (South Bank)]
✉cmwilliams.williams@btinternet.com

WILLIAMS MR CHRISTOPHER DAVID CURNOW

Park Lane Plowden
Lombard House, 4-8 Lombard Street, Newcastle Upon Tyne NE1 3AE, ☎0191 211 4087
✉clerks@parklaneplowden.co.uk
Call Date: July 1981, Gray's Inn
Pupil Supervisor, Recorder
✉christopher.williams@parklaneplowden.co.uk

WILLIAMS MR CHRISTOPHER GREGSON

Five St Andrew's Hill
5 St Andrew's Hill, London EC4V 5BZ, ☎020 7332 5400 ✉Clerks@5sah.co.uk
Call Date: July 2008, Middle Temple
Qualifications: [BA (Hons) (Manch) PgDl (Lond) MSc]

WILLIAMS MR CHRISTOPHER PAUL

Tooks Chambers
81 Farringdon Street, London EC4A 4BL, ☎020 7842 7575 ✉clerks@tooks.co.uk
Call Date: Feb 1988, Inner Temple
Pupil Supervisor
Qualifications: [LLB]
✉christopher.williams@tooks.co.uk

WILLIAMS MISS CLAIRE LOUISE

30 Park Place
Cardiff CF10 3BS, ☎029 2039 8421
✉clerks@30parkplace.law.co.uk
Call Date: July 2004, Gray's Inn
Pupil Supervisor
Qualifications: [LLB (Cardiff)]
✉clw@30parkplace.co.uk

WILLIAMS MR DAVID BASIL

4 Paper Buildings
1st Floor, 4 Paper Buildings, Temple, London EC4Y 7EX, ☎020 7427 5200
✉clerks@4pb.com
Call Date: Oct 1990, Inner Temple
Pupil Supervisor
Qualifications: [LLB (Leics)]
✉dw@4pb.com

WILLIAMS MR DAVID HENRY

Chavasse Court Chambers
18 Queen Avenue, Liverpool L2 4TX, ☎0151 229 2030
✉clerks@chavassechambers.co.uk
Call Date: Feb 1990, Gray's Inn
Recorder
Qualifications: [BA (Hons)]
✉david.williams@chavassechambers.co.uk

WILLIAMS MR DAVID HUW ANTHONY QC (2008)

18 Red Lion Court (Annexe)
Thornwood House, 102 New London Road, Chelmsford, Essex CM2 0RG, ☎01245 280880
18 Red Lion Court
London EC4A 3EB, ☎020 7520 6000
✉chambers@18rlc.co.uk
Call Date: July 1988, Inner Temple
Qualifications: [BSc (Wales) Dip Law (Lond) GRSC]
✉david.williams@18rlc.co.uk

WILLIAMS MR DAVID JOHN

Five St Andrew's Hill
5 St Andrew's Hill, London EC4V 5BZ, ☎020 7332 5400 ✉Clerks@5sah.co.uk
Call Date: July 2009, Gray's Inn
Qualifications: [LLB]
✉alisterwalker@5sah.co.uk

WILLIAMS MR EDMUND MORYS

Cloisters
1 Pump Court, Temple, London EC4Y 7AA, ☎020 7827 4000 ✉clerks@cloisters.com
Call Date: Oct 2000, Inner Temple
Pupil Supervisor
Qualifications: [BA (Hons)(Notts) CPE BVC]
✉ew@cloisters.com

WILLIAMS MR EIFION WYN

9 Park Place
9 Park Place, Cardiff, South Glamorgan CF10 3DP, ☎029 2038 2731
✉clerks@9parkplace.co.uk
Call Date: Oct 2000, Gray's Inn
Qualifications: [LLB (Cardiff)]
✉clerks@9parkplace.co.uk

WILLIAMS MISS FELICITY MAY

Tooks Chambers
81 Farringdon Street, London EC4A 4BL, ☎020 7842 7575 ✉clerks@tooks.co.uk
Call Date: Nov 2000, Lincoln's Inn
Qualifications: [LLB (Hons) (B'Ham) LLM (Durham)]

WILLIAMS MRS FIONA CLARE

East Anglian Chambers
Gresham House, 5 Museum Street, Ipswich, Suffolk IP1 1HQ, ☎01473 214481
✉ipswich@ealaw.co.uk
East Anglian Chambers
140 New London Road, Chelmsford, Essex CM2 0AW, ☎01473 214481
✉chelmsford@ealaw.co.uk

E

East Anglian Chambers
15 The Close, Norwich, Norfolk NR1 4DZ,
☎01473 214481 ✉norwich@ealaw.co.uk
Call Date: July 2009, Gray's Inn
Qualifications: [BA MA PgDL]

WILLIAMS MR GRAHAM ELLIS

Oriel Chambers
14 Water Street, Liverpool, Merseyside
L2 8TD, ☎0151 236 7191
✉clerks@orielchambers.co.uk
Oriel Chambers
18 Ribblesdale Place, Preston PR1 3NA,
☎01772 254 764
✉clerks@oriel-chambers.co.uk
Call Date: July 2002, Middle Temple
Qualifications: [LLB (Hons) (Essex)]
graham.williams@orielchambers.co.uk

WILLIAMS MR GUY DONALD IRWIN

Landmark Chambers
180 Fleet Street, London EC4A 2HG,
☎020 7430 1221
✉clerks@landmarkchambers.co.uk
Call Date: July 2000, Inner Temple
Qualifications: [BA (Oxon) CPE]
gwilliams@landmarkchambers.co.uk

E

WILLIAMS MS HEATHER JEAN QC (2006)

Doughty Street Chambers
53-54 Doughty Street, London WC1N 2LS,
☎020 7404 1313
✉enquiries@doughtystreet.co.uk
Doughty Street Chambers
Pall Mall Court, 61-67 King Street, Manchester
M2 4PD, ☎0161 618 1066
Doughty Street Chambers
5th Floor, Broad Quay House, Prince Street,
Bristol BS1 4DJ, ☎01179 058 717
Call Date: July 1985, Gray's Inn
Qualifications: [LLB (Lond)]
h.williams@doughtystreet.co.uk

Types of work: Administrative law, Civil actions against the police, Civil liberties, Discrimination, Employment

WILLIAMS MISS HELEDD LLWYD

St Philips Chambers
55 Temple Row, Birmingham B2 5LS,
☎0121 246 7000 ✉clerks@st-philips.com
Linenhall Chambers
1 Stanley Place, Chester CH1 2LU,
☎01244 348282
✉clerks@linenhallchambers.co.uk
Call Date: Oct 1999, Gray's Inn
Pupil Supervisor
Qualifications: [BA (Oxon)]
hwilliams@st-philips.com

WILLIAMS MISS HELEN ELIZABETH

29 Bedford Row Chambers
London WC1R 4HE, ☎020 7404 1044
✉clerks@29br.co.uk
Call Date: Oct 2007, Middle Temple
Qualifications: [BA (Hons) (Oxon) PgDL (Lond)]

WILLIAMS MISS HERMIONE ROSE

No5 Chambers
Greenwood House, 4-7 Salisbury Court,
London EC4Y 8AA, ☎0845 210 5555
No5 Chambers
38 Queen Square, Bristol BS1 4QS,
☎0845 210 5555
No5 Chambers
Fountain Court, Steelhouse Lane, Birmingham
B4 6DR, ☎0845 210 5555 ✉info@no5.com
Call Date: Oct 2008, Middle Temple
Qualifications: [LLB (Hons) (Lond)]

WILLIAMS MR HUGH DAVID HAYDN

13 King's Bench Walk
13 King's Bench Walk, Temple, London
EC4Y 7EN, ☎020 7353 7204
✉clerks@13kbw.co.uk
13 KBW
32 Beaumont Street, Oxford OX1 2NP,
☎01865 311066 ✉clerks@13kbw.co.uk
Call Date: July 1992, Gray's Inn
Qualifications: [BA]
hwilliams@13kbw.co.uk

WILLIAMS MR JAMES

Henderson Chambers
2 Harcourt Buildings, Temple, London
EC4Y 9DB, ☎020 7583 9020
✉clerks@hendersonchambers.co.uk
Call Date: Nov 2010, Inner Temple
Qualifications: [BA (Cantab)]

WILLIAMS MR JAMIE WYN

One Essex Court
1st Floor, Temple, London EC4Y 9AR,
☎020 7936 3030 ✉clerks@1ec.co.uk
Call Date: Nov 2006, Middle Temple
Qualifications: [BA (Hons) (Lanc) PgDip Law]
jwilliams@1ec.co.uk

WILLIAMS MS JOANNE CATHERINE

Civitas Chambers
Global Reach, Celtic Gateway, Cardiff Bay,
Cardiff CF11 0SN, ☎0845 0713 007
✉clerks@civitaslaw.com
Call Date: Oct 1999, Inner Temple
Qualifications: [LLB (Bris)]

WILLIAMS MR JOHN ALBAN

Chambers of John Alban Williams
53 Wilmington Avenue, London W4 3HA,
☎ 07956 235232 ✉ jalbanwilliams@aol.com
Call Date: Nov 1979, Middle Temple
✉ jalbanwilliams@aol.com

WILLIAMS MR JOHN LEIGHTON QC (1986)

Farrar's Building
Farrar's Building, Temple, London EC4Y 7BD,
☎ 020 7583 9241
✉ Chambers@farrarsbuilding.co.uk
Call Date: Apr 1964, Gray's Inn
Recorder
Qualifications: [MA LLB]
✉ jlwilliams@farrarsbuilding.co.uk

WILLIAMS MR JOHN ROBERT SELWYN

Atkinson Bevan Chambers
1st Floor, 2 Harcourt Buildings, Temple,
London EC4Y 9DB, ☎ 020 7353 2112
✉ clerks@2hb.co.uk
Call Date: Nov 1973, Middle Temple
Pupil Supervisor, Recorder
Qualifications: [LLB]

WILLIAMS MR JOHN WYN

Linenhall Chambers
1 Stanley Place, Chester CH1 2LU,
☎ 01244 348282
✉ clerks@linenhallchambers.co.uk
Call Date: Nov 1992, Gray's Inn
Pupil Supervisor
Qualifications: [LLB (Wales)]
✉ clerks@1stanleyplace.co.uk

WILLIAMS MISS JULIET LESLIE

Southernhay Chambers
33 Southernhay East, Exeter EX1 1NX,
☎ 01392 255777
✉ clerks@southernhaychambers.co.uk
Call Date: Oct 1998, Inner Temple
Qualifications: [LLB (Bris)]
✉ j.williams@southernhaychambers.co.uk

WILLIAMS MISS JUNE CLEO

No 8 Chambers
8 Fountain Court, Steelhouse Lane,
Birmingham B4 6DR, ☎ 0121 236 5514
✉ clerks@no8chambers.co.uk
Call Date: Nov 1999, Inner Temple
Qualifications: [LLB (Hons) (Leeds)]
✉ junewilliams@no8chambers.co.uk

WILLIAMS MR KARL

9 Park Place
9 Park Place, Cardiff, South Glamorgan
CF10 3DP, ☎ 029 2038 2731
✉ clerks@9parkplace.co.uk
Call Date: July 1982, Middle Temple
Qualifications: [LLB (Lond)]
✉ clerks@9parkplace.co.uk

WILLIAMS MR LLOYD QC (2006)

30 Park Place
Cardiff CF10 3BS, ☎ 029 2039 8421
✉ clerks@30parkplace.law.co.uk
Call Date: July 1981, Inner Temple
Recorder
Qualifications: [BA]
✉ lw@30parkplace.co.uk

WILLIAMS MISS MAIR ROSE

187 Fleet Street
London EC4A 2AT, ☎ 020 7430 7430
✉ chambers@187fleetstreet.com
Call Date: July 2010, Lincoln's Inn
Qualifications: [BA (Dub)]
✉ chambers@187fleetstreet.com

WILLIAMS MS MARCIA ANNE

KCH Garden Square
1 Oxford Street, Nottingham NG1 5BH,
☎ 0115 941 8851
✉ clerks@kchgardensquare.co.uk
Call Date: Mar 2005, Middle Temple
Qualifications: [BA (Hons) CPE]
✉ awilliams@kch.co.uk

WILLIAMS MR MARK JOHN

Queen Square Chambers
56 Queen Square, Bristol BS1 4PR,
☎ 0117 921 1966 ✉ crime@qs-c.co.uk
Call Date: Oct 1998, Gray's Inn
Qualifications: [BA (Lond)]
✉ civil@qs-c.co.uk

WILLIAMS MR MARK STEPHEN

Argent Chambers
5 Bell Yard, London WC2A 2JR,
☎ 020 7556 5500
✉ briefsin@argentchambers.co.uk
Call Date: Oct 1996, Lincoln's Inn
Qualifications: [BSC (Hons)(Surrey)]

E

WILLIAMS MR MEYRICK JOHNS

Argent Chambers
5 Bell Yard, London WC2A 2JR,
☎ 020 7556 5500
✉ briefsin@argentchambers.co.uk
Call Date: Oct 2003, Inner Temple
Qualifications: [LLB (Hons)(Edin) LLM (Lond) Dip Law (Edin)]
m.williams@argentchambers.co.uk

WILLIAMS MISS MICAILA TERESA

Optimus Chambers
The Chambers of Miss Micaila Williams, Po Box 11193, Braintree, Essex CM7 0HQ,
☎ 01376 691 885/07736 283873
Call Date: July 2004, Inner Temple
micaila@optimuschambers.co.uk

WILLIAMS MR MICHAEL RICHARD POYNTER

2 King's Bench Walk
2 King's Bench Walk, Temple, London EC4Y 7DE, ☎ 020 7353 1746
✉ clerks@2kbw.com
Call Date: Nov 2005, Inner Temple
Qualifications: [BA University of Durham CPE BPP Law School]
mwilliams@2kbw.com

WILLIAMS MR MICHAEL TUDOR

Chambers of Sarah Breach
The Old Farm House, Brook Farm, Marthall Lane, Marthall, Knutsford, Cheshire WA16 7ST, ☎ 01565 880272
✉ sbreach@btconnect.com
Call Date: Oct 2008, Middle Temple
Qualifications: [LLB (Hons)]

WILLIAMS MR NICHOLAS MICHAEL HEATHCOTE QC (2006)

12 King's Bench Walk
12 King's Bench Walk, Temple, London EC4Y 7EL, ☎ 020 7583 0811
Call Date: Nov 1976, Inner Temple
Pupil Supervisor, Recorder
Qualifications: [MA (Cantab)]
williams@12kbw.co.uk

WILLIAMS MR NICHOLAS WILLIAM EDWIN

Linenhall Chambers
1 Stanley Place, Chester CH1 2LU,
☎ 01244 348282
✉ clerks@linenhallchambers.co.uk
Call Date: Nov 1994, Inner Temple
Qualifications: [LLB (So'ton)]
clerks@1stanleyplace.co.uk

WILLIAMS MR OWEN DAVID PARKER

9 Park Place
9 Park Place, Cardiff, South Glamorgan CF10 3DP, ☎ 029 2038 2731
✉ clerks@9parkplace.co.uk
Call Date: Oct 2000, Gray's Inn
Qualifications: [LLB (Cardiff)]

WILLIAMS MR PAUL KENNETH

Old Bailey Chambers
15 Old Bailey, London EC4M 7EF,
☎ 020 3008 6404
✉ clerks@15oldbaileychambers.com
Call Date: July 1990, Inner Temple
Pupil Supervisor
Qualifications: [BA (Wales)]

WILLIAMS MR PAUL ROBERT

Park Court Chambers
16 Park Place, Leeds LS1 2SJ,
☎ 0113 243 3277
✉ clerks@parkcourtchambers.co.uk
Call Date: Oct 1994, Inner Temple
Qualifications: [BA (Hons) CPE (Lond)]
clerks@parkcourtchambers.co.uk, pwilliams@parkcourtchambers.co.uk

WILLIAMS MR PHILIP RICHARD

No5 Chambers
Greenwood House, 4-7 Salisbury Court, London EC4Y 8AA, ☎ 0845 210 5555
No5 Chambers
38 Queen Square, Bristol BS1 4QS,
☎ 0845 210 5555
No5 Chambers
Fountain Court, Steelhouse Lane, Birmingham B4 6DR, ☎ 0845 210 5555 ✉ info@no5.com
Call Date: Mar 2005, Inner Temple
Qualifications: [BSc CPE]
pw@no5.com

WILLIAMS MR RHODRI JOHN QC (2010)

30 Park Place
Cardiff CF10 3BS, ☎ 029 2039 8421
✉ clerks@30parkplace.law.co.uk
Henderson Chambers
2 Harcourt Buildings, Temple, London EC4Y 9DB, ☎ 020 7583 9020
✉ clerks@hendersonchambers.co.uk
Call Date: July 1987, Gray's Inn
Pupil Supervisor
Qualifications: [MA (Oxon) Dip Law]

E

WILLIAMS MR RHYS

Five Paper
Ground Floor, 5 Paper Buildings, Temple, London EC4Y 7HB, ☎020 7815 3200
Call Date: Nov 2007, Middle Temple
Qualifications: [LLB (Hons) (Lond) LLM (Lond)]
rhyswilliams@fivepaper.com

WILLIAMS MR RICHARD KEVIN

13 King's Bench Walk
13 King's Bench Walk, Temple, London EC4Y 7EN, ☎020 7353 7204
✉clerks@13kbw.co.uk
Call Date: July 2009, Middle Temple
Qualifications: [BA (Hons) (Leic) Grad Dip Law (Nott'm)]
clerks@13kbw.co.uk, RWilliams@13kbw.co.uk

WILLIAMS MR ROBERT BRYCHAN JAMES

Monckton Chambers
1 & 2 Raymond Buildings, Gray's Inn, London WC1R 5NR, ☎020 7405 7211
✉chambers@monckton.com
Call Date: Nov 2000, Middle Temple
Pupil Supervisor
Qualifications: [MA (Hons) (Oxon) BCL (Oxon)]
rwilliams@monckton.com

WILLIAMS MR ROBERT JAMES

Cornerstone Barristers
2-3 Gray's Inn Square, Gray's Inn, London WC1R 5JH, ☎020 7242 4986
✉chambers@2-3gis.co.uk
Call Date: July 2008, Lincoln's Inn
Qualifications: [LLB (Lond)]
rwilliams@2-3gis.co.uk

WILLIAMS MS SANDRA ALESSANDRA CAROLINE

The Chambers Of Alessandra Williams
P O Box 363, Tadworth KT20 9EJ, ☎07941 944950
✉alessandra.williams@yahoo.co.uk
Call Date: Nov 2003, Lincoln's Inn
Qualifications: [LLB (Hons) MA (Lond)]

WILLIAMS MISS SARAH LOUISE

Keating Chambers
15 Essex Street, London WC2R 3AA, ☎020 7544 2600
✉clerks@keatingchambers.com
Call Date: Oct 2008, Gray's Inn
Qualifications: [MA (Cantab) LLB]
swilliams@keatingchambers.com

WILLIAMS MR SIMON CHRISTOPHER

12 Old Square Chambers
1st Floor, 12 Old Square, Lincoln's Inn, London WC2A 3TX, ☎020 7404 0875
✉clerks@12oldsquare.com
Call Date: Nov 1999, Inner Temple
Qualifications: [BSc]

WILLIAMS MR SIMON PAUL

Radcliffe Chambers
Ground Floor, 11 New Square, Lincoln's Inn, London WC2A 3QB, ☎020 7831 0081
✉clerks@radcliffechambers.com
Call Date: Nov 1984, Inner Temple
Pupil Supervisor
Qualifications: [LLB (So'ton)]

WILLIAMS MR VINCENT ALLAN

The Chambers of Grahame Aldous QC
9 Gough Square, London EC4A 3DG, ☎020 7832 0500
✉clerks@9goughsquare.co.uk
Call Date: July 1985, Middle Temple
Pupil Supervisor
Qualifications: [BA (Cantab)]
vwilliams@9goughsquare.co.uk

WILLIAMS MISS ZILLAH ELIZABETH

Call Date: Oct 1997, Lincoln's Inn
Qualifications: [LLB (Hons)(L'pool)]
zillah.williams@hotmail.co.uk

WILLIAMS-HOWES MRS KATIE ANTOINETTE

Chambers of K A Williams-Howes
148 Lower Richmond Road, Putney, London SW15 1LU, ☎020 8704 1010
✉katie@williams-howes.com
Call Date: Nov 1993, Middle Temple
Qualifications: [BA (Hons) CPE]
katie@williams-howes.com

WILLIAMSON MR ADRIAN JOHN GERARD HUGHES QC (2002)

Keating Chambers
15 Essex Street, London WC2R 3AA, ☎020 7544 2600
✉clerks@keatingchambers.com
Call Date: Nov 1983, Middle Temple
Recorder
Qualifications: [MA (Cantab)]

E

WILLIAMSON MS AILSA BAXTER

3 Raymond Buildings
3 Raymond Buildings, Gray's Inn, London WC1R 5BH, ☎020 7400 6400
✉clerks@3rblaw.com
Call Date: Oct 1997, Inner Temple
Pupil Supervisor
Qualifications: [BA (Cantab) CPE]
ailsa.williamson@3raymondbuildings.com

WILLIAMSON MR ALISDAIR GEORGE JAMES

3 Raymond Buildings
3 Raymond Buildings, Gray's Inn, London WC1R 5BH, ☎020 7400 6400
✉clerks@3rblaw.com
Call Date: Nov 1994, Middle Temple
Pupil Supervisor
Qualifications: [MA (Oxon) DipLL (Lond)]
alisdair.williamson@3raymondbuildings.com

WILLIAMSON MR BRETT

Linenhall Chambers
1 Stanley Place, Chester CH1 2LU, ☎01244 348282
✉clerks@linenhallchambers.co.uk
Call Date: Oct 2000, Lincoln's Inn
Qualifications: [LLB (Hons)]
brettwilliamson@1stanleyplace.co.uk

WILLIAMSON MISS BRIDGET SUSAN

Enterprise Chambers
9 Old Square, Lincoln's Inn, London WC2A 3SR, ☎020 7405 9471
✉london@enterprisechambers.com
Enterprise Chambers
65 Quayside, Newcastle Upon Tyne NE1 3DE, ☎0191 222 3344
✉newcastle@enterprisechambers.com
Enterprise Chambers
43 Park Square, Leeds LS1 2NP, ☎0113 246 0391
✉leeds@enterprisechambers.com
Call Date: Feb 1993, Lincoln's Inn
Pupil Supervisor
Qualifications: [BA (Hons)]
bridgetwilliamson@enterprisechambers.com

WILLIAMSON MR GUY EVERIS

7 Bell Yard
London WC2A 2JR, ☎020 7831 0636
✉kevintarrant@btconnect.com
Call Date: Nov 2002, Middle Temple
Qualifications: [LLB (Hons) (Lond) LLM (Lond)]

WILLIAMSON MS GWEN

9 King's Bench Walk
Lower Ground Floor South, 9 King's Bench Walk, Temple, London EC4Y 7DX, ☎020 7353 9564 ✉9kbw@btconnect.com
Call Date: Oct 2006, Gray's Inn
Qualifications: [LLB]

WILLIAMSON MR NICHOLAS JOHN

Pump Court Chambers
31 Southgate Street, Winchester, Hampshire SO23 9EB, ☎01962 868 161
✉clerks@3pumpcourt.com
Pump Court Chambers
Upper Ground Floor, 3 Pump Court, Temple, London EC4Y 7AJ, ☎020 7353 0711
✉clerks@3pumpcourt.com
Pump Court Chambers
5 Temple Chambers, Temple Street, Swindon SN1 1SQ, ☎01793 539899
✉clerks@3pumpcourt.com
Call Date: Mar 2009, Middle Temple
Qualifications: [BA (Hons) (Newc) CPE]

WILLIAMSON MR OLIVER JACK

3 Serjeants Inn
London EC4Y 1BQ, ☎020 7427 5000
✉clerks@3serjeantsinn.com
Call Date: July 2008, Middle Temple
Qualifications: [M.Sci (Hons) (Lond) PgDl (Lond)]
owilliamson@3serjeantsinn.com

WILLIAMSON MR PATRICK LAWRENCE VICTOR

Kenworthy's Chambers
Arlington House, Bloom Street, Salford, Manchester M3 6AJ, ☎0161 832 4036
Call Date: Nov 1989, Inner Temple
Qualifications: [BSc (Keele)]
p.williamson@kenworthysbarristers.co.uk

WILLINK MR DAVID CHRISTOPHER

Lamb Chambers
Lamb Building, Elm Court, Temple, London EC4Y 7AS, ☎020 7797 8300
✉info@lambchambers.co.uk
Call Date: Nov 2004, Middle Temple
Qualifications: [BA (Hons) (Cantab) MA (Cantab) LLM (Wales)]
davidwillink@lambchambers.co.uk

WILLINS MR ANDREW JAN

29 Bedford Row Chambers
London WC1R 4HE, ☎020 7404 1044
✉clerks@29br.co.uk
Call Date: July 2000, Gray's Inn
Qualifications: [LLB]
awillins@29br.co.uk

E

WILLIS MR ANTONY MARTIN DEREK

Brick Court Chambers
7-8 Essex Street, London WC2R 3LD,
☎020 7379 3550 ✉clerks@brickcourt.co.uk
Call Date: Oct 2004, Middle Temple
Qualifications: [LLB]

WILLITTS MR TIMOTHY LEONARD

Cobden House Chambers
19 Quay Street, Manchester M3 3HN,
☎0161 833 6000 ✉Clerks@Cobden.co.uk
Call Date: Nov 1989, Gray's Inn
Pupil Supervisor
Qualifications: [LLB (Hons) (B'Ham)]
✉timothywillitts@yahoo.co.uk

WILLMER MR STEPHEN JAMES

Argent Chambers
5 Bell Yard, London WC2A 2JR,
☎020 7556 5500
✉briefsin@argentchambers.co.uk
Call Date: Nov 2004, Middle Temple
Qualifications: [MSc BA (Hons) PgDL]

WILLMOTT MISS FRANCES

Linenhall Chambers
1 Stanley Place, Chester CH1 2LU,
☎01244 348282
✉clerks@linenhallchambers.co.uk
Call Date: July 2008, Lincoln's Inn
Qualifications: [LLB (L'pool)]

WILLMOTT MR GARY LEIGH

2 Dr Johnson's Buildings
2 Dr Johnson's Buildings, Temple, London
EC4Y 7AY, ☎020 7936 2613
✉clerks@2drj.com
Call Date: Nov 2000, Middle Temple
Qualifications: [BA (Hons) (Oxon) CPE]

WILLMOTT MR OLIVER RICHARD SHEPHERD

Queen Square Chambers
56 Queen Square, Bristol BS1 4PR,
☎0117 921 1966 ✉crime@qs-c.co.uk
Call Date: Oct 2002, Middle Temple
Qualifications: [BA (Hons) (Dunelm)]
✉orsw@qs-c.co.uk

WILLOUGHBY MR JAMES WILLIAM MICHAEL

Dere Street Barristers
14 Toft Green, York YO1 6JT, ☎0844 3351551
✉clerks@derestreet.co.uk
Dere Street Barristers
33 Broad Chare, Newcastle Upon Tyne
NE1 3DQ, ☎0844 3351551
✉clerks@derestreet.co.uk
Call Date: Oct 2005, Middle Temple
Qualifications: [MA (Hons) (Edin)]
✉clerks@yorkchambers.co.uk

WILLS MISS ALEXANDRA ITARI

Christ Church Chambers
Mayfair Point, 34 South Molton Street, London
W1K 5RG, ☎020 7409 5278/07788 512787
Call Date: Nov 2000, Inner Temple
Qualifications: [LLB (Lond) LLM (Lond)]

WILLS MISS JANICE MARIE

18 St John Street
Manchester M3 4EA, ☎0161 278 1800
✉clerks@18sjs.com
Call Date: Oct 1991, Gray's Inn
Qualifications: [LLB]

WILLS MR JONATHAN STUART

Landmark Chambers
180 Fleet Street, London EC4A 2HG,
☎020 7430 1221
✉clerks@landmarkchambers.co.uk
Call Date: July 2006, Lincoln's Inn
Qualifications: [BA (Cantab)]
✉jwills@landmarkchambers.co.uk

WILLS-GOLDINGHAM MISS CLAIRE LOUISE MARGARET QC (2012)

Albion Chambers
Broad Street, Bristol BS1 1DR,
☎0117 927 2144
✉clerks@albionchambers.co.uk
Call Date: July 1988, Inner Temple
Pupil Supervisor
Qualifications: [LLB (B'ham)]
✉claire.wills-goldingham@albionchambers.co.uk

WILLSON MR WILLIAM

South Square
3-4 South Square, Gray's Inn, London
WC1R 5HP, ☎020 7696 9900
✉practicemanagers@southsquare.com
Call Date: Oct 2006, Lincoln's Inn
Qualifications: [MA (Oxon)]
✉williamwillson@southsquare.com

E

WILLSTEED MISS ELIZABETH LOUISE

Southernhay Chambers
33 Southernhay East, Exeter EX1 1NX,
☎01392 255777
✉clerks@southernhaychambers.co.uk
Call Date: Nov 2004, Inner Temple
Qualifications: [LLB (Hons) University of West of England Bristol]
e.willsteed@southernhaychambers.co.uk

WILMOT-SMITH MISS CLAUDIA RUTH

Quadrant Chambers
Quadrant House, 10 Fleet Street, London EC4Y 1AU, ☎020 7583 4444
✉info@quadrantchambers.com
Call Date: July 2008, Middle Temple
Qualifications: [BA (Hons) (Cantab) PgDl (Lond)]

WILMOT-SMITH MR RICHARD JAMES CROSBIE QC (1994)

39 Essex Street
London WC2R 3AT, ☎020 7832 1111
✉clerks@39essex.com
82 King Street
Manchester M2 4WQ, ☎0161 870 9969
Call Date: July 1978, Middle Temple
Recorder
Qualifications: [AB (USA)]
rws@39essex.com

WILMSHURST MR PAUL IVAN WILLIAM

12 College Place
Fauvelle Buildings, 12 College Place, Southampton SO15 2FE, ☎023 8032 0320
✉clerks@12cp.co.uk
Call Date: Oct 2007, Middle Temple
Qualifications: [BA (Hons) (Dunelm) CPE/GDL]
pwilmshurst@12cp.co.uk

WILSHIRE MR SIMON VINCENT

4 Breams Buildings
Chancery Lane, London EC4A 1HP,
☎020 7092 1900 ✉clerks@4bb.co.uk
Call Date: Oct 1994, Gray's Inn
Qualifications: [BSc]

WILSON MR ADAM

No.6 Park Square
Leeds LS1 2LW, ☎0113 245 9763
✉Tim@no6.co.uk
Call Date: Nov 1994, Inner Temple
Qualifications: [LLB (Lond)]
wilson@no6.co.uk

WILSON MR ALAN ANTHONY

Kenworthy's Chambers
Arlington House, Bloom Street, Salford, Manchester M3 6AJ, ☎0161 832 4036
Call Date: Nov 2005, Inner Temple
Qualifications: [LLB Manchester Metropolitan University]

WILSON MR ALASDAIR JOHN

Fenners Chambers
3 Madingley Road, Cambridge CB3 0EE,
☎01223 368761
✉clerks@fennerschambers.com
Call Date: Nov 1988, Gray's Inn
Pupil Supervisor
Qualifications: [LLB (Wales)]
alasdair.wilson@fennerschambers.com

WILSON MR ALASTAIR JAMES DRYSDALE QC (1987)

Hogarth Chambers
5 New Square, Lincoln's Inn, London WC2A 3RJ, ☎020 7404 0404
✉barristers@hogarthchambers.com
Call Date: July 1968, Middle Temple
Recorder
Qualifications: [MA (Cantab)]
awilson@hogarthchambers.com

WILSON MR ANDREW

One Essex Court
1st Floor, Temple, London EC4Y 9AR,
☎020 7936 3030 ✉clerks@1ec.co.uk
Call Date: Mar 2010, Inner Temple
Qualifications: [BA (York) CPE (Guildford)]

WILSON MR ANDREW JAMES

Sovereign Chambers
46 Park Place, Leeds LS1 2RY,
☎0113 245 1841
✉clerks@sovereignchambers.co.uk
Call Date: July 2005, Middle Temple
Qualifications: [BSc (Hons) Leeds PgDip Law]

WILSON MR ANDREW ROBERT

Zenith Chambers
10 Park Square, Leeds LS1 2LH,
☎0113 245 5438
✉clerks@zenithchambers.co.uk
Call Date: Nov 1995, Gray's Inn
Qualifications: [BA]
awilson@zenithchambers.co.uk

WILSON MR BRETT

Palmyra Chambers
Royal House, 46 Legh Street, Warrington
WA1 1UJ, ☎01925 444919
✉clerk@palmyrachambers.com
Call Date: July 2008, Inner Temple
Qualifications: [BSc LLB (Lond) CPE]
brett.wilson@palmyrachambers.com

WILSON MS CHARMAINE KIMBERLEY

Westgate Chambers
64 High Street, Lewes, East Sussex BN7 1XG,
☎01273 480510
✉clerks@westgate-chambers.co.uk
Call Date: July 2003, Inner Temple
Qualifications: [LLB (Hull)]
cw@westgate-chambers.co.uk

WILSON MR CHRISTOPHER JOHN

The Chambers of Grahame Aldous QC
9 Gough Square, London EC4A 3DG,
☎020 7832 0500
✉clerks@9goughsquare.co.uk
Call Date: July 1980, Gray's Inn
Pupil Supervisor, Recorder
Qualifications: [LLB (Hons)]

WILSON MR DAVID WILLIAM

18 Red Lion Court (Annexe)
Thornwood House, 102 New London Road,
Chelmsford, Essex CM2 0RG,
☎01245 280880
18 Red Lion Court
London EC4A 3EB, ☎020 7520 6000
✉chambers@18rlc.co.uk
Call Date: Oct 1996, Gray's Inn
Qualifications: [LLB]
david.wilson@18rlc.co.uk

WILSON MR GERALD SIMON JOHN

Tanfield Chambers
2-5 Warwick Court, London WC1R 5DJ,
☎020 7421 5300
✉clerks@tanfieldchambers.co.uk
Call Date: Nov 1989, Gray's Inn
Qualifications: [BA (Oxon) Dip Law]
geraldwilson@tanfieldchambers.co.uk

WILSON MR GRAEME JOHN

Furnival Chambers
32 Furnival Street, London EC4A 1JQ,
☎020 7405 3232
Call Date: Feb 1987, Inner Temple
Qualifications: [LLB (Lond)]
g_j_wilson@btinternet.com

WILSON MR GRAHAM JAMES

Gray's Inn Tax Chambers
3rd Floor, Gray's Inn Chambers, Gray's Inn,
London WC1R 5JA, ☎020 7242 2642
✉clerks@taxbar.com
Call Date: July 1975, Gray's Inn
Qualifications: [LLB (Lond) LLM (Nancy) TEP]
gjwilson@wilson.lu

Fax: +352 252741;
Out of hours telephone: +352 621 330080
URL: www.wilson.lu

Other professional qualifications: TEP

Types of work: Banking, Capital tax, Company, commercial and competition, Corporate finance, Corporation tax, EC competition law, Equity, Financial services, Income tax, Insolvency, Insurance, Share options, Succession, Trusts, Wills

Membership of foreign bars: Luxembourg

Circuit: European

Other professional experience: Chairman, STEP Benelux

Languages spoken: French

Principal Practice Address
Wilson Associates
11 Boulevard Royal
PO Box 742
L-2017
Luxembourg

Email: gjwilson@wilson.lu

Tel: +352 252740
Fax: +352 252741

WILSON MISS HANNAH

Henderson Chambers
2 Harcourt Buildings, Temple, London
EC4Y 9DB, ☎020 7583 9020
✉clerks@hendersonchambers.co.uk
Call Date: Nov 2005, Lincoln's Inn
Qualifications: [BA (Hons) (Cantab) MPhil (Cantab)]
hwilson@hendersonchambers.co.uk

WILSON MISS HELEN TRACY

Call Date: Oct 2004, Gray's Inn
Qualifications: [LLB]
helen.wilson@stjohnsbuildings.co.uk

E

WILSON MR IAN ROBERT

3 Verulam Buildings
London WC1R 5NT, ☎020 7831 8441
✉chambers@3vb.com
Call Date: Oct 1995, Middle Temple
Pupil Supervisor
Qualifications: [MA (Hons) LLM]
iwilson@3vb.com

WILSON MR JOHN ARMSTRONG QC (2011)

1 Hare Court
1 Hare Court, Temple, London EC4Y 7BE,
☎020 7797 7070 ✉clerks@1hc.com
Call Date: July 1981, Inner Temple
Pupil Supervisor
Qualifications: [MA (Cantab)]
clerks@1hc.com

WILSON MR JONATHAN CHARLES

37 Park Square Chambers
37 Park Square, Leeds LS1 2NY,
☎0113 243 9422 ✉chambers@no37.co.uk
Call Date: Mar 2005, Lincoln's Inn
Qualifications: [BA (Hons) Lond]
chambers@no37.co.uk

WILSON MR JULIAN MARTIN

11 King's Bench Walk
11 King's Bench Walk, Temple, London
EC4Y 7EQ, ☎020 7632 8500
✉clerksroom@11kbw.com
Call Date: Oct 1997, Inner Temple
Qualifications: [BA (Oxon)]
julian.wilson@11kbw.com

WILSON MS KATHARINE ELIZABETH

One Brick Court
1st Floor, One Brick Court, Temple, London
EC4Y 9BY, ☎020 7353 8845
✉clerks@onebrickcourt.com
Call Date: Nov 2005, Inner Temple
Qualifications: [BA Magdalen College University of Oxford M Phil]
kw@onebrickcourt.com

WILSON MISS KATRINA

1 High Pavement
Nottingham NG1 1HF, ☎0115 941 8218
✉clerks@1highpavement.co.uk
Call Date: July 2007, Lincoln's Inn
Qualifications: [LLB (Sheff)]
katrinawilson@1highpavement.co.uk

WILSON MR LACHLAN BAYARD

3 PB Barristers
3 Paper Buildings, Temple, London EC4Y 7EU,
☎020 7583 8055
3 PB Barristers
Royal Talbot House, 2 Victoria Street, Bristol,
Avon BS1 6BB, ☎0117 928 1520
3 PB Barristers
30 Christchurch Road, Bournemouth, Dorset
BH1 3PD, ☎01202 292102
✉clerks.bournemouth@3paper.co.uk
3 PB Barristers
4 St Peter Street, Winchester SO23 8BW,
☎01962 868884
✉clerks.winchester@3paper.co.uk
3 PB Barristers
23 Beaumont Street, Oxford OX1 2NP,
☎01865 793 736
Call Date: Oct 1996, Inner Temple
Pupil Supervisor
Qualifications: [BA (Oxon)]
lachlan.wilson@3paper.co.uk

WILSON MISS LISA MARIE

Furnival Chambers
32 Furnival Street, London EC4A 1JQ,
☎020 7405 3232
Call Date: Oct 2006, Inner Temple
Qualifications: [LLB (Wales) MA (Lond)]
lwilson@furnivallaw.co.uk

WILSON MISS MARY ELIZABETH FRANCES

Pump Court Tax Chambers
16 Bedford Row, London WC1R 4EF,
☎020 7414 8080 ✉clerks@pumptax.com
Call Date: Oct 1995, Middle Temple
Pupil Supervisor
Qualifications: [BA (Hons)]
ewilson@pumptax.com

Types of work: Capital tax, Corporation tax, Employee benefit trusts, Equity, Income tax, National Insurance, Private client, Professional negligence, Stamp duty, Trusts, VAT, Wills

WILSON MR MYLES BRENNAND

Call Date: Oct 1993, Lincoln's Inn
Qualifications: [LLB (Hons)(Leeds)]
clerk@stjohnsbuildings.co.uk

WILSON MR PAUL RICHARD

Broadway House Chambers
Broadway House, 9 Bank Street, Bradford,
West Yorkshire BD1 1TW, ☎01274 722560
✉clerks@broadwayhouse.co.uk
Call Date: Nov 1989, Lincoln's Inn
Pupil Supervisor
Qualifications: [MA (Oxon)]
prw@broadwayhouse.co.uk

WILSON MR PETER JULIAN

Sovereign Chambers
46 Park Place, Leeds LS1 2RY,
☎0113 245 1841
✉clerks@sovereignchambers.co.uk
Call Date: Oct 1995, Middle Temple
Qualifications: [MA (Hons)]
peter.wilson@sovereignchambers.co.uk

WILSON MISS REBEKAH MAXINE

Tooks Chambers
81 Farringdon Street, London EC4A 4BL,
☎020 7842 7575 ✉clerks@tooks.co.uk
Call Date: Nov 1998, Middle Temple
Qualifications: [LLB (Hons) LLM]
rebekah.wilson@tooks.co.uk

WILSON MR RICHARD CARVER QC (2003)

36 Bedford Row
London WC1R 4JH, ☎020 7421 8000
✉chambers@36bedfordrow.co.uk
Call Date: Nov 1981, Lincoln's Inn
Recorder
Qualifications: [BA (Sussex) LLM (Cambridge)]
rwilson@36bedfordrow.co.uk

WILSON MR RICHARD COLIN

3 Stone Buildings
Ground Floor, 3 Stone Buildings, Lincoln's Inn, London WC2A 3XL, ☎020 7242 4937
✉clerks@3sb.law.co.uk
Call Date: Oct 1996, Middle Temple
Pupil Supervisor
Qualifications: [LLB (Hons)(Sheff) LLM (Lond)]
rwilson@3sb.law.co.uk

WILSON MR SCOTT

Themis Chambers
Suite 14067, 145-157 St John's Street, London EC1V 4PY, ☎07967 418976
✉karentaylor@themischambers.co.uk
Call Date: Nov 1993, Lincoln's Inn
Qualifications: [LLB (Hons) (Leics)]

WILSON MISS THEA CHARLOTTE

12 King's Bench Walk
12 King's Bench Walk, Temple, London EC4Y 7EL, ☎020 7583 0811
Call Date: July 2008, Inner Temple
Qualifications: [MA (Cantab) LLM]
wilson@12kbw.co.uk

WILSON MISS VICTORIA

Goldsmith Chambers
Ground Floor, Goldsmith Building, Temple, London EC4Y 7BL, ☎020 7353 6802
✉clerks@goldsmithchambers.com
Call Date: July 2002, Gray's Inn
Qualifications: [Dip Law MA (Oxon)]
V.Wilson@goldsmithchambers.law.co.uk

WILSON-BARNES MISS LUCY EMMA

St James's Chambers
68 Quay Street, Manchester M3 3EJ,
☎0161 834 7000
✉clerks@stjameschambers.com
Zenith Chambers
10 Park Square, Leeds LS1 2LH,
☎0113 245 5438
✉clerks@zenithchambers.co.uk
Call Date: July 1989, Inner Temple
Pupil Supervisor
Qualifications: [BA (Warw)]
lucy.wilson-barnes@stjameschambers.com

WILSON-SMITH MR CHRISTOPHER QC (1986)

Outer Temple Chambers
The Outer Temple, 222 Strand, London WC2R 1BA, ☎020 7353 6381
✉clerks@outertemple.com
St John's Chambers
101 Victoria Street, Bristol BS1 6PU,
☎0117 923 4700
✉clerks@stjohnschambers.co.uk
Call Date: Nov 1965, Gray's Inn
Recorder
christopher.wilson-smithqc@outertemple.com

WILTON MR SIMON DANIEL

Hailsham Chambers
Ground Floor, 4 Paper Buildings, Temple, London EC4Y 7EX, ☎020 7643 5000
✉clerks@hailshamchambers.com
Call Date: Oct 1993, Gray's Inn
Pupil Supervisor
Qualifications: [BA (Sussex)]
simon.wilton@hailshamchambers.com

WILTSHIRE MRS HANNAH LOUISE

Albion Chambers
Broad Street, Bristol BS1 1DR,
☎0117 927 2144
✉clerks@albionchambers.co.uk
Call Date: Oct 1998, Gray's Inn
Pupil Supervisor
Qualifications: [LLB (Hons)(Lond)]
hannah.wiltshire@albionchambers.co.uk

E

WINBERG MR STEPHEN ALEXANDER

Furnival Chambers
32 Furnival Street, London EC4A 1JQ,
☎020 7405 3232
Call Date: Nov 1974, Inner Temple
Qualifications: [BA]
swinberg@furnivallaw.co.uk

WINCHESTER MR LEONARD CLIVE ALLYN

Lamb Chambers
Lamb Building, Elm Court, Temple, London
EC4Y 7AS, ☎020 7797 8300
info@lambchambers.co.uk
Call Date: July 2002, Lincoln's Inn
Qualifications: [LLB]
AllynWinchester@lambchambers.co.uk

WINDLE MISS VICTORIA KATHLEEN FITZGERALD

Blackstone Chambers
Blackstone House, Temple, London
EC4Y 9BW, ☎020 7583 1770
clerks@blackstonechambers.com
Call Date: Nov 2001, Inner Temple
Qualifications: [BA (Cantab)]
victoriawindle@blackstonechambers.com

WINDSOR MISS EMILY MAY

Falcon Chambers
Falcon Court, London EC4Y 1AA,
☎020 7353 2484
clerks@falcon-chambers.com
Call Date: Oct 1995, Gray's Inn
Pupil Supervisor
Qualifications: [BA DSU (France)]
windsor@falcon-chambers.com

Types of work: Agriculture, Arbitration, Chancery (general), Chancery (land law), Commercial litigation, Commercial property, Costs, Dispute resolution, Environment, Equity, Highways, Housing, Landlord and tenant, Professional negligence, Real property, Remedies, Trusts, Wills

WINFIELD MR JOSHUA ANSEL SIDNEY

Radcliffe Chambers
Ground Floor, 11 New Square, Lincoln's Inn,
London WC2A 3QB, ☎020 7831 0081
clerks@radcliffechambers.com
Call Date: Oct 2001, Inner Temple
Pupil Supervisor
Qualifications: [MA (Oxon) Dip in Law]
jwinfield@radcliffechambers.com

WING MR CHRISTOPHER JOHN

1 Paper Buildings
1st Floor, 1 Paper Buildings, Temple, London
EC4Y 7EP, ☎020 7353 3728
clerks@onepaper.co.uk
Call Date: July 1985, Gray's Inn
Pupil Supervisor
Qualifications: [BSc (Kent) BA]
christopherwing@onepaper.co.uk

WING MR JAMES

3 Temple Gardens
Lower Ground Floor, 3 Temple Gardens,
Temple, London EC4Y 9AU, ☎020 7353 3102
clerks@3tg.co.uk
Call Date: Oct 2003, Lincoln's Inn
Qualifications: [BA (Hons) (Oxon)]
jjw@3tg.co.uk

WINGERT MISS RACHEL THOMAS

Renaissance Chambers
5th Floor, Gray's Inn Chambers, Gray's Inn,
London WC1R 5JA, ☎020 7404 1111
clerks@renaissancechambers.co.uk
Call Date: July 1980, Middle Temple
Qualifications: [LLB (Lond) LLM (Lond) MA (Westminister) G Dip Psych]
rw@renaissancechambers.co.uk

WINGFIELD MR RICHARD CHRISTOPHER

6 King's Bench Walk
Ground Floor, 6 King's Bench Walk, Temple,
London EC4Y 7DR, ☎020 7583 0410
clerks@6kbw.com
Call Date: Oct 2009, Lincoln's Inn
Qualifications: [LLB (Nott'm)]
clerks@6kbw.com

WINN-SMITH MR MATTHEW

Lamb Chambers
Lamb Building, Elm Court, Temple, London
EC4Y 7AS, ☎020 7797 8300
info@lambchambers.co.uk
Call Date: Mar 2003, Lincoln's Inn
Qualifications: [MA (Hons) (Oxon)]
matthewwinnsmith@lambchambers.co.uk

WINSER MR CRISPIN DAVID RICHARD

Crown Office Chambers
2 Crown Office Row, Temple, London
EC4Y 7HJ, ☎020 7797 8100
mail@crownofficechambers.com
Call Date: Oct 2003, Inner Temple
Qualifications: [BA (Bristol) Dip Law (City)]
winser@crownofficechambers.com

WINSHIP MR JULIAN ABDULLA

Furnival Chambers
32 Furnival Street, London EC4A 1JQ,
☎ 020 7405 3232
Call Date: Oct 1995, Gray's Inn
Pupil Supervisor
Qualifications: [LLB]
jwinship@furnivallaw.co.uk

WINSLETT MR FRANK

Westgate Chambers
64 High Street, Lewes, East Sussex BN7 1XG,
☎ 01273 480510
✉ clerks@westgate-chambers.co.uk
Call Date: Mar 2004, Middle Temple
Pupil Supervisor

WINSTANLEY MISS ALICE BRYONY

St Philips Chambers
55 Temple Row, Birmingham B2 5LS,
☎ 0121 246 7000 ✉ clerks@st-philips.com
Call Date: Oct 2006, Lincoln's Inn
Qualifications: [LLB (Bris) LLM]
awinstanley@st-philips.com

WINSTON MISS NAOMI EMILY LOUISE

Ten Old Square
Ground Floor, Ten Old Square, Lincoln's Inn, London WC2A 3SU, ☎ 020 7405 0758
✉ clerks@tenoldsquare.com
Call Date: Oct 2006, Middle Temple
Qualifications: [LLB (Hons) (Leic)]

WINSTONE THE HON ANNE HILARY WELCH

Old Square Chambers
3 Orchard Court, St Augustine's Yard, Bristol BS1 5DP, ☎ 0117 930 5100
✉ clerks@oldsquare.co.uk
Old Square Chambers
10-11 Bedford Row, London WC1R 4BU,
☎ 020 7269 0300 ✉ clerks@oldsquare.co.uk
Call Date: Oct 1998, Lincoln's Inn
Qualifications: [LLB (Hons)(Wales)]

WINT MR EARL PETER

Chavasse Court Chambers
18 Queen Avenue, Liverpool L2 4TX,
☎ 0151 229 2030
✉ clerks@chavassechambers.co.uk
Call Date: Mar 2007, Gray's Inn
earlwint@hotmail.co.uk

WINTER MR ALEXANDER THOMAS

Maitland Chambers
7 Stone Buildings, Lincoln's Inn, London WC2A 3SZ, ☎ 020 7406 1200
✉ clerks@maitlandchambers.com
Call Date: July 2003, Middle Temple
Qualifications: [BA Hons (Oxon) MA CPE]
awinter@maitlandchambers.com

WINTER MR IAN DAVID QC (2006)

Cloth Fair Chambers
39-40 Cloth Fair, London EC1A 7NT,
☎ 020 7710 6444
✉ email@clothfairchambers.com
Call Date: July 1988, Inner Temple
Qualifications: [LLB (Hons)]
ianwinter@clothfairchambers.com

WINTER MISS LOUISE DEBORAH

New Walk Chambers
27 New Walk, Leicester, Leicestershire LE1 6TE, ☎ 0871 200 1298 / 0116 255 9144
✉ clerks@newwalkchambers.co.uk
Call Date: July 2009, Lincoln's Inn
Qualifications: [LLB (Open University)]

WINTER MISS MELANIE JANE

The Chambers of Grahame Aldous QC
9 Gough Square, London EC4A 3DG,
☎ 020 7832 0500
✉ clerks@9goughsquare.co.uk
Call Date: Oct 1996, Middle Temple
Qualifications: [LLB (Hons)(Wales)]
mwinter@9goughsquare.co.uk

WISE MR IAN QC (2010)

Doughty Street Chambers
53-54 Doughty Street, London WC1N 2LS,
☎ 020 7404 1313
✉ enquiries@doughtystreet.co.uk
Doughty Street Chambers
Pall Mall Court, 61-67 King Street, Manchester M2 4PD, ☎ 0161 618 1066
Doughty Street Chambers
5th Floor, Broad Quay House, Prince Street, Bristol BS1 4DJ, ☎ 01179 058 717
Call Date: Oct 1992, Gray's Inn
Pupil Supervisor
Qualifications: [BA]
i.wise@doughtystreet.co.uk

E

WISE MR LESLIE MICHAEL

10 King's Bench Walk
Ground Floor, 10 King's Bench Walk, Temple, London EC4Y 7EB, ☎ 020 7353 7742
✉ Chambers@10kingsbenchwalk.co.uk
Call Date: Nov 1985, Middle Temple
Pupil Supervisor
Qualifications: [FCA]
chambers@10kingsbenchwalk.co.uk

WISE MR OLIVER DACRES

Queen Elizabeth Building
3rd Floor, Queen Elizabeth Building, Temple, London EC4Y 9BS, ☎ 020 7797 7837
✉ clerks@qeb.co.uk
Call Date: July 1981, Lincoln's Inn
Pupil Supervisor
Qualifications: [MA (Cantab)]
o.wise@qeb.co.uk

WISEMAN MR ADAM PHILIP PASTERNAK

18 Red Lion Court
London EC4A 3EB, ☎ 020 7520 6000
✉ chambers@18rlc.co.uk
18 Red Lion Court (Annexe)
Thornwood House, 102 New London Road, Chelmsford, Essex CM2 0RG,
☎ 01245 280880
Call Date: Nov 1994, Inner Temple
Pupil Supervisor
Qualifications: [MSc (Exon) CPE (Lond)]
adam.wiseman@18rlc.co.uk

WISHART MR JOHN DUCKWORTH SCOTT

Chambers of Mr J D S Wishart
7 Lower Cribden Avenue, Rawtenstall, Rossendale, Lancashire BB4 6SW,
☎ 01706 220495 ✉ johnwishart@fsmail.net
Call Date: July 1974, Gray's Inn
Qualifications: [HNC (Mechanical & Production Eng)]

WITCHER MR COLIN MILES

Chambers of Marion Smullen and Kerim Fuad QC
1 Inner Temple Lane, London EC4Y 1AF,
☎ 020 7427 4400 ✉ clerks@1itl.com
Call Date: July 2010, Middle Temple
Qualifications: [LLB (Hons) (Nott'm)]
colin.witcher@1itl.com

WITCOMB MR HENRY JAMES

1 Crown Office Row
1 Crown Office Row, Temple, London EC4Y 7HH, ☎ 020 7797 7500
✉ mail@1cor.com
Call Date: Apr 1989, Lincoln's Inn
Pupil Supervisor
Qualifications: [BA (Dunelm)]
henry.witcomb@1cor.com

WITCOMBE MR RICHARD JOSHUA

Chambers of Marion Smullen and Kerim Fuad QC
1 Inner Temple Lane, London EC4Y 1AF,
☎ 020 7427 4400 ✉ clerks@1itl.com
Call Date: Oct 1997, Lincoln's Inn
Pupil Supervisor
Qualifications: [LLB (Hons)(Coventry) LLM (Lond)]

WITHERINGTON MISS GEMMA JANE

Hardwicke
New Square, Lincoln's Inn, London WC2A 3SB, ☎ 020 7242 2523
✉ enquiries@hardwicke.co.uk
Call Date: July 2008, Inner Temple
Qualifications: [BA (Hons) Dip in Law]
gemma.witherington@hardwicke.co.uk

WITHERS MISS MICHELLE JEAN MARY

30 Park Place
Cardiff CF10 3BS, ☎ 029 2039 8421
✉ clerks@30parkplace.law.co.uk
Call Date: Nov 1991, Inner Temple
Pupil Supervisor
Qualifications: [LLB (Wales)]

WITHINGTON MR ANGUS RICHARD

Henderson Chambers
2 Harcourt Buildings, Temple, London EC4Y 9DB, ☎ 020 7583 9020
✉ clerks@hendersonchambers.co.uk
Call Date: Nov 1995, Gray's Inn
Pupil Supervisor
Qualifications: [BA (Dunelm) Dip Law (Lond)]
awithington@hendersonchambers.co.uk

WITHYMAN MRS ELIZABETH RACHEL

Sovereign Chambers
46 Park Place, Leeds LS1 2RY,
☎ 0113 245 1841
✉ clerks@sovereignchambers.co.uk
Call Date: Oct 1995, Lincoln's Inn
Qualifications: [MA (Cantab)]
elizabeth.withyman@sovereignchambers.co.uk

WITHYMAN MR JAMES ANDREW

Dere Street Barristers
14 Toft Green, York YO1 6JT, ☎ 0844 3351551
✉ clerks@derestreet.co.uk
York Chambers
Rotterdam House, 116 The Quayside, Newcastle Upon Tyne NE1 3DY, ☎ 0191 206 4677
Call Date: Nov 1999, Lincoln's Inn
Qualifications: [LLB (Hons)]
✉ clerks@yorkchambers.co.uk, jwithyman@yorkchambers.co.uk

WOERNER MR STEVEN JOHN

Number 7 Harrington Street Chambers
7 Harrington Street, Liverpool L2 9YH, ☎ 0151 242 0707 ✉ clerks@7hs.co.uk
Call Date: Nov 2006, Middle Temple
Qualifications: [LLB (Hons) (Sheffield)]
✉ steven.woerner@7hs.co.uk

WOLANSKI MR ADAM MICHAEL VENANTIUS

5RB
1st Floor, 5 Raymond Buildings, Gray's Inn, London WC1R 5BP, ☎ 020 7242 2902
✉ clerks@5rb.com
Call Date: Feb 1995, Lincoln's Inn
Pupil Supervisor
Qualifications: [MA (Hons) (Cantab)]
✉ adamwolanski@5rb.com

WOLCHOVER MR CHAIM DAVID HIRSCH

7 Bell Yard
London WC2A 2JR, ☎ 020 7831 0636
✉ kevintarrant@btconnect.com
Call Date: July 1971, Gray's Inn
Pupil Supervisor

WOLFE DR DAVID FREDERICK HARRIS QC (2012)

Matrix Chambers
Griffin Building, Gray's Inn, London WC1R 5LN, ☎ 020 7404 3447
✉ matrix@matrixlaw.co.uk / lscott@matrixlaw.co.uk
Call Date: Nov 1992, Middle Temple
Pupil Supervisor
Qualifications: [BSc PhD (Cantab) Dip Law (Lond) M Eng (Manch)]
✉ davidwolfe@matrixlaw.co.uk

WOLFE MISS GEORGINA SYLVIA

5 Essex Court
1st Floor, 5 Essex Court, Temple, London EC4Y 9AH, ☎ 020 7410 2000
✉ clerks@5essexcourt.co.uk
Call Date: July 2006, Middle Temple
Qualifications: [MA (Hons) (Edin)]
✉ wolfe@5essexcourt.co.uk

WOLFE MISS MADELEINE LOUISE

Chambers of Marion Smullen and Kerim Fuad QC
1 Inner Temple Lane, London EC4Y 1AF, ☎ 020 7427 4400 ✉ clerks@1itl.com
Call Date: Oct 1998, Inner Temple
Qualifications: [BA (B'ham) CPE]
✉ clerks@1itl.com

WOLFE MS TARA KATE

Guildhall Chambers
23 Broad Street, Bristol BS1 2HG, ☎ 0117 930 9000
✉ hoc@guildhallchambers.co.uk
Call Date: Nov 2000, Inner Temple
Qualifications: [BA (Manc) CPE (Bris)]

WOLFENDEN MR PETER HAROLD

Oriel Chambers
14 Water Street, Liverpool, Merseyside L2 8TD, ☎ 0151 236 7191
✉ clerks@orielchambers.co.uk
Oriel Chambers
18 Ribblesdale Place, Preston PR1 3NA, ☎ 01772 254 764
✉ clerks@oriel-chambers.co.uk
Call Date: July 2007, Middle Temple
Qualifications: [LLB (Hons) (Manch)]
✉ peter.wolfenden@orielchambers.co.uk

WOLFF MR MICHAEL EMANUEL

Number 7 Harrington Street Chambers
7 Harrington Street, Liverpool L2 9YH, ☎ 0151 242 0707 ✉ clerks@7hs.co.uk
Call Date: June 1964, Gray's Inn
Qualifications: [LLB]
✉ michaelwolff@btinternet.com

WOLFSON MR DAVID QC (2009)

One Essex Court
Ground Floor, One Essex Court, Temple, London EC4Y 9AR, ☎ 020 7583 2000
✉ clerks@oeclaw.co.uk
Call Date: Nov 1992, Inner Temple
Qualifications: [MA (Cantab)]
✉ dwolfson@oeclaw.co.uk

E

WOLKIND MR MICHAEL IAN QC (1999)

2 Bedford Row
London WC1R 4BU, ☎ 020 7440 8888
✉ clerks@2bedfordrow.co.uk
Call Date: Nov 1976, Middle Temple
✉ mwolkind@2bedfordrow.co.uk

WOLMAN MR CLIVE RICHARD

11 Stone Buildings
11 Stone Buildings, Lincoln's Inn, London
WC2A 3TG, ☎ 020 7831 6381
✉ clerks@11sb.com
Call Date: July 2003, Middle Temple
Qualifications: [Ma (Oxon) PG Dip Law (Lond) MBA]
✉ wolman@11sb.com

WOLONIECKI MR JAN WLADYSLAW

Brick Court Chambers
7-8 Essex Street, London WC2R 3LD,
☎ 020 7379 3550 ✉ clerks@brickcourt.co.uk
Call Date: July 1983, Gray's Inn
Qualifications: [LLB (Lond)]
✉ jww@aswlaw.com

WOLSTENHOLME MISS HELEN SARAH

2 Temple Gardens
2 Temple Gardens, Temple, London
EC4Y 9AY, ☎ 020 7822 1200
✉ clerks@2tg.co.uk
Call Date: Nov 2002, Lincoln's Inn
Pupil Supervisor
Qualifications: [BA (Hons)(Oxon)]
✉ hwolstenholme@2tg.co.uk

WOLSTENHOLME MISS JANINE

Sovereign Chambers
46 Park Place, Leeds LS1 2RY,
☎ 0113 245 1841
✉ clerks@sovereignchambers.co.uk
Call Date: July 2002, Middle Temple
Qualifications: [LLB (Hons) (Sheff)]

WONG MISS NATASHA PUI-WAI

187 Fleet Street
London EC4A 2AT, ☎ 020 7430 7430
✉ chambers@187fleetstreet.com
Call Date: Nov 1993, Middle Temple
Pupil Supervisor
Qualifications: [BSc (Hons)(Kingston) CPE (Middx)]
✉ natashawong@187fleetstreet.com

WONNACOTT MR MARK ANDREW

Maitland Chambers
7 Stone Buildings, Lincoln's Inn, London
WC2A 3SZ, ☎ 020 7406 1200
✉ clerks@maitlandchambers.com
Call Date: July 1989, Lincoln's Inn
Pupil Supervisor
Qualifications: [LLB (Lond)]

WOOD MR BENJAMIN ANTHONY

Four New Square
Four New Square, Lincoln's Inn, London
WC2A 3RJ, ☎ 020 7822 2000
✉ barristers@4newsquare.com
Call Date: July 2005, Lincoln's Inn
Qualifications: [BA (Hons) (Oxon) PgDL]
✉ b.wood@4newsquare.com

WOOD MISS CAROLINE SARAH

Sovereign Chambers
46 Park Place, Leeds LS1 2RY,
☎ 0113 245 1841
✉ clerks@sovereignchambers.co.uk
Call Date: Mar 1998, Gray's Inn
Qualifications: [LLB (W'hampton)]

WOOD MISS CATHERINE QC (2011)

4 Paper Buildings
1st Floor, 4 Paper Buildings, Temple, London
EC4Y 7EX, ☎ 020 7427 5200
✉ clerks@4pb.com
Call Date: July 1985, Middle Temple
Pupil Supervisor, Recorder
Qualifications: [LLB (Lond)]
✉ cw@4pb.com

WOOD MR CHRISTOPHER MARK BRUCE

1 Hare Court
1 Hare Court, Temple, London EC4Y 7BE,
☎ 020 7797 7070 ✉ clerks@1hc.com
Call Date: Feb 1986, Middle Temple
Pupil Supervisor
Qualifications: [MA (Oxon) DESU (France)]
✉ wood@1hc.com

WOOD MR DANIEL JAMES

Ropewalk Chambers
24 The Ropewalk, Nottingham NG1 5EF,
☎ 0115 947 2581 ✉ clerks@ropewalk.co.uk
Call Date: July 2008, Lincoln's Inn
Qualifications: [BSc (Bath) LLB (Nott'm)]
✉ danielwood@ropewalk.co.uk

WOOD MR DANIEL JAMES

Number 7 Harrington Street Chambers
7 Harrington Street, Liverpool L2 9YH,
☎0151 242 0707 ✉clerks@7hs.co.uk
Call Date: July 2000, Lincoln's Inn
Qualifications: [BSc LLB (Leeds) MSc (L'pool)]
✉daniel.wood@7hs.co.uk

WOOD MR DAVID EMRYS

Charter Chambers
33 John Street, London WC1N 2AT,
☎020 7618 4400
✉clerks@charterchambers.com
Call Date: July 2007, Inner Temple
Qualifications: [MA (Oxon)]
✉david.wood@charterchambers.com

WOOD MR DEREK ALEXANDER QC (1978)

Falcon Chambers
Falcon Court, London EC4Y 1AA,
☎020 7353 2484
✉clerks@falcon-chambers.com
Call Date: Feb 1964, Middle Temple
Recorder
Qualifications: [MA BCL (Oxon)]
✉wood@falcon-chambers.com

WOOD MISS EMILY CAROLINE

Essex Court Chambers
24 Lincoln's Inn Fields, London WC2A 3EG,
☎020 7813 8000
✉clerksroom@essexcourt.net
Call Date: Oct 2006, Middle Temple
Qualifications: [BA (Hons) (Cantab) BCL (Oxon)]
✉ewood@essexcourt.net

WOOD MR GRAEME CRESSWELL

Assize Court Chambers
14 Small Street, Bristol BS1 1DE,
☎0117 926 4587 ✉carly@assize.co.uk
New Bailey Chambers
4th Floor, Corn Exchange, Fenwick Street, Liverpool, Merseyside L2 7QS,
☎0151 236 9402 ✉clerks@newbailey.com
Call Date: July 1968, Middle Temple
Pupil Supervisor
Qualifications: [MA LLM (Cantab)]

WOOD MISS HANNAH LOUISE

Call Date: July 2007, Lincoln's Inn
Qualifications: [LLB (Nott'm) BA (Sheff)]
✉clerk@stjohnsbuildings.co.uk,
hannah.wood@stjohnsbuildings.co.uk

WOOD MR JAMES ALEXANDER DOUGLAS QC (1999)

Doughty Street Chambers
53-54 Doughty Street, London WC1N 2LS,
☎020 7404 1313
✉enquiries@doughtystreet.co.uk
Doughty Street Chambers
Pall Mall Court, 61-67 King Street, Manchester M2 4PD, ☎0161 618 1066
Doughty Street Chambers
5th Floor, Broad Quay House, Prince Street, Bristol BS1 4DJ, ☎01179 058 717
Call Date: Nov 1975, Middle Temple
Recorder
Qualifications: [LLB]
✉j.wood@doughtystreet.co.uk

WOOD MISS JOANNA LINDA IRIS

Angel Chambers
Ethos Building, Kings Road, Swansea SA1 8AS,
☎01792 464623
✉clerks@angelchambers.co.uk
Call Date: Nov 1989, Inner Temple
Pupil Supervisor
Qualifications: [LLB]
✉joannawood@angelchambers.co.uk

WOOD MISS JOANNA RACHEL

1 Pump Court
Elm Court, Temple, London EC4Y 7AB,
☎020 7842 7070
✉(name)@pumpcourt.co.uk
Call Date: Oct 1996, Inner Temple
Qualifications: [LLB (Nott'm)]
✉jw@1pumpcourt.co.uk

WOOD MISS KATHERINE ANNE

Trinity Chambers
The Custom House, 39 Quayside, Newcastle Upon Tyne NE1 3DE, ☎0191 232 1927
✉info@trinitychambers.co.uk
Trinity Chambers
Multi Media Exchange, 72-80 Corporation Road, Middlesbrough TS1 2RF,
☎01642 247569
✉info@trinitychambers.co.uk
Call Date: July 2002, Middle Temple
Pupil Supervisor
Qualifications: [LLB (Hons)]
✉k.wood@trinitychambers.co.uk

WOOD MS KATIE ANNE

4 Paper Buildings
1st Floor, 4 Paper Buildings, Temple, London EC4Y 7EX, ☎020 7427 5200
✉clerks@4pb.com
Call Date: July 2001, Inner Temple
Qualifications: [LLB (Cardiff)]
✉kw@4pb.com

E

WOOD MS LANA CLAIRE

9 Stone Buildings
Lincoln's Inn, London WC2A 3NN,
☎ 020 7404 5055
✉ clerks@9stonebuildings.com
Call Date: Oct 1993, Gray's Inn
Pupil Supervisor
Qualifications: [MA (Cantab) BCL]
clerks@9stonebuildings.com

WOOD MR MARTIN JOHN

Broadway House Chambers
Broadway House, 9 Bank Street, Bradford, West Yorkshire BD1 1TW, ☎ 01274 722560
✉ clerks@broadwayhouse.co.uk
Broadway House Chambers
25 Park Square West, Leeds, West Yorkshire LS1 2PW, ☎ 0113 246 2600
✉ clerks@broadwayhouse.co.uk
Call Date: July 1973, Inner Temple
Pupil Supervisor
Qualifications: [MA (Cantab)]
mjw@broadwayhouse.co.uk

WOOD SIR MICHAEL CHARLES

20 Essex Street
London WC2R 3AL, ☎ 020 7842 1200
✉ clerks@20essexst.com
Call Date: Nov 1968, Gray's Inn
Qualifications: [MA LLB]

WOOD MR MICHAEL JOHN

Exchange Chambers
One Derby Square, Derby Square, Liverpool L2 9XX, ☎ 0151 236 7747
✉ info@exchangechambers.co.uk
Exchange Chambers
7 Ralli Courts, West Riverside, Manchester M3 5FT, ☎ 0161 833 2722
Exchange Chambers
Oxford House, Oxford Row, Leeds LS1 3BE,
☎ 0113 203 1970
✉ spencer@exchangechambers.co.uk
Call Date: Nov 1989, Lincoln's Inn
Qualifications: [BA (Sheff) DipIA (Bradford) LLB (Sheff)]

WOOD MR MICHAEL MURE QC (1999)

Chambers of Mr Michael Wood QC
21 Tonsley Place, Wandsworth, London SW18 1BH, ☎ 020 8874 3474
✉ mwoodqc@hotmail.com
Call Date: July 1976, Middle Temple
Qualifications: [LLB]
mwoodqc@hotmail.com

WOOD MISS NATALIE RACHAEL

2 King's Bench Walk
2 King's Bench Walk, Temple, London EC4Y 7DE, ☎ 020 7353 1746
✉ clerks@2kbw.com
Call Date: July 2001, Middle Temple
Qualifications: [LLB (Hons)]
nwood@2kbw.com

WOOD MISS REBECCA JANE

4 Breams Buildings
Chancery Lane, London EC4A 1HP,
☎ 020 7092 1900 ✉ clerks@4bb.co.uk
Call Date: Oct 2004, Lincoln's Inn
Qualifications: [LLB (Hons)]

WOOD MR RICHARD JAMES

9 King's Bench Walk
Lower Ground Floor South, 9 King's Bench Walk, Temple, London EC4Y 7DX,
☎ 020 7353 9564 ✉ 9kbw@btconnect.com
Call Date: Nov 2001, Middle Temple
Pupil Supervisor
Qualifications: [BSc (Hons)(Lond)]
9kbw@btconnect.com

WOOD MR RICHARD MICHAEL

East Anglian Chambers
Gresham House, 5 Museum Street, Ipswich, Suffolk IP1 1HQ, ☎ 01473 214481
✉ ipswich@ealaw.co.uk
East Anglian Chambers
140 New London Road, Chelmsford, Essex CM2 0AW, ☎ 01473 214481
✉ chelmsford@ealaw.co.uk
East Anglian Chambers
15 The Close, Norwich, Norfolk NR1 4DZ,
☎ 01473 214481 ✉ norwich@ealaw.co.uk
Call Date: Nov 1995, Gray's Inn
Pupil Supervisor
Qualifications: [BA]
richardwood@ealaw.co.uk

WOOD MISS SARAH TRACEY

Seven Bedford Row
7 Bedford Row, London WC1R 4BS,
☎ 020 7242 3555 ✉ clerks@7br.co.uk
Call Date: Oct 1996, Inner Temple
Qualifications: [LLB (Exon)]
swood@7br.co.uk

WOOD MR STEPHEN

Broadway House Chambers
Broadway House, 9 Bank Street, Bradford, West Yorkshire BD1 1TW, ☎01274 722560
✉clerks@broadwayhouse.co.uk
Broadway House Chambers
25 Park Square West, Leeds, West Yorkshire LS1 2PW, ☎0113 246 2600
✉clerks@broadwayhouse.co.uk
Call Date: Nov 1991, Inner Temple
Pupil Supervisor
Qualifications: [LLB (Hons) (Huddersfield)]
✉sw@broadwayhouse.co.uk

WOOD MR THOMAS PETER

42 Bedford Row
London WC1R 4LL, ☎020 7831 0222
✉clerks@42br.com
Call Date: Oct 2002, Lincoln's Inn
Qualifications: [LLB (Lond)]
✉thomas.wood@42br.com

WOOD MR WILLIAM JAMES QC (1998)

Brick Court Chambers
7-8 Essex Street, London WC2R 3LD, ☎020 7379 3550 ✉clerks@brickcourt.co.uk
Call Date: Nov 1980, Middle Temple
Qualifications: [BA LLM (Harvard) BCL (Oxon)]
✉William.Wood@Brickcourt.co.uk

WOODALL MR PETER

Carmelite Chambers
9 Carmelite Street, London EC4Y 0DR, ☎020 7936 6300
✉clerks@carmelitechambers.co.uk
Call Date: July 1983, Middle Temple
Pupil Supervisor
Qualifications: [LLB (Leeds)]
✉pwoodall@carmelitechambers.co.uk

WOODBRIDGE MR JULIAN GUY

1 KBW Chambers
1 King's Bench Walk, Temple, London EC4Y 7DB, ☎020 7936 1500
✉clerks@1kbw.co.uk
King's Bench Chambers
174 High Street, Lewes BN7 1YE, ☎01273 402600
Call Date: Nov 1981, Middle Temple
Pupil Supervisor
Qualifications: [LLB (Warwick)]
✉jwoodbridge@1kbw.co.uk

WOODBRIDGE MISS VICTORIA KATHLEEN

Crown Office Chambers
2 Crown Office Row, Temple, London EC4Y 7HJ, ☎020 7797 8100
✉mail@crownofficechambers.com
Call Date: Oct 1998, Lincoln's Inn
Pupil Supervisor
Qualifications: [BA (Hons)(Lond)]
✉woodbridge@crownofficechambers.com

WOODCOCK MR JONATHAN

3 Temple Gardens
Lower Ground Floor, 3 Temple Gardens, Temple, London EC4Y 9AU, ☎020 7353 3102
✉clerks@3tg.co.uk
Call Date: Nov 1981, Middle Temple
Pupil Supervisor
Qualifications: [LLB LLM (Lond)]

WOODCOCK MR ROBERT ANDREW PHILIP QC (2009)

Dere Street Barristers
33 Broad Chare, Newcastle Upon Tyne NE1 3DQ, ☎0844 3351551
✉clerks@derestreet.co.uk
KBW
The Engine House, No 1 Foundry Square, Leeds LS11 5DL, ☎0113 297 1200
✉clerks@kbwchambers.com
Kenworthy's Chambers
Arlington House, Bloom Street, Salford, Manchester M3 6AJ, ☎0161 832 4036
Call Date: Feb 1978, Inner Temple
Qualifications: [BA]

WOODCRAFT MISS ELIZABETH JANE

Tooks Chambers
81 Farringdon Street, London EC4A 4BL, ☎020 7842 7575 ✉clerks@tooks.co.uk
Call Date: July 1980, Middle Temple
Pupil Supervisor
Qualifications: [BA (Hons)(B'ham)]
✉elizabeth.woodcraft@tooks.co.uk

WOODHALL MR GARY

9 St John Street
Manchester M3 4DN, ☎0161 955 9000
✉civilclerks@9sjs.com / criminalclerks@9sjs.com
Call Date: Oct 1997, Gray's Inn
Pupil Supervisor
Qualifications: [MA (Cantab)]

E

WOODHAM MISS SAMANTHA SUSANNE

4 Paper Buildings
1st Floor, 4 Paper Buildings, Temple, London EC4Y 7EX, ☎020 7427 5200
✉clerks@4pb.com
Call Date: Nov 2006, Middle Temple
Qualifications: [BA (Cantab)]
sw@4pb.com

WOODHEAD MR GEORGE BYRON

Guildford Chambers
Stoke House, Leapale Lane, Guildford, Surrey GU1 4LY, ☎01483 539131
✉clerks@guildfordchambers.co.uk
Call Date: July 2009, Lincoln's Inn
Qualifications: [BA (Sheff) CPE UZNTU]
gwoodhead@guildfordchambers.com

WOODHOUSE MR CHARLES PHILIP

Old Square Chambers
10-11 Bedford Row, London WC1R 4BU, ☎020 7269 0300 ✉clerks@oldsquare.co.uk
Old Square Chambers
3 Orchard Court, St Augustine's Yard, Bristol BS1 5DP, ☎0117 930 5100
✉clerks@oldsquare.co.uk
Call Date: Oct 1997, Middle Temple
Pupil Supervisor
Qualifications: [LLB (Hons)(Lond)]
woodhouse@oldsquare.co.uk

WOODHOUSE MR NIGEL MARTIN

13 King's Bench Walk
13 King's Bench Walk, Temple, London EC4Y 7EN, ☎020 7353 7204
✉clerks@13kbw.co.uk
Call Date: Nov 1997, Gray's Inn
Qualifications: [LLB]
nwoodhouse@13kbw.co.uk

WOODING MR OLIVER JOHN

St John's Chambers
101 Victoria Street, Bristol BS1 6PU, ☎0117 923 4700
✉clerks@stjohnschambers.co.uk
Call Date: July 2009, Middle Temple
Qualifications: [BA (Hons) (Oxon) MSt (Oxon) Grad Dip Law]
oliver.wooding@stjohnschambers.co.uk

WOODLEY MISS SONIA QC (1996)

Furnival Chambers
32 Furnival Street, London EC4A 1JQ, ☎020 7405 3232
Call Date: July 1968, Gray's Inn

WOODS MR ALEXANDER ALAN GRAEME

187 Fleet Street
London EC4A 2AT, ☎020 7430 7430
✉chambers@187fleetstreet.com
Call Date: Oct 2007, Lincoln's Inn
Qualifications: [BA (Oxon)]
alexwoods@187fleetstreet.com

WOODS MISS CATHY LEANNE

3 Serjeants Inn
London EC4Y 1BQ, ☎020 7427 5000
✉clerks@3serjeantsinn.com
Call Date: Oct 2005, Inner Temple
Qualifications: [BA (Oxon) LLM (Pennsylvania)]
lwoods@3serjeantsinn.com

WOODS MISS DANIELLE LOUISE

15 Winckley Square
Preston PR1 3JJ, ☎01772 252828
✉clerks@15winckleysq.co.uk
Call Date: Oct 2009, Middle Temple
Qualifications: [LLB (Hons) (B'ham)]
daniellewoods@15ws.co.uk

WOODS MR GEORGE ROBERT

4 Pump Court
4 Pump Court, Temple, London EC4Y 7AN, ☎020 7842 5555
✉chambers@4pumpcourt.com
Call Date: Mar 2003, Middle Temple
Qualifications: [BA (Hons) (Oxon) CPE]
gwoods@4pumpcourt.com

WOODS MISS RACHAEL HELEN

Exchange Chambers
7 Ralli Courts, West Riverside, Manchester M3 5FT, ☎0161 833 2722
Exchange Chambers
One Derby Square, Derby Square, Liverpool L2 9XX, ☎0151 236 7747
✉info@exchangechambers.co.uk
Exchange Chambers
Oxford House, Oxford Row, Leeds LS1 3BE, ☎0113 203 1970
✉spencer@exchangechambers.co.uk
Call Date: Oct 1992, Gray's Inn
Qualifications: [LLB (Hons)]
woods@exchangechambers.co.uk

WOODS MR TERENCE MCCARTAN

187 Fleet Street
London EC4A 2AT, ☎020 7430 7430
✉chambers@187fleetstreet.com
Call Date: Nov 1989, Middle Temple
Pupil Supervisor
Qualifications: [LLB (Hons) (Lond)]
terencewoods@187fleetstreet.com

WOODWARD MISS ALISON JANE

Deans Court Chambers
24 St John Street, Manchester M3 4DF, ☎0161 214 6000 ✉clerks@deanscourt.co.uk
Deans Court Chambers
101 Walker Street, Preston PR1 2RR, ☎01772 565 600
✉preston@deanscourt.co.uk
Call Date: Oct 1992, Gray's Inn
Qualifications: [LLB (Sheff)]
✉woodward@deanscourt.co.uk

WOODWARD MR JEREMY PAUL

Pallant Chambers
12 North Pallant, Chichester, West Sussex PO19 1TQ, ☎01243 784538
✉clerks@pallantchambers.co.uk
Call Date: Oct 1996, Inner Temple
Qualifications: [LLB(Hons) (Leics)]

WOODWARD MISS JOANNE CLAIRE

9 St John Street
Manchester M3 4DN, ☎0161 955 9000
✉civilclerks@9sjs.com / criminalclerks@9sjs.com
Call Date: Nov 1989, Gray's Inn
Pupil Supervisor
Qualifications: [LLB (Hons)]

WOODWARD MR JOHN EDWARD

15 Winckley Square
Preston PR1 3JJ, ☎01772 252828
✉clerks@15winckleysq.co.uk
Call Date: Nov 1984, Lincoln's Inn
Qualifications: [LLB]

WOODWARD-CARLTON MR DAMIAN

42 Bedford Row
London WC1R 4LL, ☎020 7831 0222
✉clerks@42br.com
Call Date: Oct 1995, Inner Temple
Pupil Supervisor
Qualifications: [BSc MA (Dunelm) CPE (Lond)]
✉damian.woodward-carlton@42br.com

WOOLF MR ELIOT CHARLES ANTHONY

Outer Temple Chambers
The Outer Temple, 222 Strand, London WC2R 1BA, ☎020 7353 6381
✉clerks@outertemple.com
Call Date: Oct 1993, Inner Temple
Pupil Supervisor
Qualifications: [BA]
✉eliot.woolf@outertemple.com

WOOLF THE HON JEREMY RICHARD GEORGE

Pump Court Tax Chambers
16 Bedford Row, London WC1R 4EF, ☎020 7414 8080 ✉clerks@pumptax.com
Call Date: July 1986, Inner Temple
Pupil Supervisor
Qualifications: [BA (Sussex) LLM (Cantab)]
✉jwoolf@pumptax.com

Types of work: Capital tax, Corporation tax, Employee benefit trusts, Equity, Income tax, National Insurance, Private client, Professional negligence, Stamp duty, Trusts, VAT, Wills

WOOLF MR STEVEN JEREMY

Hardwicke
New Square, Lincoln's Inn, London WC2A 3SB, ☎020 7242 2523
✉enquiries@hardwicke.co.uk
Call Date: July 1989, Inner Temple
Pupil Supervisor
Qualifications: [LLB]
✉steven.woolf@hardwicke.co.uk

WOOLFALL MR RICHARD IAN

Sovereign Chambers
46 Park Place, Leeds LS1 2RY, ☎0113 245 1841
✉clerks@sovereignchambers.co.uk
Call Date: Nov 1992, Middle Temple
Pupil Supervisor, Recorder
Qualifications: [LLB (Hons)(Leics)]
✉richard.woolfall@sovereignchambers.co.uk

WOOLFE MR PHILIP JOHN

Monckton Chambers
1 & 2 Raymond Buildings, Gray's Inn, London WC1R 5NR, ☎020 7405 7211
✉chambers@monckton.com
Call Date: Oct 2004, Lincoln's Inn
Qualifications: [BA (Hons) Cantab BA (Oxon)]
✉pwoolfe@monckton.com

WOOLFENDEN MR IVAN PETER

Atlantic Chambers
4-6 Cook Street, Liverpool L2 9QU, ☎0151 236 4421
✉info@atlanticchambers.co.uk
Call Date: July 1985, Middle Temple
Pupil Supervisor
Qualifications: [BA(Oxon)]
✉ivanwoolfenden@atlanticchambers.co.uk

E

WOOLGAR MR DERMOT GERVASE BECKET

Crown Office Chambers
2 Crown Office Row, Temple, London EC4Y 7HJ, ☎020 7797 8100
✉mail@crownofficechambers.com
Call Date: July 1988, Inner Temple
Pupil Supervisor
Qualifications: [LLB (Manch)]
woolgar@crownofficechambers.com

WOOLHOUSE MR OLIVER DUNCAN CAMPBELL

Cornwall Street Chambers
85-87 Cornwall Street, Birmingham B3 3BY, ☎0121 233 7500
✉clerks@cornwallstreet.co.uk
Call Date: Nov 1996, Inner Temple
Qualifications: [LLB (Leics)]
oliver.woolhouse@cornwallstreet.co.uk

WOOLLEY MR DAVID RORIE QC (1980)

Landmark Chambers
180 Fleet Street, London EC4A 2HG, ☎020 7430 1221
✉clerks@landmarkchambers.co.uk
Call Date: July 1962, Middle Temple
Qualifications: [MA (Cantab)]
dwoolley@landmarkchambers.co.uk

WOOLRICH MISS SARAH

Dere Street Barristers
14 Toft Green, York YO1 6JT, ☎0844 3351551
✉clerks@derestreet.co.uk
York Chambers
Rotterdam House, 116 The Quayside, Newcastle Upon Tyne NE1 3DY, ☎0191 206 4677
Call Date: Nov 1994, Middle Temple
Pupil Supervisor
Qualifications: [LLB]
clerks@yorkchambers.co.uk

WOOSEY MISS ELIZABETH JANE

Linenhall Chambers
1 Stanley Place, Chester CH1 2LU, ☎01244 348282
✉clerks@linenhallchambers.co.uk
Call Date: July 1993, Lincoln's Inn
Pupil Supervisor
Qualifications: [LLB (Hons)]

WORDSWORTH MRS PHILIPPA LINDSEY

Zenith Chambers
10 Park Square, Leeds LS1 2LH, ☎0113 245 5438
✉clerks@zenithchambers.co.uk
Call Date: Oct 1995, Gray's Inn
Qualifications: [LLB (Manch)]
pwordsworth@zenithchambers.co.uk

WORDSWORTH MR SAMUEL SHERRATT

Essex Court Chambers
24 Lincoln's Inn Fields, London WC2A 3EG, ☎020 7813 8000
✉clerksroom@essexcourt.net
Call Date: Nov 1997, Lincoln's Inn
Qualifications: [BA (Hons)]
swordsworth@essexcourt.net

WORLOCK MR SIMON RICHARD

No5 Chambers
Fountain Court, Steelhouse Lane, Birmingham B4 6DR, ☎0845 210 5555 ✉info@no5.com
No5 Chambers
Greenwood House, 4-7 Salisbury Court, London EC4Y 8AA, ☎0845 210 5555
No5 Chambers
38 Queen Square, Bristol BS1 4QS, ☎0845 210 5555
Call Date: July 2001, Middle Temple
swa@no5.com

WORMALD MR RICHARD

3 Raymond Buildings
3 Raymond Buildings, Gray's Inn, London WC1R 5BH, ☎020 7400 6400
✉clerks@3rblaw.com
Call Date: Oct 1993, Gray's Inn
Pupil Supervisor
Qualifications: [BA (York)]
richard.wormald@3raymondbuildings.com

WORMINGTON MR TIMOTHY MICHAEL

Fountain Court Chambers
Fountain Court, Temple, London EC4Y 9DH, ☎020 7583 3335
✉chambers@fountaincourt.co.uk
Call Date: Nov 1977, Middle Temple
Qualifications: [BA FCIArb BCL (Oxon)]
tmw@fountaincourt.co.uk

WORRALL MISS ANNA MAUREEN QC (1989)

Chambers of Mr Ami Feder
Ground Floor, Lamb Building, Temple, London EC4Y 7AS, ☎020 7797 7788
✉clerks@lambbuilding.co.uk
Lamb Building
22 Ship Street, Brighton BN1 1AD,
☎01273 820490
✉admin@lambbuilding.co.uk
Chambers of Mr Ami Feder
Ground Floor, Lamb Building, Temple, London EC4Y 7AS, ☎020 7797 7788
✉clerks@lambbuilding.co.uk
Call Date: Nov 1959, Middle Temple
Recorder
Qualifications: [LLB]
✉clerks@lambbuilding.co.uk

WORRALL MR JOHN RAYMOND GUY

Zenith Chambers
10 Park Square, Leeds LS1 2LH,
☎0113 245 5438
✉clerks@zenithchambers.co.uk
Call Date: July 1984, Gray's Inn
Qualifications: [BA (Hons) LLB (Hons)]
✉jworrall@zenithchambers.co.uk

WORRALL MR PHILIP GEORGE

Kew Chambers
354 Kew Road, Kew, Surrey TW9 3DU,
☎0844 8099991
✉admin@kewchambers.co.uk
Call Date: July 2001, Gray's Inn
Qualifications: [LLB]

WORSLEY MISS CHARLOTTE HELEN GRACE

No.6 Park Square
Leeds LS1 2LW, ☎0113 245 9763
✉Tim@no6.co.uk
Call Date: Oct 2002, Middle Temple
Qualifications: [BA (Cantab) Dip Law]
✉worsley@no6.co.uk

WORSLEY MR MARK INDRA

Guildhall Chambers
23 Broad Street, Bristol BS1 2HG,
☎0117 930 9000
✉hoc@guildhallchambers.co.uk
Call Date: Nov 1994, Inner Temple
Qualifications: [LLB (Hons)(Newc)]
✉mark.worsley@guildhallchambers.co.uk

WORSLEY MR NICHOLAS FREDERICK AVERY

Zenith Chambers
10 Park Square, Leeds LS1 2LH,
☎0113 245 5438
✉clerks@zenithchambers.co.uk
Call Date: Oct 1998, Middle Temple
Pupil Supervisor
Qualifications: [MA (Cantab)]
✉nworsley@zenithchambers.co.uk

WORTHEN MR THOMAS JONATHAN

Pallant Chambers
12 North Pallant, Chichester, West Sussex PO19 1TQ, ☎01243 784538
✉clerks@pallantchambers.co.uk
Call Date: July 2007, Gray's Inn
Qualifications: [BA BCL (Oxon)]
✉tworthen@pallantchambers.co.uk

WORTHINGTON MR STEPHEN QC (2006)

12 King's Bench Walk
12 King's Bench Walk, Temple, London EC4Y 7EL, ☎020 7583 0811
Call Date: Nov 1976, Gray's Inn
Pupil Supervisor, Recorder
Qualifications: [MA (Cantab)]
✉worthington@12kbw.co.uk

WORTHLEY MR ANDREW MARK

Rougemont Chambers
Victory House, Dean Clarke Gardens, Southernhay East, Exeter EX2 4AA,
☎01392 208484
✉clerks@rougemontchambers.co.uk
Call Date: Oct 2004, Lincoln's Inn
Qualifications: [LLB (Hons) (Exon)]
✉aworthley@rougemontchambers.co.uk

WORTON MISS DAWN LOUISE

3 PB Barristers
3 Paper Buildings, Temple, London EC4Y 7EU,
☎020 7583 8055
3 PB Barristers
Royal Talbot House, 2 Victoria Street, Bristol, Avon BS1 6BB, ☎0117 928 1520
3 PB Barristers
4 St Peter Street, Winchester SO23 8BW,
☎01962 868884
✉clerks.winchester@3paper.co.uk
3 PB Barristers
23 Beaumont Street, Oxford OX1 2NP,
☎01865 793 736

E

3 PB Barristers
30 Christchurch Road, Bournemouth, Dorset BH1 3PD, ☎01202 292102
✉clerks.bournemouth@3paper.co.uk
Call Date: Oct 2000, Inner Temple
Pupil Supervisor
Qualifications: [LLB (Dunelm)]
louise.worton@3paper.co.uk

WRACK MR ROBERT NICHOLAS

Tooks Chambers
81 Farringdon Street, London EC4A 4BL, ☎020 7842 7575 ✉clerks@tooks.co.uk
Call Date: Mar 1997, Inner Temple
Pupil Supervisor
Qualifications: [MA LLB (Cantab)]
nick.wrack@tooks.co.uk

WRAGG MR JONATHAN ROBERT

Highgate Chambers
62A Great North Road, Highgate, London N6 4LT, ☎020 8340 6031
✉enquiries@highgatechambers.co.uk
Call Date: Nov 1995, Gray's Inn
Qualifications: [BMUS (Hull) Dip Law(Lond)]
enquiries@highgatechambers.co.uk

WRAIGHT MR OLIVER ROBERT

Harcourt Chambers
1st Floor, 2 Harcourt Buildings, Temple, London EC4Y 9DB, ☎0844 561 7135
Harcourt Chambers
Churchill House, 3 St Aldate's Courtyard, St Aldate's, Oxford OX1 1BN, ☎0844 561 7135
Call Date: Oct 1998, Middle Temple
Qualifications: [MA (Hons)(Cantab)]
owraight@harcourtchambers.law.co.uk

WRAIGHT MR WILLIAM MARK

2 Temple Gardens
2 Temple Gardens, Temple, London EC4Y 9AY, ☎020 7822 1200
✉clerks@2tg.co.uk
Call Date: July 2009, Lincoln's Inn
Qualifications: [BCH BA BM MA(Oxon) MRCS]
wwraight@2tg.co.uk

WRAITH MR NIGEL PATRICK

Colleton Chambers
Colleton Crescent, Exeter, Devon EX2 4DG, ☎01392 274898
✉clerks@colletonchambers.co.uk
Call Date: July 2004, Middle Temple
Qualifications: [LLB Hons (Exeter)]
nigelwraith@colletonchambers.co.uk

WREN MR ANDREW JOHN

St Mary's Family Law Chambers
26-28 High Pavement, The Lace Market, Nottingham NG1 1HN, ☎0115 950 3503
✉clerks@stmarysflc.co.uk
Call Date: July 2005, Middle Temple
Qualifications: [LLB (Hons)]
andrew.wren@stmarysflc.co.uk

WRENN MISS HELEN MARGARET

Number 7 Harrington Street Chambers
7 Harrington Street, Liverpool L2 9YH, ☎0151 242 0707 ✉clerks@7hs.co.uk
Call Date: Nov 1994, Inner Temple
Qualifications: [BA (Hons)(Leeds) CPE (Wolves)]
helen.wrenn@7hs.co.uk

WRIGHT MISS ABIGAIL MARY BARBARA

Lamb Chambers
Lamb Building, Elm Court, Temple, London EC4Y 7AS, ☎020 7797 8300
✉info@lambchambers.co.uk
Call Date: Oct 2000, Middle Temple
Qualifications: [BA (Hons) (Oxon)]
abigailwright@lambchambers.co.uk

WRIGHT MR ALASTAIR DAVID

St Johns Buildings
24a - 28 St John Street, Manchester M3 4DJ, ☎0161 214 1500
✉clerk@stjohnsbuildings.co.uk
16 Winckley Square
Preston PR1 3JJ, ☎01772 256100
St Johns Buildings Liverpool
8th Floor India Buildings, Water Street, Liverpool L2 0XG, ☎0151 243 6000
✉clerk@stjohnsbuildings.co.uk
Call Date: Oct 1991, Lincoln's Inn
Pupil Supervisor
Qualifications: [MA (Oxon) Dip Law]
alastair.wright@stjohnsbuildings.co.uk

WRIGHT MR ALEXANDER

Argent Chambers
5 Bell Yard, London WC2A 2JR, ☎020 7556 5500
✉briefsin@argentchambers.co.uk
Call Date: Nov 1997, Inner Temple
Qualifications: [LLB (Manch)]
a.wright@argentchambers.co.uk

WRIGHT MR ALEXANDER PAUL

4 Pump Court
4 Pump Court, Temple, London EC4Y 7AN, ☎ 020 7842 5555
✉ chambers@4pumpcourt.com
Call Date: July 2007, Middle Temple
Qualifications: [PGDip in Law (City) MA (Cantab)]
✉ awright@4pumpcourt.com

WRIGHT MR CALEY DENIS ALASTAIR

New Square Chambers
12 New Square, Lincoln's Inn, London WC2A 3SW, ☎ 020 7419 8000
✉ robin.hollington@newsquarechambers.co.uk
Call Date: July 2008, Lincoln's Inn
Qualifications: [BA (Oxon)]
✉ caley.wright@newsquarechambers.co.uk

WRIGHT MR COLIN JOHN

Stone Chambers
4 Field Court, Gray's Inn, London WC1R 5EF, ☎ 020 7440 6900
✉ clerks@stonechambers.com
Call Date: July 1987, Middle Temple
Qualifications: [LLB (Leics)]
✉ colin@wrightcounsel.com

WRIGHT MR FREDERICK GEORGE IAN

Crown Office Chambers
2 Crown Office Row, Temple, London EC4Y 7HJ, ☎ 020 7797 8100
✉ mail@crownofficechambers.com
Call Date: July 1989, Inner Temple
Qualifications: [BSc (Hons) Chartered Engineer DIC MSc]
✉ wright@crownofficechambers.com

WRIGHT MR IAN

Five Paper
Ground Floor, 5 Paper Buildings, Temple, London EC4Y 7HB, ☎ 020 7815 3200
Call Date: Nov 1983, Middle Temple
Pupil Supervisor
Qualifications: [BSc (Dundee) LLB (Leic)]
✉ ianwright@fivepaper.com

WRIGHT MR IAN BERNARD

Iscoed Chambers
86 St Helen's Road, Swansea SA1 4BQ, ☎ 01792 652988
✉ clerks@iscoedchambers.co.uk
Call Date: Nov 1994, Middle Temple
Pupil Supervisor
Qualifications: [LLB (Hons) (Wales)]
✉ iw@iscoedchambers.co.uk

WRIGHT MR JEREMY JOHN

2 King's Bench Walk
2 King's Bench Walk, Temple, London EC4Y 7DE, ☎ 020 7353 1746
✉ clerks@2kbw.com
Call Date: July 1970, Inner Temple
Pupil Supervisor, Recorder
Qualifications: [BA (Oxon)]
✉ jwright@2kbw.com

WRIGHT MR JONATHAN NICHOLAS

Castle Chambers
The Old Fire Station, 90 High Street, Harrow-on-the-Hill, Middlesex HA1 3LP, ☎ 020 8423 6579 ✉ info@castlechambers.net
Kings Chambers
36 Young Street, Manchester M3 3FT, ☎ 0845 034 3444
✉ clerks@kingschambers.com
Call Date: Nov 1997, Middle Temple
Qualifications: [LLB (Hons) BA]

WRIGHT MISS LISA JANINE

4 King's Bench Walk
2nd Floor, 4 King's Bench Walk, Temple, London EC4Y 7DL, ☎ 020 7822 7000
✉ clerks@4kbw.co.uk
Call Date: July 2007, Inner Temple
Qualifications: [LLB (Hons) (Hull)]
✉ ljw@4kbw.co.uk

WRIGHT MR PAUL ANDREW

Number 7 Harrington Street Chambers
7 Harrington Street, Liverpool L2 9YH, ☎ 0151 242 0707 ✉ clerks@7hs.co.uk
Call Date: Oct 2003, Inner Temple
Qualifications: [BA (Manch)]
✉ paul.wright@7hs.co.uk

WRIGHT MR PAUL WAYNE

Brick Court Chambers
7-8 Essex Street, London WC2R 3LD, ☎ 020 7379 3550 ✉ clerks@brickcourt.co.uk
Call Date: Nov 1990, Inner Temple
Qualifications: [LLB (So'ton)]
✉ Paul.Wright@Brickcourt.co.uk

E

WRIGHT MR PETER DUNCAN QC (1999)

2 Hare Court
Lower Ground, Ground, 1st & 2nd Floor, 2 Hare Court, Temple, London EC4Y 7BH, ☎ 020 7353 3982 ✉ clerks@2harecourt.com
Lincoln House Chambers
Tower 12, The Avenue North, Spinningfields, 18-22 Bridge Street, Manchester M3 3BZ, ☎ 0161 832 5701
✉ info@lincolnhousechambers.com
Call Date: July 1981, Inner Temple
Recorder
Qualifications: [LLB (Hull)]
✉ peterwright@2harecourt.com

WRIGHT MR RICHARD JAMES

No.6 Park Square
Leeds LS1 2LW, ☎ 0113 245 9763
✉ Tim@no6.co.uk
Call Date: Oct 1998, Middle Temple
Qualifications: [LLB (Hons)(Leeds)]
✉ wright@no6.co.uk

WRIGHT MISS SARAH CAROLYN

Call Date: Nov 1984, Gray's Inn
Pupil Supervisor
Qualifications: [BA]
✉ wright@paradise-sq.co.uk

WRIGHT MR STUART GRAHAM

Crown Office Row Chambers
119 Church Street, Brighton, Sussex BN1 1UD, ☎ 01273 625625
✉ clerks@1cor.com
Call Date: July 2000, Inner Temple
Pupil Supervisor
Qualifications: [LLB (Hons)]
✉ stuart.wright@1cor.com

WRIGHT MR TREVOR

Maidstone Chambers
33 Earl Street, Maidstone, Kent ME14 1PF, ☎ 01622 688592
✉ clerks@maidstonechambers.co.uk
Call Date: Nov 1992, Middle Temple
Qualifications: [LLB (Hons) (Lond)]

WRIGHT MRS YASMIN TAJDIN

Cobden House Chambers
19 Quay Street, Manchester M3 3HN, ☎ 0161 833 6000 ✉ Clerks@Cobden.co.uk
Call Date: Nov 1990, Inner Temple
Qualifications: [LLB (Hons)]
✉ clerks@cobden.co.uk

WROTTESLEY MISS ANGELA JANE

Bank House Chambers
Old Bank House, Hartshead, Sheffield S1 2EL, ☎ 0114 275 1223
✉ w.digby@bankhousechambers.co.uk
Call Date: Oct 1999, Inner Temple
Pupil Supervisor
Qualifications: [LLB (Leics)]
✉ a.wrottesley@bankhousechambers.co.uk

WYAND MR ROGER NICHOLAS LEWES QC (1997)

Hogarth Chambers
5 New Square, Lincoln's Inn, London WC2A 3RJ, ☎ 020 7404 0404
✉ barristers@hogarthchambers.com
Call Date: May 1973, Middle Temple
Recorder
Qualifications: [MA (Cantab)]
✉ rwyand@hogarthchambers.com

WYATT MR ANTHONY CHRISTOPHER PHILIP

2 Bedford Row
London WC1R 4BU, ☎ 020 7440 8888
✉ clerks@2bedfordrow.co.uk
Call Date: Mar 2002, Middle Temple
Qualifications: [LLB (Hons)]
✉ awyatt@2bedfordrow.co.uk

WYATT MR DERRICK ARTHUR QC (1993)

Brick Court Chambers
7-8 Essex Street, London WC2R 3LD, ☎ 020 7379 3550 ✉ clerks@brickcourt.co.uk
Call Date: July 1972, Lincoln's Inn
Qualifications: [MA JD (USA) LLB (Cantab)]
✉ derrick.wyatt@seh.ox.ac.uk

WYATT MISS HANNAH CAROLINE

5 King's Bench Walk
5 King's Bench Walk, Temple, London EC4Y 7DN, ☎ 020 7353 5638
✉ clerks@5kbw.co.uk
Call Date: July 2008, Middle Temple
Qualifications: [LLB (Hons) (Lancs)]
✉ hannah.wyatt@5kbw.co.uk

WYATT MR MARK

New Street Chambers
2 New Street, Leicester LE1 5NA, ☎ 0116 262 5906 ✉ clerks@2newstreet.co.uk
Call Date: July 1976, Middle Temple
Pupil Supervisor
Qualifications: [MA (Oxon)]

WYETH MR STEPHEN MICHAEL

3 PB Barristers
4 St Peter Street, Winchester SO23 8BW,
☎ 01962 868884
✉ clerks.winchester@3paper.co.uk
3 PB Barristers
23 Beaumont Street, Oxford OX1 2NP,
☎ 01865 793 736
3 PB Barristers
30 Christchurch Road, Bournemouth, Dorset BH1 3PD, ☎ 01202 292102
✉ clerks.bournemouth@3paper.co.uk
3 PB Barristers
Royal Talbot House, 2 Victoria Street, Bristol, Avon BS1 6BB, ☎ 0117 928 1520
3 PB Barristers
3 Paper Buildings, Temple, London EC4Y 7EU,
☎ 020 7583 8055
Call Date: Oct 2010, Inner Temple
Qualifications: [LLB (So'ton)]
✉ stephen.wyeth@3pb.co.uk

WYGAS MR LUKE

4 Pump Court
4 Pump Court, Temple, London EC4Y 7AN,
☎ 020 7842 5555
✉ chambers@4pumpcourt.com
Call Date: Nov 2004, Middle Temple
Qualifications: [BA (Hons) MA Eng (Cantab)]
✉ lwygas@4pumpcourt.com

WYLES MISS LUCY ANNE

2 Temple Gardens
2 Temple Gardens, Temple, London EC4Y 9AY, ☎ 020 7822 1200
✉ clerks@2tg.co.uk
Call Date: Oct 1994, Lincoln's Inn
Qualifications: [MA (Hons) Lic Spec Droit (Belgium)]
✉ lwyles@2tg.co.uk

WYLIE MR NEIL RICHARD

KCH Garden Square
1 Oxford Street, Nottingham NG1 5BH,
☎ 0115 941 8851
✉ clerks@kchgardensquare.co.uk
Call Date: Nov 1996, Gray's Inn
Pupil Supervisor
Qualifications: [LLB (Manch)]
✉ nwylie@kch.co.uk

WYNN MR TOBY

KBW
The Engine House, No 1 Foundry Square, Leeds LS11 5DL, ☎ 0113 297 1200
✉ clerks@kbwchambers.com
Call Date: July 1982, Gray's Inn
Pupil Supervisor, Recorder
Qualifications: [LLB (Lond)]
✉ tw@kbwchambers.com

WYNN MORGAN MISS CATHERINE LOWRI

Angel Chambers
Ethos Building, Kings Road, Swansea SA1 8AS,
☎ 01792 464623
✉ clerks@angelchambers.co.uk
Call Date: Oct 2010, Gray's Inn
Qualifications: [LLB]
✉ lowri.wynnmorgan@angelchambers.co.uk

WYNNE MR ALEXANDER JAMES WARREN

Littleton Chambers
3 King's Bench Walk North, Temple, London EC4Y 7HR, ☎ 020 7797 8600
✉ fschneider@littletonchambers.co.uk
Call Date: July 2002, Middle Temple
Qualifications: [MA (Cantab) LLB (Hons) (Lond) LLM (Lond)]
✉ jwynne@littletonchambers.co.uk

WYNNE MR ANDREW MARK

Call Date: Oct 2001, Lincoln's Inn
Qualifications: [LLB (Hons)(Keele)]
✉ wynne@paradise-sq.co.uk

WYNNE MR ASHLEY JOHN

No5 Chambers
Fountain Court, Steelhouse Lane, Birmingham B4 6DR, ☎ 0845 210 5555 ✉ info@no5.com
No5 Chambers
Greenwood House, 4-7 Salisbury Court, London EC4Y 8AA, ☎ 0845 210 5555
No5 Chambers
38 Queen Square, Bristol BS1 4QS,
☎ 0845 210 5555
Call Date: Nov 1990, Gray's Inn
Qualifications: [LLB (Cardiff)]
✉ aw@no5.com

WYNTER MR COLIN PETER QC (2006)

Devereux Chambers
Queen Elizabeth Building, Temple, London EC4Y 9BS, ☎ 020 7353 7534
✉ clerks@devchambers.co.uk
Call Date: Nov 1984, Inner Temple
Qualifications: [LLB MPhil]
✉ wynter@devchambers.co.uk

E

XYDIAS MR NICHOLAS

No5 Chambers
Fountain Court, Steelhouse Lane, Birmingham B4 6DR, ☎0845 210 5555 ✉info@no5.com
No5 Chambers
Greenwood House, 4-7 Salisbury Court, London EC4Y 8AA, ☎0845 210 5555
No5 Chambers
38 Queen Square, Bristol BS1 4QS, ☎0845 210 5555
Call Date: Oct 1992, Lincoln's Inn
Qualifications: [LLB(Hons)(Lond) LLM(Lond)]
nx@no5.com

YAKUBU MR EMMANUEL MAHAMA

5 Barnsbury Close
5 Barnsbury Close, New Malden, Surrey KT3 5BP, ☎020 8949 7748
✉emyakubu@aol.com
Call Date: July 1970, Middle Temple
Qualifications: [LLB (Lond)]

YANG DR ZIZHEN

Pump Court Tax Chambers
16 Bedford Row, London WC1R 4EF, ☎020 7414 8080 ✉clerks@pumptax.com
Call Date: July 2009, Lincoln's Inn
Qualifications: [BA (Hons) MA (Cantab) PhD]
zyang@pumptax.com

Types of work: Capital tax, Corporation tax, Customs, Excise, Income tax, National Insurance, Private client, Stamp duty, Tax investigations, Tax tribunal, Trusts, VAT

YAP MISS TSE YEENG

Holborn Chambers
6 Gate Street, Lincoln's Inn Fields, London WC2A 3HP, ☎020 7242 6060
Call Date: July 2003, Lincoln's Inn
Qualifications: [LLB Hons (Exon) LLM (Lond)]
clerks@holbornchambers.com

YARROW MISS CHARLOTTE ZAIRE

36 Bedford Row
London WC1R 4JH, ☎020 7421 8000
✉chambers@36bedfordrow.co.uk
Call Date: Oct 1999, Lincoln's Inn
Qualifications: [BA (Hons) Dip in Law]

YASSERI MISS YASMIN

No5 Chambers
Fountain Court, Steelhouse Lane, Birmingham B4 6DR, ☎0845 210 5555 ✉info@no5.com
No5 Chambers
Greenwood House, 4-7 Salisbury Court, London EC4Y 8AA, ☎0845 210 5555
No5 Chambers
38 Queen Square, Bristol BS1 4QS, ☎0845 210 5555
Call Date: July 2005, Inner Temple
Qualifications: [BA St Catharines College University of Cambridge]
yy@no5.com

YATES MR DAVID JAMES FRANCIS

Pump Court Tax Chambers
16 Bedford Row, London WC1R 4EF, ☎020 7414 8080 ✉clerks@pumptax.com
Call Date: July 2004, Lincoln's Inn
Qualifications: [BA PgDI MA (Cantab)]
dyates@pumptax.com

Types of work: Capital tax, Corporation tax, Equity, Income tax, National Insurance, Private client, Professional negligence, Stamp duty, Trusts, VAT, Wills

YATES MISS KATRINA MARJORIE

Landmark Chambers
180 Fleet Street, London EC4A 2HG, ☎020 7430 1221
✉clerks@landmarkchambers.co.uk
Call Date: Oct 2006, Lincoln's Inn
Qualifications: [BA (Oxon) MA (Bris)]
kyates@landmarkchambers.co.uk

YATES MR NICHOLAS GILMORE

1 Hare Court
1 Hare Court, Temple, London EC4Y 7BE, ☎020 7797 7070 ✉clerks@1hc.com
Call Date: Oct 1996, Inner Temple
Pupil Supervisor
Qualifications: [MA (Cantab) CPE (Lond)]
yates@1hc.com

YATES MISS VICTORIA CAROLINE

No5 Chambers
Greenwood House, 4-7 Salisbury Court, London EC4Y 8AA, ☎0845 210 5555
No5 Chambers
38 Queen Square, Bristol BS1 4QS, ☎0845 210 5555
No5 Chambers
Fountain Court, Steelhouse Lane, Birmingham B4 6DR, ☎0845 210 5555 ✉info@no5.com
Call Date: Nov 2006, Middle Temple
Qualifications: [LLB (Hons) (Lond)]
vy@no5.com

YEARWOOD MR JEFFREY RYEBURN

1 Mitre Court Buildings
1 Mitre Court Buildings, Temple, London EC4Y 7BS, ☎ 020 7452 8900
✉ clerks@1mcb.com
Call Date: Nov 1975, Inner Temple
Pupil Supervisor
Qualifications: [BA]
✉ jeffrey.yearwood@1mcb.com

YEATMAN MISS TRUDI ANN

13 King's Bench Walk
13 King's Bench Walk, Temple, London EC4Y 7EN, ☎ 020 7353 7204
✉ clerks@13kbw.co.uk
Call Date: July 2006, Inner Temple
Qualifications: [LLB (Oxford)]
✉ tyeatman@13kbw.co.uk

YEGINSU MR CAN VEDAT

Four New Square
Four New Square, Lincoln's Inn, London WC2A 3RJ, ☎ 020 7822 2000
✉ barristers@4newsquare.com
Call Date: July 2007, Inner Temple
Qualifications: [BA (Oxon) LLB (Lond) LLM]
✉ c.yeginsu@4newsquare.com

YELL MR NICHOLAS ANTHONY

1 Chancery Lane
London WC2A 1LF, ☎ 0845 634 6666
✉ clerks@1chancerylane.com
Call Date: July 1979, Middle Temple
Pupil Supervisor
Qualifications: [LLB (Lond)]

YEO MR COLIN ANTHONY

Renaissance Chambers
5th Floor, Gray's Inn Chambers, Gray's Inn, London WC1R 5JA, ☎ 020 7404 1111
✉ clerks@renaissancechambers.co.uk
Call Date: Mar 2002, Middle Temple
Qualifications: [BA (Hons) (Oxon)]
✉ cy@renaissancechambers.co.uk

YEO MR NICHOLAS

3 Raymond Buildings
3 Raymond Buildings, Gray's Inn, London WC1R 5BH, ☎ 020 7400 6400
✉ clerks@3rblaw.com
Call Date: Nov 1999, Inner Temple
Pupil Supervisor
Qualifications: [Dip Law BSc]

YEO MR NIK

Fountain Court Chambers
Fountain Court, Temple, London EC4Y 9DH, ☎ 020 7583 3335
✉ chambers@fountaincourt.co.uk
Call Date: Nov 2000, Middle Temple
Qualifications: [BA (Hons) LLB (Hons) (Melb) BCL (Oxon)]
✉ nyeo@fountaincourt.co.uk

YEUNG MR STUART ROY

Northampton Chambers
10 Spencer Parade, Northampton NN1 5AQ, ☎ 01604 636271
✉ clerks@northampton-chambers.co.uk
Call Date: Nov 1989, Inner Temple
Pupil Supervisor
Qualifications: [LLB]

YIP MRS AMANDA LOUISE QC (2011)

Exchange Chambers
One Derby Square, Derby Square, Liverpool L2 9XX, ☎ 0151 236 7747
✉ info@exchangechambers.co.uk
Exchange Chambers
7 Ralli Courts, West Riverside, Manchester M3 5FT, ☎ 0161 833 2722
Exchange Chambers
Oxford House, Oxford Row, Leeds LS1 3BE, ☎ 0113 203 1970
✉ spencer@exchangechambers.co.uk
Call Date: Oct 1991, Gray's Inn
Pupil Supervisor
Qualifications: [MA (Cantab)]
✉ yip@exchangechambers.co.uk

YIP MR VINCENT

Chambers of Mr Vincent Yip
4 Westbury Close, Liverpool L17 5BD, ☎ 0151 324 0880 ✉ clerks@vincentyip.co.uk
Call Date: July 1998, Gray's Inn
Qualifications: [BA (Hons) (Leic)]

YONG MISS PEARL ANNE YEN YEN

Renaissance Chambers
5th Floor, Gray's Inn Chambers, Gray's Inn, London WC1R 5JA, ☎ 020 7404 1111
✉ clerks@renaissancechambers.co.uk
Call Date: Nov 1993, Lincoln's Inn
Qualifications: [LLB (Hons)(Lond)]

E

YORKE MR RICHARD SIMEON

Coram Chambers
9-11 Fulwood Place, London WC1V 6HG,
☎ 020 7092 3700
✉ mail@coramchambers.co.uk
Call Date: Oct 2006, Middle Temple
Qualifications: [BA (Hons) (Sheff)]
✉ richardyorke@coramchambers.co.uk

YOULL MISS JOANNA ISABEL

Field Court Chambers
5 Field Court, Gray's Inn, London WC1R 5EF,
☎ 020 7405 6114 ✉ clerks@fieldcourt.co.uk
Call Date: Nov 1989, Gray's Inn
Qualifications: [LLB (Lond)]
✉ joanna.youll@fieldcourt.co.uk

YOUNG MR ANDREW CHARLES ALEXANDER

Seven Bedford Row
7 Bedford Row, London WC1R 4BS,
☎ 020 7242 3555 ✉ clerks@7br.co.uk
Call Date: Nov 2008, Lincoln's Inn
Qualifications: [BA (Oxon) CPE UCU]
✉ ayoung@7br.co.uk

YOUNG MR ANDREW GEORGE

3 Hare Court
3 Hare Court, Temple, London EC4Y 7BJ,
☎ 020 7415 7800 ✉ clerks@3harecourt.com
Call Date: July 1977, Lincoln's Inn
Pupil Supervisor
Qualifications: [BA (Oxon)]
✉ andrewyoung@3harecourt.com

YOUNG MR ANDREW PAUL

Prince Henry's Chambers
2 Tamar House, 12 Tavistock Place, London WC1H 9RD, ☎ 020 7837 1645
✉ d.harris4@btconnect.com
Call Date: Oct 1992, Lincoln's Inn
Pupil Supervisor
Qualifications: [LLB(Hons) BSc]

YOUNG MRS CHRISTINE ANN

Eighteen Carlton Crescent
Rownhams House, Rownhams, Southampton SO16 8LF, ☎ 023 8063 9001
✉ clerks@18carltoncrescent.co.uk
Call Date: Nov 1991, Inner Temple
Qualifications: [LLB (So'ton)]
✉ clerks@18carltoncrescent.co.uk

YOUNG MR CHRISTOPHER JOHN DEANS

No5 Chambers
Fountain Court, Steelhouse Lane, Birmingham B4 6DR, ☎ 0845 210 5555 ✉ info@no5.com
No5 Chambers
Greenwood House, 4-7 Salisbury Court, London EC4Y 8AA, ☎ 0845 210 5555
No5 Chambers
38 Queen Square, Bristol BS1 4QS,
☎ 0845 210 5555
Call Date: Oct 1997, Middle Temple
Qualifications: [BA (Hons)(Leeds) CPE (Lond)]
✉ cy@no5.com

YOUNG MR DAVID ANTHONY

Nine Bedford Row
9 Bedford Row, London WC1R 4AZ,
☎ 020 7489 2727
✉ clerks@9bedfordrow.co.uk
Park Court Chambers
16 Park Place, Leeds LS1 2SJ,
☎ 0113 243 3277
✉ clerks@parkcourtchambers.co.uk
Call Date: July 1986, Middle Temple
Pupil Supervisor
Qualifications: [BA (Hons) LLM (Lond)]
✉ david.young@9bedfordrow.co.uk

YOUNG MISS GUDRUN RACHAEL

2 Hare Court
Lower Ground, Ground, 1st & 2nd Floor, 2 Hare Court, Temple, London EC4Y 7BH,
☎ 020 7353 3982 ✉ clerks@2harecourt.com
Call Date: Mar 2001, Gray's Inn

YOUNG MR LEE TERENCE

Eighteen Carlton Crescent
Rownhams House, Rownhams, Southampton SO16 8LF, ☎ 023 8063 9001
✉ clerks@18carltoncrescent.co.uk
Call Date: Oct 1991, Middle Temple
Pupil Supervisor
Qualifications: [LLB (Hons)]
✉ clerks@18carltoncrescent.co.uk

YOUNG MR MARTIN FORD

9 Stone Buildings
Lincoln's Inn, London WC2A 3NN,
☎ 020 7404 5055
✉ clerks@9stonebuildings.com
Call Date: Nov 1984, Middle Temple
Pupil Supervisor
Qualifications: [LLB LLM (Lond)]
✉ myoung@9stonebuildings.com, myoung@9stonebuildings.com

YOUNG MISS RACHEL

Ropewalk Chambers
24 The Ropewalk, Nottingham NG1 5EF,
☎ 0115 947 2581 ✉ clerks@ropewalk.co.uk
Call Date: Oct 2006, Inner Temple
Qualifications: [LLB (B'ham)]
rachelyoung@ropewalk.co.uk

YOUNG MISS REBECCA LEAH

39 Park Square
Leeds LS1 2NU, ☎ 0113 245 6633
✉ seniorclerk@39parksquarechambers.co.uk
Call Date: Nov 1993, Inner Temple
Qualifications: [LLB]

YOUNG MR SIMON

Kings Chambers
36 Young Street, Manchester M3 3FT,
☎ 0845 034 3444
✉ clerks@kingschambers.com
Kings Chambers
5 Park Square East, Leeds LS1 2NE,
☎ 0845 034 3444
✉ clerks@kingschambers.com
Kings Chambers
Embassy House, 60 Church Street, Birmingham B3 2DJ, ☎ 0845 034 3444
✉ clerks@kingschambers.com
Call Date: Nov 1998, Inner Temple
Qualifications: [MA (Cantab)]
syoung@kingschambers.com

YOUNG MR STUART ANTHONY JOSEPH

Sovereign Chambers
46 Park Place, Leeds LS1 2RY,
☎ 0113 245 1841
✉ clerks@sovereignchambers.co.uk
Call Date: July 2009, Inner Temple
Qualifications: [BA (Wolves)]

YOUNG MR TIMOTHY NICHOLAS QC (1996)

20 Essex Street
London WC2R 3AL, ☎ 020 7842 1200
✉ clerks@20essexst.com
Call Date: July 1977, Gray's Inn
Qualifications: [BA BCL (Oxon)]
clerks@20essexst.com

YOUNG MR WILLIAM KIRKPATRICK MUMFORD

Outer Temple Chambers
The Outer Temple, 222 Strand, London WC2R 1BA, ☎ 020 7353 6381
✉ clerks@outertemple.com
Call Date: Oct 2008, Lincoln's Inn
Qualifications: [BA (Oxon)]

YOUNGER-BANKS MRS BRYNN LEADBITTER

Zenith Chambers
10 Park Square, Leeds LS1 2LH,
☎ 0113 245 5438
✉ clerks@zenithchambers.co.uk
Call Date: Nov 1994, Gray's Inn
Qualifications: [BA (Hons)(Dunelm) Dip Law]
byounger-banks@zenithchambers.co.uk

YOUNIS MISS SAIMA

Queen Elizabeth Building
3rd Floor, Queen Elizabeth Building, Temple, London EC4Y 9BS, ☎ 020 7797 7837
✉ clerks@qeb.co.uk
Call Date: Nov 2008, Inner Temple
Qualifications: [BA (Bris) CPE]
s.younis@qeb.co.uk

YOUSHANI MISS ELAHE

St James's Chambers
68 Quay Street, Manchester M3 3EJ,
☎ 0161 834 7000
✉ clerks@stjameschambers.com
12 King's Bench Walk
12 King's Bench Walk, Temple, London EC4Y 7EL, ☎ 020 7583 0811
Call Date: July 2005, Lincoln's Inn
Qualifications: [LLB (Hons)]
elahe.youshani@stjameschambers.com

YULE MISS STEPHANIE

Trinity Chambers
Highfield House, Moulsham Street, Chelmsford, Essex CM2 9AH,
☎ 01245 605040
✉ clerks@trinitychambers.com
Call Date: Oct 2005, Lincoln's Inn
Qualifications: [LLB (Hons) Essex)]

ZABIHI MISS TANYA

3 PB Barristers
Royal Talbot House, 2 Victoria Street, Bristol, Avon BS1 6BB, ☎ 0117 928 1520
3 PB Barristers
4 St Peter Street, Winchester SO23 8BW,
☎ 01962 868884
✉ clerks.winchester@3paper.co.uk
3 PB Barristers
3 Paper Buildings, Temple, London EC4Y 7EU,
☎ 020 7583 8055
3 PB Barristers
23 Beaumont Street, Oxford OX1 2NP,
☎ 01865 793 736

E

3 PB Barristers
30 Christchurch Road, Bournemouth, Dorset BH1 3PD, ☎01202 292102
✉clerks.bournemouth@3paper.co.uk
Call Date: Nov 1988, Gray's Inn
Qualifications: [LLB (Hons) (Middx)]
Tanya.zabihi@3pb.co.uk

ZACAROLI MR ANTONY JAMES QC (2006)

South Square
3-4 South Square, Gray's Inn, London WC1R 5HP, ☎020 7696 9900
✉practicemanagers@southsquare.com
Call Date: Nov 1987, Middle Temple
Qualifications: [BA BCL (Oxon)]
antonyzacaroli@southsquare.com

ZAFFUTO MISS ROSA

The Chambers Of Ms Rosa Zaffuto
10 Walnut Tree Close, Cheshunt, Hertfordshire EN8 8NH, ☎01992 633474
Lombard Chambers
1 Sekforde Street, Clerkenwell, London EC1R 0BE, ☎020 7107 2100
Call Date: Nov 2001, Middle Temple
Qualifications: [BA (Hons) CPE]

E

ZAHIR MR HOSSEIN

Garden Court Chambers
57-60 Lincoln's Inn Fields, London WC2A 3LJ, ☎020 7993 7600 ✉info@gclaw.co.uk
Call Date: Mar 2005, Middle Temple
Qualifications: [BA (Hons) CPE]
hosseinz@gclaw.co.uk

ZAMAN MR MOHAMMED KHALIL QC (2009)

St Philips Chambers
55 Temple Row, Birmingham B2 5LS, ☎0121 246 7000 ✉clerks@st-philips.com
Hardwicke
New Square, Lincoln's Inn, London WC2A 3SB, ☎020 7242 2523
✉enquiries@hardwicke.co.uk
Call Date: Nov 1985, Gray's Inn
Qualifications: [LLB (Warw)]
mzaman@st-philips.co.uk

ZAMAN MISS SHAZMA NAZ

37 Park Square Chambers
37 Park Square, Leeds LS1 2NY, ☎0113 243 9422 ✉chambers@no37.co.uk
Call Date: Nov 2003, Middle Temple
Qualifications: [LLB (Hons) (Leic)]
chambers@no37.co.uk

ZEITLER MISS BARBARA

3 Dr Johnson's Buildings
Ground Floor, 3 Dr Johnson's Buildings, Temple, London EC4Y 7BA, ☎020 7353 4854
✉clerks@3djb.co.uk
Call Date: Nov 2001, Lincoln's Inn
Qualifications: [BA (Hons) PhD]
BZeitler@3DJB.co.uk

ZEITLIN MR DEREK JAMES

Nine Bedford Row
9 Bedford Row, London WC1R 4AZ, ☎020 7489 2727
✉clerks@9bedfordrow.co.uk
Call Date: July 1974, Lincoln's Inn
Pupil Supervisor
Qualifications: [BSc]
derek.zeitlin@9bedfordrow.co.uk

ZELIN MR GEOFFREY ANDREW

Enterprise Chambers
9 Old Square, Lincoln's Inn, London WC2A 3SR, ☎020 7405 9471
✉london@enterprisechambers.com
Enterprise Chambers
65 Quayside, Newcastle Upon Tyne NE1 3DE, ☎0191 222 3344
✉newcastle@enterprisechambers.com
Enterprise Chambers
43 Park Square, Leeds LS1 2NP, ☎0113 246 0391
✉leeds@enterprisechambers.com
Call Date: July 1984, Middle Temple
Pupil Supervisor
Qualifications: [MA (Cantab)]
geoffreyzelin@enterprisechambers.com

Types of work: Banking, Chancery (general), Chancery (land law), Commercial property, Company, commercial and competition, Insolvency, Landlord and tenant, Partnerships, Personal insolvency, Professional negligence

ZELLICK MR ADAM DAVID RUSSELL

Fountain Court Chambers
Fountain Court, Temple, London EC4Y 9DH, ☎020 7583 3335
✉chambers@fountaincourt.co.uk
Call Date: Oct 2000, Middle Temple
Pupil Supervisor
Qualifications: [MA (Hons) (Cantab)]
az@fountaincourt.co.uk

ZENTAR DR REMY PAUL

Call Date: July 1997, Gray's Inn
Qualifications: [LLB LLM PhD (Manc)]
clerk@stjohnsbuildings.co.uk

ZENTLER-MUNRO MS RUTH DEVICA

15 New Bridge Street
London EC4V 6AU, ☎ 020 7842 1900
✉ clerks@15nbs.com
Call Date: Nov 2004, Inner Temple
Qualifications: [LLB (Durham) University of Durham LLM (International Law) University of Bris]
✉ ruth.zentlermunro@15nbs.com

ZIMBLER MISS ALEXIA

Maidstone Chambers
33 Earl Street, Maidstone, Kent ME14 1PF,
☎ 01622 688592
✉ clerks@maidstonechambers.co.uk
Call Date: Oct 1993, Lincoln's Inn
Pupil Supervisor
Qualifications: [BSc (Hons)(Lond) Dip Law (CPE) MA]
✉ azimbler@maidstonechambers.co.uk

ZOEST MS JACQUELINE AMY

Carmelite Chambers
9 Carmelite Street, London EC4Y 0DR,
☎ 020 7936 6300
✉ clerks@carmelitechambers.co.uk
Call Date: Oct 1995, Gray's Inn
Qualifications: [B.Sc]

ZORBAS MR PANAYLOTIS CHRISTOPHOROU

Argent Chambers
5 Bell Yard, London WC2A 2JR,
☎ 020 7556 5500
✉ briefsin@argentchambers.co.uk
Call Date: June 1964, Lincoln's Inn
Pupil Supervisor
✉ briefsin@argentchambers.co.uk, pz@argentchambers.co.uk

ZURAWEL MR BENJAMIN DAVID

The Chambers of Grahame Aldous QC
9 Gough Square, London EC4A 3DG,
☎ 020 7832 0500
✉ clerks@9goughsquare.co.uk
Call Date: July 2010, Inner Temple
Qualifications: [MA MPhil (Oxon) CPE]
✉ bzurawel@9goughsquare.co.uk

ZWART MR AUBERON CHRISTIAAN CONRAD

39 Essex Street
London WC2R 3AT, ☎ 020 7832 1111
✉ clerks@39essex.com
82 King Street
Manchester M2 4WQ, ☎ 0161 870 9969
Call Date: Oct 1997, Inner Temple
Qualifications: [BA BArch (Newc)]
✉ christiaan.zwart@39essex.com

PART F

Individual Barristers in Employment

This section lists those barristers who are in employment. Barristers are listed alphabetically by surname, and details include their date of call to the Bar, their Inn of Court and academic qualifications along with details of their position of employment with a full address.

ABBOTT MR STEPHEN GEORGE

Deputy Justices' Clerk, Director of Legal Services, Hmcs West Midlands, Birmingham Magistrates Court, Victoria Law Courts, Corporation Street, Birmingham, Midlands, B4 6QA, ☎0121 212 6611 Fax: 0121 212 6624, ✉stephen.abbott@hmcourts-service.gsi.gov.uk, *Call Date: July 1983, Inner Temple*
Qualifications: [LLB (Sheff) MA]

ABEYSEKERA MS SAMANTHA

Senior Legal Counsel, The Northern Trust Company, Legal Department, 50 South Lasalle Street, M-9 Chicago, Illinois, 60675, USA, ☎(312) 444-3308 Fax: (312) 444 -4675, ✉sa65@ntrs.com, *Call Date: Oct 1998, Middle Temple*
Qualifications: [LLB (Hons)(Dunelm) ALAM ASI]

ABRAHAM MISS SIRAH MARIE

5 Parkside, Epping, Essex, CM16 6SS, *Call Date: Mar 2001, Lincoln's Inn*
Qualifications: [LLB (Hons)]

ABRAHAMS MR DARREN

Steptoe and Johnson LLP, Avenue Louise 240, Box 5, 1050 Brussels, Belgium, ☎00 32 2626 0500 Fax: 00 32 2626 0510, ✉dabrahams@steptoe.com, *Call Date: July 1999, Lincoln's Inn*
Qualifications: [LLB (Hons) LLM]

ABRAHAMS MR DAVID ROBERT DUDLEY

The Bar Standards Board, 289-293 High Holborn, London, WC1V 7HZ, *Call Date: Oct 1998, Middle Temple*
Qualifications: [BA (Hons)(Cantab) CPE]

ABRAMS MR NEILL

Director of Legal Services, Ocado Group PLC, Titan Court, Ground Floor, 3 Bishop Square, Hatfield Business Park, Hatfield, AL10 9NE, ☎01707 22 7899 Fax: 01707 22 7997, ✉Neill.Abrams@ocado.com, *Call Date: Oct 1998, Inner Temple*
Qualifications: [BA (South Africa) LLB (South Africa) LLM (Cantab)]

ADAIR CAPTAIN CHRISTOPHER DOUGLAS

Directorate of Army Legal Services, Idl426, Ramillies Building, Marlborough Lines, Monxton Road, Andover, SP11 8HJ, Fax: 01264 381 905, ✉spa-team1b-so3(c)@mod.uk, LF-DALS-Group@mod.uk, *Call Date: July 2010, Gray's Inn*
Qualifications: [LLB]

ADAM MRS AMINA ALI

Associate, Pillsbury Winthrop Shaw Pittman, Tower 42, Level 23, 25 Old Broad Street, London, EC2N 1HQ, ☎020 7067 8573, ✉amina.adam@pillsburylaw.com, *Call Date: Nov 1996, Gray's Inn*
Qualifications: [LLB (Thames) LLM (Lond)]

ADAM MR JOHN

Shearman & Sterling LLP, 114 Avenue Des Champs-Elysées, Paris, France, ☎1 53 897000 Fax: 1 53 897070, ✉john.adam@shearman.com, *Call Date: July 2001, Inner Temple*
Qualifications: [LLB (Lond) Licenciatura en Derecho (Seville)]

ADAM MR MICHAEL WILLIAM

Senior Legal Officer, Department For Work and Pensions, 5th Floor, the Adelphi, 1-11 John Adam Street, London, WC2N 6HT, ✉michael.adam@dwp.gsi.gov.uk, *Call Date: Oct 1990, Middle Temple*
Qualifications: [BA (Lond) Dip Law (City)]

ADAMS MR JAMES DAVID SETON

Company Secretary, General Counsel, H R Owen PLC, Melton Court, Old Brompton Road, London, SW7 3TD, ☎020 7245 1123, *Call Date: July 1989, Middle Temple*
Qualifications: [MA (Oxon)]

ADAMS MISS KIM ROSALIND

The London Borough of Havering, Havering Town Hall, Main Road, Romford, Essex, RM1 3BD, ☎01708 432449 Fax: 01708 432482, *Call Date: Oct 1998, Inner Temple*
Qualifications: [LLB (Middx)]

ADAMS MR RICHARD IAIN

Grayson Willis Bennett Solicitors, 7 North Church Street, Sheffield, S1 1TD, ☎0114 290 9500 Fax: 0114 290 9501, ✉radams@gwbsol.co.uk, *Call Date: Nov 2006, Gray's Inn*
Qualifications: [LLB]

F

ADATIA MR KAMAL

Leicester City Council, New Walk Centre, Welford Place, Leicester, Leicestershire, LE1 6ZG, ☎0116 252 7044, ✉kamal.adatia@leicester.gov.uk, *Call Date: Nov 1995, Gray's Inn*
Qualifications: [LLB (B'ham)]

ADDISON MISS FIONA ROSALINDA

Call Date: July 1993, Inner Temple
Qualifications: [BSc (Econ) MA LLM]

ADEBOWALE MR ADEBUSOYE MICHAEL

Crown Prosecution Service, Holborn Police Station, 10 Lambs Conduit Street, Islington, London, WC1N 3NR, ☎020 3300 2200 Fax: 020 3300 2290, *Call Date: Nov 1999, Lincoln's Inn*
Qualifications: [LLB (Hons)(Leics)]

ADLINGTON MR NICHOLAS DAVID

Crown Advocate, Crown Prosecution Service, Citadel House, 58 High Street, Hull, Humberside, HU1 1QD, *Call Date: July 1988, Inner Temple*
Qualifications: [LLB (Hons)]

ADUTT MR JAMES IAN

Other, Department For Work and Pensions, Caxton House, Tothill Street, London, SW1H 9NA, *Call Date: Oct 1992, Lincoln's Inn*
Qualifications: [MA (Cantab)]

AFZAL MS SAFIRA NAZLI

Senior Crown Prosecutor, Crown Prosecution Service, Bishopsgate Police Station, 182 Bishopgate, Bishopsgate, London, EC2M 4NP, *Call Date: Oct 1998, Middle Temple*
Qualifications: [LLB (Hons)(Lond) LLM (Lond)]

AGBAMU MR ALEXANDER ONAKOMEME

Crown Prosecution Service, Snaresbrook Crown Court, 75 Hollybush Hill, Snaresbrook, London, E11 1QW, ✉alex.agbamu@cps.gsi.gov.uk, *Call Date: Nov 1988, Lincoln's Inn*
Qualifications: [LLB (Hons) (B'ham)]

AGUTU MR SOLOMON OCHAYE

HED, London Borough of Croydon, Taberner House, Park Lane, Croydon, CR9 3JS, ☎020 8726 26920, ✉Solomon.Agutu@croydon.gov.uk, *Call Date: July 1980, Inner Temple*
Qualifications: [LLB (So'ton) LLM (Lond)]

AHLUWALIA MISS SMRITI

The Swatch Group Ltd, Seevorstadt 6, Ch-2501 Biel, Switzerland, ☎00 41 32 343 6829 Fax: 00 41 32 343 6923, ✉Smriti.Ahluwalia@swatchgroup.com, *Call Date: Nov 2001, Middle Temple*
Qualifications: [LLB (Hons)]

AHMAD MR NADEEM

Call Date: Oct 1996, Gray's Inn
Qualifications: [BA (Hons)(Lond) Dip Law (Lond)]

AHMADI MISS HANNAH

Hugh James Solicitors, Hodge House, 114 -116 St Mary Street, Cardiff, CF10 1DY, Fax: 029 2038 8222, *Call Date: July 2009, Gray's Inn*
Qualifications: [LLB]

AHMED MS RACHAEL AMAYA

The Treasury Solicitors, 5th Floor, One Kemble Street, London, WC2B 4TS, *Call Date: Oct 1995, Inner Temple*
Qualifications: [LLB (Lond)]

AHMED MRS SHAHNAZ

Crown Prosecution Service, Southern House, Wellesley Grove, Croydon, Surrey, CR9 1DY, ✉shahnaz.ahmed@cps.gsi.gov.uk, *Call Date: Feb 1994, Gray's Inn*
Qualifications: [LLB (Bucks)]

AHMED MR SHARAZ HUSSNAIN

Manager, Landmark Legal LLP, Second Floor, 380-384 Harrow Road, London, W9 2HU, Fax: 020 7239 3084, ✉info@landmarklegal.net, *Call Date: Nov 2000, Lincoln's Inn*
Qualifications: [LLB (Hons)]

AHUJA MR RAJU NEIL

Senior Crown Prosecutor, Crown Prosecution Service, Building 3, Etruria Valley Office Village, Etruria, Stoke-On-Trent, Staffordshire, ST1 5RU, ☎01782 664500 / 01782 664500, ✉neil.ahuja@cps.gsi.gov.uk, *Call Date: Nov 1990, Inner Temple*
Qualifications: [LLB]

AINSLIE MRS ROSEMARY CAROLINE PATRICIA

Advocate, Senior Crown Prosecutor, Crown Prosecution Service, United House, Piccadilly, York, North Yorkshire, YO1 9PQ, ☎01904 545513, ✉Rosemary.Ainslie@cps.gsi.gov.uk, *Call Date: Nov 1990, Middle Temple*
Qualifications: [BA (Belfast) BL (Belfast)]

AIREY MR SIMON ANDREW

Dla Piper Uk LLP, 3 Noble Street, London, EC2V 7EE, ☎020 7153 7281
Fax: 020 7796 6839, ✉simon.airey@dlapiper.com, *Call Date: Nov 1989, Inner Temple*
Qualifications: [LLB (Sheff)]

AJOH MR ANTHONY AFAMEFUNE

Associate, Davis Langdon LLP, Midcity Place, 71 High Holborn, London, WC1V 6QS, ☎020 70617000 Fax: 0870 048 0965, ✉afam.ajoh@davislangdon.com, *Call Date: Feb 1994, Gray's Inn*
Qualifications: [Btech (Hons) MSc (Reading) LLB (Lond) MRICS MCIOB]

AJOSE MS OLADUNNI AYODELE

General Counsel, HED, Forensic Science Service Ltd, Trident Court, 2920 Solihull Parkway, Birmingham Business Park, Birmingham, B37 7YN, ☎0121 329 4377
Fax: 0121 329 8408, ✉Ayo.Ajose@fss.pnn.police.uk, *Call Date: Nov 1988, Middle Temple*
Qualifications: [LLB MBA MCIM Dip M]

AKHTAR MISS JABEEN

Gqs Solicitors, 288 Baldwins Lane, Hall Green, Birmingham, B28 0XB, ☎0121 733 7070 Fax: 0121 733 7071, ✉office@gqs.solicitors.co.uk, *Call Date: Nov 1999, Gray's Inn*
Qualifications: [LLB]

ALABI MR BABATUNDE OMOTOSO

Advocate, Crown Prosecution Service, Snaresbrook Crown Court, 75 Hollybush Hill, Snaresbrook, London, E11 1QW, ☎020 8929 3023 Fax: 020 8929 3031, ✉babatunde.alabi@csp.gsi.gov.uk, *Call Date: Oct 1992, Lincoln's Inn*
Qualifications: [LLB(Hons) LLM(Lond)]

ALDERMAN MR RICHARD JOHN

Serious Fraud Office, Elm House, 10-16 Elm Street, London, WC1X 0BJ, ☎020 7239 7101, ✉Andrea.Johnson@SFO.GSI.GOV.UK, *Call Date: June 1974, Gray's Inn*
Qualifications: [LLB (Lond)]

ALEXANDER MR ROBERT DOMINIC

HM Revenue and Customs, 1st Floor, South West Wing, Bush House, Strand, London, WC2B 4RD, ☎020 7438 8258
Fax: 020 7438 6219, ✉dominic.alexander@hmrc.gsi.gov.uk, *Call Date: Nov 1995, Middle Temple*
Qualifications: [BA (Hons)(Bris)]

ALFORD MR STUART ROBERT

Prosecutor, Serious Fraud Office, Elm House, 10-16 Elm Street, London, WC1X 0BJ, *Call Date: Oct 1992, Middle Temple*
Qualifications: [BSc (Hons) (Reading)]

ALI MR JAHANGIR HUSSNAIN

Crown Prosecution Service, 4/7 Prebendal Court, Oxford Road, Aylesbury, Buckinghamshire, HP19 8EY, *Call Date: Mar 2001, Lincoln's Inn*
Qualifications: [LLB (Hons)]

AL-KHOEE MS FATIMA

Buckinghamshire County Council, County Hall, Walton Street, Aylesbury, Buckinghamshire, HP20 1UA, ☎01296 383644 Fax: 01296 382538, ✉legal@bucuscc.gov.uk, *Call Date: July 2009, Lincoln's Inn*
Qualifications: [LLB (Lond) LLM (Lond)]

ALLAN MR ROBERT JOHN

Deputy Justices' Clerk, Willesden Magistrates Court, 448 High Road, Willesden, London, NW10 2DZ, ☎020 8955 0650
Fax: 020 8955 0599, *Call Date: July 1980, Lincoln's Inn*
Qualifications: [BA (Hons)]

F

ALLEN MR CHARLES LAUGHARNE

Lawyer, The Treasury Solicitors, Treasury Solicitor's Department, One Kemble Street, London, WC2B 4TS, ☎020 7238 0511 Fax: 020 7 238 6242, ✉charles.allen@defra.gsi.gov.uk, *Call Date: July 1983, Middle Temple*
Qualifications: [MA (Cantab)]

ALLEN MR CHRISTIAN DARREL

Bemobile Limited, Level 2, Bemobile Building, Section 38, Lot 2 Waigani Drive, Po Box 1055, Waigani, Ncd, Papua New Guinea, ☎00 675 764 00084 Fax: 00 675 325 9428, ✉chris.allen@bemobile.com.pg, *Call Date: Nov 1992, Inner Temple*
Qualifications: [LLB (Lancs) LLM (Nott'm)]

ALLEN MR CHRISTOPHER JOHN

Legal Adviser, Barclays Capital, 5 The North Colonnade, London, E14 4BB, ✉chris.allen@barcap.com, *Call Date: July 1998, Middle Temple*
Qualifications: [MA (Hons)(Oxon) Dip Law]

ALLEN MR DREW MARK

General Healthcare Group Ltd, 4 Thameside Centre, Kew Bridge Road, Brentford, Middlesex, TW8 0HF, ☎020 7009 4527 Fax: 020 7009 4522, ✉drew.allen@ghg.co.uk, *Call Date: Oct 2002, Lincoln's Inn*
Qualifications: [LLB]

ALLEN MISS JADE ALEXANDRA

The Treasury Solicitors, One Kemble Street, London, WC2B 4TS, ☎020 7210 3003, *Call Date: July 2005, Lincoln's Inn*
Qualifications: [BA (Hons) MA]

ALLEN MR MARK EDWARD

Director, Doosan Power Systems Ltd, Manor Royal Business Quarter, Crawley, West Sussex, RH10 9AD, ✉Mark.Allen@doosan.com, *Call Date: Nov 1999, Middle Temple*
Qualifications: [MSc (Newc)]

ALLEN MR NEIL EDWARD

Senior Lawyer, Wokingham Borough Council, Legal Services, Shute End, Wokingham, Berkshire, RG40 1WH, Fax: 0118 974 6542, ✉neil.allen@wokingham.gov.uk, *Call Date: Feb 1993, Inner Temple*
Qualifications: [LLB (Reading)]

F

ALLEN MR STUART HARRY

Crown Prosecution Service, Gemini One, Oxford Business Park South, Garsington Road, Oxford, Oxfordshire, OX4 2LL, Fax: 01865 233401, ✉stuart.allen@cps.gsi.gov.uk, *Call Date: July 2008, Middle Temple*
Qualifications: [MA MSt (Oxon) MA (Hons) (Oxon)]

ALLMAN MR JOSEPH MICHAEL

Crown Prosecution Service, Sunlight House, Quay Street, Manchester, M60 3PS, *Call Date: Nov 2006, Inner Temple*
Qualifications: [BA (Manc)]

ALLMAN MISS KIRSTY ELIZABETH

Crown Prosecution Service, Froomsgate House, Rupert Street, Bristol, BS1 2QJ, ☎0117 930 2800, *Call Date: July 2005, Inner Temple*
Qualifications: [LLB University of Durham]

ALLSOP MR ALEXANDER NIGEL MARK

Crown Prosecution Service, Argal House, Peninsula Business Park, Rydon Lane, Exeter, Devon, EX2 7NT, *Call Date: Oct 1997, Middle Temple*
Qualifications: [LLB (Reading)]

ALMEYDA MISS GENEVIEVE MARGARET MARY

Mediator, Crown Prosecution Service, Bishopsgate Police Station, 182 Bishopgate, Bishopsgate, London, EC2M 4NP, ☎020 3300 1509, ✉genevieve.almeyda@cps.gsi.gov.uk, *Call Date: Nov 1994, Inner Temple*
Qualifications: [LLB (Hons)(Lond) LLM]

AL-MUGHEIRY MR SATTAM

Crown Prosecution Service, Justinian House, Spitfire Close, Ermine Business Park, Huntingdon, Cambridgeshire, PE29 6XY, *Call Date: Oct 2005, Middle Temple*
Qualifications: [BA (Hons) (Cantab) MA (Hons) (Cantab)]

AL-YUNUSI MR ABDULLAH MUHAMMAD

Partner, MPR Solicitors LLP, 8 Red Lion Court, Alexandra Road, Hounslow, Middlesex, TW3 1JS, ☎020 8607 4660 Fax: 020 8607 4661, ✉seema@mprsolicitors.co.uk, *Call Date: Nov 1994, Inner Temple*
Qualifications: [BSc (Wales) CPE (Wolves)]

AMAEE DR ROBERT FARZIN

Covington and Burling LLP, 265 Strand, London, WC2R 1BH, ☎020 7067 2217 Fax: 020 7067 2222, *Call Date: Nov 2005, Lincoln's Inn*
Qualifications: [Phd (B'ham)]

AMAH MR STANLEY CHIKANENE

Senior Crown Prosecutor, Crown Prosecution Service, Eagle House, Ram Passage, Kingston Upon Thames, Surrey, KT1 1HH, ✉stanley.amah@cps.gsi.gov.uk, *Call Date: July 1991, Gray's Inn*
Qualifications: [BA (Nigeria) LLB (Lond)]

AMARATUNGA MRS PRAVEEN DHARSHINI

Financial Services Authority, 25 North Colonnade, Canary Wharf, London, E14 5HS, *Call Date: Oct 1995, Gray's Inn*
Qualifications: [BA (Hons) LLM Dip Int Law]

AMATINO MISS NICOLETTA

Crown Advocate, Crown Prosecution Service, Sunlight House, Quay Street, Manchester, M60 3PS, ✉nicoletta.amatino@cps.gsi.gov.uk, *Call Date: Nov 2004, Lincoln's Inn*
Qualifications: [LLB (Hons) (Sheff)]

AMES MRS TRACEY AMANDA

Crown Prosecution Service, Sunlight House, Quay Street, Manchester, M60 3PS, ✉Tracey.Ames@cps.gsi.gov.uk, *Call Date: Nov 1987, Inner Temple*
Qualifications: [LLB (Essex)]

AMIDE MR NAUSHAD CASSAM

Arora Lodhi Heath Solicitors, 170 High Street, Acton, London, W3 6QZ, ☎020 8993 9995 Fax: 020 8992 2628, ✉alh@lawyer.com, *Call Date: Nov 2003, Gray's Inn*
Qualifications: [LLB (Lond)]

AMIN MISS SAIQA

Office of the Immigration Services Commissioner, 5th Floor, Counting House, 53 Tooley Street, London, SE1 2QN, *Call Date: Nov 1991, Inner Temple*
Qualifications: [LLB (Hons) LLM]

AMIRFAZLI MISS FARINAZ

Senior Crown Prosecutor, Crown Prosecution Service, Country House, 100 New London Road, Chelmsford, Essex, CM2 0RG, *Call Date: Nov 1991, Lincoln's Inn*
Qualifications: [LLB (Hons)]

ANASTASIOU MR ANDROS

Stuart Miller and Co, 247 High Road, Wood Green, London, N22 4HF, ☎020 8888 5225 Fax: 020 8889 5871, ✉andy@stuartmillersolicitors.co.uk, *Call Date: Oct 2000, Lincoln's Inn*
Qualifications: [LLB (Hons) (Lond)]

ANDALL MR HOGARTH CHRISTOPHER

HED, Sony Computer Entertainment Europe Ltd, 10 Great Marlborough Street, London, W1F 7LP, ✉Hogarth_Andall@scee.net, *Call Date: Oct 1993, Lincoln's Inn*
Qualifications: [BA (Hons)(Oxon) LLM]

ANDERSON MR ASA

Northumbria Police Legal Department, 4th Floor, Cobalt Business Exchange, Cobalt Business Park, Cobalt Way, Newcastle Upon Tyne, NE28 9NZ, ☎01661 868 034 Fax: 01661 868 038, ✉asa.anderson.5545@northumbria.pnn.police.uk, *Call Date: July 1998, Middle Temple*
Qualifications: [LLB (Hons)(N'castle)]

ANDERSON MR CHARLES SAMUEL

Clintons Solicitors, 55 Drury Lane, London, WC2B 5RZ, ☎020 7395 8380, *Call Date: Oct 2003, Lincoln's Inn*
Qualifications: [BSc (Hons) (Lond)]

ANDERSON MR DAVID CORMACK

HM Revenue and Customs, 2nd Floor North Spur, South West Bush House, London, WC2B 4RD, ☎020 7428 6451 Fax: 020 7438 7367, ✉david.anderson3@hmrc.gsi.gov.uk, *Call Date: Oct 2005, Lincoln's Inn*
Qualifications: [LLB MSc]

ANDERSON MR IAN GEORGE

Head of Legal Services, Hull City Council, Hull City Council, Guildhall, Hull, HU1 2AA, *Call Date: July 1984, Gray's Inn*
Qualifications: [B Soc Sc MBA]

F

ANDRE MR JEAN-FRANCOIS CHARLES

Department For Transport, Zone 2/19, Great Minster House, 76 Marsham Street, London, SW1P 4DR, ☎020 7944 8662, ✉jean-francois.andre@dft.gsi.gov.uk, *Call Date: July 2001, Inner Temple*
Qualifications: [LLB (Kent)]

ANDREWS MISS GILLIAN MARGARET

Clerk, Hmcs Thames Valley, Her Majesty's Court Service Thames Valley, Reading Magistrates' Court, Civic Centre, Reading, Berkshire, RG1 7TQ, ☎01189 801 828
Fax: 01189 801 872, ✉gill.andrews@hmcourts-service.gsi.gov.uk, *Call Date: Nov 1987, Gray's Inn*
Qualifications: [DMS]

ANJOMSHOAA MS POUPAK

White & Case LLP, 5 Old Broad Street, London, EC2N 1DW, ☎020 7532 1000
Fax: 020 7532 1001, *Call Date: Oct 1996, Middle Temple*
Qualifications: [LLB (Hons)(Lond)]

ANSARI MR ASKAR HUMAYUN

Senior Lawyer, HM Revenue and Customs, Personal Tax & Nics, Room 2/C16, 100 Parliament Street, London, SW1A 2BQ, ☎020 7147 0155, *Call Date: July 1973, Middle Temple*
Qualifications: [BA (Hons)]

ANSARI MR SELMAN

Bates Wells and Braithwaite, Scandinavian House, 2-6 Cannon Street, London, EC4M 6YH, *Call Date: Oct 1997, Lincoln's Inn*
Qualifications: [BA (Hons) (LSE)]

ANSON MRS SHEKINAH ADEBISI

Other, Crown Prosecution Service, Southern House, Wellesley Grove, Croydon, CR9 1DY, *Call Date: Nov 1994, Lincoln's Inn*
Qualifications: [LLB (Hons)]

ANTONELLI MS EMMA VICTORIA JANE

Senior Crown Prosecutor, Crown Prosecution Service, Harrow Police Station, 74 Northolt Road, Harrow, Middlesex, HA2 0DN, ☎020 3300 3000, ✉Emma.Antonelli@cps.gsi.gov.uk, *Call Date: Oct 2002, Middle Temple*
Qualifications: [BA (Manch) CPE PG Dip Law]

ANWAR MR MOHAMMED AFZAL

David Phillips & Partners, 202 Stanley Road, Bootle, Merseyside, L20 3EP,
Fax: 0151 922 8298, *Call Date: Oct 2001, Lincoln's Inn*
Qualifications: [LLB (Hons) BA]

APPADOO MISS DANISTA

Gloucestershire County Council, Quayside House, Quay Street, Goucester, GL1 2TZ, ☎01452 426914, *Call Date: July 1996, Gray's Inn*
Qualifications: [BA (Hons) Dip Law]

APTED MR STEPHEN PHILIP

Manager, Crown Prosecution Service, Kingston Crown Court, Penrhyn Road, Kingston, Surrey, KT1 2BB, ☎020 8240 2678
Fax: 020 8240 2574, *Call Date: Oct 1995, Gray's Inn*
Qualifications: [LLB]

ARMSTRONG MR MARTIN ROBERT

Company Secretary, Legal Director, Philips Electronics Uk Limited, Philips Centre, Guildford Business Park, Guildford, Surrey, GU2 8XH, ☎01483 298621, ✉martin.armstrong@philips.com, *Call Date: July 1979, Inner Temple*
Qualifications: [BA (Cantab)]

ARNOLD MR PIERS JOHN

Crown Prosecution Service, Rose Court, 2 Southwark Bridge, London, SE1 9HS, ☎020 3 357 0705 Fax: 020 3 357 0723, ✉Piers.Arnold@cps.gsi.gov.uk, *Call Date: Nov 1992, Inner Temple*
Qualifications: [BA (Oxon) Dip Law MA (Oxon)]

ARON MR TIMOTHY EDWARD

Associate, Norton Rose LLP, 3 More London Riverside, London, SE1 2AQ, *Call Date: Oct 2004, Inner Temple*
Qualifications: [BA MA DIP LAW]

ARTHUR MR ROBIN ANTHONY

Managing Director, Parmentier Arthur Group Limited, 7 The Waits, St Ives, Cambridgeshire, PE27 5BY, ☎01480 465522
Fax: 01480 461221, *Call Date: Nov 1976, Gray's Inn*
Qualifications: [LLB (Lond)]

F

ASAD MISS SABEENA

Nursing and Midwifery Council, Legal Team, 23 Portland Place, London, W1B 1PZ, *Call Date: July 1989, Middle Temple*
Qualifications: [LLB (Lond)]

ASANTE MR ARIZUNA SESAY

Senior Crown Prosecutor, Crown Prosecution Service, Snaresbrook Crown Court, 75 Hollybush Hill, Snaresbrook, London, E11 1QW, ☎ 020 8530 0251, ✉ Arizuna.Asante@cps.gsi.gov.uk, *Call Date: Oct 1996, Lincoln's Inn*
Qualifications: [BSc (Hons)(W.Indies) LLB (Hons)(Warw)]

ASFAW MRS ANNE ROSE

Para-Legal, JFH Law LLP, 274a Kentish Town Road, London, NW5 2AA, ☎ 020 7428 6311 Fax: 020 7485 8948, *Call Date: July 2007, Middle Temple*
Qualifications: [BSc (Lond) PG Dip Law (Nott'm)]

ASGARIAN MISS TINA

Babbe, PO Box 69, 18-20 Smith Street, St Peter Port, Guernsey, GY1 4BL, Guernsey, Fax: 01481 711607, ✉ t.asgarian@babbelegal.com, *Call Date: Oct 1999, Lincoln's Inn*
Qualifications: [LLB (Hons)(Lond) LLM (Cantab)]

ASHBY MR PETER MARCUS

Principal Crown Prosecutor, Crown Prosecution Service, 2 Kimbrose Way, Gloucester, Gloucestershire, GL1 2DB, ☎ 01452 872400, *Call Date: Nov 1978, Middle Temple*
Qualifications: [BA (Hons)]

ASHCROFT MISS CLARE LOUISE

Taylor Haldane Barlex Solicitors, Copt House, Springfield Road, Chelmsford, Essex, CM2 6JG, ☎ 01245 493959 Fax: 01245 455590, ✉ mail@thblegal.com, *Call Date: July 2001, Middle Temple*
Qualifications: [LLB (Hons) LLM (Lond)]

ASHKAR MISS NATALIE

Derbyshire County Council, Legal Services, County Hall, Matlock, Derbyshire, DE4 3AG, *Call Date: Oct 2009, Inner Temple*
Qualifications: [LLB (Warw) LLM (Cantab)]

ASHPLANT MR ANTHONY JOHN

Legal Director, M and G Limited, Laurence Pountney Hill, London, EC4R 0HH, ☎ 020 7548 3750 Fax: 020 7548 3913, ✉ anthony.ashplant@mandg.co.uk, *Call Date: July 1977, Middle Temple*
Qualifications: [LLB Hons (Lond)]

ASHTON MISS BRIDGET LESLEY

Senior Crown Prosecutor, Crown Prosecution Service, Artillery House, Heritage Way, Droitwich, Worcestershire, WR9 8YB, ✉ Lesley.Ashton@cps.gsi.gov.uk, *Call Date: Feb 1990, Inner Temple*
Qualifications: [LLB (Hons) (Bucks)]

ASHTON MR RAGLAN HALLEY

Tuckers Solicitors, 210 Corporation Street, Birmingham, B4 6QB, ☎ 0121 236 4324 Fax: 0121 236 4364, *Call Date: Oct 1994, Lincoln's Inn*
Qualifications: [LLB (Hons)(Lond)]

ASHTON-JONES MR PHILIP

Head of Legal Services, R V Mawhood, 1st Floor, Sheraton House, Lower Road, Chorleywood, Hertfordshire, WD3 5LH, ☎ 01923 253 638 Fax: 01923 284 490, ✉ philip@ashton-jones.com, *Call Date: Nov 1986, Middle Temple*
Qualifications: [LLB (UEA)]

ASHWORTH MISS JENNY FRANCES

Health & Safety Executive, Redgrave Court, Melton Road, Bootle, Merseyside, L20 7HS, *Call Date: Oct 2002, Lincoln's Inn*
Qualifications: [BA (Manch)]

ASIF MR MOHAMMED JALIL AHKTER

Kobre & Kim LLP, 60 Gresham Street, London, EC2V 7BB, *Call Date: Nov 1988, Lincoln's Inn*
Qualifications: [MA (Cantab)]

ASKEW MR RICHARD JOHN ALDIS

Arbitrator, General Counsel, E D + F Man Holdings Ltd, Cottons Centre, Hays Lane, London, SE1 2QE, ☎ 020 7089 8000 Fax: 020 7089 8067, ✉ richard.askew@edfman.com, *Call Date: July 1978, Inner Temple*
Qualifications: [MA (Oxon) MCIArb]

F

ATHERTON-HAM MR JAMES WEST

Director, Mediator, Aggregate Industries Ltd, Bardon Hall, Copt Oak Road, Markfield, Leicestershire, LE67 9PJ, *Call Date: Oct 1994, Lincoln's Inn*
Qualifications: [LLB (Hons)]

ATHOW MR KEVIN JOHN

Legal Counsel, Bsh Home Applicances Limited, Grand Union House, Old Wolverton Road, Milton Keynes, MK12 5PT, ☎ 01908 328404, ✉ Kevin.Athow@bshg.com, *Call Date: July 1999, Inner Temple*
Qualifications: [LLB (Nott'm)]

ATHWAL MS HARBINDER KAUR

Crown Prosecution Service, Colmore Gate, 2 - 6 Colmore Row, Birmingham, West Midlands, B3 2QA, *Call Date: Oct 1999, Lincoln's Inn*
Qualifications: [LLB (Hons)(Lond)]

ATKINSON MR CHRISTOPHER DEAN

Crown Prosecution Service, 1 Hudson Quay, The Halyard, Middlesbrough, Cleveland, TS3 6RT, ☎ 01642 204500, ✉ christopher.atkinson@cps.gsi.gov.uk, *Call Date: Nov 2007, Inner Temple*
Qualifications: [LLB (Nott'm)]

ATKINSON MISS EMMA DOLORES

Crown Prosecution Service, 1 Hudson Quay, The Halyard, Middlesbrough, Cleveland, TS3 6RT, ☎ 01642 204509, *Call Date: Mar 2001, Lincoln's Inn*
Qualifications: [BA (Hons)]

ATKINSON MR MICHAEL JOHN

Crown Prosecution Service, Rose Court, 2 Southwark Bridge, London, SE1 9HS, ☎ 020 3357 0700 Fax: 020 3357 0723, *Call Date: July 2003, Inner Temple*
Qualifications: [BA (Hons) (UEA) CPE (UEA) Dip Law]

ATOGDINA MS CLAIRE

Nursing and Midwifery Council, 23 Portland Place, London, W1B 1PZ, *Call Date: Nov 2004, Lincoln's Inn*
Qualifications: [BA (Hons)]

ATTON MISS CORINNE ELISABETH

Wilmerhale, 399 Park Avenue, New York, NY 10022, USA, Fax: 212 230 8888, ✉ corinne.atton@wilmerhale.com, *Call Date: July 2002, Lincoln's Inn*
Qualifications: [BSc(Hons) (London)]

ATTRILL MR DAVID MARTIN

Bedell Group, 26 New Street, Po Box 75, St Helier, JE4 8PP, Jersey, ☎ 01534 814814 Fax: 01534 814815, ✉ david.attrill@bedellgroup.com, *Call Date: July 1988, Lincoln's Inn*
Qualifications: [LLB (Hons)]

ATWILL COMMANDER JOHN WILLIAM OWEN

Other, Royal Navy Officers, J9- Legal Advisor, Permanent Joint Headquarters, Sandy Lane, Northwood, Middlesex, HA6 3HP, ☎ 01923 955 5924, ✉ John.Atwill757@mod.uk, *Call Date: Oct 1997, Inner Temple*
Qualifications: [LLB (Hons)]

AUSTEN-PETERS MR OLUDOTUN

Head of Legal Services, G4S Secure Solutions UK Limited, 15 Carshalton Road, Sutton Park House, Sutton, Surrey, SM1 4DL, ☎ 020 8722 2317, ✉ Austen.Austen-Peters@uk.g4s.com, *Call Date: July 1983, Inner Temple*
Qualifications: [BA (Hons) LLM]

AVERILL MS SALLY FRANCES

Adviser, HED, Manager, Crown Prosecution Service, Rose Court, 2 Southwark Bridge, London, SE1 9HS, ☎ 0203 3357 0837 Fax: 0203 3357 0874, ✉ sally.averill@cps.gsi.gov.uk, *Call Date: Oct 1992, Gray's Inn*
Qualifications: [LLB (Lond) MA LLM]

AYLETT MR ANTHONY PETER MICHAEL

Legal Officer, The Treasury Solicitors, One Kemble Street, London, WC2B 4TS, ✉ anthony.aylett@tsol.gsi.gov.uk, *Call Date: May 1971, Middle Temple*
Qualifications: [LLB]

AYUB MISS SALIHA

Crown Prosecution Service, Acton Police Station, 250 Acton High Street, London, W3 9BH, *Call Date: Nov 1992, Lincoln's Inn*
Qualifications: [LLB (Hons)]

F

BABER MR WAHEED

Barrett and Nelligan Solicitors, 50 Adelaide Street, Fleetwood, Lancashire, FY7 6EE, Fax: 01253 778530, *Call Date: Nov 1999, Gray's Inn*
Qualifications: [LLB]

BACARESE MR GEORGE ALAN

Senior Crown Prosecutor, Peters & Peters Solicitors LLP, 15 Fetter Lane, London, EC4A 1BW, ☎020 7822 7777 Fax: 020 7822 7788, ✉ABacarese@petersandpeters.com, *Call Date: July 1988, Middle Temple*
Qualifications: [LLB (Hons)]

BADERIN MISS TILLY

Pricewaterhousecoopers Legal LLP, 1 Embankment Place, London, WC2N 6DX, ☎020 7212 4104, ✉tilly.baderin@pwclegal.co.uk, *Call Date: Nov 2004, Lincoln's Inn*
Qualifications: [BA (Hons)]

BAILDON MISS ANDREA LAUREN

Office of Gas and Electricity Markets (Ofgem), Office of Gas and Electricity Markets, 9 Millbank, London, SW1P 3GE, ☎020 7901 3851, ✉andrea.baildon@ofgem.gov.uk, *Call Date: Oct 2008, Middle Temple*
Qualifications: [BA (Hons) (Cantab)]

BAILEY MISS CLAUDINE HYPHA

Crown Prosecution Service, Eaton Court, 112 Oxford Road, Reading, Berkshire, RG1 7LL, *Call Date: Nov 2003, Middle Temple*
Qualifications: [LLB (Hons) (Wolves) LLM (Wolves)]

BAILEY MISS JANE ANGELA TABITHA

Deloitte LLP, 4 Brindley Place, Birmingham, B1 2HZ, Fax: 0121 695 5658, *Call Date: Oct 1993, Inner Temple*
Qualifications: [LLB]

BAILEY MR THOMAS WILLIAM

Steeles (Law) LLP, 3 The Norwich Business Park, Whiting Road, Norwich, Norfolk, NR4 6DJ, Fax: 01603 666 948, ✉tbailey@steeleslaw.co.uk, *Call Date: Oct 2005, Middle Temple*
Qualifications: [LLB (Hons)]

BAKER MR JOHN VICTOR ROBERT

Justices' Clerk, Her Majesty's Court Service, Court House, London Road, Dorking, Surrey, RH4 1SX, *Call Date: July 1981, Middle Temple*

BAKER MR STUART CHRISTOPHER

Crown Prosecution Service, Rose Court, 2 Southwark Bridge, London, SE1 9HS, ☎020 33570000, ✉stuart.baker@cps.gsi.gov.uk, *Call Date: Oct 1995, Middle Temple*
Qualifications: [LLB (Hons) (Manch)]

BAKER MR WILLIAM ARTHUR

Crown Advocate, Crown Prosecution Service, Sunlight House, Quay Street, Manchester, M60 3PS, ☎0161 848 5079 Fax: 0161 827 4824, *Call Date: Oct 1991, Middle Temple*
Qualifications: [LLB (Hons) (Lancs)]

BALJIT MISS DEBORAH CHASWAREE

ACCA, 29 Lincoln's Inn Fields, London, WC2A 3EE, ✉Deborah.Baljit@accaglobal.com, *Call Date: Oct 1999, Lincoln's Inn*
Qualifications: [LLB (Hons) Dip LAw]

BALL MR ANDREW NICHOLAS

Deputy Justices' Clerk, City of Salford Magistrates' Court, Bexley Square, Salford, M3 6DJ, ☎0161 834 9457 Fax: 0161 831 9026, ✉andrew.ball@hmcourts-service.gsi.gov.uk, *Call Date: May 1993, Middle Temple*
Qualifications: [LLB (Hons)(Wales)]

BALL MISS CLARE ESME

Department For Business, Innovation and Skills, Legal Services Group, 1 Victoria Street, London, SW1H 0ET, *Call Date: Oct 2006, Lincoln's Inn*
Qualifications: [LLB]

BALOCH DR TARIQ ALI

Freshfields Bruckhaus Deringer LLP, 65 Fleet Street, London, EC4Y 1HS, ☎020 7936 4000 Fax: 020 7832 7001, ✉tariq.baloch@freshfields.com, *Call Date: Oct 2001, Lincoln's Inn*
Qualifications: [LLB (Ho (Lond) LLM (Lond)]

F

BALONWU MR STEPHEN

HED, Bank of Ireland, Bow Bells House, 1 Bread Street, London, EC4M 9BE, ☎020 3210 6395 Fax: 020 7248 8980, ✉stephen.balonwu@boi.com, *Call Date: Oct 1993, Middle Temple*
Qualifications: [BA (Hons)(Kent)]

BAMFORD MISS SALLY

Solicitor Advocate, Oliver D'Sa Solicitors, 75-81 King Street, Leicester, LE1 6RP, *Call Date: July 2011, Lincoln's Inn*
Qualifications: [LLB (Leic)]

BAMFORTH MISS RUTH ALEXANDRA

Eversheds LLP, Bridgewater Place, Water Lane, Leeds, LS11 5DR, ☎0845 498 4749, ✉RuthBamforth@eversheds.com, *Call Date: Nov 1996, Lincoln's Inn*
Qualifications: [LLB (Hons)(Leeds) LLM (Cantab)]

BANDARA MISS YAPA MUDIYANSELAGE DHARSHINI

Fleet Hamburg LLP, Willy-Brandt Strasse 57, Hamburg, 20457, Germany, Fax: 40 5 700 70 200, ✉info@fleet-hamburg.com, *Call Date: Oct 1999, Lincoln's Inn*
Qualifications: [LLB (Hons) LLM (Bucks)]

BANGA MR BALVINDER SINGH

Financial Services Authority, The Financial Services Authority, Enforcement and Financial Crime Division - Legal Group, 25 The North Colonade, Canary Wharf, London, E14 5HS, ✉Balvinder.Banga@fsa.gov.uk, *Call Date: July 1997, Inner Temple*
Qualifications: [BA (Cantab)]

BANHAM MR MARK RICHARD MIDDLECOTT

Castle Trust Capital plc, 41 Lothbury, London, EC2R 7HG, ✉mark.banham@castletrust.co.uk, *Call Date: Nov 1994, Inner Temple*
Qualifications: [BA (Cantab) CPE]

BANKS MS DAVINA JANE

Serious Fraud Office, Elm House, 10-16 Elm Street, London, WC1X 0BJ, ☎020 7239 7433, ✉Davina.Banks@sfo.gsi.gov.uk, *Call Date: Nov 1999, Inner Temple*
Qualifications: [BA LLB (Australia)]

BANTON MISS ELAINE ROSE

Seven Bedford Row, 7 Bedford Row, London, WC1R 4BS, ☎020 7242 3555 Fax: 020 7242 2511, ✉ebanton@7br.co.uk, *Call Date: Oct 1996, Middle Temple*
Qualifications: [LLB (Hons)(Lond) MA (Lond)]

BAQRI MISS ZAHRA

Crown Prosecution Service, Sunlight House, Quay Street, Manchester, M60 3PS, ☎0161 827 4700 Fax: 0161 827 4743, ✉Zahra.baqri@cps.gsi.gov.uk, *Call Date: Nov 2010, Lincoln's Inn*
Qualifications: [LLB (Leeds)]

BARADON MR ADAM HEDLEY

Skadden, Arps, Slate, Meagher & Flom LLP, 40 Bank Street, Canary Wharf, London, E14 5DS, ☎020 7519 7000 Fax: 020 7519 7070, *Call Date: July 2006, Lincoln's Inn*
Qualifications: [BA (Hons) (Nott'm)]

BARBARY MR GEORGE NAGY

Crown Prosecution Service, Rose Court, 2 Southwark Bridge, London, SE1 9HS, *Call Date: Oct 1999, Lincoln's Inn*
Qualifications: [LLB (Hons)]

BARCLAY MR RENE JAMES

Director, Crown Prosecution Service, Rose Court, 2 Southwark Bridge, London, SE1 9HS, ☎020 3357 1013 Fax: 020 3357 0089, ✉rene.barclay@cps.gsi.gov.uk, *Call Date: July 1977, Gray's Inn*
Qualifications: [LLB (Lond)]

BARKER MR DAVID ANDREW

Southampton City Council, Southbrook Rise, 4-8 Millbrook Road East, Southampton, Hampshire, SO15 1YG, ☎023 8083 4973 Fax: 023 8083 3217, ✉david.barker@southampton.gov.uk, *Call Date: Oct 2006, Inner Temple*
Qualifications: [BSc (Bath)]

BARKER MR GRENVILLE STUART

Crown Advocate, Crown Prosecution Service, Capital Tower, Greyfriars Road, Cardiff, CF10 3PL, ✉grenville.barker@cps.gsi.gov.uk, *Call Date: Nov 1984, Middle Temple*
Qualifications: [LLB (Cardiff)]

F

BARKER MISS JENNIFER CLAIRE

Peters & Peters Solicitors LLP, 15 Fetter Lane, London, EC4A 1BW, ☎020 7822 7777, ✉JBarker@petersandpeters.com, *Call Date: Oct 2005, Inner Temple*
Qualifications: [BA Robinson College University of Cambridge CPE]

BARKER MISS JOANNE LESLEY

Crown Advocate, Crown Prosecution Service, Colmore Gate, 2 - 6 Colmore Row, Birmingham, West Midlands, B3 2QA, Fax: 0121 262 6351, ✉joanne.barker@cps.gsi.gov.uk, *Call Date: July 1998, Lincoln's Inn*
Qualifications: [BA (Hons)(Leics) CPE (Staffs)]

BARKER MR JOHN CHARLES

Partner, Ronald Fletcher Baker LLP, 326 Old Street, London, EC1V 9DR, ☎020 7613 1402, *Call Date: July 1982, Middle Temple*
Qualifications: [BA LLM (Lond)]

BARKER MR PETER ROY

Royal Navy Officers, Dnls, Mp 4.2 Leach Building, Whale Island, Portsmouth, Hampshire, PO2 8BY, *Call Date: July 2011, Middle Temple*
Qualifications: [MPhys (Hons) (Oxon) PgDL (Lond)]

BARKLEY MR ANDREW ROGER

Crown Advocate, Crown Prosecution Service, Shropshire Office, Lakeside House, Holsworth Park, Bicton Heath, Shrewsbury, Shropshire, SY3 5HJ, ☎01743 263700 Fax: 01743 263747, ✉Andrew.Barkley@cps.gsi.gov.uk, *Call Date: July 2001, Gray's Inn*
Qualifications: [LLB LLM]

BARLOW MS URSULA SUSANNE

London Borough of Hammersmith and Fulham, Hammersmith Town Hall, King Street, London, W6 9JU, ☎020 8753 2713, *Call Date: July 2001, Gray's Inn*
Qualifications: [BA (Manch) MA (Bruges)]

BARNARD MR ANTHONY CHRISTOPHER

District Crown Prosecutor, HM Crown Prosecution Service Inspectorate, 26-28 Old Queen Street, London, SW1H 9HP, *Call Date: Oct 1992, Gray's Inn*
Qualifications: [BA (UEA) Dip Law (Lond)]

BARNARD MS HELEN KAY

HM Revenue and Customs, Solicitors Office, 100 Parliament Street, London, SW1A 2BQ, ☎020 7147 0439, ✉helen.barnard@hmrc.gsi.gov.uk, *Call Date: Nov 1995, Lincoln's Inn*
Qualifications: [LLB (Hons)]

BARNARD MR JOHN DANIEL

Lewis Nedas Solicitors, 24 Camden High Street, London, NW1 0JH, ☎020 7387 2032 Fax: 020 7388 6575, ✉dbarnard@lewisnedas.co.uk, *Call Date: Mar 2003, Lincoln's Inn*
Qualifications: [BA (Hons)]

BARNETT MRS MIRANDA FLEUR

Senior Lawyer, The Treasury Solicitors, One Kemble Street, London, WC2B 4TS, ☎020 7783 8206 Fax: 020 7210 4512, ✉miranda.barnett@dcsf.gsi.gov.uk, *Call Date: Oct 1993, Lincoln's Inn*
Qualifications: [LLB (Hons)(B'ham)]

BARR MR EDWARD ROBERT

Oliver D'Sa Solicitors, 75-81 King Street, Leicester, LE1 6RP, *Call Date: Nov 1983, Inner Temple*
Qualifications: [LLB (Hons)]

BARR MR PETER ERIC PLAYFAIR

Crown Advocate, Crown Prosecution Service, 2 King Edward Court, King Edward Street, Nottingham, Nottinghamshire, NG1 1EL, *Call Date: Oct 1998, Middle Temple*
Qualifications: [B.Pharm (Lond) MA (Lond) CPE]

BARRATT MR JAMES WILLIAM

O'Melveny and Myers LLP, Warwick Court, 5 Paternoster Square, London, EC4M 7DX, ☎020 7088 0000 Fax: 020 7088 0001, ✉jbarratt@omm.com, *Call Date: Nov 2001, Middle Temple*
Qualifications: [MA (Hons) (Cantab) CPE]

BARRETT MS CATHERINE WENDY

Crown Prosecution Service, The Cooperage, 8 Gainsford Street, London, SE1 2NE, ☎020 7378 3297 Fax: 020 3300 4861, ✉Wendy.Barrett@cps.gsi.gov.uk, *Call Date: Nov 1994, Middle Temple*
Qualifications: [BA (Hons)]

BARRETT MR MICHAEL JOHN

Company Secretary, Xerox Limited, Bridge House, Oxford Road, Uxbridge, Middlesex, UB8 1HS, ☎01895 251133
Fax: 018 9584 5488, ✉john.barrett2@xerox.com, *Call Date: Nov 1991, Middle Temple*
Qualifications: [BA (Hons) (Cambs) Dip Law ACIS]

BARRETT MR PAUL JAMES

Group Legal Adviser, Home Retail Group PLC, 489-499 Avebury Boulevard, Saxon Gate West, Milton Keynes, MK9 2NW, ☎01908 600538
Fax: 01908 600721, ✉paul.barrett@homeretailgroup.com, *Call Date: Feb 1993, Lincoln's Inn*
Qualifications: [LLB (Hons)]

BARRETT MS PENELOPE JANE

Criminal Cases Review Commission, 5 St Philips Place, Birmingham, B3 2PW, *Call Date: July 1982, Middle Temple*
Qualifications: [MA (Cantab)]

BARRETT MR THOMAS DUNCAN

The Treasury Solicitors, Constitutional Law Team, Cabinet Office, Room 3/07, 1 Horseguards Road, London, SW1A 2HQ, *Call Date: July 2002, Lincoln's Inn*
Qualifications: [LLB (Hons)(London)]

BARTON MR CHARLES NEVILLE

Legal Adviser, The Treasury Solicitors, The Office of Government Commerce, 4th Floor, 1 Horse Guards Road, London, SW1A 2HQ, ☎020 7271 2781 Fax: 020 7271 1480, ✉charles.barton@ogc.gsi.gov.uk, *Call Date: July 1986, Inner Temple*
Qualifications: [LLB (Lond)]

BASARAN MRS SANDRA JUDITH

Legal Director, Think Money, Pennington House, Carolina Way, South Langworth Road, Salford Quays, Lancashire, M50 2ZY, *Call Date: July 1984, Gray's Inn*
Qualifications: [LLB (Hons)]

BASIT-AHMED MR KAASHIF

Legal Consultant, Dubai International Financial Centre, Gate Village 7, Level 2, Po Box 506546, Dubai, United Arab Emirates, ✉kaashif@jsalaw.com, *Call Date: Nov 1994, Lincoln's Inn*
Qualifications: [LLB (Hons)(Bucks) LLM (Lond)]

BASTOS G MARTIN MR PHILIP JOHN

Assistant General Counsel, Director, Ge Capital Emea, Av Des Communautes 5, Brusslels 1140, Belgium, ✉philip.bastosmartin@ge.com, *Call Date: Nov 1993, Gray's Inn*
Qualifications: [LLB (Essex) DEA (France)]

BASTOW MR ANTONY

Markel Syndicate 3000 At Lloyds, The Markel Building, 49 Leadenhall Street, London, EC3A 2EA, *Call Date: Nov 1997, Gray's Inn*
Qualifications: [BA MA]

BATTA MR VIRENSH

Department of Energy and Climate Change, 3-8 Whitehall Place, London, SW1A 2HD, *Call Date: Oct 2000, Lincoln's Inn*
Qualifications: [LLB (Hons) (Lond) BCL]

BATTLE MR JOHN GERARD STEPHEN

HED, ITN, 200 Gray's Inn Road, London, WC1X 8XZ, ☎020 7430 4766
Fax: 020 7430 4211, ✉john.battle@itn.co.uk, *Call Date: July 1985, Lincoln's Inn*
Qualifications: [LLB]

BAUM MISS VICTORIA EMMA

Ministry of Justice, 102 Petty France, London, SW1H 9AJ, ☎020 3334 3555, *Call Date: Oct 1993, Middle Temple*
Qualifications: [MA (Hons) (Oxon)]

BAYLIS MS NATALIE JAYNE

Financial Services Authority, General Counsel's Division, 25 The North Colonnade, Canary Wharf, London, E14 5HS, *Call Date: Oct 1996, Lincoln's Inn*
Qualifications: [MA (Hons)(Edin) Dip in Law]

BAYLISS MR NEIL MCKENZIE

Crown Prosecution Service, United House, Piccadilly, York, YO1 9PQ, *Call Date: July 1986, Gray's Inn*
Qualifications: [LLB (Hons)]

BAYMAN MR KEITH WILLIAM

Crown Prosecution Service, United House, Piccadilly, York, North Yorkshire, YO1 9PQ, ✉cpsdirect.enquiries@cps.gsi.gov.uk, keith.bayman@cps.gsi.gov.uk, *Call Date: July 1987, Lincoln's Inn*
Qualifications: [MA LLM (Cantab)]

F

BEACH MR NICHOLAS PETER

The Office of the Counsel to the Chairman of Committees, House of Lords, Room 22, First Floor, West Front, Palace Of Westminster, London, SW1A 0AA, *Call Date: Nov 1983, Middle Temple*
Qualifications: [BA (Hons)(Oxon)]

BEARDMORE MISS ALISON CLAIRE

Deputy Justices' Clerk, Legal Manager, Senior Legal Adviser, Stafford Magistrates' Court, The Court House, South Walls, Stafford, Stafforshire, ST16 3DW, ☎01785 275700, ✉alison.beardmore@hmcourts-service.gsi.gov.uk, *Call Date: Oct 1991, Gray's Inn*
Qualifications: [LLB (Hons) (B'ham)]

BEATTIE MR CAMERON ROBERT

Legal Manager, South Somerset Magistrates' Court, The Law Courts, Petters Way, Yeovil, Somerset, BA20 1SW, ☎01935 426281, ✉cameron.beattie@hmcts.gsi.gov.uk, *Call Date: Feb 1991, Lincoln's Inn*
Qualifications: [LLB]

BEAUMONT MR DAVID ANTHONY

Head of Legal Services, Lloyds Banking Group, 1 Lovell Park Road, Leeds, LS1 2NS, ☎0113 2357322, *Call Date: July 1987, Lincoln's Inn*
Qualifications: [BA (Durham)]

BECK MR JAMES HARRISON

The Johnson Partnership, Cannon Courtyard, Off Long Row, Nottingham, NG1 6JE, ☎0115 941 9141 Fax: 0115 947 0178, ✉mail@thejohnsonpartnership.co.uk, *Call Date: July 1989, Lincoln's Inn*
Qualifications: [BSc MSc (LSE)]

BECK MISS SANDRA MARY

Crown Prosecution Service, Eaton Court, 112 Oxford Road, Reading, Berkshire, RG1 7LL, ☎0118 951 3600 / 0118 951 3600 Fax: 0118 951 3601 / 0118 951 3601, ✉Sandra.Beck@cps.gsi.gov.uk, *Call Date: Nov 1982, Lincoln's Inn*
Qualifications: [BA]

BECKETT MS RACHEL SARA

Crown Prosecution Service, City Gate House, 185 Dyke Road, Hove, East Sussex, BN3 1TL, *Call Date: Oct 1999, Inner Temple*
Qualifications: [LLB (Lond)]

BEGUM MISS ZEENAT

Crown Prosecution Service, St Ann's Quay, 122 Quayside, Newcastle Upon Tyne, Tyne and Wear, NE1 3BD, *Call Date: July 2009, Gray's Inn*
Qualifications: [BA]

BEHZADI SPENCER MS SHAYESTEH

HED, The Treasury Solicitors, European Division, Joint Head of Eu Litigation, One Kemble Street, London, WC2B 4TS, Fax: 020 7210 3132, ✉Head_of_eu_litigation@tsol.gsi.gov.uk, *Call Date: Nov 1988, Middle Temple*
Qualifications: [LLB (Hons) LLM]

BELDAM MS ALEXANDRA GAY

Lawyer, Ministry of Justice, Criminal Appeal Office, Royal Courts of Justice, The Strand, London, WC2A 2LL, ☎020 7947 6927 Fax: 020 7947 7874, ✉Alix.Beldam@hmcourts-service.x.gsi.gov.uk, *Call Date: Nov 1981, Inner Temple*
Qualifications: [BA (Hons)]

BELL MISS ALLEGRA ANNE

Shearman Bowen and Co Solicitors, 16 Tooks Court, Cursitor Street, London, EC4A 1LB, Fax: 020 7242 3988, ✉info@shearmanbowen.co.uk, *Call Date: July 2009, Lincoln's Inn*
Qualifications: [BSc (Lond) CPE OBPP]

BELL MISS JANE ELIZABETH

Legal Adviser, Department of Social Security, New Court, 48 Carey Street, London, WC2A 2LS, *Call Date: Nov 1984, Middle Temple*
Qualifications: [BA (Oxon)]

BELL MR SIMON WILLIAM

Caseworker, The Treasury Solicitors, B5 General Public Law and Planning, One Kemble Street, London, WC2B 4TS, ☎020 7210 2957 Fax: 020 7210 3001, ✉Simon.bell@tsol.gsi.gov.uk, *Call Date: July 2003, Lincoln's Inn*
Qualifications: [LLB Hons (Kent)]

BELLAMY SIR CHRISTOPHER WILLIAM

Assistant Recorder, Linklaters, 1 Silk Street, London, EC2Y 8HQ, ✉christopher.bellamy@linklaters.com, *Call Date: July 1968, Middle Temple*
Qualifications: [MA (Oxon)]

F

BELLIS MR GARETH PAUL

Davison Flynn Duke, The Antiques Triangle, 128 Chester Street, Birkenhead, CH41 5DL, *Call Date: Nov 2000, Gray's Inn*

BELTRAMI MR EDWIN JOSEPH

Chief Crown Prosecutor, Crown Prosecution Service, Bromfield House, Ellice Way, Wrexham, Wales, LL13 7YW, ☎01978 346002 Fax: 01978 346052, ✉ed.beltrami@cps.gsi.gov.uk, *Call Date: July 1988, Middle Temple*
Qualifications: [LLB (Hons)]

BENJAMIN MR GRANT ANDREW

Jerman Simpson Pearson and Samuels Solicitors, 4a Southchurch Road, Southend On Sea, Essex, SS1 2NE, ☎01702 610 071 Fax: 01702 613 124, ✉bonem@jspssolicitors.co.uk, *Call Date: July 2002, Middle Temple*
Qualifications: [LLB (Hon) (Manch)]

BENNETT MISS ALEXANDRA CATHERINE

Legal Adviser, Stewarts Law LLP, 5 New Street Square, London, EC4A 3BF, ☎020 7822 8000 Fax: 020 7822 8080, *Call Date: Nov 1997, Inner Temple*
Qualifications: [BA (Lond) Dip Law]

BENNETT MRS CHRISTINA

Qdos Consulting Ltd, Qdos Court, Rossendale Road, Earl Shilton, Leicester, LE9 9LY, *Call Date: Mar 2000, Lincoln's Inn*
Qualifications: [LLB (Hons) (Staffs)]

BENNETT MR DAVID MARK

Crown Prosecution Service, 2 King Edward Court, King Edward Street, Nottingham, Nottinghamshire, NG1 1EL, *Call Date: Nov 2001, Gray's Inn*
Qualifications: [LLB (Westminister)]

BENNETT MR NICHOLAS

Farrer & Co, 66 Lincoln's Inn Fields, London, WC2A 3LH, *Call Date: Nov 2005, Gray's Inn*
Qualifications: [BA (Oxon)]

BENNETTS MR PHILIP JAMES

Crown Prosecution Service, The Cooperage, 8 Gainsford Street, London, SE1 2NE, *Call Date: July 1986, Lincoln's Inn*
Qualifications: [LLB (Brunel)]

BENTLEY MR BENJAMIN UVEDALE

Browne Jacobson LLP, Mowbray House, Castle Meadow Road, Nottingham, NG2 1BJ, ☎0115 908 4826 Fax: 0115 947 5246, ✉bbentley@brownejacobson.com, *Call Date: Oct 2008, Middle Temple*
Qualifications: [BA (Hons) (Cantab) Dip in Law (Nott'm) MA (Cantab) LLB (Nott'm)]

BENTLEY-THOBURN MISS LISA CLARE

HM Revenue and Customs, 100 Parliament Street, London, SW1A 2BQ, ☎020 7147 0214, ✉lisa.bentley-thoburn@hmrc.gsi.gov.uk, *Call Date: Nov 1999, Lincoln's Inn*
Qualifications: [LLB (Hons)]

BERGSTROM MISS SARAH LOUISE

Government Legal Services, Criminal Appeals Office, Royal Courts of Justice, the Strand, London, WC2A 2LL, ☎020 7947 6119, ✉dickycole@hotmail.co.uk, *Call Date: Nov 2002, Lincoln's Inn*
Qualifications: [LLB (Hons)(Plymouth)]

BERLIN MRS SALLY LOUISE

Criminal Cases Review Commission, 5 St Philips Place, Birmingham, B3 2PW, *Call Date: July 2000, Lincoln's Inn*
Qualifications: [LLB(Hons) (Wolves)]

BERRILL-COX MR ADRIAN LEIGH

Financial Services Authority, The Financial Services Authority, Enforcement and Financial Crime Division - Legal Group, 25 The North Colonade, Canary Wharf, London, E14 5HS, ☎020 7066 1212 Fax: 020 7066 1213, ✉adrian.berrill-cox@fsa.gov.uk, *Call Date: July 1986, Inner Temple*
Qualifications: [LLB (Reading)]

BEST MR DAVID MARK

Office of Comminucations (Ofcom), Riverside House, 2a Southwark Bridge Road, London, SE1 9HA, ☎020 7981 3899, ✉david.best@ofcom.org.uk, *Call Date: Mar 1997, Lincoln's Inn*
Qualifications: [LLB (Hons)(Lond)]

BESWICK MISS PHILIPPA HELENA

Linn and Associates, 175 Canterbury Street, Gillingham, Kent, ME7 5TU, ☎01634 577179, *Call Date: Nov 2003, Middle Temple*
Qualifications: [LLB (Hons) (Essex)]

BETTELEY MR JASON PAUL

Legal Officer, Deva Medical Electronics Limited, Picow Farm Court, 1 Chandlers Court, Runcorn, Cheshire, WA7 4UH, ☎01928 567 571 Fax: 01928 580 788, *Call Date: Oct 1990, Inner Temple*
Qualifications: [LLB]

BHADRESA MRS IRENE MARY

Crown Prosecution Service, Holborn Police Station, 10 Lambs Conduit Street, Islington, London, WC1N 3NR, Fax: 020 70613905, ✉irene.bhadresa@cps.gsi.gov.uk, *Call Date: May 1987, Middle Temple*
Qualifications: [LLB (Hons)]

BHAKAR MR GURVINDER SINGH

Legal Adviser, Ministry of Justice (Moj), The Courthouse, 389-397 High Street, Stratford, London, E15 4SB, ☎020 8522 5000, ✉Gurvinder.Bhakar@hmcourts-service.gsi.gov.uk, *Call Date: July 2001, Inner Temple*
Qualifications: [LLB (Hons)]

BICKERSTAFF MISS ANTHEA MARY

Legal Adviser, Osprey House, Hedgerows Business Park, Colchester Road, Chelmsford, Essex, CM2 5PF, *Call Date: Oct 1990, Gray's Inn*
Qualifications: [BA (Keele) MA (Lond)]

BIKER MR ANDREW DUNKIN

Senior Lawyer, Crown Prosecution Service, Rose Court, 2 Southwark Bridge, London, SE1 9HS, ☎020 33570262 Fax: 020 7147 7802, *Call Date: Nov 1978, Gray's Inn*
Qualifications: [MA (Cantab)]

BILAL MR SULAIMAN

JP Morgan Chase, 125 London Wall, London, EC2Y 5AJ, Fax: 020 7325 4508, ✉sulaiman.m.bilal@jpmorgan.com, *Call Date: July 2002, Middle Temple*
Qualifications: [LLB (Hons)]

BILEWYCZ MR MICHAEL DOMENICO

Managing Director, Decisis Limited, 5 St John's Lane, London, EC1M 4BH, ☎020 7250 4732 Fax: 020 7250 4733, ✉michael.bilewycz@decisis.co.uk, *Call Date: Nov 1988, Middle Temple*
Qualifications: [BA (Hons) LLM]

BINEY MR KWAMINA AUBYN

Borough Crown Prosecutor, Crown Prosecution Service, Wembley Police Station, 603 Harrow Road, Wembley, Middlesex, HA0 2HH, ☎020 33003130 Fax: 020 33003160, ✉kwame.biney@cps.gsi.gov.uk, *Call Date: July 1989, Lincoln's Inn*
Qualifications: [LLB (Ghana) Dip Law (Lond) LLM (Lond)]

BIONDI MR ALESSANDRO

Legal Adviser, Bombardier Transportation Uk, Litchchurch Lane, Derby, DE24 8AD, ✉alessandro.biondi@uk.transport.bombardier.com, *Call Date: Feb 1994, Lincoln's Inn*
Qualifications: [LLB (Hons)]

BISHOP DR PAUL KEVIN

The Treasury Solicitors, One Kemble Street, London, WC2B 4TS, ☎020 7210 3312 Fax: 020 7210 3503, ✉paul.bishop@tsol.gsi.gov.uk, *Call Date: Oct 2008, Gray's Inn*
Qualifications: [BEng PhD MSc LLB LLM]

BLACK MISS CHARLOTTE LOUISE

Forsters LLP, 31 Hill Street, London, W1J 5LS, ☎020 7863 8333 Fax: 020 7863 8444, ✉mail@forsters.co.uk, *Call Date: Oct 2006, Middle Temple*
Qualifications: [BA (Hons) (Cantab)]

BLACKBURN MISS KATHARINE ELIZABETH MARY

Blake Lapthorn Solicitors, Watchmaker Court, 33 St John's Lane, London, EC1M 4DB, ☎020 7814 6868
Fax: 020 705 2000 / 020 7814 9421, *Call Date: Oct 1998, Middle Temple*
Qualifications: [LLB (Hons)(Wales)]

BLACKBURN-LINDLEY MRS CLAIRE ANN

Chief Crown Prosecutor, Crown Prosecution Service, 7th Floor (South), Royal Liver Building, Pier Head, Liverpool, Merseyside, L3 1HN, ☎0151 239 8556 Fax: 0151 239 6410, ✉claire.lindley@cps.gsi.gov.uk, *Call Date: Nov 1986, Gray's Inn*
Qualifications: [LLB (Nott'm) LLM (Lond)]

F

BLACKETT MR ROBERT JAMES DAVID

Chadbourne and Parke LLP, Regis House, 45 King William Street, London, EC4R 9AN, *Call Date: Nov 2004, Lincoln's Inn*
Qualifications: [LLB (Hons)]

BLACKMAN MISS SHARON ANNETTE

Lawyer, Vice President, Citigroup, Citigroup Legal Department, Citigroup Centre, 33 Canada Square, Canary Wharf, London, E14 5LB, ☎ 020 7508 0760 Fax: 020 7508 0179, ✉ sharon.blackman@citi.com, *Call Date: Oct 1997, Lincoln's Inn*
Qualifications: [LLB (Brunel)]

BLACKSTOCK MS JODIE ELLEN

Justice, Eu Justice and Home Affairs, 59 Carter Lane, London, EC4V 5AQ, ☎ 020 7762 6436 Fax: 020 7329 5055, ✉ jblackstock@justice.org.uk, *Call Date: July 2003, Inner Temple*
Qualifications: [LLB (Hons) (Leic) LEC LLM]

BLAIR DR CHRISTOPHER PAUL ANTONY

The Treasury Solicitors, One Kemble Street, London, WC2B 4TS, ☎ 020 7210 3000, *Call Date: Nov 2002, Lincoln's Inn*
Qualifications: [MA (Cantab) PhD (Cantab)]

BLAIR MRS IY LEE

Court Clerk, Hmcs Cambridgeshire, Cambridgeshire Magistrates' Court Committee, Bridge Street, Peterborough, PE1 1ED, ☎ 01733 63971 Fax: 01733 313749, *Call Date: July 1989, Middle Temple*
Qualifications: [BSoc Sci (Keele)]

BLAIR MISS MARTI

Crown Advocate, Crown Prosecution Service, Justinian House, Spitfire Close, Ermine Business Park, Huntingdon, Cambridgeshire, PE29 6XY, ☎ 01223 488372, *Call Date: Mar 2002, Gray's Inn*
Qualifications: [LLB (Lond)]

BLAKE MR ALAN GEOFFREY

Crown Advocate, Crown Prosecution Service, Eaton Court, 112 Oxford Road, Reading, Berkshire, RG1 7LL, ☎ 0118 951 3600 x 3264 Fax: 0118 951 3601, ✉ alan.blake@cps.gsi.gov.uk, *Call Date: Oct 1997, Gray's Inn*
Qualifications: [BA MA (Oxon)]

BLAKEBROUGH MR PHILIP DAVID

General Dental Council, 37 Wimpole Street, London, W1G 8DQ, ☎ 0845 222 4141 Fax: 020 7224 3294, ✉ information@gdc-uk.org, *Call Date: July 1987, Middle Temple*
Qualifications: [LLB (Lond)]

BLAKE-JAMES MR HUGH DESMOND

Bailey Nicholson Grayson Solicitors & Advocates, 15 Bourne Court, Southend Road, South Woodford, IG8 8HD, *Call Date: Mar 1998, Middle Temple*
Qualifications: [BA (Hons)(Lond) CPE Dip Law (Lond)]

BLATCH MR JACOB JONATHON INIGO

Serious Fraud Office, Elm House, 10-16 Elm Street, London, WC1X 0BL, ☎ 020 7239 7272 Fax: 020 837 1173, *Call Date: Nov 1996, Inner Temple*
Qualifications: [LLB]

BLIZZARD MR DAVID JOHN MARK

Secretary, Barclaycard, Barclays Bank PLC, 1 Churchill Place, Canary Wharf, London, E14 5HP, ☎ 020 7116 2895 Fax: 020 7116 7665, ✉ david.blizzard@barclays.com, *Call Date: July 2002, Middle Temple*
Qualifications: [BA (Hons) FCIS]

BLOOR MISS BARBARA ELIZABETH

Lincolnshire Magistrates' Courts Service, The Magistrates' Court, Park Avenue, Skegness, Lincolnshire, PE25 1BH, ☎ 01754 898848 Fax: 01754 767318, ✉ barbara.bloor@hmcourts-service.gsi.gov.uk, *Call Date: July 1986, Middle Temple*
Qualifications: [BA (Lond)]

BLOOR MS LOUISE MARGARET

The Treasury Solicitors, One Kemble Street, London, WC2B 4TS, ☎ 020 7210 3000, ✉ louise.bloor@tsol.gsi.gov.uk, *Call Date: Oct 2008, Gray's Inn*
Qualifications: [BA]

BLOYCE MISS SAMANTHA JEANETTE

HM Revenue and Customs, 1st Floor, South West Bush House, London, WC2B 4RD, *Call Date: Nov 1997, Gray's Inn*
Qualifications: [LLB (Brunel)]

BLUNDEN MS ANNE-MARIE

Senior Crown Prosecutor, Crown Prosecution Service, Rose Court, 2 Southwark Bridge, London, SE1 9HS, ✉anne-marie.blunden2@cps.gsi.gov.uk, *Call Date: Nov 1992, Inner Temple*
Qualifications: [BA Dip Law (Lond)]

BODDY MR JAMES PETER

Fergusons Solicitors LLP, 11 Gough Square, London, EC4A 3DE, ☎020 7822 2999 Fax: 020 7822 2950, *Call Date: Oct 2004, Gray's Inn*
Qualifications: [BA PgDL]

BOGLE MR PAUL WAKEFIELD

Clerk, Company Secretary, Solicitor, Canterbury Christ Church University, Canterbury, Kent, CT1 1QU, ☎01227 782202 Fax: 01227 470442, ✉paul.bogle@canterbury.ac.uk, *Call Date: Oct 1995, Lincoln's Inn*
Qualifications: [LLB (Hons)(Bris)]

BOLTON SMITH MR JAMES RICHARD

Crown Prosecution Service, The Cooperage, 8 Gainsford Street, London, SE1 2NE, ☎020 7378 4242, ✉james.boltonsmith@cps.gsi.gov.uk, *Call Date: Nov 2008, Inner Temple*
Qualifications: [BA (Leeds) CPE]

BONDY MR RUPERT MARK BODEN

General Counsel, Bp PLC, 1 St James's Square, London, SW1Y 4PD, ☎020 4976 4452, ✉Rupert.Bondy@uk.bp.com, *Call Date: July 1987, Middle Temple*
Qualifications: [BA (Cantab)]

BONNELL MR MARCUS STEPHEN IESTYN LLEWELLY

Financial Services Authority, 25 The North Colannade, Canary Wharf, London, E14 8HS, *Call Date: July 1998, Gray's Inn*
Qualifications: [MA (Cantab)]

BOOCOCK MISS LISA JAYNE

Crown Prosecution Service, Sunlight House, Quay Street, Manchester, M60 3PS, *Call Date: Oct 1998, Gray's Inn*
Qualifications: [BA (Hons) (Cantab)]

BOODIA MISS ANURADHA DEVI

Crown Prosecution Service, Eagle House, Ram Passage, Kingston Upon Thames, Surrey, KT1 1HH, *Call Date: Oct 1994, Gray's Inn*
Qualifications: [LLB (Hons)]

BOONE MISS CAROLINE ANNE

Legal Adviser, Department For Transport, Zone 1/18, Great Minster House, 33 Horseferry Road, London, SW1P 4DR, ✉caroline.boone@dft.gsi.gov.uk, *Call Date: Feb 1980, Middle Temple*
Qualifications: [LLB (Soton)]

BOOTH MR JAMES ANDREW

Horwich Farrelly Solicitors, Alexander House, Talbot Road, Manchester, M16 0SP, ☎0161 214 5704, ✉james.booth@horwichfarrelly.co.uk, *Call Date: July 2006, Lincoln's Inn*
Qualifications: [BA (Dunelm)]

BOOTH MR MARTYN PARKINSON

Crown Prosecution Service, Central Police Station, Winston Churchill Avenue, Portsmouth, Hampshire, PO1 2DG, *Call Date: Oct 1996, Lincoln's Inn*
Qualifications: [LLB (Hons)(So'ton)]

BOSTON MISS JANET SUSAN

Crown Prosecution Service, Rose Court, 2 Southwark Bridge, London, SE1 9HS, ☎020 3357 0000, *Call Date: Nov 1976, Middle Temple*
Qualifications: [LLB (Lond)]

BOTTRELL MR ERIC PERRY

Manager, Department of Health, Room 523, Richmond House, 79 Whitehall, London, SW1A 2NS, ☎020 7210 6315, ✉Eric.Bottrell@DH.gsi.gov.uk, *Call Date: Mar 1997, Middle Temple*
Qualifications: [LLB (Hons) FCCA]

BOURNE MRS SHARON ELSIE MARY

Senior Crown Prosecutor, Crown Prosecution Service, 7th Floor (South), Royal Liver Building, Pier Head, Liverpool, Merseyside, L3 1HN, ✉Sharon.Bourne@cps.gsi.gov.uk, *Call Date: July 1985, Gray's Inn*
Qualifications: [LLB (L'pool)]

F

BOUSHER MR STEPHEN

HM Revenue and Customs, SLSI Team, 2nd Floor Team, North Bush, Strand, London, WC2B 4RD, ☎020 7438 6307, *Call Date: Nov 1975, Gray's Inn*
Qualifications: [LLB]

BOUSTRED MRS ANNE MARY

Luton Borough Council, Legal Services, Town Hall, Luton, Bedfordshire, LU1 2BQ, ☎01582 547497 Fax: 01582 546206, ✉anne.boustred@luton.gov.uk, *Call Date: July 1975, Inner Temple*
Qualifications: [LLB]

BOWEN MR JUSTIN

Imperial Innovations Group PLC, 52 Princes Gate, Exhibition Road, London, SW7 2PG, *Call Date: Oct 1994, Lincoln's Inn*
Qualifications: [MA (Cantab)]

BOWEN MISS MENNA GABRIELE

GSC Solicitors LLP, 31-32 Ely Place, London, EC1N 6TD, ☎020 7822 2222 Fax: 020 7822 2211, ✉mbowen@gscsolicitors.com, *Call Date: Oct 2002, Lincoln's Inn*
Qualifications: [PgDL (LGU) MA ATT CpE BA]

BOWLES MS VICKI

Stone King LLP, 13 Queen Square, Bath, BA1 2HJ, Fax: 01225 335437, ✉vb@stoneking.co.uk, *Call Date: Oct 2002, Middle Temple*
Qualifications: [LLB (Hon)(Nott'm) LLM]

BOWN MR PHILIP CLIVE

Chair, Cartwright King Solicitors, Norwich Union House, South Parade, Old Market Square, Nottingham, Nottinghamshire, NG1 2LH, ☎01159 587444 Fax: 01159 588666, ✉philip.bown@cartwrightking.co.uk, *Call Date: Nov 1974, Middle Temple*
Qualifications: [LLB FCIArb]

BOWYER MR HENRY MARTIN MITFORD

Cartwright King Solicitors, Norwich Union House, South Parade, Old Market Square, Nottingham, Nottinghamshire, NG1 2LH, ☎0115 958 7444 Fax: 0115 958 8666, ✉ck@cartwrightking.co.uk, *Call Date: Nov 1989, Inner Temple*
Qualifications: [LLB (Buck)]

BOYD MR JAMES ALUN

Crown Advocate, Crown Prosecution Service, Rose Court, 2 Southwark Bridge, London, SE1 9HS, ☎020 3357 1011 Fax: 020 3357 0056, ✉james.boyd@cps.gsi.gov.uk, *Call Date: Mar 2008, Middle Temple*
Qualifications: [BA (Hons) (Notts) PgDL (Notts)]

BOYD MISS MARIAN ELIZABETH

Crown Advocate, Senior Crown Prosecutor, Crown Prosecution Service, Priory Gate, 29 Union Street, Maidstone, Kent, ME14 1PT, ☎01622 356300 Fax: 01622 356359, *Call Date: July 1983, Middle Temple*
Qualifications: [BA]

BOYLE MR CHARLES GERARD

Nautilus International, 1 & 2 The Shrubberies, George Lane, South Woodford, London, E18 1BD, ☎020 7801 0347, ✉cboyle@nautilusint.org, *Call Date: Nov 1994, Middle Temple*
Qualifications: [LLB (Hons) (L'pool) LLM (Leics)]

BOYLE MR JAMES

Nexus Chambers, 7 New Square, Lincolns Inn, London, WC2A 3QS, ☎020 7404 1147 Fax: 020 7 9744, ✉james.boyle@nexuschambers.com, *Call Date: Nov 1999, Middle Temple*
Qualifications: [MA BA (Open) PG Dip Law PG Cert Management PG Dip Legal Pract]

BRABY-PAVITT MRS LYNNE LOUISE

Principal Lawyer, Essex Legal Services, New Bridge House, 60-68 New London Road, Chelmsford, Essex, CM2 0PD, ☎01245 506667 Fax: 01245 346994, *Call Date: Nov 1986, Gray's Inn*
Qualifications: [LLB (Hons)]

BRACKEN MR GREGORY PATRICK

Deutsche Bank AG London, Winchester House, 1 Great Winchester Street, London, EC2N 2DB, ☎020 7545 2014, ✉greg.bracken@db.com, *Call Date: Mar 2006, Middle Temple*
Qualifications: [B.Comm.(Hons) BL (Hons)]

F

BRACKEN MISS JANINE

Bench Legal Adviser, Royal Courts of Justice, Administrative Court Office, Room C323, The Strand, London, WC2A 2LL, *Call Date: Mar 2001, Middle Temple*
Qualifications: [LLB (Hons) LLM (L'Pool)]

BRADBURY MR TREVOR

Company Secretary, Interserve PLC, Interserve House, Ruscombe Park, Twyford, Reading, Berkshire, RG10 9JU, ☎0118 9320123 Fax: 0118 9320206, ✉trevor.bradbury@interserve.com, *Call Date: Nov 1995, Middle Temple*
Qualifications: [LLB (Hons) FRICS MCIArb]

BRADFORD MR TOM HENRY

Russell-Cook Solicitors, 2 Putney Hill, London, SW15 6AB, Fax: 020 8780 1194, *Call Date: July 2004, Lincoln's Inn*
Qualifications: [BA Hons (Warw) MA (Warw) PgDI (Sussex)]

BRADLEY MISS CELIA ANNE

Legal Adviser, Her Majesty's Courts and Tribunals Service, Gail House, Lower Stone Street, Maidstone, Kent, ME15 6NB, ☎01622 680050 Fax: 01622 680078, *Call Date: Feb 1992, Middle Temple*
Qualifications: [LLB (Hons)]

BRADLEY MR JOHN JOSEPH

The Directorate of Legal Services, Welsh Assembly Government, Room G05, Cathays Park, Cardiff, Wales, CF10 3NQ, ☎029 2082 3202, *Call Date: July 1998, Gray's Inn*
Qualifications: [LLB (Warw) LLM (Bruges)]

BRAICH MR STEPHEN HARMIT SINGH

Bench Legal Adviser, Northampton Magistrates' Court, Regents Pavilion, Summerhouse Road, Moulton Park, Northampton, Northamptonshire, NN3 6AS, ☎01604 497000 Fax: 01604 497010, ✉stephen.braich@hmcts.gsi.gov.uk, *Call Date: Nov 1987, Gray's Inn*
Qualifications: [LLB LLM (Cantab)]

BRAITHWAITE MR MARC DAVID

Office of Fair Trading, Fleetbank House, 2-6 Salisbury Square, London, EC4Y 8JX, ☎020 7211 8732 Fax: 020 7211 8992, ✉marc.braithwaite@oft.gsi.gov.uk, *Call Date: Oct 1997, Middle Temple*
Qualifications: [BSc (Hons)(Lond) LLB]

BRAMLEY MR STEVEN MICHAEL STUART

Legal Adviser, The Home Office, Legal Advisors Branch, Seacole, Ground Floor, 2 Marsham Street, London, SW1P 4DF, *Call Date: July 1983, Gray's Inn*
Qualifications: [LLB]

BRAMLEY MISS SUSANNAH JANE

Crown Prosecution Service, Gateway, 31 Power Close, Guildford, Surrey, GU1 1EJ, *Call Date: Oct 1997, Middle Temple*
Qualifications: [LLB (Hons)(Kingston)]

BRAMWELL MR PHILIP NICHOLAS

General Counsel, Bae Systems PLC, Stirling Square, 6 Carlton Gardens, London, SW1Y 5AD, ☎01252 383892 Fax: 01252 383992, ✉philip.bramwell@baesystems.com, *Call Date: Nov 1983, Lincoln's Inn*
Qualifications: [BA (Hons)]

BRAVINER ROMAN MR STEPHEN THOMAS

Call Date: Oct 1992, Gray's Inn
Qualifications: [BA LLM]

BRAZIL MR SHAUL DAVID

BCL Burton Copeland, 51 Lincoln's Inn Fields, London, WC2A 3LZ, ☎020 7430 2277 Fax: 020 7430 1101, ✉sbrazil@bcl.com, *Call Date: July 2003, Lincoln's Inn*
Qualifications: [BSc (Hons) (Bath)]

BREWER MISS STEPHANIE ALEXANDRIA

American Express, 60 Buckingham Palace Road, London, SW1W 0RR, ☎020 7824 6428 Fax: 020 7730 5067, ✉stephanie.a.brewer@aexp.com, *Call Date: July 2002, Middle Temple*
Qualifications: [LLB (Hons) LLM (Nott'm)]

BRICK MR NEVILLE EYRE

HED, BNP Paribas, Compliance Department, 10 Harewood Avenue, London, NW1 6AA, ☎ 020 7595 4764 Fax: 020 7595 5654, ✉ neville.brick@bnpparibas.com, *Call Date: July 1976, Gray's Inn*
Qualifications: [LLB (Lond)]

BRIDDICK MS CATHERINE ALLISON

Lecturer, Senior Legal Officer, Rights of Women, 52-54 Featherstone Street, London, EC1Y 8RT, ☎ 020 7251 6575
Fax: 020 7490 5377, ✉ cate@row.org.uk, *Call Date: July 2004, Lincoln's Inn*
Qualifications: [BA Hons (Lond) LLM (Lond)]

BRIDGE MR IAN CHARLES

No5 Chambers, Greenwood House, 4-7 Salisbury Court, London, EC4Y 8AA, ✉ ib@no5.com, *Call Date: Nov 1988, Inner Temple*
Qualifications: [LLB (Hons) (Sheff)]

BRIDGES DR PAUL WILLIAM

Director, Department For Work and Pensions, 5th Floor, the Adelphi, 1-11 John Adam Street, London, WC2N 6HT, ☎ 020 7962 8106, *Call Date: July 1984, Gray's Inn*
Qualifications: [BA PhD]

BRIDGLAND MR NICHOLAS JAMES

Scansource Europe SPRL, Avenue Du Bourget, Bourgetlaan, B-1130 Brussels, Belgium, *Call Date: Nov 2000, Lincoln's Inn*
Qualifications: [LLB (Hons) (Essex)]

BRIGHOUSE MISS SOPHIE MARIE

The Treasury Solicitors, 5th Floor, One Kemble Street, London, WC2B 4TS, ☎ 020 7210 3363 Fax: 020 7210 3410, *Call Date: Nov 2008, Lincoln's Inn*
Qualifications: [BA (Oxon) CPE OBPP]

BRINDLEY MRS VICTORIA ROSEMARY CLAIRE

Chichester Magistrates Court, 6 Market Avenue, Chichester, West Sussex, PO19 1YE, ✉ vicky.brindley@hmcourts-service.gsi.gov.uk, *Call Date: Oct 2000, Inner Temple*
Qualifications: [LLB (Cardiff)]

BRINKWORTH MR PAUL GREGORY

Serious Fraud Office, Elm House, 10-16 Elm Street, London, WC1X 0BJ, ☎ 020 7239 7313 Fax: 020 7833 5432, ✉ paul.brinkworth@sfo.gsi.gov.uk, *Call Date: Oct 1990, Lincoln's Inn*
Qualifications: [BA]

BRISTOW MISS CLARE

Director, Arup Group Limited, Legal Group, 13 Fitzroy Street, London, W1T 4BQ, ☎ 020 7755 4152 Fax: 020 7755 2762, ✉ clare.bristow@arup.com, *Call Date: Oct 1996, Lincoln's Inn*
Qualifications: [LLB (Hons)(Leeds) MA (Leeds)]

BROADHURST MR SIMON THOMAS

The Home Office, Ground Floor, Seacole House, 2 Marsham Street, London, SW1P 4DF, *Call Date: Nov 1994, Inner Temple*
Qualifications: [BA (Oxon) CPE]

BROCK MISS CAROLYN ANNE

Commercial Lawyer, BT Group PLC, Bt Australiasia Pty Limited, Bt Tower, Level 12, 1 Market Street, Sydney, Nsw 2000, Australia, ☎ +61 2 9269 1032, *Call Date: July 1987, Lincoln's Inn*
Qualifications: [LLB]

BROCKLEHURST MISS ELIZABETH ANNE

Senior Crown Prosecutor, Crown Prosecution Service, Riding Gate House, 37 Old Dover Road, Canterbury, Kent, CT1 3JG, ☎ 01227 866 020, *Call Date: July 1982, Middle Temple*
Qualifications: [BA (Lond) Dip Law]

BROMFIELD MR COLIN HUGH

Crown Prosecution Service, Rose Court, 2 Southwark Bridge, London, SE1 9HS, *Call Date: Nov 1988, Gray's Inn*
Qualifications: [LLB (Hons)]

BRONZE MR LEE CLIFFORD

Thompsons Solicitors, 23 Princess Street, Manchester, M2 4ER, ☎ 0161 615 8204 Fax: 0161 819 3581, ✉ leebronze@thompsons.law.co.uk, *Call Date: July 2007, Gray's Inn*
Qualifications: [LL.B (Manch)]

BROOKES-HOWELLS MR IAN DAVID

HED, Senior Lawyer, BT Group PLC, Commercial, Legal & Regulatory, PP HW A906 Virtual Postbox, (HOM-NZ) PO Box 200, London, N18 1ZF, ☎01977 594 717 Fax: 01926 315 336, *Call Date: July 1989, Middle Temple*
Qualifications: [LLB]

BROOKS MRS KAREN ANNE

Senior Crown Prosecutor, Crown Prosecution Service, Bolton Police Station, 10 Scholey Street, Bolton, Greater Manchester, BL2 1HX, ☎01204 543300, ✉karen.brooks@cps.gsi.gov.uk, *Call Date: July 1983, Middle Temple*
Qualifications: [LLB (Manch)]

BROOKWELL MR PAUL

Crown Prosecution Service, The Unicentre, Lords Walk, Preston, Lancashire, PR1 1DH, ☎01772 208120 Fax: 01772 208137, ✉paul.brookwell@cps.gsi.gov.uk, *Call Date: Feb 1985, Middle Temple*
Qualifications: [BA]

BROWITT MR DAVID PHILIP

Department For Transport, Legal, Zone 1/06, Great Minster House, 76 Marsham Street, London, SW1P 4DR, *Call Date: Nov 1998, Inner Temple*
Qualifications: [BA (Oxon)]

BROWN MR ANDREW CHARLES

Crown Prosecution Service, Rose Court, 2 Southwark Bridge, London, SE1 9HS, *Call Date: Nov 1982, Gray's Inn*
Qualifications: [BSc (Lond) DipL]

BROWN MR ANTHONY JOSEPH

The Home Office, Seacole House, 2 Marsham Street, London, SW1P 4DF, ✉anthony.brown@homeoffice.gsi.gov.uk, *Call Date: Nov 2010, Lincoln's Inn*
Qualifications: [BA (Oxon) MPHIL PHD (Cantab)]

BROWN MISS ARABA AKYENBA

Crown Prosecution Service, 8 Gainsford Street, The Cooperage, London, SE1 2NE, *Call Date: July 2001, Middle Temple*
Qualifications: [LLB (Hons) LLM]

BROWN MRS CHANTELLE NICOLE

Crown Prosecution Service, The Cooperage, 8 Gainsford Street, London, SE1 2NE, ✉chantelle.brown@cps.gsi.gov.uk, *Call Date: July 2006, Lincoln's Inn*
Qualifications: [BA LLB (Lond)]

BROWN MISS CHARLOTTE LEONIE

The Khan Partnership LLP, 48/49 Russell Square, London, WC1B 4JP, ☎020 7612 2530 Fax: 020 7612 2531, ✉cbrown@thekhanpartnership.com, *Call Date: July 2007, Inner Temple*
Qualifications: [LLB (Lond) LLM (Lond) ADIT]

BROWN MR DAVID CHARLES

Head of Legal Services, Birmingham City Council, Ingleby House, Legal Services, 11-14 Cannon Street, Birmingham, B2 5EN, ☎0121 464 3096 Fax: 0121 303 2293, *Call Date: Feb 1993, Middle Temple*
Qualifications: [B Sc Dip LG]

BROWN MRS ELAINE MAUDE

Legal Adviser, Office of the Public Guardian, 6th Floor Tower, Zones 6.50 - 6.53, Ministry of Justice, London, SW1H 9AJ, ☎020 33346575 / 020 3334 6575, ✉Elaine.Brown@guardianship.gsi.gov.uk, *Call Date: July 1983, Middle Temple*
Qualifications: [LLM (Lond) LLB (Lond)]

BROWN MISS GEORGINA NICOLE

The Treasury Solicitors, One Kemble Street, London, WC2B 4TS, ✉georgina.brown@tsol.gsi.gov.uk, *Call Date: Nov 2001, Middle Temple*
Qualifications: [BA (Hons) (Oxon) CPE MA (Hons)]

BROWN MR GRAHAM

Chief Crown Prosecutor, Bailey Nicholson Grayson Solicitors & Advocates, 15 Bourne Court, Southend Road, South Woodford, IG8 8HD, ☎020 8418 2400 Fax: 020 8418 2901, *Call Date: Nov 1982, Gray's Inn*
Qualifications: [BA]

BROWN MR IAN WILLIAM

Nursing and Midwifery Council, 1 Kemble Street, London, WC2B 4AN, Fax: 020 7580 3410, ✉ian.brown@nmc-uk.org, *Call Date: July 2008, Inner Temple*
Qualifications: [LLB (Nott'm)]

BROWN MR JOHN ALEXANDER

Financial Services Authority, The Financial Services Authority, Enforcement and Financial Crime Division - Legal Group, 25 The North Colonade, Canary Wharf, London, E14 5HS, ☎ 020 7066 9734, *Call Date: Nov 2002, Lincoln's Inn*
Qualifications: [LLB (Hons) (Nott'm) LLM (Cantab)]

BROWN MS MANDY

Legal Officer, Department For Work and Pensions, 5th Floor, the Adelphi, 1-11 John Adam Street, London, WC2N 6HT, ✉ Mandy. Brown@dwp.gsi.gov.uk, *Call Date: Nov 1991, Lincoln's Inn*
Qualifications: [LLB (Hons) (Essex)]

BROWN MR MARTIN FREDERICK JOHN

Senior Legal Adviser, Stoke-On-Trent Magistrates' Court, Baker Street, Fenton, Stoke-On-Trent, ST4 3BX, ☎ 01782 845353 Fax: 01782 744782, *Call Date: Feb 1990, Gray's Inn*
Qualifications: [BA (Hons) LLM]

BROWN MR MATTHEW JAMES

BT Group PLC, BT Legal PPA6, BT Centre, 81 Newgate Street, London, EC1A 7AJ, *Call Date: Nov 1994, Middle Temple*
Qualifications: [LLB (Hons)]

BROWN COMMODORE NEIL LOGAN

Royal Navy Officers, M-P 4-2 Fleet Headquarters, Sir Henry Leach Building, Whale Island, Portsmouth, Hampshire, PO2 8BY, ☎ 02392 625750 Fax: 02392 625755, *Call Date: Oct 1992, Middle Temple*
Qualifications: [LLB (Hons)(Ireland)]

BROWN MR RICHARD GORDON

Call Date: Oct 1997, Inner Temple
Qualifications: [BA (Cantab) CPE]

BROWNING MR ROBERT ANDRE

Legal Adviser, Legal Manager, Sir Robert Mcalpine Limited, Yorkshire House, Grosvenor Crescent, London, SW1X 7EP, ☎ 020 7591 3602 Fax: 020 7245 9140, ✉ r. browning@sir-robert-mcalpine.com, *Call Date: Nov 1995, Gray's Inn*
Qualifications: [LLB (Hons) FCIArb FRICS]

BROWNING MR ROBERT MARK

Ba Law, 59 Pelham Street, London, SW7 2NJ, ☎ 0870 458 4600 Fax: 0870 458 4800, ✉ balaw@onetel.com, *Call Date: Nov 1986, Inner Temple*
Qualifications: [LLB (So'ton)]

BROWNLEE MISS SHELLEY VICTORIA

Nursing and Midwifery Council, 1 Kemble Street, London, WC2B 4AN, ☎ 07793535403 / 020 7681 5857, ✉ shelley. brownlee@nmc-uk.org, *Call Date: Nov 2005, Inner Temple*
Qualifications: [LLB London School of Economics &, Political Science]

BRUCE MS NIMUE

Capsticks, 1 St George's Road, Wimbledon, London, SW19 4DR, *Call Date: Nov 1999, Gray's Inn*
Qualifications: [BA (Lond)]

BRUDENELL MISS KIM ELAINE

CVS, The Treasury Solicitors, One Kemble Street, London, WC2B 4TS, ☎ 020 7210 3252, ✉ kim.brudenell@tsol.gsi.gov.uk, *Call Date: Nov 1992, Inner Temple*
Qualifications: [BA (Hons) CPE]

BRYAN MS DEBORAH

West Sussex County Council Child Care, And Advocacy Team, Room 208, County Hall, Chichester, West Suusex, PO19 1RO, ☎ 01243 777 036 Fax: 01243 777 285, *Call Date: July 1987, Lincoln's Inn*
Qualifications: [LLB]

BRYAN MRS JAYNE MARIE

Crown Prosecution Service, Citadel House, 58 High Street, Hull, Humberside, HU1 1QD, *Call Date: Feb 1994, Gray's Inn*
Qualifications: [LLB]

BRYANT MR JEFFREY MARTIN

Crown Prosecution Service, Rose Court, 2 Southwark Bridge, London, SE1 9HS, ☎ 0203357 0434 Fax: 020 3357 0390, *Call Date: July 2001, Lincoln's Inn*
Qualifications: [LLB (Hons)]

BRYNING MR PAUL

Tuckers Solicitors, 63-65 Mosley Street, Manchester, M2 3HZ, Fax: 0161 233 4333, ✉Bryningp@TuckersSolicitors.com, *Call Date: Oct 2001, Lincoln's Inn*
Qualifications: [BA (Hons)]

BUCKENHAM MR GILES EDWARD

HED, Department For Transport, 1/12 Great Minster House, 33 Horseferry Road, London, SW1P 4DR, ☎020 7944 4753 Fax: 020 7944 6692, ✉Giles.Buckenham@dft.gsi.gov.uk, *Call Date: Feb 1995, Lincoln's Inn*
Qualifications: [BA (Hons)(Warw)]

BUCKINGHAM MISS LISE MERIE

Head of Legal Services, Her Majesty's Court Service, Court House, London Road, Dorking, Surrey, RH4 1SX, ☎01306 885544 Fax: 01306 877447, ✉lise.buckingham@hmcourts-service.gsi.gov.uk, *Call Date: Feb 1992, Gray's Inn*
Qualifications: [LLB]

BUCKSEY MR NICHOLAS RICHARD

Ricardo PLC, Shoreham Technical Centre, Shoreham-By-Sea, West Sussex, RH15 0HG, ☎01273 455 611 Fax: 01273 464 124, *Call Date: July 1995, Inner Temple*
Qualifications: [LLB]

BUCKWELL MR WILLIAM DOMINIC HEYMANSON

Solicitor Advocate, Seaco Global Ltd, 21 St Thomas Street, London, SE1 9RY, ☎020 7939 5600 Fax: 020 7939 5650, *Call Date: Oct 1993, Middle Temple*
Qualifications: [BA (Hons)]

BUGEJA MR ALBERT JOHN

Head of Legal Services, Rochford District Council, Council Offices, South Street, Rochford, Essex, SS4 1BW, ☎01702 318 130 Fax: 01702 545737, ✉albert.bugeja@rochford.gov.uk, *Call Date: Nov 1981, Lincoln's Inn*
Qualifications: [BA (Hons)]

BULL MISS ALEXANDRA RYRIE

Crown Prosecution Service, Riverside House, Riverside Way, Bedford Road, Northampton, Northamptonshire, NN1 5NX, ✉alexandra.bull@cps.gsi.gov.uk, *Call Date: Oct 1999, Middle Temple*
Qualifications: [BA (Hons)]

BULLINGHAM MS MARGARET HANNAH

Travis Perkins, Rye Hill House, Rye Hill, Northampton, NN5 7UA, ☎01604 685268 Fax: 01604 683161, *Call Date: July 2005, Middle Temple*
Qualifications: [LLB (Hons)]

BULLOCK MR ANDREW JOHN

Other, Solicitors Regulation Authority, Ipsley Court, Berrington Close, Redditch, Worcestershire, B98 0TD, ✉Andrew.Bullock@sra.org.uk, *Call Date: May 1992, Lincoln's Inn*
Qualifications: [LLB (Hons) (Manch)]

BURAK MR FRANCIS ADRIAN

Crown Prosecution Service, The Cooperage, 8 Gainsford Street, London, SE1 2NE, ☎0207 3784127 Fax: 020 3300 4861, *Call Date: Oct 2006, Middle Temple*
Qualifications: [LLB (Hons)]

BURCHILL MR JOHN ROBERT

Director, The Legal Director Limited, Level 4, One Kingdom Street, London, W2 6BD, *Call Date: Nov 1986, Middle Temple*
Qualifications: [LLB(Wales)]

BURGESS MR BRIAN NEIL

Senior Crown Prosecutor, Crown Prosecution Service, United House, Piccadilly, York, North Yorkshire, YO1 9PQ, ✉brian.burgess@cps.gsi.gov.uk, *Call Date: July 1989, Lincoln's Inn*
Qualifications: [BA (Warw)]

BURGESS MR DAVID BRIAN

Senior Crown Prosecutor, Crown Prosecution Service, Argal House, Peninsula Business Park, Rydon Lane, Exeter, Devon, EX2 7NT, *Call Date: Nov 1989, Inner Temple*
Qualifications: [LLB]

F

BURGESS MISS EMMA VICTORIA

Ministry of Justice, Zone 6.31, Legal Directorate, 102 Petty France, London, SW1H 9AJ, *Call Date: Feb 1995, Middle Temple*
Qualifications: [LLB (Hons)(Bris)]

BURGESS MR JOHN

Crown Prosecution Service, Froomsgate House, Rupert Street, Bristol, BS1 2QJ, ☎0117 930 2800 / 0117 930 2800, ✉john.burgess@cps.gsi.gov.uk, *Call Date: Oct 1997, Inner Temple*
Qualifications: [LLB (Lond)]

BURGESS MR KEITH JOHN

Company Secretary, General Counsel, Hogg Robinson Group PLC, Global House, Victoria Street, Basingstoke, Hampshire, RG21 2BT, ☎01256 312600 Fax: 01256 346999, ✉keith.burgess@hrgworldwide.com, *Call Date: Nov 1977, Inner Temple*
Qualifications: [BA FCIS]

BURKE MR CHRISTOPHER MICHAEL

The Treasury Solicitors, 3rd Floor, Ergon House, Horseferry Road, London, SW1P 2AL, ✉chris.burke@defra.gsi.gov.uk, *Call Date: July 1985, Inner Temple*
Qualifications: [BA Dip Law]

BURKE MISS VANESSA SAMANTHA

Principal Legal Officer, Department For Work and Pensions, Office of the Solicitor, New Court, 48 Carey Street, London, WC2A 2LS, *Call Date: Nov 1989, Lincoln's Inn*
Qualifications: [LLB]

BURLEY MR JAMES JOHN

Dobsons Solicitors, 27 London Road, Bromley, Kent, BR1 1DF, ✉mail@bnglaw.co.uk, *Call Date: Mar 2008, Middle Temple*
Qualifications: [LLB (Hons) (Warw)]

BURMAN MRS HELENA JEANNETTE

Deputy Justices' Clerk, Crown Prosecution Service, Queens House, 58 Victoria Street, St. Albans, Hertfordshire, AL1 3HZ, ☎01727 798700 / 01727 798700, ✉Helena.Lewer@cps.gsi.gov.uk, Helena.Burman@cps.gsi.gov.uk, *Call Date: Nov 1993, Inner Temple*
Qualifications: [BA (Lond) CPE (Lond)]

BURMAN MR KEITH WILLIAM

Deputy Justices' Clerk, Her Magestys' Courts Services, Justices' Clerk, Bromley Magistrates, 1 London Road, Bromley, Kent, BR1 1RA, *Call Date: Nov 1984, Middle Temple*
Qualifications: [Dip Mag Law]

BURN MR NICHOLAS GEORGE ORWIN

Advocate, Crown Prosecution Service, 2 Parker Court, Staffordshire Technology Park, Stafford, Staffordshire, ST18 0EZ, ☎01785 272200 Fax: 01785 272290, ✉nick.burn@cps.gsi.gov.uk, *Call Date: July 1982, Gray's Inn*
Qualifications: [BA (Hons)]

BURNHAM MR JAMES PITT

District Crown Prosecutor, Crown Prosecution Service, Basingstoke Police Station, London Road, Basingstoke, Hampshire, RG21 4AD, ☎01256 405390 Fax: 01256 405038, ✉james.burnham@cps.gsi.gov.uk, *Call Date: July 1984, Gray's Inn*
Qualifications: [LLB (Reading)]

BURNS MISS LORNA MARIE

Borough Crown Prosecutor, Crown Prosecution Service, The Cooperage, 8 Gainsford Street, London, SE1 2NE, ☎020 3300 4319 Fax: 020 3300 4333, ✉lorna.burns@cps.gsi.gov.uk, *Call Date: Nov 1986, Inner Temple*
Qualifications: [LLB (Leics)]

BURROWS MS AMANDA JANE

Crown Prosecution Service, City Gate House, 185 Dyke Road, Hove, East Sussex, BN3 1TL, ☎01273 765600 Fax: 01273 765605, *Call Date: July 2001, Middle Temple*
Qualifications: [CPE CQSW PGDip]

BURROWS MRS CAROL JANE

Senior Legal Adviser, Justices Clerks Office, The Court House, South Wells, Stafford, ST16 3DW, *Call Date: Apr 1989, Gray's Inn*
Qualifications: [LLB]

BURROWS MR ROSS OLIVER

Kb Law Solicitors, 60-2 Pitt Street, Norwich, NR3 1DF, ☎01603 617 592 Fax: 0871 528 8926, ✉rburrows@kblaw.org.uk, *Call Date: Nov 2009, Lincoln's Inn*
Qualifications: [LLB (Lond)]

F

BURTON MRS CLAIRE LOUISE

Crown Prosecution Service, Vantage Point, Ty Coch Way, Cwmbian, Gwent, NP44 7XX, ☎01633 261100, ✉ClaireL.Burton@cps.gsi.gov.uk, *Call Date: Oct 2000, Middle Temple*
Qualifications: [LLB (Hons) (Nott'm)]

BURTON MISS JANICE ELAINE

London Borough of Haringey Council, Alexandra House, 10 Station Road, Wood Green, London, N22 7TE, *Call Date: July 1991, Lincoln's Inn*
Qualifications: [LLB (Hons)]

BURTON MR MERVYN JOHN

Senior Crown Prosecutor, Crown Prosecution Service, Charing Cross Police Station, Agar Street, London, WC2N 4JP, *Call Date: July 1973, Middle Temple*
Qualifications: [BA (Hons)]

BUSH MR KEITH

Arbitrator, Recorder, 30 Park Place, 30 Park Place, Cardiff, CF10 3BS, ☎029 2039 8421 Fax: 029 2039 8725, *Call Date: July 1977, Gray's Inn*
Qualifications: [BSc MICE LLM(Lond)]

BUSHELL MR JONATHAN DAVID

Crown Advocate, Crown Prosecution Service, Capital Tower, Greyfriars Road, Cardiff, CF10 3PL, ☎02920 803807 Fax: 02920 803840, *Call Date: July 1990, Lincoln's Inn*
Qualifications: [MA (Oxon)]

BUTCHER MR MICHAEL

Bencher, Consultant, Director, Legal Officer, Veolia Water Uk PLC, Fifth Floor, Kings Place, 90 York Way, London, N1 9AG, *Call Date: July 1975, Gray's Inn*
Qualifications: [BA Hons (Keele)]

BUTLER MR EDWARD JACK GREER

Martin Murray and Associates, Chapel House, 152-156 High Street, Yiewsley, West Drayton, Middlesex, UB7 7BE, ☎01895 431 332 Fax: 01895 448 343, ✉ebutler@mmasolicitors.co.uk, *Call Date: July 2007, Middle Temple*
Qualifications: [LLB (Hons) (Exon)]

BUTLER MISS FIONA

Browne Jacobson LLP, Mowbray House, Castle Meadow Road, Nottingham, NG2 1BJ, ☎0115 976 6000 Fax: 0115 947 5246, ✉fbutler@brownejacobson.com, *Call Date: July 1999, Lincoln's Inn*
Qualifications: [LLB (Hons)(Manch)]

BUTLER MISS JUDITH LYNNE

Office of Fair Trading, Fleetbank House, 2-6 Salisbury Square, London, EC4Y 8JX, ✉judith.butler@oft.gsi.gov.uk, *Call Date: Oct 1997, Middle Temple*
Qualifications: [MA (Hons) (Oxon)]

BUTLER MISS MEGAN VERONICA

Chief Executive, HED, Financial Services Authority, The Financial Services Authority, Enforcement and Financial Crime Division - Legal Group, 25 The North Colonade, Canary Wharf, London, E14 5HS, ☎020 7066 3480, ✉megan.butler@fsa.gov.uk, *Call Date: July 1987, Inner Temple*
Qualifications: [LLB (Sheff)]

BUTT MR IRFAN SALAH

Hogan Lovells (Middle East) LLP, 19th Floor, Currency Tower, Dubai International Financial Centre, Po Box 506602, Dubia, United Arab Emirates, Fax: 4 377 9378, *Call Date: Nov 2000, Lincoln's Inn*
Qualifications: [LLB (Hons) (Reading)]

BUTT MISS NAZIA TUSNEEM

Crown Prosecution Service, Solihull Cju, Police Station, Homer Road, Solihull, B91 3QL, *Call Date: July 2003, Middle Temple*
Qualifications: [BA Hons PG Dip Law]

BUTT MR ZAHURUDDIN

Lincoln Harford Solicitors, 713 Harrow Road, Wembley, Middlesex, HA0 2LL, Fax: 020 8902 1526, *Call Date: Nov 1959, Lincoln's Inn*
Qualifications: [BA]

BUTTER MR TIMOTHY

Barclays Bank PLC, 1 Churchill Place, Canary Wharf, London, E14 5HP, ☎020 7116 5109, ✉timothy.butter@barclays.com, *Call Date: Oct 1991, Inner Temple*
Qualifications: [BA (Warw) MSc (Lond) Dip Law]

BUTTERWORTH MR ADRIAN ERNEST

HED, Gmp Securities Europe LLP, 4 Albermarble Street, London, W1S 4GA, ☎020 7467 2807, *Call Date: Nov 1995, Middle Temple*
Qualifications: [BA (Hons)(Hull) FCIS MA]

BUTTERWORTH MRS BARBARA SUSAN

Company Secretary, Legal Adviser, Secretary, Janssen Cilag Ltd, 50-100 Holmers Farm Way, High Wycombe, HP12 4EG, ✉bbutterw@its.jnj.com, *Call Date: July 1989, Lincoln's Inn*
Qualifications: [BA (York) LLB MBA LLM]

BUTTERWORTH MRS CHARLOTTE LOUISE

Protection Vessels International Limited, Unit 8 Cotswold Business Park, Millfield Lane, Caddington, Bedfordshire, LU1 4AJ, ☎01884 842878 Fax: 01884 841944, ✉charlotte.butterworth@pviltd.com, *Call Date: July 2003, Middle Temple*
Qualifications: [BMus Hons (Wales) PG Dip Law]

BYATT MR JAMES ROBERT

Crown Advocate, Crown Prosecution Service, Citadel House, 58 High Street, Hull, Humberside, HU1 1QD, ☎01482 621000, ✉james.byatt@cps.gsi.gov.uk, *Call Date: July 1983, Gray's Inn*
Qualifications: [LLB (UEA) LLB (Hons)]

BYFORD MR NEVILLE PAUL

Partner, Eversheds LLP, 1 Wood Street, London, EC2V 7WS, ☎0845 497 9797
Fax: 0845 497 4919, ✉nevillebyford@eversheds.com, *Call Date: July 1987, Inner Temple*
Qualifications: [LLB (So'ton)]

BYRNE MR DANIEL CHRISTOPHER

Bristows, 100 Victoria Embankment, London, EC4Y 0DH, ☎020 7400 8296
Fax: 020 7400 8050, ✉Daniel.Byrne@Bristows.com, *Call Date: July 2005, Inner Temple*
Qualifications: [BSc University of Durham MA University of Sheff]

BYRNE MR KEVIN MOWBRAY

Deputy Justices' Clerk, Her Majesty's Court Service, The Courthouse, N.Quay, Great Yarmouth, Norfolk, NR30 1PW, ☎01493 849800, ✉kevin.byrne@hmcourts-service.gsi.gov.uk, *Call Date: Nov 1983, Middle Temple*
Qualifications: [BA (Law)(Kent)]

BYRNE MR PHILIP OWEN JOSEPH

Brabners Chaffe Street LLP, Horton House, Exchange Road, Liverpool, L2 3YL,
Fax: 0151 600 3010, ✉philip.byrne@brabnerscs.com, *Call Date: July 1999, Middle Temple*
Qualifications: [BA (Hons) Dip in Law]

CACCIOTTI MISS MELISSA ERSILIA DOREEN

Accenture, Legal Group, Litigation & Disputes Team, 118/120 Avenue De France, Paris, 75013, France, ☎1 5323 5050
Fax: 1 5323 5323, ✉melissa.cacciotti@accenture.com, *Call Date: Oct 1997, Gray's Inn*
Qualifications: [LLB (Lancs)]

CAIN MR DANIEL JOHN

Deputy Justices' Clerk, Hmcs Suffolk, Ipswich Magistrates' Court, Elm Street, Ipswich, Suffolk, IP1 2AP, ☎01473 217261
Fax: 01473 231249, ✉Daniel.Cain@hmcts.gsi.gov.uk, *Call Date: Feb 1990, Inner Temple*
Qualifications: [LLB (Hons)]

CAIN MR FRANCIS CROFTON

Wiltshire Council, Legal Unit, Dept of Resources, County Hall, Trowbridge, Wiltshire, BA14 8JN, ☎01225 713 032
Fax: 01225 713 998, ✉frankcain@wiltshire.gov.uk, *Call Date: Oct 2006, Inner Temple*
Qualifications: [LLB (New Zealand)]

CAIN MISS NICOLA BOBBIE

Bbc Litigation Department, Room 2251, Bbc White City, 201 Wood Lane, London, W12 7TS, ✉nicola.cain@bbc.co.uk, *Call Date: July 2005, Middle Temple*
Qualifications: [LLB (Hons) Brunel LLM (Lond)]

CAISTOR MR DANIEL JOHN

Office of Fair Trading, Fleetbank House, 2-6 Salisbury Square, London, EC4Y 8JX, *Call Date: Oct 1998, Lincoln's Inn*
Qualifications: [LLB (Hons)(Leic)]

CAKEBREAD MISS SARAH ELIZABETH

Associate, Carey Olsen, Po Box 98, Carey House, Les Banques, St Peter Port, GY1 4BZ, ☎01481 732085 Fax: 01481 711052, ✉sarah.cakebread@careyolsen.com, *Call Date: July 2006, Inner Temple*
Qualifications: [LLB (Lond) LLM (Lond)]

CALLAGHAN MR LEE PATRICK

Director, General Counsel, Aviva Legal Services, Aviva PLC Group Legal, 20th Floor, St. Helen's, 1 Undershaft, London, EC3P 3DQ, *Call Date: Feb 1988, Gray's Inn*
Qualifications: [BA Dip COMP Dip EC LLM]

CALLARD MR GRAHAM MICHAEL

Lewis Silkin LLP, 5 Chancery Lane, Cliffords Inn, London, EC4A 1BL, *Call Date: Nov 2001, Middle Temple*
Qualifications: [LLB (Hons) LLM TEP MCIArb]

CALLAWAY MR IAN PAUL

Senior Crown Prosecutor, Crown Prosecution Service, Riding Gate House, 37 Old Dover Road, Canterbury, Kent, CT1 3JG, ☎01227 817236, ✉Ian.Callaway@cps.gsi.gov.uk, *Call Date: July 1987, Middle Temple*
Qualifications: [LLB (Lond)]

CALLENDER SMITH MR ROBIN

Deputy District Judge, Judge, Express Newspapers, Editorial Legal Department, 10 Lower Thames Street, London, EC3R 6EN, ✉pilgrim_wigs@msn.com, *Call Date: July 1977, Gray's Inn*
Qualifications: [LLB (Lond) LLM (Lond)]

CALLER MR MITCHELL BERNARD

Adviser, Vice President, The Chase Manhattan Bank, 125 London Wall, London, EC2Y 5AJ, ☎020 7777 4800 Fax: 020 7777 3141, ✉mitchell.caller@chase.com, *Call Date: July 1978, Middle Temple*
Qualifications: [BA (Oxon)]

CALVERT MR PHILIP ALAN

Director, Orient-Express Services Limited, Shackleton House, 4 Battle Bridge Lane, London, SE1 2HP, ☎020 7921 4107, ✉philip.calvert@orient-express.com, *Call Date: July 1977, Middle Temple*
Qualifications: [BA]

CALVERT-LEE MISS GEORGINA ELIZA JANE

Mcallister Olivarius, Thames Wharf Studios, Rainville Road, London, W6 9HA, *Call Date: Oct 1993, Middle Temple*
Qualifications: [MA (Hons)(Oxon) CPE (Lond)]

CAMERON MR ALEXANDER JAMES

Legal Officer, Extreme Group Ltd, 19 Bolsover Street, London, W1W 5NA, ☎020 7244 1000 Fax: 020 7244 0101, ✉alex@extremeinternational.com, *Call Date: Mar 1998, Lincoln's Inn*
Qualifications: [BA (Hons)(Cantab)]

CAMERON MISS VIVECA CECILE

Senior Crown Prosecutor, Crown Prosecution Service, Bexleyheath Police Station, 2 Armsberg Way, Bexleyheath, Kent, DA7 4QS, ✉viv.cameron@cps.gsi.gov.uk, *Call Date: Feb 1987, Middle Temple*
Qualifications: [LLB]

CAMPBELL MR DAVID

Kitsons Solicitors, The Forum, Barnfield Road, Exeter, Devon, EX1 1QR, ☎01392 455968 Fax: 01392 455961, *Call Date: Nov 1992, Inner Temple*
Qualifications: [LLB (Sheff)]

CAMPBELL MRS ROSEMARY VERONICA

Senior Lawyer, Barclaycard, Legal and Regulatory Compliance, Level 4, 1234 Pavilion Drive, Northampton, NN4 7SG, ✉Rose.Campbell@barclaycard.co.uk, *Call Date: July 1982, Middle Temple*
Qualifications: [LLB(L'pool)]

CANEY MR HOWARD BERNARD

Company Secretary, Legal Counsel, Quadriga Worldwide Limited, Forum One, Station Road, Theale, Berkshire, RG7 4RA, ☎0118 903 3985, *Call Date: May 1997, Lincoln's Inn*
Qualifications: [LLB (Hons)]

CANNING MR EDWARD

Senior Crown Prosecutor, Crown Prosecution Service, Argal House, Peninsula Business Park, Rydon Lane, Exeter, Devon, EX2 7NT, *Call Date: July 1985, Lincoln's Inn*
Qualifications: [BA Dip App Soc Studies DSA LRAM]

F

CANNON MR ADAM RICHARD

HED, Telegraph Media Group Limited, 111 Buckingham Palace Road, Victoria, London, SW1W 0DT, ✉Adamrichard.cannon@telegraph.co.uk, *Call Date: Oct 1997, Middle Temple*
Qualifications: [BA (Hons)(Cantab) MA (Hons) (Cantab)]

CANTY MISS NICOLA FRANCES

Harrison Grant Solicitors, 175-185 Gray's Inn Road, London, WC1X 8UE,
Fax: 020 7812 0654, ✉nicolacanty@hglaw.co.uk, *Call Date: July 2006, Inner Temple*
Qualifications: [BSc (Southampton)]

CAPGRAS MRS HANNAH REBECCA

Nursing and Midwifery Council, 23 Portland Place, London, W1B 1PZ, ✉hannah.capgras@nmc-uk.org, *Call Date: July 2004, Middle Temple*
Qualifications: [BA Hons (Oxon)]

CAPLIN MISS NINA SUZANNE

Office of Fair Trading, Fleetbank House, 2-6 Salisbury Square, London, EC4Y 8JX,
☎020 7211 8000, *Call Date: Oct 2003, Middle Temple*
Qualifications: [LLB (Hons) (Edin)]

CAPON MR JULIUS PIERS

Crown Prosecution Service, Croydon Crown Court, Altyre Road, Croydon, Surrey, CR9 5AB, *Call Date: Nov 1990, Lincoln's Inn*
Qualifications: [LLB (Newc)]

CAREY MISS MARY FRANCES

Department For Work and Pensions, Department of Health Legal Services, Floor 5, The Adelphi, 1-11 John Adam Street, London, WC2N 6HT, ✉Frances.Carey@dwp.gsi.gov.uk, *Call Date: Nov 1990, Lincoln's Inn*
Qualifications: [BA (Dub) Dip Law]

F

CAREY-YARD MR GORDON MICHAEL

Other, Metropolitan Police Service, Directorate of Legal Services, First Floor (V), New Scotland Yard, 8-10 Broadway, London, SW1H 0BG, ☎020 7230 1212
Fax: 020 7230 7571, *Call Date: Nov 1982, Gray's Inn*
Qualifications: [LLB (Lond) (Hons)]

CARLYON MR OLIVER CHARLES

London Fire and Emergency Planning Authority, 169 Union Street, London, SE1 0LL, *Call Date: July 2004, Gray's Inn*
Qualifications: [LLB (Cardiff)]

CARNEGIE MRS JANE

Department For Business, Innovation and Skills, Bay 5122, 1 Victoria Street, London, SW1H 0ET, ☎020 7215 5428, ✉jane.carnegie@bis.gsi.gov.uk, *Call Date: Oct 1998, Middle Temple*
Qualifications: [LLB (Hons)(Lond)]

CARNEY MRS JULIE ANN

Lawyer, Department For Business, Innovation and Skills, 10 Victoria Street, London, SW1H 0NN, ☎020 7215 0779 Fax: 020 7215 3221, ✉julie.carney@bis.gsi.gov.uk, *Call Date: Nov 1990, Middle Temple*
Qualifications: [LLB (Warw)]

CARPENTER MR THOMAS

Lawyer, Law Officers of the Crown, St James Chambers, Po Box 96, St Peter Port, GY1 4BY, Guernsey, ☎01481 743735
Fax: 01481 725439, ✉thomas.carpenter@gov.gg, *Call Date: July 2002, Middle Temple*
Qualifications: [LLB (Hons) (Wales)]

CARR MISS ALEXANDRIA PIRIE

The Treasury Solicitors, Hm Treasury, 1 Horse Guards Road, London, SW1A 2HQ,
☎020 7270 5000 Fax: 020 7270 5764,
✉alexandria.carr@hm-treasury.gsi.gov.uk, *Call Date: Oct 1997, Inner Temple*
Qualifications: [LLB (Nottingham)]

CARRIER MR DAVID JAMES

Justices' Clerk, Her Majesty's Courts Service, The Courthouse, Bishopgate, Norwich, Norfolk, NR3 1UP, ☎01603 679 570
Fax: 01603 679 456, ✉davidcarrier@btinternet.com, *Call Date: July 1980, Gray's Inn*
Qualifications: [DMS]

CARROLL MS ERICA ELAINE

Pensions Regulator, Napier House, Trafalgar Place, Brighton, BN1 4DW, *Call Date: Oct 2002, Inner Temple*
Qualifications: [BA (Thames Valley) CPE (Thames Valley)]

CARTER MISS DEBORAH DORIS LILY

Senior Counsel, Ace European Group Limited, The Ace Building, 100 Leadenhall Street, London, EC3A 3BP, ☎020 7173 7000 Fax: 020 7173 7800, ✉Deborah.Carter@ACEGroup.com, *Call Date: Oct 1998, Inner Temple*
Qualifications: [LLB (Soton)]

CARTER MR HAROLD MARK

Lawyer, The Home Office, Seacole House, 2 Marsham Street, London, SW1P 4DF, *Call Date: July 1984, Gray's Inn*
Qualifications: [LLB]

CARTER MR HOWARD ERNEST

General Counsel, Transport for London, 7th Floor, Winsor House, 42-50 Victoria Street, London, SW1H 0TL, ☎020 7126 4097 Fax: 020 7126 4598, ✉howardcarter@tfl.gov.uk, howard_sue@hotmail.com, *Call Date: Nov 1989, Middle Temple*
Qualifications: [LLB (Hons) (Manch) LLM MBA]

CARTER MS JANE ELIZABETH

Antony Clapp Solicitors, Holly Bank Chambers, The Oasts Business Village, Red Hill, Wateringbury, ME18 5NN, ☎01622 815 940 Fax: 01622 817 872, ✉jane.carter@antonyclappsolicitors.co.uk, *Call Date: July 2001, Inner Temple*
Qualifications: [LLB (Lond)]

CARTER MRS NATALIE JANE

Crown Prosecution Service, Sceptre House, 7-9 Castle Street, Luton, Bedfordshire, LU1 3AJ, ☎01582 816615, ✉natalie.carter@cps.gsi.gov.uk, *Call Date: Nov 1991, Inner Temple*
Qualifications: [LLB]

CARTER MR ROBERT JAMES

Associate, Other, Shell International Ltd, Shell Centre, London, SE1 7NA, ☎0207 934 4185 Fax: 44 (0) 207 934 6627, ✉bob.carter@shell.com, *Call Date: July 1995, Inner Temple*
Qualifications: [BSc (Leeds) CPE (Notts)]

CASE MR TOBY EDWARD JAMES

HM Revenue and Customs, 100 Parliament Street, London, SW1A 2BQ, ☎020 7147 3682 Fax: 020 7147 0433, ✉toby.case@hmrc.gsi.gov.uk, *Call Date: Oct 1996, Inner Temple*
Qualifications: [LLB (So'ton)]

CASELY-HAYFORD MS MARGARET HENRIETTA AUGUSTA

Solicitor, John Lewis PLC, Partnership House, Carlisle Place, London, SW1P 1BX, ☎020 7592 6306, ✉margaret.casely-hayford@johnlewis.com, *Call Date: July 1983, Gray's Inn*
Qualifications: [BA (Hons) (Oxon)]

CASEY MR PAUL

Dyfed-Powys Police, Police Headquarters, Po Box 99, Llangunnor, Carmarthen, SA31 2PF, ☎01267 226308 Fax: 01267 226217, ✉paul.casey@dyfed-powys.pnn.police.uk, *Call Date: Nov 1999, Middle Temple*
Qualifications: [LLB (Hons)(Wales)]

CAULFIELD MR PAUL ANTHONY

Partner, Pearson Caulfield Limited, Newgate Chambers, 1 Newgate Street, Newcastle Upon Tyne, NE1 5RE, ☎0191 261 8878 Fax: 0191 222 1259, ✉p.caulfield@pearson-caulfield.co.uk, *Call Date: May 1996, Middle Temple*
Qualifications: [LLB (Hons)]

CAWLEY MISS EMMA

Associate, The Treasury Solicitors, One Kemble Street, London, WC2B 4TS, ☎020 7210 3311, ✉emma.cawley@tsol.gsi.gov.uk, *Call Date: Oct 1998, Lincoln's Inn*
Qualifications: [LLB (Hons)(Aberyst)]

CAWLEY MRS SERENE CHOR JOO

Legal Manager, Principal Legal Adviser, Her Majesty's Courts and Tribunals Service, Milton Keynes Magistratesé Court, 301 Silbury Boulevard, Witan Gate East, Milton Keynes, Buckinghamshire, MK9 2AJ, ☎01908 451 130 Fax: 01908 451146, ✉serene.cawley@hmcourts-service.gsi.gov.uk, *Call Date: Nov 1990, Inner Temple*
Qualifications: [LLB (Lond) DMS MSc]

CAWSE MISS ALISON

Crown Prosecution Service, Froomsgate House, Rupert Street, Bristol, BS1 2QJ, ☎01179 678894, *Call Date: July 2007, Gray's Inn*
Qualifications: [BSc (Cardiff)]

CAYLEY MR ANDREW THOMAS

Other, Prosecutor, ECCC, Office of the Co-Prosecutors, National Road 4, Chaom Chau, Dangkao, Po Box 71, Phnom Penh, Cambodia, *Call Date: July 2007, Inner Temple*
Qualifications: [LLB (Lond) LLM (Lond)]

CHADWICK MS FIONA JANE

Department For Work and Pensions, Litigation Division, Second Floor, Caxton House, 6-12 Tothill Street, London, SW1H 9NA, Fax: 020 7962 8924, ✉fiona.reid1@dwp.gsi.gov.uk, *Call Date: July 2003, Inner Temple*
Qualifications: [BSc (Warw) CPFA CPE (College of Law)]

CHADWICK MRS KARA

Royal Navy Officers, Directorate of Naval Legal Services, Mp 4-2, Leach Building, Whale Island, Portsmouth, PO2 8BY, *Call Date: July 2007, Middle Temple*
Qualifications: [BA (Hons) (Glasgow) GDL]

CHAKRABARTI MISS SHAMI

Director, Liberty, 26-30 Strutton Ground, London, SW1P 2HR, *Call Date: Oct 1994, Middle Temple*
Qualifications: [LLB (Hons)(Lond)]

CHALLENER DUDLEY MR WILLIAM JAMES

Morgan Cullen & Ball Solicitors & Barristers LLP, 101 Bath Street, Birmingham, B4 6HG, Fax: 0121 200 3029, *Call Date: Oct 2009, Middle Temple*
Qualifications: [BSc (Hons) (Bris)]

CHAMBERLAIN MR PAUL

Special Casework Lawyer, Crown Prosecution Service, Priory Gate, 29 Union Street, Maidstone, Kent, ME14 1PT, ☎01622 356 333 Fax: 01622 356 395, ✉paul.chamberlain@cps.gsi.gov.uk, *Call Date: Nov 1993, Inner Temple*
Qualifications: [BA (Hons) CPE]

CHAMBERS MR MICHAEL

Carter and Company Solicitors, 95 Borough High Street, London, SE1 1NL, *Call Date: July 2003, Gray's Inn*
Qualifications: [BA (Sheff)]

CHAMPNESS MR ANDREW PAUL

Gloucester Police Authority, Holland House, Lansdown Road,, Cheltenham, Gloucestershire, GL51 6QH, ☎01242 276262 Fax: 01242 262521, ✉andy.champness@gloucestershire.pnn.police.uk, *Call Date: Oct 1998, Middle Temple*
Qualifications: [BSc (Hons)(Wales) Dip in Law (Bris)]

CHANDLER MR DOMINIC LEONARD MARK

Wells Burcombe LLP, 7 The Green, West Drayton, Middlesex, UB7 7PL, ☎01895 449 288 Fax: 01895 449726, *Call Date: Mar 1996, Gray's Inn*
Qualifications: [LLB]

CHANTZI MS EMILY

Barclaycard, Lcr Department, 13. B4.2, 1 Churchill Place, Canary Wharf, London, E14 5HP, ☎020 7116 2317, *Call Date: Apr 2005, Middle Temple*

CHAPLIN MR RICHARD JAMES

Assistant General Counsel, Hess Limited, Level 9, The Adelphi Building, 1-11 John Adam Street, London, WC2N 6AG, Fax: 020 7331 3004, *Call Date: Feb 1992, Middle Temple*
Qualifications: [LLB (Hons) LLM (Cantab) PgDip EC Competition Law ACIArb]

CHAPMAN MR RODERIC ALAN KEITH

Senior Crown Prosecutor, Crown Prosecution Service, 2 King Edward Court, King Edward Street, Nottingham, Nottinghamshire, NG1 1EL, ☎01158 523300 Fax: 01623 8523493, ✉rodanddianne@live.co.uk, *Call Date: Nov 1983, Middle Temple*
Qualifications: [LLB (Nott'm)]

CHARLES MR KEVIN LAURENCE

Crossland Employment Solicitors, 99 Milton Park, Abingdon, Oxon, OX14 4RY, ☎01235 841506, *Call Date: Oct 1996, Middle Temple*
Qualifications: [LLB (Hons)(Essex)]

F

CHARNLEY MR PHILIP JAMES

Crown Prosecution Service, Carmelite House, St James Court, Whitefriars, Norwich, Norfolk, NR3 1SL, ☎01603 693000
Fax: 01603 693067, ✉phil.charnley@cps.gsi.gov.uk, *Call Date: July 1983, Gray's Inn*
Qualifications: [LLB (UEA)]

CHARVONIA MR ARTHUR JAMES

Other, Waveney District Council, Waveney District Council, Town Hall, High Street, Lowestoft, Suffolk, NR32 1HS, *Call Date: Nov 1999, Middle Temple*
Qualifications: [LLB (Hons)(Lond)]

CHASTNEY MS CAROL ANNE

Crown Prosecution Service, Riding Gate House, 37 Old Dover Road, Canterbury, Kent, CT1 3JG, ☎01227 451144
Fax: DX 5350 CANTERBURY, *Call Date: Oct 1993, Gray's Inn*
Qualifications: [LLB (Hons)]

CHAUDHRY MISS SAFINA HABIB

Legal Manager, The Treasury Solicitors, 5th Floor, One Kemble Street, London, WC2B 4TS, *Call Date: Nov 1994, Lincoln's Inn*
Qualifications: [BA (Hons)]

CHAUVIN MRS JOANNE AUN LENG

Senior Legal Adviser, Richmond-Upon-Thames Magistrates' Court, Parkshot, Richmond-Upon-Thames, Surrey, TW9 2RF, ☎020 8271 2300, *Call Date: July 1982, Middle Temple*
Qualifications: [LLB (Hons)]

CHEEMA MR MOHAMMAD ABDULLAH

Crown Prosecution Service, Romford Police Station, 19 Main Road, Romford, Essex, RM1 3BJ, *Call Date: Oct 2001, Inner Temple*
Qualifications: [LLB (South Bank)]

CHELMICK MR TIMOTHY HAMAR

Pinsent Masons LLP, Level 8 Monarch Office Tower, One Sheikh Zayed Road, Dubai, United Arab Emirates, Fax: 43 739701, ✉timchelmich@pinsentmasons.com, *Call Date: Oct 2004, Lincoln's Inn*
Qualifications: [BSc (Hons)]

CHESAITES MS NICOLA

Covington and Burling LLP, 44 Avenue Des Arts, Bruxelles, B-1040, Belgium, ☎00 32 2 549 5230 Fax: 00 32 2 502 1598, ✉nchesaites@cov.com, *Call Date: July 2006, Lincoln's Inn*
Qualifications: [LLB LLM]

CHICO MR JONATHAN MICHAEL RAYMOND

Unicredit Bank AG, Moor House, 120 London Wall, London, EC2Y 5ET, ☎020 7826 1168, ✉Jonathan.Chico@unicredit.eu, *Call Date: Nov 1998, Lincoln's Inn*
Qualifications: [LLB (Hons)(Leics)]

CHIJNER MR DAVID

Partner, Fried Frank Harris Shriver and Jacobson, (Europe), 65-67 Avenue Des Champs Elyseés, 75008 Paris, France, ✉david.chijner@friedfrank.com, *Call Date: Oct 1993, Inner Temple*
Qualifications: [Dip de Droit Francais (France) BA (Kent) LLM (Italy)]

CHILESE MRS ANGELA FRANCES

HM Revenue and Customs, 1st Floor, South West Bush House, London, WC2B 4RD, *Call Date: July 2003, Inner Temple*
Qualifications: [BA (Exon) CPE (Lond)]

CHITTENDEN MR TIMOTHY PAUL

Senior Crown Prosecutor, Crown Prosecution Service, Bishopsgate Police Station, 182 Bishopgate, Bishopsgate, London, EC2M 4NP, *Call Date: Oct 1990, Gray's Inn*
Qualifications: [LLB (Lond) (Hons)]

CHITTY MRS ANNE LOUISE

Crown Advocate, Crown Prosecution Service, Gemini One, Oxford Business Park South, Garsington Road, Oxford, Oxfordshire, OX4 2LL, ☎01235 551944 / 01865 233400 / 01235 551900, ✉louise.chitty@cps.gsi.gov.uk, *Call Date: July 1983, Inner Temple*
Qualifications: [LLB (Exon)]

CHONG MR ENG LEE

Diageo, Lakeside Drive, Park Royal, London, NW10 7HQ, ☎020 8978 4881
Fax: 020 8978 1588, *Call Date: July 1988, Middle Temple*
Qualifications: [LLB (Hons) (Lond) LLM (Lond) ACCA (Affiliate) ITMA]

F

CHOO-JACKSON MRS JINNY MEI-YUIN

Legal Adviser, HSBC Bank Plc, Legal Level 22, 8 Canada Square, Canary Wharf, London, E14 5HQ, *Call Date: July 1996, Lincoln's Inn*
Qualifications: [LLB (Hons)(Leeds)]

CHOUDHURY MR ABDUS SAMAD

General Medical Council, Regent's Place, 350 Euston Road, London, NW1 3JN, *Call Date: Mar 1996, Gray's Inn*
Qualifications: [LLB]

CHOUDHURY MR BHASKAR

1st Central Insurance Management Limited, Gemini House, Mill Green Business Estate, Mill Green Road, Haywards Heath, West Sussex, RH16 1XQ, ✉bhaskar.choudhury@1stcentral.co.uk, *Call Date: Nov 1988, Lincoln's Inn*
Qualifications: [ACMA BA (Hons) LLB (Hons) AICWA MSc]

CHOUDHURY MR REZA

Islington Law Centre, 161 Hornsey Road, London, N7 6DU, ☎020 7700 7521
Fax: 020 7700 4315, ✉rezac2238@gmail.com, *Call Date: Nov 2003, Middle Temple*
Qualifications: [LLB (Hons)]

CHOUDRY MR SIKANDER RASHID

Powell, Spencer and Partners, 290 Kilburn High Road, London, NW6 2DD,
☎020 7604 5600 Fax: 020 7328 1221,
✉sikanderchoudry@psplaw.co.uk, *Call Date: Mar 2011, Lincoln's Inn*
Qualifications: [BA (Lond)]

CHRIMES MR DAVID FRANCIS WILLIAM

Advocate, Crown Prosecution Service, Queens House, 58 Victoria Street, St. Albans, Hertforshire, AL1 3HZ,
☎01727 798 700 / 01727 798 700, *Call Date: Oct 1990, Gray's Inn*
Qualifications: [LLB(Hons) (London)]

CHRISTIE MR MARTIN JAMES

Henry & Co Solicitors, 72-74 Wellington Road South, Stockport, SK1 3SU, ☎0161 477 8338, *Call Date: July 2003, Gray's Inn*
Qualifications: [BA (Bolton)]

CHRISTY MR LESLIE JAMES

Harcus Sinclair, 3 Lincoln's Inns Fields, London, WC2A 3AA, ☎020 7242 9700
Fax: 020 7539 4702, ✉leslie.christy@harcus-sinclair.co.uk, *Call Date: Nov 1999, Middle Temple*
Qualifications: [BSc(Hons) LLB MPhil (Cantab) BSc PGDip (Oxon)]

CHUNG MR MING CHIT

Director, GAM UK Limited, 12 St James' Place, London, SW1A 1NX, *Call Date: Nov 1993, Inner Temple*
Qualifications: [LLB]

CHURAMAN MISS DEBORAH SIROJINI

Lawyer, Department For Business, Innovation and Skills, 1 Victoria Street, London, SW1H 0ET, ✉debbie.churaman@bis.gsi.gov.uk, *Call Date: Nov 1984, Middle Temple*
Qualifications: [LLB]

CHURTON MR DAVID RICHARD HARDING

Morgan Stanley, Legal and Compliance Division, 20 Cabot Square, Canary Wharf, London, E14 4QW, *Call Date: Oct 1998, Middle Temple*
Qualifications: [BA (Hons)(Cantab) MA (Hons) (Cantab)]

CIECIORA MISS LOUISA JOANNA

Directorate of Army Legal Services, Trenchard Lines, Upavon, Pewsey, Wiltshire, SN9 6BE, ✉917cieci@armymail.mod.uk, *Call Date: Oct 2002, Inner Temple*
Qualifications: [LLB Hons (Sussex)]

CINA MISS CHLOE HANNAH

The Treasury Solicitors, One Kemble Street, London, WC2B 4TS, ☎020 7210 3000,
✉Chloe.Cina@tsol.gsi.gov.uk, *Call Date: Nov 2005, Middle Temple*
Qualifications: [BA (Hons)]

CLADINGBOWL MR RODNEY

Senior Crown Prosecutor, Crown Prosecution Service, Stevenage Police Station, Lytton Way, Stevenage, Hertfordshire, SG1 1HE,
✉Rodney.Cladingbowl@cps.gsi.gov.uk, *Call Date: Nov 1970, Gray's Inn*
Qualifications: [LLB (Lond)]

F

CLAPHAM MRS TINA

Legal Adviser, Ministry of Defence, Po Box 1680, London, SW1P 1ZE, *Call Date: July 1989, Inner Temple*
Qualifications: [LLB (Lancs) LLM (Leics)]

CLARK MR DAVID ANDREW

Clerk, DCOR, Nursing and Midwifery Council, 61 Aldwich, London, WC2B 4AE, ☎020 7681 5489 Fax: 020 7580 3410, *Call Date: Nov 1987, Middle Temple*
Qualifications: [LLB]

CLARK MRS ELIZABETH ANNE

District Crown Prosecutor, Crown Prosecution Service, City Gate House, 185 Dyke Road, Hove, East Sussex, BN3 1TL, ☎01273 322266 Fax: 01273 765633, ✉libby.clark@cps.gsi.gov.uk, *Call Date: July 1984, Gray's Inn*
Qualifications: [BA]

CLARK MISS SARAH LOUISE

Emery Halil and Brown Solicitors, 67 West Ham Lane, Stratford, London, E15 4PH, ☎020 8519 5500 Fax: 020 8555 9544, *Call Date: Nov 2004, Middle Temple*
Qualifications: [MA (Cantab)]

CLARKE MISS ALISON LEE

Reynolds Porter Chamberlain LLP, Tower Bridge House, St Katherine's Way, London, E1W 1AA, ☎020 3060 6000 Fax: 020 3060 7000, *Call Date: Oct 1994, Lincoln's Inn*
Qualifications: [LLB (Hons)(Leics)]

CLARKE MR ANDREW TERENCE

Bencher, General Counsel, Vice Chairman, Vice President, ExxonMobil International Limited, ExxonMobil House, Ermyn Way, Leatherhead, Surrey, KT22 8UX, ☎01372 222 530 Fax: 01372 222560, *Call Date: July 1982, Middle Temple*
Qualifications: [MA (Cantab)]

CLARKE MRS ANTOINETTE OLUWATOYIN

Senior Crown Prosecutor, Crown Prosecution Service, City Gate House, 185 Dyke Road, Hove, East Sussex, BN3 1TL, *Call Date: Nov 1986, Lincoln's Inn*
Qualifications: [BA]

CLARKE MISS FRANCESCA LOUISE

Fadiga and Co Solicitors, 2 The Boulevard, London, SW17 7BW, ☎020 8673 6699 Fax: 020 8675 5958, ✉f.clarke@fadiga.co.uk, admin@fadiga.co.uk, *Call Date: Nov 1981, Inner Temple*
Qualifications: [BA]

CLARKE MR PATRICK JAMES

Lawyer, HM Revenue and Customs, 100 Parliament Street, London, SW1A 2BQ, *Call Date: July 1975, Middle Temple*
Qualifications: [LLB]

CLARKE MR SIMON ANDREW

Cartwright King Solicitors, Norwich Union House, South Parade, Old Market Square, Nottingham, Nottinghamshire, NG1 2LH, ☎0115 958 7444, *Call Date: Oct 1997, Lincoln's Inn*
Qualifications: [LLB (Hons)(Lond)]

CLARKE-JERVOISE MISS CAROLINE SARAH

Hogan Lovells International LLP, Hogan Lovells LLP, 65 Holborn Viaduct, London, EC1A 2DY, ☎020 7296 2000 Fax: 020 7248 4212, ✉charlie.clarke-jervoise@hoganlovells.com, *Call Date: July 1986, Inner Temple*
Qualifications: [LLB]

CLEMENTS MS AMY ELIZABETH

Marine Management Organisation, Po Box 1275, Newcastle Upon Tyne, NE99 5BN, ✉amy.clements@marinemanagement.gsi.gov.uk, *Call Date: July 2004, Gray's Inn*
Qualifications: [LLB (Manch)]

CLEMENTS MR SIMON ANTHONY

HED, Crown Prosecution Service, Rose Court, 2 Southwark Bridge, London, SE1 9HS, ☎020 3357 0049 / 020 3357 0857 (PA) Fax: 020 3357 0056, *Call Date: Nov 1982, Gray's Inn*
Qualifications: [BA (Hull)]

CLEMINSON MR CRAIG DERRICK

Legal Adviser, Crown Prosecution Service, The Unicentre, Lords Walk, Preston, Lancashire, PR1 1DH, *Call Date: Oct 1993, Lincoln's Inn*
Qualifications: [LLB (Hons)(L'pool)]

CLOHERTY MR WILLIAM

Assistant General Counsel, Elavon, Inc., One Concourse Parkway, Suite 300, Atlanta, GA 30328, USA, ☎ 001 678 731 5717
Fax: 001 678 731 5861, ✉ william.cloherty@elavon.com, *Call Date: Oct 1997, Middle Temple*
Qualifications: [BA (Hons)(Sussex)]

COCCHIARA MS ANNETTE GRAZIELLA

Crown Prosecution Service, The Cooperage, 8 Gainsford Street, London, SE1 2NE, ☎ 020 7378 3280 Fax: 020 7378 4201, ✉ Annette.Cocchiara@cps.gsi.gov.uk, *Call Date: July 2007, Lincoln's Inn*
Qualifications: [LLB (Exon)]

COCHRANE MISS PAULA MARGARET

Tuckers Solicitors, 39 Warren Street, London, W1T 6AF, ☎ 020 7388 8333
Fax: 020 7330 7268, ✉ cochranep@tuckerssolicitors.com, *Call Date: July 2003, Gray's Inn*
Qualifications: [LLB (Teeside)]

COCKBURN MISS SUZANNE ESTHER

Legal Adviser, Elavon Merchant Services, Meridien House, 4th Floor, 69-71 Clarendon Road, Watford, WD17 1DS, ☎ 01923 651548, ✉ suzanne.cockburn@elavon.com, *Call Date: Mar 2002, Lincoln's Inn*
Qualifications: [LLB (Hons) (Manch) LLM (Lond)]

COCKER MR ROBERT GLENVILLE

District Crown Prosecutor, Crown Prosecution Service, County House, 100 New London Road, Chelmsford, Essex, CM2 0RG, ☎ 01245 455800, ✉ glen.cocker@cps.gsi.gov.uk, *Call Date: Nov 1977, Gray's Inn*
Qualifications: [BA]

COCKSHUTT MS EMMA ELIZABETH

Head of Legal Services, Tiger Aspect Productions Limited, Shepherdés Building Central, Charecroft Way, London, W14 0EE, ☎ 020 7434 6920 Fax: 020 8121 3420, ✉ emmacockshutt@tigeraspect.co.uk, *Call Date: Nov 1983, Inner Temple*
Qualifications: [LLB (Lond) LLB (Hons)(Lond)]

COE-SALAZAR MR ROGER GRAHAM

Chief Crown Prosecutor, Crown Prosecution Service, Priory Gate, 29 Union Street, Maidstone, Kent, ME14 1PT, *Call Date: Nov 1994, Middle Temple*
Qualifications: [LLB (Hons) LLM]

COFFER MR IAN

Principal Court Clerk, Justices' Clerk's Office, Market Street (East), Newcastle Upon Tyne, NE99 1TB, ☎ 0191 232 7326
Fax: 0191 221 0025, *Call Date: Nov 1985, Inner Temple*
Qualifications: [LLB (Lond)]

COFFEY MS RUTH CHRISTINE MAUD

Royal Courts of Justice, Judicial Office, Room C115, Royal Courts of Justice, Strand, London, WC2A 2LL, ✉ Ruth.Coffey@judiciary.gsi.gov.uk, *Call Date: Oct 2004, Inner Temple*
Qualifications: [BA (Cantab) MA (Cantab) CPE MSc]

COHEN MS HéLéNE

Tanfield Chambers, 2-5 Warwick Court, London, WC1R 5DJ, ☎ 020 7421 5300
Fax: 020 7421 5333, *Call Date: Oct 2001, Gray's Inn*

COHEN MISS LINDA

London Borough of Harrow, Po Box 2, Civic Centre, Station Road, Harrow, Middlesex, HA1 2UF, ☎ 020 8424 1289, ✉ Linda.cohen@harrow.gov.uk, *Call Date: July 1985, Middle Temple*
Qualifications: [MA (Wark)]

COHEN MS NATALIE SIMONE

The Treasury Solicitors, One Kemble Street, London, WC2B 4TS, ☎ 020 7210 3344
Fax: 020 7210 3001, *Call Date: Oct 1997, Inner Temple*
Qualifications: [LLB (Nottingham)]

COKER MS AGATHA

Pensions Regulator, Napier House, Trafalgar Place, Brighton, BN1 4DW, *Call Date: Oct 1999, Middle Temple*
Qualifications: [LLB (Hons) PG Dip]

F

COLE MISS ROXANNE HARRIET

Crown Advocate, Crown Prosecution Service, Fox Talbot House, Bellinger Close, Malmesbury Road, Chippenham, Wiltshire, SN15 1BN, ☎01249 766 138 Fax: 01249 766 159, ✉roxanne.cole@cps.gsi.gov.uk, *Call Date: Nov 2005, Gray's Inn*
Qualifications: [LLB]

COLE MR THOMAS JAMES

Department For Business, Innovation and Skills, 1 Victoria Street, London, SW1H 0ET, ✉tom.cole@bis.gsi.gov.uk, *Call Date: Oct 2007, Inner Temple*
Qualifications: [LLB (Dunelm)]

COLE MISS VANESSA ANNE

Ministry of Defence, 917, 6th Floor, Main Building, Whitehall, London, SW1A 2HB, ✉vanessa.cole908@mod.uk, *Call Date: Oct 1992, Lincoln's Inn*
Qualifications: [LLB(Hons)(Manch)]

COLEMAN MR RODNEY BERNARD

Criminal Defence Solicitors, 227/228 Strand, London, WC2R 1BE, ☎020 7353 7000 Fax: 020 7353 7111, ✉rc@criminaldefence.co.uk, *Call Date: Nov 1978, Gray's Inn*
Qualifications: [LLB (Lond)]

COLLEY MISS LOIS MARIE

Crown Prosecution Service, The Regatta, 6 Henley Buisness Park, Doddington Road, Lincoln, LN6 3QR, ✉lois.colley@cps.gsi.gov.uk, *Call Date: Oct 1996, Inner Temple*
Qualifications: [BA (Dunelm)]

COLLIE MR PETER ANDREW

Adjudicator, Fenwick Elliott LLP, Aldwych House, 71-91 Aldwych, London, WC2B 4HN, ☎020 7421 1986 Fax: 020 7421 1987, ✉pcollie@fenwickelliott.com, *Call Date: July 1994, Middle Temple*
Qualifications: [LLB (Hons)(Notts) MCIOB LCGI ACIArb]

COLLIER MISS MELANIE

Post Office Limited, 148 Old Street, London, EC1V 9HQ, *Call Date: Nov 1999, Middle Temple*
Qualifications: [MA (Hons)(Cantab)]

COLLIER-WRIGHT MR CHARLES EDWARD HURRELL

Legal Manager, Trinity Mirror PLC, 1 Canada Square, London, E14 5AP, ☎020 7293 3747 Fax: 020 7293 3613, ✉c.collier-wright@mgn.co.uk, *Call Date: July 1976, Middle Temple*
Qualifications: [MA (Oxon)]

COLLINS MR KEVIN THOMAS

Call Date: Nov 2000, Lincoln's Inn
Qualifications: [LLB (Hons) LLM]

COLLINS MISS NADIA ANOUCHKA

Department For Business, Innovation and Skills, 1 Victoria Street, London, SW1H 0ET, ☎020 7215 5000, ✉Nadia.Collins@bis.gsi.gov.uk, *Call Date: Nov 1994, Middle Temple*
Qualifications: [BA (Hons) LLM]

COLLINS MR RICHARD ALEXANDER

Director, Ugc Limited, Unipart House, Garsington Road, Cowley, Oxford, Oxfordshire, OX4 2PG, ☎01865 383643 Fax: 01865 384672, ✉richard_collins@unipart.co.uk, *Call Date: Nov 1982, Middle Temple*
Qualifications: [BA (Hons)]

COLPSTEIN MISS LISA LAYA

Deputy Chief Clerk, Her Majesty's Courts Service, Thames Magistrates' Court, 58 Bow Road, London, E3 4DJ, *Call Date: Nov 1990, Inner Temple*
Qualifications: [BA (Hons)(Kent)]

CONCEICAO MR CARLOS MANUEL

Clifford Chance LLP, 10 Upper Bank Street, London, E14 5JJ, ☎020 7006 Line, *Call Date: July 1987, Middle Temple*
Qualifications: [LLB (Hons) (Manch) MSc]

CONNELL MR ANTHONY EDWARD

Special Casework Lawyer, Crown Prosecution Service, The Cooperage, 8 Gainsford Street, London, SE1 2NE, ☎020 7378 4217, ✉anthony.connell@cps.gsi.gov.uk, *Call Date: July 1982, Gray's Inn*
Qualifications: [LLB (B'ham)]

CONNELL MISS CAROLINE ANN

Legal Adviser, The Treasury Solicitors, One Kemble Street, London, WC2B 4TS, *Call Date: July 1984, Inner Temple*
Qualifications: [LLB (Exon)]

F

CONNER MR GRAHAM

Imperial College London, Level 1 Faculty Building, Tax - Finance Division, South Kensington, London, SW7 2AZ, ☎020 7594 3315 Fax: 020 7594 8720, ✉g. conner@imperial.ac.uk, *Call Date: Feb 1995, Lincoln's Inn*
Qualifications: [LLB (Hons)]

CONNOLLY MR JOHN GERARD JOSEPH

Temple Vale and Law Solicitors, Po Box 58855, Peckham Rye, London, SE15 9AJ, ☎020 7635 0600 Fax: 020 7635 0700, *Call Date: Nov 2006, Gray's Inn*
Qualifications: [LLB]

CONROY HARRIS MRS ALEXANDRA JANE

British Association For Adoption and Fostering, Saffron House, 6-10 Kirby Street, London, EC1N 8TS, ☎020 7421 2600 Fax: 020 7421 2601, ✉Alexandra. ConroyHarris@baaf.org.uk, *Call Date: July 1989, Gray's Inn*
Qualifications: [LLB]

CONRY MR MICHAEL HARVEY

Crown Prosecution Service, Colmore Gate, 2 - 6 Colmore Row, Birmingham, West Midlands, B3 2QA, ☎0121 262 1300, ✉michael. conry@cps.gsi.gov.uk, *Call Date: July 1979, Gray's Inn*
Qualifications: [LLB (Reading)]

CONWAY MR MICHAEL DAVID

Legal Officer, Directorate of Army Legal Services, Headquaters Land Forces, Idl 426, Building 400, Moxton Road, Andover, SP11 BHJ, ✉michael.conway548@mod.uk, *Call Date: July 1982, Middle Temple*
Qualifications: [LLB (Lond)]

CONYNGHAM MR JOHN STAFFORD

Director, Legal Counsel, Control Risks Group Ltd, Cottons Centre, Cottons Lane, London, SE1 2QG, ☎020 7970 2100 Fax: 020 7970 2230, ✉john.conyngham@ control-risks.com, *Call Date: Nov 1975, Gray's Inn*
Qualifications: [LLB]

COOK MRS ADELE HAVLYNN

Crown Prosecution Service, St Vincent's House, 1 Cutler Street, Ipswich, Suffolk, IP1 1UL, ✉adele.cook@cps.gsi.gov.uk, *Call Date: Mar 1999, Inner Temple*
Qualifications: [LLB]

COOK MR JEREMY OWAIN

Head of Legal Services, Adur District Council, Legal Services, Town Hall, Chapel Road, Worthing, West Sussex, BN11 1HA, ☎01903 221028 Fax: 01903 214384, *Call Date: July 1982, Middle Temple*
Qualifications: [LLB (Hons) M Soc Sc Dip LG]

COOKE MR ARTHUR ALEXANDER CRICHTON

Department of Energy and Climate Change, 3 Whitehall Place, London, SW1A 2AW, ☎0300 068 6215, ✉alex.cooke@decc.gsi. gov.uk, *Call Date: Oct 1999, Middle Temple*
Qualifications: [BSc (Hons)(Dunelm) CPE]

COOKE MR TIMOTHY MARK ALISTER

Legal Director, Clyde & Co LLP, 3 Anson Road, #21-01 Sprigleaf Tower, 79909, Singapore, ☎6544 6500 Fax: 6544 6501, ✉post@clyde. com.sg, *Call Date: July 2000, Middle Temple*
Qualifications: [BA(Hons) (Cantab) Dip Law]

COOMANSINGH MISS ANAMARIE

Senior Crown Prosecutor, Crown Prosecution Service, Colmore Gate, 2 - 6 Colmore Row, Birmingham, West Midlands, B3 2QA, *Call Date: Nov 1987, Gray's Inn*
Qualifications: [LLB (Wales)]

COOPER MR JAMES JOSEPH

CVS, Legal Adviser, Department For Environment, Food & Rural Affairs, Ergon House, C/O Nobel House, 17 Smith Square, London, SW1P 3JR, ☎020 7238 3367, ✉james.j.cooper@defra.gsi.gov.uk, *Call Date: July 1986, Inner Temple*
Qualifications: [MA BCL (Oxon)]

COOPER MR MARK

Legal Manager, Her Majesty's Courts and Tribunals Service, Inner London & City Family Proceedings, 59-65 Wells Street, London, W1A 3AE, ☎020 7805 3415 Fax: 020 7805 3491, ✉mark.cooper@hmcourts-service.gsi.gov.uk, *Call Date: Nov 1989, Inner Temple*
Qualifications: [BA Dip Law]

F

COORAY MISS MABEL MARGARET SWYRIE

Department For Work and Pensions, 5th Floor, the Adelphi, 1-11 John Adam Street, London, WC2N 6HT, ☎020 7962 8759, ✉swyrie.cooray@dwp.gsi.gov.uk, *Call Date: Nov 2005, Middle Temple*
Qualifications: [LLB (Hons)]

CORBETT MR JAMES PATRICK

Deputy High Court Judge, Partner, Kobre & Kim LLP, 60 Gresham Street, London, EC2V 7BB, *Call Date: July 1975, Inner Temple*
Qualifications: [LLB FCIArb LLM (Exon)]

CORDINGLEY MRS EMMA LOUISE

The Directorate of Legal Services, Welsh Assembly Government, Room G05, Cathays Park, Cardiff, Wales, CF10 3NQ, *Call Date: July 2005, Lincoln's Inn*
Qualifications: [LLB (Hons) (Warwick)]

CORDINGLEY MR WILLIAM STANCLIFFE

Morgans Solicitors and Advocates, Elgin House, St Mary's Street, Cardiff, CF10 1DX, *Call Date: July 2005, Lincoln's Inn*
Qualifications: [LLB (Hons)]

CORERA MRS JANE GRACE WYN

Office of Gas and Electricity Markets (Ofgem), Office of Gas and Electricity Markets, 9 Millbank, London, SW1P 3GE, *Call Date: Nov 1994, Lincoln's Inn*
Qualifications: [BA (Hons)(Ireland) MA (Dunelm) Dip Law (Lond)]

CORNAH MS EMMA LOUISE

Tangerine Holdings Limited, Docklands, Dock Road, Lytham, Lancashire, FY8 5AQ, ☎01253 667420 Fax: 01253 667425, ✉emma@tangerineholdings.co.uk, *Call Date: Nov 1992, Inner Temple*
Qualifications: [LLB (Hons)]

COSSAR MR BRUCE JAMES

Crown Prosecution Service, Colmore Gate, 2 - 6 Colmore Row, Birmingham, West Midlands, B3 2QA, *Call Date: Oct 1995, Inner Temple*
Qualifications: [LLB (Hons)]

COTTAM DR DAVID WILLIAM

Other, Global Patent Group, TEVA UK Limited, Field House, Station Approach, Harlow, Essex, CM20 2FB, *Call Date: Nov 1997, Lincoln's Inn*
Qualifications: [BSc (Hons) (Sheff) PhD (Sheff) LLB (Hons) (City)]

COTTON MR DAVID JOSEPH

Directorate of Army Legal Services, Army Headquarters, IDL 426, Ramillies Building, Marlborough Lines, Monxton Road, Andover, Hants, SP11 8HJ, *Call Date: Nov 2003, Inner Temple*
Qualifications: [LLB (Essex)]

COTTON MISS PENELOPE JANE

The Treasury Solicitors, One Kemble Street, London, WC2B 4TS, ☎2072104551, ✉penny.cotton@tsol.gsi.gov.uk, *Call Date: Nov 1991, Middle Temple*
Qualifications: [BA (Hons) (Oxon)]

COTTRELL MISS DIANA JAYNE

Crown Prosecution Service, Princes Court, 34 York Road, Leicester, Leicestershire, LE1 5TU, ☎0116 204 6700 Fax: 0116 204 6799, *Call Date: July 2004, Gray's Inn*
Qualifications: [LLB (Hons) (Leic)]

COUNSELL MISS SARAH JANE

Crown Advocate, Crown Prosecution Service, The Cooperage, 8 Gainsford Street, London, SE1 2NE, ☎020 73784337
Fax: 020 3300 4862, ✉Sarah.Counsell@cps.gsi.gov.uk, *Call Date: July 2001, Middle Temple*
Qualifications: [BSc (Hons) CPE MA]

COURTENAY MR CHARLES PEREGRINE

Latham and Watkins LLP, 355 S. Grand Avenue, Los Angeles, California, USA, *Call Date: Nov 1999, Inner Temple*
Qualifications: [BA (Cantab)]

COURTNEY MR MARK ST JOHN

Head of Legal Services, Eseye Limited, Surrey Research Centre, 40 Occam Road, Guilford, Surrey, GU2 7YG, ✉mcourtney@eseye.com, *Call Date: July 1981, Middle Temple*
Qualifications: [LLB]

F

COUSSEY MR JAMES ROMAINE HENLEY

Lawyer, Crown Prosecution Service, Rose Court, 2 Southwark Bridge, London, SE1 9HS, *Call Date: July 1971, Middle Temple*

COVENTRY MR ROGER JAMES

Adviser, Crown Advocate, Judge, Crown Prosecution Service, Rose Court, 2 Southwark Bridge, London, SE1 9HS, *Call Date: July 1971, Gray's Inn*
Qualifications: [LLM (Lond) Dip(Lond)]

COWDREY MISS JANET ANN

Ministry of Justice, Legal Directorate, 102 Petty France, London, SW1H 9AS, *Call Date: Oct 1998, Middle Temple*
Qualifications: [LLB (Hons)(Middx)]

COWEN MR TIMOTHY ROBERT WILLIAM

General Counsel, Partner, Sidley Austin LLP, Woolgate Exchange, 25 Basinghall Street, London, EC2V 5HA, Fax: 020 7 626 7937, ✉tcowen@sidley.com, *Call Date: July 1985, Inner Temple*
Qualifications: [MA (Cantab)]

COWIE MR MATTHEW JOHN

Skadden, Arps, Slate, Meagher & Flom LLP, 40 Bank Street, Canary Wharf, London, E14 5DS, *Call Date: Nov 1995, Inner Temple*
Qualifications: [LLB (Warw) MA (Sheff)]

COWLEY MR PETER JOHN

Principal Legal Adviser, Thames Valley Magistrates' Courts Service, Waverley House, Queens Avenue, Bicester, Oxfordshire, OX26 2NZ, ☎01869 853101 Fax: 01869 853103, *Call Date: Nov 1983, Middle Temple*
Qualifications: [BA (Hons)]

COWLEY MISS SAOIRSE KEZIA

The Treasury Solicitors, One Kemble Street, London, WC2B 4TS, *Call Date: Nov 2008, Inner Temple*
Qualifications: [BA (Oxon) CPE]

COX MS LOUISE ANN

Crown Prosecution Service, Princes Court, 34 York Road, Leicester, Leicestershire, LE1 5TU, ☎0116 2046700 / 0116 204 6812 Fax: 0116 204 6701, *Call Date: Oct 2001, Inner Temple*
Qualifications: [LLB (Hons)(Brunel)]

COX MRS REBECCA JANE

Crown Prosecution Service, Basingstoke Police Station, London Road, Basingstoke, Hampshire, RG21 4AD, ☎01256 405 390, ✉rebecca.cox@cps.gsi.gov.uk, *Call Date: Nov 1994, Middle Temple*
Qualifications: [BA (Hons)]

COX MR SIMON FRANCIS

Open Society Foundation, Cambridge House, 100 Cambridge Grove, London, W6 0LE, Fax: 020 7031 0201, ✉scox@justiceinitiative.org, *Call Date: Nov 1992, Inner Temple*
Qualifications: [LLB (Wales)]

COXON MISS CLARA BEATRICE MARIA

Reading Magistrates Court, The Civic Centre, Reading, RG1 7TQ, *Call Date: July 1999, Middle Temple*
Qualifications: [BA (Hons)]

CRAVEN MR RICHARD JOHN

Enfield Chambers, 21 Natal Road, Bounds Green, London, N11 2HU, ✉richard.cohraiii@blueyonder.co.uk, *Call Date: Oct 1995, Gray's Inn*
Qualifications: [LLB]

CRAWSHAW MRS NICHOLA JANE

Legal Adviser, Uxbridge Magistrates' Court, The Court House, Harefield Road, Uxbridge, Middlesex, UB8 1PQ, ✉ncrawshaw24@hotmail.com, nichola.crawshaw1@hmcourts-service.gsi.gov.uk, *Call Date: Oct 1999, Lincoln's Inn*
Qualifications: [BSc (Hons)]

CREASY MR RICHARD ANDREW

Legal Adviser, Ministry of Justice, Zone 6.31, Legal Directorate, 102 Petty France, London, SW1H 9AJ, *Call Date: Oct 1990, Inner Temple*
Qualifications: [LLB (So'ton) LLM (Leics)]

F

CRIBB MR NICHOLAS

Crown Advocate, Crown Prosecution Service, Wood Green Crown Court, Woodall House, Lordship Lane, Wood Green, London, N22 5LF, ☎ 020 8826 4261 Fax: 020 8881 9380, ✉ Nick.Cribb@cps.gsi.gov.uk, *Call Date: July 2005, Middle Temple*
Qualifications: [LLB (Hons) City]

CRIDGE MR PHILIP JAMES

London Borough of Hackney, Hackney Town Hall, Mare Street, London, E8 1EA, ☎ 020 8356 3000, *Call Date: Nov 1992, Lincoln's Inn*
Qualifications: [LLB (Hons) LLM]

CRIGHTON MR ROBERT DAVID

General Counsel, Secretary, Port of London Authority, London River House, Royal Pier Road, Gravesend, Kent, DA12 2BG, ☎ 01474 562 272 Fax: 01474 562 398, ✉ bob.crighton@pla.co.uk, *Call Date: July 1982, Middle Temple*
Qualifications: [BA (Hons) (Leics) Dip Law (Lond)]

CRIMMINS MS RHIANNON SARA

Sa Law Chambers Solicitors Ltd, Heraldic House, 1st Floor, 160-162 Cranbrook Road, Ilford, Essex, IG1 4PE, ☎ 020 8554 0012 Fax: 020 8554 6619, ✉ info@salawchambers.com, *Call Date: Nov 1999, Gray's Inn*
Qualifications: [BA]

CRIMMINS MRS RUTH

Senior Crown Prosecutor, Oldham Council, Legal Services, Civic Centre, West Street, Oldham, OL1 1UW, *Call Date: Nov 1988, Lincoln's Inn*
Qualifications: [LLB (Hons)]

CRIMP MR MICHAEL WILLIAM JASON

Crown Prosecution Service, Cju St Vincent House - 8th Floor, 1 Cutler Street, Ipswich, Suffolk, IP1 1UL, ✉ michael.crimp@cps.gsi.gov.uk, *Call Date: Nov 1980, Gray's Inn*
Qualifications: [BA MA]

CRIPPS MISS BEVERLY MARY

Crown Prosecution Service, Sceptre House, 7-9 Castle Street, Luton, Bedfordshire, LH1 3AJ, ☎ 01582 816 600, ✉ beverly.cripps@cps.gsi.gov.uk, *Call Date: Nov 1988, Gray's Inn*
Qualifications: [BA (Hons)]

CRISPIN MR DARREN MARTYN

Crown Prosecution Service, Priory Gate, 29 Union Street, Maidstone, Kent, ME14 1PT, *Call Date: Nov 1997, Middle Temple*
Qualifications: [BA (Hons)(Dunelm)]

CROCKFORD MR GARY BRETT

Legal Consultant, Buck Consultants Limited, 160 Queen Victoria Street, London, EC4V 4AN, Fax: 020 7429 1010, ✉ gary.crockford@buckconsultants.com, *Call Date: July 1980, Inner Temple*
Qualifications: [BA]

CROFT MS CAROLINE CHARLOTTE ANN

Department of Energy and Climate Change, DECC Legal, Area 7B, 3 Whitehall Place, London, SW1A 2AW, *Call Date: Nov 1991, Gray's Inn*
Qualifications: [BA (Oxon) Dip Law]

CROFT MR FREDERICK LISTER

Department For Transport, Great Minster House, 33 Horseferry Road, London, SW1P 4DR, ✉ fred.croft@dft.gsi.gov.uk, *Call Date: July 1975, Middle Temple*
Qualifications: [MA (Oxon)]

CROFT MR PETER ANDREW

London Borough of Waltham Forest, Town Hall, Forest Road, London, E17 4JF, ☎ 020 8496 4890 Fax: 020 8523 4967, *Call Date: July 2002, Middle Temple*
Qualifications: [LLB (Hons) (Sussex)]

CROFT MRS SONIA JUNE

Crown Prosecution Service, Argal House, Peninsula Buisness Park, Rydon Lane, Exeter, Devon, EX2 7NT, ☎ 01392 356700 Fax: 01392 35 6703, ✉ sonia.croft@cps.gsi.gov.uk, *Call Date: July 2006, Inner Temple*
Qualifications: [LLB (Nottingham)]

CROOM MISS NATASHA DAWN

Reading Magistrates' Court, Civic Centre, Reading, Berkshire, RG1 7TQ, Fax: 0118 980 1873, *Call Date: Nov 1997, Gray's Inn*
Qualifications: [LLB (Hons)(Lond)]

F

CROOT MR WAYNE DAVID

Crown Prosecution Service, Capital Tower, Greyfriars Road, Cardiff, CF10 3PL, ☎029 2080 3800, *Call Date: Oct 1993, Gray's Inn*
Qualifications: [BA LLB]

CROSBIE MR JONATHAN CRAIG

Peter Bonner & Co, 8-12 Lee High Road, Lewisham, London, SE13 5LQ, ☎020 8297 9097, *Call Date: Oct 2004, Middle Temple*
Qualifications: [BA (Hons) CPE]

CROSLAND MR TIMOTHY JOHN EDWARD

Call Date: Nov 1994, Inner Temple
Qualifications: [BA (Oxon) CPE (Lond)]

CROSS MISS CLAIRE IRENE

Financial Services Authority, 25 The North Colannade, Canary Wharf, London, E14 8HS, *Call Date: Oct 2000, Inner Temple*
Qualifications: [LLB (Hons) (Leic)]

CROSSLEY MISS VANESSA ANNE

Senior Crown Prosecutor, Crown Prosecution Service, Citadel House, 58 High Street, Hull, Humberside, HU1 1QD, ✉Vanessa.Crossley2@cps.gsi.gov.uk, *Call Date: Nov 1992, Lincoln's Inn*
Qualifications: [BA (Hons)]

CROZIER MR STUART ROSS MCDONALD

Legal Adviser, Royal Navy Officers, RAF Northolt, Service Prosecting Authority, West End Road, Ruislip, Middlesex, HA4 6NG, ☎020 8842 6120, *Call Date: Nov 1991, Gray's Inn*
Qualifications: [LLB]

CULLEN MISS DEBORAH ELIZABETH

Aviva Investors Global Services Limited, No 1 Poultry, London, EC2R 8EJ, ☎020 7809 6000 Fax: 020 7809 7940, ✉information.uk@avivainvestors.com, *Call Date: Nov 1989, Gray's Inn*
Qualifications: [LLB MA CEDR]

CULLEN MR GERARD KEVIN

Parker Greed Cullen and Ball, 101 Bath Street, Birmingham, B4 6HG, ☎0121 200 3031 Fax: 0121 200 3029, *Call Date: Mar 2010, Middle Temple*
Qualifications: [LLB (B'ham)]

CULVER LIEUTENANT COLONEL MICHAEL JOHN

Directorate of Army Legal Services, Idl426, Ramillies Building, Marlborough Lines, Monxton Road, Andover, SP11 8HJ, *Call Date: Oct 1992, Middle Temple*
Qualifications: [LLB]

CUNDY MR MARK ANDREW

Doncaster Metropolitan Borough Council, Po Box 71, Copley House, Waterdale, Doncaster, DN1 3EQ, ☎01302 734688, *Call Date: Oct 1999, Lincoln's Inn*
Qualifications: [LLB (Hons)(Sheff) LLM (Sheff)]

CUNNINGHAM MR ROBERT HENRY THOMAS

Lawyer, Financial Services Authority, General Counsel's Division, 25 The North Colonnade, Canary Wharf, London, E14 5HS, *Call Date: July 2001, Gray's Inn*
Qualifications: [LLB]

CURRIE MR SEAN

Legal Manager, HMCTS, South Worcestershire Magistrates' Court, Castle Street, Worcester, WR1 3QZ, ☎01562 514000, ✉sean.currie@hmcts.gsi.gov.uk, *Call Date: Nov 1982, Middle Temple*
Qualifications: [BA (Hons) MBA]

CURTIS MR JOHN WILLIAM JAMES

Criminal Cases Review Commission, 5 St Philips Place, Birmingham, B3 2PW, *Call Date: July 1996, Middle Temple*
Qualifications: [BA (Hons)(Warw) CPE MA (B'ham)]

CURTIS MISS NICOLE DIANE

Partner, Penningtons Solicitors, Abacus House, 33 Gutter Lane, London, EC2V 8AR, ☎020 7457 3114 Fax: 020 7457 3240, *Call Date: Oct 1992, Gray's Inn*
Qualifications: [MA (Cantab)]

CURTIS MISS REBECCA LOUISE

Childcare Legal Team, Legal Services, Bristol City Council, Po Box 2156, Bristol, BS99 7PH, ☎0117 92 22076 Fax: 0117 92 23436, ✉rebecca_curtis@bristol-city.gov.uk, *Call Date: Oct 1993, Inner Temple*
Qualifications: [BSc CPE]

CURTIS MR RICHARD ANTHONY

HED, Essex Legal Service, New Bridge House, 60-68 New London Road, Chelmsford, Essex, CM2 0PD, ☎01245 506730
Fax: 01245 506769, ✉richard.curtis@essex.gov.uk, *Call Date: July 1984, Inner Temple*
Qualifications: [LLB (Wales) LLM (Lond)]

CUSH MR MARTIN STUART

Manager, Her Majesty's Courts Service, Bristol Magistrates Court, Marlborough Street, Bristol, BS1 3NU,
☎0117 943 5100 / 0117 930 2440, *Call Date: July 1981, Lincoln's Inn*
Qualifications: [BA]

CYRUS MR WILLAN JULIUS

Reading Borough Council, Civic Offices, Civic Centre, Reading, RG1 7AE, *Call Date: Nov 1984, Lincoln's Inn*
Qualifications: [BA (Hons) (Reading) DipLaw (Lond)]

DALBY MR THOMAS JAMES

Cliff Top, Valley Road, Radcliffe On Trent, Nottinghamshire, NG12 1BB, *Call Date: Oct 1995, Lincoln's Inn*
Qualifications: [LLB (Hons)(Notts) ATII]

DALESANDRO MISS SHERRY CANDICE

DWF LLP, Capital House, 85 King William Street, London, EC4N 7BL, ☎020 7645 9500
Fax: 020 7645 9501, ✉Sherry.Dalesandro@dwf.co.uk, *Call Date: July 2000, Lincoln's Inn*
Qualifications: [LLB(Hons) (Brunel)]

DALZIELL MRS RUTH MARGUERITE

Senior Crown Prosecutor, Crown Prosecution Service, Riding Gate House, 37 Old Dover Road, Cantebury, Kent, CT1 3JG,
☎01227 866 026, *Call Date: Feb 1991, Gray's Inn*
Qualifications: [LLB]

DAMAZER MISS AUDREY FAITH

Justices' Clerk, Judge, Inner London and City Family Proceedings Court, 59-65 Wells Street, London, W1A 3AE, ☎020 7805 3402/3
Fax: 020 7805 3491, ✉audrey.damazer@hmcts.gsi.gov.uk, *Call Date: Nov 1980, Gray's Inn*
Qualifications: [BA (Hons) (Law)]

DANIELS MISS TANYA COLLETTE

Legal Director, Quintiles Limited, 500 Brook Drive, Green Park, Reading, RG2 6UU,
☎0118 5450 8000, *Call Date: Nov 1985, Lincoln's Inn*
Qualifications: [LLB (Exon)]

DARLINGTON MISS FAYE LOUISE

HM Revenue and Customs, 4th Floor West, Ralli Quays, 3 Stanley Street, Manchester, M60 9LB, ☎0870 785 8503 Fax: 0870 785 8533, *Call Date: Oct 1998, Lincoln's Inn*
Qualifications: [LLB (Hons)]

DASS MR PRESTON

Crown Prosecution Service, City Gate House, 185 Dyke Road, Hove, East Sussex, BN3 1TL, *Call Date: Nov 1983, Inner Temple*
Qualifications: [BA (Kent)]

DAVEY MR NATHAN PAUL

Crown Prosecution Service, Holborn Police Station, 10 Lambs Conduit Street, Islington, London, WC1N 3NR, ☎020 7061 3937, *Call Date: July 1988, Lincoln's Inn*
Qualifications: [LLB (Hons)]

DAVID MR DERRICK HUW

Senior Crown Prosecutor, Crown Prosecution Service, Cambria House, Pentrebach Industrial Estate, Pentrebach, Merthyr Tydfil, Mid Glamorgan, CF48 4XA, ☎01443 694800, ✉huw.david@cps.gsi.gov.uk, *Call Date: July 1989, Middle Temple*
Qualifications: [LLB]

DAVIES MISS ANNE MARGARET

Crown Prosecution Service, Kingston Crown Court, Penrhyn Road, Kingston, Surrey, KT1 2BB, ☎020 8240 2500, ✉anne.davies@cps.gsi.gov.uk, *Call Date: Nov 1989, Inner Temple*
Qualifications: [LLB (Hull)]

F

DAVIES MISS CHARLOTTE ANN LOUISE

West Glamorgan Joint Childcare Legal, County Hall, Oystermouth Road, Swansea, SA1 3SN, ☎01792 636 646, ✉charlotte.beynon@swansea.gov.uk, *Call Date: July 2004, Lincoln's Inn*
Qualifications: [LLB Hons (Nott'm Trent)]

DAVIES MR DAFYDD HUW

The Directorate of Legal Services, Welsh Assembly Government, Room G05, Cathays Park, Cardiff, Wales, CF10 3NQ, ✉dhuw.davies@wales.gsi.gov.uk, *Call Date: Nov 1998, Gray's Inn*
Qualifications: [LLB (Wales)]

DAVIES MRS ELIZABETH CAROLINE SIAN

Crown Prosecution Service, Rose Court, 2 Southwark Bridge, London, SE1 9HS, *Call Date: July 1980, Gray's Inn*
Qualifications: [LLB (Bristol) MA]

DAVIES MR FREDERICK GEORGE

Deputy Justices' Clerk, Peterborough Magistrates Court, The Court House, Bridge Street, Peterborough, Cambridgeshire, PE1 1ED, ☎01733 201 311, *Call Date: July 1979, Inner Temple*
Qualifications: [BA (Hons) Law]

DAVIES DR JANE ELIZABETH

Legal Adviser, Norwich Magistrates' Court, Bishopsgate, Norwich, Norfolk, NR3 1UP, ☎01603 679 500 Fax: 01603 663 263, *Call Date: July 1983, Middle Temple*
Qualifications: [LLB PhD (B'ham)]

DAVIES MR KEITH

HED, Airbus Operations Ltd, New Filton House, P.O. Box 77, Bristol, BS99 7AR, ☎0117 9362224 Fax: 0117 9362680, ✉keith.davies@airbus.com, *Call Date: Nov 1976, Inner Temple*
Qualifications: [MA (Cantab) MIL]

DAVIES MS MANON WYNNE

The Directorate of Legal Services, Welsh Assembly Government, Room G05, Cathays Park, Cardiff, Wales, CF10 3NQ, *Call Date: Oct 1997, Inner Temple*
Qualifications: [BA (Oxon) CPE]

DAVIES MR MARC SCOTT

Directorate of Army Legal Services, Building 398, Trenchard Lines, Upavon, Pewsey, Wiltshire, SN9 6BE, ☎01980 673118, ✉marcscottdavies@yahoo.co.uk, *Call Date: July 1998, Middle Temple*
Qualifications: [LLB (Hons)(Dunelm)]

DAVIES MRS NICOLA JANE

Crown Advocate, Crown Prosecution Service, 7th Floor (South), Royal Liver Building, Pier Head, Liverpool, Merseyside, L3 1HN, ☎0151 239 6400, ✉nicky.davies@cps.gsi.gov.uk, *Call Date: July 1978, Middle Temple*
Qualifications: [MA (Oxon)]

DAVIES LIEUTENANT COLONEL PENNY MAY

Legal Adviser, Other, Directorate of Army Legal Services, CLS CSL10, Central Legal Services, 6-F-44, Main Building, Whitehall, London, SW1A 2HB, *Call Date: Oct 1995, Inner Temple*
Qualifications: [LLB (Hons)]

DAVIES MISS RACHEL

Crown Prosecution Service, Gateway, 31 Power Close, Guildford, Surrey, GU1 1EJ, ☎01483 468200 Fax: 01483 468203, ✉rachel.davies@cps.gsi.gov.uk, *Call Date: Oct 1998, Middle Temple*
Qualifications: [LLB (Hons)(Leic)]

DAVIES MISS RACHEL KATHERINE

Foreign and Commonwealth Office, Room 200a, King Charles Street, London, SW1A 2AH, *Call Date: Oct 2002, Inner Temple*
Qualifications: [LLB (Lond)]

DAVIES MRS RACHEL VALERIE

Clerk, Her Majesty's Courts and Tribunals Service, Dorset Area, the Law Courts, Park Road, Poole, Dorset, BH15 2RJ, ☎01202 745309 Fax: 01202 711999, *Call Date: July 1995, Gray's Inn*
Qualifications: [LLB]

DAVIES MR ROBERT HOWARD

Crown Prosecution Service, Colmore Gate, 2 - 6 Colmore Row, Birmingham, West Midlands, B3 2QA, *Call Date: Oct 1990, Lincoln's Inn*
Qualifications: [LLB (B'ham)]

F

DAVIES MS SAMANTHA YEMISI

Peters & Peters Solicitors LLP, 15 Fetter Lane, London, EC4A 1BW, ☎020 7822 7777 Fax: 020 7822 7788, *Call Date: July 2003, Inner Temple*
Qualifications: [BA (Cantab)]

DAVIES MR WARREN BYRON

Call Date: Nov 2006, Gray's Inn
Qualifications: [LLB]

DAVIES-EVANS MRS JANE ELEANOR

Other, Freshfields Bruckhaus Deringer LLP, 65 Fleet Street, London, EC4Y 1HS, ☎020 7785 5645 Fax: 020 7108 5645, *Call Date: Oct 2001, Middle Temple*
Qualifications: [LLB (Hons) ACA]

DAVIS MR JAMES CHARLES AYLMER

Senior Crown Prosecutor, Crown Prosecution Service, Luton Police Station, Luton, Bedfordshire, LU1 1SD, *Call Date: Nov 1990, Gray's Inn*
Qualifications: [LLB (Hons)(Essex)]

DAVIS MR JOHN ANTHONY

The Treasury Solicitors, One Kemble Street, London, WC2B 4TS, ☎020 7210 3353 Fax: 020 7210 3410, ✉john.davis@tsol.gsi.gov.uk, *Call Date: July 1983, Gray's Inn*
Qualifications: [LLB (Hull)]

DAVIS MRS LISA MARISKA

Advocate, The Royal Pharmaceutical Society, Fitness to Practise Directorate, 1 Lambeth High Street, London, SE1 7JN, ☎020 7572 2660 Fax: 020 7572 2510, *Call Date: July 2000, Middle Temple*
Qualifications: [LLB(Hons) (Keele) LLM]

DAVIS MS MARCIA PATRICIA

Hmcs Thames Valley, Milton Keynes Magistrates' Court, 301 Silbury Boulevard, Witan Gate East, Milton Keynes, Buckinghamshire, MK9 2AJ, ☎01908 451123 Fax: 01908 451146, ✉marcia.davis@hmcts.gsi.gov.uk, *Call Date: July 1992, Gray's Inn*
Qualifications: [B Ed LLB LLM Dip Edad]

DAVISON MISS CHARLOTTE ELIZABETH

Crown Prosecution Service, County House, 100 New London Road, Chelmsford, Essex, CM2 0RG, *Call Date: Nov 2003, Lincoln's Inn*
Qualifications: [LLB (Hons) (Essex)]

DAW MR CHRISTOPHER

Senior Counsel, Lincoln House Chambers, Tower 12, The Avenue North, Spinningfields, 18-22 Bridge Street, Manchester, M3 3BZ, ☎0161 832 5701 Fax: 0161 832 0839, ✉chris.daw@lincolnhousechambers.com, *Call Date: Nov 1993, Gray's Inn*
Qualifications: [LLB (Manch)]

DAWES MR ALISTAIR NICHOLAS LOUIS

Financial Services Authority, 25 The North Colonade, Canary Wharf, London, E14 5HS, ☎020 7066 1000, ✉alistair.dawes@fsa.gov.uk, *Call Date: Feb 1995, Inner Temple*
Qualifications: [BA (Cantab)]

DAWES MISS LAURA MICHELLE

Financial Services Authority, 25 The North Colonnade, Canary Wharf, London, E14 5HS, ☎020 7066 1000, ✉laura.dawes@fsa.gov.uk, *Call Date: Oct 2001, Lincoln's Inn*
Qualifications: [LLB (Hons)(Lond) MA (Lond)]

DAWSON MR MARK

Shearman and Sterling (London) LLP, 9 Appold Street, London, EC2A 2AP, ☎020 7655 5609 Fax: 020 7655 5500, ✉mark.dawson@sherman.com, *Call Date: Oct 2009, Lincoln's Inn*
Qualifications: [BA (Oxon)]

DAY MR NICHOLAS JOHN

Company Secretary, Wt Partnership, Amp House, Dingwall Road, Croydon, Surrey, CR0 2LX, ☎020 8686 0431 Fax: 020 8686 3195, ✉nicholas.day@wtpartnership.com, *Call Date: July 1982, Lincoln's Inn*
Qualifications: [BA (Lond) Dip Law FCIS]

DAY MR RICHARD CHRISTOPHER

Serious Fraud Office, Elm House, 10-16 Elm Street, London, WC1X 0BJ, ☎020 7239 7279 Fax: 020 7833 5485, *Call Date: July 1996, Gray's Inn*
Qualifications: [LLB (Middx)]

DE MISS ZOE MONICA

Lawyer, Department For Work and Pensions, 5th Floor, the Adelphi, 1-11 John Adam Street, London, WC2N 6HT, ☎020 7712 2296, ✉zoe.de@dwp.gsi.gov.uk, *Call Date: Nov 1994, Inner Temple*
Qualifications: [BA (Warw)]

DE LA MARE MISS CARA

Cambridge City Council, Market Square, Guildhall, CB2 3QJ, *Call Date: Nov 1999, Gray's Inn*
Qualifications: [LLB LLM (LSE)]

DE LACY-BROWN MR NICHOLAS JAMES

HM Revenue and Customs, 100 Parliament Street, London, SW1A 2BQ, Fax: 020 7438 9160, ✉nicholas.delacybrown@hmrc.gsi.gov.uk, *Call Date: Mar 2008, Lincoln's Inn*
Qualifications: [LLB (Lond)]

DE MAUNY MR CHRISTOPHER DAVID FRANCIS

Bird and Bird LLP, 15 Fetter Lane, London, EC4A 1JP, ☎020 7415 6000 Fax: 020 7415 6111, ✉christopher.demauny@twobirds.com, *Call Date: Nov 2006, Inner Temple*
Qualifications: [MA MSci (Cantab)]

DE MENEZES MR RAUL ANTONIO

Legal Adviser, Hmcs Dorset, The Law Courts, Stafford Road, Bournemouth, Dorset, BH1 1LA, ☎01202 711905, ✉raul.demenezes@hmcourts-service.gsi.gov.uk, *Call Date: Feb 1994, Lincoln's Inn*
Qualifications: [BA (Hons) LLM]

DE VAL MR PETER ROBERT

Legal Adviser, The BBC Trust, 180 Great Portland Street, London, W1W 5QZ, ☎020 3214 4958, ✉Peter.De.Val@bbc.co.uk, *Call Date: Nov 1988, Inner Temple*
Qualifications: [LLB MPhil (Leics)]

DEALY MR NICHOLAS JOHN

Head of Legal Services, UBS AG, One Exchange Square, 8 Connaught Place, Central, Hong Kong, ☎00 852 2971 7328 Fax: 00 852 2971 7066, ✉Nicholas.Dealy@ubs.com, *Call Date: Oct 1996, Middle Temple*
Qualifications: [BSc (Hons) CPE]

DEAN MISS ABIGAIL ELIZABETH

The Treasury Solicitors, 5th Floor, One Kemble Street, London, WC2B 4TS, ✉Abigail.Dean@cabinet-office.gsi.gov.uk, *Call Date: Oct 1995, Gray's Inn*
Qualifications: [BA]

DEAN MISS BRYONY

Crown Prosecution Service, Rose Court, 2 Southwark Bridge, London, SE1 9HS, ☎020 3 357 1047 Fax: 020 3 357 0675, ✉bryony.dean@cps.gsi.gov.uk, *Call Date: July 2007, Inner Temple*
Qualifications: [MA (Cantab)]

DEAN MR NICHOLAS

Recorder, Seven Bedford Row, 7 Bedford Row, London, WC1R 4BS, ☎020 7242 3555 Fax: 020 7242 2511, ✉ndean@7br.co.uk, *Call Date: Nov 1982, Lincoln's Inn*
Qualifications: [LLB (Leeds)]

DEANE MR VINCENT

Henry & Co Solicitors, 72-74 Wellington Road South, Stockport, SK1 3SU, *Call Date: July 1976, Lincoln's Inn*
Qualifications: [LLB]

DEBATTISTA PROF CHARLES

Stone Chambers, 4 Field Court, Gray's Inn, London, WC1R 5EF, ☎020 7440 6900 Fax: 020 7242 0197, ✉charles.debattista@stonechambers.com, *Call Date: Aug 2004, Middle Temple*
Qualifications: [MA (Oxon) BA (Hons) (Oxon)]

DEDEZADE MR TANER

Standing Counsel, Corbett and Co, George House, 2 Claremont Road, Teddington, TW11 8DG, ☎020 8614 6208 Fax: 020 8614 6222, ✉taner.d@corbett.co.uk, *Call Date: Nov 1996, Gray's Inn*
Qualifications: [LLB (Lond) DipICA FCIArb]

DEHN MR GUY JULIAN

Witness Confident, 45 Osbaldeston Road, London, N16 7DL, ☎020 8442 4251, ✉guy.dehn@witnessconfident.org, *Call Date: July 1982, Middle Temple*
Qualifications: [BA (Bris)]

DEIGH MISS FRANCESS AMA

Call Date: Nov 1993, Gray's Inn
Qualifications: [LLB]

F

DEIGHAN MISS PATRICIA CATHERINE

Crown Prosecution Service, Forest Gate Police Station, 350-360 Romford Rd, London, E7 8BS, ☎ 020 3300 1804
Fax: 020 3300 1833, ✉ patricia.deighan@cps.gsi.gov.uk, *Call Date: July 1996, Inner Temple*
Qualifications: [LLB (Hons)]

DELBOURGO MRS ANGELA MARIE

Lecturer, DR Solicitors, C/O 57 Harrington Gardens, London, SW7 4JZ, *Call Date: July 1980, Lincoln's Inn*
Qualifications: [LLM]

DEN BRINKER MISS MELANIE JANE MARGARET

Buss Murton, Wellington Gate, 7-9 Church Road, Turnbridge Wells, Kent, TN1 1HT, ☎ 01892 510 222, *Call Date: July 1984, Inner Temple*
Qualifications: [LLB (Liverpool)]

DENMAN MR DANIEL JEREMY

HED, Ministry of Justice, 102 Petty France, London, SW1H 9AJ, ☎ 020 3334 5284, ✉ daniel.denman@justice.gsi.gov.uk, *Call Date: Nov 1995, Gray's Inn*
Qualifications: [MA (Cantab)]

DENMAN MR ROBERT ELLISON

Holden and Co, 32-33 Robertson Road, Hastings, East Sussex, TN34 1HT, ☎ 01424 722 422 Fax: 01424 720 108, ✉ law@holdenandco.co.uk, *Call Date: July 1970, Gray's Inn*
Qualifications: [MA (Cantab)]

DESAI MRS SAFINA

Crown Prosecution Service, Princes Court, 34 York Road, Leicester, Leicestershire, LE1 5TU, ☎ 0116 204 6700, ✉ safina.desai@cps.gsi.gov.uk, *Call Date: Oct 2001, Middle Temple*
Qualifications: [LLB (Hons)(Lond)]

DEVINE-BAILLIE MRS FRANCESCA MARIA

Senior Crown Prosecutor, Crown Prosecution Service, United House, Piccadilly, York, North Yorkshire, YO1 9PQ, *Call Date: Feb 1984, Gray's Inn*
Qualifications: [BA (Hons)]

DHALL MR VISHAL KUMAR

Legal Services Commission, 8th Floor, 102 Petty France, London, SW1H 9AJ, *Call Date: Nov 2004, Lincoln's Inn*
Qualifications: [LLB (Hons) (Leic)]

DHANOO MR DAVID DEVANAND

Compliance Officer, Secretary, Qatar Financial Centre Authority, Po Box 23245, Doha, Qatar, ☎ 00 974 4496 8312 Fax: 00 974 4496 8310, ✉ d.dhanoo@qatarlyst.com, *Call Date: Nov 1988, Lincoln's Inn*
Qualifications: [LLB (Hons) (Lond) LLM (Lond)]

DHAR MISS SHARMISTHA

Ministry of Defence, 6.F.01, MOD Main Building, Whitehall, London, SW1A 2HB, ✉ CLS-BMSp@defence.gsi.gov.uk, *Call Date: July 2002, Middle Temple*
Qualifications: [BSc (Lond) CPE LLM (Bris)]

DHILLON MR BALKAR SINGH

Manager, Lexis Nexis (Butterworths Ltd), Halsbury House, 35 Chancery Lane, London, WC2A 1EL, *Call Date: Feb 1992, Lincoln's Inn*
Qualifications: [LLB (Hons) (Lond) LLM (Lond)]

DIAMOND MR CHE KIERON

Ministry of Defence, Dgls, Floor 7, Zone D, Main Building, Whitehall, London, SW1A 2HB, ☎ 020 7218 5249, *Call Date: Oct 1996, Inner Temple*
Qualifications: [BA (Oxon)]

DIAMOND MRS KATHARINE ELIZABETH

Department of Energy and Climate Change, DECC Legal, Area 7B, 3 Whitehall Place, London, SW1A 2AW, *Call Date: Nov 1998, Gray's Inn*
Qualifications: [LLB (L'pool)]

DIANDA DR LEE

Department For Work and Pensions, Eu, International and Echr Co-Ordination, 5th Floor, Adelphi, 1-11 John Adam Str, London, WC2N 6HT, ☎ 020 7712 2498, *Call Date: July 2003, Middle Temple*
Qualifications: [BSc Hons (Lond) PhD (Lond) PG Dip Law (Lond)]

F

DIBBLE MR KENNETH MICHAEL

Director, Charity Commission, First Floor, 30 Millbank, London, SW1P 4DU, ☎020 7674 2375 Fax: 020 7674 2309, ✉Kenneth.Dibble@charitycommission.gov.uk, *Call Date: July 1977, Lincoln's Inn*
Qualifications: [LLB LLM AIB AKC]

DICKERSON MRS SARA BETTY

Solicitors Regulation Authority, Ipsley Court, Berrington Close, Redditch, Worcestershire, B98 0TD, *Call Date: Nov 1998, Inner Temple*
Qualifications: [LLB]

DIGBY MR CHARLES SPENCER

Ronald Fletcher Baker LLP, 326 Old Street, London, EC1V 9DR, ☎020 7613 1402 Fax: 020 7613 2711, ✉info@rfblegal.co.uk, *Call Date: July 1982, Middle Temple*
Qualifications: [BA]

DILLON MISS LEAH ANNE

Leonard & Co Solicitors, 126 Shirley Road, Southampton, Hampshire, SO15 3FD, *Call Date: July 2003, Lincoln's Inn*
Qualifications: [BA (Hons)]

DILWORTH MR JOHN

Senior Crown Prosecutor, Crown Prosecution Service, The Unicentre, Lords Walk, Preston, Lancashire, PR1 1DH, ☎01772 208100, *Call Date: Nov 1987, Gray's Inn*
Qualifications: [LLB (Hons) DML]

DIMMOCK MISS JOANNA MARY

Peters & Peters Solicitors LLP, 15 Fetter Lane, London, EC4A 1BW, *Call Date: Nov 2005, Middle Temple*
Qualifications: [BA (Hons) MSc]

DINGLE MR JONATHAN CRISPIN

Chair, Mediator, Partner, The Chambers of J Dingle & H Hodgkin, 3rd Floor, 218 Strand, London, WC2R 1DR, *Call Date: July 1986, Middle Temple*
Qualifications: [LLB (Lond) MCIArb FInst CPD]

DINGWALL MR RICHARD ANDREW

Legal Adviser, The Treasury Solicitors, One Kemble Street, London, WC2B 4TS, ☎020 7210 4657, *Call Date: Oct 1991, Gray's Inn*
Qualifications: [LLB]

DIRMIKIS MISS JOANNA CLARE

Nursing and Midwifery Council, 1 Kemble Street, London, WC2B 4AN, ☎020 7681 5529 Fax: 020 7580 3917, ✉joanna.dirminkis@nmc-uk.org, *Call Date: July 2004, Middle Temple*
Qualifications: [BA (Oxon) CPE]

DIXON MRS COLETTE YVONNE

Senior Crown Prosecutor, Crown Prosecution Service, Athena House, Kettlestring Lane, Clifton Down, York, YO30 4XF, ☎01904 731700 Fax: 01904 731828, ✉Colette.Dixon@cps.gsi.gov.uk, *Call Date: Nov 1987, Lincoln's Inn*
Qualifications: [LLB]

DIXON MR DENNIS JOSEPH

Legal Officer, HM Revenue and Customs, Bush House, Strand, London, WC2B 4RD, Fax: 020 7438 7361, *Call Date: Nov 1995, Middle Temple*
Qualifications: [BA (Hons) (Cantab)]

DOBKIN MR MATTHEW JACOB

Forsters LLP, 31 Hill Street, London, W1J 5LS, Fax: 020 7863 8444, ✉enquiries@forsters.co.uk, *Call Date: Nov 2007, Gray's Inn*
Qualifications: [BA (Cantab)]

DOBSON MISS AMANDA JANE-MARIE

Wace Morgan Solicitors, 2 Belmont, Shrewsbury, Shripshire, SY1 1TD, ☎01743 280100 Fax: 01743 280111, ✉help@wmlaw.co.uk, *Call Date: Nov 1991, Inner Temple*
Qualifications: [LLB (So'ton)]

DODDS MR MALCOLM DOUGLAS

Justices' Clerk, Her Majesty's Court Service, Gail House, Lower Stone Street, Maidstone, Kent, MD15 6NB, ☎01622 680 050 Fax: 01622 680 078, *Call Date: Nov 1984, Middle Temple*
Qualifications: [BA (Kent) LLM (Manch) DMS]

DOGGART MR PIERS GRAHAM

The Treasury Solicitors, One Kemble Street, London, WC2B 4TS, ☎020 7210 4586, ✉piers.doggart@tsol.gsi.gov.uk, *Call Date: Oct 1991, Lincoln's Inn*
Qualifications: [LLB (Hons) (Leeds)]

DOGRA MISS TANYIA ANITA

Senior Crown Prosecutor, Crown Prosecution Service, Bethnal Green Police Station, Po Box 60416, London, E2 9NZ, ☎ 020 7855 8608 Fax: 020 8721 5639, ✉ tanyia.dogra@cps.gsi.gov.uk, *Call Date: Oct 1994, Gray's Inn*
Qualifications: [LLB LLM]

DOLPHIN MISS KELLY LOUISE

Criminal Cases Review Commission, 5 St Philips Place, Birmingham, B3 2PW, *Call Date: Oct 1996, Inner Temple*
Qualifications: [MA (Oxon) CPE]

DONALD MR KEITH MALCOLM HAMILTON

Director, TRS, Radius Systems, Radius House, Berristow Lane, South Normanton, Alfreton, Derbyshire, DE55 2JJ, ☎ 01773 582204 Fax: 01773 812343, ✉ keith.donald@radius-systems.com, *Call Date: July 1978, Gray's Inn*
Qualifications: [LLB (Sheff)]

DONNABELLA MISS ROSEMARY

Serious Fraud Office, Elm House, 10-16 Elm Street, London, WC1X OBJ, *Call Date: Feb 1991, Middle Temple*
Qualifications: [LLB]

DONNELLY MISS JUDITH ALISON

Clyde & Co LLP, The St Botolph Building, 138 Houndsditch, London, EC3A 7AR, Fax: 020 7876 5111, ✉ Judith.Donnelly@clydeco.com, *Call Date: Nov 1998, Gray's Inn*
Qualifications: [LLB (L'pool)]

DOOLEY MR BARRY WILLIAM

Nursing and Midwifery Council, 23 Portland Place, London, W1B 1PZ, *Call Date: July 2008, Middle Temple*
Qualifications: [BA (Hons) (Cantab)]

DOREY MS MEGAN

Directorate of Army Legal Services, Idl426, Ramillies Building, Marlborough Lines, Monxton Road, Andover, SP11 8HJ, *Call Date: July 2007, Lincoln's Inn*
Qualifications: [BA (Cantab)]

DORIS MISS SUSAN DEBORAH

Freshfields Bruckhaus Deringer LLP, 65 Fleet Street, London, EC4Y 1HS, ☎ 020 7936 4000 Fax: 020 7832 7001, ✉ susan.doris@freshfields.com, *Call Date: Oct 1998, Gray's Inn*
Qualifications: [LLB (Belfast)]

DOSANJH-PAHIL MRS GURBINDER

HED, Scottish & Southern Energy, Legal Services, 55 Vastern Road, Reading, Berkshire, RG1 8BU, *Call Date: Oct 1998, Inner Temple*
Qualifications: [LLB]

DOUBLE MR PAUL ROBERT EDGAR

City Remembrancer's Office, Guildhall, Po Box 270, London, EC2P 2EJ, ☎ 020 7332 1200 Fax: 020 7332 1895, ✉ paul.double@cityoflondon.gov.uk, *Call Date: July 1981, Middle Temple*
Qualifications: [BSc LLM]

DOW COMMANDER CLIVE STEWART

Royal Navy Officers, Naval Command Hq, Ddnls, Mp4-2, Lead Building, Whale Island, Portsmouth, Hampshire, PO2 8BY, *Call Date: July 2001, Middle Temple*
Qualifications: [BA (Hons) CPE]

DOWD MISS CARMEN JANE LOUISE

Director, S E Law Limited, 443c London Road, Davenham, Northwich, Cheshire, CW9 8HP, ☎ 01606 333533 Fax: 01606 333963, ✉ cdowd@selawlimited.com, *Call Date: July 1989, Gray's Inn*
Qualifications: [BA]

DOWELL MS NITA MARY

Senior Crown Prosecutor, Crown Prosecution Service, Llys Eirias, Heritage Gate, Abergele Road, Colwyn Bay, Denbighshire, LL29 8BW, *Call Date: July 1982, Gray's Inn*
Qualifications: [LLB (L'pool)]

DOWLING MR CARL MICHAEL

Legal Adviser, Legal Officer, The Treasury Solicitors, One Kemble Street, London, WC2B 4TS, ✉ carl.dowling@tsol.gsi.gov.uk, *Call Date: Mar 1998, Gray's Inn*
Qualifications: [LLB (Lond)]

F

DOWN MISS SARA LYDIA

The General Council of the Bar, 4th Floor, 289-293 High Holborn, London, WC1V 7HZ, ☎020 7611 1444 Fax: 020 7831 9217, ✉sdown@barstandardsboard.org.uk, *Call Date: Oct 1991, Gray's Inn*
Qualifications: [LLB (L'pool)]

DOWNING MS EMMALYNE NATASHA

Senior Crown Prosecutor, Crown Prosecution Service, Bromfield House, Ellice Way, Wrexham, Wales, LL13 7YW, *Call Date: July 2001, Inner Temple*
Qualifications: [BA (Reading) PG Dip (Bris)]

DOWTY MR IAN

McCormacks Law, Security House, 2 Romford Road, Stratford, London, E15 4BX, ☎020 7791 2000, ✉ian.dowty@mccormacks.co.uk, *Call Date: Nov 1976, Middle Temple*
Qualifications: [BA]

DOYLE MR JAMES GAVIN CHARLES

No5 Chambers, Greenwood House, 4-7 Salisbury Court, London, EC4Y 8AA, ✉jdo@no5.com, *Call Date: July 1985, Middle Temple*
Qualifications: [LLB]

DRAPER MR NORMAN HENRY

Justices' Clerk, Her Majesty's Courts Service, Justices' Clerk's Office, Ground Floor, Queen Elizabeth II Law Courts, Derby Square, Merseyside,, Liverpool, Merseyside, L2 1XA, ☎0151 471 1079 Fax: 0151 235 5180, *Call Date: Nov 1978, Inner Temple*
Qualifications: [BA (Hons)]

DRUMMOND MS SUSAN MICHELLE

Senior Crown Prosecutor, Crown Prosecution Service, Gemini One, Oxford Business Park South, Garsington Road, Oxford, Oxfordshire, OX4 2LL, ☎01296 414800, ✉susan.drummond@cps.gsi.gov.uk, *Call Date: Oct 1999, Inner Temple*
Qualifications: [LLB (Hons) (Lond)]

DU FEU MR PETER

Reeds Solicitors, 1 Cambridge Terrace, Oxford, OX1 1RR, Fax: 01865 246968, *Call Date: Nov 2001, Inner Temple*
Qualifications: [BA CPE Economic History]

DUAH MR GODFRIED O'BRIEN FISCO

Crown Advocate, Crown Prosecution Service, Cju St Vincent House - 8th Floor, 1 Cutler Street, Ipswich, Suffolk, IP1 1UL, ☎01473 282100 3506, ✉godfried.duah@cps.gsi.gov.uk, *Call Date: Oct 2000, Lincoln's Inn*
Qualifications: [BA (Hons) MPS LLB (Hons) (Wales) LLM (Wales)]

DUBLJEVIC MR ALEXANDER SALVATORE

Senior Crown Prosecutor, Crown Prosecution Service, Capital Tower, Greyfriars Road, Cardiff, Wales, CF10 3PL, ☎02920 803800 / 02920 803800, *Call Date: July 1979, Middle Temple*
Qualifications: [LLB (Hons)(Wales)]

DUFF MR GRAHAM

Jacqueline Duff and Co, Lynnholm, Thropton, Northumberland, NE65 7JE, ☎01669 621 987 Fax: 01669 621 988, ✉grahamduffone@btinternet.com, *Call Date: July 1976, Lincoln's Inn*
Qualifications: [BA PGCE]

DUFFETT MR SAMUEL OWEN SALISBURY

Department of Energy and Climate Change, DECC Legal, Area 7B, 3 Whitehall Place, London, SW1A 2AW, *Call Date: Mar 2001, Lincoln's Inn*
Qualifications: [BA (Hons) (Oxon)]

DUFFY MR DESMOND JOSEPH

Crown Prosecution Service, Oxford House, Oxford Road, Bournemouth, Dorset, BH8 8HA, ✉desmond.duffy@cps.gsi.gov.uk, *Call Date: Nov 1993, Gray's Inn*
Qualifications: [MA]

DUHS MISS ELEONOR ALICE MARY

Ministry of Justice, Selborne House, 54-60 Victoria Street, London, SW1E 6QW, ☎020 7210 8655, ✉eleonor.duhs@justice.gsi.gov.uk, *Call Date: Nov 1998, Middle Temple*
Qualifications: [BA (Hons)(Oxon)]

F

DUIVENVOORDEN MR BENEDICT LEO

HM Revenue and Customs, Somerset House, The Strand, London, WC2R 1LB, ☎020 7438 6070 Fax: 020 7438 6664, ✉benedict.duivenvoorden@hmrc.gsi.gov.uk, *Call Date: July 2000, Middle Temple*
Qualifications: [BA(Hons) (York)]

DUKE MR PAUL STUART

Khattak Solicitors, 279 Bury New Road, Whitefield, Manchester, M45 7SE, ☎0161 796 5800 Fax: 0161 796 5011, *Call Date: Nov 1989, Gray's Inn*
Qualifications: [LLB (Hons)]

DUKU MR JERRY JOHN

Pershing Limited, Capstan House, Legal Department, One Clove Crescent, East India Dock, London, E14 2BH, ☎020 7864 8703, ✉jerry.duku@pershing.co.uk, *Call Date: Oct 2003, Lincoln's Inn*
Qualifications: [LLM (LSE) LLB (Hons) (Cardiff)]

DULOVIC MR MILAN

EEF Ltd, EEF House, Queensway North, Team Valley Trading Estate, Gateshead, NE11 0NX, *Call Date: July 1982, Gray's Inn*
Qualifications: [LLB (Lond)]

DUNCAN MS DENISE

Deputy Justices' Clerk, South Western Magistrates' Court, 176a Lavender Hill, London, SW11 1JU, *Call Date: Nov 1985, Gray's Inn*
Qualifications: [LLB DMS CITP]

DUNCAN MR SIMON ROSS

Crown Advocate, Senior Crown Prosecutor, Crown Prosecution Service, 7th Floor (South), Royal Liver Building, Pier Head, Liverpool, Merseyside, L3 1HN, ☎0151 239 6400 / 0151 239 6400, *Call Date: May 1987, Lincoln's Inn*
Qualifications: [LLB]

DUNLEAVY MISS ANN GERALDINE

Company Secretary, Director, Flexible Remuneration Services Ltd, 7 Pelican Wharf, 58 Wapping Wall, Wapping, London, E1W 3SL, *Call Date: Nov 1988, Inner Temple*
Qualifications: [B Ed (Newc) LLB]

DUNN MR DARREN WILLIAM

Lawyer, Health & Safety Executive, Redgrave Court, Melton Road, Bootle, Merseyside, L20 7HS, *Call Date: Nov 1999, Inner Temple*
Qualifications: [LLB (Leics)]

DUNSEATH MISS LAURA ANN

Serious Fraud Office, Elm House, 10-16 Elm Street, London, WC1X 0BJ, ✉laura.dunseath@sfo.gsi.gov.uk, *Call Date: Mar 2009, Middle Temple*
Qualifications: [LLB (Hons)]

DUODU MR KORIEH KWABENA

David Price Solicitors and Advocates, Media Law Specialists, 21 Fleet Street, London, EC4Y 1AA, ☎020 7427 5692, *Call Date: Mar 2000, Lincoln's Inn*
Qualifications: [BA (Hons) (Lond) CPE]

DURSTON MS POLLYANN JOY

Legal Officer, Ministry of Defence, Central Legal Services, 6th Floor Zone F, Main Building, Whitehall, London, SW1A 2HP, ☎020 7218 0582, ✉Polly.Durston472@mod.uk, *Call Date: Oct 1991, Lincoln's Inn*
Qualifications: [LLB (Hons (B'ham)]

DYER MRS BARBARA ANN

Manager, Chevron (Uk Ltd), Legal Dept, 1 Westferry Circus, Canary Wharf, London, E14 4HA, ☎020 7719 3402 Fax: 020 7719 5124, ✉dyerb@chevron.com, *Call Date: Nov 1985, Inner Temple*
Qualifications: [BA (Hons)]

DYER MISS SANDRA PENELOPE

Senior Crown Prosecutor, Crown Prosecution Service, St Vincent House, 9th Floor, 1 Cutler Street, Ipswich, Suffolk, IP1 1UL, *Call Date: Nov 1983, Middle Temple*
Qualifications: [BA (Hons)]

DYER MISS SHEREEN

Fitzgerald's Solicitors, Hanover House, 72-82 High Street, Brentwood, CM14 4AP, Fax: 01277 205295, ✉coralfitzgerald@blueyonder.co.uk, *Call Date: Oct 2003, Lincoln's Inn*
Qualifications: [LLB (Hons)]

DYKE MISS LAURA JANE

Crown Prosecution Service, St Peters House, Gower Street, Derby, Derbyshire, DE1 1SB, *Call Date: Oct 2005, Gray's Inn*
Qualifications: [LLB (Keele)]

EARL MR ROBERT JAMES

Crown Prosecution Service, Southern House, Wellesley Grove, Croydon, Surrey, CR9 1DY, ☎ 020 8662 2831, ✉ robert.earl@cps.gsi.gov.uk, *Call Date: Mar 2008, Inner Temple*
Qualifications: [LLB (Lond) MA (Lond) LLM (Lond)]

EARNSHAW MR STEPHEN

FSOL, Baxter Brown McArthur, 150a Falcon Road, London, SW11 2LW, ✉ office@bbmlaw.co.uk, *Call Date: May 0, Middle Temple*
Qualifications: [LLB (Brunel)]

EASTON MR JEREMY JOHN CHARLES

Department of Energy and Climate Change, DECC Legal, Area 7B, 3 Whitehall Place, London, SW1A 2AW, *Call Date: July 2002, Gray's Inn*
Qualifications: [LLB (Brunel)]

EASTON MISS TRACY

Chief Crown Prosecutor, Crown Prosecution Service, Hawkins House, Pynes Hill, Exeter, Devon, EX2 5SS, ☎ 01392 288010 Fax: 01392 288008, *Call Date: Nov 1992, Inner Temple*
Qualifications: [BA (Hons) DipLaw]

EBBATSON MISS ELEANOR ANNE

Assistant, Senior Lawyer, HM Revenue and Customs, Solicitor's Office, 100 Parliament Street, London, SW1A 2BQ, ☎ 020 7147 0030 Fax: 020 7147 0433, *Call Date: July 1998, Gray's Inn*
Qualifications: [BA (Hons) (Oxon) Dip in Law]

EBLE MR KEITH JAMES

Legal Adviser, Directorate of Army Legal Services, Idl426, Ramillies Building, Marlborough Lines, Monxton Road, Andover, SP11 8HJ, ✉ keitheble472@mod.uk, *Call Date: Oct 1994, Lincoln's Inn*
Qualifications: [LLB (Hons)(Wales) MA (Lond)]

EDE MR RONALD GEORGE

Senior Crown Prosecutor, Ralph and Co Solicitors LLP, 20 Cliff Road, Newquay, Cornwall, TR7 1SG, Fax: 01637 875523, *Call Date: July 1981, Middle Temple*
Qualifications: [BA DMS]

EDIS MRS MARY ELIZABETH

Clyde and Co, Beaufort House, 15 St Botolph Street, London, EC3A 7NJ, ☎ 020 7876 5000 Fax: 020 7876 5111, *Call Date: July 1989, Gray's Inn*
Qualifications: [LLB (Bris)]

EDMONDS MS TAMLYN LOUISE

Lawyer, Edmonds Marshall Mcmahon Limited, 8 Red Lion Court, London, EC4A 3EB, Fax: 020 7681 2248, ✉ tamlynedmonds@emmlegal.com, *Call Date: Nov 2000, Inner Temple*
Qualifications: [LLB (Lond)]

EDWARDS MR ANGUS HEREWARD

Department For Transport, Great Minster House, 33 Horseferry Road, London, SW1P 4DR, ☎ 020 7944 4960 Fax: 020 7944 6692, ✉ angus.edwards@dft.gsi.gov.uk, *Call Date: Oct 1999, Lincoln's Inn*
Qualifications: [BA (Oxon) Dip in Law]

EDWARDS MISS BENITA AVA

London Borough of Hounslow, Civic Centre, Lampton Road, Hounslow, London, TW3 4DN, *Call Date: Oct 1997, Middle Temple*
Qualifications: [LLB (Hons)(Lond)]

EDWARDS MR DAVID CHARLES

Company Secretary, Anchor Trust, 2nd Floor, 25 Bedford Street, London, WC2E 9ES, ☎ 020 7759 9100 Fax: 020 7759 9101, ✉ david.edwards@anchor.org.uk, *Call Date: Nov 1978, Gray's Inn*
Qualifications: [LLB (Nottm)]

EDWARDS MR DAVID WILLIAM

Senior Crown Prosecutor, Crown Prosecution Service, Wood Green Crown Court, Woodall House, Lordship Lane, Wood Green, London, N22 5LF, ✉ David.Edwards2@cps.gsi.gov.uk, *Call Date: July 1988, Middle Temple*
Qualifications: [LLB (Hons)]

F

EDWARDS MISS JACQUELINE ELIZABETH ANNE

Crown Prosecution Service, 2 King Edward Court, King Edward Street, Nottingham, Nottinghamshire, NG1 1EL, ✉Jacqueline.Edwards@cps.gsi.gov.uk, *Call Date: Mar 1997, Lincoln's Inn*
Qualifications: [BA (Jnt Hons)(Keele)]

EDWARDS MISS JOANNE LOUISE

Directorate of Army Legal Services, Army Legal Services, Idl 426, Ramillies Building, Marlborough Lines, Moxton Road, Andover, SP11 8HJ, *Call Date: Nov 1996, Lincoln's Inn*
Qualifications: [LLB (Hons)]

EDWARDS MR JONATHAN LEIGHTON

Senior Crown Prosecutor, Crown Prosecution Service, Capital Tower, Greyfriars Road, Cardiff, CF10 3PL, ✉jonathan.edwards@cps.gsi.gov.uk, *Call Date: Oct 1997, Gray's Inn*
Qualifications: [LLB (Wales)]

EDWARDS MISS LUISA FRANCESCA

General Counsel, Google, Belgrave House, 76 Buckingham Palace Road, London, SW1W 9TQ, *Call Date: Oct 1992, Lincoln's Inn*
Qualifications: [MA (Hons) (Oxon) Lic Spec Dr Eur (Belgium)]

EDWARDS MR MARTIN RUSSELL

Crown Prosecution Service, United House, Piccadilly, York, North Yorkshire, YO1 9PQ, *Call Date: Nov 1992, Lincoln's Inn*
Qualifications: [LLB (Hons)]

EDWARDS MR MATTHEW JAMES

Crown Prosecution Service, Stoke Newington Police Station, 33 Stoke Newington High Street, London, N16 8DS, ☎020 87215517 Fax: 020 87215539, ✉matthew.edwards@cps.gsi.gov.uk, *Call Date: July 2005, Inner Temple*
Qualifications: [LLB (Leic)]

EDWARDS MR RICHARD HUW WYN

Crown Prosecution Service, Llys Eirias, Heritage Gate, Abergele Road, Colwyn Bay, Denbighshire, LL29 8BW, ☎01492 806800, ✉Richard.Edwards@cps.gsi.gov.uk, *Call Date: Oct 1997, Lincoln's Inn*
Qualifications: [B.Eng (Hons)(City) LLB (Hons)(Wales)]

EDWARDS MR RICHARD JOHN

Lawyer, Crown Prosecution Service, Rose Court, 2 Southwark, London, SE1 9HS, ☎020 3357 0846 Fax: 020 3357 0874, ✉johnr.edwards@cps.gsi.gov.uk, *Call Date: Nov 1994, Middle Temple*
Qualifications: [BA (Hons) MA]

EDWARDS MR SIMON DAVID

Crown Prosecution Service, Black Horse House, 8-10 Leigh Road, Eastleigh, Hampshire, SO50 9FH, *Call Date: Nov 1987, Gray's Inn*
Qualifications: [LLB (Leics)]

EDWARDS MR STEVEN JOHN

Senior Lawyer, Royal Bank of Scotland, 250 Bishopsgate, London, EC2M 4AA, ✉steven.edwards@rbs.com, *Call Date: Oct 1995, Inner Temple*
Qualifications: [HNC BA LLB LLM]

EGERTON-PETERS MR JONATHON JOSEPH

Skadden, Arps, Slate, Meagher & Flom LLP, 40 Bank Street, Canary Wharf, London, E14 5DS, ☎020 7519 7000 Fax: 020 7519 7070, ✉jonathon.egerton-peters@skadden.com, *Call Date: July 2008, Inner Temple*
Qualifications: [LLB (Lond) BCL (Oxon)]

EGOLE MISS SITA SEETA RUTH

The Treasury Solicitors, One Kemble Street, London, WC2B 4TS, ☎020 7210 2905 Fax: 020 7210 3352, *Call Date: Oct 1999, Gray's Inn*
Qualifications: [LLB (Lond)]

EISA MR WAYIL

Office of Fair Trading, Fleetbank House, 2-6 Salisbury Square, London, EC4Y 8JX, *Call Date: Oct 1998, Inner Temple*
Qualifications: [BSc (Hons) (Sussex) CPE]

ELAHI MR RIZWAN

HM Revenue and Customs, 100 Parliament Street, London, SW1A 2BQ, ☎020 3300 9375 Fax: 020 7147 0433, ✉rizwan.elahi@hmrc.gsi.gov.uk, *Call Date: May 1990, Middle Temple*
Qualifications: [LLB (Hons)]

F

ELLACOTT MR STUART IAN

Crown Prosecution Service, Oxford House, Oxford Road, Bournemouth, Dorset, BH8 8HA, ✉stuart.ellacott@cps.gsi.gov.uk, *Call Date: Nov 1989, Inner Temple*
Qualifications: [BA]

ELLINS DR JULIA ELISABETH

Financial Services Authority, The Financial Services Authority, Enforcement and Financial Crime Division - Legal Group, 25 The North Colonade, Canary Wharf, London, E14 5HS, *Call Date: Oct 1994, Gray's Inn*
Qualifications: [LLB (Lond) LLM (USA) Dr Jur (Germany)]

ELLIOTT MR CHRISTOPHER DAVID

Leeds City Council, Civic Hall, Calverley Street, Leeds, LS1 1UR, ✉christopher.elliott@leeds.gov.uk, *Call Date: July 1974, Gray's Inn*
Qualifications: [BA (Hons)]

ELLIOTT MRS LORNA

Lound Mulrenan Jefferies, 210 Bon Marche Centre, Brixton, London, SW9 8BJ, Fax: 020 7 793 4264, *Call Date: Mar 2003, Lincoln's Inn*
Qualifications: [LLB (Hons)]

ELLIOTT MS REIKO

The Bank of Tokyo-Mitsubishi UFJ, Ltd., Ropemaker Place, 25 Ropemaker Street, London, EC2Y 9AN, ☎020 7577 1829 Fax: 020 7577 1299, *Call Date: Oct 2000, Inner Temple*
Qualifications: [LLB (Lond) LLM (Lond)]

ELLIOTT CAPTAIN SPENCER FREDERICK

Directorate of Army Legal Services, RAF Northolt, Service Prosecuting Authority, West End Road, Ruislip, Middlesex, HA4 6NG, ☎020 8833 6135, ✉spa-team2b-so3-1@northolt.raf.mod.uk, *Call Date: Oct 2007, Lincoln's Inn*
Qualifications: [LLB (Lond)]

ELLIS MISS CATHERINE SIOBHAN

Harrow Council, Civic Centre, Station Road, Harrow, Middlesex, HA1 2UH, ☎020 8424 1119 Fax: 020 8424 1557, ✉catherine.ellis@harrow.gov.uk, *Call Date: July 2003, Middle Temple*
Qualifications: [LLB Hons (Sheff)]

ELLIS MRS EDWINA FRANCESCA

Principal Legal Adviser, Stratford Magistrates' Court, The Courthouse, 389-397 High Street, Stratford, London, E15 4SB, ☎020 8437 6061 Fax: 020 8437 6010, ✉edwina.ellis@hmcts.gsi.gov.uk, *Call Date: Nov 1984, Middle Temple*
Qualifications: [BA (Hons)]

ELLIS MS HELEN GRACE

Directorate of Army Legal Services, Trenchard Lines, Upavon, Pewsey, Wiltshire, SN9 6BE, ☎01980 615971 Fax: 01980 615978, *Call Date: Oct 2002, Inner Temple*
Qualifications: [LLB (Hons) (Hull) LLM (Lond)]

ELLIS MR LEE ANDREW

Call Date: Nov 2005, Lincoln's Inn
Qualifications: [BSc (Hons) (Leeds) MSc (Leeds)]

ELLIS MISS SARAH LOUISE

Simply Social Housing Solicitors, Po Box 491, Manchester, M16 6BZ, ☎08443 814734 Fax: 0161 839 8222, ✉info@simplysocialhousing.co.uk, *Call Date: July 1999, Lincoln's Inn*
Qualifications: [BA (Hons)(Reading) Dip Law]

ELLIS MR WESLEY JONATHAN

Crown Prosecution Service, Gateway, 31 Power Close, Guildford, Surrey, GU1 1EJ, ✉Jonathan.Ellis@cps.gsi.gov.uk, *Call Date: Feb 1995, Gray's Inn*
Qualifications: [MA (Cantab)]

ELLIS OWEN MISS ANGHARAD

Dickinson Dees, St Ann's Wharf, 112 Quayside, Newcastle Upon Tyne, NE99 1SB, ☎0191 279 9000 Fax: 0191 279 9100, ✉angharad.ellis-owen@dickinson-dees.com, *Call Date: Oct 2001, Lincoln's Inn*
Qualifications: [LLB (Hons) (Wales)]

ELLIS-JONES MR STEPHEN

Lightfoots LLP, 1-3 High Street, Thame, Oxfordshire, OX9 2BX, *Call Date: Nov 1992, Middle Temple*
Qualifications: [B Eng (L'pool)]

ELMAAZI MS AYAH

Financial Services Authority, 25 The North Colannade, Canary Wharf, London, E14 8HS, *Call Date: Nov 2006, Inner Temple*
Qualifications: [BA (Lond) MSc (Lond)]

F

ELMES MISS LOUISE ELISABETH

Curtis Davis Garrard LLP, 2 Roundwood Avenue, Stockley Park, Heathrow Airport, Uxbridge, UB11 1AF, ☎020 8734 2800 Fax: 020 8734 2820/21, ✉louise.elmes@cdg.co.uk, *Call Date: July 2002, Middle Temple*
Qualifications: [MA (Hons) (Cantab)]

ELOQUIN MISS SOPHIE CHANTAL

Crown Prosecution Service, Rose Court, 2 Southwark Bridge, London, SE1 9HS, ☎020 33570000, ✉sophie.eloquin@cps.gsi.gov.uk, *Call Date: July 2000, Middle Temple*
Qualifications: [BA(Hons) (Oxon) CPE]

EL-SOBKY MISS MARIAM ADEL

Senior Crown Prosecutor, Crown Prosecution Service, Southern House, Wellesley Grove, Croydon, Surrey, CR9 1DY, ☎020 8662 2846 Fax: 020 8662 2843, ✉mariam.el-sobky@cps.gsi.gov.uk, *Call Date: Mar 2001, Lincoln's Inn*
Qualifications: [LLB (Hons) LLM]

ELVY MR PHILIP JAMES

Department For Work and Pensions, 5th Floor, the Adelphi, 1-11 John Adam Street, London, WC2N 6HT, ☎020 7962 8242 Fax: 020 7962 8924, ✉philip.elvy@dwp.gsi.gov.uk, *Call Date: Oct 1997, Inner Temple*
Qualifications: [LLB (Southampton)]

EMERSON MR THOMAS PATRICK

Crown Prosecution Service, Private Office, 9th Floor, Rose Court, 2 Southwark Bridge Road, London, SE1 9HS, ☎0118 951 3600, ✉thomas.emerson@cps.gsi.gov.uk, *Call Date: July 2008, Middle Temple*
Qualifications: [LLB (Hons) (Bris)]

EMERY MISS ELIZABETH

Department For Transport, Great Minster House, Room 1/04c, 76 Marsham Street, London, SW1P 4DR, ☎020 7944 8887, ✉elizabeth.emery@dft.gsi.gov.uk, *Call Date: Nov 2006, Lincoln's Inn*
Qualifications: [LLB LLM]

EMIN MR FUAT

Crown Prosecution Service, Rose Court, 2 Southwark Bridge, London, SE1 9HS, *Call Date: Nov 1986, Inner Temple*
Qualifications: [BSc]

EMMANOUILIDOU MISS THALIA

HMCTS, Brighton and Hove Magistrates Court, Edward Street, Brighton, Sussex, BN2 0LG, ☎01273 811606, ✉t.emman@hmcourts-service.gsi.gov.uk, *Call Date: Mar 2002, Middle Temple*
Qualifications: [LLB]

EMSON MR RAYMOND NEAL

Serious Fraud Office, Elm House, 10-16 Elm Street, London, WC1X 0BJ, ✉Raymond.emson@sfo.gsi.gov.uk, *Call Date: Nov 1994, Middle Temple*
Qualifications: [B Sc (Hons) LLB (Hons) LLM]

ENGLAND MS ANGELA MARGARET

Crown Advocate, Crown Prosecution Service, Oxford House, Oxford Road, Bournemouth, Dorset, BH8 8HA, ☎01202 498700 Fax: 01202 498748, *Call Date: Oct 1999, Lincoln's Inn*
Qualifications: [LLB (Hons) MA PhD]

ENGLAND MR JAMES

Commissioner, Criminal Cases Review Commission, 5 St Philips Place, Birmingham, B3 2PW, *Call Date: July 1981, Gray's Inn*
Qualifications: [LLB (Lond)]

ENGLISH MR LAWRENCE JAMES

HED, Crown Prosecution Service, Princes Court, 34 York Road, Leicester, Leicestershire, LE1 5TU, ☎0116 204 6843 Fax: 0116 204 6843, ✉lawrence.english@cps.gsi.gov.uk, *Call Date: Nov 1988, Lincoln's Inn*
Qualifications: [LLB (Nott'm)]

ENSTON MISS NICOLA JAYNE

The Treasury Solicitors, Treasury Solicitor's Department, One Kemble Street, London, WC2B 4TS, *Call Date: Nov 1995, Lincoln's Inn*
Qualifications: [LLB (Hons)(Leic)]

ENVER MS SEREF

Justice of the Peace, Serco Home Affairs, Cavell House, St Crispins Road, Norwich, NR3 1YE, ☎01603 428318 Fax: 0870 0700321, *Call Date: July 2004, Lincoln's Inn*
Qualifications: [BA Hons (Greenwich) Dip in Applied Social Sciences MSc (Lond) CPE/LLDip BVC]

F

EPPEL MR MAX PETER LLOYD

McFaddens, City Tower, 40 Basinghall Street, London, EC2V 5DE, ☎020 7588 9080 Fax: 020 7588 8988, ✉maxeppel@mcfaddenslaw.co.uk, *Call Date: Oct 2002, Lincoln's Inn*
Qualifications: [LLB]

ERSHAD MISS JENNIFER

Chair, Thames Magistrates' Court, 58 Bow Road, London, E3 4DJ, ☎020 8271 1203, *Call Date: Oct 1994, Middle Temple*
Qualifications: [LLB (Hons)(Lond)]

ERTAN MISS FERYAL

Guney Clark and Ryan Solicitors, 58 Green Lanes, London, N16 9NH, ☎020 7275 7788 Fax: 020 7923 2554, *Call Date: Oct 2005, Gray's Inn*
Qualifications: [BA (Westminster)]

ESPINDOLA MISS MARIA-TERESA

Fce Bank PLC, Central Office, 1/426, Eagle Way, Brentwood, Essex, CM13 3AR, ☎01277 692996 Fax: 01277 692083, ✉tespindo@ford.com, *Call Date: Mar 1999, Gray's Inn*
Qualifications: [LLB (Lond)]

ESSIEN MRS OLIVE

Prosecutor, Crown Prosecution Service, United House, Piccadilly, York, North Yorkshire, YO1 9PQ, ☎020 8464 2849 Fax: 020 460 9948, ✉olive.essien@cps.gsi.gov.uk, *Call Date: July 1990, Gray's Inn*
Qualifications: [LLB]

EUBANK MISS NICOLE RUTH

The Treasury Solicitors, Bona Vacantia Division- Zone 7.03, Treasury Solicitors Department, One Kemble Street, London, WC2B 4TS, Fax: 020 7210 3104, ✉Nicole.Eubank@TSOL.GSI.GOV.UK, *Call Date: Oct 1997, Middle Temple*
Qualifications: [LLB (Hons)(Lond)]

EVANS MRS ANN

TRM, Crown Prosecution Service, Queen House, 58 Victoria Street, St. Albans, Hertfordshire, AL1 3HZ, ☎01727 798774, ✉ann.evans@cps.gsi.gov.uk, *Call Date: July 1983, Gray's Inn*

EVANS MR GARY LEE

The University of Nottingham, University Park, Nottingham, NG7 2RD, ☎01558 467890, ✉gary.evans@nottingham.ac.uk, *Call Date: Nov 1985, Inner Temple*
Qualifications: [BSc LLB MSc]

EVANS MR JEREMY MARK

Crown Prosecution Service, Citadel House, 58 High Street, Hull, Humberside, HU1 1QD, *Call Date: Nov 1998, Lincoln's Inn*
Qualifications: [LLB (Hons)(Leics)]

EVANS MISS KATHARINE

Peter Bonner & Co, 8-12 Lee High Road, Lewisham, London, SE13 5LQ, ☎020 8297 1727 Fax: 020 8297 9097, *Call Date: July 2005, Lincoln's Inn*
Qualifications: [LLB (Hons) (Lond)]

EVANS MISS LEANNE JAYNE

Hine & Associates, Hine and Associates Solicitors, 51 Amersham Road, Beaconsfield, Buckinghamshire, HP9 2HB, Fax: 01494 685584, *Call Date: July 2007, Middle Temple*
Qualifications: [LLB (Hons) (Uni of West England)]

EVANS MISS LISA CLAIRE

Law Officers of the Crown, St James Chambers, St Peter Port, GY1 4PY, Guernsey, ☎01481 743730, ✉lisa.evans@gov.gg, *Call Date: Oct 1991, Inner Temple*
Qualifications: [LLB (Hons)]

EVANS MR PETER WILLIAM

Department For Business, Innovation and Skills, Room 537, 1 Victoria Street, London, SW1H 0ET, ✉peter.evans@bis.gsi.gov.uk, *Call Date: Nov 1994, Middle Temple*
Qualifications: [MA (Hons)]

EVANS MISS SUSAN

Crown Prosecution Service, Greenfield House, 32 Scotland Street, Sheffield, South Yorkshire, S3 7DQ, ☎0114 229 8600, ✉sue.evans@cps.gsi.gov.uk, *Call Date: Nov 1992, Inner Temple*
Qualifications: [LLB (Hull)]

F

EVANS MRS ZOE

Company Secretary, General Counsel, Eusa Pharma Inc, The Magdalen Centre, Oxford Science Park, Oxford, Oxfordshire, OX4 4GA, ☎01865 784259 Fax: 01865 784253, ✉zoe.evans@eusapharma.com, *Call Date: Oct 1999, Middle Temple*
Qualifications: [ACIS LLB (Hons)]

EWEN MRS LORNA SYLVIA

Principal Crown Prosecutor, Crown Prosecution Service, Lewisham Police Station, 43 Lewisham High Street, Lewisham, London, SE13 5JZ, *Call Date: Nov 1983, Gray's Inn*
Qualifications: [BA LLM]

EWING MS MICHELLE

Financial Services Authority, General Counsel's Division, 25 The North Colonnade, Canary Wharf, London, E14 5HS, *Call Date: Oct 1994, Middle Temple*
Qualifications: [BA (Hons)(Oxon) LLM (Canada)]

EWULO MISS SOPHIA

Crown Prosecution Service, County House, 100 New London Road, Chelmsford, Essex, CM2 0RG, ✉Sophia.Ewulo@cps.gsi.gov.uk, *Call Date: July 2001, Lincoln's Inn*
Qualifications: [BA (Hons) (Cantab)]

EYEINGTON MISS LOUISE REBECCA

Legal Adviser, Department For Communities & Local Government, Zone 4/B3, Eland House, Bressenden House, London, SW1E 5DU, ✉Louise.eyeington@communities.gsi.gov.uk, *Call Date: Nov 1993, Inner Temple*
Qualifications: [LLB (Warw)]

EYLES MR ALAN JAMES

Crown Prosecution Service, Greenwich Police Station, 31 Royal Hill, Greenwich, London, SE10 8RR, *Call Date: Feb 1989, Gray's Inn*
Qualifications: [LLB]

EYRE MISS RACHEL LOUISE

Capsticks Solicitors LLP, 1 St George's Road, Wimbledon, London, SW19 4DR, ☎020 8780 4682 Fax: 020 8780 1141, ✉rachel.eyre@capstickes.com, *Call Date: Oct 2008, Lincoln's Inn*
Qualifications: [LLB (Reading)]

EYRES MR RAYMOND JOHN

Company Secretary, Director, Cummins Ltd, 49-51 Gresham Road, Staines, Middlesex, TW18 2BD, ☎01784 231505 Fax: 01784 231509, ✉raymond.j.eyres@cummins.com, *Call Date: Nov 1973, Inner Temple*
Qualifications: [LLB MBA MA]

EYSENCK MS FLEUR DAVINA RUTH

Financial Services Authority, 25 The North Colannade, Canary Wharf, London, E14 8HS, *Call Date: Oct 2003, Inner Temple*
Qualifications: [BA (Lond)]

FAIRCLOUGH DR MURRAY SIMON CHARLES

Director of Legal Services, Abbey Protection Group Limited, 17 Lansdowne Road, Croydon, Surrey, CR0 2BX, ☎020 8730 6000 Fax: 020 8730 6001, ✉m.fairclough@abbeylegal.com, *Call Date: Nov 1993, Inner Temple*
Qualifications: [LLB PhD LLM]

FALCONER OF THOROTON LORD CHARLES LESLIE

The Lord Chancellor, Recorder, Solicitor General, Gibson Dunn & Crutcher LLP, Telephone House, 2-4 Temple Avenue, London, EC4Y 0HB, ✉cfalconer@gibsondunn.com, *Call Date: July 1974, Inner Temple*
Qualifications: [MA (Cantab)]

FALSHAW MR WILLIAM FREDRICK

Senior Crown Prosecutor, Crown Prosecution Service, Riverside House, Riverside Way, Bedford Road, Northampton, Northamptonshire, NN1 5NX, *Call Date: July 1987, Inner Temple*
Qualifications: [Dip Law (Lond) BA (Hons)]

FANNING MISS CLAIRE ELIZABETH

Senior Crown Prosecutor, Crown Prosecution Service, Burnley Wharf, Manchester Road, Burnley, Lancashire, BB11 1JG, ☎01282 478500 Fax: 01282 478 502, *Call Date: Oct 1993, Lincoln's Inn*
Qualifications: [BA (Hons)(Lond) CPE (Lond)]

FARAZI MRS SEEMA ANDALIB

Fragomen LLP, 4th Floor, Holborn Gate, 330 High Holborn, London, WC1V 7PP, ☎020 3077 5110 Fax: 020 3077 5001, ✉sfarazi@fragomen.com, *Call Date: July 2001, Lincoln's Inn*
Qualifications: [LLB (Hons) LLM (Lond)]

FARGIN MISS ELEANOR MARIE

Crown Prosecution Service, Western Range, 83 London Road, Southampton, Hampshire, SO15 2AA, ☎02380 714 000, ✉ellie.fargin@cps.gsi.gov.uk, *Call Date: July 2004, Inner Temple*
Qualifications: [LLB]

FARLEY MR PETER JOHN

Company Secretary, Legal Director, Fiat Group Automobiles Uk Ltd, Fiat House, 240 Bath Road, Slough, Berkshire, SL1 4DX, ☎01753 511 431 Fax: 01753 512 393, ✉peter.farley@fiat.com, *Call Date: July 1982, Middle Temple*
Qualifications: [BA (Hons) LLM (Lond)]

FARMER MR PAUL RONALD

Dorsey and Whitney LLP, 21 Wilson Street, London, EC2M 2TD, ☎020 7588 0800, ✉farmer.paul@dorsey.com, *Call Date: July 2000, Lincoln's Inn*
Qualifications: [LLB(Hons) (MPhil) (Manch)]

FAROOQ MR MOHAMMED KHAN

Senior Lawyer, Dudley Metropolitan Borough Council, Legal and Democratic Services, 5 Ednam Road, Dudley, West Midlands, DY1 1HL, ☎01384 815371 Fax: 01384 815325, *Call Date: Oct 1993, Lincoln's Inn*
Qualifications: [LLB (Hons)(Warw)]

FARRANT MR JAMES DEREK

Other, Royal Navy Officers, Directorate of Naval Legal Services, Mp 4-2, Leach Building, Whale Island, Portsmouth, PO2 8BY, ✉261-LO@a.dii.mod.uk, *Call Date: July 2007, Gray's Inn*
Qualifications: [BA (Cantab) MA (Cantab)]

FARRER MR DAVID JOHN

Bencher, Recorder, Seven Bedford Row, 7 Bedford Row, London, WC1R 4BS, ☎020 7242 3555 Fax: 020 7242 2511, ✉dfarrer@7br.co.uk, *Call Date: Apr 1967, Middle Temple*
Qualifications: [MA (Cantab) LLB]

FARUK MR MOHAMMED OMAR

Director, Department For Work and Pensions, 5th Floor, the Adelphi, 1-11 John Adam Street, London, WC2N 6HT, ☎020 7962 8788, ✉omar.faruk@dwp.gsi.gov.uk, *Call Date: Oct 1996, Lincoln's Inn*
Qualifications: [LLB (Hons)(Lond) MBA (Cranfield)]

FAULKNER MISS ANGELA ELIZABETH

Aviva Legal Services, 4th Floor, Wellington Row, York, YO90 1WR, *Call Date: Nov 1988, Middle Temple*
Qualifications: [LLB (L'pool)]

FAWCETT MISS DONNA MARIE

Senior Crown Prosecutor, Crown Prosecution Service, 2 King Edward Court, King Edward Street, Nottingham, Nottinghamshire, NG1 1EL, ☎0115 852 3519 Fax: 0115 852 3324, ✉Donna.Fawcett@cps.gsi.gov.uk, *Call Date: Feb 1994, Gray's Inn*
Qualifications: [LLB]

FAWCETT MS SARAH JANE

Proven, 40 George Street, London, W1U 7DW, ☎020 7467 2040 Fax: 020 7786 2672, ✉sarahfawcett@provenlegal.eu, *Call Date: July 2001, Inner Temple*
Qualifications: [LLB (Lond) CPE]

FEASTER-GEE MRS TRUDY DAWN

Call Date: Oct 1993, Inner Temple
Qualifications: [LLB (Hons)(Warw) Dip Spec en Droit]

FEENEY MS CIARA

London Borough of Islington, Town Hall, 222 Upper Street, Islington, London, N1 2UD, *Call Date: Oct 2001, Lincoln's Inn*
Qualifications: [LLB (Hons)]

FELDMAN MISS LAURA

Accuracy Management Consultants, Mid-City Place, 71 High Holborn, London, WC1V 6EA, ☎020 7421 8122, ✉herve.detrogoff@accuracy.com, *Call Date: July 2009, Middle Temple*
Qualifications: [BA (Hons) (Lond) BA (Hons) (Oxon)]

F

FELIHO MRS NCHIKE CLAUDINE

Arbitrator, The Treasury Solicitors, 5th Floor, One Kemble Street, London, WC2B 4TS, *Call Date: Nov 2002, Inner Temple*
Qualifications: [LLB (Staff)]

FELL MRS ELIZABETH ANNE

Crown Prosecution Service, The Regatta, 6 Henley Buisness park, Doddington Road, Lincoln, LN6 3QR, *Call Date: Nov 2000, Inner Temple*
Qualifications: [LLB (Lancs)]

FENNER MR EDWARD HOWARD

FMW Law, 150 King Street, Hammersmith, London, W6 0QU, Fax: 020 3012 1483, ✉edward.fenner@fmwlaw.co.uk, *Call Date: Nov 2000, Middle Temple*
Qualifications: [LLB (Hons) (Lond)]

FENWICK MR DANIEL FITZGERALD

London Borough of Waltham Forest, Town Hall, Forest Road, Walthamstow, London, E17 4JA, ☎020 8496 4881, ✉daniel.fenwick@lbwf.gov.uk, *Call Date: Oct 1993, Lincoln's Inn*
Qualifications: [BA (Hons)(Manch) CPE (Manch)]

FERGUSON MISS ANDREA JANET

Dobsons Solicitors, 27 London Road, Bromley, Kent, BR1 1DF, *Call Date: Oct 2003, Middle Temple*
Qualifications: [LLB (Hons)]

FERGUSON MISS CAROLE ANNE

Call Date: Oct 1999, Lincoln's Inn
Qualifications: [BA (Hons)]

FERGUSON MISS CORINNA MAY

Liberty, Liberty House, 26-30 Strutton Ground, London, SW1P 2HR, ☎020 7378 3658 Fax: 020 7799 5306, *Call Date: July 2003, Lincoln's Inn*
Qualifications: [BA Hons (Cantab) CPE]

FERGUSON MR FRANCIS JOHN

Advocate, District Crown Prosecutor, Crown Prosecution Service, Carmelite House, St James Court, Whitefriars, Norwich, Norfolk, NR3 1SL, ☎01603 693000 Fax: 01603 693001, ✉frank.ferguson@cps.gsi.gov.uk, *Call Date: Nov 1992, Gray's Inn*
Qualifications: [BA (Hons)]

FERN MISS CAROLE LYNN

Crown Prosecution Service, Gateway, 31 Power Close, Guildford, Surrey, GU1 1EJ, ☎01483 468200 Fax: 01483 468202, ✉carole.fern@cps.gsi.gov.uk, *Call Date: July 2010, Middle Temple*
Qualifications: [BA (USA) JD (Harvard)]

FERNANDES MR NICHOLAS JOHN DAMIAN

Legal Adviser, Department For Business, Innovation and Skills, Legal Services Group, 1 Victoria Street, London, SW1H 0ET, *Call Date: Nov 1984, Lincoln's Inn*
Qualifications: [LLM LLM BA Dip French Law]

FERNANDEZ-LEE MISS KELLY JANE AMERIQITA

Jackson Parton Solicitors, 4th Floor, 1 Alie Street, London, E1 8DE, *Call Date: Nov 2002, Middle Temple*
Qualifications: [LLB (Hons)]

FERNANDO MISS CHAMALI

Sriharans Solicitors, 223 The Broadway, Southall, Middlesex, UB1 1ND, *Call Date: Nov 2002, Middle Temple*
Qualifications: [LLB (Hons) (Lond)]

FERRARI MR CESARE MARIA PRIMO

Lawyer, Department For Communities & Local Government, Legal 2, Housing Building and Land Division, Eland House, Zone 4/A4, Bressenden Place, London, SW1E 5DU, ✉Cesare.Ferrari@communities.gsi.gov.uk, *Call Date: Feb 1979, Middle Temple*
Qualifications: [BA (Oxon)]

FIELD MISS AMANDA JANE

Crown Prosecution Service, Rose Court, 2 Southwark Bridge, London, SE1 9HS, ☎020 3357 0400, ✉Amanda-Jane.Field@cps.gsi.gov.uk, *Call Date: Feb 1994, Middle Temple*
Qualifications: [MA (Ireland)]

FIELD MR MICHAEL CLIVE

Freemans, 35 Duke Street, London, W1U 1LH, ☎020 7935 3522 Fax: 020 7535 1335, ✉mf@freemanssolicitors.net, *Call Date: July 2009, Middle Temple*
Qualifications: [LLB (Hons)]

FIELDING MISS CLAIRE ELLWOOD

Crown Prosecution Service, The Cooperage, 8 Gainsford Street, London, SE1 2NE, ☎0207 3784100 Fax: 0207 3784201, ✉Claire.Mays@cps.gsi.gov.uk, *Call Date: Nov 2000, Middle Temple*
Qualifications: [LLB (Hons) (B'Ham)]

FINCH MR CHRISTOPHER

Creed Lane Law Group, 8 Creed Lane, St Pauls, London, EC4V 5BR, *Call Date: July 1975, Lincoln's Inn*
Qualifications: [LLB (Hons)]

FINLAY MR ANDREW STEVEN

CKM Solicitors, 82 Medomsley Road, Consett, County Durham, DH8 5HS, ☎0191 384 9080 Fax: 0191 384 9144, ✉durham.office@ckm-solicitors.co.uk, *Call Date: Oct 1993, Gray's Inn*
Qualifications: [LLB (Hons)(Manch)]

FINNEY MR MARK MATYAS VESZY

Director, Citigroup, Citigroup Legal Department, Citigroup Centre, 33 Canada Square, Canary Wharf, London, E14 5LB, ☎020 7508 9516 Fax: 020 7508 9116, ✉mark.finney@citigroup.com, *Call Date: Nov 1983, Gray's Inn*
Qualifications: [LLB (Reading)]

FIREMAN MR MARK PHILLIP

Kemps Solicitors, Second Floor, 19-25 Union Street, Oldham, OL1 1HA, ☎0161 633 0555 Fax: 0161 633 9905, ✉mfireman@kemps-solicitors.com, *Call Date: Feb 1986, Gray's Inn*
Qualifications: [LLB (Lond)(Hons)]

FIRMAN MISS HAYLEY JANE

Crown Prosecution Service, Colmore Gate, 2 - 6 Colmore Row, Birmingham, West Midlands, B3 2QA, ☎0121 262 1145
Fax: 0121 262 6306, *Call Date: Nov 2006, Inner Temple*
Qualifications: [LLB (Wolves)]

FIRTH MISS SHEILA RUTH

Legal Adviser, Milton Keynes Magistrates' Court, 301 Silbury Boulevard, Witan Gate East, Milton Keynes, MK9 2AJ, *Call Date: Nov 1996, Lincoln's Inn*
Qualifications: [LLB (Hons)(Hull)]

FISHER MS ANGELA PATRICIA

Criminal Cases Review Commission, 5 St Philips Place, Birmingham, B3 2PW, *Call Date: Oct 1996, Lincoln's Inn*
Qualifications: [LLB (Hons)(Brunel)]

FITTALL MISS MARIE

Crown Prosecution Service, Southampton Magistrates Unit, Western Range, 83 London Road, Southampton, Hampshire, SO15 2AA, ✉marie.fittall@cps.gsi.gov.uk, *Call Date: Oct 2003, Inner Temple*
Qualifications: [LLB (Bris)]

FITZGERALD MISS KATE MARY ANN KATHARINE GENEVI

JP Morgan Chase, 125 London Wall, London, EC2Y 5AJ, ✉kate.fitzgerald@jpmorgan.com, *Call Date: July 1988, Inner Temple*
Qualifications: [LLB (Wales) (Hons)]

FITZGERALD MRS VICTORIA MARY

The Home Office, Legal Team, 5th Floor, Becket House, 60-68 St Thomas Street, London, SE1 3QU, *Call Date: July 2007, Middle Temple*
Qualifications: [LLB (Kent)]

FITZPATRICK MRS ANTONIA SARAH

Associate, Berwin Leighton Paisner LLP, Adelaide House, London Bridge, London, EC4R 9HA, ☎020 3400 1000
Fax: 020 34001111, *Call Date: Oct 1996, Middle Temple*
Qualifications: [LLB (Hons)(Manc)]

FITZPATRICK MR DESMOND CHRISTOPHER

Manager, Toyota (Gb) PLC, Great Burgh, Burgh Heath, Epsom, Surrey, KT18 5UX, ☎0845 275 5555 Fax: 020 3166 4115, *Call Date: July 1983, Inner Temple*
Qualifications: [BA (York) Dip in law Post-graduate Dip in EC Law (Lond) Dip in Management]

FLAHERTY MS MAUREEN

Crown Prosecution Service, Harrow Crown Court, Hailsham Drive, Harrow, HA1 4TU, ☎020 8424 2294, ✉Maureen.Flaherty@cps.gsi.gov.uk, *Call Date: Nov 1995, Lincoln's Inn*
Qualifications: [BA (Hons)]

F

FLANAGAN MR JOHN

Company Secretary, Cooper Gay Sweet and Crawford Ltd, 52 Leadenhall Street, London, EC34 2EB, ☎020 7204 4854, *Call Date: Oct 1991, Middle Temple*
Qualifications: [BA (Hons) (Dunelm) DipLaw]

FLECK MISS HELEN ALEXANDRA

Nursing and Midwifery Council, Fitness to Practice, 61 Aldwych, London, WC2B 4AE, *Call Date: Oct 2005, Lincoln's Inn*
Qualifications: [BA (Hons) (Oxon)]

FLEMING MRS CAROLINE SYBIL ELIZABETH

Royal Navy Officers, Dnls, Mp 4.2 Leach Building, Whale Island, Portsmouth, Hampshire, PO2 8BY, ✉fleet-dnlsempllawson1@mod.uk, *Call Date: July 2011, Gray's Inn*
Qualifications: [MA]

FLEWERS MR JONATHAN

Legal Services Commission, Legal Department, 8th Floor, 102 Petty France, London, SW1H 9AJ, ✉jonathan.flewers@legalservices.gov.uk, *Call Date: Oct 2004, Lincoln's Inn*
Qualifications: [LLB (Hons) Essex]

FLORIDA-JAMES MR MARK

Carlton Place Law, 9 Carlton Place, Southampton, Hampshire, SO15 2EA, *Call Date: Oct 1995, Inner Temple*
Qualifications: [BA (Sussex) MPhil Dip In Law]

FLOWITT MRS NICOLA

Clerk, Legal Adviser, Justices' Clerk's Office, Old Shire Hall, Honey Hill, Bury St Edmunds, Suffolk, IP33 1HF, ☎01284 778035 Fax: 01284 778020, ✉nicola.flowitt@hmcts.gsi.gov.uk, *Call Date: Nov 1986, Inner Temple*
Qualifications: [LLB]

FODOR DR NEIL HARRIS

Crown Prosecution Service, St Ann's Quay, 122 Quayside, Newcastle Upon Tyne, Tyne and Wear, NE1 3BD, ☎0191 260 4200, ✉Neil.Fodor@cps.gsi.gov.uk, *Call Date: Nov 1991, Inner Temple*
Qualifications: [MA (Scotland) PHD (Scotland) Dip Law]

FOLEY MR CHEN EUGENE

Sedgwick, Detert, Moran and Arnold LLP, Fitzwilliam House, 10 St. Mary Axe, London, EC3A 8BF, ☎020 7929 1829 Fax: 020 7929 1808, ✉chen.foley@sdma.com, *Call Date: July 2001, Lincoln's Inn*
Qualifications: [LLB (Hons)(Lond)]

FOLEY MR JOHN SHELDON

Director, General Medical Council, Head of Registration and Certification Appeals, 3 Hardman Street, Manchester, M3 3AW, ☎01619 236552, ✉JFoley@gmc-uk.org, *Call Date: July 1981, Lincoln's Inn*
Qualifications: [LLB MBA]

FOO MR YOKE YAN

Vice President, Citigroup, Citigroup Legal Department, Citigroup Centre, 33 Canada Square, Canary Wharf, London, E14 5LB, ☎020 7508 9543 Fax: 0207508 6907, ✉sean.foo@citi.com, *Call Date: July 1989, Lincoln's Inn*
Qualifications: [BSc (Keele)]

FOOT MR KENNETH ALAN

London Borough of Newham, London Borough of Newham Legal Services, Ground Floor East Wing, Newham Dockside, 1000 Dockside Road, London, E16 2QU, ☎020 33732072 Fax: 020 84301438, ✉ken.foot@newham.gov.uk, *Call Date: Nov 2001, Lincoln's Inn*
Qualifications: [BA (Hons) MA]

FORBES MRS ANGELA JULIE

Royal Navy Officers, Directorate of Naval Legal Services, Mp 4-2, Leach Building, Whale Island, Portsmouth, PO2 8BY, Fax: 023 9262 5755, ✉angela.forbes420@mod.uk, *Call Date: Nov 2009, Middle Temple*
Qualifications: [BA (Hons) (Manch) MA (Nott'm)]

FORD MRS ALISON JEAN

Legal Adviser, Ignis Asset Management, 50 Bothwell Street, Glasgow, G2 6HR, ✉alison.ford@ignisasset.com, *Call Date: Nov 1986, Middle Temple*
Qualifications: [BA (Oxon)]

F

FOREMAN MR FREDERICK CHRISTOPHER

Company Secretary, Senior Counsel, QEB Management Services (UK) Limited, Plantation Place, 30 Fenchurch Street, London, EC3M 3BD, Fax: 020 7105 4019, *Call Date: Feb 1991, Inner Temple*
Qualifications: [LLB]

FORER MR TIMOTHY JOHN

Blake Lapthorn, New Kings Court, Chandler's Ford, Eastleigh, SO53 3LG, ☎ 023 8085 7432, *Call Date: Oct 1993, Gray's Inn*
Qualifications: [BA (Dunelm)]

FORGAARD MS ALEXANDRA KATHERINE

The Treasury Solicitors, One Kemble Street, London, WC2B 4TS, ✉ alexandra.forgaard@tsol.gsi.gov.uk, *Call Date: Nov 1997, Inner Temple*
Qualifications: [BA (Bris)]

FORREST MISS CHRISTINA

HM Revenue and Customs, South West Bush House, The Strand, London, WC2B 4RD, ☎ 020 7438 6373 Fax: 020 7438 6664, *Call Date: July 2003, Inner Temple*
Qualifications: [LLB (B'ham)]

FORSDIKE MISS CLARE LOUISE

Crown Advocate, Court Clerk, Legal Adviser, Senior Crown Prosecutor, Crown Prosecution Service, St Vincent House, 9th Floor, 1 Cutler Street, Ipswich, Suffolk, IP1 1UL, ☎ 01473 282100, *Call Date: Oct 1997, Inner Temple*
Qualifications: [LLB (Luton) (Hons)]

FORSTER MS SARAH ELIZABETH

The Law Office of George Z. Georgiou, 1st Floor, 1 Eras Street, 1060 Nicosia, Cyprus, *Call Date: Nov 2000, Inner Temple*
Qualifications: [BA CPE (UEA) LLM]

FORSYTH MISS SAMANTHA LOUISE

Crown Prosecution Service, Gateway, 31 Power Close, Surrey, Guildford, GU1 1EJ, *Call Date: July 2007, Inner Temple*
Qualifications: [LLB (Newc)]

FORTUNE MR ADAM SCOTT

Addleshaw Goddard, Milton Gste, 60 Chiswell Street, London, EC1Y 4AG, ✉ adam.fortune@addleshawgoddard.com, *Call Date: Nov 2005, Lincoln's Inn*
Qualifications: [LLB (Hons) (Bristol) LLM (Bristol)]

FORWOOD MISS GENEVRA FRANCES

White and Case LLP, 62 Rue De La Loi, Brussels, 1040, Belgium, ☎ 00 32 2 239 2620 Fax: 00 32 2 219 1626, *Call Date: Oct 2005, Middle Temple*
Qualifications: [MA (Hons) MA Dip in Law (Lond)]

FORWOOD MISS VICTORIA CLARE

Solicitor, The Treasury Solicitors, Hm Treasury, 1 Horse Guards Road, London, SW1A 2HQ, ☎ 020 7270 4362, ✉ victoria.forwood@hmtreasury.gsi.gov.uk, *Call Date: Oct 1997, Gray's Inn*
Qualifications: [BA LLM MA]

FOSTER MR ADRIAN GAVIN

Chief Crown Prosecutor, HED, Crown Prosecution Service, Rose Court, 2 Southwark Bridge, London, SE1 9HS, ☎ 0203 335 70834, ✉ Adrian.Foster@cps.gsi.gov.uk, *Call Date: Oct 1993, Inner Temple*
Qualifications: [LLB]

FOSTER MR JONATHAN ANDREW

Crown Prosecution Service, Colindale Police Station, Grahame Park Way, Colindale, London, NW9 5TW, ☎ 020 8200 2679 Fax: 020 8200 2670, ✉ jonathan.foster@cps.gsi.gov.uk, *Call Date: July 2008, Lincoln's Inn*
Qualifications: [BA (Lond)]

FOSTER MR JONATHAN ROBERT MELVILLE

Financial Services Authority, 25 The North Colannade, Canary Wharf, London, E14 8HS, *Call Date: Feb 1978, Middle Temple*
Qualifications: [BA LLM]

FOSTER MISS JULIET KATE

Directorate of Army Legal Services, Idl 426, Ramillies Buildings, Marlborough Lines, Monxton Road, Andover, SP11 8HJ, ☎01264 381 906 Fax: 01264 381 905, ✉juliet.bartlett766@mod.uk, juliet_bartlett@hotmail.com, *Call Date: Nov 1989, Middle Temple*
Qualifications: [LLB (Hons)]

FOSTER MISS KATIE

Department For Work and Pensions, Department of Health Legal Services, Floor 5, The Adelphi, 1-11 John Adam Street, London, WC2N 6HT, ☎020 7962 8012, ✉adelphi.foster-venables-jobshare@dwp.gsi.gov.uk, *Call Date: Oct 1999, Lincoln's Inn*
Qualifications: [BA (Hons)]

FOUDY MS DENISE

Company Secretary, Legal Adviser, Isode Limited, 5 Castle Business Village, 36 Station Road, Hampton, Middlesex, TW12 2BX, ☎020 8783 2963 Fax: 020 8783 9292, ✉denise.foudy@isode.com, *Call Date: July 1983, Gray's Inn*
Qualifications: [BSc (Bath) Dip Law]

FOULDS MRS SONYA LOUISE

Lawyer, Freshfields Bruckhaus Deringer LLP, 65 Fleet Street, London, EC4Y 1HS, ☎020 7716 4353, ✉sonya.foulds@freshfields.com, *Call Date: Oct 1999, Lincoln's Inn*
Qualifications: [BA (Hons) MA (Hons)]

FOWLER MR CHRISTOPHER STEPHEN

HED, Legal Counsel, BT Group PLC, BT Legal PPA6, BT Centre, 81 Newgate Street, London, EC1A 7AJ, ☎020 7778 5722, *Call Date: Feb 1994, Lincoln's Inn*
Qualifications: [LLB (Hons)]

FOWLER MISS TRACEY

Metropolitan Police Service, Directorate of Legal Services, First Floor (V), New Scotland Yard, 8-10 Broadway, London, SW1H 0BG, ☎020 7230 1212 Fax: 020 7230 7571, *Call Date: Feb 1994, Inner Temple*
Qualifications: [LLB (Lond)]

FOX MR ANDREW PATRICK

Jones Myers LLP, 5th Floor, St Paul's House, 23 Park Square, Leeds, LS1 2ND, ☎0113 246 0055 Fax: 0113 246 7446, ✉info@jonesmyers.co.uk, *Call Date: Oct 1990, Lincoln's Inn*
Qualifications: [LLB (Buck'm)]

FOX MISS CLAIRE LOUISE

Legal Officer, HMCS Essex, Her Majesty's Court Service, Osprey House, Hedgerows Business Park, Colchester Road, Springfield, Chelmsford, Essex, CM2 5PF, *Call Date: Oct 1993, Lincoln's Inn*
Qualifications: [LLB (Hons) MSc]

FOX MS VICTORIA CHARLOTTE

Director, The Electoral Commission, 3 Bunhill Road, London, EC1Y 8YZ, ✉VFox@electoralcommission.org.uk, *Call Date: Nov 1995, Middle Temple*
Qualifications: [LLB (Hons) LLM]

FOY MR JONATHAN GILES KENNEDY

Crown Prosecution Service, Snaresbrook Crown Court, 75 Hollybush Hill, Snaresbrook, London, E11 1QW, *Call Date: July 2000, Middle Temple*
Qualifications: [MA (Hons) CPE]

FRANCIS MISS ANGELA VALERIE

Waltech PLC, 54 Pont Street, London, W1F 9QY, ☎020 7025 8940, *Call Date: Nov 1989, Middle Temple*
Qualifications: [LLM LLB]

FRANCIS MS CLAIRE LOUISE

Assistant Solicitor, HM Revenue and Customs, 100 Parliament Street, London, SW1A 2BQ, ☎020 7147 3059, ✉claire.francis@hmrc.gsi.gov.uk, *Call Date: Nov 1987, Inner Temple*
Qualifications: [BA BCL (Oxon)]

FRANCIS MISS SUZANNE

Advocate, Dobsons Solicitors, 27 London Road, Bromley, Kent, BR1 1DF, *Call Date: Oct 2001, Gray's Inn*
Qualifications: [LLB (Hons)]

F

FRANCK MR RICHARD DAVID WILLIAM

Crown Prosecution Service, 2 -6 Colmore Gate, Colmore Row, Birmingham, West Midlands, B3 2QA, *Call Date: Oct 1993, Middle Temple*
Qualifications: [BA (Hons)(Bris) CPE]

FRANKHAM MR DAVID MARK

Manager, Her Majesty's Courts and Tribunals Service, Devon & Cornwall Magistrates' Courts, Trevecca Liskeard, Cornwall, ☎01752 292571 Fax: 01752 206194, ✉david.frankham@hmcourts-service.gsi.gov.uk, *Call Date: Feb 1988, Gray's Inn*
Qualifications: [MBA]

FRASER MISS FIONA ELIZABETH

Senior Lawyer, The Home Office, Seacole, Ground Floor, 2 Marsham Street, London, SW1P 4DF, ☎020 7035 1391, ✉fiona.fraser1@homeoffice.gsi.gov.uk, *Call Date: Oct 2000, Lincoln's Inn*
Qualifications: [LLB (Hons) (Reading)]

FRASER MRS SHARON LOUISE

Senior Legal Officer, City of Wakefield Metropolitan District Council, Room 116, County Hall, Bond Street, Wakefield, WF1 2QW, ☎01924 305289 Fax: 01924 305243, ✉sharonhunt@wakefield.gov.uk, *Call Date: Oct 2001, Middle Temple*
Qualifications: [LLB (Hons)(Bris) LLM (Hudds)]

FREEMAN MR JASON OLIVER JOHN

Office of Fair Trading, Fleetbank House, 2-6 Salisbury Square, London, EC4Y 8JX, ☎020 7211 8893, ✉jason.freeman@oft.gsi.gov.uk, *Call Date: Oct 2000, Inner Temple*
Qualifications: [BA (Cantab) CPE (City) MA (Cantab)]

FREEMANTLE MR CLIVE JAMES FRANCIS

Senior Crown Prosecutor, Crown Prosecution Service, St Ann's Quay, 122 Quayside, Newcastle Upon Tyne, Tyne and Wear, NE1 3BD, ☎0191 231 6264, ✉clive.freemantle@cps.gsi.gov.uk, *Call Date: July 1982, Inner Temple*
Qualifications: [BA (Hons)]

FRENCH MR ALAN VAN

Senior Crown Prosecutor, Crown Prosecution Service, Wednesfield Police Station, Alfred Squire Road, Wednesfield, West Midlands, WV11 1XU, *Call Date: July 1984, Middle Temple*
Qualifications: [LLB]

FRENCH MR MICHAEL ALAN

Principal Crown Prosecutor, Crown Prosecution Service, St Andrew's Court, 12 St Andrews Street, Plymouth, Devon, PL1 2AH, ☎01752 602700 Fax: 01752 602740, ✉Michael.French@cps.gsi.gov.uk, *Call Date: Nov 1986, Middle Temple*
Qualifications: [LLB (Nott'm)]

FRENCH MR RICHARD ANTHONY LISTER

General Counsel, Aegate Ltd, Cambridge Technology Centre, Melbourn, Hertfordshire, SG8 6DP, *Call Date: Nov 1995, Gray's Inn*
Qualifications: [BEng (Hons) Dip Law]

FREND LIEUTENANT COLONEL DAVID PETER

Directorate of Army Legal Services, Idl426, Ramillies Building, Marlborough Lines, Monxton Road, Andover, SP11 8HJ, *Call Date: Nov 1994, Inner Temple*
Qualifications: [BA (Keele)]

FREUND MR PHILIPPE

Dorsey and Whitney (Europe) LLP, 21 Wilson Street, London, EC2M 2TD, ☎020 7826 4502 Fax: 020 7588 0555, ✉freund.philippe@dorsey.com, *Call Date: July 2005, Middle Temple*
Qualifications: [MA]

FREW MISS LUCY ROSEANNE

Gide Loyrette Nouel LLP, Accounts Department, 125 Old Broad Street, London, EC2N 1AR, ☎020 7382 5686 Fax: 020 7382 5501, ✉SSchulze@GIDE.com, *Call Date: Nov 1998, Middle Temple*
Qualifications: [LLB (Hons)(Lond)]

FRITH LIEUTENANT ADELE MARIE

Royal Navy Officers, Dnls, Mp 4.2 Leach Building, Whale Island, Portsmouth, Hampshire, PO2 8BY, Fax: 02392 625 755, ✉a.frith@manw.nato.int, *Call Date: July 2010, Middle Temple*
Qualifications: [LLB (Hons) (East Anglia)]

FROST MISS GILLIAN

Ronald Fletcher Baker LLP, 326 Old Street, London, EC1V 9DR, ☎020 7613 1402, ✉g.frost@rfblegal.co.uk, *Call Date: Nov 1979, Lincoln's Inn*
Qualifications: [BA (Lond) (Hons)]

FROST MR MALCOLM EDWARD

Department For Business, Innovation and Skills, Legal Services Group, 1 Victoria Street, London, SW1H 0ET, *Call Date: Oct 2008, Lincoln's Inn*
Qualifications: [BA (Oxon) MSc]

FRY MR LAURENCE FREDERICK

Legal Manager, Jx Nippon Exploration and Production (Uk) Limited, 4th Floor, 1 Finsbury Square, London, EC2A 1AE, ☎020 7309 7695 Fax: 020 7309 7676, ✉Lfry@jx.noex.co.uk, *Call Date: Nov 1989, Middle Temple*
Qualifications: [LLB Hons (Nott'm)]

FULLER MRS ADELE SUSANNAH

Legal Adviser, RSPCA, Wilberforce Way, Southwater, Horsham, West Sussex, RH13 9RS, ✉afuller@rspca.org.uk, *Call Date: Mar 1996, Lincoln's Inn*
Qualifications: [BA (Hons)(Hull)]

FUNG MISS NORA YIN LING

Legal Adviser, Legal Director, AECOM Limited, Midcity Place, 71 High Holborn, London, WC1V 6QS, Fax: 020 7645 2099, ✉nora.fung@aecom.com, *Call Date: Nov 1993, Gray's Inn*
Qualifications: [LLB (Lond) ACIArb]

FURLEY MISS JULIA CLARE

JFH Law LLP, 274a Kentish Town Road, London, NW5 2AA, ☎020 7428 6311 Fax: 020 7485 8948, ✉jfurley@jfhlaw.co.uk, *Call Date: Oct 2000, Inner Temple*
Qualifications: [LLB (Leic)]

FURLONG MR TOMAS PATRICK KIRBY

Wilmer Hale, 49 Park Lane, London, W1K 1PS, ☎020 7645 2906, ✉tomas.furlong@wilmerhale.com, *Call Date: Oct 2009, Lincoln's Inn*
Qualifications: [BA BCL (Oxon)]

FUTTER MR DANIEL ASHER

Berrymans Lace Mawer LLP, Salisbury House, London Wall, London, EC2M 5QN, ☎020 7865 3349, ✉daniel.futter@blm-law.com, *Call Date: July 2005, Lincoln's Inn*
Qualifications: [BA (Hons)]

FUTTER MRS REBECCA LOUISE

The Home Office, Legal Adviser's Branch, Seacole, Ground Floor, 2 Marsham Street, London, SW1P 4DF, ☎020 7035 1403 Fax: 020 7035 6433, ✉rebecca.futter@homeoffice.gsi.gov.uk, *Call Date: July 2005, Gray's Inn*
Qualifications: [BA]

GABATHULER MR DAVID

Legal Adviser, Allen & Overy LLP, Allen and Overy LLP, Avenue De Tervuren 268a, Brussels, B- 1150, Belgium, ☎00 32 2 780 2222, *Call Date: Nov 1996, Inner Temple*
Qualifications: [LLB (Nott'm) LLM (Lond)]

GABAY MS SARAH JANE

Crown Advocate, Senior Crown Prosecutor, Crown Prosecution Service, Holborn Police Station, 10 Lamb's Conduit Street, Islington, London, WC1N 3NR, ☎020 7061 3900 Fax: 020 7061 3905, ✉sarah.gabay@cps.gsi.gov.uk, *Call Date: July 1999, Inner Temple*
Qualifications: [BA MA]

GADD MISS SUZANNE HEATHER

Deputy Justices' Clerk, Her Majestys Courts Service, Court Administration Office, Barley House, Sish Lane, Stevenage, Hertfordshire, SG1 3SS, ☎01438 730 431 Fax: 01438 730 435, ✉suzanne.gadd@hmcourts-service.gsi.gov.uk, *Call Date: July 1984, Lincoln's Inn*
Qualifications: [LLB]

GALLEY MR ROBERT EDWARD

Crown Prosecution Service, Jefferson House, 27 Park Place, Leeds, West Yorkshire, LS1 2SZ, *Call Date: Oct 1993, Lincoln's Inn*
Qualifications: [BSc (Econ)(Hons) CPE]

GAMBLE MR NEIL ROBERT

Associate, Lawyer, Financial Services Authority, The Financial Services Authority, Enforcement and Financial Crime Division - Legal Group, 25 The North Colonade, Canary Wharf, London, E14 5HS, ☎ 020 7066 1884 Fax: 020 7066 1099, ✉ neil.gamble@fsa.gov.uk, *Call Date: Mar 1998, Lincoln's Inn*
Qualifications: [LLB (Hons)(L'pool)]

GARBUTT MS HELEN JANE

Royal Navy Officers, Directorate of Naval Legal Services, Mp 4-2, Leach Building, Whale Island, Portsmouth, PO2 8BY, *Call Date: Oct 2005, Middle Temple*
Qualifications: [LLB (Hons) (Manch)]

GARDINER MISS CAROLYN EDITH

Crown Prosecution Service, County House, 100 New London Road, Chelmsford, Essex, CM2 0RG, *Call Date: Oct 1997, Middle Temple*
Qualifications: [BA (Hons)(Soton) CPE (Northumbria)]

GARLAND MR DAVID ROBERTSON

Dominion Petroleum Limited, Administrative Services Limited, 65 Sloane Street, London, SW1X 9SH, ☎ 020 7043 0160 Fax: 020 3043 0161, *Call Date: Nov 1986, Middle Temple*
Qualifications: [LLB AKC (Lond) LLM]

GARLAND-COLLINS MR FRANCIS

Deputy Justices' Clerk, HMCS Essex, Essex Magistrates' Court, Osprey House,Hedgerows Business Park, Colchester Road, Springfield, Chelmsford, Essex, CM2 5PF, ✉ francis.garland@hmcourtsservice.gsi.gov.uk, *Call Date: July 1974, Middle Temple*

GARN MISS JENNIFER MARY

K&L Gates LLP, Dubai International Financial Centre (Difc), Currency House, Tower 1, Level 4, Po Box 506826, Dubai, United Arab Emirates, *Call Date: Oct 2006, Lincoln's Inn*
Qualifications: [BA (Oxon)]

GARNER MISS MARGARET THERESA

Director, Director of Legal Services, Head of Legal Services, Falcon Trade Corporation, 17th Floor, 30 St Mary Avenue, London, EC3A 8BF, *Call Date: Nov 1968, Gray's Inn*

GARNHAM MR TOM EDWARD KARL

Advocate, Crown Prosecution Service, Oxford House, Oxford Road, Bournemouth, Dorset, BH8 8HA, ☎ 01202 498700 Fax: 01202 498701, ✉ tom.garnham@cps.gsi.gov.uk, *Call Date: Nov 1995, Middle Temple*
Qualifications: [BA (Hons)]

GARNIER MR EDWARD HENRY

Recorder, Solicitor General, The Treasury Solicitors, Attorney General's Office, 20 Victoria Street, London, SW1H 0NF, ☎ 020 7271 2492, ✉ privateoffice@attorneygeneral.gsi.gov.uk, *Call Date: July 1976, Middle Temple*
Qualifications: [MA (Oxon)]

GARSED MR KRISTIAN PAUL

Nursing and Midwifery Council, 61 Aldwich, London, WC2B 4AE, *Call Date: July 2006, Inner Temple*
Qualifications: [BA MA (Kent)]

GARVIN MR MICHAEL

Department of Energy and Climate Change, Area 7A/B, 3 Whitehall Place, London, SW1A 2AW, ☎ 030 0068 5637, ✉ michael.garvin@decc.gsi.gov.uk, *Call Date: Nov 1994, Inner Temple*
Qualifications: [BA (Oxon)]

GASKELL MR RICHARD CARL

Recorder, Oliver D'Sa Solicitors, 75-81 King Street, Leicester, LE1 6RP, *Call Date: July 1971, Lincoln's Inn*
Qualifications: [LLB]

GAUTAMA MISS NISHA

Legal Manager, West London Magistrates' Court, 181 Talgarth Road, London, W6 8DN ☎ 020 8700 9304, *Call Date: Nov 1988, Middle Temple*
Qualifications: [LLB (B'ham)]

GAVIN MRS MELANIE PAULINE

Ward Hadaway, 1a Tower Square, Wellington Street, Leeds, LS1 4DL, ☎ +44 (0) 113 205 6600 Fax: +44 (0) 113 205 6700, ✉ Melanie.Gavin@wardhadaway.com, *Call Date: July 1999, Lincoln's Inn*
Qualifications: [LLB (Hons)]

F

GAWNE MS ANNE MARIA

Legal Adviser, Office of Fair Trading, Fleetbank House, 2-6 Salisbury Square, London, EC4Y 8JX, ☎020 7211 8455 / 020 7211 8893 / 020 7211 8000, ✉maria.gawne@oft.gsi.gov.uk, *Call Date: Oct 1990, Middle Temple*
Qualifications: [LLB (Lond)]

GEORGE MISS ANNA

DAC Beachcroft LLP, Portwall Place, Portwall Lane, Bristol, BS99 7UD, Fax: 0117 918 2100, ✉ageorge@decbeachcroft.com, *Call Date: Nov 1999, Middle Temple*
Qualifications: [LLB(Hons)(Newc)]

GEORGE MS ELIZABETH

Leigh Day and Co, Priory House, 25 St John's Lane, London, EC1M 4LB, ☎020 7650 1374, ✉e.george@leighday.co.uk, *Call Date: Nov 2005, Inner Temple*
Qualifications: [BA University of Greenwich CPE Southbank Univer]

GEORGE MRS SARA

Partner, Stephenson Harwood, One St.Paul's Churchyard, London, EC4M 8SH, ☎020 7809 2338, ✉sara.george@sklegal.com, *Call Date: Mar 1999, Gray's Inn*
Qualifications: [MA (Oxon)]

GEORGE MRS VALERIE

Leicestershire County Council, County Hall, Glenfield, Leicester, LE3 8RA, *Call Date: July 1983, Inner Temple*
Qualifications: [LLB(Manch)]

GERAGHTY MISS TONI

Lincolnshire County Council, County Offices, Lincoln, LN1 1YP, ☎01522 552222 Fax: 01522 552138, ✉Toni.Geraghty@lincolnshire.gov.uk, *Call Date: Oct 1993, Middle Temple*
Qualifications: [LLB (Hons)(Lond)]

GERRARD MR LEE JOHN

Frisby and Co Solicitors, 26 Eastgate Street, Stafford, ST16 2LZ, ✉lee.gerrard@frisbysolicitors.co.uk, *Call Date: Mar 1996, Gray's Inn*
Qualifications: [BA (Hons)(Newc) CPE]

GERRISH MR SIMON DAVID PETER

Financial Services Authority, The Financial Services Authority, Enforcement and Financial Crime Division - Legal Group, 25 The North Colonade, Canary Wharf, London, E14 5HS, ☎020 7066 1000, *Call Date: Oct 1993, Gray's Inn*
Qualifications: [MA (Hons)(Oxon)]

GETHIN MRS SUSAN JANE

Senior Crown Prosecutor, Crown Prosecution Service, Froomsgate House, Rupert Street, Bristol, BS1 2QJ, ☎0117 930 2800, *Call Date: Oct 1990, Inner Temple*
Qualifications: [LLB (Hons)]

GHOBADIAN MR RAMEEN JOHN

Department For Business, Innovation and Skills, 1 Victoria Street, London, SW1H 0ET, *Call Date: July 2005, Middle Temple*
Qualifications: [BA (Hons) M.Phil Dip in Law]

GIBBINS MR BRIAN RICHARD

Associate, Crown Advocate, Crown Prosecution Service, Rose Court, 2 Southwark Bridge, London, SE1 9HS, ☎020 3357 0060 Fax: 020 3357 0055, ✉Brian.Gibbins@cps.gsi.gov.uk, *Call Date: Nov 1986, Middle Temple*
Qualifications: [LLB (Hons) (Lond)]

GIBBONS MR MYLES

Kent County Council, Legal Secretariat, Sessions House, County Hall, Maidstone, Kent, ME14 1XQ, *Call Date: Oct 2000, Middle Temple*
Qualifications: [LLB (Hons)(Lond) Dip Law FILEX]

GIBBS MR NIGEL JAMES

Adviser, Senior Crown Prosecutor, Crown Prosecution Service, Rose Court, 2 Southwark Bridge, London, SE1 9HS, ✉nigel.gibbs@cps.gsi.gov.uk, *Call Date: July 1985, Inner Temple*
Qualifications: [LLB (Brunel)]

GIBSON MR JOHN PHILIP ROBSON

Hill Dickinson Solicitors, 1 St Paul's Square, Liverpool, L3 9SJ, ☎0151 600 8000 Fax: 0151 600 8001, ✉john.gibson@hilldickinson.com, *Call Date: July 1990, Inner Temple*
Qualifications: [LLM BA (Hons) Pg Dip M Ed MA]

F

GIBSON MR PAUL ALBERT

Senior Crown Prosecutor, Crown Prosecution Service, Stoicklund House, Castle Street, Carlisle, CA3 8SY, ☎01228 882 900 Fax: 01228 882 910, ✉paula.gibson@cps.gsi.gov.uk, *Call Date: Nov 1998, Lincoln's Inn*
Qualifications: [LLB (Hons)(Anglia)]

GIFFIN MRS SAMANTHA CHRISTINE

Henscott Solicitors, 413 Chingford Road, Walthamstow, London, E17 5AF, *Call Date: Oct 1991, Gray's Inn*
Qualifications: [LLB (Hons) (Lond)]

GILBERT MR CARL ST. JOHN

Standard Chartered Bank, 7th Floor, Legal Department, 1 Basinghall Avenue, London, EC2V 5DD, ☎020 7885 7381 Fax: 020 7885 1381, ✉carl.gilbert@sc.com, *Call Date: Oct 1996, Middle Temple*
Qualifications: [BA (Hons)(Exon) CPE (Notts)]

GILES MISS EMMA ELISABETH

Directorate of Army Legal Services, Idl426, Ramillies Building, Marlborough Lines, Monxton Road, Andover, SP11 8HJ, ☎01980 615013 Fax: 01980 615978, ✉lf-dals-res-so1@mod.uk, *Call Date: Nov 2003, Middle Temple*
Qualifications: [LLB (Hons)]

GILHESPY MRS SONIA

Senior Crown Prosecutor, Crown Prosecution Service, East Midlands Rart, Po Box 9557, Nottingham, NG15 5BU, ☎01623 608210, ✉Sonia.Gilhespy@cps.gsi.gov.uk, *Call Date: Oct 1990, Gray's Inn*
Qualifications: [LLB (Newc)]

GILL MR INDERJEET SINGH

Dewey and Leboeuf, 1 Minster Court, Mincing Lane, London, EC3R 7YL, ☎020 7459 5079 Fax: 020 7459 5099, ✉igill@dl.com, *Call Date: July 2007, Lincoln's Inn*
Qualifications: [BA (Oxon) MA (Oxon) MA]

F

GILL MRS NARANDERJIT

Other, Travelers Insurance Company Limited, Exchequer Court, St Mary Axe, London, EC3A 8AG, ☎020 3207 6633 Fax: 020 3116 2139, ✉ngill@travelers.com, *Call Date: Nov 1988, Inner Temple*
Qualifications: [LLM (Lond) LLB]

GILTHORPE MISS CHARLOTTE EMMA TIFFANY

Director, BAA Ltd, The Compass Centre, Nelson Road, Hounslow, Middlesex, TW6 2GW, ☎020 8757 5512 Fax: 020 8745 6477, ✉emma_gilthorpe@baa.com, *Call Date: July 1996, Middle Temple*
Qualifications: [BSc (Hons)]

GIMSON MR GARETH LEE

Crown Prosecution Service, Nottingham City 2 Cju, 2 King Edward Court, King Edward Street, Nottingham, NG1 1EL, *Call Date: Nov 1998, Gray's Inn*
Qualifications: [BA (Hons)(Oxon)]

GIOVANNELLI MR DARIO ROBERTO

The Football Association, Wembley Stadium, Wembley, London, HA9 0WS, Fax: 0844 980 0625, *Call Date: Oct 2000, Inner Temple*
Qualifications: [CPE (Leeds) MA (Hons) (Edin) PG Dip Law]

GIRET MR JOSEPH JOHN BELA LESLIE

The Chambers of Mr J Giret QC, Portobello, 3 Hollycross, Crazies Hill, Reading, Berkshire, RG10 8QB, *Call Date: Feb 1985, Gray's Inn*
Qualifications: [LLB (Hons)(Warw)]

GIRVAN MR ROBERT JAMES

Crown Prosecution Service, 7th Floor (South), Royal Liver Building, Pier Head, Liverpool, Merseyside, L3 1HN, ☎0151 239 6400, ✉robert.girvan@cps.gsi.gov.uk, *Call Date: Nov 1990, Gray's Inn*
Qualifications: [LLB]

GIST MR ROBIN

Law Officers of the Crown, St James Chambers, St Peter Port, GY1 2PA, Fax: 01481 725 439, ✉robin.gist@gov.gg, *Call Date: July 2004, Gray's Inn*
Qualifications: [MSci (Lond) PgDL]

GITTINS MR DAVID JAMES

Senior Crown Prosecutor, Crown Prosecution Service, Plymouth Branch Office, St Andrews Court, 12 St Andrews Street, Plymouth, Devon, PL1 2AH, ☎01752 602700 Fax: 01752 602740, ✉David.Gittins@cps.gsi.gov.uk, *Call Date: July 1971, Inner Temple*
Qualifications: [MA (Cantab)]

GIULIANI MR MARK

Crown Prosecution Service, St Ann's Quay, 122 Quayside, Newcastle Upon Tyne, Tyne and Wear, NE1 3BD, ☎0191 383 5800
Fax: 0191 383 5801, ✉Mark.Giuliani@cps.gsi.gov.uk, *Call Date: Oct 1993, Gray's Inn*
Qualifications: [BSc (Warw)]

GLAZEBROOK MS HARAMRITA KAUR

Blackrock PM, 20 Southampton Street, London, WC2E 7QH, *Call Date: July 2009, Inner Temple*
Qualifications: [BA MA Meng (Cantab) MSc (Lond)]

GLEESON MR MARK ANTHONY JOHN

HED, Legal Director, Addleshaw Goddard LLP, Milton Gate, 60 Chiswell Street, London, EC1Y 4AG, *Call Date: Oct 1995, Middle Temple*
Qualifications: [B.Sc (Hons) (Manch)]

GLENN MISS ANGELA VERONICA

Leonard and Co Solicitors, Oakwood Court, 62 The Avenue, Southampton, Hampshire, SO17 1XS, ☎023 8023 4433
Fax: 023 8022 0460, ✉avglenn@leonardlawyers.co.uk, *Call Date: Nov 1981, Gray's Inn*
Qualifications: [BA]

GLOVER MR ANDREW SPENCER

Crown Prosecution Service, Rose Court, 2 Southwark Bridge, London, SE1 9HS, *Call Date: July 2002, Gray's Inn*
Qualifications: [BSc (Hons) Dip in Law]

GLOVER MISS JUSTINE REBECCA

Department For Work and Pensions, 5th Floor, the Adelphi, 1-11 John Adam Street, London, WC2N 6HT, *Call Date: Oct 1991, Inner Temple*
Qualifications: [LLB (Hull)]

GODDARD MR DAVID SIMON

Royal Navy Officers, Directorate of Naval Legal Services, Mp 4-2, Leach Building, Whale Island, Portsmouth, PO2 8BY, ☎02392 625739, *Call Date: July 2009, Lincoln's Inn*
Qualifications: [BA MA (Cantab) CPE COL]

GODDARD MISS LISA KATE

Crown Prosecution Service, Eaton Court, 112 Oxford Road, Reading, Berkshire, RG1 7LL, ☎0118 9513600
Fax: 0118 9513601 / 01189 513666, ✉Lisa.Goddard@cps.gsi.gov.uk, *Call Date: July 2003, Middle Temple*
Qualifications: [LLB Hons (Wales)]

GODDARD MR PAUL GERARD

Crown Prosecution Service, Edmonton Police Station, Edmonton, London, N9 0XR, *Call Date: Oct 1996, Gray's Inn*
Qualifications: [LLB (Leeds)]

GODDARD MR PETER ANDREW GEORGE

FSOL, Managing Director, Forbes Hare, Cassia Court, Camana Bay, Suite 716, 10 Market Street, Grand Cayman, KY1-9006, Cayman Islands, *Call Date: Nov 1987, Middle Temple*
Qualifications: [LLB (Wales)]

GOGO MR EMMANUEL MARKWEI KOFI

Senior Lawyer, London Borough of Newham, Legal and Democratic Services, Newham Dockside, 1000 Dockside Road, London, E16 2QU, ☎020 3373 9240 Fax: 020 8430 1435, ✉emmanuel.gogo@newham.gov.uk, *Call Date: July 1984, Middle Temple*
Qualifications: [LLB LLM]

GOLD MR BENJAMIN DANIEL

Reynolds Porter Chamberlain LLP, Tower Bridge House, St Katherine's Way, London, E1W 1AA, ☎020 3060 6000
Fax: 020 3060 7000, ✉Ben.Gold@rpc.co.uk, *Call Date: July 2005, Middle Temple*
Qualifications: [PgDip Law BA (Hons) Leeds]

GOLD MRS SALLY JANE

Cheshire East Borough Council Westfields, Middlewich Road, Sandbach, CW11 1HZ, ✉sally.gold@cheshireeast.gov.uk, *Call Date: Oct 2000, Middle Temple*
Qualifications: [BA (Hons) (Newc) CPE LLM (Wales)]

GOLDBERG MS CHARLOTTE HILARY

The Home Office, Seacole House, 2 Marsham Street, London, SW1P 4DF, ☎020 7035 1365, ✉Charlotte.Goldberg@homeoffice.gsi.gov.uk, *Call Date: Oct 1995, Gray's Inn*
Qualifications: [BA (Hons) LLM MA]

F

GOLDRING MR JONATHAN DEREK

Director, Bankside Law Ltd, Thrale House, 44-46 Southwark Street, London, SE1 1UN, ✉ jonathan.goldring@banksidelaw.com, *Call Date: Oct 1997, Middle Temple*
Qualifications: [LLB (Hons)(Lond)]

GOLDSBROUGH MS FELICITY

Mary Monson Solicitors, Coleridge Chambers, 177 Cirporation Street, 2nd Floor, Birmingham, B4 6RG, ☎ 0121 535 0012 Fax: 0121 233 2860, ✉ felicity.goldsbrough@monsons.org.uk, *Call Date: May 1997, Inner Temple*
Qualifications: [BA (Humberside)]

GOLDSMITH LORD

Debevoise and Plimpton LLP, Tower 42, Old Broad Street, London, EC2N 1HQ, ☎ 020 7786 9000 Fax: 020 7588 4180, ✉ phgoldsmith@debevoise.com, *Call Date: July 1972, Gray's Inn*
Qualifications: [MA (Cantab) LLM (Lond)]

GOLDSPINK MR JUSTIN STEPHEN

GSC Solicitors LLP, 31-32 Ely Place, London, EC1N 6TD, ☎ 020 7822 2222 Fax: 020 7822 2211, ✉ info@gscsolicitors.com, *Call Date: Nov 1994, Inner Temple*
Qualifications: [MA (Oxon) LLM (Notts)]

GOODIER MR JOHN STUART

Advocate, Crown Prosecution Service, Justinian House, Spitfire Close, Ermine Business Park, Huntingdon, Cambridgeshire, PE29 6XY, ☎ 01480 825200 Fax: 01480 825206, *Call Date: Oct 1992, Middle Temple*
Qualifications: [MA (Oxon)]

GOODMAN MR DAVID RODERICK

Deputy District Judge, Director of Legal Services, Justices' Clerk, Hmcs-The Black Country,Staffordshire & West Mercia, Stafford Magistrates' Court, The Court House, South Walls, Stafford, ST16 3DW, ☎ 01785 275 704 Fax: 01785 258508, ✉ david.goodman@hmcourts-service.gsi.gov.uk, *Call Date: Nov 1983, Gray's Inn*
Qualifications: [DML]

GOOM MS SARAH LOUISE

Director, Lawyer, The Treasury Solicitors, Attorney General's Office, 20 Victoria Street, London, SW1H 0NF, Fax: 020 7271 2453, ✉ Sarah.goom@attorneygeneral.gsi.gov.uk, *Call Date: Nov 1992, Inner Temple*
Qualifications: [BA (Kent) MPhil (Cantab)]

GORDON MR ASHLEY

Head of Legal Services, The Bank of Tokyo-Mitsubishi UFJ, Ltd., Ropemaker Place, 25 Ropemaker Street, London, EC2Y 9AN, ✉ ashley.gordon@uk.mufg.jp, *Call Date: Feb 1988, Inner Temple*
Qualifications: [BSc Dip Law (City)]

GORDON MR CLIVE STUART

Financial Services Authority, 25 The North Colannade, Canary Wharf, London, E14 8HS, *Call Date: Apr 1991, Gray's Inn*
Qualifications: [LLB (Hons) (Wales) LLM (Sussex)]

GORDON LENNOX MR HENRY CHARLES

Other, Blake Lapthorn LLP, Seacourt Tower, Westway, Oxford, Oxfordshire, OX2 0FB, ☎ 01865 254237, ✉ Henry.GordonLennox@bllaw.co.uk, *Call Date: Nov 2000, Lincoln's Inn*
Qualifications: [BSc (Hons) CPE]

GORDON-BASSETT MISS DIANNE CHERI

Crown Prosecution Service, City Gate House, 185 Dyke Road, Hove, East Sussex, BN3 1TL, *Call Date: Oct 1998, Middle Temple*
Qualifications: [LLB (Hons)(Anglia)]

GORIELY MISS TAMARA ANTHEA

Law Commission, Steel House, 11 Tothill Street, London, SW1H 9LJ, ☎ 020 3334 0281, *Call Date: Nov 1979, Middle Temple*

GORING MISS JULIA MICHELE

Department For Transport, Zone 1/18, Great Minster House, 33 Horseferry Road, London, SW1P 4DR, *Call Date: Oct 1991, Lincoln's Inn*
Qualifications: [LLB (Hons) (B'ham)]

GORNALL MR MARK ANDREW

Crown Prosecution Service, The Unicentre, Lords Walk, Preston, Lancashire, PR1 1DH, *Call Date: July 1987, Middle Temple*
Qualifications: [LLB (Hons) (Lancs)]

GOSS MR KENNETH JACK

Advocate, Crown Prosecution Service, Priory Gate, 29 Union Street, Maidstone, Kent, ME14 1PT, ☎01622 356 311 Fax: 01622 356 395, ✉Ken.Goss@cps.gsi.gov.uk, *Call Date: Nov 1985, Gray's Inn*

GOULD MISS DEBORAH SAMANTHA

Crown Prosecution Service, Colmore Gate, 2 - 6 Colmore Row, Birmingham, West Midlands, B3 2QA, ☎0121 262 1300
Fax: 0121 262 1500, *Call Date: Feb 1990, Inner Temple*
Qualifications: [LLB (Hons) (Warw)]

GOVINDARAJAH MR RABINDRANATH

Thompsons & Co Solicitors, 48a Tooting High Street, London, SW17 0RG, ✉rabin@thompsonlaw.co.uk, *Call Date: Nov 2002, Middle Temple*
Qualifications: [LLB (Hons) LLM]

GOW MISS JANE

Bailey Nicholson Grayson Solicitors & Advocates, 15 Bourne Court, Southend Road, South Woodford, IG8 8HD, ✉mail@bnglaw.co.uk, *Call Date: Oct 2000, Middle Temple*
Qualifications: [LLB (Hons) (Oxon)]

GRAHAM MS ANGELA LESLEY HELEN

Company Secretary, Legal Adviser, Petroplus Refining Teesside Ltd, Pertroplus House, St Mark's Court, Teesdale, Thornaby, TS17 6QW, ☎01642 737213, ✉angela.graham@petroplus.co.uk, *Call Date: July 1999, Lincoln's Inn*
Qualifications: [LLB (hons)(Leeds)]

GRAHAM MR JAMES HENRY FERGUS

Tyco International, Frier Platz 10, Ch - 8200, Schoffhausen, Switzerland,
☎0041 52 633 0256 Fax: 0041 52 633 0299, ✉jgraham@tyco.com, *Call Date: Nov 1994, Inner Temple*
Qualifications: [B Eng M Sc (Bris) CPE]

GRAHAM MISS ZAHRA AMINA

The Football Association, Wembley Stadium, Wembley, London, HA9 0WS,
Fax: 0844 980 0625, *Call Date: July 2008, Middle Temple*
Qualifications: [LLB (Hons) (Brunel)]

GRANDFIELD MRS JOANNA LOUISE

Mills and Reeve, Mills and Reeve LLP, 1 City Square, Leeds, LS1 2ES, *Call Date: Oct 2000, Inner Temple*
Qualifications: [MA (Hons)(Oxon) CPE (City) Dip Law]

GRANT MR NICOLAS STUART

Head of Legal Services, Sainsbury's Supermarkets Ltd, 33 Holborn, London, EC1N 2HT, ☎020 7695 6000, *Call Date: Nov 1995, Inner Temple*
Qualifications: [BA (York) MSc (Lond) Dip Law (Lond)]

GRAY MR JAMES DAVID

Edward Fail Bradshaw Waterson, 402-404 Commercial Street, London, E1 0GL, ☎020 7790 4032, ✉jamesg@efbw.co.uk, *Call Date: July 2005, Lincoln's Inn*
Qualifications: [LLB (Hons)]

GRAYSON MRS SHAMINI NAINAPPAN

Caseworker, The Treasury Solicitors, Public Law B5, One Kemble Street, London, WC2B 4TS, ☎020 7210 4514 Fax: 020 7210 3001, *Call Date: Nov 1988, Middle Temple*
Qualifications: [LLB (Leeds)]

GRAYSON MR STEPHEN ARTHUR

Senior Principal Legal Officer, Financial Services Authority, The Financial Services Authority, Enforcement and Financial Crime Division - Legal Group, 25 The North Colonade, Canary Wharf, London, E14 5HS, ✉stephen.grayson@fsa.gov.uk, *Call Date: Nov 1990, Inner Temple*
Qualifications: [BA]

GREEN MR DAVID JOHN MARK

Director, Serious Fraud Office, Elm House, 10-16 Elm Street, London, WC1X 0BJ, *Call Date: July 1979, Inner Temple*
Qualifications: [MA (Cantab)]

F

GREEN MR DAVID MICHAEL

Legal Counsel, Klesch and Company Limited, 105 Wigmore Street, London, W1U 1QY, ☎020 7529 2419 Fax: 020 7493 2525, *Call Date: Nov 1987, Middle Temple*
Qualifications: [LLB (Hons)]

GREEN MISS FRANCES

Solicitor, The General Council of the Bar, 289-293 High Holborn, London, WC1V 7HZ, *Call Date: Feb 1995, Gray's Inn*

GREEN MR SAM

McFaddens, 13-14 Orchard Street, Bristol, BS1 5EH, ☎020 7588 9080 / 0117 905 5130, ✉reception@mcfaddenslaw.co.uk, samgreen@mcfaddenslaw.co.uk, *Call Date: Oct 2000, Middle Temple*
Qualifications: [BA (Hons) (Exon) Dip in Law MSc MSc Econ (LSE)]

GREEN MR SIMON CLINTON

Covent Garden Family Law, Joel House, 19 Garrick Street, London, WC2E 9AX, ☎020 7257 6130 Fax: 020 7836 3656, ✉s.green@cgfamilylaw.co.uk, *Call Date: Mar 2003, Middle Temple*
Qualifications: [LLB (Hons) (Wales)]

GREEN MR TREVOR MITCHELL

Big Lottery Fund, 1 Plough Place, London, EC4A 1DE, ☎020 7211 1870 Fax: 020 7211 3749, ✉Trevor.Green@biglotteryfund.org.uk, *Call Date: July 2002, Middle Temple*
Qualifications: [BA (Hons) (Kent) Dip in Law(Kingston)]

GREENALD MR TIMOTHY ALEXANDER

Lawyer, Crown Prosecution Service, Sunlight House, Quay Street, Manchester, M60 3PS, ☎0161 827 4700, *Call Date: Mar 1996, Middle Temple*
Qualifications: [LLB (Hons)]

GREENLAND MRS SHERIDAN DAWN

HED, The Judicial College, Steel House, 11 Tothill Street, London, SW1H 9LJ, ✉sheridan.greenland@judiciary.gsi.gov.uk, *Call Date: July 1982, Inner Temple*
Qualifications: [LLB]

GREENWOOD MR GEOFFREY WILLIAM

Crown Prosecution Service, 7th Floor (South), Royal Liver Building, Pier Head, Liverpool, Merseyside, L3 1HN, *Call Date: July 1979, Lincoln's Inn*
Qualifications: [BA (Nottm)]

GREGORY MR MICHAEL RAYMOND

Crown Prosecution Service, United House, Piccadilly, York, North Yorkshire, YO1 9PQ, ☎01904 544465, ✉michael.gregory@cps.gsi.gov.uk, *Call Date: Oct 1996, Middle Temple*
Qualifications: [BA (Hons)(Lond) CPE]

GREINEDER DR DANIEL

Python and Peter, 9 Rue Firmin-Massot, Geneva Ch-1206, Switzerland, ☎0041 22 702 1515 Fax: 0041 22 702 1414, ✉dgreineder@pplex.ch, *Call Date: Oct 2005, Inner Temple*
Qualifications: [BA MSt DPhil Magdalen College University of Ox Dip Law (City) MA]

GREKOS MS MARTHA

Eversheds LLP, 1 Wood Street, London, EC2V 7WS, *Call Date: July 2000, Inner Temple*
Qualifications: [LLB (Bris) LLM (Cantab)]

GRETTON MS JOANNE CLAIRE

Telent Limited, Point 3, Haywood Road, Warwick, CV34 5AH, *Call Date: Nov 1997, Inner Temple*
Qualifications: [LLB (Exon)]

GREW MISS MICHELLE ROBYN

HED, Glg Partners LLP, 1 Curzon Street, London, W1J 5HB, *Call Date: Oct 1991, Middle Temple*
Qualifications: [LLB (Hons)]

GREY MR PHILIP JOHN

Director, Mills and Reeve, Mills and Reeve LLP, Francis House, 112 Hills Road, Cambridge, Cambridgeshire, CB2 1PH, ☎01223 222463 Fax: 01223 222220, ✉philip.grey@mills-reeve.com, *Call Date: Nov 1996, Gray's Inn*
Qualifications: [BA (Hons)(Cantab)]

F

GREY MR TIMOTHY JAMES CLEMENTE

Mills and Reeve, Fountain House, 130 Fenchurch Street, London, EC3M 5DJ, ☎0207 7648 9241 Fax: 0207 7648 9221, ✉tim.grey@mills-reeve.com, *Call Date: Mar 1999, Inner Temple*
Qualifications: [LLB]

GRICE MISS JOANNA HARRISON

HM Revenue and Customs, Business Tax Team, 2c/19, 100 Parliament Street, London, SW1A 2BQ, ☎020 7147 0256, *Call Date: Oct 1991, Middle Temple*
Qualifications: [MA (Hons) (Cantab)]

GRICE MR PETER ROBERT

Crown Prosecution Service, Colmore Gate, 2 - 6 Colmore Row, Birmingham, West Midlands, B3 2QA, ☎01905 825143 Fax: 01905 825102, *Call Date: July 1984, Gray's Inn*
Qualifications: [LLB (Hons)(Wolves)]

GRIERSON MR JACOB

Mcdermott, Will and Emery, 23 Rue De L'Universite, Paris, 75007, France, Fax: 1 8169 1515, ✉jgrierson@mwe.com, *Call Date: Oct 1993, Lincoln's Inn*
Qualifications: [BA (Hons) (Oxon) Dip in Law (City) MA (Belgium)]

GRIEVE MR DOMINIC CHARLES ROBERTS

Attorney, The Treasury Solicitors, Attorney General's Office, 20 Victoria Street, London, SW1H 0NF, ☎020 7271 2492, ✉privateoffice@attorneygeneral.gsi.gov.uk, *Call Date: Nov 1980, Middle Temple*
Qualifications: [BA (Oxon)]

GRIEVES-SMITH MR PETER MICHAEL

Crown Prosecution Service, Colmore Gate, 2 - 6 Colmore Row, Birmingham, West Midlands, B3 2QA, ✉Peter.Grieves-Smith@cps.gsi.gov.uk, *Call Date: Nov 1989, Middle Temple*
Qualifications: [LLB (Hons)(Leics)]

GRIFFITHS MR GARETH VAUGHAN

Lawyer, Mbna Europe Bank Limited, Business Park, Chester, Cheshire, CH4 9FB, ☎01244 672926 Fax: 01244 672044, *Call Date: Oct 1999, Lincoln's Inn*
Qualifications: [LLB (Hons)(Sheff)]

GRIFFITHS MS LOWRI MAI

The Treasury Solicitors, One Kemble Street, London, WC2B 4TS, ☎020 7210 3284 Fax: 020 7210 4512, ✉lowri.griffiths@tsol.gsi.gov.uk, *Call Date: Oct 2006, Middle Temple*
Qualifications: [LLB (Hons) (Bris) LLM]

GRIMSHAW MR DAVID

Senior Counsel, Conoco Phillips, Portman House, 2 Portman Street, London, W1H 6DU, ✉david.grimshaw@conocophillips.com, *Call Date: Nov 1975, Middle Temple*
Qualifications: [BA (Cantab) MA MBA]

GROOM MISS JOANNE PATRICIA

Derby City Council, Saxon House, Heritage Gate, Friary Street, Derby, DE1 1AN, ☎01332 643582 Fax: 01332 643617, ✉Joanne.Groom@derby.gov.uk, *Call Date: Oct 1999, Lincoln's Inn*
Qualifications: [LLB (Hons)(Staffs)]

GROUT-SMITH MR JEREMY GAYWOOD

Senior Crown Prosecutor, Crown Prosecution Service, The Unicentre, Lords Walk, Preston, Lancashire, PR1 1DH, ☎01772 208100, ✉Jeremy.Grout-Smith@cps.gsi.gov.uk, *Call Date: July 1986, Inner Temple*
Qualifications: [LLB LLM (Bris)]

GRUDZINSKA MISS ANIA JOANNA

Lansbury Worthington Solicitors, 5 King Street Cloisters, Clifton Walk, 146 King Street, Hammersmith, London, W6 0GY, *Call Date: July 2005, Inner Temple*
Qualifications: [BA Oxford Brookes University LLM University of]

GRUNDY MISS MADELEINE JANE

The Treasury Solicitors, 5th Floor, One Kemble Street, London, WC2B 4TS, *Call Date: Nov 1999, Gray's Inn*
Qualifications: [BA (Cantab)]

GUESS MR JOHN

Ministry of Justice, Zone 6.31, Legal Directorate, 102 Petty France, London, SW1H 9AJ, *Call Date: Oct 2000, Middle Temple*
Qualifications: [BA (Hons) (Oxon) CPE]

F

GUEST MR TOM

Crown Prosecution Service, Rose Court, 2 Southwark Bridge, London, SE1 9HS, ☎ 020 71477509 Fax: 020 71477734, ✉ tom.guest@cps.gsi.gov.uk, *Call Date: July 2007, Middle Temple*
Qualifications: [BA (Hons) (Cantab) MA (Cantab) LLB]

GUMPERT MR RUSSELL BENJAMIN WALLACE

Deputy District Judge, Recorder, Crown Prosecution Service, Gemini One, Oxford Business Park South, Garsington Road, Oxford, Oxfordshire, OX4 2LL, *Call Date: Feb 1987, Inner Temple*
Qualifications: [MA (Cantab)]

GUNTHER MISS ELIZABETH ANN

Pump Court Chambers, 31 Southgate Street, Winchester, Hampshire, SO23 9EB, ☎ 01962 868 161 Fax: 0845 259 3240, *Call Date: Oct 1993, Lincoln's Inn*
Qualifications: [LLB (Hons)(B'ham)]

GUPTA MR SANDEEP

Serious Fraud Office, Elm House, 10-16 Elm Street, London, WC1X 0BJ, ☎ 020 7239 7107, ✉ sandeep.gupta@sfo.gsi.gov.uk, *Call Date: July 2004, Lincoln's Inn*
Qualifications: [LLB Hons (Middlesex)]

GUY MR IAN LESLIE

COMT, Senior Lawyer, County Borough Council, Legal Services Department, Neath Port Talbot, Civic Centre, Port Talbot, SA13 1PJ, ☎ 01639 763365 Fax: 01639 763370, *Call Date: Nov 1988, Gray's Inn*
Qualifications: [BA (Hons) FRSA]

HADIK MR ANDREW JOHN WILLIAM MICHAEL

Special Casework Lawyer, Crown Prosecution Service, The Cooperage, 8 Gainsford Street, London, SE1 2NE, ☎ 020 7378 4100, ✉ Andrew.Hadik@cps.gsi.gov.uk, *Call Date: Nov 1980, Middle Temple*
Qualifications: [BA MA (Lond)]

HAFEEZ MR MOHAMMAD

Crown Advocate, Crown Prosecution Service, Colmore Gate, 2 - 6 Colmore Row, Birmingham, West Midlands, B3 2QA, ☎ 0121 262 1300 Fax: 0121 262 1319, ✉ Mohammed.hafeez@cps.gsi.gov.uk, *Call Date: Mar 2011, Middle Temple*
Qualifications: [LLB (Hons) (Lond)]

HAFEJEE MR MAHMED SALIM

Nursing and Midwifery Council, 23 Portland Place, London, W1B 1PZ, *Call Date: July 2001, Inner Temple*
Qualifications: [BA (Lond) CPE]

HAFFENDEN MRS REBEKAH RUTH

Senior Lawyer, HM Revenue and Customs, Solicitors Office, 100 Parliament Street, London, SW1A 2BQ, *Call Date: July 1987, Lincoln's Inn*
Qualifications: [LLB]

HAGGIS MR ROBERT ARTHUR

Chair, Company Secretary, Director, Buxton Corporate Services Limited, 5 The Towers, Spencer Road, Buxton, Derbyshire, SK17 9DX, ✉ rahaggis@msn.com, *Call Date: Nov 1980, Gray's Inn*
Qualifications: [BA Hons]

HALEPAS MR MICHAEL NICHOLAS

Stuart Miller Solicitors, 247 High Road, Wood Green, London, N22 8HF, *Call Date: Oct 2007, Inner Temple*
Qualifications: [BA (B'ham)]

HALES MR CHRISTOPHER JAMES

Lawyer, The Treasury Solicitors, 8.09, One Kemble Street, London, WC2B 4TS, ☎ 020 7210 2961, ✉ chris.hales@tsol.gsi.gov.uk, *Call Date: Nov 1979, Gray's Inn*
Qualifications: [BA DipLaw]

HALL MR EDMUND CHARLES DOUGLAS

Prosecutor, Room N250, Charing Cross Police Station, Agar Street, London, WC2N 4JP, *Call Date: Oct 1993, Middle Temple*
Qualifications: [BA (Hons)(Newc) CPE (Lond)]

F

HALL MISS JANET MARIE

Senior Legal Officer, Quintiles Limited, 500 Brook Drive, Green Park, Reading, RG2 6UU, ☎0118 450 8592, ✉janet.hall@quintiles.com, *Call Date: Oct 1997, Inner Temple*
Qualifications: [LLB (Hons) MA]

HALL MS JOANNE

Gordons LLP, Riverside West, Whitehall Road, Leeds, LS1 4AW, *Call Date: July 1999, Inner Temple*
Qualifications: [LLB (Sheff)]

HALL MR ROBERT ANTHONY

Crown Prosecution Service, PO Box 237, Eigth Floor, Sunlight House, Quay Street, Manchester, M60 3PS, Fax: 0161 827 4930, *Call Date: Oct 1997, Gray's Inn*
Qualifications: [LLB (Lond)]

HALPIN MR THOMAS GAVIN

Crown Prosecution Service, The Cooperage, 8 Gainsford Street, London, SE1 2NE, ☎020 7378 4341 Fax: 020 3300 4862, *Call Date: Nov 1994, Inner Temple*
Qualifications: [LLB (Lond)]

HAMADEH MR SHARIF SUBHI SEBASTIAN

Clyde & Co LLP, P.O. Box 7001, Rolex Tower, Sheikh Zayed Road, Dubai, United Arab Emirates, Fax: 4 384 4004, ✉sharif.hamedah@clydeco.ae, *Call Date: Nov 2008, Lincoln's Inn*
Qualifications: [BA (York) MPHIL (Oxon) CPE COLS]

HAMBLEY MS ELIZABETH

Efficiency and Reform Group, Cabinet Office, 1 Horse Guards Road, London, SW1A 2HQ, ☎020 7271 1378, ✉elizabeth.hambley@cabinet-office.gsi.gov.uk, *Call Date: Nov 1992, Inner Temple*
Qualifications: [LLB (Warw)]

HAMID MR HAQ EMANUL

HSN Partnership (Uk) Ltd, Grange Cottage, Womersley, Doncaster, DN6 9BW, ☎01302 787300, ✉emanulc@yahoo.co.uk, *Call Date: July 2001, Lincoln's Inn*
Qualifications: [LLB (Hons)(Lond)]

HAMILTON MISS LAURA

Shell International Ltd, Shell Centre, London, SE1 7NA, *Call Date: Nov 1987, Lincoln's Inn*
Qualifications: [BA (Lond) Dip Law (Lond)]

HAMILTON SUGDEN MRS MEREDITH THERESA

Chair, Legal Adviser, Managing Director, Hamilton Advisory Services Ltd, Hamilton House, 20 Alderberry Road, Hawarden, Cheshire, CH5 3JS, ☎01244 531143
Fax: 01244 537600, ✉MTHS@hamiltonadvisoryservices.com, *Call Date: Nov 1969, Gray's Inn*

HAMMERSLEY MISS LOUISE CLAIRE ISOBEL

Shed Media Group Ltd, 85 Grays Inn Road, London, WC1X 8TX, ☎020 7239 1047, ✉l.hammersley@shed-media.com, *Call Date: Nov 2002, Lincoln's Inn*
Qualifications: [LLB (Hons)(Lond) LLM]

HAMMOND MR MICHAEL JOHN

Senior Crown Prosecutor, Crown Prosecution Service, Athena House, Kettlestring Lane, Clifton Down, York, YO30 4XF, *Call Date: Oct 1991, Inner Temple*
Qualifications: [BSc CPE]

HAMMOND MISS TRACEY ANN

Deputy Chief Clerk, Inner London and City Family Proceedings Court, 59-65 Wells Street, London, W1A 3AE, ☎020 7805 3417, *Call Date: Feb 1989, Gray's Inn*
Qualifications: [LLB (Lond)]

HAMPER MR ANDREW JOHN PAUL

Senior Legal Counsel, Banco Santander S.A., Ciudad Grupo Santander, Encinar, Planta 0, 28660 Boadilla Del Monte, Madrid, Spain, ☎00 34 91 289 3517
Fax: 00 34 91 257 0118, ✉ajphamper@gruposantander.com, *Call Date: Oct 1991, Middle Temple*
Qualifications: [LLB (Hons) (B'ham)]

HAMPSHIRE MRS ANN CHRISTINE

Crown Advocate, Crown Prosecution Service, Argal House, Peninsula Business Park, Rydon Lane, Exeter, Devon, EX2 7NT, ☎01392 356 717 Fax: 01392 356 703, ✉ann.hampshire@cps.gsi.gov.uk, *Call Date: Nov 1983, Gray's Inn*
Qualifications: [LLB (Sheff)]

F

HAMPSON MR MICHAEL DAVID

Company Secretary, Director, General Counsel, National Express Group plc, 60 Charlotte Street, London, W1T 2NU, Fax: 020 7636 7476, ✉michael.hampson@nationalexpress.com, *Call Date: July 1985, Middle Temple*
Qualifications: [LLB (Wales) FCIS]

HANCOCK MISS STEPHANIE JANE

Crown Advocate, Crown Prosecution Service, Jefferson House, 27 Park Place, Leeds, West Yorkshire, LS1 2SZ, ☎0113 290 2700 Fax: 0113 290 2701, *Call Date: Oct 2006, Gray's Inn*
Qualifications: [BA]

HAND MR EDWARD

Crown Prosecution Service, City Gates, Southgate, Chichester, PO19 8DJ, ☎01243 523 900 Fax: 01243 523 950, ✉edward.hand@cps.gsi.gov.uk, *Call Date: July 2007, Lincoln's Inn*
Qualifications: [LLB (Notts)]

HANNA MS ELIZABETH COLETTE

Crown Prosecution Service, Bromley Police Station, High Street, Bromley, Kent, BR1 1ER, ✉colette.hanna@cps.gsi.gov.uk, *Call Date: Feb 1994, Lincoln's Inn*
Qualifications: [LLB (Hons)]

HARBON MS LESLEY EDITH

Crown Prosecution Service, Cae Bank, Tanerdy Lodge, Carmarthen, Carmarthenshire, SA31 2EZ, ☎01267 242100 Fax: 01267 242121, ✉Lesley.Harbon@cps.gsi.gov.uk, *Call Date: Nov 2001, Lincoln's Inn*
Qualifications: [LLB (Hons)]

HARBORD MRS JILLIAN

Guile Nicholas Solicitors, 43 Lodge Lane, North Finchley, London, N12 8JG, ☎020 8492 2290 Fax: 020 8445 5376, ✉sols@gnlaw.co.uk, *Call Date: Nov 2004, Gray's Inn*
Qualifications: [LLB]

HARDING MISS ANNA CATHERINE

Department For Work and Pensions, Room 4c06, Quarry House, Leeds, LS2 7UA, ✉anna.harding@dwp.gsi.gov.uk, *Call Date: Oct 1999, Middle Temple*
Qualifications: [LLB (Hons)]

HARDING MRS DEBORAH JANE

Senior Crown Prosecutor, Crown Prosecution Service, Riverside House, Riverside Way, Bedford Road, Northampton, Northamptonshire, NN1 5NX, *Call Date: Oct 1992, Inner Temple*
Qualifications: [LLB (Hons)]

HARDING MISS JENNIFER ANN

Legal Counsel, TT International, Moor House, Level 13, 120 London Wall, London, EC2Y 5ET, ☎020 7509 1261, *Call Date: Oct 1990, Middle Temple*
Qualifications: [BA (Wales)]

HARDING-ROBERTS MR PETER LANGSTON

Declan Mcsorley and Jon Lewis Solicitors, 16 Pearl Street, Cardiff, Wales, CF24 1HD, *Call Date: July 1981, Middle Temple*
Qualifications: [LLB]

HARDWICK MRS MELANIE SARAH

Senior Crown Prosecutor, Crown Prosecution Service, Southern House, Wellesley Grove, Croydon, Surrey, CR9 1DY, *Call Date: July 2001, Lincoln's Inn*
Qualifications: [LLB (Hons) (Newc)]

HARLEY MR DAVID WILLIAM

Crown Advocate, Crown Prosecution Service, Sunlight House, Quay Street, Manchester, M60 3PS, ☎0161 827 4886, *Call Date: July 1988, Middle Temple*
Qualifications: [LLB (Hons)]

HARMES MR STEPHEN DOUGLAS

Crown Advocate, Judge, Crown Prosecution Service, Capital Tower, Greyfriars Road, Cardiff, CF10 3PL, ☎02920 803988, ✉stephen.harmes@cps.gsi.gov.uk, *Call Date: Oct 1993, Gray's Inn*
Qualifications: [B Sc (Econ) (Wales)]

HAROLD MISS CAROLINE GRACE

Lawyer, The Treasury Solicitors, Employment & Commercial Contracts, One Kemble Street, London, WC2B 4TS, ☎020 7210 3100, *Call Date: July 1993, Inner Temple*
Qualifications: [LLB]

HAROLD MR FERGUS DOUGAL

Senior Crown Prosecutor, Crown Prosecution Service, Carmelite House, St James Court, Whitefriars, Norwich, Norfolk, NR3 1SL, ☎01603 693 000 Fax: 0161 693 001, *Call Date: Oct 1996, Gray's Inn*
Qualifications: [BA (Dunelm)]

HAROON MISS SARA YASMIN

John Morley and Co Solicitors, 29/31 High Street, Rainham, Kent, ME8 7HX, ☎01634 266 940 Fax: 01634 266941, ✉sara.haroon@morlaw.com, *Call Date: July 1998, Middle Temple*
Qualifications: [LLB (Hons)(Lond)]

HARPER-WARD MS VICTORIA LOUISE

The Treasury Solicitors, 5th Floor, One Kemble Street, London, WC2B 4TS, *Call Date: Oct 2004, Inner Temple*
Qualifications: [LLB (Lond)]

HARRIES MR JOHN CHRISTOPHER NICHOLAS

EEF Ltd, Engineers' House, The Promenade, Clifton Down, Bristol, BS8 3NB, *Call Date: July 2003, Inner Temple*
Qualifications: [BA (Manch) MA (Manch) MA (Leic) LLM (Leic)]

HARRINGTON MRS ELAINE

Director, Csc Computer Sciences Ltd, Royal Pavillion, Wellesley Road, Aldershot, Hampshire, GU11 1PZ, ☎01252 534550 Fax: 01252 534143, *Call Date: Nov 1996, Gray's Inn*
Qualifications: [LLB]

HARRIS MRS ALYSON

Senior Crown Prosecutor, Crown Prosecution Service, Froomsgate House, Rupert Street, Bristol, BS1 2QJ, ☎0117 302800, *Call Date: July 1979, Middle Temple*
Qualifications: [LLB (B'ham)]

HARRIS MS CHARLOTTE ROSE

Partner, Mishcon De Reya, Summit House, 12 Red Lion Square, London, WC1R 4QD, ☎020 7440 7000 Fax: 020 7404 5982, ✉charlotte.harris@mishcon.com, *Call Date: Nov 2000, Inner Temple*
Qualifications: [BA (E.Ang) CPE]

HARRIS MISS CLAIRE-LOUISE

Crown Prosecution Service, Colmore Gate, 2 - 6 Colmore Row, Birmingham, West Midlands, B3 2QA, ☎01212 121 368, *Call Date: Oct 1998, Lincoln's Inn*
Qualifications: [BA (Hons)(B'ham) CPE]

HARRIS MR IAN ROBERT BERESFORD

Crown Prosecution Service, Black Horse House, 8-10 Leigh Road, Eastleigh, Hampshire, SO50 9FH, ☎02380 673800 Fax: 02380 673857, ✉Ian.Harris@cps.gsi.gov.uk, *Call Date: July 2004, Middle Temple*

HARRIS MR JOHN DAVID

Senior Crown Prosecutor, Crown Prosecution Service, Citadel House, 58 High Street, Hull, Humberside, HU1 1QD, *Call Date: Nov 1981, Inner Temple*
Qualifications: [LLB (Hons)]

HARRIS MRS KATHLEEN JANE

Partner, Arnold and Porter (Uk) LLP, Tower 42, 25 Old Broad Street, London, EC2N 1HQ, ☎020 7786 6249 Fax: 020 7786 6249, ✉kathleen.harris@aporter.com, *Call Date: Oct 1998, Inner Temple*
Qualifications: [LLB (Thames)]

HARRIS MR MARTIN JOHN

Legal Adviser, Essex Magistrates Court, Opsrey House, Hedgerows Business Park, Colchester Road, Chelmsford, Essex, CM2 5PF, ☎01245 313300 Fax: 01245 313399, *Call Date: July 1984, Lincoln's Inn*
Qualifications: [BA]

HARRIS MISS PHILIPPA KAY

Mayer Brown International LLP, 201 Bishopsgate, London, EC2M 3AF, ✉pharris@mayerbrown.com, *Call Date: Oct 2005, Gray's Inn*
Qualifications: [LLB (Bristol)]

HARRIS MISS SALLY FIONA

Senior Principal Legal Officer, Department For Work and Pensions, 5th Floor, the Adelphi, 1-11 John Adam Street, London, WC2N 6HT, *Call Date: July 1986, Inner Temple*
Qualifications: [LLB (Hull)]

F

HARRIS MISS SARAH CHARLOTTE

Kingsley Napley LLP, 14 St John's Lane, London, EC1M 4AJ, ☎020 7814 1200 Fax: 020 7490 2288, *Call Date: July 2007, Gray's Inn*
Qualifications: [BA]

HARRISON MS ANNE DENISE

Associate, DAC Beachcroft LLP, Portwall Place, Portwall Lane, Bristol, BS99 7UD, ☎0117 918 2731 Fax: 0117 918 2100, ✉aharrison@beachcroft.co.uk, *Call Date: May 1992, Inner Temple*
Qualifications: [LLB LLM]

HARRISON MR MICHAEL JOHN

Legal Counsel, Deutsche Bank AG London, Winchester House, 1 Great Winchester Street, London, EC2N 2DB, ☎020 7547 1822 Fax: 020 7547 6554, ✉michael.harrison@db.com, *Call Date: Oct 1994, Middle Temple*
Qualifications: [MA (Hons)(Cantab)]

HARRISON MR NIGEL JEFFREY

Crown Prosecution Service, 3rd Floor, Unicentre, Preston, Lancashire, PR1 1DH, *Call Date: Nov 1985, Gray's Inn*
Qualifications: [LLB(Sheff)]

HARRISON MRS ROSALYNDE VICTORIA

Company Secretary, General Counsel, Monsoon Limited, Notting Hill Village, 1 Nicholas Road, London, W11 4AN, ☎020 3372 3000 Fax: 020 3372 3012, *Call Date: July 1981, Middle Temple*
Qualifications: [BA]

HARRISON MS SOPHIA VICTORIA

Carey Olsen, Po Box 98, Carey House, Les Banques, St Peter Port, GY1 4BZ, ☎01481 727272, *Call Date: Oct 2006, Lincoln's Inn*
Qualifications: [LLB (Lond) LLM (Law)]

HART MISS CHRISTINE JAYNE

Crown Prosecution Service, Riverside, Castle Street, Taunton, TA1 4HJ, ☎01823 425119, *Call Date: Oct 2009, Lincoln's Inn*
Qualifications: [LLB (Reading)]

HART MISS JESSICA ELLEN

Crown Prosecution Service, Sceptre House, 7-9 Castle Street, Luton, Bedfordshire, LU1 3AJ, ☎01582 816600, ✉jessica.hart@cps.gsi.gov.uk, *Call Date: Nov 2005, Inner Temple*
Qualifications: [BA Queen's College University of Cambridge]

HARTHAN MR PETER JAMES

Riverview Chambers, Hamilton House, 1 Temple Avenue, London, EC4Y 0HA, ✉peterharthan@riverviewchambers.com, *Call Date: Oct 2007, Inner Temple*
Qualifications: [BA (Oxon)]

HARTLEY MISS CATHERINE ANNE

Law Commission, Steel House, 11 Tothill Street, London, SW1H 9LJ, ☎020 3334 0244 Fax: 020 3334 0201, ✉catherine.vine@lawcommission.gsi.gov.uk, *Call Date: July 2006, Inner Temple*
Qualifications: [MA (Cantab)]

HARTLEY MR CHRISTOPHER JOHN

District Crown Prosecutor, Crown Prosecution Service, South Yorkshire Area, Greenfield House, 32 Scotland Street, Sheffield, S3 7DQ, ☎0114 229 8600, *Call Date: July 1987, Inner Temple*
Qualifications: [BA (Hons) (Kent)]

HARVEY MRS JAYNE DENISE

Vice President, Brand Events Limited, Registered In the Uk - Number 04928306, Registered Office Earls Court Exhibition, Warwick Road, London, SW5 9TA, ☎020 7471 1080 Fax: 020 7471 1090, ✉jayneh@brandevents.co.uk, *Call Date: Feb 1992, Middle Temple*
Qualifications: [LLB (Hons) LLM (Lond)]

HARVEY MISS KEELY LOUISE

Eric Robinsons Solicitors, 359 Bitterne Road, Bitterne, Southampton, SO18 1DN, ☎02380 425000, *Call Date: Oct 1999, Middle Temple*
Qualifications: [LLB (Hons)(Kent)]

HARWOOD MISS SUSAN MARY JOSEPHINE

Lawyer, The Treasury Solicitors, Queen Anne's Chambers, Dept D2b, 28 Broadway, London, SW1H 9JS, *Call Date: Nov 1988, Middle Temple*
Qualifications: [BA (Keele)]

HASSALL MR DAVID CARL

Lamb Chambers, Lamb Building, Elm Court, Temple, London, EC4Y 7AS, ☎020 7797 8300 Fax: 020 7797 8308, *Call Date: Oct 2011, Middle Temple*
Qualifications: [LLB (Hons) (Wales) LLM (Bristol) MSc (Staffs)]

HASSAN MR ROBIN ANTHONY

HED, British Sky Broadcasting Ltd, Grant Way, Isleworth, Middlesex, TW7 5QD, ☎020 7705 3387 Fax: 020 7705 3530, ✉robin.hassan@bskyb.com, *Call Date: Nov 1994, Inner Temple*
Qualifications: [LLB (Essex)]

HASSLACHER MR JAMES MICHAEL ROCHE

GT Stewart, 28 Grove Vale, London, SE22 8EF, Fax: 020 8299 6009, ✉info@gtstewart.co.uk, *Call Date: Nov 1993, Middle Temple*
Qualifications: [LLB (Hons)(Keele)]

HASWELL MR OLIVER JAMES

Crown Prosecution Service, Carmelite House, St James Court, Whitefriars, Norwich, Norfolk, NR3 1SL, ☎01603 693 000 Fax: 01603 693 001, ✉oliver.haswell@cps.gsi.gov.uk, *Call Date: July 2006, Gray's Inn*
Qualifications: [LLB (Cardiff)]

HATTON MISS THERESA JACQUELINE

Badenoch & Clark, Livery Place, 35 Livery Street, Colmore Business District, Birmingham, B3 2PB, *Call Date: Mar 1998, Lincoln's Inn*
Qualifications: [LLB (Hons)(Derby)]

HAVARD MR NIGEL GEORGE

Lawyer, Council of the City and County Of Swansea, County Hall, Oystermouth Road, Swansea, West Glamorgan, SA1 3SN, ☎01792 636 291 Fax: 01792 637 477, ✉nigel.havard@swansea.gov.uk, *Call Date: Mar 1998, Gray's Inn*
Qualifications: [BA]

HAWKINS MISS EVELYN ANN JOAN

Crown Prosecution Service, Riding Gate House, 37 Old Dover Road, Canterbury, Kent, CT1 3JG, ✉evelyn.hawkins@cps.gsi.gov.uk, *Call Date: Nov 1998, Inner Temple*
Qualifications: [LLB (Hons) (Kent)]

HAWKINS MR NICHOLAS JOHN

Associate, Revelfree Ltd, 1 Half Moon Cottages, Harewood Road, Collingham, Wetherby, West Yorkshire, LS22 5BL, ✉howkinsn1@hotmail.co.uk, *Call Date: Nov 1979, Middle Temple*
Qualifications: [MA (Oxon) Assoc IPS ACIArb]

HAWKINS MR NICHOLAS SIMON

Chief Crown Prosecutor, Crown Prosecution Service, Black Horse House, 8-10 Leigh Road, Eastleigh, Hampshire, SO50 9FH, ✉nick.hawkins@cps.gsi.gov.uk, *Call Date: Oct 1991, Inner Temple*
Qualifications: [MA (Oxon) Dip Law]

HAY MISS ELEANOR FRANCES MARGARET

The Treasury Solicitors, One Kemble Street, London, WC2B 4TS, Fax: 020 7210 4512, *Call Date: Nov 1996, Lincoln's Inn*
Qualifications: [LLB (Hons)]

HAYCOCK MRS ANNE

Legal Adviser, Reading Borough Council, Civic Offices, Civic Centre, Reading, RG1 7AE, *Call Date: Nov 1986, Gray's Inn*
Qualifications: [Dip Mag Law]

HAYE MISS MARLEEN VICTORIA

Avalon House, 3rd Floor, 57-63 Scrutton Street, London, EC2A 4PF, ☎020 7613 6134, ✉marleenhaye@hotmail.com, *Call Date: Oct 2002, Gray's Inn*
Qualifications: [LLB (Luton)]

HAYES MRS SONIA MARIE

Partnerships In Care, 2 Imperial Place, Borehamwood, Hertfordshire, WD6 1JN, ☎020 8327 1800, ✉sonia.hayes@partnershipsincare.co.uk, *Call Date: Oct 2003, Lincoln's Inn*
Qualifications: [BSc (Hons) (Lond) LLB (Hons) (Lond)]

HAYES MR TIMOTHY BARRINGTON

Pannone LLP, 123 Deansgate, Manchester, Lancashire, M3 2BU, ☎0161 909 3000 Fax: 0161 909 4444, ✉tim.hayes@pannone.co.uk, *Call Date: Oct 1996, Gray's Inn*
Qualifications: [LLB (Lond)]

F

HAYHOE MR JUSTIN OLIVER

Crown Prosecution Service, Sunlight House, Quay Street, Manchester, M60 3PS, ☎0161 827 4700, *Call Date: Oct 1994, Gray's Inn*
Qualifications: [BA]

HEAD MR JOHN SEBASTIAN

Allen & Overy LLP, One Bishops Square, London, E1 6AD, ☎020 3088 0000 Fax: 020 3088 0088, *Call Date: Nov 1987, Gray's Inn*
Qualifications: [MA (Cantab)]

HEALY MR ANTONY JULIAN

Temenos, The Banking Software Company, 71 Fenchurch Street, London, EC3M 4TD, ☎020 7423 3700 Fax: 020 7423 3815, *Call Date: July 1998, Middle Temple*
Qualifications: [LLB (Hons)]

HEARN MR STEVEN MAXWELL

Crown Prosecution Service, 2 King Edward Court, King Edward Street, Nottingham, Nottinghamshire, NG1 1EL, *Call Date: Nov 1992, Inner Temple*
Qualifications: [LLB LLM]

HEATH MISS ASHLEY EMMA LOUISE

Osborne Clark, 2 Temple Back East, Temple Quay, Bristol, BS1 6EG, ✉Ashley.Heath@osborneclarke.com, *Call Date: Oct 1997, Gray's Inn*
Qualifications: [BA (Hons) Dip LA Dip Law MLI]

HEATLEY MR RICHARD JONATHON

HED, Crown Prosecution Service, The Cooperage, 8 Gainsford Street, London, SE1 2NE, ✉richard.heatley2@cps.gsi.gov.uk, *Call Date: Nov 1989, Inner Temple*
Qualifications: [LLB (Oxon) LLM (Lond)]

HEDDERLY MR MARK ROBERT ERNEST

General Counsel, HED, Legal Counsel, Veolia Environmental Services, 8th Floor, 210 Pentonville Road, London, N1 9JY, ☎020 7812 5168 Fax: 020 7812 5161, ✉mark.hedderly@veolia.co.uk, *Call Date: Nov 1981, Lincoln's Inn*
Qualifications: [BA (Hons)(Law) LLM]

HEGER MRS LORNA BLANCHE

Prosecutor, Senior Crown Prosecutor, Crown Prosecution Service, The Cooperage, 8 Gainsford Street, London, SE1 2NE, ☎020 73784344 Fax: 020 3300 4859, ✉lorna.heger@cps.gsi.gov.uk, *Call Date: Nov 1990, Inner Temple*
Qualifications: [BA (Hons) (L'pool) Dip Law (Lond)]

HEINE MS ELEANOR LOUISE

Sedgwick, Detert, Moran and Arnold LLP, Fitzwilliam House, 10 St. Mary Axe, London, EC3A 8BF, ✉eleanor.heine@sdma.com, *Call Date: Nov 1995, Inner Temple*
Qualifications: [BA (Pennsylvania) LLB]

HELFER MISS ANNETTE

Etat de Vaud, Dept. of Obstetrics, University Hospital of Lausanne, Lausanne, Rue De Bugnon, Lausanne Ch 1011, *Call Date: July 2000, Lincoln's Inn*
Qualifications: [LLB BA (Bris)]

HEMMING MR MARTIN JOHN

Legal Adviser, Foreign and Commonwealth Office, Room 200a, King Charles Street, London, SW1A 2AH, ☎020 7008 5369, *Call Date: July 1972, Gray's Inn*
Qualifications: [MA (Cantab) LLM (Lond)]

HEMMING MISS SUSAN JANE

HED, Crown Prosecution Service, Rose Court, 2 Sourthwark Bridge, London, SE1 9HS, ☎020 3357 6539 Fax: 020 3357 0723, ✉susan.hemming@cps.gsi.gov.uk, *Call Date: July 1988, Middle Temple*
Qualifications: [LLB (Hons) (Wales)]

HENDERSON MISS CARA MCDONALD

The Home Office, Legal Advisors Branch, Seacole, Ground Floor, 2 Marsham Street, London, SW1P 4DF, *Call Date: Nov 2004, Lincoln's Inn*
Qualifications: [BA (Hons) (Oxon) PgDl]

HENDERSON MR DUNCAN ALAN RONALD

Addleshaw Goddard, Milton Gste, 60 Chiswell Street, London, EC1Y 4AG, Fax: 020 7606 4390, ✉duncan.henderson@addleshawgoddard.com, *Call Date: Oct 2003, Lincoln's Inn*
Qualifications: [BA (Hons) (Oxon)]

F

HENDERSON MRS LYNNE MCLEOD

Crown Prosecution Service, Fox Talbot House, Bellinger Close, Malmesbury Road, Chippenham, Wiltshire, SN15 1BN, ☎ 01249 766100, ✉ lynnem.henderson@cps.gsi.gov.uk, *Call Date: Nov 1993, Inner Temple*
Qualifications: [LLB (So'ton)]

HENDRY MR STUART IAIN

Euro Parking Collection PLC, Unit 6 Shepperton House, 83-93 Shepperton Road, London, N1 3DF, ☎ 020 7288 9745
Fax: 020 7288 9741, *Call Date: Oct 2001, Lincoln's Inn*
Qualifications: [LLB (Hons)]

HENDY MR ROBERT JAMES

Ministry of Justice, Criminal Appeal Office, Royal Courts of Justice, The Strand, London, WC2A 2LL, ☎ 020 7947 7171, ✉ robert.hendy@hmcourts-service.gsi.gov.uk, *Call Date: Nov 1996, Inner Temple*
Qualifications: [LLB (Lond) BCL (Oxon)]

HENLEY-PRICE MR JULIAN KENDALL

Legal Counsel, Kendso Limited, 55 Nansen Road, London, SW11 5NS, *Call Date: Feb 1994, Gray's Inn*
Qualifications: [LLB (Lond) Maitrise de Droit Prive (France)]

HENNESSY MRS EMILY ELIZABETH

Ministry of Defence, Po Box 1680, London, SW1P 1ZE, ☎ 020 7218 9048, *Call Date: Oct 1997, Middle Temple*
Qualifications: [BA (Hons) (Cantab) MA (Hons) (Cantab)]

HENNESSY MRS LISA

Crown Prosecution Service, 2 Kimbrose Way, Gloucester, Gloucestershire, GL1 4DB, ☎ 01452 872400, *Call Date: Mar 2003, Lincoln's Inn*
Qualifications: [BA (Hons) (Manch) PgDl (B'ham)]

HENRY MR DAVID

Mcdermott, Will and Emery, Avenue Des Nerviens 9-41, Brussels, 1040, Belgium, ✉ Dahenry@mwe.com, *Call Date: Oct 2006, Middle Temple*
Qualifications: [LLB (Lond) LLM]

HENRY MISS JENNIFER LORRAINE

HM Crown Prosecution Service Inspectorate, 26-28 Old Queen Street, London, SW1H 9HP, ☎ 020 7210 1141, ✉ jennifer.henry@hmcpsi.gsi.gov.uk, *Call Date: Oct 1990, Middle Temple*
Qualifications: [BA (Kent) LLM (Law)(Lond)]

HENRY MR PHILIP BRUCE

Thompsons Solicitors, 23 Princess Street, Manchester, M2 4ER, ☎ 0161 819 3500, ✉ BruceHenry@Thompsons.law.co.uk, *Call Date: Nov 1988, Middle Temple*
Qualifications: [LLB (Lond) AKC]

HENTY MRS GABRIELLE MARIE

Crown Advocate, Solicitor, Crown Prosecution Service, City Gate House, 185 Dyke Road, Hove, East Sussex, BN3 1TL, ☎ 01273 765600, ✉ gabby.henty@cps.gsi.gov.uk, *Call Date: Nov 2003, Lincoln's Inn*
Qualifications: [BA (Hons) (Manch)]

HEPBURNE SCOTT MR GEORGE WALTER

Geoff White Solicitors, 83 Victoria Road, Horley, Surrey, RH6 7QH, ☎ 01293 789958
Fax: 01293 782290, *Call Date: Oct 1999, Middle Temple*
Qualifications: [BA (Hons)(Lond) CPE]

HEPPER MR MICHAEL DAVID

Manager, Other, The Royal College of Veterinary Surgeons, Belgravia House, 62-64 Horseferry Road, London, SW1P 2AF, ☎ 020 7 2001 Fax: 020 7202 0740, ✉ m.hepper@rcvs.org.uk, *Call Date: July 2000, Gray's Inn*
Qualifications: [BA (Glas) Dip Law]

HEPTONSTALL MR SIMON ANTHONY

Crown Advocate, Crown Prosecution Service, Eaton Court, 112 Oxford Road, Reading, Berkshire, RG1 7LL, ☎ 0118 951 3600
Fax: 0118 951 3601, ✉ simon.heptonstall@cps.gsi.gov.uk, *Call Date: Nov 1999, Inner Temple*

HERON MISS SIOBHAN HEATHER

Crown Prosecution Service, Froomsgate House, Rupert Street, Bristol, BS1 2QJ, ☎ 0117 930 2800, ✉ siobhan.heron@cps.gsi.gov.uk, *Call Date: Nov 2006, Middle Temple*
Qualifications: [BA (Hons) (Sheff) PgDip Law]

F

HERSKOVIC MR DAVID JOSEPH

Kostick Hanan Herskovic LLP, 1 Egerton Road, London, N16 6UE, *Call Date: Oct 2002, Lincoln's Inn*
Qualifications: [LLB (Lond)]

HEWAGE MS RUWANI VIRGINIA

Vickers and Co Solicitors, 183 Uxbridge Road, Ealing, London, W13 9AA, ☎ 020 8579 2559 Fax: 020 8280 1091, *Call Date: July 2001, Inner Temple*
Qualifications: [LLB (Middx)]

HEWARD-MILLS MS D'YANN RACHELLE

Arbitrator, Lawyer, Linklaters, 1 Silk Street, London, EC2Y 8HQ, ☎ 020 7456 2000 Fax: 020 7456 2222, ✉ dyann.heward-mills@linklaters.com, *Call Date: Mar 2001, Middle Temple*
Qualifications: [LLB (Hons) LLM]

HEWITT MR PAUL ANTHONY

Crown Prosecution Service, Capital Tower, Greyfriars Road, Cardiff, CF10 3PL, ☎ 02920 803858, ✉ paul.hewitt@cps.gsi.gov.uk, *Call Date: Nov 2010, Gray's Inn*

HEWITT MS SUSAN ELIZABETH

Advocate, London Borough of Islington, Corporate Resources Legal Services, Division, Town Hall, Upper Street, London, N1 2UP, ☎ 020 7527 3497 Fax: 020 7527 3425, ✉ susan.hewitt@islington.gov.uk, *Call Date: Oct 1997, Lincoln's Inn*
Qualifications: [BSc (Hons) Dip in Law (Lond) FCCA]

HEXT MR CHRISTOPHER JOHN RICHARD

Senior Crown Prosecutor, Crown Prosecution Service, County House, 100 New London Road, Chelmsford, Essex, CM2 0RG, ☎ 01245 252939 Fax: 01245 494710, *Call Date: July 1986, Lincoln's Inn*
Qualifications: [LLB]

HIBBERT MR ARTHUR JOHN

Principal Crown Prosecutor, Crown Prosecution Service, Bolton Police Station, 10 Scholey Street, Bolton, Greater Manchester, BL2 1HX, ✉ john.hibbert@cps.gsi.gov.uk, *Call Date: May 1984, Middle Temple*
Qualifications: [BA (Manch)]

HICKEY MR EUGENE JAMES

Kangs Solicitors, 2 Wake Green Road, Moseley, Birmingham, B13 9EZ, Fax: 0121 449 8849, ✉ ehickey@kangssolicitors.co.uk, *Call Date: July 1988, Lincoln's Inn*
Qualifications: [LLB (Hons) (Leeds)]

HICKLING MISS SALLY BARBARA

Senior Crown Prosecutor, Crown Prosecution Service, Justonian House, Spitfire Close, Ermine Buisness Park, Huntingdon, Cambridgeshire, PE29 6XY, ☎ 01480 825 241 Fax: 01480 825 207, ✉ Sally.Hickling@cps.gsi.gov.uk, *Call Date: Oct 1993, Gray's Inn*
Qualifications: [M Soc Sci (B'ham)]

HICKMAN MS JANE

Senior Lawyer, Metropolitan Police Service, Directorate of Legal Services, First Floor (V), New Scotland Yard, 8-10 Broadway, London, SW1H 0BG, ☎ 020 7230 1212 Fax: 020 7230 7571, *Call Date: Nov 1983, Gray's Inn*
Qualifications: [BA (Lond) Dip Law]

HICKSON MISS FABIOLA ANNALIESE AMELIA

Call Date: Nov 1992, Inner Temple
Qualifications: [LLB]

HIDAKA MISS SEIKO

Allen & Overy LLP, One Bishops Square, London, E1 6AD, ☎ 020 3088 0000 Fax: 020 3088 0088, ✉ seiko.hidaka@allenovery.com, *Call Date: July 2002, Middle Temple*
Qualifications: [MA (Cantab) D.Phil (Oxon) CPE]

HIGGINSON MR ANDREW JAMES

Henry & Co Solicitors, 72-74 Wellington Road South, Stockport, SK1 3SU, ☎ 0161 477 8558 Fax: 0161 474 7667, ✉ reception@henrysolicitors.co.uk, *Call Date: Mar 2007, Middle Temple*
Qualifications: [BA (Leeds)]

HILL MR ANTHONY ALAN

Senior Crown Prosecutor, Crown Prosecution Service, Rose Court, 2 Southwark Bridge, London, SE1 9HS, *Call Date: Oct 2002, Middle Temple*
Qualifications: [MA (Oxon)]

HILL MR JASON

Law Officers of the Crown, St James Chambers, Po Box 96, St Peter Port, GY1 4BY, Guernsey, ☎01481 723 355, ✉jason.hill@gov.gg, *Call Date: Oct 1995, Lincoln's Inn*
Qualifications: [BSc (Hons)(Sheff)]

HINCHLIFFE MR PETER MICHAEL

Judge, OMB, Charities Aid Foundation, St Andrewés House, 18-20 St Andrew Street,, London, EC4A 3AY, ✉phinchliffe@cafonline.org, *Call Date: July 1982, Lincoln's Inn*
Qualifications: [LLB (Hons) (Hull)]

HINGSTON MS THERESA CLOTHILDE

Chair, Lawyer, Crown Prosecution Service, Fox Talbot House, Bellinger Close, Malmesbury Road, Chippenham, Wiltshire, SN15 1BN, ☎01249 766100
Fax: 01249 766101, ✉tessa.hingston@cps.gsi.gov.uk, *Call Date: July 1978, Inner Temple*

HIRST MR RICHARD DODSWORTH

General Counsel, Gamma Telecom Holdings Limited, Kings House, Kings Road West, Newbury, Berkshire, RG14 5BY, ✉rhirst@gammatelecom.com, rdhirst@hotmail.co.uk, *Call Date: Nov 1981, Middle Temple*
Qualifications: [MA (Oxon)]

HOCKEY MR GORDON ANDREW

HED, The Royal College of Veterinary Surgeons, Belgravia House, 62-64 Horseferry Road, London, SW1P 2AF, ✉g.hockey@rcvs.org.uk, *Call Date: Feb 1995, Lincoln's Inn*
Qualifications: [BSc (Manch)]

HODGSON MRS MARGARET

Ministry of Justice, Selborne House, 54-60 Victoria Street, London, SW1E 6QW, ☎020 7210 8553, ✉margaret.hodgson@justice.gsi.gov.uk, *Call Date: July 1978, Gray's Inn*
Qualifications: [BA]

HODGSON MR NICHOLAS

Lawyer, The Treasury Solicitors, Constitutional Law Team, Cabinet Office, Room 3/07, 1 Horseguards Road, London, SW1A 2HQ, ☎020 7276 0199, ✉nick.hodgson@cabinet-office.gsi.gov.uk, *Call Date: July 1976, Middle Temple*
Qualifications: [BA (Oxon) MA (Oxon)]

HOGG MR JONATHON

Ipc Information Systems, Tower House, 67-73 Worship Street, London, EC2A 2DZ, ☎020 7979 7200, *Call Date: Nov 2000, Middle Temple*
Qualifications: [LLB (Hons)]

HOLDEN MISS HOLLY

Crown Prosecution Service, 8th Floor, Sunllight House, Quay Street, Manchester, M60 3PP, ☎0161 827 4700, ✉Holly.Holden@cps.gsi.gov.uk, *Call Date: July 2008, Lincoln's Inn*
Qualifications: [LLB (Hons) (Manch)]

HOLDEN MR RICHARD DERRICK JAMES

DAC Beachcroft LLP, 3 Minster Court, Mincing Lane, London, EC3R 7DD, *Call Date: Nov 1996, Lincoln's Inn*
Qualifications: [BA (Hons)(Oxon)]

HOLDER MISS CLAIRE ALISON

Crown Prosecution Service, The Cooperage, 8 Gainsford Street, London, SE1 2NE, ✉claire.holder@cps.gsi.gov.uk, *Call Date: July 1978, Lincoln's Inn*
Qualifications: [MA MSc ACIS]

HOLDERNESS MR DAVID ALAN

Crown Prosecution Service, Jefferson House, 27 Park Place, Leeds, West Yorkshire, LS1 2SZ, ☎0113 290 2700 Fax: 0113 290 2701, ✉David.Holderness@cps.gsi.gov.uk, *Call Date: Nov 1991, Lincoln's Inn*
Qualifications: [BA (Hons)]

HOLDHAM MISS SUSAN PAULINE

Lawyer, Legal Manager, Ministry of Justice, Criminal Appeal Office, Royal Courts of Justice, The Strand, London, WC2A 2LL, ☎020 7947 7812, ✉susan.holdham@hmcourts-service.x.gsi.gov.uk, *Call Date: July 1983, Gray's Inn*
Qualifications: [LLB (Hons) (Bris)]

HOLIDAY MS YEWA SARAH-JANE

Manager, Criminal Cases Review Commission, 5 St Philips Place, Birmingham, B3 2PW, *Call Date: Nov 1996, Middle Temple*
Qualifications: [BA (Hons) (Cantab) LLM (Sussex) LLM (Cantab)]

F

HOLLAND MRS JOANNE PENELOPE

Crown Prosecution Service, Princes Court, 34 York Road, Leicester, Leicestershire, LE1 5TU, ☎0116 2046700 Fax: 0116 2046777, ✉joanne.holland@cps.gsi.gov.uk, *Call Date: July 1992, Middle Temple*
Qualifications: [BA (Hons) Dip Law]

HOLLAND MR RICHARD DAVID

Deputy Justices' Clerk, Her Majesty's Court Service, Chester Magistrates' Court, Grosvenor Street, Chester, Cheshire, CH1 2XA, ☎01244 405 795 Fax: 01244 405 843, *Call Date: Nov 1987, Gray's Inn*
Qualifications: [Dip Mag Law CPE]

HOLLAND MISS SARAH ELIZABETH

Legal Adviser, HM Revenue and Customs, Room 2c/25, Solicitor's Office, 100 Parliament Street, London, SW1A 2BQ, ☎020 7147 2148, *Call Date: Oct 2002, Middle Temple*
Qualifications: [LLB (Warwick)]

HOLLIER MR MARK ANTHONY

Crown Prosecution Service, Froomsgate House, Rupert Street, Bristol, BS1 2QJ, ☎0117 930 2800 Fax: 0117 930 2806, *Call Date: May 1994, Inner Temple*
Qualifications: [LLB]

HOLLINS CAPTAIN RUPERT PATRICK

Royal Navy Officers, Mp 4.2, Sir Henry Leach Building, Whale Island, Portsmouth, Hampshire, PO2 8BY, ☎02392 625742, ✉rupert.hollins241@mod.uk, *Call Date: Oct 1995, Gray's Inn*
Qualifications: [MA (Oxon)]

HOLMES MR CARL STANLEY

Call Date: July 1986, Lincoln's Inn
Qualifications: [BA]

HOLMES MISS KATHERINE LAURA

Legal Adviser, Hmcs Thames Valley, Thames Valley Magistrates' Courts Service, Waverley House, Queens Avenue, Bicester, Oxfordshire, OX26 2NZ, *Call Date: July 2001, Lincoln's Inn*
Qualifications: [LLB (Hons)]

HOLT MR MATTHEW CHRISTOPHER

Lawyer, The Treasury Solicitors, 5th Floor, One Kemble Street, London, WC2B 4TS, *Call Date: Oct 2001, Gray's Inn*
Qualifications: [BA (Oxon)]

HOODLESS MR NEIL GORDON

Senior Crown Prosecutor, Crown Prosecution Service, St Peters House, Gower Street, Derby, Derbyshire, DE1 1SB, ☎01332 614000 Fax: 01332 614111, *Call Date: Nov 1989, Middle Temple*
Qualifications: [LLB(Hons)(Essex)]

HOOK MR ANTONY JAMES

Crown Prosecution Service, Justinian House, Spitfire Close, Ermine Business Park, Huntingdon, Cambridgeshire, PE29 6XY, ☎01480 825229, ✉antony.hook@cps.gsi.gov.uk, *Call Date: Nov 2003, Inner Temple*
Qualifications: [BA (Lond)]

HOOPER MR GRAHAM BOUCHER

Justices' Clerk, Nottinghamshire Magistrates' Court, Carrington Street, Nottingham, NG2 1EE, ☎0115 955 8102 Fax: 0115 955 8104, ✉Graham.Hooper@hmcts.gsi.gov.uk, *Call Date: July 1984, Lincoln's Inn*
Qualifications: [LLB]

HOOPER MR NEAL DAVID

Senior Lawyer, British Medical Association, Legal Department, Bma House, Tavistock Square, London, WC1H 9JP, *Call Date: Nov 1993, Lincoln's Inn*
Qualifications: [LLB (Hons) (L'pool)]

HOOSE MR ROBERT

Associate, White & Case LLP, 19 Place Vendome, Paris, 75001, France, ✉rhoose@whitecase.com, *Call Date: Nov 2008, Middle Temple*
Qualifications: [BA (Hons) (Oxon)]

HOPKINS MR CHRISTOPHER NEIL

Crown Prosecution Service, 7th Floor (South), Royal Liver Building, Pier Head, Liverpool, Merseyside, L3 1HN, ☎0151 239 6400, ✉chris.hopkins@cps.gsi.gov.uk, *Call Date: Oct 1995, Gray's Inn*
Qualifications: [BA]

F

HOPKINS MR CHRISTOPHER PAUL

Pinsent Masons, 3 Colmore Circus, Queensway, Birmingham, West Midlands, B4 6BH, ☎0121 629 1779, ✉christopher.hopkins@pinsentmasons.com, chopkins78@hotmail.com, *Call Date: Oct 2003, Middle Temple*
Qualifications: [LLB(Hons)]

HOPKINS MS EMMA KATE

The Home Office, Legal Adviser's Branch, Seacole, 2 Marsham Street, London, SW1P 4DF, ☎020 7035 1383, ✉emma.hopkins@homeoffice.gsi.gov.uk, *Call Date: Oct 1995, Middle Temple*
Qualifications: [BA (Hons)]

HOPKINSON MISS JOY THERESA OLIVIA

London Borough of Lambeth, Legal Services - Room 205, Lambeth Town Hall, Brixton Hill, London, SW2 1RW, ☎020 7926 7713 Fax: 020 7926 2361, ✉jhopkinson@lambeth.gov.uk, *Call Date: Nov 1999, Middle Temple*
Qualifications: [MA (Dundee) BA (Hons)]

HOQUE MISS SANJEEDA MICHELLE

London Borough of Newham, Legal and Democratic Services, Newham Dockside, 1000 Dockside Road, London, E16 2QU, ✉Michelle.Hoque@newham.gov.uk, *Call Date: Oct 2001, Lincoln's Inn*
Qualifications: [LLB (Hons)]

HOREESORUN MRS ROOMA DEVI

Environment Agency, King's Meadow House, King's Meadow Road, Reading, Berkshire, RG1 8DQ, ☎0118 953 5703 Fax: 0118 950 9440, ✉rooma.horeesorun@environment-agency.gov.uk, *Call Date: Oct 2000, Lincoln's Inn*
Qualifications: [LLB (Hons)(Lond)]

HORNE MR ALEXANDER LEE

House of Commons, Home Affairs Section, 1 Derby Gate, London, SW1A 2DG, ☎020 7219 3666, ✉hornea@parliament.uk, *Call Date: Nov 1999, Lincoln's Inn*
Qualifications: [LLB (Hons)(Herts)]

HORWOOD MISS ANYA LOUISE

Crown Prosecution Service, 7th Floor (South), Royal Liver Building, Pier Head, Liverpool, Merseyside, L3 1HN, ☎0151 239 6400 Fax: 0151 239 6330, *Call Date: Nov 1991, Inner Temple*
Qualifications: [LLB (Lancs)]

HOSEIN MISS AISLING TARA PHILOMENA

Senior Crown Prosecutor, Crown Prosecution Service, The Cooperage, 8 Gainsford Street, London, SE1 2NE, *Call Date: Nov 1990, Middle Temple*
Qualifications: [LLB (West Indies)]

HOULDER MR BRUCE

Chair, Master of the Bench, Recorder, Service Prosecuting Authority, Director Service Prosecutions, Raf Northolt, West End Road, Ruislip, Middlesex, HA4 6NG, ☎020 8833 6100, ✉spa-hq-dsp@northolt.raf.mod.uk, *Call Date: July 1969, Gray's Inn*

HOUSE MR CHRISTOPHER

Assistant, The Treasury Solicitors, One Kemble Street, London, WC2B 4TS, ✉Christopher.House@tsol.gsi.gov.uk, *Call Date: Nov 1976, Lincoln's Inn*
Qualifications: [LLB (Lond)]

HOUSEN MS JENNIFER JACQUELINE

The Immigration Uk Partnership, 373-375 Brixton Road, London, SW9 7DE, ☎020 7043 2737 Fax: 020 7691 9558, ✉immigrationuk@cwjamaica.com, *Call Date: Oct 1999, Inner Temple*
Qualifications: [LLB (Leics)]

HOW MISS JUSTINE FIONA LYNDA

The Treasury Solicitors, One Kemble Street, London, WC2B 4TS, ☎020 7210 3594 Fax: 020 7210 3257, ✉justine.how@tsol.gsi.gov.uk, *Call Date: Oct 2001, Middle Temple*
Qualifications: [LLB (Hons)]

HOWARD MR JAMES STEVEN

Kaim Todner Ltd, 11 Bolt Court, London, EC4A 3DQ, ☎020 7353 6660 Fax: 020 7353 6661, ✉jhoward@kaimtodner.com, *Call Date: Oct 2001, Gray's Inn*
Qualifications: [LLB]

F

HOWARD-JONES MS SARAH RACHEL

Ministry of Justice, Legal Services Team, 102 Petty France, London, SW1H 9AJ, ☎020 3334 4758, *Call Date: Nov 1994, Middle Temple*
Qualifications: [BA (Hons)(Cantab)]

HOWELL MAJOR GENERAL DAVID MALCOM

Adviser, The General Chiropractic Council, 44 Wicklow Street, London, WC1X 9HL, ☎020 77135155 Fax: 020 77135844, ✉d. howell@gcc-uk.org, *Call Date: July 1973, Lincoln's Inn*
Qualifications: [LLB (Hons)]

HOWELLS MR JOHN JULIAN

Crown Advocate, Crown Prosecution Service, Froomsgate House, Rupert Street, Bristol, BS1 2QJ, *Call Date: Nov 1985, Gray's Inn*
Qualifications: [LLB (Lond)]

HOYLE MR MARK STANLEY WADIH

Arbitrator, Judge, Mediator, Professor of Law, Recorder, Sj Berwin (Mena) LLP, 3rd Floor, Suite 33, Park Place, Po Box 24482, Dubai, United Arab Emirates, ✉mark.hoyle@ sjberwin.com, *Call Date: July 1978, Inner Temple*
Qualifications: [BA (Hons) PhD FCIArb FRGS]

HUDSON MR ANDREW MICHAEL

Al Tamimi & Company, D.I.F.C Office, Building 4 East, 6th Floor, Sheikh Zayed Road, Po Box 9275, Dubai, United Arab Emirates, Fax: 4 3641 777, *Call Date: July 2002, Middle Temple*
Qualifications: [LLB (Hons) (Oxon)]

HUDSON MISS EMMA CERIL

Lawyer, Senior Lawyer, London Borough of Lewisham, Town Hall, London, SE6 4RU, ☎020 8314 6419 Fax: 020 8314 3115, ✉emma.hudson@lewisham.gov.uk, *Call Date: Nov 1992, Inner Temple*
Qualifications: [LLB (Hons) Dip L G]

HUEHNE MS EVA YIM HONG

Department For Transport, Great Minster House, Room 1/04c, 76 Marsham Street, London, SW1P 4DR, *Call Date: July 2006, Inner Temple*
Qualifications: [BA MA (Australia) BA (Cantab)]

HUGHES MR BARRY MICHAEL

Chief Crown Prosecutor, Crown Prosecution Service, Froomsgate House, Rupert Street, Bristol, BS1 2QJ, ☎0117 930 2859 Fax: 0117 930 2886, ✉barry.hughes@cps.gsi. gov.uk, *Call Date: Nov 1983, Middle Temple*
Qualifications: [LLB (Sheff)]

HUGHES MS CAROLINE BARTON

Crown Prosecution Service, Harrow Crown Court, Hailsham Drive, Harrow, HA1 4TU, ☎020 8424 2294 Fax: 020 8424 0423, ✉caroline.hughes@cps.gsi.gov.uk, *Call Date: Nov 1999, Gray's Inn*
Qualifications: [BA (Newcastle)]

HUGHES MS CLARE MARIE

TLT LLP, 20 Gresham Street, London, EC2V 7JE, Fax: 020 3 465 4001, ✉clare.hughes@ tltsolicitors.com, *Call Date: Nov 2000, Inner Temple*
Qualifications: [LLB (Leics) LLM (Lond)]

HUGHES MR DAVID MARTIN

Senior Crown Prosecutor, Crown Prosecution Service, Edmonton Police Station, Edmonton, London, N9 0XR, *Call Date: Nov 1984, Gray's Inn*
Qualifications: [LLB]

HUGHES MR GARETH BRYN

Jeffrey Green Russell Solicitors, Waverley House, 7-12 Noel Street, London, W1F 8GQ, ☎020 7339 7012 Fax: 020 7339 0252, ✉gbh@jgrlaw.co.uk, *Call Date: Nov 1984, Lincoln's Inn*
Qualifications: [LLB (Wales)]

HUGHES MRS HELEN SIAN

Senior Crown Prosecutor, Crown Prosecution Service, Rose Court, 2 Southwark Bridge, London, SE1 9HS, Fax: 020 3357 0388, ✉Helen.Hughes@cps.gsi.gov.uk, *Call Date: Oct 1993, Inner Temple*
Qualifications: [BSc (Lond) CPE]

HUGHES MRS MERRIL

Crown Advocate, Crown Prosecution Service, 4/7 Prebendal Court, Oxford Road, Aylesbury, Buckinghamshire, HP19 8EY, *Call Date: July 1984, Lincoln's Inn*
Qualifications: [LLB]

HUGHES MISS SUSAN ANN

Advocate, Lecturer, Senior Crown Prosecutor, Crown Prosecution Service, Capital Tower, Greyfriars Road, Cardiff, Wales, CF10 3PL, ☎029 2080 3800 Fax: 029 2080 3802, *Call Date: Nov 1982, Gray's Inn*
Qualifications: [LLB (Leeds)]

HUGILL MISS CHERYL DAWN

HED, HM Revenue and Customs, West Wing, S2 Somerset House, The Strand, London, WC2R 1LB, ☎020 7438 6560
Fax: 020 7084 5610, ✉cheryl.hugill@hmrc.gsi.gov.uk, *Call Date: Nov 1979, Gray's Inn*
Qualifications: [LLB (Lond)]

HULME MS AMANDA CLAIRE

Associate, Addleshaw Goddard, Milton Gste, 60 Chiswell Street, London, EC1Y 4AG, ☎020 7880 5853 Fax: 020 7606 4390, ✉amanda.hulme@addleshawgoddard.com, *Call Date: Oct 1997, Middle Temple*
Qualifications: [LLB (Hons)(Kent)]

HULME MRS SUSAN ANNE

Crown Advocate, Crown Prosecution Service, Inner London Crown Court, Session House, Newington Causeway, London, SE1 6AZ, Fax: 020 74034548, ✉susan.hulme@cps.gsi.gov.uk, *Call Date: Oct 1994, Middle Temple*
Qualifications: [BSc (Hons) ARCS (Lond) LLB (Hons)]

HUMPHREY MR MATTHEW RICHARD

Criminal Cases Review Commission, 5 St Philips Place, Birmingham, B3 2PW, *Call Date: Mar 2001, Middle Temple*
Qualifications: [LLB (Hons) (Leic) LLM (Bristol)]

HUMPHRIES MR MARK NICHOLAS

Crown Prosecution Service, Froomsgate House, Rupert Street, Bristol, BS1 2QJ, *Call Date: Oct 2000, Lincoln's Inn*
Qualifications: [LLB (Hons) (Bris)]

HUNGATE MISS CLAIRE ELIZABETH

Director, Shed Media Group Ltd, 85 Grays Inn Road, London, WC1X 8TX,
Fax: 020)20 7239 1011, ✉claire.hungate@shed-media.com, c.hungate@shed-media.com, *Call Date: Oct 1999, Middle Temple*
Qualifications: [BA (Hons)(Warw) MA]

HUNT MR JAMIE PETER LEWIS

Nursing and Midwifery Council, 1 Kemble Street, London, WC2B 4AN, *Call Date: Nov 2006, Middle Temple*
Qualifications: [LLB (Hons) (Lond)]

HUNT MR JULIAN RICHARD

Ashley Smith and Co, 4-6 Lee High Road, Lewisham, London, SE13 5LQ, ☎020 8463 0099 Fax: 020 8763 9191, *Call Date: Mar 2005, Lincoln's Inn*
Qualifications: [BA (Hons) Cantab]

HUNT MR ROBERT JAMES CAMPBELL

Royal Navy Officers, Directorate of Naval Legal Services, Mp 4-2, Leach Building, Whale Island, Portsmouth, PO2 8BY, ☎02392 625739, *Call Date: July 2007, Middle Temple*
Qualifications: [LLB]

HUNTER MR JOHN DAVID

T V Edwards LLP, Park House, 29 Mile End Road, London, E1 4TP, ☎020 7790 7000 Fax: 020 7790 5101, *Call Date: Feb 1991, Lincoln's Inn*
Qualifications: [LLB (Bucks)]

HUNTER MR PETER MICHAEL

Kaim Todner Ltd, 11 Bolt Court, London, EC4A 3DQ, ☎020 7353 6660
Fax: 020 7353 6661, ✉solicitors@kaimtodner.com, *Call Date: July 2000, Lincoln's Inn*
Qualifications: [LLB (Hons)]

HUNTER MR WILLIAM EDWARD HENRY

Crown Advocate, Crown Prosecution Service, Froomsgate House, Rupert Street, Bristol, BS1 2QJ, ☎0117 9302800, *Call Date: July 1982, Gray's Inn*
Qualifications: [BA (Hons)]

HURRELL MRS NICOLA HILDA

Oxfordshire County Council, County Hall, New Road, Oxford, OX1 1ND, ☎01865 792422 Fax: 01865 726155, *Call Date: Oct 1998, Middle Temple*
Qualifications: [LLB (Hons)(Oxon)]

F

HURTLEY MISS DIANE ELAINE

Other, HM Crown Prosecution Service Inspectorate, Crown Prosecution Service, United House, Piccadilly, York, YO1 9PQ, ☎01904 545 498, ✉diane.hurtley@cps.gsi.gov.uk, *Call Date: Oct 1990, Gray's Inn*
Qualifications: [LLB]

HUSAIN MR MAQBOOL ASKER

HED, Crown Prosecution Service, Special Crime Division, Rose Court, 2 Southwark Bridge, London, SE1 9HS, ☎020 33570019, ✉asker.husain@cps.gsi.gov.uk, *Call Date: Nov 1985, Lincoln's Inn*
Qualifications: [BA (Hons)]

HUSSAIN MR IMRAN

Altaf Solicitors, Lincoln Chambers, 227 Manningham Lane, Bradford, BD8 7HH, ☎01274 400405 Fax: 01274 400342, ✉Imran@altafsolicitors.co.uk, *Call Date: Mar 2003, Lincoln's Inn*
Qualifications: [LLB (Hons)]

HUTCHINSON MR ROBERT IAN

Crown Prosecution Service, Blackfriars Crown Court, Pocock Street, London, SE1 0BJ, *Call Date: July 2006, Middle Temple*
Qualifications: [BA (Hons) (Cantab)]

HYAMS MR DAVID IAN

easyjet Airline Company Limited, Hanger 89, London Luton Airport,, Luton, Bedfordshire, LU2 9PF, *Call Date: July 1981, Middle Temple*
Qualifications: [LLB (Lond)]

HYDE MISS KATRINA

Royal Courts of Justice, Criminal Appeal Office, Room C327, The Strand, London, WC2A 2LL, Fax: 020 7947 6345, *Call Date: Nov 2003, Middle Temple*
Qualifications: [LLB (Hons) (Dublin)]

HYDER MR STUART HENRY

Senior Counsel, Chevron (Uk Ltd), 9 Cavendish Square, London, W1G 9DF, ☎0560 109 1538, *Call Date: July 1974, Lincoln's Inn*
Qualifications: [MA (Cantab) MBA]

HYPOLITE MR MARK STEPHEN

Canon Europe Limited, 6 Roundwood Avenue, Stockley Park, Uxbridge, UB11 1JA, ☎020 8588 8000 Fax: 020 8588 8001, *Call Date: Nov 2002, Lincoln's Inn*
Qualifications: [BA (Hons)(Cantab)]

IDAN MR LIONEL

Crown Prosecution Service, Rose Court, 2 Southwark Bridge, London, SE1 9HS, ☎020 7147 7905, ✉Lionel.Idan@cps.gsi.gov.uk, *Call Date: Mar 1996, Middle Temple*
Qualifications: [LLB (Hons)]

IDRIS MISS KEMI RASHIDA

Department For Work and Pensions, Office of the Solicitor/Dh Legal Service, The Adelphi, 1-11 John Adam Street, London, WC2N 6HT, ☎020 7962 8924, *Call Date: Feb 1995, Lincoln's Inn*
Qualifications: [LLB (Hons)(Bris) LLM (London)]

IHUOMAH MISS BIBIANA CHIWUBA

Needham Poulier and Partners Solicitors, 599 High Road, London, N17 6EW, ☎020 8808 6622 Fax: 020 8808 3311, *Call Date: Nov 1986, Lincoln's Inn*
Qualifications: [LLB(Hons)]

ILES MR ADRIAN

Deputy District Judge, The Archbishops' Council., National Institutions of the Church Of England, Church House, Great Smith Street, London, SW1P 3AZ, ☎020 7898 1000, *Call Date: July 1980, Inner Temple*
Qualifications: [MA (Cantab)]

IMAN MISS SAFIA RASHID

General Pharmaceutical Council, 129 Lambeth Road, London, SE1 7BT, ☎020 3365 3478, ✉Safia.Iman@pharmacyregulation.org, *Call Date: July 2006, Gray's Inn*
Qualifications: [BSc (Manch)]

INCLEDON MRS CLAIRE FRANCES

Pembrokeshire County Council, County Hall, Haverfordwest, Pembrokeshire, SA61 1TP, ☎01437 775781 Fax: 01437 776476, ✉claire.incledon@pembrokeshire.gov.uk, *Call Date: Nov 1990, Inner Temple*
Qualifications: [LLB]

F

INGHAM MR RICHARD LEE

Crown Prosecution Service, Inner London Crown Court, Session House, Newington Causeway, London, SE1 6AZ, ☎020 357 9529 Fax: 020 7403 4548, ✉lee.ingham@cps.gsi.gov.uk, *Call Date: Nov 1994, Lincoln's Inn*
Qualifications: [LLB (Hons)(B'ham)]

INGLESE MR ANTHONY MICHAEL CHRISTOPHER

Bencher, General Counsel, Solicitor, HM Revenue and Customs, Room 2/40, 100 Parliament Street, London, SW1A 2BQ, ☎020 7147 2720, ✉anthony.inglese@hmrc.gsi.gov.uk, *Call Date: Nov 1976, Gray's Inn*
Qualifications: [MA LLB]

INWARD MS LOUISE JANE

Pension Corporation LLP, Pension Corporation, 14 Cornhill, London, EC3V 3ND, ☎020 7105 2035 Fax: 020 7105 2001, ✉inward@pensioncorporation.com, *Call Date: Nov 1995, Middle Temple*
Qualifications: [LLB (Hons)]

IP PIANG SIONG MR DANIEL JAMES

Crown Prosecution Service, Sceptre House, 7-9 Castle Street, Luton, Bedfordshire, LH1 3AJ, ✉Daniel.IpPiangSiong@cps.gsi.gov.uk, *Call Date: Nov 2002, Middle Temple*
Qualifications: [LLB (Hons)]

IQBAL MR ARIF SULTAN

Other, Solicitor, Cartwright King Solicitors, 14 Floor, Mclaren Building, 46 The Priory Queensway, Birmingham, B4 7LR, ☎0121 262 3803 Fax: 0808 168 1500, ✉arif.iqbal@cartwrightking.co.uk, *Call Date: Oct 2003, Gray's Inn*
Qualifications: [LLB (Wolv)]

IQBAL MR ZAFAR

Advocate, Director, Clyde & Co LLP, The St Botolph Building, 138 Houndsditch, London, EC3A 7AR, ☎020 7876 4426 Fax: 020 7876 5111, ✉zafar.iqbal@clydeco.com, *Call Date: Oct 1999, Middle Temple*
Qualifications: [MBA]

IRELAND MISS TERESA ANITA

Legal Adviser, National Farmer's Union, Agriculture House, Stoneleigh Park, Warwickshire, CV8 2TZ, Fax: 01567 824651, ✉teresa.ireland@nfu.org.uk, *Call Date: July 2003, Gray's Inn*
Qualifications: [BSc]

IRVINE AIR VICE MARSHAL LINDSAY JOHN

Director of Legal Services, Directorate of Legal Services (Raf), Rm 42a, Lancaster Building, Hq Air Command, Raf High Wycombe, Buckinghamshire, HP14 4UE, *Call Date: July 1983, Middle Temple*
Qualifications: [MA (Oxon) MA (Lond) FRAeS Dip Law RAF]

IRWIN MISS LORRAINE SUSAN

Higher Court Advocate, Lecturer in Law, Crown Prosecution Service, The Cooperage, 8 Gainsford Street, London, SE1 2NE, ✉Lorraine.Irwin@cps.gsi.gov.uk, *Call Date: Nov 1988, Lincoln's Inn*
Qualifications: [BA (Hons) (Kent)]

ISAACS MISS DEBORAH JANE

Call Date: Nov 1987, Lincoln's Inn
Qualifications: [MA (Oxon) Dip Law]

ISAACS MR STUART LINDSAY

Deputy High Court Judge, Recorder, Berwin Leighton Paisner, Adelaide House, London Bridge, London, EC4R 9HA, Fax: 020 3400 1111, ✉stuart.isaacsQC@blplaw.com, *Call Date: July 1975, Lincoln's Inn*
Qualifications: [MA (Cantab) Lic spec en droit eur (Belguim)]

ISGAR MR SIMON PETER DENIS

Legal Counsel, 162 Howlands Court, Commonwealth Drive, Crawley, West Sussex, RH10 1AW, *Call Date: Oct 1998, Gray's Inn*
Qualifications: [LLB (Herts)]

ISHERWOOD MR MALCOLM OLIVER

Principal Crown Prosecutor, Crown Prosecution Service, The Unicentre, Lords Walk, Preston, Lancashire, PR1 1DH, ☎01253 743 800 / 01772 208122 Fax: 01253 743843, ✉malcolm.isherwood@cps.gsi.gov.uk, *Call Date: Nov 1980, Gray's Inn*
Qualifications: [BA]

F

ISLAM MISS FAHMINA SHILPI

Crown Prosecution Service, Gateway, 31 Power Close, Guildford, Surrey, GU1 1EJ, ☎01483 468200, ✉Fahmina.Islam@cps.gsi.gov.uk, *Call Date: Nov 2005, Inner Temple*
Qualifications: [LLB (Hons)]

ISLAM MS RAHENA

Crown Prosecution Service, 8th Floor, Holborn Police Station, P.O. Box 36822, 10 Lambs Conduit Street, Islington, London, WC1N 3NR, ✉Rahena.Choudhury@cps.gsi.gov.uk, *Call Date: July 2001, Inner Temple*
Qualifications: [LLB Hons (Kingston)]

ISLAM MR ZAGLUL

Senior Legal Officer, Financial Services Authority, General Counsel's Division, 25 The North Colonnade, Canary Wharf, London, E14 5HS, *Call Date: Nov 1995, Lincoln's Inn*
Qualifications: [BSc (Hons) (Wales) Dip Law (Lond)]

ISLES MISS MARY PATRICIA THERESA

Lawyer, London Borough of Bromley, Civic Centre, Stockwell Close, Bromley, Kent, BR1 3UH, ✉mary.isles@bromley.gov.uk, *Call Date: Nov 1984, Inner Temple*
Qualifications: [BSc BA]

ISMAIL MISS BILKIS

Associate, Sj Berwin LLP, 10 Queen Street Place, London, EC4R 1BE, ☎020 7111 2913 Fax: 020 7111 2000, ✉bill.ismail@sjberwin.com, *Call Date: Oct 1998, Lincoln's Inn*
Qualifications: [LLB (Hons) LLM CTA]

IVORY MR MARTIN

Crown Prosecution Service, Carmelite House, St James Court, Whitefriars, Norwich, Norfolk, NR3 1SL, ☎01603 693000 / 01603 693 035, ✉martin.ivory@cps.gsi.gov.uk, *Call Date: Oct 1996, Gray's Inn*
Qualifications: [LLB (Lond)]

IYER MISS KATHRYN ANN

Crown Advocate, Crown Prosecution Service, Holborn Police Station, 10 Lamb's Conduit Street, Islington, London, WC1N 3NR, ☎020 7061 3600 Fax: 020 7061 3905, ✉Kathryn.Iyer@cps.gsi.gov.uk, *Call Date: Oct 2000, Middle Temple*
Qualifications: [LLB (Hons) (Dunelm)]

JACK MR ANDREW MICHAEL

The Treasury Solicitors, One Kemble Street, London, WC2B 4TS, *Call Date: Oct 1997, Middle Temple*
Qualifications: [BA (Hons)(Lond) BPhil DPhil (Oxon) CPE (Lond)]

JACKSON MR ANDREW RICHARD

Crown Prosecution Service, County House, 100 New London Road, Chelmsford, Essex, CM2 0RG, *Call Date: July 1987, Gray's Inn*
Qualifications: [LLB (Warw)]

JACKSON MR ANTHONY WARREN

International Criminal Court, Maanweg 174, 2516 AB, The Hague, Netherlands, ✉anthony.jackson@icc-cpi.int, *Call Date: Oct 1995, Inner Temple*
Qualifications: [MA (Cantab) M.Phil (Cantab) LLM]

JACKSON MRS GILLIAN WENDY

The Treasury Solicitors, 3rd Floor, Ergon House, Horseferry Road, London, SW1P 2AL, *Call Date: July 2004, Gray's Inn*
Qualifications: [BA (Cantab)]

JACKSON MR LEE ANTONY

Gherson Solicitors, 1 Great Cumberland Place, London, W1H 7AL, ☎020 7724 4488 Fax: 020 7724 4888, ✉lee@gherson.com, *Call Date: Oct 1995, Lincoln's Inn*
Qualifications: [LLB (Hons)(Lond) LLM]

JACKSON MISS VENETIA LOIS HEATHER

The Treasury Solicitors, One Kemble Street, London, WC2B 4TS, ☎020 7210 4521 Fax: 020 7210 3288 / 020 7210 3132, ✉venetia.jackson@tsol.gsi.gov.uk, *Call Date: Nov 2001, Lincoln's Inn*
Qualifications: [BA (Hons)]

JACOBS MISS SUSAN JANE

District Crown Prosecutor, Prosecutor, The Treasury Solicitors, Dept. For Environment, Food and Rural Affairs, Legal Services, Nobel House, 17 Smith Square, London, SW1P 3JR, ✉sue.jacobs@defra.gsi.gov.uk, *Call Date: Nov 1988, Gray's Inn*
Qualifications: [BA (Hons)]

F

JAGESSAR MR SONIL JAY

Punatar and Co Solicitors, 152-156 Kentish Town Road, London, NWQ 9QB, ☎020 7485 6677 Fax: 020 7485 6611, ✉lawyers@puntar.biz, *Call Date: Oct 2006, Gray's Inn*
Qualifications: [LLB]

JAGGAR MR THOMAS HATRICK

HM Revenue and Customs, 1st Floor, South West Bush House, London, WC2B 4RD, ☎020 7438 7058, ✉thomas.jaggar@hmrc.gsi.gov.uk, tom.jaggar@gmail.com, *Call Date: Mar 2007, Lincoln's Inn*
Qualifications: [LLB (Lond)]

JAKHURA MR RIAZ

Crown Prosecution Service, Acton Police Station, 250 Acton High Street, London, W3 9BH, *Call Date: Nov 2000, Lincoln's Inn*
Qualifications: [LLB (Hons)]

JAKYMEC MS JOANNE

Crown Prosecution Service, Rose Court, 2 Southwark Bridge, London, SE1 9HS, ☎020 3357 0000, ✉joanne.jakymec@cps.gsi.gov.uk, *Call Date: July 1998, Lincoln's Inn*
Qualifications: [BSc (Hons) Dip Law]

JAMES MR ANDREW JOHN

Company Secretary, Legal Counsel, Jacobs Process Limited, One Port Way, Port Solent, Portsmouth, PO6 4TZ, *Call Date: July 1983, Gray's Inn*
Qualifications: [BA]

JAMES MR ARNOLD VICTOR

Upper Tribunal Appeal Chamber, 5th Floor Rolls Buildings, 7 Rolls Buildings, Fetter Lane, London, EC4A 1NL, *Call Date: Nov 1991, Inner Temple*
Qualifications: [BSc Dip Law]

JAMES MR RODERICK MORRICE

Rowe Sparkes Partnership, First Floor, The Old Treasury, 7 Kings Road, Southsea, PO5 4DJ, ✉rjames@rowe-sparkes.co.uk, *Call Date: July 1979, Gray's Inn*
Qualifications: [BA (Cantab)]

JAMESON COMMODORE ANDREW CHARLES

Royal Navy Officers, 4th Floor, Leach Building, Whale Island, Portsmouth, Hampshire, PO2 8DY, ✉andrew.jameson903@mod.uk, *Call Date: Oct 1993, Middle Temple*
Qualifications: [LLB (Hons)(Newc)]

JAMES-STADDEN MISS JODIE CARA

Hadaway and Hadaway Solicitors, Midland Chambers, 58 Howard Street, North Shields, Tyne & Wear, NE30 1AL, ☎0191 257 0382 Fax: 0191 296 1904, ✉jodiejs@hadaway.co.uk, *Call Date: Oct 1996, Gray's Inn*
Qualifications: [LLB (Hons) (Bris)]

JAMIESON MR ANDREW

Director, Legal Adviser, I.T.I.M. Ltd, 90 Fenchurch Street, London, EC3M 4ST, *Call Date: July 1985, Middle Temple*
Qualifications: [BA (Lond) Dip Law]

JAMIESON-HESK MRS DEBRA AUDREY

Legal Adviser, Portsmouth City Council, Legal Services, Civic Offices, Guidhall Walk, Portsmouth, Hampshire, PO1 2PX, ☎023 9284 1108 Fax: 023 9283 4076, ✉Debra.Jamieson-Hesk@portsmouthcc.gov.uk, *Call Date: Nov 1996, Inner Temple*
Qualifications: [LLB (So'ton)]

JAMIL MISS AISHA

HKH Kenwright and Cox Solicitor's, 202 High Road, Ilford, Essex, IG1 1QB, *Call Date: Nov 1995, Lincoln's Inn*
Qualifications: [LLB (Hons)]

JANSARI MR NEERAJ

Commerzbank AG, 30 Gresham Street, London, EC2V 7PG, *Call Date: Oct 2001, Gray's Inn*
Qualifications: [LLB BSc]

JANUSZ MRS FRANCES MIRIAM

Principal Crown Prosecutor, Crown Prosecution Service, United House, Piccadilly, York, North Yorkshire, YO1 9PQ, ✉frances.janusz@cps.gsi.gov.uk, *Call Date: July 1979, Lincoln's Inn*
Qualifications: [BA (Reading)]

F

JARDINE DR FRANCIS STEPHEN JOHN

Legal Adviser, Morgan Stanley & Co International PLC, 20 Bank Street, Canary Wharf, London, E14 4AD, *Call Date: July 1996, Gray's Inn*
Qualifications: [BSc LLB C Eng FCCA MIMgt ACIS MIM LLM (Lond) DPhil (Sussex)]

JARZABKOWSKI MISS JULIA MARIE ANTIONETTE

Law Commission, Steel House, 11 Tothill Street, London, SW1H 9LJ, *Call Date: Oct 1993, Middle Temple*
Qualifications: [BA (Hons)(Cantab) MA (Cantab)]

JAYANATHAN MS SHAMINI

Crown Prosecution Service, Greenwich Police Station, 31 Royal Hill, Greenwich, London, SE10 8RR, *Call Date: Nov 1996, Lincoln's Inn*
Qualifications: [LLB (Hons)(Wales)]

JEFFERY MRS ELISABETH

Crown Prosecution Service, Sunlight House, Quay Street, Manchester, M60 3PS, ☎0161 827 4700 / 0161 827 4819 Fax: 0161 827 4941, ✉Liz.Jeffery@cps.gsi.gov.uk, *Call Date: Oct 1990, Middle Temple*
Qualifications: [LLB (Nott'm)(Hons)]

JEMPSON MISS VICTORIA

New Walk Chambers, 27 New Walk, Leicester, Leicestershire, LE1 6TE, *Call Date: July 2008, Middle Temple*
Qualifications: [LLB (Hons)]

JENKING-REES MR MARK

Senior Principal Legal Officer, Department For Work and Pensions, Department of Social Security, 5th Floor, the Adelphi, 1-11 John Adam Street, London, EC2N 6HT, *Call Date: May 1987, Lincoln's Inn*
Qualifications: [LLB]

JENKINS MISS ELIZABETH

Crown Prosecution Service, Sunlight House, Quay Street, Manchester, M60 3PS, ☎0161 827 4780 Fax: 0161 827 4824, ✉elizabeth.jenkins@cps.gsi.gov.uk, *Call Date: Oct 1995, Lincoln's Inn*
Qualifications: [LLB (Hons)(Newc)]

JENKINS MISS GLYNYS CERI

HM Revenue and Customs, Bush House, Strand, London, WC2B 4RD, ☎020 7438 7285, *Call Date: July 1974, Gray's Inn*
Qualifications: [LLB]

JENKINS MR PAUL CHRISTOPHER

Head of Legal Services, The Treasury Solicitors, One Kemble Street, London, WC2B 4TS, *Call Date: July 1977, Middle Temple*
Qualifications: [LLB]

JENNINGS MRS CAROLINE PATRICIA

Assistant, Deputy Justices' Clerk, Northampton Magistrates' Court, Regents Pavillion, Summerhouse Road, Moulton Park, Northampton, Northamptonshire, NN3 1AS, ☎01604 497036 Fax: 01604 497010, ✉caroline.jennings@hmcourts-service.gsi.gov.uk, *Call Date: July 1989, Middle Temple*
Qualifications: [Dip Law Dip Mag Law Dip Management Stud]

JENNINGS MR MICHAEL STUART

Crown Advocate, The Treasury Solicitors, Attorney General's Office, 20 Victoria Street, London, SW1H 0NF, ✉Michael.Jennings@attorneygeneral.gsi.gov.uk, *Call Date: Oct 1994, Gray's Inn*
Qualifications: [BA]

JENNINGS MS SALLY JANE

Novartis Vaccines and Diagnostics Inc, 350 Massachusetts Avenue, Cambridge, Ma 02139, USA, ☎001 617 871 8054 Fax: 001 617 417 1791, ✉sally.jennings@novartis.com, *Call Date: Oct 1991, Middle Temple*
Qualifications: [BA (Hons) DipLaw LLM (Lond)]

JEREMIAH MISS ELISE KIT-MARIE

2 Dr Johnson's Buildings, 2 Dr Johnson's Buildings, Temple, London, EC4Y 7AY, ☎020 7936 2613 / 0845 621 8800 Fax: 020 7353 9439, *Call Date: Nov 1999, Middle Temple*
Qualifications: [LLB (Hons)(Kingston)]

F

JEWELL MR TIMOTHY KESTER

Ministry of Justice, Legal Directorate, Post Point 6.38, 102 Petty France, London, SW1H 9AJ, ☎020 3334 4761 Fax: 020 3334 4035, ✉tim.jewell@justice.gsi.gov.uk, *Call Date: July 2000, Lincoln's Inn*
Qualifications: [LLB(Hons) MPhil (Leic)]

JEYES MR CHRISTOPHER BRYAN

Bird and Co Solicitors, 38 Kirkgate, Newark, Nottinghamshire, NG24 1AB, ☎01636 650880, ✉cjeyes@birdandco.co.uk, *Call Date: July 2005, Gray's Inn*
Qualifications: [B.Sc Brunel]

JHANGIANI MS SAPNA

Clyde & Co LLP, 3 Anson Road, #21-01 Sprigleaf Tower, 79909, Singapore, ✉sapnajethani@hotmail.com, Sapna. Jhangiani@clasisllc.com, *Call Date: Oct 1999, Lincoln's Inn*
Qualifications: [MA (Hons) Dip Law]

JOAD MISS NICOLA WARD

Senior Principal Legal Officer, HM Revenue and Customs, 100 Parliament Street, London, SW1A 2BQ, ☎020 7147 3402, ✉n_w_turner@hotmail.com, *Call Date: Nov 1983, Middle Temple*
Qualifications: [LLB (Lond)]

JOBES MRS JHARNA

Crown Prosecution Service, Citadel House, 58 High Street, Hull, Humberside, HU1 1QD, ☎01482 621035 Fax: 01482 621072, ✉Jharna.Jobes@cps.gsi.gov.uk, *Call Date: July 1982, Middle Temple*
Qualifications: [BA]

JOHAL MR INDERJIT SINGH

Solicitors Regulation Authority, Ipsley Court, Berrington Close, Redditch, Worcestershire, B98 0TD, *Call Date: Oct 1998, Inner Temple*
Qualifications: [LLB (Leic)]

JOHN-CHARLES MR LEE

CVS, HED, Lawyer, The Treasury Solicitors, 5th Floor, One Kemble Street, London, WC2B 4TS, ✉lee.john-charles@tsol.gsi.gov.uk, *Call Date: Nov 1985, Lincoln's Inn*
Qualifications: [LLB (Hons)]

JOHNSON MS BUSOLA

Crown Prosecution Service, Inner London Crown Court, Session House, Newington Causeway, London, SE1 6AZ, ✉busola. johnson@cps.gsi.gov.uk, *Call Date: Nov 1998, Inner Temple*
Qualifications: [BA (Lond) BA (Cantab) MA (Cantab)]

JOHNSON MR DAVID ANTHONY

Taylor Wessing LLP, 5 New Street Square, London, EC4A 3TW, ☎020 7300 7000 Fax: 020 7300 7100, *Call Date: July 2005, Lincoln's Inn*
Qualifications: [LLB (Hons) LLM]

JOHNSON MRS JANICE COSIE

Henscott Solicitors, 413 Chingford Road, Walthamstow, London, E17 5AF, *Call Date: Nov 1994, Inner Temple*
Qualifications: [LLB (UEA)]

JOHNSON MISS LOUISE ANNE

Crown Prosecution Service, Eaton Court, 112 Oxford Road, Reading, Berkshire, RG1 7LL, ☎0118 951 3600 / 0118 951 3600 Fax: 0118 951 3666 / 0118 951 3666, *Call Date: Nov 2002, Middle Temple*
Qualifications: [LLB (Hons)]

JOHNSON MR MATTHEW STUART

The Football Association, Wembley Stadium, Wembley, London, HA9 0WS, ☎020 8980 8200 Fax: 020 8980 5779, ✉matthew.johnson@thefa.com, *Call Date: Oct 1995, Lincoln's Inn*
Qualifications: [LLB (Hons)(Leic)]

JOHNSON MS SOPHIE LOUISE

Phone Pay Plus, Clove Building, 4 Maguire Street, London, SE1 2NQ, ✉sjohnson@ phonepayplus.org.uk, *Call Date: July 2008, Gray's Inn*
Qualifications: [LLB (Bris)]

JOHNSTON MR JAMES KENNEDY

The Treasury Solicitors, One Kemble Street, London, WC2B 4TS, *Call Date: July 2007, Middle Temple*
Qualifications: [BA (Oxon)]

F

JOHNSTON MS KAREN ANN

Pensions Regulator, Napier House, Trafalgar Place, Brighton, BN1 4DW, *Call Date: Nov 1994, Inner Temple*
Qualifications: [MA (Oxon) CPE (Lond)]

JOHNSTON MR PAUL CHARLES

Call Date: Nov 1998, Middle Temple
Qualifications: [BSc MRICS MCIArb Chartered Surveyor]

JOHNSTONE MR ANDREW MARK ST GEORGE

Holman Fenwick Willan LLP, Friary Court, 65 Crutched Friars, London, EC3N 2AE, ☎020 7264 8000 Fax: 020 7264 8888, ✉andrewmark.johnstone@hfw.com, *Call Date: July 2004, Lincoln's Inn*
Qualifications: [BA Hons (Dunelm)]

JONES MR BRIAN EDWARD

Rose and Dunn, 58 High Street, Runcorn, Cheshire, WA7 1AW, ☎01928 572030 Fax: 0870 4954 998, ✉info@rosedunn.com, *Call Date: Oct 1994, Middle Temple*
Qualifications: [LLB (Hons)]

JONES MS CATRIN HELEN

The Treasury Solicitors, Department For Culture, Media and Sport, 2-4 Cockspur Street, London, SW1Y 5DH, ☎020 7211 2278, *Call Date: Nov 1994, Lincoln's Inn*
Qualifications: [LLB (Hons)(Lancs)]

JONES MISS CHERYL LOUISE

Crown Advocate, Crown Prosecution Service, The Cooperage, 8 Gainsford Street, London, SE1 2NE, ☎020 7378 4100 Fax: 020 3300 4862, *Call Date: Oct 2001, Lincoln's Inn*
Qualifications: [MA (Hons)(Cantab)]

JONES MR DANIEL

London Borough of Hackney, Hackney Town Hall, Mare Street, London, E8 1EA, *Call Date: Oct 1997, Lincoln's Inn*

JONES MR DANIEL OSKAR

Artesian Law, 3 Bolt Court, Fleet Street, London, EC4A 3DQ, ✉daniel.jones@artesianlaw.com, *Call Date: Oct 1994, Gray's Inn*
Qualifications: [BA (Hons) CPE]

JONES MR DANIEL OWEN MALCOLM

General Counsel, Westcon Group European Operations Ltd, Chandler's House, Wilkinson Road, Cirencester, Gloucestershire, GL7 1YT, ☎07920 272274 Fax: 01753 797801, ✉daniel.jones@westcon.com, *Call Date: Nov 1995, Middle Temple*
Qualifications: [BA (Hons) LLM]

JONES MISS ELIZABETH JEAN

Call Date: July 2001, Gray's Inn
Qualifications: [LLB]

JONES MR JAMES WILLIAM

Legal Counsel, E.On Uk PLC, Westwood Way, Westwood Business Park, Coventry, CV4 8LG, ☎024 7642 4000 Fax: 024 7642 5248, ✉james.jones@pgen.com, james.jones@eon-uk.com, *Call Date: Feb 1989, Middle Temple*
Qualifications: [LLB]

JONES MISS JENNIFER CLAIRE

Judge, Harrison Clark, 5 Deansway, Worcester, WR1 2JG, ☎01905 746470, ✉jjones@harrison-clark.co.uk, *Call Date: Oct 1991, Lincoln's Inn*
Qualifications: [LLB (Hons) (B'ham)]

JONES MR JOHN NICHOLAS

Commissioner, Traffic Commissioner, Traffic Area Office, 38 George Road, Edgbaston, Birmingham, B15 1PL, ☎01432 272182, *Call Date: July 1977, Gray's Inn*
Qualifications: [LLB MCIPD MA FCILT]

JONES MR JONATHAN GUY

Solicitor, The Treasury Solicitors, 5th Floor, One Kemble Street, London, WC2B 4TS, *Call Date: July 1985, Middle Temple*
Qualifications: [BA (Durham)]

JONES MS KATHRINE MARGARET

Legal Adviser, Leeds City Council, Civic Hall, Calverley Street, Leeds, LS1 1UR, ☎0113 247 4760 Fax: 0113 247 4729, ✉KATHERINE.JONES@LEEDS.GOV.UK, *Call Date: Nov 1995, Gray's Inn*
Qualifications: [BA (Hons)]

F

JONES MISS KATHRYN ANNE

Crown Prosecution Service, Princess House, Princess Way, Swansea, South Wales, SA1 3LY, *Call Date: July 1992, Middle Temple*
Qualifications: [LLB (Hons)]

JONES MISS KRISTIN FRANCESCA DEIRDRE

Lawyer, The Treasury Solicitors, Attorney General's Office, 20 Victoria Street, London, SW1H 0NF, ☎020 7271 2416 Fax: 020 7271 2453, ✉Kristin.Jones@attorneygeneral.gsi.gov.uk, *Call Date: July 1984, Inner Temple*
Qualifications: [LLB (Nottm)]

JONES MISS LESLEY ANN

Advocate, Crown Prosecution Service, Southwark Crown Court, 1 English Grounds, London, SE1 2HU, Fax: 020 7522 7216, ✉Lesley.Jones@cps.gsi.gov.uk, *Call Date: Oct 1995, Inner Temple*
Qualifications: [LLB (Lond) (Hons)]

JONES MR MARC ROBERT

Royal Navy Officers, Directorate of Naval Legal Services, Mp 4-2, Leach Building, Whale Island, Portsmouth, PO2 8BY, ☎02392 625739, *Call Date: July 2004, Middle Temple*
Qualifications: [LLB Hons (Northumbria)]

JONES MR MICHAEL SELWYN TUDOR

Crown Prosecution Service, Capital Tower, Greyfriars Road, Cardiff, CF10 3PL, ☎029 208 03913, ✉mike.jones@cps.gsi.gov.uk, *Call Date: July 1995, Middle Temple*
Qualifications: [BA (Hons)]

JONES BRIGADIER NEIL JAMES HENRY

Directorate of Army Legal Services, Director Legal Advisory, Idl 426, Ramillies Building, Marlborough Lines, Monxton Road, Andover, SP11 8HJ, ☎01264 383082, *Call Date: Nov 1978, Gray's Inn*
Qualifications: [LLB (Newc)]

JONES MRS RHIANYDD

Crown Prosecution Service, Vantage Point, Ty Coch Way, Cwmbian, Gwent, NP44 7XX, ✉rhian.jones@cps.gsi.gov.uk, *Call Date: Oct 2001, Middle Temple*
Qualifications: [LLB (Hons)]

JONES MR RODERICK JAMES WATSON

Partner, Wainwright and Cummins Solicitors, 413a Brixton Road, London, SW9 7DG, ☎020 7737 9330 Fax: 020 7737 9331, ✉rod.jones@wainwrightcummins.co.uk, *Call Date: July 1983, Gray's Inn*
Qualifications: [BA]

JONES MRS SIAN ELIZABETH

Justices' Clerk, Teesside Law Courts, Victoria Square, Middlesbrough, TS1 2AS, ☎01642 261 611 Fax: 01642 224 010, ✉sian.jones1@hmcourts-service.gsi.gov.uk, *Call Date: July 1981, Lincoln's Inn*
Qualifications: [LLB (Hons) CTP DMS]

JONES MR SIMON DAVID

Principal Lawyer, London Borough of Hounslow, Civic Centre, Lampton Road, Hounslow, London, TW3 4DN, ✉simon.jones@hounslow.gov.uk, *Call Date: Nov 1985, Gray's Inn*
Qualifications: [LLB (Sheff)]

JONES MR STEVEN ALAN VAUGHAN

IBM United Kingdom Limited, IMB South Bank, Law Department, 76 Upper Ground, London, SE1 9PZ, ☎020 7202 3387 Fax: 020 7202 5935, ✉jones12@uk.ibm.com, *Call Date: Nov 1984, Lincoln's Inn*
Qualifications: [BA (Cantab)]

JONES MRS VANESSA

Company Secretary, Legal Adviser, Corporate Legal Solutions Limited, Norbryght Lodge, Tilburstow Hill Road, South Godstone, Surrey, RH9 8NA, *Call Date: Nov 1984, Gray's Inn*
Qualifications: [LLB (Hons) ACSA]

JORDAN MISS EMMA

Lawrence Graham LLP, 4 More London Riverside, London, SE1 2AU, ☎020 7759 6442 Fax: 020 7173 8442, ✉emma.jordan@lg-legal.com, *Call Date: Oct 2001, Lincoln's Inn*
Qualifications: [BA (Hons)(Oxon)]

JORGENSEN DR NINA HELENE BORLASE

Other, The Chinese University of Hong Kong, Faculty of Law, Room 618, 6/F, Lee Shau Kee Building, Sha Tin, Nt, Hong Kong Sar, Hong Kong, *Call Date: Oct 1999, Gray's Inn*
Qualifications: [LLB (Bristol) DPhil]

F

JOSEPH MRS CAROL SANDRA

London Borough of Hammersmith and Fulham, Hammersmith Town Hall, King Street, London, W6 9JU, ☎020 8753 2713 Fax: 020 8753 2777, ✉carol.joseph@lbhf.gov.uk, *Call Date: Nov 1983, Lincoln's Inn*
Qualifications: [BA (Lond)]

JOSHUA MR JULIAN MATHIC

Partner, Shearman & Sterling LLP, 56 Avenue Des Arts, Brussels, B1000, Belgium, Fax: 2 500 9801, *Call Date: Nov 1969, Middle Temple*
Qualifications: [MA (Cantab)]

JOSHUA MS SUSAN MARY

Director, John Wiley and Sons Ltd, The Atrium, Southern Gate, Chichester, Sussex, PO19 8SQ, ✉sjoshua@wiley.com, *Call Date: May 1993, Gray's Inn*
Qualifications: [MA]

JOSLIN MRS ELIZABETH ANNE

District Crown Prosecutor, Crown Prosecution Service, Rose Court, 2 Southwark Bridge, London, SE1 9HS, *Call Date: July 1984, Lincoln's Inn*
Qualifications: [LLB (Hons) (Lond) AKC]

JOUHAL MR SUKHRAJ

Company Secretary, General Counsel, Toyota Financial Services (Uk) PLC, Great Burgh, Burgh Heath, Epsom, Surrey, KT18 5UZ, ☎01737 365560 Fax: 01737 365567, *Call Date: Nov 1996, Inner Temple*
Qualifications: [LLB (Hons) (Lond)]

JOY MR MICHAEL TENNENT

Bladeroom Group Ltd, Stella Way, Bishops Cleeve, Cheltenham, Gloucestershire, Fax: 01242 663088, ✉mjoy@bladeroom.com, *Call Date: Nov 1997, Middle Temple*
Qualifications: [M.Chem (Oxon)]

F

JOYCE MR MARCUS

United Nations, Administrative Law Section, 9th Floor, 380 Madison Avenue, New York, USA, *Call Date: Oct 2005, Lincoln's Inn*
Qualifications: [BA (Hons) MA (Dub) CPE BVC]

JUDGE MS SOPHIE TALLULAH

HED, Crown Prosecution Service, United House, Piccadilly, York, North Yorkshire, YO1 1PQ, ☎020 8540 6085 Fax: 020 8540 6563, ✉sophie.judge@cps.gsi.gov.uk, *Call Date: Nov 1990, Inner Temple*
Qualifications: [LLB]

JUPP MR JEFFREY ERNEST

Seven Bedford Row, 7 Bedford Row, London, WC1R 4BS, ☎020 7242 3555 Fax: 020 7242 2511, ✉jjupp@7br.co.uk, *Call Date: Nov 1994, Inner Temple*
Qualifications: [BA CPE]

KALE MR SAMUEL MEANO

Legal Director, Royal Bank of Scotland Group, Bank of Scotland, Corporate Banking Legal Operations, Po Box 39900, Level 7, 155 Bishopsgate, London, EC2M 3YB, ☎020 7806 1698 Fax: 020 7012 9437, ✉samuel.kale@lloydsbanking.com, *Call Date: July 1987, Lincoln's Inn*
Qualifications: [LLB (L'pool) MA]

KAPUR MR DEEPAK KUMAR

Crown Prosecution Service, Priory Gate, 29 Union Street, Maidstone, Kent, ME14 1PT, *Call Date: July 1984, Lincoln's Inn*
Qualifications: [BA (Hons)]

KARAA MS RADHIA

Office of Fair Trading, Fleetbank House, 2-6 Salisbury Square, London, EC4Y 8JX, ☎020 7211 5869, ✉radhia.karaa@oft.gsi.gov.uk, *Call Date: Nov 1995, Inner Temple*
Qualifications: [BA (Wales) CPE (Wales)]

KARAN-APPUKUTTEN MR SHUBA

Borough Crown Prosecutor, Crown Prosecution Service, Rose Court, 2 Southwark Bridge, London, SE1 9HS, ✉shuba.karan@cps.gsi.gov.uk, *Call Date: Feb 1991, Lincoln's Inn*
Qualifications: [LLB (Warw)]

KARPINSKI MR JAN

Head of Legal Services, Bank of Ireland, Po Box 27, Broad Quay, Bristol, Avon, BS99 7AX, ☎0117 9432553 Fax: 0117 9291115, ✉jan.karpinski@boiukfs.co.uk, *Call Date: Nov 1976, Middle Temple*
Qualifications: [BA (Oxon)]

KARRAR-LEWSLEY MR ROBERT EDWARD

Al Tamimi and Co, Difc Building 4, Level 6, Po Box 9275, Sheikh Zayed Road, Dubai, United Arab Emirates, ☎+971 4 364 1641
Fax: +971 4 364 1777, *Call Date: Oct 2004, Lincoln's Inn*
Qualifications: [LLB (Hons) Lond]

KATAN MISS DEBORAH RACHEL

Senior Legal Adviser, The Treasury Solicitors, One Kemble Street, London, WC2B 4TS, ☎020 7783 8216, ✉deborah.katan@education.gsi.gov.uk, *Call Date: Nov 1983, Middle Temple*
Qualifications: [BA (Hons)]

KAUR MISS JAGDISH

Senior Crown Prosecutor, Crown Prosecution Service, Prospect West, 81 Station Road, Croydon, Surrey, CR0 2RD, ☎020 8251 5410, *Call Date: Nov 1988, Middle Temple*
Qualifications: [LLB (L'pool)]

KAUR MISS JASVINDER

Lyons Davidson Solicitors, Victoria House, 51 Victoria Street, Bristol, BS1 6AD, ☎0117 904 6000 Fax: 0117 904 6006, ✉jkaur@lyonsdavidson.co.uk, *Call Date: Oct 2004, Inner Temple*
Qualifications: [LLB (UEA)]

KAVANAGH MR DANIEL ANTONY

Senior Crown Prosecutor, Crown Prosecution Service, Chingford Police Station, Kings Head Hill, Chingford, London, E4 7EA, *Call Date: Nov 1988, Lincoln's Inn*
Qualifications: [BA (Hons) Dip Law]

KAVANAGH MR KEVIN

Principal Crown Prosecutor, Crown Prosecution Service, 2 King Edward Court, King Edward Street, Nottingham, Nottinghamshire, NG1 1EL, ☎0115 852 3300, *Call Date: July 1983, Gray's Inn*
Qualifications: [BA]

KAVANAUGH MISS CLAIRE ALISON

Ministry of Defence, Po Box 1680, London, SW1P 1ZE, *Call Date: Oct 1996, Gray's Inn*
Qualifications: [BA (Lond)]

KAY MISS NICOLA JUDITH

T V Edwards LLP, Park House, 29 Mile End Road, London, E1 4TP, *Call Date: Oct 1996, Inner Temple*
Qualifications: [BA (Hull) LLB (Wolves)]

KAYA MR HUSSEIN AHMET

HED, Department For Transport, 1/09b Great Minster House, 76 Marsham Street, London, SW1P 4DR, ☎020 7944 8882
Fax: 020 7944 4942, ✉hussein.kaya@dft.gsi.gov.uk, *Call Date: July 1977, Gray's Inn*
Qualifications: [LLB (Lond) LLM (Lond)]

KAYE MR DAVID ROBERT

Legal Counsel, Shore Capital Limited, Bond Street House, 14 Clifford Street, London, W15 4JU, ☎020 7408 4080 Fax: 020 7408 4081, *Call Date: July 2000, Gray's Inn*
Qualifications: [MA (Oxon)]

KAZI MS DILNAAZ

Lawyer, The Treasury Solicitors, 5th Floor, One Kemble Street, London, WC2B 4TS, *Call Date: July 1999, Inner Temple*
Qualifications: [BDS (Wales) Dip Law]

KEEN MS ALICIA LOUISE

Crown Prosecution Service, Central Police Station, Winston Churchill Avenue, Portsmouth, Hampshire, PO1 2DG, ☎023 9285 6210 Fax: 023 9285 5392, ✉alicia.keen@cps.gsi.gov.uk, *Call Date: Oct 2010, Inner Temple*
Qualifications: [MSc (So'ton)]

KEERY MR NEIL WILLIAM

Directorate of Army Legal Services, Idl426, Ramillies Building, Marlborough Lines, Monxton Road, Andover, SP11 8HJ, *Call Date: Oct 1997, Gray's Inn*
Qualifications: [LLB (Belfast)]

KEHOE MRS EMMA-JANE

Crown Advocate, Crown Prosecution Service, Burnley Wharf, Manchester Road, Burnley, Lancashire, BB11 1JG, ☎01282 478557
Fax: 01282 478509, *Call Date: Nov 1991, Middle Temple*
Qualifications: [LLB (Hons)]

F

KEITH MR THOMAS HAMILTON

Eversheds LLP, 1 Wood Street, London, EC2V 7WS, ☎0845 497 4681 Fax: 0845 497 4919, *Call Date: July 1983, Gray's Inn*
Qualifications: [MA (Oxon)]

KELLAM MR JAMES ANTONY PLENDERLEITH

Advocate, Crown Prosecution Service, Black Horse House, 8-10 Leigh Road, Eastleigh, Hampshire, SO5O 9FH, ☎02380 673800 Fax: 02380 673857, ✉James.Kellam@cps.gsi.gov.uk, *Call Date: Nov 1991, Inner Temple*
Qualifications: [LLB]

KELLEHER MS KATHERINE

Chambers of Mr Ami Feder, Ground Floor, Lamb Building, Temple, London, EC4Y 7AS, ☎020 7797 7788 Fax: 020 7353 0535, ✉katekelleher@lambbuilding.co.uk, clerks@lambbuilding.co.uk, *Call Date: July 2000, Lincoln's Inn*
Qualifications: [BA(Hons) (Lond)]

KELLET MR MARK ALAN

Crown Prosecution Service, Sunlight House, Quay Street, Manchester, M60 3PS, *Call Date: Oct 2000, Inner Temple*
Qualifications: [BA (Hons) (Stirling) CPE (Manch)]

KELLOW MR IAN ROBERT

HED, Qatar Investment Authority, Po Box 23224, Diplomatic Area Street, Doha, Qatar, ☎00 974 4499 5893, ✉ikellow@qia.qa, *Call Date: July 1982, Inner Temple*
Qualifications: [MBA LLB]

KELLY MISS AMANDA JANE

Crown Prosecution Service, City Gate House, 185 Dyke Road, Hove, East Sussex, BN3 1TL, ☎01273 765600, *Call Date: Oct 2003, Lincoln's Inn*
Qualifications: [MA (Hons) (Oxon)]

KELLY MRS MAUREEN ELIZABETH

Assistant Justices' Clerk, Legal Manager, Highbury Corner Magistrate's Court, 51 Holloway Road, London, N7 8JA, ☎020 7506 3112 Fax: 020 7506 3192, *Call Date: Nov 1988, Gray's Inn*
Qualifications: [BA Hons (Lond) Dip Law]

KELLY MS TARA JANE

Advocate, Senior Crown Prosecutor, Crown Prosecution Service, 2 King Edward Court, King Edward Street, Nottingham, Nottinghamshire, NG1 1EL, *Call Date: Oct 1992, Gray's Inn*
Qualifications: [LLB LLM]

KELVIN MR CARL GEORGE LESLIE STEVEN

Senior Crown Prosecutor, Crown Prosecution Service, The Cooperage, 8 Gainsford Street, London, SE1 2NE, *Call Date: Nov 1988, Middle Temple*
Qualifications: [LLB (Hons) LLM (Lond)]

KEMP MS SOPHIA KATHERINE HELENA

Kingsley Napley LLP, 14 St John's Lane, London, EC1M 4AJ, *Call Date: Nov 2004, Gray's Inn*
Qualifications: [BA (Hons)(Cantab)]

KENDAL MISS JACQUELINE JANE

Cobbetts, Verulam Gardens, 70 Gray's Inn Road, London, WC1X 8BT, ☎0845 404 4122, ✉Jacqueline.Kendal@Cobbetts.com, *Call Date: Nov 2003, Lincoln's Inn*
Qualifications: [LLB (Hons) (Lond)]

KENDALL MR MARK NOEL

Principal Crown Prosecutor, Crown Prosecution Service, Citadel House, 58 High Street, Hull, Humberside, HU1 1QD, *Call Date: Nov 1987, Inner Temple*
Qualifications: [LLB (So'ton)]

KENDRICK-PHILLIPS MRS JANE MARGARET

Credit Agricole, Broadwalk House, 5 Appold Street, London, EC2A 2DA, ☎020 7214 5000 Fax: 020 7214 5294, *Call Date: Oct 1998, Lincoln's Inn*
Qualifications: [LLB (Hons) LLM (Newc)]

KENNEDY MR ANDREW GEORGE

Legal Director, Lloyd's Register Group Services Ltd, 71 Fenchurch Street, London, EC3M 4BS, ☎020 7423 2439 Fax: 020 7709 1573, ✉andrew.kennedy@lr.org, *Call Date: July 1987, Middle Temple*
Qualifications: [BA (Kent)]

F

KENNEDY MR BRIAN JOSEPH

Dobsons Solicitors, 27 London Road, Bromley, Kent, BR1 1DF, *Call Date: Oct 1992, Middle Temple*
Qualifications: [LLB (Hons)]

KENNEDY MR PAUL GILBERT

Legal Adviser, Financial Reporting Council, 5th Floor, Aldwych House, 71-91 Aldwych, London, WC2B 4HN,
☎020 7492 2347 (Direct Line)
Fax: 020 7492 2359, ✉p.kennedy@frc.org.uk, *Call Date: Nov 1991, Lincoln's Inn*
Qualifications: [MA (Cantab) FCII ACIArb FCCA FIA]

KENNELL MR ROGER CHARLES ALEXANDER

Brown Rudnick LLP, 8 Clifford Street, London, W1S 2LQ, ☎020 7851 6029
Fax: 020 7851 6100, ✉rkennell@brownrudnick.com, *Call Date: Oct 2004, Inner Temple*
Qualifications: [BA (Oxon) LLM]

KENNERLEY MR IAN LESLIE

Silk Family Law Ltd, Keel House, Garth Heads, Newcastle Upon Tyne, NE1 2JE,
☎0191 406 5000 Fax: 0191 232 8643, ✉ian.kennerley@silkfamilylaw.co.uk, *Call Date: July 1983, Gray's Inn*
Qualifications: [BA]

KENSAH MRS ELIZABETH ABENA BAAFIA

Essex Magistrates Court, Opsrey House, Hedgerows Business Park, Colchester Road, Chelmsford, Essex, CM2 5PF, ☎01245 313300
Fax: 01245 313399, *Call Date: Nov 2000, Middle Temple*
Qualifications: [LLB (Hons) (London)]

KENT MR GRAHAM EDWARD

Department For Work and Pensions, 5th Floor, the Adelphi, 1-11 John Adam Street, London, WC2N 6HT, *Call Date: July 1975, Gray's Inn*
Qualifications: [MA (Oxon) MJur (Manch)]

KENWARD MR RICHARD FRANCIS

Crown Prosecution Service, St Peters House, Gower Street, Derby, Derbyshire, DE1 1SB, *Call Date: Oct 1990, Inner Temple*
Qualifications: [LLB]

KENYON LIEUTENANT COMMANDER CAROLYN MARIE

Royal Navy Officers, c/o Director of Naval Legal Services, Navy Command Headquarters, Mail Point 4-2, Leach Building, Whale Island, Portsmouth, Hampshire, PO2 8BY, *Call Date: July 2005, Gray's Inn*
Qualifications: [LLB]

KER MR TIMOTHY PAUL

Department For Work and Pensions, 5th Floor, the Adelphi, 1-11 John Adam Street, London, WC2N 6HT, ☎020 7962 8817, ✉tim.ker@dwp.gsi.gov.uk, *Call Date: Oct 2010, Middle Temple*
Qualifications: [MA (Hons) (Edin)]

KERR MS CLARE PATRICIA

Lawyer, Department For Work and Pensions, New Court, 48 Carey Street, London, WC2A 2LS, ☎020 7412 1358, *Call Date: Nov 1995, Middle Temple*
Qualifications: [BA (Hons) MA (Cantab)]

KERR MR JOHN STUART

Karis Law, 40 Bowling Green Lane, Clerkenwell, London, EC1R 0NE,
☎020 7415 7016 Fax: 020 7415 7017,
✉stuart.kerr@karislaw.com, *Call Date: Nov 1995, Inner Temple*
Qualifications: [MA (Edin) CPE]

KERR MR JON STEPHEN

Crown Prosecution Service, Sunlight House, Quay Street, Manchester, M60 3PS, *Call Date: Nov 2001, Middle Temple*
Qualifications: [LLB (Hons)]

KERR MR LEWIS ALLAN

CKM Solicitors, 82 Medomsley Road, Consett, County Durham, DH8 5HS, *Call Date: Nov 2010, Lincoln's Inn*
Qualifications: [LLB (Sunderland)]

KESNER MR JULIAN BRIAN

Crown Prosecution Service, 2 Kimbrose Way, Gloucester, Gloucestershire, GL1 2DB,
☎01452 872 400, ✉julian.kesner@cps.gsi.gov.uk, *Call Date: Nov 1984, Lincoln's Inn*
Qualifications: [BA LLM (Cantab)]

F

KHAIRA MISS INDERJIT KAUR

Crown Prosecution Service, Bathnal Green Police Station, Po Box 60416, Bethnal Green, London, E2 9WH, ☎020 8721 5614, ✉inderjit.khaira@cps.gsi.gov.uk, *Call Date: Mar 2005, Middle Temple*
Qualifications: [BSc (Hons) MSc]

KHAN MRS AAMINAH AMANDA MATHER

The Information Commissioner, Wycliffe House, Water Lane, Wilmslow, SK9 5AF, ☎0845 630 6060 Fax: 01625 524 510, ✉Aaminah.khan@ico.gsi.gov.uk, *Call Date: Oct 2001, Middle Temple*
Qualifications: [LLB (Hons)]

KHAN MR ANAS AHMAD

Thompson & Co Solicitors, 2-3 Hind Court, Fleet Street, London, EC4A 3DL, ☎020 7936 2427 Fax: 020 7936 2106, ✉akhan@thompsonlaw.co.uk, *Call Date: Mar 2012, Gray's Inn*

KHAN MR AVERROES ALDEBORAN KARAM

Call Date: Nov 1986, Lincoln's Inn
Qualifications: [BA (Hons) (Cantab) MA (Cantab)]

KHAN MS AYESHA

Nexus Chambers, 7 New Square, Lincolns Inn, London, WC2A 3QS, ☎020 7404 1147, ✉ayesha.khan@nexuschambers.com, *Call Date: Mar 2005, Gray's Inn*
Qualifications: [LLB (Belfast)]

KHAN MS AZRA PERVEEN

Crown Prosecution Service, Harrow Crown Court, Hailsham Drive, Harrow, HA1 4TU, *Call Date: Nov 1983, Lincoln's Inn*
Qualifications: [LLB (Hons)]

KHAN MR MOHAMMED ASHRAF

2 Bedford Row, 2 Bedford Row, London, WC1R 4BU, *Call Date: July 1999, Middle Temple*
Qualifications: [LLB (Hons) LLM]

KHAN MR NICHOLAS PAUL

European Commission Legal Sevice, Berlaymont 3/359, B-1049 Brussel, Belgium, ☎+32 2 296 0420, ✉nicholas.khan@ec.europa.eu, *Call Date: July 1983, Inner Temple*
Qualifications: [LLB (So'ton)]

KHAN MR RASAB

Khattak Solicitors, 279 Bury New Rd, Whitefield, Manchester, M45 7SE, *Call Date: Nov 2006, Lincoln's Inn*
Qualifications: [LLB (Lanc)]

KHAN MR TARIQ

Company Secretary, Legal Director, Marlin Finance Group Limited, Marlin House, 16-22 Grafton Road, Worthing, West Sussex, BN11 1QP, ☎+44 (0)1903 703 494
Fax: +44 (0) 1903 282 296, ✉tariq.khan@marlincapitaleurope.com, *Call Date: Mar 1999, Lincoln's Inn*
Qualifications: [LLB (Hons)]

KHARRAN MISS DEVI SAMANTHA

Senior Crown Prosecutor, Crown Prosecution Service, The Cooperage, 8 Gainsford Street, London, SE1 2NE, ✉devi.kharran@cps.gsi.gov.uk, *Call Date: July 1994, Lincoln's Inn*
Qualifications: [LLB (Hons)]

KHONG DR TECK MENG

GlaxoSmithKline, 980 Great West Road, Brentford, Middlesex, TW8 9GS, *Call Date: July 2000, Gray's Inn*
Qualifications: [BSc LLB(Lond) PhD]

KIELTY MS MARIANNE

Northamptonshire County Council, Legal Services, Po Box No 104, County Hall, Northampton, NN1 1AW, ☎01604 236 027
Fax: 01604 237 167, ✉mkielty@northamptonshire.gov.uk, *Call Date: Nov 1988, Gray's Inn*
Qualifications: [LLB (Hons)]

KIFF MISS LISA RACHEL

Crown Prosecution Service, Bethnal Green Police Station, Po Box 60416, London, E2 9NZ, ✉lisa.kiff@cps.gsi.gov.uk, *Call Date: Oct 2006, Inner Temple*
Qualifications: [LLB (Warw)]

KILBY MR JAMES RICHARD

Lawyer, Charity Commission, Woodfield House, Tangier, Taunton, Somerset, TA1 4BL, ✉ james.kilby@charitycommission.gsi.gov.uk, *Call Date: Nov 1979, Inner Temple*
Qualifications: [BA (Hons) (Oxon)]

KILGARRIFF MR PATRICK HERBERT

Department For Business, Innovation and Skills, Legal Services Group, 1 Victoria Street, London, SW1H 0ET, *Call Date: Nov 1986, Gray's Inn*
Qualifications: [BSc Dip Law]

KILGOUR MR PETER JAMES

Watson Woodhouse Solicitors, York House, Borough Road, Middlesbrough, TS1 2HJ, ☎ 01642 266 507 Fax: 01642 213 482, ✉ pkilgour@watsonwoodhouse.co.uk, *Call Date: July 1984, Lincoln's Inn*
Qualifications: [STB (Spain) Dip Law]

KILLICK MR JAMES RICHARD MCFADYEN

Partner, White and Case LLP, 62 Rue De La Loi, Brussels, 1040, Belgium, ☎ 0032 2 239 2552 Fax: 0032 2 219 1626, *Call Date: Oct 1996, Middle Temple*
Qualifications: [BA (Hons) (Camb) LLM (Edin)]

KINDRED MR FRANK PAUL

BT Group PLC, BT Legal PPA6, BT Centre, 81 Newgate Street, London, EC1A 7AJ, *Call Date: July 1985, Gray's Inn*
Qualifications: [BSc (Lond) MSc (Dunelm)]

KING MR PHILIP ST. LAWRENCE

The Care Quality Commission, Finsbury Tower, 103-105 Bunhill Row, London, EC1Y 8TG, ☎ 020 7448 4512, ✉ philip.king@cqc.org.uk, *Call Date: July 2002, Inner Temple*
Qualifications: [RMN MSc (Lond) LLB (Lond)]

KING MR STEVEN MCMURRAY

Mariel Irvine Solicitors, 12-13 Clerkenwell Green, London, EC1R 0QJ, ✉ king@marielirvine.com, *Call Date: Oct 2008, Middle Temple*
Qualifications: [MA (Edin)]

KINGHORN MR ANDREW DAVID

New Forest District Council, Legal Department, Appletree Court, Lyndhurst, Hampshire, SO43 7PA, ☎ 023 8028 5000 Fax: 023 8028 5555, ✉ andrew.kinghorn@nfdc.gov.uk, *Call Date: Nov 1991, Gray's Inn*
Qualifications: [LLB]

KINGSBURY MISS CAROL JAYNE

Allen and Overy LLP, One Bishops Square, London, E1 6AD, ☎ 020 3088 0000 Fax: 020 3088 0088, ✉ carol.kingsbury@allenovery.com, *Call Date: July 1984, Middle Temple*
Qualifications: [MA (Cantab)]

KINGSBURY MR SIMON ANTHONY

Managing Director, Citigroup Global Markets Limited, Citigroup Centre Cgc-17-50, Canada Square, London, E14 5LB, ☎ 020 7508 9567, ✉ simon.kingsbury@citigroup.com, *Call Date: Nov 1996, Gray's Inn*
Qualifications: [LLB (Sussex)]

KINGSLEY MR CARL WAYNE

Kingsley Brookes Solicitors Limited, 6/7 Estate Buildings, Railways Street, Hudderfield, HD1 1JY, Fax: 01484 302 870, *Call Date: Mar 2012, Inner Temple*

KINGSTON MS SARAH JANE

Crown Prosecution Service, Sunlight House, Quay Street, Manchester, M60 3PS, *Call Date: Oct 1999, Inner Temple*
Qualifications: [LLB (Hons)]

KINNEAR MRS SHERYL LORRAINE

Legal Manager, Norwich Magistrates' Court, Bishopsgate, Norwich, Norfolk, NR3 1UP, ☎ 01603 679500 Fax: 01603 663263, *Call Date: Oct 1994, Inner Temple*
Qualifications: [LLB (UEA)]

KIRK MR MATTHEW JONATHAN

The First Law Partnership Limited, 30-32 Bromham Road, Bedford, Bedfordshire, MK40 2QD, ☎ 01234 263263 Fax: 01234 263239, ✉ info@firstdefencesolicitors.co.uk, *Call Date: Mar 2001, Lincoln's Inn*
Qualifications: [BA (Hons) (Oxon) Dip in Law]

F

KIRKHAM MR KEITH

Principal Crown Prosecutor, Crown Prosecution Service, The Unicentre, Lords Walk, Preston, Lancashire, PR1 1DH, ☎01772 208100 Fax: 01772 208144, ✉keith.kirkham@cps.gsi.gov.uk, *Call Date: Feb 1985, Middle Temple*

KIRKHAM-SMITH MRS MARJORIE ANNE

Senior Crown Prosecutor, Crown Prosecution Service, 2 King Edward Court, King Edward Street, Nottingham, Nottinghamshire, NG1 1EL, *Call Date: July 1981, Middle Temple*
Qualifications: [BA (Hons)]

KIRKPATRICK MR GAVIN WARING

Crown Prosecution Service, Isleworth Crown Court, 36 Ridgeway Road, Isleworth, London, TW7 5LP, ✉gavin.kirkpatrick@cps.gsi.gov.uk, *Call Date: Nov 1981, Middle Temple*
Qualifications: [BA (Hons)]

KISANGA MR LUTHER JOSEPH

DAC Beachcroft LLP, 3 Minster Court, Mincing Lane, London, EC3R 7DD, *Call Date: July 2006, Middle Temple*
Qualifications: [LLB (Hons) (Lond)]

KITCHING MR JAMES ROBERT

Partner, Fried Frank Harris Shriver and Jacobson, (London), 99 City Road, London, EC1Y 1AX, ☎020 7972 9600 Fax: 020 7972 9602, ✉james.kitching@friedfrank.com, *Call Date: Oct 1999, Inner Temple*
Qualifications: [LLB (Lond)]

KLEIN PROF SILVIU THOMAS RUDOLF

Adjudicator, Chief Executive, Professor of Law, Specialist Engineering Contractors Group, Esca House, 34 Palace Court, Bayswater, London, W2 4JG, ☎020 7313 4920 Fax: 020 7727 9268, ✉rklein@hvca.org.uk, *Call Date: Nov 1979, Middle Temple*
Qualifications: [LLB (Hons) (Lond) Cert Ed FRSA FCIOB]

F

KLOUDA MR THOMAS JOSEPH

Crown Advocate, Crown Prosecution Service, Jefferson House, 27 Park Place, Leeds, West Yorkshire, LS1 2SZ, ☎0113 290 2700, ✉tomklouda@hotmail.com, *Call Date: Nov 1980, Middle Temple*
Qualifications: [BA LLB (Leeds)]

KNAPP MR EDWARD IAN

Crown Prosecution Service, Froomsgate House, Rupert Street, Bristol, BS1 2QJ, ☎0117 930 2849, ✉Edward.Knapp@cps.gsi.gov.uk, *Call Date: Feb 1992, Lincoln's Inn*
Qualifications: [LLB (Hons)]

KNAPPER MR DON

Crown Prosecution Service, Building 3, Etruria Valley Office Village, Etruria, Stoke-On-Trent, Staffordshire, ST1 5RU, ☎01782 664540 Fax: 01782 664501, ✉don.knapper@cps.gsi.gov.uk, *Call Date: Oct 1992, Gray's Inn*
Qualifications: [BSc (Hons) Dip Law]

KNAPTON MISS SARAH

Kings and Wood Mallesons, 13/F Gloucester Tower, The Landmark, 15 Queen's Road Central, Hong Kong, *Call Date: July 2007, Middle Temple*
Qualifications: [BA (Hons) (Leeds) PgDL (Lond)]

KNELLER MISS KAREN BELINDA

Director, Criminal Cases Review Commission, 5 St Philips Place, Birmingham, B3 2PW, *Call Date: Nov 1993, Inner Temple*
Qualifications: [BA (L'pool) LLB (Lond) MSC (Portsmouth)]

KNIBBE MR JORREN DANIEL

Osborne Clark, 2 Temple Back East, Temple Quay, Bristol, BS1 6EG, Fax: 0117 917 3005, ✉jorren.knibbe@osborneclarke.com, *Call Date: Oct 2005, Middle Temple*
Qualifications: [BA (Hons)]

KNIGHT MS JUDITH

Principal Lawyer, Clyde & Co LLP, 1 Stoke Road, Guildford, Surrey, GU1 4HW, ☎01908 691691, *Call Date: Oct 1991, Lincoln's Inn*
Qualifications: [LLB (Hons) (Notts)]

KNIGHT MR NIGEL MERLEY

Senior Crown Prosecutor, Crown Prosecution Service, Sussex Suite, 2-4 City Gates, Southgate, Chichester, West Sussex, P019 8DJ, ☎01243 523908 Fax: 01243 523950, ✉nigel.knight@cps.gsi.gov.uk, *Call Date: July 1984, Gray's Inn*
Qualifications: [LLB (UEA)]

KNIGHT MISS RACHEL ELISABETH

Crown Prosecution Service, Cambria House, Pentrebach Industrial Estate, Pentrebach, Merthyr Tydfil, Mid Glamorgan, CF48 4XA, ☎01443 694 800 Fax: 01443 694 804, *Call Date: Oct 2000, Middle Temple*
Qualifications: [LLB (Hons) (LSE)]

KNOTT MISS JUDITH MARY

Principal Crown Prosecutor, Crown Prosecution Service, Emlyn Hughes House, Abbey Road, Barrow-In-Furness, Cumbria, LA14 5QY, ☎01229 814400
Fax: 01229 814410, ✉judith.knott@cps.gsi.gov.uk, *Call Date: July 1980, Inner Temple*
Qualifications: [LLB (Hull)]

KNOTT MISS LYNSEY

Carter Osbourne Solicitors, 82 George Street, Corby, Northamptonshire, NN17 1QE, *Call Date: Oct 2006, Middle Temple*
Qualifications: [LLB (Hons) (Leic)]

KNOWLDEN MS MARTHA

Gullands Solicitors, 16 Mill Street, Maidstone, Kent, ME15 6XT, ✉m.knowlden@gullands.com, *Call Date: Nov 2000, Inner Temple*
Qualifications: [LLB (Kent)]

KNOX MR GRAEME PETER

Royal Navy Officers, HM Naval Base, Portsmouth, Hampshire, PO1 3LS, *Call Date: July 2004, Inner Temple*
Qualifications: [LLB PgDL BVC]

KNOX MR HENRY ANDREW LOISELURE

Financial Services Authority, 25 The North Colonade, Canary Wharf, London, E14 5HS, ✉henry.knox@fsa.gov.uk, *Call Date: July 2000, Gray's Inn*
Qualifications: [MA (Hons) PhD]

KODAMA MR TORU

Kowa Co Ltd, 3-7-9 Shimo-Odanaka, Nakahara-Ku, Kawasaki-Shi, Kanagawa-Ken, 211-0041, Japan, ☎00 8144 777 6790
Fax: 00 8144 777 6790, *Call Date: July 1999, Middle Temple*
Qualifications: [MA Dip in Law BS]

KODIKARA MISS SWARNA REKHA

Crown Prosecution Service, Snaresbrook Crown Court, 75 Hollybush Hill, Snaresbrook, London, E11 1QW, ☎020 8929 3011, ✉Rekha.Kodikara@cps.gsi.gov.uk, *Call Date: Nov 2000, Middle Temple*
Qualifications: [BA (Hons) (Sussex) LLM CPE]

KOHL MISS SARAH JANE

Legal Adviser, The Treasury Solicitors, 5th Floor, One Kemble Street, London, WC2B 4TS, ☎020 7210 2972, ✉Sarah.kohl@tsol.gsi.gov.uk, *Call Date: Nov 1998, Inner Temple*
Qualifications: [BA (Manch)]

KONG MISS MING-WAI

Legal Adviser, Prosecutor, Department For Business, Innovation and Skills, Legal Services, 5th Floor, 1 Victoria Street, London, SW1H OET, ☎020 7215 3124
Fax: 020 7215 3271, ✉ming.kong@bis.gsi.gov.uk, *Call Date: Oct 1997, Gray's Inn*
Qualifications: [LLB (Hons) (Lond)]

KORPAL MISS BENDNA

Crown Prosecution Service, County House, 100 New London Road, Chelmsford, Essex, CM2 0RG, ☎01245 455800, *Call Date: Nov 1997, Lincoln's Inn*
Qualifications: [BA (Hons) MSc]

KRELING MR PAUL ALEXANDER JULIAN

Senior Legal Officer, HM Revenue and Customs, Room 2c/03, Solicitor's Office, 100 Parliament Street, London, SW1A 2BQ, ☎020 7147 0341 Fax: 020 7147 0433, *Call Date: Nov 1989, Inner Temple*
Qualifications: [LLB (Exon)]

KRIKLER MISS SUSAN

Crown Prosecution Service, Queens House, 58 Victoria Street, St Albans, Hertfordshire, AL1 3HZ, *Call Date: Nov 1988, Middle Temple*
Qualifications: [BA (Oxon) Dip Law (Lond)]

F

KRON MR MICHAEL

HED, Secretary, Ministry of Justice, 102 Petty France, London, SW1H 9AJ, ☎ 020 33344764 / 020 33344764 Fax: 020 33344035 / 020 33344035, ✉ michael.kron@justice.gsi.gov.uk, *Call Date: July 1975, Lincoln's Inn*

KRONE MRS MAXINE JANE

Carter Osbourne Solicitors, 82 George Street, Corby, Northamptonshire, NN17 1QE, *Call Date: July 1980, Middle Temple*
Qualifications: [BA (Leics) (Hons)]

KUHN MR CHARLES ANTON

Energy Financing Team Ltd, 11-15 Wigmore Street, Cavendish Court, London, W1U 1PF, ☎ 020 7518 9257, ✉ charles@eft-group.net, *Call Date: Mar 2006, Inner Temple*
Qualifications: [DipLP University of Bonn]

KUMAR MR VIVEK RAJ

Attorney General's Office, 20 Victoria Street, London, SW1H 0NF, ✉ vivek.kumar@attorneygeneral.gsi.gov.uk, *Call Date: Oct 1997, Middle Temple*
Qualifications: [BA (Hons)(Cantab) CPE]

KVJATKOVSKI MS VANDA

The Treasury Solicitors, One Kemble Street, London, WC2B 4TS, *Call Date: Oct 1999, Lincoln's Inn*
Qualifications: [BA (Hons)(Dunelm) LLM (Southampton)]

KWONG MR CHEE HAY JOEY

Crown Prosecution Service, 2 King Edward Court, King Edward Street, Nottingham, Nottinghamshire, NG1 1EL, *Call Date: July 2005, Middle Temple*
Qualifications: [BA (Hons) Cantab]

LACK MR PAUL VERNON

The Kyte Group Limited, Business Design Centre, 52 Upper Street, London, N1 0QH, ✉ paul.lack@kytegroup.com, *Call Date: Oct 1993, Lincoln's Inn*
Qualifications: [LLB (Hons)]

LAFFAN MR PAUL REDMOND

Financial Services Authority, General Counsel's Division, 25 The North Colonnade, Canary Wharf, London, E14 5HS, *Call Date: Nov 2006, Middle Temple*
Qualifications: [BA (Hons)]

LAIDLAW MR STUART ROBERT

Crown Prosecution Service, Clarendon House, Laburnum Road, Wakefield, West Yorkshire, WF1 4QP, ✉ stuart.laidlaw@cps.gsi.gov.uk, *Call Date: Feb 1989, Inner Temple*
Qualifications: [LLB (B'ham)]

LAKE MR JAMES MICHAEL

Qatar Financial Centre Regulatory Authority, Enforcement Department, 14th Floor, Qfc Tower 1, Po Box 22989, Doha, Qatar, ✉ j.lake@qfcra.com, *Call Date: Oct 1999, Lincoln's Inn*
Qualifications: [LLB (Hons)(Notts)]

LAKEN MRS ELAINE ANNE

Clerk, Bristol City Council, The Council House, College Green, Bristol, BS99 7PH, ☎ 01179 223746 Fax: 01179 223436, *Call Date: July 1978, Inner Temple*

LAKIN MRS DAMARIS DOROTHY

Prosecution Team Leader, Crown Prosecution Service, The Cooperage, 8 Gainsford Street, London, SE1 2NE, ☎ 020 3300 4854 Fax: 020 3300 4861, ✉ Damaris.Lakin@cps.gsi.gov.uk, *Call Date: July 1989, Gray's Inn*
Qualifications: [BA (Hons) (Dunelm) Dip Law]

LAKIN MRS DEBORAH RACHEL

Her Majesty's Courts and Tribunals Service, Po Box 16, 14 Hamilton Terrace, Leamington Spa, Warwickshire, CV32 4XG, ☎ 01926 429133 Fax: 01926 426217, ✉ deborah.lakin@hmcourts-service.gsi.gov.uk, *Call Date: Nov 1992, Inner Temple*
Qualifications: [LLB (Hons)]

LAKIN MR MARK ANTHONY

Senior Crown Prosecutor, Crown Prosecution Service, County House, 100 New London Road, Chelmsford, Essex, CM2 0RG, ☎ 01245 455800 Fax: 01245 455928, *Call Date: July 1986, Gray's Inn*
Qualifications: [LLB]

LAM MR YUK WAI

Senior Crown Prosecutor, Crown Prosecution Service, Capital Tower, Greyfriars Road, Cardiff, CF10 3PL, ☎ 029 2080 3800 Fax: 029 2080 3802, ✉ yuk.wai-lam@cps.gsi.gov.uk, *Call Date: Oct 1999, Lincoln's Inn*
Qualifications: [LLB (Hons) LLM (Cardiff)]

LAMBE MS SHAUNEEN

Other, Lawrence and Co Solicitors, 402 - 404 Harrow Road, London, W9 2HU, ☎020 7266 4333, ✉slambe@lawsol.co.uk, *Call Date: Nov 1997, Gray's Inn*
Qualifications: [MA (Edin)]

LAMBERT MS SARA MAIR

Northumbria University, School of Law, City Campus East, Newcastle Upon Tyne, NE1 8ST, *Call Date: July 2002, Inner Temple*
Qualifications: [LLB (Cardiff)]

LAMING MS HANNAH KATE

Peters & Peters Solicitors LLP, 15 Fetter Lane, London, EC4A 1BW, ☎020 7822 7777 Fax: 020 7822 7788, ✉hlaming@petersandpeters.com, *Call Date: July 2001, Middle Temple*
Qualifications: [BSc (Hons) Dip Law]

LAMING MS NORMA YVONNE

FSOL, Essex Legal Services, New Bridge House, 60-68 New London Road, Chelmsford, Essex, CM2 0PD, ☎01245 506626 Fax: 01245 506650, ✉Norma.Laming@essex.gov.uk, *Call Date: July 1990, Middle Temple*
Qualifications: [MBA]

LAMONT MISS ALEXANDRA ELIZABETH

The Royal British Legion, Haig House, 199 Borough High Street, London, SE1 1AA, ✉alamont@britishlegion.org.uk, *Call Date: Oct 2008, Middle Temple*
Qualifications: [BA (Hons) (Cantab) Dip in Law]

LAMPTEY MISS CAROLYNE SOPHIA

Crown Prosecution Service, Rose Court, 2 Southwark Bridge, London, SE1 9HS, ☎2033570409 Fax: 2033570358, ✉carolyne.lamptey@cps.gsi.co.uk, *Call Date: Oct 2000, Middle Temple*
Qualifications: [LLB (Hons) (Lond) LLM]

LANCASTER DR DAVID EWAN

Powell Gilbert LLP, 85 Fleet Street, London, EC4Y 1AE, ✉david.lancaster@powellgilbert.com, *Call Date: July 2008, Lincoln's Inn*
Qualifications: [MBiochem (Oxon) DPhil (Oxon)]

LANCASTER MR PETER

Crown Prosecution Service, Southwark Crown Court, 1 English Grounds, London, SE1 2HU, *Call Date: Feb 1980, Lincoln's Inn*
Qualifications: [BA (Kent)]

LANE MR PAUL TIMOTHY

Legal Adviser, HMCS Kent, Sussex & Surrey, Eastbourne and Hailsham Magistrates' Court, Old Orchard Road, Eastbourne, BN21 4UN, ☎01323 727518, ✉paul.lane@hmcourts-service.gsi.gov.uk, *Call Date: Oct 1993, Inner Temple*
Qualifications: [LLB]

LANGDALE MISS RACHEL

Seven Bedford Row, 7 Bedford Row, London, WC1R 4BS, ☎020 7242 3555 Fax: 020 7242 2511, ✉rlangdale@7br.co.uk, *Call Date: Oct 1990, Middle Temple*
Qualifications: [LLB (Hons) M Phil (Cantab)]

LANGDON MISS PENELOPE JANE

Clerk, Deputy Chief Clerk, Secretary, President's Chambers, Royal Courts of Justice, Strand, London, WC2A 2LL, *Call Date: May 1981, Inner Temple*
Qualifications: [LLB (Cardiff)]

LANGFORD MRS MARION JEAN

Crown Prosecution Service, Fox Talbot House, Bellinger Close, Malmesbury Road, Chippenham, Wiltshire, SN15 1BN, ☎01249 766100 / 01249 766100, ✉Marion.Langford@cps.gsi.gov.uk, *Call Date: Nov 1996, Gray's Inn*
Qualifications: [BA (Leeds)]

LANLEHIN MISS ELIZABETH

Buckinghamshire County Council, County Hall, Walton Street, Aylesbury, Buckinghamshire, HP20 1UA, ☎01296 3839688 Fax: 01296 382421, ✉C-ELANLEHIN@buckscc.gov.uk, *Call Date: Mar 2001, Inner Temple*
Qualifications: [BA (Lond)]

LAPAZ MISS ANNIE

Legal Counsel, Macmillan Publishers Limited, The Macmillan Building, 4 Crinian Street, London, N1 9XW, ☎020 7014 4097 Fax: 020 7843 3648, ✉a.lapaz@macmillan.co.uk, *Call Date: Oct 1998, Inner Temple*
Qualifications: [LLB (Brunel)]

F

LARIZADEH MR KAMBIZ

Skadden, Arps, Slate, Meagher & Flom LLP, Skadden, Arps, Slate, Meagher and Flom (Uk) LLP, 40 Bank Street, Canary Wharf, London, E14 5DS, ☎020 7519 7169
Fax: 020 7072 7169, ✉kambiz.larizadeh@skadden.com, *Call Date: Nov 1999, Inner Temple*
Qualifications: [BA (Cantab)]

LASHMAR MRS NICOLA JANE

Eversheds LLP, Franciscan House, 51 Princes Street, Ipswich, IP1 1UR, ☎0845 497 2424
Fax: 01473 284559, ✉nicoladarvill@eversheds.com, *Call Date: Oct 1997, Inner Temple*
Qualifications: [BA (Humberside)]

LAVELL MR MARCUS CHRISTOPHER

Jeffrey Green Russell Solicitors, Waverley House, 7-12 Noel Street, London, W1F 8GQ, ✉mcl@jgrlaw.co.uk, *Call Date: July 2008, Gray's Inn*
Qualifications: [LLB (Bris)]

LAVENDER MR MICHAEL DAVID

Company Secretary, Group Legal Adviser, Legal Adviser, Asset Co PLC, 800 Field End Road, South Ruislip, Middlesex, HA4 0GH, *Call Date: Nov 1986, Lincoln's Inn*
Qualifications: [LLB (B'ham)]

LAVERS PROF ANTHONY PHILIP

Director, Professor of Law, White and Case, 5 Old Broad Street, London, EC2N 1DW, ☎020 7532 1607 Fax: 020 7532 1001, *Call Date: July 1997, Lincoln's Inn*
Qualifications: [LLB (Hons)(Lond) MPhil (So'ton) PhD FRICS MCIArb DLitt]

LAWRENCE MISS CERI JANE

DAC Beachcroft LLP, 100 Fetter Lane, London, EC4A 1BN, ☎020 7894 6228, ✉celawrence@dacbeachcroft.com, *Call Date: Oct 1998, Middle Temple*
Qualifications: [BA (Hons)(Oxon)]

LAWRENCE MR ELOGHOSA STEPHEN

Sutton Council, Legal Services, Civic Offices, St Nicholas Way, Sutton, Surrey, SM1 1EA, ☎020 8770 5056 Fax: 020 8770 5616, *Call Date: Feb 1994, Middle Temple*
Qualifications: [LLB (Hons)(Lond)]

LAWRIE MR ROBERT JAMES SEYMOUR

Finers Stephens Innocent, 179 Great Portland Street, London, W1W 5LS, ☎020 7323 4000, ✉robert.lawrie@fsilaw.com, *Call Date: Oct 2003, Inner Temple*
Qualifications: [PgDL MA (Hons) (Edin)]

LAWSON MR MATTHEW RICHARD

Crown Prosecution Service, Central Police Station, Winston Churchill Avenue, Portsmouth, Hampshire, PO1 2DG, *Call Date: Oct 1999, Lincoln's Inn*
Qualifications: [BA (Hons) CPE]

LE GALLAIS MR JAMES LYLE

Peters & Peters Solicitors LLP, 15 Fetter Lane, London, EC4A 1BW, ✉jlegallais@petersandpeters.com, *Call Date: Oct 2005, Middle Temple*
Qualifications: [BA (Hons) (Bristol)]

LE GRYS MR JAMES MARK

Crown Prosecution Service, Froomsgate House, Rupert Street, Bristol, BS1 2QJ, ☎0117 930 1355 Fax: 0117 930 1350, *Call Date: Oct 2008, Gray's Inn*
Qualifications: [BSc LLB]

LE MARCHANT MR PIERS ALFRED

General Counsel, Managing Director, Nomura International PLC, 25 Bank Street, London, E14 5LE, ✉piers.lemarchant@nomura.com, *Call Date: Nov 1987, Inner Temple*
Qualifications: [LLB (Lond)]

LEA LADY GERRY VALERIE

Legal Adviser, West Suffolk Magistrates', Old Shire Hall, Honey Hill, Bury St Edmunds, Suffolk, IP33 1HF, ☎01284 778000
Fax: 01284 778033, *Call Date: Nov 1969, Gray's Inn*
Qualifications: [BA (Hons)]

LEACH MISS JUDITH VANESSA

Withy King Solicitors, North Bailey House, New Inn Hall Street, Oxford, OX1 2EA, ☎01865 792 300 Fax: 01865 793 616, ✉judith.leach@withyking.co.uk, *Call Date: Nov 1994, Inner Temple*
Qualifications: [LLB]

F

LEACH MISS SANDRA ELIZABETH

Clerk, Legal Adviser, Her Majesty's Courts and Tribunals Service, Gail House, Lower Stone Street, Maidstone, Kent, ME15 6NB, ☎01622 680 050, *Call Date: Apr 1986, Middle Temple*
Qualifications: [LLB (Hons)]

LEADBETTER MRS ELAINE

Department For Work and Pensions, Department of Health, Legal Group, Room 7202, Government Buildings, Norcross Lane, Blackpool, Lancashire, FY5 3TA, ✉elaine.leadbetter@dwp.gsi.gov.uk, *Call Date: Mar 2002, Lincoln's Inn*
Qualifications: [MBA]

LEADER MR DANIEL

Leigh Day and Co, Priory House, 25 St John's Lane, London, EC1M 4LB, ☎020 7650 1200 Fax: 020 7253 4433, ✉dleader@leighday.co.uk, *Call Date: Nov 2001, Gray's Inn*
Qualifications: [BA (Oxon)]

LEDWIDGE MISS REBECCA KATHERINE

Crown Prosecution Service, The Cooperage, 8 Gainsford Street, London, SE1 2NE, ☎020 7378 4185, ✉Rebecca.Ledwidge@cps.gsi.gov.uk, *Call Date: July 2007, Inner Temple*
Qualifications: [BSc (Bris) MSc (Lond) GDL (BPP) BVC (BPP)]

LEE MR MARTIN JOHN

Legal Manager, Her Majesty's Court Service and Tribunal Service, Royal Courts of Justice, London, WC2A 2LL, ☎020 7073 4775 Fax: 020 7947 6031, *Call Date: Nov 1987, Lincoln's Inn*
Qualifications: [LLB (Hons)(Manc) DMS Assoc CIPD]

LEES MR DAVID SLATER

Crown Prosecution Service, Colmore Gate, 2 - 6 Colmore Row, Birmingham, West Midlands, B3 2QA, ☎0121 262 1300, ✉david.lees@cps.gsi.gov.uk, *Call Date: July 1984, Middle Temple*
Qualifications: [BA]

LEFTERIS MR MATHEOS

Stuart Miller and Co, 247 High Road, Wood Green, London, N22 4HF, ☎020 8888 5225, *Call Date: Oct 1997, Middle Temple*
Qualifications: [LLB (Hons)(Luton)]

LEFTLEY MRS SUSANNAH NICOLE

Call Date: Oct 1996, Inner Temple
Qualifications: [LLB (Bris)]

LEIST MR IAN DOUGLAS

11 Old Square, 11 Old Square, Lincoln's Inn, London, WC2A 3TS, *Call Date: July 1981, Inner Temple*
Qualifications: [BA]

LEMARIé MISS CLOTILDE

Pinsent Masons, 30 Crown Place, London, EC2A 4ES, *Call Date: Nov 2008, Lincoln's Inn*
Qualifications: [LLB (Lond)]

LEMOINE MR PHILIP ROBERT

Crown Prosecution Service, Charing Cross Police Station, Agar Street, London, WC2N 4JP, ☎020 3300 2300, *Call Date: July 2009, Middle Temple*
Qualifications: [LLB (Hons)]

LEMON MR GUY ROBERT

Head of Legal Services, Thames Valley Police Hq, Oxford Road, Kidlington, Oxford, OX5 2NX, ☎01865 846305, ✉guy.lemon@thamesvalley.pnn.police.uk, *Call Date: Nov 1995, Inner Temple*
Qualifications: [LLB (B'ham)]

LENIHAN MR MARTIN JOHN

Legal Adviser, Skanska Construction Group Ltd, Legal Dept, Maple Cross House, Denham Way, Maple Cross, Rickmansworth, Hertfordshire, WD3 9AS, ☎01923 423966 Fax: 01923 423864, ✉martin.lenihan@skanska.co.uk, *Call Date: July 1983, Middle Temple*
Qualifications: [BA LLM (Lond)]

LEONARD MS CATHERINE MARTINE

Prosecutor, Crown Prosecution Service, Special Crime Divison, Rose Court, 2 Southwark Bridge, London, SE1 9HS, ☎020 3357 0064 Fax: 020 7796 8280, ✉kate.leonard@cps.gsi.gov.uk, *Call Date: Nov 1990, Middle Temple*
Qualifications: [MA (Oxon)]

LEONARD DR EAMONN BENEDICT KNIGHTLEY

Crown Advocate, Senior Crown Prosecutor, Crown Prosecution Service, Rose Court, 2 Southwalk Bridge, London, SE1 9HS, ☎020 33571017 Fax: 020 3357 0056, ✉benedict.leonard@cps.gsi.gov.uk, *Call Date: Nov 1992, Inner Temple*
Qualifications: [BA (Dunelm) LLM (Germany) Dr Juris (Germany)]

LEONG MR GARY TAT HAU

Head of Legal Services, Serious Fraud Office, Elm House, 10-16 Elm Street, London, WC1X 0BJ, ☎020 7239 7405 Fax: 020 7833 5485, ✉gary.leong@sfo.gsi.gov.uk, *Call Date: July 1990, Gray's Inn*
Qualifications: [LLB (Hons) (Lond)]

LEREGO MISS KATHRYN MARGARET

Kaplan Altior, 2nd Floor, St David's House, Wood Street, Cardiff, CF10 1 ES, ☎029 20 451000 Fax: 029 20 459900, ✉kath.lerego@kaplan.co.uk, *Call Date: July 2004, Middle Temple*
Qualifications: [LLB Hons (Wales)]

LEVENE MR RICHARD WILLIAM OSBORNE

Higher Court Advocate, Other, Crown Prosecution Service, Froomsgate House, Rupert Street, Bristol, BS1 2QJ, ☎0117 930 2800 Fax: 0117 930 2885, ✉richard.levene@cps.gsi.gov.uk, *Call Date: July 1982, Gray's Inn*
Qualifications: [BA (Law) (Kent)]

LEVEY MRS NATASHA GILLIAN

Ofsted, Aviation House, 125 Kingsway, London, WC2B 6SE, ☎020 7421 6796, ✉Natasha.Wright@ofsted.gov.uk, *Call Date: Nov 2001, Middle Temple*
Qualifications: [LLB (Hons) (Edin)]

LEVIN MR ANDREW PAUL

Lawyer, Crown Prosecution Service, The Cooperage, 8 Gainsford Street, London, SE1 2NE, ☎020 3300 4149 Fax: 020 3300 4861, ✉Andrew.Levin@cps.gsi.gov.uk, *Call Date: July 1985, Middle Temple*
Qualifications: [BA (Hons)]

LEVINE MS IONA JAYNE

Lch Clearnet Group Limited, Aldgate House, 33 Aldgate High Street, London, EC3N 1EA, *Call Date: Feb 1982, Lincoln's Inn*

LEVITT MISS ALISON FRANCES JOSEPHINE

Principal Legal Adviser, Crown Prosecution Service, Headquarters, Rose Court, 2 Southwark Bridge, London, SE1 9HS, ☎020 3357 0882, ✉alison.levitt@cps.qsi.gov.uk, *Call Date: July 1988, Inner Temple*
Qualifications: [MA (St Andrews) Dip Law]

LEVY MR ANTHONY JULIAN

Crown Prosecution Service, 19, York Court, The Albany, Albany Park Road, Kingston Upon Thames, Surrey, KT2 5ST, ✉tony.levy@cps.gsi.gov.uk, *Call Date: Nov 1983, Middle Temple*
Qualifications: [LLB]

LEWANDOWSKA MISS KATE

Ministry of Justice, Legal Directorate 6.38, 102 Petty France, London, SW1H 9AJ, ☎020 3334 4767, *Call Date: Oct 2005, Lincoln's Inn*
Qualifications: [BA (Hons) MA CPE BVC]

LEWIN MISS MAURINE JOY

Call Date: July 1982, Middle Temple
Qualifications: [MA (Sheffield) BA (Hons)]

LEWIS MR CHARLES ELIOT

Legal Adviser, Department of Energy and Climate Change, 3 Whitehall Place, London, SW1A 2AW, *Call Date: Nov 1986, Gray's Inn*
Qualifications: [MA PhD(Cantab)]

LEWIS MRS CHRISTINA MARIE

Head of Legal Services, Hutchison 3g Uk Limited, Star House, 20 Grenfell Road, Maidenhead, Berkshire, SL6 1EH, ☎07782 326295 Fax: 01628 765 109, ✉christina.lewis@three.co.uk, *Call Date: Oct 1997, Middle Temple*
Qualifications: [LLB (Hons)(Bournem)]

LEWIS MR DAVID THOMAS

HM Revenue and Customs, Solicitor's Office, Room 2/72, 100 Parliament Street, London, SW1A 2BQ, ☎020 7147 0613
Fax: 020 7147 0433, ✉david.lewis2@hmrc.gsi.gov.uk, *Call Date: Oct 1999, Gray's Inn*
Qualifications: [BA DipLaw]

F

LEWIS MR DAVID VAUGHAN

Department For Work and Pensions, Caxton House, Tothill Street, London, SW1H 9NA, ☎020 7962 8932 / 020 7413 1469 Fax: 020 7962 8447, ✉vaughan.lewis@dwp.gsi.gov.uk, *Call Date: Mar 1999, Gray's Inn*
Qualifications: [LLB (Lond)]

LEWIS MS JACQUELINE ANN

British Waterways, 64 Clarendon Road, Watford, Hertfordshire, WD17 1DA, ✉jackie.lewis@britishwaterways.co.uk, *Call Date: Oct 1992, Lincoln's Inn*
Qualifications: [BSc(Hons)(Bris) Dip Law]

LEWIS MR JAMES HENRY

Lawyer, Crown Prosecution Service, Central Fraud Group South (Fiscal Division), 6th Floor, Rose Court, 2 Southwark Bridge, London, SE1 9HS, *Call Date: Oct 2000, Middle Temple*
Qualifications: [LLB (Hons) (UWE)]

LEWIS MR JOSEPH MORGAN

Manager, Morgan, Cullen and Ball Solicitors and Barristers, 101 Bath Street, Birmingham, B4 6HG, ☎0121 200 3031 Fax: 0121 200 3029, ✉info@pgcb.co.uk, *Call Date: July 2002, Middle Temple*
Qualifications: [BA (Hons) (Wales) CPE (Keele) LLM (Keele)]

LEWIS MISS LINDA CATHERINE

Kleymann Karpenstein and Partner, Philopsophenweg 1, Wetzlar 35578, Germany, ☎06 441 94460 Fax: 06 441 944631, *Call Date: Feb 1990, Inner Temple*
Qualifications: [BSc (Surrey) LLM]

LEWIS-NUNN MR HOWARD

Ashfords LLP, 44 Baker Street, London, W1U 7AL, ☎020 7544 2424 Fax: 020 7544 2400, ✉h.lewis-nunn@ashfords.co.uk, *Call Date: Nov 1994, Inner Temple*
Qualifications: [LLB (UEA)]

LIGERE MISS EDITE ALEXANDRA IZABELLA

Debevoise and Plimpton LLP, Tower 42, Old Broad Street, London, EC2N 1HQ, ☎020 7786 5422 Fax: 020 7588 4180, ✉eligere@debevoise.com, *Call Date: July 2000, Lincoln's Inn*
Qualifications: [LLB First (Hons) LLM (Lond)]

LIGHTMAN SIR GAVIN ANTHONY

Winston and Strawn, City Point, One Ropemaker Street, London, EC2Y 9HU, Fax: 020 7 011 8800, *Call Date: July 1963, Lincoln's Inn*
Qualifications: [LLB (Lond) LLM (USA)]

LILLYWHITE MR DAVID VICTOR

Adviser, Manager, Qbe European Operations, Plantation Place, 30 Fenchurch Street, London, EC3M 3BD, ☎020 7105 4000 Fax: 2007105 4032, *Call Date: Nov 1980, Middle Temple*
Qualifications: [LLB]

LINDNER MS BRIGITTE

Serle Court, 6 New Square, Lincoln's Inn, London, WC2A 3QS, ☎020 7242 6105 Fax: 020 7405 4004, *Call Date: Dec 1988, Lincoln's Inn*

LING MISS VICTORIA JANE

The Treasury Solicitors, One Kemble Street, London, WC2B 4TS, ☎020 7210 3000 Fax: 020 7210 3250, ✉vling@tsol.gsi.gov.uk, *Call Date: Oct 1998, Middle Temple*
Qualifications: [LLB (Hons)(Notts)]

LINNETT MRS LYNN MARIE

Court Clerk, Hmcs Thames Valley, Thames Valley Magistrates' Courts Service, Waverley House, Queens Avenue, Bicester, Oxfordshire, OX26 2NZ, ☎01869 853100 Fax: 01869 853103, ✉lynn.linnett1@hmcourts-service.gsi.gov.uk, *Call Date: Nov 1986, Gray's Inn*
Qualifications: [Dip Law]

LINSLEY MS SIOBHAN MARIE

Crown Prosecution Service, 10 Malmesbury Place, Southhampton, SO15 5FS, ☎7771870757, *Call Date: Nov 2003, Inner Temple*
Qualifications: [LLB (Essex)]

LIPSCOMB MRS MARINA LYNN

London Borough of Islington, Legal Services, Room 206, 2nd Floor, Town Hall, Upper Street, London, N1 2UD, ✉marina.lipscomb@islington.gov.uk, *Call Date: Nov 1987, Gray's Inn*
Qualifications: [BSc Econ (Hons) Dip Law]

F

LIS MISS JACQUELINE MARY

Crown Prosecution Service, Heol Penlanffos, Tanerdy, Carmarthen, Wales, SA31 2EZ, *Call Date: July 1985, Lincoln's Inn*
Qualifications: [BA Dip Law]

LISGARTEN MS BARBARA KIMPINDE

Dacorum Borough Council, Civic Centre, Marlowes, Hemel Hempstead, Hertfordshire, HP1 1HH, ☎01442 228000
Fax: 01442 228746, ✉barbara.lisgarten@dacorum.gov.uk, *Call Date: Nov 2000, Inner Temple*
Qualifications: [LLB]

LITCHFIELD MISS SARAH KATE

University of Surrey, Senate House, Guildford, Surrey, GU2 7XH, ☎01483 683764, ✉s.litchfield@surrey.ac.uk, *Call Date: Feb 1992, Gray's Inn*
Qualifications: [BA (Oxon)]

LITTLE MR GEORGE BRADBURY

HM Revenue and Customs, 2nd Floor, South West Bush House, London, WC2B 4RD, ☎020 7438 7268 Fax: 020 7438 4382, *Call Date: Nov 1987, Inner Temple*
Qualifications: [LLB (Lond)]

LIVESEY MR NICHOLAS RALPH

Department For Transport, Dept. For Transport, Accident Investigation, And Transport Security, Zone 1/03d, Great Minster House, 76 Marsham Street, London, SW1P 4DR, ☎020 7944 6460 Fax: 020 7944 2226, ✉Nicholas.livesey@dft.gsi.gov.uk, *Call Date: Nov 1991, Lincoln's Inn*
Qualifications: [BA (Hons) (Kent)]

LIXANDRU MR EMIL MIHAI

Chambers of Mr E M Lixandru, 5 Ebbett Court, Victoria Road, London, W3 6BW, *Call Date: Mar 2012, Lincoln's Inn*

LLOYD MISS CATHERINE RACHEL

Legal Adviser, Department For Business, Innovation and Skills, 1 Victoria Street, London, SW1H 0ET, ☎020 7215 5000, ✉catherine.lloyd@bis.gsi.gov.uk, *Call Date: July 2002, Middle Temple*
Qualifications: [BA (Hons) (Cantab)]

LLOYD MR DANIEL RHYS

BT Group PLC, British Telecommunications Group PLC, Bt Centre, Pp B8d, 81 Newgate Street, London, EC1A 7AJ, ✉daniel.lloyd@bt.com, *Call Date: Nov 1996, Inner Temple*
Qualifications: [BA (Wales)]

LLOYD MISS EIRLYS MORVEN SHEENA LLOYD

Ksa Group Ltd, Unit 7-8, The Chaudlery, Quayside, Berwick-Upon-Tweed, TD15 1HE, ☎01289 331 873 Fax: 01289 309 429, ✉eirlysl@ksagroup.co.uk, *Call Date: Apr 1991, Middle Temple*
Qualifications: [LLB (Edin)]

LLOYD MR JOHN DESMOND

Crown Advocate, Crown Prosecution Service, Capital Tower, Greyfriars Road, Cardiff, CF10 3PL, ☎029 2080 3800, ✉john.lloyd@cps.gsi.gov.uk, *Call Date: Nov 1987, Gray's Inn*
Qualifications: [LLB (Hons) (Wales)]

LOCKLEY MR PETER JONATHAN

Legal Adviser, Hmcts Secretariat, Upper Bond Street, Hinckley, Leicestershire, ☎01455 623030 Fax: 01509 261714, ✉peter.lockley@hmcourts-service.gsi.gov.uk, *Call Date: Mar 1998, Lincoln's Inn*
Qualifications: [BA (Hons)(Oxon)]

LODATO MR PAUL SIMON

Crown Prosecution Service, Rose Court, 2 Southwark Bridge, London, SE1 9HS, ✉Paul.Lodato@cps.gsi.gov.uk, *Call Date: Nov 2003, Middle Temple*
Qualifications: [LLB (Hons) (Wales)]

LODGE MR NICHOLAS CHARLES GARA

Chair, Bhatia Best Solicitors, 12 Carrington Street, Nottingham, NG1 7FF, ☎0115 950 3231 Fax: 0115 941 3169, ✉info@bhatiabest.co.uk, *Call Date: July 1979, Gray's Inn*
Qualifications: [BA M Theol]

LONERGAN MR PAUL HENRY

Department For Transport, Great Minster House, 33 Horseferry Road, London, SW1P 4DR, *Call Date: Oct 1991, Lincoln's Inn*
Qualifications: [MA (Cantab)]

F

LONG MISS LORINDA JOANNE

Head of Legal Services, LJL Transaction Management Limited, Willow House, 81 Imperial Road, Windsor, SL4 3RU, *Call Date: Nov 1988, Middle Temple*
Qualifications: [LLB Dip Pet Law]

LONG MR TOBIAS CHARLES

Noble Solicitors, The Point Business Centre, 1a Harrow Road, Wembley, Middlesex, HA9 6DE, ✉ t.long@noblesolicitors.co.uk, *Call Date: Nov 1988, Inner Temple*
Qualifications: [BA (UEA) DipLaw]

LONGMAN MR JONATHAN ALAN

Bray and Bray Solicitors, 1 Welford Road, Leicester, LE2 7AN, ☎ 0116 254 8871
Fax: 0870 3835023, ✉ info@braybray.co.uk, *Call Date: Nov 2004, Middle Temple*
Qualifications: [LLB (Hons)]

LONGMAN MISS ROSEMARIE JULIET

Lawtons Solicitors Ltd, Suite L, 19-25 Salisbury Square, Old Hatfield, Hertfordshire, AL9 5BT, ☎ 01707 270905
Fax: 01707 260881, ✉ RosieLongman@LawtonsLaw.co.uk, *Call Date: Nov 2002, Lincoln's Inn*
Qualifications: [BA (Hons)(Cantab) MA]

LOUGHNEY MRS SHERYL JANE

District Crown Prosecutor, Crown Prosecution Service, 2 King Edward Court, King Edward Street, Nottingham, Nottinghamshire, NG1 1EL, ☎ 01158 523477, ✉ sheryl.loughney@cps.gsi.gov.uk, *Call Date: Nov 1996, Gray's Inn*
Qualifications: [BA (Hons)(Nott'm)]

LOW MS POLLY ANN

Lawyer, Legal Services, Shire Hall, Box Res 1001, Cambridge, CB3 0AP, ☎ (01223) 714675 Fax: (01223) 717074, ✉ Polly.Low@cambridgeshire.gov.uk, *Call Date: Nov 1990, Middle Temple*
Qualifications: [LLB (Wales)]

LOWETH MR CHRIS RICHARD

Senior Lawyer, Locog Ltd, One Churchill Place, Canary Wharf, London, E14 5LN, ☎ 020 3201 2000, *Call Date: Oct 1996, Lincoln's Inn*
Qualifications: [LLB (Hons)(Lond)]

LOWSON MR NORMAN LAURENCE

Crown Prosecution Service, St Ann's Quay, 122 Quayside, Newcastle Upon Tyne, Tyne and Wear, NE1 3BD, ☎ 0191 2604236, ✉ norman.lowson@cps.gsi.gov.uk, *Call Date: July 1989, Lincoln's Inn*
Qualifications: [Dip Law]

LOWTHER MRS SAMANTHA SARAH-ANNE

Crown Prosecution Service, County House, 100 New London Road, Chelmsford, Essex, CM2 0RG, ☎ 01245 455800
Fax: 01245 455809, ✉ samantha.lowther@cps.gsi.gov.uk, *Call Date: July 1995, Lincoln's Inn*
Qualifications: [BCL BL]

LOYAL MRS JASY

Director of Legal Services, Hca International Limited, 242 Marylebone Road, London, NW1 6JL, ☎ 020 7616 4861, *Call Date: July 1984, Inner Temple*
Qualifications: [LLB LLM]

LUCAROTTI MR JOHN RICHARD KERR

Nursing and Midwifery Council, 23 Portland Place, London, W1B 1PZ, ✉ john.lucarotti@nmc-uk.org, *Call Date: July 2004, Middle Temple*
Qualifications: [BA (Lond) CPE]

LUDLAM MR GRAHAM

DAC Beachcroft LLP, 3 Minster Court, Mincing Lane, London, EC3R 7DD,
Fax: 020 7936 2020, ✉ GLudlam@dacbeachcroft.com, *Call Date: Oct 1998, Lincoln's Inn*
Qualifications: [BA (Hons)]

LUMB MR KEITH SIMON MARTIN

Crown Prosecution Service, Riverside House, Riverside Way, Bedford Road, Northampton, Northamptonshire, NN1 5NX, ✉ keith.lumb@cps.gsi.gov.uk, *Call Date: Nov 1979, Gray's Inn*
Qualifications: [LLB (Hons)]

F

LUNN MISS CHRISTINE NICOLA

Legal Adviser, Her Majesty's Courts Service, South Western Magistrates' Court, 176a Lavender Hill, London, SW11 1JU, ☎020 7805 1420, ✉Christine.lunn@hmcourts-service.gsi.gov.uk, *Call Date: Nov 1992, Lincoln's Inn*
Qualifications: [LLB (Hons)]

LUNN MR CHRISTOPHER SIMON

Other, Citigroup Global Markets Asia Ltd, 41/F. One Island East, 18 Westlands Road, Island East, Hong Kong, China, ✉christopher.lunn@citi.com, christopher.lunn@citigroup.com, *Call Date: Nov 1995, Gray's Inn*
Qualifications: [LLB (Lond)]

LUTTER MRS SUSAN

Justices' Clerk, Thames Valley Magistrates' Courts Service, Waverley House, Queens Avenue, Bicester, Oxfordshire, OX26 2NZ, *Call Date: July 1978, Gray's Inn*
Qualifications: [LLB DMS]

LYNCH MRS ANTOINETTE CASSANDRA BERNADETT

Birmingham City Council, Ingleby House, Litigation Department, 11-14 Cannon Street, Birmingham, B2 5EN, ☎0121 303 9199 Fax: 0121 303 9383, *Call Date: Nov 1994, Inner Temple*
Qualifications: [LLB (Lond)]

LYNCH MR SIMON JAMES

The Treasury Solicitors, One Kemble Street, London, WC2B 4TS, *Call Date: Oct 2006, Lincoln's Inn*
Qualifications: [BA (Oxon)]

LYNDS MR WILLIAM ALEXANDER

Deputy District Judge, Winchester City Council, City Offices, Colebrook, Winchester, SO23 9LJ, *Call Date: July 1999, Middle Temple*
Qualifications: [BA (Hons)]

LYON MRS JACQUELINE ANNE

Crown Prosecution Service, Queen House, 58 Victoria Street, St. Albans, Hertfordshire, AL1 3HZ, *Call Date: Feb 1988, Inner Temple*
Qualifications: [LLB (Hons)]

LYON MR VICTOR LAWRENCE

Recorder, Attride-Stirling and Woloniecki, Crawford House, 50 Cedar Avenue, Hm11, Po Box Hm 2879, Hamilton Hmlx, Bermuda, ☎001 441 295 6500 Fax: 001 441 294 6566, ✉vlyon@essexcourt.net, victor.lyon@aswlaw.com, *Call Date: July 1980, Gray's Inn*
Qualifications: [MA (Cantab)]

LYONS MRS RUTH

Lawyer, Department For Business, Innovation and Skills, 1 Victoria Street, London, SW1H 0ET, ✉ruth.lyons@bis.gsi.gov.uk, *Call Date: Nov 1981, Middle Temple*

LYTHGOE MR STUART GRAHAM SILVESTER

Call Date: July 1982, Gray's Inn
Qualifications: [LLB (Bris)]

MACDAID MISS MOIRA MAJELLA

Senior Crown Prosecutor, Crown Prosecution Service, Rose Court, 2 Southwark Bridge, London, SE1 9HS, ✉moira.macdaid@cps.gsi.gov.uk, *Call Date: July 1985, Gray's Inn*
Qualifications: [BA (Hons)]

MACGREGOR MR ALASTAIR RANKIN

Mediator, Criminal Cases Review Commission, 5 St Philips Place, Birmingham, B3 2PW, *Call Date: July 1974, Lincoln's Inn*
Qualifications: [MA (Oxon)]

MACK MR JAMES DAVID

Senior Legal Adviser, Office of Gas and Electricity Markets (Ofgem), Office of Gas and Electricity Markets, 9 Millbank, London, SW1P 3GE, *Call Date: Nov 2002, Middle Temple*
Qualifications: [MA (Cantab)]

MACKELVIE JUTSUM MISS JANE MARGARET LOUISE

Advocate, Crown Prosecution Service, Rose Court, 2 Southwark Bridge, London, SE1 9HS, ☎020 7023 6500 Fax: 020 7023 6501, ✉jane.mackelvie-jutsum@cps.gsi.gov.uk, *Call Date: Oct 1995, Gray's Inn*
Qualifications: [B.Sc (Wales) MSc (Lond) DIC Dip Law FGS]

F

MACKENOW LIEUTENANT HELEN REBECCA

Other, Royal Navy Officers, Directorate of Naval Legal Services, Mp 4-2, Leach Building, Whale Island, Portsmouth, PO2 8BY, *Call Date: Oct 2008, Middle Temple*
Qualifications: [LLB (Hons) (Luton)]

MACKENZIE MISS ANNA KAREEN

Maidments Solicitors Ltd, River House, 22 The Crescent, Salford, M5 4PF, Fax: 0845 017 6633, ✉anna.mackenzie@maidments.co.uk, *Call Date: Nov 1994, Lincoln's Inn*
Qualifications: [LLB (Hons)(L'pool)]

MACKESY MS TERTIA ELIZABETH

Senior Crown Prosecutor, Crown Prosecution Service, The Cooperage, 8 Gainsford Street, London, SE1 2NG, ☎020 7378 4196 Fax: 020 7378 4101, *Call Date: Nov 1993, Inner Temple*
Qualifications: [BA Dip Law (Lond)]

MACKINTOSH MR ANDREW STUART

Crown Prosecution Service, Sunlight House, Quay Street, Manchester, M60 3PS, *Call Date: Nov 1990, Middle Temple*
Qualifications: [BA (Keele) MPhil (Cantab)]

MACLAUCHLAN MR IAIN JOHN GERALD

Other, Chadwick Lawrence LLP, 13 Railway Street, Huddersfield, HD1 1JS, ☎01484 519999 Fax: 01484 468399, ✉iainmaclauchlan@chadlaw.co.uk, *Call Date: Oct 1992, Lincoln's Inn*
Qualifications: [LLB (Hons) Dip Th (Oxon)]

MACNAMARA MISS JILLIAN

Principal Crown Prosecutor, Crown Prosecution Service, Froomsgate House, Rupert Street, Bristol, BS1 2QJ, ☎0117 952 9811, ✉jill.macnamara@cps.gsi.gov.uk, *Call Date: Feb 1987, Gray's Inn*
Qualifications: [LLB (Notts)]

MACPHERSON MRS ELLORA

Senior Legal Counsel, Warnaco Inc, Linen Hall, 162-168 Regent Street, London, W1B 5TB, ☎020 3100 2909, ✉EMacPherson@warnaco.com, *Call Date: Nov 1999, Middle Temple*
Qualifications: [BSc (Hons)(City)]

MACRAE MRS ANNE GLOVER

Foster Wheeler Energy Ltd, Shinfield Park, Reading, Berkshire, RG2 9FW, ☎0118 913 8793 Fax: 0118 913 2333, ✉anne_macrae@fwuk.fwc.com, *Call Date: Nov 1989, Inner Temple*
Qualifications: [B Arch (Glas) Dip Law (City) RIBA MCIArb]

MAEHLE MRS JILLIAN MARY

Hartlepool Mind Legal Services, Crown Buildings, Tees Street, Hartlepool, TS24 8HB, ☎01429 269303 Fax: 01429 422262, *Call Date: Oct 1992, Middle Temple*
Qualifications: [BA (Hons) (Hull) CPE LLM (Dunelm)]

MAGENNIS MR BRENDAN PATRICK

Office of Fair Trading, Fleetbank House, 2-6 Salisbury Square, London, EC4Y 8JX, ☎020 7211 8995 Fax: 020 7211 8694, ✉Brendan.Magennis@oft.gsi.gov.uk, *Call Date: Nov 2010, Inner Temple*
Qualifications: [LLB (Ireland)]

MAGUIRE MISS LINDSAY JANE

Senior Legal Adviser, Legal Services, The Farmhouse, Thames Valley Police Headquarters, Kidlington, Oxfordshire, OX5 2NX, ☎01865 846305, *Call Date: Nov 1981, Gray's Inn*
Qualifications: [BA (Hons)]

MAGYAR MR NICHOLAS

Legal Adviser, Department of Energy and Climate Change, 3 Whitehall Place, London, SW1A 2AW, *Call Date: July 1986, Inner Temple*
Qualifications: [LLB (So'ton)]

MAHARAJ MR NARAINDRA

Manager, Ibm United Kingdom Limited, 1 New Square, Bedfont Lakes, Mail Point 21 Green, Feltham, Middlesex, TW14 8HB, Fax: 020 8844 6571, *Call Date: Nov 2000, Middle Temple*
Qualifications: [LLB (Hons) LLM (Lond)]

MAHONY MISS RACHEL ANN

Caseworker, Crown Prosecution Service, Charing Cross Police Station, Agar Street, London, WC2N 4JP, ☎020 3300 2313 Fax: 020 3300 2361, ✉rachel.mahony@cps.gsi.gov.uk, *Call Date: July 2007, Lincoln's Inn*
Qualifications: [BA (Staffs)]

F

MAHY MS HELEN MARGARET

Company Secretary, General Counsel, National Grid PLC, 1-3 Strand, London, WC2N 5EH, ☎020 7004 3220 Fax: 020 7004 3221, ✉helen.mahy@ngrid.com, *Call Date: July 1982, Middle Temple*
Qualifications: [LLB (Hons) (Manch) ACII]

MAINWARING MISS SAMANTHA JAYNE

Crown Prosecution Service, Cambria House, Pentrebach Industrial Estate, Pentrebach, Merthyr Tydfil, Mid Glamorgan, CF48 4XA, Fax: 01443 694804, ✉Samantha.Mainwaring@cps.gsi.gov.uk, *Call Date: Oct 2000, Lincoln's Inn*
Qualifications: [LLB (Hons) (Swansea)]

MAIR MISS CAROLINE

Bcl Burton Copeland, 51 Lincoln's Inn Fields, London, WC2A 3LZ, ☎020 7430 2277 Fax: 020 7430 1101, ✉law@bcl.com, *Call Date: Nov 2005, Middle Temple*
Qualifications: [BA (Bris) PGDL]

MAJOR MISS REBECCA CECELIA

The Treasury Solicitors, One Kemble Street, London, WC2B 4TS, ☎020 7210 3000, *Call Date: July 2003, Middle Temple*
Qualifications: [BSc (Lanc) Msc Msc PG Dip Law]

MAJUMDAR MR SOUMYA KANTI

Senior Lawyer, Crown Prosecution Service, Rose Court, 2 Southwark Bridge, London, SE1 9HS, ☎020 3357 0481 Fax: 020 3357 0388, ✉soumya.majumdar@cps.gsi.gov.uk, *Call Date: Nov 1988, Lincoln's Inn*
Qualifications: [LLB (Hons)]

MAKKAN MR SHAMSHUDDIN

Crown Advocate, Crown Prosecution Service, Bolton Police Station, 10 Scholey Street, Bolton, Greater Manchester, BL2 1HX, *Call Date: Feb 1987, Lincoln's Inn*
Qualifications: [LLB (Hons)]

MALHI MISS TAJINDER KAUR

The Treasury Solicitors, One Kemble Street, London, WC2B 4TS, ☎020 7210 3586, *Call Date: July 2004, Middle Temple*
Qualifications: [LLB (Hons)]

MALIK MR BILLAL

HM Revenue and Customs, 1st Floor, South West Bush House, London, WC2B 4RD, *Call Date: Nov 2005, Inner Temple*

MALIK MR IJAZ AHAMED

Crown Prosecution Service, Bishopsgate Police Station, 182 Bishopgate, Bishopsgate, London, EC2M 4NP, Fax: 020 3300 1598, ✉ijaz.malik@cps.gsi.gov.uk, *Call Date: Nov 1982, Gray's Inn*
Qualifications: [LLB]

MANASSI MISS XENIA POLYXENI

Luton Borough Council Legal Services, Town Hall, Luton, LU1 2BQ, Fax: 01582 546026, ✉xenia.manassi@luton.gov.uk, *Call Date: Mar 2002, Middle Temple*
Qualifications: [LLB (Hons) LLM]

MANCE MISS JESSICA MARY KEZIA

Thomas Miller & Co Ltd, 90 Fenchurch Street, London, EC3M 4ST, *Call Date: July 2002, Middle Temple*
Qualifications: [MA (Hons) (Cantab) LLM]

MANEKPORIA MS RESHMI

Berwin Leighton Paisner, Adelaide House, London Bridge, London, EC4R 9HA, ☎020 3400 1000 Fax: 020 3400 1111, ✉Reshmi.Manekporia@blplaw.com, *Call Date: Nov 2000, Inner Temple*
Qualifications: [LLB (Lond)]

MANIS MR JOHN GEORGE

Burges Salmon LLP, Narrow Quay House, Narrow Quay, Bristol, BS1 4AH, ☎0117 939 2000 Fax: 0117 902 4400, ✉john.manis@burges-salmon.com, *Call Date: Oct 2005, Gray's Inn*
Qualifications: [BA (Warwick)]

MANN MR PETER

Crown Prosecution Service, Jefferson House, 27 Park Place, Leeds, West Yorkshire, LS1 2SZ, ☎0113 290 2700 / 0113 290 2700 Fax: 0113 290 2701 / 0113 290 2701, ✉peter.mann@cps.gsi.gov.uk, *Call Date: July 1986, Middle Temple*
Qualifications: [LLB (Manch)]

F

MARK MR ANDREW BRIAN

Kyles Legal Practice Ltd, 20 Northumberland Square, North Shields, Tyne and Wear, NE30 1PX, *Call Date: Nov 1981, Inner Temple*
Qualifications: [BA (Newc)]

MARKHAM MR DAVID HAROLD

Attorney, Crown Prosecution Service, Wood Green Crown Court, Woodall House, Lordship Lane, Wood Green, London, N22 5LF, ✉David.Markham@cps.gsi.gov.uk, *Call Date: Nov 1983, Gray's Inn*
Qualifications: [BA MA]

MARKS MR STUART DAVID

Lawyer, Department For Transport, Great Minster House, 33 Horseferry Road, London, SW1P 4DR, *Call Date: July 1982, Gray's Inn*
Qualifications: [LLB (Lond)]

MARLAND MS EUNICE ELIZABETH

Royal Navy Officers, Directorate of Naval Legal Services, Mp 4-2, Leach Building, Whale Island, Portsmouth, PO2 8BY, *Call Date: July 2007, Middle Temple*
Qualifications: [BSc (Hons) (Manch) LLB]

MARLOW MS CLAIRE DEBORAH

Crown Prosecution Service, Fox Talbot House, Bellinger Close, Malmesbury Road, Chippenham, Wiltshire, SN15 1BN, ☎01249 766100, ✉claire.marlow@cps.gsi.gov.uk, *Call Date: July 1983, Gray's Inn*
Qualifications: [BA (Hons)]

MARRIOTT MR IAN LESLIE

Lawyer, Warwickshire County Council, Legal Services Division, Po Box 9, Shire Hall, Warwick, Warwickshire, CV34 4RR, ☎01926 412018 Fax: 01926 418008, ✉ianmarriott@warwickshire.gov.uk, *Call Date: Nov 1984, Middle Temple*
Qualifications: [LLB (Nott'm)]

MARSH MRS CERI LOUISE

Royal Navy Officers, Directorate of Naval Legal Services, Mp 4-2, Leach Building, Whale Island, Portsmouth, PO2 8BY, ☎02392 625739, *Call Date: July 2009, Middle Temple*
Qualifications: [BA (Hons) (Middx)]

MARSH MISS CLAIRE JUNE

Crown Prosecution Service, Sunlight House, Quay Street, Manchester, M60 3PS, ☎0161 827 4944, *Call Date: Nov 1997, Lincoln's Inn*
Qualifications: [LLB (Hons)(Manch)]

MARSH MR MARK NIGEL RICHARD BAXTER

Crown Prosecution Service, London Area Traffic Prosecution Service, 6th Floor, Marlowe House, Sidcup, Kent, DA15 7ES, ✉mark.marsh@cps.gsi.gov.uk, *Call Date: Apr 1989, Middle Temple*
Qualifications: [LLB]

MARSH MISS SUSAN AMANDA

Rundle Walker Solicitors, The Gallery, King's Wharf, The Quay, Exeter, EX2 4AN, ☎01392 209209 Fax: 01392 209208, ✉susan.marsh@rundlewalker.com, sue.marsh@rundlewalker.com, *Call Date: Oct 1998, Inner Temple*
Qualifications: [LLB Dip Law]

MARSHALL MR ANDREW

Standing Counsel, 18 Red Lion Court, 18 Red Lion Court, London, EC4A 3EB, ☎020 7520 6000 Fax: 020 7520 6248/49, ✉andrew.marshall@18rlc.co.uk, andrew.marshall@18rlc.cjsm.net, *Call Date: July 1986, Inner Temple*
Qualifications: [LLB (Lond)]

MARSHALL MR ANDREW FRANCIS

Oracle Corporation, 15 Boulevard Charles De Gaulle, Colombes, 92715, France, Fax: 15 760 2032, ✉andrew.marshall@oracle.com, *Call Date: May 1996, Gray's Inn*
Qualifications: [BA (L'pool)]

MARSHALL-CASSON MS JOANNA TAMAR

Legal Adviser, The Treasury Solicitors, 5th Floor, One Kemble Street, London, WC2B 4TS, ☎020 7271 1427, ✉joanna.marshall-casson@ogc.gsi.gov.uk, *Call Date: Nov 1990, Middle Temple*
Qualifications: [BA (Cantab) DEL (Belgium) LLM]

F

MARTIN MRS CHARAN MARGARET HELENA

The National Youth Advocacy Service, Egerton House, Tower Road, Birkenhead, Wirral, CH41 1FN, Fax: 0151 649 8701, ✉ charan.martin@nyas.net, *Call Date: Oct 1991, Inner Temple*
Qualifications: [LLB (Hons) (Leics)]

MARTIN MR GERARD

Advocate, Crown Prosecution Service, Snaresbrook Crown Court, 75 Hollybush Hill, Snaresbrook, London, E11 1QW, ☎ 020 8530 0240 Fax: 020 8530 1421, ✉ gerard.martin@cps.gsi.gov.uk, *Call Date: July 1986, Gray's Inn*
Qualifications: [LLB (Lond)]

MARTIN DR JILL ELIZABETH

Legal Adviser, Office of the Public Guardian, 6th Floor Tower, Zones 6.50 - 6.53, Ministry of Justice, London, SW1H 9AJ, *Call Date: Nov 1993, Lincoln's Inn*
Qualifications: [LLB(Hons) LLD (Lond) LLM (Lond)]

MARTIN MR RICHARD MYLES ANDREW

Knight Polson Solicitors, Criminal Defence Office, 4 Leigh Road, Eastleigh, Hampshire, SO50 9FH, ☎ 023 8064 4822
Fax: 023 8064 3951, *Call Date: Oct 1998, Middle Temple*
Qualifications: [BA (Hons)(Portsmout) CPE (York)]

MARTIN MISS ZOE VICTORIA

Crown Prosecution Service, Rose Court, 2 Southwark Bridge, London, SE1 9HS, *Call Date: Oct 1990, Gray's Inn*
Qualifications: [LLB]

MARTINS MISS YETUNDE TOKUNBO

Senior Crown Prosecutor, Crown Prosecution Service, Wembley Police Station, 603 Harrow Road, Wembley, Middlesex, HA0 2HH, *Call Date: July 1989, Middle Temple*
Qualifications: [BA (Hons)]

MASCARENHAS MRS MARGARET

Crown Prosecution Service, Queens House, 58 Victoria Street, St. Albans, Hertforshire, AL1 3HZ, ☎ 07790 701695, *Call Date: Nov 1996, Lincoln's Inn*
Qualifications: [LLB (Hons)(Middx)]

MASKREY MR SIMEON ANDREW

Deputy High Court Judge, Recorder, Seven Bedford Row, 7 Bedford Row, London, WC1R 4BS, ☎ 020 7242 3555 Fax: 020 7242 2511, ✉ smaskrey@7br.co.uk, *Call Date: July 1977, Gray's Inn*
Qualifications: [LLB]

MASON MR PHILIP JUDE

Overburys Solicitors, Overbury Steward Eaton and Woolsey, 3 Upper King Street, Norwich, NR3 1RL, Fax: 01603 632460, ✉ pmason@overburys.co.uk, *Call Date: July 1975, Gray's Inn*
Qualifications: [BA]

MASON MRS SANDRA FRANCESCA HERMIONE

Child & Child, 14 Grosvenor Crescent, London, SW1X 7EE, ✉ sandramason@childandchild.co.uk, *Call Date: July 1972, Middle Temple*
Qualifications: [BA Hons (Oxon)]

MATHARU MR JITINDER SINGH

Principal Crown Prosecutor, Crown Prosecution Service, Colmore Gate, 2 - 6 Colmore Row, Birmingham, West Midlands, B3 2QA, ☎ 0121 262 1300
Fax: 0121 262 1500, *Call Date: July 1981, Inner Temple*

MATHEW MR OSCAR JONATHAN FAIRBANK

General Medical Council, Regent's Place, 350 Euston Road, London, NW1 3JN,
Fax: 0845 357 9001, ✉ omathew@gmc-uk.org, *Call Date: July 2009, Middle Temple*
Qualifications: [MA (Hons) (Edin) Grad Dip Law (Lond)]

MATHIAS MISS ANNA

Joelson Wilson LLP, 30 Portland Place, London, W1B 1LZ, ☎ 020 7580 5721, *Call Date: Oct 1994, Lincoln's Inn*
Qualifications: [LLB (Hons)(Warw)]

MATIC MR ALEXANDER

Crown Prosecution Service, Ilford Police Station, 270-294 High Road, Ilford, Essex, IG1 1GT, *Call Date: Oct 2000, Lincoln's Inn*
Qualifications: [LLB (Hons) (Manch)]

MATTHEWS MISS KELLY SUZANNE

Crown Prosecution Service, London Traffic Unit, Marlowe House, 109 Station Road, Sidcup, DA15 7ES, ✉Kelly.matthews@cps.gsi.gov.uk, *Call Date: Oct 2004, Middle Temple*
Qualifications: [LLB (Hons) Northumbria]

MAUDE MISS VICTORIA VIOLA

Wannop and Fox Solicitors, South Pallant House, Chichester, West Sussex, PO19 1TH, ☎01243 778844, *Call Date: Oct 1995, Middle Temple*
Qualifications: [LLB (Hons)]

MAWSON MR BENEDICT

SSB Solicitors, Matrix Complex, 91 Peterborough Road, London, SW6 3BU, ☎020 7348 7630, ✉ben@ssb.co.uk, *Call Date: Mar 2002, Lincoln's Inn*
Qualifications: [BA (Hons) (Manch)]

MAXWELL MISS JOANNE

Crown Prosecution Service, Higher Court Advocate Unit, Royal Liver Building, 7th Floor, Pier Head, Liverpool, Merseyside, L3 1HN, ☎0151 239 6400, ✉jo.maxwell@cps.gsi.gov.uk, *Call Date: Nov 1999, Gray's Inn*
Qualifications: [BA (Lincs)]

MAY MR ALAN

Other, Financial Services Authority, The Financial Services Authority, Enforcement and Financial Crime Division - Legal Group, 25 The North Colonade, Canary Wharf, London, E14 5HS, *Call Date: Oct 1995, Inner Temple*
Qualifications: [LLB (Hons)(Plymouth)]

MAY SMITH MR CARL DANIEL

Crown Prosecution Service, Stoke Newington Police Station, 33 Stoke Newington High Street, London, N16 8DS, ☎020 8721 5520, ✉carl.may-smith@cps.gsi.gov.uk, *Call Date: Oct 2005, Inner Temple*
Qualifications: [LLB King's College University of London]

MAYDON MR GARY

Company Secretary, General Counsel, St. Johns Ambulance, 27 St John's Lane, London, EC1M 4BU, ☎020 7324 4027, ✉gary.maydon@nhq.sja.org.uk, *Call Date: July 1996, Middle Temple*
Qualifications: [LLB (Hons)(Lond) FCIS FCIB FFA LLM]

MAYER MR ALEXANDER TIMOTHY

Woodsford Litigation Funding Limited, Monmouth House, 87-93 Westbourne Grove, London, W2 4UL, ☎020 7313 8087, *Call Date: Nov 1997, Gray's Inn*
Qualifications: [BA (Oxon), BCL]

MAYER MRS NANCY ELAINE

Senior Lawyer, HM Revenue and Customs, Solicitors Office, 4th Floor East, Ralli Quay, Stanley Street, Manchester, M60 9LB, ☎0161 827 0160, ✉nancy.mayer@hmrc.gsi.gov.uk, *Call Date: Nov 1983, Middle Temple*
Qualifications: [LLB (Nott'm)]

MAYLIN MS KERRY FIONA

Crown Prosecution Service, Black Horse House, 8-10 Leigh Road, Eastleigh, Hampshire, SO50 9FH, ☎02380 673800, *Call Date: Oct 1994, Gray's Inn*
Qualifications: [LLB]

MAYNE MISS CAROLINE MARGARET

Other, Rotch Limited, Rotch Limited, Leconfield House, Curzon Street, London, W1J 5JA, ✉c.mayne@rotch.com, *Call Date: Nov 1984, Inner Temple*
Qualifications: [LLB (Hons) (Leics)]

MAZIBRADA MR ANDREW GRANT

Crown Prosecution Service, Croydon Crown Court, Altyre Road, Croydon, Surrey, CR9 5AB, *Call Date: Nov 1999, Middle Temple*
Qualifications: [LLB (Hons) LLM (Lond)]

MCARDLE MR KEVIN EDWARD

Legal Officer, Merck Sharp and Dohme Limited, Hertford Road, Hoddesdon, Hertfordshire, EN11 9BU, ☎01992 452509 Fax: 01992 470189, ✉kevin_mcardle@merck.com, *Call Date: Nov 1989, Middle Temple*
Qualifications: [BSc LLB]

MCCAFFERTY MS ELAINE

Metropolitan Police Service, Directorate of Legal Services, First Floor (V), New Scotland Yard, 8-10 Broadway, London, SW1H 0BG, *Call Date: July 1979, Gray's Inn*
Qualifications: [LLB (L'pool) ACIB]

F

MCCAFFREY MISS TARRYN LYNNE

Crown Prosecution Service, Southern House, Wellesley Grove, Croydon, Surrey, CR9 1DY, ☎020 8662 2848 Fax: 020 662 2828, *Call Date: Oct 2005, Gray's Inn*
Qualifications: [BA (Keele)]

MCCAHON MR DAVID JOHN

Assistant General Counsel, Barclaycard, Lcr Department, 13. B4.2, 1 Churchill Place, Canary Wharf, London, E14 5HP, ☎020 7116 6377, ✉David.McCahon@barclaycard.co.uk, *Call Date: July 1988, Middle Temple*
Qualifications: [LLB (Hons) (Reading) LLM (Cantab)]

MCCALLA MR TARQUIN JEFFREY

Artesian Law, 3 Bolt Court, Fleet Street, London, EC4A 3DQ, ✉tarquin.mccalla@artesianlaw.com, *Call Date: Oct 1994, Lincoln's Inn*
Qualifications: [BA (Hons)(Hull)]

MCCANN MISS CATRYN ANNE

Her Majesty's Courts Service, Bromley Magistrates Court, The Court House, 1 London Road, Bromley, Kent, BR1 1RA, ☎020 8437 3546 Fax: 020 8437 3506, ✉catryn.mccann@hmcourts-service.gsi.gov.uk, *Call Date: July 1988, Lincoln's Inn*
Qualifications: [LLM LLB (Hons)(Lond)]

MCCANN MR HOWARD EARLE

Environment Agency, Kings Meadow House, Kings Meadow Road, Reading, Berkshire, RG1 8DQ, ☎01189 535 536 Fax: 01189 509 440, ✉howard.mccann@environment-agency.gov.uk, *Call Date: Mar 2010, Inner Temple*
Qualifications: [Bsoc Sci LLB LLM]

MCCANN MR JOHN MICHAEL

Senior Crown Prosecutor, Crown Prosecution Service, 6th Floor, Friars House, Warwick Road, Coventry, West Midlands, CV1 2TE, *Call Date: Nov 1983, Gray's Inn*
Qualifications: [LLB (Hons)(L'pool)]

MCCARROLL MR JOHN MICHAEL

Companies House, Crown Way, Maindy, Cardiff, Glamorgan, CF14 3UZ, ☎02920 380920 Fax: 02920 380953, *Call Date: Oct 1997, Gray's Inn*
Qualifications: [LLB (Wales) ATT CTA]

MCCARTHY MR JAMIE

Uxbridge Magistrates' Court, The Court House, Harefield Road, Uxbridge, Middlesex, UB8 1PQ, ☎01895 814646 311, ✉jamie.mccarthy@hmcourts-service.gsi.gov.uk, *Call Date: July 1999, Gray's Inn*
Qualifications: [BA (Hons)]

MCCARTHY MISS NIAMH JANE

International Airlines Group, LAG, 2 World Business Centre, Newall Road, London Heathrow Airport, London, TW6 2SF, ☎020 8564 2819, ✉niamh.mccarthy@iairgroup.com, *Call Date: Nov 1991, Gray's Inn*
Qualifications: [LLB (Ireland) D'Hautes Etudes Européennes (Belgium)]

MCCARTHY MISS SARAH JOANNE

Crown Prosecution Service, Rose Court, 2 Southwark Bridge, London, SE1 9HS, ✉sarah.mccarthy@cps.gsi.gov.uk, *Call Date: Nov 2001, Middle Temple*
Qualifications: [BA (Hons) CPE]

MCCARTNEY MR PETER

Beswicks Solicitors, Alexander House, Bethesda Street, Hanley, Stoke-On-Trent, ST1 3DX, ☎01782 205000 Fax: 01782 404665, *Call Date: Nov 1983, Inner Temple*
Qualifications: [BA]

MCCONAGHY MR RICHARD JAMES

Lionel Blackman Solicitors, Upper Chambers, 7 Waterloo Road, Epsom, Surrey, KT19 8AY, ☎01372 728941 Fax: 01372 741869, *Call Date: July 2005, Gray's Inn*
Qualifications: [BA]

MCCONOCHIE MR MARK LEA

HED, Legal Adviser, Transport for London, 7th Floor, Winsor House, 42-50 Victoria Street, London, SW1H 0TL, Fax: 020 7126 4598, ✉markmcconochie@tfl.gov.uk, *Call Date: Nov 1996, Middle Temple*
Qualifications: [BPharm (Hons) MR]

MCCORMACK MISS SHELEEN ELLEN

Chair, General Pharmaceutical Council, 129 Lambeth Road, London, SE1 7BT, ☎020 3365 3417, ✉Sheleen.Mccormack@pharmacyregulation.org, *Call Date: Feb 1993, Middle Temple*
Qualifications: [LLB (Hons)(Sheff)]

F

MCCREATH MS FIONA MARY

Legal Adviser, Southampton City Council, Southbrook Rise, 4-8 Millbrook Road East, Southampton, Hampshire, SP15 1YG, ☎023 8083 3212 Fax: 020 8083 3217, ✉fiona.mccreath@southampton.gov.uk, *Call Date: Oct 1991, Gray's Inn*
Qualifications: [LLB (Lond)]

MCCULLOUGH MISS JUDITH ANN

Aa Mirsons Solicitors Ltd, Ground Floor, Temple Chambers, Temple Avenue, London, EC4Y 0HP, *Call Date: Apr 1991, Middle Temple*
Qualifications: [LLB (Hons)]

MCDONAGH MR PETER MARTIN MICHAEL

HED, Other, Prosecution Team Leader, Crown Prosecution Service, Rose Court, 2 Southwark Bridge, London, SE1 9HS, ✉peter.mcdonagh@cps.gsi.gov.uk, *Call Date: July 1981, Inner Temple*
Qualifications: [LLB]

MCDONNELL MISS ADRIANNA

ACCA, 29 Lincoln's Inn Fields, London, WC2A 3EE, *Call Date: Nov 2001, Inner Temple*
Qualifications: [LLB]

MCDONNELL MR SCOTT

Legal Officer, Directorate of Army Legal Services, Idl 426, Ramillies Buildings, Marlborough Lines, Monxton Road, Andover, SP11 8HJ, *Call Date: Oct 1994, Middle Temple*
Qualifications: [BA (Hons) CPE (Bournemouth)]

MCDOUGALL LIEUTENANT COLONEL CRAIG ALLEN

Crown Advocate, Solicitor Advocate, Crown Prosecution Service, Justinian House, Spitfire Close, Ermine Business Park, Huntingdon, Cambridgeshire, PE29 6XY, ✉craig.mcdougall@cps.gsi.gov.uk, *Call Date: Oct 2004, Middle Temple*
Qualifications: [BSc]

MCDOUGALL MR IAN PAUL

TRM, Lexis Nexis (Butterworths Ltd), 125 Park Avenue, New York, USA, *Call Date: Oct 1997, Lincoln's Inn*
Qualifications: [BA (Hons)(Hull)]

MCENTEE MR FRANCIS RICHARD

HED, Higher Court Advocate, Senior Crown Prosecutor, Crown Prosecution Service, The Unicentre, Lords Walk, Preston, Lancashire, PR1 1DH, ☎01772 208100, *Call Date: July 1987, Inner Temple*
Qualifications: [LLB]

MCEVILLY MR GERARD MARTIN

General Pharmaceutical Council, 291 Lambeth Road, London, SE1 7BT, ☎020 3365 3400, ✉gerard.m.mcevilly@hotmail.com, *Call Date: Oct 1994, Lincoln's Inn*
Qualifications: [LLB (Hons)(Wolves)]

MCFARLANE MISS SUSAN JOYCE

Legal Adviser, Mitsubishi Trust International Limited, Mitsubishi Trust House, 24 Lombard Street, London, EC3V 9AJ, ☎020 7929 2866 Fax: 020 7929 3471, *Call Date: Nov 1985, Gray's Inn*
Qualifications: [LLB (Manc) LLM (Lond) ACIS PG Cert Corporate &, Investment Law]

MCGARR MRS LINDA MARIA

Judge, Directorate of Army Legal Services, Idl 426, Ramillies Building, Marlborough Lines, Monxton Road, Andover, SP11 8HJ, ☎01264 381906 Fax: 01264 381905, *Call Date: July 1985, Lincoln's Inn*
Qualifications: [LLB (Hons)]

MCGARY MS RAEDENE

Mcgary and Co, 89 Chelverton Road, London, SW15 1RW, ☎020 8788 5145, *Call Date: Feb 1995, Middle Temple*
Qualifications: [LLB (Hons)(Lond) BA]

MCGIBBON MS SUSANNA JUSTINE

Legal Adviser, Department For Communities & Local Government, Zone 4/B3, Eland House, Bressenden House, London, SW1E 5DU, ☎0303 444 1079, ✉susanna.mcgibbon@communities.gsi.gov.uk, *Call Date: Nov 1990, Lincoln's Inn*
Qualifications: [LLB (Sheff)]

MCGINTY MRS EMMA LOUISE

Law Officers of the Crown, St James Chambers, Po Box 96, St Peter Port, GY1 4BY, Guernsey, *Call Date: July 2002, Inner Temple*
Qualifications: [LLB (Lond)]

F

MCGINTY MR KEVIN CHARLES PATRICK

Legal Adviser, Attorney General's Office, 20 Victoria Street, London, SW1H 0NF, Fax: 020 7271 2453, *Call Date: July 1982, Gray's Inn*
Qualifications: [BA]

MCGIVERN MR BILL JOSEPH

Crown Prosecution Service, Kingston Crown Court, 6-8 Penrhyn Road, Kingston Upon Thames, Surrey, KT1 2BB, *Call Date: Nov 1987, Inner Temple*
Qualifications: [LLB]

MCGOWAN-SMYTH MISS MARGARET CHRISTINE

The Home Office, Legal Advisors Branch, Seacole, Ground Floor, 2 Marsham Street, London, SW1P 4DF, *Call Date: Nov 2005, Lincoln's Inn*
Qualifications: [LLB (Hons) (Leic)]

MCGRATH DR CASEY

States of Jersey: Economic Development Department, 3rd Floor, Liberation Place, St Helier, JE1 1BB, Jersey, ☎01534 440413, ✉caseyamcgrath@gmail.com, *Call Date: Oct 2006, Lincoln's Inn*
Qualifications: [BSc (Lond) PhD (Lond)]

MCGRATH MR JOHN DERMOT

Chorley Magistratesé Court, St Thomasés Square, Chorley, Lancashire, PR7 1DS, *Call Date: Nov 1984, Gray's Inn*
Qualifications: [LLB (L'pool)]

MCGRATH MR SIMON JAMES

Merrill Lynch Commodities, Merrill Lynch Financial Centre, 2 King Edward Street, London, EC1A 1HQ, ✉Simon_McGrath@ml.com, *Call Date: Oct 1995, Inner Temple*
Qualifications: [MA (Edin) CPE (Lond)]

MCGREGOR REV ALEXANDER SCOTT

Legal Adviser, The Archbishops' Council., Church House, Great Smith Street, London, SW1P 3AZ, ✉alexander.mcgregor@churchofengland.org, *Call Date: Oct 1996, Lincoln's Inn*
Qualifications: [MA (Oxon)]

MCGREGOR MRS MENNA LYN

Clerk, The Mercers' Company, Mercers' Hall, Ironmonger Lane, London, EC2V 8HE, ✉mennam@mercers.co.uk, *Call Date: Nov 1973, Lincoln's Inn*
Qualifications: [LLB (Hons)]

MCGURK MISS BERNADETTE KATHLEEN

Crown Prosecution Service, 2 King Edward Court, King Edward Street, Nottingham, Nottinghamshire, NG1 1EL, ☎0115 8523300, ✉bernadette.mcgurk@cps.gsi.giv.uk, *Call Date: Nov 2010, Lincoln's Inn*
Qualifications: [LLB (Keele)]

MCHAFFIE MR MALCOLM BRUCE

HED, Crown Prosecution Service, Rose Court, 2 Southwark Bridge, London, SE1 9HS, ☎020 3357 0000 Fax: 020 3357 6501, ✉malcolm.mchaffie@cps.gsi.gov.uk, *Call Date: Oct 1991, Lincoln's Inn*
Qualifications: [LLB (Hons) (B'ham)]

MCINNES MR NEIL

Pinsent Masons, 30 Crown Place, London, EC2A 4ES, *Call Date: Oct 1999, Middle Temple*
Qualifications: [BA (Hons)(Cantab) Dip Law]

MCINTYRE MR KENNETH JOHN

Upper Tribunal Appeal Chamber, 5th Floor Rolls Buildings, 7 Rolls Buildings, Fetter Lane, London, EC4A 1NL, ☎020 7071 5628, ✉kenny.mcintyre@hmcts.gsi.gov.uk], *Call Date: Mar 1997, Middle Temple*
Qualifications: [BA (Hons)]

MCKIM MR IAN PATRICK

Associate, Salans LLP, Millenium Bridge House, 2 Lambeth Hill, London, EC4V 4AJ, Fax: 020 7429 6001, ✉imckim@salans.com, *Call Date: Oct 1997, Gray's Inn*
Qualifications: [LLB]

MCKINLEY MR GREGOR CHARLES

Crown Advocate, Crown Prosecution Service, Woolwich Crown Court, 2 Belmarsh Road, London, SE28 0EY, ✉gregor.mckinley@cps.gsi.gov.uk, *Call Date: Oct 1992, Gray's Inn*
Qualifications: [BA (Hons)(Ireland) Dip Law]

MCLACHLAN MR EWAN

Crown Advocate, Crown Prosecution Service, Jefferson House, 27 Park Place, Leeds, West Yorkshire, LS1 2SZ, ☎0113 290 2700, *Call Date: July 1984, Gray's Inn*
Qualifications: [LLB (Leeds)]

MCLEAN MRS MANDY RACHEL

Crown Prosecution Service, Snaresbrook Crown Court, 75 Hollybush Hill, Snaresbrook, London, E11 1QW, *Call Date: Oct 1996, Middle Temple*
Qualifications: [LLB (Hons)(Kent)]

MCMINNIES MR STEPHEN MARK

Senior Crown Prosecutor, Crown Prosecution Service, The Cooperage, 8 Gainsford Street, London, SE1 2NE, ✉stephen.mcminnies@cps.gsi.gov.uk, *Call Date: Nov 1996, Gray's Inn*
Qualifications: [LLB (Hons)(Lond)]

MCMULLEN MISS CLARE

Financial Services Authority, The Financial Services Authority, Enforcement and Financial Crime Division - Legal Group, 25 The North Colonade, Canary Wharf, London, E14 5HS, ☎020 7066 0652 Fax: 020 7066 0653, ✉clare.mcmullen@fsa.gov.uk, *Call Date: Oct 2001, Inner Temple*
Qualifications: [BA (Oxon) CPE]

MCNABB MRS HANNAH LOUISE

Her Majesty's Court Service and Tribunal Service, Royal Courts of Justice, London, WC2A 2LL, *Call Date: Nov 1999, Lincoln's Inn*
Qualifications: [LLB (Hons)(Hull)]

MCNALLY MISS SARAH ELIZABETH

Call Date: Oct 1999, Lincoln's Inn
Qualifications: [BA (Cantab)]

MCNAUGHT MR PETER GODFREY

Health & Safety Executive, Redgrave Court, Melton Road, Bootle, Merseyside, L20 7HS, ☎0151 951 3506 Fax: 0151 951 3448, ✉peter.mcnaught@hse.gsi.gov.uk, *Call Date: July 1982, Middle Temple*
Qualifications: [LLB (B'ham)]

MCREDDIE MR DUNCAN CHRISTOPHER

Vickers Chisman and Wishlade, 33 Silver Street, Stockton-On-Tees, TS18 1SX, ☎01642 615439 Fax: 01642 615014, *Call Date: Nov 2006, Lincoln's Inn*
Qualifications: [LLB (Teesside)]

MCROBB MR MARTIN FREDERICK DAVID

Advocate, Crown Prosecution Service, Windsor House, Pepper Street, Chester, Cheshire, CH1 1TD, ☎01244 408 669, *Call Date: Oct 1994, Gray's Inn*
Qualifications: [LLB (Hons)]

MCVITIE MISS JUSTINE

GHP Legal, 26-30 Grosvenor Road, Wrexham, LL11 1BU, ☎01978 291456, *Call Date: Nov 1995, Inner Temple*
Qualifications: [LLB (Lond)]

MEAD MISS VANESSA JUNE

Financial Services Authority, 25 The North Colonade, Canary Wharf, London, E14 5HS, ☎020 70668286, *Call Date: Oct 1997, Middle Temple*
Qualifications: [LLB (Hons)(Lond)]

MEADS MISS REBECCA FRANCES

Peters & Peters Solicitors LLP, 15 Fetter Lane, London, EC4A 1BW, ☎020 7822 7777 Fax: 020 7822 7788, ✉rmeads@petersandpeters.com, *Call Date: Nov 2007, Gray's Inn*
Qualifications: [LLB (Sheff)]

MEALING-MCLEOD MS SALLY

Crown Prosecution Service, Queens House, 58 Victoria Street, St Albans, Hertfordshire, AL1 3HZ, ☎01727 798700 / 01727 798700 (switchboard) Fax: 020 8422 7014, ✉sallymm@btinternet.com, sally.mealing-mcleod@cps.gsi.gov.uk, *Call Date: July 2001, Inner Temple*
Qualifications: [PGDN RGN SRN MBA]

MEANS MS KATHERINE ANNE

HM Revenue and Customs, 2nd Floor, South West Wing, Bush House, Strand, London, WC2B 4RD, ☎020 7438 6609 Fax: 020 7438 6601, ✉kate.means@hmrc.gsi.gov.uk, *Call Date: July 2008, Lincoln's Inn*
Qualifications: [BA (Sussex) LLM (Essex)]

F

MEARS MISS NAILAH ABA

Berrymans Lace Mawer LLP, Salisbury House, London Wall, London, EC2M 5QN, *Call Date: July 2004, Inner Temple*

MEEKE MR COLIN WILSON

Crown Advocate, Crown Prosecution Service, Fox Talbot House, Bellinger Close, Malmesbury Road, Chippenham, Wiltshire, SN15 1BN, ☎01249 766100 / 01249 766100 Fax: 01249 766101 / 01249 766101, ✉colin.meeke@cps.gsi.gov.uk, *Call Date: July 1983, Gray's Inn*
Qualifications: [BA (Leics)]

MEHTA MR ISMAIL

HED, Haji Abdullah Alireza & Co Ltd, Po Box 8, Jeddad, 21411, Saudi Arabia, Fax: 2 648 3923, *Call Date: Nov 1984, Gray's Inn*
Qualifications: [LLB (Hons)(Lond)]

MEIKLE MR CHRISTIAN PAUL

Crown Prosecution Service, County House, 100 New London Road, Chelmsford, Essex, CM2 0RG, *Call Date: Nov 1999, Gray's Inn*
Qualifications: [LLB (Essex)]

MEJZNER MR STEPHEN JOHN

Artesian Law, 3 Bolt Court, Fleet Street, London, EC4A 3DQ, ✉stephen.mejzner@artesianlaw.com, *Call Date: Nov 1978, Middle Temple*
Qualifications: [LLB (Sheff)]

MELNICK MISS JUDITH ANN

Justices' Clerk, City of Westminster Magistrates Court, 70 Horseferry Road, London, SW1P 2AX, ☎020 7805 1072 Fax: 020 7805 1020, *Call Date: July 1979, Middle Temple*
Qualifications: [LLB (Lond)]

MENSAH MISS HELYN

Pinsent Masons, 30 Crown Place, London, EC2A 4ES, *Call Date: Oct 1998, Lincoln's Inn*
Qualifications: [LLB (Hons)(Kingston)]

MERCER MS AMANDA

Senior Crown Prosecutor, Crown Prosecution Service, Kingston Police Station, 5-7 High Street, Kingston-Upon-Thames, KT1 1LB, ✉Amanda.Mercer@cps.gsi.fov.uk, *Call Date: July 1986, Inner Temple*
Qualifications: [LLB]

MEREDITH MR JACK EDWARD

Bj Services Company (Uk) Ltd, Badentoy Avenue, Badentoy Park, Portlethen, Aberdeen, AB12 4YB, ✉jmeredith@bjservices.co.uk, *Call Date: Nov 1996, Lincoln's Inn*
Qualifications: [LLB (Hons)(Herts)]

MEREDITH MRS KATIE ALEXANDRA JANE

Ministry of Justice, 102 Petty France, London, SW1H 9AJ, ☎020 3334 4771 Fax: 020 3334 4035, ✉katie.meredith@justice.gsi.gov.uk, *Call Date: July 2002, Lincoln's Inn*
Qualifications: [LLB (Hons)]

MERTCAN MR EROL

The Treasury Solicitors, One Kemble Street, London, WC2B 4TS, ✉erol.mertcan@tsol.gsi.gov.uk, *Call Date: Nov 1996, Gray's Inn*
Qualifications: [LLB LLM (LSE)]

MESSENT MR JOHN GEORGE DENYS

Cleary Gottlieb Steen and Hamilton LLP, 55 Basinghall Street, London, EC2V 5EH, ☎020 7614 2200 Fax: 020 7600 1698, ✉jmessent@cgsh.com, *Call Date: Oct 2007, Inner Temple*
Qualifications: [BA (Oxon) LLM (Lond)]

MEW MR GRAEME STEUART

Clyde and Co LLP, 390 Bay Street, Suite 800, Toronto, Ontario, M5H 2Y2, Canada, ☎00 1 416 366 4555 Fax: 00 1 416 366 6110, *Call Date: July 1982, Middle Temple*
Qualifications: [BA LLB (Windsor)]

MEYER-PAYSAN MISS KATJA

Manager, Senior Legal Adviser, Nerine Trust Company (Hong Kong) Limited, 3109, Tower 2, Lippo Centre, 89 Queensway, Admiralty, Hong Kong, Fax: 2 537 7624, ✉katja.meyer-paysan@nerine.com.hk, *Call Date: Nov 2001, Middle Temple*
Qualifications: [LLB (Hons)]

MIAN MS SMINAH

Director, Goldman Sachs International, Limited, 133 Fleet Street, London, EC4A 2BB, ☎020 7552 3241, ✉sminah.mian@gs.com, *Call Date: Oct 1995, Inner Temple*
Qualifications: [LLB (Newc)]

F

MICHAEL MR ANTONIOS

Solicitor, London Borough of Haringey Council, Alexandra House, 10 Station Road, Wood Green, London, N22 7TE, ☎020 8489 3659 Fax: 020 8489 3963, ✉antonios.michael@haringey.gov.uk, *Call Date: Oct 2000, Lincoln's Inn*
Qualifications: [LLB (Hons) (Lond)]

MICKLEWRIGHT MR GUY EDWARD

Blake Lapthorn Solicitors, Watchmaker Court, 33 St John's Lane, London, EC1M 4DB, ☎020 7405 2000 Fax: 020 7814 9421, ✉Guy.Micklewright@bllaw.co.uk, *Call Date: July 2004, Lincoln's Inn*
Qualifications: [BA Hons (Warw)]

MIDDLETON MS EMMA LOUISE

The Ede and Ravenscroft Group, 93 Chancery Lane, London, WC2A 1DU, *Call Date: Nov 1996, Lincoln's Inn*
Qualifications: [BA(Jnt Hons)(Dunelm) MBA (Lond)]

MIDDLETON MISS EVELYN VIOLET

Siemens Enterprise Communications Limited, Brickhill Street, Willen Lake, Milton Keynes, MK15 0DJ, ✉eve.middleton@siemens-enterprise.com, *Call Date: July 1986, Lincoln's Inn*
Qualifications: [BA (New South Wales) Dip Law]

MIDDLETON MR SEAN

Royal College of Nursing, 3 Capital Court, Bittern Road, Sowton Industrial Estate, Exeter, EX2 7FW, *Call Date: Nov 1991, Lincoln's Inn*
Qualifications: [BA (Hons) (Keele) Dip Law LLM (Germany) MA (Lond)]

MILLEDGE MR PETER NEIL

Legal Adviser, The House of Lords, Westminster, London, SW1A 0PW, ☎020 7219 3211, ✉milledgep@parliament.uk, *Call Date: July 1977, Middle Temple*
Qualifications: [LLB (Lond)]

MILLER MS HAYLEY JANE

Westfield Shoppingtowns Ltd, Midcity Place, 71 High Holborn, London, WC1V 2EA, ☎020 7061 1400 Fax: 020 7061 1525, ✉hayley.miller@westfield-uk.com, *Call Date: Oct 1995, Inner Temple*
Qualifications: [LLB (Sussex)]

MILLER MISS HELENA-JAYNE

Crown Prosecution Service, Colemore Gate, 2 - 6 Colemore Row, Birmingham, West Midlands, B3 2QA, ☎0121 262 1300, *Call Date: Nov 1989, Middle Temple*
Qualifications: [LLB Hons]

MILLER MISS SOPHIE JANE

Association of the British Pharmaceutical Industry, 7th Floor, Southside, 105 Victoria Street, London, SW1E 6QT, *Call Date: Oct 1993, Lincoln's Inn*
Qualifications: [MA (Hons) (Cantab) Dip Law Dip Counselling Skills (Bris)]

MILLIGAN MR SCOTT GREGOR

Department of Energy and Climate Change, 3 Whitehall Place, London, SW1A 2AW, ☎0300 060 4000, *Call Date: July 1975, Middle Temple*
Qualifications: [MA (Oxon)]

MILLS MRS JULIE ANN

Deputy Justices' Clerk, Bristol Magistrates Court, Marlborough Street, Bristol, BS1 3NU, ☎0117 930 2414, *Call Date: July 1986, Inner Temple*
Qualifications: [CIPD Cert in Training Practise A1 Assessor Award]

MILNER MISS LESLEY

Crown Prosecution Service, Hounslow Police Station, 3-5 Montague Road, Hounslow, London, TW3 1LB, *Call Date: Feb 1992, Middle Temple*
Qualifications: [BA (Hon) (Lond) LLB (Hons) (Lond)]

MINIHAN MR SEAN THOMAS

Buxton Ryan & Co, 15 Bell Street, Sawbridgeworth, Hertfordshire, CM21 9AR, ☎01279 723434 Fax: 01279 723835, ✉info@buxtonryan.co.uk, *Call Date: Nov 1988, Gray's Inn*
Qualifications: [LLB]

MINTY MR GARETH JOHN

Crown Prosecution Service, Central Fraud Group,6th Floor Rose Court, 2 Southwark Bridge, London, SE1 9HS, ☎020 3357 0302 Fax: 020 3357 0236, *Call Date: July 2002, Gray's Inn*
Qualifications: [LLB (Brunel)]

F

MIRRIELEES MRS ESTHER MARGARET

Other, Foreign and Commonwealth Office, Room 200a, King Charles Street, London, SW1A 2AH, ☎020 7008 4515 Fax: 020 7008 4524, ✉Esther.mirrielees@fcolaw.gsi.gov.uk, esther.mirrielees@fco.gov.uk, *Call Date: Oct 1998, Inner Temple*
Qualifications: [LLB (Lond)]

MISTRY MRS CHANDRAPRABHA

Senior Crown Prosecutor, Crown Prosecution Service, Queens House, 58 Victoria Street, St. Albans, Hertforshire, AL1 3HZ, *Call Date: July 1976, Inner Temple*

MISTRY MR HIREN BALWANT

Commercial Lawyer, Boisbois Lawyers, 4 Bond Street, St Hilier, JE5 5QR, Jersey, ☎01534 480480, ✉Hiren.Mistry@boisbois.com, *Call Date: Nov 2002, Middle Temple*
Qualifications: [LLB (Hons) (Dunelm) LLM (Lond)]

MITCALF MR RICHARD JAMES

District Crown Prosecutor, Higher Court Advocate, Principal Crown Prosecutor, Prosecution Team Leader, Crown Prosecution Service, Burnley Wharf, Manchester Road, Burnley, Lancashire, BB11 1JG, ☎01772 593038 Fax: 01282 478588, ✉Richard.Mitcalf@cps.gsi.gov.uk, *Call Date: July 1983, Gray's Inn*
Qualifications: [BA (Hons)]

MITCHELL MRS FELICITY JANE

Adjudicator, The Office of the Independent Adj. For Higher Edu, Fifth Floor, Thames Tower, Station Road, Reading, RG1 1LX, ☎0118 959 9813, ✉felicity.mitchell@oiahe.org.uk, *Call Date: Oct 1992, Middle Temple*
Qualifications: [BA (Hons) Dip Law]

MITCHELL MR JOHN WINTERBURN

Principal Crown Prosecutor, Crown Prosecution Service, The Regatta, 6 Henley Business Park, Doddington Road, Lincoln, LN6 3QR, ☎01522 585900 Fax: 01522 585958, ✉john.mitchell@cps.gsi.gov.uk, *Call Date: Nov 1984, Gray's Inn*

MITCHELL MR PAUL

Crown Prosecution Service, United House, Piccadilly, York, North Yorkshire, YO1 9PQ, ☎01904 545538, *Call Date: Nov 1994, Inner Temple*
Qualifications: [BA (York) CPE (Lond)]

MITCHELL MISS TRACEY JANE

Northampton Magistrates' Court, Regents Pavillion, Summerhouse Road, Moulton Park, Northampton, Northamptonshire, NN3 1AS, ✉tracey.mitchell1@hmcourts-service.gsi.gov.uk, *Call Date: Nov 2000, Lincoln's Inn*
Qualifications: [LLB (Hons) (Luton)]

MITHANI MR MOHAMMED RAZA

Simmons & Simmons, Middle East LLP, Po Box 506688, Dubai, United Arab Emirates, ☎(0) 4 709 6630 Fax: (0) 4 709 6601, ✉raza.mithani@simmons-simmons.com, *Call Date: Mar 2000, Lincoln's Inn*
Qualifications: [LLB (Hons) (Leics)]

MOBEDJI MR FIRDAUS JEHANGIR

Serious Fraud Office, Head of Restraint and Confiscation Unit, Serious Fraud Office, Elm House, 10-16 Elm Street, London, WC1X 0BJ, ☎020 7239 7392 Fax: 020 7833 5413, ✉philip.mobedji@sfo.gsi.gov.uk, *Call Date: July 1977, Lincoln's Inn*
Qualifications: [BA (Hons)]

MOCKETT MR GRAHAM ANDREW

Manager, Her Majesty's Courts and Tribunals Service, Richmond-Upon-Thames Magistrates' Court, Parkshot, Richmond-Upon-Thames, Surrey, TW9 2RF, ☎020 8271 2326 Fax: 020 8271 2330, *Call Date: July 1989, Middle Temple*
Qualifications: [Dip Law Dip Mag Law DMS]

MODHWADIA MISS SHITAL

Jinnah and Co Solicitors, 11 Bowling Green Street, Leicester, LE1 6AS, *Call Date: Oct 2002, Gray's Inn*
Qualifications: [LLB (Warwick)]

MOGRIDGE MR FRASER MCLEAN

Directorate of Army Legal Services, Idl426, Ramillies Building, Marlborough Lines, Monxton Road, Andover, SP11 8HJ, *Call Date: Nov 1995, Inner Temple*
Qualifications: [LLB (Soton)]

MOHAMMED MR SOHAIL SAFDAR

Kingston's Solicitors, 141-143 Benwell Lane, Newcastle Upon Tyne, NE15 6RT, ☎0191 226 0333 Fax: 0191 226 0599, ✉sohail.mohammed@kingstonlaw.com, *Call Date: Oct 2005, Inner Temple*
Qualifications: [LLB University of Dundee LLM (Northumbria)]

MOHAMMED MR TARIQUE

Crown Prosecution Service, Gateway, 31 Power Close, Guildford, Surrey, GU1 1EJ, *Call Date: Nov 2001, Lincoln's Inn*
Qualifications: [LLB (Hons) BA (Hons) Law &, Accountancy]

MOLLOY MR COLIN VINCENT

District Crown Prosecutor, Crown Prosecution Service, Building 3, Etruria Valley Office Village, Etruria, Stoke-On-Trent, Staffordshire, ST1 5RU, ☎01782 664561 Fax: 01782 664555, ✉colin.molloy@cps.gsi.gov.uk, *Call Date: Feb 1985, Middle Temple*
Qualifications: [BA (Hons)]

MOLONEY MISS LOUISE CLAIRE

Her Majesty's Courts Service, Camberwell Green Magistrates Court, 15 D'Eynsford Road, London, SE5 7UP, ✉louise.moloney@hmcourts-service.gsi.gov.uk, *Call Date: Nov 1988, Gray's Inn*
Qualifications: [BA]

MOLONEY MR NEIL ANDREW

Nursing and Midwifery Council, 61 Aldwich, London, WC2B 4AE, ☎020 7482 5800, ✉neil-moloney@nmc-uk.org, *Call Date: Oct 1999, Gray's Inn*
Qualifications: [LLB (B'ham)]

MONAGHAN MR PETER JOHN

Deputy Justices' Clerk, Hmcs Dorset, Her Majesty's Courts Service, The Law Courts, Westwey Road, Weymouth, Dorset, DT4 8BS, Fax: 01305 761418, ✉peter.monaghan@hmcourts-service.gsi.gov.uk, *Call Date: Feb 1986, Middle Temple*
Qualifications: [DML DMS]

MONK MR THOMAS JOHN

Legal Adviser, Unipart Rail Limited, Jupiter Building, First Point, Balby Court Bank, Doncaster, South Yorkshire, DN4 5JQ, *Call Date: July 1976, Middle Temple*
Qualifications: [LLB]

MONRO MISS VIJAYA

Advocate, Deputy District Judge, Senior Crown Prosecutor, Crown Prosecution Service, St Peters House, Gower Street, Derby, Derbyshire, DE1 1SB, ☎01332 621600, *Call Date: May 1990, Lincoln's Inn*
Qualifications: [BA (Hons)]

MOODY MR SEAN-ALISTAIR

Crown Prosecution Service, Rose Court, 2 Southwark Bridge, London, SE1 9HS, *Call Date: July 1999, Lincoln's Inn*
Qualifications: [LLB (Hons) LLM]

MOORE MR BENJAMIN EDWARD

Crown Prosecution Service, Jefferson House, 27 Park Place, Leeds, West Yorkshire, LS1 2SZ, ☎0113 290 2700 Fax: 0113 290 2707, ✉Ben.Moore@cps.gsi.gov.uk, *Call Date: Nov 1999, Gray's Inn*
Qualifications: [BA (York)]

MOORE MISS CATHERINE MARGARET

Crown Prosecution Service, Rose Court, 2 Southwark, London, SE1 9HS, ☎020 33570334, ✉Catherine.Moore@cps.gsi.gov.uk, *Call Date: July 2003, Lincoln's Inn*
Qualifications: [LLB Hons (Lond)]

MOORE MISS JENNIFER MARY

Crown Prosecution Service, Rose Court, 2 Southwark Bridge, London, SE1 9HS, *Call Date: Oct 1992, Gray's Inn*
Qualifications: [LLB (Brunel)]

MOORE MRS KAREN MARIE

Southwark Council, Southwark Town Hall, Strategic Services Department, 31 Peckham Road, London, SE5 8UB, ☎020 7525 5000, *Call Date: Nov 1992, Middle Temple*
Qualifications: [LLB (Hons)]

MOORE MR SEAN BARRY

Legal Adviser, Royal Navy Officers, Mp2-2 Room 220, Navy Command Headquare, Whale Island, Portsmouth, Hampshire, PO2 8DY, ☎023 9262 8717, *Call Date: Oct 1999, Inner Temple*
Qualifications: [LLB (Kent)]

F

MOORE MISS ZIMBA MICHELLE

Legal Adviser, Ernst and Young LLP, 1 More London Place, London, SE1 2AF, ☎020 7951 9547 Fax: 020 7951 4263, ✉zmoore@uk.ey.com, *Call Date: Oct 1999, Middle Temple*
Qualifications: [LLB (Hons)(LSE) LLM (LSE)]

MOORE-WILLIAMS MS ANNE ELIZABETH

Company Director, COMT, Financial Services Authority, 25 The North Colannade, Canary Wharf, London, E14 8HS, *Call Date: Oct 1992, Inner Temple*
Qualifications: [BA (Keele) LLM (Lond)]

MOORMAN MISS LUCINDA CLAIRE

Simons Muirhead and Burton, 8-9 Frith Street, Soho, London, W1D 3JB, ☎020 3206 2700 Fax: 020 3206 2800, ✉lucy.moorman@smab.co.uk, *Call Date: Nov 1992, Inner Temple*
Qualifications: [LLM (Cantab)]

MORE MS GILLIAN CATHERINE

Department For Work and Pensions, 5th Floor, the Adelphi, 1-11 John Adam Street, London, WC2N 6HT, *Call Date: Nov 1996, Middle Temple*
Qualifications: [BA (Hons)(Kent) LLM (Canada)]

MORGAN MR ALEXANDER PAUL

Department of Energy and Climate Change, DECC Legal, Area 7B, 3 Whitehall Place, London, SW1A 2AW, *Call Date: Nov 2005, Middle Temple*
Qualifications: [LLB (Hons)]

MORGAN MR ANDREW PHILIP

Crown Prosecution Service, Gemini One, Oxford Business Park South, Garsington Road, Oxford, Oxfordshire, OX4 2LL, ☎01865 233400 Fax: 01865 233401, ✉andrew.morgan@cps.gsi.gov.uk, *Call Date: Oct 1998, Gray's Inn*
Qualifications: [LLB (Wales) LLM]

MORGAN MR IESTYN NEAL

Crown Advocate, Crown Prosecution Service, Priory Gate, 29 Union Street, Maidstone, Kent, ME14 1PT, ✉www.cps.gov.uk, *Call Date: Oct 2006, Middle Temple*
Qualifications: [BA (Hons) (Oxon)]

MORGAN MRS TINA JANE

Commercial Lawyer, John Kennedy Limited, 1st Floor, Venture House, 6 Silver Court, Watchmead, Welwyn Garden City, Herts, AL7 1TS, *Call Date: Oct 1995, Middle Temple*
Qualifications: [LLB (Hons)]

MORLEY MR ALISTAIR ERIC

Department of Energy and Climate Change, DECC Legal, Area 7B, 3 Whitehall Place, London, SW1A 2AW, *Call Date: Nov 1991, Middle Temple*
Qualifications: [BA (Hons)(Lond) MPhil (Oxon)]

MORLEY MR MICHAEL AZEVEDO

Crown Prosecution Service, Sunlight House, Quay Street, Manchester, M60 3PS, ☎0161 827 4700 Fax: 0161 827 4935, *Call Date: Nov 1995, Lincoln's Inn*
Qualifications: [LLB (Hons)(Hull) LLM (Hull)]

MORLEY MR PHILIP GEORGE MYLES

Crown Prosecution Service, 1 Hudson Quay, The Halyard, Middlesbrough, Cleveland, TS3 6RT, ☎01642 204 500, *Call Date: July 2005, Middle Temple*
Qualifications: [LLB (Hons)]

MORRIS MRS HELEN ELIZABETH

Caseworker, Higher Court Advocate, Crown Prosecution Service, 7th Floor (South), Royal Liver Building, Pier Head, Liverpool, Merseyside, L3 1HN, ☎0151 239 6537 Fax: 0151 239 6127, *Call Date: Nov 1996, Gray's Inn*
Qualifications: [LLB (Lond)]

MORRIS MR JAMES BARR

Partner, Irwin Mitchell LLP, 40 Holborn Viaduct, London, EC1N 2PZ, ☎0870 1500 100 Fax: 020 7404 0208, ✉jim.morris@irwinmitchell.com, *Call Date: Oct 2004, Lincoln's Inn*
Qualifications: [B Comm (Hons) (Edin) PgDI (Leic)]

MORRIS MS JUDITH VIRGINIA

Crown Prosecution Service, Riverside Chambers, Castle Street, Taunton, Somerset, TA1 4AP, ☎01823 425100 Fax: 01823 424111, ✉judith.morris@cps.gsi.gov.uk, *Call Date: Oct 2003, Inner Temple*
Qualifications: [LLB (L'pool)]

MORRIS MR MICHAEL JOHN

DAC Beachcroft LLP, Portwall Place, Portwall Lane, Bristol, BS99 7UD, ☎0117 918 2000 Fax: 0117 918 2100, ✉mmorris@dacbeachcroft.com, *Call Date: Nov 1996, Gray's Inn*
Qualifications: [BA (Cantab)]

MORRIS MR RICHARD GIDEON

Pfizer Ireland Pharmaceuticals, Osg Building, Po Box 17, Ringaskiddy, County Cork, Ireland, ☎00 353 21 432 8405, ✉Richard.Morris@pfizer.com, *Call Date: July 1998, Gray's Inn*
Qualifications: [LLB (Derby)]

MORTIMORE MISS CLAUDIA

Department For Business, Innovation and Skills, Legal A, 5th Floor, 1 Victoria Street, London, SW1H 0ET, ✉claudia.mortimore@bis.gsi.gov.uk, *Call Date: Oct 1994, Middle Temple*
Qualifications: [LLB (Hons)(Leeds) LLM (Lond)]

MOSCROP DR JOHN JAMES

Senior Crown Prosecutor, Crown Prosecution Service, Sunlight House, Quay Street, Manchester, M60 3PS, ☎0161 908 2600 Fax: 0161 908 2608, *Call Date: July 1983, Middle Temple*
Qualifications: [BA (Manch) M Phil (Salford) Dip Lib Studs (Belfast) PhD (Leic) LLB(Hull) FRSA]

MOSES MISS REBECCA

Legal Director, Canada Life Limited, Canada Life Place, Potters Bar, Hertfordshire, EN6 5BA, ☎01707 422 312 Fax: 01707 422 372, ✉rebecca.moses@canadalife.co.uk, *Call Date: Nov 1996, Inner Temple*
Qualifications: [LLB (Hons)]

MOSESSON MISS POPPY JULIET MARDALL

Lawrence and Co Solicitors, 402 - 404 Harrow Road, London, W9 2HU, ☎020 7266 4333 Fax: 020 7289 3161, *Call Date: Oct 2005, Middle Temple*
Qualifications: [LLB (Hons) (Exeter) LLM (Nott'm)]

MOSS MISS LINDA JOAN EDNA

HM Revenue and Customs, 100 Parliament Street, London, SW1A 2BQ, *Call Date: July 2008, Lincoln's Inn*
Qualifications: [BEn (Warw) LLB]

MOSS MRS SANDRA MARIE

Manager, C. I. P. F. A, Nla Tower, 9 Floor, 12-16 Addiscombe Road, Croydon, Surrey, CR0 0XT, ☎01245 400255, *Call Date: Oct 1993, Gray's Inn*
Qualifications: [LLB (UEA)]

MOTTRAM MR PAUL RICHARD

Legal Adviser, Mgn Ltd, 1 Canada Square, Canary Wharf, London, E14 5AP, ☎020 7293 3934, *Call Date: Nov 1995, Middle Temple*
Qualifications: [LLB (Hons)]

MOVICK MRS NICOLETTE

Adviser, Borough Crown Prosecutor, Consultant, HED, Legal Adviser, Manager, Senior Crown Prosecutor, Crown Prosecution Service, Rose Court, 2 Southwark Bridge, London, SE1 9HS, ☎020 33570860 Fax: 020 33570874, ✉nicolette.movick@cps.gsi.gov.uk, *Call Date: Oct 1990, Middle Temple*
Qualifications: [LLB (Bris)]

MOWBRAY MR ANTHONY LEIGHTON

Senior Crown Prosecutor, Crown Prosecution Service, Citadel House, 58 High Street, Hull, Humberside, HU1 1QD, ✉anthony.mowbray@cps.gsi.gov.uk, *Call Date: Nov 1983, Middle Temple*
Qualifications: [LLB (Wales)]

MOYLAN MS PAULINE MARY

Rotherham Metropolitan Borough Council, Council Offices, Doncaster Gate, Doncaster Road, Rotherham, S65 1DW, *Call Date: Nov 1995, Gray's Inn*
Qualifications: [LLB]

MUIR MISS ELIZABETH MARY RUDLAND

Kj Commons and Co, 2-6 Upper Lane Street, Workington, Cumbria, CA14 4AY, ☎01900 604698 Fax: 01900 601422, ✉law@kjcommons.co.uk, *Call Date: Nov 1998, Middle Temple*
Qualifications: [BA (Hons)(Leeds)]

MULGREW MR MARTIN JOHN

Martin Murray and Associates, Chapel House, 152-156 High Street, Yiewsley, West Drayton, Middlesex, UB7 7BE, ☎01895 431332 Fax: 01895 448343, *Call Date: May 1996, Lincoln's Inn*
Qualifications: [LLB (Hons)]

F

MULHERN MISS KATHLEEN ALICE ANN

Wainwright and Cummins Solicitors, 413a Brixton Road, London, SW9 7DG, ☎ 020 7737 9339 Fax: 020 7737 9331, ✉ kathleen.mulhern@wainwrightcummins.co.uk, *Call Date: Oct 2007, Inner Temple*
Qualifications: [LLB]

MULHERN MS PAULA MARIA

Crown Prosecution Service, Fox Talbot House, Bellinger Close, Malmesbury Road, Chippenham, Wiltshire, SN15 1BN, ☎ 01249 766 100 Fax: 01249 766162, ✉ paula.mulhern@cps.gsi.gov.uk, *Call Date: Nov 2000, Inner Temple*
Qualifications: [LLB (Hons)]

MULHOLLAND MR MICHAEL JOSEPH

Avon Cosmetics Limited, Nunn Mills Road, Northampton, NN1 5PA, ☎ 01604 617274, ✉ michael.mulholland@avon.com, *Call Date: Nov 1997, Inner Temple*
Qualifications: [BA (Hull) BSc ACIB Dip Law]

MULLAN MR JAMES ANTHONY

Head of Legal Services, PRD, Emi Records Limited, 27 Wrights Lane, London, W8 5SW, ☎ 020 7752 5695 Fax: 020 7752 5696, ✉ james.mullan@emimusic.com, *Call Date: Feb 1995, Lincoln's Inn*
Qualifications: [MA (Cantab) MBA]

MULLARKEY MISS CLAIRE MARIE

Deputy Justices' Clerk, Her Majesty's Court Service, Brighton Magistrates Court, Edward Street, Brighton, Sussex, BN2 0LG, ☎ 01273 811600, ✉ claire.mullarkey@hmcourts-service.gsi.gov.uk, *Call Date: July 1998, Inner Temple*
Qualifications: [LLB (Lond)]

MULLINEAUX MRS JOANNA ELIZABETH

Senior Principal Legal Officer, Department For Work and Pensions, Legal Services, 5th Floor, Adelphi, 1-11 John Adam Street, London, WC2N 6HT, ☎ 020 7712 2476 Fax: 020 7962 8447, ✉ elizabeth.mullineaux@dwp.gsi.gov.uk, *Call Date: Oct 1999, Inner Temple*
Qualifications: [BA (B'ham) LLB Dip Law]

MUNRO MR CHRISTOPHER HAMISH

Ministry of Justice, 102 Petty France, London, SW1H 9AJ, ☎ 020 3334 4775, ✉ chris.munro@justice.gsi.gov.uk, *Call Date: Oct 1997, Gray's Inn*
Qualifications: [BA MA LLM]

MUNRO MR RANALD TORQUIL IAN

Company Secretary, General Counsel, HED, Solicitor, Chubb Insurance Company of Europe, Cottons Centre, Hays Lane, London, SE1 2QP, ☎ 020 7895 3406, ✉ rtmunro@chubb.com, *Call Date: July 1986, Gray's Inn*
Qualifications: [BA (Hons) Dip Law]

MUNTON MISS JEAN MARGARET

Crown Prosecution Service, Vantage Point, Ty Coch Way, Cwmbian, Gwent, NP44 7XX, ☎ 01633 261100 Fax: 01633 261106, ✉ jean.munton@cps.gsi.gov.uk, *Call Date: July 1983, Middle Temple*
Qualifications: [BA (Hons) DMS]

MURDOCH-DE SILVA MRS CONSTANCE ARLENE

Senior Crown Prosecutor, Crown Prosecution Service, Hammersmith Police Station, 226 Shepherds Bush Road, Hammersmith, London, W6 7NX, ☎ 020 3300 4125 Fax: 020 3300 4130, ✉ Arlene.Desilva@cps.gsi.gov.uk, *Call Date: Nov 1989, Middle Temple*
Qualifications: [BA LLB (Lond)]

MURPHIE MR IAN RICHARD

Legal Adviser, MM & K Ltd, No 1 Bengal Court, Birchin Lane, London, EC3V 9DD, ☎ 020 7283 7200 Fax: 020 7283 4119, ✉ ian.murphie@mm-k.com, *Call Date: Oct 1995, Lincoln's Inn*
Qualifications: [BA LLB (South Africa)]

MURPHY MISS CLARE FENELLA

Crown Prosecution Service, United House, Piccadilly, York, YO1 9PQ, ✉ Clare.Murphy@cps.gsi.gov.uk, *Call Date: Oct 1998, Inner Temple*
Qualifications: [LLB]

MURPHY MISS TERESA

Field Fisher Waterhouse LLP, Ibex House, The Minories, London, EC3N 1DY, ☎ 020 7861 4716, ✉ Teresa.Murphy@ffw.com, *Call Date: July 2001, Middle Temple*
Qualifications: [LLB (Hons) LLM]

MURRAY MISS CHRISTINE MARIA

Head of Legal Services, Her Majesty's Court Service, North East & N.W Hants Magistrates Court, The Court House, Civic Centre, Aldershot, GU11 1NY, ☎01252 366012 Fax: 01252 314009, ✉christine.murray1@hmcts.gsi.gov.uk, *Call Date: Oct 1992, Gray's Inn*
Qualifications: [LLB]

MURRAY MISS JEAN LENNOX

Senior Lawyer, HM Revenue and Customs, Commercial and Employment Law Team, Room 2c/17, 100 Parliament Street, London, SW1A 2BQ, ☎020 7417 3827, ✉jeana.murray@hmrc.gsi.gov.uk, *Call Date: Oct 1992, Middle Temple*
Qualifications: [LL.B (Hons) (Lond)]

MURRAY MISS SINEAD

HM Revenue and Customs, 100 Parliament Street, London, SW1A 2BQ, ☎020 7147 0494, ✉sinead.murray@hmrc.gsi.gov.uk, *Call Date: Nov 1997, Gray's Inn*
Qualifications: [LLB (Manch)]

MURRAY MS SOPHIE CORDELIA

Cartwright King Solicitors, 14 Floor, Mclaren Building, 46 The Priory Queensway, Birmingham, B4 7LR, ☎0121 262 3800 Fax: 08081 681500, ✉sophie.murray@cartwrightking.co.uk, *Call Date: Nov 2007, Lincoln's Inn*
Qualifications: [LLB (UEA)]

MURRIN MRS DENISE SELBY

Crown Advocate, Crown Prosecution Service, Charing Cross Police Station, Agar Street, London, WC2N 4JP, *Call Date: Nov 1993, Inner Temple*
Qualifications: [LLB (So'ton)]

MUSTAFA MISS MUHARNILARA

Department For Business, Innovation and Skills, 10 Victoria Street, London, SW1H 0NN, *Call Date: Nov 1999, Middle Temple*
Qualifications: [LLB (Hons)]

MUZAFFER MISS SHENAZ LEYLA

Crown Prosecution Service, Colmore Gate, 2 - 6 Colmore Row, Birmingham, West Midlands, B3 2QA, *Call Date: July 2002, Lincoln's Inn*
Qualifications: [LLB (Hons)(Nott'm)]

MYERS MR STEPHEN PAUL

Lawyer, Serious Fraud Office, Elm House, 10-16 Elm Street, London, WC1X 0BJ, *Call Date: July 1980, Middle Temple*
Qualifications: [BA (Essex)]

NADARAJAH MRS TAPASHI

Crown Prosecution Service, Queens House, 58 Victoria Street, St. Albans, Hertforshire, AL1 3HZ, ☎01727 798 724 / 01923 472414 / 01727 798 724 / 01923 472414 Fax: 01727 798 805 / 01923 472419 / 01727 798 805 / 01923 472419, ✉Tapashi.Nadarajah@cps.gsi.gov.uk, *Call Date: Nov 1989, Inner Temple*
Qualifications: [LLB (Hons)]

NAFISSI MISS SANAM LILA

The Attorney General's Office, 20 Victoria Street, London, SW1H 0NF, ✉sam.nafissi@attorneygeneral.gsi.gov.uk, *Call Date: Nov 2005, Lincoln's Inn*
Qualifications: [BA (Hons) (Nottingham)]

NAFTALIN MS EVE MICHAELA

The Treasury Solicitors, One Kemble Street, London, WC2B 4TS, ☎020 7210 3179 Fax: 020 7210 4740, ✉Eve.Naftalin@tsol.gsi.gov.uk, *Call Date: Nov 2004, Inner Temple*
Qualifications: [BA University of Leeds MSc London School of Eco]

NARWAL MISS JASWANT KAUR

Chief Crown Prosecutor, Crown Prosecution Service, City Gate House, 185 Dyke Road, Hove, East Sussex, BN3 1TL, ✉jaswant.narwal@cps.gsi.gov.uk, *Call Date: Nov 1993, Inner Temple*
Qualifications: [BA (Lancs) CPE]

NASH MS CHLOE

Legal Adviser, The Treasury Solicitors, HM Treasury, Financial Stability Team, Treasury Legal Advisers, LG/20, 1 Horse Guards Road, London, SW1A 2HQ, ☎020 7270 5441, ✉chloe.nash@hmtreasury.gsi.gov.uk, *Call Date: July 2001, Inner Temple*
Qualifications: [LLB (Lond) Diploma German Law]

F

NASSER MS AMATUL-SHAFI

The Treasury Solicitors, One Kemble Street, London, WC2B 4TS, ✉shafi.nasser@tsol.gsi.gov.uk, *Call Date: Nov 1988, Lincoln's Inn*
Qualifications: [LLB (Hons)]

NASSER MRS RUXANA

Crown Prosecution Service, Isleworth Crown Court, 36 Ridgeway Road, Isleworth, London, TW7 5LP, ✉ruxana.nasser@cps.gsi.gov.uk, *Call Date: Nov 1978, Lincoln's Inn*
Qualifications: [LLB (Hons)(Lond) PGCE]

NAUGHTON MISS REGINA MARIAN

Crown Advocate, Crown Prosecution Service, 3rd Floor, Bishopsgate Police Station, Bishopsgate, London, EC2M 4WX, *Call Date: July 1980, Gray's Inn*
Qualifications: [LLB (Brunel)]

NAWBATT MR LALCHAND

Environment Agency, Kings Meadow House, Kings Meadow Road, Reading, RG1 8TQ, ☎0118 953 5789 Fax: 0118 9509440, ✉lal.nawbatt@environment-agency.gov.uk, *Call Date: July 1972, Middle Temple*
Qualifications: [LLB (Hons)(Lond)]

NAYEE MRS MANJULA LAXMIKANT

Crown Prosecution Service, Rose Court, 2 Southwark Bridge, London, SE1 9HS, *Call Date: Nov 1988, Gray's Inn*
Qualifications: [LLB (Lond)]

NAYER MR RAVI

Fishburns Solicitors, 60 Fenchurch Street, London, EC3M 4AD, *Call Date: July 2006, Lincoln's Inn*
Qualifications: [BA (Bris) PgDL]

NAYLOR MR JONATHAN PETER

Shoosmiths, Apex Plaza, Forbury Road, Reading, Berkshire, RG1 1SH, *Call Date: Oct 1995, Lincoln's Inn*
Qualifications: [LLB (Hons)(Lond)]

NAYLOR MISS SARAH DIANE

Office of Fair Trading, Fleetbank House, 2-6 Salisbury Square, London, EC4Y 8JX, *Call Date: Nov 2005, Middle Temple*
Qualifications: [BA (Hons)]

NAYYAR MRS MONICA

Milton Keynes Council, Milton Keynes Council, Civic Offices, Saxon Gate East, Central Milton Keynes, MK9 3EJ, Fax: 01908 253 185, ✉monica.nayyar@milton-keynes.gov.uk, *Call Date: Oct 2004, Gray's Inn*
Qualifications: [LLB]

NEBHRAJANI MISS MEL

The Treasury Solicitors, One Kemble Street, London, WC2B 4TS, *Call Date: Nov 1994, Middle Temple*
Qualifications: [BA (Hons) (Dunelm) Dip Law (Lond)]

NEEDHAM MR CHRISTOPHER ERIC

Consultant, Senior Legal Adviser, Diligenta 2 Limited, Level 7, 101 Old Hall Street, Liverpool, L3 9BD, ☎0151 328 2915 Fax: 0151 328 2976, ✉Christopher.Needham@diligenta-ltd.co.uk, *Call Date: Nov 1974, Middle Temple*
Qualifications: [LLB]

NEIL DR ALLAN ROBERT WOODSIDE

Associate, Gibson Dunn & Crutcher LLP, Telephone House, 2-4 Temple Avenue, London, EC4Y 0HB, ☎020 7071 4296 Fax: 020 7070 9296, ✉aneil@gibsondunn.com, *Call Date: Oct 2001, Middle Temple*
Qualifications: [MA (Hons) PhD Dip Law]

NEILL MR JAMES HECTOR

Allen & Overy LLP, One Bishops Square, London, E1 6AD, ☎020 3088 4633 Fax: 020 3088 0088, ✉James.Neill@AllenOvery.com, *Call Date: Oct 2006, Inner Temple*
Qualifications: [BA (Oxon)]

NEJRANOWSKI MISS TESSA

Nursing and Midwifery Council, 61 Aldwych, London, WC2B 4AE, ☎020 7462 5800 Fax: 020 7580 3410, *Call Date: Oct 2005, Middle Temple*
Qualifications: [BA (Hons)]

NELL THE HON ADAM EDWARD O'NEILL

Dw F LLP, Capital House, 85 King William Street, London, EC4N 7BL, ☎020 7645 9500 Fax: 020 7645 9501, ✉enquiries@dwf.co.uk, *Call Date: Nov 1995, Gray's Inn*
Qualifications: [BA]

F

NELSON MR KEVIN PAUL

Department For Work and Pensions, Pensions, Child Maintenance and étell Us Onceé Division, 2nd Floor, Caxton House, Tothill Street, London, SW1H 9NA, ☎020 7449 5845 Fax: 020 7 3404340, ✉kevin.nelson@dwp.gsi.gov.uk, *Call Date: Mar 2001, Lincoln's Inn*
Qualifications: [LLB (Hons) (Hull)]

NEOFYTOU MR MICHAEL

Artesian Law, 3 Bolt Court, Fleet Street, London, EC4A 3DQ, ✉michael.neofytou@artesianlaw.com, *Call Date: Oct 1999, Inner Temple*
Qualifications: [LLB]

NEOFYTOU MR THOMAS

Crown Prosecution Service, Greenfield House, 32 Scotland Street, Sheffield, South Yorkshire, S3 7DQ, ☎0114 229 8600, *Call Date: Oct 1996, Lincoln's Inn*
Qualifications: [LLB (Hons)(Hudds)]

NETTELTON MR JOHN MARCUS

Credit Agricole, Broadwalk House, 5 Appold Street, London, EC2A 2DA, *Call Date: Nov 1986, Middle Temple*
Qualifications: [LLB (Hons) (Law)]

NEVILLE MS HILARY

Crown Prosecution Service, Eaton Court, 112 Oxford Road, Reading, Berkshire, RG1 7LL, ☎0118 951 3600 Fax: 0118 951 3601, ✉hilary.neville-rusby@cps.gsi.gov.uk, *Call Date: July 2004, Inner Temple*

NEWBOLD MISS REBECCA JANE

Crown Advocate, Crown Prosecution Service, Froomsgate House, Rupert Street, Bristol, BS1 2QJ, ☎0117 930 2800 / 0117 930 2800, *Call Date: Oct 1999, Middle Temple*
Qualifications: [LLB (Hons)(Coventry)]

NEWCOMBE MR RICHARD ALLAN

Chief Crown Prosecutor, Crown Prosecution Service, Sceptre House, 7-9 Castle Street, Luton, Bedfordshire, LU1 3AJ, ☎01582 816600 Fax: 01582 816678, *Call Date: July 1979, Middle Temple*
Qualifications: [LLB (Bris)]

NEWMAN MR BENEDICT GEORGE

The Attorney General's Office, 20 Victoria Street, London, SW1H 0NF, *Call Date: Nov 1991, Middle Temple*
Qualifications: [LLB (Hons)(Bris) LLM (Lond)]

NEWMAN MR RICHARD ALAN

Legal Adviser, Essex Magistrates' Court, Osprey House, Hedgerows Business Park, Colchester Road, Chelmsford, Essex, CM2 5PF, ☎01245 313 500 Fax: 01245 313 399, *Call Date: July 2000, Middle Temple*
Qualifications: [LLB(Hons)]

NG MISS JULIANA PIKWAH

Crown Prosecution Service, Rose Court, 2 Southwark Bridge, London, SE1 9HS, ☎020 3357 0000, *Call Date: July 1999, Lincoln's Inn*
Qualifications: [LLB (Hons)]

NICHOLAS MISS GEORGINA MARY

Crown Prosecution Service, 8 Gainsford Street, The Cooperage, London, SE1 2NE, ☎020 7378 4100, ✉georgina.nicholas@cps.gsi.gov.uk, *Call Date: July 1983, Gray's Inn*
Qualifications: [BA (Lond)]

NICHOLAS MR KARL PETER

G4S Secure Solutions UK Limited, 15 Carshalton Road, Sutton Park House, Sutton, Surrey, SM1 4DL, *Call Date: Nov 1999, Lincoln's Inn*
Qualifications: [LLB (Hons)(Nott'm) BA (Hons) Sussex]

NICHOLL MR GARETH CHARLES

Crown Prosecution Service, Priory Gate, 29 Union Street, Maidstone, Kent, ME14 1PT, ☎01622 356 300, ✉gareth.nicholl@cps.gsi.gov.uk, *Call Date: Mar 2008, Gray's Inn*
Qualifications: [LLB]

NICHOLLS MR MICHAEL JOHN

HED, Crown Prosecution Service, Riverside, Castle Street, Taunton, Somerset, TA1 4AP, ☎01823 425100, ✉michael.nicholls@cps.gsi.gov.uk, *Call Date: July 1978, Gray's Inn*
Qualifications: [LLB (Nott'm)]

F

NICHOLSON MR ANDREW DAVID

Deputy Justices' Clerk, Her Majesty's Courts Service, West London Magistrates' Court, 181 Talgarth Road, London, W6 8DN, ☎ 020 8700 9301, *Call Date: July 1987, Inner Temple*
Qualifications: [BA (Oxon)]

NICHOLSON MR PAUL ANDREW

Crown Prosecution Service, Jefferson House, 27 Park Place, Leeds, West Yorkshire, LS1 2SZ, Fax: 0113 290 2945, ✉ paul.nicholson@cps.gsi.gov.uk, *Call Date: Oct 1992, Lincoln's Inn*
Qualifications: [LLB(Hons)]

NICOL-GENT MR WILLIAM PHILIP TRAHAIR

Other, Guernsey Financial Services Commission, Po Box 128, Glategny Court, Glategny Esplanade, St Peter Port, GY1 3HQ, Guernsey, ☎ 01481 712706
Fax: 01481 712010, ✉ pnicol-gent@gfsc.gg, *Call Date: Oct 1991, Inner Temple*
Qualifications: [CEJFN (France) LLB (Hons) (Bucks) MRAeS]

NICOLSON MR ARIS TONY

Denning Legal Tax Planning, 10a High Street, Windsor, SL4 1LD, ☎ 01753 622544
Fax: 01753 680171, ✉ aris@denning-ltp.co.uk, *Call Date: July 1981, Gray's Inn*
Qualifications: [LLB]

NIGAR MR SUHAIL

Directus, 148a Nelson Road, Whitton, Twickenham, TW2 7BU, ☎ 020 8898 0454, ✉ directus@btinternet.com, *Call Date: July 1981, Lincoln's Inn*

NISBET MISS AIMEE LEONORA

The National Magazine Company, 72 Broadwick Street, London, W1F 9EP, ☎ 020 7439 5267 Fax: 020 7439 5646, ✉ aimee.nisbet@natmags.co.uk, aimee.nisbet@hearst.co.uk, *Call Date: Nov 2001, Inner Temple*
Qualifications: [LLB]

NIXON MR ANTHONY MICHAEL

Mediator, The Warwick Partnership Limited, 1 Stonecross, St Albans, Hertfordshire, AL1 4AA, ☎ 01727 846194 Fax: 01727 810885, ✉ anthony.nixon@warwickpartnership.co.uk, *Call Date: July 1979, Middle Temple*
Qualifications: [MA (Cantab) FCIArb DipICArb]

NIXON MISS DIANE ELEANOR

Mossfield Chambers, 90 Glenagoorland Road, Co. Tyrone, BT82 0ST, Northern Ireland, ☎ 07970 154902, *Call Date: Oct 1997, Middle Temple*
Qualifications: [BA (Hons)(Oxon)]

NIXON MISS LUCY HANNAH

Crown Prosecution Service, County House, 100 New London Road, Chelmsford, Essex, CM2 0RG, ☎ 01245 455 800
Fax: 01245 455 929, *Call Date: Nov 1982, Middle Temple*
Qualifications: [BA]

NOBEEN MISS SHAREENA SHARMEELA

Office of Fair Trading, Fleetbank House, 2-6 Salisbury Square, London, EC4Y 8JX, ✉ Shareena.Nobeen@oft.gsi.gov.uk, *Call Date: Nov 2001, Inner Temple*
Qualifications: [BA (Oxon) CPE]

NOBLE MR DAVID JONATHAN

Other, The Treasury Solicitors, Treasury Solicitor's Department, One Kemble Street, London, WC2B 4TS, ☎ 020 7210 2953
Fax: 020 7210 3503, ✉ david.noble@tsol.gsi.gov.uk, *Call Date: July 1981, Gray's Inn*
Qualifications: [M Soc Sci LLB]

NOONE MRS CHRISTINE VERONICA

Company Secretary, Lecturer, John E. Noone and Associates, 11 Queen Street, Oldham, Lancashire, OL1 1RD, ☎ 0161 627 3746
Fax: 0161 627 1056, ✉ chrisnoone22@hotmail.com, *Call Date: Nov 2001, Inner Temple*
Qualifications: [LLB (Manch)]

NORFOLK MISS BRIDGET JANE

Crown Prosecution Service, City Gate House, 185 Dyke Road, Hove, East Sussex, BN3 1TL, ✉ b.norfolk@cps.gsi.gov.uk, *Call Date: July 1989, Middle Temple*
Qualifications: [LLB (Leics)]

NORMAN MR MARK LEONARD

Legal Adviser, Tower Hamlets Legal Services, Town Hall, Mulbery Place, 5 Clove Crescent, London, E14 2BG, ☎ 020 7364 4845
Fax: 020 7364 4804, ✉ mark.norman@towerhamlets.gov.uk, *Call Date: July 1986, Inner Temple*
Qualifications: [LLB (Essex)]

NORRIS MR CHARLES JOHN

Legal Director, Department For Business, Innovation and Skills, Abbey 1, 6th Floor, 1 Victoria Street, London, SW1H 0ET, ✉ Charles.Norris@bis.gsi.gov.uk, *Call Date: July 1986, Lincoln's Inn*
Qualifications: [LLB LLM (Wales)]

NORRIS MISS REBECCA LOUISE

Milbank, Tweed, Hadley and Mccloy LLP, 10 Gresham Street, London, EC2V 7JD, ☎ 020 7615 3042 Fax: 020 7 615 3100, ✉ rnorris@milbank.com, *Call Date: July 2010, Gray's Inn*
Qualifications: [BA]

NORTH MR SIMON TIMOTHY

Principal Crown Prosecutor, Crown Prosecution Service, United House, Piccadilly, York, North Yorkshire, YO1 9PQ, *Call Date: Nov 1984, Gray's Inn*
Qualifications: [BA]

NORTHFIELD MR DAVID ANDREW

Field Fisher Waterhouse LLP, 35 Vine Street, London, EC3N 2PX, ☎ 020 7861 4924 Fax: 020 7488 0084, ✉ david.northfield@ffw.com, *Call Date: July 2005, Middle Temple*
Qualifications: [BA (Hons) Leeds PgDip Law Leeds]

NUGENT MR PETER FRANCIS

Crown Prosecution Service, The Cooperage, 8 Gainsford Street, London, SE1 2NE, ☎ 020 7378 4174, *Call Date: Feb 1994, Middle Temple*
Qualifications: [BA (Hons)(Lond)]

NUNAN MR MATTHEW DOMINIC

Manager, Other, Financial Services Authority, Enforcement and Financial Crime Division, 25 The North Colonnade, Canary Wharf, London, E14 5HS, *Call Date: July 1996, Middle Temple*
Qualifications: [LLB (Hons)(Manc)]

NUNKOO MISS SHANEE

British Medical Association, Legal Department, Bma House, Tavistock Square, London, WC1H 9JP, *Call Date: Nov 1989, Inner Temple*
Qualifications: [LLB LLM (Lond)]

NUNN MRS ALISON-MARIE

Lawyer, The Treasury Solicitors, 5th Floor, One Kemble Street, London, WC2B 4TS, ☎ 020 721 3000, *Call Date: Oct 1997, Middle Temple*
Qualifications: [MA (Cantab)]

NURSE MR LEWITT CARTER

Santander UK plc, Legal Department, 2 Triton Square, Regent's Place, London, NW1 3AN, ✉ lewitt.nurse@santandergbm.com, *Call Date: Oct 1990, Inner Temple*
Qualifications: [LLB (West Indies) LLM (Lond)]

NUTTING MRS KERRY SIOBHAN

Senior Crown Prosecutor, Crown Prosecution Service, Gateway, 31 Power Close, Guildford, Surrey, GU1 1EJ, ☎ 01483 468343 Fax: 01483 468202, ✉ kerry.nutting@cps.gsi.gov.uk, *Call Date: Nov 1993, Middle Temple*
Qualifications: [LLB (Hons)(Lond)]

NWANODI MR ANTONY CHIDI KOJO EZIHUO

Senior Principal Legal Officer, The Treasury Solicitors, One Kemble Street, London, WC2B 4TS, ✉ tony.nwanodi@tsol.gsi.gov.uk, *Call Date: Nov 1987, Gray's Inn*
Qualifications: [BA (Keele) LLB (Bucks)]

OATWAY MISS HELEN LAURA

Legal Adviser, Essex Magistrates' Courts, Osprey House, Hedgerows Business Park, Colchester Road, Springfield, Chelmsford, Essex, CM2 5PF, ☎ 01245 313000 Fax: 01245 313399, *Call Date: Oct 1997, Lincoln's Inn*
Qualifications: [LLB (Hons)]

O'BREE MR EDWARD MARK

Directorate of Army Legal Services, Trenchard Lines, Upavon, Pewsey, Wiltshire, SN9 6BE, *Call Date: Nov 2003, Middle Temple*
Qualifications: [BA (Hons) (Manch) CPE]

O'BRIEN MR ANTHONY LOUIS

Anglo-Norden Group, Orwell Terminal, Eagle Wharf, Helena Road, Ipswich, Suffolk, IP3 0BT, ☎ 01473 233244 Fax: 01473 289273, ✉ tonyobrien@anglonorden.co.uk, *Call Date: Feb 1984, Inner Temple*
Qualifications: [LLB (Lond)]

F

O'BRIEN FLIGHT LIEUTENANT JAMES PATRICK

Other, Directorate of Legal Services (Raf), Regional Legal Office, RAF Coningsby, Lincoln, LN4 4SY, *Call Date: July 2009, Middle Temple*
Qualifications: [MTh MA (Nott'm)]

O'BRIEN MR PAUL ANTHONY

Company Secretary, Addax Petroleum Services Ltd, Geneva Branch, 16, Avenue Eugene-Pittard, Po Box 265, Genera 12, CH-1211, Switzerland, ☎00 41 22 702 9482, ✉paul.obrien@addaxpetroleum.com, *Call Date: July 1981, Inner Temple*
Qualifications: [MA (Oxon)]

O'BRIEN QUINN MR HUGH DAVID

Crown Prosecution Service, Colemore Gate, 2 - 6 Colemore Row, Birmingham, West Midlands, B3 2QA, ☎0121 262 1300, *Call Date: Feb 1992, Gray's Inn*
Qualifications: [LLB (Wales)]

OCAN MS AKIDI KASALINA

Surrey County Council, Legal Services, Penhryn Road, Kingston Upon Thames, Surrey, KT1 2DN, ☎020 8541 8013
Fax: 020 8541 9115, ✉akidi.ocan@surreycc.gov.uk, *Call Date: July 1984, Middle Temple*
Qualifications: [BA]

O'CONNELL MR DAVID JAMES OLIVER

Prosecution Team Leader, Senior Crown Prosecutor, Crown Prosecution Service, Isleworth Crown Court, 36 Ridgeway Road, Isleworth, London, TW7 5LP, *Call Date: July 1988, Gray's Inn*

O'CONNOR MISS DAPHNE EVADNEY PORTIA

Pegasus, Somerville House, 16 Harborne Road, Edgbaston, B15 3AA,
☎0121 525 4862 / 0121 455 8347
Fax: 0121 455 6546, ✉poconnor@pegasusllp.co.uk, *Call Date: July 2000, Inner Temple*
Qualifications: [LLB (Wolves) LLM]

ODELL MR ALEXANDER ADRIAN LEWIS

Peters & Peters Solicitors LLP, 15 Fetter Lane, London, EC4A 1BW, *Call Date: Oct 2007, Lincoln's Inn*
Qualifications: [BA (Warw)]

O'DONNELL MR PETER JOHN

Senior Crown Prosecutor, Crown Prosecution Service, Capital Tower, Greyfriars Road, Cardiff, CF10 3PL, *Call Date: July 1983, Middle Temple*
Qualifications: [BA (Hons)]

O'DWYER MRS ANGELA MARIE

Senior Legal Adviser, Her Majesty's Courts Service, Ealing Magistrates' Court, Green Man Lane, West Ealing, London, W13 0SD, ☎020 8579 9311, *Call Date: Nov 1997, Lincoln's Inn*
Qualifications: [LLB (Hons)(Dunelm)]

O'FLAHERTY MISS NORA

HM Revenue and Customs, East Wing, Somerset House, The Strand, London, WC2R 1LB, *Call Date: Oct 1991, Lincoln's Inn*
Qualifications: [BA (Hons) (Cantab) DipLaw (Lond)]

OGBORNE MR NIGEL JOHN

Crown Advocate, Crown Prosecution Service, 4/7 Prebendal Court, Oxford Road, Aylesbury, Buckinghamshire, HP19 8EY,
Fax: 01296 414803, ✉nigel.ogborne@cps.gsi.gov.uk, *Call Date: Nov 1985, Gray's Inn*
Qualifications: [BA (Hons)]

O'HARA MISS MARIE-CLAIRE

Nabarro LLP, Lacon House, Theobald's Road, London, WC2X 8RW, *Call Date: Nov 1999, Middle Temple*
Qualifications: [BA (Hons)(Cantab) LLM]

OJUKWU MRS MARY ADA

Lawyer, London Borough of Lambeth, Borough Solicitors Office, Town Hall, Brixton Hill, London, SW2 1RW, ☎020 7926 2381
Fax: 020 7926 2313, ✉mojukwu@lambeth.gov.uk, *Call Date: Oct 1993, Lincoln's Inn*
Qualifications: [BA (Hons) MSc]

F

OKAFOR MS SARAH

Consultant, London Borough of Sutton, Civic Offices, St Nicholas Way, Sutton, Surrey, SM1 1EA, ☎020 8770 5061 Fax: 020 8770 5616, ✉Sarah.Okafor@sutton.gov.uk, *Call Date: Nov 2001, Middle Temple*
Qualifications: [BA (Hons) CpE Dip SW]

OKEZUE MISS IFEOMA CHICKA

Thurrock Borough Council, Civic Offices, New Road, Grays, Essex, RM17 6SL, Fax: 01375 652712, ✉Iobioha@thurrock.gov.uk, *Call Date: Mar 1996, Lincoln's Inn*
Qualifications: [LLB (Hons)]

OKORONKWO MR SAMUEL NWABUEZE

Capstone Sports Management Ltd, 205 Wardour Street, London, W1F 8ZJ, ☎020 7734 3435, ✉samuel@capstonesport.com, *Call Date: July 2002, Gray's Inn*
Qualifications: [MSc]

OKRAKU MISS NADIA OFEIBEA

London Borough of Lambeth, Legal Services - Room 205, Lambeth Town Hall, Brixton Hill, London, SW2 1RW, Fax: 020 7926 2361, ✉nokraku@lambeth.gov.uk, *Call Date: Oct 2000, Inner Temple*
Qualifications: [LLB (Hertfordshire)]

OLDKNOW MR CHRISTOPHER JAMES

Attorney, Microsoft Limited, Buildings 80-100, Cardinal Place, Victoria, London, SW1E 5JL, ☎0870 6010100 Fax: 00 1 425 936 7329, ✉chris.oldknow@microsoft.com, *Call Date: Oct 1995, Middle Temple*
Qualifications: [BSc (Hons) LLM Dip Law]

OLDLAND MR ANDREW RICHARD

Recorder, Michelmores LLP, Woodwater House, Pynes Hill, Exeter, Devon, EX2 5WR, ☎01392 688688 Fax: 01392 360563, ✉andrew.oldland@michelmores.com, *Call Date: Nov 1990, Inner Temple*
Qualifications: [BSc (Lond) Dip Law (Lond)]

O'LEARY MR DEAN

Al Tamimi and Co, Difc Building 4, Level 6, Po Box 9275, Sheikh Zayed Road, Dubai, United Arab Emirates, ☎00971 5730 7521, *Call Date: July 1999, Lincoln's Inn*
Qualifications: [BSc (Hons) LLM PgDL MSc (Lond) MA (Leic) MCMI]

OLIVER MRS MARCIA FRANCES

General Counsel, Visitbritain, 1 Palace Street, London, SW1E 5HE, ☎020 7578 1017 Fax: 020 7578 1001, ✉marcia.oliver@visitbritain.org, *Call Date: Nov 1984, Middle Temple*
Qualifications: [LLB (Hons)(Lond)]

OLVER MR GRAHAM DUDLEY

Other, Well House, Infrastructure Department, Church End, Southam, Priors Hardwick, Warwickshire, CV47 7SN, *Call Date: Nov 1985, Gray's Inn*
Qualifications: [BA (Warw)]

OMIDEYI MR AYO

Head of Legal Services, Phone Pay Plus, Clove Building, 4 Maguire Street, London, SE1 2NQ, ☎020 7940 7422 Fax: 020 7940 7456, ✉aomideyi@phonepayplus.org.uk, *Call Date: Nov 1999, Lincoln's Inn*
Qualifications: [LLB (Hons)]

O'NEILL MS ELIZABETH HELEN

Department of Constitutional Affairs, Criminal Appeal Office, Royal Courts of Justice, the Strand, London, WC2A 2LL, *Call Date: Nov 1984, Middle Temple*
Qualifications: [BA LLM]

O'NEILL MISS ELIZABETH MARIE

Department For Business, Innovation and Skills, 1 Victoria Street, London, SW1H 0ET, ☎020 7215 3461 Fax: 020 7215 3376, ✉elizabeth.oneill@bis.gsi.gov.uk, *Call Date: Nov 1996, Middle Temple*
Qualifications: [LLB (Hons)(Dub) BCL (Oxon) MA]

ONUMA-ELLIOTT MRS NKOLIKA ANNE

Senior Crown Prosecutor, Crown Prosecution Service, Uxbridge Police Station, 1 Warwick Place, Uxbridge, Middlesex, UB8 1PG, *Call Date: Oct 1992, Inner Temple*
Qualifications: [LLB LLM (Lond)]

ONWUAZOR MISS IFEYINWA

Department For Business, Innovation and Skills, 1 Victoria Street, London, SW1H 0ET, ☎020 7215 5438, ✉ify.onwuazor@bis.gsi.gov.uk, *Call Date: Oct 1998, Gray's Inn*
Qualifications: [LLB LLM (Lond)]

F

O'RIORDAN DR DENNIS THOMAS DELCARON

Paul Hastings (Europe) LLP, Ten Bishops Square, London, E1 6EG, ☎020 3023 5166 Fax: 020 3023 5466, ✉tomoriordan@paulhastings.com, *Call Date: Oct 1993, Inner Temple*
Qualifications: [LLB (Hons) BCL D Phil (Oxon) MA]

ORMAN MR DAVID AARON

Senior Crown Prosecutor, Crown Prosecution Service, 2 King Edward Court, King Edward Street, Nottingham, Nottinghamshire, NG1 1EL, *Call Date: Nov 2007, Lincoln's Inn*
Qualifications: [LLB (Soton)]

ORME MISS KATRINA LOUISE

Bark and Co Solicitors, Bridewell Court, 14 New Bridge Street, London, EC4V 6AG, Fax: 020 7353 1880, ✉korme@barkco.com, *Call Date: July 2008, Middle Temple*
Qualifications: [LLB (Hons) (Lond)]

ORME MR SIMON TIMOTHY

Crown Advocate, Crown Prosecution Service, United House, Piccadilly, York, North Yorkshire, YO1 1PQ, ☎01904 545534 / 01904 545534 Fax: 01904 545501 / 01904 545501, ✉simon-timothy.orme@cps.gsi.gov.uk, *Call Date: July 1986, Inner Temple*
Qualifications: [BSc (Econ)]

ORMOND MRS PHILLIPPA MARY

The Treasury Solicitors, 5th Floor, One Kemble Street, London, WC2B 4TS, ✉Phillippa.Ormond@tsol.gsi.gov.uk, *Call Date: Nov 1995, Gray's Inn*
Qualifications: [BA (Exon)]

O'ROURKE MISS SINEAD CHRISTINA

The Treasury Solicitors, One Kemble Street, London, WC2B 4TS, *Call Date: Oct 2001, Gray's Inn*
Qualifications: [BA]

O'ROURKE MR THOMAS

Dell Corporation Limited, Dell House, Cain Road, Bracknell, RG12 1LF, ☎01344 860 466, *Call Date: Nov 1991, Lincoln's Inn*
Qualifications: [BA (Hons) (Cardiff) LLB (Hons)]

ORR MISS LUCINDA EMILY

Associate, Skadden, Arps, Slate, Meagher & Flom LLP, 40 Bank Street, Canary Wharf, London, E14 5DS, *Call Date: July 2006, Gray's Inn*
Qualifications: [MA (Oxon) MSt (Oxon)]

ORR MR MATHEW LIAM

Serious Fraud Office, Elm House, 10-16 Elm Street, London, WC1X 0BJ, *Call Date: Oct 2004, Lincoln's Inn*
Qualifications: [LLB (Hons) (Lond)]

ORTON MR PAUL WALTER

The First Law Partnership Limited, 30-32 Bromham Road, Bedford, Bedfordshire, MK40 2QD, ☎01234 263263 Fax: 01234 263269, *Call Date: Nov 1988, Gray's Inn*
Qualifications: [BA (Hons)]

OSBORNE MISS CLARE ELIZABETH ANN

Legal Adviser, Gardner Leader Solicitors, White Hart House, Market Place, Newbury, Berkshire, RG14 5BA, ☎01635 508 080 Fax: 01635 521 341, *Call Date: Nov 1994, Middle Temple*
Qualifications: [BA (Hons)]

OSBORNE MISS NICOLA FRANCES

HM Revenue and Customs, 2nd Floor, North Spur, , South West Wing, Bush House, London, WC2B 4RD, ☎020 7438 6111 Fax: 020 7084 5610, ✉nikki.osborne@hmrc.gsi.gov.uk, *Call Date: Nov 1994, Lincoln's Inn*
Qualifications: [LLB (Hons)]

OUAHES MR HENNI

Law Commission, Steel House, 11 Tothill Street, London, SW1H 9LJ, Fax: 020 3334 0201, ✉henni.ouahes@lawcommission.gsi.gov.uk, *Call Date: Nov 2005, Middle Temple*
Qualifications: [BA (Oxford) BCL(Oxford)]

OUTHWAITE MR BRIAN

Senior Crown Prosecutor, Crown Prosecution Service, Greenfield House, 32 Scotland Street, Sheffield, South Yorkshire, S3 7DQ, ☎0114 229 8600, ✉Brian.Outhwaite@cps.gsi.gov.uk, *Call Date: Nov 1988, Lincoln's Inn*
Qualifications: [LLB (Hons) (Leeds)]

OUTRAM MRS LOUISE ANN

Legal Manager, Secretary, Mersey Travel, 24 Hatton Garden, Liverpool, L3 2AN, ☎0151 330 1700 Fax: 0151 330 1709, ✉louise.outram@merseytravel.gov.uk, *Call Date: July 1989, Middle Temple*
Qualifications: [BA (Keele) (Hons)]

OVEN MR PATRICK JEROME

Principal Crown Prosecutor, Crown Prosecution Service, Gateway, 31 Power Close, Guildford, Surrey, GU1 1EJ, ☎01483 468200 Fax: 01483 468303, *Call Date: Nov 1984, Gray's Inn*
Qualifications: [LLB (Manch)]

OVERS MS ESTELLE FAE

Icon Entertainment International, Charlotte Building, 17 Gresse Street, London, W1T 1QL, ☎020 7927 6900 Fax: 020 7927 6901, *Call Date: Oct 1994, Gray's Inn*
Qualifications: [BA]

OWEN MISS BECKY ELLA

Crown Prosecution Service, Bethnal Green Police Station, Po Box 60416, London, E2 9WH, ☎0803 300 4880 Fax: 020 3356 3820, ✉Becky.Owen@cps.gsi.gov.uk, *Call Date: Nov 2007, Middle Temple*
Qualifications: [LLB (Hons) (Brunel) PgDL (Lond)]

OWEN MR DAVID BENEDICT

Crown Prosecution Service, Gateway, 31 Power Close, Guildford, Surrey, GU1 1EJ, ☎01483 468200, ✉david.owen@cps.gsi.gov.uk, *Call Date: July 2008, Middle Temple*
Qualifications: [BA (Hons) (Lond)]

OWEN MISS HELEN NNONYELUM

Crown Prosecution Service, Snaresbrook Crown Court, 75 Hollybush Hill, Snaresbrook, London, E11 1QW, *Call Date: Nov 1994, Inner Temple*
Qualifications: [BA]

OWENS MR GARETH RICHARD

Chief Executive, Director, Flintshire County Council, County Hall, Mold, CH7 6NB, ✉gareth_owens@flintshire.gov.uk, *Call Date: Nov 1993, Gray's Inn*
Qualifications: [LLB (Wales)]

OWENS MISS LOUISE JEAN

Chubb Insurance Company of Europe, 106 Fenchurch Street, London, EC3M 5NB, ☎020 7895 3315 Fax: 020 7956 5922, ✉lowens@chubb.com, *Call Date: July 2005, Lincoln's Inn*
Qualifications: [LLB (Hons)]

OWUSU-AKYAW MISS JENNIFER

London Borough of Hammersmith and Fulham, Hammersmith Town Hall, King Street, London, W6 9JU, ☎020 8753 2399, ✉jennifer.owusu-akyaw@lbhf.gov.uk, *Call Date: Oct 1998, Gray's Inn*
Qualifications: [LLB (Wales)]

OYEFUSI MRS OLAYINKA

Maximux Limited, 1st Floor, Venture House, 6 Silver Court, Watchmead, Weleyn Garden City, Hertfordshire, AL7 1TS, Fax: 08456 122 061, *Call Date: Nov 2000, Lincoln's Inn*
Qualifications: [LLB (Hons)]

PAGE MR LAURENCE BERELOWITZ

Plexus Law, Peninsular House, 30-36 Monument Street, London, EC3R 8NB, ☎020 7618 0795, ✉laurence.page@plexuslaw.co.uk, *Call Date: Oct 2010, Lincoln's Inn*
Qualifications: [BSc (Lond)]

PAGE MR MATTHEW CHARLES

Senior Lawyer, Exeter City Council, Civic Centre, Paris Street, Exeter, EX1 1JN, *Call Date: Feb 1986, Middle Temple*
Qualifications: [MA (Oxon) MSc]

PAINTER MR IAN DAVID

HM Revenue and Customs, 1st Floor, Ralli Quays, 3 Stanley Street, Salford, Manchester, M60 9LB, ☎0870 785 8509 Fax: 0870 785 8538, *Call Date: Nov 1993, Lincoln's Inn*
Qualifications: [BA (Hons)]

PALLISTER MR NEIL

Senior Crown Prosecutor, Crown Prosecution Service, St Ann's Quay, 122 Quayside, Newcastle Upon Tyne, Tyne and Wear, NE1 3BD, ☎0191 260 4200, *Call Date: July 1982, Lincoln's Inn*
Qualifications: [LLB (Hull)]

F

PALMER MRS ANN

Deputy Justices' Clerk, Leicester Magistrates' Court, 15 Pocklingtons Walk, Leicester, LE1 6BT, *Call Date: July 1988, Middle Temple*
Qualifications: [BA (Hons) Assoc CIPD]

PALMER MISS GILLIAN

Trowers and Hamlins, Sceptre Court, 40 Tower Hill, London, EC3N 4DX, ☎ 020 7423 8000 Fax: 020 7423 8001, ✉ gpalmer@trowers.com, *Call Date: Feb 1993, Gray's Inn*
Qualifications: [BA]

PALMER MISS LOUISE JANE

Royal Courts of Justice, Minstry of Justice, Criminal Appeal Office, Royal Courts of Justice, the Strand, London, WC2A 2LL, ☎ 020 7947 6098, *Call Date: Mar 1998, Middle Temple*
Qualifications: [LLB (Hons)(Kent)]

PALMER MRS NICOLA JANE

Pb Legal Ltd T/A Palmer Biggs Legal, Richmond House, 13 Carfax, Horsham, West Sussex, RH12 1AQ, ☎ 01403 211211 Fax: 01403 211201, *Call Date: July 2001, Middle Temple*
Qualifications: [LLB (Hons) Dip Prof Leg Skills]

PANGRAZ MR THEODOR

Clerksroom (Taunton), Equity House, Administration Centre, Blackbrook Park Avenue, Taunton, Somerset, TA1 2PX, ☎ 0845 083 3000 Fax: 0845 083 3001, ✉ pangraz@clerksroom.com, *Call Date: Nov 2007, Middle Temple*

PARK MR IAN DAVID

Royal Navy Officers, HM Naval Base, Portsmouth, Hampshire, PO1 3LS, *Call Date: Oct 2003, Lincoln's Inn*
Qualifications: [MA]

PARKER MR CHRISTOPHER IAN

Director, Microsoft Ltd, Microsoft Campus, Thames Valley Park, Reading, Berkshire, RG6 1WG, ☎ 0118 909 3254 Fax: 0118 909 6767, ✉ chris.parker@microsoft.com, *Call Date: July 1977, Gray's Inn*
Qualifications: [LLB]

PARKER MR CHRISTOPHER JOHN GORRILL

HMG Law LLP, 126 High Street, Oxford, OX1 4DG, Fax: 01865 721263, ✉ christopher.parker@hmg-law.co.uk, *Call Date: July 1984, Inner Temple*
Qualifications: [LLB (Newc) TEP]

PARKER MISS EMMA RACHEL

The Teasury Solicitors, One Kemble Street, London, WC2B 4TS, ☎ 020 7210 2907, *Call Date: Oct 2000, Inner Temple*
Qualifications: [BA (Oxon) CPE]

PARKER MISS JANICE TERESA

Senior Legal Adviser, Her Majesty's Courts Service, Inner London and City Family Proceedings Court, 59-65 Wells Street, London, W1A 3AE, *Call Date: July 1981, Lincoln's Inn*
Qualifications: [LLB (Lond)]

PARKER MR OLIVER JOHN

Call Date: Nov 1977, Inner Temple

PARKER MISS RACHEL CLARE

Crown Prosecution Service, Burnley Wharf, Manchester Road, Burnley, Lancashire, BB11 1JG, ☎ 01282 478553 Fax: 01282 478505, ✉ rachel.parker@cps.gsi.gov.uk, *Call Date: Nov 2006, Middle Temple*
Qualifications: [LLB (Hons) (Lanc)]

PARKER MR STEPHEN ALBERT

Legal Adviser, The Treasury Solicitors, Treasury Legal Advisers, Hm Treasury, 1 Horseguards Road, London, SW1A 2HQ, ☎ 020 7270 5666, ✉ Stephen.Parker@hmtreasury.gsi.gov.uk, *Call Date: July 1982, Lincoln's Inn*
Qualifications: [MA LLB (Cantab)]

PARKINSON MRS DORREN PATRICIA

Ministry of Justice, Criminal Appeal Office, Royal Courts of Justice, The Strand, London, WC2A 2LL, ☎ 020 7947 6921, ✉ doreen.parkinson@hmcourts-service.x.gsi.gov.uk, *Call Date: Feb 1973, Inner Temple*

PARKINSON MISS HELEN ESTHER

Ministry of Justice, Criminal Appeal Office, Royal Courts of Justice, The Strand, London, WC2A 2LL, *Call Date: July 1986, Middle Temple*
Qualifications: [LLB (Hons)]

PARKS MR EDWIN ROBERT

Lecturer in Law, The Open University, Walton Hall, Milton Keynes, Buckinghamshire, MK7 6AA, ☎01908 274066, *Call Date: Nov 1999, Lincoln's Inn*
Qualifications: [BA LLB (Hons) (New Zealand) Dip Law]

PARNELL MRS MICHELE DONNA

Chair, Consultant, Judge, The Lantern Corporation Limited, Whitehall Cottage, Sandwich Bay, Kent, CT13 9PR, ✉lantern.corp@gmail.com, *Call Date: Nov 1980, Lincoln's Inn*
Qualifications: [LLB (Hons) FCIArb]

PARRINGTON MRS FRANCES ISABELLA

Oracle Corporation Uk Limited, Oracle Parkway, Thames Valley Park, Reading, Berkshire, RG6 1RA, ☎0118 924 4531, *Call Date: Oct 1991, Inner Temple*
Qualifications: [BA (Nott'm)]

PARRISH MRS MELANIE JANE

Crown Prosecution Service, Uxbridge Police Station, 1 Warwick Place, Uxbridge, Middlesex, UB8 1PG, *Call Date: Nov 1992, Middle Temple*
Qualifications: [BA (Hons)]

PARRY DR ANTHONY

The Treasury Solicitors, Hm Treasury, 1 Horse Guards Road, London, SW1A 2HQ, ☎020 7270 5601 Fax: 020 7270 5764, ✉tony.parry@hmtreasury.gsi.gov.uk, *Call Date: Feb 1971, Middle Temple*
Qualifications: [BA (Cantab) MA PhD]

PARSELL MR RICHARD ALAN

Crown Advocate, Crown Prosecution Service, 1 Hudson Quay, The Halyard, Middlesbrough, Cleveland, TS3 6RT, ☎01642 204500 Fax: 01642 204503, ✉richard.parsell@cps.gsi.gov.uk, *Call Date: July 1975, Gray's Inn*
Qualifications: [LLB (B'ham)]

PARTON MISS RUTH ALISON

Lawyer, Crown Prosecution Service, Bromley Police Station, High Street, Bromley, Kent, BR1 1ER, *Call Date: Oct 1992, Gray's Inn*
Qualifications: [LLB]

PARTRIDGE MS ELIZABETH ANN

Senior Court Clerk, HMCS Kent, Sussex & Surrey, Sussex Magistrates' Court, Bolnore Road, Haywards Heath, West Sussex, RH16 4BA, ☎01444 472643 Fax: 01444 472638, ✉elizabeth.partridge@hmcourts-service.gsi.gov.uk, *Call Date: July 1989, Gray's Inn*
Qualifications: [LLB (Soton)]

PARTRIDGE MR GRAHAM DAVID

Senior Crown Prosecutor, Crown Prosecution Service, The Cooperage, 8 Gainsford Street, London, SE1 2NE, *Call Date: Feb 1991, Gray's Inn*
Qualifications: [LLB (Lond)]

PARTRIDGE MISS SARAH LOUISE

Senior Crown Prosecutor, Crown Prosecution Service, Country House, 100 New London Road, Chelmsford, Essex, CM2 0RG, *Call Date: Oct 2000, Lincoln's Inn*
Qualifications: [LLB (Hons) (Keele)]

PARVIN MR DAVID MICHAEL

Criminal Defence Solicitors, 227/228 Strand, London, WC2R 1BE, ✉dp@criminaldefence.co.uk, *Call Date: Oct 2009, Lincoln's Inn*
Qualifications: [LLB (Lond) LLM (Lond)]

PATAKY MR CHRISTOPHER ANTAL

Nursing and Midwifery Council, 23 Portland Place, London, W1B 1PZ, *Call Date: July 2006, Gray's Inn*
Qualifications: [MSc (Lond)]

PATEL MISS AMEE

Crown Prosecution Service, The Cooperage, 8 Gainsford Street, London, SE1 2NE, ✉amee.patel@cps.gsi.gov.uk, *Call Date: July 2008, Middle Temple*
Qualifications: [BSc (Hons) (Leeds) PgDl (Notts)]

PATEL MISS HANIFA

Senior Crown Prosecutor, Crown Prosecution Service, 1st Floor, Bolton Police Station, Scholey Street, Bolton, BL2 1HX, *Call Date: Oct 1999, Lincoln's Inn*
Qualifications: [LLB (Hons)]

F

PATEL MR MAYOOR

Assistant, Lloyds Tsb Bank PLC, 125 Shaftesbury Avenue, London, WC2H 8AD, ✉ mayoor.patel@lloydstsb.co.uk, *Call Date: Feb 1989, Inner Temple*
Qualifications: [LLM (Lond) LLB (Hons)]

PATEL MR VINAY KALYAN

Legal Adviser, Dalkia PLC, Elizabeth House, 56-60 London Road, Staines, Middlesex, TW18 4BQ, ☎ 01784 496 200 Fax: 01784 496 222, ✉ Vinay.Patel@dalkia.co.uk, *Call Date: Oct 2001, Middle Temple*
Qualifications: [LLB (Hons) MSc Construction Law &, Arbitration]

PATERSON MR RICHARD CHRISTOPHER

Crown Advocate, Crown Prosecution Service, Carmelite House, St James Court, Whitefriars, Norwich, Norfolk, NR3 1SL, *Call Date: Nov 1994, Middle Temple*
Qualifications: [BA (Hons)(Lancs)]

PATROS MR GEORGE CHARLES

Partner, Charles Ross Solicitors, 17 The Grangeway, Grange Park, London, N21 2HD, ☎ 020 8370 7750 Fax: 020 8364 3260, ✉ enquiries@chatlesross.co.uk, *Call Date: Oct 2009, Middle Temple*
Qualifications: [LLB (Hon) (Lond) LLM (Kent) BSc (Hons) MCIArb]

PATTEN MRS SUSAN JANET

Director, Crown Prosecution Service, Rose Court, 2 Southwark Bridge, London, SE1 9HS, ✉ sue.patten@cps.gsi.gov.uk, *Call Date: July 1985, Middle Temple*
Qualifications: [LLB (Warw)]

PATTERSON MS NICOLE

Head of Legal Services, Express Newspapers, Editorial Legal Department, 10 Lower Thames Street, London, EC3R 6EN, ☎ 020 8612 7785 Fax: 020 8434 7967, ✉ nicole.patterson@express.co.uk, *Call Date: Nov 1995, Middle Temple*
Qualifications: [LLB (Hons)]

F

PAYNE MR GEORGE REGINALD ALEXANDER

Tuckers Solicitors, 39 Warren Street, London, W1T 6AF, ☎ 020 7388 8333
Fax: 020 7388 5888, ✉ payneg@tuckerssolicitors.com, *Call Date: July 2004, Lincoln's Inn*
Qualifications: [BSc (Hons) LLB (Hons)]

PAYNE MR TIMOTHY MARTIN

The Home Office, Legal Advisors Branch, Seacole, Ground Floor, 2 Marsham Street, London, SW1P 4DF, ✉ timothy.payne11@homeoffice.gsi.gov.uk, *Call Date: Nov 2002, Lincoln's Inn*
Qualifications: [BA (Hons)(Oxon)]

PAYNTER MR WILLIAM

Lansbury Worthington Solicitors, 5 King Street Cloisters, Clifton Walk, King Street, London, W6 0GY, ☎ 020 8563 9797
Fax: 020 8563 9798, ✉ wp@lansbury-worthington.co.uk, *Call Date: July 2002, Gray's Inn*
Qualifications: [LLB (Hull)]

PEACOCK MISS NATASHA VALERIE

Director, Regulatory Legal Solicitors, Brindley House, Engine Lane, Lye, West Midlands, DY9 7AQ, *Call Date: Oct 1995, Gray's Inn*
Qualifications: [LLB (Hons)]

PEACOCK MR NICHOLAS

Kyles Legal Practice Ltd, 20 Northumberland Square, North Shields, Tyne and Wear, NE30 1PX, ✉ nickpeacock@kyleslegalpractice.co.uk, *Call Date: Oct 1996, Gray's Inn*
Qualifications: [LLB (Coventry)]

PEARCE MISS JOANNE

Crown Prosecution Service, Riverside Chambers, Castle Street, Taunton, Somerset, TA1 4AP, ☎ 01823 425100, ✉ joanne.pearce@cps.gsi.gov.uk, *Call Date: July 2001, Gray's Inn*
Qualifications: [BA]

PEARSE MISS CHRISTINE ANNE

Director, Pricewaterhousecoopers LLP, 1 Embankment Place, London, WC2N 6RH, ☎ 01559 362352 Fax: 01559 362427, ✉ christine.pearse@uk.pwc.com, *Call Date: Oct 1996, Inner Temple*
Qualifications: [LLB (L'pool), ACA]

PEARSON MISS CARMEL LOUISE

Crown Prosecution Service, Jefferson House, 27 Park Place, Leeds, West Yorkshire, LS1 2SZ, *Call Date: Nov 2005, Inner Temple*
Qualifications: [LLB Sheffield Hallam University]

PEARSON MR PETER RODERICK PRESCOTT

Anti-Corruption Bureau, Po Box 2437, Lilongwe, Malawi, ☎00 265 01 770 167, *Call Date: July 1972, Middle Temple*
Qualifications: [LLB (Lond)]

PEARSON MRS VIVIENNE MARY

Senior Crown Prosecutor, Crown Prosecution Service, Horsham Police Station, Hurst Road, Horsham, West Sussex, RH12 2DJ, Fax: 01293 583379, ✉vivienne.pearson@sussex.pnn.police.uk, viv.pearson@cps.gsi.gov.uk, *Call Date: July 1982, Middle Temple*
Qualifications: [BA]

PEDDIE MR JONATHAN PETER

Director, Director of Litigation and Special Investigations, Barclays Bank PLC, Level 29, One Churchill Place, London, E14 5HP, ☎020 7116 9944 Fax: 01452 638 490, ✉jonathan.peddie@barclays.com, *Call Date: Nov 1994, Inner Temple*
Qualifications: [BA (So'ton) CPE (Lond)]

PEGG MAJOR JASON GEOFFREY

Assistant Deputy Coroner, Crown Advocate, Other, Crown Prosecution Service, Colmore Gate, 2 - 6 Colmore Row, Birmingham, West Midlands, B3 2QA, ☎0121 262 1300, *Call Date: Oct 1994, Gray's Inn*
Qualifications: [LLB (UEA)]

PENNELL MISS LINDSAY ALEXANDRA

Crown Prosecution Service, Portsmouth Magistrate's Unit, Crown House, Winston Churchill Avenue, Portsmouth, Hampshire, PO1 2PJ, *Call Date: Nov 1994, Inner Temple*
Qualifications: [LLB (Wales)]

PENNELS MRS CAROLINE JANE

Head of Legal Services, Gloucestershire Hospitals Nhs Foundation Trust, Cheltenham General Hospital, Sandford Road, Cheltenham, Gloucestershire, GL53 7AN, ☎08454 223555 Fax: 08454 223083, ✉caroline.pennels@glos.nhs.uk, *Call Date: Mar 1998, Middle Temple*
Qualifications: [BSc (Hons)(Lond) MSc (Lond) MA (Bris) RGN ARCM FGS]

PENNY MR JOHN CORNELIUS

Crown Prosecution Service, Froomsgate House, Rupert Street, Bristol, BS1 2QJ, ☎0117 930 2863 Fax: 0117 930 2823, ✉John.Penny@cps.gsi.gov.uk, *Call Date: Oct 1995, Middle Temple*
Qualifications: [BA (Hons)]

PERCIVAL MR RICHARD ALLIGHAN

Law Commission, Steel House, 11 Tothill Street, London, SW1H 9LJ, ☎020 3334 0261, *Call Date: Oct 1992, Gray's Inn*
Qualifications: [MA (Oxon)]

PEREIRA MS SANCHIA RACHAEL

Crown Prosecution Service, Taunton Police Station, Shuttern, Taunton, Somerset, TA1 4ET, ✉sanchia.pereira@cps.gsi.gov.uk, *Call Date: Oct 1997, Inner Temple*
Qualifications: [LLB (Sussex)]

PERERA MISS THAMALA DIOSHA

IGAS Energy Plc, 7 Down Street, London, W1J 7AJ, ✉thamala.perera@igasplc.com, *Call Date: Oct 2000, Middle Temple*
Qualifications: [LLB (Hons)(Lond)]

PEREZ MS RACHEL ANNE

Judge, Department For Transport, Zone 1/16, Great Minster House, 33 Horseferry Road, London, SW1P 4DR, *Call Date: Oct 1992, Gray's Inn*
Qualifications: [BA (Sheff) CPE (Nott'm)]

PERKS MR JOLYON ANTHONY

Crown Prosecution Service, St Ann's Quay, 122 Quayside, Newcastle Upon Tyne, Tyne and Wear, NE1 3BD, ☎0191 260 4248 Fax: 0191 231 6229, ✉jolyon.perks@cps.gsi.gov.uk, *Call Date: Nov 1994, Lincoln's Inn*
Qualifications: [BA (Hull) Dip Law (Leeds)]

F

PERRY MRS KATE MARIE

West Midlands Police Authority, Civic House, 156 Great Charles Street, Birmingham, B3 3HN, ☎0121 626 8347 Fax: 0121 626 8272, ✉kate.richards@west-midlands.pnn.police.uk, *Call Date: Nov 2007, Inner Temple*
Qualifications: [LLB (Leic)]

PESARO MISS NATASHA LUCILLE

The Treasury Solicitors, One Kemble Street, London, WC2B 4TS, ✉natasha.pesaro@tsol.gsi.gov.uk, *Call Date: Oct 2006, Lincoln's Inn*
Qualifications: [BA (Sheff)]

PETERS MR WILLIAM JOHN STEPHEN CHARLES

Directorate of Army Legal Services, Army Legal Services, Bld 398, Trenchard Lines, Upavon, Pewsey, Wiltshire, SN9 6BE, ☎01980 615013, *Call Date: Nov 1992, Lincoln's Inn*

PETHERBRIDGE MS BRIDGET

Wilmer Cutler Pickering Hale and Dorr LLP, 49 Park Lane, London, W1K 1PS, ☎020 7872 1014 Fax: 020 7839 3537, ✉Bridget.Petherbridge@wilmerhale.com, *Call Date: Nov 2002, Gray's Inn*
Qualifications: [BA (Cantab) MBA (Manch)]

PETTY MR CHRISTOPHER ROGER WILLIAM

General Counsel, University of Manchester, Oxford Road, Manchester, M13 9PZ, ✉chris.petty@manchester.ac.uk, *Call Date: Nov 1976, Middle Temple*
Qualifications: [MA (Cantab)]

PEYTON MR DANIEL LEWIS

McGuireWoods London LLP, 11 Pilgrim Street, London, EC4V 6RN, ☎020 7632 1600 Fax: 020 7632 1638, ✉dpeyton@mcguirewoods.com, *Call Date: Oct 1995, Inner Temple*
Qualifications: [LLB (Sheff) BCL (Oxon)]

PHELPS MR MARK

Call Date: Nov 1994, Lincoln's Inn
Qualifications: [BA MA (Notts) CPE (Notts)]

PHILLIPS MRS ANNE MARGARET

Senior Crown Prosecutor, Crown Prosecution Service, Priory Gate, 29 Union Street, Maidstone, Kent, ME14 1PT, ☎01622 356300, ✉anne.phillips@cps.gsi.gov.uk, *Call Date: July 1988, Middle Temple*
Qualifications: [LLB (Hons) LLM]

PHILLIPS MISS CLAUDETTE

Senior Crown Prosecutor, Crown Prosecution Service, Wembley Police Station, 603 Harrow Road, Wembley, Middlesex, HA0 2HH, *Call Date: Nov 1991, Middle Temple*
Qualifications: [BA (Hons) (Kent)]

PHILLIPS MR DAVID WHITFIELD

Directorate of Army Legal Services, SPA, Bld 85, RAF Northolt, West End Road, Ruislip, Middlesex, HA4 6NG, *Call Date: Mar 2004, Middle Temple*
Qualifications: [BA Dip in Law]

PHILLIPS MR FRASER GUY

Head of Legal Services, Legal Adviser, Legal Services Manager, Computacenter (Uk) Limited, Hatfield Avenue, Hatfield, Hertfordshire, AL10 9TW, ☎01707 639062 Fax: 01707 639959, *Call Date: Nov 1996, Gray's Inn*
Qualifications: [LLB (Swansea)]

PHILLIPS MR HOWARD MICHAEL

Crown Advocate, Crown Prosecution Service, Argal House, Peninsula Business Park, Rydon Lane, Exeter, Devon, EX2 7NT, ☎01392 356700 / 01392 356700 Fax: 01392 356703 / 01392 356703, ✉Howard.Phillips@cps.gsi.gov.uk, *Call Date: Nov 1991, Inner Temple*
Qualifications: [LLB (Reading)]

PHILLIPS MR MARK DAVID

Crown Prosecution Service, Colemore Gate, 2 - 6 Colemore Row, Birmingham, West Midlands, B3 2QA, ✉mark.phillips@cps.gsi.gov.uk, *Call Date: Apr 1991, Middle Temple*
Qualifications: [BSc Econ (Hons)]

PHILLIPS MR MICHAEL BERTRAM

Andrew Storch Solicitors, 7 Barrington Way, Reading, RG1 6EG, *Call Date: Mar 2009, Inner Temple*
Qualifications: [LLB (Nott'm)]

PHILLIPS MR MICHAEL ROLAND

Call Date: Oct 1994, Lincoln's Inn
Qualifications: [LLB (Hons)]

PHILPOTT MRS DEIRDRE PATRICIA MARY

Senior Crown Prosecutor, Crown Prosecution Service, Eaton Court, 112 Oxford Road, Reading, Berkshire, RG1 7LL, ☎0118 951 3600, *Call Date: July 1976, Gray's Inn*
Qualifications: [LLB (Lond)]

PICARDO MS CATHERINE MARY

Crown Prosecution Service, 2 King Edward Court, King Edward Street, Nottingham, Nottinghamshire, NG1 1EL, ☎0115 852 3300 Fax: 0115 852 3429, ✉Catherine.Picardo@cps.gsi.gov.uk, *Call Date: Nov 2008, Lincoln's Inn*
Qualifications: [BA MA (Cantab) CPE UZNTU]

PICCOLO MR VAUGHAN

BNP Paribas, Compliance Department, 10 Harewood Avenue, London, NW1 6AA, ☎020 7595 4026, *Call Date: Nov 1994, Inner Temple*
Qualifications: [BA (Cantab)]

PIDCOCK MR STEVEN CRAWFORD

Stuart Miller Solicitors, 247 High Road, Wood Green, London, N22 8HF, *Call Date: Nov 1996, Lincoln's Inn*
Qualifications: [LLB (Hons)(LSE)]

PIGOTT MRS SARAH-JANE

Total E&P UK Limited, Crawpeel Road, Altens, Aberdeen, AB12 3FG, *Call Date: July 1998, Inner Temple*
Qualifications: [LLB (Hons) LLM]

PIKE MR JOHN ANTHONY

Sciaroni and Associates, Po Box 1153, Phnom Penh, Cambodia, ☎77 730 883, *Call Date: Nov 2003, Lincoln's Inn*
Qualifications: [MA (Oxon)]

PIKETT MR CHRISTOPHER

Company Secretary, Director, 3m United Kingdom PLC, 3m Centre, Cain Road, Bracknell, Berkshire, RG12 8HT, ✉CPIKETT1@MMM.COM, *Call Date: Nov 1975, Middle Temple*
Qualifications: [LLB (Hons) (So'ton)]

PILCHER MS SARA KATE

Legal Officer, Crown Prosecution Service, Riding Gate House, 37 Old Dover Road, Canterbury, Kent, CT1 3JG, ☎01227 866090, ✉sarakjones@virginmedia.com, sara.pilcher@cps.gsi.gov.uk, *Call Date: Nov 1996, Gray's Inn*
Qualifications: [LLB (Brunel)]

PINION MRS DEBORAH

HMCS Essex, Essex Magistrates' Courts, Springfield Lodge, Colchester Road, Springfield, Chelmsford, Essex, CM2 5PW, ✉debbie.pinion1@hmcts.gsi.gov.uk, *Call Date: Oct 1992, Gray's Inn*
Qualifications: [LLB (Lancs)]

PINNELL MR ELLIS ANTHONY

Legal Services Commission, 8th Floor, 102 Petty France, London, SW1H 9AJ, ☎020 3545 8911 Fax: 020 3334 2234, ✉ellis.pinnell@legalservices.gsi.gov.uk, *Call Date: Oct 1998, Lincoln's Inn*
Qualifications: [LLB (Hons)]

PITBLADO MR ALASTAIR BRUCE

Official Solicitor, 81 Chancery Lane, London, WC2A 1DD, *Call Date: July 1974, Middle Temple*

PITKETHLY MR RICHARD ALEXANDER

Steel and Shamash Solicitors, 12 Baylis Road, Waterloo, London, SE1 7AA, ☎020 7803 3999 Fax: 020 7803 3900, *Call Date: Nov 1999, Gray's Inn*
Qualifications: [LLB (Lond)]

PLISKIN MISS MELANIE CLARE

HED, Crown Prosecution Service, Western Range, 83 London Road, Southampton, Hampshire, SO15 2AA, ✉Melanie.Pliskin@cps.gsi.gov.uk, *Call Date: Nov 1985, Lincoln's Inn*
Qualifications: [BA LLM (So'ton) MA (So'ton)]

POGONOWSKI MISS RUTH

Ministry of Justice, 6.38, 102 Petty France, London, SW1H 9AJ, ☎020 3334 4782, ✉ruth.pogonowski@justice.gsi.gov.uk, *Call Date: Nov 2006, Inner Temple*
Qualifications: [LLB (Brunel)]

F

POLL MRS AMANDA CLAIRE

Crown Prosecution Service, Romford Police Station, 19 Main Road, Romford, Essex, RM1 3BJ, ✉amanda.poll@cps.gsi.gov.uk, *Call Date: July 2001, Inner Temple*
Qualifications: [BSc (Bris) CPE]

POOLE MISS JOANNA CAROLINE SANDRA

Farrer & Co, 66 Lincoln's Inn Fields, London, WC2A 3LH, *Call Date: July 2005, Inner Temple*
Qualifications: [LLB King's College University of London]

POPE MR DAVID JAMES

Director, SNR Denton, 124 Chancery Lane, Clifford's Inn, London, EC4A 1BU, *Call Date: Feb 1995, Lincoln's Inn*
Qualifications: [LLB (Hons)(Edin) LLM (USA)]

POPE MR GAVIN DANIEL

Legal Counsel, Senior Legal Counsel, Novartis Pharma AG, Forum 1, Novartis Campus, Basel, Ch-4056, Switzerland, ☎0041 61 324 2314 Fax: 0041 61 324 7399, ✉gavin.pope@novartis.com, *Call Date: Oct 1999, Middle Temple*
Qualifications: [BA (Hons) (Cantab) MA (Cantab) FCIS]

POPE MR WILLIAM DAVID LONGFIELD

Wainwright and Cummins Solicitors, 413a Brixton Road, London, SW9 7DG, ☎020 7737 9330 Fax: 020 7737 9331, ✉mail@wainwrightcummins.co.uk, *Call Date: Nov 1995, Lincoln's Inn*
Qualifications: [MA (Hons)]

PORTER MISS ALEXANDRA ELIZABETH

The Treasury Solicitors, Litigation & Employment Group, One Kemble Street, London, WC2B 4TS, *Call Date: Nov 2002, Middle Temple*
Qualifications: [BA(Hons) (Cantab) CPE]

PORTER MR MARK ALEXANDER

Bae Systems PLC, Warton, Preston, Lancashire, PR4 1AX, *Call Date: July 1982, Lincoln's Inn*
Qualifications: [LLB (Hons)]

PORTER MR RYAN WALCOTT

Legal Adviser, Lloyds Tsb Corporate Markets, 10 Gresham Street, London, EC2V 7AE, ☎020 7158 1352 Fax: 020 7158 3209, ✉Ryan.Porter@lloydsbanking.com, *Call Date: July 1999, Inner Temple*
Qualifications: [BA]

PORTER MISS SARAH RUTH

Cartwright King Solicitors, Norwich Union House, South Parade, Old Market Square, Nottingham, Nottinghamshire, NG1 2LH, ☎0115 958 7444 Fax: 0115 958 8666, *Call Date: Nov 1996, Gray's Inn*
Qualifications: [LLB (Teeside) MA (Sheff)]

PORTER MR STEPHEN DAVID

Orange Business Services, Betjeman Place, 217 Bath Road, Slough, SL1 4AA, ☎020 8321 1722, ✉stephen.porter@orange-ftgroup.com, *Call Date: Feb 1992, Lincoln's Inn*
Qualifications: [LLB (Hons)]

POSNER MR RICHARD MICHAEL

Crown Prosecution Service, Froomsgate House, Rupert Street, Bristol, BS1 2QJ, ☎0117 9302800, ✉richard.posner@cps.gsi.gov.uk, *Call Date: July 1999, Lincoln's Inn*
Qualifications: [LLB (Hons)]

POSNER MR ROBERT

Legal Counsel, Other, The Electoral Commission, Trevelyan House, Great Peter Street, London, SW1P 2HW, ☎020 7271 0546 Fax: 020 7271 0505, ✉bposner@electoralcommission.org.uk, *Call Date: July 1981, Lincoln's Inn*
Qualifications: [BA (Hons) MA]

POTTER MR CHARLES ALEXANDER

Brunswick Group, 16 Lincoln's Inn Fields, London, WC2A 3ED, Fax: 020 7831 2823, ✉www.brunswickgroup.com, *Call Date: July 2007, Gray's Inn*
Qualifications: [BA (Cantab) DipLaw]

POTTER MRS IRENE WAI KENG

Intrust Limited, 33 Wigmore Street, London, W1U 1AU, ☎020 7467 2100 Fax: 020 7467 2180, ✉info@intrust.co.uk, *Call Date: July 1980, Lincoln's Inn*
Qualifications: [BA (Hons)]

POTTS MR ALEXANDER JAMES KENNETH

Sedgwick Chudleigh, E W Pearman Building, 20 Brunswick Street, Hamilton, HM10, Bermuda, Fax: 441 296 9277, ✉alex.potts@sedgwicklaw.com, *Call Date: Oct 2000, Middle Temple*
Qualifications: [BA (Hons) (Oxon) CPE]

POUS MISS KRISTEL ELISABETH MARIE

Crown Prosecution Service, Rose Court, 2 Sourthwark Bridge, London, SE1 9HS, ✉Kristel.pous@cps.gsi.gov.uk, *Call Date: Oct 2006, Middle Temple*
Qualifications: [LLB (Hons) (Essex) MA (Reading)]

POWELL MR GLYN STEPHEN

Jones Day, 21 Tudor Street, London, EC4Y 0DJ, Fax: 020 7039 5999, ✉gpowell@jonesday.com, *Call Date: Oct 1993, Middle Temple*
Qualifications: [LLB (Hons)(Lond)]

POWELL MR GUY STORER

HED, Hogan Lovells International LLP, Atlantic House, 50 Holborn Viaduct, London, EC1A 2FG, ☎020 72962637 Fax: 020 7296 2001, ✉guy.powell@hoganlovells.com, *Call Date: Nov 1982, Middle Temple*
Qualifications: [LLB]

POWELL MR IAN GEORGE

Spirit Pub Company, Sunrise House, Ninth Avenue, Burton Upon Trent, Staffordshire, DE14 3JZ, Fax: 01283 498 250, *Call Date: July 1983, Inner Temple*
Qualifications: [LLB (Sheff)]

POWELL MISS NICOLA JAYNE

Dinas Chambers, Dinas Hall, Pantdu, West Glamorgan, SA12 9BU, ☎01639 894590, *Call Date: Nov 1996, Lincoln's Inn*
Qualifications: [LLB (Hons)]

POWER MR PIERCE DECLEAN KIERAN

Wannop and Fox Solicitors, South Pallant House, Chichester, West Sussex, PO19 1TH, ☎01243 778844 Fax: 01243 788349, *Call Date: Apr 1989, Gray's Inn*
Qualifications: [BA (Hons)]

POWICK MISS ANNA

Principal Legal Officer, Department For Work and Pensions, The Adelphi, 5th Floor (Litigation Dept), 1-11 John Adam Street, London, WC2N 6HT, ✉anna.powick@dwp.gsi.gov.uk, *Call Date: Oct 1997, Middle Temple*
Qualifications: [LLB (Hons)(Leeds)]

POWSNEY MISS JENNIE ROCHELLE

In House Counsel, Greater Manchester Police, Legal Services Unit, Machester, M11 2NS, *Call Date: July 2007, Gray's Inn*

POXON MR PHILIP EDWARD

Legal Manager, Hydratight Operations Ltd, Unit 5 Coopies, Field Industrial Estate, Morpeth, Northumberland, NE61 6JT, *Call Date: July 1985, Lincoln's Inn*
Qualifications: [LLB (Newc)]

PRATLEY MRS FIONA CATHERINE

Hampshire County Council, Employment Law Team, Athelstan House, St Clement Street, Winchester, Hampshire, *Call Date: Oct 1996, Gray's Inn*
Qualifications: [BA (Dunelm) MSc (Sheff)]

PRATT MISS SARA CAROLINE

Crown Prosecution Service, Colmore Gate, 2 - 6 Colmore Row, Birmingham, West Midlands, B3 2QA, ☎0121 262 1300, *Call Date: Oct 1996, Inner Temple*
Qualifications: [LLB (Hons)]

PRENDIVILLE MR RICE IRWIN

General Counsel, Cls Services Ltd, Exchange Tower, 1 Harbour Exchange Square, London, E14 9GE, *Call Date: July 1981, Gray's Inn*

PRENTIS MRS VICTORIA MARY BOSWELL

Lawyer, The Treasury Solicitors, One Kemble Street, London, WC2B 4TS, ☎020 7210 3358, ✉victoria.prentis@tsol.gsi.gov.uk, *Call Date: Oct 1995, Middle Temple*
Qualifications: [MA (Hons)]

F

PRESCOTT MISS VICTORIA CATHERINE

Reynolds Porter Chamberlain LLP, Tower Bridge House, St Katherine's Way, London, E1W 1AA, ✉victoria.prescott@rpc.co.uk, *Call Date: July 2000, Middle Temple*
Qualifications: [BA(Hons) (Cantab)]

PRETTY MR PAUL LEONARD

Nursing and Midwifery Council, Fitness to Practice, 61 Aldwych, London, WC2B 4AE, ☎020 7462 5800, *Call Date: Nov 2004, Lincoln's Inn*
Qualifications: [LLB (Hons) (Dunelm)]

PREVEZER MS SUSAN RACHEL

Deputy High Court Judge, Mediator, Recorder, Quinn Emanuel Urquhart & Sullivan LLP, 16 Old Bailey, London, EC4M 7EG, *Call Date: July 1983, Inner Temple*
Qualifications: [MA (Cantab)]

PRICE MISS ANGHARAD MARY

Caerphilly County Borough Council, Ty Penallta, Parctredomen, Ystradmunach, CF82 7PG, ☎01443 863150 Fax: 01443 863154, ✉pricea4@caerphilly.gov.uk, *Call Date: July 2004, Middle Temple*
Qualifications: [LLB Hons (Wales)]

PRICE MR ANTHONY JOHN

Square Enix Europe, 1 Hartfield Road, Wimbledon, London, SW19 3RU, ✉anthonyp@square-enix.com, *Call Date: July 1983, Gray's Inn*
Qualifications: [BA (Hons)]

PRICE MR JONATHAN NICHOLAS

Deputy Justices' Clerk, Hmcs Northamptonshire, Northampton Magistrates' Court, Regents Pavillion, Summerhouse Road, Moulton Park, Northampton, Northamptonshire, NN3 6AS, ☎01604 497033 Fax: 01604 497010, ✉jonathan.price@hmcourts-service.gsi.gov.uk, *Call Date: Nov 1989, Inner Temple*
Qualifications: [LLB (B'ham) MBA (B'ham)]

PRICE MR NICHOLAS JOHN

Crown Prosecution Service, Colmore Gate, 2 - 6 Colmore Row, Birmingham, West Midlands, B3 2QA, ☎0121 262 1566, ✉Nick.price@cps.gsi.gov.uk, *Call Date: July 1998, Middle Temple*
Qualifications: [LLB (Hons)(Herts)]

PRICE MR ROBERT SAMUEL

Crown Prosecution Service, Building 3, Etruria Valley Office Village, Etruria, Stoke-On-Trent, Staffordshire, ST1 5RU, ☎01782 664500 / 01782 664500 / 01782 664 541 Fax: 01782 664 532, ✉robert.price@cps.gsi.gov.uk, *Call Date: Oct 1990, Middle Temple*
Qualifications: [LLB (Leics)]

PRIESTLEY MS REBECCA JANET

Lloyds Banking Group, 25 Gresham Street, London, EC2V 7HN, ☎020 7206 0770, *Call Date: Nov 1989, Middle Temple*
Qualifications: [BA (Hons) (Oxon)]

PRINCE MR RAYMOND ANDREW

London Borough of Haringey Council, Alexandra House, 10 Station Road, Wood Green, London, N22 7TR, ☎020 8489 0000 Fax: 020 8489 3963, ✉raymond.prince@haringey.gov.uk, *Call Date: July 1985, Lincoln's Inn*
Qualifications: [BA]

PRITCHARD MISS DAWN MARIE

Crown Prosecution Service, 2 King Edward Court, King Edward Street, Nottingham, Nottinghamshire, NG1 1EL, ☎0115 852 5229, *Call Date: Feb 1992, Inner Temple*
Qualifications: [LLB (Sheff)]

PRIVETT MISS ANNABEL PATRICIA

Serious Fraud Office, Elm House, 10-16 Elm Street, London, WC1X 0BJ, ☎020 7239 7365 Fax: 020 7833 5446, ✉annabel.privett@sfo.gsi.gov.uk, *Call Date: July 2002, Middle Temple*
Qualifications: [MA Hons (Edinb) Dip in Law]

PROBERT-WOOD MR TIMOTHY BLAIR

Crown Advocate, Crown Prosecution Service, Rose Court, 2 Southwark Bridge, London, SE1 9HS, ✉tim.probert-wood@cps.gsi.gov.uk, *Call Date: July 1983, Inner Temple*
Qualifications: [LLB (Hull)]

PROCTOR MISS CARMEL GAIL

Manchester City Council, Child Care Legal Services, Manchester Town Hall, Albert Square, Manchester, M60 2LA, ✉c.proctor@manchester.gov.uk, *Call Date: Oct 1997, Lincoln's Inn*
Qualifications: [LLB (Hons)(Manc)]

F

PROWSE MR DANIEL GORDON BARRINGTON

Forbes Solicitors, Ribchester House, Lancaster Road, Preston, PR1 2QL, ☎01772 220 022 Fax: 01772 220 167, ✉daniel.prowse@forbessolicitors.co.uk, *Call Date: Oct 2004, Inner Temple*
Qualifications: [LLB (Hons) (Newc)]

PRUDHOE MR TIMOTHY NIXON

Consultant, Lawyer, Kobre & Kim LLP, 60 Gresham Street, London, EC2V 7BB, *Call Date: Oct 1994, Gray's Inn*
Qualifications: [LLB (Hons)(Manc) PG Dip Law FCIArb]

PRYER MRS JULIA MARY

Crown Prosecution Service, Rose Court, 2 Southwark Bridge, London, SE1 9HS, ☎0203 3570783, *Call Date: Feb 1986, Middle Temple*
Qualifications: [BA]

PUGH MR DENZIL ANTHONY

Crown Prosecution Service, Riding Gate House, 37 Old Dover Road, Canterbury, Kent, CT1 3JG, *Call Date: July 1980, Gray's Inn*

PUGSLEY MISS ALISON JANE

The Treasury Solicitors, Hm Treasury, 1 Horse Guards Road, London, SW1A 2HQ, ☎020 7270 6384, ✉alison.pugsley@hmtreasury.gsi.gov.uk, *Call Date: Oct 1998, Middle Temple*
Qualifications: [BA (Hons)(Lond) CPE]

PULLIN MS SAMANTHA JOAN

HM Revenue and Customs, 2c. 22, Solicitor's Office, 100 Parliament Street, London, SW1A 2BQ, ☎020 7147 3244 Fax: 020 7147 2251, *Call Date: Oct 1996, Middle Temple*
Qualifications: [LLB (Hons)(Wales) LLM (Leics)]

PURDASY MR MOHAMMAD ISMAEL SHAHMEEM

The Home Office, Seacole House, 2 Marsham Street, London, SW1P 4DF, *Call Date: July 2000, Gray's Inn*
Qualifications: [LLB (Hons)]

PURVES MR MICHAEL NEIL

Senior Lawyer, HM Revenue and Customs, Hm Revenue and Customs, Room 2/72, 100 Parliament Street, London, SW1A 2BQ, ☎020 7147 3079, *Call Date: July 1989, Inner Temple*
Qualifications: [LLB (Lond)]

PURVIS MR ANDREW JOHN

Call Date: Feb 1993, Gray's Inn
Qualifications: [Bsc (Econ)(Wales) FCII]

QUENTIN MR DAVID GEOFFREY ST.CLAIR

Farrer & Co, 66 Lincoln's Inn Fields, London, WC2A 3LH, *Call Date: Oct 2004, Middle Temple*
Qualifications: [LLM MA (Hons) MPhil (Cantab) PgDip]

QUINTON MR THOMAS HENRY ALEXANDER

Halarose Limited, Goring House, Beechwood Court, Long Toll, Woodcote, Oxfordshire, RG8 0RR, ✉thomas.quinton@halarose.co.uk, *Call Date: Oct 1997, Inner Temple*
Qualifications: [BA (Hons)(LSE)]

QURESHI MISS AYESHA MAJIDA

Call Date: July 2004, Inner Temple

RADWAY MRS MARGARET LEONIE

Her Majesty's Court Service, Grantham Magistrates Court, Harlaxton Road, Grantham, Lincolnshire, NG31 7SB, *Call Date: Nov 1979, Lincoln's Inn*
Qualifications: [BA]

RAE MISS HELEN SAMANTHA

Department For Business, Innovation and Skills, Legal Service Directorate, 1 Victoria Street, London, SW1H 0ET, Fax: 020 7215 3221, *Call Date: July 2005, Lincoln's Inn*
Qualifications: [BA (Hons)]

RAFFRAY MR FREDERIC JOSEPH

Call Date: Feb 1991, Middle Temple
Qualifications: [LLB (Lond) Maitrise en Droit (Paris I)]

F

RAGNAUTH MRS JANET

Springfield University Hospital, Building 7, 61 Glenburnie Road, London, SW17 7DJ, Fax: 020 8767 6996, ✉jragnauth@springfieldlawcentre.org.uk, *Call Date: July 1991, Lincoln's Inn*
Qualifications: [LLB (Hons)]

RAGNAUTH MS PORTIA URANIE

Chief Crown Prosecutor, Crown Prosecution Service, Gateway, 31 Power Close, Surrey, Guildford, GU1 1EJ, Fax: 01483 468282, ✉portia.ragnauth@cps.gsi.gov.uk, *Call Date: July 1985, Lincoln's Inn*
Qualifications: [LLB]

RAHMAN MS KHADIJA UMBARIN

Legal Manager, Wainwright and Cummins LLP, 413a Brixton Road, London, SW9 7DG, Fax: 020 7737 9331, *Call Date: Nov 2000, Inner Temple*
Qualifications: [LLB (Westminster) LLM (Lond)]

RAI MRS SUKHVINDERJIT KAUR

The Treasury Solicitors, HM Treasury, LG/18, 1 Horse Guards Road, London, SW1A 2HQ, ☎020 7270 5277, ✉Suki.Rai@hmtreasury.gsi.gov.uk, *Call Date: Nov 2002, Gray's Inn*
Qualifications: [BA (Oxon)]

RAINFORD DR DAVID

Taylor Vinters, Merlin Place, Milton Road, Cambridge, Cambridgeshire, CB4 0DP, ☎01223 225288 Fax: 01223 425446, ✉david.rainford@taylorvinters.com, *Call Date: Oct 1997, Inner Temple*
Qualifications: [BSc (Lond) PhD (Lond) CPE]

RAJA MR AHTIQ

9 King's Bench Walk, Lower Ground Floor South, 9 King's Bench Walk, Temple, London, EC4Y 7DX, *Call Date: Oct 2007, Lincoln's Inn*
Qualifications: [LLB]

RAJA MR ANIL JAYANTILAL

Next Retail Limited, Desford Road, Enderby, Leicester, LE19 4AT, ☎0116 284 2958 Fax: 0116 284 2642, ✉anil_raja@next.co.uk, *Call Date: Mar 1996, Gray's Inn*
Qualifications: [LLB (Lond)]

RAJAH MISS REHANA

Sanlam UK Limited, St Bartholomew's House, Lewins Mead, Bristol, BS1 2NH, ☎0117 975 2164, ✉rehana.loram@merchinv.co.uk, *Call Date: Nov 1987, Middle Temple*
Qualifications: [BA(Hons) (Lond) Dip Law (Lond)]

RAJPUT MR SACHIN

Ebr Attridge LLP, The Colleen Bawn, 196 Southwark Park Road, Bermondsey, London, SE16 3RP, ☎020 7231 5166 Fax: 020 7232 6014, *Call Date: Oct 2004, Middle Temple*
Qualifications: [Dip in Law BA (Hons)]

RAMRATTAN DR HEMMA

Us Securities and Exchange Commission, 100f Street, Ne, Washington, DC 20005, USA, ☎001 202 551 4486, *Call Date: Nov 2002, Inner Temple*
Qualifications: [LLB (Exon) LLM]

RAMSAY MR JONATHAN MICHAEL

Prosecutor, Crown Prosecution Service, Rose Court, 2 Southwark Bridge, London, SE1 9HS, ☎020 3357 0000, *Call Date: July 1998, Middle Temple*
Qualifications: [LLB (Hons)(Dunelm)]

RAMSDEN MR SIMON CHRISTOPHER

The Treasury Solicitors, One Kemble Street, London, WC2B 4TS, ☎020 7210 2960 Fax: 020 7210 3214, ✉simon.ramsden@tsol.gsi.gov.uk, *Call Date: Oct 2005, Middle Temple*
Qualifications: [Dip Law BA (Hons)]

RAMSHAW MRS PHYLLIS MURIEL

HM Revenue and Customs, Business Income Profits and Structures, 100 Parliament Street, London, SW1A 2BQ, ☎0207 7147 3886 Fax: 020 7147 0433, *Call Date: Oct 2001, Gray's Inn*
Qualifications: [LLB (L'pool)]

RAMSUBHAG MR ANDREW IVAN

Crown Prosecution Service, Southern House, Wellesley Grove, Croydon, CR9 1DY, ✉andrew.ramsubhag@cps.gsi.gov.uk, *Call Date: Mar 2000, Middle Temple*
Qualifications: [LLB (Hons) (Brunel)]

RANAUTA MISS MANVINDER KAUR

Senior Crown Prosecutor, Crown Prosecution Service, Capital Tower, Greyfiars Road, Cardiff, CF10 3PL, ✉mani.ranauta@cps.gsi.gov.uk, *Call Date: May 1997, Gray's Inn*
Qualifications: [LLB]

RANCE MS EMMA JANE

J D Spicer and Co Solicitors, 140 Kilburn High Road, London, NW6 4JD, ☎020 7624 7771 Fax: 020 7328 9466, ✉Erance@jdspicer.co.uk, *Call Date: Mar 2005, Inner Temple*
Qualifications: [LLB University of Westminster]

RANCE MS GENEVIEVE

J D Spicer and Co Solicitors, 140 Kilburn High Road, London, NW6 4JD, ☎020 7624 7771 Fax: 020 7328 9466, *Call Date: Nov 2003, Inner Temple*
Qualifications: [LLB (Westminster)]

RAPPO MR PATRICK JAMES

Serious Fraud Office, Elm House, 10-16 Elm Street, London, WC1X 0BJ, ✉patrick.rappo@sfo.gsi.gov.uk, *Call Date: Nov 1995, Gray's Inn*
Qualifications: [MA (Oxon)]

RASAIAH MS SANTHA GERALDINE

Director, The Newspaper Society, St Andrew's House, 18-20 St Andrew Street, London, EC4A 3AY, ☎020 7632 7400 Fax: 020 7632 7401, *Call Date: July 1983, Middle Temple*
Qualifications: [BA (Oxon)]

RASHID MRS ALIYA

Crown Advocate, Senior Crown Prosecutor, Crown Prosecution Service, Colmore Gate, 2 - 6 Colmore Row, Birmingham, West Midlands, B3 2QA, ☎0121 262 1300, ✉aliya.rashid@cps.gsi.gov.uk, *Call Date: Oct 1994, Gray's Inn*
Qualifications: [LLB (Hons)]

RASHID MISS PARVEEN AKHTAR

Senior Crown Prosecutor, Crown Prosecution Service, Eaton Court, 112 Oxford Road, Reading, Berkshire, RG1 7LL, ☎0118 951 3600 Fax: 0118 951 3666, *Call Date: Oct 1992, Lincoln's Inn*
Qualifications: [LLB(Hons) LLM]

RATCLIFFE MR STEVEN JAMES

Nottinghamshire County Council, County Hall, West Bridgford, Nottingham, Nottinghamshire, NG2 7QP, ✉steven.ratcliffe@nottscc.gov.uk, *Call Date: Nov 1984, Gray's Inn*
Qualifications: [LLB (Hons) (Warw)]

RATHOUR MISS DELVINDER KAUR

East Sussex County Council, Po Box 2714, County Hall, St Ann's Crescent, Lewes, East Sussex, BN7 1AL, ✉delvinder.rathour@eastsussex.gov.uk, *Call Date: Nov 2005, Gray's Inn*
Qualifications: [PgDL The University of West of England]

RATTIGAN MR MICHAEL PAUL WILLIAM

Crown Prosecution Service, Kingston Crown Court, 6-8 Penrhyn Road, Kingston Upon Thames, Surrey, KT1 2BB, ✉Paul.Rattigan@cps.gsi.gov.uk, *Call Date: Oct 1991, Lincoln's Inn*
Qualifications: [LLB (Hons) (Lond)]

RAU MR RUSTUM FREDERICK

BT Group PLC, BT Legal PPA6, BT Centre, 81 Newgate Street, London, EC1A 7AJ, *Call Date: Oct 2004, Gray's Inn*
Qualifications: [BA Dip Law]

RAVAL MR ANILKUMAR HARISH

General Counsel, One Regent Capital Partners LLP, 1 Regent Street, London, SW1Y 4NS, ☎7956670256, *Call Date: Oct 1991, Lincoln's Inn*
Qualifications: [MA (Hons) (Cantab)]

RAWLINGS MR DAVID WILLIAM

Financial Reporting Council, 5th Floor, Aldwych House, 71-91 Aldwych, London, WC2B 4HN, ✉d.rawlings@frc.org.uk, *Call Date: Nov 1995, Gray's Inn*
Qualifications: [LLB (Lond)]

RAWLINS MR JEREMY JOHN

HED, Crown Prosecution Service, Rose Court, 2 Southwark Bridge, London, SE1 9HS, ☎020 3357 0825, ✉Jeremy.Rawlins@cps.gsi.gov.uk, *Call Date: Nov 1982, Middle Temple*
Qualifications: [LLB (Hons)]

F

RAWNSLEY MISS COLLETTE LIANNE

Shearman and Sterling LLP, Broadgate West, 9 Appold Street, London, EC2A 2AP, ☎+44 20 7655 5063 Fax: +44 20 7655 5375, ✉Collette.Rawnsley@Shearman.com, *Call Date: Nov 1998, Middle Temple*
Qualifications: [LLB (Hons)(Bucks)]

RAY MR BENJAMIN JAMES

The Home Office, Seacole House, 2 Marsham Street, London, SW1P 4DF, ☎020 7273 8106 Fax: 020 7273 4075, *Call Date: Nov 2002, Lincoln's Inn*
Qualifications: [LLB (Hons)(Sheff)]

RAYNE MISS TRACY REBECCA ANNE

Newcastle City Council, Legal Services, Civic Centre, Newcastle Upon Tyne, NE99 2BN, ☎0191 232 8520, ✉tracy.rayne@newcastle.gov.uk, *Call Date: July 2002, Middle Temple*
Qualifications: [LLB (Hons)]

RAYNER MISS DONNA FRANCES

HED, Crown Prosecution Service, Special Crime Division, Rose Court, 2 Southwark Bridge, London, SE1 9HS, ☎020 3357 0000, *Call Date: Nov 1988, Gray's Inn*
Qualifications: [BA (Hons)]

RAYNER MISS JACQUELINE

Senior Court Clerk, Her Majesty's Courts and Tribunals Service, Po Box 16, 14 Hamilton Terrace, Leamington Spa, Warwickshire, CV32 4XG, ✉jacky.rayner@hmcts.gsi.gov.uk, *Call Date: Nov 1991, Gray's Inn*
Qualifications: [LLB]

RAYNER MR WILLIAM NICHOLAS

General Counsel, Imperial Innovations Group PLC, 52 Princes Gate, Exhibition Road, London, SW7 2PG, *Call Date: July 2004, Lincoln's Inn*
Qualifications: [BSc Hons (Lond) MSc (Lond)]

F

RAZAQ MISS BUSHRA JABINE

HM Revenue and Customs, 2nd Floor, South West Bush House, London, WC2B 4RD, *Call Date: Mar 2003, Lincoln's Inn*
Qualifications: [LLB (Hons) (Bris)]

READING MR TIMOTHY MARK LUCAS

Chair, General Counsel, BP Legal, Building 200, Chertsey Road, Sunbury On Thames, TW16 7LN, ☎01932 774932 Fax: 01932 774 914, ✉tim.reading@uk.bp.com, *Call Date: July 1981, Lincoln's Inn*
Qualifications: [MA (Oxon)]

REDDIN LIEUTENANT COLONEL DAVID GORDON

Manager, Legal Services Commission, Special Cases Unit, 3/4th Floor, Invicta House, Trafalgar Place, Brighton, East Sussex, BN1 4FR, ☎01273 878 850 Fax: 01273 878 990, ✉david.reddin@legalservices.gsi.gov.uk, *Call Date: Nov 1982, Gray's Inn*
Qualifications: [LLB (Hons) (L'pool)]

REDDY MISS CHALLA ANUDITA

Legal Officer, Crown Prosecution Service, Jefferson House, 27 Park Place, Leeds, West Yorkshire, LS1 2SZ, *Call Date: Nov 1993, Inner Temple*
Qualifications: [BSc (Lond) CPE (Lond)]

REDFEARN MR CHARLES

General Counsel, General Counsel's Office, Export Credits Guarantee Dept, P.O. Box 2200, 2 Exchange Tower, Harbour Exchange Square, London, E14 9GS, ☎020 7512 7177 Fax: 020 7512 7052, ✉charles.redfearn@ecgd.gsi.gov.uk, *Call Date: Nov 1986, Lincoln's Inn*
Qualifications: [BA (Hons) Dip Law]

REDFORD MR ALISTAIR DAVID

Crown Prosecution Service, Colmore Gate, 2 - 6 Colmore Row, Birmingham, West Midlands, B3 2QA, ☎0121 262 1479, ✉alistair.redford@cps.gsi.gov.uk, *Call Date: Nov 1995, Gray's Inn*
Qualifications: [LLB]

REDGRAVE MR WILLIAM ALEXANDER FRANK

Baker & Partners, Po Box 842, St Helier, Jersey, JE4 0US, Jersey, *Call Date: Oct 1995, Inner Temple*
Qualifications: [BA (Hons) Dip Law]

REDMAN MR STEPHEN MICHAEL

Call Date: July 1986, Lincoln's Inn
Qualifications: [BA]

REDPATH MS LARA CATHERINE

Senior Crown Prosecutor, Crown Prosecution Service, United House, Piccadilly, York, North Yorkshire, YO1 9PQ, ☎01904 545400, *Call Date: Feb 1994, Lincoln's Inn*
Qualifications: [BA (Hons)(Oxon)]

REED COMMANDER DARREN KEITH

Royal Navy Officers, Legal Office, Room 3.73, Atlantic Building, Northwood Headquarter, Sandy Lane, Northwood, Middlesex, HA6 3HP, ☎01923 843744, ✉D.Reed@manw.nato.int, *Call Date: Oct 2003, Middle Temple*
Qualifications: [BA (Hons) (Wales)]

REED MRS MARIE GABRIELLE

Principal Crown Prosecutor, Prosecution Team Leader, Crown Prosecution Service, The Cooperage, 8 Gainsford Street, London, SE1 2NE, ✉moya.reed@cps.gsi.gov.uk, *Call Date: Nov 1972, Gray's Inn*
Qualifications: [LLB]

REEDS MR GRAHAM JOSEPH

Recorder, Crown Prosecution Service, United House, Piccadilly, York, North Yorkshire, YO1 9PQ, ☎01904 545652, *Call Date: Nov 1984, Middle Temple*
Qualifications: [LLB (Sheff)]

REES MR GARETH DAVID

Financial Reporting Council, 5th Floor, Aldwych House, 71-91 Aldwych, London, WC2B 4HN, ✉g.rees@frc-aadb.org.uk, *Call Date: July 1981, Gray's Inn*
Qualifications: [BA]

REEVES MISS ELEANOR

Employment Lawyer, O.H Parsons & Partners, 3rd Floor, Sovereign House, 212-224 Shaftsbury Avenue, London, WC2H 8PR, ✉elliereeves@ohparsons.co.uk, *Call Date: July 2004, Inner Temple*
Qualifications: [BA]

REEVES MR SIMON RICHARD

HED, Syngenta International AG, Werk Rosenthal, Schwarzwaldallee 125, Ch-4058 Basel, Switzerland, ☎00 41 61 323 8329 Fax: 00 41 61 323 9266, ✉simon.reeves@syngenta.com, *Call Date: Nov 2002, Middle Temple*
Qualifications: [LLB (Hons) (B'ham)]

REFAHI MS RANA

Birnberg Peirce and Partners, 14 Inverness Street, Camden, London, NW1 7HJ, Fax: 020 7911 0170, ✉rana@birnbergpeirce.co.uk, *Call Date: Oct 2004, Inner Temple*
Qualifications: [BA (Manch) CPE]

REGIS MR SIMON TREVOR ANDREW

Legal Officer, The Treasury Solicitors, One Kemble Street, London, WC2B 4TS, ✉simon.regis@tsol.gsi.gov.uk, *Call Date: Oct 1997, Inner Temple*
Qualifications: [BA (Warwick)]

REID MR GRAHAM MATTHEW

Reynolds Porter Chamberlain LLP, Tower Bridge House, St Katherine's Way, London, E1W 1AA, ☎020 3060 6000 Fax: 020 3060 7000, ✉graham.reid@rpc.co.uk, *Call Date: Feb 1993, Middle Temple*
Qualifications: [MA (Oxon) DipLaw (City)]

REID MRS MARY HELENE THERESA

Crown Advocate, Principal Crown Prosecutor, Crown Prosecution Service, Rose Court, 2 Southwalk Bridge, London, SE1 9HS, ☎020 3357 0000 Fax: 020 3357 0723, ✉mari.reid@cps.gsi.gov.uk, *Call Date: Nov 1982, Middle Temple*
Qualifications: [LLB (Hons)]

REID MR SIMON BENJAMIN

Department For Work and Pensions, Room 4c06, Quarry House, Leeds, LS2 7UA, ✉ben.reid@dwp.gsi.gov.uk, *Call Date: Mar 2001, Lincoln's Inn*
Qualifications: [LLB (Hons)]

REID MISS SOPHIA JANE

Department For Business, Innovation and Skills, Bay 5122, 1 Victoria Street, London, SW1H 0ET, ☎020 7215 3541, ✉sophie.reid@bis.gsi.gov.uk, *Call Date: July 2005, Middle Temple*
Qualifications: [LLB (Hons)]

REIHILL MR MARK

London Borough of Camden, Legal Services, Town Hall, Judd Street, London, WC1H 9LP, ☎020 7974 6857 Fax: 020 7974 2785, ✉Mark.Reihill@camden.gov.uk, *Call Date: Nov 1996, Gray's Inn*
Qualifications: [MA]

F

REILLY MR DANIEL EDWARD

Tang Bentley Jackson, 151 West Street, Fareham, Hampshire, ☎01329 220 401 Fax: 01329 828 347, ✉daniel@tbj.org.uk, *Call Date: Nov 1995, Middle Temple*
Qualifications: [LLB (Hons)]

REIN DR ANDREW PAUL

Senior Legal Adviser, HM Revenue and Customs, Solicitors Office, 100 Parliament Street, London, SW1A 2BQ, ☎020 7147 3379 Fax: 0207147 0344, *Call Date: Nov 1992, Middle Temple*
Qualifications: [BA (Hons) MA B Phil D Phil]

REISS MS PAMELA JANET

Crown Prosecution Service, Isleworth Crown Court, 36 Ridgeway Road, Isleworth, London, TW7 5LP, ✉pamela.reiss@cps.gsi.gov.uk, *Call Date: Oct 1999, Inner Temple*
Qualifications: [BA (Sheff) MSc (Leeds)]

RENDELL MR ANTOINE MARK JOHN

Deputy Justices' Clerk, South Somerset Magistrates' Court, The Law Courts, Petters Way, Yeovil, Somerset, BA20 1SW, ☎01935 426281 Fax: 01935 431022, *Call Date: Nov 1987, Gray's Inn*
Qualifications: [LLB (Reading)]

RENWICK MR JOHN

Senior Crown Prosecutor, Crown Prosecution Service, The Cooperage, 8 Gainsford Street, London, SE1 2NE, ☎020 73784110 Fax: 020 3300 4861, ✉jack.renwick@cps.gsi.gov.uk, *Call Date: Feb 1987, Middle Temple*
Qualifications: [LLB]

RESTELL MR PIERS NEVILLE CHARLES

Reeves and Co Solicitors, 27 High Street, Ashford, Kent, TN24 8TF, ☎01233 665 054 Fax: 0560 313 8186, ✉piers@reevesandcosolicitors.co.uk, solicitors@reevesandcosolicitors.co.uk, *Call Date: July 2002, Middle Temple*
Qualifications: [LLB (Hons)]

RESTELL MR THOMAS GEORGE

Solicitor, Reeves and Co Solicitors, 27 High Street, Ashford, Kent, TN24 8TF, ☎01233 665054 Fax: 0560 313 8186, ✉solicitors@reevesandcosolicitors.co.uk, tom@reevesandcosolicitors.co.uk, thomas@restell.com, *Call Date: Nov 1976, Middle Temple*

REVELEY MR THOMAS EDWIN

Department For Business, Innovation and Skills, Legal Services Group, 1 Victoria Street, London, SW1H 0ET, ☎020 7215 6069, ✉thomas.reveley@bis.gsi.gov.uk, *Call Date: July 2006, Lincoln's Inn*
Qualifications: [LLB (Lond) LLM (Cantab)]

RHONE MS SHIRLEY ANN

Lawyer, The Treasury Solicitors, One Kemble Street, London, WC2B 4TS, ✉Shirley.rhone@defra.gsi.gov.uk, *Call Date: Nov 1996, Gray's Inn*
Qualifications: [LLB (Lond)]

RICH MRS MARION CONSTANCE

Company Secretary, Director, The British Constructional, Steelwork Association Limited, 4 Whitehall Court, Westminster, London, SW1A 2ES, ☎020 7839 8566 Fax: 020 7976 1634, ✉rich@bcsa.org.uk, *Call Date: Nov 1978, Middle Temple*
Qualifications: [MSc FCIArb]

RICHARDS MR JONATHAN GLYN

Ministry of Defence, Po Box 1680, London, SW1P 1ZE, ☎020 7218 9048, *Call Date: Oct 1996, Middle Temple*
Qualifications: [BA (Hons)(Oxon) MA (Oxon)]

RICHARDS MR KEITH DAVID

HED, Visit Britain, 1 Palace Street, London, SW1E 5HE, *Call Date: July 1985, Middle Temple*
Qualifications: [BA (Kent)]

RICHARDS MR STEVEN JOSEPH

Department For Business, Innovation and Skills, Abbey 1, 6th Floor, 1 Victoria Street, London, SW1H 0ET, ☎020 7215 5140 Fax: 020 7215 3466, ✉steven.richards@bis.gsi.gov.uk, *Call Date: Nov 2001, Gray's Inn*
Qualifications: [BA BSc]

F

RICHARDSON MR BRIAN ALBAN

Call Date: July 2008, Inner Temple
Qualifications: [BA (Manch)]

RICHARDSON MR FRANK CAMERON

Crown Prosecution Service, Western Range, 83 London Road, Southampton, Hampshire, SO15 2AA, ☎023 80754203
Fax: 023 80714053, *Call Date: July 1981, Inner Temple*
Qualifications: [BSc (Hons) Dip Law]

RICHARDSON MR PHILIP MARTIN

Assistant Director, Nuneaton and Bedworth Borough Council, Town Hall, Coton Road, Nuneaton, Warwickshire, CV11 5AA, ☎024 7637 6233 Fax: 0870 608 9457, ✉philip.richardson@nuneatonandbedworth.gov.uk, *Call Date: July 1988, Lincoln's Inn*
Qualifications: [LLB (Hons) (Leics) MA]

RICHARDSON MISS SHEILA FRANCES

Mediator, The Warwick Partnership Limited, 1 Stonecross, St Albans, Hertfordshire, AL1 4AA, ☎01727 846194 Fax: 01727 810885, ✉sheila.richardson@warwick-partnership.co.uk, *Call Date: July 1979, Middle Temple*
Qualifications: [MA (Cantab)]

RICHINGS MR FRANCIS GORDON

Advocate, Crown Prosecution Service, Trials Unit, Riverside, Taunton, Somerset, TA1 4AP, Fax: 01823 425111, ✉Gordon.Richings@cps.gsi.gov.uk, *Call Date: May 1992, Middle Temple*
Qualifications: [BA M Phil (Cantab) LLB (Cape Town)]

RICHMOND MR DAVID ANDREW

Justices' Clerk, Her Majesty's Court Service, Justices' Clerk's Office, Fitzalan Place, Cardiff, CF24 0RZ, ☎029 20 474346
Fax: 029 20 456224, ✉david.richmond@hmcourts-service.gsi.gov.uk, *Call Date: Nov 1992, Inner Temple*
Qualifications: [LLB]

RICHTER MR RYAN ROBERT

Crown Prosecution Service, City Gate House, 185 Dyke Road, Hove, East Sussex, BN3 1TL, ✉ryan.richter@cps.gsi.gov.uk, *Call Date: Oct 1998, Lincoln's Inn*
Qualifications: [BA (Hons)]

RICKETTS MS CAROLINE MARIA BIANCA

Department of Health Solicitors, New Court, Room 487, 48 Carey Street, London, WC2A 2LS, Fax: 020 7412 1286, ✉caroline.ricketts@dwp.gsi.gov.uk, *Call Date: Nov 1992, Inner Temple*
Qualifications: [BA (Hons)(Essex) DipLaw (Lond)]

RICKS MR RICHARD MATTHEW

The First Law Partnership Limited, 30-32 Bromham Road, Bedford, Bedfordshire, MK40 2QD, ☎01234 263263 Fax: 01234 263239, ✉rricks@theflp.co.uk, *Call Date: Oct 1999, Lincoln's Inn*
Qualifications: [BA (Hons)(Leic) LLB (Hons)(Leic) LLM (Wales)]

RIDOUT MISS FRANCES VICTORIA

15 New Bridge Street, 15 New Bridge Street, London, EC4V 6AU, ☎020 7842 1900
Fax: 020 7842 1901, ✉Frances.ridout@15nbs.com, *Call Date: July 2007, Middle Temple*
Qualifications: [LLB (Hons) (Lond)]

RILEY MRS ALISON CLAIRE

Crown Advocate, Principal Crown Prosecutor, Crown Prosecution Service, Rose Court, 2 Southwark Bridge, London, SE1 9HS, ☎020 3357 0057, *Call Date: July 1981, Middle Temple*
Qualifications: [BA (Hons)]

RIMER MR MICHAEL JONATHAN FARQUHARSON

Senior Legal Adviser, Legal Services Commission, Legal Department, 8th Floor, 102 Petty France, London, SW1H 9AJ, *Call Date: Nov 1998, Lincoln's Inn*
Qualifications: [BA (Hons)(Leics) DipLaw]

RIMMER MISS CHARLOTTE ELIZABETH

Caseworker, Crown Prosecution Service, Sunlight House, Quay Street, Manchester, M60 3PS, *Call Date: Mar 2005, Gray's Inn*
Qualifications: [LLB (Durham)]

RING MR THOMAS JOSEPH

Justices' Clerk, Her Majesty's Court Service, Stratford Magistrates' Court, 389-397 High Street, London, E15 4SB, ☎020 8437 6003 Fax: 020 8437 6065, *Call Date: Nov 1987, Inner Temple*
Qualifications: [LLB]

RITCHIE MR DUNCAN JAMES

Crown Prosecution Service, Jefferson House, 27 Park Place, Leeds, West Yorkshire, LS1 2SZ, ☎0113 290 2700, ✉Duncan.Ritchie@cps.gsi.gov.uk, *Call Date: July 2004, Inner Temple*

RIZZO MISS SADIE MARIE

Advocate, Legal Adviser, Crown Prosecution Service, Oxford House, Oxford Road, Bournemouth, Dorset, BH8 8HA, ☎01202 498 700, *Call Date: Oct 2000, Gray's Inn*
Qualifications: [LLB]

ROBB MR JOHN EDMUND BOULTON

Prospect Law Limited, The Old Gun Room, Langley Priory, Diseworth, Derbyshire, DE74 2QQ, ✉er@prospectlaw.co.uk, *Call Date: Mar 1998, Gray's Inn*
Qualifications: [BA (Oxon)]

ROBERTS MR ADRIAN PAUL

Crown Prosecution Service, Eaton House, 112 Oxford Road, Reading, Berkshire, RG1 7LL, ✉adrian.roberts@cps.gsi.gov.uk, *Call Date: Feb 1993, Lincoln's Inn*
Qualifications: [LLB (Hons)]

ROBERTS MR ADRIAN PAUL

Department of Energy and Climate Change, 3 Whitehall Place, London, SW1A 2AW, ☎030 0068 6213, ✉adrian.roberts@decc.gsi.gov.uk, *Call Date: July 1988, Middle Temple*
Qualifications: [MA (Cantab)]

ROBERTS MISS AMANDA

Crown Prosecution Service, Bankside Chambers, 14 Bankside Crossfield Street, Warrington, Cheshire, WA1 1UP, ✉Amanda.Roberts@cps.gsi.gov.uk, *Call Date: Oct 2001, Inner Temple*
Qualifications: [LLB (L'Pool)]

ROBERTS MR DAVID GORDON

Crown Prosecution Service, Capital Tower, Greyfriars Road, Cardiff, CF10 3PL, *Call Date: Oct 2011, Gray's Inn*

ROBERTS MR HOWARD VINCENT

Senior Principal Legal Officer, Department For Work and Pensions, Dh Legal Services, 5th Floor, Adelphi, 1-11 John Adam Street, London, WC2N 6HT, ☎020 7962 8054 Fax: 020 7962 8441, *Call Date: July 1972, Middle Temple*
Qualifications: [LLB]

ROBERTS MRS JANE CAROL

Crown Prosecution Service, Queens House, 58 Victoria Street, St. Albans, Hertforshire, AL1 3HZ, ☎01727 798700, ✉Jane.Roberts@cps.gsi.gov.uk, *Call Date: Nov 1996, Inner Temple*
Qualifications: [BA (Oxon) MA (Kent) LLB]

ROBERTS MR NICHOLAS

Vinson & Elkins RLLP, City Point, 33rd Floor, One Ropemaker Street, London, EC2Y 9UE, ☎020 7065 6000 Fax: 020 7065 6001, ✉nroberts@velaw.com, *Call Date: Nov 2007, Gray's Inn*
Qualifications: [BA (Lond) MSt (Oxon)]

ROBERTSON MISS RACHEL DAWN

Crown Prosecution Service, Western Range, 83 London Road, Southampton, Hampshire, SO15 2AA, *Call Date: Oct 1998, Inner Temple*
Qualifications: [LLB (Soton)]

ROBERTS-PLOWMAN MRS LYNNE TRACEY

Crown Prosecution Service, 1 Hudson Quay, The Halyard, Middlesbrough, Cleveland, TS3 6RT, ☎01642 204500 Fax: 01642 204502, ✉Lynne.Roberts-Plowman@cps.gsi.gov.uk, *Call Date: July 1999, Inner Temple*
Qualifications: [LLB (Teeside)]

ROBINSON MR ALEXANDER

Assistant General Counsel, HSBC Bank Plc, Legal Level 22, 8 Canada Square, Canary Wharf, London, E14 5HQ, *Call Date: Oct 1998, Gray's Inn*
Qualifications: [BA (Hons) (Lond) LLM (Lond) CPE (Lond)]

ROBINSON MR DAVID EDWARD

Chief Crown Prosecutor, Floor 5 Rose Court, 2 Southwark Bridge, London, SE1 9HS, ☎020 7147 7519 Fax: 020 7147 7734, *Call Date: Oct 1993, Gray's Inn*
Qualifications: [BSc (So'ton)]

ROBINSON MISS EMMA MILLICENT

Call Date: May 1995, Inner Temple
Qualifications: [BA CPE]

ROBINSON MR JAMES DOUGLAS

Lawyer, The Treasury Solicitors, 5th Floor, One Kemble Street, London, WC2B 4TS, Fax: 020 7238 6242, ✉james.robinson@defra.gsi.gov.uk, *Call Date: Nov 1991, Inner Temple*
Qualifications: [LLB (Reading) LLM (Lond)]

ROBINSON MS LOUISE

HM Revenue and Customs, South West Wing, Bush House, Strand, London, WC2B 4RD, *Call Date: July 2003, Inner Temple*
Qualifications: [LLB (Lond) LLM (Bruges)]

ROBINSON MISS PENELOPE THERESE

Kent County Council, Legal Secretariat, Sessions House, County Hall, Maidstone, Kent, ME14 1XQ, ✉Penelope.robinson@kent.gov.uk, *Call Date: Nov 1986, Gray's Inn*
Qualifications: [BSc (Wales)]

ROBINSON MR ROBERT GEORGE

HM Revenue and Customs, Room F18, West Wing, Somerset House, The Strand, London, WC2R 1LB, Fax: 020 7084 5575, ✉robert.robinson@hmrc.gsi.gov.uk, *Call Date: July 2000, Inner Temple*
Qualifications: [LLB (Lond)]

ROBINSON MR SIMON ROBERT

Rnib, 105 Judd Street, London, WC1H 9NE, ☎020 7388 1266 Fax: 020 7388 2034, ✉simon.robinson@rnib.org.uk, *Call Date: Oct 1991, Lincoln's Inn*
Qualifications: [LLB (Hons) LLM]

ROBINSON MR STEVEN ANDREW

Other, Crown Prosecution Service, 50 Ludgate Hill, London, EC4M 7EX, ☎020 7273 8157, *Call Date: Nov 1985, Gray's Inn*
Qualifications: [BA]

ROBINSON MR VIVIAN

Recorder, McGuireWoods London LLP, 11 Pilgrim Street, London, EC4V 6RN, Fax: 020 7 632 1638, ✉vrobinson@mcguirewoods.com, *Call Date: July 1967, Inner Temple*
Qualifications: [BA (Cantab)]

ROBSON MR ANDREW JOHN

Company Secretary, General Counsel, Rm PLC, New Mill House, 183 Milton Park, Abingdon, Oxfordshire, OX14 4SE, ☎01235 854506 Fax: 01235 854823, *Call Date: July 1985, Inner Temple*
Qualifications: [LLB(Nott'm)]

ROBSON MISS CAROLYN

Call Date: July 2006, Lincoln's Inn
Qualifications: [BA (Cantab)]

ROBSON MR JOHN CHRISTIAN

Prosecution Team Leader, Crown Prosecution Service, The Cooperage, 8 Gainsford Street, London, SE1 2NE, ☎020 7962 2625 Fax: 020 7962 0906, *Call Date: Nov 1987, Inner Temple*
Qualifications: [MA (Carleton) BA (Lond) DipLaw]

ROBSON DR MATTHEW WILLIAM

General Counsel, Legal Director, Cpi Group, 98-102 Rue De Paris, Boulogne Billancourt, Paris, 92100, France, Fax: 0870 706 4471, ✉mrobson@cpi-group.co.uk, *Call Date: Oct 2001, Inner Temple*
Qualifications: [BSc (Lond) CPE PhD]

ROCHE MR BRENDAN KENNETH

Seven Bedford Row, 7 Bedford Row, London, WC1R 4BS, ☎020 7242 3555 Fax: 020 7242 2511, ✉broche@7br.co.uk, *Call Date: July 1989, Middle Temple*
Qualifications: [MA (Oxon) Dip Law]

RODGER MR ANDREW CHARLES JAMES

Stonehage Financial Services Ltd, 56 Conduit Street, London, W1S 2YS, ☎020 7087 0124 Fax: 020 7087 0001, *Call Date: July 1993, Gray's Inn*
Qualifications: [LLB]

F

RODGERS MR KONRAD

Cleary, Gottlieb, Steen & Hamilton LLP, City Place House, 55 Basinghall Street, London, EC2V 5EH, *Call Date: July 2007, Inner Temple*
Qualifications: [BA BCL (Oxon)]

ROGERS MRS DEBORAH ELIZABETH

Crown Prosecution Service, 20th Floor, Capital Tower, Greyfriars Road, Cardiff, CF10 3PL, ✉Deborah.Rogers@cps.gsi.gov.uk, *Call Date: July 1983, Lincoln's Inn*
Qualifications: [BA]

ROGERS MR KEVIN PATRICK

Crown Prosecution Service, Sunlight House, Quay Street, Manchester, M60 3PS, *Call Date: Nov 1985, Middle Temple*

ROGERS MR SIMON JOHN

Director, Department For Work and Pensions, Litigation Division, Second Floor, Caxton House, 6-12 Tothill Street, London, SW1H 9NA, ☎020 7962 8049, *Call Date: May 1994, Gray's Inn*
Qualifications: [BA]

ROHARD MR ADRIAN

Robin Murray & Co Solicitors, Haselmere, 4 Summerhouse Road, Dartford, Kent, DA1 2LP, ☎01322 228898 Fax: 01322 288739, *Call Date: Nov 1993, Inner Temple*
Qualifications: [LLB (Hons)]

ROLLINS MR PETER ALISTAIR

London Borough of Sutton, Civic Offices, St Nicholas Way, Sutton, Surrey, SW11 1EA, ☎020 8770 5105 Fax: 020 8770 5086, ✉peter.rollins@sutton.gov.uk, *Call Date: Oct 1999, Middle Temple*
Qualifications: [LLB (Hons)(Lond)]

ROMAN MR DAN

Partner, Kpmg LLP, Investment Management Tax, 15 Canada Square, London, E14 5GL, ☎020 7694 5726, ✉dan.roman@kpmg.co.uk, *Call Date: Oct 2000, Middle Temple*
Qualifications: [BA (Hons) MBA MA (Cantab)]

ROMER MISS EMMA EVELYN MARTINDALE

East Sussex County Council, Po Box 2714, County Hall, St Ann's Crescent, Lewes, East Sussex, BN7 1AL, ☎01273 336485 / 01272 481609 Fax: 01273 481900, ✉emma.romer@eastsussex.gov.uk, *Call Date: Nov 1992, Lincoln's Inn*
Qualifications: [BA (Hons) CPE]

ROONEY MR ADAM CHARLES

Associate, Gide Loyrette Nouel LLP, Gide Loyrette Nouel LLP, 125 Old Broad Street, London, EC2N 1AR, ☎020 7382 5616 Fax: 020 73825501, ✉arooney@gide.com, *Call Date: Oct 1997, Inner Temple*
Qualifications: [LLB (Lond)]

ROPER MISS SOPHIA

Hampshire County Council, The Castle, Winchester, SO23 8UB, ☎01962 841 841, *Call Date: Oct 1990, Middle Temple*
Qualifications: [MA (Cantab) BCL (Oxon)]

ROSE MR JONATHAN PETER

Artesian Law, 3 Bolt Court, Fleet Street, London, EC4A 3DQ, ✉jonathan.rose@artesianlaw.com, *Call Date: Nov 1986, Middle Temple*
Qualifications: [LLB (Lond)]

ROSE MR MARTIN JOHN

Director, Other, Smith and Williamson Holdings Limited, 25 Moorgate, London, EC2R 6AY, ✉martin.rose@smith.williamson.co.uk, *Call Date: July 1979, Middle Temple*
Qualifications: [LLB FSI]

ROSE MISS VICTORIA KATE

Crown Prosecution Service, Princes Court, 34 York Road, Leicester, Leicestershire, LE1 5TU, ☎0116 204 6700 Fax: 0116 204 6733, *Call Date: July 2009, Lincoln's Inn*
Qualifications: [BA (Hons) (Coventry) CPE UZDMU]

ROSE MISS VIVIEN JUDITH

Chair, Lawyer, Competition Appeal Tribunal, Victoria House, Bloomsbury Place, London, WC1A 2EB, *Call Date: July 1984, Gray's Inn*
Qualifications: [MA (Cantab) BCL (Oxon)]

F

ROSELL MRS TRACEY ALLISON GROSSER

Bibby Consulting & Support Ltd, Brunswick Court, Brunswick Street, Newcastle-Under-Lyme, Staffs, ST5 1HH, *Call Date: Nov 1987, Middle Temple*
Qualifications: [LLB ATT Assoc IPD]

ROSS MS ALISON

Senior Legal Adviser, Her Majesty's Courts Service, Willesden Magistrates Court, 448 High Road, Willesden, London, NW10 2DZ, ☎020 8955 0555, *Call Date: July 1982, Middle Temple*
Qualifications: [BA (Hons)]

ROSS MISS CAROLINE ANNE

Department of Energy and Climate Change, 3 Whitehall Place, London, SW1A 2AW, ✉caroline.ross@decc.gsi.gov.uk, *Call Date: Oct 1999, Middle Temple*
Qualifications: [BA (Hons)]

ROSS MR NEIL MARTIN

15 New Bridge Street, 15 New Bridge Street, London, EC4V 6AU, ☎020 7842 1900 Fax: 020 7842 1901, ✉neil.ross@15nbs.com, *Call Date: Oct 2006, Gray's Inn*
Qualifications: [BA]

ROTHWELL MISS CAROLYN ANN

Mediator, Suffolk County Council, Endeavour House, 8 Russell Road, Ipswich, Suffolk, IP1 2BX, ☎1473264236, ✉carolyn.rothwell@legal.suffolkcc.gov.uk, *Call Date: Oct 1991, Lincoln's Inn*
Qualifications: [LLB (Hons)]

ROUND MR SHAUN PETER

Crown Prosecution Service, The Cooperage, 8 Gainsford Street, London, SE1 2NE, ✉shaun.round@cps.gsi.gov.uk, *Call Date: July 2007, Middle Temple*
Qualifications: [LLB (Hons) (B'Ham)]

ROUSE MR TIMOTHY CARMICHAEL

Lecturer, Other, Regency Clinic, 10 Harley Street, London, WIG 9PF, ☎020 7490 0505 Fax: 020 7490 4490, *Call Date: Oct 2000, Gray's Inn*
Qualifications: [LLB (Hons) (Leic) PgD (Lond)]

ROUTRAY MISS SHONALI SRABANI

Public Concern At Work, 3rd Floor, Bank Chambers, 6-10 Borough High Street, London, SE1 9QQ, ✉sr@pcaw.co.uk, *Call Date: Mar 2006, Middle Temple*
Qualifications: [BA (Hons) (Oxon)]

ROWAN MR GREGG NICHOLAS

Herbert Smith LLP, Exchange House, Primrose Street, London, EC2A 2HS, ✉Gregg.Rowan@herbertsmith.com, *Call Date: Oct 2003, Lincoln's Inn*
Qualifications: [LLB (Hons) (Lond) BCL MPhil (Oxon) LLM]

ROWBERRY MISS CHRISTINA CHARLOTTE

Robin Murray and Co., The Old Ragged School, King Street, Chatham, Kent, ME4 4LY, ☎01634 832332 Fax: 01634 831331, *Call Date: Oct 2006, Inner Temple*
Qualifications: [LLB (Hons)]

ROWBOTTOM MR STEPHEN PETER

Environment and Housing Legal Team, Legal Democratic Services, North Tyneside Council Quadrant, The Silverlink North, Cobalt Business Park, North Tyneside, NE27 0BY, ☎0191 643 5372 Fax: 0191 643 2430, ✉peter.rowbottom@northtyneside.gov.uk, *Call Date: Feb 1983, Gray's Inn*
Qualifications: [LLB MBA]

ROWLAND MRS ALICE MARY

Eastbourne Borough Council, 1 Grove Road, Eastbourne, BN21 4TW, ☎01323 415011 Fax: 01323 415130, ✉Alice.Rowland@eastbourne.gov.uk, *Call Date: Oct 2000, Middle Temple*
Qualifications: [LLB (Hons) (Nott'm)]

ROWLAND MISS DERVILLE ANN

Central Bank of Ireland, Enforcement, Block D, Iveagh Court, Harcourt Road, Dublin 2, Ireland, ☎35312245100, ✉derville.rowland@centralbank.ie, *Call Date: Oct 1996, Inner Temple*
Qualifications: [LLB BL Dip Law]

ROXBOROUGH MR ADAM BENEDICT

Sulby House Chambers, 2 Ranford Road, Burnage, Manchester, M19 2GL, ☎0161 282 9616 Fax: 0161 282 9616, ✉adam.roxborough@sulbyhouse.com, *Call Date: July 1998, Gray's Inn*
Qualifications: [LLB (Manch) PGDipLaw]

F

ROY MR JOHN SCOTT

Legal Adviser, HSBC Bank Plc, Legal Level 22, 8 Canada Square, Canary Wharf, London, E14 5HQ, *Call Date: Feb 1991, Inner Temple*
Qualifications: [LLB (Lond)]

ROYCE-LEWIS MS CHRISTINE ALISON

Vice President, Visa Europe, Po Box 39662, London, W2 6WH, ✉roycelec@visa.com, *Call Date: Nov 1982, Middle Temple*
Qualifications: [BA MSc (Wales)]

ROZYCKI MR ALEXANDER

Fishburns Solicitors, 60 Fenchurch Street, London, EC3M 4AD, ☎020 7280 8888 Fax: 020 7280 8899, ✉rozycki@fishburnslaw.com, *Call Date: July 2005, Lincoln's Inn*
Qualifications: [BA (Hons) MA (Lond) LLB (Hons)]

RUDSTON MR NEVILLE JAMES

Hodge Jones and Allen LLP, 180 North Gower Street, London, NW1 2NB, ☎020 7874 8447 Fax: 020 7874 8304, *Call Date: Oct 2000, Middle Temple*
Qualifications: [LLB (Hons) (Lond)]

RUFFORD MR JOHN GEORGE

Director of Legal Services, Oppenheimer Europe Ltd, 6 Gracechurch Street, 1st Floor, London, EC3V 0AT, Fax: 020 7220 1931, ✉john.rufford@opco.com, *Call Date: Nov 1986, Middle Temple*
Qualifications: [LLB (Leeds)]

RUGARABAMU MS DONATA MARY

Senior Legal Officer, Organisation for the Prohibition of Chemical Weapons, Johan De Wittlaan 32, 2517 Jr,, The Hague, Netherlands, *Call Date: July 1992, Lincoln's Inn*
Qualifications: [MA LLM]

RUGHANI MISS MEETA

Call Date: Oct 2003, Inner Temple
Qualifications: [LLB (Reading)]

RUPASINGHE MR MANOJA LAKMAL

Lloyds PR Solicitors, 183 High Street, Harlesden, London, NW10 4TE, ☎020 8963 1253 Fax: 020 8963 1975, ✉Manoj@lloydpr.com, *Call Date: Mar 2001, Middle Temple*
Qualifications: [LLB (Hons) (London)]

RUSSELL MR BRIAN

Watson Woodhouse Solicitors, York House, Borough Road, Middlesbrough, TS1 2HJ, ☎01642 247656, ✉brussell@watsonwoodhouse.co.uk, *Call Date: July 1998, Lincoln's Inn*
Qualifications: [LLB (Hons)(Nott'm)]

RUSSELL MS ELIZABETH ANN MILLICENT

Senior Lawyer, Crown Prosecution Service, Rose Court, 2 Southwark Bridge, London, SE1 9HS, ☎020 33570317, ✉Elizabeth.Russell@CPS.gsi.gov.uk, *Call Date: Nov 1983, Middle Temple*
Qualifications: [BA (Hons)]

RUSSELL MR GEOFFREY DAVID

Legal Adviser, Nottinghamshire County Council, Centenary House, 1 Wilford Lane, West Bridgford, Nottingham, NG2 7QZ, ☎0115 977 3111 Fax: 0115 977 3815, ✉geoff.russell@nottscc.gov.uk, *Call Date: July 1997, Inner Temple*
Qualifications: [LLB (Nott'm)]

RUSSELL MISS JENNIFER ANNE

Crown Prosecution Service, Colmore Gate, 2 - 6 Colmore Row, Birmingham, West Midlands, B3 2QA, ☎0121 262 1671 Fax: 0121 262 1680, ✉Jenny.russell@cps.gsi.gov.uk, *Call Date: Oct 1990, Middle Temple*
Qualifications: [LLB (Hons)]

RUSSELL MRS SALLY-ANNE

Crown Prosecution Service, Southern House, Wellesley Grove, Croydon, Surrey, CR9 1DY, ✉sally-anne.russell@cps.gsi.gov.uk, *Call Date: Nov 2000, Middle Temple*
Qualifications: [BA (Hons) (Oxon)]

RUSSELL-HARGREAVES MR BARRY

Crown Prosecution Service, County House, 100 New London Road, Chelmsford, Essex, CM2 0RG, ☎01245 455800, *Call Date: Nov 1988, Middle Temple*
Qualifications: [LLB]

RYAN MISS CATHERINE MARY

Guney Clark and Ryan Solicitors, 58 Green Lanes, London, N16 9NH, ☎020 7275 7788 Fax: 020 7923 5544, *Call Date: Oct 1997, Middle Temple*
Qualifications: [LLB (Hons)(Lond)]

RYAN MISS HILARY MARGARET

Crown Prosecution Service, Southern House, Wellesley Grove, Croydon, Surrey, CR9 1DY, ☎02086 622 821 Fax: 02086 622828, ✉hilary.ryan@cps.gsi.gov.uk, *Call Date: Feb 1990, Inner Temple*
Qualifications: [LLB (Hons)]

RYAN MR MARTIN PHILIP

District Crown Prosecutor, Crown Prosecution Service, The Cooperage, 8 Gainsford Street, London, SE1 2NE, ✉martin.ryan@cps.gsi.gov.uk, *Call Date: Feb 1978, Lincoln's Inn*
Qualifications: [BA Hons]

RYAN MS MISHA JOSIE

Manchester City Council, P O Box 532, Manchester, M60 2LA, *Call Date: Nov 2003, Inner Temple*
Qualifications: [LLB (So'ton)]

RYB MISS SAMANTHA DANIELLE

The Home Office, Seacole, Ground Floor, 2 Marsham Street, London, SW1P 4DF, *Call Date: Oct 1993, Middle Temple*
Qualifications: [LLB (Hons)(Lond)]

RYDER MR DEREK

Crown Prosecution Service, 2 Kimbrose Way, Gloucester, Gloucestershire, GL1 2DB, *Call Date: May 1988, Gray's Inn*

RYLANDS MR KEITH WILLIAM

Principal Crown Prosecutor, Crown Prosecution Service, County House, 100 New London Road, Chelmsford, Essex, CM2 0RG, ☎01245 455800 Fax: 01245 490476, ✉keithrylands@hotmail.co.uk, *Call Date: July 1979, Middle Temple*
Qualifications: [LLB (Lond)]

SABATO MS MIMMA

J D Spicer and Co Solicitors, 140 Kilburn High Road, London, NW6 4JD, ☎020 7624 7771 Fax: 020 7328 9466, ✉solicitors@jdspicer.co.uk, *Call Date: Oct 2003, Inner Temple*
Qualifications: [BSc (Hons), MA (Herts) Dip Law]

SACHDEVA MR AKASH

Edwards Wildman Palmer Uk LLP, Dashwood, 69 Old Broad Street, London, EC2M 1QS, *Call Date: Mar 1997, Lincoln's Inn*
Qualifications: [LLB (Hons)]

SADD MR ROBERT CLIVE

Advocate, Crown Prosecution Service, 9th Floor, St Vincent House, 1 Cutler Street, Ipswich, Suffolk, IP1 1UL, ☎01473 282100 Fax: 01473 282103, ✉robert.sadd@cps.gsi.gov.uk, *Call Date: Oct 1990, Inner Temple*
Qualifications: [LLB (Reading)]

SADOTTI MR ROBERT JOSEPH

Mizuho International PLC, Bracken House, One Friday Street, London, EC4M 9JA, ☎020 7489 6860, ✉robert.sadotti@uk.mizuho-sc.com, *Call Date: Nov 1996, Middle Temple*
Qualifications: [BA (Hons)(Leeds)]

SAGE MISS MELANIE JANE

Crown Advocate, Crown Prosecution Service, Queens House, 58 Victoria Street, St. Albans, Hertforshire, AL1 3HZ, ☎01727 798 700, *Call Date: July 1984, Lincoln's Inn*
Qualifications: [LLB (Hons) (B'ham)]

SAHA MISS RUMA

The London Borough of Wandsworth, Wandsworth Town, Wandsworth High Street, Wandsworth, London, SW18 2PU, *Call Date: Nov 2001, Lincoln's Inn*
Qualifications: [LLB (Hons)]

SALEY MR MUHAMMAD DANYAL

Treasury Solicitor's Department, One Kemble Street, London, WC2B 4TS, *Call Date: July 2008, Lincoln's Inn*
Qualifications: [BA LLM CPE]

SAMAT MR DAREN ARMAND CAMERON

Hine & Associates, Hine and Associates Solicitors, 51 Amersham Road, Beaconsfield, Buckinghamshire, HP9 2HB, ☎01494 671 996 Fax: 01494 685 584, *Call Date: Oct 1992, Middle Temple*
Qualifications: [LLB (Hons)]

SANDEMAN MR DAVID MCEWEN

Foreign and Commonwealth Office, Room 200a, King Charles Street, London, SW1A 2AH, ✉David.Sandeman@fco.gov.uk, *Call Date: Nov 1993, Middle Temple*
Qualifications: [LLB (Hons)(Kingston)]

SANDILANDS MR RICHARD JAMES

Company Secretary, Lehman Brothers International (Europe, 25 Canada Square, London, *Call Date: July 1995, Lincoln's Inn*
Qualifications: [BA (Hons)]

SANDS MISS SARAH REBECCA

Legal Adviser, HMCTS, The Court House, 60 Pinfoldgate, Loughborough, Leicestershire, LE11 1AZ, *Call Date: Nov 1998, Middle Temple*
Qualifications: [BA (Hons) LLM (UEA)]

SANGAM MR PAUL STEPHEN JASON

Legal Manager, BBC Worldwide, 33 Foley Street, London, W1W 7TL, ✉paul.sangam@2entertain.co.uk, paul.sangam@bbc.com, *Call Date: Oct 1996, Inner Temple*
Qualifications: [LLB (Westminster)]

SANK MR JONATHAN ELLIOT

Crown Prosecution Service, Eaton Court, 112 Oxford Road, Reading, Berkshire, RG1 7LL, *Call Date: Oct 2002, Inner Temple*
Qualifications: [LLB (Essex) LLM]

SANTOMAURO MISS SARA

Financial Services Authority, The Financial Services Authority, Enforcement and Financial Crime Division - Legal Group, 25 The North Colonade, Canary Wharf, London, E14 5HS, ☎020 7066 8344, ✉Sara.Santomauro@fsa.gov.uk, *Call Date: July 2003, Middle Temple*
Qualifications: [LLB Hons (Lond)]

SARKARIA MRS NEELAM

Chair, Crown Prosecution Service, Rose Court, 2 Southwark Bridge, London, SE1 9HS, ☎020 3357 0812, ✉neelam.sarkaria@cps.gsi.gov.uk, *Call Date: Nov 1988, Gray's Inn*
Qualifications: [BA Hons MBA]

SARTOR MR ROBERT ALEXANDER

Olswang LLP, 90 High Holborn, London, WC1V 6XX, Fax: 020 7067 3999, ✉robert.sartor@olswang.com, *Call Date: Nov 2005, Inner Temple*
Qualifications: [BA University of Durham CPE Kingston University]

SAUL MR ANTHONY JOSEPH

Company Secretary, General Counsel, Statoil (Uk) Limited, One Kingdom Street, London, W2 6BD, ☎020 3204 3311
Fax: 020 3204 3362, ✉tsaul@statoil.com, *Call Date: Feb 1989, Middle Temple*
Qualifications: [LLB]

SAUL MR GUY PATRICK SELWYN

Crown Prosecution Service, Wembley Police Station, 603 Harrow Road, Wembley, Middlesex, HA0 2HH, *Call Date: Nov 1980, Lincoln's Inn*
Qualifications: [BA]

SAUNDERS MRS ALISON MARGARET

Chief Crown Prosecutor, Crown Prosecution Service, Rose Court, 2 Southwark Bridge, London, SE1 9HS, ✉alison.saunders@cps.gsi.gov.uk, *Call Date: Nov 1983, Inner Temple*
Qualifications: [LLB (Leeds)]

SAUNDERS MRS COLLEEN MARIA

Ds Legal, Eagle Tower, Cheltenham, Gloucestershire, GL50 1TA, ☎01242 517949
Fax: 01242 576496, *Call Date: Nov 1988, Inner Temple*
Qualifications: [LLB (Wales) (Hons)]

SAUNDERS MISS ELLEN AUDREY LAUREN

Porter Dodson Solicitors, Central House, Church Street, Yeovil, Somerset, BA20 1HH, ☎01935 424581 Fax: 01935 706063, *Call Date: Oct 2000, Inner Temple*
Qualifications: [BA (Hons)(Oxon) CPE (Oxford Brookes)]

SAUNDERS MR PHILIP GEORGE

Commercial Lawyer, PCNL, City Remembrancer's Office, City of London Corporation, Guildhall, London, EC2P 2EJ, ☎020 7606 3030, ✉philip.saunders@cityoflondon.gov.uk, *Call Date: Oct 1997, Lincoln's Inn*
Qualifications: [LLB (Hons)]

F

SAUTELLE-SMITH MRS HOLLY ANNE

Manches LLP, Aldwych House, 81 Aldwych, London, WC2B 4RP, ☎020 7404 4433 Fax: 020 7430 1133, ✉Holly.Lewis@manches.com, *Call Date: Nov 2008, Middle Temple*
Qualifications: [LLB (Hons) (Exon)]

SAVAGE MISS AYISHA CAROL

Crown Prosecution Service, United House, Piccadilly, York, North Yorkshire, YO1 9PQ, *Call Date: July 1995, Inner Temple*
Qualifications: [BA (Leics)]

SAVARIS MR MATHIEU NICOLAS

Ge Energy Services, C/ Rossellé I Porcel, 21, Edificio Meridian, 10 Planta, Barcelona, 8016, Spain, ☎00 34 93 312 78 21 Fax: 00 34 93 312 78 99, ✉mathieu.savaris@ge.com, *Call Date: July 2004, Middle Temple*
Qualifications: [MA Paris II (Pantheon-Assas) LLB (Hons) BCL]

SAW MISS LILY

Crown Prosecution Service, Hammersmith Police Station, 226 Shepherds Bush Road, Hammersmith, London, W6 7NX, *Call Date: Feb 1987, Middle Temple*
Qualifications: [LLB (Newc) LLM]

SAWHNEY MISS DEBBIE JANE

Official Solicitor, 81 Chancery Lane, London, WC2A 1DD, *Call Date: Nov 1987, Middle Temple*
Qualifications: [BA (Hons) (Keele)]

SAWYER MR DANIEL JAMES

Crown Prosecution Service, Central Police Station, Winston Churchill Avenue, Portsmouth, Hampshire, PO1 2DG, *Call Date: July 2001, Middle Temple*
Qualifications: [MA (Cantab)]

SCAMMELL MR IAN MICHAEL

Idt Global Ltd, Idt House, 44 Featherstone Street, London, EC1Y 8RN, ☎020 7549 6037 Fax: 020 7549 6183, ✉mscammell@idteurope.com, *Call Date: Nov 2000, Middle Temple*
Qualifications: [BA (Hons) (Manch) CPE MPhil (Manch)]

SCARBROUGH MISS CASSANDRA JANE

Nursing and Midwifery Council, 61 Aldwych, London, WC2B 4AE, ☎020 7462 5800 Fax: 020 7242 9579, *Call Date: Nov 2006, Inner Temple*
Qualifications: [BA (Oxon) LLB (Hons)]

SCATTERGOOD MR BRYAN EDWARD

Office of Fair Trading, Fleetbank House, 2-6 Salisbury Square, London, EC4Y 8JX, ☎020 7211 8697 Fax: 020 7211 8694, ✉bryan.scattergood@oft.gsi.gov.uk, *Call Date: Nov 2003, Middle Temple*
Qualifications: [BA (Hons) (Nott'm) MA (Nott'm) CPE (Sussex) LLM (Sussex)]

SCHAEFFER MISS JOANNE ABIGAIL LAIKA

DPK Management Limited, 78 Buckingham Gate, London, SW1E 6PE, *Call Date: Oct 2005, Middle Temple*
Qualifications: [BA PgDL]

SCHENCK MRS SUSAN JEAN

Senior Crown Prosecutor, Crown Prosecution Service, United House, Piccadilly, York, North Yorkshire, YO1 9PQ, *Call Date: July 1981, Gray's Inn*
Qualifications: [BA (Hons)]

SCHOLEFIELD MISS JANE ELIZABETH

Senior Crown Prosecutor, Crown Prosecution Service, The Cooperage, 8 Gainsford Street, London, SE1 2NE, ✉jane.scholefield@cps.gsi.gov.uk, *Call Date: Oct 1991, Middle Temple*
Qualifications: [BSc Dip Law]

SCHULZE MS ELLEN FRANZISKA

Pearson Education Ltd, Edinburgh Gate, Harlow, Essex, CM20 2JE, ☎01279 623 091 Fax: 01279 623 409, ✉franziska.schulze@pearson.com, *Call Date: July 2001, Inner Temple*
Qualifications: [LLB (Lond) LLM]

SCHUMACHER MR TOBIAS

Veolia Water Solutions and Technologies, Marlow International, Parkway, Marlow, Buckinghamshire, SL7 1YL, ☎01628 897243, ✉toby.schumacher@veoliawater.com, *Call Date: Nov 1997, Middle Temple*
Qualifications: [LLB (Hons)]

SCOTHERN MR PAUL JEFFERY

Crown Prosecution Service, County House, 100 New London Road, Chelmsford, Essex, CM2 0RG, ☎01245 455015, ✉Paul.scothern@cps.gsi.gov.uk, *Call Date: Mar 1999, Gray's Inn*
Qualifications: [LLB]

SCOTT MISS CAROLYN

Crown Prosecution Service, Rose Court, 2 Southwark Bridge, London, SE1 9HS, ☎020 3357 0921, ✉carolyn.scott@cps.gsi.gov.uk, *Call Date: Mar 2006, Middle Temple*
Qualifications: [LLB (Hons) (Leeds)]

SCOTT MS CHARLOTTE ELIZABETH

Crown Prosecution Service, London Area Traffic Prosecution Service, 6th Floor, Marlowe House, Sidcup, Kent, DA15 7ES, *Call Date: Nov 2005, Gray's Inn*
Qualifications: [LLB]

SCOTT MISS LAURIE

Crown Prosecution Service, St Ann's Quay, 122 Quayside, Newcastle Upon Tyne, Tyne and Wear, NE1 3BD, ☎0191 2604200, ✉laurie.hind@cps.gsi.gov.uk, *Call Date: Oct 2003, Middle Temple*
Qualifications: [LLB (Hons)]

SCOTT MISS RACHAEL ELIZABETH

Prosecution Team Leader, Crown Prosecution Service, 2 Kimbrose Way, Gloucester, Gloucestershire, GL1 2DB, ☎01452 872419 Fax: 01452 872430, ✉rachael.scott@cps.gsi.gov.uk, *Call Date: July 1989, Inner Temple*
Qualifications: [LLB(Hons)]

SCOTT MR RICHARD MICHAEL

Crown Prosecution Service, Country House, 100 New London Road, Chelmsford, Essex, CM2 0RG, ☎01245 455800 Fax: 01245 455964, *Call Date: Oct 1997, Middle Temple*
Qualifications: [LLB (Hons)(Lond) LLM (Lond)]

SCOTT MRS TRUDE KOBY

Solicitor, Crown Prosecution Service, Southern House, Wellesley Grove, Croydon, Surrey, CR9 1DY, ☎020 8662 2832 Fax: 020 8662 4411, ✉trude.scott@cps.gsi.gov.uk, *Call Date: July 2008, Gray's Inn*

SCOTT-LYNCH MISS ANDREA GEORGINA

Crown Prosecution Service, Queens House, 58 Victoria Street, St. Albans, Hertforshire, AL1 3HZ, ✉Andrea.Scottlynch@cps.gsi.gov.uk, *Call Date: Oct 1996, Inner Temple*
Qualifications: [LLB]

SCRIVEN MISS ELIZABETH MARY

Crown Prosecution Service, 4/7 Prebendal Court, Oxford Road, Aylesbury, Buckinghamshire, HP19 8EY, ☎01296 414800 Fax: 01296 414 801, ✉elizabeth.scrivens@cps.gsi.gov.uk, *Call Date: July 2003, Gray's Inn*
Qualifications: [LLB (Cardiff)]

SEABROOK MRS SADIE EMMA

Barlow Lyde and Gilbert LLP, Barlow Lyde and Gilbert LLP, Chancery Place, 50 Brown Street, Manchester, M2 2JT, ☎0844 875 8000 Fax: 0844 875 8001, ✉sseabrook@blg.co.uk, *Call Date: Nov 1999, Lincoln's Inn*
Qualifications: [LLB (Hons)]

SEAL MISS HARRIET JANE

The Treasury Solicitors, One Kemble Street, London, WC2B 4TS, ☎020 7210 3000, *Call Date: Oct 2001, Inner Temple*
Qualifications: [LLB (Durham)]

SEALY MR RICHARD CAMPBELL

Crown Prosecution Service, Bankside Chambers, 1-4 Bankside Crossfield Street, Warrington, Cheshire, WA1 1UP, ☎01925 425300 Fax: 01925 425348, *Call Date: July 1981, Lincoln's Inn*
Qualifications: [BA (Hons)]

SEARLE MS FRANCES ANNE

Legal Manager, South Western Magistrates' Court, 176a Lavender Hill, London, SW11 1JU, ✉frances.searle@hmcourts-service.gsi.gov.uk, *Call Date: Nov 1979, Gray's Inn*
Qualifications: [BA (Hons) (Lond)]

SEARLEY MISS ELEANOR NAOMI BEATRICE

Financial Services Authority, 25 The North Colonade, Canary Wharf, London, E14 5HS, ✉eleanor.searley@fsa.gov.uk, *Call Date: July 2006, Middle Temple*
Qualifications: [BA (Hons) (York) PGDL]

F

SEBASTOS MR GEORGE

Legal Counsel, Credit Suisse First Boston (Europe) Limited, One Cabot Square, London, E14 4QJ, ☎ 020 8888 8888, *Call Date: Oct 1994, Lincoln's Inn*
Qualifications: [LLB (Hons)(Lond)]

SECULER-FABER MR ANTHONY ROY

Commissioner, Legal Adviser, Secretary, Wales Probation Trust, West Glamorgan House, Orchard Street, Swansea, SA1 5AB, ☎ 01656 674 747 Fax: 01656 674 792, *Call Date: Nov 1985, Middle Temple*
Qualifications: [BSc (Wales)]

SEFTON MISS CLAIRE LOUISE

Highbury Corner Magistrates' Court, North London Administration Centre, Po Box 52693, London, N7 0AF, ✉ Claire.manning1@hmcts.gsi.gov.uk, *Call Date: Oct 1997, Inner Temple*
Qualifications: [BA (London) CPE]

SEGAL MISS ELENA

Apple, One Hanover Street, London, W1S 1YZ, ☎ 020 7184 1451 Fax: 020 7184 1315, ✉ segal.e@euro.apple.com, *Call Date: Oct 1998, Gray's Inn*
Qualifications: [BA (Oxon)]

SEGAL MR GILAD YA'ACOV

Ministry of Justice, Legal Directorate 6.38, 102 Petty France, London, SW1H 9AJ, ☎ 020 3334 4786 Fax: 020 3334 4035, *Call Date: Oct 1999, Gray's Inn*
Qualifications: [LLB (L'pool)]

SELBY MISS JANET LOUISE

Senior Crown Prosecutor, The Home Office, 5th Floor, Fry Building, 2 Marsham Street, London, SW1P 4DF, ✉ Louise.Selby2@homeoffice.gov.uk, *Call Date: July 1998, Lincoln's Inn*
Qualifications: [LLB (Hons)]

SELBY MISS KATHRYN ANN

Crown Prosecution Service, Southern House, Wellesley Grove, Croydon, Surrey, CR9 1DY, ☎ 020 8662 2840 Fax: 020 8662 4411, ✉ kathryn.selby@cps.gsi.gov.uk, *Call Date: July 2010, Inner Temple*
Qualifications: [BA (Lincoln) CPE]

SELIGMAN MR MATTHEW THOMAS ARTHUR

Steel and Shamash Solicitors, 12 Baylis Road, Waterloo, London, SE1 7AA, ☎ 020 7803 3999 Fax: 020 7803 3900, ✉ matthew.seligman@steelandshamash.co.uk, *Call Date: Oct 1994, Middle Temple*
Qualifications: [MA (Hons)(Oxon) CPE (Lond)]

SELMAN-AYETEY MS JULIA ELYSA

The Treasury Solicitors, One Kemble Street, London, WC2B 4TS, Fax: 020 7210 3503, ✉ julia.selman-ayetey@attorneygeneral.gsi.gov.uk, *Call Date: July 2007, Middle Temple*
Qualifications: [BA MPhil (Cantab)]

SELVANAYAGAM MISS RUBY

Crown Prosecution Service, Gateway, 31 Power Close, Surrey, Guildford, GU1 1EJ, *Call Date: Mar 1999, Lincoln's Inn*
Qualifications: [BA (Hons)(Exon)]

SENIOR MR RICHARD HARVEY

Fishburns Solicitors, 60 Fenchurch Street, London, EC3M 4AD, *Call Date: Nov 2001, Inner Temple*
Qualifications: [LLB (Bris)]

SENTANCE MR JOSEPH RICHARD PATTISON

Senior Crown Prosecutor, Crown Prosecution Service, Bishopsgate Police Station, 182 Bishopsgate, London, EC2M 4NP, ✉ joe.sentance@cps.gsi.gov.uk, *Call Date: Nov 1986, Inner Temple*
Qualifications: [BA(Cantab) MA (Cantab)]

SERGIDES MS EVRIDIKI

Crown Prosecution Service, Rose Court, 2 Southwark Bridge, London, SE1 9HS, ☎ 020 3357 0671 Fax: 020 3 357 0568, ✉ vicky.sergides@cps.gsi.gov.uk, *Call Date: July 1999, Inner Temple*
Qualifications: [LLB (Lond) LLM (Lond)]

SERLIN MR RICHARD ANTHONY

Department For Transport, Legal Services Directorate, Zone 51/05, Great Minster House, London, SW1P 4DR, ☎ 020 7944 8663, *Call Date: Nov 1987, Lincoln's Inn*
Qualifications: [BA (Oxon) Dip Law (City)]

SEYMOUR MR DAVID

Bencher, Legal Adviser, The Home Office, Seacole House, 2 Marsham Street, London, SW1P 4DF, ☎020 70351393 / 020 70351393 Fax: 0870 336 9006 / 0870 336 9006, ✉david.seymour@homeoffice.gsi.gov.uk, *Call Date: July 1975, Gray's Inn*
Qualifications: [MA (Oxon) LLB (Cantab)]

SHAH MRS BIJAL

Legal Counsel, Brown Brothers Harriman (London), Park House, 16-18 Finsbury Circus, London, EC2M 7EB, Fax: 020 7614 8773, *Call Date: July 1996, Middle Temple*
Qualifications: [LLB (Hons)(Lond) LLM (Keele)]

SHAH MR JILAN CHANDULAL

Conference Chambers, P.O. Box 626, Harrow, Middlesex, HA2 2DZ, ☎020 8144 0134 Fax: 0800 242 5323, *Call Date: Nov 2001, Middle Temple*
Qualifications: [BA (Hons)(Cardiff) PGDL (Leics)]

SHAH MISS RUKHSANA ANJUM

Senior Lawyer, The Treasury Solicitors, One Kemble Street, London, WC2B 4TS, *Call Date: July 1976, Middle Temple*

SHAH MISS SHEENA

Ace European Group Limited, The Ace Building, 100 Leadenhall Street, London, EC3A 3BP, *Call Date: Nov 1993, Inner Temple*
Qualifications: [LLB (Hons)(Lond) MBA]

SHAH MISS SHEILJA HARSUKHLAL

Legal Adviser, The Electoral Commission, 3 Bunhill Road, London, EC1Y 8YZ, Fax: 020 7271 0505, ✉sshah@electoralcommission.org.uk, *Call Date: Oct 1994, Middle Temple*
Qualifications: [LLB (Hons) LLM (Lond)]

SHAH MRS SHILPA

Crown Prosecution Service, Queens House, 58 Victoria Street, St. Albans, Hertforshire, AL1 3HZ, *Call Date: Oct 1996, Inner Temple*
Qualifications: [LLB]

SHAHID MISS AKSHA

Crown Prosecution Service, The Unicentre, Lords Walk, Preston, Lancashire, PR1 1DH, ☎01772 208 100, ✉aksha.shahid@cps.gsi.gov.uk, *Call Date: Nov 1999, Middle Temple*
Qualifications: [LLB (Hons)(Sheff)]

SHAMEL MISS LINDA JUSUF ZAIN

Principal Crown Prosecutor, Crown Prosecution Service, Crown Prosecution Service, Westminster Borough Unit, Charing Cross Police Station, Agar Street, London, WC2N 4JP, Fax: 020 3300 2360, *Call Date: Nov 1984, Middle Temple*
Qualifications: [LLB (Hons) MA]

SHANAHAN MR MATTHEW JOHN PAUL

The Dubai Financial Services Authority, Level 13, Po Box 75850, The Gate, Dubai, United Arab Emirates, ☎00 971 04 362 1511 Fax: 00 971 04 362 0801, ✉mshanahan@dfsa.ae, *Call Date: Nov 2006, Inner Temple*
Qualifications: [BSc (Lond) MSc (Lond)]

SHANNON MISS FIONA NIAMH

London Borough of Hackney, Hackney Town Hall, Mare Street, London, E8 1EA, *Call Date: Oct 2000, Inner Temple*
Qualifications: [BA (Cantab) CPE (City)]

SHARMA MR KISHORE

Waltons and Morse LLP, 77 Gracechurch Street, London, EC3V 0DL, ☎020 7623 4255 Fax: 020 7626 4153, ✉kxs@wamlaw.co.uk, *Call Date: Nov 1986, Gray's Inn*
Qualifications: [LLB (London)]

SHARP MR HOWARD

Law Officer's Department, Morier House, Halkatt Place, St Helier, JE2 1QD, Jersey, ☎01534 441247, *Call Date: Oct 2001, Inner Temple*
Qualifications: [BA (Warwick) CPE]

SHARP MR JONATHAN JEREMY GRANVILLE

Crown Prosecution Service, Jefferson House, 27 Park Place, Leeds, West Yorkshire, LS1 2SZ, ☎0113 290 2781 Fax: 0113 290 2701, ✉jonathan.sharp@cps.gsi.gov.uk, *Call Date: July 1987, Inner Temple*
Qualifications: [BA (Oxon) Dip Law]

SHARPLES MR JOHN MICHAEL

Hempsons Solicitors, Portland Tower, Portland Place, Manchester, M1 3LF, Fax: 0161 236 6734, *Call Date: Nov 1992, Inner Temple*
Qualifications: [LLB (Hons)]

SHARPLING MS DRUSILLA HOPE

Chief Crown Prosecutor, Hm Inspectorate of Constabulary, Bartleet House, 165a Birmingham Road, Bromsgrove, Worcestershire, B61 0DJ, Fax: 11527 882005, ✉drusilla.sharpling@hmic.gsi.gov.uk, *Call Date: July 1987, Gray's Inn*
Qualifications: [LLB (B'ham)]

SHAW MR CHARLES NOEL

Crown Prosecution Service, United House, Piccadilly, York, North Yorkshire, YO1 9PQ, *Call Date: Feb 1991, Inner Temple*
Qualifications: [MA (Cantab) MSc (Lond)]

SHAW MR DANIEL PETER

Associate, White & Case LLP, 5 Old Broad Street, London, EC2N 1DW, ☎020 7532 1000 Fax: 020 7532 1001, ✉dshaw@whitecase.com, *Call Date: Oct 2007, Gray's Inn*
Qualifications: [LLB (Keele)]

SHAW MR IAN DOUGLAS

Senior Crown Prosecutor, Crown Prosecution Service, St Peters House, Gower Street, Derby, Derbyshire, DE1 1SB, ☎01332 614031 Fax: 01332 614050, ✉ian.shaw@cps.gsi.gov.uk, *Call Date: Nov 1991, Middle Temple*
Qualifications: [BSc (Hons)]

SHAW MR JOHN MARTIN

General Counsel, Citigroup, Citigroup Legal Department 19-51, Citigroup Centre, 33 Canada Square, Canary Wharf, London, E14 5LB, ✉john.m.shaw@citi.com, *Call Date: Nov 1992, Lincoln's Inn*
Qualifications: [LLB (Hons)]

SHAW MR JONATHON

Henry & Co Solicitors, 72-74 Wellington Road South, Stockport, SK1 3SU, *Call Date: Oct 2008, Middle Temple*
Qualifications: [BA (Hons)]

SHAW MS LESLEY MARGARET

Agilent Technologies (UK) Limited, 5 Lochside Avenue, Lochside Park, Edinburgh, EH12 9DJ, ☎0131 452 0200 Fax: 0131 452 0491, *Call Date: Oct 1998, Gray's Inn*
Qualifications: [BA Dip Law]

SHAW MS MADELEINE

The Home Office, Legal Advisors Branch, Seacole, Ground Floor, 2 Marsham Street, London, SW1P 4DF, *Call Date: Nov 1999, Inner Temple*
Qualifications: [LLB (Hons)(Sussex) LLM]

SHAW MR PETER FRANCIS

Crown Prosecution Service, Queens House, 58 Victoria Street, St. Albans, Hertforshire, AL1 3HZ, *Call Date: Nov 1992, Inner Temple*
Qualifications: [LLB (Brunel)]

SHAW MR PHILIP JOHN

HM Revenue and Customs, 100 Parliament Street, London, SW1A 2BQ, ☎020 7147 2823 Fax: 020 7147 0433, ✉philip.shaw@hmrc.gsi.gov.uk, *Call Date: July 2008, Middle Temple*
Qualifications: [LLB (Hons) (Notts)]

SHAW MRS SANDRA NAN DEMBY

Director, Valiant Petroleum PLC, Albion House, Chertsey Road, Woking, Surrey, GU21 6BD, ✉sshaw@valiant-petroleum.com, *Call Date: Nov 1987, Gray's Inn*
Qualifications: [BA (USA) Juris Doctorate (USA)]

SHAW MRS SHIRLEY ANN

Solicitor, Havant Borough Council, Civic Offices, Civic Centre Road, Havant, Hampshire, PO9 2AX, ✉shirley.shaw@havant.gov.uk, *Call Date: Oct 2000, Inner Temple*
Qualifications: [LLB (Southampton)]

SHAWKAT MISS TASNIM

Head of Legal Services, Thurrock Borough Council, Civic Offices, New Road, Grays, Essex, RM17 6SL, ☎01375 652442 Fax: 01375 652782, ✉tshawkat@thurrock.gov.uk, *Call Date: Oct 1991, Inner Temple*
Qualifications: [LLB (Brunel) MA (Lond)]

SHEARS MRS ALEXANDRA FLORENCE

Royal Navy Officers, Directorate of Naval Legal Services, Mp 4-2, Leach Building, Whale Island, Portsmouth, PO2 8BY, ☎02392 628718 Fax: 02392 628658, ✉alex.shears773@mod.uk, *Call Date: July 2009, Middle Temple*
Qualifications: [BA (Hons) (Lond) Grad Dip Law]

SHEFFI MISS BOSMATH

Noble Solicitors, 26-28 Stuart Street, Luton, Bedfordshire, LU1 2SW, *Call Date: Nov 1991, Middle Temple*
Qualifications: [BA (Hons) (Kent)]

SHEFIK MISS SHERIN

The Home Office, Seacole House, 2 Marsham Street, London, SW1P 4DF, ☎020 7035 1622 Fax: 020 7035 6433, ✉sherin.shefik@homeoffice.gsi.gov.uk, *Call Date: Oct 2009, Middle Temple*
Qualifications: [LLB (Hons) (Warw)]

SHEIKH MR KHALID FADHAL-RAHMAN

Crown Prosecution Service, Haringey Borough Unit, 1 Lymington Avenue, Wood Green, London, N22 6JB, ☎020 3300 2811, ✉khalid.sheikh@cps.gsi.gov.uk, *Call Date: Feb 1993, Middle Temple*
Qualifications: [LLB (Hons)(Lond) LLM (Lond)]

SHELTON MR CHARLES JOHN MASEFIELD PATRICK

Advocate, Lansbury Worthington Solicitors, 5 King Street Cloisters, Clifton Walk, King Street, London, W6 0GY, ☎020 8563 9797 Fax: 020 8563 9798, ✉cs@lansbury-worthington.co.uk, *Call Date: Nov 2000, Middle Temple*
Qualifications: [MA (Hons) CPE]

SHENKMAN MR JONATHAN PAUL

Paul Hastings (Europe) LLP, Ten Bishops Square, London, E1 6EG, ☎020 3023 5131 Fax: 020 3023 5431, ✉jonathanshenkman@paulhastings.com, *Call Date: Oct 2001, Inner Temple*
Qualifications: [LLB (Lond)]

SHEPHERD MR JONATHAN ROBERT

Crown Prosecution Service, Eagle House, Ram Passage, Kingston Upon Thames, Surrey, KT1 1HH, *Call Date: Oct 1999, Middle Temple*
Qualifications: [LLB (Hons)(Leeds) MA]

SHEPPARD MR SAMUEL EDWARD HUGH

Special Casework Lawyer, Crown Prosecution Service, The Cooperage, 8 Gainsford Street, London, SE1 2NE, ☎020 7378 4100 Fax: 2033004861, ✉hugh.sheppard@cps.gsi.gov.uk, *Call Date: July 1976, Gray's Inn*

SHERGILL MRS RAMINDER KAUR

Malletts Solicitors, 3 Field Court, Grays Inn, London, WC1R 5EF, Fax: 020 74309 760, ✉ramindershergill@malletts.com, *Call Date: July 1998, Middle Temple*
Qualifications: [LLB (Hons)(Wolves)]

SHERGILL MISS USHA SITA

Advocate, Crown Prosecution Service, Charing Cross Police Station, Agar Street, London, WC2N 4JP, Fax: 020 74034724, ✉usha.shergill@cps.gsi.gov.uk, *Call Date: July 1984, Gray's Inn*
Qualifications: [BA (Hons)(Law)]

SHERRIFF MISS CHARLIEANN

David Phillips And Partners, 150 High Road, Chadwell Heath, Romford, Essex, RM6 6NT, *Call Date: Oct 2010, Inner Temple*
Qualifications: [LLB]

SHINER MR DAVID COLIN

Legal Adviser, Suffolk County Council, Endeavour House, 8 Russell Road, Ipswich, Suffolk, IP1 2BX, ✉david.shiner@suffolk.gov.uk, *Call Date: Nov 1990, Middle Temple*
Qualifications: [BSc (Hons)]

SHOYLEV MR KAMEN PETROV

27 Redcliffe Gardens, London, SW10 9BH, ☎020 7734 9951, *Call Date: 2010, Gray's Inn*

F

SHRIMPLIN MISS KATHERINE ANNE

Legal Director, Department For Business, Innovation and Skills, Legal Services: Prosecutions, 1 Victoria Street, London, SW1H 0ET, ☎ 020 7215 3203 Fax: 020 7215 3221, ✉ katy.shrimplin@bis.gsi.gov.uk, *Call Date: July 1984, Middle Temple*
Qualifications: [LLB (Lond)]

SHROPSHIRE MISS ALISON ELIZABETH MARY

Nspcc, Weston House, 42 Curtain Road, London, EC2A 3NH, ☎ 020 7825 2500 Fax: 020 7825 2525, ✉ alison.shropshire@nspcc.org.uk, *Call Date: Nov 1979, Lincoln's Inn*
Qualifications: [BA (CNAA) LLM (Lond)]

SHUKLA MS VINA

The Treasury Solicitors, One Kemble Street, London, WC2B 4TS, *Call Date: Nov 1992, Gray's Inn*
Qualifications: [MA (Cantab) BCL]

SIANI MR PAUL ANTHONY

Company Director, Ground Floor Office, 315 Upper Street, London, N1 2XQ, ☎ 020 7359 3669 Fax: 020 7354 1901, ✉ paul@agarfield.co.uk, *Call Date: May 1997, Inner Temple*
Qualifications: [LLB (Wales)]

SIDDIQUE LIEUTENANT COLONEL BILAL MOHAMMED

Legal Adviser, Directorate of Army Legal Services, Idl426, Ramillies Building, Marlborough Lines, Monxton Road, Andover, SP11 8HJ, *Call Date: Nov 1996, Gray's Inn*
Qualifications: [LLB LLM (Bucks)]

SIDHU MR RAVI

Lawyer, Other, Senior Crown Prosecutor, Crown Prosecution Service, Easton Court, 112 Oxford Road, Reading, Berkshire, RG1 7LL, ☎ 01189 885763 Fax: 01189 888011, ✉ ravi.sidhu@cps.gsi.gov.uk, *Call Date: Feb 1988, Inner Temple*
Qualifications: [LLB (Lancs)]

SILLIS MS LOUISE ANN

Royal Courts of Justice, Strand, London, WC2A 2LL, ☎ 020 7947 6429 Fax: 020 7947 7401, ✉ louise.sillis@hmcts.x.gsi.gov.uk, *Call Date: Nov 1994, Middle Temple*
Qualifications: [MA (Cantab)]

SIMON MISS DALE INEZ

Crown Prosecution Service, Rose Court, 2 Southwark Bridge, London, SE1 9HS, ☎ 020 3357 0550 Fax: 020 3357 0567, ✉ dale.simon@cps.gsi.gov.uk, *Call Date: Nov 1986, Inner Temple*
Qualifications: [LLB]

SIMPSON MR BRIAN ADAM

Crown Prosecution Service, Swansea Tu, Princess House, Princess Way, Swansea, SA1 3LY, ☎ 01792 452900 Fax: 01792 452930, *Call Date: Mar 1998, Middle Temple*
Qualifications: [LLB (Hons)(Essex)]

SIMPSON MS CLAIRE MARGARET LOUISE

Director, Euroclear Sa/Nv, 1 Boulevard Du Roi Albert Ii, Brussels, B-1210, Belgium, ☎ 00 322 326 7948, ✉ claire.simpson@euroclear.com, *Call Date: Oct 1999, Inner Temple*
Qualifications: [LLB (Edin'b) LLM (Bruges)]

SIMPSON MR ROBERT THOMPSON

Crown Prosecution Service, Hounslow Police Station, 3-5 Montague Road, Hounslow, London, TW3 1LB, ☎ 020 3300 4063, *Call Date: Nov 1986, Inner Temple*
Qualifications: [LLB (Manch)]

SIMPSON MISS YVONNE MICHELLE

Senior Lawyer, Cohen Cramer Solicitors, St George House, 40 Great George Street, Leeds, LS1 3DL, Fax: 0113 298 7363, ✉ Yvonne.Simpson@CohenCramer.co.uk, *Call Date: Oct 1997, Lincoln's Inn*
Qualifications: [LLB (Hons)(Manc)]

SINGH MRS KUMUD

Senior Crown Prosecutor, Crown Prosecution Service, Priory Gate, 29 Union Street, Maidstone, Kent, ME14 1PT, *Call Date: Nov 1987, Inner Temple*
Qualifications: [LLB (Hons) LLM]

SINGH MR RAJESH KUMAR

EOS Legal Limited, Amadeus House, Floral Street, London, WC2E 9DP, Fax: 020 3014 8700, ✉ rajesh.singh@eos-law.com, *Call Date: Nov 1996, Gray's Inn*
Qualifications: [MA (Cantab) LLM]

SIVELL MR COLIN PETER

Head of Legal Services, Colin Sivell Associates Ltd, 22 Tor Bryan, Ingatestone, Essex, CM4 9JZ, *Call Date: July 1979, Inner Temple*

SKILBECK MR RUPERT HUGH

Open Society Justice Initiative, 400 West 59th Street, New York, N.Y. 10019, USA, ☎001 212 548 0633 Fax: 00 1 212 548 4662, ✉rskilbeck@justiceinitiative.org, *Call Date: Mar 1996, Gray's Inn*
Qualifications: [BA (York)]

SKINNER MR CONOR WILLIAM RICHARD

BG Group, Bg Group PLC, Legal Dept, C and P, 100 Thames Valley Park Drive, Reading, Berkshire, RG6 1PT, ☎0118 929 3552, ✉Conor.Skinner@bg-group.com, *Call Date: Nov 1979, Gray's Inn*
Qualifications: [MA]

SKINNER MISS KATHERINE JOY

Assistant, Derbyshire Constabulary, Constabulary Headquarters, Butterley Hall, Ripley, Derbyshire, DE5 3RS, ☎01773 572839 Fax: 01773 572581, *Call Date: Nov 1988, Inner Temple*
Qualifications: [LLB (L'pool)]

SKINNER MR NIALL FRASER

Tuckers Solicitors, 210 Corporation Street, Birmingham, B4 6QB, ☎0121 236 4324 Fax: 0121 236 4364, ✉Skinnern@tuckerssolicitors.com, *Call Date: July 2001, Lincoln's Inn*
Qualifications: [MA (Hons) CPE]

SLANEY MISS LOUISE PAULINE

Swindon Borough Council, Civic Offices, Euclid Street, Swindon, Wiltshire, SN1 2JH, ☎01793 463019, ✉lslaney@swindon.gov.uk, *Call Date: Nov 1990, Inner Temple*
Qualifications: [LLB (Exon)]

SLATER MISS ALISON FIONA

Civil Aviation Authority, Caa House, 45-59 Kingsway, London, WC2B 6TE, Fax: 020 7453 6163 / 020 7453 6163, ✉alison.slater@caa.co.uk, *Call Date: Nov 1996, Middle Temple*
Qualifications: [LLB (Leics)]

SLATER MISS SARAH HELEN

Crown Prosecution Service, St Peters House, Gower Street, Derby, Derbyshire, DE1 1SB, ☎01332 614000, *Call Date: Oct 1996, Gray's Inn*
Qualifications: [LLB (Sussex) (Hons)]

SLEGG MR KEVIN ANDREW

Manager, Force Majeure Consulting Limited, Dunheved, 118 St Andrews Road, Coulsdon, Surrey, CR5 3HD, ☎0786 653 3354, ✉kevinslegg@bbmax.co.uk, *Call Date: Nov 1996, Middle Temple*
Qualifications: [BSc ARICS MRICS MAPM]

SMALS MR RUFUS ALEXANDER OGILVIE

Chair, General Counsel, Gkn PLC, Ipsley House, P.O. Box 55, Ipsley Church Lane, Redditch, Worcestershire, B98 0TL, ☎01527 517715 Fax: 01527 533470, ✉rufus.ogilviesmals@gkn.com, *Call Date: Nov 1973, Middle Temple*
Qualifications: [MA (Cantab) Dip Euro Integration (Amsterdam)]

SMART MISS EMMA CATHERINE ISABELLE

C/O Itv, The London Television Centre, Upper Ground, London, SE1 9LT, ☎020 7261 3915, ✉Emma.Smart@itv.com, *Call Date: Oct 1998, Inner Temple*
Qualifications: [LLB (Lond)]

SMILES MISS SARAH-JANE

Nursing and Midwifery Council, 1 Kemble Street, London, WC2B 4AN, Fax: 020 7242 9579, ✉sarah-jane.smiles@nmc-uk.org, *Call Date: Nov 2008, Middle Temple*
Qualifications: [LLB (Hons) (Lond)]

SMILLIE MR DAVID CRAIG

Clerk, Legal Adviser, Redhill Magistrates' Court, The Law Court, Hatchlands Road, Redhill, Surrey, RH1 6DH, ☎01737 765 581 Fax: 01737 778 372, ✉david.smillie@hmcourts-service.gsi.gov.uk, *Call Date: Mar 2003, Lincoln's Inn*
Qualifications: [LLB (Hons) (Lond)]

SMITH MISS AMELIE JANE

Legal Adviser, Hampshire County Council, The Castle, Winchester, SO23 8UB, ☎01962 847 208 / 01962 847 208 Fax: 01962 840 215, ✉amelie.smith@hants.gov.uk, *Call Date: Nov 1992, Lincoln's Inn*
Qualifications: [LLB (Hons)(B'ham)]

SMITH MR BARRY JAMES

Artesian Law, 3 Bolt Court, Fleet Street, London, EC4A 3DQ, *Call Date: July 2010, Middle Temple*
Qualifications: [BA (Hons) (Cantab) MPhil (Cantab)]

SMITH DR BETHANY MARIE

HM Revenue and Customs, 100 Parliament Street, London, SW1A 2BQ, ☎020 7147 2969 Fax: 020 7147 2251, ✉bethany.smith@hmrc.gsi.gov.uk, *Call Date: July 2009, Middle Temple*
Qualifications: [BSc (Hons) MA (Leic) PhD (Leic)]

SMITH MS CAROLINE SARAH

London Borough of Hounslow, Civic Centre, Lampton Road, Hounslow, London, TW3 4DN, *Call Date: July 2003, Inner Temple*
Qualifications: [BA (Newc) CPE (Northumbria)]

SMITH MR DARREN LEE

Forbes Solicitors, Ribchester House, Lancaster Road, Preston, PR1 2QL, ☎01772 220022 Fax: 01772 220158, ✉darren.lee-smith@forbessolicitors.co.uk, *Call Date: Oct 2011, Lincoln's Inn*
Qualifications: [LLB (Lancashire)]

SMITH MS DEANA KAY

Legal Adviser, City of Westminster Magistrates' Court, 70 Horseferry Road, London, SW1P 2AX, ☎020 7805 1014, *Call Date: Nov 1998, Gray's Inn*
Qualifications: [BSc (Lond) MSc (Lond)]

SMITH MISS ELIZABETH ALICE LOUISA

Bobbetts Mackan Solicitors and Advocates, 17 Berkeley Square, Clifton, Bristol, BS8 1HB, ☎0845 120 2350 Fax: 0870 421 5281, *Call Date: July 2008, Gray's Inn*
Qualifications: [LLB (Bris)]

SMITH MISS EMMA CLARE

Crown Prosecution Service, Princess House, Princess Way, Swansea, SA1 3LY, ☎01792 452 9000, *Call Date: July 2002, Gray's Inn*
Qualifications: [BA (Oxon) MA (Oxon)]

SMITH MISS HANNAH FRANCES

Edwards Hayes LLP, Temple Bar House, 23-28 Fleet Street, London, EC4Y 1AA, ☎020 7353 0011 Fax: 020 7427 7391, ✉HSmith@EdwardHayes.co.uk, *Call Date: Nov 2005, Inner Temple*
Qualifications: [LLB (LSE)]

SMITH MISS JANET MARY

Gloucester Law Centre, 75-81 Eastgate Street, Gloucester, Gloucestershire, GL1 1PN, ☎01452 423 492 Fax: 01452 387 594, *Call Date: Nov 1985, Middle Temple*
Qualifications: [LLB (Hull)]

SMITH MS JESSICA CLARE

The Treasury Solicitors, One Kemble Street, London, WC2B 4TS, ☎020 7210 3000, ✉jessica.smith@tsol.gsi.gov.uk, *Call Date: Oct 1992, Middle Temple*
Qualifications: [BA (Hons) (Dunelm) Dip Law]

SMITH MISS LISA IMOGEN

Woolley and Co Solicitors, Avon House, 23 Banbury Road, Po Box 1700, Stratford Upon Avon, CV37 7ZW, ☎01789 267377, ✉lisa.smith@family-lawfirm.co.uk, *Call Date: Oct 1994, Lincoln's Inn*
Qualifications: [LLB (Hons)(Lond)]

SMITH REV MARK WINTON

Deputy Chairman, Department For Business, Innovation and Skills, Orchard 1, 6th Floor, 1 Victoria Street, London, SW1H 0ET, ✉mark.smith@bis.gsi.gov.uk, *Call Date: July 1982, Middle Temple*
Qualifications: [BA (Dunelm)]

SMITH MR MATTHEW JAMES

The Home Office, Seacole House, 2 Marsham Street, London, SW1P 4DF, ☎020 7035 1376, ✉matthew.smith110@homeoffice.gsi.gov.uk, *Call Date: Oct 1993, Middle Temple*
Qualifications: [BA (Hons)(Oxon)]

F

SMITH MR MICHAEL DAVID

Crown Prosecution Service, Jefferson House, 27 Park Place, Leeds, West Yorkshire, LS1 2SZ, ☎ 0113 2902999, ✉ Michael.Smith@cps.gsi.gov.uk, *Call Date: Nov 2000, Middle Temple*
Qualifications: [LLB (Hons)]

SMITH DR MICHAEL ROBERT

Lawyer, Ministry of Justice, Moj Legal Corporate Advisory Team, Post Point 6.34, 102 Petty France, London, SW1H 9AJ, ☎ 020 3334 4791, ✉ Michael.Smith@justice.gsi.gov.uk, *Call Date: Nov 1987, Gray's Inn*
Qualifications: [MA Dip Law (City) PhD (Cantab)]

SMITH MR PETER STANLEY

Consultant, Old Gold Script Services, Brooklea House, Heights of Achterneed, Strathpeffer, Ross-Shire, IV14 9AE, ☎ 01997 421444 Fax: 01997 421 602, ✉ peter@oldgoldscript.co.uk, *Call Date: July 1980, Middle Temple*
Qualifications: [LLB (Hons)]

SMITH MISS PHYLLIS DAWN

Crown Prosecution Service, The Cooperage, 8 Gainsford Street, London, SE1 2NE, *Call Date: Nov 1991, Inner Temple*
Qualifications: [LLB]

SMITH MS REMI

Legal Counsel, HSBC Bank Plc, Legal Level 22, 8 Canada Square, Canary Wharf, London, E14 5HQ, Fax: 020 7991 4613, ✉ remi.smith@hsbc.com, *Call Date: Mar 1998, Gray's Inn*
Qualifications: [PG DipLaw LLB (Hons) LLM (Bris)]

SMITH MR SEAN DAVID

Harters Solicitors, 398 Caledonian Road, London, N1 1DN, ☎ 020 7607 5768, *Call Date: Oct 1995, Gray's Inn*
Qualifications: [BA (Sheff)]

SMITH MR STEPHEN HARVEY

Legal Adviser, Secretary, The Treasury Solicitors, Attorney General's Office, 20 Victoria Street, London, SW1H 0NF, *Call Date: Nov 2003, Lincoln's Inn*
Qualifications: [LLB (Hons) (Newc)]

SOBEY MISS JESSICA ANNE

Lloyds PR Solicitors, 183 High Street, Harlesden, London, NW10 4TE, ☎ 020 8963 1050 Fax: 020 8963 1975, ✉ info@lloydspr.com, *Call Date: Oct 2007, Lincoln's Inn*
Qualifications: [LLB (Swansea)]

SOFOWORA MRS PAULA BOLANLE

Zurich Financial Services, Ukgi Legal Unit, 1st Floor, 3 Minster Court, Mincing Lane, London, EC3R 7DD, ☎ 0845 300 3989
Fax: 020 7648 3670, ✉ paula.sofowora@uk.zurich.com, *Call Date: Oct 1993, Inner Temple*
Qualifications: [BA (Nigeria) LLB (Lond)]

SOLLEY MR YUSUF

The Treasury Solicitors, One Kemble Street, London, WC2B 4TS, *Call Date: July 2009, Inner Temple*
Qualifications: [LLB (Westminster) PGDip]

SOLOMON MR DANIEL IESTYN

Department For Transport, Legal Services Directorate, Zone 51/05, Great Minster House, London, SW1P 4DR, ☎ 020 7944 6640, ✉ Daniel.Solomon@dft.gsi.gov.uk, *Call Date: Oct 1996, Gray's Inn*
Qualifications: [BA (Oxon) Dip law]

SORABJI MR JOHN ROBERT

Secretary, Master of the Rolls Office, The Royal Courts of Justice, The Strand, London, WC2A 2LL, ☎ 020 7947 6852, *Call Date: Oct 2001, Inner Temple*
Qualifications: [MA (Oxon) M Phil (Manch) PgDL LLM (Lond)]

SOUTHALL MR RICHARD ANTHONY

Hierons, 2 Chester Row, London, SW1W 9JH, ☎ 020 3328 4510
Fax: 020 77305214 / 020 3328 4520, ✉ rs@hieronslaw.com, *Call Date: Nov 1983, Middle Temple*
Qualifications: [LLB (Buckingham)]

SOUTHGATE MISS MARIE DAWN

Peterborough City Council, Chief Executive's Department, Town Hall, Peterborough, PE1 1HG, ✉ marie.southgate@peterborough.gov.uk, *Call Date: Oct 1997, Lincoln's Inn*
Qualifications: [LLB (Hons)(Notts)]

SPARKES MR DUNCAN ALISTAIR

Assistant General Counsel, Bacardi - Martini B.V., 267 Route De Meyrin, Meyrin 2, 1217, Switzerland, Fax: 22 719 3722, ✉dsparkes@bacardi.com, *Call Date: Oct 1996, Middle Temple*
Qualifications: [BA (Hons)(Sheff) CPE]

SPARROW MR GARY

Crown Prosecution Service, County House, 100 New London Road, Chelmsford, Essex, CM2 0RG, ☎01245 455 800, ✉gary.sparrow@cps.gsi.gov.uk, *Call Date: July 2006, Gray's Inn*
Qualifications: [LLB]

SPEAK MR MICHAEL NORMAN

Crown Prosecution Service, Queens House, 58 Victoria Street, St. Albans, Hertforshire, AL1 3HZ, *Call Date: July 1983, Lincoln's Inn*
Qualifications: [BA (Hull) Dip Law]

SPEAK MR RICHARD GIBSON

Other, National Australia Bank Ltd, 88 Wood Street, London, EC2V 7QQ, ☎020 7710 2100, *Call Date: Nov 1992, Inner Temple*
Qualifications: [LLB]

SPECK MR CHRISTOPHER JOHN

BT Group PLC, P.O.Box 200, London, N18 1ZF, ☎0161 236 4492, *Call Date: Oct 1996, Lincoln's Inn*
Qualifications: [BSc (Hons)(Manc)]

SPEDDING MISS CATHERINE ANN

Allen Hoole Solicitors, 5 Portland Square, Bristol, BS2 8RR, *Call Date: Nov 1995, Inner Temple*
Qualifications: [LLB (Hons)]

SPELLER MR DUNCAN JAMES

Wilmer Cutler Pickering Hale and Dorr LLP, 49 Park Lane, London, W1K 1PS, ☎02078 721 084 Fax: 02078 393 537, ✉duncan.speller@wilmerhale.com, *Call Date: Nov 2001, Lincoln's Inn*
Qualifications: [BA (Hons) BCL]

SPENCE CAPTAIN ANDREI BARRY

Royal Navy Officers, Naval Command Hq, Ddnls, Mp4-2, Lead Building, Whale Island, Portsmouth, Hampshire, PO2 8BY, *Call Date: Oct 1993, Middle Temple*
Qualifications: [BSc (Hons)(Aston) CPE (Lond)]

SPENCER MR GEORGE CHARLES WELLESLEY

Adviser, Ade (Legal), British Defence Staff, British Embassy, 3100 Massachusetts Avenue Nw, Washington, DC 20008, USA, ☎001 202 5886758 Fax: 001 202 588 7887, ✉george.spencer@bdsus.mod.uk, *Call Date: Mar 1999, Gray's Inn*
Qualifications: [BSc (Lond) DPhil (Oxon) BA (Cantab)]

SPENCER MRS GERALDINE ERICA

Senior Crown Prosecutor, Crown Prosecution Service, The Cooperage, 8 Gainsford Street, London, SE1 2NE, ☎020 7378 4255 Fax: 020 7378 4302, ✉geraldine.spencer@cps.gsi.gov.uk, *Call Date: Nov 1968, Gray's Inn*

SPENCER MRS MARGARET ELIZABETH

Director, Hfl Limited, 2 Cranwell House, La Route Du Picquerel, L'lslet, GY2 4SD, Guernsey, ☎01481 722066 Fax: 01481 724308, *Call Date: Feb 1989, Gray's Inn*

SPENCER MISS MELANIE DAWN

UNISON Legal Services, Unison Centre, 130 Euston Road, London, NW1 2AY, ☎0845 355 0845 Fax: 020 7551 1163, *Call Date: July 1986, Inner Temple*
Qualifications: [BA (Leeds) Dip Law]

SPENCER MR THOMAS BENEDICT

GlaxoSmithKline, 980 Great West Road, Brentford, Middlesex, TW8 9GS, *Call Date: July 2000, Inner Temple*
Qualifications: [BA (Newc) CPE]

SPINNEY MR MARK ROBIN EUGENE

Olswang LLP, 90 High Holborn, London, WC1V 6XX, ☎020 7067 3000 Fax: 020 7067 3999, ✉mark.spinney@olswang.com, *Call Date: Nov 2010, Middle Temple*
Qualifications: [BA (Hons) (Oxon)]

SPOONER MISS CLAIRE ELIZABETH

Crown Prosecution Service, 2 Parker Court, Staffordshire Technology Park, Stafford, Staffordshire, ST18 0ZE, ✉Claire.Spooner@cps.gsi.gov.uk, *Call Date: Oct 2006, Gray's Inn*
Qualifications: [LLB]

F

SPRIGGE MR WILLIAM LIDDON

Legal Adviser, Maclay Murray & Spens, One London Wall, London, EC2Y 5AB, ✉william.sprigge@mms.co.uk, *Call Date: July 1976, Lincoln's Inn*
Qualifications: [BSc ACIS]

SPURR MR HENRY RICHARD JAMES

Hogan Lovells International LLP, Atlantic House, 50 Holborn Viaduct, London, EC1A 2FG, *Call Date: Oct 2001, Inner Temple*
Qualifications: [BA (Exon) CPE]

SPYBEY MR JAMES MATTHEW BENJAMIN

The Treasury Solicitors, 5th Floor, One Kemble Street, London, WC2B 4TS, ☎020 7210 3000, ✉james.spybey@tsol.gsi.gov.uk, *Call Date: July 2009, Middle Temple*
Qualifications: [LLB (Hons) (Dunelm)]

SQUIBB-WILLIAMS MS KAREN VICTORIA

Crown Advocate, Crown Prosecution Service, Rose Court, 2 Southwark Bridge, London, SE1 9HS, ✉Karen.Squibbwilliams@cps.gsi.gov.uk, *Call Date: Oct 1999, Gray's Inn*
Qualifications: [MA (Oxon)]

STADNIK MISS NINA

Legal Manager, Her Majesty's Courts and Tribunals Service, The Court House, Pinfold Gate, Loughborough, AL11 1AZ, ☎01509 220356, *Call Date: Nov 1986, Inner Temple*
Qualifications: [BA (Hons) Dip Law DMS]

STAHELI MRS REBECCA

Senior Legal Adviser, Civil Aviation Authority, Caa House, 45-59 Kingsway, London, WC2B 6TE, Fax: 020 7 453 6175, ✉Rebecca.staheli@caa.co.uk, *Call Date: Nov 1989, Middle Temple*
Qualifications: [BA (Cantab)]

STANISLAS MR PAUL JUNIOR

Monioro Less and Co Solicitors, 4a The Works, Bird In Hand Mews, Forest Hill, London, SE23 3HJ, ☎020 8291 7657 Fax: 020 8291 7463, ✉paul@monioroless.com, *Call Date: Feb 1989, Middle Temple*
Qualifications: [LLB]

STANLEY MR DAVID JAMES

HED, Ordnance Survey, Adanac Drive, Southampton, SO16 0AS, ☎08456 05 05 05, *Call Date: Oct 2001, Middle Temple*
Qualifications: [LLB (Hons)]

STANSFIELD MISS JANE

HED, Higher Court Advocate, Crown Prosecution Service, Queens House, 58 Victoria Street, St. Albans, Hertforshire, AL1 3HZ, ☎01727 798 700 Fax: 01727 798 804, ✉jane.stansfield@cps.gsi.gov.uk, *Call Date: July 1986, Lincoln's Inn*
Qualifications: [LLB]

STANYER MR SIMON MICHAEL

Advocate, Crown Prosecution Service, Stoke Newington Police Station, 33 Stoke Newington High Street, London, N16 8DS, ☎020 87215514 Fax: 029 87721 5539, ✉Simon.Stanyer@cps.gsi.gov.uk, *Call Date: Nov 1992, Inner Temple*
Qualifications: [LLB (Leeds)]

STARKIE MISS CLAIRE ELIZABETH

Suffolk County Council, Endeavour House, 8 Russell Road, Ipswich, Suffolk, IP1 2BX, ✉Claire.Starkie@Suffolk.gov.uk, *Call Date: Nov 1991, Lincoln's Inn*
Qualifications: [MA (Cantab)]

STARMER MR KEIR

Director of Public Prosecutions, HED, Crown Prosecution Service, Rose Court, 2 Southwark Bridge, London, SE1 9HS, *Call Date: Nov 1987, Middle Temple*
Qualifications: [LLB (Leeds) BCL (Oxon)]

START MISS VICTORIA LOUISE

Directorate of Army Legal Services, Trenchard Lines, Upavon, Pewsey, Wiltshire, SN9 6BE, Fax: 01980 615978, *Call Date: Oct 1996, Middle Temple*
Qualifications: [BA (Hons)(Oxon) LLM (Lond)]

STEEL REAR ADMIRAL DAVID GEORGE

Secretary, Royal Navy Officers, Naval Secretary and Chief of Staff (Personnel), Mail Point 3.1, Leach Building, Whale Island, Portsmouth, Hampshire, PO2 8BY, *Call Date: July 1988, Middle Temple*
Qualifications: [BA (Hons) (Dunelm) CFIPD CFILT]

F

STEEL MR STEPHEN PAUL

Crown Prosecution Service, United House, Piccadilly, York, North Yorkshire, YO1 1PQ, ✉Stephen.Steel@cps.gsi.gov.uk, *Call Date: Nov 1985, Lincoln's Inn*
Qualifications: [BSc Dip Law]

STEENE MRS ALISON DAWN

Dhl Gbs (Uk) Limited, Magna House, 18-32 London Road, Staines, TW18 4BP, Fax: 01784 871118, *Call Date: Nov 1998, Middle Temple*
Qualifications: [LLB (Hons)(Thames)]

STEPHENSON MISS HANNAH CLARE LOUISE

Nursing and Midwifery Council, 1 Kemble Street, London, WC2B 4AN, *Call Date: July 2007, Middle Temple*
Qualifications: [LLB (Hons) (Hull) LLM (Nott'm)]

STEPHENSON MR SYDNEY DINGAAN

Commerzbank AG, 30 Gresham Street, London, EC2V 7PG, *Call Date: Nov 1996, Middle Temple*
Qualifications: [LLB (Hons)(Lond)]

STERN MS ELIZABETH

Howes Percival LLP, The Guildyard, 51 Colegate, Norwich, NR3 1DD, ☎01603 281 947 Fax: 01603 617 981, ✉elizabeth.stern@howespercival.com, *Call Date: Oct 1994, Lincoln's Inn*
Qualifications: [LLB (Hons)(Lond)]

STERNBERG MS LESLI EDEN

Crown Advocate, Crown Prosecution Service, Rose Court, 2 Southwark Bridge, London, SE1 9HS, ☎020 3357 0922 Fax: 020 3357 0388, ✉lesli.sternberg@cps.gsi.gov.uk, *Call Date: Nov 1994, Gray's Inn*
Qualifications: [BA (Hons)]

STEVENS MR RICHARD DAVID SOMMERVILLE

Crown Advocate, Crown Prosecution Service, County House, 100 New London Road, Chelmsford, Essex, CM2 0RG, *Call Date: Mar 2007, Middle Temple*

STEVENSON MR BRETT CARL

National Grid, National Grid House, Warwick Technology Park, Gallows Hill, Warwick, CV34 6DA, *Call Date: July 1998, Lincoln's Inn*
Qualifications: [LLB (Hons)(Dundee)]

STEWART MR ANGUS BETHUNE

Crown Prosecution Service, Southern House, Wellesley Grove, Croydon, Surrey, CR9 1DY, ✉Angus.Stewart@cps.gsi.gov.uk, *Call Date: July 2002, Inner Temple*
Qualifications: [LLB (Kingston)]

STEWART MS EMMA JANE

Independent Police Complaints Commission, 90 High Holborn, London, WC1V 6BH, ✉emma.stewart@ipcc.gsi.gov.uk, *Call Date: Mar 2010, Middle Temple*
Qualifications: [LLB (Belfast)]

STIBBS MR MICHAEL JOHN PARKER

Legal Manager, Hmcs Suffolk, Her Majesty's Court Service, Combined Court, Old Nelson Street, Lowestoft, NR32 1HJ, *Call Date: Nov 1982, Middle Temple*
Qualifications: [BA CTP Assoc CIPD]

STIMSON MR PAUL

Crown Prosecution Service, 2 King Edward Court, King Edward Street, Nottingham, Nottinghamshire, NG1 1EL, ✉paul.stimson@cps.gsi.gov.uk, *Call Date: Nov 2003, Lincoln's Inn*
Qualifications: [LLB (Hons) (Leeds)]

STIRLING MR ANDREW FRASER

Senior Crown Prosecutor, Crown Prosecution Service, Citadel House, 58 High Street, Hull, Humberside, HU1 1QD, *Call Date: July 1985, Lincoln's Inn*
Qualifications: [LLB (Hons) (B'ham)]

STOCKBRIDGE MR ANTONY JULIAN

Royal Navy Officers, Directorate of Naval Legal Services, Mp 4-2, Leach Building, Whale Island, Portsmouth, PO2 8BY, *Call Date: Oct 2005, Middle Temple*
Qualifications: [MA (Hons) (Dundee) Dip in Law]

STOCKFORD MS CLAIRE ELIZABETH

Crowell and Moring, 11 Pilgrim Street, London, EC4V 6RN, ☎ 020 7413 0011 Fax: 020 7413 0333, ✉ cstockford@crowell.com, *Call Date: Nov 1999, Gray's Inn*
Qualifications: [LLB (Birm'h)]

STOKES MR DYLAN DANIEL

Director, Barclays Capital, 5 The North Colonnade, London, E14 4BB, ☎ 020 7773 3903 Fax: 020 7773 4922, ✉ dylan.stokes@barcap.com, *Call Date: Nov 1998, Inner Temple*
Qualifications: [BA (Dunelm) Dip Law]

STOKES MR PAUL GWYNNE

Legal Adviser, HSBC Bank Plc, Hsbc Holdings PLC, 8th Floor, Group Legal Department, 12 Calthorpe Road, Edgbaston, Birmingham, B15 1QZ, ☎ 0121 455 2709 Fax: 0121 455 2770, ✉ paulstokes@hsbc.com, *Call Date: Oct 1998, Lincoln's Inn*
Qualifications: [LLB (Hons)]

STONE MISS CAROLINE BETH

3 PB Barristers, 3 Paper Bldgs, Temple, London, EC4Y 7EU, ☎ 020 7583 8055 Fax: 020 7353 6271, ✉ caroline.stone@3pb.co.uk, *Call Date: Nov 2005, Middle Temple*
Qualifications: [BA (Hons) Cambridge MA (Hons) (Cantab)]

STONECLIFFE MISS HEIDI LORRAINE

Advocate, Solicitor, Crown Prosecution Service, Rose Court, 2 Southwark Bridge, London, SE1 9HS, ☎ 020 3357 1042, ✉ heidi.stonecliffe@cps.gsi.gov.uk, *Call Date: Oct 1996, Inner Temple*
Qualifications: [LLB LSE]

STONES MR KEITH WILLIAM

J D Spicer and Co Solicitors, 140 Kilburn High Road, London, NW6 4JD, ☎ 020 7624 7771 Fax: 020 7328 9466, *Call Date: Nov 1975, Gray's Inn*
Qualifications: [LLB]

STOPLAR MR DAVID JONATHAN ARON

Senior Legal Adviser, Civil Aviation Authority, Room K509 Caa House, 45-59 Kingsway, London, WC2B 6TE, ☎ 020 7453 6174 Fax: 020 7453 6175, ✉ david.stoplar@caa.co.uk, *Call Date: July 1982, Gray's Inn*
Qualifications: [LLB (Lond)]

STOPPS MISS NATALIE JANE

Peters & Peters Solicitors LLP, 15 Fetter Lane, London, EC4A 1BW, ☎ 020 7822 7777 Fax: 020 7822 7788, ✉ law@petersandpeters.com, *Call Date: July 2000, Gray's Inn*
Qualifications: [MA (Hons)(Cantab) CPE]

STOREY MRS BERNADETTE

Senior Crown Prosecutor, Crown Prosecution Service, Bishopsgate Police Station, 182 Bishopsgate, London, EC2M 4NP, *Call Date: Feb 1990, Lincoln's Inn*
Qualifications: [LLB Hons]

STOREY JEWKES MRS PENELOPE JOSEPHINE ELEANOR

Assistant Deputy Coroner, Cambridge City Council, Market Square, Guildhall, Cambridge, CB2 3QJ, ☎ 01223 457402 Fax: 01223 457109, ✉ Penny.jewkes@cambridge.gov.uk, *Call Date: July 1973, Lincoln's Inn*
Qualifications: [LLB]

STORR MR CHRISTOPHER KIP

Directorate of Army Legal Services, Idl426, Ramillies Building, Marlborough Lines, Monxton Road, Andover, SP11 8HJ, *Call Date: July 2006, Lincoln's Inn*
Qualifications: [LLB (Dunelm)]

STRADLING MR MICHAEL DONAT

4 Breams Buildings, Chancery Lane, London, EC4A 1HP, ☎ 020 7092 1900 Fax: 020 7092 1999, *Call Date: Nov 1998, Gray's Inn*
Qualifications: [BA (Cantab)]

STRANAGHAN MISS PATRICIA ANN

General Counsel, Legal Adviser, The Royal Bank of Scotland, Head of Technical Services, C/O Lombard North Central PLC, 3 Priness Way, Redhill, Surrey, RH1 1NP, ☎ 01737 776416 Fax: 01737 774466, *Call Date: Nov 1984, Lincoln's Inn*
Qualifications: [LLB (Hons)]

STRICKLAND MISS CLARE ELIZABETH

Other, Nursing and Midwifery Council, 61 Aldwych, London, WC2B 4AE, ☎ 020 7462 5861 Fax: 020 7242 9579, ✉ clare.strickland@nmc-uk.org, *Call Date: Oct 1995, Lincoln's Inn*
Qualifications: [LLB (Hons)(B'ham)]

F

STUART MR PAUL MAX

Cleary Gottlieb Steen & Hamilton LLP, Rue De La Loi 57, Brussels, 1040, Belgium, *Call Date: Nov 2008, Inner Temple*
Qualifications: [BA (Oxon) CPE]

STUBBING DR TAMSIN LUCY

Ministry of Justice, 102 Petty France, London, SW1H 9AJ, ☎020 3334 3555
Fax: 020 3555 4455, ✉tamsin.stubbing@justice.gsi.gov.uk, *Call Date: Oct 2004, Inner Temple*
Qualifications: [LLB (UEA) MA PhD (Sheff)]

STUBBS MR MATTHEW JAMES

CVS, Department For Communities & Local Government, Zone 4/B3, Eland House, Bressenden House, London, SW1E 5DU, *Call Date: July 1989, Inner Temple*
Qualifications: [LLB (Exon)]

SUDRA MR SURAJ BHIKHULAL

London Borough of Camden, Camden Town Hall, Judd Street, London, WC1H 9JE, ☎020 7974 4302 Fax: 020 7974 6032, ✉suraj.sudra@camden.gov.uk, *Call Date: July 2000, Inner Temple*
Qualifications: [LLB (Lond)]

SUGRUE MISS CLARE VERONICA

Director, Universal-Island Records Ltd, 364-366 Kensington High Street, London, W14 8NS, ☎020 7471 5214
Fax: 020 7471 5275, ✉claire.sugrue@umusic.com, *Call Date: Nov 1985, Middle Temple*
Qualifications: [LLB (Lond)]

SUH MRS KATHERINE LUCY

Ministry of Justice, 102 Petty France, London, SW1H 9AH, *Call Date: Oct 2000, Lincoln's Inn*
Qualifications: [BA (Hons) (Oxon) CPE]

SULLIVAN MR DALE ROBERT

Crown Prosecution Service, City Gate House, 185 Dyke Road, Hove, East Sussex, BN3 1TL, ☎01273 765600, *Call Date: Mar 1999, Inner Temple*
Qualifications: [LLB]

SULLIVAN MRS DEBRA

Mediator, Other, British American Tobacco PLC, Globe House, 4 Temple Place, London, WC2R 2PG, ☎020 7845 1546
Fax: 020 7395 0217, ✉debra_sullivan@bat.com, *Call Date: July 1988, Lincoln's Inn*
Qualifications: [LLB (Hons) (Lond) Maitrise En Droit (Paris)]

SULLIVAN MR PATRICK CLEMENT

Crown Prosecution Service, 2 Parker Court, Staffordshire Technology Park, Stafford, Staffordshire, ST18 OZE,
☎01785 272 200 / 01785 272 200
Fax: 01785 272 295 / 01785 272 295,
✉patrick.sullivan@cps.gsi.gov.uk, *Call Date: Nov 1992, Middle Temple*
Qualifications: [LLB (Hons)(Lond)]

SULLIVAN MR RORY MYLES

Pfizer Ireland Pharmaceuticals, Osg Building, Po Box 17, Ringaskiddy, County Cork, Ireland, ☎00353 21 500 8098
Fax: 00353 21 437 9877, *Call Date: Oct 1992, Gray's Inn*
Qualifications: [MA (Oxon)]

SULLIVAN MR SCOTT

Gam (Uk) Limited, 12 St James Place, London, SW1A 1NX, ☎020 7917 2279
Fax: 020 7917 2208, ✉scottsullivan@gam.com, *Call Date: Nov 1991, Inner Temple*
Qualifications: [LLB (So'ton)]

SULLIVAN MR WYNFORD MARK

Lawyer, Senior Legal Counsel, Metlife, 15 Bedford Street, Covent Garden, London, WC2E 9HE, ☎020 7557 4945,
✉msullivan1@metlife.com, *Call Date: Feb 1989, Middle Temple*
Qualifications: [LLB (Wales)]

SUMMERLIN MRS SARA HILL

Advocate, Senior Crown Prosecutor, Crown Prosecution Service, Citadel House, 58 High Street, Hull, Humberside, HU1 1QD, ☎01482 621000 Fax: 01482 621001, ✉sara.hill-summerlin@cps.gsi.gov.uk, *Call Date: Oct 1993, Gray's Inn*
Qualifications: [B Sc (Hons)]

F

SUMPTER MR GAVIN PAUL

Crown Prosecution Service, Western Range, 83 London Road, Southampton, Hampshire, SO15 2AA, ☎ 02380 714000 Fax: 02380 7144054, ✉ gavin.sumpter@cps.gsi.gov.uk, *Call Date: Nov 2006, Middle Temple*
Qualifications: [LLB (Hons) (L'pool) LLM (Leeds)]

SWAFFIELD MRS HELEN LINDA

Harrington Law Limited, High Trees House, Dewles Road, Bewdley, DY12 2RD, ☎ 01299 404802, ✉ office@harringtonlaw.co.uk, *Call Date: July 1988, Lincoln's Inn*
Qualifications: [LLB (Hons) (Leics) Dip D'et Jur (France)]

SWAIN MRS FIONA PATRICIA

Crown Prosecution Service, Greenfield House, 32 Scotland Street, Sheffield, South Yorkshire, S3 7DQ, *Call Date: July 1983, Gray's Inn*
Qualifications: [BA]

SWAN MR IAN CHRISTOPHER

Partner, Babbé, 18-20 Smith Street, Po Box 69, St Peter Port, GY1 4BL, Guernsey, ☎ +44 (0) 1481 713371 Fax: +44 (0) 1481 712245, ✉ i.swan@babbelegal.com, *Call Date: July 1985, Middle Temple*
Qualifications: [MA (Oxon)]

SWAN MS PAULINE MARY

Legal Adviser, The Copyright Licensing Agency Ltd, Saffron House, 6-10 Kirby Street, London, EC1N 8TS, ☎ 020 7400 3166 Fax: 020 7400 3101, ✉ polly.swan@cla.co.uk, *Call Date: Mar 1998, Gray's Inn*
Qualifications: [LLB (Lond)]

SWAN MR STEPHEN ANDREW JOHN

The Treasury Solicitors, 5th Floor, One Kemble Street, London, WC2B 4TS, *Call Date: July 1983, Lincoln's Inn*
Qualifications: [LLB (Hons)(Lond) MA (Lond) LLM (Lond)]

SWARTZ MR BRUCE CARLTON

Assistant, U.S Department of Justice, Criminal Division, Washington Dc 20530-0001, USA, ☎ 202-514 2333, *Call Date: July 1997, Middle Temple*
Qualifications: [BA, JD (Yale)]

SWEENEY MR STEPHEN JOSEPH

Guney Clark and Ryan Solicitors, 58 Green Lanes, London, N16 9NH, ☎ 020 7275 7788 Fax: 020 7923 2554, ✉ info@guneyclarkryan.com, *Call Date: Nov 2001, Inner Temple*
Qualifications: [BA (Hons) LLM LPC]

SWEETING MR DEREK ANTHONY

Deputy High Court Judge, Recorder, Seven Bedford Row, 7 Bedford Row, London, WC1R 4BS, ☎ 020 7242 3555 Fax: 020 7242 2511, ✉ dsweeting@7br.co.uk, *Call Date: July 1983, Middle Temple*
Qualifications: [MA (Cantab)]

SWIFT MR ANTONY

Crown Prosecution Service, Rose Court, 2 Southwark Bridge, London, SE1 9HS, ☎ 020 3357 0350 Fax: 020 357 0381/2, *Call Date: Nov 1984, Inner Temple*
Qualifications: [BA (Hons) Inst FWRI]

SWIFT MR CARL

Clark Willis Law Firm, 105 Bondgate, Darlington, DL3 7LB, ☎ 01325 281111 Fax: 01325 289800, *Call Date: July 2007, Inner Temple*
Qualifications: [BA (Cantab)]

SWIFT MR STEVEN GEOFFREY

Stephensons Solicitors, 10-14 Library Street, Wigan, WN1 1NN, ☎ 01942 777777, *Call Date: Nov 1991, Inner Temple*
Qualifications: [LLB (Lancs)]

SWINHOE MR LUKE FRANCIS

Head of Legal Services, Darlington Borough Council, Town Hall, Darlington, County Durham, DL1 5QT, ☎ 01325 388055 / 01325 388337 Fax: 01325 388318, ✉ luke.swinhoe@darlington.gov.uk, *Call Date: Nov 1987, Inner Temple*
Qualifications: [BA (Hons) DipLaw LLM]

SWORDS MR JOHN CARMEL

The Home Office, Legal Adviser's Branch, Seacole House, 2 Marsham Street, London, SW1P 4DF, ☎ 020 7035 1412 / 020 7035 1412, *Call Date: Nov 2002, Gray's Inn*
Qualifications: [BA (Manch)]

F

SYKES MR RICHARD ROBERT

HED, Partner, Mills and Reeve, Mills and Reeve LLP, 78-84 Colmore Road, Birmingham, B3 2AB, ☎0121 456 8436
Fax: 0121 456 8486, ✉richard.sykes@mills-reeve.com, *Call Date: July 1996, Inner Temple*
Qualifications: [BA (Dunelm)]

SYNMOIE MS LORRAYNE

Crown Prosecution Service, Priory Gate, 29 Union Street, Maidstone, Kent, ME14 1PT, ✉lorrayne.synmoir@cps.gsi.gov.uk, *Call Date: July 1991, Lincoln's Inn*
Qualifications: [LLB (Hons) (Hull)]

SZAGUN MISS TERESA EWA

Deputy District Judge, Director of Legal Services, Justices' Clerk, HMCS Essex, Her Majesty's Court Service, Osprey House, Hedgerows Business Park, Colchester Road, Springfield, Chelmsford, Essex, CM2 5PF, ☎01245 313500, ✉tessa.szagun@hmcts.gsi.gov.uk, *Call Date: Nov 1985, Middle Temple*
Qualifications: [BA (Hons) Dip Law]

TABBUSH MR SIMON JAMES

Law Commission, Steel House, 11 Tothill Street, London, SW1H 9LJ, ☎020 3334 0273
Fax: 020 3334 0201, ✉simon.tabbush@lawcommission.gsi.gov.uk, *Call Date: July 1979, Middle Temple*
Qualifications: [MA (Oxon)]

TAGGART MR SAMUEL NICHOLAS

Financial Services Authority, Enforcement and Financial Crime Division, 25 The North Colonnade, Canary Wharf, London, E14 5HS, ☎020 7066 6960, ✉sam.taggart@fsa.gov.uk, *Call Date: Nov 1992, Middle Temple*
Qualifications: [LLB (Hons) (Manch)]

TAGHAVI MR SHAHRAM

Lewis Silkin LLP, 5 Chancery Lane, Clifford's Inn, London, EC4A 1BL, ☎020 7074 8211
Fax: 020 7864 1715, *Call Date: Oct 1994, Gray's Inn*
Qualifications: [LLB]

TAHERI MISS ELIZABETH SARA

Kingsley Napley LLP, 14 St John's Lane, London, EC1M 4AJ, ☎020 7814 1263
Fax: 020 7490 2288, ✉etaheri@kingsleynapley.co.uk, *Call Date: July 2005, Lincoln's Inn*
Qualifications: [LLB (Hons)]

TALBOT MISS ANN-MARIE LORRAINE GUY

11 Gray's Inn Square Chambers, Chambers of Mr Ian Sen, 1st Floor South, 10/11 Gray's Inn Square, London, WC1R 5JD, ☎020 7405 6879
Fax: 020 7430 0502, ✉amtalbot@11graysinnsquare.com, *Call Date: Oct 2006, Middle Temple*
Qualifications: [BA (Hons) Dip Law]

TAMS MISS LAURA

Crown Prosecution Service, Southern House, Wellesley Grove, Croydon, CR9 1DY, ☎020 8662 2791, ✉laura.tams@cps.gsi.gov.uk, *Call Date: Oct 2006, Lincoln's Inn*
Qualifications: [LLB (L'pool)]

TAN MISS ESTHER

Legal Adviser, HMCS Norfolk, Norwich Magistrates' Court, Bishopgate, Norwich, Norfolk, NR3 1UP, ☎01603 679540
Fax: 01603 663263, ✉e.tan-worthington-chapman@hmcts.gsi.gov.uk, *Call Date: Nov 1990, Middle Temple*
Qualifications: [LLB (Bucks)]

TAN MISS STEPHANIE HUI LING

Government of Singapore Investment Corp Pte Ltd, 168 Robinson Road, 37-01 Capital Tower, 68912, Singapore, ☎00 65 6889 8960, ✉stephanietan@gic.com.sg, *Call Date: Nov 2007, Middle Temple*
Qualifications: [MA (Hons) (Cantab)]

TANNER MS LIZ ANNE

Commercial Lawyer, Director, Senior Legal Adviser, Scottish & Southern Energy, Legal Services, 55 Vastern Road, Reading, Berkshire, RG1 8BU, *Call Date: Nov 1994, Inner Temple*
Qualifications: [LLB (Wales)]

TANSER MR ANDREW JOHN

Crown Prosecution Service, 2 King Edward Court, King Edward Street, Nottingham, Nottinghamshire, NG1 1EL, ☎0115 852 3300, ✉Andrew.Tanser@cps.gsi.gov.uk, *Call Date: Oct 1996, Gray's Inn*
Qualifications: [LLB (Notts)]

TAPPER MISS LUCY OLIVIA

Reeds Solicitors, 1 Cambridge Terrace, Oxford, OX1 1RR, ☎01865 260230
Fax: 01865 246968, *Call Date: Nov 2002, Middle Temple*
Qualifications: [LLB (Hons) (Oxon)]

TAUSZ MRS DILYS KIM

Royal Courts of Justice, Administrative Court Office, The Strand, London, WC2A 2LL, ☎020 7435 5996, *Call Date: July 1974, Inner Temple*
Qualifications: [LLB (Hons)]

TAWSE MR ALISTAIR ROBERT JAMES

Chris Kallis Solicitors, 33 North Road East, Plymouth, Devon, PL4 6AY, *Call Date: July 2007, Lincoln's Inn*
Qualifications: [BSc (Plymouth)]

TAYLER MRS KERI

Hampshire County Council, Chief Executive's Department, Elizabeth 2 Court, The Castle, Winchester, SD23 8UJ, ☎01962 847353 Fax: 01962 845031, ✉keri.tayler@hants.gov.uk, *Call Date: Feb 1995, Inner Temple*
Qualifications: [LLB (So'ton)]

TAYLOR MR CHRISTOPHER PAUL

Other, Enviroment Agency, Kingfisher House, Serious Casework Group, Goldhay Way, Orton Goldhay, Peterborough, PE2 5ZR, ☎01733 464186 Fax: 01733 464487, ✉paul.taylor1@environment-agency.gov.uk, *Call Date: Oct 1990, Lincoln's Inn*
Qualifications: [LLB (Hons)]

TAYLOR MR IAN RUSSELL

Senior Legal Adviser, Office of Fair Trading, Fleetbank House, 2-6 Salisbury Square, London, EC4Y 8JX, ☎020 7211 8000, ✉ian.taylor@oft.gsi.gov.uk, *Call Date: Mar 1998, Gray's Inn*
Qualifications: [MA (Cantab)]

TAYLOR MR MICHAEL JOHN

Director, Onslow Partnership LLP, 104 William Court, 6 Hall Road, London, NW8 9PB, ☎020 7289 6585 Fax: 020 7289 6585, *Call Date: Feb 1986, Gray's Inn*
Qualifications: [BA]

TAYLOR MR RICHARD GRAHAM

Legal Adviser, Slough Magistrates' Court, Chalvey Park, Off Windsor Road, Slough, SL1 2HJ, ✉richard.taylor@hmcourts-service.gsi.gov.uk, *Call Date: Oct 1992, Gray's Inn*
Qualifications: [BA (Hons) MBA Dip Law]

TAYLOR MR SCOTT GRAHAM JOHN

John Mcaslan and Partners, 7-9 William Road, London, NW1 3ER, ☎020 7313 6000 Fax: 020 7313 6001, ✉s.taylor@mcaslan.co.uk, *Call Date: July 2002, Middle Temple*
Qualifications: [LLB (Hons) (Derby)]

TAYLOR MISS SUSAN MARY EDITH

HMRC Solicitorés Office, 100 Parliament Street, London, SW1A 2BQ, *Call Date: July 1980, Middle Temple*
Qualifications: [LLB (Leeds)]

TAYLOR-CAMARA MR ELDRED

London Borough of Barking and Dagenham, First Floor Annex, Civic Centre, Dagenham, RM10 7BN, *Call Date: July 1981, Gray's Inn*

TEAH MRS JACQUELINE MOOI HUA

Aviva Legal Services, Aviva Investors Global Services Ltd, No 1 Poultry, London, EC2R 8EJ, *Call Date: Feb 1992, Lincoln's Inn*
Qualifications: [LLB (Hons) LLM]

TEASDALE MR DAVID ANDREW

Royal Navy Officers, Dnls, Mp 4.2 Leach Building, Whale Island, Portsmouth, Hampshire, PO2 8BY, *Call Date: Nov 2007, Middle Temple*
Qualifications: [BA (Hons) (Dunelm) PgDL]

TEASDALE MR JONATHAN PAUL

Chief Executive, Lawyer, Other, Law Commission, Steel House, 11 Tothill Street, London, SW1H 9LJ, ☎020 3334 0241, ✉jonathan.teasdale@lawcommission.gsi.gov.uk, *Call Date: July 1977, Inner Temple*
Qualifications: [LARTPI LLM FRSA]

TEELUCK MR SUNIL BHISMA

The Home Office, Room Sg52, Seacole House, 2 Marsham Street, London, SW1P 4DF, ☎020 8917 2158, *Call Date: Nov 2004, Gray's Inn*
Qualifications: [LLB (Herts)]

TEHAL MR TANVIR

Serious Fraud Office, Elm House, 10-16 Elm Street, London, WC1X 0BJ, ☎020 7239 7295, ✉tanvir.tehal@sfo.gsi.gov.uk, *Call Date: Nov 1996, Middle Temple*
Qualifications: [LLB (Hons)]

TEICHMAN MRS SANDRA ANITA

Director, Pillsbury Winthrop Shaw Pittman, Tower 42, Level 23, 25 Old Broad Street, London, EC2N 1HQ, ☎020 7847 9560 Fax: 020 7847 9501, ✉sandra.teichman@pillsburylaw.com, *Call Date: Nov 1988, Middle Temple*
Qualifications: [LLB (Essex)]

TELFER MISS FREDELINDA JANE

Call Date: Feb 1995, Middle Temple
Qualifications: [Dip in Stage Management LLB (Hons)]

TEO MISS MAY MAY

Lawyer, Upper Tribunal Appeal Chamber, 5th Floor Rolls Buildings, 7 Rolls Buildings, Fetter Lane, London, EC4A 1NL, *Call Date: July 1989, Middle Temple*
Qualifications: [LLB (Hons)]

TERRY MISS MICHELLE CAMILLA

Prosecutor, London Borough of Hackney, Town Hall, 298 More Street, London, E8 1HE, ☎020 8356 6198 Fax: 020 8356 6251, *Call Date: Nov 2000, Inner Temple*
Qualifications: [LLB (Lond)]

TERRY MISS MICHELLE JANE EVELYN

Advocate, Crown Prosecution Service, Black Horse House, 8-10 Leigh Road, Eastleigh, Hampshire, SO50 9FH, ✉jane.terry@cps.gsi.gov.uk, WinchesterTrials.Unit@cps.gsi.gov.uk, *Call Date: July 1988, Lincoln's Inn*
Qualifications: [LLB (Hons)]

TETSOLA MISS AUGUSTINA

Crown Prosecution Service, City Gate House, 185 Dyke Road, Hove, East Sussex, BN3 1TL, ☎01273 765 600, *Call Date: July 1988, Lincoln's Inn*
Qualifications: [LLB (Hons) (Essex)]

TEW MR JOHN PHILIP

Crown Advocate, Senior Crown Prosecutor, Crown Prosecution Service, Froomsgate House, Rupert Street, Bristol, BS1 2QJ, ✉philip.tew@cps.gsi.gov.uk, *Call Date: Oct 1993, Lincoln's Inn*
Qualifications: [BA (Hons) LLM]

THAKOR MISS AARTI

Legal Adviser, Charity Commission, Harmsworth House, 13 Bouverie Street, London, EC4Y 8DP, ☎0845 300 0218, *Call Date: Oct 2004, Inner Temple*
Qualifications: [BA (Cantab)]

THATCHER MISS NICHOLA JANE

Head of Legal Services, Police Headquarters, Norfolk Constabulary, Jubilee House, Falconer's Chase, Wymondham, Norfolk, NR18 0WW, ☎01953 423922 Fax: 01953 423926, ✉thatchern@norfolk.pnn.police.uk, *Call Date: Nov 1992, Inner Temple*
Qualifications: [LLB (Hons)]

THATCHER MR ROGER FRANCIS

FSOL, Tosswill and Co, 260 Britxon Hill, London, SW2 1HP, ☎020 8674 9494, *Call Date: Feb 1977, Gray's Inn*
Qualifications: [Dip Criminology]

THOMAS MR DOMINIC RAPHAEL MARC

Artesian Law, 3 Bolt Court, Fleet Street, London, EC4A 3DQ, ✉dominic.thomas@artesianlaw.com, *Call Date: Nov 1998, Gray's Inn*
Qualifications: [MA (Oxon)]

THOMAS MISS KATIE

Riley Hayes Solicitors, 24 Waterloo Street, Wolverhampton, WV1 4BL, Fax: 01902 713187, *Call Date: Oct 1994, Gray's Inn*
Qualifications: [LLB]

THOMAS MISS LAURA ELIZABETH

Birketts LLP, 24-26 Museum Street, Ipswich, Suffolk, *Call Date: Oct 2001, Gray's Inn*
Qualifications: [BA (Oxon)]

THOMAS MISS VICTORIA LOUISE

Other, Directorate of Legal Services (Raf), Care of Wg Cdr V L Mckillop-Duffy, Deputy Legal Adviser, United Kingdom Joint Support Unit, Joint Force Headquarters, Brunssum, BFPO 28, Netherlands, *Call Date: Nov 1996, Inner Temple*
Qualifications: [LLB (Reading)]

THOMASSON MISS CLAIRE MARGARET MARY

Crown Advocate, Crown Prosecution Service, St Ann's Quay, 122 Quayside, Newcastle Upon Tyne, Tyne and Wear, NE1 3BD, ✉claire.thomasson@cps.gsi.gov.uk, *Call Date: Oct 1991, Gray's Inn*
Qualifications: [BA (Hons)]

THOMLINSON MR PETER ROBERT

Legal Adviser, Mitsubishi Electric Europe B.V, Travellers Lane, Hatfield, Hertfordshire, AL10 8XB, ☎01707 276100 Fax: 01707 278525, ✉peter.thomlinson@meuk.mee.com, *Call Date: July 1981, Lincoln's Inn*
Qualifications: [BA LLM]

THOMPSON MRS ANUPAMA

Nursing and Midwifery Council, 23 Portland Place, London, W1B 1PZ, ✉anupama.thompson@nmc-uk.org, *Call Date: Nov 1994, Inner Temple*
Qualifications: [LLB (Hons) (Essex)]

THOMPSON MR CEDRIC AUGUSTUS

Charles Allotey and Co Solicitors, 334 Coldharbour Lane, London, SW9 8QH, *Call Date: Nov 1984, Gray's Inn*
Qualifications: [BA (Hons)]

THOMPSON MR LYALL NORRIS

Crown Prosecution Service, Isleworth Crown Court, 36 Ridgeway Road, Isleworth, London, TW7 5LP, *Call Date: Oct 1995, Inner Temple*
Qualifications: [LLB (Aberdeen) CPE (lond)]

THOMPSON MR MARCUS ELLIOT GERARD

Walkers, 3rd Floor, 6 Gracechurch Street, London, EC3V 0AT, ☎020 7220 4979, ✉marcus.thompson@walkersglobal.com, *Call Date: Oct 1996, Inner Temple*
Qualifications: [BA (Cantab) CPE MA (Cantab)]

THOMPSON MISS MEGAN MARY ELIZABETH

HM Revenue and Customs, Room 2c/03, Solicitor's Office, 100 Parliament Street, London, SW1A 2BQ, ☎020 7147 2891, ✉megan.thompson@hmrc.gsi.gov.uk, *Call Date: Oct 2000, Middle Temple*
Qualifications: [BA (Hons) (Cantab) MA (Cantab)]

THOMPSON MISS SAMANTHA

Advocate, Crown Prosecution Service, United House, Piccadilly, York, North Yorkshire, YO1 9PQ, ☎01904 545409 Fax: 01904 545840, ✉Sam.Thompson@cps.gsi.gov.uk, *Call Date: Mar 1996, Gray's Inn*
Qualifications: [BSc (Hons)]

THOMPSON MISS SAMANTHA JADE

Kennedys, 2nd Floor, Terrington House, 13-15 Hills Road, Cambridge, CB2 1NL, *Call Date: July 2003, Middle Temple*
Qualifications: [LLB Hons (Newc)]

THOMPSTONE MISS HELEN FIONA

Ministry of Defence, CTLB SSBC - MOD, Mail Point G-M-12, Main Building, Whitehall, London, SW1A 2HB, *Call Date: Nov 1998, Middle Temple*
Qualifications: [LLB (Hons)(Lond)]

THOMSON MR BEN

Arnold and Porter (Uk) LLP, Tower 42, 25 Old Broad Street, London, EC2N 1HQ, ☎020 7786 6100 Fax: 020 7786 6299, *Call Date: Nov 2001, Middle Temple*
Qualifications: [BSc (Hons) MSc MA]

THOMSON MR JEFFREY JOHN RUDOLF

Norton Rose LLP, 3 More London Riverside, London, SE1 2AQ, ✉jef.thomson@nortonrose.com, *Call Date: Nov 2004, Inner Temple*
Qualifications: [BCOMM McGill University Montreal Canada LLB Kin]

THOMSON MR MARK ALLAN

HM Revenue and Customs, HMRC Solicitor's Office, Bush House, Strand, London, WC2B 4RD, Fax: 020 7438 9160, ✉mark.thomson1@hmrc.gsi.gov.uk, *Call Date: Oct 2006, Lincoln's Inn*
Qualifications: [MSCi (Glasgow) MSc (Oxon)]

THOMSON MRS SALLY MARGARET

Principal Crown Prosecutor, Hennessy & Hammudi Solicitors, 44 Queen's Road, Reading, Berkshire, RG1 4AU, Fax: 0118 959 6167, ✉info@hennessyandhammudi.com, *Call Date: July 1982, Gray's Inn*
Qualifications: [BA (Hons) (Keele)]

THORNE MISS SARAH LOUISE

Harringtons Solicitors, 83 Ditchling Road, Brighton, BN1 4SD, *Call Date: Feb 1995, Middle Temple*
Qualifications: [LLB (Hons)(Lond)]

THORNTON MR PHILIP CHARLES

Lexis Nexis (Butterworths Ltd), Halsbury House, 35 Chancery Lane, London, WC2A 1EL, *Call Date: Nov 1988, Middle Temple*
Qualifications: [MA (Cantab) MSc (Lond)]

THUKRAL MR RAVINDER KUMAR

Brown Rudnick LLP, 8 Clifford Street, London, W1S 2LQ, Fax: 020 7851 6100, ✉rthukral@brownrudnick.com, *Call Date: Nov 2007, Lincoln's Inn*
Qualifications: [LLB (Lond)]

TIGER MISS SAMANTHA JAYNE

Health & Safety Executive, Redgrave Court, Melton Road, Bootle, Merseyside, L20 7HS, *Call Date: Nov 2000, Lincoln's Inn*
Qualifications: [LLB (Hons) (L'Pool)]

TILT MISS MARCIA JANE MARGARET

Wiltshire Council, County Hall, Bythesea Road, Trowbridge, Wiltshire, BN14 8JN, ☎01225 713 063 Fax: 01225 713 025, ✉marciatilt@wiltshire.gov.uk, *Call Date: July 1991, Lincoln's Inn*
Qualifications: [LLB (Hons)(Wales)]

TIMSON-HUNT MR DAREN FREDERICK

Legal Adviser, HM Revenue and Customs, Solicitors Office, 100 Parliament Street, London, SW1A 2BQ, ☎020 7147 3996, *Call Date: July 2001, Lincoln's Inn*
Qualifications: [LLB (Hons) (Lond) MIEx]

TITCHARD MR DENIS JOHN

General Counsel, Legal Adviser, Kewill PLC, Bramley House, the Guildway, Old Portsmouth Road, Artington, Guildford, Surrey, GU3 1LR, ☎01483 406 055 Fax: 01483 406 001, ✉denis.titchard@kewill.com, *Call Date: Oct 2000, Gray's Inn*
Qualifications: [LLB (Westminster)]

TITCHENER MR ALAN JOHN

General Counsel, Cppgroup PLC, Holgate Park, York, YO26 4GA, ☎01904 544757, ✉John.Titchener@cpp.co.uk, *Call Date: Feb 1990, Lincoln's Inn*
Qualifications: [LLB (Hons) (Leeds)]

TIWARI MR SEAN

Adviser, Other, Vtb Capital PLC, 14 Cornhill, London, EC3V 3ND, ☎020 3334 8000 Fax: 020 3334 8900, ✉helpdesk@vtbeurope.com, *Call Date: Nov 1993, Inner Temple*
Qualifications: [BA (Oxon) Dip Law]

TODHUNTER MR STEPHEN EDWARD

Her Majesty's Courts Service, Greenwich Magistrates Court, 9 Blackhealth Road, Greenwich, London, SE10 8PE, ☎020 8276 1334 Fax: 020 8276 1397, *Call Date: Apr 1989, Lincoln's Inn*
Qualifications: [LLB (Lanc)]

TOLAN MR ANTHONY

Company Secretary, Hitachi Europe Limited, Whitebrook Park, Lower Cookham Road, Maidenhead, Berkshire, SL6 8YA, ☎01628 585000 Fax: 01628 585380, ✉tony.tolan@hitachi-eu.com, *Call Date: Nov 1974, Lincoln's Inn*
Qualifications: [BA]

TOLHURST MR ROBERT LEIGH DOUGLAS

Shearman Bowen and Co Solicitors, 16 Tooks Court, Cursitor Street, London, EC4A 1LB, ✉robert@shearmanbowen.co.uk, *Call Date: Oct 1992, Middle Temple*
Qualifications: [BA (Hons)]

TOLLAND MS ANNE MARIE

Senior Legal Adviser, South Somerset Magistrates' Court, The Law Courts, Petters Way, Yeovil, Somerset, BA20 1SW, ☎01935 426281 Fax: 01935 431022, *Call Date: July 1988, Lincoln's Inn*
Qualifications: [LLB (Hons) (Sheff)]

TOMAN MR VINCENT

Lewis Silkin LLP, 5 Chancery Lane, Cliffords Inn, London, EC4A 1BL, Fax: 020 7864 1270, ✉vince.toman@lewissilkin.com, *Call Date: Nov 1988, Inner Temple*
Qualifications: [LLB (Sheff)]

TOMANY MR DECLAN

Lawyer, Partner, Office of Gas and Electricity Markets (Ofgem), Office of Gas and Electricity Markets, 9 Millbank, London, SW1P 3GE, ☎020 7901 7015 Fax: 020 7901 7128, ✉declan.tomany@ofgem.gov.uk, *Call Date: Oct 1997, Lincoln's Inn*
Qualifications: [LLB (Hons)]

TOOGOOD MISS KATHERINE SARAH

Legal Adviser, Her Majesty's Courts Service, Westminster Magistrates Court, 181 Marylebone Road, London, NW1 5BR, Fax: 020 3103 3051, ✉katherine.toogood@hmcts.gsi.gov.uk, *Call Date: Nov 1998, Gray's Inn*
Qualifications: [LLB]

TOOLEY MR MICHAEL PHILIP

Senior Crown Prosecutor, Crown Prosecution Service, Greenfield House, 32 Scotland Street, Sheffield, South Yorkshire, S3 7DQ, ☎0114 229 8600, *Call Date: Nov 1982, Gray's Inn*
Qualifications: [LLB (Reading)]

TOWLER COMMANDER ALISON

Royal Navy Officers, M-P 4-2 Fleet Headquarters, Sir Henry Leach Building, Whale Island, Portsmouth, Hampshire, PO2 8BY, ☎023 92625866 Fax: 023 92625755, ✉alison.towler228@mod.uk, fleet-dnlscwkteamleaderso1@mod.uk, *Call Date: Oct 1995, Gray's Inn*
Qualifications: [B.Sc (Wales) PG Dip (Business Law) (Portsmouth)]

TOWNLEY MISS LYNNE

Crown Prosecution Service, Woolwich Crown Court, 2 Belmarsh Road, London, SE28 0EY, Fax: 020 8855 0514, ✉Lynne.Townley@cps.gsi.gov.uk, *Call Date: Oct 1996, Middle Temple*
Qualifications: [LLB (Hons) LLM (B'ham)]

TOWNSEND MS JACQUELINE MARY

Crown Prosecution Service, Southern House, Wellesley Grove, Croydon, Surrey, CR9 1DY, *Call Date: Nov 2002, Inner Temple*
Qualifications: [BSc (So'ton) CPE]

TOWNSEND MR JOHN CARL

Guney Clark and Ryan Solicitors, 58 Green Lanes, London, N16 9NH, ☎020 7275 7788, *Call Date: Nov 2006, Middle Temple*
Qualifications: [BA (Hons) PgDip Law]

TOWNSEND MR JOHN WILLIAM JAMES

Assistant, The Competition Commission, Victoria House, Southampton Row, London, WC1B 4AD, ☎020 7271 0100, ✉john.townsend@cc.gsi.gov.uk, *Call Date: July 2006, Lincoln's Inn*
Qualifications: [BA (Oxon) LLB LLM (Lond)]

TOWNSEND MR ROBERT

Crown Prosecution Service, The Regatta, 6 Henley Buisness Park, Doddington Road, Lincoln, LN6 3QR, ☎01522 585900 Fax: 01522 585959, ✉rob.townsend@cps.gsi.gov.uk, *Call Date: Oct 2007, Lincoln's Inn*
Qualifications: [LLB (Nott'm)]

TOWNSEND MISS STEPHANIE HOLLY BLIGH

Legal Adviser, HMCTS, Osprey House, PO Box 10754, Chelmsford, Essex, CM1 9PZ, Fax: 01245 313399, ✉stephanie.townsend1@hmcourts-service.gsi.gov.uk, stephanie.townsend1@hmcts.gsi.gov.uk, *Call Date: Oct 1998, Inner Temple*
Qualifications: [LLB MSc]

TOWNSLEY MR JON EDWARD DANIEL

Assistant Legal Adviser, Ministry of Defence, Po Box 1680, London, SW1P 1ZE, Fax: 020 7218 9039, *Call Date: Mar 1998, Middle Temple*
Qualifications: [LLB (Hons)(Sussex)]

TRAIN MR TOBY JAMES

Company Secretary, General Counsel, Head of Legal Services, Legal Director, Rexel Uk Limited, 5th Floor, Maple House, Mutton Lane, Potters Bar, Hertforshire, EN6 5BS, ✉toby.train@rexel.co.uk, *Call Date: July 2002, Middle Temple*
Qualifications: [LLB (Hons) (L'pool) LLM (Cantab)]

TRANTER MR GAVIN ANDREW

David Phillips & Partners, 202 Stanley Road, Bootle, Merseyside, L20 3EP, *Call Date: Oct 1996, Middle Temple*
Qualifications: [BA (Hons) (Cantab)]

TRAVERS MR MICHAEL GARRY

Senior Crown Prosecutor, Crown Prosecution Service, United House, Piccadilly, York, North Yorkshire, YO1 1PQ, *Call Date: July 1985, Middle Temple*
Qualifications: [LLB (L'pool)]

TREIP MR MICHAEL ANTHONY JOHN

Financial Services Authority, The Financial Services Authority, Enforcement and Financial Crime Division - Legal Group, 25 The North Colonade, Canary Wharf, London, E14 5HS, *Call Date: Nov 1995, Inner Temple*
Qualifications: [LLB (Lond) M.Phil (Cantab)]

TRIMBLE MR ANDREW MARK

Nexus Chambers, 7 New Square, Lincolns Inn, London, WC2A 3QS, ☎020 7404 1147 Fax: 020 7 9744, ✉andrew.trimble@nexuschambers.com, *Call Date: Oct 2006, Inner Temple*
Qualifications: [BA (Oxon)]

TRIPCONY MISS CLARE

Crown Prosecution Service, Central Fraud Group, Sunlight House, Quay Street, Manchester, M3 3LU, *Call Date: Oct 2007, Lincoln's Inn*
Qualifications: [LLB (Manch)]

TROUNSON MR RICHARD NOY

Lawyer, Dla Piper Uk LLP, 3 Noble Street, London, EC2V 7EE, ☎020 7796 6318 Fax: 020 7796 6588, ✉noy.trounson@dlapiper.com, *Call Date: Nov 1975, Lincoln's Inn*
Qualifications: [MA (Oxon)]

TROVATO MR DAVID ALAN

Crown Prosecution Service, Rose Court, 2 Southwark Bridge, London, SE1 9HS, Fax: 020 3357 0389, ✉David.Trovato@cps.gsi.gov.uk, *Call Date: July 2002, Middle Temple*
Qualifications: [LLB (Hons) (Nott'm)]

TRUEMAN MR SCOTT ANDREW

Ministry of Justice, Legal Directorate, 102 Petty France, London, SW1H 9AS, *Call Date: Oct 1996, Middle Temple*
Qualifications: [LLB (Hons)(Manc)]

TSE MR NICHOLAS HON KEUNG

Lawyer, Partner, Brown Rudnick LLP, 8 Clifford Street, London, W1S 2LQ, Fax: 020 7851 6100, ✉ntse@brownerudnick.com, *Call Date: Nov 1995, Inner Temple*
Qualifications: [BA (Oxon) Maitre de Lettres (France) CPE MCI Arb]

TUBB MRS ELIZABETH JANET MARY

Director, Cunnigham Lesley Loves Ltd, Suite 520, 3030 Rocky Point Drive, Florida, 33607, USA, *Call Date: Nov 1989, Middle Temple*
Qualifications: [LLB (Hons)]

TUCKER MISS CLARE ELIZABETH

Crown Advocate, Crown Prosecution Service, Gemini One, Oxford Business Park South, Garsington Road, Oxford, Oxfordshire, OX4 2LL, ☎01865 233 400 Fax: 01865 233401, ✉clare.tucker@cps.gsi.gov.uk, *Call Date: July 1982, Gray's Inn*
Qualifications: [LLB]

TUDWAY MR STEPHEN WILLIAM

Milbank, Tweed, Hadley and Mccloy, 10 Gresham Street, London, EC2V 7JD, ☎020 7615 3023, ✉SWTudway@milbank.com, *Call Date: Oct 1998, Lincoln's Inn*
Qualifications: [MA (Hons) (Oxon)]

TUMBRIDGE MR JAMES RICHARD

Gowlings (Uk) LLP, 15th Floor, 125 Old Broad Street, London, EC2N 1AR, *Call Date: Nov 2001, Lincoln's Inn*
Qualifications: [LLB (Hons)]

TURFITT MR RICHARD JAMES GRENVILLE

Commissioner, Office of the Traffic Commissioner, City House, 126-130 Hills Road, Cambridge, CB2 1NP, ☎01223 531 028 Fax: 01223 309 681, *Call Date: Oct 1993, Middle Temple*
Qualifications: [LLB (Hons)(Kingston) FCILT]

TURNBULL MISS GLENDA

Legal Adviser, Crown Prosecution Service, St Ann's Quay, 122 Quayside, Newcastle Upon Tyne, Tyne and Wear, NE1 3BD, *Call Date: July 1998, Gray's Inn*
Qualifications: [LLB (Hons)(Luton)]

F

TURNER MR ALAN RICHARD

Senior Legal Adviser, BP PLC, 1 St James's Square, London, SW1Y 4PD, ✉turnerar@bp.com, *Call Date: July 1992, Inner Temple*
Qualifications: [LLB (Hons) (Lond) BSc (Hons) (Wales)]

TURNER MISS JANET MARY

Berwin Leighton Paisner, Adelaide House, London Bridge, London, EC4R 9HA, Fax: 020 3400 1111, ✉janet.turnerQC@blplaw.com, *Call Date: Nov 1979, Middle Temple*
Qualifications: [LLB (Bris)]

TURNER MR JOSEPH SEYMOUR HUME

Assistant Deputy Coroner, Legal Adviser, Royal Navy Officers, Director Naval Legal Services, Mail Point 4-2, Sir Henry Leach Building, Whale Island, Portsmouth, PO2 8BY, ☎02392 625737, ✉joe.turner601@mod.uk, *Call Date: Oct 1997, Gray's Inn*
Qualifications: [MA (Edin) Dip Law]

TURNER MR MARCUS PHILIP ROBERT

HED, Roadrunner Music Group, Zwarteweg 10, 1412gd Naarden, Netherlands, ☎31-35-6971246 Fax: 31-35-6971394, ✉mturner@cnrentertainment.nl, *Call Date: Nov 1991, Middle Temple*
Qualifications: [LLB (Hons) (Lond)]

TURNER MR NIGEL STUART

Emms Gilmore Librson, Lancaster House, 67 New Hall Street, Birmingham, *Call Date: Nov 1990, Gray's Inn*
Qualifications: [LLB (Hons)(B'ham)]

TURNER MRS RHONDA NATALIE

Legal Adviser, The Law Society, Ipsley Court, Berrington Close, Redditch, Worcestershire, B98 0TD, ☎01527 517971 X 3182 Fax: 01527 883267, ✉natalie.turner@lawsociety.org.uk, *Call Date: Nov 1984, Middle Temple*
Qualifications: [BA(Hons)]

TURNER MISS ROWENA

Legal Counsel, Ingres Europe Ltd, 215 Bath Road, Slough, Berkshire, SL1 4AA, *Call Date: Nov 1996, Lincoln's Inn*
Qualifications: [LLB (Hons)(Lond) LLM (Wolv) FSALS]

TURNILL MR JAMES LINDSAY

Director, Department For Environment, Food & Rural Affairs, Area 3f, Ergon House, Horseferry Road, London, SW1P 2AL, ☎020 7238 0521, *Call Date: Nov 1989, Middle Temple*
Qualifications: [BA (Hons) (York) DipLaw]

TURNOCK MISS SARAH EMILY

The Home Office, Seacole, Ground Floor, 2 Marsham Street, London, SW1P 4DF, Fax: 020 7035 6433, ✉sarah.turnock@homeoffice.gsi.gov.uk, *Call Date: Oct 2007, Inner Temple*
Qualifications: [LLB (Lond)]

TUTTIETT MISS EMILY PATRICIA JAYNE

The Directorate of Legal Services, Welsh Assembly Government, Room G05, Cathays Park, Cardiff, Wales, CF10 3NQ, *Call Date: Oct 2004, Gray's Inn*
Qualifications: [LLB Wales]

TWITE MS JENNIFER ANNE RAY

Lawrence and Co Solicitors, 404 Harrow Road, London, W9 2HU, ☎020 7266 4333 Fax: 020 7289 3161, ✉jen@law.com, *Call Date: Oct 2006, Inner Temple*
Qualifications: [BA (Oxon)]

TYLER MS ELIZABETH OSYTH EYRE

Legal Officer, Senior Lawyer, Office of Fair Trading, Fleetbank House, 2-6 Salisbury Square, London, EC4Y 8JX, ☎020 7211 8986, ✉elizabeth.tyler@oft.gsi.gov.uk, *Call Date: Oct 1997, Inner Temple*
Qualifications: [BA (York) CPE (Leic)]

UDEZE MR UFONDU KARUIKI

Lawyer, Nomura House, 1 Angel Lane, London, EC4R 3AB, *Call Date: Oct 1995, Inner Temple*
Qualifications: [LLB (Plymouth) LLM]

UFF MR ALEXANDER JOHN

Shearman & Sterling LLP, 114 Avenue Des Champs-Elysées, Paris, France, ☎00 33 1 53 89 70 00 Fax: 00 33 1 53 89 70 70, ✉alexander.uff@shearman.com, *Call Date: July 1998, Gray's Inn*
Qualifications: [BA LLM]

UHLMANN MS MARIA ANNA

Principal Lawyer, London Borough of Newham, Legal Services, Town Hall, Barking Road, East Ham, London, E6 2RP, ☎020 8430 3655, ✉maria.uhlmann@newham.gov.uk, *Call Date: Nov 1982, Lincoln's Inn*
Qualifications: [LLB NVQ5 Management]

UKONU CHIEF LUKE OBIA WUCHUKWU

Legal Adviser, C I O Security Ltd, 9 Dartmouth Road, London, SE23 3HN, ☎020 8699 5555 Fax: 020 8699 9000, ✉ciosecurity@hotmail.com, *Call Date: July 2001, Gray's Inn*
Qualifications: [LLB (Lond)]

UNDERHILL MISS CAROLINE PATRICIA

Legal Adviser, Thompsons Solicitors, Congress House, Great Russell Street, London, WC1B 3LW, ☎020 7290 0000 Fax: 020 7637 0000, ✉carolineunderhill@thompsons.law.co.uk, *Call Date: July 1982, Gray's Inn*
Qualifications: [BSc (Hons)(Bris)]

UNDERWOOD MR STEPHEN CHRISTOPHER

Department For Transport, Great Minster House, Room 1/04c, 76 Marsham Street, London, SW1P 4DR, *Call Date: Nov 2008, Lincoln's Inn*
Qualifications: [LLB (So'ton) LLM (Lond)]

UPTON MR JOHN DOMINIC

Financial Services Authority, 25 The North Colannade, Canary Wharf, London, E14 8HS, *Call Date: Mar 1997, Middle Temple*
Qualifications: [MA (Hons)]

URQUHART MS MHAIRI CHRISTINE

Senior Lawyer, Crown Prosecution Service, Rose Court, 2 Southwark Bridge, London, SE1 9HS, *Call Date: Nov 1984, Gray's Inn*
Qualifications: [LLB (B'ham)]

USHER MR RICHARD IAN

Director, Morgan Stanley and Co International PLC, 25 Cabot Square, Canary Wharf, London, E14 4QW, ☎020 7677 2484 Fax: 020 7056 1138, ✉Richard.Usher@morganstanley.com, *Call Date: Oct 1996, Gray's Inn*
Qualifications: [LLB (Hons) LLM (Sheff)]

UUKELO MISS ANNA NDINELAGO TALENI

London Borough of Hillingdon, Legal Services 3e/04, Civic Centre, High Street, Uxbridge, Middlesex, UB8 1UW, ☎01895 277 028 Fax: 01895 250 784, ✉anna.uukelo@hillingdon.gov.uk, *Call Date: July 2008, Lincoln's Inn*
Qualifications: [BJUR LLB LLM]

VAHEY MR PHILIP THOMAS ANTHONY

Director of Legal Services, Justices' Clerk, HMCS Kent, Sussex & Surrey, Horsham Magistrates Court, HMCTS, Hurst Road, Horsham, West Sussex, RH12 2ET, *Call Date: Nov 1986, Inner Temple*
Qualifications: [MBA]

VALANSOT MISS CHRISTIANE

General Counsel, Investment Management Association, 65 Kingsway, London, WC2B 6TD, ☎020 7269 4647, ✉cvalansot@investmentuk.org, *Call Date: Nov 1989, Middle Temple*
Qualifications: [BA]

VALERA MISS ELIZABETH

Senior Crown Prosecutor, Crown Prosecution Service, Oxford House, Oxford Road, Bournemouth, Dorset, BH8 8HA, ☎01202 498 700, *Call Date: Oct 1991, Middle Temple*
Qualifications: [BA (Hons) (Kent)]

VALLANCE MR PHILIP IAN FERGUS

Berrymans Lace Mawer LLP, Salisbury House, London Wall, London, EC2M 5QN, ☎020 7638 2811 Fax: 020 7920 0361, *Call Date: July 1968, Inner Temple*
Qualifications: [BA (Oxon)]

VALLES MR JAIME ALBERT

Lancashire County Council, County Hall, P O Box 78, Preston, PR1 8XJ, ☎01772 533 400 Fax: 01772 533612, ✉jaime.valles@css.lancscc.gov.uk, *Call Date: Oct 1992, Middle Temple*
Qualifications: [LLM (Lond) LLB (Lancs)]

F

VAMOS MR NICHOLAS PAUL

Crown Prosecution Service, Rose Court, 2 Southwark Bridge, London, SE1 9HS, ✉nick.vamos@fco.gov.uk, *Call Date: Oct 1998, Lincoln's Inn*
Qualifications: [BA (Hons) CPE]

VAN DER STRAETEN MS LOUISE

Senior Lawyer, The Treasury Solicitors, Attorney General's Office, 20 Victoria Street, London, SW1H 0NF, Fax: 020 7271 2453, ✉louise.vanderstraeten@attorneygeneral.gsi.gov.uk, *Call Date: July 2000, Middle Temple*
Qualifications: [BSc(Hons)(Lond) FCCA]

VAN DER WAL MR DOMINIC PIET

Lawyer, The Treasury Solicitors, One Kemble Street, London, WC2B 4TS, ☎020 7210 6188 Fax: 020 7210 3214, ✉dominic.vanderwal@tsol.gsi.gov.uk, *Call Date: Oct 1996, Lincoln's Inn*
Qualifications: [LLB (Hons)(Lond)]

VANTYGHEM MR JULIEN DARREN

Clerk, Her Majesty's Courts Service, West London Magistrates' Court, 181 Talgarth Road, London, W6 8DN, ☎020 8700 9302 / 020 8700 9302, ✉julien.vantyghem@hmcourts-service.gsi.gov.uk, *Call Date: Oct 1992, Inner Temple*
Qualifications: [LLB]

VARLEY MS SARAH-JANE

M and M Solicitors, 24 King Street, Leicester, LE1 6RL, ☎0116 285 2300 Fax: 0116 285 2303, ✉contactus@mandmsolicitors.com, *Call Date: July 2001, Gray's Inn*
Qualifications: [LLB (Hons) Lancaster]

VARSANI MR DIPAN HARJI

Crown Advocate, Higher Court Advocate, Senior Crown Prosecutor, Crown Prosecution Service, Harrow Crown Court, Hailsham Drive, Harrow, HA1 4TU, Fax: 020 8424 0423, ✉Dipan.Varsani@cps.gsi.gov.uk, *Call Date: Oct 1999, Inner Temple*
Qualifications: [LLB (Hons) Mdx LLM (City)]

VATISH MRS ANJULIKA

St Law, 74 Ilford Lane, Ilford, Essex, IG1 2LA, *Call Date: Mar 2009, Gray's Inn*
Qualifications: [Transferring Solicitor]

VATVANI MISS PRIYA

Olswang LLP, 90 High Holborn, London, WC1V 6XX, ☎020 7067 3000 Fax: 020 7067 3999, ✉priya.vatvani@olswang.com, *Call Date: Nov 2002, Lincoln's Inn*
Qualifications: [BSc (Hons)(Bris)]

VAUGHAN MRS LISA LORRAINE

EEF Ltd, EEF House, Queensway North, Team Valley Trading Estate, Gateshead, NE11 0NX, *Call Date: July 2005, Middle Temple*
Qualifications: [LLB (Hons)]

VAUGHAN MRS SIAN CLAIR

Crown Prosecution Service, Heol Penlanffos, Tanerdy, Dyfed, Carmarthen, SA31 2EZ, ☎01267 242100, *Call Date: July 2002, Lincoln's Inn*
Qualifications: [LLB (Hons) MA]

VENING-RICHARDS MRS HILARY JANE

Senior Crown Prosecutor, Crown Prosecution Service, Princes Court, 34 York Road, Leicester, Leicestershire, LE1 5TU, ☎0116 2046700, ✉hilary.vening-richards@cps.gsi.gov.uk, *Call Date: Nov 1990, Middle Temple*
Qualifications: [BA]

VENKATASAMI MR KRIS

District Crown Prosecutor, Crown Prosecution Service, Rose Court, 2 Southwark Bridge, London, SE1 9HS, *Call Date: July 1989, Lincoln's Inn*
Qualifications: [LLB (Hons) MA MPhil]

VENKOV MS JOANNA

Legal Officer, The Treasury Solicitors, One Kemble Street, London, WC2B 4TS, ☎020 7210 3000, ✉Joanna.venkov@tsol.gsi.gov.uk, *Call Date: Oct 2007, Middle Temple*
Qualifications: [BA (Hons) (Oxon) LLb (Lond)]

VENTOM MR SYAN MARK

Environment Agency, Manley House, Kestrel Way, Exeter, EX2 7LQ, *Call Date: Nov 2008, Middle Temple*
Qualifications: [BSc (Hons) (Lond)]

F

VERGHIS MRS KATHRYN MARY

Principal Court Clerk, Her Majesty's Courts and Tribunals Service, Ealing Magistrates' Court, Green Man Lane, West Ealing, London, W13 0SD, *Call Date: Nov 1985, Inner Temple*
Qualifications: [LLB DMS]

VERGHIS MR MATHEW

HM Revenue and Customs, 1st Floor, South West Bush House, London, WC2B 4RD, *Call Date: Nov 1984, Inner Temple*
Qualifications: [LLB]

VIALL MISS DANIELLE NADINE

General Medical Council, Regent's Place, 350 Euston Road, London, NW1 3JN, ✉dviall@gmc-uk.org, *Call Date: July 2007, Inner Temple*
Qualifications: [BA (Lond)]

VICKERS MR PAUL ANDREW

Company Secretary, Legal Director, Trinity Mirror PLC, 1 Canada Square, London, E14 5AP, ☎020 7293 3359 Fax: 020 7293 3360, *Call Date: July 1983, Inner Temple*
Qualifications: [LLB (So'ton)]

VIDAL MS MAVELYN KATHLEEN

Duncan Lewis and Co Solicitors, 1 Kingsland High Street, London, E8 2JS, ☎020 7923 4020 Fax: 020 7923 3200, ✉mavelynv@duncanlewis.com, *Call Date: Nov 1986, Inner Temple*
Qualifications: [LLB]

VINCE MR DAVID SIBLEY

Ministry of Defence, Po Box 1680, London, SW1P 1ZE, *Call Date: Oct 1998, Middle Temple*
Qualifications: [MA (Oxon)]

VINCENT MISS RUTH

London Borough of Camden, Room 219, 2nd Floor, Town Hall, Judd Street, London, WC1H 9LP, ✉ruth.vincent@camden.gov.uk, *Call Date: Oct 1995, Gray's Inn*
Qualifications: [LLB (Manch)]

VIRDI MISS PRABHJOT KAUR

Call Date: Oct 1995, Lincoln's Inn
Qualifications: [LLB (Hons)(Leic)]

VIRTOPEANU MR GHEORGHE

The Chambers of Gheorghe Virtopeanu, 10 Clifford Road, London, E17 4JE, ☎07590 201391, *Call Date: Nov 2010, Lincoln's Inn*

VITTI MR NICHOLAS

Senior Crown Prosecutor, Crown Prosecution Service, Sunlight House, Quay Street, Manchester, M60 3PS, *Call Date: Feb 1992, Inner Temple*
Qualifications: [BA (Hons)(Sussex)]

WAGSTAFF MR MATTHEW EDWARD

CVS, Crown Prosecution Service, Rose Court, 2 Southwark Bridge, London, SE1 9HS, ☎020 3357 0326 Fax: 020 3357 0236, ✉matthew.wagstaff@cps.gsi.gov.uk, *Call Date: Oct 1993, Lincoln's Inn*
Qualifications: [LLB (Hons) (UEA)]

WAITE MR WILLIAM FRANCIS

Chief Executive, Vice President, The Risk Advisory Group PLC, Russell Square House, 10-12 Russell Square, London, WC1B 5EH, ☎020 7578 0000 Fax: 020 7578 7855, ✉bill.waite@riskadvisory.net, *Call Date: Nov 1984, Middle Temple*
Qualifications: [LLB (UEA) LLM (Lond)]

WAKEHAM MRS JANE ELIZABETH

Winckworth Sherwood LLP, Minerva House, 5 Montague Close, London, SE1 9BB, Fax: 020 7593 5099, *Call Date: Nov 1984, Middle Temple*
Qualifications: [LLB (Lond)]

WAKEHAM MR PHILIP JOHN LE MESSURIER

Horsman Solicitor's Ltd, 163 Malling Street, Lewes, East Sussex, BN7 2RB, ☎01273 474743 Fax: 01273 474896, ✉andy.horsman@horsmanloader.co.uk, *Call Date: July 1978, Middle Temple*
Qualifications: [BA]

WALCOTT MR STEPHEN JOHN

Legal Counsel, Aviva Legal Services, 5 Surrey Street, Po Box 89, Surrey Street, Norwich, NR1 3DR, *Call Date: Oct 1998, Middle Temple*
Qualifications: [BSc (Hons)(Herts) LLM]

WALEY MR SIMON FELIX

Crown Prosecution Service, Citadel House, 58 High Street, Hull, Humberside, HU1 1QD, ☎01482 621000, *Call Date: Feb 1988, Middle Temple*
Qualifications: [LLB (Exon)]

WALFORD MR JUSTIN HUGH

Legal Adviser, News Group Newspapers Ltd, 1 Virginia Street, London, E98 1LL, ☎020 7782 6832 Fax: 020 7782 6836, ✉justin.walford@newsint.co.uk, *Call Date: July 1981, Inner Temple*
Qualifications: [BA (Hons) (Sussex)]

WALKER MR ANDREW VIERSEN

Crown Prosecution Service, City Gate House, 185 Dyke Road, Hove, East Sussex, BN3 1TL, ☎01273 765600 Fax: 01273 765606, ✉andrew.walker@cps.gsi.gov.uk, *Call Date: Nov 1987, Inner Temple*
Qualifications: [BA Dip Law (Lond)]

WALKER MISS EMMA JUNE CATHERINE

Financial Services Authority, 25 The North Colannade, Canary Wharf, London, E14 8HS, ✉Emma.Walker@fsa.gov.uk, *Call Date: Nov 2000, Middle Temple*
Qualifications: [LLB (Hons)]

WALKER MISS JESSICA LOUISE HELEN

Crown Prosecution Service, Rose Court, 2 Southwark Bridge, London, SE1 9HS, ☎020 7796 8000, *Call Date: Nov 1996, Middle Temple*
Qualifications: [BA (Hons)]

WALKER MISS JILL CHRISTINE VEZEY

Registrar, Upper Tribunal Appeal Chamber, 5th Floor Rolls Buildings, 7 Rolls Buildings, Fetter Lane, London, EC4A 1NL, *Call Date: Nov 1970, Middle Temple*
Qualifications: [LLB (Hons) (Lond)]

WALKER MR PATRICK HOWARD

Deputy High Court Judge, Director, Mediator, Recorder, Squire Sanders (UK) LLP, 2 Park Lane, Leeds, LS3 1ES, ☎0113 284 7566 Fax: 0870 460 3297, ✉patrick.walker@squiresanders.com, *Call Date: July 1979, Lincoln's Inn*
Qualifications: [LLB (Sheff)]

WALKER MR PETER MAXWELL

Company Secretary, New Culture Revolution Limited, 7 Abbey Court, Clandon Gardens, London, N3 3BG, ☎020 8343 3870 Fax: 020 8343 3870, ✉writelaws@aol.com, *Call Date: July 1977, Lincoln's Inn*
Qualifications: [LLB (Lond) FFA FIAB Minst LM]

WALKER MR STUART JAMES

London Borough of Redbridge, Town Hall, Legal Services, Po Box 2, High Road, Ilford, Essex, IG1 1DD, ☎020 8708 2215, ✉stuart.walker@redbridge.gov.uk, *Call Date: Oct 1990, Gray's Inn*
Qualifications: [MA (Oxon)]

WALKER MR THOMAS ALEXANDER

Morgan Cole, Bradley Court, Park Place, Cardiff, CF1 3DP, ☎02920 385 385 Fax: 02920 385 300, ✉tom.walker@morgan-cole.com, *Call Date: Nov 2005, Middle Temple*
Qualifications: [BA (Hons) London MA City University]

WALKER MR TIMOTHY JOHN

Seven Bedford Row, 7 Bedford Row, London, WC1R 4BS, ☎020 7242 3555 Fax: 020 7242 2511, ✉twalker@7br.co.uk, *Call Date: July 1984, Inner Temple*
Qualifications: [MA (Cantab)]

WALKER-JENNINGS MR NIGEL

Spicer Finch Ltd, 5 Millbank House, Riverside Business Park, Wilmslow, Cheshire, SK9 1BJ, ✉nwj@spicerfinch.co.uk, *Call Date: Nov 1999, Inner Temple*
Qualifications: [LLB (Lancs) LLM (Manch)]

WALLACE MR ADRIAN ROBERT

Clyde & Co LLP, Chancery Place, 50 Brown Street, Manchester, M2 2JT, ☎0161 240 2724 Fax: 0844 875 8001, ✉awallace@ble.co.uk, *Call Date: July 1979, Middle Temple*
Qualifications: [BA (Cantab)]

F

WALLACE MR ALASDAIR WILLIAM MCKINNON

HED, Ministry of Justice, 102 Petty France, London, SW1H 9AJ, ✉alasdair.wallace@justice.gsi.gov.uk, *Call Date: July 1985, Gray's Inn*
Qualifications: [MA LLM]

WALLACE MR PHILIP CHRISTOPHER

Schroder Investment Management Limited, 31 Gresham Street, London, EC2V 7QA, *Call Date: Nov 1994, Gray's Inn*
Qualifications: [BA (Exon)]

WALLBANK MR MICHAEL

Assistant Deputy Coroner, Crown Advocate, Crown Prosecution Service, Newgate House, Newgate, Rochdale, Lancashire, OL16 1XD, ✉michael.wallbank@cps.gsi.gov.uk, *Call Date: Mar 2008, Gray's Inn*
Qualifications: [LLB (Hons)]

WALLEDGE MR CHRISTOPHER ROWAN

Senior Lawyer, Dartmoor National Park Authority, Hayton Road, Bovey Tracey, Newton Abbot, Devon, TQ13 9JQ, ☎01626 831068, ✉cwalledge@dartmoor-npa.gov.uk, *Call Date: Feb 1995, Inner Temple*
Qualifications: [LLB (Exon)]

WALLINGTON MR ANDREW DAVID

Senior Crown Prosecutor, Crown Prosecution Service, United House, Piccadilly, York, YO1 9PQ, ☎01969 663634 Fax: 01969 663191, *Call Date: Nov 1993, Inner Temple*
Qualifications: [BA CPE]

WALLIS MR TIMOTHY JAMES

Bishop & Sewell LLP, 59 - 60 Russell Square, London, WC1B 4HP, *Call Date: July 1979, Gray's Inn*
Qualifications: [BA]

WALSH MR GREGORY FRANCIS ANDREW

COMT, Head of Legal Services, Bupa, Anchorage 3, Anchorage Quay, Salford Quays, Manchester, M5 2XL, ☎0161 254 3510
Fax: 0161 254 3513, ✉walshgr@bupa.com, *Call Date: Feb 1991, Lincoln's Inn*
Qualifications: [LLB (L'pool)]

WALSH MISS HELEN MARGARET

Crown Prosecution Service, County House, 100 New London Road, Chelmsford, Essex, CM2 0RG, ☎01245 455800, ✉helen.walsh@cps.gsi.gov.uk, *Call Date: Oct 2007, Inner Temple*
Qualifications: [LLB (Kent)]

WALSH MR MARK HOWEL

Clyde and Co LLP, 1 Stoke Road, Guildford, Surrey, GU1 4HW, ☎01483 555555
Fax: 01483 567330, *Call Date: Oct 1996, Middle Temple*
Qualifications: [MA (Hons)(Cantab) CPE (Lond)]

WALSH MR MATTHEW PATRICK

Crown Prosecution Service, Gemini One, Oxford Business Park South, Garsington Road, Oxford, Oxfordshire, OX4 2LL, *Call Date: Oct 2000, Middle Temple*
Qualifications: [LLB]

WALSHE MRS SARAH JANE

Director, Other, Lexis Nexis (Butterworths Ltd), Halsbury House, 35 Chancery Lane, London, WC2A 1EL, ☎020 7400 2500
Fax: 020 7400 2842, ✉customer.service@lexisnexis.co.uk, *Call Date: Oct 1998, Gray's Inn*
Qualifications: [BA (B'ham)]

WALTERS MISS DINAH MARY

Crown Prosecution Service, County House, 100 New London Road, Chelmsford, Essex, CM2 0RG, ☎01245 455955
Fax: 01245 455871, ✉dinah.walters@cps.gsi.gov.uk, *Call Date: Nov 1981, Gray's Inn*
Qualifications: [LLB (B'ham)]

WALTERS MR GARETH RUPEL

Crown Prosecution Service, Colmore Gate, 2 - 6 Colmore Row, Birmingham, West Midlands, B3 2QA, *Call Date: Nov 1986, Middle Temple*
Qualifications: [LLB (Wales)]

WALTON MR ANDREW DAVID

General Counsel, Financial Risk Management Ltd, 15 Adam Street, London, WC2N 6AH, ☎020 7968 6131 Fax: 020 7808 3710, ✉andrew.walton@frmhedge.com, *Call Date: Nov 1986, Inner Temple*
Qualifications: [BA LLM]

F

WANNELL MR COLIN DOUGLAS

Legal Manager, Senior Legal Adviser, BP PLC, Legal Department, 20 Canada Square, London, E15 5NJ, ☎020 7948 5617 Fax: 020 7948 7894, ✉Colin.Wannell@uk.bp.com, *Call Date: Oct 2001, Inner Temple*
Qualifications: [BSc (Econ)(Lond) CPE FCII Dip Law]

WARD MR ALEXANDER JAMES

Royal Navy Officers, RAF Northolt, Service Prosecting Authority, West End Road, Ruislip, Middlesex, HA4 6NG, *Call Date: July 2008, Middle Temple*
Qualifications: [MA PgDl]

WARD MISS CLAIRE

Special Casework Lawyer, Crown Prosecution Service, The Cooperage, 8 Gainsford Street, London, SE1 2NE, ☎020 7 378 3281, ✉claire.ward@cps.gsi.gov.uk, *Call Date: July 1985, Lincoln's Inn*
Qualifications: [LLB (Hons)]

WARD MR DANIEL LINUS

Call Date: Oct 2006, Gray's Inn
Qualifications: [BA BCL]

WARD MR DOUGLAS JOHN

Royal Navy Officers, HMS Gloucester, Bfpo 289, HMS Nelson, Portsmouth, Hampshire, PO1 3LT, ☎02392 727617, ✉289-lo@a.dii.mod.uk, *Call Date: July 2005, Inner Temple*
Qualifications: [BSc (So'ton) CPE]

WARD MR IAN ROBERT

Legal Adviser, Ministry of Defence, Po Box 1680, London, SWIP 1ZE, *Call Date: Nov 1981, Middle Temple*
Qualifications: [BA LLM (Canada) LLB (Cantab)]

WARD MR JAMES ADAM ROBERTSON ERNEST

Crown Advocate, Crown Prosecution Service, Froomsgate House, Rupert Street, Bristol, BS1 2QJ, ☎0117 930 2800 Fax: 0117 952 9836, *Call Date: Oct 1999, Gray's Inn*
Qualifications: [BA (Hons) FTCL PgDipPLS LMUSLSM MA PgCert LS ARCM FLSM LGSM LDBC LTCL]

WARD MR PETER GRAHAM

Clerk, Dudley Magistrates' Court, The Inhedge, Dudley, DY1 1RY, ☎01384 211 415 Fax: 01384 211 415, ✉peter.ward@hmcourts-service.gsi.gov.uk, *Call Date: Nov 1987, Lincoln's Inn*
Qualifications: [LLB DMS]

WARD MR RUSSELL

Director, Inexus Services Ltd, Driscoll 2, Ellen Street, Cardiff, CF10 4BP, ☎029 20 314167 Fax: 0871 4290431, ✉russell.ward@inexus.co.uk, *Call Date: Oct 1992, Middle Temple*
Qualifications: [BSc (Hons) MA (Hons) (Cantab)]

WARDALE MISS JOANNE VICTORIA

Aon Limited, 11 Devonshire Square, Cutlers, London, EC2M 4YP, ☎020 7086 3639, ✉joanne.wardale@aon.co.uk, *Call Date: Nov 1998, Middle Temple*
Qualifications: [BA (Hons)(Cantab)]

WARD-JACKSON MR CHARLES

Crown Prosecution Service, Eaton House, 112 Oxford Road, Reading, Berkshire, RG1 7LL, *Call Date: Nov 1985, Middle Temple*
Qualifications: [BA (Edin) Dip Law]

WAREHAM MR GERARD

Crown Prosecution Service, Greenfield House, 32 Scotland Street, Sheffield, South Yorkshire, S3 7DQ, ✉gerard.wareham@cps.gsi.gov.uk, *Call Date: July 1988, Gray's Inn*
Qualifications: [BA]

WAREHAM MRS TRACEY ANN

Adviser, Crown Prosecution Service, United House, Piccadilly, York, North Yorkshire, YO1 9PQ, *Call Date: Nov 1987, Gray's Inn*
Qualifications: [LLB (Wales)]

WARMAN MR ANDREW CECIL JAMES

Senior Crown Prosecutor, Crown Prosecution Service, Bromfield House, Ellice Way, Wrexham, Wales, LL13 7YW, ☎01978 346000 Fax: 01978 346001, *Call Date: Feb 1994, Inner Temple*
Qualifications: [BSc (Wales) CPE]

WARNE MR BENJAMIN DAVID ANDREW

Crown Prosecution Service, Queens House, 58 Victoria Street, St Albans, Hertfordshire, AL1 3HZ, ✉ benwarne@hotmail.co.uk, *Call Date: July 2006, Gray's Inn*
Qualifications: [LLB (Keele)]

WARNSBY MR GRANT DARREN

Manager, BP PLC, Legal Department, 20 Canada Square, London, E14 5NJ, ☎ 020 7948 4424 Fax: 020 7948 7982, ✉ grant.warnsby@uk.bp.com, *Call Date: May 1997, Lincoln's Inn*
Qualifications: [BA (Hons)(Keele) ACA]

WARREN MR JOHN BENTON

Advocate, Crown Prosecution Service, Capital Tower, Greyfriars Road, Cardiff, Wales, CF10 3PL, ☎ 02920 803976 Fax: 02920 803900, ✉ john.warren@cps.gsi.gov.uk, *Call Date: Nov 1978, Gray's Inn*
Qualifications: [LLB (So'ton)]

WARREN MS SUSAN MARY

Her Majesty's Courts and Tribunals Service, Central Kent, Maidstone Mag Court, The Court House, Palace Avenue, Maidstone, Kent, ME15 6LL, ☎ 01622 671 041 Fax: 01622 691 800, *Call Date: July 2002, Inner Temple*
Qualifications: [BA (Sheff) CPE]

WATERS MR JONATHAN ROY

Legal Director, British Medical Association, Legal Department, Bma House, Tavistock Square, London, WC1H 9JP, *Call Date: Nov 1990, Lincoln's Inn*
Qualifications: [MCIArb LLM (Credit) MIod]

WATKIN MR DAMIAN JOHN

Allens Arthur Robinson, Deutshe Bank Place, 126 Phillip Street, Sydney, 2000, Australia, *Call Date: July 2005, Lincoln's Inn*
Qualifications: [MRICS MCIArb BSc (Hons) LLB (Hons)]

WATKINS MRS BEVERLEY ANNE

Senior Crown Prosecutor, Crown Prosecution Service, Black Horse House, 8-10 Leigh Road, Eastleigh, Hampshire, SO50 9FH, *Call Date: July 1982, Gray's Inn*
Qualifications: [BA]

WATKINS MR NOEL

Senior Crown Prosecutor, Crown Prosecution Service, Priory Gate, 29 Union Street, Maidstone, Kent, ME14 1PT, ☎ 01622 356300 Fax: 01622 356359, ✉ noel.watkins@cps.gsi.gov.uk, *Call Date: Mar 2003, Lincoln's Inn*
Qualifications: [LLB (Hons) (Cardiff)]

WATKINS DR OWEN DAVID

Lewis Silkin LLP, 5 Chancery Lane, Clifford's Inn, London, EC4A 1BL, ☎ 020 7074 8222, ✉ owen.watkins@lewissilkin.com, odwandrbs@btinternet.com, *Call Date: July 1986, Lincoln's Inn*
Qualifications: [MA MA (Lond) D Phil (Oxon)]

WATKINS MR PAUL JOHN

Lch Clearnet Group Ltd, Aldgate House, 33 Aldgate High Street, London, EC3N 1EA, ✉ paul.watkins@lchclearnet.com, *Call Date: Nov 1986, Middle Temple*
Qualifications: [LLB (Manch)]

WATSON MR NICHOLAS BRUCE

Justices' Clerk, Her Majesty's Courts and Tribunals Service, Leicester Magistrates Court, 15 Pocklingtons Walk, Leicester, LE1 6BT, ☎ 0116 257 5883 Fax: 0116 254 5851, ✉ nick.watson@hmcourts-service.gsi.gov.uk, *Call Date: July 1986, Gray's Inn*
Qualifications: [LLB LLM MBA]

WATSON MR ROY STUART

Senior Legal Adviser, Reading Magistrates Court, Civic Centre, Reading, Berkshire, RG7 7TQ, ☎ 0118 980 1800 Fax: 0118 980 1830, *Call Date: Feb 1993, Gray's Inn*
Qualifications: [BA]

WATSON-HOPKINSON MISS GHISLAINE ELIZABETH CLARE

Crown Prosecution Service, Basingstoke Police Station, London Road, Basingstoke, Hampshire, RG21 4AD, Fax: 01256 405038, ✉ G.Watson-Hopkinson@cps.gsi.gov.uk, *Call Date: Nov 1991, Inner Temple*
Qualifications: [LLB (Hons) Dip Nursing SRN]

WATTERS MR CHARLES PATRICK

General Counsel, Secretary, Charter One Groupv Ltd, The Highlands, Chiltern Hill, Chalfont St Peter, Gerrards Cross, Buckinghamshire, SL9 9TZ, *Call Date: July 1981, Middle Temple*
Qualifications: [LLB (Hons)]

F

WATTS MRS ALISON

Director of Legal Services, Justices' Clerk, Derbyshire Magistrates' Court, Magistrates Court, Tapton Lane, Chesterfield, Derbyshire, S41 7TW, ☎01246 246 505
Fax: 01246 246 510, *Call Date: July 1984, Inner Temple*
Qualifications: [LLB]

WATTS MR MARTIN WILLIAM

Financial Services Authority, The Financial Services Authority, Enforcement and Financial Crime Division - Legal Group, 25 The North Colonade, Canary Wharf, London, E14 5HS, *Call Date: Oct 1995, Middle Temple*
Qualifications: [MA (Oxon)]

WAYMAN MRS ANNE ELIZABETH

HMCS Kent, Sussex & Surrey, Croydon Magistrates' Court, Barclay Road, Croydon, CR0 1JN, *Call Date: Nov 1987, Gray's Inn*
Qualifications: [DML]

WEARE MR JONATHAN BRAN

Royal Navy Officers, HQ 3 Commando Brigade Royal Marines, Rmb Stonehouse, Plymouth, Devon, PL1 3QS, ☎01752 836281, ✉jonathan.weare763@mod.uk, *Call Date: Oct 2005, Inner Temple*
Qualifications: [BA (Hons) University of Bristol MSc University College]

WEAVER MS VICTORIA ANNE

Capsticks Solicitors LLP, 1 St George's Road, Wimbledon, London, SW19 4DR,
Fax: 020 8780 1141, ✉victoria.weaver@capsticks.com, *Call Date: July 2006, Gray's Inn*
Qualifications: [BA (Exon)]

WEBB MR ROBERT STOPFORD

Bencher, Director, Recorder, Rolls-Royce Plc, 65 Buckingham Gate, London, SW1E 6AT, ✉robert.webb@rolls-royce.com, *Call Date: July 1971, Inner Temple*
Qualifications: [LLB FRAes]

WEBER MR ROBBIE

Crown Prosecution Service, Queens House, 58 Victoria Street, St. Albans, Hertforshire, AL1 3HZ, ✉robbie.weber@cps.gsi.gov.uk, *Call Date: Oct 2000, Inner Temple*
Qualifications: [LLB (Lond)]

WEBSTER MR COLIN PETER

Deputy Justices' Clerk, The Court House, Speedwell Street, Oxford, Oxfordshire, OX1 1RZ, ☎01865 448014 Fax: 01865 448024, ✉colin.webster@hmcts.gsi.gov.uk, *Call Date: Nov 1987, Middle Temple*
Qualifications: [Dip Mag Law DMS IOSH]

WEDDERBURN MISS KIM

Legal Counsel, Curam Software, Thatch End, 3 Ilges Lane, Cholsey, Wallingford, OX10 9NT, ☎01491 201471 Fax: 01491 201471, *Call Date: Nov 1991, Middle Temple*
Qualifications: [LLB (Hons)]

WEEKS MR STEPHEN THOMAS

Call Date: July 1978, Lincoln's Inn
Qualifications: [MA (Cantab)]

WEINSTEIN MISS LINDSAY

London Borough of Brent, Brent County Council, Town Hall Annexe, Forty Lane, Wembely, Middlesex, HA9 9HD, *Call Date: Oct 1992, Middle Temple*
Qualifications: [LLB (Hons)]

WEIR MISS HEATHER ANNE

Advocate, Higher Court Advocate, Crown Prosecution Service, Jefferson House, 27 Park Place, Leeds, West Yorkshire, LS1 2SZ, ☎0113 2902700, ✉Heather.Weir@cps.gsi.gov.uk, *Call Date: July 1989, Gray's Inn*
Qualifications: [LLB (Hons)]

WEIR MISS MARION

Brockbank Curwen Cain & Hall Solicitors, 44 Duke Street, Whitehaven, Cumbria, CA28 7NR, *Call Date: July 2001, Gray's Inn*
Qualifications: [BA (Sheff)]

WEISS MISS KATIE

Crown Prosecution Service, Colindale Police Station, Grahame Park Way, Colindale, London, NW9 5TW, *Call Date: Nov 1999, Middle Temple*
Qualifications: [LLB (Hons)(Lond)]

WEITZMAN MR ADAM JOHN

Seven Bedford Row, 7 Bedford Row, London, WC1R 4BS, ☎020 7242 3555
Fax: 020 7242 2511, ✉aweitzman@7br.co.uk, *Call Date: Nov 1993, Middle Temple*
Qualifications: [BA (Hons)(Cantab) MA (Manch) CPE (Lond)]

F

WELCH MR BRYAN JAMES

Legal Director, Department For Business, Innovation and Skills, Abbey 1, 1 Victoria Street, London, SW1H 0ET, ✉bryan.welch@bis.gsi.gov.uk, *Call Date: July 1975, Inner Temple*
Qualifications: [MA (Cantab)]

WELCH MR EDWARD BRETT

The Treasury Solicitors, Department For Education, Sanctuary Buildings, Great Smith Street, London, SW1P 3BT, ☎020 7783 8219 Fax: 020 7925 6410, ✉brett.welch@education.gsi.gov.uk, *Call Date: Oct 1996, Lincoln's Inn*
Qualifications: [BA (Hons) Dip in Law CPE]

WELLING MR ROBERT DAVID

Senior Crown Prosecutor, Crown Prosecution Service, Black Horse House, 8-10 Leigh Road, Eastleigh, Hampshire, SO50 9FH, ☎02380 673800 Fax: 02380 673854, ✉rob.welling@cps.gsi.gov.uk, *Call Date: Nov 1989, Lincoln's Inn*
Qualifications: [LLB]

WELSH MISS CHARLOTTE ELIZABETH

Crown Prosecution Service, Inner London Crown Court, Session House, Newington Causeway, London, SE1 6AZ, ✉charlotte.welsh@cps.gsi.gov.uk, *Call Date: Nov 2000, Middle Temple*
Qualifications: [BA (Hons) (Manch) CPE]

WERBICKI MRS ANNE VIVIEN

HED, Lawyer, The Treasury Solicitors, One Kemble Street, London, WC2B 4TS, *Call Date: Feb 1981, Gray's Inn*
Qualifications: [LLB (Bris)]

WERHUN MR JOHN

Senior Crown Prosecutor, Crown Prosecution Service, Sunlight House, Quay Street, Manchester, M60 3PS, ☎0161 827 8398 Fax: 0161 827 4940, *Call Date: July 1982, Gray's Inn*
Qualifications: [BA (Law)]

WEST MR ANDREW PETER

Senior Crown Prosecutor, Crown Prosecution Service, United House, Piccadilly, York, North Yorkshire, YO1 9PQ, *Call Date: Nov 1995, Gray's Inn*
Qualifications: [BA (Hons)]

WEST MR DAVID JOHN COURTNEY

Head of Legal Services, United Kingdom Atomic Energy Authority, Culham Science Centre, Abingdon, Oxfordshire, OX14 3DB, ☎01235 466912, *Call Date: July 1977, Middle Temple*
Qualifications: [LLB (Hons)]

WESTON-SIMONS MR CHARLES PHILIP

Herbert Smith LLP, Exchange House, Primrose Street, London, EC2A 2HS, ☎020 7374 8000, ✉charles.weston-simons@herbertsmith.com, *Call Date: July 2006, Lincoln's Inn*
Qualifications: [BA (Cantab) CPE (City)]

WETTON MR STEPHEN LEONARD

Directorate of Legal Services (Raf), Rm 42a, Lancaster Building, Hq Air Command, Raf High Wycombe, Buckinghamshire, HP14 4UE, *Call Date: Nov 2006, Lincoln's Inn*
Qualifications: [LLB]

WHALE MR STEPHEN JOHN TREHANE

Justices' Clerk, Brecon Magistrates Clerks Office, Captains Walk, Brecon, Powys, LD3 7HS, ☎01874 622993 Fax: 01874 622441, *Call Date: Feb 1986, Gray's Inn*
Qualifications: [MBA DML]

WHEATER MISS JENNIFER CLARE

Partner, Tax Consultant, Proskauer Rose LLP, 9th Floor, 10 Bishops Square, London, E1 6EG, ☎020 7539 0600 Fax: 020 7539 0601, ✉jwheater@proskauer.com, *Call Date: Nov 1995, Inner Temple*
Qualifications: [BA (Dunelm) LLM]

WHEELER MRS ELIZABETH SARAH CLAIRE

Lawyer, Nursing and Midwifery Council, 23 Portland Place, London, W1B 1PZ, *Call Date: July 2008, Middle Temple*
Qualifications: [BA (Hons) (Manch) PgDl (Lond)]

WHEELER MISS PHILIPPA RUTH

Hewlett-Packard Europa Holding Bv, Herrenberger Str. 140, D-71034, Boeblingen, Germany, ☎0049 7031 14 2898 Fax: 0049 7031 14 1415, ✉pippa.wheeler@hp.com, *Call Date: July 1988, Inner Temple*
Qualifications: [LLB]

F

WHINCUP MISS CATHERINE ELIZABETH

Senior Crown Prosecutor, Crown Prosecution Service, Bankside Chambers, 1-4 Bankside Crossfield Street, Warrington, Cheshire, WA1 1UP, Fax: 01925 425349, ✉Catherine.Whincup@cps.gsi.gov.uk, *Call Date: Nov 1987, Middle Temple*
Qualifications: [LLB]

WHISSON-EASTWICK MR KEVIN PAUL

Crown Prosecution Service, Carmelite House, St James Court, Whitefriars, Norwich, Norfolk, NR3 1SL, *Call Date: Nov 1989, Middle Temple*
Qualifications: [BA (Hons) DipLaw]

WHITE MR BARRY JAMES

Cartwright King Solicitors, Norwich Union House, South Parade, Old Market Square, Nottingham, Nottinghamshire, NG1 2LH, ✉barry.white@cartwrightking.co.uk, *Call Date: Oct 2007, Inner Temple*
Qualifications: [LLB (Nott'm) PgDip Law (De Montfot)]

WHITE MR CHARLES DAVID

Crown Prosecution Service, Queens House, 58 Victoria Street, St Albans, Hertfordshire, AL1 3HZ, ☎01727 798700
Fax: 01727 798794, *Call Date: May 1988, Inner Temple*
Qualifications: [LLB (Hull)]

WHITE MISS GEMMA

Crown Prosecution Service, Basingstoke Police Station, London Road, Basingstoke, Hampshire, RG21 4AD, ☎01256 405390, ✉gemma.white@cps.gsi.gov.uk, *Call Date: July 2009, Inner Temple*
Qualifications: [LLB (Bris)]

WHITE MR IAIN CHARLES

Crown Prosecution Service, 1st Floor, Penhaligon House, Green Street, Truro, Cornwall, TR1 1DZ, ☎01872 243005, *Call Date: July 1986, Middle Temple*
Qualifications: [MA (Hons) (Cantab)]

WHITE MR MARTIN STEPHEN

Rogers Stirk Harbour + Partners Thames Wharf Rainville Road, London, ✉martin.w@rsh-p.com, *Call Date: July 1973, Middle Temple*
Qualifications: [BA (Cantab)]

WHITEFORD DR ELAINE ANGUS

Berwin Leighton Paisner, Adelaide House, London Bridge, London, EC4R 9HA, *Call Date: Oct 1999, Middle Temple*
Qualifications: [LLB (Hons)(Edin'b) PGDL PhD]

WHITEHEAD MR KIARON JAMES

BPI (British Recorded Music Industry) Ltd, Riverside Building, County Hall, Westminster Bridge Road, London, SE1 7JA, ☎020 7803 1300, *Call Date: Nov 1999, Middle Temple*
Qualifications: [BA (Hons)(Cantab)]

WHITEHORN MR JODY FRANCIS

Financial Services Authority, The Financial Services Authority, Enforcement and Financial Crime Division - Legal Group, 25 The North Colonade, Canary Wharf, London, E14 5HS, ☎020 7066 9194, ✉jody.whitehorn@fsa.gov.uk, *Call Date: Mar 2000, Inner Temple*
Qualifications: [LLB (S'ton)]

WHITEHOUSE MR MARTIN

District Crown Prosecutor, Principal Crown Prosecutor, Crown Prosecution Service, Charing Cross Police Station, Agar Street, London, WC2N 4JP, ✉Martin.Whitehouse@cps.gsi.gov.uk, *Call Date: Feb 1985, Middle Temple*
Qualifications: [LLB]

WHITELEY MISS MIRANDA BLYTH

Mediator, Mills and Reeve, Mills and Reeve LLP, Francis House, 112 Hills Road, Cambridge, Cambridgeshire, CB2 1PH, *Call Date: Nov 1985, Middle Temple*
Qualifications: [MA (Cantab)]

WHITLOCK MR SHAUN PEREGRINE

SLS Solicitors Limited, 3rd Floor, St John's House, 2 Queen Square, Liverpool, L1 1RH, ✉shaun.whitlock@systech-solicitors.com, *Call Date: Nov 2007, Middle Temple*
Qualifications: [MSc (Leeds) PgDL (Leeds)]

WHITTAKER MR BRIAN PAUL

Chief Crown Prosecutor, Crown Prosecution Service, 7th Floor (South), Royal Liver Building, Pier Head, Liverpool, Merseyside, L3 1HN, ☎0151 239 6439, ✉paul.whittaker@cps.gsi.gov.uk, *Call Date: July 1977, Gray's Inn*
Qualifications: [BA (Hons)]

F

WHITTAKER MR IAN DORIEN GEOFFREY

Legal Adviser, Department For Business, Innovation and Skills, 1 Victoria Street, London, SW1H 0ET, ☎ 020 7215 3130 Fax: 020 7215 3221, ✉ ian.whittaker@bis.gsi.gov.uk, *Call Date: Oct 1994, Inner Temple*
Qualifications: [MA (Oxon) DipLaw]

WHITTAKER MISS ISOBEL

6 King's Bench Walk, Ground, Third & Fourth Floors, 6 King's Bench Walk, Temple, London, EC4Y 7DR, ☎ 020 7583 0695, *Call Date: Nov 2002, Middle Temple*
Qualifications: [BA (Hons)(B'ham)]

WICKS MR IAIN GEORGE MACKENZIE

Crown Prosecution Service, Rose Court, 2 Southwark Bridge, London, SE1 9HS, ☎ 020 3357 0145, *Call Date: Nov 1990, Middle Temple*
Qualifications: [LLB (Hons)]

WIDDICOMBE MS RACHEL LUCY

Crown Prosecution Service, Sunlight House, Quay Street, Manchester, M60 3PS, *Call Date: Oct 2001, Gray's Inn*
Qualifications: [BA LLDip]

WIGNALL MS NATALIE ELIZABETH

Liverpool Football Club, Anfield Road, Liverpool, L4 0TH, ☎ 0151 264 2380 Fax: 0151 263 2730, ✉ natalie.wignall@liverpoolfc.tv, *Call Date: Oct 1992, Lincoln's Inn*
Qualifications: [LLB(Hons)]

WILKES MISS JAYNE DENISE

HED, Crown Prosecution Service, United House, Piccadilly, York, North Yorkshire, YO1 9PQ, ✉ jayne.wilkes@cps.gsi.gov.uk, *Call Date: Nov 1991, Inner Temple*
Qualifications: [LLB]

WILKINS MR NIGEL GRANVILLE

Crown Advocate, Crown Prosecution Service, Colmore Gate, 2 - 6 Colmore Row, Birmingham, West Midlands, B3 2QA, ☎ 0121 262 1300 Fax: 0121 262 6351, ✉ nigel.wilkins@cps.gsi.gov.uk, *Call Date: Feb 1974, Inner Temple*
Qualifications: [LLB]

WILKS-WOOD MRS ELIZABETH

Emirates Integrated Telecommunications PJSC, PO Box 50266, Dubai, United Arab Emirates, *Call Date: Nov 1997, Gray's Inn*
Qualifications: [LLB LLM]

WILLCOX MISS SUSAN TRACEY

Office of Fair Trading, Fleetbank House, 2-6 Salisbury Square, London, EC4Y 8JX, ✉ susan.willcox@oft.gsi.gov.uk, *Call Date: Oct 1998, Middle Temple*
Qualifications: [BA (Hons)(Cantab)]

WILLERTON MISS KATHERINE JANE

Department For Business, Innovation and Skills, 1 Victoria Street, London, SW1H 0ET, ☎ 020 7215 1022 Fax: 020 7215 3271, ✉ katherine.willerton@bis.gsi.gov.uk, *Call Date: July 2005, Inner Temple*
Qualifications: [LLB University of Manchester]

WILLEY MR STUART CHRISTOPHER

White & Case LLP, 5 Old Broad Street, London, EC2N 1DW, ☎ 020 7532 1508 Fax: 020 7532 1001, ✉ Swilley@whitecase.com, *Call Date: May 1979, Middle Temple*
Qualifications: [BA (York)]

WILLIAMS MS ALISON

Secretary, Ministry of Justice, Zone 6.31, Legal Directorate, 102 Petty France, London, SW1H 9AJ, ✉ alison.williams@justice.gsi.gov.uk, *Call Date: Oct 2001, Inner Temple*
Qualifications: [BA (Oxon)]

WILLIAMS MISS CAROLINE SARAH

Rackspace Ltd, Hyde Park Hayes, 5 Millington Road, Hayes, Middlesex, UB3 4AZ, *Call Date: Oct 1997, Gray's Inn*
Qualifications: [LLB (Hons)]

WILLIAMS MISS CHERYL ANNE

Crown Prosecution Service, Justinian House, Spitfire Close, Ermine Business Park, Huntingdon, Cambridgeshire, PE29 6XY, ☎ 01480 825286 Fax: 01480 825226, ✉ cheryla.williams@cps.gsi.gov.uk, *Call Date: July 1982, Inner Temple*
Qualifications: [BA (Oxon) LLM (Lond)]

F

WILLIAMS MR DAVID MICHAEL

Caseworker, Other, Crown Prosecution Service, Rose Court, 2 Southwark Bridge, London, SE1 9HS, *Call Date: July 1972, Inner Temple*
Qualifications: [LLB (Manch) MBA]

WILLIAMS MR HUW DAVID

Senior Legal Adviser, The Enviroment Agency, Horizon House, Deanery Road, Bristol, BS1 5AH, ☎01179 345099 Fax: 01179 34 5115, *Call Date: July 1988, Inner Temple*
Qualifications: [BA (Cantab) Dip Law]

WILLIAMS MR JONATHAN DANIEL

Gide Loyrette Nouel LLP, 26 Cours Albert 1er, Paris, France, *Call Date: Oct 2007, Middle Temple*
Qualifications: [LLB (Hons) (L'pool)]

WILLIAMS MR MICHAEL JAMES JOHN

Managing Director, Chevron (Australia), 250 St George's Terrace, Perth, WA 6000, Australia, *Call Date: Feb 1990, Gray's Inn*
Qualifications: [LLB MA]

WILLIAMS MISS NATASHA LOUISE

Head of Legal Services, Oxford Brookes University, Legal Services Department, Kennett House, Gipsy Lane, Oxford, OX3 0BP, *Call Date: Oct 1995, Gray's Inn*
Qualifications: [LLB]

WILLIAMS MR ROBERT EVAN

Other, Coffin Mew LLP, 1000 Lakeside, North Harbour, Portsmouth, Hants, PO6 3EN, ☎02392 364309, *Call Date: July 1981, Gray's Inn*
Qualifications: [LLB]

WILLIAMS MISS ROSEMARIE MAUD JOSEPHINE

Senior Crown Prosecutor, Crown Prosecution Service, The Cooperage, 8 Gainsford Street, London, SE1 2NE, ✉Rosemarie.Williams@cps.gsi.gov.uk, *Call Date: July 1978, Middle Temple*
Qualifications: [BA (Kent) LLM (Lond)]

WILLIAMS MS ROWAN ELAINE

Legal Adviser, Her Majesty's Courts and Tribunals Service, Eastbourne Magistrates Court, Orchard Road, Eastbourne, East Sussex, BN21 4UN, ☎01323 727518, ✉Rowan.williams@hmcourts-service.gsi.gov.uk, *Call Date: July 1981, Middle Temple*

WILLIAMS MISS SAMANTHA

Higher Court Advocate, Senior Crown Prosecutor, Crown Prosecution Service, United House, Piccadilly, York, North Yorkshire, YO1 9PQ, *Call Date: Oct 1992, Lincoln's Inn*
Qualifications: [LLB(Hons)(Wales)]

WILLIAMS MISS SARA HELEN

Financial Services Authority, The Financial Services Authority, Enforcement and Financial Crime Division - Legal Group, 25 The North Colonade, Canary Wharf, London, E14 5HS, *Call Date: Feb 1989, Gray's Inn*
Qualifications: [LLB (Lond)]

WILLIAMS MR SIMON DAVID

Manager, Mills and Co Solicitors, Milburn House, Dean Street, Newcastle Upon Tyne, NE1 1LE, *Call Date: Oct 1996, Gray's Inn*
Qualifications: [BA (Oxon)]

WILLIS-JONES MR WILLIAM MARK

General Counsel, Armstrong World Industries Ltd, Armstrong House, 38 Market Square, Uxbridge, Middlesex, UB8 1NG, ☎00 34 933 728 731 Fax: 00 34 933 714 072, *Call Date: Nov 1982, Middle Temple*
Qualifications: [BSc (Lond) Dip Law]

WILLSON MR JOHN

Legal Adviser, Mitsubishi Ufj Trust And, Banking Corporation, 24 Lombard Street, London, EC3V 9AJ, ☎020 7929 2323, *Call Date: July 1978, Lincoln's Inn*

WILMAN MR DAVID MARK

Sj Berwin LLP, 10 Queen Street Place, London, EC4R 1BE, ☎020 7111 2222, *Call Date: July 2001, Middle Temple*
Qualifications: [BA (Hons) CPE]

F

WILSON MR ALASTAIR GRAHAME

Grecon Management Limited, Gsc Solicitors LLP, 31-32 Ely Place, London, EC1B 6TD, ☎020 7822 2222 Fax: 020 7822 2222, ✉mbowen@gscsolicitors.com, *Call Date: July 1977, Gray's Inn*
Qualifications: [BA LLB (Cantab)]

WILSON MR ALEXANDER DAVID

Crown Prosecution Service, Priory Gate, 29 Union Street, Maidstone, Kent, ME14 1PT, ✉alex.wilson@cps.gsi.gov.uk, *Call Date: Oct 1998, Inner Temple*
Qualifications: [LLB (Dunelm)]

WILSON MRS CORINNE INEZ

Crown Prosecution Service, Greenfield House, 32 Scotland Street, Sheffield, South Yorkshire, S3 7DQ, ☎0114 229 8841, ✉corinne.wilson@cps.gsi.gov.uk, *Call Date: Mar 2011, Gray's Inn*

WILSON MR GEORGE RICHARD ROLAND

Compliance Officer, Absa Capital, 2nd Floor, 15 Alice Lane, Sandton, 2196, South Africa, ☎00 27 11 895 5110
Fax: 00 27 11 895 7831, ✉george.wilson@absacapital.com, *Call Date: Oct 1996, Middle Temple*
Qualifications: [BSc (Hons)(Lond) CPE (Lond)]

WILSON MISS HILARY MARGARET

Director, Director of Legal Services, Skanska Infrastructure Development, Condor House, 10 St Paul's Churchyard, London, EC4M 8AL, ☎020 7429 4200 Fax: 020 7429 4299, ✉hilary.wilson@skanska.se, *Call Date: Nov 1974, Gray's Inn*
Qualifications: [MA (Cantab)]

WILSON MR JAMES MASON

Crown Prosecution Service, Capital Tower, Greyfriars Road, Cardiff, CF10 3PL, ✉james.wilson@cps.gsi.gov.uk, *Call Date: Nov 1991, Inner Temple*
Qualifications: [LLB (Hons)(Leeds)]

WILSON MR JULIAN

Lawyer, Durham County Council, County Hall, Durham, County Durham, DH1 5UL, ☎0191 383 3879 Fax: 0191 383 3690, ✉julian.wilson@durham.gov.uk, *Call Date: Oct 1994, Middle Temple*
Qualifications: [BSc (Hons)(York) CPE (Northumbria)]

WILSON MS MARION JANET

Worcestershire County Council, County Hall, Spetchley Road, Worcester, WR5 2NP, ☎01905 766667 Fax: 01905 766677, ✉mwilson@worcestershire.gov.uk, *Call Date: Oct 1991, Middle Temple*
Qualifications: [LLB (Hons) (Lancs)]

WILSON MR MARK JOHN

CVS, Department For Work and Pensions, 5th Floor, the Adelphi, 1-11 John Adam Street, London, WC2N 6HT, ☎020 7712 2726, *Call Date: Apr 1991, Lincoln's Inn*
Qualifications: [LLB (Hons)]

WILSON MR SEAN

Senior Principal Legal Officer, Department For Work and Pensions, The Adelphi, 1-11 John Adam Street, WC2N 6HT, *Call Date: Oct 1998, Gray's Inn*
Qualifications: [LLB (LSE) BCL(Oxon)]

WILSON MRS SHELLEY ANNE

Senior Crown Prosecutor, Crown Prosecution Service, The Regatta, 6 Henley Buisness Park, Doddington Road, Lincoln, LN6 3QR, ☎01522 585900, ✉shelley.wilson@cps.gsi.gov.uk, *Call Date: Nov 1987, Inner Temple*
Qualifications: [BA (Kent)]

WILSON MR STEPHEN JAMES

Financial Services Authority, General Counsel's Division, 25 The North Colonnade, Canary Wharf, London, E14 5HS, *Call Date: July 1999, Inner Temple*
Qualifications: [LLB (Brunel)]

WILSON MR TERENCE JOHN

Portsmouth City Council, Civic Office, Guildhall Square, Portsmouth, PO1 2BG, *Call Date: Nov 1982, Lincoln's Inn*
Qualifications: [LLB (Leics)]

WILSON MS VICTORIA ANNE

Bath and North East Somerset Council, Bath and North East Somerset Council, Corporate And Community Law Team, Temple Way, Keywsham, BS31 1LA, *Call Date: Nov 1994, Inner Temple*
Qualifications: [BA CPE (Notts)]

WILSON THE HON WILLIAM EDWARD ALEXANDER

Company Director, FLW, Burges Salmon LLP, One Glass Wharf, Bristol, Avon, BS2 0ZX, *Call Date: Nov 1978, Middle Temple*
Qualifications: [LLM]

WINFIELD MISS GEORGINA MARY

Senior Crown Prosecutor, Crown Prosecution Service, 17th Floor, Tolworth Tower, Ewell Road, Surbiton, Surrey, KT6 7DS, ☎ 020 8335 1500 Fax: 020 8335 1600, ✉ gina.winfield@cps.gsi.gov.uk, *Call Date: Nov 1989, Middle Temple*
Qualifications: [LLB (Hons)]

WINFIELD MISS SARAH

Senior Lawyer, Metropolitan Police Service, Directorate of Legal Services, First Floor (V), New Scotland Yard, 8-10 Broadway, London, SW1H 0BG, ☎ 020 7230 1212, *Call Date: Oct 1990, Inner Temple*
Qualifications: [LLB (Hons)(Exon)]

WINKLEY MR JULIAN PATRICK

Senior Lawyer, HM Revenue and Customs, Ralli Quays, 3 Stanley Street, Salford, Manchester, M60 9LB, ☎ 0870 785 8517 Fax: 0870 785 8533, ✉ julian.winkley@hmrc.gsi.gov.uk, *Call Date: Nov 1983, Middle Temple*
Qualifications: [BA]

WINTER MRS TRACY-ELLEN

Bibby Consulting and Support, Brunswick Court, Brunswick Street, Staffordshire, ST5 1HH, ☎ 08453 100 600 Fax: 08453 100 650, ✉ tracy.winter@bibbycas.com, *Call Date: Oct 1998, Middle Temple*
Qualifications: [LLB (Hons)(Kent) BA (Hons)]

WINTERS MR EDWIN LEE

Ruffer LLP, 80 Victoria Street, London, SW1E 5JL, ☎ 020 7963 8100 Fax: 020 7963 8175, *Call Date: Nov 2004, Inner Temple*
Qualifications: [BA (Leeds)]

WINZER MR BENJAMIN CHARLES

Crown Prosecution Service, Argal House, Peninsula Business Park, Rydon Lane, Exeter, Devon, EX2 7NT, ✉ ben.winzer@cps.gsi.gov.uk, *Call Date: May 1997, Middle Temple*
Qualifications: [BA (Hons)(Bris)]

WISE MR CURT NICOLAS

Senior Legal Officer, Crown Prosecution Service, Rose Court, 2 Southwark Bridge, London, SE1 9HS, ☎ 020 3357 0327, ✉ curt.wise@cps.gsi.gov.uk, *Call Date: Nov 1983, Middle Temple*
Qualifications: [BA LLM]

WISNIEWSKA MS ROWENA

Financial Services Authority, General Counsel's Division, 25 The North Colonnade, Canary Wharf, London, E14 5HS, *Call Date: Oct 2007, Gray's Inn*

WITHEY MR RICHARD LESLIE

Crown Prosecution Service, Western Range, 83 London Road, Southampton, Hampshire, SO15 2AA, ☎ 023 8071 4000, ✉ richard.withey@cps.gsi.gov.uk, *Call Date: Oct 1996, Inner Temple*
Qualifications: [LLB]

WITHINGTON MR NEIL ROBERT

General Counsel, Legal Director, British American Tobacco PLC, Globe House, 4 Temple Place, London, WC2R 2PG, ☎ 020 7845 1000 Fax: 020 7845 2187, ✉ neil_withington@bat.com, *Call Date: July 1981, Middle Temple*
Qualifications: [MA (Oxon) BCL]

WOLCHOVER MR JOEL ALEXANDER

Department For Communities & Local Government, 4/A1, Eland House, Bressenden Place, London, SW1E 5DU, ✉ Joel.Wolchover@communities.gsi.gov.uk, *Call Date: July 2006, Middle Temple*
Qualifications: [BA (Hons) (Cantab) LLB (Hons) (Lond)]

WOLFSON MR ALEXANDER SPENCER

Crown Prosecution Service, St Peters House, Gower Street, Derby, Derbyshire, DE1 1SB, ☎ 01332 614 000, ✉ Alex.Wolfson@cps.gsi.gov.uk, *Call Date: Oct 1999, Middle Temple*
Qualifications: [LLB (Hons)]

WONG MR CHRISTOPHER YU NIEN

The Bank of New York Mellon, Legal Department, Level 24, Three Pacific Place, 1 Queen's Road East, Hong Kong, Hong Kong, Fax: 3 010 1251, ✉ christopher.wong@bnymellon.com, *Call Date: Oct 2001, Lincoln's Inn*
Qualifications: [LLB (Hons)(Leic) MSI TEP]

WONG MR GARRETH JERN KWANG

Freshfields Buckhaus Deringer LLP, 65 Fleet Street, London, EC4Y 1HT, ☎020 7936 4000 Fax: 020 7832 7001, ✉garreth.wong@freshfields.com, *Call Date: July 2002, Inner Temple*
Qualifications: [BA (Cantab) LLM (Cantab)]

WOOD MR ANDREW NIGEL MARQUIS

Deputy Justices' Clerk, Legal Manager, Her Majesty's Courts and Tribunals Service, Harrow Magistrates' Court, Rosslyn Crescent, Harrow, HA1 2JY, ☎020 8490 1334, ✉andrew.wood1@hmcourts-service.gsi.gov.uk, *Call Date: Nov 1991, Lincoln's Inn*
Qualifications: [LLB (Hons) (Hull)]

WOOD MRS CATHERINE JUDITH

South London Healthcare Nhs Trust, Stadium Road, Woolwich, London, SE18 4QH, ☎020 8836 5996 Fax: 020 8838 5771, ✉catherine.wood@nhs.net, *Call Date: Oct 2001, Inner Temple*
Qualifications: [LLB (Lond) MA (Lond)]

WOOD MR CHRISTOPHER MARK

Winter Scott, St Olave's House, Ironmonger Lane, London, EC2V 8EY, ✉cwood@winterscott.co.uk, *Call Date: Nov 2007, Inner Temple*
Qualifications: [BA (Cantab) LLM (Lond)]

WOOD MISS GAYNOR ELLEN

Assistant General Counsel, Bank of America Merrill Lynch, Merrill Lynch Financial Centre, 2 King Edward Street, London, EC1A 1HQ, ☎020 7995 6598, *Call Date: Nov 1994, Gray's Inn*
Qualifications: [LLB]

WOOD MRS JANINE SUZANNE DEAN

Crown Prosecution Service, Froomsgate House, Rupert Street, Bristol, BS1 2QJ, *Call Date: July 1983, Inner Temple*
Qualifications: [BA]

WOOD MS NICOLA SUSAN LOUISE

Crown Prosecution Service, Southern House, Wellesley Grove, Croydon, Surrey, CR9 1DY, *Call Date: July 2007, Gray's Inn*
Qualifications: [BA LLDip]

WOOD MR ROBERT

Legal Adviser, Royal Navy Officers, Directorate of Naval Legal Services, Mp 4-2, Leach Building, Whale Island, Portsmouth, PO2 8BY, *Call Date: Oct 1997, Gray's Inn*
Qualifications: [BA (Durham) Dip in Law MA]

WOOD MR SIMON RICHARD HENRY

Adams and Remers, Trinity House, School Hill, Lewes, East Sussex, BN7 2NN, ☎01273 480616 Fax: 01273 480618, ✉simon.wood@adams-remers.co.uk, *Call Date: July 1987, Middle Temple*
Qualifications: [BA (Bris) Dip Law (Lond)]

WOOD MISS SOPHIA ROSEMARY

Hine & Associates, Hine and Associates Solicitors, 51 Amersham Road, Beaconsfield, Buckinghamshire, HP9 2HB, *Call Date: Nov 2000, Middle Temple*
Qualifications: [LLB (Hons) (Brunel) LLM (Brunel)]

WOODHAM MS HEATHER MARIE

London Fire and Emergency Planning Authority, 169 Union Street, London, SE1 0LL, ☎020 8555 1200, ✉heather.woodham@london-fire.gov.uk, *Call Date: Nov 2000, Inner Temple*
Qualifications: [BA (W.Indies) CPE (Lond)]

WOODHEAD MR SIMON ANDREW

Birketts LLP, Kingfisher House, 1 Gilders Way, Off Barrack Street, Norwich, Norfolk, NR3 1UB, Fax: 01603 756555, ✉simon-woodhead@birketts.co.uk, *Call Date: Oct 1990, Lincoln's Inn*
Qualifications: [LLB (UEA)]

WOODINGS MR DAVID JON

HED, The Treasury Solicitors, Attorney General's Office, 20 Victoria Street, London, SW1H 0NF, ☎020 7271 2503, ✉David.Woodings@attorneygeneral.gsi.gov.uk, *Call Date: Oct 1992, Lincoln's Inn*
Qualifications: [BA(Hons)(Lancs) LLB(Hons)(Lond) LLM (Sussex)]

WOODMAN MR PAUL NORMAN

Senior Counsel, Northrop Grumman Law Department, Unit 5, Quinn Close, Whitley, Coventry, CV3 4LH, ☎0247 6516047 Fax: 0247 651 6049, *Call Date: Oct 1991, Inner Temple*
Qualifications: [LLB (Hull) LLM (Bris)]

F

WOODS MISS JOANNA MARY

Baker & Partners, Po Box 842, St Helier, Jersey, JE4 0US, Jersey, *Call Date: July 2003, Middle Temple*
Qualifications: [BA Hons (Cantab)]

WOOLARD MR DOMINIC JUSTIN

Alexander Solicitors & Advocates, 146 Midland Road, Luton, Bedfordshire, LU2 0BL, Fax: 01582 455435, ✉dominic.woolard@alexandersolicitors.co.uk, *Call Date: Oct 2008, Lincoln's Inn*
Qualifications: [LLB (Wales)]

WOOLLS MISS TANYA JANE

Advocate, Crown Prosecution Service, Rose Court, 2 Southwark Bridge, London, SE1 9HS, ✉Tanya.Woolls@cps.gsi.gov.uk, *Call Date: Feb 1991, Middle Temple*
Qualifications: [LLB (Hons)]

WOOTTON MISS NICOLA JANE DAWN

Crown Prosecution Service, Fox Talbot House, Bellinger Close, Malmesbury Road, Chippenham, Wiltshire, SN15 1BN, ☎01249 766 100 Fax: 01249 766 101, *Call Date: July 1995, Middle Temple*
Qualifications: [BA (Hons)]

WORMALD-CRIPPS MR DARREN WILLIAM

Head of Legal Services, Engine Lease Finance Corporation, Building 156, Shannon Free Zone, Shannon, County Clare, Ireland, *Call Date: Nov 1995, Lincoln's Inn*
Qualifications: [LLB (Hons)(Essex)]

WORRALL MRS JUDITH ELIZABETH

Legal Adviser, National Grid, National Grid House, Warwick Technology Park, Gallows Hill, Warwick, CV34 6DA, ✉judith.worrall@uk.ngrid.com, *Call Date: Oct 1992, Middle Temple*
Qualifications: [LLB (Hons) (Nott'm)]

WORRALL MISS SARA LOUISE

Solicitor, Crown Prosecution Service, Rose Court, 2 Southwark Bridge, London, SE1 9HS, *Call Date: Nov 1998, Lincoln's Inn*
Qualifications: [LLB (Hons)(B'ham) Dip French Law]

WORSLEY MRS CERIAN SHEILA

HSBC Bank Plc, Level 34, 8 Canada Square, Canary Wharf, London, E14 5HQ, *Call Date: Nov 2000, Inner Temple*
Qualifications: [LLB (Lancs)]

WRAY MR NIGEL HUBERT

Crown Prosecution Service, Jefferson House, 27 Park Place, Leeds, West Yorkshire, LS1 2SZ, ☎0113 290 2700 / 0113 290 2700 Fax: 0113 290 2701 / 0113 290 2701, ✉nigel.wray@cps.gsi.gov.uk, *Call Date: July 1986, Middle Temple*
Qualifications: [LLB(Lond)]

WRIGHT MR DANIEL EDWARD

Reeds Solicitors, 1 Cambridge Terrace, Oxford, OX1 1RR, *Call Date: Nov 2009, Gray's Inn*
Qualifications: [BA]

WRIGHT MISS GWENDOLINE AGNES

The Treasury Solicitors, One Kemble Street, London, WC2B 4TS, *Call Date: Nov 2002, Lincoln's Inn*
Qualifications: [LLB (Hons)(Lond) MA (Hons) MSc (Lond)]

WRIGHT LIEUTENANT JENNIFER SARAH

Royal Navy Officers, Operation Atalanta, European Union Naval Force, European Union Operational Headquarters, Sandy Lane, Northwood, HA6 3HP, ✉legad3@mschoa.org, *Call Date: July 2010, Middle Temple*
Qualifications: [BA (Hons) (Dundee)]

WRIGHT MR PAUL

HED, Legal Adviser, Department For Work and Pensions, 5th Floor, the Adelphi, 1-11 John Adam Street, London, WC2N 6HT, ☎020 7962 8268 Fax: 020 7962 8924, ✉paul.wright@dwp.gsi.gov.uk, *Call Date: Oct 1993, Inner Temple*
Qualifications: [BA (Manch) CPE]

WRIGHT MR SAMUEL JAMES

Directorate of Army Legal Services, IDL 426, Level 2, Zone 1, Ramillies Building, Marlborough Lines, Monxton Road, Andover, Hampshire, SP11 8HJ, ✉samueljwright@hotmail.com, samw@gcpd.gsi.gov.uk, *Call Date: Nov 2000, Middle Temple*
Qualifications: [LLB CPE]

F

WRIGHT COMMANDER STUART HUGH

Royal Navy Officers, Directorate of Naval Legal Services, Mp 4-2, Leach Building, Whale Island, Portsmouth, PO2 8BY, ✉wrights222@mod.uk, *Call Date: Oct 1995, Middle Temple*
Qualifications: [BA (Hons) LLM]

WRIGHT MR THOMAS

Crown Prosecution Service, Portsmouth Magistrate's Unit, Crown House, Winston Churchill Avenue, Portsmouth, Hampshire, PO1 2PJ, *Call Date: July 2001, Inner Temple*
Qualifications: [BA (Sheff) CPE]

WYATT MR GUY PETER JAMES

G.V. Hale and Co., 70 Waterdale, Doncaster, DN1 3BU, ☎01302 360606
Fax: 01302 360606, ✉guywyatt@btinternet.com, *Call Date: July 1981, Inner Temple*
Qualifications: [BA (Hons) (Law)]

WYETH MR MARK CHARLES

Five Paper Bldgs, 1st Floor, Five Paper Bldgs, Temple, London, EC4Y 7HB, ☎020 7583 6117, ✉mw@5pb.co.uk, *Call Date: July 1983, Inner Temple*
Qualifications: [BA (Hons) ACI Arb]

YAGNIK MS MEERA

Nelsons and Co Ltd, 83 Parkside, Wimbledon, London, SW19 5LP, *Call Date: Nov 2001, Middle Temple*
Qualifications: [LLB (Hons) (Lond)]

YALE MR MARTIN DAVID

Crown Advocate, Crown Prosecution Service, Priory Gate, 29 Union Street, Maidstone, Kent, ME14 1PT, ☎01622 356 414, ✉martin.yale@cps.gsi.gov.uk, *Call Date: July 2000, Middle Temple*
Qualifications: [LLB(Hons) (Lond) LLM]

YAMADA MR KOICHI

Adviser, Soei Patent and Law Firm, Marunouchi My Plaza 9th Floor, 1-1 Marunouchi 2-Chome, Chiyoda-Ku, Tokyo, 100-0005, Japan, ☎+81 3 6738 8001
Fax: + 81 3 6738 8004, *Call Date: Oct 2000, Inner Temple*
Qualifications: [LLB (Wolves)]

YANGYE MISS YIMINUM SOLOMONDA

Nexus Chambers, 7 New Square, Lincolns Inn, London, WC2A 3QS, ☎020 7404 1147
Fax: 020 7 9744, ✉yimi.yangye@nexuschambers.com, Yiminum_yangye@hotmail.com, *Call Date: Oct 2004, Inner Temple*
Qualifications: [LLB (Hons) (Leeds)]

YAP MR RICHARD HOONG KENG

Senior Crown Prosecutor, Crown Prosecution Service, Queens House, 58 Victoria Street, St Albans, Hertfordshire, AL1 3HZ, ☎01727 798710 / 01727 798797, ✉richard.yap@cps.gsi.gov.uk, *Call Date: July 1985, Lincoln's Inn*
Qualifications: [BA]

YARDLEY MR ROBERT HUW

Call Date: Oct 1990, Gray's Inn
Qualifications: [LLB]

YARDY MR KEITH STUART

Crown Advocate, Crown Prosecution Service, Priory Gate, 29 Union Street, Maidstone, Kent, ME14 1PT, ☎01622 356300
Fax: 01622 356359, ✉keith.yardy@cps.gsi.gov.uk, *Call Date: July 1988, Inner Temple*
Qualifications: [LLB (Lond)]

YATES MR SEAN DAVID

Po Box 123218 Dubai, Dubai, United Arab Emirates, ☎00 971 50 5151576
Fax: 00 971 2071171662, *Call Date: Nov 1996, Inner Temple*
Qualifications: [BA (Oxon) CPE]

YEAK MS CHENG MOOI

Senior Crown Prosecutor, Crown Prosecution Service, Princes Court, 34 York Road, Leicester, Leicestershire, LE1 5TU, ✉Cheng.Yeak@cps.gsi.gov.uk, *Call Date: Nov 1990, Lincoln's Inn*
Qualifications: [LLB (Bucks)]

YIP MRS AIK HOOI

Legal Adviser, Wimbledon Magistrates' Court, Alexandra Road, Wimbledon, London, SW19 7JP, ☎020 8879 9012, ✉aikhooi.yip@hmcourts-service.gsi.gov.uk, *Call Date: July 1985, Lincoln's Inn*
Qualifications: [BA (Sussex)]

YONG MR YING KEONG

The Treasury Solicitors, One Kemble Street, London, WC2B 4TS, ☎ 020 7210 3000, *Call Date: Oct 1993, Middle Temple*
Qualifications: [LLB (Hons)(Notts)]

YOUELL MR CHRISTOPHER JAMES

Advocate, Crown Prosecution Service, Carmelite House, St James Court, Whitefriars, Norwich, Norfolk, NR3 1SL,
☎ 01603 693 044 / 01603 693 044
Fax: 01603 693 075 / 01603 693 075,
✉ chris.youell@cps.gsi.gov.uk, *Call Date: Feb 1991, Gray's Inn*
Qualifications: [LLB]

YOUNG MR ANDREW DAVID

Crown Prosecution Service, Colmore Gate, 2 - 6 Colmore Row, Birmingham, West Midlands, B3 2QA, ✉ andy.young@cps.gsi.gov.uk, *Call Date: July 1986, Gray's Inn*
Qualifications: [MA (Cantab)]

YOUNG MISS SARAH JOANNA

MAS, Law Commission, Public Law Team, Steel House, 11 Tothill Street, London, SW1H 9LJ, ☎ 020 3334 0279, ✉ sarah.young@lawcommission.gsi.gov.uk, *Call Date: Oct 1992, Middle Temple*
Qualifications: [BA (Hons) (Manch) Dip Law]

YOUSEF MISS SALMA

Crown Prosecution Service, Eaton Court, 112 Oxford Road, Reading, Berkshire, RG1 7LL, *Call Date: Nov 2008, Lincoln's Inn*
Qualifications: [LLB]

YOUSUF MS FARAH

Assistant, Clerk, Legal Adviser, Her Majesty's Courts Service, Magistrates' Court Brent, Church End, 448 High Road, London, NW10 2DZ, ☎ 020 8451 7111 Fax: 020 8451 2040, *Call Date: July 1985, Lincoln's Inn*
Qualifications: [BA (Hons)]

F

ZACHARY MR JOHN GEORGE BRANSBY

Lionel Blackman Solicitors, Upper Chambers, 7 Waterloo Road, Epsom, Surrey, KT19 8AY, ☎ 01372 728941 Fax: 01372 741869, *Call Date: Oct 2005, Middle Temple*
Qualifications: [MA (Hons) Dip in Law]

ZAKARAUSKAS MR AUDRIUS PAULIUS

Quinn Emanuel Urquhart & Sullivan LLP, 16 Old Bailey, London, EC4M 7EG, *Call Date: Oct 2003, Inner Temple*
Qualifications: [BA, MA (Lithuania)]

ZAMAN MRS SAJADA

Solicitor, Her Majesty's Courts and Tribunals Service, Stockport Magistrates' Court, The Court House, Edward Street, Stockport, SK1 3UR, ☎ 0161 474 3247 Fax: 0161 477 9530, ✉ sajada.zaman@stockport.gov.uk, *Call Date: Nov 1985, Lincoln's Inn*
Qualifications: [BA]

ZATSCHLER MR CARSTEN

Chambers of Judge Schiemann, Court of Justice Of the E.C., L-2925 Luxembourg, Luxembourg, ☎ 00 352 4303 2111
Fax: 00 352 4303 2040, *Call Date: Oct 1999, Inner Temple*
Qualifications: [BA (Cantab) LLM MA (Cantab) Dip Law]

ZEB MR AURANG

Partner, Invictus Chambers, Foxhall Bc, 2 King Street, Nottingham, NG1 2 AS, ☎ 0115 845 6554 Fax: 0115 845 6554, *Call Date: Oct 2002, Lincoln's Inn*
Qualifications: [LLB (Leeds)]

ZEFFMAN MR MICHAEL

Senior Lawyer, HM Revenue and Customs, Somerset House, The Strand, London, WC2R 1LB, ✉ michael.zeffman@hmrc.gsi.gov.uk, *Call Date: July 1977, Gray's Inn*
Qualifications: [LLB (Lond)]

ZHU MR HUIJIAN

Hogan Lovells International LLP, View Building, Rue De Industrie 26, Brussels 1040, Belgium, ☎ 0032 2505 0944
Fax: 0032 2505 0996, ✉ huijian.zhu@hoganlovells.com, *Call Date: Nov 2005, Lincoln's Inn*
Qualifications: [LLB (Hons) LLM MPA (Hons)]

ZIMBRON MR RICARDO

Cleary Gottlieb Steen and Hamilton LLP, 55 Basinghall Street, London, EC2V 5EH, ☎ 020 7614 2200, ✉ ricardozimbron@gmail.com, rzimbron@cgsh.com, *Call Date: Oct 2009, Lincoln's Inn*
Qualifications: [BA (Oxon) CPE UCU]

ZIMMERN MR JONATHAN PETER

Field Fisher Waterhouse LLP, 35 Vine Street, London, EC3N 2AA, ☎020 7861 4218 Fax: 020 7488 0084, ✉jonathan.zimmern@ffw.com, *Call Date: Oct 2002, Middle Temple*
Qualifications: [MA (Edin) CPE MA (Lond)]

ZINNER MR PETER ANTHONY

Borough Crown Prosecutor, Crown Prosecution Service, Charing Cross Police Station, Agar Street, London, WC2N 4JP, ✉peter.zinner@cps.gsi.gov.uk, *Call Date: Nov 1983, Middle Temple*
Qualifications: [BA (Hons)]

ZOLLNER MR ROLAND LOUIS

Senior Crown Prosecutor, Crown Prosecution Service, Heron House, Hougoumont Avenue, Hougoumont Avenue, Liverpool, Merseyside, L22 0LL, *Call Date: July 1978, Middle Temple*
Qualifications: [BA]

ZOUQ MISS SADIA KAUSAR

Crown Prosecution Service, Sunlight House, Quay Street, Manchester, M60 3PS, ✉sadia.zouq@cps.gsi.gov.uk, *Call Date: Nov 2000, Lincoln's Inn*
Qualifications: [LLB (Hons) (Leeds) MSc (Oxon)]

F

Individual Barristers Unregistered

This section lists those barristers who are unregistered. Barristers are listed alphabetically by surname, and details include their date of call to the Bar, their Inn of Court and academic qualifications.

Note: For barristers in this section, information has been supplied by the Bar Council based on payment of the Members' Services Fee.

Abbasi *Mr Bilal Haider*
Call Date: July 2011 (Lincoln's Inn) Qualifications: LLB (Sheff)

Abdulrouf *Mr Mizan Hussein Ibn*
Call Date: Nov 2007 (Middle Temple) Qualifications: LLB (Hons) (Lond)

Abeyewickreme *Mr Sunil*
Partner, DWF LLP, Bridgewater Place, Water Lane, Leeds, LS11 5DY, Call Date: Oct 2004 (Gray's Inn) Qualifications: BSc (Dundee) LLB (Dundee)

Abraham *Mr Matthew*
Call Date: July 2012 (Lincoln's Inn)

Acton *Ms Victoria Jane*
Call Date: Oct 1995 (Inner Temple) Qualifications: BA (Kent) MPhil (Leeds) Dip Law (Lond)

Adam *Mr Steven Robert*
Call Date: July 2012 (Lincoln's Inn)

Adamson *Mr Henry Macrae*
Call Date: July 2012 (Inner Temple)

Adderley *Miss Paula Anne Lilith*
Harry B. Sands, Lobosky & Company, Po Box N-624, Fifty Shirley Street, Nassau, Bahamas, 001 242 322 2670, Call Date: July 1997 (Middle Temple) Qualifications: BA (Hons)

Adedeji *Mr Adeoye Gabriel*
Call Date: July 2012 (Middle Temple)

Adeleye *Mr Ayodeji Adeyanju*
Call Date: Mar 2012 (Middle Temple)

Afshar *Miss Zahra*
Call Date: Nov 2007 (Lincoln's Inn) Qualifications: LLB (Bris) LLM

Afzal *Miss Tahlee*
Call Date: July 2005 (Lincoln's Inn) Qualifications: LLB (Hons)

Agnew *Ms Danielle Mia*
Call Date: July 2007 (Middle Temple) Qualifications: LLB (Hons) (N'hampton)

Agnew *Mr James Fraser*
Call Date: Nov 2008 (Middle Temple) Qualifications: BA (Hons)

Agnew *Miss Rachael Maria*
Call Date: Oct 2011 (Middle Temple) Qualifications: BA (Hons) (Oxon)

Agnini *Ms Julia Kate*
Call Date: Nov 1999 (Gray's Inn) Qualifications: LLB (Leic)

Ahammed *Mrs Maharunnesa*
Call Date: Oct 2009 (Gray's Inn) Qualifications: LLB

Ah-Hen *Miss Jade Chung Li Kiao*
Call Date: July 2009 (Lincoln's Inn) Qualifications: LLB (B'ham) Licence De Droit Francais

Ahlquist *Mr Philip James*
Call Date: July 2012 (Inner Temple)

Ahluwalia *Miss Paramjit*
Call Date: Mar 2002 (Lincoln's Inn) Qualifications: BA (Hons)

Ahmad *Miss Nisha*
Call Date: Nov 2009 (Lincoln's Inn) Qualifications: BA (Lond) CPE COL

Ahmed *Mr Mahmood*
Call Date: Mar 2008 (Middle Temple) Qualifications: BSc (Hons) PgDL

Ainge *Mrs Katy*
Call Date: Nov 2002 (Lincoln's Inn) Qualifications: LLB (Hons)(Manch)

Airey *Mr Anthony Maurice*
Call Date: July 1988 (Inner Temple) Qualifications: LLB

Akers *Mr Timothy Robert*
Associate, Solicitor, Hine & Associates, Oxford Summertown Office, 285 Banbury Road, Summertown, Oxford, Oxfordshire, OX2 7HT, Call Date: July 2005 (Gray's Inn) Qualifications: LLB

Akindoyin *Miss Comfort Yetunde*
Call Date: Oct 2008 (Lincoln's Inn) Qualifications: LLB (Bris)

Akinola *Miss Abidemi*
Call Date: Nov 2007 (Inner Temple) Qualifications: LLB (Dunelm)

Akonta *Mr Victor Solomon Kudzo*
Senior Principal Legal Officer, Call Date: Nov 1975 (Inner Temple) Qualifications: MA

Akosa *Miss Nana Serwa*
Call Date: July 2012 (Middle Temple)

Akter *Miss Sumon*
Call Date: July 2008 (Lincoln's Inn) Qualifications: LLB (Sheff)

Alam *Mr Md Masud*
Call Date: Mar 2009 (Lincoln's Inn) Qualifications: LLB (Newc)

Alam *Mr Monsur*
Call Date: Nov 1999 (Lincoln's Inn) Qualifications: BSc (Dhaka) LLB (Hons) (Wolves)

Alamgir *Miss Zainab*
Call Date: Mar 2006 (Lincoln's Inn) Qualifications: LLB (Hons) (Lond)

Albery *Mr Oliver Peter*
Call Date: July 1972 (Lincoln's Inn)

Albri *Mr Bledi Edward*
Call Date: July 2012 (Lincoln's Inn)

Alhady *Mr Syed Farid*
Call Date: July 2012 (Inner Temple)

Ali *Miss Aisha*
Call Date: Oct 2006 (Lincoln's Inn) Qualifications: LLB (Sheff)

Ali *Mr Mosaddeq Ahmed*
Call Date: July 1999 (Lincoln's Inn) Qualifications: LLB (Hons)

Ali *Mrs Saleha*
Call Date: July 2012 (Gray's Inn)

Ali-Noor *Mr Sehar Izzat*
Call Date: Oct 2011 (Gray's Inn) Qualifications: LLB

Allen *Ms Heather Muriel*
Mediator, Call Date: Nov 1977 (Inner Temple) Qualifications: BA (Hons) (Lond) CEDR FRSA

Allott *Mr Stephen Anthony*
Call Date: Nov 1981 (Gray's Inn) Qualifications: MA (Cantab)

Allybokus *Mr Javed Moussa*
Call Date: July 2012 (Gray's Inn)

Amarasingham *Mr Dushyanthan*
Call Date: July 2003 (Inner Temple) Qualifications: BEng LLB (Lond)

Amarasingham *Mr Vijeya-Raghavan*
Call Date: July 2007 (Gray's Inn) Qualifications: LLB (Lond)

Ames *Mr Geoffrey Alan*
Call Date: July 1976 (Lincoln's Inn) Qualifications: BSc

Amoako Nyantakyiwa *Miss Lorraine*
Call Date: July 2008 (Lincoln's Inn) Qualifications: LLB (Lond)

Amponsah *Miss Nana Abena Antwiwaa*
Call Date: July 2012 (Lincoln's Inn)

Anderson *Miss Ella Dawn*
Call Date: Nov 2006 (Inner Temple) Qualifications: BA (Lond)

Anderson *Miss Eva-Marie*
Call Date: July 2012 (Middle Temple)

Andrew *Mrs Margaret*
Call Date: Feb 1987 (Middle Temple) Qualifications: Dip Law CPE

Angus *Mr James William*
Call Date: July 2012 (Inner Temple)

Anthony *Miss Farin Olivia*
Call Date: Mar 2004 (Middle Temple) Qualifications: LLB (Hons) (Nott'm)

Antoine *Ms Francesca Juliet Margaret*
Call Date: July 2012 (Lincoln's Inn)

Antwi-Boasiako *Mr Kwaku*
Call Date: Oct 2010 (Inner Temple) Qualifications: BPhil (B'ham) LLM PGDip Law

Anwar *Miss Nadia*
Call Date: July 2012 (Lincoln's Inn)

Appleton *Miss Katy*
Call Date: Oct 2000 (Lincoln's Inn) Qualifications: BA (Hons) (Leic)

Arefin *Mr Saleh Mohammad*
Call Date: July 2012 (Lincoln's Inn)

Argent *Miss Sophia*
Call Date: July 2007 (Lincoln's Inn) Qualifications: BA (Lond)

Armstrong *Miss Kirsty Marie*
Call Date: Oct 2008 (Inner Temple) Qualifications: LLB

Artner *Miss Petra Angelika*
Call Date: Nov 2007 (Middle Temple) Qualifications: LLM

Arzandeh *Mr Ardavan*
Call Date: July 2012 (Lincoln's Inn)

Aslam *Miss Sarah*
Call Date: Nov 2008 (Inner Temple)
Qualifications: LLB (Sheff) CPE

Aslett *Mr Charles Nicholas*
Call Date: July 2012 (Middle Temple)

Atherton *Miss Sally*
Call Date: July 1987 (Middle Temple)
Qualifications: LLB (Man)

Athill *Ms Amaya Marissa*
Call Date: July 2011 (Gray's Inn)
Qualifications: LLB

Athwal *Miss Gursharon Kaur*
The Bar Standards Board, 4th Floor, 289-293 High Holborn, London, WC1V 7HZ, 020 7611 1444, Fax: 020 7831 9217, Call Date: Nov 2008 (Lincoln's Inn) Qualifications: LLB (Leic)

G

Atkins *Mr Richard Anton*
Call Date: Nov 2006 (Middle Temple)
Qualifications: BBusSc

Atuah *Miss Velda Adobea*
Call Date: July 2012 (Lincoln's Inn)

Austen *Miss Kate Jane*
Call Date: Oct 2008 (Lincoln's Inn)
Qualifications: LLB (Huddersfield)

Austen *Mr Timothy Alexander*
Call Date: July 2012 (Lincoln's Inn)

Austin *Miss Patricia Mary*
Call Date: Nov 1955 (Gray's Inn)

Awan *Miss Zaynab*
Call Date: July 2009 (Middle Temple)
Qualifications: LLB (Hons) (Keele)

Awang Metussin *Miss Dayang Nadiah*
Call Date: July 2012 (Lincoln's Inn)

Baba *Miss Yasmin Abiba Al*
Call Date: July 2012 (Lincoln's Inn)

Bachor *Mr Kevin Damian*
Call Date: July 2012 (Inner Temple)

Baddoo *Mr Samuel Nablah*
Call Date: July 2012 (Lincoln's Inn)

Bagshaw *Mr Duncan John*
St Philips Chambers, 55 Temple Row, Birmingham, B2 5LS, Call Date: July 2003 (Lincoln's Inn) Qualifications: LLB (Hons) (B'ham)

Bailey *Mr David Peter*
Call Date: July 2012 (Middle Temple)

Bailey *Mr James John*
Call Date: July 2012 (Gray's Inn)

Bains *Ms Neenu Navpreet*
Call Date: July 2012 (Middle Temple)

Baisden *Mr Howard Ralph*
Call Date: July 1972 (Middle Temple)
Qualifications: LLM

Baker *Mr Robert John*
Call Date: Oct 1996 (Middle Temple)
Qualifications: LLB (Hons) LLM (Lond)

Bakshi *Miss Irvinder Kaur*
Arbitrator, Secretary, KSB Law Consultants Limited, 15 Woodcote Valley Road, Purley, Surrey, CR8 3AL, 020 8763 6909, Fax: 020 8763 6910/020 8711 6609, Call Date: Nov 1987 (Lincoln's Inn) Qualifications: LLB (Hons) FCIArb DipICArb

Bakshi *Miss Priya Shobhna*
Call Date: July 2012 (Middle Temple)

Ballard *Mr David Edward*
Call Date: July 1988 (Middle Temple)
Qualifications: BSc (Lond) CEng FCIArb FICE LLB MSc (Lon)

Ballard *Mr Peter*
Compton Developments, Po Box 425, Swansea, Glamorgan, SA6 8YH, 01792 315460, Fax: 01792 315513, Call Date: Nov 1976 (Middle Temple)
Qualifications: MA (Cantab) ATII MBA ACA

Balogh *Mr Christopher Thomas*
Call Date: Nov 1984 (Middle Temple)
Qualifications: MA (Cantab) MSc (Econ) DipLaw

Balonwu *Miss Nkiru*
Call Date: Oct 2001 (Lincoln's Inn)
Qualifications: LLB (Hons)(Manch)

Banerjee *Mr Anindya*
Other, Call Date: Oct 2010 (Lincoln's Inn) Qualifications: LLB (Hons) (Northumbria) PGCE (Lancaster) LLM (Cardiff)

Banerjee *Mr Baladeb*
Call Date: July 1970 (Middle Temple)
Qualifications: MA LLB

Banerjee *Mr Ranamit*
Call Date: July 2012 (Middle Temple)

Banerjee *Miss Ria Indira Tina Ava*
Call Date: July 2012 (Inner Temple)

Banjoko *Mr Alimi Ajimon*
Call Date: July 2005 (Lincoln's Inn)
Qualifications: LLB (Hons) Wolves BA (Hons) MA CFP

Bappy *Mr Shakir Uddin Ahmed*
Call Date: July 2011 (Lincoln's Inn)
Qualifications: LLB (Lond)

Baptiste *Ms Iasha Giselle*
Call Date: July 2012 (Gray's Inn)

Barber *Mr Nathaniel Paul*
Call Date: July 2012 (Gray's Inn)

Barclay *Mrs Aimee Elizabeth*
Call Date: July 2008 (Inner Temple)
Qualifications: LLB (Bris) LLM (Bris)

Barker *Mr David QC*
Judge, Master of the Bench, Recorder, Deputy High Court, Call Date: July 1954 (Inner Temple) Qualifications: LLB (Lond) LLM (USA)

Barlen *Ms Catherine Veronica*
Call Date: Oct 1990 (Inner Temple)
Qualifications: BA (Oxon) Dip Law LLM (Belgium)

Barnes *Miss Lena Jane*
Call Date: July 2012 (Inner Temple)

Barnett *Mr Jeremy Mark*
Call Date: July 2012 (Inner Temple)

Barr *Prof Alistair Robert Sanders*
Call Date: July 2012 (Middle Temple)

Barrett *Ms Rachel*
Call Date: July 2012 (Inner Temple)

Barry *Miss Margaret Mary*
The Law Libray, Distillery Building, Four Courts, Inns Quay, Dublin 7, Ireland, Call Date: Nov 1984 (Gray's Inn)
Qualifications: BA (Dublin) Dip EU Law (Dublin) MA (Dublin)

Barstow *Mr Stephen Royden*
Call Date: July 1976 (Gray's Inn)
Qualifications: MA (Cantab)

Bashford *Mr Keith*
Call Date: July 1980 (Lincoln's Inn)
Qualifications: LLB

Bastian *Mr Edward James*
Call Date: July 2007 (Inner Temple)
Qualifications: LLB (Lond)

Bates *Mr Joshua William*
Call Date: July 2012 (Inner Temple)

Batstone *Mr Rodney Karl CBE*
Call Date: June 1961 (Inner Temple)
Qualifications: MA LLB (Cantab)

Bauluck *Mr Abdullah Yusuf Ali*
Call Date: July 2012 (Middle Temple)

Bayliss *Mr Edward*
Call Date: July 2012 (Gray's Inn)

Beardsmore *Dr Valerie*
Call Date: May 1990 (Middle Temple)
Qualifications: BA (Wales) PhD (Kent)

Beattie *Mrs Amanda Jayne*
Call Date: Oct 2008 (Inner Temple)
Qualifications: BSc (Lond)

Beaty *Mr Richard John Gavin*
Call Date: July 2012 (Lincoln's Inn)

Bedwell *Mrs Sarah Elizabeth*
Call Date: Nov 1994 (Lincoln's Inn)
Qualifications: LLB (Hons)(Lond) MSc (Lond)

Bee *Miss Fiona Kayleigh*
Call Date: Nov 2011 (Lincoln's Inn)
Qualifications: LLB (Plymouth)

Beeby *Mr Ian Philip*
Solicitor, Call Date: Nov 2008 (Lincoln's Inn) Qualifications: BSc (So'ton) LLB

Beeley *Mr Mark Justin*
Solicitor Advocate, Vinson and Elkins, Citypoint (33rd Floor), 1 Ropemaker Sreet, London, EC2Y 9UE, 020 7 6046, Fax: 020 7065 6001, Call Date: Nov 2001 (Lincoln's Inn) Qualifications: LLB (Hons) (Exon) MCIArb

Beesley *Miss Sophie*
Call Date: July 2012 (Lincoln's Inn)

Begum *Mrs Hasina*
Call Date: Mar 2010 (Middle Temple) Qualifications: LLB (Bangladesh) LLM (Bangladesh) LLB (Lond)

Behanzin *Mr Tiyani*
Call Date: July 2006 (Lincoln's Inn) Qualifications: BA LLM (Nott'm) LLB (Lond)

Behbahani *Mr Khashayar*
Consultant, Solicitor, Argo House, Kilburn Park Road, London, NW6 5LF, 020 7644 0203, Fax: 020 7644 0603, Call Date: Oct 1999 (Inner Temple) Qualifications: LLB (Lond)

Bell *Miss Alice Naomi Jane*
Call Date: July 2010 (Middle Temple) Qualifications: BA (Hons) (Cantab)

Bell *Mr Matthew Andrew*
Para-Legal, Call Date: Oct 2008 (Inner Temple) Qualifications: BA (Oxon)

Bell-Paris *Miss Ayesha*
Call Date: July 2012 (Lincoln's Inn)

Belmar-Valencia *Ms Gabriela Cristina*
Call Date: Oct 2009 (Lincoln's Inn) Qualifications: LLB (Hull)

Bendall *Miss Charlotte Louise*
Call Date: July 2007 (Lincoln's Inn) Qualifications: BA (Oxon)

Benson *Mr Charles Jefferius Woodburn QC*
Call Date: Feb 1990 (Middle Temple) Qualifications: MA BA (Hons) LLM (Cantab)

Bentley *Miss Elizabeth Rose*
Call Date: Nov 2008 (Lincoln's Inn) Qualifications: LLB (Cardiff)

Benton *Mr Derek John*
Call Date: Oct 2011 (Middle Temple) Qualifications: MusB (Hons) (Manch)

Beresford *Mr John Martin Patrick*
Call Date: July 2012 (Lincoln's Inn)

Beresford-Evans *Ms Cerys*
Call Date: Nov 1995 (Middle Temple) Qualifications: LLB (Hons)

Bergin *Mr Gerard Patrick*
Adjudicator, Managing Director, Bergin Associates, 9 Barnacre Drive, Parkgate, South Wirral, Cheshire, CH64 6RJ, 0151 336 4643, Fax: 0151 336 7372, Call Date: July 1995 (Middle Temple) Qualifications: LLB (Hons) FCIOB FRICS

Berry *Miss Sophia Cordelia De Voil*
Call Date: July 2012 (Lincoln's Inn)

Bhamra *Miss Meena Kaur*
Call Date: Nov 1997 (Middle Temple) Qualifications: LLB (Hons) LLM (Hons) (Cambridge)

Bhattacharjee *Mr Partha Sarathy*
Call Date: Nov 2007 (Middle Temple) Qualifications: LLB (Hons) (Lond)

Bhatti *Mr Ahsan*
Call Date: July 2012 (Middle Temple)

Bhimjee *Mr Anwar Ali*
244 Juanita Way, San Francisco, California 94127, USA, (415) 242 1734, Call Date: July 1965 (Lincoln's Inn) Qualifications: MA FCA LLB

Bhimji *Ms Mumtaz Begum*
Call Date: July 1971 (Gray's Inn) Qualifications: LLB (Hons)

Bhowmick *Miss Anita*
Call Date: July 2012 (Inner Temple)

Bhuiyan *Mr Mohammad Dullah Rahim*
Call Date: Nov 2009 (Middle Temple) Qualifications: LLB (Hons)(Dhaka) LLB (Hons)

Bhujohory *Mr Sajjit Singh*
Call Date: July 2012 (Middle Temple)

Bibby *Mr John Benjamin*
Call Date: July 1981 (Gray's Inn) Qualifications: MA (Cantab)

Bibi *Miss Qubra*
Call Date: July 2012 (Lincoln's Inn)

Bibi *Mrs Zainab*
Call Date: July 2012 (Lincoln's Inn)

Bicknell *Mrs Louise Jean*
Managing Director, Other, Pershing Limited, Capstan House, Legal Department, One Clove Crescent, East India Dock, London, E14 2BH, 020 7864 8277, Fax: 020 7864 8499, Call Date: Nov 1984 (Middle Temple) Qualifications: BA

Bicknell *Mr Simon Michael*
Call Date: Nov 1983 (Middle Temple) Qualifications: BA (Hons)

Bierer *Mr Timothy Ryan*
Call Date: July 2012 (Inner Temple)

Birbal *Miss Savita Tamara*
Call Date: July 2012 (Inner Temple)

Bird *Mrs Penelope Hamilton*
Call Date: July 1982 (Inner Temple) Qualifications: BA

Blackman *Mr Colin*
Other, Call Date: July 1988 (Gray's Inn) Qualifications: BSc (Lond) MSc (Reading) C Phys

Blair *Miss Kathryn Hazel*
Call Date: July 2012 (Lincoln's Inn)

Blake *Mr Andrew John*
Call Date: July 2012 (Lincoln's Inn)

Blakeley *Mr John Christopher*
Call Date: July 1967 (Lincoln's Inn) Qualifications: MA

Blance *Mr Alexander James*
Call Date: July 2012 (Inner Temple)

Blythe *Mr James Benjamin*
Call Date: Nov 2011 (Lincoln's Inn) Qualifications: LLB (Newc)

Boardall *Miss Sophia Rebecca Zoe*
Call Date: July 2012 (Middle Temple)

Boardman *Mr Patrick*
Call Date: Nov 2001 (Middle Temple) Qualifications: BA (Hons)

Bogaert *Mr Peter Willy Luc*
Call Date: May 1995 (Gray's Inn) Qualifications: Licenciaat in de Rechten BA

Boodia-Canoo *Ms Nandini Shivany*
Call Date: July 2007 (Inner Temple) Qualifications: LLB (Lond)

Borge *Mr Peter Hector Paul*
Call Date: Nov 2011 (Inner Temple) Qualifications: Beng (Plymouth)

Bower *Miss Amy Madeleine*
Call Date: Nov 2005 (Lincoln's Inn) Qualifications: BA (Hons) (B'ham) GDL (B'ham)

Box *Miss Joanne Katherine*
Call Date: July 2012 (Middle Temple)

Boynes *Miss Hannah*
Call Date: July 2009 (Lincoln's Inn) Qualifications: LLB (Hudds)

Bracken *Miss Carolina Imelda Deangelis*
Call Date: July 2012 (Inner Temple)

Brad *Miss Adelina*
Call Date: July 2012 (Inner Temple)

Bradley *Mr Mark James*
Legal Adviser, Call Date: July 2004 (Middle Temple) Qualifications: BSc Hons (Leeds) PGDip Law

Bradley *Mr Paul David*
Other, Call Date: July 1979 (Gray's Inn) Qualifications: LLB (Exon)

Brady *Mr Stuart James*
Call Date: July 2012 (Middle Temple)

Braham *Ms Gillian*
Call Date: Oct 2008 (Middle Temple) Qualifications: LLB (Hons) (Lond)

Brand *Mrs Alison Jill*
Call Date: Oct 2003 (Inner Temple) Qualifications: BSc (Kingston)

Brawn *Ms Miranda Katherine*
Call Date: July 2012 (Lincoln's Inn)

Bray *Mr David William*
Call Date: Nov 2002 (Inner Temple) Qualifications: LLB (Essex) LLM

Brayley *Miss Jayne Amanda*
Call Date: July 2012 (Lincoln's Inn)

Bremang *Miss Wendy Ann Tawia*
Call Date: July 2012 (Gray's Inn)

Brewer *Miss Charlotte Jade*
Call Date: July 2012 (Inner Temple)

Bridge *Mr Mark David*
Professor of Law, M D Bridge, 3395 Cadboro Bay Road, Victoria, Bristish Columbia, CANADA, Canada, Call Date: July 1992 (Lincoln's Inn) Qualifications: LLB (Canada) BSc (Canada) LLM (Lond)

G

Brightwell *Ms Christine Lesley*
The Pension Professionals Ltd, Lombard Business Park, 8 Lombard Road, London, SW19 3TZ, 0845 076 3000, Fax: 0845 076 3011, Call Date: Oct 1999 (Gray's Inn) Qualifications: BA (Hons) (Brighton)

Brindle *Miss Elaine*
Call Date: July 1978 (Middle Temple) Qualifications: LLB (Hons) (B'ham)

Briscoe *Miss Frederica Anne*
Call Date: July 2012 (Inner Temple)

Bromley-Davenport *Mr John QC*
Recorder, Deans Court Chambers, 24 St John Street, Manchester, M3 4DF, Call Date: Feb 1972 (Gray's Inn)

Brook *Miss Kathleen*
Call Date: Nov 2006 (Lincoln's Inn) Qualifications: LLB (Herts)

Brown *Mr Roger William*
Head of Legal Services, Clarion Solicitors LLP, Britannia Chambers, 4 Oxford Place, Leeds, West Yorkshire, LS1 3AX, 0113 246 0622, Fax: 0113 246 7488, Call Date: Nov 1975 (Middle Temple) Qualifications: LLB (Manch)

Brown *Mr Steven David*
Call Date: Oct 1994 (Inner Temple) Qualifications: BA (Lond) MA (Reading) Dip Law

Bruce *Mr Israel Rondolph*
Call Date: July 2012 (Gray's Inn)

Bruckshaw *Ms Stacey*
Call Date: Nov 2009 (Gray's Inn) Qualifications: LLB

Buckley *Prof Richard Anthony*
School of Law, University of Reading, Foxhill House, Earley, Reading, RG6 7BA, Call Date: Nov 1969 (Lincoln's Inn) Qualifications: MA DCL (Oxon) DPhil (Oxon)

Budden *Dr Ian*
Legal Adviser, University of London, Senate House, Malet Street, London, WC1E 7HU, 020 7862 8000, Fax: 020 7862 8233, Call Date: July 1993 (Middle Temple) Qualifications: MA LLB Ph D

Budwal *Miss Sundeep Kaur*
Call Date: July 2012 (Inner Temple)

Bullard *Mr Ashley Roy*
Call Date: Oct 2008 (Lincoln's Inn) Qualifications: LLB (Hull) LLM (UCL)

Burge *Mr Rodney Michael*
Call Date: July 2001 (Middle Temple) Qualifications: LLB (Hons) Pg Dplm CFE

Burns *Mr Martin Oliver*
Royal Institution of Chartered Surveyors, Surveyor Court, Westwood Way, Coventry, Warwickshire, CV4 6JE, 020 7334 3805, Fax: 020 7334 3802, Call Date: July 2005 (Lincoln's Inn) Qualifications: BA (Hons) LLB (Hons)

Burslem *Ms Sarah Bryony*
Enterprise Chambers, 9 Old Square, Lincoln's Inn, London, WC2A 3SR, 020 7405 9471, Fax: 020 7242 1447, Call Date: Oct 2008 (Gray's Inn) Qualifications: LLB BCL

Burton *Mr Rhett Nicholas Page*
Call Date: July 2012 (Inner Temple)

Bushnell *Mr David Edward*
Call Date: May 1953 (Middle Temple)

Butcher *Dr Kevin John*
Call Date: Oct 2006 (Lincoln's Inn) Qualifications: BA (Oxon) MRES PhD

Butt *Ms Saiqa Jamil*
Other, Call Date: Feb 1991 (Middle Temple) Qualifications: LLB

Butterfield *Miss Lauren Elizabeth*
Call Date: Mar 2009 (Middle Temple) Qualifications: LLB (Hons) (Lond)

Buttery *Miss Alison Tracey*
Call Date: July 1997 (Lincoln's Inn) Qualifications: BA (Hons) (Hull) ACIS LLDip

Buxton *Mrs Sarah Frances*
Call Date: Nov 1992 (Inner Temple) Qualifications: LLB (Bris)

Cadbury *Miss Justine*
Queen Elizabeth Bldg, 3rd Floor, Queen Elizabeth Bldg, Temple, London, EC4Y 9BS, 020 7797 7837, Fax: 020 7353 5422, Call Date: Nov 2001 (Middle Temple) Qualifications: BA (Hons) (Bris)

Cahalan *Mr Anthony John*
Call Date: July 2012 (Middle Temple)

Caiels *Miss Laura Jayne*
Call Date: July 2008 (Middle Temple) Qualifications: LLB (Hons) (Lond)

Calcroft *Mr Christopher John*
Call Date: Oct 1996 (Middle Temple) Qualifications: BA (Hons) BArch CPE FCIArb MSc

Cam *Mr David Edward*
Company Secretary, Director, Blackpool Pleasure Beach Ltd, Ocean Boulevard, Blackpool, Lancashire, FY4 1EZ, 01253 341033, Fax: 01253 401098, Call Date: May 1981 (Middle Temple) Qualifications: BA

Camp *Miss Haley Louise*
Call Date: July 2012 (Gray's Inn)

Campbell *Mr Andrew Ian*
Call Date: July 2012 (Lincoln's Inn)

Campbell *Mr Andrew Neil*
Call Date: Nov 1988 (Middle Temple) Qualifications: MA (Cantab)

Campbell *Ms Jeniffer Lingaury*
Call Date: Nov 2007 (Gray's Inn) Qualifications: BEng Meng

Campbell *Ms Jess*
Call Date: Mar 2012 (Lincoln's Inn)

Campbell *Miss Natalie Grace*
Other, Call Date: Oct 1999 (Lincoln's Inn) Qualifications: LLB (Hons)(Kent) LLM (Bris)

Campion *Mr Donald John Martin*
Call Date: June 1956 (Gray's Inn) Qualifications: MA (Cantab)

Cann *Miss Kara Jane*
Call Date: July 2012 (Lincoln's Inn)

Cannon *Mr Nicholas Charles*
Adviser, Other, c/o Herzog Fox & Neeman, Asia House, 4 Weizmann Street, Tel Aviv 62962, Israel, 00 972 545690709, Call Date: July 1973 (Gray's Inn) Qualifications: LLB (Lond)

Cansick *Mr Allen Thomas*
Call Date: Oct 2004 (Inner Temple) Qualifications: BA (Wales) CPE (Lond)

Caplin *Dr Oliver Simon*
Call Date: July 2012 (Middle Temple)

Carballo-Williams *Miss Leila Margarita*
Call Date: Nov 2007 (Lincoln's Inn) Qualifications: BA (Lond)

Cardew *Mr Maxim Paul*
Call Date: July 2012 (Gray's Inn)

Carey *Miss Solika Shonica*
Call Date: July 2012 (Lincoln's Inn)

Carless *Mr Alexander George*
Call Date: July 2012 (Lincoln's Inn)

Carmichael *Mr Adam Jason*
Call Date: July 2010 (Inner Temple) Qualifications: LLB (So'ton)

Carmichael *Miss Sri Hannah*
Call Date: July 2012 (Inner Temple)

Caro De Sousa *Mr Pedro De Almeida Frazao*
Call Date: July 2012 (Middle Temple)

Carter *Mr Mark Hamilton*
Consultant, Carter Planning Limited, 85 Alma Road, Windsor, Berkshire, SL4 3EX, 01753 867447, Call Date: July 2000 (Middle Temple) Qualifications: BA(Hons) LLB(Hons)(Lond) MRTPI FRGS

Carter *Mr Peter André*
Call Date: July 2012 (Inner Temple)

Carter-Braine *Ms Natalie*
Amgen Ltd, 240 Cambridge Science Park, Milton Road, Cambridge, CB4 0WD, 01223 436054, Call Date: July 2008 (Gray's Inn) Qualifications: BSc (Brunel)

Cartwright *Miss Sadie Louise*
Call Date: July 2009 (Lincoln's Inn) Qualifications: LLB (L'pool)

Casserly *Mr David Anthony*
Call Date: July 2012 (Middle Temple)

Cawley-Wilkinson *Miss Sarah Ann*
Call Date: July 2010 (Middle Temple) Qualifications: LLB (Hons) (Nott'm)

Cawood *Mr Nicholas James*
Call Date: July 2012 (Inner Temple)

Chai *Mr Adrian Kho Hung*
Call Date: July 2012 (Lincoln's Inn)

Chaker *Miss Leila Sarah*
Call Date: July 2012 (Middle Temple)

Chan *Mr Che Bun Anderson*
Call Date: Nov 1997 (Gray's Inn) Qualifications: LLB LLM (Australia) GCBL PCEUL DipProjMan LLM (Lond) GCURP

Chan *Mr Tik-Hin Dickson*
Call Date: July 2012 (Lincoln's Inn)

Chandran *Miss Kalpana*
Call Date: July 2012 (Inner Temple)

Chandran *Miss Kanchana*
Call Date: July 2012 (Inner Temple)

Chapman *Mr Robin Denis*
Call Date: Mar 1998 (Middle Temple) Qualifications: LLB (Hons) BSc PGCert Adj MRICS MCIArb

Charles *Miss Deborah Ann*
6 Pump Court, 1st Floor, 6 Pump Court, Temple, London, EC4Y 7AR, Call Date: Oct 1996 (Lincoln's Inn) Qualifications: BA (Hons)(Warw) CPE (Middx)

Charlesworth *Mr Philip John*
Call Date: Nov 2003 (Gray's Inn) Qualifications: BA (Wales) MSc (Lanc)

Charnock *Mrs Elizabeth Mary*
Legal Adviser, Call Date: Oct 2006 (Middle Temple) Qualifications: LLB (Hons)

Chaudri *Mr Hashim Abid*
Call Date: July 2012 (Middle Temple)

Cheng *Miss Kitty Kit Yee*
Solicitor, Call Date: Apr 1991 (Gray's Inn) Qualifications: LLB MIL PCLL

Cheung *Mr K-John*
Lawyer, Call Date: July 1973 (Lincoln's Inn) Qualifications: BSc Dip Comp Law Dip Ch Law JD LLB

Chia *Miss Cai Jin*
Call Date: July 2012 (Inner Temple)

Chia *Mr Wilson*
Call Date: July 2012 (Lincoln's Inn)

Chichester *Mr Julian Edward Michael*
Call Date: Nov 1977 (Inner Temple)

Chilton *Miss Melorie Anne*
Chilton Media Law Limited, 8 West Street, London, WC2H 9NG, 020 7836 2764, Call Date: Nov 1980 (Gray's Inn) Qualifications: LLB (Lond) LLM (Lond)

Chin *Miss Rachel Sue-Li*
Call Date: July 2012 (Middle Temple)

Chinyama *Dr Catherine Nyaya*
Call Date: Nov 2009 (Lincoln's Inn) Qualifications: MBchB (Hons) LLM (Newc) CPE OBPP

Chiy *Dr Paul Chu*
Synergy Law Firm, PO Box 4430, Nlongkak, Yaounde, Cameroon, Call Date: Mar 2012 (Gray's Inn)

Chong *Mr Terrence Edward*
Call Date: July 2012 (Inner Temple)

Choo *Miss Lyn Pearl*
Call Date: July 2012 (Inner Temple)

Choudhary *Mr Mudassar Ishaq*
Call Date: July 2012 (Lincoln's Inn)

Choudhary *Miss Rabia*
Call Date: July 2010 (Lincoln's Inn) Qualifications: LLB (Lond)

Choudhury *Ms Roxana Idris*
Call Date: Mar 1996 (Inner Temple) Qualifications: LLB

Chowdhury *Mr Aneera Joshini*
Call Date: July 2012 (Middle Temple)

Chowdhury *Miss Fayeka Akther*
Call Date: July 2011 (Inner Temple) Qualifications: LLB (Lond)

Chowdhury *Mr Mashmoom Hoq*
Call Date: Nov 2010 (Gray's Inn) Qualifications: LLB LLM

Chowdhury *Mr Masud*
Call Date: Oct 2008 (Lincoln's Inn) Qualifications: BA (Hons) (Lond) LLPGD (Lond)

Christian *Mr Simon Joseph*
Call Date: July 2012 (Middle Temple)

Chua *Miss Meixin Sherri*
Call Date: July 2012 (Lincoln's Inn)

Chung *Mr Insu*
Call Date: Oct 2008 (Middle Temple) Qualifications: LLB (Hons) LLM (Lond)

Chung *Mr Kee Ying*
Call Date: Nov 1990 (Gray's Inn) Qualifications: LLB (Lond)

Churcher *Mr Daniel William*
Call Date: July 2012 (Gray's Inn)

Churitter *Miss Luxmi*
Call Date: July 2012 (Lincoln's Inn)

Clancey *Mr Michael Patrick*
Call Date: Mar 2011 (Middle Temple) Qualifications: BSL (USA) Jurisdoctorate (USA) LLM (USA) LLM (USA)

Clare *Ms Carina Elizabeth*
Call Date: July 2012 (Gray's Inn)

Clark *Mr Stuart Michael*
Para-Legal, Reynolds, Peter Chamberlain LLP, Tower Bridge House, St Katherine's Way, London, E1W 1AA, 020 3060 6238, Call Date: Nov 2006 (Gray's Inn) Qualifications: LLB

Clarke *Mr Brian Michael*
Call Date: July 2008 (Middle Temple) Qualifications: LLB (Hons) (Leic)

Clarke *Mr David Andrew*
Call Date: July 2012 (Middle Temple)

Clarke *Mr Dominic Tobias*
Blaney Mcmurtry, Barristers & Solicitors LLP, 20 Queen Street, West Suite 1400, Toronto, M5H 2V3, Canada, 416 593 1221, Fax: 416 593 5437, Call Date: July 1988 (Middle Temple) Qualifications: MA LLM (Cantab)

Clarke *Mr Giles Nevill*
Call Date: Nov 1976 (Middle Temple) Qualifications: MA (Cantab) PhD (Lond) CTA (Fellow)

Clarke *Miss Louise Marie*
Call Date: July 2010 (Middle Temple) Qualifications: BA (Hons) (Dunelm)

Clayton *Miss Lauren Chelsea*
Call Date: July 2012 (Gray's Inn)

Cleary *Miss Niamh*
Call Date: July 2012 (Lincoln's Inn)

Clerk *Mr William James*
Call Date: July 2012 (Middle Temple)

Clifford *Mr Shane Wesley*
Call Date: Oct 2007 (Inner Temple) Qualifications: LLB

Cobb *Miss Phoebe Florence*
Call Date: July 2012 (Gray's Inn)

Cockshott *Ms Gemma Louise*
Call Date: July 2012 (Gray's Inn)

Coe *Mr Samuel James*
Call Date: July 2012 (Lincoln's Inn)

Cohen-Lask *Miss Maia Rachel*
Call Date: July 2012 (Lincoln's Inn)

Coker *Dr William John OBE QHP*
Consultant, Call Date: July 2006 (Lincoln's Inn) Qualifications: BSc MB ChB LLB BA FRCP

Cole Roberts *Miss Alice Geraldine*
Call Date: July 2012 (Inner Temple)

Coleman *Mr Kieran Joseph*
Call Date: July 2012 (Middle Temple)

Collier *Mr Stephen John*
General Counsel, General Healthcare Group Ltd, 4 Thameside Centre, Kew Bridge Road, Brentford, Middlesex, TW8 0HF, Call Date: July 1980 (Lincoln's Inn) Qualifications: LLB (Hons) Dip Ae Law LLM

Collins *Mr Michael Geoffrey QC*
Legal Consultant, Mediator, Other, Crandall, Hanscom and Collins P.A, P.O Box 664, 10 School Street, Rockland, Maine, 04841-0664, USA, +1 207 594 4421, Fax: +1 240 363 0599, Call Date: Nov 1971 (Gray's Inn) Qualifications: LLB (Exon)

Collins *Mr Peter Lloyd*
Call Date: July 2012 (Lincoln's Inn)

Condry *Mr Samuel Nicholas*
The General Council of the Bar, 289-293 High Holborn, London, WC1V 7HZ, 020 7242 0082, Fax: 020 7831 9217, Call Date: Nov 2007 (Inner Temple) Qualifications: MA

Connah *Mr Jack Edward*
Call Date: July 2012 (Gray's Inn)

Connell *Mr William Howard*
Other, St Mary's Crecent, Third Floor, Hill Street, Douglas, Isle of Man, 01624 686 475, Call Date: July 1979 (Inner Temple) Qualifications: BA (Dunelm) LLM (Leic)

Connelly *Mr Paul Michael*
Call Date: Nov 1989 (Middle Temple) Qualifications: BSc (Exon) DipLaw M Phil (Cantab)

Consitt *Mr Jeremy David*
Solicitor, Doyle Clayton Solicitors Limited, Sovereign House, Vastern Road, Reading, RG1 8BT, 0118 351 6161, Call Date: Nov 2000 (Inner Temple) Qualifications: LLB (Hons) PG Dip

Constable *Mrs Judith*
Call Date: July 2012 (Gray's Inn)

Cook *Mr Christopher John*
Call Date: July 1975 (Gray's Inn) Qualifications: BA (Oxon)

Cook *Mr Robert*
Call Date: July 2012 (Gray's Inn)

Cooper *Mrs Laura*
Call Date: July 2009 (Middle Temple) Qualifications: LLB (Hons)

Cope *Mr Anthony James*
Call Date: Mar 2003 (Lincoln's Inn) Qualifications: LLB (Hons) (Oxon)

Copp *Dr Stephen Francis*
Associate, Solicitor, The Business School, Bournemouth University, Talbot Campus, Wallisdown, Poole, BH12 5BB, 01202 961 855, Call Date: Nov 1985 (Inner Temple) Qualifications: LLB (Exon) FHEA Hon FIIT

Coram James *Miss Clementine Lucy*
Call Date: July 2012 (Inner Temple)

Cornick *Mr Robert James*
Call Date: July 2012 (Middle Temple)

Corrah *Miss Nyansa Enmani Adebayo*
Call Date: Nov 2009 (Middle Temple) Qualifications: LLB (Hons) (Kent) LLM (Kent)

Cotter *Mr Michael James*
Call Date: Mar 2010 (Middle Temple) Qualifications: BA (So'ton) LLB (Lond)

Cotton *Mr Matthew Alexander*
Call Date: July 2008 (Gray's Inn) Qualifications: LLB (Bris)

Cowley *Mr Giles Norman James*
Call Date: July 2002 (Lincoln's Inn) Qualifications: BSc (Hons) Dip in Law

Cowling *Mr Robin John Reeves*
Call Date: July 2012 (Middle Temple)

Cownie *Prof Fiona Caird*
Professor of Law, Department of Law, Keele University, Keele, Staffordshire, ST5 5BG, 01782 734 130, Fax: 01782 733 228, Call Date: Nov 1985 (Lincoln's Inn) Qualifications: LLB (Leic) BA (Bristol) LLM (Lond)

Cracknell *Mr Douglas George*
Other, 23 Warham Road, 23 Warham Road, Otford, Sevenoaks, Kent, TN14 5PF, 01959 522325, Fax: 01959 522325, Call Date: May 1957 (Middle Temple) Qualifications: LLB

Craig *Mr Toby Alexander*
The General Council of the Bar, 4th Floor, 289-293 High Holborn, London, WC1V 7HZ, 020 7242 0082, Fax: 020 7831 9217, Call Date: July 2006 (Lincoln's Inn) Qualifications: BA (Leeds)

Crane *Miss Camilla Henley*
Call Date: July 2012 (Middle Temple)

Crane *Mr Malcolm*
Call Date: Nov 1967 (Gray's Inn) Qualifications: MA

Craney *Mr Colin John*
Consultant, Dunbar and Boardman, The Business Centre, 95 Spencer Street, Birmingham, B18 6DA, 0121 523 1130, Fax: 0121 523 1190, Call Date: July 2009 (Middle Temple) Qualifications: BSc (Hons) MBA LLB (Hons) MSc CEng CMIOSH MCMI LLM MCIBSE

Crawford *Miss Maria Clair*
Call Date: July 2012 (Middle Temple)

Crisp *Prof Peter Charles*
Call Date: Oct 1995 (Inner Temple) Qualifications: BA (Lond) CPE (Lond)

Crockford *Miss Felicity Chantelle*
Call Date: July 2010 (Lincoln's Inn) Qualifications: LLB (B'ham)

Crolley *Mrs Hellen*
Call Date: July 2012 (Inner Temple)

Cronin *Mr Ciaran*
Call Date: July 2012 (Middle Temple)

Cruickshank *Ms Dionne Alecia*
Call Date: Oct 2004 (Inner Temple) Qualifications: BA (Florida) LLB

Cryan *Mr Seén Tomés*
Call Date: July 2012 (Middle Temple)

Cuffie *Miss Kera Janella*
Call Date: July 2012 (Inner Temple)

Cushen *Mr Peter Roy*
Le Jardin, La Rue A Don, Grouville, JE3 9GB, Jersey, Call Date: July 1981 (Inner Temple) Qualifications: LLB (So'ton)

Cutting *Mr Stuart*
Call Date: Nov 2011 (Lincoln's Inn) Qualifications: LLB (Lond)

Dann *Miss Yolanda Maria*
Call Date: Nov 2003 (Lincoln's Inn) Qualifications: LLB (Hons) (Lancs)

Danny Kummar *Miss Michelle Sunita*
Call Date: July 2012 (Lincoln's Inn)

Darby *Mr Jonathan Michael*
Call Date: July 2012 (Middle Temple)

Darbyshire *Mr Gareth Carl*
Call Date: July 2012 (Middle Temple)

Dardani *Mr Lawrence*
Genoa Chambers, Piazza G.Verdi 6/9, Genoa, Italy, Fax: 010 5957705, Call Date: Nov 2010 (Inner Temple) Qualifications: LLB LLM (Italy)

Davies *Miss Ann Katharine*
Call Date: Oct 2006 (Middle Temple) Qualifications: BSc (Hons) (Manch) MA (Manch) PgDL

Davies *Mr Brett*
Call Date: July 2008 (Inner Temple) Qualifications: LLB (Teesside)

Davies *Miss Eleanor Mary*
Call Date: Oct 1998 (Inner Temple) Qualifications: BA (Sheff)

Davies *Miss Elizabeth Lindsey*
Call Date: Nov 2000 (Middle Temple) Qualifications: BA (Hons) (Nottingham

Davies *Miss Kaitlin Elizabeth*
Call Date: July 2012 (Middle Temple)

Davies *Mr Keith Frederick RD*
Call Date: July 1980 (Gray's Inn)

Davies *Mr Robin Hunkin*
Company Secretary, Director, Call Date: Nov 1960 (Inner Temple) Qualifications: LLB

Davies *Dr Vanessa Louise*
Director, The Bar Standards Board, 3rd Floor, 289-293 High Holborn, London, WC1V 7HZ, 020 7611 1444, Fax: 020 7831 9217, Call Date: Oct 2007 (Inner Temple) Qualifications: BA (Leic) PhD (Lond)

Davis *Mr Anthony Edward*
Hinshaw and Culbertson LLP, Fourth Floor, 780 Third Avenue, New York, Ny 10017, USA, 212 935 1100/(212) 935 1100, Fax: 212 471 8011/(212) 935 1166, Call Date: Nov 1970 (Lincoln's Inn) Qualifications: MA (Cantab) LLM

Davis *Mr Bernard James OBE*
Senior Lecturer, Portsmouth Business School, University of Portsmouth, Richmond Building, Portsmouth, PO1 3DE, 02392 844087, Call Date: July 1982 (Gray's Inn) Qualifications: LLB (B'ham) LLM (Portsmouth)

Davis *Miss Ceri Dawn*
Call Date: July 2009 (Middle Temple) Qualifications: BA (Hons) (Cantab)

Davis *Mr Julian Mark*
Call Date: July 1973 (Middle Temple) Qualifications: LLB

Dawood *Mr Elias*
Call Date: Nov 2011 (Lincoln's Inn) Qualifications: BA BA (Exon)

Dawson *Mr Peter Henry*
Legal Adviser, Call Date: Feb 1976 (Middle Temple) Qualifications: MA LLB (Lond)

De Wilde *Mr Gervase Edward Patrick*
Call Date: July 2012 (Lincoln's Inn)

Deal *Ms Indira Melissa*
Call Date: July 2012 (Lincoln's Inn)

Deane *Miss Tanja Katrien Thea*
Call Date: July 2012 (Inner Temple)

Dee *Mr Nicholas*
Call Date: July 1973 (Lincoln's Inn) Qualifications: BA (Hons) FCA

Deegan *Mr Marc James*
Call Date: Mar 2003 (Lincoln's Inn) Qualifications: LLB LLM

Dehinbo *Miss Olubunmi Omowunmi*
Call Date: Oct 2004 (Gray's Inn) Qualifications: BA LLB

Delaney *Mr Barry Douglas*
Call Date: Oct 1993 (Inner Temple) Qualifications: LLB (Lond)

Denham *Mr Grey*
COMT, Director, Call Date: Nov 1972 (Inner Temple) Qualifications: LLB (Lond)

Densem *Miss Julia Margaret*
Call Date: July 2007 (Inner Temple) Qualifications: BDS (Lond)

Desai *Mr Sadananda Shankrappa*
46 Parkfield Road, Harrow, Middlesex, HA2 8LB, 020 8422 2855, Call Date: July 1970 (Inner Temple) Qualifications: BA BIM Dip LLB

Deshraj *Ms Sukanya*
Call Date: July 2012 (Inner Temple)

Devine *Mr Joshua Thomas*
Call Date: July 2012 (Gray's Inn)

Dhunnoo *Mr Haresh Bhagwath Narain*
Call Date: Oct 2001 (Lincoln's Inn) Qualifications: LLB (Hons) LLM

Dian *Mr Joseph Désiré*
Call Date: July 2012 (Inner Temple)

Dillon *Mr Nicholas Jack*
Call Date: July 2012 (Lincoln's Inn)

Dingler *Miss Rebecca Elizabeth*
Call Date: Oct 2007 (Lincoln's Inn) Qualifications: LLB (Dunelm)

Doggett *Ms Abigail Sarah*
Call Date: July 2003 (Middle Temple) Qualifications: MA Hons (Cantab) BA Hons (Oxon)

Doherty *Ms Catriona*
Call Date: July 2012 (Lincoln's Inn)

Donald *Miss Charlotte Lucy*
Call Date: July 2012 (Gray's Inn)

Donnelly *Mr Barry Sean*
Call Date: Nov 1985 (Lincoln's Inn) Qualifications: MA (Cantab)

Donnison *Mr Peter Rhys*
Call Date: July 2012 (Lincoln's Inn)

Donovan *Mr Paul*
Call Date: Nov 2008 (Lincoln's Inn) Qualifications: BA(Portsmouth) CPE COL

Downey *Miss Nicola Anne*
Call Date: July 2012 (Inner Temple)

Dudley *Dr James Mark*
Call Date: July 2004 (Middle Temple) Qualifications: MA (Oxon) FRCP FRCPath MD PGDip Law

Dudley *Mrs Julia Jill*
Call Date: Nov 1982 (Middle Temple) Qualifications: Dip Law (Lond)

Duffy *Mr Simon John*
Deputy Chairman, Other, Senior Legal Officer, Call Date: Oct 1996 (Lincoln's Inn) Qualifications: BSc (Hons)(Sheff) CPE (Northumbria) MRICS Dip EC Law (Lond)

Duncan *Miss Catriona Mckinlay*
Call Date: July 2012 (Middle Temple)

Duncan *Mr William John*
Call Date: July 2012 (Gray's Inn)

Dunn *Miss Katherine Elspeth*
Call Date: Nov 1987 (Middle Temple) Qualifications: MA (Cantab)

Dunn-Walsh *Mr Patrick Jeremiah*
Call Date: July 2012 (Gray's Inn)

Dymond *Mr Anthony Simon*
Herbert Smith LLP, Exchange House, Primrose Street, London, EC2A 2HS, Call Date: Feb 1993 (Inner Temple) Qualifications: BA

Earles *Mr Charles Graham*
Solicitor, Call Date: Oct 1990 (Lincoln's Inn) Qualifications: MA (Cantab)

Easha *Miss Nusrat Bayazid*
Call Date: July 2012 (Lincoln's Inn)

Easterbrook *Miss Emma Reiko*
Her Majesty's Court Service, The Law Courts, 12 St Andrews Street, Cambridge, CB2 3AX, 01223 376049, Fax: 01223 376094, Call Date: July 2002 (Middle Temple) Qualifications: BA (Hons) (Cantab) CPE

Eastwood *Miss Niamh Catherine*
Head of Legal Services, Release, 388 Old Street, London, EC1V 9CT, 020 7729 9904, Call Date: July 2004 (Middle Temple) Qualifications: LLB Hons (LGU)

Eaton *Mr Richard Mark Cooper*
Lecturer in Law, Richard Eaton Law Training, Whisperwood, Westfield, Hastings, East Susssex, TN35 4RD, Call Date: May 1982 (Lincoln's Inn) Qualifications: LLB (Hons)

Ebrahim *Miss Aleisha-Fatéma*
Call Date: July 2012 (Middle Temple)

Edel *Mr Gary Mark*
Call Date: July 2012 (Middle Temple)

Edge *Miss Stephanie Sarah*
Call Date: July 2012 (Inner Temple)

Edinborough *Miss Amy Clare*
Call Date: July 2012 (Lincoln's Inn)

Edwards *Mr Benjamin*
Call Date: July 2007 (Middle Temple) Qualifications: LLB (Exon)

Edwards *Miss Helen Claire*
Call Date: Nov 2009 (Lincoln's Inn) Qualifications: LLB (Lancaster)

Edwards *Miss Jacqueline Anne*
Principal Lawyer, Legal Services, Surrey County Council, County Hall, Kingston-Upon-Thames, Surrey, KT1 2DN, 020 8541 9745, Fax: 020 8541 8061, Call Date: Nov 2000 (Middle Temple) Qualifications: LLB (Hons) (Lond)

Edwards *Miss Naomi Jayne*
Call Date: July 2012 (Middle Temple)

Edwards *Mr Nicholas Robin*
Call Date: July 2012 (Lincoln's Inn)

Edwards *Miss Patricia Anne*
Bencher, Call Date: July 1967 (Middle Temple) Qualifications: LLB

Edwards *Mrs Sarah Louise*
Call Date: Nov 2011 (Inner Temple) Qualifications: LLB (Wales) BCL (Oxon)

Egypt *Mr Egypt*
Cain & Abel Law Firm, 52 Trafalgar Avenue, London, SE15 6NR, Fax: 020 7701 3344, Call Date: Nov 1996 (Lincoln's Inn) Qualifications: LLB (Hons) LLM (Lond)

Ehtesham *Mr Sepehar*
Call Date: July 2010 (Lincoln's Inn) Qualifications: LLB (Lond)

Eiland *Dr Murray Lee*
Call Date: Oct 2005 (Middle Temple) Qualifications: BA DPhil MSc LLM

Ekperigin *Mr Ortisebemigho Eyimoyowa*
Call Date: Oct 2011 (Middle Temple) Qualifications: LLB (Hons) (Nigeria) LLM (Scotland)

Elahi *Mr Omer Zaheer*
Call Date: July 2012 (Inner Temple)

Elfer *Mr Jonathan Christopher*
Call Date: July 2012 (Inner Temple)

El-Hamdy *Mr Hesham Ahmed*
Call Date: Oct 2011 (Gray's Inn) Qualifications: MBBCh MSc

Elia *Miss Katerina*
Call Date: July 2012 (Lincoln's Inn)

Elkeles *Mrs Arran*
Mediator, 11 Askew Road, Moor Park, Northwood, Middlesex, HA6 2JE, 01923 827341, Call Date: July 1969 (Gray's Inn) Qualifications: Ch FCIPD MA

Elliott *Mr Benedict Edward Henry Thomas*
Call Date: July 2012 (Middle Temple)

Elliott *Miss Ebony Paula Inez*
Call Date: July 2012 (Gray's Inn)

Emele *Mr Chukwuma*
Lawyer, Legal Adviser, Call Date: Mar 2010 (Lincoln's Inn) Qualifications: LLB (Hons)

Emilianou *Mr Adam Nicholas*
Call Date: July 2001 (Lincoln's Inn) Qualifications: LLB (Hons) (Bris)

Erdeljan *Mr Branislav*
Call Date: Oct 1991 (Inner Temple) Qualifications: LLB LLM (Lond)

G

Erdem *Ms Ozge*
Call Date: July 2011 (Lincoln's Inn) Qualifications: LLB (Istanbul) LLM (Lond)

Eskander *Mr Anthony*
Call Date: July 2012 (Inner Temple)

Espley *Mr Roger Hugh Cowan*
Call Date: Oct 2009 (Inner Temple) Qualifications: BSc MBA LLB

Etienne *Mr Michael*
Call Date: July 2012 (Lincoln's Inn)

Evans *Miss Elisabeth*
Call Date: July 2012 (Lincoln's Inn)

Everitt *Miss Heather Jane*
Call Date: July 2012 (Middle Temple)

Ewing *Miss Jennifer Christine*
Call Date: Oct 2010 (Inner Temple) Qualifications: LLB (Dundee)

Faircloth *Miss Jemima Lucy*
Call Date: July 2010 (Inner Temple) Qualifications: LLB (Lond)

Fantoni *Ms Sara Ida*
Call Date: July 2012 (Gray's Inn)

Farani *Mr Farhan Khan*
Advocate, Call Date: Nov 2002 (Lincoln's Inn) Qualifications: LLB (Hons)

Fardy *Mr David Rhys*
Call Date: July 2012 (Inner Temple)

Farhad *Mr Shah Ali*
Call Date: July 2012 (Lincoln's Inn)

Farncombe *Mr Frederick Alexander Edward*
Call Date: July 2012 (Gray's Inn)

Farooq *Mr Ahmed*
Call Date: July 2012 (Inner Temple)

Farooq *Mr Faisal*
Call Date: Nov 2011 (Middle Temple) Qualifications: BA (Hons) (L'pool) PgDL (Lond)

Fawls *Mr Richard Granville*
Call Date: July 1973 (Inner Temple) Qualifications: LLB (Lond)

Fear *Miss Clare Elizabeth*
Neil Foley and Co Solicitors and Advocates, 112 Broadway, Treforest, Pontypridd, Rhondda Cynon Taff, CF37 1BE, Call Date: Mar 2010 (Middle Temple) Qualifications: LLB (Wales)

Feingold *Mr Daniel Michael*
Strategic Tax Planning, 3rd Floor, The Triangle, Exchange Square, Manchester, M4 3TR, 0161 838 5616, Fax: 0161 838 5601, Call Date: July 1983 (Middle Temple) Qualifications: BSc (Hons)

Ferguson *Mr Gerald Patrick*
Clerk, Legal Adviser, Call Date: Nov 1991 (Gray's Inn) Qualifications: BA (Dub) LLB (Lond)

Ferguson *Ms Sonia*
Call Date: July 2012 (Gray's Inn)

Ferley *Mrs Joyce Mary*
6 Arran Mews, Ealing, London, W5 3PY, 020 8993 4968, Call Date: Feb 1964 (Gray's Inn)

Fernandes Padron *Miss Melina*
Call Date: July 2012 (Lincoln's Inn)

Fernyhough *Mr Richard QC*
Deputy High Court Judge, Recorder, Keating Chambers, 15 Essex Street, London, WC2R 3AA, 020 7544 2600, Fax: 020 7544 2700, Call Date: Nov 1970 (Middle Temple) Qualifications: LLB FCIArb

Firth *Miss Georgina Elizabeth*
Call Date: Oct 1995 (Middle Temple) Qualifications: LLB (Hons) LLM

Fisher *Miss Hannah Rachel*
E.S. Shimron, I. Molho, Persky & Co., Technology Park, Bldg. 1, Manahat, Jerusalem, 96958, Israel, -6489679, Call Date: July 2010 (Gray's Inn) Qualifications: BA

Fisher *Mrs Patricia Anne*
Call Date: Nov 2009 (Inner Temple) Qualifications: BSc (Manch) MSc LLB (Ulster)

Fisher *Mr Paul Edward*
Call Date: July 2012 (Middle Temple)

Flax *Mrs Maya*
Call Date: Oct 1999 (Middle Temple) Qualifications: LLB (Hons)(Lond)

Fleming *Miss Heather Danielle*
Call Date: Nov 2009 (Inner Temple) Qualifications: MA (Glas) CPE (College of Law)

Fletcher Rogers *Mrs Helen Susan*
Call Date: July 1965 (Gray's Inn) Qualifications: LLB (Hons) (Lond)

Flindall *Miss Siri Anne*
Call Date: July 2009 (Gray's Inn) Qualifications: LLB

Floyd *Mr Robert Hamilton*
Call Date: Nov 1971 (Middle Temple) Qualifications: LLM (Lond)

Flynn *Mr Daniel James*
Call Date: July 2012 (Middle Temple)

Foong *Miss Serena Mei Kwan*
Call Date: July 2012 (Lincoln's Inn)

Forman *Mr Ian Douglas*
Mediator, Senior Legal Adviser, Call Date: Nov 1984 (Middle Temple) Qualifications: LLB (Lond)

Forman *Mr John Wilson*
Chase House, Scarletts Chase, West Bergholt, Essex, CO6 3DH, 01206 240300, Call Date: Nov 1970 (Lincoln's Inn) Qualifications: ACI Arb MILT MCIT

Forrest *Mr John George William*
Call Date: July 2011 (Inner Temple) Qualifications: LLB (Lond)

Forrester *Dr Ian Stewart*
Professor of Law, White & Case, 62 Rue De La Loi, 1040 Brussels, Belgium, 32-2 219 1620, Fax: 32-2 219 1626, Call Date: Oct 1996 (Middle Temple) Qualifications: MA MCL LLD LLB

Foster *Ms Ashley-Ann Elizabeth Robinson*
Call Date: July 2012 (Lincoln's Inn)

Fotheringham *Mrs Emma Clark*
Other, Kent Police Authority, Police Headquarters, Sutton Road, Maidstone, Kent, ME14 9BZ, 01622 690690, Call Date: Nov 1992 (Gray's Inn) Qualifications: LLB

Fountain *Miss Hannah Louise*
Call Date: July 2012 (Inner Temple)

Fox *Mrs Celia Janet Clough*
Call Date: Nov 1969 (Lincoln's Inn)

Francis *Miss Rachel Catherine*
Call Date: July 2012 (Middle Temple)

Francois *Mr Herbert Dolton*
Call Date: July 1972 (Inner Temple) Qualifications: BA (Hons)

Franklin *Mr Anthony Blen Stuart*
Senior Counsel, St James Hall Chambers, 4th Floor, 169 Phillip Street, Sydney, Nsw 2000, Australia, 00 612 9237 0500, Fax: 00 612 9237 0873, Call Date: Nov 2002 (Lincoln's Inn) Qualifications: BA LLB

Frost *Mr Peter*
Call Date: Feb 1985 (Gray's Inn) Qualifications: DML

Furneaux-Gotch *Miss Sabrina*
Call Date: Oct 2009 (Lincoln's Inn) Qualifications: LLB (Lond)

Furse *Mr Matthew Edward*
Call Date: July 2012 (Inner Temple)

Galvin *Mr Anthony Patrick John*
Call Date: Oct 2003 (Gray's Inn) Qualifications: LLB

Gandy *Mr Geoffrey Harold*
Silverwood, Oak End Way, Woodham, Surrey, KT15 3DY, 01932 343933, Call Date: Feb 1963 (Inner Temple) Qualifications: MA LLM (Cantab)

Gani *Miss Habibatou*
Call Date: July 2012 (Middle Temple)

Gardner *Mr David Christopher*
Legal Adviser, The Administrative Court Office, 2 Park Street, Cardiff, South Wales, CF10 1ET, Call Date: Mar 2006 (Lincoln's Inn) Qualifications: LLB (Hons) (Leeds)

Gardner *Miss Francesca*
Call Date: Nov 2009 (Gray's Inn) Qualifications: LLB

Gardner *Ms Laura Kate*
Call Date: July 2012 (Gray's Inn)

Gardner *Mrs Pamela Jeannette Noall*
Call Date: Nov 1974 (Inner Temple)

Gardner *Miss Sunita*
Call Date: Oct 2006 (Inner Temple) Qualifications: LLB (Wolves) LLB (Hons)

Garland *Mr Gary John Richard*
Deputy District Judge, Mediator, OMB, Deputy Chief Legal Ombudsman For England & Wales, Baskerville House, Centenary Square, Birmingham, B1 2 ND, 0121 245 3100, Call Date: Nov 1989 (Inner Temple) Qualifications: LLB (Hons) FTC

Garner *Mr Adrian John Robinson*
Advocate, Call Date: Nov 1985 (Middle Temple) Qualifications: LLB (Hons) (Bucks)

Garraway *Prof Charles Henry Barre CBE*
Professor of Law, Call Date: July 1972 (Inner Temple) Qualifications: MA (Cantab)

Garro *Mr Albert Luke*
Call Date: Nov 2011 (Middle Temple) Qualifications: LLB (Hons) (Bris)

Garside *Miss Jemma Louise*
Call Date: Nov 2009 (Middle Temple) Qualifications: BA (Hons) (Newc)

Gayle *Mr Matthew Gerald Walter*
Call Date: July 2012 (Middle Temple)

Gaymer *Mrs Vivien Murray*
Arbitrator, Mediator, Call Date: Feb 1971 (Middle Temple) Qualifications: LLB (Hons)

Geraci *Miss Sofia-Louisa*
Call Date: July 2012 (Inner Temple)

Ghani *Mr Mohammed Shehzad*
Call Date: July 2012 (Gray's Inn)

Gibson *Miss Jane Annabel Lindsay*
Call Date: Oct 2007 (Lincoln's Inn) Qualifications: BA (Dunelm)

Gilbert *Mr David Richard TD*
Consultant, Little Orchard, Littlewick Green, Maidenhead, Berkshire, SL6 3RA, 01628 828462, Fax: 01628 828462, Call Date: Feb 1957 (Middle Temple) Qualifications: MA LLM

Gill *Mr Maninder Singh*
Partner, Solicitor, Simons Muirhead and Burton, 8-9 Frith Street, Soho, London, W1D 3JB, 020 3206 2723, Call Date: Nov 1992 (Gray's Inn) Qualifications: LLB (Bris) LLM (Lond)

Gillam *Ms Yasmina Sarah*
Call Date: July 2010 (Lincoln's Inn) Qualifications: LLB (Lond) LLM (Kent) MA (kent)

Gilzean *Miss Sasha-Kay Janice*
Call Date: Oct 2011 (Inner Temple) Qualifications: LLB (Dunelm)

Glass *Mr Stephen Campbell*
Call Date: July 2012 (Middle Temple)

Glover *Mr Nigel David*
Call Date: July 1985 (Gray's Inn) Qualifications: MA (Cantab)

Glover *Mr William Ferris*
Call Date: July 2012 (Middle Temple)

Glyn-Jones *Mr Oliver Robert Lawrence*
Call Date: July 2012 (Middle Temple)

Goff *Miss Joanne Louise*
Call Date: Nov 2004 (Inner Temple) Qualifications: LLB University of Durham

Goni *Mr Mohammed Osman*
Call Date: July 2012 (Lincoln's Inn)

Good-Allen *Ms Sarah Mary Amelia*
Call Date: July 2012 (Gray's Inn)

Goodchild *Mr Graham Stuart*
Commissioner, Call Date: July 1966 (Lincoln's Inn)

Goodin *Mr Sydney Matthew Raymond*
Call Date: July 2012 (Lincoln's Inn)

Goring *Miss Georgina Lesley*
Call Date: July 2012 (Lincoln's Inn)

Gorst *Mr Alexander James Richard*
Call Date: July 2012 (Middle Temple)

Gracia *Ms Dominique*
Call Date: July 2012 (Gray's Inn)

Graham *Miss Danielle Mary Frances*
Call Date: Oct 2003 (Gray's Inn) Qualifications: BA (Leeds)

Grainger *Miss Kaleigh Michelle*
Call Date: Nov 2008 (Inner Temple) Qualifications: LLB CPE

Grainger *Mr Michael David*
Call Date: July 2012 (Inner Temple)

Grainger *Mr Norman Revell*
Call Date: July 1973 (Gray's Inn) Qualifications: PhD M Phil (York) BA DMS MA (York)

Granby *Mr Richard James*
Call Date: July 2012 (Lincoln's Inn)

Grant *Mr Michael Elliott*
Call Date: Mar 2009 (Middle Temple) Qualifications: LLB (Hons) (Newc)

Graves *Mrs Sheila May*
Company Secretary, Call Date: July 1988 (Inner Temple) Qualifications: LLB (Hons)

Greany *Mr John Richard*
Call Date: July 2012 (Middle Temple)

Grier-Mulvenna *Miss Laurie*
Call Date: Oct 2011 (Inner Temple) Qualifications: LLB (Oxon)

Griffiths *Miss Eleanor Louise*
Call Date: July 2012 (Gray's Inn)

Grytsenko *Mr Kyryl*
Call Date: July 2012 (Inner Temple)

Guerra *Miss Valene Leandra*
Call Date: July 2012 (Lincoln's Inn)

Gulzar *Mr Hamza*
Call Date: July 2012 (Lincoln's Inn)

Gumus *Miss Sibel*
Call Date: July 2012 (Lincoln's Inn)

Gupta *Miss Aastha*
Call Date: July 2012 (Lincoln's Inn)

Habbitts *Mr Robert Michael Warner*
Call Date: Oct 2010 (Inner Temple) Qualifications: LLB (Bournemouth)

Hackett *Mr Andrew Timothy Peter*
Call Date: Nov 2011 (Inner Temple) Qualifications: LLB (E.Anglia)

Haddadi *Miss Anoosh Lona*
Solicitor Advocate, Farrell Matthews and Weir, Broadway Chambers, 20 Hammersmith Broadway, London, W6 7AF, 020 8746 3771, Fax: 020 8748 7033, Call Date: July 2000 (Lincoln's Inn) Qualifications: LLB(Hons) (Leic)

Hafiz *Ms Nasreen*
Orr, Dignam & Co., Shajan Tower 2 (1st Floor), Office No 101-104, 3 Segun Bagicha, Dhaka, 1000, Bangladesh, 00 880 2 956 3950, Fax: 00 880 2 956 0257, Call Date: July 2002 (Inner Temple) Qualifications: LLB (Lond)

Haines-Nutt *Mrs Samantha*
Call Date: July 2012 (Middle Temple)

Hainsworth *Mr Paul Louis*
Call Date: Nov 2004 (Inner Temple) Qualifications: BA University of Bristol CPE College of Law Gu

Halai *Ms Vanessa*
Call Date: Nov 2008 (Gray's Inn) Qualifications: LLB

Halblander *Mr Craig James Michael*
Call Date: Nov 2004 (Lincoln's Inn) Qualifications: BA (Hons) LLB PgDl LLM

Hall *Mr Douglas Peter*
Other, Office of the Parliamentary Counsel, 36 Whitehall, London, SW1A 2AY, 020 7210 6791, Fax: 020 7210 6632, Call Date: Oct 1996 (Lincoln's Inn) Qualifications: MA (Oxon) Dip in Legal Studies

Hall *Mrs Jane*
Call Date: July 2010 (Lincoln's Inn) Qualifications: LLB (L'pool)

Halligan *Mr Brendan*
Call Date: Mar 1998 (Middle Temple) Qualifications: LLB (Hons)(Lond)

Halls *Mr Edward David Thomas*
Call Date: July 2012 (Lincoln's Inn)

Halton *Mrs Jane*
HM Revenue and Customs, 100 Parliament Street, London, SW1A 2BQ, 020 7147 2240, Call Date: Oct 2000 (Lincoln's Inn) Qualifications: MA (Oxon)

Hambly *Mr Hedley Maurice*
Call Date: Nov 1960 (Gray's Inn)

Hamill *Mr Michael Garvin*
Rah Partners LLP, 33 St Christophers Place, London, W1U 1NY, 020 7224 5345, Call Date: Nov 1989 (Inner Temple) Qualifications: LLB (Hons)

Hamilton *Miss Natasha*
Call Date: Oct 2007 (Lincoln's Inn) Qualifications: BA (Leeds) LLB

Hamlett *Mrs Rebecca Christine*
Legal Adviser, Mediator, Hibberts LLP, 144 Nantwich Road, Crewe, CW2 6BG, Call Date: July 1995 (Inner Temple) Qualifications: LLB (Staffs)

Hangchi *Mr Kevin*
Call Date: July 1997 (Middle Temple) Qualifications: BSc (Hons)

Hanniffy *Mr Rory Gerard*
Call Date: July 2012 (Middle Temple)

Hanratty *Miss Judith Christine OBE*
Chair, Call Date: Feb 1987 (Inner Temple) Qualifications: LLB LLM LLD

Hanstock *Mr Richard Simon*
Call Date: July 2012 (Gray's Inn)

Haque *Mr N.M. Ahasanul*
Call Date: July 2012 (Lincoln's Inn)

Harbidge *Mr Simon Christopher*
Call Date: Oct 2011 (Middle Temple) Qualifications: LLB (Hons) (Nott'm)

Hardaker *Ms Emma Jane Bluett Griffith*
Call Date: Nov 1998 (Inner Temple) Qualifications: BA (Oxon)

Haria-Shah *Mr Shiv Raaxeet*
Call Date: July 2012 (Middle Temple)

Harkin *Miss Bernadette Laura*
Call Date: July 2008 (Lincoln's Inn) Qualifications: LLB (Lond)

Harman *Mr Ross Michael Robert*
Call Date: July 2012 (Inner Temple)

Harris *Miss Portia Dianne*
Call Date: July 2012 (Inner Temple)

Harrison *Mrs Angela Marjorie*
South Lawn, High Road, Eastcote, Pinner, Middlesex, HA5 2HJ, 020 8866 5416, Call Date: Nov 1961 (Gray's Inn)

Hart *Mr Durand Thomas*
Call Date: Nov 2007 (Lincoln's Inn) Qualifications: BA MA (Essex)

Hart-Leverton *Mr Colin Allen QC*
Recorder, Call Date: May 1957 (Middle Temple)

Harvey-Jones *Ms Angela Catherine*
Call Date: July 2011 (Middle Temple) Qualifications: LLB (Hons) (Notts)

Harwood *Mr Michael Andrew*
Call Date: July 2012 (Middle Temple)

Harwood *Mr Tristan Charles*
Call Date: Mar 2003 (Middle Temple) Qualifications: LLB (Hons)

Hasnat *Mr Abul Khayer Mohammad*
Call Date: July 2012 (Lincoln's Inn)

Hatcher *Mr Mark*
Director, The General Council of the Bar, 4th Floor, 289-293 High Holborn, London, WC1V 7HZ, 020 7611 1369, Fax: 020 7611 1352, Call Date: Nov 1978 (Middle Temple) Qualifications: MA (Oxon) FRSA

Haut *Mr Paul James Alexander*
Shearman and Sterling LLP, Broadgate West, 9 Appold Street, London, EC2A 2AP, Call Date: Nov 2007 (Middle Temple) Qualifications: BA (Hons) (Bris) PgDL (Lond)

Hawkes *Mr Christopher Andrew*
Attorney, Ipulse, Byron House, Cambridge Business Park, Cowley Road, Cambridge, CB4 0WZ, 01223 435 256, Fax: 01223 425 258, Call Date: July 2010 (Middle Temple) Qualifications: LLB (Hons) (Sheff)

Hawley-Jones *Ms Grace Charlotte Imogen*
Call Date: Nov 2009 (Lincoln's Inn) Qualifications: LLB (UEA)

Haydon *Mr Hilary Risdon*
Call Date: June 1961 (Gray's Inn) Qualifications: MA (Cantab)

Hazell *Mr Dirk Nicholas Downing*
Call Date: July 1978 (Middle Temple) Qualifications: MA (Cantab)

Headen *Miss Margaret Bernice*
Judge, Call Date: Nov 1970 (Gray's Inn)

Healy *Mr John Pascal*
Arbitrator, Hilltown, Carrigaline, Co.Cork, Ireland, 353 21 437 1562, Call Date: Feb 1982 (Middle Temple) Qualifications: MCIArb

Heasman *Miss Victoria Margaret Anne*
Call Date: July 2012 (Inner Temple)

Hedley-Dent *Mrs Gloria CBE*
CVS, Call Date: July 1970 (Inner Temple) Qualifications: BA (Dunelm)

Heiden *Miss Katie Rose*
Call Date: July 2012 (Gray's Inn)

Heng *Mr Clive Boon Howe*
Managing Director, 17 Leedon Road, Wilmer Park, 267837, Singapore, 0065 6883 0117, Fax: 0065 6883 0153, Call Date: July 1976 (Lincoln's Inn) Qualifications: LLB (Hons) (Lond)

Henty *Miss Maria*
Call Date: July 2012 (Lincoln's Inn)

Hepburn *Ms Katrina*
5 Pump Court, Ground Floor, 5 Pump Court, Temple, London, EC4Y 7AP, 020 7353 2532, Fax: 020 7353 5321, Call Date: July 2002 (Inner Temple) Qualifications: LLB (Hons) Northumbria

Hepburn *Miss Margaret Geraldine*
Housing Ombudsman Service, 81 Aldwych, London, WC2B 4HN, 020 7421 3800, Fax: 020 7831 1942, Call Date: Oct 1992 (Lincoln's Inn) Qualifications: LLB(Hons)

Heslop *Mr Stanley William*
Call Date: July 2004 (Lincoln's Inn) Qualifications: MSc (Leeds)

Hesse-Djabatey *Mrs Leonora Akousa Kwakua*
Call Date: Nov 1988 (Gray's Inn) Qualifications: LLB (Lond)

Hetherington *Mr Stephen John*
Call Date: July 2003 (Lincoln's Inn) Qualifications: BA (California) LLB Hons (Buck'ham)

Hetherington *Miss Tessa Mary*
Matrix Chambers, Griffin Building, Gray's Inn, London, WC1R 5LN, 020 7404 3447, Fax: 020 7404 3448, Call Date: July 2004 (Lincoln's Inn) Qualifications: BA (Cantab) LLM

Heung *Miss Elaine Sau Mun*
Call Date: July 2012 (Inner Temple)

Hewson *Mr Dermot George*
Call Date: July 2012 (Middle Temple)

Hickmet *Miss Lucy Clementine Rose*
Call Date: July 2012 (Inner Temple)

Hicks *Ms Barbara Helen*
Manager, Other, Trading Standards, Ty Elai, Dinas Isaf Industrial Estate, Williamstown, Rct, Tonypandy, CF40 1NY, Call Date: July 1995 (Gray's Inn) Qualifications: LLB (Wales) DCA Diploma in Consumer Affairs

Hillemand *Miss Claudia*
Call Date: July 2009 (Lincoln's Inn) Qualifications: LLB (Belfast) LLM (Nott'm)

Hillier *Miss Lucy Anne*
Call Date: July 2012 (Inner Temple)

Hilton *Mr George Henry John*
Call Date: July 2012 (Lincoln's Inn)

Hirech *Miss Sarah Marie*
Call Date: July 2012 (Middle Temple)

Hoccom *Mr Gavin Mark*
Call Date: Oct 2010 (Inner Temple) Qualifications: LLB LLM

Hodgson *Miss Margaret Julia*
Call Date: July 1975 (Lincoln's Inn) Qualifications: LLB (Hons)(Warw)

Hogarth *Mr Isaac Louis*
Call Date: July 2011 (Gray's Inn) Qualifications: BA

Holland *Mr Richard John*
Call Date: July 2012 (Middle Temple)

Holtom *Miss Alice Lucy Joyce*
Call Date: July 2012 (Lincoln's Inn)

Homewood *Miss Morwenna Hebbaye*
Call Date: July 2010 (Lincoln's Inn) Qualifications: LLB (L'pool)

Hoque *Ms Tasmia*
Call Date: July 2012 (Lincoln's Inn)

Horner *Mr Allan Nigel Francis John*
Croft House, East Road, Oundle, Peterborough, PE8 4BZ, 01832 273888, Fax: 01832 274888, Call Date: July 1979 (Lincoln's Inn) Qualifications: ACA Pupil Supervisor

Hornyold-Strickland *Mr Francis Richard Michael*
Call Date: July 2012 (Middle Temple)

Horton *Mr Stephen Patrick*
Call Date: July 2007 (Middle Temple) Qualifications: LLB (Hons) (Lond) LLM (Lond)

Hossain *Mr Md Iqbal*
Adviser, Director, London Law Associates, 2nd Floor, 130 Whitechapel Road, London, E1 1JE, Call Date: Oct 2004 (Lincoln's Inn) Qualifications: LLB (Hons)

Hossain *Mr Mohammed Mostak*
Call Date: July 2012 (Gray's Inn)

Hossain *Ms Nuzhat Binte*
Call Date: July 2012 (Lincoln's Inn)

Hossain *Mr Syed Md. Zahangir*
Call Date: July 2012 (Inner Temple)

Hossen *Mr Mohammad Zahraan Abdullah Mohamed*
Call Date: July 2012 (Lincoln's Inn)

Howard *Mr Charles Vyvyan*
Call Date: July 2012 (Gray's Inn)

Howard *Miss Eleanor Davina Elizabeth*
Call Date: July 2012 (Gray's Inn)

Howdle *Mrs Susan Ruth*
Call Date: July 1971 (Lincoln's Inn) Qualifications: MA BCL (Oxon)

Huggins *Mr Adrian Armstrong*
Temple Chambers, 16/F One Pacific Place, 88 Queensway, Hong Kong, China, 2523 2003, Fax: 2523 6343, Call Date: Nov 1975 (Gray's Inn) Qualifications: MA (Cantab) LLM

Hughes *Mr Earle William*
Call Date: Oct 2000 (Inner Temple) Qualifications: LLB (Nott'm) FCIS

Hughes *Mrs Julie*
Director, Partner, Spoor and Fisher Jersey, Africa House, 11 Castle Street, St Helier, JE4 9TW, Jersey, 00 44 1534 838000, Fax: 00 44 1534 838001, Call Date: July 1998 (Lincoln's Inn) Qualifications: BA (Hons)(Manch) LLB (Hons)(Lond)

Hugh-Jones *Mr Michael Gwyn*
FSOL, Call Date: July 1970 (Lincoln's Inn)

Humpherson *Mr Peter James*
Call Date: Oct 2005 (Lincoln's Inn) Qualifications: LLB (Hons) (B'ham)

Humphreys *Mr Mark Edward Proctor*
Call Date: July 2012 (Middle Temple)

Hunter *Mr Joshua Mcbride*
Ministry of the Attorney General, Consitutional Law Branch, 4th Floor, 720 Bay Street, Toronto, Ontario M7a 259, Canada, Call Date: Mar 2011 (Gray's Inn)

Hunting *Mrs Linda Ann*
Call Date: July 2012 (Gray's Inn)

Hurst *Ms Catherine Elizabeth*
Call Date: July 2012 (Gray's Inn)

Husain *Miss Amna*
Call Date: July 2012 (Inner Temple)

Hussain *Mr Abad*
Call Date: July 2010 (Middle Temple) Qualifications: LLB (Hons) (Bradford)

Hussain *Mr Asim*
Call Date: Oct 2007 (Lincoln's Inn) Qualifications: LLB (Sussex)

Hussain *Mr Jabran*
Call Date: July 2010 (Lincoln's Inn) Qualifications: LLB (Leeds)

Hussain *Mr Md Anwar*
Call Date: July 2008 (Lincoln's Inn) Qualifications: LLB (Lond)

Hussain *Mr Nasir Ali*
Khan Solicitors, 24 Sunbridge Road, Bradford, BD1 2AA, 01274 301999, Fax: 01274 301998, Call Date: Mar 2009 (Lincoln's Inn) Qualifications: BA (Leeds)

Hutcheon *Dr Philip*
Legal Adviser, Call Date: July 1999 (Lincoln's Inn) Qualifications: LLB (Hons) PhD

Hyams *Mr Oliver Morris*
Call Date: July 2012 (Lincoln's Inn)

Hyde-Vaamonde *Mrs Cari Jeraldine*
Call Date: Nov 2006 (Inner Temple) Qualifications: LLB (Lond)

Idid *Miss Sharifah Alliana*
Call Date: July 2012 (Lincoln's Inn)

Ilguy *Mr Mustafa Gunes*
Call Date: July 2009 (Middle Temple) Qualifications: BA (Hons) (Lond) LLM PgDL

Ingles *Mr Christopher David*
Call Date: July 2010 (Lincoln's Inn) Qualifications: BA (Cantab)

Inman *Mr John Werner*
Call Date: July 2008 (Gray's Inn) Qualifications: BA (Manch)

Iqbal *Ms Sahar*
No 38/1, 2nd Gizri Street, Phase Iv, D.H.A., Karachi, 75500, Pakistan, 0092 332 2409569, Fax: 0092 213 5880326, Call Date: July 2009 (Lincoln's Inn) Qualifications: LLB (Lond)

Islam *Mr Md Nazrul*
Call Date: Nov 2008 (Middle Temple) Qualifications: LLB (Hons) (Lond)

Islam *Mr Md.Fakhrul*
Call Date: Nov 2008 (Middle Temple) Qualifications: LLM (Bangladesh) LLB (Hons) (Lond)

Islam *Mr Misbahul*
Call Date: Nov 1977 (Lincoln's Inn) Qualifications: MA DIA Dip M MSc

Islam *Mr Mohammad Saiful*
Call Date: July 2012 (Middle Temple)

Ivanciu-Wilkinson *Ms Lorraine Marie*
Call Date: Oct 2011 (Inner Temple) Qualifications: BA (Luton) LLB (Bucks)

Jack *Mrs Angela Margaret*
Five Paper, Ground Floor, 5 Paper Bldgs, Temple, London, EC4Y 7HB, 020 7815 3200, Fax: 020 7815 3201, Call Date: Nov 1999 (Inner Temple) Qualifications: LLB (Reading)

Jacklin *Mrs Louise*
Lecturer, Call Date: Oct 1994 (Middle Temple) Qualifications: MA (Hons)(Cantab) LLM (Cantab)

Jackson *Miss Rolly Olapeju*
Call Date: July 2011 (Gray's Inn) Qualifications: BA LLB

Jackson *Dr William Thomas*
Call Date: Nov 1975 (Lincoln's Inn) Qualifications: MRCVS FCIARb Dr Med Vet BVMS DVSM

Jagasia *Mr Jay Kumar*
Call Date: July 2012 (Lincoln's Inn)

Jaggard *Mr Andrew William*
Call Date: July 2012 (Lincoln's Inn)

Jahangeer *Mr Muhammad Fariis*
Call Date: July 2012 (Middle Temple)

Jalan *Mr Prateek*
4 Babar Road, New Delhi-110001, India, +91 11 23715651/+91 11 2371 1196, Fax: 23711197/+91 11 2371 1197, Call Date: July 1993 (Inner Temple) Qualifications: BA (Delhi) MA (Cantab) LLM (Michigan)

Jaleel *Ms Farah*
Call Date: July 2012 (Lincoln's Inn)

Jam *Mr Zeeshan Ali*
Call Date: July 2012 (Lincoln's Inn)

James *Miss Suzanne Margarete*
17 Downs Court Road, Purley, Surrey, CR8 1BE, Call Date: July 1985 (Gray's Inn) Qualifications: BA (Cantab) BA (Lond)

James *Mr Thomas William*
Call Date: Oct 2009 (Middle Temple) Qualifications: LLB (Hons) (Chester)

Jamieson *Mr Charles Donald Gardner*
Call Date: July 2012 (Inner Temple)

Jat *Mr Sew Tong*
Chair, Senior Counsel, Temple Chambers, 16/F One Pacific Place, 88 Queensway, Hong Kong, China, 852 2523 2003, Fax: 852 2810 0302, Call Date: July 1988 (Gray's Inn) Qualifications: LLB (LSE) BCL (Oxon)

Jaya Gobi *Miss Nimisha*
Call Date: July 2012 (Middle Temple)

Jeetoo *Mr Saleem Hussein Feroz Mohammad Ali*
Call Date: July 2009 (Gray's Inn) Qualifications: LLB

Jeffers *Mr Jamal Marvin*
Call Date: July 2012 (Lincoln's Inn)

Jeffreys *Mr David Alfred QC*
Call Date: Nov 1958 (Gray's Inn) Qualifications: BA (Cantab)

Jeffs *Mr Christopher Peter*

Call Date: July 2012 (Gray's Inn)

Jenkins *Mr Christopher James*
Call Date: Oct 2010 (Middle Temple) Qualifications: BA (Hons) (Sheff) LLB (Hons) (L'pool) FCA

Jenkins *Mr John David QC*
Recorder, Call Date: July 1970 (Gray's Inn) Qualifications: LLB (Lond) (Hons)

Jenkinson *Mr Richard*
Call Date: Oct 2007 (Lincoln's Inn) Qualifications: BA (Cantab)

Jiwani *Mrs Zeenat*
Call Date: Oct 2003 (Lincoln's Inn) Qualifications: LLB (Hons) (Wolves)

G

Joffe *Mr Victor Howard QC*
Call Date: Nov 1975 (Middle Temple) Qualifications: MA LLB (Cantab)

Johnson *Miss Emily Louise*
Call Date: Oct 2011 (Middle Temple) Qualifications: LLB (Hons) (B'ham)

Johnston *Mr John Leslie Kerr*
Call Date: Nov 1980 (Lincoln's Inn) Qualifications: LLB (Lond)

Johnston *Mr Matthew James*
Call Date: July 2012 (Middle Temple)

Johnston *Miss Victoria Louise*
Call Date: Oct 2010 (Middle Temple) Qualifications: LLB (Hons) (Dundee)

Jones *Miss Caroline*
Call Date: Mar 2008 (Lincoln's Inn) Qualifications: LLB (Reading)

Jones *Mr Duncan*
Call Date: July 2012 (Inner Temple)

Jones *Miss Elizabeth Ruth*
Park Lane Plowden, 19 Westgate, Leeds, LS1 2RD, 0113 228 5049, Fax: 0113 228 1500, Call Date: Oct 2000 (Middle Temple) Qualifications: LLB (Hons) (Nott'm)

Jones *Mr Geoffrey*
Call Date: July 2007 (Inner Temple) Qualifications: LLB

Jones *Prof Grant Meredith*
COMT, General Counsel, Other, Partner, Vice President, Arbitral Ltd, 350 Riverside Mansions, Milk Yard, Garnet Street, Wapping, London, E1W 3SU, Call Date: Nov 1996 (Middle Temple) Qualifications: LLB FABRP FCIArb FCCA FCA

Jones *Miss Hilary Jean*
Silwood House, Runnymede Close, Gateacre, Woolton, Liverpool, L25 5JU, Call Date: June 1951 (Middle Temple) Qualifications: LLB

Jones *Mr Ian Christopher*
Call Date: Oct 2007 (Middle Temple) Qualifications: BA (Hons) (St Andrews) MA (St Andrews) PgDL

Jones *Miss Leah Hughes*
10 Fleman Grove, West Bridgford, Nottingham, NG2 5BH, Call Date: July 2006 (Lincoln's Inn) Qualifications: LLB (Warw)

Jones *Mr Roger Kenneth*
41 Townscliffe Lane, Marple Bridge, Stockport, Cheshire, SK6 5AP, Call Date: Feb 1977 (Gray's Inn) Qualifications: BA Hons (Econ)

Jones *Miss Samantha Nicola*
Call Date: Nov 2009 (Gray's Inn) Qualifications: LLB

Jones *Ms Samantha Rochelle*
Call Date: July 2012 (Gray's Inn)

Jones *Mr Timothy Leighton*
Solicitor, Call Date: Nov 1997 (Lincoln's Inn) Qualifications: LLB (Hons)(Wales)

Jones-Crawford *Mrs Shaaron*
Call Date: July 1990 (Lincoln's Inn) Qualifications: LLB

Jong *Miss Yee Ling*
Call Date: July 2010 (Lincoln's Inn) Qualifications: LLB (Bucks)

Jordan *Mr Edward Thomas*
Call Date: Nov 2006 (Lincoln's Inn) Qualifications: BSc (So'ton)

Joseph *Miss Margaret Mary*
Advocate, Solicitor, Call Date: July 1996 (Middle Temple) Qualifications: LLB (Hons)(Lond)

Joshi *Mr Sunit Kishor*
31 Ellington Road, Hounslow, Middlesex, TW3 4HX, 020 8572 4756/001 973 779 8590, Call Date: Nov 1997 (Lincoln's Inn) Qualifications: LLB (Hons)(Nott'm)

Joyce *Miss Lucy Helen Houghton*
Call Date: July 2010 (Gray's Inn) Qualifications: BA

Kabir *Mr Abu Rahat Murshed*
Call Date: July 2009 (Lincoln's Inn) Qualifications: LLB (Northumbria)

Kainyah *Miss Rosalind Nana Emela*
Call Date: July 1988 (Gray's Inn) Qualifications: BA (Ghana) LLB (Lond) LLM (Lond)

Kalina *Mr Karl Louis*
Call Date: Nov 2007 (Inner Temple) Qualifications: LLB (Brunel)

Kallipetis *Mrs Caroline Sarah*
Call Date: July 1970 (Gray's Inn) Qualifications: LLB

Kalu *Mrs Annette Obiageli*
Lecturer, Birbeck College, University of London, School of Law, Malet Street, Bloomsbury, London, WC1E 7HX, Call Date: Oct 1997 (Gray's Inn) Qualifications: MPhil (Law) LLB (Essex)

Kammitsi *Mrs Lefkothea*
Judge, Rent Control Court, Char Mouskou, 1405, Nicosia, Cyprus, 228 65624, Fax: 226 72728, Call Date: July 1990 (Middle Temple) Qualifications: BSocSc (Keele)

Kandola *Miss Sukhveer Kaur*
Call Date: July 2012 (Inner Temple)

Kapila *Mr Varun*
Call Date: Nov 2005 (Lincoln's Inn) Qualifications: BA (Hons) GDLl

Kasabova *Miss Diyana Vladimirova*
Call Date: July 2012 (Inner Temple)

Kashefi *Mr Kirk*
Associate, Call Date: Oct 2005 (Gray's Inn) Qualifications: BSc (Lond)

Kateka *Mr Kahabuka Edward*
Call Date: Nov 2008 (Gray's Inn) Qualifications: LLB LLM

Katun *Ms Rooji*
Call Date: Nov 2008 (Gray's Inn) Qualifications: LLB

Kaudri *Mr Atif Waheed*
Caseworker, Manager, The Citizens Advice Bureau Service, The Vanstone Suite, Community Centre, 2 Allum Lane, Elstree, Hertfordshire, WD6 3PJ, 020 8327 0006, Fax: 020 8327 0006, Call Date: Mar 2008 (Lincoln's Inn) Qualifications: LLB (Lond)

Kaur *Miss Jaswinder*
Call Date: Oct 2008 (Middle Temple) Qualifications: BA (Hons) (Oxon) LLM (B'ham) PhD (B'ham)

Kavanagh *Miss Rosemary Jennifer*
Call Date: July 2012 (Lincoln's Inn)

Kay *Mr John Lawrence*
Legal Adviser, Call Date: July 1973 (Middle Temple) Qualifications: LLB LLM (Lond)

Kearns *Mr Kevin Patrick*
Call Date: July 1992 (Lincoln's Inn) Qualifications: BA (L'Pool) LLB (Lond) MA (Sheff)

Kelly *Miss Claire*
Call Date: Oct 2008 (Middle Temple) Qualifications: LLB (Belfast)

Kelly *Mr Kieran Martin*
Call Date: Oct 2010 (Lincoln's Inn) Qualifications: LLB (Northumbria)

Kelly *Mr Mark Frank*
Call Date: Nov 1997 (Gray's Inn) Qualifications: LLB

Kelly *Mr Philip James*
Call Date: May 1996 (Middle Temple) Qualifications: BA Dip legal Ed BL MSc (Dub)

Kemp *Mrs Rachael Mae*
London Borough of Brent, Brent County Council, Town Hall Annexe, Forty Lane, Wembely, Middlesex, HA9 9HD, Call Date: Nov 2008 (Inner Temple) Qualifications: LLB CPE

Kenedey *Mr Leo Saha*
Call Date: July 2012 (Lincoln's Inn)

Kent *Miss Leyla Yasemin*
Call Date: Oct 2006 (Inner Temple)
Qualifications: LLB (Keele)

Kew *Mr Michael Deslie*
Call Date: Nov 1967 (Inner Temple)
Qualifications: LLB (Lond)

Khan *Dr Inayat Ullah*
Other, Telecommuications Regulatory Authority, P.O. Box 579, Postal Code 112, Ruwi, Muscat, Sultanate of Oman, (+968) 574 232, Fax: (+968) 565 464, Call Date: Nov 1980 (Lincoln's Inn) Qualifications: LLB (Leeds) BA Dip Int Law Cert Public Admin PhD in Law (USA)

Khan *Mr Mohammad Ali Jawad*
Call Date: July 2012 (Lincoln's Inn)

Khan *Mr Tahir Mahmood*
Call Date: Nov 2009 (Gray's Inn)

Khayem *Mrs Rukia*
Call Date: Nov 2008 (Lincoln's Inn)
Qualifications: LLB

Killerby *Miss Joan Margaret*
Call Date: Nov 1967 (Inner Temple)
Qualifications: Doc De L'Universite (France)

Kilmurry *Mrs Marcia Pillay*
Legal Adviser, Exemplas Holdings Limited, 4 Bishops Square Business Park, Hatfield, Hertfordshire, AL10 9NE, 01707 398149, Call Date: Nov 2006 (Middle Temple) Qualifications: LLB (Hons) LLM PGDL BSc

Kinahan *Mrs Ann*
Director, Citizens Advice Bureau, 2nd Floor, Cobourg House, 32 Mayflower Street, Plymouth, PL1 1QX, Call Date: Nov 1981 (Inner Temple)
Qualifications: LLB

Kindell *Mr James William*
Secretary, Zotefoams plc, 675 Mitcham Road, Croydon, Surrey, CR9 3AL, Call Date: Nov 1992 (Middle Temple)
Qualifications: BSc (Hons, City) Dip in Law LLM (Surrey) ACIS

King *Miss Julie Elizabeth*
Call Date: July 2012 (Inner Temple)

Kinghorn *Miss Helen Diane*
Call Date: July 2006 (Middle Temple)
Qualifications: MA (Cantab)

Kingston *Mr John William*
Call Date: July 2012 (Gray's Inn)

Kirk *Mr Pierre Du Quesnay*
United States Navy, Naval Operation Logistics Support Centre, 1837 Morris Street, Suite 600, Norfolk Naval Base, Norfolk, Virginia, 23511, USA, Call Date: Nov 2007 (Inner Temple)
Qualifications: BA

Kirkpatrick *Mrs Krystyna Maria*
Call Date: Feb 1965 (Gray's Inn)

Kistnamah *Mr Nagesh*
Call Date: July 2012 (Lincoln's Inn)

Knight *Mr Alexander Peter Henry*
Call Date: July 2012 (Gray's Inn)

Knight *Miss Kivinee Mildred Jasmine*
Call Date: Mar 2005 (Lincoln's Inn)
Qualifications: LLB (Hons)

Knowles *Mr Philip Jonathan*
Judge, First Tier Tribunal Immigration and Asylum Chamber, Colombus House, Langstone Business Park, Chepstow Road, Newport, NP18 2LX, Call Date: July 1982 (Gray's Inn) Qualifications: LLB (Lond) DMS

Koh *Ms Caryna Ern Xinh*
Call Date: July 2012 (Inner Temple)

Koh *Mr Kenneth Zhong Wey*
Call Date: July 2012 (Inner Temple)

Kohn *Ms Nicola*
Call Date: July 2012 (Inner Temple)

Kok *Miss Wen Ying*
Call Date: July 2007 (Lincoln's Inn)
Qualifications: LLB (Lond)

Konecki *Mr Andrew Anthony*
Call Date: Nov 1991 (Lincoln's Inn)
Qualifications: LLB (Hons) MA (Lond)

Kong *Miss Yoke San*
Call Date: Nov 2008 (Lincoln's Inn)
Qualifications: LLB (Newc)

Koomson *Miss Sarsie*
Call Date: July 2012 (Middle Temple)

Korer *Mr Jeremy*
Korer Media Ltd, 28 Imber Close, Ember Lane, Esher, Surrey, KT10 8ED, Call Date: Nov 1987 (Middle Temple)
Qualifications: BA (Hons)

Kosmin *Mr Leslie Gordon QC*
Call Date: July 1976 (Middle Temple)
Qualifications: MA LLM (USA) LLM (Cantab)

Koso-Thomas *Miss Oyinda Mia*
Legal Officer, Axiom Legal, 6th Floor, 159/173 St John Street, London, EC1V 4QT, 020 7324 5300, Call Date: Nov 1990 (Middle Temple) Qualifications: LLB (So'ton) LLM

Kousari *Miss Shirin*
Call Date: Mar 2010 (Lincoln's Inn)
Qualifications: LLB (Lond)

Kuehl *Miss Lara*
Call Date: July 2012 (Lincoln's Inn)

Kullar *Mrs Richenda Margaret*
Assistant General Counsel, Wonga.com, 3-4 Prince Albert Road, London, NW1 7SN, Call Date: Feb 1993 (Gray's Inn)
Qualifications: LLB

Kumar *Mr Sanjeev*
Call Date: Nov 2003 (Lincoln's Inn)
Qualifications: LLB (Hons) (B'ham)

Kumar *Mr Sree*
Call Date: July 2009 (Middle Temple)
Qualifications: BSc (Lond) LLB (Hons) (London) LLM (Lond)

La Niece *Mr Jeremy Peter Babington*
Call Date: Nov 1973 (Middle Temple)
Qualifications: LLB

Lacey *Mr Matthew Charles*
Call Date: July 2010 (Middle Temple)
Qualifications: BA (Hons) (York)

Lagnado *Mr Lawrence*
Call Date: July 2009 (Middle Temple)
Qualifications: BA (Hons) (Manch) Grad Dip Law

Lai *Miss Fui Sim*
Securities and Futures Commission, 7th Floor, Chater House, 8 Connaught Road, Central, Hong Kong, Call Date: July 1995 (Lincoln's Inn) Qualifications: LLB (Hons)

Lai *Mr Nicholas Weng Keong*
Call Date: July 2012 (Lincoln's Inn)

Lai *Mr Wei Shiung*
Call Date: July 2012 (Lincoln's Inn)

Laithwaite *Miss Hannah Joy*
Call Date: July 2012 (Inner Temple)

Lall *Miss Jasdeep Kaur*
Call Date: Oct 2009 (Lincoln's Inn)
Qualifications: LLB (Leeds)

Lane *Mr Nicholas Hayward*
Call Date: July 2007 (Lincoln's Inn)
Qualifications: BSc (Bris) LLB

Langley *Miss Sarah Jayne*
Call Date: July 2012 (Inner Temple)

Langsdale *Miss Jane*
Call Date: Nov 1989 (Inner Temple)
Qualifications: BA Dip Law (Lond)

Larbi *Mr Michael Fianko*
Call Date: July 2004 (Lincoln's Inn)
Qualifications: LLB (Hons) (Lond) Pg Dip Environmental Law Pg Dip Legal Skills ACIArb

Last *Mr Christopher Matthew*
Call Date: Oct 2007 (Middle Temple)
Qualifications: LLB (UEA)

Lavin *Miss Danielle Rose Mary*
Call Date: July 2012 (Lincoln's Inn)

Lawrence *Miss Arlene Alison*
Legal Officer, Other, Ministry of Energy and Energy Affairs, Tower C, International Waterfront, No 1 Wrightson Road, Port-Of-Spain, West Indies, Trinidad and Tobago, 00 1 868 623 6708, Fax: 00 1 867 627 1454, Call Date: Nov 2003 (Middle Temple)
Qualifications: LLB (Hons) (Lond) Pgd Dip LEC LLM

Lawrey *Mr Keith*
Justice of the Peace, Foundation For Science & Technology, 10 Carlton House Terrace, London, SW1Y 5AH, 020 7321 2220, Fax: 020 7321 2221, Call Date: July 1972 (Gray's Inn)
Qualifications: JP MSc (Econ) FCOLLP FCIS MA LLB

Lawson *Mr Kyle William*
Call Date: July 2012 (Lincoln's Inn)

G

Le Bas *Mr Patrick Joseph*
Call Date: Oct 2006 (Lincoln's Inn) Qualifications: BA (Oxon)

Leach *Miss Helen Clare*
Call Date: July 2012 (Inner Temple)

Leach-Smith *Mrs Caryn Gail*
Gail & Associates PTE Ltd, 987 Bukit Timah Road, #04-13, Maplewoods, 589628, Singapore, Call Date: July 1988 (Lincoln's Inn) Qualifications: LLB (Hons)

Lee *Ms Delia Sze Zhen*
Call Date: July 2012 (Middle Temple)

Lee *Miss Katie Louise*
Call Date: July 2012 (Inner Temple)

Lee *Miss Nyet Fah Alyssa*
Call Date: July 1996 (Middle Temple) Qualifications: LLB (Hons)(Lond)

Lee *Miss Valerie Lingli*
Call Date: July 2006 (Middle Temple) Qualifications: LLB (Hons) (Manchester)

Lee *Miss Zhi Wei*
Call Date: July 2012 (Lincoln's Inn)

Leech *Mr Brian Walter Thomas*
Call Date: Nov 1967 (Middle Temple)

Leene *Miss Sharon Anabel*
Call Date: Oct 1996 (Gray's Inn) Qualifications: LLB (Leeds)

Lees *Mr Gordon Clifford*
Call Date: July 1979 (Gray's Inn) Qualifications: BA Dip Law

Lelliott *Mr Stephen Robert*
Arbitrator, Call Date: July 2005 (Middle Temple) Qualifications: BSc MSc DipLaw DIPPls MICE MIHT MCIWEM CEng FCIArb

Lemon *Mr Roy*
Call Date: July 1970 (Gray's Inn) Qualifications: LLB

Leong *Ms Alicia Yin San*
20 Jalam, Usj 11/3b, Subang Jaya, Selanger, Malaysia, Call Date: Oct 2008 (Lincoln's Inn) Qualifications: LLB (Reading)

Levene *Mr Edward Stanley*
Call Date: Nov 2008 (Gray's Inn) Qualifications: BA

Levy *Mr Moses Joseph*
Call Date: July 2012 (Middle Temple)

Levy *Ms Winsome*
COMT, Call Date: Oct 2003 (Gray's Inn) Qualifications: LLB

Lewin *Miss Dainele Rochelle*
Call Date: Nov 2010 (Lincoln's Inn) Qualifications: LLB (Bucks)

Lewis *Mrs Cherry Anne*
Chair, Call Date: July 1973 (Inner Temple) Qualifications: FCIArb

Lewis *Mr Robert*
Call Date: Nov 1996 (Gray's Inn) Qualifications: MA (Oxon) BCL (Oxon)

Lewis *Mr Simon James Ward*
Call Date: July 2012 (Lincoln's Inn)

Liddle *Mr Stephen Johnstone*
Call Date: July 2012 (Lincoln's Inn)

Liew *Mr Vui Khen*
Call Date: July 2012 (Middle Temple)

Liggins *Miss Caroline Elizabeth*
Call Date: July 2009 (Middle Temple) Qualifications: LLB (Hons) (South Bank)

Lim *Ms Abigail Jiunn*
Call Date: July 2012 (Gray's Inn)

Lim *Miss Shermaine Liew Mae*
Call Date: July 2012 (Inner Temple)

Lin *Miss Sandy Yuan-Yu*
Call Date: Nov 2005 (Middle Temple) Qualifications: LLB (Hons)

Lindsay *Miss Cherreem Simone*
Call Date: Oct 2011 (Gray's Inn) Qualifications: LLB

Lindsay *Ms Emma Louise*
Clerk, Simpson Thacher and Bartlett LLP, 425 Lexington Avenue, New York, Ny 10017, USA, 001 212 455 2000, Fax: 001 212 455 2502, Call Date: July 2002 (Inner Temple) Qualifications: BA (Oxon) LLM (New York)

Linton *Miss Sara Geraldine*
Call Date: Nov 1970 (Inner Temple)

Litchfield *Miss Claire*
Para-Legal, Call Date: July 2007 (Middle Temple) Qualifications: BA (Hons) (Cardiff) Dip Law

Little *Mr Bryan William*
Call Date: July 2011 (Gray's Inn) Qualifications: BA LLB

Livingston *Mr Paul Robert*
Call Date: July 2012 (Gray's Inn)

Llukaci *Mr Bonis*
Call Date: July 2012 (Inner Temple)

Lo *Mr Pui Yin*
8/F Far East Finance Centre, 16 Harcourt Road, Hong Kong, China, 2866 8233, Call Date: July 1992 (Inner Temple) Qualifications: LLB (Lond)

Lo Conte *Miss Marianna Concetta*
Call Date: July 2012 (Middle Temple)

Lockhart *Mr Robert*
Adjudicator, Call Date: July 2005 (Middle Temple) Qualifications: LLM (Newc) ARICS

Loh *Mr Gentry Guo Xiong*
Call Date: July 2012 (Lincoln's Inn)

Loizides *Mr Romanos*
Call Date: July 2012 (Gray's Inn)

Loney *Mr Keith Edward*
Chair, Call Date: Nov 1972 (Lincoln's Inn) Qualifications: LLM (Lond) FCA

Loo *Ms Jamie Huai Ning*
Call Date: July 2012 (Lincoln's Inn)

Love *Miss Kathy Lee*
General Counsel, Call Date: Nov 1977 (Gray's Inn) Qualifications: BA LLM (Cantab)

Low *Miss Belinda Chou Yen*
Call Date: July 2012 (Lincoln's Inn)

Low *Miss Yun See*
Call Date: July 2012 (Middle Temple)

Lowe *Mr Philip Raymond*
Crown Advocate, Call Date: July 1986 (Middle Temple) Qualifications: LLB (Wolves)

Luchmun *Mr Mahendranathsingh*
Call Date: Nov 2011 (Inner Temple) Qualifications: LLB LLM (Lond)

Luhar *Miss Rita Kantilal*
Solicitor, Wragge and Co. LLP, 55 Comore Road, Birmingham, B3 2AS, 0121 260 9916, Call Date: July 2000 (Lincoln's Inn) Qualifications: LLB(Hons)

Lui *Miss Phyllis Long Ning*
Call Date: July 2012 (Lincoln's Inn)

Lunt *Mr Mark Antony*
Senior Crown Prosecutor, Call Date: Nov 1984 (Inner Temple) Qualifications: LLB (Manch)

Lyon *Miss Nina Clare*
Call Date: July 2006 (Inner Temple) Qualifications: BA (Leeds) BA (Cantab)

Ma *Mr Anthony Kong-Ting*
Associate, Solicitor, Financial Services Authority, 25 The North Colonnade, Canary Wharf, London, E14 5HS, 020 7066 1000, Call Date: Oct 2008 (Inner Temple) Qualifications: BSc (B'ham) LLB (Hons)

MacChiavello *Miss Lisa Laura*
Call Date: July 2007 (Gray's Inn) Qualifications: LLB (Lond)

MacDonald *Mr Iain Ezra*
Call Date: July 2012 (Gray's Inn)

MacDonald *Mr Robert Edward*
Call Date: Nov 2005 (Middle Temple) Qualifications: LLB (Hons)

MacKay *Mr Iain Arthur*
Call Date: Nov 2004 (Middle Temple) Qualifications: LLB (Hons) (Hull)

MacKenzie *Dr Catherine Patricia*
Associate, Lecturer, Call Date: May 1995 (Inner Temple) Qualifications: MA Dip Law M Ed PhD

MacKenzie *Miss Emily*
Call Date: July 2012 (Inner Temple)

Madders *Dr Kevin John*
Call Date: July 1977 (Gray's Inn) Qualifications: LLB (Lond)

Maginn *Mr Emmett*
Call Date: Nov 2005 (Lincoln's Inn) Qualifications: LLB (Hons)

Maginnis *Miss Carol Ann*
Call Date: Oct 2009 (Gray's Inn) Qualifications: BA MSc LLB

Maguire *Mr David James*
Call Date: Nov 2008 (Lincoln's Inn)
Qualifications: LLB (Lancaster)

Maguire *Miss Helen Kate*
Call Date: July 2010 (Middle Temple)
Qualifications: LLB (Hons) (Sheff)

Maizels *Miss Heather Jill*
Call Date: July 1977 (Inner Temple)
Qualifications: MA (Cantab)

Majid *Mrs Fateha Nisha Begum*
Call Date: July 2012 (Lincoln's Inn)

Majidulla *Mr Faiz*
Call Date: Nov 2008 (Lincoln's Inn)
Qualifications: LLB (Bris)

Malik *Mr Muhammad Momin*
Call Date: July 2012 (Lincoln's Inn)

Maljik *Miss Andrea*
Call Date: July 2012 (Middle Temple)

Mangat *Mr Harneet Singh*
Call Date: Mar 2006 (Lincoln's Inn)
Qualifications: BDs (Nott'm) MSc (Nott'm) PgDl (Nott'm)

Mannan *Mr Morshed*
Call Date: July 2012 (Lincoln's Inn)

Mansell *Mr Daniel John*
Call Date: July 2012 (Middle Temple)

Mansfield *Miss Gillian*
Senior Legal Adviser, Call Date: Oct 1994 (Lincoln's Inn) Qualifications: BA (Hons)(Warw) CPE (Leeds) LLM (Sheff)

Mariappan *Mr Mogan*
Ho Mogan & Nor' Aini, 72b 1st Floor, Jalan Melati, 28400 Mentakab, Pahang Darulmakmur, Malaysia, 09-2782290/2784131, Fax: 09-2782293, Call Date: July 1993 (Inner Temple) Qualifications: LLB (Lancs) AFF AII

Markus *Mr Joseph*
Call Date: July 2012 (Inner Temple)

Marshall *Mr Albert Simon Obiri*
Call Date: Nov 1995 (Middle Temple)
Qualifications: LLB (Hons) LLM

Marshall *Miss Erica Rechelle*
Call Date: July 2012 (Middle Temple)

Martey *Mr Alastair Miles*
Call Date: July 2012 (Middle Temple)

Martin-Royle *Miss Claire Louise*
Taylor Wessing LLP, 5 New Street Square, London, EC4A 3TW, Call Date: Oct 2000 (Inner Temple) Qualifications: LLB (Cardiff)

Mason *Mr Owen Vermeylen*
Call Date: July 2009 (Middle Temple)
Qualifications: BA (Hons) (Dunelm)

Mason *Mr Peter*
Cms Cameron Mckenna LLP, 160 Aldersgate, London, EC1 A4DD, 020 7361 2209, Call Date: Nov 2006 (Gray's Inn) Qualifications: LLB CTA FCCA BSc

Mason *Mr Richard Michael*
Call Date: July 2008 (Gray's Inn)
Qualifications: LLB (Sheff)

Massam *Mr Arthur David Wright*
80a Westbury Road, Finchley, London, N12 7PD, 020 8922 3249, Call Date: Nov 1968 (Inner Temple)
Qualifications: LLB (Lond) FRPharmS

Massiah *Mr Tony Dorjee*
Call Date: July 2012 (Inner Temple)

Mateh Esua *Ms Hostencia*
Call Date: July 2012 (Middle Temple)

Matharu *Miss Amanpreet Kaur*
Call Date: July 2012 (Lincoln's Inn)

Mather *Mr Adam*
Call Date: Nov 2010 (Gray's Inn)
Qualifications: BA

Mathew *Mr Ian David*
Call Date: Nov 2008 (Middle Temple)
Qualifications: BA (Hons) (Manch) MSc (Lond)

Matthews *Miss Alexandra Anna*
Call Date: July 2012 (Middle Temple)

Mauleverer *Mr Peter Bruce QC*
Adjudicator, Recorder, Deputy High Court, P B Mauleverer, Eliot Vale House, 8 Eliott Vale, Blackheath, London, SE3 0UW, 020 8852 2070, Fax: 020 8852 4614, Call Date: July 1969 (Inner Temple) Qualifications: BA (Dunelm) FCIArb MA (Birkbeck)

Mawji *Mr Rajan*
Call Date: July 2003 (Lincoln's Inn)
Qualifications: LLB Hons (Luton) LLM

Mayhew-Arnold *Mr Michael Charles John*
Director, Osiris Privee Llc, 2903 Salzedo, Coral Gables, Florida, 33134, USA, Call Date: Nov 1983 (Inner Temple) Qualifications: LLB (Hons) (So'ton)

Maynard *Miss Sandrea Icilma*
Call Date: Oct 1998 (Inner Temple)
Qualifications: LLB (Hons)

Mazumder *Miss Nur Jahan*
Call Date: Oct 2008 (Inner Temple)
Qualifications: LLB (So'ton)

McAdden *Miss Natalie Ann*
Call Date: Nov 2006 (Middle Temple)
Qualifications: BA (Hons) (Leeds) PgDip Law (Leeds)

McBride *Mr Alexander Nathaniel James*
Call Date: Nov 2002 (Inner Temple)
Qualifications: BSc (B'ham) CPE

McCadden *Miss Sarah Josephine*
Call Date: July 2012 (Inner Temple)

McCarthy *Miss Mary Patricia Nodlaig*
Call Date: Feb 1988 (Inner Temple)
Qualifications: BL LLB (Dublin)

McCleave *Miss Ingrid Anne*
Solicitor, Shepperson Solicitors, 1 Massett Road, Horley, Surrey, RH6 7PR, Call Date: Oct 1995 (Lincoln's Inn)
Qualifications: LLB (Hons)

McCombe *Mr Duncan William Bramwell*
Call Date: July 2012 (Lincoln's Inn)

McConnell *Ms Christine Maria*
Senior Legal Adviser, Hmcs Sheffield, Legal Adviser Department, Castle Street, Sheffield, S3 8LU, 0114 276 0760, Fax: 0114 272 0129, Call Date: Oct 1999 (Gray's Inn) Qualifications: LLB (Hons)(Manch)

McConnochie *Dr Kathryn*
Mediator, Call Date: Oct 1997 (Gray's Inn) Qualifications: BSc (St Andrews) MBChB (Manc) LLB (Wales) MRCP

McDade *Miss Jenna*
Call Date: July 2008 (Lincoln's Inn)
Qualifications: LLB (Leic)

McDonald *Ms Alice Margaret*
Call Date: July 2012 (Gray's Inn)

McElroy *Mr Stephen Anthony*
Jmw Solicitors LLP, 1 Byrom Place, Spinningfields, Manchester, M3 3HG, Call Date: Oct 2007 (Lincoln's Inn)
Qualifications: LLB (Manch)

McGann *Mr Martin Terence*
Call Date: Oct 2007 (Lincoln's Inn)
Qualifications: LLB (Reading)

McGarry *Mr Paul Anthony*
Call Date: July 2012 (Middle Temple)

McGarvey *Mr Michael*
Call Date: Nov 2002 (Lincoln's Inn)
Qualifications: LLB (Bris) LLM (Bris) AIIT

McGlue *Ms Hannah Louise Caitlin*
Call Date: July 2012 (Inner Temple)

McGuigan *Ms Janine Geralyn*
Call Date: July 2012 (Gray's Inn)

McHenry *Rev Brian Edward CBE*
Call Date: July 1976 (Middle Temple)
Qualifications: MA (Oxon)

McHugo *Mr Christopher Benedict*
Call Date: Nov 1978 (Middle Temple)
Qualifications: MA (Oxon) FCA

McLaren *Mrs Denise Anne*
Call Date: July 2010 (Middle Temple)
Qualifications: LLB (Hons) (Teeside)

McLeish *Mr Robin*
Temple Chambers, 16/F One Pacific Place, 88 Queensway, Hong Kong, China, (852) 2523 2003, Fax: (852) 2810 0302, Call Date: Oct 1997 (Gray's Inn) Qualifications: MA (Oxon)

McLeod *Mr Mark Julian*
Call Date: July 2007 (Gray's Inn)
Qualifications: LLB

McLoughlin *Mr Richard Alan*
Call Date: July 2012 (Gray's Inn)

McMillan *Mr John Richard Mcfarlane*
Call Date: July 2012 (Lincoln's Inn)

McNally *Miss Tammy*
Call Date: July 2012 (Middle Temple)

McQuilkin *Miss Emily Charlotte*
Call Date: July 2012 (Inner Temple)

Meade *Miss Natasha Juliana Margaret*
Call Date: July 2012 (Lincoln's Inn)

Meakins *Mr Vincent*
Call Date: Oct 1999 (Gray's Inn) Qualifications: LLB (Nott'm)

Medici *Mr Matthew James*
Call Date: July 2012 (Inner Temple)

Mendy *Miss Madeleine Antrego*
Call Date: July 2008 (Middle Temple) Qualifications: LLB (Hons)

Mensah *Miss Marian Serwaa*
Call Date: July 2012 (Lincoln's Inn)

Merriman-Kelly *Mrs Patricia Jean FRSA*
Call Date: July 1999 (Gray's Inn) Qualifications: BA Dip Ed (L'pool) FCA (L'pool) LLB (L'pool)

Metcalfe-Mason *Miss Stephanie Ann*
Call Date: July 2010 (Middle Temple) Qualifications: BA (Hons) (UEA) LLB (Notts) Dip Law (UEA)

Miah *Miss Aysha Azmin*
Call Date: July 2012 (Inner Temple)

Mijatovic *Mr Djura*
Call Date: July 1997 (Middle Temple) Qualifications: LLB (Hons)

Milburn *Miss Laura Anne*
Henry Hyams, 7 South Parade, Leeds, LS1 5QE, Fax: 0113 2429714, Call Date: July 2010 (Gray's Inn) Qualifications: LLB

Miller *Mr George Peter*
Call Date: July 2012 (Inner Temple)

Miller *Mr Ronald Kinsman CB*
4 Liskeard Close, Chislehurst, Kent, BR7 6RT, 020 7438 664, Call Date: Nov 1953 (Gray's Inn)

Miller *Miss Sarah Elizabeth Barbara*
Stone Chambers, 4 Field Court, Gray's Inn, London, WC1R 5EF, 020 7440 6900, Fax: 020 7242 0197, Call Date: Nov 1971 (Gray's Inn)

Miller *Mr Sefton Semion*
Call Date: Oct 2011 (Middle Temple) Qualifications: LLB (Hons) (Wales)

Mills *Mr Alexander Christopher*
Call Date: July 2012 (Inner Temple)

Mills *Mr George Arthur Charles*
EXP, Call Date: Nov 1987 (Inner Temple) Qualifications: LLB (So'ton) LLM (Lond) M Phil (Cantab)

Mills *Mr Michael John Patrick*
Solicitor, Call Date: Oct 1992 (Inner Temple) Qualifications: BA (Hons)

Mirdha *Mr Mohammad Bakir Hossain*
Call Date: July 2012 (Lincoln's Inn)

Mitchell *Mr Iain Grant*
Call Date: July 2012 (Middle Temple)

Mitchell *Miss Julie Zoe*
Call Date: July 2012 (Inner Temple)

Mitchell *Miss Nathalie Keryn Maxwell*
Call Date: July 2008 (Inner Temple) Qualifications: LLB (Exon)

Mitchell *Mr Oliver James*
Call Date: July 2009 (Middle Temple) Qualifications: BA (Hons) (Oxon) LLB (Hons)

Mitchell *Mr Paul Martin Selby*
Judge, Call Date: Nov 1986 (Gray's Inn)

Mitchell *Mr Rhon Andrew*
Call Date: Oct 2011 (Middle Temple) Qualifications: LLB (Hons) (Lond)

Mitchell *Mrs Sally*
Consultant, Call Date: Oct 1990 (Inner Temple) Qualifications: LLB (Hons)

Mitchell *Mrs Tamsin Christina-Marie*
Call Date: Nov 2002 (Lincoln's Inn) Qualifications: LLB (Hons)

Mitha *Mr Abdulsultan Alibhai*
Call Date: July 1972 (Inner Temple) Qualifications: MA

Mitton *Mr John Grahame*
Call Date: Oct 2003 (Middle Temple) Qualifications: LLB (Hons)(Teesside)

Miyajima *Miss Mitsue*
8 Welbeck Street, London, W1G 9YD, 020 7577 2802, Fax: 020 7577 2872, Call Date: July 1997 (Lincoln's Inn) Qualifications: BA (Japan) ACIB LLDip (Wolves)

Moggridge *Miss Katherine Sarah Cuff*
Call Date: July 2012 (Lincoln's Inn)

Mohd Haaziq Pillay *Miss Shameen*
Call Date: July 2012 (Middle Temple)

Mohindra *Dr Raj Kumar*
Other, Call Date: Oct 1991 (Inner Temple) Qualifications: MA (Cantab) MA (Lond) BM Bch (Oxon) MRCP

Moloney *Prof Denis George Gerard OBE*
Call Date: Mar 2006 (Lincoln's Inn) Qualifications: LLB Cert PLS Dip Sol NP Dip Phil Dip Sch Phil Dip Th BTh DASE LLD

Monro *Mr Alexander James*
Call Date: Nov 2011 (Gray's Inn) Qualifications: LLB LLM

Moore *Dr Dudley John*
Lecturer in Law, Bellerbys College, 1 Billington Way, Brighton, East Sussex, BN1 4LF, 01273 339397, Fax: 01273 339201, Call Date: Oct 1996 (Middle Temple) Qualifications: BA (Hons)(Sussex) LLM MPhil MA DPhil MSc (Oxon)

Moore *Miss Naomi Charmaine*
Brent Community Law Centre, 389 High Road, Willesden, London, NW10 2JR, 020 8 208 5706, Fax: 020 8 208 5734, Call Date: Nov 2008 (Middle Temple) Qualifications: LLB (Hons)(Lond)

Moore *Miss Nicola Jean*
Other, Call Date: Nov 1993 (Lincoln's Inn) Qualifications: LLB (Hons) (Bris)

Moore *Mr Rowland Peter*
Call Date: July 1952 (Lincoln's Inn) Qualifications: LLB

Morad *Mr Jahed*
Call Date: July 2012 (Middle Temple)

Morad *Mr Yunus Casim*
Call Date: July 2012 (Gray's Inn)

Morcos *Mr Peter*
Call Date: July 2012 (Inner Temple)

Moree *Mr Kevin Alexander Carl*
Call Date: July 2012 (Lincoln's Inn)

Moree *Mr Sean*
Call Date: July 2003 (Lincoln's Inn) Qualifications: LLB Hons (Nott'm) MA (USA) Pupil Supervisor

Morgan *Miss Eloise Jane*
Call Date: July 2012 (Lincoln's Inn)

Morgan *Miss Shelagh Elizabeth*
Call Date: June 1964 (Middle Temple) Qualifications: LLB

Morris *Miss Sarah Eliza*
Call Date: July 2012 (Middle Temple)

Morrison *Dr Scott Darrel*
Call Date: July 2012 (Gray's Inn)

Moss *Miss Karen Nicola*
Call Date: Oct 2002 (Middle Temple) Qualifications: LLB (Sussex) BVC (ICSL)

Moyler *Miss Alexandra Tandy*
Call Date: July 2006 (Lincoln's Inn) Qualifications: BEng (York) PgDL

Muehl *Mrs Ruth Anna*
Call Date: Feb 1960 (Gray's Inn)

Mugabe *Miss Rumbidzai*
Call Date: July 2012 (Middle Temple)

Mughal *Ms Tahaba*
Call Date: July 2006 (Lincoln's Inn) Qualifications: MSc (Manch)

Muir Wood *Dr Alan Jamie*
Call Date: July 2012 (Inner Temple)

Mulchrone *Ms Maureen Teresa*
Call Date: Oct 2003 (Inner Temple) Qualifications: LDS RCS BDS (Lond) MBBS (Lond)

Mulligan *Ms Louise Susan*
Call Date: Oct 1999 (Gray's Inn) Qualifications: LLB (Keele)

Mullins *Mr Bruce Ashley*
Other, Jewel Beach, P.O. Box 200, Muscat, 134, Sultanate of Oman, 00 968 2469 1007, Fax: 00 968 2469 1020, Call Date: July 1980 (Lincoln's Inn) Qualifications: B Sc (Hons)(Wales)

Munang *Mrs Mariam Nelly*
Call Date: July 2012 (Lincoln's Inn)

Munro *Miss Lesley Vanessa Christianne*
Call Date: Nov 2002 (Lincoln's Inn) Qualifications: PgDL

Mure *Mr Kenneth Nisbet QC*
Chair, Advocates Library, Parliament House, Edinburgh, EH1 1RF, 0131 226 5071, Call Date: July 1990 (Gray's Inn) Qualifications: LLB (Glas) MA (Glas) FTII

Murphy *Miss Niamh May*
Call Date: Nov 2011 (Middle Temple) Qualifications: LLB (Hons) (Leeds)

Murphy *Mr Ruairi John*
Call Date: July 2012 (Lincoln's Inn)

Murray *Mrs Michelle Theresa*
Call Date: July 2012 (Inner Temple)

Musah *Mr Zakaria Tanko*
Call Date: July 2012 (Lincoln's Inn)

Mustasum *Mr Shamikh Mohammed*
Call Date: July 2011 (Lincoln's Inn) Qualifications: BSc (Manch)

Nabukeera *Miss Stella*
Call Date: Nov 2011 (Lincoln's Inn) Qualifications: Ben (B'ham) MSc (Loughborough)

Naiken *Miss Belinda*
Call Date: Oct 2002 (Gray's Inn) Qualifications: LLB (B'Ham)

Namdarkhan *Mr Abdool Karrim*
Call Date: July 2012 (Gray's Inn)

Naqvi *Mr Ali Raza*
Call Date: Mar 2006 (Lincoln's Inn) Qualifications: LLB (Hons) (Lond)

Naresh *Mr Suman*
Call Date: Nov 1972 (Inner Temple) Qualifications: MA (Cantab)

Narine *Miss Saajida*
Call Date: July 2009 (Lincoln's Inn) Qualifications: LLB (So'ton) PGDip (Cardiff)

Narshi *Miss Anjali Arvinkumar*
Call Date: July 2007 (Inner Temple) Qualifications: LLB (Leic)

Nasir *Mr Jahanzeb Khan*
Call Date: Nov 2008 (Lincoln's Inn) Qualifications: LLB

Nathaniel *Miss Leontia Mary Charmaine*
Call Date: July 2004 (Lincoln's Inn) Qualifications: LLB Hons (Wolverhampton)

Nduka-Eze *Mr Chukwuemeka Cecil*
Call Date: Oct 1990 (Middle Temple) Qualifications: LLB (Warw)

Neal *Miss Merry Anne*
Call Date: July 2012 (Middle Temple)

Nelson *Miss Jade Chantelle*
Call Date: July 2012 (Middle Temple)

Nesbitt *Miss Amy Stella*
Call Date: July 2012 (Lincoln's Inn)

Neville *Mr Shaun Anton*
Call Date: July 2010 (Middle Temple) Qualifications: LLB (Hons) (Brunel)

Newman *Mr David Ross*
Call Date: July 2008 (Middle Temple) Qualifications: LLB (Hons) (Lincoln)

Newman *Miss Lauretta*
Call Date: Nov 2005 (Inner Temple) Qualifications: LLB

Newton *Mr Clive Trevor CB*
Call Date: Nov 1969 (Middle Temple) Qualifications: LLB FCCA ACIArb

Newton *Mr David*
Call Date: Oct 2010 (Gray's Inn) Qualifications: LLB

Ng *Miss Isabella Ling Ling*
Call Date: July 2012 (Lincoln's Inn)

Ng *Mr Robert Chee Siong*
Tsim Sha Tsui Centre, 11th-12th Floor, Salisbury Road, Tsim Sha Tsui, Kowloon, Hong Kong, China, (852) 2734 8383, Fax: (852) 2369 8471, Call Date: July 1975 (Middle Temple)

Ng *Mr Soo Heng*
Call Date: July 2012 (Middle Temple)

Ng *Mr Stephen Shiu Chi*
Call Date: July 1997 (Middle Temple) Qualifications: LLB (Hons) LLM

Nicholson *Miss Juliette Frances*
Call Date: July 2012 (Lincoln's Inn)

Niemelae *Miss Chris-Marie*
Call Date: Nov 2008 (Middle Temple) Qualifications: BA MSc GDL

Nihat *Miss Senay*
Call Date: July 2012 (Inner Temple)

Noble-Mathews *Dr Priscilla Mary OStJ*
Lovehill Cottage, Trotton, Petersfield, Hampshire, GU31 5ER, 01730 816583, Fax: 01730 816583, Call Date: Feb 1953 (Middle Temple) Qualifications: BM (So'ton) Dip PALL MED FIMC (RCS ED) MA Th BTh (Hons)

Noguera *Mr Stephen Andrew*
Call Date: July 2012 (Middle Temple)

Noonan *Miss Kiran Saira*
Call Date: July 2012 (Lincoln's Inn)

Norman *Miss Victoria Marie*
Call Date: Oct 2011 (Middle Temple) Qualifications: LLB (Hons) (Manch)

Noviss *Mr Adrian Paul*
Call Date: July 2007 (Inner Temple) Qualifications: LLB (Dunelm)

Nujeerallee *Mr Rasheed*
Call Date: Oct 2008 (Gray's Inn) Qualifications: LLB LLM

Nunns *Mr Malcolm Reeve Mark MC*
Call Date: July 1969 (Middle Temple) Qualifications: LLB (Exon) FCI Arb

Nusrat *Ms Farah*
Call Date: July 2012 (Lincoln's Inn)

Nyamangunda *Mr Patrick Junior Tatenda*
Call Date: July 2012 (Inner Temple)

Oakland *Miss Natasha Wendy*
Company Secretary, Call Date: Nov 2001 (Middle Temple) Qualifications: BSc (Hons) CPE RGN

Obhrai *Mr Ashwini*
Call Date: July 2007 (Middle Temple) Qualifications: LLB (Hons) (Lond) LLM (LSE)

O'Brien *Miss Dawn Catherine*
Armstrong Solicitors, No5 Temple Square, Temple Street, Liverpool, L2 5RH, Call Date: Nov 2006 (Middle Temple) Qualifications: LLB (Hons) (L'pool)

O'Connell *Mr Michael Alfred*
Lecturer, Call Date: Nov 1966 (Inner Temple) Qualifications: BL (Dublin) MPhil

O'Connor *Miss Kate Victoria*
Call Date: July 2012 (Lincoln's Inn) Pupil Supervisor

O'Connor *Mr Simon Mark*
Norwegian Red Cross, Hausmannsgate 7, 0133 Oslo, Norway, Call Date: July 1999 (Lincoln's Inn) Qualifications: LLB (Hons)

O'Donnell *Mr John*
130 Water Street, New York, Ny 10005-1621, USA, 00 212 825 0783, Fax: 00 212 825 0890, Call Date: July 1974 (Middle Temple) Qualifications: LLB (Lond)

O'Donnell *Mr Laurence Paul*
Law Officers Department, Morier House, Hackett Place, St Helier, JE1 1DD, Jersey, 01534 441224, Call Date: Nov 2009 (Middle Temple) Qualifications: BA (Hons) (Leic)

O'Donoghue *Mr Florence*
Judge, 19 Parchment Street, Winchester, Hampshire, SO23 8AZ, 01962 852246, Call Date: Feb 1959 (Inner Temple) Qualifications: MA (Dub)

Offeh *Mr John Kofi*
Call Date: Nov 1969 (Inner Temple) Qualifications: LLB (Hons) (Lond)

Ogbeide *Miss Iyuwa Sandra*
Call Date: July 2012 (Middle Temple)

Ogg *Mr Thomas William*
Call Date: July 2012 (Inner Temple)

O'Grady *Miss Eileen Joyce*
EDT, Other, Call Date: Nov 1976 (Lincoln's Inn) Qualifications: LLB

Ohiullah *Mr Muhammad*
Orr, Dignam & Co., Shajan Tower 2 (1st Floor), Office No 101-104, 3 Segun Bagicha, Dhaka, 1000, Bangladesh, 00 880 2 956 3950, Fax: 00 880 2 956 0257, Call Date: July 1997 (Inner Temple) Qualifications: LLB (So'ton)

O'Keefe *Mrs Hilary Ann*
Call Date: Oct 2010 (Gray's Inn) Qualifications: BA

Okorefe *Miss Nancy Emuobo*
Call Date: Nov 1992 (Middle Temple) Qualifications: LLB (Hons)

Okoronkwo *Mr Samuel Nwabueze*
Call Date: 0 (Gray's Inn) Qualifications: LLB

Okpaluba *Dr Johnson Chukwuemeka*
Jacksons Solicitors, Fleet House, 8-12 New Bridg Street, London, EC4V 6AL, 020 7822 8535, Fax: 020 7822 8536, Call Date: Nov 1992 (Inner Temple) Qualifications: LLB LLM (Lond) PhD (Lond)

Oldfield *Miss Jamie Lee*
Call Date: July 2012 (Lincoln's Inn)

Oldham *Mr David Alexander Samuel*
Call Date: July 2009 (Middle Temple) Qualifications: LLB (Hons)

Olhausen *William Paul*
Call Date: Nov 1993 (Middle Temple) Qualifications: BA (Hons)(Sussex) MA (Sussex) CPE (Lond) BA (Oxon) PhD (L'pool)

Oliver *Dr Peter John*
Other, Legal Service, European Commission, Rue De Loi 200, 1049 Brussels, Belgium, 296 63 39, Fax: 296 43 08, Call Date: Nov 1977 (Middle Temple) Qualifications: BA (Cantab) LicSpec Droit European (Brussels) PhD (Cantab)

Omamalin *Mr Timothy Ian*
Call Date: July 2012 (Middle Temple)

O'Maoileoin *Mr Michael Brendan*
Arbitrator, Other, Solicitor Advocate, Moorhead James LLP, Kildare House, 3 Dorset Rise, London, EC4Y 8EN, 020 7400 5048, Fax: 020 7936 3635, Call Date: Oct 2004 (Inner Temple) Qualifications: BA (Surrey) Dip Law (Westminister)

Omar *Dr Paul Johan*
Professor of Law, Senior Lecturer, Sussex Law School, Falmer, Brighton, BN1 9SP, 01273 877061, Fax: 01273 877534, Call Date: Oct 1990 (Gray's Inn) Qualifications: LLB (Exeter) LLM (Sussex) DPhil (Sussex)

Omonua *Miss Patricia*
Call Date: Nov 2010 (Lincoln's Inn) Qualifications: LLB

O'Neill *Miss June*
Call Date: Nov 1997 (Lincoln's Inn) Qualifications: LLB (Hons)(Lond)

Ong *Miss Congning*
Call Date: July 2012 (Lincoln's Inn)

Ong *Ms Josephine Yam Hee*
Call Date: Oct 2000 (Lincoln's Inn) Qualifications: BSc (Hons)(Lond) MSc (City) LLB (Hons) (Wolves)

Ooi *Miss Mary-Ann Suan Kim*
O S Kim & Associates, 94-B Jalan Jejaka, Taman Maluri, Cheras, Kuala Lumpur, 55100, Malaysia, 00 603 92851464, Fax: 00 603 92850249, Call Date: July 2007 (Lincoln's Inn) Qualifications: LLB (Sheff)

O'Reilly *Miss Beth Melissa*
25 Bedford Row, 25 Bedford Row, London, WC1R 4HD, 020 7067 1500, Fax: 020 7067 1507, Call Date: Oct 1999 (Lincoln's Inn) Qualifications: BA (Hons)(Lond) Dip in Law

O'Rourke *Ms Maeve Maria*
Call Date: July 2012 (Lincoln's Inn)

O'Rourke *Mr Raymond John*
Call Date: Nov 1995 (Gray's Inn) Qualifications: BA MA (Dublin) LLB (Lond)

Ors *Mr Sinan*
Call Date: Nov 2006 (Gray's Inn) Qualifications: LLB

Osborne *Mr Charles Richard*
Call Date: July 2012 (Inner Temple)

Osborne *Mr David*
Call Date: Nov 2009 (Gray's Inn) Qualifications: LLB

O'Shea *Judge Michael*
Call Date: Nov 1999 (Middle Temple) Qualifications: BL (King's Inn)

Osman *Miss Sona Kaarina Pia*
Call Date: Nov 1986 (Middle Temple) Qualifications: BA(Keele) Dip Law

Oster *Mr Norman Howard*
International Law Consultant, Po Box 844, 87 Bareket Street, Shaarei Tikva, 44810, Israel, 03 936 1015, Fax: 03 906 3985, Call Date: Feb 1954 (Middle Temple)

Ottey *Dr Dominic Sean*
Call Date: Nov 2009 (Middle Temple) Qualifications: MBChB (Sheff) LLB (Hons) (Sheff) LLM (Sheff)

Ough *Dr Richard Norman*
Adjudicator, Arbitrator, Deputy Chairman, FLW, Mediator, Call Date: July 1985 (Inner Temple) Qualifications: MRCS FCIArb LRCP MBBS MSc MA MB BS MSc

Owen *Miss Denise*
No5 Chambers, Greenwood House, 4-7 Salisbury Court, London, EC4Y 8AA, Call Date: Oct 2003 (Gray's Inn) Qualifications: LLB (Exon)

Owen *Miss Kayleigh*
Call Date: July 2012 (Gray's Inn)

Owen *Mrs Mary Lisa Hacon*
Call Date: July 1972 (Gray's Inn)

Owen *Mrs Tracey Rebecca*
Company Secretary, Head of Legal Services, Call Date: July 1984 (Middle Temple) Qualifications: LLB

Owolabi *Miss Ibukun*
Call Date: Nov 2008 (Inner Temple) Qualifications: LLB (Lond) CPE

Owusu *Miss Nikita*
Call Date: July 2012 (Lincoln's Inn)

Paczko *Miss Claire Jayne*
Call Date: Oct 2007 (Inner Temple) Qualifications: BSc (Teesside) PgDL

Page *Miss Emily Victoria*
Call Date: July 2012 (Lincoln's Inn)

Page *Ms Rowena Juliet*
Call Date: July 2012 (Gray's Inn)

Pal *Miss Shaswati*
Call Date: Mar 2007 (Middle Temple) Qualifications: LLB (Hons) (Lond)

Palin *Ms Marianne Josephine*
Call Date: July 2012 (Middle Temple)

Paluch *Dr Nicholas Anthony Fleetwood*
La Gallie, Rue De La Gallie, St Peters, GY7 9ED, Guernsey, 01481 264242, Call Date: July 2007 (Lincoln's Inn) Qualifications: BSc (Lond) MBBS MRCGP GDL

Panayi *Mr Christian Alexi*
Call Date: July 2009 (Middle Temple) Qualifications: BA (Hons) (Lond) MA (Sussex) Grad Dip Law (Lond) LLB

Panter *Mrs Kerry Louise*
Call Date: July 2012 (Gray's Inn)

Pao *Mr Felix Ho Ming*
87 New Henry House, 10 Ice House Street, Central, Hong Kong, China, 2522 5494, Fax: 2810 4677, Call Date: Apr 1991 (Gray's Inn) Qualifications: LLB PCLL

Paphiti *Mr Anthony Steven*
Consultant, Legal Officer, Prosecutor, Senior Crown Prosecutor, Systems Consultant Services Ltd, Arlington House, 1025 Arlington Business Park, Theale, Reading, RG7 4SA, Call Date: Nov 1975 (Inner Temple) Qualifications: LLB (Leeds)

Paradysz *Mr Roger John*
Prosecution Team Leader, Call Date: Nov 1985 (Gray's Inn) Qualifications: BA (Hons) (Notts)

Pardal *Miss Alexandra Emilia Lucia*
Call Date: July 2012 (Inner Temple)

Parikh *Mr Romesh Chandra*
8 Shackleton Road, Southall, Middlesex, UB1 2JA, 020 8571 5091, Call Date: Nov 1975 (Middle Temple)

Partington *Miss Jessica Samantha*
Call Date: July 2008 (Middle Temple) Qualifications: BSc (Hons) (York) PgDl (Lond)

Partos *Miss Natasha Vivienne*
Call Date: July 2012 (Middle Temple)

Parveen *Miss Sonia*
Call Date: July 2012 (Lincoln's Inn)

Pasquale *Miss Shawna Lee*
Call Date: July 2012 (Lincoln's Inn)

Patel *Miss Krishma*
Call Date: July 2012 (Middle Temple)

Patterson *Miss Margaret Elizabeth*
Call Date: July 1973 (Middle Temple) Qualifications: LLB (lond)

Patzer *Mr Tomasz Dariusz*
Call Date: July 2011 (Middle Temple) Qualifications: LLB (Hons) (Lond)

Pavlovich *Mr Anthony David*
Call Date: July 2012 (Lincoln's Inn)

Payne *Mr Brian Wyndham*
Call Date: Nov 1993 (Inner Temple) Qualifications: BSc (Bris) Dip Law (Lond)

Peaa *Ms Farah Khan*
Call Date: July 2012 (Lincoln's Inn)

Peacock *Miss Louisa Jean Alice*
Call Date: July 2012 (Inner Temple)

Pearce *Mrs Kathy-Ann*
Call Date: Nov 2006 (Gray's Inn) Qualifications: LLB LLM

Pedelty *Mr Tristan Edwin Cornish*
Call Date: July 2007 (Inner Temple) Qualifications: BA (Cantab)

Peeroo *Mrs Lokeshnee*
Call Date: July 2012 (Gray's Inn)

Pendery *Ms Lisa Jane*
Call Date: July 2010 (Inner Temple) Qualifications: LLB (Leic)

Penry-Davey *Mr James Alexander*
Call Date: Nov 2004 (Inner Temple) Qualifications: LLB University of Leeds

Pereira *Miss Danielle Louise*
Call Date: July 2012 (Gray's Inn)

Perry *Dr Melissa Anne*
Call Date: July 2012 (Inner Temple)

Pershad *Mr Rohan QC*
Call Date: Oct 1991 (Lincoln's Inn) Qualifications: LLB (Hons) (Lond)

Peter *Mr David Benjamin*
Call Date: July 2012 (Lincoln's Inn)

Petrie *Miss Isabel Mary*
Call Date: July 2012 (Middle Temple)

Petryszyn *Miss Nina*
Call Date: Oct 2007 (Middle Temple) Qualifications: LLB (Hons) (Nott'm)

Philand *Mr Paul Michael*
Call Date: Oct 2007 (Inner Temple) Qualifications: BA (Wolves)

Phillips *Mr Andrew Robert Forbes*
Call Date: Nov 2011 (Inner Temple) Qualifications: LLB

Pierce *Miss Sophie Louise*
Call Date: July 2009 (Inner Temple) Qualifications: LLB (Hudds)

Pine *Miss Amie Suzanne*
Call Date: Oct 2009 (Middle Temple) Qualifications: LLB (Hons) (Cantab)

Piskolti *Miss Catherine Isabelle*
Call Date: July 2003 (Lincoln's Inn) Qualifications: LLB Hons (Leic)

Pitts *Mr Damian Stuart*
Call Date: Oct 2009 (Middle Temple) Qualifications: MA (Hons) (St. Andrews)

Place *Miss Sarah Lesley*
Call Date: Oct 2002 (Middle Temple) Qualifications: LLB (Hons) (So'ton)

Plumb *Miss Claire Martina Sarah*
Call Date: July 2012 (Lincoln's Inn)

Pobjoy *Mr Jason Mark*
Call Date: July 2012 (Inner Temple)

Polak *Miss Sabrina Rosanne*
Call Date: July 2012 (Middle Temple)

Pollitt *Miss Oriana Patricia*
Call Date: July 2008 (Middle Temple) Qualifications: BSc (Hons) (Lond) PgDl (Lond)

Pompa *Mr Adam*
Call Date: Nov 2008 (Inner Temple) Qualifications: LLB (So'ton) CPE

Poo *Miss Rachel Xiu Xian*
Call Date: July 2012 (Middle Temple)

Poole *Prof Jill*
HED, Professor of Law, Aston Law, Aston University, Birmingham, B4 7ET, 0121 204 3223, Fax: 0121 204 4915, Call Date: Feb 1992 (Lincoln's Inn) Qualifications: LLB (Hons) (Reading) LLM (Bris) FCIArb FHEA FRSA

Pooley *Miss Helen Jane*
Call Date: July 2012 (Inner Temple)

Popert *Miss Catherine Teresa Marie*
Call Date: Nov 1987 (Middle Temple) Qualifications: LLB (Lond)

Porter *Miss Esther Arabella*
Call Date: July 2007 (Lincoln's Inn) Qualifications: BA (Sheff)

Poselay *Mr Mukhtar Mohammed*
Call Date: Nov 2008 (Gray's Inn) Qualifications: LLB

Potts *Mr Richard Vivian*
Director, 1 Carey Lane, London, EC2V 8AE, 020 7776 1212, Fax: 020 7776 1201, Call Date: July 1982 (Middle Temple) Qualifications: BA FCSI

Pourgoura *Miss Vasiliki Andrea*
Call Date: Nov 2002 (Middle Temple) Qualifications: LLB (Hons) (So'ton) LLM (Lond)

Powell *Miss Charlotte Claire*
Furnival Chambers, 32 Furnival Street, London, EC4A 1JQ, 020 7405 3232, Fax: 020 7405 3322, Call Date: July 2005 (Inner Temple) Qualifications: LLB King's College University of London

Powers *Miss Jessica*
Call Date: July 2012 (Inner Temple)

Pratt *Dr Landé Nicola*
Call Date: July 2011 (Inner Temple) Qualifications: BA (Reading) DPhil (Oxon) MA (Lond)

Press *Mr Benjamin Thomas*
Call Date: Mar 2007 (Lincoln's Inn) Qualifications: LLB (Lond)

Preston *Mr Iain David*
Call Date: July 2012 (Middle Temple)

Price *Miss Catherine Emily*
Call Date: July 2012 (Middle Temple)

Price *Ms Emily Jane*
Call Date: July 2012 (Lincoln's Inn)

Price *Mr John Philip*
Chair, Call Date: July 1974 (Inner Temple) Qualifications: MA B Phil (Oxon)

Price *Mr Leolin QC CBE*
Bencher, Ten Old Square, Ground Floor, Ten Old Square, Lincoln's Inn, London, WC2A 3SU, 020 7405 0758, Fax: 020 7831 8237, Call Date: Nov 1949 (Middle Temple) Qualifications: MA(Oxon)

Procter *Miss Diana Elizabeth Cecil*
Call Date: July 1973 (Lincoln's Inn) Qualifications: BA (Lond)

Proferes *Ms Amy Linnea*
Call Date: July 2012 (Lincoln's Inn)

Prosser *Mr Henry William*
Recorder, Call Date: July 1969 (Middle Temple) Qualifications: MA

Pryer *Mr David*
Justices' Clerk, Call Date: Nov 1982 (Gray's Inn) Qualifications: MCMI FinstCPD

Pullen *Miss Hannah Louise*
Solicitor, Edward Fail Bradshaw Solicitors, 402 Commercial Road, London, E1 0LG, 020 7790 4032, Fax: 020 7790 2739, Call Date: Oct 2008 (Lincoln's Inn) Qualifications: BA (Lond)

Pullen *Mr James Oliver*
Call Date: July 2012 (Middle Temple)

Purcell-David *Mrs Nicole Beverly*
Call Date: Nov 2009 (Gray's Inn) Qualifications: LLB

Purchase *Mr Richard James William*
Call Date: July 2012 (Inner Temple)

Purnell *Mr Christopher Arthur*
Other, Call Date: July 1980 (Gray's Inn) Qualifications: MA (Oxon)

Quayum *Mr S.O.M. Rashedul*
Call Date: July 2012 (Lincoln's Inn)

Qureshi *Mr Mohammad Ishaq Afzal*
Call Date: Nov 2010 (Gray's Inn) Qualifications: LLB

Raad-Chagoury *Mrs Margaret-Catherine*
Call Date: July 2011 (Gray's Inn) Qualifications: BA LLM

Rabin *Mr Anthony Leon Philip*
Call Date: July 1978 (Middle Temple) Qualifications: LLB FCA

Rahman *Mr Habib Ur*
Liaison Office, 109-9-2, Pechs, Karachi, Pakistan, 092 21 4555244, Fax: 092 21 4310511, Call Date: June 1961 (Lincoln's Inn) Qualifications: BA

Rahman *Mr Shamsur*
Call Date: Nov 2002 (Inner Temple) Qualifications: LLB (Wolv)

Raisbeck *Mr Gareth Ewan*
Call Date: Oct 2008 (Inner Temple) Qualifications: LLB (Wales)

Rajakumaran *Mr Anthonipillai Basil*

Call Date: June 1964 (Lincoln's Inn)

Rajwana *Mr Malik Kashif Rafique*
Call Date: July 2012 (Lincoln's Inn)

Ramdenee *Mr Bishan*
Call Date: July 2012 (Lincoln's Inn)

Ramlogan *Mr Ouditnarine*
Call Date: Feb 1960 (Lincoln's Inn)

Ramos *Mr Daniel*
Call Date: July 2012 (Inner Temple)

Ramsay *Mr Edward Raymond Jonathan*
Call Date: July 2012 (Inner Temple)

Ramsey *Miss Sarah Julia*
Call Date: July 2012 (Lincoln's Inn)

Ranger *Mr Matthew Alexander*
Call Date: July 2012 (Middle Temple)

Ranjha *Mr Hassan Khalid*
Call Date: July 2012 (Inner Temple)

Ransom *Dr William Thomas Mclean*
Po Box 534, Epsom, Surrey, KT17 9ET, Call Date: Oct 1999 (Lincoln's Inn) Qualifications: MB ChB (Bris) Dip in Law (Bris)

Rasteen *Mr Daniel*
Call Date: July 2012 (Gray's Inn)

Rawat *Mr Anas Moussa Ismael*
Call Date: July 2012 (Middle Temple)

Rawlings *Mr Robert William*
Call Date: July 2012 (Lincoln's Inn)

Rawlins *Mr Anthony Jeremy*
Greenwoods Solicitors, 18 Bedford Square, London, WC1B 3JA, Call Date: July 2006 (Middle Temple) Qualifications: LLB (Hons) (Lond)

Rayner *Mr Stephen Alan*
Call Date: Nov 2004 (Lincoln's Inn) Qualifications: LLB MRICS

Raza *Mr Mohammad Ali*
Call Date: July 2005 (Lincoln's Inn) Qualifications: LLB (Hons) Dip Law

Rea *Mr Luigi Orlando Anthony*
Call Date: July 1982 (Middle Temple) Qualifications: BA (Dublin)

Rea *Mrs Tessa Louise*
Deputy District Judge, Call Date: Nov 1990 (Inner Temple) Qualifications: LLB (Hons)(Bris) LLM

Rebelo *Mr Mario Jose Reis*
Call Date: July 2008 (Inner Temple) Qualifications: Beng (Southbank)

Redford *Miss Jessica Kate*
Lecturer in Law, 3 Dr Johnson's Bldgs, Ground Floor, 3 Dr Johnson's Bldgs, Temple, London, EC4Y 7BA, 020 7353 4854, Fax: 020 7583 8784, Call Date: Nov 1994 (Inner Temple) Qualifications: BA (Hons) (Oxon) CPE

Rees *Ms Christina Elizabeth*
Call Date: Oct 1997 (Gray's Inn) Qualifications: LLB (Wales)

Rees *Mr William Patrick Charles*
Call Date: Nov 1974 (Middle Temple) Qualifications: LLB (Lond)

Regnart *Mr Horace FRAS*
Quintessence, 4 Grosvenor Avenue, Jesmond, Newcastle Upon Tyne, NE2 2NN, 0191 2810809/0191 281 0809, Call Date: July 1985 (Gray's Inn) Qualifications: LLB (Newc)

Rehman *Miss Saira*
Call Date: Oct 2008 (Lincoln's Inn) Qualifications: LLB (Wales)

Reid *Mr Horace Deighton*
Call Date: July 1975 (Lincoln's Inn) Qualifications: LLB (Lond)

Remy *Dr Michael*
Call Date: July 1999 (Lincoln's Inn) Qualifications: LLB PhD LLM MSc MBA MA

Rennie Wainwright *Mrs Karene Elisabet*
Call Date: July 2012 (Middle Temple)

Revill *Miss Deborah*
Richmond Canter Immigration Barristers, 1 Fetter Lane, London, EC4A 1BR, Call Date: July 2009 (Inner Temple) Qualifications: BA (Oxon)

Rial *Mr William Michael*
Call Date: Nov 2008 (Lincoln's Inn) Qualifications: BSc LLB (Nott'm) LLM MRPharmS MPSNI

Riaz *Mr Shahryar Fareed*
Call Date: July 2012 (Lincoln's Inn)

Ricci *Miss Ariel Elizabeth*
Call Date: July 2012 (Inner Temple)

Richardson *Mr James Anthony David*
Call Date: July 2012 (Middle Temple)

Richardson *Sophie Charlotte*
Call Date: July 2012 (Middle Temple)

Riegels *Mr Colin David*
Harney Westwood & Riegels LLP, 3rd Floor, 7 Ludgate Broadway, London, EC4V 6DX, 020 7332 5620, Fax: 020 7332 5621, Call Date: Oct 1996 (Lincoln's Inn) Qualifications: LLB (Hons)(Bris) BCL (Oxon)

Riordan *Mr Jaani*
Call Date: July 2012 (Lincoln's Inn)

Ritchie *Mr Robert Stuart*
Call Date: Oct 2008 (Middle Temple) Qualifications: BA (Hons) (Australia) LLM (Lond)

Rivett *Miss Katherine Patricia Mary*
Call Date: July 2006 (Middle Temple) Qualifications: BSc (Hons) PgDL

Roberts *Mrs Marian*
73 Dacre Park, London, SE13 5BX, 020 8852 0215, Fax: 020 8852 0215, Call Date: July 1979 (Gray's Inn) Qualifications: BA P Grad Dip

Robertson *Mr Giles William James*
Call Date: July 2012 (Lincoln's Inn)

Robertson *Mr John*
Eton Court, Flat 55, Eton Avenue, London, NW3 3HJ, 020 7586 1368, Call Date: Nov 1961 (Lincoln's Inn) Qualifications: LLB

Robinson *Miss Georgina Clare*
Call Date: July 2012 (Middle Temple)

Robinson *Mr Jason Paul*
Call Date: July 2012 (Middle Temple)

Robinson *Miss Tanya Lin*
6 Pump Court Chambers, 6-8 Mill Street, Maidstone, Kent, ME15 6XH, Call Date: Nov 1997 (Inner Temple) Qualifications: LLB (So'ton)

Robinson-Doyle *Miss Francesca Victoria*
Call Date: July 2012 (Middle Temple)

Rochat-Spechter *Mrs Alison Jean*
Associate, dfjswiss LLC, 4 Rue Charles-Bonnet, Geneva, 1206, Switzerland, Call Date: Oct 1993 (Gray's Inn) Qualifications: LLB (Bucks)

Rodger *Miss Senay Denise*
Farrar's Building, Farrar's Building, Temple, London, EC4Y 7BD, 020 7583 9241, Fax: 020 7583 0090, Call Date: Oct 1999 (Lincoln's Inn) Qualifications: LLB (Hons) MSt(Oxon)

Rogerson *Mr Daniel David*
Call Date: July 2011 (Inner Temple) Qualifications: BA, (Manch)

Rose *Dr Craig Mark*
Lexis Nexis Butterworths, Halsbury House, 35 Chancery Lane, London, WC2A 1EL, 020 7520 5349, Call Date: Nov 1994 (Lincoln's Inn) Qualifications: BA (Hons)(Bris) Ph D (Cantab)

Rose *Mr Jonathen Michael*
Call Date: July 2012 (Middle Temple)

Rosney *Miss Claire Louise*
EEF Ltd, Glazebrook Lane, Glazebrook, Warrington, Cheshire, WA3 5BN, 0161 777 2500, Fax: 0161 777 2522, Call Date: Oct 2003 (Lincoln's Inn) Qualifications: LLB (Hons) (L'pool)

Routledge *Miss Babiche Mary Johanna*
Call Date: July 2012 (Gray's Inn)

Rowland-Frank *Miss Charlotte Angharad*
Call Date: July 2009 (Inner Temple) Qualifications: LLB (Sheff)

Royston *Mr Thomas Daniel*
Call Date: July 2012 (Lincoln's Inn)

Rudman *Mr Jake Henry*
Call Date: July 2012 (Lincoln's Inn)

Sabga *Mr Colin Simon*
53 Carlos Street, Wood Brook, Port Of Spain, Trinidad and Tobago, Call Date: Oct 2011 (Inner Temple) Qualifications: LLB (Bris) LLM (Lond)

Sadeeq *Mr Irfan*
Call Date: July 2005 (Lincoln's Inn) Qualifications: BA (Hons) (Leic) LLM

Sadjadi *Miss Shahrzad*
Call Date: July 2012 (Lincoln's Inn)

Saeed *Ms Salma*
Call Date: July 2012 (Inner Temple)

Saggu *Miss Kiranjit Kaur*
Call Date: Oct 2008 (Lincoln's Inn) Qualifications: LLB (Lond)

Salehmohamed *Mr Abdool Rahim*
Call Date: July 2012 (Middle Temple)

Saley *Mrs Raisa Adam*
Call Date: July 2008 (Inner Temple) Qualifications: LLB (Lond)

Salgin *Miss Iraz Benil*
Call Date: Oct 2011 (Inner Temple) Qualifications: LLB (Sheff) LLM (Lond)

Salter *Mr Benjamin Luke*
Call Date: Oct 2011 (Inner Temple) Qualifications: BA (Leic)

Samsunder *Mrs Jayanthi Devi*
Call Date: Mar 2009 (Lincoln's Inn) Qualifications: LLB (Hons) LLM (Northumbria Uni)

Samuel *Mr Adam Wilfred*
Call Date: July 1983 (Inner Temple) Qualifications: BA (Oxon) LLM (USA) FCIArB MSFA Dip PFS

Sangha *Mr Paul*
Call Date: July 2012 (Lincoln's Inn)

Sargent *Miss Caroline Emma*
Transworld House, 100 City Road, London, EC1Y RBP, 020 7878 6912, Call Date: July 1994 (Middle Temple) Qualifications: LLB (Hons)(Lond)

Sargent *Miss Sarah Louise*
Call Date: Mar 2003 (Lincoln's Inn) Qualifications: LLB (Hons) (Hull)

Sarkar *Mr Christopher George*
Call Date: July 1996 (Inner Temple) Qualifications: BA (Oxon) CPE

Sarkis *Miss Laura Marie*
Call Date: Mar 2010 (Middle Temple) Qualifications: LLB (Lond)

Saugh *Ms Kimberly Renuka*
Call Date: Oct 2010 (Lincoln's Inn) Qualifications: LLB (Lond)

Saund *Mr Jeetinder Singh*
Call Date: Oct 2009 (Middle Temple) Qualifications: LLB (Hons) (Keele)

Saunders *Mrs Ingrid Inez*
Call Date: July 2012 (Inner Temple)

Scanlon *Mr Mark Iain*
Call Date: Nov 2007 (Inner Temple) Qualifications: LLB (Lond)

Scarborough *Miss Christi Alice*
Call Date: July 2012 (Gray's Inn)

Schmid *Mr Joachim Alexander*
Call Date: July 2012 (Lincoln's Inn)

Scott *Miss Charlotte Mary*
Call Date: July 2012 (Inner Temple)

Scouller *Mr Joshua Alexander*
Call Date: July 2012 (Gray's Inn)

Seecharan *Mr Riaz Patrick*
Call Date: Oct 2011 (Gray's Inn) Qualifications: BA LLB

Seejore *Miss Tashalee*
Call Date: July 2003 (Lincoln's Inn) Qualifications: LLB (Hons) (Kent)

Seifert *Miss Anne Miriam*
Chair, COMT, Deputy Chairman, FLW, Judge, Solicitor, Call Date: July 1975 (Inner Temple) Qualifications: FCIArb

Sen *Ms Lisa*
Call Date: July 1995 (Gray's Inn) Qualifications: BA MA (USA) LLB (Lond)

Sethi *Miss Ruhi*
Call Date: July 2012 (Middle Temple)

Setter *Mr Daniel Martin*
Call Date: July 2011 (Inner Temple) Qualifications: LLB (Lond) LLM (Lond)

Shafaat *Miss Sehreen*
Call Date: July 2012 (Middle Temple)

Shah *Mr Saleem*
Call Date: Mar 2010 (Lincoln's Inn) Qualifications: LLB LLM (Manch)

Shah *Mr Yawar Ali*
Legal Adviser, Call Date: Nov 2006 (Lincoln's Inn) Qualifications: LLB (Hons) (Bedfordshire)

Shaheen *Miss Salma*
Call Date: July 2012 (Inner Temple)

Shaikh *Mr Mohammad Rashid*
Advocate, Noori Rashid & Co Solicitors, 31a South Road, Southall, Middlesex, UB1 1SW, 020 8893 6787, Fax: 020 8893 6797, Call Date: Nov 1968 (Inner Temple) Qualifications: BA (Hons) MA LLB (India) MCI Arb

Sham *Mr Abdool Raffeek*
Call Date: Oct 2011 (Middle Temple) Qualifications: MBA (Nott'm) LLB (Hons) (Hudds)

Shanmuganathan *Mr Sivakhanthan*
Call Date: Oct 1998 (Lincoln's Inn) Qualifications: LLB (Hons)(Lond)

Sharda *Mr Manoj Kumar*
Call Date: Mar 2010 (Lincoln's Inn) Qualifications: LLB (Herts)

Sharief *Miss Lujayne Tarek Abdulkadir*
Call Date: July 2012 (Middle Temple)

Sharma *Miss Dipika Aupasna*
Call Date: July 2012 (Middle Temple)

Sharpes *Miss Amelia Jane*
Call Date: Mar 2009 (Middle Temple) Qualifications: LLB (Hons) (Surrey)

Shaw *Dr Jennifer*
Call Date: July 2011 (Middle Temple) Qualifications: BA (Hons) (Sussex) MSc (So'ton) PhD (Middlesex) PgDL (Lond)

Sheikh *Mr Asad Mushtaq*
Call Date: Nov 2011 (Lincoln's Inn) Qualifications: LLB (Manch)

Sher *Mr Jules QC*
Advocate, Deputy High Court Judge, Mediator, Call Date: July 1968 (Inner Temple) Qualifications: BCom BCL (Oxon) LLB (Rand)

Sherratt *Mr Peter Robert*
Director, Call Date: July 1985 (Inner Temple) Qualifications: BA (Oxon) LLM (Cantab)

Shirazi *Mr Gideon Chayim*
Call Date: July 2012 (Lincoln's Inn)

Shoeb *Mr Hesham Ismail Hani*
Call Date: July 2009 (Inner Temple) Qualifications: LLB (Surrey)

Shore *Ms Fiona*
Call Date: July 2012 (Gray's Inn)

Shorinde *Mr Lawrence Lanrewaju*
Redemption Chambers, 121 The Vale, Golders Green, London, NW11 8TL, Call Date: July 2001 (Lincoln's Inn) Qualifications: LLB (Hons) LLM ACIArb

Shrotri *Ms Pranjal Nitin*
Call Date: July 2012 (Gray's Inn)

Siddiqui *Mrs Nabeela*
Call Date: Mar 2003 (Lincoln's Inn) Qualifications: LLB (Hons) (Nott'm)

Sidhu *Miss Sandeep Kaur*
Call Date: July 2009 (Middle Temple) Qualifications: LLB (Hons) (Nott'm)

Sidhu *Mr Sarjeet Singh*
Messrs Sidhu & Associates, No 51-1a, Jalan 3/93, Taman Miharja, Cheras, Kuala Lumpur, 55200, Malaysia, 00 603 9282 1223, Fax: 00 603 9281 6113, Call Date: Nov 1992 (Gray's Inn) Qualifications: LLB (So'ton)

Silva-Egger *Mrs Sampathawaduge Tharoja Damsari*
Lawyer, Call Date: Nov 1980 (Lincoln's Inn) Qualifications: BA (Hons)

Silvester *Mr Stephen James*
Call Date: July 2010 (Middle Temple) Qualifications: BA (Hons) (Leic) MBA (Lond)

Silvestro *Miss Leanne*
Call Date: July 2010 (Lincoln's Inn) Qualifications: LLB (Cardiff)

Sinyor *Dr Alan David*
Call Date: Nov 2002 (Lincoln's Inn) Qualifications: BA(Hons) (Oxon) PhD (Cantab) PgDL

Siraj *Mr Someir*
Call Date: July 2011 (Lincoln's Inn) Qualifications: LLB (Bucks)

Sirikanda *Ms Miranda*
Call Date: Nov 2005 (Middle Temple) Qualifications: BA (Hons) Sheffield

Sirrieh *Miss Natasha*
Call Date: July 2012 (Inner Temple)

Skelton *Mr Guy Francis*
Call Date: July 2012 (Middle Temple)

Skilbeck *Mrs Jennifer Seth*
Call Date: Oct 1991 (Lincoln's Inn) Qualifications: BSc (Econ) MSc (Econ) Dip Law

Slater *Mr James Edwin*
Legal Adviser, Call Date: Oct 1999 (Gray's Inn) Qualifications: LLB (Lancs) MA (Salford) MPhil

Slaughter *Miss Ingrid Elizabeth*
Call Date: July 1969 (Gray's Inn) Qualifications: LLB (Lond)

Sleator-Rollinson *Miss Emma-Jane*
Call Date: July 2011 (Middle Temple) Qualifications: LLB (Hons) (Lond)

Smallbone *Mr Sammy*
Call Date: July 2008 (Middle Temple) Qualifications: BA (Hons)

Smallwood *Miss Laura Jane*
Call Date: July 1987 (Middle Temple) Qualifications: MA (Cantab) Dip Law (City)

Smith *Mr Errol*
Call Date: July 2010 (Middle Temple) Qualifications: BSc (West Indies) LLB (Hons) (Wolv)

Smith *Mr Geoffrey*
Adjudicator, Arbitrator, Mediator, PS Consulting, 58 Avenue Wagram, 75017 Paris, France, 1 44 40 21 53, Fax: 1 44 40 07 89, Call Date: Feb 1995 (Middle Temple) Qualifications: BSc (Loughborough) LLDip CDipAF CEng FICE FCIArb

Smith *Mr Jonathan*
The Bar Standards Board, 4th Floor, 289-293 High Holborn, London, WC1V 7HZ, 020 7611 1444, Fax: 020 7831 9217, Call Date: Oct 2010 (Inner Temple) Qualifications: LLB (Lond)

Smith *Mr Kayode Olatunji Kwesi*
Call Date: Mar 2010 (Lincoln's Inn) Qualifications: LLB (Lond)

Smith *Mr Mark Oliver*
Call Date: July 2012 (Lincoln's Inn)

Smith *Mr Matthew James*
Call Date: Mar 2009 (Inner Temple) Qualifications: BA (Oxon) LLM CPE (Oxon)

Smith *The Hon Mr Justice Neville Leroy*
FSOL, Judge, Call Date: July 1991 (Lincoln's Inn) Qualifications: MBA

Smith *Mr Owen David*
Call Date: July 2012 (Middle Temple)

Smith *Mr Paul Andrew*
Conyers Dill & Pearman, Clarendon House, 2 Church Street, Po Box Hm666, Hamilton, Bermuda, 441 295 1422, Fax: 441 292 4270, Call Date: July 1978 (Middle Temple) Qualifications: BA (Hons) FCIArb MA

Smith *Mr Peter Oliver*
Call Date: July 2008 (Lincoln's Inn) Qualifications: MA (Cantab) MPhil (Cantab)

Smith *Mr Philip Tudor*
Call Date: July 2012 (Middle Temple)

Smith *Dr Robert Alan Lundie*
Call Date: July 2007 (Lincoln's Inn) Qualifications: Msci (Lond) PhD (Lond) GDL (Lond) LLB (Lond)

Smithdale *Mr James David Arthur*
Call Date: July 2012 (Lincoln's Inn)

Snodgrass *Miss Caroline Jane*
Call Date: Oct 2006 (Gray's Inn) Qualifications: LLB

Snooks *Dr Steven James*
Consultant, Call Date: July 2010 (Middle Temple) Qualifications: MBBS (Lond) Doctor Medicine (Lond) LLB (Hons)

Soh *Miss Siew Sun*
Call Date: July 2012 (Middle Temple)

Solf *Miss Charlotte Elizabeth*
Call Date: July 2012 (Lincoln's Inn)

Somerville *Mr Robin John*
Call Date: July 2012 (Lincoln's Inn)

Song *Miss Vuina*
Call Date: July 2012 (Middle Temple)

Soormally *Miss Zena*
Call Date: July 2007 (Gray's Inn) Qualifications: LLB (Lond)

Sorensen *Mr Charles Frederik Daniel*
Call Date: July 2011 (Gray's Inn) Qualifications: BA MPhil

Sotomi *Mr Joseph Oluwasegun*
Call Date: Nov 2008 (Lincoln's Inn) Qualifications: LLB (Kent)

Sowdagur *Miss Sheetul*
Call Date: July 2007 (Middle Temple) Qualifications: LLB (Hons) (Newc)

Spicer *Mr David Leslie*
Call Date: July 1973 (Gray's Inn) Qualifications: LLB

Spokes *Mr John Arthur Clayton QC*
Call Date: June 1955 (Gray's Inn)

Sprenger *Mrs Polly*
Call Date: July 2012 (Lincoln's Inn)

St Cyr Clarke *Miss Natalie Lorraine*
Call Date: July 2012 (Inner Temple)

Stanford-Wood *Miss Irene Emily*
Call Date: Nov 2007 (Inner Temple) Qualifications: Bed (Leeds) Med (Leic)

Stansfield *Mr Robert Harvey*
Call Date: Nov 1991 (Inner Temple) Qualifications: BSc (Hons) DipLaw

Stanton *Miss Margaret Judith*
Call Date: July 1966 (Gray's Inn) Qualifications: BA (Hons) BSc (Hons)

Staynings *Ms Chantelle*
Call Date: July 2012 (Gray's Inn)

Stearns *Dr Elizabeth Jane Elford*
COR, Call Date: Oct 1997 (Inner Temple) Qualifications: BDS CPE (Lond) MBBS

Steel *Mr Samuel Edward*
Call Date: July 2012 (Inner Temple)

Steele *Miss Leah Yvonne*
Call Date: July 2007 (Inner Temple) Qualifications: LLB (Bris)

Steele *Mr Mervyn Anthony*
Call Date: July 2012 (Inner Temple)

Stembridge *Mr David Harry QC*
Recorder, Call Date: Nov 1955 (Gray's Inn) Qualifications: LLB

Stephenson *Mr Thomas*
Clerk, Call Date: July 1976 (Middle Temple) Qualifications: BSc PGCE

Sterling *Mr Dialo Andre*
Call Date: Oct 2010 (Middle Temple) Qualifications: BA (Hons)(West Indies) LLB (Hons) (Wales)

Stevens *Miss Ihantha Valerie Sophia*
Call Date: Oct 2010 (Middle Temple) Qualifications: LLB (Hons) (Nott'm)

Stewart *Mr David Fielding*
Call Date: Oct 2006 (Middle Temple) Qualifications: BSc (Dundee) PgDL (Hudds) LLM (Northumbria)

Stock *Ms Melissa*
Call Date: July 2012 (Lincoln's Inn)

Stockwell *Mr Sam*
Call Date: July 2012 (Middle Temple)

Stone *Ms Annette*
Call Date: Nov 2002 (Lincoln's Inn) Qualifications: LLB (Hons)(Lond)

Stone *Prof Richard Thomas Horner*
Professor of Law, Lincoln Law School, University of Lincoln, Brayford Pool, Lincoln, LN6 7TS, 01522 886915, Fax: 01522 886032, Call Date: July 1998 (Gray's Inn) Qualifications: LLB (So'ton) LLM (Hull)

Stone *Miss Virginia Mary*
Call Date: Nov 2008 (Middle Temple) Qualifications: BA (Hons) (York) PGCE (Hull)

Story *Mr David William Joseph*
Call Date: July 2012 (Lincoln's Inn)

Stouph *Mr Mark*
Director, Premier Waste Management Ltd, Prospect House, Aykley Heads, Durham, DH1 5TS, 0191 384 4000, Fax: 0191 384 5869, Call Date: July 2008 (Lincoln's Inn) Qualifications: LLB (Newc) LLM

Stratton *Miss Hannah Louise*
Call Date: July 2012 (Middle Temple)

Straw *Miss Louise Victoria*
Solicitor, Burton Copeland LLP, Astley House, Quay Street, Manchester, M3 4AS, Call Date: Nov 1987 (Gray's Inn) Qualifications: LLB (L'pool)

Stripe *Miss Rebecca Carly*
Call Date: July 2012 (Lincoln's Inn)

Strong *Miss Annemarie*
Solicitor, Call Date: July 2006 (Inner Temple) Qualifications: LLB (Bristol)

Stuart *Miss Alicia Frances Sarah*
Call Date: July 2008 (Inner Temple) Qualifications: LLB (Lond)

Subbarayan *Mr Sivaramen*
Other, 7 Saxton Street, Northampton, NN3 2SQ, 01604 727993, Fax: 01604 402104, Call Date: Mar 2005 (Lincoln's Inn) Qualifications: LLM LLB (Hons)

Sultan *Miss Nazneen*
Call Date: Nov 2001 (Lincoln's Inn) Qualifications: LLB (Hons)

Suttle *Miss Rebecca Ellen*
Call Date: July 2012 (Middle Temple)

Swan *Mr Daniel Rowan*
Call Date: July 2012 (Gray's Inn)

Swift *Miss Valeria*
5 King's Bench Walk, 5 King's Bench Walk, Temple, London, EC4Y 7DN, Call Date: Oct 2003 (Lincoln's Inn) Qualifications: LLB (Hons) (B'ham)

Sykes *Mr Martin Howard*
Call Date: May 1973 (Middle Temple) Qualifications: MA (Oxon)

Symon *Mr Terence Paul*
Call Date: Nov 2008 (Lincoln's Inn) Qualifications: BA CPE COL

Sze *Miss Sylvia Yi*
Call Date: July 2012 (Middle Temple)

Tagoe-Reinhold *Miss Clarice*
Call Date: July 2012 (Lincoln's Inn)

Tahir *Miss Zillay-I-Humma*
Employment Appeal Tribunal, Audit House, 58 Victoria Embankment, London, EC4Y 0DS, 020 7273 1083, Fax: 020 7273 1045, Call Date: July 1999 (Lincoln's Inn) Qualifications: LLB (Hons)

Tahmin *Miss Sayma*
Call Date: July 2012 (Lincoln's Inn)

Tai *Miss Siew Yen*
Call Date: July 2012 (Lincoln's Inn)

Tan *Miss Cheng Sioh*
Call Date: Nov 1970 (Middle Temple)

Tan *Mr Jia Xin*
Call Date: July 2012 (Lincoln's Inn)

Tan *Mr Kai-Lit Melvin*
Advocate, Solicitor, Call Date: July 2001 (Middle Temple) Qualifications: LLB (Hons) Dip in Law

Tan *Mr Shang Neng*
Call Date: July 2012 (Lincoln's Inn)

Tandy *Miss Sarah Ellen*
Call Date: July 2008 (Middle Temple) Qualifications: LLB (Hons) (So'ton)

Tang *Dr Zheng Sophia*
Call Date: July 2012 (Middle Temple)

Tatham *Mr Allan Francis*
Call Date: Oct 1992 (Gray's Inn) Qualifications: BA (Dunelm) BCL (Dunelm)

Taylor *Mr Daniel David*
Call Date: July 2012 (Gray's Inn)

Taylor *Miss Ellory Shelly-Ann*
Call Date: Mar 2010 (Middle Temple) Qualifications: BSc (West Indies) LLB (B'ham)

Taylor *Mr Jacob*
Call Date: July 2012 (Inner Temple)

Taylor *Ms Julie Margaret*
Call Date: Nov 2008 (Inner Temple) Qualifications: LLB (Hons) (Kent) LLM ACIArb

Taylor *Ms Melissa*
Call Date: Oct 2000 (Gray's Inn) Qualifications: BA GradDipLaw LLM Dip Law MBA

Taylor *Mr Peter William Edward QC*
Call Date: Nov 1946 (Inner Temple) Qualifications: MA

Teh *Miss Amy Bee Lin*
Call Date: July 2002 (Lincoln's Inn) Qualifications: LLB (Hons) (Manch)

Teh *Miss Chiew Yin*
Call Date: July 2012 (Middle Temple)

Tepeyurt *Mr Faruk*
Legal Adviser, Regnum Splicitors, 44 Balls Pond Road, London, N1 4AP, 020 7923 3855, Fax: 020 7241 4772, Call Date: July 2005 (Middle Temple) Qualifications: LLB (Hons) MA

Tepre *Mr Paul Kwasi*
Call Date: July 2010 (Lincoln's Inn) Qualifications: LLB (Kent)

Terry *Mrs Jennifer*
Call Date: Nov 1973 (Inner Temple) Qualifications: MSc Dip Soc Ad LLB

Tester *Mr John William Nielson*
CVS, Call Date: July 1980 (Gray's Inn) Qualifications: LLB (B'ham)

Thacker *Mr Charles Malcom Belford*
Viberts, Po Box 737, Pirovet House, Union Street, St Helier, JE4 82Q, Jersey, Call Date: Nov 1970 (Lincoln's Inn) Qualifications: MA (Hons)

Thakur *Miss Sazeeda Johora*
Call Date: July 2012 (Lincoln's Inn)

Thomas *Miss Isobel Julia*
Call Date: July 2012 (Inner Temple)

Thomas *Mr Jeremy Paul*
Call Date: July 2012 (Middle Temple)

Thomas *Miss Nicole Marie*
Call Date: July 2012 (Middle Temple)

Thomas-Mestanas *Miss Kalissa*
Call Date: Oct 2010 (Gray's Inn) Qualifications: LLB

Thompson *Mr Charles Richard*
Call Date: July 2012 (Middle Temple)

Thompson *Mrs Paula Mary*
Call Date: July 1989 (Middle Temple) Qualifications: LLB (Lond) MA (Sussex)

Thompson *Mr Peter Kenneth James QC*
St James' Church Legal Advice Centre, Muswell Hill, London, N10 3DB, 020 8883 0371, Call Date: Feb 1961 (Lincoln's Inn) Qualifications: MA LLB

Thomson *Mr Douglas Allan*
Call Date: July 2012 (Inner Temple)

Thornsby *Mr Nicholas Alexander*
Call Date: July 2012 (Middle Temple)

Timmermann *Ms Wibke Kristin*
Call Date: July 2009 (Inner Temple) Qualifications: MA (St. Andrews) MA Law (Sheff) LLM (Geneva)

Tirathdas *Mr Dilip Dayaram*
Call Date: Oct 2011 (Lincoln's Inn) Qualifications: BSc (Manch) LLB

Tite *Mrs Elizabeth*
Call Date: Nov 2008 (Lincoln's Inn) Qualifications: BSc (USA) LLB

Tiyamiyu *Mr Suraju-Deen Olatunde Lekan*
Call Date: Nov 2008 (Gray's Inn) Qualifications: LLB

Todd *Ms Susan Margaret*
St Philips Chambers, 55 Temple Row, Birmingham, B2 5LS, 0121 246 7000, Fax: 0121 246 7001, Call Date: Nov 1991 (Gray's Inn) Qualifications: BA (Cantab) MA (Sussex)

Tolson *Mr Asa Jack*
Call Date: July 2012 (Lincoln's Inn)

Toner *Mr Blair*
Call Date: July 2010 (Middle Temple) Qualifications: LLB (Hons) (Brunel)

Tonge *Mr Adrian*
Leeds City Council, 3rd Floor East, Civic Hall, Leeds, LS1 1UR, 0113 247 7869, Call Date: Mar 2005 (Gray's Inn) Qualifications: MA (Cantab)

Tookey *Mr Michael John*
Call Date: Oct 1992 (Lincoln's Inn) Qualifications: LLB (Hons)

Toole *Miss Hannah Laura*
Call Date: Oct 2011 (Inner Temple) Qualifications: LLB (Sussex)

Tosic *Mrs Helena*
Call Date: July 2012 (Gray's Inn)

Toynbee *Mrs Ann*
Mediator, Call Date: Nov 2003 (Lincoln's Inn) Qualifications: LLB (Hons) (Wales)

Trace *Miss Charlotte Emily Alice*
Call Date: July 2012 (Lincoln's Inn)

Travers *Mr Richard Ettore Nicholas*
Assistant Deputy Coroner, HM Coronerés Court, Station Approach, Woking, Surrey, GU22 7AP, Call Date: Feb 1985 (Lincoln's Inn) Qualifications: BA (Lond) Dip Law

Travis *Miss Clementine Camilla Curtis*
Call Date: July 2012 (Inner Temple)

Trevelyan *Mr Michael John*
Call Date: July 2008 (Inner Temple) Qualifications: LLB (Warw)

G

Tritton *Miss Emma-Jane*
Call Date: July 2012 (Inner Temple)

Trotter *Mr Christopher Paul*
Call Date: July 2012 (Lincoln's Inn)

Tucker *Miss Hazel Chenayi*
Quinn, Emanuel, Urquhart, Oliver & Hedges LLP, 16 Old Bailey, London, EC4M 7EG, 020 7653 2000, Call Date: Mar 2008 (Middle Temple) Qualifications: BA (Lond)

Tunnicliffe *Mrs Denise*
Call Date: Nov 2003 (Inner Temple) Qualifications: BSc (Lond) LLB (Wolves) BA

Turkan *Miss Nezire*
Call Date: July 2006 (Middle Temple) Qualifications: LLB (Hons) (Lond)

Turner *Mrs Catherine Elizabeth*
Call Date: Nov 2000 (Lincoln's Inn) Qualifications: BA (Hons) (Exon) LLB (Hons) (Bris)

Turner-Samuels *Mr David Jessel QC*
Call Date: May 1939 (Middle Temple)

Twizell *Mrs Krystina*
Call Date: Mar 2010 (Lincoln's Inn) Qualifications: LLB (Open University)

Tyler *Mr Thomas Huw*
Call Date: July 2009 (Gray's Inn) Qualifications: BA

Uddin *Mr Amal*
Call Date: July 2012 (Gray's Inn)

Uddowlla *Miss Shahema Tafader*
Call Date: July 2012 (Inner Temple)

Ujoodha *Mr Purusram*
Call Date: Nov 2011 (Lincoln's Inn) Qualifications: LLB (Notts)

Upward *Mr Patrick Charles QC*
Recorder, 4 Breams Buildings, Chancery Lane, London, EC4A 1HP, Call Date: July 1972 (Inner Temple) Qualifications: LLB (Lond)

Usman *Mr Asad Ullah*
Call Date: July 2012 (Lincoln's Inn)

Utting *Mr David William*
Director, Jisc, 1st Floor, Brettenham House (South), 5 Lancaster Place, London, WC2E 7EN, 020 3006 6036, Fax: 020 7240 5377, Call Date: July 2006 (Middle Temple) Qualifications: LLB LLM (Lond)

Uwaezuoke *Miss Uchechukwu Ogemdi*
Call Date: July 2003 (Gray's Inn) Qualifications: LLB (Hert)

Van Den Berg *Miss Nienke Elisabeth*
Call Date: July 2012 (Lincoln's Inn)

Vanderman *Mr Yaaser*
Call Date: July 2012 (Middle Temple)

Veli *Mr Rafail*
Call Date: Nov 2011 (Middle Temple) Qualifications: BSc (Canada) MBA LLB (Hons) (Lond) LLM (Lond)

Verghese-Dipple *Mrs Mary*
Lawyer, Call Date: Nov 1991 (Lincoln's Inn) Qualifications: LLB (Hons) MA

Vicary *Ms Clare Louise*
Other, The Bar Standards Board, 289-293 High Holborn, London, WC1V 7HZ, 020 7611 1444, Fax: 020 7831 9217, Call Date: July 2002 (Gray's Inn) Qualifications: LLB (B'ham)

Vignoles *Miss Laura Emily*
Call Date: July 2012 (Middle Temple)

Vincent *Mr Matthew William*
Call Date: July 2012 (Inner Temple)

Vinton *Mr Kareem Olando*
Call Date: July 2012 (Lincoln's Inn)

Voelcker *Miss Harriet Jane*
Call Date: July 2003 (Gray's Inn) Qualifications: BA (So'ton)

Voong *Miss Anna Khi*
Call Date: July 2012 (Middle Temple)

Waldron *Mr Steve*
Call Date: Nov 2006 (Gray's Inn) Qualifications: LLB

Wale *Miss Joanna-Louise*
Call Date: Nov 2001 (Lincoln's Inn) Qualifications: LLB (Hons)

Walkden *Miss Heather Louise*
Call Date: Oct 2011 (Lincoln's Inn) Qualifications: LLB (Salford)

Walker *Miss Emma Jayne*
Call Date: July 2009 (Lincoln's Inn) Qualifications: BA (London) CPE LINC

Wall *Mr Andrew Mark*
Call Date: Oct 2009 (Lincoln's Inn) Qualifications: LLB (Lancs)

Wall *Mr Andrew Martin*
Call Date: July 2012 (Middle Temple)

Wall *Mr Ian Laurence*
Call Date: Nov 1994 (Inner Temple) Qualifications: LLB LLM

Wall *Mr William*
Call Date: Nov 1985 (Inner Temple) Qualifications: BA (York) Dip Law (Lond)

Wallace *Miss Mary Joan*
Call Date: July 2007 (Gray's Inn) Qualifications: LLB (Hons) BSc (Hons) LLM (UEA)

Wallace *Prof Rebecca Mairi Maclean*
Judge, Call Date: Nov 1999 (Lincoln's Inn) Qualifications: MA LLB (Hons)(Dundee) PhD (Glas)

Waller *Ms Helen Margaret*
EXM, Call Date: Mar 1997 (Middle Temple) Qualifications: BA (Hons)

Walmsley *Mr Keith*
Legal Adviser, The London Law Agency Ltd, The Old Exchange, 12 Compton Road, Wimbledon, London, SW19 7QD, Call Date: July 1972 (Gray's Inn) Qualifications: LLB (Lond) FCIS

Walters *Mr Joshua Peter Edward*
Call Date: July 2012 (Inner Temple)

Walters *Mr Julian Charles Edward*
Call Date: Nov 2003 (Middle Temple) Qualifications: BA (Hons) (Lond) Dip. in Law

Walters *Mr Richard David Glyn*
Clerk, Secretary, Abercrave House, Abercrave, Powys, SA9 1TJ, 01639 731036, Call Date: Feb 1977 (Lincoln's Inn) Qualifications: LLB MBA

Walton *Mr Alan Roderick*
Company Secretary, Director, FLW, FSOL, Long Hazel Lodge, Long Hazel Park, High Street, Sparkford, Yeovil, BA22 7JH, 01963 440 002, Fax: 01963 440 002, Call Date: Feb 1984 (Inner Temple)

Warren *Ms Joy Nefertiri Beverley*
Call Date: July 2010 (Middle Temple) Qualifications: LLB (Hons)

Watling-Darrell *Miss Daisy Adeline*
Call Date: Oct 2009 (Inner Temple) Qualifications: BA (Sheff) CPE (N'ham)

Watson *Mr Anthony CBE*
Associate, Call Date: Nov 1976 (Lincoln's Inn) Qualifications: BSc (Econ) FSI (Hons)

Watson *Mr Matthew Edward*
Call Date: July 2012 (Inner Temple)

Watt *Mr John Gillie Mcarthur QC*
Advocate, Other, Advocates Library, Parliament House, Edinburgh, EH1 1RF, 970 328 0130, Fax: 970 328 0130, Call Date: Feb 1992 (Middle Temple) Qualifications: LLB (Edin)

Watts *Miss Charlotte Joan*
Call Date: July 2012 (Middle Temple)

Way *Mr Frederick William Patrick*
Call Date: July 2012 (Middle Temple)

Wayman *Miss Caroline Ann*
Financial Ombudsman Service, South Quay Plaza, 183 Marsh Wall, London, E14 9SR, Call Date: Mar 1998 (Middle Temple) Qualifications: LLB (Hons)

Weatherley *Mr Robert David*
Call Date: July 2011 (Middle Temple) Qualifications: LLB (Hons) (Warwick)

Webb *Mr Michael Jeffrey*
Call Date: July 2012 (Middle Temple)

Webber *Mr David Malcolm TD*
Call Date: Nov 1955 (Gray's Inn) Qualifications: MA (Cantab)

Wee *Miss Camilla Louise*
Call Date: July 2011 (Inner Temple) Qualifications: LLB (Kent) LLM (Cantab)

Wee *Mr Chin Kam*
Cassin Law LLC, 50 Raffles Place, #37-00 Singapore Land Tower, 48623, Singapore, Call Date: Nov 1999 (Middle Temple) Qualifications: LLB (Wolves) MBA (Warwick) CPA ACIS MCIM ACMA

Wee *Miss Lee Kiak*
Call Date: Nov 2001 (Middle Temple) Qualifications: LLB (Hons)

Wee Inn *Roland Sagah*
Advocate, Other, Solicitor, M/S David Allan Sagah & Teng Advocates, No 4, 1st Floor, Block A, Wisma Nation Horizon, Jalan Petanak, 93740, Malaysia, 082-232739, Fax: 082-251831, Call Date: July 1980 (Gray's Inn) Qualifications: LLB (Hons)(Lond) MPS (Australia)

Weedon *Mr Rupert Stuart*
Call Date: Mar 2006 (Middle Temple)

Weinberger *Miss Orly*
Call Date: July 2007 (Inner Temple) Qualifications: LLB (Middlesex) LLM (Lond)

Weitzman *Mr Peter QC*
Bencher, Deputy High Court Judge, President of Mental Health Tribunals, Recorder, 21 St James's Gardens, London, W11 4RE, 020 7603 4476, Call Date: July 1952 (Gray's Inn) Qualifications: MA (Oxon)

Weldensae *Miss Adiam*
Call Date: July 2010 (Middle Temple) Qualifications: LLB (Hons)(Lond)

West *Miss Alexandra Mary Lucy*
Call Date: July 2012 (Inner Temple)

West *Mr Christopher John CBE*
Call Date: July 1966 (Lincoln's Inn)

Westcott *Mr Richard Henry*
Call Date: July 1978 (Lincoln's Inn) Qualifications: FCA ACIB FTII

Weston *Mr John Anthony*
Call Date: July 2007 (Gray's Inn) Qualifications: BA

Whayman *Mr Derek Rae*
Call Date: July 2012 (Lincoln's Inn)

Wheeler *Mr Thomas Samuel*
Call Date: July 2011 (Inner Temple) Qualifications: LLB (Derby)

Whelan *Mr Dermot Gerard*
Call Date: Oct 2002 (Inner Temple) Qualifications: LLB (Lond)

White *Miss Christina Louise*
Advocate, Head of Legal Services, Para-Legal, Call Date: Oct 2007 (Gray's Inn) Qualifications: GDL (Lond) BA (Lond) LLM (So'ton)

White *Mr Ian Robert*
Legal Consultant, Call Date: Nov 1989 (Inner Temple) Qualifications: BA (Bris) Dip Law (Lond)

White *Miss Kirsty Louise*
Call Date: Nov 2011 (Inner Temple) Qualifications: LLB (Reading)

White *Mr Timothy Richard*
Call Date: Oct 1993 (Middle Temple) Qualifications: LLB (Hons) MA (Keele)

Whitehead *Mrs Louise Michelle*
Call Date: July 2009 (Middle Temple) Qualifications: LLB (Hons) (Wales)

Whitmore *Ms Alexandra Elizabeth*
Call Date: Nov 2010 (Gray's Inn) Qualifications: LLB

Whittaker *Mr Rodney Martin*
Call Date: July 1971 (Inner Temple) Qualifications: MA (Oxon)

Whybrow *Mr Christopher John QC*
Judge, Call Date: July 1965 (Inner Temple) Qualifications: LLB (Lond)

Wilcock *Miss Rhiannon Francesca Evelyn*
Call Date: July 2012 (Lincoln's Inn)

Wilfred Jr *Mr Bode*
Galadari & Associates, Al Ghubaiba Road, Po Box 7992, Bur Dubai, Dubai, United Arab Emirates, Call Date: Nov 1997 (Middle Temple) Qualifications: LLB (Hons)(Sheff) LLM (Dundee)

Will *Mr Kenneth Campbell*
Call Date: July 2012 (Inner Temple)

Williams *Mr Christopher Michael*
Call Date: Nov 1972 (Middle Temple) Qualifications: MA (Oxon)

Williams *Mr David Arthur Rhodes QC*
Po Box 405, Shortland Street, Auckland, New Zealand, 00 64 9 367 6896, Fax: 00 64 9 367 6895, Call Date: July 2003 (Lincoln's Inn) Qualifications: LLB LLM

Williams *Judge Jonathan Steuart*
Judge, Magistrate, Senior Crown Prosecutor, Judges Chambers, District Court of Nsw, Po Box K1026, Haymarket, NSW 2000, Australia, 02 9287 7446, Fax: 02 9287 7493, Call Date: May 1990 (Lincoln's Inn) Qualifications: Dip Law Dip Crim LLM

Williams *Miss Kirsty Laura*
Call Date: Nov 2011 (Middle Temple) Qualifications: BA (Hons) (Cardiff) PgDL (Lond) MA (Cardiff)

Williams *The Hon Miss Rebecca Clare*
Call Date: Feb 1995 (Inner Temple) Qualifications: MA (Oxon) M Phil (Cantab)

Williams *Mr Richard*
Call Date: Oct 2008 (Inner Temple) Qualifications: LLB (Herts)

Williams *Mr Robert Charles*
Call Date: July 1973 (Inner Temple) Qualifications: MA (Oxon)

Wilson *Mr David James*
Call Date: Oct 2007 (Middle Temple) Qualifications: LLB (Hons) (Dunelm)

Wilson *Mr John Frederick*
Call Date: July 1966 (Inner Temple) Qualifications: BA (Oxon)

Wilson *Miss Kirstie Louise*
Call Date: July 2012 (Inner Temple)

Winch *Mr John*
Arbitrator, Chair, Call Date: July 1973 (Gray's Inn) Qualifications: LLM FCIARB FCILT

Winfield *Mr Paul*
Winfield Associates Ltd, Building 3, City West, Gelderd Road, Leeds, L512 6LX, 0113 2512223, Fax: 0113 2512001, Call Date: July 2010 (Inner Temple) Qualifications: LLB (Bradford)

Wingrave *Mr Michael Vincent*
No5 Chambers, Fountain Court, Steelhouse Lane, Birmingham, B4 6DR, 0845 210 5555, Fax: 0121 606 1501, Call Date: July 2001 (Middle Temple) Qualifications: LLB (Hons)

Winny *Ms Elspeth Margaret*
Oldham Marsh Pace Flavell Solicitors, 19 High Street, Melton Mowbray, Leicestershire, LE13 0TZ, Call Date: Nov 1996 (Lincoln's Inn) Qualifications: LLB (Hons)(Lond) LLM (Lond)

Winter *Miss Sarah Joanne*
Call Date: July 2012 (Middle Temple)

Winters *Mr Matthew*
Call Date: July 2012 (Lincoln's Inn)

Woerle *Mrs Irene Mutalemwa*
Call Date: July 2012 (Gray's Inn)

Wolstenholme *Mr Alan James*
St Johns Buildings, 24a - 28 St John Street, Manchester, M3 4DJ, Call Date: July 1989 (Lincoln's Inn) Qualifications: LLB (Leeds)

Wolstenholme *Mrs Alison Jane*
Call Date: Nov 2008 (Inner Temple) Qualifications: LLB (Sheff) BVC (Sheff)

Wong *Miss Fian Ho Yan*
Call Date: Mar 2006 (Lincoln's Inn) Qualifications: LLB (Hons) (Bristol)

Wong *Miss Wei Guan*
Call Date: July 2012 (Lincoln's Inn)

Wood *Mr Christopher Douglas*
Call Date: May 1997 (Lincoln's Inn) Qualifications: BSc (Hons) MSc Dip Law MRICS MCIOB

Wood *Miss Priscilla Jane*
Call Date: Nov 1973 (Middle Temple) Qualifications: BA MLitt (Edin)

Woodhead *Miss Charlotte Cassandra*
Lecturer, School of Law, University of Warwick, Coventry, CV4 7AL, 024 7652 4162, Call Date: Oct 2002 (Middle Temple) Qualifications: LLB LLM

Woodward *Mr William Charles QC*
Deputy High Court Judge, Other, President of Mental Health Tribunals, Professor of Law, Recorder, Call Date: Feb 1964 (Inner Temple) Qualifications: BA (Oxon)

Worthington *Prof Sarah Elizabeth QC*
Call Date: Mar 2005 (Middle Temple) Qualifications: LLB (Hons) LLM PhD

Wray *Mr Benedict Semple*
Call Date: July 2009 (Middle Temple) Qualifications: LLB (Hons) (Lond)

Wray *Mr Nigel Duncan Andrew*
Call Date: Feb 1993 (Gray's Inn) Qualifications: MA (St Andrews) Dip Law (Lond)

Wright *Mr Mark*
M Wright, 12 Balmoral Close, Knutsford, WA16 8LN, Call Date: Feb 1986 (Inner Temple) Qualifications: BA

Wrightson *Ms Alexandra Katherine*
Higher Court Advocate, Solicitor, Sa Law Chambers Solicitors Ltd, Heraldic House, 1st Floor, 160-162 Cranbrook Road, Ilford, Essex, IG1 4PE, 020 8554 0012, Fax: 020 8554 6619, Call Date: July 2000 (Inner Temple) Qualifications: LLB (Lond)

Wyatt *Mr Jonathan Martin*
Adjudicator, Arbitrator, Call Date: July 1973 (Gray's Inn) Qualifications: LLB (Lond) FCIArb Dip IC Arb

Wylie-Otte *Ms Regan*
Other, 3 Um Kallek, L-5369 Schuttrange, Luxembourg, Fax: 00352 350503, Call Date: Feb 1978 (Middle Temple) Qualifications: MA LLM

Wynne *Mr Damian James*
Call Date: July 2012 (Gray's Inn)

Xu Lindsey *Mrs Cecilia Chunping*
Call Date: July 2012 (Lincoln's Inn)

Yaba *Ms Minerva David*
Call Date: Nov 2011 (Gray's Inn) Qualifications: BA

Yap *Miss Sim Yi*
Call Date: July 2004 (Lincoln's Inn) Qualifications: LLB (Hons) (UEA.) LLM

Yaqub *Mr Omar*
Call Date: Oct 1997 (Inner Temple) Qualifications: LLB (London) LLM (London)

Yazdani *Mr Humzah Qamar*
Call Date: July 2012 (Lincoln's Inn)

Yee *Miss Deborah Geat Mei*
Call Date: July 2012 (Inner Temple)

Yemi-Lawal *Mr Adekunle*
Call Date: July 2012 (Inner Temple)

Yeoh *Ms Pei Nee*
Call Date: July 2012 (Gray's Inn)

Yerrell *Miss Nicola Jane*
Legal Service of the European Commission, Rue De La Loi 200, B-1049 Bruxelles, Belgium, 32 2 295 1969, Fax: 32 2 296 5965, Call Date: Oct 1993 (Middle Temple) Qualifications: BA (Hons)(Oxon) Lic Spec en Droit Euro(Belgium)

Yin *Mr Michael Chi-Ming*
10/F New Henry House, 10 Ice House Street, Central, Hong Kong, China, Call Date: Nov 1993 (Lincoln's Inn) Qualifications: LLB (Hons)(Bris) LLM (Bris)

Youngman *Mr Brian John*
Call Date: June 1953 (Gray's Inn) Qualifications: LLB (Lond)

Younis *Miss Abda Begum*
Call Date: Oct 2011 (Middle Temple) Qualifications: BA (Hons) (B'ham)

Yu *Miss Garsin Joyce*
Financial Services Authority, 25 The North Colannade, Canary Wharf, London, E14 8HS, Call Date: July 2005 (Lincoln's Inn) Qualifications: LLB (Hons)

Zadra-Symes *Mrs Lynda Julie*
Knobbe Martens Olson & Bear, Fourteenth Floor, 2040 Main Street, Irvine, CA 92614, USA, 001 949 760 0404, Fax: 001 949 760 9502, Call Date: Nov 1989 (Inner Temple) Qualifications: LLB

Zang *Miss Clara Yeji*
Call Date: July 2012 (Middle Temple)

Zerin *Ms Ishrat*
Call Date: July 2012 (Gray's Inn)

Zhang *Mr Jianquan Andrew*
Call Date: July 2012 (Middle Temple)

PART H

Index of Languages Spoken

This section provides an index of all languages spoken by chambers and individual barristers. The languages are listed alphabetically, as are chambers and individuals.

All chambers in this section have an expanded entry in *Part D Chambers by Location* and all individual barristers in this section have an expanded entry in *Part E Individual Barristers in Private Practice*.

H

AFRIKAANS

Cornerstone Barristers
23 Essex Street
Goldsmith Chambers
Henderson Chambers
Oriel Chambers

ARABIC

2 Bedford Row
39 Essex Street
Lincoln House Chambers
Nine Bedford Row
1 Paper Buildings
3 Raymond Buildings
Wilberforce Chambers

BENGALI

187 Fleet Street
No5 Chambers
Sen, Mr Aditya Kumar
St Philips Chambers

BRITISH SIGN LANGUAGE

1 Paper Buildings

CHINESE (CANTONESE)

Argent Chambers

CHINESE (MANDARIN)

Argent Chambers
No5 Chambers
South Square
Sovereign Chambers

CROATIAN

3 Dr Johnson's Buildings

DUTCH

2 Bedford Row
Chambers of Mr Ami Feder
College Chambers
Monckton Chambers
3 Raymond Buildings

FARSI

3 Dr Johnson's Buildings

FRENCH

Arden Chambers
Argent Chambers
Badenoch, Mr James Forster
2 Bedford Row
29 Bedford Row Chambers
9-12 Bell Yard
Chambers of Mr Ami Feder
Charter Chambers
Cobden House Chambers
College Chambers
Cornerstone Barristers
Crown Office Chambers
Devereux Chambers
3 Dr Johnson's Buildings
23 Essex Street
39 Essex Street
Farrar's Building
187 Fleet Street
Goldsmith Chambers
4-5 Gray's Inn Square
Henderson Chambers
Jeans, Mr Christopher James Marwood
1 KBW Chambers
Lincoln House Chambers
Maitland Chambers
Monckton Chambers
Nine Bedford Row
No5 Chambers
Number 7 Harrington Street Chambers
13 Old Square Chambers
Oriel Chambers
1 Paper Buildings
4 Paper Buildings
Pump Court Chambers
Purdie, Mr Robert Anthony James
QEB Hollis Whiteman
3 Raymond Buildings
South Square
Sovereign Chambers
St Philips Chambers
Tanfield Chambers
Temple Garden Chambers
Three New Square IP
Trinity Chambers
Walsh, Mr Steven James Franklyn
Wilberforce Chambers
Wilson, Mr Graham James

GERMAN

Argent Chambers
2 Bedford Row
29 Bedford Row Chambers
9-12 Bell Yard
Chambers of Mr Ami Feder
Charter Chambers
College Chambers
Cornerstone Barristers
Crown Office Chambers
23 Essex Street
39 Essex Street
187 Fleet Street
Goldsmith Chambers
4-5 Gray's Inn Square
Henderson Chambers
Jeans, Mr Christopher James Marwood
1 KBW Chambers
Monckton Chambers
Nine Bedford Row
No5 Chambers
Number 7 Harrington Street Chambers
1 Paper Buildings
4 Paper Buildings
Pump Court Chambers
QEB Hollis Whiteman
3 Raymond Buildings
South Square
Sovereign Chambers
St Philips Chambers
Tanfield Chambers
Temple Garden Chambers
Wilberforce Chambers

GREEK

Argent Chambers
Cornerstone Barristers
23 Essex Street
4-5 Gray's Inn Square
Number 7 Harrington Street Chambers
QEB Hollis Whiteman

GUJARATI

Argent Chambers
9-12 Bell Yard
Cobden House Chambers
39 Essex Street
Lincoln House Chambers
Nine Bedford Row

HEBREW

2 Bedford Row
29 Bedford Row Chambers
9-12 Bell Yard
Chambers of Mr Ami Feder
College Chambers
Sovereign Chambers
Tanfield Chambers

HINDI

Argent Chambers
9-12 Bell Yard
23 Essex Street
187 Fleet Street
Lincoln House Chambers
Nine Bedford Row
No5 Chambers
Sen, Mr Aditya Kumar
South Square
St Philips Chambers

HUNGARIAN

Argent Chambers
No5 Chambers
South Square

IBO

Argent Chambers

INDONESIAN

Charter Chambers

IRISH

No5 Chambers

ITALIAN

Arden Chambers
Argent Chambers
Badenoch, Mr James Forster
2 Bedford Row
9-12 Bell Yard
Chambers of Mr Ami Feder
Charter Chambers
College Chambers
Cornerstone Barristers
Crown Office Chambers
23 Essex Street
39 Essex Street
187 Fleet Street
Goldsmith Chambers
Monckton Chambers
New Court
Nine Bedford Row
No5 Chambers
QEB Hollis Whiteman
3 Raymond Buildings
South Square
Sovereign Chambers
St Philips Chambers
Tanfield Chambers
Wilberforce Chambers

JAPANESE

Argent Chambers
Henderson Chambers
No5 Chambers
Three New Square IP

KASHMIRI

No5 Chambers

KOREAN

3 Raymond Buildings

KRIO (SIERRA LEONE)

2 Bedford Row

MALAY

Argent Chambers
Charter Chambers

MIRPURI

No5 Chambers

NORWEGIAN

1 Paper Buildings

PERSIAN

Lincoln House Chambers

PORTUGUESE

1 KBW Chambers
No5 Chambers
Tanfield Chambers

PUNJABI

9-12 Bell Yard
Chambers of Mr Ami Feder
College Chambers
23 Essex Street
Goldsmith Chambers
Lincoln House Chambers
Nine Bedford Row
No5 Chambers
South Square
Sovereign Chambers
St Philips Chambers
Temple Garden Chambers

ROMANIAN

Charter Chambers

RUSSIAN

2 Bedford Row
9-12 Bell Yard
23 Essex Street
Lincoln House Chambers

H

Monckton Chambers
Number 7 Harrington Street Chambers
13 Old Square Chambers
QEB Hollis Whiteman
St Philips Chambers
Tanfield Chambers

SERBO-CROAT

2 Bedford Row

SPANISH

Argent Chambers
29 Bedford Row Chambers
9-12 Bell Yard
Chambers of Mr Ami Feder
Charter Chambers
College Chambers
Cornerstone Barristers
Devereux Chambers
23 Essex Street
39 Essex Street
Goldsmith Chambers
4-5 Gray's Inn Square
Henderson Chambers
1 KBW Chambers
Lincoln House Chambers
Maitland Chambers
Monckton Chambers
Nine Bedford Row
No5 Chambers
13 Old Square Chambers
Oriel Chambers
4 Paper Buildings
QEB Hollis Whiteman
3 Raymond Buildings
South Square
Sovereign Chambers
St Philips Chambers
Tanfield Chambers
Temple Garden Chambers
Walsh, Mr Steven James Franklyn
Wilberforce Chambers

SWAHILI

Nine Bedford Row
No5 Chambers
Three New Square IP

SWEDISH

QEB Hollis Whiteman

TAMIL

Argent Chambers

TURKISH

No5 Chambers

URDU

Argent Chambers
9-12 Bell Yard
3 Dr Johnson's Buildings
23 Essex Street
Goldsmith Chambers
Lincoln House Chambers
No5 Chambers
Number 7 Harrington Street Chambers
3 Raymond Buildings
South Square
Sovereign Chambers
St Philips Chambers

WELSH

Argent Chambers
College Chambers
Cornerstone Barristers
Henderson Chambers
No5 Chambers
QEB Hollis Whiteman
St Philips Chambers

PART I

A-Z Index of Chambers

This section lists all the chambers from *Part D Chambers by Location* alphabetically with the Part D page reference.

I

A

B

C

D

E

F

G

J

K

L

N

O

T